INDEX TO
Encyclopedia of American Quaker Genealogy

By William Wade Hinshaw

INDEX TO
Encyclopedia of American Quaker Genealogy

By William Wade Hinshaw

GENEALOGICAL PUBLISHING Co., Inc

Published by Genealogical Publishing Co., Inc.
Library of Congress Catalogue Card Number 98-75468
International Standard Book Number 0-8063-1606-3
Made in the United States of America

Publisher's Preface

The six volumes of Hinshaw's legendary *Encyclopedia of American Quaker Genealogy* were published between 1936 and 1950, just prior to the author's death. In the nearly fifty years since its completion, the *Encyclopedia* has remained the pre-eminent reference work in Quaker genealogy. For records of birth, marriage, and death—carefully recorded in the monthly meeting records of the Carolinas, Tennessee, New Jersey, New York, Pennsylvania, Virginia, and Ohio—there simply is no substitute for Hinshaw's *Encyclopedia.* And for records of removal, showing the movement of the Quaker population from one meeting to another and from one state to the next, there is, again, no substitute for the *Encyclopedia.* Indeed, almost no class of records, religious or secular, has been kept as meticulously as the monthly meeting records of the Religious Society of Friends (Quakers), and Hinshaw's careful transcriptions of these records have left the *Encyclopedia* without any serious rival.

Still, for all its gilt-edged data and its reams and reams of vital records, the *Encyclopedia* has a flaw: it does not contain an every-name index; instead, each volume has a separate *surname* index. So not only does the researcher have to examine six separate indexes, he also has to check out every reference to a given surname—page by page. Needless to say, this is a cumbersome and tedious procedure and is certainly not in the best interest of the researcher, who for fifty years has endured this lapse with surprising fortitude.

Now, however, comes an index to Hinshaw—*the* index, one might say—and all impediments to research are immediately overcome. Here in this one mammoth volume—in a single alphabetical sequence—are the 600,000 names found in the great *Encyclopedia.* Each entry in this index contains the surname, the given name, and the volume number and page number wherein the name can be found. Simple! A straight-forward index that enables the researcher to pin down his quarry with maximum efficiency.

For those who own the *Encyclopedia,* or even individual volumes of the *Encyclopedia,* this is a godsend; for those hoping to find out if any of their ancestors appear in the *Encyclopedia,* this is as good as it gets.

INDEX TO
Encyclopedia of American Quaker Genealogy

By William Wade Hinshaw

Aames, Lloyd II, 331
Aames, Robert II, 331
Aaron, Caroline II, 279
Aaron, Caroline II, 284
Aarons, Samuel V, 19
Aaronson, Caroline II, 316
Aaronson, Caroline II, 326
Aaronson, Caroline B. II, 316
Aaronson, Charles B. II, 279
Aaronson, Elizabeth Ann II, 279
Aaronson, Hope II, 194
Aaronson, Hope II, 221
Aaronson, Mary Elizabeth II, 279
Aarson, Derek III, 162
Aarson, Hannah III, 162
Abbett, Catharine II, 450
Abbett, Elizabeth II, 450
Abbett, Elizabeth II, 596
Abbett, Henry II, 450
Abbett, Henry II, 596
Abbett, Howard II, 450
Abbett, Rebecca II, 450
Abbett, Samuel II, 830
Abbett, Timothy II, 450
Abbett, Wm. II, 450
Abbiata, Edna I, 611
Abbiata, Edna I, 629
Abbiata, Frank I, 611
Abbiata, Mary I, 611
Abbiata, Teresa I, 611
Abbiata, Theresa I, 629
Abbiate, Edna I, 629
Abbitt, Geo. VI, 805
Abbitt, Geo. W. VI, 795
Abbitt, George VI, 863
Abbitt, Isabel VI, 805
Abbot, Abel II, 191
Abbot, Elsworth V, 655
Abbot, Fay V, 317
Abbot, Fay V, 655
Abbot, James II, 779
Abbot, John B. V, 317
Abbot, Mary II, 779
Abbot, Mary V, 797
Abbot, Minnie V, 317
Abbot, Minnie V, 655
Abbot, Rebecca II, 80
Abbot, Rebecca II, 779
Abbot, Sarah V, 797
Abbot, W. Elworth V, 317
Abbot, Wm. II, 779
Abbott, ??? III, 98
Abbott, Abel II, 191
Abbott, Abijah V, 725
Abbott, Agnes III, 15
Abbott, Alice III, 15
Abbott, Amy II, 19
Abbott, Ann II, 114
Abbott, Ann II, 191
Abbott, Ann II, 203
Abbott, Ann II, 331
Abbott, Ann II, 817
Abbott, Ann A. II, 1044
Abbott, Ann A. II, 1051
Abbott, Ann A. II, 1068
Abbott, Ann A. II, 1073
Abbott, Ann Davidson VI, 795
Abbott, Ann N. II, 450
Abbott, Ann N. II, 725
Abbott, Ann R. II, 1068
Abbott, Ann R. II, 1071
Abbott, Ann R. II, 1073
Abbott, Anna Maria II, 779
Abbott, Anna Maria II, 830
Abbott, Annie III, 15
Abbott, Benjamin II, 19
Abbott, Calvin V, 725
Abbott, Casper W. II, 19
Abbott, Catharine II, 450
Abbott, Catharine W. II, 19
Abbott, Charles H. II, 450
Abbott, Charles H. II, 725
Abbott, Charles T. II, 19
Abbott, Edmund II, 331
Abbott, Edmund II, 450
Abbott, Edmund II, 830
Abbott, Edw. H. A. III, 15
Abbott, Edward II, 830
Abbott, Edward L. II, 19
Abbott, Edward L. II, 114
Abbott, Eleanor Steel II, 331
Abbott, Eleanor Steel II, 450
Abbott, Eliza Cecelia II, 1068
Abbott, Elizabeth II, 19
Abbott, Elizabeth II, 331
Abbott, Elizabeth II, 450
Abbott, Elizabeth II, 545
Abbott, Elizabeth II, 779
Abbott, Elizabeth II, 825
Abbott, Elizabeth II, 830
Abbott, Elizabeth II, 892
Abbott, Elizabeth III, 15
Abbott, Elizabeth E. II, 114
Abbott, Elizabeth E. II, 121
Abbott, Elizabeth G. VI, 1017
Abbott, Elizabeth K. IV, 1035
Abbott, Elizabeth L. II, 114
Abbott, Elizabeth Phipps II, 794
Abbott, Elizabeth S. II, 830
Abbott, Elizabeth S. II, 920
Abbott, Ella H. V, 217
Abbott, Ellen V, 217
Abbott, Ellsworth V, 655
Abbott, Elsworth V, 317
Abbott, Elsworth V, 655
Abbott, Emma Walton II, 864
Abbott, Ephraim O. II, 1068
Abbott, Ephraim O. II, 1073
Abbott, Eva V, 217
Abbott, Fay V, 317
Abbott, Fay V, 451
Abbott, Fay V, 655
Abbott, Fay V, 658
Abbott, Faye V, 317
Abbott, Frances E. M. VI, 869
Abbott, Garland VI, 813
Abbott, Garland VI, 1017
Abbott, Geo. W. VI, 795
Abbott, George II, 19
Abbott, George II, 49
Abbott, George II, 114
Abbott, George II, 121
Abbott, George II, 331
Abbott, George II, 450
Abbott, George II, 698
Abbott, George II, 725
Abbott, George II, 779
Abbott, George II, 1065
Abbott, George II, 1068
Abbott, George VI, 795
Abbott, George B. II, 1068
Abbott, George B. II, 1071
Abbott, George B. III, 15
Abbott, George, Jr. II, 114
Abbott, Hana II, 49
Abbott, Hannah II, 19
Abbott, Hannah II, 49
Abbott, Hannah II, 50
Abbott, Hannah II, 78
Abbott, Hannah II, 89
Abbott, Hannah II, 450
Abbott, Hannah II, 684
Abbott, Hannah G. II, 19
Abbott, Hannah G. II, 20
Abbott, Helen May II, 866
Abbott, Henry II, 331
Abbott, Henry II, 450
Abbott, Henry III, 15
Abbott, Henry B. II, 19
Abbott, Henry B. II, 114
Abbott, Henry B. II, 698
Abbott, Henry B. II, 725
Abbott, Howard II, 450
Abbott, Howard II, 725
Abbott, Howard II, 747
Abbott, Isaac III, 15
Abbott, Isabella III, 15
Abbott, J. B. V, 317
Abbott, James II, 49
Abbott, James II, 109
Abbott, James II, 331
Abbott, James II, 450
Abbott, James II, 690
Abbott, James II, 725
Abbott, James II, 830
Abbott, James II, 892
Abbott, James III, 15
Abbott, James Henry II, 779
Abbott, James Henry II, 830
Abbott, Jane II, 191
Abbott, Jane II, 203
Abbott, John II, 191
Abbott, John II, 203
Abbott, John II, 331
Abbott, John II, 450
Abbott, John II, 545
Abbott, John V, 725
Abbott, John V, 760
Abbott, John V, 797
Abbott, John A. II, 450
Abbott, John B. II, 450
Abbott, John B. V, 317
Abbott, John Bullock II, 450
Abbott, John Meader V, 725
Abbott, John R. II, 725
Abbott, Joseph II, 191
Abbott, Joseph II, 203
Abbott, Joseph II, 1068
Abbott, Joseph II, 1071
Abbott, Joseph II, 1073
Abbott, Joseph III, 15
Abbott, Joseph B. II, 19
Abbott, Josiah II, 19
Abbott, Josiah II, 49
Abbott, Julia Anna II, 794
Abbott, Katherine II, 114
Abbott, Lorena V, 317
Abbott, Louisa Jane II, 830
Abbott, Louisa Jane II, 892
Abbott, Lucy Ann II, 331
Abbott, Lucy Ann II, 450
Abbott, Lucy Ann II, 830
Abbott, Lydia II, 19
Abbott, Lydia III, 15
Abbott, Mar??? II, 138
Abbott, Marcy II, 20
Abbott, Margaret V, 655
Abbott, Margaret V, 705
Abbott, Margaretta II, 450
Abbott, Martha II, 19
Abbott, Martha II, 49
Abbott, Martha II, 114
Abbott, Martha II, 126
Abbott, Mary II, 19
Abbott, Mary II, 49
Abbott, Mary II, 107
Abbott, Mary II, 114
Abbott, Mary II, 331
Abbott, Mary II, 450
Abbott, Mary II, 690
Abbott, Mary II, 830
Abbott, Mary II, 892
Abbott, Mary II, 1065
Abbott, Mary III, 15
Abbott, Mary V, 725
Abbott, Mary V, 760
Abbott, Mary V, 797
Abbott, Mary Ann II, 19
Abbott, Mary Ann II, 47
Abbott, Mary Ann II, 114
Abbott, Mary Ann II, 126
Abbott, Mary Ann III, 15
Abbott, Mary H. II, 830
Abbott, Mary Isabella III, 15
Abbott, Mary Isabella III, 46
Abbott, Mercy II, 19
Abbott, Mercy II, 49
Abbott, Mercy II, 105
Abbott, Minnie V, 317
Abbott, Minnie V, 451
Abbott, Minnie V, 655
Abbott, Paul II, 450
Abbott, Rachel II, 331
Abbott, Rachel II, 830
Abbott, Rebecca II, 19
Abbott, Rebecca II, 49
Abbott, Rebecca II, 105
Abbott, Rebecca II, 138
Abbott, Rebecca II, 331
Abbott, Rebecca II, 450
Abbott, Rebecca II, 690
Abbott, Rebecca II, 725
Abbott, Rebecca II, 758
Abbott, Rebecca II, 1044
Abbott, Rebecca II, 1049
Abbott, Rebecca II, 1068
Abbott, Rebecca II, 1071
Abbott, Rebecca V, 725
Abbott, Rebecca V, 755
Abbott, Rebecca V, 797
Abbott, Rebecca V, 816
Abbott, Rebecca Ann II, 725
Abbott, Rebecca Ann II, 747
Abbott, Rebecca Ann II, 830
Abbott, Rebecca W. II, 19
Abbott, Rebecca W. II, 114
Abbott, Rebecca W. II, 125
Abbott, Rebeckah II, 49
Abbott, Rebeckah II, 58
Abbott, Rebekah II, 49
Abbott, Rebekah II, 107
Abbott, Redman II, 114
Abbott, Redman II, 725
Abbott, Richard II, 864
Abbott, Robert II, 331
Abbott, Robert III, 15
Abbott, Robert M. VI, 869
Abbott, Roy III, 15
Abbott, Roy Twining III, 15
Abbott, Roy Twining III, 46
Abbott, Ruth L. II, 114
Abbott, Ruth S. II, 19
Abbott, Ruth S. II, 114
Abbott, Ruth S. II, 121
Abbott, Ruth S. II, 698
Abbott, Ruth S. II, 725
Abbott, Samuel II, 19
Abbott, Samuel II, 20
Abbott, Samuel II, 47
Abbott, Samuel II, 49
Abbott, Samuel II, 105
Abbott, Samuel II, 114
Abbott, Samuel II, 125
Abbott, Samuel II, 126
Abbott, Samuel II, 138
Abbott, Samuel II, 331
Abbott, Samuel II, 440
Abbott, Samuel II, 450
Abbott, Samuel II, 545
Abbott, Samuel II, 684
Abbott, Samuel II, 830
Abbott, Samuel V, 725
Abbott, Samuel Edmund II, 830
Abbott, Samuel M. V, 725
Abbott, Samuel M. V, 755
Abbott, Samuel M. V, 797
Abbott, Samuel M. V, 816
Abbott, Samuel R. II, 830
Abbott, Samuel, Jr. II, 114
Abbott, Sarah II, 19
Abbott, Sarah II, 47
Abbott, Sarah II, 114
Abbott, Sarah II, 126
Abbott, Sarah II, 331
Abbott, Sarah II, 450
Abbott, Sarah II, 799
Abbott, Sarah II, 830
Abbott, Sarah V, 725
Abbott, Sarah V, 760
Abbott, Sarah V, 797
Abbott, Sarah A. VI, 795
Abbott, Sarah W. II, 19
Abbott, Sarah W. II, 114
Abbott, Sarah W. II, 125
Abbott, Sarah W. II, 126
Abbott, Susan II, 725
Abbott, Susan II, 733
Abbott, Susan II, 830
Abbott, Susan B. VI, 813
Abbott, Susan S. II, 316
Abbott, Susan S. II, 725
Abbott, Susan S. II, 747
Abbott, Susannah II, 830
Abbott, Thomas C. II, 1065
Abbott, Thomas C. II, 1068
Abbott, Thomas Middleton II, 331
Abbott, Thomas Middleton II, 450
Abbott, Timothy II, 331
Abbott, Timothy II, 450
Abbott, Timothy II, 698
Abbott, Timothy II, 725
Abbott, Timothy II, 758
Abbott, Timothy, Jr. II, 725
Abbott, W. E. V, 451
Abbott, W. Elworth V, 317
Abbott, Wd. Elizabeth II, 49
Abbott, Wd. Elizabeth II, 109
Abbott, Wd. Elizabeth II, 331
Abbott, Wd. Elizabeth Williams II, 779
Abbott, William II, 331
Abbott, William III, 15
Abbott, William VI, 467
Abbott, William Evans VI, 795
Abbott, William W. II, 698
Abbott, Wilson II, 779
Abbott, Wilson II, 830
Abbott, Wilson II, 892
Abbott, Wm. II, 19
Abbott, Wm. II, 49
Abbott, Wm. II, 107
Abbott, Wm. II, 450
Abbott, Wm. II, 690
Abbott, Wm. II, 830
Abbott, Wm. V, 725
Abbott, Wm. G. II, 19
Abbott, Wm. G. II, 49
Abbott, Wm. H. II, 830
Abbott, Wm. L. II, 725
Abbott, Wm. S. II, 779
Abbott, Wm. S. II, 794
Abbott, Wm. White II, 450
Abbott, Wm. White II, 725
Abbotts, Martha II, 114
Abbotts, Martha II, 125
Abbotts, Samuel II, 125
Abbut, Lula Parrish I, 629
Abel, Abigail IV, 509
Abel, Abigail IV, 541
Abel, Esther IV, 921
Abel, Esther IV, 999
Abel, John II, 450
Abel, Lyman IV, 921
Abel, Sally IV, 921
Abel, Wm. IV, 921
Abel, Wm. IV, 999
Abele, Emma IV, 1233
Abele, Michael IV, 1233
Abell, George Ernest II, 698
Abell, John II, 450
Abell, Richard VI, 227
Abendroth, Cordelia III, 15
Abendroth, Jno. W. III, 15
Abendroth, Mabel Maria III, 15
Abendroth, Mabel Maria III, 355
Abendroth, William Philip III, 15
Abendroth, William Philip III, 355
Aber, Minnie H. III, 162
Abernathy, Nancy W. V, 609
Abernathy, Nancy W. V, 635
Abernathy, William VI, 137
Abernathy, William D. VI, 129
Abernathy, William D. VI, 131
Abernethy, Susan III, 501
Abers, Eliza V, 451
Abers, Eliza A. V, 217
Abers, James N. V, 217
Aberson, Benjamin I, 708
Aberson, Elias I, 708
Abidan, Ebidan VI, 98
Abieatie, Theresa I, 629
Abijah, Janney VI, 749
Abit, Hana II, 49
Aborn, Mary II, 90
Aborn, Mary II, 191
Abot, John V, 725
Abot, William VI, 467
Abott, Julia Ann II, 794
Abrahams, Robert VI, 51
Abram, Ben C. IV, 1305
Abram, Edith IV, 1245
Abram, Eugene IV, 1305
Abram, Harold IV, 1305
Abram, Harold H. IV, 1245
Abram, J. H. IV, 1245
Abram, Jean IV, 1305
Abram, Luzena IV, 1245
Abram, May IV, 1245
Abram, Minnie IV, 1245
Abram, Minnie IV, 1305
Abram, Roy IV, 1245
Abram, Roy E. IV, 1305
Abram, Wm. IV, 1245
Abrams, Ethel May IV, 463
Abrams, May IV, 463
Abrams, Rev. Will IV, 463
Abrams, Rodney IV, 463
Abrams, William IV, 463
Abshire, Allen VI, 869
Abshire, Mary VI, 869
Absten, Jesse, Jr. VI, 869
Absten, Mary VI, 869
Absten, Polly VI, 869
Absten, Wd. Joshua VI, 869
Abston, Elizabeth VI, 981
Abston, Fanny VI, 913
Abston, Jesse VI, 883
Abston, Jesse VI, 889
Abston, Jesse VI, 913
Abston, Jesse VI, 975
Abston, Jesse VI, 980
Abston, Jesse VI, 981
Abston, Jesse, Jr. VI, 869
Abston, Joshua VI, 913
Abston, Joshua VI, 962
Abston, Joshua VI, 990
Abston, Lucy VI, 883
Abston, Lucy VI, 889
Abston, Mary VI, 975
Abston, Mille VI, 918
Abston, Nancy VI, 990
Abston, Sally VI, 883
Abston, Suckey VI, 980
Abston, Susannah VI, 962
Acherman, Isaiah V, 983
Achor, Ann V, 317
Achor, Bruce V, 371
Achor, Clement V, 371
Achor, Cora V. V, 317
Achor, Elizabeth V, 217
Achor, Elizabeth V, 371
Achor, Elizabeth V, 381
Achor, Elizabeth D. V, 317
Achor, Elizabeth M. V, 371
Achor, Elizabeth Minerva V, 371
Achor, Ellwood V, 217
Achor, Emma V, 371
Achor, Eunice V, 217
Achor, Eunice V, 371
Achor, Euphemia V, 317
Achor, Euphemia V, 655
Achor, Euphemia A. V, 317
Achor, Euphemia Ann V, 471
Achor, Euphemia B. V, 655
Achor, George V, 217
Achor, George V, 655
Achor, George R. V, 371
Achor, George Riley V, 217
Achor, George Riley V, 371
Achor, Georgia V, 217
Achor, John V, 317
Achor, John C. V, 655

Achor, John G. V, 655
Achor, Joseph V, 217
Achor, Joseph V, 371
Achor, Lydia Ann V, 371
Achor, Maria S. V, 655
Achor, Martha V, 217
Achor, Martha Jane V, 317
Achor, Mary J. V, 217
Achor, Mary Jane V, 217
Achor, Mary M. V, 371
Achor, Mary Margaret V, 371
Achor, Maud Miller V, 371
Achor, Mildred V, 371
Achor, Mildred Brewer V, 371
Achor, Rachel V, 317
Achor, Samuel V, 217
Achor, Samuel V, 371
Achor, Samuel D. V, 217
Achor, Samuel D. V, 371
Achor, Samuel Davis V, 371
Achor, Sarah V, 317
Achor, Sarah Ann V, 217
Achor, Sarah Ann V, 317
Achor, Sarah J. V, 371
Achor, Sarah Jane V, 217
Achor, Sarah Jane V, 371
Achor, Survetus T. V, 317
Achor, Survetus Taylor V, 317
Achor, Thomas V, 317
Achor, Thomas V, 371
Achor, Thomas C. V, 371
Achor, Thomas Claton V, 371
Achor, Thomas D. V, 317
Achor, Thomas Dillon V, 317
Achor, Wayne V, 371
Achurst, Ann VI, 15
Ackerlie, Lucy VI, 869
Ackerlie, William VI, 869
Ackerman, Chloe Olive IV, 1305
Ackerman, Irene T. IV, 1305
Ackerman, Laura O. V, 317
Ackerman, Letitia III, 211
Ackerman, Marietta III, 15
Ackerson, Henry III, 479
Ackerson, Henry III, 490
Ackerson, Phebe III, 479
Ackerson, Phebe III, 490
Ackley, David II, 331
Ackley, Elizabeth II, 331
Ackley, Elizabeth II, 450
Ackley, Elizabeth II, 779
Ackley, Elizabeth II, 815
Ackley, Flora IV, 1305
Ackley, Hannah II, 450
Ackley, Hannah II, 663
Ackley, Hannah IV, 169
Ackley, Hannah IV, 207
Ackley, Hiram III, 15
Ackley, John II, 331
Ackley, John II, 450
Ackley, John B. II, 779
Ackley, Jonathan III, 15
Ackley, Joseph II, 331
Ackley, Marcy II, 450
Ackley, Martha II, 450
Ackley, Mary IV, 169
Ackley, Mary IV, 1245
Ackley, Mercy II, 830
Ackley, Mercy II, 883
Ackley, Mordecai II, 450
Ackley, Sarah II, 450
Ackley, Thomas II, 331
Ackley, Thomas II, 450
Ackley, Thomas, Jr. II, 450
Ackley, Walter IV, 1245
Ackley, Wd. Mary A. II, 799
Ackley, William II, 331
Acklin, Eleanor II, 331
Ackroyd, John II, 450
Acley, Elizabeth II, 450
Acley, Elizabeth II, 471
Acley, Thomas II, 450
Acley, Thomas II, 471
Acord, Ann VI, 467
Acord, Ann VI, 496
Acord, Elisha VI, 496
Acord, Elizabeth VI, 496
Acord, Martha VI, 496
Acorst, Daniel I, 93
Acre, David VI, 795
Acre, Rachel V, 317
Acre, Rachel V, 342
Acre, Rhoda VI, 795
Acre, Sarah Ann V, 217
Acree, Paulina P. VI, 869
Acree, Thomas O. VI, 869
Acres, Ann VI, 13
Acton, Benjamin II, 19
Acton, Benjamin II, 24
Acton, Benjamin II, 34
Acton, Benjamin II, 47
Acton, Benjamin II, 49
Acton, Benjamin II, 78
Acton, Benjamin II, 88
Acton, Benjamin II, 94
Acton, Benjamin II, 114
Acton, Benjamin II, 116
Acton, Benjamin II, 121
Acton, Benjamin II, 122
Acton, Benjamin II, 126
Acton, Benjamin II, 142
Acton, Benjamin II, 191
Acton, Benjamin II, 256
Acton, Benjamin II, 450
Acton, Benjamin II, 516
Acton, Benjamin, Jr. II, 114
Acton, Beulah II, 127
Acton, Beulah T. II, 142
Acton, Caspar W. II, 114
Acton, Caspar W. II, 127
Acton, Casper W. II, 19
Acton, Catharine II, 19
Acton, Charles L. II, 142
Acton, Charles Lindzey II, 127
Acton, Charlotte II, 19
Acton, Charlotte II, 47
Acton, Charlotte W. II, 114
Acton, Charlotte W. II, 126
Acton, Christiana II, 19
Acton, Clement II, 19
Acton, Clement II, 49
Acton, Clement II, 88
Acton, Clement II, 114
Acton, Clement II, 127
Acton, Clement II, 133
Acton, Clement II, 142
Acton, Clement II, 149
Acton, Clement II, 779
Acton, Clement II, 797
Acton, Clement B. II, 127
Acton, Clement B. II, 142
Acton, Clement James II, 19
Acton, Clement James II, 49
Acton, Clement Jas. II, 127
Acton, Clement, Jr. II, 114
Acton, Clement, Jr. II, 142
Acton, Elizabeth II, 19
Acton, Elizabeth II, 34
Acton, Elizabeth II, 49
Acton, Elizabeth II, 78
Acton, Elizabeth II, 94
Acton, Elizabeth II, 142
Acton, Elizabeth Jones II, 127
Acton, Elizabeth T. II, 127
Acton, Elizabeth W. II, 114
Acton, Elizabeth W. II, 121
Acton, Elizabeth Wyatt II, 19
Acton, Emma II, 127
Acton, Emma II, 142
Acton, Emma II, 159
Acton, Emma J. II, 127
Acton, Emma L. II, 136
Acton, Emma T. II, 142
Acton, Emma Thompson II, 154
Acton, Frank Miller II, 127
Acton, Frank Miller II, 142
Acton, George II, 114
Acton, George II, 127
Acton, George II, 142
Acton, George II, 154
Acton, Hannah II, 19
Acton, Hannah II, 49
Acton, Hannah II, 88
Acton, Hannah II, 112
Acton, Hannah II, 114
Acton, Hannah II, 116
Acton, Hannah II, 121
Acton, Hannah II, 127
Acton, Hannah II, 142
Acton, Hannah II, 149
Acton, Hannah II, 153
Acton, Hannah II, 779
Acton, Hannah II, 797
Acton, Hannah II, 830
Acton, Hannah H. II, 19
Acton, Hannah H. II, 114
Acton, Hannah Hall II, 24
Acton, Isaac II, 19
Acton, Isaac II, 49
Acton, Isaac II, 127
Acton, Isaac II, 142
Acton, John II, 19
Acton, John II, 49
Acton, John V, 214
Acton, Joseph II, 19
Acton, Joseph II, 49
Acton, Joseph VI, 869
Acton, Joshua II, 19
Acton, Leatitia II, 47
Acton, Leatitia M. II, 19
Acton, Leatitia M. II, 114
Acton, Leatitia M. II, 126
Acton, Lidia II, 19
Acton, Lucy II, 127
Acton, Lucy II, 142
Acton, Lucy II, 158
Acton, Lucy Ann II, 127
Acton, Margaret II, 49
Acton, Margaret II, 114
Acton, Margaret II, 118
Acton, Margaret II, 811
Acton, Margaret II, 869
Acton, Margaret II, 902
Acton, Margaret M. II, 142
Acton, Margaret M. II, 149
Acton, Margaret W. II, 127
Acton, Margaret Woodnutt II, 19
Acton, Margaret Woodnutt II, 797
Acton, Mary II, 19
Acton, Mary II, 49
Acton, Mary II, 90
Acton, Mary II, 111
Acton, Mary II, 114
Acton, Mary II, 115
Acton, Mary II, 127
Acton, Mary II, 128
Acton, Mary II, 135
Acton, Mary II, 136
Acton, Mary II, 142
Acton, Mary II, 143
Acton, Mary II, 191
Acton, Mary II, 256
Acton, Mary B. II, 49
Acton, Mary E. II, 142
Acton, Mary E. II, 161
Acton, Mary H. II, 127
Acton, Mary H. II, 142
Acton, Mary Jane II, 127
Acton, Mary Jane II, 142
Acton, Mary Jane II, 153
Acton, Mary T. II, 142
Acton, Mary Thompson II, 142
Acton, Mary Thompson II, 154
Acton, Morris G. II, 142
Acton, Morris G., Jr. II, 142
Acton, Morris Goodwin II, 127
Acton, Morris Goodwin, Jr. II, 127
Acton, Polly VI, 869
Acton, Rachel G. II, 127
Acton, Rebecca II, 49
Acton, Rebecca II, 57
Acton, Rebecca II, 114
Acton, Richard M. II, 19
Acton, Richard M. II, 114
Acton, Salem II, 256
Acton, Samuel II, 19
Acton, Samuel II, 49
Acton, Samuel II, 75
Acton, Samuel II, 114
Acton, Samuel II, 127
Acton, Samuel II, 128
Acton, Samuel II, 135
Acton, Samuel II, 142
Acton, Samuel II, 143
Acton, Samuel II, 153
Acton, Sarah II, 19
Acton, Sarah II, 24
Acton, Sarah II, 34
Acton, Sarah II, 47
Acton, Sarah II, 49
Acton, Sarah II, 75
Acton, Sarah II, 114
Acton, Sarah II, 116
Acton, Sarah II, 121
Acton, Sarah II, 126
Acton, Sarah II, 127
Acton, Sarah II, 128
Acton, Sarah II, 142
Acton, Sarah II, 143
Acton, Sarah III, 207
Acton, Sarah Hall II, 133
Acton, Sarah Hall II, 142
Acton, Sarah J. II, 133
Acton, Sarah J. II, 142
Acton, Sarah Jane II, 127
Acton, Sarah Jane II, 135
Acton, Sarah Jane II, 142
Acton, Sarah Jane II, 153
Acton, Sarah Jane III, 230
Acton, Sarah L. II, 142
Acton, Sarah U. II, 114
Acton, Sarah U. II, 122
Acton, Sarah W. II, 19
Acton, Sarah W. II, 126
Acton, Sarah Wyatt II, 19
Acton, Sarah Wyatt II, 37
Acton, Sarah Wyatt II, 49
Acton, Sarah Wyatt II, 88
Acton, Sarah Wyatt II, 114
Acton, Sarah Wyatt II, 122
Acton, Susannah II, 49
Acton, Susie L. V, 214
Acton, Susy Ann II, 142
Acton, Wm. H. II, 127
Acton, Wm. Hall II, 136
Acton, Wyatt II, 127
Adair, ??? VI, 869
Adair, Mary I, 869
Adair, Sabilla Ann V, 471
Adair, Sabilla Ann V, 527
Adair, William VI, 869
Adam, Polly VI, 989
Adam, Robert VI, 989
Adam, Sarah II, 49
Adam, Sarah II, 109
Adams, ??? II, 331
Adams, A. J. V, 149
Adams, Abbigail I, 980
Adams, Abbigail I, 984
Adams, Abel III, 15
Adams, Abel III, 50
Adams, Abel III, 173
Adams, Abel III, 245
Adams, Abi V, 19
Adams, Abigail II, 165
Adams, Abigail III, 15
Adams, Abigail III, 173
Adams, Abner V, 983
Adams, Abram VI, 869
Adams, Absalom V, 217
Adams, Absalom, Jr. V, 217
Adams, Achsa V, 547
Adams, Achsah V, 576
Adams, Achsia P. V, 217
Adams, Achsie P. V, 217
Adams, Adams VI, 811
Adams, Adelia II, 786
Adams, Aggatha I, 980
Adams, Aggatha I, 990
Adams, Agnes V, 825
Adams, Ailce I, 980
Adams, Alma V, 983
Adams, Amanda II, 847
Adams, Amanda M. II, 779
Adams, Amanda M. II, 830
Adams, Amanda M. II, 847
Adams, Amanda M. II, 878
Adams, Amos V, 19
Adams, Amos P. V, 19
Adams, Andrew W. II, 830
Adams, Andrew W. II, 841
Adams, Ann I, 370
Adams, Ann I, 413
Adams, Ann I, 796
Adams, Ann I, 959
Adams, Ann I, 973
Adams, Ann I, 980
Adams, Ann II, 331
Adams, Ann II, 450
Adams, Ann II, 501
Adams, Ann II, 974
Adams, Ann II, 1038
Adams, Ann IV, 169
Adams, Ann V, 19
Adams, Ann V, 217
Adams, Ann V, 317
Adams, Ann V, 338
Adams, Ann V, 825
Adams, Ann V, 879
Adams, Ann VI, 900
Adams, Ann E. VI, 913
Adams, Ann W. VI, 869
Adams, Anna I, 973
Adams, Anna III, 15
Adams, Anna B. V, 149
Adams, Anna C. III, 15
Adams, Anna May IV, 169
Adams, Anne I, 345
Adams, Anne I, 370
Adams, Anne I, 376
Adams, Anne VI, 285
Adams, Anneah VI, 967
Adams, Arksah V, 547
Adams, Arksah V, 584
Adams, Asa L. V, 217
Adams, Aseanith J. I, 973
Adams, Azariah V, 149
Adams, Azariah J. V, 149
Adams, Bartholomew V, 872
Adams, Bell IV, 1245
Adams, Bell V, 317
Adams, Bell V, 451
Adams, Belle IV, 1245
Adams, Belle V, 217
Adams, Belle V, 317
Adams, Benjamin II, 974
Adams, Benjamin II, 1038
Adams, Benjamin V, 19
Adams, Bertha V, 471
Adams, Bertha M. V, 609
Adams, Bertha N. V, 471
Adams, Bertha W. V, 609
Adams, Betsey III, 393
Adams, Betsey III, 450
Adams, Betsey VI, 869
Adams, Betsy Ann VI, 863
Adams, Betty V, 725
Adams, Betty V, 891
Adams, Beulah IV, 169
Adams, Beulah IV, 509
Adams, Blanch V, 825
Adams, Bridget V, 726
Adams, Bulah IV, 169
Adams, C. L. VI, 806
Adams, Caroline I, 973
Adams, Caroline VI, 795
Adams, Catharine II, 127
Adams, Catharine II, 779
Adams, Catherine V, 217
Adams, Catherine H. VI, 817
Adams, Charity I, 796
Adams, Charity I, 819
Adams, Charity V, 19
Adams, Charity V, 96
Adams, Charles II, 127
Adams, Charles II, 142
Adams, Charles II, 830
Adams, Charles III, 15
Adams, Charles IV, 1233
Adams, Charles V, 19
Adams, Charles V, 217
Adams, Charles V, 825
Adams, Charles William V, 825
Adams, Charles, Jr. II, 142
Adams, Chas. II, 830
Adams, Chas. II, 878
Adams, Christian II, 331
Adams, Clara W. III, 15
Adams, Cora IV, 671
Adams, Cora V, 217
Adams, Cora A. V, 825
Adams, Cora Ann V, 825
Adams, Daniel I, 973
Adams, Daniel I, 980
Adams, David III, 15
Adams, David V, 19
Adams, David VI, 361
Adams, David VI, 795
Adams, David M. III, 286
Adams, David M. V, 655
Adams, David Paul III, 15
Adams, Deborah III, 15
Adams, Dora III, 409
Adams, Dorath I, 980
Adams, Dorath I, 987
Adams, Dorcas III, 15
Adams, Dorcas III, 173
Adams, Dr. John VI, 153
Adams, Dr. John VI, 218
Adams, Earl V, 149
Adams, Ebanezar I, 973
Adams, Ebanezar I, 980
Adams, Ebanezar I, 984
Adams, Ebenezar I, 973
Adams, Ebenezer I, 980
Adams, Edith IV, 169
Adams, Edith V, 217
Adams, Edith V, 280
Adams, Edith VI, 361
Adams, Edith S. V, 471
Adams, Edward IV, 565
Adams, Edward IV, 601
Adams, Edward IV, 1087
Adams, Edward V, 655
Adams, Edward G. IV, 363
Adams, Edward G. IV, 447
Adams, Edward G. IV, 565
Adams, Effie V, 609
Adams, Effie J. V, 471
Adams, Effie J. V, 655
Adams, Elen I, 980
Adams, Eli II, 127
Adams, Eli II, 142
Adams, Eli II, 779
Adams, Eli II, 830
Adams, Eli Adams, Jr. II, 142
Adams, Eli, Jr. II, 127
Adams, Eli, Jr. II, 830
Adams, Elias V, 217
Adams, Elias H. V, 217
Adams, Elias, Jr. V, 217
Adams, Elisabeth II, 165
Adams, Elisha VI, 869
Adams, Eliza II, 127
Adams, Eliza II, 142
Adams, Eliza II, 830
Adams, Eliza III, 15
Adams, Eliza V, 217
Adams, Eliza VI, 1021
Adams, Eliza H. III, 308
Adams, Eliza J. V, 317
Adams, Eliza Jane IV, 560
Adams, Eliza P. VI, 970

Adams, Elizabeth I, 973
Adams, Elizabeth I, 980
Adams, Elizabeth I, 998
Adams, Elizabeth III, 15
Adams, Elizabeth IV, 169
Adams, Elizabeth IV, 560
Adams, Elizabeth IV, 565
Adams, Elizabeth IV, 1201
Adams, Elizabeth V, 80
Adams, Elizabeth V, 655
Adams, Elizabeth V, 825
Adams, Elizabeth V, 872
Adams, Elizabeth V, 879
Adams, Elizabeth V, 882
Adams, Elizabeth V, 891
Adams, Elizabeth V, 934
Adams, Elizabeth VI, 795
Adams, Elizabeth VI, 810
Adams, Elizabeth VI, 847
Adams, Elizabeth VI, 864
Adams, Elizabeth VI, 869
Adams, Elizabeth VI, 915
Adams, Elizabeth VI, 937
Adams, Elizabeth VI, 979
Adams, Elizabeth L. II, 830
Adams, Elizabeth L. II, 841
Adams, Elizabeth Martha I, 973
Adams, Elizabeth S. II, 1068
Adams, Elizabeth S. III, 15
Adams, Elizabeth W. II, 1068
Adams, Ellen I, 976
Adams, Ellen I, 980
Adams, Ellen I, 987
Adams, Ellsworth IV, 169
Adams, Elma V, 983
Adams, Elmira IV, 1305
Adams, Elnor IV, 363
Adams, Elnora IV, 410
Adams, Elsworth IV, 169
Adams, Elvira IV, 1305
Adams, Emma III, 15
Adams, Emma III, 286
Adams, Emma Frances III, 15
Adams, Ephraim II, 974
Adams, Ester I, 980
Adams, Esther VI, 869
Adams, Ethel V, 149
Adams, Eunice III, 15
Adams, Eunice III, 150
Adams, Eunice V, 471
Adams, Eustacia III, 15
Adams, Eustatia II, 830
Adams, Eustatia III, 15
Adams, Eva IV, 1305
Adams, Ezra V, 19
Adams, Fam V, 19
Adams, Fanna I, 980
Adams, Fannie V, 655
Adams, Fatama I, 980
Adams, Flora V, 217
Adams, Flora V, 371
Adams, Florence N. II, 830
Adams, Frances VI, 859
Adams, Frances VI, 869
Adams, Francis VI, 818
Adams, Francis Marion V, 217
Adams, Frank M. V, 217
Adams, Franklin II, 1068
Adams, Franklyn M. V, 217
Adams, Franky VI, 869
Adams, G. Adams VI, 817
Adams, George I, 345
Adams, George I, 796
Adams, George I, 971
Adams, George I, 980
Adams, George II, 1068
Adams, George W. II, 1068
Adams, Gerta B. V, 451
Adams, Glenna M. V, 655
Adams, Grief VI, 981
Adams, Grief R. VI, 869
Adams, Hannah I, 973
Adams, Hannah III, 15
Adams, Hannah III, 50
Adams, Hannah III, 245
Adams, Hannah IV, 73
Adams, Hannah IV, 112
Adams, Hannah IV, 565
Adams, Hannah IV, 568
Adams, Hannah IV, 1087
Adams, Hannah V, 217
Adams, Hannah V, 725
Adams, Hannah VI, 361
Adams, Hannah VI, 386
Adams, Hannah VI, 398
Adams, Hannah VI, 430
Adams, Hannah C. III, 286
Adams, Harley V, 471
Adams, Harriet IV, 363
Adams, Harriet IV, 447
Adams, Harriet C. III, 15
Adams, Harriet C. III, 16
Adams, Harriett IV, 565
Adams, Harvy I, 980
Adams, Hattie V, 983
Adams, Helen III, 15
Adams, Henrietta IV, 169
Adams, Henrietta IV, 565
Adams, Henrietta IV, 1087
Adams, Henry VI, 361
Adams, Henry VI, 869
Adams, Henry VI, 891
Adams, Henry VI, 918
Adams, Henry C. III, 15
Adams, Henry Graham III, 15
Adams, Henry S. V, 217
Adams, Hetty IV, 1233
Adams, Hezakiah I, 973
Adams, Hilda Gray I, 611
Adams, Hilda Gray I, 629
Adams, Ira IV, 565
Adams, Ira L. IV, 565
Adams, Isaac V, 19
Adams, Isaac V, 217
Adams, Isaac V, 445
Adams, Isaac VI, 361
Adams, Isaac VI, 803
Adams, J. C. VI, 869
Adams, J. Clinton V, 655
Adams, J. M. V, 317
Adams, Jacob III, 393
Adams, Jacob III, 450
Adams, Jacob V, 879
Adams, James I, 345
Adams, James II, 331
Adams, James III, 15
Adams, James VI, 795
Adams, James VI, 810
Adams, James VI, 848
Adams, James VI, 869
Adams, James VI, 913
Adams, James VI, 938
Adams, James VI, 952
Adams, James VI, 954
Adams, James VI, 1001
Adams, James VI, 1012
Adams, James C. III, 15
Adams, James C. III, 16
Adams, James D. I, 611
Adams, James G. VI, 811
Adams, James Randolph I, 611
Adams, James Randolph I, 629
Adams, Jane I, 347
Adams, Jane I, 370
Adams, Jane I, 375
Adams, Jane I, 796
Adams, Jane I, 973
Adams, Jane II, 450
Adams, Jane II, 555
Adams, Jane II, 974
Adams, Jane VI, 891
Adams, Janny Alice I, 980
Adams, Janny Alice I, 998
Adams, Jason V, 19
Adams, Jean I, 345
Adams, Jearden I, 973
Adams, Jeddediah II, 191
Adams, Jeddiah V, 19
Adams, Jedediah II, 191
Adams, Jedediah II, 974
Adams, Jedediah V, 879
Adams, Jediah V, 825
Adams, Jedidiah II, 191
Adams, Jedidiah V, 825
Adams, Jennie V, 655
Adams, Jenny VI, 869
Adams, Jeremiah V, 217
Adams, Jeremiah VI, 886
Adams, Jeremiah VI, 1021
Adams, Jeremiah N. VI, 1021
Adams, Jesse I, 980
Adams, Jesse V, 19
Adams, Jesse VI, 795
Adams, Jesse VI, 818
Adams, Jesse W. V, 217
Adams, Jessie V, 983
Adams, Jinny Alice I, 980
Adams, Joan III, 16
Adams, Joan III, 72
Adams, Joane III, 15
Adams, Joel I, 959
Adams, Joel I, 961
Adams, Joel I, 973
Adams, Joel I, 980
Adams, Joel V, 879
Adams, Joel L. VI, 903
Adams, Joel L. VI, 938
Adams, Joel T. VI, 795
Adams, Joel T. VI, 873
Adams, Joel T. VI, 874
Adams, Joel T. VI, 897
Adams, Joel T. VI, 918
Adams, Joel T. VI, 941
Adams, Joel T. VI, 996
Adams, John I, 345
Adams, John I, 796
Adams, John I, 973
Adams, John I, 980
Adams, John II, 19
Adams, John II, 165
Adams, John II, 191
Adams, John II, 201
Adams, John III, 15
Adams, John III, 16
Adams, John III, 72
Adams, John IV, 565
Adams, John IV, 1127
Adams, John V, 19
Adams, John V, 217
Adams, John VI, 361
Adams, John VI, 430
Adams, John VI, 795
Adams, John VI, 800
Adams, John VI, 801
Adams, John VI, 806
Adams, John VI, 853
Adams, John VI, 949
Adams, John VI, 962
Adams, John VI, 1012
Adams, John B. IV, 1271
Adams, John G. R. James VI, 949
Adams, John H. V, 451
Adams, John L. III, 16
Adams, John L. III, 94
Adams, John M. VI, 757
Adams, John Q. VI, 859
Adams, John T. IV, 565
Adams, John T. IV, 578
Adams, John T. IV, 1087
Adams, John T. IV, 1143
Adams, John Till II, 450
Adams, John W. II, 1068
Adams, John, Jr. VI, 361
Adams, John, Jr. VI, 800
Adams, John, Jr. VI, 996
Adams, John, Sr. VI, 361
Adams, Johnny H. V, 451
Adams, Jonathan I, 345
Adams, Jonathan I, 370
Adams, Jonathan I, 376
Adams, Jonathan I, 796
Adams, Jonathan I, 959
Adams, Jonathan I, 973
Adams, Jonathan I, 980
Adams, Jonathan I, 1070
Adams, Jonathan V, 217
Adams, Jonathan V, 879
Adams, Jonathan VI, 361
Adams, Jonathan Jacob William V, 825
Adams, Jonathan, Jr. I, 980
Adams, Joseph II, 191
Adams, Joseph II, 239
Adams, Joseph V, 217
Adams, Joseph V, 445
Adams, Joseph V, 471
Adams, Joseph VI, 361
Adams, Josephine P. III, 15
Adams, Josephine Parker III, 15
Adams, Judediah, Jr. II, 974
Adams, Judith I, 980
Adams, Judith I, 998
Adams, Jurah VI, 795
Adams, Kate IV, 169
Adams, Katharine I, 345
Adams, Katie V, 217
Adams, Kezia II, 450
Adams, Kezia II, 631
Adams, Keziah II, 191
Adams, Keziah II, 450
Adams, Keziah VI, 1004
Adams, L. VI, 858
Adams, L. B. IV, 1305
Adams, Laomi V, 317
Adams, Lena V, 149
Adams, Levi V, 983
Adams, Lewis II, 127
Adams, Lewis II, 142
Adams, Lewis II, 830
Adams, Lewis III, 16
Adams, Lewis IV, 1143
Adams, Liddy VI, 869
Adams, Lidia VI, 361
Adams, Lirenna D. V, 471
Adams, Lizzie IV, 1201
Adams, Lizzie S. IV, 169
Adams, Lizzie S. IV, 191
Adams, Loami A. V, 317
Adams, Lorena D. V, 609
Adams, Lorenna D. V, 609
Adams, Loretta IV, 1233
Adams, Louis P. II, 779
Adams, Louisa V, 317
Adams, Louisa Jane IV, 639
Adams, Louisa W. VI, 915
Adams, Louretta IV, 1201
Adams, Lowell V, 655
Adams, Lucinda I, 973
Adams, Lucy VI, 869
Adams, Lucy VI, 903
Adams, Ludia I, 980
Adams, Luzena I, 980
Adams, Lydia I, 983
Adams, Lydia IV, 319
Adams, Lydia IV, 363
Adams, Lydia IV, 565
Adams, Lydia IV, 568
Adams, Lydia V, 19
Adams, Lydia VI, 361
Adams, Lydia VI, 421
Adams, Lydia VI, 430
Adams, Lydia J. IV, 424
Adams, Lynch VI, 795
Adams, Lynch VI, 864
Adams, Maggie V, 655
Adams, Maggie Beatrice I, 611
Adams, Maggie Beatrice I, 629
Adams, Maggie White I, 629
Adams, Mahala V, 217
Adams, Mahlon I, 973
Adams, Malinda T. VI, 869
Adams, Marcey III, 15
Adams, Margaret I, 345
Adams, Margaret I, 980
Adams, Margaret II, 331
Adams, Margaret IV, 565
Adams, Margaret IV, 601
Adams, Margaret V, 983
Adams, Margaret VI, 869
Adams, Margaret T. IV, 1143
Adams, Margaret W. II, 1068
Adams, Margret I, 796
Adams, Maria II, 127
Adams, Maria II, 142
Adams, Maria II, 146
Adams, Maria II, 830
Adams, Marian H. III, 16
Adams, Marian H. III, 308
Adams, Marion H. III, 16
Adams, Marjorie VI, 757
Adams, Marl. III, 15
Adams, Marlboro III, 15
Adams, Martha II, 974
Adams, Martha III, 15
Adams, Martha VI, 937
Adams, Martha Ann VI, 920
Adams, Martia I, 973
Adams, Mary I, 345
Adams, Mary I, 347
Adams, Mary I, 370
Adams, Mary I, 375
Adams, Mary I, 796
Adams, Mary I, 826
Adams, Mary I, 865
Adams, Mary I, 973
Adams, Mary I, 980
Adams, Mary II, 49
Adams, Mary II, 107
Adams, Mary II, 142
Adams, Mary II, 331
Adams, Mary II, 471
Adams, Mary II, 830
Adams, Mary II, 841
Adams, Mary II, 974
Adams, Mary II, 1038
Adams, Mary III, 15
Adams, Mary IV, 169
Adams, Mary V, 217
Adams, Mary V, 872
Adams, Mary VI, 260
Adams, Mary VI, 361
Adams, Mary VI, 401
Adams, Mary VI, 461
Adams, Mary VI, 795
Adams, Mary VI, 869
Adams, Mary A. IV, 565
Adams, Mary A. VI, 811
Adams, Mary Ann I, 980
Adams, Mary Ann V, 19
Adams, Mary Ann V, 983
Adams, Mary B. VI, 948
Adams, Mary E. V, 149
Adams, Mary J. V, 471
Adams, Mary J. V, 609
Adams, Mary Jane III, 16
Adams, Mary Jane III, 94
Adams, Mary Jane V, 217
Adams, Mary Jane V, 471
Adams, Mary L. V, 19
Adams, Mary L. V, 34
Adams, Mary L. V, 655
Adams, Mary L. C. V, 655
Adams, Mary M. V, 19
Adams, Mary P. II, 142
Adams, Mary Prudence II, 127
Adams, Mary Susan III, 16
Adams, Mary Susannah III, 15
Adams, Maryann V, 19
Adams, Matilda V, 825
Adams, Matilda V, 879
Adams, Matilda C. VI, 795
Adams, Mattie V, 983
Adams, Maud IV, 169
Adams, Mellescent V, 547
Adams, Mercy II, 191
Adams, Michael V, 217
Adams, Mildred VI, 938
Adams, Milkijah VI, 869
Adams, Millesant I, 980
Adams, Millicent I, 980
Adams, Millicent V, 19
Adams, Milly V, 471
Adams, Minny VI, 869
Adams, Moses I, 345
Adams, Moses I, 796
Adams, Mourning VI, 260
Adams, Mourning VI, 954
Adams, Nancy III, 393
Adams, Nancy III, 450
Adams, Nancy VI, 795
Adams, Nancy VI, 853
Adams, Nancy VI, 979
Adams, Nathan IV, 565
Adams, Nathan IV, 1127
Adams, Nathan VI, 853
Adams, Nathan C. IV, 565
Adams, Nathan M. I, 973
Adams, Nathaniel VI, 869
Adams, Nathaniel VI, 970
Adams, Nellie Lorea IV, 169
Adams, Neziah I, 973
Adams, Opha V, 317
Adams, Otho V, 217
Adams, Ova IV, 1201
Adams, Patience IV, 565
Adams, Patience IV, 578
Adams, Patience IV, 1087
Adams, Patience IV, 1127
Adams, Patsey Arnold VI, 795
Adams, Patsy VI, 847
Adams, Patsy VI, 869
Adams, Peggy VI, 949
Adams, Peggy Gregory VI, 795
Adams, Penelope VI, 858
Adams, Penelope VI, 991
Adams, Perthena VI, 800
Adams, Perthina VI, 801
Adams, Peter VI, 153
Adams, Peter VI, 161
Adams, Peter VI, 757
Adams, Phebe II, 191
Adams, Phebe II, 201
Adams, Phebe III, 16
Adams, Phebe V, 217
Adams, Phebe VI, 361
Adams, Phebe VI, 368
Adams, Phebe VI, 869
Adams, Phebe VI, 988
Adams, Pheeby II, 191
Adams, Phillip VI, 869
Adams, Polly VI, 902
Adams, Polly VI, 967
Adams, President John Quincy VI, 727
Adams, Prudence II, 779
Adams, Prudence II, 830
Adams, Prudence II, 878
Adams, Prudence V, 19
Adams, Rachel I, 345
Adams, Rachel I, 361
Adams, Rachel I, 370
Adams, Rachel I, 409
Adams, Rachel I, 959
Adams, Rachel I, 961
Adams, Rachel I, 973
Adams, Rachel I, 980
Adams, Rachel I, 982
Adams, Rachel I, 990
Adams, Rachel II, 191
Adams, Rachel IV, 169
Adams, Rachel IV, 565
Adams, Rachel IV, 597
Adams, Rachel IV, 1087
Adams, Rachel IV, 1127
Adams, Rachel V, 19
Adams, Rachel V, 217
Adams, Rachel V, 825
Adams, Rachel V, 879
Adams, Rachel VI, 361
Adams, Rachel VI, 399
Adams, Rachel Abigail I, 755
Adams, Rebecca I, 973
Adams, Rebecca I, 980
Adams, Rebecca II, 974
Adams, Rebecca III, 15

Adams, Rebecca V, 19
Adams, Rebecca VI, 859
Adams, Rebecca VI, 869
Adams, Rebecca Ann IV, 363
Adams, Rebecca Ann IV, 439
Adams, Rebeckah I, 980
Adams, Rebeckah I, 984
Adams, Rebekah III, 16
Adams, Rebekah III, 72
Adams, Rhoda Jane I, 973
Adams, Richard II, 450
Adams, Richard VI, 869
Adams, Richard E. VI, 817
Adams, Robert II, 331
Adams, Robert II, 441
Adams, Robert II, 450
Adams, Robert II, 501
Adams, Robert VI, 260
Adams, Robert VI, 852
Adams, Robert VI, 991
Adams, Robert, Jr. VI, 823
Adams, Robt. VI, 952
Adams, Robt. VI, 954
Adams, Rosa V, 217
Adams, Rosa B. V, 471
Adams, Rosa B. V, 609
Adams, Rosa E. V, 609
Adams, Ruetty V, 825
Adams, Ruth II, 331
Adams, Ruth II, 450
Adams, Ruth II, 974
Adams, Ruth IV, 169
Adams, Ruth IV, 605
Adams, Ruth IV, 648
Adams, Ruth V, 19
Adams, Ruth V, 825
Adams, Ruth V, 879
Adams, Ruth VI, 361
Adams, Ruth VI, 417
Adams, S??? II, 331
Adams, Sally I, 980
Adams, Sally I, 993
Adams, Sally VI, 795
Adams, Sally VI, 952
Adams, Sally Arnold VI, 795
Adams, Samuel II, 331
Adams, Samuel II, 450
Adams, Samuel II, 555
Adams, Samuel II, 974
Adams, Samuel III, 15
Adams, Samuel V, 879
Adams, Samuel VI, 795
Adams, Samuel VI, 869
Adams, Samuel VI, 920
Adams, Samuel VI, 937
Adams, Samuel VI, 948
Adams, Samuel C. V, 879
Adams, Samuel Cary V, 825
Adams, Samuel, Jr. VI, 869
Adams, Sarah I, 345
Adams, Sarah I, 796
Adams, Sarah I, 973
Adams, Sarah I, 980
Adams, Sarah I, 986
Adams, Sarah I, 990
Adams, Sarah II, 19
Adams, Sarah II, 29
Adams, Sarah II, 49
Adams, Sarah II, 57
Adams, Sarah II, 73
Adams, Sarah II, 450
Adams, Sarah III, 15
Adams, Sarah III, 16
Adams, Sarah III, 89
Adams, Sarah IV, 1127
Adams, Sarah V, 19
Adams, Sarah V, 655
Adams, Sarah VI, 361
Adams, Sarah VI, 389
Adams, Sarah VI, 900
Adams, Sarah VI, 918
Adams, Sarah VI, 949
Adams, Sarah Ann V, 217
Adams, Sarah B. V, 19
Adams, Sarah E. V, 90
Adams, Sarah E. V, 217
Adams, Sarah K. V, 891
Adams, Sarah R. V, 111
Adams, Sarrah I, 980
Adams, Sarrah I, 989
Adams, Savory V, 19
Adams, Seamary II, 450
Adams, Seamercy II, 471
Adams, See Merry II, 450
Adams, Seemercy II, 974
Adams, Seemerrie II, 450
Adams, Seemerrie II, 471
Adams, Seneth I, 973
Adams, Sidney L. IV, 1143
Adams, Simon V, 825
Adams, Siner VI, 1012
Adams, Solomon V, 825
Adams, Solomon VI, 361
Adams, Solomon W. V, 879
Adams, Stella V, 19
Adams, Susana I, 971
Adams, Susana I, 973
Adams, Susanna I, 345
Adams, Susanna I, 361
Adams, Susanna I, 370
Adams, Susanna I, 796
Adams, Susanna I, 973
Adams, Susanna V, 471
Adams, Susanna V, 609
Adams, Susanna V, 655
Adams, Susanna V, 696
Adams, Susanna VI, 361
Adams, Susanna VI, 795
Adams, Susannah I, 345
Adams, Susannah I, 347
Adams, Susannah I, 980
Adams, Susannah I, 991
Adams, Susannah II, 19
Adams, Susannah II, 29
Adams, Susannah II, 49
Adams, Susannah II, 73
Adams, Susannah III, 15
Adams, Susannah VI, 361
Adams, Susannah VI, 806
Adams, Sydney IV, 1143
Adams, Theodosia II, 19
Adams, Theodosia II, 49
Adams, Thomas I, 973
Adams, Thomas II, 331
Adams, Thomas II, 974
Adams, Thomas II, 1038
Adams, Thomas IV, 169
Adams, Thomas IV, 363
Adams, Thomas IV, 565
Adams, Thomas IV, 568
Adams, Thomas V, 19
Adams, Thomas V, 825
Adams, Thomas V, 879
Adams, Thomas VI, 361
Adams, Thomas VI, 795
Adams, Thomas VI, 869
Adams, Thomas VI, 1003
Adams, Thomas A. VI, 863
Adams, Thomas F. VI, 827
Adams, Thomas H. VI, 847
Adams, Thos G. VI, 795
Adams, Thos. V, 725
Adams, Thos. VI, 795
Adams, Thos. T. VI, 795
Adams, Uny VI, 878
Adams, Valentine V, 217
Adams, Vincent I, 980
Adams, Virgil IV, 1201
Adams, Walter J. III, 15
Adams, Walter J. III, 16
Adams, Wd. Hannah T. III, 15
Adams, Wd. Mary II, 191
Adams, Wd. Mary II, 239
Adams, Wd. Mary II, 450
Adams, William I, 345
Adams, William I, 370
Adams, William I, 796
Adams, William I, 971
Adams, William I, 973
Adams, William I, 980
Adams, William I, 982
Adams, William I, 1070
Adams, William III, 16
Adams, William IV, 169
Adams, William IV, 560
Adams, William V, 19
Adams, William V, 471
Adams, William V, 825
Adams, William V, 879
Adams, William VI, 361
Adams, William VI, 421
Adams, William VI, 795
Adams, William VI, 833
Adams, William VI, 869
Adams, William VI, 878
Adams, William VI, 900
Adams, William VI, 915
Adams, William VI, 937
Adams, William VI, 940
Adams, William Clark III, 16
Adams, William G. IV, 565
Adams, William, Jr. I, 980
Adams, William, Jr. VI, 869
Adams, William, Jr. VI, 970
Adams, William, Sr. I, 973
Adams, Wilmouth VI, 869
Adams, Wilson V, 217
Adams, Wilson V, 471
Adams, Wilson V, 609
Adams, Wilson V, 655
Adams, Wilson A. VI, 869
Adams, Wilson S. V, 609
Adams, Winney VI, 1003
Adams, Wm II, 779
Adams, Wm. I, 345
Adams, Wm. I, 347
Adams, Wm. I, 361
Adams, Wm. I, 370
Adams, Wm. II, 19
Adams, Wm. II, 29
Adams, Wm. II, 49
Adams, Wm. II, 73
Adams, Wm. II, 142
Adams, Wm. II, 450
Adams, Wm. II, 830
Adams, Wm. II, 878
Adams, Wm. III, 15
Adams, Wm. V, 547
Adams, Wm. V, 879
Adams, Wm. Clark III, 16
Adams, Wm. Clark III, 308
Adams, Wm. G. IV, 565
Adams, Wm. G. IV, 1087
Adams, Wm. J. II, 830
Adams, Wm. J. II, 841
Adams, Wm. Kinsey II, 779
Adams, Wm., Jr. II, 127
Adams, Wm., Jr. II, 142
Adams, Zacharah I, 973
Adams, Zachariah I, 980
Adams, Zachry I, 980
Adams, Zephaniah V, 217
Adams, Zimri I, 973
Adamson, Abraham I, 1103
Adamson, Abraham I, 1113
Adamson, Abraham I, 1147
Adamson, Abram I, 1113
Adamson, Abram I, 1147
Adamson, Adam I, 1113
Adamson, Adam I, 1147
Adamson, Alex VI, 729
Adamson, Alice I, 1113
Adamson, Amos II, 779
Adamson, Amy J. IV, 921
Adamson, Amy J. IV, 998
Adamson, Amy Jane IV, 921
Adamson, Ann I, 755
Adamson, Anna Mary IV, 921
Adamson, Benjamin I, 1113
Adamson, Benjamin I, 1147
Adamson, Benjamin IV, 921
Adamson, Charity I, 755
Adamson, Charity I, 796
Adamson, Charlotty I, 755
Adamson, Eleanor I, 1113
Adamson, Eleanor I, 1123
Adamson, Elizabeth I, 1113
Adamson, Elizabeth IV, 605
Adamson, Elizabeth IV, 639
Adamson, Elizabeth IV, 666
Adamson, Elizabeth IV, 918
Adamson, Elizabeth IV, 921
Adamson, Elizabeth Ann IV, 921
Adamson, Elizabeth Rebecca IV, 921
Adamson, Ellis IV, 605
Adamson, Ellis IV, 921
Adamson, Emond I, 1113
Adamson, Enos I, 1103
Adamson, Enos I, 1113
Adamson, Enos I, 1147
Adamson, Erwin IV, 605
Adamson, Esther IV, 605
Adamson, Esther IV, 666
Adamson, Evan I, 1113
Adamson, Evans I, 1147
Adamson, Franklin C. VI, 729
Adamson, George I, 127
Adamson, George I, 163
Adamson, Hannah II, 779
Adamson, Hannah II, 830
Adamson, Hannah IV, 19
Adamson, Hannah IV, 38
Adamson, Hannah IV, 605
Adamson, Hannah IV, 630
Adamson, Hannah IV, 666
Adamson, Hannah IV, 918
Adamson, Hannah IV, 921
Adamson, Hannah VI, 729
Adamson, Hannah Ann IV, 921
Adamson, Henry I, 1147
Adamson, Huldah I, 1139
Adamson, Ira I, 1113
Adamson, Isaac I, 1103
Adamson, Isaac I, 1113
Adamson, Isaac I, 1147
Adamson, Ivy I, 1113
Adamson, Jacob I, 1139
Adamson, James IV, 19
Adamson, James IV, 605
Adamson, James IV, 630
Adamson, James IV, 666
Adamson, James IV, 918
Adamson, James IV, 921
Adamson, James VI, 361
Adamson, James H. IV, 605
Adamson, Jane IV, 921
Adamson, Jane IV, 967
Adamson, Jane VI, 729
Adamson, Jane H. IV, 921
Adamson, Jesse I, 796
Adamson, Jesse I, 1089
Adamson, Jesse I, 1101
Adamson, Jesse I, 1113
Adamson, Jesse T. I, 796
Adamson, John I, 755
Adamson, John I, 796
Adamson, John I, 1089
Adamson, John I, 1103
Adamson, John I, 1113
Adamson, John I, 1139
Adamson, John I, 1147
Adamson, John IV, 605
Adamson, John IV, 623
Adamson, John IV, 921
Adamson, John W. IV, 605
Adamson, John W. IV, 918
Adamson, John W. IV, 921
Adamson, John W. IV, 1010
Adamson, Joseph I, 796
Adamson, Joseph I, 1089
Adamson, Joseph I, 1113
Adamson, Joseph II, 779
Adamson, Joseph IV, 605
Adamson, Joseph IV, 921
Adamson, Joseph L. II, 830
Adamson, Joseph L. VI, 729
Adamson, Joseph L., Jr. VI, 729
Adamson, Lewis I, 1147
Adamson, Lydia IV, 605
Adamson, Lydia IV, 921
Adamson, Lydia Ann IV, 921
Adamson, Lydia Ann IV, 939
Adamson, Lydia V. IV, 921
Adamson, Malvina IV, 921
Adamson, Margaret I, 1113
Adamson, Margaret I, 1130
Adamson, Margaret IV, 19
Adamson, Margaret IV, 59
Adamson, Margret I, 796
Adamson, Marietta IV, 921
Adamson, Martha IV, 921
Adamson, Martha IV, 1010
Adamson, Mary I, 127
Adamson, Mary I, 163
Adamson, Mary I, 370
Adamson, Mary I, 393
Adamson, Mary I, 427
Adamson, Mary I, 673
Adamson, Mary I, 755
Adamson, Mary I, 796
Adamson, Mary I, 1103
Adamson, Mary I, 1113
Adamson, Mary I, 1139
Adamson, Mary I, 1147
Adamson, Mary I, 1155
Adamson, Mary IV, 605
Adamson, Mary IV, 921
Adamson, Mary VI, 361
Adamson, Melvina IV, 921
Adamson, Mordecai I, 1103
Adamson, Mordecai I, 1113
Adamson, Mordecai I, 1147
Adamson, Nancy I, 1113
Adamson, Nathan IV, 605
Adamson, Nathan IV, 921
Adamson, Nathan IV, 998
Adamson, Nathaniel I, 755
Adamson, Nellie I, 1113
Adamson, Nelly I, 1103
Adamson, Obadiah I, 1139
Adamson, Rachel I, 1113
Adamson, Rebecca II, 779
Adamson, Rebecca IV, 605
Adamson, Rebecca IV, 630
Adamson, Rebecca IV, 918
Adamson, Rebecca IV, 921
Adamson, Rebecca IV, 1016
Adamson, Ruth I, 1113
Adamson, Ruth IV, 605
Adamson, Ruth IV, 630
Adamson, Samuel IV, 605
Adamson, Samuel IV, 921
Adamson, Samuel IV, 939
Adamson, Samuel E. IV, 605
Adamson, Sarah IV, 605
Adamson, Sarah IV, 623
Adamson, Sarah VI, 361
Adamson, Sarah VI, 366
Adamson, Sarah Ann IV, 605
Adamson, Seth I, 1103
Adamson, Seth I, 1113
Adamson, Seth I, 1139
Adamson, Seth I, 1147
Adamson, Seth I, 1155
Adamson, Simon I, 755
Adamson, Simon Wells I, 1089
Adamson, Simon, Jr. I, 1113
Adamson, Simon, Sr. I, 1113
Adamson, Solomon I, 1103
Adamson, Solomon I, 1113
Adamson, Solomon I, 1147
Adamson, Susanna I, 1113
Adamson, Susanna V, 217
Adamson, Susannah I, 1103
Adamson, Susannah I, 1113
Adamson, Susannah IV, 605
Adamson, Susannah IV, 654
Adamson, Susannah V, 217
Adamson, Tage VI, 729
Adamson, Telitha I, 755
Adamson, Thomas IV, 605
Adamson, Thomas IV, 666
Adamson, Thomas IV, 918
Adamson, Thomas IV, 921
Adamson, Thomas VI, 361
Adamson, Thos. IV, 605
Adamson, William I, 1089
Adamson, William I, 1113
Adamson, William I, 1147
Adamson, William III, 16
Adamson, William IV, 605
Adamson, William Lindley IV, 921
Adamson, Wm. IV, 605
Adamson, Wm. Lindley IV, 921
Adamson, Zibeah I, 1113
Adan, Ariadny I, 976
Aday, Josiah VI, 869
Aday, Martha VI, 869
Adbert, Beulah IV, 19
Adbert, Beulah IV, 28
Adcock, Delilah I, 370
Adcock, Delilah I, 410
Adcock, Hannah I, 443
Adcock, Hannah I, 447
Adcock, John I, 370
Adcock, Lula M. I, 370
Adcock, Martha I, 370
Adcock, Rachel I, 370
Adcock, Rachel I, 410
Adcock, Stephen I, 370
Adcock, T. M. I, 370
Adcock, Willis J. I, 370
Addams, Ann V, 19
Addams, Beede I, 1067
Addams, Elizabeth VI, 872
Addams, Hannah I, 1067
Addams, James VI, 1007
Addams, John I, 1067
Addams, John II, 191
Addams, John II, 203
Addams, John VI, 872
Addams, Jonathan I, 1067
Addams, Jonathan I, 1070
Addams, Maria II, 830
Addams, Maria II, 835
Addams, Mary I, 1067
Addams, Mary II, 49
Addams, Mary II, 107
Addams, Mary II, 331
Addams, Mercy II, 191
Addams, Peter VI, 153
Addams, Peter VI, 201
Addams, Rachel II, 191
Addams, Rachel II, 203
Addams, Ruth II, 331
Addams, Ruth V, 19
Addams, S??? II, 331
Addams, Samuel II, 331
Addams, Samuel VI, 1012
Addams, Thomas II, 331
Addams, Thomas V, 19
Addams, William I, 1066
Addams, William I, 1067
Addams, William I, 1070
Addenton, Elizabeth I, 1026
Addenton, Elizabeth I, 1031
Addenton, Henry I, 1026
Addenton, John I, 1026
Addenton, John I, 1031
Addenton, Sarah I, 1026
Addington, ??? V, 149
Addington, Alice I, 1017
Addington, Ayner J. V, 371
Addington, Elizabeth I, 1017
Addington, Elizabeth I, 1026
Addington, Elizabeth I, 1060
Addington, Elizabeth I, 1062
Addington, Elizabeth V, 19
Addington, Elizabeth V, 725
Addington, Else I, 1060
Addington, Else I, 1061
Addington, Elsie A. IV, 1305
Addington, Esther I. IV, 1305

Addington, Esther J. IV, 1305
Addington, Henry I, 1026
Addington, Henry I, 1055
Addington, Henry V, 149
Addington, James I, 1026
Addington, James I, 1055
Addington, James I, 1060
Addington, James V, 19
Addington, James V, 149
Addington, James V, 725
Addington, John I, 1017
Addington, John I, 1026
Addington, John I, 1055
Addington, John V, 19
Addington, John V, 149
Addington, John V, 725
Addington, Joseph I, 1017
Addington, Karenhappuck I, 1055
Addington, Kerenhappuck V, 149
Addington, Luther E. IV, 1305
Addington, Martha V, 149
Addington, Marthe I, 1055
Addington, Mary I, 1017
Addington, Mary I, 1026
Addington, Mary I, 1055
Addington, Mary I, 1060
Addington, Mary I, 1063
Addington, Mary V, 149
Addington, Rachel I, 1060
Addington, Rachel I, 1062
Addington, Rebecca I, 1055
Addington, Rebecca V, 149
Addington, Rebekah I, 1060
Addington, Rebekah, Jr. I, 1060
Addington, Sarah I, 1017
Addington, Sarah I, 1026
Addington, Sarah I, 1055
Addington, Sarah I, 1060
Addington, Sarah V, 19
Addington, Sarah V, 149
Addington, Sarah V, 725
Addington, Thomas I, 1017
Addington, Thomas I, 1026
Addington, Thomas I, 1055
Addington, Thomas V, 149
Addington, Widow Rebekah I, 1060
Addington, William I, 1017
Addis, Martha IV, 863
Addis, Martha IV, 878
Addison, Clyde V, 983
Addison, Eveline Pearl V, 983
Addison, John E. V, 983
Addison, Mary V, 983
Addison, Rachel M. V, 983
Addison, Samuel V, 779
Addleton, Rebecca I, 229
Addoms, Ann VI, 285
Addoms, Anne VI, 285
Adee, Anna H. III, 405
Adee, Daniel III, 393
Adee, Henry III, 393
Adee, Henry III, 404
Adee, Henry III, 459
Adee, Hobby III, 459
Adee, James III, 393
Adee, James III, 405
Adee, Jemima III, 393
Adee, Mary III, 393
Adee, Mary III, 459
Adee, Wd. Mary III, 393
Adell, Jacob IV, 1201
Adell, Mary R. IV, 1201
Adell, Rachel T. IV, 1201
Adell, Wm. T. IV, 1201
Adella, Orie IV, 1325
Aden, Morlan IV, 872
Aden, Rebecca IV, 872
Adenton, James I, 1026
Adington, James V, 725
Adington, John V, 725
Adington, Sarah V, 725
Adington, Sarah V, 775
Adison, John E. V, 983
Adison, Rachel M. V, 983
Adkerson, Anne VI, 869
Adkerson, Apphia VI, 869
Adkerson, Austin VI, 869
Adkerson, Elias VI, 869
Adkerson, Elijah VI, 869
Adkerson, Elizabeth VI, 994
Adkerson, Ellis VI, 869
Adkerson, John VI, 869
Adkerson, John VI, 996
Adkerson, Joshua VI, 869
Adkerson, Joshua VI, 994
Adkerson, Joshua VI, 996
Adkerson, Lewis VI, 869
Adkerson, Lewis VI, 875
Adkerson, Lewis VI, 940
Adkerson, Lewis VI, 954
Adkerson, Lucy VI, 996
Adkerson, Lydia VI, 955
Adkerson, Margaret VI, 869
Adkerson, Martha E. VI, 869
Adkerson, Nancy VI, 869
Adkerson, Nancy VI, 954
Adkerson, Polly VI, 940
Adkerson, Rebecca VI, 869
Adkerson, Rebeccah VI, 954
Adkerson, Reuben VI, 869
Adkerson, Rhody VI, 869
Adkerson, Sally VI, 869
Adkerson, Sarah VI, 996
Adkerson, Sibley VI, 875
Adkerson, Tabitha VI, 869
Adkerson, Thomas VI, 869
Adkerson, Wilson VI, 869
Adkins, Abigail VI, 829
Adkins, Anna IV, 1245
Adkins, James VI, 869
Adkins, Minnie IV, 1245
Adkins, Polly VI, 869
Adkins, Robin VI, 903
Adkins, Sarah VI, 903
Adkinson, Ann II, 194
Adkinson, Ann II, 225
Adkinson, Benjamin II, 194
Adkinson, Benjamin II, 225
Adkinson, Beulah II, 51
Adkinson, Ellis VI, 997
Adkinson, Ellis VI, 998
Adkinson, Hugh I, 433
Adkinson, James I, 433
Adkinson, James II, 51
Adkinson, John I, 433
Adkinson, John II, 225
Adkinson, Katey VI, 998
Adkinson, Mahlon II, 51
Adkinson, Mahlon II, 94
Adkinson, Mary I, 433
Adkinson, Mary Ann VI, 984
Adkinson, Nancy VI, 997
Adkinson, Richard II, 51
Adkinson, Ruth I, 393
Adkinson, Ruth I, 433
Adkinson, Sarah I, 433
Adkinson, Sarah II, 51
Adkinson, Sarah II, 194
Adkinson, Sarah II, 225
Adkinson, Thomas I, 372
Adkinson, Thomas I, 393
Adkinson, Thomas I, 433
Adkinson, Wilson VI, 869
Adkisson, Austin VI, 873
Adkisson, Nancy VI, 873
Adkisson, Samuel VI, 873
Adley, Jane VI, 795
Adley, Peter VI, 795
Adrich, Amos IV, 1349
Adrich, Rhoda IV, 1349
Adset, Isabella V, 547
Adset, Isabella V, 595
Adset, Mary Ann V, 547
Adsit, Elizabeth V, 471
Adsit, Elizabeth N. V, 471
Adsit, Isabella V, 471
Adsit, Isabella V, 525
Adsit, Mary Ann V, 471
Ady, Betty IV, 169
Ady, Betty IV, 218
Ady, Cherry IV, 169
Ady, Levina IV, 169
Ady, Rachel IV, 169
Ady, Rachel IV, 214
Affeck, Thomas II, 451
Affleck, Thomas II, 450
Affleck, Thomas II, 451
Afflick, Mary II, 437
Afflick, William II, 331
Agar, Philip II, 331
Agatha, Aggy VI, 238
Agee, A. J. VI, 991
Agee, Ali VI, 869
Agee, Archless VI, 870
Agee, Arkless VI, 870
Agee, B. A. VI, 870
Agee, Barbara Ann VI, 870
Agee, Betsey VI, 869
Agee, Charlotte VI, 991
Agee, Elizabeth Hurt. A. I. VI, 884
Agee, Emily B. VI, 795
Agee, James VI, 795
Agee, James VI, 869
Agee, Mary Jane VI, 870
Agee, Matthias VI, 870
Agee, Patty VI, 869
Agee, William VI, 940
Agen, Hattie IV, 1245
Agen, Mamie IV, 1245
Agie, Maggie V, 983
Agie, Oliver V, 983
Agnew, Arthur V, 149
Agnew, Elizabeth VI, 946
Agnew, Hannah IV, 319
Agnew, Hannah IV, 354
Agnew, Jane VI, 1002
Agnew, Joshua VI, 994
Agnew, Martha VI, 870
Agnew, Mary III, 16
Agnew, Mary C. VI, 946
Agnew, Nancy VI, 976
Agnew, Polly VI, 870
Agnew, Rachel VI, 994
Agnew, Rebecca VI, 988
Agnew, Sally VI, 870
Agnew, Samuel VI, 870
Agnew, Sarah VI, 967
Agnew, Sarah G. VI, 975
Agnew, Susanna VI, 870
Agnew, Tamer VI, 980
Agnew, Thomas J. VI, 870
Agnew, William VI, 870
Agnew, William VI, 946
Agnew, William VI, 975
Agnew, William VI, 988
Agnew, William, Jr. VI, 976
Agnew, William, Sr. VI, 976
Agnew, Wm. VI, 980
Agnew, Wm. VI, 1002
Agnue, Samuel VI, 870
Agur, Rebecca IV, 363
Agur, Rebecca IV, 382
Ahl, Erwin II, 127
Ahl, Pauline II, 127
Aicher, E. C. IV, 169
Aidy, Cherry IV, 169
Aidy, Cherry IV, 225
Aigee, Archless VI, 870
Aiken, ??? IV, 984
Aiken, A. F. IV, 1305
Aiken, Algeroy F. IV, 1305
Aiken, Ella IV, 921
Aiken, Ella IV, 984
Aiken, Ella A. IV, 921
Aiken, Ella C. IV, 984
Aiken, Ellen C. IV, 921
Aiken, Elmer IV, 671
Aiken, Homer IV, 671
Aiken, Homer L. IV, 671
Aiken, Judith Ann IV, 921
Aiken, Lee IV, 671
Aiken, Lydia IV, 671
Aiken, Mabel IV, 671
Aiken, Wm. IV, 921
Aiken, Wm. IV, 984
Aikens, Hannah IV, 509
Aikens, Hannah IV, 520
Aikers, Rachel V, 297
Aikers, Rachel V, 305
Ailas, Amos VI, 361
Ailes, Aaron IV, 19
Ailes, Amos IV, 19
Ailes, Amos IV, 73
Ailes, Amos V, 838
Ailes, Ann IV, 19
Ailes, Ann IV, 22
Ailes, Ann IV, 73
Ailes, Ann V, 838
Ailes, Austin M. IV, 921
Ailes, Celina IV, 921
Ailes, Curtis IV, 921
Ailes, Curtis L. IV, 921
Ailes, Curtis Lionel IV, 921
Ailes, Dr. Austin M. IV, 921
Ailes, Eugene Elsworth IV, 921
Ailes, Isaac IV, 19
Ailes, James IV, 19
Ailes, Joseph IV, 19
Ailes, Joseph IV, 73
Ailes, Marguerite IV, 921
Ailes, Marguerite M. IV, 921
Ailes, Mary IV, 19
Ailes, Mary IV, 73
Ailes, Mary IV, 87
Ailes, Mary V, 838
Ailes, Nathan Gause IV, 73
Ailes, Sarah IV, 19
Ailes, Sarah IV, 66
Ailes, Sarah IV, 73
Ailes, Stephen IV, 19
Ailsworth, Abigail IV, 1350
Aimes, Frances III, 16
Aimes, Sarah S. III, 16
Aimes, William III, 16
Ainley, Sarah III, 121
Ainscouch, Thomas IV, 169
Ainsley, Mary II, 451
Ainsley, Robert II, 451
Aires, Ann IV, 311
Aires, Milla I, 796
Aires, Symon II, 441
Airey, Anne VI, 13
Airey, Rebecca II, 830
Airey, Sally V, 472
Airhart, Sarah V, 51
Airhart, Sarah V, 92
Airl, Mary VI, 980
Airn, Ida M. IV, 169
Airs, Alce I, 870
Airs, Alice I, 870
Airs, Guylla I, 870
Airs, Milla I, 838
Airy, Betty IV, 106
Airy, Clara M. V, 825
Airy, Elizabeth IV, 73
Airy, Elizabeth IV, 110
Airy, Elizabeth V, 825
Airy, George V, 825
Airy, Harmon V, 149
Airy, John IV, 73
Airy, John IV, 106
Airy, John V, 725
Airy, John V, 825
Airy, Keziah V, 825
Airy, Lydia V, 825
Airy, Mary IV, 19
Airy, Mary IV, 73
Airy, Mary IV, 96
Airy, Mary Ann V, 825
Airy, Phebe IV, 319
Airy, Robert Cook IV, 319
Airy, Wd Mary IV, 73
Airy, Wd Mary IV, 106
Airy, William V, 825
Aisel, Thomas IV, 1245
Aisel, Winnie IV, 1245
Aitken, Beula Marie IV, 1305
Aitken, Elizabeth L. III, 16
Aitken, Elizabeth L. III, 210
Aitken, Geo. Russell IV, 1305
Aitken, George IV, 1305
Aitken, Jane III, 16
Aitken, Jane III, 190
Aitken, Jessie III, 16
Aitken, Jessie III, 190
Aitken, John III, 16
Aitken, John III, 190
Aitken, John III, 210
Aitken, Lydia III, 16
Aitken, Lydia III, 210
Aitken, Melvina W. V, 217
Aitken, Sarah IV, 1305
Aitken, Sarah A. III, 265
Aitken, Sarah Mabel IV, 1305
Aitken, Thelmo Ernestine IV, 1305
Aitkin, Ann II, 451
Aitkin, Ann II, 618
Aitkins, James F. III, 501
Akehurst, Daniel VI, 13
Akehurst, Daniel VI, 38
Akerly, ??? III, 43
Akerly, Benjamin III, 16
Akerly, Jackamiah III, 16
Akerly, Wd. Susannah III, 16
Akers, Agness VI, 795
Akers, Agness VI, 797
Akers, Ann VI, 846
Akers, Bryan VI, 795
Akers, Catharine VI, 805
Akers, Catherine VI, 795
Akers, Cynthia VI, 795
Akers, Elizabeth VI, 795
Akers, Elizabeth VI, 853
Akers, George VI, 795
Akers, George VI, 836
Akers, John VI, 795
Akers, John VI, 797
Akers, John VI, 810
Akers, John VI, 833
Akers, John VI, 846
Akers, John VI, 853
Akers, Joseph VI, 795
Akers, Madison J. VI, 870
Akers, Martha VI, 795
Akers, Mary VI, 833
Akers, Nancy VI, 795
Akers, Nancy VI, 797
Akers, Peter VI, 805
Akers, Polly VI, 795
Akers, Ruth VI, 863
Akers, Sally VI, 855
Akers, Sarah VI, 870
Akers, Simon P. VI, 795
Akers, William VI, 795
Akers, William VI, 846
Akers, William VI, 853
Akers, William VI, 863
Akers, William, Jr. VI, 853
Akers, William, Sr. VI, 855
Akey, Mary IV, 891
Akey, Mary IV, 892
Akin, Abiel III, 16
Akin, Agnes II, 331
Akin, Albert IV, 1245
Akin, Ann VI, 979
Akin, Betsy A. VI, 848
Akin, Carrie W. III, 16
Akin, Elizabeth IV, 863
Akin, Elizabeth IV, 881
Akin, Elizabeth IV, 1349
Akin, Esther IV, 1035
Akin, Henry Franklin III, 16
Akin, Isabella VI, 857
Akin, Joseph VI, 848
Akin, Joseph VI, 857
Akin, Lizzie IV, 1245
Akin, Lucy E. III, 16
Akin, Mary VI, 857
Akin, Sally VI, 857
Akin, Sylvia G. III, 16
Akin, William VI, 857
Akinson, Samuel II, 194
Akley, John II, 331
Akley, William II, 331
Alaback, John IV, 797
Alaback, Thornton IV, 797
Alan, Elizabeth I, 370
Alan, Elizabeth I, 386
Alan, Harmon I, 755
Alan, John I, 370
Alan, Joseph I, 370
Alan, Joseph I, 382
Alan, Martha I, 382
Alan, Martha I, 383
Alan, Nathan I, 370
Alan, Nathan I, 383
Alan, Peter I, 370
Alan, Peter I, 386
Alan, Phebe I, 370
Alan, Phebe I, 383
Alaxander, Sarah Ella Lecta V, 655
Alazier, Catharine IV, 992
Alazier, Catharine Alesi IV, 921
Alazier, Mary IV, 921
Alazier, Mary IV, 992
Alazier, Mathew IV, 921
Alazier, Matt IV, 992
Alban, Ann E. V, 655
Alban, Emily V, 655
Alban, Emily V, 721
Alban, James S. V, 655
Albaugh, Henry C. III, 16
Albaugh, Henry C. III, 109
Albaugh, Mary E. III, 16
Albaugh, Mary E. III, 109
Albaugh, Sarah J. III, 16
Albaugh, Sarah J. III, 109
Alberson, Elias I, 796
Alberson, Elias I, 802
Alberson, Hannah II, 451
Alberson, Jemima I, 796
Alberson, Joshua I, 697
Alberson, Joshua I, 849
Alberson, Josiah I, 697
Alberson, Josiah V, 471
Alberson, Mary I, 802
Alberson, Sarah I, 697
Alberston, Benj. III, 490
Alberston, Phebe H. III, 490
Alberton, Abigail I, 93
Alberton, Caleb I, 93
Alberton, Chalkley I, 93
Alberton, Elias I, 40
Alberton, Elihu I, 93
Alberton, Elihue I, 93
Alberton, Elisabeth I, 93
Alberton, Elizabeth I, 40
Alberton, Elizabeth I, 93
Alberton, Jane I, 93
Alberton, Jesse I, 93
Alberton, John I, 93
Alberton, Jonathan II, 451
Alberton, Joseph I, 93
Alberton, Joshua I, 93
Alberton, Josiah I, 93
Alberton, Liddea I, 93
Alberton, Mary I, 93
Alberton, Miriam I, 93
Alberton, Mirriam I, 93
Alberton, Nathan I, 93
Alberton, Penelopy I, 93
Alberton, Penninah I, 93
Alberton, Samuel I, 93
Albertson, ??? III, 377
Albertson, ??? III, 387
Albertson, ??? III, 393
Albertson, A. Raymond III, 393
Albertson, Aaron I, 34
Albertson, Aaron I, 127
Albertson, Aaron I, 128

Albertson, Aaron I, 150
Albertson, Aaron I, 181
Albertson, Aaron I, 188
Albertson, Aaron I Sup 1, 3
Albertson, Aaron I Sup 1, 4
Albertson, Aaron Morris, Jr. I, 127
Albertson, Abigail I, 34
Albertson, Abigail I, 44
Albertson, Abigail I, 127
Albertson, Abigail I, 130
Albertson, Abigail I, 181
Albertson, Abigail I, 188
Albertson, Abigail I, 743
Albertson, Abigail I, 869
Albertson, Abigail I Sup 1, 3
Albertson, Abigail I Sup 1, 5
Albertson, Abraham I, 93
Albertson, Achsah I, 188
Albertson, Achsah I, 229
Albertson, Achsah I, 233
Albertson, Achsah I, 647
Albertson, Achsah I, 673
Albertson, Acsah I, 743
Albertson, Acsah I, 755
Albertson, Adah III, 393
Albertson, Adah III, 450
Albertson, Agnes E. III, 16
Albertson, Albert I Sup 1, 3
Albertson, Alfred II, 946
Albertson, Alfred Parker I, 181
Albertson, Alice II, 946
Albertson, Alice III, 16
Albertson, Alice III, 259
Albertson, Alice V, 371
Albertson, Alice V, 547
Albertson, Alice M. II, 830
Albertson, Alice M. II, 853
Albertson, Alice Maulsby II, 830
Albertson, Alice Maulsby II, 912
Albertson, Alletta P. III, 393
Albertson, Alpheus I, 188
Albertson, Amanda R. I, 647
Albertson, Amanda Roxanna I, 673
Albertson, Amy II, 279
Albertson, Amy II, 291
Albertson, Amy II, 698
Albertson, Amy II, 725
Albertson, Amy II, 946
Albertson, Amy II, 948
Albertson, Amy II, 1085
Albertson, Amy II, 1087
Albertson, Amy II, 1088
Albertson, Amy H. II, 698
Albertson, Andrew Hoover I, 708
Albertson, Ann I, 34
Albertson, Ann I, 60
Albertson, Ann I, 181
Albertson, Ann I Sup 1, 3
Albertson, Ann I Sup 1, 4
Albertson, Ann II, 316
Albertson, Ann II, 325
Albertson, Ann II, 1068
Albertson, Ann II, 1073
Albertson, Ann II, 1083
Albertson, Anna I, 849
Albertson, Anna I, 869
Albertson, Anna II, 974
Albertson, Anna II, 1044
Albertson, Anna III, 393
Albertson, Anna Maria II, 1068
Albertson, Anna Maria II, 1082
Albertson, Anna Owen II, 780
Albertson, Anne II, 451
Albertson, Anne II, 510
Albertson, Annie H. III, 393
Albertson, Annie H. III, 403
Albertson, Anthony Benezette I, 34
Albertson, Anthony Benezette I, 81
Albertson, Arthur I, 127
Albertson, Artie L. I, 919
Albertson, Asenath I, 647
Albertson, Asenath I, 673
Albertson, Asenath A. I, 673
Albertson, Aug. III, 474
Albertson, Augustus III, 473
Albertson, Axsa I, 181
Albertson, B. I, 181
Albertson, Barbara III, 393
Albertson, Benj. III, 421
Albertson, Benj. III, 486
Albertson, Benjamin I, 34
Albertson, Benjamin I, 66
Albertson, Benjamin I, 74
Albertson, Benjamin I, 93
Albertson, Benjamin I, 111
Albertson, Benjamin I, 127
Albertson, Benjamin I, 128
Albertson, Benjamin I, 129
Albertson, Benjamin I, 155
Albertson, Benjamin I, 181
Albertson, Benjamin I, 188
Albertson, Benjamin I, 198
Albertson, Benjamin I, 708
Albertson, Benjamin I, 849
Albertson, Benjamin I, 869
Albertson, Benjamin II, 451
Albertson, Benjamin II, 698
Albertson, Benjamin II, 725
Albertson, Benjamin II, 946
Albertson, Benjamin II, 1044
Albertson, Benjamin II, 1068
Albertson, Benjamin II, 1073
Albertson, Benjamin II, 1083
Albertson, Benjamin II, 1085
Albertson, Benjamin II, 1087
Albertson, Benjamin II, 1088
Albertson, Benjamin III, 393
Albertson, Benjamin III, 421
Albertson, Benjamin III, 479
Albertson, Benjamin V, 371
Albertson, Benjamin V, 547
Albertson, Benjamin F. I, 743
Albertson, Benjamin H. I, 647
Albertson, Benjamin, Jr. I, 34
Albertson, Benjamin, Jr. I, 180
Albertson, Benjamin, Jr. I, 181
Albertson, Benjamin, Jr. I, 188
Albertson, Benjamin, Jr. II, 974
Albertson, Benjamin, Sr. I, 34
Albertson, Benjamin, Sr. I, 127
Albertson, Benjamin, Sr. I, 180
Albertson, Benjamin, Sr. I, 181
Albertson, Benjamin, Sr. I, 188
Albertson, Benjm. I, 181
Albertson, Benjn. I, 181
Albertson, Bertha I, 937
Albertson, Bertha E. I, 937
Albertson, Blanch I, 919
Albertson, Boswell I, 708
Albertson, Caroline I, 127
Albertson, Caroline I, 129
Albertson, Caroline I, 181
Albertson, Caroline I, 188
Albertson, Caroline III, 393
Albertson, Caroline III, 413
Albertson, Caroline III, 426
Albertson, Caroline III, 458
Albertson, Caroline III, 468
Albertson, Caroline III, 475
Albertson, Caroline L. III, 393
Albertson, Cath. M. III, 393
Albertson, Catharine I, 188
Albertson, Catharine I, 869
Albertson, Catherine I, 127
Albertson, Chalkey I, 188
Albertson, Chalkley I, 34
Albertson, Chalkley I, 76
Albertson, Chalkley I, 180
Albertson, Chalkley I, 181
Albertson, Chalkley I, 195
Albertson, Chalkley I, 229
Albertson, Chalkley II, 316
Albertson, Chalkley II, 325
Albertson, Chalkley II, 1044
Albertson, Chalkley II, 1068
Albertson, Chalkley II, 1073
Albertson, Chalkley V, 371
Albertson, Chalkley V, 547
Albertson, Charles I, 708
Albertson, Charles II, 725
Albertson, Charles II, 946
Albertson, Charles II, 1068
Albertson, Charles E. II, 698
Albertson, Charlotte B. III, 502
Albertson, Chockley V, 371
Albertson, Christianna II, 1068
Albertson, Christianna II, 1079
Albertson, Daniel I, 181
Albertson, Daniel I, 188
Albertson, Daniel III, 393
Albertson, Daniel III, 450
Albertson, Derick III, 393
Albertson, Derick III, 450
Albertson, Dinah III, 393
Albertson, Dinah III, 450
Albertson, Ed. C. C. I, 34
Albertson, Edgar B. V, 825
Albertson, Edith Agnes III, 16
Albertson, Edith Agnes III, 125
Albertson, Edmund I, 188
Albertson, Edmund Peele I, 181
Albertson, Edna I, 919
Albertson, Elias I, 34
Albertson, Elias I, 60
Albertson, Elias I, 63
Albertson, Elias I, 93
Albertson, Elias I, 100
Albertson, Elias I, 127
Albertson, Elias I, 181
Albertson, Elias I, 188
Albertson, Elias I, 263
Albertson, Elias I, 264
Albertson, Elias I, 267
Albertson, Elias I, 275
Albertson, Elias I, 708
Albertson, Elias I, 796
Albertson, Elias T. I, 34
Albertson, Elihu I, 34
Albertson, Elihu I, 35
Albertson, Elihu I, 107
Albertson, Elihu I, 127
Albertson, Elihu I, 188
Albertson, Elisabeth I, 34
Albertson, Elisabeth I, 53
Albertson, Elisabeth I, 66
Albertson, Elisabeth I, 76
Albertson, Elisabeth I, 81
Albertson, Elisabeth I, 127
Albertson, Elisabeth I, 128
Albertson, Elisabeth I, 162
Albertson, Elisabeth I, 180
Albertson, Elisabeth I, 188
Albertson, Elisabeth I, 200
Albertson, Elisabeth W. I, 128
Albertson, Elisabeth Waring I, 128
Albertson, Elisabeth Woring I, 188
Albertson, Elisabeth, Jr. I, 188
Albertson, Elisabeth, Sr. I, 34
Albertson, Eliza I, 188
Albertson, Eliza I, 796
Albertson, Eliza II, 1068
Albertson, Eliza II, 1073
Albertson, Elizabeth I, 34
Albertson, Elizabeth I, 162
Albertson, Elizabeth I, 181
Albertson, Elizabeth I, 188
Albertson, Elizabeth I, 199
Albertson, Elizabeth I, 229
Albertson, Elizabeth I, 267
Albertson, Elizabeth I, 299
Albertson, Elizabeth I, 673
Albertson, Elizabeth I, 680
Albertson, Elizabeth I, 697
Albertson, Elizabeth I, 708
Albertson, Elizabeth I, 849
Albertson, Elizabeth I, 869
Albertson, Elizabeth I Sup 1, 3
Albertson, Elizabeth I Sup 1, 5
Albertson, Elizabeth III, 393
Albertson, Elizabeth III, 421
Albertson, Elizabeth III, 430
Albertson, Elizabeth III, 486
Albertson, Elizabeth Ann I, 647
Albertson, Elizabeth C. III, 393
Albertson, Elizabeth C. III, 473
Albertson, Elizabeth I. I, 647
Albertson, Elizabeth J. I, 673
Albertson, Elizabeth L. II, 725
Albertson, Elizabeth R. II, 946
Albertson, Elizabeth, Jr. I, 708
Albertson, Ella III, 479
Albertson, Ella III, 486
Albertson, Ella III, 487
Albertson, Ella III, 495
Albertson, Elva IV, 463
Albertson, Elvira IV, 363
Albertson, Elvy I, 34
Albertson, Elvy I, 281
Albertson, Elvy I, 299
Albertson, Elvy I, 319
Albertson, Elvy IV, 169
Albertson, Elvy IV, 426
Albertson, Emily III, 393
Albertson, Emma III, 479
Albertson, Emma III, 502
Albertson, Esther III, 16
Albertson, Esther III, 358
Albertson, Esther III, 473
Albertson, Ethel Mary III, 393
Albertson, Eunice I, 743
Albertson, Feraby V, 340
Albertson, Ferebee I, 708
Albertson, Feriby I, 523
Albertson, Frances I, 181
Albertson, Francis I, 34
Albertson, Francis I, 127
Albertson, Francis I, 129
Albertson, Francis I, 157
Albertson, Francis I, 180
Albertson, Francis I, 188
Albertson, Frank IV, 1233
Albertson, Geo. Fitz R. III, 16
Albertson, George II, 1068
Albertson, George W. II, 1068
Albertson, Hannah I, 34
Albertson, Hannah I, 65
Albertson, Hannah I, 109
Albertson, Hannah I, 673
Albertson, Hannah I Sup 1, 3
Albertson, Hannah I Sup 1, 5
Albertson, Hannah II, 451
Albertson, Hannah II, 510
Albertson, Hannah V, 19
Albertson, Hannah V, 149
Albertson, Hannah V, 371
Albertson, Hannah V, 547
Albertson, Hannah V, 580
Albertson, Harmon Kester V, 149
Albertson, Harmon Kester V, 547
Albertson, Harriet III, 393
Albertson, Harriet III, 397
Albertson, Henry I, 523
Albertson, Henry I, 708
Albertson, Henry II, 279
Albertson, Henry II, 291
Albertson, Henry II, 698
Albertson, Henry II, 725
Albertson, Henry II, 946
Albertson, Henry II, 948
Albertson, Henry II, 1056
Albertson, Henry II, 1087
Albertson, Henry II, 1088
Albertson, Henry H. II, 948
Albertson, Henry Haines II, 946
Albertson, Henry Haines II, 1044
Albertson, Henry Haines II, 1056
Albertson, Hicks III, 393
Albertson, Hicks III, 430
Albertson, Hicks III, 473
Albertson, Howard Z. V, 825
Albertson, Huldah I, 127
Albertson, Huldah I, 188
Albertson, Ida III, 393
Albertson, Ida III, 468
Albertson, Isaac I, 127
Albertson, Isaac W. I, 647
Albertson, Isabel I, 181
Albertson, Isabel I, 188
Albertson, Isaiah V, 371
Albertson, J. Aug. III, 433
Albertson, J. Augustus III, 393
Albertson, James I, 181
Albertson, James I, 188
Albertson, Jane I, 34
Albertson, Jane I, 35
Albertson, Jane I, 42
Albertson, Jane I, 55
Albertson, Jane I, 127
Albertson, Jane I, 188
Albertson, Jane I, 708
Albertson, Jane I, 849
Albertson, Jane I, 869
Albertson, Jasper I, 919
Albertson, Jean I, 181
Albertson, Jemima I, 796
Albertson, Jesse I, 34
Albertson, Jesse I, 45
Albertson, Jesse I, 188
Albertson, Jesse I, 708
Albertson, Jno. Augustus III, 393
Albertson, Jno. Augustus III, 433
Albertson, John I, 34
Albertson, John I, 127
Albertson, John I, 162
Albertson, John I, 523
Albertson, John I, 673
Albertson, John I, 675
Albertson, John I, 708
Albertson, John I, 796
Albertson, John I, 869
Albertson, John III, 393
Albertson, John V, 547
Albertson, John Augustus III, 393
Albertson, John C. II, 725
Albertson, John C., Jr. II, 725
Albertson, Jonathan II, 451
Albertson, Jonathan II, 974
Albertson, Jonathan II, 1044
Albertson, Jonathan K. II, 974
Albertson, Jonathan K. II, 1068
Albertson, Jonathan W. I, 34
Albertson, Jordan I, 188
Albertson, Jordan I, 189
Albertson, Jordon I, 181
Albertson, Joseph I, 34
Albertson, Joseph I, 188
Albertson, Joseph I, 281
Albertson, Joseph I, 299
Albertson, Joseph I, 319
Albertson, Joseph I, 743
Albertson, Joseph I, 849
Albertson, Joseph I, 869
Albertson, Joseph I, 937
Albertson, Joseph IV, 139
Albertson, Joseph IV, 169
Albertson, Joseph IV, 363
Albertson, Joseph IV, 426
Albertson, Joseph IV, 463
Albertson, Joseph V, 371
Albertson, Joseph E. I, 919
Albertson, Joseph G. II, 725
Albertson, Joshua I, 34
Albertson, Joshua I, 127
Albertson, Joshua I, 162
Albertson, Joshua I, 165
Albertson, Joshua I, 167
Albertson, Joshua I, 188
Albertson, Joshua I, 673
Albertson, Joshua I, 708
Albertson, Joshua I, 849
Albertson, Joshua I, 869
Albertson, Joshua, Jr. I, 127
Albertson, Josiah I, 34
Albertson, Josiah I, 62
Albertson, Josiah I, 153
Albertson, Josiah I, 168
Albertson, Josiah I, 180
Albertson, Josiah I, 181
Albertson, Josiah I, 188
Albertson, Josiah I, 849
Albertson, Josiah I, 869
Albertson, Josiah V, 19
Albertson, Josiah V, 149
Albertson, Josiah V, 371
Albertson, Josiah V, 547
Albertson, Josiah V, 580
Albertson, Kezia I, 127
Albertson, Kezia I, 168
Albertson, Kezia III, 393
Albertson, Kezia III, 458
Albertson, Keziah I, 181
Albertson, Keziah I, 188
Albertson, Keziah III, 393
Albertson, Keziah III, 466
Albertson, Keziah III, 479
Albertson, Keziah III, 504
Albertson, Liddia I, 127
Albertson, Liddia I, 176
Albertson, Liddy I, 267
Albertson, Liddy I, 275
Albertson, Lilian I, 937
Albertson, Lillie May I, 919
Albertson, Lydia I, 34
Albertson, Lydia I, 76
Albertson, Lydia I, 708
Albertson, Lydia I, 869
Albertson, Lydia I Sup 1, 7
Albertson, Lydia II, 946
Albertson, Lydia H. II, 698
Albertson, Lydia M. II, 948
Albertson, Lydiah I, 849
Albertson, M ary I, 188
Albertson, Maranda I, 181
Albertson, Margaret I, 128
Albertson, Margaret I, 188
Albertson, Margaret I, 196
Albertson, Maria Balderston II, 1044
Albertson, Maria Balderston II, 1056
Albertson, Mariam I, 299
Albertson, Mark I, 181
Albertson, Mark I, 188
Albertson, Mark I, 647
Albertson, Mark I, 673
Albertson, Mark I, 743
Albertson, Mark I, 755
Albertson, Mark I, 765
Albertson, Martha I, 128
Albertson, Martha I, 154
Albertson, Martha I, 181
Albertson, Martha I, 188
Albertson, Martha I, 869
Albertson, Martha III, 393
Albertson, Martha III, 421
Albertson, Martin J. D. III, 393
Albertson, Mary I, 34
Albertson, Mary I, 35
Albertson, Mary I, 36
Albertson, Mary I, 38
Albertson, Mary I, 46
Albertson, Mary I, 63
Albertson, Mary I, 66
Albertson, Mary I, 74
Albertson, Mary I, 100
Albertson, Mary I, 111
Albertson, Mary I, 127
Albertson, Mary I, 128
Albertson, Mary I, 140
Albertson, Mary I, 142
Albertson, Mary I, 158
Albertson, Mary I, 165
Albertson, Mary I, 167
Albertson, Mary I, 181
Albertson, Mary I, 188
Albertson, Mary I, 189
Albertson, Mary I, 192
Albertson, Mary I, 201

Albertson, Mary I, 267
Albertson, Mary I, 275
Albertson, Mary I, 673
Albertson, Mary I, 675
Albertson, Mary I, 695
Albertson, Mary I, 697
Albertson, Mary I, 708
Albertson, Mary I, 796
Albertson, Mary I, 849
Albertson, Mary I, 869
Albertson, Mary I, 878
Albertson, Mary I, 937
Albertson, Mary III, 393
Albertson, Mary A. I, 919
Albertson, Mary Ann II, 946
Albertson, Mary Ann II, 1085
Albertson, Mary Ann II, 1087
Albertson, Mary Ann II, 1088
Albertson, Mary B. II, 1056
Albertson, Mary Ethel III, 433
Albertson, Mary G. E. I, 647
Albertson, Mary G. E. I, 673
Albertson, Mary P. III, 393
Albertson, Mary P. III, 473
Albertson, Mary R. II, 279
Albertson, Mary R. II, 291
Albertson, Mary R. II, 946
Albertson, Mary R. II, 948
Albertson, Mary R. II, 1044
Albertson, Mary R. II, 1087
Albertson, Mary R. II, 1088
Albertson, Mary W. II, 830
Albertson, Mary W. II, 912
Albertson, Mary W. III, 16
Albertson, Mary W. III, 259
Albertson, Mary W. III, 393
Albertson, Mary W. III, 433
Albertson, Mary W. III, 474
Albertson, Mary, Jr. I, 34
Albertson, Mary, Sr. I, 796
Albertson, Mearim I, 267
Albertson, Melicent I, 188
Albertson, Melva V, 825
Albertson, Melva Edger V, 864
Albertson, Melva S. V, 825
Albertson, Meranda I, 188
Albertson, Meranda I, 190
Albertson, Milicent I, 188
Albertson, Milicent I, 523
Albertson, Milicent I, 708
Albertson, Milicent I, 869
Albertson, Milisent I, 181
Albertson, Milisent I, 188
Albertson, Milisent I, 189
Albertson, Milisent I, 708
Albertson, Milisent I, 727
Albertson, Millicent I, 523
Albertson, Millicent I, 708
Albertson, Millisent I, 708
Albertson, Millisent I, 849
Albertson, Miriam I, 34
Albertson, Miriam I, 35
Albertson, Miriam I, 45
Albertson, Miriam I, 53
Albertson, Miriam I, 79
Albertson, Miriam I, 127
Albertson, Miriam I, 129
Albertson, Miriam I, 181
Albertson, Miriam I, 188
Albertson, Miriam I, 267
Albertson, Miriam I, 275
Albertson, Miriam I, 299
Albertson, Miriam I, 849
Albertson, Miriam I, 869
Albertson, Miriam I, 874
Albertson, Morris I, 128
Albertson, Morris I, 188
Albertson, Myron C. V, 825
Albertson, Myron Charles V, 825
Albertson, Nathan I, 34
Albertson, Nathan I, 127
Albertson, Nathan I, 181
Albertson, Nathan I, 188
Albertson, Nathan I, 198
Albertson, Nathan I, 647
Albertson, Nathan I, 673
Albertson, Nathan I, 680
Albertson, Nathaniel I, 34
Albertson, Nathaniel I, 36
Albertson, Nathaniel I, 109
Albertson, Nathaniel I, 127
Albertson, Nathaniel I, 181
Albertson, Nathaniel I, 299
Albertson, Nathaniel I Sup 1, 3
Albertson, Nathaniel I Sup 1, 5
Albertson, Nathaniell I Sup 1, 3
Albertson, Newby I, 127
Albertson, Nixon I, 127
Albertson, Nixon I, 128
Albertson, Nixon I, 188
Albertson, Nixon I, 796
Albertson, Nixon I, 869
Albertson, Patience I, 743
Albertson, Peggy I, 181
Albertson, Penina I, 34
Albertson, Penina I, 71
Albertson, Penina I, 127
Albertson, Penina IV, 169
Albertson, Peninah I, 34
Albertson, Peninah I, 127
Albertson, Peninah I, 188
Albertson, Peninah I, 197
Albertson, Peninah I, 281
Albertson, Peninah I, 796
Albertson, Peninah I, 849
Albertson, Peninah I, 869
Albertson, Peninah IV, 363
Albertson, Peninah IV, 463
Albertson, Penninah I, 708
Albertson, Penninah IV, 363
Albertson, Penninah IV, 426
Albertson, Pervis E. I, 937
Albertson, Pharaby I, 188
Albertson, Phariba I, 189
Albertson, Phebe III, 479
Albertson, Phebe III, 495
Albertson, Phebe H. III, 479
Albertson, Phebe W. III, 393
Albertson, Phebe W. III, 438
Albertson, Phebe W. III, 479
Albertson, Phebe W. III, 502
Albertson, Pheraby I, 188
Albertson, Pheraby I, 198
Albertson, Pheraby I, 708
Albertson, Phereby I, 188
Albertson, Pheriba I, 697
Albertson, Pheribe I, 523
Albertson, Pheriby I, 708
Albertson, Pheriby I, 717
Albertson, Phineas I, 188
Albertson, Phineas I, 647
Albertson, Phineas I, 673
Albertson, Phineas I, 692
Albertson, Phinehas I, 34
Albertson, Phinehas I, 79
Albertson, Phinehas I, 127
Albertson, Phinehas I, 181
Albertson, Phinehas I, 188
Albertson, Phinehas I, 673
Albertson, Phinehas I, 869
Albertson, Polly I, 127
Albertson, Polly I, 181
Albertson, Polly I, 188
Albertson, Polly I, 869
Albertson, Prichard I, 647
Albertson, Priscilla I, 849
Albertson, Priscilla I, 869
Albertson, Priscilla I, 873
Albertson, Priscilla I, 919
Albertson, Pritchar I, 755
Albertson, Pritchard I, 181
Albertson, Pritchard I, 188
Albertson, Pritchard I, 229
Albertson, Pritchard I, 233
Albertson, Pritchard I, 673
Albertson, Pritchard I, 743
Albertson, Pritchet I, 188
Albertson, Pruvis I, 937
Albertson, Purvis E. I, 919
Albertson, Rachel II, 974
Albertson, Raymond III, 393
Albertson, Raymond III, 397
Albertson, Rebecca I, 34
Albertson, Rebecca I, 79
Albertson, Rebecca I, 81
Albertson, Rebecca I, 127
Albertson, Rebecca I, 157
Albertson, Rebecca I, 180
Albertson, Rebecca I, 181
Albertson, Rebecca I, 188
Albertson, Rebecca I, 647
Albertson, Rebecca I, 673
Albertson, Rebecca I, 743
Albertson, Rebecca I, 869
Albertson, Rebecca II, 698
Albertson, Rebecca III, 393
Albertson, Rebecca V, 317
Albertson, Rebecca V, 340
Albertson, Rebecca S. II, 725
Albertson, Rebecka I, 127
Albertson, Rebeckah I, 127
Albertson, Rebeckah I, 869
Albertson, Rebekah I, 181
Albertson, Rebekah I, 188
Albertson, Rebekah I, 202
Albertson, Rhoda I, 34
Albertson, Rhoda I, 61
Albertson, Rhoda I, 107
Albertson, Rhoda I, 127
Albertson, Rhoda I, 152
Albertson, Rich. III, 393
Albertson, Richard III, 393
Albertson, Richard III, 426
Albertson, Richard III, 438
Albertson, Richard III, 479
Albertson, Richard III, 495
Albertson, Richard III, 502
Albertson, Robert Francis III, 393
Albertson, Ruby I, 937
Albertson, Ruth I, 181
Albertson, Ruth I, 919
Albertson, S. Louisa III, 393
Albertson, Sallie L. III, 393
Albertson, Samuel I, 188
Albertson, Samuel I, 200
Albertson, Samuel I, 697
Albertson, Samuel I, 708
Albertson, Sarah I, 3
Albertson, Sarah I, 34
Albertson, Sarah I, 52
Albertson, Sarah I, 62
Albertson, Sarah I, 66
Albertson, Sarah I, 93
Albertson, Sarah I, 107
Albertson, Sarah I, 127
Albertson, Sarah I, 128
Albertson, Sarah I, 150
Albertson, Sarah I, 153
Albertson, Sarah I, 155
Albertson, Sarah I, 162
Albertson, Sarah I, 181
Albertson, Sarah I, 188
Albertson, Sarah I, 189
Albertson, Sarah I, 191
Albertson, Sarah I, 196
Albertson, Sarah I, 197
Albertson, Sarah I, 202
Albertson, Sarah I, 708
Albertson, Sarah I, 849
Albertson, Sarah I, 869
Albertson, Sarah I, 892
Albertson, Sarah I Sup 1, 3
Albertson, Sarah II, 331
Albertson, Sarah II, 830
Albertson, Sarah III, 377
Albertson, Sarah III, 387
Albertson, Sarah III, 393
Albertson, Sarah III, 413
Albertson, Sarah III, 426
Albertson, Sarah III, 430
Albertson, Sarah III, 479
Albertson, Sarah A. III, 413
Albertson, Sarah A. III, 475
Albertson, Sarah Elizabeth II, 830
Albertson, Sarah Elizabeth II, 889
Albertson, Sarah Elizabeth II, 1068
Albertson, Sarah H. II, 698
Albertson, Sarah H. II, 725
Albertson, Sarah H. II, 1085
Albertson, Sarah H. III, 393
Albertson, Sarah H. III, 458
Albertson, Sarah N. III, 479
Albertson, Sarah W. III, 393
Albertson, Sarah, Jr. I, 34
Albertson, Sarah, Sr. I, 34
Albertson, Silas III, 393
Albertson, Silas III, 426
Albertson, Silas III, 458
Albertson, Silas III, 466
Albertson, Silas III, 479
Albertson, Silas III, 504
Albertson, Silas W. III, 393
Albertson, Silas W. III, 413
Albertson, Silas W. III, 468
Albertson, Silas W. III, 475
Albertson, Susanna I, 755
Albertson, Susanna I, 765
Albertson, Susanna II, 1044
Albertson, Susanna II, 1068
Albertson, Susanna S. II, 1068
Albertson, Susanna S. II, 1083
Albertson, Susannah I, 743
Albertson, Susannah I, 755
Albertson, Susannah II, 827
Albertson, Thomas I, 181
Albertson, Thomas I, 188
Albertson, Thomas I, 189
Albertson, Thomas I, 708
Albertson, Thomas Parker I, 128
Albertson, Thomas Parker I, 869
Albertson, Thompson II, 974
Albertson, Tomes I, 188
Albertson, Toms I, 128
Albertson, Toms I, 154
Albertson, Toms I, 181
Albertson, Toms I, 188
Albertson, Townsend III, 393
Albertson, W. III, 473
Albertson, Widow Elizabeth I, 267
Albertson, Widow Elizabeth I, 277
Albertson, Widow Margaret I, 198
Albertson, Widow Mary I, 181
Albertson, Widow Mary I, 195
Albertson, William I, 34
Albertson, William I, 66
Albertson, William I, 93
Albertson, William I, 127
Albertson, William I, 128
Albertson, William I, 162
Albertson, William I, 181
Albertson, William I, 189
Albertson, William I, 849
Albertson, William I, 869
Albertson, William III, 16
Albertson, William III, 259
Albertson, William III, 393
Albertson, William III, 403
Albertson, William III, 473
Albertson, William A. II, 946
Albertson, William M. I, 919
Albertson, William, Jr. I, 127
Albertson, William, Jr. I, 188
Albertson, Willmett III, 393
Albertson, Willmett III, 450
Albertson, Wm. I, 181
Albertson, Wm. II, 451
Albertson, Wm. II, 510
Albertson, Wm. II, 830
Albertson, Wm. II, 912
Albertson, Wm. II, 1044
Albertson, Wm. II, 1068
Albertson, Wm. III, 16
Albertson, Wm. III, 358
Albertson, Zachariah I, 181
Albeson, Hannah II, 451
Albeson, Wd. Hannah II, 510
Albinson, Frances II, 451
Albinson, Frances II, 603
Albinson, Wd. Hannah II, 451
Albion, Bessie Wilson I, 628
Albion, Luella Edna II, 960
Albion, William I, 628
Albord, Esau I, 93
Albord, Isaiah I, 93
Albord, Sarah I, 93
Albright, Amanda V, 547
Albright, Anna IV, 195
Albright, Carl IV, 1305
Albright, Florence IV, 1305
Albright, George VI, 802
Albright, Jos. IV, 1305
Albright, Joseph IV, 1305
Albright, Joseph C. IV, 1305
Albright, Lulu V, 983
Albright, M. V, 983
Albright, Martha II, 784
Albright, Miss ??? IV, 1305
Albright, Mrs. L. G. I, 629
Albright, Susanna II, 724
Albro, Minnie V, 655
Alcor, Ruth Palmer V, 19
Alcot, Mary V, 891
Alcot, Mary V, 915
Alcott, Mary V, 915
Alcott, Rebecca II, 813
Alcott, William V, 915
Alday, Alis II, 191
Alday, Alis II, 277
Alday, Patsy VI, 880
Alden, Ellen F. III, 199
Alden, Susan M. III, 410
Alder, David Edward V, 655
Alder, Dorothy E. V, 655
Alderman, Rebecca V, 217
Alderman, Rebecca V, 258
Alderson, Agnes II, 279
Alderson, Agnes II, 301
Alderson, Agnes V, 891
Alderson, Agness IV, 19
Alderson, Alice Ann V, 891
Alderson, Anna Mary II, 279
Alderson, Anna Mary II, 306
Alderson, Anna Mary IV, 19
Alderson, Anna Mary V, 891
Alderson, Elisabeth V, 891
Alderson, Elizabeth IV, 19
Alderson, Elizabeth V, 891
Alderson, Emma II, 279
Alderson, Emma II, 301
Alderson, Emma II, 303
Alderson, Emma II, 306
Alderson, Emma IV, 19
Alderson, Emma V, 891
Alderson, Harrison II, 165
Alderson, Harrison II, 279
Alderson, Harrison II, 301
Alderson, Harrison II, 306
Alderson, Harrison IV, 19
Alderson, Harrison V, 891
Alderson, Phebe V, 297
Alderson, Phebe V, 298
Alderson, Samuel V, 891
Alderson, Sarah Jane V, 217
Alderson, Sarah Jane V, 231
Alderson, Weeks VI, 928
Alderson, William Charles II, 279
Alderson, William Charles IV, 19
Alderson, William Chas. V, 891
Alderson, Wm. Chas. V, 891
Aldertson, Elisabeth I, 35
Aldertson, Jane I, 35
Aldertson, William I, 35
Aldred, Alice Elizabeth II, 828
Aldred, Chas. Mason II, 828
Aldred, Lucy II, 828
Aldred, Marthy W. I, 708
Aldred, Millicent M. I, 708
Aldred, Rachel I, 708
Aldreige, Gladys V, 655
Aldrich, Abigail IV, 1349
Aldrich, Abigail IV, 1366
Aldrich, Abraham IV, 1349
Aldrich, Alvah IV, 1349
Aldrich, Amadon IV, 1349
Aldrich, Amos IV, 1349
Aldrich, Amy IV, 1349
Aldrich, Amy IV, 1364
Aldrich, Amy S. IV, 1349
Aldrich, Anson H. IV, 1349
Aldrich, Asa III, 479
Aldrich, Asa IV, 1349
Aldrich, Asa W. IV, 1349
Aldrich, Bathsheba IV, 1349
Aldrich, Bathsheba IV, 1370
Aldrich, Caroline M. V, 725
Aldrich, Catharine W. III, 16
Aldrich, Catharine W. III, 267
Aldrich, Chloe IV, 1349
Aldrich, Cloe IV, 1349
Aldrich, Cynthia IV, 1349
Aldrich, Cynthia C. IV, 1349
Aldrich, David IV, 1143
Aldrich, Desire IV, 1349
Aldrich, Eli S. III, 16
Aldrich, Eli S. III, 267
Aldrich, Elias IV, 1143
Aldrich, Elisabeth IV, 1349
Aldrich, Eliza IV, 1349
Aldrich, Emma IV, 1143
Aldrich, Erastus IV, 1349
Aldrich, Esther M. II, 948
Aldrich, Esther M. II, 949
Aldrich, Freelove IV, 1349
Aldrich, Freeman IV, 1349
Aldrich, Harris H. IV, 1349
Aldrich, Huldah IV, 1349
Aldrich, Isaac IV, 1349
Aldrich, Israel Hoag IV, 1349
Aldrich, Jabez IV, 1349
Aldrich, Jacob IV, 1349
Aldrich, Jennie IV, 671
Aldrich, John Moore II, 948
Aldrich, Joseph IV, 671
Aldrich, Judah IV, 1349
Aldrich, Lavina IV, 1349
Aldrich, Lavinia II, 1087
Aldrich, Lavinia II, 1089
Aldrich, Ledia IV, 1349
Aldrich, Lyman IV, 1349
Aldrich, Lyman A. IV, 1349
Aldrich, Margaret Ann III, 16
Aldrich, Margaret Ann III, 267
Aldrich, Martha III, 479
Aldrich, Martha III, 484
Aldrich, Mary III, 479
Aldrich, Mary III, 493
Aldrich, Mary IV, 1349
Aldrich, Mary C. V, 947
Aldrich, Mary C. V, 948
Aldrich, Mary C. VI, 618
Aldrich, Mary Canby VI, 615
Aldrich, Mary E. V, 947
Aldrich, Mary Early IV, 1143
Aldrich, Mary P. IV, 1349
Aldrich, Mary P. IV, 1368
Aldrich, Merril IV, 1349
Aldrich, Mich. IV, 1349
Aldrich, Morgancy IV, 1349
Aldrich, Morganzia IV, 1349
Aldrich, Morganzy IV, 1349
Aldrich, Orrington IV, 1143
Aldrich, Oscar IV, 1143
Aldrich, Rhoda IV, 1349
Aldrich, Rhoda IV, 1382
Aldrich, Richard IV, 1370
Aldrich, Richard L. IV, 1349
Aldrich, Royal III, 484

Aldrich, Royal O. B. III, 479
Aldrich, Ruth III, 479
Aldrich, Ruth III, 493
Aldrich, Ruth IV, 1349
Aldrich, Samuel IV, 1349
Aldrich, Sarah II, 451
Aldrich, Sarah II, 517
Aldrich, Sarah IV, 1349
Aldrich, Sarah A. IV, 1349
Aldrich, Sarah A. IV, 1370
Aldrich, Savil IV, 1349
Aldrich, Savile IV, 1349
Aldrich, Stephen III, 479
Aldrich, Stephen III, 493
Aldrich, Stephen IV, 1349
Aldrich, Stephen H. IV, 1349
Aldrich, Stephen H. IV, 1366
Aldrich, Susanna IV, 1349
Aldrich, Willis IV, 1349
Aldrich, Wm. V, 725
Aldrick, Chas. V, 983
Aldrick, Mary C. V, 947
Aldrick, Savil IV, 1349
Aldridge, Alton V, 609
Aldridge, Charles V, 609
Aldridge, David V, 609
Aldridge, Elizabeth VI, 129
Aldridge, Elizabeth VI, 132
Aldridge, Eva V, 609
Aldridge, Fred V, 609
Aldridge, George Tellfair V, 655
Aldridge, Gladys V, 609
Aldridge, Gladys V, 655
Aldridge, Gladys V, 717
Aldridge, Jane V, 609
Aldridge, Joseph V, 609
Aldridge, Lena V, 609
Aldridge, Mary V, 609
Aldridge, Walmanus II, 331
Aldridge, Wm. V, 609
Aldridge, Wm. V, 717
Aldy, Mattie I, 627
Alen, Abigail I, 345
Alen, Alfred I, 345
Alen, Catharine I, 443
Alen, Elcy V, 471
Alen, Hanah II, 49
Alen, Hannah I, 345
Alen, Harmon I, 473
Alen, Herman I, 345
Alen, Ire II, 451
Alen, Jacob V, 471
Alen, Job I, 345
Alen, Joel I, 370
Alen, John I, 345
Alen, John I, 370
Alen, Martha I, 345
Alen, Miles I, 345
Alen, Nathan I, 345
Alen, Phebe I, 345
Alen, Rachel I, 345
Alen, Ruth I, 345
Alen, Samuel I, 370
Alen, Solomon I, 345
Alen, Zimri I, 345
Ales, Amos IV, 73
Ales, Ann IV, 73
Ales, Joseph IV, 73
Ales, Sarah IV, 73
Alex, Sarah VI, 495
Alexander, Agnes II, 953
Alexander, Agnes II, 956
Alexander, Agnes II, 957
Alexander, Agnes II, 1044
Alexander, Agnes II, 1047
Alexander, Agness II, 974
Alexander, Alice V, 210
Alexander, Almeda V, 210
Alexander, Andrew VI, 870
Alexander, Angeline A. I, 869
Alexander, Angie I, 229
Alexander, Angie I, 245
Alexander, Angie I, 869
Alexander, Ann VI, 870
Alexander, Ann F. VI, 862
Alexander, Anna I, 925
Alexander, Anna I, 930
Alexander, Anna E. I, 869
Alexander, Aubine V, 609
Alexander, Bee V, 210
Alexander, Carrie IV, 1305
Alexander, Catharine VI, 823
Alexander, Catherine W. VI, 845
Alexander, Charles II, 953
Alexander, Charles Ed VI, 833
Alexander, Charlotte L. VI, 852
Alexander, Chas. S. IV, 1305
Alexander, Christopher II, 953
Alexander, Clarence V, 891
Alexander, Cora Ann V, 664
Alexander, Deborah V, 210
Alexander, Deborah Sarah V, 210
Alexander, Delilah V, 664
Alexander, Dorothy Mae V, 210
Alexander, E. VI, 823
Alexander, Edna IV, 995
Alexander, Edward V, 210
Alexander, Edward B. V, 210
Alexander, Edward R. V, 210
Alexander, Elisha II, 331
Alexander, Eliza VI, 806
Alexander, Elizabeth II, 331
Alexander, Elizabeth V, 609
Alexander, Elizabeth V, 635
Alexander, Elizabeth VI, 795
Alexander, Elizabeth VI, 829
Alexander, Elizabeth VI, 849
Alexander, Elizabeth VI, 870
Alexander, Ellen B. V, 210
Alexander, Esther II, 974
Alexander, Esther II, 1036
Alexander, Esther VI, 842
Alexander, Esther VI, 873
Alexander, Florence V, 891
Alexander, Franklin B. III, 16
Alexander, Franklin F. III, 16
Alexander, Genevive Loyd V, 210
Alexander, George III, 16
Alexander, George III, 19
Alexander, George VI, 824
Alexander, Gerard VI, 814
Alexander, Gerard VI, 829
Alexander, Gladys IV, 1305
Alexander, Hannah II, 331
Alexander, Hannah II, 451
Alexander, Hannah V, 149
Alexander, Hannah V, 209
Alexander, Helen Marie V, 210
Alexander, Henrietta VI, 814
Alexander, Henry A. VI, 795
Alexander, Henry A. VI, 862
Alexander, Hester I, 370
Alexander, Hester I, 399
Alexander, Hesther I, 370
Alexander, James II, 331
Alexander, James II, 451
Alexander, James IV, 319
Alexander, James VI, 840
Alexander, James A. II, 331
Alexander, James A. II, 451
Alexander, James Adam II, 451
Alexander, Jane II, 331
Alexander, Jemima II, 953
Alexander, John VI, 325
Alexander, John VI, 800
Alexander, John VI, 803
Alexander, John VI, 805
Alexander, John VI, 806
Alexander, John VI, 810
Alexander, John VI, 826
Alexander, John VI, 829
Alexander, John VI, 831
Alexander, John VI, 836
Alexander, John VI, 840
Alexander, John VI, 843
Alexander, John VI, 845
Alexander, John VI, 849
Alexander, John VI, 852
Alexander, John VI, 853
Alexander, John VI, 857
Alexander, John VI, 859
Alexander, John VI, 861
Alexander, John VI, 866
Alexander, John VI, 867
Alexander, John VI, 870
Alexander, John VI, 894
Alexander, John VI, 976
Alexander, John D. VI, 795
Alexander, John D. VI, 811
Alexander, John D. VI, 861
Alexander, Jonathan I, 869
Alexander, Jonathan R. I, 869
Alexander, Joseph I, 925
Alexander, Joseph I, 930
Alexander, Joseph F. III, 16
Alexander, Joseph N. II, 865
Alexander, Julietta V, 210
Alexander, Lucy V, 210
Alexander, Lydia S. II, 865
Alexander, Margaret II, 953
Alexander, Margaret II, 960
Alexander, Margaret II, 974
Alexander, Margaret II, 1044
Alexander, Margaret II, 1052
Alexander, Margaret M. I, 869
Alexander, Martha III, 16
Alexander, Mary V, 210
Alexander, Mary VI, 795
Alexander, Mary G. VI, 810
Alexander, Mary G. VI, 846
Alexander, Maud IV, 1305
Alexander, Mildred V, 210
Alexander, Milow V, 210
Alexander, Minerva IV, 995
Alexander, Moses A. V, 210
Alexander, Moses, Jr. V, 210
Alexander, Nancy VI, 806
Alexander, Nellie IV, 1305
Alexander, Nellie Dar V, 210
Alexander, Nilow V, 210
Alexander, Olivia VI, 803
Alexander, Perdido I, 869
Alexander, Rachel II, 803
Alexander, Rachel II, 953
Alexander, Rachel II, 956
Alexander, Rachel II, 960
Alexander, Rachel II, 974
Alexander, Rachel II, 1047
Alexander, Rachel II, 1052
Alexander, Rachel II, 1068
Alexander, Rachel III, 16
Alexander, Rachel III, 19
Alexander, Rachel A. E. I, 869
Alexander, Rachel E. III, 16
Alexander, Rachel E. III, 19
Alexander, Rachel Perdita I, 930
Alexander, Robert I, 869
Alexander, Robert II, 953
Alexander, Robert II, 956
Alexander, Robert II, 960
Alexander, Robert II, 974
Alexander, Robert II, 1047
Alexander, Robert II, 1052
Alexander, Robert II, 1068
Alexander, Robert VI, 802
Alexander, Robert VI, 803
Alexander, Robert VI, 805
Alexander, Robert VI, 814
Alexander, Robert VI, 837
Alexander, Robert VI, 842
Alexander, Robert VI, 845
Alexander, Robert VI, 855
Alexander, Robert VI, 856
Alexander, Robert VI, 858
Alexander, Robert VI, 865
Alexander, Robert VI, 866
Alexander, Robert VI, 870
Alexander, Robert VI, 873
Alexander, Robert VI, 877
Alexander, Robert VI, 888
Alexander, Robert VI, 921
Alexander, Robert VI, 952
Alexander, Robert VI, 965
Alexander, Robert VI, 966
Alexander, Robert VI, 983
Alexander, Robert VI, 995
Alexander, Robert VI, 998
Alexander, Robert VI, 1002
Alexander, Robert VI, 1006
Alexander, Robert VI, 1007
Alexander, Robert VI, 1010
Alexander, Robert S. V, 210
Alexander, Robert W. G. I, 869
Alexander, Robt. VI, 846
Alexander, Robt. VI, 926
Alexander, Robt. VI, 931
Alexander, Robt. VI, 939
Alexander, Robt. VI, 955
Alexander, Robt. VI, 980
Alexander, Rufus V, 451
Alexander, Sally VI, 837
Alexander, Sally L. VI, 870
Alexander, Samuel III, 16
Alexander, Samuel V, 210
Alexander, Sarah II, 953
Alexander, Sarah II, 1068
Alexander, Sarah II, 1072
Alexander, Sarah III, 16
Alexander, Sarah IV, 169
Alexander, Sarah IV, 232
Alexander, Sarah VI, 870
Alexander, Sarah A. VI, 795
Alexander, Sarah A. VI, 843
Alexander, Sarah Alice V, 210
Alexander, Sarah E. I, 869
Alexander, Sarah E. I, 925
Alexander, Sarah F. II, 1068
Alexander, Sarah M. II, 953
Alexander, Sarah M. II, 1044
Alexander, Sarah M. II, 1052
Alexander, Sarah N. II, 865
Alexander, Sarah R. II, 331
Alexander, Sarah R. II, 451
Alexander, Susan IV, 1143
Alexander, Susan VI, 861
Alexander, Susan D. VI, 866
Alexander, Susie IV, 1143
Alexander, Thomas II, 331
Alexander, Thomas II, 451
Alexander, Thomas VI, 795
Alexander, Thomas VI, 798
Alexander, Thomas VI, 870
Alexander, Thomas VI, 994
Alexander, Toddy Leon V, 210
Alexander, Truman S. II, 865
Alexander, Twilight V, 664
Alexander, Velma V, 210
Alexander, W. VI, 817
Alexander, William I, 869
Alexander, William II, 953
Alexander, William VI, 829
Alexander, William VI, 835
Alexander, William B. II, 953
Alexander, William F. II, 953
Alexander, Wilson IV, 995
Alexander, Wm. IV, 1305
Alexander, Wm. V, 210
Alexander, Wm. B. II, 1044
Alexander, Wm. B. II, 1052
Alexander, Zora V, 471
Alexanders, Robert I, 869
Alexandria, ??? VI, 171
Alford, John IV, 605
Alford, John VI, 795
Alford, Mary VI, 795
Alford, Mary E. II, 830
Alford, Newell G. II, 830
Alford, R. IV, 671
Alford, Reuben G. II, 830
Alford, Sarah I, 128
Alford, Sarah I, 172
Alford, Tabitha I, 128
Alfred, Anna G. IV, 509
Alfred, Anna G. IV, 540
Alfred, Ella IV, 1305
Alfriend, Peter A. VI, 129
Alfriend, Peter A. VI, 136
Alfriend, Thomas Hunnicutt VI, 129
Algar, Marcia III, 66
Alger, Marcia III, 257
Alice, Laura A. VI, 439
Aliff, Alicia VI, 945
Aliff, Betsey VI, 870
Aliff, David VI, 870
Aliff, James VI, 870
Aliff, James VI, 918
Aliff, James VI, 945
Aliff, James VI, 1000
Aliff, Jane VI, 870
Aliff, Lucinda VI, 948
Aliff, Nancy VI, 870
Aliff, Polly VI, 870
Aliff, Sarah VI, 918
Aliff, Sophia VI, 870
Aliff, Thomas VI, 870
Aliff, William VI, 870
Aliff, William VI, 948
Aling, Margaret B. III, 101
Aling, Sarah III, 101
Aling, Silvanus III, 101
Alinn, John II, 17
Alinn, John II, 23
Alioth, ??? III, 40
Alioth, Ann Augusta III, 16
Alioth, Ann Augusta III, 40
Alioth, Chas. B. III, 16
Alison, Martha IV, 671
Alkinson, Ailse II, 194
Alkinson, Ailse II, 200
Alkinson, Mary I, 430
Allaback, Ida IV, 797
Allaback, John IV, 797
Allaback, Thornton IV, 797
Allam, Wm. H. A. IV, 1245
Allaman, Charles V, 149
Allaman, Missouri V, 149
Allamn, Bessie S. IV, 1271
Allan, Elizabeth VI, 824
Allan, Elizabeth VI, 834
Allan, Gillian VI, 834
Allan, Jackson VI, 295
Allan, Mary II, 331
Allan, Mary V, 19
Allan, Nehemiah II, 331
Allan, Rachel II, 451
Allan, Susanna VI, 295
Allan, Susanna VI, 299
Allawase, Mary II, 332
Allawase, William II, 332
Allaway, Hastings III, 16
Allaway, John III, 16
Allbright, Ruth V, 217
Allcock, Viliana I, 267
Allegre, Ann VI, 819
Allegre, Matthew VI, 819
Allen, ??? III, 484
Allen, ??? III, 491
Allen, ??? IV, 1269
Allen, ??? F. IV, 1271
Allen, A. Ward IV, 671
Allen, A. Ward IV, 1035
Allen, Aaron II, 50
Allen, Aaron IV, 363
Allen, Aaron IV, 565
Allen, Abigail I, 467
Allen, Abigail II, 165
Allen, Abigail II, 191
Allen, Abigail IV, 671
Allen, Abigail IV, 756
Allen, Abigail IV, 797
Allen, Abigail IV, 841
Allen, Abijah VI, 596
Allen, Abner II, 831
Allen, Abner II, 855
Allen, Abraham III, 393
Allen, Abraham V, 471
Allen, Achsa II, 974
Allen, Achsah II, 191
Allen, Addie M. I, 371
Allen, Adelaide III, 17
Allen, Adelaide III, 242
Allen, Adelaide L. III, 17
Allen, Adelaide L. III, 346
Allen, Adnah B. Silvin IV, 671
Allen, Adrain III, 16
Allen, Adrian III, 18
Allen, Agnes III, 17
Allen, Agnes Roberta III, 17
Allen, Agnes Roberta III, 27
Allen, Albert IV, 1349
Allen, Alex V, 19
Allen, Alfred I, 371
Allen, Alfred III, 18
Allen, Alfred Benjamin III, 16
Allen, Alice V, 149
Allen, Alice V, 200
Allen, Alice VI, 361
Allen, Alice H. V, 891
Allen, Alice V. V, 891
Allen, Alice Virginia V, 891
Allen, Alvie Ray V, 891
Allen, Amanda I, 1139
Allen, Amanda II, 720
Allen, Amelia IV, 797
Allen, Amelia IV, 802
Allen, Amelia IV, 852
Allen, Amelia VI, 870
Allen, Amos IV, 169
Allen, Amos V, 149
Allen, Amos G. IV, 319
Allen, Amos G. IV, 560
Allen, Amy I, 370
Allen, Amy I, 400
Allen, Amy I, 428
Allen, Amy III, 17
Allen, Amy IV, 19
Allen, Amy IV, 61
Allen, Amy V, 217
Allen, Amy V, 947
Allen, Amy VI, 361
Allen, Anderson M. I, 371
Allen, Andrew V, 218
Allen, Andrew J. V, 218
Allen, Ann I, 370
Allen, Ann I, 371
Allen, Ann II, 20
Allen, Ann II, 24
Allen, Ann II, 50
Allen, Ann II, 59
Allen, Ann II, 331
Allen, Ann II, 452
Allen, Ann II, 953
Allen, Ann II, 1020
Allen, Ann II, 1043
Allen, Ann II, 1044
Allen, Ann III, 479
Allen, Ann III, 491
Allen, Ann IV, 605
Allen, Ann IV, 606
Allen, Ann IV, 645
Allen, Ann IV, 891
Allen, Ann IV, 894
Allen, Ann VI, 361
Allen, Ann VI, 936
Allen, Ann A. II, 725
Allen, Ann A. II, 729
Allen, Ann F. V, 891
Allen, Ann H. III, 16
Allen, Ann H. V, 891
Allen, Ann Louisa III, 305
Allen, Ann, Jr. IV, 891
Allen, Ann, Sr. IV, 891
Allen, Anna II, 127
Allen, Anna II, 720
Allen, Anna V, 19
Allen, Anna V, 149
Allen, Anna V, 655
Allen, Anna V, 947
Allen, Anna VI, 399
Allen, Anna B. II, 142
Allen, Anna Comfort IV, 1349
Allen, Anna Tyler II, 142
Allen, Anna V. II, 132
Allen, Anna V. II, 149

Allen, Anna W. III, 16
Allen, Anna Willis III, 17
Allen, Annetta V, 547
Allen, Annetta V, 655
Allen, Anthony II, 331
Allen, Arthur L. III, 16
Allen, Arthur L. III, 252
Allen, Asenath I, 371
Allen, Asenath I, 459
Allen, Asenath E. I, 459
Allen, Asenath E. I, 473
Allen, B. C. VI, 871
Allen, Barzillai III, 16
Allen, Beatrice III, 17
Allen, Beatrice Alice III, 17
Allen, Beatrice Alice III, 275
Allen, Benj. IV, 605
Allen, Benjamin II, 331
Allen, Benjamin II, 451
Allen, Benjamin II, 452
Allen, Benjamin II, 725
Allen, Benjamin II, 779
Allen, Benjamin II, 830
Allen, Benjamin II, 831
Allen, Benjamin II, 953
Allen, Benjamin II, 968
Allen, Benjamin IV, 319
Allen, Benjamin IV, 321
Allen, Benjamin IV, 363
Allen, Benjamin IV, 560
Allen, Benjamin VI, 361
Allen, Benjamin VI, 591
Allen, Benjamin VI, 596
Allen, Benjamin VI, 603
Allen, Benjamin VI, 607
Allen, Benjamin F. IV, 1271
Allen, Benjamin, Jr. IV, 363
Allen, Bessie V, 149
Allen, Betsy IV, 363
Allen, Betsy IV, 411
Allen, Bette VI, 361
Allen, Betty VI, 361
Allen, Betty VI, 416
Allen, Betty VI, 444
Allen, Betty VI, 591
Allen, Betty VI, 597
Allen, Beulah II, 20
Allen, Beulah II, 50
Allen, Beulah V, 891
Allen, Beulah V, 899
Allen, Beulah Ann II, 20
Allen, Beulah Ann II, 114
Allen, Beulah Ann II, 127
Allen, Beulah Ann II, 142
Allen, Beulah W. II, 452
Allen, Beulah W. II, 830
Allen, Beulah W. V, 891
Allen, Beverly II, 279
Allen, Bnjamin C. IV, 891
Allen, C. C. V, 891
Allen, C. E. V, 891
Allen, Cameron H. I, 345
Allen, Caroline I, 371
Allen, Caroline I, 403
Allen, Caroline III, 16
Allen, Caroline III, 17
Allen, Caroline IV, 1271
Allen, Carolyn III, 253
Allen, Carrie IV, 671
Allen, Carrie IV, 792
Allen, Carry IV, 671
Allen, Casper Williams IV, 671
Allen, Cata V, 471
Allen, Catharine I, 371
Allen, Catharine I, 443
Allen, Catharine II, 50
Allen, Catharine II, 191
Allen, Catharine II, 831
Allen, Catharine II, 913
Allen, Catharine A. III, 16
Allen, Catharine A. III, 17
Allen, Chalmless II, 331
Allen, Chambles II, 332
Allen, Chambless II, 451
Allen, Chamles II, 114
Allen, Chamless II, 20
Allen, Chamless II, 50
Allen, Chamless II, 89
Allen, Chamlis II, 331
Allen, Chamness II, 127
Allen, Chamness II, 451
Allen, Charity I, 371
Allen, Charity I, 386
Allen, Charles I, 370
Allen, Charles I, 398
Allen, Charles II, 165
Allen, Charles II, 452
Allen, Charles II, 698
Allen, Charles II, 974
Allen, Charles II, 1044
Allen, Charles III, 18
Allen, Charles IV, 1305
Allen, Charles V, 547
Allen, Charles VI, 870
Allen, Charles VI, 878
Allen, Charles F. I, 937
Allen, Charles Francis II, 165
Allen, Charles Franklin I, 919
Allen, Charles J. II, 698
Allen, Charles L. II, 698
Allen, Charles M. II, 165
Allen, Charles M. II, 279
Allen, Charles M. II, 284
Allen, Charles M. II, 304
Allen, Charles Milton II, 279
Allen, Charles Mitton II, 279
Allen, Charles R. VI, 870
Allen, Charles W. II, 1068
Allen, Charles W. V, 149
Allen, Charles W. VI, 870
Allen, Chas. V, 983
Allen, Chas. E. IV, 1305
Allen, Chas. J. V, 655
Allen, Chas. L. V, 983
Allen, Chester V, 983
Allen, Chincy A. Ann IV, 1049
Allen, Christopher IV, 671
Allen, Christopher IV, 756
Allen, Christopher IV, 797
Allen, Christopher IV, 802
Allen, Christopher IV, 841
Allen, Christopher IV, 852
Allen, Christopher V, 891
Allen, Christopher V, 929
Allen, Christopher, Jr. IV, 671
Allen, Christopher, Jr. IV, 797
Allen, Christopher, Sr. IV, 797
Allen, Cinthy Ann IV, 606
Allen, Clarissa VI, 976
Allen, Clarissa VI, 982
Allen, Clarkson I, 459
Allen, Clary VI, 870
Allen, Clayton II, 331
Allen, Clayton II, 725
Allen, Clayton II, 779
Allen, Clayton II, 830
Allen, Clifford II, 779
Allen, Cola E. I, 937
Allen, Cola Etta I, 919
Allen, Collins II, 127
Allen, Collins II, 142
Allen, Collins II, 144
Allen, Collins B. II, 127
Allen, Collins B. II, 142
Allen, Columbus V, 891
Allen, Conelia I, 919
Allen, Cora I, 935
Allen, Cora I, 937
Allen, Cora I, 951
Allen, Cora E. I, 919
Allen, Cornelia L. IV, 1349
Allen, Cynthia IV, 605
Allen, Cynthia IV, 606
Allen, Cynthia IV, 642
Allen, Cynthia IV, 659
Allen, Cynthia Ann IV, 605
Allen, Cynthia Ann IV, 606
Allen, Cynthia Ann IV, 1049
Allen, Cynthia Ann IV, 1087
Allen, Cynthy Ann IV, 1087
Allen, Cyrus V, 947
Allen, Daniel I, 459
Allen, Daniel I, 473
Allen, Daniel IV, 319
Allen, Daniel IV, 509
Allen, Daniel IV, 526
Allen, Daniel VI, 361
Allen, Daniel A. IV, 319
Allen, Daniel B. V, 471
Allen, Daniel C. V, 547
Allen, Daniel C. V, 567
Allen, Daniel Cox I, 473
Allen, Daniel H. IV, 319
Allen, Daniel H. IV, 509
Allen, Daniel H. IV, 560
Allen, Daniel Johnson VI, 657
Allen, David II, 20
Allen, David II, 22
Allen, David II, 24
Allen, David II, 28
Allen, David II, 29
Allen, David II, 49
Allen, David II, 50
Allen, David II, 51
Allen, David II, 61
Allen, David II, 89
Allen, David II, 105
Allen, David II, 114
Allen, David II, 129
Allen, David II, 451
Allen, David II, 452
Allen, David II, 725
Allen, David II, 779
Allen, David II, 974
Allen, David II, 1043
Allen, David III, 16
Allen, David III, 35
Allen, David IV, 19
Allen, David IV, 605
Allen, David IV, 606
Allen, David IV, 642
Allen, David IV, 921
Allen, David IV, 968
Allen, David IV, 1049
Allen, David IV, 1087
Allen, David IV, 1349
Allen, David V, 471
Allen, David B. V, 471
Allen, David C. I, 1139
Allen, David Franklin II, 127
Allen, David M. IV, 605
Allen, David Palmer II, 974
Allen, David T. I, 371
Allen, David W. II, 452
Allen, Dayt V, 983
Allen, Deborah I, 370
Allen, Deborah IV, 19
Allen, Deborah IV, 68
Allen, Deborah IV, 606
Allen, Deborah IV, 659
Allen, Deborah V, 149
Allen, Deborah VI, 361
Allen, Delphina I, 1139
Allen, Diadema III, 17
Allen, Dillwyn II, 779
Allen, Dinah I, 345
Allen, Dinah I, 370
Allen, Dinah I, 421
Allen, Dinah E. I, 371
Allen, Dinah S. I, 459
Allen, Dinah S. I, 469
Allen, Dinah S. I, 473
Allen, Dinah S. I, 483
Allen, Diyt V, 983
Allen, Donald Townsend V, 891
Allen, Donald Wade IV, 671
Allen, Donald Wade IV, 792
Allen, Dorothea Elizabeth IV, 671
Allen, Dorothy IV, 605
Allen, Dorothy IV, 621
Allen, Dorothy E. IV, 606
Allen, E. Jane I, 919
Allen, Earl IV, 671
Allen, Eastburn II, 191
Allen, Eastwood II, 191
Allen, Ebanezer IV, 671
Allen, Ebenezar IV, 797
Allen, Ebenezer IV, 671
Allen, Ebenezer IV, 754
Allen, Ebenezer IV, 792
Allen, Ebenezer IV, 797
Allen, Ebinazar IV, 797
Allen, Edgar Bassett II, 127
Allen, Edith II, 20
Allen, Edith II, 331
Allen, Edmund II, 331
Allen, Edmund II, 779
Allen, Edmund II, 831
Allen, Edmund II, 911
Allen, Edmund H. II, 725
Allen, Edmund H. II, 830
Allen, Edna III, 35
Allen, Edne VI, 795
Allen, Edward II, 20
Allen, Edward II, 114
Allen, Edward V, 19
Allen, Edward V, 149
Allen, Edward VI, 361
Allen, Edward VI, 870
Allen, Edward S. III, 17
Allen, Edwin I, 1139
Allen, Effie IV, 754
Allen, Elcy V, 471
Allen, Elcy H. V, 471
Allen, Elcy H. V, 891
Allen, Elcy H. V, 893
Allen, Eleanor V, 149
Allen, Eleanor VI, 826
Allen, Eleazar N. I, 459
Allen, Eli VI, 361
Allen, Eli C. I, 459
Allen, Elias Henly I, 473
Allen, Elihu II, 974
Allen, Elihu W. II, 974
Allen, Elijah IV, 1349
Allen, Elisabeth I, 128
Allen, Elisabeth I, 145
Allen, Elisabeth I, 1113
Allen, Elisabeth I, 1129
Allen, Elisabeth II, 165
Allen, Elisabeth P. II, 279
Allen, Eliza II, 50
Allen, Eliza II, 114
Allen, Eliza II, 142
Allen, Eliza IV, 319
Allen, Eliza IV, 509
Allen, Eliza IV, 526
Allen, Eliza IV, 560
Allen, Eliza VI, 855
Allen, Eliza J. I, 371
Allen, Elizabeth I, 345
Allen, Elizabeth I, 370
Allen, Elizabeth I, 371
Allen, Elizabeth I, 381
Allen, Elizabeth I, 459
Allen, Elizabeth I, 473
Allen, Elizabeth I, 482
Allen, Elizabeth I, 647
Allen, Elizabeth I, 1113
Allen, Elizabeth I, 1139
Allen, Elizabeth I, 1147
Allen, Elizabeth II, 20
Allen, Elizabeth II, 49
Allen, Elizabeth II, 50
Allen, Elizabeth II, 58
Allen, Elizabeth II, 102
Allen, Elizabeth II, 146
Allen, Elizabeth II, 165
Allen, Elizabeth II, 451
Allen, Elizabeth II, 452
Allen, Elizabeth II, 560
Allen, Elizabeth II, 595
Allen, Elizabeth II, 648
Allen, Elizabeth II, 725
Allen, Elizabeth II, 779
Allen, Elizabeth II, 815
Allen, Elizabeth II, 827
Allen, Elizabeth II, 830
Allen, Elizabeth II, 831
Allen, Elizabeth II, 855
Allen, Elizabeth II, 953
Allen, Elizabeth II, 974
Allen, Elizabeth II, 1009
Allen, Elizabeth II, 1036
Allen, Elizabeth III, 17
Allen, Elizabeth III, 18
Allen, Elizabeth III, 393
Allen, Elizabeth III, 430
Allen, Elizabeth IV, 319
Allen, Elizabeth IV, 321
Allen, Elizabeth IV, 363
Allen, Elizabeth IV, 463
Allen, Elizabeth IV, 671
Allen, Elizabeth IV, 785
Allen, Elizabeth IV, 797
Allen, Elizabeth IV, 853
Allen, Elizabeth V, 46
Allen, Elizabeth V, 149
Allen, Elizabeth V, 156
Allen, Elizabeth V, 471
Allen, Elizabeth V, 547
Allen, Elizabeth V, 567
Allen, Elizabeth V, 879
Allen, Elizabeth V, 891
Allen, Elizabeth VI, 657
Allen, Elizabeth VI, 855
Allen, Elizabeth VI, 870
Allen, Elizabeth VI, 947
Allen, Elizabeth A. II, 725
Allen, Elizabeth A. II, 831
Allen, Elizabeth A. II, 910
Allen, Elizabeth Ackley II, 725
Allen, Elizabeth Ann III, 393
Allen, Elizabeth B. IV, 797
Allen, Elizabeth B. IV, 802
Allen, Elizabeth B. IV, 803
Allen, Elizabeth B. IV, 832
Allen, Elizabeth C. II, 1044
Allen, Elizabeth C. II, 1054
Allen, Elizabeth Cooper II, 805
Allen, Elizabeth E. II, 831
Allen, Elizabeth E. II, 892
Allen, Elizabeth Ellis II, 779
Allen, Elizabeth Ellis II, 831
Allen, Elizabeth Ellis II, 892
Allen, Elizabeth L. II, 698
Allen, Elizabeth L. II, 763
Allen, Elizabeth L. III, 17
Allen, Elizabeth L. IV, 1349
Allen, Elizabeth Milton II, 165
Allen, Elizabeth Milton II, 279
Allen, Elizabeth Milton II, 284
Allen, Elizabeth Wistar II, 127
Allen, Elizabeth Wistar II, 142
Allen, Elizabeth, Jr. IV, 363
Allen, Ella V, 149
Allen, Ellinor II, 451
Allen, Ellinor II, 515
Allen, Elma II, 128
Allen, Elmer V, 983
Allen, Elsie III, 17
Allen, Elsie Miller II, 127
Allen, Elsie Miller II, 142
Allen, Elwood I, 371
Allen, Emily V, 891
Allen, Emily V, 947
Allen, Emma I, 935
Allen, Emma I, 937
Allen, Emma II, 779
Allen, Emma V, 983
Allen, Emma A. V, 655
Allen, Emma J. I, 869
Allen, Emma Josephine I, 919
Allen, Emma L. II, 831
Allen, Emma L. II, 856
Allen, Emma Y. IV, 1305
Allen, Emmor IV, 19
Allen, Emy I, 370
Allen, Emy I, 400
Allen, Enoch II, 50
Allen, Enoch II, 127
Allen, Enoch II, 331
Allen, Enoch II, 332
Allen, Enoch II, 451
Allen, Enoch II, 725
Allen, Enoch II, 779
Allen, Enoch II, 830
Allen, Enoch II, 831
Allen, Enoch II, 876
Allen, Enoch II, 913
Allen, Enoch R. II, 20
Allen, Enoch R. II, 114
Allen, Enoch R. II, 142
Allen, Enock A. II, 50
Allen, Ephraim II, 49
Allen, Ephraim II, 83
Allen, Erall I, 919
Allen, Ester IV, 311
Allen, Ester IV, 313
Allen, Esther II, 955
Allen, Esther IV, 169
Allen, Esther IV, 509
Allen, Etta M. I, 459
Allen, Eunice III, 17
Allen, Eunice III, 335
Allen, Eunice IV, 319
Allen, Eunice IV, 323
Allen, Eunice IV, 363
Allen, Eunice VI, 361
Allen, Eunice VI, 376
Allen, Eunice VI, 593
Allen, Eva V, 983
Allen, Eva O. V, 983
Allen, Evalina I, 371
Allen, Eve IV, 1349
Allen, Eveline I, 371
Allen, Evelyn I, 919
Allen, Evia I, 937
Allen, Experience III, 17
Allen, Experience III, 118
Allen, Fanney V, 893
Allen, Fannie K. V, 149
Allen, Fanny VI, 873
Allen, Fanny H. V, 471
Allen, Fanny L. I, 869
Allen, Florence III, 17
Allen, Florence III, 66
Allen, Ford II, 128
Allen, Frances II, 331
Allen, Frances VI, 870
Allen, Francis II, 279
Allen, Francis H. V, 19
Allen, Francis H. V, 891
Allen, Francis H. V, 940
Allen, Francis Hayes V, 891
Allen, Frank II, 127
Allen, Franklin I, 371
Allen, Franklin I, 459
Allen, Franklin II, 114
Allen, Franklin II, 127
Allen, Franklin II, 142
Allen, Franklin II, 331
Allen, Franklin II, 725
Allen, Franklin II, 830
Allen, Franklin II, 831
Allen, Frederick VI, 153
Allen, Frederick J. III, 17
Allen, Frederick J. III, 27
Allen, Frederick Jerome III, 17
Allen, Frederick William IV, 1349
Allen, Freelove III, 393
Allen, Geneva V, 891
Allen, George II, 827
Allen, George III, 393
Allen, George III, 394
Allen, George V, 655
Allen, George B. II, 279
Allen, George B. II, 286
Allen, George B. II, 698
Allen, George C. III, 17
Allen, George L. III, 17
Allen, George Tappan III, 18
Allen, George W. I, 919
Allen, Georgia I, 937
Allen, Gilbert III, 17

Allen, Gladys IV, 1340
Allen, Gordon Elthan IV, 671
Allen, Grace Johnson V, 891
Allen, Hanah II, 49
Allen, Hannah I, 346
Allen, Hannah I, 370
Allen, Hannah I, 371
Allen, Hannah I, 373
Allen, Hannah I, 381
Allen, Hannah I, 386
Allen, Hannah I, 391
Allen, Hannah I, 430
Allen, Hannah I, 457
Allen, Hannah I, 459
Allen, Hannah I, 473
Allen, Hannah I, 673
Allen, Hannah II, 20
Allen, Hannah II, 28
Allen, Hannah II, 49
Allen, Hannah II, 50
Allen, Hannah II, 61
Allen, Hannah II, 64
Allen, Hannah II, 68
Allen, Hannah II, 70
Allen, Hannah II, 83
Allen, Hannah II, 100
Allen, Hannah II, 104
Allen, Hannah II, 114
Allen, Hannah II, 115
Allen, Hannah II, 138
Allen, Hannah II, 191
Allen, Hannah II, 253
Allen, Hannah II, 331
Allen, Hannah II, 332
Allen, Hannah II, 451
Allen, Hannah II, 532
Allen, Hannah II, 586
Allen, Hannah II, 680
Allen, Hannah II, 698
Allen, Hannah II, 790
Allen, Hannah II, 794
Allen, Hannah II, 830
Allen, Hannah II, 831
Allen, Hannah II, 913
Allen, Hannah III, 17
Allen, Hannah IV, 19
Allen, Hannah IV, 23
Allen, Hannah IV, 319
Allen, Hannah IV, 321
Allen, Hannah IV, 323
Allen, Hannah IV, 363
Allen, Hannah IV, 605
Allen, Hannah IV, 642
Allen, Hannah IV, 797
Allen, Hannah IV, 891
Allen, Hannah IV, 922
Allen, Hannah IV, 968
Allen, Hannah VI, 361
Allen, Hannah VI, 591
Allen, Hannah VI, 607
Allen, Hannah A. II, 114
Allen, Hannah A. II, 116
Allen, Hannah A. II, 142
Allen, Hannah A. II, 149
Allen, Hannah B. II, 132
Allen, Hannah C. I, 371
Allen, Hannah D. II, 127
Allen, Hannah D. II, 142
Allen, Hannah D. II, 144
Allen, Hannah D. II, 149
Allen, Hannah E. I, 371
Allen, Hannah E. II, 831
Allen, Hannah E. II, 911
Allen, Hannah G. II, 20
Allen, Hannah G. IV, 891
Allen, Hannah G., Jr. II, 20
Allen, Hannah J. I, 460
Allen, Hannah J. I, 473
Allen, Hannah J. I, 474
Allen, Hannah L. I, 371
Allen, Hannah L. II, 114
Allen, Hannah L. V, 149
Allen, Hannah Metta I, 459
Allen, Hannah P. II, 50
Allen, Hannah P. II, 830
Allen, Hannah P. II, 831
Allen, Hannah, Jr. IV, 363
Allen, Harmon I, 345
Allen, Harmon I, 473
Allen, Harmon I, 755
Allen, Harmony V, 19
Allen, Harmony V, 149
Allen, Harmony V, 947
Allen, Harmony VI, 361
Allen, Harriet III, 16
Allen, Harriet III, 17
Allen, Harriet IV, 1271
Allen, Harrison I, 371
Allen, Hartwick VI, 795
Allen, Harvey I, 919
Allen, Helen N. V, 891
Allen, Helen Nancy V, 891
Allen, Henry II, 165
Allen, Henry II, 191
Allen, Henry II, 253
Allen, Henry III, 17
Allen, Henry III, 393
Allen, Henry III, 430
Allen, Henry H. IV, 1349
Allen, Henry L. II, 698
Allen, Herbert IV, 797
Allen, Herman I, 370
Allen, Herman I, 371
Allen, Herman I, 457
Allen, Herman I, 473
Allen, Herman I, 755
Allen, Hetty Hall II, 127
Allen, Hezekiah I, 459
Allen, Hezekiah B. I, 473
Allen, Hirman I, 473
Allen, Hope II, 50
Allen, Hope II, 104
Allen, Hope II, 191
Allen, Hope II, 451
Allen, Hope II, 831
Allen, Howard II, 779
Allen, Howard A. IV, 605
Allen, Howard A. IV, 621
Allen, Hubert V, 891
Allen, Hubert Emerson V, 891
Allen, Hugh I, 345
Allen, Hugh I, 1113
Allen, Hugh I, 1147
Allen, Hugh Sharp II, 974
Allen, Ida IV, 1271
Allen, Ida M. V, 609
Allen, Inez B. III, 16
Allen, Inez B. III, 252
Allen, Ira II, 50
Allen, Ira II, 451
Allen, Ira II, 831
Allen, Ira II, 913
Allen, Ire II, 451
Allen, Irene J. II, 967
Allen, Irene J. IV, 820
Allen, Isaac I, 345
Allen, Isaac III, 17
Allen, Isaac IV, 19
Allen, Isaac IV, 169
Allen, Isaac IV, 363
Allen, Isaac IV, 560
Allen, Isaac IV, 605
Allen, Isaac IV, 606
Allen, Isaac IV, 632
Allen, Isaac IV, 921
Allen, Isaac V, 471
Allen, Isaac VI, 361
Allen, Isaac H. III, 16
Allen, Isaac H. III, 17
Allen, Isaac H. III, 284
Allen, Isaac W. V, 891
Allen, Isaac William V, 891
Allen, Isaac Wm. V, 891
Allen, Isaphine V, 609
Allen, J. W. I, 937
Allen, Jackson V, 19
Allen, Jackson V, 149
Allen, Jackson V, 164
Allen, Jackson V, 947
Allen, Jackson VI, 295
Allen, Jackson VI, 361
Allen, Jackson VI, 367
Allen, Jackson VI, 444
Allen, Jackson VI, 591
Allen, Jackson VI, 597
Allen, Jacob I, 371
Allen, Jacob III, 17
Allen, Jacob IV, 363
Allen, Jacob V, 471
Allen, Jacob V, 879
Allen, Jacob H. III, 305
Allen, Jacob H. IV, 363
Allen, Jacob H. IV, 463
Allen, Jacob H. V, 891
Allen, Jamaica II, 451
Allen, James I, 207
Allen, James I, 213
Allen, James I, 345
Allen, James I, 370
Allen, James I, 647
Allen, James I, 919
Allen, James I, 935
Allen, James I, 1113
Allen, James I, 1137
Allen, James I, 1139
Allen, James I, 1147
Allen, James II, 49
Allen, James II, 68
Allen, James II, 102
Allen, James II, 331
Allen, James II, 441
Allen, James IV, 19
Allen, James IV, 169
Allen, James IV, 509
Allen, James IV, 605
Allen, James IV, 892
Allen, James V, 655
Allen, James VI, 153
Allen, James VI, 361
Allen, James VI, 622
Allen, James VI, 643
Allen, James VI, 855
Allen, James VI, 870
Allen, James VI, 969
Allen, James A. I, 473
Allen, James A. I, 474
Allen, James A. I, 869
Allen, James C. I, 1113
Allen, James C. I, 1129
Allen, James C. I, 1139
Allen, James C. I, 1147
Allen, James M. IV, 169
Allen, James M. IV, 560
Allen, James M. H. III, 17
Allen, James M. H. III, 66
Allen, James M. H. III, 217
Allen, James, Junr. I, 1147
Allen, Jane I, 355
Allen, Jane I, 371
Allen, Jane I, 388
Allen, Jane II, 953
Allen, Jane II, 1026
Allen, Jane III, 17
Allen, Jane III, 159
Allen, Jane IV, 319
Allen, Jane IV, 330
Allen, Jane IV, 363
Allen, Jane IV, 565
Allen, Jane V, 825
Allen, Jas. W. III, 17
Allen, Jean I, 370
Allen, Jeane I, 370
Allen, Jedediah II, 20
Allen, Jedediah II, 50
Allen, Jedediah II, 51
Allen, Jedediah II, 114
Allen, Jedediah II, 138
Allen, Jedediah II, 331
Allen, Jedediah II, 452
Allen, Jedediah II, 779
Allen, Jedediah II, 830
Allen, Jedediah III, 18
Allen, Jedediah T. II, 20
Allen, Jedediah T. II, 49
Allen, Jedediah T. II, 50
Allen, Jedediah, Jr. II, 20
Allen, Jedediah, Jr. II, 50
Allen, Jedidiah II, 20
Allen, Jedidiah II, 100
Allen, Jedidiah II, 165
Allen, Jedidiah II, 451
Allen, Jedidiah II, 452
Allen, Jehu I, 345
Allen, Jehu IV, 319
Allen, Jehu IV, 331
Allen, Jehu IV, 363
Allen, Jehu IV, 560
Allen, Jennie IV, 797
Allen, Jenny VI, 889
Allen, Jeremiah II, 20
Allen, Jeremiah II, 49
Allen, Jeremiah II, 114
Allen, Jeremiah II, 451
Allen, Jeremiah VI, 870
Allen, Jeremiah C. I, 459
Allen, Jerome V, 891
Allen, Jerome Frederick III, 17
Allen, Jesse I, 370
Allen, Jesse IV, 605
Allen, Jesse IV, 606
Allen, Jesse IV, 645
Allen, Jesse IV, 1305
Allen, Jesse E. III, 17
Allen, Jesse M. IV, 605
Allen, Jesse M. IV, 649
Allen, Jesse M. VI, 685
Allen, Jesse, Jr. IV, 606
Allen, Jessie M. V, 891
Allen, Jessie W. V, 891
Allen, Jessie Wasterman V, 891
Allen, Jessie Westerman V, 929
Allen, Joanna I, 345
Allen, Joanna I, 1113
Allen, Joanna I, 1122
Allen, Joanna IV, 169
Allen, Joanna IV, 247
Allen, Joanna IV, 509
Allen, Joanna IV, 560
Allen, Job I, 371
Allen, Job I, 459
Allen, Job I, 473
Allen, Job I, 934
Allen, Job D. V, 547
Allen, Jobe V, 149
Allen, Jobe Harmon I, 459
Allen, Joel I, 370
Allen, Joel I, 371
Allen, Joel A. V, 609
Allen, Johannah I, 370
Allen, Johannah I, 1113
Allen, John I, 345
Allen, John I, 346
Allen, John I, 370
Allen, John I, 371
Allen, John I, 421
Allen, John I, 457
Allen, John I, 459
Allen, John I, 467
Allen, John I, 473
Allen, John I, 673
Allen, John I, 676
Allen, John I, 1075
Allen, John II, 191
Allen, John II, 224
Allen, John II, 242
Allen, John II, 331
Allen, John II, 451
Allen, John II, 452
Allen, John II, 725
Allen, John II, 953
Allen, John II, 974
Allen, John II, 997
Allen, John II, 1009
Allen, John II, 1036
Allen, John III, 17
Allen, John III, 393
Allen, John III, 394
Allen, John III, 415
Allen, John III, 483
Allen, John IV, 19
Allen, John IV, 605
Allen, John IV, 606
Allen, John IV, 891
Allen, John V, 371
Allen, John V, 547
Allen, John V, 725
Allen, John VI, 361
Allen, John VI, 795
Allen, John VI, 870
Allen, John VI, 947
Allen, John VI, 978
Allen, John VI, 988
Allen, John B. Ackley II, 452
Allen, John C. II, 698
Allen, John C. II, 763
Allen, John C. V, 891
Allen, John C., Jr. II, 698
Allen, John C., Jr. II, 725
Allen, John Carlin III, 17
Allen, John Christopher C. V, 891
Allen, John Curlin III, 275
Allen, John D. I, 371
Allen, John G. I, 473
Allen, John G. I, 869
Allen, John Gurney I, 473
Allen, John H. I, 371
Allen, John H. II, 720
Allen, John M. I, 473
Allen, John Mercer IV, 605
Allen, John Mercer IV, 606
Allen, John Mercer IV, 1049
Allen, John Mercer IV, 1087
Allen, John Milten IV, 363
Allen, John Milton IV, 363
Allen, John Milton IV, 463
Allen, John R. I, 371
Allen, John W. I, 371
Allen, John W. I, 919
Allen, John W. I, 935
Allen, John, Jr. I, 371
Allen, John, Jr. IV, 606
Allen, John, Jr. VI, 596
Allen, Jonathan IV, 605
Allen, Jonathan IV, 606
Allen, Jonathan IV, 1049
Allen, Jonathan IV, 1087
Allen, Jonathan VI, 596
Allen, Jonathan S. I, 371
Allen, Josep I, 473
Allen, Joseph I, 345
Allen, Joseph I, 370
Allen, Joseph I, 371
Allen, Joseph I, 457
Allen, Joseph I, 459
Allen, Joseph I, 473
Allen, Joseph II, 20
Allen, Joseph II, 49
Allen, Joseph II, 50
Allen, Joseph II, 104
Allen, Joseph II, 114
Allen, Joseph II, 138
Allen, Joseph II, 331
Allen, Joseph II, 332
Allen, Joseph II, 451
Allen, Joseph II, 1044
Allen, Joseph IV, 19
Allen, Joseph IV, 23
Allen, Joseph IV, 68
Allen, Joseph IV, 605
Allen, Joseph V, 19
Allen, Joseph V, 149
Allen, Joseph V, 217
Allen, Joseph V, 280
Allen, Joseph VI, 376
Allen, Joseph VI, 440
Allen, Joseph VI, 591
Allen, Joseph VI, 592
Allen, Joseph VI, 593
Allen, Joseph VI, 596
Allen, Joseph VI, 602
Allen, Joseph VI, 607
Allen, Joseph A. IV, 671
Allen, Joseph E. I, 371
Allen, Joseph Edward III, 17
Allen, Joseph J. I, 473
Allen, Joseph M. II, 20
Allen, Joseph M. II, 50
Allen, Joseph M. II, 142
Allen, Joseph P. IV, 671
Allen, Joseph P. IV, 762
Allen, Joseph P. V, 891
Allen, Joseph W. III, 16
Allen, Joseph W. III, 17
Allen, Joseph Walker III, 17
Allen, Joseph Warren V, 371
Allen, Joseph, Jr. V, 149
Allen, Joseph, Jr. VI, 361
Allen, Joseph, Jr. VI, 591
Allen, Josephine I, 937
Allen, Josephine V, 609
Allen, Josephine M. V, 149
Allen, Joshua II, 331
Allen, Joshua IV, 19
Allen, Joshua IV, 117
Allen, Joshua VI, 361
Allen, Joshua G. II, 698
Allen, Josiah II, 830
Allen, Josiah II, 831
Allen, Josiah J. II, 831
Allen, Josiah J. II, 892
Allen, Josiah Johnson II, 725
Allen, Josiah Johnson II, 779
Allen, Judiah II, 50
Allen, Judidiah II, 50
Allen, Judidiah II, 68
Allen, Judith VI, 521
Allen, Judith VI, 526
Allen, Judith VI, 563
Allen, Judith VI, 757
Allen, Judith VI, 760
Allen, Judith VI, 779
Allen, Judith VI, 794
Allen, Julia I, 345
Allen, Julia I, 371
Allen, Julia I, 1139
Allen, Julia III, 17
Allen, Julias VI, 153
Allen, Julias VI, 205
Allen, Julias VI, 219
Allen, Julius C. I, 473
Allen, Katharine I, 371
Allen, Katharine I, 1139
Allen, Katherine S. VI, 795
Allen, Kesiah V, 217
Allen, Keturah M. II, 830
Allen, Kittie V, 983
Allen, L. E. IV, 671
Allen, L. Ebbert IV, 671
Allen, L. Ebbert IV, 792
Allen, L. Margaret V, 891
Allen, Laetitia W. II, 830
Allen, Latitia W. II, 831
Allen, Latitia W. II, 876
Allen, Laura V, 983
Allen, Laura E. V, 983
Allen, Laura Peninah V, 891
Allen, Lavenia I, 370
Allen, Lawrence V, 891
Allen, Leah VI, 361
Allen, Leah VI, 375
Allen, Lemuel IV, 1349
Allen, Leroy IV, 671
Allen, Leticia I, 345
Allen, Letitia I, 923
Allen, Letitia II, 779
Allen, Lettice II, 20
Allen, Lettice II, 50
Allen, Lettice II, 142
Allen, Lettice II, 452
Allen, Lettice II, 779
Allen, Lettice II, 830
Allen, Lettice II, 831
Allen, Lettitia II, 50
Allen, Levi N. I, 459
Allen, Lidya II, 49

Allen, Lidya II, 104
Allen, Lillian II, 128
Allen, Lindley IV, 319
Allen, Linzy J. I, 459
Allen, Lizzie II, 779
Allen, Lora V, 983
Allen, Lott VI, 596
Allen, Lottie IV, 1143
Allen, Louis I, 937
Allen, Louisa I, 473
Allen, Louisa I, 869
Allen, Louisa I, 935
Allen, Louisa IV, 319
Allen, Louisa J. I, 919
Allen, Louisa Jaene I, 371
Allen, Lowell IV, 671
Allen, Lucinda I, 1139
Allen, Lucinda V, 609
Allen, Lydia I, 267
Allen, Lydia I, 268
Allen, Lydia I, 345
Allen, Lydia I, 371
Allen, Lydia I, 386
Allen, Lydia II, 20
Allen, Lydia II, 114
Allen, Lydia II, 125
Allen, Lydia II, 331
Allen, Lydia II, 451
Allen, Lydia II, 648
Allen, Lydia IV, 605
Allen, Lydia IV, 632
Allen, Lydia IV, 671
Allen, Lydia IV, 762
Allen, Lydia V, 149
Allen, Lydia V, 891
Allen, Lydia VI, 361
Allen, Lydia VI, 591
Allen, Lydia H. IV, 891
Allen, Lydia M. V, 891
Allen, Lydia M. V, 929
Allen, Lydia Maria V, 471
Allen, Mabel Loretta IV, 169
Allen, Mabel S. VI, 729
Allen, Magdaline VI, 892
Allen, Mahala B. V, 217
Allen, Mahala B. V, 280
Allen, Malinda I, 345
Allen, Malinda I, 371
Allen, Malinda I, 406
Allen, Malinda V, 19
Allen, Malinda V, 891
Allen, Malinda V, 940
Allen, Malinda W. V, 891
Allen, Margaret II, 49
Allen, Margaret II, 61
Allen, Margaret II, 132
Allen, Margaret II, 165
Allen, Margaret II, 279
Allen, Margaret II, 304
Allen, Margaret III, 393
Allen, Margaret III, 394
Allen, Margaret V, 149
Allen, Margaret Elizabeth III, 17
Allen, Margret II, 49
Allen, Maria II, 331
Allen, Maria III, 17
Allen, Maria III, 38
Allen, Maria Louisa III, 207
Allen, Marion III, 17
Allen, Marion III, 346
Allen, Marion L. V, 655
Allen, Marion S. V, 547
Allen, Marmaduke II, 953
Allen, Martha I, 370
Allen, Martha I, 371
Allen, Martha I, 457
Allen, Martha I, 459
Allen, Martha I, 473
Allen, Martha I, 478
Allen, Martha I, 673
Allen, Martha I, 676
Allen, Martha II, 50
Allen, Martha II, 165
Allen, Martha II, 191
Allen, Martha II, 279
Allen, Martha II, 304
Allen, Martha II, 830
Allen, Martha II, 831
Allen, Martha IV, 605
Allen, Martha IV, 606
Allen, Martha IV, 640
Allen, Martha IV, 644
Allen, Martha IV, 671
Allen, Martha IV, 797
Allen, Martha V, 471
Allen, Martha A. I, 459
Allen, Martha A. I, 473
Allen, Martha A. I, 481
Allen, Martha D. II, 698
Allen, Martin III, 17
Allen, Martin D. III, 17
Allen, Martin D. III, 242
Allen, Martin D. III, 346
Allen, Mary I, 345
Allen, Mary I, 370
Allen, Mary I, 371
Allen, Mary I, 389
Allen, Mary I, 397
Allen, Mary I, 459
Allen, Mary I, 473
Allen, Mary I, 480
Allen, Mary I, 934
Allen, Mary I, 1113
Allen, Mary I, 1125
Allen, Mary I, 1139
Allen, Mary II, 20
Allen, Mary II, 22
Allen, Mary II, 24
Allen, Mary II, 49
Allen, Mary II, 50
Allen, Mary II, 54
Allen, Mary II, 114
Allen, Mary II, 115
Allen, Mary II, 122
Allen, Mary II, 129
Allen, Mary II, 130
Allen, Mary II, 142
Allen, Mary II, 154
Allen, Mary II, 191
Allen, Mary II, 242
Allen, Mary II, 279
Allen, Mary II, 286
Allen, Mary II, 331
Allen, Mary II, 441
Allen, Mary II, 451
Allen, Mary II, 452
Allen, Mary II, 508
Allen, Mary II, 518
Allen, Mary II, 533
Allen, Mary II, 562
Allen, Mary II, 633
Allen, Mary II, 680
Allen, Mary II, 698
Allen, Mary II, 818
Allen, Mary II, 824
Allen, Mary II, 830
Allen, Mary II, 831
Allen, Mary II, 932
Allen, Mary II, 974
Allen, Mary II, 979
Allen, Mary II, 989
Allen, Mary II, 1018
Allen, Mary II, 1023
Allen, Mary II, 1044
Allen, Mary II, 1068
Allen, Mary III, 17
Allen, Mary III, 393
Allen, Mary III, 419
Allen, Mary III, 430
Allen, Mary IV, 319
Allen, Mary IV, 340
Allen, Mary IV, 363
Allen, Mary IV, 605
Allen, Mary IV, 649
Allen, Mary IV, 671
Allen, Mary IV, 797
Allen, Mary IV, 844
Allen, Mary IV, 1152
Allen, Mary V, 19
Allen, Mary V, 31
Allen, Mary V, 53
Allen, Mary V, 149
Allen, Mary V, 153
Allen, Mary V, 193
Allen, Mary V, 200
Allen, Mary VI, 361
Allen, Mary VI, 444
Allen, Mary VI, 603
Allen, Mary VI, 685
Allen, Mary VI, 870
Allen, Mary VI, 936
Allen, Mary A. I, 430
Allen, Mary Ann I, 371
Allen, Mary Ann II, 779
Allen, Mary Ann III, 246
Allen, Mary Ann IV, 319
Allen, Mary Ann IV, 331
Allen, Mary Ann IV, 560
Allen, Mary Ann IV, 606
Allen, Mary Ann IV, 608
Allen, Mary Anna III, 17
Allen, Mary B. II, 50
Allen, Mary B. II, 452
Allen, Mary B. II, 725
Allen, Mary B. II, 746
Allen, Mary B. V, 73
Allen, Mary C. V, 609
Allen, Mary D. II, 279
Allen, Mary E. II, 698
Allen, Mary Elizabeth IV, 1349
Allen, Mary Elizabeth V, 891
Allen, Mary Elizabeth V, 939
Allen, Mary Griffin II, 127
Allen, Mary Griffin II, 142
Allen, Mary J. I, 371
Allen, Mary Jane I, 371
Allen, Mary Jane I, 922
Allen, Mary Jane I, 934
Allen, Mary Jane IV, 169
Allen, Mary L. V, 547
Allen, Mary L. V, 655
Allen, Mary Louisa III, 17
Allen, Mary Louisa III, 284
Allen, Mary Louise III, 284
Allen, Mary Matilda III, 17
Allen, Mary R. II, 50
Allen, Mary Ruth IV, 792
Allen, Mary S. V, 471
Allen, Mary W. II, 1068
Allen, Mary W. III, 17
Allen, Mary W. III, 305
Allen, Mary W. IV, 671
Allen, Mary W. IV, 1349
Allen, Mary White II, 452
Allen, Mason W. II, 331
Allen, Mason Ward II, 331
Allen, Matilda I, 371
Allen, Matilda I, 388
Allen, Matilda I, 1113
Allen, Matilda I, 1129
Allen, Matilda I, 1139
Allen, Matilda I, 1147
Allen, Matilda Ann V, 371
Allen, Matildah I, 371
Allen, Matthew II, 191
Allen, Maud IV, 671
Allen, Melinda I, 371
Allen, Mercy Ackley II, 725
Allen, Mercy Ann II, 725
Allen, Mercy Ann II, 731
Allen, Mercy Ann II, 830
Allen, Mercy Ann II, 843
Allen, Meribah V, 825
Allen, Meribah V, 856
Allen, Metta T. I, 459
Allen, Michael II, 132
Allen, Miles T. I, 459
Allen, Miller II, 331
Allen, Milly VI, 931
Allen, Milly VI, 952
Allen, Milton I, 371
Allen, Minnie I, 937
Allen, Minnie III, 17
Allen, Miriam Borden III, 17
Allen, Miriam T. II, 831
Allen, Miriam T. II, 855
Allen, Miriam Tilton II, 790
Allen, Mirriam Borden III, 17
Allen, Moses IV, 319
Allen, Moses IV, 330
Allen, Moses IV, 363
Allen, Moses IV, 565
Allen, Moses VI, 361
Allen, Myrtie V, 983
Allen, Myrtle IV, 211
Allen, Myrtle IV, 671
Allen, Myrtle IV, 1271
Allen, Myrtle IV, 1305
Allen, Myrtle V, 983
Allen, Myrtle O. IV, 671
Allen, Myrtle O. IV, 1305
Allen, N. Penrose II, 831
Allen, N. Penrose Allen II, 856
Allen, Nancy I, 370
Allen, Nancy I, 371
Allen, Nancy I, 457
Allen, Nancy I, 473
Allen, Nancy V, 825
Allen, Nancy VI, 870
Allen, Nancy VI, 997
Allen, Nancy C. I, 371
Allen, Nancy E. I, 371
Allen, Nannie I, 934
Allen, Narcissa IV, 319
Allen, Nathan I, 345
Allen, Nathan I, 370
Allen, Nathan I, 371
Allen, Nathan I, 459
Allen, Nathan I, 473
Allen, Nathan II, 191
Allen, Nathan IV, 605
Allen, Nathan F. I, 371
Allen, Nathan J. I, 459
Allen, Nathan J. I, 473
Allen, Nathaniel I, 459
Allen, Nathaniel II, 331
Allen, Nathaniel II, 332
Allen, Nathaniel II, 451
Allen, Nathaniel II, 518
Allen, Nathaniel II, 633
Allen, Nathaniel II, 636
Allen, Nathaniel II, 680
Allen, Nathaniel, Jr. II, 451
Allen, Nathaniel, Sr. II, 331
Allen, Nathaniell II, 332
Allen, Nehemiah I, 1075
Allen, Nehemiah II, 331
Allen, Nehemiah II, 332
Allen, Nehemiah II, 451
Allen, Nehemiah II, 466
Allen, Nehemiah II, 518
Allen, Nehemiah II, 562
Allen, Nehemiah II, 633
Allen, Nehemiah II, 636
Allen, Nehemiah II, 680
Allen, Nehemiah III, 17
Allen, Nehemiah III, 393
Allen, Nehemiah, Jr. II, 451
Allen, Nehemiah, Jr. II, 586
Allen, Ner II, 50
Allen, Ner II, 104
Allen, Newton I, 371
Allen, Nicholas II, 974
Allen, Nicolas II, 974
Allen, Nixon Henly I, 473
Allen, Nora L. I, 869
Allen, Norwood Penrose II, 831
Allen, Olive III, 393
Allen, Olive M. V, 547
Allen, Olive M. V, 655
Allen, Oliver VI, 526
Allen, Orilla B. V, 655
Allen, Orpha IV, 19
Allen, Orpha IV, 605
Allen, Orrilla B. V, 547
Allen, Orville M. V, 609
Allen, Owega V, 317
Allen, Owen VI, 889
Allen, Pamela III, 17
Allen, Pamela III, 189
Allen, Pamelia III, 393
Allen, Patience VI, 596
Allen, Paulina III, 18
Allen, Pauline III, 17
Allen, Paune III, 96
Allen, Penrose II, 779
Allen, Peter I, 345
Allen, Peter I, 370
Allen, Peter I, 371
Allen, Peter, Jr. I, 371
Allen, Phebe I, 345
Allen, Phebe I, 346
Allen, Phebe I, 370
Allen, Phebe I, 371
Allen, Phebe I, 381
Allen, Phebe I, 396
Allen, Phebe I, 421
Allen, Phebe II, 798
Allen, Phebe III, 17
Allen, Phebe IV, 605
Allen, Phebe IV, 606
Allen, Phebe IV, 891
Allen, Phebe IV, 894
Allen, Phebe IV, 1143
Allen, Phebe IV, 1150
Allen, Phebe V, 19
Allen, Phebe V, 99
Allen, Phebe VI, 870
Allen, Phebe C. I, 371
Allen, Phebe H. V, 19
Allen, Phebe H. V, 99
Allen, Phebe J. IV, 73
Allen, Phebe J. IV, 117
Allen, Phebe J. IV, 671
Allen, Phebe J. IV, 788
Allen, Phebe W. IV, 1349
Allen, Phila II, 50
Allen, Philip IV, 363
Allen, Philip V, 879
Allen, Philip V, 891
Allen, Phillip IV, 363
Allen, Phillip IV, 463
Allen, Phillip V, 879
Allen, Polly VI, 873
Allen, Preston V, 149
Allen, Priscilla II, 451
Allen, Priscilla II, 653
Allen, Rachel I, 345
Allen, Rachel I, 370
Allen, Rachel I, 371
Allen, Rachel I, 388
Allen, Rachel I, 420
Allen, Rachel I, 459
Allen, Rachel I, 467
Allen, Rachel II, 20
Allen, Rachel II, 50
Allen, Rachel II, 127
Allen, Rachel II, 142
Allen, Rachel II, 144
Allen, Rachel II, 331
Allen, Rachel II, 451
Allen, Rachel II, 452
Allen, Rachel II, 455
Allen, Rachel II, 545
Allen, Rachel II, 683
Allen, Rachel II, 974
Allen, Rachel II, 1026
Allen, Rachel IV, 1305
Allen, Rachel VI, 818
Allen, Rachel VI, 1013
Allen, Rachel B. II, 142
Allen, Rachel H. IV, 1305
Allen, Rachel J. I, 459
Allen, Rachel W. II, 331
Allen, Rachel W. II, 831
Allen, Rachel W. II, 876
Allen, Rachel Ward II, 779
Allen, Rachel Ward II, 800
Allen, Rachel, Jr. II, 50
Allen, Ralfe II, 49
Allen, Ralph II, 50
Allen, Ralph V, 609
Allen, Ray IV, 792
Allen, Rebecca I, 345
Allen, Rebecca I, 370
Allen, Rebecca I, 371
Allen, Rebecca I, 398
Allen, Rebecca I, 457
Allen, Rebecca I, 480
Allen, Rebecca I, 647
Allen, Rebecca I, 1139
Allen, Rebecca I, 1147
Allen, Rebecca I, 1154
Allen, Rebecca II, 20
Allen, Rebecca II, 22
Allen, Rebecca II, 24
Allen, Rebecca II, 28
Allen, Rebecca II, 29
Allen, Rebecca II, 43
Allen, Rebecca II, 49
Allen, Rebecca II, 50
Allen, Rebecca II, 51
Allen, Rebecca II, 57
Allen, Rebecca II, 70
Allen, Rebecca II, 73
Allen, Rebecca II, 89
Allen, Rebecca II, 105
Allen, Rebecca II, 106
Allen, Rebecca II, 114
Allen, Rebecca II, 120
Allen, Rebecca II, 191
Allen, Rebecca II, 224
Allen, Rebecca II, 331
Allen, Rebecca II, 332
Allen, Rebecca II, 451
Allen, Rebecca II, 466
Allen, Rebecca II, 698
Allen, Rebecca II, 974
Allen, Rebecca II, 997
Allen, Rebecca III, 17
Allen, Rebecca III, 66
Allen, Rebecca III, 217
Allen, Rebecca IV, 169
Allen, Rebecca IV, 258
Allen, Rebecca IV, 311
Allen, Rebecca IV, 313
Allen, Rebecca IV, 319
Allen, Rebecca V, 19
Allen, Rebecca V, 947
Allen, Rebecca V, 983
Allen, Rebecca VI, 361
Allen, Rebecca VI, 371
Allen, Rebecca VI, 622
Allen, Rebecca VI, 643
Allen, Rebecca C. V, 19
Allen, Rebecca E. V, 19
Allen, Rebecca E. V, 45
Allen, Rebecca G. II, 20
Allen, Rebecca L. V, 547
Allen, Rebecca L. V, 655
Allen, Rebecca S. II, 698
Allen, Rebecca S. II, 763
Allen, Rebecca S., Jr. II, 698
Allen, Rebecca T. II, 20
Allen, Rebecca W. II, 165
Allen, Rebecca Warren II, 331
Allen, Rebecca Warren II, 332
Allen, Rebeccah I, 473
Allen, Rebeccah I, 1113
Allen, Rebeccah II, 191
Allen, Rebeccah II, 242
Allen, Rebeckah II, 50
Allen, Rebeckah II, 105
Allen, Rebeckah II, 332
Allen, Rebeckah II, 953
Allen, Rebeckah II, 974
Allen, Rebeckah V, 149
Allen, Rebekah I, 370
Allen, Rebekah I, 473
Allen, Rebekah I, 480
Allen, Rebekah II, 451
Allen, Rebekah II, 636
Allen, Rebekah VI, 361
Allen, Reuben IV, 169
Allen, Reuben IV, 509

Allen, Reuben IV, 560
Allen, Reuben VI, 813
Allen, Reubin VI, 795
Allen, Rhesa VI, 361
Allen, Richard II, 20
Allen, Richard II, 114
Allen, Richard II, 331
Allen, Richard II, 332
Allen, Richard II, 451
Allen, Richard II, 533
Allen, Richard III, 17
Allen, Richard III, 393
Allen, Richard IV, 671
Allen, Richard IV, 797
Allen, Richard V, 19
Allen, Richard B. II, 127
Allen, Richard B. II, 142
Allen, Richard I. II, 279
Allen, Richard I. II, 286
Allen, Richard J. II, 279
Allen, Robenia III, 17
Allen, Robenia III, 96
Allen, Robert II, 332
Allen, Robert VI, 892
Allen, Robert Thomas II, 332
Allen, Robert Warren V, 891
Allen, Roy IV, 671
Allen, Rufus G. I, 459
Allen, Ruth I, 459
Allen, Ruth I, 465
Allen, Ruth I, 471
Allen, Ruth I, 473
Allen, Ruth I, 476
Allen, Ruth I, 485
Allen, Ruth I, 1139
Allen, Ruth II, 20
Allen, Ruth II, 50
Allen, Ruth II, 89
Allen, Ruth V, 19
Allen, Ruth V, 149
Allen, Ruth V, 164
Allen, Ruth VI, 361
Allen, Ruth VI, 591
Allen, Ruthann IV, 169
Allen, Ruthann IV, 560
Allen, Ruthanna III, 32
Allen, Ruthanna IV, 509
Allen, Ruthanna L. II, 698
Allen, S. Catherine V, 217
Allen, Salley VI, 926
Allen, Sallie I, 919
Allen, Sally I, 371
Allen, Sally I, 427
Allen, Sally Ann IV, 605
Allen, Sally Ann IV, 606
Allen, Sally Ann IV, 624
Allen, Saml I, 345
Allen, Sampson I, 345
Allen, Sampson I, 371
Allen, Samuel I, 345
Allen, Samuel I, 370
Allen, Samuel I, 371
Allen, Samuel I, 459
Allen, Samuel I, 473
Allen, Samuel I, 482
Allen, Samuel I, 673
Allen, Samuel II, 20
Allen, Samuel II, 50
Allen, Samuel II, 114
Allen, Samuel II, 115
Allen, Samuel II, 127
Allen, Samuel II, 144
Allen, Samuel II, 191
Allen, Samuel II, 331
Allen, Samuel II, 332
Allen, Samuel II, 451
Allen, Samuel II, 452
Allen, Samuel II, 698
Allen, Samuel II, 725
Allen, Samuel II, 830
Allen, Samuel II, 953
Allen, Samuel II, 974
Allen, Samuel II, 982
Allen, Samuel II, 1020
Allen, Samuel II, 1026
Allen, Samuel II, 1035
Allen, Samuel II, 1043
Allen, Samuel III, 393
Allen, Samuel IV, 19
Allen, Samuel IV, 363
Allen, Samuel IV, 463
Allen, Samuel V, 547
Allen, Samuel V, 879
Allen, Samuel V, 891
Allen, Samuel VI, 361
Allen, Samuel A. II, 20
Allen, Samuel A. II, 114
Allen, Samuel Austin II, 20
Allen, Samuel C. II, 127
Allen, Samuel C. II, 142
Allen, Samuel C. II, 144
Allen, Samuel Leeds II, 698
Allen, Samuel P. II, 127
Allen, Samuel P. II, 132
Allen, Samuel P. II, 142
Allen, Samuel P. II, 144
Allen, Samuel P. II, 149
Allen, Samuel, Jr. II, 114
Allen, Samuel, Jr. II, 725
Allen, Samuel, Jr. II, 974
Allen, Samuel, Jr. II, 982
Allen, Samuel, Jr. II, 1035
Allen, Sarah I, 345
Allen, Sarah I, 370
Allen, Sarah I, 919
Allen, Sarah I, 935
Allen, Sarah I, 1113
Allen, Sarah I, 1139
Allen, Sarah I, 1147
Allen, Sarah II, 20
Allen, Sarah II, 50
Allen, Sarah II, 51
Allen, Sarah II, 89
Allen, Sarah II, 114
Allen, Sarah II, 127
Allen, Sarah II, 142
Allen, Sarah II, 144
Allen, Sarah II, 155
Allen, Sarah II, 332
Allen, Sarah II, 451
Allen, Sarah II, 698
Allen, Sarah II, 725
Allen, Sarah II, 779
Allen, Sarah II, 830
Allen, Sarah II, 953
Allen, Sarah II, 968
Allen, Sarah II, 974
Allen, Sarah II, 982
Allen, Sarah II, 1009
Allen, Sarah II, 1035
Allen, Sarah II, 1043
Allen, Sarah III, 17
Allen, Sarah III, 18
Allen, Sarah III, 393
Allen, Sarah III, 394
Allen, Sarah III, 447
Allen, Sarah IV, 19
Allen, Sarah IV, 30
Allen, Sarah IV, 363
Allen, Sarah IV, 509
Allen, Sarah IV, 510
Allen, Sarah IV, 605
Allen, Sarah IV, 632
Allen, Sarah IV, 642
Allen, Sarah IV, 671
Allen, Sarah IV, 762
Allen, Sarah IV, 891
Allen, Sarah IV, 892
Allen, Sarah IV, 921
Allen, Sarah V, 19
Allen, Sarah V, 149
Allen, Sarah V, 164
Allen, Sarah V, 471
Allen, Sarah V, 947
Allen, Sarah V, 950
Allen, Sarah VI, 361
Allen, Sarah VI, 591
Allen, Sarah VI, 795
Allen, Sarah VI, 870
Allen, Sarah VI, 878
Allen, Sarah A. I, 473
Allen, Sarah A. I, 474
Allen, Sarah A. II, 968
Allen, Sarah Ann II, 20
Allen, Sarah Ann II, 114
Allen, Sarah Ann II, 725
Allen, Sarah C. II, 953
Allen, Sarah D. II, 698
Allen, Sarah E. I, 459
Allen, Sarah E. II, 1044
Allen, Sarah Elizabeth II, 698
Allen, Sarah G. I, 371
Allen, Sarah H. I, 371
Allen, Sarah J. I, 207
Allen, Sarah J. I, 213
Allen, Sarah J. I, 229
Allen, Sarah J. I, 371
Allen, Sarah J. IV, 671
Allen, Sarah J. IV, 754
Allen, Sarah J. IV, 792
Allen, Sarah Jane III, 17
Allen, Sarah Jane IV, 797
Allen, Sarah Jane VI, 870
Allen, Sarah K. IV, 606
Allen, Sarah K. IV, 922
Allen, Sarah K. IV, 968
Allen, Sarah L. I, 869
Allen, Sarah M. V, 547
Allen, Sarah M. V, 655
Allen, Sarah N. II, 114
Allen, Sarah N. II, 142
Allen, Sarah N. II, 155
Allen, Sidney II, 279
Allen, Sidney II, 286
Allen, Sidney II, 698
Allen, Simon I, 345
Allen, Smith V, 983
Allen, Solomon I, 370
Allen, Solomon I, 371
Allen, Solomon I, 386
Allen, Solomon V, 19
Allen, Solomon V, 149
Allen, Solomon V, 217
Allen, Solomon V, 947
Allen, Solomon VI, 361
Allen, Solomon Howland V, 893
Allen, Solomon V. I, 371
Allen, Solomon, Jr. I, 371
Allen, Stanley S. I, 459
Allen, Stephen III, 18
Allen, Stephen III, 35
Allen, Stephen G. IV, 1349
Allen, Susan III, 479
Allen, Susan III, 483
Allen, Susan III, 484
Allen, Susan IV, 1349
Allen, Susan D. III, 393
Allen, Susan H. III, 17
Allen, Susan W. III, 16
Allen, Susan W. III, 17
Allen, Susan W. III, 284
Allen, Susanna I, 345
Allen, Susanna I, 370
Allen, Susanna IV, 922
Allen, Susanna IV, 968
Allen, Susanna VI, 591
Allen, Susanna E. I, 371
Allen, Susannah I, 370
Allen, Susannah I, 1113
Allen, Susannah II, 451
Allen, Susannah II, 508
Allen, Susannah V, 825
Allen, Susannah VI, 361
Allen, Susannah VI, 591
Allen, Susannah VI, 592
Allen, Susannah M. II, 953
Allen, Sybbel Jenkins IV, 117
Allen, Tacey I, 459
Allen, Thomas I, 345
Allen, Thomas I, 370
Allen, Thomas I, 371
Allen, Thomas I, 919
Allen, Thomas II, 332
Allen, Thomas VI, 361
Allen, Thomas VI, 416
Allen, Thomas VI, 870
Allen, Thomas C. I, 473
Allen, Thomas Lancaster II, 953
Allen, Thomas M. I, 459
Allen, Thomas N. I, 1113
Allen, Thomas N. I, 1129
Allen, Thomas N. I, 1147
Allen, Thomas Norris I, 1147
Allen, Thos. IV, 605
Allen, Thos. N. I, 1139
Allen, Tristam III, 18
Allen, Tristram IV, 1349
Allen, Unice IV, 319
Allen, Unice IV, 363
Allen, Unice VI, 361
Allen, Unice VI, 591
Allen, Unice VI, 607
Allen, Vashty II, 49
Allen, Vashty II, 93
Allen, Verna IV, 671
Allen, Vida E. IV, 1245
Allen, Viola E. IV, 1305
Allen, Violetta III, 394
Allen, Violetta III, 415
Allen, Walker IV, 565
Allen, Walter III, 17
Allen, Walter III, 18
Allen, Walter IV, 1271
Allen, Walter J. M. I, 459
Allen, Walter Jay I, 473
Allen, Walton IV, 319
Allen, Walton IV, 363
Allen, Walton IV, 565
Allen, Walton IV, 1271
Allen, Ward IV, 671
Allen, Warren V, 891
Allen, Warren Daniel V, 891
Allen, Wd. Elinor II, 331
Allen, Wd. Eliza III, 17
Allen, Wd. Hannah II, 20
Allen, Wd. Margaret II, 974
Allen, Wd. Mary III, 16
Allen, Wd. Rebecca II, 191
Allen, Wd. Rebecca II, 974
Allen, Wd. Rebecca II, 1043
Allen, Welmet I, 371
Allen, Welmet I, 402
Allen, Welmet I, 459
Allen, Welmet I, 473
Allen, Wesley I, 345
Allen, Wesley I, 371
Allen, Wesley V, 19
Allen, Wesley V, 149
Allen, Westlay VI, 361
Allen, Widower Walter III, 18
Allen, William I, 345
Allen, William I, 370
Allen, William I, 371
Allen, William I, 459
Allen, William I, 473
Allen, William I, 647
Allen, William I, 1139
Allen, William II, 20
Allen, William II, 127
Allen, William II, 332
Allen, William II, 441
Allen, William II, 953
Allen, William II, 974
Allen, William II, 989
Allen, William II, 1043
Allen, William III, 18
Allen, William IV, 19
Allen, William IV, 30
Allen, William IV, 319
Allen, William IV, 363
Allen, William IV, 565
Allen, William VI, 361
Allen, William VI, 834
Allen, William VI, 870
Allen, William VI, 873
Allen, William VI, 878
Allen, William VI, 952
Allen, William VI, 997
Allen, William VI, 1013
Allen, William A. III, 18
Allen, William E. II, 698
Allen, William F. V, 19
Allen, William LeRoy V, 891
Allen, William M. I, 459
Allen, William N. II, 779
Allen, William Pettit II, 165
Allen, Willie V, 983
Allen, Winney VI, 870
Allen, Wm. I, 355
Allen, Wm. I, 370
Allen, Wm. I, 381
Allen, Wm. II, 50
Allen, Wm. II, 114
Allen, Wm. II, 191
Allen, Wm. II, 830
Allen, Wm. II, 974
Allen, Wm. II, 1009
Allen, Wm. II, 1044
Allen, Wm. II, 1068
Allen, Wm. IV, 169
Allen, Wm. B. III, 17
Allen, Wm. B. III, 305
Allen, Wm. E. II, 725
Allen, Wm. Franklin V, 371
Allen, Wm. H. A. IV, 1245
Allen, Wm. Large II, 974
Allen, Wm. Leroy V, 891
Allen, Wm. N. II, 142
Allen, Wm. N. II, 831
Allen, Wm. N. II, 892
Allen, Wm. Nicholson II, 142
Allen, Wm. Nicholson II, 155
Allen, Wm. T. V, 19
Allen, Wm. W. II, 830
Allen, Wm. Young III, 17
Allen, Wm. Young III, 96
Allen, Wm., Jr. II, 50
Allen, Zachariah I, 370
Allen, Zachariah II, 191
Allen, Zacheriah V, 825
Allen, Zechariah V, 825
Allen, Zimri I, 370
Allen, Zimri I, 371
Allen-Brown, Esther VI, 622
Allenson, Elizabeth II, 165
Allenson, Elizabeth II, 191
Allenson, Ellen II, 165
Allenson, Joseph II, 165
Allenson, Joseph II, 191
Allenson, Martha II, 279
Allenson, Mary II, 191
Allenson, Peter II, 165
Allenson, Rebecca II, 279
Allenson, Samuel II, 191
Allenson, Sybil II, 191
Allenson, William II, 165
Allenson, William J. II, 279
Allent, Edith II, 331
Alleson, Elizabeth II, 192
Alleson, Elizabeth II, 257
Alleson, Elizabeth II, 260
Alleson, Joseph II, 192
Alleson, Joseph II, 257
Alleson, Richard II, 192
Alleson, Richard II, 260
Alley, ??? III, 318
Alley, Alexander III, 18
Alley, Alexander W. III, 219
Alley, Amos III, 18
Alley, Barbara Jane III, 18
Alley, Benj. R. V, 892
Alley, Benjamin R. V, 891
Alley, Caroline III, 18
Alley, Deborah III, 479
Alley, Doshia VI, 895
Alley, Edward T. III, 18
Alley, Eleanor Graves III, 18
Alley, Eleanor Graves III, 219
Alley, Eliz. III, 346
Alley, Eliz. III, 464
Alley, Elizabeth III, 18
Alley, Elizabeth III, 394
Alley, Elizabeth III, 454
Alley, Elizabeth C. III, 394
Alley, Elizabeth C. III, 451
Alley, Elizabeth W. III, 18
Alley, Emily III, 18
Alley, Emily F. III, 18
Alley, Emily T. III, 18
Alley, Enos III, 18
Alley, Enos III, 394
Alley, Enos III, 479
Alley, Enos III, 503
Alley, Enos III, 504
Alley, Enos VI, 153
Alley, George B. III, 394
Alley, H. VI, 895
Alley, H. VI, 919
Alley, H. VI, 982
Alley, H. VI, 1015
Alley, Henry F. V, 891
Alley, Jericho III, 18
Alley, Jericho III, 394
Alley, John III, 394
Alley, Josephine III, 18
Alley, Josephine III, 394
Alley, Louisa III, 394
Alley, Louise III, 18
Alley, Louise III, 348
Alley, Lydia III, 18
Alley, Lydia III, 394
Alley, Lydia III, 454
Alley, Lydia V, 892
Alley, Lydia T. III, 172
Alley, Lydia T. III, 318
Alley, Lynn III, 479
Alley, Mary III, 18
Alley, Mary III, 348
Alley, Mary III, 394
Alley, Mary III, 459
Alley, Mary Anna III, 394
Alley, Rebecca III, 18
Alley, Rebecca III, 394
Alley, Rebecca III, 479
Alley, Rebecca III, 503
Alley, Rebecca III, 504
Alley, Rebecca VI, 153
Alley, Richard V, 891
Alley, Robert W. III, 18
Alley, Robert W. III, 479
Alley, Rowland III, 172
Alley, Ruth V, 891
Alley, Samuel III, 479
Alley, Sarah III, 172
Alley, Sarah Elizabeth III, 18
Alley, Sarah Elizabeth III, 346
Alley, Sarah Elizabeth III, 394
Alley, Sarah Elizabeth III, 464
Alley, Saul III, 18
Alley, Saul III, 348
Alley, Saul III, 394
Alley, Saul III, 459
Alley, Sidney III, 18
Alley, Sidney III, 454
Alley, Sidney B. III, 18
Alley, Sidney B. III, 346
Alley, Sidney B. III, 394
Alley, Sidney B. III, 451
Alley, Sidney B. III, 453
Alley, Sidney B. III, 464
Alley, Sidney B. III, 479
Alley, T. W. VI, 795
Alley, William III, 18
Alley, William III, 394
Alley, William L. III, 18
Alley, William S. III, 394
Allford, Tabitha I, 128
Allford, Tabitha I, 172
Allgood, Eliza R. VI, 853
Allgood, Winny A. VI, 855
Allibone, ??? II, 332
Allibone, Benjamin IV, 73
Allibone, Elias IV, 73
Allibone, Elizabeth II, 784
Allibone, Esther II, 452

Allibone, Hesther II, 452
Allibone, Phebe IV, 73
Allibone, Sarah II, 452
Allibone, Thomas II, 332
Allibone, Thomas II, 452
Allibone, Wm. II, 452
Allicott, Latitia II, 995
Allicott, Latitia II, 1000
Allicott, Nathaniel II, 995
Allicott, Nathaniel II, 1000
Alligre, Elizabeth VI, 887
Alligre, Mary VI, 870
Alligre, Mathew VI, 870
Alligre, Mathew VI, 887
Alligre, William VI, 887
Alliman, Charles V, 149
Allin, Betty VI, 361
Allin, Betty VI, 462
Allin, Elisabeth I, 128
Allin, Hannah II, 191
Allin, Jackson VI, 462
Allin, John II, 191
Allin, Kesiah V, 217
Allin, Kesiah V, 252
Allin, Margret II, 49
Allin, Margret II, 65
Allin, Mary II, 331
Allin, Mary VI, 361
Allin, Mary VI, 462
Allin, Ralfe II, 49
Allin, Ralfe II, 65
Allin, Richard II, 331
Alling, Abraham III, 402
Alling, Elizabeth II, 332
Alling, Freelove III, 393
Alling, John III, 415
Alling, Martha III, 402
Alling, Mary II, 332
Alling, Mary III, 402
Alling, Nemiah II, 332
Alling, Violetta III, 394
Alling, Violetta III, 415
Allingham, Richard V, 983
Allingham, Sarah V, 983
Allinson, Anna B. II, 279
Allinson, Anna Bernice II, 165
Allinson, Bernice II, 725
Allinson, Bernice III, 18
Allinson, Beulah II, 279
Allinson, Beulah II, 294
Allinson, Charles II, 279
Allinson, David II, 165
Allinson, David II, 191
Allinson, David II, 192
Allinson, David II, 279
Allinson, David II, 294
Allinson, David II, 452
Allinson, Edward P. II, 165
Allinson, Edward P. II, 279
Allinson, Eleanor II, 191
Allinson, Eleanor II, 271
Allinson, Elisabeth II, 165
Allinson, Elizabeth II, 165
Allinson, Elizabeth II, 191
Allinson, Elizabeth II, 207
Allinson, Elizabeth II, 262
Allinson, Elizabeth II, 725
Allinson, Elizabeth S. II, 316
Allinson, Elizabeth S. II, 325
Allinson, Ellen II, 165
Allinson, Emily L. II, 279
Allinson, Francis G. II, 279
Allinson, Francis Greenleaf II, 165
Allinson, Gertrude II, 165
Allinson, Gertrude II, 279
Allinson, Gertrude II, 304
Allinson, Hetty II, 279
Allinson, James II, 165
Allinson, James II, 191
Allinson, James II, 725
Allinson, James III, 18
Allinson, John II, 191
Allinson, John II, 279
Allinson, John C. II, 191
Allinson, John C. II, 192
Allinson, John C. II, 279
Allinson, John C. II, 294
Allinson, John C. III, 18
Allinson, John Cooper II, 165
Allinson, Joseph II, 165
Allinson, Joseph II, 191
Allinson, Joseph II, 262
Allinson, Joseph West II, 165
Allinson, Lucy A. II, 279
Allinson, Lucy Ann II, 279
Allinson, Lucy Ann II, 294
Allinson, Margaret II, 191
Allinson, Margaret II, 279
Allinson, Margaret II, 298
Allinson, Martha II, 165
Allinson, Martha II, 180
Allinson, Martha II, 191
Allinson, Martha II, 279
Allinson, Martha II, 298
Allinson, Martha II, 452
Allinson, Martha II, 656
Allinson, Mary II, 165
Allinson, Mary II, 191
Allinson, Mary II, 259
Allinson, Peter II, 165
Allinson, Peter II, 169
Allinson, Peter II, 191
Allinson, Peter II, 271
Allinson, Rebecca II, 279
Allinson, Rebecca III, 18
Allinson, Rebecca W. II, 279
Allinson, Rebecca W. II, 304
Allinson, Samuel II, 165
Allinson, Samuel II, 180
Allinson, Samuel II, 191
Allinson, Samuel II, 192
Allinson, Samuel II, 262
Allinson, Samuel II, 279
Allinson, Samuel II, 298
Allinson, Samuel II, 452
Allinson, Samuel II, 656
Allinson, Samuel III, 18
Allinson, Samuel C. III, 18
Allinson, Samuel, Jr. II, 725
Allinson, Sarah II, 165
Allinson, Sarah II, 191
Allinson, Sarah II, 452
Allinson, Sarah II, 789
Allinson, Sarah II, 827
Allinson, Sibyl II, 165
Allinson, Sibyl II, 279
Allinson, Susanna II, 192
Allinson, Susanna D. II, 165
Allinson, Susanna Dillwyn II, 452
Allinson, Susanna Dillwyn II, 656
Allinson, Susannah II, 191
Allinson, Sybil II, 191
Allinson, Thomas II, 165
Allinson, Thomas II, 191
Allinson, Thomas II, 259
Allinson, Wd. Margaret II, 180
Allinson, Wd. Rebecca W. II, 165
Allinson, William II, 165
Allinson, William II, 191
Allinson, William G. II, 279
Allinson, William J. II, 165
Allinson, William J. II, 279
Allinson, William J. II, 304
Allinson, William W. II, 279
Allinson, Wm. II, 191
Allis, Caleb III, 18
Allis, Caleb III, 26
Allis, Caleb W. III, 18
Allis, Frances J. III, 18
Allis, Frances J. III, 26
Allis, Latitia W. III, 18
Allis, Letitia III, 26
Allis, Letitia W. III, 18
Allison, ??? IV, 671
Allison, Abraham V, 725
Allison, Abram V, 779
Allison, Adesda IV, 926
Allison, Amelia V, 19
Allison, Andrew V, 725
Allison, Anna V, 805
Allison, Anne V, 797
Allison, Benjamin V, 725
Allison, Caleb V, 725
Allison, Cora V, 655
Allison, David W. V, 725
Allison, Desda IV, 922
Allison, Dr. Nathaniel S. VI, 757
Allison, Elizabeth II, 192
Allison, Elizabeth VI, 521
Allison, Elizabeth VI, 757
Allison, Frances II, 452
Allison, Frances VI, 757
Allison, George IV, 671
Allison, George IV, 765
Allison, George W. IV, 671
Allison, Gulielma Sanders V, 19
Allison, Hannah V, 725
Allison, James V, 655
Allison, James V, 725
Allison, James V, 761
Allison, James V, 779
Allison, John III, 394
Allison, John V, 725
Allison, John V, 779
Allison, John Sanders V, 19
Allison, John, Jr. II, 192
Allison, Jonathan V, 725
Allison, Jonathan V, 779
Allison, Joseph II, 192
Allison, Joseph II, 199
Allison, Mahlon IV, 671
Allison, Margaret I, 1026
Allison, Margaret I, 1028
Allison, Martha IV, 671
Allison, Martha Sanders V, 19
Allison, Mary II, 192
Allison, Mary II, 208
Allison, Mary II, 234
Allison, Mary IV, 671
Allison, Mary IV, 696
Allison, Mary J. IV, 926
Allison, Philip IV, 926
Allison, Priscilla V, 725
Allison, Rachel II, 50
Allison, Rebecca IV, 671
Allison, Rebecca IV, 765
Allison, Rebecca V, 725
Allison, Richard II, 192
Allison, Richard II, 234
Allison, Richard B. VI, 795
Allison, Samuel L. IV, 671
Allison, Samuel L. IV, 674
Allison, Samuel Sanders V, 19
Allison, Sarah II, 199
Allison, Sarah II, 452
Allison, Sarah II, 685
Allison, Sarah IV, 671
Allison, Sarah IV, 674
Allison, Sarah IV, 765
Allison, Sarah V, 725
Allison, Sarah V, 761
Allison, Sarah V, 797
Allison, Sarah VI, 795
Allison, Sarah L. IV, 671
Allison, Sarah, Sr. V, 725
Allison, Susannah II, 192
Allison, Susannah II, 194
Allison, Thomas II, 192
Allison, Thomas V, 725
Allison, Wd. Elizabeth II, 169
Allison, William V, 779
Allison, Wm. V, 725
Alllen, Catharine I, 443
Alllen, Hannah I, 443
Alllen, Rebecca I, 443
Alllen, Solomon I, 443
Allman, Abigail IV, 671
Allman, Abner IV, 671
Allman, Albert R. IV, 671
Allman, Ann W. IV, 671
Allman, Ann W. IV, 960
Allman, Ann W. IV, 961
Allman, Anna W. IV, 960
Allman, Bessie IV, 1271
Allman, Beulah E. IV, 463
Allman, Bulah Elma IV, 463
Allman, David IV, 671
Allman, Dora IV, 1271
Allman, Earl IV, 1271
Allman, Ebenezer IV, 1271
Allman, Elizabeth IV, 463
Allman, Ellen II, 779
Allman, Emmet M. IV, 671
Allman, Esther C. IV, 671
Allman, Esther W. IV, 922
Allman, Esther W. IV, 960
Allman, Hannah II, 452
Allman, Hannah II, 666
Allman, Hannah IV, 463
Allman, Hannah IV, 607
Allman, Hannah IV, 614
Allman, Hannah IV, 671
Allman, Hannah VI, 361
Allman, Hannah Hammons IV, 671
Allman, Hannah M. IV, 671
Allman, Hannah Maria IV, 463
Allman, Hannah Maria IV, 471
Allman, Hannah Maria IV, 671
Allman, Hannah Mariah IV, 671
Allman, Israil IV, 671
Allman, Jasper IV, 1271
Allman, Jehu IV, 671
Allman, Jesse IV, 922
Allman, Jesse IV, 960
Allman, John II, 779
Allman, John IV, 463
Allman, John IV, 1271
Allman, John P. IV, 922
Allman, Jos. IV, 471
Allman, Joseph IV, 463
Allman, Joseph IV, 671
Allman, Luanna C. IV, 922
Allman, Lucy Ann IV, 1201
Allman, Lucy Ann IV, 1217
Allman, Lydia IV, 463
Allman, Lydia IV, 671
Allman, Lydia IV, 922
Allman, Margaret IV, 1271
Allman, Mary F. IV, 463
Allman, Mary S. IV, 671
Allman, Meader IV, 607
Allman, Meader IV, 922
Allman, Medre IV, 922
Allman, Samuel Henry II, 779
Allman, Sarah IV, 671
Allman, Susanna IV, 922
Allman, Susannah IV, 607
Allman, Tacy IV, 671
Allman, Tacy M. IV, 671
Allman, Thomas IV, 671
Allman, Thomas IV, 1271
Allman, Thos. II, 779
Allman, Webster IV, 671
Allman, Webster A. IV, 671
Allman, Webster Alison IV, 607
Allman, Webster Alison IV, 922
Allman, Webster Allison IV, 922
Allman, William IV, 922
Allman, Wm. IV, 463
Allmon, Aaron IV, 606
Allmon, Aaron IV, 607
Allmon, Abigail IV, 606
Allmon, Abigail IV, 612
Allmon, Abigail IV, 863
Allmon, Abner IV, 606
Allmon, Abner IV, 607
Allmon, Abner IV, 630
Allmon, Albert J. IV, 607
Allmon, Albert R. IV, 607
Allmon, Albert Robert IV, 607
Allmon, Alfred C. IV, 607
Allmon, Alfred Clarence IV, 607
Allmon, Ann IV, 606
Allmon, Ann IV, 607
Allmon, Ann IV, 666
Allmon, Ann W. IV, 169
Allmon, Ann W. IV, 215
Allmon, Ann W. IV, 401
Allmon, Ann W. IV, 606
Allmon, Ann W. IV, 627
Allmon, Ann W. IV, 628
Allmon, Ann W. IV, 633
Allmon, Ann W. IV, 738
Allmon, Anna Pricilla IV, 626
Allmon, Beulah E. IV, 463
Allmon, Charles F. IV, 607
Allmon, Chas. Franklin IV, 607
Allmon, David IV, 671
Allmon, Ebenezer IV, 606
Allmon, Ebenezer IV, 607
Allmon, Ebenezer IV, 646
Allmon, Ebenezer IV, 649
Allmon, Eli IV, 606
Allmon, Eli IV, 607
Allmon, Elizabeth IV, 463
Allmon, Elizabeth IV, 471
Allmon, Elizabeth IV, 606
Allmon, Elizabeth IV, 646
Allmon, Elizabeth J. IV, 626
Allmon, Emmet M. IV, 607
Allmon, Emmit IV, 607
Allmon, Ephraim IV, 606
Allmon, Ephraim IV, 607
Allmon, Esther II, 701
Allmon, Esther IV, 606
Allmon, Esther IV, 612
Allmon, Esther IV, 613
Allmon, Esther IV, 681
Allmon, George IV, 606
Allmon, Hannah IV, 463
Allmon, Hannah IV, 606
Allmon, Hannah IV, 607
Allmon, Hannah IV, 611
Allmon, Hannah IV, 613
Allmon, Hannah IV, 627
Allmon, Hannah IV, 665
Allmon, Hannah VI, 361
Allmon, Hannah M. IV, 671
Allmon, Hannah Mary IV, 607
Allmon, Hannah W. IV, 607
Allmon, Isaac IV, 606
Allmon, Isaac IV, 607
Allmon, Israel IV, 606
Allmon, Israel IV, 607
Allmon, Israil IV, 671
Allmon, James IV, 606
Allmon, James IV, 607
Allmon, James IV, 1201
Allmon, James B. IV, 606
Allmon, James B. IV, 607
Allmon, James B. IV, 1201
Allmon, Jehu IV, 606
Allmon, Jehu IV, 607
Allmon, Jehu IV, 611
Allmon, Jehu IV, 627
Allmon, Jesse IV, 606
Allmon, Jesse IV, 607
Allmon, Jno. IV, 606
Allmon, John IV, 463
Allmon, John IV, 471
Allmon, John IV, 606
Allmon, John IV, 607
Allmon, John IV, 613
Allmon, John IV, 665
Allmon, Joseph IV, 463
Allmon, Joseph IV, 606
Allmon, Joseph IV, 607
Allmon, Levi IV, 606
Allmon, Levi IV, 607
Allmon, Levi IV, 1201
Allmon, Lewis J. IV, 626
Allmon, Luanna C. IV, 606
Allmon, Luanna C. IV, 607
Allmon, Luanna C. IV, 635
Allmon, Lucinda Ann IV, 607
Allmon, Lucinda Ann IV, 630
Allmon, Lucy Ann IV, 606
Allmon, Lucy Ann IV, 607
Allmon, Lucy Ann IV, 1201
Allmon, Lydia IV, 463
Allmon, Lydia IV, 606
Allmon, Lydia IV, 607
Allmon, Lydia IV, 633
Allmon, Lydia IV, 663
Allmon, Margaret IV, 606
Allmon, Margaret IV, 607
Allmon, Margaret IV, 1271
Allmon, Mary IV, 606
Allmon, Mary IV, 607
Allmon, Mary IV, 654
Allmon, Mary IV, 1201
Allmon, Mary L. IV, 607
Allmon, Mary Ruanna IV, 1201
Allmon, Meader IV, 606
Allmon, Meader IV, 607
Allmon, Meader IV, 616
Allmon, Meader IV, 635
Allmon, Morris Cope IV, 606
Allmon, Phebe IV, 606
Allmon, Phebe IV, 607
Allmon, Phebe IV, 620
Allmon, Phebe IV, 1201
Allmon, Phebe Ann IV, 606
Allmon, Phebe Ann IV, 1201
Allmon, Phebe Elma IV, 607
Allmon, Phebe Elma IV, 632
Allmon, Phebe Elma IV, 863
Allmon, Phebe Elma IV, 872
Allmon, Phebe Elma IV, 1201
Allmon, Rachel IV, 606
Allmon, Rachel IV, 607
Allmon, Rachel IV, 626
Allmon, Rebecca IV, 607
Allmon, Rebecca IV, 646
Allmon, Rebecca IV, 649
Allmon, Rebeccah IV, 606
Allmon, Ruth IV, 607
Allmon, Ruth IV, 626
Allmon, Samuel IV, 606
Allmon, Samuel IV, 607
Allmon, Sarah IV, 121
Allmon, Sarah IV, 606
Allmon, Sarah IV, 607
Allmon, Sarah IV, 611
Allmon, Silas IV, 606
Allmon, Silas IV, 607
Allmon, Silas IV, 632
Allmon, Silas IV, 863
Allmon, Silas IV, 872
Allmon, Silas IV, 1201
Allmon, Susanna IV, 607
Allmon, Susannah IV, 607
Allmon, Susannah IV, 616
Allmon, Susannah H. IV, 606
Allmon, Susannah H. IV, 635
Allmon, Tacy M. IV, 607
Allmon, Tacy M. IV, 623
Allmon, Thomas IV, 606
Allmon, Thomas IV, 607
Allmon, Thomas IV, 612
Allmon, Thomas IV, 863
Allmon, Thos. IV, 606
Allmon, Webster IV, 607
Allmon, Webster A. IV, 607
Allmon, Webster A. IV, 623
Allmon, Webster Alison IV, 607
Allmon, Webster Allison IV, 606
Allmon, Webster Allison IV, 607
Allmon, William IV, 606
Allmon, William IV, 607
Allmon, William IV, 663
Allmon, Wilmer J. IV, 607
Allmon, Wilmer Joseph IV, 606
Allmon, Wm. IV, 463
Allmon, Wm. IV, 606
Allmond, Elizabeth VI, 870
Allmond, John VI, 870
Allmond, Susanna VI, 795
Allmond, William VI, 795
Allot, Ann, Jr. II, 995
Alloway, Elizabeth II, 332

Alloway, Elizabeth II, 452
Alloway, Elizabeth II, 657
Alloway, Mary II, 332
Alloway, Mary VI, 362
Alloway, Mary VI, 456
Alloway, Sarah II, 332
Alloway, Sarah IV, 169
Alloway, William II, 332
Alloway, Wm. II, 452
Alloway, Wm. II, 657
Allred, Anna Maude Tetley I, 611
Allred, D. E. I, 629
Allred, David I, 611
Allred, David E. I, 629
Allred, David Edgar I, 611
Allred, David Edgar I, 629
Allred, Edgar I, 629
Allred, Edgar Turner I, 611
Allred, Edgar Turner I, 629
Allred, Edward I, 629
Allred, Edward I, 641
Allred, Epsie I, 611
Allred, Epsie H. I, 629
Allred, Hannah I, 611
Allred, Ida Martitia I, 621
Allred, Joseph Myrick I, 629
Allred, Joseph Wyrick I, 611
Allred, Litetia I, 614
Allred, Margaret I, 629
Allred, Martha I, 611
Allred, Martha I, 629
Allred, Martha I, 641
Allred, Martha T. I, 629
Allred, Martin J. I, 921
Allred, Martitia I, 621
Allred, Mary Ann I, 921
Allred, Philip Morrison I, 611
Allred, Rachel I, 473
Allred, Sam'l I, 629
Allred, Sarah I, 629
Allred, Sarah Hendricks I, 611
Allred, Susan I, 931
Allred, Susan J. I, 929
Allred, Susan Janina I, 921
Allred, William I, 611
Allred, William F. I, 621
Allredd, Edward I, 629
Allredd, Martha I, 629
Allsup, Thomas II, 332
Ally, Amos VI, 467
Alman, Albert R. IV, 671
Alman, Ebeneezer IV, 19
Alman, Emmet M. IV, 671
Alman, Hannah IV, 19
Alman, Jesse IV, 19
Alman, John IV, 19
Alman, Luanna C. IV, 922
Alman, Mary S. IV, 671
Alman, Meader IV, 922
Alman, Medre IV, 922
Alman, Susanna IV, 922
Alman, Tacy IV, 671
Alman, Thomas IV, 19
Alman, Webster A. IV, 671
Alman, Webster Alison IV, 922
Alman, Webster Allison IV, 922
Alman, William IV, 19
Alment, Elisabeth II, 452
Alment, John II, 452
Almon, Ebeneezer IV, 19
Almon, Ebenezer IV, 606
Almon, Elizabeth IV, 463
Almon, Hannah IV, 19
Almon, Hannah IV, 606
Almon, Jehu IV, 606
Almon, Jesse IV, 19
Almon, Jesse IV, 606
Almon, Jno. IV, 606
Almon, John IV, 19
Almon, John IV, 606
Almon, Luanna C. IV, 607
Almon, Sarah IV, 644
Almon, Sarah IV, 671
Almon, Thomas IV, 19
Almon, Thos. IV, 606
Almon, William IV, 19
Almon, Wm. IV, 606
Almond, Anna VI, 857
Almond, Elisabeth I, 1067
Almond, Eliza A. VI, 860
Almond, Elizabeth VI, 795
Almond, Hannah IV, 19
Almond, Harden VI, 795
Almond, Harris I, 1067
Almond, Harris I, 1070
Almond, James VI, 795
Almond, Jane VI, 795
Almond, John VI, 795
Almond, Judith I, 1067
Almond, Lydia VI, 795
Almond, Mariah VI, 795
Almond, Mary VI, 795
Almond, Mary VI, 860
Almond, Matthew I, 1067
Almond, Matthew I, 1070
Almond, Matthew V, 471
Almond, Molly VI, 795
Almond, Polly VI, 795
Almond, Rebeckah I, 1067
Almond, Reuben VI, 795
Almond, Sterling VI, 795
Almond, Susanna VI, 795
Almond, William VI, 795
Almond, William, Jr. VI, 795
Almy, Catharine III, 394
Almy, Catharine III, 457
Alred, Lydia I, 927
Alred, Millicent M. I, 708
Alred, Rachel I, 755
Alricks, Susanna II, 452
Alricks, Susanna II, 500
Alson, Mandales IV, 169
Alsop, Ann III, 394
Alsop, Ann III, 395
Alsop, Ann III, 475
Alsop, Bernice II, 725
Alsop, David G. III, 151
Alsop, Elizabeth II, 332
Alsop, Elizabeth II, 452
Alsop, Elizabeth II, 725
Alsop, Elizabeth Billings III, 18
Alsop, Elizabeth Billings III, 19
Alsop, Esther III, 18
Alsop, Esther III, 32
Alsop, Esther III, 151
Alsop, Esther K. III, 18
Alsop, Esther K. III, 151
Alsop, George M. II, 192
Alsop, George M. II, 698
Alsop, George M. II, 725
Alsop, George Morris II, 452
Alsop, George N. II, 279
Alsop, Hannah II, 452
Alsop, Hannah II, 475
Alsop, Hannah III, 18
Alsop, Hannah III, 394
Alsop, Hannah III, 398
Alsop, Henry II, 698
Alsop, Jacob II, 452
Alsop, James II, 725
Alsop, Jeanes II, 452
Alsop, John II, 332
Alsop, John II, 452
Alsop, John III, 18
Alsop, John III, 394
Alsop, John, Jr. II, 332
Alsop, Leah II, 452
Alsop, Leah Ann II, 452
Alsop, Mary II, 452
Alsop, Mary II, 475
Alsop, Mary III, 18
Alsop, Mary III, 394
Alsop, Mary III, 475
Alsop, Othniel II, 452
Alsop, Othniel II, 475
Alsop, Phebe III, 394
Alsop, Rachel II, 452
Alsop, Rebecca II, 452
Alsop, Richard III, 18
Alsop, Richard III, 394
Alsop, Richard III, 398
Alsop, Richard III, 425
Alsop, Richard III, 475
Alsop, Richard III, 476
Alsop, Richard, Jr. III, 394
Alsop, Richard, Jr. III, 395
Alsop, Richard, Jr. III, 429
Alsop, Richard, Jr. III, 432
Alsop, Robert II, 452
Alsop, Robert III, 18
Alsop, Ruhama John II, 725
Alsop, Samuel II, 452
Alsop, Samuel, Jr. III, 18
Alsop, Samuel, Jr. III, 32
Alsop, Samuel, Jr. III, 151
Alsop, Sarah III, 18
Alsop, Sarah III, 394
Alsop, Sarah III, 398
Alsop, Sarah III, 425
Alsop, Sarah III, 428
Alsop, Sarah III, 429
Alsop, Sarah III, 432
Alsop, Sarah Jenkings II, 779
Alsop, Scrivener II, 452
Alsop, Scrivener II, 475
Alsop, Susan K. III, 18
Alsop, Susan Kit III, 18
Alsop, Susan Kite III, 32
Alsop, Susanna III, 18
Alsop, Susannah III, 394
Alsop, Susannah III, 396
Alsop, Thomas II, 332
Alsop, Thomas III, 394
Alsop, Thomas III, 396
Alsop, Thomas Jenkins III, 18
Alsop, Wd. Sarah III, 429
Alsop, Wd. Sarah Mott III, 394
Alsop, William K. III, 18
Alsop, William K., Jr. III, 19
Alsop, Wm. II, 452
Alsop, Wm. Jeans II, 452
Alsop, Wm. K. III, 18
Alsopp, Richard III, 18
Alsopp, Susanna III, 18
Alsover, Anna II, 836
Alston, Thomas IV, 19
Alstone, Thomas IV, 19
Altemus, Almira II, 779
Altemus, Almira II, 831
Altemus, Ann D. II, 452
Altemus, Ann Maria II, 831
Altemus, Anna Maria II, 831
Altemus, Carrie II, 779
Altemus, Carrie II, 831
Altemus, Carrie II, 895
Altemus, Edward II, 779
Altemus, Edward E. II, 831
Altemus, Edward E. II, 839
Altemus, Ella II, 831
Altemus, Ella II, 942
Altemus, Everett II, 779
Altemus, Fannie C. II, 831
Altemus, Frances II, 452
Altemus, Frances II, 725
Altemus, Francis II, 779
Altemus, Francis II, 831
Altemus, Francis II, 845
Altemus, Francis II, 904
Altemus, Francis S. II, 831
Altemus, Francis S. II, 895
Altemus, Francis Swayne II, 779
Altemus, Hannah II, 452
Altemus, Hannah II, 725
Altemus, Hannah B. II, 779
Altemus, Hannah B. II, 831
Altemus, Henry C. II, 831
Altemus, Henry C. II, 845
Altemus, Henry Clay II, 779
Altemus, Hiram II, 779
Altemus, Hiram II, 831
Altemus, Isaac II, 332
Altemus, Isaac II, 452
Altemus, Isaac II, 725
Altemus, Isaac II, 779
Altemus, Isaac II, 831
Altemus, James C. II, 779
Altemus, James C. II, 831
Altemus, Jane C. II, 831
Altemus, Maria II, 452
Altemus, Maria II, 725
Altemus, Marshall II, 725
Altemus, Marshall II, 831
Altemus, Marshel II, 452
Altemus, Martha II, 779
Altemus, Martha II, 831
Altemus, Martha II, 845
Altemus, Martha II, 895
Altemus, Martha II, 904
Altemus, Martha N. II, 779
Altemus, Martha N. II, 831
Altemus, Martha N. II, 839
Altemus, Mary S. II, 831
Altemus, Mary S. II, 839
Altemus, Mary S. II, 917
Altemus, Sarah Ann II, 332
Altemus, Sarah Ann II, 831
Altemus, Sarah Ann II, 904
Altemus, Sarah Goldson II, 779
Altemus, Sarah Goldson II, 831
Altemus, Sarah Goldson II, 845
Altemus, Willameta Calver II, 779
Alter, Emma Kille IV, 922
Alter, Joanna IV, 868
Alter, Mary Emma Kille IV, 922
Alter, Newton IV, 922
Altermus, Fannie C. II, 831
Altermus, Fannie C. II, 860
Altermus, James C. II, 831
Altermus, James C. II, 860
Altha, Ada V, 983
Altha, John B. V, 983
Altha, Sarah V, 983
Altha, Wm. V, 983
Althen, William IV, 1245
Alther, Louisa M. IV, 671
Altimas, Ann D. II, 452
Altimus, Maria II, 725
Alton, Mary II, 332
Alton, Samuel II, 332
Altrich, Sarah II, 332
Altrup, Blandina Ellen Lutz VI, 615
Altrup, Blandina Ellen Lutz VI, 662
Alverson, James VI, 870
Alverson, Mary I, 937
Alverson, Mary VI, 870
Alvin, Eliza IV, 404
Alvis, David VI, 795
Alvis, David VI, 862
Alvis, David VI, 867
Alvis, Elizabeth VI, 795
Alvis, Frances VI, 795
Alvis, Frank V, 471
Alvis, George VI, 795
Alvis, George VI, 819
Alvis, Hannah VI, 795
Alvis, John VI, 795
Alvis, Joyassa VI, 836
Alvis, Lotsey VI, 795
Alvis, Mary VI, 795
Alvis, Mary VI, 867
Alvis, Sally VI, 795
Alvis, Samuel VI, 795
Alway, Esther III, 19
Alway, Francis I, 267
Alway, Hester III, 19
Alway, Hester Ann III, 19
Alway, Jerome III, 19
Alway, John III, 19
Alway, Norman III, 19
Alway, Virginia III, 19
Always, Hester Ann III, 19
Always, Jerome III, 19
Always, John III, 19
Always, Norman III, 19
Always, Virginia III, 19
Alwine, Homer P. IV, 363
Alwine, Ida M. IV, 363
Alwine, Ida M. IV, 402
Alwine, Ida May IV, 363
Amadon, Ann E. IV, 1143
Amatt, George III, 479
Amatt, James III, 479
Amatt, Mary III, 479
Ambach, Edwin T. V, 892
Ambern, Lydia I, 796
Ambern, Lydia I, 802
Ambern, Rebekah I, 1007
Ambert, Rebekah I, 1010
Ambler, Ann II, 831
Ambler, Ann II, 893
Ambler, Chalkley II, 779
Ambler, Charles E. II, 831
Ambler, Chester W. II, 831
Ambler, Edward II, 779
Ambler, Elizabeth II, 20
Ambler, Elizabeth II, 50
Ambler, Elizabeth C. II, 698
Ambler, George R. II, 698
Ambler, Jesse Hamilton II, 831
Ambler, Jesse Hamilton II, 886
Ambler, John II, 332
Ambler, John II, 452
Ambler, Joseph II, 332
Ambler, Joseph II, 452
Ambler, Joseph II, 565
Ambler, Joseph II, 831
Ambler, Joseph II, 893
Ambler, Josephine H. II, 698
Ambler, Josephine H. II, 725
Ambler, Lidya II, 50
Ambler, Lidya II, 51
Ambler, Lillian II, 779
Ambler, Louis B. II, 831
Ambler, Louisa II, 807
Ambler, Louisa II, 831
Ambler, Louisa II, 893
Ambler, Lucy H. VI, 795
Ambler, Lydia II, 20
Ambler, Lydia II, 808
Ambler, Mahala V, 983
Ambler, Mary II, 332
Ambler, Mary II, 779
Ambler, Mary H. II, 831
Ambler, Pamela F. II, 831
Ambler, Peter II, 20
Ambler, Peter II, 50
Ambler, Robert II, 831
Ambler, Robert II, 886
Ambler, Sarah II, 50
Ambler, Sarah II, 51
Ambler, Sarah II, 100
Ambler, Sarah II, 332
Ambler, Sarah II, 565
Ambler, Sarah Conrow II, 831
Ambler, Sarah Conrow II, 886
Ambler, Sarah W. II, 831
Ambler, Sarah W. II, 886
Ambler, Thomas II, 831
Ambler, Thomas VI, 729
Ambler, Thomas VI, 795
Ambrose, Alice VI, 7
Ambrose, Alice VI, 9
Ambrose, Ambrose VI, 820
Ambrose, William II, 441
Ambrose, Wm. V, 983
Amburn, Arthur I, 1147
Amburn, Earnest I, 1147
Amburn, Ernest I, 1147
Amburn, Esther I, 796
Amburn, Floyd I, 1147
Amburn, H. H. I, 1147
Amburn, Henry H. I, 1147
Amburn, Lucy I, 1147
Amburn, Lydia I, 796
Amburn, Othineal I, 1147
Amburn, Phebe I, 796
Amburn, Susanah I, 1147
Amburn, Susannah I, 1147
Amburn, Theophalis I, 1147
Amen, Anne VI, 870
Amen, John VI, 870
Amer, Agnes II, 795
Amer, Agnes II, 831
Amer, Agnes II, 866
Amer, Sarah Ann II, 831
Ames, Alice C. II, 831
Ames, Almon IV, 1214
Ames, Amanda IV, 1214
Ames, Clarence V, 655
Ames, Clarence V, 674
Ames, Cleo V, 695
Ames, George I Sup 1, 3
Ames, George I Sup 1, 4
Ames, Jessie V, 655
Ames, Margaret P. II, 831
Ames, Margaret P. II, 911
Ames, Mary Amanda IV, 1201
Ames, Mary Jane IV, 1214
Ames, Matilda V, 310
Ames, Sarah S. II, 725
Ames, Susannah I Sup 1, 3
Ames, Virginia V, 655
Ames, Virginia V, 674
Amess, ??? III, 298
Amess, Pearl B. III, 19
Amess, Pearl B. III, 298
Amick, Maggie IV, 1143
Amies, Alice C. II, 831
Amies, Alice C. II, 844
Amies, Alice Evans II, 779
Amies, Robert C. III, 19
Amine, John IV, 1271
Amler, Peter II, 50
Ammerman, Margaret III, 19
Ammons, Prudence I, 523
Amonett, Jacob VI, 796
Amonett, Susannah VI, 796
Amos, Abraham II, 452
Amos, Anna VI, 993
Amos, Anthony II, 332
Amos, Anthony II, 974
Amos, Caroline VI, 153
Amos, Clara III, 19
Amos, Clara Louise III, 19
Amos, Clara Louise III, 353
Amos, Elizabeth VI, 870
Amos, Francis VI, 153
Amos, George V, 655
Amos, George Howard III, 19
Amos, George Howard III, 353
Amos, George Oliver III, 19
Amos, Godfrey III, 19
Amos, Hannah II, 452
Amos, James VI, 926
Amos, Jeanne Louise C. III, 19
Amos, Martha IV, 363
Amos, Martha IV, 385
Amos, Mary VI, 153
Amos, Matilda V, 297
Amos, Matilda V, 310
Amos, Nicho VI, 153
Amos, Sarah III, 19
Amos, Susan IV, 505
Amos, Susanna IV, 463
Amos, Susanna IV, 501
Amos, Susanna IV, 505
Amos, Susannah IV, 363
Amos, Susannah IV, 458
Amos, Thomas VI, 153
Amos, William VI, 870
Amos, William Willets III, 19
Amos, Wilson VI, 870
Amos, Wm. IV, 458
Amoss, Caroline VI, 153
Amoss, Susannah IV, 363
Amoss, Thomas VI, 153
Ampey, Frankey VI, 990
Amsbaugh, Olie IV, 1143
Amscough, Jane IV, 169
Amscough, Maggie IV, 169
Amspoker, Margaret IV, 1271
Amspoker, Samuel IV, 1271

Amyx, Andrew VI, 881
Amyx, Eleanor VI, 1010
Amyx, James VI, 870
Amyx, Nancy VI, 870
Anabe, Anna M. V, 149
Anabe, D. W. V, 149
Anabe, Daniel W. V, 149
Anabe, Eunice V, 149
Anabe, Katie V, 149
Anabe, Katie B. V, 149
Anabe, Lillian V, 149
Anabe, Lillian S. V, 149
Anabe, Olive V. V, 149
Anabe, Ollie V. V, 149
Anabe, Sarah A. V, 149
Anabe, Sarah J. V, 149
Anabee, Anna M. V, 149
Anabee, D. W. V, 149
Anabee, Daniel W. V, 149
Anabee, Katie B. V, 149
Anabee, Lillian V, 149
Anabee, Lillian S. V, 149
Anabee, Ollie V. V, 149
Anabee, Sarah A. V, 149
Anabel, ??? IV, 77
Anbertson, Lydda I, 35
Ancher, Henry E. II, 1085
Ancher, Henry E. II, 1087
Ancher, Henry E. II, 1088
Ancher, Mary W. II, 1087
Ancher, Mary W. II, 1088
Anchurtz, Chas. V, 983
Anchurtz, Ellen V, 983
Anchurtz, Mary V, 983
Ancker, Henry E. II, 1087
Ancker, Mary W. II, 1087
Anda, Daniel IV, 1271
Anda, Eliza IV, 1271
Anders, Foster V, 655
Anders, Foster V, 710
Anders, Viola V, 655
Anders, Viola V, 710
Anderson, Abigail I, 35
Anderson, Abigail I, 42
Anderson, Abigail I, 79
Anderson, Abigail I, 182
Anderson, Abigail I, 189
Anderson, Abigail I, 192
Anderson, Abigail V, 779
Anderson, Abigail V, 792
Anderson, Abigail V, 797
Anderson, Abigail V, 819
Anderson, Abner D. V, 218
Anderson, Ada VI, 51
Anderson, Agness VI, 810
Anderson, Agness VI, 871
Anderson, Albert I, 1113
Anderson, Albert H. I, 1103
Anderson, Alden IV, 1271
Anderson, Alexander II, 332
Anderson, Alexander II, 452
Anderson, Alexander J. V, 983
Anderson, Alfred M. VI, 871
Anderson, Alice II, 452
Anderson, Alice II, 1068
Anderson, Allie V, 218
Anderson, Almira L. VI, 990
Anderson, Alta Ruth I, 919
Anderson, Amanda IV, 1305
Anderson, Andrew IV, 672
Anderson, Andrew B. VI, 729
Anderson, Anita I, 934
Anderson, Anita I, 937
Anderson, Anita I, 949
Anderson, Ann I, 180
Anderson, Ann I, 181
Anderson, Ann I, 189
Anderson, Ann II, 974
Anderson, Ann II, 1026
Anderson, Ann VI, 965
Anderson, Ann VI, 985
Anderson, Ann J. T. VI, 1020
Anderson, Ann Meriwether VI, 870
Anderson, Anna VI, 310
Anderson, Anna Corina I, 919
Anderson, Anna E. I, 869
Anderson, Anna E. I, 879
Anderson, Anna Maie I, 621
Anderson, Anna R. I, 919
Anderson, Anne I, 189
Anderson, Anne VI, 153
Anderson, Anne VI, 310
Anderson, Anne Jane II, 786
Anderson, Annie I, 335
Anderson, Annie I, 919
Anderson, Annie A. I, 933
Anderson, Arenith I, 1113
Anderson, Arta A. I, 920
Anderson, Asenath I, 1113
Anderson, Asenath H. I, 1103
Anderson, B. C. VI, 871
Anderson, B. Frank I, 937
Anderson, B. H. V, 609
Anderson, Benjamin I, 128
Anderson, Benjamin I, 149
Anderson, Benjamin I, 181
Anderson, Benjamin I, 182
Anderson, Benjamin I, 189
Anderson, Benjamin I, 849
Anderson, Benjamin I, 869
Anderson, Benjamin Frank I, 919
Anderson, Bessie I, 919
Anderson, Betsey VI, 871
Anderson, Betsy VI, 295
Anderson, Betsy VI, 343
Anderson, Betty I, 35
Anderson, Betty I, 69
Anderson, Betty I, 128
Anderson, Betty I, 162
Anderson, Bevan Braithwaite I, 919
Anderson, Binjamin F. I, 869
Anderson, Bridget I, 473
Anderson, Bridget I, 869
Anderson, Bridget I, 919
Anderson, Bridget B. I, 473
Anderson, Bridget B. I, 755
Anderson, Bridget B. I, 765
Anderson, Bridget B. I, 796
Anderson, Bridget B. I, 869
Anderson, Bridget B. I, 891
Anderson, Bridget C. I, 849
Anderson, Bud I, 335
Anderson, Caroline IV, 1305
Anderson, Carrie M. I, 937
Anderson, Carrie May I, 919
Anderson, Carrie May I, 937
Anderson, Catherine VI, 845
Anderson, Cecilia II, 811
Anderson, Cecilia II, 831
Anderson, Cecilia II, 869
Anderson, Cecilia II, 902
Anderson, Celah V, 947
Anderson, Celia V, 947
Anderson, Celia V, 961
Anderson, Celia VI, 871
Anderson, Charles I, 937
Anderson, Charles IV, 169
Anderson, Charles V, 371
Anderson, Charles V, 655
Anderson, Charles Earnest V, 218
Anderson, Charles F. I, 937
Anderson, Charles Foster I, 919
Anderson, Charles Frank I, 919
Anderson, Charles J. VI, 998
Anderson, Charles W. V, 20
Anderson, Clark I, 1113
Anderson, Clark W. I, 1103
Anderson, Cora I, 523
Anderson, Cora I, 931
Anderson, Cora I, 933
Anderson, Cora W. VI, 227
Anderson, Cora Worth I, 583
Anderson, Corina I, 919
Anderson, Corina I, 922
Anderson, Corina L. I, 937
Anderson, Corinna I, 919
Anderson, Corinna I, 920
Anderson, Correnna A. I, 849
Anderson, Daniel I, 919
Anderson, Daniel I, 920
Anderson, Daniel I, 933
Anderson, Daniel B. I, 473
Anderson, Daniel B. I, 755
Anderson, Daniel B. I, 765
Anderson, Daniel B. I, 796
Anderson, Daniel B. I, 849
Anderson, Daniel B. I, 869
Anderson, Daniel B. I, 919
Anderson, Daniel B. I, 937
Anderson, David VI, 976
Anderson, David VI, 1010
Anderson, David N. VI, 871
Anderson, Deborah IV, 863
Anderson, Deborah IV, 864
Anderson, Deborah IV, 1201
Anderson, Dollie V, 218
Anderson, Dolly VI, 796
Anderson, Dorothy IV, 363
Anderson, Dorothy IV, 368
Anderson, Dorothy E. V, 655
Anderson, Dorothy E. V, 670
Anderson, Dorothy Frances I, 937
Anderson, Dorothy Francis I, 920
Anderson, Doshea VI, 848
Anderson, Doshey VI, 910
Anderson, E. Jane V, 218
Anderson, E. W. VI, 990
Anderson, Edith IV, 1305
Anderson, Edith VI, 295
Anderson, Edith VI, 328
Anderson, Edith Marie IV, 1305
Anderson, Edwin E. III, 16
Anderson, Edwin E. III, 19
Anderson, Eli I, 1103
Anderson, Eli I, 1113
Anderson, Eli V, 471
Anderson, Eli V, 534
Anderson, Eli, Jr. V, 471
Anderson, Elijah I, 1103
Anderson, Elijah I, 1113
Anderson, Elijah V, 150
Anderson, Elijah V, 471
Anderson, Elijah V, 947
Anderson, Elijah, Jr. V, 947
Anderson, Elimiah VI, 947
Anderson, Elisabeth I, 34
Anderson, Elisabeth I, 35
Anderson, Elisabeth I, 37
Anderson, Elisabeth I, 48
Anderson, Elisabeth I, 52
Anderson, Elisabeth I, 65
Anderson, Elisabeth I, 75
Anderson, Elisabeth I, 76
Anderson, Elisabeth I, 189
Anderson, Elisha VI, 871
Anderson, Eliza W. VI, 919
Anderson, Eliza W. VI, 1020
Anderson, Elizabeth I, 100
Anderson, Elizabeth I, 182
Anderson, Elizabeth I, 934
Anderson, Elizabeth I Sup 1, 3
Anderson, Elizabeth I Sup 1, 5
Anderson, Elizabeth II, 1044
Anderson, Elizabeth II, 1054
Anderson, Elizabeth IV, 33
Anderson, Elizabeth IV, 607
Anderson, Elizabeth IV, 612
Anderson, Elizabeth IV, 1305
Anderson, Elizabeth V, 371
Anderson, Elizabeth V, 471
Anderson, Elizabeth V, 983
Anderson, Elizabeth VI, 295
Anderson, Elizabeth VI, 763
Anderson, Elizabeth VI, 780
Anderson, Elizabeth VI, 861
Anderson, Elizabeth VI, 870
Anderson, Elizabeth VI, 871
Anderson, Elizabeth VI, 882
Anderson, Elizabeth VI, 916
Anderson, Elizabeth A. VI, 796
Anderson, Elizabeth A. VI, 976
Anderson, Elizabeth I. VI, 796
Anderson, Elizabeth W. VI, 729
Anderson, Elizabeth W. VI, 763
Anderson, Elizabeth W. VI, 781
Anderson, Elizabeth W. VI, 919
Anderson, Elizabeth W. VI, 998
Anderson, Ella I, 629
Anderson, Ella I, 637
Anderson, Ella I, 919
Anderson, Ella I, 937
Anderson, Ella V, 655
Anderson, Ella Belle I, 937
Anderson, Ella Corinna I, 920
Anderson, Ellen C. I, 937
Anderson, Ellen Corinna I, 937
Anderson, Ellen M. V, 725
Anderson, Elmer E. V, 451
Anderson, Emma May I, 919
Anderson, Emma May I, 937
Anderson, Enos Albert Doan I, 229
Anderson, Ester II, 51
Anderson, Ester II, 61
Anderson, Esther III, 19
Anderson, Esther III, 377
Anderson, Ethel Ines I, 929
Anderson, Etta Belle I, 920
Anderson, Etta Belle I, 937
Anderson, Etta Pearl I, 920
Anderson, Eunice I, 931
Anderson, Eva IV, 1245
Anderson, Flora I, 937
Anderson, Flora I, 939
Anderson, Flora Jane I, 922
Anderson, Florence I, 937
Anderson, Florence May I, 919
Anderson, Frances VI, 917
Anderson, Frances VI, 998
Anderson, Frances A. VI, 871
Anderson, Frances H. VI, 871
Anderson, Francis VI, 834
Anderson, Francis Russel V, 725
Anderson, Frank V, 150
Anderson, Frank P. I, 937
Anderson, Franklin Pleas I, 919
Anderson, Frederick IV, 1305
Anderson, Geneva IV, 1245
Anderson, Geneva IV, 1255
Anderson, George I, 335
Anderson, George II, 332
Anderson, George V, 609
Anderson, George V, 725
Anderson, George Edwin V, 725
Anderson, Hannah I, 35
Anderson, Hannah I, 61
Anderson, Hannah I, 105
Anderson, Hannah I, 849
Anderson, Hannah I, 869
Anderson, Hannah I, 888
Anderson, Hannah II, 51
Anderson, Hannah II, 61
Anderson, Hannah II, 76
Anderson, Hannah V, 19
Anderson, Hannah V, 108
Anderson, Hannah V, 947
Anderson, Hannah VI, 870
Anderson, Hannah VI, 1002
Anderson, Hannah A. V, 218
Anderson, Hannah E. V, 218
Anderson, Harriett J. I, 869
Anderson, Harvey V, 150
Anderson, Hattie I, 869
Anderson, Hattie I, 881
Anderson, Hattie V, 547
Anderson, Hattie E. VI, 680
Anderson, Hazel I, 937
Anderson, Henry I, 1113
Anderson, Henry VI, 204
Anderson, Henry T. I, 1103
Anderson, Hester II, 20
Anderson, Isaac I, 182
Anderson, Isaac IV, 865
Anderson, Israel III, 19
Anderson, J. C. VI, 871
Anderson, J. J. III, 19
Anderson, J. W. V, 150
Anderson, Jabez VI, 871
Anderson, Jacob II, 51
Anderson, Jacob VI, 813
Anderson, Jacob VI, 893
Anderson, Jacob VI, 910
Anderson, Jacob VI, 942
Anderson, Jacob H. VI, 871
Anderson, James II, 127
Anderson, James II, 142
Anderson, James II, 441
Anderson, James II, 811
Anderson, James II, 831
Anderson, James II, 902
Anderson, James II, 1068
Anderson, James III, 19
Anderson, James IV, 1245
Anderson, James V, 218
Anderson, James V, 947
Anderson, James V, 961
Anderson, James VI, 796
Anderson, James VI, 833
Anderson, James C. V, 218
Anderson, James C. VI, 796
Anderson, James C. VI, 803
Anderson, James C. VI, 817
Anderson, James C. VI, 861
Anderson, James L. VI, 894
Anderson, James P. VI, 802
Anderson, James T. VI, 871
Anderson, James T. VI, 877
Anderson, James T. VI, 1017
Anderson, James, Jr. III, 19
Anderson, James, Jr. III, 377
Anderson, Jane I, 34
Anderson, Jane I, 35
Anderson, Jane I, 189
Anderson, Jane I, 202
Anderson, Jane I, 869
Anderson, Jane III, 19
Anderson, Jane III, 394
Anderson, Jane III, 415
Anderson, Jane V, 20
Anderson, Jane V, 34
Anderson, Jane V, 655
Anderson, Jane E. I, 849
Anderson, Jane E. I, 925
Anderson, Jane R. VI, 796
Anderson, Jane, Jr. III, 19
Anderson, Jennie IV, 672
Anderson, Jenny VI, 1010
Anderson, Jeremiah VI, 848
Anderson, Jeremiah E. VI, 796
Anderson, Jesse I, 335
Anderson, Jesse VI, 870
Anderson, Jesse VI, 871
Anderson, Jesse VI, 947
Anderson, Jesse Moore I, 796
Anderson, Joel I, 849
Anderson, Joel C. VI, 871
Anderson, Joel G. I, 869
Anderson, Joel G. I, 919
Anderson, Joel G. I, 925
Anderson, Joel P. V, 471
Anderson, Joel S. I, 849
Anderson, John I, 35
Anderson, John I, 52
Anderson, John I, 61
Anderson, John I, 85
Anderson, John I, 105
Anderson, John I, 128
Anderson, John I, 180
Anderson, John I, 181
Anderson, John I, 182
Anderson, John I, 189
Anderson, John I, 191
Anderson, John I, 229
Anderson, John I, 335
Anderson, John I Sup 1, 3
Anderson, John I Sup 1, 5
Anderson, John IV, 169
Anderson, John IV, 865
Anderson, John IV, 1245
Anderson, John IV, 1305
Anderson, John V, 150
Anderson, John V, 471
Anderson, John VI, 295
Anderson, John VI, 310
Anderson, John VI, 796
Anderson, John VI, 870
Anderson, John VI, 871
Anderson, John VI, 872
Anderson, John VI, 883
Anderson, John VI, 890
Anderson, John VI, 998
Anderson, John Gray, Jr. I, 621
Anderson, John J. III, 267
Anderson, John J. III, 309
Anderson, John M. I, 849
Anderson, John McKay II, 786
Anderson, John N. VI, 919
Anderson, John N. VI, 1013
Anderson, John W. V, 150
Anderson, John W. V, 655
Anderson, John W. V, 983
Anderson, John, Jr. VI, 861
Anderson, Joseph I, 34
Anderson, Joseph I, 35
Anderson, Joseph I, 75
Anderson, Joseph I, 87
Anderson, Joseph I, 100
Anderson, Joseph I, 128
Anderson, Joseph I, 182
Anderson, Joseph I, 189
Anderson, Joseph I, 240
Anderson, Joseph IV, 865
Anderson, Joseph V, 725
Anderson, Joseph Gerald IV, 672
Anderson, Joseph Irvin V, 725
Anderson, Joseph J. V, 983
Anderson, Josephine V, 609
Anderson, Joshua I, 128
Anderson, Joshua I, 181
Anderson, Joshua I, 189
Anderson, Joshua I, 744
Anderson, Joshua I, 796
Anderson, Joshua I, 849
Anderson, Joshua I, 869
Anderson, Joshua I, 874
Anderson, Joshua I, 879
Anderson, Joshua I, 919
Anderson, Joshua I, 922
Anderson, Joshua II, 452
Anderson, Josiah VI, 922
Anderson, Josias VI, 870
Anderson, Jubal VI, 871
Anderson, Judith VI, 871
Anderson, Judith E. VI, 818
Anderson, Juilianna V, 518
Anderson, Julianna V, 471
Anderson, Junette V, 609
Anderson, Junius I, 937
Anderson, Junius L. I, 849
Anderson, Junius S. I, 919
Anderson, Justine VI, 796
Anderson, Leah I, 35
Anderson, Leah I, 73
Anderson, Leah I, 869
Anderson, Lefy Anna IV, 1201
Anderson, Lena I, 920
Anderson, Lena I, 937
Anderson, Lindsey VI, 871
Anderson, Liza A. IV, 1201
Anderson, Lizzie I, 920
Anderson, Louisa IV, 1245
Anderson, Lowella H. I, 849
Anderson, Lucinda VI, 803
Anderson, Lucy B. VI, 866
Anderson, Luella I, 937
Anderson, Luella I, 945

Anderson, Lydda I, 65
Anderson, Lydia V, 200
Anderson, Lydia C. I, 937
Anderson, Lydia Cora I, 919
Anderson, Lydia Dougherty II, 786
Anderson, Lydia Jane V, 371
Anderson, Mabel V, 150
Anderson, Magdalena V, 915
Anderson, Mahala IV, 1245
Anderson, Margaret I, 929
Anderson, Margaret IV, 19
Anderson, Margaret IV, 33
Anderson, Margaret V, 609
Anderson, Margaret Anita I, 920
Anderson, Maria G. VI, 991
Anderson, Marie V, 725
Anderson, Martha V, 19
Anderson, Martha V, 20
Anderson, Martha V, 123
Anderson, Martha V, 547
Anderson, Martha VI, 871
Anderson, Martha Ann I, 229
Anderson, Martha I. VI, 917
Anderson, Martha J. VI, 818
Anderson, Martha Ruth V, 471
Anderson, Mary I, 34
Anderson, Mary I, 35
Anderson, Mary I, 65
Anderson, Mary I, 76
Anderson, Mary I, 85
Anderson, Mary I, 128
Anderson, Mary I, 146
Anderson, Mary I, 149
Anderson, Mary I, 180
Anderson, Mary I, 181
Anderson, Mary I, 182
Anderson, Mary I, 189
Anderson, Mary I, 197
Anderson, Mary I, 744
Anderson, Mary I, 849
Anderson, Mary I, 869
Anderson, Mary I, 875
Anderson, Mary I, 919
Anderson, Mary II, 332
Anderson, Mary II, 452
Anderson, Mary II, 829
Anderson, Mary III, 19
Anderson, Mary III, 56
Anderson, Mary III, 361
Anderson, Mary III, 394
Anderson, Mary III, 415
Anderson, Mary IV, 1245
Anderson, Mary V, 20
Anderson, Mary V, 150
Anderson, Mary V, 218
Anderson, Mary V, 471
Anderson, Mary V, 534
Anderson, Mary V, 609
Anderson, Mary V, 947
Anderson, Mary VI, 295
Anderson, Mary VI, 327
Anderson, Mary VI, 328
Anderson, Mary VI, 332
Anderson, Mary VI, 870
Anderson, Mary VI, 871
Anderson, Mary A. I, 849
Anderson, Mary A. I, 937
Anderson, Mary A. I, 941
Anderson, Mary Almina I, 925
Anderson, Mary An I, 937
Anderson, Mary Ann II, 332
Anderson, Mary Annetta IV, 672
Anderson, Mary C. I, 869
Anderson, Mary E. I, 937
Anderson, Mary E. VI, 882
Anderson, Mary J. VI, 871
Anderson, Mary Jane III, 19
Anderson, Mary Jane III, 377
Anderson, Mary Jane IV, 1201
Anderson, Mary Jane V, 947
Anderson, Mary L. VI, 919
Anderson, Mary L. VI, 991
Anderson, Mary M. V, 20
Anderson, Mathew IV, 169
Anderson, Matilda VI, 861
Anderson, Melissa Urton V, 655
Anderson, Meriam I, 35
Anderson, Meriam I, 87
Anderson, Minerva J. V, 983
Anderson, Minnie I, 920
Anderson, Miriam I, 34
Anderson, Miriam I, 35
Anderson, Miriam I, 182
Anderson, Miriam I, 189
Anderson, Miriam I, 796
Anderson, Miriam I, 827
Anderson, Miriam Rachel I, 919
Anderson, Mollie I, 335
Anderson, Mourning I, 35
Anderson, Mourning I, 53
Anderson, Mourning I, 100
Anderson, Mrs. Anna IV, 1305
Anderson, Mrs. C. D. IV, 1305
Anderson, Mrs. Elizabeth VI, 919
Anderson, Mrs. Fred IV, 1305
Anderson, Mrs. Jessie IV, 672
Anderson, Mrs. Minnie I, 937
Anderson, Mrs. Minnie I, 940
Anderson, Myrtle Corina I, 919
Anderson, Nancy VI, 861
Anderson, Nancy VI, 871
Anderson, Nancy VI, 872
Anderson, Nancy A. I, 849
Anderson, Nancy A. I, 869
Anderson, Nancy Lee VI, 796
Anderson, Nancy R. IV, 169
Anderson, Nancy S. VI, 872
Anderson, Nannie I, 920
Anderson, Nannie I, 934
Anderson, Nannie I, 937
Anderson, Nannie A. I, 919
Anderson, Nannie A. I, 937
Anderson, Nathan I, 937
Anderson, Nathan M. I, 849
Anderson, Nathan M. I, 869
Anderson, Nellie I, 937
Anderson, Nellie Lee I, 919
Anderson, Nellie R. I, 934
Anderson, Nelson VI, 977
Anderson, Nettie IV, 672
Anderson, Neva Stanfield V, 150
Anderson, Noah E. V, 547
Anderson, Norma I, 919
Anderson, Norma I, 937
Anderson, Orphy VI, 295
Anderson, Otey VI, 998
Anderson, Parintha I, 937
Anderson, Parintha I, 945
Anderson, Paulina H. VI, 919
Anderson, Peggy VI, 870
Anderson, Peggy VI, 872
Anderson, Peggy VI, 976
Anderson, Penelope E. VI, 871
Anderson, Peninah I, 189
Anderson, Peninah I, 200
Anderson, Penninah I, 35
Anderson, Penninah I, 43
Anderson, Penninah I, 180
Anderson, Penninah I, 182
Anderson, Penninah I, 189
Anderson, Penninah I, 194
Anderson, Peter III, 19
Anderson, Peter III, 394
Anderson, Peter III, 415
Anderson, Peter H. III, 19
Anderson, Phebe III, 19
Anderson, Phebe Baset II, 51
Anderson, Phebe Jane IV, 672
Anderson, Philip P. V, 150
Anderson, Phillip P. V, 150
Anderson, Polly VI, 861
Anderson, Polly VI, 871
Anderson, Priscilla V, 149
Anderson, Rachel I, 612
Anderson, Rachel I, 744
Anderson, Rachel I, 849
Anderson, Rachel I, 869
Anderson, Rachel I, 874
Anderson, Rachel I, 888
Anderson, Rachel I, 919
Anderson, Rachel I, 937
Anderson, Rachel III, 19
Anderson, Rachel IV, 1245
Anderson, Rachel V, 218
Anderson, Rachel V, 819
Anderson, Rachel VI, 295
Anderson, Rachel VI, 328
Anderson, Rachel A. I, 869
Anderson, Rachel E. I, 869
Anderson, Rachel E. I, 872
Anderson, Rachel E. III, 16
Anderson, Rachel E. III, 19
Anderson, Ravian VI, 796
Anderson, Rebecca E. I, 869
Anderson, Rebecca Elizabeth I, 869
Anderson, Reuben V, 947
Anderson, Richard VI, 295
Anderson, Richard VI, 328
Anderson, Richard VI, 870
Anderson, Richard VI, 871
Anderson, Richard VI, 882
Anderson, Richard VI, 1017
Anderson, Richard H. VI, 796
Anderson, Richard H. VI, 871
Anderson, Richard H. VI, 882
Anderson, Richard H. VI, 932
Anderson, Richard H. VI, 954
Anderson, Richard H. VI, 977
Anderson, Richard, Sr. VI, 882
Anderson, Rilla IV, 1245
Anderson, Robert VI, 834
Anderson, Robert VI, 870
Anderson, Robert VI, 965
Anderson, Robert B. I, 849
Anderson, Robert B. I, 869
Anderson, Robert B. I, 937
Anderson, Robert Barcley I, 869
Anderson, Robert Duane V, 725
Anderson, Robert W. V, 371
Anderson, Robt. C. VI, 796
Anderson, Roy IV, 672
Anderson, Roy Andrew IV, 672
Anderson, Roy Stanton I, 919
Anderson, Rufus I, 919
Anderson, Rufus I, 937
Anderson, Rufus K. I, 937
Anderson, Russel V, 471
Anderson, Russell V, 471
Anderson, Ruth I, 849
Anderson, Ruth V, 451
Anderson, Ruth V, 947
Anderson, Ruth V, 961
Anderson, Ruth Almina I, 925
Anderson, Ruth C. I, 869
Anderson, Ruth C. I, 905
Anderson, Ruth E. I, 869
Anderson, Ruth Ella I, 937
Anderson, Ruth Ella I, 950
Anderson, Ruth Ophelia I, 919
Anderson, S. B. I, 929
Anderson, Salley VI, 942
Anderson, Sally VI, 803
Anderson, Sally VI, 818
Anderson, Sally VI, 845
Anderson, Sally VI, 870
Anderson, Sally VI, 871
Anderson, Sally VI, 976
Anderson, Samuel I, 34
Anderson, Samuel I, 35
Anderson, Samuel I, 37
Anderson, Samuel I, 73
Anderson, Samuel I, 85
Anderson, Samuel I, 182
Anderson, Samuel I, 919
Anderson, Samuel II, 332
Anderson, Samuel II, 452
Anderson, Samuel II, 1068
Anderson, Samuel IV, 865
Anderson, Samuel A. IV, 1201
Anderson, Samuel C. I, 849
Anderson, Samuel C. I, 869
Anderson, Samuel G. I, 937
Anderson, Samuel S. B. VI, 871
Anderson, Samuel U. II, 332
Anderson, Sarah I, 35
Anderson, Sarah I, 52
Anderson, Sarah I, 57
Anderson, Sarah I, 85
Anderson, Sarah I, 128
Anderson, Sarah I, 182
Anderson, Sarah I, 189
Anderson, Sarah I, 196
Anderson, Sarah I, 592
Anderson, Sarah I, 594
Anderson, Sarah I, 796
Anderson, Sarah I, 810
Anderson, Sarah II, 452
Anderson, Sarah II, 685
Anderson, Sarah II, 974
Anderson, Sarah II, 1017
Anderson, Sarah III, 19
Anderson, Sarah IV, 1305
Anderson, Sarah V, 218
Anderson, Sarah V, 264
Anderson, Sarah VI, 848
Anderson, Sarah VI, 859
Anderson, Sarah VI, 871
Anderson, Sarah VI, 890
Anderson, Sarah Ann VI, 998
Anderson, Sarah G. VI, 798
Anderson, Sarah Isabelle V, 451
Anderson, Sarah Jane VI, 871
Anderson, Sarah M. IV, 1201
Anderson, Sena VI, 871
Anderson, Simon II, 20
Anderson, Stella I, 920
Anderson, Stella I, 937
Anderson, Sterling VI, 795
Anderson, Sterling VI, 810
Anderson, Sterling C. VI, 795
Anderson, Sterling C. VI, 798
Anderson, Sterling C. VI, 866
Anderson, Sue V, 983
Anderson, Susan III, 267
Anderson, Susan III, 309
Anderson, Susan VI, 832
Anderson, Susan L. VI, 833
Anderson, Susanna II, 332
Anderson, Susanna II, 452
Anderson, Susanna VI, 962
Anderson, Susannah V, 19
Anderson, Susannah V, 947
Anderson, Thelma I, 920
Anderson, Thelma I, 937
Anderson, Thomas I, 920
Anderson, Thomas I, 934
Anderson, Thomas II, 20
Anderson, Thomas II, 51
Anderson, Thomas II, 76
Anderson, Thomas IV, 1201
Anderson, Thomas VI, 357
Anderson, Thomas A. H. VI, 871
Anderson, Thomas E. I, 849
Anderson, Thomas E. I, 869
Anderson, Thomas E. I, 919
Anderson, Thomas J. V, 218
Anderson, Thomas J. VI, 871
Anderson, Thomas Jefferson VI, 870
Anderson, Thomas Nathan I, 920
Anderson, Thomas T. V, 471
Anderson, Thos. E. I, 937
Anderson, Thos. J. VI, 988
Anderson, Thos. J. VI, 991
Anderson, Troy I, 925
Anderson, Vena IV, 1271
Anderson, Vera E. I, 937
Anderson, Vera Elzena I, 920
Anderson, Vinnie Edna V, 725
Anderson, Viola I, 937
Anderson, Viola May I, 919
Anderson, Walter I, 937
Anderson, Walter IV, 169
Anderson, Walter E., Jr. I, 920
Anderson, Walter E., Jr. I, 937
Anderson, Walter Eugene I, 919
Anderson, Walter Eugene I, 920
Anderson, Wd. Ann VI, 870
Anderson, Wd. Elizabeth VI, 729
Anderson, Wd. Elizabeth VI, 781
Anderson, Wd. Mary II, 452
Anderson, Wd. Susan III, 19
Anderson, Widow Anne I, 191
Anderson, William I, 48
Anderson, William I, 182
Anderson, William I, 189
Anderson, William I, 755
Anderson, William I, 931
Anderson, William I, 934
Anderson, William I, 937
Anderson, William I, 940
Anderson, William II, 1068
Anderson, William IV, 33
Anderson, William V, 218
Anderson, William VI, 295
Anderson, William VI, 823
Anderson, William VI, 870
Anderson, William VI, 871
Anderson, William VI, 872
Anderson, William VI, 890
Anderson, William VI, 917
Anderson, William VI, 942
Anderson, William VI, 976
Anderson, William B. VI, 802
Anderson, William H. VI, 871
Anderson, William H. L. VI, 871
Anderson, William I. VI, 796
Anderson, William T. I, 849
Anderson, William T. I, 869
Anderson, William Thomas I, 869
Anderson, William Thomas I, 919
Anderson, William Thomas I, 920
Anderson, William Watson VI, 872
Anderson, William, Sr. VI, 872
Anderson, Willis Jeptha I, 919
Anderson, Wm. IV, 1245
Anderson, Wm. V, 150
Anderson, Wm. V, 819
Anderson, Wm. VI, 861
Anderson, Wm. B. VI, 809
Anderson, Wm. H. V, 19
Anderson, Wm. H. V, 655
Anderson, Wm. H. VI, 1020
Anderson, Wm. T. I, 937
Anderton, Samuel II, 452
Anderton, Wd. Mary II, 452
Andree, Helen V, 892
Andres, Pheby II, 51
Andreson, Hannah II, 51
Andreson, Jacob II, 51
Andreson, Jacob II, 54
Andreson, Phebe II, 54
Andreson, Phebe Baset II, 51
Andreson, Thomas II, 51
Andrew, Aaron I, 433
Andrew, Aaron I, 443
Andrew, Aaron I, 743
Andrew, Aaron V, 471
Andrew, Abigail V, 20
Andrew, Albert B. I, 443
Andrew, Albert C. I, 433
Andrew, Alfred I, 743
Andrew, Alfred I, 755
Andrew, Amanda J. T. V, 547
Andrew, Amanda Jane T. V, 548
Andrew, Americus J. V, 547
Andrew, Americus J. V, 548
Andrew, Andy Tate V, 471
Andrew, Ann I, 372
Andrew, Ann I, 433
Andrew, Ann V, 372
Andrew, Anna I, 673
Andrew, Anna I, 689
Andrew, Anna I, 743
Andrew, Anna I, 755
Andrew, Anna V, 371
Andrew, Anna V, 372
Andrew, Anna V, 397
Andrew, Anna V, 471
Andrew, Anna V, 547
Andrew, Anna V, 576
Andrew, Anna D. V, 547
Andrew, Anna D. V, 548
Andrew, Anna Elias V, 372
Andrew, Anne I, 443
Andrew, Anne V, 547
Andrew, Aron I, 443
Andrew, Arrie Jane V, 371
Andrew, Asenath I, 443
Andrew, Asenath I, 451
Andrew, Aseneth I, 433
Andrew, Braxton I, 433
Andrew, Braxton I, 443
Andrew, Caroline V, 472
Andrew, Caroline V, 547
Andrew, Caroline V, 548
Andrew, Caroline V, 655
Andrew, Catharine I, 372
Andrew, Catharine I, 433
Andrew, Catharine I, 443
Andrew, Charles Emmet V, 372
Andrew, Charles Emmett V, 372
Andrew, Clarinda V, 371
Andrew, Clarissa V, 548
Andrew, Clarkson I, 433
Andrew, Clifton G. V, 372
Andrew, Clinton R. V, 548
Andrew, Cyrus V, 548
Andrew, David I, 372
Andrew, David I, 382
Andrew, David S. I, 743
Andrew, David S. I, 755
Andrew, Debora J. I, 433
Andrew, Deborah I, 346
Andrew, Deborah I, 360
Andrew, Deborah I, 372
Andrew, Deborah I, 384
Andrew, Deborah I, 399
Andrew, Delilah V, 471
Andrew, Delilah V, 547
Andrew, Delilah V, 556
Andrew, Delilah V, 665
Andrew, Earl J. V, 372
Andrew, Eden V, 547
Andrew, Eden V, 548
Andrew, Eleanor I, 443
Andrew, Eli V, 471
Andrew, Eli V, 472
Andrew, Elias V, 371
Andrew, Eliza Jane V, 547
Andrew, Elizabeth V, 371
Andrew, Elizabeth V, 372
Andrew, Elizabeth V, 386
Andrew, Elizabeth V, 548
Andrew, Elizabeth V, 655
Andrew, Ella I, 433
Andrew, Ellen V, 317
Andrew, Ellen V, 471
Andrew, Elvira J. I, 433
Andrew, Elvira J. I, 443
Andrew, Elwood I, 443
Andrew, Elwood V, 548
Andrew, Elwood G. V, 547
Andrew, Elwood G. V, 655
Andrew, Emily V, 710
Andrew, Erminnie V, 372
Andrew, Eugenia A. I, 743
Andrew, Frances V, 432
Andrew, Frances V, 547
Andrew, Frances V, 548
Andrew, Frances A. V, 371
Andrew, Frances A. V, 372
Andrew, Frances Green V, 548
Andrew, Fred V, 371
Andrew, George I, 743
Andrew, George M. I, 372
Andrew, George R. I, 743
Andrew, Grace V, 372
Andrew, Grace V, 427
Andrew, Hannah I, 346
Andrew, Hannah I, 360
Andrew, Hannah I, 372

Andrew, Hannah I, 382
Andrew, Hannah I, 384
Andrew, Hannah I, 399
Andrew, Hannah I, 407
Andrew, Hannah I, 431
Andrew, Hannah I, 433
Andrew, Hannah I, 443
Andrew, Hannah I, 447
Andrew, Hannah I, 673
Andrew, Hannah I, 678
Andrew, Hannah I, 743
Andrew, Hannah I, 796
Andrew, Hannah V, 471
Andrew, Hannah V, 547
Andrew, Hannah V, 570
Andrew, Hannah V, 575
Andrew, Hannah V, 576
Andrew, Hannah V, 678
Andrew, Hannah E. V, 548
Andrew, Hannah Elma V, 547
Andrew, Hannah Elma V, 548
Andrew, Hannah F. I, 433
Andrew, Hannah F. I, 443
Andrew, Hannah Isabel V, 372
Andrew, Hannah Isabella V, 371
Andrew, Hannah Jane I, 372
Andrew, Hannah M. I, 743
Andrew, Henery I, 796
Andrew, Henery I, 830
Andrew, Henry I, 372
Andrew, Henry I, 433
Andrew, Henry I, 443
Andrew, Henry V, 371
Andrew, Henry V, 372
Andrew, Henry V, 399
Andrew, Henry V, 471
Andrew, Henry V, 472
Andrew, Henry V, 547
Andrew, Ida V, 317
Andrew, Ida V, 372
Andrew, Ida May V, 317
Andrew, Ira V, 547
Andrew, Ira V, 548
Andrew, Ira V, 655
Andrew, Isaac I, 372
Andrew, Isaac I, 433
Andrew, Isaac I, 443
Andrew, Isaac V, 547
Andrew, Isaac H. V, 547
Andrew, Isaac N. I, 433
Andrew, Jacob I, 372
Andrew, Jacob I, 433
Andrew, Jacob I, 443
Andrew, Jacob II, 453
Andrew, Jacob V, 371
Andrew, Jacob V, 372
Andrew, Jacob V, 432
Andrew, Jacob V, 547
Andrew, Jacob H. V, 371
Andrew, Jacob H. V, 548
Andrew, James I, 433
Andrew, James I, 443
Andrew, James A. I, 433
Andrew, James Gilbert V, 371
Andrew, James Rileigh V, 371
Andrew, Jamiah I, 443
Andrew, Jamiah I, 453
Andrew, Jane I, 346
Andrew, Jane I, 357
Andrew, Jane I, 372
Andrew, Jane I, 433
Andrew, Jane I, 443
Andrew, Jane I, 455
Andrew, Jane I, 796
Andrew, Jane I, 830
Andrew, Jane V, 371
Andrew, Jane V, 372
Andrew, Jane V, 399
Andrew, Jane V, 471
Andrew, Jane V, 472
Andrew, Jane V, 547
Andrew, Jehu V, 471
Andrew, Jehu V, 472
Andrew, Jemima I, 443
Andrew, Jesse V, 471
Andrew, Jesse F. V, 471
Andrew, John I, 346
Andrew, John I, 360
Andrew, John I, 372
Andrew, John I, 399
Andrew, John I, 433
Andrew, John I, 443
Andrew, John II, 453
Andrew, John V, 20
Andrew, John V, 471
Andrew, John V, 472
Andrew, John V, 547
Andrew, John V, 548
Andrew, John B. V, 547
Andrew, John B. V, 548
Andrew, John E. V, 372
Andrew, John Milton V, 371
Andrew, John T. V, 548
Andrew, John Thomas V, 547
Andrew, John Thomas V, 548
Andrew, John, Jr. V, 547
Andrew, Jonathan V, 371
Andrew, Jonathan V, 372
Andrew, Jonathan V, 386
Andrew, Jonathan V, 547
Andrew, Joseph I, 443
Andrew, Joseph V, 371
Andrew, Joseph V, 372
Andrew, Joseph V, 547
Andrew, Joseph M. V, 372
Andrew, Kesiah I, 443
Andrew, Leanna I, 372
Andrew, Leanna C. I, 372
Andrew, Leanna Elzena I, 433
Andrew, Lillian V, 317
Andrew, Lillian A. V, 432
Andrew, Lillian C. V, 371
Andrew, Lizzie M. V, 371
Andrew, Louisa V, 547
Andrew, Louisa V, 548
Andrew, Louisa V, 577
Andrew, Lucy IV, 598
Andrew, Lydia V, 547
Andrew, Lydia Ann V, 371
Andrew, Lydia Ann V, 372
Andrew, Lydia Ann V, 378
Andrew, Mable V, 371
Andrew, Margaret IV, 169
Andrew, Margaret IV, 241
Andrew, Margaret E. V, 372
Andrew, Margaret Ellen V, 372
Andrew, Martha I, 433
Andrew, Martha E. I, 443
Andrew, Martha Jane V, 371
Andrew, Martha Jane V, 372
Andrew, Martha Jane V, 547
Andrew, Mary I, 372
Andrew, Mary I, 405
Andrew, Mary I, 433
Andrew, Mary I, 443
Andrew, Mary V, 20
Andrew, Mary V, 371
Andrew, Mary V, 472
Andrew, Mary V, 490
Andrew, Mary V, 547
Andrew, Mary V, 597
Andrew, Mary V, 655
Andrew, Mary V, 662
Andrew, Mary B. V, 548
Andrew, Mary C. I, 433
Andrew, Mary C. I, 443
Andrew, Mary E. V, 387
Andrew, Mary E. V, 547
Andrew, Mary E. V, 548
Andrew, Mary Ellen V, 548
Andrew, Mary Emily V, 655
Andrew, Mary Jane V, 547
Andrew, Mary Jane V, 591
Andrew, Mary R. V, 548
Andrew, Mary Ruth V, 547
Andrew, Miles V, 548
Andrew, Milton V, 317
Andrew, Milton V, 372
Andrew, Nancy I, 443
Andrew, Nancy V, 547
Andrew, Nancy V, 548
Andrew, Nancy Elizabeth V, 547
Andrew, Nancy Elizabeth V, 548
Andrew, Nancy Ellen V, 317
Andrew, Nancy Jane V, 371
Andrew, Nancy Jane V, 548
Andrew, Nathan F. I, 673
Andrew, Nathan F. I, 689
Andrew, Nathan F. I, 743
Andrew, Nathan F. I, 755
Andrew, Nettie V, 472
Andrew, Otis L. V, 372
Andrew, Paul V, 655
Andrew, Paul J. V, 655
Andrew, Rachel I, 372
Andrew, Rachel I, 433
Andrew, Rachel I, 443
Andrew, Rachel Ann V, 372
Andrew, Rebecca I, 755
Andrew, Rebeckah I, 755
Andrew, Robert I, 346
Andrew, Robert I, 357
Andrew, Robert I, 372
Andrew, Robert I, 405
Andrew, Robert I, 433
Andrew, Robert I, 443
Andrew, Robert V, 20
Andrew, Robert V, 371
Andrew, Robert V, 471
Andrew, Robert V, 472
Andrew, Robert V, 547
Andrew, Robert V, 548
Andrew, Robert VI, 467
Andrew, Robert E. V, 371
Andrew, Robt. I, 346
Andrew, Rodema Tamar I, 443
Andrew, Ruth I, 743
Andrew, Ruth I, 755
Andrew, Ruth I, 764
Andrew, Ruth V, 20
Andrew, Ruth V, 371
Andrew, Ruth V, 378
Andrew, Ruth V, 386
Andrew, Ruth V, 387
Andrew, Ruth V, 471
Andrew, Ruth V, 547
Andrew, Ruth V, 567
Andrew, Ruth V, 655
Andrew, Ruth D. V, 471
Andrew, Ruth E. V, 547
Andrew, Ruth Ella V, 548
Andrew, Ruth Ellen V, 547
Andrew, Ruth Ellen V, 548
Andrew, Sallie F. I, 372
Andrew, Sallie Foushe I, 372
Andrew, Samuel I, 346
Andrew, Samuel I, 433
Andrew, Samuel I, 443
Andrew, Samuel I, 743
Andrew, Samuel V, 471
Andrew, Samuel V, 547
Andrew, Samuel V, 548
Andrew, Samuel C. V, 371
Andrew, Samuel, Jr. V, 547
Andrew, Sarah I, 346
Andrew, Sarah I, 357
Andrew, Sarah I, 372
Andrew, Sarah I, 433
Andrew, Sarah I, 443
Andrew, Sarah I, 743
Andrew, Sarah II, 453
Andrew, Sarah V, 371
Andrew, Sarah V, 372
Andrew, Sarah V, 547
Andrew, Sarah VI, 467
Andrew, Sarah Emily V, 548
Andrew, Sarah J. I, 433
Andrew, Sarah, Jr. I, 443
Andrew, Sophronia I, 443
Andrew, Sophronia I, 450
Andrew, Stanton V, 472
Andrew, Susan I, 433
Andrew, Susan I, 443
Andrew, Susanna V, 372
Andrew, Susanna V, 548
Andrew, Susannah V, 371
Andrew, Susannah V, 547
Andrew, Susannah V, 583
Andrew, Susannah V, 693
Andrew, Susannah V, 947
Andrew, Thomas I, 755
Andrew, Thomas C. I, 743
Andrew, Thomas Ellwood V, 372
Andrew, Thomas F. I, 372
Andrew, Thomas F. I, 433
Andrew, Thomas F. I, 443
Andrew, Unity I, 433
Andrew, Walter T. V, 548
Andrew, William I, 346
Andrew, William I, 433
Andrew, William I, 443
Andrew, William I, 673
Andrew, William I, 678
Andrew, William I, 743
Andrew, William I, 796
Andrew, William V, 20
Andrew, William V, 371
Andrew, William V, 372
Andrew, William V, 471
Andrew, William V, 547
Andrew, William G. V, 371
Andrew, William G. V, 372
Andrew, William H. V, 548
Andrew, William Henry V, 371
Andrew, William Henry V, 372
Andrew, William Henry V, 547
Andrew, William J. I, 433
Andrew, William P. V, 371
Andrew, William W. I, 743
Andrew, Wilson Hobbs V, 547
Andrew, Wm. I, 399
Andrew, Wm. V, 378
Andrew, Wm. V, 386
Andrew, Wm. V, 387
Andrew, Wm. V, 567
Andrew, Wm. Andrew I, 346
Andrew, Wm. G. V, 372
Andrew, Wm. H. V, 655
Andrew, Wm. Henry V, 547
Andrews, Abraham VI, 807
Andrews, Almina E. I, 936
Andrews, Alta I, 920
Andrews, Amy VI, 1009
Andrews, Ann II, 51
Andrews, Ann II, 192
Andrews, Ann II, 453
Andrews, Ann II, 572
Andrews, Ann II, 658
Andrews, Ann IV, 922
Andrews, Ann IV, 946
Andrews, Ann VI, 51
Andrews, Ann Eliza V, 983
Andrews, Ann Maria VI, 131
Andrews, Anna Maria VI, 51
Andrews, Anna Maria VI, 129
Andrews, Anna Maria VI, 131
Andrews, Arrena IV, 363
Andrews, Arthur III, 19
Andrews, Benajah II, 192
Andrews, Benajah II, 453
Andrews, Benajah II, 572
Andrews, Benajah W. II, 832
Andrews, Benejah II, 192
Andrews, Benj. Kendal II, 453
Andrews, Benj. Kendal II, 658
Andrews, Benjamin II, 332
Andrews, Benjamin II, 453
Andrews, Benjamin IV, 922
Andrews, Benjamin VI, 153
Andrews, Benjamin C. IV, 922
Andrews, Benjamin C. IV, 931
Andrews, Brice V, 218
Andrews, Calvin V, 218
Andrews, Caroline II, 127
Andrews, Caroline Virginia VI, 51
Andrews, Catharine I, 372
Andrews, Catharine I, 413
Andrews, Charlotte IV, 1201
Andrews, Chesley VI, 871
Andrews, Clarissa II, 51
Andrews, Clarissa II, 115
Andrews, Clarissa II, 127
Andrews, Cornelia Hawkins III, 19
Andrews, Daniel IV, 169
Andrews, Daniel IV, 266
Andrews, Daniel IV, 922
Andrews, Daniel IV, 953
Andrews, Daniel IV, 976
Andrews, Daniel IV, 988
Andrews, Daniel VI, 129
Andrews, Daniel VI, 153
Andrews, Daniel VI, 166
Andrews, Daniel VI, 170
Andrews, David V, 297
Andrews, Deborah IV, 922
Andrews, Deborah IV, 1201
Andrews, Deborah IV, 1218
Andrews, Deborah M. IV, 1201
Andrews, Deborah M. IV, 1221
Andrews, Delilah V, 471
Andrews, Edna IV, 922
Andrews, Edna VI, 153
Andrews, Edna VI, 166
Andrews, Edna VI, 170
Andrews, Edward II, 192
Andrews, Edward II, 204
Andrews, Edward II, 332
Andrews, Edward II, 452
Andrews, Edward II, 513
Andrews, Edward III, 19
Andrews, Edward Bird II, 453
Andrews, Edwin Z. V, 983
Andrews, Eldenna III, 19
Andrews, Eleanor III, 19
Andrews, Eleanor B. III, 264
Andrews, Eleazer IV, 922
Andrews, Eleazer VI, 153
Andrews, Elisabeth II, 452
Andrews, Elisabeth II, 453
Andrews, Elisabeth II, 513
Andrews, Eliza IV, 922
Andrews, Eliza J. IV, 922
Andrews, Eliza L. IV, 922
Andrews, Eliza L. IV, 1143
Andrews, Elizabeth I, 299
Andrews, Elizabeth I, 303
Andrews, Elizabeth II, 20
Andrews, Elizabeth II, 51
Andrews, Elizabeth II, 115
Andrews, Elizabeth II, 127
Andrews, Elizabeth II, 192
Andrews, Elizabeth II, 221
Andrews, Elizabeth II, 332
Andrews, Elizabeth II, 452
Andrews, Elizabeth II, 453
Andrews, Elizabeth II, 513
Andrews, Elizabeth II, 611
Andrews, Elizabeth II, 831
Andrews, Elizabeth II, 876
Andrews, Elizabeth II, 974
Andrews, Elizabeth II, 1002
Andrews, Elizabeth III, 185
Andrews, Elizabeth IV, 922
Andrews, Elizabeth IV, 953
Andrews, Elizabeth VI, 97
Andrews, Elizabeth VI, 129
Andrews, Elizabeth VI, 136
Andrews, Elizabeth H. III, 19
Andrews, Elizabeth H. III, 185
Andrews, Elizabeth Holbert III, 19
Andrews, Elizabeth P. VI, 871
Andrews, Elizabeth T. II, 831
Andrews, Elizabeth T. II, 876
Andrews, Ellen V, 317
Andrews, Ellen V, 471
Andrews, Ellen V, 490
Andrews, Ellen B. II, 832
Andrews, Ellen Bernard II, 779
Andrews, Ellena III, 264
Andrews, Emelen W. III, 19
Andrews, Emelene W. III, 157
Andrews, Emeline W. III, 19
Andrews, Emeline W. III, 185
Andrews, Emeline W. III, 290
Andrews, Estella I, 611
Andrews, Estella V. I, 629
Andrews, Esther II, 51
Andrews, Esther II, 453
Andrews, Fleet W. IV, 1143
Andrews, Flete IV, 1143
Andrews, Frances VI, 871
Andrews, Frances Lloyd II, 831
Andrews, Frances Serrill II, 779
Andrews, Frances T. VI, 796
Andrews, Francis I, 611
Andrews, Frank C. II, 832
Andrews, Gabriella E. VI, 872
Andrews, Geo. F. III, 19
Andrews, Geo. R. III, 19
Andrews, Geo. R. III, 185
Andrews, Geo. R. III, 290
Andrews, George II, 127
Andrews, George R. III, 19
Andrews, George Rutt III, 19
Andrews, George Rutt, Jr. III, 19
Andrews, George T. III, 19
Andrews, Hannah I, 796
Andrews, Hannah II, 20
Andrews, Hannah II, 192
Andrews, Hannah II, 453
Andrews, Hannah II, 698
Andrews, Hannah III, 19
Andrews, Hannah V, 218
Andrews, Hannah V, 232
Andrews, Hannah V, 297
Andrews, Hannah V, 471
Andrews, Hannah B. IV, 922
Andrews, Hannah L. II, 831
Andrews, Hannah, Jr. II, 453
Andrews, Helen III, 19
Andrews, Henery I, 796
Andrews, Henry V, 472
Andrews, Hester II, 51
Andrews, Hester II, 77
Andrews, Hester II, 98
Andrews, Hester II, 192
Andrews, Hester II, 204
Andrews, Hester III, 19
Andrews, Irena IV, 565
Andrews, Irene IV, 598
Andrews, Isaac II, 20
Andrews, Isaac II, 192
Andrews, Isaac II, 452
Andrews, Isaac II, 453
Andrews, Isaac II, 513
Andrews, Isaac R. IV, 922
Andrews, J. Lesley I, 920
Andrews, J. William I, 629
Andrews, Jacob II, 20
Andrews, Jacob II, 51
Andrews, Jacob II, 192
Andrews, Jacob II, 453
Andrews, Jacob III, 19
Andrews, Jacob Andrews II, 22
Andrews, James II, 20
Andrews, James II, 51
Andrews, James II, 127
Andrews, James II, 779
Andrews, James II, 831
Andrews, James II, 832
Andrews, James II, 876
Andrews, James IV, 922
Andrews, James A. VI, 796
Andrews, James, Jr. II, 779
Andrews, James, Jr. II, 832
Andrews, Jane I, 372
Andrews, Jane I, 399
Andrews, Jane I, 796
Andrews, Jane III, 19
Andrews, Jane VI, 97
Andrews, Jane VI, 112
Andrews, Jane VI, 807

Andrews, Jeremiah II, 20
Andrews, Jeremiah II, 51
Andrews, Jettie Gertrude I, 936
Andrews, Jno. Lesley I, 920
Andrews, Joel IV, 1201
Andrews, John II, 453
Andrews, John IV, 169
Andrews, John IV, 922
Andrews, John IV, 946
Andrews, John V, 471
Andrews, John V, 725
Andrews, John VI, 51
Andrews, John VI, 97
Andrews, John VI, 102
Andrews, John VI, 103
Andrews, John VI, 112
Andrews, John VI, 129
Andrews, John VI, 140
Andrews, John VI, 153
Andrews, John VI, 796
Andrews, John E. V, 983
Andrews, John F. IV, 922
Andrews, John H. III, 19
Andrews, John H. IV, 922
Andrews, John H. VI, 153
Andrews, John Henry II, 779
Andrews, John Hunt II, 779
Andrews, John L. IV, 1143
Andrews, John L. IV, 1201
Andrews, John S. IV, 922
Andrews, John W. I, 611
Andrews, John William I, 611
Andrews, John, Jr. VI, 129
Andrews, John, Jr. VI, 153
Andrews, John, Jr. VI, 166
Andrews, John, Jr. VI, 170
Andrews, John, Sr. VI, 153
Andrews, Jon. I, 629
Andrews, Joseph III, 19
Andrews, Joseph VI, 51
Andrews, Joseph VI, 97
Andrews, Joseph VI, 129
Andrews, Joseph VI, 131
Andrews, Joseph VI, 136
Andrews, Joseph B. II, 831
Andrews, Joseph Butler IV, 922
Andrews, Joseph Oliver VI, 51
Andrews, Joshua II, 453
Andrews, Joshua IV, 922
Andrews, Josiah II, 20
Andrews, Josiah II, 51
Andrews, Josiah II, 831
Andrews, Josiah II, 832
Andrews, Josiah II, 876
Andrews, Josiah R. II, 780
Andrews, Ketura II, 453
Andrews, Keturah II, 332
Andrews, Keturah II, 832
Andrews, Keturah T. II, 831
Andrews, Keturah T. II, 832
Andrews, Keziah Arnold VI, 796
Andrews, Leanna I, 372
Andrews, Leanna C. I, 372
Andrews, Lindley IV, 922
Andrews, Lindley IV, 1143
Andrews, Lindley M. IV, 1201
Andrews, Louise I, 630
Andrews, Louise Boren I, 629
Andrews, Lucy IV, 363
Andrews, Lucy IV, 565
Andrews, Lucy IV, 598
Andrews, Lucy A. VI, 807
Andrews, Lydia II, 192
Andrews, Lydia V, 548
Andrews, M. E. VI, 950
Andrews, M. E. VI, 1020
Andrews, Magdaline IV, 620
Andrews, Malinda IV, 565
Andrews, Malinda IV, 598
Andrews, Margaret IV, 169
Andrews, Margaret IV, 922
Andrews, Margaret IV, 976
Andrews, Margaret V, 218
Andrews, Margaret M. VI, 871
Andrews, Margery V, 218
Andrews, Margery V, 258
Andrews, Mark VI, 871
Andrews, Mark VI, 948
Andrews, Martha II, 51
Andrews, Martha II, 97
Andrews, Martha II, 137
Andrews, Martha II, 779
Andrews, Martha IV, 922
Andrews, Martha IV, 1201
Andrews, Martha IV, 1204
Andrews, Martha VI, 97
Andrews, Martha VI, 129
Andrews, Martha VI, 131
Andrews, Martha B. IV, 922
Andrews, Martha Bunting II, 832
Andrews, Mary I, 643
Andrews, Mary II, 20
Andrews, Mary II, 51
Andrews, Mary II, 97
Andrews, Mary II, 115
Andrews, Mary II, 127
Andrews, Mary II, 137
Andrews, Mary II, 192
Andrews, Mary II, 198
Andrews, Mary II, 779
Andrews, Mary III, 19
Andrews, Mary III, 370
Andrews, Mary IV, 19
Andrews, Mary IV, 58
Andrews, Mary IV, 169
Andrews, Mary IV, 266
Andrews, Mary IV, 922
Andrews, Mary IV, 931
Andrews, Mary IV, 976
Andrews, Mary IV, 988
Andrews, Mary V, 297
Andrews, Mary V, 298
Andrews, Mary V, 566
Andrews, Mary VI, 129
Andrews, Mary VI, 136
Andrews, Mary E. III, 19
Andrews, Mary Emily VI, 51
Andrews, Mary F. I, 611
Andrews, Mary F. I, 629
Andrews, Mary F. I, 643
Andrews, Mary H. II, 127
Andrews, Mary Jane IV, 1201
Andrews, Mary R. IV, 922
Andrews, Mary R. IV, 953
Andrews, Mary T. III, 19
Andrews, Mary Willits I, 629
Andrews, Mathew II, 332
Andrews, Mattie IV, 922
Andrews, Melissa D. VI, 950
Andrews, Milton VI, 796
Andrews, Miriam IV, 922
Andrews, Mordica III, 19
Andrews, Mosby Arnold VI, 796
Andrews, Nancy VI, 872
Andrews, Nancy Trent VI, 796
Andrews, Nathan D. I, 611
Andrews, Nathan D. I, 629
Andrews, Nathan D. I, 643
Andrews, Nehemiah II, 192
Andrews, Nettie V, 472
Andrews, Obediah VI, 796
Andrews, Ollie V, 609
Andrews, Patsy VI, 796
Andrews, Paul V, 701
Andrews, Permilia Jane VI, 51
Andrews, Peter II, 20
Andrews, Peter II, 51
Andrews, Peter II, 97
Andrews, Peter II, 127
Andrews, Peter II, 137
Andrews, Peter II, 192
Andrews, Peter II, 204
Andrews, Peter II, 279
Andrews, Peter II, 332
Andrews, Peter II, 453
Andrews, Peter II, 572
Andrews, Peter III, 19
Andrews, Phebe II, 20
Andrews, Phebe II, 22
Andrews, Phebe II, 51
Andrews, Phebe II, 192
Andrews, Pheby II, 51
Andrews, Philo III, 19
Andrews, Polly IV, 363
Andrews, Polly H. VI, 97
Andrews, Polly H. VI, 99
Andrews, Price V, 218
Andrews, Rachel V, 983
Andrews, Rachel A. V, 983
Andrews, Rebecca II, 831
Andrews, Rebecca VI, 948
Andrews, Richard IV, 363
Andrews, Richard IV, 565
Andrews, Richard IV, 922
Andrews, Richard IV, 1201
Andrews, Richard V, 892
Andrews, Richard H. IV, 1201
Andrews, Richard H. V, 892
Andrews, Richardson II, 453
Andrews, Robert V, 20
Andrews, Robert V, 469
Andrews, Robert V, 471
Andrews, Robert V, 490
Andrews, Robert V, 725
Andrews, Robert VI, 97
Andrews, Robert VI, 129
Andrews, Robert VI, 860
Andrews, Robert Pitfield Willits I, 629
Andrews, Rodney V, 218
Andrews, Ruth V, 701
Andrews, Sallie F. I, 372
Andrews, Sallie Foushe I, 372
Andrews, Sally S. VI, 871
Andrews, Samuel II, 20
Andrews, Samuel II, 22
Andrews, Samuel II, 51
Andrews, Samuel II, 192
Andrews, Samuel II, 453
Andrews, Samuel III, 19
Andrews, Samuel III, 370
Andrews, Samuel IV, 922
Andrews, Samuel IV, 1271
Andrews, Samuel V, 471
Andrews, Samuel A. IV, 922
Andrews, Samuel A. IV, 1143
Andrews, Samuel A. IV, 1201
Andrews, Sara Louise III, 19
Andrews, Sarah II, 332
Andrews, Sarah II, 453
Andrews, Sarah IV, 169
Andrews, Sarah IV, 922
Andrews, Sarah IV, 946
Andrews, Sarah V, 297
Andrews, Sarah V, 308
Andrews, Sarah VI, 51
Andrews, Sarah VI, 97
Andrews, Sarah VI, 102
Andrews, Sarah VI, 103
Andrews, Sarah VI, 129
Andrews, Sarah VI, 153
Andrews, Sarah VI, 166
Andrews, Sarah VI, 170
Andrews, Sarah C. IV, 922
Andrews, Sarah C. VI, 129
Andrews, Sarah C. VI, 153
Andrews, Sarah Crew IV, 922
Andrews, Sarah Emily V, 594
Andrews, Sarah Louise III, 19
Andrews, Sarah Louise III, 290
Andrews, Sarah M. IV, 1201
Andrews, Sarah Rively II, 779
Andrews, Simon II, 51
Andrews, Simon II, 77
Andrews, Stokes I, 869
Andrews, Susanna IV, 922
Andrews, Susanna IV, 933
Andrews, Susannah II, 779
Andrews, Susannah VI, 51
Andrews, Susannah Lloyd II, 832
Andrews, Tabitha II, 192
Andrews, Tabitha II, 453
Andrews, Tabitha II, 508
Andrews, Thomas II, 51
Andrews, Thomas II, 192
Andrews, Thomas II, 332
Andrews, Thomas II, 452
Andrews, Thomas II, 611
Andrews, Thomas IV, 1201
Andrews, Thomas V, 297
Andrews, Thomas VI, 872
Andrews, Thomas VI, 1010
Andrews, Thomas Elwood IV, 922
Andrews, Thomas J. I, 936
Andrews, Thos. VI, 948
Andrews, Timothy II, 332
Andrews, Timothy II, 453
Andrews, W. E. VI, 51
Andrews, Wd. Elizabeth II, 20
Andrews, Wd. Hannah II, 332
Andrews, William I, 629
Andrews, William I, 630
Andrews, William I, 796
Andrews, William IV, 922
Andrews, William V, 471
Andrews, William V, 725
Andrews, William E. VI, 796
Andrews, William F. IV, 922
Andrews, William James IV, 922
Andrews, William M. VI, 872
Andrews, William W. VI, 871
Andrews, William W. VI, 872
Andrews, William W. VI, 948
Andrews, William W. VI, 950
Andrews, Wm. II, 142
Andrews, Wm. V, 983
Andrews, Wm. Arthur III, 264
Andrews, Wm. F. IV, 922
Andrews, Wm. H. II, 127
Andrews, Wm. H. II, 142
Andrews, Wm. L. IV, 1201
Andrews, Wm. P. IV, 1201
Andrews, Wm. W. VI, 980
Andros, Daniel IV, 922
Andrus, Isaac II, 192
Andy, William V, 825
Anesly, Elizabeth, Jr. II, 453
Anesly, Esther II, 453
Anesly, Hester II, 453
Aness, Albie VI, 227
Anesworth, Bell V, 983
Angel, Archibald VI, 796
Angel, Burton VI, 920
Angel, Burton VI, 1013
Angel, Clara Hazel I, 920
Angel, Daisy Elizabeth I, 920
Angel, Delia I, 920
Angel, Delia I, 937
Angel, Elizabeth I, 920
Angel, Elizabeth VI, 1007
Angel, Ellis VI, 871
Angel, Howard W. I, 920
Angel, James VI, 993
Angel, Jane Inge VI, 796
Angel, Jesse I, 920
Angel, Joseph VI, 796
Angel, Luther H. I, 920
Angel, Mary Ann VI, 796
Angel, Nancy VI, 1007
Angel, Nancy A. VI, 796
Angel, Paul Webster I, 920
Angel, Peggy VI, 871
Angel, Polly VI, 818
Angel, Rhoda VI, 818
Angel, Richard VI, 796
Angel, Sally VI, 920
Angel, W. L. I, 937
Angel, William VI, 1007
Angel, William H. I, 920
Angel, William Luther I, 920
Angel, Zachariah VI, 796
Angel, Zachariah VI, 873
Angel, Zachariah VI, 877
Angel, Zachariah VI, 891
Angel, Zachariah VI, 920
Angelis, Gideon III, 20
Angell, Augustus III, 20
Angell, Charles I, 523
Angell, Charles H. III, 20
Angell, Eliza III, 20
Angell, Joseph Thorn III, 20
Angell, Margaret III, 20
Angell, Mary I, 523
Angell, Mary I, 565
Angell, Mary A. III, 20
Angell, Maud M. III, 20
Angell, Milton I, 870
Angell, William H. III, 20
Angely, Mary I, 1047
Angely, Mary I, 1048
Angevine, Almira III, 20
Angevine, Almira III, 30
Angevine, Almira B. III, 20
Angevine, Ann III, 20
Angevine, Behia III, 20
Angevine, Bethia III, 20
Angevine, Bethia III, 30
Angevine, Bethia III, 48
Angevine, Bethia Coleman III, 20
Angevine, Bethia Y. III, 20
Angevine, Bethia Y. III, 78
Angevine, Bethia Y. III, 201
Angevine, Caroline III, 20
Angevine, David III, 20
Angevine, Fannie III, 20
Angevine, Frances III, 20
Angevine, Frank III, 20
Angevine, Frank III, 30
Angevine, Frank III, 48
Angevine, Frank III, 78
Angevine, Frank III, 201
Angevine, Frank, Jr. III, 20
Angevine, Gilbert III, 20
Angevine, Henry III, 20
Angevine, Laura W. III, 20
Angevine, Mary III, 20
Angevine, Mary Louise III, 20
Angevine, Mary Louise III, 201
Anglea, Burton VI, 878
Anglea, Hartwell VI, 818
Anglea, Nancy Ann VI, 878
Anglea, Sarah VI, 871
Anglea, William VI, 871
Anglea, William VI, 1007
Anglemire, Joseph IV, 899
Angler, Katherine VI, 858
Anglin, Catharine I, 1047
Anglin, Elijah I, 1047
Anglin, Henry I, 1047
Anglin, John I, 1047
Anglin, Mary I, 1047
Anglin, Nathan I, 1047
Anglin, Susannah I, 1047
Angus, ??? III, 185
Angus, Catharine III, 185
Angus, Mary Ann IV, 797
Angus, Mary Ann IV, 855
Angus, Thomas III, 185
Anjavine, Rebecca II, 699
Annadown, Hannah A. II, 725
Annadown, Hannah A. II, 727
Annadown, Susanna II, 453
Annadown, Susanna II, 667
Annas, Eliza II, 192
Annas, Eliza II, 234
Annas, Nathaniel Ible II, 192
Annesley, Elizabeth II, 453
Annesley, Elizabeth II, 534
Annesley, Elizabeth II, 634
Annesley, Elizabeth, Jr. II, 453
Annesley, Esther II, 453
Annesley, Hester II, 453
Annesley, Joseph II, 453
Annesley, Joseph II, 534
Annesley, Joseph II, 634
Annesley, Mary II, 332
Annesley, Mary II, 453
Annesley, Robert II, 453
Annesley, Robert II, 634
Annesley, Wd. Mary II, 453
Annesley, Wd. Mary II, 634
Anngolo, Hester VI, 872
Annis, Elizabeth II, 332
Annis, Elizabeth II, 453
Annis, Elizabeth II, 561
Annis, James II, 332
Annis, John II, 332
Annis, Lydia II, 453
Annis, Lydia II, 483
Annis, Mary II, 332
Annis, Mary II, 453
Annis, Meribah II, 974
Annis, Meribah II, 999
Annis, Patience II, 332
Annis, Sarah II, 332
Annis, Sarah II, 453
Annis, Thomas II, 332
Annis, William II, 332
Annis, Wm. II, 332
Annisly, Mary II, 453
Annisly, Robert II, 453
Anniss, Elizabeth II, 332
Anniss, James II, 332
Anniss, John II, 441
Anniss, Patience II, 332
Anniss, Wm. II, 332
Annshutis, Mary V, 983
Anrim, Hannah III, 20
Anrim, John III, 20
Anschurts, Chas. V, 983
Anscombe, Francis C. I, 629
Anscombe, Margaret I, 629
Anscombe, Prof. Francis I, 629
Ansevin, Imogene Thornburg V, 218
Ansley, Esther II, 667
Anson, Alice J. V, 548
Anson, Ellsworth V, 983
Anson, George H. V, 548
Anson, Grace V, 609
Anson, Hannah V, 548
Anson, Icy V, 983
Anson, Jesse V, 20
Anson, Lovesy IV, 139
Anson, Lydia V, 547
Anson, Lydia V, 548
Anson, Lydia H. V, 548
Anson, Margaret V, 20
Anson, Margaret Ruth V, 20
Anson, Marion L. V, 20
Anson, Marion Lewis V, 20
Anson, Mary A. V, 548
Anson, Minnie B. V, 548
Anson, Patience IV, 139
Anson, Sallie V, 685
Anson, Semer E. V, 548
Anson, Susan L. V, 548
Anson, Willis A. V, 548
Antam, Daniel VI, 591
Antam, Elizabeth VI, 591
Antam, Esther VI, 591
Antam, Jesse VI, 591
Antam, Susannah VI, 591
Anthony, ??? III, 231
Anthony, ??? VI, 153
Anthony, ??? VI, 194
Anthony, ??? VI, 223
Anthony, ??? VI, 283
Anthony, ??? VI, 348
Anthony, Abner VI, 796
Anthony, Abner VI, 839
Anthony, Abner VI, 870
Anthony, Abner VI, 871
Anthony, Abner VI, 873
Anthony, Abner VI, 874
Anthony, Abner VI, 875
Anthony, Abner VI, 880
Anthony, Abner VI, 881
Anthony, Abner VI, 884
Anthony, Abner VI, 885
Anthony, Abner VI, 886
Anthony, Abner VI, 887
Anthony, Abner VI, 891
Anthony, Abner VI, 892
Anthony, Abner VI, 897

Anthony, Abner VI, 898
Anthony, Abner VI, 901
Anthony, Abner VI, 902
Anthony, Abner VI, 904
Anthony, Abner VI, 906
Anthony, Abner VI, 907
Anthony, Abner VI, 910
Anthony, Abner VI, 912
Anthony, Abner VI, 914
Anthony, Abner VI, 915
Anthony, Abner VI, 921
Anthony, Abner VI, 922
Anthony, Abner VI, 924
Anthony, Abner VI, 926
Anthony, Abner VI, 928
Anthony, Abner VI, 931
Anthony, Abner VI, 933
Anthony, Abner VI, 936
Anthony, Abner VI, 938
Anthony, Abner VI, 942
Anthony, Abner VI, 947
Anthony, Abner VI, 949
Anthony, Abner VI, 950
Anthony, Abner VI, 953
Anthony, Abner VI, 955
Anthony, Abner VI, 958
Anthony, Abner VI, 959
Anthony, Abner VI, 962
Anthony, Abner VI, 964
Anthony, Abner VI, 965
Anthony, Abner VI, 966
Anthony, Abner VI, 967
Anthony, Abner VI, 969
Anthony, Abner VI, 971
Anthony, Abner VI, 972
Anthony, Abner VI, 973
Anthony, Abner VI, 978
Anthony, Abner VI, 980
Anthony, Abner VI, 989
Anthony, Abner VI, 995
Anthony, Abner VI, 998
Anthony, Abner VI, 1001
Anthony, Abner VI, 1004
Anthony, Abner VI, 1006
Anthony, Abner VI, 1008
Anthony, Abner VI, 1010
Anthony, Abner VI, 1012
Anthony, Abner VI, 1014
Anthony, Abner VI, 1015
Anthony, Abner VI, 1016
Anthony, Abner VI, 1020
Anthony, Abner, Jr. VI, 871
Anthony, Adner VI, 937
Anthony, Alice I, 647
Anthony, Alice I, 673
Anthony, Alice I, 755
Anthony, Alice I, 770
Anthony, Almerid V, 297
Anthony, Almira VI, 871
Anthony, Ann VI, 153
Anthony, Ann VI, 227
Anthony, Ann VI, 871
Anthony, Ann Goode VI, 796
Anthony, Ann W. VI, 153
Anthony, Ann W. VI, 164
Anthony, Anna VI, 153
Anthony, Anna VI, 164
Anthony, Anna VI, 227
Anthony, Anna R. III, 20
Anthony, C. V, 902
Anthony, Carrie III, 231
Anthony, Catharine L. VI, 1001
Anthony, Charles I, 959
Anthony, Charles I, 1003
Anthony, Charles I, 1007
Anthony, Charles V, 20
Anthony, Charles V, 106
Anthony, Charles V, 218
Anthony, Charles V, 317
Anthony, Charles V, 372
Anthony, Charles V, 892
Anthony, Charles VI, 153
Anthony, Charles VI, 154
Anthony, Charles VI, 190
Anthony, Charles VI, 194
Anthony, Charles VI, 227
Anthony, Charles VI, 295
Anthony, Charles VI, 349
Anthony, Charles VI, 353
Anthony, Charles VI, 799
Anthony, Charles VI, 931
Anthony, Charlotte I, 673
Anthony, Charlotte I, 691
Anthony, Charlotte V, 20
Anthony, Charlotte V, 103
Anthony, Charlotte V, 922
Anthony, Charlotte VI, 295
Anthony, Charlotte VI, 349
Anthony, Chas. V, 892
Anthony, Chas. V, 904
Anthony, Christopher I, 1089
Anthony, Christopher V, 20
Anthony, Christopher V, 112
Anthony, Christopher V, 317
Anthony, Christopher V, 825
Anthony, Christopher V, 889
Anthony, Christopher V, 892
Anthony, Christopher V, 922
Anthony, Christopher VI, 97
Anthony, Christopher VI, 153
Anthony, Christopher VI, 164
Anthony, Christopher VI, 227
Anthony, Christopher VI, 260
Anthony, Christopher VI, 295
Anthony, Christopher VI, 327
Anthony, Christopher VI, 330
Anthony, Christopher VI, 333
Anthony, Christopher VI, 341
Anthony, Christopher VI, 348
Anthony, Christopher VI, 349
Anthony, Christopher VI, 350
Anthony, Christopher VI, 352
Anthony, Christopher VI, 839
Anthony, Christopher, Jr. V, 317
Anthony, Christopher, Jr. VI, 153
Anthony, Christopher, Jr. VI, 164
Anthony, Christopher, Jr. VI, 227
Anthony, Christopher, Jr. VI, 349
Anthony, Clark V, 218
Anthony, Clark V, 297
Anthony, Clark VI, 227
Anthony, Cynthia I, 870
Anthony, Cynthia I, 882
Anthony, Daniel V, 730
Anthony, Daniel VI, 729
Anthony, Daniel VI, 786
Anthony, Daniel VI, 787
Anthony, Edward Clark V, 892
Anthony, Edwin C. V, 892
Anthony, Edwin Clark V, 892
Anthony, Elija V, 20
Anthony, Eliza I, 1003
Anthony, Eliza V, 20
Anthony, Eliza V, 123
Anthony, Eliza V, 317
Anthony, Elizabeth I, 647
Anthony, Elizabeth I, 1003
Anthony, Elizabeth I, 1007
Anthony, Elizabeth V, 20
Anthony, Elizabeth V, 106
Anthony, Elizabeth V, 317
Anthony, Elizabeth V, 326
Anthony, Elizabeth V, 372
Anthony, Elizabeth V, 432
Anthony, Elizabeth V, 892
Anthony, Elizabeth V, 904
Anthony, Elizabeth VI, 153
Anthony, Elizabeth VI, 190
Anthony, Elizabeth VI, 194
Anthony, Elizabeth VI, 295
Anthony, Elizabeth VI, 297
Anthony, Elizabeth VI, 349
Anthony, Elizabeth VI, 353
Anthony, Elizabeth VI, 796
Anthony, Elizabeth A. VI, 894
Anthony, Emelia VI, 871
Anthony, Emelia L. VI, 931
Anthony, Eva I, 613
Anthony, Eva E. I, 618
Anthony, Hannah III, 173
Anthony, Hannah III, 297
Anthony, Hannah V, 902
Anthony, Hannah VI, 295
Anthony, Hannah VI, 324
Anthony, Hannah VI, 327
Anthony, Hannah VI, 349
Anthony, Hannah VI, 352
Anthony, Harriet V, 725
Anthony, Harriet V, 730
Anthony, Harriet V, 731
Anthony, Harriet V, 797
Anthony, Henrietta I, 1003
Anthony, Henrietta V, 20
Anthony, Henrietta V, 317
Anthony, Henrietta P. V, 106
Anthony, Henrietta P. V, 145
Anthony, Henrietta P. V, 317
Anthony, Henrietta P. V, 352
Anthony, Henry VI, 796
Anthony, Henry VI, 871
Anthony, Hope I, 673
Anthony, J. Milton I, 673
Anthony, Jacob I, 673
Anthony, James I, 647
Anthony, James I, 673
Anthony, James I, 684
Anthony, James I, 691
Anthony, James VI, 227
Anthony, James VI, 796
Anthony, James VI, 871
Anthony, James VI, 964
Anthony, James C. I, 618
Anthony, James C. I, 647
Anthony, Jane I, 618
Anthony, Jane V, 218
Anthony, Jane VI, 154
Anthony, Jane VI, 227
Anthony, Jane L. VI, 796
Anthony, Jane L. VI, 871
Anthony, Jane W. V, 317
Anthony, Jane W. V, 341
Anthony, Jane Wood V, 317
Anthony, Jane Wood V, 892
Anthony, Jane Wood VI, 227
Anthony, Jno. VI, 920
Anthony, John VI, 330
Anthony, John VI, 820
Anthony, John VI, 860
Anthony, John VI, 871
Anthony, John VI, 942
Anthony, John VI, 1001
Anthony, John A. VI, 798
Anthony, John A. VI, 815
Anthony, Johnathan I, 690
Anthony, Jonathan I, 647
Anthony, Jonathan I, 673
Anthony, Jonathan I, 676
Anthony, Jonathan G. I, 673
Anthony, Jordan VI, 295
Anthony, Jordan VI, 349
Anthony, Jos. VI, 194
Anthony, Joseph V, 20
Anthony, Joseph V, 150
Anthony, Joseph V, 317
Anthony, Joseph V, 341
Anthony, Joseph V, 372
Anthony, Joseph V, 892
Anthony, Joseph VI, 15
Anthony, Joseph VI, 153
Anthony, Joseph VI, 154
Anthony, Joseph VI, 227
Anthony, Joseph VI, 282
Anthony, Joseph VI, 295
Anthony, Joseph VI, 326
Anthony, Joseph VI, 890
Anthony, Joseph VI, 894
Anthony, Joseph VI, 896
Anthony, Judeth I, 1003
Anthony, Judith V, 20
Anthony, Judith V, 297
Anthony, Judith V, 317
Anthony, Judith V, 363
Anthony, Judith V, 372
Anthony, Judith V, 424
Anthony, Judith VI, 153
Anthony, Judith VI, 260
Anthony, Judith VI, 295
Anthony, Laura I, 929
Anthony, Lillian III, 94
Anthony, Lucinda IV, 678
Anthony, Lucinda IV, 1246
Anthony, Lydia I, 623
Anthony, Lydia I, 647
Anthony, Lydia I, 673
Anthony, Lydia I, 690
Anthony, Lydia Ann III, 20
Anthony, Mark VI, 796
Anthony, Mark VI, 871
Anthony, Mark VI, 931
Anthony, Mark VI, 1001
Anthony, Martha III, 20
Anthony, Martha Haden VI, 796
Anthony, Mary I, 647
Anthony, Mary I, 673
Anthony, Mary V, 20
Anthony, Mary V, 112
Anthony, Mary V, 892
Anthony, Mary V, 902
Anthony, Mary V, 922
Anthony, Mary VI, 97
Anthony, Mary VI, 295
Anthony, Mary VI, 322
Anthony, Mary VI, 327
Anthony, Mary VI, 349
Anthony, Mary VI, 350
Anthony, Mary VI, 351
Anthony, Mary VI, 352
Anthony, Mary VI, 890
Anthony, Mary Ann VI, 227
Anthony, Mary Ann VI, 964
Anthony, Mary C. VI, 1010
Anthony, Mary E. VI, 871
Anthony, Mary J. V, 892
Anthony, Micajah VI, 871
Anthony, Millicent VI, 871
Anthony, Millicent VI, 964
Anthony, Molley VI, 342
Anthony, Molly VI, 295
Anthony, Molly VI, 341
Anthony, Moreman V, 892
Anthony, Narcissa V, 150
Anthony, Narcissa V, 173
Anthony, Narcissa V, 892
Anthony, Narcissa H. V, 892
Anthony, Obed I, 647
Anthony, Obed I, 673
Anthony, Obed I, 684
Anthony, Ovilla V, 297
Anthony, Parsons V, 218
Anthony, Parsons VI, 295
Anthony, Patience II, 453
Anthony, Penelope V, 20
Anthony, Penelope V, 317
Anthony, Penelope V, 892
Anthony, Penelope VI, 295
Anthony, Penelope VI, 321
Anthony, Penelope VI, 349
Anthony, Phebe I, 523
Anthony, Phebe I, 647
Anthony, Phebe I, 673
Anthony, Phebe I, 676
Anthony, Polly C. VI, 820
Anthony, Rachel V, 20
Anthony, Rachel V, 112
Anthony, Rachel V, 145
Anthony, Rachel V, 297
Anthony, Rachel V, 317
Anthony, Rachel V, 318
Anthony, Rachel V, 892
Anthony, Rachel VI, 295
Anthony, Rachel VI, 349
Anthony, Rhoda V, 20
Anthony, Rhoda V, 150
Anthony, Rhoda V, 218
Anthony, Rhoda V, 297
Anthony, Rhoda V, 312
Anthony, Rhoda V, 317
Anthony, Rhoda V, 341
Anthony, Rhoda V, 892
Anthony, Rhoda VI, 153
Anthony, Rhoda VI, 154
Anthony, Rhoda VI, 227
Anthony, Rhoda VI, 282
Anthony, Rhoda VI, 295
Anthony, Rhoda M. V, 317
Anthony, Rhoda Moorman V, 317
Anthony, Rhoda Mourman V, 892
Anthony, Ruth V, 297
Anthony, Sally I, 1003
Anthony, Sally V, 20
Anthony, Sally V, 317
Anthony, Sally VI, 871
Anthony, Samuel V, 218
Anthony, Samuel V, 317
Anthony, Samuel V, 892
Anthony, Samuel VI, 154
Anthony, Samuel VI, 227
Anthony, Samuel VI, 295
Anthony, Samuel VI, 349
Anthony, Samuel P. V, 892
Anthony, Samuel Parson V, 317
Anthony, Samuel Parsons V, 317
Anthony, Samuel Parsons VI, 153
Anthony, Samuel Parsons VI, 227
Anthony, Sarah I, 684
Anthony, Sarah V, 317
Anthony, Sarah V, 331
Anthony, Sarah V, 372
Anthony, Sarah V, 424
Anthony, Sarah V, 892
Anthony, Sarah VI, 295
Anthony, Sarah VI, 349
Anthony, Sarah VI, 350
Anthony, Sarah VI, 351
Anthony, Sarah VI, 729
Anthony, Sarah VI, 860
Anthony, Sarah VI, 896
Anthony, Sarah VI, 1001
Anthony, Sarah E. VI, 729
Anthony, Sarah E. VI, 734
Anthony, Sarah E. VI, 786
Anthony, Sarah E. VI, 787
Anthony, Sarah H. VI, 796
Anthony, Sarah L. VI, 796
Anthony, Snelson VI, 796
Anthony, Susan V, 725
Anthony, Susan V, 754
Anthony, Susan Evans V, 20
Anthony, Susan Evans V, 317
Anthony, Susan Evans V, 892
Anthony, Susannah V, 725
Anthony, Susannah V, 730
Anthony, Susannah V, 773
Anthony, Susannah VI, 798
Anthony, Thomas V, 218
Anthony, Thomas V, 297
Anthony, Thomas VI, 154
Anthony, Thomas VI, 227
Anthony, Thomas C. V, 317
Anthony, Thomas Clark V, 317
Anthony, Thomas Clarke VI, 153
Anthony, Thomas P. V, 150
Anthony, Thos. C. V, 363
Anthony, Thos. P. V, 173
Anthony, Thos. W. VI, 1010
Anthony, Widow Mary I, 691
Anthony, Widow Mary Way I, 684
Antill, Abigail II, 453
Antill, Abigail II, 574
Antill, Abigail II, 575
Antonio, John II, 782
Antonio, Noami II, 782
Antony, Anna VI, 295
Antony, James VI, 295
Antony, Mary Ann VI, 295
Antony, Rhoda V, 20
Antram, ??? VI, 595
Antram, Aaron II, 193
Antram, Aaron II, 226
Antram, Aaron IV, 672
Antram, Aaron V, 20
Antram, Aaron V, 548
Antram, Aaron A. II, 193
Antram, Aaron L. V, 20
Antram, Aaron L., Jr. V, 20
Antram, Abigail II, 192
Antram, Abigail II, 193
Antram, Ada V, 655
Antram, Ada V, 675
Antram, Ann II, 192
Antram, Ann II, 193
Antram, Ann V, 20
Antram, Ann V, 548
Antram, Ann VI, 362
Antram, Anna II, 193
Antram, Anna II, 276
Antram, Anna E. V, 150
Antram, Anne II, 193
Antram, Anslem V, 20
Antram, Anslum V, 20
Antram, Arthur V, 150
Antram, Arthur D. V, 609
Antram, Azubah II, 193
Antram, Azubah II, 198
Antram, Barbara N. V, 20
Antram, Bathsheba II, 192
Antram, Bathsheba II, 196
Antram, Bell V, 655
Antram, Benajah II, 193
Antram, Benjamin IV, 672
Antram, Benjmin IV, 672
Antram, Bernise II, 193
Antram, Brightie L. V, 20
Antram, Caleb II, 193
Antram, Caleb IV, 73
Antram, Caleb IV, 74
Antram, Caleb IV, 78
Antram, Caleb VI, 362
Antram, Caleb VI, 387
Antram, Caleb VI, 591
Antram, Caleb VI, 595
Antram, Caleb VI, 596
Antram, Carrie V, 609
Antram, Carrie E. V, 609
Antram, Carrie E. V, 655
Antram, Catharine V, 609
Antram, Charity II, 193
Antram, Charity II, 235
Antram, Charity V, 20
Antram, Charity V, 548
Antram, Charity Ann V, 20
Antram, Charles West II, 279
Antram, Chas. II, 193
Antram, Daniel II, 192
Antram, Daniel II, 193
Antram, Daniel V, 20
Antram, Daniel VI, 362
Antram, Daniel VI, 600
Antram, David II, 193
Antram, David V, 20
Antram, Deborah IV, 73
Antram, Ebenezer II, 192
Antram, Edith II, 193
Antram, Edmund V, 20
Antram, Edmund V, 548
Antram, Edward V, 20
Antram, Edward V, 96
Antram, Edward V, 979
Antram, Elisabeth II, 192
Antram, Elisabeth II, 193
Antram, Elisabeth II, 229
Antram, Eliza V, 150
Antram, Elizabeth II, 192
Antram, Elizabeth II, 193
Antram, Elizabeth II, 226
Antram, Elizabeth II, 239
Antram, Elizabeth IV, 73
Antram, Elizabeth IV, 672
Antram, Elizabeth V, 150
Antram, Elizabeth V, 548
Antram, Elizabeth VI, 362
Antram, Elizabeth VI, 591
Antram, Elizabeth D. IV, 672
Antram, Elizabeth H. IV, 672
Antram, Esther II, 193

Antram, Esther VI, 362
Antram, Esther VI, 591
Antram, Frances II, 192
Antram, Frances II, 193
Antram, Frances IV, 672
Antram, Francis IV, 672
Antram, Frank W. V, 609
Antram, Godfrey II, 193
Antram, Hannah II, 193
Antram, Hannah III, 20
Antram, Hannah IV, 672
Antram, Hannah V, 979
Antram, Hannah VI, 362
Antram, Hannah VI, 387
Antram, Hannah VI, 595
Antram, Hannah D. IV, 672
Antram, Hiram V, 548
Antram, Hiram V, 609
Antram, I. H. V, 20
Antram, I. M. V, 20
Antram, Ida M. V, 20
Antram, Isaac II, 192
Antram, Isaac II, 193
Antram, Isaac H. V, 20
Antram, James II, 192
Antram, James II, 193
Antram, James V, 979
Antram, James VI, 362
Antram, Jane II, 192
Antram, Jane II, 193
Antram, Jane Ridgway II, 192
Antram, Jesse II, 193
Antram, Jesse VI, 362
Antram, John II, 192
Antram, John II, 193
Antram, John II, 226
Antram, John II, 235
Antram, John IV, 73
Antram, John IV, 672
Antram, John V, 20
Antram, John V, 655
Antram, John VI, 362
Antram, John VI, 591
Antram, John M. V, 609
Antram, John, Jr. II, 192
Antram, John, Jr. V, 548
Antram, Jonathan Harvey V, 20
Antram, Joseph II, 165
Antram, Joseph II, 193
Antram, Joseph II, 276
Antram, Joseph V, 372
Antram, Joseph V; 548
Antram, Joseph V, 560
Antram, Joshua II, 193
Antram, Joshua IV, 73
Antram, Joshua V, 372
Antram, Joshua V, 548
Antram, Laura E. V, 20
Antram, Levi II, 193
Antram, Lucinda V, 372
Antram, Lydia II, 193
Antram, Lydia VI, 362
Antram, Lydia Davis V, 372
Antram, Lydia Martha V, 20
Antram, Margaret II, 165
Antram, Margaret II, 193
Antram, Margaret II, 198
Antram, Margaret V, 150
Antram, Maria IV, 73
Antram, Maria IV, 93
Antram, Marie V, 20
Antram, Martha II, 192
Antram, Martha II, 193
Antram, Martha II, 276
Antram, Martha IV, 73
Antram, Martha IV, 78
Antram, Martha V, 20
Antram, Martha VI, 362
Antram, Martha D. V, 20
Antram, Mary II, 192
Antram, Mary II, 193
Antram, Mary II, 209
Antram, Mary II, 270
Antram, Mary IV, 73
Antram, Mary IV, 78
Antram, Mary IV, 117
Antram, Mary V, 150
Antram, Mary V, 548
Antram, Mary V, 560
Antram, Mary V, 609
Antram, Mary VI, 362
Antram, Mary VI, 386
Antram, Mary C. V, 150
Antram, Mary H. V, 20
Antram, Mercy II, 192
Antram, Micajah T. V, 20
Antram, Orville Paris V, 609
Antram, Patience II, 193
Antram, Pindar II, 1044
Antram, Priscilla II, 192
Antram, Priscilla II, 193
Antram, Priscilla II, 226
Antram, Prudence II, 192
Antram, Prudence II, 193
Antram, Rachel II, 192
Antram, Rachel II, 193
Antram, Rachel VI, 600
Antram, Rebecca II, 193
Antram, Rebecca Ann V, 609
Antram, Rebecca Ann V, 648
Antram, Robert II, 193
Antram, Robert II, 229
Antram, Robert G. II, 193
Antram, Sarah I, 523
Antram, Sarah I, 525
Antram, Sarah II, 192
Antram, Sarah II, 193
Antram, Sarah II, 229
Antram, Sarah IV, 73
Antram, Sarah IV, 74
Antram, Sarah V, 472
Antram, Sarah VI, 362
Antram, Sarah VI, 363
Antram, Sarah VI, 462
Antram, Sarah VI, 467
Antram, Sarah VI, 591
Antram, Sarah VI, 595
Antram, Sarah VI, 596
Antram, Sarah Ann V, 20
Antram, Sarah Ann V, 135
Antram, Sarah Church II, 193
Antram, Susanna II, 193
Antram, Susannah II, 192
Antram, Susannah II, 193
Antram, Susannah VI, 600
Antram, Thomas II, 192
Antram, Thomas II, 193
Antram, Thomas V, 20
Antram, Thomas, Jr. II, 193
Antram, Thos., Jr. II, 192
Antram, W. H. V, 20
Antram, William II, 193
Antram, William Henry V, 20
Antram, Zachariah II, 165
Antram, Zachariah II, 193
Antram, Zachariah II, 198
Antram, Zachary II, 192
Antram, Zalinda V, 20
Antram, Zalinda V, 96
Antrem, Caleb VI, 591
Antrem, Elizabeth VI, 591
Antrem, Esther VI, 591
Antrem, Hannah IV, 899
Antrem, Jesse VI, 591
Antrem, John IV, 672
Antrim, ??? IV, 861
Antrim, ??? V, 443
Antrim, Aaron II, 193
Antrim, Aaron II, 200
Antrim, Aaron II, 279
Antrim, Aaron IV, 672
Antrim, Aaron V, 67
Antrim, Aaron V, 472
Antrim, Aaron A. II, 279
Antrim, Aaron L. V, 20
Antrim, Abigail II, 135
Antrim, Abigail II, 193
Antrim, Abigail II, 257
Antrim, Abigail II, 260
Antrim, Aden V, 218
Antrim, Adier II, 165
Antrim, Ann II, 165
Antrim, Ann II, 193
Antrim, Ann II, 453
Antrim, Ann IV, 607
Antrim, Ann IV, 863
Antrim, Ann V, 20
Antrim, Ann V, 472
Antrim, Ann VI, 395
Antrim, Ann VI, 591
Antrim, Anne II, 241
Antrim, Barbara N. V, 20
Antrim, Benajah II, 115
Antrim, Benajah II, 165
Antrim, Benajah II, 193
Antrim, Benajah II, 279
Antrim, Benjamin IV, 733
Antrim, Benjamin IV, 922
Antrim, Benjamin V, 218
Antrim, Benjmin IV, 672
Antrim, Bernise II, 193
Antrim, Caleb IV, 73
Antrim, Caleb IV, 78
Antrim, Caleb VI, 362
Antrim, Caleb VI, 379
Antrim, Caleb VI, 591
Antrim, Caleb, Jr. IV, 73
Antrim, Charity Ann V, 20
Antrim, Charity Ann V, 118
Antrim, Charity Ann V, 472
Antrim, Charles West II, 279
Antrim, Daniel II, 192
Antrim, Daniel IV, 607
Antrim, Daniel V, 297
Antrim, Daniel V, 304
Antrim, Daniel VI, 591
Antrim, David II, 165
Antrim, David V, 20
Antrim, Deborah IV, 73
Antrim, Deborah IV, 78
Antrim, Deborah V, 472
Antrim, Deborah V, 541
Antrim, Edmond V, 472
Antrim, Edna K. III, 20
Antrim, Eliza V, 218
Antrim, Elizabeth II, 193
Antrim, Elizabeth II, 200
Antrim, Elizabeth IV, 19
Antrim, Elizabeth IV, 73
Antrim, Elizabeth IV, 607
Antrim, Elizabeth IV, 715
Antrim, Elizabeth IV, 863
Antrim, Elizabeth IV, 922
Antrim, Elizabeth V, 157
Antrim, Elizabeth V, 472
Antrim, Elizabeth V, 548
Antrim, Elizabeth V, 587
Antrim, Elizabeth VI, 413
Antrim, Elizabeth VI, 591
Antrim, Elizabeth VI, 604
Antrim, Elizabeth D. IV, 672
Antrim, Elizabeth D. IV, 733
Antrim, Elizabeth H. IV, 672
Antrim, Elizabeth L. III, 20
Antrim, Elizabeth, Jr. VI, 591
Antrim, Esther IV, 19
Antrim, Esther IV, 38
Antrim, Esther IV, 73
Antrim, Esther VI, 591
Antrim, Frances II, 165
Antrim, Frances II, 193
Antrim, Georgiana II, 780
Antrim, Godfrey II, 165
Antrim, Hannah II, 165
Antrim, Hannah II, 180
Antrim, Hannah II, 193
Antrim, Hannah II, 197
Antrim, Hannah II, 453
Antrim, Hannah II, 506
Antrim, Hannah II, 790
Antrim, Hannah II, 974
Antrim, Hannah II, 1044
Antrim, Hannah II, 1068
Antrim, Hannah III, 20
Antrim, Hannah IV, 797
Antrim, Hannah IV, 810
Antrim, Hannah V, 967
Antrim, Hannah W. II, 453
Antrim, Hannah W. II, 506
Antrim, Hannah, Jr. II, 453
Antrim, Harriet Stockton II, 790
Antrim, Hiram V, 472
Antrim, Hiram V, 609
Antrim, Iaac II, 332
Antrim, Isaac II, 165
Antrim, Isaac II, 453
Antrim, Isaac II, 506
Antrim, Isaac II, 780
Antrim, Isaac II, 832
Antrim, Isaac II, 974
Antrim, Isaac II, 1044
Antrim, Isaac II, 1068
Antrim, Isaac H. V, 20
Antrim, Isaac, Jr. II, 453
Antrim, James II, 165
Antrim, James II, 192
Antrim, James II, 453
Antrim, James IV, 863
Antrim, James VI, 362
Antrim, James P. IV, 607
Antrim, Jane II, 193
Antrim, Jane II, 207
Antrim, Jane II, 209
Antrim, Jesse IV, 73
Antrim, Jesse VI, 591
Antrim, Jno. II, 165
Antrim, Job II, 165
Antrim, Job IV, 1269
Antrim, John II, 165
Antrim, John II, 180
Antrim, John II, 192
Antrim, John II, 193
Antrim, John II, 245
Antrim, John II, 790
Antrim, John IV, 19
Antrim, John IV, 73
Antrim, John IV, 797
Antrim, John IV, 810
Antrim, John V, 20
Antrim, John V, 218
Antrim, John V, 472
Antrim, John VI, 362
Antrim, John VI, 395
Antrim, John VI, 413
Antrim, John VI, 591
Antrim, Jonathan Harvey V, 20
Antrim, Joseph II, 165
Antrim, Joseph II, 453
Antrim, Joseph V, 218
Antrim, Joseph V, 472
Antrim, Joseph Kirby II, 780
Antrim, Joshua IV, 73
Antrim, Joshua V, 472
Antrim, Joshua VI, 591
Antrim, Levi IV, 607
Antrim, Levi VI, 591
Antrim, Louisa V, 218
Antrim, Lucinda V, 218
Antrim, Lucinda V, 317
Antrim, Lucinda V, 349
Antrim, Luicnda V, 218
Antrim, Lydia II, 193
Antrim, Lydia II, 200
Antrim, Lydia IV, 1271
Antrim, Lydia IV, 1279
Antrim, Lydia IV, 1285
Antrim, Lydia Martha V, 20
Antrim, Margaret II, 165
Antrim, Maria IV, 73
Antrim, Marian II, 780
Antrim, Martha IV, 73
Antrim, Martha IV, 78
Antrim, Martha V, 20
Antrim, Martha VI, 379
Antrim, Martha W. V, 67
Antrim, Mary II, 192
Antrim, Mary II, 193
Antrim, Mary II, 245
Antrim, Mary II, 1068
Antrim, Mary IV, 73
Antrim, Mary Ann II, 974
Antrim, Mary Ann II, 1044
Antrim, Mary Ann II, 1068
Antrim, Micajah T. V, 20
Antrim, P. Daniel IV, 863
Antrim, Patience II, 193
Antrim, Pindar II, 780
Antrim, Pindar II, 1044
Antrim, Pinder II, 974
Antrim, Pinder II, 1068
Antrim, Priscilla II, 165
Antrim, Priscilla II, 180
Antrim, Prudence II, 165
Antrim, Rachel V, 218
Antrim, Rachel VI, 591
Antrim, Rachel VI, 600
Antrim, Richard II, 1044
Antrim, Richard II, 1068
Antrim, Richard Birdsal II, 1068
Antrim, Richard Burdsal II, 1068
Antrim, Richard Burdsall II, 974
Antrim, Robert G. II, 279
Antrim, Robert G. II, 698
Antrim, Robert G. II, 725
Antrim, Samuel N. II, 115
Antrim, Samuel N. II, 279
Antrim, Sarah II, 115
Antrim, Sarah II, 165
Antrim, Sarah II, 193
Antrim, Sarah II, 214
Antrim, Sarah II, 275
Antrim, Sarah II, 279
Antrim, Sarah II, 1044
Antrim, Sarah II, 1068
Antrim, Sarah IV, 73
Antrim, Sarah V, 297
Antrim, Sarah V, 304
Antrim, Sarah V, 472
Antrim, Sarah VI, 362
Antrim, Sarah VI, 413
Antrim, Sarah VI, 469
Antrim, Sarah VI, 591
Antrim, Sarah B. II, 832
Antrim, Sarah B. II, 974
Antrim, Susanna II, 974
Antrim, Susanna II, 1044
Antrim, Susanna II, 1068
Antrim, Susannah II, 192
Antrim, Susannah IV, 616
Antrim, Susannah VI, 591
Antrim, Thomas II, 165
Antrim, Thomas II, 453
Antrim, Thomas IV, 1269
Antrim, Thomas V, 20
Antrim, Thomas V, 218
Antrim, Thomas V, 445
Antrim, Thomas, Jr. II, 193
Antrim, Wd Hannah IV, 797
Antrim, William II, 165
Antrim, Zachariah II, 165
Antrobus, Benj. II, 453
Antrobus, Joseph II, 453
Antrom, Frances II, 192
Antrom, Frances II, 204
Antrom, Isaac II, 165
Antrom, John II, 192
Antrom, John II, 204
Antrum, Adier II, 165
Antrum, Ann II, 165
Antrum, Ann II, 192
Antrum, Ann II, 213
Antrum, Ann II, 241
Antrum, Ann V, 20
Antrum, Charity Ann V, 20
Antrum, David II, 165
Antrum, Ebenezer II, 192
Antrum, Elisabeth II, 192
Antrum, Elisabeth II, 216
Antrum, Elizabeth II, 192
Antrum, Frances II, 165
Antrum, Godfrey II, 165
Antrum, Ida M. V, 20
Antrum, Isaac II, 165
Antrum, Isaac II, 192
Antrum, Isaac II, 203
Antrum, Isaac II, 213
Antrum, Isaac II, 253
Antrum, James II, 192
Antrum, James II, 193
Antrum, James II, 453
Antrum, Jane II, 192
Antrum, Jane II, 253
Antrum, Jane Ridgway II, 192
Antrum, Jesse II, 193
Antrum, Job II, 165
Antrum, John II, 165
Antrum, John II, 192
Antrum, John II, 216
Antrum, John II, 227
Antrum, John II, 241
Antrum, John, Jr. II, 192
Antrum, Martha II, 192
Antrum, Martha II, 246
Antrum, Mary II, 192
Antrum, Mary II, 240
Antrum, Mary II, 258
Antrum, Mercy II, 192
Antrum, Mercy II, 203
Antrum, Priscilla II, 192
Antrum, Priscilla II, 227
Antrum, Prudence II, 165
Antrum, Rachel II, 192
Antrum, Rachel II, 213
Antrum, Sarah II, 165
Antrum, Sarah II, 192
Antrum, Sarah II, 213
Antrum, Sarah II, 266
Antrum, Thomas II, 165
Antrum, Thomas II, 192
Antrum, Thomas II, 213
Antrum, Thomas II, 246
Antrum, Thomas II, 258
Antrum, Thomas II, 266
Antrum, Thos., Jr. II, 192
Antrum, William II, 165
Anwyler, Elizabeth Moon V, 150
Apel, Anna IV, 1320
Apel, Bernard IV, 1325
Apel, Bernbord IV, 1320
Apel, Conrad IV, 1305
Apel, Gretchen IV, 1325
Apel, Laura IV, 1305
Apel, Laura IV, 1319
Apel, Lora IV, 1305
Apel, Margaret IV, 1320
Apel, Mary II, 51
Apel, Mary IV, 1325
Appel, Henry II, 51
Apperson, Anthony VI, 871
Apperson, Susan A. VI, 865
Apperson, Washington VI, 865
Apperson, Widower Susannah VI, 871
Apple, Henry II, 51
Apple, Henry II, 65
Apple, John Henry II, 453
Apple, Mary II, 51
Apple, Mary II, 65
Apple, Mary II, 453
Apple, Mary II, 633
Appleby, Catharine III, 394
Appleby, Catharine III, 429
Appleby, Deborah III, 394
Appleby, Epinetus III, 394
Appleby, John III, 394
Appleby, Mary F. VI, 444
Appleby, Samuel W. VI, 444
Appleby, Sarah III, 394
Appleby, Sarah III, 429
Appleby, Thomas III, 394
Appleby, Thomas III, 429
Applegarth, Martha IV, 169
Applegate, Anna L. V, 726
Applegate, Anna Leona V, 726
Applegate, Bridget V, 726

Applegate, Caroline E. V, 726
Applegate, Catharine Diana V, 725
Applegate, Chas. Robert V, 725
Applegate, Clarkson Andrew V, 726
Applegate, Cornelia Edith V, 725
Applegate, Elizabeth II, 193
Applegate, Elizabeth II, 206
Applegate, Elizabeth V, 725
Applegate, Emma V, 725
Applegate, Emma Alice V, 726
Applegate, Frances V, 726
Applegate, Frances Elizabeth V, 725
Applegate, Hannah V, 725
Applegate, Hannah V, 726
Applegate, Henry V, 725
pplegate, Henry D. V, 726
pplegate, Henry Dorsey V, 725
pplegate, Herbert V, 726
pplegate, John V, 725
pplegate, John V, 726
pplegate, Lilly Florence V, 726
pplegate, Lucinda V, 725
pplegate, Lucinda V, 726
pplegate, Mary Caroline V, 725
pplegate, Matilda Emma V, 725
pplegate, Matilda M. V, 726
pplegate, Myra Anna V, 725
pplegate, Retta I, 612
pplegate, Ritta I, 625
pplegate, Robert V, 725
pplegate, Robert Charles V, 726
pplegate, Robert Chas. V, 725
pplegate, Samuel P. V, 726
pplegate, Samuel Pearson V, 726
pplegate, Stephen Herbert V, 726
pplegate, Thos. V, 726
pplegate, Thos. Adams V, 725
pplegate, William H. V, 726
pplegate, Wm. Herschel V, 725
ppleton, Edward G. II, 1068
ppleton, Florence II, 1068
ppleton, George W. II, 780
ppleton, George W. II, 1068
ppleton, Hannah G. II, 1068
ppleton, Jane II, 51
ppleton, Jane II, 78
ppleton, Jane II, 127
ppleton, Jane II, 139
ppleton, Jane II, 143
ppleton, Jos. II, 139
ppleton, Joseph II, 127
ppleton, Lewis II, 143
ppleton, Lewis R. II, 143
ppleton, Lewis R. II, 1068
ppleton, Ruth II, 139
ppleton, Ruth II, 143
ppleton, Ruth W. II, 127
ppleton, Ruth W. II, 143
ppleton, Ruth W. II, 159
ppleton, Ruth Wright II, 135
ppleton, Sarah II, 127
ppleton, Sarah II, 143
ppleton, Sarah II, 161
pplewhite, Orpha I, 299
pplewhite, Orpha I, 317
pshear, Elizabeth VI, 871
pshear, Leroy VI, 871
ptee, Ann II, 453
ptee, Ann II, 678
rabella, Margaret III, 275
rabella, Thos. III, 275
rahood, Josephine IV, 1271
rasmith, Elizabeth V, 218
rbor, Ann III, 298
rbuckle, Hannah II, 454
rbuckle, James II, 332
rbuckle, James II, 454
rbuckle, Sarah IV, 922
rbuckle, Sarah IV, 1014
rchabald, John III, 332
rchabald, Mary III, 332
rchbold, Sarah II, 454
rchdeacon, Ann M. V, 548
rchdeacon, Bertha V, 548
rchdeacon, Bertha H. V, 548
rchdeacon, Bruce V, 548
rchdeacon, Bruce Burdette V, 548
chdeacon, Ellen R. V, 20
chdeacon, George V, 20
chdeacon, George H. V, 548
chdeacon, George, Jr. V, 20
chdeacon, Hurley V, 548
chdeacon, Joanna V, 20
chdeacon, Mary V, 20
hdeacon, N. V, 548
Archdeacon, Rachel V, 20
Archer, Abigail III, 292
Archer, Abigail Jane III, 20
Archer, Alfred III, 20
Archer, Alice B. II, 832
Archer, Allenor VI, 362
Archer, Beulah II, 193
Archer, Elenor VI, 362
Archer, Eliz. M. III, 20
Archer, Eliz. M. III, 66
Archer, Elizabeth II, 332
Archer, Elizabeth II, 454
Archer, Elizabeth II, 629
Archer, Elizabeth II, 698
Archer, Evaline IV, 169
Archer, Florence III, 20
Archer, Florence III, 66
Archer, Isaac H. III, 20
Archer, Isaac H. III, 66
Archer, James B. III, 20
Archer, Jane III, 20
Archer, Jane III, 377
Archer, Jonah III, 20
Archer, Joseph II, 698
Archer, Josiah III, 20
Archer, Josiah III, 314
Archer, Lovet II, 193
Archer, Martha II, 332
Archer, Mary II, 193
Archer, Mary II, 260
Archer, Mary III, 20
Archer, Mary W. II, 698
Archer, Methsibah II, 193
Archer, Phebe III, 20
Archer, Phebe T. III, 292
Archer, Rebecca II, 193
Archer, Rebecca II, 454
Archer, Rebecca II, 812
Archer, Richard III, 20
Archer, Samuel II, 193
Archer, Samuel II, 332
Archer, Samuel II, 454
Archer, Samuel II, 698
Archer, Samuel W. II, 698
Archer, Sarah III, 20
Archer, Sarah III, 216
Archer, Sarah A. III, 216
Archer, Stephen III, 20
Archer, Thomas II, 193
Archer, Thomas III, 20
Archer, Thomas III, 292
Archer, Wd. Anna III, 20
Archibald, Agnes IV, 1143
Archibald, Araminta III, 20
Archibald, John III, 20
Archibald, Martha E. III, 20
Archibald, Mary III, 20
Archley, Thomas II, 441
Archpool, Sarah II, 454
Archpool, Sarah II, 552
Archut, Charles II, 698
Archut, Charlotte II, 698
Archut, Sarah II, 698
Archut, Sarah C. II, 725
Archut, William II, 698
Archut, Wm. II, 725
Archute, Sarah C. II, 725
Archute, Wm. II, 725
Arding, Wd. Abigail III, 20
Arey, Rebecca II, 832
Arey, Wd. Rebecca Dallas II, 780
Arey, Wm. II, 780
Argo, Eva V, 983
Argo, Smith IV, 1271
Arington, Sally VI, 865
Arinson, Benjamin II, 194
Arinson, Hope II, 194
Aris, Elizabeth I, 656
Aris, Mary VI, 362
Arison, Jane W. III, 394
Arison, Jane W. III, 459
Armbruster, Eliza Ann II, 795
Armbruster, Sarah II, 51
Armbruster, Sarah II, 110
Arment, A. E. V, 150
Arment, Donald V, 150
Arment, John V, 150
Arment, Mary V, 150
Armentrout, Christian VI, 871
Armentrout, Sally VI, 871
Armetage, Mary II, 974
Armetage, Mary II, 1026
Armetage, Samuel II, 974
Armetage, Samuel II, 1026
Armfield, Ann I, 343
Armfield, Ann I, 372
Armfield, Bell I, 855
Armfield, Elizabeth I, 523
Armfield, Esther I, 611
Armfield, G. William I, 611
Armfield, Isaac I, 523
Armfield, J. H. I, 629
Armfield, Jane I, 620
Armfield, Jane I, 621
Armfield, Jonathan I, 523
Armfield, Jos. H. I, 629
Armfield, Jos. H., Jr. I, 629
Armfield, Joseph I, 624
Armfield, Joseph H. I, 629
Armfield, Joseph H. I, 639
Armfield, Joseph Henry I, 611
Armfield, Lydia B. I, 796
Armfield, Lydia B. I, 816
Armfield, Martitia I, 592
Armfield, Mary I, 523
Armfield, Mary V, 788
Armfield, Robert I, 523
Armfield, Sarah I, 523
Armfield, Sarah I, 545
Armfield, Vivian I, 611
Armfield, Vivian I, 629
Armfield, Vivian I, 639
Armfield, Vivian A. I, 624
Armfield, William I, 523
Armfield, William, II I, 523
Armistead, Addison VI, 848
Armistead, Amanda M. VI, 829
Armistead, Ann VI, 838
Armistead, Ann VI, 865
Armistead, Catharine VI, 867
Armistead, Cona VI, 856
Armistead, Elizabeth VI, 862
Armistead, Frances VI, 856
Armistead, Francis VI, 862
Armistead, Harriet P. VI, 865
Armistead, John S. VI, 838
Armistead, Lucy C. VI, 838
Armistead, Nancy VI, 817
Armistead, Robert VI, 823
Armistead, Robert VI, 838
Armistead, Robert VI, 856
Armistead, Robert VI, 871
Armistead, S. M. VI, 795
Armistead, S. M. VI, 806
Armistead, Samuel VI, 829
Armistead, Samuel VI, 838
Armistead, Samuel VI, 843
Armistead, Samuel VI, 865
Armistead, Samuel VI, 867
Armistead, Samuel M. VI, 805
Armistead, Samuel M. VI, 846
Armistead, Sarah M. VI, 817
Armistead, Susanna VI, 823
Armistead, Susanna VI, 871
Armistead, William VI, 871
Armit, Samuel II, 454
Armitage, Anna III, 20
Armitage, Anna III, 93
Armitage, Anna IV, 1305
Armitage, Anna IV, 1329
Armitage, Annie I, 622
Armitage, Annie I, 629
Armitage, Annie II, 712
Armitage, Charles IV, 672
Armitage, Charles IV, 1021
Armitage, Charles IV, 1023
Armitage, Charls IV, 1023
Armitage, Chas IV, 1025
Armitage, Dearborn IV, 672
Armitage, Edward II, 780
Armitage, Edward II, 832
Armitage, Eleanor V, 20
Armitage, Eleanor V, 825
Armitage, Eleanor V, 872
Armitage, Eliza Jane IV, 1023
Armitage, Eliza Jane IV, 1031
Armitage, Elma J. IV, 1023
Armitage, Grace V, 20
Armitage, Grace V, 825
Armitage, Hannah II, 825
Armitage, Henry D. IV, 1023
Armitage, Henry D. IV, 1031
Armitage, Jane IV, 672
Armitage, Jane IV, 1023
Armitage, Jane IV, 1025
Armitage, Mark V, 20
Armitage, Oliver IV, 672
Armitage, Phebe IV, 672
Armitage, Phebe IV, 922
Armitage, Phebe IV, 923
Armitage, Phebe IV, 1023
Armitage, Phebe IV, 1026
Armitage, Rachel IV, 672
Armitage, Rachel IV, 923
Armitage, Rachel IV, 1023
Armitage, Rachel IV, 1025
Armitage, Sarah III, 20
Armitage, Sarah IV, 672
Armitage, Sarah IV, 1021
Armitage, Sarah IV, 1023
Armitage, Sarah A. III, 93
Armitage, Seth III, 20
Armitage, Seth III, 93
Armitage, Walter W. I, 629
Armitage, Zebidee IV, 672
Armitt, Ann II, 332
Armitt, Eliza II, 675
Armitt, Elizabeth II, 332
Armitt, Elizabeth II, 441
Armitt, Elizabeth II, 454
Armitt, Elizabeth II, 556
Armitt, Elizabeth II, 582
Armitt, Hannah II, 332
Armitt, Jeremiah II, 332
Armitt, John II, 332
Armitt, John II, 454
Armitt, John II, 516
Armitt, John II, 556
Armitt, Joseph II, 332
Armitt, Joseph II, 454
Armitt, Joseph II, 474
Armitt, Joseph II, 582
Armitt, Joseph II, 675
Armitt, Mary II, 332
Armitt, Mary II, 350
Armitt, Mary II, 454
Armitt, Mary II, 516
Armitt, Mary, Jr. II, 454
Armitt, Mary, Jr. II, 474
Armitt, Richard II, 332
Armitt, Richard II, 454
Armitt, Richard II, 566
Armitt, Samuel II, 332
Armitt, Samuel II, 454
Armitt, Sarah II, 332
Armitt, Sarah II, 454
Armitt, Sarah II, 584
Armitt, Sarah II, 626
Armitt, Sarah II, 685
Armitt, Sophia II, 332
Armitt, Sophia II, 454
Armitt, Sophia II, 566
Armitt, Stephen II, 332
Armitt, Stephen II, 333
Armitt, Stephen II, 454
Armitt, Stephen II, 556
Armitt, Stephen II, 584
Armitt, Stephen II, 685
Armitt, Thomas II, 332
Armitt, Thomas II, 441
Armitt, Thomas II, 454
Armitt, Thomas II, 582
Armitt, Wd. Elizabeth II, 454
Armitt, Wd. Sophia II, 332
Armond, Sarah I, 128
Armour, Mary I, 128
Armour, Mary I, 708
Armour, Mary L. III, 20
Armour, Ruth I, 128
Armour, Samuel I, 128
Armour, William I, 128
Armour, William I, 708
Arms, Barbara VI, 871
Arms, Effie IV, 1153
Arms, Josiah VI, 871
Arms, Josiah VI, 876
Arms, Lizzie IV, 463
Arms, Lucy VI, 871
Arms, Mrs. George A. VI, 729
Arms, Sarah VI, 871
Arms, William VI, 871
Armstead, James M. VI, 796
Armstead, Justine VI, 796
Armstead, Lucy Cannifax VI, 796
Armstead, Lydia VI, 841
Armstead, Mary Lewis VI, 796
Armstead, Sam VI, 841
Armstead, Samuel VI, 796
Armstead, William VI, 796
Armsted, Gill VI, 154
Armstrong, ??? III, 131
Armstrong, Alice III, 131
Armstrong, Alice IV, 672
Armstrong, Alice IV, 863
Armstrong, Alice V, 865
Armstrong, Alice Anna IV, 608
Armstrong, Alice H. III, 20
Armstrong, Alice L. II, 726
Armstrong, Allis Anna IV, 863
Armstrong, Alvine Isaac IV, 863
Armstrong, Ambrose VI, 872
Armstrong, Amora V, 548
Armstrong, Andrew VI, 941
Armstrong, Ann IV, 608
Armstrong, Ann IV, 672
Armstrong, Ann IV, 877
Armstrong, Ann IV, 923
Armstrong, Ann VI, 871
Armstrong, Ann Eliza IV, 672
Armstrong, Anna IV, 607
Armstrong, Anna IV, 663
Armstrong, Anna ??? IV, 863
Armstrong, Anne IV, 672
Armstrong, Anne Eliza IV, 863
Armstrong, B. J. C. IV, 463
Armstrong, Benjamin VI, 842
Armstrong, Benjamin VI, 856
Armstrong, Bennet IV, 607
Armstrong, Bennet IV, 608
Armstrong, Bennet IV, 877
Armstrong, Bennett IV, 607
Armstrong, Bennett IV, 608
Armstrong, Bennett IV, 619
Armstrong, Bennett IV, 863
Armstrong, Bennett IV, 899
Armstrong, Bennett VI, 632
Armstrong, Carmel IV, 608
Armstrong, Christian II, 454
Armstrong, Christian II, 472
Armstrong, Dasey IV, 672
Armstrong, Dawsey IV, 607
Armstrong, Dawsey IV, 609
Armstrong, Dawsey IV, 627
Armstrong, Dawsey IV, 863
Armstrong, Dawsey IV, 899
Armstrong, Dawsy IV, 608
Armstrong, Deborah IV, 608
Armstrong, Deborah IV, 619
Armstrong, Deborah IV, 797
Armstrong, Deborah IV, 809
Armstrong, Deborah IV, 858
Armstrong, Deborah IV, 899
Armstrong, Deborah Elma IV, 607
Armstrong, Dorcas IV, 672
Armstrong, Dorcas IV, 863
Armstrong, Edith IV, 672
Armstrong, Edith IV, 863
Armstrong, Edwin VI, 842
Armstrong, Eliza IV, 608
Armstrong, Eliza Ann IV, 672
Armstrong, Elizabeth IV, 121
Armstrong, Elizabeth IV, 123
Armstrong, Elizabeth IV, 607
Armstrong, Elizabeth IV, 608
Armstrong, Elizabeth IV, 619
Armstrong, Elizabeth IV, 672
Armstrong, Elizabeth IV, 877
Armstrong, Elizabeth ??? IV, 863
Armstrong, Ellis K. V, 655
Armstrong, Elma IV, 672
Armstrong, Elma IV, 863
Armstrong, Elma C. IV, 608
Armstrong, Elma C. IV, 622
Armstrong, Emeline IV, 608
Armstrong, Emeline IV, 617
Armstrong, Emily IV, 608
Armstrong, Emily IV, 647
Armstrong, Emily IV, 863
Armstrong, Emily Jane IV, 863
Armstrong, Emily Jane IV, 877
Armstrong, Emmeline C. IV, 863
Armstrong, Emmely IV, 608
Armstrong, Fanny VI, 842
Armstrong, Frank V, 983
Armstrong, Geo. V, 983
Armstrong, George V, 983
Armstrong, Hannah IV, 608
Armstrong, Hannah IV, 622
Armstrong, Hannah IV, 672
Armstrong, Hannah IV, 899
Armstrong, Hannah IV, 907
Armstrong, Hannah IV, 918
Armstrong, Ida May VI, 740
Armstrong, Ida May VI, 790
Armstrong, Israel IV, 608
Armstrong, Israel IV, 650
Armstrong, Israel IV, 863
Armstrong, Isral IV, 672
Armstrong, James IV, 121
Armstrong, James IV, 607
Armstrong, James IV, 608
Armstrong, James IV, 619
Armstrong, James IV, 631
Armstrong, James IV, 634
Armstrong, James IV, 643
Armstrong, James IV, 672
Armstrong, James IV, 797
Armstrong, James IV, 809
Armstrong, James IV, 857
Armstrong, James IV, 858
Armstrong, James IV, 899
Armstrong, James IV, 906
Armstrong, James IV, 907
Armstrong, James IV, 914
Armstrong, James IV, 918
Armstrong, James IV, 923
Armstrong, James VI, 632
Armstrong, James C. IV, 607
Armstrong, James C. IV, 608
Armstrong, James C. IV, 899
Armstrong, James E. II, 698
Armstrong, Jane II, 698
Armstrong, Jane IV, 863

Armstrong, Jane VI, 872
Armstrong, Jane Emily IV, 607
Armstrong, Jane Emily IV, 608
Armstrong, Jane Emily IV, 899
Armstrong, Jefferson IV, 907
Armstrong, Joel IV, 672
Armstrong, Joel IV, 923
Armstrong, John II, 441
Armstrong, John IV, 607
Armstrong, John IV, 672
Armstrong, John IV, 797
Armstrong, John IV, 899
Armstrong, John IV, 923
Armstrong, John VI, 872
Armstrong, John C. IV, 607
Armstrong, John W. IV, 607
Armstrong, John W. IV, 608
Armstrong, John W. IV, 610
Armstrong, John W. IV, 672
Armstrong, Joseph II, 698
Armstrong, Joseph IV, 607
Armstrong, Joseph IV, 608
Armstrong, Joseph IV, 650
Armstrong, Joseph IV, 672
Armstrong, Joseph IV, 863
Armstrong, Joseph IV, 880
Armstrong, Joseph IV, 899
Armstrong, Joseph IV, 907
Armstrong, Joshua IV, 608
Armstrong, Joshua IV, 672
Armstrong, Joshua IV, 863
Armstrong, Judith A. IV, 1035
Armstrong, Judith Ann IV, 923
Armstrong, Juliann IV, 170
Armstrong, Juliann IV, 239
Armstrong, Layfiett V, 983
Armstrong, Lenora V, 372
Armstrong, Lewis IV, 923
Armstrong, Lucinda IV, 923
Armstrong, Lucinda IV, 942
Armstrong, Lucinda C. IV, 607
Armstrong, Lucinda C. IV, 608
Armstrong, Lucinda C. IV, 923
Armstrong, Lydia IV, 608
Armstrong, Lydia IV, 672
Armstrong, Lydia IV, 923
Armstrong, Lydia Ann IV, 797
Armstrong, M. Russell IV, 1035
Armstrong, Malinda V, 983
Armstrong, Marjorie Wistar IV, 1305
Armstrong, Martha IV, 607
Armstrong, Martha IV, 608
Armstrong, Martha IV, 672
Armstrong, Martha IV, 863
Armstrong, Martha IV, 899
Armstrong, Martha A. IV, 608
Armstrong, Martha A. IV, 646
Armstrong, Martha Jane IV, 907
Armstrong, Mary II, 333
Armstrong, Mary III, 20
Armstrong, Mary IV, 607
Armstrong, Mary IV, 631
Armstrong, Mary IV, 672
Armstrong, Mary IV, 797
Armstrong, Mary IV, 863
Armstrong, Mary IV, 877
Armstrong, Mary IV, 899
Armstrong, Mary IV, 906
Armstrong, Mary IV, 914
Armstrong, Mary IV, 918
Armstrong, Mary IV, 1087
Armstrong, Mary IV, 1105
Armstrong, Mary V, 983
Armstrong, Mary VI, 960
Armstrong, Mary Ann IV, 606
Armstrong, Mary Ann IV, 608
Armstrong, Mary Ann IV, 672
Armstrong, Mary Ann IV, 863
Armstrong, Mary Ann IV, 899
Armstrong, Mary Ann IV, 923
Armstrong, Mary Ann IV, 937
Armstrong, Mary E. V, 983
Armstrong, Mary E. VI, 872
Armstrong, Maryann IV, 608
Armstrong, Melissa IV, 627
Armstrong, Micajah Russel IV, 923
Armstrong, Milton IV, 608
Armstrong, Nancy VI, 872
Armstrong, Nancy VI, 960
Armstrong, Nathan IV, 608
Armstrong, Nathan IV, 672
Armstrong, Nathan IV, 863
Armstrong, Nathan IV, 899
Armstrong, Nathan Edgar IV, 608
Armstrong, Nathan Edgar IV, 863
Armstrong, Nathan Elmer IV, 863
Armstrong, Nathan H. IV, 607
Armstrong, Nathan H. IV, 608
Armstrong, Nathan H. IV, 622
Armstrong, Nathan H. IV, 863
Armstrong, Nathan H. IV, 866
Armstrong, Nathan H. IV, 899
Armstrong, Nathan H., Jr. IV, 608
Armstrong, Nathan, Jr. IV, 863
Armstrong, Olin J. IV, 923
Armstrong, Olin J. IV, 1035
Armstrong, Olin L. IV, 923
Armstrong, Oscar Allen IV, 672
Armstrong, Oscar Allen IV, 863
Armstrong, Peggy VI, 872
Armstrong, Phebe IV, 607
Armstrong, Phebe IV, 608
Armstrong, Phebe IV, 626
Armstrong, Phebe IV, 643
Armstrong, Phebe IV, 672
Armstrong, Phebe IV, 899
Armstrong, Phebe IV, 907
Armstrong, Phebe B. IV, 672
Armstrong, Phebe B. IV, 863
Armstrong, Polly VI, 856
Armstrong, R. Lewis IV, 1035
Armstrong, Rachel IV, 672
Armstrong, Rachel IV, 899
Armstrong, Rachel Ann IV, 607
Armstrong, Rebecca IV, 607
Armstrong, Rebecca IV, 608
Armstrong, Rebecca IV, 622
Armstrong, Rebecca IV, 672
Armstrong, Rebecca IV, 863
Armstrong, Rebecca IV, 866
Armstrong, Rebecca IV, 899
Armstrong, Rebecca IV, 923
Armstrong, Rebecca IV, 960
Armstrong, Rebecca VI, 991
Armstrong, Robert IV, 672
Armstrong, Robert IV, 919
Armstrong, Robert IV, 923
Armstrong, Robert VI, 872
Armstrong, Russell IV, 923
Armstrong, Russell V, 705
Armstrong, Ruth IV, 121
Armstrong, Ruth IV, 607
Armstrong, Ruth IV, 608
Armstrong, Ruth IV, 634
Armstrong, Ruth IV, 643
Armstrong, Ruth IV, 672
Armstrong, Ruth IV, 863
Armstrong, Ruth IV, 899
Armstrong, Ruth IV, 906
Armstrong, Ruth IV, 907
Armstrong, Ruth VI, 632
Armstrong, Ruth A. IV, 608
Armstrong, Ruth A. IV, 657
Armstrong, Ruth Anna IV, 672
Armstrong, Ruth Anna IV, 863
Armstrong, Samuel IV, 121
Armstrong, Samuel IV, 123
Armstrong, Samuel IV, 607
Armstrong, Samuel IV, 608
Armstrong, Samuel IV, 617
Armstrong, Samuel IV, 663
Armstrong, Samuel IV, 672
Armstrong, Samuel IV, 863
Armstrong, Samuel IV, 877
Armstrong, Sarah IV, 607
Armstrong, Sarah IV, 608
Armstrong, Sarah IV, 610
Armstrong, Sarah IV, 634
Armstrong, Sarah IV, 650
Armstrong, Sarah IV, 672
Armstrong, Sarah IV, 797
Armstrong, Sarah IV, 823
Armstrong, Sarah IV, 880
Armstrong, Sarah IV, 899
Armstrong, Sarah IV, 907
Armstrong, Sarah IV, 914
Armstrong, Sarah IV, 923
Armstrong, Sarah VI, 872
Armstrong, Sarah Ann IV, 627
Armstrong, Sarah Emily IV, 607
Armstrong, Sarah Emily IV, 609
Armstrong, Sarah Emily IV, 672
Armstrong, Sarah Emily IV, 863
Armstrong, Sarah J. IV, 672
Armstrong, Sarah J. IV, 735
Armstrong, Sarah Josephine IV, 608
Armstrong, Sarah Josephine IV, 641
Armstrong, Sarah P. IV, 672
Armstrong, Sarah P. IV, 923
Armstrong, Sina IV, 608
Armstrong, Sina IV, 650
Armstrong, Sina IV, 863
Armstrong, Sinia IV, 672
Armstrong, Thomas IV, 607
Armstrong, Thomas IV, 672
Armstrong, Thomas IV, 863
Armstrong, Thomas VI, 872
Armstrong, Titus IV, 672
Armstrong, Titus IV, 899
Armstrong, Uree Ann IV, 1143
Armstrong, Uree Ann IV, 1170
Armstrong, Vesta V, 655
Armstrong, Vesta V, 705
Armstrong, W. C. V, 150
Armstrong, Wd Deborah IV, 797
Armstrong, William II, 472
Armstrong, William IV, 608
Armstrong, William IV, 863
Armstrong, William IV, 899
Armstrong, William IV, 923
Armstrong, William VI, 871
Armstrong, William VI, 872
Armstrong, William VI, 961
Armstrong, William VI, 991
Armstrong, Wm. IV, 607
Armstrong, Wm. IV, 672
Armstrong, Wm. IV, 923
Arnall, Edward II, 194
Arnel, David II, 225
Arnel, Hannah II, 225
Arnell, David II, 194
Arnell, Edward II, 194
Arnell, Hannah II, 194
Arnell, Mary II, 454
Arnell, Mary II, 459
Arnet, Anderson IV, 363
Arnet, Elizabeth I, 911
Arnet, Thomas IV, 363
Arnett, Alben I, 909
Arnett, Allie I, 642
Arnett, Calvin I, 909
Arnett, Charlotte I, 909
Arnett, David V, 472
Arnett, Elizabeth I, 909
Arnett, Elizabeth I, 911
Arnett, Hannah V, 20
Arnett, Hannah V, 78
Arnett, Jeremiah V, 726
Arnett, Jesse I, 796
Arnett, Jesse I, 845
Arnett, Jesse I, 911
Arnett, John Hartas III, 21
Arnett, Malinda I, 909
Arnett, Margaret I, 796
Arnett, Margaret I, 845
Arnett, Margaret I, 911
Arnett, Martha W. V, 472
Arnett, Rachel V, 20
Arnett, Rachel V, 472
Arnett, Rachel V, 490
Arnett, Rachel V, 544
Arnett, Sarah I, 796
Arnett, Sarah V, 20
Arnett, Sarah V, 150
Arnett, Sarah V, 544
Arnett, Thomas I, 796
Arnett, Thomas I, 907
Arnett, Thomas I, 911
Arnett, Thomas V, 20
Arnett, Thomas V, 78
Arnett, Thomas V, 472
Arnett, Thomas V, 490
Arnett, Thomas V, 544
Arnett, Valentine I, 796
Arnett, Valentine V, 544
Arnett, Vanentine V, 20
Arnett, Willis I, 909
Arnett, Willis I, 911
Arney, Ann II, 454
Arney, Ann W. II, 454
Arney, Ann W. II, 656
Arney, Barclay II, 454
Arney, Barkley II, 454
Arney, Barkley II, 656
Arney, Benjamin II, 656
Arney, Beulah II, 454
Arney, Beulah Charlotte II, 454
Arney, Charlotte II, 279
Arney, Charlotte II, 454
Arney, Daniel II, 454
Arney, Daniel II, 656
Arney, Elizabeth II, 454
Arney, Elizabeth II, 656
Arney, Martha II, 193
Arney, Olive IV, 1305
Arney, Thomas IV, 1305
Arney, Thos. A. IV, 1305
Arniss, Polly VI, 796
Arniss, Thos. B. VI, 796
Arnol, Asa I, 93
Arnol, Benjamin I, 93
Arnol, Elizabeth I, 93
Arnol, Joseph I, 93
Arnol, Mary I, 93
Arnol, Rebekah I, 93
Arnol, Sarah I, 93
Arnol, Thomas I, 93
Arnol, William I, 93
Arnold, ??? I, 279
Arnold, ??? III, 21
Arnold, ??? IV, 917
Arnold, ??? V, 147
Arnold, Alex A. VI, 950
Arnold, Alexander A. VI, 872
Arnold, Alexander A. VI, 999
Arnold, Alfred IV, 170
Arnold, Alice M. III, 21
Arnold, Almary C. VI, 948
Arnold, Amanda III, 21
Arnold, Amanda IV, 363
Arnold, Amanda IV, 388
Arnold, Amanda Jane IV, 363
Arnold, Amos I, 128
Arnold, Amy III, 20
Arnold, Amy A. III, 208
Arnold, Anderson I, 870
Arnold, Anderson IV, 565
Arnold, Anderson V, 21
Arnold, Andrew VI, 657
Arnold, Angelina C. VI, 796
Arnold, Ann G. VI, 810
Arnold, Anna I, 281
Arnold, Anna I, 299
Arnold, Anna V, 607
Arnold, Anna V, 609
Arnold, Anna M. V, 609
Arnold, Anna M. V, 650
Arnold, Anna Mary IV, 1023
Arnold, Asa I, 128
Arnold, Asa I, 170
Arnold, Asa IV, 363
Arnold, Asa IV, 565
Arnold, Asa IV, 590
Arnold, Asenath W. IV, 899
Arnold, Asenath W. IV, 906
Arnold, Benj. C. III, 140
Arnold, Benjamin I, 35
Arnold, Benjamin I, 39
Arnold, Benjamin I, 93
Arnold, Benjamin I, 128
Arnold, Benjamin I, 281
Arnold, Benjamin I, 299
Arnold, Benjamin I, 308
Arnold, Benjamin I, 313
Arnold, Benjamin C. III, 20
Arnold, Benjamin C. III, 21
Arnold, Bessie III, 73
Arnold, Bethula IV, 565
Arnold, Bethula IV, 1049
Arnold, Bethula IV, 1060
Arnold, Beverly VI, 796
Arnold, Beverly VI, 822
Arnold, Binjo I, 281
Arnold, Blanche IV, 170
Arnold, Caleb IV, 170
Arnold, Caleb IV, 363
Arnold, Caleb IV, 406
Arnold, Carrie III, 21
Arnold, Celia I, 281
Arnold, Celia I, 299
Arnold, Celia I, 306
Arnold, Charity I, 281
Arnold, Charity I, 299
Arnold, Charles III, 21
Arnold, Clementine A. G. VI, 912
Arnold, Cora Ellen May IV, 363
Arnold, David II, 194
Arnold, Delaney R. VI, 796
Arnold, Delany R. VI, 813
Arnold, Dorcas III, 20
Arnold, Dorcas III, 21
Arnold, Dorcas III, 141
Arnold, Dorotha IV, 170
Arnold, Dutchess III, 21
Arnold, Eber J. V, 150
Arnold, Edward II, 194
Arnold, Edward IV, 672
Arnold, Edward VI, 796
Arnold, Edwin A. II, 726
Arnold, Edwin A. II, 832
Arnold, Edwin A. IV, 673
Arnold, Eleanor V, 150
Arnold, Elinor II, 454
Arnold, Eliz. III, 333
Arnold, Eliza Ann VI, 884
Arnold, Elizabeth I, 128
Arnold, Elizabeth I, 169
Arnold, Elizabeth I, 281
Arnold, Elizabeth I, 299
Arnold, Elizabeth I, 309
Arnold, Elizabeth II, 454
Arnold, Elizabeth III, 21
Arnold, Elizabeth III, 38
Arnold, Elizabeth III, 333
Arnold, Elizabeth IV, 363
Arnold, Elizabeth IV, 365
Arnold, Elizabeth IV, 398
Arnold, Elizabeth IV, 566
Arnold, Elizabeth IV, 1087
Arnold, Elizabeth IV, 1103
Arnold, Elizabeth VI, 801
Arnold, Ellen May IV, 363
Arnold, Ellen May IV, 385
Arnold, Elsie I, 870
Arnold, Emma V, 150
Arnold, Emma V, 218
Arnold, Emma V, 372
Arnold, Ephraim III, 479
Arnold, Eugene V, 150
Arnold, Eugenia III, 21
Arnold, Eugenia III, 268
Arnold, Francis V, 983
Arnold, Gabriella E. VI, 872
Arnold, George VI, 797
Arnold, Hannah I, 870
Arnold, Hannah II, 194
Arnold, Hannah III, 21
Arnold, Hannah IV, 363
Arnold, Hannah IV, 565
Arnold, Hannah IV, 583
Arnold, Hannah IV, 590
Arnold, Hannah IV, 672
Arnold, Hannah IV, 917
Arnold, Hannah V, 983
Arnold, Hattie IV, 1305
Arnold, Henry IV, 363
Arnold, Henry IV, 1349
Arnold, Huldah I, 281
Arnold, Huldah I, 299
Arnold, Huldah I, 316
Arnold, Isaac I, 281
Arnold, Isaac I, 299
Arnold, Isaac V, 218
Arnold, J. H. V, 983
Arnold, Jacob I, 281
Arnold, Jacob I, 299
Arnold, Jacob III, 21
Arnold, Jacob IV, 1349
Arnold, James IV, 363
Arnold, James IV, 565
Arnold, James Hadly IV, 363
Arnold, Jane III, 140
Arnold, Jane III, 233
Arnold, Jane V, 150
Arnold, Jane V, 472
Arnold, Jane V, 510
Arnold, Jane A. III, 141
Arnold, Jemima I, 93
Arnold, Jennie V, 983
Arnold, Jeremiah I, 281
Arnold, Jeremiah I, 299
Arnold, Jesse I, 281
Arnold, Jesse I, 299
Arnold, Jesse V, 150
Arnold, Jesse V, 472
Arnold, Jesse V, 510
Arnold, Jno. VI, 833
Arnold, John III, 21
Arnold, John IV, 565
Arnold, John IV, 672
Arnold, John IV, 673
Arnold, John V, 150
Arnold, John V, 372
Arnold, John V, 983
Arnold, John VI, 796
Arnold, John VI, 800
Arnold, John VI, 801
Arnold, John VI, 810
Arnold, John VI, 822
Arnold, John VI, 830
Arnold, John VI, 851
Arnold, John R. III, 21
Arnold, John R. III, 268
Arnold, John W. IV, 672
Arnold, John Wright IV, 672
Arnold, John, Jr. V, 150
Arnold, Jonathan I, 93
Arnold, Jos. J. III, 73
Arnold, Jos., Jr. III, 21
Arnold, Joseph I, 35
Arnold, Joseph I, 60
Arnold, Joseph I, 128
Arnold, Joseph I, 281
Arnold, Joseph I, 299
Arnold, Joseph I, 306
Arnold, Joseph III, 20
Arnold, Joseph III, 21
Arnold, Joseph III, 141
Arnold, Joseph IV, 19
Arnold, Joseph IV, 137
Arnold, Joseph IV, 164
Arnold, Joseph IV, 363
Arnold, Joseph IV, 565
Arnold, Joseph IV, 600
Arnold, Joseph IV, 1049
Arnold, Joseph IV, 1060
Arnold, Joseph, Jr. III, 21

Arnold, Joseph, Jr. III, 141
Arnold, Joseph, Jr. III, 333
Arnold, Josephine III, 21
Arnold, Josephine III, 73
Arnold, Judith P. VI, 851
Arnold, Juliann VI, 800
Arnold, Lena V, 150
Arnold, Leona V, 150
Arnold, Levi III, 21
Arnold, Levi IV, 672
Arnold, Levi IV, 673
Arnold, Lottie IV, 170
Arnold, Lucy VI, 796
Arnold, Lydia IV, 73
Arnold, Lydia IV, 90
Arnold, Lydia V, 21
Arnold, Lydia V, 101
Arnold, Lydia Ann IV, 608
Arnold, Lydia Ann IV, 672
Arnold, Lydia Ann IV, 673
Arnold, Lydia Ann IV, 797
Arnold, Lydia Ann IV, 814
Arnold, Lydia Ann IV, 899
Arnold, Lydia Ann IV, 1087
Arnold, Lydia Ann IV, 1097
Arnold, Lydia Ann V, 983
Arnold, Mabelle Thorne III, 21
Arnold, Maggie S. IV, 170
Arnold, Mahala V, 150
Arnold, Malinda IV, 899
Arnold, Margaret D. VI, 796
Arnold, Margaret D. VI, 872
Arnold, Maria IV, 363
Arnold, Maria A. IV, 363
Arnold, Maria A. IV, 565
Arnold, Maria A. IV, 566
Arnold, Mary I, 35
Arnold, Mary I, 63
Arnold, Mary I, 72
Arnold, Mary I, 93
Arnold, Mary I, 128
Arnold, Mary I, 281
Arnold, Mary I, 299
Arnold, Mary I, 306
Arnold, Mary I, 708
Arnold, Mary I, 870
Arnold, Mary III, 21
Arnold, Mary IV, 19
Arnold, Mary IV, 565
Arnold, Mary IV, 1049
Arnold, Mary V, 150
Arnold, Mary VI, 872
Arnold, Mary J. III, 20
Arnold, Mary J. III, 21
Arnold, Mary J. III, 140
Arnold, Mary J. V, 983
Arnold, Mary Jay I, 1026
Arnold, Mary Jay V, 21
Arnold, Mary M. III, 21
Arnold, Mary R. VI, 657
Arnold, Mary, Jr. I, 128
Arnold, Matilda VI, 796
Arnold, Matilda VI, 833
Arnold, Matilda VI, 872
Arnold, Michael I, 281
Arnold, Michael I, 299
Arnold, Milicent Rosalie IV, 364
Arnold, Milicent Rosaline IV, 408
Arnold, Milly Roselee IV, 363
Arnold, Miriam I, 35
Arnold, Miriam I, 63
Arnold, Miriam I, 93
Arnold, Miriam I, 128
Arnold, Miriam I, 162
Arnold, Miriam I, 299
Arnold, Miriam I, 708
Arnold, Miriam I, 870
Arnold, Mosby VI, 869
Arnold, Mosby VI, 884
Arnold, Mosby VI, 899
Arnold, Mosby VI, 912
Arnold, Mosby VI, 931
Arnold, Mosby VI, 947
Arnold, Mosby VI, 948
Arnold, Mosby VI, 949
Arnold, Mosby VI, 961
Arnold, Mosby VI, 963
Arnold, Mosby VI, 972
Arnold, Mosby VI, 979
Arnold, Mosby VI, 1001
Arnold, Moseby VI, 872
Arnold, Moses VI, 796
Arnold, Moses VI, 802
Arnold, Moses VI, 818
Arnold, Moses VI, 864
Arnold, Moses VI, 872
Arnold, Moses VI, 968
Arnold, Mosley VI, 880
Arnold, Mosley VI, 957
Arnold, Mosley VI, 966
Arnold, Mosley VI, 984
Arnold, Mosley VI, 1008
Arnold, Mosley VI, 1019
Arnold, Mossby VI, 872
Arnold, Nancy V, 150
Arnold, Nancy V, 372
Arnold, Nancy VI, 872
Arnold, Nathan I, 281
Arnold, Nathan I, 299
Arnold, Nathan I, 309
Arnold, Nathan IV, 363
Arnold, Nathan IV, 565
Arnold, Noah P. Hartley IV, 363
Arnold, Orville IV, 170
Arnold, Patsy VI, 796
Arnold, Pauline IV, 672
Arnold, Pegga I, 299
Arnold, Peggy I, 281
Arnold, Penina IV, 19
Arnold, Peninah I, 281
Arnold, Peninah I, 299
Arnold, Peninah I, 310
Arnold, Penninah I, 299
Arnold, Phebe IV, 170
Arnold, Phebe IV, 363
Arnold, Phebe IV, 406
Arnold, Phebe Delora Dazelln IV, 363
Arnold, Phebe E. IV, 363
Arnold, Phebe E. IV, 454
Arnold, Piety I, 281
Arnold, Piety I, 299
Arnold, Rachel I, 1026
Arnold, Rachel I, 1032
Arnold, Rachel IV, 672
Arnold, Rachel IV, 673
Arnold, Rachel IV, 794
Arnold, Rachel IV, 797
Arnold, Rachel IV, 899
Arnold, Rachel IV, 917
Arnold, Rachel IV, 1120
Arnold, Rachel IV, 1127
Arnold, Rachel V, 21
Arnold, Rachel V, 150
Arnold, Raiford I, 281
Arnold, Raiford I, 299
Arnold, Rebecca I, 128
Arnold, Rebecca I, 155
Arnold, Rebecca I, 281
Arnold, Rebecca I, 299
Arnold, Rebecca I, 304
Arnold, Rebecca IV, 463
Arnold, Rebecca IV, 486
Arnold, Rebecca VI, 657
Arnold, Rebeckah I, 299
Arnold, Rebekah I, 93
Arnold, Rhoda IV, 170
Arnold, Rhoda IV, 363
Arnold, Richard II, 194
Arnold, Richard III, 21
Arnold, Ruth IV, 363
Arnold, Ruth V, 656
Arnold, Ruth Dodd IV, 565
Arnold, Samuel I, 281
Arnold, Samuel IV, 672
Arnold, Samuel IV, 1305
Arnold, Sarah I, 35
Arnold, Sarah I, 39
Arnold, Sarah I, 60
Arnold, Sarah I, 93
Arnold, Sarah I, 128
Arnold, Sarah I, 281
Arnold, Sarah I, 299
Arnold, Sarah I, 306
Arnold, Sarah II, 194
Arnold, Sarah III, 21
Arnold, Sarah III, 333
Arnold, Sarah IV, 19
Arnold, Sarah IV, 139
Arnold, Sarah IV, 164
Arnold, Sarah IV, 600
Arnold, Sarah IV, 672
Arnold, Sarah IV, 1349
Arnold, Sarah VI, 944
Arnold, Sarah E. III, 21
Arnold, Sarah E. III, 73
Arnold, Sarah E. III, 100
Arnold, Sarah E. III, 333
Arnold, Sarah Eliz. III, 21
Arnold, Sarah Elizabeth III, 21
Arnold, Sarah Elizabeth III, 141
Arnold, Sarah G. VI, 830
Arnold, Sarah Jane V, 150
Arnold, Seneca IV, 1349
Arnold, Stephen IV, 899
Arnold, Susan VI, 796
Arnold, Susanah I, 870
Arnold, Susanna I, 299
Arnold, Susanna I, 870
Arnold, Susanna IV, 363
Arnold, Susanna IV, 565
Arnold, Susanna IV, 590
Arnold, Susanna V, 21
Arnold, Susannah I, 128
Arnold, Susannah I, 170
Arnold, Susannah I, 299
Arnold, Susannah I, 708
Arnold, Susannah I, 870
Arnold, Susannah I, 1060
Arnold, Susannah IV, 363
Arnold, Susannah IV, 565
Arnold, Susannah G. VI, 796
Arnold, Thomas I, 128
Arnold, Thomas I, 870
Arnold, Thomas IV, 363
Arnold, Thomas IV, 365
Arnold, Thomas IV, 398
Arnold, Thomas IV, 566
Arnold, Thomas V, 21
Arnold, Thos. T. III, 21
Arnold, Truman Dewitt V, 656
Arnold, Typhena Belinda IV, 899
Arnold, Vanona IV, 1305
Arnold, Versa V, 656
Arnold, Washington VI, 796
Arnold, William I, 35
Arnold, William I, 63
Arnold, William I, 72
Arnold, William I, 93
Arnold, William I, 128
Arnold, William I, 155
Arnold, William I, 281
Arnold, William I, 299
Arnold, William I, 306
Arnold, William I, 316
Arnold, William I, 708
Arnold, William IV, 363
Arnold, William VI, 796
Arnold, William Cannon I, 299
Arnold, William, Jr. I, 93
Arnold, William, Sr. I, 93
Arnold, Wm. IV, 565
Arnold, Wm. IV, 1049
Arnold, Wm. VI, 872
Arnold, Wyatt VI, 833
Arnold, Wyatt VI, 851
Arnold, Zenas S. III, 21
Arnold, Zilpha I, 299
Arnold, Zilphia I, 281
Arnoll, Mary II, 454
Arnoll, Mary II, 459
Arnoll, Richard II, 194
Arnoll, Richard II, 207
Arnoll, Sarah II, 194
Arnoll, Sarah II, 207
Arnott, Anna I, 1076
Arnott, Elizabeth V, 825
Arnott, Elizabeth V, 869
Arnott, Elizabeth T. V, 825
Arnott, Homer V, 297
Arnould, Benjamin I, 128
Arnould, Elizabeth I, 122
Arnould, William I, 122
Arns, Effie IV, 1153
Arold, Anderson IV, 601
Arold, Bethula IV, 601
Aronson, Anna T. II, 291
Aronson, Benjamin II, 194
Aronson, Elizabeth Ann II, 279
Aronson, Elizabeth Ann II, 291
Aronson, Hope II, 194
Arp, Bettie I, 1147
Arp, Martha I, 1147
Arp, Mary I, 1147
Arp, Polly Ann I, 1147
Arp, Squire I, 1147
Arrasmith, Abner V, 218
Arrasmith, Charles V, 218
Arrasmith, Elizabeth V, 218
Arrasmith, Hannah V, 218
Arrasmith, John V, 218
Arrasmith, Josie B. V, 218
Arrasmith, Lincoln V, 218
Arrasmith, Reed V, 218
Arrasmith, Sarah E. V, 218
Arriet, John Hartas III, 21
Arrihood, Joseph IV, 1271
Arrihood, Josephine IV, 1271
Arrington, Adler VI, 796
Arrington, Adler VI, 818
Arrington, Adler VI, 861
Arrington, Ann VI, 944
Arrington, Catharine VI, 796
Arrington, Charles VI, 796
Arrington, Charles VI, 812
Arrington, Charles VI, 838
Arrington, Christopher VI, 872
Arrington, Daniel VI, 796
Arrington, David VI, 872
Arrington, Doshia VI, 871
Arrington, Doshia VI, 872
Arrington, Doshia VI, 893
Arrington, Edmond VI, 944
Arrington, Edmund VI, 893
Arrington, Edmund VI, 944
Arrington, Elizabeth VI, 796
Arrington, Elizabeth VI, 812
Arrington, Elizabeth VI, 871
Arrington, Frances VI, 872
Arrington, Hampton VI, 872
Arrington, Hester VI, 872
Arrington, James W. VI, 872
Arrington, Jesse VI, 796
Arrington, Jesse R. VI, 796
Arrington, John VI, 796
Arrington, John VI, 831
Arrington, Judith VI, 872
Arrington, Judith W. VI, 818
Arrington, Keziah VI, 872
Arrington, Lydia VI, 872
Arrington, Mariah VI, 893
Arrington, Martha VI, 872
Arrington, Martha E. VI, 796
Arrington, Mary VI, 872
Arrington, Mary M. VI, 943
Arrington, Nancy S. VI, 872
Arrington, Parham VI, 1005
Arrington, Patsey VI, 796
Arrington, Patty VI, 796
Arrington, Peter VI, 872
Arrington, Polly VI, 861
Arrington, Polly VI, 871
Arrington, Richard VI, 872
Arrington, Richard VI, 944
Arrington, Sally VI, 796
Arrington, Sarah VI, 944
Arrington, Sarah B. VI, 796
Arrington, Thomas VI, 872
Arrington, Thomas L. VI, 795
Arrington, Thomas L. VI, 805
Arrington, Thos. L. VI, 796
Arrington, Wesley VI, 872
Arrington, William VI, 796
Arrington, William VI, 820
Arrington, William P. VI, 872
Arrosmith, Grace V, 664
Arrowsmith, Golda V, 683
Arrowsmith, Goldam V, 656
Arrowsmith, Goldie V, 656
Arrowsmith, Grace V, 656
Arrowsmith, Hannah V, 218
Arskin, Ann II, 691
Arskine, Ann II, 454
Arson, Dereck III, 21
Arson, Hannah III, 21
Arter, Mary VI, 1009
Arter, Thomas VI, 968
Arther, Agness V, 218
Arther, Anne VI, 872
Arther, Barnabas VI, 872
Arther, Benjamin VI, 872
Arther, Catharine VI, 988
Arther, Charlotte VI, 873
Arther, Frances VI, 873
Arther, Granvil VI, 873
Arther, Greenville VI, 873
Arther, Lewis VI, 988
Arther, Lewsey VI, 924
Arther, Martha VI, 872
Arther, Sarah VI, 296
Arther, Sarah VI, 342
Arther, William VI, 872
Arther, William, Jr. VI, 872
Arthers, Clark IV, 170
Arthur, A. A. VI, 989
Arthur, Admire VI, 873
Arthur, Albert VI, 873
Arthur, Almira VI, 871
Arthur, Angeline L. VI, 989
Arthur, Ann V, 297
Arthur, Ann V, 306
Arthur, Ann V, 318
Arthur, Ann VI, 847
Arthur, Ann VI, 863
Arthur, Ann VI, 872
Arthur, Anne VI, 872
Arthur, Baldin D. VI, 796
Arthur, Baldwin VI, 798
Arthur, Baldwin D. VI, 801
Arthur, Barnabas VI, 796
Arthur, Barnabas VI, 803
Arthur, Barnabas VI, 846
Arthur, Barnabas VI, 847
Arthur, Barnabas VI, 855
Arthur, Barnabas VI, 872
Arthur, Benj. VI, 946
Arthur, Benjamin VI, 296
Arthur, Benjamin VI, 342
Arthur, Benjamin VI, 872
Arthur, Benjamin VI, 987
Arthur, Benjamin VI, 1020
Arthur, Bertha V, 656
Arthur, Betsey VI, 872
Arthur, Betsy VI, 926
Arthur, Brice VI, 877
Arthur, C. A. V, 548
Arthur, C. W. V, 548
Arthur, Caleb VI, 872
Arthur, Cary VI, 873
Arthur, Catharine VI, 855
Arthur, Catharine VI, 873
Arthur, Catharine Mackey VI, 796
Arthur, Charlotte VI, 872
Arthur, Charlotte VI, 873
Arthur, David VI, 872
Arthur, Dosha VI, 964
Arthur, Edmund VI, 803
Arthur, Edmund VI, 813
Arthur, Edmund VI, 814
Arthur, Edmund VI, 846
Arthur, Edmund VI, 847
Arthur, Edmund VI, 848
Arthur, Edmund VI, 855
Arthur, Edwin V, 318
Arthur, Edwin P. V, 656
Arthur, Eli VI, 872
Arthur, Eli VI, 996
Arthur, Elias VI, 873
Arthur, Eliza VI, 906
Arthur, Elizabeth VI, 796
Arthur, Elizabeth VI, 815
Arthur, Elizabeth VI, 872
Arthur, Elizabeth VI, 873
Arthur, Elizabeth VI, 934
Arthur, Elizabeth VI, 961
Arthur, Elizabeth VI, 968
Arthur, Elizabeth VI, 990
Arthur, Elizabeth A. VI, 847
Arthur, Emily VI, 873
Arthur, Emily J. VI, 873
Arthur, Frances VI, 872
Arthur, Frances VI, 873
Arthur, Frances VI, 899
Arthur, Granvil VI, 873
Arthur, Greenville VI, 873
Arthur, Henry VI, 872
Arthur, James VI, 796
Arthur, James VI, 814
Arthur, James VI, 872
Arthur, James VI, 900
Arthur, James VI, 934
Arthur, James VI, 989
Arthur, Jane VI, 987
Arthur, Janetty VI, 873
Arthur, Jemima VI, 796
Arthur, Jenny VI, 872
Arthur, Jenny VI, 899
Arthur, Joanna VI, 872
Arthur, Joannah VI, 941
Arthur, John VI, 796
Arthur, John VI, 855
Arthur, John VI, 860
Arthur, John VI, 872
Arthur, John VI, 895
Arthur, John VI, 906
Arthur, John VI, 998
Arthur, John VI, 1005
Arthur, John VI, 1012
Arthur, John, Sr. VI, 906
Arthur, Joseph VI, 796
Arthur, Joseph VI, 864
Arthur, Joseph VI, 941
Arthur, Lacy VI, 947
Arthur, Larkin VI, 872
Arthur, Larkin VI, 906
Arthur, Larkin VI, 964
Arthur, Laura E. V, 317
Arthur, Laura E. V, 343
Arthur, Lewis VI, 872
Arthur, Lewis VI, 937
Arthur, Lewis VI, 961
Arthur, Lewis VI, 1007
Arthur, Lewis C. VI, 871
Arthur, Lewis C. VI, 872
Arthur, Lewis C. VI, 989
Arthur, Lilly Ann VI, 872
Arthur, Lindsay VI, 873
Arthur, Locky VI, 872
Arthur, Lucinda VI, 796
Arthur, Lucy VI, 814
Arthur, Lucy VI, 872
Arthur, Malinda VI, 873
Arthur, Martha VI, 798
Arthur, Martha VI, 872
Arthur, Martha VI, 906
Arthur, Martha A. V, 318
Arthur, Martha A. VI, 814
Arthur, Mary VI, 872
Arthur, Mary VI, 968
Arthur, Mary VI, 986
Arthur, Mary E. V, 317
Arthur, Mary Emeline VI, 998
Arthur, Matilda C. VI, 846
Arthur, Melinda VI, 898

Arthur, Meredith VI, 978
Arthur, Meredith Dixon VI, 873
Arthur, Meridth VI, 873
Arthur, Milly VI, 797
Arthur, Milly VI, 872
Arthur, Mrs. Ursela VI, 872
Arthur, Nancy VI, 837
Arthur, Nancy VI, 872
Arthur, Nancy VI, 925
Arthur, Nancy VI, 935
Arthur, Nancy VI, 1008
Arthur, Pamelia VI, 803
Arthur, Phebe VI, 873
Arthur, Phebe A. III, 21
Arthur, Phebe Ann III, 21
Arthur, Polley VI, 895
Arthur, Polly VI, 796
Arthur, Polly VI, 985
Arthur, Rebecca VI, 947
Arthur, Sally VI, 837
Arthur, Sally VI, 864
Arthur, Sally VI, 872
Arthur, Sally VI, 895
Arthur, Sally VI, 1005
Arthur, Sarah VI, 796
Arthur, Sarah VI, 853
Arthur, Sarah VI, 872
Arthur, Sarah VI, 899
Arthur, Sarah VI, 946
Arthur, Sarah D. VI, 937
Arthur, Sarah J. VI, 850
Arthur, Sarah Jane VI, 899
Arthur, Stephen VI, 931
Arthur, Susanna VI, 873
Arthur, Susanna VI, 925
Arthur, Tabbitha VI, 820
Arthur, Tabitha VI, 873
Arthur, Thomas VI, 872
Arthur, Thomas VI, 873
Arthur, Thomas VI, 898
Arthur, Thomas VI, 906
Arthur, Thomas VI, 935
Arthur, Thomas VI, 947
Arthur, Thomas, Jr. VI, 946
Arthur, Thos., Sr. VI, 984
Arthur, Timandra VI, 873
Arthur, Tyree VI, 873
Arthur, Ursela VI, 872
Arthur, Usley VI, 968
Arthur, Ussilla VI, 985
Arthur, W. A. IV, 1245
Arthur, William VI, 796
Arthur, William VI, 815
Arthur, William VI, 847
Arthur, William VI, 853
Arthur, William VI, 872
Arthur, William VI, 873
Arthur, William VI, 906
Arthur, William VI, 926
Arthur, William B. VI, 873
Arthur, William J. VI, 873
Arthur, William, Jr. VI, 872
Arthur, Willis VI, 872
Arthur, Winny VI, 906
Arthur, Zenas VI, 906
Arthur, Zenus VI, 873
Arthurs, W. A. IV, 1245
Artis, Frazier H. IV, 1271
Artois, Rebecca W. III, 21
Arundel, Alfred II, 698
Arundel, Alfred II, 718
Arundel, Ann VI, 501
Arundel, Kate II, 698
Arundel, Kate II, 718
Arundel, Winifred II, 698
Arundel, Winifred II, 718
Arville, Emma M. V, 892
Arville, John J. V, 892
Arwin, John II, 194
Arwing, John II, 194
Ary, Carrie V, 609
Ary, Clara M. V, 825
Ary, Clara M. V, 831
Ary, Corwin V, 472
Ary, Elsie V, 609
Ary, Elsie V, 648
Ary, Goldie V, 472
Ary, Guy V, 472
Ary, Mary IV, 19
Ary, Nannie V, 150
Ary, Sally V, 472
Ary, Sally V, 473
Ary, Wm. V, 609
Asa, Abraham VI, 596
Asa, Esther VI, 596
Asa, Jonah VI, 596
Asberry, Elizabeth VI, 955
Asberry, Fanny VI, 873
Asberry, James VI, 873
Asberry, James VI, 879
Asberry, Jane VI, 954
Asberry, Jane VI, 997
Asberry, Nancy VI, 873
Asberry, Nancy VI, 954
Asberry, Rhoda VI, 891
Asberry, Sally VI, 879
Asborne, John II, 333
Asborne, Martin II, 333
Asburry, Nancy VI, 877
Asburry, Sophia VI, 877
Asbury, Daniel VI, 891
Asbury, George VI, 873
Asbury, George VI, 997
Asbury, James VI, 896
Asbury, James VI, 902
Asbury, James VI, 946
Asbury, James VI, 978
Asbury, Mary VI, 873
Asbury, Nancy VI, 841
Asbury, Nancy VI, 913
Asbury, Nancy VI, 946
Asbury, Rhoda VI, 896
Asbury, Rutha VI, 913
Asbury, Sally VI, 902
Asbury, Thomas VI, 955
Ash, Abigail II, 454
Ash, Abigail II, 518
Ash, Barrett V, 984
Ash, Caleb II, 780
Ash, Caleb II, 832
Ash, Caleb II, 920
Ash, Caroline Margaret II, 698
Ash, Christopher VI, 873
Ash, Edward III, 21
Ash, Elizabeth II, 454
Ash, Elizabeth II, 726
Ash, Even II, 333
Ash, George II, 698
Ash, Hannah Shinn II, 780
Ash, Hannah Shinn II, 832
Ash, Helen II, 832
Ash, Helen II, 840
Ash, Henry C. II, 832
Ash, Henry C. II, 840
Ash, Henry Caleb II, 780
Ash, Jane II, 46
Ash, Joshua II, 333
Ash, Joshua II, 726
Ash, Joshua W. II, 454
Ash, Joshua W. II, 698
Ash, Joshua W. II, 726
Ash, Joshua, Jr. II, 454
Ash, Margaret G. II, 832
Ash, Margaret Gibbons II, 780
Ash, Margaret L. II, 698
Ash, Martha II, 919
Ash, Martha IV, 1349
Ash, Martha IV, 1350
Ash, Mary II, 291
Ash, Mary II, 780
Ash, Mary II, 787
Ash, Mary II, 832
Ash, Mary II, 920
Ash, Mary G. II, 698
Ash, Mary G. II, 726
Ash, Mary H. II, 726
Ash, Mary Hannah II, 698
Ash, Mary Hannah II, 726
Ash, Mary Schofield II, 780
Ash, Matthew II, 780
Ash, Matthew II, 787
Ash, Matthew II, 832
Ash, Matthew II, 920
Ash, Matthew F. II, 780
Ash, Matthew Franklin II, 832
Ash, Nancy VI, 873
Ash, Oliver Howard II, 780
Ash, Rebecca II, 454
Ash, Rebecca II, 587
Ash, Rebecca II, 780
Ash, Rebecca II, 832
Ash, Rebecca II, 920
Ash, Samuel II, 441
Ash, Samuel Earl II, 780
Ash, Samuel Garrett II, 698
Ash, Samuel S. II, 832
Ash, Samuel Shinn II, 780
Ash, Samuel Shinn II, 832
Ash, Sarah II, 441
Ash, Sarah II, 454
Ash, Sarah J. II, 832
Ash, Sarah Jane II, 780
Ash, Wd. Jane II, 787
Ash, Wm. G. II, 698
Ash, Wm. G. II, 726
Ashard, Thomas II, 333
Ashba, Frank D. IV, 463
Ashba, Frank D. IV, 673
Ashba, Rev. Frank D. IV, 463
Ashbaugh, Orianna IV, 1201
Ashbaugh, Orianna IV, 1225
Ashberry, George VI, 873
Ashberry, Mary VI, 873
Ashbey, Ellen V, 879
Ashborn, Benjamin II, 333
Ashborn, Jeremiah II, 333
Ashborn, John II, 333
Ashborn, Martin II, 333
Ashborn, Mary II, 333
Ashborn, Sarah II, 333
Ashborne, Sarah II, 333
Ashbourn, Charles I, 1096
Ashbourn, Daniel I, 1096
Ashbourn, Isaac I, 1096
Ashbourn, Sarah II, 975
Ashbourn, William I, 1096
Ashbourn, William II, 1042
Ashbourn, Wm. II, 975
Ashbridge, Aaron II, 194
Ashbridge, Aaron II, 266
Ashbridge, Aaron II, 333
Ashbridge, Ann II, 454
Ashbridge, Ann II, 455
Ashbridge, Ann II, 556
Ashbridge, Ann II, 780
Ashbridge, Ann II, 832
Ashbridge, Ann II, 862
Ashbridge, Ann, Jr. II, 832
Ashbridge, Elizabeth II, 194
Ashbridge, Elizabeth II, 266
Ashbridge, George II, 454
Ashbridge, George Garret II, 455
Ashbridge, Hannah II, 454
Ashbridge, Jane II, 454
Ashbridge, John II, 454
Ashbridge, Joseph II, 333
Ashbridge, Joseph II, 454
Ashbridge, Priscilla II, 454
Ashbridge, Priscilla II, 585
Ashbridge, Priscilla Jones II, 454
Ashbridge, Rebecca II, 454
Ashbridge, Rebecca II, 557
Ashbridge, Sarah II, 454
Ashbridge, Sarah II, 455
Ashbridge, Sarah II, 780
Ashbridge, Sarah II, 832
Ashbridge, Thomasin II, 455
Ashbridge, Wm. II, 454
Ashbrook, Ernest IV, 1143
Ashbrook, Frank IV, 1143
Ashbrook, Mary IV, 1143
Ashbrook, Maurice II, 797
Ashbrook, Mrs. Frank IV, 1143
Ashburn, Hannah II, 455
Ashburn, Hannah II, 482
Ashburn, Jacob II, 975
Ashburn, Jeremiah II, 333
Ashburn, John II, 953
Ashburn, John II, 975
Ashburn, Martin II, 333
Ashburn, Mary II, 333
Ashburn, Mary II, 455
Ashburn, Mary II, 463
Ashburn, Sarah II, 953
Ashburn, Sarah II, 975
Ashburn, Thomas II, 455
Ashburn, Thomas II, 482
Ashburn, William II, 953
Ashburn, Wm. II, 975
Ashburn, Wm., Jr. II, 975
Ashburne, Jacob II, 975
Ashburne, Wm., Jr. II, 975
Ashburnham, Hannah II, 333
Ashburnham, Hannah II, 455
Ashburnham, Hannah II, 485
Ashburnham, Hannah, Jr. II, 455
Ashburnham, Mary II, 333
Ashburnham, Thomas II, 333
Ashbury, Elizabeth VI, 978
Ashbury, Martha VI, 997
Ashbury, Thomas VI, 997
Ashby, Abigail II, 455
Ashby, Hudson III, 21
Ashby, William III, 21
Ashby, Wm. II, 455
Ashe, Sarah II, 454
Ashe, Sarah II, 651
Ashead, Amos II, 168
Ashead, Amos II, 279
Ashead, Amos II, 280
Ashead, Amos IV, 364
Ashead, Amos IV, 673
Ashead, Avalinda IV, 673
Ashead, Benjamin S. IV, 673
Ashead, Dudley Fawcett IV, 673
Ashead, Elizabeth T. IV, 364
Ashead, Elizabeth T. IV, 400
Ashead, Elizabeth T. IV, 402
Ashead, Elizabeth T. IV, 673
Ashead, Ellinor II, 168
Ashead, Hannah IV, 170
Ashead, Hannah IV, 225
Ashead, Hannah IV, 364
Ashead, Hannah IV, 673
Ashead, Hannah S. IV, 170
Ashead, Ira II, 115
Ashead, Ira II, 280
Ashead, J. Moris IV, 673
Ashead, J. Morris IV, 364
Ashead, J. Morris IV, 400
Ashead, J. Morris IV, 673
Ashead, Joseph B. II, 166
Ashead, Joseph B. II, 279
Ashead, Joseph B. II, 280
Ashead, Joseph Howard IV, 673
Ashead, Lydia II, 168
Ashead, Mary R. IV, 673
Ashead, Oliver P. IV, 673
Ashead, Rebecca II, 166
Ashead, Rebecca II, 279
Ashead, Rebecca II, 280
Ashead, Sarah II, 279
Ashead, Sarah II, 280
Ashead, Sarah B. IV, 792
Ashead, Sarah Edith IV, 673
Asher, Alexander VI, 796
Asher, Betsy VI, 796
Asher, Deborah IV, 1271
Asher, Deborah IV, 1291
Asher, Donald IV, 1305
Asher, Elizabeth IV, 1245
Asher, Elizabeth VI, 857
Asher, Elizabeth VI, 858
Asher, Elizabeth VI, 861
Asher, Frances VI, 796
Asher, Harry IV, 1305
Asher, James VI, 796
Asher, James VI, 824
Asher, James VI, 861
Asher, Jane VI, 858
Asher, Janes VI, 858
Asher, John VI, 832
Asher, John VI, 852
Asher, John VI, 858
Asher, John, Jr. VI, 796
Asher, John, Jr. VI, 853
Asher, Lloyd F. IV, 1245
Asher, Mary IV, 1305
Asher, Mary VI, 858
Asher, Merrill IV, 1305
Asher, Myrtle IV, 1305
Asher, Nancy T. VI, 824
Asher, Polly VI, 796
Asher, Sarah VI, 852
Asher, Theda A. IV, 1245
Asher, Thomas IV, 1245
Asher, Willie IV, 1305
Asher, Wm. IV, 1305
Asherton, Charles II, 165
Asherton, John II, 333
Asherton, Mary II, 165
Asheworth, Elizabeth H. I, 708
Asheworth, Martha F. I, 708
Asheworth, W. R. I, 708
Asheworth, Walter C. I, 708
Ashford, Deborah IV, 863
Ashford, Deborah IV, 885
Ashford, Hannah I, 1060
Ashford, Hannah I, 1061
Ashford, Rebekah VI, 467
Ashford, Rebekah VI, 540
Ashford, Sarah IV, 863
Ashford, Sarah IV, 880
Ashley, Anthony I, 1113
Ashley, Florence V, 926
Ashley, Margaret IV, 1143
Ashley, Martha II, 441
Ashley, Mary II, 441
Ashley, Rachel I, 1113
Ashley, Rachel I, 1128
Ashline, Anna VI, 739
Ashmalhan, Mary II, 333
Ashmalhan, Thomas II, 333
Ashman, Charles IV, 170
Ashman, Elizabeth IV, 170
Ashmead, Abigail IV, 19
Ashmead, Abigail IV, 24
Ashmead, James II, 441
Ashmead, Joseph II, 441
Ashmead, Mary II, 333
Ashmead, Mary II, 455
Ashmead, Mary II, 597
Ashmead, Nicholas II, 441
Ashmead, Sarah II, 441
Ashmead, Thomas II, 441
Ashmead, William II, 441
Ashmond, Dina IV, 170
Ashton, Albert H. IV, 170
Ashton, Albert H. IV, 609
Ashton, Ann II, 953
Ashton, Ann II, 975
Ashton, Ann II, 1002
Ashton, Anna Matilda II, 822
Ashton, Barak IV, 170
Ashton, Barak IV, 509
Ashton, Barak IV, 608
Ashton, Barak IV, 609
Ashton, Barak IV, 647
Ashton, Barak IV, 656
Ashton, Barak IV, 693
Ashton, Barak IV, 807
Ashton, Barak IV, 863
Ashton, Barak IV, 876
Ashton, Barok IV, 673
Ashton, Caty Longshore IV, 863
Ashton, Charlotte II, 726
Ashton, D. Ida IV, 923
Ashton, Deborah II, 953
Ashton, Deborah II, 975
Ashton, Deborah II, 978
Ashton, Dorothy II, 455
Ashton, Dorothy II, 975
Ashton, Dorothy IV, 509
Ashton, Dorothy H. IV, 797
Ashton, Dorothy S. IV, 509
Ashton, Dorothy S. IV, 553
Ashton, Dorothy S. IV, 797
Ashton, Dorothy S. IV, 846
Ashton, Edward II, 333
Ashton, Eleanor II, 51
Ashton, Elisabeth II, 455
Ashton, Elisabeth II, 470
Ashton, Eliza IV, 170
Ashton, Eliza IV, 608
Ashton, Eliza IV, 643
Ashton, Eliza IV, 863
Ashton, Eliza IV, 864
Ashton, Eliza IV, 883
Ashton, Eliza A. IV, 647
Ashton, Eliza F. IV, 509
Ashton, Eliza F. IV, 534
Ashton, Eliza F. IV, 609
Ashton, Eliza G. IV, 170
Ashton, Eliza G. IV, 246
Ashton, Eliza G. IV, 261
Ashton, Eliza G. IV, 608
Ashton, Eliza G. IV, 609
Ashton, Eliza M. IV, 608
Ashton, Eliza Margaret IV, 673
Ashton, Elizabeth II, 51
Ashton, Elizabeth II, 75
Ashton, Elizabeth II, 333
Ashton, Elizabeth II, 455
Ashton, Elizabeth IV, 863
Ashton, Esther II, 333
Ashton, Geo. W. IV, 797
Ashton, George II, 333
Ashton, George II, 455
Ashton, Hannah II, 455
Ashton, Hannah II, 461
Ashton, Hannah II, 953
Ashton, Hannah II, 975
Ashton, Hannah II, 1003
Ashton, Harman J. IV, 170
Ashton, Harmon J. IV, 609
Ashton, Harmond J. IV, 170
Ashton, Ida IV, 608
Ashton, Ida IV, 611
Ashton, Ida B. IV, 923
Ashton, Ida D. IV, 960
Ashton, Isaac II, 333
Ashton, Isaac II, 461
Ashton, Isabel II, 953
Ashton, Jacob IV, 608
Ashton, Jacob IV, 863
Ashton, Jacob IV, 864
Ashton, Jacob F. IV, 608
Ashton, Jacob F. IV, 864
Ashton, Jane IV, 170
Ashton, Jane IV, 509
Ashton, Jane IV, 608
Ashton, Jane IV, 609
Ashton, Jane IV, 647
Ashton, Jane IV, 656
Ashton, Jane IV, 673
Ashton, Jane IV, 693
Ashton, Jane IV, 807
Ashton, Jane IV, 863
Ashton, Jane IV, 876
Ashton, John II, 266
Ashton, John II, 333
Ashton, John II, 953
Ashton, John II, 975
Ashton, John Lacy II, 975
Ashton, John Shackamaxon II, 194
Ashton, Joseph II, 333
Ashton, Justin Ann IV, 863
Ashton, Justine Ann IV, 864
Ashton, Liddia II, 975
Ashton, Lydia II, 455
Ashton, Lydia III, 21
Ashton, Margaret II, 817
Ashton, Margaret IV, 863
Ashton, Margaret IV, 864

Ashton, Margaret IV, 880
Ashton, Margaret IV, 1179
Ashton, Mariam IV, 673
Ashton, Martha II, 953
Ashton, Martha IV, 608
Ashton, Martha IV, 673
Ashton, Martha IV, 863
Ashton, Martha IV, 864
Ashton, Martha IV, 875
Ashton, Martha IV, 880
Ashton, Martha ??? IV, 863
Ashton, Martha S. IV, 656
Ashton, Martha Williams II, 455
Ashton, Mary II, 333
Ashton, Mary II, 953
Ashton, Mary II, 975
Ashton, Mary II, 981
Ashton, Mary II, 1009
Ashton, Mary IV, 863
Ashton, Mary IV, 864
Ashton, Mary IV, 886
Ashton, Mary IV, 1143
Ashton, Mary IV, 1195
Ashton, Patience II, 194
Ashton, Patience II, 266
Ashton, Peter II, 333
Ashton, Peter II, 455
Ashton, Phebe IV, 401
Ashton, Phebe IV, 608
Ashton, Phebe IV, 673
Ashton, Phebe IV, 715
Ashton, Phebe IV, 800
Ashton, Phebe IV, 863
Ashton, Phebe Y. IV, 608
Ashton, Phebe Y. IV, 617
Ashton, Phebe Y. IV, 639
Ashton, Phebe Y. IV, 678
Ashton, Phebe Y. IV, 693
Ashton, Phebe Y. IV, 730
Ashton, Phebe Y. IV, 797
Ashton, Phebe Y. IV, 807
Ashton, Philip II, 333
Ashton, Rachel II, 975
Ashton, Rachel II, 1009
Ashton, Rachel IV, 863
Ashton, Rachel IV, 864
Ashton, Rachel IV, 884
Ashton, Rena J. IV, 170
Ashton, Rena J. IV, 609
Ashton, Rena Jane IV, 170
Ashton, Rena Jane IV, 261
Ashton, Richard IV, 170
Ashton, Richard IV, 246
Ashton, Richard IV, 608
Ashton, Richard IV, 609
Ashton, Richard IV, 643
Ashton, Richard IV, 673
Ashton, Richard S. IV, 261
Ashton, Richard S. IV, 608
Ashton, Richard S. IV, 863
Ashton, Robert II, 65
Ashton, Samuel II, 333
Ashton, Sarah II, 51
Ashton, Sarah II, 113
Ashton, Sarah II, 333
Ashton, Sarah II, 399
Ashton, Sarah II, 455
Ashton, Sarah II, 526
Ashton, Susan II, 803
Ashton, Susannah II, 51
Ashton, Susannah II, 65
Ashton, Susannah II, 975
Ashton, Susannah II, 1018
Ashton, Thomas II, 333
Ashton, Thomas II, 726
Ashton, Thomas II, 953
Ashton, Thomas II, 975
Ashton, Thomas II, 978
Ashton, Thomas II, 1003
Ashton, Thomas II, 1009
Ashton, Thomas IV, 863
Ashton, Thomas IV, 864
Ashton, Thomas IV, 880
Ashton, Thomas L. IV, 608
Ashton, Thomas L. IV, 609
Ashton, Thomas L. IV, 611
Ashton, Thomas S. IV, 863
Ashton, William II, 953
Ashton, William IV, 864
Ashton, William B. IV, 170
Ashton, William B. IV, 609
Ashton, William L. IV, 509
Ashton, William L. IV, 609
Ashton, William L. IV, 863
Ashton, Wm. B. IV, 170
Ashton, Wm. L. IV, 509
Ashton, Wm. L. IV, 534
Ashton, Wm. L. IV, 608
Ashton, Wm. L. IV, 797
Ashton, Wm. Marsh IV, 863
Ashton, Zebulon II, 975
Ashurst, Josiah VI, 873
Ashurst, Rebeckah VI, 873
Ashwell, Amelia Frances VI, 976
Ashwell, Charlotte VI, 873
Ashwell, Daniel VI, 873
Ashwell, Daniel VI, 952
Ashwell, Daniel VI, 957
Ashwell, Daniel VI, 963
Ashwell, Daniel VI, 976
Ashwell, Daniel J. VI, 873
Ashwell, Elenor VI, 873
Ashwell, Elizabeth VI, 952
Ashwell, Emeline VI, 873
Ashwell, Emeline VI, 976
Ashwell, Evelina VI, 971
Ashwell, Fanny VI, 873
Ashwell, James VI, 873
Ashwell, James VI, 922
Ashwell, Jane VI, 963
Ashwell, Janetty VI, 873
Ashwell, John VI, 873
Ashwell, John VI, 881
Ashwell, John VI, 952
Ashwell, John VI, 963
Ashwell, John, Jr. VI, 873
Ashwell, John, Sr. VI, 976
Ashwell, Julian H. VI, 922
Ashwell, Little Mary VI, 873
Ashwell, Matilda VI, 873
Ashwell, Meredith VI, 873
Ashwell, Nancy VI, 976
Ashwell, Nelly VI, 952
Ashwell, Pleasant T. VI, 873
Ashwell, Polly VI, 873
Ashwell, Sarah VI, 873
Ashwell, Sarah J. VI, 976
Ashwell, Sarah Jane VI, 870
Ashwell, Thomas VI, 870
Ashwell, Thomas VI, 873
Ashwell, William VI, 873
Ashwell, William M. VI, 976
Ashworth, Agnes I, 614
Ashworth, Elizabeth H. I, 708
Ashworth, Martha F. I, 708
Aske, Sarah II, 455
Askew, ??? III, 21
Askew, ??? IV, 364
Askew, Abigail IV, 355
Askew, Abigail E. IV, 355
Askew, Angelina I, 240
Askew, Ann IV, 319
Askew, Anna IV, 355
Askew, Anthony VI, 796
Askew, Anthony VI, 804
Askew, Anthony VI, 837
Askew, Benjamin IV, 170
Askew, Benjamin IV, 319
Askew, Benjamin IV, 355
Askew, Benjamin IV, 364
Askew, Catharine VI, 837
Askew, Catherine VI, 797
Askew, Catherine E. VI, 797
Askew, Childress VI, 796
Askew, Clarissa IV, 319
Askew, Clarissa IV, 344
Askew, Clarissa R. IV, 364
Askew, David IV, 355
Askew, Edward II, 780
Askew, Edward II, 832
Askew, Elizabeth II, 832
Askew, Elizabeth II, 856
Askew, Elizabeth IV, 319
Askew, Elizabeth IV, 344
Askew, Elizabeth VI, 796
Askew, Elizabeth VI, 804
Askew, Elizabeth A. VI, 797
Askew, Elizabeth S. IV, 364
Askew, Eunice IV, 355
Askew, Fanny Conard II, 780
Askew, Grace VI, 856
Askew, Hannah IV, 139
Askew, Hannah IV, 319
Askew, Hannah IV, 358
Askew, Hannah IV, 359
Askew, Hannah IV, 364
Askew, Hannah Elizabeth II, 780
Askew, Hervey IV, 355
Askew, Isaac IV, 319
Askew, Isaac IV, 355
Askew, Isaac IV, 364
Askew, Isaac Blackfan IV, 364
Askew, James III, 21
Askew, James VI, 797
Askew, James D. VI, 797
Askew, James D. VI, 816
Askew, Jane I, 207
Askew, Jane I, 229
Askew, Jane I, 240
Askew, Jane VI, 796
Askew, Jennie VI, 796
Askew, John II, 455
Askew, John IV, 355
Askew, John VI, 362
Askew, John, Jr. IV, 355
Askew, Joseph II, 455
Askew, Joseph II, 832
Askew, Joseph IV, 319
Askew, Joseph IV, 364
Askew, Joseph S. IV, 355
Askew, Joseph W. II, 832
Askew, Margaret I, 229
Askew, Margaret I, 240
Askew, Margaret IV, 319
Askew, Margaret IV, 364
Askew, Margaret Ann I, 229
Askew, Margaret Hall I, 207
Askew, Martha IV, 139
Askew, Martha IV, 164
Askew, Martha IV, 319
Askew, Martha IV, 326
Askew, Martha IV, 354
Askew, Martha IV, 359
Askew, Martha IV, 364
Askew, Mary IV, 170
Askew, Mary IV, 319
Askew, Mary IV, 355
Askew, Mary IV, 364
Askew, Mary C. II, 780
Askew, Moses I, 240
Askew, Nicholas I, 207
Askew, Nicholas I, 229
Askew, Palinah VI, 334
Askew, Parker IV, 139
Askew, Parker IV, 170
Askew, Parker IV, 319
Askew, Parker IV, 354
Askew, Parker IV, 358
Askew, Parker IV, 364
Askew, Parker W. IV, 364
Askew, Parker, Jr. IV, 319
Askew, Pauline VI, 296
Askew, Pauline VI, 796
Askew, Peter Hatton IV, 364
Askew, Pleasant VI, 837
Askew, Polly VI, 796
Askew, Rachel Ann II, 780
Askew, Rachel C. II, 832
Askew, Rebecca IV, 170
Askew, Rebecca IV, 319
Askew, Rebecca IV, 335
Askew, Rebecca IV, 354
Askew, Rebecca IV, 364
Askew, Rebecca W. IV, 319
Askew, Rebecca W. IV, 326
Askew, Rebecca W. IV, 364
Askew, Rebecca W. IV, 1087
Askew, Rebecca W. IV, 1093
Askew, Samuel IV, 319
Askew, Samuel IV, 364
Askew, Sarah IV, 319
Askew, Sarah IV, 333
Askew, Sarah IV, 364
Askew, Sarah V, 656
Askew, Sarah V, 692
Askew, Semira L. IV, 355
Askew, Susanna C. II, 832
Askew, Susanna C. II, 848
Askew, Tarlton W. VI, 796
Askew, Walter E. IV, 355
Askew, Watson VI, 797
Askew, William III, 21
Askew, William IV, 139
Askew, William IV, 319
Askew, William IV, 364
Askew, William VI, 362
Askew, William VI, 796
Askew, William VI, 856
Askew, Wm. IV, 164
Askew, Wm. IV, 326
Askew, Wm. IV, 359
Askin, I. Henry II, 801
Askin, Louisa II, 801
Aspden, Dorothy II, 333
Aspden, Mathias II, 333
Aspden, Matthias II, 455
Aspden, Rebecca II, 333
Aspden, Rebecca II, 455
Aspdin, Rebecca II, 455
Aspery, Mary II, 441
Assaub, Joseph II, 780
Asson, William II, 441
Asten, George II, 441
Asten, John II, 441
Asten, Thomas II, 441
Astin, George II, 441
Astin, Margaret II, 441
Astin, William II, 441
Aston, Ann A. V, 963
Aston, Benjamin V, 963
Aston, Edward Warder V, 963
Aston, Elizabeth V, 963
Aston, George II, 455
Aston, George V, 963
Aston, James T. V, 963
Aston, Jeremiah Warder V, 963
Aston, Joseph II, 333
Aston, Mary Aston V, 963
Aston, Sarah II, 333
Aston, Thomas II, 441
Aston, Ursila II, 441
Aston, William V, 963
Atchison, Benjamin V, 472
Atchison, Charles V, 472
Atchison, Elmer V, 472
Atchison, Emma V, 472
Atchison, Harry V, 472
Atchison, Louisa Ethel V, 472
Atchison, Maud V, 472
Atchison, Mildred V, 472
Atchison, Mrs. ??? V, 472
Atchison, Roxie V, 472
Atha, Ada V, 983
Atha, Sarah IV, 1271
Atha, Washington IV, 1271
Athe, John V, 218
Athe, Mary V, 218
Ather, Emma IV, 1245
Atherton, Abigail II, 333
Atherton, Abigail II, 455
Atherton, Abigail II, 612
Atherton, Ann IV, 19
Atherton, Ann IV, 73
Atherton, Ann IV, 364
Atherton, Ann IV, 509
Atherton, Ann IV, 560
Atherton, Boah IV, 364
Atherton, Boaz IV, 19
Atherton, Boaz IV, 69
Atherton, Boaz IV, 319
Atherton, Boaz IV, 509
Atherton, Boaz IV, 560
Atherton, Charles II, 165
Atherton, Charles II, 280
Atherton, Charles II, 298
Atherton, Charles II, 333
Atherton, Charles II, 455
Atherton, Charles II, 1068
Atherton, Charles III, 21
Atherton, Charles, Jr. II, 1068
Atherton, David IV, 364
Atherton, David IV, 509
Atherton, David IV, 560
Atherton, Deborah P. II, 165
Atherton, Deborah P. II, 280
Atherton, Deborah P. III, 21
Atherton, Elizabeth II, 280
Atherton, Elizabeth II, 298
Atherton, Elizabeth II, 780
Atherton, Elizabeth II, 832
Atherton, Elizabeth II, 1068
Atherton, Elizabeth IV, 364
Atherton, Elizabeth IV, 509
Atherton, Elizabeth IV, 560
Atherton, Elizabeth V. II, 1068
Atherton, Frances IV, 19
Atherton, Francis IV, 73
Atherton, Geo. II, 194
Atherton, George II, 780
Atherton, George II, 832
Atherton, George II, 898
Atherton, Hannah II, 194
Atherton, Hannah II, 455
Atherton, Hannah II, 595
Atherton, Hannah II, 598
Atherton, Hannah II, 612
Atherton, Hannah II, 832
Atherton, Hannah E. II, 165
Atherton, Hannah S. II, 832
Atherton, Hannah S. II, 898
Atherton, Hannah, Jr. II, 455
Atherton, Henry II, 194
Atherton, Henry II, 280
Atherton, Henry II, 298
Atherton, Henry II, 333
Atherton, Henry II, 455
Atherton, Henry II, 595
Atherton, Henry II, 598
Atherton, Henry II, 612
Atherton, Henry II, 1068
Atherton, Henry IV, 19
Atherton, Henry IV, 73
Atherton, Henry H. II, 165
Atherton, Humphrey II, 194
Atherton, Humphrey II, 333
Atherton, Humphrey II, 455
Atherton, Humphrey II, 612
Atherton, Isaac II, 194
Atherton, John II, 1068
Atherton, Maery II, 1068
Atherton, Marahda IV, 364
Atherton, Mary II, 165
Atherton, Mary II, 280
Atherton, Mary II, 298
Atherton, Mary II, 455
Atherton, Mary III, 21
Atherton, Mary IV, 19
Atherton, Mary IV, 69
Atherton, Mary IV, 73
Atherton, Mary IV, 103
Atherton, Mary IV, 319
Atherton, Mary IV, 364
Atherton, Mary IV, 509
Atherton, Mary IV, 560
Atherton, Matthew II, 832
Atherton, Mira II, 333
Atherton, Nathan II, 455
Atherton, Nathan II, 832
Atherton, Nathan Atkinson II, 455
Atherton, Rebecca II, 455
Atherton, Rebecca II, 832
Atherton, Reuben IV, 364
Atherton, Reuben IV, 560
Atherton, Reuben R. IV, 364
Atherton, Reuben R. IV, 509
Atherton, Reuben Ross IV, 509
Atherton, Richard IV, 19
Atherton, Richard IV, 139
Atherton, Richard IV, 364
Atherton, Richard IV, 509
Atherton, Richard IV, 560
Atherton, Ross IV, 364
Atherton, Ross IV, 560
Atherton, Ruth II, 455
Atherton, Ruth II, 595
Atherton, Ruth II, 809
Atherton, Ruth Charles II, 194
Atherton, Sarah II, 455
Atherton, Sarah II, 780
Atherton, Sarah II, 832
Atherton, Susan II, 898
Atherton, Susan T. II, 832
Atherton, Susanna II, 455
Atherton, Susanna II, 598
Atherton, Susannah II, 194
Atherton, Thomas II, 165
Atherton, Thomas II, 1068
Atherton, Thomas IV, 19
Atherton, Thomas IV, 73
Athey, Rosa V, 984
Athreton, Maranda IV, 365
Athreton, Richard IV, 365
Athy, Andrew J. V, 984
Athy, Jennie V, 984
Athy, Rosa V, 984
Atkerson, Frankey VI, 932
Atkerson, John VI, 932
Atkerson, Martha VI, 97
Atkerson, Reuben VI, 869
Atkeson, Hope II, 194
Atkeson, Hope II, 258
Atkeson, Jane II, 194
Atkeson, Jane II, 235
Atkeson, Joseph II, 194
Atkeson, Mary II, 194
Atkeson, Mary II, 260
Atkeson, Michal II, 194
Atkeson, Michal II, 236
Atkeson, Michal II, 258
Atkeson, Rachel II, 194
Atkeson, Rachel II, 236
Atkeson, Thomas II, 194
Atkeson, Thomas II, 235
Atkeson, Thomas V, 472
Atkins, ??? III, 117
Atkins, Amelia III, 117
Atkins, Amelia Anne III, 21
Atkins, Amelia Anne III, 117
Atkins, Anna E. IV, 1245
Atkins, Anne J. IV, 170
Atkins, Charles D. III, 21
Atkins, Charles Elgar III, 117
Atkins, Cora I, 920
Atkins, Cora Peggy I, 920
Atkins, Duglass II, 441
Atkins, James L. R. VI, 873
Atkins, John E. I, 920
Atkins, John E. I, 937
Atkins, John Edward I, 920
Atkins, Kathleen III, 21
Atkins, Kathleen III, 117
Atkins, Louise C. III, 117
Atkins, Minnie IV, 1245
Atkins, Mrs. S. L. I, 937
Atkins, Nancy Jane I, 920
Atkins, Peter III, 117
Atkins, Phebe A. III, 21
Atkins, Phebe Ann III, 21
Atkins, Savannah L. I, 920
Atkins, Susan G. VI, 873
Atkins, William III, 21
Atkins, William III, 117
Atkins, William B. III, 117
Atkins, Wm. VI, 61

Atkinson, ??? IV, 170
Atkinson, ??? VI, 154
Atkinson, Aaron IV, 1271
Atkinson, Aaron VI, 13
Atkinson, Abigail II, 194
Atkinson, Abigail II, 216
Atkinson, Abigail II, 1043
Atkinson, Abigail IV, 1271
Atkinson, Abigail V, 150
Atkinson, Abigail V, 472
Atkinson, Abigail V, 947
Atkinson, Abner I, 459
Atkinson, Adin II, 194
Atkinson, Ailse II, 194
Atkinson, Alice V, 218
Atkinson, Alice V, 226
Atkinson, Alice V, 472
Atkinson, Alice V, 609
Atkinson, Amos II, 456
Atkinson, Amos II, 780
Atkinson, Amos II, 832
Atkinson, Amos III, 21
Atkinson, Amos III, 218
Atkinson, Ann I, 346
Atkinson, Ann I, 372
Atkinson, Ann I, 426
Atkinson, Ann I, 443
Atkinson, Ann I, 450
Atkinson, Ann II, 194
Atkinson, Ann II, 280
Atkinson, Ann II, 726
Atkinson, Ann II, 780
Atkinson, Ann II, 832
Atkinson, Ann II, 975
Atkinson, Ann IV, 170
Atkinson, Ann V, 21
Atkinson, Ann VI, 97
Atkinson, Ann VI, 154
Atkinson, Ann Eliza II, 780
Atkinson, Ann Eliza II, 832
Atkinson, Ann White VI, 97
Atkinson, Anna II, 194
Atkinson, Anna II, 316
Atkinson, Anna II, 833
Atkinson, Anna E. IV, 1245
Atkinson, Anna H. III, 21
Atkinson, Anna H. III, 347
Atkinson, Anna K. II, 308
Atkinson, Anna Mary IV, 170
Atkinson, Anna Owen II, 780
Atkinson, Anne IV, 364
Atkinson, Anne VI, 154
Atkinson, Anne H. II, 833
Atkinson, Anne H. II, 937
Atkinson, Annie K. II, 833
Atkinson, Annie K. II, 937
Atkinson, Barclay II, 780
Atkinson, Barclay G. II, 832
Atkinson, Benjamin I, 372
Atkinson, Benjamin II, 194
Atkinson, Benjamin II, 195
Atkinson, Benjamin II, 280
Atkinson, Benjamin II, 308
Atkinson, Benjamin II, 780
Atkinson, Benjamin H. II, 308
Atkinson, Benjamin H. II, 316
Atkinson, Beulah II, 51
Atkinson, Beulah II, 103
Atkinson, Beulah T. VI, 615
Atkinson, Beulah Thomas VI, 615
Atkinson, Beulah Thomas VI, 636
Atkinson, Budd II, 308
Atkinson, Budd II, 316
Atkinson, Bula II, 456
Atkinson, Caleb II, 194
Atkinson, Caleb II, 195
Atkinson, Caleb II, 241
Atkinson, Caleb II, 256
Atkinson, Caleb II, 267
Atkinson, Caleb II, 280
Atkinson, Caleb II, 308
Atkinson, Caleb II, 314
Atkinson, Caleb II, 316
Atkinson, Caleb F. II, 195
Atkinson, Caroline IV, 170
Atkinson, Catharine II, 456
Atkinson, Catharine IV, 170
Atkinson, Catharine IV, 221
Atkinson, Catharine IV, 258
Atkinson, Catharine IV, 509
Atkinson, Catharine IV, 710
Atkinson, Catharine VI, 985
Atkinson, Catherine IV, 204
Atkinson, Cephas IV, 1271
Atkinson, Cephas V, 472
Atkinson, Cephas V, 609
Atkinson, Cephas V, 947
Atkinson, Cephis V, 947
Atkinson, Cephus V, 150
Atkinson, Cephus V, 472
Atkinson, Cephus V, 947
Atkinson, Chalkley II, 832
Atkinson, Champion II, 115
Atkinson, Champion II, 140
Atkinson, Champion II, 195
Atkinson, Champion II, 241
Atkinson, Champion II, 308
Atkinson, Champion II, 316
Atkinson, Charity I, 346
Atkinson, Charles IV, 346
Atkinson, Charles V, 472
Atkinson, Charles V, 520
Atkinson, Charles V, 609
Atkinson, Charles C. II, 195
Atkinson, Charlotte M. III, 21
Atkinson, Chas. V, 609
Atkinson, Chas. F. III, 21
Atkinson, Christopher II, 333
Atkinson, Clara A. D. VI, 615
Atkinson, Clara A. D. VI, 636
Atkinson, Clara E. V, 609
Atkinson, Clara Emma V, 609
Atkinson, Clayton V, 892
Atkinson, Clayton G. II, 456
Atkinson, Clothilda VI, 124
Atkinson, Clotilda VI, 97
Atkinson, Daniel IV, 139
Atkinson, Daniel IV, 170
Atkinson, Daniel IV, 171
Atkinson, Daniel IV, 212
Atkinson, Daniel IV, 364
Atkinson, Daniel IV, 377
Atkinson, David I, 1043
Atkinson, David V, 472
Atkinson, David V, 609
Atkinson, David A. V, 609
Atkinson, David Coulson IV, 673
Atkinson, David H. V, 609
Atkinson, Deborah C. II, 195
Atkinson, Deborah Clark II, 195
Atkinson, Dorothy II, 441
Atkinson, Dorothy III, 394
Atkinson, Dorothy III, 440
Atkinson, Dorothy VI, 154
Atkinson, Dorothy VI, 188
Atkinson, Edith I, 1043
Atkinson, Edith II, 280
Atkinson, Edith II, 301
Atkinson, Edith IV, 170
Atkinson, Edith IV, 248
Atkinson, Edith IV, 258
Atkinson, Edith IV, 923
Atkinson, Edith IV, 925
Atkinson, Edith R. II, 308
Atkinson, Edith R. II, 316
Atkinson, Edith R. II, 324
Atkinson, Edward VI, 615
Atkinson, Edward VI, 636
Atkinson, Edward VI, 873
Atkinson, Edward Haviland III, 21
Atkinson, Edwin Corlies II, 780
Atkinson, Edy IV, 170
Atkinson, Eleanor III, 394
Atkinson, Eleanor III, 440
Atkinson, Elihu I, 346
Atkinson, Elisa II, 195
Atkinson, Elisa II, 241
Atkinson, Elisa VI, 148
Atkinson, Elisa VI, 154
Atkinson, Elisa, Junior VI, 154
Atkinson, Elisa, Senior VI, 154
Atkinson, Eliza II, 194
Atkinson, Eliza II, 195
Atkinson, Eliza II, 818
Atkinson, Eliza IV, 923
Atkinson, Eliza IV, 1004
Atkinson, Eliza Ann II, 280
Atkinson, Eliza Ann II, 300
Atkinson, Eliza P. V, 892
Atkinson, Elizabeth I, 346
Atkinson, Elizabeth I, 1043
Atkinson, Elizabeth II, 140
Atkinson, Elizabeth II, 143
Atkinson, Elizabeth II, 145
Atkinson, Elizabeth II, 165
Atkinson, Elizabeth II, 194
Atkinson, Elizabeth II, 195
Atkinson, Elizabeth II, 213
Atkinson, Elizabeth II, 221
Atkinson, Elizabeth II, 235
Atkinson, Elizabeth II, 280
Atkinson, Elizabeth II, 308
Atkinson, Elizabeth II, 316
Atkinson, Elizabeth II, 333
Atkinson, Elizabeth II, 456
Atkinson, Elizabeth II, 570
Atkinson, Elizabeth II, 780
Atkinson, Elizabeth II, 975
Atkinson, Elizabeth IV, 170
Atkinson, Elizabeth IV, 923
Atkinson, Elizabeth IV, 1350
Atkinson, Elizabeth IV, 1377
Atkinson, Elizabeth VI, 936
Atkinson, Elizabeth Ann II, 456
Atkinson, Elizabeth B. II, 143
Atkinson, Elizabeth Borton II, 785
Atkinson, Elizabeth H. II, 308
Atkinson, Elizabeth H. II, 316
Atkinson, Elizabeth P. V, 892
Atkinson, Ellen F. I, 611
Atkinson, Elsie III, 21
Atkinson, Elsie III, 154
Atkinson, Emily S. II, 832
Atkinson, Emily Sharpless II, 832
Atkinson, Emma Jane IV, 170
Atkinson, Emma S. II, 833
Atkinson, Emma S. II, 876
Atkinson, Empson II, 51
Atkinson, Empson II, 103
Atkinson, Esther II, 165
Atkinson, Esther II, 194
Atkinson, Esther II, 280
Atkinson, Esther II, 801
Atkinson, Esther V, 609
Atkinson, Esther V, 642
Atkinson, Esther Ann VI, 615
Atkinson, Esther Ann VI, 695
Atkinson, Esther C. II, 140
Atkinson, Esther F. V, 609
Atkinson, Evan II, 280
Atkinson, Ezekiel II, 975
Atkinson, Ezekiel II, 997
Atkinson, Francis B. III, 394
Atkinson, Francis B. III, 440
Atkinson, Francis W. III, 154
Atkinson, Francis Whitmer III, 21
Atkinson, Francis Whitmer, Jr. III, 21
Atkinson, Frank Stanley II, 780
Atkinson, Gennet II, 975
Atkinson, Geo. IV, 923
Atkinson, George II, 145
Atkinson, George II, 280
Atkinson, George II, 316
Atkinson, George F. II, 143
Atkinson, George T. II, 143
Atkinson, George W. II, 308
Atkinson, George W. II, 316
Atkinson, George W. II, 833
Atkinson, George W. II, 937
Atkinson, Haines II, 195
Atkinson, Hannah I, 346
Atkinson, Hannah I, 372
Atkinson, Hannah I, 373
Atkinson, Hannah I, 387
Atkinson, Hannah I, 459
Atkinson, Hannah I, 473
Atkinson, Hannah II, 165
Atkinson, Hannah II, 194
Atkinson, Hannah II, 195
Atkinson, Hannah II, 226
Atkinson, Hannah II, 232
Atkinson, Hannah II, 247
Atkinson, Hannah II, 256
Atkinson, Hannah II, 258
Atkinson, Hannah II, 308
Atkinson, Hannah II, 316
Atkinson, Hannah II, 455
Atkinson, Hannah II, 456
Atkinson, Hannah II, 630
Atkinson, Hannah II, 975
Atkinson, Hannah II, 999
Atkinson, Hannah IV, 673
Atkinson, Hannah IV, 923
Atkinson, Hannah IV, 968
Atkinson, Hannah IV, 1201
Atkinson, Hannah IV, 1212
Atkinson, Hannah IV, 1213
Atkinson, Hannah V, 218
Atkinson, Hannah V, 239
Atkinson, Hannah V, 609
Atkinson, Hannah VI, 467
Atkinson, Hannah Alice V, 609
Atkinson, Hannah Ann II, 280
Atkinson, Hannah Ann II, 288
Atkinson, Hannah T. II, 780
Atkinson, Hannah T. II, 832
Atkinson, Harvey I, 372
Atkinson, Helen III, 21
Atkinson, Henry I, 346
Atkinson, Henry I, 372
Atkinson, Henry I, 1043
Atkinson, Henry II, 780
Atkinson, Henry II, 832
Atkinson, Henry IV, 923
Atkinson, Henry IV, 1016
Atkinson, Henry C. II, 833
Atkinson, Henry C. II, 876
Atkinson, Henry W. II, 195
Atkinson, Hettie Ann II, 784
Atkinson, Hope II, 194
Atkinson, Hope II, 258
Atkinson, Howard M. VI, 615
Atkinson, Hugh I, 346
Atkinson, Hugh I, 372
Atkinson, Hugh I, 373
Atkinson, Hugh I, 459
Atkinson, Hugh I, 473
Atkinson, Huldah I, 611
Atkinson, Isaac I, 1043
Atkinson, Isaac II, 441
Atkinson, Isaac II, 801
Atkinson, Isaac II, 953
Atkinson, Isaac II, 975
Atkinson, Isaac II, 1002
Atkinson, Isaac V, 150
Atkinson, Isaac V, 472
Atkinson, Isaac V, 947
Atkinson, Isaac W. V, 609
Atkinson, Isaac Wm. V, 609
Atkinson, Isabella III, 21
Atkinson, Isabella III, 218
Atkinson, Isaiah II, 280
Atkinson, Isaiah II, 308
Atkinson, Isaiah II, 316
Atkinson, Isaiah E. II, 316
Atkinson, James I, 346
Atkinson, James I, 372
Atkinson, James II, 51
Atkinson, James II, 194
Atkinson, James II, 280
Atkinson, James II, 333
Atkinson, James II, 455
Atkinson, James II, 975
Atkinson, James V, 472
Atkinson, James VI, 940
Atkinson, Jane II, 194
Atkinson, Jane II, 333
Atkinson, Jane II, 456
Atkinson, Jane II, 570
Atkinson, Jane II, 953
Atkinson, Jane II, 975
Atkinson, Jane II, 979
Atkinson, Jane II, 1039
Atkinson, Jane IV, 1271
Atkinson, Jane V, 218
Atkinson, Jane V, 472
Atkinson, Jane V, 609
Atkinson, Jane V, 947
Atkinson, Jane VI, 154
Atkinson, Jennet II, 194
Atkinson, Jennet II, 210
Atkinson, Jesse V, 472
Atkinson, Jesse V, 609
Atkinson, Jessie IV, 923
Atkinson, Jessie IV, 1016
Atkinson, Job II, 194
Atkinson, Joel II, 456
Atkinson, Joel II, 539
Atkinson, Joel II, 661
Atkinson, Joel II, 780
Atkinson, Joel II, 832
Atkinson, Joel II, 853
Atkinson, John I, 346
Atkinson, John I, 372
Atkinson, John I, 426
Atkinson, John I, 430
Atkinson, John I, 443
Atkinson, John I, 459
Atkinson, John II, 143
Atkinson, John II, 145
Atkinson, John II, 192
Atkinson, John II, 194
Atkinson, John II, 195
Atkinson, John II, 217
Atkinson, John II, 258
Atkinson, John II, 308
Atkinson, John II, 316
Atkinson, John II, 333
Atkinson, John II, 456
Atkinson, John II, 570
Atkinson, John II, 780
Atkinson, John II, 832
Atkinson, John II, 833
Atkinson, John II, 876
Atkinson, John II, 937
Atkinson, John III, 21
Atkinson, John III, 347
Atkinson, John IV, 1271
Atkinson, John V, 218
Atkinson, John V, 472
Atkinson, John V, 609
Atkinson, John V, 947
Atkinson, John VI, 97
Atkinson, John VI, 124
Atkinson, John VI, 154
Atkinson, John VI, 188
Atkinson, John Hopkins III, 21
Atkinson, John M. III, 21
Atkinson, Jonathan II, 194
Atkinson, Jonathan II, 226
Atkinson, Jonathan III, 21
Atkinson, Joseph II, 194
Atkinson, Joseph II, 210
Atkinson, Joseph II, 333
Atkinson, Joseph II, 456
Atkinson, Joseph II, 630
Atkinson, Joseph II, 953
Atkinson, Joseph II, 975
Atkinson, Joseph II, 1026
Atkinson, Joseph IV, 1271
Atkinson, Joseph V, 21
Atkinson, Joseph V, 472
Atkinson, Joseph V, 947
Atkinson, Joseph B. II, 876
Atkinson, Joseph Burr II, 780
Atkinson, Joseph Burr II, 832
Atkinson, Joseph H. V, 892
Atkinson, Joseph Hendrickson V, 892
Atkinson, Joseph M. II, 832
Atkinson, Joseph Middleton II, 780
Atkinson, Joshua I, 372
Atkinson, Joshua VI, 924
Atkinson, Joshua VI, 978
Atkinson, Joshua VI, 985
Atkinson, Joshua Reeve II, 51
Atkinson, Josiah VI, 615
Atkinson, Josiah VI, 695
Atkinson, Kesiah II, 194
Atkinson, Kesiah II, 308
Atkinson, Kezia II, 280
Atkinson, Keziah II, 194
Atkinson, Keziah IV, 170
Atkinson, Keziah IV, 198
Atkinson, Laura II, 780
Atkinson, Leah II, 194
Atkinson, Lee W. IV, 923
Atkinson, Levi IV, 1271
Atkinson, Levi V, 150
Atkinson, Levi V, 472
Atkinson, Levi V, 609
Atkinson, Levi V, 947
Atkinson, Lititia II, 975
Atkinson, Lititia II, 977
Atkinson, Louisa D. VI, 51
Atkinson, Louisa D. VI, 89
Atkinson, Louise III, 21
Atkinson, Louise III, 218
Atkinson, Lydia I, 346
Atkinson, Lydia I, 459
Atkinson, Lydia I, 473
Atkinson, Lydia II, 456
Atkinson, Lydia II, 780
Atkinson, Lydia V, 472
Atkinson, Lydia V, 520
Atkinson, Lydia V, 609
Atkinson, Lydia V, 947
Atkinson, Lydia Ann II, 832
Atkinson, Lydia Ann II, 878
Atkinson, Lydia S. II, 832
Atkinson, Lydia S. II, 937
Atkinson, Lydia Sharpless II, 832
Atkinson, Lydia T. II, 788
Atkinson, Mabel L. IV, 923
Atkinson, Mahlon II, 51
Atkinson, Mahlon II, 100
Atkinson, Mahlon II, 165
Atkinson, Mahlon II, 456
Atkinson, Malinda IV, 914
Atkinson, Margaret II, 194
Atkinson, Margaret II, 953
Atkinson, Margaret II, 975
Atkinson, Margaret IV, 1271
Atkinson, Margaret IV, 1282
Atkinson, Margaret V, 472
Atkinson, Margaret V, 520
Atkinson, Margaret V, 892
Atkinson, Margaret V, 947
Atkinson, Margaretta II, 833
Atkinson, Margret II, 333
Atkinson, Maria IV, 673
Atkinson, Maria IV, 765
Atkinson, Maria IV, 923
Atkinson, Maria IV, 944
Atkinson, Maria IV, 968
Atkinson, Maria IV, 981
Atkinson, Maria IV, 1004
Atkinson, Martha I, 1043
Atkinson, Martha II, 194
Atkinson, Martha II, 206
Atkinson, Martha II, 456
Atkinson, Martha V, 21
Atkinson, Martha VI, 97
Atkinson, Martha VI, 104
Atkinson, Martha Rekestraw II, 456
Atkinson, Mary I, 346

Atkinson, Mary I, 372
Atkinson, Mary I, 430
Atkinson, Mary I, 443
Atkinson, Mary I, 445
Atkinson, Mary I, 459
Atkinson, Mary II, 165
Atkinson, Mary II, 194
Atkinson, Mary II, 195
Atkinson, Mary II, 226
Atkinson, Mary II, 250
Atkinson, Mary II, 265
Atkinson, Mary II, 267
Atkinson, Mary II, 270
Atkinson, Mary II, 314
Atkinson, Mary II, 333
Atkinson, Mary II, 456
Atkinson, Mary II, 780
Atkinson, Mary II, 832
Atkinson, Mary II, 876
Atkinson, Mary II, 953
Atkinson, Mary II, 975
Atkinson, Mary II, 1002
Atkinson, Mary IV, 139
Atkinson, Mary IV, 170
Atkinson, Mary IV, 177
Atkinson, Mary IV, 212
Atkinson, Mary IV, 923
Atkinson, Mary IV, 975
Atkinson, Mary V, 21
Atkinson, Mary VI, 729
Atkinson, Mary Alice IV, 923
Atkinson, Mary Ann II, 115
Atkinson, Mary Ann II, 118
Atkinson, Mary Ann II, 195
Atkinson, Mary Ann II, 280
Atkinson, Mary Ann II, 308
Atkinson, Mary Ann II, 316
Atkinson, Mary Ann IV, 170
Atkinson, Mary Jane II, 833
Atkinson, Mary M. V, 609
Atkinson, Mary S. II, 832
Atkinson, Mary, Jr. I, 443
Atkinson, Matilda IV, 923
Atkinson, Melinda IV, 899
Atkinson, Michael II, 194
Atkinson, Michal II, 194
Atkinson, Michal II, 258
Atkinson, Miles K. II, 308
Atkinson, Miles K. II, 316
Atkinson, Mills IV, 1271
Atkinson, Mills V, 947
Atkinson, Minnie II, 309
Atkinson, Moses IV, 1377
Atkinson, Moses V, 472
Atkinson, Nancy V, 947
Atkinson, Nancy VI, 857
Atkinson, Nanny IV, 170
Atkinson, Nanny IV, 287
Atkinson, Nanny IV, 364
Atkinson, Nathan I, 1043
Atkinson, Nathan II, 456
Atkinson, Nathan Atherton II, 456
Atkinson, Nellie V, 21
Atkinson, Patience II, 194
Atkinson, Patience II, 209
Atkinson, Phinias II, 456
Atkinson, Priscilla VI, 615
Atkinson, Priscilla VI, 695
Atkinson, Rachel I, 1043
Atkinson, Rachel II, 194
Atkinson, Rachel II, 195
Atkinson, Rachel II, 280
Atkinson, Rachel II, 308
Atkinson, Rachel II, 451
Atkinson, Rachel II, 455
Atkinson, Rachel II, 647
Atkinson, Rachel II, 780
Atkinson, Rachel II, 832
Atkinson, Rachel II, 953
Atkinson, Rachel II, 975
Atkinson, Rachel II, 993
Atkinson, Rachel II, 997
Atkinson, Rachel II, 1029
Atkinson, Rachel IV, 170
Atkinson, Rachel IV, 171
Atkinson, Rachel IV, 257
Atkinson, Rachel IV, 364
Atkinson, Rachel IV, 456
Atkinson, Rachel IV, 673
Atkinson, Rachel IV, 695
Atkinson, Rachel IV, 923
Atkinson, Rachel IV, 944
Atkinson, Rachel A. II, 316
Atkinson, Rachel M. IV, 170
Atkinson, Rachel M. IV, 221
Atkinson, Rachel S. II, 832
Atkinson, Rachel W. II, 316
Atkinson, Rachel W. II, 324
Atkinson, Rebecca I, 372
Atkinson, Rebecca I, 399
Atkinson, Rebecca II, 195
Atkinson, Rebecca II, 456
Atkinson, Rebecca II, 483
Atkinson, Rebecca II, 780
Atkinson, Rebecca II, 832
Atkinson, Rebecca II, 853
Atkinson, Rebecca II, 953
Atkinson, Rebecca II, 975
Atkinson, Rebecca II, 1003
Atkinson, Rebecca IV, 463
Atkinson, Rebecca IV, 502
Atkinson, Rebecca IV, 923
Atkinson, Rebecca IV, 1016
Atkinson, Rebecca VI, 558
Atkinson, Rebecca A. IV, 710
Atkinson, Rebecca A. VI, 467
Atkinson, Rebecca A. VI, 558
Atkinson, Rebecca M. II, 832
Atkinson, Rebecca Middleton II, 780
Atkinson, Rebecca S. II, 195
Atkinson, Rebecca W. IV, 170
Atkinson, Rebecca W. IV, 204
Atkinson, Rebecca W. IV, 364
Atkinson, Rebecca W. IV, 394
Atkinson, Reuben VI, 985
Atkinson, Reuben VI, 1014
Atkinson, Reuben Watkins VI, 129
Atkinson, Rhoda VI, 924
Atkinson, Richard II, 51
Atkinson, Robert I, 346
Atkinson, Robert I, 372
Atkinson, Robert I, 443
Atkinson, Robert I, 445
Atkinson, Robert II, 165
Atkinson, Robert II, 195
Atkinson, Robert II, 456
Atkinson, Robert IV, 673
Atkinson, Robert V, 472
Atkinson, Robert VI, 97
Atkinson, Robert VI, 104
Atkinson, Robert VI, 154
Atkinson, Robert E. VI, 615
Atkinson, Robert Edward VI, 615
Atkinson, Robert Edward VI, 636
Atkinson, Robert, Sr. VI, 188
Atkinson, Roger VI, 154
Atkinson, Ruth I, 346
Atkinson, Ruth I, 372
Atkinson, Ruth I, 420
Atkinson, Ruth I, 1043
Atkinson, Ruth IV, 170
Atkinson, Ruth IV, 253
Atkinson, Ruth IV, 258
Atkinson, Ruth IV, 1271
Atkinson, Ruth V, 947
Atkinson, Ruth Eleanor VI, 729
Atkinson, Sabilla IV, 364
Atkinson, Sabilla Smith IV, 377
Atkinson, Samuel I, 346
Atkinson, Samuel I, 372
Atkinson, Samuel I, 399
Atkinson, Samuel I, 1026
Atkinson, Samuel I, 1047
Atkinson, Samuel II, 165
Atkinson, Samuel II, 194
Atkinson, Samuel II, 226
Atkinson, Samuel II, 456
Atkinson, Samuel II, 953
Atkinson, Samuel II, 975
Atkinson, Samuel IV, 673
Atkinson, Samuel C. II, 195
Atkinson, Samuel C. II, 456
Atkinson, Samuel Clark II, 832
Atkinson, Samuel Doan II, 975
Atkinson, Samuel, Jr. II, 194
Atkinson, Sarah I, 346
Atkinson, Sarah I, 372
Atkinson, Sarah I, 412
Atkinson, Sarah II, 51
Atkinson, Sarah II, 65
Atkinson, Sarah II, 100
Atkinson, Sarah II, 103
Atkinson, Sarah II, 115
Atkinson, Sarah II, 194
Atkinson, Sarah II, 195
Atkinson, Sarah II, 241
Atkinson, Sarah II, 256
Atkinson, Sarah II, 267
Atkinson, Sarah II, 280
Atkinson, Sarah II, 308
Atkinson, Sarah II, 314
Atkinson, Sarah II, 316
Atkinson, Sarah II, 327
Atkinson, Sarah II, 455
Atkinson, Sarah II, 456
Atkinson, Sarah II, 616
Atkinson, Sarah II, 953
Atkinson, Sarah II, 975
Atkinson, Sarah II, 1002
Atkinson, Sarah II, 1026
Atkinson, Sarah IV, 609
Atkinson, Sarah IV, 622
Atkinson, Sarah IV, 673
Atkinson, Sarah IV, 742
Atkinson, Sarah IV, 923
Atkinson, Sarah IV, 981
Atkinson, Sarah IV, 1035
Atkinson, Sarah IV, 1087
Atkinson, Sarah IV, 1377
Atkinson, Sarah VI, 978
Atkinson, Sarah A. II, 832
Atkinson, Sarah A. II, 853
Atkinson, Sarah Allinson II, 780
Atkinson, Sarah B. II, 280
Atkinson, Sarah C. II, 195
Atkinson, Sarah H. VI, 615
Atkinson, Sarah J. IV, 923
Atkinson, Sarah Jane V, 609
Atkinson, Sarah W. II, 316
Atkinson, Sophia VI, 985
Atkinson, Susan Jane VI, 873
Atkinson, Susanna II, 456
Atkinson, Susanna V, 472
Atkinson, Susannah II, 192
Atkinson, Susannah II, 194
Atkinson, Susannah II, 217
Atkinson, Susannah II, 258
Atkinson, Susannah II, 456
Atkinson, Susannah II, 630
Atkinson, Susannah V, 472
Atkinson, Susannah V, 609
Atkinson, T. IV, 170
Atkinson, Temple V, 609
Atkinson, Thadeus V, 984
Atkinson, Theodosia II, 308
Atkinson, Theodosia II, 316
Atkinson, Theophilus Morlan IV, 673
Atkinson, Thomas I, 346
Atkinson, Thomas I, 372
Atkinson, Thomas I, 1043
Atkinson, Thomas II, 194
Atkinson, Thomas II, 195
Atkinson, Thomas II, 258
Atkinson, Thomas II, 280
Atkinson, Thomas II, 441
Atkinson, Thomas II, 456
Atkinson, Thomas II, 630
Atkinson, Thomas II, 953
Atkinson, Thomas IV, 139
Atkinson, Thomas IV, 170
Atkinson, Thomas IV, 364
Atkinson, Thomas IV, 1271
Atkinson, Thomas V, 472
Atkinson, Thomas V, 609
Atkinson, Thomas VI, 154
Atkinson, Thomas VI, 183
Atkinson, Thomas VI, 939
Atkinson, Thomas VI, 984
Atkinson, Thomas E. IV, 170
Atkinson, Thomas F. IV, 1271
Atkinson, Thomas L. V, 218
Atkinson, Thomas L. V, 609
Atkinson, Thos. IV, 170
Atkinson, Thos. V, 947
Atkinson, Thos. VI, 936
Atkinson, Thos. C. II, 832
Atkinson, Walter II, 780
Atkinson, Warner II, 165
Atkinson, Warner II, 195
Atkinson, Warner IV, 673
Atkinson, Warner IV, 765
Atkinson, Warner IV, 923
Atkinson, Warner IV, 944
Atkinson, Warner IV, 968
Atkinson, Warner IV, 981
Atkinson, Warner IV, 1004
Atkinson, Wd. Ann II, 780
Atkinson, Wd. Hannah II, 333
Atkinson, Wd. Sarah II, 165
Atkinson, Wd. Sarah II, 1043
Atkinson, Wd. Susanna II, 456
Atkinson, Wd. Susanna II, 630
Atkinson, William I, 346
Atkinson, William I, 1043
Atkinson, William II, 194
Atkinson, William II, 210
Atkinson, William II, 213
Atkinson, William II, 258
Atkinson, William II, 280
Atkinson, William II, 333
Atkinson, William II, 953
Atkinson, William IV, 170
Atkinson, William IV, 258
Atkinson, William IV, 364
Atkinson, William IV, 1271
Atkinson, William V, 472
Atkinson, William V, 609
Atkinson, William VI, 129
Atkinson, William VI, 143
Atkinson, William E. II, 316
Atkinson, William H. I, 611
Atkinson, William, Jr. II, 953
Atkinson, Wilson VI, 985
Atkinson, Wm Corlies II, 780
Atkinson, Wm. II, 455
Atkinson, Wm. II, 456
Atkinson, Wm. II, 483
Atkinson, Wm. II, 616
Atkinson, Wm. II, 647
Atkinson, Wm. II, 975
Atkinson, Wm. II, 1002
Atkinson, Wm. II, 1029
Atkinson, Wm. IV, 204
Atkinson, Wm. IV, 221
Atkinson, Wm. IV, 287
Atkinson, Wm. IV, 710
Atkinson, Wm. IV, 1271
Atkinson, Wm. V, 947
Atkinson, Wm. VI, 188
Atkinson, Wm. H. II, 832
Atkinson, Wm. Hill II, 832
Atkison, Dieney VI, 873
Atkison, Kesiah II, 194
Atkison, Kesiah II, 210
Atkison, Washington VI, 873
Atkisson, Burwell VI, 873
Atkisson, Dieney VI, 873
Atkisson, Elizabeth B. II, 143
Atkisson, Ellen VI, 227
Atkisson, George T. II, 143
Atkisson, Hector VI, 829
Atkisson, Huldah I, 629
Atkisson, Huldah I, 637
Atkisson, Huldah VI, 227
Atkisson, Huldah Minthorn VI, 227
Atkisson, Murlin VI, 227
Atkisson, Nancy VI, 873
Atkisson, Polly VI, 829
Atkisson, Samuel VI, 873
Atkisson, Washington VI, 873
Atkisson, William I, 629
Atkisson, William VI, 227
Atkisson, William VI, 829
Atkisson, William H. I, 629
Atkisson, William H. I, 637
Atkisson, William Henry I, 629
Atkisson, William Henry VI, 227
Atkyson, Elisabeth VI, 955
Atkyson, John VI, 955
Atlee, Alfred J. II, 833
Atlee, Alfred Jessup II, 780
Atlee, Anna II, 780
Atlee, Anna II, 833
Atlee, Anna II, 838
Atlee, Annie L. II, 780
Atlee, Caroline II, 780
Atlee, Caroline II, 790
Atlee, Caroline II, 833
Atlee, Charles II, 780
Atlee, Charlotte White V, 892
Atlee, Clara II, 780
Atlee, Clara II, 833
Atlee, Clara II, 838
Atlee, Dr. Edwin P. II, 806
Atlee, Edith W. II, 833
Atlee, Edith Willits II, 780
Atlee, Edwin V, 892
Atlee, Edwin A. II, 780
Atlee, Edwin A. II, 833
Atlee, Edwin A. V, 892
Atlee, Edwin Anthony II, 780
Atlee, Edwin Augustus II, 780
Atlee, Edwin I. II, 833
Atlee, Edwin J. II, 833
Atlee, Edwin P. II, 833
Atlee, Edwin Pitt II, 780
Atlee, Eliza II, 1068
Atlee, Eliza II, 1083
Atlee, Eliza W. II, 828
Atlee, Eliza W. II, 833
Atlee, Elizabeth Jane V, 892
Atlee, George B. II, 780
Atlee, George B. II, 833
Atlee, George B. II, 838
Atlee, Hannah Bullock II, 780
Atlee, Joshua II, 780
Atlee, Joshua II, 833
Atlee, Joshua Woolston II, 833
Atlee, Joshua Woolston II, 838
Atlee, Margaret II, 780
Atlee, Margaret II, 833
Atlee, Margaret V, 892
Atlee, Margaret C. II, 833
Atlee, Margaret Collins II, 780
Atlee, Margaret S. V, 892
Atlee, Margaret, Sr. II, 833
Atlee, Margaret, Sr. V, 892
Atlee, Martaret V, 892
Atlee, Richard J. V, 892
Atlee, Richard Jordan II, 726
Atlee, Richard Jordon V, 892
Atlee, Sarah Jane II, 780
Atlee, Sarah T. II, 833
Atlee, Thomas Scattergood V, 892
Atlee, Thos. Scattergood V, 892
Atlee, Wd. Margaret Bullock II, 806
Atley, Ada V, 984
Atlie, Elizabeth III, 191
Atmore, Ann II, 195
Atmore, Ann II, 456
Atmore, Caleb I, 35
Atmore, Caleb II, 195
Atmore, Caleb II, 456
Atmore, Elizabeth II, 456
Atmore, Isaac I, 35
Atmore, Isaac I, 78
Atmore, Isaac II, 333
Atmore, Isaac II, 456
Atmore, Jonathan II, 333
Atmore, Jonathan II, 456
Atmore, Margaret I, 35
Atmore, Margaret I, 78
Atmore, Margaret II, 456
Atmore, Marshall II, 456
Atmore, Mary II, 456
Atmore, Rachel II, 456
Atmore, Samuel II, 333
Atmore, Sarah II, 333
Atmore, Thomas II, 333
Atmore, Thomas II, 456
Atmore, Wd. Margaret II, 456
Atmore, William II, 333
Atmore, Wm. II, 456
Atterbury, Cath. B. III, 83
Atterbury, Hudson III, 21
Atterbury, James III, 21
Attic, Lillie V, 726
Attmore, Ann II, 195
Attmore, Ann II, 239
Attmore, Ann II, 333
Attmore, Ann II, 639
Attmore, Caleb I, 35
Attmore, Caleb II, 239
Attmore, Caleb II, 333
Attmore, Caleb II, 456
Attmore, Caleb II, 639
Attmore, Elizabeth II, 333
Attmore, Elizabeth II, 456
Attmore, Elizabeth II, 594
Attmore, Hannah III, 171
Attmore, Isaac II, 333
Attmore, Jonathan II, 333
Attmore, Jonathan II, 456
Attmore, Jonathan II, 594
Attmore, Margaret II, 546
Attmore, Marshall II, 456
Attmore, Marshall II, 698
Attmore, Mary II, 333
Attmore, Mary II, 456
Attmore, Mary II, 639
Attmore, Mary II, 662
Attmore, Rachel II, 456
Attmore, Rachel II, 594
Attmore, Samuel II, 333
Attmore, Sarah II, 333
Attmore, Thomas II, 333
Attmore, Thomas II, 456
Attmore, Thomas II, 662
Attmore, Wd. Margaret II, 456
Attmore, William II, 333
Attmore, Wm. II, 456
Attmore, Wm. II, 662
Atwaide, Hester III, 132
Atwater, Bertha A. IV, 615
Atwater, Harriet H. III, 21
Atwater, Harriet H. III, 62
Atwater, Jane Louisa III, 62
Atwater, Jane Louise III, 21
Atwater, Jane Louse III, 21
Atwater, Jeremiah W. III, 21
Atwater, Jeremiah W. III, 62
Atwater, Levi H. IV, 615
Atwater, Louisa C. III, 21
Atwater, Mary M. IV, 615
Atwater, Samuel IV, 615
Atwater, Sarah E. IV, 1201
Atwater, Wm. C. III, 21
Atwater, Wm. C. III, 62
Atwood, Ann I, 1
Atwood, Ann I, 35
Atwood, Ann I, 64
Atwood, Ann II, 333
Atwood, Clarence C. IV, 171
Atwood, Hazel IV, 171
Atwood, Lillian IV, 171
Atwood, William II, 333
Atwood, Wm. II, 456
Atyea, Vernor IV, 1233
Audi, Aneesie III, 22

Audi, Badeah III, 22
Augburn, Eliza B. V, 548
Augburn, Henry Marshal V, 548
Augburn, Isaac Samuel V, 548
Augsbarger, Amy Ann V, 825
Augsbarger, Elijah V, 825
Augsbarger, Jane V, 825
Augsbarger, Jennie L. V, 825
Augspurger, Jennie L. V, 825
Augustine, Joseph III, 22
Augustine, Joseph III, 216
Augustine, Louisa III, 22
Augustine, Louisa III, 216
Augustus, Fred'k III, 283
Augustus, George III, 202
Auker, Ella IV, 1201
Auld, Eva M. III, 343
Auld, Josiah VI, 990
Auld, Lee IV, 171
Auldey, Sally VI, 880
Ault, Amy IV, 171
Ault, Amy IV, 311
Ault, Anna V, 451
Ault, Charles IV, 1201
Ault, Clarence IV, 1201
Ault, Elizabeth V, 451
Ault, Fernanda IV, 1201
Ault, Lydia IV, 1201
Ault, M. F. IV, 1201
Ault, Mamie Bell IV, 1201
Ault, Marion IV, 1201
Ault, Noah IV, 1201
Ault, Paul IV, 1201
Ault, Rosa IV, 171
Auman, Arlige C. I, 937
Aunspaugh, Caroline VI, 1016
Aunspaugh, Daniel VI, 932
Aunspaugh, Daniel VI, 952
Aunspaugh, Daniel VI, 956
Aunspaugh, Daniel VI, 1022
Aunspaugh, Danl. VI, 914
Aunspaugh, Elizabeth VI, 873
Aunspaugh, Fred E. VI, 912
Aunspaugh, Frederick VI, 873
Aunspaugh, Lucy VI, 912
Aunspaugh, Peter F. VI, 911
Aunspaugh, Peter F. VI, 999
Aunspaugh, Reuben Parker VI, 873
Aurens, Emma II, 717
Ausbarger, ??? V, 834
Ausbarger, Jane V, 834
Ausborn, Matthew I, 452
Auspaugh, Elizabeth VI, 1003
Auspaugh, Frederick VI, 1003
Austen, Edward II, 333
Austen, Mary II, 333
Austen, Samuel II, 333
Austen, Thomas II, 333
Austill, Joseph II, 456
Austin, Abram VI, 874
Austin, Abram VI, 937
Austin, Adeline VI, 818
Austin, America VI, 874
Austin, Amos II, 165
Austin, Amos II, 166
Austin, Amos II, 195
Austin, Amos II, 225
Austin, Amos II, 280
Austin, Ann VI, 870
Austin, Ann Elizabeth VI, 874
Austin, Baby IV, 1306
Austin, Behethaland VI, 971
Austin, Benjamin I, 1075
Austin, Benjamin II, 333
Austin, Beulah Ann II, 280
Austin, Beulah Ann II, 300
Austin, Caleb IV, 1269
Austin, Catherine VI, 797
Austin, Chapman VI, 154
Austin, Chapman VI, 187
Austin, Charlotte VI, 898
Austin, Chas. IV, 1306
Austin, Chas. R. IV, 1305
Austin, Clarkson II, 136
Austin, Constance VI, 831
Austin, Dr. G. M. V, 656
Austin, Dr. J. M. V, 656
Austin, Dr. William VI, 796
Austin, Edw. B. III, 435
Austin, Edward II, 127
Austin, Edward II, 333
Austin, Edward II, 456
Austin, Edward B. III, 435
Austin, Elisabeth II, 456
Austin, Eliza Ann VI, 1014
Austin, Eliza L. VI, 881
Austin, Elizabeth II, 195
Austin, Elizabeth II, 227
Austin, Elizabeth II, 280
Austin, Elizabeth V, 656
Austin, Elizabeth V, 704
Austin, Elizabeth VI, 797
Austin, Elizabeth VI, 910
Austin, Elma V, 656
Austin, Esther VI, 869
Austin, Esther VI, 873
Austin, Esther VI, 982
Austin, Faith V, 656
Austin, Fanny VI, 873
Austin, Francis II, 166
Austin, Francis II, 195
Austin, Francis II, 279
Austin, Francis II, 280
Austin, Francis, Jr. II, 195
Austin, G. M. V, 656
Austin, Grace III, 435
Austin, H. G. IV, 1143
Austin, H. J. IV, 1143
Austin, Hannah II, 456
Austin, Hannah IV, 891
Austin, Hannah IV, 892
Austin, Henrietta II, 833
Austin, Henrietta T. II, 833
Austin, Henrietta T. II, 857
Austin, Henrietta Troth II, 791
Austin, Isaac V, 21
Austin, Isaac D. V, 21
Austin, James II, 456
Austin, James IV, 891
Austin, James IV, 892
Austin, James V, 150
Austin, James V, 892
Austin, James VI, 797
Austin, James VI, 858
Austin, James VI, 910
Austin, James E. V, 150
Austin, James H. VI, 964
Austin, John II, 333
Austin, John II, 456
Austin, John II, 565
Austin, John VI, 873
Austin, John B. V, 656
Austin, John M. VI, 874
Austin, John T. VI, 796
Austin, Jonas VI, 931
Austin, Joshua V, 21
Austin, Lena V, 656
Austin, Lena V, 714
Austin, Lidia II, 50
Austin, Lidia II, 51
Austin, Lidya II, 50
Austin, Lidya II, 51
Austin, Lockey VI, 797
Austin, Luckey VI, 854
Austin, Lucy Ann V, 21
Austin, Lucy Ann C. V, 21
Austin, Lucy T. III, 435
Austin, Lulu V, 656
Austin, Lulu V, 695
Austin, Lydia II, 20
Austin, Lydia II, 127
Austin, Lydia II, 456
Austin, Lydia II, 616
Austin, Lydia V, 892
Austin, Lydia A. V, 218
Austin, Lydia A. V, 451
Austin, Marietta III, 223
Austin, Martha II, 456
Austin, Martha VI, 937
Austin, Martha N. VI, 797
Austin, Mary II, 166
Austin, Mary II, 195
Austin, Mary II, 269
Austin, Mary II, 280
Austin, Mary II, 305
Austin, Mary II, 333
Austin, Mary II, 456
Austin, Mary II, 460
Austin, Mary II, 565
Austin, Mary II, 833
Austin, Mary V, 548
Austin, Mary V, 593
Austin, Mary V, 656
Austin, Mary VI, 924
Austin, Mary Ann II, 136
Austin, Mary Augusta II, 136
Austin, Mary Berry II, 780
Austin, Mary Berry II, 791
Austin, Mary E. VI, 979
Austin, Mary S. VI, 874
Austin, Miles VI, 797
Austin, Moses VI, 924
Austin, Moses VI, 931
Austin, Moses VI, 961
Austin, Mourning VI, 797
Austin, Nancy VI, 797
Austin, Nancy VI, 873
Austin, Nancy VI, 931
Austin, Nancy A. VI, 1016
Austin, Nicholas II, 333
Austin, Nicholas II, 456
Austin, Nicholas II, 487
Austin, Olive E. V, 451
Austin, Pamelia VI, 858
Austin, Peter VI, 873
Austin, Polly VI, 838
Austin, Priscilla V, 21
Austin, Prudence V, 21
Austin, Rachel II, 166
Austin, Rachel II, 195
Austin, Rachel II, 280
Austin, Rachel V, 21
Austin, Rachel V, 39
Austin, Rachel V, 64
Austin, Rachel G. III, 22
Austin, Rebecca II, 166
Austin, Rebecca II, 279
Austin, Rebecca II, 280
Austin, Rebecca II, 780
Austin, Rebecca V, 21
Austin, Rebecca V, 48
Austin, Richard II, 780
Austin, Richard VI, 797
Austin, Richard VI, 873
Austin, Richard VI, 931
Austin, Robert VI, 806
Austin, Robert VI, 898
Austin, Robert A. VI, 874
Austin, Robert A. VI, 1014
Austin, Ruth V, 372
Austin, Sally VI, 873
Austin, Sally VI, 980
Austin, Sally Ann II, 833
Austin, Samantha V, 656
Austin, Samantha L. V, 548
Austin, Samuel II, 20
Austin, Samuel II, 50
Austin, Samuel II, 51
Austin, Samuel II, 127
Austin, Samuel II, 333
Austin, Samuel II, 456
Austin, Samuel II, 565
Austin, Samuel, Jr. II, 51
Austin, Sarah II, 20
Austin, Sarah II, 50
Austin, Sarah II, 51
Austin, Sarah II, 127
Austin, Sarah II, 165
Austin, Sarah II, 166
Austin, Sarah II, 195
Austin, Sarah II, 225
Austin, Sarah II, 833
Austin, Sarah II, 834
Austin, Sarah VI, 797
Austin, Sarah VI, 873
Austin, Sarah P. II, 316
Austin, Sarah P. II, 324
Austin, Septimus II, 333
Austin, Simeon VI, 831
Austin, Simson VI, 824
Austin, Susan II, 316
Austin, Susan VI, 796
Austin, Susan N. VI, 874
Austin, Susanna II, 316
Austin, Susanna II, 456
Austin, Susanna II, 487
Austin, Thomas II, 165
Austin, Thomas II, 333
Austin, Thomas VI, 869
Austin, Thomas VI, 873
Austin, Thomas VI, 971
Austin, Thomas VI, 980
Austin, Thomas VI, 1016
Austin, Thomas E. VI, 979
Austin, Thomas W. II, 280
Austin, Thos. W. VI, 797
Austin, Turza H. VI, 797
Austin, Wd. Jane II, 333
Austin, William II, 333
Austin, William VI, 797
Austin, William VI, 870
Austin, William VI, 873
Austin, William N. VI, 873
Austin, William N. VI, 979
Austin, Wilmerton II, 166
Austin, Wm Kersey Austin II, 780
Austin, Wm. II, 136
Austin, Wm. Kersey II, 791
Austin, Wm. N. VI, 1014
Austin, Wm. N. VI, 1016
Austin, Wm. W. VI, 898
Avenport, Eliz. D. III, 65
Averet, James H. VI, 797
Averet, Mary King VI, 797
Averett, Mary K. VI, 855
Averett, William B. VI, 831
Averill, Elmina L. III, 479
Averill, Gulia III, 479
Averill, Julia M. III, 479
Averill, Sidney III, 479
Averill, Willis P. III, 479
Averitt, Elissif C. VI, 874
Averitt, Lewis H. VI, 874
Avery, Amanda III, 285
Avery, Amanda III, 294
Avery, Carrie IV, 1306
Avery, Carrie G. IV, 1306
Avery, Hannah II, 195
Avery, John II, 780
Avery, Mary Ivins II, 780
Avery, Mary W. II, 833
Avery, Mary W. II, 1068
Avery, Sarah II, 195
Avery, Stephen II, 780
Avery, Wd. Mary II, 780
Avey, Mrs. ??? VI, 919
Avice, Mary IV, 454
Avis, Mehitabel I, 236
Avis, Peninah I, 35
Avis, Peninah I, 46
Avondale, Henrietta II, 887
Avory, John I, 35
Axaline, Clyde V, 372
Axaline, Clyde V, 892
Axaline, Homer V, 372
Axaline, Moreton Homer V, 892
Axaline, Rachel V, 372
Axaline, Rachel A. V, 372
Axaline, Rachel A. V, 892
Axhuff, Josiah VI, 874
Axhuff, Rebeckah VI, 874
Axhuft, Josiah VI, 873
Axhuft, Rebeckah VI, 873
Ayars, Cornelia II, 129
Ayars, Ella II, 127
Ayars, Ella D. II, 160
Ayars, Ella Finlaw II, 128
Ayars, George II, 129
Ayars, Helen Elizabeth II, 128
Ayars, Helen Elizabeth II, 160
Ayars, Maurice B. II, 127
Ayars, Maurice B. II, 160
Ayars, Maurice Waddington II, 128
Ayars, Nella G. II, 128
Ayars, Nella G. II, 129
Ayars, Wm. Finlaw II, 143
Ayars, Wm. Finlaw II, 160
Ayars, Wm. Finlaw, Jr. II, 128
Aycock, Mary I, 299
Aycock, Mary I, 317
Aydlet, Rebecca I, 523
Aydlott, Jemmima I, 523
Aydlott, Rebecca I, 523
Aydlott, Rebeckah I, 600
Aydlott, Rebeckah I, 605
Ayers, Alce I, 870
Ayers, Alice I, 870
Ayers, Amy IV, 1350
Ayers, Andrew IV, 1143
Ayers, Anna IV, 1245
Ayers, Anna A. II, 854
Ayers, Annie E. IV, 1245
Ayers, Arthur G. V, 656
Ayers, Arthur G. V, 659
Ayers, Betsey VI, 874
Ayers, Charles IV, 1245
Ayers, David IV, 1350
Ayers, Denitia VI, 992
Ayers, Easter VI, 931
Ayers, Elijah VI, 874
Ayers, Elizabeth IV, 1350
Ayers, Elizabeth A. VI, 874
Ayers, Elizabeth A. VI, 992
Ayers, Ella D. II, 143
Ayers, Ella Finlaw II, 143
Ayers, Elme J. VI, 874
Ayers, Emanuel W. VI, 874
Ayers, Florence S. V, 656
Ayers, Florence S. V, 692
Ayers, Gincy VI, 874
Ayers, Guylla I, 870
Ayers, Guylla I, 890
Ayers, Hannah VI, 920
Ayers, Hannah VI, 934
Ayers, Helen Elizabeth II, 143
Ayers, Helen W. II, 143
Ayers, Henrietta VI, 874
Ayers, James VI, 874
Ayers, James VI, 934
Ayers, James W. VI, 874
Ayers, James, Sr. VI, 931
Ayers, Job IV, 1350
Ayers, Joel I, 935
Ayers, John IV, 1143
Ayers, John IV, 1350
Ayers, John VI, 869
Ayers, John VI, 870
Ayers, John VI, 871
Ayers, John VI, 872
Ayers, John VI, 875
Ayers, John VI, 876
Ayers, John VI, 877
Ayers, John VI, 878
Ayers, John VI, 879
Ayers, John VI, 880
Ayers, John VI, 881
Ayers, John VI, 882
Ayers, John VI, 884
Ayers, John VI, 886
Ayers, John VI, 887
Ayers, John VI, 888
Ayers, John VI, 889
Ayers, John VI, 890
Ayers, John VI, 891
Ayers, John VI, 892
Ayers, John VI, 894
Ayers, John VI, 895
Ayers, John VI, 896
Ayers, John VI, 897
Ayers, John VI, 900
Ayers, John VI, 901
Ayers, John VI, 902
Ayers, John VI, 903
Ayers, John VI, 906
Ayers, John VI, 907
Ayers, John VI, 908
Ayers, John VI, 909
Ayers, John VI, 911
Ayers, John VI, 912
Ayers, John VI, 914
Ayers, John VI, 915
Ayers, John VI, 917
Ayers, John VI, 919
Ayers, John VI, 920
Ayers, John VI, 921
Ayers, John VI, 922
Ayers, John VI, 924
Ayers, John VI, 925
Ayers, John VI, 926
Ayers, John VI, 927
Ayers, John VI, 929
Ayers, John VI, 930
Ayers, John VI, 931
Ayers, John VI, 932
Ayers, John VI, 933
Ayers, John VI, 934
Ayers, John VI, 935
Ayers, John VI, 936
Ayers, John VI, 937
Ayers, John VI, 938
Ayers, John VI, 939
Ayers, John VI, 941
Ayers, John VI, 942
Ayers, John VI, 943
Ayers, John VI, 944
Ayers, John VI, 945
Ayers, John VI, 946
Ayers, John VI, 947
Ayers, John VI, 948
Ayers, John VI, 949
Ayers, John VI, 952
Ayers, John VI, 953
Ayers, John VI, 954
Ayers, John VI, 956
Ayers, John VI, 957
Ayers, John VI, 958
Ayers, John VI, 959
Ayers, John VI, 960
Ayers, John VI, 961
Ayers, John VI, 962
Ayers, John VI, 963
Ayers, John VI, 964
Ayers, John VI, 965
Ayers, John VI, 966
Ayers, John VI, 967
Ayers, John VI, 968
Ayers, John VI, 969
Ayers, John VI, 971
Ayers, John VI, 972
Ayers, John VI, 973
Ayers, John VI, 977
Ayers, John VI, 978
Ayers, John VI, 980
Ayers, John VI, 981
Ayers, John VI, 982
Ayers, John VI, 984
Ayers, John VI, 985
Ayers, John VI, 986
Ayers, John VI, 987
Ayers, John VI, 988
Ayers, John VI, 989
Ayers, John VI, 990
Ayers, John VI, 991
Ayers, John VI, 993
Ayers, John VI, 995
Ayers, John VI, 996
Ayers, John VI, 998
Ayers, John VI, 1000
Ayers, John VI, 1001
Ayers, John VI, 1002
Ayers, John VI, 1003
Ayers, John VI, 1004

Ayers, John VI, 1005
Ayers, John VI, 1006
Ayers, John VI, 1008
Ayers, John VI, 1009
Ayers, John VI, 1013
Ayers, John VI, 1014
Ayers, John VI, 1015
Ayers, John VI, 1016
Ayers, John VI, 1017
Ayers, John VI, 1020
Ayers, John VI, 1021
Ayers, John C. VI, 154
Ayers, John C. VI, 211
Ayers, John L. VI, 874
Ayers, John N. VI, 874
Ayers, John W. VI, 872
Ayers, John W. VI, 976
Ayers, John W. VI, 992
Ayers, Josiah IV, 1143
Ayers, Lindsay VI, 873
Ayers, Lunsford VI, 888
Ayers, Lydia IV, 1196
Ayers, M. VI, 874
Ayers, Margaret V, 656
Ayers, Margaret VI, 877
Ayers, Marshal VI, 920
Ayers, Martha I, 935
Ayers, Mary IV, 1143
Ayers, Mary VI, 992
Ayers, Mary VI, 1009
Ayers, Mary C. VI, 965
Ayers, Mary Cathron VI, 877
Ayers, Mary H. VI, 874
Ayers, Mary Jane VI, 874
Ayers, Mary Louise V, 656
Ayers, Mary Louise V, 659
Ayers, Masten J. VI, 874
Ayers, Maston VI, 874
Ayers, Maurice B. II, 143
Ayers, Nancy VI, 874
Ayers, Nancy VI, 911
Ayers, Nancy VI, 934
Ayers, Pauline V, 656
Ayers, Polly VI, 972
Ayers, Sadie IV, 1245
Ayers, Sadie E. IV, 1245
Ayers, Sally VI, 874
Ayers, Samuel II, 51
Ayers, Samuel VI, 874
Ayers, Samuel VI, 931
Ayers, Samuel J. VI, 874
Ayers, Sarah B. VI, 874
Ayers, Sarah Jane V, 21
Ayers, Sarah Jane V, 34
Ayers, Sarah Jane VI, 920
Ayers, Sarah M. I, 932
Ayers, Sarah M. I, 935
Ayers, Seth V, 34
Ayers, Sibert VI, 874
Ayers, Stephen IV, 1350
Ayers, Susan L. VI, 874
Ayers, Talbert VI, 874
Ayers, Thomas IV, 1143
Ayers, Thomas IV, 1245
Ayers, Uriah VI, 874
Ayers, Wm. II, 143
Ayers, Wm. B. VI, 874
Ayers, Wm. B. VI, 965
Ayers, Wm. B. VI, 992
Ayers, Wm. Finlaw II, 143
Ayers, Wm. M. V, 656
Ayers, Wm. M. V, 692
Ayles, Amos IV, 33
Ayles, Ann IV, 33
Ayles, Mary IV, 19
Ayles, Mary IV, 33
Aylesworth, Abigail IV, 1350
Aylesworth, Edwin IV, 1350
Aylesworth, Edwin P. IV, 1350
Aylesworth, Robert IV, 1350
Aylesworth, Rosanna IV, 1350
Aylesworth, Susanna IV, 1350
Aylesworth, Warner IV, 1350
Aylsworth, Abigail IV, 1350
Aylsworth, Belinda Louisa IV, 1350
Aylsworth, Edwin IV, 1350
Aylsworth, Edwin P. IV, 1350
Aylsworth, Francis Marion IV, 1350
Aylsworth, Frebon Maria IV, 1350
Aylsworth, Gulielma IV, 1350
Aylsworth, Robert IV, 1350
Aylsworth, Rosanna IV, 1350
Aylsworth, Susan IV, 1350
Aylsworth, Susanna IV, 1350
Aylsworth, Warner IV, 1350
Aylsworth, Warner B. IV, 1350
Ayre, Anna A. II, 833
Ayres, Andrew IV, 1143
Ayres, Andrew F. IV, 1143
Ayres, Asa II, 219
Ayres, Belle IV, 1143
Ayres, Betsey VI, 874
Ayres, Daniel VI, 11
Ayres, David IV, 1350
Ayres, Dianna VI, 1006
Ayres, Elizabeth IV, 1350
Ayres, Elizabeth IV, 1374
Ayres, Elizabeth VI, 1015
Ayres, Elme J. VI, 874
Ayres, Emanuel W. VI, 936
Ayres, Frances A. VI, 797
Ayres, Gincy VI, 874
Ayres, Hannah VI, 963
Ayres, Helen IV, 1143
Ayres, Isham VI, 797
Ayres, Izabell VI, 945
Ayres, James VI, 874
Ayres, James VI, 949
Ayres, James VI, 958
Ayres, James VI, 1007
Ayres, James VI, 1015
Ayres, John IV, 1143
Ayres, John VI, 873
Ayres, John VI, 959
Ayres, John VI, 997
Ayres, John VI, 1007
Ayres, John VI, 1008
Ayres, John E. IV, 1143
Ayres, Josiah IV, 1143
Ayres, Levi II, 219
Ayres, Luna VI, 958
Ayres, Lydia IV, 1143
Ayres, Mary II, 333
Ayres, Mary IV, 1143
Ayres, Masten J. VI, 874
Ayres, Nanny VI, 945
Ayres, Nathaniel VI, 296
Ayres, Rachel VI, 1007
Ayres, Rebecca II, 266
Ayres, Rebecca IV, 20
Ayres, Rebecca IV, 38
Ayres, Ruth VI, 949
Ayres, Samuel VI, 874
Ayres, Sarah IV, 200
Ayres, Susan L. VI, 874
Ayres, Talbert VI, 874
Ayres, Thomas II, 219
Ayres, Thomas IV, 1143
Ayres, Willam, Sr. V, 218
Ayrs, ??? VI, 293
Ayrs, Nathaniel VI, 296
Ayrs, Richard II, 975
Ayrs, Richard II, 981

B???, Hannah III, 369
Ba???, Mark II, 138
Ba???, Rachel II, 138
Ba???, Rachel Ann II, 138
Bab, Mary I, 523
Bab, Mary I, 552
Babb, Albert V, 150
Babb, Albert V, 656
Babb, Alice Ann V, 472
Babb, Allie V, 150
Babb, Alpheus V, 472
Babb, Alpheus W. V, 472
Babb, Amelia IV, 171
Babb, Ann IV, 319
Babb, Ann IV, 349
Babb, Anna V, 150
Babb, Anna V, 656
Babb, Anna VI, 51
Babb, Anna VI, 52
Babb, Anna VI, 81
Babb, Anna VI, 82
Babb, Anna B. V, 473
Babb, Anna Barbara V, 656
Babb, Anne V, 472
Babb, Annie V, 656
Babb, Annie M. VI, 51
Babb, Benj. F. VI, 81
Babb, Benj. F. VI, 82
Babb, Benj. F. VI, 89
Babb, Benj. T. VI, 51
Babb, Benjamin F. VI, 51
Babb, Benjamin F. VI, 52
Babb, Bertha V, 472
Babb, Bertha VI, 52
Babb, Besty VI, 51
Babb, Bettie VI, 91
Babb, Burly M. V, 472
Babb, Burtha E. V, 472
Babb, Calvin M. V, 656
Babb, Carey Henry V, 656
Babb, Caroline V, 656
Babb, Catherine VI, 51
Babb, Charles F. V, 656
Babb, Charles O. V, 656
Babb, Charles White VI, 51
Babb, Charley V, 472
Babb, Charlie W. V, 472
Babb, Chas. F. V, 656
Babb, Clara Louisa V, 472
Babb, Clayton V, 472
Babb, Clinton V, 150
Babb, Clinton V, 472
Babb, Clinton V, 656
Babb, Clyde V, 472
Babb, Clyde VI, 51
Babb, Cornelius VI, 82
Babb, Cornelius T. VI, 51
Babb, Cornelius T. VI, 81
Babb, Daniel J. V, 656
Babb, David V, 656
Babb, Deborah Bertha I, 35
Babb, Deborah Bertha I, 84
Babb, Deborah Bertha VI, 51
Babb, Deborah Bertha VI, 89
Babb, Deborah Bertha White VI, 52
Babb, Dr. Benjamin F. VI, 51
Babb, E. L. V, 473
Babb, Edwin Loyd VI, 51
Babb, Eli V, 472
Babb, Eli V, 548
Babb, Eli V, 656
Babb, Eliza V, 472
Babb, Eliza W. V, 656
Babb, Elizabeth V, 318
Babb, Elizabeth V, 472
Babb, Elizabeth V, 656
Babb, Elizabeth VI, 51
Babb, Elizabeth VI, 67
Babb, Elizabeth VI, 362
Babb, Elizabeth VI, 435
Babb, Elizabeth VI, 454
Babb, Elizabeth F. VI, 51
Babb, Elizabeth F. VI, 52
Babb, Elizabeth F. VI, 81
Babb, Elizabeth F. VI, 83
Babb, Ella E. V, 150
Babb, Elwood VI, 51
Babb, Emma F. II, 787
Babb, Emmerson M. VI, 51
Babb, Enoch L. VI, 51
Babb, Enoch L. VI, 52
Babb, Esther V, 150
Babb, Esther V, 656
Babb, Eugene J. VI, 51
Babb, Eva V, 150
Babb, Eva V, 656
Babb, Florence Bell V, 984
Babb, Frank V, 656
Babb, Geneva E. VI, 51
Babb, Geneva M. VI, 51
Babb, Geneva M. VI, 54
Babb, Geneva M. VI, 55
Babb, Gertrude VI, 51
Babb, Grace VI, 362
Babb, Grace VI, 419
Babb, Gulia I, 35
Babb, Gulia I, 39
Babb, Gulielma I, 3
Babb, Hannah V, 656
Babb, Hannah V, 702
Babb, Hannah VI, 51
Babb, Hannah C. VI, 51
Babb, Hannah C. VI, 52
Babb, Hannah C. VI, 55
Babb, Hannah O. V, 656
Babb, Harriett V, 656
Babb, Harriett M. V, 656
Babb, Hattie Harley V, 472
Babb, Henry V, 472
Babb, Herbert Harlan VI, 51
Babb, Howard VI, 227
Babb, Howard W. VI, 51
Babb, Howard W. VI, 227
Babb, Isaiah V, 472
Babb, Israel V, 472
Babb, James VI, 51
Babb, Jane V, 472
Babb, Jane V, 538
Babb, Jasper V, 656
Babb, John VI, 51
Babb, John VI, 52
Babb, John VI, 54
Babb, John VI, 67
Babb, John VI, 68
Babb, John VI, 81
Babb, John E. VI, 51
Babb, John E. VI, 52
Babb, John E. VI, 81
Babb, John E. VI, 82
Babb, John H. VI, 51
Babb, John H. VI, 55
Babb, John Stanley VI, 51
Babb, John Way II, 780
Babb, Johnetta VI, 51
Babb, Josiah I, 3
Babb, Judith VI, 51
Babb, Judith VI, 52
Babb, Judith VI, 91
Babb, Lelia F. VI, 51
Babb, Lelia F. VI, 81
Babb, Lelia F. VI, 82
Babb, Lewis A. IV, 171
Babb, Livingston H. VI, 51
Babb, Lorena VI, 82
Babb, Lorena P. VI, 81
Babb, Lorena Pearl VI, 51
Babb, Lula May VI, 81
Babb, Lulu M. VI, 51
Babb, Lulu May VI, 51
Babb, Lulu May VI, 82
Babb, Lydia VI, 362
Babb, Lydia VI, 383
Babb, Lydia Ann V, 472
Babb, Margaret VI, 91
Babb, Marietta V, 472
Babb, Marion E. V, 656
Babb, Marion S. V, 656
Babb, Martha IV, 311
Babb, Martha IV, 313
Babb, Martha VI, 51
Babb, Martha VI, 52
Babb, Martha VI, 54
Babb, Martha VI, 81
Babb, Martha A. VI, 51
Babb, Mary I, 1026
Babb, Mary V, 150
Babb, Mary V, 656
Babb, Mary VI, 428
Babb, Mary Emma V, 472
Babb, Mary L. VI, 51
Babb, Mary L. VI, 52
Babb, Mata V, 472
Babb, May V, 150
Babb, Nancy VI, 51
Babb, Nancy VI, 67
Babb, Nancy VI, 68
Babb, Nancy J. VI, 51
Babb, Nancy J. VI, 52
Babb, Nelie A. IV, 171
Babb, Nicholas D. V, 150
Babb, Oriana V, 472
Babb, Oriana V, 548
Babb, Orianna V, 472
Babb, Orianna V, 473
Babb, Orianna V, 656
Babb, Orville Clinton V, 472
Babb, Peggy VI, 51
Babb, Phebe K. II, 833
Babb, Philip VI, 362
Babb, Philip VI, 428
Babb, Ralph Gregory V, 984
Babb, Rebecca V, 656
Babb, Rowland H. VI, 51
Babb, Ruth C. V, 656
Babb, Ruth C. V, 698
Babb, Sampson II, 698
Babb, Sarah V, 656
Babb, Sarah A. V, 472
Babb, Sarah Ann V, 472
Babb, Thomas VI, 357
Babb, Thomas, Jr. VI, 362
Babb, Vedith V, 150
Babb, Vedith V, 656
Babb, Viola V, 656
Babb, Wd. Phebe Harper II, 780
Babb, Wilbur T. V, 656
Babb, William VI, 51
Babb, Wm. R. V, 656
Babb, Wm. R., Jr. V, 656
Babbitt, Catharine W. V, 892
Babbitt, Eliz. G. III, 22
Babbitt, Eliz. G. III, 53
Babbitt, Isaac N., Jr. III, 22
Babbitt, Isaac N., Jr. III, 53
Babbitt, Mary Rogers III, 22
Babbitt, Mary Rogers III, 53
Babbitt, Rebecca II, 780
Babbitt, Rebecca T. II, 833
Babbitt, Rebecca T. II, 933
Babbitt, Wm Walker II, 780
Babcock, Belle H. IV, 1306
Babcock, Benjamin V, 33
Babcock, Benjamin V, 135
Babcock, Chas. IV, 1306
Babcock, Chas. H. IV, 1306
Babcock, Chris G. VI, 874
Babcock, Elizabeth III, 22
Babcock, Eva Stanton III, 50
Babcock, Helena III, 22
Babcock, Hudson III, 22
Babcock, Joshua S. III, 50
Babcock, Julia V, 135
Babcock, Julia A. V, 21
Babcock, Julia E. VI, 874
Babcock, Juliann V, 21
Babcock, Maria C. IV, 463
Babcock, Mary II, 457
Babcock, Rachel V, 21
Babcock, Rachel V, 33
Babcock, Saphrona IV, 1143
Babcock, Sarah III, 50
Babcock, Sarah V, 33
Babcock, Sarah V, 135
Babcock, Sophoronia IV, 1143
Babcock, William IV, 1143
Babcock, Wm. J. IV, 1143
Baber, Bitsey VI, 874
Baber, Catherine VI, 924
Baber, Charles III, 220
Baber, Edward VI, 857
Baber, Elizabeth III, 220
Baber, Elizabeth VI, 874
Baber, George VI, 823
Baber, George VI, 874
Baber, George VI, 997
Baber, Henrietta VI, 957
Baber, James VI, 797
Baber, James VI, 874
Baber, James VI, 906
Baber, James VI, 933
Baber, John VI, 797
Baber, Judith VI, 823
Baber, Lucy VI, 874
Baber, Lucy VI, 967
Baber, Margaret VI, 874
Baber, Mary VI, 855
Baber, Mary VI, 1022
Baber, Matilda Ann VI, 960
Baber, Milly VI, 797
Baber, Nancy VI, 858
Baber, Peggy VI, 874
Baber, Polly VI, 874
Baber, Polly VI, 997
Baber, Robt. VI, 913
Baber, Sally VI, 797
Baber, Thomas VI, 874
Baber, Thomas VI, 960
Baber, Wd. Jane VI, 913
Baber, William VI, 826
Baber, William VI, 858
Baber, William VI, 874
Baber, William VI, 913
Baber, William VI, 924
Baber, William VI, 997
Baber, William VI, 1016
Baber, William L. VI, 957
Baber, Wilmouth Ann VI, 933
Baber, Wm. VI, 833
Bablin, Susannah II, 821
Babock, Rachel V, 21
Babridge, ??? III, 22
Babridge, Emma III, 22
Babridge, Mary III, 22
Babson, Betsey III, 71
Babson, Betsey III, 313
Bach, Catharine III, 394
Bach, Elizabeth III, 394
Bach, Jacob III, 394
Bach, Philip III, 394
Bach, Theodore III, 394
Bach, William III, 394
Bachloffer, Louisa III, 118
Bachman, Jessie H. III, 22
Backenstoe, Nannie V, 451
Backer, Eliza III, 22
Backer, Florence E. VI, 405
Backer, Jacob III, 22
Backes, Margaret B. IV, 364
Backes, Margaret B. IV, 376
Backhouse, Eliz. III, 22
Backhouse, Jamima VI, 507
Backhouse, John VI, 507
Backhouse, Kennet VI, 467
Backhouse, Mary VI, 467
Backhouse, Strange VI, 467
Backhouse, Thomas III, 22
Backhouse, Thomas VI, 467
Backhouse, Wm. III, 22
Backman, Ruth IV, 20
Backnyer, Katie IV, 1245
Backus, Amanda N. III, 22
Backus, Frederick B. III, 22
Backus, Margaret B. II, 953
Backus, Rebecca Fitzhugh III, 79
Bacock, Elijah VI, 942
Bacock, Elizabeth VI, 942
Bacon, ??? III, 22
Bacon, ??? III, 294
Bacon, Ada V, 218
Bacon, Ann II, 20
Bacon, Ann II, 21
Bacon, Ann II, 52
Bacon, Ann II, 166
Bacon, Ann II, 195
Bacon, Ann II, 699
Bacon, Ann II, 726

Bacon, Ann II, 975
Bacon, Ann II, 998
Bacon, Ann C. II, 726
Bacon, Ann C. II, 777
Bacon, Ann E. II, 698
Bacon, Ann H. II, 115
Bacon, Ann H. II, 126
Bacon, Ann T. II, 52
Bacon, Anna II, 698
Bacon, Annie E. II, 833
Bacon, Annie E. II, 851
Bacon, Caroline B. II, 726
Bacon, Caroline B. II, 777
Bacon, Caroline W. II, 698
Bacon, Caroline W. II, 726
Bacon, Caroline Warder II, 726
Bacon, Charles II, 20
Bacon, Charles II, 21
Bacon, Charles II, 52
Bacon, Charles II, 113
Bacon, Charles H. II, 128
Bacon, Charles Warden II, 457
Bacon, Charles Warder II, 334
Bacon, Chas. II, 20
Bacon, Chas. II, 52
Bacon, Chas. II, 69
Bacon, Chas. II, 75
Bacon, Daniel II, 166
Bacon, Daniel II, 195
Bacon, Daniel II, 199
Bacon, Daniel, Jr. II, 195
Bacon, David II, 20
Bacon, David II, 21
Bacon, David II, 51
Bacon, David II, 52
Bacon, David II, 333
Bacon, David II, 334
Bacon, David II, 457
Bacon, David II, 519
Bacon, David II, 610
Bacon, David II, 644
Bacon, David II, 670
Bacon, David V, 947
Bacon, Deborah II, 21
Bacon, Dorcas II, 21
Bacon, Edith V, 656
Bacon, Edith V, 671
Bacon, Edmond II, 20
Bacon, Edmond II, 51
Bacon, Eleanor II, 21
Bacon, Eleanor II, 52
Bacon, Eleanor II, 75
Bacon, Elisabeth II, 166
Bacon, Elizabeth II, 20
Bacon, Elizabeth II, 21
Bacon, Elizabeth II, 51
Bacon, Elizabeth II, 52
Bacon, Elizabeth II, 65
Bacon, Elizabeth II, 70
Bacon, Elizabeth II, 72
Bacon, Elizabeth II, 96
Bacon, Elizabeth II, 103
Bacon, Elizabeth II, 111
Bacon, Elizabeth II, 113
Bacon, Elizabeth II, 115
Bacon, Elizabeth II, 117
Bacon, Elizabeth II, 128
Bacon, Elizabeth II, 143
Bacon, Elizabeth II, 195
Bacon, Elizabeth II, 246
Bacon, Elizabeth II, 261
Bacon, Elizabeth II, 333
Bacon, Elizabeth II, 334
Bacon, Elizabeth II, 457
Bacon, Elizabeth II, 469
Bacon, Elizabeth II, 531
Bacon, Elizabeth II, 563
Bacon, Elizabeth II, 587
Bacon, Elizabeth II, 644
Bacon, Elizabeth II, 691
Bacon, Elizabeth II, 698
Bacon, Elizabeth II, 953
Bacon, Elizabeth Ann II, 128
Bacon, Elizabeth H. II, 280
Bacon, Elizabeth H. II, 301
Bacon, Elizabeth H. II, 698
Bacon, Elizabeth S. II, 166
Bacon, Elizabeth Warder II, 726
Bacon, Ellis William II, 833
Bacon, Ellis Williams II, 851
Bacon, Elonar II, 21
Bacon, Elonar II, 51
Bacon, Elonar II, 64
Bacon, Esther II, 21
Bacon, Fanny H. III, 22
Bacon, Fanny H. III, 182
Bacon, Francis II, 114
Bacon, Francis II, 115
Bacon, Francis II, 726
Bacon, Francis Rogers V, 656
Bacon, Francis Rogers V, 671
Bacon, George II, 114
Bacon, George II, 115
Bacon, George V, 218
Bacon, George B. II, 698
Bacon, George B. III, 22
Bacon, George B. III, 182
Bacon, George Vance II, 334
Bacon, George Vaux II, 457
Bacon, Grace II, 51
Bacon, Grace II, 66
Bacon, Grace II, 112
Bacon, Hannah II, 20
Bacon, Hannah II, 21
Bacon, Hannah II, 52
Bacon, Hannah II, 92
Bacon, Hannah II, 114
Bacon, Hannah II, 115
Bacon, Hannah II, 128
Bacon, Hannah II, 136
Bacon, Hannah II, 334
Bacon, Hannah II, 457
Bacon, Hannah II, 519
Bacon, Hannah II, 815
Bacon, Hannah V, 21
Bacon, Hannah V, 77
Bacon, Hannah H. II, 698
Bacon, Hannah H. II, 699
Bacon, Hannah H. II, 726
Bacon, Harriet II, 726
Bacon, Harriet M. II, 726
Bacon, Harriet M. II, 766
Bacon, Helen II, 953
Bacon, Helen II, 1044
Bacon, Helen Atkinson II, 833
Bacon, Helen Atkinson II, 851
Bacon, J. Murray II, 698
Bacon, J. Murry II, 166
Bacon, James VI, 52
Bacon, Jane E. H. II, 1044
Bacon, Jane Eves II, 953
Bacon, Jane H. II, 726
Bacon, Jane Haines II, 726
Bacon, Jesse II, 21
Bacon, Jesse II, 52
Bacon, Jesse II, 92
Bacon, Job II, 21
Bacon, Job II, 52
Bacon, Job II, 106
Bacon, Job II, 115
Bacon, Job II, 126
Bacon, Job II, 334
Bacon, Job II, 457
Bacon, Job II, 587
Bacon, Job II, 655
Bacon, Job II, 698
Bacon, John II, 20
Bacon, John II, 21
Bacon, John II, 51
Bacon, John II, 52
Bacon, John II, 92
Bacon, John II, 96
Bacon, John II, 101
Bacon, John II, 106
Bacon, John II, 108
Bacon, John II, 111
Bacon, John II, 115
Bacon, John II, 126
Bacon, John II, 128
Bacon, John II, 136
Bacon, John II, 195
Bacon, John II, 249
Bacon, John II, 261
Bacon, John II, 280
Bacon, John II, 301
Bacon, John II, 333
Bacon, John II, 334
Bacon, John II, 441
Bacon, John II, 457
Bacon, John II, 531
Bacon, John II, 587
Bacon, John II, 670
Bacon, John II, 698
Bacon, John II, 726
Bacon, John II, 770
Bacon, John II, 777
Bacon, John II, 815
Bacon, John G. V, 947
Bacon, John L. II, 128
Bacon, John Murray II, 280
Bacon, John Murray II, 301
Bacon, John S. II, 143
Bacon, John, Jr. II, 52
Bacon, Joseph II, 20
Bacon, Joseph II, 21
Bacon, Joseph II, 51
Bacon, Joseph II, 76
Bacon, Joseph II, 128
Bacon, Joseph II, 333
Bacon, Joseph II, 457
Bacon, Joseph II, 682
Bacon, Joseph II, 975
Bacon, Joseph VI, 52
Bacon, Joseph K. II, 698
Bacon, Joseph Y. V, 947
Bacon, Josiah II, 52
Bacon, Josiah II, 726
Bacon, Josiah II, 777
Bacon, Katharine II, 115
Bacon, Katharine II, 126
Bacon, Katharine W. II, 115
Bacon, Katherine W. II, 115
Bacon, Latitia II, 51
Bacon, Latitia II, 54
Bacon, Lavinia III, 22
Bacon, Lavinia III, 182
Bacon, Luce II, 51
Bacon, Luce II, 66
Bacon, Lucy Shipley II, 698
Bacon, Lydall VI, 169
Bacon, Lydall VI, 175
Bacon, Lyddall VI, 154
Bacon, Lyddall VI, 174
Bacon, Lyddall VI, 187
Bacon, Lydia II, 21
Bacon, Lydia II, 52
Bacon, Lydia II, 128
Bacon, Lydia Ann II, 953
Bacon, Lydia S. II, 143
Bacon, Margaret II, 21
Bacon, Margaret II, 51
Bacon, Margaret II, 76
Bacon, Margaret Haines II, 699
Bacon, Margaret Haines II, 726
Bacon, Margaret, Jr. II, 51
Bacon, Margaret, Jr. II, 87
Bacon, Mark B. II, 953
Bacon, Mark B. II, 1044
Bacon, Martha II, 21
Bacon, Martha II, 37
Bacon, Martha II, 52
Bacon, Martha II, 66
Bacon, Martha II, 92
Bacon, Martha II, 136
Bacon, Martha II, 334
Bacon, Martha II, 457
Bacon, Martha II, 794
Bacon, Martha II, 815
Bacon, Martha II, 820
Bacon, Mary I, 35
Bacon, Mary I, 68
Bacon, Mary II, 20
Bacon, Mary II, 21
Bacon, Mary II, 51
Bacon, Mary II, 52
Bacon, Mary II, 73
Bacon, Mary II, 101
Bacon, Mary II, 106
Bacon, Mary II, 108
Bacon, Mary II, 115
Bacon, Mary II, 121
Bacon, Mary II, 195
Bacon, Mary II, 260
Bacon, Mary II, 333
Bacon, Mary II, 334
Bacon, Mary II, 457
Bacon, Mary II, 519
Bacon, Mary II, 531
Bacon, Mary II, 587
Bacon, Mary II, 610
Bacon, Mary II, 644
Bacon, Mary II, 655
Bacon, Mary II, 670
Bacon, Mary II, 672
Bacon, Mary II, 704
Bacon, Mary II, 713
Bacon, Mary V, 947
Bacon, Mary Alice II, 953
Bacon, Mary Ann II, 280
Bacon, Mary Ann II, 301
Bacon, Mary Ann II, 334
Bacon, Mary Ann II, 457
Bacon, Mary Ann II, 698
Bacon, Mary Ann II, 726
Bacon, Mary Ann II, 770
Bacon, Mary Ann, Jr. II, 726
Bacon, Mary B. II, 121
Bacon, Mary, Jr. II, 457
Bacon, Mary, Jr. II, 655
Bacon, Matilda R. III, 22
Bacon, Matilda Ruthland III, 294
Bacon, Murray II, 726
Bacon, Murry II, 726
Bacon, Naomi II, 114
Bacon, Naomi II, 115
Bacon, Pary V, 984
Bacon, Perry C. V, 984
Bacon, Priscilla II, 21
Bacon, Priscilla II, 115
Bacon, Priscilla II, 117
Bacon, Priscilla II, 121
Bacon, Prudence II, 21
Bacon, Prudence II, 52
Bacon, Rachel II, 20
Bacon, Rachel II, 21
Bacon, Rachel II, 51
Bacon, Rachel II, 52
Bacon, Rachel II, 64
Bacon, Rachel II, 334
Bacon, Rachel II, 698
Bacon, Rebecca II, 21
Bacon, Rebecca II, 52
Bacon, Rebecca II, 86
Bacon, Rebecca II, 133
Bacon, Rebecca II, 166
Bacon, Rebecca II, 195
Bacon, Rebecca II, 199
Bacon, Rebecca II, 249
Bacon, Rebecca II, 333
Bacon, Rebecca II, 457
Bacon, Rebecca V, 947
Bacon, Rebecca Ann V, 947
Bacon, Rebeckah II, 20
Bacon, Rebeckah II, 52
Bacon, Rebeckah II, 69
Bacon, Rebeckah II, 75
Bacon, Richard II, 21
Bacon, Richard II, 51
Bacon, Richard II, 52
Bacon, Richard II, 457
Bacon, Richard Marshall II, 698
Bacon, Richard W. II, 726
Bacon, Rowland Haines II, 953
Bacon, Rowland Haines II, 1044
Bacon, Ruth II, 21
Bacon, Ruth II, 52
Bacon, Ruth II, 56
Bacon, Ruth II, 106
Bacon, Samuel II, 20
Bacon, Samuel II, 21
Bacon, Samuel II, 51
Bacon, Samuel II, 457
Bacon, Samuel A. II, 953
Bacon, Sarah II, 52
Bacon, Sarah II, 92
Bacon, Sarah II, 108
Bacon, Sarah II, 334
Bacon, Sarah II, 441
Bacon, Sarah II, 457
Bacon, Sarah II, 682
Bacon, Sarah II, 698
Bacon, Sarah VI, 240
Bacon, Sarah E. II, 726
Bacon, Sarah E. II, 770
Bacon, Sarah Eliza II, 726
Bacon, Sarah Minturn II, 726
Bacon, Sarah S. II, 52
Bacon, Sarah S. II, 115
Bacon, Sophia Matilda II, 698
Bacon, Susan Prior II, 791
Bacon, Thomas II, 20
Bacon, Thomas II, 21
Bacon, Thomas II, 51
Bacon, Thomas II, 52
Bacon, Thomas II, 64
Bacon, Thomas II, 115
Bacon, Thomas II, 117
Bacon, Thomas II, 128
Bacon, Thomas II, 143
Bacon, Thomas D. II, 128
Bacon, Thomas D. II, 143
Bacon, Thomas L. II, 117
Bacon, Thomas S. II, 115
Bacon, Thos. II, 21
Bacon, Thos. II, 52
Bacon, Thos. II, 113
Bacon, Thos. II, 115
Bacon, Thos. L. II, 115
Bacon, Thos. P. II, 833
Bacon, Thos. P. II, 851
Bacon, Thos. S. II, 115
Bacon, Thos. S. II, 121
Bacon, Wd. Mary II, 111
Bacon, William H. II, 698
Bacon, Wm. H. II, 699
Bacon, Wm. H. II, 726
Bacon, Wm. Henry II, 726
Badcock, Alexander II, 441
Badcock, Elizabeth II, 457
Badcock, Elizabeth II, 536
Badcock, Elizabeth III, 22
Badcock, Hannah II, 457
Badcock, Hannah II, 575
Badcock, Henry II, 334
Badcock, Henry II, 457
Badcock, Mary II, 334
Badcock, Mary II, 441
Badcock, Mary II, 457
Badcock, Mary II, 582
Badcock, Mary, Jr. II, 457
Badcock, Thomas II, 441
Badcocke, Henry II, 334
Badcocke, Mary II, 334
Badcoke, Henry II, 457
Badcoke, Henry II, 473
Badcoke, Mary II, 457
Badcoke, Mary II, 473
Bader, John Valentine IV, 609
Badger, Geo. F. III, 295
Badger, Myrtle L. VI, 681
Badger, Wd. Catherine L. II, 79
Badgley, Anthony III, 22
Badgley, Anthony III, 144
Badgley, Anthony, Sr. III, 22
Badgley, Cash V, 451
Badgley, Cassius V, 451
Badgley, George V, 726
Badgley, Olive V, 451
Badgley, Phebe III, 22
Badgley, Phebe III, 144
Baels, John I, 525
Baer, Altey V, 984
Baer, Elijah V, 984
Baer, Eliza V, 984
Baer, Henry Clinton V, 726
Baer, Hettie V, 984
Baer, Jacob V, 984
Baer, Jennie V, 984
Baer, John A. V, 984
Baer, John C. V, 984
Baer, Kenneth L. V, 984
Baer, Lendal V, 984
Baer, Lilas V, 984
Baer, Martha L. V, 984
Baer, Mary V, 984
Baer, Mary E. V, 984
Baer, Minnie May V, 984
Baer, Paul Harold V, 984
Baer, Pearl Dean V, 984
Baer, Rachel V, 984
Baer, Reta Jane V, 984
Baer, Richard L. V, 984
Baer, Ruth Ellen V, 984
Baer, Samuel V, 984
Baer, Susan V, 726
Baer, Thomas V, 984
Baer, Wesley V, 984
Baer, Wm. E. V, 984
Bagbey, Elizabeth VI, 986
Bagbey, William VI, 986
Bagby, Agness VI, 797
Bagby, Elizabeth VI, 797
Bagby, Elizabeth VI, 815
Bagby, Hannah VI, 797
Bagby, John W. VI, 797
Bagby, John W. VI, 848
Bagby, Lewis G. VI, 797
Bagby, Lewis G. VI, 840
Bagby, Lucius G. VI, 807
Bagby, Martha J. VI, 815
Bagby, Mary VI, 816
Bagby, Matthew VI, 822
Bagby, Nancy VI, 797
Bagby, Nancy VI, 830
Bagby, Pamelia VI, 822
Bagby, Pleasant VI, 797
Bagby, Rachel VI, 797
Bagby, Reuben VI, 797
Bagby, Reuben VI, 815
Bagby, Reuben VI, 816
Bagby, William VI, 797
Bagby, William L. VI, 847
Bagford, Carrie Jenson V, 150
Bagg, Henry R. Cooper II, 833
Bagg, Jessie II, 833
Bagg, Jessie II, 852
Baggass, Mary VI, 467
Baggass, Mary VI, 547
Bagget, Sarah I, 220
Baggott, Chas. E. III, 22
Baggott, Estelle M. III, 22
Baggott, Eugenia L. III, 22
Bagley, Ann I, 3
Bagley, Anna I, 35
Bagley, Anne I, 189
Bagley, Barnabe I, 189
Bagley, Betty I, 35
Bagley, Betty I, 61
Bagley, Betty I, 93
Bagley, Elisabeth I, 189
Bagley, Elisabeth I, 193
Bagley, Elvy I, 128
Bagley, Ephraim I, 189
Bagley, Ephrim I, 93
Bagley, Hannah I, 128
Bagley, Hannah I, 141
Bagley, Hannah I, 145
Bagley, Hannah I, 184
Bagley, Hannah I, 189
Bagley, John I, 3
Bagley, John I, 35
Bagley, John I, 93
Bagley, John I, 180
Bagley, Jonathan I, 93
Bagley, Joseph I, 3

Bagley, Joseph I, 35
Bagley, Joseph I, 189
Bagley, Margaret I, 189
Bagley, Margaret I, 198
Bagley, Margaret Ann I, 3
Bagley, Margaret Ann I, 189
Bagley, Mary I, 35
Bagley, Mary I, 50
Bagley, Mary I, 128
Bagley, Mary I, 145
Bagley, Mary I, 189
Bagley, Mary I, 200
Bagley, Mary Ann V, 218
Bagley, Milisent I, 188
Bagley, Milisent I, 189
Bagley, Miriam I, 189
Bagley, Nathan I, 93
Bagley, Nathan I, 128
Bagley, Nathan I, 145
Bagley, Nathan I, 184
Bagley, Nathan I, 189
Bagley, Nathan I, 198
Bagley, Nathan I, 200
Bagley, Nathan, Jr. I, 189
Bagley, Phariby I, 189
Bagley, Phariby I, 200
Bagley, Sarah I, 189
Bagley, Sarah I, 197
Bagley, Thomas I, 35
Bagley, Urilla V, 984
Bagley, William I, 35
Bagley, William I, 93
Bagley, William I, 189
Bagley, William V, 218
Bagly, Betty I, 35
Bagly, Betty I, 67
Bagly, Elvy I, 128
Bagly, Elvy I, 168
Bagly, Hannah I, 194
Bagly, William I, 35
Bagly, William I, 67
Bagnall, Ann II, 457
Bagnall, Benjamin II, 457
Bagnall, Benjamin, Jr. II, 457
Bagnall, Ellin II, 52
Bagnall, Ellin II, 93
Bagnall, Robert II, 457
Bagnell, Benjamin II, 334
Bagnell, Thomas II, 334
Bagsham, Catharine IV, 1306
Bagshaw, Catharine IV, 1313
Bagwell, Benjamin II, 334
Bagwell, Catherine VI, 985
Bagwell, Drury VI, 985
Bagwell, Joseph II, 334
Bagwell, Mary W. I, 226
Bagwell, Richard VI, 874
Bagwell, Sarah VI, 874
Bahan, Mary Flora V, 656
Bahan, William V, 656
Bahl, Lewis A. IV, 171
Bahl, Martha L. IV, 171
Bahler, Annie L. III, 22
Bahler, Annie L. III, 180
Bahler, Elsie Margarita III, 22
Bahler, Elsie Margarita III, 180
Bahler, Martin III, 22
Bahler, Martin III, 180
Bailace, Sally VI, 797
Bailace, William VI, 797
Bailes, Ann I, 526
Bailes, Daniel III, 22
Bailes, George III, 22
Bailes, Hannah VI, 363
Bailes, Hannah VI, 433
Bailes, Hester I, 980
Bailes, Jemima I, 870
Bailes, Jemima I, 875
Bailes, Mary I, 374
Bailes, Mary I, 423
Bailes, Rosannah III, 22
Bailey, ??? III, 22
Bailey, ??? III, 212
Bailey, ??? IV, 795
Bailey, ??? VI, 95
Bailey, Abidan V, 473
Bailey, Abidan VI, 97
Bailey, Abidan VI, 98
Bailey, Abidan VI, 101
Bailey, Abidan VI, 120
Bailey, Abidan VI, 154
Bailey, Abidan VI, 190
Bailey, Abidan VI, 194
Bailey, Abiden V, 473
Bailey, Abidon IV, 366
Bailey, Abidon V, 473
Bailey, Abigail IV, 364
Bailey, Abigail IV, 365
Bailey, Abigail IV, 366
Bailey, Abigail IV, 395
Bailey, Abigail IV, 566
Bailey, Abigail IV, 673
Bailey, Abigail IV, 1049
Bailey, Abigail IV, 1087
Bailey, Abigail VI, 97
Bailey, Abigail VI, 130
Bailey, Abigail F. IV, 171
Bailey, Abigail F. IV, 566
Bailey, Abigail F. IV, 572
Bailey, Abigail F. IV, 1049
Bailey, Abner VI, 797
Bailey, Abraham IV, 171
Bailey, Absalom VI, 98
Bailey, Absalom VI, 108
Bailey, Achsah IV, 364
Bailey, Achsah IV, 365
Bailey, Achsah IV, 367
Bailey, Achsah IV, 371
Bailey, Achsah IV, 566
Bailey, Achsah IV, 567
Bailey, Achsah IV, 576
Bailey, Achsan IV, 566
Bailey, Adaline IV, 171
Bailey, Adaline IV, 366
Bailey, Adaline IV, 438
Bailey, Adderson Mills V, 610
Bailey, Addie S. V, 656
Bailey, Adelaide V, 929
Bailey, Adeline IV, 365
Bailey, Agness VI, 865
Bailey, Albert V, 610
Bailey, Albert V, 611
Bailey, Albert V, 797
Bailey, Albert A. V, 726
Bailey, Albert H. IV, 365
Bailey, Albert I. V, 656
Bailey, Albert J. V, 611
Bailey, Alfred Bracken IV, 366
Bailey, Alfred L. IV, 366
Bailey, Alfred S. IV, 368
Bailey, Allen IV, 171
Bailey, Allen IV, 365
Bailey, Allen IV, 366
Bailey, Allen IV, 390
Bailey, Allen IV, 427
Bailey, Allen IV, 442
Bailey, Allen IV, 446
Bailey, Allen V, 610
Bailey, Allen G. VI, 797
Bailey, Alma Elizabeth V, 656
Bailey, Almeda IV, 365
Bailey, Almeda V, 473
Bailey, Almeda V, 610
Bailey, Almeda VI, 296
Bailey, Almedia IV, 171
Bailey, Almedia IV, 367
Bailey, Almedia IV, 395
Bailey, Almedia IV, 567
Bailey, Almedia IV, 595
Bailey, Almedia V, 318
Bailey, Almedia V, 353
Bailey, Almedia V, 473
Bailey, Almedia V, 534
Bailey, Almedia V, 610
Bailey, Almedia V, 636
Bailey, Almedia V, 797
Bailey, Almedia V, 967
Bailey, Almedia VI, 130
Bailey, Almedia VI, 141
Bailey, Almedia VI, 296
Bailey, Almedia Granderson Edwin V, 610
Bailey, Almira P. IV, 1143
Bailey, Almira S. V, 893
Bailey, Almira S. V, 895
Bailey, Alpha V, 726
Bailey, Alta IV, 1306
Bailey, Alva C. IV, 171
Bailey, Alva C. IV, 282
Bailey, Alva C. IV, 365
Bailey, Alva C. IV, 366
Bailey, Alva C. IV, 368
Bailey, Alva C. IV, 444
Bailey, Alvah B. IV, 1143
Bailey, Alvin V, 318
Bailey, Alvin Arthur V, 318
Bailey, Amelia IV, 509
Bailey, Amos II, 977
Bailey, Amos IV, 673
Bailey, Amos V, 473
Bailey, Amos V, 656
Bailey, Amos H. V, 610
Bailey, Amy IV, 367
Bailey, Ann I, 489
Bailey, Ann II, 781
Bailey, Ann II, 977
Bailey, Ann IV, 141
Bailey, Ann IV, 171
Bailey, Ann IV, 319
Bailey, Ann IV, 365
Bailey, Ann IV, 367
Bailey, Ann IV, 373
Bailey, Ann IV, 413
Bailey, Ann IV, 445
Bailey, Ann IV, 509
Bailey, Ann IV, 510
Bailey, Ann IV, 560
Bailey, Ann IV, 565
Bailey, Ann IV, 566
Bailey, Ann IV, 567
Bailey, Ann IV, 595
Bailey, Ann IV, 673
Bailey, Ann IV, 797
Bailey, Ann IV, 816
Bailey, Ann IV, 923
Bailey, Ann IV, 1127
Bailey, Ann V, 21
Bailey, Ann V, 297
Bailey, Ann V, 318
Bailey, Ann VI, 52
Bailey, Ann VI, 97
Bailey, Ann VI, 98
Bailey, Ann VI, 99
Bailey, Ann VI, 110
Bailey, Ann VI, 111
Bailey, Ann VI, 118
Bailey, Ann VI, 119
Bailey, Ann VI, 130
Bailey, Ann VI, 369
Bailey, Ann VI, 370
Bailey, Ann VI, 467
Bailey, Ann VI, 732
Bailey, Ann B. IV, 797
Bailey, Ann B. IV, 837
Bailey, Ann Elizabeth V, 726
Bailey, Anna II, 457
Bailey, Anna II, 698
Bailey, Anna II, 699
Bailey, Anna II, 718
Bailey, Anna II, 726
Bailey, Anna II, 833
Bailey, Anna IV, 172
Bailey, Anna IV, 366
Bailey, Anna IV, 367
Bailey, Anna IV, 368
Bailey, Anna IV, 428
Bailey, Anna IV, 674
Bailey, Anna IV, 700
Bailey, Anna IV, 1049
Bailey, Anna IV, 1084
Bailey, Anna VI, 130
Bailey, Anna VI, 140
Bailey, Anna C. II, 698
Bailey, Anna C. II, 699
Bailey, Anna E. IV, 366
Bailey, Anna E. IV, 389
Bailey, Anna E. IV, 923
Bailey, Anna H. II, 699
Bailey, Anna Jean V, 318
Bailey, Anna M. VI, 736
Bailey, Anna M. VI, 792
Bailey, Anna S. II, 699
Bailey, Anna S. II, 726
Bailey, Anne IV, 673
Bailey, Anne IV, 1023
Bailey, Anne B. IV, 673
Bailey, Annie IV, 365
Bailey, Ansalem V, 318
Bailey, Ansalem, Jr. V, 297
Bailey, Ansalum V, 318
Bailey, Anselm VI, 15
Bailey, Anselm VI, 97
Bailey, Anselm VI, 98
Bailey, Anselm VI, 110
Bailey, Anselm, Jr. VI, 97
Bailey, Anselm, Jr. VI, 98
Bailey, Anselm, Jr. VI, 111
Bailey, Armager VI, 130
Bailey, Arminger VI, 52
Bailey, Arminger VI, 99
Bailey, Arthur de Kamp III, 22
Bailey, Asenath IV, 171
Bailey, Asenath IV, 365
Bailey, Asenath IV, 366
Bailey, Asenath IV, 427
Bailey, Asenath IV, 509
Bailey, Asenath V, 473
Bailey, Asenath V, 610
Bailey, Asenath Elma IV, 510
Bailey, Asenath Elma IV, 522
Bailey, Asenath Elma IV, 566
Bailey, Asenath Elma IV, 575
Bailey, Barak IV, 364
Bailey, Barak IV, 365
Bailey, Barak IV, 450
Bailey, Barak VI, 98
Bailey, Barbara I, 469
Bailey, Barclay V, 611
Bailey, Barclay Thomas V, 610
Bailey, Barsheba I, 129
Bailey, Bartham B. II, 780
Bailey, Barthsheba I, 129
Bailey, Bartram B. II, 833
Bailey, Bathsheba V, 21
Bailey, Bell V, 656
Bailey, Belle V, 611
Bailey, Belle V, 656
Bailey, Benj. VI, 97
Bailey, Benj. VI, 98
Bailey, Benjamin I, 372
Bailey, Benjamin I, 1137
Bailey, Benjamin I, 1139
Bailey, Benjamin I, 1147
Bailey, Benjamin IV, 171
Bailey, Benjamin IV, 364
Bailey, Benjamin IV, 565
Bailey, Benjamin IV, 572
Bailey, Benjamin IV, 590
Bailey, Benjamin IV, 1087
Bailey, Benjamin V, 797
Bailey, Benjamin VI, 97
Bailey, Benjamin VI, 99
Bailey, Benjamin VI, 101
Bailey, Benjamin VI, 154
Bailey, Benjamin F. IV, 566
Bailey, Benjamin H. V, 610
Bailey, Benjamin Hamilton V, 610
Bailey, Benjamin, Jr. VI, 98
Bailey, Benjamin, Sr. VI, 98
Bailey, Bernice May V, 548
Bailey, Betcy IV, 407
Bailey, Bethany IV, 365
Bailey, Bethany IV, 408
Bailey, Bethany VI, 97
Bailey, Bethiah IV, 373
Bailey, Betsy IV, 366
Bailey, Betsy VI, 862
Bailey, Borden IV, 1049
Bailey, Borden IV, 1087
Bailey, Borden IV, 1127
Bailey, Brackin IV, 171
Bailey, Braxton VI, 874
Bailey, Burden IV, 367
Bailey, Burden IV, 1049
Bailey, Caleb I, 489
Bailey, Caleb IV, 171
Bailey, Caleb IV, 565
Bailey, Caleb IV, 566
Bailey, Caleb VI, 467
Bailey, Caleb Kirk V, 473
Bailey, Calibourne VI, 824
Bailey, Carl J. V, 548
Bailey, Caroline I, 697
Bailey, Caroline I, 708
Bailey, Caroline V, 336
Bailey, Caroline Yarnall V, 892
Bailey, Catharine I, 647
Bailey, Catharine I, 673
Bailey, Catharine I, 678
Bailey, Catharine I, 697
Bailey, Catharine I, 708
Bailey, Catharine VI, 874
Bailey, Catharine H. VI, 807
Bailey, Catherine V, 21
Bailey, Charity IV, 365
Bailey, Charity IV, 382
Bailey, Charity IV, 445
Bailey, Charity IV, 566
Bailey, Charles III, 22
Bailey, Charles IV, 171
Bailey, Charles IV, 365
Bailey, Charles IV, 367
Bailey, Charles IV, 674
Bailey, Charles IV, 923
Bailey, Charles VI, 874
Bailey, Charles A. IV, 1087
Bailey, Charles Addison IV, 1049
Bailey, Charles F. IV, 923
Bailey, Charles F. IV, 924
Bailey, Charles H. III, 22
Bailey, Charles H. III, 266
Bailey, Charles Lloyd IV, 366
Bailey, Charles W. W. II, 128
Bailey, Charles W. W. II, 143
Bailey, Charles W. White II, 143
Bailey, Charles W. White II, 151
Bailey, Charlotte VI, 797
Bailey, Chas. IV, 1035
Bailey, Chas. VI, 874
Bailey, Chas. Addison IV, 1087
Bailey, Chas. F. IV, 1035
Bailey, Chas. H. III, 145
Bailey, Chester M. IV, 923
Bailey, Christian II, 781
Bailey, Christian II, 1001
Bailey, Christiana II, 833
Bailey, Christiana II, 977
Bailey, Christianna II, 726
Bailey, Christina II, 457
Bailey, Christopher V, 218
Bailey, Christopher V, 318
Bailey, Christopher VI, 296
Bailey, Claiborne VI, 797
Bailey, Claibourne VI, 832
Bailey, Claibourne VI, 837
Bailey, Clara IV, 365
Bailey, Clara IV, 366
Bailey, Clara IV, 375
Bailey, Clara Grace V, 893
Bailey, Clara Olive V, 218
Bailey, Clara Olive V, 318
Bailey, Clarkson IV, 509
Bailey, Clifford IV, 366
Bailey, Clifton D. V, 656
Bailey, Clifton Dennis V, 610
Bailey, Clinton V, 611
Bailey, Corwin V, 656
Bailey, Corwin A. V, 656
Bailey, Corwin Allen V, 610
Bailey, Cyrus VI, 797
Bailey, Daniel I, 489
Bailey, Daniel III, 22
Bailey, Daniel IV, 368
Bailey, Daniel IV, 565
Bailey, Daniel IV, 567
Bailey, Daniel V, 21
Bailey, Daniel V, 372
Bailey, Daniel V, 403
Bailey, Daniel V, 469
Bailey, Daniel V, 473
Bailey, Daniel V, 499
Bailey, Daniel V, 609
Bailey, Daniel V, 610
Bailey, Daniel V, 626
Bailey, Daniel V, 628
Bailey, Daniel V, 629
Bailey, Daniel V, 637
Bailey, Daniel VI, 97
Bailey, Daniel VI, 129
Bailey, Daniel VI, 296
Bailey, Daniel VI, 467
Bailey, Daniel, Jr. V, 610
Bailey, Daniel, Jr. V, 651
Bailey, David I, 35
Bailey, David I, 93
Bailey, David I, 94
Bailey, David I, 129
Bailey, David I, 489
Bailey, David I, 523
Bailey, David I, 647
Bailey, David I, 673
Bailey, David I, 697
Bailey, David I, 708
Bailey, David IV, 364
Bailey, David IV, 365
Bailey, David IV, 367
Bailey, David IV, 1049
Bailey, David V, 21
Bailey, David V, 372
Bailey, David V, 406
Bailey, David V, 473
Bailey, David V, 610
Bailey, David V, 630
Bailey, David V, 635
Bailey, David V, 636
Bailey, David V, 726
Bailey, David V, 893
Bailey, David V, 967
Bailey, David VI, 15
Bailey, David VI, 97
Bailey, David VI, 129
Bailey, David VI, 130
Bailey, David VI, 135
Bailey, David VI, 138
Bailey, David VI, 141
Bailey, David VI, 874
Bailey, David VI, 997
Bailey, David Branson IV, 366
Bailey, David D. V, 473
Bailey, David Elwood IV, 1087
Bailey, David H. V, 610
Bailey, David H. V, 656
Bailey, David H. V, 893
Bailey, David M. V, 610
Bailey, Deborah II, 977
Bailey, Deborah II, 985
Bailey, Deborah V, 967
Bailey, Deborah V, 979
Bailey, Deborah VI, 52
Bailey, Deborah VI, 130
Bailey, Delisha IV, 673
Bailey, Delitha IV, 141
Bailey, Delitha IV, 171
Bailey, Delitha IV, 364
Bailey, Delitha IV, 365
Bailey, Delitha IV, 373
Bailey, Delitha V, 616
Bailey, Delitha VI, 97
Bailey, Delitha VI, 98
Bailey, Delitha VI, 99
Bailey, Delitha VI, 111
Bailey, Delitha VI, 130
Bailey, Delitha VI, 296
Bailey, Delitha Ann V, 610

Bailey, Delitha Ann V, 726
Bailey, Delitha Ann V, 732
Bailey, Delithia V, 610
Bailey, Dempsey IV, 171
Bailey, Dempsey IV, 367
Bailey, Dempsey IV, 389
Bailey, Dempsey IV, 700
Bailey, Demsey IV, 365
Bailey, Dillwyn G. IV, 509
Bailey, Diza Ann IV, 364
Bailey, Donald III, 22
Bailey, Dorcas I, 647
Bailey, Dorcas I, 673
Bailey, Dorcas I, 682
Bailey, Dorcas I, 697
Bailey, Dorothy IV, 363
Bailey, Dorothy IV, 368
Bailey, Dorothy M. IV, 366
Bailey, Ebidan VI, 98
Bailey, Edgar IV, 1143
Bailey, Edgar P. IV, 1143
Bailey, Edith IV, 366
Bailey, Edith E. V, 610
Bailey, Edith Griffith V, 893
Bailey, Edith Irene IV, 1143
Bailey, Edith M. IV, 171
Bailey, Edith M. IV, 179
Bailey, Edith M. IV, 368
Bailey, Edith M. IV, 371
Bailey, Edmond IV, 171
Bailey, Edmond IV, 364
Bailey, Edmond IV, 566
Bailey, Edmond VI, 97
Bailey, Edmond VI, 98
Bailey, Edmond VI, 99
Bailey, Edmond VI, 125
Bailey, Edmond VI, 130
Bailey, Edmond J. VI, 797
Bailey, Edmund IV, 171
Bailey, Edmund IV, 364
Bailey, Edmund IV, 365
Bailey, Edmund IV, 366
Bailey, Edmund IV, 385
Bailey, Edmund IV, 509
Bailey, Edmund IV, 565
Bailey, Edmund IV, 566
Bailey, Edmund IV, 581
Bailey, Edmund IV, 584
Bailey, Edmund IV, 591
Bailey, Edmund IV, 595
Bailey, Edmund IV, 673
Bailey, Edmund IV, 797
Bailey, Edmund IV, 819
Bailey, Edmund VI, 15
Bailey, Edmund VI, 98
Bailey, Edmund VI, 121
Bailey, Edmund VI, 125
Bailey, Edmund J. IV, 797
Bailey, Edmund J. IV, 798
Bailey, Edmund, Jr. IV, 567
Bailey, Edna A. IV, 366
Bailey, Edna A. IV, 446
Bailey, Edny Strong VI, 797
Bailey, Edward II, 718
Bailey, Edward IV, 1087
Bailey, Edward IV, 1127
Bailey, Edward VI, 98
Bailey, Edward E. IV, 1087
Bailey, Edward French IV, 366
Bailey, Edward H. IV, 923
Bailey, Edward P. IV, 673
Bailey, Edward P. IV, 1023
Bailey, Edwin IV, 365
Bailey, Edwin IV, 367
Bailey, Edwin IV, 1087
Bailey, Edwin V, 473
Bailey, Edwin Frazier V, 610
Bailey, Edwin H. IV, 171
Bailey, Edwin M. IV, 365
Bailey, Edwin M. IV, 366
Bailey, Edwin M. IV, 368
Bailey, Edwin M. IV, 387
Bailey, Eldene IV, 673
Bailey, Eli IV, 567
Bailey, Eli C. IV, 566
Bailey, Elihu IV, 365
Bailey, Elijah I, 372
Bailey, Elijah I, 408
Bailey, Elijah VI, 15
Bailey, Elijah VI, 97
Bailey, Elijah VI, 98
Bailey, Elijah VI, 102
Bailey, Elijah VI, 115
Bailey, Elijah VI, 117
Bailey, Elijah T. V, 473
Bailey, Elisabeth I, 129
Bailey, Elisabeth I, 158
Bailey, Elisabeth IV, 609
Bailey, Elisha IV, 566
Bailey, Eliza I, 129
Bailey, Eliza I, 132
Bailey, Eliza IV, 366
Bailey, Eliza IV, 674
Bailey, Eliza V, 797
Bailey, Eliza VI, 98
Bailey, Eliza VI, 129
Bailey, Eliza VI, 130
Bailey, Eliza VI, 296
Bailey, Eliza VI, 844
Bailey, Eliza Ann V, 473
Bailey, Eliza Ann V, 893
Bailey, Eliza D. IV, 367
Bailey, Eliza D. IV, 394
Bailey, Eliza Jane IV, 1143
Bailey, Eliza S. IV, 364
Bailey, Elizabeth II, 143
Bailey, Elizabeth II, 457
Bailey, Elizabeth II, 470
Bailey, Elizabeth II, 699
Bailey, Elizabeth II, 780
Bailey, Elizabeth II, 781
Bailey, Elizabeth IV, 139
Bailey, Elizabeth IV, 141
Bailey, Elizabeth IV, 171
Bailey, Elizabeth IV, 192
Bailey, Elizabeth IV, 195
Bailey, Elizabeth IV, 241
Bailey, Elizabeth IV, 319
Bailey, Elizabeth IV, 325
Bailey, Elizabeth IV, 363
Bailey, Elizabeth IV, 364
Bailey, Elizabeth IV, 365
Bailey, Elizabeth IV, 366
Bailey, Elizabeth IV, 367
Bailey, Elizabeth IV, 374
Bailey, Elizabeth IV, 375
Bailey, Elizabeth IV, 385
Bailey, Elizabeth IV, 390
Bailey, Elizabeth IV, 394
Bailey, Elizabeth IV, 414
Bailey, Elizabeth IV, 426
Bailey, Elizabeth IV, 428
Bailey, Elizabeth IV, 438
Bailey, Elizabeth IV, 441
Bailey, Elizabeth IV, 450
Bailey, Elizabeth IV, 463
Bailey, Elizabeth IV, 509
Bailey, Elizabeth IV, 510
Bailey, Elizabeth IV, 560
Bailey, Elizabeth IV, 565
Bailey, Elizabeth IV, 566
Bailey, Elizabeth IV, 567
Bailey, Elizabeth IV, 570
Bailey, Elizabeth IV, 590
Bailey, Elizabeth IV, 609
Bailey, Elizabeth IV, 673
Bailey, Elizabeth IV, 713
Bailey, Elizabeth IV, 797
Bailey, Elizabeth IV, 805
Bailey, Elizabeth IV, 933
Bailey, Elizabeth IV, 1049
Bailey, Elizabeth IV, 1080
Bailey, Elizabeth IV, 1087
Bailey, Elizabeth IV, 1088
Bailey, Elizabeth V, 21
Bailey, Elizabeth V, 84
Bailey, Elizabeth V, 218
Bailey, Elizabeth V, 297
Bailey, Elizabeth V, 307
Bailey, Elizabeth V, 318
Bailey, Elizabeth V, 348
Bailey, Elizabeth V, 473
Bailey, Elizabeth V, 475
Bailey, Elizabeth V, 610
Bailey, Elizabeth V, 611
Bailey, Elizabeth V, 616
Bailey, Elizabeth V, 630
Bailey, Elizabeth V, 635
Bailey, Elizabeth V, 651
Bailey, Elizabeth V, 726
Bailey, Elizabeth V, 892
Bailey, Elizabeth V, 893
Bailey, Elizabeth V, 901
Bailey, Elizabeth V, 908
Bailey, Elizabeth V, 923
Bailey, Elizabeth V, 967
Bailey, Elizabeth VI, 97
Bailey, Elizabeth VI, 98
Bailey, Elizabeth VI, 99
Bailey, Elizabeth VI, 101
Bailey, Elizabeth VI, 125
Bailey, Elizabeth VI, 129
Bailey, Elizabeth VI, 130
Bailey, Elizabeth VI, 296
Bailey, Elizabeth VI, 343
Bailey, Elizabeth VI, 393
Bailey, Elizabeth VI, 797
Bailey, Elizabeth VI, 806
Bailey, Elizabeth VI, 862
Bailey, Elizabeth VI, 867
Bailey, Elizabeth A. M. II, 280
Bailey, Elizabeth A. M. II, 296
Bailey, Elizabeth Ann V, 610
Bailey, Elizabeth Ann V, 620
Bailey, Elizabeth B. V, 893
Bailey, Elizabeth B. V, 896
Bailey, Elizabeth B. V, 917
Bailey, Elizabeth B. VI, 393
Bailey, Elizabeth Griffith V, 892
Bailey, Elizabeth Griffith V, 901
Bailey, Elizabeth Griffith V, 944
Bailey, Elizabeth Jr. IV, 171
Bailey, Elizabeth Jr. IV, 241
Bailey, Elizabeth L. II, 457
Bailey, Elizabeth L. II, 726
Bailey, Elizabeth M. IV, 171
Bailey, Elizabeth R. VI, 829
Bailey, Elizabeth S. II, 334
Bailey, Elizabeth S. IV, 171
Bailey, Elizabeth S. IV, 366
Bailey, Elizabeth S., Jr. IV, 366
Bailey, Elizabeth White II, 128
Bailey, Elizabeth, Jr. IV, 673
Bailey, Elizabeth, Jr. IV, 797
Bailey, Elizabeth, Sr. V, 610
Bailey, Ellen V, 611
Bailey, Ellen M. II, 143
Bailey, Ellen M. II, 151
Bailey, Ellis IV, 20
Bailey, Ellis IV, 73
Bailey, Ellwood IV, 1087
Bailey, Elma IV, 438
Bailey, Elma IV, 510
Bailey, Elma V, 318
Bailey, Elmer V, 611
Bailey, Elmer V, 656
Bailey, Elmira IV, 463
Bailey, Elmira V, 892
Bailey, Elmira V, 893
Bailey, Elmira V, 895
Bailey, Elmira S. IV, 463
Bailey, Elmira S. V, 893
Bailey, Elsie V, 656
Bailey, Elsie V, 689
Bailey, Elvira IV, 171
Bailey, Elvira IV, 509
Bailey, Elvira IV, 510
Bailey, Elvira IV, 545
Bailey, Elvira IV, 566
Bailey, Elvira IV, 567
Bailey, Elvira IV, 593
Bailey, Elvira P. IV, 510
Bailey, Elvira P. IV, 550
Bailey, Elvira P. IV, 566
Bailey, Elvira P. IV, 567
Bailey, Elwood IV, 319
Bailey, Elwood IV, 367
Bailey, Elwood IV, 1049
Bailey, Emma V, 611
Bailey, Emma V, 984
Bailey, Emmer IV, 319
Bailey, Emmer, Jr. V, 967
Bailey, Emmer, Sr. V, 967
Bailey, Emmor II, 52
Bailey, Emmor II, 457
Bailey, Emmor IV, 171
Bailey, Emmor IV, 192
Bailey, Emmor IV, 195
Bailey, Emmor IV, 241
Bailey, Emmor IV, 319
Bailey, Emmor IV, 509
Bailey, Emmor IV, 560
Bailey, Emmor IV, 565
Bailey, Emmor IV, 566
Bailey, Emmor V, 21
Bailey, Emmor V, 120
Bailey, Emmor V, 892
Bailey, Emmor S. V, 21
Bailey, Emmor, Jr. IV, 509
Bailey, Enoch II, 977
Bailey, Enos II, 977
Bailey, Enos V, 610
Bailey, Enos P. V, 611
Bailey, Ephraim I, 129
Bailey, Ernest IV, 368
Bailey, Ervin G. IV, 923
Bailey, Esther V, 797
Bailey, Ethel IV, 673
Bailey, Ethel IV, 923
Bailey, Ethel IV, 1035
Bailey, Ethel E. IV, 366
Bailey, Ethel E. IV, 390
Bailey, Ethel S. IV, 1035
Bailey, Euphemia V, 893
Bailey, Euphemia V, 917
Bailey, Euphenia F. V, 892
Bailey, Eva V, 611
Bailey, Eva L. IV, 366
Bailey, Eva L. IV, 390
Bailey, Eva L. IV, 427
Bailey, Eva L. IV, 442
Bailey, Eva L. IV, 446
Bailey, Evan IV, 367
Bailey, Evan P. II, 833
Bailey, Even IV, 365
Bailey, Exum IV, 364
Bailey, Exum IV, 566
Bailey, Exum IV, 1143
Bailey, Exum V, 967
Bailey, Exum VI, 97
Bailey, Exum VI, 99
Bailey, Exum VI, 109
Bailey, Exum VI, 130
Bailey, Exum VI, 135
Bailey, Exum VI, 140
Bailey, Exum VI, 296
Bailey, Exum VI, 301
Bailey, Ezra IV, 171
Bailey, Ezra IV, 463
Bailey, Ezra IV, 797
Bailey, Ezra IV, 805
Bailey, Ezra IV, 857
Bailey, Ezra V, 892
Bailey, Ezra V, 893
Bailey, Ezra V, 923
Bailey, Faith I, 372
Bailey, Faith IV, 591
Bailey, Faith VI, 97
Bailey, Faith VI, 99
Bailey, Fanney V, 611
Bailey, Fanny IV, 171
Bailey, Fanny IV, 365
Bailey, Fanny IV, 367
Bailey, Florence E. V, 336
Bailey, Florence Eleanor IV, 366
Bailey, Frances IV, 366
Bailey, Francis C. IV, 1023
Bailey, Frank C. V, 548
Bailey, Frank R. V, 548
Bailey, Franky VI, 874
Bailey, G. Wilson IV, 368
Bailey, Geo. IV, 923
Bailey, Geo. S. V, 893
Bailey, Geo. W. IV, 933
Bailey, George II, 698
Bailey, George II, 699
Bailey, George III, 22
Bailey, George IV, 565
Bailey, George IV, 567
Bailey, George IV, 673
Bailey, George IV, 923
Bailey, George IV, 1049
Bailey, George IV, 1087
Bailey, George IV, 1143
Bailey, George V, 473
Bailey, George V, 610
Bailey, George V, 616
Bailey, George V, 643
Bailey, George E. IV, 1143
Bailey, George L. V, 21
Bailey, George M. IV, 367
Bailey, George M. IV, 566
Bailey, George M. IV, 567
Bailey, George M. IV, 1087
Bailey, George W. IV, 566
Bailey, George W. IV, 567
Bailey, George W. IV, 923
Bailey, George W. IV, 1271
Bailey, Georgia III, 22
Bailey, Georgia III, 266
Bailey, German VI, 797
Bailey, Granderson V, 611
Bailey, Grandison V, 611
Bailey, Gulia VI, 52
Bailey, Gulie VI, 97
Bailey, Gulielma I, 1139
Bailey, Gulielma V, 610
Bailey, Gwenn E. V, 611
Bailey, H. K. V, 656
Bailey, H. K. V, 714
Bailey, Hannah II, 195
Bailey, Hannah II, 977
Bailey, Hannah II, 1020
Bailey, Hannah IV, 171
Bailey, Hannah IV, 319
Bailey, Hannah IV, 333
Bailey, Hannah IV, 364
Bailey, Hannah IV, 509
Bailey, Hannah IV, 560
Bailey, Hannah IV, 565
Bailey, Hannah IV, 673
Bailey, Hannah IV, 710
Bailey, Hannah IV, 713
Bailey, Hannah IV, 797
Bailey, Hannah IV, 1049
Bailey, Hannah IV, 1087
Bailey, Hannah IV, 1127
Bailey, Hannah IV, 1140
Bailey, Hannah V, 297
Bailey, Hannah V, 641
Bailey, Hannah Jane II, 781
Bailey, Hannah Jane II, 833
Bailey, Hannah L. IV, 509
Bailey, Hannah Lavina IV, 509
Bailey, Hannah Mary V, 610
Bailey, Hannah Mary V, 611
Bailey, Hannah Mary V, 614
Bailey, Harding IV, 673
Bailey, Harlan V, 656
Bailey, Harmon Eugene IV, 366
Bailey, Harriet IV, 171
Bailey, Harriet IV, 198
Bailey, Harriet IV, 367
Bailey, Harriet IV, 390
Bailey, Harriet IV, 1049
Bailey, Harriet IV, 1087
Bailey, Harriet IV, 1127
Bailey, Harriet Ellis V, 896
Bailey, Harriet Ellis V, 944
Bailey, Harriett IV, 171
Bailey, Harriett IV, 1127
Bailey, Harriett Ellis V, 893
Bailey, Harris IV, 1143
Bailey, Harris W. IV, 1143
Bailey, Harrison V, 984
Bailey, Harry IV, 1143
Bailey, Harry Rhodes III, 22
Bailey, Helen Margaret IV, 366
Bailey, Henery I, 129
Bailey, Henery I, 158
Bailey, Henery IV, 566
Bailey, Henry I, 129
Bailey, Henry I, 489
Bailey, Henry IV, 139
Bailey, Henry IV, 171
Bailey, Henry IV, 319
Bailey, Henry IV, 330
Bailey, Henry IV, 363
Bailey, Henry IV, 364
Bailey, Henry IV, 365
Bailey, Henry IV, 367
Bailey, Henry IV, 385
Bailey, Henry IV, 565
Bailey, Henry IV, 566
Bailey, Henry IV, 587
Bailey, Henry IV, 1049
Bailey, Henry IV, 1080
Bailey, Henry IV, 1087
Bailey, Henry IV, 1127
Bailey, Henry V, 21
Bailey, Henry VI, 98
Bailey, Herbert IV, 366
Bailey, Herbert IV, 368
Bailey, Herbert J. IV, 366
Bailey, Herman T. V, 548
Bailey, Hester Harris IV, 1245
Bailey, Hezekiah IV, 171
Bailey, Hezekiah IV, 364
Bailey, Hezekiah IV, 365
Bailey, Hezekiah IV, 374
Bailey, Hezekiah IV, 394
Bailey, Hezekiah IV, 438
Bailey, Hezekiah IV, 441
Bailey, Hezekiah V, 901
Bailey, Hezekiah VI, 393
Bailey, Hezekiah B. IV, 463
Bailey, Hezekiah B. V, 892
Bailey, Hezekiah B. V, 893
Bailey, Hezekiah B. V, 896
Bailey, Hezekiah B. V, 908
Bailey, Hezekiah B. V, 917
Bailey, Hezekiah B. VI, 393
Bailey, Hiram IV, 366
Bailey, Hiram IV, 367
Bailey, Hiram V, 21
Bailey, Hiram V, 473
Bailey, Hoopes IV, 673
Bailey, Hoopes IV, 797
Bailey, Hoops IV, 609
Bailey, Hoops IV, 673
Bailey, Hoops IV, 797
Bailey, Hoops IV, 837
Bailey, Hoops IV, 1021
Bailey, Hoops IV, 1023
Bailey, Howard Edmund IV, 797
Bailey, Howard H. IV, 673
Bailey, Huldah VI, 15
Bailey, Huldah VI, 98
Bailey, Huldah VI, 99
Bailey, Huldah VI, 121
Bailey, Ida IV, 172
Bailey, Ida IV, 509
Bailey, Ida IV, 511
Bailey, Ira IV, 367
Bailey, Ira W. IV, 364
Bailey, Irvin IV, 1143
Bailey, Irvin C. IV, 923
Bailey, Irving IV, 510
Bailey, Irving IV, 567
Bailey, Irving C. IV, 566
Bailey, Irving E. IV, 509
Bailey, Irving E. IV, 510
Bailey, Irving E. IV, 522
Bailey, Irving E. IV, 566
Bailey, Irving E. IV, 567

Bailey, Irving G. IV, 575
Bailey, Isaac IV, 171
Bailey, Isaac IV, 367
Bailey, Isaac IV, 509
Bailey, Isaac IV, 566
Bailey, Isaac IV, 673
Bailey, Isaac H. IV, 566
Bailey, Isaac H. IV, 567
Bailey, Isaac Hoover IV, 171
Bailey, Isaiah V, 610
Bailey, Israel II, 195
Bailey, Israel II, 977
Bailey, Issachar IV, 565
Bailey, J. H. V, 611
Bailey, Jabez II, 781
Bailey, Jabez II, 794
Bailey, Jacob I, 1102
Bailey, Jacob I, 1113
Bailey, Jacob IV, 171
Bailey, Jacob IV, 367
Bailey, Jacob IV, 566
Bailey, James I, 229
Bailey, James II, 334
Bailey, James IV, 367
Bailey, James IV, 565
Bailey, James IV, 566
Bailey, James IV, 567
Bailey, James IV, 570
Bailey, James IV, 601
Bailey, James IV, 673
Bailey, James IV, 797
Bailey, James IV, 1049
Bailey, James IV, 1071
Bailey, James IV, 1087
Bailey, James IV, 1127
Bailey, James V, 473
Bailey, James V, 797
Bailey, James VI, 97
Bailey, James VI, 797
Bailey, James VI, 822
Bailey, James VI, 874
Bailey, James E. IV, 171
Bailey, James E. IV, 566
Bailey, James E. IV, 567
Bailey, James E. IV, 571
Bailey, James E. IV, 797
Bailey, James E. IV, 798
Bailey, James E. V, 726
Bailey, James E. V, 797
Bailey, James Edwin V, 21
Bailey, James Edwin V, 473
Bailey, James Edwin VI, 296
Bailey, James M. VI, 867
Bailey, James W. V, 610
Bailey, James, Sr. II, 334
Bailey, Jane I, 372
Bailey, Jane I, 408
Bailey, Jane IV, 171
Bailey, Jane IV, 172
Bailey, Jane IV, 364
Bailey, Jane IV, 365
Bailey, Jane IV, 367
Bailey, Jane IV, 431
Bailey, Jane IV, 441
Bailey, Jane IV, 565
Bailey, Jane IV, 567
Bailey, Jane IV, 598
Bailey, Jane IV, 707
Bailey, Jane V, 318
Bailey, Jane V, 614
Bailey, Jane V, 984
Bailey, Jane VI, 97
Bailey, Jane VI, 99
Bailey, Jane F. IV, 1127
Bailey, Jane F. IV, 1135
Bailey, Jane N. VI, 115
Bailey, Jeanette V, 656
Bailey, Jeanette V, 714
Bailey, Jehu IV, 171
Bailey, Jehu IV, 281
Bailey, Jehu IV, 365
Bailey, Jehu IV, 565
Bailey, Jehu IV, 566
Bailey, Jehu IV, 567
Bailey, Jehu IV, 797
Bailey, Jehu IV, 1049
Bailey, Jehu??? IV, 566
Bailey, Jephtha IV, 172
Bailey, Jephthah IV, 566
Bailey, Jeptha IV, 365
Bailey, Jeptha IV, 367
Bailey, Jeptha IV, 510
Bailey, Jeptha IV, 566
Bailey, Jeptha IV, 567
Bailey, Jepthah IV, 567
Bailey, Jere VI, 52
Bailey, Jeremiah VI, 52
Bailey, Jesse II, 781
Bailey, Jesse IV, 139
Bailey, Jesse IV, 172
Bailey, Jesse IV, 364
Bailey, Jesse IV, 365
Bailey, Jesse IV, 366
Bailey, Jesse IV, 367
Bailey, Jesse IV, 373
Bailey, Jesse IV, 381
Bailey, Jesse IV, 386
Bailey, Jesse IV, 395
Bailey, Jesse IV, 398
Bailey, Jesse IV, 409
Bailey, Jesse IV, 421
Bailey, Jesse IV, 427
Bailey, Jesse IV, 430
Bailey, Jesse IV, 509
Bailey, Jesse IV, 510
Bailey, Jesse IV, 554
Bailey, Jesse IV, 609
Bailey, Jesse IV, 673
Bailey, Jesse IV, 797
Bailey, Jesse IV, 1049
Bailey, Jesse IV, 1087
Bailey, Jesse VI, 96
Bailey, Jesse VI, 97
Bailey, Jesse VI, 98
Bailey, Jesse VI, 99
Bailey, Jesse VI, 129
Bailey, Jesse VI, 130
Bailey, Jesse VI, 135
Bailey, Jesse VI, 797
Bailey, Jesse VI, 818
Bailey, Jesse M. IV, 172
Bailey, Jesse S. IV, 365
Bailey, Jesse S. IV, 366
Bailey, Jesse S. IV, 368
Bailey, Jesse S., Jr. IV, 366
Bailey, Jesse W. IV, 364
Bailey, Jesse W. IV, 367
Bailey, Jesse, Jr. IV, 364
Bailey, Joanna V, 610
Bailey, Joannah I, 129
Bailey, Joannah I, 130
Bailey, Joannah V, 610
Bailey, Joannah V, 637
Bailey, Joel IV, 171
Bailey, Joel IV, 172
Bailey, Joel IV, 319
Bailey, Joel IV, 365
Bailey, Joel IV, 367
Bailey, Joel IV, 377
Bailey, Joel IV, 445
Bailey, Joel IV, 509
Bailey, Joel IV, 534
Bailey, Joel IV, 565
Bailey, Joel IV, 566
Bailey, Joel IV, 567
Bailey, Joel IV, 591
Bailey, Joel IV, 1087
Bailey, Joel IV, 1105
Bailey, Joel IV, 1127
Bailey, John I, 35
Bailey, John I, 129
Bailey, John I, 647
Bailey, John I, 673
Bailey, John I, 678
Bailey, John I, 682
Bailey, John I, 695
Bailey, John I, 697
Bailey, John I, 708
Bailey, John II, 195
Bailey, John II, 977
Bailey, John IV, 172
Bailey, John IV, 365
Bailey, John IV, 367
Bailey, John IV, 509
Bailey, John IV, 566
Bailey, John IV, 567
Bailey, John IV, 673
Bailey, John IV, 1049
Bailey, John V, 21
Bailey, John V, 218
Bailey, John V, 318
Bailey, John V, 473
Bailey, John V, 929
Bailey, John VI, 97
Bailey, John VI, 154
Bailey, John VI, 296
Bailey, John VI, 467
Bailey, John VI, 491
Bailey, John VI, 797
Bailey, John VI, 807
Bailey, John VI, 829
Bailey, John H. V, 318
Bailey, John H. VI, 812
Bailey, John H. VI, 856
Bailey, John H. VI, 920
Bailey, John Henry IV, 367
Bailey, John Henry IV, 1049
Bailey, John Henry IV, 1087
Bailey, John Hervey IV, 1049
Bailey, John L. IV, 923
Bailey, John Quincey IV, 510
Bailey, John, Sr. I, 128
Bailey, John, Sr. I, 130
Bailey, Jonathan V, 372
Bailey, Jonathan V, 404
Bailey, Jonathan V, 610
Bailey, Jonathan V, 611
Bailey, Jonathan V, 621
Bailey, Jonathan V, 967
Bailey, Jonathan VI, 130
Bailey, Jonathan VI, 797
Bailey, Joseph II, 195
Bailey, Joseph II, 457
Bailey, Joseph II, 699
Bailey, Joseph IV, 172
Bailey, Joseph IV, 364
Bailey, Joseph IV, 365
Bailey, Joseph IV, 367
Bailey, Joseph IV, 509
Bailey, Joseph IV, 545
Bailey, Joseph IV, 550
Bailey, Joseph IV, 566
Bailey, Joseph IV, 567
Bailey, Joseph IV, 576
Bailey, Joseph IV, 593
Bailey, Joseph IV, 609
Bailey, Joseph IV, 673
Bailey, Joseph IV, 713
Bailey, Joseph IV, 797
Bailey, Joseph V, 297
Bailey, Joseph V, 318
Bailey, Joseph V, 372
Bailey, Joseph V, 473
Bailey, Joseph V, 610
Bailey, Joseph VI, 15
Bailey, Joseph VI, 97
Bailey, Joseph VI, 109
Bailey, Joseph VI, 122
Bailey, Joseph VI, 129
Bailey, Joseph VI, 130
Bailey, Joseph B. V, 473
Bailey, Joseph E. IV, 367
Bailey, Joseph E. IV, 510
Bailey, Joseph E. IV, 566
Bailey, Joseph E. IV, 567
Bailey, Joseph G. VI, 98
Bailey, Joseph J. V, 892
Bailey, Joseph L. II, 699
Bailey, Joseph Oscar IV, 366
Bailey, Joseph S. IV, 509
Bailey, Joseph Sidingham IV, 673
Bailey, Joseph Sydenham IV, 509
Bailey, Joseph Sydenham IV, 673
Bailey, Joseph, Jr. VI, 112
Bailey, Joseph, Sr. VI, 97
Bailey, Joseph, Sr. VI, 99
Bailey, Josephine IV, 366
Bailey, Joshua II, 457
Bailey, Joshua II, 699
Bailey, Joshua II, 726
Bailey, Joshua II, 781
Bailey, Joshua IV, 364
Bailey, Joshua IV, 365
Bailey, Joshua IV, 367
Bailey, Joshua IV, 390
Bailey, Joshua IV, 1143
Bailey, Joshua IV, 1195
Bailey, Joshua V, 967
Bailey, Joshua V, 969
Bailey, Joshua V, 979
Bailey, Joshua VI, 52
Bailey, Joshua VI, 97
Bailey, Joshua VI, 98
Bailey, Joshua VI, 122
Bailey, Joshua VI, 130
Bailey, Joshua VI, 296
Bailey, Joshua L. II, 833
Bailey, Joshua S. II, 334
Bailey, Joshua, Jr. II, 334
Bailey, Joshua, Jr. II, 457
Bailey, Joshua, Jr. II, 726
Bailey, Joshua, Jr. II, 781
Bailey, Joshua, Jr. II, 833
Bailey, Josiah IV, 373
Bailey, Josiah V, 21
Bailey, Josiah V, 610
Bailey, Josiah V, 629
Bailey, Josiah V, 641
Bailey, Josiah V, 646
Bailey, Josiah V, 797
Bailey, Josiah VI, 97
Bailey, Josiah VI, 129
Bailey, Josiah VI, 296
Bailey, Josiah VI, 297
Bailey, Josiah H. V, 473
Bailey, Josiah H. V, 610
Bailey, Josiah H. V, 611
Bailey, Juanita V, 656
Bailey, Judith IV, 572
Bailey, Judith V, 297
Bailey, Judith V, 318
Bailey, Judith V, 473
Bailey, Judith V, 531
Bailey, Judith VI, 97
Bailey, Judith VI, 99
Bailey, Judith VI, 106
Bailey, Judith VI, 296
Bailey, Katharine III, 22
Bailey, Katherine III, 212
Bailey, Katie V, 548
Bailey, Katie C. V, 548
Bailey, Kiziah VI, 815
Bailey, Laban IV, 365
Bailey, Laban IV, 367
Bailey, Laban IV, 1087
Bailey, Lambert R. V, 726
Bailey, Latitia II, 1044
Bailey, Laura II, 699
Bailey, Laura IV, 366
Bailey, Laura IV, 1143
Bailey, Laura E. IV, 171
Bailey, Laura E. IV, 172
Bailey, Laura E. IV, 282
Bailey, Laura E. IV, 368
Bailey, Laura E. IV, 444
Bailey, Laura L. IV, 1143
Bailey, Laura May IV, 923
Bailey, Lavina IV, 1087
Bailey, Lavina IV, 1127
Bailey, Lavina IV, 1130
Bailey, Lee VI, 859
Bailey, Lemuel VI, 98
Bailey, Lemuel VI, 99
Bailey, Lemuel, Jr. VI, 99
Bailey, Leone V, 318
Bailey, Leroy C. IV, 1143
Bailey, Leslie W. V, 726
Bailey, Lester Wm. IV, 366
Bailey, Letitia II, 977
Bailey, Levina IV, 1127
Bailey, Lewis IV, 566
Bailey, Lillian IV, 365
Bailey, Lillian IV, 366
Bailey, Lillian V, 548
Bailey, Lillian M. IV, 366
Bailey, Lillian M. IV, 387
Bailey, Lindley IV, 172
Bailey, Lindley IV, 365
Bailey, Lindley IV, 367
Bailey, Lindley IV, 566
Bailey, Lindley IV, 1087
Bailey, Lindley M. V, 610
Bailey, Lindley P. IV, 171
Bailey, Lindley P. IV, 365
Bailey, Lindley P. IV, 366
Bailey, Lindley P. IV, 375
Bailey, Lindley P. IV, 428
Bailey, Lindley P. IV, 441
Bailey, Lindley P., Jr. IV, 366
Bailey, Lizzie V, 611
Bailey, Lloyd II, 334
Bailey, Lloyd II, 457
Bailey, Lloyd II, 833
Bailey, Lois IV, 673
Bailey, Lois IV, 1035
Bailey, Lois Lansdowne II, 128
Bailey, Lois Lansdowne II, 143
Bailey, Lois Marie IV, 923
Bailey, Louella V, 611
Bailey, Louisa VI, 130
Bailey, Louisa VI, 296
Bailey, Louisa VI, 301
Bailey, Louisa VI, 302
Bailey, Loyd II, 726
Bailey, Loyd II, 781
Bailey, Lucinda IV, 365
Bailey, Lucreasy Daniel VI, 797
Bailey, Lucretia Bell V, 656
Bailey, Lucretia Bell V, 721
Bailey, Lucretia M. IV, 1023
Bailey, Lucy IV, 139
Bailey, Lucy IV, 172
Bailey, Lucy IV, 365
Bailey, Lucy IV, 426
Bailey, Lucy IV, 565
Bailey, Lucy IV, 572
Bailey, Lucy IV, 590
Bailey, Lucy IV, 1233
Bailey, Lucy V, 473
Bailey, Lucy V, 475
Bailey, Lucy V, 610
Bailey, Lucy V, 611
Bailey, Lucy VI, 97
Bailey, Lucy VI, 99
Bailey, Lucy VI, 102
Bailey, Lucy VI, 797
Bailey, Lucy VI, 818
Bailey, Lucy VI, 868
Bailey, Lucy VI, 874
Bailey, Luella V, 656
Bailey, Luther G. V, 611
Bailey, Lydenham IV, 509
Bailey, Lydia II, 781
Bailey, Lydia II, 826
Bailey, Lydia IV, 172
Bailey, Lydia IV, 364
Bailey, Lydia IV, 365
Bailey, Lydia IV, 367
Bailey, Lydia IV, 386
Bailey, Lydia IV, 427
Bailey, Lydia IV, 443
Bailey, Lydia IV, 509
Bailey, Lydia IV, 534
Bailey, Lydia IV, 554
Bailey, Lydia IV, 565
Bailey, Lydia IV, 566
Bailey, Lydia IV, 575
Bailey, Lydia IV, 595
Bailey, Lydia IV, 609
Bailey, Lydia IV, 797
Bailey, Lydia IV, 1049
Bailey, Lydia IV, 1087
Bailey, Lydia IV, 1105
Bailey, Lydia IV, 1127
Bailey, Lydia IV, 1140
Bailey, Lydia V, 610
Bailey, Lydia V, 616
Bailey, Lydia V, 643
Bailey, Lydia V, 967
Bailey, Lydia V, 969
Bailey, Lydia C. IV, 798
Bailey, Lydia C. V, 893
Bailey, Lydia C. V, 979
Bailey, Lydia H. IV, 365
Bailey, Lydia H. IV, 367
Bailey, Lydia J. IV, 172
Bailey, Lydia Jane IV, 365
Bailey, Lydia Jane IV, 367
Bailey, Lydia Jane IV, 1049
Bailey, Lydia Jane IV, 1087
Bailey, Lydia M. IV, 366
Bailey, Lydia M. IV, 368
Bailey, Lydia Pamelia IV, 509
Bailey, Lydia Pamelia IV, 673
Bailey, Lydia, Jr. IV, 172
Bailey, M. Gertrude V, 893
Bailey, Mabel Gertrude V, 893
Bailey, Mabel Sarah IV, 959
Bailey, Mable Gertrude V, 893
Bailey, Mahala IV, 366
Bailey, Mahala IV, 367
Bailey, Mahala IV, 1087
Bailey, Mahala VI, 129
Bailey, Mahala VI, 833
Bailey, Mahala R. IV, 364
Bailey, Mahlon IV, 365
Bailey, Mahlon IV, 366
Bailey, Mahlon IV, 382
Bailey, Mahlon IV, 445
Bailey, Mahlon IV, 566
Bailey, Mahlon G. V, 610
Bailey, Marah VI, 812
Bailey, Marahda IV, 364
Bailey, Maranda IV, 364
Bailey, Maranda IV, 365
Bailey, Maranda IV, 441
Bailey, Marander IV, 139
Bailey, Margaret IV, 73
Bailey, Margaret IV, 121
Bailey, Margaret IV, 171
Bailey, Margaret IV, 172
Bailey, Margaret IV, 192
Bailey, Margaret IV, 365
Bailey, Margaret IV, 366
Bailey, Margaret IV, 385
Bailey, Margaret IV, 459
Bailey, Margaret IV, 463
Bailey, Margaret IV, 469
Bailey, Margaret IV, 509
Bailey, Margaret IV, 531
Bailey, Margaret IV, 565
Bailey, Margaret IV, 566
Bailey, Margaret IV, 581
Bailey, Margaret IV, 584
Bailey, Margaret IV, 591
Bailey, Margaret IV, 595
Bailey, Margaret IV, 797
Bailey, Margaret IV, 819
Bailey, Margaret IV, 1087
Bailey, Margaret IV, 1122
Bailey, Margaret IV, 1127
Bailey, Margaret IV, 1128
Bailey, Margaret VI, 98
Bailey, Margaret VI, 130
Bailey, Margaret M. VI, 856
Bailey, Margaret Rebecca IV, 171
Bailey, Margaret Whitfield VI, 97
Bailey, Maria IV, 172
Bailey, Maria IV, 364
Bailey, Maria IV, 365
Bailey, Maria IV, 367
Bailey, Maria IV, 405
Bailey, Maria IV, 566
Bailey, Maria IV, 820
Bailey, Maria IV, 1087

Bailey, Maria V, 401
Bailey, Maria V, 610
Bailey, Maria V, 656
Bailey, Maria VI, 130
Bailey, Maria VI, 132
Bailey, Maria VI, 302
Bailey, Maria A. IV, 319
Bailey, Maria A. IV, 330
Bailey, Maria A. IV, 565
Bailey, Maria A. IV, 566
Bailey, Maria A. VI, 859
Bailey, Maria E. IV, 319
Bailey, Maria S. V, 656
Bailey, Maria T. V, 610
Bailey, Mariah VI, 97
Bailey, Mariah VI, 797
Bailey, Mariam IV, 567
Bailey, Mariam IV, 575
Bailey, Mariana V, 610
Bailey, Marianna V, 404
Bailey, Marion IV, 400
Bailey, Mark II, 985
Bailey, Marmaduke Brackney V, 218
Bailey, Marshall II, 781
Bailey, Marshall IV, 1127
Bailey, Marshall J. II, 781
Bailey, Marshall J. II, 833
Bailey, Martha I, 1139
Bailey, Martha II, 457
Bailey, Martha II, 593
Bailey, Martha II, 699
Bailey, Martha III, 394
Bailey, Martha IV, 171
Bailey, Martha IV, 172
Bailey, Martha IV, 176
Bailey, Martha IV, 281
Bailey, Martha IV, 319
Bailey, Martha IV, 365
Bailey, Martha IV, 367
Bailey, Martha IV, 377
Bailey, Martha IV, 509
Bailey, Martha IV, 511
Bailey, Martha IV, 560
Bailey, Martha IV, 565
Bailey, Martha IV, 566
Bailey, Martha IV, 567
Bailey, Martha IV, 576
Bailey, Martha IV, 593
Bailey, Martha IV, 601
Bailey, Martha IV, 797
Bailey, Martha IV, 1087
Bailey, Martha IV, 1121
Bailey, Martha IV, 1271
Bailey, Martha V, 318
Bailey, Martha V, 473
Bailey, Martha V, 609
Bailey, Martha V, 610
Bailey, Martha V, 637
Bailey, Martha V, 984
Bailey, Martha VI, 97
Bailey, Martha VI, 98
Bailey, Martha VI, 99
Bailey, Martha VI, 119
Bailey, Martha VI, 121
Bailey, Martha VI, 129
Bailey, Martha VI, 130
Bailey, Martha VI, 142
Bailey, Martha VI, 806
Bailey, Martha VI, 822
Bailey, Martha A. IV, 1143
Bailey, Martha Griffith V, 892
Bailey, Martha J. VI, 830
Bailey, Martha L. II, 718
Bailey, Martha L. IV, 171
Bailey, Martha L. IV, 172
Bailey, Martha Leone V, 318
Bailey, Martha Leone V, 342
Bailey, Martha Louise IV, 366
Bailey, Martha R. VI, 874
Bailey, Martha S. IV, 566
Bailey, Martha Yancie VI, 804
Bailey, Mary I, 129
Bailey, Mary I, 647
Bailey, Mary I, 697
Bailey, Mary I, 708
Bailey, Mary I, 730
Bailey, Mary II, 143
Bailey, Mary II, 334
Bailey, Mary II, 781
Bailey, Mary II, 977
Bailey, Mary II, 985
Bailey, Mary II, 1039
Bailey, Mary III, 22
Bailey, Mary III, 497
Bailey, Mary IV, 139
Bailey, Mary IV, 141
Bailey, Mary IV, 171
Bailey, Mary IV, 172
Bailey, Mary IV, 195
Bailey, Mary IV, 319
Bailey, Mary IV, 330
Bailey, Mary IV, 364
Bailey, Mary IV, 365
Bailey, Mary IV, 366
Bailey, Mary IV, 367
Bailey, Mary IV, 373
Bailey, Mary IV, 377
Bailey, Mary IV, 381
Bailey, Mary IV, 386
Bailey, Mary IV, 398
Bailey, Mary IV, 401
Bailey, Mary IV, 405
Bailey, Mary IV, 431
Bailey, Mary IV, 441
Bailey, Mary IV, 509
Bailey, Mary IV, 565
Bailey, Mary IV, 566
Bailey, Mary IV, 567
Bailey, Mary IV, 569
Bailey, Mary IV, 572
Bailey, Mary IV, 587
Bailey, Mary IV, 599
Bailey, Mary IV, 673
Bailey, Mary IV, 1049
Bailey, Mary IV, 1080
Bailey, Mary IV, 1087
Bailey, Mary V, 21
Bailey, Mary V, 117
Bailey, Mary V, 120
Bailey, Mary V, 218
Bailey, Mary V, 318
Bailey, Mary V, 372
Bailey, Mary V, 403
Bailey, Mary V, 406
Bailey, Mary V, 473
Bailey, Mary V, 499
Bailey, Mary V, 609
Bailey, Mary V, 610
Bailey, Mary V, 626
Bailey, Mary V, 628
Bailey, Mary V, 629
Bailey, Mary V, 637
Bailey, Mary V, 651
Bailey, Mary V, 684
Bailey, Mary V, 967
Bailey, Mary VI, 42
Bailey, Mary VI, 97
Bailey, Mary VI, 98
Bailey, Mary VI, 99
Bailey, Mary VI, 104
Bailey, Mary VI, 109
Bailey, Mary VI, 111
Bailey, Mary VI, 113
Bailey, Mary VI, 118
Bailey, Mary VI, 124
Bailey, Mary VI, 129
Bailey, Mary VI, 130
Bailey, Mary VI, 296
Bailey, Mary VI, 467
Bailey, Mary VI, 491
Bailey, Mary VI, 803
Bailey, Mary VI, 818
Bailey, Mary VI, 830
Bailey, Mary VI, 833
Bailey, Mary VI, 863
Bailey, Mary Abba V, 629
Bailey, Mary Alma IV, 366
Bailey, Mary Alma IV, 442
Bailey, Mary Ann IV, 171
Bailey, Mary Ann IV, 172
Bailey, Mary Ann IV, 319
Bailey, Mary Ann IV, 365
Bailey, Mary Ann IV, 366
Bailey, Mary Ann IV, 367
Bailey, Mary Ann IV, 406
Bailey, Mary Ann IV, 673
Bailey, Mary Ann IV, 797
Bailey, Mary Ann IV, 1087
Bailey, Mary Ann IV, 1127
Bailey, Mary Ann IV, 1137
Bailey, Mary Ann VI, 797
Bailey, Mary Anna IV, 171
Bailey, Mary Anna IV, 172
Bailey, Mary Anna IV, 179
Bailey, Mary Anna IV, 366
Bailey, Mary Anna IV, 367
Bailey, Mary Anna IV, 371
Bailey, Mary Anna V, 610
Bailey, Mary Anna V, 611
Bailey, Mary B. V, 610
Bailey, Mary B. V, 646
Bailey, Mary Byram V, 508
Bailey, Mary Byram Baily V, 473
Bailey, Mary Byrum V, 21
Bailey, Mary Byrum V, 473
Bailey, Mary Byrum VI, 296
Bailey, Mary C. IV, 80
Bailey, Mary C. V, 610
Bailey, Mary E. V, 656
Bailey, Mary Elizabeth II, 128
Bailey, Mary Elizabeth II, 143
Bailey, Mary Elizabeth II, 151
Bailey, Mary Elizabeth IV, 366
Bailey, Mary Ella V, 892
Bailey, Mary Ellen V, 893
Bailey, Mary Emily IV, 673
Bailey, Mary Emily IV, 1023
Bailey, Mary Emily IV, 1028
Bailey, Mary Hilliard II, 128
Bailey, Mary Hilliard, Jr. II, 143
Bailey, Mary J. V, 372
Bailey, Mary J. V, 610
Bailey, Mary J. V, 611
Bailey, Mary J. V, 620
Bailey, Mary Jane IV, 365
Bailey, Mary Jane IV, 367
Bailey, Mary Jane IV, 1087
Bailey, Mary Jane V, 610
Bailey, Mary M. II, 833
Bailey, Mary M. II, 862
Bailey, Mary M. VI, 797
Bailey, Mary M. C. VI, 859
Bailey, Mary Mitchel IV, 509
Bailey, Mary Nanville V, 726
Bailey, Mary R. IV, 509
Bailey, Mary Ruth IV, 139
Bailey, Mary T. V, 641
Bailey, Mary, Jr. VI, 1016
Bailey, Mary, Sr. VI, 1016
Bailey, Maryann IV, 1087
Bailey, Mathen VI, 97
Bailey, Matilda IV, 364
Bailey, Matilda IV, 365
Bailey, Matilda IV, 366
Bailey, Matilda IV, 430
Bailey, Matilda IV, 566
Bailey, Matilda IV, 673
Bailey, Matilda VI, 130
Bailey, Matther IV, 365
Bailey, Matthew IV, 373
Bailey, Matthew Wood IV, 365
Bailey, Matthews IV, 364
Bailey, May V, 726
Bailey, Melissa IV, 566
Bailey, Mellie V, 150
Bailey, Melvina IV, 172
Bailey, Melvina IV, 365
Bailey, Melvina IV, 394
Bailey, Mercy II, 977
Bailey, Mercy II, 1013
Bailey, Micajah IV, 139
Bailey, Micajah IV, 171
Bailey, Micajah IV, 364
Bailey, Micajah IV, 365
Bailey, Micajah IV, 366
Bailey, Micajah IV, 405
Bailey, Micajah IV, 431
Bailey, Micajah IV, 441
Bailey, Micajah IV, 509
Bailey, Micajah IV, 566
Bailey, Micajah V, 610
Bailey, Micajah V, 611
Bailey, Micajah V, 893
Bailey, Micajah V, 907
Bailey, Micajah V, 967
Bailey, Micajah VI, 96
Bailey, Micajah VI, 97
Bailey, Micajah VI, 99
Bailey, Micajah VI, 106
Bailey, Micajah VI, 111
Bailey, Micajah VI, 113
Bailey, Micajah VI, 130
Bailey, Michael VI, 98
Bailey, Michael VI, 99
Bailey, Michal IV, 366
Bailey, Michal VI, 97
Bailey, Michal VI, 98
Bailey, Michal VI, 130
Bailey, Michal VI, 139
Bailey, Michel IV, 365
Bailey, Michel IV, 367
Bailey, Michel IV, 382
Bailey, Michel IV, 395
Bailey, Michel VI, 129
Bailey, Michel VI, 130
Bailey, Michl VI, 98
Bailey, Miffraim VI, 807
Bailey, Miffraim VI, 827
Bailey, Miffraim VI, 860
Bailey, Miffram VI, 797
Bailey, Milicent IV, 172
Bailey, Milisent I, 647
Bailey, Milisent I, 697
Bailey, Millicent IV, 566
Bailey, Millicent IV, 581
Bailey, Millicent IV, 715
Bailey, Millicent IV, 819
Bailey, Millicent IV, 841
Bailey, Millicent IV, 844
Bailey, Millisent I, 708
Bailey, Milten IV, 365
Bailey, Milton IV, 365
Bailey, Milton IV, 367
Bailey, Milton IV, 377
Bailey, Milton IV, 565
Bailey, Milton IV, 566
Bailey, Milton IV, 567
Bailey, Minnie Howell V, 656
Bailey, Miriam IV, 566
Bailey, Miriam VI, 97
Bailey, Miriam VI, 98
Bailey, Miriam VI, 108
Bailey, Moses V, 297
Bailey, Moses V, 797
Bailey, Mourning VI, 97
Bailey, Mourning VI, 154
Bailey, Mourning VI, 190
Bailey, Mourning VI, 194
Bailey, Mrs. W. H. V, 548
Bailey, Myrtle D. IV, 1143
Bailey, Nace VI, 874
Bailey, Nancey VI, 874
Bailey, Nancy IV, 172
Bailey, Nancy IV, 365
Bailey, Nancy IV, 366
Bailey, Nancy IV, 367
Bailey, Nancy IV, 409
Bailey, Nancy IV, 1087
Bailey, Nancy VI, 129
Bailey, Nancy VI, 797
Bailey, Nancy VI, 839
Bailey, Nancy VI, 863
Bailey, Nancy VI, 874
Bailey, Nancy C. VI, 797
Bailey, Nathan I, 489
Bailey, Nathan II, 833
Bailey, Nathan IV, 566
Bailey, Nathan IV, 1087
Bailey, Nathan V, 218
Bailey, Nathan V, 473
Bailey, Nathan V, 825
Bailey, Nathan V, 879
Bailey, Nathan VI, 467
Bailey, Nathan H. V, 610
Bailey, Neil V, 657
Bailey, Nell V, 656
Bailey, Nelson VI, 874
Bailey, Nelson VI, 1016
Bailey, Nunnery VI, 797
Bailey, Oakley H. IV, 1023
Bailey, Oliver IV, 171
Bailey, Oliver IV, 366
Bailey, Oliver IV, 797
Bailey, Oliver B. IV, 368
Bailey, Oliver B. IV, 444
Bailey, Oliver B. IV, 797
Bailey, Oliver B. IV, 844
Bailey, Oliver Bracken IV, 366
Bailey, Oliver Brackin IV, 171
Bailey, Oliver S. IV, 172
Bailey, Oscar IV, 923
Bailey, Oscar J. IV, 171
Bailey, Oscar J. IV, 179
Bailey, Oscar J. IV, 365
Bailey, Oscar J. IV, 366
Bailey, Oscar J. IV, 367
Bailey, Oscar J. IV, 368
Bailey, Oscar J. IV, 371
Bailey, Oscar Wilson IV, 171
Bailey, Oscar Wilson IV, 172
Bailey, Oscar Wilson IV, 366
Bailey, Oscar Wilson IV, 368
Bailey, Osmond II, 977
Bailey, Ozmond II, 195
Bailey, Ozro Whitaker V, 893
Bailey, Patience VI, 97
Bailey, Patience VI, 98
Bailey, Patience VI, 99
Bailey, Patience VI, 122
Bailey, Paul IV, 673
Bailey, Paul Chester IV, 923
Bailey, Paul Chester IV, 1035
Bailey, Paulina VI, 874
Bailey, Peggy VI, 797
Bailey, Penelope VI, 797
Bailey, Peninah IV, 366
Bailey, Peninah IV, 371
Bailey, Peninah VI, 97
Bailey, Penninah VI, 99
Bailey, Penninah VI, 123
Bailey, Pennock IV, 609
Bailey, Pennock IV, 797
Bailey, Penock IV, 673
Bailey, Permelia IV, 566
Bailey, Permelia IV, 570
Bailey, Permelia VI, 98
Bailey, Peterson VI, 97
Bailey, Pharaba IV, 364
Bailey, Pharaba IV, 566
Bailey, Pharaba VI, 98
Bailey, Pharabi IV, 386
Bailey, Pharaby IV, 365
Bailey, Pharaby IV, 565
Bailey, Phareba IV, 365
Bailey, Phares Compton V, 726
Bailey, Phariba IV, 366
Bailey, Phariba IV, 373
Bailey, Phariba IV, 381
Bailey, Phariba IV, 395
Bailey, Phariba IV, 430
Bailey, Phariba IV, 591
Bailey, Phebe II, 977
Bailey, Phebe IV, 171
Bailey, Phebe IV, 367
Bailey, Phebe IV, 426
Bailey, Phebe IV, 560
Bailey, Phebe IV, 566
Bailey, Phebe IV, 567
Bailey, Phebe IV, 578
Bailey, Phebe V, 21
Bailey, Phebe V, 120
Bailey, Phebe V, 218
Bailey, Phebe V, 276
Bailey, Phebe V, 610
Bailey, Phebe V, 613
Bailey, Phebe V, 907
Bailey, Phebe W. IV, 509
Bailey, Phebe W. IV, 510
Bailey, Phebe W. IV, 532
Bailey, Pheraba IV, 365
Bailey, Phereby VI, 99
Bailey, Pheriba IV, 574
Bailey, Pheriba IV, 673
Bailey, Pheriba VI, 130
Bailey, Pheruba VI, 99
Bailey, Philip VI, 874
Bailey, Philip, Sr. VI, 1016
Bailey, Phillip VI, 874
Bailey, Polly VI, 797
Bailey, Polly VI, 818
Bailey, Polly H. VI, 97
Bailey, Polly H. VI, 99
Bailey, Priscilla IV, 172
Bailey, Priscilla IV, 365
Bailey, Priscilla IV, 367
Bailey, Priscilla IV, 445
Bailey, Priscilla IV, 566
Bailey, Priscilla VI, 98
Bailey, Prudence IV, 172
Bailey, Prudence IV, 365
Bailey, Prudence IV, 367
Bailey, R. C. IV, 179
Bailey, Rachel II, 781
Bailey, Rachel IV, 171
Bailey, Rachel IV, 172
Bailey, Rachel IV, 364
Bailey, Rachel IV, 367
Bailey, Rachel IV, 375
Bailey, Rachel IV, 423
Bailey, Rachel IV, 432
Bailey, Rachel IV, 435
Bailey, Rachel IV, 458
Bailey, Rachel IV, 509
Bailey, Rachel IV, 565
Bailey, Rachel IV, 566
Bailey, Rachel IV, 587
Bailey, Rachel IV, 589
Bailey, Rachel IV, 609
Bailey, Rachel IV, 673
Bailey, Rachel IV, 674
Bailey, Rachel IV, 781
Bailey, Rachel IV, 797
Bailey, Rachel IV, 1049
Bailey, Rachel IV, 1127
Bailey, Rachel IV, 1135
Bailey, Rachel V, 21
Bailey, Rachel V, 473
Bailey, Rachel VI, 97
Bailey, Rachel VI, 98
Bailey, Rachel VI, 99
Bailey, Rachel VI, 105
Bailey, Rachel VI, 106
Bailey, Rachel Ann II, 833
Bailey, Rachel C. III, 23
Bailey, Rachel Orynthia Nealy V, 893
Bailey, Rachel W. IV, 365
Bailey, Ralph W. IV, 366
Bailey, Randal IV, 609
Bailey, Randal IV, 797
Bailey, Randel IV, 797
Bailey, Randel IV, 799
Bailey, Raymon C. IV, 368
Bailey, Raymon C. IV, 371
Bailey, Raymond C. IV, 171
Bailey, Raymond C. IV, 366
Bailey, Rebecca II, 699
Bailey, Rebecca IV, 95
Bailey, Rebecca IV, 171
Bailey, Rebecca IV, 365
Bailey, Rebecca IV, 366
Bailey, Rebecca IV, 368
Bailey, Rebecca IV, 382
Bailey, Rebecca IV, 426

Bailey, Rebecca IV, 444
Bailey, Rebecca IV, 459
Bailey, Rebecca IV, 509
Bailey, Rebecca IV, 565
Bailey, Rebecca IV, 593
Bailey, Rebecca IV, 673
Bailey, Rebecca IV, 797
Bailey, Rebecca V, 21
Bailey, Rebecca V, 372
Bailey, Rebecca V, 473
Bailey, Rebecca V, 610
Bailey, Rebecca V, 726
Bailey, Rebecca V, 797
Bailey, Rebecca VI, 97
Bailey, Rebecca Adamson IV, 691
Bailey, Rebecca Alice IV, 367
Bailey, Rebecca Alice IV, 1049
Bailey, Rebecca Alice IV, 1087
Bailey, Rebecca Ann V, 797
Bailey, Rebecca B. IV, 797
Bailey, Rebecca B. IV, 844
Bailey, Rebecca L. V, 967
Bailey, Rebecca Louisa V, 979
Bailey, Rebecca Mary V, 610
Bailey, Rebecca S. IV, 172
Bailey, Rebecca S. IV, 366
Bailey, Rebecca S. IV, 368
Bailey, Rebecca Steer IV, 798
Bailey, Rebecca T. IV, 509
Bailey, Rebecca T. V, 404
Bailey, Rebecca T. V, 610
Bailey, Rebecca T. V, 611
Bailey, Rebecca T. V, 621
Bailey, Rebeckah IV, 366
Bailey, Rebeckah VI, 97
Bailey, Rebeckah VI, 99
Bailey, Rebeckah VI, 105
Bailey, Rebekah IV, 408
Bailey, Reuben IV, 73
Bailey, Rev. Charles IV, 673
Bailey, Rhoda IV, 367
Bailey, Rhoda IV, 567
Bailey, Rhoda IV, 1049
Bailey, Rhoda IV, 1071
Bailey, Rhoda IV, 1087
Bailey, Rhoda V, 984
Bailey, Rhoda VI, 797
Bailey, Robert IV, 172
Bailey, Robert IV, 319
Bailey, Robert IV, 367
Bailey, Robert IV, 673
Bailey, Robert IV, 1049
Bailey, Robert IV, 1087
Bailey, Robert V, 797
Bailey, Robert VI, 98
Bailey, Robert VI, 797
Bailey, Robert B. V, 473
Bailey, Robert B. V, 475
Bailey, Robert B. V, 610
Bailey, Robert B. V, 611
Bailey, Robert Barclay V, 473
Bailey, Robert Barclay VI, 296
Bailey, Robert C. IV, 364
Bailey, Robert H. IV, 365
Bailey, Robert H. IV, 367
Bailey, Robert S. VI, 99
Bailey, Roland A. IV, 366
Bailey, Rosanna III, 22
Bailey, Rosannah III, 22
Bailey, Rosella IV, 171
Bailey, Rosella IV, 176
Bailey, Rosella IV, 567
Bailey, Rueben II, 780
Bailey, Russell W. V, 548
Bailey, Ruth I, 94
Bailey, Ruth I, 129
Bailey, Ruth I, 130
Bailey, Ruth I, 229
Bailey, Ruth I, 253
Bailey, Ruth I, 489
Bailey, Ruth IV, 172
Bailey, Ruth IV, 364
Bailey, Ruth IV, 365
Bailey, Ruth IV, 367
Bailey, Ruth IV, 385
Bailey, Ruth IV, 426
Bailey, Ruth IV, 566
Bailey, Ruth IV, 567
Bailey, Ruth IV, 673
Bailey, Ruth IV, 797
Bailey, Ruth V, 21
Bailey, Ruth VI, 98
Bailey, Ruth VI, 111
Bailey, Ruth Anna IV, 445
Bailey, Ruth Anna IV, 566
Bailey, Ruthanna IV, 566
Bailey, Ruthanna IV, 591
Bailey, Ruthetta IV, 923
Bailey, Ruthetta IV, 933
Bailey, S. M. IV, 172
Bailey, Sally IV, 171
Bailey, Sally V, 473
Bailey, Sally VI, 797
Bailey, Sally L. VI, 904
Bailey, Sally S. VI, 799
Bailey, Samantha V, 372
Bailey, Samuel II, 195
Bailey, Samuel II, 726
Bailey, Samuel IV, 139
Bailey, Samuel IV, 171
Bailey, Samuel IV, 198
Bailey, Samuel IV, 364
Bailey, Samuel IV, 367
Bailey, Samuel IV, 390
Bailey, Samuel IV, 1049
Bailey, Samuel IV, 1087
Bailey, Samuel IV, 1127
Bailey, Samuel V, 548
Bailey, Samuel VI, 97
Bailey, Samuel VI, 105
Bailey, Samuel VI, 110
Bailey, Samuel VI, 111
Bailey, Samuel VI, 118
Bailey, Samuel G. IV, 172
Bailey, Samuel G. IV, 567
Bailey, Samuel L. II, 457
Bailey, Samuel L. II, 726
Bailey, Samuel L. II, 833
Bailey, Samuel Oscar V, 548
Bailey, Samuel P. II, 726
Bailey, Samuel P. II, 833
Bailey, Samuel T. II, 143
Bailey, Samuel T. II, 151
Bailey, Sara C. IV, 797
Bailey, Sarah I, 129
Bailey, Sarah I, 131
Bailey, Sarah II, 195
Bailey, Sarah II, 334
Bailey, Sarah II, 457
Bailey, Sarah II, 699
Bailey, Sarah II, 812
Bailey, Sarah II, 977
Bailey, Sarah II, 1041
Bailey, Sarah IV, 171
Bailey, Sarah IV, 172
Bailey, Sarah IV, 201
Bailey, Sarah IV, 365
Bailey, Sarah IV, 366
Bailey, Sarah IV, 367
Bailey, Sarah IV, 412
Bailey, Sarah IV, 421
Bailey, Sarah IV, 454
Bailey, Sarah IV, 510
Bailey, Sarah IV, 565
Bailey, Sarah IV, 566
Bailey, Sarah IV, 567
Bailey, Sarah IV, 570
Bailey, Sarah IV, 571
Bailey, Sarah IV, 572
Bailey, Sarah IV, 601
Bailey, Sarah IV, 673
Bailey, Sarah IV, 797
Bailey, Sarah IV, 808
Bailey, Sarah IV, 1049
Bailey, Sarah IV, 1087
Bailey, Sarah IV, 1127
Bailey, Sarah IV, 1134
Bailey, Sarah V, 218
Bailey, Sarah V, 318
Bailey, Sarah V, 401
Bailey, Sarah V, 473
Bailey, Sarah V, 479
Bailey, Sarah V, 610
Bailey, Sarah V, 629
Bailey, Sarah VI, 52
Bailey, Sarah VI, 60
Bailey, Sarah VI, 97
Bailey, Sarah VI, 98
Bailey, Sarah VI, 101
Bailey, Sarah VI, 102
Bailey, Sarah VI, 105
Bailey, Sarah VI, 110
Bailey, Sarah VI, 112
Bailey, Sarah VI, 117
Bailey, Sarah VI, 118
Bailey, Sarah VI, 129
Bailey, Sarah VI, 130
Bailey, Sarah VI, 797
Bailey, Sarah VI, 812
Bailey, Sarah VI, 867
Bailey, Sarah A. VI, 822
Bailey, Sarah A. VI, 835
Bailey, Sarah Ann IV, 172
Bailey, Sarah Ann IV, 365
Bailey, Sarah Ann IV, 367
Bailey, Sarah Ann IV, 377
Bailey, Sarah Ann IV, 426
Bailey, Sarah Ann IV, 566
Bailey, Sarah Ann IV, 590
Bailey, Sarah Ann IV, 797
Bailey, Sarah Ann IV, 799
Bailey, Sarah E. IV, 389
Bailey, Sarah E. IV, 700
Bailey, Sarah E. IV, 1143
Bailey, Sarah E. IV, 1195
Bailey, Sarah E. V, 548
Bailey, Sarah E. V, 611
Bailey, Sarah E. V, 967
Bailey, Sarah E. V, 979
Bailey, Sarah Elma IV, 367
Bailey, Sarah Elma IV, 439
Bailey, Sarah Elma IV, 509
Bailey, Sarah Elma IV, 550
Bailey, Sarah Emily V, 610
Bailey, Sarah F. IV, 367
Bailey, Sarah F. IV, 567
Bailey, Sarah H. IV, 365
Bailey, Sarah Lavada IV, 366
Bailey, Sarah Lavada IV, 368
Bailey, Sarah M. IV, 365
Bailey, Sarah M. IV, 368
Bailey, Sarah M. IV, 567
Bailey, Sarah Maria IV, 1127
Bailey, Sarah Maria IV, 1137
Bailey, Sarah V. IV, 1049
Bailey, Sarah W. II, 781
Bailey, Sarah Woodward VI, 369
Bailey, Sary VI, 797
Bailey, Savage VI, 822
Bailey, Savage VI, 867
Bailey, Savage VI, 874
Bailey, Sidenham IV, 509
Bailey, Sidney IV, 172
Bailey, Sidney IV, 367
Bailey, Sidney IV, 565
Bailey, Sidney IV, 566
Bailey, Sidney V, 218
Bailey, Sidney V, 611
Bailey, Sidney Leona IV, 1023
Bailey, Sidney M. V, 218
Bailey, Sidney M. V, 473
Bailey, Sidney M. V, 611
Bailey, Silas IV, 172
Bailey, Silas IV, 365
Bailey, Silas IV, 367
Bailey, Silviah V, 610
Bailey, Silviah V, 636
Bailey, Silviah VI, 129
Bailey, Silviah VI, 138
Bailey, Silviah Caroline V, 610
Bailey, Sina IV, 172
Bailey, Sina IV, 566
Bailey, Sina IV, 1087
Bailey, Sina IV, 1103
Bailey, Smith M. IV, 172
Bailey, Stanton V, 21
Bailey, Stella V, 473
Bailey, Stella V, 641
Bailey, Stella V, 657
Bailey, Stephen IV, 139
Bailey, Stephen IV, 171
Bailey, Stephen IV, 172
Bailey, Stephen IV, 176
Bailey, Stephen IV, 364
Bailey, Stephen IV, 366
Bailey, Stephen IV, 423
Bailey, Stephen IV, 426
Bailey, Stephen IV, 511
Bailey, Stephen IV, 565
Bailey, Stephen IV, 566
Bailey, Stephen IV, 567
Bailey, Stephen IV, 589
Bailey, Stephen VI, 97
Bailey, Stephen VI, 102
Bailey, Stephen VI, 129
Bailey, Susan V, 21
Bailey, Susan A. V, 892
Bailey, Susan A. V, 907
Bailey, Susan Ann IV, 365
Bailey, Susan Antoinette V, 656
Bailey, Susann IV, 365
Bailey, Susanna I, 128
Bailey, Susanna I, 130
Bailey, Susanna IV, 367
Bailey, Susanna IV, 373
Bailey, Susanna IV, 509
Bailey, Susanna IV, 566
Bailey, Susanna IV, 581
Bailey, Susanna IV, 1049
Bailey, Susanna IV, 1087
Bailey, Susanna V, 21
Bailey, Susanna V, 218
Bailey, Susanna VI, 97
Bailey, Susanna VI, 296
Bailey, Susanna VI, 297
Bailey, Susanna VI, 853
Bailey, Susanna VI, 874
Bailey, Susannah I, 128
Bailey, Susannah II, 457
Bailey, Susannah IV, 345
Bailey, Susannah IV, 365
Bailey, Susannah IV, 367
Bailey, Susannah IV, 373
Bailey, Susannah IV, 391
Bailey, Susannah IV, 523
Bailey, Susannah IV, 591
Bailey, Susannah IV, 1049
Bailey, Susannah V, 21
Bailey, Susannah V, 473
Bailey, Susannah V, 508
Bailey, Susannah V, 610
Bailey, Susannah V, 611
Bailey, Susannah V, 612
Bailey, Susannah V, 628
Bailey, Susannah V, 646
Bailey, Susannah V, 893
Bailey, Susannah Brackney V, 610
Bailey, Susannah Farmer IV, 509
Bailey, Susannah W. VI, 797
Bailey, Suzannah IV, 139
Bailey, Sydenham IV, 509
Bailey, Sydnie M. V, 473
Bailey, Sylvia V, 610
Bailey, Sylvia V, 630
Bailey, Sylvia V, 893
Bailey, Sylvia V, 929
Bailey, Sylvia V, 967
Bailey, Sylvia VI, 130
Bailey, Tabitha IV, 171
Bailey, Tabitha IV, 319
Bailey, Tabitha IV, 345
Bailey, Tabitha IV, 365
Bailey, Tabitha IV, 367
Bailey, Tabitha IV, 423
Bailey, Tabitha IV, 565
Bailey, Tabitha IV, 567
Bailey, Tabitha IV, 591
Bailey, Tabitha IV, 592
Bailey, Tabitha IV, 593
Bailey, Tabitha IV, 1049
Bailey, Tabitha IV, 1087
Bailey, Tabitha IV, 1143
Bailey, Tabitha V, 967
Bailey, Tabitha VI, 99
Bailey, Tabitha VI, 113
Bailey, Tabitha VI, 129
Bailey, Tabitha VI, 135
Bailey, Tabitha VI, 296
Bailey, Tabitha VI, 301
Bailey, Tacy II, 977
Bailey, Tacy II, 1019
Bailey, Talbert IV, 1087
Bailey, Talbott IV, 1127
Bailey, Talitha IV, 366
Bailey, Talitha IV, 565
Bailey, Talitha IV, 566
Bailey, Talitha IV, 576
Bailey, Talitha IV, 579
Bailey, Talitha IV, 589
Bailey, Tamar IV, 1127
Bailey, Telitha IV, 567
Bailey, Telitha IV, 578
Bailey, Temperance VI, 797
Bailey, Temperance VI, 817
Bailey, Thamer V, 318
Bailey, Thamer V, 336
Bailey, Thomas II, 977
Bailey, Thomas II, 1039
Bailey, Thomas IV, 509
Bailey, Thomas IV, 673
Bailey, Thomas V, 218
Bailey, Thomas V, 297
Bailey, Thomas V, 318
Bailey, Thomas V, 473
Bailey, Thomas VI, 113
Bailey, Thomas VI, 154
Bailey, Thomas VI, 296
Bailey, Thomas VI, 343
Bailey, Thomas VI, 797
Bailey, Thomas VI, 810
Bailey, Thomas VI, 839
Bailey, Thomas VI, 859
Bailey, Thomas VI, 865
Bailey, Thomas VI, 868
Bailey, Thomas C. IV, 510
Bailey, Thomas F. IV, 367
Bailey, Thomas F. IV, 566
Bailey, Thomas F. IV, 567
Bailey, Thomas Flanner IV, 1087
Bailey, Thomas L. II, 726
Bailey, Thomas S. II, 334
Bailey, Thomas T. IV, 1087
Bailey, Thos. VI, 186
Bailey, Thos. VI, 817
Bailey, Thos. Chalkley V, 797
Bailey, Thos. E. V, 610
Bailey, Thos. L. II, 833
Bailey, Tilitha IV, 364
Bailey, Tilitha IV, 426
Bailey, Tilton H. IV, 1143
Bailey, Townsend III, 497
Bailey, Tyral VI, 98
Bailey, Unity IV, 923
Bailey, Uriah IV, 171
Bailey, Uriah IV, 172
Bailey, Uriah IV, 345
Bailey, Uriah IV, 364
Bailey, Uriah IV, 365
Bailey, Uriah IV, 366
Bailey, Uriah IV, 367
Bailey, Uriah IV, 391
Bailey, Uriah IV, 509
Bailey, Uriah IV, 523
Bailey, Uriah IV, 567
Bailey, Uriah IV, 591
Bailey, Uriah IV, 673
Bailey, Uriah IV, 1049
Bailey, Uriah IV, 1087
Bailey, Uriah VI, 98
Bailey, Uriah VI, 130
Bailey, Ursula VI, 99
Bailey, Veda V, 473
Bailey, Veda V, 657
Bailey, Victory A. V, 336
Bailey, Vincent VI, 875
Bailey, W. A. V, 657
Bailey, Wakefield I, 489
Bailey, Wakefield VI, 467
Bailey, Walter IV, 673
Bailey, Walter IV, 1035
Bailey, Walter E. V, 548
Bailey, Walter Rollen IV, 923
Bailey, Warren Oliver IV, 171
Bailey, Warren Oliver IV, 172
Bailey, Warren Oliver IV, 366
Bailey, Warren Oliver IV, 368
Bailey, Wd Sarah IV, 365
Bailey, Wd. Georgia III, 22
Bailey, Wd. Georgia III, 145
Bailey, Wd. Sarah VI, 129
Bailey, Wiley IV, 366
Bailey, Wiley IV, 367
Bailey, Wiley S. IV, 364
Bailey, William II, 195
Bailey, William II, 781
Bailey, William IV, 171
Bailey, William IV, 565
Bailey, William IV, 566
Bailey, William IV, 567
Bailey, William IV, 1087
Bailey, William V, 610
Bailey, William VI, 52
Bailey, William VI, 97
Bailey, William VI, 105
Bailey, William VI, 130
Bailey, William VI, 296
Bailey, William VI, 797
Bailey, William VI, 853
Bailey, William B. VI, 52
Bailey, William B. VI, 129
Bailey, William E. VI, 369
Bailey, William Forster V, 893
Bailey, William J. IV, 923
Bailey, William L. II, 699
Bailey, William L. IV, 172
Bailey, William L. IV, 566
Bailey, William, Sr. VI, 96
Bailey, William, Sr. VI, 99
Bailey, Wilson IV, 366
Bailey, Wilson V, 401
Bailey, With IV, 566
Bailey, With??? IV, 566
Bailey, Wm. II, 781
Bailey, Wm. IV, 201
Bailey, Wm. IV, 365
Bailey, Wm. IV, 382
Bailey, Wm. IV, 408
Bailey, Wm. IV, 426
Bailey, Wm. IV, 566
Bailey, Wm. IV, 572
Bailey, Wm. IV, 1049
Bailey, Wm. IV, 1087
Bailey, Wm. V, 657
Bailey, Wm. V, 979
Bailey, Wm. VI, 96
Bailey, Wm. A. V, 656
Bailey, Wm. B. V, 548
Bailey, Wm. Binford VI, 98
Bailey, Wm. Foster V, 893
Bailey, Wm. J. IV, 923
Bailey, Wm. L. II, 726
Bailey, Wm. L. II, 833
Bailey, Wm. L. IV, 567
Bailey, Wm. M. VI, 848
Bailey, Wm. Penn IV, 673
Bailey, Wm. Penn IV, 1023
Bailey, Wm. T. II, 151
Bailey, Wm. V. V, 548
Bailey, Wm., Sr. VI, 99
Bailey, Wood Jones VI, 803
Bailey, Wyat IV, 366
Bailey, Wyatt VI, 97
Bailey, Wyla VI, 129
Bailey, Yancy VI, 797

Bailey, Yarnall IV, 609
Bailey, Yarnall IV, 673
Bailey, Yarnel IV, 797
Bailey, Yarnell IV, 797
Bailey, Zachariah IV, 139
Bailey, Zachariah IV, 364
Bailey, Zachariah IV, 366
Bailey, Zachariah IV, 367
Bailey, Zachariah VI, 97
Bailey, Zachariah VI, 99
Bailey, Zachariah VI, 129
Bailey, Zachariah VI, 130
Bailey, Zacheriah VI, 124
Baileyy, Mary C. IV, 73
Baileyy, Rebecca IV, 73
Bailiff, Able V, 473
Bailiff, Addie V, 657
Bailiff, Alida I, 372
Bailiff, Allie I, 372
Bailiff, Amos V, 473
Bailiff, Amos V, 657
Bailiff, Ann V, 473
Bailiff, Ann V, 477
Bailiff, Anna Mariah V, 548
Bailiff, Charlotte A. I, 372
Bailiff, Daniel V, 473
Bailiff, Daniel V, 548
Bailiff, David V, 548
Bailiff, Elijah V, 548
Bailiff, Eliza V, 548
Bailiff, Eliza Ann V, 473
Bailiff, Eliza Ann V, 548
Bailiff, Elizabeth V, 473
Bailiff, Frederick I, 372
Bailiff, Jesse E. I, 372
Bailiff, Joel V, 473
Bailiff, Jones I, 372
Bailiff, Joshua V, 473
Bailiff, Joshua M. V, 548
Bailiff, Judith V, 473
Bailiff, Judith V, 484
Bailiff, Leah V, 473
Bailiff, Lydia V, 473
Bailiff, Lydia V, 519
Bailiff, Malida I, 372
Bailiff, Malinda I, 372
Bailiff, Margaret V, 473
Bailiff, Marion M. I, 372
Bailiff, Martha I, 443
Bailiff, Martha I, 445
Bailiff, Martha V, 473
Bailiff, Mary V, 473
Bailiff, Mary V, 484
Bailiff, Nathan I, 372
Bailiff, Newton I, 372
Bailiff, Newton J. I, 372
Bailiff, Polly V, 473
Bailiff, Robert I, 372
Bailiff, Robert W. I, 372
Bailiff, Sally V, 472
Bailiff, Sally V, 473
Bailiff, Sally Elizabeth V, 473
Bailiff, Sarah V, 473
Bailiff, Sarah V, 542
Bailiff, Sarah V, 544
Bailiff, Susanna V, 473
Bailiff, Susanna V, 534
Bailiff, Thomas V, 473
Bailiff, Thomas V, 544
Bailiff, Thomas V, 548
Bailiff, Vandalia S. I, 372
Bailiff, Vandelia I, 372
Bailiff, William I, 372
Bailiss, Elizabeth VI, 812
Bailor, ??? II, 334
Bailous, William VI, 857
Bails, Ann I, 526
Bails, Ann I, 870
Bails, Ann I, 902
Bails, Catherine I, 1080
Bails, Catron V, 24
Bails, Charity I, 1080
Bails, Curtis V, 24
Bails, Daniel I, 1089
Bails, Elihu I, 1080
Bails, Elihu I, 1089
Bails, Elizabeth I, 1089
Bails, Elizabeth Ann V, 24
Bails, Eunice V, 24
Bails, Hannah I, 1080
Bails, Hannah I, 1089
Bails, Hannah I, 1092
Bails, Isaac V, 24
Bails, Jacob I, 1089
Bails, Jacob V, 24
Bails, Jane V, 24
Bails, Jesse I, 526
Bails, John I, 525
Bails, John I, 526
Bails, John I, 536
Bails, John I, 550
Bails, John I, 1089
Bails, John B. I, 1080
Bails, John Boater I, 1089
Bails, John Boater V, 24
Bails, Jonathan V, 24
Bails, Joseph I, 1080
Bails, Lois I, 1080
Bails, Lois V, 24
Bails, Lowes I, 1080
Bails, Martha I, 1007
Bails, Mary V, 24
Bails, Nathan I, 1080
Bails, Nathan V, 24
Bails, Polly VI, 890
Bails, Rachel I, 374
Bails, Rachel I, 550
Bails, Rachel I, 1080
Bails, Rachel V, 24
Bails, Ruth I, 1115
Bails, Sam'l I, 1089
Bails, Sarah I, 443
Bails, Sarah I, 525
Bails, Sarah I, 536
Bails, Sarah I, 1080
Bails, Sarah V, 24
Bails, Solomon I, 1080
Bails, Solomon I, 1089
Bails, Solomon, Jr. I, 1080
Bails, Susannah V, 24
Bails, Thomas I, 525
Bails, William I, 526
Bails, William I, 1089
Bails, William I, 1114
Baily, Amos V, 473
Baily, Ann IV, 673
Baily, Anna II, 457
Baily, Anna II, 726
Baily, Anna II, 833
Baily, Anne B. IV, 673
Baily, Asenath V, 473
Baily, Asenath V, 536
Baily, Bartram B. II, 833
Baily, Bathsheba I, 299
Baily, Caroline A. II, 833
Baily, Caroline A. II, 853
Baily, Christiana II, 833
Baily, Daniel I, 523
Baily, David I, 523
Baily, David I, 959
Baily, Edith II, 977
Baily, Edward P. IV, 673
Baily, Edward, Jr. II, 977
Baily, Elizabeth I, 96
Baily, Elizabeth I, 281
Baily, Elizabeth I, 299
Baily, Elizabeth IV, 609
Baily, Elizabeth IV, 673
Baily, Elizabeth V, 326
Baily, Elizabeth VI, 296
Baily, Elizabeth A. II, 280
Baily, Elizabeth A. II, 296
Baily, Elizabeth A. M. II, 280
Baily, Elizabeth B. V, 899
Baily, Elizabeth L. II, 726
Baily, Elizabeth S. II, 280
Baily, Elizabeth S. II, 296
Baily, Elizabeth, Jr. IV, 673
Baily, Ellis IV, 20
Baily, Emmor V, 117
Baily, Esther II, 977
Baily, Evan P. II, 833
Baily, Frederick L. II, 833
Baily, Frederick L. II, 853
Baily, George IV, 673
Baily, Hannah IV, 20
Baily, Hannah IV, 42
Baily, Hannah IV, 673
Baily, Hannah Jane II, 833
Baily, Harding IV, 673
Baily, Harding IV, 710
Baily, Hellen C. IV, 1350
Baily, Henry I, 281
Baily, Henry I, 959
Baily, Henry V, 21
Baily, Henry M. IV, 1350
Baily, Hezekiah B. V, 899
Baily, Hiram V, 21
Baily, Hiram V, 131
Baily, Hiram V, 473
Baily, Hoopes IV, 673
Baily, Howard H. IV, 673
Baily, James IV, 170
Baily, Jesse I, 281
Baily, Jesse IV, 609
Baily, Jesse IV, 660
Baily, John I, 35
Baily, John II, 977
Baily, John V, 21
Baily, John VI, 296
Baily, Joseph IV, 609
Baily, Joseph IV, 673
Baily, Joshua II, 457
Baily, Joshua II, 726
Baily, Joshua II, 833
Baily, Joshua D. II, 833
Baily, Joshua L. II, 833
Baily, Joshua L. II, 853
Baily, Joshua, Jr. II, 833
Baily, Josiah VI, 296
Baily, Latitia II, 1044
Baily, Linda R. VI, 856
Baily, Lititia II, 975
Baily, Lititia II, 977
Baily, Lloyd II, 833
Baily, Loyd II, 280
Baily, Loyd II, 296
Baily, Loyd II, 726
Baily, Lucretia M. IV, 710
Baily, Lydia IV, 609
Baily, Lydia IV, 660
Baily, Lydia IV, 1350
Baily, Margaret IV, 73
Baily, Marshall J. II, 833
Baily, Mary I, 129
Baily, Mary I, 281
Baily, Mary V, 117
Baily, Mary V, 326
Baily, Mary VI, 296
Baily, Mary Ann II, 833
Baily, Mary Ann IV, 673
Baily, Mary B. V, 473
Baily, Mary B. V, 532
Baily, Mary Ella V, 899
Baily, Mary Emily IV, 673
Baily, Millisent I, 708
Baily, Millisent I, 722
Baily, Nathan II, 833
Baily, Nathan V, 473
Baily, Nathan V, 825
Baily, Phebe V, 120
Baily, Rachel IV, 170
Baily, Rachel IV, 673
Baily, Rachel V, 21
Baily, Rachel V, 131
Baily, Rachel Ann II, 833
Baily, Randal IV, 609
Baily, Rebecca V, 21
Baily, Rebecca V, 474
Baily, Reuben IV, 73
Baily, Rose I, 262
Baily, Ruth I, 281
Baily, Ruth I, 523
Baily, Samuel II, 195
Baily, Samuel L. II, 280
Baily, Samuel L. II, 296
Baily, Samuel L. II, 457
Baily, Samuel L. II, 726
Baily, Samuel L. II, 833
Baily, Samuel P. II, 833
Baily, Sarah II, 246
Baily, Sarah II, 457
Baily, Sarah II, 517
Baily, Stanton I, 959
Baily, Susanna VI, 296
Baily, Theodate II, 833
Baily, Theodate II, 853
Baily, Thomas V, 326
Baily, Thomas VI, 296
Baily, Thomas VI, 349
Baily, Thomas L. II, 726
Baily, Thomas L. II, 833
Baily, Thos. L. II, 833
Baily, William II, 246
Baily, Wm. L. II, 726
Baily, Wm. L. II, 833
Baily, Wm. Penn IV, 673
Bain, Almedia IV, 368
Bain, Almedia IV, 567
Bain, Ann IV, 1049
Bain, Ann IV, 1076
Bain, Anna IV, 1049
Bain, Elijah IV, 571
Bain, Elijah IV, 1049
Bain, John IV, 73
Bain, John IV, 368
Bain, John IV, 1049
Bain, Lavina IV, 368
Bain, Lydia Ann IV, 1049
Bain, Martha IV, 567
Bain, Martha IV, 1049
Bain, Mary IV, 368
Bain, Rhoda IV, 368
Bain, Rhoda IV, 571
Bain, Rhoda VI, 100
Bain, Rhoda VI, 102
Bain, Sarah IV, 368
Bain, Sarah IV, 567
Bain, Sarah IV, 571
Bain, Sarah IV, 1092
Bain, William III, 22
Bainard, Esther IV, 924
Bainbridge, James II, 334
Bainbridge, John II, 334
Bainbridge, John II, 975
Bainbridge, John II, 989
Bainbridge, Mary Philips III, 22
Bainbridge, Rachel II, 334
Bainbridge, Sarah II, 975
Bainbridge, Sarah II, 989
Baine, Sarah IV, 572
Bainebridge, John II, 975
Baines, Elin II, 977
Baines, Elin II, 994
Baines, Ellinor II, 994
Baines, Isaac V, 979
Baines, Nancy V, 23
Baines, Robert T. II, 461
Baines, Sarah V, 979
Bains, Deborah II, 975
Bains, Deborah II, 978
Bair, David IV, 1202
Bair, Hettie V, 984
Bair, Jacob V, 984
Bair, Mary E. V, 984
Bair, Rachel V, 984
Baird, Ann V, 29
Baird, Earl W. IV, 1245
Baird, Esther IV, 1306
Baird, Frank IV, 1035
Baird, Ida IV, 1035
Baird, L. E. IV, 1245
Baird, Lennard E. IV, 1245
Baird, Lorena IV, 1035
Baird, Lydia Ann V, 21
Baird, Lydia Ann V, 29
Baird, Mrs. Frank IV, 1035
Baird, Ray H. IV, 1245
Baird, Warren IV, 1245
Baisley, DeWitt C. E. III, 394
Baisley, Edward N. III, 394
Baisley, Edward N. III, 450
Baisley, Evelyn O. III, 394
Baisley, Howard N. III, 394
Baisley, Mary W. III, 394
Baisley, Mary W. III, 450
Baiten, Charles VI, 52
Baiten, Charles VI, 55
Baiten, Charles VI, 76
Baiten, Eliza VI, 52
Baiten, Eliza VI, 76
Baiten, Martha VI, 55
Baits, James VI, 100
Baits, James VI, 111
Bake, Gilbert IV, 463
Bake, Gilbert H. IV, 463
Bake, Margaret IV, 463
Baken, John S. II, 143
Baken, Joseph II, 975
Baker, ??? III, 23
Baker, ??? IV, 1350
Baker, ??? IV, 1351
Baker, Aaron II, 334
Baker, Aaron III, 22
Baker, Aaron III, 23
Baker, Aaron III, 268
Baker, Aaron T. IV, 1351
Baker, Abel VI, 516
Baker, Abel T. IV, 1368
Baker, Abigail IV, 1369
Baker, Abraham VI, 797
Baker, Abraham VI, 870
Baker, Abraham VI, 871
Baker, Abraham VI, 875
Baker, Abraham VI, 940
Baker, Abram VI, 1017
Baker, Abram. VI, 878
Baker, Absolam VI, 875
Baker, Absolam VI, 986
Baker, Addison V, 372
Baker, Alice VI, 729
Baker, Almeda I, 1113
Baker, Amasa V, 297
Baker, Amasa V, 302
Baker, Amasa V, 305
Baker, Amasa V, 318
Baker, Amba V, 297
Baker, Amos IV, 319
Baker, Amos V, 318
Baker, Amy II, 52
Baker, Amy II, 54
Baker, Andrew D. V, 984
Baker, Ann II, 334
Baker, Ann IV, 559
Baker, Ann Mary II, 953
Baker, Anna II, 833
Baker, Anna II, 888
Baker, Anna IV, 1368
Baker, Anna V, 150
Baker, Anna VI, 729
Baker, Anna VI, 759
Baker, Anna VI, 762
Baker, Anna VI, 929
Baker, Anna D. V, 372
Baker, Anna D. V, 400
Baker, Anna Delilah V, 372
Baker, Anna H. III, 23
Baker, Anna H. V, 947
Baker, Anna H. V, 953
Baker, Anna P. V, 947
Baker, Anna T. II, 833
Baker, Annie V, 984
Baker, Annie D. V, 372
Baker, Annie S. II, 833
Baker, Annie S. II, 926
Baker, Anny VI, 883
Baker, Asa III, 394
Baker, Asa IV, 1351
Baker, Augustus IV, 1306
Baker, Basil VI, 873
Baker, Basil VI, 929
Baker, Basil VI, 935
Baker, Basil VI, 947
Baker, Basil VI, 1007
Baker, Basil VI, 1013
Baker, Benezet IV, 609
Baker, Benezet IV, 674
Baker, Benezett IV, 674
Baker, Benjamin II, 953
Baker, Benjamin III, 22
Baker, Benjamin IV, 1351
Baker, Benjamin J. IV, 1351
Baker, Bertha IV, 674
Baker, Bessie V, 984
Baker, Betsey IV, 1350
Baker, Betsey IV, 1351
Baker, Betsey IV, 1368
Baker, Betsey VI, 875
Baker, Betsey VI, 940
Baker, Betsy IV, 1368
Baker, Betsy VI, 874
Baker, Betsy VI, 930
Baker, Beulah T. III, 220
Baker, Branton V, 21
Baker, Brenton V, 947
Baker, Brinton V, 150
Baker, Burwell W. VI, 878
Baker, Caroline C. Colvin IV, 674
Baker, Caroline S. Colvin IV, 674
Baker, Catharine III, 22
Baker, Catharine VI, 729
Baker, Charles IV, 1271
Baker, Charles IV, 1369
Baker, Charles W. I, 937
Baker, Chas. Gilbert V, 657
Baker, Clara V, 548
Baker, Clara E. IV, 924
Baker, Claudin I, 299
Baker, Cloe Jane IV, 1350
Baker, Cynthia IV, 1350
Baker, Cynthia W. IV, 1350
Baker, Daisy VI, 729
Baker, Daniel III, 22
Baker, Daniel VI, 154
Baker, Daniel VI, 875
Baker, Daniel I. IV, 1351
Baker, David IV, 1350
Baker, David IV, 1351
Baker, David IV, 1368
Baker, David VI, 615
Baker, David P. II, 833
Baker, David P. II, 871
Baker, David S. IV, 1350
Baker, David S. IV, 1351
Baker, David S. IV, 1368
Baker, David W. IV, 1350
Baker, David W. IV, 1351
Baker, Deborah III, 394
Baker, Deborah III, 421
Baker, Deborah III, 479
Baker, Deborah III, 485
Baker, Delilah V, 547
Baker, Dicia H. V, 893
Baker, Dobel II, 458
Baker, Dobel III, 22
Baker, Dobel III, 23
Baker, Dobel III, 316
Baker, Dobel III, 350
Baker, Douglas VI, 797
Baker, Earl V, 657
Baker, Earl R. V, 657
Baker, Earle V, 657
Baker, Edna V, 984
Baker, Edward B. II, 133
Baker, Elcy H. V, 891
Baker, Elcy H. V, 893
Baker, Elcy H. A. V, 22
Baker, Elijah VI, 875
Baker, Elisabeth IV, 1350
Baker, Eliza IV, 607
Baker, Eliza IV, 609
Baker, Eliza IV, 634
Baker, Eliza IV, 674
Baker, Eliza IV, 924
Baker, Eliza R. IV, 674

Baker, Elizabeth II, 334
Baker, Elizabeth II, 457
Baker, Elizabeth II, 458
Baker, Elizabeth II, 464
Baker, Elizabeth II, 473
Baker, Elizabeth II, 699
Baker, Elizabeth II, 953
Baker, Elizabeth II, 975
Baker, Elizabeth II, 1038
Baker, Elizabeth III, 22
Baker, Elizabeth III, 23
Baker, Elizabeth III, 268
Baker, Elizabeth III, 394
Baker, Elizabeth III, 407
Baker, Elizabeth III, 430
Baker, Elizabeth IV, 320
Baker, Elizabeth IV, 609
Baker, Elizabeth IV, 674
Baker, Elizabeth IV, 1306
Baker, Elizabeth IV, 1351
Baker, Elizabeth V, 297
Baker, Elizabeth VI, 467
Baker, Elizabeth VI, 729
Baker, Elizabeth VI, 875
Baker, Elizabeth VI, 990
Baker, Elizabeth B. II, 726
Baker, Elizabeth Bartram II, 726
Baker, Elizabeth Bartram II, 749
Baker, Elizabeth M. IV, 1368
Baker, Elizabeth R. II, 458
Baker, Elizabeth W. IV, 674
Baker, Elizabeth, Jr. II, 975
Baker, Ella V, 657
Baker, Elmira V, 984
Baker, Elsey H. V, 893
Baker, Elsie VI, 729
Baker, Elvira VI, 797
Baker, Emanuel V, 984
Baker, Emma IV, 1233
Baker, Emma V, 726
Baker, Enoch N. V, 984
Baker, Enos V, 297
Baker, Esther II, 457
Baker, Esther II, 458
Baker, Esther II, 546
Baker, Esther IV, 1350
Baker, Esther O. IV, 1351
Baker, Esther O. IV, 1368
Baker, Esther P. IV, 1350
Baker, Esther P. IV, 1351
Baker, Ethel R. VI, 615
Baker, Eugene II, 833
Baker, Florence H. V, 947
Baker, Frances Susie V, 657
Baker, Francis Augustus V, 372
Baker, Frank V, 657
Baker, Frank Leonidas V, 549
Baker, Frank M. V, 548
Baker, Frank M. V, 657
Baker, Fred IV, 1233
Baker, Geo. C. III, 23
Baker, Geo. H. V, 297
Baker, Geo. H. V, 299
Baker, Geo. W. III, 23
Baker, George II, 458
Baker, George II, 781
Baker, George IV, 1233
Baker, George IV, 1368
Baker, George IV, 1369
Baker, George V, 297
Baker, George V, 318
Baker, George V, 548
Baker, George VI, 880
Baker, George C. III, 23
Baker, George C. III, 210
Baker, George Corlies III, 22
Baker, George Dobel III, 23
Baker, George H. IV, 319
Baker, George H. V, 297
Baker, George H. V, 318
Baker, George Howard III, 23
Baker, George Lukens VI, 729
Baker, George S. II, 833
Baker, George S. II, 926
Baker, George W. II, 19
Baker, George W. II, 698
Baker, George W. II, 726
Baker, George W. II, 749
Baker, Gilbert III, 23
Baker, Glover VI, 296
Baker, Glover VI, 874
Baker, Glover VI, 875
Baker, Hannah II, 458
Baker, Hannah II, 833
Baker, Hannah II, 953
Baker, Hannah III, 510
Baker, Hannah IV, 609
Baker, Hannah IV, 634
Baker, Hannah IV, 864
Baker, Hannah IV, 873
Baker, Hannah IV, 1368
Baker, Hannah V, 297
Baker, Hannah V, 313
Baker, Hannah VI, 296
Baker, Hannah VI, 310
Baker, Hannah VI, 615
Baker, Hannah VI, 632
Baker, Hannah VI, 635
Baker, Hannah VI, 638
Baker, Hannah VI, 874
Baker, Hannah D. III, 22
Baker, Hannah D. III, 23
Baker, Hannah D. III, 100
Baker, Hannah D. III, 349
Baker, Hannah D. III, 350
Baker, Hannah M. III, 23
Baker, Hannah W. III, 23
Baker, Harlan VI, 615
Baker, Harlan VI, 632
Baker, Harlan VI, 635
Baker, Harlan VI, 638
Baker, Harley V, 549
Baker, Harley V, 657
Baker, Harriet III, 23
Baker, Harrison W. VI, 875
Baker, Harrison W. VI, 967
Baker, Harvey VI, 875
Baker, Henry II, 458
Baker, Henry II, 726
Baker, Henry II, 953
Baker, Henry II, 975
Baker, Henry IV, 1350
Baker, Henry IV, 1351
Baker, Henry V, 984
Baker, Henry VI, 875
Baker, Henry J. VI, 729
Baker, Henry Judson VI, 729
Baker, Henry Judson VI, 759
Baker, Henry Judson VI, 762
Baker, Hester II, 334
Baker, Hester II, 975
Baker, Hester II, 1041
Baker, Homer Richard V, 657
Baker, Horace L. IV, 1350
Baker, Ida V, 984
Baker, Isaac III, 23
Baker, Isaac IV, 609
Baker, Isaac IV, 674
Baker, Isaac R. IV, 609
Baker, Isaac S. IV, 1350
Baker, Isaac S. IV, 1351
Baker, Isaac S. IV, 1368
Baker, Israel IV, 1369
Baker, Israel H. I, 1147
Baker, Israel H. IV, 1350
Baker, Jacob III, 23
Baker, Jacob IV, 924
Baker, Jacob IV, 1350
Baker, Jacob IV, 1351
Baker, James II, 133
Baker, James II, 833
Baker, James VI, 929
Baker, James VI, 1007
Baker, James B. II, 133
Baker, James T. II, 833
Baker, James Truman II, 726
Baker, James, Jr. IV, 139
Baker, Jas. III, 424
Baker, Jemima III, 424
Baker, Jennie V, 548
Baker, Jennie V, 657
Baker, Jennie V, 984
Baker, Jesse III, 23
Baker, Jesse IV, 607
Baker, Jesse IV, 609
Baker, Jesse IV, 634
Baker, Jesse IV, 674
Baker, Jesse IV, 1351
Baker, Jesse IV, 1368
Baker, Jesse V, 984
Baker, Jesse C. IV, 609
Baker, Jesse C. IV, 674
Baker, Jesse P. IV, 674
Baker, Jessie B. V, 947
Baker, John II, 334
Baker, John II, 457
Baker, John II, 546
Baker, John II, 953
Baker, John III, 23
Baker, John IV, 1350
Baker, John V, 297
Baker, John V, 318
Baker, John V, 984
Baker, John VI, 990
Baker, John L. IV, 1351
Baker, John Milton IV, 1369
Baker, John R. V, 657
Baker, John S. II, 143
Baker, John S. IV, 1350
Baker, John S. IV, 1351
Baker, John S. IV, 1368
Baker, John T. IV, 319
Baker, John W. I, 3
Baker, John W. I, 35
Baker, John Y. V, 318
Baker, Joseph II, 133
Baker, Joseph II, 334
Baker, Joseph II, 441
Baker, Joseph II, 457
Baker, Joseph II, 458
Baker, Joseph II, 611
Baker, Joseph II, 953
Baker, Joseph III, 22
Baker, Joseph III, 23
Baker, Joseph III, 350
Baker, Joseph IV, 319
Baker, Joseph V, 297
Baker, Joseph V, 318
Baker, Joseph C. III, 23
Baker, Joseph Engle II, 797
Baker, Joseph M. V, 984
Baker, Joseph Second IV, 1369
Baker, Joshua II, 457
Baker, Joshua V, 21
Baker, Joshua V, 22
Baker, Joshua V, 947
Baker, Joshua VI, 467
Baker, Joshua, Jr. II, 457
Baker, Judson VI, 762
Baker, Julia A. II, 833
Baker, Julia A. II, 871
Baker, Julia Ann IV, 1351
Baker, Katharine Nehrenst IV, 1306
Baker, Keziah II, 457
Baker, Laura E. I, 1147
Baker, Lee V, 657
Baker, Leonidas V, 548
Baker, Leonidas V, 657
Baker, Leonidas Frank V, 657
Baker, Levi IV, 1350
Baker, Levicy VI, 875
Baker, Lewis IV, 609
Baker, Lewis IV, 674
Baker, Lewis Judson VI, 729
Baker, Lewis W. R. IV, 609
Baker, Lidia II, 953
Baker, Lodema S. IV, 1368
Baker, Lorenzo IV, 1368
Baker, Louisa II, 833
Baker, Louisa II, 926
Baker, Louise M. III, 23
Baker, Lovicy J. VI, 878
Baker, Lucy IV, 1350
Baker, Lucy IV, 1351
Baker, Lydia II, 458
Baker, Lydia IV, 320
Baker, Lydia IV, 674
Baker, Lydia IV, 1351
Baker, Lydia IV, 1369
Baker, Lydia V, 297
Baker, Lydia V, 308
Baker, Lydia V, 318
Baker, Lydia Ann IV, 1350
Baker, Lydia Ann IV, 1369
Baker, Lydia Ann V, 297
Baker, Maggie V, 984
Baker, Margaret II, 458
Baker, Margaret II, 792
Baker, Margaret II, 975
Baker, Margaret II, 978
Baker, Margaret II, 1033
Baker, Margaret V, 297
Baker, Margaret V, 299
Baker, Margaret VI, 615
Baker, Margaret VI, 638
Baker, Margaret C. III, 23
Baker, Margaret Corlies III, 23
Baker, Margaret H. II, 458
Baker, Margaret Head II, 458
Baker, Margaret Head II, 464
Baker, Margarett II, 115
Baker, Margarett II, 120
Baker, Margarett II, 975
Baker, Margaretta M. VI, 615
Baker, Marietta IV, 1002
Baker, Marietta S. IV, 924
Baker, Marietta S. IV, 1002
Baker, Martha I, 1113
Baker, Martha II, 133
Baker, Martha III, 23
Baker, Martha III, 394
Baker, Martha III, 421
Baker, Martha III, 479
Baker, Martha V, 893
Baker, Martha V, 984
Baker, Martha VI, 681
Baker, Martha Ann IV, 1368
Baker, Mary III, 133
Baker, Mary II, 953
Baker, Mary II, 975
Baker, Mary III, 23
Baker, Mary III, 316
Baker, Mary III, 394
Baker, Mary III, 416
Baker, Mary IV, 319
Baker, Mary IV, 1350
Baker, Mary IV, 1351
Baker, Mary V, 297
Baker, Mary V, 302
Baker, Mary V, 318
Baker, Mary V, 984
Baker, Mary VI, 154
Baker, Mary VI, 159
Baker, Mary VI, 296
Baker, Mary VI, 310
Baker, Mary VI, 467
Baker, Mary VI, 521
Baker, Mary VI, 870
Baker, Mary VI, 874
Baker, Mary VI, 900
Baker, Mary VI, 940
Baker, Mary A. IV, 1351
Baker, Mary A. IV, 1368
Baker, Mary Ann II, 133
Baker, Mary Ann III, 22
Baker, Mary Ann IV, 1350
Baker, Mary Ann IV, 1351
Baker, Mary B. III, 210
Baker, Mary C. III, 22
Baker, Mary C. III, 23
Baker, Mary C. III, 350
Baker, Mary D. IV, 1143
Baker, Mary D. VI, 615
Baker, Mary D. VI, 632
Baker, Mary Ellen VI, 615
Baker, Mary Ellen VI, 624
Baker, Mary Ellen VI, 625
Baker, Mary Eugenia VI, 729
Baker, Mary H. II, 833
Baker, Mary Jane IV, 1351
Baker, Mary M. IV, 1369
Baker, Mary Rosamond II, 833
Baker, Mary Rosamond II, 871
Baker, Matilda VI, 1007
Baker, Mattie IV, 798
Baker, Mattie V, 984
Baker, May Ollie V, 984
Baker, Mercey IV, 1350
Baker, Mercy IV, 1350
Baker, Meta Almeda V, 372
Baker, Millicent II, 133
Baker, Minerva N. VI, 875
Baker, Minnie V, 657
Baker, Minnie F. VI, 729
Baker, Miriam V, 984
Baker, Molly III, 416
Baker, Moses IV, 674
Baker, Moses IV, 1350
Baker, Moses IV, 1351
Baker, Moses C. IV, 1350
Baker, Moses C. IV, 1351
Baker, Moses D. IV, 1351
Baker, Mrs. Della V, 726
Baker, Myra T. III, 220
Baker, Nancy V, 553
Baker, Nancy VI, 870
Baker, Nancy VI, 875
Baker, Naomi Ann V, 802
Baker, Nathan II, 457
Baker, Nathan II, 953
Baker, Nathan V, 297
Baker, Nathan V, 318
Baker, Nathan VI, 467
Baker, Nathan, Jr. VI, 467
Baker, Nathaniel IV, 1350
Baker, Nathaniel IV, 1351
Baker, Nayl V, 21
Baker, Nayl V, 947
Baker, Nehemiah Colvin IV, 674
Baker, Neil V, 22
Baker, Nelly VI, 875
Baker, Newsom II, 458
Baker, Olive May IV, 1306
Baker, Ophelia V, 984
Baker, Orin IV, 1350
Baker, Oscar Robert VI, 729
Baker, Patience I, 796
Baker, Patience I, 812
Baker, Peter II, 975
Baker, Peter II, 1038
Baker, Phebe II, 975
Baker, Phebe II, 1022
Baker, Phebe V, 21
Baker, Phebe V, 22
Baker, Phebe V, 88
Baker, Phebe C. III, 23
Baker, Phebe C. III, 210
Baker, Phila A. IV, 924
Baker, Philena G. IV, 20
Baker, Philena G. IV, 35
Baker, Pleasant VI, 1017
Baker, Polley IV, 1350
Baker, Polly IV, 1350
Baker, Rachel II, 458
Baker, Rachel II, 650
Baker, Rachel II, 659
Baker, Rachel II, 953
Baker, Rachel II, 975
Baker, Rachel II, 984
Baker, Rachel II, 1034
Baker, Rachel III, 23
Baker, Rachel IV, 1306
Baker, Rachel V, 21
Baker, Rachel V, 22
Baker, Rachel V, 86
Baker, Rachel V, 297
Baker, Rachel V, 317
Baker, Rachel V, 318
Baker, Rachel V, 984
Baker, Rachel VI, 467
Baker, Rachel C. III, 23
Baker, Rachel C. III, 350
Baker, Raymond V, 611
Baker, Raymond Leslie VI, 615
Baker, Raymond Leslie VI, 624
Baker, Raymond Leslie VI, 625
Baker, Rebecca I, 980
Baker, Rebecca II, 334
Baker, Rebecca VI, 875
Baker, Rebecca VI, 900
Baker, Rebecca Ann II, 133
Baker, Rebeckah II, 975
Baker, Rebeckah II, 1039
Baker, Reuben V, 891
Baker, Reuben VI, 615
Baker, Rhoda II, 52
Baker, Rhoda II, 133
Baker, Richard II, 334
Baker, Richard II, 458
Baker, Richard III, 23
Baker, Richard III, 394
Baker, Richard III, 421
Baker, Richard III, 479
Baker, Richard V, 21
Baker, Richard V, 22
Baker, Richard V, 947
Baker, Richard H. II, 458
Baker, Richard Harris II, 458
Baker, Richard Mace II, 458
Baker, Richard Mace II, 975
Baker, Riley V, 984
Baker, Robert II, 457
Baker, Robert II, 611
Baker, Robert III, 23
Baker, Robert VI, 296
Baker, Robert VI, 874
Baker, Robert VI, 925
Baker, Robert A. VI, 615
Baker, Robert Allison VI, 615
Baker, Robert Allison VI, 632
Baker, Robert Allison VI, 635
Baker, Robert Haydock III, 23
Baker, Robert White III, 23
Baker, Rosamond Mary II, 797
Baker, Rueben V, 893
Baker, Rufus IV, 1350
Baker, Ruth H. II, 698
Baker, Ruth H. II, 726
Baker, Ruth H. II, 749
Baker, Ruth S. II, 19
Baker, Ruth S. II, 698
Baker, Sallie I, 299
Baker, Sally VI, 875
Baker, Sally Ann III, 23
Baker, Sam, Sr. VI, 870
Baker, Sam., Sr. VI, 940
Baker, Samuel II, 334
Baker, Samuel II, 457
Baker, Samuel II, 458
Baker, Samuel II, 464
Baker, Samuel II, 546
Baker, Samuel II, 726
Baker, Samuel II, 749
Baker, Samuel II, 953
Baker, Samuel II, 975
Baker, Samuel II, 989
Baker, Samuel II, 999
Baker, Samuel II, 1034
Baker, Samuel II, 1039
Baker, Samuel III, 22
Baker, Samuel III, 23
Baker, Samuel V, 548
Baker, Samuel V, 549
Baker, Samuel V, 657
Baker, Samuel V, 984
Baker, Samuel VI, 516
Baker, Samuel VI, 874
Baker, Samuel Henry III, 23
Baker, Samuel N. II, 334
Baker, Samuel W. V, 657
Baker, Samuel, Jr. II, 458
Baker, Samuel, Jr. II, 975
Baker, Sarah II, 334
Baker, Sarah II, 457

Baker, Sarah II, 510
Baker, Sarah II, 821
Baker, Sarah II, 953
Baker, Sarah II, 975
Baker, Sarah II, 1005
Baker, Sarah II, 1039
Baker, Sarah III, 22
Baker, Sarah III, 429
Baker, Sarah IV, 319
Baker, Sarah IV, 1350
Baker, Sarah IV, 1351
Baker, Sarah V, 21
Baker, Sarah V, 22
Baker, Sarah V, 297
Baker, Sarah V, 302
Baker, Sarah V, 305
Baker, Sarah V, 318
Baker, Sarah V, 947
Baker, Sarah VI, 467
Baker, Sarah VI, 481
Baker, Sarah VI, 514
Baker, Sarah VI, 516
Baker, Sarah VI, 517
Baker, Sarah VI, 519
Baker, Sarah VI, 520
Baker, Sarah VI, 521
Baker, Sarah VI, 522
Baker, Sarah VI, 523
Baker, Sarah VI, 538
Baker, Sarah VI, 661
Baker, Sarah VI, 666
Baker, Sarah VI, 668
Baker, Sarah VI, 729
Baker, Sarah VI, 735
Baker, Sarah VI, 759
Baker, Sarah VI, 797
Baker, Sarah VI, 1017
Baker, Sarah A. III, 394
Baker, Sarah E. II, 833
Baker, Sarah E. II, 871
Baker, Sarah Emily IV, 607
Baker, Sarah Emily IV, 609
Baker, Sarah Emily IV, 863
Baker, Sarah H. III, 23
Baker, Sarah H. IV, 1350
Baker, Sarah H. IV, 1351
Baker, Sarah H. IV, 1368
Baker, Sarah Haydock III, 22
Baker, Sarah Jane IV, 1350
Baker, Sharpless III, 23
Baker, Sharpless L. III, 161
Baker, Siddie V, 984
Baker, Socrates IV, 1369
Baker, Stephen III, 23
Baker, Stephen III, 394
Baker, Stephen III, 429
Baker, Stephen IV, 1369
Baker, Stephen Z. IV, 1369
Baker, Susanna II, 334
Baker, Susanna II, 457
Baker, Susanna II, 611
Baker, Susanna V, 22
Baker, Susanna V, 85
Baker, Susanna Bessie V, 657
Baker, Susannah II, 611
Baker, Susannah II, 833
Baker, Susannah V, 297
Baker, Susannah V, 305
Baker, Susannah V, 318
Baker, Sylvia IV, 1350
Baker, Tamar III, 23
Baker, Thomas II, 1005
Baker, Thomas IV, 1143
Baker, Thomas IV, 1351
Baker, Thomas V, 21
Baker, Thomas Betts II, 975
Baker, Thomas C. VI, 615
Baker, Thomas C. VI, 635
Baker, Thomas L. Colvin IV, 674
Baker, Thomas S. Baker IV, 674
Baker, Thos. II, 821
Baker, Thos. IV, 1306
Baker, Thos. A. IV, 1306
Baker, Tredwell III, 510
Baker, Valentine VI, 729
Baker, W. H. IV, 1233
Baker, Walter J. V, 150
Baker, Wd. Alender VI, 986
Baker, Wd. Ann III, 394
Baker, Wd. Lydia II, 821
Baker, Wd. Sharpless III, 27
Baker, Wd. Susannah T. II, 781
Baker, William III, 23
Baker, William IV, 1351
Baker, William IV, 1369
Baker, William V, 297
Baker, William VI, 521
Baker, William VI, 875
Baker, William Dobel III, 22
Baker, William H. V, 21
Baker, Willis Croasdale VI, 615
Baker, Wm. II, 458
Baker, Wm. IV, 674
Baker, Wm. V, 947
Baker, Wm. V, 984
Baker, Wm. Anderson V, 657
Baker, Wm. N. IV, 609
Baker, Wm. N. IV, 674
Baker, Wm. R. V, 947
Bakers, Esther II, 510
Bakewell, Robert II, 441
Balance, Anna II, 976
Balance, Catherine II, 976
Balance, John II, 976
Balance, Joseph II, 976
Balance, Mary II, 976
Balance, Rachel II, 976
Balance, Simeon II, 976
Balance, Susannah II, 976
Balanger, Henry IV, 368
Balard, Jane V, 549
Balard, Mary I, 797
Balard, Mary I, 802
Balard, Mary V, 549
Balard, Mary V, 567
Balard, Susannah H. V, 549
Balard, Susannah H. V, 578
Balckburn, Rachel IV, 47
Balckburn, William IV, 47
Balderson, Catharine IV, 172
Balderson, David II, 976
Balderson, Deborah II, 1035
Balderson, Deborah IV, 172
Balderson, Deborah IV, 185
Balderson, Deborah IV, 368
Balderson, Deborah IV, 1049
Balderson, Deborah, Jr. IV, 172
Balderson, Elizabeth II, 1014
Balderson, Ellen II, 1070
Balderson, Emily W. VI, 772
Balderson, Esther IV, 172
Balderson, Esther IV, 1049
Balderson, Hannah II, 976
Balderson, Isabella II, 1070
Balderson, Isaiah II, 976
Balderson, John II, 976
Balderson, John II, 1035
Balderson, John P. V, 893
Balderson, Jonathan IV, 172
Balderson, Joseph IV, 172
Balderson, Letitia II, 1068
Balderson, Lydia II, 976
Balderson, Lydia Ray V, 893
Balderson, Mary II, 976
Balderson, Mary IV, 172
Balderson, Mary L. II, 1045
Balderson, Mordecai IV, 172
Balderson, Mordecai, Jr. IV, 172
Balderson, Rachel II, 976
Balderson, Rachel S. V, 893
Balderson, Robert Fitfield II, 1045
Balderson, Ruth II, 1045
Balderson, Sidney IV, 1049
Balderson, Sidney IV, 1061
Balderson, Timothy II, 976
Balderson, Wm. II, 1045
Balderston, Abner II, 954
Balderston, Ann II, 954
Balderston, Ann II, 976
Balderston, Ann II, 982
Balderston, Ann II, 987
Balderston, Ann II, 1027
Balderston, Ann III, 23
Balderston, Ann Brown II, 954
Balderston, Annie II, 954
Balderston, Annie II, 1044
Balderston, C. Canby II, 726
Balderston, Canby II, 730
Balderston, Catharine IV, 172
Balderston, Catharine C. II, 726
Balderston, Catharine C. II, 730
Balderston, Catherine II, 726
Balderston, Catherine II, 731
Balderston, Charles W. II, 953
Balderston, D. Newlin II, 834
Balderston, David II, 976
Balderston, David II, 1044
Balderston, David II, 1068
Balderston, Deborah II, 975
Balderston, Deborah II, 976
Balderston, Deborah II, 982
Balderston, Deborah II, 1016
Balderston, Deborough II, 976
Balderston, Deborough II, 1027
Balderston, Edward II, 953
Balderston, Edward II, 954
Balderston, Edward II, 1044
Balderston, Elizabeth II, 458
Balderston, Elizabeth II, 576
Balderston, Elizabeth II, 726
Balderston, Elizabeth II, 731
Balderston, Elizabeth II, 953
Balderston, Elizabeth II, 954
Balderston, Elizabeth II, 965
Balderston, Elizabeth II, 975
Balderston, Elizabeth II, 976
Balderston, Elizabeth II, 1044
Balderston, Elizabeth II, 1056
Balderston, Elizabeth B. II, 953
Balderston, Elizabeth Lloyd II, 954
Balderston, Elizabeth P. II, 1044
Balderston, Emily W. VI, 749
Balderston, Fanny B. II, 833
Balderston, George II, 954
Balderston, George II, 1044
Balderston, George W. II, 954
Balderston, George W. II, 1045
Balderston, George W. II, 1050
Balderston, Hannah II, 458
Balderston, Hannah II, 576
Balderston, Hannah II, 976
Balderston, Hannah II, 1016
Balderston, Hannah II, 1044
Balderston, Henry II, 1055
Balderston, Hugh VI, 229
Balderston, Isaiah II, 699
Balderston, Isaiah II, 976
Balderston, Isaiah II, 1044
Balderston, James II, 1044
Balderston, Jane II, 976
Balderston, John II, 458
Balderston, John II, 576
Balderston, John II, 954
Balderston, John II, 965
Balderston, John II, 975
Balderston, John II, 976
Balderston, John II, 982
Balderston, John II, 1011
Balderston, John II, 1016
Balderston, John II, 1027
Balderston, John B. II, 953
Balderston, John B. II, 954
Balderston, John B. II, 961
Balderston, John B. II, 976
Balderston, John B. II, 987
Balderston, John B. II, 1046
Balderston, John B. II, 1052
Balderston, John B. II, 1056
Balderston, John B. II, 1068
Balderston, John Brown II, 954
Balderston, John D. II, 976
Balderston, John D. II, 1044
Balderston, John L. II, 1044
Balderston, John P. V, 893
Balderston, John W. II, 954
Balderston, Jonathan II, 976
Balderston, Joshua II, 976
Balderston, Julia O. III, 23
Balderston, Latitia II, 954
Balderston, Latitia II, 965
Balderston, Letitia II, 953
Balderston, Letitia II, 961
Balderston, Letitia II, 976
Balderston, Letitia II, 987
Balderston, Letitia II, 1046
Balderston, Letitia II, 1052
Balderston, Letitia II, 1056
Balderston, Letitia II, 1068
Balderston, Lloyd II, 726
Balderston, Lloyd II, 730
Balderston, Lloyd II, 731
Balderston, Lloyd II, 954
Balderston, Lloyd II, 1068
Balderston, Llyod II, 1044
Balderston, Lydia II, 976
Balderston, Lydia Ray V, 893
Balderston, Mahlon II, 976
Balderston, Marcellus II, 699
Balderston, Margaret A. VI, 229
Balderston, Maria II, 719
Balderston, Maria II, 720
Balderston, Maria II, 954
Balderston, Maria II, 1044
Balderston, Mark II, 726
Balderston, Mark II, 731
Balderston, Mark II, 954
Balderston, Mark II, 976
Balderston, Mark II, 982
Balderston, Mark II, 987
Balderston, Mark II, 1044
Balderston, Mark Brown II, 954
Balderston, Martha II, 954
Balderston, Martha II, 1044
Balderston, Martha Ann II, 699
Balderston, Martha Ann VI, 229
Balderston, Martha Ann VI, 393
Balderston, Mary II, 954
Balderston, Mary II, 961
Balderston, Mary II, 976
Balderston, Mary II, 1052
Balderston, Mary Ann II, 726
Balderston, Mary Anna II, 726
Balderston, Mary L. II, 1045
Balderston, Mary P. II, 953
Balderston, Mary Tacie II, 1044
Balderston, Mary Tacie II, 1055
Balderston, Merab II, 976
Balderston, Merab II, 1044
Balderston, Oliver II, 953
Balderston, Oliver II, 976
Balderston, Phebe II, 976
Balderston, Phebe II, 1011
Balderston, Phebe II, 1044
Balderston, Pitfield II, 954
Balderston, Rachel II, 975
Balderston, Rachel II, 976
Balderston, Rachel II, 1011
Balderston, Rachel II, 1034
Balderston, Rachel II, 1037
Balderston, Rachel II, 1044
Balderston, Rachel E. II, 699
Balderston, Rachel S. V, 893
Balderston, Robert II, 954
Balderston, Robert Fitfield II, 1045
Balderston, Ruth II, 954
Balderston, Ruth II, 1045
Balderston, Samuel F. II, 699
Balderston, Samuel F. VI, 393
Balderston, Sarah II, 954
Balderston, Sarah II, 975
Balderston, Sarah II, 976
Balderston, Sarah II, 1037
Balderston, Sarah II, 1044
Balderston, Sarah II, 1054
Balderston, Sarah II, 1055
Balderston, Sarah A. II, 1044
Balderston, Sarah Brown II, 954
Balderston, Sarah C. II, 954
Balderston, Sarah C. II, 1045
Balderston, Sarah Cadwallader II, 1044
Balderston, Sarah Cadwallader II, 1050
Balderston, Sarah W. II, 954
Balderston, Sarah W. II, 1044
Balderston, Sarah W. II, 1046
Balderston, Timothy II, 976
Balderston, Timothy II, 1011
Balderston, Timothy II, 1034
Balderston, Timothy II, 1037
Balderston, William II, 954
Balderston, William Henry II, 954
Balderston, Wm. II, 976
Balderston, Wm. II, 1044
Balderston, Wm. II, 1045
Balderston, Wm. II, 1046
Balderston, Wm. II, 1055
Balderston, Wm. II, 1068
Balderston, Wm. III, 23
Balderston, Wm. Henry II, 1044
Balderstone, Mary IV, 172
Baldeston, John D. II, 1044
Baldeston, Martha II, 1044
Baldwin, ??? V, 315
Baldwin, Alfred IV, 1144
Baldwin, Alfred Eugene IV, 1144
Baldwin, Alice C. III, 23
Baldwin, Alice C. III, 292
Baldwin, Alva V, 984
Baldwin, Alvin C. IV, 1035
Baldwin, Amanda IV, 1271
Baldwin, Ann I, 489
Baldwin, Ann I, 523
Baldwin, Ann I, 550
Baldwin, Ann I, 562
Baldwin, Ann I, 577
Baldwin, Ann II, 787
Baldwin, Ann II, 954
Baldwin, Ann II, 976
Baldwin, Ann II, 1025
Baldwin, Ann III, 23
Baldwin, Ann III, 377
Baldwin, Ann V, 22
Baldwin, Ann V, 44
Baldwin, Anna I, 489
Baldwin, Anna I, 524
Baldwin, Anna I, 554
Baldwin, Anna III, 394
Baldwin, Anna III, 448
Baldwin, Anna V, 22
Baldwin, Anna E. IV, 924
Baldwin, Anna L. II, 834
Baldwin, Anna L. II, 923
Baldwin, Anna Lukens II, 781
Baldwin, Anna W. III, 23
Baldwin, Annie III, 23
Baldwin, Arcadia I, 489
Baldwin, Arcady I, 523
Baldwin, Asa I, 489
Baldwin, Benj. III, 23
Baldwin, Benj. III, 52
Baldwin, Benj. III, 265
Baldwin, Benjamin II, 787
Baldwin, Benjamin III, 23
Baldwin, Benjamin III, 394
Baldwin, Benjamin IV, 1144
Baldwin, Benjamin IV, 1201
Baldwin, Bennie IV, 1201
Baldwin, Bertha Hatton IV, 1144
Baldwin, Bessie V, 451
Baldwin, Caleb I, 775
Baldwin, Caleb II, 834
Baldwin, Caleb II, 923
Baldwin, Catharine II, 458
Baldwin, Catharine III, 394
Baldwin, Catharine IV, 1035
Baldwin, Catharine V, 297
Baldwin, Catharine V, 310
Baldwin, Catherine V, 219
Baldwin, Charity I, 673
Baldwin, Charity I, 682
Baldwin, Charity I, 796
Baldwin, Charity V, 297
Baldwin, Charity V, 312
Baldwin, Charles I, 489
Baldwin, Charles I, 523
Baldwin, Charles I, 1066
Baldwin, Charles I, 1070
Baldwin, Charles I, 1071
Baldwin, Charles IV, 1144
Baldwin, Charles B. IV, 1144
Baldwin, Charles P. IV, 1272
Baldwin, Charles R. IV, 1144
Baldwin, Charlotte I, 775
Baldwin, Charlotte I, 796
Baldwin, Chas. B. IV, 1271
Baldwin, Chloe IV, 1144
Baldwin, Chloe H. IV, 1144
Baldwin, Christian I, 523
Baldwin, Christian I, 524
Baldwin, Christian I, 1072
Baldwin, Clark IV, 1272
Baldwin, Dallas IV, 1201
Baldwin, Daniel I, 489
Baldwin, Daniel I, 523
Baldwin, Daniel I, 527
Baldwin, Daniel I, 673
Baldwin, Daniel I, 682
Baldwin, Daniel I, 775
Baldwin, Daniel I, 796
Baldwin, Daniel I, 847
Baldwin, Daniel I, 959
Baldwin, Daniel I, 1070
Baldwin, Daniel I, 1072
Baldwin, Daniel V, 297
Baldwin, Daniel, Jr. I, 523
Baldwin, David I, 489
Baldwin, David I, 775
Baldwin, David I, 796
Baldwin, David IV, 139
Baldwin, David IV, 320
Baldwin, David V, 22
Baldwin, David V, 984
Baldwin, Davis IV, 320
Baldwin, Dorcas I, 523
Baldwin, Dorcas I, 959
Baldwin, Dorcas I, 960
Baldwin, Edith I, 489
Baldwin, Edna M. IV, 1272
Baldwin, Eleanor II, 1043
Baldwin, Eleanor M. IV, 1271
Baldwin, Elias I, 489
Baldwin, Elisabeth I, 489
Baldwin, Eliz. III, 23
Baldwin, Eliz. III, 52
Baldwin, Eliz. III, 265
Baldwin, Eliza C. III, 23
Baldwin, Eliza Jane I, 775
Baldwin, Elizabeth I, 489
Baldwin, Elizabeth I, 523
Baldwin, Elizabeth I, 524
Baldwin, Elizabeth I, 534
Baldwin, Elizabeth I, 536
Baldwin, Elizabeth I, 553
Baldwin, Elizabeth I, 775
Baldwin, Elizabeth I, 796
Baldwin, Elizabeth II, 787
Baldwin, Elizabeth II, 1043
Baldwin, Elizabeth III, 23
Baldwin, Elizabeth III, 281
Baldwin, Elizabeth III, 377
Baldwin, Elizabeth III, 394
Baldwin, Elizabeth III, 462
Baldwin, Elizabeth III, 479
Baldwin, Elizabeth V, 218
Baldwin, Elizabeth V, 250
Baldwin, Elizabeth V, 318
Baldwin, Ella M. IV, 1271
Baldwin, Ellwood I, 775
Baldwin, Elmore V, 984
Baldwin, Emma A. II, 834

Baldwin, Emma A. II, 923
Baldwin, Emma K. IV, 1144
Baldwin, Enos I, 489
Baldwin, Enos I, 523
Baldwin, Enos I, 796
Baldwin, Enos I, 959
Baldwin, Enos IV, 1271
Baldwin, Enos V, 22
Baldwin, Enos V, 78
Baldwin, Enos V, 219
Baldwin, Ens I, 523
Baldwin, Ernest V, 451
Baldwin, Esther III, 23
Baldwin, Esther III, 479
Baldwin, Everett G. IV, 1035
Baldwin, Faith IV, 260
Baldwin, Florence Mary III, 354
Baldwin, Florence May III, 23
Baldwin, Fred V, 451
Baldwin, George Chalkley I, 775
Baldwin, Gertie IV, 1144
Baldwin, Gilbert III, 394
Baldwin, Hannah I, 489
Baldwin, Hannah I, 523
Baldwin, Hannah I, 524
Baldwin, Hannah I, 673
Baldwin, Hannah I, 755
Baldwin, Hannah I, 775
Baldwin, Hannah I, 796
Baldwin, Hannah I, 820
Baldwin, Hannah I, 827
Baldwin, Hannah I, 841
Baldwin, Hannah I, 870
Baldwin, Hannah I, 899
Baldwin, Hannah I, 959
Baldwin, Hannah I, 1101
Baldwin, Hannah II, 458
Baldwin, Hannah II, 489
Baldwin, Hannah III, 23
Baldwin, Hannah III, 265
Baldwin, Hannah IV, 1271
Baldwin, Hannah V, 22
Baldwin, Hannah V, 215
Baldwin, Hannah V, 218
Baldwin, Hannah V, 297
Baldwin, Hannah V, 318
Baldwin, Helen Cordelia V, 451
Baldwin, Henry I, 523
Baldwin, Henry I, 959
Baldwin, Henry I, 1113
Baldwin, Henry III, 394
Baldwin, Henry N. IV, 1306
Baldwin, Herold IV, 1144
Baldwin, Hezekiah I, 775
Baldwin, I. W. V, 150
Baldwin, Ida IV, 1306
Baldwin, Ida B. IV, 1306
Baldwin, Isaac I, 775
Baldwin, Isaac I, 796
Baldwin, Isaiah I, 489
Baldwin, Isaiah I, 523
Baldwin, Isaiah I, 524
Baldwin, J. W. V, 150
Baldwin, James C. T. III, 23
Baldwin, James C. T. III, 292
Baldwin, Jamima III, 23
Baldwin, Jamima III, 52
Baldwin, Jane I, 775
Baldwin, Jane I, 796
Baldwin, Jane I, 809
Baldwin, Jane IV, 1271
Baldwin, Jane IV, 1286
Baldwin, Jemima I, 673
Baldwin, Jemima I, 773
Baldwin, Jemima I, 775
Baldwin, Jemima I, 796
Baldwin, Jemima I, 797
Baldwin, Jemima III, 23
Baldwin, Jemima III, 189
Baldwin, Jemime I, 523
Baldwin, Jemime I, 570
Baldwin, Jennie IV, 1201
Baldwin, Jericho III, 23
Baldwin, Jess V, 22
Baldwin, Jesse I, 489
Baldwin, Jesse I, 523
Baldwin, Jesse I, 755
Baldwin, Jesse I, 775
Baldwin, Jesse I, 796
Baldwin, Jesse I, 797
Baldwin, Jesse I, 799
Baldwin, Jesse I, 827
Baldwin, Jesse I, 841
Baldwin, Jesse I, 959
Baldwin, Jesse I, 1101
Baldwin, Jesse III, 23
Baldwin, Jesse III, 281
Baldwin, Jesse III, 377
Baldwin, Jesse III, 394
Baldwin, Jesse III, 462
Baldwin, Jesse III, 479
Baldwin, Jesse IV, 1201
Baldwin, Jesse IV, 1271
Baldwin, Jesse V, 22
Baldwin, Jesse V, 215
Baldwin, Jesse V, 219
Baldwin, Jesse V, 297
Baldwin, Jesse V, 310
Baldwin, Jesse V, 318
Baldwin, Jesse, Jr. III, 23
Baldwin, John I, 489
Baldwin, John I, 523
Baldwin, John I, 570
Baldwin, John I, 673
Baldwin, John I, 773
Baldwin, John I, 775
Baldwin, John I, 796
Baldwin, John I, 959
Baldwin, John I, 960
Baldwin, John II, 458
Baldwin, John II, 672
Baldwin, John II, 781
Baldwin, John II, 834
Baldwin, John II, 923
Baldwin, John II, 954
Baldwin, John II, 976
Baldwin, John II, 981
Baldwin, John II, 997
Baldwin, John II, 1025
Baldwin, John II, 1043
Baldwin, John IV, 1271
Baldwin, John VI, 875
Baldwin, John C. I, 775
Baldwin, John Wesley IV, 1201
Baldwin, John, Jr. I, 796
Baldwin, John, Jr. II, 976
Baldwin, Jonathan I, 489
Baldwin, Jonathan I, 775
Baldwin, Joseph I, 489
Baldwin, Joseph II, 976
Baldwin, Joseph II, 1043
Baldwin, Joseph IV, 1144
Baldwin, Joseph IV, 1271
Baldwin, Joseph IV, 1272
Baldwin, Joseph VI, 467
Baldwin, Joseph C. IV, 1144
Baldwin, Joseph Cloud II, 458
Baldwin, Joseph T. II, 726
Baldwin, Josephine V, 150
Baldwin, Joshua II, 976
Baldwin, Joshua II, 981
Baldwin, Joshua III, 23
Baldwin, Josiah I, 489
Baldwin, Josiah I, 524
Baldwin, Josiah I, 581
Baldwin, Josiah I, 600
Baldwin, Josiah I, 601
Baldwin, Josiah I, 605
Baldwin, Judith I, 775
Baldwin, Kitty III, 394
Baldwin, Lavina H. IV, 1144
Baldwin, Lemuel IV, 1271
Baldwin, Lena V, 451
Baldwin, Lennie V, 984
Baldwin, Lewis C. IV, 1271
Baldwin, Louise IV, 1201
Baldwin, Ludia I, 489
Baldwin, Lydia I, 524
Baldwin, Lydia I, 581
Baldwin, Lydia I, 601
Baldwin, Malind I, 755
Baldwin, Malinda I, 755
Baldwin, Malinda I, 762
Baldwin, Malinda I, 796
Baldwin, Margaret I, 489
Baldwin, Margaret I, 524
Baldwin, Margaret I, 673
Baldwin, Margaret I, 682
Baldwin, Margaret I, 775
Baldwin, Margaret I, 796
Baldwin, Margaret I, 797
Baldwin, Margaret I, 799
Baldwin, Margaret II, 1043
Baldwin, Margaret IV, 139
Baldwin, Margaret IV, 320
Baldwin, Margaret V, 218
Baldwin, Margaret VI, 362
Baldwin, Margaret VI, 385
Baldwin, Margret I, 807
Baldwin, Maria IV, 1272
Baldwin, Martha M. IV, 1144
Baldwin, Martha M. IV, 1272
Baldwin, Martha W. IV, 1035
Baldwin, Mary I, 489
Baldwin, Mary I, 523
Baldwin, Mary I, 527
Baldwin, Mary I, 578
Baldwin, Mary I, 959
Baldwin, Mary I, 1070
Baldwin, Mary I, 1111
Baldwin, Mary II, 976
Baldwin, Mary II, 1010
Baldwin, Mary II, 1043
Baldwin, Mary III, 23
Baldwin, Mary III, 394
Baldwin, Mary III, 479
Baldwin, Mary IV, 139
Baldwin, Mary IV, 172
Baldwin, Mary IV, 320
Baldwin, Mary IV, 609
Baldwin, Mary IV, 648
Baldwin, Mary IV, 1271
Baldwin, Mary Ann I, 524
Baldwin, Mary Ann I, 560
Baldwin, Mary Ann III, 510
Baldwin, Mary C. IV, 1272
Baldwin, Mary Emma IV, 1271
Baldwin, Mary M. IV, 1035
Baldwin, Matilda I, 1113
Baldwin, Matilda I, 1114
Baldwin, Matilda IV, 1271
Baldwin, Mercy II, 976
Baldwin, Mercy II, 981
Baldwin, Mercy II, 1024
Baldwin, Meribah IV, 981
Baldwin, Merihab IV, 924
Baldwin, Milton I, 489
Baldwin, Milton I, 601
Baldwin, Miriam V, 297
Baldwin, Nathan I, 489
Baldwin, Nathan I, 524
Baldwin, Nathan I, 673
Baldwin, Nathan I, 682
Baldwin, Nathan I, 755
Baldwin, Nathan I, 762
Baldwin, Nathan I, 775
Baldwin, Nathan I, 796
Baldwin, Newton I, 775
Baldwin, Olive V, 297
Baldwin, Olive V, 304
Baldwin, Oren A. V, 451
Baldwin, Phebe III, 23
Baldwin, Phebe III, 330
Baldwin, Phebe VI, 362
Baldwin, Phebe VI, 424
Baldwin, Phinehas V, 318
Baldwin, Priscilla IV, 320
Baldwin, Priscilla IV, 357
Baldwin, Rachel II, 997
Baldwin, Rachel II, 1043
Baldwin, Rebecca I, 1113
Baldwin, Rebecca I, 1134
Baldwin, Rebecca II, 1009
Baldwin, Rebecca II, 1043
Baldwin, Rebecca III, 394
Baldwin, Rebecca VI, 459
Baldwin, Rebecca VI, 460
Baldwin, Rebekah I, 1113
Baldwin, Rees IV, 139
Baldwin, Rees Ellis IV, 320
Baldwin, Richard III, 394
Baldwin, Richard V, 22
Baldwin, Richard V, 297
Baldwin, Ruth VI, 615
Baldwin, Ruth VI, 626
Baldwin, Samuel R. VI, 459
Baldwin, Samuel R. VI, 460
Baldwin, Sarah I, 489
Baldwin, Sarah I, 523
Baldwin, Sarah I, 559
Baldwin, Sarah I, 775
Baldwin, Sarah I, 796
Baldwin, Sarah I, 834
Baldwin, Sarah I, 1070
Baldwin, Sarah I, 1071
Baldwin, Sarah II, 541
Baldwin, Sarah II, 976
Baldwin, Sarah II, 997
Baldwin, Sarah II, 1002
Baldwin, Sarah II, 1003
Baldwin, Sarah II, 1043
Baldwin, Sarah III, 23
Baldwin, Sarah III, 479
Baldwin, Sarah IV, 1144
Baldwin, Sarah IV, 1271
Baldwin, Sarah IV, 1286
Baldwin, Sarah V, 22
Baldwin, Sarah V, 78
Baldwin, Sarah V, 297
Baldwin, Sarah V, 318
Baldwin, Sarah V, 353
Baldwin, Sarah, Jr. II, 976
Baldwin, Sarah, Jr. II, 999
Baldwin, Selah III, 510
Baldwin, Sophah V, 297
Baldwin, Sophia I, 489
Baldwin, Sophia V, 22
Baldwin, Sophia V, 318
Baldwin, Sophia VI, 875
Baldwin, Stephen IV, 1144
Baldwin, Stephen IV, 1272
Baldwin, Stephen H. IV, 1271
Baldwin, Susanna I, 1070
Baldwin, Susannah I, 489
Baldwin, Susannah I, 1113
Baldwin, Susannah VI, 362
Baldwin, Susannah VI, 422
Baldwin, Susannah VI, 797
Baldwin, Susannah VI, 835
Baldwin, Thomas I, 489
Baldwin, Thomas I, 523
Baldwin, Thomas I, 601
Baldwin, Thomas III, 23
Baldwin, Thomas IV, 139
Baldwin, Thomas IV, 320
Baldwin, Thomas IV, 1272
Baldwin, Thomas C. III, 23
Baldwin, Thomas W. I, 489
Baldwin, Thos. II, 834
Baldwin, Uriah I, 489
Baldwin, Uriah I, 523
Baldwin, Uriah I, 524
Baldwin, Uriah I, 673
Baldwin, Uriah I, 796
Baldwin, Uriah I, 820
Baldwin, Uriah I, 959
Baldwin, Uriah IV, 1271
Baldwin, Uriah V, 22
Baldwin, Uriah V, 218
Baldwin, Uriah V, 297
Baldwin, W. Clark IV, 1272
Baldwin, Walter I, 523
Baldwin, Walter I, 959
Baldwin, Walter IV, 1306
Baldwin, Walter V, 22
Baldwin, Walter V, 297
Baldwin, Walter E. IV, 1306
Baldwin, Wd. Hannah II, 489
Baldwin, William I, 343
Baldwin, William I, 372
Baldwin, William I, 489
Baldwin, William I, 523
Baldwin, William I, 524
Baldwin, William I, 550
Baldwin, William I, 775
Baldwin, William I, 796
Baldwin, William I, 959
Baldwin, William II, 954
Baldwin, William IV, 1271
Baldwin, William V, 22
Baldwin, William V, 218
Baldwin, William V, 219
Baldwin, William V, 250
Baldwin, William S. III, 23
Baldwin, Wm. II, 976
Baldwin, Wm. IV, 1201
Baldwin, Wm. IV, 1271
Baldwin, Wm. IV, 1272
Baldwin, Wm. VI, 362
Baldwin, Wm. H. IV, 1144
Baldwin, Wm. H. IV, 1201
Baldwin, Wm. H. IV, 1272
Baldwin, Wm. K. IV, 1272
Baldwin, Wm. Lukens II, 781
Baldwin, Zebulon VI, 797
Baldwind, Jesse, Jr. III, 281
Bale, Susanna II, 458
Bale, Susanna II, 550
Bale, Thomas II, 458
Bale, Thomas II, 550
Baleau, Phreeby IV, 1087
Baleau, Phreeby IV, 1109
Baleau, Rebecca IV, 1087
Balen, Hannah Elizabeth V, 219
Balen, Hannah Elizabeth V, 274
Balenger, James I, 1089
Balenger, Joshua II, 52
Balenger, Lydia I, 1089
Balenger, Mary C. IV, 464
Balenger, Samuel IV, 464
Balentine, Margaret I, 870
Balentine, Margaret I, 888
Baler, James VI, 875
Baler, Margarett VI, 875
Bales, Abigail I, 1103
Bales, Abigail I, 1115
Bales, Abigail I, 1116
Bales, Abijeh V, 24
Bales, Abraham I, 1079
Bales, Abraham V, 24
Bales, Ada V, 657
Bales, Ada V, 705
Bales, Allen I, 526
Bales, Allen I, 870
Bales, Anderson T. I, 1147
Bales, Ann I, 870
Bales, Ann I, 894
Bales, Ann I, 1103
Bales, Anna I, 955
Bales, Anne I, 870
Bales, Anne I, 884
Bales, Asa H. I, 955
Bales, Asher I, 526
Bales, Asher I, 1103
Bales, Asher I, 1114
Bales, Bowater I, 955
Bales, Bowater I, 966
Bales, Bowater V, 221
Bales, Caleb I, 1079
Bales, Catherine I, 1079
Bales, Daniel I, 1089
Bales, Daniel V, 24
Bales, David I, 525
Bales, David I, 1079
Bales, David Morgan I, 1103
Bales, David, Jr. I, 1079
Bales, Eliaser I, 870
Bales, Eliaser I, 894
Bales, Elizabeth I, 955
Bales, Elizabeth I, 966
Bales, Elizabeth I, 1079
Bales, Elizabeth I, 1103
Bales, Elizabeth I, 1107
Bales, Elizabeth V, 24
Bales, Elizabeth E. V, 657
Bales, Elizabeth E. V, 695
Bales, Elizabeth Haines V, 473
Bales, Elwood Williams I, 1103
Bales, Emery V, 657
Bales, Emery V, 695
Bales, Emery R. V, 657
Bales, Emory V, 657
Bales, Eunice V, 221
Bales, Evan Lewis I, 1107
Bales, George I, 1103
Bales, Hannah I, 1079
Bales, Hannah I, 1103
Bales, Hannah I, 1115
Bales, Hannah I, 1123
Bales, Hannah V, 24
Bales, Hannah V, 53
Bales, Henry I, 1103
Bales, Henry I, 1114
Bales, Henry Wilson I, 955
Bales, Hester I, 980
Bales, Huldah I, 1103
Bales, Ilo V, 657
Bales, Ilo H. V, 657
Bales, Isaac I, 1089
Bales, Isaac I, 1103
Bales, Isaac V, 221
Bales, Isaac Hammer I, 1079
Bales, Jacob I, 955
Bales, Jacob I, 1079
Bales, Jacob I, 1089
Bales, Jacob I, 1103
Bales, Jacob I, 1114
Bales, Jacob Willis I, 955
Bales, James C. I, 1147
Bales, Jane V, 221
Bales, Jane V, 657
Bales, Jane VI, 995
Bales, Jemima I, 955
Bales, Jerusha I, 1079
Bales, Jesse I, 870
Bales, Jesse I, 1103
Bales, John I, 1089
Bales, John I, 1103
Bales, John I, 1107
Bales, John I, 1114
Bales, John B. V, 221
Bales, John Boeter I, 1089
Bales, John Carter I, 1103
Bales, John, Jr. I, 1114
Bales, Jonathan I, 1089
Bales, Jonathan V, 221
Bales, Joseph D. IV, 463
Bales, Katherine I, 1103
Bales, Levi I, 1103
Bales, Lois V, 221
Bales, Lorena V, 657
Bales, Lorena V, 670
Bales, Lucy VI, 874
Bales, Lydia I, 1103
Bales, Mahetabel V, 24
Bales, Margaret I, 526
Bales, Margaret I, 562
Bales, Martha I, 708
Bales, Martha I, 712
Bales, Martha Ellen V, 150
Bales, Mary I, 955
Bales, Mary I, 1103
Bales, Mary V, 221
Bales, Mary Elizabeth V, 657
Bales, Mary Jane I, 1103
Bales, Nace VI, 874
Bales, Nathan I, 955
Bales, Nathan I, 980
Bales, Nathan V, 221
Bales, Nathan Williams I, 955
Bales, Owen I, 1103
Bales, Parnel I, 526
Bales, Parnel I, 1114
Bales, Patsy P. I, 955
Bales, Phila A. I, 870

Bales, Phila A. I, 885
Bales, Pleasant M. I, 1103
Bales, Polly I, 1103
Bales, Polly VI, 945
Bales, Rachel I, 374
Bales, Rachel I, 526
Bales, Rachel I, 708
Bales, Rachel I, 870
Bales, Rachel I, 877
Bales, Rachel I, 1079
Bales, Rachel I, 1103
Bales, Rachel I, 1115
Bales, Rebecca Ann V, 473
Bales, Robert I, 1103
Bales, Ruth I, 1103
Bales, Ruth V, 221
Bales, Ruth V, 222
Bales, Samuel I, 1079
Bales, Samuel H. I, 1147
Bales, Sarah V, 221
Bales, Seth I, 1103
Bales, Solomon I, 1089
Bales, Susanna I, 504
Bales, Susanna I, 526
Bales, Susanna I, 1107
Bales, Susannah I, 1103
Bales, Thomas I, 1079
Bales, Thomas I, 1103
Bales, Thomas IV, 320
Bales, Thomas V, 657
Bales, Thomas V, 705
Bales, Thomas U. V, 657
Bales, Thos. V, 657
Bales, Viola V. V, 612
Bales, Walter I, 1103
Bales, William I, 1103
Bales, William I, 1115
Bales, William, Jr. I, 1114
Bales, Wm. I, 1103
Bales, Wm. I, 1112
Bales, Wm. Chas. V, 657
Bales, Zimri V, 473
Baley, Abiden V, 473
Baley, Ann II, 977
Baley, David I, 1007
Baley, Eliza IV, 674
Baley, Elizabeth IV, 463
Baley, Elizabeth IV, 465
Baley, Elizabeth V, 218
Baley, Henry IV, 465
Baley, James II, 334
Baley, James, Sr. II, 334
Baley, Jehu IV, 584
Baley, John II, 441
Baley, John VI, 362
Baley, Judith V, 297
Baley, Martha II, 441
Baley, Martha III, 394
Baley, Martha IV, 584
Baley, Mary II, 334
Baley, Mary II, 441
Baley, Mary II, 977
Baley, Mary IV, 465
Baley, Mary V, 218
Baley, Patience VI, 45
Baley, Phebe II, 977
Baley, Phebe VI, 362
Baley, Phebe VI, 437
Baley, Rachel VI, 362
Baley, Randal IV, 797
Baley, Ruth I, 1007
Baley, Sarah II, 334
Baley, Sinah IV, 584
Baley, Thomas II, 441
Baley, Thomas II, 977
Baley, Tyral VI, 45
Balgee, Rebecca IV, 369
Baliff, Nathan I, 372
Balinger, Abraham V, 826
Balinger, Hannah V, 826
Balinger, Hannah M. V, 879
Balinger, Henry II, 166
Balinger, Isaac V, 826
Balinger, Isaac H. V, 826
Balinger, John, Jr. II, 53
Balinger, Mary II, 166
Balinger, Mary VI, 468
Balinger, Mary Ann V, 826
Balinger, Samuel V, 826
Balinger, Sarah V, 826
Balinger, Thomas II, 166
Ball, ??? IV, 924
Ball, Abigail IV, 463
Ball, Abigail IV, 464
Ball, Abigail IV, 489
Ball, Abigail IV, 1049
Ball, Abigail IV, 1070
Ball, Abigail IV, 1127
Ball, Abigail IV, 1136
Ball, Ada IV, 1004
Ball, Albert V, 984
Ball, Alfred VI, 591
Ball, Alice Ann IV, 463
Ball, Alice Ann IV, 464
Ball, Alice Ann IV, 1049
Ball, Alice Ann IV, 1065
Ball, Allen IV, 675
Ball, Amos IV, 1049
Ball, Amos P. IV, 1127
Ball, Amos P. IV, 1131
Ball, Ann IV, 20
Ball, Ann IV, 73
Ball, Ann IV, 89
Ball, Ann IV, 675
Ball, Ann VI, 467
Ball, Atlantic II, 458
Ball, Atlantic IV, 674
Ball, Atlantic IV, 703
Ball, Atlantic IV, 924
Ball, Barclay Lee VI, 615
Ball, Benjamin IV, 674
Ball, Benjamin IV, 675
Ball, Benjamin IV, 924
Ball, Benjamin IV, 977
Ball, Benjamin Franklin IV, 674
Ball, Cassandra IV, 172
Ball, Cassandra IV, 464
Ball, Charity IV, 1144
Ball, Charles IV, 674
Ball, Charles IV, 675
Ball, Charles S. II, 781
Ball, Charles S. II, 834
Ball, Charlotee VI, 469
Ball, Charlotte VI, 560
Ball, Charlotte E. VI, 467
Ball, Charlotte E. VI, 469
Ball, Chas. S. II, 834
Ball, Clarence II, 781
Ball, Cynthiann IV, 1127
Ball, Cynthiann IV, 1131
Ball, David IV, 20
Ball, David IV, 463
Ball, David IV, 464
Ball, David IV, 491
Ball, David IV, 674
Ball, David IV, 758
Ball, David IV, 1049
Ball, David IV, 1051
Ball, David IV, 1064
Ball, David IV, 1065
Ball, David IV, 1070
Ball, David IV, 1127
Ball, David F. IV, 674
Ball, David Thomas IV, 674
Ball, David U. IV, 172
Ball, Deborah II, 781
Ball, Deborah II, 834
Ball, Deborah M. II, 834
Ball, Edward VI, 476
Ball, Eliza IV, 74
Ball, Eliza IV, 113
Ball, Eliza IV, 1351
Ball, Eliza VI, 468
Ball, Elizabeth I, 870
Ball, Elizabeth I, 890
Ball, Elizabeth IV, 463
Ball, Elizabeth IV, 474
Ball, Elizabeth IV, 671
Ball, Elizabeth IV, 674
Ball, Elizabeth IV, 675
Ball, Elizabeth IV, 677
Ball, Elizabeth IV, 792
Ball, Elizabeth IV, 798
Ball, Elizabeth IV, 830
Ball, Elizabeth IV, 864
Ball, Elizabeth VI, 467
Ball, Elizabeth VI, 531
Ball, Elizabeth Ball IV, 674
Ball, Elizabeth H. VI, 468
Ball, Elizabeth H. VI, 729
Ball, Elizabeth J. II, 834
Ball, Elizabeth J. II, 896
Ball, Elizabeth L. IV, 675
Ball, Elizabeth L. IV, 798
Ball, Ellen VI, 468
Ball, Elvira IV, 1351
Ball, Emily Ann VI, 615
Ball, Evelyn Joyce VI, 615
Ball, Florence E. VI, 615
Ball, Florence E. VI, 671
Ball, Florence E. VI, 672
Ball, Gaynor IV, 464
Ball, Gaynor IV, 1049
Ball, Gaynor IV, 1051
Ball, Gaynor IV, 1090
Ball, Genevieve VI, 615
Ball, George IV, 924
Ball, George IV, 1004
Ball, George W. I, 755
Ball, Gertrude V, 984
Ball, Hanna P. IV, 930
Ball, Hannah II, 458
Ball, Hannah IV, 674
Ball, Hannah IV, 675
Ball, Hannah IV, 703
Ball, Hannah IV, 864
Ball, Hannah IV, 924
Ball, Hannah IV, 977
Ball, Hannah VI, 467
Ball, Hannah VI, 492
Ball, Hannah P. IV, 674
Ball, Hannah P. IV, 864
Ball, Hannah P. IV, 871
Ball, Hannah P. IV, 924
Ball, Hannal L. IV, 674
Ball, Helen IV, 924
Ball, Henry IV, 172
Ball, Henry IV, 463
Ball, Henry IV, 464
Ball, Henry VI, 467
Ball, Henry C. IV, 172
Ball, Henry C. IV, 1087
Ball, Iden IV, 20
Ball, Iden IV, 73
Ball, James IV, 20
Ball, James IV, 73
Ball, James IV, 74
Ball, James IV, 172
Ball, James IV, 474
Ball, James IV, 476
Ball, James IV, 487
Ball, James IV, 488
Ball, James IV, 498
Ball, James IV, 505
Ball, James IV, 674
Ball, James V, 150
Ball, James VI, 467
Ball, James VI, 550
Ball, James P. IV, 172
Ball, James R. IV, 172
Ball, James R. IV, 286
Ball, James R. IV, 463
Ball, James R. IV, 464
Ball, James R. IV, 498
Ball, James R. IV, 1087
Ball, Jane IV, 172
Ball, Jane IV, 463
Ball, Jane IV, 674
Ball, Jane IV, 675
Ball, Jane VI, 467
Ball, Jane E. IV, 1233
Ball, Jane E. IV, 1241
Ball, Jas. IV, 463
Ball, Jeremiah V, 984
Ball, Jesse IV, 20
Ball, Jesse IV, 64
Ball, Jesse IV, 73
Ball, Jesse IV, 113
Ball, Jesse, Jr. IV, 73
Ball, Joel IV, 20
Ball, Joel IV, 73
Ball, John II, 458
Ball, John II, 834
Ball, John IV, 20
Ball, John IV, 73
Ball, John IV, 89
Ball, John IV, 674
Ball, John IV, 675
Ball, John VI, 467
Ball, John VI, 468
Ball, John VI, 500
Ball, John VI, 729
Ball, John Manning IV, 674
Ball, Joseph II, 458
Ball, Joseph IV, 20
Ball, Joseph IV, 73
Ball, Joseph IV, 172
Ball, Joseph IV, 674
Ball, Joseph IV, 675
Ball, Joseph IV, 792
Ball, Joseph IV, 798
Ball, Joseph IV, 830
Ball, Joseph IV, 924
Ball, Joseph IV, 930
Ball, Joseph Ailes IV, 20
Ball, Joseph Allen IV, 674
Ball, Joseph P. IV, 675
Ball, Joseph P. VI, 729
Ball, Joseph Parkins VI, 468
Ball, Joseph Parkins VI, 729
Ball, Joseph R. IV, 674
Ball, Joshua L. IV, 674
Ball, Joshua L. IV, 675
Ball, Judith II, 458
Ball, Julian IV, 1049
Ball, Julian IV, 1065
Ball, Julian IV, 1127
Ball, Juliann IV, 463
Ball, Juliann IV, 464
Ball, Juliann IV, 491
Ball, Juliann IV, 1049
Ball, Juliann IV, 1051
Ball, Juliann IV, 1064
Ball, Juliann IV, 1070
Ball, Lemuel IV, 1351
Ball, Lizzie IV, 172
Ball, Lizzie IV, 403
Ball, Lucinda Sackett IV, 674
Ball, Lydia IV, 675
Ball, Lydia IV, 741
Ball, Lydia Montgomery IV, 674
Ball, Lysle VI, 469
Ball, M. E. V, 984
Ball, Margaret IV, 20
Ball, Margaret IV, 73
Ball, Margaret IV, 89
Ball, Maria IV, 1201
Ball, Maria VI, 591
Ball, Martha IV, 172
Ball, Martha IV, 463
Ball, Martha IV, 488
Ball, Martha IV, 674
Ball, Martha IV, 675
Ball, Martha VI, 468
Ball, Martha VI, 476
Ball, Mary IV, 172
Ball, Mary IV, 463
Ball, Mary IV, 464
Ball, Mary IV, 474
Ball, Mary V, 150
Ball, Mary VI, 467
Ball, Mary VI, 468
Ball, Mary VI, 469
Ball, Mary VI, 475
Ball, Mary VI, 476
Ball, Mary VI, 500
Ball, Mary VI, 514
Ball, Mary VI, 537
Ball, Mary VI, 538
Ball, Mary VI, 542
Ball, Mary VI, 550
Ball, Mary VI, 555
Ball, Mary VI, 556
Ball, Mary VI, 623
Ball, Mary Ann IV, 172
Ball, Mary Ann IV, 286
Ball, Mary Ann IV, 463
Ball, Mary Ann IV, 464
Ball, Mary Ann IV, 498
Ball, Mary Ann IV, 1087
Ball, Mary C. G. VI, 684
Ball, Mary Cassander IV, 1087
Ball, Mary Cassandra IV, 172
Ball, Mary, Jr. VI, 468
Ball, McFarling VI, 468
Ball, Mercy IV, 20
Ball, Mercy IV, 64
Ball, Mercy IV, 73
Ball, Mercy IV, 113
Ball, N. E. V, 984
Ball, Naomi II, 712
Ball, Naomi IV, 463
Ball, Naomi IV, 487
Ball, Naomi IV, 738
Ball, Nathan II, 458
Ball, Nathan IV, 674
Ball, Nathan IV, 675
Ball, Nathan IV, 703
Ball, Nathan IV, 924
Ball, Nellie IV, 924
Ball, Nellie IV, 1004
Ball, Nellie Katherine VI, 615
Ball, Nettie IV, 1306
Ball, Pauline V, 984
Ball, Phebe VI, 468
Ball, Phebe Faust IV, 1245
Ball, Prudence II, 52
Ball, Rachel IV, 463
Ball, Rachel IV, 498
Ball, Rachel IV, 674
Ball, Rachel IV, 675
Ball, Rachel IV, 758
Ball, Rachel V, 150
Ball, Rebecca IV, 463
Ball, Rebecca IV, 505
Ball, Rebecca Eastburn VI, 615
Ball, Rebeccah IV, 463
Ball, Robert Braden VI, 615
Ball, Rodney VI, 615
Ball, Rodney VI, 671
Ball, Rodney VI, 672
Ball, Ruth IV, 463
Ball, Ruth IV, 464
Ball, Ruth IV, 476
Ball, Ruth IV, 487
Ball, Ruth IV, 488
Ball, Ruth IV, 498
Ball, Ruth IV, 505
Ball, Ruth IV, 531
Ball, Ruth IV, 584
Ball, Ruth IV, 1049
Ball, Ruth IV, 1064
Ball, Samuel IV, 674
Ball, Samuel C. IV, 674
Ball, Samuel C. IV, 675
Ball, Samuel S. IV, 864
Ball, Samuel S. IV, 871
Ball, Samuel Sackett IV, 674
Ball, Sarah IV, 19
Ball, Sarah IV, 20
Ball, Sarah IV, 73
Ball, Sarah IV, 172
Ball, Sarah IV, 265
Ball, Sarah IV, 671
Ball, Sarah IV, 674
Ball, Sarah VI, 591
Ball, Sarah Allison IV, 674
Ball, Sarah Ann II, 834
Ball, Sarah Ann IV, 674
Ball, Sarah Ann IV, 675
Ball, Sarah Ann IV, 864
Ball, Sarah H. IV, 674
Ball, Sarah H. IV, 675
Ball, Sarahann IV, 864
Ball, Smuel Sackett IV, 674
Ball, Susanna IV, 20
Ball, Susannah IV, 73
Ball, Susannah IV, 74
Ball, Susannah IV, 463
Ball, Susannah VI, 468
Ball, Susannah VI, 591
Ball, Susannah VI, 729
Ball, Thaddeus I. IV, 1351
Ball, Thadeus IV, 1351
Ball, Thomas IV, 20
Ball, Thomas IV, 139
Ball, Thomas IV, 674
Ball, Thomas IV, 675
Ball, Thomas IV, 864
Ball, Thomas L. IV, 674
Ball, Thos. IV, 671
Ball, Thos. IV, 674
Ball, W. C. V, 984
Ball, W. E. V, 984
Ball, Walter II, 781
Ball, Walter II, 834
Ball, Wd. Susannah VI, 467
Ball, Wd. Susannah VI, 729
Ball, William VI, 537
Ball, William James VI, 729
Ball, William Lloyd VI, 615
Ball, Wm. VI, 996
Ball, Wm. James VI, 468
Ballance, Anna II, 976
Ballance, Catharine II, 976
Ballance, Catherine II, 976
Ballance, Dorithy II, 976
Ballance, Dorothy II, 455
Ballance, Dorothy II, 458
Ballance, Dorothy II, 976
Ballance, John II, 334
Ballance, John II, 976
Ballance, Joseph II, 976
Ballance, Joseph II, 1085
Ballance, Liddia II, 976
Ballance, Lydia Ashton II, 458
Ballance, Mary II, 976
Ballance, Mary II, 1015
Ballance, Rachel II, 334
Ballance, Rachel II, 976
Ballance, Sarah II, 334
Ballance, Simeon II, 976
Ballance, Susanna II, 976
Ballance, Susannah II, 976
Ballangee, Eve II, 458
Ballangee, Isaac II, 458
Ballanger, James IV, 320
Ballanger, John II, 253
Ballanger, John IV, 320
Ballanger, Lydia IV, 267
Ballanger, Lydia IV, 500
Ballanger, Mary II, 253
Ballanger, Mary VI, 468
Ballanger, Rachel VI, 468
Ballanger, Rebecca IV, 320
Ballanger, Wm. IV, 500
Ballantine, Julia I, 870
Ballantine, Margaret I, 870
Ballard, ??? VI, 223
Ballard, ??? VI, 283
Ballard, ??? VI, 348
Ballard, Aaron V, 219
Ballard, Aaron V, 298
Ballard, Abigail V, 298
Ballard, Achilles III, 23
Ballard, Achilles V, 22
Ballard, Achilles V, 318
Ballard, Achsah I, 592
Ballard, Achsah I, 597
Ballard, Achsah V, 826
Ballard, Achsah P. V, 825
Ballard, Adam V, 474
Ballard, Addison V, 22
Ballard, Addison V, 318
Ballard, Addison B. V, 22

Ballard, Aden V, 298
Ballard, Aden V, 311
Ballard, Adin V, 298
Ballard, Adison V, 318
Ballard, Ahira I, 1003
Ballard, Ahira V, 22
Ballard, Ahira V, 474
Ballard, Alanson VI, 1011
Ballard, Alice V, 151
Ballard, Alice V, 549
Ballard, Alice V, 657
Ballard, Alice V, 825
Ballard, Alice V, 846
Ballard, Alice E. V, 510
Ballard, Allen V, 475
Ballard, Allen V, 657
Ballard, Almeda H. V, 657
Ballard, Almeda Hester V, 657
Ballard, Almedia V, 151
Ballard, Almeida V, 825
Ballard, Alpheus V, 151
Ballard, Alpheus V, 474
Ballard, Alpheus V, 475
Ballard, Amaziah V, 304
Ballard, Amos I, 1079
Ballard, Amos V, 22
Ballard, Amos V, 219
Ballard, Amos V, 372
Ballard, Amos V, 474
Ballard, Amos V, 475
Ballard, Amos V, 549
Ballard, Amos V, 657
Ballard, Amos VI, 227
Ballard, Amos VI, 296
Ballard, Amos VI, 297
Ballard, Amos VI, 875
Ballard, Amos Underwood V, 510
Ballard, Amy IV, 172
Ballard, Ann I, 775
Ballard, Ann V, 474
Ballard, Ann V, 525
Ballard, Ann V, 595
Ballard, Ann VI, 227
Ballard, Ann VI, 228
Ballard, Ann VI, 268
Ballard, Ann VI, 269
Ballard, Ann VI, 270
Ballard, Anna V, 372
Ballard, Anna V, 657
Ballard, Anne V, 474
Ballard, Annie V, 549
Ballard, Ansalom V, 298
Ballard, Ansolemn I, 955
Ballard, Anthony I, 959
Ballard, Anthony IV, 1306
Ballard, Anthony VI, 296
Ballard, Anthony VI, 349
Ballard, Archar I, 955
Ballard, Archar I, 959
Ballard, Archer I, 489
Ballard, Archer I, 959
Ballard, Archer I, 970
Ballard, Archer V, 219
Ballard, Asa I, 959
Ballard, Asa V, 151
Ballard, Asa V, 474
Ballard, Asa V, 549
Ballard, Asa V, 825
Ballard, Asa VI, 296
Ballard, Asa VI, 349
Ballard, Asa M. V, 893
Ballard, Asa N. V, 318
Ballard, Asa N. V, 474
Ballard, Asa N. V, 611
Ballard, Asa N. V, 893
Ballard, Asenath V, 318
Ballard, Asenath V, 611
Ballard, Asenath B. V, 318
Ballard, Barbara V, 474
Ballard, Barbara V, 525
Ballard, Barbarah V, 474
Ballard, Barclay V, 22
Ballard, Barclay V, 318
Ballard, Barclay VI, 228
Ballard, Barclay VI, 296
Ballard, Barclay VI, 297
Ballard, Barclay VI, 349
Ballard, Barkley V, 22
Ballard, Barkley V, 318
Ballard, Barlcay VI, 296
Ballard, Bartlett VI, 227
Ballard, Bartlett VI, 297
Ballard, Bartly I, 1003
Ballard, Benajah I, 1079
Ballard, Benajah V, 459
Ballard, Benajah V, 474
Ballard, Benajah V, 475
Ballard, Benajah V, 657
Ballard, Benajah V, 825
Ballard, Benajah V, 849
Ballard, Benejah V, 22
Ballard, Benjamin I, 797
Ballard, Bertha E. V, 657
Ballard, Bessie IV, 1306
Ballard, Bessie T. IV, 1306
Ballard, Bessie T. V, 657
Ballard, Betsey VI, 875
Ballard, Betsy V, 298
Ballard, Betsy VI, 297
Ballard, Betsy VI, 302
Ballard, Betsy VI, 319
Ballard, Betsy VI, 326
Ballard, Betty VI, 227
Ballard, Betty VI, 296
Ballard, Byram I, 955
Ballard, Byram VI, 227
Ballard, Byram VI, 285
Ballard, Byrom I, 953
Ballard, Byrom I, 959
Ballard, Byrom I, 1003
Ballard, Byrom I, 1007
Ballard, Byrom I, 1008
Ballard, Byrom VI, 227
Ballard, Byrom VI, 228
Ballard, Byrom VI, 296
Ballard, Byrom VI, 297
Ballard, Byrom VI, 315
Ballard, Byrom VI, 321
Ballard, Byrom VI, 349
Ballard, Byron V, 298
Ballard, Byron VI, 304
Ballard, Byrum I, 489
Ballard, Byrum I, 959
Ballard, Byrum I, 961
Ballard, Byrum VI, 296
Ballard, Caroline V, 22
Ballard, Caroline V, 62
Ballard, Caroline V, 726
Ballard, Caroline VI, 227
Ballard, Catharine V, 474
Ballard, Catharine V, 726
Ballard, Catharine E. VI, 890
Ballard, Catherine V, 22
Ballard, Catherine V, 825
Ballard, Catherine V, 872
Ballard, Charles Brooke VI, 297
Ballard, Chistopher VI, 321
Ballard, Christopher Hiatt I, 524
Ballard, Claborn J. VI, 875
Ballard, Claborn J. VI, 1002
Ballard, Claiborne J. VI, 890
Ballard, Clermont O. V, 473
Ballard, Daniel V, 474
Ballard, David I, 489
Ballard, David I, 524
Ballard, David I, 525
Ballard, David I, 953
Ballard, David I, 955
Ballard, David I, 959
Ballard, David I, 1003
Ballard, David I, 1007
Ballard, David I, 1079
Ballard, David V, 22
Ballard, David V, 151
Ballard, David V, 318
Ballard, David V, 345
Ballard, David V, 354
Ballard, David V, 474
Ballard, David V, 493
Ballard, David V, 510
Ballard, David V, 549
Ballard, David V, 825
Ballard, David V, 829
Ballard, David VI, 227
Ballard, David VI, 228
Ballard, David VI, 285
Ballard, David Ballard VI, 228
Ballard, David F. V, 318
Ballard, David F. V, 474
Ballard, David F. V, 611
Ballard, David, Jr. V, 474
Ballard, Davis I, 956
Ballard, Deborah I, 490
Ballard, Deborah I, 955
Ballard, Delilah IV, 172
Ballard, Delphin VI, 227
Ballard, Delphin VI, 285
Ballard, Dina I, 959
Ballard, Dinah I, 955
Ballard, Dinah I, 1001
Ballard, Dinah I, 1003
Ballard, Dinah I, 1007
Ballard, Dinah V, 474
Ballard, Dinah V, 542
Ballard, Dinah V, 549
Ballard, Dinah V, 605
Ballard, Donald V, 475
Ballard, E. Ann V, 22
Ballard, E. Ann V, 66
Ballard, Edeteth I, 1079
Ballard, Edeth I, 955
Ballard, Edith I, 1007
Ballard, Edith I, 1010
Ballard, Edith I, 1079
Ballard, Edith V, 151
Ballard, Edith V, 161
Ballard, Edith V, 298
Ballard, Edith V, 302
Ballard, Edith V, 474
Ballard, Edith V, 482
Ballard, Edith V, 537
Ballard, Edna Marie V, 151
Ballard, Edna Marie V, 657
Ballard, Elaner I, 1007
Ballard, Elaner I, 1011
Ballard, Eleanor V, 474
Ballard, Eleanor V, 657
Ballard, Eleanor VI, 15
Ballard, Eleanor VI, 227
Ballard, Eleanor VI, 228
Ballard, Eleanor VI, 296
Ballard, Eleanor VI, 297
Ballard, Eleanor VI, 304
Ballard, Elenor VI, 349
Ballard, Elisabeth V, 475
Ballard, Elizabeth I, 489
Ballard, Elizabeth I, 490
Ballard, Elizabeth I, 524
Ballard, Elizabeth I, 566
Ballard, Elizabeth I, 775
Ballard, Elizabeth I, 797
Ballard, Elizabeth I, 811
Ballard, Elizabeth I, 955
Ballard, Elizabeth I, 956
Ballard, Elizabeth I, 959
Ballard, Elizabeth I, 960
Ballard, Elizabeth I, 1001
Ballard, Elizabeth I, 1003
Ballard, Elizabeth I, 1007
Ballard, Elizabeth I, 1008
Ballard, Elizabeth I, 1079
Ballard, Elizabeth I, 1089
Ballard, Elizabeth I, 1093
Ballard, Elizabeth V, 22
Ballard, Elizabeth V, 111
Ballard, Elizabeth V, 151
Ballard, Elizabeth V, 171
Ballard, Elizabeth V, 188
Ballard, Elizabeth V, 215
Ballard, Elizabeth V, 219
Ballard, Elizabeth V, 220
Ballard, Elizabeth V, 245
Ballard, Elizabeth V, 298
Ballard, Elizabeth V, 308
Ballard, Elizabeth V, 318
Ballard, Elizabeth V, 372
Ballard, Elizabeth V, 474
Ballard, Elizabeth V, 492
Ballard, Elizabeth V, 549
Ballard, Elizabeth V, 611
Ballard, Elizabeth V, 644
Ballard, Elizabeth V, 657
Ballard, Elizabeth V, 825
Ballard, Elizabeth V, 826
Ballard, Elizabeth V, 846
Ballard, Elizabeth VI, 227
Ballard, Elizabeth VI, 295
Ballard, Elizabeth VI, 297
Ballard, Elizabeth VI, 302
Ballard, Elizabeth VI, 319
Ballard, Elizabeth VI, 349
Ballard, Elizabeth VI, 875
Ballard, Elizabeth Ann V, 22
Ballard, Elizabeth Ann VI, 297
Ballard, Elizabeth Anthony VI, 296
Ballard, Elizabeth Bunch VI, 228
Ballard, Elizabeth Edith V, 298
Ballard, Elizabeth Jane V, 826
Ballard, Ellroy V, 657
Ballard, Elroy V, 151
Ballard, Elroy V, 657
Ballard, Elva V, 372
Ballard, Elva V, 549
Ballard, Elva V, 657
Ballard, Emily M. VI, 972
Ballard, Emma V, 657
Ballard, Enoch I, 489
Ballard, Enoch I, 1089
Ballard, Enoch V, 474
Ballard, Enrich I, 1079
Ballard, Ernest IV, 172
Ballard, Eunice I, 1003
Ballard, Eunice V, 474
Ballard, Eva V, 510
Ballard, Evaline V, 318
Ballard, Eveline V, 611
Ballard, Fereby V, 473
Ballard, Frances I, 489
Ballard, Frances I, 955
Ballard, Frances I, 959
Ballard, Frances I, 960
Ballard, Frances VI, 227
Ballard, Frances VI, 285
Ballard, Fred W. IV, 1306
Ballard, Fred W. V, 151
Ballard, Fred W. V, 657
Ballard, Fred Wayne IV, 1306
Ballard, Fred Wayne V, 151
Ballard, Frederick V, 22
Ballard, Garman I, 489
Ballard, Garman I, 524
Ballard, Garman I, 953
Ballard, Garman VI, 297
Ballard, George B. VI, 875
Ballard, George B. VI, 969
Ballard, German I, 959
Ballard, Granderson B. V, 22
Ballard, Granderson Butterworth VI, 297
Ballard, Grandison Butterworth V, 22
Ballard, Grant IV, 172
Ballard, Hannah I, 1007
Ballard, Hannah I, 1010
Ballard, Hannah V, 22
Ballard, Hannah V, 130
Ballard, Hannah V, 473
Ballard, Hannah V, 474
Ballard, Hannah V, 510
Ballard, Hannah V, 533
Ballard, Hannah V, 611
Ballard, Hannah V, 647
Ballard, Hannah V, 826
Ballard, Hannah VI, 349
Ballard, Hannah Ann V, 22
Ballard, Hellen L. V, 22
Ballard, Ideteth V, 22
Ballard, Isaac V, 474
Ballard, Israel V, 611
Ballard, Israel V, 826
Ballard, J. Alansen B. VI, 897
Ballard, Jacob V, 474
Ballard, James I, 797
Ballard, James VI, 296
Ballard, James VI, 297
Ballard, James VI, 302
Ballard, James VI, 319
Ballard, Jane I, 797
Ballard, Jane V, 474
Ballard, Jane V, 549
Ballard, Jarman I, 955
Ballard, Jarmen I, 959
Ballard, Jarmen I, 963
Ballard, Jehu V, 474
Ballard, Jehu V, 726
Ballard, Jehu V, 757
Ballard, Jerman I, 524
Ballard, Jerman I, 955
Ballard, Jerman I, 1007
Ballard, Jerman V, 219
Ballard, Jerman V, 298
Ballard, Jesse I, 1003
Ballard, Jesse V, 298
Ballard, Jesse V, 474
Ballard, Jesse V, 519
Ballard, Jesse V, 549
Ballard, Jesse D. V, 657
Ballard, Jesse F. V, 473
Ballard, Jesse F. V, 474
Ballard, Jesse F. V, 543
Ballard, Jesse F. V, 549
Ballard, Jesse F. V, 605
Ballard, Joel V, 151
Ballard, Joel V, 474
Ballard, Joel V, 825
Ballard, John I, 489
Ballard, John I, 955
Ballard, John I, 959
Ballard, John I, 1003
Ballard, John I, 1007
Ballard, John V, 22
Ballard, John V, 151
Ballard, John V, 473
Ballard, John V, 474
Ballard, John V, 657
Ballard, John VI, 929
Ballard, John Harvey V, 475
Ballard, Johnson VI, 296
Ballard, Johnson VI, 875
Ballard, Johnson VI, 1002
Ballard, Jonathan V, 22
Ballard, Jonathan V, 474
Ballard, Jonathan V, 549
Ballard, Jordan V, 473
Ballard, Jordan V, 474
Ballard, Jordan V, 475
Ballard, Jordan W. V, 151
Ballard, Jordon V, 474
Ballard, Joseph I, 489
Ballard, Joseph I, 959
Ballard, Joseph I, 960
Ballard, Joseph I, 1007
Ballard, Joseph V, 151
Ballard, Joseph V, 188
Ballard, Joseph V, 474
Ballard, Joseph V, 475
Ballard, Joseph V, 549
Ballard, Joseph V, 825
Ballard, Joseph V, 846
Ballard, Judith I, 524
Ballard, Judith I, 542
Ballard, Judith I, 1007
Ballard, Judith I, 1008
Ballard, Judith VI, 227
Ballard, Judith VI, 296
Ballard, Judith VI, 297
Ballard, Judith VI, 349
Ballard, Judith Douglass VI, 228
Ballard, Judith F. V, 474
Ballard, Judith F. V, 480
Ballard, Judith F. V, 549
Ballard, Judith F. V, 554
Ballard, Judith Johnson VI, 228
Ballard, Julia A. I, 592
Ballard, Juliana V, 825
Ballard, Juliann V, 474
Ballard, Julianna V, 151
Ballard, Levina V, 298
Ballard, Levina V, 304
Ballard, Lilla IV, 172
Ballard, Louisa V, 318
Ballard, Louisa V, 324
Ballard, Louisa V, 657
Ballard, Lucina V, 510
Ballard, Lucinda V, 657
Ballard, Lydia I, 489
Ballard, Lydia I, 955
Ballard, Lydia I, 959
Ballard, Lydia I, 965
Ballard, Lydia I, 1003
Ballard, Lydia I, 1079
Ballard, Lydia V, 22
Ballard, Lydia V, 48
Ballard, Lydia V, 67
Ballard, Lydia V, 151
Ballard, Lydia V, 459
Ballard, Lydia V, 473
Ballard, Lydia V, 474
Ballard, Lydia V, 475
Ballard, Lydia V, 487
Ballard, Lydia V, 549
Ballard, Lydia V, 572
Ballard, Lydia V, 573
Ballard, Lydia V, 611
Ballard, Lydia V, 645
Ballard, Lydia V, 826
Ballard, Lydia VI, 296
Ballard, Lydia VI, 297
Ballard, Lydia VI, 319
Ballard, Lydia VI, 324
Ballard, Lydia J. V, 510
Ballard, Manarve I, 1089
Ballard, Mannerva V, 485
Ballard, Marah VI, 297
Ballard, Marie V, 700
Ballard, Martha I, 955
Ballard, Martha I, 959
Ballard, Martha I, 960
Ballard, Martha I, 1003
Ballard, Martha I, 1007
Ballard, Martha V, 22
Ballard, Martha V, 151
Ballard, Martha V, 474
Ballard, Martha V, 549
Ballard, Martha V, 657
Ballard, Martha F. V, 151
Ballard, Martha Jane VI, 875
Ballard, Mary I, 489
Ballard, Mary I, 524
Ballard, Mary I, 775
Ballard, Mary I, 797
Ballard, Mary I, 811
Ballard, Mary I, 955
Ballard, Mary I, 956
Ballard, Mary I, 959
Ballard, Mary I, 963
Ballard, Mary I, 980
Ballard, Mary I, 1001
Ballard, Mary I, 1007
Ballard, Mary I, 1012
Ballard, Mary III, 23
Ballard, Mary V, 298
Ballard, Mary V, 318
Ballard, Mary V, 354
Ballard, Mary V, 474
Ballard, Mary V, 493
Ballard, Mary V, 525
Ballard, Mary V, 543
Ballard, Mary V, 549
Ballard, Mary V, 611
Ballard, Mary V, 657
Ballard, Mary V, 726
Ballard, Mary V, 757
Ballard, Mary V, 825

Ballard, Mary V, 826
Ballard, Mary V, 829
Ballard, Mary V, 834
Ballard, Mary V, 836
Ballard, Mary V, 893
Ballard, Mary VI, 227
Ballard, Mary VI, 228
Ballard, Mary VI, 285
Ballard, Mary VI, 296
Ballard, Mary VI, 297
Ballard, Mary VI, 303
Ballard, Mary VI, 349
Ballard, Mary VI, 479
Ballard, Mary A. VI, 875
Ballard, Mary Alice V, 474
Ballard, Mary Embree VI, 297
Ballard, Mary J. V, 549
Ballard, Mary J. V, 657
Ballard, Mary Jane V, 611
Ballard, Mary Jane V, 633
Ballard, Mary Jane V, 657
Ballard, Mary M. V, 474
Ballard, Mary N. VI, 890
Ballard, Mary P. VI, 1002
Ballard, Mary Stanley V, 826
Ballard, Mary T. V, 22
Ballard, Mary T. VI, 897
Ballard, Mary W. VI, 972
Ballard, Matilda V, 474
Ballard, Matilda V, 508
Ballard, Meda V, 658
Ballard, Menerva I, 489
Ballard, Micajah V, 22
Ballard, Micajah VI, 875
Ballard, Micajah VI, 979
Ballard, Minerva I, 1079
Ballard, Minerva I, 1089
Ballard, Minerva V, 22
Ballard, Minerva V, 318
Ballard, Minerva V, 474
Ballard, Minerva V, 485
Ballard, Moorman I, 489
Ballard, Moorman I, 524
Ballard, Moorman I, 953
Ballard, Moorman I, 1077
Ballard, Moorman I, 1079
Ballard, Moorman I, 1089
Ballard, Moorman V, 22
Ballard, Moorman V, 318
Ballard, Moorman VI, 227
Ballard, Moorman VI, 228
Ballard, Moorman VI, 285
Ballard, Moreman I, 1089
Ballard, Morman I, 1089
Ballard, Morman V, 469
Ballard, Moses I, 1003
Ballard, Mouring VI, 297
Ballard, Mourman V, 474
Ballard, Mourning V, 475
Ballard, Mourning V, 500
Ballard, Mourning V, 549
Ballard, Mourning VI, 227
Ballard, Mourning VI, 334
Ballard, Nadine V, 475
Ballard, Nancy I, 797
Ballard, Nancy I, 809
Ballard, Nancy V, 22
Ballard, Nancy V, 219
Ballard, Nancy V, 298
Ballard, Nancy V, 300
Ballard, Nancy V, 473
Ballard, Nancy VI, 297
Ballard, Nancy VI, 302
Ballard, Nancy VI, 875
Ballard, Nathan I, 489
Ballard, Nathan I, 524
Ballard, Nathan I, 775
Ballard, Nathan I, 797
Ballard, Nathan I, 955
Ballard, Nathan I, 959
Ballard, Nathan I, 960
Ballard, Nathan I, 1003
Ballard, Nathan I, 1007
Ballard, Nathan V, 22
Ballard, Nathan V, 474
Ballard, Nathan V, 825
Ballard, Nathan V, 872
Ballard, Nathan, Jr. V, 474
Ballard, Nina V, 151
Ballard, Olive V, 372
Ballard, Olive V, 474
Ballard, Olive V, 549
Ballard, Olive V, 657
Ballard, Olive E. V, 657
Ballard, Ormie V, 549
Ballard, Penina III, 23
Ballard, Pharaba G. V, 474
Ballard, Pharaba G. V, 543
Ballard, Phariba J. V, 474
Ballard, Phariba J. V, 549
Ballard, Phariba J. V, 605
Ballard, Phariby V, 549
Ballard, Phebe I, 955
Ballard, Phebe I, 1007
Ballard, Phebe V, 219
Ballard, Phebe V, 297
Ballard, Phebe V, 298
Ballard, Phebe V, 311
Ballard, Phebe V, 318
Ballard, Phebe V, 452
Ballard, Phebe V, 474
Ballard, Phebe V, 475
Ballard, Phebe V, 479
Ballard, Phebe V, 490
Ballard, Phebe V, 549
Ballard, Phebe V, 632
Ballard, Phebe V, 657
Ballard, Phebe V, 726
Ballard, Phebe V, 825
Ballard, Phebe V, 826
Ballard, Phebe V, 849
Ballard, Phebe A. V, 549
Ballard, Phebe Alice V, 372
Ballard, Phebe Alice V, 657
Ballard, Phebe Ann V, 474
Ballard, Phebe Ann V, 549
Ballard, Phebe Anslum V, 298
Ballard, Phebeann V, 473
Ballard, Pheraba V, 474
Ballard, Pheriba V, 549
Ballard, Pheriba J. V, 549
Ballard, Philip I, 959
Ballard, Philip I, 1003
Ballard, Philip VI, 296
Ballard, Phillip VI, 349
Ballard, Polly VI, 875
Ballard, Priscilla V, 318
Ballard, Priscilla V, 345
Ballard, Priscilla V, 474
Ballard, Priscilla V, 510
Ballard, Priscilla V, 611
Ballard, Prudence I, 592
Ballard, Rachel I, 955
Ballard, Rachel I, 959
Ballard, Rachel I, 963
Ballard, Rachel I, 970
Ballard, Rachel I, 1007
Ballard, Rachel V, 22
Ballard, Rachel V, 219
Ballard, Rachel V, 298
Ballard, Rachel V, 318
Ballard, Rachel V, 474
Ballard, Rachel VI, 296
Ballard, Rachel VI, 297
Ballard, Rachel VI, 332
Ballard, Rachel VI, 333
Ballard, Rebecca I, 592
Ballard, Rebecca I, 1007
Ballard, Rebecca I, 1089
Ballard, Rebecca I, 1093
Ballard, Rebecca V, 22
Ballard, Rebecca V, 151
Ballard, Rebecca V, 213
Ballard, Rebecca V, 298
Ballard, Rebecca V, 372
Ballard, Rebecca V, 452
Ballard, Rebecca V, 459
Ballard, Rebecca V, 473
Ballard, Rebecca V, 474
Ballard, Rebecca V, 475
Ballard, Rebecca V, 480
Ballard, Rebecca V, 543
Ballard, Rebecca V, 544
Ballard, Rebecca V, 549
Ballard, Rebecca V, 657
Ballard, Rebecca V, 825
Ballard, Rebecca J. V, 151
Ballard, Rebecca Jane V, 151
Ballard, Rebecca Jane V, 475
Ballard, Rebeccah I, 1079
Ballard, Rebeckah I, 1089
Ballard, Reva V, 475
Ballard, Rhoda I, 489
Ballard, Rhoda I, 956
Ballard, Rhoda I, 959
Ballard, Rhoda I, 962
Ballard, Rhoda I, 1003
Ballard, Rhoda V, 22
Ballard, Rhoda V, 474
Ballard, Rhoda V, 493
Ballard, Rhoda V, 562
Ballard, Richard VI, 227
Ballard, Rleanor V, 219
Ballard, Roy V, 510
Ballard, Ruth I, 299
Ballard, Ruth I, 301
Ballard, Ruth I, 489
Ballard, Ruth I, 1003
Ballard, Ruth I, 1007
Ballard, Ruth I, 1008
Ballard, Ruth I, 1079
Ballard, Ruth V, 22
Ballard, Ruth V, 58
Ballard, Ruth V, 474
Ballard, S. G. IV, 172
Ballard, Salley VI, 349
Ballard, Sallie M. V, 657
Ballard, Sally Mary V, 475
Ballard, Samuel I, 524
Ballard, Samuel I, 592
Ballard, Samuel I, 1003
Ballard, Samuel V, 22
Ballard, Samuel V, 474
Ballard, Samuel V, 826
Ballard, Samuel VI, 296
Ballard, Samuel Jorden I, 1003
Ballard, Samuel M. V, 22
Ballard, Samuel Moorman V, 22
Ballard, Samuel Moorman VI, 297
Ballard, Sarah I, 524
Ballard, Sarah I, 564
Ballard, Sarah I, 775
Ballard, Sarah I, 797
Ballard, Sarah I, 849
Ballard, Sarah I, 959
Ballard, Sarah I, 961
Ballard, Sarah I, 1003
Ballard, Sarah I, 1007
Ballard, Sarah I, 1013
Ballard, Sarah IV, 1306
Ballard, Sarah V, 22
Ballard, Sarah V, 151
Ballard, Sarah V, 188
Ballard, Sarah V, 298
Ballard, Sarah V, 318
Ballard, Sarah V, 474
Ballard, Sarah V, 549
Ballard, Sarah V, 574
Ballard, Sarah V, 825
Ballard, Sarah V, 829
Ballard, Sarah VI, 227
Ballard, Sarah VI, 285
Ballard, Sarah VI, 296
Ballard, Sarah VI, 297
Ballard, Sarah VI, 315
Ballard, Sarah VI, 349
Ballard, Sarah VI, 353
Ballard, Sarah A. VI, 1002
Ballard, Sarah Jane V, 22
Ballard, Sarah T. V, 22
Ballard, Simeon I, 489
Ballard, Simeon I, 1079
Ballard, Simeon V, 22
Ballard, Simon V, 474
Ballard, Simon V, 525
Ballard, Spencer I, 1079
Ballard, Spencer I, 1089
Ballard, Spencer I, 1093
Ballard, Spencer V, 22
Ballard, Spencer V, 452
Ballard, Spencer V, 474
Ballard, Spencer V, 544
Ballard, Spencer V, 825
Ballard, Spenser I, 489
Ballard, Stephen V, 219
Ballard, Stephen V, 298
Ballard, Stephen VI, 875
Ballard, Susan V, 611
Ballard, Susan M. V, 22
Ballard, Susan M. V, 72
Ballard, Susan Maria V, 22
Ballard, Susanna I, 524
Ballard, Susanna I, 775
Ballard, Susanna I, 797
Ballard, Susanna I, 824
Ballard, Susanna V, 21
Ballard, Susanna V, 151
Ballard, Susanna V, 219
Ballard, Susanna VI, 296
Ballard, Susanna VI, 297
Ballard, Susannah V, 266
Ballard, Susannah V, 474
Ballard, Susannah V, 503
Ballard, Susannah V, 825
Ballard, Susannah VI, 227
Ballard, Susannah H. V, 503
Ballard, Susannah H. V, 549
Ballard, Thomas I, 489
Ballard, Thomas I, 490
Ballard, Thomas I, 524
Ballard, Thomas I, 775
Ballard, Thomas I, 797
Ballard, Thomas I, 953
Ballard, Thomas I, 955
Ballard, Thomas I, 959
Ballard, Thomas V, 22
Ballard, Thomas V, 318
Ballard, Thomas VI, 227
Ballard, Thomas VI, 228
Ballard, Thomas VI, 285
Ballard, Thomas VI, 296
Ballard, Thomas VI, 349
Ballard, Thomas VI, 353
Ballard, Thomas Beals I, 524
Ballard, Thomas C. V, 549
Ballard, Thomas Chalkley V, 473
Ballard, Thomas Chalkley V, 474
Ballard, Thomas Chalkley V, 549
Ballard, Thomas Elroy V, 151
Ballard, Thomas Elwood V, 474
Ballard, Thos. I, 490
Ballard, Thos. I, 956
Ballard, Unice V, 474
Ballard, Unice V, 542
Ballard, Uriah V, 298
Ballard, Willa V, 151
Ballard, Willa V, 657
Ballard, Willa Elsie V, 151
Ballard, Willard M. IV, 172
Ballard, William I, 489
Ballard, William I, 524
Ballard, William I, 775
Ballard, William I, 797
Ballard, William I, 955
Ballard, William I, 959
Ballard, William I, 1003
Ballard, William V, 219
Ballard, William V, 318
Ballard, William V, 473
Ballard, William V, 474
Ballard, William V, 490
Ballard, William V, 549
Ballard, William V, 726
Ballard, William VI, 227
Ballard, William VI, 228
Ballard, William VI, 268
Ballard, William VI, 270
Ballard, William VI, 285
Ballard, William VI, 295
Ballard, William VI, 296
Ballard, William VI, 297
Ballard, William VI, 302
Ballard, William VI, 305
Ballard, William VI, 332
Ballard, William VI, 333
Ballard, William VI, 349
Ballard, William VI, 1001
Ballard, William A. V, 151
Ballard, William Amos Mourning VI, 297
Ballard, William F. V, 22
Ballard, William F. V, 130
Ballard, William F. V, 473
Ballard, William F. V, 533
Ballard, William Frederick V, 22
Ballard, William Frederick VI, 297
Ballard, William Hiatt I, 524
Ballard, William R. V, 510
Ballard, William, Jr. I, 797
Ballard, Willis IV, 1306
Ballard, Wm. V, 298
Ballard, Wm. V, 318
Ballard, Wm. V, 611
Ballard, Wm. Alpheus V, 151
Ballazell, Benjamin V, 984
Ballazell, Lydia V, 984
Ballence, Dorithy II, 976
Ballence, Dorothy II, 975
Ballence, Dorothy II, 976
Ballence, Liddia II, 976
Ballenger, Abigail I, 538
Ballenger, Abigail IV, 1272
Ballenger, Abigail IV, 1290
Ballenger, Abraham V, 23
Ballenger, Adaline IV, 1272
Ballenger, Amy II, 53
Ballenger, Amy II, 56
Ballenger, Anna I, 1114
Ballenger, Anna V, 789
Ballenger, Anne I, 1114
Ballenger, Barshebe II, 53
Ballenger, Benjamin T. V, 797
Ballenger, Cassandra IV, 172
Ballenger, Cassandra IV, 296
Ballenger, Catharine I, 1103
Ballenger, Charity I, 1104
Ballenger, Daniel IV, 368
Ballenger, Dorothy I, 1114
Ballenger, Elizabeth II, 52
Ballenger, Elizabeth II, 53
Ballenger, Elizabeth II, 74
Ballenger, Elizabeth II, 115
Ballenger, Elizabeth II, 116
Ballenger, Elizabeth II, 195
Ballenger, Elizabeth II, 216
Ballenger, Ellwood II, 316
Ballenger, Esther II, 196
Ballenger, Esther II, 834
Ballenger, Evan I, 1114
Ballenger, Frances VI, 869
Ballenger, Hannah I, 490
Ballenger, Hannah I, 492
Ballenger, Hannah I, 1101
Ballenger, Hannah I, 1103
Ballenger, Hannah I, 1109
Ballenger, Hannah II, 334
Ballenger, Hannah II, 834
Ballenger, Hannah II, 888
Ballenger, Hannah V, 23
Ballenger, Henry I, 343
Ballenger, Henry I, 490
Ballenger, Henry I, 492
Ballenger, Henry I, 1104
Ballenger, Henry I, 1114
Ballenger, Henry II, 52
Ballenger, Henry II, 541
Ballenger, Henry IV, 368
Ballenger, Henry VI, 463
Ballenger, Iddings V, 797
Ballenger, Isaac II, 458
Ballenger, Isaac II, 834
Ballenger, Isaac V, 23
Ballenger, Jacob II, 196
Ballenger, Jacob II, 834
Ballenger, Jacob II, 888
Ballenger, Jacob H. II, 834
Ballenger, Jacob, Jr. II, 834
Ballenger, James I, 1089
Ballenger, James I, 1102
Ballenger, James I, 1114
Ballenger, James V, 726
Ballenger, James V, 789
Ballenger, James W. V, 797
Ballenger, Jesse I, 1089
Ballenger, Jesse I, 1114
Ballenger, Jesse V, 726
Ballenger, Jesse V, 773
Ballenger, Jesse V, 797
Ballenger, John I, 1114
Ballenger, John II, 53
Ballenger, John II, 56
Ballenger, John V, 797
Ballenger, Johnathan I, 1114
Ballenger, Jonathan I, 1089
Ballenger, Jonathan I, 1114
Ballenger, Jonathan V, 22
Ballenger, Jonathan V, 797
Ballenger, Joseph II, 196
Ballenger, Joshua II, 52
Ballenger, Joshua II, 67
Ballenger, Joshua V, 22
Ballenger, Joshua V, 151
Ballenger, Josiah VI, 357
Ballenger, Josiah VI, 463
Ballenger, Keziah II, 825
Ballenger, Lydia I, 1089
Ballenger, Lydia I, 1102
Ballenger, Lydia I, 1104
Ballenger, Lydia I, 1114
Ballenger, Lydia V, 726
Ballenger, Lydia V, 789
Ballenger, Lydia V, 797
Ballenger, Lydis V, 797
Ballenger, Mabel IV, 1272
Ballenger, Martha I, 1103
Ballenger, Mary I, 343
Ballenger, Mary I, 1089
Ballenger, Mary I, 1096
Ballenger, Mary I, 1104
Ballenger, Mary II, 53
Ballenger, Mary II, 56
Ballenger, Mary II, 115
Ballenger, Mary Ann V, 23
Ballenger, Mary Ann V, 879
Ballenger, Mary Ann V, 885
Ballenger, Moses I, 1089
Ballenger, Moses I, 1101
Ballenger, Moses I, 1103
Ballenger, Moses I, 1104
Ballenger, Moses, Jr. I, 1114
Ballenger, Myrtle IV, 1272
Ballenger, Naomi II, 52
Ballenger, Naomi II, 67
Ballenger, Phebe V, 797
Ballenger, Priscilla II, 834
Ballenger, Priscilla II, 887
Ballenger, Priscilla II, 888
Ballenger, Rachel I, 343
Ballenger, Rebecca I, 490
Ballenger, Rebecca I, 492
Ballenger, Rebecca V, 726
Ballenger, Rebeckah V, 726
Ballenger, Rebeckah V, 773
Ballenger, Rebekah II, 458
Ballenger, Rebekah II, 541
Ballenger, Richard VI, 875
Ballenger, Sally VI, 875
Ballenger, Samuel II, 52
Ballenger, Samuel II, 74
Ballenger, Samuel IV, 1272
Ballenger, Samuel V, 23
Ballenger, Sarah I, 1114
Ballenger, Sarah II, 53

Ballenger, Sarah II, 196
Ballenger, Sarah V, 22
Ballenger, Sarah V, 826
Ballenger, Sarah V, 831
Ballenger, Sarah Ann II, 316
Ballenger, Sarah Ann II, 326
Ballenger, Sarah S. II, 834
Ballenger, Sarah W. VI, 869
Ballenger, Thomas I, 1104
Ballenger, Thomas I, 1114
Ballenger, Thomas II, 195
Ballenger, Thomas II, 216
Ballenger, Widow Abigail I, 524
Ballenger, William I, 1104
Ballenger, William I, 1114
Ballenger, Wm. II, 53
Ballenger, Wm. II, 56
Ballentine, Alice V, 219
Ballentine, Burch V, 219
Ballentine, Elizabeth V, 219
Ballentine, Erma V, 219
Ballentine, Esther V, 219
Ballentine, Lavon V, 219
Ballentine, Oakley V, 219
Ballentine, Olive V, 219
Ballentine, Reba V, 219
Ballentine, Ruth V, 219
Ballews, Sarah VI, 796
Balliner, Cassandra VI, 469
Balliner, Edith VI, 469
Balliner, Elizabeth VI, 469
Balliner, Mary VI, 469
Balliner, Rebecca VI, 469
Balliner, Samuel VI, 469
Balliner, William VI, 469
Ballinger, ??? III, 24
Ballinger, ??? V, 754
Ballinger, ??? VI, 788
Ballinger, Abigail I, 524
Ballinger, Abigail V, 879
Ballinger, Abigail V, 880
Ballinger, Abraham II, 195
Ballinger, Abraham II, 196
Ballinger, Abraham V, 23
Ballinger, Abraham V, 826
Ballinger, Abraham V, 879
Ballinger, Abraham V, 880
Ballinger, Abraham H. V, 879
Ballinger, Amariah II, 52
Ballinger, Amariah II, 53
Ballinger, Amy II, 53
Ballinger, Anita Moon VI, 730
Ballinger, Ann I, 1017
Ballinger, Ann I, 1103
Ballinger, Ann VI, 468
Ballinger, Ann VI, 729
Ballinger, Anna Eliza VI, 773
Ballinger, Anna Eliza VI, 774
Ballinger, Anna Maria VI, 730
Ballinger, Arilla I, 638
Ballinger, Arilla Osborne I, 629
Ballinger, Atlantic II, 458
Ballinger, Aurilla I, 623
Ballinger, Aurilla I, 638
Ballinger, Barshebe II, 53
Ballinger, Benjamin II, 781
Ballinger, Betsy Ann Cyrene I, 524
Ballinger, Beulah V, 826
Ballinger, Beulah V, 879
Ballinger, Beulah V, 880
Ballinger, Caroline VI, 729
Ballinger, Caroline VI, 730
Ballinger, Caroline VI, 767
Ballinger, Caroline VI, 793
Ballinger, Carrie I, 524
Ballinger, Casander IV, 464
Ballinger, Cassandra IV, 172
Ballinger, Cassandra IV, 464
Ballinger, Cassandra IV, 501
Ballinger, Cassandra VI, 468
Ballinger, Cassandra VI, 545
Ballinger, Cassandra VI, 562
Ballinger, Charity I, 524
Ballinger, Charity I, 959
Ballinger, Charles VI, 729
Ballinger, Charles VI, 742
Ballinger, Charles VI, 762
Ballinger, Charles VI, 773
Ballinger, Charles VI, 774
Ballinger, Charles VI, 788
Ballinger, Charles VI, 791
Ballinger, Cyrus C. I, 524
Ballinger, Daniel II, 53
Ballinger, Daniel IV, 139
Ballinger, Daniel VI, 468
Ballinger, David L. II, 308
Ballinger, David R. II, 308
Ballinger, David Walton VI, 730
Ballinger, David Walton VI, 767
Ballinger, David Walton VI, 788
Ballinger, Deborah II, 52
Ballinger, Deborah II, 62
Ballinger, Dora I, 524
Ballinger, Dora I, 615
Ballinger, Edith IV, 464
Ballinger, Edith IV, 493
Ballinger, Edna H. II, 308
Ballinger, Edw. III, 24
Ballinger, Edward III, 23
Ballinger, Edward III, 24
Ballinger, Edward III, 59
Ballinger, Edward III, 250
Ballinger, Edward Gibbs VI, 729
Ballinger, Edward, Jr. III, 24
Ballinger, Elijah I, 490
Ballinger, Eliza III, 23
Ballinger, Eliza III, 24
Ballinger, Eliza III, 250
Ballinger, Eliza P. III, 24
Ballinger, Eliza P. III, 59
Ballinger, Elizabeth II, 52
Ballinger, Elizabeth II, 53
Ballinger, Elizabeth II, 86
Ballinger, Elizabeth II, 115
Ballinger, Elizabeth II, 195
Ballinger, Elizabeth III, 24
Ballinger, Elizabeth V, 826
Ballinger, Elizabeth V, 879
Ballinger, Elizabeth V, 887
Ballinger, Elizabeth VI, 444
Ballinger, Elizabeth VI, 468
Ballinger, Elizabeth VI, 920
Ballinger, Elizabeth D. II, 781
Ballinger, Elizabeth H. II, 308
Ballinger, Elwood II, 196
Ballinger, Elwood II, 280
Ballinger, Emeline I, 615
Ballinger, Emeline I, 622
Ballinger, Emeline I, 624
Ballinger, Emma V, 879
Ballinger, Enoch II, 53
Ballinger, Esther II, 31
Ballinger, Esther II, 196
Ballinger, Esther II, 834
Ballinger, Esther III, 23
Ballinger, Esther III, 24
Ballinger, Esther Sarah II, 52
Ballinger, Evan I, 1017
Ballinger, Even I, 1103
Ballinger, Florence G. VI, 730
Ballinger, Florence Helen II, 308
Ballinger, Grace II, 195
Ballinger, Hannah I, 343
Ballinger, Hannah I, 490
Ballinger, Hannah I, 524
Ballinger, Hannah I, 537
Ballinger, Hannah I, 578
Ballinger, Hannah I, 959
Ballinger, Hannah I, 1017
Ballinger, Hannah I, 1026
Ballinger, Hannah I, 1029
Ballinger, Hannah I, 1103
Ballinger, Hannah II, 52
Ballinger, Hannah II, 53
Ballinger, Hannah II, 85
Ballinger, Hannah II, 195
Ballinger, Hannah II, 196
Ballinger, Hannah II, 334
Ballinger, Hannah II, 458
Ballinger, Hannah V, 23
Ballinger, Hannah V, 826
Ballinger, Hannah V, 879
Ballinger, Hannah V, 885
Ballinger, Hannah VI, 468
Ballinger, Hannah VI, 585
Ballinger, Hannah VI, 788
Ballinger, Hannah M. V, 886
Ballinger, Henry I, 343
Ballinger, Henry I, 372
Ballinger, Henry I, 490
Ballinger, Henry I, 524
Ballinger, Henry I, 959
Ballinger, Henry II, 52
Ballinger, Henry II, 195
Ballinger, Henry II, 229
Ballinger, Henry VI, 358
Ballinger, Henry VI, 463
Ballinger, Henry VI, 468
Ballinger, Henry VI, 469
Ballinger, Henry VI, 545
Ballinger, Henry VI, 585
Ballinger, Henry VI, 609
Ballinger, Hephsiba II, 53
Ballinger, Hephzibah II, 53
Ballinger, Hephzibah II, 62
Ballinger, Hester II, 53
Ballinger, Hester II, 77
Ballinger, Hope II, 21
Ballinger, Hope II, 52
Ballinger, Hope II, 53
Ballinger, Hope II, 84
Ballinger, Isaac I, 1017
Ballinger, Isaac I, 1026
Ballinger, Isaac II, 195
Ballinger, Isaac II, 196
Ballinger, Isaac II, 458
Ballinger, Isaac III, 23
Ballinger, Isaac V, 23
Ballinger, Isaac V, 826
Ballinger, Isaac V, 879
Ballinger, Isaac H. II, 195
Ballinger, Isaac H. II, 196
Ballinger, Isaac H. V, 826
Ballinger, Isaac H. V, 879
Ballinger, Isaac K. V, 879
Ballinger, Isaac K. V, 880
Ballinger, Jacob I, 1017
Ballinger, Jacob I, 1026
Ballinger, Jacob II, 21
Ballinger, Jacob II, 196
Ballinger, Jacob II, 458
Ballinger, Jacob II, 781
Ballinger, Jacob II, 834
Ballinger, Jacob III, 24
Ballinger, James I, 1017
Ballinger, James I, 1026
Ballinger, James I, 1103
Ballinger, James II, 195
Ballinger, James Elizabeth III, 24
Ballinger, Jane V, 885
Ballinger, Jane Eliz. III, 59
Ballinger, Jane Elizabeth III, 24
Ballinger, Jemima II, 53
Ballinger, Jemima VI, 729
Ballinger, Jemima Ann VI, 730
Ballinger, Jemima Ann VI, 732
Ballinger, Jemima Ann VI, 788
Ballinger, Jesse I, 524
Ballinger, Jesse I, 1103
Ballinger, Jesse V, 22
Ballinger, Jessie F. VI, 730
Ballinger, Jessie Freemont VI, 730
Ballinger, Jessie Freemont VI, 767
Ballinger, John I, 490
Ballinger, John I, 524
Ballinger, John I, 1017
Ballinger, John I, 1103
Ballinger, John I, 1114
Ballinger, John II, 52
Ballinger, John II, 53
Ballinger, John II, 85
Ballinger, John II, 195
Ballinger, John V, 826
Ballinger, John V, 879
Ballinger, John VI, 468
Ballinger, John VI, 729
Ballinger, John VI, 730
Ballinger, John VI, 767
Ballinger, John VI, 788
Ballinger, John Roland VI, 730
Ballinger, John Wm. II, 52
Ballinger, John, Jr. II, 53
Ballinger, Jonathan I, 524
Ballinger, Jonathan I, 1017
Ballinger, Jonathan I, 1103
Ballinger, Jonathan V, 22
Ballinger, Joseph II, 196
Ballinger, Joseph I. III, 24
Ballinger, Joseph J. II, 196
Ballinger, Joseph L. III, 24
Ballinger, Joseph T. II, 196
Ballinger, Joshua II, 52
Ballinger, Joshua V, 22
Ballinger, Joshua V, 151
Ballinger, Josiah I, 1017
Ballinger, Josiah I, 1026
Ballinger, Josiah I, 1103
Ballinger, Josiah II, 52
Ballinger, Josiah VI, 358
Ballinger, Josiah VI, 440
Ballinger, Josiah VI, 444
Ballinger, Josiah VI, 463
Ballinger, Josiah VI, 609
Ballinger, Julia I, 524
Ballinger, Julia Anna M. VI, 730
Ballinger, Julia Anna M. VI, 762
Ballinger, Juliette I, 615
Ballinger, Laura I, 628
Ballinger, Laura A. E. I, 524
Ballinger, Levi II, 308
Ballinger, Levi VI, 729
Ballinger, Levi VI, 730
Ballinger, Levi VI, 732
Ballinger, Levi VI, 788
Ballinger, Louisa S. VI, 788
Ballinger, Lucy I, 623
Ballinger, Luzena I, 524
Ballinger, Lyda I, 1103
Ballinger, Lydia I, 524
Ballinger, Lydia I, 579
Ballinger, Lydia I, 1017
Ballinger, Lydia IV, 464
Ballinger, Lydia IV, 493
Ballinger, Lydia IV, 501
Ballinger, Lydia VI, 562
Ballinger, Maria L. VI, 729
Ballinger, Maria L. VI, 730
Ballinger, Maria L. VI, 742
Ballinger, Maria L. VI, 791
Ballinger, Martha I, 490
Ballinger, Martha I, 524
Ballinger, Martha I, 577
Ballinger, Martha I, 959
Ballinger, Martha II, 314
Ballinger, Martha VI, 468
Ballinger, Martha VI, 767
Ballinger, Mary I, 372
Ballinger, Mary I, 490
Ballinger, Mary I, 524
Ballinger, Mary I, 536
Ballinger, Mary I, 1017
Ballinger, Mary I, 1103
Ballinger, Mary II, 53
Ballinger, Mary II, 115
Ballinger, Mary II, 195
Ballinger, Mary II, 229
Ballinger, Mary IV, 172
Ballinger, Mary IV, 464
Ballinger, Mary V, 22
Ballinger, Mary VI, 440
Ballinger, Mary VI, 468
Ballinger, Mary VI, 585
Ballinger, Mary Alice VI, 729
Ballinger, Mary Alice VI, 730
Ballinger, Mary Alice VI, 791
Ballinger, Mary Ann II, 195
Ballinger, Mary Ann II, 196
Ballinger, Mary Ann V, 22
Ballinger, Mary Ann V, 23
Ballinger, Mary Ann V, 826
Ballinger, Mary Ann V, 879
Ballinger, Mary Ann V, 881
Ballinger, Mary C. IV, 464
Ballinger, Mary E. III, 24
Ballinger, Mary Olive V, 879
Ballinger, Md. Hannah VI, 468
Ballinger, Md. Lydia VI, 469
Ballinger, Melinda I, 490
Ballinger, Milton I, 623
Ballinger, Moses I, 490
Ballinger, Moses I, 524
Ballinger, Moses I, 959
Ballinger, Moses VI, 468
Ballinger, Naomi I, 628
Ballinger, Naomi II, 52
Ballinger, Naomi II, 80
Ballinger, Naomi P. I, 524
Ballinger, Naomi P. I, 533
Ballinger, Nereus I, 524
Ballinger, Nereus A. I, 615
Ballinger, Patience VI, 444
Ballinger, Permelia L. VI, 972
Ballinger, Priscilla II, 458
Ballinger, Priscilla II, 805
Ballinger, Priscilla II, 834
Ballinger, Priscilla III, 24
Ballinger, Priscilla V, 879
Ballinger, Priscilla V, 884
Ballinger, Priscilla VI, 615
Ballinger, Priscilla VI, 695
Ballinger, Rachel I, 372
Ballinger, Rachel I, 490
Ballinger, Rachel I, 524
Ballinger, Rachel VI, 468
Ballinger, Rachel Ann V, 826
Ballinger, Rachel Ann V, 879
Ballinger, Rebecca I, 524
Ballinger, Rebecca I, 528
Ballinger, Rebecca IV, 172
Ballinger, Rebecca IV, 288
Ballinger, Rebecca IV, 464
Ballinger, Rebecca IV, 500
Ballinger, Rebecca VI, 729
Ballinger, Rebecca VI, 730
Ballinger, Rebecca VI, 788
Ballinger, Rebecca N. VI, 730
Ballinger, Rebecca N. VI, 742
Ballinger, Rebecca Walton VI, 767
Ballinger, Rebeckah I, 490
Ballinger, Rebeckah VI, 468
Ballinger, Rebekah I, 524
Ballinger, Rebekah I, 550
Ballinger, Rebekah II, 458
Ballinger, Richard C. II, 280
Ballinger, Ruth I, 524
Ballinger, Ruth V, 754
Ballinger, S. W. VI, 920
Ballinger, Samuel II, 52
Ballinger, Samuel II, 196
Ballinger, Samuel IV, 464
Ballinger, Samuel V, 23
Ballinger, Samuel V, 826
Ballinger, Samuel V, 879
Ballinger, Samuel VI, 468
Ballinger, Sarah I, 1017
Ballinger, Sarah I, 1103
Ballinger, Sarah II, 53
Ballinger, Sarah II, 196
Ballinger, Sarah II, 314
Ballinger, Sarah III, 24
Ballinger, Sarah V, 22
Ballinger, Sarah V, 826
Ballinger, Sarah VI, 371
Ballinger, Sarah VI, 372
Ballinger, Sarah VI, 440
Ballinger, Sarah VI, 468
Ballinger, Sarah VI, 553
Ballinger, Sarah VI, 621
Ballinger, Sarah VI, 623
Ballinger, Sarah VI, 685
Ballinger, Sarah VI, 730
Ballinger, Sarah VI, 734
Ballinger, Sarah VI, 769
Ballinger, Sarah Elma V, 879
Ballinger, Sarah Elma V, 882
Ballinger, Sarah H. V, 879
Ballinger, Sarah H. V, 880
Ballinger, Sarah S. II, 834
Ballinger, Sarah W. VI, 972
Ballinger, Thomas I, 524
Ballinger, Thomas I, 959
Ballinger, Thomas II, 195
Ballinger, Thomas II, 458
Ballinger, Wd. Esther II, 781
Ballinger, Wd. Jemima Ann VI, 730
Ballinger, Widow Abigail I, 524
Ballinger, William I, 490
Ballinger, William I, 524
Ballinger, William I, 959
Ballinger, William IV, 172
Ballinger, William IV, 464
Ballinger, William VI, 371
Ballinger, William VI, 468
Ballinger, William VI, 545
Ballinger, William VI, 562
Ballinger, William Pearsall III, 24
Ballinger, William, Jr. VI, 468
Ballinger, William, Jr. VI, 562
Ballinger, Wm. II, 53
Ballinger, Wm. IV, 464
Ballinger, Wm. IV, 493
Ballinger, Wm. IV, 501
Ballinger, Wm. V, 879
Ballinger, Wm. VI, 468
Ballinger, Wm. Ellis V, 879
Ballinger, Yancy I, 628
Ballinger, Zacheus II, 21
Ballinger, Zacheus II, 53
Ballinger, Zacheus II, 84
Balloon, Maria IV, 1306
Balloon, Mary IV, 1306
Ballord, Thomas VI, 227
Ballow, Charles VI, 797
Ballow, Elizabeth VI, 941
Ballow, Esther VI, 941
Ballow, Letitia M. VI, 797
Ballszell, Benjamin V, 984
Ballszell, Lydia V, 984
Ballyhagan, Wm. II, 458
Balmer, Ann VI, 52
Balon, Hannah Elizabeth V, 219
Balon, John V, 219
Balor, James VI, 875
Balor, Lucy VI, 875
Balor, Margarett VI, 875
Balston, Ann II, 334
Balston, Thomas II, 334
Balt, Anna Maria III, 88
Balten, Aaron IV, 172
Balten, Amy IV, 172
Balten, Ira IV, 172
Balten, Jesse IV, 172
Balten, Lydia IV, 172
Balten, Priscilla IV, 172
Balten, Rhoda IV, 172
Balten, Ruth IV, 172
Balten, Samuel IV, 172
Balten, Sara IV, 172
Baltimore, Broomell VI, 416
Baltimore, Rebecca J. VI, 416
Baltzell, Alta V, 984
Baltzell, Benjamin V, 984
Baltzell, Bessie V, 984
Baltzell, L. A. V, 984
Baltzell, Lydia V, 984
Balwin, Rachel V, 726
Balwin, Richard V, 984
Baly, Ann II, 977

Baly, David I, 267
Baly, Lucy VI, 874
Baly, Nace VI, 874
Balyard, Caroline V, 726
Balyard, Catharine V, 726
Balyeat, Addie V, 984
Balyeat, Adie V, 984
Balyeat, Ida V, 984
Balyeat, Mable V, 984
Balyeat, Mollie V, 984
Balyeat, Olive V, 984
Bamer, James II, 441
Banander, Anna I, 999
Bancher, Francelia III, 89
Bancker, Frederick A. III, 24
Bancker, Mary E. III, 24
Banckson, John II, 334
Banckson, Joseph II, 334
Bancroft, Agnes V. II, 834
Bancroft, Agnes V. II, 913
Bancroft, Anna II, 834
Bancroft, Anna P. II, 834
Bancroft, Anna P. II, 850
Bancroft, Anne S. II, 781
Bancroft, Anne S. II, 834
Bancroft, Catharine M. IV, 173
Bancroft, Charles II, 781
Bancroft, Charles II, 834
Bancroft, Edward II, 781
Bancroft, Edward II, 834
Bancroft, Edward II, 850
Bancroft, Elizabeth II, 781
Bancroft, Elizabeth II, 809
Bancroft, Elizabeth II, 812
Bancroft, Elizabeth R. II, 834
Bancroft, Esther II, 781
Bancroft, Esther II, 834
Bancroft, Harvey II, 781
Bancroft, Harvey II, 834
Bancroft, Henry II, 781
Bancroft, Hugh II, 781
Bancroft, J. Sellers II, 834
Bancroft, James R. II, 834
Bancroft, James Ronaldson II, 781
Bancroft, John II, 781
Bancroft, John II, 809
Bancroft, John II, 834
Bancroft, John Sellers II, 781
Bancroft, John, Jr. II, 834
Bancroft, John, Jr. II, 927
Bancroft, Joseph IV, 173
Bancroft, Joseph W. II, 834
Bancroft, Lena Olive IV, 173
Bancroft, Lucretia II, 781
Bancroft, Lydia II, 808
Bancroft, Margaret II, 781
Bancroft, Margaret II, 834
Bancroft, Margaret B. II, 834
Bancroft, Margaret B. II, 927
Bancroft, Martha II, 781
Bancroft, Martha II, 791
Bancroft, Martha II, 809
Bancroft, Mary II, 808
Bancroft, Mary II, 834
Bancroft, Mary S. II, 834
Bancroft, Mary S. II, 850
Bancroft, Napoleon II, 834
Bancroft, Powell II, 781
Bancroft, Rachel II, 781
Bancroft, Rebecca II, 781
Bancroft, Rebecca II, 834
Bancroft, Rebecca W. II, 781
Bancroft, Rebecca W. II, 834
Bancroft, Rebecca Worrel II, 781
Bancroft, Sarah II, 833
Bancroft, Sarah II, 834
Bancroft, Sarah III, 76
Bancroft, Sarah III, 96
Bancroft, Sarah III, 202
Bancroft, Susan II, 781
Bancroft, Susan II, 834
Bancroft, Susann II, 927
Bancroft, Susanna II, 834
Bancroft, Susannah II, 781
Bancroft, Susannah II, 834
Bancroft, Thos. II, 808
Bancroft, Thos. B. II, 834
Bancroft, Thos. B. II, 913
Bancroft, Wd. Mary II, 781
Bancroft, Wd. Rebecca W. II, 834
Bancroft, Wilfred II, 781
Bancroft, Wm. II, 781
Bancroft, Wm. II, 834
Bancroft, Wm. C. II, 834
Bandenhausen, Mathilde C. III, 202
Bandy, Cornelius VI, 875
Bandy, Elizabeth VI, 875
Bandy, Elizabeth VI, 940
Bandy, Frances VI, 875
Bandy, George VI, 875
Bandy, George VI, 940
Bandy, George VI, 968
Bandy, George VI, 1013
Bandy, Harriet E. VI, 875
Bandy, James VI, 875
Bandy, Judith VI, 875
Bandy, Maney VI, 875
Bandy, ManeyBrown VI, 875
Bandy, Mary Elizabeth VI, 875
Bandy, Matthew VI, 875
Bandy, Nancy VI, 875
Bandy, Nancy VI, 940
Bandy, Nancy VI, 968
Bandy, Narcissas VI, 950
Bandy, Polly VI, 875
Bandy, Polly VI, 888
Bandy, Reubin VI, 875
Bandy, Rhoda VI, 1013
Bandy, Richard VI, 940
Bandy, Richard VI, 968
Bandy, Richard H. VI, 875
Bandy, Richard H. VI, 950
Bandy, Ritchard VI, 888
Bandy, Sally VI, 875
Bandy, Samuel VI, 875
Bandy, Samuel VI, 888
Bandy, Samuel W. VI, 875
Bandy, Sibley VI, 875
Bandy, Thomas VI, 875
Bandy, Thomas VI, 940
Bandy, Thomas L. VI, 875
Bandy, Thomas L. VI, 1022
Bandy, William VI, 875
Bane, Abner VI, 362
Bane, Almedia IV, 567
Bane, Ann II, 334
Bane, Ann IV, 311
Bane, Ann IV, 314
Bane, Anna IV, 567
Bane, Anna IV, 1049
Bane, Elijah IV, 567
Bane, Elijah IV, 1049
Bane, John IV, 567
Bane, John IV, 1049
Bane, Lavina IV, 567
Bane, Lavina IV, 570
Bane, Margaret, Jr. II, 836
Bane, Martha IV, 567
Bane, Martha IV, 1049
Bane, Mary III, 395
Bane, Mary IV, 567
Bane, Mary IV, 570
Bane, Mary W. II, 836
Bane, Mordecai III, 394
Bane, Nathan III, 394
Bane, Nathan III, 401
Bane, Parthania VI, 362
Bane, Rachel VI, 362
Bane, Rhoda IV, 567
Bane, Sarah IV, 567
Baner, Charlotte Anna III, 24
Baner, Dr. William J. III, 24
Baner, Dr. Wm. J. III, 124
Baner, Hannah II, 784
Baner, Isaac III, 24
Baner, Isaac V, 893
Baner, Joseph S. V, 893
Baner, Marinna III, 24
Baner, Martha III, 24
Baner, Martha III, 124
Baner, Oriella Eugenia III, 24
Baner, Sarah III, 24
Baner, Sarah V, 893
Baner, Walter III, 24
Baner, Wm. I. V, 893
Baner, Wm. J. V, 893
Banes, Hannah V, 23
Banes, Hannah V, 475
Banes, Isaac V, 23
Banes, Isaac V, 475
Banes, Maria M. VI, 935
Banes, Nancy V, 23
Banes, Thomas V, 475
Banes, Watson V, 475
Banes, Wilson V, 475
Bangam, Agnes V, 475
Bangam, Benjamin V, 475
Bangam, Elizabeth V, 475
Bangam, Lucy Humphrey V, 475
Bangam, Martha V, 475
Bangam, Mary V, 475
Bangam, Zachariah M. V, 475
Bangham, Agnes V, 475
Bangham, Agnes V, 611
Bangham, Agnes V, 616
Bangham, Agnes V, 797
Bangham, Agnes V, 801
Bangham, Alberta V, 657
Bangham, Anna V, 151
Bangham, Anna V, 657
Bangham, Anna Lucy V, 549
Bangham, Anna Lucy V, 657
Bangham, Benj. VI, 797
Bangham, Benjamin V, 475
Bangham, Benjamin V, 549
Bangham, Benjamin V, 610
Bangham, Benjamin V, 611
Bangham, Benjamin V, 616
Bangham, Benjamin V, 623
Bangham, Benjamin V, 635
Bangham, Benjamin V, 947
Bangham, Caroline Elizabeth V, 611
Bangham, Cyrus V, 151
Bangham, Cyrus V, 549
Bangham, Cyrus V, 657
Bangham, Elizabeth II, 458
Bangham, Elizabeth II, 465
Bangham, Elizabeth IV, 20
Bangham, Elizabeth V, 475
Bangham, Elizabeth V, 611
Bangham, Elizabeth VI, 297
Bangham, Elizabeth VI, 315
Bangham, Elizabeth VI, 469
Bangham, Elizabeth C. V, 151
Bangham, Elizabeth C. V, 657
Bangham, Ella M. V, 549
Bangham, Ella M. V, 657
Bangham, Esther V, 549
Bangham, Esther V, 580
Bangham, Esther C. V, 689
Bangham, Humphrey II, 458
Bangham, Humphrey II, 465
Bangham, Humphrey V, 611
Bangham, Humphrey VI, 297
Bangham, Humphrey VI, 315
Bangham, Humphrey VI, 469
Bangham, Humphrey I. V, 947
Bangham, Humphrey I. V, 950
Bangham, Humphrey John VI, 834
Bangham, Isabella V, 611
Bangham, Jane V, 475
Bangham, Jane V, 491
Bangham, Jane W. V, 611
Bangham, Jane W. V, 647
Bangham, John V, 151
Bangham, John V, 657
Bangham, John VI, 310
Bangham, John VI, 816
Bangham, John C. V, 151
Bangham, John C. V, 549
Bangham, John C. V, 611
Bangham, John C. V, 657
Bangham, Jonathan V, 475
Bangham, Jonathan V, 491
Bangham, Jonathan V, 611
Bangham, Jonathan V, 647
Bangham, Jonathan V, 649
Bangham, Jonathan P. V, 611
Bangham, Lavina V, 549
Bangham, Levina V, 657
Bangham, Loren E. V, 657
Bangham, Lovina V, 151
Bangham, Lovina V, 657
Bangham, Lucy V, 475
Bangham, Lucy V, 610
Bangham, Lucy V, 611
Bangham, Lucy V, 616
Bangham, Lucy V, 623
Bangham, Lucy V, 635
Bangham, Lucy V, 947
Bangham, Lucy VI, 797
Bangham, Lucy Ann V, 611
Bangham, Lucy Humphrey V, 475
Bangham, Lydia V, 657
Bangham, Lydia M. V, 151
Bangham, Mabel E. V, 151
Bangham, Mabel E. V, 657
Bangham, Martha V, 475
Bangham, Martha V, 611
Bangham, Martha V, 635
Bangham, Martha VI, 297
Bangham, Martha VI, 315
Bangham, Martha A. V, 611
Bangham, Martha A. V, 647
Bangham, Martha A. V, 649
Bangham, Martha Ann V, 611
Bangham, Mary V, 475
Bangham, Mary V, 611
Bangham, Mary V, 947
Bangham, Mary V, 950
Bangham, Mary E. V, 657
Bangham, Nancy V, 611
Bangham, Nancy V, 616
Bangham, Rachel V, 573
Bangham, Rachel V, 611
Bangham, Rachel H. V, 611
Bangham, Rachel M. V, 611
Bangham, Rachel M. V, 623
Bangham, Tacy VI, 834
Bangham, Thomas E. V, 611
Bangham, William Francis V, 611
Bangham, William J. V, 151
Bangham, Wm. V, 657
Bangham, Wm. J. V, 151
Bangham, Wm. J. V, 657
Bangham, Zachariah M. V, 475
Bangham, Zachariah M. V, 611
Banghm, Margaret P. I, 241
Banghum, Lucy V, 473
Banghum, Mary V, 475
Banghum, Mary V, 505
Bangs, Wm. P. II, 726
Bangum, Mary V, 726
Banham, Agnes V, 665
Banister, Anne VI, 875
Banister, David V, 726
Banister, Isaac VI, 875
Banister, James VI, 875
Banister, James VI, 1002
Banister, Judy Wear VI, 875
Banister, Mary VI, 875
Banister, Peggy VI, 875
Banister, Rachel Jones VI, 875
Banister, Sally VI, 1002
Banister, William VI, 875
Banister, Wm. VI, 875
Bank, Elsie III, 24
Bank, Elsie III, 290
Bank, Levi VI, 936
Bank, Willis III, 24
Bankhorn, Elisabeth I, 129
Bankhorn, Elisabeth I, 153
Banks, Annie L. III, 395
Banks, Caroline M. III, 395
Banks, Cynthia III, 395
Banks, Cynthia VI, 730
Banks, Daniel VI, 730
Banks, Daniel G. III, 395
Banks, Daniel G. III, 415
Banks, Daniel G. VI, 730
Banks, Daniel G. VI, 747
Banks, Daniel N. III, 395
Banks, Deborah II, 334
Banks, Edward O. V, 984
Banks, Elizabeth VI, 875
Banks, Gulielma M. V, 219
Banks, Hempstead VI, 730
Banks, James V, 451
Banks, Jemima VI, 875
Banks, John VI, 875
Banks, John VI, 965
Banks, John L. V, 984
Banks, Julielma M. V, 219
Banks, Julielma M. V, 229
Banks, Maria III, 395
Banks, Maria III, 415
Banks, Maria VI, 730
Banks, Maria VI, 747
Banks, Martha VI, 965
Banks, Mary VI, 926
Banks, Myrta V, 451
Banks, Nathan III, 395
Banks, Nathan O. III, 395
Banks, Nathan O. VI, 730
Banks, Orlinder VI, 965
Banks, Rebecca C. III, 395
Banks, Ruby I, 24
Banks, Samuel VI, 875
Banks, Samuel VI, 965
Banks, Sarah J. V, 451
Banks, Sarah Jane V, 451
Banks, Sidney V, 451
Banks, Willis III, 24
Bankson, Andrew II, 334
Bankson, Deborah A. V, 219
Bankson, Elizabeth V, 219
Bankson, Elizabeth V, 318
Bankson, Elizabeth V, 445
Bankson, Elizabeth V, 549
Bankson, Elizabeth E. V, 219
Bankson, Elizabeth E. V, 549
Bankson, Esther II, 458
Bankson, Esther II, 484
Bankson, Esther II, 588
Bankson, Esther V, 219
Bankson, Esther V, 318
Bankson, Esther V, 359
Bankson, Esther E. V, 219
Bankson, Isaac V, 219
Bankson, Isaac V, 318
Bankson, Isaac V, 319
Bankson, Isaac E. V, 219
Bankson, Jacob II, 334
Bankson, Joel V, 219
Bankson, John II, 334
Bankson, Joseph II, 334
Bankson, Lewis C. V, 219
Bankson, Lydia V, 219
Bankson, Lydia V, 318
Bankson, Lydia V, 339
Bankson, Lydia C. V, 219
Bankson, Marian V, 318
Bankson, Martha II, 334
Bankson, Mary II, 334
Bankson, Mary Ann V, 219
Bankson, Mary Ann V, 318
Bankson, Mary Ann V, 549
Bankson, Mary Ann V, 558
Bankson, Peter II, 334
Bankson, Ruth V, 219
Bankson, Ruth V, 318
Bankson, Ruth V, 549
Bankson, Ruth C. V, 219
Bankson, Ruth C. V, 549
Bankson, Ruth C. V, 581
Bankson, Susannah V, 219
Bankson, Susannah V, 318
Bankson, William V, 219
Bankson, William V, 318
Bankson, William V, 549
Banloff, Ann II, 334
Bannan, Mary E. III, 60
Bannan, Mary E. III, 373
Banner, Elizabeth II, 976
Banner, Elizabeth II, 992
Banner, Wm. Darby II, 976
Banner, Wm. J. V, 893
Banning, Alpheus V, 984
Banning, Mary V, 984
Banning, Mary J. V, 984
Bannister, Betty VI, 981
Bannister, James VI, 981
Bannister, Mary II, 458
Banoldwon, Ann II, 954
Banoldwon, John II, 954
Banseter, Anna M. IV, 1245
Bant, John II, 459
Bantingham, Rachel E. II, 729
Bantoft, Ann II, 459
Banton, Manervy VI, 847
Banton, Pieter II, 334
Banton, Rebecca II, 334
Bantum, Peter II, 441
Bantz, O. Perry V, 298
Banyon, Arthur Ware III, 24
Banyon, Helen Ware III, 24
Banyon, Helen Ware III, 312
Banyon, Herbert III, 24
Banyon, Herbert III, 312
Bara, Annie VI, 279
Bara, Robert II, 441
Barba, Israel IV, 675
Barba, Israel Barba IV, 745
Barba, Lydia IV, 675
Barba, Lydia IV, 745
Barbee, Allie I, 623
Barbee, Clarence I, 373
Barbee, Clarence D. I, 372
Barbee, Daisie J. I, 372
Barbee, Edward VI, 875
Barbee, Elizabeth I, 373
Barbee, Elizabeth VI, 875
Barbee, Ernest I, 373
Barbee, Ernest V. I, 372
Barbee, Hilda I, 937
Barbee, John I, 373
Barbee, John V, 726
Barbee, John M. I, 372
Barbee, Leroy C. I, 373
Barbee, Lidda VI, 797
Barbee, William VI, 797
Barbee, Winnie I, 920
Barber, Aaron I, 129
Barber, Abigail, Jr. II, 53
Barber, Abigail, Jr. II, 65
Barber, Abraham II, 21
Barber, Abraham II, 53
Barber, Abraham IV, 74
Barber, Abraham IV, 173
Barber, Abraham IV, 320
Barber, Abraham IV, 330
Barber, Abraham IV, 386
Barber, Abraham IV, 510
Barber, Abraham IV, 519
Barber, Abraham IV, 529
Barber, Abraham IV, 609
Barber, Abraham IV, 675
Barber, Abraham IV, 676
Barber, Abraham IV, 712
Barber, Abraham IV, 782
Barber, Abraham IV, 791
Barber, Abraham IV, 792
Barber, Abraham IV, 924
Barber, Abraham VI, 469
Barber, Abram IV, 173
Barber, Abram IV, 203
Barber, Abram IV, 675
Barber, Acenath IV, 567
Barber, Acenath IV, 572
Barber, Alanson D. IV, 1233

Barber, Albert II, 128
Barber, Albert II, 143
Barber, Albert B. IV, 1035
Barber, Ales IV, 719
Barber, Alice IV, 675
Barber, Alice IV, 719
Barber, Alice IV, 798
Barber, Alice IV, 843
Barber, Alice IV, 924
Barber, Alice IV, 1023
Barber, Alonzo III, 24
Barber, Alonzo D. IV, 1233
Barber, Ambrose II, 53
Barber, Ambrose II, 781
Barber, Angeline IV, 798
Barber, Angeline IV, 853
Barber, Ann II, 53
Barber, Ann II, 56
Barber, Ann II, 128
Barber, Ann II, 819
Barber, Ann IV, 74
Barber, Ann IV, 173
Barber, Ann IV, 223
Barber, Ann IV, 228
Barber, Ann IV, 242
Barber, Ann IV, 289
Barber, Ann IV, 320
Barber, Ann IV, 510
Barber, Ann IV, 529
Barber, Ann IV, 675
Barber, Ann IV, 708
Barber, Ann IV, 739
Barber, Ann IV, 798
Barber, Ann IV, 1023
Barber, Ann IV, 1027
Barber, Ann VI, 469
Barber, Ann VI, 831
Barber, Ann B. IV, 791
Barber, Ann L. IV, 675
Barber, Ann L. IV, 798
Barber, Ann L. IV, 847
Barber, Ann S. II, 143
Barber, Ann S. II, 834
Barber, Ann S. II, 920
Barber, Ann S. II, 921
Barber, Anna IV, 675
Barber, Anna IV, 676
Barber, Anna Mary IV, 798
Barber, Anne IV, 173
Barber, Anne IV, 510
Barber, Annetta G. IV, 1245
Barber, Annie IV, 676
Barber, Annie IV, 724
Barber, Annie Mary IV, 798
Barber, Aquilla II, 21
Barber, Aquilla II, 53
Barber, Aquilla II, 80
Barber, Aron VI, 52
Barber, Aron VI, 76
Barber, Asa IV, 510
Barber, Asenath IV, 510
Barber, Asenath IV, 519
Barber, Asenith IV, 510
Barber, Barbery II, 53
Barber, Barclay IV, 675
Barber, Barclay IV, 924
Barber, Barclay IV, 1023
Barber, Benj. W. IV, 675
Barber, Benjamin IV, 510
Barber, Benjamin IV, 675
Barber, Benjamin IV, 676
Barber, Benjamin IV, 924
Barber, Benjamin IV, 1087
Barber, Benjamin W. IV, 676
Barber, Bertis, Jr. II, 143
Barber, Blanche IV, 1306
Barber, Burtis II, 53
Barber, Burtis II, 128
Barber, Burtis II, 143
Barber, Burtis II, 144
Barber, Burtis II, 781
Barber, Burtis II, 834
Barber, Burtis II, 872
Barber, Burton II, 128
Barber, Carl IV, 1245
Barber, Charles II, 143
Barber, Charles IV, 464
Barber, Charles IV, 1245
Barber, Charles VI, 813
Barber, Charles C. II, 143
Barber, Clarkson IV, 1023
Barber, Cornelias VI, 469
Barber, Cornelius IV, 74
Barber, Cornelius IV, 173
Barber, Cornelius IV, 510
Barber, Daniel II, 21
Barber, Daniel II, 53
Barber, David II, 21
Barber, Della V, 612
Barber, Doritha IV, 173
Barber, Dorothy IV, 74
Barber, Dorothy IV, 173
Barber, Dorothy IV, 223
Barber, Dorthy IV, 173
Barber, Drucilla IV, 791
Barber, Drusilla IV, 675
Barber, Drusilla IV, 676
Barber, Drusilla IV, 712
Barber, Drusilla IV, 782
Barber, Drusilla IV, 792
Barber, Drusilla IV, 924
Barber, Edith IV, 675
Barber, Edith IV, 924
Barber, Edith IV, 979
Barber, Edith IV, 1023
Barber, Edith IV, 1029
Barber, Edward II, 834
Barber, Edward VI, 875
Barber, Elija II, 21
Barber, Elijah II, 53
Barber, Elisabeth I, 35
Barber, Elisabeth I, 55
Barber, Elisha VI, 797
Barber, Eliza VI, 730
Barber, Elizabeth II, 53
Barber, Elizabeth II, 64
Barber, Elizabeth II, 79
Barber, Elizabeth II, 143
Barber, Elizabeth II, 781
Barber, Elizabeth IV, 74
Barber, Elizabeth IV, 173
Barber, Elizabeth IV, 242
Barber, Elizabeth IV, 368
Barber, Elizabeth IV, 399
Barber, Elizabeth IV, 510
Barber, Elizabeth IV, 535
Barber, Elizabeth IV, 675
Barber, Elizabeth IV, 676
Barber, Elizabeth IV, 798
Barber, Elizabeth IV, 819
Barber, Elizabeth VI, 875
Barber, Elizabeth A. IV, 1023
Barber, Elizabeth A. IV, 1027
Barber, Elizabeth C. II, 128
Barber, Elizabeth C. II, 143
Barber, Elizabeth C. IV, 798
Barber, Elizabeth E. IV, 798
Barber, Elizabeth I. M. VI, 875
Barber, Elizabeth M. II, 834
Barber, Elizabeth M. II, 898
Barber, Elizabeth Marshall II, 809
Barber, Ellen III, 24
Barber, Ellin II, 459
Barber, Ellin II, 665
Barber, Elma J. IV, 1023
Barber, Elmy IV, 675
Barber, Emaline IV, 676
Barber, Emaline IV, 706
Barber, Emily I, 35
Barber, Emily I, 48
Barber, Emma J. II, 834
Barber, Emma J. II, 920
Barber, Emma Jane II, 128
Barber, Emma Jane II, 143
Barber, Emma Jane II, 819
Barber, Emma Jane II, 834
Barber, Emmaline IV, 675
Barber, Emmor IV, 675
Barber, Esther I, 129
Barber, Esther M. II, 834
Barber, Esther M. II, 905
Barber, Ezekiel IV, 675
Barber, Ezekiel IV, 1023
Barber, Ezekiel IV, 1027
Barber, Frances L. IV, 1233
Barber, George II, 954
Barber, George V, 549
Barber, George W. II, 128
Barber, George W. II, 143
Barber, George W. V, 549
Barber, Guly Elma II, 143
Barber, Hannah II, 21
Barber, Hannah II, 53
Barber, Hannah II, 80
Barber, Hannah II, 103
Barber, Hannah II, 109
Barber, Hannah II, 111
Barber, Hannah II, 113
Barber, Hannah II, 128
Barber, Hannah II, 143
Barber, Hannah II, 144
Barber, Hannah II, 147
Barber, Hannah IV, 675
Barber, Hannah IV, 719
Barber, Hannah IV, 782
Barber, Hannah IV, 924
Barber, Hannah IV, 963
Barber, Hannah IV, 1011
Barber, Hannah IV, 1023
Barber, Hannah IV, 1029
Barber, Hannah G. IV, 675
Barber, Hannah M. IV, 1351
Barber, Hannah Mather IV, 1351
Barber, Hartwell IV, 798
Barber, Hartwell IV, 1351
Barber, Heartwell IV, 798
Barber, Henrietta VI, 836
Barber, Henrietta B. II, 921
Barber, Henrietta S. II, 921
Barber, Henry II, 53
Barber, Henry II, 103
Barber, Henry II, 143
Barber, Henry IV, 1023
Barber, Henry V, 437
Barber, Henry A. II, 128
Barber, Henry A. II, 316
Barber, Henry A. II, 834
Barber, Henry A. II, 898
Barber, Henry A. II, 899
Barber, Howard G. II, 921
Barber, Hulda Jane IV, 798
Barber, Hulda Jane IV, 810
Barber, Irene VI, 798
Barber, Isaac I, 35
Barber, Isaac II, 21
Barber, Isaac II, 53
Barber, Isaac II, 143
Barber, Isaac II, 781
Barber, Isaac II, 834
Barber, Isaac IV, 74
Barber, Isaac IV, 609
Barber, Isaac IV, 675
Barber, Isaac IV, 719
Barber, Isaac IV, 775
Barber, Isaac IV, 798
Barber, Isaac IV, 843
Barber, Isaac IV, 924
Barber, Isaac IV, 1023
Barber, Isaac A. II, 128
Barber, Isaac A. II, 143
Barber, Isaac E. IV, 798
Barber, Isaac Elwood IV, 798
Barber, Isaac, Jr. II, 53
Barber, Isaac, Jr. II, 84
Barber, Isaac, Jr. IV, 675
Barber, Isabel IV, 924
Barber, Isabell IV, 924
Barber, Israel IV, 675
Barber, Israel IV, 676
Barber, Israel IV, 924
Barber, Israel IV, 983
Barber, Jacob II, 21
Barber, Jacob II, 53
Barber, Jacob II, 81
Barber, Jacob IV, 74
Barber, Jacob IV, 368
Barber, Jacob IV, 609
Barber, Jacob IV, 675
Barber, Jacob IV, 676
Barber, Jacob IV, 770
Barber, Jacob IV, 798
Barber, Jacob IV, 924
Barber, James II, 21
Barber, James II, 53
Barber, James II, 459
Barber, James II, 954
Barber, James IV, 173
Barber, James IV, 675
Barber, Jane II, 21
Barber, Jane II, 53
Barber, Jane IV, 74
Barber, Jane IV, 510
Barber, Jane IV, 532
Barber, Jane IV, 609
Barber, Jane IV, 675
Barber, Jane IV, 781
Barber, Jane IV, 924
Barber, Jane VI, 797
Barber, Jane VI, 831
Barber, Jane VI, 875
Barber, Jean II, 21
Barber, Jean II, 53
Barber, Jennet IV, 924
Barber, Jennet IV, 940
Barber, Joel I, 35
Barber, Joel I, 79
Barber, Joel I, 189
Barber, John II, 21
Barber, John II, 53
Barber, John II, 90
Barber, John II, 128
Barber, John II, 143
Barber, John II, 920
Barber, John E. IV, 1023
Barber, John W. II, 143
Barber, John W. II, 834
Barber, John W. II, 920
Barber, John W. Barber II, 921
Barber, John Wright II, 819
Barber, Jonathan II, 21
Barber, Jonathan II, 53
Barber, Jonathan II, 334
Barber, Jonathan VI, 730
Barber, Joseph I, 35
Barber, Joseph II, 21
Barber, Joseph II, 53
Barber, Joseph IV, 675
Barber, Joseph IV, 924
Barber, Joseph VI, 779
Barber, Joseph B. II, 128
Barber, Joseph B. II, 143
Barber, Joseph Bertis II, 143
Barber, Joseph W. IV, 798
Barber, Julianna VI, 852
Barber, Laura B. II, 834
Barber, Laura B. Shinn II, 921
Barber, Levi A. IV, 675
Barber, Levi Arnold IV, 675
Barber, Levi Arnold IV, 924
Barber, Liddy II, 21
Barber, Lillian I, 920
Barber, Lottie IV, 1035
Barber, Louisa Hill II, 921
Barber, Lovisa II, 21
Barber, Lovisa II, 53
Barber, Lovisa II, 83
Barber, Lucinda V, 437
Barber, Lucy VI, 813
Barber, Lulu IV, 1306
Barber, Lydia I, 35
Barber, Lydia I, 61
Barber, Lydia II, 53
Barber, Lydia II, 97
Barber, Lydia IV, 675
Barber, Lydia IV, 676
Barber, Lydia IV, 924
Barber, Lydia IV, 983
Barber, Lydia Ann II, 128
Barber, Lydia Ann II, 143
Barber, Lydia F. II, 128
Barber, Lydia F. II, 143
Barber, Lydia F. II, 147
Barber, Marcy II, 53
Barber, Marcy II, 77
Barber, Margaret IV, 1087
Barber, Margaret IV, 1103
Barber, Margaret H. IV, 1087
Barber, Martha II, 954
Barber, Martha VI, 852
Barber, Martha E. IV, 798
Barber, Martha Ellen IV, 798
Barber, Martha J. II, 834
Barber, Martha J. II, 872
Barber, Mary I, 35
Barber, Mary I, 73
Barber, Mary II, 21
Barber, Mary II, 53
Barber, Mary II, 54
Barber, Mary II, 60
Barber, Mary II, 67
Barber, Mary II, 84
Barber, Mary II, 128
Barber, Mary II, 834
Barber, Mary II, 872
Barber, Mary III, 24
Barber, Mary IV, 74
Barber, Mary IV, 368
Barber, Mary IV, 386
Barber, Mary IV, 510
Barber, Mary IV, 609
Barber, Mary IV, 675
Barber, Mary IV, 770
Barber, Mary IV, 775
Barber, Mary IV, 786
Barber, Mary IV, 924
Barber, Mary VI, 52
Barber, Mary VI, 76
Barber, Mary VI, 730
Barber, Mary A. IV, 675
Barber, Mary Ann II, 21
Barber, Mary Ann II, 53
Barber, Mary Ann II, 91
Barber, Mary Ann IV, 368
Barber, Mary Ann IV, 609
Barber, Mary Ann IV, 675
Barber, Mary Ann IV, 716
Barber, Mary Ann IV, 775
Barber, Mary Ann IV, 798
Barber, Mary Ann IV, 924
Barber, Mary Ann IV, 962
Barber, Mary C. II, 128
Barber, Mary C. II, 143
Barber, Mary C. II, 834
Barber, Mary C. II, 841
Barber, Mary Emma IV, 1023
Barber, Mary N. IV, 676
Barber, Mary N. IV, 756
Barber, Mary N. IV, 924
Barber, Mary S. IV, 675
Barber, Mary S. IV, 676
Barber, Maryann IV, 74
Barber, Matthew VI, 797
Barber, Melissa IV, 1023
Barber, Mercy II, 128
Barber, Mercy II, 143
Barber, Mercy II, 144
Barber, Milicent I, 189
Barber, Milicent I, 195
Barber, Minnie IV, 1245
Barber, Minnie N. IV, 1245
Barber, Miriam I, 35
Barber, Miriam I, 48
Barber, Miriam L. IV, 1306
Barber, Moses I, 35
Barber, Moses I, 55
Barber, Moses I, 73
Barber, Moses I, 189
Barber, Mourning I, 35
Barber, Mourning I, 79
Barber, Naomi IV, 173
Barber, Naomi IV, 510
Barber, Naomi IV, 515
Barber, Naomy IV, 173
Barber, Penina I, 129
Barber, Pennina I, 129
Barber, Phebe II, 53
Barber, Phebe II, 108
Barber, Phebe II, 834
Barber, Phebe II, 899
Barber, Phebe IV, 1144
Barber, Phebe IV, 1147
Barber, Phebe A. II, 834
Barber, Pleasant VI, 798
Barber, Pleasant VI, 875
Barber, Priscilla Gulielma II, 781
Barber, Rachel II, 799
Barber, Rachel IV, 173
Barber, Rachel IV, 193
Barber, Rachel IV, 199
Barber, Rachel IV, 203
Barber, Rachel IV, 320
Barber, Rachel IV, 330
Barber, Rachel IV, 386
Barber, Rachel IV, 510
Barber, Rachel IV, 519
Barber, Rachel IV, 529
Barber, Rachel IV, 675
Barber, Rachel IV, 719
Barber, Rachel IV, 924
Barber, Rachel IV, 963
Barber, Randal VI, 831
Barber, Rebecca II, 53
Barber, Rebecca IV, 74
Barber, Rebecca IV, 609
Barber, Rebecca IV, 675
Barber, Rebecca IV, 739
Barber, Rebecca IV, 772
Barber, Rebecca IV, 924
Barber, Rebecca IV, 979
Barber, Rebeckah II, 21
Barber, Rebekah II, 53
Barber, Rebekah II, 81
Barber, Rebekah II, 90
Barber, Rosalie V, 437
Barber, Ruth II, 53
Barber, Ruth II, 78
Barber, Ruth IV, 675
Barber, Ruth Anna IV, 1023
Barber, Samuel I, 189
Barber, Samuel II, 21
Barber, Samuel II, 53
Barber, Samuel II, 128
Barber, Samuel III, 24
Barber, Samuel IV, 74
Barber, Samuel IV, 173
Barber, Samuel IV, 223
Barber, Samuel IV, 228
Barber, Samuel IV, 242
Barber, Samuel IV, 289
Barber, Samuel IV, 320
Barber, Samuel IV, 368
Barber, Samuel IV, 399
Barber, Samuel IV, 510
Barber, Samuel IV, 798
Barber, Samuel IV, 819
Barber, Samuel IV, 853
Barber, Samuel IV, 1023
Barber, Samuel IV, 1029
Barber, Samuel VI, 469
Barber, Samuel B. II, 143
Barber, Samuel C. II, 143
Barber, Samuel, Jr. IV, 510
Barber, Sarah I, 35
Barber, Sarah I, 43
Barber, Sarah I, 129
Barber, Sarah I, 189
Barber, Sarah II, 21
Barber, Sarah II, 53
Barber, Sarah II, 73
Barber, Sarah IV, 74
Barber, Sarah IV, 173
Barber, Sarah IV, 228
Barber, Sarah IV, 675
Barber, Sarah IV, 719

Barber, Sarah IV, 792
Barber, Sarah IV, 798
Barber, Sarah IV, 840
Barber, Sarah IV, 924
Barber, Sarah IV, 963
Barber, Sarah VI, 469
Barber, Sarah E. V, 549
Barber, Sarah S. IV, 1023
Barber, Sarah, Jr. I, 35
Barber, Sarah, Jr. I, 129
Barber, Sarah, Jr. I, 189
Barber, Susanna IV, 173
Barber, Susannah II, 21
Barber, Susannah IV, 173
Barber, Susannah IV, 510
Barber, Susannah VI, 797
Barber, Thomas II, 53
Barber, Thomas II, 78
Barber, Thomas VI, 875
Barber, Thomas, Jr. II, 53
Barber, Thos. II, 21
Barber, Thos. II, 53
Barber, Thos. II, 54
Barber, Thos., Jr. II, 53
Barber, Thos., Jr. II, 65
Barber, William I, 35
Barber, William II, 143
Barber, William IV, 173
Barber, William IV, 510
Barber, William VI, 797
Barber, William M. IV, 1023
Barber, Witsey V, 984
Barber, Wm. II, 21
Barber, Wm. II, 53
Barber, Wm. II, 128
Barber, Wm. II, 143
Barber, Wm. II, 144
Barber, Wm. II, 147
Barber, Wm. IV, 510
Barber, Wm., Jr. II, 128
Barber, Zac. I, 189
Barbey, Aline G. III, 395
Barbour, Alvin Gray VI, 764
Barbour, Carmen VI, 764
Barbour, Lucinda VI, 852
Barbour, Margaret VI, 764
Barbour, Patsy VI, 852
Barbour, Sally VI, 897
Barbur, Hannah II, 53
Barbur, Hannah II, 78
Barclay, Hannah IV, 1144
Barclay, Hannah B. IV, 1176
Barclay, Joshua Clebborn II, 334
Barcleft, Sarah I, 129
Barcliff, Sarah I, 129
Barcraft, Lydia IV, 464
Barcraft, Rebecca IV, 464
Barcroft, ??? VI, 726
Barcroft, Elizabeth IV, 283
Barcroft, George VI, 730
Barcroft, John VI, 730
Barcroft, John Woodward VI, 730
Barcroft, Jos. IV, 283
Barcroft, Joseph IV, 173
Barcroft, Rebecca IV, 464
Barcroft, Rebecca IV, 491
Barcroft, Ruth II, 692
Barcroft, Sarah IV, 283
Barcroft, Sarah W. VI, 730
Barcus, Beulah V, 23
Barcus, Beulah V, 77
Barcus, Emma IV, 464
Barcus, Emma L. IV, 464
Barcus, John IV, 464
Barcus, Leela IV, 173
Barcus, Levi IV, 173
Bard, Catherine IV, 676
Bard, Elizabeth IV, 676
Bard, Emery IV, 676
Bard, George IV, 676
Bard, Hannah II, 976
Bard, Mary IV, 676
Bard, Mary IV, 720
Barden, Dennison R. II, 835
Barden, Margaret L. II, 835
Barden, Margaret T. II, 835
Barden, Mary Hill II, 835
Bardin, Arthur VI, 285
Bardin, Dennison R. II, 835
Bardin, Dennison R. II, 887
Bardin, Margaret L. II, 835
Bardin, Margaret L. II, 887
Bardin, Mary Hill II, 835
Bardin, Mary Hill II, 887
Bardizbanian, Dorothy III, 24
Bardizbanian, Elizabeth III, 24
Bardizbanian, Esther III, 24
Bardizbanian, Vartan III, 24
Bardo, Esther IV, 924
Bardsley, Edith II, 699
Bardsley, Edith II, 726
Bardsley, Edith II, 727
Bardsley, Elizabeth II, 699
Bardsley, Elizabeth II, 726
Bardsley, Elizabeth II, 727
Bardsley, Joseph II, 699
Bardsley, Joseph II, 726
Bardsley, Joseph II, 727
Bardsley, Mary V, 372
Bardy, Mary V, 151
Bare, Barbara VI, 871
Bare, Katherine IV, 679
Bare, Mary VI, 871
Barefiel, Demaris V, 298
Barefield, Damarice I, 1007
Barefield, Damaris I, 797
Barefield, Damaris V, 298
Barefield, Jonathan V, 298
Barefield, Mary I, 797
Barefield, Milesent I, 797
Barefield, Milicent I, 1007
Barefield, Milley V, 298
Barefield, Millicent V, 298
Barefield, Miriam I, 797
Barefield, Sarah I, 797
Barett, Esther IV, 558
Barfell, Othias IV, 1245
Barfell, Sadie V, 984
Barfell, Sarah V, 984
Barfell, Thomas V, 984
Barfield, Charity I, 1067
Barfield, Damaris I, 299
Barfield, Daniel I, 299
Barfield, Demaris I, 775
Barfield, Demaris I, 1067
Barfield, Demsey I, 281
Barfield, Demsey I, 1067
Barfield, Jonathan I, 1067
Barfield, Mary I, 281
Barfield, Mary I, 299
Barfield, Mary I, 775
Barfield, Mary I, 1067
Barfield, Milicent I, 281
Barfield, Milicent I, 299
Barfield, Milicent I, 1067
Barfield, Milley V, 298
Barfield, Millisent I, 775
Barfield, Miriam I, 281
Barfield, Miriam I, 299
Barfield, Miriam I, 300
Barfield, Miriam I, 775
Barfield, Miriam I, 1067
Barfield, Ruth I, 1067
Barfield, Sarah I, 775
Barfield, Sarah I, 1067
Barfield, Solomon I, 281
Barfield, Solomon I, 299
Barfield, Solomon I, 300
Barfield, Solomon I, 775
Barfield, Solomon I, 1066
Barfield, Solomon I, 1067
Barfield, William I, 281
Barfield, William I, 775
Barfield, William I, 1067
Barger, John VI, 908
Barger, Joseph II, 459
Barger, Maggie IV, 987
Barger, Mary II, 459
Barger, Molly VI, 908
Barger, Nancy IV, 987
Barger, Sprogle II, 334
Barger, Thomas II, 459
Barger, Wm. IV, 987
Bargher, Christian Franklin VI, 875
Bargher, John VI, 875
Barick, Jane V, 221
Barick, Jane V, 262
Baright, ??? III, 24
Baright, Augusta Ellen III, 24
Baright, Augustin III, 24
Baright, Augustin, Jr. III, 24
Baright, Augustine III, 250
Baright, Edward III, 24
Baright, Edward P. III, 24
Baright, Edward R. III, 24
Baright, Eleanor III, 24
Baright, Eliza P. III, 24
Baright, George P. III, 24
Baright, John III, 24
Baright, Martha Ann III, 24
Baright, Mary III, 24
Baright, Mary III, 250
Baright, Sarah Eliza III, 24
Baright, Sophia III, 24
Baright, Sophia E. III, 24
Baright, Walter III, 24
Baright, William P. III, 24
Barker, Abel V, 726
Barker, Abigail II, 196
Barker, Abigail II, 227
Barker, Abner I, 346
Barker, Abner I, 349
Barker, Abner I, 373
Barker, Abner I, 460
Barker, Abner I, 461
Barker, Abner I, 473
Barker, Abner I, 474
Barker, Abner I, 673
Barker, Abner I, 685
Barker, Abner I, 708
Barker, Abner I, 1067
Barker, Abner I, 1070
Barker, Abner A. I, 474
Barker, Abraham II, 334
Barker, Abraham II, 898
Barker, Abraham III, 24
Barker, Abraham III, 25
Barker, Abraham III, 241
Barker, Achsah I, 461
Barker, Aletha B. II, 965
Barker, Alexander I, 920
Barker, Alice II, 714
Barker, Allen I, 474
Barker, Allen I, 708
Barker, Allen I, 1067
Barker, Allen I, 1070
Barker, Alpheus E. I, 524
Barker, Amelia Ann I, 460
Barker, Amy I, 373
Barker, Amy I, 382
Barker, Amy I, 460
Barker, Amy I, 474
Barker, Amy Catharine I, 461
Barker, Amy R. I, 708
Barker, Anderson M. I, 460
Barker, Andrew Signourey III, 24
Barker, Andrew Signourey III, 25
Barker, Angelina I, 461
Barker, Angelina I, 708
Barker, Ann I, 461
Barker, Ann I, 474
Barker, Ann III, 395
Barker, Ann III, 453
Barker, Ann Mifflin III, 24
Barker, Anna I, 474
Barker, Anna I, 476
Barker, Anna III, 25
Barker, Anna Hazard III, 24
Barker, Anne I, 460
Barker, Annie I, 629
Barker, Annie III, 25
Barker, Annie III, 267
Barker, Annie Lee I, 611
Barker, Annie White I, 629
Barker, Arminta I, 621
Barker, Arminta A. I, 629
Barker, Arminta Ann I, 611
Barker, Arminta Ann I, 743
Barker, Arta A. I, 920
Barker, Arthur J. I, 937
Barker, Arthur James I, 920
Barker, Asa III, 407
Barker, Asaph H. I, 708
Barker, Asaph H. I, 731
Barker, Asenath I, 459
Barker, Asenath I, 462
Barker, Asenath I, 474
Barker, Asenath I, 477
Barker, Benj. I, 611
Barker, Benjamin I, 460
Barker, Benjamin I, 621
Barker, Benjamin C. I, 621
Barker, Benjamin S. I, 461
Barker, Benjamin S. I, 474
Barker, Benjamin S. I, 611
Barker, Benjamin S. I, 743
Barker, Benjamin S. I, 755
Barker, Beulah II, 835
Barker, Beulah II, 931
Barker, Beulah T. II, 835
Barker, Beulah T. III, 30
Barker, Biddy I, 459
Barker, Bridget I, 919
Barker, Caleb I, 460
Barker, Caleb I, 797
Barker, Caleb II, 166
Barker, Caleb II, 334
Barker, Caleb II, 781
Barker, Caleb II, 796
Barker, Caleb II, 823
Barker, Caleb II, 835
Barker, Caleb II, 915
Barker, Caleb II, 931
Barker, Caleb III, 25
Barker, Caleb III, 240
Barker, Calvin I, 524
Barker, Caroline III, 25
Barker, Caroline S. IV, 1351
Barker, Catharine I, 461
Barker, Catharine I, 474
Barker, Catharine I, 476
Barker, Catharine I, 647
Barker, Catharine I, 755
Barker, Catharine IV, 638
Barker, Catharine VI, 955
Barker, Charles I, 461
Barker, Charles VI, 154
Barker, Clara I, 524
Barker, Claud IV, 1306
Barker, Claud L. IV, 1306
Barker, Claud L. IV, 1331
Barker, Claude L. IV, 1306
Barker, Cyrus I, 461
Barker, Cyrus I, 474
Barker, D. Luther I, 937
Barker, Daniel I, 346
Barker, Daniel I, 459
Barker, Daniel I, 460
Barker, Daniel I, 473
Barker, Daniel I, 474
Barker, Daniel I, 479
Barker, Daniel I, 755
Barker, Daniel I, 775
Barker, Daniel I, 797
Barker, Daniel I, 869
Barker, Daniel I, 870
Barker, Daniel J. I, 797
Barker, Daniel S. I, 797
Barker, Daniel S. I, 830
Barker, Darius F. I, 980
Barker, David I, 460
Barker, David I, 474
Barker, David I, 673
Barker, David I, 686
Barker, David I, 755
Barker, David III, 25
Barker, David III, 441
Barker, David D. III, 25
Barker, David D. III, 156
Barker, David D. III, 395
Barker, David L. I, 920
Barker, David Luther I, 920
Barker, David O. I, 920
Barker, David O. III, 441
Barker, Deborah A. V, 241
Barker, Deborah Ann I, 613
Barker, Deborah Ann V, 219
Barker, Deborah Wharton II, 835
Barker, Deborah Wharton II, 898
Barker, Della IV, 1245
Barker, Dematris A. VI, 876
Barker, Dinah I, 460
Barker, Dorcas I, 373
Barker, Dorcas I, 427
Barker, E. I, 647
Barker, E. Benjamin I, 524
Barker, Edgar T. I, 611
Barker, Edith I, 460
Barker, Edith I, 471
Barker, Edith I, 524
Barker, Edith I, 755
Barker, Edith I, 760
Barker, Edith III, 267
Barker, Edith F. II, 727
Barker, Edith F. II, 756
Barker, Edna A. VI, 934
Barker, Edna L. I, 647
Barker, Edney I, 463
Barker, Edward II, 835
Barker, Edward II, 921
Barker, Edward VI, 954
Barker, Edward D. II, 835
Barker, Edward D. II, 842
Barker, Edwin VI, 875
Barker, Effie I, 621
Barker, Effie I, 629
Barker, Effie M. I, 629
Barker, Effie Margaret I, 611
Barker, Elander VI, 875
Barker, Eli I, 460
Barker, Eli I, 611
Barker, Eli I, 629
Barker, Eli I, 635
Barker, Eli P. I, 611
Barker, Eli Penn I, 743
Barker, Eli W. I, 474
Barker, Elias I, 461
Barker, Elias I, 708
Barker, Eligah VI, 871
Barker, Elihu I, 460
Barker, Elihu I, 473
Barker, Elihu I, 474
Barker, Elijah VI, 876
Barker, Elijah VI, 1022
Barker, Elisabeth I, 474
Barker, Elisha I, 708
Barker, Eliz. III, 109
Barker, Eliz. H. III, 25
Barker, Eliz. H. III, 241
Barker, Eliza I, 708
Barker, Eliza III, 341
Barker, Eliza A. I, 708
Barker, Eliza A. I, 731
Barker, Eliza B. III, 25
Barker, Elizabeth I, 346
Barker, Elizabeth I, 373
Barker, Elizabeth I, 384
Barker, Elizabeth I, 391
Barker, Elizabeth I, 421
Barker, Elizabeth I, 427
Barker, Elizabeth I, 457
Barker, Elizabeth I, 459
Barker, Elizabeth I, 460
Barker, Elizabeth I, 461
Barker, Elizabeth I, 468
Barker, Elizabeth I, 473
Barker, Elizabeth I, 474
Barker, Elizabeth I, 629
Barker, Elizabeth I, 755
Barker, Elizabeth I, 763
Barker, Elizabeth I, 797
Barker, Elizabeth II, 166
Barker, Elizabeth II, 196
Barker, Elizabeth II, 231
Barker, Elizabeth II, 255
Barker, Elizabeth II, 459
Barker, Elizabeth II, 537
Barker, Elizabeth II, 699
Barker, Elizabeth II, 727
Barker, Elizabeth II, 756
Barker, Elizabeth III, 24
Barker, Elizabeth III, 25
Barker, Elizabeth III, 137
Barker, Elizabeth VI, 871
Barker, Elizabeth VI, 988
Barker, Elizabeth D. II, 196
Barker, Elizabeth D. II, 227
Barker, Elizabeth E. I, 797
Barker, Elizabeth E. I, 824
Barker, Elizabeth Ellison III, 25
Barker, Elizabeth Emily I, 459
Barker, Elizabeth Rachel II, 835
Barker, Elizabeth Rachel II, 921
Barker, Ella IV, 676
Barker, Ellis B. II, 699
Barker, Ellis B. II, 727
Barker, Ellis B. II, 756
Barker, Elma J. I, 647
Barker, Elma R. I, 524
Barker, Elzena I, 460
Barker, Elzena I, 797
Barker, Emely I, 797
Barker, Emey I, 346
Barker, Emily III, 25
Barker, Emily III, 240
Barker, Emma I, 920
Barker, Emma IV, 676
Barker, Emma IV, 798
Barker, Emma IV, 830
Barker, Enoch I, 346
Barker, Enoch I, 373
Barker, Enoch I, 384
Barker, Enoch I, 443
Barker, Enoch I, 445
Barker, Enoch I, 457
Barker, Enoch I, 459
Barker, Enoch I, 460
Barker, Enoch I, 461
Barker, Enoch I, 473
Barker, Enoch I, 474
Barker, Enoch I, 755
Barker, Enoch I, 765
Barker, Enoch I, 797
Barker, Erastus B. III, 25
Barker, Erastus B. III, 156
Barker, Ester E. I, 743
Barker, Estes III, 241
Barker, Esther I, 460
Barker, Esther I, 611
Barker, Esther I, 621
Barker, Esther II, 53
Barker, Esther II, 108
Barker, Esther E. I, 611
Barker, Esther E. I, 629
Barker, Esther Lewis II, 459
Barker, Esther Pauline I, 621
Barker, Ethel I, 937
Barker, Ethel I, 946
Barker, Ezra I, 461
Barker, Ezra I, 474
Barker, Ezra IV, 676
Barker, Ezra IV, 798
Barker, F. M. VI, 869
Barker, F. M. VI, 872
Barker, F. M. VI, 890
Barker, F. M. VI, 893
Barker, F. M. VI, 905
Barker, F. M. VI, 910
Barker, F. M. VI, 912
Barker, F. M. VI, 913
Barker, F. M. VI, 916
Barker, F. M. VI, 919
Barker, F. M. VI, 922
Barker, F. M. VI, 923

Barker, F. M. VI, 940
Barker, F. M. VI, 943
Barker, F. M. VI, 946
Barker, F. M. VI, 951
Barker, F. M. VI, 970
Barker, F. M. VI, 971
Barker, F. M. VI, 973
Barker, F. M. VI, 975
Barker, F. M. VI, 977
Barker, F. M. VI, 978
Barker, F. M. VI, 989
Barker, F. M. VI, 1000
Barker, F. M. VI, 1003
Barker, F. M. VI, 1004
Barker, F. M. VI, 1005
Barker, F. M. VI, 1016
Barker, F. M. VI, 1018
Barker, F. M. VI, 1019
Barker, Fannie I, 625
Barker, Fanny I, 473
Barker, Fanny I, 708
Barker, Fanny I, 724
Barker, Fany I, 461
Barker, Fidella I, 937
Barker, Fidella H. I, 920
Barker, Florence II, 699
Barker, Frances I, 708
Barker, Francis M. VI, 876
Barker, Francis M. VI, 934
Barker, Genieve IV, 676
Barker, George T. II, 835
Barker, George T. II, 915
Barker, George Thos. II, 781
Barker, Gurney I, 629
Barker, Gurney I, 631
Barker, Gurney S. I, 611
Barker, Gurney Seth I, 743
Barker, Hannah I, 346
Barker, Hannah I, 370
Barker, Hannah I, 372
Barker, Hannah I, 373
Barker, Hannah I, 384
Barker, Hannah I, 421
Barker, Hannah I, 460
Barker, Hannah I, 461
Barker, Hannah I, 472
Barker, Hannah I, 474
Barker, Hannah I, 481
Barker, Hannah I, 673
Barker, Hannah I, 708
Barker, Hannah I, 870
Barker, Hannah I, 1067
Barker, Hannah II, 699
Barker, Hannah C. I, 647
Barker, Hannah J. I, 460
Barker, Hannah J. I, 473
Barker, Hannah J. I, 474
Barker, Hannah M. I, 474
Barker, Hannah M. I, 755
Barker, Harvey IV, 676
Barker, Henry Hopkins III, 24
Barker, Homer Allen I, 611
Barker, Horatio I, 980
Barker, Horatio C. I, 980
Barker, Howard Edward II, 835
Barker, Howard Edward II, 921
Barker, Huldah I, 461
Barker, Huldah I, 474
Barker, Huldah I, 755
Barker, Ida V, 984
Barker, Ida V, 985
Barker, Ida C. I, 647
Barker, Ida Ethel V, 985
Barker, Isaac I, 346
Barker, Isaac I, 373
Barker, Isaac I, 384
Barker, Isaac I, 460
Barker, Isaac I, 461
Barker, Isaac I, 474
Barker, Isaac II, 459
Barker, Isaac IV, 1021
Barker, Isaac V, 726
Barker, Isaac, Sr. I, 314
Barker, Jacob III, 24
Barker, Jacob V, 726
Barker, James II, 334
Barker, James II, 459
Barker, James IV, 139
Barker, James VI, 861
Barker, James VI, 876
Barker, Jane Payn VI, 876
Barker, Jerome A. I, 920
Barker, Jesse I, 314
Barker, Jesse Elisabeth I, 611
Barker, Jesse Elizabeth I, 937
Barker, Jessie C. I, 920
Barker, Jessie Elizabeth I, 939
Barker, Jessie Elizabeth Cecil I, 629
Barker, Jincey VI, 875
Barker, Jno. II, 166
Barker, Job I, 461
Barker, Joel I, 461
Barker, John I, 346
Barker, John I, 373
Barker, John I, 427
Barker, John I, 443
Barker, John I, 457
Barker, John I, 460
Barker, John I, 461
Barker, John I, 471
Barker, John I, 472
Barker, John I, 473
Barker, John I, 474
Barker, John I, 476
Barker, John I, 673
Barker, John I, 685
Barker, John I, 708
Barker, John I, 755
Barker, John I, 760
Barker, John I, 870
Barker, John I, 892
Barker, John II, 53
Barker, John II, 108
Barker, John II, 166
Barker, John II, 196
Barker, John II, 231
Barker, John II, 255
Barker, John II, 459
Barker, John VI, 100
Barker, John VI, 955
Barker, John D. I, 474
Barker, John Gurney I, 460
Barker, John Newbold III, 25
Barker, John Rodman II, 835
Barker, John, Jr. I, 474
Barker, Jonathan I, 461
Barker, Joseph I, 937
Barker, Joseph II, 699
Barker, Joseph VI, 875
Barker, Joseph D. I, 460
Barker, Joseph D. I, 755
Barker, Joseph D. I, 797
Barker, Joseph Daniel I, 797
Barker, Joseph E. I, 920
Barker, Joseph E. I, 937
Barker, Joseph E. I, 950
Barker, Joseph Rudd III, 25
Barker, Josephine I, 870
Barker, Joshua II, 166
Barker, Joshua II, 196
Barker, Joshua II, 252
Barker, Joshua II, 255
Barker, Joshua III, 90
Barker, Julia III, 25
Barker, Julia III, 395
Barker, Julia III, 441
Barker, Julia A. III, 25
Barker, Julia A. III, 156
Barker, Julia A. III, 276
Barker, Julia Anna III, 395
Barker, Julia Anna III, 441
Barker, Junius I, 920
Barker, K. M. I, 931
Barker, Katharine I, 474
Barker, Katharine IV, 1306
Barker, Katherine IV, 1331
Barker, Kezia I, 460
Barker, Kezia I, 673
Barker, Keziah I, 460
Barker, Keziah I, 474
Barker, Keziah I, 673
Barker, Keziah I, 686
Barker, Keziah I, 755
Barker, La Rue IV, 676
Barker, LaRue IV, 798
Barker, Larwell Lamborn IV, 798
Barker, Laura A. I, 797
Barker, Laura Ann I, 797
Barker, Lawrence IV, 676
Barker, Lawrence IV, 798
Barker, Lawrence La Rue IV, 676
Barker, Lewis C. I, 613
Barker, Lewis C. V, 241
Barker, Louisa I, 870
Barker, Louisa I, 937
Barker, Louisa A. I, 797
Barker, Louisa A. I, 830
Barker, Louise I, 920
Barker, Luanna I, 460
Barker, Luanna I, 474
Barker, Luatta I, 920
Barker, Lucie II, 842
Barker, Lucie H. II, 835
Barker, Lucinda I, 980
Barker, Lucy H. II, 835
Barker, Lucy H. II, 921
Barker, Luelma I, 335
Barker, Luelma I, 338
Barker, Luelma I, 870
Barker, Luther I, 937
Barker, Luther IV, 798
Barker, Luther IV, 830
Barker, Lyda I, 708
Barker, Lydia I, 346
Barker, Lydia I, 349
Barker, Lydia I, 373
Barker, Lydia I, 457
Barker, Lydia I, 459
Barker, Lydia I, 460
Barker, Lydia I, 461
Barker, Lydia I, 473
Barker, Lydia I, 474
Barker, Lydia I, 479
Barker, Lydia I, 673
Barker, Lydia I, 685
Barker, Lydia I, 708
Barker, Lydia I, 755
Barker, Lydia I, 775
Barker, Lydia I, 797
Barker, Lydia I, 869
Barker, Lydia I, 870
Barker, Lydia I, 1067
Barker, Lydia VI, 798
Barker, Lydia J. II, 965
Barker, Lydia Jane I, 797
Barker, Lynn III, 241
Barker, M. Luther IV, 676
Barker, M. Luther IV, 798
Barker, Maggie I, 613
Barker, Mahala S. VI, 988
Barker, Mahlon I, 460
Barker, Mahlon C. I, 459
Barker, Mahlon C. I, 460
Barker, Mahlon C. I, 474
Barker, Mahlon C. I, 483
Barker, Mahlon C. I, 755
Barker, Margaret I, 373
Barker, Margaret I, 461
Barker, Margaret I, 474
Barker, Margaret I, 476
Barker, Margaret I, 743
Barker, Margaret I, 755
Barker, Margaret II, 196
Barker, Margaret II, 217
Barker, Margaret II, 515
Barker, Margaret A. I, 524
Barker, Margaret B. III, 25
Barker, Margaret B. III, 241
Barker, Margaret C. II, 835
Barker, Margaret C. III, 23
Barker, Margaret C. III, 25
Barker, Margaret Ellison II, 459
Barker, Margaret Frances I, 611
Barker, Margaret Washington II, 796
Barker, Margorie Beth I, 611
Barker, Maria III, 25
Barker, Maria Louisa III, 25
Barker, Maria Louisa III, 156
Barker, Maria Louise III, 25
Barker, Maria M. II, 289
Barker, Marion II, 824
Barker, Martha II, 166
Barker, Martha II, 196
Barker, Martha II, 231
Barker, Martha II, 252
Barker, Martha II, 255
Barker, Martha VI, 876
Barker, Martha Elen I, 460
Barker, Martha Emma IV, 798
Barker, Martha L. I, 755
Barker, Mary I, 349
Barker, Mary I, 373
Barker, Mary I, 384
Barker, Mary I, 427
Barker, Mary I, 443
Barker, Mary I, 460
Barker, Mary I, 461
Barker, Mary I, 467
Barker, Mary I, 468
Barker, Mary I, 471
Barker, Mary I, 473
Barker, Mary I, 474
Barker, Mary I, 479
Barker, Mary I, 481
Barker, Mary I, 486
Barker, Mary I, 673
Barker, Mary I, 685
Barker, Mary I, 708
Barker, Mary I, 1067
Barker, Mary II, 166
Barker, Mary II, 459
Barker, Mary III, 25
Barker, Mary IV, 173
Barker, Mary VI, 100
Barker, Mary VI, 154
Barker, Mary VI, 203
Barker, Mary VI, 850
Barker, Mary A. I, 524
Barker, Mary Ellen IV, 676
Barker, Mary Ellen IV, 798
Barker, Mary L. I, 920
Barker, Mary, Jr. I, 229
Barker, Matilda I, 980
Barker, Matilda I, 986
Barker, Matthew I, 373
Barker, Matthew I, 384
Barker, Matthew I, 460
Barker, Matthew I, 474
Barker, Matthew I, 1067
Barker, Mattie J. I, 920
Barker, Maurice Byron I, 621
Barker, May III, 25
Barker, Merrit II, 965
Barker, Milicent I, 460
Barker, Milicent I, 474
Barker, Milicent I, 481
Barker, Mira T. III, 25
Barker, Miriam III, 241
Barker, Moses VI, 876
Barker, Myra I, 937
Barker, Myra T. III, 25
Barker, N. Egbert I, 920
Barker, Nancy Ann I, 474
Barker, Nancy Ann I, 755
Barker, Nancy J. I, 474
Barker, Nancy J. F. I, 980
Barker, Nancy Jane I, 460
Barker, Nancy Jane I, 755
Barker, Nancy Jane I, 760
Barker, Naomi Ann V, 797
Barker, Narcissa I, 920
Barker, Nathan I, 314
Barker, Nathan I, 346
Barker, Nathan I, 373
Barker, Nathan I, 384
Barker, Nathan I, 460
Barker, Nathan I, 461
Barker, Nathan I, 473
Barker, Nathan I, 474
Barker, Nathan I, 481
Barker, Nathan I, 708
Barker, Nathan I, 1067
Barker, Nathan I, 1070
Barker, Nereus M. I, 460
Barker, Nereus M. I, 797
Barker, Nichless I, 708
Barker, Nichless I, 724
Barker, Nicholas I, 346
Barker, Nicholas I, 373
Barker, Nicholas I, 460
Barker, Nicholas I, 461
Barker, Nicholas I, 473
Barker, Nicholas I, 474
Barker, Nicholas I, 476
Barker, Nicholas I, 647
Barker, Nicholas I, 673
Barker, Nicholas I, 708
Barker, Nicholas I, 870
Barker, Nicholas I, 1067
Barker, Nicholas I, 1070
Barker, Nicholas, Sr. I, 461
Barker, O. B. I, 629
Barker, Ola IV, 1245
Barker, Ora I, 611
Barker, Ora I, 629
Barker, Ora I, 635
Barker, Paris C. I, 629
Barker, Paris Clarkson I, 611
Barker, Paris Clarkson I, 743
Barker, Patience I, 463
Barker, Patience II, 196
Barker, Patience II, 208
Barker, Peleg III, 25
Barker, Penina I, 129
Barker, Peter II, 166
Barker, Peter II, 196
Barker, Peter II, 227
Barker, Peter II, 459
Barker, Peter II, 537
Barker, Phebe I, 373
Barker, Phebe I, 460
Barker, Phebe I, 474
Barker, Phebe I, 483
Barker, Phebe I, 755
Barker, Phebe I, 765
Barker, Phebe I, 797
Barker, Phebe I, 1067
Barker, Phebe III, 90
Barker, Phebe III, 395
Barker, Phebe M. I, 755
Barker, Pheby I, 708
Barker, Phillis May I, 611
Barker, Phinehas I, 314
Barker, Priscilla III, 24
Barker, Rachel I, 460
Barker, Rachel I, 461
Barker, Rachel M. II, 835
Barker, Rachel Moore II, 835
Barker, Rachel Morse II, 835
Barker, Rachel W. II, 835
Barker, Rachel W. II, 915
Barker, Rachel W. II, 931
Barker, Rachel Wilson II, 781
Barker, Rachel Wilson II, 796
Barker, Raymond Dewees II, 699
Barker, Raymond Robert II, 699
Barker, Rebecca I, 373
Barker, Rebecca I, 459
Barker, Rebecca I, 460
Barker, Rebecca IV, 609
Barker, Rebecca IV, 637
Barker, Rebecca T. III, 25
Barker, Rebecca T. III, 30
Barker, Reuben I, 460
Barker, Richard II, 459
Barker, Richard II, 537
Barker, Richard H. III, 25
Barker, Robert III, 395
Barker, Robert III, 407
Barker, Robert H. III, 25
Barker, Roberth III, 25
Barker, Rosa May I, 611
Barker, Rufus J. I, 647
Barker, Ruth I, 346
Barker, Ruth I, 373
Barker, Ruth I, 384
Barker, Ruth I, 460
Barker, Ruth I, 461
Barker, Ruth I, 473
Barker, Ruth I, 474
Barker, Ruth I, 479
Barker, Ruth I, 481
Barker, Ruth I, 647
Barker, Ruth I, 673
Barker, Ruth I, 708
Barker, Ruth I, 870
Barker, Ruth I, 892
Barker, Ruth I, 1067
Barker, S. Calvin II, 727
Barker, S. Calvin II, 756
Barker, S. Ethel I, 931
Barker, S. G. III, 267
Barker, Sally VI, 876
Barker, Samuel I, 373
Barker, Samuel I, 460
Barker, Samuel I, 474
Barker, Samuel III, 395
Barker, Samuel III, 453
Barker, Samuel N. I, 524
Barker, Sarah I, 459
Barker, Sarah I, 460
Barker, Sarah I, 461
Barker, Sarah I, 473
Barker, Sarah I, 476
Barker, Sarah I, 797
Barker, Sarah I, 870
Barker, Sarah I, 919
Barker, Sarah I, 935
Barker, Sarah III, 24
Barker, Sarah IV, 638
Barker, Sarah VI, 861
Barker, Sarah VI, 954
Barker, Sarah VI, 1022
Barker, Sarah A. I, 473
Barker, Sarah A. I, 474
Barker, Sarah E. I, 937
Barker, Sarah E. I, 950
Barker, Sarah E. A. F. I, 980
Barker, Sarah Jane I, 460
Barker, Sarah Jane I, 474
Barker, Sarah K. I, 474
Barker, Sarah Keziah I, 460
Barker, Sarah Louisa I, 474
Barker, Sarah Louisa I, 920
Barker, Sarah W. II, 898
Barker, Serena I, 708
Barker, Seth I, 460
Barker, Seth I, 461
Barker, Seth I, 474
Barker, Seth I, 476
Barker, Seth I, 743
Barker, Seth I, 755
Barker, Seth C. I, 474
Barker, Seth C. I, 755
Barker, Seth C. I, 760
Barker, Shadrach III, 25
Barker, Sibyl E. I, 647
Barker, Simeon I, 461
Barker, Simeon I, 474
Barker, Simeon I, 481
Barker, Simeon I, 647
Barker, Simeon I, 673
Barker, Simon I, 373
Barker, Simon I, 421
Barker, Simon I, 457
Barker, Simon I, 461
Barker, Simon I, 474
Barker, Sirrena I, 708
Barker, Sirrine I, 461
Barker, Sofihia I, 474
Barker, Solomon E. I, 755
Barker, Solomon E. I, 759
Barker, Solomon Elwood I, 460

Barker, Sophia I, 443
Barker, Sophia I, 460
Barker, Sophia I, 797
Barker, Sopia I, 445
Barker, Stella IV, 1245
Barker, Susan VI, 876
Barker, Susan H. II, 835
Barker, Susan R. II, 835
Barker, Susan R. II, 915
Barker, Susan Rotch II, 781
Barker, Susana M. I, 980
Barker, Susannah I, 460
Barker, Susannah I, 468
Barker, Susannah I, 474
Barker, Sybel J. I, 755
Barker, Syble J. I, 759
Barker, T. Hazan III, 24
Barker, T. Ridgway II, 835
Barker, Tamer I, 460
Barker, Tamer I, 469
Barker, Tamer I, 474
Barker, Thamer I, 373
Barker, Thamer I, 384
Barker, Thamer I, 457
Barker, Thamer I, 460
Barker, Thamer I, 474
Barker, Thamer I, 482
Barker, Thomas I, 920
Barker, Thomas V, 726
Barker, Thomas C. I, 931
Barker, Thomas Hazard III, 25
Barker, Thomas L. I, 461
Barker, Thomas L. I, 708
Barker, Thomas Low I, 708
Barker, Thomas Ridgway II, 835
Barker, Thomas S. I, 524
Barker, Thomas S. I, 708
Barker, Thos. IV, 638
Barker, Thos. Ridgway II, 835
Barker, Vera I, 920
Barker, Vera I, 937
Barker, Wade II, 53
Barker, Wade II, 54
Barker, Waid II, 459
Barker, Wd. Abigail II, 166
Barker, Wd. Phebe III, 407
Barker, Wd. Sharpless III, 27
Barker, Wharton III, 23
Barker, Wharton III, 25
Barker, Widow Bridget B. I, 869
Barker, Widow Bridget B. Anderson I, 870
Barker, William I, 314
Barker, William I, 980
Barker, William II, 166
Barker, William II, 196
Barker, William II, 208
Barker, William II, 252
Barker, William III, 25
Barker, William IV, 676
Barker, William VI, 798
Barker, William VI, 876
Barker, William C. III, 25
Barker, William C. III, 267
Barker, William Capres I, 460
Barker, William E. I, 797
Barker, William Hapgood III, 25
Barker, William R. II, 334
Barker, Wilmington I, 755
Barker, Wm. C. II, 835
Barker, Wm. C. II, 931
Barker, Wm. C. III, 25
Barker, Wm. C. III, 30
Barker, Wm. Hapgood III, 25
Barkhous, Frederick IV, 1306
Barkhouse, Frederick IV, 676
Barkhurst, Lelah IV, 173
Barkhurst, Mary E. IV, 464
Barklay, Barclay VI, 296
Barklay, James VI, 296
Barklay, Johnson VI, 296
Barklay, Judith VI, 296
Barklay, Lydia VI, 296
Barklay, Samuel VI, 296
Barklay, Susanna VI, 296
Barklay, Thomas VI, 296
Barksdale, Ann VI, 228
Barksdale, Ann VI, 256
Barksdale, Cleavers VI, 876
Barksdale, Douglas VI, 228
Barksdale, John VI, 876
Barksdale, Mary VI, 876
Barksdale, Nancy VI, 228
Barksdale, Susanna VI, 876
Barlett, Marell V, 612
Barlett, Martha IV, 1234
Barley, A. J. IV, 676
Barley, Amanda IV, 926
Barley, Barak IV, 139
Barley, Benjamin IV, 676
Barley, Benjamin W. IV, 924
Barley, Bethany IV, 139
Barley, Beuford IV, 139
Barley, Charles IV, 676
Barley, Charles IV, 924
Barley, James IV, 676
Barley, James A. IV, 676
Barley, Joseph IV, 926
Barley, Lucy IV, 139
Barley, Martha IV, 139
Barley, Mary IV, 676
Barley, Michael IV, 139
Barley, Permilia IV, 139
Barley, Rebecca IV, 139
Barley, Rebecca IV, 676
Barley, Rebecca J. IV, 924
Barley, Susannah IV, 139
Barley, Wm. IV, 139
Barley, Wyatt IV, 139
Barlow, Alvaretta Josephine V, 612
Barlow, Alzina W. V, 658
Barlow, Angeline V, 612
Barlow, Annie V, 658
Barlow, Bessie V, 658
Barlow, Charles V, 612
Barlow, Chas. H. V, 612
Barlow, Edith VI, 861
Barlow, Elgina V, 658
Barlow, Elizabeth VI, 821
Barlow, Fred J. V, 658
Barlow, George F. V, 612
Barlow, Harry V, 612
Barlow, Henry C. V, 658
Barlow, James VI, 730
Barlow, James M. V, 612
Barlow, Jane VI, 821
Barlow, Lewis Stanley V, 612
Barlow, Margaret V, 612
Barlow, Maria VI, 730
Barlow, Martha A. V, 612
Barlow, Mary VI, 815
Barlow, Mattie A. V, 612
Barlow, Miriam V, 658
Barlow, Susan Mary V, 612
Barlow, Susanna VI, 154
Barlow, Susanna VI, 170
Barlow, Thomas VI, 815
Barlow, Thomas VI, 821
Barlow, Thomas VI, 861
Barmore, Emeline III, 25
Barmore, Hannah III, 25
Barmore, Henry III, 25
Barmore, Lydia III, 303
Barmore, Maria III, 25
Barmore, Mary III, 267
Barmore, Philip III, 25
Barnaba, Ann IV, 676
Barnaba, Clarkson IV, 676
Barnaba, James IV, 676
Barnaba, Rachel IV, 676
Barnabe, Ann IV, 676
Barnabe, Catharine IV, 676
Barnabe, Catherine IV, 676
Barnabe, Clarkson IV, 676
Barnabe, Howard IV, 676
Barnabe, James IV, 676
Barnabe, James, Jr. IV, 676
Barnabe, Joseph IV, 676
Barnabe, Laura IV, 676
Barnabe, Lea IV, 676
Barnabe, Leander IV, 676
Barnabe, Lee IV, 676
Barnabe, Louiza IV, 676
Barnabe, Rachel IV, 676
Barnabe, Samuel P. IV, 676
Barnabe, Stephen IV, 676
Barnabee, Joseph IV, 676
Barnaby, Ann IV, 676
Barnaby, Ann IV, 754
Barnaby, Ann IV, 1021
Barnaby, Anna Jane IV, 1023
Barnaby, Bitters VI, 11
Barnaby, Catherine IV, 1021
Barnaby, Catherine IV, 1023
Barnaby, Clarkson IV, 1021
Barnaby, Emeline IV, 1023
Barnaby, Howard IV, 1023
Barnaby, James IV, 676
Barnaby, James IV, 1021
Barnaby, James IV, 1023
Barnaby, James, Jr. IV, 676
Barnaby, James, Jr. IV, 767
Barnaby, Laura IV, 676
Barnaby, Laura IV, 767
Barnaby, Lee IV, 676
Barnaby, Lee IV, 1021
Barnaby, Lee IV, 1023
Barnaby, Leonard IV, 1023
Barnaby, Louisa IV, 1023
Barnaby, Rachel IV, 1023
Barnaby, Rachel IV, 1028
Barnaby, Rachel M. IV, 1021
Barnaby, Samantha IV, 1023
Barnaby, Samuel P. IV, 1023
Barnaby, Stephen IV, 1021
Barnaby, Stephen IV, 1023
Barnaby, Zilpah IV, 1023
Barnaby, Zilpah T. IV, 864
Barnaby, Zilpah T. IV, 884
Barnaby, Zilpha IV, 1021
Barnard, ??? III, 26
Barnard, Aaron G. I, 490
Barnard, Abigail IV, 1144
Barnard, Abigail IV, 1151
Barnard, Amy I, 525
Barnard, Amy I, 558
Barnard, Amy I, 673
Barnard, Ann I, 525
Barnard, Ann I, 980
Barnard, Ann V, 475
Barnard, Ann V, 516
Barnard, Ann V, 779
Barnard, Anna I, 490
Barnard, Anna I, 525
Barnard, Anna I, 647
Barnard, Anna I, 775
Barnard, Anna I, 797
Barnard, Anna I, 804
Barnard, Anna I, 810
Barnard, Anna I, 980
Barnard, Anna I, 999
Barnard, Anna III, 25
Barnard, Anna III, 26
Barnard, Anna III, 307
Barnard, Anna V, 298
Barnard, Anna VI, 298
Barnard, Anne VI, 298
Barnard, Asa I, 775
Barnard, Asa I, 797
Barnard, Asa I, 825
Barnard, Asa I, 907
Barnard, Asa I, 911
Barnard, Barachiah I, 673
Barnard, Barzilla VI, 298
Barnard, Barzillari VI, 298
Barnard, Benjamin I, 525
Barnard, Benjamin I, 673
Barnard, Benjamin III, 25
Barnard, Benjamin III, 26
Barnard, Benjamin VI, 298
Barnard, Benjamin VI, 864
Barnard, Caroline Theodosia III, 395
Barnard, Catharine I, 773
Barnard, Catharine I, 775
Barnard, Catharine I, 797
Barnard, Catharine I, 980
Barnard, Catharine V, 726
Barnard, Catharine V, 779
Barnard, Charles III, 26
Barnard, Charles H. III, 26
Barnard, Christopher I, 775
Barnard, Christopher I, 980
Barnard, Cornelius L. III, 26
Barnard, Cromwell II, 459
Barnard, Cromwell, Jr. II, 727
Barnard, David IV, 1144
Barnard, Dinah I, 775
Barnard, Dinah I, 797
Barnard, Doris L. IV, 676
Barnard, Edward III, 26
Barnard, Elisha I, 797
Barnard, Elisha VI, 864
Barnard, Elizabeth I, 647
Barnard, Elizabeth I, 673
Barnard, Elizabeth I, 676
Barnard, Elizabeth I, 684
Barnard, Elizabeth I, 775
Barnard, Elizabeth I, 980
Barnard, Elizabeth I, 998
Barnard, Elizabeth I, 1114
Barnard, Elizabeth I, 1118
Barnard, Elizabeth V, 298
Barnard, Elizabeth V, 469
Barnard, Elizabeth V, 475
Barnard, Elizabeth V, 516
Barnard, Elizabeth V, 920
Barnard, Elizabeth VI, 298
Barnard, Elizabeth Hicks II, 790
Barnard, Eunice I, 525
Barnard, Eunice I, 673
Barnard, Eunice VI, 298
Barnard, Ford B. III, 395
Barnard, Ford B. III, 475
Barnard, Frances I, 973
Barnard, Francis I, 773
Barnard, Francis I, 775
Barnard, Francis I, 797
Barnard, Francis I, 980
Barnard, Francis V, 779
Barnard, Francis Marsh VI, 798
Barnard, Francis, Jr. I, 524
Barnard, Francis, Jr. I, 980
Barnard, Francis, Sr. I, 971
Barnard, Frederic I, 525
Barnard, Frederick I, 525
Barnard, Frederick I, 541
Barnard, Frederick I, 1089
Barnard, Frederick I, 1114
Barnard, George I, 647
Barnard, George III, 26
Barnard, George V, 298
Barnard, George VI, 297
Barnard, George VI, 298
Barnard, Gilbert VI, 297
Barnard, Gilbert VI, 298
Barnard, Hannah I, 647
Barnard, Hannah I, 980
Barnard, Hannah V, 298
Barnard, Harrison III, 395
Barnard, Hepzabeth I, 825
Barnard, Huldah I, 775
Barnard, Huldah I, 797
Barnard, Huldah I, 825
Barnard, Huldah I, 907
Barnard, Huldah I, 911
Barnard, Huldah IV, 1144
Barnard, Huldah H. IV, 1144
Barnard, James I, 775
Barnard, James I, 980
Barnard, Jamima I, 775
Barnard, Jamima I, 797
Barnard, Jamima I, 822
Barnard, Jane I, 980
Barnard, Jane IV, 304
Barnard, Jane VI, 798
Barnard, Jemimah I, 1114
Barnard, Jethro I, 647
Barnard, Jethro I, 775
Barnard, Jethro I, 980
Barnard, Job VI, 298
Barnard, Job VI, 345
Barnard, John I, 673
Barnard, John I, 775
Barnard, John V, 298
Barnard, John T. III, 395
Barnard, John T. III, 483
Barnard, Jonathan I, 490
Barnard, Joseph I, 647
Barnard, Joseph II, 781
Barnard, Judith I, 525
Barnard, Judith I, 541
Barnard, Judith I, 1114
Barnard, Kennett II, 316
Barnard, Levina I, 797
Barnard, Libni I, 525
Barnard, Libni I, 558
Barnard, Lotty V, 794
Barnard, Love I, 647
Barnard, Love I, 673
Barnard, Love I, 980
Barnard, Love V, 298
Barnard, Love VI, 298
Barnard, Lucinda I, 673
Barnard, Lucinday I, 673
Barnard, Lucinday I, 684
Barnard, Lucretia M. II, 810
Barnard, Lucretia M. II, 835
Barnard, Lucretia M. II, 900
Barnard, Lucy VI, 298
Barnard, Lucy VI, 304
Barnard, Lydda I, 525
Barnard, Lydda I, 541
Barnard, Lydia I, 490
Barnard, Lydia I, 525
Barnard, Lydia I, 647
Barnard, Lydia I, 775
Barnard, Lydia I, 1114
Barnard, Lydia V, 788
Barnard, Lydia V, 893
Barnard, Lydia V, 899
Barnard, Mara R. IV, 1144
Barnard, Margaret I, 525
Barnard, Margaret I, 647
Barnard, Margaret I, 673
Barnard, Margaret I, 679
Barnard, Margaret I, 773
Barnard, Margaret I, 775
Barnard, Margaret I, 797
Barnard, Margaret I, 907
Barnard, Margaret Shepard III, 395
Barnard, Margaret Shephard III, 475
Barnard, Martha II, 786
Barnard, Martha III, 304
Barnard, Martha V, 779
Barnard, Martha V, 781
Barnard, Mary I, 647
Barnard, Mary I, 673
Barnard, Mary I, 775
Barnard, Mary I, 797
Barnard, Mary I, 804
Barnard, Mary I, 846
Barnard, Mary I, 911
Barnard, Mary I, 912
Barnard, Mary I, 980
Barnard, Mary II, 316
Barnard, Mary II, 322
Barnard, Mary II, 781
Barnard, Mary III, 26
Barnard, Mary III, 395
Barnard, Mary III, 483
Barnard, Mary V, 298
Barnard, Mary A. VI, 864
Barnard, Mary Emma III, 395
Barnard, Mary L. II, 835
Barnard, Mary R. IV, 1144
Barnard, Mary S. III, 158
Barnard, Matilda I, 525
Barnard, Matilda I, 797
Barnard, Matilda I, 911
Barnard, Metilda I, 541
Barnard, Millicent I, 980
Barnard, Obed I, 490
Barnard, Obed I, 525
Barnard, Obed I, 647
Barnard, Obed I, 673
Barnard, Obed I, 676
Barnard, Obed I, 679
Barnard, Obed W. IV, 1144
Barnard, Patsy VI, 830
Barnard, Paul I, 490
Barnard, Paul I, 525
Barnard, Phebe I, 647
Barnard, Phebe I, 673
Barnard, Phebe I, 693
Barnard, Phebe I, 775
Barnard, Phebe I, 797
Barnard, Phebe III, 26
Barnard, Phebe III, 251
Barnard, Phebe IV, 1144
Barnard, Ralph IV, 676
Barnard, Rebecah I, 980
Barnard, Rebecca I, 775
Barnard, Rebecca I, 980
Barnard, Rebecca I, 992
Barnard, Rebecca V, 779
Barnard, Rebecca V, 794
Barnard, Rebeckah I, 797
Barnard, Rehubin F. VI, 809
Barnard, Reuben I, 980
Barnard, Reuben VI, 298
Barnard, Reubin VI, 798
Barnard, Rheubin F. VI, 859
Barnard, Rueben VI, 298
Barnard, Ruth V, 23
Barnard, Ruth V, 893
Barnard, Ruth V, 920
Barnard, Ruth H. IV, 1144
Barnard, Samuel I, 980
Barnard, Samuel V, 726
Barnard, Samuel V, 779
Barnard, Sarah II, 781
Barnard, Sarah IV, 306
Barnard, Sarah IV, 1144
Barnard, Sarah D. II, 835
Barnard, Sarah D. II, 900
Barnard, Seth IV, 1144
Barnard, Shubael I, 490
Barnard, Shubael I, 525
Barnard, Shuball V, 788
Barnard, Simon II, 781
Barnard, Simon II, 835
Barnard, Simon II, 900
Barnard, Smith VI, 298
Barnard, Thadeus IV, 1144
Barnard, Thomas I, 775
Barnard, Thomas III, 26
Barnard, Thos. V, 920
Barnard, Thos. Upham III, 395
Barnard, Timothy I, 524
Barnard, Timothy I, 673
Barnard, Timothy VI, 298
Barnard, Timothy VI, 798
Barnard, Timothy VI, 830
Barnard, Tristim I, 971
Barnard, Tristram I, 524
Barnard, Tristram I, 525
Barnard, Tristram I, 773
Barnard, Tristram I, 775
Barnard, Tristram I, 797
Barnard, Tristram I, 911
Barnard, Tristram I, 1053
Barnard, Trustram I, 525
Barnard, Trustram I, 541
Barnard, Uriah I, 647
Barnard, Uriah I, 673
Barnard, Uriah I, 684
Barnard, Uriah I, 980
Barnard, Uriah V, 298
Barnard, Uriah VI, 298
Barnard, Valentine III, 26
Barnard, Verne Joshua III, 395

Barnard, Wd. Mary II, 781
Barnard, Widow Levina I, 797
Barnard, William I, 525
Barnard, William I, 541
Barnard, William I, 647
Barnard, William I, 673
Barnard, William I, 775
Barnard, William I, 797
Barnard, William I, 911
Barnard, William II, 316
Barnard, William II, 322
Barnard, William VI, 298
Barnard, William A. VI, 862
Barnard, William G. IV, 1144
Barnard, Wm. II, 781
Barnard, Wm. V, 298
Barnard, Wm. V, 779
Barnard, Wm. C. V, 779
Barnard, Wm. G. IV, 1144
Barnart, John VI, 228
Barneba, Catharine IV, 676
Barneba, Howard IV, 676
Barneba, Louiza IV, 676
Barneba, Stephen IV, 676
Barneby, Bittus VI, 12
Barned, Ellen D. III, 395
Barned, Geo. R. III, 395
Barned, Hester Wilcox III, 395
Barnell, Sally VI, 851
Barnem, Lavina I, 797
Barnem, Lavinia I, 798
Barner, Frances J. III, 18
Barnerd, Anna VI, 298
Barnerd, Barzilla VI, 298
Barnerd, Barzillari VI, 298
Barnerd, Benjamin VI, 298
Barnerd, Elizabeth VI, 298
Barnerd, Eunice VI, 298
Barnerd, George VI, 297
Barnerd, George VI, 298
Barnerd, Gilbert VI, 297
Barnerd, Gilbert VI, 298
Barnerd, Job VI, 298
Barnerd, Love VI, 298
Barnerd, Rueben VI, 298
Barnerd, Timothy VI, 298
Barnerd, Uriah VI, 298
Barnerd, William VI, 298
Barnes, ??? III, 25
Barnes, ??? III, 26
Barnes, ??? VI, 39
Barnes, Aaron III, 26
Barnes, Abigail I, 1047
Barnes, Alathea III, 25
Barnes, Alice IV, 676
Barnes, Ann III, 26
Barnes, Ann III, 360
Barnes, Ann Eliza III, 26
Barnes, Ann Eliza III, 303
Barnes, Anna III, 26
Barnes, Anna III, 147
Barnes, Anna B. III, 147
Barnes, Anna E. IV, 1144
Barnes, Anna Elvira IV, 1144
Barnes, Anna M. C. III, 26
Barnes, Annie P. III, 26
Barnes, Annie P. III, 339
Barnes, Annie Pancoast III, 339
Barnes, Avy VI, 81
Barnes, Charles IV, 676
Barnes, Charlotte IV, 437
Barnes, Daniel II, 459
Barnes, Daniel F. II, 781
Barnes, David IV, 139
Barnes, David IV, 320
Barnes, David IV, 368
Barnes, David H. III, 26
Barnes, David H. III, 147
Barnes, Donna Rose IV, 676
Barnes, E. S. I, 920
Barnes, Earl V, 219
Barnes, Earnest V, 451
Barnes, Edith II, 459
Barnes, Edith II, 587
Barnes, Edward IV, 173
Barnes, Edwin I, 283
Barnes, Elias IV, 437
Barnes, Eliz. III, 350
Barnes, Eliza II, 781
Barnes, Eliza II, 835
Barnes, Eliza II, 884
Barnes, Eliza III, 26
Barnes, Elizabeth II, 334
Barnes, Elizabeth II, 459
Barnes, Elizabeth II, 506
Barnes, Elizabeth II, 699
Barnes, Elizabeth II, 976
Barnes, Elizabeth VI, 876
Barnes, Elizabeth W. II, 976
Barnes, Ella I, 616
Barnes, Ellen III, 26
Barnes, Emily III, 26
Barnes, Emily III, 303
Barnes, Emily IV, 437
Barnes, Emma I, 611
Barnes, Emma I, 938
Barnes, Emsley I, 708
Barnes, Eshter Syng II, 727
Barnes, Esther II, 767
Barnes, Esther L. II, 835
Barnes, Esther S. II, 835
Barnes, Esther S. II, 923
Barnes, Esther Syng II, 727
Barnes, Fannie Meda Lee I, 611
Barnes, Felix IV, 676
Barnes, Frances J. III, 26
Barnes, George III, 26
Barnes, George A. IV, 173
Barnes, George E. IV, 173
Barnes, Gertrude IV, 926
Barnes, Goldie Blackburn IV, 676
Barnes, Grace W. VI, 731
Barnes, Grace Winder VI, 730
Barnes, Grace Winder VI, 762
Barnes, Grace Winder VI, 769
Barnes, Grace Winder VI, 794
Barnes, Griffith C. IV, 1144
Barnes, Griffith L. IV, 1144
Barnes, Hannah II, 459
Barnes, Hannah II, 622
Barnes, Hannah II, 727
Barnes, Hannah II, 835
Barnes, Hannah II, 1031
Barnes, Hannah III, 26
Barnes, Hannah B. II, 835
Barnes, Hannah B. II, 933
Barnes, Hannah G. III, 26
Barnes, Hannah L. II, 1045
Barnes, Hannah L. II, 1046
Barnes, Henry III, 26
Barnes, Henry III, 303
Barnes, Henry IV, 139
Barnes, Henry IV, 368
Barnes, Henry W. III, 26
Barnes, Hester A. IV, 173
Barnes, Hope IV, 437
Barnes, Ida IV, 676
Barnes, Isaac II, 976
Barnes, Isaac IV, 437
Barnes, Isaac V, 23
Barnes, J. S. I, 611
Barnes, James I, 373
Barnes, James I, 387
Barnes, James II, 835
Barnes, James II, 884
Barnes, James IV, 320
Barnes, James IV, 368
Barnes, James IV, 676
Barnes, Jane VI, 15
Barnes, Jesse W. IV, 1144
Barnes, Jno. VI, 93
Barnes, John II, 54
Barnes, John II, 334
Barnes, John II, 441
Barnes, John II, 454
Barnes, John II, 459
Barnes, John II, 506
Barnes, John III, 26
Barnes, John IV, 139
Barnes, John IV, 1144
Barnes, John VI, 27
Barnes, John VI, 28
Barnes, John VI, 41
Barnes, John A. III, 26
Barnes, John A. III, 293
Barnes, John A. III, 295
Barnes, Johnson VI, 81
Barnes, Jonathan IV, 437
Barnes, Joseph III, 26
Barnes, Joseph III, 339
Barnes, Joseph V. IV, 1144
Barnes, Joshua II, 54
Barnes, Josiah III, 26
Barnes, Josiah III, 119
Barnes, Josiah F. III, 26
Barnes, Julia III, 25
Barnes, Julia A. III, 25
Barnes, Julia A. III, 156
Barnes, Katherine II, 441
Barnes, L. Olin I, 611
Barnes, Letitia III, 354
Barnes, Lorenzo V, 151
Barnes, Louisa VI, 52
Barnes, Louisa VI, 81
Barnes, Lucy Ann IV, 173
Barnes, Lucy Ann IV, 236
Barnes, Lydia II, 459
Barnes, Lydia II, 727
Barnes, Lydia II, 781
Barnes, Lydia II, 835
Barnes, Lydia III, 303
Barnes, Lydia, Jr. II, 459
Barnes, Lydia, Jr. II, 781
Barnes, Mada Lee Bingham I, 629
Barnes, Maggie IV, 173
Barnes, Mahlon IV, 437
Barnes, Maida Bingham I, 629
Barnes, Margaret V, 151
Barnes, Marion IV, 368
Barnes, Martha II, 976
Barnes, Martha II, 982
Barnes, Martha B. II, 976
Barnes, Mary I, 299
Barnes, Mary I, 309
Barnes, Mary II, 454
Barnes, Mary II, 459
Barnes, Mary II, 727
Barnes, Mary II, 781
Barnes, Mary II, 835
Barnes, Mary II, 976
Barnes, Mary II, 1031
Barnes, Mary III, 26
Barnes, Mary III, 350
Barnes, Mary IV, 139
Barnes, Mary IV, 173
Barnes, Mary IV, 368
Barnes, Mary IV, 437
Barnes, Mary IV, 676
Barnes, Mary IV, 1068
Barnes, Mary A. IV, 676
Barnes, Mary Anna II, 781
Barnes, Mary Anna II, 835
Barnes, Mary F. III, 26
Barnes, Mary L. IV, 173
Barnes, Meriam IV, 173
Barnes, Merian IV, 368
Barnes, Merion IV, 368
Barnes, Merion IV, 436
Barnes, Miriam IV, 567
Barnes, Nancy I, 283
Barnes, Nancy M. I, 283
Barnes, Naomi III, 26
Barnes, Naomi C. III, 147
Barnes, Nathan IV, 437
Barnes, Olan I, 629
Barnes, Olin I, 619
Barnes, Olive IV, 676
Barnes, Phebe III, 26
Barnes, Phebe III, 119
Barnes, Phebe III, 347
Barnes, Phebe Ann III, 26
Barnes, Phebe Ann III, 339
Barnes, Phebe C. III, 293
Barnes, Phebe C. III, 295
Barnes, Polly VI, 865
Barnes, Rachel II, 459
Barnes, Rachel II, 692
Barnes, Rachel IV, 368
Barnes, Rachel IV, 370
Barnes, Rachel IV, 1118
Barnes, Rachel IV, 1144
Barnes, Rachel W. IV, 1144
Barnes, Rebecca II, 506
Barnes, Rebecca II, 699
Barnes, Rebeckah II, 54
Barnes, Rebeckah II, 441
Barnes, Rena IV, 173
Barnes, Richard II, 54
Barnes, Richard II, 441
Barnes, Richard II, 459
Barnes, Richard II, 506
Barnes, Robert III, 350
Barnes, Robert III, 360
Barnes, Robert S. III, 26
Barnes, Robert T. II, 459
Barnes, Ruth II, 196
Barnes, Ruth II, 244
Barnes, Ruth IV, 437
Barnes, Ruth Anna VI, 730
Barnes, Ruth Anna VI, 762
Barnes, Sally VI, 832
Barnes, Samuel I, 629
Barnes, Samuel II, 334
Barnes, Samuel II, 459
Barnes, Samuel II, 976
Barnes, Samuel IV, 1144
Barnes, Samuel H. IV, 1144
Barnes, Samuel H. IV, 1190
Barnes, Samuel W. II, 459
Barnes, Sarah I, 373
Barnes, Sarah I, 387
Barnes, Sarah I, 708
Barnes, Sarah I, 920
Barnes, Sarah II, 459
Barnes, Sarah IV, 1088
Barnes, Sarah IV, 1093
Barnes, Sarah IV, 1122
Barnes, Sarah IV, 1144
Barnes, Sarah IV, 1190
Barnes, Sarah V, 23
Barnes, Sarah VI, 52
Barnes, Sarah VI, 64
Barnes, Sarah Ann IV, 368
Barnes, Sarah Ann IV, 457
Barnes, Sarah Elizabeth IV, 173
Barnes, Sarah Elizabeth IV, 226
Barnes, Sarah F. III, 26
Barnes, Sarah M. III, 26
Barnes, Susan H. II, 781
Barnes, Susan Jane III, 26
Barnes, Susan N. II, 835
Barnes, Susan N. II, 884
Barnes, Susan N. Jones II, 835
Barnes, Thomas I, 708
Barnes, Thomas II, 334
Barnes, Thomas II, 459
Barnes, Thomas II, 727
Barnes, Thomas II, 781
Barnes, Thomas II, 835
Barnes, Thomas II, 976
Barnes, Thomas IV, 437
Barnes, Thomas VI, 876
Barnes, Thomas C. II, 781
Barnes, Thomas, Jr. II, 976
Barnes, Thomas, Jr. II, 1031
Barnes, Thos. II, 835
Barnes, Thos. C. II, 835
Barnes, Titus IV, 437
Barnes, Virginia I, 611
Barnes, Virginia Maie I, 619
Barnes, W. T. I, 920
Barnes, Walter III, 26
Barnes, Wd. Mary II, 334
Barnes, Wd. Phebe C. III, 26
Barnes, William IV, 173
Barnes, William V, 23
Barnes, William A. III, 26
Barnes, William B. III, 26
Barnes, Willis A. III, 18
Barnes, Willis A. III, 26
Barnes, Wm. Jeffreys VI, 730
Barnes, Wm. Jeffreys VI, 762
Barnet, Abraham II, 459
Barnet, Athanations V, 151
Barnet, Athenacions V, 151
Barnet, Benj. VI, 798
Barnet, David I, 1059
Barnet, Elisha VI, 798
Barnet, Elizabeth II, 166
Barnet, Hannah I, 1059
Barnet, Hannah V, 151
Barnet, Isaac II, 335
Barnet, Isaac II, 459
Barnet, James V, 23
Barnet, Jane I, 971
Barnet, Jesse V, 23
Barnet, Jesse VI, 849
Barnet, Jethro I, 870
Barnet, John I, 981
Barnet, John II, 335
Barnet, Lydia I, 525
Barnet, Lydia II, 459
Barnet, Martha B. VI, 798
Barnet, Mary V, 298
Barnet, Mary V, 299
Barnet, Mary V, 475
Barnet, Mary M. VI, 798
Barnet, Mary N. VI, 798
Barnet, Phebe II, 459
Barnet, Rachel VI, 851
Barnet, Richard II, 166
Barnet, Samson IV, 74
Barnet, Stephen IV, 74
Barnet, Theodate V, 23
Barnet, Thomas I, 981
Barnet, Thomas V, 23
Barnet, Walter V, 612
Barnet, William II, 166
Barnet, William II, 335
Barnet, William V, 23
Barnett, ??? III, 26
Barnett, ??? III, 238
Barnett, Abraham II, 459
Barnett, Abraham II, 543
Barnett, Amos V, 475
Barnett, Amos Curtis V, 612
Barnett, Ann VI, 829
Barnett, Ann Mildred Wilson Thos. V, 612
Barnett, Anna VI, 228
Barnett, Anna VI, 842
Barnett, Arthanacis I, 980
Barnett, Arthanacis I, 981
Barnett, Arthanantoush VI, 251
Barnett, Arthanatious VI, 228
Barnett, Arthanatoush VI, 228
Barnett, Arthenations V, 612
Barnett, Asa IV, 864
Barnett, Athanasius I, 981
Barnett, Athanasius VI, 228
Barnett, Athanations V, 151
Barnett, Catharine V, 160
Barnett, Catharine V, 612
Barnett, Daniel P. II, 835
Barnett, David IV, 29
Barnett, David VI, 876
Barnett, Elizabeth I, 981
Barnett, Elizabeth II, 196
Barnett, Elizabeth II, 222
Barnett, Elizabeth V, 473
Barnett, Elizabeth V, 475
Barnett, Elizabeth V, 612
Barnett, Elizabeth VI, 228
Barnett, Elizabeth VI, 251
Barnett, Flora IV, 864
Barnett, Frances R. VI, 876
Barnett, Hannah F. II, 835
Barnett, Hutchins VI, 228
Barnett, Isaac II, 335
Barnett, Isaac II, 459
Barnett, Isaac II, 543
Barnett, Isaac V, 612
Barnett, James I, 973
Barnett, James V, 23
Barnett, James V, 475
Barnett, James V. V, 612
Barnett, Jane I, 981
Barnett, Jane V, 23
Barnett, Jane V, 475
Barnett, Jane V, 612
Barnett, Jane VI, 228
Barnett, Jane VI, 251
Barnett, Jane, Sr. V, 612
Barnett, Jesse I, 973
Barnett, Jesse I, 980
Barnett, Jesse V, 23
Barnett, Jesse V, 473
Barnett, Jesse V, 475
Barnett, Jesse V, 612
Barnett, Jesse VI, 228
Barnett, John I, 980
Barnett, John I, 981
Barnett, John II, 335
Barnett, John V, 475
Barnett, John V, 612
Barnett, John VI, 228
Barnett, John VI, 251
Barnett, Jonathan V, 612
Barnett, Joseph V, 612
Barnett, Love VI, 298
Barnett, Lucy VI, 304
Barnett, Lydia II, 459
Barnett, Lydia II, 543
Barnett, Margaret V, 612
Barnett, Martha VI, 228
Barnett, Mary II, 835
Barnett, Mary III, 26
Barnett, Mary III, 238
Barnett, Mary IV, 20
Barnett, Mary IV, 29
Barnett, Mary V, 298
Barnett, Mary V, 475
Barnett, Mary V, 501
Barnett, Mary VI, 228
Barnett, Melesent V, 475
Barnett, Melissa Ann V, 612
Barnett, Millicent VI, 228
Barnett, Nancy V, 475
Barnett, Nancy VI, 228
Barnett, Nancy VI, 842
Barnett, Obediance VI, 228
Barnett, Rachel IV, 29
Barnett, Ruth V, 612
Barnett, Samson IV, 74
Barnett, Samuel W. VI, 876
Barnett, Sarah V, 122
Barnett, Sarah V, 298
Barnett, Sarah V, 305
Barnett, Sarah A. VI, 876
Barnett, Theodate I, 973
Barnett, Theodate I, 981
Barnett, Theodate I, 999
Barnett, Theodate V, 23
Barnett, Theodate V, 475
Barnett, Theodate V, 612
Barnett, Thomas I, 973
Barnett, Thomas I, 981
Barnett, Thomas I, 999
Barnett, Thomas V, 23
Barnett, Thomas V, 475
Barnett, Thomas V, 612
Barnett, Thomas F. II, 835
Barnett, Walter V, 612
Barnett, William I, 973
Barnett, William V, 23
Barnett, William V, 475
Barnett, William V, 612
Barnette, Benj. VI, 798
Barnette, Timothy VI, 818
Barney, Albert C. III, 26
Barney, Ann Eliza III, 26
Barney, Avis III, 26
Barney, Avis III, 27
Barney, Avis III, 109

Barney, Avis M. III, 26
Barney, Avis M. III, 27
Barney, Benjamin I, 525
Barney, Benjamin III, 26
Barney, Caroline III, 26
Barney, Caroline III, 27
Barney, Charles III, 26
Barney, Charles III, 27
Barney, Charles Gorham III, 26
Barney, Charles Gorham III, 27
Barney, Chas. III, 109
Barney, Eliza Ann III, 26
Barney, Eliza Ann III, 27
Barney, Eliza Ann III, 109
Barney, Frances Augusta III, 27
Barney, John, Sr. II, 335
Barney, Josiah Macy III, 26
Barney, Josiah Macy III, 27
Barney, Lydia III, 27
Barney, Mary V, 297
Barney, Mary V, 298
Barney, Mary N. III, 26
Barney, Mary N. III, 27
Barney, Mary N. III, 86
Barney, Mary N. III, 338
Barney, Mary Powell III, 27
Barney, Sarah II, 459
Barney, Susan Rebecca III, 27
Barney, William H. III, 27
Barney, William H. III, 86
Barney, William Henry III, 26
Barney, William Henry III, 27
Barney, Wm. H. III, 26
Barnhard, Alice IV, 173
Barnhard, Alice IV, 247
Barnhard, Catharine V, 779
Barnhard, Francis V, 779
Barnhard, Jane IV, 173
Barnhard, Sarah IV, 173
Barnhardt, Henry V, 726
Barnhardt, Icy V, 726
Barnhardt, Ida May V, 726
Barnhardt, J. W. Dorsey V, 726
Barnhardt, Nettie V, 726
Barnhardt, Noah V, 726
Barnhardt, Sarah V, 726
Barnhardt, Sarah V, 779
Barnhart, Genevra Mary IV, 173
Barnhart, Hattie IV, 173
Barnhart, Jacob IV, 1351
Barnhart, James IV, 173
Barnhart, Lydia IV, 1351
Barnhart, Mary Geneva IV, 173
Barnhart, William IV, 173
Barnhill, Celeste Terrill V, 373
Barns, Abigail I, 373
Barns, Abigail I, 1047
Barns, Ann I, 373
Barns, Ann I, 418
Barns, Anne I, 356
Barns, Brinsley I, 347
Barns, Brinsley I, 356
Barns, Charity I, 365
Barns, Edith II, 459
Barns, Elizabeth I, 347
Barns, Elizabeth I, 356
Barns, Elizabeth I, 373
Barns, Elizabeth I, 419
Barns, Elizabeth I, 1026
Barns, Elizabeth I, 1047
Barns, Elizabeth I Sup 1, 3
Barns, Elizabeth II, 21
Barns, Ephraim II, 21
Barns, Henry IV, 368
Barns, Hepzibah II, 21
Barns, Jacob I, 373
Barns, Jacob I, 1047
Barns, James I, 373
Barns, James I, 1047
Barns, Jeremiah I, 373
Barns, Jeremiah I, 1047
Barns, Jeremiah I Sup 1, 3
Barns, Jerimiah I, 373
Barns, John I Sup 1, 11
Barns, John II, 21
Barns, John II, 54
Barns, John A. III, 230
Barns, Jonathan I, 373
Barns, Jonathan I, 419
Barns, Jonathan, Jr. I, 373
Barns, Joseph II, 21
Barns, Joseph II, 54
Barns, Joseph II, 135
Barns, Joshua I, 373
Barns, Joshua II, 21
Barns, Joshua II, 54
Barns, Lourana I, 373
Barns, Lowrana I, 373
Barns, Lowranna I, 346
Barns, Lurana I, 365
Barns, Lurena I, 346
Barns, Maria M. VI, 935
Barns, Mary I, 347
Barns, Mary I, 373
Barns, Mary I, 402
Barns, Mary I, 1047
Barns, Mary Jane II, 135
Barns, Olive I, 373
Barns, Olive I, 1047
Barns, Phebe Ann II, 135
Barns, Phebe C. III, 230
Barns, Rache I, 1047
Barns, Rebecca II, 54
Barns, Rebeckah II, 21
Barns, Rebeckah II, 54
Barns, Rebekah I, 373
Barns, Rebekah I, 387
Barns, Richard II, 21
Barns, Richard II, 54
Barns, Samuel I, 373
Barns, Samuel I, 1047
Barns, Samuel II, 21
Barns, Samuel VI, 798
Barns, Sarah I, 373
Barns, Sarah I, 419
Barns, Sarah I, 423
Barns, Sarah II, 21
Barns, Sarah II, 54
Barns, Seth I, 373
Barns, Tabitha VI, 798
Barns, Thomas I, 365
Barnsides, Elizabeth I, 983
Barnsides, Elizabeth I, 988
Barnum, David L. III, 27
Barnum, David Lane III, 229
Barnum, Ezekiel III, 27
Barnum, Ida III, 229
Barnum, Peter C. III, 353
Barnum, Phebe C. III, 27
Barr, Beulah II, 459
Barr, David VI, 876
Barr, Eliza IV, 173
Barr, Elizabeth IV, 676
Barr, Elizabeth E. IV, 676
Barr, Elizabeth E. IV, 768
Barr, Lizzie V, 219
Barr, Mary E. V, 985
Barr, Mary Oldinger VI, 876
Barr, Robert VI, 406
Barr, Sidney VI, 362
Barr, Sidney VI, 406
Barr, Sidney VI, 407
Barra, Filipino III, 27
Barra, Gertrude III, 161
Barra, Gertude III, 27
Barra, Gesto III, 27
Barra, Henry N. III, 27
Barra, James J. III, 23
Barra, James J. III, 27
Barra, James J. III, 161
Barra, Marietta III, 27
Barracks, Mary VI, 298
Barracks, Mary VI, 343
Barracks, Moore VI, 850
Barracks, Polly VI, 298
Barracks, Russell VI, 298
Barracks, Sarah D. VI, 850
Barracks, William J. VI, 850
Barraclif, Aaron II, 21
Barraclif, Ann II, 21
Barraclif, Aron II, 21
Barraclif, George II, 21
Barraclif, John II, 21
Barraclif, Leatitia II, 21
Barraclif, Leatitiah II, 21
Barraclif, Prudence II, 21
Barraclif, Ruth II, 21
Barracliff, Ann II, 21
Barracliff, Ann II, 54
Barracliff, Ann II, 108
Barracliff, Ann II, 954
Barracliff, John II, 21
Barracliff, John II, 51
Barracliff, John II, 54
Barracliff, John II, 57
Barracliff, John II, 108
Barracliff, John II, 954
Barracliff, Latitia II, 51
Barracliff, Latitia II, 54
Barracliff, Prudence II, 54
Barracliff, Prudence II, 57
Barracliff, Prudence II, 99
Barracliff, Ruth II, 54
Barracliff, Ruth II, 97
Barracliff, Ruth II, 954
Barracliff, William II, 954
Barracliffe, Ann II, 976
Barracliffe, Ann II, 985
Barracliffe, Wm. II, 976
Barracliffe, Wm. II, 985
Barras, John II, 977
Barras, John II, 1027
Barrat, Mary V, 726
Barratt, Elizabeth II, 54
Barratt, Elizabeth II, 62
Barratt, Lydia VI, 363
Barrell, Elsie Josephine VI, 731
Barrell, Fred A. VI, 731
Barrell, Winifred VI, 731
Barrere, Helen V, 658
Barrere, Helen V, 694
Barret, Absalom III, 395
Barret, Agnes Roberta III, 17
Barret, Amy IV, 173
Barret, Arthur I, 1026
Barret, Belinda IV, 510
Barret, Benjamin I, 1026
Barret, Benjamin I Sup 1, 10
Barret, Calista IV, 1144
Barret, Daisie V, 985
Barret, Daisy V, 985
Barret, Deborah III, 395
Barret, Eleanor V, 23
Barret, Elisha IV, 1144
Barret, Elizabeth V, 475
Barret, Geo. IV, 1144
Barret, Hannah IV, 121
Barret, Hannah IV, 125
Barret, Isaac IV, 1144
Barret, Isaac Slocum IV, 1144
Barret, Jacob I, 1026
Barret, Jacob V, 475
Barret, James I, 1089
Barret, James VI, 363
Barret, James E. III, 17
Barret, Jemime I, 1026
Barret, John I, 1026
Barret, John VI, 154
Barret, John VI, 363
Barret, John B. IV, 1144
Barret, John R. V, 23
Barret, Joseph I, 1026
Barret, Joseph I Sup 1, 10
Barret, Lydia I, 1026
Barret, Mahala IV, 1144
Barret, Mahala M. IV, 1144
Barret, Mahalah M. IV, 1144
Barret, Maria IV, 1144
Barret, Mariah IV, 1144
Barret, Mary VI, 155
Barret, Mary VI, 390
Barret, Mary J. III, 17
Barret, Mary J. III, 395
Barret, Mary J. III, 459
Barret, Mary L. IV, 1144
Barret, Merriet H. IV, 1144
Barret, Rachel IV, 798
Barret, Rachel IV, 849
Barret, Rhoda I, 1026
Barret, Richard VI, 390
Barret, Roda VI, 363
Barret, Samuel III, 459
Barret, Samuel A. III, 395
Barret, Sarah IV, 1144
Barret, Slocumb IV, 1144
Barrett, ??? III, 27
Barrett, ??? III, 30
Barrett, A. H. V, 221
Barrett, Abbie V, 452
Barrett, Abi V, 221
Barrett, Abi V, 255
Barrett, Abi V, 451
Barrett, Abi V, 658
Barrett, Adam V, 221
Barrett, Agnes Roberta III, 27
Barrett, Albert IV, 320
Barrett, Albert IV, 510
Barrett, Alfred V, 220
Barrett, Alfred V, 451
Barrett, Amon V, 221
Barrett, Amon Edward V, 221
Barrett, Amos VI, 362
Barrett, Amy IV, 248
Barrett, Amy IV, 320
Barrett, Amy IV, 510
Barrett, Amy V, 23
Barrett, Amy V, 298
Barrett, Amy VI, 363
Barrett, Ann II, 459
Barrett, Ann II, 578
Barrett, Ann IV, 320
Barrett, Ann IV, 510
Barrett, Ann IV, 551
Barrett, Ann Maria V, 220
Barrett, Anna I, 525
Barrett, Anna V, 219
Barrett, Anna V, 220
Barrett, Anna V, 247
Barrett, Anna V, 257
Barrett, Anna V, 373
Barrett, Anna V, 398
Barrett, Anna V, 451
Barrett, Anna V, 468
Barrett, Anna M. V, 220
Barrett, Anna M. V, 293
Barrett, Anna M. V, 468
Barrett, Anna R. V, 467
Barrett, Annie G. II, 835
Barrett, Arther VI, 363
Barrett, Arthur I, 1026
Barrett, Arthur IV, 320
Barrett, Arthur IV, 510
Barrett, Arthur V, 221
Barrett, Arthur VI, 363
Barrett, Athanasious V, 151
Barrett, Athanasious V, 188
Barrett, Augusta V, 221
Barrett, Austa E. V, 221
Barrett, Austie V, 221
Barrett, Avanella V, 151
Barrett, B. H. V, 221
Barrett, Baldin IV, 173
Barrett, Baldin IV, 285
Barrett, Baldwin IV, 320
Barrett, Baldwin IV, 510
Barrett, Baldwin IV, 553
Barrett, Belinda IV, 320
Barrett, Belinda IV, 510
Barrett, Belinda IV, 516
Barrett, Benjamin I, 1026
Barrett, Benjamin V, 23
Barrett, Benjamin V, 220
Barrett, Benjamin V, 221
Barrett, Benjamin V, 451
Barrett, Benjamin V, 452
Barrett, Benjamin VI, 362
Barrett, Benjamin VI, 363
Barrett, Benjamin VI, 430
Barrett, Bertha V, 221
Barrett, Bertha V, 452
Barrett, Bertha VI, 363
Barrett, Bertha B. V, 220
Barrett, Bertha O. V, 221
Barrett, Bertha V. VI, 363
Barrett, Bessie VI, 363
Barrett, Bessie M. III, 27
Barrett, Bessie M. III, 100
Barrett, Byrdia V, 452
Barrett, C. Leslie V, 220
Barrett, C. Maynard V, 451
Barrett, Calista V, 23
Barrett, Caroline E. V, 151
Barrett, Carrie Bertha V, 220
Barrett, Carrie E. V, 151
Barrett, Catherine V, 220
Barrett, Charles E. VI, 363
Barrett, Charles Lee II, 459
Barrett, Chas. Vernon V, 220
Barrett, Clara B. V, 151
Barrett, Clara Bell V, 221
Barrett, Clara C. V, 220
Barrett, Clara C. V, 451
Barrett, Clara L. V, 221
Barrett, Clarabel V, 151
Barrett, Clarabel V, 174
Barrett, Clarence V, 221
Barrett, Claude V, 221
Barrett, Claude E. V, 221
Barrett, Clinton Delos V, 220
Barrett, Cora V, 451
Barrett, Cyrus V, 452
Barrett, Daniel V, 219
Barrett, Daniel V, 220
Barrett, Daniel V, 229
Barrett, David IV, 74
Barrett, David IV, 320
Barrett, David IV, 510
Barrett, David V, 219
Barrett, David V, 220
Barrett, David V, 256
Barrett, David V, 451
Barrett, David V, 466
Barrett, David VI, 362
Barrett, David VI, 363
Barrett, David VI, 367
Barrett, David VI, 374
Barrett, David Barrett V, 220
Barrett, Davis V, 451
Barrett, Deborah VI, 363
Barrett, Delila V, 220
Barrett, Delila V, 265
Barrett, Delilah V, 219
Barrett, Delilah V, 220
Barrett, Delilah V, 373
Barrett, Delilah V, 417
Barrett, Delilah V, 451
Barrett, Denson V, 219
Barrett, Denson V, 220
Barrett, Denson V, 451
Barrett, Denson V, 452
Barrett, Denson V, 658
Barrett, Don C. V, 151
Barrett, Don Carlos V, 151
Barrett, E. Iona V, 451
Barrett, Earnest Clifford V, 151
Barrett, Eddie V, 221
Barrett, Edgar V, 451
Barrett, Edith V, 451
Barrett, Edith V, 452
Barrett, Edward III, 27
Barrett, Eleanor V, 23
Barrett, Eleanor V, 219
Barrett, Eleanor V, 220
Barrett, Eleanor V, 240
Barrett, Eleanor V, 276
Barrett, Eleanor VI, 362
Barrett, Eleanor VI, 363
Barrett, Eleanor VI, 380
Barrett, Eleanor VI, 403
Barrett, Eleanor F. III, 27
Barrett, Elenor V, 220
Barrett, Eli V, 219
Barrett, Eli S. V, 220
Barrett, Eli S. V, 221
Barrett, Elias M. V, 220
Barrett, Elinor VI, 362
Barrett, Eliza V, 219
Barrett, Eliza V, 220
Barrett, Elizabeth II, 54
Barrett, Elizabeth II, 104
Barrett, Elizabeth IV, 320
Barrett, Elizabeth IV, 510
Barrett, Elizabeth IV, 536
Barrett, Elizabeth IV, 864
Barrett, Elizabeth V, 219
Barrett, Elizabeth V, 220
Barrett, Elizabeth V, 221
Barrett, Elizabeth V, 466
Barrett, Elizabeth V, 475
Barrett, Elizabeth V, 657
Barrett, Elizabeth VI, 362
Barrett, Elizabeth VI, 363
Barrett, Elizabeth VI, 391
Barrett, Elizabeth VI, 409
Barrett, Elizabeth VI, 451
Barrett, Ella V, 151
Barrett, Ella M. V, 151
Barrett, Ella M. V, 549
Barrett, Ella M. V, 574
Barrett, Ellen V, 221
Barrett, Ellenor V, 219
Barrett, Ellinor VI, 430
Barrett, Ellis V, 23
Barrett, Ellis V, 219
Barrett, Ellis V, 220
Barrett, Ellis V, 257
Barrett, Ellis V, 451
Barrett, Ellis V, 468
Barrett, Ellis VI, 363
Barrett, Elsa V, 452
Barrett, Elsie V, 451
Barrett, Emily VI, 363
Barrett, Emily VI, 731
Barrett, Emily J. VI, 363
Barrett, Emily J. VI, 419
Barrett, Emily Reynolds VI, 744
Barrett, Emma V, 451
Barrett, Emma A. V, 221
Barrett, Enos V, 220
Barrett, Enos J. V, 221
Barrett, Enos J. V, 451
Barrett, Enos Jewry V, 220
Barrett, Ernest Clifford V, 151
Barrett, Esther IV, 320
Barrett, Esther IV, 510
Barrett, Ethel V, 452
Barrett, Ethel Kathleen V, 658
Barrett, Etta V, 451
Barrett, Ezekiel V, 319
Barrett, Fannie V, 452
Barrett, Fannie Ray III, 27
Barrett, Fannie Ray III, 109
Barrett, Frances V, 451
Barrett, Frank V, 221
Barrett, Frank V, 452
Barrett, Frank V, 658
Barrett, Freddie V, 151
Barrett, Frederick Enos V, 451
Barrett, Frederick W. V, 151
Barrett, Frederick Weller V, 152
Barrett, Geo. W. V, 451
Barrett, Geo. W. V, 467
Barrett, George III, 27
Barrett, George V, 23
Barrett, George VI, 1004
Barrett, George E. V, 451
Barrett, George Edgar V, 220
Barrett, Georgianna V, 658
Barrett, Georgianna V, 682
Barrett, Georgie V, 221
Barrett, Gideon V, 221
Barrett, Gideon F. V, 221
Barrett, Glenn V, 221
Barrett, Hannah IV, 74
Barrett, Hannah V, 220

Barrett, Hannah V, 229
Barrett, Hannah V, 451
Barrett, Hannah VI, 363
Barrett, Harry Milton V, 220
Barrett, Harry Wraymond V, 220
Barrett, Helen V, 221
Barrett, Hellen V, 658
Barrett, Hester V, 220
Barrett, Hibbard II, 781
Barrett, Homer V, 451
Barrett, Horace Leslie V, 451
Barrett, Hubert V, 221
Barrett, Hubert V, 658
Barrett, Hubert A. V, 658
Barrett, Hubert A. V, 661
Barrett, Hurbert A. V, 658
Barrett, I. W. V, 151
Barrett, Immer IV, 510
Barrett, Ione V, 221
Barrett, Isaac III, 27
Barrett, Isaac M. V, 23
Barrett, Isaac M. V, 151
Barrett, Isaac M. V, 166
Barrett, Isaac M. V, 174
Barrett, J. Arthur V, 221
Barrett, Jacob I, 1026
Barrett, Jacob V, 219
Barrett, Jacob V, 475
Barrett, Jacob VI, 363
Barrett, Jacob, Jr. I, 1026
Barrett, James I, 1026
Barrett, James I, 1077
Barrett, James I, 1089
Barrett, James III, 27
Barrett, James V, 220
Barrett, James V, 221
Barrett, James VI, 362
Barrett, James VI, 363
Barrett, James VI, 425
Barrett, James VI, 459
Barrett, James VI, 469
Barrett, James C. III, 27
Barrett, James G. V, 221
Barrett, James G. V, 451
Barrett, James G. V, 452
Barrett, James J. V, 451
Barrett, James R. VI, 363
Barrett, James T. III, 100
Barrett, Jane V, 151
Barrett, Jane V, 221
Barrett, Jane VI, 826
Barrett, Jeannette III, 27
Barrett, Jemime I, 1026
Barrett, Jennie B. V, 248
Barrett, Jennie M. V, 151
Barrett, Jeremiah VI, 363
Barrett, Jesse V, 23
Barrett, Jesse V, 219
Barrett, Jesse V, 220
Barrett, Jesse V, 451
Barrett, Jesse VI, 363
Barrett, Jesse W. V, 221
Barrett, Jesse William V, 220
Barrett, Jessie V, 452
Barrett, John I, 1026
Barrett, John I, 1038
Barrett, John II, 335
Barrett, John II, 441
Barrett, John IV, 864
Barrett, John V, 23
Barrett, John V, 151
Barrett, John V, 219
Barrett, John V, 221
Barrett, John V, 248
Barrett, John V, 451
Barrett, John VI, 362
Barrett, John VI, 363
Barrett, John VI, 416
Barrett, John Chandler V, 220
Barrett, John R. V, 23
Barrett, John R. V, 151
Barrett, Jonas V, 221
Barrett, Jonas T. V, 221
Barrett, Jonathan I, 1026
Barrett, Jonathan V, 23
Barrett, Jonathan V, 215
Barrett, Jonathan V, 219
Barrett, Jonathan V, 220
Barrett, Jonathan V, 235
Barrett, Jonathan V, 257
Barrett, Jonathan V, 373
Barrett, Jonathan VI, 362
Barrett, Jonathan VI, 391
Barrett, Joseph I, 1026
Barrett, Joseph I Sup 1, 10
Barrett, Joseph II, 335
Barrett, Joseph IV, 510
Barrett, Joseph V, 219
Barrett, Joseph V, 451
Barrett, Joseph VI, 363
Barrett, Joseph C. V, 221
Barrett, Joseph M. V, 220
Barrett, Joseph M. V, 263
Barrett, Josephine V, 262
Barrett, Josephine A. V, 221
Barrett, Laura V, 221
Barrett, Lavena V, 451
Barrett, Lavinia V, 221
Barrett, Lawrence V, 151
Barrett, Lawrence Doan V, 220
Barrett, Lawrence H. V, 151
Barrett, Leah VI, 363
Barrett, Leslie V, 221
Barrett, Leslie V, 451
Barrett, Levi V, 23
Barrett, Levi V, 219
Barrett, Levi V, 220
Barrett, Levi V, 236
Barrett, Levi V, 247
Barrett, Levi V, 265
Barrett, Levi V, 268
Barrett, Levi V, 373
Barrett, Levi V, 417
Barrett, Levi VI, 363
Barrett, Lida V, 221
Barrett, Lida V, 451
Barrett, Lora V, 221
Barrett, Louise V, 221
Barrett, Lucile V, 658
Barrett, Lucy E. III, 27
Barrett, Lucy E. III, 100
Barrett, Lucy E. III, 109
Barrett, Lula V, 221
Barrett, Lydia I, 525
Barrett, Lydia I, 1026
Barrett, Lydia V, 23
Barrett, Lydia V, 219
Barrett, Lydia V, 220
Barrett, Lydia V, 235
Barrett, Lydia V, 268
Barrett, Lydia V, 307
Barrett, Lydia V, 373
Barrett, Lydia V, 423
Barrett, Lydia V, 452
Barrett, Lydia VI, 362
Barrett, Lydia VI, 363
Barrett, Lydia VI, 413
Barrett, Lydia VI, 423
Barrett, Lydia Ann V, 452
Barrett, M. Corrine V, 151
Barrett, M. Corrinn V, 151
Barrett, M. E. V, 221
Barrett, M. Ella V, 221
Barrett, Mabel E. V, 451
Barrett, Madge IV, 1306
Barrett, Maggie V, 451
Barrett, Mahala V, 23
Barrett, Mahala V, 220
Barrett, Mahala V, 373
Barrett, Mahala V, 417
Barrett, Mahala M. V, 23
Barrett, Mahala M. V, 129
Barrett, Malinda V, 220
Barrett, Malinda V, 280
Barrett, Malinda V, 451
Barrett, Margaret IV, 173
Barrett, Margaret IV, 320
Barrett, Margaret IV, 510
Barrett, Margaret V, 151
Barrett, Margaret V, 188
Barrett, Margaret V, 219
Barrett, Margaret V, 220
Barrett, Margaret V, 451
Barrett, Margaret Ellen Ellis V, 220
Barrett, Maria V, 23
Barrett, Maria V, 32
Barrett, Maria V, 219
Barrett, Mariah V, 220
Barrett, Mariell V, 23
Barrett, Martha Ellen V, 221
Barrett, Mary IV, 20
Barrett, Mary IV, 74
Barrett, Mary IV, 173
Barrett, Mary IV, 226
Barrett, Mary IV, 320
Barrett, Mary IV, 510
Barrett, Mary IV, 536
Barrett, Mary IV, 1245
Barrett, Mary IV, 1306
Barrett, Mary V, 151
Barrett, Mary V, 166
Barrett, Mary V, 174
Barrett, Mary V, 221
Barrett, Mary V, 248
Barrett, Mary V, 451
Barrett, Mary V, 452
Barrett, Mary V, 469
Barrett, Mary V, 612
Barrett, Mary V, 633
Barrett, Mary V, 658
Barrett, Mary V, 695
Barrett, Mary V, 797
Barrett, Mary VI, 362
Barrett, Mary VI, 363
Barrett, Mary VI, 391
Barrett, Mary VI, 416
Barrett, Mary VI, 469
Barrett, Mary A. V, 451
Barrett, Mary Ann IV, 173
Barrett, Mary Ann IV, 285
Barrett, Mary Ann IV, 510
Barrett, Mary Ann IV, 553
Barrett, Mary B. VI, 363
Barrett, Mary Bell VI, 363
Barrett, Mary Coffin V, 452
Barrett, Mary Coffin V, 658
Barrett, Mary E. V, 220
Barrett, Mary E. V, 221
Barrett, Mary E. V, 263
Barrett, Mary Ellen V, 151
Barrett, Mary Guthrie V, 221
Barrett, Mary J. III, 27
Barrett, Mary J. V, 221
Barrett, Mary Jane III, 27
Barrett, Mary Jane V, 451
Barrett, Mary L. V, 23
Barrett, Mary Louise V, 658
Barrett, Mary Walton IV, 798
Barrett, Mary, Jr. VI, 363
Barrett, Marybelle V, 166
Barrett, Maryelle V, 151
Barrett, Maryelle V, 166
Barrett, Maud V, 221
Barrett, Maude V, 221
Barrett, May Swayne V, 151
Barrett, Melicent V, 220
Barrett, Melinda IV, 320
Barrett, Mildred V, 151
Barrett, Milford V, 151
Barrett, Milicent V, 220
Barrett, Milicent V, 256
Barrett, Millicent V, 220
Barrett, Millicent V, 451
Barrett, Millicent V, 466
Barrett, Milton V, 219
Barrett, Milton V, 220
Barrett, Milton V, 373
Barrett, Milton V, 417
Barrett, Minerva V, 475
Barrett, Minerva Jane V, 220
Barrett, Minerva Jane V, 475
Barrett, Minerva Jane V, 537
Barrett, Minnie V, 221
Barrett, Mordecai V, 220
Barrett, Nancey VI, 1004
Barrett, Nancy V, 221
Barrett, Nancy V, 451
Barrett, Nancy Ellen V, 221
Barrett, Nathan IV, 798
Barrett, Nathan VI, 363
Barrett, Nathan Walton IV, 20
Barrett, Nellie V, 452
Barrett, Nora V, 452
Barrett, Pearl V, 452
Barrett, Phebe V, 221
Barrett, Phebe V, 373
Barrett, Phebe V, 451
Barrett, Phebe V, 797
Barrett, Phebe VI, 362
Barrett, Phebe VI, 363
Barrett, Phebe VI, 430
Barrett, Phebe VI, 459
Barrett, Phebe VI, 469
Barrett, Phebe L. V, 221
Barrett, Phebe L. V, 658
Barrett, Phebe M. III, 27
Barrett, Phoebe V, 221
Barrett, R. E. V, 151
Barrett, R. P. V, 221
Barrett, Rachel II, 54
Barrett, Rachel IV, 20
Barrett, Rachel IV, 74
Barrett, Rachel IV, 320
Barrett, Rachel IV, 510
Barrett, Rachel IV, 798
Barrett, Rachel V, 23
Barrett, Rachel V, 219
Barrett, Rachel V, 220
Barrett, Rachel V, 235
Barrett, Rachel V, 257
Barrett, Rachel V, 373
Barrett, Rachel V, 459
Barrett, Rachel VI, 362
Barrett, Rachel VI, 363
Barrett, Rachel VI, 374
Barrett, Rachel VI, 425
Barrett, Rachel VI, 453
Barrett, Rachel A. V, 451
Barrett, Rachel Ann V, 220
Barrett, Rachel Barrett IV, 20
Barrett, Ralph E. V, 451
Barrett, Rebecca V, 220
Barrett, Rebecca J. V, 221
Barrett, Rebecca L. V, 947
Barrett, Rebecca S. V, 23
Barrett, Reuben Putman V, 658
Barrett, Rhoda I, 1026
Barrett, Rhoda I, 1038
Barrett, Rhoda V, 221
Barrett, Rhoda V, 451
Barrett, Rhoda V, 467
Barrett, Rhoda VI, 362
Barrett, Rhoda VI, 363
Barrett, Rhoda VI, 416
Barrett, Rhoda VI, 444
Barrett, Richard V, 23
Barrett, Richard V, 215
Barrett, Richard V, 219
Barrett, Richard V, 220
Barrett, Richard V, 276
Barrett, Richard V, 280
Barrett, Richard V, 295
Barrett, Richard VI, 362
Barrett, Richard VI, 363
Barrett, Richard C. V, 221
Barrett, Richard Cyrus V, 451
Barrett, Richard Cyrus V, 658
Barrett, Richard L. V, 221
Barrett, Richard L. V, 451
Barrett, Richard Warren V, 451
Barrett, Richard Warren V, 658
Barrett, Richard, Jr. V, 298
Barrett, Robert W. V, 220
Barrett, Roda VI, 363
Barrett, Rosa V, 23
Barrett, Rosa B. IV, 320
Barrett, Rosa B. IV, 357
Barrett, Rosa B. P. V, 658
Barrett, Rose V, 658
Barrett, Rose Eugenia V, 221
Barrett, Roxie V, 221
Barrett, Roy V, 221
Barrett, Rueben P. V, 221
Barrett, Russell V, 221
Barrett, Ruth IV, 510
Barrett, Ruth V, 221
Barrett, Ruth Anna V, 221
Barrett, Sallie V, 221
Barrett, Sally V, 219
Barrett, Sanford VI, 731
Barrett, Sarah IV, 74
Barrett, Sarah IV, 173
Barrett, Sarah IV, 311
Barrett, Sarah IV, 313
Barrett, Sarah IV, 320
Barrett, Sarah IV, 509
Barrett, Sarah IV, 510
Barrett, Sarah V, 23
Barrett, Sarah V, 215
Barrett, Sarah V, 219
Barrett, Sarah V, 220
Barrett, Sarah V, 276
Barrett, Sarah V, 451
Barrett, Sarah VI, 362
Barrett, Sarah VI, 363
Barrett, Sarah VI, 425
Barrett, Sarah VI, 455
Barrett, Sarah VI, 731
Barrett, Sarah VI, 1004
Barrett, Sarah E. V, 451
Barrett, Sarah Elizabeth V, 452
Barrett, Sarah Elizabeth V, 658
Barrett, Sarah Eunice V, 220
Barrett, Sarah Lucile V, 658
Barrett, Sarah Lucile V, 661
Barrett, Sarah Lydia V, 373
Barrett, Sidney V, 298
Barrett, Sidney V, 310
Barrett, Sidney VI, 363
Barrett, Sidney VI, 381
Barrett, Silas V, 219
Barrett, Slocum V, 23
Barrett, Stanley V, 451
Barrett, Stephen VI, 744
Barrett, Stephens VI, 731
Barrett, Susanna V, 220
Barrett, Susanna V, 373
Barrett, Susannah V, 219
Barrett, Susannah V, 236
Barrett, Susannah V, 247
Barrett, Susannah V, 268
Barrett, Susannah V, 373
Barrett, Swayne V, 151
Barrett, Sydney V, 23
Barrett, T. S. V, 151
Barrett, T. Swayne V, 151
Barrett, Thomas II, 54
Barrett, Thomas II, 104
Barrett, Thomas IV, 173
Barrett, Thomas IV, 320
Barrett, Thomas IV, 510
Barrett, Thomas V, 451
Barrett, Thomas VI, 362
Barrett, Thomas VI, 363
Barrett, Thomas VI, 391
Barrett, Thomas VI, 451
Barrett, Thomas S. V, 23
Barrett, Thomas Swayne V, 151
Barrett, Thos. IV, 173
Barrett, Thos. Swayne V, 23
Barrett, Thos., Jr. IV, 510
Barrett, Uriah IV, 320
Barrett, Uriah IV, 510
Barrett, Virginia F. V, 451
Barrett, Virginia Frances V, 451
Barrett, Vivian Maurine V, 220
Barrett, W. O. Vernon V, 452
Barrett, Walter V, 452
Barrett, Walter C. V, 451
Barrett, Warden IV, 173
Barrett, Warden IV, 226
Barrett, Warden IV, 320
Barrett, Warden IV, 510
Barrett, Warden IV, 536
Barrett, Warren V, 452
Barrett, Wd. Anne Gibson II, 781
Barrett, William IV, 320
Barrett, William IV, 510
Barrett, William VI, 362
Barrett, William VI, 363
Barrett, William VI, 413
Barrett, William VI, 453
Barrett, William VI, 469
Barrett, William Austin V, 220
Barrett, William Carry V, 220
Barrett, William Curry V, 220
Barrett, William W. V, 451
Barrett, Winifred IV, 510
Barrett, Winifred IV, 555
Barrett, Winnefred IV, 320
Barrett, Wm. V, 451
Barrett, Wm. Elmer V, 658
Barrett, Wyman R. III, 27
Barrette, Frank V, 221
Barrettes, John II, 335
Barrick, Aaron Chalfont V, 221
Barrick, Elizabeth V, 221
Barrick, Elizabeth V, 285
Barrick, Elizabeth V, 319
Barrick, Elizabeth V, 323
Barrick, Elizabeth Barrick V, 221
Barrick, Jane V, 221
Barrick, John V, 319
Barrick, John Timberlake V, 221
Barrick, Mary V, 323
Barrick, Nancy V, 221
Barrick, Nancy V, 319
Barrick, Russel V, 323
Barrick, Russell VI, 876
Barrick, Sally VI, 876
Barricks, John W. VI, 798
Barricks, Louisa VI, 798
Barricks, Mary A. VI, 803
Barricks, Mary Ann VI, 798
Barricks, Mary I. VI, 798
Barricks, Moore VI, 798
Barricks, Moore VI, 803
Barricks, Polly VI, 298
Barricks, Polly VI, 798
Barricks, Rhoda VI, 798
Barricks, Russell VI, 298
Barricks, Russell VI, 798
Barricks, Susanna VI, 798
Barricks, William VI, 798
Barricks, William VI, 819
Barringer, Ella I, 621
Barringer, Ella I, 622
Barringer, Ella I, 629
Barringer, Ella I, 637
Barringer, Geo. L. V, 893
Barringer, George L. V, 893
Barringer, Margaret I, 621
Barringer, Sarah IV, 924
Barringer, Sarah IV, 988
Barringer, Susan V, 893
Barrington, Benjamin III, 27
Barrington, Bethia M. IV, 1197
Barrington, Bethia M. IV, 1198
Barrington, Charles Burdick III, 27
Barrington, Elizabeth IV, 1144
Barrington, Elizabeth IV, 1184
Barrington, Elizabeth W. IV, 1144
Barrington, Elizabeth W. IV, 1189
Barrington, George IV, 1144
Barrington, Hannah IV, 1144
Barrington, Jane III, 27
Barrington, Jennie III, 27
Barrington, Joseph IV, 1144
Barrington, Joseph IV, 1184
Barrington, Joseph VI, 991
Barrington, Kate III, 27
Barrington, Mark IV, 1144
Barrington, Robert Walker III, 27

Barrington, Ruth IV, 1144
Barrington, Sarah III, 27
Barrington, Thomas IV, 1144
Barrington, Thos. IV, 1189
Barrington, William Thomas III, 27
Barrit, Jacob VI, 363
Barritt, James VI, 363
Barrix, Elizabeth V, 221
Barrix, Elizabeth V, 228
Barron, Alice I, 981
Barron, Edward F. III, 27
Barron, Edward F. III, 329
Barron, Elizabeth I, 981
Barron, Elizabeth III, 27
Barron, Elizabeth III, 329
Barron, Elizabeth E. III, 27
Barron, Margaret III, 27
Barron, Margaret III, 329
Barron, Sarah I, 93
Barrot, Elizabeth II, 21
Barrot, Gwen II, 21
Barrot, James I, 1026
Barrot, Phebe VI, 363
Barrot, Thos. II, 21
Barrott, Ann II, 196
Barrott, Ann II, 263
Barrough, Annie G. II, 146
Barroughs, Rachel I, 525
Barrow, Abigail III, 27
Barrow, Ann I, 23
Barrow, Anna I, 25
Barrow, Anna J. III, 27
Barrow, Anne I, 36
Barrow, Anne I, 78
Barrow, Arrodi I, 36
Barrow, Caroline J. III, 27
Barrow, Caroline K. III, 27
Barrow, Charles Henry III, 28
Barrow, Delilah I, 36
Barrow, Delilah I, 46
Barrow, Edmund Prior III, 27
Barrow, Edmund Prior III, 28
Barrow, Edward III, 28
Barrow, Eleanor III, 27
Barrow, Eleanor P. III, 27
Barrow, Elizabeth I Sup 1, 3
Barrow, Elizabeth I Sup 1, 6
Barrow, Elizabeth I Sup 1, 8
Barrow, Elizabeth III, 27
Barrow, Elizabeth III, 28
Barrow, Elizabeth K. III, 27
Barrow, Elizabeth M. III, 27
Barrow, Elizabeth Moode III, 395
Barrow, Elizabeth Moode III, 438
Barrow, Eri I, 36
Barrow, George I Sup 1, 3
Barrow, George I Sup 1, 6
Barrow, George III, 28
Barrow, Hannah III, 27
Barrow, Henry III, 27
Barrow, Henry III, 184
Barrow, Henry H. III, 27
Barrow, Henry H. III, 28
Barrow, James I Sup 1, 3
Barrow, Jane I Sup 1, 7
Barrow, Jeane I, 36
Barrow, Jeane I, 55
Barrow, John I, 36
Barrow, John I, 47
Barrow, John I, 66
Barrow, John I, 87
Barrow, John I, 101
Barrow, John I Sup 1, 3
Barrow, John I Sup 1, 6
Barrow, John I Sup 1, 8
Barrow, John III, 27
Barrow, John III, 28
Barrow, John III, 160
Barrow, John III, 339
Barrow, John III, 395
Barrow, John D. III, 28
Barrow, John Denson I, 36
Barrow, John Dodgson III, 28
Barrow, John, Jr. I, 36
Barrow, John, Jr. I Sup 1, 8
Barrow, John, Jr. III, 27
Barrow, John, Jr. III, 28
Barrow, John, Jr. III, 395
Barrow, John, Jr. III, 438
Barrow, Joseph I, 36
Barrow, Joseph I, 46
Barrow, Joseph I, 189
Barrow, Joseph I, 193
Barrow, Joseph I Sup 1, 3
Barrow, Joseph I Sup 1, 5
Barrow, Joseph I Sup 1, 7
Barrow, Joseph, Jr. I, 36
Barrow, Joseph, Jr. I, 129
Barrow, Joseph, Jr. I, 132
Barrow, Joseph, Sr. I, 36
Barrow, Joseph, Sr. I, 129
Barrow, Joseph, Sr. I, 165
Barrow, Lemuel I, 36
Barrow, Margaret I, 36
Barrow, Margaret I, 47
Barrow, Margaret I, 71
Barrow, Margaret I, 189
Barrow, Margret I Sup 1, 8
Barrow, Martha I, 36
Barrow, Mary III, 27
Barrow, Mary III, 28
Barrow, Mary III, 339
Barrow, Mary III, 395
Barrow, Mary K. III, 27
Barrow, Mary K. III, 184
Barrow, Mary L. III, 28
Barrow, Orpah I, 36
Barrow, Orpah I, 78
Barrow, Rachel I Sup 1, 8
Barrow, Rebecca III, 27
Barrow, Rebecca III, 160
Barrow, Rebecca H. III, 28
Barrow, Rebekah I Sup 1, 8
Barrow, Robert II, 335
Barrow, Sarah I, 36
Barrow, Sarah I, 51
Barrow, Sarah I, 66
Barrow, Sarah I, 71
Barrow, Sarah I, 87
Barrow, Sarah I, 129
Barrow, Sarah I, 132
Barrow, Sarah I, 162
Barrow, Sarah I Sup 1, 3
Barrow, Sarah I Sup 1, 5
Barrow, Sarah I Sup 1, 8
Barrow, Stephen I, 36
Barrow, Thomas III, 28
Barrow, Thomas W. III, 27
Barrow, Widow Jane I, 101
Barrow, Widow Margaret I, 193
Barrow, Widow Sarah I, 165
Barrow, William I, 36
Barrow, William I, 129
Barrow, William III, 28
Barrows, Laura L. III, 424
Barrows, Laura L. III, 471
Barry, ??? III, 211
Barry, E. E. IV, 1201
Barry, Elizabeth II, 459
Barry, Elizabeth II, 460
Barry, Esther III, 28
Barry, Esther Lenora IV, 1245
Barry, H. E. IV, 1245
Barry, Hannah M. IV, 1201
Barry, Hazel IV, 1201
Barry, Hazel Bell IV, 1245
Barry, Hazel E. IV, 1201
Barry, Jessie B. IV, 1245
Barry, John III, 28
Barry, Joseph II, 335
Barry, Laurence A. IV, 1201
Barry, Lawrence IV, 1201
Barry, Levallen II, 459
Barry, Lottie Pearl IV, 1201
Barry, Margaret II, 459
Barry, Margaret II, 460
Barry, Margaret II, 498
Barry, Mary II, 335
Barry, Mary II, 459
Barry, Phila A. III, 28
Barry, Phila A. III, 29
Barry, Rebecca III, 28
Barry, Sally Ann III, 211
Barry, Samuel II, 781
Barry, Samuel J. III, 77
Barry, Sarah II, 335
Barry, Sarah II, 459
Barry, Tacy II, 459
Barry, Tacy II, 460
Barry, Walter II, 335
Barry, Walter III, 77
Barry, William III, 28
Barry, Wm. III, 29
Barshaw, Pleasant VI, 731
Barson, Rachel II, 460
Barson, Rachel II, 627
Barsto, Mary Ann VI, 847
Barston, Amy II, 977
Barstow, Amy II, 1001
Bartee, Frances VI, 1009
Bartee, Richard D. VI, 1017
Bartee, Sarah I, 36
Bartee, Sarah I, 68
Barten, Edward II, 196
Barten, Edward II, 220
Barten, Edward II, 276
Barten, John II, 196
Barten, Mary II, 196
Barten, Mary II, 220
Barten, Sarah II, 196
Barten, Sarah II, 276
Barterum, Darby II, 196
Barterum, Elisabeth II, 196
Barterum, Elisabeth II, 261
Bartham, Frances Miller VI, 731
Bartham, Thomas VI, 731
Barthelow, Eva IV, 1035
Barthelow, John IV, 1035
Barthelow, John W. IV, 1035
Barthelow, Mary IV, 511
Barthelow, Mary IV, 541
Barthlow, Eva IV, 1035
Barthlow, John IV, 1035
Bartholemew, Grace IV, 1035
Bartholf, James V, 221
Bartholf, Rebecca V, 221
Bartholomew, Berrilla B. VI, 774
Bartholomew, Emma II, 835
Bartholomew, George II, 335
Bartholomew, George II, 460
Bartholomew, Howard I, 275
Bartholomew, Mary II, 460
Bartholomew, Mary II, 977
Bartholomew, Mary II, 984
Bartholomew, Ruth I, 275
Bartholomew, Sarah Ann VI, 774
Bartie, John L. VI, 839
Bartin, Edward II, 276
Bartin, Mary E. IV, 1164
Bartin, Sarah II, 196
Bartin, Sarah II, 250
Bartin, Sarah II, 276
Bartlet, William VI, 93
Bartlett, Adaline IV, 1088
Bartlett, Adaline IV, 1095
Bartlett, Agnes IV, 1145
Bartlett, Agnes IV, 1238
Bartlett, Agnes IV, 1242
Bartlett, Agnes McCollon IV, 1233
Bartlett, Alfred IV, 1145
Bartlett, Alfred H. IV, 1233
Bartlett, Ann IV, 1233
Bartlett, Ann B. IV, 1145
Bartlett, Ann B. IV, 1233
Bartlett, Ann B. IV, 1239
Bartlett, Ann B. IV, 1242
Bartlett, Ann P. IV, 1145
Bartlett, Ann P. IV, 1233
Bartlett, Anna Glover II, 280
Bartlett, Anna Glover II, 301
Bartlett, Anna Mary IV, 1233
Bartlett, Annie O. IV, 1233
Bartlett, Armett IV, 1242
Bartlett, Ballard VI, 252
Bartlett, Caleb Hunt IV, 74
Bartlett, Deliverence IV, 1145
Bartlett, Della IV, 1306
Bartlett, Edith Louisa III, 28
Bartlett, Edward III, 28
Bartlett, Edward III, 48
Bartlett, Eliza IV, 1231
Bartlett, Elizabeth D. IV, 1145
Bartlett, Elizabeth D. IV, 1167
Bartlett, Elizabeth D. IV, 1233
Bartlett, Elizabeth Louisa III, 28
Bartlett, Elizabeth Louisa III, 48
Bartlett, Ellen B. IV, 1145
Bartlett, Ellen B. IV, 1233
Bartlett, Emily IV, 1145
Bartlett, Emma IV, 1233
Bartlett, Emma Laura IV, 1233
Bartlett, Ernest Russell III, 28
Bartlett, Eva II, 311
Bartlett, Fannie I, 335
Bartlett, Frank IV, 1242
Bartlett, George V, 985
Bartlett, George J. IV, 1242
Bartlett, George James IV, 1145
Bartlett, George James IV, 1233
Bartlett, Harriett G. IV, 1233
Bartlett, Hattie G. IV, 1233
Bartlett, Henrietta IV, 1145
Bartlett, J. Henry II, 727
Bartlett, J. Henry V, 23
Bartlett, James IV, 1144
Bartlett, James IV, 1145
Bartlett, James IV, 1233
Bartlett, James IV, 1242
Bartlett, Jane W. II, 727
Bartlett, Jarvis H. II, 280
Bartlett, Jarvis H. II, 301
Bartlett, John III, 28
Bartlett, John Kemp II, 835
Bartlett, John Kemp III, 28
Bartlett, Joseph IV, 74
Bartlett, Joseph IV, 1145
Bartlett, Joseph IV, 1167
Bartlett, Joseph IV, 1233
Bartlett, Joseph B. IV, 1233
Bartlett, Joseph Bartlett IV, 74
Bartlett, Josh W. III, 28
Bartlett, Judith VI, 252
Bartlett, Lavinia IV, 1145
Bartlett, Lizzie Louisa III, 28
Bartlett, Martha Culver IV, 1242
Bartlett, Martha W. IV, 1145
Bartlett, Martha W. IV, 1233
Bartlett, Martha W. IV, 1242
Bartlett, Mary Ann IV, 1088
Bartlett, Mary Ann IV, 1110
Bartlett, Mary Elizabeth III, 28
Bartlett, Mary H. IV, 1088
Bartlett, Mary H. IV, 1115
Bartlett, Mary P. IV, 1145
Bartlett, Mary P. IV, 1233
Bartlett, Matilda P. II, 280
Bartlett, Matilda P. II, 301
Bartlett, Mrs. Della IV, 1306
Bartlett, Nathan IV, 1145
Bartlett, Phebe Ann IV, 1144
Bartlett, Phebe Ann IV, 1145
Bartlett, Phebe Ann IV, 1231
Bartlett, Phebe Ann IV, 1233
Bartlett, Phebe Ann IV, 1242
Bartlett, Phebe M. III, 28
Bartlett, Rhoda Hunt IV, 74
Bartlett, Rhoda M. IV, 74
Bartlett, Rohda M. IV, 94
Bartlett, Samuel Pharo II, 280
Bartlett, Samuel Pharo II, 301
Bartlett, Sarah II, 460
Bartlett, Sarah II, 643
Bartlett, Sarah III, 28
Bartlett, Sarah IV, 73
Bartlett, Sarah IV, 74
Bartlett, Sarah A. V, 23
Bartlett, Sarah A. V, 120
Bartlett, Sarah Elizabeth III, 28
Bartlett, Sattie V, 120
Bartlett, Susan Jane IV, 1145
Bartlett, Susan Jane IV, 1242
Bartlett, Susan Jane Williams IV, 1242
Bartlett, Susan M. III, 28
Bartlett, Thomas II, 460
Bartlett, Thomas III, 28
Bartlett, Walter VI, 41
Bartlett, Willets G. IV, 1233
Bartlett, William III, 28
Bartley, Eleaner I, 361
Bartley, Eleanor I, 428
Bartley, Francis IV, 609
Bartley, John I, 361
Bartley, Mary I, 361
Bartlit, Miriam I, 299
Bartlit, Miriam I, 314
Bartlow, Cora IV, 1233
Bartlow, Eldora IV, 1272
Bartlow, George IV, 1233
Bartlow, John L. IV, 1272
Bartlow, Mina IV, 1233
Bartly, Elizabeth I, 373
Bartly, Elizabeth I, 387
Bartly, Francis IV, 609
Bartman, Benjamin IV, 880
Bartman, Hannah IV, 880
Barto, Alice C. IV, 1233
Barton, ??? III, 36
Barton, ??? III, 366
Barton, Aaron II, 192
Barton, Aaron II, 196
Barton, Aaron II, 268
Barton, Aaron II, 977
Barton, Alce VI, 886
Barton, Alice IV, 755
Barton, Alice IV, 1145
Barton, Alice C. V, 23
Barton, Alice E. V, 893
Barton, Allice IV, 1145
Barton, Altie IV, 368
Barton, Altie IV, 402
Barton, Amerrilla VI, 876
Barton, Amy S. II, 727
Barton, Ann II, 166
Barton, Ann II, 196
Barton, Ann II, 199
Barton, Ann II, 204
Barton, Ann V, 23
Barton, Anna III, 28
Barton, Anna III, 93
Barton, Anna V, 23
Barton, Anna V, 101
Barton, Anna VI, 876
Barton, Anna Irene III, 28
Barton, Anna Irene III, 296
Barton, Anna M. III, 296
Barton, Anna M. C. III, 259
Barton, Annie III, 28
Barton, Bashebe II, 699
Barton, Bathsheba II, 192
Barton, Bathsheba II, 196
Barton, Bathsheba II, 460
Barton, Benjamin II, 335
Barton, Betsey VI, 876
Barton, Betsy VI, 876
Barton, Beulah II, 699
Barton, Brer VI, 883
Barton, Bur VI, 1004
Barton, Ceziah VI, 876
Barton, Daniel II, 166
Barton, Daniel III, 28
Barton, David II, 196
Barton, David II, 977
Barton, David VI, 875
Barton, David VI, 876
Barton, David VI, 899
Barton, David VI, 954
Barton, Dr. Joshua L. III, 28
Barton, E. Farnham III, 28
Barton, Edmond VI, 876
Barton, Edmond VI, 907
Barton, Edmond VI, 950
Barton, Edmond VI, 995
Barton, Edmund VI, 882
Barton, Edward II, 166
Barton, Edward II, 196
Barton, Edward II, 214
Barton, Edward II, 268
Barton, Edward II, 977
Barton, Edward V, 23
Barton, Elijah VI, 798
Barton, Elijah VI, 876
Barton, Elisha VI, 876
Barton, Elisha VI, 954
Barton, Eliz. III, 28
Barton, Eliz. III, 67
Barton, Eliza I, 931
Barton, Eliza J. II, 727
Barton, Elizabeth I, 981
Barton, Elizabeth I, 1007
Barton, Elizabeth I, 1008
Barton, Elizabeth II, 196
Barton, Elizabeth II, 977
Barton, Elizabeth VI, 876
Barton, Emma IV, 1145
Barton, Frances IV, 864
Barton, Frances IV, 883
Barton, George V, 985
Barton, George John III, 361
Barton, Hannah II, 166
Barton, Hannah II, 196
Barton, Hannah V, 985
Barton, Hester II, 196
Barton, Imo Shaw IV, 1201
Barton, Isaac II, 196
Barton, Isaac II, 460
Barton, Isaac II, 699
Barton, Jacob V, 23
Barton, James II, 460
Barton, James III, 28
Barton, James IV, 676
Barton, James IV, 755
Barton, James VI, 876
Barton, James R. I, 921
Barton, Jane II, 196
Barton, Jane II, 727
Barton, Jean VI, 876
Barton, Jesse III, 28
Barton, Jesse III, 259
Barton, Jesse III, 296
Barton, Jessie III, 28
Barton, Jessie Emma III, 28
Barton, Jessie Emma III, 259
Barton, Job V, 26
Barton, Jobal VI, 876
Barton, Joel VI, 876
Barton, John II, 166
Barton, John II, 196
Barton, John II, 204
Barton, John II, 699
Barton, John III, 28
Barton, John III, 67
Barton, John IV, 174
Barton, John Nelson IV, 174
Barton, Jonathan II, 166
Barton, Jonathan II, 196
Barton, Jonathan II, 257
Barton, Joseph VI, 876
Barton, Joseph Collings V, 826
Barton, Joseph Collins V, 826
Barton, Joshua L. III, 81
Barton, Jubal VI, 954
Barton, Judith VI, 876
Barton, Loretta IV, 676
Barton, Lucinda VI, 876
Barton, Lucy III, 28
Barton, Lucy III, 67
Barton, Lucy VI, 989
Barton, Lula Angeline I, 931
Barton, Lydia II, 493
Barton, M. ??? III, 28
Barton, Margaret II, 196
Barton, Margaret II, 204

Barton, Maria II, 830
Barton, Maria II, 835
Barton, Maria III, 28
Barton, Maria W. III, 81
Barton, Martha I, 921
Barton, Martha V, 826
Barton, Martha VI, 876
Barton, Martha C. II, 699
Barton, Martha C. II, 727
Barton, Martha C. V, 826
Barton, Martha R. III, 361
Barton, Mary II, 166
Barton, Mary II, 196
Barton, Mary II, 197
Barton, Mary II, 198
Barton, Mary II, 257
Barton, Mary II, 335
Barton, Mary II, 460
Barton, Mary II, 699
Barton, Mary II, 977
Barton, Mary III, 28
Barton, Mary IV, 676
Barton, Mary V, 23
Barton, Mary V, 826
Barton, Mary VI, 876
Barton, Mary E. IV, 755
Barton, May Geneva I, 921
Barton, Meribah II, 196
Barton, Mina Jewell I, 921
Barton, Nancy VI, 955
Barton, Nina I, 938
Barton, Obediah VI, 908
Barton, Patience II, 977
Barton, Patience V, 23
Barton, Patience V, 88
Barton, Phebe G. III, 28
Barton, Phebe Jane III, 28
Barton, Phebe Jane III, 36
Barton, Polly VI, 899
Barton, Rebecca II, 699
Barton, Rebecca V, 826
Barton, Rebecca VI, 876
Barton, Rebeccah V, 826
Barton, Reuben III, 28
Barton, Richard III, 93
Barton, Rufus J. I, 931
Barton, Ruth I, 373
Barton, Ruth I, 424
Barton, Sally VI, 798
Barton, Sally VI, 875
Barton, Sally VI, 876
Barton, Sally Haldron VI, 908
Barton, Samuel II, 699
Barton, Samuel V, 23
Barton, Samuel V, 826
Barton, Sarah II, 166
Barton, Sarah II, 196
Barton, Sarah II, 199
Barton, Sarah II, 204
Barton, Sarah II, 214
Barton, Sarah II, 268
Barton, Sarah II, 335
Barton, Sarah II, 460
Barton, Sarah II, 727
Barton, Sarah II, 977
Barton, Sarah V, 23
Barton, Sarah VI, 876
Barton, Sarah Ann III, 366
Barton, Sarah L. V, 985
Barton, Siller Witt. VI, 876
Barton, Susanna II, 196
Barton, Susanna VI, 1004
Barton, Susannah II, 196
Barton, Susannah II, 335
Barton, Susannah IV, 511
Barton, Susannah IV, 521
Barton, Sydney V, 23
Barton, Thomas II, 166
Barton, Thomas II, 196
Barton, Thomas II, 199
Barton, Thomas II, 335
Barton, Thomas II, 977
Barton, Thomas VI, 876
Barton, Thomas VI, 892
Barton, Unicea VI, 954
Barton, Valentine VI, 876
Barton, Vilet VI, 883
Barton, William V, 23
Barton, William VI, 875
Barton, William VI, 984
Barton, Wm. II, 977
Bartow, Della I, 870
Bartram, Ann II, 460
Bartram, Ann II, 491
Bartram, Anna E. II, 939
Bartram, Caleb II, 335
Bartram, Eliza M. II, 460
Bartram, Elizabeth II, 460
Bartram, Elizabeth II, 476
Bartram, Elizabeth II, 708
Bartram, Elizabeth II, 709
Bartram, Elizabeth II, 780
Bartram, Elizabeth M. II, 460
Bartram, Elizabeth W. II, 835
Bartram, Ellen H. II, 835
Bartram, Ellen H. II, 928
Bartram, Emily II, 835
Bartram, Emily II, 886
Bartram, Emma II, 835
Bartram, Emma II, 886
Bartram, Emma K. II, 835
Bartram, Florence E. I, 629
Bartram, Frances Miller VI, 782
Bartram, Hannah II, 460
Bartram, Howard II, 939
Bartram, Isaac II, 335
Bartram, Isaac II, 460
Bartram, Isaac II, 513
Bartram, Isaac II, 649
Bartram, Isaac L. II, 835
Bartram, Isaac L. II, 886
Bartram, Isaac L., Jr. II, 835
Bartram, Isaac L., Jr. II, 886
Bartram, Isaac, Jr. II, 335
Bartram, Isaac, Jr. II, 460
Bartram, Isaac, Jr. II, 649
Bartram, Isaac, Jr. II, 835
Bartram, James II, 460
Bartram, Jane II, 460
Bartram, Jane II, 592
Bartram, John II, 335
Bartram, John II, 460
Bartram, John II, 476
Bartram, John II, 513
Bartram, John Henry II, 835
Bartram, John Henry II, 939
Bartram, John Lewis I, 629
Bartram, Lucy T. II, 835
Bartram, Lucy Taylor II, 835
Bartram, Lucy Taylor II, 928
Bartram, Margaret II, 335
Bartram, Martha II, 335
Bartram, Mary II, 335
Bartram, Mary II, 456
Bartram, Mary II, 460
Bartram, Mary Hayes II, 835
Bartram, Mary Hayes II, 939
Bartram, Moses II, 460
Bartram, Moses II, 476
Bartram, Rebecca S. II, 835
Bartram, Sarah II, 335
Bartram, Sarah II, 460
Bartram, Sarah II, 463
Bartram, Sarah II, 513
Bartram, Sarah II, 621
Bartram, Sarah II, 649
Bartram, Sarah S. II, 460
Bartram, Sarah S. II, 608
Bartram, T. Elwood II, 835
Bartram, Thomas II, 460
Bartram, Thomas II, 491
Bartram, Thomas VI, 782
Bartram, William Shipley II, 335
Bartram, Wm. II, 835
Bartram, Wm. II, 928
Bartram, Wm. H. II, 460
Bartram, Wm. S. II, 460
Bartree, Mary VI, 876
Bartree, William VI, 876
Bartrom, Sarah II, 335
Bartrum, Margaret II, 335
Barvis, Margaret II, 977
Barvis, Sarah II, 977
Barwis, Agnes II, 954
Barwis, Agnes II, 977
Barwis, Elizabeth II, 954
Barwis, Elizabeth II, 977
Barwis, Joseph II, 954
Barwis, Joseph II, 977
Barwis, Joseph II, 1045
Barwis, Joseph II, 1068
Barwis, Margaret II, 954
Barwis, Margaret II, 977
Barwis, Mary II, 954
Barwis, Mary II, 977
Barwis, Mary II, 1038
Barwis, Sarah II, 954
Barwis, Sarah II, 977
Barwis, Sarah II, 1040
Barwis, Thomas II, 954
Barwis, Thomas II, 977
Barwise, Margaret V, 152
Baset, Mary II, 54
Baset, Phebe II, 54
Basett, Abigal II, 54
Bash, Allie M. IV, 1145
Bash, Willie M. IV, 1145
Bash???, Amanda VI, 996
Basham, Archer VI, 876
Basham, Caroline VI, 876
Basham, Caroline VI, 902
Basham, Caroline VI, 904
Basham, Caroline VI, 969
Basham, David VI, 875
Basham, David VI, 876
Basham, Doshia VI, 876
Basham, Dosiah Ann VI, 887
Basham, Eleanor VI, 985
Basham, Elender VI, 871
Basham, Elender VI, 876
Basham, Elijah VI, 887
Basham, Elisha VI, 876
Basham, Elizabeth VI, 876
Basham, Elizabeth VI, 924
Basham, Elizabeth VI, 959
Basham, Jane VI, 969
Basham, Joel VI, 877
Basham, John VI, 877
Basham, John VI, 985
Basham, Jonathan VI, 876
Basham, Katy VI, 881
Basham, Katy VI, 1019
Basham, Lucinda VI, 876
Basham, Lucy VI, 876
Basham, Mahala VI, 876
Basham, Margaret VI, 877
Basham, Nancy VI, 939
Basham, Nancy VI, 1003
Basham, Nathan VI, 876
Basham, Nathan VI, 985
Basham, Nathaniel VI, 871
Basham, Nelson VI, 876
Basham, Polly VI, 876
Basham, Rebecca Ann V, 221
Basham, Sena VI, 871
Basham, Sophia VI, 877
Basham, Suckey VI, 880
Basham, Susan J. VI, 877
Basham, Susanna VI, 1003
Basham, Warner VI, 876
Basham, William VI, 876
Basham, William VI, 877
Basham, William VI, 959
Basham, Winna Jons. VI, 876
Bashand, Julian VI, 978
Bashand, Mary Ann VI, 978
Bashaw, Alzana M. IV, 899
Bashaw, Catharine IV, 924
Bashaw, Catharine E. IV, 924
Bashaw, Catherine E. IV, 965
Bashaw, Clyde Leonard IV, 924
Bashaw, George IV, 924
Bashaw, Herbert IV, 924
Bashaw, John Herbert IV, 924
Bashaw, Lemuel IV, 924
Bashaw, Lemuel R. IV, 924
Bashaw, Leon H. IV, 899
Bashaw, Leslie D. IV, 899
Bashaw, Lucretia P. IV, 798
Bashaw, Lucretia P. IV, 838
Bashaw, Lucretia P. IV, 899
Bashaw, Lunsford IV, 899
Bashaw, Ottiwell W. IV, 924
Bashaw, R. Odell IV, 899
Basher, Delilah V, 319
Bashman, Amy VI, 876
Bashman, Bartlett VI, 876
Bashman, Elijah VI, 876
Bashman, Nancy VI, 876
Bashman, Rachel VI, 876
Bashman, Vardiman VI, 876
Bashore, Charles V, 655
Bashore, Charles V, 658
Bashore, Fay V, 655
Bashore, Fay V, 658
Bashore, Mary Louise V, 658
Basit, Mary II, 54
Basit, Rachel II, 54
Basit, Rachel II, 87
Basket, Ruth I, 373
Basmajian, David III, 28
Basmajian, Gadar III, 28
Basmajian, Gadar III, 278
Basmajian, Mary III, 28
Basmajian, Sarkis III, 188
Basmajian, Sarkis III, 278
Basmajian, Sarkis T. III, 28
Basmajian, Vargin M. III, 28
Basnett, Elizabeth II, 460
Basnett, Hannah II, 197
Basnett, Hannah II, 250
Basnett, Richard II, 460
Basnett, Richard II, 527
Bason, Charity VI, 364
Bass, Betsey R. VI, 798
Bass, Clara V, 985
Bass, Elizabeth VI, 836
Bass, Elizabeth VI, 862
Bass, F. L. VI, 802
Bass, F. S. VI, 801
Bass, Francis I, 299
Bass, Frederick VI, 846
Bass, Frederick VI, 853
Bass, Frederick VI, 864
Bass, Hannah I, 373
Bass, James V, 985
Bass, James VI, 864
Bass, James A. VI, 853
Bass, Joan II, 441
Bass, John II, 441
Bass, John S. VI, 816
Bass, Josiah VI, 798
Bass, Josiah VI, 840
Bass, Josiah VI, 862
Bass, Julian VI, 853
Bass, Lizzie L. IV, 1306
Bass, Lizzie Lillian IV, 1306
Bass, Lula I, 335
Bass, Martha L. VI, 846
Bass, Mary VI, 864
Bass, Mary C. VI, 798
Bass, Mary E. V, 985
Bass, Missouri VI, 802
Bass, Nancy VI, 798
Bass, Nancy H. VI, 801
Bass, Peter VI, 798
Bass, Peter VI, 839
Bass, Polly VI, 811
Bass, Rebeckah VI, 840
Bass, Rowland G. VI, 796
Bass, Rowland G. VI, 798
Bass, Susan VI, 846
Bass, Thomas M. VI, 813
Bass, Thos. M. VI, 798
Bass, Trecia I, 328
Bass, Trecy I, 328
Basset, Abigail II, 54
Basset, Amy II, 52
Basset, Amy II, 54
Basset, Ann II, 54
Basset, Ann W. IV, 609
Basset, Ann W. IV, 637
Basset, Burwell VI, 155
Basset, Burwell VI, 186
Basset, Charles D. IV, 609
Basset, Charles D. IV, 637
Basset, Charles D. IV, 677
Basset, Davis II, 335
Basset, Elisha II, 460
Basset, Grace II, 460
Basset, Isaac II, 460
Basset, John II, 335
Basset, Mary II, 54
Basset, Patrick A. VI, 877
Basset, Phebe II, 54
Basset, Rachel II, 54
Basset, Rachel II, 78
Basset, Rebecca II, 54
Basset, Rebecca II, 72
Basset, Sarah S. II, 727
Basset, Susan M. II, 727
Basset, Susanna II, 727
Basset, Susanna II, 752
Basset, Zebedee II, 54
Basset, Zebedee II, 78
Bassett, ??? III, 29
Bassett, Abigail II, 21
Bassett, Abigail II, 22
Bassett, Abigail II, 54
Bassett, Abigail II, 129
Bassett, Abigail II, 159
Bassett, Abigail II, 335
Bassett, Abigail II, 460
Bassett, Abigail II, 559
Bassett, Abigal II, 54
Bassett, Adelia IV, 1351
Bassett, Adelia IV, 1384
Bassett, Albert II, 21
Bassett, Albert II, 22
Bassett, Albert II, 115
Bassett, Albert II, 128
Bassett, Albert II, 129
Bassett, Albert II, 144
Bassett, Amanda II, 22
Bassett, Amanda II, 128
Bassett, Amanda II, 129
Bassett, Amanda IV, 174
Bassett, Amey II, 54
Bassett, Amey II, 84
Bassett, Amey II, 460
Bassett, Amy II, 54
Bassett, Ann II, 21
Bassett, Ann II, 22
Bassett, Ann II, 54
Bassett, Ann II, 103
Bassett, Ann II, 144
Bassett, Ann II, 154
Bassett, Ann II, 159
Bassett, Ann II, 460
Bassett, Ann E. II, 129
Bassett, Ann Elizabeth II, 128
Bassett, Ann Elizabeth II, 144
Bassett, Ann T. II, 144
Bassett, Ann T. II, 153
Bassett, Ann W. IV, 609
Bassett, Ann W. IV, 676
Bassett, Ann W. IV, 677
Bassett, Ann W. IV, 725
Bassett, Anna II, 128
Bassett, Anna II, 145
Bassett, Anna II, 151
Bassett, Anna II, 836
Bassett, Anna E. II, 129
Bassett, Anna E. II, 145
Bassett, Anna E. II, 836
Bassett, Anna Elgar II, 145
Bassett, Anna Elgar II, 781
Bassett, Anna Elizabeth II, 129
Bassett, Anna Elizabeth II, 153
Bassett, Anna L. II, 129
Bassett, Anna T. II, 129
Bassett, Anne II, 128
Bassett, Anne Thompson II, 145
Bassett, Anne Thompson II, 152
Bassett, Annie II, 152
Bassett, Annie Elkinton II, 145
Bassett, Annie S. II, 144
Bassett, Annie S. II, 159
Bassett, Artamas IV, 1351
Bassett, Artemas IV, 1351
Bassett, Arthur E. II, 836
Bassett, Arthur Edward II, 781
Bassett, B. Allen II, 128
Bassett, B. Allen II, 129
Bassett, B. Allen II, 144
Bassett, B. Allen II, 145
Bassett, Benj. II, 127
Bassett, Benj. II, 129
Bassett, Benj. II, 132
Bassett, Benjamin II, 22
Bassett, Benjamin II, 115
Bassett, Benjamin II, 128
Bassett, Benjamin II, 142
Bassett, Benjamin II, 143
Bassett, Benjamin II, 144
Bassett, Benjamin II, 149
Bassett, Benjamin Allen II, 144
Bassett, Beulah II, 54
Bassett, Beulah II, 335
Bassett, Beulah II, 460
Bassett, Burrell VI, 186
Bassett, Burwell VI, 174
Bassett, Caspar II, 43
Bassett, Charles II, 128
Bassett, Charles IV, 609
Bassett, Charles D. IV, 609
Bassett, Charles D. IV, 677
Bassett, Charles D. IV, 725
Bassett, Charles Edwin II, 128
Bassett, Charles Edwin II, 144
Bassett, Charles Edwin II, 149
Bassett, Charles S. II, 144
Bassett, Chas. D. IV, 676
Bassett, Clara Allen II, 129
Bassett, Clara Anna II, 145
Bassett, Clara Anna II, 146
Bassett, Clemence A. II, 144
Bassett, Clemence A. II, 151
Bassett, Clement II, 128
Bassett, Clement II, 144
Bassett, Clement II, 145
Bassett, Clement II, 147
Bassett, Cornelia II, 129
Bassett, Cornelia II, 144
Bassett, Cornelia II, 160
Bassett, Cornelia B. II, 140
Bassett, Daniel II, 21
Bassett, Daniel II, 54
Bassett, Daniel II, 74
Bassett, Daniel II, 84
Bassett, Daniel II, 99
Bassett, Daniel, Jr. II, 21
Bassett, Daniel, Jr. II, 54
Bassett, Daniel, Jr. II, 87
Bassett, David II, 21
Bassett, David II, 22
Bassett, David II, 54
Bassett, David II, 127
Bassett, David II, 128
Bassett, David II, 129
Bassett, David II, 142
Bassett, David II, 143
Bassett, David II, 144
Bassett, David II, 149
Bassett, David II, 150
Bassett, David II, 151
Bassett, David II, 460
Bassett, David II, 559
Bassett, David IV, 1351
Bassett, David F. II, 22
Bassett, David S. II, 460
Bassett, David, Jr. II, 115
Bassett, Davis II, 22
Bassett, Davis II, 54
Bassett, Davis II, 129

Bassett, Davis II, 135
Bassett, Davis II, 144
Bassett, Davis II, 335
Bassett, Davis II, 460
Bassett, Davis II, 515
Bassett, Deborah II, 22
Bassett, Deborah II, 808
Bassett, Deborah, Jr. II, 54
Bassett, Deborah, Jr. II, 67
Bassett, E. Russell II, 128
Bassett, E. Russell II, 129
Bassett, E. Smith II, 144
Bassett, E. Smith II, 145
Bassett, E. Smith II, 152
Bassett, Edward H. II, 115
Bassett, Edward H. II, 128
Bassett, Edward H. II, 129
Bassett, Edward H. II, 144
Bassett, Edward H. II, 159
Bassett, Edward Hicks II, 22
Bassett, Edward Hicks II, 129
Bassett, Edwin II, 129
Bassett, Edwin II, 139
Bassett, Edwin II, 144
Bassett, Edwin Russell, Jr. II, 128
Bassett, Elisha II, 21
Bassett, Elisha II, 22
Bassett, Elisha II, 39
Bassett, Elisha II, 54
Bassett, Elisha II, 89
Bassett, Elisha II, 115
Bassett, Elisha II, 128
Bassett, Elisha II, 129
Bassett, Elisha II, 130
Bassett, Elisha II, 136
Bassett, Elisha II, 144
Bassett, Elisha II, 145
Bassett, Elisha II, 147
Bassett, Elisha II, 151
Bassett, Elisha II, 152
Bassett, Elisha II, 158
Bassett, Elisha II, 460
Bassett, Elisha II, 515
Bassett, Elisha II, 836
Bassett, Elisha, Jr. II, 54
Bassett, Elisha, Jr. II, 115
Bassett, Elisha, Jr. II, 144
Bassett, Elisha, Jr. II, 158
Bassett, Eliza W. II, 727
Bassett, Elizabeth II, 22
Bassett, Elizabeth II, 54
Bassett, Elizabeth II, 74
Bassett, Elizabeth II, 115
Bassett, Elizabeth II, 126
Bassett, Elizabeth II, 129
Bassett, Elizabeth II, 140
Bassett, Elizabeth II, 146
Bassett, Elizabeth A. II, 146
Bassett, Elizabeth Allen II, 129
Bassett, Elizabeth Allen II, 145
Bassett, Elizabeth F. II, 144
Bassett, Elizabeth F. II, 161
Bassett, Elizabeth N. II, 22
Bassett, Elizabeth N. II, 115
Bassett, Elizabeth N. II, 128
Bassett, Elizabeth N. II, 144
Bassett, Elizabeth N. II, 149
Bassett, Elizabeth, II, 149
Bassett, Elizabeth, Jr. II, 54
Bassett, Elizabeth, Jr. II, 99
Bassett, Ellen I, 623
Bassett, Ellen I, 936
Bassett, Ellen M. I, 14
Bassett, Elma II, 128
Bassett, Emerson II, 128
Bassett, Emmerson II, 144
Bassett, Evi Smith II, 129
Bassett, Evi Smith II, 144
Bassett, Evi Smith II, 159
Bassett, F. Milton II, 145
Bassett, Fannie III, 377
Bassett, Fannie III, 389
Bassett, Francis IV, 1351
Bassett, Frank L. II, 129
Bassett, Frank Miller II, 128
Bassett, Franklin IV, 1306
Bassett, Franklin G. II, 145
Bassett, Franklin L. II, 129
Bassett, Franklin L. II, 144
Bassett, Franklin L. II, 781
Bassett, Franklin L. II, 836
Bassett, Franklin Lippincott II, 145
Bassett, Fred II, 128
Bassett, Fred II, 129
Bassett, Frederick II, 128
Bassett, Frederick II, 145
Bassett, Geo. G. II, 145
Bassett, George G. II, 129
Bassett, George Grier II, 145
Bassett, George H. II, 144
Bassett, Gideon Scull II, 21
Bassett, Grace II, 22
Bassett, Grace II, 54
Bassett, Grace II, 96
Bassett, Grace II, 112
Bassett, Grace II, 460
Bassett, Hannah II, 22
Bassett, Hannah II, 24
Bassett, Hannah II, 54
Bassett, Hannah II, 55
Bassett, Hannah II, 60
Bassett, Hannah II, 71
Bassett, Hannah II, 115
Bassett, Hannah II, 128
Bassett, Hannah II, 129
Bassett, Hannah II, 143
Bassett, Hannah II, 144
Bassett, Hannah II, 152
Bassett, Hannah Ann II, 128
Bassett, Hannah Ann II, 129
Bassett, Hannah Ann II, 130
Bassett, Hannah Ann II, 144
Bassett, Hannah Ann II, 145
Bassett, Hannah Ann II, 147
Bassett, Hannah Ann II, 151
Bassett, Hannah Ann II, 158
Bassett, Hannah D. II, 127
Bassett, Hannah D. II, 142
Bassett, Hannah D. II, 144
Bassett, Hannah P. II, 128
Bassett, Hannah P. II, 129
Bassett, Hannah P. II, 143
Bassett, Hannah P. II, 144
Bassett, Hannah P. II, 155
Bassett, Hannah P. II, 159
Bassett, Hannah P. S. II, 129
Bassett, Hannah S. II, 117
Bassett, Hannah S. II, 128
Bassett, Hannah S. II, 145
Bassett, Harriet II, 128
Bassett, Harriet II, 129
Bassett, Harriet II, 144
Bassett, Harriet II, 158
Bassett, Helen II, 781
Bassett, Henry II, 128
Bassett, Henry II, 129
Bassett, Henry II, 144
Bassett, Henry II, 145
Bassett, Henry II, 152
Bassett, Henry II, 158
Bassett, Henry IV, 676
Bassett, Hephsiba II, 54
Bassett, Hephsiba II, 82
Bassett, Herbert T. II, 781
Bassett, Herbert T. II, 836
Bassett, Hope II, 460
Bassett, Howard II, 128
Bassett, Howard II, 144
Bassett, Howard II, 151
Bassett, Isaac II, 22
Bassett, Isaac II, 54
Bassett, Isaac II, 67
Bassett, Isaac II, 460
Bassett, James II, 54
Bassett, James Alvin IV, 609
Bassett, James Alvin IV, 676
Bassett, James Alvin IV, 677
Bassett, John II, 22
Bassett, John II, 129
Bassett, John II, 335
Bassett, John IV, 676
Bassett, John T. II, 115
Bassett, John T. II, 129
Bassett, John T. II, 132
Bassett, John T. II, 140
Bassett, John T. II, 144
Bassett, John T. II, 149
Bassett, John T. II, 153
Bassett, Jonas F. II, 22
Bassett, Jos. II, 128
Bassett, Jos. II, 133
Bassett, Joseph II, 22
Bassett, Joseph II, 24
Bassett, Joseph II, 50
Bassett, Joseph II, 54
Bassett, Joseph II, 60
Bassett, Joseph II, 70
Bassett, Joseph II, 111
Bassett, Joseph II, 128
Bassett, Joseph II, 129
Bassett, Joseph II, 132
Bassett, Joseph II, 140
Bassett, Joseph II, 141
Bassett, Joseph II, 142
Bassett, Joseph II, 143
Bassett, Joseph II, 144
Bassett, Joseph II, 145
Bassett, Joseph II, 146
Bassett, Joseph II, 147
Bassett, Joseph II, 149
Bassett, Joseph II, 161
Bassett, Joseph B. IV, 1035
Bassett, Joseph, Jr. II, 55
Bassett, Joseph, Jr. II, 115
Bassett, Joseph, Jr. II, 143
Bassett, Joseph, Jr. II, 144
Bassett, Joseph, Jr. II, 149
Bassett, Joseph, Jr. II, 161
Bassett, Joshua II, 159
Bassett, Josiah II, 22
Bassett, Josiah II, 54
Bassett, Josiah II, 68
Bassett, Josiah II, 128
Bassett, Josiah II, 143
Bassett, Josiah II, 335
Bassett, Josiah II, 460
Bassett, Josiah II, 727
Bassett, Josiah II, 781
Bassett, Josiah II, 836
Bassett, L. Anna II, 128
Bassett, L. Ida II, 145
Bassett, Leo J. V, 658
Bassett, Leo J. V, 705
Bassett, Lewis D. II, 128
Bassett, Lewis S. II, 145
Bassett, Lillie IV, 1306
Bassett, Louise V, 658
Bassett, Louise V, 705
Bassett, Lydia II, 22
Bassett, Lydia II, 55
Bassett, Lydia II, 70
Bassett, Lydia II, 115
Bassett, Lydia II, 128
Bassett, Lydia II, 129
Bassett, Lydia II, 133
Bassett, Lydia II, 140
Bassett, Lydia II, 141
Bassett, Lydia II, 143
Bassett, Lydia II, 144
Bassett, Lydia II, 161
Bassett, Lydia II, 710
Bassett, Lydia Amanda II, 129
Bassett, Lydia Amanda II, 143
Bassett, Lydia Ann II, 144
Bassett, Lydia F. II, 144
Bassett, Lydia F. II, 161
Bassett, Lydia Freidland II, 829
Bassett, Lydia S. II, 128
Bassett, Margaret Griscom II, 129
Bassett, Margaret Griscom II, 145
Bassett, Margery IV, 1351
Bassett, Margery Ann II, 699
Bassett, Maria II, 128
Bassett, Mariah II, 144
Bassett, Mariah II, 156
Bassett, Marianna II, 128
Bassett, Marianna II, 139
Bassett, Marianna II, 144
Bassett, Marianna II, 146
Bassett, Marianna II, 149
Bassett, Mark II, 21
Bassett, Mark S. II, 699
Bassett, Martha B. II, 129
Bassett, Martha B. II, 135
Bassett, Martha B. II, 144
Bassett, Martha Jane II, 128
Bassett, Martha V. II, 129
Bassett, Martha V. II, 144
Bassett, Mary II, 21
Bassett, Mary II, 22
Bassett, Mary II, 24
Bassett, Mary II, 50
Bassett, Mary II, 53
Bassett, Mary II, 54
Bassett, Mary II, 60
Bassett, Mary II, 62
Bassett, Mary II, 70
Bassett, Mary II, 111
Bassett, Mary II, 114
Bassett, Mary II, 115
Bassett, Mary II, 117
Bassett, Mary II, 127
Bassett, Mary II, 128
Bassett, Mary II, 129
Bassett, Mary II, 132
Bassett, Mary II, 136
Bassett, Mary II, 142
Bassett, Mary II, 143
Bassett, Mary II, 144
Bassett, Mary II, 147
Bassett, Mary II, 149
Bassett, Mary II, 150
Bassett, Mary II, 158
Bassett, Mary II, 335
Bassett, Mary II, 460
Bassett, Mary A. II, 129
Bassett, Mary A. II, 145
Bassett, Mary Ann II, 22
Bassett, Mary Ann II, 55
Bassett, Mary Ann II, 115
Bassett, Mary Ann II, 129
Bassett, Mary Ann II, 143
Bassett, Mary Anna II, 128
Bassett, Mary Anna II, 129
Bassett, Mary Augusta II, 144
Bassett, Mary Augusta II, 147
Bassett, Mary B. II, 129
Bassett, Mary B. II, 144
Bassett, Mary E. II, 128
Bassett, Mary E. II, 139
Bassett, Mary E. II, 144
Bassett, Mary E. II, 150
Bassett, Mary G. II, 143
Bassett, Mary Jane II, 159
Bassett, Mary L. II, 159
Bassett, Mary M. II, 129
Bassett, Mary M. II, 132
Bassett, Mary M. II, 144
Bassett, Mary M. II, 149
Bassett, Mary McIlvain II, 129
Bassett, Mary N. II, 115
Bassett, Mary T. II, 129
Bassett, Mary T. II, 144
Bassett, Mary T. II, 151
Bassett, Mary Wistar II, 43
Bassett, Maurice H. II, 144
Bassett, Minnie IV, 174
Bassett, Minnie IV, 1306
Bassett, Morrice II, 144
Bassett, Morris II, 22
Bassett, Morris H. II, 129
Bassett, Nathan II, 95
Bassett, Nathan II, 699
Bassett, Nathan II, 727
Bassett, Nathan IV, 1351
Bassett, Nathan H. IV, 609
Bassett, Nathan H. IV, 676
Bassett, Nathan H. IV, 677
Bassett, Nathan H. IV, 1351
Bassett, Nathan H. IV, 1384
Bassett, Nella G. II, 128
Bassett, Nella G. II, 129
Bassett, Norman H. II, 129
Bassett, Norman H. II, 145
Bassett, Norman H. II, 781
Bassett, Norman H. II, 836
Bassett, Norman Hallowell II, 145
Bassett, Paul II, 335
Bassett, Phebe II, 20
Bassett, Phebe II, 22
Bassett, Phebe II, 54
Bassett, Phebe II, 58
Bassett, Phebe IV, 798
Bassett, Rachel II, 54
Bassett, Rachel II, 127
Bassett, Rachel II, 128
Bassett, Rachel II, 142
Bassett, Rachel II, 144
Bassett, Rachel II, 335
Bassett, Rachel II, 460
Bassett, Rachel II, 836
Bassett, Rebecca II, 19
Bassett, Rebecca II, 22
Bassett, Rebecca II, 43
Bassett, Rebecca II, 46
Bassett, Rebecca II, 47
Bassett, Rebecca II, 54
Bassett, Rebecca II, 55
Bassett, Rebecca II, 111
Bassett, Rebecca II, 115
Bassett, Rebecca II, 128
Bassett, Rebecca II, 129
Bassett, Rebecca II, 130
Bassett, Rebecca II, 143
Bassett, Rebecca II, 144
Bassett, Rebecca II, 146
Bassett, Rebecca S. II, 144
Bassett, Rebecca S. II, 152
Bassett, Rebecca S. II, 158
Bassett, Rebecca White II, 460
Bassett, Rebeckah II, 39
Bassett, Rebekah II, 54
Bassett, Rebekah White II, 54
Bassett, Reuben II, 335
Bassett, Rhoda I, 14
Bassett, Richard II, 128
Bassett, Richard II, 129
Bassett, Richard II, 144
Bassett, Richard II, 166
Bassett, Ruth IV, 676
Bassett, Ruth, Jr. II, 87
Bassett, Samuel II, 21
Bassett, Samuel II, 22
Bassett, Samuel II, 54
Bassett, Samuel II, 55
Bassett, Samuel II, 115
Bassett, Samuel II, 144
Bassett, Samuel, Jr. II, 54
Bassett, Sarah II, 22
Bassett, Sarah II, 37
Bassett, Sarah II, 54
Bassett, Sarah II, 68
Bassett, Sarah II, 84
Bassett, Sarah II, 92
Bassett, Sarah II, 95
Bassett, Sarah II, 99
Bassett, Sarah II, 115
Bassett, Sarah II, 128
Bassett, Sarah II, 129
Bassett, Sarah II, 132
Bassett, Sarah II, 143
Bassett, Sarah II, 144
Bassett, Sarah II, 149
Bassett, Sarah II, 150
Bassett, Sarah II, 895
Bassett, Sarah IV, 1351
Bassett, Sarah IV, 1384
Bassett, Sarah Ann II, 128
Bassett, Sarah Ann II, 132
Bassett, Sarah Ann II, 144
Bassett, Sarah Ann II, 149
Bassett, Sarah S. II, 727
Bassett, Sarah T. II, 144
Bassett, Sarah T. II, 159
Bassett, Sarah, Jr. IV, 1351
Bassett, Steven IV, 174
Bassett, Susan II, 132
Bassett, Susan M. II, 129
Bassett, Susan M. II, 140
Bassett, Susan M. II, 144
Bassett, Susan M. II, 149
Bassett, Susan M. II, 153
Bassett, Susan M. II, 727
Bassett, Susanna II, 727
Bassett, Thompson II, 128
Bassett, Vashti II, 127
Bassett, Vashti II, 142
Bassett, Vashti II, 144
Bassett, Walter II, 144
Bassett, Walter S. II, 128
Bassett, Walter S. II, 144
Bassett, Wd. Mary II, 515
Bassett, Wd. Sarah B. II, 136
Bassett, William I, 14
Bassett, William IV, 1351
Bassett, William Judson IV, 1351
Bassett, William W. III, 29
Bassett, Winifred IV, 1306
Bassett, Wm. II, 20
Bassett, Wm. II, 22
Bassett, Wm. II, 54
Bassett, Wm. II, 55
Bassett, Wm. II, 460
Bassett, Wm. II, 836
Bassett, Wm. Henry II, 727
Bassett, Zebedee II, 54
Bassham, Florentine VI, 932
Bassitt, Ann II, 460
Bassitt, Beulah II, 460
Bassitt, Daniel II, 54
Bassitt, Rebekah II, 54
Bassitt, Rebekah II, 91
Bassnett, Elizabeth II, 197
Bassnett, Hannah II, 197
Bassnett, Sarah II, 197
Bast, Jose IV, 174
Baster, Birdie L. IV, 1306
Baster, Joseph IV, 1306
Baster, Joseph C. IV, 1306
Bastock, Mrs. Ruth IV, 1306
Batchelor, Daniel VI, 731
Batchelor, Jane II, 460
Batchelor, Jane II, 671
Batchford, Martha C. V, 893
Bateman, Alexander VI, 877
Bateman, Amanda VI, 877
Bateman, Ann V, 23
Bateman, Ann V, 144
Bateman, Anne VI, 877
Bateman, Azel VI, 877
Bateman, Azel VI, 1002
Bateman, Benjamin VI, 877
Bateman, Benjamin VI, 894
Bateman, Benjamin VI, 1011
Bateman, Caroline IV, 1272
Bateman, Caroline V, 893
Bateman, Caroline S. V, 893
Bateman, Caroline S. V, 897
Bateman, Deborah V, 23
Bateman, Deborah V, 79
Bateman, Deborah V, 221
Bateman, Deborah V, 251
Bateman, Deborah V, 965
Bateman, Deborah V, 979
Bateman, Doshia VI, 1002
Bateman, Edward S. IV, 1272
Bateman, Edward S. V, 893
Bateman, Elizabeth V, 23
Bateman, Elizabeth V, 86
Bateman, Elizabeth V, 144

Bateman, Elizabeth VI, 894
Bateman, Elizabeth VI, 1002
Bateman, Elizabeth B. V, 23
Bateman, Elizabeth B. V, 91
Bateman, Ellwood V, 23
Bateman, Frances VI, 860
Bateman, Hannah IV, 1272
Bateman, Hannah V, 23
Bateman, Hannah V, 893
Bateman, Hannah V, 967
Bateman, Hannah V, 978
Bateman, Hopkins VI, 877
Bateman, Jacob V, 23
Bateman, Jane VI, 895
Bateman, Jenny VI, 894
Bateman, Joel V, 979
Bateman, Joel VI, 877
Bateman, Joel Mahlon V, 23
Bateman, John IV, 1272
Bateman, John V, 23
Bateman, John V, 79
Bateman, John V, 251
Bateman, John V, 967
Bateman, John V, 978
Bateman, John V, 979
Bateman, John VI, 860
Bateman, John VI, 877
Bateman, John F. V, 897
Bateman, John T. V, 23
Bateman, John T. V, 893
Bateman, John T. V, 967
Bateman, John T. V, 977
Bateman, Lida S. IV, 1272
Bateman, Lydia V, 23
Bateman, Lydia V, 967
Bateman, Lydia V, 978
Bateman, Lydia V, 979
Bateman, Lydia A. V, 967
Bateman, Lydia B. V, 967
Bateman, Lydia B. V, 977
Bateman, Lydia S. V, 893
Bateman, Lydia S. V, 897
Bateman, Mahlon IV, 1272
Bateman, Mahlon V, 23
Bateman, Mahlon V, 967
Bateman, Mary Ann IV, 1272
Bateman, Mary Ann V, 23
Bateman, Mary Ann V, 893
Bateman, Mary Ann V, 967
Bateman, Mary Ann V, 979
Bateman, Mary Anna IV, 1272
Bateman, Mary Anna V, 967
Bateman, Mary Ella V, 893
Bateman, Nancy VI, 877
Bateman, Nancy VI, 895
Bateman, Oliver H. V, 893
Bateman, Oliver W. IV, 1272
Bateman, Oliver W. V, 893
Bateman, Oney VI, 877
Bateman, Rachel V, 23
Bateman, Rachel V, 86
Bateman, Rachel V, 967
Bateman, Rachel V, 978
Bateman, Rachel Elizabeth V, 23
Bateman, Rachel J. V, 319
Bateman, Rachel J. V, 363
Bateman, Rachel, Sr. V, 967
Bateman, Reuben VI, 895
Bateman, Sarah VI, 877
Bateman, Susan S. IV, 1272
Bateman, Susanna VI, 877
Bateman, William V, 23
Bateman, William V, 86
Bateman, William V, 144
Bateman, William VI, 877
Bateman, Wm. V, 967
Baterman, Rachel V, 23
Baterman, Rachel V, 104
Bates, ??? III, 29
Bates, ??? III, 113
Bates, Abigail II, 33
Bates, Abram. Henry VI, 1003
Bates, Agnes VI, 158
Bates, Agness VI, 157
Bates, Alexandria VI, 156
Bates, Alfred V, 985
Bates, Alice E. III, 29
Bates, Alpha Nettie IV, 944
Bates, Amos II, 22
Bates, Amos P. IV, 174
Bates, Andrew I, 443
Bates, Anice V, 549
Bates, Ann IV, 218
Bates, Ann IV, 464
Bates, Ann VI, 155
Bates, Ann VI, 156
Bates, Ann VI, 161
Bates, Ann VI, 190
Bates, Ann VI, 194
Bates, Ann VI, 229
Bates, Ann VI, 280
Bates, Ann Scott IV, 272
Bates, Anna IV, 174
Bates, Anna VI, 155
Bates, Anna VI, 157
Bates, Anna VI, 238
Bates, Annie IV, 1035
Bates, Benj. IV, 464
Bates, Benj., Jr. VI, 238
Bates, Benjamin IV, 174
Bates, Benjamin IV, 230
Bates, Benjamin IV, 464
Bates, Benjamin IV, 924
Bates, Benjamin VI, 15
Bates, Benjamin VI, 155
Bates, Benjamin VI, 156
Bates, Benjamin VI, 157
Bates, Benjamin VI, 184
Bates, Benjamin VI, 209
Bates, Benjamin VI, 228
Bates, Benjamin VI, 229
Bates, Benjamin VI, 238
Bates, Benjamin VI, 264
Bates, Benjamin VI, 272
Bates, Benjamin VI, 731
Bates, Benjamin Jordan VI, 156
Bates, Benjamin L. IV, 174
Bates, Benjamin L. IV, 464
Bates, Benjamin Spence VI, 228
Bates, Benjamin Spence VI, 229
Bates, Benjamin, Jr. VI, 156
Bates, Benjamin, Jr. VI, 194
Bates, Benjamin, Jr. VI, 229
Bates, Benjamin, Jr. VI, 239
Bates, Benjamin, Sr. VI, 155
Bates, Bersheba VI, 157
Bates, Caroline VI, 156
Bates, Caroline Matilda VI, 156
Bates, Caroline Matilda VI, 220
Bates, Caroline Matilda VI, 229
Bates, Catharine II, 22
Bates, Catharine A. IV, 174
Bates, Catherine VI, 157
Bates, Catherine VI, 229
Bates, Cathrine II, 55
Bates, Charity I, 1114
Bates, Charity I, 1120
Bates, Charles VI, 156
Bates, Charles E. III, 29
Bates, Charles Frederick VI, 157
Bates, Charles Frederick VI, 229
Bates, Charles Stebbins III, 254
Bates, Charlotte VI, 877
Bates, Curles PM VI, 155
Bates, Daniel I, 525
Bates, Deborah III, 32
Bates, Deborah IV, 174
Bates, Deborah IV, 464
Bates, Deborah IV, 475
Bates, Deborah VI, 157
Bates, Deborah VI, 228
Bates, Deborah VI, 229
Bates, Deborah VI, 244
Bates, Deborah VI, 245
Bates, Deborah VI, 731
Bates, Deborah H. IV, 174
Bates, Deborah H. IV, 281
Bates, Deborah H. VI, 155
Bates, Edward IV, 181
Bates, Edward IV, 924
Bates, Edward VI, 15
Bates, Edward VI, 155
Bates, Edward VI, 156
Bates, Edward VI, 164
Bates, Edward VI, 180
Bates, Edward VI, 184
Bates, Edward VI, 228
Bates, Edward S. VI, 229
Bates, Elisha IV, 174
Bates, Elisha IV, 218
Bates, Elisha IV, 224
Bates, Elisha IV, 281
Bates, Elisha VI, 15
Bates, Elisha VI, 155
Bates, Elisha VI, 156
Bates, Elisha VI, 157
Bates, Elisha VI, 164
Bates, Elisha VI, 180
Bates, Elisha Henry VI, 157
Bates, Elisha Henry VI, 229
Bates, Eliza V, 373
Bates, Eliza V, 658
Bates, Elizabeth II, 22
Bates, Elizabeth II, 55
Bates, Elizabeth II, 461
Bates, Elizabeth III, 29
Bates, Elizabeth III, 479
Bates, Elizabeth IV, 174
Bates, Elizabeth IV, 181
Bates, Elizabeth VI, 100
Bates, Elizabeth VI, 110
Bates, Elizabeth VI, 130
Bates, Elizabeth VI, 155
Bates, Elizabeth VI, 156
Bates, Elizabeth VI, 157
Bates, Elizabeth VI, 171
Bates, Elizabeth VI, 176
Bates, Elizabeth VI, 180
Bates, Elizabeth VI, 229
Bates, Elizabeth VI, 798
Bates, Elizabeth VI, 877
Bates, Elizabeth VI, 999
Bates, Elizabeth H. IV, 464
Bates, Elizabeth R. III, 113
Bates, Elizabeth, Sr. II, 22
Bates, Ellwood Heacock II, 836
Bates, Emelia VI, 967
Bates, Emma P. IV, 174
Bates, Exekiah II, 55
Bates, Ezekiah II, 22
Bates, Fleming IV, 174
Bates, Fleming VI, 155
Bates, Fleming VI, 156
Bates, Fleming VI, 157
Bates, Fleming VI, 188
Bates, Fleming VI, 228
Bates, Fleming VI, 229
Bates, Fleming VI, 234
Bates, Fleming VI, 239
Bates, Fleming VI, 244
Bates, Fleming VI, 249
Bates, Fleming VI, 731
Bates, Fleming VI, 737
Bates, Fleming VI, 798
Bates, Fleming VI, 821
Bates, Fleming VI, 826
Bates, Fleming VI, 839
Bates, Fleming E. VI, 229
Bates, Fleming, Jr. VI, 229
Bates, Francis Rosalie IV, 1035
Bates, Frank T. VI, 230
Bates, Geo. IV, 925
Bates, Geo. Anson III, 29
Bates, George VI, 155
Bates, George VI, 171
Bates, George VI, 176
Bates, Grace VI, 155
Bates, Hannah II, 696
Bates, Hannah II, 977
Bates, Hannah IV, 174
Bates, Hannah VI, 155
Bates, Hannah VI, 156
Bates, Hannah VI, 157
Bates, Hannah VI, 188
Bates, Hannah VI, 228
Bates, Hannah VI, 229
Bates, Hannah VI, 272
Bates, Hannah VI, 731
Bates, Harmony V, 947
Bates, Harriett IV, 925
Bates, Henrico VI, 155
Bates, Henrietta VI, 155
Bates, Henrietta VI, 162
Bates, Henrietta VI, 229
Bates, Henrietta M. VI, 157
Bates, Henrietta M. VI, 162
Bates, Henrietta M. VI, 264
Bates, Henrietta Maria VI, 132
Bates, Henrietta Maria VI, 155
Bates, Henrietta Maria VI, 156
Bates, Henrietta Maria VI, 161
Bates, Henrietta Maria VI, 162
Bates, Henrietta Maria VI, 228
Bates, Henriette Maria VI, 130
Bates, Henry IV, 944
Bates, Henry VI, 877
Bates, Hezekiah II, 55
Bates, Ida May IV, 464
Bates, Idamay IV, 464
Bates, Ira B. IV, 1035
Bates, Isaac III, 29
Bates, Isaac Ashton II, 696
Bates, J. IV, 1246
Bates, J. W. IV, 1306
Bates, Jacob VI, 230
Bates, James IV, 464
Bates, James VI, 8
Bates, James VI, 13
Bates, James VI, 15
Bates, James VI, 100
Bates, James VI, 110
Bates, James VI, 155
Bates, James VI, 156
Bates, James VI, 157
Bates, James VI, 161
Bates, James VI, 184
Bates, James VI, 188
Bates, James VI, 190
Bates, James VI, 194
Bates, James VI, 229
Bates, James Oldden II, 22
Bates, James Oldden II, 461
Bates, James Olden II, 55
Bates, James W. VI, 798
Bates, James, Jr. VI, 157
Bates, Jane III, 244
Bates, Jane III, 395
Bates, Jane III, 431
Bates, Jane V, 985
Bates, Jeannette III, 29
Bates, Jeannette III, 254
Bates, Jeannette A. III, 254
Bates, Jesse J. IV, 924
Bates, John II, 55
Bates, John VI, 8
Bates, John VI, 12
Bates, John VI, 13
Bates, John VI, 15
Bates, John VI, 155
Bates, John VI, 156
Bates, John VI, 176
Bates, John VI, 201
Bates, John VI, 877
Bates, John R. VI, 228
Bates, John Stebbins III, 29
Bates, John, Jr. VI, 155
Bates, John, Jr. VI, 176
Bates, Jos. IV, 464
Bates, Jos. D. IV, 504
Bates, Joseph II, 33
Bates, Joseph II, 335
Bates, Joseph II, 977
Bates, Joseph III, 29
Bates, Joseph D. IV, 174
Bates, Joseph Denson IV, 464
Bates, Joseph Denson VI, 155
Bates, Joseph Denson VI, 157
Bates, Joshua IV, 174
Bates, Joshua IV, 464
Bates, Joshua VI, 155
Bates, Julia VI, 877
Bates, Julia A. IV, 174
Bates, Julia A. IV, 264
Bates, Julia Ann IV, 174
Bates, Juliann IV, 174
Bates, Katy VI, 966
Bates, Lemuel VI, 228
Bates, Lemuel VI, 229
Bates, Lemuel VI, 731
Bates, Lemuel VI, 877
Bates, Lemuel VI, 934
Bates, Lemuel VI, 999
Bates, Lewis VI, 877
Bates, Lillian M. II, 836
Bates, Lillian M. II, 874
Bates, Lucretia II, 335
Bates, Lucy VI, 157
Bates, Lucy VI, 228
Bates, Lucy VI, 872
Bates, Lucy H. IV, 174
Bates, Lucy H. VI, 155
Bates, Lulu V, 985
Bates, Lydia IV, 174
Bates, Lydia IV, 230
Bates, Lydia IV, 464
Bates, Lydia IV, 483
Bates, Lydia IV, 505
Bates, Lydia VI, 188
Bates, Lydia Ann IV, 925
Bates, Lydia J. IV, 924
Bates, Maggie W. VI, 230
Bates, Margaret IV, 174
Bates, Margaret IV, 181
Bates, Margaret VI, 155
Bates, Margaret VI, 157
Bates, Margaret VI, 228
Bates, Margaret VI, 230
Bates, Martha IV, 174
Bates, Martha IV, 368
Bates, Martha VI, 155
Bates, Martha VI, 157
Bates, Martha VI, 228
Bates, Martha VI, 229
Bates, Martha VI, 263
Bates, Martha VI, 280
Bates, Martha VI, 968
Bates, Martha Ann VI, 157
Bates, Martha Ann VI, 229
Bates, Mary II, 22
Bates, Mary II, 55
Bates, Mary II, 460
Bates, Mary II, 543
Bates, Mary II, 866
Bates, Mary II, 905
Bates, Mary IV, 174
Bates, Mary IV, 224
Bates, Mary IV, 232
Bates, Mary IV, 1246
Bates, Mary IV, 1306
Bates, Mary VI, 155
Bates, Mary VI, 156
Bates, Mary VI, 157
Bates, Mary VI, 178
Bates, Mary VI, 209
Bates, Mary VI, 229
Bates, Mary VI, 877
Bates, Mary VI, 959
Bates, Mary VI, 998
Bates, Mary Alice IV, 174
Bates, Mary Ann IV, 944
Bates, Mary E. IV, 464
Bates, Mary Elizabeth IV, 464
Bates, Mary Elizabeth IV, 677
Bates, Mary F. VI, 228
Bates, Mary Frances III, 254
Bates, Mary M. IV, 174
Bates, Mary Morton VI, 155
Bates, Mary P. IV, 464
Bates, Mary P. IV, 504
Bates, Mary W. IV, 464
Bates, Mary Wood IV, 464
Bates, Matilda Jordan IV, 174
Bates, Matilda Jordan VI, 155
Bates, Matilda Jordan VI, 157
Bates, Mauda V, 985
Bates, Maudie V, 985
Bates, Mercy II, 33
Bates, Mercy II, 55
Bates, Micajah VI, 155
Bates, Micajah VI, 157
Bates, Micajah VI, 178
Bates, Micajah VI, 196
Bates, Micajah VI, 228
Bates, Micajah VI, 229
Bates, Micajah VI, 230
Bates, Micajah VI, 272
Bates, Mollie VI, 229
Bates, Molly VI, 920
Bates, Moore VI, 157
Bates, Moore VI, 158
Bates, Myra A. III, 29
Bates, Nancy I, 1114
Bates, Nancy I, 1126
Bates, Nancy VI, 230
Bates, Nancy VI, 798
Bates, Nathan P. IV, 174
Bates, Nathan Pusey IV, 174
Bates, Nathan Pusey IV, 464
Bates, Nellie IV, 1035
Bates, Oliver IV, 174
Bates, Oliver L. IV, 174
Bates, Ora May IV, 1035
Bates, Orville IV, 1246
Bates, Pattie A. VI, 229
Bates, Paul IV, 1246
Bates, Paul IV, 1306
Bates, Phebe II, 55
Bates, Raymond IV, 1246
Bates, Raymond IV, 1306
Bates, Rebecca II, 22
Bates, Rebecca II, 55
Bates, Rebecca II, 145
Bates, Rebecca IV, 174
Bates, Rebecca VI, 155
Bates, Rebecca VI, 157
Bates, Rebecca VI, 158
Bates, Rebeckah II, 55
Bates, Richmond VI, 229
Bates, Sally I. Clark VI, 228
Bates, Samuel VI, 877
Bates, Sarah II, 335
Bates, Sarah III, 395
Bates, Sarah IV, 174
Bates, Sarah IV, 218
Bates, Sarah IV, 224
Bates, Sarah IV, 281
Bates, Sarah VI, 15
Bates, Sarah VI, 155
Bates, Sarah VI, 156
Bates, Sarah VI, 176
Bates, Sarah VI, 188
Bates, Sarah VI, 201
Bates, Sarah Ann IV, 174
Bates, Sarah C. IV, 464
Bates, Sarah Catherine IV, 464
Bates, Sarah I. VI, 229
Bates, Sarah I. VI, 234
Bates, Sarah I. VI, 235
Bates, Sarah J. IV, 174
Bates, Sarah J. VI, 157
Bates, Sarah Jordan IV, 174
Bates, Sarah Jordan VI, 155
Bates, Sarah Jordan VI, 156
Bates, Sarah Jordan VI, 157
Bates, Sarah Jordan VI, 209
Bates, Sibyl IV, 924
Bates, Sibyl IV, 1011
Bates, Skimino VI, 157
Bates, Spence VI, 731
Bates, Susan VI, 250
Bates, Susan F. Hubbard VI, 228
Bates, Susan L. IV, 174
Bates, Susan R. III, 29
Bates, Susan R. VI, 250
Bates, Susanna F. VI, 249

Bates, Susanna Fleming VI, 155
Bates, Susanna P. IV, 174
Bates, Susanna P. IV, 464
Bates, Susannah VI, 155
Bates, Susannah VI, 176
Bates, Susannah VI, 250
Bates, Susannah Fleming VI, 156
Bates, Susannah R. VI, 229
Bates, Susannah, Jr. VI, 155
Bates, Tace IV, 464
Bates, Tace VI, 155
Bates, Tace VI, 157
Bates, Tace VI, 228
Bates, Tace VI, 229
Bates, Tace VI, 238
Bates, Tace VI, 239
Bates, Tace C. VI, 229
Bates, Tace C. VI, 237
Bates, Tace Crew VI, 228
Bates, Tace Elizabeth VI, 229
Bates, Tacy IV, 174
Bates, Tacy IV, 237
Bates, Tacy IV, 464
Bates, Tacy IV, 483
Bates, Tacy E. VI, 229
Bates, Tacy E. VI, 263
Bates, Thomas IV, 174
Bates, Thomas VI, 156
Bates, Thomas VI, 220
Bates, Thomas VI, 229
Bates, Thomas Fleming VI, 155
Bates, Thomas W. IV, 174
Bates, Thomas W. IV, 464
Bates, Unity VI, 228
Bates, Unity VI, 229
Bates, Unity VI, 239
Bates, Unity VI, 244
Bates, Unity VI, 249
Bates, Unity VI, 731
Bates, Unity VI, 737
Bates, Unity, Sr. VI, 229
Bates, Violet B. VI, 877
Bates, W. G. IV, 1246
Bates, W. J. IV, 1246
Bates, W. J. IV, 1306
Bates, Walter G. VI, 230
Bates, Wd. Elizabeth VI, 156
Bates, Wd. Sarah VI, 156
Bates, William IV, 174
Bates, William IV, 464
Bates, William VI, 155
Bates, William VI, 157
Bates, William VI, 877
Bates, William VI, 920
Bates, William VI, 966
Bates, William VI, 967
Bates, William I. VI, 798
Bates, William J. IV, 174
Bates, William Jordan VI, 155
Bates, William S. IV, 174
Bates, William S. VI, 229
Bates, William Savery IV, 464
Bates, William Savery VI, 228
Bates, William, Jr. VI, 877
Bates, William, Sr. VI, 968
Bates, Wm. II, 22
Bates, Wm. II, 55
Bates, Wm. IV, 174
Bates, Wm. VI, 887
Bates, Wm. VI, 998
Bates, Wm. Rolly Crouch VI, 872
Bates, Wm. S. IV, 483
Bates, Wm. S. IV, 505
Bates, Wm. Savory IV, 464
Bates, Wm., Sr. VI, 967
Batey, Sarah J. V, 707
Batfy, Abigail III, 427
Batfy, David III, 427
Bath, Bertha V, 658
Bath, Bertha V, 703
Bath, Bessie G. V, 475
Bath, Dorothy V, 658
Bath, Edwin J. V, 475
Bath, Elizabeth V, 475
Bath, Elizabeth V, 658
Bath, Fred C. V, 475
Bath, Fred C. V, 658
Bath, Frederic V, 475
Bath, Harry F. V, 475
Bath, J. Harold V, 475
Bath, J. Harroll V, 658
Bath, Lydia V, 475
Bath, Rachel K. V, 658
Bath, Rata V, 658
Bath, Rata K. V, 475
Bath, Robert V, 658
Bath, Robert K. V, 475
Bath, Robert K. V, 658
Bath, Russell V, 152
Bath, William II, 335
Batley, Susanna H. IV, 397
Baton, Frank VI, 11
Bats, John VI, 8
Batt, John II, 166
Battan, Emely T. V, 947
Battan, Kersy R. V, 947
Battan, Martha Alma V, 947
Battan, Orlando G. V, 947
Battan, Samuel R. V, 947
Batte, Eliza II, 197
Batte, Elizabeth II, 197
Battelle, ??? III, 238
Battelle, Catharine B. III, 29
Battelle, Catharine B. III, 238
Battelle, Eliza III, 29
Battelle, Lindley III, 29
Battels, Clarence IV, 1306
Batten, Abigail IV, 924
Batten, Abigail Jr. IV, 901
Batten, Ann I, 1028
Batten, Ann IV, 139
Batten, Ann IV, 641
Batten, Ann IV, 677
Batten, Ann IV, 798
Batten, Ann V, 23
Batten, Ann V, 789
Batten, Ann, Jr. IV, 139
Batten, Benjamin IV, 924
Batten, Catharine V, 779
Batten, Catherine IV, 798
Batten, Catherine V, 779
Batten, David IV, 677
Batten, Eli IV, 262
Batten, Eli IV, 677
Batten, Elizabeth IV, 641
Batten, Elizabeth IV, 677
Batten, Espy IV, 798
Batten, Ezra IV, 677
Batten, Fanney IV, 677
Batten, Hannah IV, 924
Batten, Hannah C. IV, 938
Batten, John IV, 224
Batten, John IV, 641
Batten, John IV, 677
Batten, Jonathan IV, 798
Batten, Jonathan IV, 840
Batten, Joseph II, 727
Batten, Joshua IV, 677
Batten, Lydia IV, 677
Batten, Miriam IV, 798
Batten, Phebe IV, 262
Batten, Priscilla IV, 798
Batten, Priscilla IV, 840
Batten, Rachel I, 373
Batten, Richard I, 1026
Batten, Richard I, 1028
Batten, Richard IV, 139
Batten, Richard IV, 798
Batten, Richard V, 152
Batten, Richard V, 779
Batten, Richard, Jr. I, 1026
Batten, Richards, Jr. V, 23
Batten, Robert IV, 677
Batten, Robert IV, 901
Batten, Robert IV, 924
Batten, Sarah D. IV, 224
Batten, Susanna I, 373
Batterson, Lewis II, 781
Batterson, Lewis II, 836
Batterson, Malinda II, 703
Batterson, Sarah II, 781
Batterson, Susan II, 836
Battes, Elizabeth VI, 798
Battes, James VI, 798
Battey, Abigail III, 395
Battey, Anna III, 29
Battey, Anna III, 187
Battey, Anna III, 308
Battey, Anna G. III, 29
Battey, Anna G. III, 265
Battey, Anna K. III, 29
Battey, Caroline III, 106
Battey, Caroline L. III, 29
Battey, Caroline L. III, 307
Battey, Caroline L. III, 308
Battey, Daniel III, 395
Battey, Deborah IV, 609
Battey, Deborah IV, 614
Battey, Deborah C. IV, 609
Battey, Deborah C. IV, 677
Battey, Elbert L. Cope IV, 677
Battey, Elizabeth K. III, 29
Battey, Esther III, 28
Battey, Esther III, 29
Battey, Herman J. IV, 368
Battey, Isabella H. IV, 368
Battey, Jaell II, 55
Battey, Jaell II, 88
Battey, Janet III, 29
Battey, Jesse III, 29
Battey, Jesse B. III, 28
Battey, Jonathan III, 29
Battey, Jonathan III, 187
Battey, Jonathan III, 265
Battey, Lavina H. IV, 609
Battey, Lavina H. IV, 621
Battey, Lois C. III, 29
Battey, Lois Margaret IV, 368
Battey, Louisa III, 266
Battey, Lucinda IV, 609
Battey, Lucinda IV, 617
Battey, Lucinda IV, 621
Battey, Lydia K. III, 29
Battey, Lydia K. III, 265
Battey, Malinda IV, 609
Battey, Malinda E. IV, 617
Battey, Malinda E. IV, 677
Battey, Malinda E. IV, 694
Battey, Mary IV, 1351
Battey, Mary B. IV, 609
Battey, Mary K. III, 29
Battey, Mary R. IV, 609
Battey, Melinda E. IV, 609
Battey, Mifflin IV, 677
Battey, Phila A. III, 28
Battey, Phila A. III, 29
Battey, Rachel E. IV, 320
Battey, Rachel E. IV, 347
Battey, Ralph D. IV, 368
Battey, Rhoda III, 29
Battey, Rhoda B. III, 29
Battey, Richard Chester IV, 368
Battey, Rudderah II, 55
Battey, Rudderah II, 88
Battey, Ruth A. III, 187
Battey, Ruth H. III, 29
Battey, Ruth Osborn III, 29
Battey, Sarah IV, 677
Battey, Susanna H. IV, 959
Battey, Susannah IV, 980
Battey, Susannah H. IV, 714
Battey, Thomas IV, 614
Battey, Thomas C. IV, 609
Battey, Thomas C. IV, 617
Battey, Thomas C. IV, 621
Battey, Walter IV, 677
Battey, William A. III, 29
Battey, William A., Jr. III, 29
Battey, William J. III, 29
Battick, Dinah I, 373
Battick, Dinah I, 399
Battie, Eliza II, 197
Battie, Elizabeth II, 197
Battie, Walter IV, 677
Battin, Aaron IV, 174
Battin, Abigail IV, 20
Battin, Abigail IV, 610
Battin, Abigail IV, 677
Battin, Abigail IV, 798
Battin, Abigail IV, 891
Battin, Abigail IV, 899
Battin, Abigail IV, 1021
Battin, Abigail IV, 1023
Battin, Abigail Jr. IV, 899
Battin, Amelia M. II, 948
Battin, Amelia M. II, 1087
Battin, Amelia M. II, 1088
Battin, Amelia W. II, 1085
Battin, Amos IV, 1023
Battin, Amy IV, 174
Battin, Amy IV, 311
Battin, Ann I, 1017
Battin, Ann IV, 20
Battin, Ann IV, 54
Battin, Ann IV, 174
Battin, Ann IV, 311
Battin, Ann IV, 677
Battin, Ann IV, 798
Battin, Ann IV, 891
Battin, Ann IV, 899
Battin, Ann IV, 900
Battin, Ann IV, 1023
Battin, Ann B. IV, 677
Battin, Ann B. IV, 700
Battin, Ann, Jr. IV, 798
Battin, Ann, Jr. IV, 899
Battin, Anna IV, 677
Battin, Asa IV, 899
Battin, Benjamin IV, 677
Battin, Benjamin IV, 891
Battin, Benjamin IV, 899
Battin, Benjamin IV, 924
Battin, Benjamin IV, 1023
Battin, Benjamin C. IV, 1023
Battin, Benjmain IV, 893
Battin, Betsy IV, 899
Battin, C. Sumner IV, 1023
Battin, Catharine I, 1017
Battin, Catharine II, 1085
Battin, Catharine II, 1087
Battin, Catharine II, 1088
Battin, Catharine IV, 609
Battin, Catharine IV, 787
Battin, Catharine IV, 899
Battin, Catherine IV, 677
Battin, Catherine IV, 798
Battin, Charles Sumner V, 947
Battin, Cynthia II, 948
Battin, Cynthia II, 949
Battin, Cynthia II, 1087
Battin, Cynthia II, 1088
Battin, David IV, 20
Battin, David IV, 677
Battin, David IV, 798
Battin, David IV, 899
Battin, David IV, 914
Battin, David IV, 1023
Battin, David C. IV, 677
Battin, Edith Dell IV, 1024
Battin, Edith Dell IV, 1029
Battin, Eli IV, 20
Battin, Eli IV, 174
Battin, Eli IV, 610
Battin, Eli IV, 677
Battin, Eli IV, 798
Battin, Eli IV, 837
Battin, Eli IV, 857
Battin, Elizabeth IV, 20
Battin, Elizabeth IV, 677
Battin, Elizabeth IV, 798
Battin, Elizabeth IV, 1023
Battin, Elva IV, 1023
Battin, Elva IV, 1029
Battin, Elvira IV, 899
Battin, Emely T. V, 947
Battin, Emily IV, 1023
Battin, Emily IV, 1031
Battin, Emily T. IV, 175
Battin, Emily T. IV, 677
Battin, Emily Tomlinson IV, 174
Battin, Ephraim Ann V, 947
Battin, Epsey IV, 899
Battin, Epsey IV, 915
Battin, Espy IV, 798
Battin, Ezra IV, 20
Battin, Ezra IV, 677
Battin, Ezra IV, 798
Battin, Fanney IV, 677
Battin, Fannie IV, 899
Battin, Fanny IV, 20
Battin, Fanny IV, 677
Battin, Fanny IV, 798
Battin, Fanny IV, 849
Battin, Franklin IV, 1023
Battin, Hannah IV, 677
Battin, Hannah IV, 899
Battin, Hannah C. IV, 677
Battin, Hannah C. IV, 690
Battin, Hannah C. IV, 1023
Battin, Hannah G. IV, 677
Battin, Hannah G. IV, 891
Battin, Hannah G. IV, 893
Battin, Hannah G. IV, 1023
Battin, Howard IV, 899
Battin, James I, 1017
Battin, James IV, 798
Battin, Jane IV, 174
Battin, Jane IV, 610
Battin, Jane IV, 798
Battin, Jane IV, 908
Battin, Jane IV, 1023
Battin, Jane W. IV, 610
Battin, Jane W. IV, 899
Battin, Jesse IV, 174
Battin, John I, 1017
Battin, John IV, 20
Battin, John IV, 54
Battin, John IV, 174
Battin, John IV, 609
Battin, John IV, 677
Battin, John IV, 798
Battin, John IV, 857
Battin, John IV, 897
Battin, John IV, 899
Battin, John IV, 900
Battin, John IV, 1023
Battin, John, Jr. IV, 174
Battin, John, Jr. IV, 798
Battin, Jonathan I, 1017
Battin, Jonathan IV, 609
Battin, Jonathan IV, 798
Battin, Joseph II, 727
Battin, Joseph IV, 1023
Battin, Joshua II, 948
Battin, Joshua II, 1087
Battin, Joshua II, 1088
Battin, Joshua IV, 20
Battin, Joshua IV, 677
Battin, Joshua IV, 798
Battin, Josiah IV, 1023
Battin, Kersey R. IV, 677
Battin, Kersy R. V, 947
Battin, Lucinda IV, 899
Battin, Lucinda M. IV, 677
Battin, Lydia IV, 20
Battin, Lydia IV, 174
Battin, Lydia IV, 677
Battin, Lydia IV, 798
Battin, Lydia IV, 840
Battin, Lydia Ann IV, 1023
Battin, Lydia H. IV, 1023
Battin, Margaret IV, 798
Battin, Margaret IV, 851
Battin, Marshall II, 1087
Battin, Marshall II, 1088
Battin, Martha Alma IV, 677
Battin, Martha Alma V, 947
Battin, Martha Elma IV, 677
Battin, Mary II, 788
Battin, Mary II, 1087
Battin, Mary II, 1088
Battin, Mary IV, 677
Battin, Mary IV, 899
Battin, Mary A. IV, 1023
Battin, Mary A. IV, 1029
Battin, Mary A. V, 947
Battin, Minor IV, 899
Battin, Miriam IV, 798
Battin, Miriam IV, 899
Battin, Nathan IV, 174
Battin, Orlando G. V, 947
Battin, Orlando Sumner II, 946
Battin, Orlando T. IV, 677
Battin, Oscar IV, 1306
Battin, Oscar L. IV, 1306
Battin, Phebe IV, 174
Battin, Phebe IV, 610
Battin, Phebe IV, 798
Battin, Phebe IV, 837
Battin, Phebe IV, 899
Battin, Priscilla IV, 174
Battin, Priscilla IV, 311
Battin, Priscilla IV, 798
Battin, Priscilla IV, 899
Battin, Rachel I, 373
Battin, Rachel I, 384
Battin, Rachel IV, 1023
Battin, Rachel G. IV, 677
Battin, Rhoda IV, 174
Battin, Rhoda IV, 311
Battin, Richard I, 1017
Battin, Richard I, 1026
Battin, Richard IV, 20
Battin, Richard IV, 787
Battin, Richard IV, 798
Battin, Richard IV, 857
Battin, Richard IV, 899
Battin, Richard, Jr. I, 1026
Battin, Richard, Jr. IV, 677
Battin, Robert IV, 20
Battin, Robert IV, 677
Battin, Robert IV, 798
Battin, Robert IV, 891
Battin, Robert IV, 899
Battin, Robert IV, 1021
Battin, Robert IV, 1023
Battin, Ruth IV, 174
Battin, Ruth IV, 175
Battin, Ruth IV, 254
Battin, Ruth IV, 677
Battin, Ruth Anna IV, 899
Battin, Ruthanna IV, 677
Battin, Ruthanna IV, 900
Battin, Samuel II, 727
Battin, Samuel II, 1085
Battin, Samuel II, 1087
Battin, Samuel II, 1088
Battin, Samuel IV, 174
Battin, Samuel R. IV, 677
Battin, Samuel R. IV, 1023
Battin, Samuel R. IV, 1031
Battin, Samuel R. V, 947
Battin, Sarah IV, 20
Battin, Sarah IV, 56
Battin, Sarah IV, 174
Battin, Sarah IV, 274
Battin, Sarah IV, 610
Battin, Sarah IV, 900
Battin, Sarah IV, 914
Battin, Sarah Ann IV, 899
Battin, Sarah Ann IV, 1023
Battin, Sarah D. IV, 174
Battin, Sarah D. IV, 677
Battin, Sarah D. IV, 899
Battin, Sumner IV, 1029
Battin, Tace IV, 174
Battin, Tacy IV, 311
Battin, Thomas IV, 174
Battin, Thomas IV, 677
Battin, Thomas IV, 1023
Battin, William IV, 899
Battin, Winslow L. IV, 1023
Battin, Winslow L. IV, 1024
Battin, Winslow L. IV, 1029
Battle, Ann I, 229

Battle, Charity Battle I, 229
Battle, Henry Horn I, 229
Battle, Jacob I, 229
Battle, Joel Horn I, 229
Battle, Phebe Ricks I, 229
Batton, ??? IV, 795
Batton, Ann I, 1047
Batton, Ann IV, 894
Batton, Cathren I, 1047
Batton, Elizabeth IV, 832
Batton, James I, 1047
Batton, John I, 1047
Batton, John IV, 894
Batton, Jonathan I, 1047
Batton, Priscilla IV, 311
Batton, Rachel I, 350
Batton, Rachel I, 373
Batton, Richard I, 1026
Batton, Richard I, 1047
Batton, Samuel I, 350
Batton, Samuel II, 727
Batton, Samuel IV, 320
Batton, Sarah IV, 320
Batts, Alton I, 219
Batts, Ann IV, 45
Batts, Margaret Helen I, 219
Batts, Thomas VI, 289
Battson, Ann II, 461
Battson, Ann II, 690
Battson, Peter Wishart II, 461
Battson, Thomas II, 461
Battson, Thomas II, 690
Batty, Abigail III, 395
Batty, Abigail III, 479
Batty, Daniel III, 395
Batty, Herman J. IV, 368
Batty, Isabelle H. IV, 368
Batty, Jael II, 35
Batty, John III, 479
Batty, Lois Margaret IV, 368
Batty, M. Irene IV, 368
Batty, Mary III, 479
Batty, Mary III, 481
Batty, Mary IV, 1351
Batty, Mary R. IV, 609
Batty, Rachel E. IV, 320
Batty, Rachel E. IV, 347
Batty, Ralph D. IV, 368
Batty, Richard II, 35
Batty, Richard Chester IV, 368
Batty, Samuel Franklin IV, 368
Baty, Elizabeth II, 461
Batzli, David IV, 925
Batzli, Mabel IV, 925
Baucher, Francelia III, 94
Baucker, Sally Ann III, 479
Bauer, Albert III, 29
Bauer, Isaac V, 23
Bauer, Isaac V, 967
Bauer, Jonathan V, 23
Bauer, Jonathan J. V, 967
Bauer, Joseph V, 967
Bauer, Lydia V, 23
Bauer, Lydia V, 967
Bauer, Lydia V, 969
Bauer, Ruth II, 698
Bauer, Sarah V, 23
Bauer, Wm. J. V, 967
Bauford, Demarquis VI, 885
Bauford, Mary Ann VI, 885
Baugh, Bartlet VI, 804
Baugh, Bartlett VI, 807
Baugh, Betsy VI, 807
Baugh, Betsy H. VI, 798
Baugh, Elizabeth VI, 855
Baugh, John VI, 804
Baugh, John VI, 860
Baugh, Lucy B. VI, 804
Baugh, Mary A. VI, 860
Baugh, Richard VI, 798
Baugh, Thomas VI, 829
Baugham, Gertrude H. V, 612
Baugham, John C. V, 658
Baugham, Mabel V, 916
Baugham, Mary V, 481
Baugham, Mary VI, 310
Baugham, Mary VI, 816
Baugham, Milisent I, 229
Baugham, Mille C. I, 229
Baugham, Rachel M. V, 549
Baugham, Rachel M. V, 567
Baughan, Anna VI, 798
Baughan, Benj. VI, 798
Baughan, Henry VI, 798
Baughan, Lucy VI, 798
Baughan, Patsy VI, 798
Baughan, Richard VI, 798
Baughan, Thomas VI, 798
Baughan, William John VI, 1011
Baughm, Ann E. I, 215
Baughm, Anna I, 207
Baughm, Anna I, 229
Baughm, Anna E. I, 229
Baughm, Anne E. I, 239
Baughm, Elizabeth I, 207
Baughm, Elizabeth I, 229
Baughm, Ella F. I, 229
Baughm, Frances R. I, 229
Baughm, Frances Rebecca I, 207
Baughm, Frances Rebecca I, 212
Baughm, Jesse I, 207
Baughm, John I, 207
Baughm, John I, 229
Baughm, Jordan I, 215
Baughm, Jordan I, 229
Baughm, Jordon I, 207
Baughm, Jordon I, 212
Baughm, Jordon I, 229
Baughm, Joseph I, 207
Baughm, Jourdan I, 229
Baughm, Lydia Jordon I, 207
Baughm, Margaret P. I, 229
Baughm, Margaret Priscilla I, 207
Baughm, Martha I, 207
Baughm, Martha I, 212
Baughm, Martha I, 215
Baughm, Martha I, 229
Baughm, Martha I, 241
Baughm, Martha Jane I, 207
Baughm, Milercent I, 207
Baughm, Milicent I, 207
Baughm, Milicent I, 229
Baughm, Milisent I, 229
Baughm, Mille C. I, 229
Baughm, Noah I, 207
Baughm, Noah I, 229
Baughm, Rachel I, 207
Baughm, Rachel I, 229
Baughm, William Jordon I, 207
Baughm, William Jourdan I, 229
Baughman, Andrew V, 985
Baughman, Elizabeth V, 630
Baughman, Elizabeth V, 893
Baughman, Emanuel IV, 798
Baughman, Emma IV, 798
Baughman, Florence IV, 798
Baughman, Mabel V, 893
Baughman, Mariah V, 985
Baughman, W. J. V, 893
Baughman, Zachariah M. V, 630
Baughn, Addaline C. VI, 941
Baughn, Dosha VI, 877
Baughn, Elizabeth N. VI, 929
Baughn, Frances A. VI, 911
Baughn, John VI, 877
Baughn, John VI, 941
Baughn, Kate V, 612
Baughn, Theodacia C. N. VI, 929
Baughorn, Wm. VI, 807
Baulden, Richard V, 984
Bauldin, John VI, 877
Bauldin, Richard V, 984
Bauldin, Sophia VI, 877
Baum, Anna I, 207
Baum, Elizabeth I, 207
Baum, Frances R. I, 229
Baum, Frances R. I, 234
Baum, Frances Rebecca I, 207
Baum, Jesse I, 207
Baum, John I, 207
Baum, John I, 229
Baum, Jordan I, 229
Baum, Jordon I, 207
Baum, Joseph I, 207
Baum, Lydia Jordon I, 207
Baum, Margaret Priscilla I, 207
Baum, Martha I, 207
Baum, Martha Jane I, 207
Baum, Mary Jane IV, 677
Baum, Mary Jane IV, 721
Baum, Milercent I, 207
Baum, Noah I, 207
Baum, William Jordon I, 207
Bauman, Berdena Ella IV, 925
Bauman, Elmer IV, 925
Bauman, Ethel Irene IV, 925
Bauman, Iva IV, 925
Bauman, Iva Ola IV, 925
Bauman, Lester John IV, 925
Bauman, Walter IV, 1246
Baums, Jordan I, 229
Baums, Jourdan I, 229
Baums, Martha I, 229
Bausch, Pauline III, 479
Bausch, Robert III, 479
Bauser, Frank V, 152
Bauwis, ??? III, 116
Bauwis, Deborah III, 29
Bauwis, Deborah III, 116
Bauwis, Geo. III, 29
Bauwis, Sarah III, 29
Bavander, Anna I, 982
Bawler, Joshua II, 441
Bawler, Mary II, 441
Bawls, Charlie V, 728
Bawls, Ellie V, 728
Bawls, John V, 728
Bawls, Nettie V, 728
Bax, Henry V, 967
Baxla, Abe V, 612
Baxla, Rose V, 612
Baxley, Ellen III, 29
Baxley, Ellen III, 84
Baxley, Ellwood III, 29
Baxley, R. III, 84
Baxley, Sarah P. III, 29
Baxter, ??? III, 29
Baxter, Alonzo V, 985
Baxter, Anne VI, 877
Baxter, B. F. V, 985
Baxter, Betsy IV, 900
Baxter, Betsy IV, 910
Baxter, Catharine V, 985
Baxter, Deborah IV, 799
Baxter, Deborah IV, 900
Baxter, Geo. VI, 877
Baxter, Glen V, 985
Baxter, Hattie V, 985
Baxter, J. V, 475
Baxter, James I, 611
Baxter, John I, 525
Baxter, John I, 611
Baxter, Maria III, 29
Baxter, Mary II, 461
Baxter, Mary II, 683
Baxter, Mary V, 24
Baxter, Mary V, 475
Baxter, Mary C. III, 60
Baxter, Mary C. III, 61
Baxter, Mary F. I, 611
Baxter, Nancy C. V, 985
Baxter, Philip III, 29
Baxter, Philip Arestus III, 29
Baxter, Robert III, 29
Baxter, Sarah I, 611
Baxter, Sarah IV, 567
Baxter, Sarah IV, 586
Baxton, Sarah S. V, 985
Bay, Elizabeth II, 461
Bay, Elizabeth II, 462
Bay, Florence W. IV, 368
Bay, Florence W. IV, 453
Bay, Hugh II, 335
Bay, John V, 221
Bayard, Bell C. IV, 677
Bayard, Charles V, 658
Bayard, Isabella C. IV, 925
Bayard, Lenna V, 658
Bayard, Martha Isabella IV, 925
Bayer, Adam J. VI, 884
Bayer, Doctor ??? VI, 885
Bayer, Joseph VI, 828
Bayer, Joseph VI, 877
Bayer, Landonia C. VI, 885
Bayer, Michael VI, 877
Bayer, Nancy VI, 877
Bayer, Polley VI, 877
Bayerd, Belle IV, 1306
Bayes, Grace II, 335
Bayes, Joseph VI, 877
Bayes, Mary II, 335
Bayes, Nancy VI, 877
Bayham, Edwin F. V, 612
Bayham, George V, 452
Bayham, George V, 612
Bayham, George C. V, 612
Bayham, James O. V, 612
Bayham, Lena M. V, 612
Bayham, Mary Alice V, 612
Bayham, Olen J. V, 612
Bayham, William A. V, 658
Bayles, John VI, 877
Bayles, Rhoda VI, 877
Bayles, Ruth V, 476
Bayles, Ruth V, 490
Bayless, Anna V, 658
Bayless, Anna V, 671
Bayless, Helen V, 475
Bayless, Helen Myrtle V, 658
Bayless, Helen Myrtle V, 667
Bayless, Marie V, 475
Bayless, Roy V, 475
Bayless, Sallie I, 1147
Bayley, Ann II, 977
Bayley, Ann II, 1000
Bayley, Christina II, 457
Bayley, David I, 523
Bayley, David I, 581
Bayley, Edith II, 977
Bayley, Edward II, 977
Bayley, Edward II, 1000
Bayley, Elizabeth L. II, 457
Bayley, Ephraim I, 129
Bayley, James IV, 1049
Bayley, John Hervey IV, 1049
Bayley, Joseph II, 457
Bayley, Joshua, Jr. II, 457
Bayley, Lydia IV, 1049
Bayley, Mercy II, 977
Bayley, Mercy II, 994
Bayley, Mercy II, 1012
Bayley, Merriot II, 977
Bayley, Milley VI, 902
Bayley, Rebecca Alice IV, 1049
Bayley, Ruth I, 581
Bayley, Samuel II, 977
Bayley, Susannah V, 21
Bayley, Thomas II, 1012
Bayley, Thomas VI, 42
Bayley, Thomas, Jr. II, 977
Baylies, ??? III, 29
Baylies, Caroline Corinne V, 24
Baylies, Carrie Corinne V, 24
Baylies, Maria III, 29
Baylies, Rachel B. V, 24
Baylies, Rachel B. V, 33
Baylies, Rachel B. V, 71
Baylies, Rachel M. B. V, 24
Baylies, Rosannah III, 102
Baylies, Wd. Rosannah III, 29
Bayliff, Abel V, 475
Bayliff, Able V, 473
Bayliff, Allie I, 623
Bayliff, Amos V, 475
Bayliff, Anna V, 475
Bayliff, Daniel V, 473
Bayliff, Daniel V, 475
Bayliff, Daniel V, 476
Bayliff, Elizabeth V, 473
Bayliff, Elizabeth V, 534
Bayliff, Joel V, 476
Bayliff, Jones I, 372
Bayliff, Joshua V, 473
Bayliff, Joshua V, 475
Bayliff, Joshua V, 476
Bayliff, Judith V, 475
Bayliff, Leah V, 473
Bayliff, Leah V, 475
Bayliff, Leah V, 490
Bayliff, Leah V, 544
Bayliff, Lydia V, 476
Bayliff, Margaret V, 475
Bayliff, Margaret V, 476
Bayliff, Marion M. I, 623
Bayliff, Martha V, 473
Bayliff, Martha V, 475
Bayliff, Mary V, 473
Bayliff, Mary V, 475
Bayliff, Nancy A. I, 623
Bayliff, Polly V, 475
Bayliff, Sarah V, 473
Bayliff, Sarah V, 475
Bayliff, Sarah V, 476
Bayliff, Sarah V, 544
Bayliff, Thomas V, 475
Bayliff, Thomas V, 476
Bayliff, Thomas V, 544
Baylis, ??? III, 29
Baylis, Celia M. III, 29
Baylis, Charles W. III, 29
Baylis, Charles William III, 29
Baylis, Charles Wm. III, 29
Baylis, Chas. W. III, 29
Baylis, Chas. W. III, 259
Baylis, Chas. W. III, 324
Baylis, Chas. Wm. III, 190
Baylis, Clara R. III, 259
Baylis, Clara Remsen III, 29
Baylis, Clara Remson III, 29
Baylis, Clifford W. III, 29
Baylis, Daniel III, 29
Baylis, Daniel S. III, 29
Baylis, Elma III, 29
Baylis, Elma III, 324
Baylis, Elma C. III, 29
Baylis, Elma C. III, 259
Baylis, Elma C. III, 324
Baylis, Elma W. III, 29
Baylis, Elma W. III, 324
Baylis, Elma Willets III, 29
Baylis, Elsie E. III, 29
Baylis, Franklin III, 29
Baylis, Helen III, 29
Baylis, Helen III, 190
Baylis, Isaac W. III, 29
Baylis, John VI, 877
Baylis, Maria III, 29
Baylis, Rosanna III, 29
Baylis, Rosannah III, 29
Baylis, Ruth VI, 877
Baylis, Wd. Rosannah III, 29
Bayliss, Charles W. III, 353
Bayliss, Elma C. III, 353
Bayliss, John VI, 798
Bayliss, Ruth VI, 798
Bayly, Amos II, 977
Bayly, Ann II, 954
Bayly, Ann II, 977
Bayly, Ann II, 1000
Bayly, Ann II, 1022
Bayly, Ann II, 1024
Bayly, Catherine V, 21
Bayly, Christiana II, 977
Bayly, Deborah II, 977
Bayly, Deborah II, 1035
Bayly, Edith II, 954
Bayly, Edith II, 977
Bayly, Edith II, 1019
Bayly, Edward II, 954
Bayly, Edward II, 977
Bayly, Edward II, 1000
Bayly, Edward II, 1006
Bayly, Edward II, 1022
Bayly, Edward II, 1023
Bayly, Edward, Jr. II, 954
Bayly, Edward, Jr. II, 977
Bayly, Edward, Jr. II, 1024
Bayly, Elizabeth II, 977
Bayly, Elizabeth II, 983
Bayly, Enoch II, 977
Bayly, Enos II, 977
Bayly, Esther II, 977
Bayly, Hannah II, 977
Bayly, Hannah II, 1042
Bayly, Israel II, 977
Bayly, John II, 977
Bayly, John II, 1019
Bayly, Joseph II, 977
Bayly, Lacy II, 977
Bayly, Latitia II, 977
Bayly, Latitia II, 1023
Bayly, Letitia II, 977
Bayly, Marcy II, 977
Bayly, Marcy II, 1023
Bayly, Martha II, 977
Bayly, Martha II, 1006
Bayly, Mary II, 954
Bayly, Mary II, 977
Bayly, Mary II, 997
Bayly, Mary II, 1006
Bayly, Mercy II, 954
Bayly, Mercy II, 977
Bayly, Merriot II, 977
Bayly, Osmond II, 977
Bayly, Ozmonde II, 977
Bayly, Phebe II, 977
Bayly, Pleasant II, 954
Bayly, Rebecca IV, 143
Bayly, Samuel II, 977
Bayly, Sarah II, 977
Bayly, Sarah II, 1019
Bayly, Sarah II, 1040
Bayly, Suzannah IV, 143
Bayly, Tacy II, 954
Bayly, Tamer II, 977
Bayly, Tamer II, 1035
Bayly, Thomas II, 954
Bayly, Thomas II, 977
Bayly, Thomas, Jr. II, 977
Bayly, William II, 954
Bayly, Wm. II, 977
Bayly, Wm. IV, 143
Bayman, Sally VI, 926
Bayn, Elizabeth II, 255
Bayne, Betsey VI, 877
Bayne, Elizabeth II, 197
Bayne, Elizabeth VI, 877
Bayne, Griffin VI, 877
Bayne, Henry T. VI, 469
Bayne, Margaret II, 836
Bayne, Mary II, 836
Bayne, Mary VI, 469
Bayne, Nancy J. VI, 877
Bayne, Phebe VI, 469
Bayne, Phebe VI, 556
Bayne, Thomas VI, 877
Baynes, Bryan II, 954
Baynes, Deborah II, 977
Baynes, Deborah II, 978
Baynes, Elin II, 977
Baynes, Elinor II, 978
Baynes, Ellin II, 954
Baynes, Gabriel II, 978
Baynes, Gabriell II, 977
Baynes, Hannah II, 784
Baynes, James II, 836
Baynes, James II, 843
Baynes, Jennet II, 461
Baynes, John Beezer II, 843
Baynes, John Beezor II, 836
Baynes, John H. V, 24
Baynes, John H. V, 893
Baynes, John H. V, 894
Baynes, Margaret II, 836

Baynes, Margaret, Jr. II, 836
Baynes, Martha II, 836
Baynes, Martha II, 843
Baynes, Mary II, 836
Baynes, Mary II, 864
Baynes, Mary W. II, 794
Baynes, Mary W. II, 836
Baynes, Miriam II, 836
Baynes, Miriam II, 843
Baynes, Robert T. II, 461
Baynes, Thomas II, 461
Bays, Betsy Ann VI, 966
Bays, John P. VI, 966
Bays, Rebecca V, 894
Bays, Rebecca V, 925
Bayse, Amos VI, 877
Bayse, Polly VI, 877
Beach, Ada M. V, 184
Beach, Adda Maria V, 152
Beach, Addra Maria V, 152
Beach, Adra M. V, 89
Beach, Barbara III, 29
Beach, Barbara III, 32
Beach, Charles V, 152
Beach, Charles A. V, 152
Beach, Charlotte VI, 560
Beach, Charlotte E. VI, 467
Beach, Demas V, 689
Beach, Elta Lorena V, 152
Beach, Erskine IV, 677
Beach, George V, 152
Beach, Harrison V, 152
Beach, Harry IV, 677
Beach, Inez IV, 1035
Beach, Iva Catherine IV, 677
Beach, Jas. Harvey III, 395
Beach, John II, 441
Beach, John Henry III, 29
Beach, John Henry III, 30
Beach, Joseph VI, 469
Beach, Louisa Annie III, 29
Beach, Louisa Annie III, 30
Beach, Luella V, 152
Beach, Lysle VI, 467
Beach, Lysle VI, 469
Beach, Lysle VI, 560
Beach, Martha Jane V, 152
Beach, Martha S. III, 395
Beach, Mary IV, 677
Beach, Mary Ann V, 152
Beach, Mary Emily III, 395
Beach, Mary Emily III, 431
Beach, Mattie V, 152
Beach, Minta P. III, 29
Beach, Minta P. III, 32
Beach, Rachel Ann V, 152
Beach, Samuel V, 152
Beach, Samuel Foster V, 152
Beach, Sarah VI, 230
Beach, Sarah E. V, 152
Beach, Sarah Ellen V, 152
Beach, Silema VI, 469
Beach, Silema VI, 560
Beach, Silena VI, 469
Beach, Thomas VI, 230
Beacham, Anna V, 152
Beacham, Asa V, 152
Beacham, Charles I, 798
Beacham, Curtis I, 798
Beacham, Elizabeth I, 798
Beacham, Ellick I, 798
Beacham, Henry I, 798
Beacham, John I, 798
Beacham, Levi I, 798
Beacham, Martha V, 962
Beacham, Matthew I, 798
Beacham, Milcha I, 798
Beacham, Noah V, 152
Beacham, Rachel M. V, 152
Beacham, Russ I, 798
Beacham, Wesley V, 152
Beacham, William I, 798
Beacham, William V, 152
Beacham, Willis V, 152
Beachboard, Benjamin VI, 877
Beachboard, Elizabeth VI, 877
Beachum, Elizabeth I, 798
Beachum, Milcha I, 798
Beadle, ??? V, 832
Beadle, Anna IV, 1145
Beadle, David IV, 1145
Beadle, David, Jr. IV, 1145
Beadle, Reading A. V, 832
Beadley, Flora V, 985
Beagle, Mordecai III, 30
Beagle, William III, 30
Beak, ??? III, 30
Beak, Alce II, 335
Beak, Alfred Latcham III, 30
Beak, Elizabeth II, 335
Beak, Grace II, 335
Beak, John II, 335
Beak, Mary II, 980
Beak, Will II, 978
Beak, William II, 335
Beak, Wm. II, 335
Beakes, Alce II, 335
Beakes, Edmond II, 461
Beakes, Edmond II, 576
Beakes, Elizabeth II, 335
Beakes, Elizabeth II, 461
Beakes, Elizabeth II, 978
Beakes, Mary II, 978
Beakes, Stacey II, 978
Beakes, Wd. Elizabeth II, 576
Beakes, William II, 335
Beakes, Wm. II, 978
Beakman, Rachel IV, 1351
Beaks, Abraham II, 954
Beaks, Abraham II, 978
Beaks, Edmond II, 461
Beaks, Elizabeth II, 335
Beaks, Elizabeth II, 461
Beaks, Elizabeth II, 978
Beaks, Grace II, 978
Beaks, Johanah II, 954
Beaks, Mary II, 954
Beaks, Mary II, 978
Beaks, Mary II, 979
Beaks, Mary II, 999
Beaks, Nathan II, 461
Beaks, Nathan II, 463
Beaks, Ruth II, 954
Beaks, Ruth II, 978
Beaks, Ruth II, 1029
Beaks, Samuel II, 954
Beaks, Samuel II, 978
Beaks, Samuel II, 979
Beaks, Sarah II, 461
Beaks, Sarah II, 463
Beaks, Sarah II, 464
Beaks, Stacey II, 978
Beaks, Stacy II, 461
Beaks, Stacy II, 954
Beaks, Stacy II, 978
Beaks, Stephen II, 978
Beaks, Stephen II, 979
Beaks, Walter II, 954
Beaks, Will II, 978
Beaks, William II, 952
Beaks, William II, 954
Beaks, Wm. II, 335
Beaks, Wm. II, 461
Beaks, Wm. II, 694
Beaks, Wm. II, 978
Beaks, Wm. II, 1029
Beal, Alexander II, 978
Beal, Alexander II, 1033
Beal, Ann IV, 610
Beal, Catharine IV, 175
Beal, Elizabeth V, 222
Beal, Elizabeth V, 246
Beal, Elizabeth VI, 490
Beal, Emma V, 179
Beal, Frederick D. IV, 175
Beal, Grace V, 894
Beal, Grace V, 931
Beal, Grace VI, 615
Beal, Hannah IV, 607
Beal, Hannah IV, 610
Beal, Hannah IV, 631
Beal, Hannah IV, 667
Beal, Hannah V, 222
Beal, Hannah V, 947
Beal, Hannah V, 967
Beal, Hannah, Jr. VI, 469
Beal, Henrietta V, 612
Beal, Henrietta V, 639
Beal, Henrietta V, 726
Beal, Henrietta P. V, 612
Beal, Honour VI, 52
Beal, Ida IV, 175
Beal, Isaac B. VI, 615
Beal, Jacob VI, 490
Beal, Joab V, 476
Beal, Jos. H. I, 624
Beal, Joseph IV, 607
Beal, Joseph IV, 631
Beal, Joseph IV, 667
Beal, Joseph VI, 615
Beal, Joseph Otis IV, 1351
Beal, Joshua II, 461
Beal, Margaret IV, 20
Beal, Margaret IV, 27
Beal, Margaret VI, 615
Beal, Maria Mildred IV, 677
Beal, Mariah Mildred IV, 610
Beal, Martha II, 978
Beal, Mary IV, 175
Beal, Mary VI, 363
Beal, Mary VI, 366
Beal, Mary VI, 419
Beal, Pamelia Maria IV, 610
Beal, Pamelia Mariah IV, 677
Beal, Pemela Maria IV, 610
Beal, Pemela Maria IV, 659
Beal, Phebe II, 978
Beal, Pheby II, 1035
Beal, Rachel IV, 610
Beal, Rachel IV, 631
Beal, Rachel IV, 1351
Beal, Rachel V, 222
Beal, Rachel S. IV, 1351
Beal, Ronie Lovanna I, 624
Beal, Ruth IV, 1351
Beal, Samuel I, 1089
Beal, Samuel IV, 175
Beal, Sarah II, 461
Beal, Sarah II, 978
Beal, Sarah II, 1033
Beal, Sarah IV, 607
Beal, Sarah IV, 610
Beal, Sarah VI, 490
Beal, Susan IV, 1351
Beal, Susan IV, 1355
Beal, Susanna II, 461
Beal, Susie IV, 175
Beal, Thomas II, 978
Beal, Thos. II, 978
Beal, Thos. II, 1035
Beal, Viola V. V, 612
Beal, William IV, 1351
Beal, William V, 222
Beal, William VI, 363
Beal, William VI, 364
Beal, William VI, 366
Beal, William VI, 419
Beal, William James IV, 1351
Beal, Wm. II, 1035
Beale, Abigail N. III, 30
Beale, Abigail Nicholson III, 30
Beale, Alexander II, 197
Beale, Alexander II, 255
Beale, Andrew II, 335
Beale, Ann VI, 469
Beale, Ann VI, 470
Beale, Ann VI, 484
Beale, Ann R. VI, 877
Beale, Anthony VI, 484
Beale, Bowater VI, 469
Beale, Caleb III, 30
Beale, Charles T. VI, 877
Beale, Daniel VI, 470
Beale, Edward, Jr. VI, 484
Beale, Eliza VI, 74
Beale, Elizabeth VI, 469
Beale, Elizabeth VI, 470
Beale, Elizabeth VI, 529
Beale, Elizabeth VI, 674
Beale, Elizabeth N. III, 30
Beale, Esther VI, 484
Beale, Grace VI, 469
Beale, Hannah II, 197
Beale, Hannah II, 255
Beale, Hannah V, 967
Beale, Hannah VI, 364
Beale, Hannah VI, 469
Beale, Hannah VI, 470
Beale, Hannah VI, 484
Beale, Hannah VI, 529
Beale, Hannah Beale VI, 674
Beale, Hannah, Jr. VI, 469
Beale, Hannah, Jr. VI, 470
Beale, Isaac VI, 469
Beale, Jacob VI, 470
Beale, James VI, 484
Beale, John VI, 469
Beale, John VI, 470
Beale, John VI, 484
Beale, Jos. H. III, 30
Beale, Joseph VI, 364
Beale, Joseph VI, 469
Beale, Joseph VI, 484
Beale, Joseph VI, 529
Beale, Joseph VI, 674
Beale, Joseph H. III, 30
Beale, Joseph H. III, 97
Beale, Joseph H. III, 241
Beale, Joseph Hoare III, 30
Beale, Joshua II, 461
Beale, Limerick III, 30
Beale, Manhattanville III, 30
Beale, Margaret III, 30
Beale, Margaret III, 97
Beale, Margaret VI, 470
Beale, Margaret VI, 636
Beale, Martha VI, 469
Beale, Martha VI, 529
Beale, Mary III, 30
Beale, Mary III, 97
Beale, Mary III, 241
Beale, Mary VI, 364
Beale, Mary VI, 367
Beale, Mary VI, 469
Beale, Mary VI, 470
Beale, Mary N. III, 30
Beale, Mary Sarah VI, 470
Beale, Mercy VI, 364
Beale, Mercy VI, 469
Beale, Mercy VI, 470
Beale, Nancy VI, 469
Beale, Pamela Maria VI, 470
Beale, Patience VI, 470
Beale, Philip VI, 364
Beale, Philip VI, 470
Beale, Prudence VI, 469
Beale, Rachel VI, 364
Beale, Rachel VI, 469
Beale, Rachel VI, 470
Beale, Samuel VI, 469
Beale, Sarah VI, 364
Beale, Sarah VI, 469
Beale, Thomas VI, 469
Beale, Thomas VI, 470
Beale, Thomas VI, 484
Beale, William VI, 364
Beale, William VI, 470
Beale, William Henry III, 30
Beale, Wm. VI, 470
Beales, Abigail I, 1115
Beales, Abraham I, 490
Beales, Abram I, 1115
Beales, Allen I, 870
Beales, Ann I, 490
Beales, Ann I, 525
Beales, Ann I, 526
Beales, Ann I, 552
Beales, Ann I, 554
Beales, Anna I, 526
Beales, Anna I, 534
Beales, Bowater I, 490
Beales, Caleb I, 526
Beales, Caleb I, 534
Beales, Catherine I, 1089
Beales, Charity I, 1089
Beales, Curtis I, 490
Beales, Daniel I, 490
Beales, Daniel I, 525
Beales, Daniel I, 552
Beales, Daniel V, 284
Beales, Daniel V, 362
Beales, David, Sr. I, 1079
Beales, Elihu I, 1147
Beales, Elizabeth I, 490
Beales, Elizabeth I, 525
Beales, Elizabeth I, 527
Beales, Elizabeth I, 1115
Beales, Elizabeth V, 222
Beales, Eunice Beils I, 490
Beales, Evelin I, 1115
Beales, Hannah I, 526
Beales, Hannah I, 1080
Beales, Hannah VI, 363
Beales, Hannah VI, 364
Beales, Isaac I, 1080
Beales, Isaac VI, 364
Beales, Isaac B. VI, 364
Beales, Jacob I, 490
Beales, Jacob I, 1115
Beales, Jacob V, 222
Beales, James I, 490
Beales, Jesse I, 490
Beales, John I, 490
Beales, John I, 525
Beales, John I, 554
Beales, John V, 222
Beales, John VI, 364
Beales, John VI, 467
Beales, John Bowater I, 490
Beales, John Bowater I, 525
Beales, John Bowater I, 528
Beales, John Bowater I, 953
Beales, Joseph I, 526
Beales, Joseph I, 1080
Beales, Joseph VI, 364
Beales, Joseph, Sr. I, 1080
Beales, Laura Jane I, 1115
Beales, Lois I, 490
Beales, Lois I, 525
Beales, Lois I, 528
Beales, Lydia I, 525
Beales, Lydia I, 544
Beales, Lydia I, 1115
Beales, Margaret I, 525
Beales, Margaret I, 1115
Beales, Martha I, 1115
Beales, Martha Ellen I, 1115
Beales, Martha Jane I, 1115
Beales, Mary I, 490
Beales, Mary I, 525
Beales, Mary I, 553
Beales, Mary I, 1080
Beales, Mary V, 369
Beales, Mary V, 373
Beales, Mary VI, 363
Beales, Mary VI, 364
Beales, Mary VI, 469
Beales, Mary Elizabeth I, 1115
Beales, Mary J. I, 1115
Beales, Mary Malinda I, 1115
Beales, Mercy VI, 364
Beales, Nathan I, 490
Beales, Nathan I, 849
Beales, Nathan I, 1115
Beales, Patience I, 490
Beales, Patience I, 525
Beales, Patience I, 530
Beales, Phebe I, 490
Beales, Phebe I, 525
Beales, Phebe I, 552
Beales, Philip VI, 364
Beales, Polly VI, 956
Beales, Priscilla I, 490
Beales, Rache I, 870
Beales, Rachel I, 525
Beales, Rachel I, 542
Beales, Rachel I, 849
Beales, Rachel I, 870
Beales, Rachel I, 1115
Beales, Rachel I, 1135
Beales, Rachel V, 221
Beales, Rachel V, 284
Beales, Rachel VI, 364
Beales, Ruth I, 490
Beales, Ruth I, 525
Beales, Ruth I, 552
Beales, Ruth I, 849
Beales, Sarah I, 490
Beales, Sarah I, 523
Beales, Sarah I, 525
Beales, Sarah I, 1115
Beales, Sarah VI, 363
Beales, Sarah VI, 364
Beales, Sarah VI, 462
Beales, Sarah VI, 467
Beales, Sarah VI, 469
Beales, Sarah Ann I, 1115
Beales, Sollomon V, 373
Beales, Solomon I, 1089
Beales, Solomon V, 222
Beales, Susann I, 526
Beales, Susanna I, 490
Beales, Susanna I, 525
Beales, Susanna I, 552
Beales, Susanna I, 554
Beales, Susannah V, 284
Beales, Susannah V, 362
Beales, Thomas I, 343
Beales, Thomas I, 490
Beales, Thomas I, 523
Beales, Thomas I, 525
Beales, Thomas I, 849
Beales, Thomas VI, 363
Beales, Thomas VI, 462
Beales, Thomas VI, 467
Beales, Thomas VI, 469
Beales, Unice V, 24
Beales, Unice V, 130
Beales, Widow Rachel I, 849
Beales, William I, 490
Beales, William I, 525
Beales, William I, 542
Beales, William VI, 363
Beales, William VI, 364
Beales, William, Jr. VI, 364
Beall, Francis Asbury V, 879
Beall, Grace VI, 615
Beall, Hannah VI, 364
Beall, Henrietta V, 726
Beall, Henrietta P. V, 612
Beall, Isaac VI, 364
Beall, Isaac VI, 469
Beall, Isaac B. VI, 364
Beall, Isaac B. VI, 615
Beall, Isaac B. VI, 731
Beall, Joseph VI, 615
Beall, Margaret VI, 615
Beall, Mary V, 826
Beall, Mary V, 866
Beall, Mary H. V, 879
Beall, Mercy VI, 440
Beall, Rachel VI, 364
Beall, Sarah M. V, 879
Beall, Sarah M. V, 885
Beall, William VI, 364
Beall, William H. V, 726
Beall, William, Jr. VI, 364
Bealls, Daniel V, 373
Bealock, J. John I, 373
Bealor, Ann VI, 364
Bealor, Elizabeth VI, 364
Bealor, Elizabeth VI, 453
Bealor, John VI, 364
Beals, ??? I, 1139
Beals, ??? V, 443

Beals, Aaron I, 526
Beals, Aaron I, 708
Beals, Aaron I, 959
Beals, Aaron H. I, 1079
Beals, Aaron H. I, 1090
Beals, Abigail I, 1080
Beals, Abigail I, 1114
Beals, Abigail I, 1115
Beals, Abigail I, 1128
Beals, Abigal I, 1129
Beals, Abijah I, 955
Beals, Abijah I, 1080
Beals, Abijah V, 222
Beals, Abijah B. I, 1080
Beals, Abijeh V, 24
Beals, Abner I, 1079
Beals, Abner I, 1081
Beals, Abner I, 1089
Beals, Abner I, 1090
Beals, Abraham I, 955
Beals, Abraham I, 959
Beals, Abraham I, 1114
Beals, Abraham V, 24
Beals, Abraham V, 221
Beals, Abram I, 1079
Beals, Abram I, 1090
Beals, Abram I, 1103
Beals, Abram I, 1115
Beals, Abram I, 1120
Beals, Abram I, 1129
Beals, Addie I, 1148
Beals, Albert I, 1148
Beals, Alexander J. I, 1147
Beals, Alfred I, 1081
Beals, Allen I, 526
Beals, Allen I, 849
Beals, Allen I, 870
Beals, Amos I, 1079
Beals, Amos I, 1090
Beals, Amos V, 373
Beals, Amy V, 373
Beals, Amy V, 434
Beals, Anderson T. I, 1079
Beals, Anderson T. I, 1090
Beals, Anderson T. I, 1147
Beals, Anderson T. I, 1153
Beals, Andrew J. I, 1147
Beals, Andrew Jones I, 1080
Beals, Andy Jones I, 1090
Beals, Anliza I, 1139
Beals, Ann I, 525
Beals, Ann I, 526
Beals, Ann I, 870
Beals, Ann I, 1079
Beals, Ann I, 1085
Beals, Ann I, 1090
Beals, Ann I, 1114
Beals, Ann I, 1147
Beals, Ann V, 24
Beals, Ann V, 319
Beals, Ann V, 373
Beals, Ann R. VI, 877
Beals, Anna I, 526
Beals, Anna I, 849
Beals, Anna I, 870
Beals, Anna I, 955
Beals, Anna Tatum I, 1139
Beals, Anne I, 870
Beals, Asa I, 955
Beals, Asa I, 959
Beals, Asaph Hiatt V, 24
Beals, Asbury I, 1080
Beals, Asbury I, 1083
Beals, Asenath I, 870
Beals, Asenath I, 955
Beals, Asenath I, 959
Beals, Asenath I, 960
Beals, Asher I, 525
Beals, Asher I, 526
Beals, Asher I, 648
Beals, Asher I, 959
Beals, Asher I, 1114
Beals, Bethiah V, 221
Beals, Bethiel Matilda V, 222
Beals, Boheter V, 445
Beals, Bowater I, 343
Beals, Bowater I, 373
Beals, Bowater I, 525
Beals, Bowater I, 526
Beals, Bowater I, 648
Beals, Bowater I, 849
Beals, Bowater I, 870
Beals, Bowater I, 955
Beals, Bowater I, 956
Beals, Bowater I, 959
Beals, Bowater V, 221
Beals, Bowater VI, 469
Beals, Caleb I, 525
Beals, Caleb I, 526
Beals, Caleb I, 648
Beals, Caleb I, 849
Beals, Caleb I, 870
Beals, Caleb I, 959
Beals, Caleb I, 1089
Beals, Caleb I, 1090
Beals, Caleb I, 1114
Beals, Calvin I, 1079
Beals, Caroline I, 1079
Beals, Catharine V, 373
Beals, Catharine Emaline I, 1103
Beals, Catharine Emeline I, 1147
Beals, Catherine I, 1079
Beals, Catherine I, 1089
Beals, Catherine I, 1090
Beals, Catherine I, 1115
Beals, Catherine Emaline I, 1139
Beals, Catron V, 24
Beals, Charity I, 956
Beals, Charity I, 959
Beals, Charity I, 964
Beals, Charity I, 1089
Beals, Charity I, 1095
Beals, Charity V, 373
Beals, Charity V, 396
Beals, Charles T. VI, 877
Beals, Curtis V, 24
Beals, Curtis V, 373
Beals, Curtis V, 445
Beals, Cynthia I, 1080
Beals, Cynthia I, 1090
Beals, Cynthia I, 1115
Beals, Cyrena I, 1090
Beals, Daniel I, 490
Beals, Daniel I, 525
Beals, Daniel I, 959
Beals, Daniel I, 1079
Beals, Daniel I, 1083
Beals, Daniel I, 1085
Beals, Daniel I, 1089
Beals, Daniel I, 1090
Beals, Daniel I, 1139
Beals, Daniel I, 1147
Beals, Daniel V, 24
Beals, Daniel V, 221
Beals, Daniel V, 222
Beals, Daniel V, 284
Beals, Daniel V, 373
Beals, Daniel, Jr. V, 222
Beals, David I, 525
Beals, David I, 1080
Beals, David I, 1089
Beals, David I, 1090
Beals, David I, 1093
Beals, David I, 1095
Beals, David I, 1097
Beals, David I, 1098
Beals, David I, 1115
Beals, David V, 373
Beals, David M. I, 1080
Beals, David, Jr. I, 1090
Beals, David, Senior I, 1079
Beals, David, Sr. I, 1089
Beals, Delwin I, 959
Beals, Dilwin I, 526
Beals, Dinah V, 24
Beals, Dinah V, 101
Beals, Dinah V, 373
Beals, Dinah V, 419
Beals, Eda I, 1080
Beals, Elbert I, 1079
Beals, Eleazar I, 526
Beals, Eleazar I, 870
Beals, Eleazer I, 648
Beals, Eli I, 1079
Beals, Eli I, 1090
Beals, Eli V, 373
Beals, Eliaser I, 870
Beals, Elihu I, 1089
Beals, Elihu I, 1090
Beals, Elihu I, 1147
Beals, Elihu Odle I, 1080
Beals, Eliza I, 1090
Beals, Eliza I, 1147
Beals, Elizabeth I, 490
Beals, Elizabeth I, 525
Beals, Elizabeth I, 959
Beals, Elizabeth I, 1080
Beals, Elizabeth I, 1083
Beals, Elizabeth I, 1089
Beals, Elizabeth I, 1090
Beals, Elizabeth I, 1114
Beals, Elizabeth I, 1115
Beals, Elizabeth I, 1124
Beals, Elizabeth V, 24
Beals, Elizabeth V, 221
Beals, Elizabeth V, 222
Beals, Elizabeth V, 284
Beals, Elizabeth V, 319
Beals, Elizabeth V, 356
Beals, Elizabeth V, 373
Beals, Elizabeth Ann V, 24
Beals, Elizabeth J. I, 1147
Beals, Elizabeth J. I, 1153
Beals, Elizabeth Jane I, 1139
Beals, Ellis I, 1079
Beals, Ellis I, 1089
Beals, Emaline I, 1079
Beals, Emaline I, 1090
Beals, Emaline I, 1092
Beals, Endema I, 1081
Beals, Enoch I, 1079
Beals, Enoch I, 1090
Beals, Enos I, 1079
Beals, Enos I, 1080
Beals, Esther I, 959
Beals, Esther I, 962
Beals, Esther V, 221
Beals, Esther V, 298
Beals, Esther V, 300
Beals, Esther V, 373
Beals, Esther V, 378
Beals, Eunice V, 24
Beals, Eunice V, 221
Beals, Evaline I, 1090
Beals, Evelin I, 1115
Beals, Eveline I, 1080
Beals, Frank I, 1148
Beals, Franklin King I, 1139
Beals, Frederick I, 1080
Beals, G. H. I, 1148
Beals, George I, 1148
Beals, George M. I, 1079
Beals, Gulielma I, 1115
Beals, Hannah I, 490
Beals, Hannah I, 525
Beals, Hannah I, 526
Beals, Hannah I, 547
Beals, Hannah I, 648
Beals, Hannah I, 651
Beals, Hannah I, 959
Beals, Hannah I, 970
Beals, Hannah I, 1080
Beals, Hannah I, 1081
Beals, Hannah I, 1082
Beals, Hannah I, 1089
Beals, Hannah I, 1090
Beals, Hannah I, 1095
Beals, Hannah I, 1114
Beals, Hannah I, 1115
Beals, Hannah I, 1147
Beals, Hannah V, 24
Beals, Hannah V, 222
Beals, Hannah V, 373
Beals, Hannah Eliza I, 1080
Beals, Harriet I, 1090
Beals, Harriet I, 1096
Beals, Harriett I, 920
Beals, Harriett I, 1079
Beals, Henry I, 1114
Beals, Henry I, 1115
Beals, Henry Powel I, 1089
Beals, Hester J. I, 1139
Beals, Huldah I, 1115
Beals, Huldah I, 1129
Beals, Ida IV, 175
Beals, Isaac I, 1089
Beals, Isaac I, 1115
Beals, Isaac I, 1134
Beals, Isaac V, 24
Beals, Isaac V, 221
Beals, Isaac V, 445
Beals, Isaac B. V, 476
Beals, Isaac Hammer I, 1079
Beals, Isaac Hammer I, 1090
Beals, J. F. I, 1139
Beals, J. H. I, 1148
Beals, J. J. Hall I, 1148
Beals, J. Perry I, 1148
Beals, Jacob I, 490
Beals, Jacob I, 648
Beals, Jacob I, 955
Beals, Jacob I, 959
Beals, Jacob I, 1077
Beals, Jacob I, 1079
Beals, Jacob I, 1080
Beals, Jacob I, 1089
Beals, Jacob I, 1090
Beals, Jacob I, 1096
Beals, Jacob I, 1114
Beals, Jacob I, 1115
Beals, Jacob I, 1129
Beals, Jacob I, 1147
Beals, Jacob I, 1158
Beals, Jacob V, 24
Beals, Jacob V, 132
Beals, Jacob V, 221
Beals, Jacob V, 222
Beals, Jacob V, 319
Beals, Jacob V, 373
Beals, Jacob V, 396
Beals, Jacob Alexander I, 1080
Beals, Jacob Alexander I, 1090
Beals, Jacob C. V, 373
Beals, Jacob L. I, 1148
Beals, Jacob Leason I, 1139
Beals, Jacob, Jr. I, 1090
Beals, Jacob, Jr. V, 373
Beals, Jacob, Sr. I, 1080
Beals, James C. I, 1090
Beals, James C. I, 1103
Beals, James C. I, 1115
Beals, James C. I, 1129
Beals, James C. I, 1139
Beals, James C. I, 1147
Beals, James Calvin I, 1080
Beals, James Dicks I, 525
Beals, James F. I, 1139
Beals, James F. I, 1147
Beals, James F. I, 1148
Beals, James M. I, 1079
Beals, James M. I, 1090
Beals, James S. I, 1139
Beals, James S. I, 1148
Beals, Jane I, 1090
Beals, Jane V, 24
Beals, Jane V, 221
Beals, Jane V, 246
Beals, Jemima I, 849
Beals, Jemima I, 870
Beals, Jemima I, 959
Beals, Jemima I, 963
Beals, Jephtha David I, 1103
Beals, Jerusha I, 1090
Beals, Jerusha I, 1095
Beals, Jesse I, 526
Beals, Jesse I, 648
Beals, Jesse I, 849
Beals, Jesse I, 870
Beals, Jesse I, 1079
Beals, Jesse V, 24
Beals, Jesse V, 101
Beals, Jesse V, 221
Beals, Jesse V, 319
Beals, Jesse V, 373
Beals, Jesse V, 419
Beals, Jesse, Jr. V, 373
Beals, Jessy I, 1103
Beals, Joab V, 476
Beals, Job I, 1090
Beals, Job S. I, 1079
Beals, Joel V, 373
Beals, John I, 443
Beals, John I, 490
Beals, John I, 525
Beals, John I, 526
Beals, John I, 648
Beals, John I, 651
Beals, John I, 652
Beals, John I, 673
Beals, John I, 675
Beals, John I, 695
Beals, John I, 849
Beals, John I, 870
Beals, John I, 959
Beals, John I, 1007
Beals, John I, 1009
Beals, John I, 1079
Beals, John I, 1080
Beals, John I, 1081
Beals, John I, 1089
Beals, John I, 1114
Beals, John I, 1115
Beals, John I, 1128
Beals, John V, 24
Beals, John V, 215
Beals, John V, 221
Beals, John V, 222
Beals, John V, 315
Beals, John V, 369
Beals, John V, 373
Beals, John V, 378
Beals, John V, 445
Beals, John VI, 357
Beals, John VI, 364
Beals, John VI, 469
Beals, John VI, 575
Beals, John VI, 581
Beals, John VI, 877
Beals, John VI, 945
Beals, John B. V, 221
Beals, John B. V, 222
Beals, John B. V, 246
Beals, John Boater I, 1089
Beals, John Boater V, 24
Beals, John Boeter I, 1089
Beals, John Bowater I, 525
Beals, John Bowater I, 959
Beals, John Bowater I, 1077
Beals, John, Jr. I, 526
Beals, John, Jr. I, 645
Beals, John, Jr. I, 648
Beals, John, Jr. I, 1114
Beals, John, Jr. I, 1115
Beals, John, Jr. V, 319
Beals, John, Jr. V, 373
Beals, John, Sr. I, 1114
Beals, Jonathan I, 526
Beals, Jonathan I, 708
Beals, Jonathan I, 1079
Beals, Jonathan I, 1089
Beals, Jonathan I, 1090
Beals, Jonathan V, 24
Beals, Jonathan V, 221
Beals, Jonathan V, 222
Beals, Joseph I, 526
Beals, Joseph I, 1080
Beals, Joseph I, 1082
Beals, Joseph I, 1089
Beals, Joseph I, 1090
Beals, Joseph I, 1115
Beals, Joseph I, 1147
Beals, Joseph Alexander I, 1139
Beals, Joseph Perry I, 1139
Beals, Joseph, Sr. I, 1090
Beals, Junetta I, 1079
Beals, Katherine V, 221
Beals, Katherine V, 373
Beals, Kezia I, 1080
Beals, Keziah I, 1095
Beals, Keziah I, 1147
Beals, Keziah I, 1158
Beals, L. H. I, 1147
Beals, L. H. I, 1148
Beals, Laura Jane I, 1115
Beals, Lemuel V, 373
Beals, Lenora G. I, 1139
Beals, Lida I, 1158
Beals, Lindley Hoag I, 1090
Beals, Lindley Hoag I, 1139
Beals, Lindly H. I, 1147
Beals, Lindly Hoegg I, 1080
Beals, Lois I, 525
Beals, Lois V, 24
Beals, Lois V, 215
Beals, Lois V, 221
Beals, Lois V, 246
Beals, Lola Maud I, 1139
Beals, Louisa I, 870
Beals, Louisa I, 1079
Beals, Louisa I, 1080
Beals, Louisa I, 1081
Beals, Lucinda V, 373
Beals, Lucinda Isabel I, 1139
Beals, Luiza T. I, 1139
Beals, Lydia I, 525
Beals, Lydia I, 673
Beals, Lydia I, 690
Beals, Lydia I, 849
Beals, Lydia I, 870
Beals, Lydia I, 1079
Beals, Lydia I, 1080
Beals, Lydia I, 1090
Beals, Lydia I, 1103
Beals, Lydia I, 1114
Beals, Lydia I, 1115
Beals, Lydia I, 1122
Beals, Lydia V, 24
Beals, Lydia V, 222
Beals, Lydia V, 319
Beals, Lydia V, 373
Beals, Lydia V, 419
Beals, Mahala V, 373
Beals, Mahetabel V, 24
Beals, Mahlon Addison I, 1080
Beals, Malissa Ann I, 1139
Beals, Margaret I, 490
Beals, Margaret I, 525
Beals, Margaret I, 526
Beals, Margaret I, 548
Beals, Margaret I, 648
Beals, Margaret I, 652
Beals, Margaret I, 680
Beals, Margaret I, 1080
Beals, Margaret I, 1089
Beals, Margaret I, 1090
Beals, Margaret I, 1115
Beals, Margaret Jane I, 1080
Beals, Margaret Jane I, 1147
Beals, Martha I, 708
Beals, Martha I, 955
Beals, Martha I, 1007
Beals, Martha I, 1082
Beals, Martha I, 1115
Beals, Martha I, 1139
Beals, Martha Elizabeth I, 1139
Beals, Martha Ellen I, 1115
Beals, Martha Jane I, 1115
Beals, Mary I, 374
Beals, Mary I, 490
Beals, Mary I, 525
Beals, Mary I, 526
Beals, Mary I, 673
Beals, Mary I, 675
Beals, Mary I, 870
Beals, Mary I, 955

Beals, Mary I, 1007
Beals, Mary I, 1009
Beals, Mary I, 1080
Beals, Mary I, 1083
Beals, Mary I, 1089
Beals, Mary I, 1090
Beals, Mary I, 1093
Beals, Mary I, 1114
Beals, Mary I, 1115
Beals, Mary I, 1127
Beals, Mary I, 1134
Beals, Mary I, 1139
Beals, Mary I, 1143
Beals, Mary I, 1145
Beals, Mary I, 1147
Beals, Mary IV, 175
Beals, Mary V, 24
Beals, Mary V, 132
Beals, Mary V, 221
Beals, Mary V, 222
Beals, Mary V, 230
Beals, Mary V, 373
Beals, Mary V, 378
Beals, Mary V, 445
Beals, Mary A. I, 1139
Beals, Mary Adeline I, 1080
Beals, Mary Ann I, 1079
Beals, Mary Elizabeth I, 1115
Beals, Mary Elizabeth I, 1139
Beals, Mary J. I, 1115
Beals, Mary Jane V, 373
Beals, Mary Jane V, 420
Beals, Mary Malinda I, 1115
Beals, Matilda V, 373
Beals, Mehetabel I, 1114
Beals, Mehetabel V, 222
Beals, Mehitabel V, 221
Beals, Mehitable I, 955
Beals, Mehitable I, 959
Beals, Metilda V, 221
Beals, Milton I, 849
Beals, Miriam I, 1080
Beals, Miriam Elizabeth I, 1080
Beals, Mollie I, 1148
Beals, Mollie A. I, 1081
Beals, Nancy I, 1079
Beals, Nancy I, 1090
Beals, Nancy I, 1095
Beals, Nancy V, 373
Beals, Nancy V, 433
Beals, Nancy Lee I, 1148
Beals, Nathan I, 373
Beals, Nathan I, 870
Beals, Nathan I, 955
Beals, Nathan I, 959
Beals, Nathan I, 962
Beals, Nathan I, 963
Beals, Nathan I, 1079
Beals, Nathan I, 1080
Beals, Nathan I, 1090
Beals, Nathan I, 1115
Beals, Nathan V, 24
Beals, Nathan V, 221
Beals, Nathan V, 222
Beals, Nathan V, 319
Beals, Nathan V, 445
Beals, Nathan H. I, 1079
Beals, Newton I, 1079
Beals, Newton I, 1090
Beals, Olive Catherine I, 1080
Beals, Parnel I, 525
Beals, Parnel I, 526
Beals, Parnel I, 959
Beals, Parnel I, 1114
Beals, Parnell I, 648
Beals, Patience I, 490
Beals, Patience I, 525
Beals, Patience I, 959
Beals, Peter I, 648
Beals, Phebe I, 525
Beals, Phebe Ann I, 849
Beals, Phila A. I, 870
Beals, Pleasant M. I, 1115
Beals, Prescilla I, 1114
Beals, Priscilla I, 525
Beals, Priscilla I, 548
Beals, Priscilla I, 955
Beals, Priscilla I, 959
Beals, Priscilla I, 1114
Beals, Priscilla V, 24
Beals, Priscilla V, 221
Beals, Priscilla V, 274
Beals, Prisila V, 221
Beals, Prudence I, 525
Beals, Prudence I, 581
Beals, Prudence VI, 469
Beals, Prudence VI, 581
Beals, Rache I, 870
Beals, Rachel I, 374
Beals, Rachel I, 490
Beals, Rachel I, 525
Beals, Rachel I, 526
Beals, Rachel I, 536
Beals, Rachel I, 648
Beals, Rachel I, 652
Beals, Rachel I, 673
Beals, Rachel I, 708
Beals, Rachel I, 849
Beals, Rachel I, 870
Beals, Rachel I, 959
Beals, Rachel I, 969
Beals, Rachel I, 1079
Beals, Rachel I, 1080
Beals, Rachel I, 1081
Beals, Rachel I, 1089
Beals, Rachel I, 1090
Beals, Rachel I, 1093
Beals, Rachel I, 1101
Beals, Rachel I, 1103
Beals, Rachel I, 1114
Beals, Rachel I, 1115
Beals, Rachel I, 1126
Beals, Rachel I, 1129
Beals, Rachel V, 24
Beals, Rachel V, 221
Beals, Rachel V, 222
Beals, Rachel V, 373
Beals, Rachel Elizabeth I, 1090
Beals, Rebecca I, 1079
Beals, Rebecca I, 1103
Beals, Rebecca I, 1115
Beals, Rebeckah I, 1080
Beals, Rhoda I, 1079
Beals, Rhoda I, 1085
Beals, Rhoda I, 1090
Beals, Rhoda I, 1095
Beals, Rhoda VI, 877
Beals, Rhoda Camline I, 1080
Beals, Rhyly I, 1079
Beals, Richard V, 373
Beals, Riley I, 1079
Beals, Robert I, 1115
Beals, Rufus J. I, 1148
Beals, Rufus Jones I, 1139
Beals, Ruth I, 525
Beals, Ruth I, 547
Beals, Ruth I, 870
Beals, Ruth I, 1080
Beals, Ruth I, 1090
Beals, Ruth I, 1096
Beals, Ruth I, 1115
Beals, Ruth I, 1129
Beals, Ruth V, 221
Beals, Ruth V, 222
Beals, Ruth V, 319
Beals, Ruth V, 445
Beals, Ruth V, 476
Beals, Ruth Emeline I, 1080
Beals, Sallie D. I, 870
Beals, Sallie D. I, 889
Beals, Sally I, 849
Beals, Sally I, 870
Beals, Sam'l I, 1089
Beals, Samuel I, 1080
Beals, Samuel I, 1089
Beals, Samuel IV, 175
Beals, Samuel V, 373
Beals, Samuel H. I, 1090
Beals, Samuel H. I, 1139
Beals, Samuel H. I, 1147
Beals, Samuel Holton I, 1080
Beals, Sarah I, 343
Beals, Sarah I, 373
Beals, Sarah I, 443
Beals, Sarah I, 445
Beals, Sarah I, 490
Beals, Sarah I, 525
Beals, Sarah I, 648
Beals, Sarah I, 673
Beals, Sarah I, 675
Beals, Sarah I, 956
Beals, Sarah I, 959
Beals, Sarah I, 1079
Beals, Sarah I, 1080
Beals, Sarah I, 1090
Beals, Sarah I, 1103
Beals, Sarah I, 1114
Beals, Sarah I, 1115
Beals, Sarah I, 1120
Beals, Sarah I, 1139
Beals, Sarah I, 1147
Beals, Sarah V, 24
Beals, Sarah V, 215
Beals, Sarah V, 221
Beals, Sarah V, 222
Beals, Sarah V, 445
Beals, Sarah VI, 469
Beals, Sarah VI, 581
Beals, Sarah VI, 586
Beals, Sarah A. I, 1139
Beals, Sarah Allen I, 1147
Beals, Sarah Ann I, 1115
Beals, Sarah Catherine I, 1080
Beals, Sarah J. I, 1090
Beals, Sarah J. I, 1100
Beals, Sarah Jane I, 849
Beals, Sarah Jane I, 1079
Beals, Sarah Josie I, 1139
Beals, Sarah Ruth I, 1080
Beals, Sarah, Jr. I, 959
Beals, Serena I, 1079
Beals, Seth I, 1114
Beals, Seth I, 1115
Beals, Sollomon V, 373
Beals, Solomon I, 373
Beals, Solomon I, 374
Beals, Solomon I, 526
Beals, Solomon I, 708
Beals, Solomon I, 1089
Beals, Solomon I, 1095
Beals, Solomon I, 1098
Beals, Solomon V, 222
Beals, Solomon, Sr. I, 1080
Beals, Sophronia I, 1079
Beals, Sophronia I, 1090
Beals, Susanah I, 1129
Beals, Susanah I, 1139
Beals, Susanah I, 1147
Beals, Susann I, 526
Beals, Susanna I, 443
Beals, Susanna I, 525
Beals, Susanna I, 526
Beals, Susanna I, 648
Beals, Susanna I, 673
Beals, Susanna I, 870
Beals, Susanna I, 1114
Beals, Susanna I, 1115
Beals, Susanna I, 1121
Beals, Susanna I, 1124
Beals, Susanna V, 24
Beals, Susannah I, 525
Beals, Susannah I, 1103
Beals, Susannah I, 1115
Beals, Susannah V, 24
Beals, Susannah V, 284
Beals, Susannah V, 319
Beals, Susannah V, 373
Beals, Susie IV, 175
Beals, Tabitha V, 24
Beals, Tabitha V, 60
Beals, Tabitha V, 132
Beals, Thomas I, 343
Beals, Thomas I, 487
Beals, Thomas I, 490
Beals, Thomas I, 525
Beals, Thomas I, 528
Beals, Thomas I, 569
Beals, Thomas I, 673
Beals, Thomas I, 959
Beals, Thomas I, 1080
Beals, Thomas I, 1089
Beals, Thomas I, 1090
Beals, Thomas I, 1114
Beals, Thomas V, 24
Beals, Thomas V, 221
Beals, Thomas V, 373
Beals, Thomas V, 433
Beals, Thomas A. I, 1079
Beals, Thomas Elwood I, 1080
Beals, Thomas, Jr. I, 525
Beals, Thos. I, 959
Beals, Walter I, 1115
Beals, Wd. Sarah VI, 575
Beals, Widow Keziah I, 1158
Beals, William I, 373
Beals, William I, 443
Beals, William I, 445
Beals, William I, 490
Beals, William I, 525
Beals, William I, 526
Beals, William I, 645
Beals, William I, 648
Beals, William I, 673
Beals, William I, 708
Beals, William I, 709
Beals, William I, 849
Beals, William I, 870
Beals, William I, 953
Beals, William I, 955
Beals, William I, 959
Beals, William I, 1079
Beals, William I, 1080
Beals, William I, 1081
Beals, William I, 1089
Beals, William I, 1101
Beals, William I, 1114
Beals, William I, 1115
Beals, William I, 1134
Beals, William V, 222
Beals, William VI, 358
Beals, William VI, 463
Beals, William VI, 609
Beals, William P. I, 1080
Beals, William P. I, 1081
Beals, William, Jr. I, 526
Beals, William, Jr. I, 1114
Beals, William, Sr. I, 1114
Beals, Wm. I, 548
Beals, Wm. I, 1081
Beals, Wm. I, 1090
Beals, Wryley H. I, 1090
Beaman, Cornelius I, 709
Beaman, Ebenezer III, 30
Beaman, Francis I, 229
Beaman, Francis, Jr. I, 229
Beaman, Francis, Sr. I, 229
Beaman, Franciss I, 229
Beaman, Grace IV, 1246
Beaman, Hannah III, 30
Beaman, James I, 229
Beaman, James I, 256
Beaman, Maria I, 229
Beaman, Mary I, 229
Beaman, Mary I, 256
Beaman, Mary I, 709
Beaman, Ozias I, 229
Beaman, Sarah I, 299
Beaman, Sarah I, 314
Beaman, Sarah Jane I, 229
Beaman, Synth I, 229
Beamer, Betty V, 152
Beamer, Betty V, 173
Beamer, Caroline V, 985
Beamer, Geo. V, 985
Beamer, George V, 985
Beamer, Nancy I, 981
Beamer, Nancy I, 992
Beamer, Wm. V, 985
Beamish, William V, 24
Beamon, Francis I, 299
Beamon, Harriet Edna I, 207
Beamon, James I, 207
Beamon, James I, 229
Beamon, Keziah I, 299
Beamon, Margaret Isabela I, 207
Beamon, Maria I, 207
Beamon, Maria I, 229
Beamon, Martha I, 299
Beamon, Martha I, 301
Beamon, Mary I, 299
Beamon, Mary Ann I, 207
Beamon, Ozias I, 229
Beamon, Polly I, 299
Beamon, Sarah I, 299
Beamon, Sarah Jane I, 207
Beamon, Synth I, 229
Beamon, Synthia I, 207
Beamon, Synthia I, 208
Beamont, James II, 335
Beamont, John II, 335
Beams, Wm. VI, 177
Bean, Abner VI, 364
Bean, Alexander I, 350
Bean, Alson I, 673
Bean, Alson J. I, 475
Bean, Alson J. I, 673
Bean, Annie J. II, 836
Bean, Bessie I, 938
Bean, Charles Armitage IV, 677
Bean, Dicey I, 475
Bean, Dicy I, 461
Bean, E. T. I, 921
Bean, Edgar C. I, 461
Bean, Effie M. I, 475
Bean, Effie M. I, 673
Bean, Elizabeth IV, 675
Bean, Elizabeth IV, 677
Bean, Elvin A. I, 475
Bean, Elvira VI, 364
Bean, Elvira VI, 388
Bean, Flora Bessie I, 921
Bean, Gulielma VI, 364
Bean, Gulielma VI, 388
Bean, Hannah I, 673
Bean, Hannah E. I, 475
Bean, Hannah Jenkins VI, 364
Bean, Ivory I, 921
Bean, James VI, 388
Bean, Jane Estelle VI, 364
Bean, Jane Estelle VI, 439
Bean, Jean I, 350
Bean, John Wesley I, 921
Bean, Levi IV, 320
Bean, Margaret V, 319
Bean, Mary I, 350
Bean, Mary Ann II, 792
Bean, Mary Ann V, 549
Bean, Mary Ann V, 595
Bean, Nicholas II, 792
Bean, Rachel VI, 364
Bean, Rachel VI, 409
Bean, Sarah IV, 677
Bean, Susan II, 792
Bean, Thomas I, 461
Bean, Wesley I, 938
Beans, Absalom VI, 616
Beans, Alice VI, 583
Beans, Amos VI, 470
Beans, Amos VI, 616
Beans, Amos VI, 671
Beans, Ann II, 978
Beans, Ann II, 1032
Beans, Ann II, 1045
Beans, Annie J. II, 836
Beans, Benjamin II, 803
Beans, Benjamin II, 954
Beans, Benjamin II, 978
Beans, Benjamin II, 983
Beans, Benjamin II, 1007
Beans, Benjamin II, 1021
Beans, Benjamin II, 1040
Beans, Benjamin II, 1045
Beans, Charles II, 954
Beans, Charles II, 957
Beans, Charles II, 971
Beans, Charles II, 978
Beans, Charles II, 983
Beans, Charles II, 1049
Beans, Charles II, 1051
Beans, Charles II, 1062
Beans, Charles II, 1085
Beans, Charles D. II, 954
Beans, Charles D. II, 1045
Beans, Charles D. II, 1049
Beans, Edward B. II, 954
Beans, Elin II, 994
Beans, Elizabeth II, 978
Beans, Elizabeth II, 1040
Beans, Elizabeth II, 1045
Beans, Elizabeth IV, 864
Beans, Elizabeth VI, 616
Beans, Elizabeth VI, 671
Beans, Ellinor II, 978
Beans, Ellinor II, 994
Beans, Emma VI, 615
Beans, Emma VI, 616
Beans, Emma VI, 671
Beans, Emma VI, 672
Beans, Hannah II, 954
Beans, Hannah II, 1045
Beans, Hannah II, 1062
Beans, Hannah V, 476
Beans, Hannah VI, 470
Beans, Hannah VI, 615
Beans, Hannah VI, 616
Beans, Hannah VI, 634
Beans, Hannah VI, 648
Beans, Hannah, Jr. VI, 616
Beans, Isaac V, 476
Beans, Isaiah VI, 616
Beans, Jacob II, 978
Beans, Jacob II, 1032
Beans, James VI, 470
Beans, James VI, 616
Beans, Jane IV, 864
Beans, Jane IV, 865
Beans, Jane IV, 885
Beans, Jane S. II, 1045
Beans, John VI, 616
Beans, Jonathan II, 978
Beans, Jonathan II, 1040
Beans, Levi IV, 320
Beans, Levi IV, 610
Beans, Levi VI, 616
Beans, Lydia II, 954
Beans, Lydia II, 957
Beans, Lydia W. II, 1045
Beans, Lydia W. II, 1049
Beans, Mahlon II, 782
Beans, Mary II, 803
Beans, Mary II, 836
Beans, Mary II, 954
Beans, Mary II, 978
Beans, Mary II, 983
Beans, Mary II, 1021
Beans, Mary II, 1040
Beans, Mary II, 1045
Beans, Mary II, 1051
Beans, Mary II, 1068
Beans, Mary II, 1069
Beans, Mary IV, 610
Beans, Mary IV, 613
Beans, Mary IV, 626
Beans, Mary Elizabeth II, 1045
Beans, Mary T. II, 954
Beans, Mary T. II, 1045
Beans, Mary T. II, 1049
Beans, Rachel II, 978
Beans, Rachel II, 1021
Beans, Rachel VI, 616
Beans, Rachel VI, 648
Beans, Rachel C. II, 954
Beans, Rebekah VI, 470
Beans, Rebekah VI, 616
Beans, Ruth II, 782

Beans, Ruth II, 836
Beans, Ruth VI, 616
Beans, Ruth Anna VI, 730
Beans, Ruth Anna VI, 762
Beans, Samuel VI, 635
Beans, Sarah II, 782
Beans, Sarah II, 946
Beans, Sarah II, 954
Beans, Sarah II, 957
Beans, Sarah II, 971
Beans, Sarah II, 978
Beans, Sarah II, 983
Beans, Sarah II, 1032
Beans, Sarah II, 1040
Beans, Sarah II, 1045
Beans, Sarah II, 1049
Beans, Sarah II, 1051
Beans, Sarah II, 1062
Beans, Sarah IV, 672
Beans, Sarah IV, 677
Beans, Sarah VI, 635
Beans, Sarah Ellen II, 803
Beans, Sarah W. II, 1045
Beans, Sarah Warner II, 808
Beans, Seneca II, 978
Beans, Seneca II, 1045
Beans, Thomas V, 476
Beans, Timothy VI, 470
Beans, Timothy VI, 616
Beans, Timothy, Jr. VI, 616
Beans, Watson T. V, 476
Beans, William II, 954
Beans, William VI, 470
Beans, William VI, 635
Beans, Wilson J. V, 476
Beans, Wm. II, 1045
Beans, Wm. VI, 615
Beans, Wm. VI, 616
Beans, Wm. VI, 634
Beans, Wm. VI, 635
Beans, Wm. VI, 648
Beans, Wm., Jr. VI, 616
Bear, David IV, 1201
Bear, Elijah V, 984
Bear, Eliza V, 984
Bear, Gladdis V, 152
Bear, Jacob V, 984
Bear, John A. V, 984
Bear, John C. V, 984
Bear, Mary V, 984
Bear, Mary E. V, 984
Bear, Rachel Minerva V, 24
Bear, Rachel Minerva V, 47
Bear, Samuel V, 152
Bear, Samuel V, 984
Bear, Sarah II, 461
Bear, Sarah II, 506
Beard, Aaron I, 776
Beard, Aaron I, 798
Beard, Abigail I, 648
Beard, Abigail I, 775
Beard, Abraham I, 1148
Beard, Adam VI, 877
Beard, Adam VI, 900
Beard, Adam VI, 909
Beard, Adeline I, 798
Beard, Agatha I, 526
Beard, Agatha I, 540
Beard, Agatha I, 775
Beard, Agatha I, 798
Beard, Aggy VI, 940
Beard, Agnes I, 776
Beard, Agnest I, 798
Beard, Alice I, 871
Beard, Alice I, 1115
Beard, Amos I, 776
Beard, Amos I, 798
Beard, Amos Elwood V, 549
Beard, Ann VI, 878
Beard, Ann Elizabeth VI, 878
Beard, Anthony I, 526
Beard, Anthony I, 540
Beard, Anthony I, 775
Beard, Anthony I, 776
Beard, Anthony I, 798
Beard, Bathsheba Elmina I, 775
Beard, Benj. I, 490
Beard, Benjamin I, 775
Beard, Benjamin I, 798
Beard, Benjamin F. I, 798
Beard, Betsey VI, 1018
Beard, Charles IV, 1145
Beard, Charles Edward VI, 878
Beard, Charlotte I, 648
Beard, Charlotte I, 674
Beard, Charlotte I, 691
Beard, Cynthia I, 798
Beard, Cynthia I, 845
Beard, David I, 490
Beard, David I, 648
Beard, David I, 674
Beard, David I, 775
Beard, David I, 776
Beard, David I, 781
Beard, David I, 797
Beard, David I, 798
Beard, David I, 840
Beard, David F. VI, 878
Beard, David, Sr. I, 798
Beard, Dolly I, 849
Beard, Dolly I, 871
Beard, Edgar V, 452
Beard, Edith I, 648
Beard, Elam I, 798
Beard, Elijah VI, 877
Beard, Elizabeth I, 648
Beard, Elizabeth I, 674
Beard, Elizabeth I, 678
Beard, Elizabeth I, 797
Beard, Elizabeth I, 802
Beard, Elizabeth I, 849
Beard, Elizabeth I, 870
Beard, Elizabeth I, 871
Beard, Elizabeth V, 222
Beard, Elizabeth VI, 877
Beard, Elizabeth VI, 878
Beard, Elizabeth VI, 1003
Beard, Elizabeth VI, 1018
Beard, Elmina Bathsheba I, 798
Beard, Elum I, 776
Beard, Elwood V, 376
Beard, Elwood V, 658
Beard, Elwood V, 894
Beard, Enoch I, 648
Beard, Eunice I, 526
Beard, Eunice I, 541
Beard, Eunice I, 648
Beard, Eunice I, 674
Beard, Eunice I, 776
Beard, Eunice I, 797
Beard, Eva V, 727
Beard, Frances G. VI, 963
Beard, Franklin I, 776
Beard, George I, 526
Beard, George I, 578
Beard, George I, 648
Beard, George I, 674
Beard, George I, 686
Beard, George I, 691
Beard, George I, 775
Beard, George I, 776
Beard, George I, 797
Beard, George I, 798
Beard, George I, 871
Beard, George IV, 1145
Beard, Granville L. VI, 878
Beard, Hannah I, 648
Beard, Hannah I, 674
Beard, Hannah I, 678
Beard, Hannah I, 686
Beard, Hannah I, 849
Beard, Hannah I, 871
Beard, Hannah I, 1101
Beard, Hannah I, 1115
Beard, Hannah IV, 1145
Beard, Hannah V, 319
Beard, Harvey VI, 877
Beard, Harvey VI, 913
Beard, Hazel V, 152
Beard, Hiram I, 798
Beard, Hiram V, 726
Beard, Hugh V, 726
Beard, Hugh VI, 877
Beard, Hyram I, 776
Beard, Isaac I, 648
Beard, Isaac I, 870
Beard, Isabel I, 674
Beard, Isabel I, 686
Beard, Israel V, 726
Beard, Jabes VI, 878
Beard, Jabez VI, 1018
Beard, Jacob V, 376
Beard, Jacob V, 545
Beard, Jacob V, 549
Beard, Jacob V, 658
Beard, James I, 798
Beard, James VI, 932
Beard, James Madison I, 775
Beard, James, Jr. I, 798
Beard, Jane I, 648
Beard, Jane I, 776
Beard, Jane I, 849
Beard, Jane I, 871
Beard, Jane I, 1115
Beard, Jesse I, 648
Beard, Jesse I, 798
Beard, Jesse I, 870
Beard, Jesse I, 871
Beard, Jesse A. V, 826
Beard, Jesse Adison I, 775
Beard, Jettie V, 222
Beard, John I, 648
Beard, John I, 674
Beard, John I, 678
Beard, John I, 798
Beard, John I, 849
Beard, John I, 870
Beard, John I, 1148
Beard, John IV, 1145
Beard, John VI, 1003
Beard, John Foster I, 775
Beard, John O. VI, 878
Beard, John, Jr. I, 871
Beard, John, Jr. V, 726
Beard, Jonathan I, 776
Beard, Jonathan I, 798
Beard, Jonathan G. I, 776
Beard, Katheren II, 197
Beard, Katheren II, 207
Beard, Katherine II, 197
Beard, Laura V, 658
Beard, Laura Ann V, 376
Beard, Laura Ann V, 549
Beard, Lavina I, 526
Beard, Lavina I, 541
Beard, Lavina I, 797
Beard, Lavinia I, 776
Beard, Lavinia I, 798
Beard, Levina I, 776
Beard, Levina I, 797
Beard, Levinah I, 490
Beard, Levinah I, 773
Beard, Lidia I, 776
Beard, Lizzie V, 376
Beard, Lizzie V, 894
Beard, Lovicy J. VI, 878
Beard, Luther V, 894
Beard, Luther A. V, 376
Beard, Luther H. V, 894
Beard, Lydia I, 648
Beard, Lydia I, 776
Beard, Lydia I, 798
Beard, Lydia I, 812
Beard, Lydia I, 838
Beard, Lydia V, 222
Beard, Lydia T. I, 781
Beard, Mahala I, 798
Beard, Mahala I, 806
Beard, Margaret VI, 877
Beard, Margarett VI, 899
Beard, Margery I, 871
Beard, Margit VI, 940
Beard, Margret VI, 900
Beard, Margret VI, 1018
Beard, Maria IV, 1145
Beard, Mariah IV, 1201
Beard, Martha I, 526
Beard, Martha I, 578
Beard, Martha I, 648
Beard, Martha I, 674
Beard, Martha I, 776
Beard, Martha I, 778
Beard, Martha I, 798
Beard, Martha I, 816
Beard, Martha I, 849
Beard, Martha I, 870
Beard, Martha I, 871
Beard, Martha I, 911
Beard, Martha I, 912
Beard, Martha I, 1115
Beard, Martha V, 727
Beard, Martha A. I, 798
Beard, Martha A. I, 808
Beard, Martha Ann VI, 878
Beard, Martha Armilla I, 775
Beard, Mary I, 526
Beard, Mary I, 648
Beard, Mary I, 674
Beard, Mary I, 691
Beard, Mary I, 775
Beard, Mary I, 797
Beard, Mary I, 798
Beard, Mary I, 817
Beard, Mary I, 830
Beard, Mary I, 871
Beard, Mary II, 826
Beard, Mary VI, 877
Beard, Mary Ann V, 222
Beard, Melinda I, 648
Beard, Meriva Jane I, 775
Beard, Miriam I, 776
Beard, Miriam I, 798
Beard, Miriam I, 840
Beard, N. B. V, 222
Beard, Nancy V, 376
Beard, Nancy VI, 877
Beard, Nancy VI, 913
Beard, Nantucket I, 526
Beard, Nathan I, 648
Beard, Nathan I, 776
Beard, Nathan I, 798
Beard, Nathan IV, 1145
Beard, Obed I, 648
Beard, Oliver IV, 1145
Beard, Pamelia V, 376
Beard, Pamelia V, 549
Beard, Patric I, 1148
Beard, Patrick I, 648
Beard, Patrick I, 870
Beard, Patrick I, 871
Beard, Patrick I, 1090
Beard, Patrick I, 1101
Beard, Patrick I, 1115
Beard, Patrick I, 1148
Beard, Paul I, 648
Beard, Paul I, 674
Beard, Paul I, 686
Beard, Permelia V, 549
Beard, Permelia V, 658
Beard, Phebe I, 776
Beard, Phebe I, 798
Beard, Phebe I, 844
Beard, Pleasant VI, 877
Beard, Polley I, 776
Beard, Polly I, 778
Beard, Polly I, 797
Beard, Polly I, 798
Beard, Polly I, 801
Beard, Polly I, 816
Beard, Polly VI, 899
Beard, Polly E. VI, 1011
Beard, Rachel I, 648
Beard, Rachel I, 776
Beard, Rachel I, 778
Beard, Rachel I, 849
Beard, Rachel I, 871
Beard, Rachel I, 897
Beard, Rebecca I, 776
Beard, Rebecca I, 781
Beard, Rebecca I, 797
Beard, Rebecca I, 798
Beard, Rebecca I, 801
Beard, Rebecca I, 819
Beard, Rebecca IV, 320
Beard, Rebekah I, 798
Beard, Reuben I, 526
Beard, Reuben I, 776
Beard, Reuben I, 797
Beard, Reuben I, 817
Beard, Richard I, 526
Beard, Richard I, 674
Beard, Richard I, 776
Beard, Richard I, 797
Beard, Richard I, 798
Beard, Robert VI, 877
Beard, Robert B. VI, 878
Beard, Robert M. VI, 878
Beard, Robert M. VI, 963
Beard, Robt. M. VI, 1011
Beard, Rosanna Jane V, 549
Beard, Ruben I, 798
Beard, Ruth I, 776
Beard, Ruth I, 798
Beard, Ruth I, 844
Beard, Rutha VI, 877
Beard, Sally VI, 878
Beard, Samuel VI, 877
Beard, Samuel VI, 880
Beard, Samuel VI, 913
Beard, Sarah I, 626
Beard, Sarah I, 648
Beard, Sarah I, 674
Beard, Sarah I, 682
Beard, Sarah I, 776
Beard, Sarah I, 798
Beard, Sarah I, 812
Beard, Sarah I, 849
Beard, Sarah I, 870
Beard, Sarah I, 886
Beard, Sarah II, 55
Beard, Sarah VI, 877
Beard, Sarah Delilah V, 549
Beard, Sherburn I, 526
Beard, Solomon I, 776
Beard, Solomon I, 798
Beard, Sophira VI, 900
Beard, Susan I, 626
Beard, Susan I, 627
Beard, Susan I, 776
Beard, Susan I, 798
Beard, Susan I, 837
Beard, Susannah Elma V, 549
Beard, Thomas I, 648
Beard, Thomas I, 674
Beard, Thomas I, 678
Beard, Thomas I, 849
Beard, Thomas I, 870
Beard, Thomas I, 871
Beard, Thomas V, 726
Beard, Thomas Clarkson I, 648
Beard, Webster IV, 1145
Beard, Widow Levina I, 797
Beard, Widow Martha I, 816
Beard, William I, 526
Beard, William I, 541
Beard, William I, 648
Beard, William I, 776
Beard, William I, 778
Beard, William I, 797
Beard, William I, 798
Beard, William I, 816
Beard, William I, 870
Beard, William I, 871
Beard, William I, 897
Beard, William II, 166
Beard, William II, 197
Beard, William II, 244
Beard, William V, 726
Beard, William S. I, 626
Beard, William S. I, 776
Beard, William S. I, 798
Beard, William, Jr. I, 798
Beard, Wm. I, 490
Beardmore, Rebecca IV, 368
Beardmore, Rebecca IV, 393
Beardsley, Alexander II, 335
Beardsley, Alexander II, 461
Beardsley, Arthur II, 782
Beardsley, Arthur II, 836
Beardsley, C. H. IV, 1145
Beardsley, Charlotte S. VI, 748
Beardsley, Charlotte Stole VI, 731
Beardsley, Charlotte Stole VI, 748
Beardsley, Clara II, 836
Beardsley, Clara D. II, 836
Beardsley, Covington S. IV, 1145
Beardsley, Emma L. II, 836
Beardsley, Emma Lynn II, 836
Beardsley, Esther IV, 1145
Beardsley, Ethel II, 782
Beardsley, Ethel II, 836
Beardsley, Jared VI, 731
Beardsley, Jared VI, 748
Beardsley, Laura II, 836
Beardsley, Martha C. IV, 175
Beardsley, Martha C. IV, 190
Beardsley, Mary II, 535
Beardsley, Mary VI, 731
Beardsley, Mary VI, 748
Beardsley, Mary Emma II, 782
Beardsley, Wd. Margrett II, 335
Bearfield, Jonathan I, 1070
Bearfield, Maries I, 1070
Bearfield, Milly I, 1070
Bearfield, Solomon I, 1070
Bearline, Amanda Salina IV, 1272
Beary, Cynthia V, 319
Beary, Cyrus A. V, 319
Beary, Sarah Ann V, 319
Beary, Sarah Ann V, 349
Beary, Sarah Ann V, 373
Beary, Sarah Ann V, 612
Beasley, Abner II, 55
Beasley, Almira III, 30
Beasley, Almira B. III, 20
Beasley, Benjamin II, 55
Beasley, Dr. Crawford III, 20
Beasley, Dr. Crawford D. III, 30
Beasley, Eliz. III, 30
Beasley, John II, 110
Beasley, John VI, 878
Beasley, Keziah VI, 878
Beasley, Lester W. III, 30
Beasley, Mary II, 55
Beasley, Mary II, 110
Beasley, Mary F. V, 967
Beasley, Mary F. V, 968
Beasley, Rhoda A. V, 968
Beasley, Robert I, 1
Beasley, Robert I Sup 1, 3
Beasley, Sarah VI, 878
Beasley, Susannah II, 110
Beasley, Thomas Mason II, 110
Beasley, Wm. II, 55
Beason, Amaziah IV, 20
Beason, Amiziah I, 1104
Beason, Amoriah V, 948
Beason, Ann I, 526
Beason, Ann I, 557
Beason, Aseaneth I, 799
Beason, Ayles I, 871
Beason, Benjamin I, 799
Beason, Benjamin V, 779
Beason, Betsy V, 794
Beason, Carmel IV, 799
Beason, Caroline V, 476
Beason, Catharine I, 799
Beason, Charity I, 799
Beason, Charity IV, 610
Beason, Charity IV, 799
Beason, Daniel W. V, 476
Beason, Darius I, 1104

Beason, Darius IV, 20
Beason, Darius V, 152
Beason, Dorcas I, 526
Beason, Edward IV, 610
Beason, Edward IV, 799
Beason, Edward V, 24
Beason, Elihugh V, 948
Beason, Elisha IV, 610
Beason, Elisha IV, 799
Beason, Elisha IV, 857
Beason, Elizabeth I, 799
Beason, Elizabeth I, 836
Beason, Elizabeth I, 981
Beason, Elizabeth V, 826
Beason, Elma I, 871
Beason, Ester V, 948
Beason, Eunice I, 592
Beason, Eunice V, 826
Beason, Hannah I, 799
Beason, Henry IV, 610
Beason, Henry IV, 799
Beason, Igal I, 1104
Beason, Igal IV, 20
Beason, Igal V, 152
Beason, Igal V, 948
Beason, Isaac, Jr. I, 799
Beason, Isabel I, 871
Beason, Isabel I, 1104
Beason, Isabel IV, 20
Beason, Jacob IV, 71
Beason, Jane I, 799
Beason, Jane I, 846
Beason, Jane I, 981
Beason, Jane V, 476
Beason, Jemima I, 981
Beason, Jemima I, 996
Beason, Jesse IV, 610
Beason, Jesse IV, 799
Beason, Jesse V, 779
Beason, Joel V, 476
Beason, John I, 526
Beason, John IV, 20
Beason, John IV, 610
Beason, John IV, 799
Beason, Joseph I, 981
Beason, Julias Madison I, 799
Beason, Luisa I, 799
Beason, Malon IV, 678
Beason, Margaret I, 799
Beason, Margaret V, 152
Beason, Margaret V, 948
Beason, Mariam V, 793
Beason, Mariam V, 794
Beason, Martha I, 799
Beason, Martha I, 839
Beason, Martha V, 476
Beason, Mary I, 799
Beason, Mary I, 803
Beason, Mary I, 826
Beason, Mary I, 839
Beason, Mary I, 981
Beason, Mary V, 373
Beason, Mary V, 794
Beason, Mehetable I, 709
Beason, Mildred M. I, 799
Beason, Molly I, 799
Beason, Nancy Alice I, 799
Beason, Nathaniel I, 799
Beason, Paul V, 24
Beason, Percy V, 24
Beason, Phebe I, 799
Beason, Phebe I, 800
Beason, Phebe I, 802
Beason, Phebe IV, 678
Beason, Phebe IV, 759
Beason, Priscilla I, 799
Beason, Priscilla I, 836
Beason, Rachel I, 798
Beason, Rachel I, 799
Beason, Rachel I, 1104
Beason, Rachel IV, 20
Beason, Rachel IV, 610
Beason, Rachel IV, 799
Beason, Rachel IV, 820
Beason, Rebecca IV, 925
Beason, Rebecca IV, 977
Beason, Rebeckah V, 222
Beason, Rebeckah V, 291
Beason, Richard VI, 365
Beason, Rosanna IV, 20
Beason, Rosannah I, 1104
Beason, Ruth I, 799
Beason, Sadie V, 24
Beason, Sarah I, 799
Beason, Sarah I, 827
Beason, Sarah I, 981
Beason, Sarah IV, 610
Beason, Sarah IV, 799
Beason, Seth V, 826
Beason, Tristram V, 779
Beason, William I, 799
Beason, William I, 981
Beason, Wilmot I, 799
Beason, Wilmot I, 809
Beasor, Asa VI, 470
Beasor, Dinah VI, 470
Beasor, Edith VI, 470
Beasor, Elizabeth VI, 470
Beasor, Gulielma VI, 470
Beasor, Jno. VI, 470
Beasor, John II, 464
Beasor, John II, 684
Beasor, John VI, 470
Beaston, Amanda V, 985
Beaston, Christine H. II, 129
Beaston, Elizabeth II, 715
Beaston, Frank V, 985
Beaston, Frank S. II, 129
Beaston, Grace II, 129
Beat, John, Jr. III, 30
Beaton, Charles VI, 52
Beaton, Edward H. VI, 52
Beaton, Edward Hunter VI, 52
Beaton, Eliza VI, 52
Beaton, Eliza J. VI, 52
Beaton, Eliza J. VI, 67
Beaton, Eliza Jane VI, 52
Beaton, Ella VI, 52
Beaton, Franklin VI, 52
Beaton, John VI, 52
Beaton, John VI, 67
Beaton, Lucy VI, 52
Beaton, Lucy A. VI, 52
Beaton, Martha VI, 52
Beaton, Mary A. VI, 52
Beaton, Mary Lena VI, 52
Beaton, Pearl VI, 91
Beaton, Pearly VI, 52
Beaton, Peqrly VI, 52
Beaton, Robert VI, 52
Beaton, William VI, 52
Beats, Emma L. V, 452
Beats, Jacob II, 441
Beats, Rachel II, 441
Beattie, Eunice III, 30
Beattie, Eunice III, 121
Beattie, Gertrude III, 30
Beattie, Gertrude B. III, 121
Beattie, Herbert III, 30
Beattie, James W. III, 30
Beattie, James W. III, 121
Beatty, Catherine II, 335
Beatty, Dora May V, 549
Beatty, Eliza II, 197
Beatty, Irene IV, 368
Beatty, Irene IV, 389
Beatty, Jay V, 985
Beatty, Mary II, 335
Beatty, Rachel II, 978
Beatty, Rachel II, 986
Beaty, Eliza II, 197
Beaty, Elizabeth II, 197
Beaty, Elizabeth II, 461
Beaty, Herman J. IV, 368
Beaty, Irene IV, 368
Beaty, Isabella H. IV, 368
Beaty, Isabelle H. IV, 368
Beaty, Jane I, 981
Beaty, Jay V, 985
Beaty, Kate V, 985
Beaty, Levi R. V, 985
Beaty, Lois Margaret IV, 368
Beaty, M. Irene IV, 368
Beaty, Mary II, 335
Beaty, Ralph D. IV, 368
Beaty, Richard Chester IV, 368
Beaty, Samuel Franklin IV, 368
Beaty, Susannah IV, 368
Beaty, Susannah IV, 439
Beauchamp, Alice I, 1070
Beauchamp, Alice I, 1071
Beauchamp, Amelia V, 961
Beauchamp, Ann V, 961
Beauchamp, Anna V, 947
Beauchamp, Asa V, 948
Beauchamp, Caleb I, 776
Beauchamp, Caleb I, 1067
Beauchamp, Charles I, 776
Beauchamp, Charles I, 1067
Beauchamp, Charles I, 1070
Beauchamp, Clark V, 948
Beauchamp, Curtis I, 776
Beauchamp, Curtis I, 1067
Beauchamp, Elick I, 1070
Beauchamp, Elick I, 1071
Beauchamp, Elizabeth I, 776
Beauchamp, Elizabeth I, 1067
Beauchamp, Elizabeth I, 1070
Beauchamp, Elleck I, 776
Beauchamp, Elleck I, 1067
Beauchamp, Ellick I, 1070
Beauchamp, Henry I, 776
Beauchamp, Henry I, 1067
Beauchamp, Henry I, 1070
Beauchamp, John I, 776
Beauchamp, John I, 1067
Beauchamp, John I, 1070
Beauchamp, Levi I, 776
Beauchamp, Levi I, 1067
Beauchamp, Levi I, 1070
Beauchamp, Lovina V, 948
Beauchamp, Lovina V, 960
Beauchamp, Martha V, 948
Beauchamp, Mary V, 948
Beauchamp, Mathew I, 776
Beauchamp, Mathew I, 1070
Beauchamp, Matthew I, 1067
Beauchamp, Milcah I, 776
Beauchamp, Milcar I, 1067
Beauchamp, Milley I, 1070
Beauchamp, Milley I, 1072
Beauchamp, Russ I, 776
Beauchamp, Russ I, 1067
Beauchamp, William I, 776
Beauchamp, William I, 1066
Beauchamp, William I, 1067
Beauchamp, William I, 1070
Beauchamp, William I, 1072
Beauchamp, William V, 222
Beauchamp, William, Jr. I, 1070
Beauchamp, Wm. V, 961
Beauchamps, Matthew V, 727
Beauley, Nathan II, 336
Beaumont, Henry F. VI, 798
Beaumont, James II, 335
Beaumont, John II, 335
Beaumont, John II, 978
Beaumont, Neomy II, 335
Beaumont, Rebeccah VI, 364
Beaumont, Sarah II, 978
Beaumont, Sarah G. VI, 798
Beaumount, Rebeckah VI, 591
Beauvais, Ida III, 94
Beaver, A. J. V, 985
Beaver, Hazel IV, 1246
Beaver, Jane VI, 1000
Beaver, John V, 985
Beaver, Lucinda V, 985
Beaver, Mahlon II, 782
Beaver, May II, 782
Beaver, Miriam V, 550
Beaver, Miriam V, 594
Beaver, Rachel IV, 1127
Beaver, Rachel IV, 1132
Beaverman, Joshua IV, 1347
Beavirge, David II, 461
Beavo, Eliza V, 985
Beavo, Joseph V, 985
Beavo, Minnie V, 985
Beawr, Elizabeth V, 319
Beawr, Elma V, 319
Beawr, Frank V, 319
Beawr, Margaret A. V, 319
Beawr???, Elizabeth V, 319
Beawr???, Elma V, 319
Beawr???, Frank V, 319
Beawr???, Margaret A. V, 319
Becham, Jesse L. VI, 832
Bechmann, Selma VI, 771
Bechtol, Estella V, 985
Bechtol, Israel V, 985
Bechtol, Israel V. V, 985
Bechtol, John V, 985
Bechtol, Lizzie V, 985
Bechtol, Lizzy V, 985
Bechtol, Louise V, 985
Bechtol, Stella V, 985
Beck, ??? IV, 1085
Beck, Aaron IV, 799
Beck, Abigail IV, 925
Beck, Abigail IV, 960
Beck, Abigail IV, 1035
Beck, Abigail H. IV, 925
Beck, Abigail H. IV, 1035
Beck, Ada Mae IV, 1035
Beck, Adah IV, 799
Beck, Adah IV, 900
Beck, Adam III, 30
Beck, Adam III, 280
Beck, Adam Mason V, 222
Beck, Agnes Rhoda IV, 1035
Beck, Albert IV, 799
Beck, Alfred H. IV, 799
Beck, Ann IV, 20
Beck, Ann IV, 69
Beck, Ann IV, 320
Beck, Ann IV, 325
Beck, Ann IV, 368
Beck, Ann IV, 567
Beck, Ann IV, 571
Beck, Ann IV, 799
Beck, Ann VI, 470
Beck, Ann VI, 477
Beck, Ann M. E. VI, 821
Beck, Anna II, 836
Beck, Anna M. IV, 993
Beck, Anna Mary IV, 1035
Beck, Austin Allen III, 30
Beck, Avine IV, 799
Beck, Bessie III, 30
Beck, Bessie M. III, 27
Beck, Bessie M. III, 30
Beck, Camille III, 27
Beck, Chas. H. IV, 1035
Beck, Cornelia I, 924
Beck, Dwight M. IV, 1035
Beck, Earl W. IV, 1035
Beck, Edward IV, 20
Beck, Edward IV, 69
Beck, Edward IV, 677
Beck, Edward IV, 799
Beck, Edward VI, 470
Beck, Edward Ivins Eastburn II, 836
Beck, Eliza IV, 567
Beck, Elizabeth IV, 320
Beck, Elizabeth IV, 368
Beck, Elizabeth IV, 369
Beck, Elizabeth IV, 390
Beck, Elizabeth IV, 511
Beck, Elizabeth IV, 567
Beck, Elizabeth IV, 799
Beck, Elizabeth IV, 840
Beck, Elizabeth IV, 1049
Beck, Elizabeth IV, 1109
Beck, Elizabeth IV, 1122
Beck, Ellen R. IV, 1035
Beck, Ervine P. IV, 799
Beck, Esther IV, 799
Beck, Esther IV, 800
Beck, Esther Ruth IV, 799
Beck, Esther Ruth IV, 800
Beck, Frances IV, 850
Beck, George I, 959
Beck, Grace IV, 567
Beck, Grace IV, 1049
Beck, Grace IV, 1088
Beck, Grace IV, 1109
Beck, Grace C. IV, 368
Beck, Grace E. IV, 567
Beck, Hallie A. IV, 1035
Beck, Hannah I, 798
Beck, Hannah II, 193
Beck, Hannah II, 197
Beck, Hannah II, 461
Beck, Helen D. III, 30
Beck, Helen D. III, 212
Beck, Isaac IV, 799
Beck, Isaac IV, 850
Beck, Isaac IV, 925
Beck, Isaac E. IV, 1035
Beck, Isaac Edwin IV, 1035
Beck, J. Marion IV, 1035
Beck, J. W. IV, 1035
Beck, James III, 30
Beck, James V, 985
Beck, James C. VI, 821
Beck, James S. III, 30
Beck, James T. III, 27
Beck, James T. III, 30
Beck, Jamima IV, 799
Beck, Jamima IV, 811
Beck, Jehu I, 798
Beck, Jemima IV, 368
Beck, Jemima IV, 677
Beck, Jemimah IV, 567
Beck, Jemimah IV, 580
Beck, Jesse IV, 320
Beck, Jesse IV, 368
Beck, Jesse IV, 369
Beck, Jesse IV, 390
Beck, Jesse IV, 511
Beck, Jesse IV, 567
Beck, Jesse IV, 1049
Beck, Jesse IV, 1088
Beck, Jesse IV, 1109
Beck, Jesse IV, 1122
Beck, John I, 776
Beck, John I, 798
Beck, John I, 924
Beck, John I, 959
Beck, John I, 966
Beck, John I, 1007
Beck, John I, 1047
Beck, John IV, 20
Beck, John IV, 368
Beck, John IV, 567
Beck, John IV, 571
Beck, John IV, 677
Beck, John IV, 799
Beck, John IV, 1088
Beck, John V, 985
Beck, John D. V, 985
Beck, John W. IV, 1035
Beck, John, Jr. IV, 368
Beck, John, Jr. IV, 567
Beck, John, Sr. IV, 1088
Beck, Jonas M. IV, 925
Beck, Jonas M. IV, 1035
Beck, Jones M. IV, 960
Beck, Joseph Middleton I, 798
Beck, L. Ray I, 923
Beck, L. Sarah IV, 567
Beck, Lawrence IV, 175
Beck, Lettie Ray I, 924
Beck, Lucy B. III, 27
Beck, Lucy E. III, 30
Beck, Lucy E. III, 100
Beck, Luiza IV, 799
Beck, Lydia IV, 20
Beck, Lydia IV, 23
Beck, Lydia IV, 139
Beck, Lydia IV, 320
Beck, Lydia IV, 326
Beck, Lydia IV, 368
Beck, Lydia IV, 571
Beck, Lydia IV, 761
Beck, Lydia Ann IV, 368
Beck, Mabel O. V, 222
Beck, Mable V, 222
Beck, Mariah IV, 799
Beck, Mariah IV, 850
Beck, Marie III, 30
Beck, Marie III, 280
Beck, Marion IV, 925
Beck, Marion IV, 1035
Beck, Martha IV, 368
Beck, Martha IV, 567
Beck, Martha IV, 589
Beck, Mary III, 30
Beck, Mary IV, 20
Beck, Mary IV, 677
Beck, Mary IV, 799
Beck, Mary IV, 843
Beck, Mary IV, 849
Beck, Mary Jane V, 222
Beck, Mary P. IV, 368
Beck, Mattie Mozelle I, 938
Beck, Milicent IV, 1035
Beck, Miliscent IV, 925
Beck, Nathan IV, 799
Beck, Paul IV, 20
Beck, Paul IV, 677
Beck, Paul IV, 799
Beck, Phebe I, 374
Beck, Phebe I, 425
Beck, Phebe I, 776
Beck, Phebe IV, 20
Beck, Phebe IV, 67
Beck, Phebe IV, 368
Beck, Phebe IV, 567
Beck, Phebe IV, 799
Beck, Phebe IV, 853
Beck, Phebe B. IV, 799
Beck, Phebia Sally Jemima IV, 368
Beck, Preston IV, 20
Beck, Preston IV, 67
Beck, Preston IV, 677
Beck, Preston IV, 799
Beck, Preston IV, 908
Beck, Preston, Jr. IV, 799
Beck, Preston, Jr. IV, 849
Beck, Prexton, Sr. IV, 799
Beck, Rachel I, 959
Beck, Rachel I, 966
Beck, Rachel I, 1007
Beck, Rachel IV, 20
Beck, Rachel IV, 311
Beck, Rachel IV, 368
Beck, Rachel IV, 369
Beck, Rachel IV, 511
Beck, Rachel IV, 567
Beck, Rachel IV, 571
Beck, Rachel IV, 677
Beck, Rachel IV, 799
Beck, Rachel IV, 814
Beck, Rachel IV, 1049
Beck, Rachel IV, 1088
Beck, Rachel IV, 1122
Beck, Rachel E. IV, 368
Beck, Rachel E. IV, 567
Beck, Richard IV, 20
Beck, Richard IV, 677
Beck, Richard IV, 799
Beck, Rosa IV, 1035
Beck, Rosella IV, 1035
Beck, Rosetta IV, 925
Beck, Rosetta IV, 1035
Beck, Ruth IV, 20
Beck, Ruth IV, 69
Beck, Ruth IV, 677
Beck, Ruth IV, 799
Beck, Sally IV, 368
Beck, Samuel IV, 320

Beck, Sarah IV, 20
Beck, Sarah IV, 67
Beck, Sarah IV, 567
Beck, Sarah IV, 586
Beck, Sarah IV, 677
Beck, Sarah IV, 799
Beck, Sarah IV, 823
Beck, Sarah IV, 841
Beck, Sarah IV, 842
Beck, Sarah IV, 908
Beck, Sarah IV, 1049
Beck, Sarah IV, 1088
Beck, Sarah IV, 1102
Beck, Sarah Ann IV, 797
Beck, Sarah Ann IV, 799
Beck, Sarah, Jr. IV, 799
Beck, Susanna I, 374
Beck, Sylvester IV, 799
Beck, Tessie C. V, 658
Beck, Tessie C. V, 701
Beck, Vanaga IV, 799
Beck, Venajah H. IV, 799
Beck, Wally III, 30
Beck, Wally III, 395
Beck, Wally III, 442
Beck, Wally B. III, 280
Beck, Walter C. I, 938
Beck, Walter S. III, 30
Beck, Walter S. III, 212
Beck, Wesley F. IV, 1035
Beck, William IV, 799
Beck, Wm. I. IV, 799
Beck, Zebulon IV, 799
Beckenby, Alfred B. I, 526
Becker, Amelia III, 322
Becker, Amelia Louise III, 30
Becker, Amelia Louise III, 323
Becker, Caroline III, 292
Becker, Frederick III, 30
Becker, Fredericka III, 323
Becker, William III, 30
Becker, William III, 323
Beckerdike, Gideon II, 979
Beckerdite, Clara I, 924
Beckerdite, Elizabeth I, 924
Beckerdite, Franklin I, 743
Beckerdite, John F. I, 755
Beckerdite, John R. I, 755
Beckerdite, John T. I, 743
Beckerdite, John T. I, 755
Beckerdite, Marinda I, 938
Beckerdite, Pleasant F. I, 755
Beckerton, Sarah II, 461
Becket, Martha II, 55
Becket, Martha II, 109
Becket, Mary II, 978
Becket, Mary II, 980
Becket, Mary III, 30
Becket, Susannah V, 611
Becket, Susannah V, 612
Beckett, Clara M. V, 24
Beckett, Clara M. V, 95
Beckett, Susannah V, 612
Beckford, Elizabeth V, 612
Beckford, Elizabeth V, 622
Beckham, Caleb II, 335
Beckham, Elizabeth VI, 865
Beckham, James VI, 865
Beckham, James C. VI, 865
Beckham, Jesse I. VI, 798
Beckham, Jesse L. VI, 798
Beckham, Philadelphia VI, 798
Beckham, Rachel II, 335
Beckham, Sally VI, 798
Beckham, Sarah VI, 798
Beckham, William VI, 798
Beckirdite, Jane I, 921
Beckirdite, John I, 921
Beckirdite, Marinda I, 921
Beckit, Martha II, 17
Beckit, Mary III, 42
Beckitt, Lucy II, 461
Beckitt, Lucy II, 660
Beckitt, Wm. II, 461
Beckitt, Wm. II, 660
Beckly, Samuel II, 197
Beckner, Augusta V, 985
Beckner, Elizabeth VI, 936
Beckner, James VI, 878
Beckner, Jefferson VI, 905
Beckner, Narcissa E. VI, 878
Beckner, Susanna VI, 878
Beckner, William VI, 878
Becknor, James VI, 901
Becknor, Jane VI, 901
Beckwith, ??? III, 30
Beckwith, ??? III, 174
Beckwith, Abbie L. III, 30
Beckwith, Abbie L. III, 174
Beckwith, Abbie M. IV, 1233
Beckwith, Aletha IV, 1035
Beckwith, Cecelia C. IV, 1246
Beckwith, Charles O. IV, 1246
Beckwith, Cybella C. IV, 1246
Beckwith, Ellen Jane IV, 1246
Beckwith, Erwin G. IV, 1233
Beckwith, Frank IV, 1307
Beckwith, J. A. IV, 1306
Beckwith, John IV, 1306
Beckwith, John A. IV, 1307
Beckwith, Mary IV, 1306
Beckwith, Minnie IV, 1307
Beckwith, Mrs. Minnie IV, 1306
Beckwith, Rosa IV, 1145
Becner, Nancy V, 319
Beddle, Absolom I, 374
Beddle, Ruth I, 374
Beddy, John II, 461
Bedel, Amy III, 472
Bedell, ??? III, 30
Bedell, Abby III, 479
Bedell, Ada M. III, 373
Bedell, Albert Boone II, 789
Bedell, Albert J. IV, 768
Bedell, Almira J. III, 479
Bedell, Amanda III, 479
Bedell, Amelia II, 727
Bedell, Amelia IV, 369
Bedell, Anetta K. II, 699
Bedell, Anetta K. II, 727
Bedell, Anna Elizabeth IV, 768
Bedell, Annetta K. II, 727
Bedell, Benajah III, 395
Bedell, Caleb C. III, 30
Bedell, Caleb C. III, 248
Bedell, Caleb C. III, 373
Bedell, Caty III, 58
Bedell, Caty III, 240
Bedell, Charles III, 479
Bedell, Charles H. III, 479
Bedell, Clara Esther IV, 677
Bedell, Clara Esther IV, 768
Bedell, Clarence L. III, 30
Bedell, Clarence Woolten II, 789
Bedell, Cynthia IV, 369
Bedell, Elbert III, 479
Bedell, Eliz. III, 210
Bedell, Eliz. III, 230
Bedell, Elizabeth III, 395
Bedell, Elizabeth III, 479
Bedell, Elizabeth IV, 1049
Bedell, Ella May III, 30
Bedell, Ella May III, 248
Bedell, Elwood IV, 369
Bedell, Emma II, 789
Bedell, Hannah III, 395
Bedell, Helen Trump II, 789
Bedell, Henry III, 479
Bedell, Howard II, 789
Bedell, Howard R. III, 30
Bedell, Isaac III, 479
Bedell, Jane III, 30
Bedell, Jane III, 479
Bedell, Jehiel III, 395
Bedell, Jennie III, 30
Bedell, Jennie Rhoda III, 30
Bedell, Jesse R. IV, 677
Bedell, Joseph III, 395
Bedell, Joseph III, 479
Bedell, Joseph III, 491
Bedell, Joseph Darnell II, 789
Bedell, Joseph Henry II, 789
Bedell, Joseph Wallace II, 789
Bedell, Jotham III, 30
Bedell, Kazia II, 699
Bedell, Lavinia Robinson II, 789
Bedell, Lewis III, 30
Bedell, Lindley H. II, 699
Bedell, Lindley H. II, 727
Bedell, Lydia II, 699
Bedell, Lydia Evans II, 727
Bedell, Mahlon IV, 369
Bedell, Martha III, 30
Bedell, Martha III, 248
Bedell, Martha III, 373
Bedell, Martha III, 479
Bedell, Martha III, 491
Bedell, Martha R. III, 30
Bedell, Mary III, 395
Bedell, Mary III, 474
Bedell, Matilda Howard II, 789
Bedell, Mordecai III, 395
Bedell, Otis T. III, 30
Bedell, Phebe M. III, 479
Bedell, Rachel III, 395
Bedell, Rachel III, 479
Bedell, Rachel III, 491
Bedell, Rachel W. III, 479
Bedell, Rhoda III, 479
Bedell, Rosella IV, 1035
Bedell, Samuel III, 479
Bedell, Samuel IV, 369
Bedell, Sarah III, 479
Bedell, Sarah III, 493
Bedell, Sarah E. IV, 369
Bedell, Sarah E. IV, 427
Bedell, Sarah Etta IV, 369
Bedell, Sarah J. II, 699
Bedell, Sarah J. II, 727
Bedell, William III, 395
Bedell, William P. IV, 369
Bedell, Wm. II, 789
Bedell, Wm. II, 836
Bedell, Wm. III, 474
Bedell, Wm. P. II, 699
Bedell, Wm., Jr. II, 836
Bedford, Abigail G. II, 461
Bedford, Abigail G. II, 471
Bedford, Abigail G. II, 727
Bedford, Ann II, 335
Bedford, Ann II, 461
Bedford, Isaac II, 461
Bedford, Isaac II, 727
Bedford, Isaac II, 836
Bedford, Jane II, 461
Bedford, Jane II, 727
Bedford, Jane II, 836
Bedford, Joseph II, 335
Bedford, Joseph II, 461
Bedford, Joseph Atkinson II, 461
Bedford, Mary VI, 296
Bedford, Peter II, 335
Bedford, Samuel II, 836
Bedford, Sarah II, 335
Bedford, Sarah II, 461
Bedford, Sarah II, 727
Bedford, Sarah II, 742
Bedford, Sarah P. II, 836
Bedford, Sarah P. II, 907
Bedford, Savery II, 836
Bedford, Susanna II, 335
Bedford, Susanna II, 461
Bedford, Thomas II, 335
Bedford, Thomas II, 461
Bedford, Thomas II, 727
Bedford, Thomas, Jr. II, 461
Bedford, Thos. II, 836
Bedford, Thos., Jr. II, 836
Bedford, Wm. Savory II, 836
Bedgood, Deborough I, 189
Bedgood, Deborough I, 200
Bedgood, Mary I, 129
Bedgood, William I, 129
Bedle, Benajah III, 395
Bedle, Eldenna III, 19
Bedle, Ellena III, 264
Bedle, Hannah III, 395
Bedle, Jehiel III, 395
Bedle, Joseph III, 395
Bedle, Mary III, 395
Bedle, Mordecai III, 395
Bedle, Rachel III, 395
Bedle, William III, 395
Bedsalt, Elisha I, 374
Bedsalt, John I, 374
Bedsalt, John I, 375
Bedsalt, Mary I, 374
Bedsalt, Sarah I, 374
Bedsalt, Sarah I, 375
Bedselt, Sarah I, 374
Bedselt, Sarah I, 375
Bedson, Mary II, 335
Bedson, Samuel II, 335
Bedson, Thomas II, 335
Bedward, Catharine II, 685
Bedward, Catherine II, 461
Bedward, James Whitten II, 461
Bedward, Jane II, 461
Bedward, Katherine II, 461
Bedward, Mary Preston II, 461
Bedward, Wm. II, 461
Bedward, Wm. II, 685
Bedwort, Katherine II, 461
Bedwort, Kathrine II, 685
Beebe, Annette Rosalie VI, 757
Beebe, Annette Rosalie VI, 773
Beebe, Nancy IV, 1145
Beebe, Nancy IV, 1156
Beeby, Dan II, 461
Beech, Elizabeth IV, 1272
Beech, Harry IV, 677
Beechler, Elizabeth V, 850
Beechler, Ira V, 826
Beechler, Ira V, 850
Beechler, Lizzie V, 826
Beechler, Mahalah Elizabeth V, 826
Beede, Abraham IV, 925
Beede, Anna Winslow IV, 751
Beede, Jonathan IV, 751
Beede, Mary IV, 751
Beedee, Abram IV, 678
Beedle, Abigail II, 336
Beedle, Ann II, 336
Beedle, Barbara II, 336
Beedle, David, Jr. IV, 1145
Beedle, Drusilla V, 152
Beedle, Elizabeth II, 336
Beedle, John II, 336
Beedle, Minnie V, 152
Beedle, Ruth I, 1041
Beedles, Fannie VI, 677
Beedles, Mr. ??? VI, 677
Beedy, Abraham IV, 799
Beedy, Abraham IV, 851
Beedy, Abraham IV, 891
Beedy, Amy IV, 891
Beedy, Eli IV, 891
Beedy, Hannah IV, 799
Beedy, Hannah IV, 851
Beedy, Hannah IV, 891
Beedy, Olive Ann IV, 891
Beeks, Stacy II, 461
Beel, Martha II, 978
Beele, Ellen VI, 52
Beele, Ellen VI, 61
Beele, Harrison VI, 61
Beell, Mary I, 871
Beell, Miriam I, 871
Beemam, Francis I, 229
Beemam, James I, 229
Beeman, ??? I, 279
Beeman, Francis, Sr. I, 229
Beeman, Mary I, 229
Beeman, Mary I, 299
Beeman, Mary I, 709
Beeman, Ozias I, 229
Beeman, Polly I, 299
Beeman, Polly I, 314
Beeman, Rebecah VI, 364
Beens, Elizabeth IV, 675
Beens, Mary IV, 610
Beer, Charley V, 985
Beer, Martha V, 698
Beer, Rachel V, 985
Beers, Clara II, 836
Beers, Clara II, 888
Beers, Edwin C. II, 836
Beers, Edwin C. II, 888
Beers, Laura A. IV, 369
Beers, Laura A. IV, 388
Beers, Louisa V, 152
Beers, Sophia II, 836
Beers, Sophia II, 888
Beers, Wm. R. II, 836
Beers, Wm. R. II, 888
Beery, Cyrus A. V, 319
Beery, Daniel V, 222
Beery, Edwin V, 222
Beery, Hazel V, 727
Beesan, Anne V, 298
Beesan, Anne V, 308
Beesley, Aber II, 129
Beesley, Abner II, 22
Beesley, Abner II, 55
Beesley, Abner II, 92
Beesley, Abner II, 129
Beesley, Abner II, 130
Beesley, Abner II, 140
Beesley, Benjamin II, 22
Beesley, Benjamin II, 55
Beesley, Charlotte II, 22
Beesley, Charlotte II, 115
Beesley, Hannah II, 22
Beesley, Hannah II, 55
Beesley, Hannah II, 111
Beesley, Hannah W. II, 115
Beesley, John Wistar II, 22
Beesley, John Wister II, 115
Beesley, Mary II, 22
Beesley, Mary II, 55
Beesley, Mary II, 92
Beesley, Mary II, 111
Beesley, Mary II, 115
Beesley, Mary II, 129
Beesley, Mary II, 130
Beesley, Maurice II, 22
Beesley, Maurice II, 55
Beesley, Maurice II, 111
Beesley, Morris II, 22
Beesley, Rachel II, 55
Beesley, Rachel II, 92
Beesley, Rachel II, 115
Beesley, Rachel II, 129
Beesley, Susannah II, 22
Beesley, Theophilus II, 115
Beesley, Theophilus E. II, 22
Beesley, Theophilus E. II, 55
Beesley, Theophilus E. II, 111
Beesley, Theophilus E. II, 115
Beesley, Thomas II, 129
Beesley, Thomas M. II, 115
Beesley, Thomas M. II, 145
Beesley, Thomas Mason II, 22
Beesley, Wm. II, 22
Beesley, Wm. II, 55
Beesley, Wm. G. II, 55
Beesley, Wm. G. II, 92
Beesley, Wm. G. II, 115
Beesley, Wm. G. II, 129
Beesom, Elmer G. V, 727
Beesom, John V, 727
Beeson, Abigail I, 674
Beeson, Abner I, 776
Beeson, Abner I, 799
Beeson, Absalom I, 649
Beeson, Absalom I, 799
Beeson, Absolem I, 776
Beeson, Alice I, 649
Beeson, Alice I, 661
Beeson, Alice I, 674
Beeson, Alice I, 871
Beeson, Alice I, 889
Beeson, Alice I, 931
Beeson, Alice VI, 365
Beeson, Alice VI, 377
Beeson, Alice U. I, 924
Beeson, Allen V, 948
Beeson, Amasa I, 491
Beeson, Amasa I, 776
Beeson, Amasa I, 798
Beeson, Amasa I, 799
Beeson, Amasa I, 953
Beeson, Amasa I, 955
Beeson, Amasa I, 959
Beeson, Amasa V, 222
Beeson, Amasa V, 298
Beeson, Amasy I, 526
Beeson, Amaziah I, 1102
Beeson, Amaziah I, 1115
Beeson, Amaziah IV, 20
Beeson, Amaziah V, 948
Beeson, Amizah V, 948
Beeson, Amiziah V, 948
Beeson, Amoriah V, 948
Beeson, Ann I, 491
Beeson, Ann I, 526
Beeson, Ann IV, 175
Beeson, Ann IV, 610
Beeson, Ann IV, 623
Beeson, Ann IV, 641
Beeson, Ann IV, 649
Beeson, Ann IV, 864
Beeson, Ann V, 222
Beeson, Ann V, 298
Beeson, Ann V, 300
Beeson, Ann V, 308
Beeson, Ann VI, 364
Beeson, Ann VI, 372
Beeson, Anna IV, 320
Beeson, Anna IV, 351
Beeson, Anna IV, 678
Beeson, Anna V, 222
Beeson, Anna Corinia I, 743
Beeson, Anne V, 298
Beeson, Annie V, 894
Beeson, Armilla I, 649
Beeson, Asahel I, 491
Beeson, Aseaneth I, 799
Beeson, Ayles I, 871
Beeson, Benj. I, 490
Beeson, Benj. I, 491
Beeson, Benj. I, 645
Beeson, Benj. I, 959
Beeson, Benjamin I, 343
Beeson, Benjamin I, 374
Beeson, Benjamin I, 491
Beeson, Benjamin I, 526
Beeson, Benjamin I, 556
Beeson, Benjamin I, 648
Beeson, Benjamin I, 649
Beeson, Benjamin I, 674
Beeson, Benjamin I, 680
Beeson, Benjamin I, 776
Beeson, Benjamin I, 798
Beeson, Benjamin I, 799
Beeson, Benjamin I, 840
Beeson, Benjamin I, 907
Beeson, Benjamin I, 955
Beeson, Benjamin I, 959
Beeson, Benjamin IV, 351
Beeson, Benjamin V, 222
Beeson, Benjamin V, 298
Beeson, Benjamin V, 779
Beeson, Benjamin VI, 364
Beeson, Benjamin, Jr. I, 799
Beeson, Bethia I, 526
Beeson, Bethia I, 556
Beeson, Bethia I, 955
Beeson, Bethia I, 959
Beeson, Bethiah I, 491
Beeson, Bethiah I, 648
Beeson, Bethiah V, 298
Beeson, Betsy V, 779
Beeson, Betsy V, 794

Beeson, Betsy V, 948
Beeson, Betty I, 491
Beeson, Binjamin I, 487
Beeson, Callie I, 611
Beeson, Callie I, 612
Beeson, Callie P. V, 727
Beeson, Cara E. V, 727
Beeson, Caroline V, 222
Beeson, Caroline V, 476
Beeson, Caroline V, 894
Beeson, Catharine I, 776
Beeson, Catharine I, 798
Beeson, Catharine I, 799
Beeson, Catharine I, 907
Beeson, Catharine IV, 623
Beeson, Charity I, 491
Beeson, Charity I, 649
Beeson, Charity I, 776
Beeson, Charity I, 799
Beeson, Charity I, 801
Beeson, Charity I, 955
Beeson, Charity I, 959
Beeson, Charity I, 960
Beeson, Charity IV, 175
Beeson, Charity IV, 201
Beeson, Charity IV, 610
Beeson, Charity IV, 829
Beeson, Charity VI, 364
Beeson, Charity VI, 400
Beeson, Charity VI, 437
Beeson, Charity VI, 470
Beeson, Charles I, 799
Beeson, Charles V, 222
Beeson, Charrity IV, 610
Beeson, Chas. V, 894
Beeson, Clara May IV, 698
Beeson, Cordelia V, 727
Beeson, Cordelia Jane V, 727
Beeson, Daniel H. V, 476
Beeson, Daniel W. V, 222
Beeson, Daniel W. V, 476
Beeson, Darias V, 948
Beeson, Darius IV, 20
Beeson, David I, 649
Beeson, David I, 776
Beeson, David I, 799
Beeson, David L. I, 674
Beeson, Dinah I, 491
Beeson, Dinah I, 674
Beeson, Dinah I, 682
Beeson, Dorcas I, 526
Beeson, Edward I, 491
Beeson, Edward I, 776
Beeson, Edward I, 799
Beeson, Edward I, 801
Beeson, Edward IV, 175
Beeson, Edward IV, 610
Beeson, Edward V, 24
Beeson, Edward VI, 364
Beeson, Edward VI, 365
Beeson, Edward VI, 400
Beeson, Edward VI, 421
Beeson, Edward VI, 433
Beeson, Edward VI, 453
Beeson, Edward VI, 470
Beeson, Edward VI, 530
Beeson, Edward, Jr. I, 799
Beeson, Edward, Jr. VI, 365
Beeson, Edward, Sr. VI, 470
Beeson, Edwin V, 319
Beeson, Eleazar I, 649
Beeson, Eli V, 948
Beeson, Elihugh V, 948
Beeson, Elisha IV, 175
Beeson, Elisha IV, 610
Beeson, Eliza J. IV, 200
Beeson, Elizabeth I, 490
Beeson, Elizabeth I, 491
Beeson, Elizabeth I, 526
Beeson, Elizabeth I, 564
Beeson, Elizabeth I, 649
Beeson, Elizabeth I, 661
Beeson, Elizabeth I, 674
Beeson, Elizabeth I, 692
Beeson, Elizabeth I, 776
Beeson, Elizabeth I, 798
Beeson, Elizabeth I, 799
Beeson, Elizabeth I, 801
Beeson, Elizabeth I, 981
Beeson, Elizabeth IV, 610
Beeson, Elizabeth IV, 660
Beeson, Elizabeth V, 222
Beeson, Elizabeth V, 779
Beeson, Elizabeth V, 826
Beeson, Elizabeth V, 868
Beeson, Elizabeth V, 874
Beeson, Elizabeth V, 894
Beeson, Elizabeth E. I, 755
Beeson, Elizabeth E. I, 770
Beeson, Elizabeth E. I, 850
Beeson, Elizabeth E. I, 871
Beeson, Elizabeth Ellen I, 743
Beeson, Elizabeth T. V, 222
Beeson, Elizabeth T. V, 894
Beeson, Elma I, 871
Beeson, Elmer V, 727
Beeson, Elmer G. V, 727
Beeson, Elwood I, 649
Beeson, Emma F. V, 727
Beeson, Ephraim L. IV, 369
Beeson, Ephraim Lycurgas IV, 610
Beeson, Erwin IV, 369
Beeson, Ester V, 948
Beeson, Eunice I, 674
Beeson, Eunice V, 826
Beeson, Eunice V, 837
Beeson, Frances I, 491
Beeson, Frances I, 526
Beeson, Frances I, 556
Beeson, Frank V, 727
Beeson, Geneva Beatrice I, 923
Beeson, Hannabel A. V, 894
Beeson, Hannah I, 374
Beeson, Hannah I, 491
Beeson, Hannah I, 648
Beeson, Hannah I, 649
Beeson, Hannah I, 674
Beeson, Hannah I, 679
Beeson, Hannah I, 682
Beeson, Hannah I, 799
Beeson, Hannah I, 803
Beeson, Hannah I, 811
Beeson, Hannah IV, 20
Beeson, Hannah IV, 36
Beeson, Hannah IV, 925
Beeson, Hannah IV, 926
Beeson, Hannah V, 826
Beeson, Hannah P. I, 374
Beeson, Hannah P. I, 415
Beeson, Hannah P. I, 674
Beeson, Hannibal V, 222
Beeson, Hannibal V, 894
Beeson, Hansel I, 629
Beeson, Hansel Clarkson I, 611
Beeson, Hansel E. I, 611
Beeson, Hansel E. I, 612
Beeson, Henry I, 648
Beeson, Henry I, 871
Beeson, Henry I, 959
Beeson, Henry IV, 36
Beeson, Henry IV, 74
Beeson, Henry IV, 175
Beeson, Henry IV, 181
Beeson, Henry IV, 201
Beeson, Henry IV, 610
Beeson, Henry IV, 667
Beeson, Henry VI, 470
Beeson, Henry H. I, 743
Beeson, Henry H. I, 755
Beeson, Henry H. I, 849
Beeson, Henry H. I, 850
Beeson, Henry H. I, 871
Beeson, Hepsibah V, 779
Beeson, Hepsibah V, 789
Beeson, Hezekiah I, 649
Beeson, Hezekiah I, 674
Beeson, Hezekiah I, 687
Beeson, Hiram I, 649
Beeson, Ida I, 931
Beeson, Igal IV, 20
Beeson, Igal V, 948
Beeson, Igar V, 948
Beeson, Isaac I, 490
Beeson, Isaac I, 491
Beeson, Isaac I, 526
Beeson, Isaac I, 565
Beeson, Isaac I, 645
Beeson, Isaac I, 648
Beeson, Isaac I, 649
Beeson, Isaac I, 674
Beeson, Isaac I, 683
Beeson, Isaac I, 776
Beeson, Isaac I, 799
Beeson, Isaac I, 802
Beeson, Isaac I, 871
Beeson, Isaac I, 923
Beeson, Isaac I, 924
Beeson, Isaac K. I, 674
Beeson, Isaac Newlin I, 649
Beeson, Isaac Newton V, 826
Beeson, Isaac W. I, 674
Beeson, Isaac, Jr. I, 649
Beeson, Isaac, Jr. I, 799
Beeson, Isaac, Sr. I, 526
Beeson, Isaac, Sr. VI, 364
Beeson, Isabel I, 491
Beeson, Isabel I, 526
Beeson, Isabel I, 565
Beeson, Isabel I, 649
Beeson, Isabel I, 674
Beeson, Isabel I, 675
Beeson, Isabel I, 871
Beeson, Isabel IV, 20
Beeson, Isabel V, 948
Beeson, Isabell I, 871
Beeson, Isabell V, 948
Beeson, Isabella I, 1115
Beeson, Isaiah I, 871
Beeson, Ithamer I, 799
Beeson, J. Henry I, 612
Beeson, J. Henry I, 629
Beeson, J. W. I, 931
Beeson, Jacob I, 799
Beeson, Jacob IV, 200
Beeson, Jacob IV, 610
Beeson, Jacob VI, 365
Beeson, Jacob VI, 470
Beeson, James VI, 365
Beeson, Jane I, 491
Beeson, Jane I, 649
Beeson, Jane I, 674
Beeson, Jane I, 776
Beeson, Jane I, 777
Beeson, Jane I, 799
Beeson, Jane I, 871
Beeson, Jane I, 981
Beeson, Jane IV, 351
Beeson, Jane V, 222
Beeson, Jane V, 476
Beeson, Jane VI, 364
Beeson, Jane VI, 365
Beeson, Jane VI, 400
Beeson, Jane VI, 421
Beeson, Jane VI, 433
Beeson, Jane VI, 437
Beeson, Jane VI, 456
Beeson, Jane VI, 470
Beeson, Jane VI, 530
Beeson, Jane O. I, 743
Beeson, Jane O. I, 755
Beeson, Jane O. I, 849
Beeson, Jane O. I, 850
Beeson, Jane R. VI, 396
Beeson, Janes R. VI, 364
Beeson, Jean VI, 364
Beeson, Jehu I, 648
Beeson, Jehu I, 674
Beeson, Jehu I, 799
Beeson, Jemima I, 776
Beeson, Jene I, 776
Beeson, Jenne V, 779
Beeson, Jenny I, 526
Beeson, Jenny I, 565
Beeson, Jesse I, 649
Beeson, Jesse I, 692
Beeson, Jesse I, 799
Beeson, Jesse IV, 74
Beeson, Jesse IV, 117
Beeson, Jesse IV, 175
Beeson, Jesse IV, 610
Beeson, Jesse V, 779
Beeson, Jesse VI, 365
Beeson, Joel V, 476
Beeson, Joel Wright V, 222
Beeson, Joel Wright V, 476
Beeson, John I, 374
Beeson, John I, 491
Beeson, John I, 526
Beeson, John IV, 20
Beeson, John IV, 175
Beeson, John IV, 610
Beeson, John IV, 667
Beeson, John IV, 678
Beeson, John V, 222
Beeson, John V, 727
Beeson, John V, 894
Beeson, John V, 948
Beeson, John VI, 364
Beeson, John VI, 470
Beeson, John VI, 534
Beeson, John Brooks I, 776
Beeson, John F. I, 611
Beeson, John F. I, 612
Beeson, John F. I, 755
Beeson, John Franklin I, 743
Beeson, John Henry V, 727
Beeson, John Howard V, 727
Beeson, John O. IV, 610
Beeson, John O. IV, 678
Beeson, John O. IV, 710
Beeson, John S. IV, 369
Beeson, John Schooley IV, 678
Beeson, Jonathan I, 491
Beeson, Jonathan I, 526
Beeson, Jonathan I, 755
Beeson, Jonathan I, 762
Beeson, Jonathan I, 959
Beeson, Joseph I, 491
Beeson, Joseph I, 776
Beeson, Joseph I, 777
Beeson, Joseph I, 799
Beeson, Joseph V, 779
Beeson, Joseph V, 789
Beeson, Julia V, 948
Beeson, Julian VI, 365
Beeson, Julian VI, 437
Beeson, Julias Madison I, 799
Beeson, Juliet VI, 365
Beeson, Lazarus I, 649
Beeson, Lewis VI, 365
Beeson, Lewis R. VI, 365
Beeson, Lorohame I, 674
Beeson, Lorohame I, 679
Beeson, Louisa I, 924
Beeson, Louisa Jane I, 923
Beeson, Luisa I, 799
Beeson, Luiza I, 649
Beeson, Lydia I, 649
Beeson, Lydia IV, 200
Beeson, Lydia V, 298
Beeson, Lydia V, 309
Beeson, Lydia V, 948
Beeson, Mabel IV, 710
Beeson, Maggie Belle V, 727
Beeson, Mahlon IV, 610
Beeson, Malon IV, 678
Beeson, Margaret I, 648
Beeson, Margaret I, 649
Beeson, Margaret I, 674
Beeson, Margaret I, 675
Beeson, Margaret I, 680
Beeson, Margaret I, 796
Beeson, Margaret I, 799
Beeson, Margaret V, 948
Beeson, Mariam I, 755
Beeson, Mariam V, 779
Beeson, Mariam V, 794
Beeson, Martha I, 649
Beeson, Martha I, 776
Beeson, Martha I, 799
Beeson, Martha I, 817
Beeson, Martha IV, 864
Beeson, Martha IV, 883
Beeson, Martha V, 222
Beeson, Martha V, 293
Beeson, Martha V, 476
Beeson, Martha VI, 364
Beeson, Martha VI, 421
Beeson, Martha VI, 453
Beeson, Martha VI, 470
Beeson, Martha VI, 530
Beeson, Martha VI, 534
Beeson, Martha Jane I, 743
Beeson, Mary I, 374
Beeson, Mary I, 491
Beeson, Mary I, 526
Beeson, Mary I, 567
Beeson, Mary I, 649
Beeson, Mary I, 674
Beeson, Mary I, 687
Beeson, Mary I, 691
Beeson, Mary I, 776
Beeson, Mary I, 798
Beeson, Mary I, 799
Beeson, Mary I, 801
Beeson, Mary I, 802
Beeson, Mary I, 813
Beeson, Mary I, 839
Beeson, Mary I, 909
Beeson, Mary I, 955
Beeson, Mary I, 959
Beeson, Mary I, 981
Beeson, Mary I, 992
Beeson, Mary IV, 74
Beeson, Mary IV, 117
Beeson, Mary IV, 175
Beeson, Mary IV, 181
Beeson, Mary IV, 200
Beeson, Mary IV, 201
Beeson, Mary IV, 610
Beeson, Mary IV, 667
Beeson, Mary V, 222
Beeson, Mary V, 298
Beeson, Mary V, 311
Beeson, Mary V, 779
Beeson, Mary V, 794
Beeson, Mary V, 826
Beeson, Mary VI, 364
Beeson, Mary VI, 453
Beeson, Mary VI, 534
Beeson, Mary Abigail I, 743
Beeson, Mary Ann V, 222
Beeson, Mary Ann V, 285
Beeson, Mary Walker VI, 364
Beeson, Mattie V, 319
Beeson, Mattie J. I, 620
Beeson, Mehetable I, 709
Beeson, Mehitable I, 374
Beeson, Mehitable I, 648
Beeson, Mehitable I, 709
Beeson, Mehitable I, 955
Beeson, Mehitable I, 959
Beeson, Merab I, 649
Beeson, Meriah I, 649
Beeson, Messer VI, 364
Beeson, Micajah VI, 364
Beeson, Micajah VI, 365
Beeson, Micajah VI, 396
Beeson, Micajah VI, 437
Beeson, Mildred I, 649
Beeson, Mildred M. I, 799
Beeson, Mildred Marceila I, 923
Beeson, Milley V, 298
Beeson, Milley V, 299
Beeson, Miriam I, 491
Beeson, Miriam I, 755
Beeson, Miriam I, 762
Beeson, Miriam V, 779
Beeson, Molly I, 799
Beeson, Nancy V, 948
Beeson, Nancy Alice I, 799
Beeson, Nathaniel I, 799
Beeson, Nathaniel VI, 364
Beeson, Nathel I, 526
Beeson, Nell M. I, 611
Beeson, Nell Mae I, 630
Beeson, Nellie Gretchel I, 611
Beeson, Nellie Gretchen I, 630
Beeson, Nellie V. V, 727
Beeson, Patience VI, 364
Beeson, Patience VI, 396
Beeson, Patience VI, 437
Beeson, Paul V, 24
Beeson, Peeter VI, 364
Beeson, Percy V, 24
Beeson, Peter VI, 470
Beeson, Phebe I, 491
Beeson, Phebe I, 773
Beeson, Phebe I, 776
Beeson, Phebe I, 798
Beeson, Phebe I, 799
Beeson, Phebe I, 836
Beeson, Phebe IV, 610
Beeson, Phebe IV, 667
Beeson, Phebe IV, 678
Beeson, Phebe VI, 545
Beeson, Phebe S. IV, 369
Beeson, Phebe S. IV, 610
Beeson, Pheby IV, 610
Beeson, Priscilla I, 649
Beeson, Priscilla I, 799
Beeson, Pugh VI, 364
Beeson, Rachel I, 491
Beeson, Rachel I, 526
Beeson, Rachel I, 627
Beeson, Rachel I, 649
Beeson, Rachel I, 674
Beeson, Rachel I, 675
Beeson, Rachel I, 685
Beeson, Rachel I, 776
Beeson, Rachel I, 798
Beeson, Rachel I, 799
Beeson, Rachel IV, 20
Beeson, Rachel IV, 175
Beeson, Rachel IV, 610
Beeson, Rachel IV, 657
Beeson, Rachel V, 948
Beeson, Rachel VI, 470
Beeson, Rachel VI, 471
Beeson, Rachel Armatta IV, 369
Beeson, Rebecca I, 674
Beeson, Rebecca I, 683
Beeson, Rebecca I, 776
Beeson, Rebecca I, 799
Beeson, Rebecca I, 833
Beeson, Rebecca IV, 175
Beeson, Rebecca IV, 181
Beeson, Rebecca IV, 610
Beeson, Rebecca IV, 641
Beeson, Rebecca IV, 864
Beeson, Rebecca IV, 872
Beeson, Rebecca H. IV, 369
Beeson, Rebecca H. IV, 864
Beeson, Rebeckah V, 222
Beeson, Rhoda W. I, 799
Beeson, Richard I, 487
Beeson, Richard I, 491
Beeson, Richard I, 526
Beeson, Richard I, 645
Beeson, Richard I, 649
Beeson, Richard I, 674
Beeson, Richard I, 776
Beeson, Richard I, 798
Beeson, Richard I, 799
Beeson, Richard I, 909
Beeson, Richard I, 911
Beeson, Richard I, 959
Beeson, Richard IV, 610
Beeson, Richard IV, 623
Beeson, Richard IV, 641
Beeson, Richard IV, 649
Beeson, Richard IV, 864
Beeson, Richard V, 222
Beeson, Richard V, 298

Beeson, Richard V, 299
Beeson, Richard VI, 357
Beeson, Richard VI, 358
Beeson, Richard VI, 359
Beeson, Richard VI, 364
Beeson, Richard VI, 365
Beeson, Richard VI, 470
Beeson, Richard VI, 609
Beeson, Richard H. IV, 369
Beeson, Richard H. IV, 610
Beeson, Richard H. IV, 864
Beeson, Richard H. IV, 872
Beeson, Richard, Jr. I, 526
Beeson, Richard, Jr. VI, 364
Beeson, Richard, Jr. VI, 372
Beeson, Richard, Jr. VI, 390
Beeson, Richard, Jr. VI, 424
Beeson, Richard, Sr. VI, 364
Beeson, Roda W. I, 799
Beeson, Roda W. I, 819
Beeson, Rosaltha V. IV, 710
Beeson, Rosanna IV, 20
Beeson, Roseanne V, 948
Beeson, Ruel V, 222
Beeson, Ruth I, 491
Beeson, Ruth I, 526
Beeson, Ruth I, 571
Beeson, Ruth I, 799
Beeson, Ruth IV, 610
Beeson, Ruth IV, 617
Beeson, Ruth Anna IV, 610
Beeson, Ruthanna W. IV, 369
Beeson, Sadie V, 24
Beeson, Sally I, 649
Beeson, Samantha E. V, 319
Beeson, Samuel I, 649
Beeson, Samuel I, 776
Beeson, Samuel I, 799
Beeson, Samuel I, 801
Beeson, Samuel I, 871
Beeson, Sarah I, 776
Beeson, Sarah I, 799
Beeson, Sarah IV, 175
Beeson, Sarah IV, 610
Beeson, Sarah IV, 667
Beeson, Sarah V, 794
Beeson, Sarah Jane I, 674
Beeson, Seth I, 649
Beeson, Seth I, 661
Beeson, Seth I, 674
Beeson, Seth I, 871
Beeson, Seth I, 889
Beeson, Seth V, 826
Beeson, Seth V, 868
Beeson, Sidney I, 871
Beeson, Silas I, 799
Beeson, Silas I, 819
Beeson, Simmons I, 777
Beeson, Smith IV, 610
Beeson, Smith H. IV, 610
Beeson, Susanna II, 309
Beeson, Susanna V, 948
Beeson, Susannah V, 948
Beeson, Susannahh VI, 364
Beeson, Tacy VI, 365
Beeson, Temple Stuart I, 799
Beeson, Thomas I, 798
Beeson, Thomas I, 799
Beeson, Thos. I, 491
Beeson, Tristram V, 779
Beeson, Vera M. I, 931
Beeson, Waid I, 871
Beeson, Welmet I, 526
Beeson, Welmet I, 577
Beeson, Welmet I, 776
Beeson, Welmet I, 799
Beeson, William I, 343
Beeson, William I, 374
Beeson, William I, 491
Beeson, William I, 526
Beeson, William I, 564
Beeson, William I, 571
Beeson, William I, 648
Beeson, William I, 649
Beeson, William I, 674
Beeson, William I, 685
Beeson, William I, 755
Beeson, William I, 776
Beeson, William I, 777
Beeson, William I, 799
Beeson, William V, 222
Beeson, William V, 298
Beeson, William V, 319
Beeson, William V, 779
Beeson, William V, 826
Beeson, William V, 874
Beeson, William Bull I, 799
Beeson, William C. V, 319
Beeson, William S. I, 755
Beeson, William S. I, 850
Beeson, William Sidney I, 743
Beeson, William, Jr. I, 799
Beeson, William, Jr. I, 811
Beeson, William, Sr. I, 674
Beeson, Wilmet I, 491
Beeson, Wilmot I, 799
Beeson, Wm. I, 487
Beeson, Wm. I, 491
Beeson, Wm. I, 565
Beeson, Wm. V, 298
Beeson, Wm. V, 311
Beeson, Wm. V, 779
Beeson, Wm. C. V, 319
Beeson, Zachariah I, 649
Beeson, Zenis V, 948
Beeson, Zeruah I, 674
Beeson, Zeruah I, 692
Beeson, Zeruiah I, 649
Beeson, Zesonos V, 948
Beeson, Zipporah I, 649
Beet, Albert V, 152
Beetchart, Elsie I, 620
Beetle, Catharine II, 336
Beetle, Elizabeth II, 55
Beetle, Elizabeth II, 64
Beetle, Elizabeth II, 336
Beetle, Esther II, 22
Beetle, Esther II, 45
Beetle, James II, 594
Beetle, John II, 22
Beetle, John II, 55
Beetle, John II, 64
Beetle, John II, 336
Beetle, Mary II, 580
Beetle, Rebecca J. II, 594
Beetle, Samuel II, 580
Beetle, Samuel II, 594
Beetle, Thomas II, 594
Beetle, Wm. II, 580
Beets, William VI, 155
Begely, Charles II, 55
Begely, Charles II, 63
Begely, Wd. Ann II, 55
Begely, Wd. Ann II, 63
Beggs, Anna Plummer IV, 369
Begley, Ada II, 810
Begley, Ada II, 836
Begley, Ada II, 900
Begley, Chas. P. II, 836
Begley, Chas. Pickering II, 836
Begley, E. Maude II, 885
Begley, Eva II, 836
Begley, Mary II, 836
Begley, Mary P. II, 836
Begley, Mary P. II, 842
Begley, Mary P. III, 51
Begley, Maude II, 836
Begley, Sarah II, 782
Begley, Sarah II, 836
Begley, Sarah P. II, 842
Begley, Sarah P. II, 885
Begley, Sarah P. II, 900
Begley, Sarah Phipps II, 782
Begley, Thos. II, 782
Begley, Thos. II, 836
Begley, Thos. II, 900
Begley, Thos. J. II, 836
Begley, Thos. J. II, 842
Begley, Thos. S. II, 836
Begley, Thos. S. II, 842
Begley, Thos. S. II, 885
Begley, Thos. S. II, 900
Begley, Thos. Smith II, 782
Behm, Esther II, 836
Behm, Esther II, 872
Behm, Freda IV, 1307
Behur, Charley V, 985
Beighle, Samuel V, 612
Beightler, Estie IV, 1272
Beihards, Esther IV, 864
Beins, Elizabeth II, 1045
Beird, Edmund VI, 940
Beird, James P. VI, 940
Beird, Mary Ann V, 222
Beird, Mary Jane VI, 940
Beird, Robert VI, 877
Beird, Sarah VI, 877
Beirson, Hannah IV, 19
Beirson, Hannah IV, 23
Beiser, Cecelia VI, 616
Beiser, Cecilia VI, 670
Beiser, Celia K. VI, 616
Beiser, Geo. VI, 616
Beiser, Gulielma P. VI, 616
Beistle, Rebecca P. II, 836
Belange, Mary II, 196
Belange, Mary II, 197
Belange, Thomas II, 196
Belange, Thomas II, 197
Belangee, Aaron IV, 320
Belangee, Aaron IV, 369
Belangee, Grace II, 197
Belangee, Grace IV, 139
Belangee, Grace IV, 369
Belangee, Isaac II, 458
Belangee, James II, 197
Belangee, James IV, 139
Belangee, James IV, 320
Belangee, James IV, 369
Belangee, Jane Penington IV, 320
Belangee, Jane Wilson P. IV, 320
Belangee, John IV, 320
Belangee, John IV, 369
Belangee, Mary IV, 139
Belangee, Mary IV, 320
Belangee, Rebecca IV, 320
Belangee, Rebecca IV, 369
Belas, Mary V, 985
Belch, David II, 441
Belch, Jonathan II, 441
Belcher, Doshie I, 1148
Belcher, Edw. III, 30
Belcher, Edward B. III, 25
Belcher, Edward B. III, 30
Belcher, Edward H. III, 30
Belcher, Ester I, 1148
Belcher, Esther I, 1148
Belcher, Hattie I, 1148
Belcher, Hugh I, 1148
Belcher, Hugh L. I, 1148
Belcher, Lora May I, 1148
Belcher, Margaret III, 30
Belcher, Olivia III, 25
Belcher, Rebecca T. III, 25
Belcher, Rebecca T. III, 30
Belcher, Richard H. III, 25
Belcher, Robert I, 1148
Belcher, Rosa Bell I, 1148
Belden, Abigail III, 30
Belden, Henry F. III, 30
Belden, Horace III, 30
Belden, Phebe III, 30
Belden, Sarah III, 30
Belden, Sarah III, 121
Belden, Thomas W. III, 30
Belevue, Sarah Florenza II, 521
Belfew, Mary I, 709
Belfew, Mary I, 718
Belford, James V, 222
Belford, John V, 319
Belford, John W. V, 319
Belford, Maria V, 222
Belford, Sarah A. V, 222
Belfred, Maria V, 222
Belfred, Maria V, 244
Belin, Sarah VI, 481
Beling, Aelian A. III, 31
Beling, Aelian Arnold III, 30
Beling, Aelian Arnold III, 182
Beling, John K. III, 30
Beling, John Kingsman III, 30
Beling, John Kingsman III, 31
Beling, Mabel III, 30
Beling, Mabel A. J. III, 31
Beling, Mabel Asche III, 30
Beling, Mabel Asche III, 182
Beling, Maria III, 30
Beling, Wm. Wright III, 30
Belk, Nettie IV, 1246
Belknap, August III, 180
Belknap, Augusta Julia III, 31
Belknap, Jessie III, 31
Belknap, Jessie III, 180
Belknap, Julia III, 180
Bell, ??? III, 31
Bell, ??? III, 113
Bell, A. III, 73
Bell, Abigail I, 850
Bell, Abigail I, 871
Bell, Abraham III, 31
Bell, Abraham III, 32
Bell, Abraham III, 73
Bell, Abraham III, 377
Bell, Abraham IV, 1145
Bell, Abraham, Jr. III, 31
Bell, Abraham, Jr. III, 377
Bell, Abram V, 948
Bell, Ada IV, 941
Bell, Agnes VI, 157
Bell, Agnes VI, 173
Bell, Agnes VI, 230
Bell, Agness I, 960
Bell, Agness VI, 158
Bell, Agness VI, 174
Bell, Alexander V, 222
Bell, Alexander V, 948
Bell, Alfred VI, 878
Bell, Alfred A. VI, 878
Bell, Alfred A. VI, 926
Bell, Alfred A. VI, 943
Bell, Alfred A. VI, 976
Bell, Alice I, 267
Bell, Alice II, 462
Bell, Alice II, 588
Bell, Alice M. IV, 511
Bell, Alice M. IV, 555
Bell, Alvada V, 684
Bell, Ann II, 335
Bell, Ann II, 462
Bell, Ann II, 568
Bell, Ann III, 31
Bell, Ann III, 202
Bell, Ann IV, 1127
Bell, Ann VI, 157
Bell, Ann VI, 158
Bell, Ann VI, 190
Bell, Ann VI, 194
Bell, Ann Eliza III, 31
Bell, Ann Eliza IV, 1352
Bell, Ann Eliza IV, 1355
Bell, Ann Lawrence III, 377
Bell, Ann T. III, 31
Bell, Anna IV, 309
Bell, Anna Mary IV, 309
Bell, Annie L. III, 377
Bell, Annie L. III, 385
Bell, Anthony VI, 230
Bell, Arthur IV, 175
Bell, Arthur IV, 1145
Bell, Arthur E. III, 395
Bell, Arthur E. III, 447
Bell, Arthur Ernest III, 31
Bell, Arthur Hallock Bell III, 31
Bell, Ashley VI, 230
Bell, Barbara II, 462
Bell, Bell VI, 216
Bell, Belle V, 985
Bell, Bertha B. IV, 1307
Bell, Bessie III, 31
Bell, Bessie III, 32
Bell, Bessie Margaret III, 32
Bell, Brinton C. III, 377
Bell, Caroline I, 94
Bell, Caroline I, 127
Bell, Caroline I, 129
Bell, Caroline I, 181
Bell, Caroline Jackson III, 377
Bell, Carrie J. III, 377
Bell, Carrie J. III, 384
Bell, Catharine IV, 925
Bell, Cecilia VI, 230
Bell, Cecilia VI, 251
Bell, Charles III, 31
Bell, Charles IV, 175
Bell, Charles V, 658
Bell, Charlotte V, 894
Bell, Charlotte V, 939
Bell, Charlotte Wakefield III, 31
Bell, Charlotte Wakefield V, 894
Bell, Chas. H. V, 658
Bell, Chrissie III, 395
Bell, Chrissie III, 445
Bell, Christiana III, 445
Bell, Cicly VI, 230
Bell, Cisley VI, 230
Bell, Clara IV, 1233
Bell, D. S. IV, 1233
Bell, David III, 31
Bell, David S. IV, 1233
Bell, Deborah II, 335
Bell, Deborah II, 462
Bell, Deborah II, 612
Bell, Deborah R. III, 32
Bell, Dorothy IV, 1352
Bell, Dorothy VI, 798
Bell, Earnest W. III, 445
Bell, Edith III, 278
Bell, Edith IV, 923
Bell, Edith IV, 925
Bell, Edith IV, 1307
Bell, Edmund V, 894
Bell, Edna Donnelly IV, 678
Bell, Eliz. D. III, 32
Bell, Eliza II, 724
Bell, Eliza III, 31
Bell, Eliza III, 100
Bell, Eliza IV, 1355
Bell, Eliza Greer III, 31
Bell, Eliza H. III, 377
Bell, Eliza H. III, 384
Bell, Eliza H. III, 385
Bell, Elizabeth II, 335
Bell, Elizabeth II, 461
Bell, Elizabeth II, 462
Bell, Elizabeth III, 31
Bell, Elizabeth VI, 157
Bell, Elizabeth VI, 218
Bell, Elizabeth VI, 219
Bell, Elizabeth VI, 471
Bell, Elizabeth VI, 878
Bell, Elizabeth Agnes V, 894
Bell, Elizabeth Kirk IV, 678
Bell, Elizabeth L. III, 74
Bell, Elizabeth M. III, 31
Bell, Elizabeth Margaret III, 186
Bell, Ella III, 32
Bell, Ella V, 152
Bell, Ella E. III, 32
Bell, Ella E. III, 169
Bell, Ella E. III, 377
Bell, Ella E. III, 381
Bell, Elma IV, 20
Bell, Elma IV, 64
Bell, Evelina B. VI, 878
Bell, Francis IV, 1307
Bell, Francis H. VI, 878
Bell, Francis Hilliard III, 31
Bell, Francis Hilliard III, 32
Bell, Francis I. III, 31
Bell, Franklin II, 727
Bell, Frederick D. III, 31
Bell, Frederick I. III, 31
Bell, Friendless I, 709
Bell, Georbe VI, 157
Bell, George VI, 197
Bell, George VI, 217
Bell, George VI, 230
Bell, George Thomas III, 31
Bell, George, Jr. VI, 157
Bell, George, Jr. VI, 218
Bell, George, Jr. VI, 219
Bell, George, Jr. VI, 230
Bell, George, Sr. VI, 157
Bell, Gilbert III, 31
Bell, Gilbert Easten III, 31
Bell, Gladis V, 985
Bell, Gladys May V, 985
Bell, Glenn V, 985
Bell, Grace II, 335
Bell, Grace V, 985
Bell, Grove V, 684
Bell, Hannah II, 461
Bell, Hannah III, 31
Bell, Hannah III, 32
Bell, Hannah III, 38
Bell, Hannah III, 69
Bell, Hannah III, 84
Bell, Hannah V, 222
Bell, Hannah V, 948
Bell, Hannah A. II, 725
Bell, Hannah A. II, 727
Bell, Hannah Booth III, 31
Bell, Hannah C. III, 31
Bell, Hannah C. V, 894
Bell, Hannah Christy V, 894
Bell, Hannah Christy, Jr. III, 31
Bell, Hannah Christy, Jr. V, 894
Bell, Hannah Nancy V, 222
Bell, Harriet III, 31
Bell, Harriet IV, 175
Bell, Harriet B. VI, 878
Bell, Harry IV, 1145
Bell, Harry Gaylord V, 985
Bell, Harry Hilary, Jr. III, 186
Bell, Henry II, 462
Bell, Henry II, 568
Bell, Henry III, 31
Bell, Henry IV, 1233
Bell, Henry VI, 798
Bell, Henry Hilary III, 31
Bell, Henry Hilary III, 32
Bell, Henry Hilary, Jr. III, 31
Bell, Herbert Hallock III, 31
Bell, Hulda I, 267
Bell, Hulda I, 276
Bell, Huldah I, 267
Bell, Ida IV, 678
Bell, Ida VI, 365
Bell, Ida VI, 441
Bell, Ida VI, 452
Bell, Ines V, 985
Bell, Irven IV, 925
Bell, Irvin IV, 925
Bell, Irvin G. IV, 925
Bell, Isaac II, 335
Bell, Isaac V, 476
Bell, Isabell IV, 720
Bell, Isabella Wakefield III, 31
Bell, Isabella Wakefield V, 894
Bell, Isaiah II, 461
Bell, Isaiah II, 727
Bell, Isaiah, Jr. II, 727
Bell, J. Franklin III, 39
Bell, J. P. VI, 294
Bell, J. R. I, 630
Bell, Jacob II, 55
Bell, Jacob II, 335
Bell, Jacob II, 462
Bell, Jacob II, 568
Bell, Jacob II, 601
Bell, Jacob III, 31
Bell, Jacob Harvey III, 31
Bell, Jacob Harvey III, 74
Bell, James I, 264
Bell, James II, 709

Bell, James IV, 720
Bell, James VI, 157
Bell, James VI, 798
Bell, James VI, 930
Bell, James C. III, 31
Bell, James C., Jr. III, 31
Bell, James C., Jr. III, 100
Bell, James Christy III, 31
Bell, James Raine I, 612
Bell, James W. I, 612
Bell, Jane II, 709
Bell, Jane V, 222
Bell, Jane Hough III, 377
Bell, Jemima III, 31
Bell, Jemima VI, 157
Bell, Jemima VI, 217
Bell, Jennie V, 985
Bell, Jesse I, 850
Bell, Jesse IV, 175
Bell, Joanna VI, 158
Bell, Joanna VI, 230
Bell, Joanna VI, 276
Bell, John I, 93
Bell, John I, 94
Bell, John I, 129
Bell, John I, 132
Bell, John I, 850
Bell, John I, 871
Bell, John II, 462
Bell, John II, 806
Bell, John III, 31
Bell, John III, 38
Bell, John III, 84
Bell, John V, 222
Bell, John V, 658
Bell, John V, 894
Bell, John V, 948
Bell, John VI, 157
Bell, John VI, 158
Bell, John VI, 191
Bell, John VI, 195
Bell, John VI, 216
Bell, John VI, 230
Bell, John VI, 276
Bell, John Wetherhead III, 31
Bell, Jonathan II, 335
Bell, Jos. D. III, 31
Bell, Joseph II, 462
Bell, Josephine Mary A. III, 32
Bell, Josiah I, 94
Bell, Josiah I, 129
Bell, Josiah I, 871
Bell, Josiah II, 462
Bell, Josiah II, 727
Bell, Katherine VI, 930
Bell, Katherine L. III, 395
Bell, Katherine L. III, 447
Bell, LaDoyt Versile V, 985
Bell, Lancaster I, 129
Bell, Lancelot I, 36
Bell, Lancelot I, 94
Bell, Lancelot I, 129
Bell, Lancelot I, 154
Bell, Lancelot I, 181
Bell, Lancelot I, 871
Bell, Laura V, 985
Bell, Leana I, 612
Bell, Lelia I, 622
Bell, Lena IV, 1246
Bell, Lester L. V, 985
Bell, Lilian Flora I, 479
Bell, Lilly Jessie V, 642
Bell, Lorna V, 658
Bell, Lorna V, 684
Bell, Lottie V, 985
Bell, Louisa VI, 230
Bell, Lucretia V, 658
Bell, Lydia I, 129
Bell, Lydia I, 850
Bell, Lydia I, 871
Bell, Lydia V, 24
Bell, Lydia V, 122
Bell, Lynah P. VI, 798
Bell, Margaret I, 36
Bell, Margaret I, 87
Bell, Margaret I, 94
Bell, Margaret I, 129
Bell, Margaret I, 850
Bell, Margaret I, 871
Bell, Margaret II, 335
Bell, Margaret II, 461
Bell, Margaret IV, 20
Bell, Margaret IV, 27
Bell, Margaret R. III, 31
Bell, Margaret R. III, 113
Bell, Maria IV, 864
Bell, Maria IV, 877
Bell, Marl III, 31
Bell, Marl. III, 32
Bell, Marquis E. V, 985
Bell, Martha II, 806
Bell, Martha III, 395
Bell, Martha III, 447
Bell, Martha IV, 610
Bell, Martha IV, 678
Bell, Martha IV, 864
Bell, Martha V, 550
Bell, Martha V, 580
Bell, Martha V, 658
Bell, Martha VI, 157
Bell, Martha VI, 230
Bell, Martha VI, 798
Bell, Martha Ellen V, 658
Bell, Mary I, 36
Bell, Mary I, 77
Bell, Mary I, 94
Bell, Mary I, 129
Bell, Mary I, 149
Bell, Mary I, 871
Bell, Mary II, 55
Bell, Mary II, 335
Bell, Mary II, 412
Bell, Mary II, 461
Bell, Mary II, 462
Bell, Mary II, 614
Bell, Mary III, 31
Bell, Mary III, 377
Bell, Mary IV, 1307
Bell, Mary V, 222
Bell, Mary V, 985
Bell, Mary VI, 157
Bell, Mary VI, 158
Bell, Mary VI, 191
Bell, Mary VI, 194
Bell, Mary VI, 216
Bell, Mary VI, 365
Bell, Mary VI, 930
Bell, Mary A. I, 207
Bell, Mary A. I, 214
Bell, Mary Ann II, 806
Bell, Mary C. III, 31
Bell, Mary C. III, 73
Bell, Mary C. P. IV, 320
Bell, Mary C. P. IV, 347
Bell, Mary Christy III, 31
Bell, Mary Christy III, 377
Bell, Mary J. VI, 878
Bell, Mary Jane V, 222
Bell, Mary Jane V, 948
Bell, Mary L. III, 31
Bell, Mary L. VI, 158
Bell, Mary Lewin III, 31
Bell, Mary Lewin III, 207
Bell, Matilda V, 985
Bell, Melina R. III, 32
Bell, Melissa III, 377
Bell, Melissa R. III, 377
Bell, Michael VI, 827
Bell, Minerva J. IV, 1307
Bell, Minnie IV, 720
Bell, Minnie V, 490
Bell, Miriam I, 94
Bell, Miriam I, 127
Bell, Miriam I, 129
Bell, Miriam I, 154
Bell, Miriam I, 871
Bell, Moore I, 959
Bell, Moore VI, 157
Bell, Moore VI, 173
Bell, Moore VI, 174
Bell, Moses IV, 464
Bell, Moses B. IV, 464
Bell, Mrs. ??? IV, 490
Bell, Musedora A. VI, 878
Bell, Myriam I, 129
Bell, Nance P. VI, 878
Bell, Nancy V, 222
Bell, Nancy V, 948
Bell, Nannie III, 31
Bell, Nannie III, 202
Bell, Nannie III, 311
Bell, Nannie I. III, 31
Bell, Nannie T. III, 31
Bell, Nannie T. III, 207
Bell, Nathan VI, 157
Bell, Nathan VI, 190
Bell, Nathan VI, 230
Bell, Nettie IV, 1246
Bell, Olive V, 658
Bell, Olivia Horner III, 32
Bell, Orville P. VI, 878
Bell, Pearl Dean V, 985
Bell, Philena IV, 1145
Bell, Philip Thomas III, 31
Bell, Pleasants VI, 230
Bell, R. E. V, 985
Bell, Rachel II, 461
Bell, Rachel II, 462
Bell, Rachel Jemima IV, 1145
Bell, Rachell II, 461
Bell, Raine A. I, 612
Bell, Rebecca I, 94
Bell, Rebecca I, 129
Bell, Rebecca I, 871
Bell, Rebecca III, 31
Bell, Rebecca V, 222
Bell, Rebecca V, 229
Bell, Rebecca V, 948
Bell, Rebecca VI, 157
Bell, Rebecca A. II, 727
Bell, Rebecca B. III, 73
Bell, Rebecca Furnass IV, 1145
Bell, Rebecca H. III, 31
Bell, Rebecca Harvey III, 31
Bell, Rebeckah I, 871
Bell, Rebeckah I, 960
Bell, Rebeckah VI, 158
Bell, Rebeckah VI, 163
Bell, Richard II, 197
Bell, Richard II, 462
Bell, Richard IV, 1145
Bell, Richard V, 658
Bell, Richard V, 684
Bell, Richard Clifford V, 985
Bell, Richard E. V, 985
Bell, Robert I, 800
Bell, Robert III, 377
Bell, Robert III, 384
Bell, Robert VI, 230
Bell, Robert G. VI, 878
Bell, Robert G. VI, 958
Bell, Robert W. IV, 1145
Bell, Ruth III, 39
Bell, Sam V, 985
Bell, Samuel II, 335
Bell, Samuel II, 412
Bell, Samuel II, 461
Bell, Samuel V, 985
Bell, Samuel VI, 157
Bell, Samuel VI, 230
Bell, Samuel L. II, 727
Bell, Samuel Thos. IV, 1145
Bell, Sarah I, 93
Bell, Sarah I, 94
Bell, Sarah I, 129
Bell, Sarah I, 132
Bell, Sarah I, 871
Bell, Sarah II, 462
Bell, Sarah II, 465
Bell, Sarah VI, 798
Bell, Sarah Ann IV, 864
Bell, Sarah Melissa IV, 1145
Bell, Scisley VI, 230
Bell, Sisley VI, 230
Bell, Sisley VI, 253
Bell, Susan II, 709
Bell, Susan III, 32
Bell, Susan Evernghim III, 31
Bell, Susan Kit III, 18
Bell, Susan Kite III, 32
Bell, Susley VI, 230
Bell, Tacey III, 31
Bell, Thomas I, 94
Bell, Thomas I, 129
Bell, Thomas I, 871
Bell, Thomas III, 31
Bell, Thomas VI, 976
Bell, Thomas A. III, 32
Bell, Thomas C. III, 377
Bell, Thomas C. III, 385
Bell, Thomas Christy III, 31
Bell, Thos. C. III, 384
Bell, Virginia V, 658
Bell, Virginia V, 985
Bell, Wd. Sarah VI, 157
Bell, Wesley Glen V, 985
Bell, Wilbur Harold V, 985
Bell, Wilhelmina III, 31
Bell, Wilhelmina V, 894
Bell, William III, 31
Bell, William III, 32
Bell, William III, 69
Bell, William III, 169
Bell, William III, 377
Bell, William VI, 798
Bell, William Brown III, 18
Bell, William Edmund III, 31
Bell, William F. I, 709
Bell, William Haydock III, 32
Bell, William Lawrence III, 377
Bell, Winslow III, 32
Bell, Winslow M. III, 31
Bell, Winslow M., Jr. III, 32
Bell, Winslow Manly III, 31
Bell, Wm. III, 31
Bell, Wm. III, 202
Bell, Wm. III, 207
Bell, Wm. III, 311
Bell, Wm. V, 894
Bell, Wm. Brown III, 32
Bell, Wm. Edmond V, 894
Bell, Wm. G. IV, 925
Bell, Wm. L. VI, 878
Bellamy, Anea VI, 1010
Bellamy, Benjamin VI, 878
Bellamy, Betsey Ann VI, 974
Bellamy, Clarence IV, 1246
Bellamy, Elizabeth VI, 878
Bellamy, Fanny VI, 878
Bellamy, Florence IV, 1246
Bellamy, Frances VI, 878
Bellamy, Magdalen VI, 983
Bellamy, Matthew VI, 878
Bellamy, Maude IV, 1246
Bellamy, Perlina VI, 983
Bellamy, Samuel VI, 974
Bellamy, Samuel VI, 1010
Bellamy, Sarah IV, 1246
Bellamy, Sarah VI, 1010
Bellamy, William B. VI, 878
Bellange, Grace II, 197
Bellange, Isaac II, 197
Bellange, James II, 197
Bellange, James IV, 369
Bellange, Mary II, 197
Bellange, Thomas II, 197
Bellangee, Hannah II, 795
Bellangee, Jane Wilson P. IV, 320
Bellas, Edgar L. II, 782
Bellas, Isaac H. II, 782
Bellatta, Naomi R. II, 836
Bellatta, Naomi R. II, 914
Bellatti, Joshua II, 782
Bellatti, Noami II, 782
Bellatti, Rosanna II, 782
Belle, Ida IV, 678
Belle, Mrs. John IV, 1332
Belle, Sarah III, 169
Belle, Selma III, 133
Beller, Adaline V, 152
Bellerby, Isaac II, 462
Bellis, Mariah V, 985
Bellis, Mary V, 985
Bellish, Magdalen II, 462
Bellish, Wd. Magdalen II, 608
Bellman, Isaac Wilson VI, 27
Bellman, John VI, 27
Bellman, John VI, 37
Bellman, Sarah VI, 27
Bellman, Sarah VI, 37
Belloes, John II, 336
Belloes, Martha II, 336
Belloes, Mary II, 336
Belloes, Mathew II, 336
Belloes, Mathias II, 336
Belloes, Maudlin II, 336
Belloes, Maudling II, 336
Belloes, Rebecka II, 336
Bellong, Berry II, 336
Bellong, John II, 336
Bellonge, Eve II, 458
Bellonge, Eve II, 504
Bellout, Marie IV, 1307
Bellow, Martha II, 336
Bellow, Mathew II, 336
Bellows, Ann II, 462
Bellows, Ann II, 510
Bellows, Edith II, 699
Bellows, Edith II, 727
Bellows, Elizabeth II, 699
Bellows, Elizabeth II, 726
Bellows, Elizabeth II, 727
Bellows, Grace III, 84
Bellows, John II, 699
Bellows, John II, 727
Bellows, Magdalen II, 462
Bellows, Matthias II, 462
Bellows, Matthias II, 674
Bellows, Maudlin II, 462
Bellows, Meda V, 658
Bellows, Philip II, 699
Bellows, Philip II, 727
Bellson, Mary VI, 27
Bellvieu, Sarah Florenza II, 462
Bellware, James II, 441
Belm, Elfreda IV, 1307
Belm, Freda IV, 1307
Belman, Esther I, 94
Belman, Esther I, 129
Belman, Esther I, 171
Belman, Jane I, 94
Belman, John I, 1
Belman, John I, 36
Belman, John I, 85
Belman, John I, 94
Belman, John I, 129
Belman, John I, 167
Belman, John I Sup 1, 7
Belman, Mary I, 94
Belman, Mary I, 129
Belman, Robert I, 94
Belman, Ruth I, 94
Belman, Sarah I, 36
Belman, Sarah I, 85
Belman, Sarah I, 94
Belman, Sarah I, 129
Belman, Sarah I, 156
Belman, William I, 94
Belmont, Hannah IV, 413
Belong, Chora IV, 1276
Belong, Wm. IV, 1276
Belson, ??? VI, 39
Belson, Edmond VI, 27
Belson, Edmond VI, 28
Belson, Edmond VI, 31
Belson, Edmond VI, 35
Belson, Edmond VI, 37
Belson, Edmond VI, 40
Belson, Elizabeth VI, 22
Belson, Elizabeth VI, 27
Belson, Elizabeth VI, 36
Belson, Elizabeth Small VI, 27
Belson, Frederick III, 32
Belson, Jean VI, 27
Belson, Jean VI, 35
Belson, Mary VI, 27
Belson, Mary VI, 28
Belson, Mary VI, 31
Belson, Mary VI, 35
Belson, Mary VI, 36
Belson, Mary VI, 37
Belson, William IV, 1352
Belston, Henry V, 768
Belston, Minerva V, 768
Belston, Susan V, 768
Belt, Anna V, 152
Belt, Catherine V, 152
Belt, Corddlia IV, 1145
Belt, Edward V, 152
Belt, Forest J. V, 152
Belt, Forrest J. V, 152
Belt, Green IV, 1145
Belt, John IV, 1145
Belt, John VI, 616
Belt, Rosella Riley V, 152
Belt, W. E. V, 152
Belten, Daisy I, 630
Belton, Bertha I, 633
Belton, Carson I, 633
Belton, Carson H., Jr. I, 633
Belton, Daisy I, 612
Belton, Daisy I, 630
Belton, Daisy I, 633
Belton, Emery P. I, 633
Belton, Francis I, 633
Belton, George F. I, 630
Belton, George F. I, 633
Belton, George Franklin I, 612
Belton, Hannah I, 633
Belton, James I, 612
Belton, Lithey I, 612
Belton, Mary IV, 1246
Belton, Sarah II, 55
Belton, Sarah II, 336
Beltz, Levi V, 985
Beltz, Lewis V, 985
Belue, Susannah V, 779
Beman, Rebecka VI, 591
Bemis, Daniel IV, 1233
Bemis, Kitty IV, 1233
Bemo, Thomas W. II, 699
Benadict, Eliza T. IV, 925
Benagh, James VI, 850
Benagh, James VI, 867
Benarfa, Julia IV, 1307
Benbo, Charles I, 527
Benbo, Edward I, 1026
Benbo, John I, 527
Benbo, Mary I, 523
Benbo, Mary I, 527
Benbo, Mary I, 800
Benbo, Mary I, 836
Benbo, Paris Shrader I, 527
Benbo, Sarah I, 526
Benbo, Sarah I, 554
Benbo, Sarah VI, 251
Benbo, Sophia I, 526
Benbow, Aaron V, 476
Benbow, Able I, 491
Benbow, Admiral I, 491
Benbow, Alexander I, 981
Benbow, Andrew Murrow I, 587
Benbow, Ann I, 374
Benbow, Ann I, 491
Benbow, Ann I, 526
Benbow, Ann I, 527
Benbow, Ann I, 561
Benbow, Ann I, 600
Benbow, Ann I, 601
Benbow, Ann I, 602
Benbow, Ann I, 605
Benbow, Ann I, 607
Benbow, Ann I, 626
Benbow, Ann I, 973
Benbow, Ann I, 981

Benbow, Anna I, 527
Benbow, Anna I, 587
Benbow, Anna I, 601
Benbow, Anna I, 605
Benbow, Anna C. I, 592
Benbow, Anna C. I, 605
Benbow, Anna R. I, 630
Benbow, Anne I, 612
Benbow, Annie I, 617
Benbow, Annie I, 630
Benbow, Annie B. I, 630
Benbow, Annie Maie I, 612
Benbow, Annie Maud I, 615
Benbow, Arcada I, 374
Benbow, Arcada I, 424
Benbow, Aron I, 601
Benbow, Barclay V, 24
Benbow, Bartly V, 24
Benbow, Benj. I, 491
Benbow, Benjamin I, 374
Benbow, Benjamin I, 526
Benbow, Benjamin I, 527
Benbow, Benjamin I, 600
Benbow, Benjamin I, 674
Benbow, Benjamin I, 680
Benbow, Benjamin I, 687
Benbow, Benjamin V, 24
Benbow, Benjamin V, 476
Benbow, Benjamin, Jr. I, 601
Benbow, Benjamin, Jr. I, 605
Benbow, Benjamin, Sr. I, 601
Benbow, Berkly I, 1026
Benbow, Bessie I, 626
Benbow, Catharine I, 491
Benbow, Catharine I, 527
Benbow, Catharine I, 551
Benbow, Caty Ann I, 491
Benbow, Charity I, 491
Benbow, Charity I, 527
Benbow, Charity I, 561
Benbow, Charity V, 222
Benbow, Charity V, 476
Benbow, Charles I, 267
Benbow, Charles I, 328
Benbow, Charles I, 491
Benbow, Charles I, 526
Benbow, Charles I, 527
Benbow, Charles I, 586
Benbow, Charles I, 587
Benbow, Charles I, 601
Benbow, Charles I, 605
Benbow, Charles I, 674
Benbow, Charles I, 973
Benbow, Charles Clinton I, 587
Benbow, Charles D. I, 527
Benbow, Charles D. I, 612
Benbow, Charles David I, 612
Benbow, Charles E. I, 981
Benbow, Charles H. I, 433
Benbow, Charles K. I, 433
Benbow, Charles R. I, 587
Benbow, Charles Rufus I, 612
Benbow, Charles T. I, 587
Benbow, Charles T. I, 592
Benbow, Charles Thomas I, 587
Benbow, Clara V, 727
Benbow, Clara A. I, 612
Benbow, Clarance I, 630
Benbow, Clarence Oliver I, 612
Benbow, David I, 491
Benbow, David I, 527
Benbow, David I, 561
Benbow, David I, 600
Benbow, David I, 601
Benbow, DeWit Clinton I, 630
Benbow, DeWitt Clinton I, 612
Benbow, Dewitt Clinton I, 612
Benbow, DeWitte Clinton I, 592
Benbow, Earnest I, 587
Benbow, Edward I, 374
Benbow, Edward I, 1026
Benbow, Edward V, 24
Benbow, Edward V, 145
Benbow, Edward P. I, 630
Benbow, Edward Perry I, 612
Benbow, Edward Perry I, 630
Benbow, Edward Perry, Jr. I, 612
Benbow, Elam I, 491
Benbow, Elisabeth Caroline I, 612
Benbow, Elizabeth I, 374
Benbow, Elizabeth I, 491
Benbow, Elizabeth I, 527
Benbow, Elizabeth I, 573
Benbow, Elizabeth I, 577
Benbow, Elizabeth I, 612
Benbow, Elizabeth I, 630
Benbow, Elizabeth V, 24
Benbow, Elizabeth H. I, 433
Benbow, Elizabeth Hellen I, 433
Benbow, Ella I, 527
Benbow, Ella Anna I, 587
Benbow, Ella G. I, 527
Benbow, Ella G. I, 535
Benbow, Ella G. I, 587
Benbow, Evan I, 601
Benbow, Evan I, 973
Benbow, Evan I, 981
Benbow, Evan I, 1026
Benbow, Evan V, 24
Benbow, Evan V, 136
Benbow, Evan V, 145
Benbow, Evan V, 222
Benbow, Evan V, 476
Benbow, Even I, 491
Benbow, Flora Jane I, 587
Benbow, Hannah I, 491
Benbow, Hannah I, 527
Benbow, Hannah I, 572
Benbow, Hannah I, 601
Benbow, Hannah Ann I, 973
Benbow, Hannah Ann I, 981
Benbow, Hannah Ann I, 984
Benbow, James I, 491
Benbow, James I, 527
Benbow, James I, 601
Benbow, James I, 605
Benbow, James I, 612
Benbow, James E. I, 587
Benbow, Jesse I, 527
Benbow, Jesse I, 587
Benbow, Jesse I, 592
Benbow, Jesse I, 605
Benbow, Jesse I, 617
Benbow, Jesse J. I, 587
Benbow, Jesse J. I, 592
Benbow, Jessie Kyle I, 587
Benbow, John I, 491
Benbow, John I, 527
Benbow, John I, 561
Benbow, John I, 601
Benbow, John I, 973
Benbow, John V, 222
Benbow, John V, 476
Benbow, John M. Clark I, 587
Benbow, John T. I, 587
Benbow, Jonathan Ruffin I, 587
Benbow, Josephine I, 587
Benbow, Julean I, 587
Benbow, Julia I, 587
Benbow, Julia I, 592
Benbow, Julia I, 595
Benbow, Julia Pearl I, 587
Benbow, Julia Pearl I, 612
Benbow, Juliann I, 587
Benbow, Kitty I, 587
Benbow, Letha I, 491
Benbow, Ludia I, 527
Benbow, Lydia I, 491
Benbow, Lydia I, 527
Benbow, Lydia I, 600
Benbow, Lydia I, 601
Benbow, Lydia I, 674
Benbow, Lydia I, 687
Benbow, Maria V, 24
Benbow, Maria V, 136
Benbow, Maria V, 145
Benbow, Mariam I, 527
Benbow, Marium I, 601
Benbow, Mary I, 328
Benbow, Mary I, 329
Benbow, Mary I, 374
Benbow, Mary I, 433
Benbow, Mary I, 526
Benbow, Mary I, 527
Benbow, Mary I, 561
Benbow, Mary I, 586
Benbow, Mary I, 587
Benbow, Mary I, 592
Benbow, Mary I, 601
Benbow, Mary I, 602
Benbow, Mary I, 605
Benbow, Mary I, 612
Benbow, Mary I, 674
Benbow, Mary I, 800
Benbow, Mary I, 1026
Benbow, Mary V, 24
Benbow, Mary V, 95
Benbow, Mary V, 145
Benbow, Mary E. I, 587
Benbow, Mary H. I, 433
Benbow, Mary K. I, 443
Benbow, Mary Lou I, 626
Benbow, Mary Roxana I, 800
Benbow, Mattie M. I, 615
Benbow, Mc Kay I, 587
Benbow, McCoy I, 592
Benbow, Meriam I, 491
Benbow, Merriam I, 527
Benbow, Merriam I, 561
Benbow, Miriam I, 491
Benbow, Miriam V, 222
Benbow, Miriam V, 476
Benbow, Moses V, 476
Benbow, Nancy I, 605
Benbow, Oliver I, 587
Benbow, Oliver C. I, 630
Benbow, Oliver Coffin I, 612
Benbow, P. S. I, 587
Benbow, Paris I, 443
Benbow, Paris I, 586
Benbow, Paris I, 592
Benbow, Paris I, 612
Benbow, Paris S. I, 328
Benbow, Paris S. I, 329
Benbow, Paris S. I, 433
Benbow, Paris S. I, 443
Benbow, Paris S. I, 587
Benbow, Paris S. I, 800
Benbow, Paris Shrader I, 527
Benbow, Parshall V, 24
Benbow, Pearl I, 630
Benbow, Powel I, 374
Benbow, Priscilla I, 617
Benbow, Priscilla I, 628
Benbow, Priscilla Jain I, 587
Benbow, Rachel I, 527
Benbow, Rachel I, 601
Benbow, Rachel I, 605
Benbow, Rachel I, 674
Benbow, Rachel I, 680
Benbow, Rachel I, 973
Benbow, Rachel V, 24
Benbow, Rachel V, 136
Benbow, Rachel A. I, 981
Benbow, Rachel A. I, 998
Benbow, Rancelar I, 587
Benbow, Reuben I, 592
Benbow, Roxana I, 612
Benbow, Ruth A. I, 587
Benbow, Sarah I, 374
Benbow, Sarah I, 390
Benbow, Sarah I, 526
Benbow, Sarah I, 527
Benbow, Sarah E. I, 587
Benbow, Sophia I, 374
Benbow, Sophia I, 491
Benbow, Sophia I, 526
Benbow, Sophia I, 563
Benbow, Stephen IV, 1149
Benbow, Susan I, 612
Benbow, Susan E. I, 587
Benbow, Susan Josephine I, 587
Benbow, Susanah I, 507
Benbow, Susanna I, 605
Benbow, Susannah I, 601
Benbow, Susannah I, 606
Benbow, Therza I, 491
Benbow, Thomas I, 374
Benbow, Thomas I, 491
Benbow, Thomas I, 526
Benbow, Thomas I, 527
Benbow, Thomas I, 561
Benbow, Thomas I, 572
Benbow, Thomas I, 587
Benbow, Thomas I, 592
Benbow, Thomas I, 601
Benbow, Thomas I, 605
Benbow, Thomas I, 973
Benbow, Thomas I, 981
Benbow, Thomas A. I, 601
Benbow, Thomas Elexander I, 973
Benbow, Thomas J. I, 587
Benbow, Thomas J. I, 592
Benbow, Thomas Kenneday I, 433
Benbow, Thos. Alexander I, 981
Benbow, Tomis I, 981
Benbow, Walter V, 727
Benbow, Walter J. I, 587
Benbow, Walter J. I, 592
Benbow, William I, 491
Benbow, William I, 527
Benbow, William I, 551
Benbow, William I, 587
Benbow, William I, 600
Benbow, William I, 626
Benbow, William E. I, 527
Benbow, William E. I, 535
Benbow, William E. I, 587
Benbow, Wm. E. I, 615
Benbow, Wm. Stanley I, 491
Benceni, Henry C. I, 871
Benda, Barbara IV, 1307
Benden, Anna K. V, 658
Benden, Bertha L. V, 658
Benden, Marie E. V, 658
Benden, Pierce E. V, 658
Benden, Robert W. V, 658
Bender, Barbara IV, 1307
Bender, Ida A. Harmon V, 152
Bender, Josiah VI, 731
Bender, Julianna VI, 731
Bender, Julianna VI, 791
Bender, Margaret VI, 791
Bender, Mary II, 462
Bender, Rhea V, 727
Bender, Wd. Margaret VI, 731
Bender, Wilson VI, 731
Bending, Lora IV, 1201
Bendure, Miriam IV, 1088
Bendure, Miriam IV, 1093
Benedal, Henry IV, 464
Benedict, ??? III, 32
Benedict, ??? III, 282
Benedict, ??? IV, 1141
Benedict, Aaron IV, 175
Benedict, Aaron IV, 1145
Benedict, Aaron IV, 1148
Benedict, Aaron IV, 1187
Benedict, Aaron IV, 1215
Benedict, Aaron D. IV, 1202
Benedict, Aaron L. IV, 1145
Benedict, Aaron L. IV, 1146
Benedict, Aaron L. IV, 1147
Benedict, Aaron L. IV, 1168
Benedict, Aaron L. IV, 1187
Benedict, Aaron L. IV, 1194
Benedict, Aden S. IV, 1145
Benedict, Aden S. IV, 1146
Benedict, Aden S. IV, 1147
Benedict, Aden S. IV, 1148
Benedict, Aden S. IV, 1162
Benedict, Aden S. IV, 1202
Benedict, Adessa T. IV, 1146
Benedict, Adessa T. IV, 1147
Benedict, Adessa T. IV, 1187
Benedict, Adin L. IV, 1202
Benedict, Adin S. IV, 1148
Benedict, Agnes S. IV, 1146
Benedict, Albert A. IV, 1148
Benedict, Albert S. IV, 1145
Benedict, Alice IV, 175
Benedict, Allen IV, 1146
Benedict, Allen IV, 1147
Benedict, Almira P. IV, 1147
Benedict, Alse IV, 1145
Benedict, Alse IV, 1146
Benedict, Alse IV, 1161
Benedict, Amelia F. IV, 678
Benedict, Amelia F. IV, 767
Benedict, Amelia F. IV, 1146
Benedict, Amelia F. IV, 1147
Benedict, Amelia F. IV, 1187
Benedict, Amos IV, 1147
Benedict, Amy IV, 1145
Benedict, Amy IV, 1147
Benedict, Amy IV, 1148
Benedict, Amy IV, 1160
Benedict, Amy IV, 1173
Benedict, Amy IV, 1187
Benedict, Amy V, 152
Benedict, Amy V, 967
Benedict, Ann IV, 1145
Benedict, Ann IV, 1197
Benedict, Ann IV, 1202
Benedict, Anna IV, 1145
Benedict, Anna IV, 1146
Benedict, Anna IV, 1147
Benedict, Anna IV, 1155
Benedict, Anna Billa IV, 1147
Benedict, Anne IV, 1197
Benedict, Annis IV, 1146
Benedict, Annis O. IV, 1148
Benedict, Asa A. IV, 1145
Benedict, Asa A. IV, 1148
Benedict, Carlos Christie IV, 1147
Benedict, Carlos Christy IV, 678
Benedict, Carlos Christy IV, 1148
Benedict, Caroline IV, 1146
Benedict, Caroline A. IV, 1148
Benedict, Caroline A. IV, 1187
Benedict, Caroline D. IV, 1154
Benedict, Catherine IV, 1146
Benedict, Cecelia IV, 1202
Benedict, Cecilia IV, 1202
Benedict, Charity T. IV, 1146
Benedict, Charles IV, 121
Benedict, Charles IV, 1145
Benedict, Charles IV, 1147
Benedict, Charles A. IV, 1146
Benedict, Charles Bowring IV, 1147
Benedict, Charles Edward IV, 1147
Benedict, Clarinda IV, 1145
Benedict, Clarinda IV, 1147
Benedict, Clarinda IV, 1171
Benedict, Cora IV, 1148
Benedict, Cynthia IV, 1145
Benedict, Cynthia IV, 1146
Benedict, Cynthia IV, 1147
Benedict, Cynthia IV, 1162
Benedict, Cyrus IV, 121
Benedict, Cyrus IV, 124
Benedict, Cyrus IV, 464
Benedict, Cyrus IV, 925
Benedict, Cyrus IV, 1145
Benedict, Cyrus IV, 1147
Benedict, Cyrus IV, 1148
Benedict, Cyrus V, 967
Benedict, Cyrus S. IV, 1146
Benedict, Cyrus S. V, 152
Benedict, Daniel IV, 175
Benedict, Daniel IV, 1145
Benedict, Daniel IV, 1146
Benedict, Daniel IV, 1147
Benedict, Daniel IV, 1148
Benedict, Daniel IV, 1160
Benedict, Daniel IV, 1173
Benedict, Daniel IV, 1187
Benedict, Daniel IV, 1194
Benedict, David IV, 1145
Benedict, David IV, 1147
Benedict, Deborah S. IV, 1146
Benedict, Direxa IV, 1155
Benedict, Direxa H. IV, 1146
Benedict, Direxa H. IV, 1148
Benedict, Dorcas IV, 1146
Benedict, Edgar N. IV, 1148
Benedict, Edward A. IV, 678
Benedict, Edward A. IV, 1146
Benedict, Edward A. IV, 1147
Benedict, Edward A. IV, 1148
Benedict, Edward A. IV, 1163
Benedict, Elbert L. IV, 1147
Benedict, Eli IV, 1145
Benedict, Eli IV, 1146
Benedict, Eli IV, 1147
Benedict, Eli IV, 1202
Benedict, Eliza IV, 925
Benedict, Eliza IV, 1012
Benedict, Eliza IV, 1146
Benedict, Eliza IV, 1202
Benedict, Eliza IV, 1272
Benedict, Eliza G. IV, 1147
Benedict, Eliza G. IV, 1148
Benedict, Eliza M. IV, 1148
Benedict, Eliza T. IV, 464
Benedict, Eliza T. IV, 925
Benedict, Eliza T. IV, 998
Benedict, Eliza T. IV, 1202
Benedict, Elizabeth IV, 175
Benedict, Elizabeth IV, 1145
Benedict, Elizabeth IV, 1147
Benedict, Elizabeth IV, 1149
Benedict, Elizabeth IV, 1172
Benedict, Elizabeth IV, 1195
Benedict, Elizabeth IV, 1202
Benedict, Elizabeth VI, 616
Benedict, Elizabeth VI, 620
Benedict, Elizabeth Ann IV, 925
Benedict, Elizabeth Ann IV, 1202
Benedict, Elizabeth Ann IV, 1226
Benedict, Elizabeth Penelope IV, 1147
Benedict, Elizabeth Penelope IV, 1149
Benedict, Ella IV, 1202
Benedict, Ella Heverlo IV, 1148
Benedict, Ella M. IV, 678
Benedict, Ella W. IV, 1146
Benedict, Ellen IV, 1148
Benedict, Ellen IV, 1202
Benedict, Ellen IV, 1227
Benedict, Ellen W. IV, 1148
Benedict, Ellen W. IV, 1202
Benedict, Elnora IV, 1190
Benedict, Elwood IV, 1146
Benedict, Elwood IV, 1148
Benedict, Elwood V, 152
Benedict, Emelina IV, 1146
Benedict, Emeline IV, 1146
Benedict, Emeline IV, 1173
Benedict, Emma III, 194
Benedict, Emma III, 259
Benedict, Esther IV, 175
Benedict, Esther IV, 1015
Benedict, Esther IV, 1145
Benedict, Esther IV, 1146
Benedict, Esther IV, 1147
Benedict, Esther IV, 1154
Benedict, Esther IV, 1194
Benedict, Esther IV, 1215
Benedict, Esther IV, 1272
Benedict, Esther IV, 1299
Benedict, Esther L. IV, 1145
Benedict, Esther L. IV, 1202
Benedict, Esther L. IV, 1215
Benedict, Ethel IV, 1148
Benedict, Ezra IV, 1146
Benedict, Ezra IV, 1147
Benedict, Ezra IV, 1154

Benedict, Ezra IV, 1160
Benedict, Fannie IV, 1148
Benedict, Fannie E. IV, 1147
Benedict, Fannie E. IV, 1148
Benedict, Flora IV, 1202
Benedict, Florence IV, 1147
Benedict, Florence A. IV, 1148
Benedict, Florilia IV, 1202
Benedict, Francis M. IV, 1148
Benedict, Francis Marion IV, 1148
Benedict, Frederick M. IV, 1146
Benedict, Frederick M. IV, 1148
Benedict, G. Grafton IV, 1148
Benedict, George Dilwin IV, 1147
Benedict, George Lewis IV, 1147
Benedict, Gideon IV, 1147
Benedict, Grace IV, 1146
Benedict, Grace IV, 1173
Benedict, Grace IV, 1194
Benedict, Grace M. IV, 1147
Benedict, Grafton IV, 1148
Benedict, Greenleaf W. IV, 1147
Benedict, Griffen Grafton IV, 1227
Benedict, Griffes Grafton IV, 1202
Benedict, Griffith IV, 1146
Benedict, Griffith Grafton IV, 1146
Benedict, Hannah IV, 121
Benedict, Hannah IV, 124
Benedict, Hannah IV, 925
Benedict, Hannah IV, 1145
Benedict, Hannah IV, 1147
Benedict, Hannah IV, 1160
Benedict, Hannah C. IV, 1148
Benedict, Hannah G. IV, 925
Benedict, Hannah G. IV, 1202
Benedict, Harvey IV, 1145
Benedict, Harvey IV, 1147
Benedict, Harvey IV, 1148
Benedict, Harvey IV, 1202
Benedict, Harvey IV, 1233
Benedict, Harvy IV, 1146
Benedict, Harvy IV, 1191
Benedict, Henry IV, 464
Benedict, Henry IV, 925
Benedict, Henry IV, 998
Benedict, Henry IV, 1145
Benedict, Henry IV, 1146
Benedict, Henry IV, 1147
Benedict, Henry IV, 1148
Benedict, Henry IV, 1202
Benedict, Henry IV, 1272
Benedict, Henry B. III, 32
Benedict, Henry O. IV, 1148
Benedict, Hugh IV, 1148
Benedict, Hugh Conray IV, 1147
Benedict, Huldah IV, 1146
Benedict, Ira IV, 1147
Benedict, Israel IV, 1146
Benedict, Israel IV, 1148
Benedict, Israel V, 152
Benedict, Jane IV, 1147
Benedict, Jane IV, 1148
Benedict, Jane IV, 1153
Benedict, Jemima IV, 1146
Benedict, Jemima IV, 1148
Benedict, John IV, 1145
Benedict, John IV, 1147
Benedict, John IV, 1160
Benedict, John IV, 1173
Benedict, John IV, 1187
Benedict, John IV, 1202
Benedict, John L. IV, 1146
Benedict, Jonathan IV, 1146
Benedict, Jonathan IV, 1208
Benedict, Jonathan G. IV, 1202
Benedict, Jonathan G. IV, 1226
Benedict, Jonathan S. IV, 1202
Benedict, Jonathan Stanley IV, 678
Benedict, Joseph C. IV, 925
Benedict, Joseph Cope IV, 925
Benedict, Kate IV, 1163
Benedict, Kate IV, 1182
Benedict, Katharine IV, 1147
Benedict, Katharine IV, 1148
Benedict, Katie O. IV, 1147
Benedict, Katie O. IV, 1148
Benedict, Laetitia IV, 1146
Benedict, Laura E. IV, 1148
Benedict, Lavina IV, 1148
Benedict, Lavina IV, 1154
Benedict, Lavina IV, 1231
Benedict, Lavina IV, 1233
Benedict, Lavina B. IV, 1146
Benedict, Lavina H. IV, 1146
Benedict, Lavinia B. IV, 1191
Benedict, Leenora IV, 1148
Benedict, Lelia IV, 1182
Benedict, Leonard V, 152
Benedict, Lester IV, 1146
Benedict, Lester P. IV, 1148
Benedict, Lester Wm. IV, 1148
Benedict, Levering IV, 1148
Benedict, Levi IV, 1202
Benedict, Levius IV, 1147
Benedict, Levius A. IV, 1147
Benedict, Lewis IV, 1145
Benedict, Lewis A. IV, 1147
Benedict, Linton W. IV, 1146
Benedict, Linton W. IV, 1148
Benedict, Livius A. IV, 1146
Benedict, Livius A. IV, 1148
Benedict, Livius A. IV, 1168
Benedict, Louisa IV, 1146
Benedict, Louisa IV, 1148
Benedict, Louisa IV, 1202
Benedict, Louisa M. IV, 1148
Benedict, Lovina B. IV, 1148
Benedict, Lovina B. IV, 1202
Benedict, Lovina B. IV, 1233
Benedict, Lydia IV, 1145
Benedict, Lydia L. IV, 1147
Benedict, Lydia L. IV, 1168
Benedict, Lydia S. IV, 1146
Benedict, Malisse V, 152
Benedict, Margaret J. IV, 1233
Benedict, Margaret Jane IV, 1146
Benedict, Marie IV, 1148
Benedict, Martha IV, 175
Benedict, Martha IV, 925
Benedict, Martha IV, 937
Benedict, Martha IV, 1146
Benedict, Martha IV, 1152
Benedict, Martha E. IV, 1148
Benedict, Martha E. IV, 1202
Benedict, Martha W. IV, 1147
Benedict, Mary IV, 678
Benedict, Mary IV, 1147
Benedict, Mary IV, 1148
Benedict, Mary IV, 1152
Benedict, Mary B. IV, 1148
Benedict, Mary Elnora IV, 1147
Benedict, Mary Jane IV, 925
Benedict, Mary Jane IV, 989
Benedict, Mary Jane IV, 1272
Benedict, Mary K. IV, 1147
Benedict, Mary R. IV, 1148
Benedict, Matilda IV, 1145
Benedict, Matilda IV, 1197
Benedict, May IV, 1147
Benedict, Melissa IV, 1146
Benedict, Melissa V, 967
Benedict, Mellise V, 152
Benedict, Merrell IV, 1147
Benedict, Mordecai J. IV, 1146
Benedict, Mordecai J. IV, 1147
Benedict, Mordecai J. IV, 1148
Benedict, Moses IV, 1146
Benedict, N. Edgar IV, 1148
Benedict, Nellie Ruthamie IV, 1147
Benedict, Nicholas IV, 1145
Benedict, Nicholas IV, 1147
Benedict, Odessa T. IV, 1148
Benedict, Orlando IV, 1146
Benedict, Orlando IV, 1233
Benedict, Penelope IV, 799
Benedict, Penelope IV, 1147
Benedict, Penelope IV, 1148
Benedict, Penelope IV, 1168
Benedict, Penelope J. IV, 1147
Benedict, Penelope J. IV, 1148
Benedict, Peter IV, 1146
Benedict, Phebe IV, 175
Benedict, Phebe IV, 1144
Benedict, Phebe IV, 1145
Benedict, Phebe IV, 1146
Benedict, Phebe IV, 1147
Benedict, Phebe IV, 1153
Benedict, Phebe IV, 1165
Benedict, Phebe IV, 1197
Benedict, Phebe IV, 1202
Benedict, Phebe V, 152
Benedict, Phebe A. IV, 1146
Benedict, Phebe A. IV, 1148
Benedict, Phebe A. IV, 1156
Benedict, Phebe Alice IV, 1146
Benedict, Phebe Ann IV, 1146
Benedict, Phebe Ann IV, 1148
Benedict, Phebe D. IV, 1146
Benedict, Phebe Ellen IV, 1146
Benedict, Phebe Ellen IV, 1148
Benedict, Phebe Ellen V, 152
Benedict, Phebe H. IV, 1146
Benedict, Phebe H. IV, 1147
Benedict, Phebe H. IV, 1168
Benedict, Phebe H. IV, 1187
Benedict, Phebe H. IV, 1194
Benedict, Phebe Jr. IV, 1160
Benedict, Phebe N. IV, 1147
Benedict, Phebe, Jr. IV, 1147
Benedict, Polly IV, 1146
Benedict, Polly IV, 1184
Benedict, Preston H. IV, 1146
Benedict, Preston H. IV, 1147
Benedict, Rachel IV, 1145
Benedict, Rachel IV, 1146
Benedict, Rachel IV, 1147
Benedict, Rachel IV, 1148
Benedict, Rachel IV, 1187
Benedict, Rachel V, 727
Benedict, Rachel V, 765
Benedict, Rachel E. IV, 1148
Benedict, Rachel J. P. IV, 1147
Benedict, Rachel J. P. IV, 1148
Benedict, Ramona Leila IV, 1147
Benedict, Rebecca C. IV, 925
Benedict, Rebecca C. IV, 1202
Benedict, Reuben IV, 175
Benedict, Reuben IV, 1146
Benedict, Reuben IV, 1147
Benedict, Reuben IV, 1148
Benedict, Robert IV, 1146
Benedict, Robert IV, 1148
Benedict, Robert IV, 1152
Benedict, Rolland IV, 1148
Benedict, Rollin Gretchel IV, 1147
Benedict, Ruth IV, 1146
Benedict, Ruth IV, 1147
Benedict, Ruth IV, 1153
Benedict, Ruth IV, 1154
Benedict, Ruth IV, 1160
Benedict, Ruth IV, 1202
Benedict, Ruth IV, 1208
Benedict, Ruth Catharine IV, 1147
Benedict, Ruth Della IV, 1148
Benedict, Ruth Esther IV, 1163
Benedict, Ruth Milicent IV, 1148
Benedict, Ruth Millicent IV, 1147
Benedict, S. Levering IV, 1147
Benedict, Sarah III, 282
Benedict, Sarah IV, 175
Benedict, Sarah IV, 232
Benedict, Sarah IV, 1145
Benedict, Sarah IV, 1146
Benedict, Sarah IV, 1147
Benedict, Sarah IV, 1148
Benedict, Sarah IV, 1160
Benedict, Sarah IV, 1162
Benedict, Sarah IV, 1165
Benedict, Sarah IV, 1182
Benedict, Sarah IV, 1197
Benedict, Sarah V, 152
Benedict, Sarah Evaline IV, 1146
Benedict, Sarah Evaline IV, 1148
Benedict, Sarah Evaline IV, 1202
Benedict, Sarah Eveline IV, 1202
Benedict, Sarah Jane IV, 1146
Benedict, Sarah M. IV, 1146
Benedict, Sarah M. IV, 1161
Benedict, Silvester IV, 1146
Benedict, Silvester IV, 1202
Benedict, Susan IV, 1147
Benedict, Susan IV, 1148
Benedict, Susan IV, 1163
Benedict, Susan Adelaide IV, 1146
Benedict, Susan Adelaide Coney IV, 1148
Benedict, Susan Coney IV, 1202
Benedict, Susan H. IV, 678
Benedict, Susan H. IV, 1148
Benedict, Susana IV, 1202
Benedict, Susana IV, 1208
Benedict, Susanna IV, 1146
Benedict, Susanna IV, 1202
Benedict, Susannah IV, 1147
Benedict, Susannah IV, 1202
Benedict, Sylvester IV, 1145
Benedict, Sylvester IV, 1146
Benedict, Sylvester IV, 1147
Benedict, Sylvester IV, 1202
Benedict, Theodore IV, 1146
Benedict, Theodore IV, 1147
Benedict, Theodore IV, 1148
Benedict, Theodore H. IV, 1148
Benedict, Walter IV, 1147
Benedict, Walter A. IV, 1148
Benedict, Walter I. IV, 1182
Benedict, Walter L. IV, 1163
Benedict, Walter Levering IV, 1147
Benedict, Walter Pearl IV, 1147
Benedict, Wd. Sarah III, 32
Benedict, Willard IV, 1147
Benedict, William IV, 175
Benedict, William IV, 1145
Benedict, William IV, 1146
Benedict, William IV, 1147
Benedict, William II IV, 1147
Benedict, William J. IV, 1146
Benedict, Wiman H. C. IV, 1146
Benedict, Wm. IV, 1146
Benedict, Wm. IV, 1148
Benedict, Wm. IV, 1153
Benedict, Wm. IV, 1161
Benedict, Wm. IV, 1165
Benedict, Wm. IV, 1184
Benedict, Wm. G. IV, 1202
Benedict, Wm. H. IV, 1147
Benedict, Wm. H. IV, 1148
Benedict, Wm. J. IV, 1148
Benegar, Cyrus Wister V, 222
Benegar, Ellis Ellsworth V, 222
Benegar, George V, 222
Benegar, James Wesley V, 222
Benegar, Lee Clark V, 222
Benegar, Mary Jane V, 222
Benegar, Mary Jane V, 223
Benet, Rebecca II, 197
Benet, Rebecca II, 257
Benet, Ruthann IV, 560
Benezet, Anthony II, 336
Benezet, Anthony II, 462
Benezet, Anthony II, 590
Benezet, J. Stephen II, 462
Benezet, J. Stephen II, 590
Benezet, Joyce II, 336
Benezet, Joyce II, 462
Benezet, Joyce II, 590
Benezet, Mary II, 336
Benezet, Sarah III, 32
Benezet, Wd. Joyce II, 336
Benezett, Anthony II, 197
Benezett, Anthony II, 336
Benezett, Joice II, 197
Benezett, Joyce II, 197
Benezett, Joyce II, 336
Benfield, Abby IV, 678
Benfield, Cora IV, 678
Benfield, Joel IV, 678
Benford, Peter VI, 221
Benford, Rebekah I, 230
Benford, Rebekah I, 251
Benham, Mary V, 24
Benham, Mary V, 658
Benine, Hannah V, 879
Benine, James V, 879
Benine, Stephen Bogue V, 879
Benington, Margaret II, 978
Benington, Samuel II, 280
Benjamin, Caroline VI, 745
Benjamin, Francis, Sr. VI, 745
Bennbow, Powel I, 374
Benner, Ellen IV, 925
Benner, Ellen IV, 941
Benner, Mary II, 462
Benner, Mary II, 660
Benner, Samantha IV, 966
Bennet, Abel P. IV, 1272
Bennet, Able IV, 1272
Bennet, Alexander II, 197
Bennet, Allen IV, 678
Bennet, Ann VI, 365
Bennet, Caroline II, 462
Bennet, Esther Ann IV, 1272
Bennet, Franklin L. IV, 1272
Bennet, James II, 462
Bennet, Jane II, 462
Bennet, Mahalah Ann V, 948
Bennet, Mahalah Ann V, 949
Bennet, Margaret V, 948
Bennet, Margaret V, 951
Bennet, Maria Ann II, 837
Bennet, Mary II, 462
Bennet, Mary II, 534
Bennet, Mary IV, 812
Bennet, Mary VI, 365
Bennet, Mary L. IV, 1272
Bennet, May IV, 1307
Bennet, Nancy A. IV, 1272
Bennet, Paris IV, 1016
Bennet, Phebe II, 462
Bennet, Rachel IV, 369
Bennet, Rachel IV, 423
Bennet, Rebecca II, 197
Bennet, Rebecca II, 272
Bennet, Rebecca II, 978
Bennet, Rebecca IV, 1202
Bennet, Rebecca IV, 1211
Bennet, Ruth I, 674
Bennet, Samuel V, 986
Bennet, Sarah II, 197
Bennet, Sarah II, 462
Bennet, Sarah Jane V, 476
Bennet, Susanna II, 462
Bennet, Thomas Williams II, 197
Bennet, Titus II, 462
Bennet, Titus VI, 365
Bennet, Wd. Rebecca II, 1038
Bennet, William, Jr. IV, 74
Benneth, Susan VI, 626
Bennett, ??? VI, 39
Bennett, ??? VI, 519
Bennett, ??? VI, 522
Bennett, Abigail III, 406
Bennett, Abner VI, 878
Bennett, Addie Catherine IV, 92
Bennett, Albert V, 153
Bennett, Albert L. V, 152
Bennett, Alfred R. II, 837
Bennett, Alfred Richards II, 782
Bennett, Alfred White II, 782
Bennett, Allen IV, 678
Bennett, Amelia IV, 797
Bennett, Amos IV, 74
Bennett, Amy III, 406
Bennett, Ann II, 336
Bennett, Ann II, 441
Bennett, Ann II, 727
Bennett, Ann II, 827
Bennett, Ann II, 836
Bennett, Ann II, 940
Bennett, Ann IV, 511
Bennett, Ann V, 476
Bennett, Ann V, 486
Bennett, Ann V, 894
Bennett, Ann V, 948
Bennett, Ann VI, 365
Bennett, Ann VI, 444
Bennett, Ann VI, 447
Bennett, Ann VI, 878
Bennett, Ann Elisa IV, 799
Bennett, Ann Eliza V, 948
Bennett, Ann Elizabeth III, 32
Bennett, Anna V, 727
Bennett, Anna May V, 658
Bennett, Barbara III, 29
Bennett, Barbara III, 32
Bennett, Belle V, 826
Bennett, Benj. III, 418
Bennett, Benjamin III, 32
Bennett, Benjamin III, 164
Bennett, Caroline II, 462
Bennett, Caroline II, 727
Bennett, Caroline II, 836
Bennett, Caroline II, 837
Bennett, Caroline V, 948
Bennett, Caroline V, 949
Bennett, Cephas J. IV, 74
Bennett, Cephus G. V, 894
Bennett, Charles Henry II, 782
Bennett, Charles Henry II, 837
Bennett, Christena V, 986
Bennett, Christopher L. VI, 808
Bennett, Clara V, 152
Bennett, Clarence M. II, 837
Bennett, Daniel R. II, 836
Bennett, Daniel R. II, 837
Bennett, Daniel R. IV, 369
Bennett, Daniel R. IV, 447
Bennett, Daniel Richards II, 33
Bennett, Daniel Richards II, 46
Bennett, Daniel Richards II, 72
Bennett, Daniel Richards II, 78
Bennett, Daniel Richards II, 83
Bennett, Delilah III, 32
Bennett, Dorcas VI, 230
Bennett, Edgar V, 152
Bennett, Edith J. IV, 74
Bennett, Edmond II, 336
Bennett, Edmond II, 624
Bennett, Edmund II, 462
Bennett, Edward II, 727
Bennett, Edward II, 836
Bennett, Edward II, 837
Bennett, Edward II, 978
Bennett, Edward II, 989
Bennett, Edward VI, 158
Bennett, Edward VI, 203
Bennett, Edward VI, 204
Bennett, Elisabeth II, 624
Bennett, Elisha IV, 20
Bennett, Elisha IV, 74
Bennett, Elisha V, 894
Bennett, Eliza III, 32
Bennett, Eliza Collings II, 782
Bennett, Eliza D. III, 170
Bennett, Eliza H. III, 32
Bennett, Elizabeth III, 395
Bennett, Elizabeth III, 475
Bennett, Elizabeth IV, 20
Bennett, Elizabeth IV, 74
Bennett, Elizabeth IV, 101
Bennett, Elizabeth V, 894
Bennett, Elizabeth V, 948
Bennett, Elizabeth VI, 471
Bennett, Elizabeth VI, 510
Bennett, Elizabeth VI, 878

Bennett, Ellen IV, 925
Bennett, Ellen IV, 1246
Bennett, Elmina IV, 799
Bennett, Elmira V, 948
Bennett, Emily IV, 74
Bennett, Emla IV, 74
Bennett, Emly IV, 74
Bennett, Emma T. III, 32
Bennett, Emma T. III, 164
Bennett, Emma T. III, 418
Bennett, Esther IV, 1352
Bennett, Esther Louisa VI, 707
Bennett, Esther Louise VI, 616
Bennett, Esther Louise VI, 702
Bennett, Etta V, 152
Bennett, Etta V, 153
Bennett, F. Paul IV, 925
Bennett, Franklin T. II, 837
Bennett, Franklin Taylor II, 782
Bennett, Frederick V, 452
Bennett, Frederick VI, 707
Bennett, Frederick Dewey VI, 616
Bennett, Frederick Dewey VI, 702
Bennett, Geo. Wilson V, 152
Bennett, George IV, 1246
Bennett, George IV, 1352
Bennett, George E. IV, 678
Bennett, George V. III, 32
Bennett, George W. V, 153
Bennett, Grace IV, 74
Bennett, Grace IV, 101
Bennett, Grace A. III, 32
Bennett, Grace A. III, 164
Bennett, Grace A. III, 418
Bennett, Hannah IV, 799
Bennett, Hannah J. IV, 799
Bennett, Hannah J. IV, 857
Bennett, Hannah J. V, 826
Bennett, Hannah J. V, 840
Bennett, Harry III, 32
Bennett, Harry III, 223
Bennett, Hattie V, 727
Bennett, Helen Elizabeth V, 152
Bennett, Hellen V, 153
Bennett, Henry II, 336
Bennett, Henry II, 727
Bennett, Henry II, 836
Bennett, Henry II, 837
Bennett, Henry V, 860
Bennett, Henry L. V, 894
Bennett, Henry S. IV, 74
Bennett, Henry S. V, 894
Bennett, Hiram IV, 925
Bennett, Hiram L. IV, 925
Bennett, Horace Coleman II, 782
Bennett, Howard VI, 798
Bennett, Howard VI, 858
Bennett, Humphrey II, 501
Bennett, Ida III, 32
Bennett, Ida May III, 223
Bennett, Ila I, 938
Bennett, Ila I, 942
Bennett, Isaac IV, 74
Bennett, Isaac IV, 96
Bennett, Isabella II, 837
Bennett, Isabella III, 32
Bennett, Isabella V, 948
Bennett, Isabella E. IV, 925
Bennett, Isaleeta IV, 925
Bennett, Isaletta IV, 800
Bennett, Isaletta IV, 925
Bennett, J. B. V, 894
Bennett, Jabez II, 837
Bennett, Jabez V, 223
Bennett, Jabez V, 948
Bennett, Jacob II, 462
Bennett, Jacob II, 562
Bennett, Jacob V, 476
Bennett, James II, 462
Bennett, James II, 837
Bennett, James III, 406
Bennett, James IV, 74
Bennett, James IV, 799
Bennett, James Allen IV, 175
Bennett, James Crawford V, 152
Bennett, James Crawford V, 153
Bennett, James H. II, 336
Bennett, James H. II, 462
Bennett, James L. II, 837
Bennett, James L. V, 948
Bennett, James Lee V, 222
Bennett, Jane II, 336
Bennett, Jane II, 462
Bennett, Jane II, 782
Bennett, Jane II, 837
Bennett, Jane II, 928
Bennett, John IV, 610
Bennett, John V, 826
Bennett, John A. V, 826
Bennett, John Anderson V, 826
Bennett, John R. VI, 878
Bennett, Joseph II, 837
Bennett, Joseph IV, 1352
Bennett, Joseph V, 222
Bennett, Joseph V, 298
Bennett, Joseph V, 948
Bennett, Joseph Jeones II, 782
Bennett, Joseph Morgan II, 462
Bennett, Joseph W. V, 949
Bennett, Kennett IV, 799
Bennett, L. S. IV, 925
Bennett, Laura V, 727
Bennett, Lauretta D. IV, 800
Bennett, Lavisa IV, 1136
Bennett, Lea II, 837
Bennett, Lea IV, 799
Bennett, Lea IV, 812
Bennett, Lea V, 948
Bennett, Leander W. III, 32
Bennett, Lee IV, 799
Bennett, Lee IV, 800
Bennett, Lee V, 948
Bennett, Lee S. IV, 800
Bennett, Lee S. IV, 925
Bennett, Leonard Parker VI, 616
Bennett, Leonard Parker VI, 702
Bennett, Lewis G. IV, 175
Bennett, Lewis Griscom III, 29
Bennett, Lewis Griscom III, 32
Bennett, Linden IV, 74
Bennett, Lloyd D. IV, 74
Bennett, Louisa IV, 74
Bennett, Louisa IV, 82
Bennett, Louisa IV, 1127
Bennett, Louisa IV, 1136
Bennett, Louise I, 938
Bennett, Louiza IV, 74
Bennett, Lucile V, 153
Bennett, Lucy IV, 1352
Bennett, Lucy VI, 809
Bennett, Lydia IV, 511
Bennett, Lydia IV, 925
Bennett, Lydia V, 948
Bennett, Lydia Ann IV, 925
Bennett, Mahala V, 948
Bennett, Mahala Ann II, 837
Bennett, Mahala Ann V, 222
Bennett, Mahalah Ann II, 837
Bennett, Mahalah Ann V, 948
Bennett, Major General ??? VI, 41
Bennett, Margaret V, 948
Bennett, Margaret VI, 616
Bennett, Margaret VI, 702
Bennett, Margaret C. IV, 74
Bennett, Margaret C. IV, 96
Bennett, Margaret C. V, 894
Bennett, Marget M. V, 985
Bennett, Maria IV, 74
Bennett, Maria IV, 96
Bennett, Maria A. IV, 369
Bennett, Maria A. IV, 447
Bennett, Maria Ann II, 782
Bennett, Maria Ann II, 837
Bennett, Maria J. IV, 74
Bennett, Mariah IV, 74
Bennett, Martha II, 336
Bennett, Martha VI, 158
Bennett, Martha VI, 203
Bennett, Martha VI, 204
Bennett, Mary I, 299
Bennett, Mary I, 311
Bennett, Mary II, 462
Bennett, Mary II, 501
Bennett, Mary III, 32
Bennett, Mary IV, 799
Bennett, Mary IV, 1246
Bennett, Mary IV, 1352
Bennett, Mary V, 222
Bennett, Mary V, 236
Bennett, Mary V, 894
Bennett, Mary V, 948
Bennett, Mary V, 949
Bennett, Mary Elizabeth II, 837
Bennett, Mary Ellen V, 236
Bennett, Mary Etta V, 986
Bennett, Mary F. V, 948
Bennett, Mary I. IV, 799
Bennett, Mary L. IV, 74
Bennett, Mary L. V, 894
Bennett, Mary Lucile V, 152
Bennett, Mary W. VI, 878
Bennett, Matilda P. II, 837
Bennett, Mildred V, 153
Bennett, Mildred Gertrude V, 152
Bennett, Minerva V, 476
Bennett, Minerva Isabel V, 687
Bennett, Nancy V, 860
Bennett, Nimrod V, 826
Bennett, Nimrod T. VI, 731
Bennett, Paul IV, 800
Bennett, Paul IV, 925
Bennett, Phebe II, 462
Bennett, Phebe III, 395
Bennett, Phebe III, 475
Bennett, Phebe IV, 610
Bennett, Phebe IV, 800
Bennett, Phebe IV, 825
Bennett, Phebe IV, 925
Bennett, Phebe VI, 519
Bennett, Phebe VI, 522
Bennett, Phebe Y. IV, 925
Bennett, Prince IV, 1352
Bennett, Prince, Jr. IV, 1352
Bennett, R. Grant III, 32
Bennett, Rachel II, 336
Bennett, Rachel II, 462
Bennett, Rachel II, 727
Bennett, Rachel II, 782
Bennett, Rachel II, 827
Bennett, Rachel II, 836
Bennett, Rachel II, 837
Bennett, Rachel II, 940
Bennett, Rachel III, 138
Bennett, Rachel IV, 369
Bennett, Rachel V, 948
Bennett, Rachel VI, 996
Bennett, Rachel B. IV, 369
Bennett, Rebecca II, 978
Bennett, Rebecca IV, 799
Bennett, Rebecca IV, 805
Bennett, Remus E. V, 986
Bennett, Retta IV, 800
Bennett, Reuben VI, 878
Bennett, Reuben Grant III, 32
Bennett, Reuben Grant III, 170
Bennett, Richard II, 336
Bennett, Richard VI, 39
Bennett, Roliff III, 32
Bennett, Rosamond VI, 798
Bennett, Ruben VI, 878
Bennett, Ruben Grant IV, 175
Bennett, Russell V, 153
Bennett, Russell Leonard V, 152
Bennett, Ruth Allen III, 32
Bennett, Ruth Allen IV, 175
Bennett, Ruthanna III, 32
Bennett, Ruthanna IV, 74
Bennett, S. F. IV, 1246
Bennett, Sallie E. VI, 841
Bennett, Sally VI, 878
Bennett, Sammie IV, 800
Bennett, Samuel V, 986
Bennett, Samuel H. IV, 800
Bennett, Samuel H. V, 985
Bennett, Sarah II, 336
Bennett, Sarah II, 462
Bennett, Sarah V, 826
Bennett, Sarah A. V, 894
Bennett, Sarah Ann IV, 74
Bennett, Sarah Catherine V, 153
Bennett, Sarah E. VI, 731
Bennett, Sarah J. V, 860
Bennett, Sarah Jane V, 476
Bennett, Sarah Jane V, 826
Bennett, Sarah R. V, 826
Bennett, Sarah W. VI, 471
Bennett, Sarah W. VI, 473
Bennett, Sarah W. VI, 510
Bennett, Sarah W. VI, 513
Bennett, Sarah W. VI, 658
Bennett, Smith IV, 511
Bennett, Snyder VI, 510
Bennett, Stephen IV, 1352
Bennett, Sue V, 851
Bennett, Susan VI, 616
Bennett, Susanna II, 462
Bennett, Susanna VI, 471
Bennett, Susanna VI, 616
Bennett, Susannah II, 462
Bennett, Susannah II, 562
Bennett, Susannah VI, 798
Bennett, Sydnor VI, 471
Bennett, Sydnor VI, 555
Bennett, T. Paul IV, 925
Bennett, Thomas IV, 511
Bennett, Thomas VI, 878
Bennett, Thos. F. VI, 798
Bennett, Titus II, 336
Bennett, Titus II, 462
Bennett, Titus II, 727
Bennett, Titus II, 782
Bennett, Titus II, 827
Bennett, Titus II, 836
Bennett, Titus II, 837
Bennett, Titus II, 940
Bennett, Titus IV, 369
Bennett, Titus VI, 471
Bennett, Veda V, 153
Bennett, Veda Alice V, 152
Bennett, Velma V, 153
Bennett, Velma V, 182
Bennett, Velma May V, 152
Bennett, Wd. Elizabeth II, 336
Bennett, William II, 336
Bennett, William III, 395
Bennett, William III, 475
Bennett, William IV, 74
Bennett, William IV, 511
Bennett, William VI, 878
Bennett, William C. IV, 74
Bennett, William, Jr. IV, 74
Bennett, Wm. II, 501
Bennett, Wm. IV, 101
Bennett, Wm. C. V, 894
Bennette, John VI, 130
Bennezett, Mary II, 336
Bennezett, Wd. Joyce II, 336
Bennington, Ann II, 703
Bennington, Camilla V, 153
Bennington, Elisabeth I, 617
Bennington, Jesse V, 153
Bennington, John II, 703
Bennington, John II, 967
Bennington, Phebe II, 703
Bennington, Phebe II, 967
Bennington, Rachel B. II, 967
Bennington, Samuel II, 280
Bennington, Stark VI, 855
Bennit, Mary VI, 365
Bennit, Mary VI, 436
Bennit, Samuel H. V, 985
Bennit, Titus II, 462
Bennitt, Alexander II, 197
Bennitt, Alexander II, 274
Bennitt, Edmond II, 336
Bennitt, Elizabeth II, 274
Bennitt, Isabella E. IV, 925
Bennitt, Jane II, 336
Bennitt, L. S. IV, 925
Bennitt, Martha II, 336
Bennitt, Sarah II, 197
Bennitt, Sarah II, 274
Bennitt, Sarah II, 336
Bennitt, T. Paul IV, 925
Bennitt, Wd. Elizabeth II, 336
Bennitt, William II, 336
Benns, Margaret Ann IV, 960
Benschoter, Ann IV, 1148
Benschoter, Ann IV, 1176
Bensine, Luzena I, 800
Bensine, Luzena I, 831
Benson, ??? III, 32
Benson, ??? III, 125
Benson, ??? III, 321
Benson, Alice I, 1047
Benson, Alice I, 1049
Benson, Alice II, 462
Benson, Alice II, 526
Benson, Catharine IV, 678
Benson, Catherine IV, 1246
Benson, Catherine V, 153
Benson, Charity V, 153
Benson, Clara III, 32
Benson, Clara III, 125
Benson, Clara III, 321
Benson, Clark V, 24
Benson, Clark V, 153
Benson, Deborah V, 826
Benson, Deborah V, 879
Benson, Deborah V, 881
Benson, Elijah V, 153
Benson, Elizabeth V, 24
Benson, Elizabeth V, 153
Benson, Elizabeth VI, 878
Benson, Ester II, 336
Benson, Esther II, 336
Benson, Esther V, 153
Benson, George II, 462
Benson, George V, 153
Benson, Hannah II, 336
Benson, Harry IV, 1148
Benson, Harvey C. V, 153
Benson, Henry V, 24
Benson, Henry V, 153
Benson, Henry V, 173
Benson, Hester V, 24
Benson, Irvine H. VI, 878
Benson, Isaac V, 153
Benson, James I, 1026
Benson, James I, 1060
Benson, James V, 24
Benson, James V, 153
Benson, Jane I, 1047
Benson, John II, 336
Benson, John II, 462
Benson, John II, 526
Benson, John III, 32
Benson, John V, 153
Benson, Jonathan V, 153
Benson, Jonathan V, 155
Benson, Jonothan V, 24
Benson, Josiah IV, 678
Benson, Josiah IV, 1246
Benson, Julia IV, 369
Benson, Julia IV, 377
Benson, Levi IV, 377
Benson, Levi L. IV, 369
Benson, Lucinda V, 153
Benson, Margaret V, 153
Benson, Margaret V, 173
Benson, Martha IV, 678
Benson, Martha IV, 1246
Benson, Martha V, 153
Benson, Mary II, 336
Benson, Mary II, 462
Benson, Mary IV, 1246
Benson, Mary V, 24
Benson, Mary V, 149
Benson, Mary V, 153
Benson, Mary V, 183
Benson, Mary Ann V, 153
Benson, Mary D. IV, 369
Benson, Mary D. IV, 402
Benson, Rachel IV, 377
Benson, Rachel L. IV, 369
Benson, Rachel L. IV, 387
Benson, Robert I, 1047
Benson, Robert IV, 678
Benson, Robert IV, 1246
Benson, Robert V, 153
Benson, Ruth IV, 678
Benson, Ruth IV, 1246
Benson, Ruth V, 153
Benson, Ruth V, 155
Benson, Ruth V, 826
Benson, Ruth V, 869
Benson, Ruth T. V, 826
Benson, Samuel V, 24
Benson, Samuel V, 153
Benson, Sarah V, 153
Benson, Sarah E. V, 153
Benson, Tabitha C. IV, 369
Benson, Tabitha C. IV, 387
Benson, Thomas V, 24
Benson, Thomas V, 153
Benson, Thomas V, 183
Benson, Vesper Marguerite V, 153
Benson, William I, 1047
Benson, William I Sup 1, 11
Benson, William IV, 1246
Benson, William V, 24
Benson, William V, 153
Benson, William V, 476
Benson, William, Jr. I, 1047
Benson, Wm. IV, 678
Benston, James I, 115
Benston, Rosannah I, 115
Benston, Rosannah I, 129
Benston, Rosannah I, 162
Benthall, Nora I, 212
Bentley, Alice Anna II, 837
Bentley, Ann IV, 900
Bentley, Anna IV, 800
Bentley, Anna IV, 900
Bentley, Archie V, 613
Bentley, Benj. V, 612
Bentley, Benjamin V, 612
Bentley, Bernice III, 32
Bentley, Caleb VI, 471
Bentley, Caleb VI, 474
Bentley, Caleb VI, 475
Bentley, Caleb VI, 731
Bentley, Charles C. V, 612
Bentley, Chas. V, 612
Bentley, Clarence V, 612
Bentley, Cora L. II, 837
Bentley, Cora Lea II, 782
Bentley, Cyrus V, 612
Bentley, Cyrus C. V, 612
Bentley, Daisey V, 658
Bentley, Daisy V, 658
Bentley, Daisy F. V, 658
Bentley, Deborah IV, 900
Bentley, Deborah R. IV, 800
Bentley, Delbert Morris V, 658
Bentley, Edith Helen III, 202
Bentley, Elias Russell V, 612
Bentley, Elizabeth V, 223
Bentley, Elizabeth V, 612
Bentley, Elizabeth G. IV, 900
Bentley, Ellen W. II, 837
Bentley, Ellen W. II, 909
Bentley, Ellen Widdefield II, 782
Bentley, Emma V, 612
Bentley, Emma V, 640
Bentley, Ervin V, 658
Bentley, Ervin I. V, 658
Bentley, Franklin H. IV, 800
Bentley, Franklin H. IV, 900
Bentley, George VI, 878
Bentley, George Taylor II, 782

Bentley, George Taylor II, 837
Bentley, Geretty V, 612
Bentley, Granville S. IV, 800
Bentley, Granville S. IV, 900
Bentley, Hannah II, 782
Bentley, Hannah II, 837
Bentley, Hannah II, 909
Bentley, Hannah IV, 900
Bentley, Hannah B. IV, 800
Bentley, Hannah H. IV, 20
Bentley, Hannah H. IV, 43
Bentley, Hannah H. IV, 900
Bentley, Henrietta T. VI, 731
Bentley, Henry II, 837
Bentley, Henry H. II, 837
Bentley, Henry H. II, 909
Bentley, Henry Hirst II, 782
Bentley, Hiram II, 782
Bentley, Hiram II, 837
Bentley, Hiram II, 909
Bentley, Inez H. V, 613
Bentley, Isaiah V, 153
Bentley, Isaiah V, 612
Bentley, Isaiah Jeremiah Jesse V, 612
Bentley, Jeanette V, 153
Bentley, Jeremiah V, 612
Bentley, Jeretta V, 612
Bentley, Jesse V, 612
Bentley, John III, 32
Bentley, John III, 362
Bentley, John IV, 74
Bentley, John E. IV, 900
Bentley, John E. V, 612
Bentley, Joseph VI, 471
Bentley, Joseph VI, 475
Bentley, Joseph E. IV, 800
Bentley, Katie F. V, 612
Bentley, Lydia I, 1007
Bentley, Lydia V, 223
Bentley, Lydia V, 445
Bentley, Mabel V, 153
Bentley, Mabel M. V, 153
Bentley, Mable V, 153
Bentley, Mable V, 612
Bentley, Malinda V, 615
Bentley, Margaret Sarah VI, 474
Bentley, Maria IV, 800
Bentley, Maria IV, 900
Bentley, Maria IV, 905
Bentley, Mary III, 32
Bentley, Mary III, 362
Bentley, Mary VI, 471
Bentley, Mary VI, 475
Bentley, Mary E. V, 612
Bentley, Mary Thomas VI, 471
Bentley, Milan II, 782
Bentley, Milan II, 837
Bentley, Morris V, 658
Bentley, Ottie V, 612
Bentley, Raymond II, 837
Bentley, Rebecca W. II, 837
Bentley, Richard T. VI, 731
Bentley, Richard Thomas VI, 471
Bentley, Russell V, 612
Bentley, Ruth IV, 678
Bentley, Ruth Ann IV, 737
Bentley, Ruthanna II, 782
Bentley, Sally V, 612
Bentley, Sally V, 625
Bentley, Samuel S. II, 837
Bentley, Sarah V, 612
Bentley, Sarah VI, 471
Bentley, Sarah E. V, 612
Bentley, Susanna IV, 74
Bentley, Thomas M. IV, 800
Bentley, Thomas M. IV, 900
Bentley, Thos. Moore II, 782
Bentley, Uny VI, 878
Bentley, Viola V, 612
Bentley, Walter V, 612
Bently, Caleb VI, 630
Bently, Lydia I, 1012
Bently, Rebecca I, 299
Bently, Rebecca I, 315
Benton, Amy J. IV, 175
Benton, Amy J. S. IV, 175
Benton, Ann V, 727
Benton, Anne V, 894
Benton, Heber C. IV, 175
Benton, Mary IV, 1272
Benton, Nancy V, 894
Benton, Nancy V, 904
Benton, Nancy VI, 928
Benton, Oliver V, 904
Benton, Samuel IV, 1272
Benton, Woodson H. VI, 327
Benton, Woodson H. VI, 829
Bentson, Arvilla IV, 1307
Bentz, Sarah V, 658
Benwell, Thomas Riggs III, 32
Beoser, Caleb II, 336
Bera, Sarah Ann V, 319
Berber, Isabel IV, 953
Bercham, Joseph I, 605
Berchett, Robert VI, 130
Berdan, Will Wiseman III, 101
Berdmore, Thomas II, 441
Beren, Anna II, 441
Beren, Mary II, 441
Beren, William II, 441
Berg, Hannah C. II, 728
Berg, Hannah C. II, 755
Berg, Hazel IV, 1246
Berg, Hazel IV, 1307
Berg, Hazel L. IV, 1307
Bergen, ??? III, 377
Bergen, Edith H. IV, 1024
Bergen, Edith R. IV, 1024
Bergen, Grace IV, 175
Bergen, Maria III, 395
Bergen, Maria III, 437
Bergen, Sarah III, 32
Bergen, Sarah III, 43
Bergen, Sarah III, 377
Bergen, Walter B. IV, 678
Bergen, Winifred E. III, 190
Bergen, Winifred E. III, 292
Berger, ??? III, 32
Berger, Dessa IV, 1035
Berger, Dessie IV, 1035
Berger, Enoch V, 373
Berger, Fanny V, 373
Berger, Floren V, 373
Berger, Hester III, 32
Berger, James V, 24
Berger, Louisa IV, 966
Berger, Ora West V, 373
Berger, Peter III, 395
Berger, Ruth V, 153
Berger, Timothy III, 32
Berger, Ursula III, 395
Berges, Joseph IV, 1051
Bergett, William IV, 464
Bergner, Eliza V, 727
Bergner, Mabel V, 727
Bergner, Mary V, 988
Bergner, Nettie V, 986
Berk, Melia A. V, 826
Berk, Melva Amy V, 834
Berk, Stephen V, 834
Berkeley, Gov. ??? VI, 40
Berkeley, Gov. ??? VI, 41
Berkeley, Governor ??? VI, 48
Berkeley, Sir William VI, 6
Berkeley, William VI, 9
Berkerdite, Fannie I, 924
Berkerdite, W. J. I, 924
Berkes, Betsy A. VI, 961
Berkhart, Edgar V, 581
Berkingoff, Alex III, 32
Berkingoff, David III, 32
Berkingoff, Esther III, 32
Berkingoff, Helen III, 32
Berkshire, Hannah R. V, 986
Berlin, Ancil V, 659
Berlin, Cora V, 659
Berlin, Dessie V, 658
Berlin, Espy V, 659
Berlin, Mary V, 659
Berlin, Mary E. V, 658
Berlin, Nola V, 659
Berlin, Nolia V, 659
Berlin, Vinta V, 659
Berlin, Wm. V, 659
Bernard, Abba V, 319
Bernard, Abbie V, 319
Bernard, Abijah III, 32
Bernard, Aleta V, 319
Bernard, Anna V, 298
Bernard, Benj. VI, 798
Bernard, Benjamin VI, 325
Bernard, Benjamin VI, 829
Bernard, Benoni I, 267
Bernard, Beth V, 319
Bernard, Catharine I, 980
Bernard, Charles V, 319
Bernard, Charles O. V, 319
Bernard, Charles Rodney V, 319
Bernard, Chas. B. V, 319
Bernard, Chas. O. V, 319
Bernard, Columbia V, 319
Bernard, Cora V, 319
Bernard, Cora B. V, 319
Bernard, Edwin V, 319
Bernard, Elijah V, 319
Bernard, Elizabeth V, 298
Bernard, Elizabeth V, 311
Bernard, Elizabeth VI, 878
Bernard, Ella V, 319
Bernard, Eunice VI, 298
Bernard, Eunice VI, 325
Bernard, Eunice VI, 829
Bernard, Frederic V, 298
Bernard, Frederick V, 298
Bernard, G. W. V, 319
Bernard, Geo. W. V, 319
Bernard, George V, 298
Bernard, George V, 319
Bernard, George W. V, 319
Bernard, George W., Jr. V, 319
Bernard, Georgia V, 319
Bernard, Hannah V, 298
Bernard, Harriet V, 319
Bernard, Harriet C. V, 319
Bernard, Harriet J. V, 319
Bernard, Hopy Ann VI, 878
Bernard, Howard VI, 52
Bernard, Howard S. VI, 52
Bernard, James E. V, 319
Bernard, James Everett V, 319
Bernard, James K. V, 319
Bernard, Jamima V, 298
Bernard, Jamima V, 300
Bernard, Jane V, 319
Bernard, Jane Emily V, 319
Bernard, Jane Emily V, 339
Bernard, Jemima V, 298
Bernard, Joanna V, 319
Bernard, John V, 298
Bernard, John V, 319
Bernard, John VI, 52
Bernard, John B. V, 319
Bernard, John K. VI, 878
Bernard, John R. V, 319
Bernard, Joseph IV, 1307
Bernard, Joseph VI, 798
Bernard, Jud V, 319
Bernard, Judson V, 319
Bernard, Keziah V, 319
Bernard, Laura May V, 319
Bernard, Lettice II, 816
Bernard, Lettuce II, 788
Bernard, Love V, 298
Bernard, Lucinda E. VI, 878
Bernard, Lucy VI, 798
Bernard, Lydia II, 807
Bernard, Lydia V, 298
Bernard, Lydia V, 307
Bernard, Martha A. V, 319
Bernard, Martha Smith VI, 798
Bernard, Mary I, 797
Bernard, Mary I, 825
Bernard, Mary V, 298
Bernard, Mattie V, 319
Bernard, Myrtle V, 319
Bernard, Oscar E. V, 319
Bernard, Pauline E. VI, 878
Bernard, Rebecca VI, 878
Bernard, Sally VI, 897
Bernard, Sarah VI, 52
Bernard, Sarah J. V, 319
Bernard, Silas G. VI, 878
Bernard, Subal V, 298
Bernard, Thomas V, 319
Bernard, Thomas J. V, 319
Bernard, Thomas Judson V, 319
Bernard, Thomas V. VI, 878
Bernard, Timothy VI, 325
Bernard, Timothy VI, 829
Bernard, Trustram I, 525
Bernard, Uriah V, 298
Bernard, Wm. V, 298
Bernard, Wm. V. VI, 878
Bernecod, John II, 441
Bernerd, Frederic I, 525
Bernerd, Reuben VI, 298
Bernet, Hannah V, 151
Bernet, Martha VI, 832
Bernet, Mary VI, 832
Bernett, Eliza IV, 466
Beroman, Eliz. III, 110
Beroman, Eliz. III, 243
Beroman, Elizabeth III, 243
Berrett, Ann II, 441
Berry, Aaron VI, 365
Berry, Agnes IV, 140
Berry, Agnes IV, 369
Berry, Albert IV, 175
Berry, Ann II, 824
Berry, Ann IV, 140
Berry, Ann IV, 369
Berry, Anna IV, 369
Berry, Anna IV, 454
Berry, Anna IV, 1272
Berry, Anna IV, 1327
Berry, Anna E. IV, 175
Berry, Anna McCann IV, 1307
Berry, Ascenath IV, 175
Berry, Asenath IV, 139
Berry, Asenath IV, 140
Berry, Asenath IV, 151
Berry, Belle V, 223
Berry, Benjamin II, 463
Berry, Benjamin II, 581
Berry, Beulah IV, 21
Berry, Beulah IV, 140
Berry, Beulah VI, 365
Berry, Braxton C. IV, 139
Berry, Catharine VI, 471
Berry, Catherine VI, 556
Berry, Charles I, 674
Berry, Charles W. I, 649
Berry, Chas. III, 50
Berry, Culberson IV, 140
Berry, Cynthia V, 319
Berry, Cyrus IV, 139
Berry, Cyrus IV, 140
Berry, David IV, 21
Berry, David IV, 137
Berry, David IV, 139
Berry, David IV, 140
Berry, David IV, 143
Berry, David IV, 175
Berry, David IV, 279
Berry, David IV, 369
Berry, David IV, 678
Berry, David VI, 365
Berry, Dorothy Everett VI, 365
Berry, Dorothy Everett Berry VI, 365
Berry, E. Willard VI, 365
Berry, Eddie N. IV, 175
Berry, Edward John IV, 140
Berry, Edward Lewis VI, 365
Berry, Edward Wilber VI, 365
Berry, Edward Willard VI, 365
Berry, Eliza Ann IV, 175
Berry, Eliza Ann IV, 229
Berry, Elizabeth I, 374
Berry, Elizabeth II, 463
Berry, Elizabeth III, 32
Berry, Elizabeth IV, 139
Berry, Elizabeth VI, 365
Berry, Elizabeth Ann IV, 369
Berry, Elizabeth Anna IV, 369
Berry, Elizabeth Anna IV, 425
Berry, Esther IV, 139
Berry, Esther IV, 799
Berry, Esther IV, 800
Berry, Esther Ruth IV, 140
Berry, Esther Ruth IV, 799
Berry, Esther Ruth IV, 800
Berry, Frank V, 986
Berry, George IV, 175
Berry, George W. I, 674
Berry, George W. F. I, 674
Berry, George W. L. I, 649
Berry, George W. L. I, 674
Berry, Hanna M. IV, 1202
Berry, Hannah II, 463
Berry, Hannah III, 50
Berry, Hannah IV, 21
Berry, Hannah IV, 139
Berry, Hannah IV, 140
Berry, Hannah IV, 143
Berry, Hannah IV, 164
Berry, Hannah IV, 369
Berry, Hannah VI, 365
Berry, Hannah VI, 397
Berry, Ida IV, 175
Berry, Isaac VI, 980
Berry, Israel IV, 139
Berry, Jacob II, 837
Berry, James II, 463
Berry, James II, 581
Berry, James II, 782
Berry, Jane II, 463
Berry, Jane II, 962
Berry, Jennie IV, 175
Berry, Jesse IV, 139
Berry, Jesse IV, 140
Berry, Jesse IV, 175
Berry, Jesse W. IV, 139
Berry, Jesse W. C. I, 649
Berry, Jesse W. C. I, 674
Berry, Job II, 463
Berry, John V, 223
Berry, John VI, 365
Berry, John, Jr. VI, 365
Berry, Jordan IV, 139
Berry, Joseph II, 462
Berry, Joseph VI, 365
Berry, Joseph J. G. I, 649
Berry, Joseph J. G. I, 674
Berry, Josiah Rogers VI, 365
Berry, Julianna IV, 140
Berry, Julianna IV, 142
Berry, Julianna IV, 175
Berry, July Anna IV, 311
Berry, Laura A. IV, 140
Berry, Laura A. IV, 142
Berry, Libbie V, 986
Berry, Libby V, 986
Berry, Little VI, 927
Berry, Llewellin II, 462
Berry, Llewellyn II, 463
Berry, Lundy III, 32
Berry, Lydia I, 649
Berry, Lydia I, 674
Berry, Lydia VI, 365
Berry, Lydia C. I, 674
Berry, Lydia K. I, 649
Berry, Madison G. IV, 139
Berry, Mancil IV, 1272
Berry, Margaret II, 462
Berry, Margaret II, 463
Berry, Margaret II, 486
Berry, Margaret II, 498
Berry, Margaret VI, 365
Berry, Martha IV, 175
Berry, Martha IV, 511
Berry, Martha H. IV, 140
Berry, Martha H. IV, 162
Berry, Martha J. A. I, 649
Berry, Martha Jane I, 674
Berry, Martha Jane Armilla I, 674
Berry, Mary I, 933
Berry, Mary II, 462
Berry, Mary II, 463
Berry, Mary IV, 139
Berry, Mary IV, 140
Berry, Mary IV, 149
Berry, Mary IV, 156
Berry, Mary IV, 175
Berry, Mary IV, 279
Berry, Mary IV, 369
Berry, Mary IV, 1272
Berry, Mary Susan VI, 365
Berry, Mary Willard B. VI, 365
Berry, Moses II, 463
Berry, Naomi II, 462
Berry, Naomi II, 535
Berry, Nicholas III, 32
Berry, Orpha V, 264
Berry, Otto C. V, 613
Berry, Patience IV, 74
Berry, Patience VI, 365
Berry, Patience VI, 383
Berry, Phebe IV, 21
Berry, Phebe VI, 365
Berry, Rachel IV, 139
Berry, Rachel IV, 140
Berry, Rachel IV, 156
Berry, Rachel IV, 163
Berry, Rachel IV, 175
Berry, Rachel VI, 365
Berry, Rachel VI, 372
Berry, Rebecca II, 798
Berry, Rees IV, 140
Berry, Reese IV, 139
Berry, Reese IV, 142
Berry, Reese IV, 175
Berry, Reese T. IV, 140
Berry, Reese T. IV, 162
Berry, Ruth II, 463
Berry, Ruth Hannah IV, 140
Berry, Sally Ann III, 32
Berry, Samuel II, 837
Berry, Samuel IV, 21
Berry, Samuel IV, 74
Berry, Samuel IV, 139
Berry, Samuel IV, 140
Berry, Samuel IV, 149
Berry, Samuel IV, 175
Berry, Samuel IV, 369
Berry, Samuel VI, 365
Berry, Samuel VI, 591
Berry, Samuel Stedman VI, 365
Berry, Samuel, Jr. IV, 369
Berry, Sarah II, 463
Berry, Sarah II, 581
Berry, Sarah II, 782
Berry, Sarah II, 837
Berry, Sarah IV, 140
Berry, Sarah IV, 369
Berry, Sarah VI, 365
Berry, Sarah VI, 409
Berry, Sarah Ann III, 32
Berry, Sarah Ann IV, 567
Berry, Susanna IV, 1049
Berry, Susanna IV, 1066
Berry, Susannah II, 336
Berry, Susannah II, 782
Berry, Sylvia IV, 1148
Berry, Tacy II, 463
Berry, Tacy II, 687
Berry, Theodore IV, 140
Berry, Thomas IV, 21
Berry, Thomas IV, 139
Berry, Thomas IV, 140
Berry, Thomas IV, 156
Berry, Thomas IV, 163
Berry, Thomas IV, 175

Berry, Thomas IV, 369
Berry, Thomas VI, 365
Berry, Thomas R. V, 613
Berry, Thomas W. IV, 139
Berry, Thos. IV, 140
Berry, Walter II, 336
Berry, Walter S. V, 613
Berry, Willard VI, 365
Berry, William IV, 140
Berry, William IV, 369
Berry, William VI, 365
Berry, Wm. II, 978
Berry, Wm. II, 1034
Berry, Wm. IV, 1272
Berson, Jane IV, 185
Bert, Daniel IV, 320
Bert, Sarah IV, 320
Bertholf, James V, 221
Bertier, Sarah II, 460
Bertier, Sarah II, 463
Bertine, Elizabeth III, 32
Berton, Elizabeth I, 921
Berton, Herbert Purdy I, 921
Berton, John I, 921
Berton, John Wilson I, 921
Berton, Samira I, 921
Bertram, Alice IV, 175
Bertram, John P. IV, 175
Bertram, John Pennington IV, 175
Bertram, Louise Marie IV, 175
Bertram, William H. IV, 175
Bertram, Wm. H. IV, 175
Bertrum, Alice IV, 175
Bertrum, Alice IV, 262
Bertsche, Auguste III, 32
Bertsche, Bertha III, 32
Bertsche, Bertha III, 363
Bertsche, Carl Victor III, 32
Bertsche, Carl Victor III, 363
Bertsche, Edithe Claire III, 32
Bertsche, Edwin Carl III, 32
Bertsche, Mathilde III, 32
Bertsche, Wm. Irving III, 32
Besch, Dorothy G. IV, 1320
Besch, Helen V, 659
Besch, Helen L. V, 659
Besch, Lester IV, 1307
Besch, Lester IV, 1320
Besch, Lester John IV, 1307
Besch, M. Zora V, 659
Beseley, John VI, 878
Beseley, Keziah VI, 878
Beseley, Sarah VI, 878
Besell, Hannah II, 337
Besell, John II, 337
Besell, William II, 337
Besom, Cordelia V, 727
Besom, Frank V, 727
Beson, Amasa V, 222
Beson, Benjamin V, 222
Beson, Hannah I, 674
Beson, Igal V, 152
Beson, Isaac I, 674
Beson, Martha I, 815
Beson, Richard V, 222
Beson, Silas I, 799
Beson, William V, 222
Bess, Charity IV, 175
Bessill, Hannah II, 463
Besson, Bessie F. I, 921
Bessonet, John III, 32
Bessonet, John P. III, 32
Best, Banks VI, 878
Best, Bettie I, 1148
Best, Catharine I, 1148
Best, Charles I, 871
Best, Charlie B. I, 871
Best, Deborah VI, 616
Best, Deborah VI, 634
Best, Drewsiller VI, 989
Best, Druzilla VI, 884
Best, Elizabeth VI, 878
Best, Elizabeth VI, 884
Best, Fredric I, 1148
Best, Hiram T. IV, 925
Best, Jacob IV, 925
Best, Janny VI, 878
Best, John VI, 807
Best, John VI, 1008
Best, John M. I, 871
Best, John McLean I, 871
Best, Josie I, 1148
Best, Levi VI, 878
Best, Levi VI, 884
Best, Levi VI, 926
Best, Levi VI, 965
Best, Levi VI, 989
Best, Lillian III, 463
Best, Lydia Ann IV, 925
Best, Media I, 1148
Best, Mildred M. I, 871
Best, Olney I, 1148
Best, Ottie May I, 1148
Best, Patsey VI, 878
Best, Polly VI, 1008
Best, Samuel VI, 878
Best, Samuel VI, 1008
Best, Sarah IV, 925
Best, Sarah VI, 926
Best, William Allen I, 871
Best, William Bascom I, 1148
Best, Willie I, 871
Beswick, Aaron II, 978
Betbly, ??? III, 32
Betbly, Lorenzo III, 32
Betell, Josiah II, 336
Beth, Eliz M. III, 145
Beth, Jane Maria III, 281
Bethel, Helena II, 463
Bethel, Helena II, 487
Bethel, Mary IV, 511
Bethel, Mary IV, 528
Bethel, Wm. II, 463
Bethel, Wm. II, 487
Betheny, Joseph VI, 591
Bets, William I, 960
Betson, Elizabeth II, 336
Betson, Thomas II, 336
Betson, Thomas II, 461
Betsy, Elizabeth VI, 558
Betsy, Elizabeth VI, 584
Betteridge, Francis II, 441
Betteridge, William II, 441
Betterson, Benjamin II, 336
Betterson, Sarah II, 336
Betterton, Ann II, 336
Betterton, Ann II, 463
Betterton, Ann II, 506
Betterton, B??? II, 336
Betterton, Benj. II, 463
Betterton, Benj. II, 506
Betterton, Benjamin II, 336
Betterton, Benjamin II, 463
Betterton, Benjamin II, 667
Betterton, Chalkley II, 336
Betterton, Charles II, 463
Betterton, Charlotte VI, 798
Betterton, Delilah V, 409
Betterton, Hannah II, 336
Betterton, Hannah II, 463
Betterton, Hannah II, 631
Betterton, Jacob II, 336
Betterton, Jacob II, 463
Betterton, Martha II, 336
Betterton, Mary II, 336
Betterton, Mary II, 455
Betterton, Mary II, 463
Betterton, Mary II, 506
Betterton, Mary II, 667
Betterton, Nancy Jane V, 409
Betterton, Rachel II, 463
Betterton, Rachel II, 656
Betterton, Rebecca II, 336
Betterton, Rebecca II, 368
Betterton, Rebecca II, 463
Betterton, Rebecca II, 536
Betterton, Rebecca II, 557
Betterton, Sarah II, 336
Betterton, Sarah II, 463
Betterton, Sarah II, 491
Betterton, Thomas VI, 798
Betterton, William II, 336
Betterton, William II, 463
Betterton, Wm. II, 463
Betterton, Wm. V, 409
Betterton, Wm. G. V, 894
Bettie, Elizabeth VI, 81
Bettis, Bird IV, 900
Bettis, Evylin IV, 900
Bettis, Grace IV, 900
Bettis, Harry IV, 900
Bettis, Leonard IV, 900
Bettis, Lottie IV, 900
Bettis, Manten IV, 900
Bettle, Abigail II, 336
Bettle, Abigail II, 463
Bettle, Abigail II, 473
Bettle, Abigail II, 594
Bettle, Ann II, 336
Bettle, Ann II, 463
Bettle, Ann II, 491
Bettle, Ann II, 699
Bettle, Barbara II, 336
Bettle, Catharine II, 336
Bettle, Edward II, 336
Bettle, Edward II, 463
Bettle, Edward II, 464
Bettle, Edward II, 512
Bettle, Edward II, 699
Bettle, Edward II, 728
Bettle, Eliza Ann II, 464
Bettle, Eliza Ann II, 512
Bettle, Eliza Ann II, 699
Bettle, Elizabeth II, 336
Bettle, Elizabeth II, 463
Bettle, Elizabeth II, 618
Bettle, Esther II, 46
Bettle, Esther II, 336
Bettle, Everhard IV, 21
Bettle, Hannah II, 463
Bettle, Hannah II, 491
Bettle, Helen Biddle II, 837
Bettle, Helen Biddle II, 869
Bettle, James II, 463
Bettle, James II, 464
Bettle, James II, 512
Bettle, Jane II, 336
Bettle, Jane II, 463
Bettle, Jane II, 699
Bettle, Jane II, 728
Bettle, Jane II, 770
Bettle, Jane, Jr. II, 699
Bettle, John II, 46
Bettle, John II, 336
Bettle, John II, 463
Bettle, John II, 467
Bettle, John II, 497
Bettle, John II, 594
Bettle, Joseph II, 463
Bettle, Josiah II, 336
Bettle, Josiah II, 463
Bettle, Lydia II, 336
Bettle, Lydia II, 463
Bettle, Lydia II, 467
Bettle, Martha II, 463
Bettle, Martha II, 582
Bettle, Martha II, 652
Bettle, Martha II, 699
Bettle, Martha II, 728
Bettle, Mary II, 463
Bettle, Mary S. II, 837
Bettle, Mary S. II, 869
Bettle, Rachel II, 463
Bettle, Rachel II, 633
Bettle, Rachel II, 782
Bettle, Rebecca II, 463
Bettle, Rebecca II, 699
Bettle, Rebecca J. II, 464
Bettle, Rebecca J. II, 728
Bettle, Samuel II, 336
Bettle, Samuel II, 440
Bettle, Samuel II, 461
Bettle, Samuel II, 463
Bettle, Samuel II, 464
Bettle, Samuel II, 491
Bettle, Samuel II, 501
Bettle, Samuel II, 512
Bettle, Samuel II, 525
Bettle, Samuel II, 837
Bettle, Samuel II, 869
Bettle, Samuel D. II, 463
Bettle, Samuel, Jr. II, 463
Bettle, Samuel, Jr. II, 501
Bettle, Samuel, Jr. II, 728
Bettle, Samuel, Sr. II, 699
Bettle, Sarah II, 336
Bettle, Sarah II, 440
Bettle, Sarah II, 461
Bettle, Sarah II, 463
Bettle, Sarah II, 497
Bettle, Sarah II, 501
Bettle, Sarah II, 699
Bettle, Thomas II, 464
Bettle, Thomas II, 699
Bettle, William II, 336
Bettle, William II, 699
Bettle, Wm. II, 461
Bettle, Wm. II, 463
Bettle, Wm. II, 728
Bettle, Wm. II, 837
Bettle, Wm. II, 869
Betton, Eliza IV, 1246
Betton, Ella IV, 1246
Betton, Mary IV, 1246
Betts, ??? III, 29
Betts, ??? III, 118
Betts, Aaron I, 1007
Betts, Aaron I, 1010
Betts, Aaron V, 223
Betts, Aaron V, 369
Betts, Aaron V, 373
Betts, Aaron V, 374
Betts, Aaron V, 433
Betts, Aaron VI, 298
Betts, Aaron VI, 471
Betts, Aaron Homer V, 374
Betts, Aaron S. V, 373
Betts, Agnes IV, 1307
Betts, Albert V, 374
Betts, Albert Lawrence V, 374
Betts, Alice II, 728
Betts, Alice E. III, 29
Betts, Alice Eliza II, 464
Betts, Alice Eliza II, 837
Betts, Ann I, 1007
Betts, Ann I, 1010
Betts, Ann II, 441
Betts, Ann III, 394
Betts, Ann III, 395
Betts, Ann IV, 21
Betts, Ann V, 223
Betts, Ann V, 373
Betts, Ann V, 441
Betts, Anna II, 837
Betts, Anna II, 841
Betts, Anna V, 373
Betts, Anna V, 374
Betts, Anna C. V, 374
Betts, Anna H. V, 374
Betts, Anna L. II, 837
Betts, Anna T. II, 837
Betts, Anne I, 1007
Betts, Anne III, 33
Betts, Anthony III, 377
Betts, Anthony III, 479
Betts, Anthony III, 485
Betts, B. Franklin II, 837
Betts, B. Franklin, Jr. II, 837
Betts, Banister VI, 100
Betts, Bannaster VI, 100
Betts, Benjamin II, 822
Betts, Benjamin II, 837
Betts, Benjamin Franklin II, 782
Betts, Bertie IV, 1272
Betts, C. C. V, 374
Betts, C. Walter II, 837
Betts, Caroline V, 374
Betts, Caroline V, 406
Betts, Caroline V, 407
Betts, Caroline V, 659
Betts, Caroline J. V, 659
Betts, Carrie IV, 1272
Betts, Catharine II, 837
Betts, Catharine II, 866
Betts, Catharine Foulke II, 742
Betts, Charles Arthur V, 374
Betts, Charles E. III, 29
Betts, Charles M. II, 837
Betts, Charles M., Jr. II, 782
Betts, Chas M. II, 865
Betts, Chas. M. II, 837
Betts, Christopher V, 223
Betts, Christopher V, 249
Betts, Christopher V, 373
Betts, Christopher V, 374
Betts, Christopher V, 402
Betts, Christopher V, 406
Betts, Christopher W. V, 373
Betts, Daniel Webster V, 374
Betts, Deborah III, 32
Betts, Deborah III, 33
Betts, Deborah III, 118
Betts, Dollie IV, 1272
Betts, Edward II, 837
Betts, Edward II, 943
Betts, Edward T. II, 837
Betts, Edward T., Jr. II, 837
Betts, Edward Trump II, 782
Betts, Eliz M. III, 284
Betts, Eliza II, 728
Betts, Elizabeth II, 978
Betts, Elizabeth II, 992
Betts, Elizabeth II, 998
Betts, Elizabeth II, 1020
Betts, Elizabeth III, 29
Betts, Elizabeth III, 33
Betts, Elizabeth III, 479
Betts, Elizabeth IV, 678
Betts, Elizabeth V, 374
Betts, Elizabeth V, 407
Betts, Elizabeth V, 659
Betts, Elizabeth B. II, 1045
Betts, Elizabeth P. II, 782
Betts, Ellen S. II, 782
Betts, Ellen S. II, 837
Betts, Emila V, 407
Betts, Emily II, 803
Betts, Emily II, 820
Betts, Enoch IV, 21
Betts, Ernest F. II, 782
Betts, Esther II, 978
Betts, Esther II, 1045
Betts, Ethel II, 782
Betts, Eva Beth V, 374
Betts, Evaline V, 374
Betts, Franklin II, 865
Betts, Geo. Anson III, 29
Betts, George II, 1020
Betts, George V, 407
Betts, George E. V, 374
Betts, Grace II, 464
Betts, Grace II, 728
Betts, Grace II, 782
Betts, Grace II, 787
Betts, Grace II, 837
Betts, Grace II, 841
Betts, Grace II, 893
Betts, Grace II, 937
Betts, Grace II, 978
Betts, Grace II, 979
Betts, Grace IV, 1272
Betts, Hannah II, 837
Betts, Hannah II, 978
Betts, Hannah II, 998
Betts, Hannah Lownes II, 782
Betts, Hattie P. V, 550
Betts, Helen D. II, 837
Betts, Helen D. II, 865
Betts, Helen F. II, 837
Betts, Helen M. VI, 731
Betts, Helen M. VI, 739
Betts, Helen M. VI, 770
Betts, Hezekiah I, 960
Betts, Hezekiah VI, 298
Betts, Hezekiah VI, 299
Betts, Hezekiah VI, 471
Betts, Homer V, 374
Betts, Horner V, 374
Betts, Hurome IV, 1352
Betts, Isaac III, 29
Betts, Israel III, 395
Betts, James E. V, 374
Betts, James E. V, 659
Betts, James Edwin V, 374
Betts, James P. V, 373
Betts, Jane III, 33
Betts, Jane III, 377
Betts, Jane III, 395
Betts, Jane III, 431
Betts, Jane V, 407
Betts, Jane M. III, 254
Betts, Jane M. III, 357
Betts, Jeannette III, 29
Betts, John II, 280
Betts, John II, 782
Betts, John V, 550
Betts, John VI, 298
Betts, John VI, 471
Betts, John H. V, 374
Betts, John M. C. VI, 731
Betts, John Stebbins III, 29
Betts, Jonathan, Jr. II, 55
Betts, Joseph II, 1045
Betts, Joseph III, 29
Betts, Joseph III, 33
Betts, Joseph V, 407
Betts, LeRoy IV, 1307
Betts, Leroy Lewis IV, 1307
Betts, Letitia III, 483
Betts, Lillie V, 374
Betts, Lizzie V, 374
Betts, Lizzie V, 659
Betts, Lizzie Russel V, 659
Betts, Lot V, 407
Betts, Louisa G. II, 837
Betts, Louisa G. II, 865
Betts, Lucy C. II, 837
Betts, Lucy Campbell II, 782
Betts, Lydia II, 813
Betts, Lydia IV, 21
Betts, Lydia IV, 59
Betts, Lydia V, 223
Betts, Lydia V, 249
Betts, Lydia V, 374
Betts, Lydia V, 402
Betts, Lydia V, 406
Betts, Lydia C. VI, 681
Betts, Lydia Luella V, 374
Betts, Madison V, 374
Betts, Madison V, 406
Betts, Madison V, 659
Betts, Margaret II, 978
Betts, Margaret II, 1045
Betts, Margaret IV, 21
Betts, Margaret IV, 61
Betts, Margaret IV, 1272
Betts, Margaret Head II, 458
Betts, Margaret Head II, 464
Betts, Marguerite II, 782
Betts, Martha II, 1020
Betts, Martha Emily V, 374
Betts, Mary I, 1001
Betts, Mary I, 1007
Betts, Mary II, 458
Betts, Mary II, 464
Betts, Mary II, 782
Betts, Mary II, 822
Betts, Mary II, 837
Betts, Mary II, 893
Betts, Mary II, 908
Betts, Mary II, 943
Betts, Mary II, 978
Betts, Mary II, 988
Betts, Mary II, 1045

Betts, Mary III, 357
Betts, Mary III, 479
Betts, Mary III, 485
Betts, Mary IV, 582
Betts, Mary IV, 1024
Betts, Mary IV, 1030
Betts, Mary V, 223
Betts, Mary V, 373
Betts, Mary V, 374
Betts, Mary V, 407
Betts, Mary V, 476
Betts, Mary V, 659
Betts, Mary VI, 298
Betts, Mary VI, 471
Betts, Mary VI, 543
Betts, Mary Elizabeth VI, 731
Betts, Mary Elizabeth VI, 739
Betts, Mary Jane V, 373
Betts, Mary L. II, 464
Betts, Mary L. II, 1045
Betts, Mary Olevia V, 374
Betts, Mary Rodman II, 837
Betts, Mary Seal II, 837
Betts, Mary Seal II, 943
Betts, Mercy II, 978
Betts, Mercy II, 1012
Betts, Mercy VI, 553
Betts, Meriam II, 978
Betts, Merriam II, 978
Betts, Merriam II, 1012
Betts, Mertie May II, 837
Betts, Mertie May II, 843
Betts, Missouri V, 374
Betts, Morris C. VI, 731
Betts, Morris C. VI, 739
Betts, Morris Cotsgrave VI, 731
Betts, Morris Cotsgrave VI, 770
Betts, Mount Pleasant VI, 299
Betts, Myra A. III, 29
Betts, Nancy V, 433
Betts, Norman S. II, 782
Betts, Patience V, 407
Betts, Pemberton S. II, 837
Betts, Pemberton Smith II, 782
Betts, Phebe II, 441
Betts, Priscilla V, 373
Betts, Priscilla V, 374
Betts, Priscilla V, 433
Betts, Priscilla E. V, 373
Betts, Rachel II, 978
Betts, Rachel II, 988
Betts, Rachel II, 1023
Betts, Rachel II, 1043
Betts, Rachel VI, 298
Betts, Rachel VI, 471
Betts, Rachel Alice V, 374
Betts, Rebecca V, 407
Betts, Rebecca A. V, 374
Betts, Rebecca A. V, 406
Betts, Rebecca Ann V, 374
Betts, Rebecca C. II, 782
Betts, Rebecca C. II, 837
Betts, Rebecca P. II, 837
Betts, Rebecca P. II, 919
Betts, Richard II, 978
Betts, Richard III, 33
Betts, Richard K. II, 837
Betts, Richard K. II, 841
Betts, Richard K. II, 893
Betts, Richard Kinsey II, 464
Betts, Richard Kinsey II, 728
Betts, Richard Kinsey II, 782
Betts, Richard Kinsey II, 837
Betts, Russel V, 374
Betts, Ruth Ann, Jr. II, 837
Betts, Ruth Anna II, 782
Betts, Ruth Anna II, 837
Betts, Ruth Anna II, 937
Betts, Sadie V, 374
Betts, Sallie IV, 678
Betts, Samuel II, 978
Betts, Samuel II, 979
Betts, Samuel III, 483
Betts, Samuel C. II, 464
Betts, Samuel C. II, 728
Betts, Samuel C. II, 787
Betts, Samuel C. II, 837
Betts, Samuel C. II, 841
Betts, Samuel C. II, 893
Betts, Samuel C. II, 937
Betts, Samuel Carey II, 782
Betts, Samuel Cary II, 837
Betts, Samuel D. II, 728
Betts, Sarah II, 728
Betts, Sarah II, 782
Betts, Sarah III, 33
Betts, Sarah III, 377
Betts, Sarah III, 479
Betts, Sarah IV, 21
Betts, Sarah IV, 51
Betts, Sarah Ann II, 280
Betts, Sarah Ann II, 298
Betts, Sarah Ann III, 33
Betts, Sarah Ann IV, 21
Betts, Sarah Ellin V, 374
Betts, Sarah Emaline V, 374
Betts, Sarah H. II, 464
Betts, Sarah Harvey II, 787
Betts, Sarah Harvey II, 837
Betts, Sarah K. II, 837
Betts, Sarah Kirk II, 822
Betts, Sarah W. II, 837
Betts, Sarah W. II, 896
Betts, Silas III, 357
Betts, Simes II, 978
Betts, Simes II, 1023
Betts, Sims II, 1043
Betts, Stephen II, 336
Betts, Stephen II, 978
Betts, Stephen II, 998
Betts, Stephen III, 33
Betts, Stephen V, 407
Betts, Stephen, Jr. II, 978
Betts, Stephen, Jr. II, 998
Betts, Susan V, 374
Betts, Susan R. III, 29
Betts, Susanna I, 1007
Betts, Susanna I, 1012
Betts, Susanna VI, 298
Betts, Susanna VI, 471
Betts, Susannah II, 978
Betts, Susannah III, 33
Betts, Susannah V, 373
Betts, Susannah VI, 298
Betts, T. E. IV, 1307
Betts, Thomas II, 458
Betts, Thomas II, 464
Betts, Thomas II, 978
Betts, Thomas II, 1045
Betts, Thomas III, 33
Betts, Thomas Wade V, 374
Betts, Thomas Wade V, 659
Betts, Wade V, 374
Betts, Walter G. V, 374
Betts, William I, 960
Betts, William I, 1007
Betts, William III, 33
Betts, William V, 223
Betts, William V, 373
Betts, William V, 407
Betts, William VI, 298
Betts, William VI, 340
Betts, William VI, 471
Betts, William VI, 543
Betts, William A. M. V, 374
Betts, William C. V, 374
Betts, William S. V, 374
Betts, William, Jr. VI, 299
Betts, Wm. V, 441
Betts, Wm. A. M. V, 374
Betts, Wm. C. II, 464
Betts, Wm. C. II, 728
Betts, Wm. C. II, 837
Betts, Wm. C. II, 937
Betts, Wm. C. V, 374
Betts, Wm. Carey II, 782
Betts, Wm. P. II, 837
Betts, Wm. P. II, 843
Betts, Zachariah II, 458
Betts, Zachariah II, 464
Betts, Zachariah II, 978
Betts, Zachariah II, 979
Betts, Zachariah II, 988
Betts, Zachariah II, 1012
Bettson, Ann II, 336
Bettson, Elizabeth II, 336
Bettson, Sarah II, 336
Bettson, Thomas II, 336
Bettson, Thomas, Jr. II, 336
Betty, Elizabeth VI, 543
Bettz, Hattie P. V, 550
Betz, Abraham VI, 878
Betz, Agnes IV, 1307
Betz, Berlinda W. VI, 878
Betz, Henry IV, 695
Betz, LeRoy IV, 1307
Betz, Leroy Lewis IV, 1307
Betz, Mary Ann IV, 695
Betz, Nettie IV, 695
Betz, Sallie IV, 678
Betz, T. E. IV, 1307
Betz, William VI, 878
Beuhler, Myrtle V, 613
Beuhler, Myrtle V, 632
Beulah, Isaac II, 464
Beulah, John II, 464
Beulah, Nathaniel II, 464
Beulah, Rachel II, 464
Bevan, ??? IV, 137
Bevan, Aaron IV, 511
Bevan, Abel IV, 511
Bevan, Abel V, 298
Bevan, Abel V, 476
Bevan, Abel V, 550
Bevan, Amora V, 550
Bevan, Ann II, 336
Bevan, Ann II, 464
Bevan, Anna V, 550
Bevan, Anna A. V, 550
Bevan, Anne II, 501
Bevan, Anora V, 550
Bevan, Anora V, 659
Bevan, Aubrey II, 464
Bevan, Benj. II, 464
Bevan, Bessie E. V, 550
Bevan, Betty Jean V, 659
Bevan, Carlton A. V, 550
Bevan, Charlotte V, 476
Bevan, Charlotte V, 550
Bevan, Charlotte F. V, 476
Bevan, Charlotte T. V, 476
Bevan, Charlotte T. V, 550
Bevan, David II, 336
Bevan, David IV, 511
Bevan, David C. IV, 511
Bevan, Donald Herbert V, 550
Bevan, Edward E. V, 550
Bevan, Edward Emmet V, 894
Bevan, Edward Emmett V, 894
Bevan, Edward Emmitt V, 550
Bevan, Eleanor II, 464
Bevan, Eleanor IV, 140
Bevan, Eleanor IV, 511
Bevan, Eleanor IV, 537
Bevan, Eleanor VI, 365
Bevan, Elizabeth IV, 369
Bevan, Elizabeth IV, 511
Bevan, Elizabeth V, 298
Bevan, Elizabeth V, 476
Bevan, Ella V, 577
Bevan, Ella H. V, 550
Bevan, Elwood Emet V, 550
Bevan, Emma V, 476
Bevan, Emmet V, 550
Bevan, Emmet V, 659
Bevan, Emmet Eugene V, 550
Bevan, Emmett V, 550
Bevan, Eunice IV, 320
Bevan, Eunice IV, 328
Bevan, Eunice IV, 369
Bevan, Eunice IV, 511
Bevan, Eunice IV, 517
Bevan, Euphenia A. V, 476
Bevan, Eva V, 550
Bevan, Evan VI, 365
Bevan, Florence Emma V, 550
Bevan, Frank V, 550
Bevan, Frank V, 659
Bevan, Franklin V, 550
Bevan, Franklin V, 894
Bevan, Geneva W. V, 550
Bevan, Gulielma IV, 511
Bevan, Hannah L. V, 476
Bevan, Hannah Louisa V, 476
Bevan, Hannah Louisa V, 550
Bevan, Hansel Malinda V, 476
Bevan, Harlan J. V, 550
Bevan, Horace V, 550
Bevan, Horace L. V, 476
Bevan, Horace L. V, 550
Bevan, Hugh Isaac V, 550
Bevan, Jacob II, 441
Bevan, James H. V, 894
Bevan, Jane IV, 511
Bevan, Jane V, 550
Bevan, Jane V, 659
Bevan, Jane V, 894
Bevan, John IV, 140
Bevan, John IV, 511
Bevan, John V, 298
Bevan, John V, 476
Bevan, John VI, 365
Bevan, Joseph IV, 369
Bevan, Joseph IV, 511
Bevan, Joseph A. IV, 399
Bevan, Joseph A. IV, 511
Bevan, Joseph A. IV, 528
Bevan, Joseph Gurney VI, 569
Bevan, Lewis IV, 511
Bevan, Lewis V, 476
Bevan, Lewis V, 550
Bevan, Lewis V, 659
Bevan, Lewis V, 677
Bevan, Lewis V, 894
Bevan, Lewis H. V, 550
Bevan, Lewis H. V, 659
Bevan, Lewis H. V, 894
Bevan, Lewis, Jr. V, 550
Bevan, Lucille R. V, 550
Bevan, Lula V, 550
Bevan, Lydia IV, 140
Bevan, Lydia IV, 511
Bevan, Lydia V, 298
Bevan, Lydia V, 476
Bevan, Lydia VI, 365
Bevan, Lydia VI, 440
Bevan, Lydia Ann IV, 369
Bevan, Lydia Ann IV, 511
Bevan, Lydia E. V, 476
Bevan, Lydia Ellen V, 476
Bevan, Lydia Ellen V, 550
Bevan, Maria IV, 369
Bevan, Maria IV, 399
Bevan, Maria IV, 511
Bevan, Maria IV, 528
Bevan, Mariah IV, 511
Bevan, Martha IV, 369
Bevan, Martha IV, 511
Bevan, Martha IV, 545
Bevan, Martha VI, 365
Bevan, Martha VI, 368
Bevan, Mary II, 464
Bevan, Mary II, 501
Bevan, Mary II, 526
Bevan, Mary IV, 511
Bevan, Mary V, 476
Bevan, Mary V, 550
Bevan, Mary E. IV, 511
Bevan, Mary Elizabeth IV, 511
Bevan, Mary Genevieve V, 550
Bevan, Mary J. V, 476
Bevan, Mary Jane V, 476
Bevan, Mary Jane V, 492
Bevan, Mary Jane V, 550
Bevan, Mary Jane V, 613
Bevan, Mary Jane V, 622
Bevan, Mina J. V, 659
Bevan, Myra F. V, 550
Bevan, Nancy IV, 511
Bevan, Nancy IV, 524
Bevan, Naomi IV, 320
Bevan, Naomi IV, 369
Bevan, Naomi IV, 511
Bevan, Naomi IV, 539
Bevan, Naomi V, 550
Bevan, Naomi V, 659
Bevan, Naomi V, 677
Bevan, Naomi H. V, 550
Bevan, Naomi Hadley V, 659
Bevan, Nida E. V, 550
Bevan, Nina V, 577
Bevan, Nina E. V, 550
Bevan, Orlando V, 550
Bevan, Orlando V, 577
Bevan, Orlando V, 659
Bevan, Orlando V, 894
Bevan, Orlando Franklin V, 550
Bevan, Orville V, 550
Bevan, Orville V, 659
Bevan, Orville Mary Louise V, 550
Bevan, Owen IV, 140
Bevan, Owen IV, 511
Bevan, Owen V, 298
Bevan, Owen V, 476
Bevan, Owen V, 550
Bevan, Owen VI, 365
Bevan, Phamy Ann V, 476
Bevan, Phamy Ann V, 550
Bevan, Phamyann IV, 511
Bevan, Phanny Ann V, 476
Bevan, Phany Ann V, 550
Bevan, Phemia VI, 365
Bevan, Phineas R. V, 476
Bevan, Phinehas R. V, 550
Bevan, Ralph V, 550
Bevan, Ralph A. V, 550
Bevan, Reba Jane V, 659
Bevan, Robert V, 476
Bevan, Robert V, 550
Bevan, Samuel II, 197
Bevan, Samuel IV, 320
Bevan, Samuel IV, 511
Bevan, Samuel V, 298
Bevan, Samuel V, 476
Bevan, Samuel VI, 365
Bevan, Samuel VI, 455
Bevan, Sarah II, 55
Bevan, Sarah II, 85
Bevan, Sarah II, 464
Bevan, Sarah Elizabeth V, 476
Bevan, Stacey V, 550
Bevan, Stacy IV, 140
Bevan, Stacy IV, 320
Bevan, Stacy IV, 328
Bevan, Stacy IV, 369
Bevan, Stacy IV, 378
Bevan, Stacy IV, 511
Bevan, Stacy V, 298
Bevan, Stacy V, 476
Bevan, Stacy V, 550
Bevan, Stacy VI, 365
Bevan, Stacy VI, 440
Bevan, Stacy Ewing IV, 511
Bevan, Stacy, Jr. IV, 320
Bevan, Susanna II, 55
Bevan, Susanna II, 197
Bevan, Susanna IV, 140
Bevan, Susanna IV, 511
Bevan, Susannah II, 197
Bevan, Susannah IV, 369
Bevan, Susannah VI, 365
Bevan, Susannah VI, 455
Bevan, Wm. O. V, 659
Bevans, Ann II, 464
Bevans, Aubrey II, 464
Bevans, Elizabeth IV, 511
Bevans, Elizabeth IV, 548
Bevans, Jane IV, 547
Bevans, Stacy IV, 547
Bevellymen, Mr. Arthur IV, 1307
Bevellymen, Mrs. ??? IV, 1307
Bevely, Clementina I, 210
Bever, John V, 986
Bever, Lucinda V, 986
Beverhammer, A. J. V, 986
Beveridge, David II, 464
Beveridge, Mary II, 464
Beveridge, Mary II, 516
Beverly, Anthony VI, 798
Beverly, Jane VI, 798
Beverly, Mary I, 709
Bevin, Phame VI, 365
Bevin, Phame VI, 426
Bevin, Samuel II, 22
Bevin, Samuel II, 197
Bevin, Samuel II, 206
Bevin, Sarah II, 55
Bevin, Susanna II, 197
Bevin, Susanna II, 206
Bevin, Susannah II, 22
Bevington, Walter IV, 175
Bevington, Walter B. IV, 175
Bewen, Robert II, 336
Bewen, Thomas II, 336
Bewley, ??? III, 395
Bewley, Ann Mary V, 894
Bewley, Anna V, 894
Bewley, Anna Mary V, 894
Bewley, Arthur V, 894
Bewley, Arthur V, 912
Bewley, C. Arthur V, 894
Bewley, Charles Arthur V, 894
Bewley, Chas. Arthur V, 894
Bewley, Clifton II, 728
Bewley, Edward Caroll V, 894
Bewley, Fanny V, 894
Bewley, Frederick Winslow V, 894
Bewley, Geo. V, 894
Bewley, George V, 894
Bewley, George, Jr. V, 894
Bewley, Gilbert II, 699
Bewley, Gilbert II, 728
Bewley, Helen Margaret V, 894
Bewley, Isaac II, 464
Bewley, Isaac II, 488
Bewley, Isabella V, 894
Bewley, Isabelle V, 894
Bewley, Isabelle V, 912
Bewley, Isabelle H. V, 894
Bewley, John II, 782
Bewley, John II, 838
Bewley, Mary V, 894
Bewley, Mary Ann V, 894
Bewley, Mary Ann V, 898
Bewley, Mary E. V, 894
Bewley, Minnie V, 894
Bewley, Nathan II, 336
Bewley, Nathan II, 464
Bewley, Nathan II, 488
Bewley, Rachel II, 464
Bewley, Rachel II, 488
Bewley, Rebecca II, 336
Bewley, Sarah II, 464
Bewley, Susannah II, 782
Bewley, Susannah II, 838
Bewley, Thomas V, 894
Bewley, Thomas, Jr. V, 894
Bewley, Thos. V, 894
Bewley, Thos. Wm. V, 894
Bewley, Wm. II, 728
Bewly, Ann Mary V, 894
Bewly, Anna V, 894
Bewly, Edward Caroll V, 894
Bewly, George V, 894
Bewly, Isaac II, 464
Bewly, Mary V, 894
Bewly, Nathan II, 464
Bewly, Rachel II, 464
Bewly, Sarah II, 464
Beyer, Jacob V, 24
Beyer, Margaret V, 24
Beyrie, Edwin V, 452
Bezer, Asa II, 464
Bezer, Asa VI, 470

Bezer, Asaph II, 464
Bezer, Dinah II, 464
Bezer, Dinah VI, 470
Bezer, Edith II, 464
Bezer, Elisabeth II, 464
Bezer, Elizabeth II, 464
Bezer, Gulielma II, 464
Bezer, John II, 464
Bezer, John VI, 470
Bezor, Asaph II, 464
Bezor, Dinah II, 464
Bezor, Dinah VI, 486
Bezor, Edith II, 464
Bezor, Edith VI, 470
Bezor, Edith VI, 481
Bezor, Elisabeth II, 464
Bezor, Elizabeth VI, 470
Bezor, Elizabeth VI, 480
Bezor, Gulielma II, 464
Bezor, Gulielma VI, 470
Bezor, Gulielma VI, 486
Bezor, John II, 464
Bezor, John VI, 486
Bians, Ann II, 978
Biardot, Alice III, 132
Bias, Clarence V, 659
Bias, Jennings V, 659
Bib, Rebecka II, 441
Bib, Thomas II, 441
Bibb, Ann II, 441
Bibb, Bunner II, 441
Bibb, Ruth II, 441
Bibb, Thomas II, 441
Bibb, Wd. Ruth II, 441
Bibby, Bridget II, 464
Bibby, Bridget II, 562
Bible, Anna III, 398
Bible, Elizabeth III, 398
Bibles, Ann III, 487
Bichart, Elizabeth V, 476
Bichart, Jacob V, 476
Bickat, William VI, 365
Bickel, Anna M. V, 986
Bickel, Annie V, 986
Bickel, Annie M. V, 986
Bickel, Annie M. V, 995
Bickel, Denard W. V, 986
Bickel, Eliza V, 986
Bickel, Fassett V, 986
Bickenstaff, Hannah III, 33
Bicker, Annie V, 986
Bickerdike, Esther II, 979
Bickerdike, Gideon II, 979
Bickerdike, Jael II, 979
Bickerdike, Jael II, 980
Bickerdike, Mary II, 978
Bickerdike, Mary II, 979
Bickerson, Ann II, 336
Bickerson, Sarah II, 336
Bickerstaff, Hannah III, 41
Bickerton, Ann II, 337
Bickerton, Benjamin II, 337
Bicket, Clara V, 24
Bicket, Clara V, 95
Bickett, Donald V, 659
Bickett, Donald V, 703
Bickett, Kathryn V, 659
Bickett, Kathryn V, 703
Bickham, Abel II, 464
Bickham, Abiah II, 464
Bickham, Caleb II, 337
Bickham, Caleb II, 464
Bickham, Elizabeth II, 838
Bickham, Elizabeth II, 893
Bickham, Elizabeth II, 905
Bickham, Elizabeth Hopper II, 838
Bickham, Joseph II, 464
Bickham, Rachel II, 464
Bickham, Sarah II, 337
Bickham, Sarah II, 782
Bickham, Sarah II, 838
Bickham, Thomas II, 464
Bickhart, Anna L. V, 659
Bickhart, Elizabeth V, 476
Bickhart, Elizabeth V, 659
Bickhart, Jacob V, 476
Bickhart, Jacob V, 659
Bickley, Abraham II, 166
Bickley, Abraham II, 197
Bickley, Abraham II, 252
Bickley, Abraham II, 261
Bickley, Abraham II, 337
Bickley, Abraham II, 464
Bickley, Abraham II, 550
Bickley, Dorothy II, 197
Bickley, Dorothy II, 237
Bickley, Dorothy II, 261
Bickley, Eliza II, 197
Bickley, Eliza II, 252
Bickley, Elizabeth II, 166
Bickley, Elizabeth II, 197
Bickley, Elizabeth II, 337
Bickley, Hannah II, 464
Bickley, Hannah II, 526
Bickley, Hannah M. II, 838
Bickley, Hannah M. II, 899
Bickley, Mary II, 464
Bickley, Mary II, 669
Bickley, Mary IV, 1233
Bickley, Mary E. IV, 1233
Bickley, Samuel II, 197
Bickley, Samuel II, 252
Bickley, Susanna II, 464
Bickley, Susanna II, 550
Bickley, Susannah II, 197
Bickley, Susannah III, 33
Bickley, Thomas II, 166
Bickley, William II, 166
Bickley, William C. III, 33
Bicknell, Alvin Bicknel II, 838
Bicknell, Clarence W. II, 838
Bicknell, Edith Linda II, 838
Bicknell, Elizabeth R. II, 838
Bicknell, Ella R. II, 838
Bicknell, Harold S. II, 838
Bicknell, Jennie H. II, 838
Bicknell, John T. II, 838
Bicknell, Lilian P. II, 838
Bicknell, Ralph II, 838
Bicknell, Sarah A. II, 838
Bicknell, Wm. W. II, 838
Bickner, Augustus V, 986
Bickner, Catharine E. IV, 1272
Bickner, Charles J. IV, 1272
Biddle, Abigail II, 464
Biddle, Absolom I, 374
Biddle, Alice M. II, 853
Biddle, Ann II, 464
Biddle, Ann II, 465
Biddle, Ann II, 686
Biddle, Anna II, 465
Biddle, Anna II, 728
Biddle, Anna II, 756
Biddle, Anna II, 780
Biddle, Anna II, 782
Biddle, Anna II, 783
Biddle, Anna II, 794
Biddle, Anna II, 833
Biddle, Anna II, 838
Biddle, Anna II, 899
Biddle, Anna M. II, 838
Biddle, Anna M. II, 894
Biddle, Anna Mary II, 783
Biddle, Anna Mary II, 838
Biddle, Anna Mary II, 894
Biddle, Anna Mary II, 921
Biddle, Anna McIlvain II, 838
Biddle, Anne II, 465
Biddle, Anne II, 663
Biddle, Anne II, 699
Biddle, Anne II, 728
Biddle, Anne II, 838
Biddle, Anne, Jr. II, 465
Biddle, Caroline C. II, 838
Biddle, Caroline Cooper II, 782
Biddle, Charles II, 780
Biddle, Charles Miller II, 782
Biddle, Charlotte II, 197
Biddle, Chas. M. II, 833
Biddle, Chas. M. II, 838
Biddle, Chas. M. II, 852
Biddle, Chas. M. II, 894
Biddle, Clement II, 337
Biddle, Clement II, 464
Biddle, Clement II, 465
Biddle, Clement II, 634
Biddle, Clement II, 728
Biddle, Clement II, 782
Biddle, Clement II, 838
Biddle, Clement II, 899
Biddle, Clement II, 927
Biddle, Clement II, 933
Biddle, Clement M. II, 838
Biddle, Clement M. II, 889
Biddle, Clement M., Jr. II, 782
Biddle, Clement M., Jr. II, 838
Biddle, Clement Miller II, 782
Biddle, Clement, Jr. II, 465
Biddle, Clement, Jr. II, 728
Biddle, Clement, Jr. II, 838
Biddle, Edward II, 337
Biddle, Edward C. II, 728
Biddle, Edward Taggart II, 838
Biddle, Edward Taggart II, 899
Biddle, Eliza III, 83
Biddle, Elizabeth II, 337
Biddle, Elizabeth II, 465
Biddle, Elizabeth II, 699
Biddle, Elizabeth II, 728
Biddle, Elizabeth II, 741
Biddle, Elizabeth II, 794
Biddle, Elizabeth II, 838
Biddle, Elizabeth II, 852
Biddle, Elizabeth B. II, 838
Biddle, Elizabeth B. II, 864
Biddle, Elizabeth C. II, 728
Biddle, Elizabeth C. II, 741
Biddle, Elizabeth E. II, 789
Biddle, Elizabeth E. II, 838
Biddle, Elizabeth E. II, 852
Biddle, Elizabeth Y. II, 853
Biddle, Elizabeth, Jr. II, 465
Biddle, Emily III, 33
Biddle, Frances II, 337
Biddle, Frances II, 699
Biddle, Frances II, 728
Biddle, Frances II, 741
Biddle, Frances III, 33
Biddle, Frances C. II, 838
Biddle, Frances C. II, 869
Biddle, Frances Canby II, 797
Biddle, Francis II, 337
Biddle, Grace IV, 1307
Biddle, Hannah II, 737
Biddle, Hannah II, 782
Biddle, Hannah II, 833
Biddle, Hannah II, 838
Biddle, Hannah II, 894
Biddle, Hannah B. II, 838
Biddle, Hannah B. II, 864
Biddle, Hannah Gillam Albertson II, 853
Biddle, Hannah N. II, 838
Biddle, Hannah N. II, 940
Biddle, Helen II, 782
Biddle, Helen II, 797
Biddle, Helen IV, 175
Biddle, Helen IV, 219
Biddle, Helen B. II, 838
Biddle, Helen B. II, 929
Biddle, Henry C. II, 838
Biddle, Henry C. II, 894
Biddle, Henry Canby II, 783
Biddle, Henry Canby, Jr. II, 783
Biddle, Hugh McIlvain II, 783
Biddle, James C. II, 728
Biddle, James Canby II, 337
Biddle, James Marsh II, 1069
Biddle, James Marsh II, 1073
Biddle, Jane II, 337
Biddle, Jane II, 464
Biddle, Jane II, 465
Biddle, Jane II, 1069
Biddle, Jane II, 1073
Biddle, John II, 337
Biddle, John II, 464
Biddle, John II, 465
Biddle, John II, 497
Biddle, John II, 611
Biddle, John II, 634
Biddle, John II, 728
Biddle, John II, 741
Biddle, John R. II, 465
Biddle, John R. II, 1069
Biddle, John Rowen II, 465
Biddle, John W. II, 699
Biddle, Joseph II, 337
Biddle, Joseph II, 728
Biddle, Joseph, Jr. II, 197
Biddle, Lillian II, 783
Biddle, Lucy II, 782
Biddle, Lucy II, 838
Biddle, Lucy II, 889
Biddle, Lydia II, 464
Biddle, Lydia II, 782
Biddle, Lydia II, 1069
Biddle, Lydia II, 1073
Biddle, Lydia C. II, 838
Biddle, Lydia C. II, 889
Biddle, Lydia, Jr. II, 838
Biddle, Margaret II, 337
Biddle, Martha II, 337
Biddle, Martha II, 465
Biddle, Martha II, 728
Biddle, Martha II, 782
Biddle, Martha II, 838
Biddle, Mary II, 197
Biddle, Mary II, 259
Biddle, Mary II, 337
Biddle, Mary II, 464
Biddle, Mary II, 465
Biddle, Mary II, 728
Biddle, Mary II, 782
Biddle, Mary II, 783
Biddle, Mary II, 786
Biddle, Mary II, 838
Biddle, Mary II, 863
Biddle, Mary II, 899
Biddle, Mary II, 942
Biddle, Mary B. II, 838
Biddle, Mary B. II, 927
Biddle, Mary B. III, 33
Biddle, Mary S. II, 737
Biddle, Owen II, 337
Biddle, Owen II, 464
Biddle, Owen II, 465
Biddle, Owen II, 663
Biddle, Owen II, 667
Biddle, Owen II, 782
Biddle, Owen II, 838
Biddle, Owen II, 933
Biddle, Owen, Jr. II, 465
Biddle, Rachel II, 465
Biddle, Rachel II, 728
Biddle, Rachel II, 756
Biddle, Rachel II, 838
Biddle, Rachel II, 899
Biddle, Rachel IV, 800
Biddle, Rachel C. II, 838
Biddle, Rachel C. II, 942
Biddle, Rachel M. II, 838
Biddle, Rachel M. II, 940
Biddle, Rebecca II, 337
Biddle, Rebecca II, 464
Biddle, Rebecca II, 465
Biddle, Rebecca II, 699
Biddle, Rebecca II, 728
Biddle, Rebecca Field II, 699
Biddle, Rebecca Owen II, 465
Biddle, Rebecca Owen II, 667
Biddle, Robert II, 465
Biddle, Robert II, 783
Biddle, Robert II, 794
Biddle, Robert II, 838
Biddle, Robert II, 894
Biddle, Robert II, 899
Biddle, Robert Ralston II, 783
Biddle, Robert, Jr. II, 782
Biddle, Robert, Jr. II, 838
Biddle, Ruth I, 374
Biddle, Ruth I, 400
Biddle, Samuel II, 337
Biddle, Samuel II, 699
Biddle, Samuel II, 728
Biddle, Sandwith II, 737
Biddle, Sarah II, 197
Biddle, Sarah II, 337
Biddle, Sarah II, 440
Biddle, Sarah II, 464
Biddle, Sarah II, 465
Biddle, Sarah II, 611
Biddle, Sarah II, 620
Biddle, Sarah II, 663
Biddle, Sarah II, 667
Biddle, Sarah II, 728
Biddle, Sarah II, 736
Biddle, Sarah II, 782
Biddle, Sarah II, 838
Biddle, Sarah II, 933
Biddle, Sarah Ann II, 316
Biddle, Sarah Anna II, 316
Biddle, Sarah Anna II, 324
Biddle, Sarah S. II, 838
Biddle, Sarah S. II, 933
Biddle, Sarah Saunders II, 782
Biddle, Sharon Hill II, 838
Biddle, Susan W. II, 838
Biddle, Susan W. II, 927
Biddle, Tacey II, 464
Biddle, Thomas II, 197
Biddle, Thomas II, 337
Biddle, Thomas II, 465
Biddle, William II, 337
Biddle, William II, 464
Biddle, William C. II, 465
Biddle, William C. III, 33
Biddle, William Canby, Jr. II, 782
Biddle, Wm. II, 611
Biddle, Wm. II, 699
Biddle, Wm. II, 728
Biddle, Wm. II, 741
Biddle, Wm. A. II, 853
Biddle, Wm. C. II, 465
Biddle, Wm. C. II, 782
Biddle, Wm. C. II, 838
Biddle, Wm. C. II, 869
Biddle, Wm. C. II, 942
Biddle, Wm. Canby II, 838
Biddle, Wm. Canby II, 899
Biddle, Wm. Canby II, 940
Biddle, Wm. J. II, 853
Biddle, Wm. W. II, 838
Biddle, Wm. W. III, 33
Biddle, Wm. Walter II, 838
Biddle, Wm. Walter II, 899
Biddlecomb, William V, 550
Biddlecum, Anna M. V. V, 550
Biddlecum, Homer V, 550
Biddlecum, Homer G. V, 550
Biddlecum, Jason V, 550
Biddlecum, Martha V, 550
Biddlecum, William V, 550
Biddlecum, Wm. V, 550
Biddock, Dinah I, 374
Biddock, Mary I, 374
Bidgood, Ann II, 954
Bidgood, Ann II, 979
Bidgood, Anna J. IV, 1307
Bidgood, Burough II, 1043
Bidgood, Elizabeth II, 979
Bidgood, Elizabeth II, 980
Bidgood, Elizabeth II, 1043
Bidgood, Essther II, 979
Bidgood, Esther II, 954
Bidgood, Esther II, 979
Bidgood, Esther II, 1019
Bidgood, Esther II, 1043
Bidgood, Geo. R. IV, 1307
Bidgood, Hannah II, 954
Bidgood, Hannah II, 979
Bidgood, Hannah II, 1001
Bidgood, Hannah II, 1008
Bidgood, Helen M. IV, 1307
Bidgood, Isabella IV, 1307
Bidgood, J. W. IV, 1307
Bidgood, James Thornton II, 465
Bidgood, Joseph II, 465
Bidgood, Joseph II, 1043
Bidgood, Lucy II, 1043
Bidgood, Mae IV, 1307
Bidgood, Mae E. IV, 1307
Bidgood, Mary II, 954
Bidgood, Mary II, 974
Bidgood, Mary II, 979
Bidgood, May IV, 1307
Bidgood, Mrs. Anna J. IV, 1307
Bidgood, Paul W. IV, 1307
Bidgood, Phebe II, 979
Bidgood, Phebe II, 1035
Bidgood, Pheby II, 954
Bidgood, Richard II, 954
Bidgood, Richard II, 979
Bidgood, Richard II, 995
Bidgood, Richard II, 1001
Bidgood, Richard II, 1043
Bidgood, Samuel II, 954
Bidgood, Samuel II, 1043
Bidgood, Samuel Burrows II, 465
Bidgood, Samuel Burrows VI, 731
Bidgood, Sarah II, 954
Bidgood, Sarah II, 979
Bidgood, Sarah II, 984
Bidgood, Thornton II, 1043
Bidgood, Wd. Hannah II, 979
Bidgood, Wd. Hannah II, 1043
Bidgood, William II, 954
Bidgood, William II, 1043
Bidgood, Wm. II, 979
Bidgood, Wm. II, 1008
Bidgood, Wm. II, 1035
Bidgood, Wm. IV, 1307
Bidgood, Wm., Jr. II, 979
Bidlake, Frank S. IV, 1307
Bidlake, George L. IV, 1307
Bidlake, Sarah A. IV, 1307
Bidock, Dinah I, 374
Bidwell, Charles Hawley II, 960
Bidwell, Luella II, 960
Bidwell, Luella II, 1052
Bidwell, Luella Edna II, 960
Bield, Alexander II, 979
Bield, Ann II, 979
Bield, Ann II, 1035
Bield, Thomas II, 979
Bield, Thomas Watson II, 979
Biele, Alma III, 33
Biele, Alma III, 202
Biele, Charles F. III, 33
Biele, Charles F. III, 202
Biele, Friedericke III, 33
Biele, Friedericke Prediger III, 202
Bierer, Evangeline VI, 377
Bierer, Wm. VI, 377
Bierly, Elizabeth Julia II, 731
Biernson, Thormod II, 838
Biernson, Tormod II, 838
Bierson, Thormod II, 838
Bigbie, Frances W. VI, 878
Bigbie, Lucy G. VI, 878
Bigbie, Martha W. VI, 883
Bigbie, William VI, 878
Bigbie, William VI, 883
Bigby, Frances W. VI, 798
Bigby, William VI, 798
Bigelow, Ann III, 273
Bigelow, Chas. C. III, 316
Bigelow, Laura E. III, 316
Bigelow, Laura P. VI, 913
Bigelow, Mary III, 316
Bigelow, Mary Eastman III, 316
Bigford, Sarah V, 894

Bigford, Sarah V, 912
Bigger, David VI, 878
Bigger, David W. VI, 878
Bigger, Nancy Ann VI, 878
Bigger, Polly E. VI, 878
Biggers, Matilda VI, 299
Biggers, Matilda VI, 338
Biggs, ??? VI, 12
Biggs, Dora IV, 1148
Biggs, Emmerine V, 24
Biggs, Grace V, 659
Biggs, Jesse IV, 1272
Biggs, John VI, 11
Biggs, John VI, 12
Biggs, Lucy T. VI, 798
Biggs, Lula M. IV, 1202
Biggs, Lulu IV, 1202
Biggs, M. J. IV, 1202
Biggs, Mary V, 659
Biggs, Mary E. IV, 1202
Biggs, Meaker J. IV, 1202
Biggs, Ralph V, 24
Biggs, Robert VI, 798
Bigham, Vora V, 986
Bigham, Wm. V, 986
Bigland, Amos III, 33
Bigley, Susannah III, 33
Bigley, William C. III, 33
Biglow, Sarah V, 986
Bigoney, Eva P. III, 33
Bigoney, I. F. V, 25
Bigoney, Jos. Warley III, 33
Bigoney, Phebe W. III, 33
Bigony, Howard V, 25
Bigony, I. F. V, 25
Bigony, Ira F. V, 25
Bigwell, Sarah IV, 175
Bigwood, Hannah II, 999
Bigwood, Wm. II, 999
Bikerdike, Mary II, 979
Bilbro, Caroline W. VI, 879
Bilbro, Eva I, 622
Bilbro, Fanny VI, 879
Bilbro, Henry C. I, 612
Bilbro, James VI, 879
Bilbro, John VI, 879
Bilbro, John R. I, 615
Bilbro, John Richardson I, 612
Bilbro, John Richardson I, 622
Bilbro, John Richardson I, 630
Bilbro, Kate I, 615
Bilbro, Kate I, 630
Bilbro, Kate I, 632
Bilbro, Katharine I, 612
Bilbro, Katharine I, 630
Bilbro, Lillian I, 630
Bilbro, Lillian I, 631
Bilbro, Martha Rhodema I, 622
Bilbro, Martha Rhodena I, 612
Bilbro, Mary A. I, 612
Bilbro, Mary Lelia I, 630
Bilbro, Mary Lilia I, 612
Bilbro, Mary M. VI, 879
Bilbro, Mildred Jane VI, 879
Bilbro, Rodema I, 615
Bilbro, Rodema I, 630
Bilbro, Rodema Spencer I, 630
Bilbro, Rosa Lillian I, 612
Bilbro, Rosa Lillian I, 630
Bilbro, William VI, 879
Bilbro, William P. VI, 879
Bilderback, Alpheus II, 129
Bilderback, E. A. V, 374
Bilderback, Edwin V, 374
Bilderback, Francis II, 129
Bilderback, John Edgar II, 129
Bilderback, John Edgar II, 145
Bilderback, Jonathan II, 127
Bilderback, Jonathan II, 129
Bilderback, Joseph II, 129
Bilderback, Joseph II, 145
Bilderback, Lucy Ann II, 127
Bilderback, Margaret II, 129
Bilderback, Margaret II, 145
Bilderback, Mary Jane II, 127
Bilderback, Rachel W. II, 129
Bilderback, Rachel W. II, 145
Bilderback, Sarah II, 55
Bilderback, Sarah II, 129
Bilderback, Sarah Virginia II, 129
Bilderback, Temperance II, 127
Bilderback, Temperance II, 129
Bilderback, Virginia II, 145
Bilderhack, Sarah II, 108
Biles, Ann II, 337
Biles, Ann II, 465
Biles, Ann II, 967
Biles, Ann II, 979
Biles, Ann II, 1021
Biles, Ann II, 1041
Biles, Ann VI, 516
Biles, Ann VI, 586
Biles, Ann Mary II, 979
Biles, Charles II, 465
Biles, Charles II, 568
Biles, Charles II, 687
Biles, Charles II, 979
Biles, Elizabeth II, 978
Biles, Elizabeth II, 979
Biles, Elizabeth III, 33
Biles, Elizabeth III, 47
Biles, George II, 337
Biles, George II, 954
Biles, George II, 979
Biles, Grace II, 465
Biles, Grace II, 687
Biles, Grace II, 782
Biles, Grace II, 787
Biles, Grace II, 978
Biles, Grace II, 979
Biles, Hannah II, 465
Biles, Hannah II, 979
Biles, Hannah II, 1005
Biles, Jane II, 954
Biles, Joanna II, 465
Biles, Joanna II, 601
Biles, Joanna II, 654
Biles, Johanah II, 978
Biles, Johanah II, 979
Biles, John II, 539
Biles, John II, 954
Biles, John II, 979
Biles, Jonathan II, 337
Biles, Jonathan II, 465
Biles, Jonathan II, 539
Biles, Lambert II, 954
Biles, Langhorn II, 337
Biles, Langhorne II, 979
Biles, Martha II, 465
Biles, Martha II, 568
Biles, Martha II, 674
Biles, Martha II, 979
Biles, Mary II, 337
Biles, Mary II, 954
Biles, Mary II, 979
Biles, Phebe II, 465
Biles, Phebe II, 623
Biles, Rebecca VI, 660
Biles, Rebeckah II, 979
Biles, Rebeckah II, 1005
Biles, Rebeckah VI, 514
Biles, Rebeckah VI, 519
Biles, Rebekah VI, 517
Biles, Ruth II, 465
Biles, Ruth II, 539
Biles, Ruth II, 954
Biles, Ruth II, 979
Biles, Samuel II, 337
Biles, Samuel II, 465
Biles, Samuel II, 568
Biles, Samuel II, 954
Biles, Sarah II, 337
Biles, Sarah II, 967
Biles, Sarah II, 979
Biles, Sarah II, 998
Biles, Sarah III, 33
Biles, Susannah II, 465
Biles, Susannah II, 601
Biles, Thomas II, 954
Biles, Thomas II, 979
Biles, Wd. Martha II, 465
Biles, William II, 952
Biles, William II, 954
Biles, William II, 967
Biles, William II, 975
Biles, William II, 979
Biles, Wm. II, 978
Biles, Wm. II, 979
Biles, Wm. II, 1005
Biles, Wm., Jr. II, 979
Billangey, Jno. II, 55
Billin, Amy III, 33
Billin, Charles W. III, 33
Billin, Charles W. III, 162
Billin, Enock, Jr. III, 33
Billin, Eugene P. III, 33
Billin, Eugene P. III, 221
Billin, Eugene Percival III, 33
Billin, George III, 33
Billin, George III, 302
Billin, Gertrude III, 33
Billin, Gertrude III, 162
Billin, Ida R. III, 33
Billin, Jane II, 337
Billin, Jessie III, 221
Billin, John II, 337
Billin, Virgina III, 33
Billin, Virgina T. III, 33
Billin, Virginia T. III, 302
Billingly, Rachel IV, 540
Billings, Bathsheba III, 33
Billings, Catherine B. III, 33
Billings, Charles W. III, 33
Billings, Charles W. III, 349
Billings, Daniel III, 33
Billings, Daniel III, 361
Billings, Hester M. III, 33
Billings, James III, 33
Billings, Jeremiah III, 33
Billings, John III, 33
Billings, Maria F. III, 33
Billings, Maria T. III, 349
Billings, Mary B. III, 33
Billings, Mary B. III, 349
Billings, Rachel S. II, 280
Billings, Rachel S. II, 281
Billings, Rachel S. II, 301
Billings, Robt. B. III, 33
Billings, Sarah III, 33
Billings, Stephen III, 33
Billings, Stephen B. III, 349
Billings, Susan B. P. III, 33
Billingsby, James IV, 320
Billingsby, Margaret IV, 320
Billingsby, Ruth IV, 320
Billingsby, Sarah IV, 320
Billingsby, William IV, 320
Billingsly, Elijah IV, 511
Billingsly, Elizabeth VI, 27
Billingsly, George VI, 27
Billingsly, James IV, 320
Billingsly, James IV, 511
Billingsly, Margaret IV, 320
Billingsly, Margaret IV, 511
Billingsly, Rachel IV, 511
Billingsly, Ruth IV, 511
Billingsly, Samuel K. IV, 511
Billingsly, Sarah IV, 320
Billingsly, Sarah IV, 338
Billingsly, Sarah IV, 511
Billingsly, William IV, 320
Billingsly, William IV, 511
Billingsly, William P. IV, 511
Billingsly, Wm. IV, 338
Billins, Daniel III, 33
Billins, John III, 33
Billips, Nancy VI, 886
Billmyer, Lucy Ann IV, 1201
Billops, Nancy VI, 886
Bills, Alanson III, 33
Bills, Alice I, 981
Bills, Alice I, 989
Bills, Ann II, 1017
Bills, Clarissa III, 33
Bills, Daniel I, 527
Bills, Daniel I, 777
Bills, Daniel I, 800
Bills, Daniel I, 971
Bills, Daniel I, 981
Bills, Daniel I Sup 1, 10
Bills, David III, 33
Bills, Deborah I, 777
Bills, Deborah I, 800
Bills, Deborah I, 971
Bills, Deborah I, 981
Bills, Deborah I, 992
Bills, Elizabeth I, 777
Bills, Elizabeth I, 800
Bills, Elizabeth I, 826
Bills, Gershom I, 777
Bills, Hannah I, 777
Bills, Hannah I, 800
Bills, Hannah I, 807
Bills, Isaac I, 777
Bills, Isaac I, 800
Bills, Isaac I, 981
Bills, Johanah II, 166
Bills, John I, 981
Bills, Jonathan I, 981
Bills, Mary I, 800
Bills, Mary I, 820
Bills, Mary I, 981
Bills, Mary I, 992
Bills, Patience I, 777
Bills, Patience I, 981
Bills, Patience I, 988
Bills, Rachel I, 777
Bills, Rachel I, 800
Bills, Rebecah II, 166
Bills, Sarah I, 777
Bills, Sarah I, 800
Bills, Sarah I, 981
Bills, Sarah I, 991
Bills, Susanna I, 800
Bills, Susanna I, 820
Bills, Thomas I, 981
Bills, Thomas III, 33
Bills, William I, 777
Bills, William I, 800
Bills, William I, 820
Bills, William I, 981
Bills, William II, 166
Bilton, Samuel II, 337
Binder, Aaron IV, 1307
Binder, Aaron Chas. IV, 1307
Binegar, Ellis E. V, 223
Binegar, James W. V, 223
Binegar, Johnson V, 223
Binegar, Lois Todhunter V, 452
Binegar, Mary J. V, 320
Binegar, Mary J. V, 452
Binegar, Mary Jane V, 223
Binegar, Mary Jane V, 255
Binegar, Ulysses N. V, 223
Bines, Kitturah VI, 879
Bines, Presley VI, 879
Bines, Ruth II, 52
Bines, Ruth II, 56
Binford, Abbie T. IV, 926
Binford, Abbie T. IV, 953
Binford, Abigail IV, 926
Binford, Abigail IV, 953
Binford, Adesda IV, 926
Binford, Agnes VI, 158
Binford, Agnes VI, 159
Binford, Agnes VI, 162
Binford, Agnes VI, 199
Binford, Agness VI, 100
Binford, Agness VI, 131
Binford, Agness VI, 143
Binford, Agness VI, 159
Binford, Agness VI, 162
Binford, Albert J. IV, 927
Binford, Albert Judson IV, 926
Binford, Alfred IV, 926
Binford, Alfred L. IV, 926
Binford, Allison J. IV, 926
Binford, Amanda IV, 926
Binford, Amanda IV, 984
Binford, Angelina I, 230
Binford, Angelina I, 253
Binford, Anjelina I, 207
Binford, Ann I, 230
Binford, Ann VI, 100
Binford, Ann VI, 160
Binford, Ann Maria VI, 131
Binford, Ann, Jr. VI, 131
Binford, Anna I, 230
Binford, Anna Maria VI, 129
Binford, Anna Maria VI, 131
Binford, Anne V, 967
Binford, Anne V, 970
Binford, Aquila VI, 66
Binford, Aquila VI, 100
Binford, Aquila VI, 158
Binford, Aquilla IV, 925
Binford, Aquilla IV, 926
Binford, Aquilla IV, 970
Binford, Aquilla VI, 53
Binford, Aquilla VI, 100
Binford, Aquilla VI, 104
Binford, Aquilla VI, 130
Binford, Aquilla VI, 131
Binford, Aquilla VI, 134
Binford, Aquilla VI, 138
Binford, Aquilla VI, 159
Binford, Aquilla VI, 189
Binford, Aquilla VI, 192
Binford, Asa I, 230
Binford, Ashbell I, 230
Binford, Benajah I, 207
Binford, Benajah I, 230
Binford, Benjamin I, 230
Binford, Benjamin IV, 925
Binford, Benjamin VI, 53
Binford, Benjamin VI, 58
Binford, Benjamin VI, 100
Binford, Benjamin VI, 131
Binford, Benjamin VI, 160
Binford, Benjamin J. IV, 926
Binford, Benjamin J. IV, 927
Binford, Betty Kinsey VI, 159
Binford, Burly I, 230
Binford, Caleb IV, 926
Binford, Chappel VI, 100
Binford, Chappel VI, 111
Binford, Chappell VI, 100
Binford, Chappell VI, 131
Binford, Charlotte Ann VI, 130
Binford, Charlotte Ann VI, 132
Binford, David IV, 926
Binford, David Bailey VI, 131
Binford, Deborah IV, 926
Binford, Delbert IV, 926
Binford, Desda IV, 922
Binford, Desda Allison IV, 927
Binford, Drury VI, 117
Binford, Earnest IV, 926
Binford, Eli Hill VI, 158
Binford, Elijah I, 230
Binford, Elisabeth I, 230
Binford, Elisabeth I Sup 1, 3
Binford, Elisabeth Peninah I, 230
Binford, Elisabeth Peninah I, 258
Binford, Elisha I, 230
Binford, Elizabeth I, 207
Binford, Elizabeth I Sup 1, 4
Binford, Elizabeth IV, 800
Binford, Elizabeth IV, 925
Binford, Elizabeth IV, 926
Binford, Elizabeth IV, 965
Binford, Elizabeth VI, 53
Binford, Elizabeth VI, 58
Binford, Elizabeth VI, 91
Binford, Elizabeth VI, 100
Binford, Elizabeth VI, 121
Binford, Elizabeth VI, 131
Binford, Elizabeth VI, 154
Binford, Elizabeth VI, 158
Binford, Elizabeth VI, 159
Binford, Elizabeth VI, 160
Binford, Elizabeth VI, 169
Binford, Elizabeth Ann IV, 926
Binford, Elizabeth Hill VI, 158
Binford, Elizabeth M. IV, 926
Binford, Elizabeth M. IV, 970
Binford, Elwood V, 967
Binford, Ernest F. IV, 926
Binford, Florence IV, 926
Binford, Frances VI, 160
Binford, Gertrude IV, 926
Binford, Gertrude Barnes IV, 927
Binford, Guli VI, 100
Binford, Guli Elma VI, 100
Binford, Gulielma M. VI, 132
Binford, Gulielma Maria VI, 131
Binford, Hanah I, 229
Binford, Hannah I, 207
Binford, Hannah I, 230
Binford, Hannah IV, 369
Binford, Hannah IV, 567
Binford, Hannah IV, 925
Binford, Hannah IV, 926
Binford, Hannah VI, 158
Binford, Hannah VI, 160
Binford, Hannah VI, 165
Binford, Hannah VI, 168
Binford, Hannah, Sr. I, 230
Binford, Howard A. IV, 926
Binford, Huldah VI, 158
Binford, Huldah VI, 159
Binford, Huldah VI, 191
Binford, Isaac Summer IV, 926
Binford, Iva IV, 926
Binford, James I, 129
Binford, James I, 207
Binford, James I, 229
Binford, James I, 230
Binford, James V, 223
Binford, James V, 967
Binford, James V, 970
Binford, James VI, 100
Binford, James VI, 119
Binford, James VI, 121
Binford, James VI, 130
Binford, James VI, 131
Binford, James VI, 133
Binford, James VI, 137
Binford, James VI, 138
Binford, James VI, 154
Binford, James VI, 158
Binford, James VI, 159
Binford, James VI, 160
Binford, James VI, 162
Binford, James VI, 165
Binford, James VI, 168
Binford, James VI, 171
Binford, James VI, 183
Binford, James L. I, 230
Binford, James L. VI, 131
Binford, James L. VI, 158
Binford, James L. VI, 160
Binford, James L. VI, 191
Binford, James L. VI, 195
Binford, James Ladd I, 207
Binford, James Ladd I, 230
Binford, James, Jr. I, 207
Binford, James, Jr. VI, 159
Binford, James, Jr. VI, 160
Binford, Jane I, 230
Binford, Jane VI, 100
Binford, Jane VI, 131
Binford, Jared I, 230
Binford, Jesse IV, 925
Binford, John I, 207
Binford, John I, 229
Binford, John I, 230
Binford, John I, 252
Binford, John IV, 925
Binford, John V, 967
Binford, John VI, 158
Binford, John VI, 159
Binford, John VI, 160
Binford, John VI, 162

Binford, John VI, 165
Binford, John VI, 169
Binford, John VI, 172
Binford, John VI, 174
Binford, John VI, 199
Binford, John VI, 213
Binford, John Stanto, Jr. VI, 131
Binford, John, Jr. VI, 159
Binford, John, Jr. VI, 172
Binford, Jonathan VI, 100
Binford, Joseph I, 230
Binford, Joseph IV, 925
Binford, Joseph IV, 926
Binford, Joseph IV, 965
Binford, Joseph VI, 158
Binford, Joseph VI, 160
Binford, Joseph VI, 191
Binford, Joseph VI, 195
Binford, Joseph B. IV, 926
Binford, Joseph Bayley IV, 926
Binford, Joseph Emerson IV, 926
Binford, Joshua I, 207
Binford, Joshua I, 230
Binford, Joshua I, 253
Binford, Joshua IV, 925
Binford, Joshua IV, 926
Binford, Joshua IV, 927
Binford, Josiah IV, 464
Binford, Josiah Cook VI, 131
Binford, Judah I, 207
Binford, Judeth I, 230
Binford, Judith IV, 927
Binford, Judith VI, 159
Binford, Judith VI, 189
Binford, Julia IV, 926
Binford, Kezia I, 207
Binford, Lemuel VI, 100
Binford, Lewellyn J. IV, 927
Binford, Louelwin IV, 926
Binford, Lucie A. IV, 678
Binford, Lucy IV, 678
Binford, Lucy IV, 926
Binford, Lucy IV, 927
Binford, Lucy E. IV, 926
Binford, Lucy E. IV, 940
Binford, Lydia I, 230
Binford, Lydia I, 253
Binford, Margaret I, 229
Binford, Margaret IV, 925
Binford, Margaret IV, 926
Binford, Margaret IV, 965
Binford, Margaret IV, 999
Binford, Margaret VI, 158
Binford, Margaret VI, 160
Binford, Margaret VI, 191
Binford, Margaret VI, 195
Binford, Margaret Ann IV, 926
Binford, Margeritt VI, 162
Binford, Maria IV, 926
Binford, Maria IV, 1014
Binford, Mariah IV, 926
Binford, Mariam IV, 926
Binford, Martha I, 207
Binford, Martha I, 230
Binford, Martha I, 252
Binford, Martha IV, 828
Binford, Martha IV, 925
Binford, Martha IV, 926
Binford, Martha IV, 970
Binford, Martha VI, 15
Binford, Martha VI, 100
Binford, Martha VI, 102
Binford, Martha VI, 107
Binford, Martha VI, 111
Binford, Martha VI, 129
Binford, Martha VI, 130
Binford, Martha VI, 131
Binford, Martha VI, 135
Binford, Martha VI, 140
Binford, Martha VI, 158
Binford, Martha VI, 159
Binford, Martha VI, 160
Binford, Martha VI, 162
Binford, Martha VI, 183
Binford, Martha Binford IV, 800
Binford, Martha, Jr. VI, 131
Binford, Martha, Sr. VI, 131
Binford, Mary I, 230
Binford, Mary IV, 925
Binford, Mary VI, 15
Binford, Mary VI, 53
Binford, Mary VI, 58
Binford, Mary VI, 100
Binford, Mary VI, 101
Binford, Mary VI, 104
Binford, Mary VI, 110
Binford, Mary VI, 111
Binford, Mary VI, 113
Binford, Mary VI, 130
Binford, Mary VI, 131
Binford, Mary VI, 134
Binford, Mary VI, 135
Binford, Mary VI, 138
Binford, Mary VI, 154
Binford, Mary VI, 158
Binford, Mary VI, 159
Binford, Mary VI, 160
Binford, Mary VI, 165
Binford, Mary VI, 168
Binford, Mary VI, 172
Binford, Mary VI, 173
Binford, Mary VI, 189
Binford, Mary VI, 190
Binford, Mary VI, 192
Binford, Mary VI, 193
Binford, Mary Peebles VI, 117
Binford, Mary, Jr. VI, 158
Binford, Mary, Jr. VI, 160
Binford, Mary, Jr. VI, 191
Binford, Mary, Jr. VI, 195
Binford, Mason I, 230
Binford, Mason Bloyed I, 230
Binford, Meriam I, 230
Binford, Micajah I, 129
Binford, Micajah I, 151
Binford, Micajah I, 207
Binford, Micajah I, 230
Binford, Micajah I, 253
Binford, Micajah M. III, 33
Binford, Michael IV, 926
Binford, Michal VI, 100
Binford, Michal VI, 131
Binford, Miriam I, 129
Binford, Miriam I, 151
Binford, Miriam I, 230
Binford, Miriam I, 247
Binford, Miriam IV, 925
Binford, Miriam IV, 970
Binford, Miriam H. VI, 131
Binford, Miriam H. VI, 134
Binford, Nathan I, 230
Binford, O. F. IV, 927
Binford, Oliver IV, 926
Binford, Oliver VI, 53
Binford, Oliver Clarkson IV, 926
Binford, Oliver F. IV, 926
Binford, Oliver F. IV, 927
Binford, Oliver Florin IV, 926
Binford, Oliver Florin IV, 927
Binford, Oliver J. IV, 926
Binford, Oliver L. IV, 926
Binford, Oliver L. IV, 927
Binford, Parker Willis IV, 926
Binford, Parmilia VI, 158
Binford, Paul Sears VI, 131
Binford, Pearl IV, 678
Binford, Pearl IV, 927
Binford, Penelope VI, 53
Binford, Penelope VI, 131
Binford, Peninah V, 967
Binford, Penninah VI, 131
Binford, Penninah VI, 138
Binford, Peter I, 230
Binford, Peter IV, 925
Binford, Peter IV, 926
Binford, Peter IV, 927
Binford, Peter IV, 999
Binford, Peter VI, 15
Binford, Peter VI, 100
Binford, Peter VI, 102
Binford, Peter VI, 107
Binford, Peter VI, 110
Binford, Peter VI, 111
Binford, Peter VI, 114
Binford, Peter VI, 129
Binford, Peter VI, 131
Binford, Peter VI, 141
Binford, Peter VI, 158
Binford, Peter VI, 159
Binford, Peter VI, 162
Binford, Peter VI, 221
Binford, Peter, Jr. IV, 926
Binford, Peter, Jr. IV, 1014
Binford, Philena Pearl IV, 926
Binford, Polly I, 230
Binford, Prince George VI, 158
Binford, Priscilla VI, 100
Binford, Priscilla VI, 101
Binford, Priscilla VI, 110
Binford, Priscilla VI, 111
Binford, Priscilla VI, 116
Binford, Priscilla VI, 159
Binford, Rachel I, 1148
Binford, Rachel VI, 221
Binford, Rebeckah VI, 100
Binford, Rebeckah VI, 158
Binford, Rebeckah VI, 159
Binford, Rebeckah VI, 162
Binford, Rebekah I, 230
Binford, Richard V, 967
Binford, Robert I, 230
Binford, Robert IV, 925
Binford, Robert IV, 926
Binford, Robert VI, 53
Binford, Robert VI, 58
Binford, Robert VI, 100
Binford, Robert VI, 129
Binford, Robert VI, 131
Binford, Robert VI, 158
Binford, Robert VI, 160
Binford, Ruth VI, 100
Binford, Ruth VI, 158
Binford, Ruth VI, 160
Binford, Ruth VI, 165
Binford, Samuel IV, 925
Binford, Samuel IV, 926
Binford, Samuel VI, 15
Binford, Samuel VI, 100
Binford, Samuel VI, 101
Binford, Samuel VI, 113
Binford, Samuel VI, 130
Binford, Samuel A. VI, 158
Binford, Samuel Alford IV, 926
Binford, Samuel Alfred IV, 925
Binford, Samuel Alfred IV, 926
Binford, Samuel Alfred IV, 970
Binford, Samuel Alfred VI, 160
Binford, Sarah I, 230
Binford, Sarah I, 253
Binford, Sarah IV, 926
Binford, Sarah VI, 100
Binford, Sarah VI, 101
Binford, Sarah VI, 114
Binford, Sarah VI, 158
Binford, Sarah VI, 159
Binford, Sarah VI, 160
Binford, Sarah VI, 189
Binford, Sarah VI, 192
Binford, Sarah VI, 194
Binford, Susanna Zelinda VI, 53
Binford, Susannah VI, 158
Binford, Susannah VI, 159
Binford, Susannah VI, 160
Binford, Susannah VI, 172
Binford, Susannah VI, 174
Binford, Susannah R. III, 33
Binford, Tabitha VI, 101
Binford, Thaddeus IV, 926
Binford, Thomas I, 229
Binford, Thomas I, 230
Binford, Thomas I Sup 1, 3
Binford, Thomas I Sup 1, 4
Binford, Thomas V, 967
Binford, Thomas VI, 100
Binford, Thomas VI, 158
Binford, Thomas VI, 159
Binford, Thomas VI, 160
Binford, Thomas VI, 161
Binford, Thomas VI, 165
Binford, Thomas VI, 168
Binford, Thomas VI, 169
Binford, Thomas VI, 171
Binford, Thomas VI, 189
Binford, Thomas VI, 190
Binford, Thomas Johnson IV, 800
Binford, Thos. VI, 105
Binford, Thos. Elwood V, 967
Binford, Wd. Priscilla VI, 100
Binford, Wd. Priscilla Hunnicutt VI, 111
Binford, Widow Martha I, 230
Binford, William I, 230
Binford, William VI, 53
Binford, William VI, 100
Binford, William VI, 117
Binford, William VI, 159
Binford, William VI, 160
Binford, William A. VI, 53
Binford, William H. IV, 925
Binford, Wm. IV, 926
Binford, Wm. VI, 212
Binford, Wm. H. IV, 926
Bing, Jane II, 441
Bingaman, David V, 153
Bingamon, David V, 153
Binger, Lillian IV, 1307
Binger, Mary J. V, 320
Binger, Mary Jane V, 320
Bingham, ??? IV, 603
Bingham, Agnes V, 797
Bingham, Bridget II, 197
Bingham, Bridget II, 270
Bingham, Catharine IV, 1049
Bingham, Catharine IV, 1063
Bingham, Dorothy II, 699
Bingham, Elizabeth I, 709
Bingham, Elizabeth II, 465
Bingham, Emeline M. III, 34
Bingham, Emmeline M. III, 292
Bingham, Fannie Meda Lee I, 611
Bingham, Henderson I, 871
Bingham, Humphrey II, 465
Bingham, J. L. I, 709
Bingham, Jason Lee I, 611
Bingham, John C. I, 709
Bingham, Jordon I, 226
Bingham, Margaret I, 226
Bingham, Martha I, 226
Bingham, Mary V, 797
Bingham, Maud III, 475
Bingham, Sarah Vuncannon I, 611
Bingham, William A. I, 709
Bingham, William G. H. VI, 867
Bingham, William H. VI, 835
Bingman, Sarah IV, 175
Bingman, Sarah IV, 295
Binkard, Judith V, 779
Binkley, Charles V, 550
Binkley, Charles H. V, 550
Binkley, Earl Wright IV, 1307
Binkley, Earle IV, 1307
Binkley, Eva V, 550
Binkley, Florence IV, 1307
Binkley, Florence Farrow IV, 1307
Binkley, Henry V, 550
Binkley, Irene V, 550
Binkley, John Howard V, 550
Binkley, Mary V, 550
Binkley, Mary C. V, 550
Binnegar, Elizabeth VI, 366
Binnegar, Elizabeth VI, 456
Binney, Kathryn III, 396
Binney, Sam C. III, 396
Binney, Sam'l III, 396
Binney, Samuel M. III, 396
Binns, Abza J. IV, 176
Binns, Addison IV, 176
Binns, Addison IV, 177
Binns, Addison H. IV, 177
Binns, Albert John IV, 678
Binns, Albert John IV, 800
Binns, Alfred Watson III, 34
Binns, Alice IV, 75
Binns, Alice IV, 121
Binns, Alice IV, 1352
Binns, Alice R. IV, 800
Binns, Alice Rebecca IV, 177
Binns, Alice Rebecca IV, 641
Binns, Alice Rebecca IV, 678
Binns, Alice Rebecca IV, 800
Binns, Alice Rebecca IV, 831
Binns, Allice IV, 176
Binns, Alza J. IV, 177
Binns, Alza J. IV, 282
Binns, Amos IV, 75
Binns, Amos IV, 121
Binns, Amos IV, 176
Binns, Amos IV, 177
Binns, Amos IV, 1246
Binns, Amos G. IV, 177
Binns, Ann IV, 75
Binns, Ann IV, 117
Binns, Ann IV, 176
Binns, Ann H. IV, 927
Binns, Ann H. IV, 941
Binns, Arthur IV, 176
Binns, Arthur H. IV, 177
Binns, Arthur H. IV, 184
Binns, Arthur H. IV, 369
Binns, Arthur H. IV, 375
Binns, Arthur H. IV, 511
Binns, Arthur H. IV, 678
Binns, Arthur H. IV, 744
Binns, Arthur H. IV, 791
Binns, Arthur W. M. II, 699
Binns, Arthur W. M. II, 728
Binns, Arthur W. M. IV, 800
Binns, Balinda IV, 812
Binns, Belinda IV, 176
Binns, Belinda IV, 195
Binns, Belinda IV, 222
Binns, Belinda IV, 369
Binns, Belinda IV, 678
Binns, Belinda IV, 699
Binns, Belinda IV, 789
Binns, Belinda IV, 800
Binns, Belinda IV, 856
Binns, Belinda IV, 1127
Binns, Belinda IV, 1133
Binns, Belinda H. IV, 176
Binns, Belinda H. IV, 1127
Binns, Bertha A. IV, 176
Binns, Bertha A. IV, 183
Binns, Bertha M. IV, 176
Binns, Caroline IV, 176
Binns, Caroline IV, 180
Binns, Caroline H. IV, 176
Binns, Charles IV, 75
Binns, Charles IV, 121
Binns, Charles IV, 1246
Binns, Charles IV, 1352
Binns, Charles H. IV, 176
Binns, Charles S. IV, 1246
Binns, Clara IV, 176
Binns, Clara IV, 177
Binns, Clarence H. II, 699
Binns, Clarence H. II, 728
Binns, Clarence H. IV, 800
Binns, Clarkson IV, 176
Binns, Daniel IV, 121
Binns, Daniel IV, 1352
Binns, David IV, 75
Binns, David IV, 96
Binns, David IV, 117
Binns, David IV, 121
Binns, David IV, 175
Binns, David IV, 176
Binns, David IV, 179
Binns, David IV, 183
Binns, David IV, 198
Binns, David IV, 212
Binns, David IV, 213
Binns, David IV, 511
Binns, David IV, 800
Binns, David IV, 813
Binns, David IV, 1127
Binns, David E. IV, 276
Binns, David M. IV, 176
Binns, David M. IV, 177
Binns, David S. IV, 177
Binns, David, Jr. IV, 75
Binns, David, Jr. IV, 177
Binns, David, Sr. IV, 176
Binns, Dorothy A. IV, 369
Binns, Dorothy A. IV, 511
Binns, Dorothy A. IV, 678
Binns, Edith K. II, 728
Binns, Edith Margaret IV, 177
Binns, Edith Margaret IV, 179
Binns, Edith Margaret IV, 800
Binns, Edith T. IV, 176
Binns, Edith T. IV, 282
Binns, Edward IV, 75
Binns, Edward IV, 177
Binns, Edward T. II, 699
Binns, Edward T. II, 728
Binns, Edward T. IV, 176
Binns, Edward T. IV, 177
Binns, Edward T. IV, 179
Binns, Edward T. IV, 800
Binns, Eliza IV, 75
Binns, Eliza IV, 105
Binns, Eliza IV, 177
Binns, Eliza IV, 231
Binns, Eliza M. IV, 75
Binns, Eliza M. IV, 94
Binns, Eliza M. IV, 176
Binns, Eliza M. IV, 226
Binns, Eliza R. IV, 176
Binns, Elizabeth IV, 121
Binns, Elizabeth IV, 127
Binns, Elizabeth IV, 176
Binns, Elizabeth IV, 1352
Binns, Elma IV, 694
Binns, Elza R. IV, 176
Binns, Elza R. IV, 214
Binns, Esther IV, 800
Binns, Esther L. II, 699
Binns, Esther L. II, 728
Binns, Esther L. IV, 177
Binns, Esther L. IV, 179
Binns, Esther L. IV, 800
Binns, Esther Mary IV, 678
Binns, Frances S. IV, 511
Binns, Frances S. IV, 678
Binns, Frances S. IV, 744
Binns, Francis S. IV, 369
Binns, Franklin IV, 176
Binns, Gertrude R. IV, 176
Binns, Gibson IV, 75
Binns, Gibson IV, 121
Binns, Gibson IV, 124
Binns, Gibson IV, 175
Binns, Gibson IV, 176
Binns, Gibson IV, 177
Binns, Gibson IV, 271
Binns, Gibson IV, 678
Binns, Gibson IV, 756
Binns, Gladys Marie IV, 176
Binns, Hannah IV, 121
Binns, Hannah IV, 176
Binns, Hannah IV, 177
Binns, Hannah IV, 1352
Binns, Hannah G. IV, 177
Binns, Henry IV, 176
Binns, Hervey IV, 177
Binns, Hervey J. IV, 176
Binns, Howard IV, 176
Binns, Ida IV, 172
Binns, Ida IV, 176
Binns, Ida IV, 264
Binns, Ida IV, 509

Binns, Ida IV, 511
Binns, Ida Mary IV, 176
Binns, Ida Mary IV, 177
Binns, J. Alfred IV, 369
Binns, J. H. IV, 282
Binns, J. Hervey IV, 176
Binns, J. Hervey IV, 177
Binns, J. Howard IV, 176
Binns, James IV, 121
Binns, James IV, 127
Binns, James IV, 176
Binns, James IV, 1352
Binns, James Harvey IV, 176
Binns, James Hervey IV, 172
Binns, James Hervey IV, 177
Binns, James Hervey IV, 264
Binns, James Hervey IV, 509
Binns, James Hervey IV, 511
Binns, Jesse C. IV, 121
Binns, John IV, 75
Binns, John IV, 121
Binns, John IV, 127
Binns, John IV, 176
Binns, John IV, 177
Binns, John IV, 800
Binns, John IV, 831
Binns, John IV, 1352
Binns, John A. IV, 176
Binns, John A. IV, 177
Binns, John A. IV, 191
Binns, John A. IV, 641
Binns, John A. IV, 678
Binns, John A. IV, 693
Binns, John A. IV, 800
Binns, John Edward IV, 369
Binns, John Edward IV, 678
Binns, John Ernest II, 699
Binns, Jonathan IV, 21
Binns, Jonathan IV, 75
Binns, Jonathan IV, 94
Binns, Jonathan IV, 121
Binns, Jonathan IV, 171
Binns, Jonathan IV, 176
Binns, Jonathan IV, 177
Binns, Jonathan IV, 180
Binns, Jonathan IV, 214
Binns, Jonathan IV, 226
Binns, Jonathan IV, 231
Binns, Jonathan IV, 289
Binns, Jonathan IV, 567
Binns, Jonathan IV, 678
Binns, Jonathan Alfred IV, 678
Binns, Jos. IV, 856
Binns, Jos. P. IV, 195
Binns, Joseph IV, 121
Binns, Joseph IV, 177
Binns, Joseph IV, 800
Binns, Joseph IV, 812
Binns, Joseph IV, 1352
Binns, Joseph IV, 1373
Binns, Joseph H. II, 728
Binns, Joseph H. IV, 800
Binns, Joseph H. IV, 1352
Binns, Joseph P. II, 699
Binns, Joseph P. IV, 176
Binns, Joseph P. IV, 222
Binns, Joseph P. IV, 369
Binns, Joseph P. IV, 678
Binns, Joseph P. IV, 699
Binns, Joseph P. IV, 789
Binns, Joseph P. IV, 1127
Binns, Joseph P. IV, 1133
Binns, Joseph R. IV, 177
Binns, Lilla Aurelia IV, 177
Binns, Lillie Aurelia IV, 1246
Binns, Lizzie IV, 800
Binns, Lizzie A. IV, 176
Binns, Lizzie A. IV, 179
Binns, Lizzie A. IV, 183
Binns, Lizzie A. IV, 276
Binns, Lizzie A. IV, 800
Binns, Lizzie S. IV, 177
Binns, Luella IV, 176
Binns, Luella IV, 177
Binns, Margaret IV, 75
Binns, Margaret IV, 96
Binns, Margaret IV, 117
Binns, Margaret IV, 121
Binns, Margaret IV, 133
Binns, Margaret IV, 176
Binns, Margaret IV, 177
Binns, Margaret Ann IV, 176
Binns, Margaret Ann IV, 177
Binns, Margaret Ann IV, 213
Binns, Margaret, Sr. IV, 176
Binns, Mariana IV, 176
Binns, Mariana IV, 177
Binns, Mariana IV, 195
Binns, Mariana IV, 567
Binns, Mariana IV, 573
Binns, Mariana D. IV, 176
Binns, Mariana D. IV, 177
Binns, Marry C. IV, 812
Binns, Martha IV, 176
Binns, Martha IV, 271
Binns, Martha IV, 289
Binns, Martha IV, 756
Binns, Martha IV, 1352
Binns, Martha D. IV, 678
Binns, Martha R. IV, 176
Binns, Martha V. IV, 121
Binns, Martha V. IV, 124
Binns, Martha V. IV, 177
Binns, Martha V. IV, 678
Binns, Mary III, 34
Binns, Mary IV, 75
Binns, Mary IV, 121
Binns, Mary IV, 175
Binns, Mary IV, 177
Binns, Mary IV, 401
Binns, Mary IV, 800
Binns, Mary IV, 949
Binns, Mary IV, 1147
Binns, Mary Anna D. IV, 567
Binns, Mary C. IV, 176
Binns, Mary C. IV, 195
Binns, Mary C. IV, 369
Binns, Mary C. IV, 699
Binns, Mary C. IV, 856
Binns, Mary E. IV, 177
Binns, Mary E. IV, 191
Binns, Mary E. IV, 641
Binns, Mary E. IV, 678
Binns, Mary E. IV, 693
Binns, Mary E. IV, 800
Binns, Mary E. IV, 831
Binns, Mary E. IV, 843
Binns, Mary E. IV, 1246
Binns, Mary Edith IV, 176
Binns, Mary Edith IV, 276
Binns, Mary H. IV, 177
Binns, Mary H. IV, 581
Binns, Mary H. IV, 800
Binns, Mary H. IV, 807
Binns, Mary H. IV, 813
Binns, Mary H. IV, 819
Binns, Mary H. IV, 832
Binns, Mary K. IV, 176
Binns, Mary K. IV, 198
Binns, Mary P. IV, 176
Binns, Mary P. IV, 231
Binns, Mich. IV, 1352
Binns, Mildred M. IV, 369
Binns, Mildred M. IV, 511
Binns, Mildred M. IV, 678
Binns, Mildred M. IV, 791
Binns, Mira H. IV, 176
Binns, Mira H. IV, 177
Binns, Mrs. Mary IV, 119
Binns, Oliver IV, 176
Binns, Oliver IV, 177
Binns, Oliver H. IV, 176
Binns, Oliver H. IV, 1246
Binns, Oliver W. IV, 195
Binns, Oliver W. IV, 567
Binns, Oliver W. IV, 573
Binns, Priscilla IV, 1352
Binns, Rachel S. IV, 176
Binns, Rachel S. IV, 177
Binns, Rachel S. IV, 179
Binns, Rachel S. IV, 800
Binns, Rachel S. IV, 801
Binns, Rebecca IV, 176
Binns, Rebecca IV, 177
Binns, Rebecca IV, 198
Binns, Rebecca IV, 212
Binns, Rebecca IV, 264
Binns, Rebecca IV, 813
Binns, Rebecca IV, 1127
Binns, Rebecca IV, 1246
Binns, Rebecca A. IV, 177
Binns, Rebecca H. IV, 213
Binns, Rebecca H. IV, 511
Binns, Richard IV, 75
Binns, Richard IV, 121
Binns, Richard IV, 175
Binns, Richard T. IV, 1352
Binns, Robert IV, 121
Binns, Rollin IV, 1352
Binns, Rosella IV, 171
Binns, Rosella IV, 176
Binns, Rosella IV, 214
Binns, Rosella IV, 289
Binns, Rosella IV, 567
Binns, Ruth IV, 75
Binns, Ruth IV, 88
Binns, Ruth IV, 121
Binns, Ruth IV, 175
Binns, Ruth IV, 176
Binns, Ruth Marjorie IV, 176
Binns, Sarah IV, 75
Binns, Sarah IV, 96
Binns, Sarah IV, 121
Binns, Sarah IV, 123
Binns, Sarah IV, 177
Binns, Sarah IV, 234
Binns, Sarah IV, 256
Binns, Sarah IV, 1352
Binns, Sarah A. IV, 121
Binns, Sarah A. IV, 127
Binns, Sarah Ann IV, 121
Binns, Sarah C. IV, 1352
Binns, Sarah C. IV, 1373
Binns, Sarah D. IV, 1352
Binns, Susannah L. IV, 1352
Binns, Tacie M. IV, 369
Binns, Tacie M. IV, 375
Binns, Tacie M. IV, 511
Binns, Tacie M. IV, 678
Binns, Tacie M. IV, 744
Binns, Tacie M. IV, 791
Binns, Tacy M. IV, 177
Binns, Tacy M. IV, 184
Binns, Tacy M. IV, 369
Binns, Tacy M. IV, 511
Binns, Thomas IV, 176
Binns, Thomas IV, 177
Binns, Thomas C. IV, 176
Binns, Thomas H. IV, 177
Binns, Thos. H. IV, 176
Binns, Thos. H. IV, 282
Binns, Virginia Louise IV, 176
Binns, William III, 34
Binns, William IV, 75
Binns, William IV, 88
Binns, William IV, 121
Binns, William IV, 175
Binns, William IV, 176
Binns, William C. IV, 511
Binns, Willis J. IV, 176
Binns, Willis J. IV, 183
Binns, Wilson IV, 121
Binns, Wilson IV, 177
Binns, Wilson IV, 1352
Binns, Wm. IV, 75
Binns, Wm. IV, 121
Binns, Wm. IV, 176
Binns, Wm. IV, 177
Binns, Wm. C. IV, 177
Binns, Zelinga II, 699
Biram, Alfred Griffin V, 827
Biram, Augustus Franklin V, 827
Biram, Axom E. V, 827
Biram, Benjamin F. V, 827
Biram, Benjamin Franklin V, 827
Biram, Caleb P. V, 827
Biram, Caleb Parker V, 827
Biram, Eli V, 827
Biram, Elliott V, 827
Biram, Emaline Isabella V, 827
Biram, Emaline Isobella V, 827
Biram, Emmaline Isabella V, 827
Biram, Exum V, 827
Biram, Exum Elliott V, 826
Biram, Harriet Eliza V, 827
Biram, Harriet Elizabeth V, 827
Biram, Jemima V, 826
Biram, Jemima V, 827
Biram, Jemima Elliott Meriam V, 826
Biram, John Wesley V, 827
Biram, Martha Maria V, 827
Biram, Miram V, 827
Biram, Miriam V, 827
Biram, Nathan V, 826
Biram, Nathan V, 827
Biram, Orpah V, 827
Biram, Robert V, 827
Biram, William V, 827
Biram, William, Jr. V, 827
Birch, Ella I, 873
Birch, Florence V, 153
Birch, George A. V, 153
Birch, Lenora I, 873
Birch, Martha E. III, 323
Birch, Sarah IV, 369
Birch, Sarah IV, 401
Birchall, Caleb II, 337
Birchall, Caleb II, 465
Birchall, Elizabeth II, 337
Birchall, Franklin II, 337
Birchall, Hannah II, 337
Birchall, James II, 337
Birchall, James II, 465
Birchall, John II, 337
Birchall, John II, 465
Birchall, Lydia II, 465
Birchall, Rebecca II, 337
Birchall, Rebekah II, 337
Birchall, Rebekah II, 465
Birchall, Robert II, 337
Bircham, James II, 197
Bircham, Joseph I, 802
Birchell, Caleb II, 465
Birchfield, Alce II, 337
Birchfield, Alice II, 337
Birchfield, Alice II, 465
Birchfield, Alice II, 480
Birchfield, Alice II, 533
Birchfield, Aron II, 337
Birchfield, Elizabeth T. VI, 879
Birchfield, Mathew II, 337
Birchfield, Matthew II, 465
Birchfield, Matthew II, 533
Birchfield, Tabitha II, 337
Birchfield, William VI, 879
Birchum, Emely I, 983
Birchum, Emely I, 998
Bird, ??? II, 699
Bird, ??? III, 58
Bird, Albreak II, 979
Bird, Albrick II, 465
Bird, Alice IV, 177
Bird, Amelia II, 718
Bird, Amelia II, 797
Bird, Amelia II, 819
Bird, Amy III, 58
Bird, Ann III, 58
Bird, Benjamin V. VI, 879
Bird, Betsey VI, 879
Bird, Betsy Ann III, 34
Bird, Catharine VI, 879
Bird, Catharine VI, 924
Bird, Catherine G. III, 34
Bird, Caty VI, 938
Bird, Christie B. V, 727
Bird, Daisy I. III, 34
Bird, Daisy I. III, 213
Bird, Dr. Orphens III, 34
Bird, Dr. Orpheus Brainard III, 339
Bird, Eliza III, 34
Bird, Elizabeth II, 442
Bird, Elizabeth III, 58
Bird, Elizabeth VI, 879
Bird, Elizabeth VI, 901
Bird, Ella Leslie II, 844
Bird, Ella Leslie II, 913
Bird, Ella R. III, 58
Bird, Evelyn III, 58
Bird, Frances II, 465
Bird, Frances Emma III, 34
Bird, Geo. VI, 799
Bird, Geo. Radcliffe III, 58
Bird, George V, 727
Bird, George W. V, 727
Bird, Hannah III, 58
Bird, Hannah VI, 879
Bird, Henry L. III, 34
Bird, Isaac II, 465
Bird, Isaac IV, 196
Bird, James III, 58
Bird, John II, 442
Bird, John VI, 799
Bird, John VI, 879
Bird, John VI, 891
Bird, John VI, 938
Bird, John VI, 991
Bird, Joseph III, 58
Bird, Levina VI, 879
Bird, Lucilla K. III, 34
Bird, Luke VI, 870
Bird, Luke VI, 879
Bird, Luke VI, 901
Bird, Luke VI, 914
Bird, Luke VI, 915
Bird, Luke VI, 924
Bird, Luke VI, 938
Bird, Luke VI, 973
Bird, Luke VI, 1001
Bird, Lydia I, 800
Bird, Lydia I, 823
Bird, Margaret III, 58
Bird, Marrietta III, 34
Bird, Mary IV, 196
Bird, Mathew III, 34
Bird, Matilda IV, 177
Bird, Matilda IV, 196
Bird, Matilda IV, 370
Bird, Matilda IV, 387
Bird, Matilda IV, 1092
Bird, Matthew III, 34
Bird, Philip G. II, 844
Bird, Philip G. II, 913
Bird, Philip G. III, 58
Bird, Rachel II, 979
Bird, Rebecca II, 728
Bird, Rebecca II, 731
Bird, Richard III, 58
Bird, Richard VI, 825
Bird, Richard VI, 840
Bird, Robert II, 442
Bird, Sally VI, 879
Bird, Sarah II, 462
Bird, Sarah II, 465
Bird, Sarah III, 34
Bird, Sarah VI, 840
Bird, Sarah M. III, 34
Bird, Sarah M. III, 339
Bird, Susan VI, 799
Bird, Susanna VI, 825
Bird, Thomas II, 699
Bird, Thomas III, 58
Bird, Thomas VI, 879
Bird, Vista L. V, 223
Bird, Washington VI, 799
Bird, William VI, 879
Bird, Wm. III, 34
Birdsal, Albert A. V, 477
Birdsal, Hannah G. V, 25
Birdsal, Jane V, 948
Birdsal, Jane V, 949
Birdsal, Mary Ann V, 25
Birdsal, Mary B. V, 477
Birdsal, Mary T. V, 477
Birdsal, R. V, 25
Birdsal, Rachel V, 25
Birdsal, Ruth V, 25
Birdsal, Samuel V, 25
Birdsal, Thomas B. V, 477
Birdsall, ??? II, 197
Birdsall, ??? III, 37
Birdsall, ??? III, 102
Birdsall, Abigail III, 36
Birdsall, Abraham III, 34
Birdsall, Abraham Y. III, 34
Birdsall, Adelia III, 35
Birdsall, Adrian IV, 1352
Birdsall, Agnes III, 36
Birdsall, Albert III, 34
Birdsall, Albert III, 35
Birdsall, Albert V, 477
Birdsall, Albert A. V, 477
Birdsall, Alice Jane IV, 1352
Birdsall, Alice S. III, 337
Birdsall, Alvin Charles II, 838
Birdsall, Alvin T. III, 34
Birdsall, Alvira V, 894
Birdsall, Amasa VI, 617
Birdsall, Amos III, 34
Birdsall, Amy III, 34
Birdsall, Amy III, 35
Birdsall, Amy III, 123
Birdsall, Amy III, 396
Birdsall, Amy Anna III, 34
Birdsall, Amy Anna III, 102
Birdsall, Andrew III, 35
Birdsall, Andrew III, 37
Birdsall, Andrew V, 25
Birdsall, Andrew V, 477
Birdsall, Andrew VI, 615
Birdsall, Andrew VI, 616
Birdsall, Andrew VI, 617
Birdsall, Andrew VI, 618
Birdsall, Andrew VI, 630
Birdsall, Andrew VI, 641
Birdsall, Angeline A. III, 35
Birdsall, Ann III, 34
Birdsall, Ann III, 35
Birdsall, Ann III, 53
Birdsall, Ann IV, 1233
Birdsall, Ann V, 477
Birdsall, Ann VI, 366
Birdsall, Ann VI, 616
Birdsall, Ann VI, 618
Birdsall, Ann Brown VI, 618
Birdsall, Ann C. III, 34
Birdsall, Ann M. IV, 1167
Birdsall, Anna III, 35
Birdsall, Anna III, 337
Birdsall, Anna IV, 1148
Birdsall, Anna IV, 1167
Birdsall, Anna V, 94
Birdsall, Anna V, 477
Birdsall, Anna VI, 471
Birdsall, Anna VI, 616
Birdsall, Anna VI, 619
Birdsall, Anna VI, 641
Birdsall, Anna C. III, 35
Birdsall, Anna D. IV, 1352
Birdsall, Anna W. III, 34
Birdsall, Anna Wood III, 36
Birdsall, Anne IV, 1352
Birdsall, Annie V, 477
Birdsall, Arthur Wood III, 34
Birdsall, Arthur Wood III, 36
Birdsall, Asael E. IV, 1352
Birdsall, Avis III, 34
Birdsall, Avis III, 497
Birdsall, Avis C. III, 35
Birdsall, Avis C. III, 36
Birdsall, Avis C. III, 110
Birdsall, Avis C. III, 480
Birdsall, Avis C. III, 497
Birdsall, Avis S. III, 35

Birdsall, Benj. III, 396
Birdsall, Benjamin III, 34
Birdsall, Benjamin III, 35
Birdsall, Benjamin III, 396
Birdsall, Benjamin III, 420
Birdsall, Benjamin VI, 366
Birdsall, Benjamin VI, 617
Birdsall, Benjamin VI, 618
Birdsall, Benjamin VI, 619
Birdsall, Benjamin VI, 675
Birdsall, Benjamin VI, 714
Birdsall, Benjamin, Jr. VI, 471
Birdsall, Benjamin, Jr. VI, 509
Birdsall, Benjamin, Jr. VI, 510
Birdsall, Benjamin, Jr. VI, 617
Birdsall, Benjamin, Jr. VI, 618
Birdsall, Benjamin, Jr. VI, 621
Birdsall, Benjamin, Jr. VI, 658
Birdsall, Betsey VI, 619
Birdsall, Betsey Elizabeth VI, 471
Birdsall, Carolina III, 337
Birdsall, Caroline III, 34
Birdsall, Caroline III, 36
Birdsall, Caroline III, 127
Birdsall, Caroline III, 309
Birdsall, Caroline III, 310
Birdsall, Caroline III, 337
Birdsall, Caroline III, 363
Birdsall, Carrie L. III, 337
Birdsall, Catherine Mailor III, 34
Birdsall, Charle Thomas III, 34
Birdsall, Charles III, 36
Birdsall, Charles G. III, 34
Birdsall, Charles M. V, 477
Birdsall, Charles Thomas III, 35
Birdsall, Charles W. VI, 471
Birdsall, Charles W. VI, 617
Birdsall, Charlotte M. III, 35
Birdsall, Charlotte Mary III, 34
Birdsall, Clara E. III, 36
Birdsall, Cornelia III, 36
Birdsall, Daniel III, 396
Birdsall, Daniel III, 415
Birdsall, Daniel III, 452
Birdsall, Daniel IV, 1352
Birdsall, Daniel V, 477
Birdsall, Daniel V, 894
Birdsall, Daniel L. III, 36
Birdsall, Daniel Thornton III, 34
Birdsall, Daniel Thornton III, 36
Birdsall, David III, 34
Birdsall, David III, 36
Birdsall, David III, 38
Birdsall, David III, 272
Birdsall, David IV, 1352
Birdsall, David V, 894
Birdsall, David VI, 617
Birdsall, David VI, 618
Birdsall, David VI, 623
Birdsall, David VI, 658
Birdsall, David VI, 705
Birdsall, David H. VI, 617
Birdsall, David H. VI, 618
Birdsall, David H. VI, 622
Birdsall, David H. VI, 625
Birdsall, David H. VI, 704
Birdsall, David H. VI, 705
Birdsall, David Waldo VI, 622
Birdsall, Deborah III, 34
Birdsall, Deborah VI, 471
Birdsall, Deborah B. VI, 509
Birdsall, Deborah B. VI, 510
Birdsall, Deborah B. VI, 617
Birdsall, Deborah B. VI, 618
Birdsall, Deborah B. VI, 658
Birdsall, Deborah B. VI, 675
Birdsall, Diantha IV, 1352
Birdsall, Dr. Ashahel H. III, 34
Birdsall, Dr. Stephen T. III, 36
Birdsall, Edgar III, 34
Birdsall, Edgar III, 36
Birdsall, Edmund L. III, 36
Birdsall, Edna III, 35
Birdsall, Edward IV, 1352
Birdsall, Edward V, 25
Birdsall, Edward V, 477
Birdsall, Edward VI, 616
Birdsall, Edward VI, 617
Birdsall, Edward S. III, 34
Birdsall, Eleanor C. III, 34
Birdsall, Eleanor C. III, 35
Birdsall, Eleanor C. III, 334
Birdsall, Eleanor H. III, 36
Birdsall, Eli VI, 617
Birdsall, Eli Whitson VI, 617
Birdsall, Elias G. III, 34
Birdsall, Elijah II, 197
Birdsall, Elisabeth G. I, 624
Birdsall, Eliz III, 36
Birdsall, Eliza Ann III, 34
Birdsall, Eliza Hough VI, 617
Birdsall, Eliza Hough VI, 675
Birdsall, Elizabeth III, 34
Birdsall, Elizabeth III, 35
Birdsall, Elizabeth III, 36
Birdsall, Elizabeth III, 87
Birdsall, Elizabeth III, 396
Birdsall, Elizabeth III, 404
Birdsall, Elizabeth III, 420
Birdsall, Elizabeth V, 477
Birdsall, Elizabeth V, 503
Birdsall, Elizabeth VI, 366
Birdsall, Elizabeth VI, 617
Birdsall, Elizabeth VI, 618
Birdsall, Elizabeth H. III, 36
Birdsall, Elizabeth M. II, 699
Birdsall, Elizabeth M. III, 34
Birdsall, Elizabeth M. III, 35
Birdsall, Elizabeth T. III, 35
Birdsall, Elizabeth T. III, 123
Birdsall, Elizabeth Y. III, 36
Birdsall, Ellen VI, 617
Birdsall, Ellwood III, 34
Birdsall, Elmira V, 894
Birdsall, Emeline III, 35
Birdsall, Emeline III, 80
Birdsall, Emeline C. VI, 230
Birdsall, Emeline Collins VI, 230
Birdsall, Ernest Wood III, 34
Birdsall, Ernest Wood III, 36
Birdsall, Estelle III, 337
Birdsall, Esther III, 34
Birdsall, Esther III, 35
Birdsall, Esther III, 266
Birdsall, Evalina IV, 1352
Birdsall, Evelina IV, 1352
Birdsall, Evelyn Westervelt III, 34
Birdsall, Evelyn Westervelt III, 36
Birdsall, Florence III, 34
Birdsall, Florence III, 371
Birdsall, Florence E. III, 334
Birdsall, Florence Eleanor III, 35
Birdsall, Folio VI, 617
Birdsall, Folio VI, 618
Birdsall, Frances III, 34
Birdsall, Frances Chase III, 203
Birdsall, Frances E. III, 34
Birdsall, Francis Chase III, 203
Birdsall, Frank Chase III, 34
Birdsall, Frank Chase III, 35
Birdsall, Geo H. III, 34
Birdsall, Geo. H. III, 34
Birdsall, Geo. H. III, 112
Birdsall, Geo. H., Jr. III, 34
Birdsall, Geo. H., Jr. III, 36
Birdsall, Geo. H., Jr. III, 203
Birdsall, Geo. H., Jr. III, 334
Birdsall, George III, 35
Birdsall, George V, 477
Birdsall, George VI, 616
Birdsall, George VI, 617
Birdsall, George F. III, 36
Birdsall, George F. V, 477
Birdsall, George H. III, 36
Birdsall, George H. III, 56
Birdsall, George H. III, 266
Birdsall, George H., Jr. III, 35
Birdsall, George Harold III, 203
Birdsall, George Henry III, 34
Birdsall, George Henry III, 35
Birdsall, George R. III, 35
Birdsall, Gertrude J. VI, 617
Birdsall, Gertrude J. VI, 622
Birdsall, Gertrude J. VI, 625
Birdsall, Gertrude J. VI, 626
Birdsall, Gertrude J. VI, 670
Birdsall, Gideon M. II, 281
Birdsall, Grace V, 477
Birdsall, Gula Elma IV, 1352
Birdsall, Gulielma IV, 1352
Birdsall, Hannah III, 396
Birdsall, Hannah IV, 1352
Birdsall, Hannah V, 477
Birdsall, Hannah V, 894
Birdsall, Hannah V, 948
Birdsall, Hannah V, 958
Birdsall, Hannah VI, 366
Birdsall, Hannah VI, 471
Birdsall, Hannah VI, 565
Birdsall, Hannah VI, 617
Birdsall, Hannah VI, 618
Birdsall, Hannah VI, 619
Birdsall, Hannah VI, 641
Birdsall, Hannah A. V, 477
Birdsall, Hannah Almirah V, 477
Birdsall, Hannah C. III, 351
Birdsall, Hannah G. V, 25
Birdsall, Harriet IV, 1352
Birdsall, Harriet M. IV, 1352
Birdsall, Henry III, 35
Birdsall, Henry III, 36
Birdsall, Henry III, 480
Birdsall, Henry C. III, 35
Birdsall, Henry Y. III, 37
Birdsall, Henry Young III, 35
Birdsall, Herbert Gardner VI, 622
Birdsall, Isaac III, 35
Birdsall, Isaac III, 396
Birdsall, Isaac IV, 1352
Birdsall, Israel IV, 1352
Birdsall, J. III, 110
Birdsall, Jacob III, 34
Birdsall, Jacob III, 35
Birdsall, Jacob III, 123
Birdsall, James I, 624
Birdsall, James II, 728
Birdsall, James III, 34
Birdsall, James III, 37
Birdsall, James IV, 1352
Birdsall, James IV, 1366
Birdsall, James V, 477
Birdsall, James A. III, 35
Birdsall, James A. V, 477
Birdsall, James Albert V, 894
Birdsall, James F. III, 35
Birdsall, James F. III, 36
Birdsall, James F. III, 110
Birdsall, James F. III, 480
Birdsall, James F. III, 497
Birdsall, James L. III, 35
Birdsall, James M. E. III, 35
Birdsall, Jane V, 948
Birdsall, Jane H. IV, 1352
Birdsall, Jas. III, 396
Birdsall, Jas. III, 404
Birdsall, Jas. F. III, 497
Birdsall, Jericho III, 34
Birdsall, Jericho III, 35
Birdsall, Jerusha III, 34
Birdsall, Jerusha III, 35
Birdsall, Jerusha III, 36
Birdsall, Jerusha III, 480
Birdsall, Jesse III, 35
Birdsall, Jesse III, 80
Birdsall, Jesse IV, 1352
Birdsall, Jesse, Jr. IV, 1352
Birdsall, Joana III, 415
Birdsall, Joanah III, 396
Birdsall, Joel II, 838
Birdsall, Joel VI, 366
Birdsall, Joel VI, 617
Birdsall, Joel VI, 618
Birdsall, Johannah III, 452
Birdsall, John VI, 471
Birdsall, John VI, 616
Birdsall, John VI, 617
Birdsall, John VI, 618
Birdsall, John VI, 619
Birdsall, John VI, 624
Birdsall, John VI, 658
Birdsall, John VI, 723
Birdsall, John Brown VI, 618
Birdsall, John P. III, 35
Birdsall, John Wm. III, 35
Birdsall, Jonathan III, 35
Birdsall, Jonathan III, 161
Birdsall, Jonathan III, 351
Birdsall, Jonathan IV, 1352
Birdsall, Jonathan M. III, 35
Birdsall, Joseph IV, 1352
Birdsall, Joseph V, 477
Birdsall, Joseph VI, 616
Birdsall, Joseph VI, 617
Birdsall, Joseph Edgar III, 36
Birdsall, Josephine IV, 1352
Birdsall, Josephine IV, 1379
Birdsall, Josiah III, 34
Birdsall, Lavenia VI, 471
Birdsall, Lavenia VI, 619
Birdsall, Lavinia III, 35
Birdsall, Lawrence Edgar II, 838
Birdsall, Leah VI, 471
Birdsall, Leah VI, 619
Birdsall, Levenia V, 477
Birdsall, Levinia III, 35
Birdsall, Levinia V, 477
Birdsall, Levinia V, 480
Birdsall, Lewis W. IV, 1352
Birdsall, Lidia V, 25
Birdsall, Lilian Eloise III, 36
Birdsall, Lillian H. VI, 617
Birdsall, Lillian H. VI, 618
Birdsall, Lillian H. VI, 622
Birdsall, Lillian H. VI, 626
Birdsall, Lindley IV, 1352
Birdsall, Lindley Hoag III, 34
Birdsall, Lindley Hoag, Jr. III, 203
Birdsall, Lois B. III, 35
Birdsall, Louisa W. III, 35
Birdsall, Louisa W. III, 36
Birdsall, Louise III, 35
Birdsall, Louise III, 37
Birdsall, Lydia III, 35
Birdsall, Lydia III, 297
Birdsall, Lydia V, 477
Birdsall, Lydia V, 894
Birdsall, Lydia V, 895
Birdsall, Lydia VI, 615
Birdsall, Lydia VI, 616
Birdsall, Lydia VI, 617
Birdsall, Lydia VI, 618
Birdsall, Lydia VI, 630
Birdsall, Lydia Ann III, 36
Birdsall, Mabel III, 36
Birdsall, Mabel V, 477
Birdsall, Mack, Henry Q. III, 36
Birdsall, Margaret III, 34
Birdsall, Margaret III, 36
Birdsall, Margaret III, 365
Birdsall, Margaret VI, 617
Birdsall, Margaret VI, 618
Birdsall, Margaret T. VI, 619
Birdsall, Margaret T. VI, 657
Birdsall, Margaret T. VI, 714
Birdsall, Maria D. IV, 1352
Birdsall, Mariah IV, 1352
Birdsall, Martha III, 34
Birdsall, Martha III, 35
Birdsall, Martha III, 36
Birdsall, Martha III, 37
Birdsall, Martha III, 91
Birdsall, Martha III, 351
Birdsall, Martha V, 25
Birdsall, Martha V, 477
Birdsall, Martha VI, 616
Birdsall, Martha VI, 617
Birdsall, Martha Malecca V, 894
Birdsall, Martha Melissa V, 477
Birdsall, Martha S. III, 36
Birdsall, Martha W. III, 35
Birdsall, Martha W. III, 91
Birdsall, Mary II, 699
Birdsall, Mary III, 32
Birdsall, Mary III, 35
Birdsall, Mary III, 36
Birdsall, Mary III, 147
Birdsall, Mary III, 161
Birdsall, Mary III, 168
Birdsall, Mary III, 219
Birdsall, Mary III, 223
Birdsall, Mary III, 272
Birdsall, Mary III, 280
Birdsall, Mary III, 371
Birdsall, Mary III, 396
Birdsall, Mary IV, 1352
Birdsall, Mary VI, 366
Birdsall, Mary VI, 471
Birdsall, Mary VI, 616
Birdsall, Mary VI, 617
Birdsall, Mary VI, 618
Birdsall, Mary VI, 619
Birdsall, Mary VI, 624
Birdsall, Mary VI, 630
Birdsall, Mary VI, 658
Birdsall, Mary VI, 723
Birdsall, Mary A. III, 35
Birdsall, Mary Ann III, 35
Birdsall, Mary Ann V, 25
Birdsall, Mary Ann V, 477
Birdsall, Mary Ann V, 500
Birdsall, Mary Ann V, 501
Birdsall, Mary Anna VI, 617
Birdsall, Mary B. III, 35
Birdsall, Mary B. III, 36
Birdsall, Mary B. III, 37
Birdsall, Mary B. III, 349
Birdsall, Mary B. V, 477
Birdsall, Mary B. V, 534
Birdsall, Mary C. V, 948
Birdsall, Mary C. VI, 618
Birdsall, Mary Canby VI, 615
Birdsall, Mary Canby VI, 616
Birdsall, Mary Canby VI, 617
Birdsall, Mary D. III, 36
Birdsall, Mary D. III, 215
Birdsall, Mary E. V, 477
Birdsall, Mary E. V, 947
Birdsall, Mary Elizabeth VI, 617
Birdsall, Mary Ellen VI, 618
Birdsall, Mary Ellen VI, 635
Birdsall, Mary Elma I, 624
Birdsall, Mary Elma IV, 1352
Birdsall, Mary Etta VI, 617
Birdsall, Mary Hannah III, 396
Birdsall, Mary Jane III, 35
Birdsall, Mary P. III, 35
Birdsall, Mary P. III, 161
Birdsall, Mary S. III, 36
Birdsall, Mary T. V, 477
Birdsall, Mattie C. III, 34
Birdsall, Mercy III, 36
Birdsall, Mercy III, 396
Birdsall, Moses T. III, 34
Birdsall, Nancy III, 34
Birdsall, Nancy IV, 1352
Birdsall, Nathan III, 36
Birdsall, Nathan D. III, 36
Birdsall, Nehemiah III, 35
Birdsall, Patty M. V, 477
Birdsall, Phebe III, 34
Birdsall, Phebe III, 36
Birdsall, Phebe III, 37
Birdsall, Phebe III, 56
Birdsall, Phebe III, 112
Birdsall, Phebe III, 203
Birdsall, Phebe III, 266
Birdsall, Phebe III, 272
Birdsall, Phebe V, 25
Birdsall, Phebe V, 477
Birdsall, Phebe V, 894
Birdsall, Phebe A. V, 895
Birdsall, Phebe A. III, 56
Birdsall, Phebe Ann III, 36
Birdsall, Phebe Ann IV, 1352
Birdsall, Phebe Anna III, 35
Birdsall, Phebe Anna III, 56
Birdsall, Phebe G. III, 28
Birdsall, Phebe G. III, 36
Birdsall, Phebe Jane III, 36
Birdsall, Phebe S. III, 35
Birdsall, Phebe S. III, 36
Birdsall, Phebe S. III, 110
Birdsall, Philena III, 35
Birdsall, Philena III, 351
Birdsall, Priscilla V, 25
Birdsall, Priscilla V, 477
Birdsall, Priscilla V, 894
Birdsall, Priscilla V, 895
Birdsall, R. V, 25
Birdsall, R. Hannah VI, 617
Birdsall, Rachel V, 25
Birdsall, Rachel V, 477
Birdsall, Rachel V, 511
Birdsall, Rachel V, 526
Birdsall, Rachel VI, 471
Birdsall, Rachel VI, 565
Birdsall, Rachel VI, 616
Birdsall, Rachel VI, 617
Birdsall, Rachel VI, 618
Birdsall, Rachel VI, 619
Birdsall, Rachel VI, 624
Birdsall, Rachel VI, 630
Birdsall, Rachel VI, 641
Birdsall, Rachel VI, 675
Birdsall, Rachel VI, 697
Birdsall, Rachel VI, 708
Birdsall, Rachel VI, 724
Birdsall, Rachel Ann VI, 617
Birdsall, Rachel Hannah VI, 617
Birdsall, Rachel L. V, 477
Birdsall, Rachel P. V, 477
Birdsall, Rachel P. VI, 616
Birdsall, Rachel P. VI, 617
Birdsall, Rachel Thornton III, 36
Birdsall, Rachel Y. III, 36
Birdsall, Rachel Y. III, 215
Birdsall, Ralph VI, 625
Birdsall, Ralph Birdsall VI, 622
Birdsall, Rebecca VI, 617
Birdsall, Rebecca VI, 618
Birdsall, Rebecca VI, 619
Birdsall, Rebecca VI, 622
Birdsall, Rebecca VI, 625
Birdsall, Rebecca VI, 627
Birdsall, Rebecca VI, 675
Birdsall, Rebecca VI, 714
Birdsall, Rebecca VI, 723
Birdsall, Rebecca VI, 733
Birdsall, Rebecca VI, 734
Birdsall, Rebecca Alice VI, 617
Birdsall, Rebecca Alice VI, 618
Birdsall, Rebecca Alice VI, 622
Birdsall, Rebecca Alice VI, 623
Birdsall, Rebecca Mary VI, 618
Birdsall, Rebecca Mary VI, 619
Birdsall, Rebecca Mary VI, 657
Birdsall, Reuben III, 36
Birdsall, Reuben III, 223
Birdsall, Reuben L. III, 34
Birdsall, Reuben L. III, 36
Birdsall, Reuben L. III, 87
Birdsall, Reuben, Jr. III, 36
Birdsall, Richard III, 36
Birdsall, Richard IV, 1352
Birdsall, Robert III, 35
Birdsall, Robert Bland III, 35
Birdsall, Rosannah III, 396
Birdsall, Rosannah III, 408
Birdsall, Rosannah III, 467
Birdsall, Ruth V, 25

Birdsall, Ruth V, 136
Birdsall, Ruth V, 477
Birdsall, Ruth V, 480
Birdsall, Ruth V, 537
Birdsall, Ruth VI, 471
Birdsall, Ruth VI, 618
Birdsall, Ruth VI, 619
Birdsall, Ruth VI, 697
Birdsall, Ruth Hannah VI, 617
Birdsall, Ruth Hannah VI, 618
Birdsall, Ruth Hannah VI, 625
Birdsall, Ruth Hannah VI, 704
Birdsall, Ruth Hannah, Jr. VI, 705
Birdsall, S. Josephine III, 36
Birdsall, Sally IV, 1352
Birdsall, Sally IV, 1375
Birdsall, Samuel III, 34
Birdsall, Samuel III, 36
Birdsall, Samuel III, 121
Birdsall, Samuel III, 337
Birdsall, Samuel III, 396
Birdsall, Samuel V, 25
Birdsall, Samuel V, 477
Birdsall, Samuel V, 500
Birdsall, Samuel VI, 471
Birdsall, Samuel VI, 619
Birdsall, Sarah III, 34
Birdsall, Sarah III, 36
Birdsall, Sarah III, 71
Birdsall, Sarah III, 95
Birdsall, Sarah III, 111
Birdsall, Sarah III, 161
Birdsall, Sarah III, 223
Birdsall, Sarah III, 396
Birdsall, Sarah III, 452
Birdsall, Sarah V, 25
Birdsall, Sarah V, 477
Birdsall, Sarah V, 894
Birdsall, Sarah VI, 617
Birdsall, Sarah VI, 618
Birdsall, Sarah VI, 623
Birdsall, Sarah VI, 658
Birdsall, Sarah VI, 705
Birdsall, Sarah F. III, 34
Birdsall, Sarah Frances III, 36
Birdsall, Sarah J. III, 111
Birdsall, Sarah Jane III, 35
Birdsall, Sarah Jane III, 112
Birdsall, Sarah Jane III, 377
Birdsall, Sarah M. IV, 1352
Birdsall, Sarah S. III, 36
Birdsall, Sarah W. III, 36
Birdsall, Scipio IV, 1352
Birdsall, Solomon III, 34
Birdsall, Solomon III, 36
Birdsall, Stephen III, 16
Birdsall, Stephen III, 35
Birdsall, Susan III, 121
Birdsall, Susan III, 396
Birdsall, Susan III, 404
Birdsall, Susan A. III, 121
Birdsall, Susan Ann III, 36
Birdsall, Susan H. III, 34
Birdsall, Susan R. III, 337
Birdsall, Sylvia III, 36
Birdsall, Thomas II, 783
Birdsall, Thomas III, 34
Birdsall, Thomas III, 396
Birdsall, Thomas V, 25
Birdsall, Thomas V, 477
Birdsall, Thomas V, 534
Birdsall, Thomas VI, 471
Birdsall, Thomas VI, 616
Birdsall, Thomas VI, 617
Birdsall, Thomas VI, 619
Birdsall, Thomas B. V, 477
Birdsall, Thomas H. III, 35
Birdsall, Thomas H. III, 36
Birdsall, Thomas H. III, 37
Birdsall, Thomas W. III, 36
Birdsall, Thomas W. III, 365
Birdsall, Thomas W. V, 477
Birdsall, Thomas W. VI, 616
Birdsall, Thomas W. VI, 617
Birdsall, Thomas W. C. V, 477
Birdsall, Thomas Whitson VI, 617
Birdsall, Thornton III, 34
Birdsall, Thos. II, 838
Birdsall, Thos. V, 894
Birdsall, Thos. H. III, 34
Birdsall, Thos. W. III, 34
Birdsall, Timothy IV, 1352
Birdsall, Tracy V, 477
Birdsall, Vera V, 477
Birdsall, Wd. Charity Farrington III, 396
Birdsall, Wd. Elizabeth III, 34
Birdsall, Wd. Mary III, 16
Birdsall, Whiteson VI, 630
Birdsall, Whitson V, 25
Birdsall, Whitson VI, 471
Birdsall, Whitson VI, 565
Birdsall, Whitson VI, 616
Birdsall, Whitson VI, 617
Birdsall, Whitson VI, 618
Birdsall, Whitson VI, 624
Birdsall, Whitson VI, 630
Birdsall, Whitson VI, 641
Birdsall, Whitson VI, 675
Birdsall, Whitson VI, 697
Birdsall, Whitson VI, 708
Birdsall, Whitson, Sr. VI, 618
Birdsall, Widow Deborah B. VI, 621
Birdsall, Widow Rebecca VI, 621
Birdsall, Wilfred Thomas II, 838
Birdsall, William II, 699
Birdsall, William III, 36
Birdsall, William III, 215
Birdsall, William IV, 1352
Birdsall, William V, 25
Birdsall, William V, 136
Birdsall, William V, 477
Birdsall, William V, 480
Birdsall, William V, 537
Birdsall, William VI, 366
Birdsall, William VI, 471
Birdsall, William VI, 565
Birdsall, William VI, 618
Birdsall, William VI, 619
Birdsall, William B. IV, 1352
Birdsall, William Edwin III, 35
Birdsall, William Edwin III, 36
Birdsall, William George VI, 618
Birdsall, William H. V, 25
Birdsall, William H. V, 477
Birdsall, William H. VI, 471
Birdsall, William J. III, 35
Birdsall, William J. IV, 1352
Birdsall, William J. IV, 1379
Birdsall, William N. III, 35
Birdsall, William Pennington VI, 619
Birdsall, Willis IV, 1352
Birdsall, Wm. III, 91
Birdsall, Wm. V, 477
Birdsall, Wm. VI, 471
Birdsall, Wm. VI, 617
Birdsall, Wm. VI, 619
Birdsall, Wm. VI, 708
Birdsall, Wm. B. IV, 1352
Birdsall, Wm. Edward Walling III, 35
Birdsall, Wm. Edward Walling III, 36
Birdsall, Wm. G. VI, 714
Birdsall, Wm. George VI, 617
Birdsall, Wm. George VI, 619
Birdsall, Wm. George VI, 657
Birdsall, Wm. George VI, 714
Birdsall, Wm. H. V, 477
Birdsall, Wm. Pennington VI, 618
Birdsall, Wm. W. II, 838
Birdsall, Wm., Jr. III, 34
Birdsall, Wm., Jr. III, 363
Birdsall, Zada V, 477
Birdsall, Zadoc III, 36
Birdsall, Zadock M. III, 34
Birdsall, Zady V, 25
Birdsall, Zady V, 894
Birdsall, Zephamiah IV, 1167
Birdsall, Zephaniah III, 36
Birdsall, Zephaniah III, 37
Birdsall, Zephaniah III, 349
Birdsall, Zephaniah IV, 1148
Birdsall, Zephaniah IV, 1233
Birdsall, Zepheniah III, 34
Birdsel, Andrew V, 477
Birdsel, Edward V, 477
Birdsel, George V, 477
Birdsel, Joseph V, 477
Birdsel, Levina V, 300
Birdsel, Martha V, 477
Birdsel, Rachel P. V, 477
Birdsel, Thomas W. V, 477
Birdsell, Ann M. IV, 1148
Birdsell, Anna IV, 1148
Birdsell, Boswell IV, 1246
Birdsell, Byron F. IV, 1246
Birdsell, Cole IV, 1246
Birdsell, Daniel IV, 1366
Birdsell, Edna IV, 1246
Birdsell, Harriet M. IV, 1366
Birdsell, Jane F. IV, 1148
Birdsell, John IV, 1246
Birdsell, Lena IV, 1246
Birdsell, Maria D. IV, 1366
Birdsell, William IV, 1246
Birdsell, Zephaniah IV, 1148
Birdshall, Elizabeth I, 932
Birdshall, Hannah VI, 708
Birdshall, James I, 932
Birdshall, Mary Ellen I, 932
Birdson, Lucinda VI, 53
Birdsong, Lucinda VI, 53
Birge, Frances IV, 1233
Birge, Zelma IV, 1233
Birkbeck, Morris II, 466
Birkell, John III, 37
Birket, Benjamin III, 37
Birkhead, Susanna IV, 560
Birkhead, Susanna IV, 562
Birkill, John III, 37
Birkley, Abraham II, 197
Birkley, Abraham II, 222
Birkley, Elizabeth II, 197
Birkley, Elizabeth II, 222
Birks, John VI, 907
Birks, John Partree VI, 995
Birks, Mary VI, 995
Birmingham, Betty VI, 810
Birmingham, John II, 337
Birmingham, Thomas II, 337
Birr, Mary II, 203
Birrell, George IV, 686
Birrell, Margaret IV, 686
Birum, Alfred I, 39
Birum, Augustus I, 39
Birum, Cader I, 39
Birum, Caleb I, 39
Birum, Edwin I, 39
Birum, Eli I, 39
Birum, Emaline Isabella V, 827
Birum, Exum I, 39
Birum, Jemmima I, 39
Birum, John I, 39
Birum, Kader I, 39
Birum, Martha Maria V, 827
Birum, Miram V, 827
Birum, Miriam I, 39
Birum, Moses I, 39
Birum, Nathan I, 39
Birum, Orpah I, 39
Birum, Robert I, 39
Birum, Sibba I, 39
Birum, William I, 39
Bise, John VI, 970
Bise, Polly VI, 970
Bisel, Eliza Vore IV, 1149
Bisher, Mary Louise V, 656
Bisher, Mary Louise V, 659
Bishon, Margaret V, 986
Bishop, Abigail I, 265
Bishop, Abigail I, 267
Bishop, Abigail I, 276
Bishop, Abigail II, 115
Bishop, Abigail II, 166
Bishop, Abram T. IV, 679
Bishop, Amos IV, 611
Bishop, Amy Ann V, 374
Bishop, Ann II, 115
Bishop, Ann II, 166
Bishop, Ann II, 197
Bishop, Ann II, 242
Bishop, Ann II, 281
Bishop, Ann II, 293
Bishop, Ann III, 480
Bishop, Ann IV, 611
Bishop, Ann V, 25
Bishop, Ann V, 70
Bishop, Ann VI, 879
Bishop, Anna I, 267
Bishop, Anna I, 299
Bishop, Anna L. IV, 679
Bishop, Anne II, 197
Bishop, Arete C. III, 37
Bishop, Avice I, 265
Bishop, Benjamin I, 265
Bishop, Chas. Sumner IV, 1272
Bishop, Christopher II, 197
Bishop, David IV, 610
Bishop, David IV, 611
Bishop, David IV, 631
Bishop, Delila E. IV, 679
Bishop, Edward II, 281
Bishop, Edward III, 37
Bishop, Edward B. II, 166
Bishop, Edward B. II, 281
Bishop, Edward H. II, 166
Bishop, Elenor F. VI, 807
Bishop, Elisa R. II, 166
Bishop, Eliz. III, 37
Bishop, Eliza II, 166
Bishop, Eliza II, 197
Bishop, Eliza II, 281
Bishop, Eliza II, 299
Bishop, Eliza IV, 611
Bishop, Eliza R. II, 281
Bishop, Eliza R. II, 294
Bishop, Elizabeth I, 265
Bishop, Elizabeth I, 267
Bishop, Elizabeth I, 268
Bishop, Elizabeth I, 276
Bishop, Elizabeth I, 299
Bishop, Elizabeth I, 302
Bishop, Elizabeth II, 197
Bishop, Elizabeth II, 466
Bishop, Elizabeth II, 979
Bishop, Elizabeth IV, 370
Bishop, Elizabeth IV, 568
Bishop, Elizabeth VI, 366
Bishop, Elizabeth VI, 422
Bishop, Emaline II, 281
Bishop, Emaline II, 293
Bishop, Ezekiel I, 281
Bishop, Ezekiel I, 300
Bishop, Fanny IV, 678
Bishop, Fanny IV, 679
Bishop, Fanny J. IV, 679
Bishop, H. III, 37
Bishop, Hanah I, 36
Bishop, Hannah I, 52
Bishop, Hannah I, 265
Bishop, Hannah I, 267
Bishop, Hannah I, 272
Bishop, Hannah I, 275
Bishop, Hannah I, 281
Bishop, Hannah I, 299
Bishop, Hannah II, 166
Bishop, Hannah II, 197
Bishop, Hannah II, 198
Bishop, Hannah II, 229
Bishop, Hannah II, 281
Bishop, Hannah IV, 610
Bishop, Hannah IV, 611
Bishop, Hannah IV, 927
Bishop, Hannah IV, 1272
Bishop, Hannah VI, 366
Bishop, Hannah VI, 471
Bishop, Hannah VI, 500
Bishop, Hannah VI, 591
Bishop, Hannah VI, 596
Bishop, Hannah H. II, 166
Bishop, Harriet E. IV, 679
Bishop, Henry I, 265
Bishop, Henry VI, 366
Bishop, Henry H. IV, 678
Bishop, Isaac II, 197
Bishop, Isaac II, 213
Bishop, Isaac II, 237
Bishop, Isaac T. IV, 679
Bishop, Jacob IV, 678
Bishop, Jacob IV, 679
Bishop, Jacob R. IV, 679
Bishop, James I, 265
Bishop, James I, 267
Bishop, James I, 275
Bishop, James I, 281
Bishop, James I, 299
Bishop, James I, 300
Bishop, James I, 302
Bishop, James IV, 568
Bishop, James S. VI, 879
Bishop, Jesse IV, 568
Bishop, Jesse Brooks VI, 366
Bishop, Jessie Brooke VI, 366
Bishop, Job II, 166
Bishop, Job II, 197
Bishop, Job II, 281
Bishop, Job II, 299
Bishop, Job VI, 366
Bishop, John I, 36
Bishop, John I, 52
Bishop, John I, 265
Bishop, John I, 267
Bishop, John I, 281
Bishop, John I, 299
Bishop, John I, 300
Bishop, John I, 301
Bishop, John I, 310
Bishop, John II, 197
Bishop, John II, 229
Bishop, John II, 699
Bishop, John II, 728
Bishop, John IV, 511
Bishop, John V, 374
Bishop, John VI, 366
Bishop, John VI, 471
Bishop, John VI, 591
Bishop, John C. IV, 679
Bishop, John R. II, 466
Bishop, Jonathan VI, 366
Bishop, Jonathan VI, 471
Bishop, Jonathan VI, 500
Bishop, Jonathan VI, 591
Bishop, Jonathan VI, 596
Bishop, Jonathan VI, 904
Bishop, Joseph I, 265
Bishop, Joseph I, 267
Bishop, Joseph I, 268
Bishop, Joseph I, 276
Bishop, Joseph II, 115
Bishop, Joseph II, 198
Bishop, Joseph III, 37
Bishop, Joseph IV, 21
Bishop, Joseph IV, 140
Bishop, Joseph IV, 370
Bishop, Joseph IV, 454
Bishop, Joseph IV, 568
Bishop, Joseph VI, 366
Bishop, Joseph VI, 591
Bishop, Joseph F. IV, 679
Bishop, Joseph R. II, 166
Bishop, Joseph R. II, 197
Bishop, Joseph R. II, 229
Bishop, Joseph R. II, 281
Bishop, Josiah VI, 366
Bishop, Josiah VI, 591
Bishop, Levi II, 115
Bishop, Lidia I, 299
Bishop, Louisa IV, 370
Bishop, Louisa IV, 1272
Bishop, Louisa H. II, 166
Bishop, Louise Newbold VI, 366
Bishop, Lucia II, 337
Bishop, Lucy II, 166
Bishop, Lucy II, 197
Bishop, Lydia I, 267
Bishop, Lydia I, 276
Bishop, Lydia IV, 611
Bishop, Lydia IV, 644
Bishop, Lydia IV, 891
Bishop, Lydia IV, 927
Bishop, Lydia IV, 979
Bishop, Lydia IV, 1024
Bishop, Lydia IV, 1307
Bishop, Lydia Alma VI, 366
Bishop, Lydia H. II, 166
Bishop, Lydia H. II, 281
Bishop, Lydia H. II, 304
Bishop, Lydia Randall V, 374
Bishop, Margaretta H. V, 223
Bishop, Maria VI, 366
Bishop, Martha IV, 611
Bishop, Martha IV, 1049
Bishop, Martha VI, 460
Bishop, Martha E. VI, 366
Bishop, Martha E. VI, 460
Bishop, Martha H. IV, 511
Bishop, Martha L. VI, 366
Bishop, Martha M. IV, 511
Bishop, Martha M. IV, 534
Bishop, Martha W. VI, 366
Bishop, Mary I, 265
Bishop, Mary I, 267
Bishop, Mary I, 299
Bishop, Mary I, 302
Bishop, Mary I, 527
Bishop, Mary I, 542
Bishop, Mary II, 166
Bishop, Mary II, 197
Bishop, Mary II, 213
Bishop, Mary II, 229
Bishop, Mary II, 237
Bishop, Mary II, 281
Bishop, Mary II, 728
Bishop, Mary II, 963
Bishop, Mary IV, 370
Bishop, Mary IV, 454
Bishop, Mary IV, 568
Bishop, Mary IV, 590
Bishop, Mary IV, 611
Bishop, Mary IV, 631
Bishop, Mary IV, 891
Bishop, Mary IV, 892
Bishop, Mary VI, 366
Bishop, Mary VI, 390
Bishop, Mary VI, 591
Bishop, Mary VI, 596
Bishop, Mary Ann VI, 904
Bishop, Mary C. L. II, 699
Bishop, Mary E. IV, 679
Bishop, Mary H. II, 166
Bishop, Mary L. II, 281
Bishop, Mary L. II, 294
Bishop, Mary Louisa II, 166
Bishop, Mary M. II, 166
Bishop, Mary M. II, 281
Bishop, Maud Wright VI, 366
Bishop, Miriam I, 265
Bishop, Miriam I, 267
Bishop, Miriam I, 268
Bishop, Naomi IV, 21
Bishop, Naomi IV, 59
Bishop, Nicholas IV, 610
Bishop, Nicholas IV, 927
Bishop, Patience VI, 366
Bishop, Patience VI, 471
Bishop, Patience VI, 500
Bishop, Patience VI, 591
Bishop, Patience VI, 596
Bishop, Phebe I, 267

Bishop, Phebe I, 277
Bishop, Phebe III, 480
Bishop, Phebe III, 491
Bishop, Phebe J. IV, 679
Bishop, Rachel I, 281
Bishop, Rachel I, 299
Bishop, Rachel I, 310
Bishop, Rachel II, 281
Bishop, Ralph Elding V, 613
Bishop, Rebecca I, 267
Bishop, Rebecca II, 197
Bishop, Rebecca II, 206
Bishop, Rebecca F. IV, 511
Bishop, Rebecca Field II, 699
Bishop, Rhoda IV, 311
Bishop, Robert V, 25
Bishop, Robert Ridgway II, 197
Bishop, Ruth I, 300
Bishop, Ruth I, 301
Bishop, Ruth II, 197
Bishop, Sam'l Perkins III, 37
Bishop, Samuel III, 480
Bishop, Samuel III, 491
Bishop, Samuel VI, 366
Bishop, Sarah I, 267
Bishop, Sarah II, 197
Bishop, Sarah II, 223
Bishop, Sarah II, 281
Bishop, Sarah II, 299
Bishop, Sarah IV, 611
Bishop, Sarah IV, 891
Bishop, Sarah VI, 366
Bishop, Sarah VI, 445
Bishop, Sarah B. IV, 1024
Bishop, Sarah B. IV, 1026
Bishop, Selia I, 300
Bishop, Shepherd V, 374
Bishop, Silas I, 281
Bishop, Silas I, 300
Bishop, Stephen IV, 21
Bishop, Stephen VI, 366
Bishop, Susan IV, 611
Bishop, Susan IV, 640
Bishop, Thomas I, 300
Bishop, Thomas II, 166
Bishop, Thomas II, 466
Bishop, Thomas IV, 611
Bishop, Thomas IV, 891
Bishop, Thomas VI, 366
Bishop, Thomas VI, 591
Bishop, Victoria IV, 679
Bishop, Wd. Hannah II, 166
Bishop, William I, 281
Bishop, William I, 300
Bishop, William II, 166
Bishop, William II, 197
Bishop, William II, 281
Bishop, William II, 299
Bishop, William IV, 611
Bishop, William IV, 644
Bishop, William IV, 679
Bishop, William IV, 891
Bishop, William IV, 927
Bishop, William IV, 1024
Bishop, William VI, 366
Bishop, William VI, 460
Bishop, William B. VI, 366
Bishop, William D. VI, 366
Bishop, William D. VI, 460
Bishop, William R. II, 166
Bishop, William R. II, 281
Bishop, William Ridgway II, 166
Bishop, Willis C. IV, 1307
Bishop, Wm. II, 115
Bishop, Wm. II, 294
Bishop, Wm. IV, 511
Bishop, Wm. IV, 534
Bishop, Wm. IV, 979
Bishop, Wm. R. II, 294
Bisop, Hanah I, 36
Bisop, Hannah I, 52
Bisop, John I, 36
Bisop, John I, 52
Bispham, Abigail II, 198
Bispham, Abigail V, 25
Bispham, Ann II, 466
Bispham, Ann II, 717
Bispham, Ann Pearson II, 466
Bispham, Benjamin II, 56
Bispham, Benjamin II, 198
Bispham, Charles II, 466
Bispham, Charles II, 728
Bispham, Elizabeth II, 166
Bispham, Elizabeth II, 466
Bispham, Elizabeth V, 25
Bispham, Elizabeth V, 115
Bispham, Elizabeth V, 137
Bispham, Hannah II, 198
Bispham, Hannah II, 244
Bispham, Hannah V, 25
Bispham, Hannah V, 100
Bispham, Hannah V, 101
Bispham, Jane L. II, 728
Bispham, Jane L. II, 764
Bispham, Jane S. II, 728
Bispham, Jerusha V, 25
Bispham, John II, 166
Bispham, John II, 198
Bispham, John II, 244
Bispham, John II, 466
Bispham, John, Jr. II, 198
Bispham, John, Jr. II, 466
Bispham, Jonah V, 25
Bispham, Joseph II, 166
Bispham, Joseph II, 176
Bispham, Joseph II, 198
Bispham, Joseph II, 337
Bispham, Joseph II, 466
Bispham, Joseph V, 25
Bispham, Joseph Mutton III, 37
Bispham, Joseph, Jr. II, 728
Bispham, Joshua II, 337
Bispham, Joshua II, 466
Bispham, Josiah V, 25
Bispham, Lydia II, 783
Bispham, Lydia II, 838
Bispham, Margaret II, 166
Bispham, Margaret II, 198
Bispham, Mary Ann II, 281
Bispham, Rebecca II, 466
Bispham, Samuel II, 466
Bispham, Sarah II, 56
Bispham, Sarah II, 198
Bispham, Sarah II, 466
Bispham, Sarah II, 582
Bispham, Stacy II, 337
Bispham, Stacy II, 466
Bispham, Susanna II, 466
Bispham, Susannah II, 466
Bispham, Susannah II, 618
Bispham, Thomas II, 198
Bispham, Thomas V, 25
Bispham, Wd. Elizabeth II, 176
Bispham, William II, 337
Bispham, William V, 25
Bispham, Wm. II, 466
Bispham, Wm. Lippincott II, 466
Bisphim, William V, 25
Bissel, Hannah II, 466
Bissel, Hannah II, 679
Bissel, Wm. II, 466
Bissel, Wm. II, 679
Bissell, Abigail I, 300
Bissell, Abigail I, 309
Bissell, Abigail II, 466
Bissell, Abigail II, 540
Bissell, Hannah II, 337
Bissell, Hannah II, 466
Bissell, Hannah II, 509
Bissell, Hannah II, 612
Bissell, James II, 337
Bissell, John II, 337
Bissell, John II, 466
Bissell, John II, 612
Bissell, Joseph II, 337
Bissell, Margaret II, 337
Bissell, Mary II, 337
Bissell, Samuel II, 337
Bissell, Samuel II, 466
Bissell, Samuel II, 540
Bissell, Sarah II, 337
Bissell, Thomas II, 337
Bissell, Wd. Abigail II, 614
Bissell, Wd. Hannah II, 337
Bissell, Wd. Margaret II, 466
Bissell, Wd. Margaret II, 612
Bissell, William II, 337
Bissell, Wm. II, 466
Bissell, Wm. II, 509
Bissell, Wm. II, 612
Bitle, John II, 337
Bitler, Mary IV, 170
Bitler, Mary IV, 177
Bittick, Mary I, 800
Bittle, Ann II, 337
Bittle, Elisabeth II, 466
Bittle, Elisabeth II, 618
Bittle, Elizabeth II, 337
Bittle, Hannah II, 466
Bittle, Hannah II, 679
Bittle, John II, 337
Bittle, John II, 338
Bittle, Joseph II, 337
Bittle, Joseph VI, 879
Bittle, Josiah II, 338
Bittle, Judith VI, 963
Bittle, Mary II, 337
Bittle, Mary II, 338
Bittle, Mary VI, 879
Bittle, Mary VI, 963
Bittle, Rachel II, 466
Bittle, Robert II, 338
Bittle, Samuel II, 338
Bittle, Samuel II, 466
Bittle, Thomas II, 338
Bittle, William II, 338
Bitzer, Virginia VI, 619
Bitzer, Virginia VI, 651
Bivan, Ellen Jane IV, 1272
Bivan, Jane IV, 1272
Bivan, Stacy IV, 1272
Biven, Abel V, 476
Biven, Abel V, 491
Biven, Charlotte V, 476
Biven, Charlotte V, 491
Biven, Elizabeth V, 476
Biven, Elizabeth V, 494
Biven, Jane V, 550
Biven, Jane V, 568
Biven, John V, 476
Biven, Maria IV, 369
Biven, Mary V, 476
Biven, Mary V, 500
Biven, Owen V, 476
Biven, Owen V, 500
Biven, Samuel V, 476
Bivens, Banister T. I, 1148
Bivens, C. T. I, 1148
Bivens, Carter I, 1148
Bivens, Emily Melviney I, 1148
Bivens, Etter I, 1148
Bivens, James Walter I, 1148
Bivens, John I, 1148
Bivens, Julia I, 1148
Bivens, Melvina I, 1148
Bivens, Mollie I, 1148
Bivens, Otterey I, 1148
Bivens, Rachel M. I, 1148
Bivens, Sarah I, 1148
Bivens, Washington I, 1148
Bivins, C. T. I, 1148
Bivins, Carter I, 1148
Bivins, Etter I, 1148
Bivins, Julia I, 1148
Blachard, Ephraim I, 111
Blachard, Isabel I, 111
Blachley, Cornelius Camden II, 979
Black, ??? III, 37
Black, Alfred III, 37
Black, Allen V, 374
Black, Allen V, 550
Black, Allen E. V, 374
Black, Allis II, 166
Black, Alonza VI, 799
Black, Andrew VI, 896
Black, Andrew VI, 969
Black, Ann T. II, 308
Black, Ann T. II, 316
Black, Ann T. II, 838
Black, Benjamin VI, 879
Black, Betsey VI, 840
Black, Betsy V, 25
Black, Betsy V, 48
Black, Betsy VI, 830
Black, Betsy VI, 858
Black, Caroline II, 308
Black, Caroline II, 316
Black, Catharine VI, 799
Black, Catharine VI, 807
Black, Christian II, 198
Black, Christiana II, 56
Black, Christiana II, 84
Black, Christiana II, 198
Black, Clarence V, 727
Black, Clarissa V, 374
Black, Clarissa V, 550
Black, Clayton IV, 121
Black, Daniel C. VI, 969
Black, Daniel M. VI, 799
Black, Delila V, 797
Black, Delila V, 802
Black, Dinah IV, 177
Black, Doris IV, 679
Black, Edward II, 166
Black, Edward II, 198
Black, Edward II, 248
Black, Edward III, 37
Black, Edwin II, 308
Black, Edwin II, 316
Black, Eleanor IV, 679
Black, Elenor II, 838
Black, Elizabeth II, 56
Black, Elizabeth II, 115
Black, Elizabeth II, 198
Black, Elizabeth II, 281
Black, Elizabeth II, 466
Black, Elizabeth II, 507
Black, Elizabeth VI, 870
Black, Elizabeth VI, 969
Black, Elizabeth L. VI, 799
Black, Ella V, 986
Black, Elvira VI, 799
Black, Emily N. II, 308
Black, Ethel J. V, 727
Black, Franklin II, 308
Black, Franklin II, 316
Black, Franklin II, 838
Black, Geo. Edward IV, 679
Black, George Edward IV, 679
Black, Greenville VI, 799
Black, Hannah II, 129
Black, Hannah II, 145
Black, Hattie V, 727
Black, Hope II, 198
Black, James VI, 799
Black, James VI, 879
Black, Jane VI, 812
Black, Jean VI, 879
Black, Jenny VI, 879
Black, Jenny VI, 969
Black, Job II, 56
Black, Job II, 198
Black, Job III, 37
Black, John II, 56
Black, John II, 84
Black, John II, 198
Black, John II, 338
Black, John VI, 799
Black, John VI, 801
Black, John VI, 812
Black, John VI, 814
Black, John VI, 829
Black, John VI, 830
Black, John VI, 831
Black, John VI, 837
Black, John VI, 848
Black, John VI, 858
Black, John VI, 879
Black, John A. V, 374
Black, John N. VI, 822
Black, John R. IV, 177
Black, John W. VI, 812
Black, John, Jr. III, 37
Black, Joseph II, 466
Black, Joseph R. V, 374
Black, Judith VI, 808
Black, Kitty VI, 837
Black, Laura Dryden IV, 679
Black, Laura Marguerite IV, 679
Black, Lora Ella IV, 1246
Black, Malinda C. V, 374
Black, Margaret VI, 799
Black, Margaret A. V, 374
Black, Margaret Ann V, 374
Black, Martha VI, 799
Black, Martha Ellis II, 826
Black, Martha J. VI, 812
Black, Mary II, 56
Black, Mary II, 84
Black, Mary II, 196
Black, Mary II, 198
Black, Mary II, 248
Black, Mary VI, 799
Black, Mary VI, 801
Black, Mary VI, 808
Black, Mary E. V, 374
Black, Mary T. II, 308
Black, Mary T. II, 316
Black, Mary T. II, 317
Black, Mary Taylor II, 838
Black, Matilda V, 550
Black, Matilda VI, 879
Black, Matilda C. V, 374
Black, Mattie I, 630
Black, Mattie I, 636
Black, Mattie May I, 620
Black, Michael VI, 848
Black, Michael VI, 879
Black, Mildred Rosser VI, 799
Black, Nancy VI, 879
Black, Newbold II, 838
Black, Oma L. V, 374
Black, Pearl V, 986
Black, Peggy Irvine VI, 799
Black, Percilla L. V, 986
Black, Percilla Lucile V, 986
Black, Polly VI, 799
Black, Polly VI, 827
Black, Polly VI, 829
Black, Polly VI, 969
Black, Robert W. V, 374
Black, Robina VI, 799
Black, Ruth Matilda V, 374
Black, Sally VI, 811
Black, Sally VI, 831
Black, Samuel II, 466
Black, Samuel VI, 969
Black, Samuel L. III, 37
Black, Sarah II, 198
Black, Sarah II, 466
Black, Sarah III, 37
Black, Sarah A. V, 374
Black, Sarah Ann II, 308
Black, Sarah Ann II, 316
Black, Sarah, Jr. II, 466
Black, Susan VI, 848
Black, Thomas II, 196
Black, Thomas II, 198
Black, Thomas II, 316
Black, Thomas III, 37
Black, Thomas VI, 811
Black, Thomas VI, 840
Black, Thomas N. II, 316
Black, Thomas Newbold II, 316
Black, Thomas Newbole II, 308
Black, Thos. II, 838
Black, William II, 166
Black, William II, 198
Black, William II, 316
Black, William III, 37
Black, William VI, 799
Black, William VI, 829
Black, William VI, 830
Black, William VI, 860
Black, William H. V, 374
Black, William Henry II, 308
Black, William Henry II, 316
Black, William M. VI, 799
Black, William, Jr. II, 308
Black, William, Jr. II, 316
Black, Wm. II, 466
Black, Wm. H. V, 374
Black, Wm. Henry II, 838
Black, Wm. Henry II, 839
Black, Wm., Jr. II, 466
Black, Wm., Jr. II, 838
Black, Wm., Sr. II, 838
Blackbourn, John IV, 506
Blackbourn, Moses IV, 506
Blackbourn, Rebecca II, 466
Blackbourn, Rebecca II, 653
Blackbourn, Thomas IV, 679
Blackbourne, Rachel II, 466
Blackbourne, Wd. Rachel II, 608
Blackburn, Abbie T. IV, 612
Blackburn, Abbie T. IV, 679
Blackburn, Abbie T. IV, 680
Blackburn, Abby J. IV, 611
Blackburn, Abel H. IV, 21
Blackburn, Abel H. IV, 611
Blackburn, Abel H. IV, 612
Blackburn, Abel H. IV, 679
Blackburn, Abel Hewitt IV, 611
Blackburn, Abigail II, 338
Blackburn, Addie IV, 1272
Blackburn, Albert E. II, 839
Blackburn, Alex III, 396
Blackburn, Alex. III, 447
Blackburn, Alexander III, 37
Blackburn, Alexander III, 295
Blackburn, Alexander III, 396
Blackburn, Alexander III, 422
Blackburn, Alexander VI, 982
Blackburn, Alexander M. III, 396
Blackburn, Alice B. IV, 612
Blackburn, Alice B. IV, 644
Blackburn, Alice M. IV, 679
Blackburn, Alice Marie IV, 679
Blackburn, Alice Marie IV, 746
Blackburn, Alice Marie IV, 800
Blackburn, Alice Marie IV, 836
Blackburn, Amelia V, 223
Blackburn, Amy IV, 21
Blackburn, Amy IV, 49
Blackburn, Amy IV, 59
Blackburn, Amy IV, 121
Blackburn, Amy IV, 135
Blackburn, Amy IV, 611
Blackburn, Amy Hannah IV, 21
Blackburn, Andrew IV, 680
Blackburn, Andrew VI, 954
Blackburn, Andrew VI, 982
Blackburn, Ann II, 338
Blackburn, Ann IV, 21
Blackburn, Ann IV, 39
Blackburn, Ann IV, 65
Blackburn, Ann IV, 75
Blackburn, Ann IV, 104
Blackburn, Ann IV, 121
Blackburn, Ann IV, 135
Blackburn, Ann IV, 611
Blackburn, Ann IV, 679
Blackburn, Ann IV, 776
Blackburn, Ann IV, 927
Blackburn, Ann IV, 1127
Blackburn, Ann V, 967
Blackburn, Ann VI, 230
Blackburn, Ann D. V, 25
Blackburn, Ann Lorena IV, 792
Blackburn, Anna IV, 121
Blackburn, Anna IV, 127
Blackburn, Anna IV, 611
Blackburn, Anna IV, 679
Blackburn, Anna IV, 1272

Blackburn, Anna V, 25
Blackburn, Anna B. III, 37
Blackburn, Anna B. IV, 615
Blackburn, Anna D. V, 25
Blackburn, Anna D. V, 57
Blackburn, Anna E. IV, 611
Blackburn, Anna E. IV, 612
Blackburn, Anna Lorena IV, 680
Blackburn, Anna P. IV, 611
Blackburn, Anne IV, 611
Blackburn, Anne IV, 679
Blackburn, Annie E. IV, 135
Blackburn, Annie E. IV, 611
Blackburn, Annie E. IV, 679
Blackburn, Annie E. IV, 680
Blackburn, Anthony IV, 21
Blackburn, Anthony VI, 366
Blackburn, Arthur IV, 611
Blackburn, Arthur IV, 612
Blackburn, Arthur IV, 679
Blackburn, Arthur IV, 927
Blackburn, Arthur IV, 928
Blackburn, Barbe IV, 679
Blackburn, Barbee IV, 679
Blackburn, Barbee IV, 721
Blackburn, Barbee IV, 927
Blackburn, Barbee IV, 939
Blackburn, Barbee IV, 946
Blackburn, Barbee IV, 966
Blackburn, Barbee IV, 976
Blackburn, Barbee IV, 1014
Blackburn, Barbee, Jr. IV, 927
Blackburn, Barbeee IV, 927
Blackburn, Barby VI, 230
Blackburn, Bazileel IV, 1026
Blackburn, Benjamin II, 338
Blackburn, Benjamin H. IV, 1024
Blackburn, Benjamin H. IV, 1026
Blackburn, Bertha V, 25
Blackburn, Bertha V, 76
Blackburn, Bertha H. V, 25
Blackburn, Caroline IV, 21
Blackburn, Caroline IV, 611
Blackburn, Caroline IV, 612
Blackburn, Caroline IV, 679
Blackburn, Caroline H. II, 964
Blackburn, Caroline H. IV, 679
Blackburn, Caroline Hoagland IV, 679
Blackburn, Caroline Hoagland IV, 735
Blackburn, Charles IV, 21
Blackburn, Charles IV, 135
Blackburn, Charles IV, 464
Blackburn, Charles IV, 611
Blackburn, Charles IV, 635
Blackburn, Charles IV, 639
Blackburn, Charles IV, 1127
Blackburn, Charles IV, 1133
Blackburn, Charles V, 25
Blackburn, Charles V, 727
Blackburn, Charles G. V, 25
Blackburn, Charles G. V, 76
Blackburn, Charles M. IV, 506
Blackburn, Chas. IV, 496
Blackburn, Chas. IV, 611
Blackburn, Chas. IV, 614
Blackburn, Chas. IV, 615
Blackburn, Chas. IV, 927
Blackburn, Christo II, 338
Blackburn, Christopher II, 338
Blackburn, Christopher II, 466
Blackburn, Christopher II, 499
Blackburn, Cyrus L. IV, 927
Blackburn, Daniel IV, 21
Blackburn, Daniel IV, 121
Blackburn, Daniel IV, 135
Blackburn, Daniel IV, 611
Blackburn, Daniel IV, 630
Blackburn, David IV, 21
Blackburn, David IV, 611
Blackburn, David IV, 679
Blackburn, David IV, 764
Blackburn, David IV, 765
Blackburn, David IV, 927
Blackburn, David IV, 956
Blackburn, David VI, 230
Blackburn, Deborah IV, 21
Blackburn, Deborah IV, 75
Blackburn, Deborah IV, 99
Blackburn, Deborah IV, 506
Blackburn, Deborah VI, 366
Blackburn, Dora IV, 611
Blackburn, Dora IV, 927
Blackburn, Doris Margaret IV, 1307
Blackburn, Dosia Esther IV, 680
Blackburn, Dr. Elisha IV, 1307
Blackburn, Dr. Wm. J. IV, 679
Blackburn, Drell IV, 1272
Blackburn, Edith IV, 611
Blackburn, Edith IV, 612
Blackburn, Edward IV, 611
Blackburn, Edward IV, 680
Blackburn, Eleanor IV, 1024
Blackburn, Elias V, 25
Blackburn, Elias V, 57
Blackburn, Elisha IV, 612
Blackburn, Elisha IV, 669
Blackburn, Elisha IV, 680
Blackburn, Elisha B. IV, 611
Blackburn, Eliza W. IV, 611
Blackburn, Elizabeth II, 964
Blackburn, Elizabeth IV, 21
Blackburn, Elizabeth IV, 26
Blackburn, Elizabeth IV, 65
Blackburn, Elizabeth IV, 611
Blackburn, Elizabeth IV, 615
Blackburn, Elizabeth IV, 679
Blackburn, Elizabeth IV, 721
Blackburn, Elizabeth IV, 735
Blackburn, Elizabeth IV, 746
Blackburn, Elizabeth IV, 780
Blackburn, Elizabeth IV, 800
Blackburn, Elizabeth IV, 816
Blackburn, Elizabeth IV, 836
Blackburn, Elizabeth IV, 927
Blackburn, Elizabeth IV, 936
Blackburn, Elizabeth IV, 939
Blackburn, Elizabeth IV, 946
Blackburn, Elizabeth IV, 956
Blackburn, Elizabeth IV, 966
Blackburn, Elizabeth IV, 976
Blackburn, Elizabeth IV, 977
Blackburn, Elizabeth IV, 993
Blackburn, Elizabeth IV, 998
Blackburn, Elizabeth IV, 1014
Blackburn, Elizabeth VI, 230
Blackburn, Elizabeth VI, 879
Blackburn, Elizabeth B. IV, 800
Blackburn, Elizabeth B. IV, 1035
Blackburn, Elizabeth C. IV, 679
Blackburn, Elizabeth E. IV, 679
Blackburn, Ella IV, 1272
Blackburn, Ella IV, 1297
Blackburn, Emily IV, 608
Blackburn, Emily IV, 611
Blackburn, Emily IV, 635
Blackburn, Emily IV, 923
Blackburn, Emily IV, 927
Blackburn, Emily H. IV, 612
Blackburn, Emily H. IV, 679
Blackburn, Emily H. IV, 928
Blackburn, Emma IV, 680
Blackburn, Emma IV, 927
Blackburn, Emma IV, 928
Blackburn, Emma V, 223
Blackburn, Esther IV, 927
Blackburn, Finley IV, 21
Blackburn, Finley IV, 75
Blackburn, Finley IV, 121
Blackburn, Florence VI, 982
Blackburn, Franklin V, 223
Blackburn, George IV, 21
Blackburn, George IV, 121
Blackburn, George IV, 611
Blackburn, George IV, 679
Blackburn, George IV, 681
Blackburn, George V, 223
Blackburn, George R. IV, 611
Blackburn, George R. IV, 612
Blackburn, George R. IV, 679
Blackburn, Hannah IV, 135
Blackburn, Hannah IV, 611
Blackburn, Hannah IV, 679
Blackburn, Hannah IV, 927
Blackburn, Hannah IV, 976
Blackburn, Hannah IV, 1202
Blackburn, Hannah IV, 1272
Blackburn, Hannah IV, 1297
Blackburn, Hannah J. IV, 611
Blackburn, Hannah L. IV, 1272
Blackburn, Hannah M. IV, 927
Blackburn, Harold C. IV, 679
Blackburn, Harold C. IV, 680
Blackburn, Harold E. IV, 679
Blackburn, Harriet Goldie IV, 680
Blackburn, Henrietta F. IV, 611
Blackburn, Henry IV, 611
Blackburn, Henry IV, 612
Blackburn, Henry IV, 927
Blackburn, Henry IV, 998
Blackburn, Henry H. IV, 927
Blackburn, Hiram V, 25
Blackburn, Horace A. V, 223
Blackburn, Howard IV, 611
Blackburn, Howard IV, 680
Blackburn, Iazer IV, 506
Blackburn, Ida IV, 608
Blackburn, Ida IV, 611
Blackburn, Ida IV, 612
Blackburn, Ida IV, 679
Blackburn, Ida IV, 927
Blackburn, Ida B. IV, 923
Blackburn, Ida E. IV, 612
Blackburn, Inetta P. IV, 611
Blackburn, Isaac IV, 21
Blackburn, Isaac V, 967
Blackburn, Isabella III, 37
Blackburn, Isabella IV, 927
Blackburn, Isabella Emily IV, 927
Blackburn, Isabella Emily IV, 940
Blackburn, Isabelle III, 295
Blackburn, Isabelle III, 396
Blackburn, Isabelle III, 438
Blackburn, Isabelle III, 447
Blackburn, Isaiah P. III, 37
Blackburn, James IV, 21
Blackburn, James IV, 506
Blackburn, James IV, 680
Blackburn, James IV, 927
Blackburn, James IV, 928
Blackburn, James IV, 939
Blackburn, James IV, 1024
Blackburn, James VI, 366
Blackburn, James C. IV, 927
Blackburn, James C. IV, 936
Blackburn, James C. IV, 945
Blackburn, James C. IV, 998
Blackburn, James Crew IV, 679
Blackburn, James Crew VI, 230
Blackburn, Jane IV, 1026
Blackburn, Jean III, 396
Blackburn, Jean Gertrude III, 396
Blackburn, Jean Gertrude III, 422
Blackburn, Jesse IV, 21
Blackburn, Jessie V, 223
Blackburn, Jessie H. IV, 611
Blackburn, Jessie H. IV, 639
Blackburn, Joell II, 338
Blackburn, John II, 338
Blackburn, John IV, 21
Blackburn, John IV, 506
Blackburn, John IV, 611
Blackburn, John IV, 679
Blackburn, John IV, 1307
Blackburn, John V, 967
Blackburn, John B. IV, 21
Blackburn, John Hollingsworth IV, 680
Blackburn, Jonathan IV, 21
Blackburn, Jonathan IV, 121
Blackburn, Jonathan IV, 611
Blackburn, Jonathan IV, 612
Blackburn, Jonathan IV, 635
Blackburn, Jonathan VI, 879
Blackburn, Jonathan K. IV, 608
Blackburn, Jonathan K. IV, 612
Blackburn, Jonathan K. IV, 679
Blackburn, Jonathan K. IV, 923
Blackburn, Jonathan K. IV, 927
Blackburn, Jonathan K. IV, 928
Blackburn, Joseph II, 338
Blackburn, Joseph IV, 21
Blackburn, Joseph IV, 611
Blackburn, Joseph IV, 927
Blackburn, Joseph V, 967
Blackburn, Joseph VI, 366
Blackburn, Joseph H. IV, 928
Blackburn, Joseph Thomas IV, 800
Blackburn, Judith A. IV, 927
Blackburn, Judith Ann IV, 927
Blackburn, Judith Ann IV, 998
Blackburn, Julia Etta IV, 927
Blackburn, Julia Etta IV, 928
Blackburn, Julia Etta IV, 985
Blackburn, Julietta IV, 612
Blackburn, Julietta IV, 651
Blackburn, Julius VI, 879
Blackburn, Katherine IV, 679
Blackburn, Keziah IV, 465
Blackburn, Keziah IV, 506
Blackburn, Laura Susan IV, 927
Blackburn, Lewis IV, 927
Blackburn, Lillie V, 223
Blackburn, Lorena IV, 679
Blackburn, Louisa IV, 680
Blackburn, Louisa IV, 927
Blackburn, Louisa IV, 977
Blackburn, Louisa S. IV, 679
Blackburn, Luesa IV, 927
Blackburn, Lydia IV, 21
Blackburn, Lydia IV, 75
Blackburn, Lydia IV, 116
Blackburn, Lydia IV, 135
Blackburn, Lydia IV, 611
Blackburn, Lydia B. IV, 1026
Blackburn, M. Elizabeth IV, 612
Blackburn, Mabel M. IV, 679
Blackburn, Mabel M. IV, 680
Blackburn, Maja W. IV, 927
Blackburn, Marg. H. III, 396
Blackburn, Margaret III, 396
Blackburn, Margaret IV, 464
Blackburn, Margaret IV, 679
Blackburn, Margaret IV, 764
Blackburn, Margaret IV, 765
Blackburn, Margaret IV, 800
Blackburn, Margaret IV, 810
Blackburn, Margaret IV, 927
Blackburn, Margaret IV, 946
Blackburn, Margaret IV, 956
Blackburn, Margaret VI, 230
Blackburn, Margaret A. IV, 939
Blackburn, Margaret E. III, 295
Blackburn, Margaret E. III, 447
Blackburn, Margaret L. IV, 680
Blackburn, Margaret S. III, 37
Blackburn, Maria A. IV, 506
Blackburn, Mariah A. IV, 491
Blackburn, Maro IV, 927
Blackburn, Martha II, 780
Blackburn, Martha IV, 21
Blackburn, Martha IV, 135
Blackburn, Martha IV, 611
Blackburn, Martha IV, 625
Blackburn, Martha IV, 679
Blackburn, Martha IV, 709
Blackburn, Martha IV, 927
Blackburn, Martha H. IV, 927
Blackburn, Mary IV, 75
Blackburn, Mary IV, 99
Blackburn, Mary IV, 121
Blackburn, Mary IV, 177
Blackburn, Mary IV, 518
Blackburn, Mary IV, 611
Blackburn, Mary IV, 612
Blackburn, Mary IV, 679
Blackburn, Mary IV, 680
Blackburn, Mary IV, 800
Blackburn, Mary IV, 853
Blackburn, Mary IV, 927
Blackburn, Mary IV, 939
Blackburn, Mary IV, 984
Blackburn, Mary IV, 1014
Blackburn, Mary VI, 230
Blackburn, Mary VI, 954
Blackburn, Mary A. IV, 977
Blackburn, Mary Alice IV, 611
Blackburn, Mary Ann V, 25
Blackburn, Mary Ann V, 61
Blackburn, Mary E. IV, 464
Blackburn, Mary E. IV, 496
Blackburn, Mary E. IV, 506
Blackburn, Mary Elizabeth IV, 679
Blackburn, Mary Elma IV, 370
Blackburn, Mary Elma IV, 378
Blackburn, Mary Elma IV, 611
Blackburn, Mary Elma IV, 614
Blackburn, Mary Eva IV, 496
Blackburn, Mary F. IV, 1024
Blackburn, Mary F. IV, 1026
Blackburn, Mary P. IV, 927
Blackburn, Mary S. IV, 1024
Blackburn, Matilda E. IV, 630
Blackburn, Maud IV, 464
Blackburn, Miles IV, 1272
Blackburn, Miles O. IV, 1272
Blackburn, Miles O. IV, 1297
Blackburn, Mira Halliday II, 839
Blackburn, Moses IV, 75
Blackburn, Moses IV, 99
Blackburn, Moses IV, 121
Blackburn, Moses IV, 464
Blackburn, Moses IV, 506
Blackburn, Mott. IV, 679
Blackburn, Mr. ??? IV, 680
Blackburn, Mrs. ??? IV, 680
Blackburn, Mrs. ??? V, 727
Blackburn, Myra J. IV, 611
Blackburn, Myra J. IV, 612
Blackburn, Myra J. IV, 679
Blackburn, Myra J. IV, 680
Blackburn, Nancy IV, 679
Blackburn, Nathan IV, 21
Blackburn, Nathan IV, 75
Blackburn, Nathan IV, 121
Blackburn, Nathan IV, 611
Blackburn, Nathan M. IV, 121
Blackburn, Nathan M. IV, 124
Blackburn, Nathan M. IV, 135
Blackburn, Nathan M. IV, 611
Blackburn, Nathan M. IV, 679
Blackburn, Nathan W. IV, 21
Blackburn, Olive IV, 611
Blackburn, Phebe IV, 611
Blackburn, Philip Conklin III, 37
Blackburn, Phinly VI, 366
Blackburn, Polly IV, 679
Blackburn, Polly Maria IV, 679
Blackburn, Polly Maria IV, 781
Blackburn, Prudence VI, 879
Blackburn, Rachel II, 338
Blackburn, Rachel II, 466
Blackburn, Rachel II, 499
Blackburn, Rachel IV, 21
Blackburn, Rachel IV, 33
Blackburn, Rachel IV, 75
Blackburn, Rachel IV, 99
Blackburn, Rachel V, 967
Blackburn, Rachel VI, 366
Blackburn, Rachel H. IV, 21
Blackburn, Rachel H. IV, 33
Blackburn, Rachel H. IV, 611
Blackburn, Rachel H. IV, 679
Blackburn, Rachel H. IV, 708
Blackburn, Rachel H. IV, 709
Blackburn, Rachel W. IV, 121
Blackburn, Rachel W. IV, 122
Blackburn, Rachel W. IV, 679
Blackburn, Rachel W. IV, 681
Blackburn, Rebecca II, 466
Blackburn, Rebecca IV, 21
Blackburn, Rebecca IV, 75
Blackburn, Rebecca IV, 124
Blackburn, Rebecca IV, 611
Blackburn, Rebecca IV, 679
Blackburn, Rebecca IV, 927
Blackburn, Rebecca IV, 936
Blackburn, Rebecca IV, 939
Blackburn, Rebecca IV, 945
Blackburn, Rebecca IV, 998
Blackburn, Rebecca M. IV, 121
Blackburn, Rebecca M. IV, 135
Blackburn, Rebecca M. IV, 611
Blackburn, Rebeckah II, 338
Blackburn, Roland IV, 928
Blackburn, Roland IV, 985
Blackburn, Rolland IV, 611
Blackburn, Rolland IV, 612
Blackburn, Rolland IV, 651
Blackburn, Rolland IV, 927
Blackburn, Rolland IV, 928
Blackburn, Ruth III, 447
Blackburn, Ruth IV, 21
Blackburn, Ruth IV, 59
Blackburn, Ruth IV, 927
Blackburn, Ruth IV, 939
Blackburn, S. Denzil IV, 464
Blackburn, Samuel IV, 21
Blackburn, Sara C. IV, 927
Blackburn, Sarah III, 337
Blackburn, Sarah IV, 121
Blackburn, Sarah IV, 506
Blackburn, Sarah IV, 607
Blackburn, Sarah IV, 611
Blackburn, Sarah IV, 614
Blackburn, Sarah IV, 635
Blackburn, Sarah IV, 679
Blackburn, Sarah IV, 680
Blackburn, Sarah IV, 764
Blackburn, Sarah IV, 780
Blackburn, Sarah IV, 1026
Blackburn, Sarah IV, 1127
Blackburn, Sarah IV, 1133
Blackburn, Sarah VI, 230
Blackburn, Sarah Ann IV, 679
Blackburn, Sarah Ann IV, 800
Blackburn, Sarah Ann IV, 825
Blackburn, Sarah Ann IV, 927
Blackburn, Sarah Ann IV, 966
Blackburn, Sarah C. IV, 611
Blackburn, Sarah C. IV, 615
Blackburn, Sarah C. IV, 639
Blackburn, Sarah C. IV, 1127
Blackburn, Sarah Ellen IV, 939
Blackburn, Sarah Ellen IV, 1005
Blackburn, Sarah H. IV, 611
Blackburn, Sarah H. IV, 612
Blackburn, Sarah H. IV, 667
Blackburn, Sarah J. IV, 680
Blackburn, Sarah Jane IV, 927
Blackburn, Sarah Jane IV, 951
Blackburn, Sarah M. IV, 927
Blackburn, Sarah S. II, 728
Blackburn, Sarah S. II, 765
Blackburn, Sidney V, 57
Blackburn, Smith IV, 679
Blackburn, Susanna B. IV, 506
Blackburn, Temperance IV, 679
Blackburn, Temperance IV, 800
Blackburn, Temperance IV, 1016
Blackburn, Temperance VI, 230
Blackburn, Temperance B. IV, 927
Blackburn, Temperancee IV, 927
Blackburn, Thomas IV, 21
Blackburn, Thomas IV, 75

Blackburn, Thomas IV, 121
Blackburn, Thomas IV, 464
Blackburn, Thomas IV, 607
Blackburn, Thomas IV, 611
Blackburn, Thomas IV, 679
Blackburn, Thomas IV, 680
Blackburn, Thomas IV, 780
Blackburn, Thomas IV, 1026
Blackburn, Thomas IV, 1149
Blackburn, Thomas V, 967
Blackburn, Thomas VI, 230
Blackburn, Thomas VI, 231
Blackburn, Thomas VI, 366
Blackburn, Thos. IV, 121
Blackburn, Thos. IV, 679
Blackburn, Thos. V, 967
Blackburn, Uree IV, 927
Blackburn, Uree IV, 945
Blackburn, Virginia IV, 669
Blackburn, Virginia IV, 680
Blackburn, Virginia L. IV, 1307
Blackburn, Warren Stookesberry IV, 611
Blackburn, Washington V, 25
Blackburn, Wiliam, Jr. IV, 38
Blackburn, Willard IV, 518
Blackburn, Willard C. IV, 611
Blackburn, William IV, 21
Blackburn, William IV, 59
Blackburn, William IV, 611
Blackburn, William IV, 1026
Blackburn, William V, 223
Blackburn, William H. IV, 667
Blackburn, William H. IV, 927
Blackburn, William J. IV, 612
Blackburn, William J. IV, 615
Blackburn, William J., Jr. IV, 680
Blackburn, William J., Jr. IV, 792
Blackburn, William J., Sr. II, 964
Blackburn, William, Jr. IV, 21
Blackburn, Wm H. IV, 927
Blackburn, Wm. IV, 121
Blackburn, Wm. IV, 127
Blackburn, Wm. IV, 135
Blackburn, Wm. IV, 611
Blackburn, Wm. IV, 679
Blackburn, Wm. IV, 927
Blackburn, Wm. IV, 1127
Blackburn, Wm. V, 967
Blackburn, Wm. H. IV, 611
Blackburn, Wm. H. IV, 977
Blackburn, Wm. Henry IV, 927
Blackburn, Wm. J. IV, 611
Blackburn, Wm. J. IV, 679
Blackburn, Wm. J. IV, 735
Blackburn, Wm. J. IV, 746
Blackburn, Wm. J. IV, 836
Blackburn, Wm. J., Jr. IV, 679
Blackburn, Wm. S. IV, 939
Blackburn, Wm., Jr. IV, 679
Blackburn, Zachariah IV, 21
Blackburn, Zachariah IV, 75
Blackburn, Zacheriah VI, 366
Blackburne, Christo II, 338
Blackburne, Christopher II, 466
Blackburne, Finley IV, 75
Blackburne, John II, 338
Blackburne, Rachel II, 338
Blackchief, Helen II, 702
Blackenship, Hudson VI, 807
Blackenship, Jesse VI, 807
Blackenship, Nancy VI, 934
Blackenship, Obedience VI, 807
Blackey, Jael II, 979
Blackey, Ruth II, 1035
Blackey, Wm. II, 1035
Blackey, Wm., Jr. II, 979
Blackfan, Edward II, 824
Blackfan, Eleanor II, 466
Blackfan, Eleanor II, 691
Blackfan, Eleanor II, 979
Blackfan, Eleanor II, 1040
Blackfan, Joseph II, 1040
Blackfan, Margaret II, 1040
Blackfan, Martha II, 822
Blackfan, Martha II, 824
Blackfan, Merab II, 1040
Blackfan, Rebecca II, 451
Blackfan, Rebecca II, 466
Blackfan, Rebeckah II, 979
Blackfan, Thomas II, 466
Blackfan, Wm. II, 466
Blackfan, Wm. II, 691
Blackfan, Wm. II, 979
Blackfan, Wm. II, 1040
Blackford, Elizabeth II, 466
Blackford, Martha C. III, 37
Blackford, Mary II, 466
Blackford, Samuel II, 56
Blackford, Samuel II, 466
Blackford, Sarah, Jr. II, 466
Blackham, Ann II, 338
Blackham, Mary II, 467
Blackham, Mary II, 659
Blackham, Rebecca II, 338
Blackham, Rebecka II, 599
Blackham, Rebeckah II, 466
Blackham, Richard II, 198
Blackham, Richard II, 338
Blackham, Richard II, 466
Blackham, Richard II, 467
Blackham, Richard II, 599
Blackham, Richard II, 659
Blackham, Wd. Sarah II, 467
Blackham, Wd. Sarah II, 659
Blackison, Ann IV, 465
Blackiston, Ann IV, 465
Blackledge, Aaron IV, 178
Blackledge, Aaron IV, 568
Blackledge, Abraham IV, 21
Blackledge, Abraham VI, 366
Blackledge, Amy II, 467
Blackledge, Ann IV, 177
Blackledge, Ann IV, 178
Blackledge, Ann IV, 226
Blackledge, Ann IV, 568
Blackledge, Ann W. IV, 800
Blackledge, Asa IV, 370
Blackledge, Asa IV, 432
Blackledge, Asa IV, 568
Blackledge, Asa Hartley IV, 177
Blackledge, Asa Hartley IV, 178
Blackledge, Asa Hartley IV, 568
Blackledge, Benjamin IV, 800
Blackledge, Blain IV, 178
Blackledge, Blanch IV, 178
Blackledge, Charles D. IV, 800
Blackledge, David IV, 178
Blackledge, David IV, 568
Blackledge, David IV, 800
Blackledge, Elizabeth II, 467
Blackledge, Elizabeth IV, 21
Blackledge, Elizabeth IV, 177
Blackledge, Elizabeth IV, 178
Blackledge, Elizabeth IV, 370
Blackledge, Elizabeth IV, 395
Blackledge, Elizabeth IV, 568
Blackledge, Elizabeth, Jr. IV, 568
Blackledge, Esther IV, 177
Blackledge, Esther IV, 178
Blackledge, Esther IV, 292
Blackledge, Esther IV, 568
Blackledge, Hannah IV, 565
Blackledge, Hannah IV, 568
Blackledge, Hannah IV, 800
Blackledge, Hiram IV, 800
Blackledge, Isaac IV, 21
Blackledge, Isaac IV, 800
Blackledge, Isaac IV, 857
Blackledge, Isaac VI, 366
Blackledge, Israel IV, 177
Blackledge, James IV, 21
Blackledge, James VI, 366
Blackledge, Jason R. IV, 800
Blackledge, Joanna II, 467
Blackledge, Joanna IV, 680
Blackledge, Johanna Dorothy II, 467
Blackledge, John IV, 21
Blackledge, John IV, 177
Blackledge, John IV, 370
Blackledge, John IV, 565
Blackledge, John IV, 568
Blackledge, Joseph IV, 21
Blackledge, Joseph IV, 612
Blackledge, Joseph IV, 680
Blackledge, Joseph IV, 714
Blackledge, Joseph IV, 800
Blackledge, Joseph IV, 1000
Blackledge, Levi IV, 21
Blackledge, Levi VI, 366
Blackledge, Margaret IV, 800
Blackledge, Margaret IV, 857
Blackledge, Margaret VI, 366
Blackledge, Martha IV, 21
Blackledge, Martha IV, 800
Blackledge, Martha VI, 366
Blackledge, Mary II, 467
Blackledge, Mary IV, 21
Blackledge, Mary IV, 320
Blackledge, Mary IV, 680
Blackledge, Mary IV, 800
Blackledge, Ora IV, 178
Blackledge, Phebe IV, 320
Blackledge, Phebe IV, 370
Blackledge, Rachel II, 467
Blackledge, Rachel II, 728
Blackledge, Rachel IV, 140
Blackledge, Rachel IV, 178
Blackledge, Rachel IV, 368
Blackledge, Rachel IV, 370
Blackledge, Rachel IV, 568
Blackledge, Rachel IV, 612
Blackledge, Rachel IV, 680
Blackledge, Rachel IV, 714
Blackledge, Rachel IV, 800
Blackledge, Rebecca II, 467
Blackledge, Rhoda IV, 1000
Blackledge, Robert II, 467
Blackledge, Robert IV, 21
Blackledge, Robert IV, 178
Blackledge, Robert IV, 568
Blackledge, Robert IV, 680
Blackledge, Robert IV, 800
Blackledge, Robert H. IV, 177
Blackledge, Robert H. IV, 292
Blackledge, Robert H. IV, 568
Blackledge, Ruth IV, 800
Blackledge, Samuel IV, 21
Blackledge, Samuel IV, 177
Blackledge, Samuel IV, 178
Blackledge, Sarah IV, 21
Blackledge, Sarah IV, 177
Blackledge, Sarah IV, 178
Blackledge, Sarah IV, 320
Blackledge, Sarah IV, 346
Blackledge, Sarah IV, 370
Blackledge, Sarah IV, 395
Blackledge, Sarah IV, 432
Blackledge, Sarah IV, 568
Blackledge, Sarah VI, 361
Blackledge, Sarah VI, 366
Blackledge, Susanna IV, 370
Blackledge, Susanna IV, 448
Blackledge, Thomas II, 467
Blackledge, Thomas IV, 21
Blackledge, Thomas IV, 320
Blackledge, Thomas IV, 346
Blackledge, Thomas IV, 370
Blackledge, Thomas IV, 800
Blackledge, Thomas VI, 366
Blackledge, Thomas G. IV, 612
Blackledge, Thomas G. IV, 800
Blackledge, Thos. G. IV, 121
Blackledge, William IV, 21
Blackledge, William IV, 177
Blackledge, William IV, 178
Blackledge, William IV, 370
Blackledge, William IV, 568
Blackledge, William VI, 366
Blackledge, Wm. IV, 395
Blackledge, Wm. IV, 568
Blacklege, Abraham IV, 21
Blacklege, Charles IV, 928
Blacklege, Hannah IV, 928
Blacklege, James IV, 21
Blacklege, Joseph IV, 21
Blacklege, Joseph IV, 928
Blacklege, Levi IV, 21
Blacklege, Margaret IV, 67
Blacklege, Martha IV, 21
Blacklege, Martha IV, 67
Blacklege, Rhoda IV, 928
Blacklege, Rhoda S. IV, 928
Blacklege, Thomas IV, 67
Blacklege, William IV, 21
Blackley, Bayard P. V, 895
Blackley, James VI, 879
Blackley, Nancy VI, 879
Blackley, Salley VI, 879
Blacklidge, Asa Hartley IV, 568
Blacklidge, Benjamin II, 338
Blacklidge, Elizabeth IV, 568
Blacklidge, Johanna Dorothy II, 467
Blacklidge, Johanna Dorothy II, 673
Blacklidge, John IV, 568
Blacklidge, Joseph IV, 612
Blacklidge, Joseph IV, 800
Blacklidge, Rachel IV, 800
Blacklidge, Robert II, 467
Blacklidge, Robert II, 673
Blacklidge, Sarah IV, 320
Blacklidge, Sarah IV, 568
Blacklidge, Thomas II, 467
Blacklidge, Thomas II, 673
Blacklidge, Thomas IV, 320
Blacklidge, Thomas IV, 800
Blacklidge, Thomas G. IV, 121
Blacklidge, Thos. G. IV, 121
Blacklidge, William IV, 568
Blackmarr, Ann IV, 1149
Blackmarr, Ann IV, 1233
Blackmarr, Ann E. IV, 1149
Blackmarr, Anna IV, 1149
Blackmarr, Anna IV, 1233
Blackmarr, Byron D. IV, 1149
Blackmarr, Byron D. IV, 1233
Blackmarr, Byron D. Oliette IV, 1149
Blackmarr, Byron Deloss IV, 1233
Blackmarr, Edwin IV, 1149
Blackmarr, Edwin IV, 1233
Blackmarr, Lorenzo IV, 1149
Blackmarr, Melvin Lorenzo IV, 1149
Blackmarr, Olette IV, 1233
Blackmarr, Oliett IV, 1233
Blackmarr, Oliette IV, 1149
Blackmarr, Rosina IV, 1149
Blackmarr, Rosina F. IV, 1149
Blackmer, Ann IV, 1149
Blackmer, Byron D. Oliette IV, 1149
Blackmer, Edwin IV, 1149
Blackmer, Lorenzo IV, 1149
Blackmer, Melvin Lorenzo IV, 1149
Blackmer, Rosina IV, 1149
Blackmore, Ann IV, 1197
Blackmore, Anna IV, 1149
Blackmore, Anna IV, 1191
Blackmore, Carrie V, 797
Blackmore, Clifford V, 797
Blackmore, Ethel IV, 178
Blackmore, Forest V, 797
Blackmore, Henry V, 797
Blacksan, Thomas II, 466
Blackshaw, Elizabeth II, 955
Blackshaw, Elizabeth II, 979
Blackshaw, Martha II, 955
Blackshaw, Martha II, 979
Blackshaw, Mary II, 955
Blackshaw, Mary II, 979
Blackshaw, Mary II, 995
Blackshaw, Mary II, 1010
Blackshaw, Nehemiah II, 955
Blackshaw, Nehemiah II, 979
Blackshaw, Nehemiah II, 1010
Blackshaw, Nehemiah II, 1036
Blackshaw, Phebe II, 955
Blackshaw, Phebe II, 979
Blackshaw, Phebe II, 1036
Blackshaw, Pheby II, 979
Blackshaw, Rebecca II, 955
Blackshaw, Rebecca II, 979
Blackshaw, Rebecca II, 1036
Blackshaw, Sarah II, 955
Blackshay, Pheby II, 979
Blackshay, Pheby II, 1007
Blackston, Ann V, 895
Blackston, William II, 338
Blackwell, ??? III, 222
Blackwell, Adelaide I, 623
Blackwell, Betsy VI, 879
Blackwell, Charles G. III, 37
Blackwell, Col. Robt. III, 396
Blackwell, Cornelius VI, 731
Blackwell, Dionetia VI, 923
Blackwell, Drusilla V. VI, 879
Blackwell, Elizabeth VI, 879
Blackwell, Elizabeth S. III, 37
Blackwell, Elizabeth S. III, 222
Blackwell, Elizabeth S. VI, 731
Blackwell, Hannah III, 222
Blackwell, Joseph VI, 879
Blackwell, Marian II, 780
Blackwell, Mary III, 394
Blackwell, Mary III, 396
Blackwell, Moses VI, 879
Blackwell, Moses, Jr. VI, 923
Blackwell, Moses, Senr. VI, 923
Blackwell, Moses, Sr. VI, 879
Blackwell, Nancy VI, 879
Blackwell, Robt. III, 394
Blackwell, Susannah III, 394
Blackwell, Susannah III, 396
Blackwell, Susannah VI, 879
Blackwell, Thomas VI, 879
Blackwell, Viney VI, 879
Blackwood, Frances II, 134
Blackwood, Rebeckah II, 56
Blackwood, Rebeckah II, 88
Blade, ??? III, 407
Blade, John III, 396
Blade, Sarah III, 396
Blade, Sarah III, 407
Blades, George VI, 879
Blades, Henry III, 37
Blades, Nancy VI, 879
Blades, Wd. Elizabeth III, 37
Blady, ??? III, 37
Blady, John III, 37
Blain, Joseph III, 37
Blain, Lucinda N. V, 948
Blair, ??? V, 153
Blair, Abigail I, 871
Blair, Abigail J. I, 851
Blair, Abigail J. I, 872
Blair, Abigail P. I, 850
Blair, Abigail P. I, 851
Blair, Abigail P. I, 871
Blair, Abigail P. I, 887
Blair, Abner I, 649
Blair, Abner I, 850
Blair, Abner I, 871
Blair, Ada I, 851
Blair, Addison I, 872
Blair, Adison J. I, 850
Blair, Adolphus E. I, 850
Blair, Adolphus E. I, 872
Blair, Allen J. I, 938
Blair, Alta L. I, 850
Blair, Alva V, 153
Blair, Alva C. V, 153
Blair, Alzena I, 374
Blair, Ann I, 850
Blair, Anna I, 625
Blair, Anna I, 932
Blair, Anna E. I, 871
Blair, Anna E. I, 899
Blair, Anna J. I, 850
Blair, Anna J. I, 872
Blair, Anna Jane I, 872
Blair, Annie I, 624
Blair, Annie I, 929
Blair, Annie E. I, 624
Blair, Annie E. I, 864
Blair, Annie M. I, 850
Blair, Annie Margaret I, 872
Blair, Augustine I, 850
Blair, Augustine W. I, 850
Blair, Beatrice Gertrude I, 929
Blair, Belle V, 199
Blair, Benjamin F. I, 850
Blair, Benjamin F. I, 869
Blair, Benjamin F. I, 872
Blair, Benjamin Franklin I, 612
Blair, Charlotte I, 921
Blair, Charlotte V, 153
Blair, Charlotte V, 199
Blair, Clarkson I. I, 564
Blair, Clorinda C. A. I, 851
Blair, Colbert I, 674
Blair, Colbert Enos I, 872
Blair, Cynthia I, 872
Blair, D. Humboldt I, 850
Blair, David IV, 1202
Blair, David H. I, 851
Blair, Delila I, 871
Blair, Della M. I, 527
Blair, Della M. I, 564
Blair, Della N. I, 850
Blair, Delphina M. I, 872
Blair, Eddie I, 938
Blair, Edward Pugh I, 612
Blair, Edward Pugh I, 630
Blair, Edwin M. I, 921
Blair, Edwin McMain I, 938
Blair, Eleanor I, 938
Blair, Eliza I, 850
Blair, Eliza I, 872
Blair, Elizabeth I, 850
Blair, Elizabeth I, 864
Blair, Elizabeth I, 871
Blair, Elizabeth I, 872
Blair, Elizabeth I, 903
Blair, Elva Jane I, 851
Blair, Elwood I, 938
Blair, Emily I, 921
Blair, Emily A. I, 850
Blair, Emily A. I, 872
Blair, Emily A. I, 894
Blair, Emma I, 851
Blair, Emma I, 938
Blair, Emma V, 153
Blair, Emma V, 320
Blair, Emma J. V, 153
Blair, Emma L. V, 659
Blair, Emma Lewis V, 659
Blair, Enos I, 527
Blair, Enos I, 649
Blair, Enos I, 674
Blair, Enos I, 684
Blair, Enos I, 850
Blair, Enos I, 871
Blair, Enos I, 931
Blair, Enos A. I, 872
Blair, Enos, Jr. I, 871
Blair, Estelle I, 612
Blair, Esther I, 938
Blair, Esther I, 942
Blair, Eunice I, 527
Blair, Eunice I, 850
Blair, Eunice I, 872
Blair, Eunice I, 931
Blair, Eva E. V, 895
Blair, Evelyn I, 938
Blair, F. S. I, 527
Blair, Florance Annie I, 931
Blair, Florence I, 938
Blair, Florence Elizabeth I, 872
Blair, Florence Elizabeth I, 921

Blair, Franklin I, 850
Blair, Franklin S. I, 230
Blair, Franklin S. I, 527
Blair, Franklin S. I, 549
Blair, Franklin S. I, 850
Blair, Franklin S. I, 871
Blair, Franklin S. I, 872
Blair, Fred I, 938
Blair, Fred C. I, 938
Blair, Fred C. I, 942
Blair, Frederick Clinton I, 921
Blair, Gertrude I, 922
Blair, Gertrude I, 938
Blair, Gertrude I, 945
Blair, Hannah I, 649
Blair, Hannah I, 674
Blair, Hannah I, 684
Blair, Hannah I, 850
Blair, Hannah I, 871
Blair, Hannah I, 872
Blair, Hannah I, 880
Blair, Hannah I, 905
Blair, Hannah I, 919
Blair, Hannah E. I, 850
Blair, Hannah E. I, 872
Blair, Henderson I, 921
Blair, I. Clarkson I, 527
Blair, I. Clarkson I, 850
Blair, Isaac C. I, 850
Blair, Isaac C. I, 871
Blair, J. Addison I, 850
Blair, J. Addison I, 921
Blair, J. Parker I, 850
Blair, J. Winston I, 850
Blair, J. Winston I, 938
Blair, James I, 931
Blair, Jane I, 649
Blair, Jane I, 850
Blair, Jane I, 871
Blair, Jane I, 903
Blair, Jane VI, 799
Blair, Jane O. I, 755
Blair, Jesse I, 649
Blair, Jesse I, 850
Blair, Jesse I, 871
Blair, Jesse C. I, 850
Blair, Jesse C. I, 871
Blair, Jesse C. I, 872
Blair, Jesse M. I, 850
Blair, Jesse M. I, 872
Blair, Jesse Milton I, 872
Blair, Jesse W. I, 850
Blair, Jesse W. I, 872
Blair, John I, 850
Blair, John I, 864
Blair, John I, 871
Blair, John II, 979
Blair, John II, 980
Blair, John A. I, 850
Blair, John A. I, 872
Blair, John A. I, 894
Blair, John Addison I, 872
Blair, John Anderson I, 921
Blair, John J. I, 851
Blair, John S. I, 850
Blair, Joseph I, 931
Blair, Joseph C. I, 929
Blair, Joseph F. I, 929
Blair, Joseph F. I, 938
Blair, Joseph Felix I, 921
Blair, Josephine III, 140
Blair, Josiah I, 649
Blair, Josiah I, 850
Blair, Josiah I, 871
Blair, Josiah Millikan I, 872
Blair, Julius O. I, 850
Blair, Julius O. I, 872
Blair, Kate C. I, 850
Blair, Laura I, 929
Blair, Leathia I, 929
Blair, Lena May I, 872
Blair, Leonidas T. I, 850
Blair, Leonidas T. I, 872
Blair, Linzy I, 871
Blair, Lucinda White I, 872
Blair, Luella IV, 1149
Blair, Luella IV, 1202
Blair, Lydia M. I, 527
Blair, Maggie I, 1148
Blair, Manetta M. I, 872
Blair, Maria I, 929
Blair, Marie V, 153
Blair, Marietta I, 622
Blair, Marietta M. I, 851
Blair, Martha I, 618
Blair, Martha I, 619
Blair, Martha I, 621
Blair, Martha I, 622
Blair, Martha I, 649
Blair, Martha I, 850
Blair, Martha I, 871
Blair, Martha I, 872
Blair, Martha I, 885
Blair, Martha I, 903
Blair, Martha I, 921
Blair, Martha C. I, 850
Blair, Martha E. I, 851
Blair, Martha M. I, 618
Blair, Martha M. I, 872
Blair, Martha N. I, 851
Blair, Martha U. I, 872
Blair, Martha White I, 938
Blair, Mary I, 612
Blair, Mary I, 630
Blair, Mary I, 850
Blair, Mary I, 871
Blair, Mary I, 872
Blair, Mary I, 894
Blair, Mary I, 938
Blair, Mary E. I, 850
Blair, Mary E. I, 871
Blair, Mary E. I, 872
Blair, Mary E. I, 901
Blair, Mary Hunter I, 612
Blair, Mary R. I, 850
Blair, Mary Roella I, 872
Blair, Mattie I, 872
Blair, Mattie I, 893
Blair, Mattie E. I, 872
Blair, Mildred I, 872
Blair, Miriam I, 931
Blair, Miriam C. I, 850
Blair, Mollie I, 850
Blair, Mollie I, 872
Blair, Nancy I, 871
Blair, Nathan I, 850
Blair, Nathan I, 871
Blair, Nathan I, 872
Blair, Olive Jane I, 850
Blair, Parker J. I, 872
Blair, Rachel I, 612
Blair, Rachel E. I, 850
Blair, Rachel E. I, 851
Blair, Rachel E. I, 869
Blair, Rachel E. I, 872
Blair, Rebecca II, 338
Blair, Rebecca IV, 75
Blair, Rebecca V, 895
Blair, Rebekah IV, 75
Blair, Ruth I, 850
Blair, Ruth I, 871
Blair, Ruth V, 659
Blair, Ruth C. I, 850
Blair, S. J. I, 938
Blair, Sallie E. I, 527
Blair, Sallie E. I, 549
Blair, Samuel I, 894
Blair, Samuel C. I, 850
Blair, Samuel H. I, 851
Blair, Sarah I, 649
Blair, Sarah I, 674
Blair, Sarah I, 850
Blair, Sarah I, 871
Blair, Sarah I, 872
Blair, Sarah I, 885
Blair, Sarah V, 320
Blair, Sarah V, 357
Blair, Sarah A. I, 851
Blair, Sarah Ann I, 871
Blair, Sarah Ann I, 878
Blair, Sarah Jane I, 612
Blair, Sarah R. I, 851
Blair, Sarah R. I, 872
Blair, Sidney J. I, 929
Blair, Sidney T. I, 850
Blair, Sidney T. I, 872
Blair, Sollomon J. I, 850
Blair, Solomon I, 649
Blair, Solomon I, 850
Blair, Solomon I, 871
Blair, Solomon J. I, 850
Blair, Solomon J. I, 851
Blair, Susan I, 931
Blair, Susan III, 138
Blair, Susan III, 275
Blair, Susan J. I, 929
Blair, Susan Janina I, 921
Blair, Thomas A. I, 851
Blair, Thomas A. I, 872
Blair, Thomas A. M. I, 851
Blair, Thomas Allen I, 612
Blair, Thomas Allen I, 872
Blair, Thomas English I, 612
Blair, Thos. English I, 630
Blair, Veturia T. I, 850
Blair, W. E. I, 630
Blair, Walter I, 630
Blair, Walter E. I, 630
Blair, Walter Elihu I, 612
Blair, Wiley C. I, 850
Blair, Wiley C. I, 872
Blair, William I, 630
Blair, William A. I, 850
Blair, William A. I, 851
Blair, William J. I, 612
Blair, William J. I, 630
Blair, William J. I, 851
Blair, William J. I, 872
Blair, William P. I, 850
Blair, William P. N. I, 872
Blair, William Wesley I, 612
Blair, Winston VI, 799
Blair, Wm. Ervin V, 153
Blair, Wm. H. V, 199
Blair, Wm. J. I, 630
Blair, Wm. Wesley I, 630
Blair, Zebedee F. I, 850
Blair, Zimri I, 475
Blake, Amy III, 98
Blake, Araminta I, 527
Blake, Arthur IV, 178
Blake, Bartholomew VI, 879
Blake, Betsy VI, 930
Blake, Edward II, 338
Blake, Eliza I, 614
Blake, Elizabeth II, 338
Blake, Elizabeth VI, 799
Blake, John II, 338
Blake, John VI, 25
Blake, John VI, 27
Blake, John VI, 32
Blake, Mary IV, 178
Blake, Mary VI, 879
Blake, Mary E. IV, 178
Blake, O. Jary V, 986
Blake, Reuben VI, 879
Blake, Sally VI, 879
Blake, Sarah II, 338
Blake, Wd. Hannah II, 338
Blake, William VI, 799
Blakeley, Daniel V, 659
Blakeley, Imogene V, 659
Blakeley, John A. V, 659
Blakemore, Juliann IV, 465
Blakemore, Juliann IV, 486
Blaker, Abraham VI, 471
Blaker, Abraham VI, 472
Blaker, Abraham VI, 619
Blaker, Agnes II, 980
Blaker, Agness II, 980
Blaker, Amos VI, 472
Blaker, Amos VI, 619
Blaker, David VI, 472
Blaker, David VI, 619
Blaker, John VI, 911
Blaker, Joseph VI, 471
Blaker, Joseph VI, 472
Blaker, Joseph VI, 619
Blaker, Paul, Jr. II, 1045
Blaker, Peter VI, 471
Blaker, Peter VI, 472
Blaker, Peter VI, 619
Blaker, Sarah VI, 472
Blaker, Sarah VI, 619
Blakes, Mary II, 979
Blakes, Stacey II, 979
Blakey, Anna I. II, 839
Blakey, Anna I. II, 881
Blakey, Elizabeth II, 822
Blakey, Elizabeth II, 980
Blakey, Elizabeth II, 1035
Blakey, Elizabeth G. II, 839
Blakey, Ernest L. II, 839
Blakey, Henry W. II, 839
Blakey, Jael II, 980
Blakey, Jael II, 1018
Blakey, Jane II, 980
Blakey, Jane II, 988
Blakey, John W. II, 839
Blakey, Jonathan II, 980
Blakey, Joseph II, 1036
Blakey, Joshua II, 814
Blakey, Joshua II, 980
Blakey, Joshua II, 985
Blakey, Joshua II, 1035
Blakey, Joshua II, 1036
Blakey, Joshua III, 37
Blakey, Letitia S. II, 839
Blakey, Lucille M. II, 881
Blakey, Lydia II, 839
Blakey, Lydia II, 881
Blakey, Margaret II, 955
Blakey, Marianna II, 839
Blakey, Mary II, 980
Blakey, Mary II, 985
Blakey, Mary Anna II, 839
Blakey, Paxson II, 783
Blakey, Pleasant VI, 799
Blakey, Rachel II, 881
Blakey, Rachel II, 980
Blakey, Rachel II, 1045
Blakey, Rachel Moon II, 814
Blakey, Rebecca II, 814
Blakey, Rebecca II, 980
Blakey, Rebecca II, 985
Blakey, Rebecca II, 1036
Blakey, Ruth II, 980
Blakey, Sally VI, 799
Blakey, Sarah II, 980
Blakey, Sarah II, 1035
Blakey, Sarah II, 1036
Blakey, Sarah L. II, 839
Blakey, Thos. II, 839
Blakey, Thos. II, 881
Blakey, Wd. Letitia II, 783
Blakey, William II, 955
Blakey, Wm. II, 467
Blakey, Wm. II, 980
Blakey, Wm. H. II, 839
Blakey, Wm. Henry II, 839
Blakey, Wm. Henry II, 881
Blakey, Wm. T. II, 839
Blakey, Wm., Jr. II, 467
Blakey, Wm., Jr. II, 980
Blakey, Wm., Jr. II, 1035
Blanchard, Aaron I, 36
Blanchard, Aaron I, 48
Blanchard, Aaron I, 207
Blanchard, Aaron I, 281
Blanchard, Aaron II, 467
Blanchard, Aaron Booth II, 469
Blanchard, Ailee I, 36
Blanchard, Ailee I, 50
Blanchard, Albert B. V, 827
Blanchard, Albert B. V, 895
Blanchard, Alice I, 281
Blanchard, Almira S. V, 893
Blanchard, Almira S. V, 895
Blanchard, Caroline C. III, 37
Blanchard, Caroline C. III, 337
Blanchard, Chas. Henry III, 37
Blanchard, Chas. Henry III, 337
Blanchard, Clarissa IV, 1352
Blanchard, Daliah I, 207
Blanchard, Eli V, 827
Blanchard, Elie I, 230
Blanchard, Elisha Stubbs V, 827
Blanchard, Elizabeth II, 22
Blanchard, Elizabeth II, 56
Blanchard, Elizabeth II, 109
Blanchard, Elizabeth V, 827
Blanchard, Elizabeth V, 850
Blanchard, Elizabeth V, 895
Blanchard, Elmira V, 893
Blanchard, Elmira V, 895
Blanchard, Emma Luella V, 827
Blanchard, Ephraim I, 36
Blanchard, Ephraim I, 50
Blanchard, Ephraim I, 129
Blanchard, Ephraim I, 230
Blanchard, Ephraim I, 231
Blanchard, Ephraim, Jr. I, 230
Blanchard, Ephraim, Sr. I, 230
Blanchard, Ephriam I, 230
Blanchard, Ezra V, 895
Blanchard, Hannah III, 37
Blanchard, Helah V, 868
Blanchard, Helen V, 827
Blanchard, Helia V, 827
Blanchard, Helia V, 866
Blanchard, Hiram V, 827
Blanchard, Isabel I, 129
Blanchard, Isabella I, 230
Blanchard, Isabella I, 239
Blanchard, Isbeal I, 129
Blanchard, Jane II, 22
Blanchard, Jane II, 56
Blanchard, Jane II, 467
Blanchard, Jean II, 56
Blanchard, Jemima II, 467
Blanchard, Jemima II, 469
Blanchard, Jemima II, 565
Blanchard, Jesse I, 207
Blanchard, Jesse I, 230
Blanchard, Jesse I, 281
Blanchard, Jesse I, 300
Blanchard, Jesse I, 311
Blanchard, John IV, 1352
Blanchard, Jonathan I, 36
Blanchard, Jonathan I, 230
Blanchard, Jonathan I, 250
Blanchard, Jonathan I, 281
Blanchard, Jonathan I, 300
Blanchard, Josiah I, 230
Blanchard, Julia I, 207
Blanchard, Laura Bell V, 827
Blanchard, Lenore III, 37
Blanchard, Lenore III, 301
Blanchard, Margret II, 22
Blanchard, Marth Jane V, 861
Blanchard, Martha Jane V, 827
Blanchard, Mary I, 207
Blanchard, Mary I, 215
Blanchard, Mary I, 230
Blanchard, Mary I, 300
Blanchard, Mary I, 311
Blanchard, Mary II, 22
Blanchard, Mary H. III, 37
Blanchard, Mary H. III, 337
Blanchard, Mary R. III, 37
Blanchard, Mary R. III, 265
Blanchard, Micajah I, 36
Blanchard, Miles I, 281
Blanchard, Miles I, 300
Blanchard, Miliscent I, 129
Blanchard, Millicent I, 230
Blanchard, Millicent I, 258
Blanchard, Noah V, 868
Blanchard, Pauline Ayers V, 659
Blanchard, Peninah I, 230
Blanchard, Peninah I, 250
Blanchard, Peninah I, 258
Blanchard, Peninnah I, 230
Blanchard, Peninnah I, 239
Blanchard, Philip II, 22
Blanchard, Phillip II, 22
Blanchard, Pinninah I, 129
Blanchard, Rachel V, 827
Blanchard, Rebecca V, 827
Blanchard, Robert Lewis V, 827
Blanchard, Robert Louis V, 827
Blanchard, Rodger I, 207
Blanchard, Ruth V, 868
Blanchard, Sallie J. I, 230
Blanchard, Samuel IV, 1352
Blanchard, Saphire I, 36
Blanchard, Saphire I, 48
Blanchard, Sarah I, 207
Blanchard, Sarah I, 230
Blanchard, Sarah I, 281
Blanchard, Sarah I, 300
Blanchard, Sarah J. I, 207
Blanchard, Sarah J. I, 230
Blanchard, Sarah W. II, 700
Blanchard, Sarah W. II, 701
Blanchard, Stephen V, 25
Blanchard, Susanna I, 230
Blanchard, Susannah I, 230
Blanchard, Susannah I, 231
Blanchard, Uriah I, 300
Blanchard, William V, 827
Blanchard, William H. Granville V, 827
Blanchard, William Henry Granville V, 827
Blanchard, Wm. III, 37
Blanchard, Wm. III, 265
Blanche, Mrs. ??? VI, 890
Blancheon, Eleanor IV, 900
Blancher, Jane II, 467
Blancher, Jane II, 471
Blanchet, Izbel I, 36
Blanchet, Izbel I, 76
Blanchford, Isbeal I, 129
Bland, Abraham II, 441
Bland, Edward VI, 289
Bland, Isaac II, 441
Bland, Louise III, 35
Bland, Louise III, 37
Bland, Susanna II, 338
Bland, Susanna II, 441
Blaney, Eliza Ann IV, 121
Blaney, Eliza Ann IV, 122
Blaney, Jesse IV, 1202
Blankenburg, Emma L. II, 783
Blankenburg, George II, 783
Blankenburg, Julia R. II, 783
Blankenburg, Louis II, 783
Blankenburg, Lucretia M. II, 839
Blankenburg, Lucretia M. II, 891
Blankenburg, Lucretia Mott II, 783
Blankenburg, Marian II, 783
Blankenburg, Rudolph II, 783
Blankenburg, Rudolph II, 839
Blankenburg, Rudolph II, 891
Blankenburg, Sophie II, 783
Blankenship, A. VI, 858
Blankenship, A. VI, 860
Blankenship, Aaron VI, 879
Blankenship, Abel VI, 879
Blankenship, Abel VI, 989
Blankenship, Abraham VI, 879
Blankenship, Abraham VI, 917
Blankenship, Abraham VI, 1006
Blankenship, Abraham VI, 1022
Blankenship, Ann VI, 902
Blankenship, Ben VI, 961
Blankenship, Benj. VI, 945
Blankenship, Benjamin VI, 879
Blankenship, Catharine VI, 830
Blankenship, Christena VI, 879
Blankenship, David VI, 1004
Blankenship, Edith VI, 799
Blankenship, Edmond VI, 998

Blankenship, Edmund VI, 858
Blankenship, Eliza VI, 995
Blankenship, Elizabeth VI, 879
Blankenship, Elizabeth VI, 945
Blankenship, Elizabeth VI, 1006
Blankenship, Gabriella VI, 859
Blankenship, Gilbert W. I, 1148
Blankenship, Hudson VI, 837
Blankenship, Hudson VI, 860
Blankenship, James VI, 859
Blankenship, Jane I, 1148
Blankenship, Joel VI, 860
Blankenship, Joel K. VI, 860
Blankenship, John VI, 879
Blankenship, John A. VI, 835
Blankenship, Jos. VI, 937
Blankenship, Joseph VI, 809
Blankenship, Joseph VI, 918
Blankenship, Joseph VI, 944
Blankenship, Josh. VI, 998
Blankenship, Lawson VI, 879
Blankenship, Lawson VI, 966
Blankenship, Lawson VI, 1022
Blankenship, Levi VI, 799
Blankenship, Levi VI, 830
Blankenship, Luney VI, 879
Blankenship, Lusanny VI, 902
Blankenship, Martha VI, 860
Blankenship, Martha VI, 918
Blankenship, Martha Ann I, 1148
Blankenship, Martha L. VI, 799
Blankenship, Mary VI, 858
Blankenship, Mary VI, 995
Blankenship, Mason VI, 917
Blankenship, Michael J. VI, 880
Blankenship, Milly VI, 945
Blankenship, Nancey VI, 969
Blankenship, Nancey Emeline VI, 1006
Blankenship, Nancy VI, 860
Blankenship, Nancy VI, 1016
Blankenship, Patience VI, 879
Blankenship, Phebe VI, 807
Blankenship, Polly VI, 799
Blankenship, Polly VI, 879
Blankenship, Polly VI, 891
Blankenship, Polly VI, 998
Blankenship, Prudence VI, 837
Blankenship, Rhoda VI, 879
Blankenship, Rhoda VI, 961
Blankenship, Rowland VI, 799
Blankenship, Rowland VI, 835
Blankenship, Sally VI, 860
Blankenship, Sally VI, 937
Blankenship, Sarah VI, 1011
Blankenship, Sarah Ann VI, 880
Blankenship, Sarah E. VI, 835
Blankenship, Susan VI, 809
Blankenship, Susanne VI, 1022
Blankenship, William VI, 945
Blankenship, Zachariah VI, 860
Blankinship, Archibald VI, 799
Blankinship, Archibald VI, 825
Blankinship, Benj. VI, 799
Blankinship, Edith VI, 799
Blankinship, Elijah VI, 799
Blankinship, Elizabeth VI, 799
Blankinship, Elizabeth VI, 825
Blankinship, Elvira VI, 799
Blankinship, Gilbert W. I, 1148
Blankinship, Henry VI, 799
Blankinship, Hester Ann VI, 799
Blankinship, Hudson VI, 799
Blankinship, Hudson VI, 825
Blankinship, Hudson VI, 829
Blankinship, Hudson H. VI, 799
Blankinship, Jane I, 1148
Blankinship, Jane VI, 799
Blankinship, Jeremiah VI, 837
Blankinship, Jesse VI, 799
Blankinship, Joel VI, 799
Blankinship, Joel VI, 821
Blankinship, Joel H. VI, 829
Blankinship, Joel H. VI, 860
Blankinship, John A. VI, 799
Blankinship, John H. VI, 843
Blankinship, Judith VI, 799
Blankinship, Leauraney VI, 829
Blankinship, Levi VI, 799
Blankinship, Martha Ann I, 1148
Blankinship, Martha L. VI, 799
Blankinship, Mary VI, 799
Blankinship, Mary A. VI, 829
Blankinship, Mary P. VI, 809
Blankinship, Nancy VI, 799
Blankinship, Nancy VI, 821
Blankinship, Polly VI, 799
Blankinship, Prudence VI, 799
Blankinship, Roland B. VI, 802
Blankinship, Rowland VI, 799
Blankinship, William H. VI, 799
Blankinship, Zachariah VI, 799
Blankley, Sarah II, 198
Blankley, Sarah II, 233
Blanks, Elizabeth Frances VI, 900
Blanks, Jane VI, 845
Blanks, Obadiah VI, 900
Blanks, Robert VI, 845
Blanshard, Alice I, 207
Blanshard, Ephraim I, 207
Blanshard, Ephraim, Jr. I, 207
Blanshard, Jane II, 56
Blanshard, Jane II, 93
Blanshard, Jesse I, 207
Blanshard, Miliscent I, 129
Blanshard, Miliscent I, 170
Blanshard, Pinninah I, 129
Blanshard, Pinninah I, 170
Blansher, Jean II, 56
Blanshon, Eleanor IV, 900
Blanshon, Eleanor IV, 903
Blansit, Ephraim I, 121
Blansit, Isbell I, 121
Blanton, Elizabeth W. VI, 837
Blanton, Fannie V, 25
Blanton, Marvin V, 25
Blanvelt, ??? III, 34
Blanvelt, Elizabeth M. III, 34
Blanvelt, Elizabeth M. III, 37
Blanvelt, Geo. H. III, 37
Blanvelt, Phebe III, 37
Blanvelt, Wd. ??? III, 201
Blany, Katherine II, 441
Blany, Richard II, 338
Blarcom, Anna III, 411
Blarcom, Herman Van III, 411
Blare, Ezikal VI, 880
Blare, Mary VI, 366
Blare, Mary VI, 453
Blare, Matilda VI, 880
Blare, Nathan I, 871
Blasdell, James III, 37
Blasdell, James H., Jr. III, 37
Blasdell, Martha III, 37
Blatchford, Martha V, 895
Blatchford, Martha V, 901
Blatchford, Martha C. V, 895
Blatchford, Martha S. V, 895
Blatchley, Bayard P. III, 37
Blatchley, Cornelius Camden II, 979
Blatchley, Cornelius Camden III, 37
Blatchley, Ebenezer D. III, 37
Blatscher, John IV, 1307
Blayblock, Bessie White I, 640
Blayblock, Evelyn I, 640
Blayblock, Henry I, 640
Blaylock, Bessie I, 630
Blaylock, Evelyn Register I, 630
Blaylock, Henry I, 630
Blckburn, Chas. IV, 491
Blckburn, Mary E. IV, 491
Bleakmore, Frank IV, 178
Blessing, Ane I, 130
Blessing, Anna V, 153
Blessing, Anne I, 91
Blessing, Anne I, 146
Blessing, Earl S. V, 659
Blessing, Earl S. V, 715
Blessing, Francis A. V, 153
Blessing, John V, 153
Blessing, Mary V, 659
Blessing, Mary V, 715
Blight, Martha II, 467
Blight, Martha II, 532
Blinston, Mary II, 467
Blinston, Mary II, 611
Bliss, Eleanor A. III, 157
Bliss, Elizabeth II, 198
Bliss, Elizabeth II, 273
Bliss, George II, 198
Bliss, George II, 273
Bliss, Marion V, 659
Bliss, Marion V, 721
Bliss, Mildred V, 659
Bliss, Mildred V, 721
Blissing, Isabella III, 70
Blith, Sarah II, 467
Blith, Sarah II, 563
Blizzard, Betsy I, 527
Blizzard, Elizabeth I, 527
Blizzard, Elizabeth V, 298
Blizzard, Elizabeth V, 299
Blocksom, Ann IV, 370
Blocksom, Ann V, 223
Blocksom, Elizabeth IV, 370
Blocksom, Elizabeth V, 153
Blocksom, James IV, 370
Blocksom, James V, 153
Blocksom, Jerusha Johnson V, 223
Blocksom, Maria IV, 370
Blocksom, Maria V, 153
Blocksom, Mary IV, 370
Blocksom, Mary V, 153
Blocksom, Mary V, 223
Blocksom, Nancy V, 153
Blocksom, Priscilla IV, 370
Blocksom, Priscilla V, 153
Blocksom, Richard VI, 231
Blocksom, Sarah IV, 370
Blocksom, Sarah V, 153
Blocksom, Unity V, 223
Blocksom, William IV, 370
Blocksom, William V, 153
Blocksome, Ann IV, 320
Blocksome, Elizabeth IV, 320
Blocksome, James IV, 320
Blocksome, Maria IV, 320
Blocksome, Maria V, 948
Blocksome, Mary IV, 320
Blocksome, Priscilla IV, 320
Blocksome, Sarah IV, 320
Blocksome, William IV, 320
Blohm, Chas. A. IV, 1307
Blohm, Chas. N. IV, 1307
Blondeau, Elizabeth II, 198
Bloodgood, Elizabeth III, 37
Bloodgood, Francis III, 37
Bloodgood, George III, 37
Bloodgood, Joseph III, 37
Bloodgood, Lilian W. II, 839
Bloodgood, Lillian W. II, 839
Bloodgood, Lillian W. II, 858
Bloodgood, Rebecca III, 37
Bloodgood, Samuel III, 37
Bloodgood, Sarah III, 37
Bloodgood, Sarah M. III, 37
Bloodgood, Wm. W. II, 839
Bloodgood, Wm. W. II, 858
Bloom, Ella V, 659
Bloom, Eunice V, 659
Bloom, Frank Preston II, 314
Bloom, Leah II, 314
Bloom, Mary Elizabeth II, 314
Bloom, Melissa V, 659
Bloom, Wm. V, 613
Bloomer, Nellie III, 37
Bloomer, Sarah V, 25
Bloomer, Sarah V, 107
Bloomer, Susan II, 839
Bloomfield, Rachel IV, 75
Bloomfield, Rachel IV, 97
Bloomfield, Susanna IV, 75
Bloomfield, Susanna IV, 97
Blosser, Lizzie V, 986
Blosser, Mamie IV, 1246
Blosser, Merle IV, 1246
Blosser, Thelma IV, 1246
Blossom, Clara B. V, 827
Blossom, Harriet V, 659
Blossom, Harriett V, 671
Blossom, Julia Ann V, 873
Blossom, Keziah V, 827
Blossom, Keziah V, 873
Blossom, Paul V, 659
Blossom, Paul V, 671
Blossom, Perry V, 873
Blosson, Electa V, 986
Blount, Ann O. VI, 804
Blount, Bessie Melvina IV, 1035
Blount, Charles VI, 827
Blount, Charles VI, 865
Blount, Charles Garfield IV, 1035
Blount, Chas. VI, 803
Blount, Chas. T., Sr. VI, 843
Blount, Esther F. IV, 1035
Blount, George H. IV, 1035
Blount, Lucy VI, 843
Blount, Maria P. VI, 865
Blount, Mary VI, 803
Blount, Susan M. VI, 827
Blount, Wm. J. IV, 1035
Blovelt, Sarah IV, 445
Blovert, Sarah IV, 370
Blovit, Rhoda M. V, 986
Blowers, Alice IV, 821
Blowers, Andrew IV, 370
Blowers, Andrew IV, 1049
Blowers, Andrew J. IV, 178
Blowers, Andrew J. IV, 370
Blowers, Andrew J. IV, 406
Blowers, Ann IV, 178
Blowers, Ann IV, 370
Blowers, Ann IV, 402
Blowers, Ann D. IV, 370
Blowers, Blanche IV, 370
Blowers, Eliza B. IV, 370
Blowers, Eliza B. IV, 382
Blowers, Eliza B. IV, 1049
Blowers, Eliza B. IV, 1052
Blowers, Eliza Blanche IV, 370
Blowers, Ethel IV, 1088
Blowers, Ethel IV, 1091
Blowers, Etta IV, 1246
Blowers, Hosetta IV, 370
Blowers, Hosetta IV, 1246
Blowers, Hosetta B. IV, 370
Blowers, Hosetta B. IV, 437
Blowers, Ida IV, 370
Blowers, Ida IV, 395
Blowers, Ida R. IV, 370
Blowers, Jephtha IV, 178
Blowers, Jeptha IV, 370
Blowers, Jeptha D. IV, 370
Blowers, Jeptha D. IV, 382
Blowers, Jeptha D. IV, 1049
Blowers, Jeptha D. IV, 1052
Blowers, Lucinda IV, 370
Blowers, Mary IV, 370
Blowers, Mary Ethel IV, 370
Blowers, Rachel IV, 178
Blowers, Rachel IV, 370
Blowers, Rachel IV, 382
Blowers, Rebecca IV, 178
Blowers, Rebecca IV, 370
Blowers, Rebecca IV, 387
Blowers, Rebecca IV, 406
Blowers, Rebecca IV, 1049
Blowers, Rebecca D. IV, 370
Blowers, Rebecca S. IV, 370
Blowers, Rebecca S. IV, 373
Blowers, Rebecca, Jr. IV, 178
Blowers, Salah Alice IV, 370
Blowers, Sarah A. IV, 370
Blowers, Sarah A. IV, 406
Blowers, Sarah Alice IV, 178
Blowers, Sarah Alice IV, 406
Blowvelt, Rhoda M. V, 986
Bloxam, Ann IV, 140
Bloxam, Ann IV, 151
Bloxam, Charles IV, 140
Bloxam, Elizabeth IV, 140
Bloxam, Gideon Johnson IV, 140
Bloxam, Jerusha IV, 140
Bloxam, Mary IV, 140
Bloxam, Obediah IV, 140
Bloxam, Richard IV, 140
Bloxam, Unity IV, 140
Bloxom, Ann IV, 140
Bloxom, Ann IV, 370
Bloxom, Ann V, 153
Bloxom, Ann V, 194
Bloxom, Ann VI, 299
Bloxom, Anna V, 153
Bloxom, Charles V, 153
Bloxom, Charles VI, 299
Bloxom, Elizabeth IV, 140
Bloxom, Elizabeth IV, 370
Bloxom, Elizabeth V, 25
Bloxom, Elizabeth V, 153
Bloxom, Gideon Johnson V, 153
Bloxom, Gregory V, 153
Bloxom, Gregory VI, 299
Bloxom, James IV, 140
Bloxom, James V, 153
Bloxom, Maria IV, 370
Bloxom, Maria V, 153
Bloxom, Mary IV, 140
Bloxom, Mary IV, 370
Bloxom, Mary V, 153
Bloxom, Mary V, 959
Bloxom, Meriah IV, 140
Bloxom, Nancy V, 153
Bloxom, Obediah VI, 299
Bloxom, Priscilla IV, 370
Bloxom, Priscilla V, 153
Bloxom, Richard V, 153
Bloxom, Richard VI, 231
Bloxom, Richard VI, 299
Bloxom, Richard VI, 318
Bloxom, Richard, Jr. VI, 299
Bloxom, Sarah IV, 370
Bloxom, Sarah V, 153
Bloxom, Sarah V, 948
Bloxom, Sarah V, 959
Bloxom, Sarah VI, 318
Bloxom, William IV, 370
Bloxom, William V, 153
Bloxom, Wm. IV, 140
Bloxom, Wm. V, 153
Bloxom, Wm. V, 959
Bloxsom, Ann IV, 140
Bloxsom, Ann V, 223
Bloxsom, Ann VI, 231
Bloxsom, Ann VI, 299
Bloxsom, Ann VI, 325
Bloxsom, Ann Elizabeth V, 223
Bloxsom, Ann Smith VI, 299
Bloxsom, Anna V, 948
Bloxsom, Chales V, 223
Bloxsom, Charles IV, 140
Bloxsom, Charles V, 223
Bloxsom, Charles V, 948
Bloxsom, Charles VI, 299
Bloxsom, Elizabeth IV, 140
Bloxsom, Elizabeth V, 25
Bloxsom, Elizabeth V, 948
Bloxsom, Elizabeth V, 955
Bloxsom, Elizabeth VI, 231
Bloxsom, Elizabeth VI, 299
Bloxsom, Gideon IV, 140
Bloxsom, Gideon V, 223
Bloxsom, Gideon VI, 231
Bloxsom, Gideon VI, 299
Bloxsom, Gideon Johnson IV, 140
Bloxsom, Gideon Johnson V, 223
Bloxsom, Gregory V, 223
Bloxsom, Gregory VI, 231
Bloxsom, Gregory VI, 299
Bloxsom, Gregory VI, 817
Bloxsom, James IV, 140
Bloxsom, James V, 223
Bloxsom, James V, 948
Bloxsom, James VI, 299
Bloxsom, Jerusha IV, 140
Bloxsom, Jerusha Johnson V, 223
Bloxsom, John Davis VI, 231
Bloxsom, Johnson V, 223
Bloxsom, Maria V, 948
Bloxsom, Mariah Priscilla V, 223
Bloxsom, Mary IV, 140
Bloxsom, Mary V, 223
Bloxsom, Mary V, 948
Bloxsom, Mary VI, 231
Bloxsom, Mary VI, 299
Bloxsom, Mary VI, 301
Bloxsom, Meriah IV, 140
Bloxsom, Meriah VI, 299
Bloxsom, Obadiah VI, 231
Bloxsom, Obediah IV, 140
Bloxsom, Obediah VI, 299
Bloxsom, Polly VI, 299
Bloxsom, Polly VI, 799
Bloxsom, Richard IV, 140
Bloxsom, Richard V, 223
Bloxsom, Richard VI, 231
Bloxsom, Richard VI, 299
Bloxsom, Richard VI, 322
Bloxsom, Richard VI, 325
Bloxsom, Richard VI, 799
Bloxsom, Richard VI, 845
Bloxsom, Richard Obidiah V, 223
Bloxsom, Richard, Jr. VI, 299
Bloxsom, Sarah V, 948
Bloxsom, Sarah VI, 231
Bloxsom, Sarah VI, 299
Bloxsom, Sarah VI, 323
Bloxsom, Thomas VI, 299
Bloxsom, Unity IV, 140
Bloxsom, Unity V, 223
Bloxsom, William V, 223
Bloxsom, William VI, 231
Bloxsom, William VI, 299
Bloxsom, William VI, 301
Bloxsom, William VI, 325
Bloxsom, Wm. IV, 140
Bloxson Johnson, Sarah IV, 151
Bloxson, Ann VI, 325
Bloxson, Richard VI, 325
Bloyed, Mason I, 230
Bluckburn, Abel H. IV, 39
Bluckburn, Caroline IV, 39
Blue, Cora D. IV, 1272
Blue, Wm. M. IV, 1272
Blumstead, Elisabeth II, 467
Blumstead, Elisabeth II, 510
Blundin, Martha N. II, 779
Blundin, Martha N. II, 831
Blundin, Martha N. II, 839
Blunston, James II, 779
Blunston, Mary II, 467
Blunston, Mary II, 611
Blunt, Edmund III, 38
Blunt, Edmund III, 53
Blunt, Eugene III, 38
Blunt, Eugene III, 53
Blunt, Lulu V, 153
Blunt, Mary IV, 928
Bly, Elizabeth IV, 1111
Bly, John II, 441
Bly, Jonas IV, 1111
Bly, Martha IV, 1111
Blythe, Albert VI, 58
Blythe, Alice VI, 53
Blythe, Alice VI, 91
Blythe, Archer VI, 53
Blythe, Archer VI, 54

Blythe, Archer VI, 64
Blythe, Benjamin F. VI, 53
Blythe, Bennie VI, 53
Blythe, Bertha VI, 53
Blythe, Butler VI, 54
Blythe, Charlie IV, 801
Blythe, Cleveland VI, 53
Blythe, Clifton VI, 53
Blythe, Clifton VI, 54
Blythe, Clifton C. VI, 53
Blythe, Ella VI, 64
Blythe, Ellen J. VI, 53
Blythe, Emmett McKenny VI, 53
Blythe, Eva Mary VI, 53
Blythe, Flournoy VI, 53
Blythe, Flournoy VI, 54
Blythe, Frank IV, 801
Blythe, Franklin VI, 53
Blythe, Franklin VI, 54
Blythe, George VI, 53
Blythe, George VI, 74
Blythe, Hendricks VI, 53
Blythe, Hendrix VI, 54
Blythe, James R. VI, 53
Blythe, Jane VI, 53
Blythe, Jane VI, 54
Blythe, Jane VI, 91
Blythe, Jane, Sr. VI, 91
Blythe, Jennie Smith VI, 53
Blythe, Jennie Smith VI, 54
Blythe, Jesse VI, 53
Blythe, Jesse VI, 54
Blythe, Jesse VI, 77
Blythe, Jesse VI, 88
Blythe, Jesse, Jr. VI, 53
Blythe, Jesse, Jr. VI, 54
Blythe, John VI, 54
Blythe, Josephine VI, 91
Blythe, Keeton VI, 53
Blythe, Keeton VI, 54
Blythe, Lala VI, 53
Blythe, Lela VI, 53
Blythe, Levina VI, 53
Blythe, Levina VI, 54
Blythe, Levina VI, 88
Blythe, Lillie G. VI, 53
Blythe, Lilly VI, 91
Blythe, Lucy IV, 801
Blythe, Mallory VI, 53
Blythe, Mallory VI, 58
Blythe, Mallory Edward VI, 53
Blythe, Maria VI, 53
Blythe, Martha A. VI, 53
Blythe, Martha A. VI, 74
Blythe, Mary A. VI, 53
Blythe, Mary E. VI, 53
Blythe, Mary E. VI, 64
Blythe, Mary E. VI, 91
Blythe, Mary Jane VI, 53
Blythe, Mary Jane VI, 54
Blythe, Mary Jane VI, 77
Blythe, Millie VI, 64
Blythe, Mitchel VI, 53
Blythe, Mitchel VI, 54
Blythe, Mitchell VI, 54
Blythe, Nancy VI, 53
Blythe, Nancy VI, 58
Blythe, Nancy VI, 91
Blythe, Nancy Wester VI, 53
Blythe, Nannie Jane VI, 53
Blythe, Rebecca I, 214
Blythe, Rebecca VI, 53
Blythe, Rebecca VI, 54
Blythe, Rebecca VI, 64
Blythe, Rebecca VI, 65
Blythe, Rebecca VI, 87
Blythe, Rebecca VI, 91
Blythe, Robert VI, 53
Blythe, Robert VI, 54
Blythe, Robert VI, 64
Blythe, Robert VI, 91
Blythe, Robert Lee Butler VI, 54
Blythe, Robert, Jr. VI, 54
Blythe, Rosa VI, 53
Blythe, Rosa VI, 58
Blythe, Sallie VI, 53
Blythe, Sankey Sherman VI, 53
Blythe, Sarah II, 467
Blythe, Sarah II, 558
Blythe, Tazewell J. VI, 53
Blythe, Thomas A. VI, 53
Blythe, Viney VI, 91
Blythe, William VI, 53
Blythe, William VI, 54
Blythe, William A. VI, 53
Blythe, William Albert VI, 53
Blythe, William N. VI, 53
Blythe, William N. VI, 54
Blythe, Willie VI, 53
Blythe, Wm. VI, 53
Blythe, Wm. Albert, Jr. VI, 53
Blythe, Wm. Luther VI, 53
Boa, Keziah VI, 828
Boa, Marian B. VI, 846
Boa, Susan VI, 846
Boa, Thomas VI, 828
Boag, Jesse I, 37
Boak, Ellen VI, 366
Boak, Ellen VI, 412
Boak, Mary VI, 366
Boak, Mary VI, 383
Boalt, Charlotte IV, 1233
Boalton, Joseph IV, 801
Boalton, Sarah IV, 801
Boan, Lydia Ann IV, 1049
Boans, B. F. I, 300
Board, Absalum VI, 1014
Board, Absolum VI, 895
Board, Adaline VI, 965
Board, Caroline M. VI, 948
Board, Clarinda V, 659
Board, Cleopatra VI, 880
Board, Eleanor VI, 974
Board, Elijah VI, 943
Board, Elizabeth VI, 880
Board, Elizabeth VI, 900
Board, Elizabeth A. A. VI, 880
Board, Emila V, 659
Board, Emily V, 659
Board, Francis VI, 875
Board, Francis VI, 880
Board, Francis VI, 881
Board, Francis VI, 960
Board, Francis VI, 975
Board, Francis H. VI, 948
Board, G. B. VI, 970
Board, James VI, 880
Board, James VI, 974
Board, James VI, 993
Board, James VI, 998
Board, James E. VI, 948
Board, James, Jr. VI, 880
Board, Jane VI, 975
Board, Jemima VI, 875
Board, Jemima VI, 997
Board, John VI, 880
Board, John VI, 893
Board, John VI, 905
Board, John VI, 943
Board, John VI, 948
Board, John VI, 953
Board, John VI, 958
Board, John VI, 959
Board, John VI, 965
Board, John VI, 975
Board, John VI, 977
Board, John VI, 997
Board, John, Jr. VI, 938
Board, John, Sr. VI, 944
Board, John, Sr. VI, 965
Board, John, Sr. VI, 987
Board, L. A. V, 659
Board, Lettice VI, 880
Board, Lucy VI, 880
Board, Lucy Ann V, 659
Board, Mariah VI, 880
Board, Nancy VI, 880
Board, Nancy VI, 959
Board, Nancy VI, 993
Board, Nancy VI, 1014
Board, Nathan VI, 936
Board, Patsy VI, 880
Board, Peggy VI, 944
Board, Polly VI, 895
Board, Polly VI, 938
Board, Salley VI, 880
Board, Sarah VI, 895
Board, Sarah F. VI, 948
Board, Sarah Jane VI, 987
Board, Sophia VI, 943
Board, Stephen VI, 875
Board, Stephen VI, 880
Board, Stephen VI, 938
Board, Suckey VI, 880
Board, Susan Ann VI, 977
Board, Thomas VI, 880
Board, William VI, 880
Board, William VI, 895
Board, William VI, 900
Board, William VI, 959
Board, William VI, 993
Board, William, Sr. VI, 974
Board, Wm. V, 659
Boardman, George II, 338
Boardman, Phebe III, 38
Boatman, Anna Ridgeway V, 320
Boatman, Sarah M. V, 223
Boatright, Ann VI, 1009
Boatright, Anne VI, 861
Boatright, Easter VI, 816
Boatright, Francis VI, 944
Boatright, Isaiah VI, 944
Boatright, James VI, 816
Boatright, James VI, 818
Boatright, James VI, 861
Boatright, James VI, 864
Boatright, Jenny VI, 864
Boatright, Locky VI, 818
Boatright, William VI, 1009
Boatright, William VI, 1017
Boatwright, Daniel VI, 799
Boatwright, James VI, 799
Boatwright, James W. VI, 799
Boatwright, Rhoda VI, 799
Boatwright, Sarah W. VI, 799
Boatwright, Sophie VI, 799
Boaz, Ann VI, 851
Boaz, Charles VI, 812
Boaz, Charles H. VI, 802
Boaz, Chas. H. VI, 799
Boaz, David P. VI, 799
Boaz, Edmund VI, 799
Boaz, Eliza VI, 839
Boaz, Isabella VI, 799
Boaz, James VI, 299
Boaz, James VI, 799
Boaz, James VI, 800
Boaz, James VI, 814
Boaz, James VI, 851
Boaz, Joseph P. VI, 799
Boaz, Lockey L. VI, 799
Boaz, Louisa VI, 816
Boaz, Nelly VI, 799
Boaz, Penelope VI, 799
Boaz, Phebe VI, 803
Boaz, Rhoda VI, 799
Boaz, Robert VI, 803
Boaz, Robert I. VI, 799
Boaz, Robert I. VI, 867
Boaz, Russell VI, 799
Boaz, Russell VI, 839
Boaz, Russell VI, 849
Boaz, Russell VI, 851
Boaz, Winnefred VI, 799
Bobbet, Marinda V, 986
Bobbet, William VI, 874
Bobbete, Bitsey VI, 874
Bobbett, Bessie V, 986
Bobbett, Betsey VI, 875
Bobbett, Elizabeth VI, 880
Bobbett, Hattie V, 986
Bobbett, Marinda V, 986
Bobbett, Nancy VI, 880
Bobbett, Peter VI, 880
Bobbett, Randolph VI, 880
Bobbett, William R. VI, 891
Bobbett, Wm. H. V, 986
Bobbit, W. VI, 1016
Bobbitt, Humphrey VI, 799
Bobbitt, Lucile V, 550
Bobbitt, Lucy George VI, 799
Bobbitt, Nancy VI, 1016
Bobhit, Elma I, 612
Bobhit, Joseph E. I, 612
Boblet, Jacob VI, 1002
Boblet, Michael VI, 1002
Boblett, John VI, 880
Boblett, Lydia VI, 880
Boblett, Mary VI, 880
Boblett, Racheal VI, 880
Boblett, William R. VI, 880
Bobletts, Frances Ann VI, 891
Bobletz, Elizabeth VI, 880
Bobletz, George VI, 880
Bobletz, Mary VI, 1002
Bobletz, Peter VI, 904
Bobletz, William VI, 916
Boblitz, Elizabeth VI, 880
Boblitz, George VI, 880
Boblitz, Henry VI, 880
Boblitz, John VI, 880
Boblitz, Sarah VI, 880
Boblitz, Susan VI, 880
Boblitz, William VI, 880
Bobson, Humphrey VI, 799
Bobson, Humphrey VI, 821
Bobson, Humphrey VI, 822
Bobson, Lucy VI, 799
Bobson, Lucy VI, 821
Bobson, Sylvia VI, 821
Bocker, Caroline III, 295
Bockus, Ann III, 38
Bocock, Catherine VI, 881
Bocock, Cleopatra VI, 996
Bocock, Elijah VI, 919
Bocock, Elijah VI, 948
Bocock, Johnston VI, 881
Bocock, Judith VI, 919
Bocock, Mary V, 153
Bocock, Mary Sears V, 948
Bocock, Morning VI, 996
Bocock, Nancy V, 223
Bocock, Nancy V, 253
Bocock, Nancy VI, 922
Bocock, Penelope V, 613
Bocock, Penelope V, 643
Bocock, Penelope V, 948
Bocock, Sally VI, 881
Bocock, Samuel VI, 881
Bocock, Samuel VI, 922
Bocock, Samuel VI, 996
Bocock, Waddy VI, 881
Bococock, William VI, 946
Bodby, Ann VI, 12
Boddie, ??? VI, 24
Boddie, John B. VI, 39
Boddy, John II, 338
Boddy, John II, 467
Boden, Edward III, 38
Boden, James S. III, 38
Boden, James S. III, 158
Boden, Martha III, 38
Boden, Moses B. III, 172
Boden, Phebe C. III, 38
Boden, Phebe C. III, 158
Boden, Phebe C. III, 172
Bodenhamer, Harold R. IV, 178
Bodenhamer, John A. IV, 178
Bodenhamer, John Myron IV, 178
Bodenhamer, Mary IV, 178
Bodenhamer, Mary IV, 282
Bodenhamer, Miriam O. IV, 178
Bodenhamer, Rowan O. IV, 178
Bodenhamer, Rowan O. IV, 282
Bodine, ??? II, 189
Bodine, Mary E. II, 189
Bodine, Mary E. II, 281
Bodine, Mary E. II, 307
Bodine, Mary E. II, 316
Bodine, Mary E. II, 327
Bodine, Roy V, 727
Bodine, Vesta V, 727
Bodkin, Rebecca Jane Haworth V, 659
Bodley, Rebecca V, 895
Bodley, Sarah E. V, 895
Bodsford, Elizabeth I, 933
Boe, Mary IV, 680
Boekenhauer, Jan Wm. II, 467
Boeraem, Timothy III, 38
Bogan, Anna V, 551
Bogan, Anna V, 660
Bogan, Anna Elizabeth V, 551
Bogan, Anna Elizabeth V, 659
Bogan, Annie Mary V, 374
Bogan, Annie Mary V, 551
Bogan, Bertie F. V, 659
Bogan, Bessie B. V, 551
Bogan, Bessie Bell V, 551
Bogan, Bessie Bell V, 660
Bogan, Calista Emiline V, 597
Bogan, Catharine VI, 366
Bogan, Catharine VI, 413
Bogan, Clara V, 551
Bogan, Clara Bell V, 659
Bogan, Dorothy Louise V, 154
Bogan, Edgar V, 25
Bogan, Edgar V, 154
Bogan, Edith Grace V, 659
Bogan, Edward V, 25
Bogan, Elizabeth V, 154
Bogan, Ella J. V, 25
Bogan, Elnora V, 374
Bogan, Elnora V, 551
Bogan, Elnora V, 659
Bogan, Evan V, 25
Bogan, Evan V, 154
Bogan, Evan O. V, 25
Bogan, Evan O. V, 154
Bogan, Evan V. V, 154
Bogan, Geo. W. V, 659
Bogan, George V, 551
Bogan, George W. V, 551
Bogan, Hannah V, 374
Bogan, Hannah V, 551
Bogan, Hannah V, 659
Bogan, Hannah O. V, 374
Bogan, Harriet V, 597
Bogan, Ida V, 551
Bogan, Ina May V, 154
Bogan, Inez V, 551
Bogan, Iva May V, 154
Bogan, J. Rendell V, 551
Bogan, J. Waller V, 551
Bogan, J. Walter V, 551
Bogan, J. Walter V, 660
Bogan, John V, 551
Bogan, John V, 597
Bogan, John A. V, 551
Bogan, Jonny A. V, 660
Bogan, Leila N. V, 154
Bogan, Lelah V, 213
Bogan, Lelia V, 25
Bogan, Lelia N. V, 25
Bogan, Lina V, 551
Bogan, Lina V, 562
Bogan, Lizzie V, 551
Bogan, Lucile V, 154
Bogan, Marianna V, 154
Bogan, Marianne V, 154
Bogan, Marianne V, 160
Bogan, Marjorie C. V, 154
Bogan, Martha V, 551
Bogan, Martha J. V, 551
Bogan, Martha Olive V, 551
Bogan, Martha Olive V, 660
Bogan, Mary V, 154
Bogan, Mary V, 213
Bogan, Mary E. V, 25
Bogan, Mary O. V, 25
Bogan, Mary O. V, 154
Bogan, Meredith V, 551
Bogan, Mr. ??? V, 299
Bogan, Mrs. ??? V, 299
Bogan, Nancy J. V, 660
Bogan, Nellie V, 155
Bogan, Nellie V, 551
Bogan, Nellie May V, 659
Bogan, Nina V, 551
Bogan, Olive V, 325
Bogan, Olive V, 551
Bogan, Olive V, 660
Bogan, Olive V, 665
Bogan, Priscilla V, 551
Bogan, Raleigh L. V, 25
Bogan, Raleigh L. V, 154
Bogan, Raleigh Leon V, 154
Bogan, Raleigh Leon V, 160
Bogan, Robert C. V, 154
Bogan, Robert Compton V, 154
Bogan, Robert W. V, 551
Bogan, Rolla V, 25
Bogan, Rosa V, 551
Bogan, Ruth Anna V, 551
Bogan, Vernon Leroy V, 551
Bogan, Vernon Leroy V, 659
Bogan, Virginia V, 551
Bogan, W. E. V, 154
Bogan, W. E. V, 213
Bogan, Walter V, 551
Bogan, Walter V, 659
Bogan, Walter Elwood V, 551
Bogan, Willard V, 25
Bogan, William E. V, 374
Bogan, William E. V, 551
Bogan, William E. V, 659
Bogan, Zoe V, 477
Bogardus, Anna C. III, 38
Bogardus, Eliz. F. III, 38
Bogardus, Elizabeth III, 38
Bogardus, Elizabeth V, 26
Bogardus, Elizabeth V, 57
Bogardus, Elizabeth F. III, 38
Bogardus, Elizabeth F. V, 26
Bogardus, James III, 38
Bogardus, James F. III, 38
Bogardus, James Furnas III, 38
Bogardus, James N. V, 26
Bogardus, Joseph III, 38
Bogardus, Joseph V, 26
Bogardus, Joseph A. III, 38
Bogardus, Joseph A. V, 26
Bogardus, Joseph A. V, 57
Bogardus, Joseph Lannin III, 38
Bogart, Amy Avis III, 38
Bogart, Dr. Jos. III, 396
Bogart, Dr. Jos. H. III, 445
Bogart, Elsie III, 38
Bogart, Ethelene III, 396
Bogart, Ethelene III, 445
Bogart, George Henry III, 38
Bogart, Hannah Ella III, 38
Bogart, Jane III, 396
Bogart, Jane III, 445
Bogart, Keturah Seaman III, 38
Bogart, Martha S. III, 38
Bogart, Mary III, 38
Bogart, Peter Titus III, 38
Bogart, Rachel III, 38
Bogart, Rudolphus III, 38
Bogart, Rudolphus Ritzema III, 38
Bogart, Wealty Jane III, 38
Boge, Jesse I, 36
Boge, Job I, 36
Boge, Jonathan, Jr. IV, 512
Boge, Joseph I, 36
Boge, Rachel I, 36
Boge, Rachel I, 67
Boge, Robert I, 36
Boge, Robert I, 67
Bogeman, Caroline III, 280
Bogemann, Caroline III, 118
Bogen, George W. V, 551
Bogen, Lina V, 551

Bogert, Amy Avis III, 38
Bogert, Charlotte III, 103
Bogert, Charlotte R. III, 38
Bogert, Elsie III, 38
Bogert, Elsie III, 82
Bogert, Elsie C. III, 38
Bogert, Elsie C. III, 103
Bogert, Elsie C. III, 358
Bogert, George Henry III, 38
Bogert, Hannah Ella III, 38
Bogert, Helen III, 38
Bogert, Helen III, 357
Bogert, Helen III, 358
Bogert, Henry III, 38
Bogert, Keturah Seaman III, 38
Bogert, Martha S. III, 38
Bogert, Mary III, 38
Bogert, Peter Titus III, 38
Bogert, Rachel III, 38
Bogert, Rudolphus III, 38
Bogert, Rudolphus III, 103
Bogert, Rudolphus R. III, 38
Bogert, Rudolphus R. III, 358
Bogert, Rudolphus Ritzema III, 38
Bogert, Rudolphus Ritzema III, 82
Bogert, Wealty Jane III, 38
Bogess, Sarah V, 452
Boggass, Mary VI, 467
Bogger, John I, 130
Boggess, David V, 452
Boggess, Mattie V, 452
Boggess, Sarah V, 452
Boggs, Ann II, 467
Boggs, Ann II, 699
Boggs, Ann II, 783
Boggs, Francis II, 467
Boggs, Francis II, 728
Boggs, Francis II, 783
Boggs, Francis II, 839
Boggs, Henry I, 374
Boggs, James II, 783
Boggs, Jane I, 374
Boggs, Mary VI, 880
Boggs, Mary Ann I, 374
Boggs, Nathan I, 374
Boggs, Nathan P. I, 374
Boggs, Phebe I, 374
Boggs, Robert VI, 880
Boggs, Sally VI, 880
Boggs, Sarah II, 783
Boggs, Sarah Ann II, 467
Boggs, Thomas II, 467
Boggs, William VI, 880
Boggus, David V, 452
Bogleman, Ella IV, 928
Bogleman, Ella Mae IV, 928
Bogleman, Monroe IV, 928
Bogleman, Rose IV, 928
Bogue, ??? I, 279
Bogue, Aaron I, 189
Bogue, Alfred V, 827
Bogue, Alfred V, 879
Bogue, Alfred V, 887
Bogue, Alice I, 267
Bogue, Amos V, 827
Bogue, Ann I, 36
Bogue, Ann I, 37
Bogue, Ann I, 77
Bogue, Ann I, 190
Bogue, Ann I, 300
Bogue, Ann V, 879
Bogue, Ann W. I, 709
Bogue, Anna I, 37
Bogue, Anna I, 281
Bogue, Anna I, 709
Bogue, Anna I, 738
Bogue, Anna V, 827
Bogue, Anna V, 845
Bogue, Barnaba I, 281
Bogue, Barnabas I, 300
Bogue, Benjamin I, 130
Bogue, Benjamin I, 281
Bogue, Benjamin I, 282
Bogue, Benjamin I, 300
Bogue, Benjamin I, 314
Bogue, Benjamin V, 827
Bogue, Benjamin V, 879
Bogue, Benjamin E. V, 827
Bogue, Catharine I, 267
Bogue, Catharine IV, 465
Bogue, Catharine IV, 497
Bogue, Catherine IV, 21
Bogue, Charity I, 281
Bogue, Charles V, 827
Bogue, Charles V, 879
Bogue, Christian I, 36
Bogue, Christian I, 37
Bogue, Christian I, 74
Bogue, Christiana I, 5
Bogue, Creesey I, 37
Bogue, Creesey I, 41
Bogue, Daniel IV, 321
Bogue, Daniel IV, 512
Bogue, Daniel E. IV, 512
Bogue, Deborah I, 36
Bogue, Deborah I, 52
Bogue, Delwin I, 37
Bogue, Dilwin V, 827
Bogue, Dilwyn V, 827
Bogue, Dilwyn V, 845
Bogue, Duke I, 36
Bogue, Duke I, 37
Bogue, Duke I, 70
Bogue, Duke I, 189
Bogue, Duke I, 709
Bogue, Edith IV, 321
Bogue, Edith IV, 512
Bogue, Edith A. IV, 512
Bogue, Elinor I, 36
Bogue, Elinor I, 68
Bogue, Elinor I Sup 1, 7
Bogue, Elisabeth I, 35
Bogue, Elisabeth I, 36
Bogue, Elisabeth I, 37
Bogue, Elisabeth I, 56
Bogue, Elisabeth I, 62
Bogue, Elisabeth I, 67
Bogue, Elisabeth I, 130
Bogue, Elisabeth I, 147
Bogue, Elisabeth I, 180
Bogue, Elisabeth I, 189
Bogue, Elisabeth I, 193
Bogue, Elisabeth, Jr. I, 189
Bogue, Elisabeth, Jr. I, 199
Bogue, Elizabeth I, 190
Bogue, Elizabeth I, 709
Bogue, Elizabeth I, 733
Bogue, Elizabeth IV, 512
Bogue, Elizabeth V, 827
Bogue, Elizabeth V, 828
Bogue, Elizabeth V, 879
Bogue, Elvira V, 827
Bogue, Elvira V, 879
Bogue, Elviry V, 828
Bogue, Elviry V, 837
Bogue, Fanny IV, 75
Bogue, Gillian I, 37
Bogue, Gillian I, 51
Bogue, Gula I, 267
Bogue, Gulia I, 282
Bogue, Hannah V, 828
Bogue, Hannah V, 879
Bogue, Hannah, Jr. I, 267
Bogue, Hudah I, 37
Bogue, Hudah I, 63
Bogue, Huldah IV, 321
Bogue, Huldah IV, 351
Bogue, Huldah IV, 465
Bogue, Huldy IV, 21
Bogue, Isaac I, 36
Bogue, Isaac I, 71
Bogue, James Benine V, 879
Bogue, James Bonign V, 828
Bogue, Jane I, 130
Bogue, Jane I, 133
Bogue, Jane I, 190
Bogue, Jean I, 130
Bogue, Jemima I, 37
Bogue, Jemima I, 189
Bogue, Jemima I, 197
Bogue, Jesse I, 36
Bogue, Jesse I, 37
Bogue, Jesse I, 61
Bogue, Jesse I, 189
Bogue, Jesse I, 267
Bogue, Jesse I, 281
Bogue, Jesse I, 282
Bogue, Jesse I, 300
Bogue, Jesse V, 827
Bogue, Jesse, Jr. I, 300
Bogue, Job I, 36
Bogue, Job I, 37
Bogue, Job I, 62
Bogue, Job I, 130
Bogue, Job I, 189
Bogue, Job I, 267
Bogue, Job IV, 21
Bogue, Job IV, 321
Bogue, Job IV, 327
Bogue, Job IV, 465
Bogue, Job IV, 512
Bogue, Job V, 827
Bogue, Job V, 861
Bogue, Job V, 879
Bogue, Joel IV, 512
Bogue, Joel H. IV, 512
Bogue, John I, 37
Bogue, John I, 80
Bogue, John I, 130
Bogue, John I, 189
Bogue, John I, 190
Bogue, John I, 709
Bogue, John IV, 21
Bogue, John IV, 370
Bogue, John IV, 512
Bogue, John V, 827
Bogue, John V, 879
Bogue, John W. V, 879
Bogue, John, Sr. I, 37
Bogue, Jonathan I, 37
Bogue, Jonathan I, 189
Bogue, Jonathan I, 281
Bogue, Jonathan IV, 75
Bogue, Jonathan IV, 140
Bogue, Jonathan IV, 321
Bogue, Jonathan IV, 327
Bogue, Jonathan IV, 370
Bogue, Jonathan IV, 465
Bogue, Jonathan IV, 511
Bogue, Jonathan IV, 512
Bogue, Jonathan, Jr. IV, 512
Bogue, Joseph I, 36
Bogue, Joseph I, 62
Bogue, Joseph I, 130
Bogue, Joseph I, 282
Bogue, Joseph V, 827
Bogue, Joseph V, 845
Bogue, Joseph V, 861
Bogue, Joseph V, 879
Bogue, Joshua I, 3
Bogue, Joshua I, 190
Bogue, Joshua IV, 864
Bogue, Josiah I, 36
Bogue, Josiah I, 37
Bogue, Josiah I, 77
Bogue, Josiah I, 189
Bogue, Josiah I, 267
Bogue, Josiah I, 281
Bogue, Josiah I, 282
Bogue, Josiah I, 300
Bogue, Josiah I, 318
Bogue, Josiah IV, 351
Bogue, Josiah V, 827
Bogue, Josiah V, 879
Bogue, Judith I, 36
Bogue, Judith I, 71
Bogue, Kezia I, 37
Bogue, Kezia I, 61
Bogue, Kezia I, 130
Bogue, Kezia V, 827
Bogue, Keziah I, 152
Bogue, Keziah V, 879
Bogue, Keziah V, 887
Bogue, Leah I, 281
Bogue, Leah I, 300
Bogue, Leah I, 314
Bogue, Linford I, 3
Bogue, Lyddia I, 37
Bogue, Lyddia I, 52
Bogue, Lydia I, 36
Bogue, Lydia I, 37
Bogue, Lydia I, 45
Bogue, Lydia I, 80
Bogue, Lydia I, 189
Bogue, Lydia I, 190
Bogue, Lydia I, 196
Bogue, Lydia I, 709
Bogue, Malachi IV, 21
Bogue, Malachi Jolly IV, 21
Bogue, Margaret I, 36
Bogue, Margaret I, 56
Bogue, Margaret V, 879
Bogue, Margret I, 37
Bogue, Mariam V, 879
Bogue, Marium V, 827
Bogue, Marium V, 861
Bogue, Mark I, 37
Bogue, Mark I, 73
Bogue, Mark I, 130
Bogue, Mark I, 133
Bogue, Mark I, 189
Bogue, Mark I, 190
Bogue, Mark I, 267
Bogue, Mark IV, 77
Bogue, Mark IV, 321
Bogue, Mark IV, 370
Bogue, Mark IV, 511
Bogue, Mark IV, 512
Bogue, Martha I, 37
Bogue, Martha I, 190
Bogue, Martha I, 709
Bogue, Martha I, 738
Bogue, Mary I, 34
Bogue, Mary I, 36
Bogue, Mary I, 37
Bogue, Mary I, 38
Bogue, Mary I, 62
Bogue, Mary I, 130
Bogue, Mary I, 189
Bogue, Mary I, 190
Bogue, Mary I, 197
Bogue, Mary I, 267
Bogue, Mary I, 282
Bogue, Mary I, 300
Bogue, Mary I, 318
Bogue, Mary IV, 21
Bogue, Mary IV, 351
Bogue, Mary V, 827
Bogue, Mary V, 845
Bogue, Mary V, 861
Bogue, Mary V, 879
Bogue, Mary Ann IV, 321
Bogue, Mary Ann IV, 327
Bogue, Mary Ann IV, 370
Bogue, Mary Ann IV, 512
Bogue, Mary Sarah Elizabeth Miriam Ann V, 827
Bogue, Mary, Jr. I, 189
Bogue, Mary, Jr. I, 200
Bogue, Maryann IV, 511
Bogue, Meriam IV, 465
Bogue, Meriam IV, 495
Bogue, Minnie I, 3
Bogue, Miriam I, 36
Bogue, Miriam I, 38
Bogue, Miriam I, 51
Bogue, Miriam I, 68
Bogue, Miriam I, 189
Bogue, Miriam I, 190
Bogue, Miriam I, 196
Bogue, Miriam I, 300
Bogue, Miriam I, 302
Bogue, Miriam IV, 21
Bogue, Miriam IV, 321
Bogue, Mirriam I, 37
Bogue, Moses Melton IV, 75
Bogue, Moses, Jr. I, 37
Bogue, Newby I, 37
Bogue, Newby I, 63
Bogue, Newby I, 130
Bogue, Newby V, 827
Bogue, Newby V, 879
Bogue, Peggy V, 827
Bogue, Phariby I, 186
Bogue, Phebe IV, 512
Bogue, Pheriba I, 37
Bogue, Pheriba I, 68
Bogue, Philip IV, 21
Bogue, Piety I, 281
Bogue, Rachel I, 36
Bogue, Rachel I, 190
Bogue, Rebecca I, 281
Bogue, Rhoda I, 267
Bogue, Robert I, 36
Bogue, Robert I, 37
Bogue, Robert I, 189
Bogue, Robert I, 190
Bogue, Robert I, 267
Bogue, Robert IV, 321
Bogue, Robert IV, 512
Bogue, Robert, Sr. I, 37
Bogue, Ruth I, 36
Bogue, Ruth I, 61
Bogue, Ruth I, 267
Bogue, Ruth IV, 75
Bogue, Ruth IV, 77
Bogue, Ruth IV, 321
Bogue, Ruth IV, 370
Bogue, Ruth IV, 511
Bogue, Ruth IV, 512
Bogue, Sadie III, 190
Bogue, Sadie III, 301
Bogue, Samuel I, 130
Bogue, Samuel I, 147
Bogue, Samuel I, 189
Bogue, Samuel V, 827
Bogue, Sarah I, 36
Bogue, Sarah I, 37
Bogue, Sarah I, 38
Bogue, Sarah I, 61
Bogue, Sarah I, 67
Bogue, Sarah I, 70
Bogue, Sarah I, 73
Bogue, Sarah I, 130
Bogue, Sarah I, 189
Bogue, Sarah I, 267
Bogue, Sarah I, 268
Bogue, Sarah I, 281
Bogue, Sarah I, 282
Bogue, Sarah I, 300
Bogue, Sarah I, 308
Bogue, Sarah I, 709
Bogue, Sarah I, 718
Bogue, Sarah IV, 75
Bogue, Sarah IV, 77
Bogue, Sarah IV, 321
Bogue, Sarah IV, 327
Bogue, Sarah IV, 370
Bogue, Sarah IV, 511
Bogue, Sarah IV, 512
Bogue, Sarah V, 827
Bogue, Sarah V, 828
Bogue, Sarah V, 861
Bogue, Sarah V, 879
Bogue, Sarah VI, 27
Bogue, Sarah VI, 28
Bogue, Sarah Ann V, 827
Bogue, Sarah Ann V, 828
Bogue, Sarah Bogue IV, 140
Bogue, Sarah Elizabeth IV, 512
Bogue, Sarah, Jr. I, 189
Bogue, Sarah, Sr. I, 300
Bogue, Simons I, 37
Bogue, Stephen I, 37
Bogue, Stephen V, 827
Bogue, Stephen V, 828
Bogue, Stephen V, 837
Bogue, Stephen V, 879
Bogue, Thomas I, 130
Bogue, Thomas I, 189
Bogue, Thomas I, 190
Bogue, William I, 36
Bogue, William I, 37
Bogue, William I, 52
Bogue, William I, 56
Bogue, William I, 68
Bogue, William I, 130
Bogue, William I, 190
Bogue, William I, 267
Bogue, William I Sup 1, 7
Bogue, William V, 827
Bogue, William V, 828
Bogue, William VI, 27
Bogue, William VI, 28
Bogue, William Melton IV, 75
Bogue, Wm. V, 879
Bogue, Zachariah I, 282
Bohack, Catharine III, 396
Bohack, Catharine III, 442
Bohack, Christian III, 396
Bohack, Christian III, 442
Boham, Bell V, 986
Boham, Charity V, 986
Boham, Effie V, 986
Boham, Etta IV, 1149
Boham, George IV, 1149
Boham, John V, 986
Boham, Lewis V, 986
Boham, Maggie IV, 1149
Boham, Rosa IV, 1149
Boham, Sada V, 986
Boham, Thomas IV, 1149
Boham, Tina IV, 1149
Bohannon, Dinah I, 981
Bohannon, Dinah I, 993
Bohanon, Vesta I, 627
Bohner, Edward IV, 816
Bohner, Edward IV, 956
Bohner, Lena IV, 816
Bohner, Lena M. IV, 956
Bohner, Magdalena IV, 816
Bohner, Magdalena IV, 956
Bohnert, Albert IV, 1307
Bohre, Willie V, 727
Bohse, Willie V, 727
Bohyer, Alexander V, 987
Boice, John II, 339
Boice, John W. I, 231
Boice, Mary IV, 612
Boice, Mary IV, 617
Boies, Charles Dwight VI, 366
Boies, Elizabeth Bainbridge VI, 366
Boies, Ortow Henry VI, 366
Boile, Charity IV, 928
Boile, Lenora S. IV, 928
Boile, Wm. IV, 928
Boileau, Rebecca IV, 1087
Boileau, Rebecca IV, 1088
Boiles, Elizabeth V, 462
Boiles, Mary V, 462
Boiles, Neal V, 462
Boils, Bell V, 452
Boils, Elizabeth V, 452
Boils, Neal V, 452
Boing, Grace II, 56
Boise, Beatrice VI, 405
Boise, Charles Dwight VI, 405
Boise, Jemima I, 38
Boisseau, John VI, 131
Boisseau, John VI, 132
Boisseau, John G. VI, 131
Boisseau, John G. VI, 132
Boisseau, Sarah J. VI, 54
Bok, Mary III, 346
Bokelman, Ella IV, 928
Boker, ??? III, 38
Boker, Aaron II, 783
Boker, Aaron II, 839
Boker, Aaron III, 23
Boker, Caroline III, 38
Boker, Martha II, 783
Boker, Martha II, 839

Boker, Martha III, 23
Boker, Martha III, 38
Boker, Martha R. II, 839
Boker, Mary II, 467
Boker, Sarah II, 467
Boland, Calvin IV, 178
Boland, Jennie IV, 178
Bolden, Fanny VI, 913
Bolden, Jane IV, 140
Bolden, Jane IV, 153
Bolden, Rachel H. II, 728
Bolden, Rachel H. II, 753
Bolderson, Elizabeth II, 975
Bolderson, John II, 975
Bolderson, John II, 976
Bolderson, Rachel II, 975
Bolderson, Sarah II, 975
Boldie, Charity V, 797
Boldie, Goldie V, 797
Boldie, Sylvia V, 797
Boldie, Thomas V, 797
Boldin, George II, 839
Boldin, George II, 892
Boldin, Rachel Hunt II, 839
Boldin, Rachel Hunt II, 892
Bolding, Charity V, 797
Bolding, Mary II, 339
Bolding, Sylvia V, 797
Bolding, Thomas V, 797
Bolding, William II, 339
Boldkins, Jack IV, 178
Bolds, Lucy VI, 947
Bolen, Jane VI, 472
Bolen, Jane VI, 490
Boles, Amy IV, 370
Boles, Ann I, 161
Boles, Ann Pike I, 131
Boles, David I, 131
Boles, David I, 153
Boles, George IV, 731
Boles, John IV, 370
Boles, Rebecca IV, 731
Boles, Rorena V, 660
Boles, Thomas IV, 370
Boles, Willetta IV, 731
Boley, Benja. R. VI, 985
Boley, Benjamin R. VI, 880
Boley, Elizabeth VI, 867
Boley, Elizabeth VI, 985
Boley, Evelina VI, 880
Boley, Gabarilla E. VI, 880
Boley, Harriet VI, 922
Boley, Harriet A. R. VI, 972
Boley, Irene VI, 826
Boley, John VI, 799
Boley, John VI, 880
Boley, John VI, 922
Boley, Louvinia G. VI, 880
Boley, Martha VI, 972
Boley, Nancy VI, 819
Boley, Permelia A. VI, 880
Boley, Pleasant VI, 880
Boley, Presly VI, 972
Boley, Prestly VI, 913
Boley, Rebecca VI, 799
Boley, Sally VI, 1017
Boley, William VI, 880
Bolger, Alice IV, 680
Bolger, Alice IV, 688
Bolin, John W. VI, 880
Bolin, Nancy VI, 880
Boling, Martha J. I, 614
Bolinger, Della V, 986
Bolinger, Ruth V, 755
Bolinger, Ruth V, 774
Boll, Charles V, 727
Boll, Charlie V, 727
Boll, Edna V, 727
Boll, Estella V, 727
Boll, Esther V, 727
Boll, Lois V, 727
Boll, Nettie V, 727
Boll, Rubey V, 727
Boll, Ruby V, 727
Boll, Sadie V, 727
Boll, Sarah V, 727
Boll, Stella V, 727
Boll, Wilber V, 727
Boll, Wilbur V, 727
Bolland, Anthony F. IV, 1307
Bolland, Sarah K. IV, 1307
Boller, ??? III, 248
Boller, Mary III, 248
Bolling, Ann E. VI, 880
Bolling, Archibald VI, 851
Bolling, Archibald VI, 880
Bolling, Archibald, Sr. VI, 840
Bolling, Edward VI, 799
Bolling, Edward VI, 811
Bolling, Elizabeth VI, 799
Bolling, Elizabeth VI, 851
Bolling, John VI, 158
Bolling, John VI, 177
Bolling, John VI, 200
Bolling, Sarah VI, 840
Bolling, William VI, 978
Bollock, Josie V, 986
Bolten, Elizabeth Ives II, 728
Bolten, Isaac II, 467
Bolten, Rebecca II, 467
Bolton, Abel G. II, 839
Bolton, Abel J. II, 468
Bolton, Abel J. II, 783
Bolton, Abel James III, 38
Bolton, Abraham II, 192
Bolton, Abraham II, 198
Bolton, Alfred II, 22
Bolton, Alfred II, 115
Bolton, Ann II, 22
Bolton, Ann II, 495
Bolton, Anna E. II, 839
Bolton, Anna Emlen II, 839
Bolton, Anna M. II, 22
Bolton, Anna M. II, 115
Bolton, Aquila II, 468
Bolton, Aquila M. IV, 140
Bolton, Aquilla II, 467
Bolton, Aquilla II, 468
Bolton, Aquilla II, 728
Bolton, Aquilla M. II, 468
Bolton, Aquilla M. IV, 178
Bolton, Aquilla Massey II, 468
Bolton, Azubah II, 198
Bolton, Benjamin II, 22
Bolton, Beulah II, 839
Bolton, Beulah Shinn II, 281
Bolton, Charles II, 22
Bolton, Clifton II, 783
Bolton, Clifton II, 839
Bolton, Daniel B. II, 917
Bolton, Deborah II, 467
Bolton, Deborah II, 537
Bolton, Edward II, 167
Bolton, Edward II, 198
Bolton, Edward II, 467
Bolton, Edward II, 979
Bolton, Edward II, 980
Bolton, Edward, Jr. II, 198
Bolton, Eleanor II, 467
Bolton, Eling II, 198
Bolton, Elizabeth II, 22
Bolton, Elizabeth II, 115
Bolton, Elizabeth II, 198
Bolton, Elizabeth II, 281
Bolton, Elizabeth II, 839
Bolton, Elizabeth II, 979
Bolton, Elizabeth II, 980
Bolton, Elizabeth Ives II, 728
Bolton, Elizabeth, Jr. II, 467
Bolton, Ellen II, 839
Bolton, Ellen M. II, 281
Bolton, Ellen M. II, 728
Bolton, Ellen M. II, 839
Bolton, Ellen W. II, 728
Bolton, Evan IV, 682
Bolton, Everad II, 338
Bolton, Everard II, 338
Bolton, Everard II, 467
Bolton, Everard II, 468
Bolton, Everard II, 639
Bolton, Everard, Jr. II, 468
Bolton, Gideon L. II, 115
Bolton, Gideon S. II, 22
Bolton, Hannah II, 22
Bolton, Hannah II, 198
Bolton, Hannah II, 467
Bolton, Hannah II, 492
Bolton, Hannah IV, 178
Bolton, Hannah N. II, 115
Bolton, Hannah S. II, 468
Bolton, Hannah S. II, 584
Bolton, Hannah S. II, 728
Bolton, Henry C. II, 839
Bolton, Henry Corbit II, 783
Bolton, Isaac II, 198
Bolton, Isaac II, 338
Bolton, Isaac II, 467
Bolton, Isaac II, 468
Bolton, James II, 198
Bolton, James II, 467
Bolton, James IV, 178
Bolton, James IV, 1202
Bolton, James M. II, 468
Bolton, James Pilling II, 955
Bolton, Jane II, 22
Bolton, Jane II, 338
Bolton, Jehu IV, 178
Bolton, Jesse II, 22
Bolton, John Smith II, 22
Bolton, Joseph II, 167
Bolton, Joseph II, 198
Bolton, Joseph II, 281
Bolton, Joseph II, 467
Bolton, Joseph II, 955
Bolton, Joseph Lafayette II, 281
Bolton, Joseph R. II, 468
Bolton, Joseph R. II, 783
Bolton, Joseph R. II, 839
Bolton, Joseph R., Jr. II, 783
Bolton, Joseph R., Jr. II, 839
Bolton, Joseph, Jr. II, 198
Bolton, Joshua II, 467
Bolton, Joshua IV, 140
Bolton, Levi II, 980
Bolton, Levi IV, 178
Bolton, Lydia II, 22
Bolton, Lydia II, 463
Bolton, Lydia II, 467
Bolton, Mabel Alden II, 955
Bolton, Mark T. II, 22
Bolton, Mary II, 192
Bolton, Mary II, 198
Bolton, Mary II, 839
Bolton, Mary III, 38
Bolton, Mary III, 220
Bolton, Mary IV, 928
Bolton, Mary Lavinia II, 281
Bolton, Mary S. II, 831
Bolton, Mary S. II, 839
Bolton, Mary S. II, 917
Bolton, Massey II, 467
Bolton, Orpah IV, 178
Bolton, Orpha IV, 178
Bolton, Permela I, 527
Bolton, Phebe II, 198
Bolton, Rachel II, 22
Bolton, Rachel II, 115
Bolton, Rachel II, 338
Bolton, Rachel II, 468
Bolton, Rachel II, 495
Bolton, Rachel II, 584
Bolton, Rachel II, 728
Bolton, Rachel II, 789
Bolton, Rachel II, 955
Bolton, Rebecca II, 338
Bolton, Rebecca II, 467
Bolton, Rebecca II, 639
Bolton, Rebecca J. II, 839
Bolton, Rebeckah II, 467
Bolton, Rebekah II, 467
Bolton, Rhoda II, 467
Bolton, Richard II, 22
Bolton, Richard Burr II, 281
Bolton, Ruth Alden II, 955
Bolton, Samuel II, 22
Bolton, Samuel II, 115
Bolton, Samuel II, 338
Bolton, Samuel II, 467
Bolton, Samuel II, 468
Bolton, Samuel II, 486
Bolton, Samuel II, 492
Bolton, Samuel II, 495
Bolton, Samuel II, 584
Bolton, Samuel II, 728
Bolton, Samuel II, 783
Bolton, Samuel II, 789
Bolton, Samuel II, 839
Bolton, Samuel Howell II, 281
Bolton, Sarah II, 167
Bolton, Sarah II, 198
Bolton, Sarah II, 201
Bolton, Sarah II, 338
Bolton, Sarah II, 467
Bolton, Sarah II, 468
Bolton, Sarah II, 495
Bolton, Sarah II, 789
Bolton, Sarah II, 955
Bolton, Sarah IV, 801
Bolton, Sarah E. II, 783
Bolton, Sarah E. II, 839
Bolton, Sarah J. II, 783
Bolton, Sarah Jones II, 839
Bolton, Thomas II, 22
Bolton, Thomas II, 198
Bolton, Thomas II, 467
Bolton, Thomas II, 980
Bolton, Thomas L. II, 115
Bolton, Thomas S. II, 22
Bolton, Wd. Rachel II, 338
Bolton, William II, 198
Boltwood, Richard V, 986
Boltz, Anna V, 26
Boltz, Anna B. V, 26
Boltz, Anna B. V, 144
Boltz, Ella V, 26
Boltz, Frederick VI, 880
Boltz, Kathrine VI, 880
Boly, Presly VI, 972
Bolyn, Sarah VI, 619
Bolyn, Sarah VI, 657
Boman, Ann IV, 465
Boman, Ann V, 26
Boman, Ann V, 61
Boman, Elvire I, 527
Boman, Jesse I, 592
Boman, Sarah I, 800
Boman, Sarah I, 840
Boman, William I, 592
Bombarger, Hazel IV, 1149
Bombarger, Hazel Gertrude IV, 1149
Bomberger, Hazel IV, 1149
Bomberger, Susannah II, 338
Bomberger, Susannah II, 468
Bomberger, Susannah II, 595
Bomberger, William II, 338
Bomstead, Dorothy II, 468
Bomstead, Dorothy II, 558
Bond, ??? III, 38
Bond, ??? III, 370
Bond, ??? VI, 299
Bond, ??? VI, 348
Bond, Abel I, 982
Bond, Abigail I, 37
Bond, Abigail I, 127
Bond, Abigail I, 130
Bond, Abigail IV, 900
Bond, Abigail IV, 914
Bond, Abigail Moor V, 299
Bond, Abner IV, 140
Bond, Abner IV, 321
Bond, Abner IV, 370
Bond, Abner VI, 349
Bond, Abner VI, 363
Bond, Abner VI, 366
Bond, Abner VI, 367
Bond, Abner VI, 368
Bond, Abner VI, 398
Bond, Abner, Jr. IV, 370
Bond, Abraham III, 396
Bond, Abraham VI, 349
Bond, Alcinda IV, 321
Bond, Alcinda IV, 322
Bond, Alesannah II, 338
Bond, Alice VI, 299
Bond, Alice VI, 349
Bond, Alice VI, 355
Bond, Alice W. VI, 472
Bond, Alinda IV, 370
Bond, Allen IV, 140
Bond, Allen IV, 321
Bond, Allen IV, 322
Bond, Allen IV, 370
Bond, Allen VI, 299
Bond, Allen VI, 349
Bond, Allen VI, 367
Bond, Allen VI, 591
Bond, Allen VI, 594
Bond, Allen VI, 880
Bond, Allen Beal VI, 367
Bond, Allen, Jr. IV, 321
Bond, Amasa V, 299
Bond, Amelia I, 981
Bond, Amelia I, 996
Bond, Amos Peaslee VI, 367
Bond, Andrew J. VI, 880
Bond, Ann I, 491
Bond, Ann I, 527
Bond, Ann I, 562
Bond, Ann I, 773
Bond, Ann I, 777
Bond, Ann I, 800
Bond, Ann I, 872
Bond, Ann I, 881
Bond, Ann I, 955
Bond, Ann I, 973
Bond, Ann I, 981
Bond, Ann I, 982
Bond, Ann I, 988
Bond, Ann I, 1007
Bond, Ann II, 468
Bond, Ann II, 955
Bond, Ann II, 980
Bond, Ann VI, 367
Bond, Ann VI, 510
Bond, Ann VI, 1007
Bond, Ann E. VI, 471
Bond, Ann E. VI, 472
Bond, Ann E. VI, 491
Bond, Ann E. VI, 509
Bond, Ann E. VI, 510
Bond, Ann E. VI, 512
Bond, Ann E. VI, 566
Bond, Ann E. VI, 567
Bond, Ann E. VI, 617
Bond, Ann E. VI, 658
Bond, Ann M. VI, 366
Bond, Ann M. VI, 367
Bond, Ann M. VI, 368
Bond, Ann M. VI, 417
Bond, Ann Sidwell VI, 367
Bond, Anna I, 777
Bond, Anna I, 800
Bond, Anna I, 802
Bond, Anna I, 971
Bond, Anna I, 973
Bond, Anna I, 981
Bond, Anna I, 982
Bond, Anna I, 989
Bond, Anna I, 992
Bond, Anna V, 320
Bond, Anne I, 973
Bond, Anne II, 468
Bond, Annie G. II, 145
Bond, Aquilla Janney VI, 367
Bond, Artilissa I, 927
Bond, Asa VI, 366
Bond, Asa VI, 367
Bond, Asa VI, 472
Bond, Asa VI, 513
Bond, Asa L. V, 299
Bond, Asa M VI, 710
Bond, Asa M. VI, 473
Bond, Asa M. VI, 619
Bond, Asa Moore II, 839
Bond, Asa Moore VI, 472
Bond, Asa Moore VI, 572
Bond, Asa Moore VI, 619
Bond, Asa Moore VI, 713
Bond, Asa Moore, Jr. II, 783
Bond, Asa Moore, Jr. VI, 472
Bond, Benj. I, 491
Bond, Benj. V, 452
Bond, Benj. Eli S. II, 129
Bond, Benjamin I, 527
Bond, Benjamin I, 777
Bond, Benjamin I, 800
Bond, Benjamin I, 845
Bond, Benjamin I, 851
Bond, Benjamin I, 872
Bond, Benjamin I, 955
Bond, Benjamin I, 960
Bond, Benjamin I, 1003
Bond, Benjamin I, 1007
Bond, Benjamin I, 1115
Bond, Benjamin IV, 178
Bond, Benjamin IV, 370
Bond, Benjamin V, 26
Bond, Benjamin V, 154
Bond, Benjamin V, 945
Bond, Benjamin VI, 295
Bond, Benjamin VI, 299
Bond, Benjamin VI, 349
Bond, Benjamin VI, 591
Bond, Benjamin Eli S. II, 145
Bond, Bridget Hadley I, 981
Bond, Caleb I, 973
Bond, Caleb I, 981
Bond, Calvin I, 927
Bond, Caroline VI, 472
Bond, Caroline Damon VI, 367
Bond, Caroline Damon VI, 417
Bond, Caroline S. II, 145
Bond, Carrie VI, 507
Bond, Carrie VI, 655
Bond, Charity I, 491
Bond, Charity I, 800
Bond, Charity I, 955
Bond, Charity I, 959
Bond, Charity I, 960
Bond, Charity I, 1007
Bond, Charity V, 299
Bond, Charles II, 115
Bond, Charles II, 129
Bond, Charles II, 145
Bond, Charles V, 727
Bond, Charles H. V, 727
Bond, Charlotta W. II, 145
Bond, Charlotte I, 800
Bond, Charlotte I, 819
Bond, Charlotte I, 971
Bond, Charlotte I, 973
Bond, Charlotte I, 974
Bond, Charlotte I, 981
Bond, Charlotte II, 129
Bond, Charlotte II, 145
Bond, Charlotte V, 26
Bond, Charlotte W. II, 145
Bond, Charlotte W. II, 151
Bond, Cornelia III, 396
Bond, Dairus V, 26
Bond, Daniel I, 973
Bond, Daniel V, 320
Bond, Daniel V, 341
Bond, Darius I, 955
Bond, David Lupton, Jr. VI, 367
Bond, Deborah VI, 472
Bond, Deborah VI, 474
Bond, Dorcas I, 959
Bond, Dorcas I, 960
Bond, Edward I, 491
Bond, Edward I, 527
Bond, Edward I, 562
Bond, Edward I, 773
Bond, Edward I, 777

Bond, Edward I, 800
Bond, Edward I, 851
Bond, Edward I, 872
Bond, Edward I, 881
Bond, Edward I, 960
Bond, Edward I, 973
Bond, Edward I, 981
Bond, Edward I, 982
Bond, Edward I, 988
Bond, Edward I, 1003
Bond, Edward I, 1007
Bond, Edward V, 26
Bond, Edward V, 154
Bond, Edward V, 223
Bond, Edward V, 320
Bond, Edward V, 445
Bond, Edward V, 948
Bond, Edward VI, 299
Bond, Edward VI, 331
Bond, Edward VI, 349
Bond, Edward VI, 355
Bond, Edward VI, 367
Bond, Edward VI, 472
Bond, Edward VI, 555
Bond, Edward VI, 556
Bond, Edward VI, 591
Bond, Edward L. VI, 367
Bond, Edward L. VI, 368
Bond, Edward Lupton, Jr. VI, 367
Bond, Edward Lupton, Sr. VI, 429
Bond, Edward, Jr. I, 800
Bond, Edward, Jr. I, 973
Bond, Edward, Jr. I, 981
Bond, Edward, Jr. V, 154
Bond, Edward, Sr. V, 948
Bond, Edwin II, 145
Bond, Elbert B. I, 974
Bond, Eleanor VI, 366
Bond, Eleanor VI, 395
Bond, Eli IV, 370
Bond, Elisabeth I, 37
Bond, Elisabeth I, 59
Bond, Elisabeth I, 87
Bond, Eliza IV, 370
Bond, Elizabeth I, 491
Bond, Elizabeth I, 525
Bond, Elizabeth I, 527
Bond, Elizabeth I, 650
Bond, Elizabeth I, 955
Bond, Elizabeth I, 960
Bond, Elizabeth I, 970
Bond, Elizabeth I, 973
Bond, Elizabeth I, 981
Bond, Elizabeth I, 991
Bond, Elizabeth I, 1000
Bond, Elizabeth I, 1003
Bond, Elizabeth I, 1115
Bond, Elizabeth I, 1125
Bond, Elizabeth II, 56
Bond, Elizabeth II, 115
Bond, Elizabeth II, 129
Bond, Elizabeth II, 143
Bond, Elizabeth II, 145
Bond, Elizabeth II, 151
Bond, Elizabeth II, 468
Bond, Elizabeth IV, 140
Bond, Elizabeth IV, 178
Bond, Elizabeth IV, 304
Bond, Elizabeth IV, 319
Bond, Elizabeth IV, 321
Bond, Elizabeth IV, 351
Bond, Elizabeth IV, 366
Bond, Elizabeth IV, 928
Bond, Elizabeth V, 154
Bond, Elizabeth V, 895
Bond, Elizabeth VI, 349
Bond, Elizabeth VI, 367
Bond, Elizabeth VI, 472
Bond, Elizabeth VI, 474
Bond, Elizabeth VI, 509
Bond, Elizabeth VI, 527
Bond, Elizabeth VI, 536
Bond, Elizabeth VI, 564
Bond, Elizabeth VI, 565
Bond, Elizabeth VI, 572
Bond, Elizabeth VI, 619
Bond, Elizabeth VI, 713
Bond, Elizabeth VI, 731
Bond, Elizabeth VI, 781
Bond, Elizabeth VI, 880
Bond, Elizabeth K. II, 839
Bond, Elizabeth K. II, 861
Bond, Elizabeth M. II, 145
Bond, Elizabeth M. VI, 472
Bond, Elizabeth Powell II, 839
Bond, Elizabeth S. II, 145
Bond, Elizabeth T. P. II, 145
Bond, Elizabeth, Jr. VI, 472
Bond, Elizabeth, Jr. VI, 536
Bond, Elizabeth, Jr. VI, 555
Bond, Ellen VI, 472
Bond, Ellen VI, 519
Bond, Ellen C. VI, 472
Bond, Elzena I, 974
Bond, Emily VI, 880
Bond, Enos I, 982
Bond, Ester IV, 321
Bond, Ester IV, 332
Bond, Esther IV, 370
Bond, Eunice V, 26
Bond, Eunice V, 320
Bond, Exum S. I, 37
Bond, Frances Malinda V, 779
Bond, Frances Malinda V, 783
Bond, George VI, 799
Bond, George M. II, 856
Bond, George M. II, 864
Bond, Gideon Peaslee VI, 367
Bond, Grace L. VI, 368
Bond, Grace Lillian VI, 367
Bond, Grace Lillian VI, 460
Bond, Hanna VI, 299
Bond, Hanna Lippincott VI, 429
Bond, Hannah I, 1003
Bond, Hannah I, 1007
Bond, Hannah I, 1009
Bond, Hannah II, 56
Bond, Hannah II, 115
Bond, Hannah II, 129
Bond, Hannah II, 468
Bond, Hannah II, 470
Bond, Hannah II, 955
Bond, Hannah II, 1045
Bond, Hannah V, 26
Bond, Hannah V, 154
Bond, Hannah VI, 349
Bond, Hannah VI, 366
Bond, Hannah VI, 367
Bond, Hannah VI, 390
Bond, Hannah VI, 391
Bond, Hannah VI, 395
Bond, Hannah VI, 421
Bond, Hannah VI, 436
Bond, Hannah VI, 472
Bond, Hannah C. II, 145
Bond, Hannah L. VI, 368
Bond, Hannah Lippincott VI, 367
Bond, Hariett A. VI, 472
Bond, Henry III, 38
Bond, Hope II, 145
Bond, Hope II, 151
Bond, Howell M. VI, 368
Bond, Howell McPherson VI, 367
Bond, Isaac I, 650
Bond, Isaac I, 955
Bond, Isaac I, 960
Bond, Isaac VI, 299
Bond, Isaac VI, 349
Bond, Isaac VI, 366
Bond, Isaac VI, 472
Bond, Isaac VI, 591
Bond, Isaac VI, 606
Bond, Isaac B. VI, 472
Bond, Isaac, Jr. VI, 591
Bond, Isom Robert I, 982
Bond, Israel VI, 349
Bond, Israel VI, 880
Bond, James II, 468
Bond, James VI, 880
Bond, James VI, 938
Bond, James L. VI, 472
Bond, Jane I, 374
Bond, Jane I, 404
Bond, Jane I, 649
Bond, Jane I, 650
Bond, Jane I, 674
Bond, Jane I, 777
Bond, Jane I, 800
Bond, Jane II, 129
Bond, Jane II, 468
Bond, Jane III, 38
Bond, Jane IV, 178
Bond, Jane IV, 304
Bond, Jane V, 299
Bond, Jean I, 374
Bond, Jedadiah I, 872
Bond, Jedidiah I, 851
Bond, Jemima I, 37
Bond, Jemima I, 58
Bond, Jesse I, 777
Bond, Jesse I, 800
Bond, Jesse I, 973
Bond, Jesse I, 974
Bond, Jesse I, 981
Bond, Jesse I, 1003
Bond, Jesse I, 1007
Bond, Jesse I, 1008
Bond, Jesse II, 56
Bond, Jesse II, 115
Bond, Jesse II, 129
Bond, Jesse II, 143
Bond, Jesse II, 145
Bond, Jesse II, 151
Bond, Jesse II, 468
Bond, Jesse V, 26
Bond, Jesse V, 727
Bond, Jesse C. II, 129
Bond, Jesse E. II, 839
Bond, Jesse E. II, 861
Bond, Job I, 37
Bond, Job I, 73
Bond, Joel I, 650
Bond, John I, 37
Bond, John I, 57
Bond, John I, 475
Bond, John I, 491
Bond, John I, 649
Bond, John I, 674
Bond, John I, 777
Bond, John I, 800
Bond, John I, 819
Bond, John I, 955
Bond, John I, 971
Bond, John I, 973
Bond, John I, 981
Bond, John I, 982
Bond, John I, 987
Bond, John I, 992
Bond, John I, 996
Bond, John I, 1003
Bond, John II, 468
Bond, John II, 474
Bond, John IV, 140
Bond, John IV, 321
Bond, John V, 26
Bond, John V, 297
Bond, John V, 727
Bond, John VI, 349
Bond, John VI, 363
Bond, John VI, 366
Bond, John VI, 367
Bond, John VI, 391
Bond, John VI, 416
Bond, John VI, 419
Bond, John VI, 421
Bond, John A. J. V, 374
Bond, John L. VI, 366
Bond, John L. VI, 367
Bond, John L. VI, 368
Bond, John L. VI, 417
Bond, John Lupton VI, 367
Bond, John Lupton VI, 404
Bond, John, Jr. I, 973
Bond, Jonathan I, 851
Bond, Jonathan I, 872
Bond, Jonathan IV, 321
Bond, Jonathan IV, 370
Bond, Joseph I, 475
Bond, Joseph I, 476
Bond, Joseph I, 491
Bond, Joseph I, 527
Bond, Joseph I, 650
Bond, Joseph I, 674
Bond, Joseph I, 777
Bond, Joseph I, 800
Bond, Joseph I, 828
Bond, Joseph I, 955
Bond, Joseph I, 960
Bond, Joseph I, 973
Bond, Joseph I, 981
Bond, Joseph I, 1003
Bond, Joseph I, 1115
Bond, Joseph II, 468
Bond, Joseph II, 955
Bond, Joseph II, 980
Bond, Joseph IV, 140
Bond, Joseph IV, 319
Bond, Joseph IV, 321
Bond, Joseph IV, 332
Bond, Joseph IV, 370
Bond, Joseph V, 26
Bond, Joseph V, 154
Bond, Joseph VI, 349
Bond, Joseph VI, 366
Bond, Joseph VI, 367
Bond, Joseph VI, 395
Bond, Joseph VI, 414
Bond, Joseph VI, 472
Bond, Joseph VI, 474
Bond, Joseph VI, 509
Bond, Joseph VI, 527
Bond, Joseph VI, 536
Bond, Joseph VI, 564
Bond, Joseph VI, 565
Bond, Joseph VI, 572
Bond, Joseph VI, 619
Bond, Joseph VI, 713
Bond, Joseph VI, 731
Bond, Joseph VI, 781
Bond, Joseph R. II, 129
Bond, Joshua I, 777
Bond, Joshua I, 973
Bond, Joshua I, 981
Bond, Joshua I, 984
Bond, Joshua I, 1007
Bond, Joshua I, 1008
Bond, Joshua VI, 349
Bond, Josiah II, 145
Bond, Josiah II, 151
Bond, Josiah II, 783
Bond, Josiah II, 839
Bond, Josiah II, 862
Bond, Josiah II, 923
Bond, Josiah H. II, 839
Bond, Julia Ann V, 551
Bond, Julia Ann V, 585
Bond, Kezia I, 491
Bond, Kezia I, 492
Bond, Kezia I, 800
Bond, Kezia I, 955
Bond, Kezia I, 1007
Bond, Keziah I, 777
Bond, Keziah I, 800
Bond, Keziah I, 832
Bond, Laura VI, 472
Bond, Laura VI, 560
Bond, Leah VI, 366
Bond, Leah VI, 390
Bond, Leah VI, 391
Bond, Leah Moor V, 299
Bond, Leonora II, 839
Bond, Leonora II, 923
Bond, Livina I, 37
Bond, Lizzie W. II, 839
Bond, Lucretia M. II, 839
Bond, Lucretia M. II, 861
Bond, Lucy Jane V, 660
Bond, Lydia I, 973
Bond, Lydia II, 56
Bond, Lydia II, 129
Bond, Lydia II, 143
Bond, Lydia II, 145
Bond, Lydia V, 26
Bond, Lydia V, 452
Bond, Lydia VI, 349
Bond, Lydia VI, 366
Bond, Lydia VI, 419
Bond, Lydia VI, 591
Bond, Maden I, 960
Bond, Maden I, 981
Bond, Mahala VI, 1007
Bond, Maiden I, 491
Bond, Maiden I, 492
Bond, Maiden I, 777
Bond, Maiden I, 800
Bond, Maiden I, 955
Bond, Maiden I, 958
Bond, Maiden I, 1007
Bond, Marg't VI, 366
Bond, Margaret I, 491
Bond, Margaret I, 927
Bond, Margaret II, 145
Bond, Margaret IV, 140
Bond, Margaret V, 297
Bond, Margaret V, 299
Bond, Margaret VI, 349
Bond, Margaret VI, 366
Bond, Margaret C. VI, 404
Bond, Margaret E. VI, 367
Bond, Margaret H. II, 145
Bond, Marget VI, 367
Bond, Margret I, 960
Bond, Margret II, 160
Bond, Marry I, 960
Bond, Marry I, 967
Bond, Martha I, 491
Bond, Martha I, 650
Bond, Martha I, 674
Bond, Martha I, 777
Bond, Martha I, 800
Bond, Martha I, 955
Bond, Martha I, 959
Bond, Martha I, 960
Bond, Martha I, 1007
Bond, Martha I, 1115
Bond, Martha II, 145
Bond, Martha II, 151
Bond, Martha II, 783
Bond, Martha II, 839
Bond, Martha II, 862
Bond, Martha VI, 299
Bond, Martha VI, 938
Bond, Martha Ann VI, 1018
Bond, Martha H. II, 839
Bond, Martha S. II, 129
Bond, Martha W. VI, 938
Bond, Mary I, 37
Bond, Mary I, 57
Bond, Mary I, 475
Bond, Mary I, 491
Bond, Mary I, 800
Bond, Mary I, 819
Bond, Mary I, 845
Bond, Mary I, 851
Bond, Mary I, 872
Bond, Mary I, 955
Bond, Mary I, 958
Bond, Mary I, 960
Bond, Mary I, 969
Bond, Mary I, 973
Bond, Mary I, 981
Bond, Mary I, 982
Bond, Mary I, 987
Bond, Mary I, 1003
Bond, Mary I, 1007
Bond, Mary II, 839
Bond, Mary II, 955
Bond, Mary III, 38
Bond, Mary V, 26
Bond, Mary V, 154
Bond, Mary V, 223
Bond, Mary V, 320
Bond, Mary V, 341
Bond, Mary V, 445
Bond, Mary V, 948
Bond, Mary V, 959
Bond, Mary VI, 299
Bond, Mary VI, 331
Bond, Mary VI, 349
Bond, Mary VI, 363
Bond, Mary VI, 366
Bond, Mary VI, 367
Bond, Mary VI, 472
Bond, Mary VI, 591
Bond, Mary VI, 880
Bond, Mary Ann II, 839
Bond, Mary Ann II, 873
Bond, Mary Annis VI, 472
Bond, Mary Beal VI, 367
Bond, Mary Beal VI, 398
Bond, Mary D. V, 613
Bond, Mary D. V, 650
Bond, Mary E. II, 839
Bond, Mary E. II, 861
Bond, Mary Eachus II, 793
Bond, Mary Elizabeth II, 129
Bond, Mary Elizabeth II, 145
Bond, Mary Emma VI, 367
Bond, Mary Hannah II, 129
Bond, Mary Hough I, 981
Bond, Mary Jane VI, 979
Bond, Mary S. II, 129
Bond, Mary S. II, 145
Bond, Mary S. VI, 884
Bond, Mary T. VI, 472
Bond, Mary T. VI, 567
Bond, Mary, Sr. V, 948
Bond, Matilda VI, 880
Bond, Mille I, 973
Bond, Miriam Moor V, 299
Bond, Mordecai I, 955
Bond, Mordicai V, 26
Bond, Moses I, 1003
Bond, Moses V, 26
Bond, Moses V, 154
Bond, Mr. Walker McClun VI, 359
Bond, Mrs. Walker McClun VI, 359
Bond, Nancy Jane I, 982
Bond, Naoma I, 981
Bond, Naoma I, 982
Bond, Naomi I, 475
Bond, Naomi I, 476
Bond, Nathan I, 492
Bond, Nathan I, 800
Bond, Nathan I, 851
Bond, Nathan I, 872
Bond, Nathan I, 955
Bond, Nathan I, 960
Bond, Nathan I, 973
Bond, Nathan I, 982
Bond, Nathan I, 1003
Bond, Nathan Robert V, 727
Bond, Nicholas II, 839
Bond, P. J. VI, 919
Bond, Parvin V, 986
Bond, Parvin W. V, 986
Bond, Patience I, 491
Bond, Patience I, 800
Bond, Patience I, 955
Bond, Patience I, 1007
Bond, Patsey VI, 799
Bond, Penelope I, 37
Bond, Penelope I, 73
Bond, Phebe I, 1001
Bond, Phebe I, 1003
Bond, Phebe I, 1007
Bond, Phebe I, 1008
Bond, Phebe V, 727
Bond, Phebe J. III, 38
Bond, Phebe J. III, 370
Bond, Phinehas II, 468

Bond, Pleasant VI, 884
Bond, Pleasant VI, 979
Bond, Pretlow I, 37
Bond, Pretlow I, 87
Bond, Rach. A. VI, 368
Bond, Rachel I, 955
Bond, Rachel I, 960
Bond, Rachel I, 963
Bond, Rachel I, 973
Bond, Rachel I, 981
Bond, Rachel I, 982
Bond, Rachel I, 984
Bond, Rachel I, 987
Bond, Rachel II, 786
Bond, Rachel V, 26
Bond, Rachel V, 297
Bond, Rachel VI, 366
Bond, Rachel VI, 367
Bond, Rachel VI, 391
Bond, Rachel VI, 416
Bond, Rachel VI, 472
Bond, Rachel A. VI, 367
Bond, Rachel A. VI, 398
Bond, Rachel Ann VI, 472
Bond, Rachel Ann VI, 533
Bond, Rachel B. VI, 472
Bond, Rachel B. VI, 527
Bond, Rebecca I, 777
Bond, Rebecca I, 974
Bond, Rebecca I, 982
Bond, Rebecca I, 987
Bond, Rebecca II, 824
Bond, Rebecca IV, 140
Bond, Rebecca IV, 321
Bond, Rebecca IV, 322
Bond, Rebeckah VI, 349
Bond, Rebeckah VI, 367
Bond, Rebekah I, 1007
Bond, Rebekah VI, 591
Bond, Rebekah VI, 606
Bond, Rees II, 636
Bond, Reuben VI, 880
Bond, Reuben VI, 1008
Bond, Reuben VI, 1018
Bond, Rhoda I, 982
Bond, Rhoda I, 989
Bond, Rhoda VI, 969
Bond, Richard II, 115
Bond, Richard II, 129
Bond, Richard II, 145
Bond, Robert I, 1003
Bond, Robert VI, 366
Bond, Robert VI, 367
Bond, Robt. VI, 472
Bond, Rosa V, 477
Bond, Rosanna V, 374
Bond, Ruth I, 491
Bond, Ruth I, 800
Bond, Ruth I, 955
Bond, Ruth I, 981
Bond, Ruth I, 1003
Bond, Ruth I, 1007
Bond, Ruth I, 1008
Bond, Ruth V, 26
Bond, Ruth V, 154
Bond, Ruth V, 213
Bond, Ruth VI, 299
Bond, Ruth VI, 349
Bond, Samuel I, 491
Bond, Samuel I, 525
Bond, Samuel I, 527
Bond, Samuel I, 953
Bond, Samuel I, 955
Bond, Samuel I, 959
Bond, Samuel I, 960
Bond, Samuel II, 338
Bond, Samuel II, 468
Bond, Samuel II, 474
Bond, Samuel II, 955
Bond, Samuel III, 38
Bond, Samuel V, 223
Bond, Samuel V, 299
Bond, Samuel VI, 366
Bond, Samuel VI, 367
Bond, Samuel VI, 424
Bond, Samuel VI, 472
Bond, Samuel VI, 536
Bond, Samuel H. II, 129
Bond, Samuel L. VI, 472
Bond, Samuel, Jr. I, 960
Bond, Sarah I, 37
Bond, Sarah I, 60
Bond, Sarah I, 491
Bond, Sarah I, 800
Bond, Sarah I, 828
Bond, Sarah I, 973
Bond, Sarah I, 982
Bond, Sarah II, 468
Bond, Sarah II, 474
Bond, Sarah III, 396
Bond, Sarah IV, 140
Bond, Sarah IV, 321
Bond, Sarah IV, 322
Bond, Sarah IV, 370
Bond, Sarah IV, 933
Bond, Sarah V, 26
Bond, Sarah V, 74
Bond, Sarah V, 75
Bond, Sarah V, 223
Bond, Sarah V, 224
Bond, Sarah V, 299
Bond, Sarah V, 374
Bond, Sarah V, 452
Bond, Sarah V, 948
Bond, Sarah VI, 299
Bond, Sarah VI, 349
Bond, Sarah VI, 366
Bond, Sarah VI, 367
Bond, Sarah VI, 409
Bond, Sarah VI, 424
Bond, Sarah VI, 472
Bond, Sarah VI, 536
Bond, Sarah VI, 557
Bond, Sarah VI, 591
Bond, Sarah VI, 594
Bond, Sarah A. VI, 473
Bond, Sarah A. VI, 513
Bond, Sarah Alice VI, 472
Bond, Sarah Alice VI, 572
Bond, Sarah Alice VI, 619
Bond, Sarah Alice VI, 710
Bond, Sarah Alice VI, 713
Bond, Sarah E. VI, 473
Bond, Sarah E. VI, 513
Bond, Sarah Elizabeth VI, 472
Bond, Sarah Elizabeth VI, 619
Bond, Sarah J. V, 374
Bond, Sarah L. VI, 368
Bond, Sarah Stone VI, 556
Bond, Selena I, 974
Bond, Silas, Jr. IV, 370
Bond, Stephen I, 491
Bond, Stephen I, 492
Bond, Stephen I, 527
Bond, Stephen I, 777
Bond, Stephen I, 800
Bond, Stephen I, 955
Bond, Stephen I, 958
Bond, Stephen I, 960
Bond, Stephen I, 981
Bond, Susana II, 468
Bond, Susana II, 636
Bond, Susanah I, 955
Bond, Susanna I, 1003
Bond, Susanna I, 1007
Bond, Susanna II, 338
Bond, Susanna V, 948
Bond, Susanna VI, 299
Bond, Susanna VI, 591
Bond, Susannah V, 26
Bond, Susannah V, 154
Bond, Susannah V, 948
Bond, Susannah V, 955
Bond, Susannah VI, 349
Bond, Susannah VI, 591
Bond, Susily VI, 349
Bond, Tabitha I, 851
Bond, Tabitha I, 872
Bond, Tamsin VI, 472
Bond, Tamsin VI, 536
Bond, Thamasin VI, 536
Bond, Thamazin VI, 472
Bond, Thomas I, 491
Bond, Thomas I, 960
Bond, Thomas I, 967
Bond, Thomas II, 129
Bond, Thomas II, 145
Bond, Thomas II, 151
Bond, Thomas II, 338
Bond, Thomas II, 468
Bond, Thomas II, 636
Bond, Thomas II, 699
Bond, Thomas III, 38
Bond, Thomas VI, 367
Bond, Thomas M. VI, 473
Bond, Thomas M. VI, 731
Bond, Thomas P. II, 115
Bond, Thomas P. II, 129
Bond, Thomas P. II, 145
Bond, Thomas P. II, 151
Bond, Thos. II, 783
Bond, Thos. H. VI, 473
Bond, Unice I, 955
Bond, Walker M. VI, 368
Bond, Walker McC. VI, 368
Bond, Walker McClun VI, 367
Bond, Walker McClun VI, 460
Bond, Walker McClunn VI, 417
Bond, Walter Hilliard II, 129
Bond, Wd. Elizabeth Moore VI, 472
Bond, Widow Abigail I, 37
Bond, Widow Abigail I, 60
Bond, William I, 37
Bond, William I, 59
Bond, William I, 127
Bond, William I, 130
Bond, William I, 491
Bond, William I, 650
Bond, William I, 777
Bond, William I, 800
Bond, William I, 819
Bond, William I, 973
Bond, William I, 974
Bond, William I, 981
Bond, William I, 982
Bond, William I, 1000
Bond, William V, 26
Bond, William V, 727
Bond, William P. VI, 979
Bond, William S. VI, 472
Bond, Wilter II, 145
Bond, Wm. Allen VI, 366
Bond, Wrig VI, 938
Bond, Wright VI, 880
Bond, Wright VI, 929
Bond, Wright VI, 969
Bond, Wright VI, 1007
Bond, Zimri V, 551
Bond, Zimri V, 585
Bonden, Myrtle IV, 1246
Bonderant, Sarah M. VI, 881
Bonderant, William W. VI, 881
Bondrant, John VI, 854
Bondrant, Nancy VI, 854
Bonds, Benjamin I, 1090
Bonds, Elizabeth I, 37
Bonds, Isaac I, 1090
Bonds, Joel I, 1090
Bonds, John I, 1090
Bonds, Joseph I, 1090
Bonds, Rachel I, 37
Bonds, Rachel I, 69
Bonds, William I, 37
Bonds, William I, 1090
Bondurant, Ann B. VI, 799
Bondurant, Anna May IV, 987
Bondurant, Cassie E. IV, 987
Bondurant, Celia VI, 880
Bondurant, Elizabeth VI, 841
Bondurant, Elizabeth VI, 862
Bondurant, Elizabeth VI, 880
Bondurant, Elizabeth Jane VI, 881
Bondurant, Ephraim VI, 862
Bondurant, Ephrain VI, 880
Bondurant, Ephriam VI, 950
Bondurant, Fanny VI, 1002
Bondurant, James VI, 880
Bondurant, Jesse VI, 880
Bondurant, Jesse G. VI, 881
Bondurant, John IV, 987
Bondurant, John VI, 950
Bondurant, John VI, 1002
Bondurant, John P. VI, 881
Bondurant, John W. S. VI, 880
Bondurant, Joseph VI, 880
Bondurant, Joseph VI, 947
Bondurant, Little Bary VI, 979
Bondurant, Littleberry VI, 880
Bondurant, Littleberry VI, 946
Bondurant, Lydia VI, 950
Bondurant, Martha Ann VI, 881
Bondurant, Mary VI, 880
Bondurant, Mary VI, 881
Bondurant, Mary VI, 946
Bondurant, Mary A. VI, 814
Bondurant, Matilda VI, 880
Bondurant, Nancy VI, 880
Bondurant, Peggy VI, 880
Bondurant, Polly VI, 947
Bondurant, Sally VI, 979
Bondurant, Sarah M. VI, 881
Bondurant, Silas F. VI, 881
Bondurant, Susanna VI, 880
Bondurant, Tabitha VI, 946
Bondurant, Thomas VI, 880
Bondurant, Thomas VI, 968
Bondurant, William VI, 799
Bondurant, William VI, 862
Bondurant, William W. VI, 881
Bone, Allen V, 154
Bone, Ann V, 473
Bone, Ann V, 477
Bone, Benjamin IV, 178
Bone, Callie V, 477
Bone, Christopher VI, 881
Bone, Earl V, 154
Bone, Eliza V, 477
Bone, Ella Mary V, 477
Bone, Glenna V, 154
Bone, Herman V, 154
Bone, James C. V, 477
Bone, Jennie IV, 178
Bone, Kelly V, 477
Bone, Lincoln V, 477
Bone, Lucian V, 477
Bone, Parthena J. VI, 881
Bone, Pinkney IV, 178
Bone, Raymond V, 154
Bone, Ruth V, 154
Bone, Sarah IV, 370
Bone, Sarah Jane IV, 178
Bone, Susan V, 477
Bone, Waller E. IV, 178
Bone, Wm. V, 154
Bonecuter, Phebe VI, 368
Bonecuter, Phebe VI, 461
Bonecutter, Phebe V, 223
Bonecutter, Phebe V, 255
Bonecutter, Phebe VI, 368
Bonel, Hannah II, 198
Bonel, Hannah II, 227
Boner, Magdalena IV, 801
Boner, Sarah IV, 928
Boner, Sarah IV, 951
Bones, Mary II, 468
Bones, Mary B. III, 38
Bones, William III, 38
Bonfield, Wilma Evylin V, 660
Bonham, B. Franklin II, 839
Bonham, Benjamin II, 839
Bonham, Benjamin F. II, 839
Bonham, Ephraim IV, 680
Bonham, Esther II, 783
Bonham, Esther II, 839
Bonham, Jonathan Addison II, 783
Bonham, Jonathan K. II, 839
Bonham, Jonathan Kinsey II, 783
Bonham, Joseph II, 783
Bonham, Joseph A. II, 839
Bonham, Letitia II, 783
Bonham, Mary E. II, 783
Bonham, Mary E. II, 839
Bonham, Nannie V, 223
Bonham, Ruth II, 468
Bonham, Ruth II, 470
Bonine, Ann I, 1081
Bonine, Ann I, 1139
Bonine, Daniel I, 1077
Bonine, Daniel I, 1081
Bonine, Daniel I, 1090
Bonine, Daniel I, 1104
Bonine, Daniel I, 1115
Bonine, Daniel I, 1137
Bonine, Daniel I, 1139
Bonine, Daniel I, 1148
Bonine, David I, 1081
Bonine, David I, 1090
Bonine, David I, 1115
Bonine, David I, 1139
Bonine, David I, 1148
Bonine, David I, 1163
Bonine, Elizabeth I, 1116
Bonine, Isaac I, 1081
Bonine, Isaac I, 1090
Bonine, Isaac I, 1115
Bonine, Isaac I, 1139
Bonine, Isaac I, 1148
Bonine, James I, 1081
Bonine, James I, 1115
Bonine, James I, 1139
Bonine, Liddia I, 1139
Bonine, Lydia I, 1116
Bonine, Mary I, 1081
Bonine, Mary I, 1090
Bonine, Mary I, 1104
Bonine, Mary I, 1116
Bonine, Mary I, 1137
Bonine, Mary I, 1139
Bonine, Mary I, 1148
Bonine, Prudence I, 1148
Bonine, Prudence I, 1163
Bonine, Rachel I, 1081
Bonine, Rachel I, 1090
Bonine, Rachel I, 1116
Bonine, Rachel I, 1139
Bonine, Rachel I, 1148
Bonine, Rebeccah I, 1081
Bonine, Rebeccah I, 1116
Bonine, Rebeckah I, 1139
Bonine, Rebekah I, 1090
Bonine, Rebekah I, 1116
Bonine, Rebekah I, 1122
Bonine, Thomas I, 1104
Bonine, Thomas I, 1139
Bonn, John IV, 1246
Bonn, John Wesley IV, 1246
Bonn, Mary IV, 1246
Bonnel, Frances II, 468
Bonnel, Frances II, 485
Bonnel, Francis II, 468
Bonnel, Robert II, 468
Bonnel, Robert II, 485
Bonnel, Samuel II, 338
Bonnel, Sarah II, 338
Bonnell, Eliza V, 986
Bonnell, Frances II, 468
Bonnell, Francis II, 468
Bonnell, James II, 338
Bonnell, John V, 986
Bonnell, Lona V, 986
Bonnell, Loretta V, 986
Bonnell, Maggie V, 986
Bonnell, Robert II, 468
Bonnell, Robert II, 667
Bonnell, Samuel II, 338
Bonnell, Samuel II, 468
Bonnell, Samuel II, 667
Bonnell, Sarah II, 338
Bonnell, Sarah II, 468
Bonnell, Sarah II, 667
Bonner, Charles IV, 680
Bonner, Deborah III, 38
Bonner, Ed V, 830
Bonner, Ella V, 828
Bonner, Ella G. V, 830
Bonner, Hanah V, 154
Bonner, Hanah V, 198
Bonnér, Leah I, 37
Bonner, Leah I, 56
Bonner, Maria III, 38
Bonner, Rachel A. II, 840
Bonner, Ragan V, 154
Bonner, Ragan E. V, 154
Bonner, Sadie IV, 1035
Bonner, Sarah IV, 1035
Bonner, Thelma IV, 680
Bonnet, Rebeckah I, 709
Bonnet, Rebeckah I, 735
Bonny, ??? II, 338
Bonny, Frances II, 338
Bonny, Hester II, 338
Bonny, James II, 338
Bonny, Mary II, 338
Bonny, Robert II, 338
Bonny, Thomas II, 338
Bons, Abigail I, 130
Bonsal, Abraham II, 783
Bonsal, Charles Albert II, 840
Bonsal, Chas. Albert II, 840
Bonsal, Eleanor Harrison II, 78
Bonsal, Eliza II, 281
Bonsal, Eliza II, 840
Bonsal, Eliza Hunt II, 815
Bonsal, Elizabeth II, 783
Bonsal, Ellenor H. II, 840
Bonsal, Gannah E. II, 840
Bonsal, Hannah Bunting II, 785
Bonsal, Hannah E. II, 783
Bonsal, Helen II, 840
Bonsal, Isaac II, 783
Bonsal, Isaac II, 785
Bonsal, Joshua W. IV, 681
Bonsal, Martha B. II, 840
Bonsal, Martha Bartram II, 783
Bonsal, Martha L. II, 840
Bonsal, Mary II, 783
Bonsal, Mary II, 785
Bonsal, Mary II, 840
Bonsal, Mary II, 1045
Bonsal, Mary L. II, 840
Bonsal, Mary Laycock II, 783
Bonsal, Mary M. II, 840
Bonsal, Mary W. II, 840
Bonsal, Mary Walton II, 783
Bonsal, Mary Wyatt II, 840
Bonsal, Naomi P. II, 840
Bonsal, Naomi Passmore II, 815
Bonsal, Phebe VI, 368
Bonsal, Phebe VI, 381
Bonsal, Philip II, 468
Bonsal, Rebecca M. VI, 368
Bonsal, Rebecca M. VI, 460
Bonsal, Ruth II, 840
Bonsal, Sally II, 840
Bonsal, Samuel Newbold V, 895
Bonsal, Sarah II, 840
Bonsal, Sarah W. II, 840
Bonsal, T. Vincent II, 840
Bonsal, Thomas II, 281
Bonsal, Thos. II, 840
Bonsal, Thos. L. II, 840
Bonsal, Thos. Laycock II, 815
Bonsal, Vincent II, 840
Bonsal, Vincent Philip VI, 368
Bonsal, William C. VI, 460
Bonsal, Wm. II, 840
Bonsall, Abraham II, 783
Bonsall, Abraham IV, 178
Bonsall, Abraham IV, 680
Bonsall, Abraham IV, 681
Bonsall, Abraham IV, 740

Bonsall, Amey II, 468
Bonsall, Amos IV, 680
Bonsall, Amy II, 338
Bonsall, Amy II, 468
Bonsall, Ann IV, 724
Bonsall, Ann Jr. IV, 681
Bonsall, Anna II, 468
Bonsall, Anna II, 544
Bonsall, Anna IV, 680
Bonsall, Anna IV, 681
Bonsall, Anna V, 895
Bonsall, Anna V, 907
Bonsall, Anna C. IV, 612
Bonsall, Anna C. IV, 682
Bonsall, Anna S. IV, 681
Bonsall, Anna S. IV, 682
Bonsall, Annie IV, 612
Bonsall, Annie C. IV, 612
Bonsall, Annie E. IV, 682
Bonsall, Annie H. IV, 667
Bonsall, Annie H. IV, 682
Bonsall, Annie H. IV, 687
Bonsall, Bella IV, 682
Bonsall, Benjamin II, 338
Bonsall, Benjamin II, 469
Bonsall, Benjamin, Jr. II, 468
Bonsall, Benjamin, Jr. II, 469
Bonsall, Caroline IV, 1050
Bonsall, Caroline B. III, 190
Bonsall, Caroline F. IV, 757
Bonsall, Caroline W. IV, 681
Bonsall, Charles II, 468
Bonsall, Charles IV, 680
Bonsall, Daniel IV, 680
Bonsall, Daniel IV, 681
Bonsall, Daniel IV, 724
Bonsall, Daniel IV, 760
Bonsall, David IV, 681
Bonsall, Deborah IV, 680
Bonsall, Deborah IV, 740
Bonsall, Deborah G. IV, 680
Bonsall, Ed IV, 681
Bonsall, Edward II, 198
Bonsall, Edward II, 245
Bonsall, Edward II, 338
Bonsall, Edward II, 468
Bonsall, Edward II, 533
Bonsall, Edward IV, 178
Bonsall, Edward IV, 531
Bonsall, Edward IV, 680
Bonsall, Edward IV, 681
Bonsall, Edward IV, 702
Bonsall, Edward IV, 704
Bonsall, Edward IV, 719
Bonsall, Edward IV, 722
Bonsall, Edward IV, 729
Bonsall, Edward IV, 770
Bonsall, Edward IV, 784
Bonsall, Edward H. II, 338
Bonsall, Edward H. II, 468
Bonsall, Edward H. II, 469
Bonsall, Edward S. IV, 681
Bonsall, Edward William IV, 681
Bonsall, Edward Wm. IV, 681
Bonsall, Edwin IV, 680
Bonsall, Elazan IV, 681
Bonsall, Elazan IV, 752
Bonsall, Eleanor Harrison II, 783
Bonsall, Elisa V, 895
Bonsall, Elisa V, 898
Bonsall, Elisa V, 904
Bonsall, Eliza II, 281
Bonsall, Eliza II, 305
Bonsall, Eliza IV, 681
Bonsall, Eliza IV, 682
Bonsall, Eliza IV, 765
Bonsall, Eliza IV, 864
Bonsall, Eliza IV, 867
Bonsall, Eliza Jane II, 828
Bonsall, Elizabeth II, 469
Bonsall, Elizabeth II, 783
Bonsall, Elizabeth IV, 680
Bonsall, Elizabeth R. IV, 681
Bonsall, Emmor IV, 680
Bonsall, Emmor IV, 681
Bonsall, Evan IV, 680
Bonsall, Evan IV, 757
Bonsall, Evan IV, 1050
Bonsall, Gibbons IV, 681
Bonsall, Hannah II, 198
Bonsall, Hannah II, 245
Bonsall, Hannah II, 468
Bonsall, Hannah II, 469
Bonsall, Hannah II, 533
Bonsall, Hannah II, 697
Bonsall, Hannah IV, 612
Bonsall, Hannah IV, 679
Bonsall, Hannah IV, 680
Bonsall, Hannah IV, 681
Bonsall, Hannah IV, 702
Bonsall, Hannah IV, 704
Bonsall, Hannah IV, 719
Bonsall, Hannah IV, 728
Bonsall, Hannah IV, 729
Bonsall, Hannah E. II, 783
Bonsall, Hannah E. IV, 681
Bonsall, Hannah Emma IV, 681
Bonsall, Hannah F. IV, 680
Bonsall, Hannah F. IV, 681
Bonsall, Hannah J. IV, 681
Bonsall, Helen II, 832
Bonsall, Henry IV, 680
Bonsall, Henry L. II, 468
Bonsall, Henry L. II, 469
Bonsall, Isaac II, 198
Bonsall, Isaac II, 245
Bonsall, Isaac II, 468
Bonsall, Isaac II, 544
Bonsall, Isaac II, 783
Bonsall, Isaac IV, 178
Bonsall, Isaac IV, 612
Bonsall, Isaac IV, 679
Bonsall, Isaac IV, 680
Bonsall, Isaac IV, 681
Bonsall, Isaac IV, 702
Bonsall, Isaac V, 895
Bonsall, Isaac E. IV, 612
Bonsall, Isaac E. IV, 667
Bonsall, Isaac E. IV, 681
Bonsall, Isaac E. IV, 682
Bonsall, Isaac E. IV, 687
Bonsall, Isaac E., Jr. IV, 680
Bonsall, Isaac, Jr. IV, 681
Bonsall, Isabella IV, 681
Bonsall, Isabella IV, 682
Bonsall, James II, 338
Bonsall, James II, 469
Bonsall, James IV, 681
Bonsall, James G. IV, 680
Bonsall, James G. IV, 681
Bonsall, James Gibbons IV, 178
Bonsall, James R. IV, 681
Bonsall, Jane II, 468
Bonsall, Jane II, 486
Bonsall, Jane V, 895
Bonsall, Joel S. IV, 680
Bonsall, Joel S. IV, 681
Bonsall, John II, 468
Bonsall, John IV, 680
Bonsall, John Saunders VI, 732
Bonsall, Jonathan II, 712
Bonsall, Jonathan IV, 680
Bonsall, Jonathan IV, 681
Bonsall, Jonathan IV, 682
Bonsall, Joseph II, 468
Bonsall, Joseph II, 486
Bonsall, Joseph IV, 680
Bonsall, Joseph V, 895
Bonsall, Joseph V, 898
Bonsall, Joseph V, 904
Bonsall, Joseph VI, 368
Bonsall, Joseph VI, 371
Bonsall, Joseph E. IV, 682
Bonsall, Joseph Scarrett IV, 681
Bonsall, Joshua IV, 680
Bonsall, Joshua IV, 681
Bonsall, Joshua W. IV, 681
Bonsall, Joshua W. IV, 752
Bonsall, Laura II, 712
Bonsall, Laura IV, 681
Bonsall, Laura IV, 767
Bonsall, Laura R. IV, 681
Bonsall, Laura R. IV, 682
Bonsall, Levi IV, 680
Bonsall, Levi IV, 681
Bonsall, Lewis IV, 681
Bonsall, Lewis H. IV, 1050
Bonsall, Lydia II, 338
Bonsall, Lydia II, 469
Bonsall, Mark IV, 680
Bonsall, Mark IV, 681
Bonsall, Mark IV, 728
Bonsall, Martha IV, 178
Bonsall, Martha IV, 680
Bonsall, Martha IV, 681
Bonsall, Martha IV, 760
Bonsall, Martha VI, 368
Bonsall, Martha VI, 371
Bonsall, Martha Bartram II, 783
Bonsall, Martha D. IV, 681
Bonsall, Martha D. IV, 772
Bonsall, Martha L. II, 840
Bonsall, Martha L. II, 888
Bonsall, Martha Newbold II, 468
Bonsall, Martha W. IV, 680
Bonsall, Mary II, 198
Bonsall, Mary II, 245
Bonsall, Mary II, 468
Bonsall, Mary II, 469
Bonsall, Mary II, 606
Bonsall, Mary II, 783
Bonsall, Mary II, 840
Bonsall, Mary V, 895
Bonsall, Mary C. V, 895
Bonsall, Mary C. V, 904
Bonsall, Mary Ellen IV, 681
Bonsall, Mary H. II, 469
Bonsall, Mary H. II, 697
Bonsall, Mary Laycock II, 783
Bonsall, Mary M. II, 840
Bonsall, Mary Newbold II, 198
Bonsall, Mary Walton II, 783
Bonsall, Mercy II, 468
Bonsall, Mercy II, 544
Bonsall, Mercy V, 895
Bonsall, Philip II, 468
Bonsall, Philip II, 469
Bonsall, Philip II, 697
Bonsall, Priscilla IV, 680
Bonsall, Priscilla IV, 681
Bonsall, Priscilla IV, 713
Bonsall, Rachel IV, 178
Bonsall, Rachel IV, 531
Bonsall, Rachel IV, 680
Bonsall, Rachel IV, 719
Bonsall, Rachel IV, 722
Bonsall, Rachel IV, 755
Bonsall, Rachel IV, 770
Bonsall, Rachel IV, 784
Bonsall, Rachel W. IV, 121
Bonsall, Rachel W. IV, 122
Bonsall, Rachel W. IV, 679
Bonsall, Rachel W. IV, 680
Bonsall, Rachel W. IV, 681
Bonsall, Rachel W. IV, 728
Bonsall, Rachel W. IV, 770
Bonsall, Rebecca IV, 178
Bonsall, Rebecca IV, 211
Bonsall, Rebecca IV, 531
Bonsall, Rebecca IV, 680
Bonsall, Rebecca IV, 681
Bonsall, Rebecca IV, 722
Bonsall, Rebecca VI, 368
Bonsall, Rebecca VI, 371
Bonsall, Rebecca VI, 731
Bonsall, Rebecca Eva IV, 681
Bonsall, Rebecca Eva IV, 682
Bonsall, Rebecca Eva IV, 1050
Bonsall, Rebecca H. IV, 680
Bonsall, Rebecca M. VI, 731
Bonsall, Rebecca W. II, 712
Bonsall, Reuben II, 468
Bonsall, Richard II, 338
Bonsall, Richard II, 468
Bonsall, Richard II, 533
Bonsall, Richard IV, 680
Bonsall, Richard S. IV, 681
Bonsall, Richard S. IV, 1050
Bonsall, Robert IV, 682
Bonsall, Ruth II, 840
Bonsall, Samuel Newbold II, 468
Bonsall, Samuel Newbold V, 895
Bonsall, Sarah II, 338
Bonsall, Sarah II, 801
Bonsall, Sarah IV, 680
Bonsall, Sarah IV, 681
Bonsall, Sarah IV, 702
Bonsall, Sarah W. II, 840
Bonsall, Sidney II, 468
Bonsall, Sidney V, 895
Bonsall, Sidney A. II, 719
Bonsall, Sidney Ann IV, 681
Bonsall, Sidney Ann IV, 704
Bonsall, Spencer II, 338
Bonsall, Spencer II, 469
Bonsall, Stephen II, 469
Bonsall, Stephen II, 697
Bonsall, Thaddeus C. V, 895
Bonsall, Thomas II, 469
Bonsall, Thomas IV, 680
Bonsall, Thomas IV, 681
Bonsall, Thomas L. II, 728
Bonsall, Thos. L. II, 469
Bonsall, Thos. L. II, 840
Bonsall, William IV, 682
Bonsall, William C. VI, 368
Bonsall, William C. VI, 731
Bonsall, William J. IV, 681
Bonsall, William J. IV, 682
Bonsall, William Milhous II, 338
Bonsall, Wm. IV, 680
Bonsall, Wm. IV, 765
Bonsall, Wm. C. VI, 731
Bonsall, Wm. F. IV, 1050
Bonsall, Wm. T. IV, 681
Bonsel, Mary Jane IV, 321
Bonsel, Mary Jane IV, 337
Bonsel, William C. VI, 368
Bonsell, Edward IV, 178
Bonsell, Isaac V, 895
Bonsell, Joseph V, 895
Bonsell, Joseph VI, 368
Bonsell, Martha VI, 368
Bonsell, Mary C. V, 895
Bonsell, Naomi P. VI, 368
Bonsell, Phebe VI, 361
Bonsell, Phebe VI, 368
Bonsell, Rebecca IV, 534
Bonsell, Rebecca VI, 368
Bonsell, Rebecca M. VI, 368
Bonsell, Rebekah VI, 368
Bonsell, Thomas L. VI, 368
Bonsell, Vincent Philip VI, 368
Bonsell, William C. VI, 368
Bonsh, Eliza Jane I, 30
Bonsh, John I, 30
Bonsier, Mary W. IV, 1149
Bonsil, Joseph VI, 368
Bonsil, Martha VI, 365
Bonsil, Martha VI, 368
Bonswel, Martha IV, 178
Bonwell, Nathaniel V, 320
Bonyer, Nettie M. IV, 1308
Boocker, Edward VI, 231
Boocock, ??? III, 329
Boocock, Elias III, 38
Boocock, Jane III, 38
Boocock, Mary C. III, 38
Boocock, Mary C. III, 329
Boody, Alvino III, 38
Boody, Alvino III, 334
Boody, Anna L. III, 38
Boody, Anna L. III, 334
Boody, Margery H. III, 334
Boody, Margery Hill III, 38
Booge, William I Sup 1, 3
Booher, Albert V, 986
Booher, Bessie V, 986
Booher, Chas. V, 986
Booher, Elizabeth V, 986
Booher, Ella V, 986
Booher, Elsie V, 986
Booher, Emma V, 986
Booher, James V, 986
Booher, Robert V, 986
Booher, Sarah E. V, 986
Booher, Wm. V, 986
Book, Enna IV, 682
Book, Frederick II, 198
Book, Henry III, 38
Book, John II, 198
Book, John H. II, 198
Book, Oliver IV, 682
Book, Oliver VI, 231
Book, William V, 154
Book, Wm. S. II, 728
Booker, ??? III, 38
Booker, Aaron III, 38
Booker, Araminta VI, 799
Booker, Daniel P. VI, 799
Booker, Fayette VI, 853
Booker, George V, 727
Booker, Helen III, 19
Booker, Jacob VI, 881
Booker, James V, 986
Booker, James N. VI, 799
Booker, James N. VI, 825
Booker, John VI, 881
Booker, John VI, 939
Booker, Martha VI, 799
Booker, Mary C. III, 38
Booker, Mildred A. VI, 881
Booker, Nancy VI, 799
Booker, Nancy VI, 881
Booker, Nellie V, 727
Booker, Peter VI, 799
Booker, Rosa I, 938
Booker, Sophia VI, 881
Booker, Susan VI, 825
Booker, William T. VI, 881
Booker, Wm. G. I, 938
Bookhout, Tallman C. III, 426
Bookwalter, Emma VI, 732
Bookwalter, Emma VI, 751
Bookwalter, Evaline V, 154
Bookwalter, Evaline V, 828
Bookwalter, Lewis VI, 732
Bookwalter, Lewis VI, 751
Bookwalter, Ruth VI, 732
Bookwalter, Ruth VI, 751
Bool, Everett IV, 1272
Bool, Jesse I, 800
Boom, Agnes II, 469
Boom, Agnes II, 601
Boon, Ada E. I, 621
Boon, Agnes II, 601
Boon, Ann IV, 864
Boon, Ann IV, 884
Boon, Anna I, 872
Boon, Anna S. V, 26
Boon, Anna S. V, 53
Boon, Anne I, 872
Boon, Arnold V, 26
Boon, Arnold VI, 619
Boon, Betsey Elizabeth VI, 619
Boon, Chalkley IV, 801
Boon, Charles I, 872
Boon, Charles V, 223
Boon, Charles V, 452
Boon, Dorcas I, 872
Boon, Dorcas V, 223
Boon, Driver I, 872
Boon, Edward II, 338
Boon, Eliza L. VI, 881
Boon, Elizabeth I, 872
Boon, Elizabeth VI, 382
Boon, Ellen V, 26
Boon, Esther IV, 801
Boon, Hannah II, 115
Boon, Hannah II, 117
Boon, Hannah V, 26
Boon, Hannah VI, 619
Boon, Isaac IV, 801
Boon, Isaiah VI, 619
Boon, Jacob Thomas IV, 682
Boon, James IV, 682
Boon, James IV, 801
Boon, James F. VI, 881
Boon, James W. I, 230
Boon, James, Jr. II, 469
Boon, Jeremiah II, 469
Boon, Jesse Thomas IV, 682
Boon, John I, 872
Boon, John I, 897
Boon, John, Jr. I, 872
Boon, Joshua James IV, 682
Boon, Maria L. IV, 682
Boon, Maria L. IV, 777
Boon, Mary IV, 178
Boon, Mary IV, 311
Boon, Phebe Jane IV, 801
Boon, Rachel I, 872
Boon, Rebecca II, 469
Boon, Rebecca IV, 682
Boon, Rebecca Jane I, 230
Boon, Sarah I, 872
Boon, Sarah I, 897
Boon, Sarah VI, 473
Boon, Stephen I, 872
Boon, Thomas IV, 801
Boon, William I, 230
Boon, William B. V, 828
Boone, Abigail VI, 489
Boone, Abigail VI, 541
Boone, Anna S. VI, 732
Boone, Anne VI, 473
Boone, Anne S. V, 967
Boone, Anne S. V, 969
Boone, Arnold V, 42
Boone, Arnold V, 969
Boone, Arnold VI, 473
Boone, Arnold VI, 508
Boone, Arnold VI, 619
Boone, Arnold VI, 633
Boone, Arnold VI, 634
Boone, Arnold VI, 656
Boone, Arnold VI, 700
Boone, Arnold VI, 703
Boone, Arnold VI, 726
Boone, Arnold VI, 732
Boone, Arnold VI, 738
Boone, Arnold VI, 749
Boone, Arnold VI, 777
Boone, Betsey VI, 732
Boone, Betsey Elizabeth VI, 619
Boone, Betsy VI, 700
Boone, Chalkley IV, 682
Boone, Elisabeth II, 469
Boone, Eliza N. VI, 473
Boone, Eliza N. VI, 510
Boone, Elizabeth II, 469
Boone, Elizabeth II, 483
Boone, Elizabeth VI, 473
Boone, Elizabeth VI, 508
Boone, Elizabeth VI, 619
Boone, Elizabeth VI, 633
Boone, Elizabeth VI, 634
Boone, Elizabeth VI, 656
Boone, Elizabeth VI, 677
Boone, Elizabeth VI, 721
Boone, Elizabeth VI, 732
Boone, Elizabeth VI, 737
Boone, Elizabeth VI, 738
Boone, Elizabeth VI, 749
Boone, Elizabeth VI, 777
Boone, Ellen V, 26
Boone, Ellen V, 42
Boone, Ellen VI, 732
Boone, Esther IV, 682
Boone, Esther IV, 725
Boone, Esther VI, 473
Boone, Esther VI, 665
Boone, Esther Boone VI, 665
Boone, Geo. VI, 665
Boone, George II, 469

Boone, George II, 483
Boone, George VI, 473
Boone, George VI, 665
Boone, George, Jr. VI, 665
Boone, Hannah IV, 682
Boone, Hannah IV, 734
Boone, Hannah V, 42
Boone, Hannah V, 969
Boone, Hannah VI, 473
Boone, Hannah VI, 520
Boone, Hannah VI, 541
Boone, Hannah VI, 619
Boone, Hannah VI, 634
Boone, Hannah VI, 665
Boone, Hannah VI, 700
Boone, Hannah VI, 732
Boone, Hannah VI, 754
Boone, Hannah VI, 777
Boone, Hannah S. VI, 656
Boone, Hannah Shoemaker VI, 508
Boone, Hannah Shoemaker VI, 619
Boone, Hannah Shoemaker VI, 732
Boone, Hannah Shoemaker VI, 749
Boone, Hesekiah VI, 473
Boone, Hezekiah II, 469
Boone, Isaac IV, 725
Boone, Isaiah VI, 473
Boone, Isaiah VI, 520
Boone, Isaiah VI, 541
Boone, Isaiah VI, 619
Boone, Isaiah VI, 665
Boone, Isaiah VI, 666
Boone, Isaiah VI, 700
Boone, Isaiah VI, 732
Boone, Isaiah VI, 754
Boone, Isaiah VI, 777
Boone, Isaiah Boone VI, 665
Boone, Jacob VI, 665
Boone, Jacob T. IV, 682
Boone, Jacob Thomas IV, 682
Boone, James IV, 682
Boone, James, Jr. II, 469
Boone, Jeremiah II, 198
Boone, Jeremiah II, 254
Boone, Jeremiah II, 469
Boone, Jeremiah VI, 473
Boone, Jesse T. IV, 682
Boone, Jesse Thomas IV, 682
Boone, Joshua J. IV, 682
Boone, Joshua James IV, 682
Boone, Maria L. IV, 682
Boone, Mary II, 469
Boone, Mary IV, 682
Boone, Mary IV, 734
Boone, Mary VI, 473
Boone, Mary VI, 666
Boone, Mary VI, 749
Boone, Mary VI, 755
Boone, Mary R. II, 316
Boone, Mary R. II, 324
Boone, Mary R. II, 840
Boone, Mary Spencer VI, 732
Boone, Mordecai VI, 473
Boone, Mordicai VI, 473
Boone, Phebe Jane IV, 682
Boone, Phebe Jane IV, 725
Boone, Rebecca II, 198
Boone, Rebecca II, 254
Boone, Rebecca II, 469
Boone, Rebecca IV, 682
Boone, Ruth VI, 665
Boone, Ruth Hannah VI, 665
Boone, Samuel II, 469
Boone, Samuel II, 483
Boone, Samuel Spencer VI, 732
Boone, Sarah II, 198
Boone, Sarah II, 254
Boone, Sarah II, 469
Boone, Sarah II, 483
Boone, Sarah VI, 473
Boone, Sarah VI, 541
Boone, Sarah Elizabeth VI, 665
Boone, Stella IV, 1272
Boone, Susanna VI, 473
Boone, Susanna VI, 519
Boone, Susanna VI, 665
Boone, Susanna VI, 732
Boone, Susanna Boone VI, 665
Boone, Susannah VI, 520
Boone, Susannah VI, 619
Boone, Susannah VI, 665
Boone, Susannah VI, 666
Boone, Susannah VI, 668
Boone, Susannah VI, 703
Boone, Susannah VI, 732
Boone, Susannah VI, 754
Boone, Thomas IV, 682
Boone, Thomas VI, 473
Boone, Victor O. VI, 473
Boone, Victor O. VI, 510
Boone, William I, 230
Boone, William II, 198
Boone, William II, 254
Boone, William VI, 473
Boone, Wm. II, 469
Boone, Wm. VI, 541
Boop, Joseph IV, 485
Boop, Julia IV, 485
Boop, Sarah IV, 485
Boor, Sarah II, 338
Boor, William II, 338
Booraem, Timothy III, 38
Booram, Aaron VI, 971
Booram, Hannah VI, 971
Booram, John VI, 928
Boorbach, Abigail III, 198
Boot, Jemima V, 154
Booth, Anderson VI, 818
Booth, Anderson VI, 838
Booth, Ann II, 22
Booth, Ann II, 53
Booth, Ann II, 56
Booth, Ann III, 38
Booth, Ann III, 237
Booth, Ann VI, 882
Booth, Anne S. III, 396
Booth, Anne S. III, 399
Booth, Aron VI, 368
Booth, Benja. VI, 873
Booth, Benjamin IV, 75
Booth, Curtis V, 223
Booth, Daisy May IV, 1246
Booth, David III, 34
Booth, David III, 38
Booth, David III, 84
Booth, David V, 223
Booth, David S. III, 38
Booth, Eliza Ann III, 31
Booth, Eliza Ann III, 34
Booth, Eliza Ann III, 38
Booth, Eliza Ann III, 84
Booth, Elizabeth II, 22
Booth, Elizabeth II, 56
Booth, Elizabeth II, 91
Booth, Elizabeth II, 812
Booth, Elizabeth II, 905
Booth, Elizabeth IV, 22
Booth, Elizabeth VI, 881
Booth, Fanny VI, 873
Booth, George IV, 1035
Booth, George V, 223
Booth, George VI, 881
Booth, George C. IV, 1035
Booth, George S. II, 166
Booth, George S. II, 281
Booth, Hannah III, 38
Booth, Hannah III, 84
Booth, Jane II, 22
Booth, Jane II, 56
Booth, Jane II, 72
Booth, Jane II, 469
Booth, Jane II, 535
Booth, Jemima II, 467
Booth, Jemima II, 469
Booth, John II, 281
Booth, John VI, 881
Booth, John VI, 1017
Booth, John Henry V, 223
Booth, Joseph VI, 368
Booth, Joshua VI, 881
Booth, Judey VI, 1017
Booth, Judith A. C. VI, 838
Booth, Lizzie V, 223
Booth, Lucinde IV, 928
Booth, Lucinde IV, 940
Booth, Lucy Ann VI, 881
Booth, Maggie V, 223
Booth, Mariam V. R. III, 396
Booth, Marion IV, 1149
Booth, Mary II, 166
Booth, Mary IV, 22
Booth, Mary IV, 40
Booth, Mary VI, 368
Booth, Mary Ann IV, 22
Booth, Mary Ann IV, 54
Booth, Mary M. II, 281
Booth, Minora IV, 1307
Booth, Pauline Broomal IV, 682
Booth, Peter VI, 881
Booth, Prudence VI, 830
Booth, Prudence VI, 881
Booth, Richard II, 22
Booth, Richard II, 53
Booth, Richard II, 56
Booth, Richard VI, 931
Booth, Robert IV, 75
Booth, Ruth II, 22
Booth, Ruth II, 56
Booth, Sarah II, 22
Booth, Sarah II, 56
Booth, Sarah II, 67
Booth, Sarah Farley VI, 931
Booth, Susan IV, 864
Booth, Susan IV, 885
Booth, Theodoshia II, 281
Booth, Theodoshia Mershon II, 281
Booth, Thomas II, 166
Booth, Thomas II, 281
Booth, Thomas II, 728
Booth, Thomas VI, 873
Booth, Thos. II, 469
Booth, Tomsey VI, 881
Booth, Vincent R. III, 396
Booth, Vincent Vergin Rave III, 396
Booth, Vincent Virgin Rave III, 399
Booth, William VI, 830
Booth, William VI, 881
Booth, Wm. II, 469
Boothe, Agness VI, 881
Boothe, Anderson VI, 799
Boothe, Anderson VI, 838
Boothe, Anna I, 527
Boothe, Benjamin IV, 75
Boothe, Benjamin VI, 881
Boothe, Charity VI, 881
Boothe, David VI, 881
Boothe, Elizabeth IV, 178
Boothe, Elizabeth VI, 881
Boothe, James VI, 881
Boothe, Jane II, 469
Boothe, John VI, 881
Boothe, John D. VI, 881
Boothe, Joshua VI, 881
Boothe, Katy VI, 881
Boothe, Kesia VI, 881
Boothe, Letitia J. VI, 838
Boothe, Lucy Ann VI, 881
Boothe, Lucy M. VI, 895
Boothe, Nancy VI, 799
Boothe, Nancy VI, 917
Boothe, Patsy VI, 881
Boothe, Peter VI, 881
Boothe, Polly VI, 881
Boothe, Polly VI, 967
Boothe, Prudence VI, 881
Boothe, Rachel VI, 881
Boothe, Richard VI, 881
Boothe, Stephen VI, 881
Boothe, Suky VI, 881
Boothe, Susanna VI, 886
Boothe, Temperance VI, 881
Boothe, Tomsey VI, 881
Boothe, William VI, 881
Boothe, William VI, 917
Boothe, William VI, 967
Bootle, Deborah II, 980
Bootle, Deborah II, 1033
Boots, Araminto II, 338
Boots, Bessie V, 208
Boots, Bessie May V, 154
Boots, Estella V, 154
Boots, Estella Olive V, 154
Boots, Jemima V, 154
Boots, Leroy Cline V, 154
Boots, Margaret II, 338
Boots, Pearl Cline V, 154
Boots, Rhoda V, 223
Boots, Rhoda V, 263
Boots, Thelma Rose V, 154
Boots, Wm. V, 154
Booz, Cassandra II, 980
Booz, Cassandra II, 1012
Booz, Sarah II, 980
Booz, Sarah II, 981
Boram, Aaron IV, 42
Boram, Aaron IV, 864
Boram, Aaron IV, 878
Boram, Allen VI, 299
Boram, Ann IV, 22
Boram, Ann IV, 42
Boram, Aron IV, 22
Boram, Cassander IV, 864
Boram, Cassandra IV, 22
Boram, Cassandra IV, 864
Boram, Cassandra IV, 880
Boram, Catherine VI, 299
Boram, Elizabeth IV, 22
Boram, Elizabeth IV, 42
Boram, Elizabeth IV, 65
Boram, Elizabeth IV, 864
Boram, Elizabeth IV, 878
Boram, Elizabeth IV, 885
Boram, Frances IV, 22
Boram, Frances IV, 864
Boram, Frances IV, 878
Boram, John IV, 22
Boram, Judith VI, 299
Boram, Katey VI, 299
Boram, Mary IV, 22
Boram, Mary IV, 28
Boram, Mary IV, 864
Boram, Mary IV, 885
Boram, Mary E. V, 223
Boram, Mary E. V, 282
Boram, Nathan IV, 22
Boram, Nathan IV, 864
Boram, Obed VI, 299
Boram, Richard IV, 22
Boram, Richard IV, 864
Boram, Sarah VI, 299
Bordals, Sarah III, 39
Bordan, Esther I, 267
Borden, Amey II, 56
Borden, Amey II, 98
Borden, Amos IV, 75
Borden, Amy II, 53
Borden, Amy II, 56
Borden, Ann II, 199
Borden, Archibald IV, 75
Borden, Archibald V, 26
Borden, Archibald V, 895
Borden, Asher II, 56
Borden, Benjamin I, 267
Borden, Benjamin III, 39
Borden, Benjamin VI, 357
Borden, C. A. V, 452
Borden, Charles II, 199
Borden, Charlotte IV, 75
Borden, Dinah II, 166
Borden, Dinah II, 469
Borden, Dinah II, 501
Borden, Dudley V, 320
Borden, Edward V, 879
Borden, Edward V, 895
Borden, Edward W. II, 145
Borden, Eliza II, 199
Borden, Elizabeth II, 56
Borden, Elizabeth II, 166
Borden, Elizabeth II, 199
Borden, Elizabeth II, 268
Borden, Elizabeth IV, 75
Borden, Elizabeth V, 26
Borden, Elizabeth V, 895
Borden, Elizabeth Ann II, 199
Borden, Esther I, 267
Borden, Francis II, 469
Borden, Gideon S. V, 880
Borden, Hannah I, 130
Borden, Hannah I, 267
Borden, Henrietta V, 880
Borden, Hope I, 267
Borden, Hope I, 275
Borden, Jacob V, 895
Borden, James I, 130
Borden, Jane III, 39
Borden, Jane E. III, 39
Borden, Jane Eliza III, 149
Borden, Job IV, 75
Borden, Joel IV, 75
Borden, John II, 338
Borden, John VI, 830
Borden, John VI, 841
Borden, Joseph I, 130
Borden, Joseph I, 267
Borden, Katharine I, 267
Borden, Katharine I, 277
Borden, Levi IV, 75
Borden, Levi IV, 93
Borden, Mary II, 22
Borden, Mary II, 56
Borden, Mary II, 199
Borden, Mary II, 338
Borden, Mary IV, 22
Borden, Mary IV, 75
Borden, Mary V, 26
Borden, Mary V, 895
Borden, Mary Ann IV, 75
Borden, Milburn V, 320
Borden, Myrtle V, 452
Borden, Peter II, 56
Borden, Peter V, 26
Borden, Peter V, 478
Borden, Reuben IV, 75
Borden, Rhoda IV, 75
Borden, Rhoda IV, 93
Borden, Ruth I, 267
Borden, Ruth II, 115
Borden, Ruth II, 118
Borden, Samuel II, 166
Borden, Sarah II, 196
Borden, Sarah II, 199
Borden, Sarah III, 39
Borden, Sidney V, 895
Borden, Susan W. II, 1069
Borden, Susanna I, 128
Borden, Susanna I, 130
Borden, Susanna II, 56
Borden, Susannah I, 130
Borden, Susannah I, 157
Borden, Sydney V, 895
Borden, Tacy II, 199
Borden, Thomas II, 56
Borden, Thomas II, 129
Borden, Thomas II, 199
Borden, Thomas P. D. II, 145
Borden, Thos. II, 53
Borden, Thos. II, 56
Borden, Thos. II, 98
Borden, Walter Henry III, 39
Borden, Walter Henry III, 149
Borden, Wilburn V, 320
Borden, William I, 130
Borden, William I, 157
Borden, William I, 263
Borden, William I, 264
Borden, William I, 267
Borden, William II, 199
Borden, William V, 895
Borden, Wm. L. III, 39
Border, Constance IV, 1246
Border, Ray IV, 1246
Borders, Rebecca VI, 620
Borders, Rebecca VI, 638
Borders, Rossie IV, 1202
Bordin, Thomas II, 199
Bordner, Jacob IV, 178
Bordon, Edward W. II, 129
Bordon, John II, 338
Bordon, Mary II, 338
Bordon, Rebecca II, 129
Bordon, Samuel II, 129
Bordon, Thomas II, 129
Bordson, Bennet I, 800
Borem, Rebecca VI, 473
Borem, Rebecca VI, 502
Borem, Timothy III, 38
Borem, Timothy T. III, 39
Boren, Eunice I, 527
Boren, Louise I, 630
Boren, Nancy I, 527
Boren, Nancy I, 592
Boren, Polly I, 527
Borgee, Secrinka III, 103
Borgeson, Adele III, 39
Borgeson, Adele III, 335
Borgeson, Mary III, 39
Borgeson, Oscar III, 39
Borgeson, Oscar III, 335
Borgeson, William III, 39
Boring, Anna I, 1148
Boring, Blount H. I, 1148
Boring, Carl V, 660
Boring, Carl M. V, 660
Boring, Corda V, 660
Boring, Damarris V, 660
Boring, Damarris M. V, 477
Boring, David Bowles VI, 620
Boring, Demaris M. V, 660
Boring, Elisabeth I, 1148
Boring, Elizabeth IV, 1149
Boring, Elizabeth VI, 616
Boring, Elizabeth VI, 620
Boring, Elizabeth Penelope IV, 1147
Boring, Elizabeth Penelope IV, 1149
Boring, Evelyn Jane V, 660
Boring, H. H. V, 986
Boring, Hartsel I, 1148
Boring, Ida I, 1148
Boring, J. Robert I, 1148
Boring, James R. I, 1148
Boring, Lula I, 1148
Boring, Madge I, 1148
Boring, Mollie I, 1148
Boring, Mollie B. I, 1148
Boring, Nathaniel I, 1148
Boring, Nellie I, 1148
Boring, Phebe I, 799
Boring, Phebe I, 800
Boring, R. E. I, 1148
Boring, Ralph I, 1148
Boring, Ralph IV, 1147
Boring, Ralph IV, 1149
Boring, Ralph Hartsell VI, 616
Boring, Ralph Hartsell VI, 620
Boring, Richard Levering VI, 620
Boring, Robert I, 1148
Boring, Robert E. I, 1148
Boring, Ruth I, 1148
Boring, Ruth Mary VI, 620
Boring, Samantha V, 986
Borland, Alexr. VI, 937
Borland, Rachel V, 986
Borntrager, Allen I, 612
Borntrager, Mary I, 612
Borntrager, Sarah Kate I, 612
Boroff, Allie V, 986

Boroff, Mattie V, 986
Boroff, Ollie V, 986
Boroff, Viola V, 986
Borom, Judith VI, 299
Borough, Benjamin F. I, 475
Borough, Elizabeth II, 59
Borough, Jacob II, 840
Borough, Nancy I, 711
Boroughs, Amos II, 1028
Boroughs, Anna I, 374
Boroughs, Josephine I, 374
Boroughs, Josephine V. I, 374
Boroughs, Margaret II, 986
Boroughs, Margaret II, 1000
Boroughs, Zacharias I, 374
Borradaike, Sarah Ann V, 880
Borradail, Sarah II, 167
Borradaile, Anne II, 271
Borradaile, Elizabeth II, 199
Borradaile, John II, 166
Borradaile, John II, 199
Borradaile, John II, 222
Borradaile, Mary II, 271
Borradaile, Priscilla V, 880
Borradaile, Rebecca II, 199
Borradaile, Sarah II, 166
Borradaile, Sarah II, 199
Borradaile, Sarah II, 222
Borradaile, Sarah II, 271
Borradaile, Sarah Ann V, 880
Borradaile, Thomas II, 271
Borradaile, William II, 199
Borradaill, John II, 195
Borradaill, Rebecca II, 195
Borradaill, Rebecca II, 199
Borradaille, Arthur II, 166
Borradaille, Frampton II, 166
Borradaille, John II, 166
Borradaille, Joseph II, 166
Borradaille, Rebecca II, 166
Borradaille, Sarah II, 166
Borradaille, Sarah II, 167
Borradaille, William II, 166
Borradall, Sarah II, 199
Borram, John VI, 971
Borras, Mary II, 56
Borriff, Mattie V, 986
Borring, Hartsel I, 1148
Borrodail, Sarah II, 199
Borrodaile, Elizabeth V, 859
Borrodaile, Sarah V, 859
Borrow, Josiah VI, 881
Borrow, Mary VI, 881
Borrowdail, Elizabeth II, 199
Borrowdail, Elizabeth II, 251
Borrows, John II, 986
Borrows, John II, 1027
Borrows, Mary II, 986
Borrows, Mary II, 1027
Borst, Maria III, 125
Borten, Ann II, 64
Borten, Edward V, 26
Borten, Emmeline V, 26
Borten, James V, 26
Borten, Job V, 26
Borten, John II, 64
Borten, Mary V, 26
Borten, Mary Ann V, 26
Borten, Rebecca V, 26
Borten, Rebecca W. II, 281
Borten, Rebecca W. II, 294
Borten, Sydney V, 895
Borton, Aaron II, 115
Borton, Aaron V, 949
Borton, Aaron Job V, 949
Borton, Abigail IV, 770
Borton, Abigail V, 879
Borton, Abigail V, 880
Borton, Abraham II, 338
Borton, Abraham II, 469
Borton, Alda O. V, 613
Borton, Alice II, 131
Borton, Alice II, 1057
Borton, Alice A. IV, 1024
Borton, Altie T. IV, 370
Borton, Angeline IV, 682
Borton, Ann II, 56
Borton, Ann II, 116
Borton, Ann II, 118
Borton, Ann II, 167
Borton, Ann II, 199
Borton, Ann II, 469
Borton, Ann IV, 891
Borton, Ann V, 26
Borton, Ann V, 102
Borton, Ann VI, 729
Borton, Aron II, 115
Borton, Asa IV, 1272
Borton, Asa V, 948
Borton, Asa V, 949
Borton, Asahel II, 116
Borton, Benjamin IV, 140
Borton, Benjamin IV, 371
Borton, Benjamin, Jr. IV, 371
Borton, Bethuel IV, 1352
Borton, Beulah V, 26
Borton, Beulah V, 948
Borton, Beulah V, 949
Borton, Charity IV, 140
Borton, Charles Walter II, 281
Borton, Daniel IV, 801
Borton, Daniel D. IV, 801
Borton, Daniel Davis IV, 801
Borton, David IV, 801
Borton, Deborah II, 281
Borton, Deborah W. II, 281
Borton, Deborah W. II, 283
Borton, Edward V, 26
Borton, Edward V, 28
Borton, Edward V, 613
Borton, Edward V, 895
Borton, Edward V, 967
Borton, Edward D. V, 967
Borton, Edwin II, 139
Borton, Elizabeth II, 56
Borton, Elizabeth II, 115
Borton, Elizabeth II, 116
Borton, Elizabeth II, 124
Borton, Elizabeth II, 189
Borton, Elizabeth II, 199
Borton, Elizabeth II, 229
Borton, Elizabeth II, 281
Borton, Elizabeth II, 313
Borton, Elizabeth II, 314
Borton, Elizabeth II, 780
Borton, Elizabeth II, 817
Borton, Elizabeth II, 980
Borton, Elizabeth IV, 1272
Borton, Elizabeth V, 26
Borton, Elizabeth V, 895
Borton, Elizabeth V, 948
Borton, Elizabeth V, 949
Borton, Elizabeth V, 952
Borton, Elizabeth V, 955
Borton, Elizabeth A. L. II, 116
Borton, Elizabeth Acton II, 121
Borton, Elizabeth Ann V, 949
Borton, Elizabeth Ann V, 956
Borton, Elizabeth C. II, 281
Borton, Elizabeth L. V, 949
Borton, Ellwood T. II, 469
Borton, Ellwood T. II, 840
Borton, Ellwood Thomas II, 783
Borton, Elsie B. IV, 370
Borton, Elsie B. IV, 371
Borton, Elsie B. IV, 451
Borton, Elsie Bell IV, 370
Borton, Elton V, 880
Borton, Elwood V, 949
Borton, Elwood F. II, 338
Borton, Elwood T. II, 840
Borton, Emaline V, 967
Borton, Emeline V, 967
Borton, Emily II, 139
Borton, Emily W. II, 167
Borton, Emily W. II, 281
Borton, Emily W. II, 283
Borton, Emma IV, 928
Borton, Emma C. IV, 801
Borton, Emma C. IV, 928
Borton, Emmaline IV, 682
Borton, Emmeline V, 26
Borton, Esther II, 199
Borton, Ezra IV, 682
Borton, Ezra IV, 719
Borton, Ezra IV, 891
Borton, Ezra IV, 1024
Borton, Ezra IV, 1031
Borton, George B. II, 167
Borton, George B. II, 281
Borton, George B. II, 283
Borton, George B. II, 306
Borton, George R. II, 121
Borton, George Ross IV, 928
Borton, George W. II, 281
Borton, George W. II, 710
Borton, George Wills II, 121
Borton, George Wills II, 167
Borton, Gertrude L. II, 116
Borton, Hanah Ann V, 26
Borton, Hanna II, 116
Borton, Hanna II, 118
Borton, Hannah II, 199
Borton, Hannah II, 338
Borton, Hannah II, 469
Borton, Hannah II, 820
Borton, Hannah IV, 770
Borton, Hannah V, 880
Borton, Hannah Ann V, 948
Borton, Hannah Ann V, 949
Borton, Hannah Ann V, 958
Borton, Hannah K. II, 469
Borton, Hannah K. II, 676
Borton, Hannah M. II, 115
Borton, Hannahann V, 26
Borton, Hope II, 821
Borton, Ira IV, 1272
Borton, Ira V, 948
Borton, Ira V, 949
Borton, Isaac IV, 928
Borton, Jacob II, 469
Borton, Jacob II, 676
Borton, Jacob V, 26
Borton, Jacob V, 895
Borton, James IV, 371
Borton, James V, 26
Borton, James C. II, 167
Borton, James C. II, 281
Borton, James S. V, 967
Borton, Jane II, 167
Borton, Jane IV, 682
Borton, Jane IV, 928
Borton, Jane IV, 963
Borton, Jane V, 967
Borton, Jane A. IV, 891
Borton, Jane D. IV, 682
Borton, Jane D. IV, 719
Borton, Jane D. IV, 891
Borton, Jemima II, 167
Borton, Jemima II, 281
Borton, Jemima II, 305
Borton, Jemima II, 307
Borton, Jemima II, 469
Borton, Jemima II, 676
Borton, Jemima V, 880
Borton, Jemima VI, 788
Borton, Jemima Ann VI, 730
Borton, Jemima Ann VI, 732
Borton, Jemima Ann VI, 788
Borton, Jennie Gertrude IV, 370
Borton, Jesse R. V, 613
Borton, Job II, 115
Borton, Job IV, 1352
Borton, Job V, 26
Borton, Job V, 102
Borton, Job V, 949
Borton, Job V, 967
Borton, Joel, Jr. II, 115
Borton, John II, 56
Borton, John II, 131
Borton, John II, 167
Borton, John II, 189
Borton, John II, 199
Borton, John II, 204
Borton, John II, 281
Borton, John II, 305
Borton, John II, 306
Borton, John II, 307
Borton, John II, 710
Borton, John II, 980
Borton, John IV, 770
Borton, John IV, 1352
Borton, John VI, 732
Borton, John VI, 788
Borton, John Howard II, 167
Borton, John W. II, 167
Borton, John, Jr. II, 281
Borton, Joseph II, 167
Borton, Joseph II, 281
Borton, Joseph II, 283
Borton, Joseph II, 303
Borton, Joseph II, 313
Borton, Joseph IV, 371
Borton, Joseph H. II, 281
Borton, Joseph Harvey II, 167
Borton, Joseph Harvey II, 281
Borton, Joseph N. II, 281
Borton, Joseph O. IV, 371
Borton, Joseph Orville IV, 370
Borton, Joshua II, 199
Borton, Joshua II, 229
Borton, Joshua II, 281
Borton, Keturah II, 281
Borton, Keturah II, 306
Borton, Keturah IV, 140
Borton, Keturah IV, 162
Borton, Leah Ellen V, 613
Borton, Levi II, 199
Borton, Levi II, 229
Borton, Lucy II, 131
Borton, Lydia II, 115
Borton, Mabel II, 139
Borton, Maria V, 967
Borton, Maria V, 974
Borton, Maria Merritt V, 949
Borton, Marian V, 26
Borton, Martha II, 189
Borton, Martha II, 281
Borton, Martha II, 307
Borton, Martha II, 710
Borton, Martha IV, 140
Borton, Martha Ann IV, 1352
Borton, Martha W. II, 167
Borton, Mary II, 117
Borton, Mary II, 281
Borton, Mary II, 338
Borton, Mary II, 469
Borton, Mary II, 783
Borton, Mary II, 840
Borton, Mary IV, 371
Borton, Mary IV, 448
Borton, Mary V, 26
Borton, Mary V, 28
Borton, Mary V, 895
Borton, Mary V, 928
Borton, Mary V, 967
Borton, Mary A. II, 840
Borton, Mary A. II, 917
Borton, Mary Anderson II, 1045
Borton, Mary Anderson II, 1057
Borton, Mary Ann V, 26
Borton, Mary Ann V, 967
Borton, Mary C. V, 828
Borton, Mary H. III, 270
Borton, Mary J. II, 281
Borton, Mary J. II, 303
Borton, Mary W. II, 840
Borton, Mary, Jr. II, 469
Borton, Mercy IV, 682
Borton, Mercy IV, 891
Borton, Miriam V, 26
Borton, Miriam V, 948
Borton, Miriam V, 949
Borton, Mirriam IV, 1272
Borton, Obediah II, 199
Borton, Obediah II, 204
Borton, Orville A. IV, 371
Borton, Orville G. IV, 370
Borton, Orville J. V, 613
Borton, Rachel II, 167
Borton, Rachel II, 281
Borton, Rachel IV, 371
Borton, Rachel IV, 419
Borton, Rachel V, 880
Borton, Rachel W. II, 281
Borton, Rachel W. II, 1045
Borton, Rachel W. II, 1057
Borton, Rebecca V, 26
Borton, Rebecca V, 28
Borton, Rebecca D. II, 338
Borton, Rebecca D. II, 469
Borton, Rebecca W. II, 167
Borton, Rebecca W. II, 281
Borton, Rebecca W. II, 710
Borton, Reuben IV, 140
Borton, Reuben IV, 371
Borton, Sallie III, 361
Borton, Samuel II, 116
Borton, Samuel IV, 682
Borton, Samuel IV, 891
Borton, Samuel C. IV, 1352
Borton, Sarah II, 167
Borton, Sarah II, 199
Borton, Sarah II, 281
Borton, Sarah II, 283
Borton, Sarah II, 303
Borton, Sarah II, 313
Borton, Sarah II, 823
Borton, Sarah V, 26
Borton, Sarah V, 948
Borton, Sarah A. II, 281
Borton, Sarah A. II, 305
Borton, Sarah B. IV, 1024
Borton, Sarah B. IV, 1027
Borton, Sarah Ellen IV, 370
Borton, Sarah H. II, 199
Borton, Sarah J. II, 281
Borton, Susan IV, 928
Borton, Susan W. II, 121
Borton, Susan W. II, 281
Borton, Susan W. II, 283
Borton, Susanah II, 199
Borton, Susanah II, 204
Borton, Susanna II, 167
Borton, Susanna II, 281
Borton, Susanna II, 306
Borton, Susannah II, 199
Borton, Sydney V, 26
Borton, Sydney V, 895
Borton, Thomas II, 115
Borton, Thomas II, 167
Borton, Thomas II, 820
Borton, Thomas V, 948
Borton, Uriah II, 167
Borton, Uriah II, 281
Borton, Uriah II, 1045
Borton, Uriah II, 1057
Borton, Vashti IV, 371
Borton, Vashti IV, 385
Borton, Walter II, 167
Borton, Walter IV, 371
Borton, Walter E. IV, 371
Borton, Walter Eugene IV, 370
Borton, Wilford A. IV, 370
Borton, William II, 189
Borton, William II, 199
Borton, William IV, 1272
Borton, William J. II, 281
Borton, William Jessup II, 167
Borton, William W. V, 26
Borton, Wm, Jr. II, 116
Borton, Wm. II, 840
Borton, Wm. V, 949
Borton, Wm. Jessup II, 1045
Borton, Wm. Jessup II, 1057
Borton, Wm. S. II, 917
Borton, Wm. W. II, 840
Borton, Wm. W. V, 948
Borum, Aaron IV, 864
Borum, Alice V, 223
Borum, Allen VI, 299
Borum, Anna V, 224
Borum, Cassander IV, 864
Borum, Catherine V, 223
Borum, Catherine VI, 299
Borum, Elizabeth IV, 864
Borum, Eva M. V, 224
Borum, Frances IV, 864
Borum, Jane V, 224
Borum, Jane V, 293
Borum, John V, 268
Borum, Judith V, 223
Borum, Judith V, 268
Borum, Judith VI, 299
Borum, Katherine V, 223
Borum, Katherine V, 268
Borum, Mary IV, 864
Borum, Mary IV, 885
Borum, Mary E. V, 223
Borum, Mary E. V, 224
Borum, Nathan IV, 864
Borum, Obed V, 224
Borum, Obed VI, 299
Borum, Obed A. V, 223
Borum, Richard IV, 864
Borum, Ruth E. V, 224
Borum, Ruth E. V, 283
Borum, Sarah V, 223
Borum, Sarah VI, 299
Borum, Sarah J. V, 224
Borum, Sarah J. V, 285
Bose, John II, 441
Bose, Rachel II, 441
Bosemand, Hannah I, 374
Bosher, William VI, 857
Bosher, William VI, 864
Boss, Ann II, 338
Boss, Barbara II, 469
Boss, Barbara II, 699
Boss, Elizabeth II, 56
Boss, Elizabeth II, 105
Boss, Elizabeth II, 338
Boss, Elizabeth II, 441
Boss, Elizabeth II, 457
Boss, Elizabeth II, 469
Boss, James II, 338
Boss, James II, 469
Boss, Lydia IV, 75
Boss, Lydia IV, 88
Boss, Miriam I, 300
Boss, Peter II, 441
Boss, Susanna II, 469
Boss, Susanna II, 699
Boss, William II, 338
Boss, William II, 699
Bossert, Ella J. II, 313
Bossert, Philip E. Jochen II, 313
Bossert, Susanna T. II, 313
Bosswick, Francis II, 199
Bostick, John IV, 22
Bostick, John VI, 799
Bostick, Keziah IV, 22
Bostick, Lardner IV, 22
Bostick, Mary IV, 22
Bostick, Mary IV, 76
Bostick, Mary IV, 102
Bostick, Sally S. VI, 799
Bostick, William G. VI, 817
Boston, Henry VI, 11
Boston, Maud V, 154
Bostwick, Bettie IV, 1246
Bostwick, Birdie IV, 1246
Bostwick, Caroline III, 39
Bostwick, Catharine M. II, 281
Bostwick, Catharine M. II, 282
Bostwick, Catharine M. III, 39
Bostwick, Catharine W. II, 281
Bostwick, David S. III, 39
Bostwick, Elizabeth III, 39
Bostwick, George F. III, 39
Bostwick, George T. III, 39
Bostwick, Harry IV, 1246
Bostwick, Isaiah III, 39
Bostwick, Isaiah T. III, 39
Bostwick, James M. III, 39

Bostwick, John II, 281
Bostwick, John II, 720
Bostwick, John II, 728
Bostwick, John II, 770
Bostwick, John III, 39
Bostwick, John, Jr. III, 39
Bostwick, Josiah III, 39
Bostwick, Lemuel III, 39
Bostwick, Martha II, 712
Bostwick, Martha W. II, 718
Bostwick, Martha W. II, 720
Bostwick, Martha W. II, 728
Bostwick, Martha W. II, 770
Bostwick, Martha W. III, 39
Bostwick, Martha Willis III, 39
Bostwick, Mary II, 720
Bostwick, Mary II, 728
Bostwick, Mary II, 770
Bostwick, Mary III, 39
Bostwick, Mary Anna F. II, 281
Bostwick, Mary Anna T. III, 39
Bostwick, Mary F. III, 39
Bostwick, Mary T. III, 39
Bostwick, Maryanna F. II, 281
Bostwick, Maryanna F. III, 39
Bostwick, William F. III, 39
Boswel, Elizabeth I, 709
Boswel, Elizabeth I, 723
Boswel, Ezra I, 709
Boswel, Ezra I, 723
Boswel, Isaac I, 709
Boswell, ??? IV, 1085
Boswell, Abraham I, 130
Boswell, Abram I, 130
Boswell, Abram I, 168
Boswell, Alice V, 660
Boswell, Alice C. V, 660
Boswell, Alice Cora V, 660
Boswell, Amos I, 37
Boswell, Ann I, 130
Boswell, Ann I, 137
Boswell, Ann I, 168
Boswell, Ann I, 282
Boswell, Ann I, 300
Boswell, Ann I, 301
Boswell, Anna IV, 371
Boswell, Anne IV, 178
Boswell, Anne IV, 568
Boswell, Anne IV, 583
Boswell, Asenath IV, 371
Boswell, Asenath IV, 385
Boswell, Asenath IV, 512
Boswell, Asenath IV, 568
Boswell, Barnabas I, 94
Boswell, Barnabas I, 709
Boswell, Barnabe I, 130
Boswell, Barnaby I, 131
Boswell, Benjamin IV, 178
Boswell, Benjamin IV, 371
Boswell, Benjamin IV, 385
Boswell, Benjamin IV, 512
Boswell, Benjamin IV, 568
Boswell, Benjamin, Jr. IV, 568
Boswell, Benjamin, Sr. IV, 178
Boswell, Delilah I, 709
Boswell, Dempsey IV, 568
Boswell, Dempsey IV, 583
Boswell, Dempsey IV, 599
Boswell, Dempsey IV, 1050
Boswell, Demsey I, 94
Boswell, Demsey I, 130
Boswell, Demsey IV, 140
Boswell, Demsey IV, 153
Boswell, Demsey IV, 371
Boswell, Demsey IV, 1050
Boswell, Demsey IV, 1088
Boswell, Densey IV, 568
Boswell, Dorathy I, 130
Boswell, Dorothy I, 94
Boswell, Elihu IV, 1050
Boswell, Elihu IV, 1088
Boswell, Elisabeth I, 37
Boswell, Elisabeth I, 61
Boswell, Elisabeth I, 130
Boswell, Eliza IV, 568
Boswell, Eliza IV, 591
Boswell, Eliza IV, 1050
Boswell, Eliza IV, 1088
Boswell, Eliza IV, 1098
Boswell, Elizabeth I, 94
Boswell, Elizabeth I, 130
Boswell, Elizabeth I, 155
Boswell, Elizabeth I, 697
Boswell, Elizabeth I, 709
Boswell, Elizabeth I, 734
Boswell, Elizabeth IV, 22
Boswell, Elizabeth IV, 371
Boswell, Elizabeth IV, 568
Boswell, Elizabeth IV, 1050
Boswell, Elizabeth IV, 1088
Boswell, Elizabeth IV, 1105
Boswell, Elizabeth IV, 1106
Boswell, Elizabeth VI, 881
Boswell, Ellen IV, 1088
Boswell, Ephraim I, 300
Boswell, Ezra I, 94
Boswell, Ezra I, 130
Boswell, Ezra I, 709
Boswell, Ezra IV, 22
Boswell, Ezra V, 26
Boswell, George I, 94
Boswell, George I, 130
Boswell, George IV, 1102
Boswell, Hannah I, 130
Boswell, Hannah I, 164
Boswell, Hannah IV, 512
Boswell, Hannah IV, 514
Boswell, Hannah IV, 568
Boswell, Hannah IV, 569
Boswell, Huldah I, 94
Boswell, Huldah I, 130
Boswell, Huldah I, 709
Boswell, Huldah I, 736
Boswell, Ichabod I, 130
Boswell, Ichabod I, 300
Boswell, Ichabod I, 301
Boswell, Isaac I, 94
Boswell, Isaac I, 130
Boswell, Isaac I, 155
Boswell, Isaac I, 697
Boswell, Isaac I, 709
Boswell, Isaac IV, 371
Boswell, Isaac IV, 568
Boswell, Isaac IV, 1050
Boswell, Isaac IV, 1088
Boswell, Isaack I, 94
Boswell, Isabel I, 130
Boswell, Isabel I, 141
Boswell, Isabel I, 153
Boswell, Isabella F. V, 660
Boswell, Isabelle V, 660
Boswell, Isabelle F. V, 660
Boswell, J. Chobud I, 94
Boswell, James IV, 178
Boswell, Jane I, 94
Boswell, Jean I, 94
Boswell, Jean I, 709
Boswell, Jeremiah P. IV, 1088
Boswell, Jesse I, 94
Boswell, Jesse I, 130
Boswell, Jesse IV, 22
Boswell, Jesse IV, 371
Boswell, Jesse IV, 568
Boswell, Jesse IV, 591
Boswell, Jesse IV, 1050
Boswell, Jesse IV, 1088
Boswell, Joanna I, 130
Boswell, Joannah I, 129
Boswell, Joannah I, 130
Boswell, Joanne I, 94
Boswell, John I, 37
Boswell, John I, 61
Boswell, John I, 130
Boswell, John I, 155
Boswell, John I, 300
Boswell, John I, 312
Boswell, John IV, 371
Boswell, John IV, 568
Boswell, John IV, 1246
Boswell, John H. IV, 568
Boswell, John, Jr. VI, 921
Boswell, Jonathan IV, 140
Boswell, Joseph I, 264
Boswell, Joseph I, 282
Boswell, Joseph IV, 568
Boswell, Joseph IV, 1050
Boswell, Joseph IV, 1088
Boswell, Joseph V, 224
Boswell, Joseph V, 660
Boswell, Joseph H. V, 660
Boswell, Joshua I, 37
Boswell, Joshua I, 94
Boswell, Joshua I, 130
Boswell, Joshua I, 154
Boswell, Joshua I, 697
Boswell, Joshua I, 709
Boswell, Judith I, 130
Boswell, Lavina IV, 1088
Boswell, Lavina IV, 1105
Boswell, Lavina V, 224
Boswell, Lavina E. V, 224
Boswell, Lavina E. V, 660
Boswell, Levi I, 94
Boswell, Levi I, 709
Boswell, Levi IV, 1088
Boswell, Levi V, 660
Boswell, Levi M. V, 660
Boswell, Levina V, 660
Boswell, Levina E. V, 660
Boswell, Love I, 709
Boswell, Lydda I, 94
Boswell, Lydia I, 130
Boswell, Lydia I, 164
Boswell, Lydia IV, 371
Boswell, Lydia IV, 568
Boswell, Lydia IV, 599
Boswell, Margaret I, 94
Boswell, Margaret I, 300
Boswell, Mariam I, 697
Boswell, Mariam I, 709
Boswell, Martha IV, 321
Boswell, Martha E. V, 660
Boswell, Martha Ellen V, 660
Boswell, Mary I, 37
Boswell, Mary I, 66
Boswell, Mary I, 94
Boswell, Mary I, 130
Boswell, Mary I, 697
Boswell, Mary I, 709
Boswell, Mary I, 720
Boswell, Mary IV, 140
Boswell, Mary IV, 153
Boswell, Mary IV, 371
Boswell, Mary IV, 568
Boswell, Mary IV, 583
Boswell, Mary IV, 598
Boswell, Mary IV, 599
Boswell, Mary IV, 1050
Boswell, Mary IV, 1088
Boswell, Mary IV, 1127
Boswell, Mary IV, 1140
Boswell, Mary M. V, 660
Boswell, Meriam I, 709
Boswell, Milicent I, 94
Boswell, Milicent I, 130
Boswell, Milicent I, 300
Boswell, Milicent I, 301
Boswell, Milicent I, 312
Boswell, Milicent IV, 1050
Boswell, Milicent IV, 1088
Boswell, Milicent IV, 1093
Boswell, Miriam I, 94
Boswell, Miriam I, 130
Boswell, Miriam I, 154
Boswell, Miriam I, 282
Boswell, Miriam I, 300
Boswell, Miriam I, 709
Boswell, Nancy VI, 921
Boswell, Nathan M. IV, 568
Boswell, Peninah I, 282
Boswell, Peninah I, 1007
Boswell, Peninah IV, 366
Boswell, Peninah IV, 371
Boswell, Penninah I, 300
Boswell, Penninah IV, 140
Boswell, Pharaby I, 130
Boswell, Pharaby I, 709
Boswell, Pharibe I, 697
Boswell, Phebe IV, 371
Boswell, Phebe IV, 568
Boswell, Phebe IV, 1050
Boswell, Phebe IV, 1088
Boswell, Phebe IV, 1105
Boswell, Pheribi I, 94
Boswell, Rachel I, 94
Boswell, Rachel I, 130
Boswell, Rachel I, 151
Boswell, Rachel IV, 371
Boswell, Rachel IV, 382
Boswell, Rachel IV, 568
Boswell, Rachel IV, 1050
Boswell, Rachel IV, 1088
Boswell, Rachel IV, 1093
Boswell, Rachel IV, 1105
Boswell, Rachel IV, 1122
Boswell, Rachel V, 660
Boswell, Rebecca IV, 178
Boswell, Rebecca IV, 371
Boswell, Rebecca IV, 1050
Boswell, Rebecca IV, 1087
Boswell, Rebecca IV, 1088
Boswell, Rebecca IV, 1102
Boswell, Rebecca Anna IV, 568
Boswell, Rebeckah IV, 371
Boswell, Ruth I, 94
Boswell, Ruth I, 129
Boswell, Ruth I, 130
Boswell, Ruth I, 282
Boswell, Ruth I, 300
Boswell, Ruth I, 1007
Boswell, Ruth IV, 140
Boswell, Ruth IV, 371
Boswell, Ruth IV, 568
Boswell, Ruth IV, 1050
Boswell, Ruth IV, 1088
Boswell, Ruth IV, 1122
Boswell, Samuel I, 130
Boswell, Samuel I, 697
Boswell, Samuel I, 709
Boswell, Samuel IV, 568
Boswell, Sarah I, 94
Boswell, Sarah I, 300
Boswell, Sarah IV, 371
Boswell, Sarah IV, 568
Boswell, Sarah IV, 573
Boswell, Sarah B. IV, 1088
Boswell, Sarah B. IV, 1102
Boswell, Sarah B. IV, 1107
Boswell, Selah I, 709
Boswell, Seth I, 130
Boswell, Simion I, 130
Boswell, Simon I, 37
Boswell, Simon I, 130
Boswell, Simon I, 137
Boswell, Simon I, 282
Boswell, Susanna IV, 568
Boswell, Susanna IV, 587
Boswell, Susannah IV, 568
Boswell, Susannah L. IV, 568
Boswell, Susannah L. IV, 592
Boswell, Symon I, 130
Boswell, Thomas I, 94
Boswell, Thomas I, 129
Boswell, Thomas I, 130
Boswell, Thomas I, 151
Boswell, Thomas I, 190
Boswell, Thomas I, 300
Boswell, Thomas IV, 140
Boswell, Thomas IV, 178
Boswell, William I, 94
Boswell, William I, 130
Boswell, William I, 709
Boswell, William II, 339
Boswell, William IV, 178
Boswell, William IV, 371
Boswell, William IV, 512
Boswell, William IV, 568
Boswell, William VI, 881
Boswell, Wilson IV, 1050
Boswell, Wilson D. IV, 1088
Boswell, Wm. IV, 140
Boswell, Wm. IV, 371
Boswell, Wm. IV, 382
Boswell, Wm. IV, 514
Boswell, Wm. IV, 568
Boswell, Wm. IV, 569
Boswell, Wm. IV, 592
Boswell, Wm. IV, 1050
Boswell, Wm. IV, 1088
Boswell, Wm. IV, 1093
Boswell, Wm. IV, 1105
Boswell, Wm. IV, 1122
Boswell, Zadoc IV, 140
Boswell, Zadock I, 94
Boswell, Zadock I, 129
Boswell, Zadock I, 130
Boswell, Zadock I, 131
Boswell, Zadock IV, 371
Boswell, Zadok IV, 371
Boswell, Zilpha I, 300
Boswell, Zodak IV, 371
Boswell, Zodock I, 94
Boswell, Zodock I, 131
Boswell, Zodock I, 282
Boswell, Zodok I, 130
Boswick, Aaron II, 980
Bosworth, Clifford Eugene V, 660
Botelar, Elizabeth VI, 865
Botelar, James VI, 865
Botelar, Sally VI, 797
Botelar, Thomas VI, 849
Botelar, Thomas VI, 865
Botelar, Thos. VI, 797
Botelar, William VI, 799
Botelar, William VI, 837
Boteler, Henry VI, 800
Boteler, Keziah VI, 800
Boteler, Mary VI, 849
Boteler, Sarah VI, 800
Boteler, William VI, 800
Boteler, William, Jr. VI, 800
Boteler, Wm. VI, 849
Botomes, Abner VI, 838
Botomes, Susanna VI, 838
Bott, Amelia VI, 123
Bott, Elizabeth VI, 101
Bott, Elizabeth VI, 123
Bott, Francis VI, 123
Bott, Frederick VI, 881
Bott, Frederick VI, 895
Bott, Fredk. VI, 895
Bott, James VI, 799
Bott, Jane VI, 123
Bott, Jemima VI, 123
Bott, Martha VI, 881
Bott, Susanna VI, 101
Bott, Susanna VI, 123
Bott, Susannah VI, 123
Bott, Susannah VI, 160
Bott, Susannah VI, 203
Bott, Tabitha VI, 120
Bott, Tabitha VI, 131
Bott, Tabitha VI, 135
Bott, Tabitha VI, 141
Bott, Thomas VI, 123
Bott, William VI, 15
Bott, William VI, 95
Bott, William VI, 101
Bott, William VI, 120
Bott, William VI, 123
Bott, William VI, 131
Bott, William VI, 160
Bott, William VI, 177
Bott, Wm. VI, 123
Bott, Wm. VI, 203
Bottin, Elinor II, 978
Bottin, Elinor II, 980
Bottin, Gabriel Baynes II, 980
Bottom, Ann Sears VI, 113
Bottom, Jesse VI, 113
Bottom, Mary VI, 101
Bottom, Mary VI, 113
Bottom, William VI, 113
Bottomley, Hannah IV, 22
Bottomley, Hannah IV, 32
Bottomley, Hannah IV, 76
Bottomley, Hannah IV, 122
Botts, Alex VI, 800
Botts, Etta V, 660
Botts, Francis M. V, 374
Botts, Francis M. V, 375
Botts, Frank V, 375
Botts, George V, 374
Botts, George W. V, 374
Botts, Henry V, 375
Botts, Isaac N. V, 374
Botts, Isaac N. V, 375
Botts, James H. V, 374
Botts, James H. V, 375
Botts, Jane V, 407
Botts, Joseph V, 374
Botts, Letitia V, 375
Botts, Lutitia V, 375
Botts, Lydia V, 374
Botts, Mary E. V, 374
Botts, Mary E. V, 375
Botts, Noah V, 375
Botts, Noah M. V, 374
Botts, Noah M. V, 375
Botts, Sarah V, 407
Botts, Susan F. VI, 800
Botts, William V, 375
Botts, Williamson V, 407
Botts, Wm. V, 660
Bouden, Susan II, 801
Bouey, Eva IV, 1307
Boug, Mark I, 189
Bouge, Aaron I, 189
Bouge, Hannah V, 879
Bouge, Jesse I, 189
Bouge, John I, 190
Bouge, Joseph V, 827
Bouge, Josiah V, 827
Bouge, Mark I, 189
Bouge, Mark I, 190
Bouge, Mary V, 827
Bouge, Thomas I, 190
Boughman, Ury Etta IV, 1127
Boughman, Ury Etta IV, 1135
Boughton, John VI, 813
Boughton, John VI, 845
Boughton, Judith VI, 844
Bould, Mary II, 469
Bould, Mary II, 565
Bould, Samuel II, 469
Bould, Samuel II, 565
Bould, Sarah II, 339
Boulden, Eleanor H. III, 357
Boulderson, Deborah II, 1035
Bouldin, James E. VI, 881
Bouldin, Malinda VI, 881
Bouldin, Mary I, 930
Boulding, Ann II, 339
Boulding, Ann II, 441
Boulding, Elizabeth II, 339
Boulding, Elizabeth II, 441
Boulding, Mary II, 339
Boulding, Mary II, 469
Boulding, William II, 339
Boulding, William II, 441
Boulding, Wm. II, 339
Boulding, Wm. II, 469
Boulds, Elizabeth II, 339
Boulds, Sarah II, 339
Boulter, Anne II, 339
Boulter, Benj. II, 339
Boulton, Abigail II, 980
Boulton, Abigail IV, 606
Boulton, Abigail IV, 612
Boulton, Ann IV, 612
Boulton, Anna IV, 667
Boulton, Anne IV, 612
Boulton, Azubah II, 193
Boulton, Azubah II, 198
Boulton, Azubah IV, 682

Boulton, Charles IV, 682
Boulton, Charles IV, 1202
Boulton, Daniel IV, 612
Boulton, Daniel IV, 648
Boulton, Daniel IV, 682
Boulton, Daniel IV, 928
Boulton, Daniel IV, 981
Boulton, Deborah II, 985
Boulton, Dinah IV, 612
Boulton, Edmund II, 167
Boulton, Edward II, 167
Boulton, Edward II, 198
Boulton, Edward II, 210
Boulton, Edward II, 247
Boulton, Edward II, 467
Boulton, Edward II, 567
Boulton, Edward II, 980
Boulton, Edward, Jr. II, 198
Boulton, Eleanor II, 467
Boulton, Eleanor II, 567
Boulton, Elizabeth II, 167
Boulton, Elizabeth II, 198
Boulton, Elizabeth II, 270
Boulton, Elizabeth II, 980
Boulton, Elizabeth IV, 612
Boulton, Elizabeth IV, 682
Boulton, Elizabeth IV, 1202
Boulton, Ellen II, 167
Boulton, Ellen M. II, 728
Boulton, Esther IV, 612
Boulton, Esther IV, 648
Boulton, Esther IV, 682
Boulton, Esther IV, 928
Boulton, Esther IV, 981
Boulton, Evan IV, 682
Boulton, Hannah II, 167
Boulton, Hannah II, 193
Boulton, Hannah II, 198
Boulton, Hannah II, 270
Boulton, Hannah II, 980
Boulton, Hannah II, 1037
Boulton, Hannah IV, 178
Boulton, Hannah IV, 606
Boulton, Hannah IV, 612
Boulton, Hannah IV, 682
Boulton, Hannah IV, 928
Boulton, Isaac II, 167
Boulton, Isaac II, 198
Boulton, Isaac II, 338
Boulton, James II, 167
Boulton, James II, 980
Boulton, James II, 1037
Boulton, James IV, 178
Boulton, James IV, 606
Boulton, James IV, 612
Boulton, James IV, 682
Boulton, James IV, 928
Boulton, James IV, 1202
Boulton, John IV, 682
Boulton, Joseph II, 167
Boulton, Joseph II, 198
Boulton, Joseph II, 980
Boulton, Joseph II, 985
Boulton, Joseph IV, 682
Boulton, Joseph IV, 801
Boulton, Joseph Lafayette II, 281
Boulton, Joseph, Jr. II, 193
Boulton, Joseph, Jr. II, 198
Boulton, Joseph, Jr. IV, 682
Boulton, Levi II, 980
Boulton, Levi IV, 178
Boulton, Levi IV, 250
Boulton, Levi IV, 612
Boulton, Levi IV, 644
Boulton, Levi IV, 667
Boulton, Levi IV, 682
Boulton, Margaret IV, 682
Boulton, Margaret IV, 685
Boulton, Mary II, 198
Boulton, Mary II, 210
Boulton, Mary IV, 612
Boulton, Mary IV, 682
Boulton, Mary IV, 744
Boulton, Mary IV, 928
Boulton, Mary IV, 981
Boulton, Mary IV, 1202
Boulton, Mary Ann IV, 682
Boulton, Mennor II, 167
Boulton, Orpah IV, 178
Boulton, Orpah IV, 612
Boulton, Orpah IV, 644
Boulton, Orpha IV, 178
Boulton, Orpha IV, 250
Boulton, Orphah IV, 682
Boulton, Phebe II, 167
Boulton, Phebe II, 198
Boulton, Phebe IV, 612
Boulton, Phebe IV, 667
Boulton, Rachel II, 980
Boulton, Rachel II, 985
Boulton, Rachel IV, 612
Boulton, Rebecca IV, 612
Boulton, Rebecca IV, 682
Boulton, Reuben IV, 612
Boulton, Richard Burr II, 281
Boulton, Samuel II, 338
Boulton, Samuel Howell II, 281
Boulton, Sarah II, 167
Boulton, Sarah II, 198
Boulton, Sarah II, 247
Boulton, Sarah II, 980
Boulton, Sarah II, 985
Boulton, Sarah IV, 612
Boulton, Sarah IV, 682
Boulton, Sarah IV, 683
Boulton, Sarah IV, 801
Boulton, Sarah IV, 804
Boulton, Sarah IV, 928
Boulton, Thomas II, 198
Boulton, Thomas II, 980
Boulton, William II, 167
Boulton, William II, 193
Boulton, William II, 198
Boulton, William II, 270
Boulton, William IV, 612
Boulton, William IV, 682
Boulton, William IV, 744
Boulton, William IV, 928
Boulton, William IV, 1202
Boulton, Wm. IV, 612
Boulton, Wm. IV, 682
Boulton, Wm. IV, 981
Boulton, Wm. IV, 1202
Boun, Abraham II, 980
Bound, Abigail II, 339
Bound, George II, 339
Bound, Samuel II, 192
Bound, Sarah II, 192
Bound, Sarah II, 199
Bounds, Grace II, 980
Bounds, Mary II, 980
Bourden, Peter V, 478
Bouren, Julia III, 165
Bourn, Jesse VI, 881
Bourn, Polly VI, 881
Bourne, Benj. II, 469
Bourne, Jesse II, 339
Bourne, Jesse II, 469
Bourne, Thos. VI, 473
Bourton, Ann II, 196
Bourton, Ann II, 199
Bourton, Elizabeth II, 199
Bourton, Elizabeth II, 275
Bourton, Ester II, 227
Bourton, Esther II, 199
Bourton, Hannah II, 199
Bourton, Hannah II, 208
Bourton, Jane II, 167
Bourton, John II, 167
Bourton, John II, 199
Bourton, William II, 199
Bourton, William II, 208
Bouse, Susannah VI, 848
Bousen, Julia III, 166
Boush, Aletha I, 37
Boush, Eliza Jane I, 3
Boush, John I, 3
Boush, John I, 37
Boush, John Ira I, 3
Boush, Martha Jane Eunice I, 3
Boush, Mary Lithia I, 3
Boush, Rose Ellen I, 3
Boutellau, Emma III, 154
Boutellau, Gustave III, 154
Boutelleau, Edmund III, 39
Boutelleau, Emma III, 39
Boutelleau, Gustave III, 39
Bouton, ??? III, 39
Bouvier, Eliza II, 840
Bouvier, Eliza II, 909
Bouvier, Elizabeth II, 784
Bouvier, Elizabeth II, 840
Bouvier, Elizabeth IV, 76
Bouvier, Hannah IV, 76
Bouvier, Hannah M. II, 840
Bouvier, Hannah M. II, 909
Bouvier, Hannah Mary II, 840
Bouvier, Hannah Mary IV, 76
Bouvier, John II, 469
Bouvier, John II, 840
Bouvier, John II, 909
Bouvier, Judge John II, 784
Bovendor, Anna I, 982
Bovendor, Rachel I, 982
Bowater, Caleb I, 953
Bowater, John II, 469
Bowater, Mary II, 469
Bowater, Sarah VI, 467
Bowater, Sarah VI, 469
Bowater, Sarah VI, 581
Bowater, Sumner I, 953
Bowater, Thomas I, 953
Bowcock, Catherine VI, 881
Bowcock, Chris VI, 800
Bowcock, Elijah VI, 881
Bowcock, Johnston VI, 881
Bowcock, Martha VI, 881
Bowcock, Micajah L. VI, 881
Bowcock, Mornig VI, 881
Bowcock, Mourin VI, 881
Bowcock, Nancy VI, 320
Bowcock, Nancy VI, 345
Bowcock, Nancy VI, 800
Bowcock, Nancy VI, 948
Bowcock, Penelope V, 948
Bowcock, Polly VI, 881
Bowcock, Rhoda Ann VI, 881
Bowcock, Sally VI, 881
Bowcock, Samuel VI, 881
Bowcock, Samuel VI, 988
Bowcock, Waddy VI, 881
Bowcock, William J. VI, 881
Bowden, Almedie VI, 54
Bowden, Almedie VI, 81
Bowden, Charles III, 39
Bowden, Elias VI, 54
Bowden, Elias VI, 81
Bowden, Franklin VI, 54
Bowden, Myrtle IV, 1246
Bowden, Temperance VI, 54
Bowden, Temperance VI, 81
Bowden, William VI, 54
Bowder, Wd. Sarah II, 469
Bowen, Addie IV, 1246
Bowen, Allie V. I, 630
Bowen, Alta I, 612
Bowen, Alta I, 630
Bowen, Alta Vera I, 612
Bowen, Alta Vera I, 630
Bowen, Ann II, 56
Bowen, Ann II, 57
Bowen, Ann Bur II, 700
Bowen, Archie IV, 1246
Bowen, Benjamin II, 339
Bowen, Carl T. I, 612
Bowen, Carl T. I, 630
Bowen, Dora Munay I, 612
Bowen, Edward IV, 1307
Bowen, Elizabeth Hooten II, 470
Bowen, Emily IV, 1307
Bowen, Frances II, 282
Bowen, George V, 224
Bowen, George E. I, 612
Bowen, George E. I, 625
Bowen, Grace I, 625
Bowen, Grace II, 56
Bowen, Grace II, 66
Bowen, John II, 339
Bowen, John B. VI, 881
Bowen, John H. Creason II, 470
Bowen, Joseph II, 339
Bowen, Kirby V. I, 612
Bowen, Kirby V. I, 630
Bowen, Marjorie I, 612
Bowen, Martha II, 659
Bowen, Mary V, 880
Bowen, Mary V, 881
Bowen, Mary Ann II, 470
Bowen, Mayme I, 630
Bowen, Patty VI, 881
Bowen, Rachel II, 470
Bowen, Rebecca II, 700
Bowen, Rebecca Walter II, 470
Bowen, Rebeccah VI, 473
Bowen, Rebekah VI, 544
Bowen, Retta I, 612
Bowen, Ritta I, 625
Bowen, Robert IV, 1246
Bowen, Robert J. IV, 1246
Bowen, Sarah II, 56
Bowen, Sarah II, 64
Bowen, Spencer V, 224
Bowen, Vera I, 630
Bowen, Virginia II, 145
Bowen, Wd. Martha II, 470
Bowen, Wm. II, 470
Bower, Albert D. IV, 930
Bower, Cora Alverda IV, 930
Bower, Elizabeth J. IV, 930
Bower, Emily IV, 1308
Bower, Mary IV, 1247
Bower, Mary VI, 368
Bower, Mary VI, 417
Bower, Mary Rebecca II, 840
Bower, Mary W. II, 840
Bower, Mary W. II, 917
Bower, Milford IV, 1308
Bower, Phebe II, 840
Bower, Phebe Allen II, 784
Bower, Samuel Y. II, 840
Bower, Susannah E. II, 840
Bower, Wm. S. II, 784
Bowerman, Abigail IV, 1353
Bowerman, Abigail IV, 1357
Bowerman, Abigail IV, 1366
Bowerman, Abigail IV, 1385
Bowerman, Abraham IV, 1353
Bowerman, Ada Ann IV, 1353
Bowerman, Adah Ann IV, 1353
Bowerman, Alice IV, 1353
Bowerman, Alice IV, 1383
Bowerman, Allice IV, 1353
Bowerman, Amy IV, 1353
Bowerman, Amy IV, 1357
Bowerman, Amy IV, 1361
Bowerman, Amy W. IV, 1353
Bowerman, Arthur III, 39
Bowerman, Arthur Lindley III, 39
Bowerman, Benjamin III, 39
Bowerman, Charles IV, 1353
Bowerman, Dorcas IV, 1353
Bowerman, Dorras IV, 1353
Bowerman, Dr. Albert III, 314
Bowerman, Dr. Albert C. III, 39
Bowerman, Edith M. III, 39
Bowerman, Edith M. III, 54
Bowerman, Elvira IV, 1353
Bowerman, Esther IV, 1353
Bowerman, Esther M. IV, 1353
Bowerman, Eunice IV, 1353
Bowerman, Florence IV, 864
Bowerman, Florence IV, 1149
Bowerman, Florence M. IV, 1149
Bowerman, Francis Marion I, 1148
Bowerman, George H. IV, 1353
Bowerman, Gertrude III, 39
Bowerman, Gideon H. III, 39
Bowerman, Harley IV, 864
Bowerman, Harley IV, 1149
Bowerman, Herbert Clyde III, 39
Bowerman, Howard IV, 864
Bowerman, Howard Roy IV, 1149
Bowerman, Isaac IV, 1353
Bowerman, J. Philip III, 39
Bowerman, J. Philip III, 54
Bowerman, Jane IV, 1353
Bowerman, John W. IV, 1353
Bowerman, Joseph IV, 1353
Bowerman, Joseph IV, 1357
Bowerman, Joseph IV, 1361
Bowerman, Joseph IV, 1374
Bowerman, Joshua IV, 1353
Bowerman, Joshua IV, 1357
Bowerman, Joshua IV, 1366
Bowerman, Joshua C. IV, 1353
Bowerman, Joshua C. IV, 1385
Bowerman, Lilian III, 39
Bowerman, Lilian III, 314
Bowerman, Lydia III, 314
Bowerman, Margaret IV, 1353
Bowerman, Margaret IV, 1366
Bowerman, Maria IV, 1353
Bowerman, Maria IV, 1374
Bowerman, Maria IV, 1375
Bowerman, Martha IV, 1353
Bowerman, Mary III, 39
Bowerman, Mary A. III, 39
Bowerman, Mary Alice III, 39
Bowerman, Mary C. III, 39
Bowerman, Mary Odell IV, 1375
Bowerman, Mary Winifred III, 39
Bowerman, Mary Winifred III, 54
Bowerman, Maude IV, 1149
Bowerman, Maude A. IV, 1149
Bowerman, Moses IV, 1353
Bowerman, Nancy IV, 1353
Bowerman, Pamilia IV, 1353
Bowerman, Pamilia IV, 1385
Bowerman, Peleg H. IV, 1353
Bowerman, Phebe A. I, 527
Bowerman, Philip Ivan III, 39
Bowerman, Roselinda IV, 1353
Bowerman, Samuel IV, 1353
Bowerman, Unice IV, 1353
Bowerman, Walter III, 39
Bowerman, Walter Gregory III, 39
Bowerman, Zilpha IV, 1353
Bowermaster, Mary V, 154
Bowers, Austie E. V, 154
Bowers, Austin V, 154
Bowers, Benjamin V, 224
Bowers, Benjamin F. V, 224
Bowers, Carrie T. IV, 178
Bowers, Christian II, 1001
Bowers, Christiana II, 980
Bowers, Clara M. IV, 801
Bowers, Clara M. IV, 839
Bowers, David M. V, 224
Bowers, Emeline F. V, 727
Bowers, Flora V, 452
Bowers, George M. V, 224
Bowers, George W. V, 224
Bowers, Helen H. II, 784
Bowers, Henrietta Arabella V, 452
Bowers, Henry H. V, 224
Bowers, Hezekiah D. V, 727
Bowers, Isaac II, 470
Bowers, Jacob V, 727
Bowers, James V, 987
Bowers, James G. V, 320
Bowers, L. A. V, 154
Bowers, Leonard VI, 851
Bowers, Lester V, 154
Bowers, Lydia IV, 1050
Bowers, Lydia IV, 1060
Bowers, Martha V, 727
Bowers, Martha Ellen V, 727
Bowers, Mary I, 443
Bowers, Mary I, 445
Bowers, Mary IV, 1024
Bowers, Mary V, 830
Bowers, Mary Ann V, 828
Bowers, Mary Ann V, 860
Bowers, Mary Olivia II, 1069
Bowers, Mary Olivia II, 1078
Bowers, Mary Rebecca II, 840
Bowers, Melissa IV, 1024
Bowers, Melissa IV, 1027
Bowers, Melissa IV, 1031
Bowers, Nellie V, 154
Bowers, Phebe II, 840
Bowers, Phebe II, 872
Bowers, Phebe Allen II, 784
Bowers, Precila V, 987
Bowers, Priscilla V, 987
Bowers, Rosamond II, 1069
Bowers, Rosamond II, 1073
Bowers, Rosamond L. II, 1069
Bowers, Samuel L. IV, 1024
Bowers, Samuel Y. II, 840
Bowers, Sarah V, 224
Bowers, Sarah E. V, 224
Bowers, Sarah Ellen V, 224
Bowers, Sophia VI, 800
Bowers, Susan V, 987
Bowers, Susanna E. II, 316
Bowers, Susanna E. II, 321
Bowers, Susannah E. II, 840
Bowers, William VI, 800
Bowers, William Irvin IV, 1027
Bowers, Wm. Irvin IV, 1031
Bowers, Wm. Irving IV, 1024
Bowers, Wm. S. II, 784
Bowersock, Rebecca IV, 900
Bowersock, Rebecca IV, 910
Bowes, Alice Cowgill II, 840
Bowes, Susan Alston II, 840
Bowes, Susan C. II, 840
Bowes, Timothy J. II, 840
Boweter, John II, 469
Boweter, John VI, 11
Boweter, John VI, 23
Boweter, John VI, 41
Boweter, John VI, 146
Bowin, Elizabeth S. II, 316
Bowker, Lee IV, 727
Bowker, Margaret T. II, 308
Bowker, Mary IV, 727
Bowker, Ruth E. II, 308
Bowker, William II, 308
Bowker, Wilma IV, 727
Bowland, Alfred I, 475
Bowlen, Clark VI, 316
Bowlen, Sally VI, 960
Bowles, Abigail II, 470
Bowles, Ada Virginia I, 925
Bowles, Alex VI, 882
Bowles, Alisha A. VI, 1002
Bowles, Amanda J. VI, 1011
Bowles, Amy IV, 321
Bowles, Benjamin VI, 876
Bowles, Benjamin VI, 882
Bowles, Benjamin VI, 947
Bowles, Benjamin H. VI, 1002
Bowles, Benjamin J. VI, 1011
Bowles, Benjn. VI, 918
Bowles, Bersheba I, 94
Bowles, Betsey VI, 882
Bowles, Daisy I, 938
Bowles, Daisy Lillian I, 921
Bowles, David I, 94
Bowles, David I, 131
Bowles, David I, 1148
Bowles, David I, 1149
Bowles, David A. I, 925
Bowles, Dorcas R. I, 1148
Bowles, Elisha VI, 871
Bowles, Elisha VI, 875
Bowles, Elisha VI, 954
Bowles, Elisha VI, 1002
Bowles, Elisha VI, 1017

Bowles, Elisha A. VI, 882
Bowles, Elizabeth II, 457
Bowles, Elizabeth II, 470
Bowles, Elizabeth IV, 321
Bowles, Elizabeth VI, 620
Bowles, Elizabeth VI, 639
Bowles, Elizabeth VI, 871
Bowles, Elizabeth B. VI, 918
Bowles, Ephraim I, 94
Bowles, Ephraim Overman V, 728
Bowles, Fannie I, 617
Bowles, Fanny I, 630
Bowles, Frances VI, 882
Bowles, George Fox I, 94
Bowles, Grace V, 895
Bowles, Grace V, 931
Bowles, Green B. VI, 962
Bowles, Hannah IV, 321
Bowles, Hannah IV, 353
Bowles, Henry T. VI, 882
Bowles, Ida May I, 1149
Bowles, Irvine S. VI, 882
Bowles, Isaac Overman I, 94
Bowles, James E. VI, 962
Bowles, James H. I, 1148
Bowles, James Harvey I, 1149
Bowles, James M. I, 921
Bowles, James T. VI, 882
Bowles, Jane VI, 881
Bowles, Jane VI, 882
Bowles, Jincey VI, 875
Bowles, John IV, 321
Bowles, John VI, 881
Bowles, John VI, 882
Bowles, John VI, 904
Bowles, John VI, 927
Bowles, John VI, 1016
Bowles, John S. VI, 1011
Bowles, Josiah I, 94
Bowles, Kezia I, 131
Bowles, Keziah I, 94
Bowles, Keziah I, 107
Bowles, Keziah I, 131
Bowles, Lillie I, 921
Bowles, Lockey VI, 882
Bowles, Lucy VI, 811
Bowles, Lucy H. VI, 1016
Bowles, Luther G. I, 1148
Bowles, Luther G. I, 1149
Bowles, Lyda I, 1149
Bowles, Lydia I, 1148
Bowles, Lydia I, 1149
Bowles, Martha E. VI, 882
Bowles, Mary II, 470
Bowles, Mary II, 564
Bowles, Mary VI, 330
Bowles, Mary VI, 952
Bowles, Mary A. E. VI, 962
Bowles, Mary C. I, 1148
Bowles, Mary E. VI, 882
Bowles, Mary N. I, 925
Bowles, Miles I, 94
Bowles, Nancy VI, 882
Bowles, Nancy VI, 904
Bowles, Polly VI, 945
Bowles, Polly VI, 1002
Bowles, Robert VI, 882
Bowles, Ruth V, 224
Bowles, Ruth N. I, 1148
Bowles, Sally VI, 871
Bowles, Samuel II, 339
Bowles, Sarah VI, 882
Bowles, Sarah A. VI, 1002
Bowles, Sarah B. VI, 882
Bowles, Suckey VI, 882
Bowles, Susan VI, 1000
Bowles, Susanna IV, 179
Bowles, Thomas IV, 321
Bowles, Thos. IV, 321
Bowles, Zenith VI, 1017
Bowlin, Achsah IV, 367
Bowlin, Achsah IV, 371
Bowlin, Alfred I, 475
Bowlin, Mary IV, 371
Bowlin, Mary IV, 439
Bowling, Archibald, Jr. VI, 829
Bowling, Blair VI, 968
Bowling, Blair D. VI, 882
Bowling, Harriett J. VI, 968
Bowling, John D. VI, 800
Bowling, John W. VI, 882
Bowling, Joseph VI, 896
Bowling, Joseph VI, 957
Bowling, Juriah VI, 800
Bowling, Letty VI, 858
Bowling, Margaret H. VI, 882
Bowling, Martha II, 470
Bowling, Martha II, 676
Bowling, Mary Jane VI, 968
Bowling, Peggy VI, 896
Bowling, Robert VI, 827
Bowls, Ada E. V, 728
Bowls, Amy IV, 321
Bowls, Amy IV, 344
Bowls, Ann Pike I, 131
Bowls, Charlie V, 728
Bowls, David I, 131
Bowls, David I, 154
Bowls, David I, 1148
Bowls, David V, 728
Bowls, David, Jr. V, 728
Bowls, Dorcas R. I, 1148
Bowls, Elizabeth IV, 321
Bowls, Ellie V, 728
Bowls, Ephraim O. I, 131
Bowls, Ephraim Overman V, 728
Bowls, George Fox V, 728
Bowls, Hannah IV, 371
Bowls, Hannah IV, 445
Bowls, James I, 131
Bowls, James H. I, 1148
Bowls, John V, 728
Bowls, Jonah V, 320
Bowls, Joseph II, 199
Bowls, Joseph V, 728
Bowls, Kezia I, 131
Bowls, Keziah I, 131
Bowls, Keziah I, 153
Bowls, Keziah I, 154
Bowls, Lizzie IV, 178
Bowls, Luther G. I, 1148
Bowls, Lydia I, 1148
Bowls, Lydia I, 1149
Bowls, Mary C. I, 1148
Bowls, Nettie V, 728
Bowls, Ruth V, 320
Bowls, Ruth N. I, 1148
Bowls, Sophia V, 728
Bowls, Susanna IV, 179
Bowls, Thomas IV, 321
Bowls, Thomas IV, 344
Bowls, Thos. IV, 321
Bowls, Wilber J. V, 728
Bowls, William V, 320
Bowlsby, M. Abby III, 265
Bowlsby, M. Abby III, 277
Bowman, Abigail II, 470
Bowman, Achsah IV, 928
Bowman, Achsah L. IV, 1127
Bowman, Alfred C. V, 320
Bowman, Alice II, 788
Bowman, Ann I, 527
Bowman, Ann I, 587
Bowman, Ann II, 470
Bowman, Ann II, 794
Bowman, Ann IV, 179
Bowman, Ann IV, 222
Bowman, Ann IV, 465
Bowman, Ann IV, 683
Bowman, Ann IV, 801
Bowman, Ann IV, 847
Bowman, Ann IV, 1127
Bowman, Ann IV, 1128
Bowman, Ann IV, 1138
Bowman, Ann V, 26
Bowman, Anna I, 492
Bowman, Anna I, 527
Bowman, Anna I, 586
Bowman, Anna I, 592
Bowman, Anna I, 596
Bowman, Anna I, 800
Bowman, Anna I, 911
Bowman, Anna II, 794
Bowman, Anna II, 864
Bowman, Anna IV, 465
Bowman, Anna M. I, 592
Bowman, Anna M. I, 909
Bowman, Anna Maria I, 911
Bowman, Anna Mariah I, 755
Bowman, Annas I, 748
Bowman, Anne IV, 465
Bowman, Annes I, 492
Bowman, Annie M. V, 551
Bowman, Annis I, 527
Bowman, Annis I, 546
Bowman, C. W. IV, 683
Bowman, Carrie V, 551
Bowman, Charles P. IV, 1088
Bowman, Chas. IV, 1088
Bowman, Cleopatree I, 527
Bowman, Cyrees I, 587
Bowman, Cyrus I, 492
Bowman, Cyrus I, 911
Bowman, E. IV, 1127
Bowman, Edmond I, 755
Bowman, Edmond F. I, 587
Bowman, Edmund I, 527
Bowman, Edmund I, 586
Bowman, Edmund I, 587
Bowman, Edmund I, 592
Bowman, Edmund I, 909
Bowman, Edmund I, 911
Bowman, Elisabeth F. IV, 1354
Bowman, Eliza I, 909
Bowman, Eliza V, 551
Bowman, Elizabeth IV, 179
Bowman, Elizabeth IV, 243
Bowman, Elizabeth IV, 463
Bowman, Elizabeth IV, 465
Bowman, Elizabeth IV, 497
Bowman, Elizabeth IV, 928
Bowman, Elizabeth IV, 1088
Bowman, Elizabeth IV, 1127
Bowman, Elizabeth IV, 1128
Bowman, Elizabeth IV, 1354
Bowman, Elizabeth L. IV, 928
Bowman, Elizabeth L. IV, 1088
Bowman, Elizabeth L. IV, 1118
Bowman, Elizabeth S. IV, 1088
Bowman, Elizabeth S. IV, 1354
Bowman, Elvira I, 527
Bowman, Elvira I, 592
Bowman, Elvire I, 527
Bowman, Emmor IV, 1088
Bowman, Emmor IV, 1127
Bowman, Emmor IV, 1128
Bowman, Esther II, 470
Bowman, Eunion I, 592
Bowman, Floretta V, 551
Bowman, Frank V, 551
Bowman, George I, 492
Bowman, George I, 587
Bowman, George I, 911
Bowman, George A. I, 909
Bowman, George W. I, 592
Bowman, Hannah II, 470
Bowman, Hannah II, 648
Bowman, Harvey IV, 1088
Bowman, Hattie V, 987
Bowman, Henry II, 470
Bowman, Henry II, 648
Bowman, Henry IV, 1088
Bowman, Henry IV, 1127
Bowman, Irea V, 551
Bowman, Isaac II, 470
Bowman, Isaac IV, 140
Bowman, Isaac IV, 179
Bowman, Isaac IV, 222
Bowman, Isaac IV, 465
Bowman, Isaac IV, 683
Bowman, Isaac IV, 801
Bowman, Isaac IV, 1088
Bowman, Isaac IV, 1127
Bowman, Isaac IV, 1354
Bowman, Israel VI, 882
Bowman, James IV, 463
Bowman, James IV, 465
Bowman, James IV, 1088
Bowman, James IV, 1127
Bowman, James VI, 160
Bowman, James VI, 161
Bowman, James A. IV, 1088
Bowman, James Arthur IV, 1088
Bowman, Jancey VI, 882
Bowman, Jane II, 470
Bowman, Jane VI, 15
Bowman, Jean II, 470
Bowman, Jean II, 648
Bowman, Jesse I, 492
Bowman, Jesse I, 527
Bowman, Jesse I, 529
Bowman, Jesse I, 587
Bowman, Jesse I, 592
Bowman, Jesse I, 909
Bowman, Jesse I, 911
Bowman, John II, 470
Bowman, John V, 26
Bowman, John Edmund I, 527
Bowman, John G. VI, 368
Bowman, John G. VI, 394
Bowman, John Gardiner VI, 368
Bowman, John Gardner VI, 368
Bowman, John H. V, 26
Bowman, John Spencer IV, 1354
Bowman, John V. IV, 1088
Bowman, John, Jr. IV, 880
Bowman, Joseph IV, 179
Bowman, Joseph IV, 465
Bowman, Joseph IV, 497
Bowman, Joseph IV, 801
Bowman, Joseph IV, 1354
Bowman, Joseph V, 551
Bowman, Joseph H. IV, 1354
Bowman, Joshua Frank IV, 801
Bowman, Joshua R. II, 1069
Bowman, Lavada IV, 1035
Bowman, Leo L. VI, 368
Bowman, Levi I, 492
Bowman, Levi I, 587
Bowman, Levi I, 592
Bowman, Levi I, 911
Bowman, Lincoln Griest VI, 368
Bowman, Lucinda I, 909
Bowman, Lucy IV, 928
Bowman, Lucy IV, 1008
Bowman, Maggie V, 551
Bowman, Margaret II, 339
Bowman, Margaret II, 470
Bowman, Margaret IV, 864
Bowman, Margaret IV, 879
Bowman, Margaret Gardner VI, 368
Bowman, Martha I, 587
Bowman, Martha I, 909
Bowman, Martha III, 39
Bowman, Mary I, 527
Bowman, Mary I, 529
Bowman, Mary I, 909
Bowman, Mary I, 911
Bowman, Mary III, 39
Bowman, Mary IV, 179
Bowman, Mary V, 551
Bowman, Mary Elizabeth VI, 368
Bowman, Mary Mott II, 788
Bowman, Maud IV, 1149
Bowman, May V, 551
Bowman, Milton I, 587
Bowman, Myrlie V, 551
Bowman, Oneta B. V, 320
Bowman, Paul V, 320
Bowman, Pauline V, 320
Bowman, Phebe I, 800
Bowman, Phebe I, 840
Bowman, Phebe I, 911
Bowman, Phebe I, 913
Bowman, Phebe IV, 1088
Bowman, Phebe IV, 1127
Bowman, Phebe IV, 1354
Bowman, Phebe V, 26
Bowman, Phebe S. I, 755
Bowman, Phebe S. I, 909
Bowman, Phebe S. I, 911
Bowman, Phillip VI, 882
Bowman, Rachel IV, 1088
Bowman, Rachel IV, 1354
Bowman, Rachel B. IV, 1088
Bowman, Rachel B. IV, 1092
Bowman, Rebecca I, 492
Bowman, Rebecca III, 91
Bowman, Rebecca III, 118
Bowman, Rebecca E. V, 551
Bowman, Rebekah I, 587
Bowman, Richard I, 492
Bowman, Richard I, 527
Bowman, Richard I, 586
Bowman, Richard I, 587
Bowman, Richard I, 592
Bowman, Richard I, 911
Bowman, Richard I, 913
Bowman, Richard II, 339
Bowman, Richard II, 470
Bowman, Richard IV, 179
Bowman, Richard IV, 465
Bowman, Roger II, 339
Bowman, Roger II, 470
Bowman, Roger II, 648
Bowman, Rufus I, 527
Bowman, Ruth II, 470
Bowman, Ruth IV, 122
Bowman, Ruth IV, 123
Bowman, Sally I, 587
Bowman, Sally I, 909
Bowman, Samuel V, 551
Bowman, Samuel S. V, 551
Bowman, Sarah I, 492
Bowman, Sarah I, 587
Bowman, Sarah I, 592
Bowman, Sarah I, 755
Bowman, Sarah I, 800
Bowman, Sarah I, 819
Bowman, Sarah I, 911
Bowman, Sarah I, 913
Bowman, Sarah I, 1026
Bowman, Sarah V, 551
Bowman, Sarah C. IV, 801
Bowman, Susannah IV, 801
Bowman, Thomas II, 470
Bowman, Thomas II, 729
Bowman, Thomas IV, 801
Bowman, Thomas IV, 847
Bowman, Thomas IV, 928
Bowman, Thomas IV, 1127
Bowman, Thomas IV, 1138
Bowman, Thomas IV, 1354
Bowman, Thomas I. IV, 1127
Bowman, Thomas I. IV, 1128
Bowman, Thos. IV, 179
Bowman, Thos. IV, 243
Bowman, Thos. I. IV, 1128
Bowman, Valeria V, 551
Bowman, Valira V, 551
Bowman, Virginia VI, 368
Bowman, Virginia VI, 394
Bowman, Virginia G. VI, 368
Bowman, Virginia Preston VI, 368
Bowman, W. O. V, 728
Bowman, Walter IV, 683
Bowman, Walter IV, 801
Bowman, William I, 492
Bowman, William I, 527
Bowman, William I, 586
Bowman, William I, 587
Bowman, William I, 592
Bowman, William I, 748
Bowman, William I, 800
Bowman, William I, 819
Bowman, William I, 911
Bowman, William F. IV, 1354
Bowman, William J. I, 592
Bowman, William, Jr. I, 586
Bowman, William, Jr. I, 587
Bowman, Wm. F. IV, 1088
Bowman, Wm. T. IV, 1088
Bown, Abraham II, 980
Bown, John II, 978
Bown, John II, 980
Bown, Philip II, 167
Bown, Samuel II, 978
Bown, Samuel II, 980
Bown, Thomasine II, 167
Bown, Wd. Mary II, 980
Bowne, ??? III, 40
Bowne, ??? III, 43
Bowne, ??? III, 261
Bowne, Abigail II, 167
Bowne, Abigail II, 199
Bowne, Abigail II, 262
Bowne, Abigail II, 470
Bowne, Abigail II, 529
Bowne, Abigail III, 39
Bowne, Abigail III, 40
Bowne, Abigail III, 41
Bowne, Abigail III, 42
Bowne, Abigail III, 43
Bowne, Abigail III, 54
Bowne, Abigail III, 72
Bowne, Abigail III, 110
Bowne, Abigail III, 145
Bowne, Abigail III, 191
Bowne, Abigail III, 360
Bowne, Abigail III, 377
Bowne, Abigail III, 396
Bowne, Abigail III, 436
Bowne, Abigail III, 470
Bowne, Abigail VI, 473
Bowne, Abigail VI, 550
Bowne, Agnes III, 377
Bowne, Alexander Murray III, 43
Bowne, Alfred II, 312
Bowne, Alice III, 200
Bowne, Amelia III, 42
Bowne, Amelia C. III, 43
Bowne, Amy III, 40
Bowne, Amy III, 41
Bowne, Amy III, 42
Bowne, Amy III, 146
Bowne, Amy III, 201
Bowne, Amy III, 272
Bowne, Ann III, 40
Bowne, Ann III, 41
Bowne, Ann III, 42
Bowne, Ann III, 118
Bowne, Ann III, 264
Bowne, Ann Augusta III, 16
Bowne, Ann Augusta III, 40
Bowne, Ann Augusta III, 42
Bowne, Anna III, 41
Bowne, Anna III, 199
Bowne, Anne III, 41
Bowne, Anne III, 377
Bowne, Anne III, 383
Bowne, Annie Laura VI, 662
Bowne, Benjamin III, 40
Bowne, Benjamin III, 42
Bowne, Benjamin III, 43
Bowne, Benjamin III, 377
Bowne, Benjamin III, 378
Bowne, Caleb III, 200
Bowne, Caleb L. III, 200
Bowne, Caroline III, 40
Bowne, Caroline III, 192
Bowne, Caroline III, 238
Bowne, Caroline III, 273
Bowne, Caroline III, 321
Bowne, Caroline III, 377
Bowne, Catharine III, 40
Bowne, Catharine III, 41
Bowne, Catharine III, 238
Bowne, Catharine III, 377
Bowne, Catharine III, 396
Bowne, Catharine S. III, 377
Bowne, Catherine III, 389
Bowne, Charles W. III, 200

Bowne, Child III, 42
Bowne, Cornell III, 378
Bowne, Cornell III, 389
Bowne, Cow Neck III, 42
Bowne, Daniel III, 40
Bowne, Daniel III, 127
Bowne, Daniel III, 303
Bowne, Daniel III, 396
Bowne, Deborah III, 40
Bowne, Deborah III, 43
Bowne, Deborah III, 378
Bowne, Dinah III, 41
Bowne, Dinah III, 118
Bowne, Dinah III, 250
Bowne, Dinah III, 396
Bowne, Dinah III, 459
Bowne, Dorothy III, 40
Bowne, Dorothy III, 41
Bowne, Dorothy III, 43
Bowne, Dorothy III, 126
Bowne, Duanes III, 40
Bowne, Edward III, 40
Bowne, Edward Hicks III, 377
Bowne, Edward S. III, 40
Bowne, Edward S. III, 59
Bowne, Edward S. III, 396
Bowne, Edward S. III, 398
Bowne, Effingham III, 199
Bowne, Eleonor III, 171
Bowne, Eliz. III, 40
Bowne, Eliz. III, 42
Bowne, Eliz. F. III, 353
Bowne, Eliza III, 40
Bowne, Eliza III, 41
Bowne, Eliza III, 43
Bowne, Eliza III, 325
Bowne, Eliza III, 377
Bowne, Eliza III, 378
Bowne, Eliza III, 380
Bowne, Eliza III, 386
Bowne, Eliza VI, 662
Bowne, Eliza VI, 701
Bowne, Eliza VI, 753
Bowne, Eliza VI, 779
Bowne, Eliza B. III, 331
Bowne, Eliza F. III, 377
Bowne, Eliza F. III, 387
Bowne, Eliza H. III, 40
Bowne, Eliza H. III, 43
Bowne, Eliza H. III, 237
Bowne, Eliza P. III, 42
Bowne, Eliza. III, 42
Bowne, Eliza. III, 208
Bowne, Elizabeth III, 40
Bowne, Elizabeth III, 41
Bowne, Elizabeth III, 42
Bowne, Elizabeth III, 43
Bowne, Elizabeth III, 60
Bowne, Elizabeth III, 80
Bowne, Elizabeth III, 102
Bowne, Elizabeth III, 145
Bowne, Elizabeth III, 171
Bowne, Elizabeth III, 179
Bowne, Elizabeth III, 199
Bowne, Elizabeth III, 254
Bowne, Elizabeth III, 260
Bowne, Elizabeth III, 321
Bowne, Elizabeth III, 353
Bowne, Elizabeth III, 377
Bowne, Elizabeth III, 378
Bowne, Elizabeth III, 396
Bowne, Elizabeth III, 410
Bowne, Elizabeth III, 438
Bowne, Elizabeth III, 455
Bowne, Elizabeth VI, 473
Bowne, Elizabeth VI, 550
Bowne, Elizabeth F. III, 40
Bowne, Elizabeth F. III, 353
Bowne, Elizabeth F. III, 396
Bowne, Elizabeth F. III, 467
Bowne, Elizabeth H. III, 40
Bowne, Elizabeth H. III, 41
Bowne, Elizabeth H. III, 340
Bowne, Elizabeth L. III, 42
Bowne, Elizabeth S. II, 316
Bowne, Elizabeth S. II, 320
Bowne, Elizabeth T. III, 199
Bowne, Elizabeth T. III, 387
Bowne, Elizabeth W. III, 199
Bowne, Ellen III, 200
Bowne, Emily III, 16
Bowne, Emily L. III, 40
Bowne, Emily L. III, 42
Bowne, Emily L. III, 43
Bowne, Emily L. III, 74
Bowne, Emy III, 42
Bowne, Esther II, 199
Bowne, Esther III, 42
Bowne, Esther III, 272
Bowne, George II, 167
Bowne, George II, 199
Bowne, George II, 262
Bowne, George II, 470
Bowne, George III, 42
Bowne, George F. III, 40
Bowne, George F. III, 377
Bowne, Gulielma III, 40
Bowne, Gulielma III, 42
Bowne, Hannah III, 33
Bowne, Hannah III, 39
Bowne, Hannah III, 40
Bowne, Hannah III, 41
Bowne, Hannah III, 42
Bowne, Hannah III, 43
Bowne, Hannah III, 56
Bowne, Hannah III, 74
Bowne, Hannah III, 80
Bowne, Hannah III, 116
Bowne, Hannah III, 118
Bowne, Hannah III, 145
Bowne, Hannah III, 199
Bowne, Hannah III, 200
Bowne, Hannah III, 250
Bowne, Hannah III, 254
Bowne, Hannah III, 260
Bowne, Hannah III, 293
Bowne, Hannah III, 319
Bowne, Hannah III, 328
Bowne, Hannah III, 377
Bowne, Hannah III, 386
Bowne, Hannah III, 396
Bowne, Hannah III, 397
Bowne, Hannah III, 410
Bowne, Hannah III, 436
Bowne, Hannah III, 438
Bowne, Hannah III, 455
Bowne, Hannah III, 470
Bowne, Hannah III, 474
Bowne, Hannah H. III, 378
Bowne, Hannah S. III, 40
Bowne, Hannah S. III, 42
Bowne, Harold Herbert III, 396
Bowne, Haydock III, 288
Bowne, Helen III, 396
Bowne, Helen Isabel III, 396
Bowne, Helen Isabel III, 416
Bowne, Herbert S. III, 396
Bowne, Herbert S. III, 416
Bowne, Hugh H. III, 42
Bowne, Isaac III, 40
Bowne, Isaac W. III, 377
Bowne, Isaac W. III, 389
Bowne, Isaac Willett III, 43
Bowne, Isaac Willett III, 378
Bowne, Jacob III, 32
Bowne, Jacob III, 40
Bowne, Jacob III, 43
Bowne, Jacob III, 396
Bowne, Jacob III, 397
Bowne, Jacob III, 449
Bowne, Jacob III, 474
Bowne, James II, 199
Bowne, James II, 339
Bowne, James II, 470
Bowne, James II, 529
Bowne, James III, 43
Bowne, James III, 192
Bowne, James III, 238
Bowne, James III, 273
Bowne, James III, 321
Bowne, James III, 377
Bowne, Jane III, 40
Bowne, Jane III, 41
Bowne, Jane III, 145
Bowne, Jane III, 237
Bowne, Jane P. III, 42
Bowne, Janet Isabel III, 396
Bowne, Jas. III, 40
Bowne, Jemima III, 41
Bowne, Jemima III, 311
Bowne, Jemima III, 396
Bowne, Jemima III, 467
Bowne, Jemima H. III, 40
Bowne, Jemima H. III, 43
Bowne, Jemima H. III, 340
Bowne, Johanna, Sr. III, 396
Bowne, John II, 504
Bowne, John II, 583
Bowne, John III, 33
Bowne, John III, 39
Bowne, John III, 40
Bowne, John III, 41
Bowne, John III, 42
Bowne, John III, 43
Bowne, John III, 72
Bowne, John III, 75
Bowne, John III, 118
Bowne, John III, 126
Bowne, John III, 146
Bowne, John III, 199
Bowne, John III, 250
Bowne, John III, 254
Bowne, John III, 260
Bowne, John III, 313
Bowne, John III, 360
Bowne, John III, 375
Bowne, John III, 377
Bowne, John III, 383
Bowne, John III, 396
Bowne, John III, 410
Bowne, John III, 436
Bowne, John III, 438
Bowne, John III, 455
Bowne, John III, 459
Bowne, John III, 470
Bowne, John L. III, 41
Bowne, John L. III, 42
Bowne, John L. III, 43
Bowne, John L. III, 237
Bowne, John P. III, 377
Bowne, John R. III, 40
Bowne, John R. III, 41
Bowne, John S. III, 42
Bowne, John Willet III, 378
Bowne, John Willett III, 43
Bowne, Jonathan Morrell III, 273
Bowne, Jordan III, 388
Bowne, Joseph II, 199
Bowne, Joseph II, 470
Bowne, Joseph III, 41
Bowne, Joseph III, 201
Bowne, Joseph III, 234
Bowne, Joshua III, 40
Bowne, Josiah III, 40
Bowne, Josiah III, 41
Bowne, Josiah III, 189
Bowne, Josiah VI, 473
Bowne, Josiah Q. III, 43
Bowne, Judith III, 41
Bowne, Judith III, 234
Bowne, Judith III, 273
Bowne, Lindley III, 43
Bowne, Lindley M. III, 41
Bowne, Lindley M. III, 377
Bowne, M. III, 43
Bowne, Mable J. II, 312
Bowne, Margaret III, 41
Bowne, Margaret III, 42
Bowne, Margaret III, 159
Bowne, Margaret III, 198
Bowne, Margaret III, 359
Bowne, Margaret III, 396
Bowne, Maria III, 41
Bowne, Maria B. III, 43
Bowne, Mariah F. III, 377
Bowne, Martha III, 396
Bowne, Martha III, 397
Bowne, Martha III, 480
Bowne, Martha III, 506
Bowne, Martha J. III, 450
Bowne, Martha Johanna III, 41
Bowne, Martha Johanna III, 313
Bowne, Martha V. III, 480
Bowne, Martha V. III, 506
Bowne, Martha W. III, 396
Bowne, Mary II, 470
Bowne, Mary II, 529
Bowne, Mary III, 30
Bowne, Mary III, 40
Bowne, Mary III, 41
Bowne, Mary III, 42
Bowne, Mary III, 43
Bowne, Mary III, 74
Bowne, Mary III, 75
Bowne, Mary III, 115
Bowne, Mary III, 127
Bowne, Mary III, 146
Bowne, Mary III, 159
Bowne, Mary III, 171
Bowne, Mary III, 189
Bowne, Mary III, 200
Bowne, Mary III, 250
Bowne, Mary III, 269
Bowne, Mary III, 272
Bowne, Mary III, 313
Bowne, Mary III, 377
Bowne, Mary III, 378
Bowne, Mary III, 383
Bowne, Mary III, 388
Bowne, Mary III, 396
Bowne, Mary III, 397
Bowne, Mary III, 400
Bowne, Mary III, 456
Bowne, Mary A. III, 41
Bowne, Mary A. III, 42
Bowne, Mary A. III, 43
Bowne, Mary A. III, 72
Bowne, Mary Ann III, 200
Bowne, Mary Anna III, 40
Bowne, Mary M. III, 480
Bowne, Mary R. III, 40
Bowne, Mary R. III, 192
Bowne, Mathew VI, 473
Bowne, Matilda III, 41
Bowne, Matilda III, 42
Bowne, Matthew III, 41
Bowne, Matthew III, 42
Bowne, Matthew VI, 473
Bowne, Matthew VI, 550
Bowne, Matthew Franklin VI, 473
Bowne, Matthew Franklin VI, 523
Bowne, Mk. John III, 116
Bowne, Moses III, 40
Bowne, Myrtle II, 312
Bowne, Naomi III, 40
Bowne, Naomi III, 42
Bowne, Naomi III, 129
Bowne, Naomi III, 199
Bowne, Nathan III, 43
Bowne, Penelope III, 40
Bowne, Penelope III, 41
Bowne, Penelope III, 42
Bowne, Penelope III, 43
Bowne, Penelope III, 208
Bowne, Penelope III, 264
Bowne, Penelope III, 266
Bowne, Penelope III, 456
Bowne, Philip II, 199
Bowne, Philip III, 43
Bowne, Philip III, 377
Bowne, Philip III, 378
Bowne, Philip III, 380
Bowne, Philip, Jr. III, 377
Bowne, Phillip III, 387
Bowne, Rahway III, 42
Bowne, Rebecca III, 388
Bowne, Rich. D. III, 16
Bowne, Rich. M. III, 396
Bowne, Richard II, 199
Bowne, Richard II, 470
Bowne, Richard III, 40
Bowne, Richard III, 41
Bowne, Richard III, 42
Bowne, Richard III, 46
Bowne, Richard III, 208
Bowne, Richard III, 264
Bowne, Richard VI, 473
Bowne, Richard H. III, 40
Bowne, Richard H. III, 42
Bowne, Richard H. III, 43
Bowne, Richard H. III, 74
Bowne, Richard L. III, 200
Bowne, Richard M. III, 41
Bowne, Richard M. III, 43
Bowne, Richard M. III, 396
Bowne, Richard M. III, 480
Bowne, Richard R. III, 200
Bowne, Robert II, 199
Bowne, Robert II, 262
Bowne, Robert II, 470
Bowne, Robert III, 41
Bowne, Robert III, 42
Bowne, Robert III, 80
Bowne, Robert III, 145
Bowne, Robert III, 159
Bowne, Robert III, 198
Bowne, Robert III, 200
Bowne, Robert III, 396
Bowne, Robert VI, 473
Bowne, Robert H. III, 41
Bowne, Robert H. III, 42
Bowne, Robert H. III, 43
Bowne, Robert L. III, 40
Bowne, Robert L. III, 42
Bowne, Robert M. III, 42
Bowne, Robert Martin III, 41
Bowne, Robert Martin VI, 473
Bowne, Robert S. III, 42
Bowne, Robert W. III, 200
Bowne, Robt. III, 42
Bowne, Robt. L. III, 40
Bowne, Robt. L. III, 199
Bowne, Robt. L. III, 272
Bowne, Rowland R. III, 42
Bowne, Ruth III, 41
Bowne, Samuel II, 199
Bowne, Samuel II, 470
Bowne, Samuel II, 529
Bowne, Samuel III, 30
Bowne, Samuel III, 39
Bowne, Samuel III, 40
Bowne, Samuel III, 41
Bowne, Samuel III, 42
Bowne, Samuel III, 43
Bowne, Samuel III, 54
Bowne, Samuel III, 56
Bowne, Samuel III, 89
Bowne, Samuel III, 102
Bowne, Samuel III, 115
Bowne, Samuel III, 126
Bowne, Samuel III, 145
Bowne, Samuel III, 171
Bowne, Samuel III, 191
Bowne, Samuel III, 200
Bowne, Samuel III, 250
Bowne, Samuel III, 293
Bowne, Samuel III, 319
Bowne, Samuel III, 377
Bowne, Samuel III, 386
Bowne, Samuel III, 397
Bowne, Samuel III, 456
Bowne, Samuel VI, 473
Bowne, Samuel VI, 550
Bowne, Samuel Smith II, 199
Bowne, Samuel, Jr. III, 42
Bowne, Sarah II, 199
Bowne, Sarah II, 217
Bowne, Sarah III, 40
Bowne, Sarah III, 41
Bowne, Sarah III, 42
Bowne, Sarah III, 43
Bowne, Sarah III, 56
Bowne, Sarah III, 122
Bowne, Sarah III, 200
Bowne, Sarah III, 201
Bowne, Sarah III, 231
Bowne, Sarah III, 303
Bowne, Sarah III, 319
Bowne, Sarah III, 377
Bowne, Sarah III, 378
Bowne, Sarah III, 396
Bowne, Sarah III, 398
Bowne, Sarah III, 456
Bowne, Sarah E. III, 42
Bowne, Sarah H. III, 40
Bowne, Sarah H. III, 41
Bowne, Sarah H. III, 59
Bowne, Sarah W. III, 43
Bowne, Sarah, Jr. III, 42
Bowne, Sarah, Jr. III, 126
Bowne, Scott III, 43
Bowne, Scott III, 261
Bowne, Scott III, 378
Bowne, Scott H. III, 43
Bowne, Scott H. III, 377
Bowne, Sidney III, 41
Bowne, Sidney III, 43
Bowne, Sidney III, 93
Bowne, Sidney VI, 473
Bowne, Sidney B. III, 40
Bowne, Sidney B. III, 41
Bowne, Sidney B. III, 43
Bowne, Sidney B. III, 340
Bowne, Sidney B. III, 396
Bowne, Sidney B. III, 467
Bowne, Sidney B. III, 480
Bowne, Sidney B. III, 506
Bowne, Sidney F. III, 43
Bowne, Sidney R. III, 40
Bowne, Sidney R. III, 43
Bowne, Stephen III, 378
Bowne, Stephen C. III, 377
Bowne, Susan II, 316
Bowne, Susanna II, 199
Bowne, Susanna II, 308
Bowne, Susannah II, 281
Bowne, Susannah Smith III, 40
Bowne, Thomas II, 199
Bowne, Thomas II, 282
Bowne, Thomas II, 308
Bowne, Thomas III, 40
Bowne, Thomas III, 41
Bowne, Thomas III, 42
Bowne, Thomas III, 43
Bowne, Thomas III, 74
Bowne, Thomas III, 171
Bowne, Thomas III, 328
Bowne, Thomas III, 397
Bowne, Thomas III, 456
Bowne, Thomas B. III, 43
Bowne, Thomas C. III, 42
Bowne, Thomas C. III, 43
Bowne, Thomas P. III, 43
Bowne, Thomas P. III, 377
Bowne, Thomas Pearsall III, 43
Bowne, Thomazin II, 199
Bowne, Thos. III, 41
Bowne, Walter III, 43
Bowne, Walter III, 321
Bowne, Wd. Elizabeth III, 40
Bowne, Wd. Elizabeth III, 189
Bowne, Wd. Grace II, 1043
Bowne, Wd. Grace III, 42
Bowne, Wd. Grace III, 89
Bowne, Wd. Hannah III, 456
Bowne, Wd. Judith III, 273
Bowne, Widow Elizabeth VI, 523
Bowne, Willet III, 377
Bowne, Willet III, 378
Bowne, Willett III, 43
Bowne, Willett III, 272
Bowne, William III, 41
Bowne, William III, 42

Bowne, William III, 43
Bowne, William III, 189
Bowne, William III, 269
Bowne, William III, 353
Bowne, William III, 377
Bowne, William III, 378
Bowne, William VI, 473
Bowne, William H. III, 41
Bowne, William H. III, 42
Bowne, William H. III, 43
Bowne, William H. III, 72
Bowne, William L. III, 200
Bowne, William N. III, 43
Bowne, William T. III, 43
Bowne, William W. III, 377
Bowne, William W. III, 378
Bowne, Winfield G. III, 171
Bowne, Wm. III, 40
Bowne, Wm. III, 377
Bowne, Wm. W. III, 377
Bowner, ??? III, 17
Bownie, Grace II, 339
Bowns, Esther II, 199
Bowren, Frances II, 282
Bowren, Nancy I, 592
Bowron, ??? III, 119
Bowron, Agnes III, 43
Bowron, Agnes III, 262
Bowron, Alice III, 43
Bowron, Alice III, 262
Bowron, Almira III, 44
Bowron, Ann Elizabeth III, 43
Bowron, Ann Elizabeth III, 44
Bowron, Anna M. III, 44
Bowron, Anna Maria III, 44
Bowron, Anna Maria III, 167
Bowron, Deborah III, 44
Bowron, Deborah III, 76
Bowron, Deborah C. III, 43
Bowron, Dr. John S. III, 44
Bowron, Dr. John S. III, 195
Bowron, Eliza III, 44
Bowron, Elizabeth M. III, 43
Bowron, Elizabeth M. III, 44
Bowron, Freelove G. III, 43
Bowron, George W. III, 44
Bowron, Hannah III, 43
Bowron, Hannah III, 44
Bowron, Hannah C. III, 43
Bowron, Hannah C. III, 44
Bowron, Henry C. III, 43
Bowron, Henry C. III, 44
Bowron, Henry C. III, 76
Bowron, Henry S. III, 43
Bowron, Henry S. III, 44
Bowron, Jacob III, 44
Bowron, Job B. III, 44
Bowron, John III, 44
Bowron, John S. III, 120
Bowron, John S. III, 121
Bowron, Joshua III, 43
Bowron, Joshua III, 262
Bowron, Joshua W. III, 44
Bowron, Joshua W. III, 167
Bowron, Josiah III, 44
Bowron, Josiah F. III, 44
Bowron, Maria Amelia III, 44
Bowron, Maria Amelia III, 195
Bowron, Maria Amelia III, 320
Bowron, Maria M. III, 44
Bowron, Maria M. III, 119
Bowron, Mary III, 44
Bowron, Mary A. III, 121
Bowron, Mary Augusta III, 44
Bowron, Mary M. III, 43
Bowron, Mary M. III, 44
Bowron, Mary S. III, 44
Bowron, Sarah III, 44
Bowron, Sarah III, 76
Bowron, Sarah III, 121
Bowron, Sarah III, 195
Bowron, Sarah B. III, 44
Bowron, Sarah S. III, 44
Bowron, Sarah S. III, 120
Bowron, Thomas C. III, 44
Bowron, Thomas Tom III, 44
Bowron, Watson III, 44
Bowron, Watson A. III, 43
Bowron, Watson A. III, 44
Bowron, Watson B. III, 44
Bowron, William III, 44
Bowron, William Henry H. III, 44
Bowron, William L. III, 44
Bowron, Wm. III, 44
Bowron, Wm. L. III, 43
Bowron, Wm. L. III, 44
Bowron, Wm. Moss II, 729
Bowser, Della V, 551
Bowser, DeWitt V, 551
Bowser, Elijah V, 551
Bowser, Frank V, 154
Bowyer, Adam VI, 882
Bowyer, Adam VI, 983
Bowyer, Adam VI, 1019
Bowyer, Drusilla V. VI, 879
Bowyer, Elisabeth II, 470
Bowyer, Elizabeth VI, 882
Bowyer, Elizabeth A. VI, 882
Bowyer, Elizabeth Ann VI, 983
Bowyer, Elizabeth M. VI, 882
Bowyer, Herbert Mead IV, 1308
Bowyer, Isaac VI, 882
Bowyer, John II, 470
Bowyer, John II, 677
Bowyer, John H. VI, 1014
Bowyer, John M. VI, 882
Bowyer, Joseph VI, 882
Bowyer, Joseph VI, 932
Bowyer, Laura IV, 1308
Bowyer, Maggie V, 660
Bowyer, Maggie V, 828
Bowyer, Margaret V, 613
Bowyer, Margaret V, 660
Bowyer, Margaret V, 828
Bowyer, Martha II, 470
Bowyer, Mary VI, 982
Bowyer, Mary, Sr. VI, 982
Bowyer, Michael VI, 909
Bowyer, Nancy VI, 882
Bowyer, Polly VI, 963
Bowyer, Polly VI, 1019
Bowyer, Rebekah II, 470
Bowyer, Ruth II, 470
Bowyer, Sarah II, 339
Bowyer, Sarah II, 470
Bowyer, Sarah II, 473
Bowyer, Sarah II, 677
Bowyer, Thomas B. VI, 882
Bowyers, Elisabeth II, 455
Bowyers, Elisabeth II, 470
Bowyers, Elisabeth Ashton II, 686
Bowyers, Martha II, 470
Bowyers, Mary VI, 912
Bowyers, Nettie IV, 1308
Box, Josiah II, 980
Box, Thomas II, 980
Boxley, Lucy VI, 231
Boyce, ??? II, 339
Boyce, Alethea I, 207
Boyce, Angie Dora I, 231
Boyce, Ann II, 470
Boyce, Ann II, 512
Boyce, Anna IV, 1354
Boyce, Benjamin IV, 1354
Boyce, Bertha Louisa I, 231
Boyce, Bertha N. I, 207
Boyce, Beulah II, 700
Boyce, Beulah II, 729
Boyce, Catharine IV, 1354
Boyce, Christian V, 797
Boyce, Deborah IV, 612
Boyce, Deborah IV, 863
Boyce, Deborah IV, 864
Boyce, Dora A. I, 207
Boyce, Dora Angie I, 207
Boyce, Elisabeth IV, 612
Boyce, Elizabeth IV, 607
Boyce, Elizabeth IV, 612
Boyce, Ester F. I, 207
Boyce, Harvey J. I, 207
Boyce, Henry IV, 1354
Boyce, Isaac IV, 612
Boyce, James II, 339
Boyce, James II, 470
Boyce, James II, 512
Boyce, Jane II, 339
Boyce, Jane II, 470
Boyce, Jane II, 700
Boyce, Jane IV, 612
Boyce, Jemima I, 38
Boyce, Jesse W. I, 207
Boyce, Jesse William I, 207
Boyce, John I, 37
Boyce, John I, 38
Boyce, John I, 86
Boyce, John II, 339
Boyce, John IV, 612
Boyce, John W. I, 207
Boyce, John W. I, 211
Boyce, John W. I, 231
Boyce, John William I, 207
Boyce, John, Jr. I, 38
Boyce, John, Sr. I, 38
Boyce, Joseph I, 38
Boyce, Joshua IV, 612
Boyce, Joshua IV, 864
Boyce, Knowles IV, 1354
Boyce, Lulie V, 797
Boyce, M. Lula I, 207
Boyce, Margaret II, 700
Boyce, Martha Lula I, 207
Boyce, Mary II, 339
Boyce, Mary II, 470
Boyce, Mary IV, 612
Boyce, Mary E. I, 207
Boyce, Mary Edna I, 211
Boyce, Minerva I, 38
Boyce, Minerva I, 49
Boyce, Moses I, 37
Boyce, Mosses I, 38
Boyce, Nancy I, 207
Boyce, Nannie I, 207
Boyce, Rachel I, 38
Boyce, Rachel I, 86
Boyce, Richard II, 339
Boyce, Richard IV, 612
Boyce, Richard D. II, 700
Boyce, Robert IV, 612
Boyce, Robert IV, 864
Boyce, Ruth I, 38
Boyce, Ruth I, 86
Boyce, Sallie Jane I, 231
Boyce, Samuel II, 339
Boyce, Sarah II, 470
Boyce, Sarah II, 512
Boyce, Sarah II, 700
Boyce, Sarah IV, 612
Boyce, Sarah Jane I, 207
Boyce, Smyrna IV, 1354
Boyce, Susan IV, 1354
Boyce, Susannah IV, 612
Boyce, Susannah IV, 651
Boyce, Timothy IV, 612
Boyce, Wilbur V, 797
Boyce, Wilbur L. V, 797
Boyce, William I, 207
Boyce, William II, 339
Boyce, Wm. II, 470
Boyce, Wm. II, 512
Boyd, ??? VI, 882
Boyd, A. C. V, 987
Boyd, Adam V, 797
Boyd, Agness VI, 971
Boyd, Andrew L. VI, 882
Boyd, Ann I, 872
Boyd, Ann I, 889
Boyd, Ann V, 728
Boyd, Ann V, 797
Boyd, Ann VI, 882
Boyd, Anna V, 797
Boyd, Benj. F. III, 397
Boyd, Benj. F. III, 408
Boyd, Catharine VI, 800
Boyd, Charles VI, 882
Boyd, Christiana III, 44
Boyd, Cora V, 987
Boyd, Daniel III, 44
Boyd, Daniel VI, 473
Boyd, Elizabeth III, 44
Boyd, Elizabeth III, 397
Boyd, Elizabeth III, 408
Boyd, Elizabeth IV, 321
Boyd, Elizabeth IV, 348
Boyd, Elizabeth V, 320
Boyd, Elizabeth V, 797
Boyd, Elizabeth VI, 953
Boyd, Elizabeth VI, 961
Boyd, Gaylord V, 987
Boyd, Hannah II, 468
Boyd, Hannah II, 470
Boyd, Hannah VI, 882
Boyd, Harold V, 987
Boyd, Harold J. V, 987
Boyd, Helen II, 167
Boyd, Helen II, 282
Boyd, Helen V, 987
Boyd, Hunter VI, 392
Boyd, Isaac III, 44
Boyd, James III, 44
Boyd, James VI, 879
Boyd, James VI, 882
Boyd, James VI, 953
Boyd, James VI, 991
Boyd, Jane IV, 22
Boyd, Jane IV, 67
Boyd, Jane VI, 882
Boyd, Jean VI, 879
Boyd, John VI, 800
Boyd, John A. IV, 1308
Boyd, John T. V, 375
Boyd, John T. V, 551
Boyd, Jonathan D. V, 797
Boyd, Jonathan D. V, 821
Boyd, Josephus III, 44
Boyd, Lester V, 987
Boyd, Lois E. V, 987
Boyd, Lucy VI, 963
Boyd, Lucy M. VI, 800
Boyd, Mahala VI, 882
Boyd, Margaret II, 282
Boyd, Margaret VI, 982
Boyd, Martha IV, 371
Boyd, Martha IV, 378
Boyd, Martha VI, 975
Boyd, Mary I, 872
Boyd, Mary IV, 371
Boyd, Mary IV, 417
Boyd, Mary Ann II, 729
Boyd, Mary Ann II, 736
Boyd, Mary B. V, 797
Boyd, Mary B. V, 821
Boyd, Mary Ruth V, 660
Boyd, Milley VI, 953
Boyd, Mrs. Ann E. VI, 882
Boyd, Nancy VI, 882
Boyd, Nellie V, 987
Boyd, Nettie IV, 686
Boyd, Opal W. V, 660
Boyd, Oscar V, 660
Boyd, Paul Fisher V, 660
Boyd, Peter III, 44
Boyd, Phebe III, 397
Boyd, Phebe III, 408
Boyd, Philip VI, 988
Boyd, Rachel I, 674
Boyd, Rachel I, 872
Boyd, Rachel I, 905
Boyd, Robert I, 872
Boyd, Robert R. V, 987
Boyd, Ruth IV, 76
Boyd, Ruth IV, 122
Boyd, Ruth IV, 129
Boyd, Ruth M. IV, 122
Boyd, Ruth M. IV, 683
Boyd, Sarah IV, 76
Boyd, Sarah IV, 122
Boyd, Sarah IV, 612
Boyd, Sarah IV, 636
Boyd, Sarah Esther III, 44
Boyd, Susan II, 167
Boyd, Susan II, 282
Boyd, Susan III, 44
Boyd, Susan VI, 627
Boyd, Susan VI, 686
Boyd, Susan VI, 769
Boyd, Susanna II, 1045
Boyd, Susanna II, 1064
Boyd, Susanna VI, 882
Boyd, Susannah V, 375
Boyd, Susannah V, 421
Boyd, Walter E. V, 987
Boyd, Wd. Martha VI, 882
Boyd, Widow Ann I, 872
Boyd, Wilhelmina IV, 683
Boyd, William VI, 368
Boyd, William VI, 882
Boyd, William VI, 953
Boyd, William VI, 955
Boyd, William VI, 961
Boyd, William VI, 971
Boyd, Wm. VI, 975
Boyde, Ann V, 728
Boyden, Daniel II, 339
Boyden, James II, 199
Boyden, James II, 254
Boyden, James II, 339
Boyden, James II, 470
Boyden, James II, 629
Boyden, Mary II, 470
Boyden, Mary II, 629
Boyden, Mary II, 651
Boyden, Merriam II, 339
Boyden, Miriam II, 199
Boyden, Miriam II, 254
Boyed, Wilhelmina IV, 683
Boyed, Wilhelmina IV, 737
Boyer, Adam VI, 815
Boyer, Adam VI, 882
Boyer, Adam VI, 942
Boyer, Adex V, 987
Boyer, Alexander V, 987
Boyer, Alice M. II, 1045
Boyer, Alice M. II, 1059
Boyer, Ann M. VI, 964
Boyer, Ann W. VI, 932
Boyer, Auther II, 56
Boyer, Clyde Edward II, 1045
Boyer, Clyde Edward II, 1059
Boyer, Dora O. V, 728
Boyer, Elizabeth II, 455
Boyer, Elizabeth VI, 882
Boyer, Emily II, 840
Boyer, Emily II, 858
Boyer, Hannah II, 56
Boyer, Hannah II, 99
Boyer, Harvey C. V, 728
Boyer, Herbert Mead IV, 1308
Boyer, Isaac VI, 882
Boyer, Jacob V, 26
Boyer, Jacob V, 987
Boyer, Jane III, 44
Boyer, Jerome L. II, 840
Boyer, Jerome L. II, 858
Boyer, Jesse V, 987
Boyer, Jessie V, 987
Boyer, John II, 441
Boyer, John M. VI, 882
Boyer, Joseph V, 828
Boyer, Joseph VI, 882
Boyer, Joseph VI, 1011
Boyer, Laura IV, 1308
Boyer, Louisa V, 987
Boyer, Lydia V, 987
Boyer, Margaret V, 828
Boyer, Mary V, 987
Boyer, Mary Elizabeth II, 1045
Boyer, Mary Elizabeth II, 1059
Boyer, Michael VI, 882
Boyer, Michael VI, 942
Boyer, Nancy VI, 815
Boyer, Nancy VI, 882
Boyer, Nettie IV, 1308
Boyer, Nettie M. IV, 1308
Boyer, Patsey VI, 882
Boyer, Paulina Ann VI, 964
Boyer, Phebe V, 987
Boyer, Phoeba V, 987
Boyer, Ralph R. II, 1045
Boyer, Ralph R. II, 1059
Boyer, Rebekah II, 470
Boyer, Rebekah II, 678
Boyer, Rhoda VI, 942
Boyer, Ruth II, 468
Boyer, Ruth II, 470
Boyer, Samuel V, 987
Boyer, Sarah II, 56
Boyer, Sarah II, 70
Boyer, Sarah II, 441
Boyer, Sarah II, 470
Boyer, Susan E. II, 840
Boyer, Susan E. II, 858
Boyer, William II, 441
Boyer, Wm. McHose II, 840
Boyer, Wm. McHose II, 858
Boyers, Minnie V, 660
Boyes, Adam J. VI, 908
Boyes, Archibald Michael II, 470
Boyes, John II, 470
Boyes, John II, 672
Boyes, Mary II, 470
Boyes, Mary II, 672
Boyes, Richard II, 470
Boyes, Robert VI, 148
Boyes, Robert VI, 161
Boykin, Colonel Francis M. VI, 48
Boykin, Colonel Francis M. VI, 54
Boykin, Frances VI, 79
Boyle, Alexander VI, 882
Boyle, Alexander VI, 982
Boyle, Betsy VI, 882
Boyle, Charity IV, 928
Boyle, Charity IV, 967
Boyle, Charity E. IV, 928
Boyle, David VI, 882
Boyle, Elizabeth II, 339
Boyle, Elizabeth IV, 928
Boyle, Elnora IV, 928
Boyle, Elnora G. VI, 882
Boyle, Hannah II, 470
Boyle, Hannah II, 561
Boyle, Irene T. IV, 928
Boyle, Irma IV, 928
Boyle, James II, 339
Boyle, James A. VI, 882
Boyle, James T. IV, 928
Boyle, Jamima VI, 925
Boyle, Jeremiah H. VI, 800
Boyle, John II, 339
Boyle, John VI, 882
Boyle, John VI, 925
Boyle, John VI, 945
Boyle, Joseph VI, 882
Boyle, L. Homer IV, 928
Boyle, Lenora S. IV, 928
Boyle, Lester IV, 928
Boyle, Lewis II, 339
Boyle, Lewis Homer IV, 928
Boyle, Liza VI, 882
Boyle, Martha A. VI, 800
Boyle, Martha Ann VI, 882
Boyle, Mary II, 339
Boyle, Mary J. IV, 928
Boyle, Merritt Alfred III, 44
Boyle, Merritt Alfred III, 171
Boyle, Myrtle IV, 928
Boyle, Myrtle Naomi IV, 928
Boyle, Olive IV, 928
Boyle, Otley IV, 928
Boyle, Otley V. IV, 928
Boyle, Peter II, 339
Boyle, Rachal VI, 882
Boyle, Rebecca III, 44

Boyle, Rebecca III, 171
Boyle, Robert VI, 882
Boyle, Robert VI, 911
Boyle, Robert R. IV, 928
Boyle, Sally VI, 925
Boyle, Sarah II, 339
Boyle, Sarah III, 44
Boyle, Sarah E. IV, 179
Boyle, Sarah E. VI, 882
Boyle, Stephen S. III, 44
Boyle, Thomas VI, 882
Boyle, Wellington H. II, 729
Boyle, William II, 339
Boyle, Wm. IV, 928
Boyles, Alexander VI, 882
Boyles, Alexr. VI, 1022
Boyles, Anne VI, 1022
Boyles, Bell V, 452
Boyles, David VI, 882
Boyles, J. Van I, 938
Boyles, Jane VI, 368
Boyles, Jane VI, 403
Boyles, L. Homer IV, 928
Boyles, Lester IV, 928
Boyles, Myrtle I, 938
Boyles, Rachal VI, 882
Boyles, Thomas II, 339
Boyls, James H. I, 328
Boynden, James II, 256
Boynden, Miriam II, 256
Boys, Joshua IV, 864
Boys, Richard IV, 612
Boys, Timothy IV, 612
Boyse, Mary II, 339
Boyse, Samuel II, 339
Boyseau, Sarah VI, 91
Bozwell, Barney VI, 1014
Bozwell, Fanny VI, 1014
Bozwell, Geo. VI, 987
Bozwell, Jean VI, 882
Bozwell, William VI, 882
Brabson, Mary VI, 368
Brace, Anna V, 154
Bracken, Alice M. IV, 179
Bracken, Anna IV, 171
Bracken, Anna IV, 708
Bracken, Anna S. II, 729
Bracken, Anna S. II, 765
Bracken, Anna S. IV, 203
Bracken, Anna S. IV, 225
Bracken, Anna S. IV, 412
Bracken, Anna Street II, 700
Bracken, Asaph Wood IV, 1050
Bracken, Caleb IV, 22
Bracken, Caleb IV, 76
Bracken, Caleb IV, 179
Bracken, Caleb IV, 512
Bracken, Caleb IV, 928
Bracken, Caroline Virginia II, 700
Bracken, Deborah IV, 512
Bracken, Edith M. IV, 368
Bracken, Edith M. IV, 371
Bracken, Edward F. II, 729
Bracken, Edward F. II, 765
Bracken, Edwin P. II, 700
Bracken, Elisha IV, 22
Bracken, Elisha IV, 179
Bracken, Elisha IV, 200
Bracken, Elisha IV, 281
Bracken, Elisha IV, 512
Bracken, Elisha IV, 513
Bracken, Esther IV, 200
Bracken, Esther IV, 512
Bracken, Esther L. IV, 800
Bracken, Lemual IV, 512
Bracken, Lindley IV, 225
Bracken, Lindley IV, 412
Bracken, Lindley M. II, 700
Bracken, Lindley M. II, 729
Bracken, Lindley M. II, 765
Bracken, Lindley M. IV, 171
Bracken, Lindley M. IV, 203
Bracken, Lindley M. IV, 708
Bracken, Lois II, 700
Bracken, Lois Sellew II, 729
Bracken, Martha IV, 412
Bracken, Martha VI, 666
Bracken, Martha B. IV, 179
Bracken, Martha B. IV, 228
Bracken, Martha H. IV, 225
Bracken, Martha H. IV, 371
Bracken, Mary IV, 76
Bracken, Mary IV, 512
Bracken, Mary IV, 865
Bracken, Mary IV, 880
Bracken, Mary IV, 928
Bracken, Mary Ann IV, 171
Bracken, Mary Ann IV, 366
Bracken, Mary Anna IV, 366
Bracken, Mary Anna IV, 371
Bracken, Mary H. IV, 512
Bracken, Ogden J. IV, 177
Bracken, Ogden J. IV, 800
Bracken, Phebe IV, 179
Bracken, Phebe IV, 281
Bracken, Phebe IV, 512
Bracken, Phebe IV, 513
Bracken, Phebe IV, 1050
Bracken, Phebe IV, 1083
Bracken, Rachel IV, 22
Bracken, Rachel S. IV, 177
Bracken, Rachel S. IV, 800
Bracken, Rebecca IV, 22
Bracken, Rebecca IV, 67
Bracken, Rebecca IV, 179
Bracken, Rebecca IV, 281
Bracken, Rebecca IV, 444
Bracken, Rebecca IV, 451
Bracken, Rebecca IV, 512
Bracken, Rebecca IV, 768
Bracken, Rebecca IV, 786
Bracken, Rebecca IV, 844
Bracken, Rebecca VI, 578
Bracken, Rebecca VI, 719
Bracken, Sarah IV, 22
Bracken, Sarah IV, 67
Bracken, Sarah VI, 578
Bracken, Sarah J. II, 700
Bracken, Sarah J. II, 729
Bracken, Solomon IV, 22
Bracken, Solomon IV, 67
Bracken, Solomon VI, 578
Bracken, Virginia Lois II, 729
Bracken, Virginia Lois II, 765
Brackens, Sarah I, 982
Brackens, Sarah I, 991
Bracket, Edward V, 895
Bracket, Geo V, 895
Bracket, Gustavus V, 895
Bracket, Jane V, 895
Bracket, Margaret V, 895
Bracket, Moses V, 895
Bracket, Rueben V, 895
Brackett, Abbie III, 480
Brackett, Abbie III, 491
Brackett, Charles III, 480
Brackett, Charles III, 491
Brackett, Ila I, 938
Brackett, Jane V, 895
Brackett, Jane V, 905
Brackett, Robert P. I, 938
Brackett, Rueben V, 895
Brackin, Alice M. IV, 179
Brackin, Anna IV, 179
Brackin, Anna IV, 683
Brackin, Anna S. IV, 179
Brackin, Anna S. IV, 191
Brackin, Anna S. IV, 683
Brackin, Anna Street II, 700
Brackin, Caleb IV, 22
Brackin, Caleb IV, 51
Brackin, Caleb IV, 179
Brackin, Caleb IV, 683
Brackin, Deborah IV, 179
Brackin, Drusilla IV, 179
Brackin, Edith IV, 366
Brackin, Edith M. IV, 171
Brackin, Edith M. IV, 179
Brackin, Edith Margaret IV, 179
Brackin, Edith Margaret IV, 801
Brackin, Edward F. IV, 179
Brackin, Edward T. IV, 179
Brackin, Elisha IV, 179
Brackin, Elisha IV, 273
Brackin, Elisha IV, 306
Brackin, Elisha IV, 512
Brackin, Elisha IV, 683
Brackin, Elisha IV, 704
Brackin, Esther IV, 179
Brackin, Esther IV, 191
Brackin, Esther IV, 273
Brackin, Esther IV, 306
Brackin, Esther IV, 512
Brackin, Esther IV, 683
Brackin, Esther IV, 704
Brackin, Esther C. IV, 179
Brackin, Esther L. II, 699
Brackin, Esther L. IV, 177
Brackin, Esther L. IV, 179
Brackin, Lemual IV, 512
Brackin, Lemuel II, 699
Brackin, Lemuel IV, 179
Brackin, Lemuel IV, 530
Brackin, Lindley IV, 179
Brackin, Lindley M. II, 700
Brackin, Lindley M. IV, 179
Brackin, Lindley M. IV, 191
Brackin, Lindley M. IV, 683
Brackin, Martha IV, 179
Brackin, Martha IV, 228
Brackin, Martha H. IV, 179
Brackin, Mary II, 699
Brackin, Mary IV, 76
Brackin, Mary IV, 179
Brackin, Mary IV, 512
Brackin, Mary IV, 530
Brackin, Mary Ann IV, 179
Brackin, Mary Anna IV, 171
Brackin, Mary Anna IV, 179
Brackin, Mary Anna IV, 366
Brackin, Ogden J. IV, 171
Brackin, Ogden J. IV, 179
Brackin, Ogden J. IV, 801
Brackin, Phebe IV, 179
Brackin, Phebe IV, 306
Brackin, Rachel IV, 51
Brackin, Rachel S. IV, 171
Brackin, Rachel S. IV, 179
Brackin, Rachel S. IV, 801
Brackin, Rebecca IV, 22
Brackin, Rebecca IV, 51
Brackin, Rebecca IV, 179
Brackin, Rebecca IV, 430
Brackin, Rebecca IV, 683
Brackin, Rebecca IV, 844
Brackin, Richard IV, 179
Brackin, Richard F. IV, 179
Brackin, Sara J. IV, 179
Brackin, Sarah IV, 22
Brackin, Sarah IV, 179
Brackin, Sarah IV, 273
Brackin, Sarah J. II, 700
Brackin, Sarah J. II, 729
Brackin, Sarah J. IV, 179
Brackin, Solomon IV, 22
Brackner, Susannah V, 607
Brackney, Albert M. V, 660
Brackney, Albert N. V, 660
Brackney, Anna C. V, 613
Brackney, Anna H. V, 660
Brackney, Callie Mary V, 613
Brackney, Charles V, 477
Brackney, Charlotte V, 477
Brackney, Charlotte B. V, 660
Brackney, Chas. E. V, 660
Brackney, Clara V, 660
Brackney, Clarice V, 660
Brackney, Clarice V, 716
Brackney, Edwin V, 613
Brackney, Eli V, 224
Brackney, Eli V, 613
Brackney, Eli V, 660
Brackney, Elizabeth V, 224
Brackney, Fanny V, 660
Brackney, Geo. V, 570
Brackney, Geo. V, 613
Brackney, Geo. V, 660
Brackney, Geo. Wm. V, 660
Brackney, George V, 551
Brackney, George V, 613
Brackney, George V, 660
Brackney, George Howard V, 613
Brackney, Hazel Smith V, 661
Brackney, Ida V, 224
Brackney, Ida V, 613
Brackney, Ida Ann V, 660
Brackney, John V, 477
Brackney, John V, 613
Brackney, John V, 660
Brackney, John William V, 477
Brackney, Joseph V, 224
Brackney, Joseph V, 613
Brackney, Joseph V, 660
Brackney, Judith V, 551
Brackney, Judith V, 570
Brackney, Judith A. V, 613
Brackney, Judith Ann V, 551
Brackney, Judith Ann V, 613
Brackney, Judith Ann V, 660
Brackney, Kate V, 660
Brackney, Katie B. V, 661
Brackney, Lauren V, 660
Brackney, Lauren V, 716
Brackney, Lewis V, 660
Brackney, Lewis C. V, 660
Brackney, Lewis Calvin V, 613
Brackney, Lillian V, 477
Brackney, Lillian V, 660
Brackney, Loren V, 477
Brackney, Loren V, 660
Brackney, Loren V, 661
Brackney, Louis V, 660
Brackney, Louis C. V, 613
Brackney, Mahlon V, 224
Brackney, Mahlon V, 477
Brackney, Mahlon V, 613
Brackney, Mahlon V, 660
Brackney, Mahlon H. V, 613
Brackney, Mahlon H. V, 660
Brackney, Marmaduke V, 224
Brackney, Marmaduke V, 613
Brackney, Marmaduke V, 636
Brackney, Marmaduke V, 660
Brackney, Martha V, 660
Brackney, Mary V, 613
Brackney, Mary V, 646
Brackney, May L. V, 660
Brackney, Phebe V, 613
Brackney, Phebe Bailey V, 224
Brackney, Pleasant V, 224
Brackney, Pleasant V, 613
Brackney, Pleasant V, 660
Brackney, Rachel V, 224
Brackney, Rachel V, 320
Brackney, Rachel V, 353
Brackney, Rachel V, 613
Brackney, Rachel V, 650
Brackney, Rachel V, 660
Brackney, Rachel V, 981
Brackney, Rachel A. V, 613
Brackney, Rachel A. V, 636
Brackney, Ruth V, 477
Brackney, Ruth V, 660
Brackney, S. A. V, 660
Brackney, S. Allen V, 660
Brackney, Sally V, 613
Brackney, Sally V, 660
Brackney, Sally Mary V, 224
Brackney, Sarah M. V, 660
Brackney, Sarah Mabel V, 613
Brackney, Sarah Mable V, 613
Brackney, Stacy Allen V, 613
Brackney, Susan V, 613
Brackney, Susanna V, 224
Brackney, Susanna V, 613
Brackney, Susanna V, 660
Brackney, Susannah V, 613
Brackney, Susannah V, 624
Brackney, Susannah V, 636
Brackney, Susannah V, 660
Brackney, Tella V, 660
Brackney, Tella F. V, 660
Brackney, U. C. V, 660
Brackney, Uriah Clifford V, 660
Brackon, William II, 441
Bracks, L. Clay I, 1149
Bracy, Ann VI, 45
Bracy, Francis VI, 45
Bradberry, John I, 300
Bradberry, Mary I, 300
Bradberry, Mary I, 308
Bradbury, ??? III, 202
Bradbury, Abraham III, 44
Bradbury, Ann III, 44
Bradbury, Anna C. V, 26
Bradbury, Hannah III, 44
Bradbury, Juliet III, 135
Bradbury, Martha III, 44
Bradbury, Naomi III, 44
Bradbury, Phebe III, 44
Bradbury, Phebe III, 202
Bradbury, Rebecca V, 895
Bradbury, Rebecca V, 943
Bradbury, Ruth III, 44
Bradbury, Ruth III, 76
Bradbury, William III, 44
Braddley, Collins VI, 800
Braddley, Delilih P. VI, 800
Braddley, Henry H. VI, 800
Braddley, John VI, 800
Braddley, Lucy VI, 800
Braddley, Margaret VI, 800
Braddley, Margaret M. VI, 800
Braddley, Nancy VI, 800
Braddley, Stephen VI, 800
Braddley, Wm. VI, 800
Braddoc, Raymon V, 26
Braddock, Amanda V, 26
Braddock, Bathsheba II, 315
Braddock, Dewayne V, 26
Braddock, Frank V, 26
Braddock, Fred V, 26
Braddock, Jennie V, 26
Braddock, Lydia S. II, 316
Braddock, Lydia S. II, 325
Braddock, Milton II, 470
Braddock, Priscilla V, 26
Braddock, Raymon V, 26
Braddock, Rehoboam II, 315
Braddock, Warren K. V, 26
Bradds, Alva V, 613
Bradds, Estie V, 613
Bradds, John V, 613
Bradds, John W. V, 613
Bradds, Rebecca V, 613
Braden, Elizabeth VI, 473
Braden, Elizabeth VI, 581
Braden, Jonathan VI, 581
Braden, Juliet V, 320
Braden, Lewis Neill VI, 581
Braden, Lydia VI, 581
Braden, Mary VI, 581
Braden, Mary E. VI, 581
Braden, Mary Ruth VI, 581
Braden, Noble VI, 474
Braden, Noble S. VI, 581
Braden, Sarah VI, 581
Bradfford, Elizabeth VI, 934
Bradfford, Sally VI, 934
Bradfield, ??? VI, 299
Bradfield, Adah IV, 856
Bradfield, Amy IV, 612
Bradfield, Amy IV, 630
Bradfield, Ann VI, 368
Bradfield, Anna VI, 368
Bradfield, Anna VI, 620
Bradfield, Benjamin VI, 299
Bradfield, Benjamin VI, 300
Bradfield, Benjamin VI, 620
Bradfield, Benjamin VI, 705
Bradfield, Carey IV, 865
Bradfield, Carey V, 320
Bradfield, Cary V, 320
Bradfield, Cinthe I, 1007
Bradfield, Cynthia I, 960
Bradfield, Cynthia IV, 22
Bradfield, Cynthia IV, 865
Bradfield, Cynthia V, 320
Bradfield, Cynthia VI, 299
Bradfield, Cynthia VI, 300
Bradfield, Cynthia VI, 304
Bradfield, Elias IV, 865
Bradfield, Elias V, 320
Bradfield, Elizabeth VI, 474
Bradfield, Elizabeth VI, 540
Bradfield, Elizabeth VI, 544
Bradfield, Elizabeth VI, 620
Bradfield, Hannah V, 224
Bradfield, Hannah V, 289
Bradfield, Hannah VI, 299
Bradfield, Hannah VI, 474
Bradfield, Hannah VI, 620
Bradfield, Hannah VI, 800
Bradfield, John I, 960
Bradfield, John I, 1007
Bradfield, John IV, 22
Bradfield, John IV, 865
Bradfield, John VI, 299
Bradfield, John VI, 300
Bradfield, John VI, 620
Bradfield, John VI, 800
Bradfield, Jonas IV, 865
Bradfield, Jonas V, 320
Bradfield, Jonathan VI, 620
Bradfield, Joseph II, 339
Bradfield, Joseph VI, 299
Bradfield, Joseph VI, 300
Bradfield, Joseph VI, 304
Bradfield, Mary I, 1007
Bradfield, Mary IV, 22
Bradfield, Mary IV, 865
Bradfield, Mary V, 320
Bradfield, Rachel II, 339
Bradfield, Rachel IV, 865
Bradfield, Rachel V, 320
Bradfield, Rachel V, 321
Bradfield, Rachel VI, 368
Bradfield, Rachel VI, 616
Bradfield, Rachel VI, 617
Bradfield, Rachel VI, 618
Bradfield, Rachel VI, 620
Bradfield, Rachel VI, 630
Bradfield, Rachel VI, 641
Bradfield, Rachel VI, 697
Bradfield, Rachel VI, 705
Bradfield, Rachel VI, 708
Bradfield, Rebecca Phillips VI, 474
Bradfield, Samuel IV, 865
Bradfield, Samuel V, 320
Bradfield, Sarah Catherine V, 224
Bradfield, Sidney VI, 620
Bradfield, Synthia VI, 300
Bradfield, Tamer V, 320
Bradfield, Tamer V, 327
Bradfield, Thomas VI, 299
Bradfield, Thomas VI, 300
Bradfield, Thomas VI, 620
Bradfield, Uri VI, 620
Bradford, Adah IV, 917
Bradford, Alce II, 339
Bradford, Alice II, 339
Bradford, Charles IV, 1247
Bradford, Cleora Della V, 154
Bradford, Della V, 154
Bradford, Eleanor IV, 917
Bradford, Elizabeth II, 471
Bradford, Frances I, 374
Bradford, Frances I, 389
Bradford, Joseph IV, 917
Bradford, Nancy VI, 889
Bradford, Priscilla II, 339
Bradford, Priscilla II, 471

Bradford, Priscilla II, 613
Bradford, Rachell II, 339
Bradford, Rena IV, 1247
Bradford, Sarah V, 154
Bradford, Sarah E. V, 154
Bradford, Sissily II, 339
Bradford, Susanna V, 154
Bradford, Susanna V, 205
Bradford, Tacy II, 729
Bradford, Tacy II, 735
Bradford, Thomas II, 339
Bradford, Thomas II, 471
Bradford, Thomas II, 613
Bradford, Thomas IV, 22
Bradford, Thomas VI, 161
Bradford, Thomas VI, 1018
Bradford, Willis V, 154
Bradford, Wm. II, 471
Bradfute, Archd. VI, 931
Bradfute, Elizabeth VI, 942
Bradfute, Lilly VI, 931
Bradfute, Robert VI, 882
Bradfute, Robert VI, 985
Bradfute, Robt. VI, 942
Bradfute, Sarah VI, 882
Bradley, ??? III, 368
Bradley, Albert III, 44
Bradley, Albert B. III, 234
Bradley, Ann III, 368
Bradley, Anna V, 26
Bradley, Anna V, 130
Bradley, Anna VI, 179
Bradley, Anna R. III, 44
Bradley, Anna R. III, 101
Bradley, Annie V, 26
Bradley, Annie V, 224
Bradley, Annie V, 234
Bradley, Archibald VI, 882
Bradley, Catharine VI, 936
Bradley, Claud S. I, 231
Bradley, Collins VI, 807
Bradley, Collins VI, 824
Bradley, Cora A. I, 231
Bradley, Eliza Ann VI, 882
Bradley, Elizabeth VI, 824
Bradley, Elizabeth VI, 871
Bradley, Elizabeth VI, 940
Bradley, Fannie III, 44
Bradley, Fannie III, 234
Bradley, Flora IV, 1149
Bradley, Flora D. V, 987
Bradley, Floyd H. III, 44
Bradley, Floyd H. III, 101
Bradley, George L. I, 231
Bradley, Gladys IV, 1149
Bradley, Harriett VI, 882
Bradley, Hazel III, 101
Bradley, Hazel B. III, 44
Bradley, Henrietta VI, 960
Bradley, Henry H. VI, 800
Bradley, James H. VI, 883
Bradley, Jane VI, 813
Bradley, Jemima VI, 882
Bradley, Jesse VI, 300
Bradley, Jesse VI, 882
Bradley, Jesse VI, 973
Bradley, Jesse VI, 983
Bradley, John VI, 161
Bradley, John VI, 169
Bradley, John VI, 170
Bradley, John VI, 179
Bradley, John VI, 210
Bradley, John VI, 800
Bradley, John VI, 940
Bradley, John W. VI, 801
Bradley, John W. VI, 813
Bradley, Joseph VI, 882
Bradley, Joshua VI, 882
Bradley, Judith VI, 801
Bradley, Lemuel Crew VI, 179
Bradley, Lucy VI, 882
Bradley, Margaret VI, 800
Bradley, Margaret M. VI, 800
Bradley, Martha VI, 971
Bradley, Martha VI, 973
Bradley, Mary III, 45
Bradley, Mary VI, 801
Bradley, Mary VI, 807
Bradley, Mary VI, 815
Bradley, Milton V, 26
Bradley, Minnie P. I, 231
Bradley, Miram VI, 883
Bradley, Nettie I, 231
Bradley, Peter VI, 883
Bradley, Peter R. I, 231
Bradley, Philah III, 99
Bradley, Rachel I, 374
Bradley, Rachel I, 674
Bradley, Rachel I, 689
Bradley, Rachel I, 792
Bradley, Rachel I, 800
Bradley, Richard I, 527
Bradley, Richard VI, 873
Bradley, Richard VI, 882
Bradley, Richard VI, 960
Bradley, Sally VI, 882
Bradley, Sarah I, 800
Bradley, Sarah VI, 811
Bradley, Sarah VI, 882
Bradley, Sarah VI, 960
Bradley, Sarah E. I, 231
Bradley, Stephen VI, 800
Bradley, Stephen VI, 811
Bradley, Susanna VI, 300
Bradley, Susanna VI, 339
Bradley, Susanna VI, 882
Bradley, Temperance Jane VI, 883
Bradley, Thomas VI, 916
Bradley, Thomas Edward V, 26
Bradley, Thurza Ann P. VI, 883
Bradley, William I, 231
Bradley, William VI, 161
Bradley, William VI, 811
Bradley, William VI, 865
Bradley, William VI, 871
Bradley, William VI, 882
Bradley, William VI, 883
Bradley, William VI, 916
Bradley, William VI, 936
Bradley, Wm. J. III, 44
Bradley, Wm. J. III, 101
Bradley, Zella V, 26
Bradly, Rachel I, 374
Bradly, Sarah I, 800
Bradly, Sarah I, 801
Bradner, Mary Virginia I, 619
Bradock, Theodore E. V, 154
Bradrick, Beulah IV, 140
Bradrick, Beulah IV, 321
Bradrick, Beulah V, 27
Bradrick, Eliza IV, 1190
Bradrick, Elizabeth IV, 1149
Bradrick, Paul IV, 1149
Bradrick, Paul IV, 1190
Bradrick, Sarah IV, 1190
Bradshaw, ??? I, 19
Bradshaw, ??? V, 661
Bradshaw, ??? V, 678
Bradshaw, Achsa VI, 81
Bradshaw, Adelaide W. VI, 54
Bradshaw, Albert E. IV, 1035
Bradshaw, Alfred Ricks VI, 55
Bradshaw, Alice I, 335
Bradshaw, Alice VI, 55
Bradshaw, Amos VI, 55
Bradshaw, Amy VI, 54
Bradshaw, Amy VI, 55
Bradshaw, Angelina IV, 1149
Bradshaw, Ann E. VI, 54
Bradshaw, Ann E. VI, 55
Bradshaw, Anna B. VI, 54
Bradshaw, August R. VI, 54
Bradshaw, August R. VI, 55
Bradshaw, Bell VI, 55
Bradshaw, Benj. VI, 70
Bradshaw, Benj. VI, 88
Bradshaw, Benjamin V, 987
Bradshaw, Benjamin VI, 55
Bradshaw, Bettie VI, 55
Bradshaw, Bettie D. VI, 54
Bradshaw, Bettie D. VI, 55
Bradshaw, C. Bell VI, 54
Bradshaw, Cora L. VI, 54
Bradshaw, Cora L. VI, 55
Bradshaw, Daisey IV, 1035
Bradshaw, Daisy IV, 1035
Bradshaw, Damaris E. VI, 54
Bradshaw, David L. VI, 54
Bradshaw, David L. VI, 55
Bradshaw, Diana VI, 54
Bradshaw, Diana VI, 82
Bradshaw, Dora J. VI, 54
Bradshaw, Dora J. VI, 57
Bradshaw, Edward A. VI, 55
Bradshaw, Elijah Nortfleet VI, 54
Bradshaw, Eliza I, 527
Bradshaw, Eliza IV, 1308
Bradshaw, Eliza J. IV, 1308
Bradshaw, Eliza Jane I, 527
Bradshaw, Elizabeth VI, 55
Bradshaw, Elizabeth VI, 67
Bradshaw, Elizabeth A. VI, 54
Bradshaw, Elizabeth A. VI, 55
Bradshaw, Elizabeth A. VI, 58
Bradshaw, Elizabeth A. VI, 67
Bradshaw, Ella L. VI, 54
Bradshaw, Ella L. VI, 55
Bradshaw, Franklin VI, 55
Bradshaw, Geneva M. VI, 51
Bradshaw, Geneva M. VI, 54
Bradshaw, Geneva M. VI, 55
Bradshaw, Goodwin VI, 54
Bradshaw, Goodwin VI, 55
Bradshaw, Goodwin VI, 58
Bradshaw, Goodwin VI, 67
Bradshaw, Hallie V, 661
Bradshaw, Harley V, 477
Bradshaw, Helen IV, 1308
Bradshaw, James IV, 683
Bradshaw, James IV, 928
Bradshaw, James VI, 55
Bradshaw, James J. VI, 54
Bradshaw, James K. VI, 54
Bradshaw, James M. VI, 51
Bradshaw, James M. VI, 54
Bradshaw, James M. VI, 55
Bradshaw, Jas. M. VI, 51
Bradshaw, Jephtha J. VI, 54
Bradshaw, Joel D. VI, 52
Bradshaw, Joel D. VI, 54
Bradshaw, Joel D. VI, 55
Bradshaw, John VI, 54
Bradshaw, John VI, 55
Bradshaw, John Babb VI, 55
Bradshaw, John Pretlow VI, 55
Bradshaw, Joseph M. VI, 54
Bradshaw, Joseph M. VI, 55
Bradshaw, Joseph M. VI, 75
Bradshaw, Joseph Pretlow VI, 55
Bradshaw, Junius Parker VI, 54
Bradshaw, Laura A. VI, 54
Bradshaw, Laura A. VI, 55
Bradshaw, Laura A. VI, 76
Bradshaw, Levi I, 335
Bradshaw, Lewis II, 784
Bradshaw, Linwood L. VI, 54
Bradshaw, Linwood L. VI, 55
Bradshaw, Lizzie VI, 54
Bradshaw, Lizzie B. VI, 54
Bradshaw, Lizzie Bell VI, 55
Bradshaw, Louisa II, 970
Bradshaw, Louisa II, 1057
Bradshaw, Louisa II, 1061
Bradshaw, Lucile VI, 54
Bradshaw, Lucile VI, 55
Bradshaw, Lucile J. VI, 54
Bradshaw, Lucile J. VI, 55
Bradshaw, Luther VI, 54
Bradshaw, Luther VI, 55
Bradshaw, Mahlon IV, 1149
Bradshaw, Margaret L. VI, 54
Bradshaw, Martha VI, 52
Bradshaw, Martha VI, 54
Bradshaw, Martha VI, 55
Bradshaw, Martha VI, 76
Bradshaw, Martha VI, 81
Bradshaw, Mary I, 335
Bradshaw, Mary I, 936
Bradshaw, Mary V, 987
Bradshaw, Mary VI, 55
Bradshaw, Mary VI, 75
Bradshaw, Mary A. VI, 54
Bradshaw, Mary Agnes VI, 81
Bradshaw, Mary Ann IV, 683
Bradshaw, Mary Ann IV, 685
Bradshaw, Mary L. VI, 54
Bradshaw, Mary N. I, 19
Bradshaw, Maryann IV, 683
Bradshaw, Mordicai VI, 54
Bradshaw, Mordicai VI, 55
Bradshaw, Murdoc VI, 54
Bradshaw, Murdoc VI, 55
Bradshaw, Murdoc VI, 76
Bradshaw, Murdoc VI, 81
Bradshaw, Murdoc VI, 82
Bradshaw, Nancy A. VI, 54
Bradshaw, Nancy A. VI, 55
Bradshaw, Nancy A. VI, 58
Bradshaw, Nancy Alice VI, 55
Bradshaw, Nancy R. VI, 54
Bradshaw, Nancy R. VI, 55
Bradshaw, Nancy R. VI, 69
Bradshaw, Nannie K. VI, 91
Bradshaw, Nettie I, 1149
Bradshaw, R. Lee VI, 54
Bradshaw, Rebecca IV, 683
Bradshaw, Rebecca IV, 928
Bradshaw, Rebecca T. IV, 683
Bradshaw, Rebecca T. IV, 721
Bradshaw, Rebecca T. IV, 928
Bradshaw, Rebecca T. IV, 964
Bradshaw, Robert B. VI, 54
Bradshaw, Robert B. VI, 55
Bradshaw, Robert B. VI, 69
Bradshaw, Ruth E. I, 443
Bradshaw, Ruth E. VI, 55
Bradshaw, Sarah IV, 683
Bradshaw, Sarah IV, 928
Bradshaw, Sarah IV, 953
Bradshaw, Sarah D. VI, 55
Bradshaw, Sarah F. IV, 683
Bradshaw, Sarah F. IV, 707
Bradshaw, Susanna II, 840
Bradshaw, Susannah II, 784
Bradshaw, Theda IV, 1036
Bradshaw, Thomas II, 471
Bradshaw, Thomas VI, 55
Bradshaw, Townsend IV, 683
Bradshaw, Townsend IV, 928
Bradshaw, Townsend IV, 1024
Bradshaw, Watson VI, 81
Bradshaw, William IV, 683
Bradshaw, William IV, 1024
Bradshaw, William Harris VI, 55
Bradshaw, Wm. IV, 928
Bradstreet, Arbie Mills V, 154
Bradstreet, Eliza V, 26
Bradt, ??? IV, 1036
Bradt, Maria III, 121
Bradt, Maria III, 363
Bradway, Aaron II, 22
Bradway, Aaron II, 23
Bradway, Aaron II, 57
Bradway, Aaron II, 93
Bradway, Aaron II, 105
Bradway, Aaron, Jr. II, 57
Bradway, Abigail II, 57
Bradway, Abigail II, 74
Bradway, Abigail V, 26
Bradway, Abigail V, 27
Bradway, Achsa Ann II, 57
Bradway, Achsah Ann II, 145
Bradway, Achsas Ann II, 116
Bradway, Adna II, 23
Bradway, Aletha IV, 1035
Bradway, Alvin H. IV, 683
Bradway, Amy IV, 801
Bradway, Ann II, 23
Bradway, Ann II, 56
Bradway, Ann II, 57
Bradway, Ann II, 84
Bradway, Anna II, 23
Bradway, Anna II, 57
Bradway, Anna II, 145
Bradway, Anna IV, 801
Bradway, Anna IV, 844
Bradway, Anne II, 23
Bradway, Annie A. IV, 801
Bradway, Annie A. IV, 832
Bradway, Annie E. IV, 801
Bradway, Beaulah II, 57
Bradway, Beulah II, 316
Bradway, Beulah V, 27
Bradway, Beulah V, 137
Bradway, Bulah II, 308
Bradway, Bulah II, 316
Bradway, Carl IV, 1036
Bradway, Charles W. IV, 683
Bradway, David II, 23
Bradway, David II, 57
Bradway, David II, 70
Bradway, David II, 81
Bradway, David W. II, 57
Bradway, Dorcas II, 57
Bradway, Dorcas V, 27
Bradway, Ebenezer II, 57
Bradway, Edna II, 146
Bradway, Edward II, 17
Bradway, Edward II, 23
Bradway, Edward II, 56
Bradway, Edward II, 57
Bradway, Edward II, 62
Bradway, Edward II, 70
Bradway, Edward II, 81
Bradway, Edward II, 108
Bradway, Edward Y. IV, 683
Bradway, Edward, Jr. II, 57
Bradway, Elizabeth II, 23
Bradway, Elizabeth II, 56
Bradway, Elizabeth II, 57
Bradway, Elizabeth II, 70
Bradway, Elizabeth II, 77
Bradway, Elizabeth II, 81
Bradway, Elizabeth II, 82
Bradway, Elizabeth II, 101
Bradway, Elizabeth II, 108
Bradway, Elizabeth II, 112
Bradway, Elizabeth II, 115
Bradway, Elizabeth II, 116
Bradway, Elizabeth IV, 801
Bradway, Elizabeth IV, 805
Bradway, Elizabeth IV, 835
Bradway, Elizabeth IV, 837
Bradway, Elizabeth V, 27
Bradway, Elizabeth H. II, 784
Bradway, Emeline IV, 612
Bradway, Emeline IV, 643
Bradway, Emeline IV, 667
Bradway, Ezra IV, 667
Bradway, Franklin II, 129
Bradway, Franklin II, 146
Bradway, Grace II, 23
Bradway, Grace II, 57
Bradway, Grace II, 84
Bradway, Grace II, 105
Bradway, Hannah II, 23
Bradway, Hannah II, 57
Bradway, Hannah II, 70
Bradway, Hannah II, 145
Bradway, Hannah II, 147
Bradway, Hannah II, 784
Bradway, Herman D. IV, 801
Bradway, Herman W. IV, 801
Bradway, Irene H. IV, 683
Bradway, Isaac II, 784
Bradway, Isaac II, 840
Bradway, James II, 23
Bradway, James II, 57
Bradway, James II, 62
Bradway, James II, 69
Bradway, James IV, 801
Bradway, James C. IV, 801
Bradway, James L. W. IV, 683
Bradway, James L. W. IV, 801
Bradway, James L. W. IV, 816
Bradway, James Lewis II, 57
Bradway, James W. IV, 801
Bradway, James W. IV, 832
Bradway, Jas. C. IV, 801
Bradway, John II, 23
Bradway, John II, 57
Bradway, John II, 74
Bradway, John V, 26
Bradway, John V, 27
Bradway, Jonathan II, 23
Bradway, Jonathan II, 57
Bradway, Jonathan II, 90
Bradway, Jonathan II, 132
Bradway, Jonathan II, 146
Bradway, Jonathan J. II, 130
Bradway, Jonathan J. II, 146
Bradway, Jonathan J. II, 149
Bradway, Jonathan P. II, 146
Bradway, Jonathan P. II, 149
Bradway, Jonathan, Jr. II, 57
Bradway, Jonathan, Jr. II, 101
Bradway, Jono V, 26
Bradway, Joshua II, 22
Bradway, Joshua II, 23
Bradway, Josiah II, 57
Bradway, Josiah II, 130
Bradway, Josiah V, 27
Bradway, Judson Hilliard II, 130
Bradway, Kasby II, 23
Bradway, Lida Frances II, 129
Bradway, Lida Francis II, 146
Bradway, Lindley Ellis IV, 801
Bradway, Lydia II, 132
Bradway, Lydia A. II, 146
Bradway, Lydia A. II, 149
Bradway, Lydia Ann II, 130
Bradway, Lydia Ann II, 146
Bradway, Lydia P. II, 146
Bradway, Lydia P. II, 149
Bradway, Lydia, Jr. II, 130
Bradway, Mark II, 23
Bradway, Mark II, 57
Bradway, Mark II, 77
Bradway, Mark II, 102
Bradway, Mark II, 308
Bradway, Mark II, 316
Bradway, Mark D. IV, 612
Bradway, Mark D. IV, 667
Bradway, Martha II, 57
Bradway, Martha II, 102
Bradway, Martha II, 130
Bradway, Martha II, 145
Bradway, Martha II, 146
Bradway, Martha II, 147
Bradway, Martha II, 308
Bradway, Martha II, 316
Bradway, Martha D. II, 130
Bradway, Mary II, 22
Bradway, Mary II, 23
Bradway, Mary II, 43
Bradway, Mary II, 56
Bradway, Mary II, 57
Bradway, Mary II, 62
Bradway, Mary II, 101
Bradway, Mary II, 105
Bradway, Mary II, 109
Bradway, Mary II, 133
Bradway, Mary IV, 667
Bradway, Mary B. II, 57
Bradway, Mary B. II, 102
Bradway, Mary J. IV, 801
Bradway, Mary Jane IV, 683
Bradway, Mary Jane IV, 801
Bradway, Mary Jane Gamble IV, 801
Bradway, Mary R. IV, 683
Bradway, Nathan II, 23
Bradway, Nathan II, 57
Bradway, Phebe Jane IV, 683

Bradway, Prudence II, 54
Bradway, Prudence II, 57
Bradway, Rachel II, 23
Bradway, Rachel II, 57
Bradway, Rachel II, 59
Bradway, Rachel II, 784
Bradway, Rachel IV, 844
Bradway, Rachel Ann II, 784
Bradway, Rachel S. IV, 801
Bradway, Rachel S. IV, 837
Bradway, Rebecca II, 49
Bradway, Rebecca II, 57
Bradway, Rebecca II, 784
Bradway, Rebecca II, 840
Bradway, Rebecca O. II, 840
Bradway, Rebeckah II, 22
Bradway, Rebeckah II, 57
Bradway, Rebeckah II, 72
Bradway, Rebekah II, 57
Bradway, Rebekah II, 81
Bradway, Richard II, 57
Bradway, Ruth II, 23
Bradway, Ruth II, 57
Bradway, Ruth II, 62
Bradway, Ruth II, 69
Bradway, Samuel II, 23
Bradway, Samuel Fogg II, 57
Bradway, Samuel Gamble IV, 683
Bradway, Sarah II, 23
Bradway, Sarah II, 43
Bradway, Sarah II, 56
Bradway, Sarah II, 57
Bradway, Sarah II, 62
Bradway, Sarah II, 75
Bradway, Sarah II, 76
Bradway, Sarah II, 93
Bradway, Sarah II, 108
Bradway, Sarah B. II, 133
Bradway, Susan D. II, 130
Bradway, Susanna II, 57
Bradway, Susanna II, 90
Bradway, Susannah II, 23
Bradway, Susannah II, 56
Bradway, Susannah II, 57
Bradway, Susannah II, 94
Bradway, Susannah II, 116
Bradway, Susannah II, 130
Bradway, Tacy II, 57
Bradway, Thomas II, 57
Bradway, Thomas II, 83
Bradway, Thomas V, 27
Bradway, Thos. II, 23
Bradway, Thos. II, 784
Bradway, Vernon A. II, 130
Bradway, Waddington II, 23
Bradway, Waddington II, 129
Bradway, Waddington II, 145
Bradway, Waddington II, 147
Bradway, Waddington II, 784
Bradway, Washington II, 784
Bradway, Wd. Elizabeth H. II, 784
Bradway, Wd. Susan Allebone II, 784
Bradway, William II, 43
Bradway, William V, 27
Bradway, Wm. II, 23
Bradway, Wm. II, 56
Bradway, Wm. II, 57
Bradway, Wm. II, 76
Bradway, Wm. II, 112
Bradway, Wm. II, 133
Bradway, Wm. IV, 801
Bradway, Wm. F. IV, 801
Bradway, Wm. T. IV, 837
Bradway, Wm. T. IV, 844
Bradway, Wm., Jr. II, 57
Bradway, Wm., Jr. II, 109
Bradwell, Fred I, 630
Brady, Barthens I, 1149
Brady, Beulah IV, 179
Brady, Catharine E. I, 374
Brady, Charity IV, 1149
Brady, Charity IV, 1177
Brady, Denvard I, 335
Brady, Dorinda F. III, 45
Brady, Dorinda F. III, 124
Brady, Edward III, 45
Brady, Ellen I, 374
Brady, Emeline III, 45
Brady, Emeline C. III, 45
Brady, Esther Ann I, 374
Brady, Harriet III, 45
Brady, Harriet A. III, 45
Brady, James IV, 1177
Brady, John I, 374
Brady, John III, 45
Brady, John T. H. III, 45
Brady, John T. H. III, 124
Brady, Lewis IV, 179
Brady, Lydia III, 327
Brady, Lydia C. III, 45
Brady, Lydia C. III, 124
Brady, Margaret I, 374
Brady, Margaret Ann I, 374
Brady, Mary I, 374
Brady, Mary V, 154
Brady, Mary VI, 883
Brady, Mary Ann I, 374
Brady, Ruth I, 470
Brady, Ruth S. I, 475
Brady, Ruthanna IV, 1050
Brady, Ruthanna IV, 1056
Brady, Sarah IV, 1177
Brady, Susan B. III, 45
Brady, Susan B. III, 124
Brady, Thomas III, 45
Brady, Thomas VI, 883
Brafford, Betsy VI, 883
Brafford, Catharine VI, 883
Brafford, Charles VI, 883
Brafford, Elizabeth VI, 883
Brafford, Nath'l VI, 883
Brafford, Nathan VI, 965
Brafford, Patsy VI, 889
Brafford, Polly VI, 965
Brafford, Samuel VI, 883
Brafford, Thomas VI, 883
Brafford, Thomas VI, 889
Braford, Jenny VI, 928
Brag, Clarissa V, 613
Brag, Clarissa V, 629
Brag, Roger II, 57
Bragdon, Elizabeth W. II, 840
Bragdon, Elizabeth W. II, 844
Bragg, Ann V, 154
Bragg, Ann V, 613
Bragg, Ann V, 728
Bragg, Ann V, 895
Bragg, Ann V, 896
Bragg, Ann V, 916
Bragg, Clarissa V, 613
Bragg, Elizabeth V, 896
Bragg, Henry III, 45
Bragg, Isaac III, 45
Bragg, Isaac V, 895
Bragg, Isaac W. V, 728
Bragg, Isaac William V, 728
Bragg, Isaac Wm. V, 895
Bragg, James V, 728
Bragg, James V, 895
Bragg, Jane V, 728
Bragg, Margaret V, 895
Bragg, Margaret V, 916
Bragg, Roger II, 57
Bragg, Roger III, 397
Bragg, Susannah II, 339
Bragg, Thomas V, 916
Bragg, Thos. V, 896
Bragg, Wm. V, 895
Braidley, Angelina IV, 371
Braidley, Angelina IV, 445
Braidy, Charity IV, 1149
Braiey, Elizabeth VI, 45
Braiey, Mary VI, 45
Brailes, Eleanor I, 756
Brailes, Fatima Jane I, 756
Brailes, Mary Ann I, 756
Brailes, Sarah Elizabeth I, 756
Brain, Cora IV, 929
Brainard, Bessie IV, 771
Brainard, Dr. Orphens III, 34
Brainard, Emma IV, 1308
Brainard, Franklin IV, 179
Brainard, Franklin IV, 180
Brainard, Geo. IV, 1308
Brainard, Mary Beals I, 1149
Braise, Elizabeth VI, 27
Braise, Elizabeth VI, 37
Braise, Francis VI, 27
Braise, Francis VI, 37
Braithwaite, James II, 980
Brake, John IV, 1273
Brake, Laura IV, 1273
Brake, Laura J. IV, 1273
Braken, Ogden J. IV, 801
Braken, Rachel S. IV, 801
Brakin, Martha H. IV, 371
Brakin, Martha H. IV, 412
Brakin, Mary Anna IV, 367
Brakin, Mary Anna IV, 371
Braman, Hannah II, 199
Braman, Hannah II, 259
Braman, Jesse IV, 1354
Braman, Martha IV, 1354
Braman, Martha IV, 1386
Braman, Nancy IV, 1354
Braman, Samuel IV, 1354
Bramblett, Ann VI, 952
Bramblett, Anna VI, 968
Bramblett, Anna VI, 981
Bramblett, Anny VI, 907
Bramblett, Caleb VI, 908
Bramblett, Caleb F. VI, 883
Bramblett, Caleb F. VI, 908
Bramblett, Caroline Ann VI, 908
Bramblett, Elizabeth VI, 908
Bramblett, Elkanah VI, 883
Bramblett, Frances VI, 883
Bramblett, Harriet VI, 948
Bramblett, James VI, 883
Bramblett, James VI, 889
Bramblett, James VI, 910
Bramblett, James VI, 927
Bramblett, Jesse A. VI, 883
Bramblett, Jesse A. VI, 948
Bramblett, Jesse A. VI, 968
Bramblett, Lucy VI, 883
Bramblett, Lucy VI, 952
Bramblett, Lucy VI, 968
Bramblett, Lydda VI, 981
Bramblett, Mary F. VI, 968
Bramblett, Matilda VI, 884
Bramblett, Matilda VI, 1011
Bramblett, Mildred A. VI, 883
Bramblett, Milley VI, 883
Bramblett, Milley VI, 927
Bramblett, Molly VI, 907
Bramblett, Polly VI, 874
Bramblett, Reuben VI, 874
Bramblett, Reuben VI, 883
Bramblett, Reuben VI, 884
Bramblett, Reuben VI, 908
Bramblett, Sally VI, 883
Bramblett, Sally VI, 908
Bramblett, William VI, 952
Bramblett, William VI, 968
Brame, Thos. R. VI, 920
Bramlet, Elizabeth VI, 885
Bramlett, Reuben VI, 883
Bramlett, Sally VI, 883
Bramwell, Sarah IV, 613
Bramwell, Sarah IV, 661
Branam, Allice V, 987
Branam, Ellsworth V, 987
Branam, John P. V, 987
Branam, Montesco V, 987
Branam, Monteto V, 987
Branam, Nancha V, 987
Branam, Wesley V, 987
Branam, Wesley E. V, 987
Branam, Wm. V, 987
Branam, Wm. A. V, 987
Branch, Adeline R. VI, 932
Branch, Ella L. VI, 54
Branch, Ella L. VI, 55
Branch, Fleming VI, 852
Branch, Frances VI, 883
Branch, Harriet E. VI, 863
Branch, James VI, 883
Branch, James VI, 918
Branch, James VI, 923
Branch, Jane VI, 883
Branch, Jenny VI, 883
Branch, John VI, 856
Branch, Lucy VI, 922
Branch, Martha VI, 883
Branch, Mary VI, 731
Branch, Mary VI, 748
Branch, Mary VI, 964
Branch, Mary VI, 1009
Branch, Nancy VI, 826
Branch, Nancy VI, 932
Branch, Olive VI, 922
Branch, Oliver VI, 975
Branch, Pleasant VI, 883
Branch, Salley VI, 923
Branch, Samuel VI, 863
Branch, Susannah VI, 800
Branch, Susannah VI, 923
Branch, Virlinche VI, 975
Branch, William VI, 817
Branch, Wilson VI, 800
Brand, John II, 339
Brand, Martha II, 339
Brand, Mary II, 339
Brand, Mary II, 471
Brand, Mary II, 515
Brand, Mary II, 528
Brand, Wd. Mary II, 471
Brand, Wd. Mary II, 515
Branda, Alice D. V, 27
Brandeis, Anna III, 347
Branden, Elizabeth VI, 580
Brandenberg, Elsie V, 987
Brandenburg, A. F. V, 728
Brandenburg, Calvin E. V, 661
Brandenburg, Flora E. V, 375
Brandenburg, Fowler V, 728
Brandenburg, Frank V, 375
Brandenburg, Frank V, 551
Brandenburg, Frank V, 661
Brandenburg, George E. V, 375
Brandenburg, Hittie A. V, 551
Brandenburg, Katie V, 661
Brandenburg, Kittie V, 551
Brandenburg, Kitty V, 375
Brandenburg, Kitty Ann V, 375
Brandenburg, Laura V, 375
Brandenburg, Laura V, 551
Brandenburg, Laura V, 661
Brandenburg, Laura B. V, 551
Brandenburg, Laura Z. V, 375
Brandenburg, Lawrence V, 375
Brandenburg, Lawrence V, 551
Brandenburg, Lawrence V, 661
Brandenburg, Margaret V. V, 154
Brandenburg, Mary V, 375
Brandenburg, Mary V, 551
Brandenburg, Mary V, 661
Brandenburg, Mary A. V, 375
Brandenburg, Moses V, 375
Brandenburg, Moses D. V, 375
Brandenburg, Moses D. V, 551
Brandenburg, Moses D. V, 661
Brandenburg, Raymond W. V, 375
Brandenburg, Rebecca V, 375
Brandenburg, Rebecca V, 551
Brandenburg, Rebecca V, 661
Brandenburg, Rebecca A. V, 375
Brandenburg, Rebecca A. V, 551
Brandenburg, Rhoda V, 779
Brandenburg, Rodney V, 375
Brandenburg, Rodney V, 551
Brandenburg, Rodney V, 661
Brandenburg, Susan Myrtle V, 375
Brandenburg, Templin V, 375
Brandenburg, Templin V, 551
Brandenburg, Templin V, 661
Brandenburg, W. L. V, 154
Brandenburgh, Flora E. V, 375
Brandenburgh, Frank V, 375
Brandenburgh, George E. V, 375
Brandenburgh, Kitty V, 375
Brandenburgh, Kitty Ann V, 375
Brandenburgh, Laura V, 375
Brandenburgh, Laura Z. V, 375
Brandenburgh, Lawrence V, 375
Brandenburgh, Mary V, 375
Brandenburgh, Mary A. V, 375
Brandenburgh, Moses V, 375
Brandenburgh, Moses D. V, 375
Brandenburgh, Raymond W. V, 375
Brandenburgh, Rebecca V, 375
Brandenburgh, Rebecca A. V, 375
Brandenburgh, Rodney V, 375
Brandenburgh, Susan Myrtle V, 375
Brandenburgh, Templin V, 375
Branderburgh, Ann V, 731
Brandly, Luke II, 980
Brandon, Ann IV, 76
Brandon, Ann IV, 103
Brandon, Eliza IV, 180
Brandreth, Cathren II, 57
Brandreth, Daniel II, 57
Brandreth, Deborah II, 57
Brandreth, Deborah II, 99
Brandreth, Elizabeth II, 57
Brandreth, Elizabeth II, 107
Brandreth, Mary III, 45
Brandreth, Mary III, 163
Brandreth, Timothy II, 57
Brandreth, Timothy III, 45
Brandreth, Timothy III, 163
Brandt, Albertus II, 441
Brandt, Albertus III, 45
Brandt, Albertus III, 310
Brandt, Jacob II, 441
Brandt, Maria III, 45
Brandt, Susanna II, 441
Brandt, Susanna, Jr. III, 45
Brandt, Susannah, Jr. III, 310
Brandt, William III, 45
Brandwith, Cathren II, 57
Brandwith, Daniel II, 57
Brandwith, Timothy II, 57
Branin, Abigail IV, 683
Branin, Abigail IV, 760
Branin, Abigail IV, 801
Branin, Charles II, 339
Branin, Charles II, 461
Branin, Charles II, 471
Branin, Cornelia I, 933
Branin, Elijah IV, 683
Branin, Elizabeth II, 199
Branin, Elizabeth II, 282
Branin, Ezra IV, 683
Branin, Ezra IV, 801
Branin, Hannah IV, 683
Branin, Hannah IV, 801
Branin, Mahlon IV, 683
Branin, Mahlon IV, 801
Branin, Mahlon IV, 1024
Branin, Nathaniel IV, 683
Branin, Nathaniel IV, 801
Branin, Nathaniel IV, 1024
Branin, Rachel IV, 683
Branin, Rachel IV, 801
Branin, Rachel IV, 1024
Branin, Rachel IV, 1025
Branin, Susanna IV, 683
Branin, Susanna IV, 801
Branin, Susannah IV, 683
Branin, Susannah IV, 763
Braning, Elizabeth II, 199
Brann, Catharine V, 477
Brann, Catharine V, 613
Brann, Catharine V, 661
Brann, Clement V, 661
Brann, Clement L. V, 661
Brann, Clifford V, 477
Brann, Clifford V, 661
Brann, Emma J. V, 477
Brann, Harriett V, 661
Brann, Harriett V, 700
Brann, Harriett M. V, 661
Brann, Irene V, 661
Brann, Irene M. V, 661
Brann, James V, 477
Brann, James V, 661
Brann, James W. V, 477
Brann, Joe Edwin V, 661
Brann, Marcy Ann V, 661
Brann, Maria V, 477
Brann, Maria V, 668
Brann, Maria E. V, 661
Brann, Mercie A. V, 477
Brann, Mercie A. V, 551
Brann, Mercie A. V, 556
Brann, Mercy Ann V, 477
Brann, Roscoe V, 477
Brann, Roscoe V, 661
Brann, Roscoe C. V, 661
Brann, Ruth Esther V, 661
Brann, Samuel L. V, 477
Brannen, Charles II, 471
Brannen, Elizabeth II, 471
Brannen, Ezra IV, 929
Brannen, Mahlon IV, 929
Brannen, Malon IV, 929
Brannen, Mary IV, 22
Brannen, Mary VI, 368
Brannen, Nathaniel IV, 929
Brannen, Rachel IV, 929
Brannen, Rachel IV, 951
Brannen, Susan IV, 929
Brannen, Susanna IV, 929
Brannen, Susanna IV, 995
Branner, Elizabeth II, 471
Branner, George II, 471
Branner, Sarah II, 840
Brannin, Abigail IV, 801
Brannin, Ezra IV, 683
Brannin, Ezra IV, 801
Brannin, Ezra IV, 929
Brannin, Ezra IV, 1021
Brannin, Hannah IV, 801
Brannin, Mahlon IV, 683
Brannin, Mahlon IV, 801
Brannin, Mahlon IV, 1024
Brannin, Malon IV, 929
Brannin, Nathaniel IV, 683
Brannin, Nathaniel IV, 801
Brannin, Nathaniel IV, 929
Brannin, Rachel IV, 683
Brannin, Rachel IV, 801
Brannin, Rachel IV, 929
Brannin, Susan IV, 929
Brannin, Susanna IV, 683
Brannin, Susanna IV, 801
Branning, Achsah III, 45
Branning, Mary III, 45
Branning, Mary D. III, 45
Branning, William C. III, 45
Brannon, Abigail IV, 683
Brannon, Alexander V, 661
Brannon, Alfred I, 630
Brannon, Alfred Brook I, 612
Brannon, Alfred Brook I, 630
Brannon, Alfred C. I, 630
Brannon, Alfred Cleveland I, 612
Brannon, Alfred Cleveland I, 630
Brannon, Bessie I, 628
Brannon, Bessie I, 630
Brannon, Bessie I, 938
Brannon, Bessie Wooters I, 630
Brannon, Charles Wm. V, 320
Brannon, Davis I, 630
Brannon, Davis I, 938
Brannon, Frank V, 661
Brannon, Frankey VI, 936

Brannon, Hannah IV, 683
Brannon, Hazel V, 661
Brannon, J. K. I, 630
Brannon, Joseph H. Camp V, 661
Brannon, Kate I, 630
Brannon, Kate Borntrager I, 612
Brannon, M. Davis I, 630
Brannon, Martha I, 612
Brannon, Martha I, 628
Brannon, Martha I, 630
Brannon, Martha E. I, 612
Brannon, Martha E. I, 630
Brannon, Martha E. I, 938
Brannon, Monrovia I, 630
Brannon, Monrovy I, 938
Brannon, Olympus VI, 1006
Brannon, Rachel VI, 888
Brannon, Robie I, 630
Brannon, Rovy I, 938
Brannon, Sarah Kate I, 612
Brannon, Sarah Kate I, 630
Brannon, Thomas I, 612
Brannon, Thomas A. I, 630
Brannon, Thomas Benjamin V, 27
Brannon, William Henry I, 612
Brannon, William Henry I, 628
Brannstein, Anna III, 373
Branon, Alfred Brook I, 630
Branon, Bessie I, 643
Branon, Bessie May I, 921
Branon, Bethshabah VI, 999
Branon, Esther IV, 180
Branon, Esther IV, 300
Branon, Henry I, 921
Branon, Kate I, 630
Branon, Laurence VI, 999
Branon, M. Davis I, 921
Branon, Martha V, 556
Branon, Martha Elizabeth I, 921
Branon, Monrovy Frost I, 921
Branon, Rovy I, 938
Bransen, Lydia Jane IV, 1115
Bransford, Thomas A. VI, 852
Branson, ??? V, 443
Branson, Aaron I, 528
Branson, Aaron IV, 22
Branson, Aaron IV, 27
Branson, Aaron IV, 76
Branson, Aaron IV, 82
Branson, Aaron IV, 122
Branson, Aaron IV, 513
Branson, Aaron IV, 520
Branson, Aaron IV, 539
Branson, Aaron VI, 474
Branson, Abigail IV, 140
Branson, Abigail IV, 180
Branson, Abigail IV, 321
Branson, Abigail IV, 371
Branson, Abigail IV, 507
Branson, Abigail IV, 512
Branson, Abigail IV, 513
Branson, Abigail IV, 557
Branson, Abigail V, 224
Branson, Abner I, 709
Branson, Abner IV, 180
Branson, Abner IV, 683
Branson, Abraham IV, 22
Branson, Abraham IV, 180
Branson, Abraham IV, 289
Branson, Abraham IV, 305
Branson, Abraham IV, 321
Branson, Abraham V, 27
Branson, Abraham VI, 368
Branson, Abraham VI, 369
Branson, Abraham VI, 370
Branson, Abraham VI, 387
Branson, Abraham VI, 435
Branson, Abraham VI, 455
Branson, Abraham D. IV, 165
Branson, Abraham D. VI, 370
Branson, Abraham W. IV, 180
Branson, Abraham W. IV, 289
Branson, Abram VI, 369
Branson, Ailse II, 194
Branson, Ailse II, 200
Branson, Albert IV, 513
Branson, Albert D. IV, 513
Branson, Alice II, 200
Branson, Allison IV, 1123
Branson, Alpheus IV, 1354
Branson, Amelia IV, 141
Branson, Amos V, 828
Branson, Amos V, 838
Branson, Amos V, 839
Branson, Amy IV, 321
Branson, Amy IV, 355
Branson, Amy IV, 371
Branson, Amy IV, 554
Branson, Ann III, 397
Branson, Ann III, 409
Branson, Ann IV, 180
Branson, Ann IV, 289
Branson, Ann IV, 305
Branson, Ann IV, 512
Branson, Ann IV, 513
Branson, Ann V, 27
Branson, Ann VI, 369
Branson, Ann VI, 370
Branson, Ann VI, 387
Branson, Ann VI, 474
Branson, Ann VI, 592
Branson, Ann VI, 732
Branson, Ann B. VI, 368
Branson, Ann B. VI, 370
Branson, Ann Bailey VI, 369
Branson, Ann Bailey VI, 732
Branson, Ann Bailey VI, 739
Branson, Ann Baily VI, 370
Branson, Ann Eliza IV, 513
Branson, Ann Eliza IV, 528
Branson, Ann Mary II, 729
Branson, Ann S. Vanlaw IV, 1088
Branson, Ann W. IV, 180
Branson, Anna II, 200
Branson, Anna III, 45
Branson, Anna IV, 140
Branson, Anna IV, 141
Branson, Anna IV, 180
Branson, Anna IV, 321
Branson, Anna IV, 354
Branson, Anna V, 949
Branson, Anna V, 950
Branson, Anna Florence III, 45
Branson, Anna L. IV, 371
Branson, Anna L. IV, 451
Branson, Anna M. II, 708
Branson, Anna M. III, 45
Branson, Anna M. III, 182
Branson, Anna M. IV, 180
Branson, Anna M. IV, 536
Branson, Anna Mary II, 700
Branson, Anna Mary II, 729
Branson, Anna Mary II, 744
Branson, Anna Mary IV, 513
Branson, Anna Mary IV, 534
Branson, Anna S. V, 949
Branson, Anne L. IV, 180
Branson, Anne L. IV, 512
Branson, Anne Mary IV, 513
Branson, Anner VI, 443
Branson, Annie L. IV, 513
Branson, Annie L. IV, 555
Branson, Aquila IV, 523
Branson, Aquilla IV, 512
Branson, Aquilla IV, 513
Branson, Asa IV, 180
Branson, Asa IV, 275
Branson, Asa IV, 321
Branson, Asa IV, 371
Branson, Asa IV, 512
Branson, Asa IV, 513
Branson, Asa IV, 516
Branson, Asa VI, 370
Branson, Asa, Jr. IV, 513
Branson, Benj. IV, 213
Branson, Benjamin IV, 180
Branson, Benjamin IV, 512
Branson, Benjamin VI, 369
Branson, Benjamin VI, 474
Branson, Bessie I, 612
Branson, Bessie I, 613
Branson, Bulah VI, 592
Branson, Bulay VI, 592
Branson, Byron Monroe I, 612
Branson, Byron Russell I, 612
Branson, Byron Russell I, 613
Branson, Cadiz O. III, 45
Branson, Carey C. I, 650
Branson, Caroline IV, 176
Branson, Caroline IV, 180
Branson, Caroline IV, 213
Branson, Caroline IV, 513
Branson, Caroline VI, 381
Branson, Catharine IV, 149
Branson, Catharine IV, 165
Branson, Catharine IV, 513
Branson, Catharine IV, 530
Branson, Catherine VI, 369
Branson, Catherine VI, 435
Branson, Cathrine VI, 369
Branson, Charity V, 224
Branson, Charity VI, 369
Branson, Charles IV, 180
Branson, Charles David VI, 369
Branson, Charles David VI, 370
Branson, Charles David Hopewell VI, 732
Branson, Charles F. III, 45
Branson, Charles F. III, 182
Branson, Charles F., Jr. III, 45
Branson, Charlotte S. IV, 180
Branson, Chester D. I, 650
Branson, Daniel H. IV, 513
Branson, David I, 492
Branson, David I, 960
Branson, David II, 200
Branson, David II, 703
Branson, David IV, 276
Branson, David IV, 321
Branson, David IV, 355
Branson, David IV, 512
Branson, David IV, 513
Branson, David IV, 521
Branson, David IV, 528
Branson, David IV, 529
Branson, David IV, 531
Branson, David IV, 534
Branson, David IV, 550
Branson, David IV, 718
Branson, David IV, 1088
Branson, David IV, 1090
Branson, David V, 224
Branson, David V, 375
Branson, David V, 445
Branson, David V, 853
Branson, David V, 875
Branson, David VI, 592
Branson, David W. VI, 368
Branson, David W. VI, 369
Branson, David W. VI, 370
Branson, David, Jr. V, 828
Branson, Deborah IV, 512
Branson, Dorothy Holmes VI, 732
Branson, Dorothy Holmes VI, 791
Branson, E. Caroline VI, 369
Branson, E. Caroline VI, 370
Branson, E. Caroline VI, 383
Branson, Edith VI, 369
Branson, Edith VI, 370
Branson, Edith VI, 732
Branson, Edith VI, 747
Branson, Eleanor IV, 1088
Branson, Eleanor Jane I, 674
Branson, Eleanor Jane I, 692
Branson, Elen I, 650
Branson, Elenor IV, 1088
Branson, Elenor IV, 1123
Branson, Elenor P. IV, 513
Branson, Eli I, 346
Branson, Eli I, 374
Branson, Eli I, 375
Branson, Eli I, 465
Branson, Eli I, 650
Branson, Eli I, 697
Branson, Eli I, 709
Branson, Elias IV, 180
Branson, Elinor Jane I, 612
Branson, Elisabeth II, 282
Branson, Elisha VI, 370
Branson, Elisha S. IV, 512
Branson, Eliza IV, 140
Branson, Eliza IV, 141
Branson, Eliza IV, 180
Branson, Eliza IV, 256
Branson, Eliza IV, 321
Branson, Eliza IV, 512
Branson, Eliza IV, 513
Branson, Eliza IV, 557
Branson, Eliza IV, 558
Branson, Eliza IV, 683
Branson, Eliza IV, 746
Branson, Eliza IV, 1088
Branson, Eliza IV, 1118
Branson, Eliza IV, 1123
Branson, Eliza V, 949
Branson, Eliza J. IV, 180
Branson, Eliza J. IV, 255
Branson, Eliza Jane IV, 180
Branson, Eliza W. V, 949
Branson, Eliza W. V, 950
Branson, Elizabeth I, 346
Branson, Elizabeth I, 375
Branson, Elizabeth I, 380
Branson, Elizabeth I, 650
Branson, Elizabeth I, 674
Branson, Elizabeth I, 685
Branson, Elizabeth I, 755
Branson, Elizabeth I, 760
Branson, Elizabeth I, 800
Branson, Elizabeth II, 199
Branson, Elizabeth II, 200
Branson, Elizabeth IV, 141
Branson, Elizabeth IV, 149
Branson, Elizabeth IV, 180
Branson, Elizabeth IV, 290
Branson, Elizabeth IV, 321
Branson, Elizabeth IV, 371
Branson, Elizabeth IV, 379
Branson, Elizabeth IV, 512
Branson, Elizabeth IV, 513
Branson, Elizabeth IV, 518
Branson, Elizabeth IV, 530
Branson, Elizabeth IV, 797
Branson, Elizabeth V, 27
Branson, Elizabeth V, 224
Branson, Elizabeth V, 828
Branson, Elizabeth VI, 368
Branson, Elizabeth VI, 369
Branson, Elizabeth VI, 370
Branson, Elizabeth VI, 380
Branson, Elizabeth VI, 453
Branson, Elizabeth VI, 592
Branson, Elizabeth VI, 595
Branson, Elizabeth VI, 598
Branson, Elizabeth VI, 732
Branson, Elizabeth A. VI, 369
Branson, Elizabeth Frances VI, 376
Branson, Elizabeth R. IV, 513
Branson, Elizabeth S. IV, 180
Branson, Elizabeth S. IV, 289
Branson, Ellen I, 709
Branson, Ellen M. VI, 369
Branson, Ellen M. VI, 732
Branson, Ellen M. VI, 774
Branson, Ellen M. VI, 791
Branson, Elma II, 712
Branson, Elma IV, 76
Branson, Elma IV, 122
Branson, Elma IV, 513
Branson, Elma IV, 683
Branson, Elma P. IV, 513
Branson, Elma P. IV, 537
Branson, Elvira IV, 180
Branson, Elvira B. IV, 180
Branson, Elvira B. IV, 237
Branson, Emily J. I, 346
Branson, Emma V, 375
Branson, Emma J. II, 703
Branson, Emma J. IV, 513
Branson, Emma J. IV, 521
Branson, Emma Jane IV, 513
Branson, Esther VI, 474
Branson, Eunice I, 492
Branson, Eunice I, 709
Branson, Eunice VI, 369
Branson, Eunice VI, 459
Branson, Florence VI, 771
Branson, Florence Bell VI, 370
Branson, Florence D. III, 397
Branson, Florence Dell III, 409
Branson, Florence Dell VI, 369
Branson, Florence Dell VI, 370
Branson, Florence Dell VI, 383
Branson, Florence Dell VI, 732
Branson, Florence Dell VI, 739
Branson, Florence Dell VI, 747
Branson, Frances IV, 22
Branson, Frances IV, 27
Branson, Frances IV, 76
Branson, Frances IV, 82
Branson, Frances IV, 122
Branson, Frances IV, 520
Branson, Frances IV, 539
Branson, Francis W. IV, 513
Branson, George III, 45
Branson, George VI, 474
Branson, Gulielmah IV, 512
Branson, Hannah I, 492
Branson, Hannah I, 709
Branson, Hannah I, 726
Branson, Hannah V, 224
Branson, Hannah V, 445
Branson, Hannah VI, 474
Branson, Hannah VI, 592
Branson, Hannah Priscilla IV, 321
Branson, Hannah Priscilla IV, 333
Branson, Hannah Priscilla IV, 338
Branson, Henry I, 346
Branson, Henry I, 374
Branson, Henry I, 382
Branson, Henry I, 709
Branson, Henry M. I, 709
Branson, Henry W. III, 45
Branson, Henry, Jr. I, 709
Branson, Herman W. I, 650
Branson, Hopy IV, 1354
Branson, Hortense S. IV, 180
Branson, Howard IV, 513
Branson, Isaac IV, 22
Branson, Isaac IV, 141
Branson, Isaac IV, 180
Branson, Isaac IV, 192
Branson, Isaac IV, 321
Branson, Isaac IV, 371
Branson, Isaac V, 445
Branson, Isaac VI, 369
Branson, Isaac VI, 370
Branson, Isaac Elsworth IV, 321
Branson, Isaac L. IV, 512
Branson, Isaac L. IV, 513
Branson, Isaiah IV, 141
Branson, Isaiah IV, 371
Branson, Isaiah IV, 416
Branson, Isaiah IV, 513
Branson, Isaiah IV, 538
Branson, Isaiah VI, 474
Branson, Isaiah J. IV, 513
Branson, Israel IV, 512
Branson, Israel IV, 513
Branson, Israel IV, 549
Branson, J. Howard II, 729
Branson, Jacob I, 492
Branson, Jacob I, 960
Branson, Jacob II, 700
Branson, Jacob IV, 22
Branson, Jacob IV, 140
Branson, Jacob IV, 180
Branson, Jacob IV, 371
Branson, Jacob IV, 507
Branson, Jacob IV, 512
Branson, Jacob IV, 513
Branson, Jacob IV, 547
Branson, Jacob IV, 555
Branson, Jacob IV, 669
Branson, Jacob IV, 683
Branson, Jacob IV, 728
Branson, Jacob V, 27
Branson, Jacob V, 224
Branson, Jacob VI, 369
Branson, Jacob VI, 592
Branson, Jacob VI, 598
Branson, Jacob VI, 655
Branson, Jacob, Jr. IV, 513
Branson, Jacob, Sr. IV, 512
Branson, James II, 282
Branson, James VI, 474
Branson, James Lawton IV, 512
Branson, James M. I, 346
Branson, James, Jr. II, 282
Branson, Jane I, 374
Branson, Jane I, 382
Branson, Jane I, 528
Branson, Jane I, 650
Branson, Jane I, 674
Branson, Jane I, 709
Branson, Jane I, 735
Branson, Jane I, 755
Branson, Jane I, 1090
Branson, Jane IV, 321
Branson, Jane IV, 330
Branson, Jane IV, 512
Branson, Jane IV, 513
Branson, Jane IV, 518
Branson, Jane IV, 549
Branson, Jane IV, 552
Branson, Jane IV, 1088
Branson, Jane V, 27
Branson, Jane V, 224
Branson, Jane V, 375
Branson, Jane VI, 592
Branson, Jeane I, 492
Branson, Jemima I, 346
Branson, Jemima I, 375
Branson, Jemima I, 383
Branson, Jemima I, 461
Branson, Jeremiah S. I, 675
Branson, Jesse IV, 512
Branson, Jesse IV, 513
Branson, Jesse IV, 547
Branson, Jesse IV, 1088
Branson, Jesse IV, 1354
Branson, Jesse V, 853
Branson, Jesse K. V, 375
Branson, Jesse R. V, 375
Branson, John I, 346
Branson, John I, 375
Branson, John I, 492
Branson, John I, 650
Branson, John I, 675
Branson, John I, 755
Branson, John II, 200
Branson, John II, 246
Branson, John IV, 180
Branson, John IV, 321
Branson, John IV, 355
Branson, John IV, 512
Branson, John IV, 513
Branson, John IV, 557
Branson, John VI, 368
Branson, John VI, 369
Branson, John VI, 370
Branson, John VI, 387
Branson, John VI, 474
Branson, John C. I, 650
Branson, John C. IV, 180
Branson, John Clarkson I, 612
Branson, John D. IV, 1088
Branson, John H. IV, 180

Branson, John Hirst IV, 141
Branson, John J. IV, 512
Branson, John P. I, 650
Branson, John Vanlaw IV, 1088
Branson, John W. IV, 512
Branson, Jonathan II, 194
Branson, Jonathan II, 200
Branson, Jonathan IV, 180
Branson, Jonathan E. IV, 512
Branson, Jonathan Ellis IV, 513
Branson, Jonathan W. VI, 369
Branson, Jonathan W. VI, 370
Branson, Jonathan W. VI, 381
Branson, Jonathan W. VI, 383
Branson, Jos. VI, 369
Branson, Joseph I, 346
Branson, Joseph I, 374
Branson, Joseph I, 375
Branson, Joseph I, 800
Branson, Joseph III, 45
Branson, Joseph IV, 180
Branson, Joseph IV, 371
Branson, Joseph IV, 512
Branson, Joseph IV, 513
Branson, Joseph VI, 367
Branson, Joseph VI, 369
Branson, Joseph VI, 370
Branson, Joseph VI, 422
Branson, Joseph VI, 460
Branson, Joseph VI, 474
Branson, Joseph VI, 620
Branson, Joseph VI, 732
Branson, Joseph VI, 749
Branson, Joseph A. I, 650
Branson, Joseph A. I, 675
Branson, Joseph Addison I, 612
Branson, Joseph Addison I, 613
Branson, Joseph C. I, 346
Branson, Joseph H. II, 700
Branson, Joseph H. II, 708
Branson, Joseph H. II, 712
Branson, Joseph H. II, 729
Branson, Joseph H. II, 744
Branson, Joseph H. IV, 512
Branson, Joseph H. IV, 513
Branson, Joseph H. IV, 683
Branson, Joseph H. IV, 801
Branson, Joseph H. IV, 845
Branson, Joseph H. VI, 369
Branson, Joseph H. VI, 370
Branson, Joseph Holmes VI, 370
Branson, Joseph Holmes VI, 732
Branson, Joseph Holmes VI, 774
Branson, Joseph Holmes VI, 791
Branson, Joseph Holmes, Jr. VI, 732
Branson, Joseph Howard II, 700
Branson, Joseph Howard II, 729
Branson, Josephine IV, 321
Branson, Joshua E. II, 471
Branson, Josiah IV, 512
Branson, Josiah VI, 387
Branson, Jula Ellen IV, 513
Branson, Julia E. II, 729
Branson, Julia E. IV, 513
Branson, Julia Ellen II, 700
Branson, Julia Ellen II, 729
Branson, Julian H. IV, 512
Branson, Julian H. IV, 513
Branson, Julian H. IV, 683
Branson, Julian H. IV, 728
Branson, Juliann IV, 683
Branson, Juliann H. II, 700
Branson, Juliann H. II, 729
Branson, Juliann H. IV, 180
Branson, Juliann H. IV, 514
Branson, Juliann H. IV, 555
Branson, Laura IV, 1354
Branson, Laurence IV, 513
Branson, Levi I, 346
Branson, Levi I, 374
Branson, Levi I, 375
Branson, Levi I, 612
Branson, Levi I, 800
Branson, Levi I, 828
Branson, Levi IV, 512
Branson, Levi IV, 513
Branson, Levi IV, 683
Branson, Levi Angelica IV, 512
Branson, Levi Clark I, 650
Branson, Levi T. I, 709
Branson, Levi, Jr. I, 375
Branson, Levy I, 346
Branson, Levy I, 374
Branson, Levy I, 408
Branson, Lillian VI, 369
Branson, Lindley IV, 180
Branson, Lindley M. III, 45
Branson, Lineal II, 200
Branson, Lizzie IV, 513
Branson, Lizzie M. IV, 180
Branson, Lizzie M. IV, 278
Branson, Lizzie M. IV, 513
Branson, Lizzie M. IV, 550
Branson, Lizzie S. IV, 180
Branson, Lois I, 492
Branson, Lois I, 525
Branson, Lois I, 528
Branson, Loretta M. IV, 180
Branson, Lucy IV, 180
Branson, Lucy IV, 289
Branson, Lydia I, 346
Branson, Lydia I, 375
Branson, Lydia I, 382
Branson, Lydia I, 466
Branson, Lydia I, 709
Branson, Lydia I, 729
Branson, Lydia III, 45
Branson, Lydia IV, 141
Branson, Lydia IV, 321
Branson, Lydia IV, 355
Branson, Lydia IV, 371
Branson, Lydia IV, 512
Branson, Lydia IV, 513
Branson, Lydia IV, 531
Branson, Lydia IV, 547
Branson, Lydia IV, 1088
Branson, Lydia IV, 1090
Branson, Lydia VI, 474
Branson, Lydia E. IV, 512
Branson, Lydia E. IV, 1088
Branson, Lydia E. IV, 1104
Branson, Lydia Elizabeth IV, 1088
Branson, Lydia Emma V, 828
Branson, Lydia Jane IV, 321
Branson, Lydia Jane IV, 512
Branson, Lydia Jane IV, 513
Branson, Lydia Jane IV, 1088
Branson, Lydia Jane IV, 1090
Branson, Lydia Jr. IV, 523
Branson, Lydia Vanlaw IV, 321
Branson, Lydia, Jr. IV, 513
Branson, Lyndall II, 200
Branson, Lyndall II, 255
Branson, Margaret I, 619
Branson, Margaret D. I, 465
Branson, Margaret D. I, 675
Branson, Margaret D. I, 677
Branson, Maria IV, 180
Branson, Maria IV, 305
Branson, Maria IV, 321
Branson, Maria IV, 409
Branson, Maria VI, 370
Branson, Mariah IV, 180
Branson, Mariah IV, 305
Branson, Mariah IV, 321
Branson, Mariah VI, 370
Branson, Mariam IV, 321
Branson, Martha II, 200
Branson, Martha II, 246
Branson, Martha IV, 512
Branson, Martha IV, 513
Branson, Martha VI, 368
Branson, Martha VI, 369
Branson, Martha VI, 387
Branson, Martha H. IV, 513
Branson, Martha H. IV, 531
Branson, Martha H. IV, 1128
Branson, Martha H. IV, 1133
Branson, Mary I, 346
Branson, Mary I, 374
Branson, Mary I, 375
Branson, Mary I, 408
Branson, Mary I, 465
Branson, Mary I, 627
Branson, Mary I, 650
Branson, Mary I, 674
Branson, Mary I, 697
Branson, Mary I, 709
Branson, Mary I, 719
Branson, Mary II, 200
Branson, Mary II, 441
Branson, Mary II, 796
Branson, Mary IV, 180
Branson, Mary IV, 311
Branson, Mary IV, 321
Branson, Mary IV, 346
Branson, Mary IV, 371
Branson, Mary IV, 512
Branson, Mary IV, 513
Branson, Mary IV, 516
Branson, Mary IV, 554
Branson, Mary IV, 1004
Branson, Mary V, 224
Branson, Mary V, 375
Branson, Mary V, 420
Branson, Mary V, 828
Branson, Mary V, 853
Branson, Mary V, 875
Branson, Mary VI, 369
Branson, Mary VI, 370
Branson, Mary VI, 387
Branson, Mary VI, 388
Branson, Mary VI, 453
Branson, Mary VI, 474
Branson, Mary VI, 576
Branson, Mary VI, 732
Branson, Mary VI, 771
Branson, Mary Ann IV, 180
Branson, Mary E. IV, 180
Branson, Mary E. VI, 370
Branson, Mary Elizabeth IV, 512
Branson, Mary Elizabeth V, 839
Branson, Mary Elizabeth VI, 369
Branson, Mary Elizabeth VI, 732
Branson, Mary Ellen IV, 513
Branson, Mary Ellen IV, 514
Branson, Mary Ellen IV, 683
Branson, Mary Emma V, 375
Branson, Mary Jane IV, 180
Branson, Mary Jane IV, 283
Branson, Mary Jane IV, 366
Branson, Mary Jane IV, 512
Branson, Mary Jane IV, 513
Branson, Mary Jane IV, 552
Branson, Mary Jane V, 375
Branson, Mary Jane V, 436
Branson, Mary L. IV, 1123
Branson, Mary Lizzie V, 828
Branson, Mary R. IV, 512
Branson, Meriam II, 57
Branson, Milton IV, 683
Branson, Mira D. IV, 513
Branson, Miriam II, 57
Branson, Miriam II, 90
Branson, Miriam IV, 512
Branson, Miriam IV, 513
Branson, Miriam IV, 523
Branson, Miriam VI, 370
Branson, Miriam M. I, 346
Branson, Moses II, 200
Branson, Myra D. IV, 513
Branson, Myra D. IV, 529
Branson, Myra D. IV, 683
Branson, Myra D. IV, 718
Branson, Nancy IV, 321
Branson, Nancy IV, 512
Branson, Nancy IV, 513
Branson, Nancy IV, 524
Branson, Nancy IV, 1354
Branson, Nancy VI, 369
Branson, Nancy VI, 370
Branson, Nancy VI, 403
Branson, Nancy VI, 620
Branson, Nancy VI, 656
Branson, Nancy VI, 657
Branson, Nancy VI, 732
Branson, Nancy VI, 749
Branson, Nancy H. VI, 370
Branson, Nancy H. VI, 620
Branson, Nancy W. VI, 370
Branson, Naomi Albert V, 828
Branson, Nath'l VI, 369
Branson, Nathan I, 709
Branson, Nathan V, 224
Branson, Nathan V, 445
Branson, Nathan VI, 620
Branson, Nathaniel VI, 369
Branson, Nathaniel VI, 370
Branson, Nathaniel B. VI, 369
Branson, Nathaniel B. VI, 370
Branson, Nathaniel B. VI, 403
Branson, Nathaniel B. VI, 620
Branson, Nathaniel B. VI, 656
Branson, Nathaniel B. VI, 657
Branson, Nathaniel B. VI, 732
Branson, Nathaniel B. VI, 749
Branson, Oliver IV, 76
Branson, Oliver J. IV, 135
Branson, Patience I, 612
Branson, Phebe IV, 141
Branson, Phebe IV, 180
Branson, Phebe IV, 512
Branson, Phebe IV, 513
Branson, Phineas A. VI, 369
Branson, Phineas A. VI, 370
Branson, Pickering IV, 321
Branson, Priscilla V, 299
Branson, Priscilla V, 302
Branson, Priscilla V, 828
Branson, Priscilla V, 838
Branson, Priscilla V, 839
Branson, Rachel I, 346
Branson, Rachel I, 375
Branson, Rachel I, 424
Branson, Rachel I, 618
Branson, Rachel I, 800
Branson, Rachel I, 828
Branson, Rachel II, 721
Branson, Rachel IV, 180
Branson, Rachel IV, 275
Branson, Rachel IV, 289
Branson, Rachel IV, 512
Branson, Rachel IV, 513
Branson, Rachel IV, 549
Branson, Rachel IV, 950
Branson, Rachel V, 27
Branson, Rachel V, 853
Branson, Rachel VI, 369
Branson, Rachel VI, 592
Branson, Rachel VI, 597
Branson, Rachel VI, 598
Branson, Rachel B. IV, 549
Branson, Rachel Ellen IV, 683
Branson, Rachel Elma IV, 180
Branson, Ray H. I, 650
Branson, Rebecca I, 346
Branson, Rebecca I, 374
Branson, Rebecca II, 200
Branson, Rebecca II, 255
Branson, Rebecca II, 282
Branson, Rebecca IV, 22
Branson, Rebecca IV, 140
Branson, Rebecca IV, 180
Branson, Rebecca IV, 275
Branson, Rebecca IV, 371
Branson, Rebecca IV, 512
Branson, Rebecca IV, 683
Branson, Rebecca V, 27
Branson, Rebecca Ann IV, 76
Branson, Rebecca Ann IV, 122
Branson, Rebecca Ann IV, 371
Branson, Rebecca Ann IV, 513
Branson, Rebecca Anna IV, 383
Branson, Rebecca Anna IV, 513
Branson, Rebecca Anna IV, 520
Branson, Rebecca G. IV, 513
Branson, Rebecka VI, 592
Branson, Rebeckah II, 200
Branson, Rebeckah VI, 598
Branson, Rebekah I, 343
Branson, Rebekah I, 374
Branson, Rebekah I, 416
Branson, Rebekah VI, 474
Branson, Rees IV, 180
Branson, Rees IV, 221
Branson, Rees IV, 255
Branson, Rees IV, 305
Branson, Rees IV, 321
Branson, Rees IV, 683
Branson, Rees VI, 369
Branson, Rees VI, 370
Branson, Rees VI, 383
Branson, Rees Ruth Downing VI, 369
Branson, Reese IV, 683
Branson, Richard IV, 76
Branson, Richard IV, 122
Branson, Richard IV, 513
Branson, Richard IV, 514
Branson, Richard C. I, 709
Branson, Robert I, 492
Branson, Robert III, 45
Branson, Robert VI, 370
Branson, Robert VI, 592
Branson, Russell W. IV, 180
Branson, Ruth IV, 180
Branson, Ruth IV, 200
Branson, Ruth IV, 221
Branson, Ruth IV, 255
Branson, Ruth IV, 305
Branson, Ruth IV, 311
Branson, Ruth IV, 321
Branson, Ruth IV, 683
Branson, Ruth V, 27
Branson, Ruth V, 299
Branson, Ruth VI, 369
Branson, Ruth VI, 370
Branson, Ruth VI, 383
Branson, Ruth VI, 474
Branson, Ruth Anna IV, 513
Branson, Ruth Anna S. II, 729
Branson, Ruth Doing VI, 369
Branson, Ruth Doing VI, 370
Branson, Ruth Doing VI, 732
Branson, Ruth Hannah VI, 369
Branson, Ruth Hannah VI, 422
Branson, Ruthanna II, 700
Branson, Ruthanna II, 708
Branson, Ruthanna II, 712
Branson, Ruthanna IV, 513
Branson, Ruthanna IV, 683
Branson, Ruthanna IV, 801
Branson, Ruthanna IV, 845
Branson, Ruthanna G. II, 729
Branson, Ruthanna G. II, 744
Branson, Ruthanna S. IV, 801
Branson, Ruthanna Stratton IV, 836
Branson, Samuel II, 58
Branson, Samuel IV, 76
Branson, Samuel IV, 512
Branson, Samuel IV, 513
Branson, Samuel IV, 536
Branson, Samuel IV, 683
Branson, Samuel V, 299
Branson, Samuel V, 304
Branson, Samuel C. IV, 1088
Branson, Sarah I, 375
Branson, Sarah II, 200
Branson, Sarah II, 247
Branson, Sarah II, 339
Branson, Sarah IV, 22
Branson, Sarah IV, 141
Branson, Sarah IV, 156
Branson, Sarah IV, 180
Branson, Sarah IV, 192
Branson, Sarah IV, 321
Branson, Sarah IV, 512
Branson, Sarah IV, 513
Branson, Sarah IV, 528
Branson, Sarah IV, 531
Branson, Sarah IV, 718
Branson, Sarah VI, 369
Branson, Sarah VI, 370
Branson, Sarah VI, 387
Branson, Sarah VI, 455
Branson, Sarah VI, 474
Branson, Sarah VI, 592
Branson, Sarah VI, 595
Branson, Sarah A. IV, 180
Branson, Sarah A. IV, 513
Branson, Sarah A. IV, 514
Branson, Sarah A. IV, 536
Branson, Sarah A. V, 224
Branson, Sarah A. V, 299
Branson, Sarah A. V, 304
Branson, Sarah Ann IV, 180
Branson, Sarah Ann IV, 192
Branson, Sarah Ann IV, 560
Branson, Sarah Ann VI, 369
Branson, Sarah Ann VI, 370
Branson, Sarah Ann VI, 376
Branson, Sarah B. II, 703
Branson, Sarah B. IV, 276
Branson, Sarah B. IV, 513
Branson, Sarah B. IV, 534
Branson, Sarah E. I, 475
Branson, Sarah E. I, 650
Branson, Sarah E. I, 675
Branson, Sarah Elizabeth I, 612
Branson, Sarah Elizabeth I, 613
Branson, Sarah G. IV, 371
Branson, Sarah G. IV, 416
Branson, Sarah G. IV, 513
Branson, Sarah G. IV, 538
Branson, Sarah H. IV, 521
Branson, Sarah H. IV, 529
Branson, Sarah H. IV, 531
Branson, Sarah H. IV, 550
Branson, Sarah M. IV, 22
Branson, Sibyl I, 618
Branson, Sibyl I, 626
Branson, Sibyl I, 650
Branson, Sibyl I, 709
Branson, Sibyle I, 709
Branson, Sibyle I, 721
Branson, Sina Ann IV, 683
Branson, Sinah Ann IV, 683
Branson, Smith IV, 321
Branson, Smith IV, 330
Branson, Smith IV, 371
Branson, Smith IV, 512
Branson, Smith IV, 513
Branson, Smith IV, 518
Branson, Smith IV, 549
Branson, Smith IV, 552
Branson, Smith IV, 1088
Branson, Smith IV, 1118
Branson, Smith IV, 1123
Branson, Smith, Jr. IV, 512
Branson, Stacy II, 200
Branson, Stacy V, 828
Branson, Susan IV, 76
Branson, Susan G. IV, 122
Branson, Susan G. IV, 513
Branson, Susan G. IV, 539
Branson, Susannah IV, 512
Branson, Susannah IV, 513
Branson, Susannah VI, 474
Branson, Sylvanus IV, 1354
Branson, Tacy VI, 367
Branson, Tacy VI, 369
Branson, Tacy VI, 370
Branson, Tacy VI, 383
Branson, Tacy VI, 422
Branson, Tacy VI, 460
Branson, Tacy VI, 620
Branson, Tacy VI, 732
Branson, Tacy VI, 749
Branson, Tacy Wright VI, 369
Branson, Thamasin H. VI, 369
Branson, Thamasin H. VI, 454
Branson, Thomas I, 343

Branson, Thomas I, 346
Branson, Thomas I, 374
Branson, Thomas I, 375
Branson, Thomas I, 492
Branson, Thomas I, 525
Branson, Thomas I, 528
Branson, Thomas I, 674
Branson, Thomas I, 685
Branson, Thomas I, 709
Branson, Thomas I, 960
Branson, Thomas II, 199
Branson, Thomas II, 200
Branson, Thomas IV, 76
Branson, Thomas IV, 140
Branson, Thomas IV, 141
Branson, Thomas IV, 321
Branson, Thomas IV, 1088
Branson, Thomas V, 27
Branson, Thomas V, 224
Branson, Thomas V, 375
Branson, Thomas V, 445
Branson, Thomas V, 828
Branson, Thomas V, 949
Branson, Thomas V, 950
Branson, Thomas VI, 357
Branson, Thomas VI, 369
Branson, Thomas VI, 370
Branson, Thomas VI, 592
Branson, Thomas H. IV, 513
Branson, Thomas H. VI, 369
Branson, Thomas H. VI, 454
Branson, Thomas W. IV, 122
Branson, Thomas W. IV, 513
Branson, Thomas, Jr. VI, 369
Branson, Thomasin H. V, 949
Branson, Thomasin H. VI, 370
Branson, Thomasin H. Walker VI, 370
Branson, Thos. IV, 354
Branson, Thos. V, 436
Branson, Unice VI, 369
Branson, Unice VI, 592
Branson, Walter J. II, 700
Branson, Walter J. II, 729
Branson, Walter J. IV, 513
Branson, Walter J. IV, 683
Branson, Wd. Mary V, 853
Branson, William II, 200
Branson, William II, 339
Branson, William II, 441
Branson, William IV, 180
Branson, William IV, 321
Branson, William IV, 512
Branson, William IV, 531
Branson, William VI, 368
Branson, William VI, 369
Branson, William VI, 370
Branson, William VI, 453
Branson, William VI, 592
Branson, William VI, 595
Branson, William VI, 598
Branson, William D. IV, 180
Branson, William D. IV, 256
Branson, William D. IV, 683
Branson, William E. IV, 512
Branson, William E. VI, 369
Branson, William E. VI, 370
Branson, William E. VI, 383
Branson, William E. VI, 732
Branson, William E. VI, 739
Branson, William E. VI, 747
Branson, William G. IV, 180
Branson, William Gurney V, 828
Branson, William P. VI, 369
Branson, William P. VI, 376
Branson, Willis V, 375
Branson, Wm. IV, 683
Branson, Wm. D. IV, 746
Branson, Wm. E. III, 397
Branson, Wm. E. III, 409
Branson, Wm. E. IV, 513
Branson, Wm. E. VI, 732
Branson, Wm. E. VI, 771
Branson, Wm. M. III, 45
Branson, Wm. M. III, 182
Branson, Wm. W. IV, 180
Branston, Mary II, 441
Branston, Nathaniel II, 441
Branston, Rachel II, 441
Branston, William II, 441
Brant, Albertus II, 339
Brant, Albertus II, 441
Brant, Elizabeth IV, 845
Brant, Jacob II, 441
Brant, Mary II, 339
Brant, Susan II, 339
Brant, Susannah II, 441
Brantingham, A. Elizabeth IV, 1036
Brantingham, Abby II, 700
Brantingham, Abby Louise II, 700
Brantingham, Abby S. II, 729
Brantingham, Abby S. II, 732
Brantingham, Adna IV, 929
Brantingham, Alace A. IV, 803
Brantingham, Alfred II, 700
Brantingham, Alfred II, 720
Brantingham, Alfred IV, 801
Brantingham, Alfred IV, 803
Brantingham, Alfred IV, 845
Brantingham, Alfred IV, 900
Brantingham, Alfred IV, 929
Brantingham, Alfred J. IV, 802
Brantingham, Alfred W. IV, 929
Brantingham, Alice IV, 802
Brantingham, Alice IV, 803
Brantingham, Alice IV, 809
Brantingham, Alice IV, 929
Brantingham, Alice IV, 945
Brantingham, Alice A. IV, 802
Brantingham, Alice A. IV, 809
Brantingham, Alice A. IV, 929
Brantingham, Alice A. IV, 945
Brantingham, Alice C. IV, 803
Brantingham, Allen C. IV, 802
Brantingham, Allen C. IV, 803
Brantingham, Alma IV, 929
Brantingham, Alma IV, 961
Brantingham, Angelina IV, 929
Brantingham, Angeline IV, 929
Brantingham, Angeline IV, 956
Brantingham, Ann II, 700
Brantingham, Ann II, 720
Brantingham, Ann IV, 803
Brantingham, Ann IV, 807
Brantingham, Ann IV, 845
Brantingham, Ann IV, 900
Brantingham, Ann M. IV, 851
Brantingham, Ann M. IV, 929
Brantingham, Anna IV, 801
Brantingham, Anna IV, 803
Brantingham, Anna IV, 809
Brantingham, Anna IV, 833
Brantingham, Anna IV, 845
Brantingham, Anna IV, 945
Brantingham, Anna C. IV, 802
Brantingham, Anna E. IV, 803
Brantingham, Anna E. IV, 929
Brantingham, Anna M. IV, 568
Brantingham, Anna M. IV, 577
Brantingham, Anna M. IV, 802
Brantingham, Anna M. IV, 803
Brantingham, Anna M. IV, 813
Brantingham, Anna M. IV, 846
Brantingham, Arthur IV, 929
Brantingham, Arthur IV, 1036
Brantingham, Barclay IV, 802
Brantingham, C. Wilmer II, 700
Brantingham, C. Wilmer II, 729
Brantingham, C. Wilmer IV, 684
Brantingham, C. Wilmer IV, 802
Brantingham, C. Wilmer IV, 803
Brantingham, Charles IV, 802
Brantingham, Charles IV, 803
Brantingham, Cyrus II, 700
Brantingham, Cyrus IV, 801
Brantingham, Cyrus IV, 802
Brantingham, Cyrus IV, 803
Brantingham, Cyrus IV, 830
Brantingham, Deborah II, 200
Brantingham, Deborah II, 267
Brantingham, E. Anetta II, 711
Brantingham, E. Anetta IV, 684
Brantingham, E. Anetta IV, 733
Brantingham, E. Annetta IV, 803
Brantingham, Edward IV, 929
Brantingham, Elisha H. IV, 802
Brantingham, Elisha K. II, 700
Brantingham, Elisha K. II, 729
Brantingham, Elisha K. II, 732
Brantingham, Elisha K. IV, 683
Brantingham, Elisha K. IV, 733
Brantingham, Elisha K. IV, 803
Brantingham, Elisha K. IV, 833
Brantingham, Elizabeth IV, 691
Brantingham, Elizabeth IV, 801
Brantingham, Elizabeth IV, 802
Brantingham, Elizabeth IV, 803
Brantingham, Elizabeth IV, 811
Brantingham, Elizabeth IV, 845
Brantingham, Elizabeth IV, 846
Brantingham, Elizabeth IV, 900
Brantingham, Elizabeth IV, 929
Brantingham, Elizabeth B. IV, 797
Brantingham, Elizabeth B. IV, 802
Brantingham, Elizabeth B. IV, 803
Brantingham, Elizabeth B. IV, 832
Brantingham, Ella IV, 1036
Brantingham, Ella C. IV, 1036
Brantingham, Ella Coppock IV, 803
Brantingham, Ellen II, 294
Brantingham, Ellen IV, 929
Brantingham, Ellen IV, 975
Brantingham, Ellen C. IV, 929
Brantingham, Elma IV, 802
Brantingham, Elma IV, 803
Brantingham, Elma IV, 845
Brantingham, Elma IV, 846
Brantingham, Elsie IV, 929
Brantingham, Elsie IV, 1010
Brantingham, Emma Annetta IV, 802
Brantingham, Esther IV, 802
Brantingham, Esther IV, 929
Brantingham, Florence IV, 929
Brantingham, Frank IV, 929
Brantingham, G. Alfrod IV, 802
Brantingham, Geo. IV, 801
Brantingham, Geo. IV, 802
Brantingham, Geo. L. IV, 797
Brantingham, Geo. L. IV, 832
Brantingham, George II, 471
Brantingham, George IV, 683
Brantingham, George IV, 684
Brantingham, George IV, 801
Brantingham, George IV, 802
Brantingham, George IV, 929
Brantingham, George IV, 946
Brantingham, George IV, 992
Brantingham, George L. IV, 803
Brantingham, George Lydia IV, 802
Brantingham, George, Jr. IV, 802
Brantingham, George, Jr. IV, 843
Brantingham, George, Jr. IV, 929
Brantingham, Grace IV, 929
Brantingham, Grace IV, 945
Brantingham, Grace C. IV, 802
Brantingham, Grace C. IV, 803
Brantingham, Grace C. IV, 929
Brantingham, Hannah II, 471
Brantingham, Hannah III, 45
Brantingham, Hannah III, 96
Brantingham, Hannah IV, 683
Brantingham, Hannah IV, 684
Brantingham, Hannah IV, 802
Brantingham, Hannah IV, 843
Brantingham, Hannah IV, 929
Brantingham, Hannah IV, 946
Brantingham, Hannah IV, 992
Brantingham, Hannah C. II, 946
Brantingham, Hannah C. IV, 684
Brantingham, Hannah C. IV, 929
Brantingham, Hannah D. II, 715
Brantingham, Hannah D. II, 720
Brantingham, Hannah D. IV, 802
Brantingham, Hannah D. IV, 803
Brantingham, Hannah D. IV, 845
Brantingham, Hannah D. IV, 846
Brantingham, Hannah D. IV, 900
Brantingham, Hervey IV, 803
Brantingham, Hugh IV, 683
Brantingham, Isabel IV, 929
Brantingham, Isabella IV, 929
Brantingham, Jacob III, 45
Brantingham, James IV, 803
Brantingham, James IV, 929
Brantingham, James IV, 1036
Brantingham, James Arthur IV, 803
Brantingham, James Arthur IV, 929
Brantingham, James H. IV, 802
Brantingham, James H. IV, 803
Brantingham, James H. IV, 929
Brantingham, James Harvey IV, 802
Brantingham, James Wilmer II, 700
Brantingham, Jary IV, 1003
Brantingham, Jesse Lareau IV, 802
Brantingham, John IV, 929
Brantingham, John R. IV, 929
Brantingham, Jos. IV, 802
Brantingham, Jos. IV, 845
Brantingham, Joseph II, 167
Brantingham, Joseph II, 186
Brantingham, Joseph II, 200
Brantingham, Joseph II, 267
Brantingham, Joseph II, 471
Brantingham, Joseph III, 45
Brantingham, Joseph IV, 684
Brantingham, Joseph IV, 801
Brantingham, Joseph IV, 803
Brantingham, Joseph IV, 811
Brantingham, Joseph IV, 846
Brantingham, Joseph IV, 851
Brantingham, Joseph IV, 853
Brantingham, Joseph IV, 929
Brantingham, Joseph C. IV, 802
Brantingham, Joseph C. IV, 929
Brantingham, Joseph C. IV, 945
Brantingham, Joseph Masters II, 729
Brantingham, Joshua IV, 802
Brantingham, Joshua IV, 803
Brantingham, Joshua IV, 817
Brantingham, Joshua IV, 830
Brantingham, Joshua IV, 900
Brantingham, Joshua Clifford IV, 802
Brantingham, Leslie Raymond IV, 802
Brantingham, Lizzie T. IV, 1202
Brantingham, Lydia IV, 180
Brantingham, Lydia IV, 290
Brantingham, Lydia IV, 568
Brantingham, Lydia IV, 801
Brantingham, Lydia IV, 802
Brantingham, Lydia IV, 803
Brantingham, Lydia IV, 811
Brantingham, Lydia IV, 845
Brantingham, Lydia IV, 848
Brantingham, Lydia IV, 853
Brantingham, Lydia IV, 929
Brantingham, Lydia Rachel II, 700
Brantingham, M. P. IV, 1308
Brantingham, Margaret IV, 683
Brantingham, Margaret IV, 684
Brantingham, Margaret IV, 723
Brantingham, Margaret IV, 929
Brantingham, Martin IV, 683
Brantingham, Martin IV, 684
Brantingham, Martin IV, 723
Brantingham, Martin IV, 929
Brantingham, Martin IV, 1308
Brantingham, Mary II, 720
Brantingham, Mary IV, 683
Brantingham, Mary IV, 803
Brantingham, Mary IV, 929
Brantingham, Mary IV, 1308
Brantingham, Mary A. II, 700
Brantingham, Mary A. II, 729
Brantingham, Mary A. II, 732
Brantingham, Mary A. IV, 683
Brantingham, Mary A. IV, 684
Brantingham, Mary A. IV, 733
Brantingham, Mary A. IV, 802
Brantingham, Mary Anna IV, 929
Brantingham, Mary C. II, 720
Brantingham, Mary C. IV, 802
Brantingham, Mary C. IV, 847
Brantingham, Mary E. IV, 803
Brantingham, Mary Elizabeth II, 700
Brantingham, Mary Esther IV, 803
Brantingham, Mary M. IV, 803
Brantingham, Mary M. IV, 830
Brantingham, Mary Morlan IV, 802
Brantingham, Phebe II, 471
Brantingham, Phebe IV, 683
Brantingham, Phebe IV, 684
Brantingham, Phebe IV, 801
Brantingham, Phebe IV, 803
Brantingham, Phebe IV, 929
Brantingham, Phebe D. IV, 803
Brantingham, Polly Maria IV, 802
Brantingham, Polly Marie IV, 802
Brantingham, Rachel IV, 801
Brantingham, Rachel IV, 802
Brantingham, Rachel IV, 803
Brantingham, Rachel IV, 830
Brantingham, Rachel IV, 845
Brantingham, Rachel IV, 929
Brantingham, Rachel E. II, 700
Brantingham, Rachel E. II, 729
Brantingham, Rachel E. IV, 802
Brantingham, Rachel K. IV, 802
Brantingham, Rebecca IV, 929
Brantingham, Rebecca IV, 946
Brantingham, Rhoda IV, 802
Brantingham, Rhoda IV, 929
Brantingham, Roselia IV, 929
Brantingham, Roselia IV, 992
Brantingham, Sally IV, 992
Brantingham, Samuel IV, 929
Brantingham, Sara IV, 255
Brantingham, Sara IV, 802
Brantingham, Sara IV, 809
Brantingham, Sara IV, 844
Brantingham, Sara K. IV, 802
Brantingham, Sarah II, 200
Brantingham, Sarah II, 267
Brantingham, Sarah II, 700
Brantingham, Sarah II, 702
Brantingham, Sarah III, 45
Brantingham, Sarah III, 290
Brantingham, Sarah IV, 802
Brantingham, Sarah IV, 803
Brantingham, Sarah IV, 817
Brantingham, Sarah IV, 830
Brantingham, Sarah IV, 929
Brantingham, Sarah IV, 945
Brantingham, Sarah H. IV, 802
Brantingham, Sarah H. IV, 929
Brantingham, Sarah H. IV, 978
Brantingham, Sarah Hopper IV, 684
Brantingham, Sarah Hopper IV, 802
Brantingham, Sarah M. II, 186
Brantingham, Sarah R. IV, 803
Brantingham, Sina IV, 451
Brantingham, Sina IV, 568
Brantingham, Sina IV, 577
Brantingham, Sina IV, 803
Brantingham, Sina IV, 832
Brantingham, Sina IV, 833
Brantingham, Sina IV, 843
Brantingham, Sina IV, 851
Brantingham, Thomas III, 45
Brantingham, Wilford T. IV, 802
Brantingham, William II, 700
Brantingham, William IV, 801
Brantingham, William IV, 802
Brantingham, William IV, 803
Brantingham, William IV, 929
Brantingham, William Chappell II, 700
Brantingham, Wilmer II, 732
Brantingham, Wilson IV, 803
Brantingham, Wilson IV, 929
Brantingham, Wilson IV, 945
Brantingham, Wilson Crawford IV, 802
Brantingham, Wilson J. IV, 802
Brantingham, Wilson J. IV, 803
Brantingham, Wm. II, 729
Brantingham, Wm. IV, 802
Brantingham, Wm. IV, 803
Brantingham, Wm. IV, 807
Brantingham, Wm. IV, 809
Brantingham, Wm. IV, 845
Brantingham, Wm. IV, 929
Brantingham, Wm. IV, 945
Brantingham, Wm. S. IV, 803
Brantley, Bettie D. VI, 55
Brantley, Charles C. VI, 55
Brantley, Hannah VI, 51
Brantley, Hannah C. VI, 52
Brantley, Hannah C. VI, 55
Brantley, Jane VI, 55
Brantley, John VI, 42
Brantley, Josie VI, 55
Brantley, Josie VI, 69
Brantley, Luther H. VI, 55
Brantley, Luther H. VI, 69
Brantley, Mary B. VI, 55
Brantley, Orris VI, 55
Brantley, Robert Raymond VI, 55
Brantley, William E. VI, 55
Brantly, Bettie D. VI, 55
Brantly, Charles C. VI, 55
Brantly, Hannah VI, 91
Brantly, Hannah C. VI, 51
Brantly, James C. I, 240
Brantly, Jane I, 231
Brantly, Jane I, 234
Brantly, Jane VI, 51
Brantly, Jane C. I, 231
Brantly, Orris VI, 51
Brantly, Pattie I, 921
Branton, Jacob I, 375
Braselton, Elizabeth I, 1116
Braselton, Lydia I, 1116
Braselton, Lydia I, 1132
Braselton, William I, 1116
Brasey, Francis VI, 55
Brasey, Francis VI, 63
Brasey, Mary VI, 63
Brasey, Mary Edmunds VI, 55
Brashare, Margaret VI, 24
Brashare, Margaret VI, 40
Brashare, Margarett VI, 27
Brashare, Robert VI, 27
Brasier, John I, 38
Brasselton, Abigail I, 1116
Brasselton, Elizabeth I, 1116
Brasselton, Hannah I, 1116
Brasselton, Hannah I, 1126
Brasselton, Lydia I, 1116
Brasselton, William I, 1116
Brassey, Patience VI, 45
Brastow, Lewis Cornetti II, 784

Brastow, Louis Cornetti II, 784
Brastow, Mary W. II, 840
Brastow, Mary Wooley II, 784
Braswell, J. T. I, 938
Braswell, John H. I, 921
Braswell, Lenton Jones I, 921
Braswell, Pattie I, 921
Bratain, Anna I, 800
Bratain, Jonathan I, 800
Bratain, Mary I, 800
Bratain, Robert I, 800
Bratcher, Benjamin VI, 131
Bratcher, Benjamin VI, 143
Bratcher, Betsey VI, 927
Bratcher, Canady VI, 923
Bratcher, John VI, 883
Bratcher, John VI, 912
Bratcher, John VI, 927
Bratcher, Nancey VI, 883
Bratcher, Polly VI, 982
Bratcher, Susanna VI, 923
Bratcher, Tempy VI, 912
Brathwit, Margret II, 58
Brathwit, Margret II, 96
Bratingham, Alfred IV, 811
Bratingham, Ann IV, 811
Bratingham, Elizabeth IV, 811
Bratingham, Mary IV, 847
Bratingham, Rachel IV, 846
Bratingham, Rhoda IV, 811
Bratingham, Wm. IV, 811
Brats, John VI, 27
Bratt, Frank IV, 1247
Brattain, Jonathan V, 828
Brattain, Martha I, 873
Brattain, Martha I, 892
Brattain, Paul I, 873
Brattan, Anna I, 800
Bratten, Anna V, 828
Bratten, Susanna IV, 900
Bratten, Susanna IV, 904
Brattin, Anna V, 828
Brattin, Jonathan V, 828
Brattin, Martha I, 872
Brattin, Robert I, 800
Brattin, Robert V, 828
Bratton, Ann V, 27
Bratton, Anna I, 800
Bratton, Benjamin I, 650
Bratton, Jerusha III, 292
Bratton, John I, 650
Bratton, Jonathan V, 27
Bratton, Martha I, 650
Bratton, Mary I, 492
Bratton, Mary I, 528
Bratton, Mary I, 562
Bratton, Mary I, 650
Bratton, Mary I, 800
Bratton, Millikan I, 650
Bratton, Paul I, 650
Bratton, Rachel I, 650
Bratton, Robert I, 492
Bratton, Robert I, 528
Bratton, Robert I, 562
Bratton, Robert I, 650
Bratton, William I, 492
Braum, Grace W. V, 895
Braun, Emilia III, 189
Braun, Emilia III, 303
Brauner, George II, 784
Brauner, Wd. Sarah II, 784
Braxton, Hannah I, 444
Braxton, Hannah I, 449
Braxton, Mary I, 375
Braxton, Mary I, 404
Braxton, Mary I, 443
Braxton, Nancy I, 617
Braxton, Thomas I, 443
Braxton, Thomas I, 449
Bray, Abijah I, 851
Bray, Abijah I, 960
Bray, Abijah I, 982
Bray, Abijah V, 27
Bray, Abijah V, 155
Bray, Edward I, 528
Bray, Edward I, 851
Bray, Edward I, 872
Bray, Edward I, 960
Bray, Edward I, 982
Bray, Edward I, 1026
Bray, Edward I, 1055
Bray, Edward V, 27
Bray, Edward V, 155
Bray, Ellen Reading II, 784
Bray, Francelia II, 840
Bray, Francelia II, 915
Bray, Francelia Williams II, 817
Bray, Francelia Williams VI, 772
Bray, Francelia Williams VI, 773
Bray, Frencelia Williams VI, 732
Bray, Henery I, 851
Bray, Henry I, 375
Bray, Henry I, 528
Bray, Henry I, 555
Bray, Henry I, 800
Bray, Henry I, 872
Bray, Henry I, 960
Bray, Henry I, 982
Bray, Henry I, 1026
Bray, Henry I, 1055
Bray, Henry V, 27
Bray, Henry V, 154
Bray, Henry V, 155
Bray, Henry, Jr. I, 982
Bray, Heziah V, 27
Bray, Jemima I, 375
Bray, Jemima I, 800
Bray, Jemima I, 851
Bray, Jemima I, 872
Bray, Jemima I, 902
Bray, Jemima I, 1055
Bray, Jemima V, 154
Bray, Jemimah I, 872
Bray, John I, 851
Bray, John I, 872
Bray, John I, 960
Bray, John I, 982
Bray, John I, 1026
Bray, John I, 1055
Bray, John V, 154
Bray, Joseph I, 851
Bray, Joseph I, 872
Bray, Joseph I, 960
Bray, Joseph I, 982
Bray, Joseph I, 1055
Bray, Joseph V, 27
Bray, Joseph V, 155
Bray, Kezia I, 375
Bray, Kezia I, 528
Bray, Kezia I, 555
Bray, Kezia I, 851
Bray, Kezia I, 982
Bray, Kezia I, 1007
Bray, Keziah I, 375
Bray, Keziah I, 800
Bray, Keziah I, 851
Bray, Keziah I, 872
Bray, Keziah I, 1053
Bray, Keziah I, 1055
Bray, Keziah I, 1060
Bray, Keziah V, 27
Bray, Keziah V, 154
Bray, Lucy V, 477
Bray, Lucy V, 533
Bray, Maccy V, 27
Bray, Mary I, 375
Bray, Mary I, 382
Bray, Mary I, 851
Bray, Mary I, 872
Bray, Mary I, 982
Bray, Mary I, 1055
Bray, Mary II, 784
Bray, Mary V, 27
Bray, Mary V, 37
Bray, Mary V, 155
Bray, Massey I, 851
Bray, Massey V, 155
Bray, Rachel I, 375
Bray, Rachel I, 405
Bray, Richard I, 851
Bray, Richard I, 872
Bray, Richard I, 960
Bray, Richard I, 982
Bray, Richard I, 1055
Bray, Richard V, 27
Bray, Richard V, 155
Bray, Sarah I, 375
Bray, Sarah I, 851
Bray, Sarah I, 872
Bray, Sarah I, 974
Bray, Sarah I, 982
Bray, Sarah I, 1055
Bray, Sarah V, 27
Bray, Sarah V, 129
Bray, Sarah V, 155
Bray, Sarah VI, 474
Bray, Sarah VI, 533
Bray, Sarah, Jr. I, 375
Bray, Susannah I, 375
Bray, Susannah I, 392
Bray, Wilson II, 784
Brayman, Nancy IV, 1354
Braynton, Patience III, 45
Brayton, Isaac IV, 684
Brazelton, Abigail I, 1115
Brazelton, Abigail I, 1116
Brazelton, Elizabeth I, 528
Brazelton, Elizabeth I, 551
Brazelton, Hannah I, 777
Brazelton, Isaac I, 492
Brazelton, Isaac I, 777
Brazelton, Isaac I, 872
Brazelton, Isaac I, 960
Brazelton, Jacob I, 492
Brazelton, Jacob I, 777
Brazelton, Jane I, 777
Brazelton, Jean I, 492
Brazelton, John I, 492
Brazelton, John I, 528
Brazelton, John I, 777
Brazelton, John I, 800
Brazelton, John VI, 474
Brazelton, Samuel I, 492
Brazelton, Samuel I, 777
Brazelton, Samuel I, 872
Brazelton, Samuel I, 960
Brazelton, Sarah I, 492
Brazelton, Sarah I, 528
Brazelton, Sarah I, 773
Brazelton, Sarah I, 777
Brazelton, Sarah I, 800
Brazelton, Sarah I, 801
Brazelton, Sarah I, 836
Brazelton, Sarah VI, 474
Brazelton, Sarah VI, 559
Brazelton, William I, 492
Brazelton, William I, 528
Brazelton, William I, 777
Brazelton, William I, 800
Brazelton, William I, 872
Brazelton, William I, 960
Brazelton, William I, 1116
Brazelton, William, Jr. I, 800
Brazelton, Wm. I, 1115
Brazelton, Wm. VI, 474
Brazelton, Wm. VI, 559
Brazier, Anna IV, 1308
Brazier, Effie IV, 1247
Brazier, John I, 38
Brazil, Charles E. V, 661
Brazil, Chas. D. V, 661
Brazil, Jennie V, 661
Brazil, Jesse V, 661
Brazil, John M. V, 661
Brazil, Sarah V, 661
Brazilton, Sarah I, 801
Brazilton, Sarah V, 27
Brazleton, Alexander I, 1102
Brazleton, William I, 1102
Breach, John II, 441
Bread, William I, 91
Breading, Mary I, 801
Breaknall, Lee V, 320
Brear, Abel III, 45
Brear, Abigail II, 840
Brear, Ann II, 840
Brear, Elizabeth P. III, 45
Brear, Mark II, 784
Brear, Mark II, 840
Brear, Mary II, 840
Brear, Sarah II, 840
Brear, Sarah T. II, 784
Brear, Sarah, Jr. II, 840
Brearley, Ann II, 998
Brearly, Ann II, 980
Breck, Isabel Mary III, 309
Breck, Isabel Mary III, 332
Breckenridge, Cary VI, 883
Breckenridge, Emma W. VI, 883
Breckman, Sue F. I, 921
Breden, Nancy VI, 161
Breden, Nancy VI, 221
Bredfield, Rachel VI, 471
Breece, Elizabeth S. II, 1045
Breece, Elizabeth S. II, 1064
Breece, Louisa P. IV, 1202
Breed, Chloe Ann IV, 1202
Breed, Chloe Ann IV, 1215
Breed, Daniel III, 45
Breed, Daniel, Jr. III, 40
Breed, Daniel, Jr. III, 45
Breed, Ebenezer II, 471
Breed, Ebenezer II, 589
Breed, Elizabeth II, 339
Breed, Elizabeth II, 700
Breed, Elizabeth H. II, 471
Breed, Elizabeth H. II, 589
Breed, Elizabeth H. II, 729
Breed, Ella Amelia III, 45
Breed, Gulielma III, 40
Breed, Hannah Lynn III, 45
Breed, Margaret V, 27
Breed, Margaret V, 141
Breed, Mary II, 471
Breed, Mary II, 589
Breed, Mary III, 45
Breed, Mary Estelle III, 45
Breed, Mary Esther III, 195
Breed, Mary Jane II, 700
Breed, Mary Jane II, 729
Breed, Preston Hamilton III, 195
Breed, Richard IV, 1202
Breed, Robert L. III, 45
Breed, Samuel II, 339
Breed, Samuel II, 729
Breed, Samuel D. II, 471
Breed, Samuel D. II, 589
Breed, Samuel D. II, 700
Breed, Samuel D. II, 729
Breed, Samuel Derby II, 471
Breed, Sarah Maddock II, 339
Breed, Sarah Maddock II, 729
Breed, Stephen IV, 1202
Breed, Stephen IV, 1215
Breed, William Maddock II, 700
Breed, Wm. Maddock II, 729
Breedin, Boston II, 58
Breedin, Nathaniel II, 58
Breedin, Nathaniel II, 75
Breedin, Sarah II, 58
Breedin, Sarah II, 75
Breeding, Eminto I, 801
Breeding, Ida V, 987
Breeding, John I, 801
Breeding, Margaret I, 801
Breeding, Mary I, 801
Breedlove, Lizzie V, 477
Breedlove, Mary V, 477
Brees, Hannah IV, 1202
Brees, Hannah IV, 1228
Breese, E. Marshall V, 896
Breese, Hannah IV, 1202
Breese, Hannah B. IV, 1202
Breese, Hannah B. IV, 1218
Breese, Louisa P. IV, 1202
Breese, Marshall E. V, 896
Breese, Peninah V, 896
Breeze, Peninah V, 896
Brehart, Abigail II, 339
Brehart, John II, 339
Brehm, Rosa IV, 1247
Breidenhart, Sarah Elizabeth II, 698
Breintall, John II, 598
Breintnal, David II, 521
Breintnal, Jane II, 471
Breintnal, Jane II, 521
Breintnall, Anna II, 472
Breintnall, Anna II, 598
Breintnall, David II, 472
Breintnall, David II, 576
Breintnall, David II, 649
Breintnall, Elizabeth II, 450
Breintnall, Esther II, 340
Breintnall, Esther II, 471
Breintnall, Esther II, 613
Breintnall, Jane II, 340
Breintnall, Jane II, 472
Breintnall, John II, 450
Breintnall, John II, 471
Breintnall, John II, 574
Breintnall, John II, 579
Breintnall, John II, 649
Breintnall, Joseph II, 340
Breintnall, Joseph II, 471
Breintnall, Joseph II, 613
Breintnall, Mary II, 574
Breintnall, Rachel II, 579
Breintnall, Sarah II, 471
Breintnall, Sarah II, 576
Breintnall, Susanah II, 471
Breintnall, Susanah II, 649
Breintnell, David II, 200
Breintnell, David II, 258
Breintnell, Hannah II, 200
Breintnell, Hannah II, 258
Breintnell, John II, 200
Breintnell, John II, 258
Brelsford, Benjamin II, 980
Brelsford, Benjamin II, 1017
Brelsford, Benjamin, Jr. II, 981
Brelsford, Daniel II, 980
Brelsford, Elizabeth II, 1065
Brelsford, Elizabeth II, 1069
Brelsford, Esther II, 980
Brelsford, Esther II, 1026
Brelsford, Hannah II, 981
Brelsford, Hannah II, 988
Brelsford, Hannah, Jr. II, 981
Brelsford, Hannah, Jr. II, 1001
Brelsford, James V, 27
Brelsford, Jane V, 27
Brelsford, Jane V, 132
Brelsford, John II, 980
Brelsford, John II, 981
Brelsford, Judith II, 980
Brelsford, Martha II, 980
Brelsford, Martha II, 1017
Brelsford, Martha Brown II, 980
Brelsford, Mary II, 980
Brelsford, Mary II, 981
Brelsford, Mary II, 1014
Brelsford, Mary II, 1027
Brelsford, Phebe II, 981
Brelsford, Phebe II, 1036
Brelsford, Rachel II, 980
Brelsford, Rachel II, 1027
Brelsford, Rebecca II, 1069
Brelsford, Rebecca V, 27
Brelsford, Rebecca V, 121
Brelsford, Samuel II, 980
Brelsford, Samuel II, 1027
Brelsford, Sarah II, 980
Brelsford, Sarah II, 981
Brelsford, Susannah II, 980
Brelsford, Wm. II, 980
Brelsford, Wm. II, 1027
Breman, Anna II, 441
Breman, Joseph II, 441
Bremer, Edith IV, 929
Breneman, John IV, 1233
Brener, Esther IV, 929
Brener, Esther IV, 1002
Brennaman, Alice H. IV, 180
Brenner, Catharine IV, 1036
Brenner, Catharine E. IV, 1036
Brenner, Clarence IV, 1308
Brenner, Edward J. IV, 1308
Brenner, Elmira IV, 930
Brenner, Elmira IV, 1002
Brenner, Esther IV, 929
Brenner, Harold IV, 1308
Brenner, Philip IV, 930
Brent, Behethaline VI, 915
Brent, Elizabeth VI, 851
Brent, Nathen VI, 851
Brentnal, David II, 471
Brentnall, David II, 339
Brentnall, David II, 467
Brentnall, David II, 471
Brentnall, Jane II, 467
Brentnall, Jane II, 471
Bresard, Elizabeth IV, 465
Bresler, Andrew V, 987
Bresler, Annie V, 987
Bresler, Chas. V, 987
Bresler, Elizabeth V, 987
Bresler, Ellen V, 987
Bresler, Emma V, 987
Bresler, Emma J. V, 987
Bresler, Flora V, 987
Bresler, Florence V, 998
Bresler, Geo. V, 987
Bresler, George V, 987
Bresler, Mable V, 987
Bresler, Marion V, 987
Bresler, Mary V, 987
Bresler, Minnie V, 987
Bresler, Nancy V, 987
Bresler, S. M. V, 987
Bresock, James F. IV, 180
Bressie, ??? VI, 39
Bressie, Elizabeth VI, 27
Bressie, Francis VI, 27
Bressie, Hugh VI, 27
Bressie, Hugh VI, 28
Bressie, Hugh VI, 37
Bressie, Sara VI, 28
Bressie, Sarah VI, 27
Bressie, Susanna VI, 15
Bressie, Susanna VI, 41
Bressie, Wd. Susanna VI, 27
Bressie, William VI, 8
Bressie, William VI, 15
Bressie, William VI, 27
Bressie, William VI, 41
Bressler, Annie V, 987
Bressler, Chas. V, 987
Bressler, Emma V, 987
Bressler, George V, 987
Bressler, Marion V, 987
Bressler, Mary V, 987
Bressler, Minnie V, 987
Bressler, Nancy V, 987
Bressock, James F. IV, 180
Bressock, Joseph Frederick IV, 180
Bressy, William VI, 41
Brestler, Elizabeth V, 987
Bresy, Susanna VI, 31
Brett, Daniel II, 471
Brett, John II, 471
Brett, John II, 574
Brett, Mary II, 471
Brett, Mary II, 574
Brett, Wd. Mary II, 471
Bretz, Albert IV, 1247
Bretz, George A. IV, 1247
Breuninger, Esther L. VI, 620
Breuninger, Esther L. VI, 665
Breuninger, Esther L. VI, 667
Breuninger, Lewis E. VI, 620
Breuninger, Lewis E. VI, 665
Breuninger, Sadie VI, 620
Breuninger, Sadie VI, 665

Brevan, John II, 441
Brevet, John Webster V, 27
Brevitt, John W. V, 949
Brevitt, John Webster V, 27
Brewer, Ann II, 471
Brewer, Ann II, 700
Brewer, Ann IV, 76
Brewer, Ann IV, 180
Brewer, Ann IV, 321
Brewer, Ann IV, 514
Brewer, Ann IV, 537
Brewer, Ann A. II, 725
Brewer, Ann A. II, 729
Brewer, Anna V, 658
Brewer, Bertha I, 625
Brewer, Bertha I, 630
Brewer, Bertha I, 640
Brewer, Catherine VI, 927
Brewer, Clara V, 613
Brewer, Clara V, 661
Brewer, Daniel B. V, 728
Brewer, Daniel H. VI, 883
Brewer, David F. V, 320
Brewer, David Franklin V, 320
Brewer, Dennis V, 613
Brewer, Dora V, 661
Brewer, Dorcus I, 982
Brewer, Edna May V, 661
Brewer, Elias IV, 22
Brewer, Elias IV, 23
Brewer, Elias IV, 76
Brewer, Elias IV, 265
Brewer, Eliza E. V, 613
Brewer, Elizabeth V, 320
Brewer, Elizabeth C. VI, 883
Brewer, Erma V, 728
Brewer, Etta V, 320
Brewer, Eva M. V, 613
Brewer, Eva M. V, 661
Brewer, Eva Mary V, 728
Brewer, Eva May V, 661
Brewer, Fanny VI, 800
Brewer, Franklin Lundy V, 661
Brewer, Geo. E. I, 625
Brewer, George II, 471
Brewer, George V, 728
Brewer, George E. I, 630
Brewer, George E. I, 640
Brewer, George O. V, 728
Brewer, Hannah IV, 76
Brewer, Hannah IV, 180
Brewer, Hannah IV, 321
Brewer, Hannah IV, 514
Brewer, Hazel V, 661
Brewer, Ida May V, 613
Brewer, Irvin V, 613
Brewer, Irvin V, 661
Brewer, Jane I, 375
Brewer, Jane I, 390
Brewer, Joel V, 320
Brewer, John IV, 76
Brewer, John IV, 180
Brewer, John IV, 321
Brewer, John IV, 514
Brewer, John V, 320
Brewer, John H. VI, 800
Brewer, John H. VI, 804
Brewer, John H. VI, 806
Brewer, John W. V, 320
Brewer, John W. VI, 839
Brewer, John Wm. V, 320
Brewer, Lovetta V, 613
Brewer, Mariah VI, 841
Brewer, Marie V, 613
Brewer, Martha II, 981
Brewer, Martha II, 984
Brewer, Martha IV, 76
Brewer, Martha IV, 180
Brewer, Martha IV, 321
Brewer, Martha IV, 514
Brewer, Martha IV, 515
Brewer, Martha V, 320
Brewer, Mary II, 981
Brewer, Mary II, 984
Brewer, Mary IV, 22
Brewer, Mary IV, 23
Brewer, Mary IV, 71
Brewer, Mary IV, 76
Brewer, Mary IV, 180
Brewer, Mary IV, 265
Brewer, Mary IV, 321
Brewer, Mary Nell V, 661
Brewer, Mary, Jr. IV, 514
Brewer, Mattie V, 320
Brewer, Miller V, 613
Brewer, Miller V, 661
Brewer, Miller T. V, 613
Brewer, Millte T. V, 661
Brewer, Peter V, 155
Brewer, Peter J. V, 155
Brewer, Phebe IV, 180
Brewer, Phebe IV, 265
Brewer, Phebe IV, 514
Brewer, Phebe IV, 1202
Brewer, Phebe IV, 1220
Brewer, Rachel II, 471
Brewer, Rachel IV, 76
Brewer, Rachel IV, 180
Brewer, Rachel IV, 321
Brewer, Rachel C. VI, 839
Brewer, Richard IV, 76
Brewer, Richard IV, 180
Brewer, Richard IV, 321
Brewer, Richard IV, 514
Brewer, Sarah II, 282
Brewer, Sarah IV, 76
Brewer, Sarah IV, 180
Brewer, Sarah IV, 514
Brewer, Sarah IV, 1050
Brewer, Susanna V, 728
Brewer, Susanna V, 773
Brewer, Thomas II, 339
Brewer, Thos. Roy V, 613
Brewer, Vedith V, 661
Brewer, Vedith V, 714
Brewer, Vedith L. V, 661
Brewer, Walter II, 981
Brewer, Walter II, 984
Brewer, William II, 339
Brewer, William VI, 839
Brewer, William VI, 841
Brewer, William A. V, 728
Brewer, Wm. II, 471
Brewinger, Esther VI, 667
Brewinger, L. E. VI, 667
Brewster, ??? III, 397
Brewster, E. Franklin III, 45
Brewster, E. Franklin III, 216
Brewster, E. Franklin VI, 764
Brewster, Eliz. III, 46
Brewster, Elizabeth III, 46
Brewster, Elizabeth III, 235
Brewster, Elizabeth Mott III, 480
Brewster, Emily III, 45
Brewster, Fanny May III, 397
Brewster, Hannah A. IV, 1202
Brewster, Isaac III, 480
Brewster, Isaac III, 482
Brewster, Isaac H. III, 397
Brewster, John H. III, 45
Brewster, John O. IV, 1202
Brewster, Mary E. III, 46
Brewster, Matilda III, 46
Brewster, Samuel III, 46
Brewster, Sarah III, 480
Brewster, Sarah III, 482
Brewster, Sarah R. III, 45
Brewster, Wd. Sarah R. III, 221
Brewster, Wd. Sarah R. VI, 764
Breyley, James IV, 1308
Breyley, Rose IV, 1308
Brian, Abraham II, 200
Brian, Abraham II, 220
Brian, Benj. II, 200
Brian, Benjamin II, 200
Brian, Benjamin II, 264
Brian, Benjamin II, 475
Brian, Charity II, 200
Brian, Eliza II, 282
Brian, Elizabeth II, 200
Brian, Elizabeth II, 227
Brian, Esther II, 200
Brian, Garner I, 971
Brian, Garner I, 982
Brian, Hern II, 200
Brian, Heron II, 200
Brian, Heron II, 216
Brian, Mary II, 200
Brian, Mary II, 216
Brian, Mary II, 220
Brian, Mary II, 247
Brian, Mary II, 264
Brian, Mary II, 475
Brian, Mary II, 609
Brian, Moses II, 475
Brian, Moses II, 609
Brian, Nathan I, 268
Brian, Rebecca II, 176
Brian, Rebecca II, 200
Brian, Rebecca II, 229
Brian, Rebeckah II, 167
Brian, Rhoda VI, 300
Brian, Samuel II, 200
Brian, Samuel II, 475
Brian, Susana II, 200
Brian, Susanna II, 475
Brian, Thomas II, 167
Brian, Thomas II, 176
Brian, Thomas II, 200
Brian, Thomas II, 220
Brian, Thomas II, 229
Brian, Thomas II, 475
Brian, Thomas II, 609
Brian, Thomas, Jr. II, 475
Brian, Uriah II, 200
Briant, Benj. II, 200
Briant, Charles VI, 161
Briant, David V, 896
Briant, Elizabeth I, 492
Briant, Elizabeth I, 982
Briant, Ellener I, 268
Briant, Ellener I, 273
Briant, Gardner I, 492
Briant, Gardner I, 953
Briant, Garner I, 982
Briant, Hannah I, 492
Briant, Hannah I, 982
Briant, Heron II, 200
Briant, James IV, 383
Briant, Jane IV, 383
Briant, John I, 529
Briant, John I, 953
Briant, Lydia I, 982
Briant, Lydia I, 1007
Briant, Lydia I, 1013
Briant, Martha I, 268
Briant, Martha I, 276
Briant, Nathan I, 268
Briant, Nicholas I, 268
Briant, Nicholas I, 273
Briant, Rebecca II, 200
Briant, Rebecca II, 209
Briant, Rebeccah I, 982
Briant, Rebekah I, 1007
Briant, Tamer IV, 383
Briant, Thomas II, 200
Briant, Thomas II, 209
Brice, B. VI, 942
Brice, Catharine VI, 1013
Brice, Eunice V, 30
Brice, Eunice V, 103
Brice, James G. V, 896
Brice, Maggie V, 896
Brice, Margaretta V, 896
Brick, Abigail II, 58
Brick, Ann II, 23
Brick, Ann II, 30
Brick, Ann II, 58
Brick, Ann II, 61
Brick, Ann II, 75
Brick, Ann II, 89
Brick, Ann II, 98
Brick, Anna II, 23
Brick, Anna II, 58
Brick, Anna II, 80
Brick, Anna II, 101
Brick, Anna W. II, 58
Brick, Anna W. II, 101
Brick, Arthur Roberts II, 145
Brick, Arthur Roberts II, 146
Brick, Clara Anna II, 145
Brick, Clara Anna II, 146
Brick, David II, 58
Brick, David S. II, 58
Brick, Deborah II, 23
Brick, Deborah II, 130
Brick, Deborah S. II, 116
Brick, Deborah S. II, 146
Brick, Deborah S. II, 840
Brick, Edgar II, 145
Brick, Edgar II, 146
Brick, Edward II, 23
Brick, Edward II, 116
Brick, Edward K. II, 58
Brick, Elizabeth II, 23
Brick, Elizabeth II, 58
Brick, Elizabeth II, 93
Brick, Elizabeth II, 100
Brick, Elizabeth II, 112
Brick, Elma Ann II, 58
Brick, Elma Ann II, 75
Brick, Hannah II, 23
Brick, Hannah II, 58
Brick, Hannah II, 76
Brick, Hannah II, 82
Brick, Jane II, 58
Brick, Jane II, 68
Brick, Jean II, 23
Brick, John II, 23
Brick, John II, 30
Brick, John II, 58
Brick, John II, 729
Brick, John E. II, 58
Brick, John R. II, 471
Brick, John R. II, 729
Brick, John, Jr. II, 58
Brick, John, Jr. II, 89
Brick, Joseph II, 23
Brick, Joseph II, 49
Brick, Joseph II, 58
Brick, Joseph II, 94
Brick, Joseph II, 100
Brick, Joseph R. II, 58
Brick, Martha II, 23
Brick, Martha II, 58
Brick, Martha II, 94
Brick, Martha II, 100
Brick, Martha R. II, 58
Brick, Martha Reeve II, 58
Brick, Mary II, 23
Brick, Mary II, 30
Brick, Mary II, 58
Brick, Mary II, 75
Brick, Mary II, 981
Brick, Rebecca II, 23
Brick, Rebecca II, 58
Brick, Rebecca II, 80
Brick, Rebecca A. II, 80
Brick, Rebeckah II, 23
Brick, Rebeckah II, 49
Brick, Rebeckah II, 58
Brick, Richard II, 981
Brick, Ruth II, 23
Brick, Ruth II, 58
Brick, Ruth II, 93
Brick, Ruth II, 471
Brick, Ruth II, 631
Brick, Samuel II, 23
Brick, Samuel II, 58
Brick, Samuel II, 80
Brick, Samuel II, 98
Brick, Samuel II, 101
Brick, Samuel II, 116
Brick, Samuel R. II, 58
Brick, Samuel, Jr. II, 116
Brick, Susan R. II, 145
Brick, Susan R. II, 146
Brick, Susanna II, 981
Brick, Wd. Ann II, 786
Brickard, Mary VI, 835
Brickeen, John VI, 800
Brickeen, Perthena VI, 800
Brickenhoof, Mary V, 987
Brickenn, Lucy VI, 1001
Bricker, Jason R. IV, 1000
Bricker, Mary IV, 1000
Bricker, Mary V, 728
Bricker, Mary A. C. IV, 1000
Bricker, Mary A. E. IV, 927
Bricker, Mary A. E. IV, 981
Bricker, Mary A. E. IV, 1000
Bricker, Susan L. IV, 1000
Brickhouse, George VI, 6
Brickhouse, George VI, 11
Brickky, Jane VI, 883
Brickky, John VI, 883
Bricky, Elizabeth VI, 988
Bridabaugh, P. W. IV, 1308
Briddell, Francis VI, 27
Bridenbaugh, Christiana V, 728
Bridenbaugh, Christiana C. V, 728
Bridenbaugh, Elmer V, 728
Bridenbaugh, Elmor V, 728
Bridenbaugh, Flora V, 728
Bridenbaugh, Henry V, 728
Bridenbaugh, Jane V, 728
Bridenbaugh, Lydia V, 728
Bridenbaugh, Paul V, 728
Bridenbaugh, Rachel V, 728
Bridenbaugh, Sarah V, 728
Bridenbough, Christina C. V, 739
Bridenstein, Samuel IV, 684
Bridenstine, Samuel IV, 684
Bridge, James M., Jr. IV, 865
Bridge, Thomas II, 471
Bridgeland, Caroline VI, 962
Bridgeland, Harriet VI, 962
Bridger, Col. ??? VI, 22
Bridgers, Katharine I, 926
Bridgers, Susannah I, 231
Bridges, ??? V, 147
Bridges, Bessie III, 480
Bridges, Bessie III, 497
Bridges, Bessie VI, 752
Bridges, Carrie Louisa I, 613
Bridges, Carrie Louise I, 618
Bridges, Charles I, 1017
Bridges, Charles I, 1026
Bridges, Charles V, 27
Bridges, Charles V, 50
Bridges, Daniel Floyd I, 618
Bridges, Daniel T. I, 613
Bridges, David VI, 800
Bridges, Eddy V, 27
Bridges, Ede I, 1017
Bridges, Edith V, 50
Bridges, George I, 375
Bridges, George III, 397
Bridges, George III, 480
Bridges, George III, 497
Bridges, Jemima V, 27
Bridges, Jemima V, 50
Bridges, Jesse I, 1017
Bridges, Jesse V, 27
Bridges, John I, 1017
Bridges, John I, 1026
Bridges, Louise Henley I, 630
Bridges, Martha VI, 800
Bridges, Mary I, 1017
Bridges, Mary VI, 370
Bridges, Mary VI, 383
Bridges, Reta III, 397
Bridges, Sarah F. III, 397
Bridges, Sarah F. III, 480
Bridges, Sarah F. III, 497
Bridges, Susannah I, 230
Bridges, Susannah I, 231
Bridges, William I, 1017
Bridges, William I, 1026
Bridget, Betty V, 725
Bridgman, John C. V, 155
Bridgman, Mary E. V, 155
Bridle, Ffrancis VI, 48
Bridle, Francis VI, 48
Bridnal, Hannah II, 200
Bridnal, John II, 200
Bridsall, Wm. W. II, 838
Brien, ??? III, 160
Brien, ??? III, 161
Brien, Ann S. VI, 800
Brien, Elijah VI, 800
Brien, Elisha VI, 800
Brien, Ely VI, 825
Brien, Ignatius J. III, 82
Brien, Isaac III, 161
Brien, Isaac, Jr. III, 161
Brien, James III, 46
Brien, John III, 161
Brien, John W. III, 161
Brien, Lucy VI, 800
Brien, Margaret J. III, 161
Brien, Maria Ann III, 161
Brien, Mary A. III, 46
Brien, Mary J. III, 82
Brien, Phebe VI, 825
Brien, Sarah III, 161
Brien, Sarah Jane III, 46
Brien, Sarah Jane III, 160
Brien, Troy III, 161
Brien, Walter III, 161
Brien, William III, 161
Brien, William Moode III, 161
Brien, William W. III, 161
Brient, Mabel VI, 1015
Brientnal, Ann II, 472
Brientnal, Hannah II, 471
Brientnall, Ann II, 472
Brientnall, Anna II, 472
Brientnall, Catharine II, 471
Brientnall, David II, 339
Brientnall, David II, 471
Brientnall, David II, 472
Brientnall, David, Jr. II, 471
Brientnall, David, Jr. II, 613
Brientnall, Elizabeth II, 339
Brientnall, Elizabeth II, 471
Brientnall, Esther II, 339
Brientnall, Esther II, 340
Brientnall, Esther II, 471
Brientnall, George II, 340
Brientnall, George II, 471
Brientnall, George II, 472
Brientnall, Grace II, 471
Brientnall, Grace II, 613
Brientnall, Hannah II, 339
Brientnall, Hannah II, 471
Brientnall, Jane II, 339
Brientnall, Jane II, 340
Brientnall, Jane II, 471
Brientnall, Jane II, 472
Brientnall, Jane II, 542
Brientnall, Jane Harper II, 471
Brientnall, John II, 339
Brientnall, John II, 340
Brientnall, John II, 471
Brientnall, John II, 472
Brientnall, Joseph II, 340
Brientnall, Joseph II, 471
Brientnall, Latitia II, 472
Brientnall, Latitia II, 668
Brientnall, Martha II, 340
Brientnall, Martha II, 472
Brientnall, Martha II, 587
Brientnall, Mary II, 471
Brientnall, Rachel II, 471
Brientnall, Rebekah II, 471
Brientnall, Rebekah II, 683
Brientnall, Sarah II, 340
Brientnall, Sarah II, 471
Brientnall, Sarah II, 472
Brientnall, Sarah II, 689
Brientnall, Susanah II, 471
Brientnall, Susanna II, 340
Brientnall, Thomas II, 340

Brientnall, William II, 340
Briesch, Charles Matson II, 140
Briesch, Harriet II, 140
Briesch, Sarah Jane II, 140
Brigg, Martha T. IV, 1019
Brigg, Mary, Jr. II, 472
Brigg, Wm., Jr. IV, 1019
Brigges, Mary VI, 15
Briggs, ??? VI, 95
Briggs, A. M. I, 921
Briggs, Abel V, 661
Briggs, Abigail II, 981
Briggs, Abigail II, 1069
Briggs, Abigail IV, 514
Briggs, Abigail IV, 515
Briggs, Abigail IV, 613
Briggs, Abigail IV, 628
Briggs, Abigail IV, 629
Briggs, Abigail IV, 684
Briggs, Abigail IV, 715
Briggs, Abner II, 58
Briggs, Abraham II, 1045
Briggs, Abraham II, 1069
Briggs, Abram II, 981
Briggs, Alanson C. III, 46
Briggs, Almarine W. II, 1069
Briggs, Alpheus I, 938
Briggs, Alpheus M. I, 801
Briggs, Alpheus M. I, 938
Briggs, Alpheus Maston I, 921
Briggs, Amos II, 981
Briggs, Amos II, 1069
Briggs, Amos II, 1081
Briggs, Amos IV, 514
Briggs, Amos IV, 515
Briggs, Ann II, 981
Briggs, Ann IV, 321
Briggs, Ann IV, 371
Briggs, Ann IV, 514
Briggs, Ann IV, 548
Briggs, Ann IV, 684
Briggs, Ann IV, 1050
Briggs, Ann IV, 1088
Briggs, Ann IV, 1104
Briggs, Ann VI, 101
Briggs, Anna IV, 515
Briggs, Anna Maria II, 1069
Briggs, Ascenith II, 1045
Briggs, Benjamin II, 981
Briggs, Benjamin IV, 181
Briggs, Benjamin IV, 321
Briggs, Benjamin IV, 322
Briggs, Benjamin IV, 371
Briggs, Benjamin IV, 372
Briggs, Benjamin IV, 514
Briggs, Benjamin IV, 515
Briggs, Benjamin IV, 1050
Briggs, Benjamin IV, 1089
Briggs, Bertha May I, 801
Briggs, Betsy IV, 514
Briggs, Betsy IV, 531
Briggs, Betsy IV, 534
Briggs, Betsy IV, 542
Briggs, Betsy IV, 550
Briggs, Blanch IV, 684
Briggs, Blanch IV, 967
Briggs, Blanche IV, 966
Briggs, Callie V, 987
Briggs, Caroline E. II, 800
Briggs, Charity C. III, 46
Briggs, Charles M. V, 614
Briggs, Clayton Albert IV, 930
Briggs, Cora Almeda IV, 930
Briggs, Cora Alverda IV, 930
Briggs, Cynthia IV, 514
Briggs, David IV, 1050
Briggs, Deborah VI, 472
Briggs, Deborah VI, 474
Briggs, Dorothy II, 975
Briggs, Edward III, 46
Briggs, Edward B. VI, 693
Briggs, Eliza IV, 514
Briggs, Eliza IV, 552
Briggs, Elizabeth II, 472
Briggs, Elizabeth IV, 181
Briggs, Elizabeth IV, 321
Briggs, Elizabeth IV, 322
Briggs, Elizabeth IV, 371
Briggs, Elizabeth IV, 372
Briggs, Elizabeth IV, 421
Briggs, Elizabeth IV, 514
Briggs, Elizabeth IV, 515
Briggs, Elizabeth IV, 529
Briggs, Elizabeth IV, 541
Briggs, Elizabeth IV, 552
Briggs, Elizabeth IV, 930
Briggs, Elizabeth VI, 99
Briggs, Elizabeth VI, 101
Briggs, Elizabeth C. IV, 930
Briggs, Elizabeth C. IV, 936
Briggs, Elizabeth H. IV, 514
Briggs, Elvina IV, 1089
Briggs, Elwood R. IV, 515
Briggs, Emily I, 592
Briggs, Emily V, 614
Briggs, Emily A. I, 592
Briggs, Emily H. II, 1069
Briggs, Emily M. V, 614
Briggs, Esther II, 981
Briggs, Esther IV, 76
Briggs, Esther IV, 141
Briggs, Esther IV, 180
Briggs, Esther IV, 181
Briggs, Esther IV, 321
Briggs, Esther IV, 371
Briggs, Esther IV, 435
Briggs, Esther IV, 436
Briggs, Esther IV, 457
Briggs, Esther IV, 465
Briggs, Esther IV, 514
Briggs, Esther IV, 534
Briggs, Esther IV, 548
Briggs, Esther IV, 684
Briggs, Esther IV, 1050
Briggs, Esther IV, 1089
Briggs, Esther IV, 1128
Briggs, Esther S. IV, 514
Briggs, Ethel V, 661
Briggs, Eugene Leroy I, 921
Briggs, Eugene Leroy, Jr. I, 921
Briggs, Evan IV, 514
Briggs, Evan IV, 515
Briggs, Francena II, 1045
Briggs, Frances II, 472
Briggs, Frances II, 802
Briggs, Frances III, 46
Briggs, Frances III, 183
Briggs, Frances J. III, 46
Briggs, Franklin I, 921
Briggs, Franklin V, 614
Briggs, George II, 200
Briggs, George II, 472
Briggs, George III, 46
Briggs, George IV, 181
Briggs, George IV, 321
Briggs, George IV, 322
Briggs, George IV, 372
Briggs, George IV, 514
Briggs, George IV, 515
Briggs, George V, 987
Briggs, George G. IV, 514
Briggs, George G. IV, 684
Briggs, George Green IV, 76
Briggs, George Green IV, 141
Briggs, George Green IV, 181
Briggs, George Green IV, 321
Briggs, George Green IV, 684
Briggs, Gurney I, 938
Briggs, Hannah II, 472
Briggs, Hannah II, 795
Briggs, Hannah III, 95
Briggs, Hannah III, 96
Briggs, Hannah IV, 465
Briggs, Hannah IV, 469
Briggs, Hannah IV, 512
Briggs, Hannah IV, 514
Briggs, Hannah IV, 519
Briggs, Hannah IV, 568
Briggs, Hannah IV, 569
Briggs, Hannah VI, 474
Briggs, Hannah C. IV, 465
Briggs, Hannah C. IV, 514
Briggs, Hannah T. II, 1069
Briggs, Hannah T. II, 1082
Briggs, Harriet IV, 515
Briggs, Harriett IV, 514
Briggs, Hazel I, 921
Briggs, Hazel I, 938
Briggs, Hazel I. I, 938
Briggs, Hazel I. I, 942
Briggs, Henry II, 981
Briggs, Henry IV, 321
Briggs, Henry IV, 465
Briggs, Henry IV, 514
Briggs, Henry IV, 531
Briggs, Henry IV, 534
Briggs, Henry IV, 542
Briggs, Henry IV, 550
Briggs, Henry IV, 556
Briggs, Henry IV, 628
Briggs, Henry IV, 684
Briggs, Henry IV, 715
Briggs, Henry VI, 55
Briggs, Henry VI, 67
Briggs, Henry VI, 80
Briggs, Henry C. I, 801
Briggs, Henry Clay I, 801
Briggs, Henry S. II, 308
Briggs, Henry S. II, 317
Briggs, Ila A. I, 801
Briggs, Isaac IV, 612
Briggs, Isaac IV, 613
Briggs, Isaac VI, 474
Briggs, Isaac VI, 726
Briggs, Isla A. H. I, 801
Briggs, Israel IV, 141
Briggs, Israel IV, 181
Briggs, Israel IV, 321
Briggs, Israel IV, 371
Briggs, Israel IV, 514
Briggs, Israel IV, 1088
Briggs, Israel S. IV, 684
Briggs, Israel S. IV, 1050
Briggs, Israel S. IV, 1088
Briggs, Israel S. IV, 1089
Briggs, Israel Shreeve IV, 684
Briggs, Israel Shreeve IV, 769
Briggs, Israel Shreve IV, 76
Briggs, Israel Shreve IV, 180
Briggs, Israel Shreve IV, 684
Briggs, J. Emery V, 551
Briggs, J. Gurney I, 938
Briggs, J. Gurney I, 942
Briggs, J. Gurney, Jr. I, 921
Briggs, James II, 981
Briggs, James II, 1031
Briggs, James II, 1045
Briggs, James II, 1069
Briggs, James II, 1082
Briggs, James VI, 101
Briggs, James H. IV, 181
Briggs, Jane IV, 514
Briggs, Jane IV, 548
Briggs, Jane IV, 1089
Briggs, Jesse IV, 514
Briggs, Jesse IV, 515
Briggs, Jessie IV, 1273
Briggs, Job IV, 181
Briggs, Job IV, 321
Briggs, Job IV, 465
Briggs, Job IV, 514
Briggs, Job IV, 515
Briggs, Job IV, 548
Briggs, Job IV, 684
Briggs, Job IV, 1050
Briggs, Job IV, 1088
Briggs, John I, 630
Briggs, John II, 981
Briggs, John IV, 684
Briggs, John IV, 803
Briggs, John IV, 1089
Briggs, John V, 614
Briggs, John Gurney I, 921
Briggs, John J. IV, 803
Briggs, John N. V, 614
Briggs, John Rufus I, 613
Briggs, John S. IV, 514
Briggs, John S. IV, 1050
Briggs, John S. IV, 1088
Briggs, John S. IV, 1109
Briggs, John Story II, 308
Briggs, John Story II, 317
Briggs, John, Jr. IV, 684
Briggs, Jonathan IV, 321
Briggs, Jonathan IV, 322
Briggs, Jonathan IV, 371
Briggs, Jonathan IV, 372
Briggs, Jonathan IV, 421
Briggs, Jonathan IV, 514
Briggs, Jonathan IV, 515
Briggs, Jonathan IV, 541
Briggs, Jonathan IV, 930
Briggs, Jonathan IV, 966
Briggs, Jonathan IV, 1010
Briggs, Jonathan T. IV, 181
Briggs, Jonathan T. IV, 465
Briggs, Jonathan T. IV, 684
Briggs, Jonathan Taylor IV, 181
Briggs, Jonathan Taylor IV, 684
Briggs, Jordan IV, 514
Briggs, Joseph II, 340
Briggs, Joseph II, 472
Briggs, Joseph II, 981
Briggs, Joseph II, 1045
Briggs, Joseph III, 397
Briggs, Joseph IV, 514
Briggs, Joshua II, 308
Briggs, Joshua B. II, 316
Briggs, Joshua B. II, 317
Briggs, Josiah IV, 181
Briggs, Josiah IV, 321
Briggs, Josiah IV, 322
Briggs, Josiah IV, 371
Briggs, Josiah IV, 372
Briggs, Josiah IV, 514
Briggs, Josiah IV, 515
Briggs, Julia IV, 803
Briggs, Julia IV, 818
Briggs, Juliah IV, 803
Briggs, Keziah IV, 514
Briggs, L. Alice I, 630
Briggs, Latitia II, 1045
Briggs, Latitia, Jr. II, 1045
Briggs, Laurra Alice I, 613
Briggs, Lee V, 614
Briggs, Lena Burdeen IV, 930
Briggs, Leona B. IV, 930
Briggs, Leroy I, 938
Briggs, Lewis Yancy V, 613
Briggs, Lindley IV, 1089
Briggs, Lindley H. IV, 1050
Briggs, Liza Ann IV, 514
Briggs, Louise I, 921
Briggs, Louise I, 938
Briggs, Luceta IV, 514
Briggs, Lucile V, 658
Briggs, Lucile V, 661
Briggs, Lydia IV, 514
Briggs, Lydia C. III, 46
Briggs, Margaret II, 981
Briggs, Margaret V, 614
Briggs, Margaret Ragan I, 921
Briggs, Maria IV, 76
Briggs, Maria IV, 141
Briggs, Maria IV, 181
Briggs, Maria IV, 514
Briggs, Maria IV, 531
Briggs, Maria IV, 534
Briggs, Maria IV, 684
Briggs, Mariah IV, 321
Briggs, Mariah IV, 465
Briggs, Mariah IV, 514
Briggs, Mariah IV, 684
Briggs, Martha II, 1045
Briggs, Martha IV, 514
Briggs, Martha IV, 515
Briggs, Martha IV, 542
Briggs, Martha IV, 546
Briggs, Martha T. IV, 930
Briggs, Martha, Jr. II, 1045
Briggs, Mary I, 801
Briggs, Mary I, 921
Briggs, Mary I, 938
Briggs, Mary II, 472
Briggs, Mary II, 975
Briggs, Mary II, 981
Briggs, Mary II, 1031
Briggs, Mary II, 1045
Briggs, Mary II, 1069
Briggs, Mary III, 46
Briggs, Mary III, 187
Briggs, Mary III, 229
Briggs, Mary IV, 321
Briggs, Mary IV, 322
Briggs, Mary IV, 371
Briggs, Mary IV, 372
Briggs, Mary IV, 514
Briggs, Mary IV, 515
Briggs, Mary IV, 537
Briggs, Mary IV, 612
Briggs, Mary IV, 640
Briggs, Mary IV, 684
Briggs, Mary IV, 769
Briggs, Mary IV, 966
Briggs, Mary IV, 1050
Briggs, Mary IV, 1088
Briggs, Mary VI, 101
Briggs, Mary VI, 370
Briggs, Mary Ann II, 805
Briggs, Mary Ann IV, 514
Briggs, Mary Ann IV, 541
Briggs, Mary Bessie I, 801
Briggs, Mary E. IV, 930
Briggs, Mary E. IV, 1010
Briggs, Mary E. V, 614
Briggs, Mary Elizabeth IV, 1089
Briggs, Mary Estella V, 661
Briggs, Mary Etta V, 614
Briggs, Mary Hazel I, 921
Briggs, Mary R. IV, 465
Briggs, Mary R. IV, 491
Briggs, Mary R. IV, 514
Briggs, Mary Sue I, 921
Briggs, Mary, Jr. II, 472
Briggs, Matthew Jones VI, 55
Briggs, Miller IV, 181
Briggs, Moses I, 38
Briggs, Mourning VI, 131
Briggs, Mourning VI, 143
Briggs, Myrtle V, 661
Briggs, Nathaniel VI, 55
Briggs, Nathaniel VI, 101
Briggs, Nellie V, 551
Briggs, Nellie Marie V, 661
Briggs, Nellie Marie V, 721
Briggs, Oresia Caroline V, 613
Briggs, Phebe I, 921
Briggs, Phebe IV, 512
Briggs, Phebe IV, 514
Briggs, Phebe IV, 552
Briggs, Phebe IV, 559
Briggs, Phebe L. IV, 515
Briggs, Phebe S. IV, 514
Briggs, Phineas II, 1069
Briggs, Phineas II, 1082
Briggs, Phinehas II, 981
Briggs, Phinehas II, 1031
Briggs, Priscilla VI, 101
Briggs, Priscilla VI, 104
Briggs, R. Joy I, 630
Briggs, Rachel IV, 465
Briggs, Rachel IV, 482
Briggs, Rachel IV, 1088
Briggs, Rachel IV, 1089
Briggs, Rachel IV, 1109
Briggs, Ralph V, 27
Briggs, Ralph V, 614
Briggs, Rebecca I, 592
Briggs, Rebecca II, 308
Briggs, Rebecca II, 981
Briggs, Rebecca IV, 514
Briggs, Rebecca IV, 543
Briggs, Rebecca IV, 550
Briggs, Rebecca IV, 684
Briggs, Rebecca IV, 803
Briggs, Rebecca V, 613
Briggs, Rebecca V, 614
Briggs, Rebecca V, 661
Briggs, Rebecca Ann IV, 684
Briggs, Rebecca M. IV, 321
Briggs, Rebecca M. IV, 465
Briggs, Rebecca M. IV, 684
Briggs, Rebecca Moorehead IV, 181
Briggs, Rebecca Moorhead IV, 181
Briggs, Rebecca Morehead IV, 684
Briggs, Regina Joy I, 613
Briggs, Robert IV, 321
Briggs, Robert M. IV, 321
Briggs, Robert M. IV, 514
Briggs, Robert M. IV, 515
Briggs, Ronald V, 661
Briggs, Ronald C. V, 661
Briggs, Ronald Cast V, 661
Briggs, Rosella IV, 953
Briggs, Rosella M. IV, 1010
Briggs, Samuel II, 472
Briggs, Samuel II, 975
Briggs, Samuel II, 981
Briggs, Samuel IV, 180
Briggs, Samuel IV, 321
Briggs, Samuel IV, 512
Briggs, Samuel IV, 514
Briggs, Samuel IV, 529
Briggs, Samuel IV, 541
Briggs, Samuel IV, 552
Briggs, Samuel M. IV, 465
Briggs, Samuel M. IV, 514
Briggs, Samuel M. IV, 552
Briggs, Samuel M. IV, 559
Briggs, Samuel M. IV, 684
Briggs, Samuel Miller IV, 76
Briggs, Samuel Miller IV, 141
Briggs, Samuel Miller IV, 181
Briggs, Samuel Miller IV, 684
Briggs, Sarah II, 308
Briggs, Sarah II, 316
Briggs, Sarah II, 981
Briggs, Sarah II, 1031
Briggs, Sarah II, 1034
Briggs, Sarah II, 1045
Briggs, Sarah II, 1069
Briggs, Sarah II, 1081
Briggs, Sarah III, 46
Briggs, Sarah IV, 372
Briggs, Sarah IV, 436
Briggs, Sarah IV, 514
Briggs, Sarah V, 661
Briggs, Sarah VI, 101
Briggs, Sarah B. IV, 181
Briggs, Sarah J. IV, 181
Briggs, Sarah Lucile V, 658
Briggs, Sarah Lucile V, 661
Briggs, Sarah M. IV, 321
Briggs, Sarah M. IV, 322
Briggs, Sarah M. IV, 372
Briggs, Sarah M. IV, 514
Briggs, Sarah M. IV, 515
Briggs, Sarah O. V, 614
Briggs, Sarah S. IV, 371
Briggs, Sarah S. IV, 457
Briggs, Sarah S. IV, 514
Briggs, Sarah S. IV, 900
Briggs, Sarah S. IV, 918
Briggs, Sarah T. II, 1069
Briggs, Sarah T. II, 1081
Briggs, Sarah T. IV, 181
Briggs, Sarah W. IV, 372
Briggs, Sarah W. IV, 515
Briggs, Sarah, Jr. II, 1045
Briggs, Sarahann IV, 1089
Briggs, Shreeve IV, 141
Briggs, Shreve IV, 181

Briggs, Stanton V, 987
Briggs, Stephen IV, 514
Briggs, Stephen IV, 541
Briggs, Story II, 981
Briggs, Susan II, 308
Briggs, Susan II, 316
Briggs, Susan II, 317
Briggs, Susan II, 1045
Briggs, Susanna II, 981
Briggs, Susanna II, 1069
Briggs, Tacey II, 1069
Briggs, Tacey II, 1082
Briggs, Talitha IV, 715
Briggs, Talitha Ann IV, 514
Briggs, Talitha Ann IV, 556
Briggs, Talitha Ann IV, 628
Briggs, Theo. S. III, 46
Briggs, Theodore S. II, 1069
Briggs, Thomas IV, 514
Briggs, Thomas IV, 515
Briggs, Thomas Franklin V, 613
Briggs, Thos. V, 614
Briggs, Uriah Pearson V, 613
Briggs, Velma L. IV, 930
Briggs, Velma Loretta IV, 930
Briggs, Virgil D. IV, 930
Briggs, Virgil Duane IV, 930
Briggs, W. Alpheus I, 921
Briggs, Wendell V, 551
Briggs, Willard V, 551
Briggs, William IV, 76
Briggs, William IV, 180
Briggs, William IV, 181
Briggs, William IV, 321
Briggs, William IV, 372
Briggs, William IV, 457
Briggs, William IV, 465
Briggs, William IV, 514
Briggs, William IV, 515
Briggs, William IV, 534
Briggs, William IV, 684
Briggs, William J. V, 613
Briggs, William L. V, 613
Briggs, Wilmer A. III, 46
Briggs, Wilmer A. III, 183
Briggs, Wm. IV, 141
Briggs, Wm. IV, 371
Briggs, Wm. IV, 465
Briggs, Wm. IV, 469
Briggs, Wm. IV, 482
Briggs, Wm. IV, 514
Briggs, Wm. IV, 515
Briggs, Wm. IV, 519
Briggs, Wm. IV, 537
Briggs, Wm. IV, 548
Briggs, Wm. IV, 684
Briggs, Wm. IV, 1050
Briggs, Wm. IV, 1088
Briggs, Wm. V, 614
Briggs, Wm. J. V, 614
Briggs, Wm., Jr. IV, 515
Briggs, Wm., Jr. IV, 930
Briggs, Yardley II, 308
Briggs, Yardley II, 316
Brigham, Charles II, 472
Brigham, Charles II, 632
Brigham, Hannah II, 632
Brigham, John S. VI, 800
Brigham, Margaret VI, 800
Brigham, Wm. V, 987
Bright, Adaley Willis VI, 953
Bright, Alba Flanders VI, 941
Bright, Celia VI, 1020
Bright, Charles VI, 931
Bright, Charles A. I, 1149
Bright, Charles G. I, 1149
Bright, Charles, Jr. VI, 883
Bright, Charles, Jr. VI, 983
Bright, Charles, Sr. VI, 983
Bright, Edward VI, 883
Bright, Edward VI, 1020
Bright, Edward C. VI, 956
Bright, Edwin C. VI, 883
Bright, Edwin C. VI, 964
Bright, Edwin C. VI, 1005
Bright, Emily M. VI, 956
Bright, Emma III, 15
Bright, Emma III, 46
Bright, Ernest V, 375
Bright, Grant III, 15
Bright, Grant III, 46
Bright, Henrietta IV, 22
Bright, Henrietta IV, 33
Bright, James II, 340
Bright, James II, 472
Bright, Jemima VI, 983
Bright, John III, 203
Bright, Joseph VI, 883
Bright, Joseph VI, 953
Bright, Joshua VI, 883
Bright, Joshua VI, 956
Bright, Joshua VI, 982
Bright, Joshua VI, 1020
Bright, Louisa M. VI, 1005
Bright, Makaska I, 1149
Bright, Margaret W. VI, 956
Bright, Margaret W. VI, 971
Bright, Martha W. VI, 883
Bright, Mary IV, 141
Bright, Mary IV, 181
Bright, Mary IV, 461
Bright, Mary Ann VI, 883
Bright, Mary Ann VI, 910
Bright, Mary Ann VI, 1020
Bright, Mary Isabella III, 15
Bright, Mary Isabella III, 46
Bright, Nancey VI, 941
Bright, Nancy VI, 883
Bright, Orlena I, 1149
Bright, Peggy VI, 883
Bright, Rebecca IV, 33
Bright, Samuel I, 1149
Bright, Samuel H. I, 1149
Bright, Sarah VI, 883
Bright, William IV, 33
Brightmen, Susanna II, 472
Brightmen, Susanna II, 694
Brighton, Hiram V, 987
Brightwell, Jane F. VI, 812
Brightwell, Margaret VI, 800
Brightwell, Obediah VI, 812
Brightwell, Susanna II, 694
Brightwell, William VI, 800
Brightwen, Susanna II, 694
Brigs, Callie V, 987
Brigs, James II, 981
Briles, Dan H. I, 756
Briles, Eleanor I, 756
Briles, Fatima Jane I, 756
Briles, Gilbert Hargrave I, 938
Briles, Henry I, 743
Briles, Henry I, 756
Briles, Jacob I, 743
Briles, James F. I, 756
Briles, Lena I, 921
Briles, Mary Ann I, 756
Briles, Sarah Elizabeth I, 756
Briles, Solomon I, 756
Briles, William O. I, 756
Brilewin, William II, 340
Brill, Elizabeth VI, 1010
Brill, Esther IV, 1128
Brill, Esther IV, 1138
Brille, Anny VI, 883
Brille, Catherine VI, 883
Brille, Henry VI, 883
Brille, John VI, 883
Brim, Catharine Virginia I, 872
Brim, Jemima Edna I, 872
Brim, Madison I, 872
Brim, Nancy Ann I, 872
Brimble, Cicely II, 472
Brimble, Cicely II, 583
Brimble, Cissley II, 472
Brimble, Cissley II, 499
Brimble, Elizabeth II, 340
Brimble, Giles II, 340
Brimble, Giles II, 472
Brimble, Giles II, 583
Brimble, John II, 472
Brimble, John II, 583
Brimley, Cissley II, 499
Brin, Jackson I, 38
Brin, Martha I, 38
Brin, Martha I, 58
Brindenstein, Amanda C. IV, 1247
Brindle, Addie V, 478
Brindle, Addie V, 661
Brindle, Alma V, 478
Brindle, Alma V, 661
Brindle, Elizabeth I, 982
Brindle, Elizabeth I, 988
Brindle, Margret I, 982
Brindle, Margret I, 999
Bringhurst, Ann Barbera II, 340
Bringhurst, Anna II, 472
Bringhurst, Anna II, 624
Bringhurst, Deborah II, 340
Bringhurst, Elizabeth II, 340
Bringhurst, Elizabeth II, 472
Bringhurst, Elizabeth II, 509
Bringhurst, James II, 340
Bringhurst, James II, 472
Bringhurst, James II, 624
Bringhurst, John II, 340
Bringhurst, John II, 472
Bringhurst, John II, 509
Bringhurst, John II, 526
Bringhurst, John II, 624
Bringhurst, John George II, 340
Bringhurst, John, Jr. II, 472
Bringhurst, Joseph II, 340
Bringhurst, Joseph II, 472
Bringhurst, Joseph, Jr. II, 472
Bringhurst, Mary II, 340
Bringhurst, Mary II, 472
Bringhurst, Mary II, 526
Bringhurst, Morjana II, 340
Bringhurst, Rosannah II, 340
Bringhurst, Rosina II, 340
Bringhurst, Rosina Elizabeth II, 340
Bringhurst, Sarah Ann II, 472
Bringhurst, Sarah Anna II, 472
Bringhurst, Sarah Anna II, 536
Bringhurst, Wd. Mary II, 340
Brinhart, John II, 340
Brink, Daniel P. IV, 1308
Brink, Mrs. S. M. IV, 1247
Brinkerhoff, Abm. III, 46
Brinkerhoff, Chas. C. II, 840
Brinkerhoff, Chas. C. II, 875
Brinkerhoff, Emma II, 840
Brinkerhoff, Emma II, 875
Brinkerhoff, Emma H. II, 841
Brinkerhoff, Emma H. III, 46
Brinkerhoff, George S. III, 46
Brinkerhoff, George S. III, 282
Brinkerhoff, Jane E. III, 46
Brinkerhoff, Martha H. III, 46
Brinkerhoff, Martha H. III, 282
Brinkley, Edith I, 592
Brinkley, Lizzie VI, 55
Brinkly, Lizzie VI, 64
Brinkman, ??? III, 46
Brinkman, ??? III, 98
Brinkman, Cornelia III, 46
Brinkman, Cornelia III, 98
Brinn, Jackson I, 38
Brinn, Martha I, 38
Brinnel, Ann II, 981
Brinson, Thomas II, 340
Brint, Nicholas I, 264
Brint, Nicklas I, 263
Brintnal, Hannah II, 339
Brintnall, Catharine II, 471
Brintnall, Catharine II, 481
Brintnall, David II, 339
Brintnall, David II, 471
Brintnall, Elizabeth II, 339
Brintnall, Hannah II, 200
Brintnall, Hannah II, 339
Brintnall, Jane II, 339
Brintnall, John II, 339
Brintnall, John II, 340
Brintnall, Susanna II, 340
Brinton, A. Adelaide II, 841
Brinton, Ann III, 399
Brinton, Anna Adelaide II, 841
Brinton, Anna Hoopes IV, 515
Brinton, Elizabeth L. II, 830
Brinton, Elizabeth L. II, 841
Brinton, Esther III, 473
Brinton, Geo. F. II, 841
Brinton, George II, 830
Brinton, George II, 841
Brinton, George F. II, 830
Brinton, George F. II, 841
Brinton, George F. II, 920
Brinton, George Fawkes II, 784
Brinton, Gulielma II, 948
Brinton, Hannah S. II, 841
Brinton, Hannah Smith II, 784
Brinton, Helen E. II, 841
Brinton, Helen E. II, 920
Brinton, James III, 400
Brinton, John IV, 122
Brinton, John IV, 123
Brinton, John F. II, 729
Brinton, John French Wilson IV, 515
Brinton, Joseph P. II, 729
Brinton, Letitia S. II, 784
Brinton, Letitia S. II, 841
Brinton, Lydia A. IV, 1273
Brinton, Mary E. II, 784
Brinton, Mary E. L. II, 830
Brinton, Mary E. L. II, 841
Brinton, Mary E. L. II, 920
Brinton, Ruth Hoops III, 46
Brinton, Ruth Hoops III, 253
Brinton, Samuel C. II, 841
Brinton, Sarah IV, 122
Brinton, Sarah IV, 123
Brinton, Sarah Ann IV, 122
Brinton, Sarah Ann IV, 123
Brinton, Susan II, 948
Brinton, Thomas III, 400
Brinton, William II, 948
Brinton, Wm. II, 472
Brinton, Wm. P. IV, 122
Brion, Mary II, 200
Brion, Mary II, 240
Brisco, Alice IV, 181
Brisco, Alice IV, 230
Briscoe, Wm. II, 893
Brishmuth, Hannah B. II, 838
Brison, Alfred III, 46
Brison, Clifford Scarnell III, 46
Brison, Eliz. III, 46
Brister, Mary I, 231
Brister, Mary I, 239
Bristley, Harry IV, 1273
Bristley, Mary IV, 1273
Bristley, Maud IV, 1273
Bristley, Phillip IV, 1273
Bristol, Ann II, 340
Bristol, Elizabeth II, 340
Bristol, Elizabeth II, 472
Bristol, Elizabeth II, 594
Bristol, Jacob II, 340
Bristol, Jacob II, 472
Bristol, Mary II, 472
Bristol, Mrs. George IV, 1308
Bristol, Sarah II, 472
Bristol, Tacy II, 472
Bristol, Thomas II, 340
Bristol, Thomas S. II, 340
Bristoll, Thomas II, 340
Bristoll, Thomas S. II, 340
Bristow, Caroline I, 335
Bristow, George Clement III, 46
Bristow, Martha VI, 89
Bristow, Martha P. VI, 89
Bristow, Mary II, 472
Bristow, Mary II, 565
Bristow, Mattie VI, 89
Bristow, Mattie VI, 91
Bristow, Mattie P. VI, 55
Bristow, Richard VI, 89
Bristow, Richard A. VI, 55
Bristow, Richard A. VI, 89
Brists, Wd. Mary II, 472
Britain, Alice VI, 579
Britain, Benjamin I, 487
Britain, Benjamin I, 528
Britan, Joseph I, 605
Brite, Mary IV, 465
Brite, Mary IV, 470
Brite, Rebecca IV, 470
Brite, Wm. Jones IV, 470
Briths, ??? III, 243
Briths, Hannah Marie III, 243
Briton, Rebecca I, 492
Britt, ??? III, 46
Britt, Ann Louisa III, 46
Britt, Benjamin III, 46
Britt, Eleanor I, 444
Britt, Eleanor I, 452
Britt, Emma III, 46
Britt, Hannah III, 46
Britt, Hannah Maria III, 46
Britt, Henry F. I, 335
Britt, Marietta III, 361
Britt, Mary II, 200
Britt, Mary II, 450
Britt, Mary II, 471
Britt, Mary II, 540
Britt, Mary II, 974
Britt, Mary II, 981
Britt, Seemercy Adam II, 981
Britt, Stephen III, 46
Britt, Wd. Mary II, 450
Brittain, Alice I, 267
Brittain, Alice I, 275
Brittain, Ann I, 528
Brittain, Ann I, 550
Brittain, Benjamin I, 524
Brittain, Benjamin I, 528
Brittain, Benjamin VI, 370
Brittain, Hannah I, 528
Brittain, Hannah I, 550
Brittain, James II, 340
Brittain, Jane I, 873
Brittain, Jemima I, 528
Brittain, John II, 340
Brittain, Jonathan I, 873
Brittain, Lydia I, 528
Brittain, Lydia I, 535
Brittain, Mahala I, 528
Brittain, Mahala I, 532
Brittain, Martha I, 872
Brittain, Martha I, 873
Brittain, Mary I, 873
Brittain, Melinda I, 528
Brittain, Millicen I, 528
Brittain, Moses O. I, 212
Brittain, Moses O. I, 231
Brittain, Paul I, 873
Brittain, Rebecca I, 524
Brittain, Rebecca I, 528
Brittain, Robert I, 873
Brittain, Samira I, 212
Brittain, Sarah II, 981
Brittain, Sarah II, 1000
Brittain, William I, 267
Brittain, William I, 275
Brittain, William I, 524
Brittain, William I, 528
Brittain, William I, 535
Brittan, Cintha I, 756
Brittan, Rebecca I, 528
Brittan, Samuel VI, 370
Brittan, Sarah VI, 370
Brittanie, Lyonell II, 952
Britten, Jacob II, 472
Britten, John II, 472
Britten, Susanna II, 472
Brittin, Joseph I, 492
Britton, Benjamin VI, 370
Britton, Charles I, 8
Britton, Charles I, 207
Britton, Charles I, 231
Britton, Charles M. I, 231
Britton, Charles Wesley I, 208
Britton, Chas. I, 208
Britton, Edna I, 208
Britton, Edna I, 215
Britton, Edna F. I, 208
Britton, Elizabeth Ann I, 207
Britton, Esther J. I, 208
Britton, Esther J. I, 211
Britton, Florence E. III, 510
Britton, Jacob II, 340
Britton, Jacob II, 472
Britton, James II, 340
Britton, James Thomas I, 208
Britton, Jane I, 6
Britton, Jesse W. I, 231
Britton, John II, 340
Britton, John II, 472
Britton, John H. I, 208
Britton, John H. I, 231
Britton, Jonathan VI, 370
Britton, Joseph I, 605
Britton, Joseph Edgar I, 208
Britton, King J. I, 208
Britton, King J. I, 211
Britton, King Jesse I, 208
Britton, Lydia Jane V, 375
Britton, Lydia Jane V, 421
Britton, Marcilla I, 222
Britton, Margaret Edna I, 208
Britton, Mariam I, 231
Britton, Mariam I, 240
Britton, Marium I, 208
Britton, Mary I, 208
Britton, Mary Eliza I, 208
Britton, Mary Eliza I, 231
Britton, Mary Frances I, 208
Britton, Melinda I, 528
Britton, Millicen I, 528
Britton, Miriam I, 207
Britton, Miriam I, 231
Britton, Moses O. I, 208
Britton, Moses O. I, 215
Britton, Moses O. I, 231
Britton, Nancy Emma I, 208
Britton, Nathan T. I, 231
Britton, Nathan Thomas I, 208
Britton, Pheriba I, 207
Britton, Rebecca I, 490
Britton, Samariah I, 208
Britton, Samuel VI, 370
Britton, Sarah II, 340
Britton, Sarah VI, 370
Britton, Sarah Ann I, 231
Britton, Sarah Jane I, 8
Britton, Sarah Jane I, 208
Britton, Sarah Jane I, 231
Britton, Sarah Jane I, 234
Britton, Susanna II, 472
Britton, Thomas I, 208
Britton, Thomas II, 46
Britts, ??? III, 46
Britts, Hannah Maria III, 46
Brizendine, Polly VI, 800
Brizendine, Thomas VI, 800
Brizentine, Clabourn VI, 800
Brizentine, Dezena VI, 800
Brizentine, Elizabeth VI, 800
Brizentine, John VI, 800
Brizentine, Labourn VI, 800
Brizentine, Polly VI, 800
Brizentine, Sarah VI, 800
Brizentine, Thomas VI, 800
Brizintine, Claibourne VI, 828
Broadbent, Harrietta III, 280
Broadgate, Christian II, 333
Broadgate, Christian II, 340
Broadgate, Christian II, 454
Broadgate, Christian II, 472
Broadgate, John II, 340
Broadgate, John II, 472

Broadgate, Mary II, 333
Broadgate, Mary II, 472
Broadgate, Mary II, 656
Broadgate, Sarah II, 472
Broadgate, Sarah II, 535
Broadgate, Thomas II, 340
Broadgate, Thomas II, 454
Broadgate, Thomas II, 472
Broadgate, William II, 340
Broadhead, Anna III, 46
Broadhead, Anna III, 184
Broadhead, Jeptha III, 46
Broadhead, Jeptha III, 184
Broadhead, Mary III, 46
Broadhead, Mary III, 184
Broadhead, Rebecca II, 340
Broadhead, Simon Edghill II, 340
Broadhent, Harrietta III, 322
Broadhurst, Caroline Laing II, 828
Broadhurst, Elizabeth IV, 181
Broadhurst, Elizabeth IV, 294
Broadhurst, Joseph II, 828
Broadhurst, Rachel H. II, 828
Broadnix, Sarah II, 981
Broadrick, Beulah V, 27
Broadrick, Samuel IV, 1273
Broadruff, Hannah G. IV, 181
Broadrup, Cornelius IV, 181
Broadrup, Hannah IV, 181
Broadrup, Hannah G. IV, 181
Broadrupt, Hannah IV, 181
Broadway, Beaulah II, 57
Broadway, Catharine III, 46
Broadway, Dorcas II, 57
Broadway, Elizabeth II, 57
Broadway, John II, 57
Broadway, Jonathan II, 57
Broadway, Josiah II, 57
Broadway, Josiah V, 27
Broadway, Wm. II, 57
Broadwell, Fred I, 938
Broadwell, Frederick I, 921
Broadwell, James I, 921
Broadwell, Josephine I, 921
Broadwick, Beulah V, 27
Brobeck, Carrie E. IV, 1247
Brobeck, Joseph IV, 1247
Brochden, Elisabeth II, 473
Brock, ??? VI, 95
Brock, Abigail II, 473
Brock, Abigail IV, 515
Brock, Abigail VI, 101
Brock, Abigail VI, 102
Brock, Abigail VI, 117
Brock, Abigail VI, 138
Brock, Alex. VI, 56
Brock, Alice VI, 370
Brock, Alice VI, 440
Brock, Alice VI, 592
Brock, Ann IV, 322
Brock, Ann IV, 345
Brock, Ann IV, 515
Brock, Ann IV, 558
Brock, Ann IV, 569
Brock, Anne IV, 515
Brock, Burwell VI, 101
Brock, Catharine IV, 322
Brock, Catharine IV, 515
Brock, Catherine IV, 322
Brock, Catherine IV, 345
Brock, Charity I, 1026
Brock, Charity I, 1028
Brock, Charity V, 153
Brock, Charity V, 155
Brock, Charity V, 181
Brock, Charity V, 191
Brock, Charity V, 478
Brock, Chas. II, 784
Brock, Daniel VI, 370
Brock, David IV, 322
Brock, David IV, 515
Brock, Elias I, 1026
Brock, Elijah V, 155
Brock, Elijah V, 478
Brock, Elizabeth II, 975
Brock, Elizabeth II, 981
Brock, Elizabeth IV, 322
Brock, Elizabeth IV, 569
Brock, Franklin VI, 56
Brock, George I, 1026
Brock, George I, 1028
Brock, George V, 153
Brock, George V, 181
Brock, George V, 191
Brock, Isaiah B. IV, 930
Brock, Jacob VI, 370
Brock, James IV, 372
Brock, James IV, 569
Brock, James IV, 573
Brock, James VI, 56
Brock, James VI, 97
Brock, James VI, 98
Brock, James VI, 101
Brock, James VI, 102
Brock, James VI, 117
Brock, James VI, 131
Brock, James VI, 140
Brock, James, Jr. IV, 372
Brock, Jane IV, 22
Brock, Jane IV, 322
Brock, Jane IV, 515
Brock, Jane IV, 521
Brock, Jane IV, 569
Brock, Jane VI, 370
Brock, Jane VI, 428
Brock, Jane VI, 440
Brock, Jane VI, 592
Brock, Jas. VI, 100
Brock, Jas. T. VI, 56
Brock, Jean VI, 370
Brock, Jesse IV, 569
Brock, Joel IV, 181
Brock, Joel IV, 569
Brock, John II, 472
Brock, John II, 473
Brock, John II, 641
Brock, John II, 981
Brock, John II, 1024
Brock, John IV, 22
Brock, John IV, 141
Brock, John IV, 322
Brock, John IV, 515
Brock, John IV, 569
Brock, John VI, 370
Brock, John VI, 406
Brock, John VI, 428
Brock, John VI, 440
Brock, John VI, 592
Brock, John Nathan IV, 22
Brock, John Nathan VI, 592
Brock, Jonathan VI, 370
Brock, Jonathan VI, 592
Brock, Jos. VI, 56
Brock, Joseph T. VI, 56
Brock, Keturah I, 1058
Brock, Keturah V, 155
Brock, Keturah V, 181
Brock, Kiturah V, 478
Brock, Lucinda V, 155
Brock, Lucinda V, 182
Brock, Lucinda V, 478
Brock, Lucy VI, 97
Brock, Lucy VI, 98
Brock, Lucy VI, 102
Brock, Lydia II, 841
Brock, Lydia B. II, 784
Brock, Lydia Jane IV, 569
Brock, Malona V, 155
Brock, Malona V, 191
Brock, Martha IV, 372
Brock, Martha IV, 569
Brock, Martha IV, 573
Brock, Martha VI, 56
Brock, Martha VI, 100
Brock, Martha VI, 101
Brock, Martha VI, 102
Brock, Martha VI, 131
Brock, Martha VI, 140
Brock, Martha A. VI, 91
Brock, Martha Ann IV, 181
Brock, Martha Ann IV, 569
Brock, Mary II, 200
Brock, Mary II, 201
Brock, Mary II, 472
Brock, Mary II, 473
Brock, Mary IV, 322
Brock, Mary IV, 515
Brock, Mary IV, 566
Brock, Mary IV, 569
Brock, Mary IV, 598
Brock, Mary E. V, 614
Brock, Mary Jane IV, 181
Brock, Massey II, 473
Brock, Massey II, 678
Brock, Nancy VI, 800
Brock, Nannie VI, 56
Brock, Nannie VI, 91
Brock, Naomi IV, 510
Brock, Naomi IV, 515
Brock, Nathan VI, 370
Brock, Nathan VI, 592
Brock, Nathen VI, 592
Brock, Oddy IV, 22
Brock, Oddy VI, 370
Brock, Oddy VI, 592
Brock, Penina IV, 573
Brock, Peninah IV, 181
Brock, Peninah IV, 372
Brock, Peninah IV, 383
Brock, Peninah IV, 569
Brock, Penninah IV, 569
Brock, Penninah IV, 584
Brock, Pharaby VI, 101
Brock, Pharaby VI, 102
Brock, Rachel VI, 370
Brock, Rebecca IV, 181
Brock, Rebecca IV, 569
Brock, Rhoda VI, 100
Brock, Rhoda VI, 101
Brock, Rhoda VI, 102
Brock, Richard II, 981
Brock, Richard II, 1025
Brock, Robert IV, 372
Brock, Robert IV, 383
Brock, Robert IV, 569
Brock, Robert IV, 573
Brock, Rose III, 66
Brock, Rose III, 108
Brock, Ruth V, 153
Brock, Ruth V, 155
Brock, Ruth V, 478
Brock, Sallie VI, 56
Brock, Sally VI, 56
Brock, Sarah II, 472
Brock, Sarah IV, 322
Brock, Sarah IV, 372
Brock, Sarah IV, 515
Brock, Sarah IV, 569
Brock, Sarah IV, 573
Brock, Sarah VI, 56
Brock, Sarah VI, 97
Brock, Sarah VI, 98
Brock, Sarah VI, 101
Brock, Sarah VI, 102
Brock, Sarah VI, 117
Brock, Stephen IV, 322
Brock, Stephen IV, 345
Brock, Stephen IV, 515
Brock, Stephen IV, 569
Brock, Stephen VI, 370
Brock, Stephen VI, 592
Brock, Susanna V, 155
Brock, Susanna V, 176
Brock, Susannah II, 981
Brock, Susannah II, 1025
Brock, Susannah V, 478
Brock, Wd. Sarah II, 473
Brock, William IV, 181
Brock, William IV, 569
Brock, Wm. II, 472
Brock, Wm. II, 473
Brock, Wm. IV, 569
Brock, Wrenny VI, 800
Brockden, Ann II, 340
Brockden, Charles II, 340
Brockden, Charles II, 473
Brockden, Charles, Jr. II, 340
Brockden, Elisabeth II, 473
Brockden, Elizabeth II, 340
Brockden, Elizabeth II, 473
Brockden, Elizabeth II, 517
Brockden, John II, 340
Brockden, Mary II, 473
Brockden, Rebecca II, 340
Brockden, Rebeccah II, 340
Brockden, Richard II, 340
Brockden, Shumah II, 340
Brockelbank, Caleb III, 46
Brockelbank, Lillian III, 46
Brockelbank, Marie III, 46
Brockelesby, Peter IV, 1247
Brocklesby, Peter IV, 1247
Broddnix, Sarah II, 981
Broderick, Elizabeth IV, 1149
Broderick, Elizabeth IV, 1157
Broderick, Elizabeth IV, 1273
Broderick, Elizabeth IV, 1277
Broderick, Isaac V, 728
Broderick, Mary V, 987
Broderick, Nancy IV, 1273
Broderick, Nanie IV, 1273
Broderick, Nannie M. V, 728
Broderick, Paul IV, 1149
Broderick, Paul IV, 1157
Broderick, Rebecca IV, 1149
Broderick, Rebecca IV, 1161
Broderick, Samuel IV, 1273
Broderick, Samuel J. V, 728
Brodey, Mary I, 1026
Brodey, Mary I, 1028
Brodrick, Carrie V, 728
Brodrick, Eliza IV, 1149
Brodrick, Elizabeth IV, 1149
Brodrick, Isaac V, 728
Brodrick, Nancy IV, 1149
Brodrick, Nancy IV, 1175
Brodrick, Nannie M. V, 728
Brodrick, Paul IV, 1149
Brodrick, Paul IV, 1175
Brodrick, Phebe V, 728
Brodrick, Phebe V, 738
Brodrick, Rebecca IV, 1149
Brodrick, Samuel IV, 1273
Brodrick, Samuel V, 728
Brodrick, Samuel J. V, 728
Brodrick, Sarah IV, 1149
Brodrick, Sarah IV, 1175
Brodrick, Sarah V, 728
Brodrick, Sarah V, 773
Brodrick, Sarah Gilbert V, 738
Brodrick, Thomas V, 738
Brodrick, Walter V, 728
Brodshaw, Harley V, 477
Brodwell, Fred I, 938
Brogan, Alice IV, 900
Brogan, Amos IV, 906
Brogan, Anna Elizabeth V, 551
Brogan, Anna L. IV, 918
Brogan, Bertha IV, 1008
Brogan, Bertha Thomas IV, 930
Brogan, Betha H. IV, 930
Brogan, C. IV, 914
Brogan, Charles IV, 900
Brogan, Charles M. IV, 900
Brogan, Emma IV, 803
Brogan, Emma IV, 900
Brogan, Emma IV, 1024
Brogan, Enna IV, 855
Brogan, J. Rendell V, 551
Brogan, J. Walter V, 551
Brogan, Jeanette IV, 900
Brogan, Jeannet Orr IV, 930
Brogan, John II, 784
Brogan, John IV, 930
Brogan, John A. V, 551
Brogan, Lillian IV, 900
Brogan, Mary IV, 900
Brogan, Mary IV, 918
Brogan, Mary J. IV, 906
Brogan, Meredith V, 551
Brogan, Morris IV, 900
Brogan, Morris IV, 918
Brogan, Philena IV, 906
Brogan, Priscilla V, 551
Brogan, R. IV, 914
Brogan, Rachel IV, 803
Brogan, Rachel IV, 1024
Brogan, Rosa V, 551
Brogan, Ruth E. IV, 914
Brogan, Sarah Plummer II, 784
Brogan, Virgil C. IV, 900
Brogan, Virginia V, 551
Brogan, Walter Elwood V, 551
Brogan, Wayne J. IV, 900
Brogden, David F. I, 335
Brogden, Naomi I, 335
Brogden, William R. I, 328
Brogdon, Charles II, 340
Brogdon, Emelia I, 300
Brogdon, Emelia I, 312
Brogdon, Susanna II, 340
Broho, Abigail II, 463
Broho, Abigail II, 473
Broho, Albina II, 473
Broiler, Clennie W. IV, 1202
Broiler, Cyrus IV, 1247
Broiler, Cyrus M. IV, 1247
Broiler, Myrtle IV, 1202
Broiler, Rosa IV, 1247
Broiler, Rose IV, 1247
Broiler, S. N. IV, 1247
Broiler, Sadie IV, 1247
Broiles, Mary Ann I, 756
Brokaw, Elizabeth IV, 515
Brokaw, Elizabeth IV, 524
Brokaw, Ethel IV, 1202
Brokaw, Mary IV, 1089
Brokaw, Mary IV, 1102
Broller, Rosa IV, 1247
Brollier, C. W. IV, 1202
Brollier, Candice IV, 1202
Brollier, Clennie W. IV, 1202
Brollier, Cyrus M. IV, 1247
Brollier, Dona IV, 1202
Brollier, Lewis C. IV, 1202
Brollier, Lewis Levi IV, 1202
Brollier, Mary IV, 1202
Brollier, Myrtle IV, 1202
Brollier, Rosa IV, 1247
Brollier, Sadie IV, 1247
Brollier, W. Clennie IV, 1202
Bromell, Elizabeth VI, 770
Bromhaul, Elizabeth V, 478
Bromley, Ellen II, 700
Bromley, John II, 700
Bromley, Sarah II, 968
Bromley, Susan II, 700
Bromley, William II, 473
Bromwell, Beulah II, 473
Bromwell, David II, 473
Bromwell, Deborah II, 473
Bromwell, Hannah II, 473
Bromwell, Jacob II, 473
Bromwell, Jacob II, 526
Bromwell, Mary II, 473
Bromwell, Mary II, 526
Bromwell, Wd. Mary II, 340
Bromwell, William II, 340
Bromwell, Wm. II, 473
Bromwell, Wm. II, 526
Bromwell, Wm. II, 539
Bronson, Eliza V, 661
Bronson, Elizabeth I, 414
Bronson, Elizabeth V, 375
Bronson, Joseph I, 414
Bronson, Mary Belle V, 661
Bronson, Seler N. V, 614
Broodhurst, Samuel I, 300
Broodruff, Cornelius IV, 181
Broodwell, Walter I, 300
Brook, Abraham III, 47
Brook, Abraham V, 478
Brook, Alice Maude VI, 733
Brook, Alice Maude VI, 743
Brook, Ann IV, 76
Brook, Ann IV, 83
Brook, Ann Eliza P. IV, 745
Brook, Ann Eliza Pleasant IV, 684
Brook, Ann H. II, 841
Brook, Basil IV, 919
Brook, Basil IV, 930
Brook, Bazil IV, 684
Brook, Caroline IV, 930
Brook, Caroline IV, 1008
Brook, Caroline V, 478
Brook, Caroline Elizabeth V, 478
Brook, Charity V, 27
Brook, Charles III, 46
Brook, Charles VI, 300
Brook, Deborah IV, 684
Brook, Deborah IV, 689
Brook, Deborah IV, 930
Brook, Elizabeth II, 200
Brook, Elizabeth II, 277
Brook, Elizabeth III, 47
Brook, Elizabeth III, 397
Brook, Elizabeth V, 478
Brook, Elizah V, 27
Brook, Esther IV, 684
Brook, Gerard IV, 684
Brook, Gilpin V, 478
Brook, Hannah VI, 620
Brook, Hannah VI, 639
Brook, Hannah Pancoast IV, 684
Brook, Henry V, 478
Brook, Henry Howard V, 478
Brook, Hester IV, 684
Brook, Isaiah B. IV, 684
Brook, Isaiah B. IV, 689
Brook, Isaiah Boone IV, 684
Brook, James IV, 684
Brook, James IV, 930
Brook, James B. V, 478
Brook, Jane I, 801
Brook, Jane I, 821
Brook, Jane IV, 930
Brook, Joanna II, 473
Brook, Kathleen Maude VI, 733
Brook, Kathleen Maude VI, 743
Brook, Keturah V, 27
Brook, Lucinda V, 27
Brook, Lydia V, 478
Brook, Lydia L. V, 478
Brook, Lydia Maria V, 478
Brook, Margaret V, 478
Brook, Mary III, 47
Brook, Mary IV, 76
Brook, Mary IV, 87
Brook, Mary VI, 161
Brook, Mary VI, 620
Brook, Olive K. VI, 231
Brook, Paulina S. IV, 684
Brook, Paulina S. IV, 725
Brook, Phebe III, 47
Brook, Rachel IV, 930
Brook, Ralph II, 340
Brook, Roger VI, 620
Brook, Ruth V, 27
Brook, Samuel II, 340
Brook, Samuel V, 478
Brook, Samuel Robert VI, 161
Brook, Sarah V, 478
Brook, Susanah V, 27
Brook, Thomas II, 340
Brook, Walter George VI, 733
Brook, Walter George VI, 743
Brook, William V, 478
Brookbanck, Richard II, 340
Brookbank, Elizabeth VI, 621
Brookbank, Elizabeth VI, 659
Brookbank, Hannah VI, 621
Brookbank, Hannah VI, 659
Brookbank, Mary II, 340

Brookbank, Richard II, 340
Brooke, ??? III, 47
Brooke, ??? VI, 726
Brooke, Abraham III, 46
Brooke, Abraham III, 397
Brooke, Abraham III, 410
Brooke, Abraham III, 419
Brooke, Abraham IV, 891
Brooke, Abraham V, 478
Brooke, Alfred IV, 891
Brooke, Alice VI, 782
Brooke, Alice VI, 792
Brooke, Amos VI, 474
Brooke, Amy III, 397
Brooke, Amy III, 446
Brooke, Amy S. III, 46
Brooke, Ann IV, 684
Brooke, Ann Eliza P. IV, 930
Brooke, Ann Eliza Pleasant IV, 684
Brooke, Basil IV, 684
Brooke, Basil IV, 930
Brooke, Basil IV, 981
Brooke, Bazil IV, 684
Brooke, Boyer II, 473
Brooke, Boyer II, 787
Brooke, Caroline IV, 891
Brooke, Charles III, 397
Brooke, Charles III, 419
Brooke, Charles III, 446
Brooke, Charles A. III, 397
Brooke, David II, 340
Brooke, Deborah IV, 684
Brooke, Deborah VI, 474
Brooke, Deborah VI, 481
Brooke, Deborah VI, 532
Brooke, Dorothy VI, 474
Brooke, Edna IV, 1323
Brooke, Edward IV, 891
Brooke, Edward IV, 893
Brooke, Elijah III, 47
Brooke, Elisa P. IV, 684
Brooke, Eliza P. VI, 564
Brooke, Eliza P. VI, 783
Brooke, Elizabeth III, 397
Brooke, Elizabeth IV, 891
Brooke, Elizabeth V, 478
Brooke, Elizabeth VI, 474
Brooke, Elizabeth VI, 545
Brooke, Elizabeth VI, 564
Brooke, Elizabeth VI, 733
Brooke, Elizabeth W. III, 46
Brooke, Esther IV, 684
Brooke, Esther IV, 924
Brooke, Gerard IV, 684
Brooke, Gerard IV, 930
Brooke, Gerard VI, 630
Brooke, Gilpin IV, 891
Brooke, Hanna P. IV, 930
Brooke, Hannah IV, 891
Brooke, Hannah IV, 893
Brooke, Hannah IV, 924
Brooke, Hannah V, 794
Brooke, Hannah VI, 474
Brooke, Hannah VI, 481
Brooke, Hannah VI, 517
Brooke, Hannah VI, 519
Brooke, Hannah Braxton VI, 994
Brooke, Hannah Pancoast IV, 684
Brooke, Harriet IV, 891
Brooke, Henrietta VI, 471
Brooke, Henry IV, 891
Brooke, Henry V, 478
Brooke, Hester IV, 684
Brooke, Hester IV, 930
Brooke, Isaiah B. IV, 684
Brooke, Isaiah Boone IV, 684
Brooke, James I, 375
Brooke, James IV, 684
Brooke, James IV, 924
Brooke, James VI, 474
Brooke, James VI, 481
Brooke, James VI, 519
Brooke, James VI, 532
Brooke, James B. IV, 891
Brooke, James, Jr. VI, 517
Brooke, Jane Gray IV, 684
Brooke, Jane Grey IV, 684
Brooke, John VI, 733
Brooke, Lolina IV, 930
Brooke, Lu III, 47
Brooke, Lu III, 210
Brooke, Lydia II, 787
Brooke, Lydia III, 46
Brooke, Lydia III, 397
Brooke, Lydia IV, 891
Brooke, Lydia V, 896
Brooke, Lydia Maria IV, 891
Brooke, Lydia S. IV, 891
Brooke, Margaret IV, 891
Brooke, Margaret V, 478
Brooke, Margaret Sarah VI, 474
Brooke, Mary III, 47
Brooke, Mary IV, 891
Brooke, Mary VI, 471
Brooke, Mary VI, 474
Brooke, Mary VI, 532
Brooke, Mary VI, 536
Brooke, Mary VI, 620
Brooke, Mary VI, 676
Brooke, Mary VI, 677
Brooke, Mary VI, 733
Brooke, Mary B. III, 397
Brooke, Mary B. III, 410
Brooke, Mary H. III, 46
Brooke, Mary M. IV, 891
Brooke, Mary P. VI, 733
Brooke, Mary P. VI, 740
Brooke, Mary, Jr. VI, 474
Brooke, Nell III, 47
Brooke, Nell III, 210
Brooke, Orson H. III, 47
Brooke, Orson Holloway III, 210
Brooke, Paulina S. IV, 684
Brooke, Phebe III, 46
Brooke, Phebe III, 397
Brooke, Phebe III, 410
Brooke, Phebe III, 419
Brooke, Phebe H. III, 46
Brooke, Phebe H. III, 397
Brooke, Pollina Snowden IV, 684
Brooke, Rachel IV, 930
Brooke, Rachel IV, 981
Brooke, Richard VI, 630
Brooke, Rizpah IV, 1323
Brooke, Robert II, 470
Brooke, Roger II, 473
Brooke, Roger VI, 471
Brooke, Roger VI, 474
Brooke, Roger VI, 532
Brooke, Roger VI, 676
Brooke, Roger VI, 733
Brooke, Roger VI, 740
Brooke, Roger, Jr. VI, 474
Brooke, Ruth Anna IV, 684
Brooke, Samuel IV, 891
Brooke, Samuel V, 478
Brooke, Samuel VI, 474
Brooke, Samuel VI, 733
Brooke, Sarah II, 470
Brooke, Sarah II, 473
Brooke, Sarah III, 397
Brooke, Sarah IV, 891
Brooke, Sarah V, 478
Brooke, Sarah VI, 471
Brooke, Sarah VI, 474
Brooke, Sarah VI, 733
Brooke, Sarah VI, 740
Brooke, Sarah H. III, 46
Brooke, Sarah H. III, 397
Brooke, Sarah P. VI, 474
Brooke, Sarah W. III, 397
Brooke, Wd. Hannah II, 787
Brooke, William IV, 891
Brooke, William V, 478
Brooke, Wm. IV, 1323
Brooke, Wm. VI, 475
Brooker, Grace E. IV, 1308
Brooker, Helen IV, 1308
Brooker, Rizpah IV, 1308
Brooker, Thelma IV, 1308
Brooker, W. Malchom IV, 1308
Brooker, Wm. IV, 1308
Brooker, Wm. L. IV, 1308
Brookes, Charles VI, 300
Brookes, Robert VI, 304
Brookins, Ruth IV, 1233
Brooks, ??? III, 47
Brooks, ??? III, 128
Brooks, ??? III, 230
Brooks, A. E. IV, 1308
Brooks, Abner VI, 231
Brooks, Abraham III, 46
Brooks, Abraham III, 47
Brooks, Abraham III, 440
Brooks, Abrm. III, 440
Brooks, Adaline IV, 613
Brooks, Adam II, 23
Brooks, Adam II, 116
Brooks, Adam II, 200
Brooks, Adam II, 282
Brooks, Adam II, 729
Brooks, Adam II, 761
Brooks, Addy II, 784
Brooks, Adeline L. II, 841
Brooks, Adeline L. II, 912
Brooks, Alexandria III, 47
Brooks, Alice VI, 410
Brooks, Alice Maude VI, 733
Brooks, Ambrose VI, 231
Brooks, Amy S. III, 46
Brooks, Ann II, 200
Brooks, Ann II, 473
Brooks, Ann II, 481
Brooks, Ann II, 1069
Brooks, Ann III, 47
Brooks, Ann V, 728
Brooks, Ann Eliza P. IV, 930
Brooks, Ann Eliza Pleasant IV, 930
Brooks, Ann H. II, 841
Brooks, Anna II, 837
Brooks, Anna II, 841
Brooks, Anne V, 728
Brooks, Anne V, 743
Brooks, Arnold IV, 930
Brooks, Arnold IV, 1203
Brooks, Barbara Ethel I, 938
Brooks, Barbary VI, 800
Brooks, Basil IV, 930
Brooks, Benjamin V, 728
Brooks, Benjamin V, 774
Brooks, Benjamin VI, 800
Brooks, Benjamin W. VI, 833
Brooks, Bertha Kate I, 921
Brooks, Bowyer II, 340
Brooks, Boyer II, 473
Brooks, Calvin V, 798
Brooks, Caroline IV, 930
Brooks, Carrie III, 47
Brooks, Carrie III, 304
Brooks, Catharine III, 46
Brooks, Catharine IV, 1373
Brooks, Catharine VI, 801
Brooks, Catherine IV, 1354
Brooks, Charity I, 777
Brooks, Charity I, 799
Brooks, Charity I, 801
Brooks, Charity V, 27
Brooks, Charles II, 441
Brooks, Charles II, 1069
Brooks, Charles II, 1080
Brooks, Charles III, 46
Brooks, Charles III, 68
Brooks, Charles VI, 300
Brooks, Charles F. III, 47
Brooks, Charles F. III, 298
Brooks, Charles Franklin VI, 732
Brooks, Charles T. III, 46
Brooks, Charles T. III, 47
Brooks, Charlotte Hallowell III, 47
Brooks, Daniel V, 728
Brooks, Daniel V, 774
Brooks, Daniel O. I, 1026
Brooks, Daniel Offley I, 528
Brooks, Daniel Ofley I, 1017
Brooks, David I, 492
Brooks, David I, 528
Brooks, David I, 777
Brooks, David I, 801
Brooks, David I, 911
Brooks, David I, 913
Brooks, David II, 340
Brooks, David II, 473
Brooks, David II, 493
Brooks, David VI, 231
Brooks, David VI, 371
Brooks, David VI, 441
Brooks, David VI, 592
Brooks, David Mendenhall I, 801
Brooks, David Singletary I, 1017
Brooks, David Singleterry I, 528
Brooks, Deborah I, 801
Brooks, Deborah I, 828
Brooks, Deborah I, 911
Brooks, Deborah II, 282
Brooks, Deborah IV, 930
Brooks, Deborah IV, 1203
Brooks, Deborah C. II, 282
Brooks, Deborah C. II, 729
Brooks, Dora V, 798
Brooks, E. A. IV, 1308
Brooks, Eada VI, 867
Brooks, Eadith IV, 372
Brooks, Edmundson II, 340
Brooks, Edward II, 200
Brooks, Edward II, 340
Brooks, Edward II, 473
Brooks, Edward II, 481
Brooks, Edward II, 656
Brooks, Eleanor M. III, 46
Brooks, Eleanor M. III, 47
Brooks, Eleanor M. III, 298
Brooks, Eleanor M. VI, 732
Brooks, Elijah III, 47
Brooks, Elijah VI, 811
Brooks, Elisabeth II, 473
Brooks, Elisabeth Louise I, 613
Brooks, Eliz. T. III, 47
Brooks, Elizabeth I, 347
Brooks, Elizabeth I, 375
Brooks, Elizabeth I, 406
Brooks, Elizabeth I, 492
Brooks, Elizabeth I, 528
Brooks, Elizabeth I, 777
Brooks, Elizabeth I, 799
Brooks, Elizabeth I, 801
Brooks, Elizabeth I, 1016
Brooks, Elizabeth I, 1017
Brooks, Elizabeth I, 1026
Brooks, Elizabeth I, 1030
Brooks, Elizabeth II, 193
Brooks, Elizabeth II, 200
Brooks, Elizabeth II, 340
Brooks, Elizabeth II, 441
Brooks, Elizabeth II, 458
Brooks, Elizabeth II, 473
Brooks, Elizabeth II, 656
Brooks, Elizabeth II, 837
Brooks, Elizabeth II, 841
Brooks, Elizabeth II, 1069
Brooks, Elizabeth II, 1080
Brooks, Elizabeth III, 47
Brooks, Elizabeth III, 440
Brooks, Elizabeth IV, 1308
Brooks, Elizabeth V, 728
Brooks, Elizabeth VI, 231
Brooks, Elizabeth VI, 733
Brooks, Elizabeth VI, 755
Brooks, Elizabeth VI, 800
Brooks, Elizabeth VI, 819
Brooks, Elizabeth VI, 826
Brooks, Elizabeth VI, 838
Brooks, Elizabeth VI, 973
Brooks, Elizabeth J. V, 797
Brooks, Elizabeth S. II, 1069
Brooks, Elizabeth W. III, 46
Brooks, Elizah V, 27
Brooks, Ella J. V, 27
Brooks, Elmer L. I, 1149
Brooks, Elmira V, 820
Brooks, Elmira F. V, 797
Brooks, Elvira V, 797
Brooks, Emma R. V, 798
Brooks, Erica May III, 47
Brooks, Ester I, 911
Brooks, Esther I, 911
Brooks, Esther II, 340
Brooks, Esther IV, 22
Brooks, Esther IV, 181
Brooks, Esther IV, 372
Brooks, Esther IV, 930
Brooks, Esther Mendenhall I, 801
Brooks, Ethel I, 613
Brooks, Ethel I, 630
Brooks, Ethel I, 643
Brooks, Evaline VI, 850
Brooks, Eveline Turner I, 938
Brooks, Ezekiel VI, 800
Brooks, Ezekiel VI, 847
Brooks, Ezekiel VI, 860
Brooks, Fannie I, 620
Brooks, Fanny VI, 800
Brooks, Frances VI, 801
Brooks, Frances A. V. VI, 850
Brooks, Francis VI, 839
Brooks, Frona Maria III, 46
Brooks, Frona Marie VI, 732
Brooks, Garnet IV, 1308
Brooks, Garnet J. IV, 1308
Brooks, Geo. Washington IV, 930
Brooks, Gerard IV, 930
Brooks, Gilpin V, 478
Brooks, Green VI, 800
Brooks, Hanah V, 728
Brooks, Hanna P. IV, 930
Brooks, Hannah I, 1026
Brooks, Hannah I, 1039
Brooks, Hannah I, 1047
Brooks, Hannah I, 1050
Brooks, Hannah II, 340
Brooks, Hannah II, 473
Brooks, Hannah II, 784
Brooks, Hannah II, 841
Brooks, Hannah II, 912
Brooks, Hannah II, 981
Brooks, Hannah II, 1040
Brooks, Hannah IV, 1203
Brooks, Hannah V, 27
Brooks, Hannah E. V, 798
Brooks, Hannah P. IV, 1203
Brooks, Hannah Pancoast IV, 930
Brooks, Hannah Pauline IV, 930
Brooks, Hannah Pauline IV, 933
Brooks, Harry I, 613
Brooks, Hebsibah S. II, 116
Brooks, Helen L. III, 47
Brooks, Henry I, 630
Brooks, Henry I, 643
Brooks, Henry V, 728
Brooks, Henry VI, 883
Brooks, Henry B. V, 798
Brooks, Henry Iverson I, 613
Brooks, Henry J. V, 798
Brooks, Hephsibah II, 116
Brooks, Hephzibah II, 282
Brooks, Hepsibah S. II, 200
Brooks, Hepzibah II, 729
Brooks, Hepzibah II, 761
Brooks, Hepzibah S. II, 282
Brooks, Hester IV, 930
Brooks, Hester IV, 992
Brooks, Hezekiah VI, 800
Brooks, Hiram VI, 801
Brooks, Howard III, 47
Brooks, Isaac II, 441
Brooks, Isaac IV, 613
Brooks, Isaac V, 798
Brooks, Isaiah B. IV, 930
Brooks, Isaiah B. IV, 1203
Brooks, Isaiah Boon IV, 930
Brooks, J. R. I, 938
Brooks, James I, 375
Brooks, James I, 528
Brooks, James I, 1015
Brooks, James I, 1016
Brooks, James I, 1017
Brooks, James I, 1026
Brooks, James I, 1037
Brooks, James I, 1149
Brooks, James II, 340
Brooks, James II, 841
Brooks, James IV, 22
Brooks, James IV, 930
Brooks, James V, 27
Brooks, James V, 784
Brooks, James VI, 231
Brooks, James VI, 800
Brooks, James VI, 801
Brooks, James VI, 833
Brooks, James VI, 850
Brooks, James B. II, 841
Brooks, James B. II, 912
Brooks, James B. V, 967
Brooks, James B. V, 968
Brooks, James Baynes II, 784
Brooks, James D. I, 1149
Brooks, James S. II, 1069
Brooks, James, Jr. IV, 930
Brooks, James, Jr. VI, 800
Brooks, James, Sr. VI, 800
Brooks, Jane I, 375
Brooks, Jane I, 777
Brooks, Jane I, 801
Brooks, Jane I, 838
Brooks, Jane IV, 930
Brooks, Jane VI, 231
Brooks, Jane VI, 800
Brooks, Jane VI, 801
Brooks, Jane Grey IV, 930
Brooks, Jean I, 982
Brooks, Jeane I, 492
Brooks, Jesse I, 777
Brooks, Jesse I, 801
Brooks, Jesse I, 911
Brooks, Jesse V, 728
Brooks, Jesse VI, 800
Brooks, Joab I, 1017
Brooks, Joab I, 1026
Brooks, Joanna II, 473
Brooks, Joel I, 347
Brooks, Joel I, 375
Brooks, Joel I, 430
Brooks, Joel I, 801
Brooks, Joel E. IV, 372
Brooks, John I, 347
Brooks, John I, 375
Brooks, John I, 492
Brooks, John I, 777
Brooks, John I, 799
Brooks, John I, 801
Brooks, John I, 828
Brooks, John I, 838
Brooks, John I, 907
Brooks, John I, 911
Brooks, John I, 1017
Brooks, John I, 1026
Brooks, John II, 116
Brooks, John II, 193
Brooks, John II, 200
Brooks, John II, 282
Brooks, John II, 340
Brooks, John II, 473
Brooks, John II, 784
Brooks, John II, 837
Brooks, John II, 841
Brooks, John II, 912
Brooks, John II, 1069
Brooks, John II, 1080
Brooks, John V, 27
Brooks, John V, 728
Brooks, John V, 797
Brooks, John VI, 733

Brooks, John VI, 800
Brooks, John VI, 801
Brooks, John A. II, 116
Brooks, John Adams II, 282
Brooks, John E. VI, 800
Brooks, John Edward V, 27
Brooks, John G. III, 47
Brooks, John Graham III, 47
Brooks, John J. V, 797
Brooks, John R. I, 921
Brooks, Johnson V, 27
Brooks, Joseph Head II, 729
Brooks, Judith I, 801
Brooks, Judith I, 911
Brooks, Juliann VI, 800
Brooks, Julianna II, 784
Brooks, Julianna II, 841
Brooks, Juriah VI, 819
Brooks, Kathleen Maude VI, 733
Brooks, Keturah V, 27
Brooks, Kitty VI, 800
Brooks, Larkin V, 728
Brooks, Lawrence G. III, 47
Brooks, Lawrence G. III, 148
Brooks, Leah H. III, 47
Brooks, Leanna VI, 801
Brooks, Leannah VI, 800
Brooks, Lemuel V, 797
Brooks, Lenora B. IV, 1308
Brooks, Leroy M. VI, 801
Brooks, Lewsey VI, 800
Brooks, Lolina IV, 930
Brooks, Lu III, 47
Brooks, Lucinda V, 27
Brooks, Lucy VI, 808
Brooks, Lucy A. I, 1149
Brooks, Lucy B. V, 27
Brooks, Lyda I, 911
Brooks, Lydia I, 911
Brooks, Lydia I, 913
Brooks, Lydia II, 193
Brooks, Lydia II, 200
Brooks, Lydia II, 282
Brooks, Lydia II, 317
Brooks, Lydia II, 784
Brooks, Lydia II, 841
Brooks, Lydia III, 46
Brooks, Lydia V, 478
Brooks, Lydia V, 896
Brooks, Lydia V, 898
Brooks, Lydia L. V, 478
Brooks, Malinda V, 774
Brooks, Malinda V, 798
Brooks, Manson V, 797
Brooks, Margaret II, 841
Brooks, Margaret II, 870
Brooks, Margaret Hurley II, 870
Brooks, Martha I, 528
Brooks, Martha I, 777
Brooks, Martha I, 801
Brooks, Martha I, 822
Brooks, Martha I, 873
Brooks, Martha I, 1016
Brooks, Martha II, 340
Brooks, Martha II, 473
Brooks, Martha II, 493
Brooks, Martha II, 543
Brooks, Martha IV, 22
Brooks, Martha IV, 372
Brooks, Martha VI, 800
Brooks, Martha VI, 801
Brooks, Martha A. VI, 231
Brooks, Martha Ann VI, 850
Brooks, Martin V, 797
Brooks, Martin V, 798
Brooks, Martin V, 820
Brooks, Mary I, 347
Brooks, Mary I, 375
Brooks, Mary I, 385
Brooks, Mary I, 411
Brooks, Mary I, 430
Brooks, Mary I, 492
Brooks, Mary I, 777
Brooks, Mary I, 799
Brooks, Mary I, 801
Brooks, Mary I, 810
Brooks, Mary I, 911
Brooks, Mary I, 1017
Brooks, Mary I, 1026
Brooks, Mary II, 282
Brooks, Mary II, 340
Brooks, Mary II, 441
Brooks, Mary II, 473
Brooks, Mary II, 841
Brooks, Mary III, 46
Brooks, Mary III, 47
Brooks, Mary III, 68
Brooks, Mary IV, 22
Brooks, Mary IV, 30
Brooks, Mary IV, 372
Brooks, Mary IV, 1354
Brooks, Mary IV, 1358
Brooks, Mary V, 27
Brooks, Mary V, 728
Brooks, Mary V, 743
Brooks, Mary VI, 161
Brooks, Mary VI, 231
Brooks, Mary VI, 251
Brooks, Mary VI, 371
Brooks, Mary VI, 451
Brooks, Mary VI, 733
Brooks, Mary A. W. II, 116
Brooks, Mary Anettie I, 1149
Brooks, Mary Ann W. II, 116
Brooks, Mary Ann Wing II, 282
Brooks, Mary Ann Wing II, 815
Brooks, Mary Anne II, 200
Brooks, Mary Elizabeth IV, 181
Brooks, Mary H. III, 46
Brooks, Mary J. IV, 372
Brooks, Mary Jane I, 613
Brooks, Mary Jane V, 797
Brooks, Mary L. III, 47
Brooks, Mary M. IV, 892
Brooks, Mary M. VI, 811
Brooks, Mary P. V, 27
Brooks, Mary P. VI, 733
Brooks, Matthew I, 347
Brooks, Matthew I, 375
Brooks, May VI, 801
Brooks, Melinda V, 779
Brooks, Melinda V, 792
Brooks, Melinda V, 797
Brooks, Melinda V, 820
Brooks, Mildred VI, 800
Brooks, Mildred VI, 833
Brooks, Miles VI, 801
Brooks, Milly V, 798
Brooks, Milly P. V, 797
Brooks, Mordecai IV, 930
Brooks, Morgan III, 46
Brooks, Morgan VI, 732
Brooks, Nancy VI, 822
Brooks, Naomi II, 58
Brooks, Naomy II, 58
Brooks, Naomy II, 66
Brooks, Nell III, 47
Brooks, Nellie Adelia I, 613
Brooks, Nelson VI, 800
Brooks, Nelson VI, 816
Brooks, Nelson VI, 838
Brooks, Nimrod I, 1017
Brooks, Nimrod I, 1026
Brooks, Nimrod V, 27
Brooks, Nimrod V, 728
Brooks, Noah V, 779
Brooks, Noah V, 792
Brooks, Noah V, 797
Brooks, Noah V, 798
Brooks, Noah V, 820
Brooks, Olive K. VI, 231
Brooks, Oliver VI, 231
Brooks, Orson H. III, 47
Brooks, Patience V, 797
Brooks, Pauline E. VI, 800
Brooks, Pauline Snowden IV, 930
Brooks, Peter VI, 850
Brooks, Peter VI, 919
Brooks, Phebe III, 46
Brooks, Phebe III, 47
Brooks, Phebe III, 440
Brooks, Phebe H. III, 46
Brooks, Phebe Jane III, 46
Brooks, Phebe Jane III, 47
Brooks, Phebe Jane III, 128
Brooks, Philip VI, 231
Brooks, Phillip VI, 231
Brooks, Powhatan VI, 800
Brooks, Powhatan VI, 801
Brooks, Powhatan VI, 808
Brooks, Powhatan VI, 819
Brooks, Powhatan VI, 867
Brooks, Priscilla V, 728
Brooks, Priscilla V, 769
Brooks, Priscilla V, 774
Brooks, Rachel IV, 930
Brooks, Rachel VI, 883
Brooks, Ralph II, 340
Brooks, Ralph Edward V, 27
Brooks, Rebecca II, 729
Brooks, Rebecca II, 761
Brooks, Rebecca Price II, 729
Brooks, Rhoda VI, 800
Brooks, Rhoda Thomas V, 798
Brooks, Richard II, 841
Brooks, Robert VI, 300
Brooks, Robert VI, 321
Brooks, Robert VI, 973
Brooks, Robt. VI, 907
Brooks, Robt. VI, 941
Brooks, Roger II, 473
Brooks, Roger IV, 1308
Brooks, Roger VI, 733
Brooks, Rose VI, 800
Brooks, Ruth IV, 372
Brooks, Ruth V, 27
Brooks, Ruth Ana IV, 741
Brooks, Ruth Anna IV, 684
Brooks, Ruth P. V, 797
Brooks, Salla I, 1017
Brooks, Sallie I, 921
Brooks, Sally VI, 850
Brooks, Sally VI, 907
Brooks, Sally D. III, 47
Brooks, Sampkin VI, 801
Brooks, Samuel I, 801
Brooks, Samuel I, 982
Brooks, Samuel II, 340
Brooks, Samuel II, 441
Brooks, Samuel IV, 892
Brooks, Samuel VI, 733
Brooks, Samuel VI, 800
Brooks, Samuel H. II, 1069
Brooks, Samuel R. VI, 231
Brooks, Samuel Robert VI, 161
Brooks, Samuel Robert VI, 231
Brooks, Samuel Robert VI, 251
Brooks, Sarah I, 492
Brooks, Sarah I, 773
Brooks, Sarah I, 777
Brooks, Sarah I, 801
Brooks, Sarah I, 822
Brooks, Sarah I, 1017
Brooks, Sarah I, 1026
Brooks, Sarah I, 1032
Brooks, Sarah I, 1037
Brooks, Sarah II, 340
Brooks, Sarah II, 473
Brooks, Sarah III, 46
Brooks, Sarah III, 47
Brooks, Sarah IV, 892
Brooks, Sarah VI, 231
Brooks, Sarah VI, 300
Brooks, Sarah VI, 371
Brooks, Sarah VI, 441
Brooks, Sarah VI, 733
Brooks, Sarah VI, 800
Brooks, Sarah D. VI, 231
Brooks, Sarah H. III, 46
Brooks, Sary V, 784
Brooks, Silas II, 116
Brooks, Silas II, 729
Brooks, Silas G. II, 729
Brooks, Silas S. II, 116
Brooks, Silas S. II, 729
Brooks, Silas S. II, 761
Brooks, Stephen III, 47
Brooks, Stephen H. III, 47
Brooks, Stephen H. III, 304
Brooks, Susan V, 728
Brooks, Susan L. VI, 231
Brooks, Susan L. VI, 259
Brooks, Susan M. III, 47
Brooks, Susan M. III, 148
Brooks, Susanah V, 27
Brooks, Susanna VI, 231
Brooks, Susanna VI, 259
Brooks, Susanna VI, 800
Brooks, Susannah I, 1017
Brooks, Susannah I, 1026
Brooks, Susannah I, 1036
Brooks, Susannah II, 781
Brooks, Susannah II, 981
Brooks, Susannah V, 728
Brooks, Susannah V, 733
Brooks, Susannah V, 734
Brooks, Susannah VI, 231
Brooks, Susannah Lightfoot VI, 231
Brooks, Tacy IV, 22
Brooks, Tacy IV, 372
Brooks, Teacy IV, 372
Brooks, Thomas I, 921
Brooks, Thomas II, 340
Brooks, Thomas II, 473
Brooks, Thomas II, 493
Brooks, Thomas II, 543
Brooks, Thomas VI, 800
Brooks, Thomas Lindley V, 797
Brooks, Ursly VI, 973
Brooks, Vashti I, 1017
Brooks, Walter III, 47
Brooks, Walter F. IV, 1308
Brooks, Walter George VI, 733
Brooks, Walter T. IV, 1308
Brooks, Widow Deborah I, 828
Brooks, Widow Mary I, 375
Brooks, William II, 193
Brooks, William II, 200
Brooks, William II, 317
Brooks, William II, 340
Brooks, William II, 672
Brooks, William IV, 22
Brooks, William IV, 30
Brooks, William IV, 372
Brooks, William V, 478
Brooks, William VI, 371
Brooks, William VI, 800
Brooks, William VI, 850
Brooks, William VI, 867
Brooks, William Howard I, 613
Brooks, William T. V, 27
Brooks, Wm. II, 473
Brooks, Wm. II, 493
Brooks, Wm. II, 784
Brooks, Wm. II, 841
Brooks, Zachariah VI, 800
Brooks, Zachariah VI, 801
Brooksby, Ann II, 473
Brooksby, Ann II, 621
Brooksby, Catherine II, 473
Brooksby, Catherine II, 523
Brooksby, Mary II, 473
Brooksby, Rachel II, 473
Brookshir, Thomas I, 528
Brookshire, Charity I, 710
Brookshire, Manering I, 710
Brookshire, Mary I, 492
Brookshire, Mary I, 528
Brookshire, Mary I, 532
Brookshire, Mary I, 710
Brookshire, Mauning I, 710
Brookshire, Thomas I, 492
Brookshire, Thomas I, 528
Brookshire, Thomas I, 532
Brookshire, Thomas I, 709
Brookshire, Thomas I, 710
Broom, Elizabeth II, 441
Broom, George J. IV, 1036
Broom, John II, 441
Broom, Margrett II, 441
Broom, Thomas II, 441
Broomal, Effie IV, 684
Broomal, Effie IV, 787
Broomal, Mrs. Effie IV, 787
Broomal, Pauline IV, 803
Broomal, R. W. IV, 787
Broomall, Effie IV, 684
Broomall, Elizabeth IV, 803
Broomall, Ethel B. III, 72
Broomall, Gertrude IV, 803
Broomall, Glenn IV, 684
Broomall, Hannah IV, 803
Broomall, John Paul III, 72
Broomall, Lida IV, 684
Broomall, Lida IV, 803
Broomall, Luella IV, 803
Broomall, Lydia IV, 803
Broomall, Lydia IV, 850
Broomall, Minerva IV, 372
Broomall, Orpha IV, 372
Broomall, Pauline IV, 684
Broomall, Pauline IV, 803
Broomall, Phebe IV, 803
Broomall, R. W. IV, 684
Broomall, Rachel IV, 803
Broomall, Raymond IV, 684
Broomall, Raymond IV, 803
Broomall, S. J. IV, 684
Broomall, Sarah IV, 613
Broomall, Sarah IV, 803
Broomall, Sarah B. IV, 613
Broomall, Sarah T. IV, 613
Broomall, Sarah T. IV, 803
Broomall, Sheridan IV, 803
Broomall, Sheridan J. IV, 803
Broomall, Vernon IV, 684
Broomall, Vernon IV, 803
Broome, Margaret II, 824
Broomell, Esther VI, 371
Broomell, Ethel B. III, 47
Broomell, Geo. Lupton III, 47
Broomell, Hannah P. III, 47
Broomell, John VI, 371
Broomell, John Paul III, 47
Broomell, Rebecca J. III, 47
Broomell, Rebecca J. VI, 371
Broomell, Rebecca J. VI, 417
Broomell, Seneca P. III, 47
Broomell, Seneca P. VI, 371
Broomell, Seneca P. VI, 417
Broomhall, Amy IV, 372
Broomhall, Amy IV, 569
Broomhall, Amy IV, 592
Broomhall, Amy J. IV, 322
Broomhall, Ann IV, 76
Broomhall, Ann IV, 109
Broomhall, Arminda IV, 322
Broomhall, Arminda IV, 372
Broomhall, Arminda IV, 569
Broomhall, Barclay IV, 322
Broomhall, Barclay IV, 328
Broomhall, Barclay IV, 438
Broomhall, Barkley IV, 322
Broomhall, Barkley IV, 372
Broomhall, Bartley IV, 141
Broomhall, Bartley VI, 349
Broomhall, Bartty VI, 349
Broomhall, Berkley IV, 372
Broomhall, Elihu IV, 322
Broomhall, Elizabeth IV, 322
Broomhall, Elizabeth IV, 333
Broomhall, Elizabeth V, 478
Broomhall, Enos IV, 141
Broomhall, Enos IV, 322
Broomhall, Enos IV, 372
Broomhall, Enos IV, 569
Broomhall, Enos VI, 349
Broomhall, Enos J. IV, 372
Broomhall, Enos. J. IV, 322
Broomhall, Hannah IV, 76
Broomhall, Hannah IV, 372
Broomhall, Hannah VI, 475
Broomhall, Hannah VI, 555
Broomhall, Isaac IV, 141
Broomhall, Isaac IV, 322
Broomhall, Isaac VI, 349
Broomhall, James IV, 76
Broomhall, James IV, 141
Broomhall, James IV, 321
Broomhall, James IV, 322
Broomhall, James VI, 349
Broomhall, Jane IV, 141
Broomhall, Jane IV, 322
Broomhall, Jane IV, 359
Broomhall, Jane VI, 349
Broomhall, Joanna IV, 141
Broomhall, Joanna IV, 322
Broomhall, Joanna IV, 341
Broomhall, Joanna VI, 349
Broomhall, Joanna Susanna VI, 349
Broomhall, Joanna W. IV, 322
Broomhall, Johanna W. IV, 340
Broomhall, John IV, 181
Broomhall, John IV, 372
Broomhall, John, Jr. IV, 372
Broomhall, Lydia IV, 438
Broomhall, Lydia J. IV, 372
Broomhall, Mahlon IV, 76
Broomhall, Mahlon IV, 109
Broomhall, Martha IV, 141
Broomhall, Martha IV, 322
Broomhall, Martha IV, 337
Broomhall, Martha VI, 349
Broomhall, Minerva IV, 372
Broomhall, Minerva IV, 431
Broomhall, Olinda IV, 322
Broomhall, Olinda IV, 345
Broomhall, Orpha IV, 322
Broomhall, Orpha IV, 372
Broomhall, Orpha IV, 458
Broomhall, Orphah IV, 372
Broomhall, Phebe IV, 141
Broomhall, Phebe IV, 322
Broomhall, Phebe IV, 372
Broomhall, Phebe IV, 569
Broomhall, Phebe VI, 349
Broomhall, Rachel V, 478
Broomhall, Rachel V, 508
Broomhall, Rebecca IV, 321
Broomhall, Rebecca IV, 322
Broomhall, Rebecca IV, 372
Broomhall, Rebecca IV, 438
Broomhall, Rebeckah IV, 322
Broomhall, Rebeckah IV, 328
Broomhall, Sarah IV, 141
Broomhall, Sarah IV, 515
Broomhall, Sarah IV, 525
Broomhall, Sarah VI, 349
Broomhall, Sarah B. IV, 613
Broomhall, Sarah B. IV, 661
Broomhall, Susan IV, 343
Broomhall, Susanna IV, 141
Broomhall, Susanna IV, 322
Broomhall, Thomas IV, 372
Broomhall, Townsend IV, 372
Broomhall, Townsend IV, 569
Broomhall, Webb IV, 372
Broomhall, William IV, 372
Broomhall, William E. IV, 322
Broomhall, William E. IV, 372
Broomhall, Wm. IV, 569
Broomwell, Henry II, 841
Broomwell, Luella IV, 803
Broomwell, Sheridan J. IV, 803
Brosins, Phebe IV, 684
Brosius, Adaline IV, 685
Brosius, Adaline IV, 1024
Brosius, Alice IV, 1024
Brosius, Amos IV, 684
Brosius, Amos IV, 685
Brosius, Amos Preston IV, 684
Brosius, Amos Preston IV, 685
Brosius, Amos Preston IV, 1024

Brosius, Anna M. VI, 733
Brosius, Anna M. VI, 791
Brosius, Arthur IV, 1024
Brosius, Arvine IV, 1024
Brosius, Caleb M. II, 784
Brosius, Caleb M. II, 841
Brosius, Chalkley IV, 684
Brosius, Chalkley IV, 1024
Brosius, Charles IV, 684
Brosius, Charles IV, 685
Brosius, Charles IV, 1024
Brosius, Charles S. II, 841
Brosius, Charlotte IV, 930
Brosius, Chas. S. II, 841
Brosius, Clarkson II, 841
Brosius, Clayton IV, 930
Brosius, Colvin M. IV, 1036
Brosius, Dalton IV, 1024
Brosius, Dalton Arvine IV, 685
Brosius, David L. IV, 684
Brosius, David L. IV, 685
Brosius, David L. IV, 1024
Brosius, Dora E. III, 341
Brosius, Edgar E. IV, 1036
Brosius, Edward Hicks IV, 684
Brosius, Edward Hicks IV, 685
Brosius, Edward Hicks IV, 1024
Brosius, Eliza VI, 883
Brosius, Ellen M. II, 841
Brosius, Emily IV, 1036
Brosius, Emma M. IV, 930
Brosius, Enos IV, 684
Brosius, Enos IV, 1024
Brosius, Enos H. IV, 1036
Brosius, Esther IV, 1021
Brosius, Esther IV, 1024
Brosius, Esther C. IV, 684
Brosius, Esther C. IV, 685
Brosius, Getchel IV, 1024
Brosius, Hannah IV, 1024
Brosius, Harper IV, 684
Brosius, Harper IV, 685
Brosius, Harper IV, 1021
Brosius, Harper IV, 1024
Brosius, Henry IV, 1024
Brosius, Herbert M. II, 784
Brosius, Jane IV, 930
Brosius, Jane IV, 1001
Brosius, Jane A. IV, 930
Brosius, Jane A. IV, 1273
Brosius, Jane W. IV, 930
Brosius, Jane W. IV, 1036
Brosius, John VI, 883
Brosius, Joseph II, 841
Brosius, Joseph II, 860
Brosius, Joseph IV, 684
Brosius, Joseph IV, 1024
Brosius, Joseph P. II, 841
Brosius, Joseph P. II, 860
Brosius, Laura Jane IV, 685
Brosius, Laura Jane IV, 1024
Brosius, Mariam IV, 930
Brosius, Marian M. II, 841
Brosius, Marion II, 784
Brosius, Marion M. II, 841
Brosius, Marium IV, 930
Brosius, Marium IV, 1036
Brosius, Martin IV, 1024
Brosius, Mary IV, 685
Brosius, Mary IV, 1024
Brosius, Mary A. II, 841
Brosius, Mary L. IV, 684
Brosius, Mary L. IV, 685
Brosius, Mary P. II, 787
Brosius, Mary P. II, 841
Brosius, Mary P. II, 846
Brosius, Mary W. II, 841
Brosius, Mary W. II, 860
Brosius, Miriam IV, 930
Brosius, Phebe IV, 684
Brosius, Phebe IV, 685
Brosius, Phebe IV, 1024
Brosius, Phebe G. IV, 684
Brosius, Phebe G. IV, 1021
Brosius, Rachel P. II, 841
Brosius, Rachel P. II, 860
Brosius, Robert Hilles IV, 685
Brosius, Robert Hillis IV, 684
Brosius, Robert Hillis IV, 685
Brosius, Samuel IV, 930
Brosius, Samuel IV, 1016
Brosius, Samuel IV, 1024
Brosius, Samuel G. IV, 1036
Brosius, Samuel Gatchel IV, 684
Brosius, Samuel Martin VI, 733
Brosius, Samuel Martin VI, 791
Brosius, Sumner II, 841
Brosius, Sumner G. II, 784
Brosius, Sumner G. II, 841
Brosius, W. O. IV, 1036
Brosius, Wd. Mary A. II, 841
Brosius, William IV, 1024
Brosius, William H. IV, 685
Brosius, William H. IV, 1024
Brosius, Wm. IV, 684
Brosius, Wm. Henry IV, 684
Broth, Amanda M. IV, 1308
Broth, Cora A. IV, 1308
Broth, Daisy E. IV, 1308
Broth, Everet H. IV, 1308
Brothers, Abigail I, 710
Brothers, Abigail I, 777
Brothers, Abigail I, 801
Brothers, Abigail I, 830
Brothers, Ann I, 131
Brothers, Ann I, 158
Brothers, Caleb I, 94
Brothers, Caleb I, 131
Brothers, Debero I, 94
Brothers, Deborah I, 131
Brothers, Durant I, 94
Brothers, Durant I, 131
Brothers, Durant I, 137
Brothers, Durent I, 801
Brothers, Elisabeth I, 94
Brothers, Elisabeth I, 131
Brothers, Elisabeth I, 149
Brothers, Jesse I, 131
Brothers, Jesse I, 801
Brothers, Job I, 94
Brothers, Job I, 131
Brothers, Job I, 149
Brothers, Lemuel I, 94
Brothers, Lemuel I, 131
Brothers, Mariah Elma I, 777
Brothers, Mary I, 94
Brothers, Mary I, 131
Brothers, Mary I, 134
Brothers, Mary Ann I, 710
Brothers, Mary Ann I, 777
Brothers, Mary Ann I, 801
Brothers, Melissa Jane I, 777
Brothers, Milisent I, 131
Brothers, Milisent I, 133
Brothers, Nathan I, 131
Brothers, Nathan I, 710
Brothers, Nathan I, 777
Brothers, Nathan I, 801
Brothers, Nathan I, 830
Brothers, Rebecca Amanda I, 777
Brothers, Rebecca Amanda I, 801
Brothers, Richard I, 94
Brothers, Richard I, 131
Brothers, Samuel I, 129
Brothers, Samuel I, 131
Brothers, Sarah I, 129
Brothers, Sarah I, 131
Brothers, Sarah I, 137
Brothers, Sarah I, 158
Brothers, Sarah I, 300
Brothers, Sarah I, 801
Brothers, Sarah Roxana I, 777
Brothers, Sarah Roxanah I, 710
Brothers, Sarah Roxanna I, 801
Brothers, Susanna I, 94
Brothers, Susannah I, 131
Brothers, Zachariah I, 94
Brothers, Zachariah I, 131
Brotherton, Grace III, 47
Brotherton, Jacob II, 784
Brotherton, Jacob L. II, 841
Brotherton, Lydia II, 784
Brotherton, Mary Ann Tucker II, 784
Brotherton, Sarah II, 784
Brotherton, Sarah B. II, 841
Brotherton, Thos. II, 784
Brottin, Rachel I, 867
Brougard, Sarah II, 200
Brougard, Sarah II, 262
Brough, James S. IV, 1247
Brought, ??? III, 47
Brought, Raymond III, 47
Broughwhite, Prudance II, 88
Broughwhite, Prudence II, 58
Brouwer, Mary III, 47
Brow, John V, 478
Brow, John V, 480
Brow, Jordan II, 340
Brow, Mary W. V, 478
Brow, Mary W. V, 480
Brow, Thomas II, 340
Brow, Thomas II, 441
Browder, Amy V, 320
Browder, E. H. V, 320
Browder, Edward V, 320
Browder, Harmon V, 320
Browder, Henrietta V, 320
Browder, Mildred V, 320
Browell, Elizabeth VI, 772
Brower, ??? III, 47
Brower, Alice V, 896
Brower, Alice V, 968
Brower, Alice V, 978
Brower, Anna Hazard III, 47
Brower, Jane I, 475
Brower, Lydia I, 475
Brower, Mary III, 486
Brower, Ruth Ann IV, 1354
Brower, Viola V, 828
Brown, ??? I, 33
Brown, ??? III, 49
Brown, ??? III, 50
Brown, ??? III, 141
Brown, ??? III, 365
Brown, ??? IV, 1047
Brown, ??? IV, 1303
Brown, ??? V, 315
Brown, ??? V, 375
Brown, ??? V, 754
Brown, ??? V, 823
Brown, ??? V, 877
Brown, ??? VI, 623
Brown, A. E. V, 987
Brown, A. H. V, 729
Brown, A. W. I, 232
Brown, Aaron I, 268
Brown, Aaron I, 271
Brown, Aaron I, 276
Brown, Aaron II, 596
Brown, Aaron IV, 23
Brown, Aaron IV, 137
Brown, Aaron IV, 181
Brown, Aaron IV, 465
Brown, Aaron V, 949
Brown, Aaron VI, 621
Brown, Aaron VI, 938
Brown, Aaron H. III, 480
Brown, Aaron L. III, 47
Brown, Aaron L. III, 48
Brown, Aaron L. III, 49
Brown, Aaron L. III, 164
Brown, Aaron W. V, 28
Brown, Aaron W. V, 31
Brown, Aaron W. V, 478
Brown, Abba IV, 182
Brown, Abby IV, 930
Brown, Abby IV, 931
Brown, Abby IV, 934
Brown, Abby W. II, 700
Brown, Abby W. II, 730
Brown, Abi II, 981
Brown, Abi II, 982
Brown, Abi II, 1018
Brown, Abi II, 1037
Brown, Abia II, 474
Brown, Abia W. IV, 930
Brown, Abia W. IV, 934
Brown, Abia Wm. IV, 931
Brown, Abiah W. IV, 182
Brown, Abiah W. IV, 930
Brown, Abiatham II, 1045
Brown, Abiatham II, 1051
Brown, Abigail I, 209
Brown, Abigail I, 231
Brown, Abigail I, 256
Brown, Abigail I, 528
Brown, Abigail I, 577
Brown, Abigail II, 58
Brown, Abigail II, 167
Brown, Abigail II, 201
Brown, Abigail II, 475
Brown, Abigail II, 660
Brown, Abigail II, 964
Brown, Abigail II, 1045
Brown, Abigail II, 1055
Brown, Abigail IV, 181
Brown, Abigail IV, 322
Brown, Abigail IV, 372
Brown, Abigail IV, 465
Brown, Abigail IV, 900
Brown, Abigail IV, 1050
Brown, Abigail IV, 1089
Brown, Abigail V, 829
Brown, Abigail V, 880
Brown, Abigail VI, 475
Brown, Abigail VI, 476
Brown, Abigail VI, 551
Brown, Abigail Livezey II, 596
Brown, Abigail W. II, 340
Brown, Abigail W. II, 729
Brown, Abigail W. II, 955
Brown, Abigail, Jr. V, 880
Brown, Abijah William IV, 182
Brown, Abner IV, 613
Brown, Abner IV, 804
Brown, Abner VI, 592
Brown, Abner VI, 622
Brown, Abner VI, 643
Brown, Abrah W. IV, 181
Brown, Abraham I, 131
Brown, Abraham II, 167
Brown, Abraham II, 191
Brown, Abraham II, 201
Brown, Abraham II, 211
Brown, Abraham II, 341
Brown, Abraham II, 474
Brown, Abraham II, 670
Brown, Abraham II, 955
Brown, Abraham II, 982
Brown, Abraham II, 1046
Brown, Abraham V, 29
Brown, Abraham V, 729
Brown, Abraham V, 829
Brown, Abraham V, 830
Brown, Abraham V, 874
Brown, Abraham V, 880
Brown, Abraham VI, 592
Brown, Abraham VI, 623
Brown, Abraham H. V, 881
Brown, Abram II, 955
Brown, Abram IV, 1089
Brown, Ada I, 1149
Brown, Ada V, 661
Brown, Ada C. V, 661
Brown, Adaline Julia IV, 1273
Brown, Addie IV, 1273
Brown, Aggy VI, 1021
Brown, Agnes Ann IV, 322
Brown, Agnes Ann IV, 336
Brown, Agnes Ann IV, 372
Brown, Agnes Ann IV, 410
Brown, Agness VI, 801
Brown, Agness W. VI, 801
Brown, Albert I, 208
Brown, Albert I, 221
Brown, Albert V, 155
Brown, Albert VI, 621
Brown, Albert Eli V, 880
Brown, Albert J. I, 208
Brown, Albert J. V, 661
Brown, Albert Russel V, 614
Brown, Albert S. VI, 622
Brown, Albert W. I, 208
Brown, Albert W. I, 231
Brown, Albert W. I, 232
Brown, Albert W. I, 252
Brown, Alberta J. VI, 621
Brown, Alberta J. VI, 688
Brown, Alcy VI, 1018
Brown, Alexander I, 131
Brown, Alexander II, 341
Brown, Alexander VI, 883
Brown, Alexander VI, 884
Brown, Alfert J. V, 661
Brown, Alfred I, 777
Brown, Alfred IV, 1203
Brown, Alfred V, 661
Brown, Alfred A. VI, 884
Brown, Alice III, 47
Brown, Alice IV, 76
Brown, Alice IV, 685
Brown, Alice V, 29
Brown, Alice V, 155
Brown, Alice V, 829
Brown, Alice V, 830
Brown, Alice V, 831
Brown, Alice V, 896
Brown, Alice VI, 592
Brown, Alice H. II, 982
Brown, Alice H. II, 1017
Brown, Alice L. IV, 1308
Brown, Alice L. IV, 1323
Brown, Alice T. V, 830
Brown, Alice V. VI, 372
Brown, Allen V, 27
Brown, Allen V, 28
Brown, Allen VI, 592
Brown, Allen K. V, 28
Brown, Almina IV, 930
Brown, Almira IV, 685
Brown, Almira IV, 930
Brown, Alpheus J. I, 262
Brown, Althea V, 661
Brown, Alva V, 987
Brown, Alva C. V, 551
Brown, Ama IV, 1273
Brown, Ambrose I, 1149
Brown, Amie A. II, 116
Brown, Amie A. II, 126
Brown, Amos R. IV, 930
Brown, Amy II, 474
Brown, Amy II, 517
Brown, Amy III, 49
Brown, Amy IV, 181
Brown, Amy IV, 372
Brown, Amy IV, 613
Brown, Amy IV, 667
Brown, Amy IV, 685
Brown, Amy IV, 852
Brown, Amy IV, 891
Brown, Amy IV, 893
Brown, Amy IV, 930
Brown, Amy IV, 1014
Brown, Amy IV, 1050
Brown, Amy IV, 1293
Brown, Ann I, 131
Brown, Ann I, 347
Brown, Ann I, 375
Brown, Ann I, 376
Brown, Ann I, 411
Brown, Ann I, 492
Brown, Ann I, 528
Brown, Ann I, 650
Brown, Ann I, 801
Brown, Ann I, 971
Brown, Ann I, 974
Brown, Ann I, 982
Brown, Ann I, 986
Brown, Ann I, 1017
Brown, Ann I, 1026
Brown, Ann I, 1043
Brown, Ann II, 23
Brown, Ann II, 24
Brown, Ann II, 50
Brown, Ann II, 59
Brown, Ann II, 130
Brown, Ann II, 167
Brown, Ann II, 201
Brown, Ann II, 202
Brown, Ann II, 263
Brown, Ann II, 340
Brown, Ann II, 474
Brown, Ann II, 568
Brown, Ann II, 729
Brown, Ann II, 826
Brown, Ann II, 955
Brown, Ann II, 956
Brown, Ann II, 976
Brown, Ann II, 981
Brown, Ann II, 982
Brown, Ann II, 989
Brown, Ann II, 992
Brown, Ann II, 1000
Brown, Ann II, 1042
Brown, Ann II, 1046
Brown, Ann II, 1051
Brown, Ann II, 1058
Brown, Ann II, 1069
Brown, Ann II, 1078
Brown, Ann III, 48
Brown, Ann IV, 19
Brown, Ann IV, 22
Brown, Ann IV, 23
Brown, Ann IV, 41
Brown, Ann IV, 59
Brown, Ann IV, 76
Brown, Ann IV, 114
Brown, Ann IV, 122
Brown, Ann IV, 181
Brown, Ann IV, 182
Brown, Ann IV, 685
Brown, Ann IV, 786
Brown, Ann IV, 803
Brown, Ann IV, 804
Brown, Ann IV, 853
Brown, Ann IV, 865
Brown, Ann IV, 882
Brown, Ann IV, 891
Brown, Ann IV, 900
Brown, Ann IV, 906
Brown, Ann IV, 930
Brown, Ann IV, 931
Brown, Ann V, 27
Brown, Ann V, 28
Brown, Ann V, 29
Brown, Ann V, 224
Brown, Ann V, 728
Brown, Ann V, 830
Brown, Ann V, 844
Brown, Ann V, 873
Brown, Ann V, 880
Brown, Ann V, 888
Brown, Ann VI, 359
Brown, Ann VI, 364
Brown, Ann VI, 372
Brown, Ann VI, 373
Brown, Ann VI, 374
Brown, Ann VI, 470
Brown, Ann VI, 476
Brown, Ann VI, 477
Brown, Ann VI, 505
Brown, Ann VI, 556
Brown, Ann VI, 616
Brown, Ann VI, 621
Brown, Ann VI, 622
Brown, Ann VI, 623
Brown, Ann VI, 624
Brown, Ann VI, 625
Brown, Ann VI, 626
Brown, Ann VI, 627
Brown, Ann VI, 638
Brown, Ann VI, 650
Brown, Ann VI, 656
Brown, Ann VI, 674

Brown, Ann VI, 677
Brown, Ann VI, 678
Brown, Ann VI, 680
Brown, Ann VI, 683
Brown, Ann VI, 684
Brown, Ann VI, 686
Brown, Ann VI, 697
Brown, Ann VI, 801
Brown, Ann VI, 883
Brown, Ann VI, 974
Brown, Ann VI, 982
Brown, Ann Allen II, 24
Brown, Ann Allen II, 116
Brown, Ann B. II, 730
Brown, Ann B. II, 732
Brown, Ann B. II, 1046
Brown, Ann B. II, 1051
Brown, Ann C. II, 146
Brown, Ann C. II, 475
Brown, Ann Eliza II, 953
Brown, Ann Eliza II, 954
Brown, Ann Eliza II, 955
Brown, Ann Eliza II, 1046
Brown, Ann Eliza II, 1052
Brown, Ann Eliza II, 1058
Brown, Ann Eliza III, 49
Brown, Ann Eliza V, 29
Brown, Ann Eliza V, 478
Brown, Ann Elizabeth VI, 623
Brown, Ann H. VI, 449
Brown, Ann H. VI, 462
Brown, Ann Humphrey VI, 733
Brown, Ann Humphrey VI, 793
Brown, Ann J. II, 955
Brown, Ann Lovett II, 956
Brown, Ann R. IV, 930
Brown, Ann W. V, 874
Brown, Ann W. V, 880
Brown, Ann W. V, 888
Brown, Ann, Jr. II, 981
Brown, Anna I, 268
Brown, Anna I, 276
Brown, Anna I, 528
Brown, Anna I, 801
Brown, Anna I, 1149
Brown, Anna II, 234
Brown, Anna II, 842
Brown, Anna II, 955
Brown, Anna II, 1046
Brown, Anna III, 47
Brown, Anna III, 178
Brown, Anna IV, 23
Brown, Anna IV, 181
Brown, Anna V, 828
Brown, Anna V, 829
Brown, Anna V, 871
Brown, Anna V, 949
Brown, Anna VI, 624
Brown, Anna VI, 884
Brown, Anna C. III, 49
Brown, Anna C. III, 270
Brown, Anna F. II, 842
Brown, Anna F. II, 857
Brown, Anna F. IV, 1308
Brown, Anna H. VI, 372
Brown, Anna H. VI, 621
Brown, Anna H. VI, 638
Brown, Anna Hannah IV, 181
Brown, Anna L. II, 730
Brown, Anna L. II, 765
Brown, Anna M. I, 208
Brown, Anna Mary I, 232
Brown, Anna Mary I, 250
Brown, Anna Mary K. I, 219
Brown, Anna May I, 208
Brown, Anna S. II, 730
Brown, Anna S. II, 734
Brown, Anna Stewardson II, 341
Brown, Anna Stewardson II, 729
Brown, Anna W. II, 308
Brown, Anne I, 347
Brown, Anne I, 370
Brown, Anne I, 376
Brown, Anne II, 955
Brown, Anne II, 982
Brown, Anne II, 1044
Brown, Anne II, 1045
Brown, Anne V, 478
Brown, Anne F. III, 56
Brown, Anne F. III, 218
Brown, Annetta V, 28
Brown, Annetta V, 48
Brown, Annetta H. V, 29
Brown, Annie I, 20
Brown, Annie I, 208
Brown, Annie V, 551
Brown, Annie VI, 56
Brown, Annie VI, 74
Brown, Annie A. II, 47
Brown, Annie B. I, 873
Brown, Annie D. I, 938
Brown, Annie E. V, 551
Brown, Annie Florence I, 922
Brown, Annie Gertrude II, 841
Brown, Annie Gertrude II, 928
Brown, Annie Laura VI, 733
Brown, Annie Laura VI, 753
Brown, Annie Laura VI, 757
Brown, Annie Laura VI, 764
Brown, Annie Lauria VI, 621
Brown, Annie Laurie VI, 662
Brown, Annie M. I, 232
Brown, Annie M. V, 28
Brown, Annie Mary V, 29
Brown, Annie S. III, 49
Brown, Annie S. VI, 372
Brown, Annie Stuart I, 938
Brown, Araba VI, 1013
Brown, Arah V, 830
Brown, Arch V, 452
Brown, Archibald VI, 839
Brown, Archibald F. III, 480
Brown, Aria V, 831
Brown, Arin V, 478
Brown, Armitt II, 474
Brown, Aron V, 28
Brown, Arthur II, 201
Brown, Ary V, 829
Brown, Asa IV, 181
Brown, Asa IV, 613
Brown, Asa IV, 804
Brown, Asa IV, 1273
Brown, Asa IV, 1292
Brown, Asa V, 949
Brown, Asa V, 958
Brown, Asenath I, 1081
Brown, Asenath IV, 410
Brown, Asher II, 167
Brown, Asher II, 201
Brown, Asher V, 27
Brown, Asher V, 28
Brown, Asher V, 52
Brown, Asher V, 86
Brown, Asher V, 97
Brown, Asher V, 122
Brown, Asher V, 968
Brown, Asher, Sr. V, 27
Brown, Asher, Sr. V, 28
Brown, Atlantic IV, 685
Brown, Atlantic IV, 794
Brown, Atlantic IV, 930
Brown, Augustus VI, 818
Brown, Axey IV, 372
Brown, Azariah V, 478
Brown, B. P. I, 232
Brown, Bannona V, 987
Brown, Barclay II, 201
Brown, Barclay II, 282
Brown, Barclay II, 317
Brown, Barclay II, 340
Brown, Barclay II, 475
Brown, Barclay V, 829
Brown, Barclay V, 880
Brown, Barclay V, 885
Brown, Barkley V, 880
Brown, Basil H. II, 842
Brown, Basil H. II, 857
Brown, Bathsheba IV, 685
Brown, Bathsheba IV, 895
Brown, Bathsheba V, 828
Brown, Bathsheba V, 830
Brown, Bathsheba V, 880
Brown, Bathsheba V, 886
Brown, Bathshebe IV, 891
Brown, Behia III, 20
Brown, Bella III, 49
Brown, Belle V, 896
Brown, Benj. IV, 372
Brown, Benj. V, 728
Brown, Benj. V, 968
Brown, Benj. P. I, 208
Brown, Benj. P. I, 209
Brown, Benj. P. I, 215
Brown, Benjamin II, 201
Brown, Benjamin II, 253
Brown, Benjamin II, 317
Brown, Benjamin II, 340
Brown, Benjamin II, 341
Brown, Benjamin II, 474
Brown, Benjamin II, 982
Brown, Benjamin II, 1045
Brown, Benjamin IV, 181
Brown, Benjamin IV, 1050
Brown, Benjamin IV, 1247
Brown, Benjamin IV, 1273
Brown, Benjamin V, 28
Brown, Benjamin V, 38
Brown, Benjamin V, 44
Brown, Benjamin V, 829
Brown, Benjamin V, 830
Brown, Benjamin V, 880
Brown, Benjamin V, 881
Brown, Benjamin VI, 592
Brown, Benjamin Brelsford II, 981
Brown, Benjamin Chapman V, 28
Brown, Benjamin Ferguson II, 474
Brown, Benjamin Lancaster V, 830
Brown, Benjamin P. I, 211
Brown, Benjamin P. I, 232
Brown, Benjamin P. I, 235
Brown, Benjamin P. II, 308
Brown, Benjamin P. II, 317
Brown, Benjamin P. II, 1045
Brown, Benjamin P. II, 1069
Brown, Benjamin Prichard I, 208
Brown, Benjamin Pritchard I, 208
Brown, Benjamin S. IV, 181
Brown, Benjamin, Jr. II, 982
Brown, Bera I, 938
Brown, Bernard VI, 476
Brown, Bernice III, 49
Brown, Bert V, 452
Brown, Bertha A. I, 232
Brown, Bertha A. I, 255
Brown, Bertha Ann I, 225
Brown, Bertha J. VI, 622
Brown, Bertha J. VI, 626
Brown, Bertha J. VI, 628
Brown, Bertha J. VI, 631
Brown, Bertha J. VI, 635
Brown, Bertha J. VI, 671
Brown, Bertha J. VI, 702
Brown, Bertie G. V, 452
Brown, Bessie IV, 1203
Brown, Bessie V, 452
Brown, Bessie H. I, 262
Brown, Bessie I. V, 452
Brown, Bethia III, 48
Brown, Betsey VI, 884
Brown, Betsey A. VI, 824
Brown, Betsy I, 1043
Brown, Betsy VI, 475
Brown, Betsy VI, 937
Brown, Betty VI, 591
Brown, Betty VI, 946
Brown, Beulah II, 54
Brown, Beulah II, 58
Brown, Beulah II, 167
Brown, Beulah II, 201
Brown, Beulah II, 282
Brown, Beulah II, 291
Brown, Beulah V, 28
Brown, Beulah V, 828
Brown, Beulah V, 829
Brown, Beulah V, 830
Brown, Beulah V, 854
Brown, Beulah V, 879
Brown, Beulah V, 880
Brown, Beulah G. V, 880
Brown, Blanch I, 930
Brown, Blanch IV, 1203
Brown, Blanch V, 225
Brown, Blanch V, 552
Brown, Blanche V, 225
Brown, Boyd Janney VI, 627
Brown, Boyd Janney VI, 734
Brown, Boyer Brooks II, 474
Brown, Burn V, 155
Brown, Burr VI, 621
Brown, Burr VI, 627
Brown, Burr VI, 682
Brown, Bushrod VI, 627
Brown, Bushrod VI, 710
Brown, Bushrod VI, 712
Brown, Caleb II, 841
Brown, Caleb II, 866
Brown, Caleb III, 47
Brown, Caleb III, 49
Brown, Callaway VI, 884
Brown, Calvin I, 462
Brown, Calvin I, 468
Brown, Calvin I, 470
Brown, Canby II, 730
Brown, Carolina III, 47
Brown, Caroline III, 48
Brown, Caroline III, 151
Brown, Caroline V, 452
Brown, Caroline V, 830
Brown, Caroline V, 831
Brown, Caroline V, 844
Brown, Caroline V, 856
Brown, Caroline V, 949
Brown, Caroline V, 951
Brown, Caroline E. II, 841
Brown, Caroline E. V, 28
Brown, Caroline E. V, 52
Brown, Caroline Elizabeth II, 784
Brown, Caroline Elizabeth V, 28
Brown, Caroline H. II, 730
Brown, Caroline H. II, 742
Brown, Caroline H. II, 841
Brown, Caroline H. II, 866
Brown, Caroline J. III, 47
Brown, Caroline J. III, 50
Brown, Caroline Willets VI, 628
Brown, Carrie IV, 685
Brown, Carrie IV, 1308
Brown, Carrie IV, 1336
Brown, Carrie Gulielma I, 33
Brown, Carrie M. IV, 1273
Brown, Carroll S. VI, 372
Brown, Cassandra VI, 371
Brown, Cassandra VI, 621
Brown, Cassandra VI, 678
Brown, Cassandra VI, 685
Brown, Cassandria VI, 426
Brown, Cate II, 473
Brown, Catharin I, 208
Brown, Catharine I, 231
Brown, Catharine I, 235
Brown, Catharine I, 528
Brown, Catharine I, 873
Brown, Catharine I, 877
Brown, Catharine III, 49
Brown, Catharine III, 50
Brown, Catharine IV, 322
Brown, Catharine IV, 804
Brown, Catharine IV, 811
Brown, Catharine V, 30
Brown, Catharine VI, 475
Brown, Catharine VI, 485
Brown, Catharine VI, 621
Brown, Catharine VI, 857
Brown, Catharine VI, 883
Brown, Catharine VI, 884
Brown, Catharine F. I, 211
Brown, Catharine M. II, 281
Brown, Catharine M. II, 282
Brown, Catharine M. II, 700
Brown, Catharine M. II, 730
Brown, Catherine I, 1081
Brown, Catherine II, 473
Brown, Catherine V, 28
Brown, Catherine VI, 371
Brown, Catherine VI, 475
Brown, Catherine VI, 633
Brown, Catherine VI, 734
Brown, Cecelia VI, 373
Brown, Cecelia H. VI, 621
Brown, Cecelia H. VI, 627
Brown, Cecelia H. VI, 710
Brown, Cecelia H. VI, 712
Brown, Ceiley I, 592
Brown, Celia I, 873
Brown, Celia VI, 1020
Brown, Charity II, 841
Brown, Charity III, 47
Brown, Charity III, 49
Brown, Charity III, 50
Brown, Charles II, 474
Brown, Charles II, 955
Brown, Charles II, 982
Brown, Charles II, 1012
Brown, Charles II, 1017
Brown, Charles II, 1019
Brown, Charles III, 47
Brown, Charles IV, 1203
Brown, Charles IV, 1273
Brown, Charles V, 375
Brown, Charles V, 551
Brown, Charles VI, 372
Brown, Charles VI, 476
Brown, Charles VI, 859
Brown, Charles A. V, 28
Brown, Charles A. V, 29
Brown, Charles A. V, 30
Brown, Charles D. VI, 622
Brown, Charles E. I, 232
Brown, Charles E. V, 224
Brown, Charles Edward I, 208
Brown, Charles Edward I, 209
Brown, Charles F. V, 28
Brown, Charles L. IV, 803
Brown, Charles M. VI, 372
Brown, Charles M. VI, 374
Brown, Charles M. VI, 712
Brown, Charles Murphy VI, 621
Brown, Charles Murphy VI, 624
Brown, Charles Murphy VI, 710
Brown, Charles Oscar V, 830
Brown, Charles Oscar V, 831
Brown, Charles W. III, 50
Brown, Charlina I, 938
Brown, Charlotte II, 955
Brown, Charlotte II, 982
Brown, Charlotte II, 1012
Brown, Charlotte II, 1017
Brown, Charlotte II, 1019
Brown, Charlotte II, 1046
Brown, Charlotte II, 1053
Brown, Charlotte II, 1069
Brown, Charlotte II, 1073
Brown, Charlotte VI, 801
Brown, Chas. IV, 1308
Brown, Chas. M. IV, 1308
Brown, Chester V, 29
Brown, Christian II, 473
Brown, Christian II, 638
Brown, Christian II, 982
Brown, Christian VI, 516
Brown, Christiana II, 981
Brown, Christiann II, 341
Brown, Christy III, 49
Brown, Clara V, 614
Brown, Clara Esther V, 29
Brown, Clara L. VI, 648
Brown, Clara Louisa VI, 621
Brown, Clara Louisa VI, 628
Brown, Clara Louisa VI, 648
Brown, Clara M. V, 825
Brown, Clara M. V, 831
Brown, Clare V, 661
Brown, Clarence Elnathan IV, 182
Brown, Clarence P. III, 50
Brown, Clayburn VI, 883
Brown, Clayton I, 1055
Brown, Clayton II, 167
Brown, Clayton II, 201
Brown, Clayton V, 28
Brown, Clayton V, 94
Brown, Clayton V, 155
Brown, Clayton V, 159
Brown, Clayton V, 828
Brown, Clayton V, 829
Brown, Clayton V, 830
Brown, Clayton V, 831
Brown, Clayton V, 880
Brown, Clayton E. V, 829
Brown, Clayton N. V, 829
Brown, Clayton, Jr. V, 831
Brown, Clayton, Jr. V, 880
Brown, Clayton, Jr. V, 881
Brown, Clement V, 478
Brown, Cleveland IV, 1203
Brown, Clinton V, 224
Brown, Constant VI, 884
Brown, Content I, 376
Brown, Content I, 398
Brown, Cora V, 661
Brown, Cora B. V, 551
Brown, Cornelia I, 930
Brown, Cornelia I, 932
Brown, Cosmelia J. VI, 627
Brown, Cosmelia J. VI, 659
Brown, Cosmelia Janney VI, 621
Brown, Cosmelia Janney VI, 658
Brown, Courtney I, 221
Brown, Curtin IV, 1336
Brown, Cyrene I, 802
Brown, Cyrene I, 805
Brown, D. H. V, 729
Brown, Daiid VI, 591
Brown, Daisy VI, 621
Brown, Daisy VI, 650
Brown, Daisy VI, 651
Brown, Dana V, 661
Brown, Dana V, 693
Brown, Dana T. V, 661
Brown, Daniel I, 268
Brown, Daniel I, 375
Brown, Daniel I, 923
Brown, Daniel II, 441
Brown, Daniel IV, 181
Brown, Daniel IV, 186
Brown, Daniel IV, 1128
Brown, Daniel V, 551
Brown, Daniel VI, 349
Brown, Daniel VI, 350
Brown, Daniel VI, 371
Brown, Daniel VI, 372
Brown, Daniel VI, 387
Brown, Daniel VI, 434
Brown, Daniel VI, 568
Brown, Daniel VI, 592
Brown, Daniel VI, 599
Brown, Daniel VI, 848
Brown, Daniel VI, 883
Brown, Daniel VI, 884
Brown, Daniel VI, 901
Brown, Daniel VI, 959
Brown, Daniel C. III, 47
Brown, Daniel C. III, 329
Brown, Daniel H. V, 320
Brown, Daniel H. VI, 855
Brown, Daniel L. II, 955
Brown, Daniel L. II, 1046
Brown, Daniel L. II, 1051
Brown, Daniel N. V, 896
Brown, Daniel T. VI, 458

Brown, Daniel W. I, 756
Brown, David I, 209
Brown, David I, 960
Brown, David II, 54
Brown, David II, 58
Brown, David II, 474
Brown, David II, 955
Brown, David II, 964
Brown, David II, 982
Brown, David II, 1045
Brown, David II, 1046
Brown, David II, 1049
Brown, David II, 1055
Brown, David II, 1058
Brown, David II, 1069
Brown, David IV, 181
Brown, David IV, 685
Brown, David IV, 786
Brown, David IV, 804
Brown, David IV, 853
Brown, David IV, 930
Brown, David IV, 1273
Brown, David V, 27
Brown, David V, 28
Brown, David V, 102
Brown, David V, 224
Brown, David V, 829
Brown, David V, 831
Brown, David VI, 371
Brown, David VI, 372
Brown, David VI, 373
Brown, David VI, 448
Brown, David VI, 457
Brown, David VI, 467
Brown, David VI, 477
Brown, David VI, 546
Brown, David VI, 558
Brown, David VI, 568
Brown, David VI, 592
Brown, David VI, 601
Brown, David VI, 602
Brown, David VI, 603
Brown, David VI, 621
Brown, David VI, 622
Brown, David VI, 623
Brown, David VI, 626
Brown, David VI, 638
Brown, David VI, 651
Brown, David VI, 702
Brown, David VI, 706
Brown, David VI, 710
Brown, David VI, 729
Brown, David VI, 733
Brown, David VI, 776
Brown, David VI, 884
Brown, David Eugene VI, 733
Brown, David Eugene VI, 741
Brown, David F. VI, 621
Brown, David H. IV, 900
Brown, David H. VI, 617
Brown, David H. VI, 618
Brown, David H. VI, 621
Brown, David H. VI, 622
Brown, David H. VI, 625
Brown, David H. VI, 627
Brown, David H. VI, 733
Brown, David H. VI, 734
Brown, David Henry VI, 374
Brown, David Henry VI, 626
Brown, David Henry VI, 627
Brown, David J. II, 1046
Brown, David John II, 955
Brown, David M. V, 880
Brown, David Percival VI, 624
Brown, David S. III, 47
Brown, David S. III, 48
Brown, David S. III, 268
Brown, David S., Jr. III, 48
Brown, David Waldo VI, 733
Brown, David Waldo VI, 764
Brown, David, Sr. VI, 476
Brown, David, Sr. VI, 592
Brown, David, Sr. VI, 599
Brown, Deborah I, 208
Brown, Deborah I, 347
Brown, Deborah I, 376
Brown, Deborah I, 430
Brown, Deborah I, 756
Brown, Deborah I, 974
Brown, Deborah II, 802
Brown, Deborah IV, 613
Brown, Deborah IV, 655
Brown, Deborah IV, 803
Brown, Deborah IV, 804
Brown, Deborah V, 829
Brown, Deborah V, 874
Brown, Deborah V, 880
Brown, Deborah VI, 597
Brown, Deborah E. IV, 804
Brown, Deborah E. IV, 833
Brown, Deborah Elizabeth IV, 803
Brown, Delbert VI, 622
Brown, Delbert Franklin VI, 622
Brown, Denise V, 829
Brown, Dinah V, 28
Brown, Dinah V, 31
Brown, Dinah V, 42
Brown, Dinah V, 97
Brown, Dinah VI, 359
Brown, Dinah VI, 721
Brown, Donald Leslie VI, 621
Brown, Dora I, 922
Brown, Dorcas II, 474
Brown, Doris Ellingwood VI, 628
Brown, Doris Ellingwood VI, 702
Brown, Dorothea W. III, 47
Brown, Dorothea W. III, 50
Brown, Dorothy W. I, 208
Brown, Dorris V. I, 262
Brown, Douglas Summers VI, 294
Brown, Dr. E. W. V, 321
Brown, Dr. Edward W. V, 321
Brown, Dr. Sanger M. III, 49
Brown, E. A. V, 452
Brown, E. C. L. VI, 884
Brown, E. Garnet IV, 182
Brown, Earl V, 478
Brown, Earl Waldo VI, 733
Brown, Ebanezar I, 376
Brown, Ebanor IV, 76
Brown, Ebenezar VI, 875
Brown, Ebenezar VI, 1009
Brown, Ebenezer II, 474
Brown, Ebunazar I, 347
Brown, Edgar V, 320
Brown, Edgar Allen IV, 181
Brown, Edith VI, 622
Brown, Edith VI, 631
Brown, Edith Adelaide V, 552
Brown, Edith W. VI, 884
Brown, Edmund VI, 801
Brown, Edmund VI, 822
Brown, Edmund VI, 853
Brown, Edmund VI, 854
Brown, Edmund VI, 861
Brown, Edna V, 224
Brown, Edna V, 321
Brown, Edna V, 706
Brown, Edna VI, 622
Brown, Edna Alice VI, 622
Brown, Edna Alice VI, 627
Brown, Edna Alice VI, 631
Brown, Edward I, 267
Brown, Edward I, 268
Brown, Edward I, 300
Brown, Edward III, 47
Brown, Edward III, 365
Brown, Edward V, 987
Brown, Edward VI, 592
Brown, Edward VI, 618
Brown, Edward VI, 621
Brown, Edward VI, 622
Brown, Edward VI, 623
Brown, Edward VI, 706
Brown, Edward VI, 801
Brown, Edward VI, 818
Brown, Edward Balderston II, 1046
Brown, Edward H. III, 47
Brown, Edward H. III, 48
Brown, Edward H. III, 271
Brown, Edward H. III, 290
Brown, Edward Roland VI, 628
Brown, Edward Roland VI, 631
Brown, Edward T. III, 47
Brown, Edwin VI, 373
Brown, Edwin J. II, 841
Brown, Edwin J. II, 866
Brown, Edwin J. IV, 803
Brown, Edwin J. IV, 804
Brown, Edwin J. V, 949
Brown, Edwin L. II, 841
Brown, Edwin Lewis II, 784
Brown, Edwin Lewis II, 841
Brown, Edwin Lewis II, 864
Brown, Edwin Mahlon VI, 617
Brown, Edwin Mahlon VI, 618
Brown, Edwin Mahlon VI, 622
Brown, Edwin Mahlon VI, 626
Brown, Edwin P. I, 208
Brown, Edwin P. I, 209
Brown, Edwin P. I, 232
Brown, Edwin P. III, 50
Brown, Edwin P., Jr. I, 208
Brown, Edy VI, 923
Brown, Effie A. V, 661
Brown, Effie Afton V, 661
Brown, Effingham III, 47
Brown, Eleanor IV, 803
Brown, Eleanor IV, 1308
Brown, Eleanor VI, 372
Brown, Eleanor VI, 558
Brown, Eleanor VI, 733
Brown, Eleanor VI, 776
Brown, Eleanor E. VI, 477
Brown, Eleanor E. VI, 628
Brown, Eleanor E. VI, 655
Brown, Eleazar IV, 17
Brown, Eleazar IV, 613
Brown, Eleazer IV, 22
Brown, Eleazer IV, 30
Brown, Eleazer IV, 71
Brown, Eleazer IV, 76
Brown, Eleazer IV, 100
Brown, Eleazer IV, 122
Brown, Eleazer IV, 125
Brown, Eleazer IV, 804
Brown, Eleazer VI, 372
Brown, Eleazer, Jr. IV, 76
Brown, Elenor I, 982
Brown, Elgar II, 23
Brown, Elgar II, 58
Brown, Elgar II, 86
Brown, Elgar II, 130
Brown, Elgar V, 224
Brown, Elgar V, 249
Brown, Elgar V, 299
Brown, Elgar V, 320
Brown, Elgar V, 452
Brown, Elgar, Jr. V, 223
Brown, Elgar, Jr. V, 224
Brown, Elgar, Jr. V, 452
Brown, Eli I, 801
Brown, Eli I, 960
Brown, Eli V, 155
Brown, Eli V, 829
Brown, Eli V, 830
Brown, Eli V, 831
Brown, Eli V, 987
Brown, Eli F. VI, 621
Brown, Eli S. V, 831
Brown, Elias I, 528
Brown, Elias I, 529
Brown, Elihu IV, 1273
Brown, Elijah II, 341
Brown, Elijah II, 454
Brown, Elijah II, 474
Brown, Elijah III, 47
Brown, Elijah V, 452
Brown, Elijah VI, 475
Brown, Elinor E. VI, 627
Brown, Elisabeth I, 231
Brown, Elisabeth I, 244
Brown, Elisabeth V, 29
Brown, Elisabeth V, 779
Brown, Elisabeth VI, 372
Brown, Elisabeth H. I, 232
Brown, Elisabeth H. I, 249
Brown, Elisan VI, 371
Brown, Elisan VI, 734
Brown, Elisha II, 23
Brown, Elisha II, 59
Brown, Elisha II, 116
Brown, Elisha II, 340
Brown, Elisha II, 474
Brown, Elisha II, 477
Brown, Elisha II, 521
Brown, Elisha II, 596
Brown, Elisha V, 829
Brown, Elisha V, 830
Brown, Elisha V, 844
Brown, Elisha S. V, 831
Brown, Eliz'h T. VI, 425
Brown, Eliza I, 1149
Brown, Eliza IV, 685
Brown, Eliza V, 452
Brown, Eliza V, 551
Brown, Eliza V, 896
Brown, Eliza V, 906
Brown, Eliza VI, 371
Brown, Eliza VI, 372
Brown, Eliza VI, 373
Brown, Eliza VI, 444
Brown, Eliza VI, 556
Brown, Eliza VI, 584
Brown, Eliza VI, 621
Brown, Eliza VI, 622
Brown, Eliza VI, 623
Brown, Eliza VI, 638
Brown, Eliza VI, 651
Brown, Eliza VI, 702
Brown, Eliza VI, 706
Brown, Eliza VI, 734
Brown, Eliza VI, 989
Brown, Eliza Ann IV, 1050
Brown, Eliza Ann IV, 1089
Brown, Eliza Ann V, 478
Brown, Eliza Ann VI, 884
Brown, Eliza E. V, 949
Brown, Eliza J. II, 955
Brown, Eliza L. II, 1046
Brown, Eliza L. II, 1051
Brown, Eliza M. II, 201
Brown, Eliza M. II, 475
Brown, Eliza N. VI, 471
Brown, Eliza N. VI, 475
Brown, Eliza N. VI, 510
Brown, Eliza N. VI, 512
Brown, Eliza T. IV, 685
Brown, Eliza T. IV, 745
Brown, Eliza Updegraff IV, 465
Brown, Eliza Updegraff IV, 685
Brown, Eliza Updegraff IV, 900
Brown, Elizabeth I, 131
Brown, Elizabeth I, 492
Brown, Elizabeth I, 528
Brown, Elizabeth I, 537
Brown, Elizabeth I, 583
Brown, Elizabeth I, 650
Brown, Elizabeth I, 801
Brown, Elizabeth I, 960
Brown, Elizabeth I, 1007
Brown, Elizabeth I, 1008
Brown, Elizabeth I, 1043
Brown, Elizabeth I, 1081
Brown, Elizabeth I, 1090
Brown, Elizabeth II, 24
Brown, Elizabeth II, 35
Brown, Elizabeth II, 50
Brown, Elizabeth II, 58
Brown, Elizabeth II, 59
Brown, Elizabeth II, 89
Brown, Elizabeth II, 116
Brown, Elizabeth II, 167
Brown, Elizabeth II, 201
Brown, Elizabeth II, 209
Brown, Elizabeth II, 227
Brown, Elizabeth II, 250
Brown, Elizabeth II, 253
Brown, Elizabeth II, 341
Brown, Elizabeth II, 473
Brown, Elizabeth II, 474
Brown, Elizabeth II, 475
Brown, Elizabeth II, 517
Brown, Elizabeth II, 660
Brown, Elizabeth II, 672
Brown, Elizabeth II, 700
Brown, Elizabeth II, 729
Brown, Elizabeth II, 789
Brown, Elizabeth II, 824
Brown, Elizabeth II, 826
Brown, Elizabeth II, 955
Brown, Elizabeth II, 981
Brown, Elizabeth II, 982
Brown, Elizabeth II, 1042
Brown, Elizabeth II, 1045
Brown, Elizabeth II, 1054
Brown, Elizabeth III, 47
Brown, Elizabeth III, 48
Brown, Elizabeth III, 50
Brown, Elizabeth III, 164
Brown, Elizabeth III, 178
Brown, Elizabeth III, 223
Brown, Elizabeth IV, 17
Brown, Elizabeth IV, 22
Brown, Elizabeth IV, 23
Brown, Elizabeth IV, 30
Brown, Elizabeth IV, 34
Brown, Elizabeth IV, 76
Brown, Elizabeth IV, 86
Brown, Elizabeth IV, 122
Brown, Elizabeth IV, 125
Brown, Elizabeth IV, 131
Brown, Elizabeth IV, 181
Brown, Elizabeth IV, 186
Brown, Elizabeth IV, 269
Brown, Elizabeth IV, 322
Brown, Elizabeth IV, 346
Brown, Elizabeth IV, 465
Brown, Elizabeth IV, 803
Brown, Elizabeth IV, 900
Brown, Elizabeth IV, 933
Brown, Elizabeth IV, 1050
Brown, Elizabeth IV, 1083
Brown, Elizabeth IV, 1089
Brown, Elizabeth IV, 1123
Brown, Elizabeth IV, 1137
Brown, Elizabeth IV, 1273
Brown, Elizabeth IV, 1279
Brown, Elizabeth V, 28
Brown, Elizabeth V, 31
Brown, Elizabeth V, 94
Brown, Elizabeth V, 100
Brown, Elizabeth V, 102
Brown, Elizabeth V, 224
Brown, Elizabeth V, 321
Brown, Elizabeth V, 478
Brown, Elizabeth V, 504
Brown, Elizabeth V, 783
Brown, Elizabeth V, 798
Brown, Elizabeth V, 829
Brown, Elizabeth V, 830
Brown, Elizabeth V, 831
Brown, Elizabeth V, 839
Brown, Elizabeth V, 862
Brown, Elizabeth V, 880
Brown, Elizabeth V, 887
Brown, Elizabeth V, 968
Brown, Elizabeth V, 979
Brown, Elizabeth VI, 349
Brown, Elizabeth VI, 371
Brown, Elizabeth VI, 372
Brown, Elizabeth VI, 373
Brown, Elizabeth VI, 437
Brown, Elizabeth VI, 442
Brown, Elizabeth VI, 475
Brown, Elizabeth VI, 476
Brown, Elizabeth VI, 477
Brown, Elizabeth VI, 480
Brown, Elizabeth VI, 491
Brown, Elizabeth VI, 505
Brown, Elizabeth VI, 544
Brown, Elizabeth VI, 548
Brown, Elizabeth VI, 549
Brown, Elizabeth VI, 552
Brown, Elizabeth VI, 555
Brown, Elizabeth VI, 556
Brown, Elizabeth VI, 584
Brown, Elizabeth VI, 587
Brown, Elizabeth VI, 592
Brown, Elizabeth VI, 618
Brown, Elizabeth VI, 621
Brown, Elizabeth VI, 622
Brown, Elizabeth VI, 623
Brown, Elizabeth VI, 624
Brown, Elizabeth VI, 625
Brown, Elizabeth VI, 626
Brown, Elizabeth VI, 627
Brown, Elizabeth VI, 628
Brown, Elizabeth VI, 637
Brown, Elizabeth VI, 650
Brown, Elizabeth VI, 655
Brown, Elizabeth VI, 665
Brown, Elizabeth VI, 682
Brown, Elizabeth VI, 683
Brown, Elizabeth VI, 684
Brown, Elizabeth VI, 688
Brown, Elizabeth VI, 689
Brown, Elizabeth VI, 690
Brown, Elizabeth VI, 691
Brown, Elizabeth VI, 696
Brown, Elizabeth VI, 697
Brown, Elizabeth VI, 699
Brown, Elizabeth VI, 703
Brown, Elizabeth VI, 710
Brown, Elizabeth VI, 714
Brown, Elizabeth VI, 718
Brown, Elizabeth VI, 764
Brown, Elizabeth VI, 801
Brown, Elizabeth VI, 813
Brown, Elizabeth VI, 822
Brown, Elizabeth VI, 828
Brown, Elizabeth VI, 829
Brown, Elizabeth VI, 879
Brown, Elizabeth VI, 884
Brown, Elizabeth VI, 914
Brown, Elizabeth VI, 917
Brown, Elizabeth VI, 923
Brown, Elizabeth VI, 940
Brown, Elizabeth VI, 943
Brown, Elizabeth VI, 959
Brown, Elizabeth VI, 986
Brown, Elizabeth VI, 995
Brown, Elizabeth VI, 1010
Brown, Elizabeth A. V, 829
Brown, Elizabeth A. V, 830
Brown, Elizabeth Ann IV, 1273
Brown, Elizabeth B. II, 116
Brown, Elizabeth B. II, 124
Brown, Elizabeth B. II, 953
Brown, Elizabeth C. VI, 625
Brown, Elizabeth C. VI, 721
Brown, Elizabeth C. VI, 884
Brown, Elizabeth H. I, 208
Brown, Elizabeth H. I, 221
Brown, Elizabeth H. II, 730
Brown, Elizabeth H. II, 784
Brown, Elizabeth H. II, 841
Brown, Elizabeth H. V, 29
Brown, Elizabeth H. V, 30
Brown, Elizabeth H. V, 551
Brown, Elizabeth H. V, 968
Brown, Elizabeth Helena I, 232
Brown, Elizabeth Helena I, 249
Brown, Elizabeth Hurt. A. I. VI, 884
Brown, Elizabeth J. V, 828
Brown, Elizabeth J. V, 830
Brown, Elizabeth J. V, 831
Brown, Elizabeth Jane VI, 884
Brown, Elizabeth K. II, 1046
Brown, Elizabeth K. II, 1052
Brown, Elizabeth L. II, 955
Brown, Elizabeth Louisa III, 48

Brown, Elizabeth M. II, 475
Brown, Elizabeth N. IV, 182
Brown, Elizabeth P. II, 955
Brown, Elizabeth P. II, 1044
Brown, Elizabeth P. II, 1046
Brown, Elizabeth R. V, 28
Brown, Elizabeth R. V, 478
Brown, Elizabeth S. II, 729
Brown, Elizabeth S. II, 730
Brown, Elizabeth S. II, 734
Brown, Elizabeth S. II, 745
Brown, Elizabeth T. IV, 1203
Brown, Elizabeth T. VI, 372
Brown, Elizabeth T. VI, 373
Brown, Elizabeth T. VI, 624
Brown, Elizabeth T. VI, 625
Brown, Elizabeth T. VI, 710
Brown, Elizabeth Updegraff IV, 465
Brown, Elizabeth W. V, 63
Brown, Elizabeth W. V, 551
Brown, Elizabeth W. V, 568
Brown, Elizabeth Waln II, 700
Brown, Elizabeth Waln II, 730
Brown, Elizabeth Wilkins V, 27
Brown, Ella IV, 1233
Brown, Ella V, 457
Brown, Ella V, 478
Brown, Ella V, 614
Brown, Ella G. V, 830
Brown, Ella G. VI, 627
Brown, Ella G. VI, 707
Brown, Ella Gardner VI, 622
Brown, Ella Gardner VI, 703
Brown, Ella L. III, 341
Brown, Ella N. V, 478
Brown, Ella V. I, 873
Brown, Ellen I, 38
Brown, Ellen I, 84
Brown, Ellen III, 48
Brown, Ellen IV, 1273
Brown, Ellen IV, 1275
Brown, Ellen E. VI, 508
Brown, Ellen Jane V, 28
Brown, Ellen Jane V, 29
Brown, Ellie V, 452
Brown, Ellie Louisa III, 49
Brown, Elma L. V, 224
Brown, Elmira V, 28
Brown, Elmira L. V, 29
Brown, Elmira L. V, 30
Brown, Elnathan IV, 182
Brown, Elnathan P. IV, 182
Brown, Elnathan P. IV, 465
Brown, Elsie III, 48
Brown, Elsie VI, 686
Brown, Elsie VI, 733
Brown, Elsie VI, 769
Brown, Elsie VI, 773
Brown, Elsie C. III, 357
Brown, Elsie Palmer VI, 627
Brown, Elsie Palmer VI, 733
Brown, Elsie Palmer VI, 734
Brown, Elsie Palmer, Jr. VI, 773
Brown, Elsie Palmer, Jr. VI, 774
Brown, Elva Wright V, 661
Brown, Ely I, 777
Brown, Emeline V, 880
Brown, Emila III, 50
Brown, Emily I, 626
Brown, Emily VI, 624
Brown, Emily Alice VI, 621
Brown, Emily Alice VI, 710
Brown, Emily Alice VI, 712
Brown, Emma I, 923
Brown, Emma I, 933
Brown, Emma IV, 1273
Brown, Emma IV, 1308
Brown, Emma IV, 1328
Brown, Emma V, 452
Brown, Emma V, 453
Brown, Emma V, 661
Brown, Emma C. IV, 933
Brown, Emma E. V, 28
Brown, Emma E. V, 29
Brown, Emma F. III, 49
Brown, Emma J. IV, 685
Brown, Emma L. I, 262
Brown, Emma L. V, 452
Brown, Emma Laura V, 224
Brown, Enoch V, 829
Brown, Enoch V, 831
Brown, Enoch VI, 477
Brown, Enoch S. IV, 803
Brown, Enoch S. IV, 804
Brown, Enoch S. IV, 850
Brown, Enos F. V, 830
Brown, Enos F. V, 831
Brown, Ernest L. II, 700
Brown, Ernest L. II, 730
Brown, Ernest L., Jr. II, 700
Brown, Ernest Lancaster II, 700
Brown, Ernest T. II, 754
Brown, Essie I, 938
Brown, Ester I, 980
Brown, Ester II, 341
Brown, Esther II, 23
Brown, Esther II, 956
Brown, Esther II, 981
Brown, Esther III, 48
Brown, Esther IV, 76
Brown, Esther IV, 569
Brown, Esther IV, 597
Brown, Esther IV, 1247
Brown, Esther V, 28
Brown, Esther V, 86
Brown, Esther V, 987
Brown, Esther VI, 371
Brown, Esther VI, 392
Brown, Esther VI, 393
Brown, Esther VI, 448
Brown, Esther VI, 457
Brown, Esther VI, 460
Brown, Esther VI, 468
Brown, Esther VI, 475
Brown, Esther VI, 501
Brown, Esther VI, 554
Brown, Esther VI, 568
Brown, Esther VI, 626
Brown, Esther VI, 710
Brown, Esther Ann IV, 804
Brown, Esther Ann V, 28
Brown, Esther Ann V, 29
Brown, Esther Ann V, 130
Brown, Esther Ann VI, 374
Brown, Esther Ann VI, 621
Brown, Esther Ann VI, 626
Brown, Esther Ann VI, 627
Brown, Esther Brown IV, 803
Brown, Esther F. III, 49
Brown, Esther F. III, 96
Brown, Esther H. III, 49
Brown, Esther J. V, 52
Brown, Esther J. V, 97
Brown, Esther J. V, 375
Brown, Ethan A. V, 28
Brown, Ethan A. V, 48
Brown, Ethel G. II, 308
Brown, Ethelred VI, 884
Brown, Ethelred VI, 917
Brown, Eunice I, 461
Brown, Eunice I, 462
Brown, Eunice I, 468
Brown, Eunice I, 470
Brown, Eunice I, 475
Brown, Eva VI, 372
Brown, Eva J. IV, 1308
Brown, Eva Jennie III, 48
Brown, Eva Jennie III, 93
Brown, Eva K. S. V, 831
Brown, Eva Keziah V, 864
Brown, Eva P. II, 841
Brown, Eva P. II, 928
Brown, Eva S. III, 50
Brown, Evaline IV, 1149
Brown, Evan V, 29
Brown, Evan H. V, 30
Brown, Evan H. V, 968
Brown, Evan H. V, 979
Brown, Evan Henry V, 29
Brown, Evan Henry V, 968
Brown, Everett L. I, 225
Brown, Everett L. I, 232
Brown, Everett L. I, 255
Brown, Ezra II, 201
Brown, Fam IV, 1273
Brown, Fannie VI, 765
Brown, Fannie M. I, 262
Brown, Fannie R. III, 49
Brown, Fanny VI, 801
Brown, Fayett VI, 719
Brown, Fern Louise IV, 1308
Brown, Florence III, 48
Brown, Florence III, 223
Brown, Florence E. IV, 685
Brown, Florence Edna III, 48
Brown, Florence Edna III, 351
Brown, Florence K. I, 630
Brown, Florence Omega I, 613
Brown, Folio VI, 621
Brown, Folio VI, 622
Brown, Folio VI, 623
Brown, Folio VI, 624
Brown, Folio VI, 625
Brown, Folio VI, 626
Brown, Folio VI, 628
Brown, Frances I, 528
Brown, Frances II, 700
Brown, Frances VI, 884
Brown, Frances VI, 986
Brown, Frances Brown II, 730
Brown, Frances E. III, 49
Brown, Frances J. I, 873
Brown, Francinia VI, 621
Brown, Francinia VI, 623
Brown, Francinia VI, 651
Brown, Francis Foster IV, 76
Brown, Francis Foster IV, 803
Brown, Francis J. VI, 624
Brown, Frank V, 452
Brown, Frank V, 478
Brown, Frank V, 614
Brown, Frank O. III, 48
Brown, Franklin II, 700
Brown, Franklin II, 730
Brown, Franklin III, 48
Brown, Franklin III, 93
Brown, Frederica VI, 622
Brown, Frederick IV, 1273
Brown, Frederick J. VI, 624
Brown, Frederick M. III, 49
Brown, Fredericka VI, 622
Brown, G. L. VI, 943
Brown, Gardner D. III, 49
Brown, Garnet IV, 182
Brown, Garrett VI, 884
Brown, Geneva V, 452
Brown, Geo. E. III, 47
Brown, Geo. E. III, 151
Brown, Geo. Evans III, 48
Brown, Geo. Evans III, 223
Brown, George II, 23
Brown, George II, 24
Brown, George II, 59
Brown, George II, 167
Brown, George II, 955
Brown, George II, 956
Brown, George II, 981
Brown, George II, 982
Brown, George II, 1041
Brown, George II, 1042
Brown, George II, 1052
Brown, George III, 48
Brown, George V, 224
Brown, George V, 880
Brown, George V, 949
Brown, George VI, 475
Brown, George VI, 883
Brown, George Betts III, 48
Brown, George E. III, 48
Brown, George Edward III, 48
Brown, George M. II, 1046
Brown, George N. V, 321
Brown, George Thomas VI, 884
Brown, George W. II, 952
Brown, George W. II, 953
Brown, George W. II, 954
Brown, George W. II, 955
Brown, George W. II, 1044
Brown, George W. II, 1046
Brown, George W. II, 1058
Brown, George W. III, 48
Brown, George W. V, 321
Brown, George W. V, 829
Brown, George, Jr. II, 981
Brown, Gertrude Elizabeth VI, 622
Brown, Gertrude J. VI, 617
Brown, Gertrude J. VI, 625
Brown, Gertrude J. VI, 626
Brown, Gertrude J. VI, 670
Brown, Gideon III, 48
Brown, Gilbert III, 48
Brown, Gladys II, 700
Brown, Gladys II, 754
Brown, Godwin M. I, 232
Brown, Godwin Moore I, 208
Brown, Golda III, 447
Brown, Golda III, 475
Brown, Grace I, 375
Brown, Grace IV, 181
Brown, Grace V, 224
Brown, Grace V, 299
Brown, Grace V, 309
Brown, Grace V, 320
Brown, Grace V, 321
Brown, Grace V, 828
Brown, Grace VI, 371
Brown, Grace VI, 373
Brown, Grace VI, 416
Brown, Grace Ann II, 719
Brown, Granville L. VI, 884
Brown, Gulia Elma VI, 621
Brown, Gulielma I, 974
Brown, Gulielma V, 224
Brown, Gulielma V, 830
Brown, Gulielma Penn VI, 622
Brown, Gulielma Penn VI, 652
Brown, Gulielma Penn VI, 654
Brown, Gulielma Penn VI, 749
Brown, Gulilema Pann VI, 628
Brown, Gurney L. I, 262
Brown, Gustavus II, 341
Brown, H. VI, 555
Brown, Hampton V, 28
Brown, Hannah I, 208
Brown, Hannah I, 209
Brown, Hannah I, 231
Brown, Hannah I, 246
Brown, Hannah I, 343
Brown, Hannah I, 347
Brown, Hannah I, 365
Brown, Hannah I, 375
Brown, Hannah I, 376
Brown, Hannah I, 420
Brown, Hannah I, 592
Brown, Hannah I, 801
Brown, Hannah I, 960
Brown, Hannah I, 974
Brown, Hannah I, 1081
Brown, Hannah I, 1089
Brown, Hannah I, 1090
Brown, Hannah II, 24
Brown, Hannah II, 116
Brown, Hannah II, 124
Brown, Hannah II, 130
Brown, Hannah II, 201
Brown, Hannah II, 211
Brown, Hannah II, 341
Brown, Hannah II, 452
Brown, Hannah II, 473
Brown, Hannah II, 475
Brown, Hannah II, 825
Brown, Hannah II, 956
Brown, Hannah II, 981
Brown, Hannah II, 982
Brown, Hannah II, 992
Brown, Hannah II, 1015
Brown, Hannah II, 1018
Brown, Hannah IV, 182
Brown, Hannah IV, 613
Brown, Hannah IV, 803
Brown, Hannah IV, 804
Brown, Hannah IV, 808
Brown, Hannah IV, 931
Brown, Hannah IV, 1203
Brown, Hannah IV, 1273
Brown, Hannah IV, 1286
Brown, Hannah V, 28
Brown, Hannah V, 29
Brown, Hannah V, 94
Brown, Hannah V, 798
Brown, Hannah V, 828
Brown, Hannah V, 829
Brown, Hannah V, 830
Brown, Hannah V, 831
Brown, Hannah V, 880
Brown, Hannah V, 949
Brown, Hannah VI, 349
Brown, Hannah VI, 371
Brown, Hannah VI, 373
Brown, Hannah VI, 377
Brown, Hannah VI, 378
Brown, Hannah VI, 438
Brown, Hannah VI, 475
Brown, Hannah VI, 518
Brown, Hannah VI, 519
Brown, Hannah VI, 520
Brown, Hannah VI, 522
Brown, Hannah VI, 557
Brown, Hannah VI, 571
Brown, Hannah VI, 572
Brown, Hannah VI, 587
Brown, Hannah VI, 592
Brown, Hannah VI, 599
Brown, Hannah VI, 622
Brown, Hannah VI, 624
Brown, Hannah VI, 627
Brown, Hannah VI, 639
Brown, Hannah VI, 643
Brown, Hannah VI, 646
Brown, Hannah VI, 652
Brown, Hannah VI, 664
Brown, Hannah VI, 665
Brown, Hannah VI, 666
Brown, Hannah VI, 667
Brown, Hannah VI, 685
Brown, Hannah VI, 697
Brown, Hannah VI, 698
Brown, Hannah VI, 710
Brown, Hannah VI, 711
Brown, Hannah VI, 712
Brown, Hannah VI, 713
Brown, Hannah VI, 714
Brown, Hannah VI, 718
Brown, Hannah VI, 883
Brown, Hannah A. III, 49
Brown, Hannah A. V, 48
Brown, Hannah Ann V, 28
Brown, Hannah Ann V, 29
Brown, Hannah Ann V, 30
Brown, Hannah Ann V, 37
Brown, Hannah Ann V, 881
Brown, Hannah B. IV, 1273
Brown, Hannah B. IV, 1292
Brown, Hannah B. V, 949
Brown, Hannah B. V, 958
Brown, Hannah C. II, 130
Brown, Hannah C. II, 146
Brown, Hannah C. II, 157
Brown, Hannah C. II, 317
Brown, Hannah C. IV, 739
Brown, Hannah Craft II, 201
Brown, Hannah E. I, 1081
Brown, Hannah E. I, 1090
Brown, Hannah E. I, 1140
Brown, Hannah G. II, 317
Brown, Hannah H. IV, 930
Brown, Hannah J. V, 29
Brown, Hannah J. V, 31
Brown, Hannah J. VI, 637
Brown, Hannah J. VI, 710
Brown, Hannah Janney VI, 475
Brown, Hannah Janney VI, 571
Brown, Hannah Janney VI, 622
Brown, Hannah Janney VI, 641
Brown, Hannah Janney VI, 652
Brown, Hannah Janney VI, 653
Brown, Hannah Janney VI, 689
Brown, Hannah Janney VI, 711
Brown, Hannah Janney VI, 713
Brown, Hannah L. II, 1045
Brown, Hannah L. II, 1046
Brown, Hannah L. IV, 685
Brown, Hannah L. V, 880
Brown, Hannah M. VI, 696
Brown, Hannah Maria VI, 374
Brown, Hannah Maria VI, 623
Brown, Hannah Maria VI, 626
Brown, Hannah Maria VI, 627
Brown, Hannah Maria VI, 696
Brown, Hannah Mary VI, 623
Brown, Hannah Mary VI, 638
Brown, Hannah P. V, 949
Brown, Hannah P. VI, 623
Brown, Hannah P. VI, 625
Brown, Hannah P. VI, 721
Brown, Hannah P. VI, 723
Brown, Hannah S. VI, 475
Brown, Hannah S. VI, 538
Brown, Hannah S. VI, 623
Brown, Hannah S. VI, 677
Brown, Hannah W. II, 1046
Brown, Hannah W. II, 1049
Brown, Hannah, Jr. II, 981
Brown, Hannah, Jr. VI, 373
Brown, Hannay VI, 626
Brown, Hanney VI, 571
Brown, Harding II, 1046
Brown, Hardy I, 268
Brown, Harman IV, 900
Brown, Harmon IV, 900
Brown, Harmon H. IV, 803
Brown, Harriet II, 955
Brown, Harriet II, 1046
Brown, Harriet VI, 853
Brown, Harriet VI, 986
Brown, Harriet Calrissa III, 50
Brown, Harriett IV, 1203
Brown, Harrold VI, 477
Brown, Harry III, 48
Brown, Harry III, 351
Brown, Harry V, 321
Brown, Harry Arthur VI, 801
Brown, Harvey IV, 900
Brown, Harvey V, 829
Brown, Hattie V, 829
Brown, Hazel IV, 1247
Brown, Helen I, 215
Brown, Helen III, 50
Brown, Helen V, 225
Brown, Helen V, 661
Brown, Helen M. V, 661
Brown, Henry I, 375
Brown, Henry I, 376
Brown, Henry II, 116
Brown, Henry IV, 465
Brown, Henry V, 224
Brown, Henry V, 830
Brown, Henry V, 831
Brown, Henry VI, 464
Brown, Henry VI, 468
Brown, Henry VI, 501
Brown, Henry VI, 800
Brown, Henry VI, 801
Brown, Henry VI, 811
Brown, Henry VI, 824
Brown, Henry VI, 841
Brown, Henry VI, 842
Brown, Henry VI, 857
Brown, Henry VI, 862
Brown, Henry VI, 893
Brown, Henry VI, 939
Brown, Henry VI, 953
Brown, Henry VI, 986

Brown, Henry VI, 1018
Brown, Henry C. VI, 621
Brown, Henry D. III, 50
Brown, Henry Franklin III, 48
Brown, Henry Franklin III, 357
Brown, Henry H. II, 700
Brown, Henry Haines II, 730
Brown, Henry P. II, 841
Brown, Henry P. II, 928
Brown, Henry T. III, 48
Brown, Henry Tatnall II, 700
Brown, Henry Tatnall, Jr. II, 700
Brown, Henry W. VI, 621
Brown, Henry, Jr. VI, 884
Brown, Herbert Raymond IV, 181
Brown, Hervey IV, 685
Brown, Hester II, 956
Brown, Hester II, 981
Brown, Hester S. VI, 621
Brown, Hester S. VI, 624
Brown, Hester S. VI, 702
Brown, Hester S. VI, 704
Brown, Hester??? II, 956
Brown, Hezekiah I, 267
Brown, Hezekiah VI, 884
Brown, Hillary VI, 801
Brown, Hiram IV, 685
Brown, Hiram W. IV, 685
Brown, Holmes Ellis Yeakly VI, 372
Brown, Homer V, 321
Brown, Honor II, 200
Brown, Honor II, 207
Brown, Horatio Franklin V, 880
Brown, Horton IV, 174
Brown, Horton IV, 181
Brown, Houk I, 1149
Brown, Howard II, 1046
Brown, Howard VI, 622
Brown, Howard C. I, 262
Brown, Howard Townsend VI, 622
Brown, Howard Townsend VI, 628
Brown, Howard Townsend VI, 671
Brown, Howell VI, 622
Brown, Hubbard VI, 798
Brown, Hubbard VI, 801
Brown, Hubbard VI, 838
Brown, Hudson II, 596
Brown, Hugh VI, 733
Brown, Hugh VI, 734
Brown, Hugh Edward IV, 685
Brown, Hulda II, 308
Brown, Hulda II, 317
Brown, Huldah IV, 685
Brown, Huldah IV, 739
Brown, Hunter Smith VI, 372
Brown, Ignatius I, 1149
Brown, Ira I, 1081
Brown, Ira IV, 181
Brown, Ira IV, 1273
Brown, Ira IV, 1291
Brown, Irenia VI, 884
Brown, Irving III, 20
Brown, Irving III, 48
Brown, Isaac I, 209
Brown, Isaac I, 231
Brown, Isaac I, 586
Brown, Isaac I, 592
Brown, Isaac I, 650
Brown, Isaac I, 777
Brown, Isaac I, 960
Brown, Isaac I, 974
Brown, Isaac I, 1081
Brown, Isaac I, 1090
Brown, Isaac I, 1139
Brown, Isaac I, 1149
Brown, Isaac II, 116
Brown, Isaac II, 341
Brown, Isaac II, 473
Brown, Isaac II, 1046
Brown, Isaac III, 48
Brown, Isaac IV, 76
Brown, Isaac IV, 175
Brown, Isaac IV, 181
Brown, Isaac IV, 182
Brown, Isaac IV, 260
Brown, Isaac IV, 269
Brown, Isaac IV, 372
Brown, Isaac IV, 569
Brown, Isaac IV, 1050
Brown, Isaac IV, 1083
Brown, Isaac IV, 1089
Brown, Isaac IV, 1123
Brown, Isaac IV, 1128
Brown, Isaac IV, 1137
Brown, Isaac IV, 1273
Brown, Isaac V, 28
Brown, Isaac V, 224
Brown, Isaac V, 299
Brown, Isaac V, 320
Brown, Isaac V, 452
Brown, Isaac V, 829
Brown, Isaac V, 830
Brown, Isaac V, 831
Brown, Isaac V, 880
Brown, Isaac VI, 368
Brown, Isaac VI, 371
Brown, Isaac VI, 373
Brown, Isaac VI, 449
Brown, Isaac VI, 458
Brown, Isaac VI, 460
Brown, Isaac VI, 468
Brown, Isaac VI, 470
Brown, Isaac VI, 476
Brown, Isaac VI, 548
Brown, Isaac VI, 552
Brown, Isaac VI, 583
Brown, Isaac VI, 592
Brown, Isaac VI, 621
Brown, Isaac VI, 623
Brown, Isaac VI, 624
Brown, Isaac VI, 683
Brown, Isaac VI, 685
Brown, Isaac VI, 688
Brown, Isaac VI, 723
Brown, Isaac VI, 734
Brown, Isaac VI, 769
Brown, Isaac B. II, 24
Brown, Isaac B. II, 116
Brown, Isaac B. II, 1069
Brown, Isaac D. III, 48
Brown, Isaac D. III, 50
Brown, Isaac H. III, 49
Brown, Isaac L. IV, 685
Brown, Isaac L. VI, 623
Brown, Isaac R. V, 224
Brown, Isaac W. V, 881
Brown, Isaac, Jr. VI, 373
Brown, Isaac, Jr. VI, 479
Brown, Isaac, Jr. VI, 623
Brown, Isaac, Sr. VI, 623
Brown, Isabella V, 908
Brown, Isadira E. Platt II, 730
Brown, Isadora V, 614
Brown, Isadora E. II, 720
Brown, Isadora E. II, 769
Brown, Isadora E. P. II, 730
Brown, Isadora E. Platt II, 700
Brown, Isadora Elizabeth II, 700
Brown, Isadora Elizabeth II, 720
Brown, Isadora Elizabeth Platt II, 769
Brown, Isaiah IV, 23
Brown, Isaiah VI, 372
Brown, Isaiah VI, 476
Brown, Isaiah J. V, 887
Brown, Isaiah M. V, 828
Brown, Isaiah M. V, 886
Brown, Isham C. VI, 884
Brown, Isiah V, 880
Brown, Isiah M. V, 880
Brown, Israel II, 23
Brown, Israel II, 59
Brown, Israel II, 146
Brown, Israel II, 474
Brown, Israel V, 28
Brown, Israel V, 829
Brown, Israel V, 830
Brown, Israel VI, 592
Brown, Israel E. II, 116
Brown, Israel E. II, 130
Brown, Ivah E. V, 798
Brown, Iwadora Elizabeth Platt II, 730
Brown, J. Edward VI, 622
Brown, J. Frank V, 478
Brown, J. H. I, 232
Brown, J. Israel VI, 476
Brown, J. J. I, 232
Brown, J. Morton II, 730
Brown, J. Morton II, 769
Brown, J. Virginia VI, 372
Brown, J. W. III, 50
Brown, Jabez VI, 884
Brown, Jacob I, 376
Brown, Jacob I, 492
Brown, Jacob I, 528
Brown, Jacob I, 801
Brown, Jacob I, 971
Brown, Jacob I, 974
Brown, Jacob I, 982
Brown, Jacob I Sup 1, 9
Brown, Jacob II, 282
Brown, Jacob II, 291
Brown, Jacob II, 341
Brown, Jacob II, 982
Brown, Jacob III, 48
Brown, Jacob III, 50
Brown, Jacob IV, 372
Brown, Jacob V, 728
Brown, Jacob V, 829
Brown, Jacob V, 830
Brown, Jacob V, 852
Brown, Jacob V, 880
Brown, Jacob V, 949
Brown, Jacob VI, 623
Brown, Jacob VI, 625
Brown, Jacob VI, 718
Brown, Jacob VI, 721
Brown, Jacob H. II, 308
Brown, Jacob Leeds II, 308
Brown, Jacob R. II, 167
Brown, Jacob R. II, 201
Brown, Jacob Ridgway II, 167
Brown, Jacob Ridgway II, 596
Brown, Jacob, Jr. I, 982
Brown, James I, 487
Brown, James I, 528
Brown, James I, 529
Brown, James I, 645
Brown, James I, 650
Brown, James I, 777
Brown, James I, 801
Brown, James I, 802
Brown, James I, 960
Brown, James I, 1047
Brown, James I, 1081
Brown, James I, 1090
Brown, James II, 23
Brown, James II, 24
Brown, James II, 47
Brown, James II, 59
Brown, James II, 116
Brown, James II, 124
Brown, James II, 126
Brown, James II, 167
Brown, James II, 200
Brown, James II, 201
Brown, James II, 207
Brown, James II, 214
Brown, James II, 341
Brown, James II, 454
Brown, James II, 474
Brown, James II, 475
Brown, James IV, 181
Brown, James IV, 1149
Brown, James IV, 1273
Brown, James V, 224
Brown, James VI, 357
Brown, James VI, 371
Brown, James VI, 516
Brown, James VI, 623
Brown, James VI, 643
Brown, James VI, 796
Brown, James VI, 815
Brown, James VI, 840
Brown, James VI, 884
Brown, James VI, 982
Brown, James VI, 984
Brown, James VI, 1006
Brown, James C. Key I, 1149
Brown, James Jones I, 528
Brown, James M. I, 208
Brown, James M. I, 219
Brown, James M. I, 232
Brown, James M. I, 250
Brown, James M. III, 480
Brown, James M. VI, 843
Brown, James M. VI, 884
Brown, James T. VI, 884
Brown, James W. I, 232
Brown, James Walter I, 209
Brown, James, Jr. I, 801
Brown, James, Jr. I, 960
Brown, James, Jr. VI, 884
Brown, James, Sr. I, 777
Brown, Jane I, 208
Brown, Jane I, 209
Brown, Jane I, 217
Brown, Jane I, 223
Brown, Jane I, 231
Brown, Jane I, 232
Brown, Jane I, 254
Brown, Jane I, 300
Brown, Jane I, 347
Brown, Jane I, 370
Brown, Jane I, 375
Brown, Jane I, 376
Brown, Jane I, 377
Brown, Jane I, 801
Brown, Jane I, 971
Brown, Jane I, 974
Brown, Jane I, 982
Brown, Jane I, 983
Brown, Jane I, 994
Brown, Jane II, 167
Brown, Jane II, 201
Brown, Jane II, 341
Brown, Jane II, 474
Brown, Jane II, 981
Brown, Jane II, 1000
Brown, Jane III, 49
Brown, Jane III, 82
Brown, Jane IV, 23
Brown, Jane IV, 182
Brown, Jane IV, 465
Brown, Jane IV, 685
Brown, Jane IV, 900
Brown, Jane IV, 931
Brown, Jane IV, 1231
Brown, Jane V, 29
Brown, Jane V, 123
Brown, Jane V, 375
Brown, Jane V, 614
Brown, Jane V, 661
Brown, Jane V, 798
Brown, Jane V, 829
Brown, Jane V, 830
Brown, Jane V, 831
Brown, Jane V, 948
Brown, Jane V, 949
Brown, Jane VI, 372
Brown, Jane VI, 373
Brown, Jane VI, 884
Brown, Jane VI, 897
Brown, Jane VI, 979
Brown, Jane C. IV, 930
Brown, Jane C. VI, 371
Brown, Jane C. VI, 734
Brown, Jane E. I, 208
Brown, Jane E. I, 215
Brown, Jane E. I, 232
Brown, Jane E. I, 235
Brown, Jane E. III, 49
Brown, Jane Eliza I, 211
Brown, Jane F. IV, 1233
Brown, Jane L. VI, 796
Brown, Jane L. VI, 871
Brown, Jane M. VI, 801
Brown, Jane P. I, 209
Brown, Jane Virginia VI, 618
Brown, Jane Virginia VI, 622
Brown, Jane Virginia VI, 625
Brown, Jane Virginia VI, 626
Brown, Jane Virginia VI, 627
Brown, Jane Virginia VI, 628
Brown, Jane Virginia VI, 702
Brown, Jane Virginia VI, 711
Brown, Jane Virginia VI, 712
Brown, Janet VI, 627
Brown, Janet VI, 734
Brown, Janet VI, 889
Brown, Jasper V, 614
Brown, Jeams I, 528
Brown, Jean I, 492
Brown, Jean VI, 372
Brown, Jeanette Ellen VI, 734
Brown, Jehu IV, 1273
Brown, Jennie IV, 1273
Brown, Jennie E. V, 614
Brown, Jere I, 232
Brown, Jeremiah I, 209
Brown, Jeremiah I, 231
Brown, Jeremiah I, 267
Brown, Jeremiah I, 353
Brown, Jeremiah I, 375
Brown, Jeremiah I, 376
Brown, Jeremiah I, 528
Brown, Jeremiah II, 341
Brown, Jeremiah II, 475
Brown, Jeremiah II, 660
Brown, Jeremiah II, 700
Brown, Jeremiah II, 729
Brown, Jeremiah II, 730
Brown, Jeremiah II, 734
Brown, Jeremiah II, 745
Brown, Jeremiah IV, 613
Brown, Jeremiah IV, 655
Brown, Jeremiah IV, 803
Brown, Jeremiah IV, 804
Brown, Jeremiah IV, 882
Brown, Jeremiah VI, 371
Brown, Jeremiah, Jr. IV, 613
Brown, Jeremiah, Jr. IV, 804
Brown, Jerry I, 208
Brown, Jerry I, 211
Brown, Jesse I, 131
Brown, Jesse I, 151
Brown, Jesse I, 207
Brown, Jesse I, 208
Brown, Jesse I, 209
Brown, Jesse I, 226
Brown, Jesse I, 231
Brown, Jesse I, 232
Brown, Jesse I, 239
Brown, Jesse I, 246
Brown, Jesse I, 613
Brown, Jesse I, 756
Brown, Jesse I, 982
Brown, Jesse II, 58
Brown, Jesse IV, 1273
Brown, Jesse VI, 372
Brown, Jesse VI, 617
Brown, Jesse VI, 884
Brown, Jesse VI, 901
Brown, Jesse VI, 958
Brown, Jesse VI, 1020
Brown, Jesse B. I, 208
Brown, Jesse H. I, 232
Brown, Jesse H. VI, 618
Brown, Jesse H. VI, 621
Brown, Jesse H. VI, 623
Brown, Jesse H. VI, 651
Brown, Jesse H., Jr. VI, 622
Brown, Jesse H., Jr. VI, 623
Brown, Jesse Harper I, 209
Brown, Jesse L. V, 299
Brown, Jesse S. V, 224
Brown, Jesse T. I, 208
Brown, Jesse Thomas I, 209
Brown, Jessie Robinson V, 831
Brown, Jno. II, 201
Brown, Jno. II, 263
Brown, Joan II, 201
Brown, Joan II, 441
Brown, Joanna I, 1140
Brown, Job II, 50
Brown, Job II, 58
Brown, Joel I, 347
Brown, Joel I, 376
Brown, Joel I, 528
Brown, Joel I, 710
Brown, Joel I, 982
Brown, Joel IV, 1273
Brown, Joel V, 28
Brown, Joel V, 224
Brown, Joel V, 320
Brown, Joel VI, 372
Brown, Joel VI, 373
Brown, Joel VI, 592
Brown, Joel VI, 599
Brown, John I, 131
Brown, John I, 209
Brown, John I, 231
Brown, John I, 256
Brown, John I, 268
Brown, John I, 300
Brown, John I, 777
Brown, John I, 801
Brown, John I, 802
Brown, John I, 805
Brown, John I, 922
Brown, John I, 960
Brown, John I, 982
Brown, John I, 1043
Brown, John I, 1047
Brown, John I, 1090
Brown, John II, 167
Brown, John II, 200
Brown, John II, 201
Brown, John II, 224
Brown, John II, 340
Brown, John II, 341
Brown, John II, 473
Brown, John II, 474
Brown, John II, 475
Brown, John II, 730
Brown, John II, 750
Brown, John II, 773
Brown, John II, 955
Brown, John II, 956
Brown, John II, 974
Brown, John II, 981
Brown, John II, 982
Brown, John II, 999
Brown, John II, 1000
Brown, John II, 1015
Brown, John II, 1019
Brown, John II, 1037
Brown, John II, 1042
Brown, John II, 1045
Brown, John II, 1046
Brown, John II, 1050
Brown, John II, 1069
Brown, John III, 47
Brown, John III, 48
Brown, John III, 178
Brown, John IV, 181
Brown, John IV, 356
Brown, John IV, 372
Brown, John IV, 417
Brown, John IV, 669
Brown, John IV, 1273
Brown, John IV, 1286
Brown, John V, 26
Brown, John V, 27
Brown, John V, 35
Brown, John V, 80
Brown, John V, 102
Brown, John V, 478
Brown, John V, 828
Brown, John V, 829

Brown, John V, 830
Brown, John V, 831
Brown, John V, 848
Brown, John V, 854
Brown, John V, 857
Brown, John V, 880
Brown, John V, 987
Brown, John VI, 371
Brown, John VI, 372
Brown, John VI, 373
Brown, John VI, 437
Brown, John VI, 442
Brown, John VI, 468
Brown, John VI, 477
Brown, John VI, 505
Brown, John VI, 551
Brown, John VI, 552
Brown, John VI, 556
Brown, John VI, 592
Brown, John VI, 618
Brown, John VI, 621
Brown, John VI, 622
Brown, John VI, 623
Brown, John VI, 624
Brown, John VI, 629
Brown, John VI, 638
Brown, John VI, 650
Brown, John VI, 666
Brown, John VI, 674
Brown, John VI, 677
Brown, John VI, 678
Brown, John VI, 683
Brown, John VI, 688
Brown, John VI, 697
Brown, John VI, 801
Brown, John VI, 802
Brown, John VI, 805
Brown, John VI, 813
Brown, John VI, 820
Brown, John VI, 831
Brown, John VI, 840
Brown, John VI, 847
Brown, John VI, 861
Brown, John VI, 883
Brown, John VI, 884
Brown, John VI, 943
Brown, John VI, 996
Brown, John VI, 1021
Brown, John A. I, 930
Brown, John A. II, 841
Brown, John A. II, 928
Brown, John A. V, 29
Brown, John B. II, 1069
Brown, John C. IV, 322
Brown, John C. IV, 1089
Brown, John C. VI, 884
Brown, John D. VI, 621
Brown, John D. VI, 623
Brown, John D. VI, 702
Brown, John D. VI, 704
Brown, John F. V, 478
Brown, John F. V, 614
Brown, John F. V, 987
Brown, John Farnum II, 700
Brown, John Farnum II, 730
Brown, John Frank V, 614
Brown, John Franklin V, 29
Brown, John Franklin V, 30
Brown, John Franklin V, 614
Brown, John Franklin V, 968
Brown, John Franklin V, 979
Brown, John G. VI, 373
Brown, John H. VI, 556
Brown, John H. VI, 624
Brown, John H. VI, 625
Brown, John H. VI, 654
Brown, John H. VI, 679
Brown, John H. VI, 697
Brown, John H. VI, 801
Brown, John H. VI, 843
Brown, John Harmon VI, 625
Brown, John I. VI, 372
Brown, John I. VI, 374
Brown, John I. VI, 390
Brown, John I., Jr. VI, 372
Brown, John I., Jr. VI, 374
Brown, John J. IV, 182
Brown, John L. III, 48
Brown, John L. VI, 949
Brown, John M. II, 59
Brown, John M. II, 201
Brown, John M. V, 880
Brown, John M. VI, 884
Brown, John Mahlon II, 201
Brown, John Mason II, 23
Brown, John Miller II, 23
Brown, John Morton II, 700
Brown, John Morton II, 720
Brown, John R. V, 829
Brown, John R. V, 831
Brown, John S. IV, 613
Brown, John S. IV, 804
Brown, John S. IV, 1308
Brown, John W. VI, 884
Brown, John William VI, 625
Brown, John, Jr. II, 976
Brown, John, Jr. II, 982
Brown, John, Jr. II, 1000
Brown, John, Jr. V, 29
Brown, John, Jr. V, 880
Brown, John, Jr. VI, 801
Brown, Johnathan I, 982
Brown, Joice II, 341
Brown, Joicey VI, 884
Brown, Jonah I, 231
Brown, Jonas V, 825
Brown, Jonas V, 829
Brown, Jonas P. V, 829
Brown, Jonas P. V, 830
Brown, Jonathan I, 974
Brown, Jonathan I, 1043
Brown, Jonathan II, 341
Brown, Jonathan II, 982
Brown, Jonathan IV, 685
Brown, Jonathan IV, 803
Brown, Jonathan IV, 804
Brown, Jonathan IV, 1203
Brown, Jonathan IV, 1225
Brown, Jonathan V, 28
Brown, Jonathan V, 729
Brown, Jonathan V, 828
Brown, Jonathan V, 829
Brown, Jonathan V, 830
Brown, Jonathan V, 831
Brown, Jonathan V, 880
Brown, Jonathan VI, 597
Brown, Jonathan VI, 627
Brown, Jonathan B. II, 955
Brown, Jonathan P. II, 308
Brown, Jonathan P. II, 317
Brown, Jonathan Taylor VI, 476
Brown, Jordan I, 232
Brown, Jordon I, 232
Brown, Jos. IV, 322
Brown, Joseph I, 347
Brown, Joseph I, 375
Brown, Joseph I, 376
Brown, Joseph I, 411
Brown, Joseph I, 492
Brown, Joseph I, 528
Brown, Joseph I, 555
Brown, Joseph I, 801
Brown, Joseph I, 960
Brown, Joseph I, 974
Brown, Joseph I, 1047
Brown, Joseph II, 24
Brown, Joseph II, 35
Brown, Joseph II, 50
Brown, Joseph II, 58
Brown, Joseph II, 59
Brown, Joseph II, 116
Brown, Joseph II, 130
Brown, Joseph II, 167
Brown, Joseph II, 201
Brown, Joseph II, 209
Brown, Joseph II, 226
Brown, Joseph II, 234
Brown, Joseph II, 253
Brown, Joseph II, 276
Brown, Joseph II, 282
Brown, Joseph II, 307
Brown, Joseph II, 340
Brown, Joseph II, 341
Brown, Joseph II, 473
Brown, Joseph II, 475
Brown, Joseph II, 729
Brown, Joseph II, 841
Brown, Joseph II, 955
Brown, Joseph II, 981
Brown, Joseph II, 982
Brown, Joseph II, 1012
Brown, Joseph II, 1065
Brown, Joseph II, 1069
Brown, Joseph III, 48
Brown, Joseph III, 49
Brown, Joseph III, 232
Brown, Joseph IV, 17
Brown, Joseph IV, 23
Brown, Joseph IV, 65
Brown, Joseph IV, 76
Brown, Joseph IV, 92
Brown, Joseph IV, 181
Brown, Joseph IV, 372
Brown, Joseph IV, 685
Brown, Joseph IV, 891
Brown, Joseph IV, 893
Brown, Joseph IV, 895
Brown, Joseph IV, 1273
Brown, Joseph V, 28
Brown, Joseph V, 31
Brown, Joseph V, 97
Brown, Joseph V, 100
Brown, Joseph V, 452
Brown, Joseph V, 828
Brown, Joseph V, 829
Brown, Joseph V, 830
Brown, Joseph V, 831
Brown, Joseph V, 841
Brown, Joseph V, 844
Brown, Joseph V, 880
Brown, Joseph VI, 349
Brown, Joseph VI, 372
Brown, Joseph VI, 476
Brown, Joseph VI, 592
Brown, Joseph A. V, 452
Brown, Joseph B. II, 186
Brown, Joseph B. III, 49
Brown, Joseph C. III, 48
Brown, Joseph C. V, 880
Brown, Joseph E. II, 24
Brown, Joseph E. II, 59
Brown, Joseph E. II, 130
Brown, Joseph E. II, 146
Brown, Joseph E. VI, 624
Brown, Joseph Edward VI, 623
Brown, Joseph Elgar II, 116
Brown, Joseph England II, 473
Brown, Joseph F. V, 829
Brown, Joseph F. V, 830
Brown, Joseph F. V, 880
Brown, Joseph F. V, 881
Brown, Joseph Frances II, 130
Brown, Joseph G. V, 828
Brown, Joseph G. V, 880
Brown, Joseph G. V, 888
Brown, Joseph Hood II, 473
Brown, Joseph J. I, 209
Brown, Joseph J. I, 232
Brown, Joseph J. V, 29
Brown, Joseph John I, 209
Brown, Joseph John V, 28
Brown, Joseph M. III, 48
Brown, Joseph M. VI, 884
Brown, Joseph Morris I, 231
Brown, Joseph R. II, 201
Brown, Joseph Ridgway II, 167
Brown, Joseph Ridgway II, 201
Brown, Joseph Tucker V, 729
Brown, Joseph W. IV, 1089
Brown, Joseph W. VI, 476
Brown, Joseph W. VI, 577
Brown, Joseph, Jr. II, 201
Brown, Joseph, Jr. II, 981
Brown, Joseph, Jr. II, 1004
Brown, Joseph, Jr. II, 1069
Brown, Joseph, Jr. VI, 476
Brown, Joshua I, 209
Brown, Joshua I, 231
Brown, Joshua I, 1017
Brown, Joshua I, 1027
Brown, Joshua II, 955
Brown, Joshua II, 982
Brown, Joshua II, 1012
Brown, Joshua II, 1046
Brown, Joshua II, 1051
Brown, Joshua II, 1054
Brown, Joshua II, 1069
Brown, Joshua IV, 76
Brown, Joshua IV, 803
Brown, Joshua IV, 804
Brown, Joshua IV, 900
Brown, Joshua IV, 906
Brown, Joshua V, 320
Brown, Joshua V, 729
Brown, Joshua V, 798
Brown, Joshua VI, 592
Brown, Joshua VI, 624
Brown, Joshua VI, 884
Brown, Joshua H. IV, 900
Brown, Joshua K. IV, 900
Brown, Joshua Pancoast VI, 628
Brown, Joshua Pancoast VI, 635
Brown, Joshua Sharpless II, 730
Brown, Joshua W. III, 28
Brown, Joshua W. III, 48
Brown, Joshua W. III, 129
Brown, Joshua W. III, 355
Brown, Joshua Wm. III, 48
Brown, Josiah I, 206
Brown, Josiah I, 209
Brown, Josiah I, 231
Brown, Josiah I, 240
Brown, Josiah I, 1026
Brown, Josiah III, 48
Brown, Josiah IV, 141
Brown, Josiah IV, 181
Brown, Josiah IV, 1050
Brown, Josiah VI, 373
Brown, Josiah VI, 476
Brown, Josiah VI, 511
Brown, Josiah VI, 558
Brown, Josiah VI, 624
Brown, Josiah White I, 38
Brown, Josiah, Jr. I, 209
Brown, Joycy VI, 884
Brown, Juana VI, 884
Brown, Judith I, 232
Brown, Judith I, 974
Brown, Judith V, 949
Brown, Judith VI, 623
Brown, Judith VI, 625
Brown, Judith VI, 718
Brown, Judith VI, 721
Brown, Judith VI, 801
Brown, Judith VI, 862
Brown, Judith VI, 947
Brown, Julda II, 308
Brown, Julia VI, 484
Brown, Julia A. I, 1149
Brown, Julia A. IV, 1273
Brown, Kath. L. III, 48
Brown, Kathleen V, 375
Brown, Kemston I, 1017
Brown, Kenneth IV, 1203
Brown, Kenneth IV, 1308
Brown, Kennett Taylor VI, 625
Brown, Kezia V, 831
Brown, Keziah V, 829
Brown, Keziah V, 830
Brown, Keziah V, 831
Brown, Keziah V, 848
Brown, Keziah V, 866
Brown, Kirk I, 1053
Brown, Kissiah VI, 801
Brown, Laetitia II, 982
Brown, Landon VI, 989
Brown, Laroy IV, 1149
Brown, Laura IV, 1273
Brown, Laura Jane VI, 621
Brown, Lavinia III, 48
Brown, Leah IV, 22
Brown, Leah IV, 38
Brown, Leah VI, 372
Brown, Leah VI, 476
Brown, Leah VI, 624
Brown, Leah VI, 694
Brown, Leatitia L. V, 880
Brown, Lenora V, 155
Brown, Lenora V, 661
Brown, Leo R. IV, 1308
Brown, Leon R. VI, 372
Brown, Leon R. VI, 374
Brown, Leona P. V, 551
Brown, LeRoy IV, 1308
Brown, Leslie IV, 1203
Brown, Leslie VI, 615
Brown, Leslie VI, 625
Brown, Leslie R. VI, 372
Brown, Leslie R. VI, 621
Brown, Leslie R. VI, 624
Brown, Leslie R. VI, 697
Brown, Leslie R. VI, 710
Brown, Leslie Russell III, 48
Brown, Letitia I, 923
Brown, Levi II, 982
Brown, Levi IV, 803
Brown, Levi IV, 1203
Brown, Levi V, 829
Brown, Levi V, 880
Brown, Levi K. VI, 357
Brown, Levi K. VI, 727
Brown, Lewis II, 784
Brown, Lewis IV, 465
Brown, Lewis VI, 801
Brown, Lewis A. I, 873
Brown, Lewis H. II, 784
Brown, Lewis W. I, 1090
Brown, Lewis W. I, 1140
Brown, Lewis W. I, 1149
Brown, Lewis W. II, 308
Brown, Lewis W. II, 317
Brown, Lewis W. II, 321
Brown, Lewis Whinery I, 1081
Brown, Lewis Wilson VI, 373
Brown, Lidia V, 880
Brown, Lidia V, 881
Brown, Lillian I, 938
Brown, Lillian H. VI, 617
Brown, Lillian H. VI, 618
Brown, Lillian H. VI, 622
Brown, Lillian H. VI, 626
Brown, Lillie V, 987
Brown, Lily M. VI, 372
Brown, Linden F. IV, 1273
Brown, Lizette I, 930
Brown, Lizzie IV, 1149
Brown, Lizzie VI, 372
Brown, Lizzie Louisa III, 28
Brown, Locky VI, 939
Brown, Lois VI, 56
Brown, Lois R. VI, 372
Brown, Lois R. VI, 374
Brown, Loranah I, 350
Brown, Lorance I, 528
Brown, Lorence I, 974
Brown, Louella Frances VI, 624
Brown, Louella Frances VI, 627
Brown, Louella Frances VI, 650
Brown, Louesia VI, 448
Brown, Louie V, 452
Brown, Louie M. V, 551
Brown, Louisa V, 155
Brown, Louisa VI, 371
Brown, Louisa VI, 373
Brown, Louisa VI, 448
Brown, Louisa VI, 476
Brown, Louisa VI, 565
Brown, Louisa VI, 568
Brown, Louisa Elizabeth III, 48
Brown, Louisa F. III, 49
Brown, Louise V, 830
Brown, Lowrena I, 801
Brown, Lozena I, 347
Brown, Lucia II, 473
Brown, Lucia III, 47
Brown, Lucia III, 151
Brown, Lucia C. III, 48
Brown, Lucile IV, 1308
Brown, Lucinda V, 949
Brown, Lucy VI, 805
Brown, Lucy VI, 847
Brown, Lucy VI, 848
Brown, Lucy VI, 860
Brown, Lucy VI, 884
Brown, Lucy VI, 901
Brown, Lucy VI, 914
Brown, Lucy VI, 948
Brown, Lucy VI, 996
Brown, Lucy VI, 1009
Brown, Lucy Ann VI, 884
Brown, Lucy C. VI, 801
Brown, Lucy J. VI, 855
Brown, Lucy M. VI, 800
Brown, Lucy S. VI, 372
Brown, Lucy V. VI, 372
Brown, Lula I, 208
Brown, Lula I, 209
Brown, Lula II, 791
Brown, Lula II, 842
Brown, Lula II, 857
Brown, Lula M. I, 232
Brown, Lurana I, 376
Brown, Lurenah I, 376
Brown, Lusce II, 341
Brown, Lusena I, 376
Brown, Lutitia A. I, 470
Brown, Luzaney I, 982
Brown, Lyda VI, 476
Brown, Lydi VI, 624
Brown, Lydia I, 221
Brown, Lydia I, 1043
Brown, Lydia II, 167
Brown, Lydia II, 201
Brown, Lydia II, 226
Brown, Lydia II, 341
Brown, Lydia II, 475
Brown, Lydia III, 397
Brown, Lydia IV, 20
Brown, Lydia IV, 23
Brown, Lydia IV, 322
Brown, Lydia IV, 336
Brown, Lydia IV, 804
Brown, Lydia IV, 891
Brown, Lydia V, 28
Brown, Lydia V, 155
Brown, Lydia V, 159
Brown, Lydia V, 224
Brown, Lydia V, 225
Brown, Lydia V, 828
Brown, Lydia V, 829
Brown, Lydia V, 830
Brown, Lydia V, 831
Brown, Lydia V, 836
Brown, Lydia V, 857
Brown, Lydia V, 881
Brown, Lydia VI, 373
Brown, Lydia VI, 476
Brown, Lydia VI, 571
Brown, Lydia VI, 583
Brown, Lydia VI, 587
Brown, Lydia VI, 592
Brown, Lydia VI, 624
Brown, Lydia VI, 629
Brown, Lydia VI, 641
Brown, Lydia VI, 686
Brown, Lydia VI, 691
Brown, Lydia VI, 708
Brown, Lydia VI, 710
Brown, Lydia VI, 711
Brown, Lydia VI, 712
Brown, Lydia VI, 723
Brown, Lydia Ann V, 21
Brown, Lydia Ann V, 28
Brown, Lydia Ann V, 29
Brown, Lydia C. I, 613

Brown, Lydia D. V, 880
Brown, Lydia E. V, 155
Brown, Lydia J. I, 208
Brown, Lydia J. I, 231
Brown, Lydia J. I, 232
Brown, Lydia J. I, 252
Brown, Lydia Jane I, 208
Brown, Lydia Janney VI, 658
Brown, Lydia N. V, 321
Brown, Lydia N. VI, 621
Brown, Lydia N. VI, 626
Brown, Lydia N. VI, 627
Brown, Lydia N. VI, 667
Brown, Lydia Neill VI, 733
Brown, Lydia Neill VI, 753
Brown, Lydia W. V, 321
Brown, Lydia W. VI, 700
Brown, Lydia W. VI, 713
Brown, M. Ellen I, 232
Brown, M. Ellen I, 260
Brown, M. Geneva I, 208
Brown, Mabel IV, 219
Brown, Mabel V, 321
Brown, Mabel V, 729
Brown, Macy II, 474
Brown, Magdalen II, 474
Brown, Magdalen II, 504
Brown, Magdalene II, 474
Brown, Maggie V, 321
Brown, Mahala VI, 861
Brown, Mahlon II, 981
Brown, Mahlon II, 1061
Brown, Mahlon V, 29
Brown, Mahlon V, 155
Brown, Mahlon V, 829
Brown, Mahlon V, 830
Brown, Mahlon V, 831
Brown, Mahlon VI, 372
Brown, Mahlon VI, 476
Brown, Mahlon VI, 623
Brown, Mahlon Oscar VI, 621
Brown, Mahlon S. II, 341
Brown, Malcolm V, 987
Brown, Malinda P. II, 841
Brown, Malinda Phebe II, 811
Brown, Malinda Phebe II, 841
Brown, Malinda Phebe II, 903
Brown, Maltilda I, 1139
Brown, Mamie Dean VI, 734
Brown, Manly VI, 889
Brown, Marcy II, 981
Brown, Marcy II, 987
Brown, Margaret I, 208
Brown, Margaret I, 209
Brown, Margaret I, 227
Brown, Margaret I, 231
Brown, Margaret I, 375
Brown, Margaret I, 376
Brown, Margaret I, 382
Brown, Margaret I, 408
Brown, Margaret I, 492
Brown, Margaret I, 528
Brown, Margaret I, 563
Brown, Margaret I, 974
Brown, Margaret I, 1043
Brown, Margaret I, 1081
Brown, Margaret I, 1089
Brown, Margaret I, 1090
Brown, Margaret I, 1149
Brown, Margaret II, 23
Brown, Margaret II, 59
Brown, Margaret II, 341
Brown, Margaret II, 475
Brown, Margaret IV, 76
Brown, Margaret IV, 122
Brown, Margaret IV, 174
Brown, Margaret IV, 181
Brown, Margaret IV, 682
Brown, Margaret IV, 685
Brown, Margaret IV, 803
Brown, Margaret V, 321
Brown, Margaret V, 829
Brown, Margaret V, 830
Brown, Margaret V, 853
Brown, Margaret V, 863
Brown, Margaret V, 949
Brown, Margaret V, 954
Brown, Margaret VI, 371
Brown, Margaret VI, 372
Brown, Margaret VI, 387
Brown, Margaret VI, 449
Brown, Margaret VI, 476
Brown, Margaret VI, 477
Brown, Margaret VI, 552
Brown, Margaret VI, 622
Brown, Margaret VI, 623
Brown, Margaret VI, 628
Brown, Margaret VI, 631
Brown, Margaret VI, 733
Brown, Margaret VI, 759
Brown, Margaret VI, 801
Brown, Margaret VI, 953
Brown, Margaret A. I, 226
Brown, Margaret A. I, 231
Brown, Margaret A. I, 255
Brown, Margaret Ann I, 208
Brown, Margaret C. I, 208
Brown, Margaret C. I, 232
Brown, Margaret C. I, 258
Brown, Margaret Ellen I, 23
Brown, Margaret Ellen I, 209
Brown, Margaret Ellen I, 628
Brown, Margaret H. VI, 801
Brown, Margaret W. II, 308
Brown, Margaret W. V, 949
Brown, Margaret, Jr. IV, 76
Brown, Margarett VI, 373
Brown, Margaretta II, 340
Brown, Margaretta II, 475
Brown, Margaretta II, 729
Brown, Margaretta K. V, 30
Brown, Margerat VI, 372
Brown, Margery VI, 484
Brown, Marget VI, 372
Brown, Maria I, 1090
Brown, Maria V, 831
Brown, Maria V, 850
Brown, Maria VI, 458
Brown, Maria VI, 624
Brown, Maria VI, 654
Brown, Maria VI, 678
Brown, Maria VI, 682
Brown, Maria VI, 683
Brown, Maria Priscilla VI, 625
Brown, Maria Priscilla VI, 628
Brown, Maria Priscilla VI, 681
Brown, Maria Priscilla VI, 682
Brown, Mariah V, 829
Brown, Mariah V, 830
Brown, Mariah VI, 625
Brown, Mariah S. V, 830
Brown, Mariane I, 268
Brown, Marianna III, 47
Brown, Marianna III, 365
Brown, Marianna V, 30
Brown, Marium I, 1081
Brown, Martha I, 209
Brown, Martha I, 231
Brown, Martha I, 375
Brown, Martha I, 381
Brown, Martha I, 801
Brown, Martha I, 1047
Brown, Martha II, 58
Brown, Martha II, 186
Brown, Martha II, 303
Brown, Martha II, 473
Brown, Martha II, 474
Brown, Martha II, 484
Brown, Martha II, 513
Brown, Martha II, 955
Brown, Martha II, 956
Brown, Martha II, 964
Brown, Martha II, 971
Brown, Martha II, 976
Brown, Martha II, 981
Brown, Martha II, 982
Brown, Martha II, 1041
Brown, Martha II, 1046
Brown, Martha II, 1055
Brown, Martha II, 1061
Brown, Martha V, 661
Brown, Martha V, 829
Brown, Martha V, 830
Brown, Martha V, 863
Brown, Martha V, 886
Brown, Martha V, 888
Brown, Martha V, 987
Brown, Martha VI, 371
Brown, Martha VI, 372
Brown, Martha VI, 373
Brown, Martha VI, 425
Brown, Martha VI, 440
Brown, Martha VI, 457
Brown, Martha VI, 468
Brown, Martha VI, 470
Brown, Martha VI, 476
Brown, Martha VI, 477
Brown, Martha VI, 592
Brown, Martha VI, 624
Brown, Martha VI, 625
Brown, Martha VI, 628
Brown, Martha VI, 629
Brown, Martha VI, 646
Brown, Martha VI, 734
Brown, Martha VI, 791
Brown, Martha VI, 801
Brown, Martha Ann V, 29
Brown, Martha Ann V, 880
Brown, Martha Ann V, 886
Brown, Martha Ann VI, 624
Brown, Martha Ann VI, 625
Brown, Martha Ann VI, 684
Brown, Martha Ann VI, 685
Brown, Martha Ann VI, 755
Brown, Martha Ann VI, 757
Brown, Martha B. II, 971
Brown, Martha Elizabeth VI, 685
Brown, Martha G. VI, 873
Brown, Martha G. VI, 884
Brown, Martha J. I, 614
Brown, Martha Jane VI, 621
Brown, Martha Jane VI, 622
Brown, Martha Jane VI, 623
Brown, Martha Jane VI, 624
Brown, Martha Jane VI, 625
Brown, Martha Jane VI, 626
Brown, Martha Jane VI, 627
Brown, Martha Jane VI, 635
Brown, Martha Jane VI, 638
Brown, Martha Jane VI, 648
Brown, Martha Jane VI, 652
Brown, Martha Jane VI, 686
Brown, Martha Jane VI, 719
Brown, Martha Jane VI, 721
Brown, Martha Jane VI, 884
Brown, Martha S. S. I, 873
Brown, Martha T. VI, 801
Brown, Martha, Jr. II, 982
Brown, Martha, Jr. II, 1000
Brown, Marthann V, 28
Brown, Martie V, 452
Brown, Mary I, 23
Brown, Mary I, 208
Brown, Mary I, 209
Brown, Mary I, 268
Brown, Mary I, 271
Brown, Mary I, 347
Brown, Mary I, 350
Brown, Mary I, 353
Brown, Mary I, 370
Brown, Mary I, 375
Brown, Mary I, 376
Brown, Mary I, 412
Brown, Mary I, 492
Brown, Mary I, 587
Brown, Mary I, 592
Brown, Mary I, 756
Brown, Mary I, 777
Brown, Mary I, 801
Brown, Mary I, 802
Brown, Mary I, 819
Brown, Mary I, 873
Brown, Mary I, 902
Brown, Mary I, 935
Brown, Mary I, 971
Brown, Mary I, 974
Brown, Mary I, 982
Brown, Mary I, 988
Brown, Mary I, 1043
Brown, Mary I, 1047
Brown, Mary I, 1048
Brown, Mary I, 1089
Brown, Mary I, 1090
Brown, Mary II, 23
Brown, Mary II, 24
Brown, Mary II, 58
Brown, Mary II, 59
Brown, Mary II, 93
Brown, Mary II, 116
Brown, Mary II, 167
Brown, Mary II, 200
Brown, Mary II, 201
Brown, Mary II, 214
Brown, Mary II, 276
Brown, Mary II, 282
Brown, Mary II, 293
Brown, Mary II, 308
Brown, Mary II, 317
Brown, Mary II, 319
Brown, Mary II, 341
Brown, Mary II, 457
Brown, Mary II, 473
Brown, Mary II, 474
Brown, Mary II, 504
Brown, Mary II, 638
Brown, Mary II, 670
Brown, Mary II, 675
Brown, Mary II, 700
Brown, Mary II, 729
Brown, Mary II, 730
Brown, Mary II, 739
Brown, Mary II, 955
Brown, Mary II, 956
Brown, Mary II, 981
Brown, Mary II, 982
Brown, Mary II, 1004
Brown, Mary II, 1012
Brown, Mary II, 1013
Brown, Mary II, 1018
Brown, Mary II, 1045
Brown, Mary II, 1046
Brown, Mary II, 1050
Brown, Mary II, 1053
Brown, Mary II, 1069
Brown, Mary III, 47
Brown, Mary III, 48
Brown, Mary III, 76
Brown, Mary III, 214
Brown, Mary III, 290
Brown, Mary III, 329
Brown, Mary IV, 22
Brown, Mary IV, 23
Brown, Mary IV, 65
Brown, Mary IV, 76
Brown, Mary IV, 100
Brown, Mary IV, 181
Brown, Mary IV, 182
Brown, Mary IV, 260
Brown, Mary IV, 372
Brown, Mary IV, 465
Brown, Mary IV, 515
Brown, Mary IV, 544
Brown, Mary IV, 569
Brown, Mary IV, 685
Brown, Mary IV, 930
Brown, Mary IV, 931
Brown, Mary IV, 1050
Brown, Mary IV, 1089
Brown, Mary IV, 1273
Brown, Mary V, 27
Brown, Mary V, 28
Brown, Mary V, 29
Brown, Mary V, 35
Brown, Mary V, 49
Brown, Mary V, 100
Brown, Mary V, 102
Brown, Mary V, 122
Brown, Mary V, 155
Brown, Mary V, 224
Brown, Mary V, 249
Brown, Mary V, 299
Brown, Mary V, 320
Brown, Mary V, 321
Brown, Mary V, 375
Brown, Mary V, 452
Brown, Mary V, 478
Brown, Mary V, 728
Brown, Mary V, 729
Brown, Mary V, 754
Brown, Mary V, 798
Brown, Mary V, 828
Brown, Mary V, 829
Brown, Mary V, 830
Brown, Mary V, 831
Brown, Mary V, 841
Brown, Mary V, 852
Brown, Mary V, 854
Brown, Mary V, 857
Brown, Mary V, 871
Brown, Mary V, 880
Brown, Mary V, 887
Brown, Mary VI, 359
Brown, Mary VI, 371
Brown, Mary VI, 372
Brown, Mary VI, 373
Brown, Mary VI, 374
Brown, Mary VI, 377
Brown, Mary VI, 378
Brown, Mary VI, 384
Brown, Mary VI, 402
Brown, Mary VI, 406
Brown, Mary VI, 426
Brown, Mary VI, 431
Brown, Mary VI, 434
Brown, Mary VI, 442
Brown, Mary VI, 448
Brown, Mary VI, 455
Brown, Mary VI, 464
Brown, Mary VI, 467
Brown, Mary VI, 471
Brown, Mary VI, 475
Brown, Mary VI, 476
Brown, Mary VI, 477
Brown, Mary VI, 511
Brown, Mary VI, 540
Brown, Mary VI, 550
Brown, Mary VI, 555
Brown, Mary VI, 556
Brown, Mary VI, 558
Brown, Mary VI, 562
Brown, Mary VI, 568
Brown, Mary VI, 592
Brown, Mary VI, 616
Brown, Mary VI, 617
Brown, Mary VI, 618
Brown, Mary VI, 619
Brown, Mary VI, 621
Brown, Mary VI, 624
Brown, Mary VI, 626
Brown, Mary VI, 628
Brown, Mary VI, 635
Brown, Mary VI, 642
Brown, Mary VI, 658
Brown, Mary VI, 673
Brown, Mary VI, 682
Brown, Mary VI, 683
Brown, Mary VI, 697
Brown, Mary VI, 723
Brown, Mary VI, 795
Brown, Mary VI, 801
Brown, Mary VI, 807
Brown, Mary VI, 815
Brown, Mary VI, 818
Brown, Mary VI, 822
Brown, Mary VI, 831
Brown, Mary VI, 889
Brown, Mary VI, 893
Brown, Mary VI, 918
Brown, Mary VI, 982
Brown, Mary VI, 996
Brown, Mary A. I, 217
Brown, Mary A. I, 231
Brown, Mary A. I, 232
Brown, Mary A. I, 242
Brown, Mary A. I, 756
Brown, Mary A. I, 770
Brown, Mary A. IV, 728
Brown, Mary A. V, 224
Brown, Mary A. V, 696
Brown, Mary A. VI, 372
Brown, Mary A. VI, 374
Brown, Mary A. VI, 439
Brown, Mary A. VI, 801
Brown, Mary Ann I, 209
Brown, Mary Ann I, 232
Brown, Mary Ann I, 756
Brown, Mary Ann IV, 372
Brown, Mary Ann IV, 417
Brown, Mary Ann IV, 683
Brown, Mary Ann IV, 685
Brown, Mary Ann IV, 1128
Brown, Mary Ann IV, 1273
Brown, Mary Ann IV, 1286
Brown, Mary Ann V, 28
Brown, Mary Ann V, 29
Brown, Mary Ann V, 72
Brown, Mary Ann V, 97
Brown, Mary Ann V, 224
Brown, Mary Ann V, 227
Brown, Mary Ann V, 299
Brown, Mary Ann V, 551
Brown, Mary Ann V, 585
Brown, Mary Ann V, 828
Brown, Mary Ann V, 829
Brown, Mary Ann V, 830
Brown, Mary Ann V, 831
Brown, Mary Ann V, 860
Brown, Mary Ann V, 862
Brown, Mary Ann V, 880
Brown, Mary Ann V, 881
Brown, Mary Ann V, 883
Brown, Mary Ann V, 968
Brown, Mary Ann VI, 624
Brown, Mary Ann VI, 625
Brown, Mary Ann VI, 626
Brown, Mary Ann VI, 681
Brown, Mary Ann VI, 683
Brown, Mary Anna II, 700
Brown, Mary Anna II, 726
Brown, Mary Anna II, 730
Brown, Mary Anna III, 365
Brown, Mary Anna VI, 624
Brown, Mary Atlantic IV, 930
Brown, Mary B. I, 215
Brown, Mary B. III, 48
Brown, Mary B. III, 214
Brown, Mary Brown V, 728
Brown, Mary C. I, 1081
Brown, Mary C. I, 1090
Brown, Mary C. I, 1140
Brown, Mary C. II, 834
Brown, Mary C. II, 841
Brown, Mary C. II, 842
Brown, Mary C. III, 48
Brown, Mary C. V, 28
Brown, Mary C. V, 122
Brown, Mary C. VI, 855
Brown, Mary Churchman III, 47
Brown, Mary E. I, 232
Brown, Mary E. I, 239
Brown, Mary E. II, 341
Brown, Mary E. II, 730
Brown, Mary E. II, 745
Brown, Mary E. II, 955
Brown, Mary E. II, 1045
Brown, Mary E. II, 1046
Brown, Mary E. III, 48
Brown, Mary E. III, 223
Brown, Mary E. IV, 613
Brown, Mary E. IV, 649
Brown, Mary E. V, 28
Brown, Mary E. V, 80
Brown, Mary E. V, 551
Brown, Mary E. V, 880
Brown, Mary E. V, 881

Brown, Mary E. VI, 372
Brown, Mary E. VI, 374
Brown, Mary E. VI, 666
Brown, Mary E. VI, 682
Brown, Mary E. VI, 688
Brown, Mary E. VI, 949
Brown, Mary E., Jr. VI, 372
Brown, Mary Eliza IV, 1273
Brown, Mary Eliza IV, 1283
Brown, Mary Elizabeth I, 208
Brown, Mary Elizabeth II, 729
Brown, Mary Elizabeth V, 28
Brown, Mary Elizabeth V, 880
Brown, Mary Elizabeth VI, 621
Brown, Mary Elizabeth VI, 624
Brown, Mary Elizabeth VI, 625
Brown, Mary Elizabeth VI, 627
Brown, Mary Elizabeth VI, 679
Brown, Mary Elizabeth VI, 680
Brown, Mary Ella VI, 390
Brown, Mary Ellen V, 375
Brown, Mary Ellen V, 421
Brown, Mary Ellen VI, 374
Brown, Mary Ellen VI, 615
Brown, Mary Ellen VI, 624
Brown, Mary Ellen VI, 625
Brown, Mary Ellen VI, 626
Brown, Mary Emily IV, 182
Brown, Mary Emily V, 29
Brown, Mary Emma VI, 622
Brown, Mary Emma VI, 624
Brown, Mary Emma VI, 625
Brown, Mary Emma VI, 626
Brown, Mary Emma VI, 627
Brown, Mary Emma VI, 631
Brown, Mary Emma VI, 636
Brown, Mary Emma VI, 650
Brown, Mary Emma VI, 691
Brown, Mary Esther VI, 476
Brown, Mary Esther VI, 548
Brown, Mary Esther VI, 555
Brown, Mary Esther VI, 556
Brown, Mary Esther VI, 567
Brown, Mary Esther VI, 623
Brown, Mary Esther VI, 624
Brown, Mary Esther VI, 625
Brown, Mary Esther VI, 688
Brown, Mary Esther VI, 697
Brown, Mary F. II, 700
Brown, Mary F. II, 730
Brown, Mary F. IV, 804
Brown, Mary F. IV, 1203
Brown, Mary F. IV, 1225
Brown, Mary F. VI, 807
Brown, Mary Francina VI, 623
Brown, Mary H. II, 700
Brown, Mary H. II, 730
Brown, Mary H. II, 773
Brown, Mary H. III, 50
Brown, Mary H. III, 263
Brown, Mary H. III, 294
Brown, Mary H. IV, 560
Brown, Mary H. IV, 803
Brown, Mary H. IV, 804
Brown, Mary H. IV, 850
Brown, Mary H. V, 830
Brown, Mary H. VI, 702
Brown, Mary Hannah VI, 625
Brown, Mary Hannah VI, 626
Brown, Mary Hannah VI, 628
Brown, Mary Hannah VI, 686
Brown, Mary Hannah VI, 693
Brown, Mary Hannah VI, 702
Brown, Mary Hannah VI, 704
Brown, Mary Hannah VI, 707
Brown, Mary Hannah VI, 723
Brown, Mary J. I, 675
Brown, Mary J. I, 682
Brown, Mary J. I, 873
Brown, Mary Jane III, 48
Brown, Mary Jane V, 224
Brown, Mary L. II, 308
Brown, Mary L. II, 317
Brown, Mary L. II, 321
Brown, Mary L. III, 48
Brown, Mary L. III, 49
Brown, Mary L. V, 452
Brown, Mary Letitia VI, 625
Brown, Mary Letitia VI, 627
Brown, Mary Letitia VI, 691
Brown, Mary Louisa IV, 1089
Brown, Mary Lydia V, 28
Brown, Mary Lydia V, 224
Brown, Mary M. V, 887
Brown, Mary M. VI, 476
Brown, Mary M. VI, 884
Brown, Mary Maria V, 478
Brown, Mary Maria V, 496
Brown, Mary Matthews VI, 371
Brown, Mary Moore II, 474
Brown, Mary P. III, 271
Brown, Mary P. VI, 677
Brown, Mary Parr VI, 625
Brown, Mary Platt II, 1046
Brown, Mary Platt II, 1056
Brown, Mary R. II, 700
Brown, Mary R. II, 841
Brown, Mary R. II, 955
Brown, Mary R. II, 1045
Brown, Mary R. II, 1069
Brown, Mary R. III, 47
Brown, Mary R. III, 48
Brown, Mary Ruth I, 528
Brown, Mary S. II, 317
Brown, Mary S. IV, 181
Brown, Mary S. VI, 884
Brown, Mary T. II, 730
Brown, Mary T. II, 750
Brown, Mary T. II, 773
Brown, Mary T. III, 47
Brown, Mary T. V, 949
Brown, Mary T. V, 960
Brown, Mary U. V, 880
Brown, Mary Virginia VI, 624
Brown, Mary Virginia VI, 625
Brown, Mary W. II, 700
Brown, Mary W. V, 28
Brown, Mary W. V, 29
Brown, Mary W. V, 478
Brown, Mary Waln II, 700
Brown, Mary Waln II, 730
Brown, Mary Waln II, 776
Brown, Mary Waln Wistar II, 730
Brown, Mary Wistar II, 700
Brown, Mary, Jr. I, 231
Brown, Mary, Jr. I, 250
Brown, Mary, Jr. II, 454
Brown, Mary, Jr. II, 474
Brown, Mary, Jr. II, 500
Brown, Mary, Jr. VI, 592
Brown, Maryann V, 28
Brown, Maryann V, 44
Brown, Matilda I, 1081
Brown, Matilda I, 1090
Brown, Matilda I, 1149
Brown, Matilda II, 784
Brown, Matilda II, 841
Brown, Matilda II, 864
Brown, Matilda VI, 476
Brown, Matilda VI, 577
Brown, Matilda VI, 884
Brown, Matilda C. VI, 951
Brown, Matthias M. III, 48
Brown, Mattie V, 375
Brown, Mattie E. V, 452
Brown, Mattie Lila VI, 56
Brown, May V, 693
Brown, May M. V, 661
Brown, Mehitabebel VI, 753
Brown, Mehitabel VI, 733
Brown, Mellie IV, 1308
Brown, Melva IV, 1203
Brown, Mercer I, 1043
Brown, Mercer I, 1047
Brown, Mercer V, 27
Brown, Mercer V, 28
Brown, Mercer V, 122
Brown, Mercer V, 828
Brown, Mercer V, 830
Brown, Mercer VI, 476
Brown, Mercer VI, 477
Brown, Mercy II, 955
Brown, Mercy II, 976
Brown, Mercy II, 981
Brown, Mercy II, 982
Brown, Mercy II, 1046
Brown, Mercy II, 1051
Brown, Mercy Ann II, 955
Brown, Mercy Ann II, 1069
Brown, Mercy E. II, 955
Brown, Meriem VI, 372
Brown, Merriam V, 28
Brown, Merritt J. III, 48
Brown, Merritt J. III, 49
Brown, Mertie M. V, 551
Brown, Messer VI, 476
Brown, Miami IV, 23
Brown, Michoes V, 729
Brown, Mildred G. VI, 842
Brown, Mildred Rosebud VI, 733
Brown, Mildred Rosebud VI, 741
Brown, Milford E. IV, 1308
Brown, Milicent II, 116
Brown, Milicent II, 124
Brown, Milisant II, 116
Brown, Miller II, 24
Brown, Miller II, 59
Brown, Millicent II, 24
Brown, Millicent II, 47
Brown, Millicent II, 126
Brown, Milly VI, 884
Brown, Milo V, 831
Brown, Milo O. V, 830
Brown, Minnie I, 938
Brown, Minnie I, 949
Brown, Minnie E. I, 475
Brown, Miriam I, 208
Brown, Miriam I, 231
Brown, Miriam I, 258
Brown, Miriam I, 300
Brown, Miriam I, 1081
Brown, Miriam I, 1090
Brown, Miriam I, 1094
Brown, Miriam IV, 23
Brown, Miriam IV, 181
Brown, Miriam IV, 186
Brown, Miriam IV, 465
Brown, Miriam VI, 371
Brown, Miriam VI, 373
Brown, Miriam G. VI, 458
Brown, Mordecai III, 48
Brown, Morgan I, 528
Brown, Morrison VI, 849
Brown, Moses I, 209
Brown, Moses I, 231
Brown, Moses I, 268
Brown, Moses I, 376
Brown, Moses I, 492
Brown, Moses I, 801
Brown, Moses I, 974
Brown, Moses I, 982
Brown, Moses II, 475
Brown, Moses II, 700
Brown, Moses II, 730
Brown, Moses II, 739
Brown, Moses II, 982
Brown, Moses III, 48
Brown, Moses IV, 23
Brown, Moses V, 29
Brown, Moses V, 829
Brown, Moses V, 880
Brown, Moses VI, 625
Brown, Moses, Jr. II, 730
Brown, Mrs. Anna IV, 1308
Brown, Mrs. Carrie L. IV, 1308
Brown, Mrs. Wm. Henry IV, 1247
Brown, Myrta VI, 733
Brown, Myrta VI, 734
Brown, Myrta May VI, 733
Brown, Myrta May VI, 764
Brown, Myrtle VI, 622
Brown, Myrtle VI, 628
Brown, Myrtle Elizabeth VI, 733
Brown, Myrtle Elizabeth VI, 764
Brown, Myrtle O. IV, 1149
Brown, Nancy I, 1017
Brown, Nancy IV, 1203
Brown, Nancy IV, 1226
Brown, Nancy V, 388
Brown, Nancy V, 729
Brown, Nancy V, 771
Brown, Nancy V, 798
Brown, Nancy V, 949
Brown, Nancy VI, 373
Brown, Nancy VI, 801
Brown, Nancy VI, 809
Brown, Nancy VI, 812
Brown, Nancy VI, 884
Brown, Nancy VI, 990
Brown, Nancy E. I, 232
Brown, Nannie IV, 1149
Brown, Naomi IV, 181
Brown, Naomi V, 729
Brown, Naomi VI, 599
Brown, Naomi VI, 682
Brown, Nathan II, 982
Brown, Nathan III, 49
Brown, Nathan IV, 17
Brown, Nathan IV, 71
Brown, Nathan IV, 76
Brown, Nathan IV, 181
Brown, Nathan IV, 372
Brown, Nathan IV, 465
Brown, Nathan IV, 613
Brown, Nathan IV, 667
Brown, Nathan IV, 685
Brown, Nathan IV, 852
Brown, Nathan IV, 930
Brown, Nathan IV, 1014
Brown, Nathan VI, 372
Brown, Nathan VI, 624
Brown, Nathan VI, 625
Brown, Nathan VI, 626
Brown, Nathan VI, 627
Brown, Nathan VI, 656
Brown, Nathan VI, 680
Brown, Nathan VI, 683
Brown, Nathan VI, 684
Brown, Nathan VI, 686
Brown, Nathan T. VI, 721
Brown, Nathan Townsend VI, 625
Brown, Nathan Townsend VI, 721
Brown, Nathanial III, 47
Brown, Nathaniel II, 24
Brown, Nathaniel II, 341
Brown, Nathaniel II, 441
Brown, Nathaniel II, 473
Brown, Nathaniel II, 474
Brown, Nathaniel II, 513
Brown, Nathaniel II, 638
Brown, Nathaniel III, 47
Brown, Nathaniel III, 49
Brown, Nathaniel V, 830
Brown, Nathaniel V, 880
Brown, Nathaniel B. II, 24
Brown, Nathaniel B. II, 116
Brown, Nathaniel B. II, 124
Brown, Nathaniel H. II, 700
Brown, Nathaniel H. II, 726
Brown, Nathaniel H. II, 729
Brown, Nathaniel H. II, 730
Brown, Nathaniel H. II, 750
Brown, Nathaniel H. II, 773
Brown, Nathaniel Howland II, 700
Brown, Nathaniel Howland II, 730
Brown, Nathaniel M. III, 49
Brown, Nathaniel M. V, 828
Brown, Nathaniel M. V, 829
Brown, Nathaniel M. V, 854
Brown, Nathaniel M. V, 881
Brown, Nathaniel M. V, 885
Brown, Nathaniel M. VI, 884
Brown, Nathaniel N. VI, 631
Brown, Nehemiah V, 829
Brown, Nellie I, 209
Brown, Nellie IV, 1247
Brown, Nellie VI, 624
Brown, Nellie VI, 628
Brown, Nellie VI, 635
Brown, Nellie G. I, 262
Brown, Ner V, 29
Brown, Newel V, 28
Brown, Newel V, 29
Brown, Newell V, 80
Brown, Newell VI, 666
Brown, Newton V, 829
Brown, Newton V, 831
Brown, Nicholas VI, 373
Brown, Nicholas VI, 733
Brown, Nicholas VI, 759
Brown, Nicolas V, 728
Brown, Nixon G. V, 949
Brown, Nixon G. VI, 623
Brown, Nixon G. VI, 625
Brown, Nixon G. VI, 721
Brown, Nixon G. VI, 723
Brown, Noah E. I, 262
Brown, Norman Hadley V, 551
Brown, Obadiah I, 873
Brown, Olive IV, 1273
Brown, Olive IV, 1282
Brown, Olive VI, 627
Brown, Olive VI, 734
Brown, Oliver V, 29
Brown, Oliver V, 880
Brown, Oliver M. VI, 373
Brown, Oliver R. IV, 803
Brown, Oliver R. IV, 804
Brown, Oliver W. V, 28
Brown, Olnie I, 938
Brown, Omar IV, 1273
Brown, Omer Jesse I, 613
Brown, Omer Jesse I, 630
Brown, Otilla V, 987
Brown, Pamela III, 397
Brown, Pamela III, 411
Brown, Parthenia VI, 839
Brown, Paschal VI, 884
Brown, Patience I, 353
Brown, Patience I. III, 480
Brown, Patricia III, 70
Brown, Patsey VI, 882
Brown, Paul II, 341
Brown, Paul II, 474
Brown, Paul II, 475
Brown, Paul IV, 1203
Brown, Paul Howard V, 661
Brown, Peace III, 49
Brown, Pearl I. VI, 372
Brown, Pearl I. VI, 374
Brown, Peggy V, 828
Brown, Pennell C. III, 49
Brown, Percy VI, 624
Brown, Peter II, 341
Brown, Peter II, 474
Brown, Peter II, 523
Brown, Phebe I, 777
Brown, Phebe I, 801
Brown, Phebe I, 1043
Brown, Phebe I, 1047
Brown, Phebe II, 54
Brown, Phebe II, 58
Brown, Phebe II, 167
Brown, Phebe II, 191
Brown, Phebe II, 201
Brown, Phebe II, 282
Brown, Phebe II, 307
Brown, Phebe II, 474
Brown, Phebe II, 602
Brown, Phebe II, 841
Brown, Phebe II, 866
Brown, Phebe II, 982
Brown, Phebe III, 49
Brown, Phebe III, 167
Brown, Phebe III, 480
Brown, Phebe IV, 76
Brown, Phebe IV, 322
Brown, Phebe IV, 613
Brown, Phebe IV, 685
Brown, Phebe IV, 803
Brown, Phebe IV, 804
Brown, Phebe IV, 829
Brown, Phebe IV, 865
Brown, Phebe IV, 882
Brown, Phebe V, 28
Brown, Phebe V, 155
Brown, Phebe V, 828
Brown, Phebe V, 829
Brown, Phebe V, 830
Brown, Phebe V, 831
Brown, Phebe V, 861
Brown, Phebe V, 880
Brown, Phebe V, 968
Brown, Phebe V, 976
Brown, Phebe V, 987
Brown, Phebe VI, 371
Brown, Phebe VI, 372
Brown, Phebe VI, 373
Brown, Phebe VI, 476
Brown, Phebe VI, 477
Brown, Phebe VI, 546
Brown, Phebe VI, 592
Brown, Phebe VI, 603
Brown, Phebe VI, 625
Brown, Phebe VI, 626
Brown, Phebe VI, 682
Brown, Phebe VI, 683
Brown, Phebe Ann III, 47
Brown, Phebe Ann III, 48
Brown, Phebe Ann III, 49
Brown, Phebe Ann III, 204
Brown, Phebe Ann IV, 685
Brown, Phebe Ann IV, 804
Brown, Phebe Ann V, 851
Brown, Phebe Broomall IV, 804
Brown, Phebe C. IV, 1089
Brown, Phebe E. V, 880
Brown, Phebe G. VI, 683
Brown, Phebe J. V, 224
Brown, Phebe Jane V, 224
Brown, Phebe Jane V, 278
Brown, Phebe W. III, 47
Brown, Phebe W. III, 49
Brown, Phebe W. V, 155
Brown, Phebe W. V, 829
Brown, Phebe W. V, 831
Brown, Phebe, Jr. IV, 804
Brown, Philepena I, 492
Brown, Philip II, 167
Brown, Philipina I, 801
Brown, Philipiney I, 873
Brown, Philipiney I, 877
Brown, Phillipine I, 528
Brown, Phillis VI, 801
Brown, Phineas V, 829
Brown, Phineas V, 831
Brown, Pleasant IV, 322
Brown, Pleasant IV, 338
Brown, Pleasant VI, 884
Brown, Polly I, 208
Brown, Polly I, 231
Brown, Polly I, 239
Brown, Polly I, 797
Brown, Polly I, 801
Brown, Polly I, 1047
Brown, Polly VI, 827
Brown, Polly VI, 848
Brown, Polly VI, 883
Brown, Polly VI, 884
Brown, Polly VI, 996
Brown, Polly L. VI, 915
Brown, Pondexter VI, 801
Brown, Preserve II, 201
Brown, Preserve II, 341
Brown, Preserve II, 474
Brown, Preserve, Jr. II, 341
Brown, Preserve, Jr. II, 474
Brown, Preston VI, 801
Brown, Priscilla I, 209
Brown, Priscilla I, 231
Brown, Priscilla I, 233
Brown, Priscilla II, 341

Brown, Priscilla II, 473
Brown, Priscilla II, 474
Brown, Priscilla II, 614
Brown, Priscilla II, 678
Brown, Priscilla III, 49
Brown, Priscilla V, 828
Brown, Priscilla V, 831
Brown, Priscilla V, 880
Brown, Priscilla M. V, 880
Brown, Priscilla W. II, 167
Brown, Priscilla W. II, 282
Brown, Priscilla W. II, 291
Brown, Prophet IV, 76
Brown, Prophet IV, 613
Brown, Prophet IV, 654
Brown, Prophet IV, 804
Brown, Prophet IV, 865
Brown, Quackey VI, 801
Brown, R. Brown VI, 829
Brown, Rachel I, 131
Brown, Rachel I, 208
Brown, Rachel I, 209
Brown, Rachel I, 231
Brown, Rachel I, 246
Brown, Rachel I, 347
Brown, Rachel I, 375
Brown, Rachel I, 424
Brown, Rachel I, 492
Brown, Rachel I, 801
Brown, Rachel I, 974
Brown, Rachel I, 980
Brown, Rachel I, 982
Brown, Rachel I, 986
Brown, Rachel I, 1081
Brown, Rachel I, 1090
Brown, Rachel I, 1092
Brown, Rachel II, 201
Brown, Rachel II, 253
Brown, Rachel II, 729
Brown, Rachel II, 730
Brown, Rachel II, 982
Brown, Rachel II, 1014
Brown, Rachel III, 49
Brown, Rachel III, 171
Brown, Rachel III, 258
Brown, Rachel IV, 22
Brown, Rachel IV, 54
Brown, Rachel IV, 181
Brown, Rachel IV, 372
Brown, Rachel IV, 613
Brown, Rachel IV, 804
Brown, Rachel V, 29
Brown, Rachel V, 138
Brown, Rachel V, 224
Brown, Rachel V, 321
Brown, Rachel V, 478
Brown, Rachel V, 828
Brown, Rachel V, 829
Brown, Rachel V, 830
Brown, Rachel V, 880
Brown, Rachel VI, 365
Brown, Rachel VI, 372
Brown, Rachel VI, 470
Brown, Rachel VI, 476
Brown, Rachel VI, 592
Brown, Rachel VI, 599
Brown, Rachel VI, 625
Brown, Rachel VI, 637
Brown, Rachel VI, 909
Brown, Rachel Airy V, 830
Brown, Rachel Ann IV, 182
Brown, Rachel Ann V, 320
Brown, Rachel Arah V, 831
Brown, Rachel Caroline V, 29
Brown, Rachel N. VI, 371
Brown, Rachel N. VI, 734
Brown, Rachel S. III, 48
Brown, Rachel S. III, 355
Brown, Ralph I, 613
Brown, Ralph VI, 625
Brown, Ralph Birdsall VI, 617
Brown, Ralph Birdsall VI, 626
Brown, Ralph Birdsall VI, 670
Brown, Ralph R. VI, 617
Brown, Ralph W. III, 96
Brown, Ralph Wolcott III, 49
Brown, Ray Wilber IV, 1308
Brown, Rebecca I, 131
Brown, Rebecca I, 151
Brown, Rebecca I, 208
Brown, Rebecca I, 209
Brown, Rebecca I, 226
Brown, Rebecca I, 231
Brown, Rebecca I, 232
Brown, Rebecca I, 475
Brown, Rebecca I, 528
Brown, Rebecca I, 552
Brown, Rebecca I, 592
Brown, Rebecca I, 756
Brown, Rebecca I, 797
Brown, Rebecca I, 801
Brown, Rebecca I, 802
Brown, Rebecca I, 1047
Brown, Rebecca I, 1140
Brown, Rebecca II, 23
Brown, Rebecca II, 24
Brown, Rebecca II, 58
Brown, Rebecca II, 59
Brown, Rebecca II, 201
Brown, Rebecca II, 214
Brown, Rebecca II, 282
Brown, Rebecca II, 299
Brown, Rebecca II, 452
Brown, Rebecca II, 474
Brown, Rebecca II, 477
Brown, Rebecca II, 568
Brown, Rebecca II, 700
Brown, Rebecca II, 726
Brown, Rebecca II, 730
Brown, Rebecca II, 750
Brown, Rebecca II, 784
Brown, Rebecca II, 811
Brown, Rebecca II, 955
Brown, Rebecca II, 964
Brown, Rebecca II, 982
Brown, Rebecca II, 1012
Brown, Rebecca III, 47
Brown, Rebecca IV, 23
Brown, Rebecca IV, 39
Brown, Rebecca IV, 57
Brown, Rebecca IV, 76
Brown, Rebecca IV, 175
Brown, Rebecca IV, 181
Brown, Rebecca IV, 269
Brown, Rebecca IV, 654
Brown, Rebecca IV, 1273
Brown, Rebecca IV, 1291
Brown, Rebecca IV, 1293
Brown, Rebecca V, 26
Brown, Rebecca V, 28
Brown, Rebecca V, 52
Brown, Rebecca V, 102
Brown, Rebecca V, 224
Brown, Rebecca V, 321
Brown, Rebecca V, 728
Brown, Rebecca V, 729
Brown, Rebecca V, 828
Brown, Rebecca V, 829
Brown, Rebecca V, 830
Brown, Rebecca V, 831
Brown, Rebecca V, 858
Brown, Rebecca V, 862
Brown, Rebecca V, 880
Brown, Rebecca V, 968
Brown, Rebecca VI, 368
Brown, Rebecca VI, 371
Brown, Rebecca VI, 372
Brown, Rebecca VI, 373
Brown, Rebecca VI, 422
Brown, Rebecca VI, 617
Brown, Rebecca VI, 618
Brown, Rebecca VI, 622
Brown, Rebecca VI, 625
Brown, Rebecca VI, 627
Brown, Rebecca VI, 733
Brown, Rebecca VI, 734
Brown, Rebecca Alice VI, 617
Brown, Rebecca Alice VI, 618
Brown, Rebecca Alice VI, 622
Brown, Rebecca Alice VI, 623
Brown, Rebecca B. II, 1046
Brown, Rebecca B. II, 1051
Brown, Rebecca E. VI, 622
Brown, Rebecca F. II, 708
Brown, Rebecca F. II, 955
Brown, Rebecca G. II, 730
Brown, Rebecca G. II, 742
Brown, Rebecca G. II, 841
Brown, Rebecca G. II, 866
Brown, Rebecca G. II, 903
Brown, Rebecca J. I, 1090
Brown, Rebecca J. I, 1140
Brown, Rebecca J. II, 1046
Brown, Rebecca J. II, 1061
Brown, Rebecca J. VI, 625
Brown, Rebecca J. VI, 626
Brown, Rebecca J. VI, 681
Brown, Rebecca J. VI, 683
Brown, Rebecca Jane I, 1081
Brown, Rebecca K. VI, 624
Brown, Rebecca K. VI, 625
Brown, Rebecca K. VI, 679
Brown, Rebecca M. VI, 372
Brown, Rebecca R. VI, 422
Brown, Rebecca T. II, 1046
Brown, Rebecca W. II, 167
Brown, Rebecca W. II, 282
Brown, Rebecca W. VI, 371
Brown, Rebecca W. VI, 734
Brown, Rebeccah V, 830
Brown, Rebeckah I, 528
Brown, Rebeckah I, 777
Brown, Rebeckah II, 58
Brown, Rebeckah IV, 181
Brown, Rebekah IV, 76
Brown, Reuben II, 167
Brown, Reuben II, 201
Brown, Reuben II, 475
Brown, Reuben L. III, 49
Brown, Reuben Ross IV, 23
Brown, Reuben S. VI, 949
Brown, Reva V, 155
Brown, Rhoda II, 341
Brown, Rhoda III, 49
Brown, Rhoda V, 829
Brown, Rhoda V, 830
Brown, Rhoda V, 831
Brown, Rhoda V, 837
Brown, Rhoda VI, 884
Brown, Rhoda VI, 891
Brown, Rhodam VI, 884
Brown, Rhodham T. VI, 884
Brown, Richard I, 131
Brown, Richard I, 347
Brown, Richard I, 350
Brown, Richard I, 375
Brown, Richard I, 376
Brown, Richard I, 492
Brown, Richard I, 528
Brown, Richard I, 756
Brown, Richard I, 801
Brown, Richard I, 974
Brown, Richard I, 982
Brown, Richard I, 1043
Brown, Richard I, 1047
Brown, Richard II, 167
Brown, Richard II, 201
Brown, Richard II, 250
Brown, Richard II, 253
Brown, Richard II, 473
Brown, Richard II, 1058
Brown, Richard V, 28
Brown, Richard V, 828
Brown, Richard V, 829
Brown, Richard V, 830
Brown, Richard V, 857
Brown, Richard V, 863
Brown, Richard V, 871
Brown, Richard VI, 372
Brown, Richard VI, 373
Brown, Richard VI, 470
Brown, Richard VI, 475
Brown, Richard VI, 476
Brown, Richard VI, 483
Brown, Richard VI, 524
Brown, Richard VI, 540
Brown, Richard VI, 548
Brown, Richard VI, 572
Brown, Richard VI, 622
Brown, Richard VI, 624
Brown, Richard VI, 625
Brown, Richard VI, 627
Brown, Richard VI, 683
Brown, Richard VI, 690
Brown, Richard VI, 714
Brown, Richard VI, 862
Brown, Richard VI, 884
Brown, Richard B. VI, 372
Brown, Richard F. III, 270
Brown, Richard G. VI, 801
Brown, Richard G. VI, 807
Brown, Richard G. VI, 824
Brown, Richard G. VI, 842
Brown, Richard H. VI, 56
Brown, Richard H. VI, 74
Brown, Richard Henry VI, 623
Brown, Richard Henry VI, 625
Brown, Richard J. II, 955
Brown, Richard J. II, 1046
Brown, Richard R. III, 480
Brown, Richard R. VI, 373
Brown, Richard R. VI, 374
Brown, Richard R. VI, 425
Brown, Richard R., Jr. VI, 372
Brown, Richard R., Jr. VI, 374
Brown, Richard R., Jr. VI, 624
Brown, Richard R., Jr. VI, 625
Brown, Richard R., Jr. VI, 626
Brown, Richard R., Sr. VI, 372
Brown, Richard R., Sr. VI, 374
Brown, Richard R., Sr. VI, 625
Brown, Richard T. III, 49
Brown, Richard Waln II, 700
Brown, Richard, Jr. V, 830
Brown, Richard, Jr. VI, 544
Brown, Richard, Jr. VI, 623
Brown, Richard, Jr. VI, 625
Brown, Richard, Jr. VI, 626
Brown, Richard, Jr. VI, 628
Brown, Richard, Jr. VI, 682
Brown, Richard, Jr. VI, 689
Brown, Richard, Jr. VI, 699
Brown, Robert II, 167
Brown, Robert II, 1069
Brown, Robert V, 829
Brown, Robert V, 830
Brown, Robert E. I, 873
Brown, Robert G. VI, 477
Brown, Robert Garfield VI, 477
Brown, Robert J. V, 661
Brown, Robert L. I, 873
Brown, Robert Lewis VI, 733
Brown, Robert M. V, 661
Brown, Robert M. VI, 801
Brown, Robert Maxwell V, 661
Brown, Robert P. II, 700
Brown, Robert P. II, 955
Brown, Robert P. II, 1046
Brown, Robert S. II, 1046
Brown, Robert S. II, 1065
Brown, Robert S. II, 1069
Brown, Rodham VI, 996
Brown, Rosa E. V, 29
Brown, Rosanna E. V, 29
Brown, Rosella VI, 615
Brown, Rosella VI, 621
Brown, Rosella VI, 624
Brown, Rosella VI, 625
Brown, Rosella VI, 697
Brown, Rosella VI, 710
Brown, Rowland I, 227
Brown, Roxanah I, 462
Brown, Roxie I, 212
Brown, Ruby IV, 1319
Brown, Ruby P. IV, 1308
Brown, Russel E. VI, 372
Brown, Ruth I, 347
Brown, Ruth I, 375
Brown, Ruth I, 492
Brown, Ruth I, 801
Brown, Ruth I, 827
Brown, Ruth I, 1081
Brown, Ruth I, 1090
Brown, Ruth I, 1091
Brown, Ruth II, 201
Brown, Ruth II, 475
Brown, Ruth IV, 76
Brown, Ruth IV, 465
Brown, Ruth IV, 685
Brown, Ruth IV, 891
Brown, Ruth IV, 1273
Brown, Ruth IV, 1277
Brown, Ruth IV, 1287
Brown, Ruth V, 28
Brown, Ruth V, 59
Brown, Ruth V, 97
Brown, Ruth V, 829
Brown, Ruth V, 830
Brown, Ruth VI, 372
Brown, Ruth VI, 592
Brown, Ruth VI, 615
Brown, Ruth VI, 626
Brown, Ruth Anna II, 167
Brown, Ruth Anna II, 282
Brown, Ruth Anna VI, 374
Brown, Ruth Anna VI, 626
Brown, Ruth Anna VI, 627
Brown, Ruth E. VI, 372
Brown, Ruth E. VI, 374
Brown, Ruth Elizabeth VI, 626
Brown, Ruth Elizabeth VI, 627
Brown, Ruth Elizabeth VI, 691
Brown, Ruth Hanna VI, 622
Brown, Ruth Hannah V, 949
Brown, Ruth Hannah VI, 623
Brown, Ruth Hannah VI, 624
Brown, Ruth Hannah VI, 625
Brown, Ruth Hannah VI, 626
Brown, Ruth Hannah VI, 670
Brown, Ruth Isabelle V, 551
Brown, Ruth W. II, 167
Brown, Ruth W. II, 201
Brown, Ruth W. II, 282
Brown, Ruth W. II, 291
Brown, Ruthanna II, 282
Brown, Sadie V, 452
Brown, Sadie V, 830
Brown, Saida V, 452
Brown, Sallie II, 805
Brown, Sally V, 798
Brown, Sally VI, 827
Brown, Sally VI, 851
Brown, Sally VI, 880
Brown, Sally VI, 975
Brown, Sally W. VI, 884
Brown, Sam'l I, 1090
Brown, Sammuel I, 528
Brown, Sammuel I, 537
Brown, Samuel I, 208
Brown, Samuel I, 209
Brown, Samuel I, 347
Brown, Samuel I, 375
Brown, Samuel I, 492
Brown, Samuel I, 529
Brown, Samuel I, 650
Brown, Samuel I, 960
Brown, Samuel I, 1015
Brown, Samuel I, 1017
Brown, Samuel I, 1026
Brown, Samuel I, 1047
Brown, Samuel I, 1081
Brown, Samuel I, 1089
Brown, Samuel I, 1090
Brown, Samuel I, 1139
Brown, Samuel I, 1149
Brown, Samuel II, 167
Brown, Samuel II, 201
Brown, Samuel II, 202
Brown, Samuel II, 214
Brown, Samuel II, 341
Brown, Samuel II, 452
Brown, Samuel II, 474
Brown, Samuel II, 477
Brown, Samuel II, 500
Brown, Samuel II, 504
Brown, Samuel II, 955
Brown, Samuel II, 956
Brown, Samuel II, 976
Brown, Samuel II, 981
Brown, Samuel II, 989
Brown, Samuel II, 1018
Brown, Samuel II, 1037
Brown, Samuel II, 1041
Brown, Samuel II, 1045
Brown, Samuel III, 48
Brown, Samuel III, 49
Brown, Samuel III, 171
Brown, Samuel III, 258
Brown, Samuel IV, 23
Brown, Samuel IV, 76
Brown, Samuel IV, 181
Brown, Samuel IV, 803
Brown, Samuel IV, 804
Brown, Samuel IV, 930
Brown, Samuel IV, 1233
Brown, Samuel IV, 1273
Brown, Samuel V, 27
Brown, Samuel V, 28
Brown, Samuel V, 30
Brown, Samuel V, 52
Brown, Samuel V, 53
Brown, Samuel V, 59
Brown, Samuel V, 63
Brown, Samuel V, 224
Brown, Samuel V, 299
Brown, Samuel V, 320
Brown, Samuel V, 321
Brown, Samuel V, 551
Brown, Samuel V, 568
Brown, Samuel V, 728
Brown, Samuel V, 729
Brown, Samuel V, 783
Brown, Samuel V, 798
Brown, Samuel V, 828
Brown, Samuel V, 829
Brown, Samuel V, 830
Brown, Samuel V, 831
Brown, Samuel V, 839
Brown, Samuel V, 863
Brown, Samuel V, 880
Brown, Samuel V, 882
Brown, Samuel V, 968
Brown, Samuel V, 979
Brown, Samuel VI, 349
Brown, Samuel VI, 371
Brown, Samuel VI, 372
Brown, Samuel VI, 373
Brown, Samuel VI, 476
Brown, Samuel VI, 622
Brown, Samuel VI, 625
Brown, Samuel VI, 626
Brown, Samuel VI, 643
Brown, Samuel VI, 801
Brown, Samuel VI, 884
Brown, Samuel C. V, 155
Brown, Samuel C. V, 829
Brown, Samuel C. V, 831
Brown, Samuel C. VI, 623
Brown, Samuel E. VI, 372
Brown, Samuel E. VI, 374
Brown, Samuel E. VI, 439
Brown, Samuel Elgar, Jr. VI, 372
Brown, Samuel H. III, 49
Brown, Samuel H. V, 829
Brown, Samuel Howell VI, 622
Brown, Samuel L. V, 224
Brown, Samuel N VI, 628
Brown, Samuel N. VI, 622
Brown, Samuel N. VI, 626
Brown, Samuel N. VI, 627
Brown, Samuel N. VI, 635
Brown, Samuel N. VI, 681
Brown, Samuel N. VI, 682
Brown, Samuel N. VI, 683
Brown, Samuel P VI, 626

Brown, Samuel P VI, 627
Brown, Samuel P. IV, 1149
Brown, Samuel P. VI, 618
Brown, Samuel P. VI, 622
Brown, Samuel P. VI, 625
Brown, Samuel P. VI, 626
Brown, Samuel P. VI, 628
Brown, Samuel P. VI, 702
Brown, Samuel P. VI, 711
Brown, Samuel P. VI, 712
Brown, Samuel S. V, 829
Brown, Samuel S. V, 830
Brown, Samuel Smith II, 167
Brown, Samuel W. III, 49
Brown, Samuel, Jr. I, 529
Brown, Samuel, Jr. I, 960
Brown, Samuel, Jr. I, 1027
Brown, Samuel, Jr. II, 784
Brown, Samuel, Jr. II, 811
Brown, Samuel, Jr. V, 728
Brown, Samuel, Jr. V, 729
Brown, Samuel, Jr. V, 798
Brown, Samuel, Jr. VI, 683
Brown, Samuel, Sr. I, 1027
Brown, Samuel, Sr. V, 728
Brown, Sandford III, 49
Brown, Sarah I, 208
Brown, Sarah I, 209
Brown, Sarah I, 231
Brown, Sarah I, 240
Brown, Sarah I, 268
Brown, Sarah I, 300
Brown, Sarah I, 347
Brown, Sarah I, 374
Brown, Sarah I, 375
Brown, Sarah I, 376
Brown, Sarah I, 380
Brown, Sarah I, 383
Brown, Sarah I, 777
Brown, Sarah I, 801
Brown, Sarah I, 805
Brown, Sarah I, 982
Brown, Sarah I, 994
Brown, Sarah I, 1043
Brown, Sarah I, 1047
Brown, Sarah I, 1055
Brown, Sarah I, 1140
Brown, Sarah II, 23
Brown, Sarah II, 58
Brown, Sarah II, 59
Brown, Sarah II, 86
Brown, Sarah II, 130
Brown, Sarah II, 198
Brown, Sarah II, 201
Brown, Sarah II, 308
Brown, Sarah II, 340
Brown, Sarah II, 468
Brown, Sarah II, 473
Brown, Sarah II, 474
Brown, Sarah II, 475
Brown, Sarah II, 477
Brown, Sarah II, 552
Brown, Sarah II, 668
Brown, Sarah II, 700
Brown, Sarah II, 954
Brown, Sarah II, 955
Brown, Sarah II, 964
Brown, Sarah II, 974
Brown, Sarah II, 982
Brown, Sarah II, 997
Brown, Sarah II, 1012
Brown, Sarah II, 1045
Brown, Sarah II, 1046
Brown, Sarah II, 1049
Brown, Sarah II, 1054
Brown, Sarah II, 1055
Brown, Sarah II, 1058
Brown, Sarah III, 28
Brown, Sarah III, 48
Brown, Sarah III, 49
Brown, Sarah III, 99
Brown, Sarah III, 129
Brown, Sarah III, 232
Brown, Sarah III, 259
Brown, Sarah IV, 22
Brown, Sarah IV, 23
Brown, Sarah IV, 76
Brown, Sarah IV, 92
Brown, Sarah IV, 181
Brown, Sarah IV, 465
Brown, Sarah IV, 613
Brown, Sarah IV, 685
Brown, Sarah IV, 801
Brown, Sarah IV, 803
Brown, Sarah IV, 804
Brown, Sarah IV, 852
Brown, Sarah IV, 853
Brown, Sarah IV, 891
Brown, Sarah IV, 893
Brown, Sarah IV, 895
Brown, Sarah IV, 930
Brown, Sarah IV, 1014
Brown, Sarah IV, 1050
Brown, Sarah V, 27
Brown, Sarah V, 28
Brown, Sarah V, 38
Brown, Sarah V, 102
Brown, Sarah V, 155
Brown, Sarah V, 159
Brown, Sarah V, 223
Brown, Sarah V, 224
Brown, Sarah V, 321
Brown, Sarah V, 452
Brown, Sarah V, 729
Brown, Sarah V, 779
Brown, Sarah V, 783
Brown, Sarah V, 798
Brown, Sarah V, 825
Brown, Sarah V, 826
Brown, Sarah V, 828
Brown, Sarah V, 829
Brown, Sarah V, 830
Brown, Sarah V, 831
Brown, Sarah V, 841
Brown, Sarah V, 845
Brown, Sarah V, 848
Brown, Sarah V, 854
Brown, Sarah V, 880
Brown, Sarah V, 881
Brown, Sarah V, 882
Brown, Sarah V, 884
Brown, Sarah V, 885
Brown, Sarah V, 949
Brown, Sarah V, 968
Brown, Sarah V, 987
Brown, Sarah VI, 371
Brown, Sarah VI, 372
Brown, Sarah VI, 373
Brown, Sarah VI, 404
Brown, Sarah VI, 442
Brown, Sarah VI, 449
Brown, Sarah VI, 451
Brown, Sarah VI, 460
Brown, Sarah VI, 462
Brown, Sarah VI, 467
Brown, Sarah VI, 468
Brown, Sarah VI, 475
Brown, Sarah VI, 476
Brown, Sarah VI, 477
Brown, Sarah VI, 479
Brown, Sarah VI, 483
Brown, Sarah VI, 516
Brown, Sarah VI, 538
Brown, Sarah VI, 544
Brown, Sarah VI, 546
Brown, Sarah VI, 548
Brown, Sarah VI, 551
Brown, Sarah VI, 555
Brown, Sarah VI, 556
Brown, Sarah VI, 558
Brown, Sarah VI, 572
Brown, Sarah VI, 577
Brown, Sarah VI, 583
Brown, Sarah VI, 591
Brown, Sarah VI, 592
Brown, Sarah VI, 593
Brown, Sarah VI, 601
Brown, Sarah VI, 602
Brown, Sarah VI, 603
Brown, Sarah VI, 621
Brown, Sarah VI, 622
Brown, Sarah VI, 623
Brown, Sarah VI, 624
Brown, Sarah VI, 625
Brown, Sarah VI, 626
Brown, Sarah VI, 627
Brown, Sarah VI, 628
Brown, Sarah VI, 649
Brown, Sarah VI, 679
Brown, Sarah VI, 680
Brown, Sarah VI, 682
Brown, Sarah VI, 683
Brown, Sarah VI, 685
Brown, Sarah VI, 689
Brown, Sarah VI, 690
Brown, Sarah VI, 710
Brown, Sarah VI, 711
Brown, Sarah VI, 714
Brown, Sarah VI, 718
Brown, Sarah VI, 723
Brown, Sarah VI, 729
Brown, Sarah VI, 733
Brown, Sarah VI, 734
Brown, Sarah VI, 769
Brown, Sarah VI, 776
Brown, Sarah VI, 801
Brown, Sarah VI, 840
Brown, Sarah VI, 880
Brown, Sarah VI, 883
Brown, Sarah VI, 884
Brown, Sarah VI, 927
Brown, Sarah VI, 958
Brown, Sarah VI, 970
Brown, Sarah VI, 989
Brown, Sarah A. V, 224
Brown, Sarah Ann II, 1046
Brown, Sarah Ann IV, 613
Brown, Sarah Ann IV, 804
Brown, Sarah Ann V, 224
Brown, Sarah Ann V, 299
Brown, Sarah Ann V, 829
Brown, Sarah Ann V, 831
Brown, Sarah Ann V, 869
Brown, Sarah Ann VI, 618
Brown, Sarah Ann VI, 621
Brown, Sarah Ann VI, 622
Brown, Sarah Ann VI, 623
Brown, Sarah Ann VI, 626
Brown, Sarah Ann VI, 675
Brown, Sarah Ann VI, 688
Brown, Sarah Ann VI, 689
Brown, Sarah Ann VI, 690
Brown, Sarah Ann VI, 695
Brown, Sarah Ann VI, 701
Brown, Sarah Ann VI, 884
Brown, Sarah Ann Elizabeth VI, 371
Brown, Sarah B. II, 317
Brown, Sarah C. II, 841
Brown, Sarah C. III, 49
Brown, Sarah C. V, 828
Brown, Sarah Clark III, 50
Brown, Sarah Clark III, 141
Brown, Sarah E. IV, 182
Brown, Sarah E. V, 829
Brown, Sarah E. V, 830
Brown, Sarah E. V, 987
Brown, Sarah Elizabeth VI, 625
Brown, Sarah Elizabeth VI, 626
Brown, Sarah Elizabeth VI, 682
Brown, Sarah Elizabeth VI, 699
Brown, Sarah F. III, 28
Brown, Sarah F. III, 48
Brown, Sarah G. II, 201
Brown, Sarah G. II, 282
Brown, Sarah G. II, 475
Brown, Sarah G. II, 729
Brown, Sarah G. II, 771
Brown, Sarah G. Twoney II, 729
Brown, Sarah H. III, 49
Brown, Sarah H. III, 181
Brown, Sarah H. III, 258
Brown, Sarah H. V, 299
Brown, Sarah H. V, 313
Brown, Sarah H. V, 320
Brown, Sarah H. V, 879
Brown, Sarah H. V, 880
Brown, Sarah H. VI, 372
Brown, Sarah H. VI, 373
Brown, Sarah H. VI, 448
Brown, Sarah H. VI, 568
Brown, Sarah J. I, 232
Brown, Sarah J. I, 252
Brown, Sarah J. V, 224
Brown, Sarah J. V, 881
Brown, Sarah Jane I, 209
Brown, Sarah Jane I, 223
Brown, Sarah Jane V, 224
Brown, Sarah Jane V, 949
Brown, Sarah Jane VI, 623
Brown, Sarah L. II, 955
Brown, Sarah L. II, 1069
Brown, Sarah L. V, 29
Brown, Sarah L. V, 139
Brown, Sarah M. VI, 943
Brown, Sarah N. V, 830
Brown, Sarah N. V, 880
Brown, Sarah N. VI, 371
Brown, Sarah N. VI, 734
Brown, Sarah S. III, 47
Brown, Sarah S. VI, 626
Brown, Sarah W. I, 873
Brown, Sarah W. II, 954
Brown, Sarah W. II, 955
Brown, Sarah W. II, 964
Brown, Sarah W. II, 1044
Brown, Sarah W. II, 1046
Brown, Sarah W. II, 1069
Brown, Sarah W. III, 49
Brown, Sarah W. VI, 373
Brown, Sarah, Sr. II, 1045
Brown, Sary VI, 891
Brown, Selah I, 592
Brown, Seth I, 777
Brown, Seth V, 28
Brown, Seth V, 29
Brown, Seth V, 72
Brown, Seth V, 829
Brown, Shadrach S. V, 224
Brown, Shadrack VI, 883
Brown, Shadrack VI, 884
Brown, Shadrick VI, 860
Brown, Sherman IV, 182
Brown, Sherman H. IV, 182
Brown, Sibyl L. I, 262
Brown, Sidney F. V, 661
Brown, Silas IV, 372
Brown, Simon I, 974
Brown, Simon W. V, 224
Brown, Sinah IV, 515
Brown, Sinah IV, 520
Brown, Sinthia VI, 1020
Brown, Sirena I, 802
Brown, Sisley VI, 592
Brown, Sol. I, 1149
Brown, Solomon I, 974
Brown, Solomon I, 982
Brown, Solomon I, 1081
Brown, Solomon I, 1090
Brown, Solomon I, 1139
Brown, Solomon I, 1140
Brown, Solomon I, 1144
Brown, Solomon I, 1149
Brown, Solomon I, 1157
Brown, Sophia II, 186
Brown, Sophia Robinson VI, 476
Brown, Sophronia I, 209
Brown, Sophronia R. I, 232
Brown, Sophronia R. I, 802
Brown, Spicer II, 341
Brown, Spotswood VI, 884
Brown, Stacy II, 982
Brown, Stark VI, 883
Brown, Stephen III, 49
Brown, Stephen IV, 372
Brown, Stephen IV, 410
Brown, Stephen IV, 685
Brown, Stephen IV, 739
Brown, Stephen VI, 372
Brown, Stephen VI, 477
Brown, Stephen C. III, 49
Brown, Stewart III, 49
Brown, Susan III, 49
Brown, Susan IV, 1308
Brown, Susan VI, 587
Brown, Susan VI, 616
Brown, Susan VI, 625
Brown, Susan VI, 626
Brown, Susan VI, 654
Brown, Susan VI, 679
Brown, Susan A. II, 841
Brown, Susan F. I, 873
Brown, Susan H. I, 335
Brown, Susan J. II, 955
Brown, Susan J. II, 967
Brown, Susan J. II, 1046
Brown, Susan J. II, 1051
Brown, Susan J. II, 1058
Brown, Susan Parthenia VI, 626
Brown, Susan Parthenia VI, 628
Brown, Susan Parthenia VI, 700
Brown, Susan Parthenia VI, 719
Brown, Susan R. III, 49
Brown, Susan S. II, 730
Brown, Susan S. V, 881
Brown, Susan Sansom II, 729
Brown, Susana I, 209
Brown, Susann II, 201
Brown, Susanna I, 231
Brown, Susanna I, 236
Brown, Susanna I, 801
Brown, Susanna I, 974
Brown, Susanna I, 982
Brown, Susanna I, 986
Brown, Susanna II, 234
Brown, Susanna II, 276
Brown, Susanna II, 474
Brown, Susanna II, 602
Brown, Susanna IV, 181
Brown, Susanna IV, 296
Brown, Susanna IV, 1273
Brown, Susanna IV, 1286
Brown, Susanna V, 28
Brown, Susanna V, 29
Brown, Susanna V, 100
Brown, Susanna V, 844
Brown, Susanna VI, 471
Brown, Susanna VI, 592
Brown, Susanna VI, 624
Brown, Susanna VI, 884
Brown, Susanna A. VI, 828
Brown, Susanna R. II, 282
Brown, Susanna R. II, 710
Brown, Susanna Sansom II, 341
Brown, Susannah I, 347
Brown, Susannah I, 873
Brown, Susannah I, 902
Brown, Susannah II, 167
Brown, Susannah II, 201
Brown, Susannah II, 209
Brown, Susannah II, 226
Brown, Susannah II, 253
Brown, Susannah II, 282
Brown, Susannah II, 307
Brown, Susannah II, 474
Brown, Susannah II, 829
Brown, Susannah II, 955
Brown, Susannah II, 981
Brown, Susannah II, 982
Brown, Susannah II, 1000
Brown, Susannah II, 1042
Brown, Susannah III, 49
Brown, Susannah IV, 804
Brown, Susannah IV, 825
Brown, Susannah IV, 1273
Brown, Susannah V, 831
Brown, Susannah V, 849
Brown, Susannah VI, 371
Brown, Susannah VI, 372
Brown, Susannah VI, 387
Brown, Susannah VI, 434
Brown, Susannah VI, 477
Brown, Susannah VI, 535
Brown, Susannah VI, 542
Brown, Susannah VI, 569
Brown, Susannah VI, 592
Brown, Susannah VI, 602
Brown, Susannah VI, 769
Brown, Susannah VI, 771
Brown, Susannah L. V, 831
Brown, Susannah R. II, 167
Brown, Susannah R. II, 282
Brown, Susie IV, 1203
Brown, Sydney V, 661
Brown, T. Janney VI, 627
Brown, T. Wister II, 700
Brown, Tabby VI, 994
Brown, Tabitha VI, 873
Brown, Tabitha VI, 883
Brown, Tabitha VI, 884
Brown, Tacy IV, 372
Brown, Tacy IV, 417
Brown, Tacy IV, 569
Brown, Tacy IV, 586
Brown, Tacy VI, 622
Brown, Tacy VI, 688
Brown, Tamar V, 754
Brown, Tamer V, 829
Brown, Tamer V, 880
Brown, Tamer VI, 626
Brown, Tamer VI, 674
Brown, Tamson W. IV, 803
Brown, Tarlton VI, 801
Brown, Thaddeus II, 340
Brown, Thelma V, 225
Brown, Theodata Pope VI, 625
Brown, Theodore IV, 182
Brown, Thomas I, 131
Brown, Thomas I, 347
Brown, Thomas I, 370
Brown, Thomas I, 375
Brown, Thomas I, 376
Brown, Thomas I, 492
Brown, Thomas I, 528
Brown, Thomas I, 563
Brown, Thomas I, 801
Brown, Thomas I, 974
Brown, Thomas I, 982
Brown, Thomas I, 988
Brown, Thomas I, 1081
Brown, Thomas I, 1090
Brown, Thomas I, 1094
Brown, Thomas II, 58
Brown, Thomas II, 93
Brown, Thomas II, 167
Brown, Thomas II, 341
Brown, Thomas II, 473
Brown, Thomas II, 504
Brown, Thomas II, 568
Brown, Thomas II, 826
Brown, Thomas II, 955
Brown, Thomas II, 971
Brown, Thomas II, 981
Brown, Thomas II, 982
Brown, Thomas III, 49
Brown, Thomas III, 204
Brown, Thomas IV, 76
Brown, Thomas IV, 86
Brown, Thomas IV, 803
Brown, Thomas IV, 804
Brown, Thomas IV, 1273
Brown, Thomas V, 28
Brown, Thomas V, 224
Brown, Thomas V, 551
Brown, Thomas V, 729
Brown, Thomas V, 830
Brown, Thomas V, 949
Brown, Thomas VI, 371
Brown, Thomas VI, 372
Brown, Thomas VI, 455
Brown, Thomas VI, 470
Brown, Thomas VI, 618
Brown, Thomas VI, 621
Brown, Thomas VI, 622
Brown, Thomas VI, 623

Brown, Thomas VI, 625
Brown, Thomas VI, 626
Brown, Thomas VI, 627
Brown, Thomas VI, 655
Brown, Thomas VI, 682
Brown, Thomas VI, 683
Brown, Thomas VI, 696
Brown, Thomas VI, 702
Brown, Thomas VI, 703
Brown, Thomas VI, 710
Brown, Thomas VI, 714
Brown, Thomas VI, 734
Brown, Thomas VI, 882
Brown, Thomas VI, 884
Brown, Thomas VI, 909
Brown, Thomas VI, 947
Brown, Thomas VI, 953
Brown, Thomas VI, 974
Brown, Thomas VI, 990
Brown, Thomas C. II, 700
Brown, Thomas Chalkley II, 201
Brown, Thomas Chalkley II, 475
Brown, Thomas Clarkson V, 829
Brown, Thomas H. I, 1081
Brown, Thomas H. I, 1090
Brown, Thomas H. I, 1140
Brown, Thomas H. III, 49
Brown, Thomas H., Jr. III, 49
Brown, Thomas J. VI, 800
Brown, Thomas Janney VI, 686
Brown, Thomas Janney VI, 733
Brown, Thomas Janney VI, 769
Brown, Thomas Janney VI, 773
Brown, Thomas K. II, 730
Brown, Thomas Kite II, 700
Brown, Thomas L. IV, 1203
Brown, Thomas Lucius IV, 1203
Brown, Thomas M. VI, 622
Brown, Thomas Magdalen II, 474
Brown, Thomas Mc herson VI, 627
Brown, Thomas R. VI, 940
Brown, Thomas S. II, 730
Brown, Thomas Stewardson II, 700
Brown, Thomas Stewardson II, 729
Brown, Thomas W. VI, 884
Brown, Thomas W. VI, 943
Brown, Thomas Wistar II, 341
Brown, Thomas Wistar II, 730
Brown, Thomas Wistar II, 739
Brown, Thomas, Jr. I, 528
Brown, Thomas, Jr. I, 974
Brown, Thomas, Jr. I, 982
Brown, Thomas, Jr. II, 474
Brown, Thomas, Jr. III, 49
Brown, Thomas, Sen. I, 1081
Brown, Thomasine II, 167
Brown, Thomson V, 831
Brown, Thornton Edward III, 47
Brown, Thos. I, 347
Brown, Thos. II, 24
Brown, Thos. IV, 900
Brown, Thos. V, 728
Brown, Thos. VI, 477
Brown, Thos. VI, 683
Brown, Thos. H. III, 47
Brown, Thos. H. III, 48
Brown, Thos. H. III, 49
Brown, Thos. H. III, 167
Brown, Thos. O. VI, 927
Brown, Thos. S. IV, 1273
Brown, Thos. S. IV, 1283
Brown, Thurman J. V, 224
Brown, Tilton II, 341
Brown, Timothy IV, 76
Brown, Timothy IV, 803
Brown, Timothy IV, 804
Brown, Timothy IV, 825
Brown, Timothy VI, 372
Brown, Uriah I, 1026
Brown, V. Kenneth IV, 1308
Brown, Valeria V, 831
Brown, Valeria Jane V, 830
Brown, Vernon I, 630
Brown, Vernon Lee I, 613
Brown, Vernon Lee I, 630
Brown, Vernon Lee III, 49
Brown, Vernon Luther I, 613
Brown, Victor I, 938
Brown, Victor Hugo I, 922
Brown, Vilet VI, 883
Brown, Vinta V, 452
Brown, Viola Mary V, 29
Brown, Violet VI, 884
Brown, Violetta II, 982
Brown, Violetta II, 1023
Brown, Virgin II, 167
Brown, Virgin II, 201
Brown, Virgin II, 224
Brown, Virgin V, 28
Brown, Virgin V, 614
Brown, Virgin V, 643
Brown, Virgin V, 828
Brown, Virgin V, 829
Brown, Virgin V, 830
Brown, Virgin V, 854
Brown, Virgin V, 880
Brown, Virginia V, 949
Brown, Virginia C. V, 949
Brown, Virginia Neill VI, 627
Brown, Virginia Neill VI, 734
Brown, Virtin V, 29
Brown, W. Brewer III, 50
Brown, W. G. VI, 825
Brown, W. J. I, 232
Brown, W. J. I, 260
Brown, W. Jordan I, 23
Brown, W. P. IV, 1203
Brown, Walker VI, 884
Brown, Walker VI, 886
Brown, Walker VI, 907
Brown, Walter I, 131
Brown, Walter I, 209
Brown, Walter I, 231
Brown, Walter I, 232
Brown, Walter I, 246
Brown, Walter IV, 356
Brown, Walter IV, 1308
Brown, Walter V, 321
Brown, Walter C. VI, 622
Brown, Walter C. VI, 624
Brown, Walter C. VI, 625
Brown, Walter C. VI, 626
Brown, Walter C. VI, 627
Brown, Walter C. VI, 631
Brown, Walter C. VI, 636
Brown, Walter C. VI, 650
Brown, Walter C. VI, 691
Brown, Walter Clayton VI, 626
Brown, Walter Clayton VI, 627
Brown, Walter Clayton VI, 636
Brown, Walter Clayton VI, 691
Brown, Walter H. IV, 1247
Brown, Walter J. I, 208
Brown, Walter J. I, 209
Brown, Walter J. I, 232
Brown, Walter J., Jr. I, 209
Brown, Walter J., Jr. I, 232
Brown, Walter Jay I, 208
Brown, Walter W. IV, 1247
Brown, Walter W. IV, 1308
Brown, Warner VI, 627
Brown, Wd. Catharine III, 47
Brown, Wd. Elizabeth IV, 76
Brown, Wd. Elizabeth H. II, 784
Brown, Wd. Magdalen II, 341
Brown, Wd. Mary V, 830
Brown, Wd. Mary VI, 476
Brown, Wd. Naomi VI, 592
Brown, Wd. Phebe III, 508
Brown, Wd. Sarah II, 341
Brown, Wd. Sarah II, 474
Brown, Wd. Sarah II, 523
Brown, Wd. Sarah E. V, 839
Brown, Wd. Susanna II, 167
Brown, Wd. Susannah VI, 467
Brown, Whittier VI, 622
Brown, Whittier B. VI, 622
Brown, Whittier B. VI, 734
Brown, Widow Esther Allen VI, 622
Brown, Widow Esther Allen VI, 643
Brown, Widow Mary VI, 551
Brown, Widow Mary M. Scott VI, 511
Brown, Widow May I, 528
Brown, Widow Rebecca VI, 621
Brown, Wiiliam IV, 891
Brown, Wilbur V, 881
Brown, Wilbur H. I, 262
Brown, Will VI, 795
Brown, William I, 131
Brown, William I, 208
Brown, William I, 209
Brown, William I, 231
Brown, William I, 232
Brown, William I, 254
Brown, William I, 343
Brown, William I, 347
Brown, William I, 375
Brown, William I, 376
Brown, William I, 492
Brown, William I, 528
Brown, William I, 586
Brown, William I, 592
Brown, William I, 777
Brown, William I, 801
Brown, William I, 960
Brown, William I, 971
Brown, William I, 974
Brown, William I, 982
Brown, William I, 1043
Brown, William I, 1081
Brown, William I, 1090
Brown, William II, 167
Brown, William II, 201
Brown, William II, 226
Brown, William II, 282
Brown, William II, 341
Brown, William II, 981
Brown, William II, 982
Brown, William II, 1041
Brown, William III, 48
Brown, William III, 49
Brown, William III, 214
Brown, William III, 397
Brown, William IV, 76
Brown, William IV, 181
Brown, William IV, 182
Brown, William IV, 685
Brown, William IV, 930
Brown, William V, 28
Brown, William V, 224
Brown, William V, 320
Brown, William V, 321
Brown, William V, 551
Brown, William V, 614
Brown, William V, 828
Brown, William V, 829
Brown, William V, 830
Brown, William V, 831
Brown, William VI, 56
Brown, William VI, 371
Brown, William VI, 372
Brown, William VI, 373
Brown, William VI, 377
Brown, William VI, 406
Brown, William VI, 416
Brown, William VI, 442
Brown, William VI, 444
Brown, William VI, 477
Brown, William VI, 491
Brown, William VI, 505
Brown, William VI, 540
Brown, William VI, 555
Brown, William VI, 558
Brown, William VI, 571
Brown, William VI, 622
Brown, William VI, 623
Brown, William VI, 624
Brown, William VI, 626
Brown, William VI, 627
Brown, William VI, 658
Brown, William VI, 665
Brown, William VI, 686
Brown, William VI, 733
Brown, William VI, 801
Brown, William VI, 879
Brown, William VI, 883
Brown, William VI, 891
Brown, William VI, 914
Brown, William A. II, 341
Brown, William A. III, 50
Brown, William C. VI, 679
Brown, William E. V, 551
Brown, William H. I, 232
Brown, William H. II, 308
Brown, William H. II, 317
Brown, William H. IV, 685
Brown, William H. V, 321
Brown, William H. VI, 367
Brown, William H. VI, 371
Brown, William H. VI, 372
Brown, William H. VI, 373
Brown, William H. VI, 374
Brown, William H. VI, 457
Brown, William H. VI, 462
Brown, William H. VI, 625
Brown, William H. VI, 719
Brown, William H. VI, 721
Brown, William H. VI, 801
Brown, William H. VI, 884
Brown, William H. VI, 951
Brown, William H. VI, 986
Brown, William H. VI, 989
Brown, William Hardy VI, 733
Brown, William Hardy VI, 753
Brown, William Henry I, 209
Brown, William Henry II, 955
Brown, William Henry VI, 622
Brown, William Henry VI, 625
Brown, William Henry VI, 628
Brown, William Henry VI, 682
Brown, William Holmes VI, 625
Brown, William Hunt VI, 371
Brown, William Hunt VI, 538
Brown, William Hunt VI, 734
Brown, William Hunt VI, 769
Brown, William Hunt VI, 791
Brown, William J. I, 231
Brown, William J. I, 232
Brown, William J. I, 756
Brown, William J. I, 770
Brown, William J. I, 1090
Brown, William J. I, 1139
Brown, William J. I, 1149
Brown, William Johnson I, 1081
Brown, William Jordon I, 208
Brown, William Jordon I, 209
Brown, William K. VI, 801
Brown, William K. VI, 842
Brown, William K. VI, 857
Brown, William K. VI, 860
Brown, William L. II, 317
Brown, William Lawson V, 614
Brown, William M. III, 50
Brown, William Penn IV, 1203
Brown, William R. II, 341
Brown, William S. II, 308
Brown, William S. II, 700
Brown, William T. I, 208
Brown, William T. V, 661
Brown, William Townsend VI, 622
Brown, William Townsend VI, 702
Brown, William V. V, 829
Brown, William, Jr. I, 375
Brown, William, Jr. I, 376
Brown, William, Jr. I, 982
Brown, William, Jr. II, 282
Brown, William, Jr. VI, 373
Brown, William, Jr. VI, 587
Brown, William, Sr. VI, 373
Brown, Willie VI, 56
Brown, Willie N. I, 209
Brown, Wilson VI, 855
Brown, Wilson S. VI, 371
Brown, Wilson S. VI, 734
Brown, Wm Townsend VI, 702
Brown, Wm. I, 217
Brown, Wm. I, 223
Brown, Wm. I, 347
Brown, Wm. I, 365
Brown, Wm. I, 375
Brown, Wm. I, 376
Brown, Wm. II, 58
Brown, Wm. II, 116
Brown, Wm. II, 468
Brown, Wm. II, 473
Brown, Wm. II, 474
Brown, Wm. II, 602
Brown, Wm. II, 660
Brown, Wm. II, 686
Brown, Wm. II, 982
Brown, Wm. II, 1046
Brown, Wm. IV, 76
Brown, Wm. IV, 804
Brown, Wm. IV, 930
Brown, Wm. IV, 933
Brown, Wm. V, 299
Brown, Wm. V, 320
Brown, Wm. V, 321
Brown, Wm. V, 661
Brown, Wm. V, 880
Brown, Wm. V, 949
Brown, Wm. VI, 430
Brown, Wm. VI, 470
Brown, Wm. VI, 475
Brown, Wm. VI, 477
Brown, Wm. VI, 511
Brown, Wm. VI, 556
Brown, Wm. VI, 571
Brown, Wm. VI, 587
Brown, Wm. VI, 621
Brown, Wm. VI, 626
Brown, Wm. VI, 650
Brown, Wm. VI, 665
Brown, Wm. VI, 667
Brown, Wm. VI, 683
Brown, Wm. VI, 711
Brown, Wm. VI, 712
Brown, Wm. VI, 718
Brown, Wm. A. II, 729
Brown, Wm. A. II, 730
Brown, Wm. B. VI, 476
Brown, Wm. B. VI, 753
Brown, Wm. Barker III, 50
Brown, Wm. C. VI, 621
Brown, Wm. C. VI, 625
Brown, Wm. C. VI, 626
Brown, Wm. C. VI, 682
Brown, Wm. C. VI, 690
Brown, Wm. C. VI, 710
Brown, Wm. C. VI, 711
Brown, Wm. Clayton VI, 621
Brown, Wm. H. IV, 1308
Brown, Wm. H. VI, 374
Brown, Wm. H. VI, 621
Brown, Wm. H. VI, 623
Brown, Wm. H. VI, 624
Brown, Wm. H. VI, 626
Brown, Wm. H. VI, 635
Brown, Wm. H. VI, 638
Brown, Wm. H. VI, 648
Brown, Wm. H. VI, 652
Brown, Wm. H. VI, 686
Brown, Wm. H. VI, 719
Brown, Wm. Henry II, 130
Brown, Wm. Henry II, 1046
Brown, Wm. Henry II, 1052
Brown, Wm. Henry VI, 681
Brown, Wm. Herbert VI, 628
Brown, Wm. Herbert VI, 702
Brown, Wm. K. VI, 810
Brown, Wm. L. V, 614
Brown, Wm. R. II, 475
Brown, Wm. S. II, 1069
Brown, Wm. T. II, 24
Brown, Wm. T. V, 614
Brown, Wm. Thomas II, 841
Brown, Wm. Thomas J. II, 841
Brown, Wm. Townsend VI, 622
Brown, Wm. Townsend VI, 626
Brown, Wm. Townsend VI, 628
Brown, Wm. Townsend VI, 631
Brown, Wm. Townsend VI, 635
Brown, Wm. V. V, 879
Brown, Wm. V. V, 880
Brown, Wm. W. IV, 1308
Brown, Wm. W. IV, 1323
Brown, Wm. Weston IV, 803
Brown, Wm. Weston IV, 804
Brown, Wm., Jr. II, 58
Brown, Wm., Jr. II, 474
Brown, Wm., Jr. II, 568
Brown, Wm., Jr. V, 614
Brown, Wm., Jr. VI, 518
Brown, Yardley T. VI, 374
Brown, Yardley T. VI, 477
Brown, Yardley T. VI, 508
Brown, Yardley T. VI, 626
Brown, Yardley T. VI, 627
Brown, Yardley T. VI, 628
Brown, Yardley T. VI, 655
Brown, Zachariah VI, 946
Brown, Zacharias IV, 1269
Brown, Zacheus IV, 181
Brown, Zacheus IV, 1273
Brown, Zacheus IV, 1286
Brown, Zeri V, 831
Brown, Zeri H. V, 830
Brown, Zeri H. V, 831
Brown, Zimri V, 829
Brown-McPherson, Elizabeth VI, 754
Brown-Parkins, Susannah VI, 729
Browne, Annie Laura VI, 662
Browne, Annie Laura VI, 733
Browne, Catharine VI, 475
Browne, J. J. III, 219
Browne, John VI, 29
Browne, Joseph II, 58
Browne, Mary II, 341
Browne, Mary II, 473
Browne, Mary II, 1069
Browne, Mary R. II, 841
Browne, Mary R. II, 1045
Browne, Mehitabel VI, 733
Browne, Mr. Thomas VI, 9
Browne, Mrs. Wm. Henry IV, 1247
Browne, Nathaniel II, 341
Browne, Rebecca II, 474
Browne, Rose III, 219
Browne, Sarah II, 473
Browne, Susanna VI, 11
Browne, Thomas VI, 11
Browne, Viola III, 18
Browne, Viola III, 219
Browne, William Hardy VI, 73
Browne, Wm., Jr. II, 474
Brownel, Eliza IV, 1355
Brownel, Phebe IV, 1355
Brownell, Ann Eliza IV, 1352
Brownell, Ann Eliza IV, 1354
Brownell, Ann Eliza IV, 1355
Brownell, Charles IV, 1355
Brownell, Charles Stuart IV, 1354
Brownell, David Sands IV, 135
Brownell, Elijah IV, 1354
Brownell, Elijah IV, 1355
Brownell, Elisabeth IV, 1354
Brownell, Elizabeth II, 341
Brownell, Elizabeth IV, 1355
Brownell, Elizabeth Margaret IV, 1354
Brownell, Franklin IV, 1354
Brownell, Franklin IV, 1355
Brownell, Hannah IV, 1355

Brownell, Hannah M. IV, 1354
Brownell, Hannah M. IV, 1355
Brownell, Hannah M. IV, 1380
Brownell, James Russel IV, 1354
Brownell, James Russel IV, 1355
Brownell, Joseph IV, 1355
Brownell, Joseph S. IV, 1354
Brownell, Judith IV, 1354
Brownell, Judith IV, 1355
Brownell, Laura Jane IV, 1355
Brownell, Lindley M. IV, 1354
Brownell, Mary IV, 1354
Brownell, Mary IV, 1355
Brownell, Milton IV, 1354
Brownell, Phebe IV, 1354
Brownell, Phebe IV, 1355
Brownell, Phebe S. IV, 1355
Brownell, Roby Jane IV, 1355
Brownell, Sands IV, 1354
Brownell, Sands IV, 1355
Brownell, Sands IV, 1380
Brownell, Shadrack IV, 1354
Brownell, Susan IV, 1351
Brownell, Susan IV, 1354
Brownell, Susan IV, 1355
Brownell, Thomas IV, 1354
Brownell, Thomas IV, 1355
Brownell, Walter IV, 1354
Brownell, Walter E. IV, 1354
Brownell, William IV, 1354
Brownell, William Aikens IV, 1354
Brownfield, Allenor VI, 374
Brownfield, Eilizabeth VI, 389
Brownfield, Elizabeth VI, 374
Browning, Alice I, 951
Browning, Alma Eugenie III, 50
Browning, Ann VI, 593
Browning, Ann VI, 601
Browning, Betsey VI, 885
Browning, Caleb VI, 885
Browning, Clarence P. III, 261
Browning, Clarence Perry III, 50
Browning, Elizabeth II, 475
Browning, Eunice III, 50
Browning, Eunice III, 261
Browning, Eva B. III, 50
Browning, Eva S. III, 261
Browning, Eva Stanton III, 50
Browning, Julia Ann III, 50
Browning, Lydia V, 224
Browning, Lydia V, 225
Browning, Marion E. III, 50
Browning, Martha F. III, 50
Browning, Mary III, 50
Browning, Mary III, 123
Browning, Oscar III, 50
Browning, Oscar F. III, 50
Browning, Oscar F. III, 123
Browning, Paul Babcock III, 50
Browning, Perry M. III, 50
Browning, Robert Stanton III, 50
Brownlow, Benjamin I, 605
Brownlow, Jane II, 475
Brownlow, Mary II, 842
Brownlow, Mary H. II, 842
Browns, Clara R. III, 140
Browns, Esther S. III, 140
Browns, George S. III, 140
Browns, Henry R. III, 140
Browns, Mary E. III, 140
Browns, Thos H. III, 140
Brownson, Wd. Eunice III, 50
Browse, Annie S. III, 49
Broxsom, Ann VI, 323
Broxsom, James VI, 323
Broxsom, Sarah VI, 323
Broxsom, William, Jr. VI, 323
Broyler, S. N. IV, 1247
Brubaker, Clara Jane V, 729
Brubaker, Edith N. II, 842
Brubaker, Edith N. II, 903
Brubaker, James V, 729
Brubaker, Lula V, 729
Bruce, Albert VI, 885
Bruce, Alfred VI, 885
Bruce, Ambrose VI, 885
Bruce, Ann II, 475
Bruce, Ann VI, 374
Bruce, Balsaroe VI, 801
Bruce, Catharine VI, 885
Bruce, Charles V, 478
Bruce, Charles M. V, 478
Bruce, Coleman VI, 801
Bruce, David VI, 884
Bruce, David VI, 885
Bruce, Elizabeth I, 268
Bruce, Elizabeth I, 275
Bruce, Elizabeth II, 453
Bruce, Elizabeth II, 475
Bruce, Elizabeth II, 478
Bruce, Elizabeth VI, 962
Bruce, Elizabeth Bruce II, 475
Bruce, Emeline IV, 465
Bruce, Eunice V, 30
Bruce, Eunice V, 103
Bruce, Frances VI, 884
Bruce, George IV, 465
Bruce, George VI, 374
Bruce, George VI, 453
Bruce, George VI, 962
Bruce, George K. VI, 885
Bruce, George O. IV, 465
Bruce, Jane VI, 374
Bruce, Jane VI, 421
Bruce, Jane VI, 885
Bruce, Jane A. E. VI, 885
Bruce, Jerusha VI, 885
Bruce, Jerusha Jane VI, 885
Bruce, John IV, 182
Bruce, Lydia VI, 374
Bruce, Lydia VI, 410
Bruce, Martha Jane IV, 1128
Bruce, Martha Jane IV, 1132
Bruce, Mary I, 797
Bruce, Mary I, 802
Bruce, Mary VI, 374
Bruce, Mary Annesley II, 475
Bruce, Milly VI, 885
Bruce, Morton VI, 802
Bruce, Mrs. F. H. IV, 1308
Bruce, Nancy VI, 885
Bruce, Patience VI, 885
Bruce, Rachel VI, 374
Bruce, Sarah VI, 374
Bruce, Sarah VI, 453
Bruce, Sarah VI, 1000
Bruce, Susanna IV, 569
Bruce, Susanna IV, 579
Bruce, Thomas VI, 944
Bruce, Treva IV, 1308
Bruce, Veny VI, 930
Bruce, William VI, 884
Bruce, William VI, 885
Bruce, William VI, 930
Bruce, William D. VI, 885
Bruck, Catharine II, 475
Bruck, Catharine IV, 685
Bruck, Catharine IV, 804
Bruck, Catharone IV, 804
Bruck, Catherine II, 341
Bruck, Catherine IV, 804
Bruck, David Townsend IV, 804
Bruck, Edwin II, 341
Bruck, Edwin IV, 804
Bruck, Edwin A. Atlee II, 475
Bruck, Eliza II, 475
Bruck, Elizabeth II, 341
Bruck, Elizabeth IV, 804
Bruck, Francis A. II, 341
Bruck, Francis Anthony II, 475
Bruck, Katharine IV, 804
Bruck, Louisa IV, 804
Bruck, Ollita IV, 804
Bruck, W. A. II, 341
Bruck, William A. II, 341
Bruck, William A. IV, 685
Bruck, William A. IV, 804
Bruck, Wm. II, 475
Bruck, Wm. IV, 804
Bruck, Wm. A. II, 475
Bruck, Wm. A. IV, 804
Brudehan, Angelina IV, 1149
Brudehan, Mahlon IV, 1149
Bruer, Anne VI, 1017
Bruer, Richard VI, 1000
Bruer, Richard VI, 1017
Bruer, Sackvill VI, 161
Bruer, Sackvill VI, 219
Bruer, Sackville VI, 205
Bruey, Alfred IV, 1036
Bruey, Alice IV, 1036
Bruey, August IV, 1036
Bruey, Gladys Victoria IV, 1036
Bruey, Helen Mae IV, 1036
Bruey, Mary Ann IV, 1036
Bruff, Adna Louisa IV, 931
Bruff, Anna Louisa IV, 931
Bruff, Anna M. IV, 686
Bruff, Anna M. IV, 746
Bruff, Anna M. IV, 931
Bruff, Anna M. IV, 983
Bruff, Anna Marie IV, 931
Bruff, Beulah IV, 931
Bruff, Charles II, 475
Bruff, Charles III, 50
Bruff, Charles III, 245
Bruff, Charles IV, 685
Bruff, Charles IV, 931
Bruff, Charles, Jr. III, 50
Bruff, Chas. III, 50
Bruff, Christopher III, 50
Bruff, Christopher IV, 685
Bruff, Edward Ogden IV, 931
Bruff, Elizabeth IV, 931
Bruff, Elizabeth IV, 973
Bruff, Esther IV, 931
Bruff, Hannah III, 50
Bruff, Hannah III, 245
Bruff, Hannah IV, 685
Bruff, Hannah IV, 931
Bruff, Hannah IV, 1015
Bruff, Harison P. III, 50
Bruff, Harrison III, 15
Bruff, Henrietta IV, 931
Bruff, James IV, 746
Bruff, James B. IV, 685
Bruff, James B. IV, 686
Bruff, James B. IV, 743
Bruff, James B. IV, 922
Bruff, James B. IV, 941
Bruff, James B. IV, 973
Bruff, James B. IV, 983
Bruff, James B. IV, 1015
Bruff, James B., Jr. IV, 931
Bruff, James Berry III, 50
Bruff, James Morris IV, 931
Bruff, James Russell IV, 931
Bruff, Jessie F. IV, 931
Bruff, Jessie H. IV, 931
Bruff, Joseph IV, 685
Bruff, Joseph IV, 746
Bruff, Joseph IV, 931
Bruff, Joseph IV, 983
Bruff, Joseph Carroll IV, 931
Bruff, Lydia IV, 746
Bruff, Lydia IV, 931
Bruff, Lydia IV, 983
Bruff, Lydia B. IV, 685
Bruff, Lydia B. IV, 686
Bruff, Lydia B. IV, 746
Bruff, Lydia B. IV, 931
Bruff, Martha H. IV, 931
Bruff, Mary III, 50
Bruff, Mary IV, 685
Bruff, Mary IV, 922
Bruff, Mary IV, 931
Bruff, Phebe III, 15
Bruff, Phebe Ann III, 50
Bruff, Phebe P. III, 50
Bruff, Richard P. III, 50
Bruff, Sarah IV, 685
Bruff, Sarah IV, 743
Bruff, Sarah IV, 746
Bruff, Sarah IV, 922
Bruff, Sarah IV, 931
Bruff, Sarah IV, 941
Bruff, Sarah IV, 973
Bruff, Sarah IV, 983
Bruff, Sarah IV, 1015
Bruff, Sibyl IV, 931
Bruff, Sibyl IV, 940
Bruff, Susan IV, 931
Bruff, Wd. Hannah F. III, 50
Bruff, Wd. Hannah T. III, 15
Bruff, Wm. C. IV, 931
Bruff, Wm. Cortland IV, 931
Bruff, Wm. L. V, 896
Bruho, Albina II, 473
Bruho, Albina II, 482
Bruling, Zella V, 987
Brumbaugh, ??? VI, 294
Brumbaugh, Eva V, 729
Brumbaugh, Mrsl Pearl V, 729
Brumbaugh, Pearl V, 729
Brumfield, Cynthia VI, 801
Brumfield, Elisha VI, 801
Brumfield, James VI, 801
Brumfield, Mary VI, 801
Brumwell, Mary Eva I, 938
Brumwell, Mary Eva I, 943
Brun, Paschal VI, 1020
Brunbaugh, Eva V, 729
Brunbaugh, Mrsl Pearl V, 729
Brunbaugh, Pearl V, 729
Brunch, Elizabeth C. VI, 883
Brunck, Loretta III, 50
Brundage, Mary Amanda III, 82
Brundage, Mary Amando III, 166
Brundage, Sarah E. III, 174
Brune, Wilhelmina VI, 787
Brunell, Carrie IV, 1203
Brunell, Cora IV, 1203
Brunell, Mildred IV, 1203
Brunell, Nettie IV, 1203
Brunell, Paul IV, 1203
Brunell, Perry IV, 1203
Bruner, Henry IV, 1247
Bruner, John IV, 1247
Brunner, ??? III, 50
Brunner, Annie III, 50
Brunner, Elizabeth II, 475
Brunner, Henry III, 50
Bruno, Helen Mae V, 896
Brunson, Cortland V, 661
Brunson, Courtland V, 661
Brunson, Eliza V, 661
Brunson, Elizabeth V, 375
Brunson, Elizabeth V, 419
Brunson, Mariah W. V, 614
Brunson, Mariah W. V, 635
Brunson, Mary Belle V, 661
Bruscbanks, Anna VI, 885
Bruscbanks, Edward VI, 885
Bruse, Mary I, 802
Brush, Charles II, 341
Brush, Cornelius III, 50
Brush, Elizabeth III, 480
Brush, Elizabeth III, 502
Brush, Mary II, 341
Brush, Mary III, 50
Brwon, James VI, 994
Bryan, ??? III, 160
Bryan, ??? III, 161
Bryan, Achilles G. V, 552
Bryan, Agnes VI, 818
Bryan, Agness VI, 795
Bryan, Andrew VI, 795
Bryan, Andrew VI, 885
Bryan, Andrew W. VI, 815
Bryan, Ann II, 475
Bryan, Ann II, 476
Bryan, Ann V, 729
Bryan, Anna E. V, 662
Bryan, Anne VI, 801
Bryan, Benjamin II, 341
Bryan, Benjamin II, 475
Bryan, Benjamin II, 476
Bryan, Benjamin II, 488
Bryan, Benjamin, Jr. II, 476
Bryan, Bridget VI, 801
Bryan, Caroline H. II, 311
Bryan, Catharine VI, 801
Bryan, Catharine VI, 807
Bryan, Catharine VI, 851
Bryan, Catharine VI, 885
Bryan, Charity II, 200
Bryan, Charity IV, 954
Bryan, Clara Belle V, 662
Bryan, Daniel E. VI, 801
Bryan, Darby III, 50
Bryan, Eli VI, 826
Bryan, Elijah III, 50
Bryan, Elizabeth II, 341
Bryan, Elizabeth II, 696
Bryan, Elizabeth V, 729
Bryan, Elizabeth VI, 801
Bryan, Elizabeth VI, 834
Bryan, Elizabeth VI, 844
Bryan, Emily IV, 944
Bryan, Frances VI, 801
Bryan, Hannah S. IV, 947
Bryan, Haram IV, 954
Bryan, Henry W. VI, 885
Bryan, Ida V, 662
Bryan, Isaac III, 161
Bryan, Isaac, Jr. III, 161
Bryan, Jamaica III, 50
Bryan, James II, 476
Bryan, James V, 478
Bryan, James VI, 815
Bryan, Jane VI, 810
Bryan, Jane VI, 885
Bryan, Jessie V, 662
Bryan, Jessie V, 678
Bryan, John I, 209
Bryan, John III, 161
Bryan, John VI, 795
Bryan, John VI, 801
Bryan, John VI, 810
Bryan, John VI, 811
Bryan, John VI, 818
Bryan, John VI, 834
Bryan, John W. III, 161
Bryan, John Woodward V, 552
Bryan, John, Jr. VI, 324
Bryan, John, Jr. VI, 829
Bryan, John, Jr. VI, 851
Bryan, John, Jr. VI, 885
Bryan, John, Sr. VI, 807
Bryan, Josie V, 662
Bryan, Laura Tyra V, 662
Bryan, Lawson VI, 885
Bryan, Letha M. V, 552
Bryan, Letha Marie V, 552
Bryan, Louisa V, 662
Bryan, Lydia I, 1007
Bryan, Margaret I, 209
Bryan, Margaret II, 475
Bryan, Margaret II, 476
Bryan, Margaret J. III, 161
Bryan, Marguerite Francella V, 552
Bryan, Maria Ann III, 161
Bryan, Martha II, 476
Bryan, Martha II, 594
Bryan, Martha IV, 931
Bryan, Martha IV, 954
Bryan, Mary II, 200
Bryan, Mary II, 341
Bryan, Mary II, 475
Bryan, Mary II, 476
Bryan, Mary II, 488
Bryan, Mary II, 509
Bryan, Mary II, 696
Bryan, Mary IV, 947
Bryan, Mary Ann V, 729
Bryan, Mary J. VI, 885
Bryan, Morgan VI, 357
Bryan, Morgan VI, 609
Bryan, Morrison VI, 300
Bryan, Morrison VI, 325
Bryan, Morrison VI, 801
Bryan, Morrison VI, 810
Bryan, Morrison VI, 834
Bryan, Moses II, 475
Bryan, Nancy VI, 856
Bryan, Nicholas I, 131
Bryan, Nicholas I, 166
Bryan, Phebe II, 475
Bryan, Phebe II, 476
Bryan, Polly V, 478
Bryan, Polly VI, 815
Bryan, Rebecca VI, 885
Bryan, Reece VI, 818
Bryan, Reese VI, 801
Bryan, Reese VI, 833
Bryan, Reese VI, 834
Bryan, Reese VI, 859
Bryan, Rev. A. G. V, 552
Bryan, Rhoda VI, 300
Bryan, Rhoda VI, 325
Bryan, Rhoda VI, 801
Bryan, S. K. V, 662
Bryan, S. K. V, 694
Bryan, Samuel II, 475
Bryan, Samuel II, 546
Bryan, Sarah II, 220
Bryan, Sarah II, 341
Bryan, Sarah II, 475
Bryan, Sarah II, 476
Bryan, Sarah II, 546
Bryan, Sarah III, 161
Bryan, Sarah J. I, 232
Bryan, Sarah J. I, 238
Bryan, Sarah Jane III, 50
Bryan, Sarah Jane III, 160
Bryan, Susanna II, 341
Bryan, Susanna II, 475
Bryan, Susannah II, 475
Bryan, Susannah II, 547
Bryan, Susannah VI, 374
Bryan, Susannah VI, 397
Bryan, Thomas II, 200
Bryan, Thomas II, 220
Bryan, Thomas II, 341
Bryan, Thomas II, 475
Bryan, Thomas II, 488
Bryan, Thomas II, 546
Bryan, Thomas II, 547
Bryan, Thomas II, 696
Bryan, Thomas, Jr. II, 475
Bryan, Troy III, 161
Bryan, Walter III, 161
Bryan, William II, 341
Bryan, William III, 161
Bryan, William Eugene V, 552
Bryan, William Moode III, 161
Bryan, William W. III, 161
Bryan, William, Jr. III, 50
Bryan, Wm. IV, 947
Bryan, Wm. Eugene V, 552
Bryant, ??? II, 441
Bryant, ??? III, 50
Bryant, ??? III, 140
Bryant, Abraham II, 200
Bryant, Adeline III, 50
Bryant, Adeline III, 345
Bryant, Alexander V, 896
Bryant, Alice II, 476
Bryant, Alice IV, 372
Bryant, Allen I, 1003
Bryant, Allen V, 225
Bryant, Allen V, 321
Bryant, Ann II, 476
Bryant, Ann V, 896
Bryant, Anna V, 896
Bryant, Arthur I, 232
Bryant, Arthur I, 279
Bryant, Arthur I, 300
Bryant, Austin VI, 978
Bryant, Auther I, 300
Bryant, Baley V, 225
Bryant, Benjamin II, 200
Bryant, Benjamin II, 476

Bryant, Betsey VI, 801
Bryant, Beulah I, 1007
Bryant, Beulah V, 445
Bryant, Catharine I, 300
Bryant, Catharine I, 317
Bryant, Charity VI, 881
Bryant, Charles III, 50
Bryant, Charles Wesley IV, 372
Bryant, Daniel Paine I, 960
Bryant, Daniel Payne I, 1003
Bryant, David I, 974
Bryant, David V, 896
Bryant, David B. V, 896
Bryant, David H. V, 896
Bryant, Eleaner I, 268
Bryant, Eleanor I, 268
Bryant, Eli IV, 1234
Bryant, Elijah IV, 984
Bryant, Elijah VI, 978
Bryant, Elisabeth I, 206
Bryant, Elizabeth I, 268
Bryant, Elizabeth I, 280
Bryant, Elizabeth I, 282
Bryant, Elizabeth I, 300
Bryant, Elizabeth I, 310
Bryant, Elizabeth I, 974
Bryant, Elizabeth I, 1003
Bryant, Elizabeth I, 1007
Bryant, Elizabeth II, 476
Bryant, Elizabeth IV, 182
Bryant, Elizabeth IV, 373
Bryant, Elizabeth IV, 424
Bryant, Elizabeth IV, 984
Bryant, Elizabeth V, 896
Bryant, Elizabeth H. VI, 801
Bryant, Ellener I, 268
Bryant, Esther III, 493
Bryant, Esther IV, 373
Bryant, Gardner I, 960
Bryant, Garner I, 529
Bryant, Garner I, 535
Bryant, Garner I, 960
Bryant, Garner I, 974
Bryant, Garner I, 1003
Bryant, Garrar I, 960
Bryant, George F. V, 896
Bryant, George H. II, 476
Bryant, Hannah I, 529
Bryant, Hannah I, 535
Bryant, Hannah I, 974
Bryant, Hannah I, 1003
Bryant, Hannah I, 1007
Bryant, Hannah C. V, 896
Bryant, Harriet Emma IV, 372
Bryant, Heron II, 200
Bryant, Isaac IV, 182
Bryant, Jacob I, 960
Bryant, Jacob I, 974
Bryant, James II, 476
Bryant, James III, 50
Bryant, James IV, 182
Bryant, James IV, 373
Bryant, James V, 896
Bryant, Jane IV, 372
Bryant, Jane V, 896
Bryant, Jane D. IV, 372
Bryant, Jane Vernon IV, 372
Bryant, Jenny IV, 372
Bryant, Jenny IV, 450
Bryant, Jesse III, 493
Bryant, Jesse D. IV, 372
Bryant, Joel IV, 373
Bryant, John I, 267
Bryant, John I, 268
Bryant, John I, 529
Bryant, John I, 960
Bryant, John I, 974
Bryant, John III, 345
Bryant, John IV, 372
Bryant, John IV, 373
Bryant, John IV, 395
Bryant, John IV, 569
Bryant, John V, 896
Bryant, John VI, 801
Bryant, John L. IV, 372
Bryant, John Thomas IV, 372
Bryant, John Yarnall II, 476
Bryant, Joseph II, 476
Bryant, Lewis VI, 828
Bryant, Lillie IV, 372
Bryant, Lucinda IV, 372
Bryant, Lydia I, 267
Bryant, Lydia I, 268
Bryant, Lydia I, 960
Bryant, Lydia I, 974
Bryant, Lydia I, 1007
Bryant, Lydia V, 896
Bryant, Lydia V, 926
Bryant, Mable VI, 885
Bryant, Mahala I, 1007
Bryant, Margaret I, 1007
Bryant, Margaret I, 1013
Bryant, Margaret IV, 1308
Bryant, Martha I, 268
Bryant, Martha IV, 465
Bryant, Martha IV, 472
Bryant, Martha IV, 1149
Bryant, Martha IV, 1181
Bryant, Martha A. V, 896
Bryant, Mary I, 300
Bryant, Mary I, 307
Bryant, Mary I, 1003
Bryant, Mary I, 1007
Bryant, Mary II, 200
Bryant, Mary II, 341
Bryant, Mary IV, 182
Bryant, Mary IV, 372
Bryant, Mary IV, 373
Bryant, Mary IV, 395
Bryant, Mary V, 896
Bryant, Mary VI, 801
Bryant, Mary Ann V, 896
Bryant, Mary Ellen IV, 1308
Bryant, Mary Louisa IV, 372
Bryant, Mehala I, 1003
Bryant, Mordecai II, 476
Bryant, Moses II, 476
Bryant, Nance VI, 885
Bryant, Nancy I, 960
Bryant, Nancy I, 1003
Bryant, Nancy I, 1007
Bryant, Nathan I, 268
Bryant, Nicholas I, 38
Bryant, Nicholas I, 268
Bryant, Nicholas I, 960
Bryant, Patience VI, 885
Bryant, Phebe M. III, 50
Bryant, Phebe M. III, 140
Bryant, Polly VI, 978
Bryant, Priscilla I, 960
Bryant, Priscilla I, 966
Bryant, Rachel IV, 372
Bryant, Rachel IV, 373
Bryant, Rachel IV, 395
Bryant, Rachel IV, 426
Bryant, Rachel IV, 569
Bryant, Rachel IV, 580
Bryant, Rebecca I, 974
Bryant, Rebecca V, 896
Bryant, Rebeckah I, 529
Bryant, Rebeckah I, 535
Bryant, Rebecker I, 268
Bryant, Rebekah I, 1007
Bryant, Reece VI, 801
Bryant, Rees VI, 801
Bryant, Robert II, 441
Bryant, Robert IV, 1234
Bryant, Roseine IV, 372
Bryant, S. J. IV, 1234
Bryant, Sally I, 1003
Bryant, Sally I, 1007
Bryant, Samuel II, 200
Bryant, Samuel II, 476
Bryant, Sarah VI, 885
Bryant, Sarah Emily IV, 984
Bryant, Sarah J. I, 232
Bryant, Tamar J. IV, 182
Bryant, Tamar Jane IV, 373
Bryant, Tamar Jane IV, 410
Bryant, Tamer I, 1007
Bryant, Thomas I, 960
Bryant, Thomas I, 966
Bryant, Thomas I, 974
Bryant, Thomas I, 1003
Bryant, Thomas II, 476
Bryant, Thomas V, 896
Bryant, Thomas VI, 801
Bryant, Thomas VI, 885
Bryant, Tiberius J. II, 476
Bryant, Wd. Mary II, 476
Bryant, William I, 960
Bryant, William I, 974
Bryant, William IV, 182
Bryant, William IV, 372
Bryant, William IV, 373
Bryant, William IV, 426
Bryant, William V, 896
Bryant, William VI, 801
Bryarly, Mary VI, 374
Bryarly, Mary VI, 418
Brydell, Francis VI, 27
Brydell, Francis VI, 28
Brydell, Mary VI, 27
Brydell, Mary VI, 28
Bryen, Mary Ellen IV, 182
Bryen, Mary Ellen IV, 209
Bryles, Henry I, 756
Bryles, Solomon I, 756
Bryon, Mary E. V, 614
Bryon, Mary E. V, 647
Bryson, ??? III, 50
Bryson, James II, 341
Bryson, John III, 50
Bryson, Margaret III, 50
Bryson, Rebecca Hardy III, 50
Buaughn, Doshea VI, 885
Buaughn, John VI, 885
Buby, Bridgett II, 476
Bucey, Lewis IV, 686
Bucey, Rhoda IV, 686
Buchan, Elizabeth VI, 859
Buchan, James C. VI, 859
Buchanan, Anne VI, 885
Buchanan, Charles IV, 182
Buchanan, Chas. IV, 1308
Buchanan, Content K. IV, 1355
Buchanan, Eleanor L. VI, 231
Buchanan, Elizabeth VI, 885
Buchanan, Frances III, 121
Buchanan, Frances III, 320
Buchanan, Grace II, 167
Buchanan, Grace II, 201
Buchanan, Grace IV, 182
Buchanan, James VI, 231
Buchanan, James VI, 885
Buchanan, James VI, 997
Buchanan, James M. VI, 923
Buchanan, Jane II, 167
Buchanan, Margaretta IV, 931
Buchanan, Margaretta IV, 940
Buchanan, Mary IV, 182
Buchanan, Stephen IV, 465
Buchanan, Theodore VI, 885
Buchanan, V. W. IV, 182
Buchanan, Victoria IV, 465
Buchanan, William IV, 182
Buchannan, Abigail III, 50
Buchannan, Grace II, 476
Buchannan, Mary VI, 734
Buchannon, John VI, 628
Buchannon, Mary VI, 628
Buchanon, Amanda I, 934
Buchanon, Amanda C. I, 930
Buchanon, Mary II, 790
Buchanon, Mary Ann I, 930
Buchanon, William I, 930
Bucher, Hannah II, 59
Bucher, James II, 59
Bucher, Sarah V, 987
Bucher, Thomas II, 59
Buchfield, John VI, 801
Buchfield, Martha VI, 801
Buchram, Sally I, 1008
Buck, Andrew IV, 1150
Buck, Carrie S. IV, 1149
Buck, Charlotte VI, 58
Buck, Cornelius VI, 161
Buck, Dorothy IV, 1150
Buck, Eleonor IV, 515
Buck, Eleonor IV, 518
Buck, Esther IV, 1308
Buck, Francis M. IV, 1150
Buck, Frank M. IV, 1149
Buck, George IV, 804
Buck, Harry IV, 1036
Buck, Helen IV, 1308
Buck, Henry IV, 686
Buck, Israel IV, 1149
Buck, James II, 476
Buck, James III, 51
Buck, James IV, 1308
Buck, Jane VI, 56
Buck, Jane VI, 58
Buck, John IV, 686
Buck, John IV, 732
Buck, John IV, 804
Buck, John IV, 830
Buck, John IV, 931
Buck, John IV, 1021
Buck, John IV, 1024
Buck, John VI, 478
Buck, John W. IV, 1024
Buck, Jonathan IV, 931
Buck, Jonathan IV, 1024
Buck, Josiah IV, 1024
Buck, Lewis Dawson IV, 804
Buck, Lottie V, 987
Buck, Lucy V, 552
Buck, Lucy V, 571
Buck, Margaret II, 827
Buck, Marium IV, 1024
Buck, Martha IV, 804
Buck, Mary Anna IV, 1024
Buck, Maud IV, 1150
Buck, May IV, 1036
Buck, Merriam IV, 931
Buck, Miriam IV, 686
Buck, Miriam IV, 732
Buck, Miriam IV, 804
Buck, Miriam IV, 830
Buck, Miriam IV, 1021
Buck, Miriam VI, 478
Buck, Moses IV, 804
Buck, Nathan IV, 931
Buck, Nathan IV, 1024
Buck, Phebe IV, 76
Buck, Phebe IV, 92
Buck, Phebe IV, 686
Buck, Phebe IV, 1143
Buck, Phebe IV, 1149
Buck, Phebe IV, 1150
Buck, Phebe IV, 1177
Buck, Philip IV, 804
Buck, Rachel IV, 686
Buck, Rachel Marietta IV, 1150
Buck, Ralph Marion IV, 1150
Buck, Rebecca IV, 1024
Buck, Serepta Caroline IV, 1150
Buck, Verda IV, 1150
Buck, Verda D. IV, 1149
Buck, Virgil IV, 1150
Buck, Virgil P. IV, 1149
Buck, William VI, 58
Buckaloo, Chas. II, 842
Buckaloo, Chas. II, 922
Buckaloo, Clarence M. II, 842
Buckaloo, Clarence M. II, 922
Buckaloo, Laura II, 842
Buckaloo, Laura II, 922
Buckaloo, Lucy II, 842
Buckaloo, Lucy II, 922
Buckanan, Mary IV, 182
Buckbee, Isaac II, 341
Buckbee, Isaac II, 476
Buckbee, Isaac II, 512
Buckbee, Isaac II, 589
Buckbee, Isaac II, 818
Buckbee, Isaac II, 916
Buckbee, John II, 476
Buckbee, John II, 641
Buckbee, Rachel II, 341
Buckbee, Rachel II, 476
Buckbee, Rachel II, 512
Buckbee, Rachel II, 589
Buckbee, Rachel II, 641
Buckbee, Sarah II, 476
Buckbee, Sarah II, 512
Buckbee, Sarah II, 589
Buckbee, Wd. Rachel II, 476
Buckbee, Wd. Rachel II, 818
Buckels, Dora Royce V, 987
Buckenham, Joseph I, 347
Bucker, Sally Ann III, 495
Buckey, Elizabeth L. VI, 734
Buckey, Elizabeth L. VI, 777
Buckey, Elizabeth S. VI, 734
Buckey, George Shoemaker VI, 734
Buckhannon, John VI, 593
Buckhannon, Mary VI, 374
Buckholdt, Robert IV, 1036
Buckhouse, Thomas III, 51
Buckhout, Adaline III, 51
Buckhout, Adaline III, 215
Buckhout, Jane H. III, 215
Buckhout, John J. III, 215
Buckhout, Peter III, 51
Buckhout, Peter III, 215
Buckhout, William B. III, 51
Buckien, Katie IV, 1247
Buckingham, Alice II, 476
Buckingham, Alice II, 568
Buckingham, Ansalom I, 529
Buckingham, Ansalom I, 545
Buckingham, James I, 376
Buckingham, Jane I, 592
Buckingham, Jane I, 596
Buckingham, Jane V, 831
Buckingham, John I, 376
Buckingham, Joseph I, 376
Buckingham, Joseph I, 413
Buckingham, Joshua I, 376
Buckingham, Joshua I, 414
Buckingham, Lela I, 587
Buckingham, Levi I, 529
Buckingham, Levi I, 545
Buckingham, Levi I, 586
Buckingham, Levi I, 592
Buckingham, Levi I, 596
Buckingham, Levi, Jr. I, 586
Buckingham, Levi, Jr. I, 587
Buckingham, Levi, Sr. I, 587
Buckingham, Lucie S. III, 277
Buckingham, Margery I, 376
Buckingham, Margery I, 404
Buckingham, Margery I, 413
Buckingham, Margery Piggott I, 376
Buckingham, Mary I, 376
Buckingham, Mary I, 389
Buckingham, Mary Ann IV, 182
Buckingham, Peter IV, 182
Buckingham, Rachel I, 376
Buckingham, Rachel I, 414
Buckingham, Rachel I, 529
Buckingham, Rachel I, 587
Buckingham, Rachel B. I, 376
Buckingham, Rebeka I, 592
Buckingham, Sarah I, 529
Buckingham, Sarah I, 586
Buckingham, Sarah I, 587
Buckingham, Sarah I, 592
Buckingham, Sarah I, 594
Buckingham, Sarah II, 476
Buckingham, Sarah IV, 912
Buckingham, Selah I, 529
Buckingham, Wd. Sarah II, 569
Buckler, Betsey VI, 801
Buckler, Harry VI, 801
Buckles, Caroline V, 987
Buckles, Dora V, 987
Buckles, Dora Royce V, 987
Buckles, Mary IV, 23
Buckles, Mary IV, 39
Buckles, Mary VI, 374
Buckles, Mary VI, 401
Buckles, Nellie V, 987
Bucklew, Mary VI, 478
Buckley, Abraham II, 476
Buckley, Albert Coulson V, 896
Buckley, Albert Coulson V, 944
Buckley, Ann II, 341
Buckley, Ann II, 476
Buckley, Ann II, 730
Buckley, Ann II, 956
Buckley, Ann II, 1043
Buckley, Ann III, 51
Buckley, Anna III, 51
Buckley, Anna III, 199
Buckley, Anna III, 366
Buckley, Anne III, 51
Buckley, Bessie Miars V, 478
Buckley, Deborah II, 956
Buckley, Deborah II, 1043
Buckley, Deborah III, 51
Buckley, Effingham Laurence III, 51
Buckley, Elizabeth II, 341
Buckley, Elizabeth II, 1043
Buckley, Elizabeth III, 51
Buckley, Elizabeth B. III, 324
Buckley, Elizabeth W. III, 51
Buckley, Elizabeth W. III, 330
Buckley, Elizabeth Williams II, 956
Buckley, Elizabeth Williams III, 51
Buckley, Enion Williams II, 956
Buckley, Hannah II, 476
Buckley, Hannah II, 529
Buckley, Harriet Ellis V, 896
Buckley, Harriet Ellis V, 944
Buckley, Harry V, 662
Buckley, Harry V, 722
Buckley, Henry VI, 885
Buckley, Isaac II, 476
Buckley, Jacob III, 51
Buckley, Jane L. III, 51
Buckley, Jane Lawrence III, 51
Buckley, John III, 51
Buckley, John Lawrence III, 51
Buckley, Joseph II, 341
Buckley, Joseph II, 476
Buckley, Joseph II, 593
Buckley, Joseph J. B. VI, 801
Buckley, Lucretia V, 662
Buckley, Lucretia V, 722
Buckley, Lucy V, 896
Buckley, Mary II, 341
Buckley, Mary II, 956
Buckley, Mary II, 982
Buckley, Mary II, 1018
Buckley, Mary II, 1043
Buckley, Mary III, 51
Buckley, Mary III, 330
Buckley, Mary Anna II, 982
Buckley, Mary Anna III, 51
Buckley, Mary Anna III, 366
Buckley, Nancy H. VI, 801
Buckley, Pauline Macy V, 729
Buckley, Peter III, 51
Buckley, Phebe III, 51
Buckley, Phineas II, 341
Buckley, Phineas II, 956
Buckley, Phineas II, 982
Buckley, Phineas II, 1043
Buckley, Phineas III, 51
Buckley, Phineas III, 330
Buckley, Phineas Henry III, 51
Buckley, Phineas William III, 51
Buckley, Phinehas II, 476
Buckley, Phinehas II, 982
Buckley, Phinias II, 982
Buckley, Rachel II, 476
Buckley, Rebeckah II, 956

uckley, Ruth II, 476
uckley, Ruth II, 956
uckley, Ruth II, 982
uckley, Samuel II, 341
uckley, Sarah II, 341
uckley, Sarah II, 476
uckley, Sarah II, 593
uckley, Sarah II, 956
uckley, Sarah II, 1043
uckley, Sarah III, 51
uckley, Sarah, Jr. II, 476
uckley, Susanna L. VI, 885
uckley, Thomas II, 341
uckley, Thomas II, 476
uckley, Thomas II, 529
uckley, Thomas II, 956
uckley, Thomas II, 1043
uckley, Thomas III, 51
uckley, Thomas III, 199
uckley, Thomas III, 366
uckley, Thos. III, 51
uckley, Wd. Hannah II, 476
uckley, William II, 341
uckley, William III, 51
uckley, William L. III, 51
uckley, Wm. II, 476
uckley, Wm. C. V, 896
uckly, Mary II, 982
uckly, Phinias II, 982
uckman, Abden II, 983
uckman, Abden II, 984
uckman, Abden II, 1042
uckman, Abdon II, 786
uckman, Abdon II, 983
uckman, Abdon II, 1046
uckman, Abdon, Jr. II, 1046
uckman, Achsah II, 1046
uckman, Acsah II, 983
uckman, Aldon II, 983
uckman, Alexandria VI, 478
uckman, Amelia II, 842
uckman, Amos II, 956
uckman, Amos II, 983
uckman, Amos J. II, 836
uckman, Amos J. II, 842
uckman, Ann C. II, 784
uckman, Ann H. II, 1046
uckman, Ann H. II, 1060
uckman, Anna II, 983
uckman, Anna IV, 943
uckman, Anna C. II, 927
uckman, Benjamin II, 956
uckman, Benjamin II, 982
uckman, Benjamin II, 983
uckman, Benjamin II, 1046
uckman, Benjamin B. II, 842
uckman, Benjamin Brougham II, 784
uckman, Bertha Schooley VI, 734
uckman, Cadwalader II, 983
uckman, Caroline Cox VI, 734
uckman, Catharine II, 836
uckman, Catharine II, 842
uckman, Charles II, 983
uckman, Chas. II, 826
uckman, Chas. II, 842
uckman, Chas. II, 936
uckman, Chas. H. II, 836
uckman, Chas. H. II, 842
uckman, Chas. H. III, 189
uckman, Chas. M. III, 51
uckman, Christiana Hughes VI, 737
uckman, Christina Hughes VI, 734
uckman, Christina Hughes VI, 737
uckman, David II, 983
uckman, David II, 1008
uckman, David II, 1037
uckman, David, Jr. II, 983
uckman, Deborah II, 983
uckman, Dilworth VI, 478
uckman, Dilworth VI, 556
uckman, Dilworth VI, 734
uckman, Dilworth VI, 742
uckman, Donald Albert III, 51
uckman, Edmund II, 983
uckman, Edna III, 51
uckman, Edna III, 189
uckman, Eleanor II, 983
uckman, Eleanor D. VI, 769
uckman, Eleanor Douglas VI, 734
uckman, Eleanor Douglas VI, 769
uckman, Elisabeth II, 1034
uckman, Eliza II, 983
uckman, Elizabeth II, 976
uckman, Elizabeth II, 977
Buckman, Elizabeth II, 982
Buckman, Elizabeth II, 983
Buckman, Elizabeth II, 984
Buckman, Elizabeth II, 1030
Buckman, Elizabeth II, 1046
Buckman, Elizabeth II, 1069
Buckman, Elizabeth P. II, 842
Buckman, Elizabeth P. II, 936
Buckman, Elizabeth P. II, 983
Buckman, Elizabeth Pearson II, 826
Buckman, Elizabeth, Jr. II, 1046
Buckman, Ellen II, 703
Buckman, Ellen II, 983
Buckman, Ellen II, 1046
Buckman, Ellen II, 1064
Buckman, Elliott Moore VI, 734
Buckman, Emaline VI, 478
Buckman, Emeline VI, 734
Buckman, Emeline VI, 742
Buckman, Emma J. II, 784
Buckman, Emmaline VI, 556
Buckman, Esther II, 983
Buckman, Esther II, 1008
Buckman, Esther II, 1037
Buckman, Frances II, 810
Buckman, Frances VI, 734
Buckman, Francis II, 983
Buckman, Geo. W. V, 988
Buckman, George II, 1046
Buckman, George C. II, 956
Buckman, Grace II, 983
Buckman, Grace IV, 182
Buckman, Grace IV, 201
Buckman, Hannah II, 784
Buckman, Hannah II, 954
Buckman, Hannah II, 956
Buckman, Hannah II, 978
Buckman, Hannah II, 982
Buckman, Hannah II, 983
Buckman, Hannah II, 1031
Buckman, Hannah II, 1032
Buckman, Hannah II, 1046
Buckman, Hannah, Jr. II, 984
Buckman, Hannah, Jr. II, 1042
Buckman, Harden II, 1069
Buckman, Harding II, 983
Buckman, Harding II, 984
Buckman, Harding II, 1046
Buckman, Harding II, 1060
Buckman, Harding IV, 931
Buckman, Harriet II, 983
Buckman, Harriet II, 1046
Buckman, Harriet II, 1064
Buckman, Henry II, 983
Buckman, Henry II, 984
Buckman, Henry II, 1069
Buckman, Henry C. II, 956
Buckman, Horace D. VI, 737
Buckman, Horace Dilworth VI, 734
Buckman, Horace Dilworth VI, 737
Buckman, Ina III, 299
Buckman, Ina F. III, 51
Buckman, Jacob II, 982
Buckman, Jacob II, 1031
Buckman, James II, 784
Buckman, James II, 802
Buckman, James II, 927
Buckman, James II, 965
Buckman, James II, 983
Buckman, James II, 984
Buckman, James II, 986
Buckman, James II, 1003
Buckman, James II, 1005
Buckman, James II, 1017
Buckman, James II, 1020
Buckman, James II, 1069
Buckman, James, Jr. II, 983
Buckman, Jane II, 983
Buckman, Jane II, 995
Buckman, Jesse II, 956
Buckman, Jesse II, 982
Buckman, Jesse II, 983
Buckman, Jesse II, 1031
Buckman, John II, 956
Buckman, John II, 983
Buckman, John II, 1009
Buckman, John II, 1037
Buckman, John II, 1046
Buckman, John B. II, 956
Buckman, John Balderston II, 983
Buckman, John, Jr. II, 983
Buckman, John, Jr. II, 1046
Buckman, Jonathan II, 810
Buckman, Jonathan II, 983
Buckman, Jonathan II, 1008
Buckman, Jonathan II, 1032
Buckman, Jonathan Fell II, 983
Buckman, Jonathan, Jr. II, 983
Buckman, Joseph II, 982
Buckman, Joseph II, 988
Buckman, Joseph II, 1046
Buckman, Joseph VI, 478
Buckman, Joshua II, 927
Buckman, Joshua II, 983
Buckman, Joshua V. II, 984
Buckman, Joshua Vansant II, 982
Buckman, Julian II, 983
Buckman, Juliann II, 965
Buckman, Juliann II, 983
Buckman, Juliann II, 984
Buckman, Juliann II, 1017
Buckman, Laetitia II, 983
Buckman, Latitia II, 1046
Buckman, Latitia II, 1060
Buckman, Leticia II, 983
Buckman, Leticia II, 1003
Buckman, Levi II, 1046
Buckman, Lucy Gillingham VI, 734
Buckman, Lydia II, 983
Buckman, Lydia II, 984
Buckman, Lydia II, 1019
Buckman, Lydia IV, 891
Buckman, Lydia IV, 893
Buckman, Macie S. II, 956
Buckman, Mahlon II, 983
Buckman, Mahlon II, 1032
Buckman, Marce II, 1046
Buckman, Margaret II, 786
Buckman, Margaret II, 983
Buckman, Margaret II, 1009
Buckman, Margaret II, 1046
Buckman, Margaret Harrold VI, 734
Buckman, Margaretta C. II, 842
Buckman, Margaretta C. II, 936
Buckman, Margaretta C. II, 1046
Buckman, Margaretta Carey II, 826
Buckman, Margret II, 983
Buckman, Mariana VI, 556
Buckman, Marianna VI, 478
Buckman, Marianna VI, 557
Buckman, Marianna VI, 734
Buckman, Marianna VI, 769
Buckman, Marianna VI, 776
Buckman, Martha II, 927
Buckman, Martha II, 982
Buckman, Martha II, 988
Buckman, Martha II, 1046
Buckman, Martha B. II, 956
Buckman, Mary II, 842
Buckman, Mary II, 956
Buckman, Mary II, 962
Buckman, Mary II, 982
Buckman, Mary II, 983
Buckman, Mary II, 984
Buckman, Mary II, 1020
Buckman, Mary II, 1031
Buckman, Mary II, 1046
Buckman, Mary II, 1053
Buckman, Mary II, 1061
Buckman, Mary II, 1069
Buckman, Mary IV, 939
Buckman, Mary Ann II, 1046
Buckman, Mary Ann VI, 734
Buckman, Mary B. III, 51
Buckman, Mary B. III, 189
Buckman, Mary C. II, 842
Buckman, Mary K. II, 784
Buckman, Mary P. II, 836
Buckman, Mary P. II, 842
Buckman, Mary P. III, 51
Buckman, Mary, Jr. II, 982
Buckman, May II, 983
Buckman, Mercy II, 956
Buckman, Mercy II, 983
Buckman, Mercy II, 1046
Buckman, Mercy II, 1060
Buckman, Mercy IV, 931
Buckman, Morris II, 983
Buckman, Morris II, 1046
Buckman, Oliver II, 983
Buckman, Phebe II, 956
Buckman, Phebe II, 982
Buckman, Phebe II, 1007
Buckman, Phineas II, 1003
Buckman, Phinehas II, 983
Buckman, Phinehas II, 1010
Buckman, Pricilla II, 983
Buckman, Priscilla II, 956
Buckman, Priscilla II, 982
Buckman, Priscilla II, 984
Buckman, Rachel II, 805
Buckman, Rachel II, 983
Buckman, Rachel II, 991
Buckman, Rachel II, 1008
Buckman, Rachel II, 1019
Buckman, Rachel II, 1025
Buckman, Rachel II, 1037
Buckman, Rachel II, 1046
Buckman, Rebecca II, 784
Buckman, Rebecca II, 842
Buckman, Rebecca II, 851
Buckman, Rebecca VI, 478
Buckman, Robert II, 983
Buckman, Robert II, 984
Buckman, Ruth II, 983
Buckman, Ruth II, 1040
Buckman, Samuel II, 784
Buckman, Samuel II, 956
Buckman, Samuel II, 983
Buckman, Samuel II, 984
Buckman, Samuel II, 1042
Buckman, Samuel B. II, 1046
Buckman, Samuel Harold VI, 556
Buckman, Samuel Harrold VI, 478
Buckman, Samuel Harrold VI, 557
Buckman, Samuel Harrold VI, 734
Buckman, Samuel Harrold VI, 769
Buckman, Samuel Harrold VI, 776
Buckman, Samuel R. II, 1047
Buckman, Samuel Satterthwait II, 983
Buckman, Samuel, Jr. II, 1046
Buckman, Sarah II, 784
Buckman, Sarah II, 786
Buckman, Sarah II, 802
Buckman, Sarah II, 810
Buckman, Sarah II, 842
Buckman, Sarah II, 954
Buckman, Sarah II, 956
Buckman, Sarah II, 957
Buckman, Sarah II, 965
Buckman, Sarah II, 971
Buckman, Sarah II, 978
Buckman, Sarah II, 982
Buckman, Sarah II, 983
Buckman, Sarah II, 984
Buckman, Sarah II, 986
Buckman, Sarah II, 1003
Buckman, Sarah II, 1005
Buckman, Sarah II, 1008
Buckman, Sarah II, 1017
Buckman, Sarah II, 1020
Buckman, Sarah II, 1031
Buckman, Sarah II, 1032
Buckman, Sarah II, 1042
Buckman, Sarah II, 1046
Buckman, Sarah II, 1069
Buckman, Sarah Ann II, 784
Buckman, Sarah Ann II, 962
Buckman, Sarah Ann II, 984
Buckman, Sarah Ann II, 1053
Buckman, Sarah, Jr. II, 983
Buckman, Sarah, Jr. II, 984
Buckman, Sarah, Jr. II, 1005
Buckman, Sarah, Jr. II, 1046
Buckman, Selina E. IV, 1024
Buckman, Selma E. IV, 1024
Buckman, Spencer II, 1069
Buckman, Spencer W. II, 1065
Buckman, Stacy II, 983
Buckman, Susanna II, 1046
Buckman, Susanna IV, 943
Buckman, Susannah II, 983
Buckman, Susannah II, 1010
Buckman, Tacy II, 983
Buckman, Thomas II, 956
Buckman, Thomas II, 962
Buckman, Thomas II, 982
Buckman, Thomas II, 983
Buckman, Thomas II, 984
Buckman, Thomas II, 1031
Buckman, Thomas II, 1046
Buckman, Thomas II, 1053
Buckman, Thomas Smith III, 51
Buckman, Thomas Smith III, 299
Buckman, Thomas Story II, 982
Buckman, Thos. IV, 943
Buckman, Thos. L. II, 842
Buckman, Timothy II, 956
Buckman, William II, 201
Buckman, William II, 202
Buckman, William II, 954
Buckman, William II, 956
Buckman, William II, 983
Buckman, William E. II, 956
Buckman, William, Jr. II, 202
Buckman, Wm. II, 978
Buckman, Wm. II, 982
Buckman, Wm. II, 983
Buckman, Wm. II, 984
Buckman, Wm. II, 986
Buckman, Wm. II, 1010
Buckman, Wm. E. II, 1046
Buckmaster, Elizabeth II, 59
Buckmaster, Elizabeth II, 65
Buckmyer, Anna IV, 1247
Bucknell, Lydia E. II, 700
Bucknell, Lydia E. II, 730
Bucknell, Malinda II, 704
Bucknell, Mary II, 704
Bucknell, Mary II, 738
Bucknell, Mary B. II, 700
Bucknell, Mary R. II, 730
Bucknell, Mary Russell II, 730
Bucknell, Rebecca II, 956
Bucknell, Rebecca Gaskill II, 700
Bucknell, Rebecca Russell II, 730
Bucknell, Rebeckah Gaskill II, 704
Bucknell, Rebekah R. II, 730
Bucknell, Rebekah R. II, 738
Bucknell, Samuel II, 700
Bucknell, Samuel II, 704
Bucknell, Samuel II, 730
Bucknell, Samuel II, 738
Bucknell, Samuel II, 956
Bucknell, Samuel R. II, 700
Bucknell, Samuel R. II, 956
Bucknell, Samuel Rooker II, 730
Buckner, Alice I, 444
Buckner, Alise I, 444
Buckner, Allis I, 433
Buckner, Ann V, 478
Buckner, Anne VI, 885
Buckner, Asenath Caroline I, 434
Buckner, Elizabeth VI, 795
Buckner, Elizabeth A. VI, 801
Buckner, Henry I, 433
Buckner, Henry C. I, 376
Buckner, Henry M. I, 376
Buckner, Irene I, 444
Buckner, Jane I, 434
Buckner, Jesse I, 376
Buckner, Jesse I, 399
Buckner, Jesse I, 433
Buckner, Jesse I, 444
Buckner, Jesse D. I, 444
Buckner, Jesse D. I, 448
Buckner, Jesse Franklin I, 434
Buckner, John VI, 801
Buckner, John Milton I, 433
Buckner, Martha J. I, 444
Buckner, Mary Ann I, 433
Buckner, Mary Catharine I, 399
Buckner, Mary Catharine I, 444
Buckner, Mary Catharine I, 448
Buckner, Mary Catherine I, 376
Buckner, Molly VI, 885
Buckner, Patrick VI, 801
Buckner, Patrick VI, 885
Buckner, Patsy VI, 801
Buckner, Perthina VI, 801
Buckner, Polly VI, 848
Buckner, Rena I, 376
Buckner, Sally P. VI, 801
Buckner, Sarah Catharine I, 433
Buckner, Thomas I, 444
Buckner, Thomas Newton I, 434
Buckner, William VI, 801
Buckner, William Madison I, 434
Buckwell, Caroly C. III, 51
Buckwell, Carolyn C. III, 51
Buckwell, Carolyn C. III, 135
Buckwell, Carrie III, 51
Buckwell, Carrie E. III, 51
Buckwell, Carrie E. III, 83
Buckwell, Carrie E. III, 135
Buckwell, Carrie E. III, 195
Buckwell, Donald III, 51
Buckwell, Helen C. III, 51
Buckwell, Helen C. III, 195
Buckwell, Helen Cook III, 51
Buckwell, James F. III, 51
Buckwell, James F. III, 83
Buckwell, Jas. F. III, 51
Buckwell, Jas. F. III, 135
Buckwell, Jas. F. III, 195
Buckwell, Ruth III, 51
Buckwell, Ruth Elizabeth III, 51
Bucy, Lewis IV, 686
Bucy, Rhoda IV, 686
Bud, Benjamin II, 341
Bud, James II, 341
Bud, Jane II, 341
Bud, John II, 341
Bud, John II, 342
Bud, John II, 441
Bud, John II, 442
Bud, Joseph II, 341
Bud, Joseph II, 342

Bud, Martha II, 341
Bud, Martha II, 441
Bud, Mary II, 341
Bud, Mary II, 342
Bud, Miriam Say II, 341
Bud, Miriam Say II, 342
Bud, Paul C. II, 341
Bud, Priscilla II, 341
Bud, Rachel II, 341
Bud, Rebecca II, 341
Bud, Rebecka II, 341
Bud, Rebecka II, 342
Bud, Rebecka II, 442
Bud, Rebeckah II, 441
Bud, Rebeckah II, 442
Bud, Rebekah II, 441
Bud, Samuel II, 341
Bud, Sarah II, 442
Bud, Susanna II, 442
Bud, Thomas II, 442
Bud, Thomas Say II, 341
Bud, Thomas, Jr. II, 441
Bud, Thomas, Sr. II, 442
Budd, Ann II, 167
Budd, Ann II, 282
Budd, Ann II, 297
Budd, Ann II, 341
Budd, Ann II, 477
Budd, Ann II, 533
Budd, Ann E. V, 452
Budd, Ann S. II, 730
Budd, Ann Say II, 784
Budd, Ann Say II, 842
Budd, Anne Eliza V, 452
Budd, Benjamin II, 341
Budd, Benjamin II, 477
Budd, Berry V, 452
Budd, Catharine II, 202
Budd, Charles II, 477
Budd, Charles II, 730
Budd, David V, 988
Budd, Elizabeth II, 282
Budd, Elizabeth II, 460
Budd, Elizabeth II, 476
Budd, Emma Rose II, 786
Budd, Ida V, 988
Budd, James II, 341
Budd, Jane II, 341
Budd, Jennie V, 452
Budd, John II, 341
Budd, John II, 342
Budd, John II, 441
Budd, Joseph II, 341
Budd, Joseph II, 342
Budd, Joseph II, 476
Budd, Joseph II, 477
Budd, Joseph II, 491
Budd, Joseph II, 506
Budd, Joseph II, 533
Budd, Joseph II, 566
Budd, Joseph II, 628
Budd, Joseph II, 694
Budd, Joseph Benjamin II, 477
Budd, Leroy W. V, 452
Budd, Mahlon II, 476
Budd, Mahlon II, 477
Budd, Mahlon VI, 102
Budd, Martha II, 341
Budd, Martha II, 441
Budd, Martha II, 477
Budd, Martha II, 628
Budd, Martha C. II, 477
Budd, Martha C. II, 491
Budd, Mary II, 59
Budd, Mary II, 167
Budd, Mary II, 341
Budd, Mary II, 342
Budd, Mary II, 441
Budd, Mary II, 477
Budd, Mary V, 452
Budd, Melvin W. V, 452
Budd, Miriam Say II, 341
Budd, Miriam Say II, 342
Budd, Orlan V, 452
Budd, Orley V, 988
Budd, Otice V, 452
Budd, Otis V, 452
Budd, Paul C. II, 341
Budd, Paul C. II, 477
Budd, Paul E. II, 477
Budd, Polly V, 988
Budd, Priscilla II, 341
Budd, Priscilla II, 477
Budd, Priscilla II, 491
Budd, Priscilla II, 628
Budd, Rachel II, 170
Budd, Rachel II, 341
Budd, Rachel II, 476
Budd, Rachel II, 477
Budd, Rachel II, 491
Budd, Rachel II, 506
Budd, Rachel III, 80
Budd, Rebecca II, 202
Budd, Rebecca II, 256
Budd, Rebecca II, 264
Budd, Rebecca II, 282
Budd, Rebecca II, 307
Budd, Rebecca II, 341
Budd, Rebecca II, 342
Budd, Rebecca II, 476
Budd, Rebecca II, 477
Budd, Rebecca II, 506
Budd, Rebecca II, 533
Budd, Rebecca II, 566
Budd, Rebecca II, 694
Budd, Rebecca III, 80
Budd, Rebecka II, 341
Budd, Rebecka II, 342
Budd, Rebeckah II, 441
Budd, Rose II, 167
Budd, Ruth II, 167
Budd, Samuel II, 341
Budd, Samuel II, 477
Budd, Sarah II, 476
Budd, Sarah II, 604
Budd, Stacey II, 202
Budd, Stacy II, 202
Budd, Stacy II, 476
Budd, Stacy II, 477
Budd, Susannah II, 167
Budd, Thomas II, 167
Budd, Thomas II, 342
Budd, Thomas II, 442
Budd, Thomas II, 460
Budd, Thomas II, 476
Budd, Thomas II, 477
Budd, Thomas II, 491
Budd, Thomas II, 533
Budd, Thomas II, 694
Budd, Thomas III, 80
Budd, Thomas Say II, 341
Budd, Thomas, Jr. II, 202
Budd, Thomas, Jr. II, 441
Budd, Wd Priscilla II, 628
Budd, Wd. Priscilla II, 477
Budd, William II, 167
Bueannan, Abigail III, 51
Buenger, Lillian IV, 1308
Buffen, John II, 202
Buffet, Wm. H. IV, 1309
Buffin, Abigail II, 202
Buffin, Ann II, 201
Buffin, Ann II, 202
Buffin, Grace II, 202
Buffin, Grace II, 267
Buffin, Hannah II, 167
Buffin, Hannah II, 202
Buffin, Jane II, 167
Buffin, John II, 167
Buffin, John II, 202
Buffin, John, Jr. II, 202
Buffin, John, Jr. II, 223
Buffin, Mary II, 167
Buffin, Mary II, 202
Buffin, Mary II, 206
Buffin, Mary II, 261
Buffin, Micall II, 202
Buffin, Michall II, 202
Buffin, Rachel II, 202
Buffin, Rachel II, 223
Buffin, Richard II, 167
Buffin, Richard II, 202
Buffin, Sarah II, 202
Buffin, Sarah II, 269
Buffing, Micall II, 202
Buffing, Micall II, 207
Buffing, Rachel II, 202
Buffingham, Margery V, 790
Buffington, Esther V, 739
Buffington, Hannah II, 477
Buffington, Isabel III, 51
Buffington, Joseph V, 225
Buffington, Lea W. II, 700
Buffington, Lea W. II, 730
Buffington, Lee W. II, 730
Buffington, Lee W. II, 744
Buffington, Marjorie V, 760
Buffington, Martha IV, 514
Buffington, Martha IV, 515
Buffington, Mary II, 477
Buffington, Mary II, 656
Buffington, Mary II, 730
Buffington, Mifflen M. V, 225
Buffington, Mifflin V, 225
Buffington, Mifflin F. V, 552
Buffington, Mifflin M. V, 225
Buffington, Mifflin M. V, 321
Buffington, Mifflin M. V, 552
Buffington, Peter VI, 374
Buffington, Rachel II, 730
Buffington, Rachel II, 744
Buffington, Rebecca II, 730
Buffington, Rebecca Leonora II, 700
Buffington, Sarah I, 1047
Buffington, Sarah II, 817
Buffington, Sarah II, 826
Buffington, Sarah IV, 23
Buffington, Sarah IV, 49
Buffington, Sarah V, 794
Buffington, Sarah VI, 374
Buffington, Sarah R. II, 700
Buffington, Sarah R. II, 730
Buffington, Sarah R. II, 744
Buffington, William H. II, 700
Buffington, William Hallowell II, 700
Buffington, Wm. II, 730
Buffington, Wm. II, 744
Buffinton, Hannah II, 477
Buffinton, Joseph V, 225
Buffinton, Mifflin M. V, 225
Buffitt, Wm. IV, 1308
Buffitt, Wm. H. IV, 1309
Buffkin, Bathsheba IV, 515
Buffkin, Bathsheba V, 155
Buffkin, Guli Elma V, 155
Buffkin, John IV, 515
Buffkin, John V, 155
Buffkin, Julia Elma IV, 515
Buffkin, Leaven I, 131
Buffkin, Levin VI, 7
Buffkin, Levin VI, 28
Buffkin, Levn VI, 27
Buffkin, Priscilla I, 119
Buffkin, Priscilla I, 131
Buffkin, Priscilla I, 167
Buffkin, Rebecca S. IV, 373
Buffkin, Ruth IV, 515
Buffkin, Ruth V, 155
Buffkin, Sarah IV, 515
Buffkin, Sarah V, 155
Buffkin, Thomas IV, 141
Buffkin, Thomas IV, 515
Buffkin, Thomas V, 155
Buffkin, Warner IV, 515
Buffkin, Warner V, 155
Buffkins, Michal II, 202
Bufflin, John II, 275
Buffum, Ann III, 193
Buffum, Arnold III, 51
Buffum, B. III, 192
Buffum, Benjamin III, 51
Buffum, Benjamin III, 192
Buffum, Caleb VI, 161
Buffum, David III, 51
Buffum, Eleanor III, 192
Buffum, Eleanor IV, 931
Buffum, Eleanor IV, 936
Buffum, Elizabeth III, 193
Buffum, Ellen III, 51
Buffum, Ellen III, 192
Buffum, Ellen K. III, 51
Buffum, Horace II, 477
Buffum, John III, 193
Buffum, John Bowne III, 193
Buffum, Joseph III, 193
Buffum, Mary III, 193
Buffum, Rebecca III, 51
Buffum, Rebecca V, 896
Buffum, Rebecca B. II, 730
Buffum, Rebecca B. II, 768
Buffum, Samuel III, 193
Buffum, Susan Ann III, 51
Bufkin, ??? VI, 39
Bufkin, Ann I, 33
Bufkin, Bathsheba IV, 515
Bufkin, Bathsheba V, 949
Bufkin, Bettie I, 18
Bufkin, Betty VI, 300
Bufkin, Cresilla I, 3
Bufkin, Dorrithy VI, 27
Bufkin, Dorrithy VI, 33
Bufkin, Edith I, 38
Bufkin, Edith I, 52
Bufkin, Elisabeth I, 3
Bufkin, Elisabeth I, 38
Bufkin, Gulielma V, 949
Bufkin, Gulyelma IV, 515
Bufkin, Henry I, 38
Bufkin, Henry M. I, 3
Bufkin, John I, 3
Bufkin, John I, 38
Bufkin, John IV, 515
Bufkin, John V, 949
Bufkin, John Q. I, 38
Bufkin, Julia Elma IV, 515
Bufkin, Leaven VI, 27
Bufkin, Leavn VI, 33
Bufkin, Leovin VI, 8
Bufkin, Martha I, 3
Bufkin, Mary I Sup 1, 3
Bufkin, Mary I Sup 1, 5
Bufkin, Nancy I, 3
Bufkin, Nancy I, 18
Bufkin, Nancy I, 38
Bufkin, Nancy I, 75
Bufkin, Pharaba I, 33
Bufkin, Pharabe I, 3
Bufkin, Phariba I, 38
Bufkin, Ralph I, 38
Bufkin, Ralph I Sup 1, 3
Bufkin, Ralph I Sup 1, 5
Bufkin, Ralph I Sup 1, 6
Bufkin, Rebecca S. IV, 370
Bufkin, Robert I, 3
Bufkin, Robert I, 33
Bufkin, Robert VI, 300
Bufkin, Ruth IV, 515
Bufkin, Ruth V, 949
Bufkin, Ruth V, 968
Bufkin, Samuel I, 3
Bufkin, Samuel I, 18
Bufkin, Samuel I, 38
Bufkin, Samuel IV, 182
Bufkin, Samuel IV, 515
Bufkin, Sarah I, 38
Bufkin, Sarah I, 55
Bufkin, Sarah IV, 515
Bufkin, Sarah V, 949
Bufkin, Thomas IV, 515
Bufkin, Thomas IV, 686
Bufkin, Thomas V, 949
Bufkin, Thomas V, 968
Bufkin, Thomas VI, 56
Bufkin, Warner IV, 515
Bufkin, Warner V, 949
Bufkin, Wd. Dorrithy VI, 31
Bufkins, Bathsheba IV, 322
Bufkins, Ruth IV, 322
Bufkins, Ruth IV, 326
Bufkins, Samuel IV, 322
Bufkins, Thomas IV, 322
Bufkins, Thomas IV, 326
Buford, A. L. VI, 976
Buford, Abraham VI, 885
Buford, Abraham VI, 911
Buford, Abraham VI, 929
Buford, Abraham VI, 997
Buford, Abram VI, 899
Buford, Betsey VI, 971
Buford, Betty VI, 885
Buford, Betty VI, 990
Buford, Demarquis VI, 885
Buford, Elizabeth VI, 885
Buford, Elizabeth VI, 911
Buford, Elizabeth VI, 914
Buford, Elnor VI, 885
Buford, Frances VI, 885
Buford, Frances J. VI, 915
Buford, Henry VI, 879
Buford, Henry VI, 885
Buford, Henry VI, 945
Buford, Henry VI, 947
Buford, Henry VI, 971
Buford, James VI, 885
Buford, James VI, 990
Buford, James H. VI, 894
Buford, Jane VI, 885
Buford, John VI, 885
Buford, John VI, 890
Buford, John VI, 914
Buford, John VI, 916
Buford, John VI, 930
Buford, John VI, 944
Buford, John VI, 948
Buford, John VI, 991
Buford, Judith VI, 990
Buford, Julia Ann VI, 991
Buford, Julian R. VI, 997
Buford, Juliann VI, 947
Buford, Lucinda VI, 911
Buford, Lucinda VI, 1013
Buford, Martha H. VI, 936
Buford, Mary VI, 885
Buford, Mary Ann VI, 885
Buford, Mary M. VI, 929
Buford, Matilda VI, 1013
Buford, Mildred Blackburn VI, 899
Buford, Mildred E. VI, 886
Buford, Milly VI, 916
Buford, Morning VI, 810
Buford, Nancy VI, 885
Buford, Nancy VI, 930
Buford, Nancy VI, 952
Buford, Paschal VI, 885
Buford, Paschal VI, 886
Buford, Paschal VI, 899
Buford, Paschal VI, 911
Buford, Paschal VI, 945
Buford, Paschal VI, 992
Buford, Paschal VI, 997
Buford, Permelia VI, 920
Buford, Perthania VI, 1012
Buford, Philip VI, 885
Buford, Polly VI, 916
Buford, Polly M. VI, 945
Buford, Prudence VI, 879
Buford, R. D. VI, 878
Buford, Rhody VI, 885
Buford, Rodah VI, 948
Buford, Simeon VI, 915
Buford, Simeon VI, 952
Buford, Sophia VI, 885
Buford, William VI, 885
Buford, William VI, 911
Buford, William VI, 990
Buford, William, Jr. VI, 993
Bugby, John W. VI, 815
Bugg, Jesse VI, 885
Bugg, Molly VI, 885
Buher, Robert V, 988
Buhrman, Lucille V, 155
Buhrman, Wilbur V, 155
Buhrman, Wm. Wilbur V, 155
Buik, James III, 51
Bukley, Abraham II, 476
Bukston, Ellen II, 59
Bukston, Ellen II, 102
Bukston, Hannah II, 59
Bukston, Samuel Stretch II, 59
Bukston, Sarah II, 59
Bukston, Simon II, 59
Bukston, Simon II, 102
Buley, Christopher VI, 934
Buley, Matilda VI, 957
Buley, Sarah VI, 934
Bulger, Anna IV, 414
Bulger, Annie D. II, 709
Bulger, Annie D. II, 715
Bulkley, Ann II, 342
Bulkley, Anne II, 477
Bulkley, Anne II, 537
Bulkley, Anne II, 567
Bulkley, Caroline III, 51
Bulkley, Caroline III, 257
Bulkley, Jacob III, 51
Bulkley, Peter III, 51
Bulkley, Peter III, 52
Bulkley, Phebe III, 51
Bulkley, Phebe III, 52
Bulkley, Ruth III, 52
Bulkley, Samuel II, 342
Bulkley, Samuel II, 477
Bulkley, Samuel II, 567
Bulkley, Thomas II, 342
Bulkley, William III, 51
Bull, Anna III, 52
Bull, Anna B. III, 346
Bull, Daniel VI, 374
Bull, David Millburn VI, 374
Bull, Deborah II, 477
Bull, Ebenezer III, 52
Bull, Ebenezer III, 346
Bull, Ebenezer III, 397
Bull, Ebenezer III, 405
Bull, Elijah I, 777
Bull, Elizabeth I, 777
Bull, Elizabeth I, 797
Bull, Elizabeth I, 802
Bull, Irving F. IV, 182
Bull, Jane III, 52
Bull, Jane III, 157
Bull, Jane III, 346
Bull, Jane III, 397
Bull, Jane III, 405
Bull, Jesse I, 674
Bull, Jesse I, 675
Bull, Jesse I, 777
Bull, Jesse I, 802
Bull, Job I, 777
Bull, John I, 777
Bull, John I, 802
Bull, John VI, 1015
Bull, John David VI, 374
Bull, John Millburn VI, 374
Bull, Jonah VI, 374
Bull, Jonathan I, 777
Bull, Joseph I, 674
Bull, Joseph I, 675
Bull, Joseph I, 777
Bull, Joseph I, 802
Bull, Lydia VI, 373
Bull, Lydia VI, 374
Bull, Margaret I, 674
Bull, Margaret I, 675
Bull, Martha III, 397
Bull, Martha III, 405
Bull, Mary I, 777
Bull, Mary I, 802
Bull, Mary I, 841
Bull, Mary VI, 374
Bull, Mary VI, 423
Bull, Mary Ann IV, 686

ull, Mary Ann IV, 711
ull, Mary Beeson I, 802
ull, Rachel I, 674
ull, Rachel I, 675
ull, Rachel VI, 374
ull, Rachel VI, 415
ull, Richard I, 777
ull, Richard I, 802
ull, Richard VI, 374
ull, Richard VI, 415
ull, Robert I, 1027
ull, Robert VI, 374
ull, Robert VI, 423
ull, Robert Millburn VI, 374
ull, Sarah I, 1027
ull, Sarah III, 157
ull, Sarah VI, 374
ull, Sarah VI, 423
ull, Sarah Lydia Hannah VI, 374
ull, Thomas I, 777
ull, Thomas I, 797
ull, Thomas I, 802
ull, Wd. Sarah VI, 423
ull, William I, 777
ull, William I, 802
ull, William Talbolt I, 777
ulla, Archie N. I, 710
ulla, Clarissa I, 760
ulla, Daniel Webster I, 614
ulla, Grace I, 938
ulla, Gulia I, 873
ulla, James R. I, 873
ulla, James Ruffin I, 873
ulla, Joseph C. I, 710
ulla, Leena I, 614
ulla, Lilyan I, 938
ulla, Litetia I, 614
ulla, Lois I, 873
ulla, Lydia L. I, 710
ulla, Lydia L. I, 719
ulla, Matthew I, 300
ulla, Milicent I, 710
ulla, Milicent I, 733
ulla, Mrs. T. J. I, 938
ulla, Sarah I, 932
ulla, Sarah Charlotte I, 932
ulla, T. J. I, 938
ulla, Watson W. I, 932
ullar, Thomas, Jr. I, 529
ullard, Alexander II, 342
ullard, Elizabeth I, 710
ullard, Elizabeth I, 721
ullard, John, Jr. IV, 1355
ullen, Ada Ruth V, 478
ullen, Claybourne V, 478
ullen, Elvert V, 478
ullen, Elvert L. V, 478
ullen, Estella V, 478
ullen, Harold William V, 552
ullen, Harold William V, 662
ullen, Harold Wm. V, 552
ullen, Herbert L. V, 478
ullen, Hubert Lee V, 552
ullen, Hubert Lee V, 662
ullen, I. C. V, 552
ullen, Isaac Claybourne V, 552
ullen, Isaac Clayhorn V, 552
ullen, Isaac Clayton V, 662
ullen, James II, 442
ullen, James Ansther V, 478
ullen, James Arthur V, 552
ullen, John Spencer V, 552
ullen, John Spencer V, 662
ullen, Martha II, 442
ullen, Mary Estella V, 552
ullen, Mary Estelle V, 662
ullen, Ruth Ida V, 552
ullen, Virgil Byron V, 552
ullen, Virgil Byron V, 662
uller, Elizabeth VI, 161
uller, Gulia I, 873
uller, Gulia I, 890
uller, James VI, 161
uller, James R. I, 873
uller, James Ruffin I, 873
uller, Lois I, 873
uller, Lois I, 890
uller, Wd. ??? VI, 161
ullezer, ??? V, 877
ullin, Elvert V, 478
ulloch, Charles II, 730
ulloch, Mary L. II, 730
ullock, Abigail II, 477
ullock, Amos II, 130
ullock, Amos II, 168
ullock, Amos II, 202
ullock, Amos II, 272
ullock, Amos II, 475
ullock, Amos II, 477
ullock, Ann VI, 808
Bullock, Anna E. II, 805
Bullock, Annie II, 130
Bullock, Annie II, 146
Bullock, Anthony II, 827
Bullock, Anthony S. II, 168
Bullock, Charles II, 730
Bullock, Charles Peck II, 202
Bullock, Charles Peck II, 282
Bullock, David II, 146
Bullock, David II, 168
Bullock, David II, 477
Bullock, David B. II, 137
Bullock, David B. II, 146
Bullock, David B. II, 156
Bullock, David Barton II, 130
Bullock, Edith II, 342
Bullock, Edith II, 477
Bullock, Edith Wood II, 827
Bullock, Edward II, 202
Bullock, Edward II, 984
Bullock, Edward II, 1047
Bullock, Edward II, 1069
Bullock, Eliza VI, 801
Bullock, Elizabeth II, 59
Bullock, Elizabeth II, 74
Bullock, Elizabeth II, 130
Bullock, Elizabeth II, 168
Bullock, Elizabeth II, 202
Bullock, Elizabeth II, 282
Bullock, Elizabeth III, 52
Bullock, Elizabeth III, 119
Bullock, Elizabeth VI, 892
Bullock, Elizabeth S. II, 202
Bullock, Elizabeth Sharp II, 138
Bullock, George II, 342
Bullock, George II, 477
Bullock, George II, 692
Bullock, Hannah II, 130
Bullock, Hannah II, 137
Bullock, Hannah II, 146
Bullock, Hannah II, 156
Bullock, Hannah II, 202
Bullock, Hannah II, 827
Bullock, Hannah VI, 874
Bullock, Isaac II, 59
Bullock, Isaac II, 74
Bullock, Isaac II, 202
Bullock, Isaac II, 984
Bullock, Isaac II, 1047
Bullock, Isaac II, 1069
Bullock, Isaac, Jr. II, 984
Bullock, James P. VI, 801
Bullock, James P. VI, 806
Bullock, James P. VI, 845
Bullock, James P. VI, 854
Bullock, John II, 59
Bullock, John II, 74
Bullock, John II, 202
Bullock, John II, 272
Bullock, John II, 1047
Bullock, John II, 1069
Bullock, John VI, 808
Bullock, John VI, 995
Bullock, Jonathan II, 1047
Bullock, Jonathan II, 1069
Bullock, Jonus VI, 806
Bullock, Joseph II, 477
Bullock, Joshua II, 202
Bullock, Joshua II, 842
Bullock, Josiah VI, 805
Bullock, Josiah VI, 821
Bullock, Josiah VI, 829
Bullock, Josias VI, 892
Bullock, Latitia II, 1047
Bullock, Letitia II, 1069
Bullock, Lidia II, 202
Bullock, Lydia II, 168
Bullock, Lydia II, 202
Bullock, Lydia II, 272
Bullock, Margaret II, 202
Bullock, Margaret II, 272
Bullock, Margaret II, 282
Bullock, Margaret II, 298
Bullock, Margaret II, 317
Bullock, Margaret II, 475
Bullock, Margaret II, 477
Bullock, Margaret II, 842
Bullock, Margaret Collins II, 780
Bullock, Margaretta II, 282
Bullock, Martha Ann VI, 995
Bullock, Mary II, 477
Bullock, Mary II, 541
Bullock, Mary L. II, 752
Bullock, Mona IV, 182
Bullock, Nancey VI, 874
Bullock, Nancy VI, 845
Bullock, Patience III, 52
Bullock, Patience III, 119
Bullock, Patterson VI, 845
Bullock, Patty VI, 805
Bullock, Priscilla I, 756
Bullock, Priscilla I, 764
Bullock, Rachel II, 59
Bullock, Rachel II, 74
Bullock, Samuel II, 202
Bullock, Samuel II, 282
Bullock, Sarah II, 475
Bullock, Sarah II, 477
Bullock, Sarah II, 842
Bullock, Sarah II, 984
Bullock, Sarah II, 986
Bullock, Sarah II, 1047
Bullock, Sarah II, 1069
Bullock, Sarah VI, 45
Bullock, Sarah VI, 46
Bullock, Sarah Ann II, 1047
Bullock, Sarah Ann II, 1069
Bullock, Susan II, 130
Bullock, Susan II, 137
Bullock, Susan E. II, 146
Bullock, Susan E. II, 156
Bullock, Susanna VI, 829
Bullock, Thomas I, 38
Bullock, William II, 202
Bullock, William II, 282
Bullock, William III, 397
Bullock, Wm. II, 477
Bulls, Franklin VI, 56
Bulls, Irvin VI, 56
Bulow, Adolph S. III, 397
Bulow, Maria Barbara III, 397
Bumbaugh, Charles Claud IV, 686
Bumbaugh, Drusilla IV, 686
Bumbaugh, Drusilla S. IV, 686
Bumbaugh, Drusilla S. IV, 736
Bumbaugh, Etta IV, 686
Bumbaugh, George IV, 686
Bumbaugh, George H. IV, 686
Bumpass, Elizabeth VI, 814
Bumpass, William VI, 814
Bumpass, William VI, 867
Bumpass, Wm. VI, 986
Bumpus, Lucie II, 842
Bumpus, Lucie H. II, 835
Bumstead, Dorothy II, 477
Bumstead, Elizabeth II, 477
Bumstide, Dorothy II, 477
Bumstide, Elizabeth II, 477
Bun, Temperance I, 301
Bun, Temperance I, 302
Bun, William II, 342
Bunce, John II, 477
Bunce, Richard II, 477
Bunch, ??? VI, 223
Bunch, ??? VI, 283
Bunch, Ann VI, 232
Bunch, Ann VI, 300
Bunch, Betsy VI, 933
Bunch, Catharine VI, 903
Bunch, Charles VI, 232
Bunch, Charles VI, 933
Bunch, Elizabeth VI, 231
Bunch, Elizabeth C. VI, 883
Bunch, George VI, 232
Bunch, George VI, 885
Bunch, George VI, 932
Bunch, Hannah VI, 231
Bunch, Hannah VI, 885
Bunch, James VI, 231
Bunch, James VI, 232
Bunch, James VI, 300
Bunch, James VI, 880
Bunch, James VI, 886
Bunch, James VI, 896
Bunch, James VI, 903
Bunch, James VI, 911
Bunch, James VI, 980
Bunch, James VI, 990
Bunch, James VI, 994
Bunch, Joseph VI, 886
Bunch, Katuri I, 38
Bunch, Margery VI, 232
Bunch, Martha VI, 231
Bunch, Mary VI, 231
Bunch, Mary VI, 232
Bunch, Mary VI, 285
Bunch, Mary VI, 300
Bunch, Mary VI, 872
Bunch, Mary VI, 886
Bunch, Mitchell VI, 886
Bunch, Molley VI, 232
Bunch, Nancy VI, 232
Bunch, Nancy VI, 911
Bunch, Nancy VI, 980
Bunch, Polly VI, 911
Bunch, Priscilla VI, 232
Bunch, Priscilla VI, 990
Bunch, Rebecca VI, 231
Bunch, Ruth VI, 886
Bunch, Samuel VI, 231
Bunch, Samuel VI, 232
Bunch, Samuel VI, 285
Bunch, Samuel, Jr. VI, 232
Bunch, Sarah VI, 232
Bunch, Susanna VI, 231
Bunch, Susanna VI, 886
Bunch, Susannah VI, 896
Bunch, Walter VI, 883
Bunda, Axey I, 301
Bunda, Axey I, 306
Bunda, Dempsey I, 960
Bunda, Gulielma I, 911
Bunda, Gulielma I, 913
Bunda, Leah I, 873
Bunda, Mary I, 873
Bunda, Moses I, 960
Bunda, Thomas I, 960
Bunda, Thomas E. I, 911
Bunda, William I, 960
Bunday, Ely I, 711
Bunde, John I, 97
Bunde, Joseph I, 97
Bunde, Mary I, 97
Bunde, William I, 97
Bunden, Louisa I, 529
Bunden, Louisa I, 581
Bunderant, Celia Ann VI, 914
Bunderant, James VI, 914
Bunderin, Martha I, 802
Bunderin, Martha I, 840
Bundram, Phebe I, 799
Bundram, Phebe I, 802
Bundrant, Cuzzy VI, 995
Bundrant, John VI, 995
Bundrant, Martha S. VI, 927
Bundron, Louisa I, 529
Bundrun, Celia VI, 918
Bundurant, Jesse G. VI, 881
Bundurant, Joel VI, 990
Bundurant, Joseph VI, 880
Bundurant, Littleberry VI, 880
Bundurant, Littleberry VI, 990
Bundurant, Lucy VI, 990
Bundurant, Martha Ann VI, 881
Bundurant, Mary VI, 880
Bundurant, Mildred VI, 1017
Bundurant, Nancy VI, 880
Bundurant, Nancy VI, 1017
Bundurant, Peggy VI, 880
Bundurant, Tabitha VI, 884
Bundurant, Thomas VI, 880
Bundurant, Zelpah VI, 1006
Bundy, ??? I, 279
Bundy, ??? IV, 375
Bundy, ??? IV, 550
Bundy, ??? IV, 1085
Bundy, ??? IV, 1125
Bundy, ??? V, 375
Bundy, Aaron I, 97
Bundy, Aaron IV, 444
Bundy, Aaron Morris, Sr. I, 132
Bundy, Abbie IV, 569
Bundy, Abbie IV, 574
Bundy, Abel IV, 1096
Bundy, Abel Trueblood I, 132
Bundy, Abigail I, 265
Bundy, Abigail I, 268
Bundy, Abigail IV, 23
Bundy, Abigail IV, 77
Bundy, Abigail IV, 141
Bundy, Abigail IV, 163
Bundy, Abigail IV, 183
Bundy, Abigail IV, 300
Bundy, Abigail IV, 569
Bundy, Abigail IV, 1050
Bundy, Abigail IV, 1051
Bundy, Abigail IV, 1071
Bundy, Abigail IV, 1081
Bundy, Abigail P. II, 722
Bundy, Abraham I, 38
Bundy, Abraham I, 74
Bundy, Abraham I, 132
Bundy, Abraham I, 172
Bundy, Abraham I, 180
Bundy, Abraham I, 182
Bundy, Abraham I, 190
Bundy, Abraham I, 710
Bundy, Abraham I, 802
Bundy, Abram I, 802
Bundy, Achsa I, 710
Bundy, Achsah I, 182
Bundy, Achsah I, 190
Bundy, Achsah I, 710
Bundy, Achsah I, 802
Bundy, Achsah IV, 376
Bundy, Achsah IV, 569
Bundy, Achsah IV, 570
Bundy, Achsah IV, 574
Bundy, Achsah IV, 582
Bundy, Achsah IV, 1050
Bundy, Achsah IV, 1051
Bundy, Achsah IV, 1056
Bundy, Achsah IV, 1058
Bundy, Achsah IV, 1089
Bundy, Achsah IV, 1096
Bundy, Achsah Embree IV, 1089
Bundy, Achsah R. IV, 183
Bundy, Achsah R. IV, 515
Bundy, Adaline IV, 1090
Bundy, Adaline W. IV, 1089
Bundy, Adaline W. IV, 1111
Bundy, Adella May V, 155
Bundy, Agnes M. IV, 376
Bundy, Agnes May IV, 374
Bundy, Albert H. IV, 375
Bundy, Aletha I, 924
Bundy, Alice IV, 410
Bundy, Alice D. IV, 376
Bundy, Alice D. IV, 420
Bundy, Alise IV, 1273
Bundy, Allen IV, 183
Bundy, Allen IV, 373
Bundy, Allen IV, 375
Bundy, Allen E. IV, 183
Bundy, Almeda IV, 374
Bundy, Alsie B. V, 155
Bundy, Alva V, 155
Bundy, Amanda IV, 183
Bundy, Amanda IV, 374
Bundy, Amanda IV, 376
Bundy, Amanda IV, 394
Bundy, Amos IV, 1089
Bundy, Amos IV, 1101
Bundy, Amy B. IV, 376
Bundy, Amy B. IV, 430
Bundy, Ann I, 95
Bundy, Ann I, 131
Bundy, Ann I, 142
Bundy, Ann I, 144
Bundy, Ann I, 167
Bundy, Ann II, 709
Bundy, Ann IV, 141
Bundy, Ann IV, 142
Bundy, Ann IV, 182
Bundy, Ann IV, 183
Bundy, Ann IV, 191
Bundy, Ann IV, 216
Bundy, Ann IV, 294
Bundy, Ann IV, 365
Bundy, Ann IV, 373
Bundy, Ann IV, 374
Bundy, Ann IV, 375
Bundy, Ann IV, 381
Bundy, Ann IV, 393
Bundy, Ann IV, 458
Bundy, Ann IV, 1050
Bundy, Ann V, 299
Bundy, Ann V, 302
Bundy, Ann T. IV, 141
Bundy, Anna I, 873
Bundy, Anna I, 1003
Bundy, Anna II, 705
Bundy, Anna IV, 183
Bundy, Anna IV, 366
Bundy, Anna IV, 374
Bundy, Anna IV, 375
Bundy, Anna IV, 376
Bundy, Anna IV, 387
Bundy, Anna IV, 389
Bundy, Anna IV, 393
Bundy, Anna IV, 441
Bundy, Anna IV, 570
Bundy, Anna V, 299
Bundy, Anna C. I, 529
Bundy, Anna D. IV, 390
Bundy, Anna M. IV, 183
Bundy, Anna M. IV, 285
Bundy, Anna M. IV, 686
Bundy, Anna M. IV, 770
Bundy, Anna M. IV, 772
Bundy, Anna Maria IV, 183
Bundy, Anna Maria IV, 376
Bundy, Anna Maria IV, 452
Bundy, Anna Mary IV, 182
Bundy, Anna Mary IV, 698
Bundy, Anna Mary IV, 749
Bundy, Anna Rebecca IV, 375
Bundy, Anna S. IV, 374
Bundy, Anna S. IV, 383
Bundy, Anne I, 131
Bundy, Anne IV, 374
Bundy, Anne IV, 569
Bundy, Anne IV, 576
Bundy, Anne C. I, 529
Bundy, Anne Maria IV, 373
Bundy, Annie I, 232
Bundy, Annie IV, 375
Bundy, Arthur H. IV, 183
Bundy, Asenath IV, 182
Bundy, Asenath IV, 183
Bundy, Asenath IV, 213
Bundy, Asenath IV, 243
Bundy, Asenath IV, 374

Bundy, Asenath IV, 375
Bundy, Asenath IV, 377
Bundy, Asenath IV, 386
Bundy, Asenath IV, 614
Bundy, Asenath IV, 687
Bundy, Asenath IV, 1050
Bundy, Asenath IV, 1051
Bundy, Asenath IV, 1089
Bundy, Asenath H. IV, 184
Bundy, Asenith IV, 183
Bundy, Aurora E. IV, 374
Bundy, Aurora E. IV, 375
Bundy, Aurora E. IV, 390
Bundy, Axey I, 301
Bundy, Bailey IV, 183
Bundy, Bailey IV, 373
Bundy, Bailey IV, 376
Bundy, Bathia IV, 23
Bundy, Bathia IV, 77
Bundy, Bathia IV, 141
Bundy, Bathia IV, 163
Bundy, Bathiah I, 268
Bundy, Bathiah IV, 142
Bundy, Bathiah IV, 161
Bundy, Bathiah IV, 182
Bundy, Bathiah IV, 373
Bundy, Beniamon I, 96
Bundy, Benj. IV, 182
Bundy, Benj. IV, 280
Bundy, Benj. IV, 374
Bundy, Benjamin I, 94
Bundy, Benjamin I, 95
Bundy, Benjamin I, 96
Bundy, Benjamin I, 129
Bundy, Benjamin I, 132
Bundy, Benjamin I, 133
Bundy, Benjamin I, 137
Bundy, Benjamin I, 190
Bundy, Benjamin I, 265
Bundy, Benjamin I, 268
Bundy, Benjamin I, 778
Bundy, Benjamin IV, 23
Bundy, Benjamin IV, 76
Bundy, Benjamin IV, 77
Bundy, Benjamin IV, 122
Bundy, Benjamin IV, 141
Bundy, Benjamin IV, 182
Bundy, Benjamin IV, 183
Bundy, Benjamin IV, 216
Bundy, Benjamin IV, 365
Bundy, Benjamin IV, 373
Bundy, Benjamin IV, 435
Bundy, Benjamin IV, 515
Bundy, Benjamin IV, 569
Bundy, Benjamin IV, 1050
Bundy, Benjamin IV, 1089
Bundy, Benjamin IV, 1107
Bundy, Benjamin IV, 1128
Bundy, Bertha IV, 183
Bundy, Bertha IV, 375
Bundy, Bertha IV, 416
Bundy, Bertha A. IV, 176
Bundy, Bertha A. IV, 183
Bundy, Bertha A. IV, 375
Bundy, Bertha R. IV, 375
Bundy, Bertha R. IV, 416
Bundy, Bertram H. IV, 374
Bundy, Bertram H. IV, 376
Bundy, Bethia IV, 141
Bundy, Bethia IV, 1050
Bundy, Bethia IV, 1051
Bundy, Bethiah I, 265
Bundy, Bethiah I, 268
Bundy, Bethiah I, 274
Bundy, Bethiah IV, 163
Bundy, Bethiah IV, 182
Bundy, Bethiah IV, 183
Bundy, Bethiah IV, 1083
Bundy, Bethial IV, 183
Bundy, C. Ellis IV, 376
Bundy, Cabbal I, 132
Bundy, Caleb I, 36
Bundy, Caleb I, 38
Bundy, Caleb I, 52
Bundy, Caleb I, 86
Bundy, Caleb I, 91
Bundy, Caleb I, 92
Bundy, Caleb I, 94
Bundy, Caleb I, 95
Bundy, Caleb I, 96
Bundy, Caleb I, 97
Bundy, Caleb I, 131
Bundy, Caleb I, 132
Bundy, Caleb I, 133
Bundy, Caleb I, 134
Bundy, Caleb I, 144
Bundy, Caleb I, 146
Bundy, Caleb I, 154
Bundy, Caleb I, 185
Bundy, Caleb I, 190
Bundy, Caleb I, 232
Bundy, Caleb I, 710
Bundy, Caleb I, 851
Bundy, Caleb I, 873
Bundy, Caleb I, 1003
Bundy, Caleb IV, 373
Bundy, Caleb IV, 374
Bundy, Caleb IV, 404
Bundy, Caleb IV, 438
Bundy, Caleb IV, 1050
Bundy, Caleb IV, 1051
Bundy, Caleb V, 299
Bundy, Caleb L. IV, 374
Bundy, Caleb Trueblood I, 132
Bundy, Caleb, Jr. I, 132
Bundy, Caleb, Sr. I, 95
Bundy, Caleb, Sr. I, 96
Bundy, Caleb, Sr. I, 132
Bundy, Callop I, 96
Bundy, Callop I, 97
Bundy, Caroline I, 1003
Bundy, Caroline V, 299
Bundy, Carver T. IV, 375
Bundy, Carver T. IV, 431
Bundy, Chalkey L. IV, 214
Bundy, Chalkley IV, 183
Bundy, Chalkley IV, 373
Bundy, Chalkley IV, 374
Bundy, Chalkley IV, 375
Bundy, Chalkley IV, 386
Bundy, Chalkley IV, 404
Bundy, Chalkley IV, 441
Bundy, Chalkley IV, 1089
Bundy, Chalkley IV, 1097
Bundy, Chalkley A. IV, 176
Bundy, Chalkley Clinton IV, 374
Bundy, Chalkley L. IV, 183
Bundy, Chalkley L. IV, 184
Bundy, Chalkley L. IV, 375
Bundy, Chalkley L. IV, 376
Bundy, Chalkley L. IV, 569
Bundy, Chalkley, Jr. IV, 183
Bundy, Charity IV, 373
Bundy, Charity IV, 374
Bundy, Charity IV, 441
Bundy, Charles I, 95
Bundy, Charles I, 96
Bundy, Charles I, 97
Bundy, Charles I, 133
Bundy, Charles I, 134
Bundy, Charles I, 143
Bundy, Charles I, 190
Bundy, Charles I, 198
Bundy, Charles IV, 182
Bundy, Charles IV, 183
Bundy, Charles IV, 184
Bundy, Charles IV, 322
Bundy, Charles IV, 374
Bundy, Charles IV, 375
Bundy, Charles IV, 376
Bundy, Charles IV, 392
Bundy, Charles IV, 411
Bundy, Charles Francis IV, 410
Bundy, Chas. I, 134
Bundy, Chester M. IV, 184
Bundy, Chester M. IV, 804
Bundy, Christopher I, 95
Bundy, Christopher I, 132
Bundy, Christopher I, 133
Bundy, Christopher I, 675
Bundy, Christopher I, 679
Bundy, Christopher I, 697
Bundy, Christopher I, 710
Bundy, Christopher I, 802
Bundy, Cidney IV, 570
Bundy, Clara IV, 366
Bundy, Clara IV, 375
Bundy, Clara IV, 579
Bundy, Clara Elma IV, 374
Bundy, Clara L. IV, 375
Bundy, Clarence IV, 375
Bundy, Clarence E. IV, 183
Bundy, Clarence E. IV, 184
Bundy, Clarence E. IV, 376
Bundy, Clarhs IV, 183
Bundy, Clarkson IV, 374
Bundy, Clarkson IV, 1089
Bundy, Clifford C. IV, 183
Bundy, Clifford C. IV, 184
Bundy, Clifford C. IV, 196
Bundy, Clifford C. IV, 569
Bundy, Clifford C. IV, 574
Bundy, Clifford C. IV, 575
Bundy, Clifford Carver IV, 375
Bundy, Clifford J. IV, 375
Bundy, Clifford M. IV, 183
Bundy, Clinton IV, 569
Bundy, Clinton T. IV, 375
Bundy, Clinton T. IV, 376
Bundy, Damaris I, 300
Bundy, Damaris I, 309
Bundy, Damaris V, 299
Bundy, Daniel W. I, 778
Bundy, David I, 132
Bundy, David I, 300
Bundy, David I, 301
Bundy, David I, 309
Bundy, David IV, 182
Bundy, David IV, 183
Bundy, David IV, 184
Bundy, David IV, 373
Bundy, David IV, 569
Bundy, David IV, 1050
Bundy, David IV, 1051
Bundy, David IV, 1058
Bundy, David IV, 1089
Bundy, David IV, 1128
Bundy, David Embree IV, 1051
Bundy, Debora M. IV, 299
Bundy, Deborah IV, 182
Bundy, Deborah IV, 183
Bundy, Deborah IV, 285
Bundy, Deborah IV, 374
Bundy, Deborah IV, 404
Bundy, Deborah IV, 438
Bundy, Deborah IV, 441
Bundy, Deborah IV, 1050
Bundy, Deborah IV, 1051
Bundy, Deborah H. IV, 374
Bundy, Deborah H. IV, 404
Bundy, Deborah M. IV, 184
Bundy, Deborah M. IV, 289
Bundy, Deborah M. IV, 770
Bundy, Deborah M. IV, 931
Bundy, Deborah M. IV, 971
Bundy, Deborah M. IV, 1012
Bundy, Deborah N. IV, 183
Bundy, Delitha IV, 122
Bundy, Delitha IV, 141
Bundy, Delitha IV, 182
Bundy, Delitha IV, 216
Bundy, Delitha IV, 280
Bundy, Delitha IV, 365
Bundy, Delitha IV, 373
Bundy, Delitha IV, 374
Bundy, Delitha IV, 375
Bundy, Delitha IV, 515
Bundy, Demcy I, 190
Bundy, Dempcey I, 95
Bundy, Dempsey I, 134
Bundy, Dempsey I, 960
Bundy, Dempsey IV, 183
Bundy, Dempsey IV, 374
Bundy, Demsey I, 38
Bundy, Demsey I, 95
Bundy, Demsey I, 132
Bundy, Demsey I, 133
Bundy, Demsey I, 190
Bundy, Demsey I, 300
Bundy, Demsey IV, 373
Bundy, Demsey IV, 374
Bundy, Demsey IV, 375
Bundy, Demsey IV, 376
Bundy, Demsey IV, 381
Bundy, Demsey IV, 393
Bundy, Demsey IV, 439
Bundy, Demsey IV, 515
Bundy, Demsey IV, 550
Bundy, Demsy I, 1007
Bundy, Deney I, 983
Bundy, Densey IV, 458
Bundy, Dianna I, 873
Bundy, Dillwyn IV, 183
Bundy, Dillwyn C. II, 953
Bundy, Dillwyn C. IV, 374
Bundy, Dillwyn C. IV, 375
Bundy, Donald IV, 183
Bundy, Dortha M. IV, 375
Bundy, Edith IV, 374
Bundy, Edith IV, 376
Bundy, Edith IV, 441
Bundy, Edith IV, 1089
Bundy, Edith L. IV, 1089
Bundy, Edith M. IV, 375
Bundy, Edmon IV, 182
Bundy, Edmond IV, 183
Bundy, Edmund IV, 182
Bundy, Edmund IV, 183
Bundy, Edmund IV, 285
Bundy, Edmund IV, 289
Bundy, Edmund IV, 299
Bundy, Edmund IV, 770
Bundy, Edmund IV, 1012
Bundy, Edna A. IV, 375
Bundy, Edna Dorothy IV, 183
Bundy, Edom T. V, 375
Bundy, Edom T. V, 376
Bundy, Edom Talbot V, 375
Bundy, Effie Ann IV, 122
Bundy, Effie Ann IV, 182
Bundy, Effie Ann IV, 183
Bundy, Effie Anna IV, 183
Bundy, Elden J. IV, 183
Bundy, Eldon C. IV, 376
Bundy, Eldon J. IV, 184
Bundy, Eldon J. IV, 376
Bundy, Eleanor I, 38
Bundy, Eleanor I, 96
Bundy, Eleanor I, 268
Bundy, Elener I, 300
Bundy, Elenor I, 132
Bundy, Elenor I, 160
Bundy, Eli I, 133
Bundy, Eli I, 710
Bundy, Eli IV, 373
Bundy, Eli IV, 374
Bundy, Eli IV, 375
Bundy, Eli IV, 386
Bundy, Eli IV, 423
Bundy, Eli IV, 450
Bundy, Eli IV, 1089
Bundy, Elias I, 94
Bundy, Elias I, 95
Bundy, Elias I, 134
Bundy, Elias I, 190
Bundy, Elias I, 198
Bundy, Elias IV, 373
Bundy, Elias IV, 375
Bundy, Elias IV, 569
Bundy, Elias IV, 1050
Bundy, Elias IV, 1089
Bundy, Elias IV, 1115
Bundy, Elias IV, 1128
Bundy, Elijah IV, 441
Bundy, Eliner I, 300
Bundy, Elinor I, 132
Bundy, Elisabeth I, 38
Bundy, Elisabeth I, 52
Bundy, Elisabeth I, 96
Bundy, Elisabeth I, 131
Bundy, Elisabeth I, 132
Bundy, Elisabeth I, 133
Bundy, Elisabeth I, 143
Bundy, Elisabeth I, 147
Bundy, Elisabeth I, 190
Bundy, Elisabeth I, 232
Bundy, Eliza I, 129
Bundy, Eliza I, 132
Bundy, Eliza I, 873
Bundy, Eliza IV, 441
Bundy, Eliza A. V, 614
Bundy, Eliza Ann I, 778
Bundy, Eliza Ann V, 614
Bundy, Elizabeth I, 95
Bundy, Elizabeth I, 96
Bundy, Elizabeth I, 97
Bundy, Elizabeth I, 131
Bundy, Elizabeth I, 132
Bundy, Elizabeth I, 134
Bundy, Elizabeth I, 142
Bundy, Elizabeth I, 144
Bundy, Elizabeth I, 167
Bundy, Elizabeth I, 182
Bundy, Elizabeth I, 267
Bundy, Elizabeth I, 268
Bundy, Elizabeth I, 300
Bundy, Elizabeth I, 710
Bundy, Elizabeth I, 711
Bundy, Elizabeth I, 802
Bundy, Elizabeth I, 838
Bundy, Elizabeth I, 851
Bundy, Elizabeth I, 873
Bundy, Elizabeth I, 932
Bundy, Elizabeth I, 938
Bundy, Elizabeth II, 705
Bundy, Elizabeth II, 953
Bundy, Elizabeth IV, 183
Bundy, Elizabeth IV, 365
Bundy, Elizabeth IV, 374
Bundy, Elizabeth IV, 375
Bundy, Elizabeth IV, 393
Bundy, Elizabeth IV, 411
Bundy, Elizabeth IV, 412
Bundy, Elizabeth IV, 438
Bundy, Elizabeth IV, 441
Bundy, Elizabeth IV, 569
Bundy, Elizabeth IV, 687
Bundy, Elizabeth IV, 1050
Bundy, Elizabeth IV, 1051
Bundy, Elizabeth IV, 1128
Bundy, Elizabeth C. V, 729
Bundy, Elizabeth C. V, 757
Bundy, Elizabeth D. IV, 122
Bundy, Elizabeth D. IV, 182
Bundy, Elizabeth D. IV, 183
Bundy, Elizabeth D. IV, 184
Bundy, Elizabeth D. IV, 186
Bundy, Elizabeth D. IV, 804
Bundy, Elizabeth D. IV, 805
Bundy, Elizabeth R. I, 922
Bundy, Elizabeth R. IV, 375
Bundy, Elizabeth R. IV, 1089
Bundy, Ella V, 155
Bundy, Ellen I, 95
Bundy, Ellen I, 134
Bundy, Ellen IV, 183
Bundy, Ellen IV, 374
Bundy, Ellen IV, 376
Bundy, Ellen IV, 1089
Bundy, Ellen M. IV, 182
Bundy, Ellen M. IV, 183
Bundy, Ellen M. IV, 243
Bundy, Ellis I, 38
Bundy, Ellis I, 96
Bundy, Ellis I, 268
Bundy, Ellis IV, 375
Bundy, Elmer A. V, 155
Bundy, Elmer E. IV, 376
Bundy, Elmer Elsworth IV, 374
Bundy, Elmer J. IV, 182
Bundy, Elmer J. IV, 183
Bundy, Elmer J. IV, 184
Bundy, Elmira IV, 122
Bundy, Elva IV, 375
Bundy, Elvira IV, 183
Bundy, Elwood I, 802
Bundy, Ely I, 711
Bundy, Emila IV, 373
Bundy, Emily IV, 183
Bundy, Emily IV, 374
Bundy, Emily IV, 393
Bundy, Emlen IV, 1050
Bundy, Emlen IV, 1051
Bundy, Emlen IV, 1089
Bundy, Emlen IV, 1128
Bundy, Emma IV, 183
Bundy, Emma IV, 374
Bundy, Emma IV, 376
Bundy, Emma Almira IV, 122
Bundy, Emma Almira IV, 183
Bundy, Emma L. IV, 375
Bundy, Ephraim I, 710
Bundy, Ephraim I, 711
Bundy, Ephram I, 697
Bundy, Ernest D. IV, 375
Bundy, Ernest J. IV, 375
Bundy, Esther IV, 374
Bundy, Esther IV, 376
Bundy, Esther IV, 386
Bundy, Esther IV, 1089
Bundy, Esther IV, 1128
Bundy, Esther M. IV, 183
Bundy, Esther M. IV, 1203
Bundy, Ethel IV, 686
Bundy, Ethel E. IV, 375
Bundy, Eva L. IV, 375
Bundy, Evaline IV, 374
Bundy, Evalyn C. IV, 375
Bundy, Evalyn C. IV, 431
Bundy, Exum IV, 373
Bundy, Exum IV, 569
Bundy, Exum IV, 600
Bundy, Exum IV, 1050
Bundy, Exum IV, 1089
Bundy, Exum IV, 1128
Bundy, Ezekiel IV, 183
Bundy, Ezekiel IV, 373
Bundy, Ezekiel IV, 374
Bundy, Ezekiel IV, 375
Bundy, Ezekiel IV, 390
Bundy, Ezekiel IV, 411
Bundy, Ezekiel IV, 431
Bundy, Ezekiel IV, 441
Bundy, Ezekiel IV, 443
Bundy, Ezekiel IV, 1089
Bundy, Ezekiel IV, 1128
Bundy, Ezra Embree IV, 1051
Bundy, Foster IV, 184
Bundy, Francis IV, 411
Bundy, Francis Iral IV, 410
Bundy, Frank E. V, 614
Bundy, Frank Woodward IV, 56
Bundy, Frederick IV, 183
Bundy, Frederick R. IV, 184
Bundy, Frederick R. IV, 366
Bundy, Frederick R. IV, 375
Bundy, Frederick R. IV, 376
Bundy, Gedion I, 95
Bundy, George I, 38
Bundy, George I, 48
Bundy, George I, 60
Bundy, George I, 95
Bundy, George I, 96
Bundy, George I, 133
Bundy, George Rix I, 95
Bundy, George Wilson IV, 375
Bundy, Gideon I, 36
Bundy, Gideon I, 38
Bundy, Gideon I, 95
Bundy, Gideon I, 131
Bundy, Gideon I, 132
Bundy, Gideon I, 133
Bundy, Gideon I, 300
Bundy, Gideon I, 315
Bundy, Gideon I, 675

Bundy, Gideon I, 710
Bundy, Gideon I, 713
Bundy, Gulia I, 35
Bundy, Gulia I, 39
Bundy, Gulia I, 301
Bundy, Gulielma I, 3
Bundy, Gulielma I, 96
Bundy, Gulielma I, 133
Bundy, Gulielma I, 149
Bundy, Gulielma I, 802
Bundy, Gulielma I, 911
Bundy, Hannah I, 38
Bundy, Hannah I, 95
Bundy, Hannah I, 96
Bundy, Hannah I, 132
Bundy, Hannah I, 133
Bundy, Hannah I, 148
Bundy, Hannah I, 153
Bundy, Hannah I, 185
Bundy, Hannah I, 268
Bundy, Hannah I, 300
Bundy, Hannah I, 710
Bundy, Hannah I, 777
Bundy, Hannah I, 802
Bundy, Hannah IV, 183
Bundy, Hannah IV, 1050
Bundy, Hannah IV, 1051
Bundy, Hannah IV, 1089
Bundy, Hannah IV, 1114
Bundy, Hannah IV, 1138
Bundy, Hannah V, 299
Bundy, Hannah Bundy I, 267
Bundy, Hannah H. IV, 374
Bundy, Hannah S. IV, 1089
Bundy, Hannah S. IV, 1115
Bundy, Hannah S. IV, 1128
Bundy, Harmon I, 930
Bundy, Harold IV, 411
Bundy, Harriet IV, 1090
Bundy, Harriet IV, 1115
Bundy, Harrold L. IV, 410
Bundy, Harvey W. IV, 374
Bundy, Helen IV, 183
Bundy, Helen E. IV, 411
Bundy, Henry IV, 374
Bundy, Henry IV, 376
Bundy, Henry IV, 1089
Bundy, Henry IV, 1090
Bundy, Henry C. IV, 1273
Bundy, Henry C. V, 155
Bundy, Henry Keton I, 131
Bundy, Herbert F. IV, 183
Bundy, Himelies M. I, 851
Bundy, Hiram V, 155
Bundy, Howard C. IV, 375
Bundy, Hulda I, 697
Bundy, Huldah I, 96
Bundy, Huldah I, 132
Bundy, Huldah I, 133
Bundy, Huldah I, 143
Bundy, Huldah I, 182
Bundy, Huldah I, 650
Bundy, Huldah I, 675
Bundy, Huldah I, 679
Bundy, Huldah I, 695
Bundy, Huldah I, 710
Bundy, Huldah I, 873
Bundy, Hulday I, 133
Bundy, Huldy I, 132
Bundy, Huldy I, 143
Bundy, Isaac I, 132
Bundy, Isaac V, 614
Bundy, Isaac C. IV, 1089
Bundy, Isaac C. IV, 1128
Bundy, Isaac C. V, 614
Bundy, Israel IV, 176
Bundy, Jabez I, 697
Bundy, Jabez I, 711
Bundy, Jabez I, 851
Bundy, Jabez I, 873
Bundy, Jacob Lewis IV, 23
Bundy, James I, 95
Bundy, James I, 132
Bundy, James V, 299
Bundy, James V, 375
Bundy, James Alexander V, 376
Bundy, Jane I, 38
Bundy, Jane I, 68
Bundy, Jane I, 95
Bundy, Jane I, 96
Bundy, Jane I, 119
Bundy, Jane I, 120
Bundy, Jane I, 130
Bundy, Jane I, 131
Bundy, Jane I, 132
Bundy, Jane I, 133
Bundy, Jane I, 146
Bundy, Jane I, 167
Bundy, Jane I, 268
Bundy, Jane IV, 182
Bundy, Jane V, 375
Bundy, Jane V, 376
Bundy, Jane V, 420
Bundy, Jean I, 96
Bundy, Jean I, 97
Bundy, Jean I, 131
Bundy, Jean I, 146
Bundy, Jean I, 282
Bundy, Jean I, 300
Bundy, Jefferson IV, 183
Bundy, Jefferson IV, 374
Bundy, Jefferson IV, 376
Bundy, Jehu I, 38
Bundy, Jehu I, 50
Bundy, Jehu I, 95
Bundy, Jehu I, 132
Bundy, Jehu I, 133
Bundy, Jehu I, 710
Bundy, Jemima I, 96
Bundy, Jemima I, 132
Bundy, Jemima I, 145
Bundy, Jephtha IV, 183
Bundy, Jeptha IV, 374
Bundy, Jeptha IV, 375
Bundy, Jeptha IV, 383
Bundy, Jeremiah I, 38
Bundy, Jeremiah I, 95
Bundy, Jeremiah I, 132
Bundy, Jeremiah I, 133
Bundy, Jeremiah I, 232
Bundy, Jeremiah I, 802
Bundy, Jesse I, 95
Bundy, Jesse I, 133
Bundy, Jesse I, 134
Bundy, Jesse I, 190
Bundy, Jesse I, 202
Bundy, Jesse I, 873
Bundy, Jesse IV, 122
Bundy, Jesse IV, 183
Bundy, Jesse IV, 184
Bundy, Jesse IV, 376
Bundy, Jesse C. IV, 182
Bundy, Jesse M. I, 232
Bundy, Jesse M. I, 234
Bundy, Jesse M. I, 529
Bundy, Jesse M. I, 778
Bundy, Jesse M. II, 709
Bundy, Jessee I, 96
Bundy, Jessee I, 97
Bundy, Joan I, 96
Bundy, Joan I, 97
Bundy, Joel I, 132
Bundy, Joel IV, 183
Bundy, Joel IV, 376
Bundy, Joel IV, 400
Bundy, Joel IV, 1050
Bundy, Joel IV, 1051
Bundy, Joel IV, 1056
Bundy, Joel IV, 1089
Bundy, Joel Bundy IV, 1051
Bundy, Joel D. IV, 374
Bundy, Joel D. IV, 375
Bundy, Joel H. IV, 374
Bundy, John I, 38
Bundy, John I, 53
Bundy, John I, 94
Bundy, John I, 95
Bundy, John I, 96
Bundy, John I, 131
Bundy, John I, 132
Bundy, John I, 133
Bundy, John I, 134
Bundy, John I, 144
Bundy, John I, 145
Bundy, John I, 190
Bundy, John I, 232
Bundy, John I, 710
Bundy, John I, 711
Bundy, John I, 778
Bundy, John I, 802
Bundy, John I, 830
Bundy, John I, 960
Bundy, John I, 1007
Bundy, John I, 1012
Bundy, John II, 705
Bundy, John IV, 183
Bundy, John IV, 373
Bundy, John IV, 374
Bundy, John IV, 375
Bundy, John IV, 376
Bundy, John IV, 387
Bundy, John IV, 389
Bundy, John IV, 393
Bundy, John IV, 423
Bundy, John IV, 428
Bundy, John IV, 441
Bundy, John IV, 448
Bundy, John IV, 569
Bundy, John IV, 570
Bundy, John IV, 576
Bundy, John IV, 1050
Bundy, John V, 299
Bundy, John V, 375
Bundy, John D. IV, 183
Bundy, John D. IV, 374
Bundy, John Elwood I, 778
Bundy, John H. IV, 374
Bundy, John H. IV, 375
Bundy, John H. IV, 387
Bundy, John LeRoy IV, 410
Bundy, John M. V, 375
Bundy, John M. V, 376
Bundy, John Symons, Sr. I, 132
Bundy, John Townsend IV, 183
Bundy, John Wood IV, 597
Bundy, John Woolman I, 911
Bundy, Jonathan I, 94
Bundy, Jonathan I, 95
Bundy, Jonathan I, 133
Bundy, Jonathan I, 873
Bundy, Jonathan IV, 373
Bundy, Jonathan IV, 569
Bundy, Jonathan IV, 570
Bundy, Jonathan IV, 574
Bundy, Jonathan IV, 582
Bundy, Jonathan IV, 1050
Bundy, Jonathan IV, 1051
Bundy, Jonathan IV, 1089
Bundy, Jonathan Barefield V, 299
Bundy, Jordan I, 190
Bundy, Jordon I, 182
Bundy, Joseph I, 36
Bundy, Joseph I, 38
Bundy, Joseph I, 96
Bundy, Joseph I, 132
Bundy, Joseph I, 133
Bundy, Joseph I, 142
Bundy, Joseph I, 160
Bundy, Joseph I, 697
Bundy, Joseph I, 710
Bundy, Joseph I, 711
Bundy, Joseph I, 851
Bundy, Joseph I, 873
Bundy, Joseph I, 892
Bundy, Joseph I, 922
Bundy, Joseph IV, 23
Bundy, Joseph IV, 141
Bundy, Joseph IV, 182
Bundy, Joseph IV, 183
Bundy, Joseph IV, 375
Bundy, Joseph IV, 569
Bundy, Joseph IV, 1050
Bundy, Joseph IV, 1128
Bundy, Joseph E. V, 375
Bundy, Joseph Edwin V, 375
Bundy, Joseph Edwin V, 376
Bundy, Joseph Embree IV, 1051
Bundy, Joseph H. I, 134
Bundy, Joseph H. I, 778
Bundy, Joseph H. I, 802
Bundy, Joseph Henley I, 95
Bundy, Joseph Henley I, 132
Bundy, Joseph J. V, 729
Bundy, Joseph J. V, 757
Bundy, Joseph S. IV, 374
Bundy, Joseph T. IV, 183
Bundy, Joseph Townsend IV, 1050
Bundy, Josephine IV, 182
Bundy, Josephine IV, 183
Bundy, Josephine IV, 299
Bundy, Josephine IV, 784
Bundy, Josephine IV, 931
Bundy, Josephine IV, 1013
Bundy, Josephine B. IV, 184
Bundy, Josephine B. IV, 1012
Bundy, Joshua I, 38
Bundy, Joshua I, 96
Bundy, Joshua I, 129
Bundy, Joshua I, 132
Bundy, Joshua I, 133
Bundy, Joshua I, 157
Bundy, Joshua I, 160
Bundy, Joshua I, 268
Bundy, Joshua I, 873
Bundy, Joshua IV, 23
Bundy, Joshua IV, 98
Bundy, Joshua IV, 141
Bundy, Joshua IV, 183
Bundy, Josiah I, 38
Bundy, Josiah I, 39
Bundy, Josiah I, 93
Bundy, Josiah I, 95
Bundy, Josiah I, 96
Bundy, Josiah I, 98
Bundy, Josiah I, 132
Bundy, Josiah I, 133
Bundy, Josiah I, 134
Bundy, Josiah I, 143
Bundy, Josiah I, 147
Bundy, Josiah I, 150
Bundy, Josiah I, 167
Bundy, Josiah I, 169
Bundy, Josiah I, 265
Bundy, Josiah I, 268
Bundy, Josiah I, 274
Bundy, Josiah I, 873
Bundy, Josiah IV, 23
Bundy, Josiah IV, 76
Bundy, Josiah IV, 77
Bundy, Josiah IV, 137
Bundy, Josiah IV, 141
Bundy, Josiah IV, 142
Bundy, Josiah IV, 161
Bundy, Josiah IV, 163
Bundy, Josiah IV, 182
Bundy, Josiah IV, 183
Bundy, Josiah IV, 184
Bundy, Josiah IV, 213
Bundy, Josiah IV, 243
Bundy, Josiah IV, 373
Bundy, Josiah IV, 376
Bundy, Josiah IV, 569
Bundy, Josiah IV, 1050
Bundy, Josiah IV, 1051
Bundy, Josiah IV, 1128
Bundy, Josiah Bundy I, 132
Bundy, Josiah Morris I, 873
Bundy, Josiah W. IV, 375
Bundy, Josiah, Jr. I, 96
Bundy, Josiah, Jr. I, 133
Bundy, Josiah, Sr. I, 96
Bundy, Judith I, 802
Bundy, Julia I, 802
Bundy, Karen I, 38
Bundy, Karen I, 48
Bundy, Karen I, 133
Bundy, Keran I, 38
Bundy, Laura R. IV, 182
Bundy, Laura R. IV, 183
Bundy, Laurence G. IV, 804
Bundy, Lawrence G. IV, 183
Bundy, Lawrence G. IV, 184
Bundy, Lawrence G. IV, 804
Bundy, Leah I, 710
Bundy, Leah I, 873
Bundy, Leah I, 875
Bundy, Lemuel Morris I, 133
Bundy, Leslie Da IV, 410
Bundy, Lewis S. IV, 183
Bundy, Liddah I, 97
Bundy, Lillian IV, 375
Bundy, Lindley IV, 183
Bundy, Lindley IV, 369
Bundy, Lindley IV, 374
Bundy, Lindley IV, 375
Bundy, Lindley IV, 376
Bundy, Lindley IV, 393
Bundy, Lindley IV, 410
Bundy, Lindley IV, 411
Bundy, Lindley IV, 416
Bundy, Lindley IV, 678
Bundy, Lindley IV, 686
Bundy, Lindley IV, 1128
Bundy, Lindley M. V, 375
Bundy, Lindley Murry V, 375
Bundy, Lindley Murry V, 376
Bundy, Lisbon V, 376
Bundy, Lizza I, 38
Bundy, Lizzie A. IV, 176
Bundy, Lizzie A. IV, 183
Bundy, Lizzie A. IV, 275
Bundy, Lizzie D. IV, 183
Bundy, Louisa IV, 184
Bundy, Louisa IV, 410
Bundy, Louisa C. V, 155
Bundy, Louisa D. IV, 183
Bundy, Louisa D. IV, 282
Bundy, Lucinda IV, 141
Bundy, Lucinda IV, 182
Bundy, Lucinda IV, 183
Bundy, Lucinda IV, 374
Bundy, Lucinda IV, 375
Bundy, Lucinda IV, 404
Bundy, Lucinda IV, 1051
Bundy, Lucinda IV, 1067
Bundy, Lucinda IV, 1128
Bundy, Lucinda IV, 1129
Bundy, Luella IV, 176
Bundy, Luella IV, 183
Bundy, Luella IV, 214
Bundy, Luella IV, 375
Bundy, Luella IV, 376
Bundy, Luella IV, 569
Bundy, Luella H. IV, 176
Bundy, Luella H. IV, 183
Bundy, Lyda I, 95
Bundy, Lyda I, 96
Bundy, Lyda I, 102
Bundy, Lydda I, 38
Bundy, Lydda I, 45
Bundy, Lyddia I, 132
Bundy, Lyddia I, 147
Bundy, Lydia I, 38
Bundy, Lydia I, 50
Bundy, Lydia I, 96
Bundy, Lydia I, 131
Bundy, Lydia I, 132
Bundy, Lydia I, 133
Bundy, Lydia I, 165
Bundy, Lydia I, 167
Bundy, Lydia I, 282
Bundy, Lydia I, 301
Bundy, Lydia I, 710
Bundy, Lydia I, 719
Bundy, Lydia I, 796
Bundy, Lydia I, 802
Bundy, Lydia I, 1007
Bundy, Lydia I, 1008
Bundy, Lydia I, 1012
Bundy, Lydia IV, 141
Bundy, Lydia IV, 156
Bundy, Lydia IV, 569
Bundy, Lydia IV, 570
Bundy, Lydia IV, 1050
Bundy, Lydia IV, 1051
Bundy, Lydia V, 375
Bundy, Lydia M. IV, 1089
Bundy, Lydia M. IV, 1119
Bundy, Lyman IV, 184
Bundy, Lyman E. IV, 182
Bundy, Mabel Anna IV, 410
Bundy, Margaret I, 95
Bundy, Margaret I, 133
Bundy, Margaret I, 134
Bundy, Margaret I, 161
Bundy, Margaret I, 650
Bundy, Margaret I, 675
Bundy, Margaret I, 679
Bundy, Margaret I, 695
Bundy, Margaret I, 697
Bundy, Margaret I, 710
Bundy, Margaret I, 726
Bundy, Margaret I, 802
Bundy, Margaret IV, 183
Bundy, Margaret IV, 375
Bundy, Margaret IV, 376
Bundy, Margaret IV, 423
Bundy, Margaret A. I, 134
Bundy, Margaret A. I, 176
Bundy, Margaret Ann I, 95
Bundy, Margaret B. II, 953
Bundy, Margaret B. IV, 364
Bundy, Margaret B. IV, 376
Bundy, Margaret H. IV, 184
Bundy, Margaret H. IV, 375
Bundy, Margaret H. IV, 376
Bundy, Marget I, 710
Bundy, Marget I, 722
Bundy, Maria IV, 374
Bundy, Maria IV, 375
Bundy, Maria IV, 411
Bundy, Maria IV, 431
Bundy, Maria IV, 443
Bundy, Maria IV, 1089
Bundy, Maria IV, 1109
Bundy, Mariah I, 300
Bundy, Mariah IV, 373
Bundy, Mariah IV, 374
Bundy, Mariah IV, 390
Bundy, Mariam I, 95
Bundy, Mariam I, 697
Bundy, Mariam I, 710
Bundy, Mariam I, 718
Bundy, Marie IV, 183
Bundy, Marion V, 375
Bundy, Mark I, 38
Bundy, Martha I, 95
Bundy, Martha I, 133
Bundy, Martha I, 134
Bundy, Martha I, 137
Bundy, Martha IV, 182
Bundy, Martha IV, 183
Bundy, Martha IV, 1050
Bundy, Martha IV, 1089
Bundy, Martha A. V, 375
Bundy, Martha A. V, 376
Bundy, Martha A. Elizabeth I, 778
Bundy, Martha Ann IV, 183
Bundy, Martha Ann IV, 373
Bundy, Martha Ann IV, 374
Bundy, Martha Ann IV, 431
Bundy, Martitia J. I, 802
Bundy, Martitia J. I, 840
Bundy, Mary I, 1
Bundy, Mary I, 3
Bundy, Mary I, 34
Bundy, Mary I, 36
Bundy, Mary I, 38
Bundy, Mary I, 68
Bundy, Mary I, 90
Bundy, Mary I, 95
Bundy, Mary I, 96
Bundy, Mary I, 97

Bundy, Mary I, 98
Bundy, Mary I, 104
Bundy, Mary I, 132
Bundy, Mary I, 133
Bundy, Mary I, 134
Bundy, Mary I, 137
Bundy, Mary I, 146
Bundy, Mary I, 148
Bundy, Mary I, 150
Bundy, Mary I, 162
Bundy, Mary I, 167
Bundy, Mary I, 168
Bundy, Mary I, 175
Bundy, Mary I, 182
Bundy, Mary I, 190
Bundy, Mary I, 232
Bundy, Mary I, 268
Bundy, Mary I, 282
Bundy, Mary I, 300
Bundy, Mary I, 301
Bundy, Mary I, 315
Bundy, Mary I, 650
Bundy, Mary I, 673
Bundy, Mary I, 675
Bundy, Mary I, 697
Bundy, Mary I, 710
Bundy, Mary I, 711
Bundy, Mary I, 718
Bundy, Mary I, 735
Bundy, Mary I, 778
Bundy, Mary I, 796
Bundy, Mary I, 802
Bundy, Mary I, 830
Bundy, Mary I, 845
Bundy, Mary I, 873
Bundy, Mary I, 895
Bundy, Mary I, 911
Bundy, Mary I, 930
Bundy, Mary I, 1003
Bundy, Mary I, 1007
Bundy, Mary I, 1008
Bundy, Mary I Sup 1, 3
Bundy, Mary I Sup 1, 7
Bundy, Mary IV, 23
Bundy, Mary IV, 45
Bundy, Mary IV, 76
Bundy, Mary IV, 77
Bundy, Mary IV, 98
Bundy, Mary IV, 122
Bundy, Mary IV, 141
Bundy, Mary IV, 156
Bundy, Mary IV, 182
Bundy, Mary IV, 183
Bundy, Mary IV, 364
Bundy, Mary IV, 365
Bundy, Mary IV, 373
Bundy, Mary IV, 374
Bundy, Mary IV, 375
Bundy, Mary IV, 376
Bundy, Mary IV, 380
Bundy, Mary IV, 386
Bundy, Mary IV, 394
Bundy, Mary IV, 428
Bundy, Mary IV, 435
Bundy, Mary IV, 437
Bundy, Mary IV, 569
Bundy, Mary IV, 570
Bundy, Mary IV, 582
Bundy, Mary IV, 592
Bundy, Mary IV, 1050
Bundy, Mary IV, 1051
Bundy, Mary IV, 1071
Bundy, Mary IV, 1101
Bundy, Mary V, 155
Bundy, Mary V, 299
Bundy, Mary V, 310
Bundy, Mary V, 375
Bundy, Mary A. IV, 375
Bundy, Mary Alice IV, 375
Bundy, Mary Alma IV, 375
Bundy, Mary Ann IV, 182
Bundy, Mary C. IV, 183
Bundy, Mary C. IV, 376
Bundy, Mary C. IV, 440
Bundy, Mary Caleb IV, 374
Bundy, Mary Caleb IV, 453
Bundy, Mary D. IV, 375
Bundy, Mary D. IV, 387
Bundy, Mary Delphina I, 778
Bundy, Mary E. I, 39
Bundy, Mary E. IV, 375
Bundy, Mary E. IV, 392
Bundy, Mary E. IV, 569
Bundy, Mary E. IV, 1090
Bundy, Mary E. IV, 1097
Bundy, Mary E. IV, 1098
Bundy, Mary E. IV, 1273
Bundy, Mary E. V, 155
Bundy, Mary Elizabeth IV, 374
Bundy, Mary Ellen IV, 375
Bundy, Mary H. IV, 1051
Bundy, Mary J. II, 709
Bundy, Mary Jane I, 232
Bundy, Mary Jane I, 234
Bundy, Mary Jane I, 529
Bundy, Mary Jane II, 719
Bundy, Mary Jane IV, 183
Bundy, Mary Jane IV, 373
Bundy, Mary Jane IV, 374
Bundy, Mary Jane IV, 443
Bundy, Mary Lina IV, 184
Bundy, Mary Maria IV, 374
Bundy, Mary Myrtle I, 930
Bundy, Mary P. II, 719
Bundy, Mary P. IV, 374
Bundy, Mary P. IV, 399
Bundy, Mary P. IV, 441
Bundy, Mary P. IV, 453
Bundy, Mary R. IV, 411
Bundy, Mary Ruanna IV, 410
Bundy, Mary, Jr. I, 300
Bundy, Mary, Jr. I, 710
Bundy, Marylina IV, 182
Bundy, Mathew IV, 183
Bundy, Mathew IV, 376
Bundy, Matthew IV, 373
Bundy, Mattie V, 155
Bundy, Maud IV, 804
Bundy, Meliscent I, 132
Bundy, Meliscent IV, 1089
Bundy, Mellie D. V, 155
Bundy, Melva IV, 375
Bundy, Melvina IV, 374
Bundy, Meriam I, 710
Bundy, Meriam I, 723
Bundy, Mertie L. V, 155
Bundy, Micajah M. I, 873
Bundy, Milicent I, 300
Bundy, Milicent I, 301
Bundy, Milicent IV, 1050
Bundy, Milicent IV, 1051
Bundy, Milicent IV, 1119
Bundy, Miliscent I, 94
Bundy, Milisent I, 131
Bundy, Milisent I, 132
Bundy, Milisent I, 133
Bundy, Milisent IV, 373
Bundy, Milisent IV, 569
Bundy, Millicent I, 300
Bundy, Millicent I, 311
Bundy, Millicent I, 1007
Bundy, Millicent IV, 569
Bundy, Millicent IV, 1050
Bundy, Millicent IV, 1089
Bundy, Millicent V, 299
Bundy, Milton IV, 1089
Bundy, Miriam I, 36
Bundy, Miriam I, 38
Bundy, Miriam I, 95
Bundy, Miriam I, 96
Bundy, Miriam I, 97
Bundy, Miriam I, 132
Bundy, Miriam I, 133
Bundy, Miriam I, 182
Bundy, Miriam I, 190
Bundy, Miriam I, 299
Bundy, Miriam I, 300
Bundy, Miriam I, 650
Bundy, Miriam I, 675
Bundy, Mordecai I, 851
Bundy, Mordecai I, 873
Bundy, Mordecai I, 924
Bundy, Mordecai I, 932
Bundy, Mordecai M. I, 922
Bundy, Mordica IV, 1071
Bundy, Mornen I, 802
Bundy, Morning I, 190
Bundy, Morning I, 710
Bundy, Morris I, 134
Bundy, Moses I, 38
Bundy, Moses I, 68
Bundy, Moses I, 95
Bundy, Moses I, 132
Bundy, Moses I, 133
Bundy, Moses I, 143
Bundy, Moses I, 182
Bundy, Moses I, 190
Bundy, Moses I, 265
Bundy, Moses I, 268
Bundy, Moses I, 300
Bundy, Moses I, 710
Bundy, Moses I, 711
Bundy, Moses I, 873
Bundy, Moses I, 960
Bundy, Moses IV, 23
Bundy, Moses IV, 76
Bundy, Moses IV, 77
Bundy, Moses IV, 141
Bundy, Moses IV, 182
Bundy, Moses IV, 183
Bundy, Moses IV, 294
Bundy, Moses IV, 570
Bundy, Moses IV, 1050
Bundy, Moses IV, 1089
Bundy, Mournen I, 182
Bundy, Mourning I, 38
Bundy, Mourning I, 74
Bundy, Mourning I, 96
Bundy, Mourning I, 132
Bundy, Mourning I, 190
Bundy, Mourning I, 802
Bundy, Mourning IV, 98
Bundy, Myra IV, 375
Bundy, Myra IV, 383
Bundy, Myrtle IV, 376
Bundy, Myrtle IV, 423
Bundy, Myrtle K. IV, 184
Bundy, Myrtle R. IV, 183
Bundy, Myrtle R. IV, 376
Bundy, Nancy I, 95
Bundy, Nancy I, 96
Bundy, Nancy I, 134
Bundy, Nancy I, 137
Bundy, Nancy I, 873
Bundy, Nancy I, 904
Bundy, Nancy J. V, 375
Bundy, Nancy Jane V, 375
Bundy, Naomi I, 132
Bundy, Naomi I, 172
Bundy, Nathan I, 29
Bundy, Nathan I, 94
Bundy, Nathan I, 95
Bundy, Nathan I, 96
Bundy, Nathan I, 97
Bundy, Nathan I, 132
Bundy, Nathan I, 133
Bundy, Nathan I, 134
Bundy, Nathan I, 149
Bundy, Nathan I, 182
Bundy, Nathan I, 190
Bundy, Nathan I, 710
Bundy, Nathan I, 802
Bundy, Nathan I, 873
Bundy, Nathan IV, 183
Bundy, Nathan IV, 373
Bundy, Nathan IV, 374
Bundy, Nathan IV, 375
Bundy, Nathan IV, 376
Bundy, Nathan IV, 386
Bundy, Nathan IV, 441
Bundy, Nathan IV, 1050
Bundy, Nathan IV, 1089
Bundy, Nathan IV, 1090
Bundy, Nathan H. IV, 374
Bundy, Nathan H. IV, 383
Bundy, Nathan W. IV, 376
Bundy, Nathan W. IV, 390
Bundy, Nehemiah IV, 183
Bundy, Nehemiah M. IV, 182
Bundy, Nehemiah Matson IV, 141
Bundy, Nehemiah Matson IV, 183
Bundy, Nehemiah Matson IV, 1050
Bundy, Nellie IV, 1273
Bundy, Nelly IV, 23
Bundy, O. W. IV, 275
Bundy, Olive IV, 990
Bundy, Olive R. IV, 183
Bundy, Olive R. IV, 184
Bundy, Olive R. IV, 302
Bundy, Olive R. IV, 931
Bundy, Olive R. IV, 1014
Bundy, Oliver IV, 182
Bundy, Oliver IV, 183
Bundy, Oliver W. IV, 183
Bundy, Oliver W. IV, 184
Bundy, Oliver W. IV, 804
Bundy, Orange L. V, 375
Bundy, Orange Lisbon V, 376
Bundy, Oscar W. IV, 183
Bundy, Oscar W. IV, 184
Bundy, Patsey I, 182
Bundy, Penelope I, 4
Bundy, Penelope I, 39
Bundy, Penelope I, 134
Bundy, Penelope I, 778
Bundy, Penelopy I, 3
Bundy, Penina IV, 1050
Bundy, Peninah I, 94
Bundy, Peninah I, 95
Bundy, Peninah I, 133
Bundy, Peninah I, 150
Bundy, Peninah I, 168
Bundy, Peninah I, 182
Bundy, Peninah I, 190
Bundy, Peninah I, 192
Bundy, Peninah IV, 569
Bundy, Peninah IV, 570
Bundy, Peninah IV, 1051
Bundy, Peninah IV, 1089
Bundy, Peninah IV, 1128
Bundy, Pennina IV, 373
Bundy, Penninah I, 95
Bundy, Penninah I, 96
Bundy, Penninah I, 133
Bundy, Penninah I, 134
Bundy, Penninah I, 137
Bundy, Penninah I, 697
Bundy, Penninah I, 710
Bundy, Penninah IV, 1050
Bundy, Penninah IV, 1051
Bundy, Penny I, 134
Bundy, Pharabe I, 96
Bundy, Pharaby I, 133
Bundy, Pharaby I, 150
Bundy, Pharaby IV, 183
Bundy, Pharaby IV, 376
Bundy, Phariba IV, 593
Bundy, Pheriba I, 134
Bundy, Pheriba I, 190
Bundy, Pheriba I, 198
Bundy, Pheriba IV, 374
Bundy, Pheriba IV, 435
Bundy, Polly I, 873
Bundy, Priscilla I, 697
Bundy, Priscilla I, 711
Bundy, Priscilla I, 851
Bundy, Priscilla I, 869
Bundy, Priscilla I, 873
Bundy, Priscilla I, 919
Bundy, Priscilla V, 729
Bundy, Prudence IV, 373
Bundy, Prudence IV, 374
Bundy, Prudence IV, 458
Bundy, R. Elizabeth I, 922
Bundy, Rachel I, 95
Bundy, Rachel I, 132
Bundy, Rachel I, 133
Bundy, Rachel I, 154
Bundy, Rachel I, 697
Bundy, Rachel I, 710
Bundy, Rachel I, 711
Bundy, Rachel I, 713
Bundy, Rachel I, 778
Bundy, Rachel I, 802
Bundy, Rachel I, 851
Bundy, Rachel I, 873
Bundy, Rachel I, 892
Bundy, Rachel II, 59
Bundy, Rachel IV, 182
Bundy, Rachel IV, 183
Bundy, Rachel IV, 184
Bundy, Rachel IV, 289
Bundy, Rachel IV, 290
Bundy, Rachel IV, 373
Bundy, Rachel IV, 375
Bundy, Rachel IV, 376
Bundy, Rachel IV, 381
Bundy, Rachel IV, 1089
Bundy, Rachel IV, 1107
Bundy, Rachel IV, 1128
Bundy, Rachel E. I, 922
Bundy, Rachel E. IV, 182
Bundy, Rachel E. IV, 183
Bundy, Rachel E. IV, 289
Bundy, Rachel P. IV, 1089
Bundy, Rachel P. IV, 1115
Bundy, Rachel R. IV, 176
Bundy, Ralph A. IV, 375
Bundy, Rebecca I, 3
Bundy, Rebecca I, 39
Bundy, Rebecca I, 51
Bundy, Rebecca I, 133
Bundy, Rebecca I, 711
Bundy, Rebecca I, 726
Bundy, Rebecca I, 802
Bundy, Rebecca I, 911
Bundy, Rebecca I, 1003
Bundy, Rebecca I, 1007
Bundy, Rebecca I, 1012
Bundy, Rebecca IV, 183
Bundy, Rebecca IV, 374
Bundy, Rebecca IV, 376
Bundy, Rebecca IV, 386
Bundy, Rebecca IV, 400
Bundy, Rebecca IV, 442
Bundy, Rebecca IV, 1089
Bundy, Rebecca IV, 1096
Bundy, Rebecca IV, 1122
Bundy, Rebecca V, 225
Bundy, Rebecca V, 299
Bundy, Rebecca V, 375
Bundy, Rebecca D. IV, 374
Bundy, Rebecca D. IV, 375
Bundy, Rebecca D. IV, 441
Bundy, Rebecca D. IV, 442
Bundy, Rebecca H. IV, 374
Bundy, Rebecca H. IV, 375
Bundy, Rebecca H. IV, 377
Bundy, Rebecca H. IV, 613
Bundy, Rebecca H. IV, 614
Bundy, Rebecca H. IV, 687
Bundy, Rebecca W. IV, 374
Bundy, Rebecca W. IV, 376
Bundy, Rebecca W. IV, 515
Bundy, Rebecca W. IV, 550
Bundy, Rebecca W. IV, 1090
Bundy, Rebeckah I, 1008
Bundy, Rebeckah V, 299
Bundy, Rebekah I, 1003
Bundy, Reuben I, 95
Bundy, Reuben I, 133
Bundy, Reuben I, 710
Bundy, Rhoda I, 710
Bundy, Rhoda I, 777
Bundy, Rhoda I, 802
Bundy, Rhoda I, 805
Bundy, Ricks I, 134
Bundy, Rix I, 3
Bundy, Rix I, 4
Bundy, Rix I, 39
Bundy, Rix I, 95
Bundy, Rix I, 96
Bundy, Rix I, 134
Bundy, Robert IV, 1050
Bundy, Rola Vail IV, 410
Bundy, Ruana IV, 183
Bundy, Ruanna IV, 183
Bundy, Ruanna IV, 184
Bundy, Ruanna IV, 283
Bundy, Ruanna IV, 369
Bundy, Ruanna IV, 375
Bundy, Ruanna IV, 376
Bundy, Ruanna IV, 393
Bundy, Ruanna IV, 410
Bundy, Ruanna IV, 411
Bundy, Ruanna IV, 416
Bundy, Ruanna IV, 444
Bundy, Ruanna IV, 678
Bundy, Ruanna IV, 686
Bundy, Ruben I, 710
Bundy, Rufina R. I, 932
Bundy, Russel C. IV, 374
Bundy, Russel C. IV, 376
Bundy, Ruth I, 38
Bundy, Ruth I, 53
Bundy, Ruth I, 95
Bundy, Ruth I, 97
Bundy, Ruth I, 115
Bundy, Ruth I, 132
Bundy, Ruth I, 133
Bundy, Ruth I, 137
Bundy, Ruth I, 149
Bundy, Ruth I, 182
Bundy, Ruth I, 190
Bundy, Ruth I, 199
Bundy, Ruth I, 265
Bundy, Ruth I, 268
Bundy, Ruth IV, 23
Bundy, Ruth IV, 77
Bundy, Ruth IV, 141
Bundy, Ruth IV, 161
Bundy, Ruth IV, 183
Bundy, Ruth IV, 294
Bundy, Ruth IV, 366
Bundy, Ruth IV, 373
Bundy, Ruth IV, 375
Bundy, Ruth IV, 387
Bundy, Ruth IV, 423
Bundy, Ruth IV, 428
Bundy, Ruth IV, 441
Bundy, Ruth IV, 569
Bundy, Ruth IV, 1050
Bundy, Ruth IV, 1051
Bundy, Ruth IV, 1083
Bundy, Ruth IV, 1089
Bundy, Ruth IV, 1114
Bundy, Ruth IV, 1138
Bundy, Ruth Ann IV, 182
Bundy, Ruth Anna IV, 373
Bundy, Ruth W. IV, 1128
Bundy, Ruthanna IV, 183
Bundy, Ruthanna IV, 374
Bundy, Ruthanna IV, 376
Bundy, Ruthanna IV, 423
Bundy, Ruthanna IV, 1050
Bundy, Ruthanna IV, 1089
Bundy, Ruthanna IV, 1128
Bundy, Ruthanna IV, 1136
Bundy, Sally IV, 569
Bundy, Sally IV, 600
Bundy, Sally IV, 1050
Bundy, Sally IV, 1089
Bundy, Sally IV, 1128
Bundy, Sally C. I, 851
Bundy, Samira Emeline I, 778
Bundy, Samuel I, 90
Bundy, Samuel I, 92
Bundy, Samuel I, 95
Bundy, Samuel I, 97
Bundy, Samuel I, 104
Bundy, Samuel I, 131
Bundy, Samuel I, 132
Bundy, Samuel I, 133
Bundy, Samuel I, 143

Bundy, Samuel I, 146
Bundy, Samuel I, 166
Bundy, Samuel I, 182
Bundy, Samuel I, 190
Bundy, Samuel I, 199
Bundy, Samuel I, 650
Bundy, Samuel I, 675
Bundy, Samuel I, 679
Bundy, Samuel I, 695
Bundy, Samuel I, 697
Bundy, Samuel I, 710
Bundy, Samuel I, 777
Bundy, Samuel I, 802
Bundy, Samuel I, 805
Bundy, Samuel IV, 1050
Bundy, Samuel IV, 1128
Bundy, Samuel V, 729
Bundy, Samuel C. I, 778
Bundy, Samuel Moore I, 95
Bundy, Samuel, Jr. I, 97
Bundy, Samuel, Sr. I, 97
Bundy, Samuel, Sr. I, 131
Bundy, Sara C. IV, 375
Bundy, Sarah I, 3
Bundy, Sarah I, 4
Bundy, Sarah I, 29
Bundy, Sarah I, 36
Bundy, Sarah I, 38
Bundy, Sarah I, 39
Bundy, Sarah I, 41
Bundy, Sarah I, 60
Bundy, Sarah I, 86
Bundy, Sarah I, 93
Bundy, Sarah I, 94
Bundy, Sarah I, 95
Bundy, Sarah I, 96
Bundy, Sarah I, 97
Bundy, Sarah I, 118
Bundy, Sarah I, 129
Bundy, Sarah I, 132
Bundy, Sarah I, 133
Bundy, Sarah I, 134
Bundy, Sarah I, 153
Bundy, Sarah I, 167
Bundy, Sarah I, 182
Bundy, Sarah I, 190
Bundy, Sarah I, 198
Bundy, Sarah I, 268
Bundy, Sarah I, 276
Bundy, Sarah I, 300
Bundy, Sarah I, 301
Bundy, Sarah I, 313
Bundy, Sarah I, 650
Bundy, Sarah I, 697
Bundy, Sarah I, 710
Bundy, Sarah I, 715
Bundy, Sarah I, 735
Bundy, Sarah I, 802
Bundy, Sarah I, 851
Bundy, Sarah I, 873
Bundy, Sarah I, 928
Bundy, Sarah I Sup 1, 3
Bundy, Sarah IV, 122
Bundy, Sarah IV, 141
Bundy, Sarah IV, 182
Bundy, Sarah IV, 183
Bundy, Sarah IV, 186
Bundy, Sarah IV, 280
Bundy, Sarah IV, 322
Bundy, Sarah IV, 365
Bundy, Sarah IV, 373
Bundy, Sarah IV, 374
Bundy, Sarah IV, 375
Bundy, Sarah IV, 376
Bundy, Sarah IV, 383
Bundy, Sarah IV, 386
Bundy, Sarah IV, 392
Bundy, Sarah IV, 394
Bundy, Sarah IV, 404
Bundy, Sarah IV, 409
Bundy, Sarah IV, 423
Bundy, Sarah IV, 441
Bundy, Sarah IV, 450
Bundy, Sarah IV, 515
Bundy, Sarah IV, 569
Bundy, Sarah IV, 570
Bundy, Sarah IV, 768
Bundy, Sarah IV, 1050
Bundy, Sarah IV, 1089
Bundy, Sarah IV, 1101
Bundy, Sarah IV, 1128
Bundy, Sarah IV, 1136
Bundy, Sarah V, 375
Bundy, Sarah A. IV, 375
Bundy, Sarah Alice IV, 183
Bundy, Sarah Alice IV, 374
Bundy, Sarah Ann I, 134
Bundy, Sarah Ann IV, 77
Bundy, Sarah Ann IV, 122
Bundy, Sarah Ann IV, 124
Bundy, Sarah Ann IV, 182
Bundy, Sarah Ann IV, 183
Bundy, Sarah Ann IV, 184
Bundy, Sarah Ann IV, 191
Bundy, Sarah Ann IV, 687
Bundy, Sarah C. IV, 375
Bundy, Sarah C. IV, 410
Bundy, Sarah C. IV, 411
Bundy, Sarah D. IV, 1089
Bundy, Sarah E. I, 29
Bundy, Sarah J. I, 938
Bundy, Sarah Jane I, 778
Bundy, Sarah Jinnette I, 924
Bundy, Sarah L. IV, 183
Bundy, Sarah Louisa IV, 282
Bundy, Sarah Louisa IV, 374
Bundy, Sarah Louisa IV, 376
Bundy, Sarah M. IV, 570
Bundy, Sarah M. IV, 1051
Bundy, Sarah S. IV, 141
Bundy, Sarah S. IV, 156
Bundy, Sarah T. IV, 570
Bundy, Sarah T. IV, 595
Bundy, Sarah W. IV, 1128
Bundy, Sary I, 132
Bundy, Sension I, 134
Bundy, Sension I, 190
Bundy, Sension I, 202
Bundy, Sidney IV, 374
Bundy, Sidney IV, 376
Bundy, Sidney IV, 448
Bundy, Sidney IV, 569
Bundy, Sidney IV, 597
Bundy, Sina IV, 804
Bundy, Sina H. IV, 183
Bundy, Sina H. IV, 275
Bundy, Sina H. IV, 804
Bundy, Sinah H. IV, 184
Bundy, Stanton I, 265
Bundy, Stanton I, 268
Bundy, Stanton IV, 23
Bundy, Stanton IV, 76
Bundy, Stanton IV, 77
Bundy, Stanton IV, 141
Bundy, Stanton IV, 183
Bundy, Stanton IV, 365
Bundy, Stanton IV, 373
Bundy, Stanton IV, 375
Bundy, Stephen IV, 1128
Bundy, Stephen Edgar IV, 183
Bundy, Stephen Edgar IV, 374
Bundy, Stephen Scott I, 131
Bundy, Stephen T. IV, 1089
Bundy, Stephen T. IV, 1128
Bundy, Susan IV, 183
Bundy, Susana I, 133
Bundy, Susanah I, 132
Bundy, Susanah I, 133
Bundy, Susanna I, 232
Bundy, Susanna I, 265
Bundy, Susanna I, 268
Bundy, Susanna IV, 23
Bundy, Susanna IV, 77
Bundy, Susanna IV, 141
Bundy, Susanna IV, 163
Bundy, Susanna IV, 182
Bundy, Susanna IV, 183
Bundy, Susanna IV, 322
Bundy, Susanna IV, 1050
Bundy, Susanna IV, 1051
Bundy, Susanna IV, 1079
Bundy, Susannah I, 38
Bundy, Susannah I, 132
Bundy, Susannah I, 232
Bundy, Susannah IV, 77
Bundy, Susannah IV, 141
Bundy, Susannah IV, 183
Bundy, Susannah IV, 373
Bundy, Susannah IV, 376
Bundy, Susannah IV, 458
Bundy, Tabitha IV, 374
Bundy, Tabitha IV, 386
Bundy, Tabitha IV, 444
Bundy, Tabitha D. IV, 184
Bundy, Tabitha D. IV, 215
Bundy, Tabitha D. IV, 282
Bundy, Tabitha D. IV, 375
Bundy, Tabitha D. IV, 400
Bundy, Tacie M. IV, 369
Bundy, Tacie M. IV, 375
Bundy, Tacie M. IV, 678
Bundy, Tacie M. IV, 744
Bundy, Tacy M. IV, 177
Bundy, Tacy M. IV, 184
Bundy, Tacy M. IV, 375
Bundy, Talitha IV, 183
Bundy, Tamer I, 131
Bundy, Tamer I, 166
Bundy, Theodore R. IV, 410
Bundy, Thomas I, 39
Bundy, Thomas I, 96
Bundy, Thomas I, 97
Bundy, Thomas I, 133
Bundy, Thomas I, 134
Bundy, Thomas I, 190
Bundy, Thomas I, 300
Bundy, Thomas I, 301
Bundy, Thomas I, 697
Bundy, Thomas I, 710
Bundy, Thomas I, 960
Bundy, Thomas IV, 183
Bundy, Thomas IV, 373
Bundy, Thomas IV, 376
Bundy, Thomas IV, 569
Bundy, Thomas IV, 570
Bundy, Thomas IV, 1050
Bundy, Thomas IV, 1051
Bundy, Thomas IV, 1083
Bundy, Thomas IV, 1089
Bundy, Thomas IV, 1119
Bundy, Thomas IV, 1128
Bundy, Thomas Clarkson IV, 375
Bundy, Thomas Clarkson IV, 376
Bundy, Thomas E. I, 911
Bundy, Thomas Elwood I, 911
Bundy, Thomas Elwood IV, 1089
Bundy, Thomas W. IV, 569
Bundy, Thomas, Jr. IV, 373
Bundy, Thomas, Jr. IV, 1050
Bundy, Thos. IV, 1114
Bundy, Thos. IV, 1138
Bundy, Thos. Clarkson IV, 381
Bundy, Thos. W. IV, 574
Bundy, Toll I, 132
Bundy, Townsend IV, 141
Bundy, Townsend IV, 1050
Bundy, W. Henry IV, 1089
Bundy, Wallace J. IV, 183
Bundy, Wallace J. IV, 184
Bundy, Wallace J. IV, 282
Bundy, Wallace Wayne IV, 183
Bundy, Walter IV, 410
Bundy, Walter A. IV, 375
Bundy, Walter A. V, 155
Bundy, Walter M. IV, 410
Bundy, Walter T. IV, 182
Bundy, Walter T. IV, 183
Bundy, Wauneta IV, 575
Bundy, Wauneta R. IV, 183
Bundy, Wauneta R. IV, 184
Bundy, Wauneta R. IV, 570
Bundy, Wauneta R. IV, 574
Bundy, Wauneta Rosetta IV, 184
Bundy, Wauneta Rosetta IV, 196
Bundy, Wauneta Rosetta IV, 569
Bundy, Wd. Sarah IV, 374
Bundy, Widow Ascention I, 95
Bundy, Widow Elizabeth I, 132
Bundy, Widow Lydia I, 710
Bundy, Widow Mary I, 132
Bundy, Widow Mary I, 145
Bundy, Widow Mourning I, 157
Bundy, Widow Sarah I, 132
Bundy, Widow Sarah I, 160
Bundy, Willard L. IV, 375
Bundy, William I, 1
Bundy, William I, 34
Bundy, William I, 38
Bundy, William I, 39
Bundy, William I, 68
Bundy, William I, 95
Bundy, William I, 96
Bundy, William I, 97
Bundy, William I, 131
Bundy, William I, 132
Bundy, William I, 134
Bundy, William I, 144
Bundy, William I, 148
Bundy, William I, 282
Bundy, William I, 301
Bundy, William I, 313
Bundy, William I, 650
Bundy, William I, 697
Bundy, William I, 710
Bundy, William I, 711
Bundy, William I, 873
Bundy, William I, 875
Bundy, William I, 960
Bundy, William I, 1003
Bundy, William I, 1008
Bundy, William I Sup 1, 3
Bundy, William I Sup 1, 4
Bundy, William I Sup 1, 7
Bundy, William IV, 141
Bundy, William IV, 182
Bundy, William IV, 183
Bundy, William IV, 184
Bundy, William IV, 191
Bundy, William IV, 365
Bundy, William IV, 373
Bundy, William IV, 374
Bundy, William IV, 375
Bundy, William IV, 376
Bundy, William IV, 377
Bundy, William IV, 383
Bundy, William IV, 386
Bundy, William IV, 428
Bundy, William IV, 458
Bundy, William IV, 569
Bundy, William IV, 614
Bundy, William IV, 1050
Bundy, William IV, 1051
Bundy, William V, 155
Bundy, William A. I, 39
Bundy, William C. IV, 373
Bundy, William C. IV, 1089
Bundy, William E. IV, 183
Bundy, William E. IV, 373
Bundy, William E. IV, 376
Bundy, William J. IV, 375
Bundy, William P. I, 778
Bundy, William P. I, 802
Bundy, William P. I, 840
Bundy, William P. IV, 183
Bundy, William P. IV, 374
Bundy, William S. V, 375
Bundy, William Walter I, 778
Bundy, Willis I, 182
Bundy, Willis IV, 410
Bundy, Willis J. IV, 176
Bundy, Willis M. IV, 183
Bundy, Willis M. IV, 184
Bundy, Willis M. IV, 376
Bundy, Wilmer L. IV, 183
Bundy, Wilmer L. IV, 184
Bundy, Wilmer L. IV, 375
Bundy, Wilson IV, 182
Bundy, Wilson IV, 183
Bundy, Wilson IV, 275
Bundy, Wilson IV, 373
Bundy, Wilson C. IV, 374
Bundy, Wilson H. IV, 374
Bundy, Wm. I Sup 1, 3
Bundy, Wm. IV, 122
Bundy, Wm. IV, 124
Bundy, Wm. IV, 156
Bundy, Wm. IV, 186
Bundy, Wm. IV, 364
Bundy, Wm. IV, 373
Bundy, Wm. IV, 374
Bundy, Wm. IV, 375
Bundy, Wm. IV, 394
Bundy, Wm. IV, 441
Bundy, Wm. IV, 515
Bundy, Wm. IV, 569
Bundy, Wm. IV, 592
Bundy, Wm. IV, 687
Bundy, Wm. IV, 1050
Bundy, Wm. IV, 1089
Bundy, Wm. V, 299
Bundy, Wm. C. IV, 376
Bundy, Wm. C. IV, 441
Bundy, Wm. C. IV, 1089
Bundy, Wm. H. IV, 1273
Bundy, Wm. H. V, 155
Bundy, Wm. Henry IV, 1089
Bundy, Wm. M. IV, 687
Bundy, Wm. P. IV, 282
Bundy, Wm. P. IV, 386
Bundy, Zadoc IV, 1050
Bundy, Zadoc V, 225
Bundy, Zadoc V, 375
Bundy, Zadock I, 95
Bundy, Zadock I, 132
Bundy, Zadock IV, 569
Bundy, Zadock V, 299
Bundy, Zadock V, 375
Bundy, Zadock G. IV, 1089
Bundy, Zadok IV, 1089
Bundy, Zadok IV, 1122
Bundy, Zodak I, 1007
Bundy, Zodak I, 1008
Bundy, Zodak I, 1012
Bundy, Zodock I, 1003
Bune, Jones II, 342
Bunker, ??? III, 52
Bunker, Abel III, 52
Bunker, Abigail III, 52
Bunker, Abigail III, 53
Bunker, Abigail III, 209
Bunker, Abishai III, 52
Bunker, Abraham I, 492
Bunker, Abraham I, 529
Bunker, Abraham III, 23
Bunker, Abraham III, 52
Bunker, Abraham VI, 300
Bunker, Abram I, 529
Bunker, Abram I, 800
Bunker, Abram I, 802
Bunker, Absalom T. I, 824
Bunker, Absalom Tatum I, 824
Bunker, Alex C. III, 497
Bunker, Alex. C. III, 52
Bunker, Alexander C. III, 52
Bunker, Alexander C. III, 53
Bunker, Alexander C. III, 480
Bunker, Alexander C. III, 498
Bunker, Alice III, 52
Bunker, Alice III, 209
Bunker, Alice IV, 1150
Bunker, Alice IV, 1151
Bunker, Alice A. III, 210
Bunker, Alice L. III, 52
Bunker, Alice L. III, 53
Bunker, Alice M. IV, 1151
Bunker, Almira III, 53
Bunker, Almira III, 323
Bunker, Almira S. III, 52
Bunker, Ann I, 529
Bunker, Ann IV, 1203
Bunker, Ann IV, 1355
Bunker, Anna I, 492
Bunker, Anna I, 529
Bunker, Anna I, 800
Bunker, Anna I, 802
Bunker, Anna S. III, 52
Bunker, Anna S. III, 53
Bunker, Arthur III, 77
Bunker, Avis III, 78
Bunker, Avis III, 253
Bunker, Barzilai III, 52
Bunker, Barzilla III, 52
Bunker, Barzillai III, 52
Bunker, Benjamin F. III, 52
Bunker, Bethuel III, 52
Bunker, Borden II, 776
Bunker, Byron IV, 1150
Bunker, Byron IV, 1151
Bunker, Caroline III, 52
Bunker, Charles III, 53
Bunker, Charles West III, 77
Bunker, Charlotte III, 77
Bunker, Clyde IV, 1150
Bunker, Clyde IV, 1151
Bunker, Comfort IV, 1150
Bunker, Cora IV, 1150
Bunker, Cornelia IV, 1355
Bunker, Cyrus E. III, 52
Bunker, David I, 492
Bunker, David I, 493
Bunker, David IV, 1150
Bunker, David IV, 1203
Bunker, David O. IV, 1151
Bunker, Deborah III, 52
Bunker, Deborah III, 215
Bunker, Deborah III, 216
Bunker, Deborah III, 299
Bunker, Deborah III, 357
Bunker, Deborah IV, 1355
Bunker, Dora James IV, 1151
Bunker, Edw. S. III, 52
Bunker, Edw. S. III, 53
Bunker, Edw. S. III, 210
Bunker, Edward H. III, 52
Bunker, Edward S. III, 52
Bunker, Edward S. III, 209
Bunker, Edwin IV, 1151
Bunker, Edwin M. IV, 1150
Bunker, Edwin M. IV, 1203
Bunker, Edwin M. IV, 1247
Bunker, Edwin M. IV, 1273
Bunker, Edwin N. IV, 1203
Bunker, Elihu III, 52
Bunker, Elihu III, 53
Bunker, Elihu IV, 184
Bunker, Elihu IV, 322
Bunker, Elihu IV, 1150
Bunker, Elihu IV, 1151
Bunker, Elihu IV, 1203
Bunker, Elihu S. III, 52
Bunker, Elise III, 52
Bunker, Elisha IV, 1151
Bunker, Eliz. S. III, 202
Bunker, Eliz. S. III, 335
Bunker, Eliza III, 78
Bunker, Eliza III, 79
Bunker, Eliza III, 181
Bunker, Eliza IV, 1355
Bunker, Elizabeth III, 52
Bunker, Elizabeth IV, 1151
Bunker, Elizabeth IV, 1203
Bunker, Elizabeth J. IV, 1150
Bunker, Elizabeth Jane IV, 1150
Bunker, Ella IV, 1151
Bunker, Elmer IV, 1151
Bunker, Elmora IV, 1150
Bunker, Elsie III, 52
Bunker, Elwood IV, 1150
Bunker, Elwood IV, 1151
Bunker, Emaline I, 824
Bunker, Emeline IV, 1150
Bunker, Emeline IV, 1173
Bunker, Emilia IV, 1150
Bunker, Emily B. III, 77
Bunker, Eunice I, 492

Bunker, Eunice I, 529
Bunker, Eunice I, 576
Bunker, Eunice III, 52
Bunker, Eunice III, 53
Bunker, Eunice III, 76
Bunker, Eunice III, 77
Bunker, Eunice III, 336
Bunker, Eunice Anna III, 77
Bunker, Eunice C. III, 52
Bunker, Eunice C. III, 53
Bunker, Eunice C. III, 480
Bunker, Eva IV, 1151
Bunker, Eva Fay IV, 1151
Bunker, Francis W. III, 77
Bunker, Frederick E. III, 52
Bunker, George III, 52
Bunker, Hannah IV, 184
Bunker, Hannah IV, 322
Bunker, Hannah IV, 1150
Bunker, Hannah IV, 1203
Bunker, Hannah R. IV, 1150
Bunker, Harold III, 52
Bunker, Hattie IV, 1150
Bunker, Hattie IV, 1151
Bunker, Helen M. IV, 1203
Bunker, Hellen IV, 1203
Bunker, Henry I, 873
Bunker, Henry IV, 1150
Bunker, Henry IV, 1203
Bunker, Henry P. IV, 1203
Bunker, Henry William III, 52
Bunker, Hephzibah III, 52
Bunker, Hephzibah III, 53
Bunker, Hepzibah III, 52
Bunker, Heradiah III, 77
Bunker, Hezediah III, 77
Bunker, Isaac IV, 184
Bunker, Isaac IV, 322
Bunker, Isaac IV, 1150
Bunker, Isaac L. IV, 1150
Bunker, Isaac S. IV, 1150
Bunker, Isaac, Jr. IV, 1150
Bunker, Isidore E. IV, 1203
Bunker, James I, 873
Bunker, Jamima III, 23
Bunker, Jamima III, 52
Bunker, Jane IV, 1150
Bunker, Jemima III, 52
Bunker, Jethro IV, 1150
Bunker, Jethro IV, 1151
Bunker, Jethro IV, 1203
Bunker, Jethro IV, 1355
Bunker, John I, 492
Bunker, John I, 529
Bunker, John IV, 1150
Bunker, John V, 729
Bunker, John V, 794
Bunker, Jonathan IV, 1150
Bunker, Joseph IV, 1150
Bunker, Judith I, 492
Bunker, Judith I, 493
Bunker, Judith I, 529
Bunker, Judith I, 802
Bunker, Judith III, 52
Bunker, Judith C. III, 295
Bunker, Judith C. III, 315
Bunker, Julia III, 52
Bunker, Julia IV, 1150
Bunker, Justin IV, 1150
Bunker, Justin H. IV, 1150
Bunker, Katie IV, 1150
Bunker, Kezia I, 492
Bunker, Lena III, 77
Bunker, Lenora C. IV, 1151
Bunker, Lester P. IV, 1203
Bunker, Lewis III, 53
Bunker, Lida IV, 1150
Bunker, Lindley IV, 1203
Bunker, Lindley H. IV, 1151
Bunker, Lindley H. IV, 1203
Bunker, Lucretia IV, 1151
Bunker, Lucy IV, 184
Bunker, Lucy IV, 322
Bunker, Lucy IV, 1150
Bunker, Lucy IV, 1180
Bunker, Lucy Howard III, 52
Bunker, Lulu IV, 1151
Bunker, Lydia I, 493
Bunker, Lydia I, 529
Bunker, Lydia III, 52
Bunker, Lydia III, 76
Bunker, Lydia III, 215
Bunker, Lydia IV, 1150
Bunker, Lydia IV, 1203
Bunker, Lydia IV, 1220
Bunker, Lydia B. III, 77
Bunker, Lydia C. III, 52
Bunker, Lydia C. III, 53
Bunker, Margaret III, 77
Bunker, Maria III, 52
Bunker, Mariam III, 52
Bunker, Mariam III, 53
Bunker, Mariann II, 776
Bunker, Marie Louise III, 53
Bunker, Marnilva IV, 1203
Bunker, Marvin IV, 1150
Bunker, Mary I, 492
Bunker, Mary I, 529
Bunker, Mary III, 52
Bunker, Mary III, 53
Bunker, Mary III, 209
Bunker, Mary III, 497
Bunker, Mary IV, 1150
Bunker, Mary IV, 1151
Bunker, Mary A. IV, 1247
Bunker, Mary Ann IV, 1355
Bunker, Mary C. III, 52
Bunker, Mary C. III, 53
Bunker, Mary D. IV, 1150
Bunker, Mary P. III, 52
Bunker, Mary P. III, 480
Bunker, Mary P. III, 498
Bunker, Matilda IV, 1150
Bunker, Matilda IV, 1195
Bunker, May IV, 1151
Bunker, Mehitable IV, 1150
Bunker, Merab III, 52
Bunker, Mila IV, 1150
Bunker, Mila IV, 1185
Bunker, Milia IV, 1150
Bunker, Milia IV, 1185
Bunker, Minerva IV, 1150
Bunker, Minerva IV, 1151
Bunker, Minnie IV, 1151
Bunker, Mira IV, 1150
Bunker, Mira IV, 1156
Bunker, Mirriam III, 52
Bunker, Mirriam III, 53
Bunker, Nancy IV, 1150
Bunker, Nancy IV, 1151
Bunker, Nellie IV, 1203
Bunker, Obed I, 492
Bunker, Obed I, 529
Bunker, Obed I, 1070
Bunker, Obed III, 52
Bunker, Paul III, 52
Bunker, Paul III, 53
Bunker, Paul III, 204
Bunker, Paul III, 323
Bunker, Peleg IV, 184
Bunker, Peleg IV, 322
Bunker, Peleg IV, 1150
Bunker, Phebe I, 492
Bunker, Phebe III, 52
Bunker, Phebe A. III, 53
Bunker, Phebe Anna III, 52
Bunker, Phebe Anna III, 53
Bunker, Phebe Anna III, 210
Bunker, Phebe Anna III, 298
Bunker, Phebe Anna III, 323
Bunker, Phebe G. III, 52
Bunker, Phebe G. III, 204
Bunker, Phebe J. III, 53
Bunker, Prince III, 53
Bunker, Rachel I, 802
Bunker, Rachel I, 824
Bunker, Rachel IV, 1150
Bunker, Rachel F. III, 53
Bunker, Rebecca II, 477
Bunker, Rebecca III, 53
Bunker, Rebecca IV, 1355
Bunker, Rebecca V, 794
Bunker, Reuben I, 492
Bunker, Reuben I, 529
Bunker, Reuben I, 802
Bunker, Reuben I Sup 1, 9
Bunker, Reuben III, 52
Bunker, Reuben III, 53
Bunker, Reuben III, 209
Bunker, Reuben IV, 184
Bunker, Reuben IV, 322
Bunker, Reuben IV, 1150
Bunker, Reuben IV, 1203
Bunker, Rhoda I, 493
Bunker, Rhoda I, 529
Bunker, Rhoda I, 541
Bunker, Robert III, 52
Bunker, Robert III, 53
Bunker, Robert IV, 1156
Bunker, Robert A. III, 52
Bunker, Robert A. IV, 1150
Bunker, Robert M. III, 77
Bunker, Robert S. III, 52
Bunker, Robert S. III, 53
Bunker, Robert T. III, 53
Bunker, Robert W. IV, 1150
Bunker, Rosanna IV, 1150
Bunker, Rose IV, 1151
Bunker, Ruben I, 492
Bunker, Ruben I, 493
Bunker, Ruth I, 824
Bunker, Ruth B. II, 776
Bunker, Sally I, 873
Bunker, Sally III, 77
Bunker, Sanaford IV, 1151
Bunker, Sanford IV, 1150
Bunker, Sarah III, 52
Bunker, Sarah A. III, 77
Bunker, Sarah P. IV, 1150
Bunker, Sarah P. IV, 1175
Bunker, Silas III, 52
Bunker, Silas III, 215
Bunker, Silas III, 299
Bunker, Silas III, 357
Bunker, Silas IV, 1150
Bunker, Silas IV, 1203
Bunker, Silvia IV, 1151
Bunker, Slocum IV, 1150
Bunker, Slocum IV, 1195
Bunker, Slocum H. IV, 1150
Bunker, Sophia IV, 1150
Bunker, Susan IV, 1150
Bunker, Susanna C. IV, 1150
Bunker, Susanna C. IV, 1175
Bunker, Susannah C. IV, 1175
Bunker, Sylvia IV, 1150
Bunker, Sylvia IV, 1151
Bunker, T. Homer III, 77
Bunker, Thomas I, 492
Bunker, Thomas I, 493
Bunker, Thomas III, 77
Bunker, Thomas IV, 1150
Bunker, Timothy III, 52
Bunker, Timothy III, 53
Bunker, Timothy M. III, 77
Bunker, Timothy W. III, 52
Bunker, Timothy W. III, 53
Bunker, Timothy W. III, 76
Bunker, Timothy W. III, 480
Bunker, Virgil IV, 1151
Bunker, Welmet V, 794
Bunker, William III, 52
Bunker, William III, 53
Bunker, William A. III, 53
Bunker, William Henry III, 53
Bunker, William Henry III, 77
Bunker, William I. III, 52
Bunker, William R. IV, 1150
Bunker, Wm. II, 776
Bunker, Wm. III, 52
Bunker, Wm. R. IV, 1151
Bunker, Zenas I, 492
Bunker, Zenas I, 529
Bunker, Zephaniah III, 77
Bunn, Anna B. III, 53
Bunn, Anna B. III, 345
Bunn, David M. III, 53
Bunn, Eliza I, 301
Bunn, Elizabeth II, 442
Bunn, J. S. I, 301
Bunn, Jane III, 53
Bunn, John McDowell III, 53
Bunn, John McDowell III, 345
Bunn, Mary II, 442
Bunn, Temperance I, 301
Bunnell, Nellie V, 155
Buntain, Annie V, 662
Buntain, Clinton V, 662
Buntain, Mary V, 662
Buntain, Susanna V, 662
Bunting, ??? II, 168
Bunting, Abigail II, 168
Bunting, Abigail II, 202
Bunting, Abner II, 784
Bunting, Alice II, 478
Bunting, Alice II, 784
Bunting, Alice II, 842
Bunting, Alice III, 53
Bunting, Alice III, 139
Bunting, Alice Elizabeth III, 53
Bunting, Amos II, 477
Bunting, Amos II, 785
Bunting, Amos II, 984
Bunting, Amos II, 985
Bunting, Ann II, 168
Bunting, Ann II, 202
Bunting, Ann II, 842
Bunting, Ann II, 984
Bunting, Ann II, 985
Bunting, Ann II, 1017
Bunting, Ann II, 1021
Bunting, Ann Maria III, 511
Bunting, Anna II, 784
Bunting, Anna II, 843
Bunting, Anna II, 985
Bunting, Anna II, 1047
Bunting, Anna II, 1069
Bunting, Anna IV, 184
Bunting, Annie Moore II, 922
Bunting, Archie M. I, 613
Bunting, Archie M. I, 631
Bunting, Arrington I, 613
Bunting, Arrington I, 616
Bunting, Arrington I, 631
Bunting, Arrington I, 711
Bunting, Arthur L. II, 785
Bunting, Arthur Levis II, 843
Bunting, Arthur Levis II, 928
Bunting, Arthur S. I, 613
Bunting, Asa II, 984
Bunting, Barter B. I, 631
Bunting, Baxter B. I, 613
Bunting, Benjamin II, 956
Bunting, Benjamin II, 984
Bunting, Bessie B. II, 843
Bunting, Bessie B. II, 926
Bunting, Bessie L. II, 784
Bunting, Blakey II, 842
Bunting, Charles T. III, 53
Bunting, Charles T. III, 233
Bunting, Chas. T. III, 53
Bunting, Christian II, 981
Bunting, Christian II, 984
Bunting, Christian II, 1001
Bunting, Daniel II, 342
Bunting, Daniel II, 956
Bunting, Daniel II, 977
Bunting, Daniel II, 984
Bunting, Daniel II, 985
Bunting, Daniel C., Jr. II, 984
Bunting, Daniel, Jr. II, 984
Bunting, David II, 956
Bunting, David II, 984
Bunting, David II, 1000
Bunting, David S. II, 842
Bunting, Eliza I, 613
Bunting, Eliza II, 781
Bunting, Elizabeth I, 711
Bunting, Elizabeth II, 202
Bunting, Elizabeth II, 218
Bunting, Elizabeth II, 257
Bunting, Elizabeth II, 781
Bunting, Elizabeth II, 785
Bunting, Elizabeth II, 842
Bunting, Elizabeth II, 984
Bunting, Elizabeth II, 985
Bunting, Elizabeth II, 1000
Bunting, Elizabeth II, 1017
Bunting, Elizabeth III, 53
Bunting, Elizabeth III, 480
Bunting, Elizabeth III, 486
Bunting, Elizabeth III, 510
Bunting, Elizabeth A. II, 784
Bunting, Elizabeth B. II, 842
Bunting, Elizabeth B. II, 886
Bunting, Elizabeth H. II, 842
Bunting, Elizabeth H. II, 849
Bunting, Elizabeth Hallowell II, 784
Bunting, Elizabeth J. I, 756
Bunting, Elizabeth L. II, 784
Bunting, Elizabeth M. III, 53
Bunting, Elizabeth S. II, 842
Bunting, Elizabeth S. II, 849
Bunting, Elizabeth T. II, 842
Bunting, Elizabeth Tomkins II, 784
Bunting, Ella Frances III, 53
Bunting, Emma I, 631
Bunting, Emma Cornelia I, 613
Bunting, Emma Cornelia I, 616
Bunting, Esther II, 984
Bunting, Esther II, 1012
Bunting, Esther Syng II, 804
Bunting, Eugene III, 38
Bunting, Eugene III, 53
Bunting, Frank Carl I, 613
Bunting, Frederick L. II, 785
Bunting, Grace Woodfine I, 613
Bunting, Hannah II, 168
Bunting, Hannah II, 202
Bunting, Hannah II, 210
Bunting, Hannah II, 253
Bunting, Hannah II, 477
Bunting, Hannah II, 956
Bunting, Hannah II, 984
Bunting, Hannah II, 1029
Bunting, Hannah Clothier II, 784
Bunting, Hannah L. II, 842
Bunting, Hannah L. II, 843
Bunting, Hannah L. II, 928
Bunting, Hannah Rhoads II, 784
Bunting, Helen II, 784
Bunting, Helen II, 842
Bunting, Helen II, 894
Bunting, Henrietta Barron II, 785
Bunting, Isaac II, 202
Bunting, Isaac II, 257
Bunting, Isaac II, 477
Bunting, Isaac II, 956
Bunting, Israel II, 984
Bunting, Jabez II, 784
Bunting, Jabez II, 793
Bunting, Jacob S. II, 842
Bunting, Jacob S. II, 849
Bunting, Jacob Smith II, 784
Bunting, Jacob T. II, 842
Bunting, James, Jr. II, 785
Bunting, James, Jr. II, 842
Bunting, James, Jr. VI, 478
Bunting, Jane II, 168
Bunting, Jane II, 202
Bunting, Jane E. III, 480
Bunting, Jane E. III, 486
Bunting, Jane R. III, 53
Bunting, Jennie R. III, 233
Bunting, Jeremiah II, 168
Bunting, Jeremiah II, 202
Bunting, Jeremiah II, 205
Bunting, Jeremiah II, 985
Bunting, Jeremiah II, 1017
Bunting, Jessie Aurelia I, 613
Bunting, John II, 168
Bunting, John II, 282
Bunting, John II, 477
Bunting, John II, 842
Bunting, John II, 861
Bunting, John II, 956
Bunting, John II, 981
Bunting, John II, 984
Bunting, John II, 1001
Bunting, John II, 1017
Bunting, John Gibson McIlvain II, 784
Bunting, John H. II, 842
Bunting, John Hunt II, 785
Bunting, John, Jr. II, 985
Bunting, Jonathan II, 984
Bunting, Jonathan II, 1006
Bunting, Joseph II, 168
Bunting, Joseph II, 784
Bunting, Joseph II, 842
Bunting, Joseph II, 956
Bunting, Joseph II, 979
Bunting, Joseph II, 984
Bunting, Joseph II, 1012
Bunting, Joseph II, 1014
Bunting, Joseph III, 53
Bunting, Joseph M. II, 784
Bunting, Joseph M. II, 842
Bunting, Joseph M. II, 849
Bunting, Joseph M. II, 886
Bunting, Joseph N. III, 53
Bunting, Joseph N. III, 139
Bunting, Joseph S. II, 842
Bunting, Joseph S. II, 843
Bunting, Joseph S. II, 928
Bunting, Joseph Shallcross II, 784
Bunting, Joseph Shallcross II, 785
Bunting, Joseph, Jr. II, 842
Bunting, Joseph, Jr. II, 886
Bunting, Joshua II, 785
Bunting, Joshua II, 956
Bunting, Joshua II, 981
Bunting, Josiah II, 477
Bunting, Josiah II, 478
Bunting, Josiah II, 784
Bunting, Josiah II, 842
Bunting, Kezia R. II, 842
Bunting, Kezia R. II, 861
Bunting, Kezia Reeves II, 784
Bunting, Latitia II, 985
Bunting, Latitia II, 1032
Bunting, Latitia II, 1047
Bunting, Laura W. I, 631
Bunting, Leatitia II, 984
Bunting, Leatitia II, 985
Bunting, Leonora III, 53
Bunting, Leticia II, 985
Bunting, Letitia II, 1069
Bunting, Letitia A. II, 843
Bunting, Letitia A. II, 928
Bunting, Liddia II, 984
Bunting, Liddia II, 1001
Bunting, Lura Watson I, 613
Bunting, Lydia II, 984
Bunting, Lydia II, 1037
Bunting, Margaret II, 342
Bunting, Margaret II, 477
Bunting, Margaret II, 627
Bunting, Margaret II, 785
Bunting, Margaret II, 984
Bunting, Margaret II, 985
Bunting, Margaret II, 1038
Bunting, Margaret VI, 374
Bunting, Margaret S. II, 969
Bunting, Margarett II, 984
Bunting, Margery II, 168
Bunting, Margery II, 202
Bunting, Margery II, 980
Bunting, Margery II, 984
Bunting, Margery II, 985

Bunting, Margery II, 1017
Bunting, Margery II, 1032
Bunting, Margery II, 1041
Bunting, Martha II, 477
Bunting, Martha II, 654
Bunting, Martha II, 779
Bunting, Martha II, 785
Bunting, Martha II, 842
Bunting, Martha II, 984
Bunting, Martha Ella I, 613
Bunting, Mary II, 168
Bunting, Mary II, 202
Bunting, Mary II, 276
Bunting, Mary II, 277
Bunting, Mary II, 308
Bunting, Mary II, 317
Bunting, Mary II, 342
Bunting, Mary II, 785
Bunting, Mary II, 842
Bunting, Mary II, 843
Bunting, Mary II, 894
Bunting, Mary II, 977
Bunting, Mary II, 980
Bunting, Mary II, 981
Bunting, Mary II, 984
Bunting, Mary II, 985
Bunting, Mary II, 1047
Bunting, Mary II, 1069
Bunting, Mary E. I, 613
Bunting, Mary E. I, 616
Bunting, Mary E. I, 631
Bunting, Mary Gibson II, 785
Bunting, Mary Hibberd Tomlinson II, 807
Bunting, Mary M. III, 299
Bunting, Mary S. II, 784
Bunting, Mary W. II, 202
Bunting, Mary W. II, 205
Bunting, Mary, Jr. II, 202
Bunting, Mattie E. I, 631
Bunting, May II, 922
Bunting, Mrs. Rosetta I, 631
Bunting, Naomi II, 956
Bunting, Naomi II, 985
Bunting, Nettie I, 613
Bunting, Newbury III, 53
Bunting, Phebe II, 956
Bunting, Phebe L. III, 53
Bunting, Phebe L. III, 299
Bunting, Phebe M. III, 53
Bunting, Phebe M. III, 233
Bunting, Philip II, 784
Bunting, Philip Syng II, 781
Bunting, Priscilla II, 956
Bunting, Priscilla II, 982
Bunting, Priscilla II, 984
Bunting, Priscilla II, 1028
Bunting, Rachel II, 956
Bunting, Rachel II, 969
Bunting, Rachel II, 984
Bunting, Rachel II, 991
Bunting, Rachel C. II, 842
Bunting, Rachel Coale II, 785
Bunting, Rachel S. II, 842
Bunting, Rebecca II, 956
Bunting, Rebecca II, 984
Bunting, Rebecca II, 1001
Bunting, Rebecca II, 1006
Bunting, Rebecca C. VI, 747
Bunting, Rebecca Humphreys II, 817
Bunting, Rebecca R. II, 842
Bunting, Rebecca R. II, 861
Bunting, Rosetta I, 613
Bunting, S. Arthur I, 613
Bunting, Samuel II, 168
Bunting, Samuel II, 202
Bunting, Samuel II, 210
Bunting, Samuel II, 253
Bunting, Samuel II, 276
Bunting, Samuel II, 477
Bunting, Samuel II, 654
Bunting, Samuel II, 842
Bunting, Samuel II, 956
Bunting, Samuel II, 969
Bunting, Samuel II, 982
Bunting, Samuel II, 985
Bunting, Samuel II, 1001
Bunting, Samuel II, 1017
Bunting, Samuel II, 1029
Bunting, Samuel II, 1032
Bunting, Samuel II, 1037
Bunting, Samuel II, 1038
Bunting, Samuel II, 1041
Bunting, Samuel II, 1069
Bunting, Samuel C. II, 835
Bunting, Samuel C. II, 842
Bunting, Samuel C. II, 884
Bunting, Samuel Chas. II, 784
Bunting, Samuel J. II, 784
Bunting, Samuel J. II, 842
Bunting, Samuel J. II, 843
Bunting, Samuel J. II, 894
Bunting, Samuel J., Jr. II, 843
Bunting, Samuel S. II, 842
Bunting, Samuel T. II, 842
Bunting, Samuel, Jr. II, 202
Bunting, Samuel, Jr. II, 210
Bunting, Samuel, Jr. II, 276
Bunting, Samuel, Jr. II, 956
Bunting, Samuel, Jr. II, 984
Bunting, Samuel, Jr. II, 991
Bunting, Sarah I, 1047
Bunting, Sarah II, 168
Bunting, Sarah II, 202
Bunting, Sarah II, 218
Bunting, Sarah II, 225
Bunting, Sarah II, 230
Bunting, Sarah II, 282
Bunting, Sarah II, 784
Bunting, Sarah II, 821
Bunting, Sarah II, 842
Bunting, Sarah II, 886
Bunting, Sarah II, 956
Bunting, Sarah II, 979
Bunting, Sarah II, 984
Bunting, Sarah II, 985
Bunting, Sarah II, 996
Bunting, Sarah II, 1012
Bunting, Sarah II, 1029
Bunting, Sarah H. II, 842
Bunting, Sarah Howard II, 477
Bunting, Sarah K. II, 842
Bunting, Sarah Louisa III, 53
Bunting, Sarah S. II, 842
Bunting, Septeme II, 202
Bunting, Septeme II, 210
Bunting, Septima II, 202
Bunting, Septima II, 984
Bunting, Septima II, 985
Bunting, Septima II, 991
Bunting, Septima II, 1038
Bunting, Solomon I, 613
Bunting, Solomon I, 631
Bunting, Solomon I, 711
Bunting, Solomon IV, 184
Bunting, Susannah II, 894
Bunting, Susannah L. II, 842
Bunting, Theodore B. I, 631
Bunting, Theodore Barclay I, 613
Bunting, Theodore M. V, 614
Bunting, Thomas II, 168
Bunting, Thomas II, 202
Bunting, Thomas II, 218
Bunting, Thomas C. II, 843
Bunting, Thomas Stapler, Jr. II, 985
Bunting, Thomasin II, 984
Bunting, Thos. Croswell II, 785
Bunting, Timothy II, 956
Bunting, Timothy II, 984
Bunting, Wd. Elizabeth II, 168
Bunting, Wd. Elizabeth II, 784
Bunting, Wd. Kezia II, 793
Bunting, Wd. Sarah III, 53
Bunting, William II, 168
Bunting, William II, 202
Bunting, William II, 785
Bunting, William II, 956
Bunting, William III, 53
Bunting, William Hill II, 785
Bunting, Wilmot III, 480
Bunting, Wilmot III, 486
Bunting, Wm. II, 477
Bunting, Wm. II, 785
Bunting, Wm. II, 842
Bunting, Wm. II, 980
Bunting, Wm. II, 984
Bunting, Wm. II, 985
Bunting, Wm. II, 1017
Bunting, Wm. II, 1032
Bunting, Wm. II, 1041
Bunting, Wm. III, 53
Bunting, Wm. III, 299
Bunting, Wm. Skipwith II, 922
Bunting, Wm. Skipworth II, 843
Bunton, Job II, 975
Bunton, John II, 342
Bunton, Letta V, 452
Buoyer, Phoeba V, 987
Buoyer, Samuel V, 987
Bur, Ann IV, 641
Bur, Sarah IV, 641
Bur, Wm. IV, 641
Buradaile, John II, 199
Burbank, Lilla III, 409
Burcaw, Allen A. V, 988
Burcaw, Eva V, 988
Burcaw, Lenora V, 988
Burcaw, Norma V, 988
Burcaw, Sarah A. V, 988
Burcaw, W. L. V, 988
Burch, Ed VI, 153
Burch, Ed VI, 161
Burch, Edward VI, 173
Burch, Eli VI, 337
Burch, Eli VI, 847
Burch, Ella I, 873
Burch, Florence V, 478
Burch, George V, 478
Burch, George A. V, 478
Burch, Harriet I, 873
Burch, Joshua II, 342
Burch, Lenora I, 873
Burch, Leonora I, 873
Burch, Lou I, 873
Burch, Lou I, 900
Burch, Lulo I, 873
Burch, Mary Ellan I, 873
Burch, Rebecah I, 983
Burch, Rebecah I, 991
Burch, Sidney A. I, 873
Burch, Sidney, Jr. I, 873
Burch, Simeon VI, 982
Burch, Sophronia I, 873
Burchal, John II, 465
Burchal, Lydia II, 465
Burchal, Sarah IV, 804
Burchal, Sarah IV, 835
Burchall, Caleb II, 337
Burchall, Hannah II, 337
Burchall, James II, 337
Burchall, John II, 465
Burchall, Rebecca II, 337
Burchall, Robert II, 337
Burcham, Aaron I, 983
Burcham, Amelia I, 983
Burcham, Amelia I, 1000
Burcham, Ann II, 202
Burcham, Betsey Elevina I, 802
Burcham, Calvin Evans I, 529
Burcham, Elizabeth I, 493
Burcham, Elizabeth I, 529
Burcham, Elizabeth I, 959
Burcham, Elizabeth I, 960
Burcham, Elizabeth II, 202
Burcham, Elizabeth Elvina I, 529
Burcham, Emely I, 983
Burcham, Henry I, 802
Burcham, Henry II, 202
Burcham, Henry L. I, 983
Burcham, Henry L. I, 1000
Burcham, Isbel I, 960
Burcham, James II, 202
Burcham, John I, 529
Burcham, John I, 960
Burcham, Joseph I, 493
Burcham, Joseph I, 529
Burcham, Joseph I, 605
Burcham, Joseph I, 802
Burcham, Joseph I, 960
Burcham, Joseph I, 965
Burcham, Levi I, 960
Burcham, Levi I, 1008
Burcham, Lydia I, 493
Burcham, Lydia I, 529
Burcham, Lydia Scott I, 529
Burcham, Margaret II, 202
Burcham, Mary I, 493
Burcham, Mary I, 527
Burcham, Mary I, 529
Burcham, Mary I, 605
Burcham, Mary I, 802
Burcham, Mary Jr. I, 960
Burcham, Mary Jr. I, 965
Burcham, Mary Prat I, 529
Burcham, Nancy I, 1008
Burcham, Reuben I, 493
Burcham, Reuben I, 960
Burcham, Roseanna I, 529
Burcham, Ruben I, 529
Burcham, Ruth I, 493
Burcham, Ruth I, 529
Burcham, Sally I, 529
Burcham, Sally I, 802
Burcham, Sally I, 1008
Burcham, Sally I, 1012
Burcham, Sally Salinus I, 529
Burcham, Sarah I, 960
Burcham, Sarah Selinah I, 605
Burcham, Sarah Selinah I, 607
Burcham, Selina I, 802
Burcham, Shepherd I, 493
Burcham, Shepherd W. I, 529
Burcham, Shepherd Ward I, 529
Burcham, Sheppard I, 529
Burcham, Shubel I, 960
Burcham, Susannah I, 960
Burcham, William I, 493
Burcham, William I, 529
Burchel, Sarah IV, 804
Burchell, Caleb II, 337
Burchem, Ruth I, 529
Burchet, Edwd VI, 199
Burchet, EdWd. VI, 161
Burchfield, John VI, 801
Burchfield, John VI, 917
Burchfield, Lucy VI, 917
Burchfield, Margaret I, 1149
Burchfield, Martha VI, 801
Burchfield, Sally VI, 917
Burchim, Mary I, 529
Burchim, Mary I, 545
Burchum, Ann II, 256
Burchum, Henry II, 202
Burchum, Henry II, 227
Burchum, Margaret II, 202
Burchum, Margaret II, 227
Burd, Albrick II, 465
Burd, Alexander II, 442
Burd, Clem VI, 797
Burd, Edmund VI, 797
Burd, Elizabeth II, 442
Burd, Elvira VI, 797
Burd, Isaac II, 465
Burd, Jane II, 442
Burd, John II, 442
Burd, Martha Hill VI, 885
Burd, Robert II, 442
Burd, Thomas II, 442
Burd, Valentine II, 442
Burd, Wd. Mary II, 442
Burd, William, Jr. VI, 885
Burdall, Ann III, 53
Burden, Amos IV, 75
Burden, Amos IV, 77
Burden, Ann II, 342
Burden, Ann IV, 23
Burden, Ann IV, 686
Burden, Anna IV, 686
Burden, Anna K. V, 662
Burden, Bertha L. V, 662
Burden, Charlotte IV, 75
Burden, Charlotte IV, 77
Burden, Charlotte IV, 891
Burden, Charlotte IV, 892
Burden, David IV, 23
Burden, David IV, 686
Burden, Edward V, 479
Burden, Elizabeth II, 56
Burden, Elizabeth II, 93
Burden, Elizabeth III, 53
Burden, Elizabeth III, 93
Burden, Elizabeth IV, 75
Burden, Elizabeth IV, 77
Burden, Flora V, 662
Burden, Francis II, 478
Burden, Frank V, 479
Burden, Franklin V, 478
Burden, George II, 478
Burden, Grace II, 342
Burden, Hannah II, 342
Burden, Hannah IV, 23
Burden, Hannah IV, 686
Burden, Hannah IV, 726
Burden, Job IV, 23
Burden, Job IV, 75
Burden, Job IV, 686
Burden, Job IV, 726
Burden, Job IV, 764
Burden, Joel IV, 23
Burden, Joel IV, 75
Burden, Joel IV, 77
Burden, Joel IV, 686
Burden, John II, 342
Burden, John II, 478
Burden, Joseph Kite II, 478
Burden, Katherine II, 342
Burden, Laura V, 478
Burden, Levi IV, 23
Burden, Levi IV, 75
Burden, Levi IV, 77
Burden, Levi IV, 686
Burden, Levi IV, 723
Burden, Lydia IV, 23
Burden, Lydia IV, 686
Burden, Marie E. V, 662
Burden, Marmaduke II, 342
Burden, Mary II, 342
Burden, Mary II, 442
Burden, Mary II, 478
Burden, Mary II, 843
Burden, Mary IV, 23
Burden, Mary IV, 686
Burden, Mary IV, 726
Burden, Mary IV, 764
Burden, Mary V, 988
Burden, Mary Ann IV, 75
Burden, Mary Ann IV, 77
Burden, Mary Ann IV, 891
Burden, Mary Kite II, 785
Burden, Peter IV, 77
Burden, Peter V, 478
Burden, Pierce H. V, 662
Burden, Rachel IV, 686
Burden, Reuben IV, 23
Burden, Reuben IV, 75
Burden, Reuben IV, 77
Burden, Reuben IV, 686
Burden, Rhoda IV, 75
Burden, Rhoda IV, 77
Burden, Rhoda IV, 686
Burden, Rhoda IV, 723
Burden, Rhody IV, 686
Burden, Robert W. V, 662
Burden, Ruth II, 478
Burden, Ruth II, 608
Burden, Sam V, 479
Burden, Samuel II, 342
Burden, Samuel III, 53
Burden, Samuel III, 93
Burden, Sarah II, 342
Burden, Sarah II, 478
Burden, Sarah IV, 23
Burden, Sarah IV, 686
Burden, Sarah IV, 764
Burden, Susanna II, 342
Burden, Susanna II, 478
Burden, Susanna W. II, 1069
Burden, Susannah II, 478
Burden, Thomas II, 56
Burden, Thomas II, 203
Burden, Thomas II, 342
Burden, Thomas II, 442
Burder, John, Sr. II, 342
Burdet, Jarvis VI, 886
Burdet, Nancy VI, 886
Burdett, Betsy L. VI, 886
Burdett, David IV, 184
Burdett, Edith P. III, 53
Burdett, Edith P. III, 269
Burdett, Howard J. III, 53
Burdett, Jarvis VI, 886
Burdett, Jennie III, 53
Burdett, John VI, 886
Burdett, Joseph III, 53
Burdett, Joseph Henry III, 53
Burdett, Joseph Henry III, 269
Burdett, Mary IV, 184
Burdett, Nancy IV, 184
Burdett, Nancy VI, 886
Burdett, Polley VI, 886
Burdett, Richard VI, 886
Burdett, William IV, 184
Burdett, Wm. H. IV, 184
Burdette, David IV, 184
Burdette, Nancy IV, 184
Burdette, William IV, 184
Burdg, ??? V, 155
Burdg, Adella May V, 155
Burdg, Albert IV, 865
Burdg, Albert IV, 932
Burdg, Elmer A. V, 155
Burdg, Hannah IV, 23
Burdg, Hannah IV, 122
Burdg, Hannah IV, 865
Burdg, Hannah IV, 885
Burdg, Hannah IV, 932
Burdg, Hannah IV, 1011
Burdg, Henry IV, 376
Burdg, Hiram IV, 865
Burdg, Hiram IV, 932
Burdg, Hiram V, 155
Burdg, Jacob IV, 23
Burdg, Jacob IV, 77
Burdg, Jacob IV, 99
Burdg, Jacob IV, 122
Burdg, Jacob IV, 865
Burdg, Jacob IV, 885
Burdg, Jacob IV, 932
Burdg, Jacob IV, 978
Burdg, Judith IV, 77
Burdg, Levi IV, 978
Burdg, Lewis IV, 23
Burdg, Lewis IV, 122
Burdg, Lewis IV, 865
Burdg, Lewis IV, 932
Burdg, Louisa C. V, 155
Burdg, Martha IV, 122
Burdg, Martha IV, 865
Burdg, Martha IV, 932
Burdg, Mary IV, 23
Burdg, Mary IV, 122
Burdg, Mary IV, 865
Burdg, Mary IV, 932
Burdg, Mary IV, 978
Burdg, Meriam IV, 122
Burdg, Miriam IV, 51
Burdg, Miriam IV, 77
Burdg, Miriam IV, 99
Burdg, Miriam IV, 122
Burdg, Miriam IV, 865
Burdg, Miriam IV, 885
Burdg, Miriam IV, 932
Burdg, Miriam IV, 978

Burdg, Oliver IV, 23
Burdg, Oliver IV, 122
Burdg, Oliver IV, 865
Burdg, Olover IV, 932
Burdg, Peter IV, 77
Burdg, Sarah IV, 978
Burdg, Walter A. V, 155
Burdg, William IV, 23
Burdg, William IV, 865
Burdg, Wm. IV, 122
Burdg, Wm. IV, 932
Burdge, Albert IV, 77
Burdge, Albert IV, 932
Burdge, Albert IV, 1242
Burdge, Almira IV, 932
Burdge, Beulah II, 478
Burdge, Beulah II, 557
Burdge, Bracken IV, 932
Burdge, Braden IV, 932
Burdge, Elizabeth II, 478
Burdge, Elizabeth II, 557
Burdge, Ella L. III, 53
Burdge, Ella L. III, 182
Burdge, Ezra IV, 932
Burdge, Franklin III, 53
Burdge, Franklin III, 182
Burdge, Hannah IV, 931
Burdge, Hannah IV, 932
Burdge, Harriet III, 53
Burdge, Harriet III, 182
Burdge, Hiram IV, 932
Burdge, Ira III, 53
Burdge, Ira III, 182
Burdge, Jacob IV, 77
Burdge, Jacob IV, 931
Burdge, Jacob IV, 932
Burdge, Jane M. IV, 932
Burdge, Jane M. IV, 964
Burdge, Jesse C. V, 896
Burdge, Jno. IV, 1309
Burdge, John IV, 932
Burdge, John IV, 1309
Burdge, Jonathan D. V, 896
Burdge, Levi IV, 932
Burdge, Lewis IV, 931
Burdge, Lewis IV, 932
Burdge, Martha IV, 124
Burdge, Martha IV, 932
Burdge, Martin IV, 932
Burdge, Mary IV, 931
Burdge, Mary IV, 932
Burdge, Miriam IV, 77
Burdge, Miriam IV, 103
Burdge, Miriam IV, 931
Burdge, Miriam IV, 932
Burdge, Oliver IV, 931
Burdge, Oliver IV, 932
Burdge, Oliver IV, 964
Burdge, Olover IV, 932
Burdge, Philena IV, 932
Burdge, Samantha IV, 932
Burdge, Samuel II, 478
Burdge, Samuel II, 557
Burdge, Sarah IV, 932
Burdge, Sarah IV, 1309
Burdge, William IV, 931
Burdge, William IV, 932
Burdge, Wm. IV, 124
Burdge, Wm. IV, 932
Burdick, Betsy L. VI, 886
Burdick, David J. III, 22
Burdick, David J. III, 53
Burdick, David M. III, 53
Burdick, John VI, 886
Burdick, Julia C. III, 53
Burdick, Mary Rogers III, 22
Burdick, Mary Rogers III, 53
Burdick, Nancy II, 967
Burdick, Polley VI, 886
Burdick, Richard VI, 886
Burdin, Elizabeth V, 26
Burdin, Elizabeth V, 30
Burdin, Elizabeth V, 72
Burdin, Flora V, 662
Burdin, Mary V, 26
Burdin, Mary V, 30
Burdin, Mary V, 137
Burdon, John W. V, 156
Burdon, Mary II, 342
Burdon, Thomas II, 342
Burdsal, Andrew IV, 891
Burdsal, Edward V, 25
Burdsal, Elijah II, 203
Burdsal, Elizabeth II, 985
Burdsal, Elizabeth II, 987
Burdsal, Jacob II, 203
Burdsal, Jacob II, 204
Burdsal, Jane II, 203
Burdsal, Jane II, 204
Burdsal, Keziah II, 203
Burdsal, Lydia II, 203
Burdsal, Mary Ann V, 25
Burdsal, Mary C. IV, 891
Burdsal, Rachel V, 25
Burdsal, Rachel V, 116
Burdsal, Samuel V, 25
Burdsal, Sarah II, 203
Burdsal, William H. V, 25
Burdsal, Wills II, 203
Burdsall, Abraham III, 34
Burdsall, Abraham Y. III, 34
Burdsall, Albert III, 34
Burdsall, Alvin T. III, 34
Burdsall, Amos III, 34
Burdsall, Amy III, 34
Burdsall, Amy Anna III, 34
Burdsall, Ann III, 34
Burdsall, Ann III, 53
Burdsall, Ann C. III, 34
Burdsall, Anna W. III, 34
Burdsall, Arthur Wood III, 34
Burdsall, Avis III, 34
Burdsall, Benjamin III, 34
Burdsall, Caroline III, 34
Burdsall, Catherine Mailor III, 34
Burdsall, Charle Thomas III, 34
Burdsall, Charles G. III, 34
Burdsall, Charlotte Mary III, 34
Burdsall, Daniel Thornton III, 34
Burdsall, David III, 34
Burdsall, Deborah III, 34
Burdsall, Dr. Ashahel H. III, 34
Burdsall, Edgar III, 34
Burdsall, Edward S. III, 34
Burdsall, Eleanor C. III, 34
Burdsall, Elias G. III, 34
Burdsall, Eliza Ann III, 34
Burdsall, Elizabeth III, 34
Burdsall, Elizabeth M. III, 34
Burdsall, Ellwood III, 34
Burdsall, Ernest Wood III, 34
Burdsall, Esther III, 34
Burdsall, Evelyn Westervelt III, 34
Burdsall, Fanny III, 53
Burdsall, Florence III, 34
Burdsall, Frances III, 34
Burdsall, Frances III, 53
Burdsall, Frances III, 276
Burdsall, Frances E. III, 34
Burdsall, Frank Chase III, 34
Burdsall, Geo H. III, 34
Burdsall, Geo. H. III, 34
Burdsall, Geo. H., Jr. III, 34
Burdsall, George Henry III, 34
Burdsall, Jacob III, 34
Burdsall, James III, 34
Burdsall, Jane C. III, 53
Burdsall, Jane C. III, 276
Burdsall, Jericho III, 34
Burdsall, Jerusha III, 34
Burdsall, Josiah III, 34
Burdsall, Lindley Hoag III, 34
Burdsall, Margaret III, 34
Burdsall, Martha III, 34
Burdsall, Mary III, 53
Burdsall, Mary III, 54
Burdsall, Mattie C. III, 34
Burdsall, Moses T. III, 34
Burdsall, Nancy III, 34
Burdsall, Phebe III, 34
Burdsall, Phebe M. III, 53
Burdsall, Phebe M. III, 233
Burdsall, Reuben L. III, 34
Burdsall, Richard III, 53
Burdsall, Richard III, 276
Burdsall, Richard, Jr. III, 54
Burdsall, Samuel III, 34
Burdsall, Sarah III, 34
Burdsall, Sarah F. III, 34
Burdsall, Solomon III, 34
Burdsall, Susan H. III, 34
Burdsall, Thomas III, 34
Burdsall, Thornton III, 34
Burdsall, Thos. H. III, 34
Burdsall, Thos. W. III, 34
Burdsall, Wd. Elizabeth III, 34
Burdsall, Wm., Jr. III, 34
Burdsall, Zadock M. III, 34
Burdsall, Zepheniah III, 34
Bure, Esther III, 28
Burford, Elizabeth VI, 886
Burford, John W. VI, 886
Burford, Philip VI, 886
Burford, Sarah VI, 300
Burford, Sarah B. VI, 886
Burg, Hazel IV, 1247
Burg, Henry IV, 1247
Burg, Jeffery II, 985
Burgandine, Polly VI, 898
Burgantine, Hannah VI, 968
Burgantine, Marget VI, 968
Burgardine, Margaret VI, 898
Burgd, Jacob IV, 51
Burgd, Judith IV, 51
Burge, Albert IV, 23
Burge, Albert IV, 77
Burge, Albert IV, 865
Burge, Albert IV, 932
Burge, Ann II, 478
Burge, Beaulah II, 478
Burge, Beaulah II, 650
Burge, Beulah II, 342
Burge, Beulah II, 630
Burge, Bracken IV, 932
Burge, Charles V, 376
Burge, Charles V, 552
Burge, Charles C. V, 662
Burge, Chas. C. V, 552
Burge, Chas. C. V, 896
Burge, Cora V, 896
Burge, Elizabeth II, 342
Burge, Elizabeth II, 478
Burge, Elizabeth II, 658
Burge, Elizabeth II, 843
Burge, Ezra IV, 932
Burge, George II, 478
Burge, George II, 836
Burge, George II, 843
Burge, Hannah IV, 23
Burge, Hannah IV, 865
Burge, Hannah IV, 931
Burge, Hiram IV, 932
Burge, Isaac II, 478
Burge, J. D. V, 552
Burge, Jacob IV, 23
Burge, Jacob IV, 77
Burge, Jacob IV, 865
Burge, Jacob IV, 900
Burge, Jacob IV, 931
Burge, James II, 478
Burge, Jane V, 552
Burge, Jesse V, 552
Burge, Jesse C. V, 552
Burge, Jesse C. V, 662
Burge, Jesse C. V, 896
Burge, Jesse Clyde V, 376
Burge, John II, 342
Burge, John IV, 932
Burge, Jonathan D. V, 552
Burge, Jonathan D. V, 662
Burge, Jonathan D. V, 896
Burge, Jonathan S. V, 896
Burge, Judith IV, 23
Burge, Judith IV, 77
Burge, Lewis IV, 23
Burge, Lewis IV, 865
Burge, Lewis IV, 900
Burge, Lewis IV, 931
Burge, Lewis IV, 932
Burge, Martha II, 478
Burge, Martha II, 836
Burge, Martha II, 843
Burge, Martha IV, 865
Burge, Martha IV, 932
Burge, Martha V, 552
Burge, Martha V, 662
Burge, Martha J. V, 552
Burge, Martha J. V, 662
Burge, Martha J. V, 896
Burge, Martha Jane V, 376
Burge, Mary II, 478
Burge, Mary IV, 23
Burge, Mary IV, 865
Burge, Mary IV, 900
Burge, Mary IV, 931
Burge, Meriam IV, 23
Burge, Miriam IV, 23
Burge, Miriam IV, 77
Burge, Miriam IV, 865
Burge, Miriam IV, 900
Burge, Miriam IV, 931
Burge, Miriam IV, 932
Burge, Octavia VI, 801
Burge, Oliver IV, 23
Burge, Oliver IV, 865
Burge, Oliver IV, 900
Burge, Oliver IV, 931
Burge, Peter IV, 77
Burge, Philena IV, 932
Burge, Samantha IV, 932
Burge, Samuel II, 342
Burge, Samuel II, 478
Burge, Samuel II, 630
Burge, Samuel II, 650
Burge, Sarah II, 478
Burge, Sarah II, 836
Burge, Sarah II, 843
Burge, Sarah IV, 77
Burge, Sarah IV, 113
Burge, Sarah IV, 932
Burge, Sarah Coates II, 342
Burge, Sarah Coates II, 478
Burge, Sarah Coates II, 630
Burge, Wd. Judith IV, 36
Burge, William II, 342
Burge, William IV, 23
Burge, William IV, 865
Burge, William IV, 931
Burge, William IV, 932
Burge, William L. VI, 801
Burge, Wm. II, 478
Burge, Wm. II, 650
Burge, Wm. II, 658
Burgendine, John VI, 909
Burgendine, Margaret VI, 909
Burger, ??? III, 307
Burger, Andew V, 376
Burger, Catharine III, 54
Burger, Daniel II, 985
Burger, Daniel II, 986
Burger, Deborah III, 54
Burger, Deborah III, 307
Burger, Francis III, 307
Burger, Hester Falconer III, 54
Burger, John III, 307
Burger, Joseph II, 342
Burger, Lydia II, 985
Burger, Lydia II, 986
Burger, M. Antoinette III, 54
Burger, Mildred Leora IV, 932
Burger, Nicholas III, 54
Burger, Rachel F. III, 54
Burger, Rebeckah II, 985
Burger, Rebeckah II, 986
Burger, Stephen D. III, 54
Burger, Timothy H. III, 54
Burger, Timothy H. III, 307
Burger, Walter IV, 932
Burges, Agnes II, 1069
Burges, Agness II, 985
Burges, Amos II, 282
Burges, Amos II, 980
Burges, Amos II, 985
Burges, Amos II, 1047
Burges, Amos II, 1069
Burges, Amos, Jr. II, 1047
Burges, Ann II, 985
Burges, Ann II, 986
Burges, Ann II, 1047
Burges, Ann IV, 465
Burges, Ann, Jr. II, 1047
Burges, Charles II, 986
Burges, Daniel II, 977
Burges, Daniel II, 978
Burges, Daniel II, 980
Burges, Daniel II, 985
Burges, Daniel II, 986
Burges, Daniel II, 988
Burges, Daniel II, 1001
Burges, Daniel II, 1014
Burges, Daniel II, 1017
Burges, Daniel II, 1021
Burges, Daniel II, 1029
Burges, Daniel II, 1069
Burges, Daniel V, 225
Burges, Daniel VI, 478
Burges, Deborah II, 977
Burges, Deborah II, 985
Burges, Deborah II, 986
Burges, Dorathy II, 985
Burges, Dorothy II, 985
Burges, Dorothy II, 1029
Burges, Edith II, 985
Burges, Edith II, 1001
Burges, Elin II, 956
Burges, Elizabeth I, 983
Burges, Elizabeth II, 986
Burges, Elizabeth VI, 895
Burges, Ellin II, 956
Burges, Ellwood II, 986
Burges, George II, 986
Burges, George, Jr. II, 985
Burges, Hampton II, 1047
Burges, Hannah II, 985
Burges, Hannah II, 988
Burges, Hannah II, 1039
Burges, Hugh II, 985
Burges, Israel II, 985
Burges, Israel II, 1047
Burges, James M. II, 986
Burges, Jane I, 983
Burges, Jane L. I, 983
Burges, Jane L. I, 990
Burges, Jeffrey II, 985
Burges, John II, 956
Burges, John II, 985
Burges, John II, 994
Burges, John IV, 465
Burges, Jonathan II, 986
Burges, Jonathan V, 226
Burges, Joseph II, 977
Burges, Joseph II, 985
Burges, Joseph II, 1014
Burges, Joseph II, 1039
Burges, Joseph II, 1069
Burges, Joseph IV, 465
Burges, Joseph VI, 478
Burges, Leah II, 985
Burges, Leticia V, 225
Burges, Lydia II, 977
Burges, Lydia II, 980
Burges, Lydia II, 985
Burges, Lydia II, 988
Burges, Lydia II, 1001
Burges, Lydia II, 1017
Burges, Lydia II, 1047
Burges, Lydia II, 1069
Burges, Lydia VI, 478
Burges, Lydia, Jr. II, 1047
Burges, Margaret II, 978
Burges, Margaret II, 985
Burges, Margaret II, 986
Burges, Margaret II, 1021
Burges, Margaret II, 1022
Burges, Mary II, 956
Burges, Mary II, 985
Burges, Mary II, 994
Burges, Mary II, 1047
Burges, Mary Jane I, 983
Burges, Moses II, 985
Burges, Moses VI, 478
Burges, Phebe II, 1047
Burges, Priscilla II, 956
Burges, Priscilla II, 984
Burges, Priscilla II, 985
Burges, Rachel II, 985
Burges, Rachel II, 986
Burges, Rachel II, 1017
Burges, Rachel II, 1022
Burges, Rebecca II, 986
Burges, Samuel II, 956
Burges, Samuel II, 985
Burges, Samuel II, 986
Burges, Samuel II, 993
Burges, Sarah II, 956
Burges, Sarah II, 980
Burges, Sarah II, 985
Burges, Sarah II, 986
Burges, Sarah II, 993
Burges, Sarah II, 1004
Burges, Sarah II, 1014
Burges, Sarah II, 1017
Burges, Sarah II, 1047
Burges, Sarah II, 1069
Burges, Sarah VI, 478
Burges, Sarah M. II, 1047
Burges, Thamer I, 232
Burges, William VI, 895
Burges, Wm. II, 985
Burges, Wm. II, 986
Burges, Wm. II, 1022
Burgess, ??? III, 39
Burgess, ??? III, 54
Burgess, ??? III, 98
Burgess, Aaron V, 225
Burgess, Aaron B. V, 30
Burgess, Aaron B. V, 226
Burgess, Abigail II, 478
Burgess, Adda Irma IV, 1090
Burgess, Adda Irma IV, 1128
Burgess, Adeliza VI, 301
Burgess, Agnes II, 956
Burgess, Agnes II, 1069
Burgess, Agnes III, 54
Burgess, Albert Lewis IV, 1090
Burgess, Albert Louis IV, 1128
Burgess, Amos II, 168
Burgess, Amos II, 282
Burgess, Amos II, 785
Burgess, Amos II, 956
Burgess, Amos II, 1047
Burgess, Amos II, 1069
Burgess, Amos II, 1070
Burgess, Amos II, 1080
Burgess, Amos IV, 1051
Burgess, Amos IV, 1090
Burgess, Amos IV, 1128
Burgess, Amos IV, 1136
Burgess, Ann II, 478
Burgess, Ann II, 956
Burgess, Ann II, 985
Burgess, Ann IV, 465
Burgess, Ann IV, 1051
Burgess, Ann V, 225
Burgess, Ann VI, 300
Burgess, Ann Eliza V, 225
Burgess, Ann Elizabeth IV, 105
Burgess, Ann, Jr. II, 1047
Burgess, Anna V, 225
Burgess, Anna V, 280
Burgess, Anna V, 729
Burgess, Anna VI, 301
Burgess, Anna Eliza V, 226

Burgess, Anna Mable IV, 1090
Burgess, Anna Mable IV, 1128
Burgess, Anna S. II, 1070
Burgess, Anne IV, 465
Burgess, Anne V, 225
Burgess, Annie I, 232
Burgess, Asa VI, 300
Burgess, Benjamin Hampton II, 1070
Burgess, Benjamin Hampton II, 1079
Burgess, Benjamin Hamton II, 1070
Burgess, Benjamin Hamton II, 1071
Burgess, Betsy VI, 300
Burgess, Betsy VI, 313
Burgess, Betty V, 30
Burgess, Betty V, 63
Burgess, Betty V, 225
Burgess, Betty VI, 300
Burgess, Betty VI, 301
Burgess, Betty VI, 314
Burgess, Beverly V, 225
Burgess, Beverly V, 226
Burgess, Beverly V, 453
Burgess, Beverly V, 462
Burgess, Beverly VI, 300
Burgess, Caroline IV, 1051
Burgess, Catharine II, 1065
Burgess, Catharine II, 1070
Burgess, Catharine II, 1071
Burgess, Catharine II, 1079
Burgess, Catharine II, 1083
Burgess, Catherine Ann II, 1070
Burgess, Cathrin Ann II, 1065
Burgess, Charles IV, 23
Burgess, Charles IV, 1051
Burgess, Charles VI, 886
Burgess, Chas. IV, 1128
Burgess, Christopher VI, 300
Burgess, Clarkson IV, 184
Burgess, Clarkson IV, 304
Burgess, Clarkson IV, 465
Burgess, Clarkson IV, 1051
Burgess, Clarkson IV, 1082
Burgess, Clarkson IV, 1090
Burgess, Clarkson IV, 1128
Burgess, Claudia II, 1065
Burgess, Daniel II, 956
Burgess, Daniel II, 985
Burgess, Daniel II, 1040
Burgess, Daniel II, 1069
Burgess, Daniel IV, 1051
Burgess, Daniel V, 225
Burgess, Daniel V, 226
Burgess, Daniel V, 253
Burgess, Daniel V, 280
Burgess, Daniel V, 452
Burgess, Daniel V, 453
Burgess, Daniel VI, 300
Burgess, Daniel VI, 301
Burgess, Daniel VI, 332
Burgess, David IV, 1051
Burgess, David V, 729
Burgess, David Bryant V, 896
Burgess, Deborah II, 985
Burgess, Deborah II, 1040
Burgess, Deborah V, 225
Burgess, Deborah VI, 300
Burgess, Deborah VI, 301
Burgess, Drucilla V, 225
Burgess, Drucilla VI, 300
Burgess, Druscilla VI, 301
Burgess, Drusilla V, 225
Burgess, Edith Lina V, 729
Burgess, Edmund K. II, 843
Burgess, Edward VI, 963
Burgess, Edwin K. II, 785
Burgess, Edwin K. II, 843
Burgess, Edwin K. II, 1070
Burgess, Eli V, 225
Burgess, Eli V, 226
Burgess, Eli V, 453
Burgess, Eli M. V, 453
Burgess, Elin II, 956
Burgess, Elisha H. V, 30
Burgess, Elizabeth II, 785
Burgess, Elizabeth II, 1070
Burgess, Elizabeth II, 1080
Burgess, Elizabeth IV, 465
Burgess, Elizabeth IV, 1051
Burgess, Elizabeth IV, 1090
Burgess, Elizabeth IV, 1128
Burgess, Elizabeth V, 30
Burgess, Elizabeth V, 48
Burgess, Elizabeth V, 67
Burgess, Elizabeth V, 68
Burgess, Elizabeth V, 225
Burgess, Elizabeth V, 244
Burgess, Elizabeth V, 552
Burgess, Elizabeth V, 573
Burgess, Elizabeth V, 574
Burgess, Elizabeth V, 896
Burgess, Elizabeth VI, 300
Burgess, Elizabeth VI, 301
Burgess, Elizabeth G. IV, 1090
Burgess, Elizabeth J. IV, 1128
Burgess, Elizabeth L. IV, 1051
Burgess, Elizabeth L. IV, 1073
Burgess, Elizabeth L. IV, 1137
Burgess, Elizabeth P. IV, 1051
Burgess, Elizabeth P. IV, 1128
Burgess, Elizabeth S. II, 1070
Burgess, Ellin II, 956
Burgess, Elliza V, 225
Burgess, Ellwood IV, 1128
Burgess, Elwood IV, 465
Burgess, Elwood IV, 1049
Burgess, Elwood IV, 1051
Burgess, Elwood IV, 1090
Burgess, Elwood IV, 1128
Burgess, Elwood IV, 1132
Burgess, Elwood IV, 1138
Burgess, Emerson Elwood IV, 1128
Burgess, Emily V, 225
Burgess, Emily V, 226
Burgess, Emma E. V, 453
Burgess, Emma Elva V, 225
Burgess, Emmar Lewis V, 729
Burgess, Emmor IV, 1090
Burgess, Ephraim Morgan V, 896
Burgess, Ethel Julia IV, 1090
Burgess, Ethel Julia IV, 1128
Burgess, Eunice Julia IV, 1090
Burgess, Eunice M. V, 453
Burgess, Gaynor IV, 1049
Burgess, Gaynor IV, 1051
Burgess, Gaynor IV, 1090
Burgess, Gaynor IV, 1128
Burgess, Gaynor IV, 1132
Burgess, Gaynor V, 729
Burgess, Gaynor P. IV, 1138
Burgess, George I, 232
Burgess, George, Jr. II, 985
Burgess, Gertrude II, 1065
Burgess, Grace IV, 1128
Burgess, Grace VI, 300
Burgess, Grace VI, 336
Burgess, Hampton II, 1047
Burgess, Hamptonetta II, 1065
Burgess, Hamptonetta II, 1070
Burgess, Harvey V, 453
Burgess, Harvey A. V, 453
Burgess, Harvey Ellen V, 225
Burgess, Hiram II, 1065
Burgess, Hiram II, 1070
Burgess, Hiram II, 1071
Burgess, Hiram II, 1083
Burgess, Hiram, Jr. II, 1070
Burgess, Horace II, 1065
Burgess, Hugh II, 985
Burgess, Hugh VI, 334
Burgess, Ida M. V, 453
Burgess, Irene V, 729
Burgess, Isaac V, 30
Burgess, Isaac W. V, 30
Burgess, Isaiah P. II, 1070
Burgess, Israel II, 956
Burgess, Israel II, 985
Burgess, Israel III, 54
Burgess, J. J. I, 209
Burgess, James V, 225
Burgess, James VI, 802
Burgess, James VI, 886
Burgess, Jane II, 203
Burgess, Jane II, 237
Burgess, Jane II, 478
Burgess, Jane B. II, 478
Burgess, Jeffrey II, 985
Burgess, Jennie Giralda II, 1065
Burgess, Jerry VI, 301
Burgess, Jesse V, 30
Burgess, Jesse V, 48
Burgess, Jesse V, 225
Burgess, Jesse V, 552
Burgess, Jesse V, 573
Burgess, Jesse V, 896
Burgess, Jesse VI, 300
Burgess, Jesse H. V, 30
Burgess, Jesse Harvey V, 30
Burgess, Jessy VI, 301
Burgess, Joel IV, 1051
Burgess, Joel IV, 1128
Burgess, John II, 953
Burgess, John II, 956
Burgess, John IV, 184
Burgess, John IV, 465
Burgess, John IV, 492
Burgess, John IV, 1051
Burgess, John IV, 1076
Burgess, John V, 30
Burgess, John V, 225
Burgess, John V, 226
Burgess, John VI, 300
Burgess, John VI, 301
Burgess, John VI, 334
Burgess, John Burgess IV, 1051
Burgess, John H. V, 453
Burgess, John J. I, 232
Burgess, John J. I, 250
Burgess, John L. V, 225
Burgess, John P. IV, 1051
Burgess, John T. V, 30
Burgess, John T. V, 68
Burgess, John T. V, 552
Burgess, John T. V, 574
Burgess, John Thompkins V, 225
Burgess, John Tompkins V, 30
Burgess, Jonathan V, 225
Burgess, Jonathan V, 226
Burgess, Jonathan VI, 300
Burgess, Jonathan VI, 301
Burgess, Jordan V, 225
Burgess, Jordan V, 452
Burgess, Jos. IV, 465
Burgess, Joseph II, 956
Burgess, Joseph II, 967
Burgess, Joseph II, 1022
Burgess, Joseph II, 1069
Burgess, Joseph IV, 465
Burgess, Joseph IV, 1051
Burgess, Joseph V, 219
Burgess, Joseph V, 225
Burgess, Joseph V, 253
Burgess, Joseph V, 306
Burgess, Joseph V, 376
Burgess, Joseph V, 452
Burgess, Joseph V, 453
Burgess, Joseph V, 474
Burgess, Joseph V, 479
Burgess, Joseph VI, 300
Burgess, Joseph VI, 301
Burgess, Joseph VI, 336
Burgess, Joseph C. V, 225
Burgess, Joseph C. VI, 300
Burgess, Joseph C. VI, 318
Burgess, Joseph C. VI, 319
Burgess, Joseph C. VI, 326
Burgess, Joseph H. V, 30
Burgess, Joseph H. V, 225
Burgess, Joseph H. V, 255
Burgess, Joseph H. V, 299
Burgess, Joseph H. V, 376
Burgess, Judith E. V, 453
Burgess, Julia A. IV, 1128
Burgess, Julia A. IV, 1132
Burgess, Julia Ann IV, 1051
Burgess, Julia Ann IV, 1128
Burgess, Juliet V, 30
Burgess, Juliet V, 225
Burgess, Juliet V, 255
Burgess, Juliett V, 299
Burgess, Juliett V, 306
Burgess, Kansas V, 30
Burgess, Leticia V, 225
Burgess, Letitia V, 30
Burgess, Letitia VI, 300
Burgess, Letitia VI, 301
Burgess, Lloyd Penrose IV, 1090
Burgess, Lloyd Penrose IV, 1128
Burgess, Louis A. IV, 1051
Burgess, Lydia II, 956
Burgess, Lydia II, 1069
Burgess, Lydia V, 453
Burgess, Lydia V, 462
Burgess, Lydia Ann IV, 1051
Burgess, Lydia Ann V, 225
Burgess, Lydia Ann V, 226
Burgess, Lydia Ann V, 269
Burgess, Mahala V, 225
Burgess, Mahala V, 253
Burgess, Mahala L. V, 30
Burgess, Malinda V, 225
Burgess, Malinda V, 226
Burgess, Malinda V, 453
Burgess, Malinda V, 462
Burgess, Margaret II, 798
Burgess, Margaret II, 953
Burgess, Margaret II, 956
Burgess, Margaret II, 985
Burgess, Margaret II, 1070
Burgess, Margaret II, 1079
Burgess, Margaret IV, 184
Burgess, Margaret IV, 465
Burgess, Margaret IV, 492
Burgess, Margaret IV, 1051
Burgess, Margaret IV, 1076
Burgess, Margaret IV, 1090
Burgess, Margaret IV, 1127
Burgess, Margaret IV, 1128
Burgess, Margaret V, 225
Burgess, Margaret VI, 300
Burgess, Martha V, 30
Burgess, Martha V, 65
Burgess, Martha V, 225
Burgess, Martha V, 226
Burgess, Martha V, 280
Burgess, Martha VI, 300
Burgess, Martha VI, 301
Burgess, Martha VI, 318
Burgess, Martha VI, 319
Burgess, Martha VI, 326
Burgess, Martha Ann V, 30
Burgess, Martha Ann V, 48
Burgess, Mary I, 232
Burgess, Mary I, 244
Burgess, Mary II, 719
Burgess, Mary II, 730
Burgess, Mary II, 785
Burgess, Mary II, 843
Burgess, Mary II, 956
Burgess, Mary II, 1070
Burgess, Mary IV, 438
Burgess, Mary IV, 465
Burgess, Mary IV, 679
Burgess, Mary IV, 820
Burgess, Mary IV, 1051
Burgess, Mary IV, 1076
Burgess, Mary IV, 1090
Burgess, Mary V, 30
Burgess, Mary V, 67
Burgess, Mary V, 136
Burgess, Mary V, 225
Burgess, Mary V, 552
Burgess, Mary V, 573
Burgess, Mary VI, 300
Burgess, Mary VI, 301
Burgess, Mary Alice IV, 1051
Burgess, Mary Alice IV, 1128
Burgess, Mary Alice IV, 1138
Burgess, Mary Ann II, 827
Burgess, Mary Ann II, 1070
Burgess, Mary Ann II, 1083
Burgess, Mary B. V, 452
Burgess, Mary E. V, 30
Burgess, Mary Emily V, 30
Burgess, Mary Emily V, 552
Burgess, Mary Emily V, 896
Burgess, Mary Emma IV, 1051
Burgess, Mary Emma IV, 1128
Burgess, Mary G. V, 30
Burgess, Mary G. V, 71
Burgess, Mary H. V, 225
Burgess, Mary H. V, 244
Burgess, Mary J. III, 54
Burgess, Mary L. II, 1070
Burgess, Mary P. II, 1070
Burgess, Mary P. II, 1071
Burgess, Mary Winifred III, 39
Burgess, Mary Winifred III, 54
Burgess, Mary, Jr. II, 1070
Burgess, Mary, Jr. V, 599
Burgess, Maud V, 453
Burgess, Moses II, 985
Burgess, Moses V, 30
Burgess, Moses V, 225
Burgess, Moses V, 552
Burgess, Moses VI, 300
Burgess, Moses VI, 301
Burgess, Nancy VI, 802
Burgess, Nancy VI, 886
Burgess, Nathan IV, 1051
Burgess, Nathan IV, 1073
Burgess, Nathan IV, 1090
Burgess, Nathan IV, 1128
Burgess, Nathan IV, 1137
Burgess, Olive D. V, 226
Burgess, Olive D. V, 237
Burgess, Oliver V, 225
Burgess, Ozella C. I, 209
Burgess, Ozella C. I, 232
Burgess, Ozella C. I, 250
Burgess, Penelope V, 225
Burgess, Penelope V, 253
Burgess, Phebe II, 956
Burgess, Phebe V, 219
Burgess, Phebe V, 225
Burgess, Phebe V, 452
Burgess, Phebe V, 453
Burgess, Phebe V, 456
Burgess, Phebe V, 474
Burgess, Phebe V, 479
Burgess, Polly VI, 886
Burgess, Polly VI, 998
Burgess, Priscilla II, 956
Burgess, Rachel II, 953
Burgess, Rachel II, 956
Burgess, Rachel II, 960
Burgess, Rachel II, 965
Burgess, Rachel II, 967
Burgess, Rachel II, 985
Burgess, Rachel II, 1022
Burgess, Rachel II, 1069
Burgess, Rachel II, 1080
Burgess, Rachel V, 225
Burgess, Rachel VI, 886
Burgess, Rachel A. IV, 1128
Burgess, Rachel A. IV, 1136
Burgess, Rachel Ann IV, 1090
Burgess, Ralph VI, 161
Burgess, Rebecca II, 956
Burgess, Rebecca V, 452
Burgess, Rebecca Ann V, 225
Burgess, Robert I, 232
Burgess, Robert II, 478
Burgess, Robert V, 453
Burgess, Ruht VI, 300
Burgess, Ruth V, 225
Burgess, Ruth V, 253
Burgess, Ruth V, 280
Burgess, Ruth V, 452
Burgess, Ruth V, 453
Burgess, Ruth V, 454
Burgess, Ruth VI, 300
Burgess, Ruth VI, 301
Burgess, Ruth VI, 332
Burgess, Samuel II, 956
Burgess, Samuel II, 985
Burgess, Samuel II, 1028
Burgess, Samuel V, 225
Burgess, Samuel V, 226
Burgess, Samuel VI, 802
Burgess, Sarah II, 168
Burgess, Sarah II, 282
Burgess, Sarah II, 956
Burgess, Sarah II, 967
Burgess, Sarah II, 1022
Burgess, Sarah II, 1047
Burgess, Sarah II, 1069
Burgess, Sarah IV, 465
Burgess, Sarah IV, 1051
Burgess, Sarah V, 30
Burgess, Sarah V, 225
Burgess, Sarah V, 226
Burgess, Sarah V, 238
Burgess, Sarah V, 275
Burgess, Sarah V, 292
Burgess, Sarah V, 673
Burgess, Sarah VI, 301
Burgess, Sarah Abbie IV, 1051
Burgess, Sarah Abbie IV, 1090
Burgess, Sarah Abbie IV, 1128
Burgess, Sarah H. II, 843
Burgess, Sarah H. II, 1070
Burgess, Sarah Harvey V, 30
Burgess, Sarah Jane IV, 1090
Burgess, Sarah L. II, 1070
Burgess, Sarah M. II, 1047
Burgess, Sarah Terry VI, 300
Burgess, Simeon II, 1070
Burgess, Spencer V, 225
Burgess, Spencer W. V, 452
Burgess, Susan IV, 184
Burgess, Susan IV, 304
Burgess, Susan IV, 1051
Burgess, Susan IV, 1082
Burgess, Susan IV, 1128
Burgess, Susan W. IV, 1051
Burgess, Susanna VI, 802
Burgess, Susanna VI, 886
Burgess, Tacy V, 30
Burgess, Tacy V, 63
Burgess, Tacy V, 225
Burgess, Tacy VI, 300
Burgess, Tacy VI, 301
Burgess, Tacy Gennette V, 599
Burgess, Tacy Jennet V, 225
Burgess, Tacy Jennett V, 280
Burgess, Tacy Jennette V, 552
Burgess, Tacy Jennette V, 599
Burgess, Thaddeus II, 1065
Burgess, Thamer I, 232
Burgess, Thomas II, 168
Burgess, Thomas II, 203
Burgess, Thomas II, 237
Burgess, Thomas II, 342
Burgess, Thomas II, 478
Burgess, Thomas V, 30
Burgess, Thomas V, 63
Burgess, Thomas V, 225
Burgess, Thomas V, 244
Burgess, Thomas VI, 300
Burgess, Thomas VI, 312
Burgess, Thomas VI, 313
Burgess, Thomas VI, 314
Burgess, Thomas VI, 341
Burgess, Thomas VI, 886
Burgess, Thomas H. V, 30
Burgess, Thomas H. V, 71
Burgess, Thomas S. II, 1070
Burgess, Thos. H. V, 552
Burgess, Valena V, 30
Burgess, Valena V, 225

Burgess, Valena V, 226
Burgess, Valeria III, 54
Burgess, Valeria III, 98
Burgess, Wd. Jane II, 168
Burgess, White V, 599
Burgess, William V, 225
Burgess, William V, 226
Burgess, William VI, 886
Burgess, William H. I, 232
Burgess, William H. V, 30
Burgess, Willis IV, 1051
Burgess, Willis I. IV, 1128
Burgess, Willis J. IV, 1128
Burgess, Winney Caudle VI, 886
Burgess, Wm. II, 1069
Burgess, Wm. II, 1080
Burgett, Eva Carter V, 376
Burgett, William IV, 465
Burgh, Elizabeth VI, 27
Burgh, Elizabeth VI, 28
Burgh, Elizabeth VI, 31
Burgh, Margaret VI, 28
Burgh, Margaret VI, 31
Burgh, Moarning VI, 28
Burgh, William VI, 28
Burgh, William VI, 31
Burgher, Andew V, 376
Burgher, Elemor V, 376
Burghtler, Dell IV, 1273
Burgis, Ann II, 976
Burgis, Anne V, 225
Burgis, Ruth V, 225
Burgis, Sarah V, 225
Burgis, Susannah VI, 963
Burgiss, Ann II, 478
Burgiss, Thomas II, 203
Burgiss, Thomas II, 478
Burglas, George T. VI, 886
Burglas, N. L. VI, 886
Burgner, Caroline V, 988
Burgner, Eliza V, 727
Burgner, Jacob V, 988
Burgner, M??? V, 988
Burgner, Mary V, 988
Burgner, Mary M. V, 988
Burgner, Nettie V, 988
Burgoine, Susanna V, 988
Burgraff, Mary IV, 1161
Burgurnal, Alma M. V, 30
Burgurnal, Alma M. V, 107
Burgy, Annie IV, 184
Burgy, Bertha IV, 1311
Burgy, Christiana IV, 1319
Burgy, Cora IV, 1309
Burgy, Cora IV, 1311
Burgy, Cora M. IV, 1309
Burgy, Cora M. IV, 1311
Burgy, Harry IV, 184
Burgy, John IV, 1319
Burgy, Lorenzo IV, 1311
Burgy, Sophia IV, 1319
Burgy, Sophia Ann IV, 1309
Burham, James II, 275
Burhaus, Mary IV, 1309
Buris, Deborough V, 226
Buris, Rachel I, 960
Burk, Abigail IV, 1144
Burk, Abigail IV, 1151
Burk, Albert IV, 184
Burk, Charles A. IV, 184
Burk, Cora IV, 184
Burk, Elizabeth III, 105
Burk, Etta Mendenhall I, 613
Burk, Hannah IV, 1151
Burk, Harry V, 988
Burk, Mary V, 896
Burk, Mary V, 927
Burk, Mary V, 988
Burk, Rachel IV, 322
Burk, Ralph IV, 184
Burk, Wilbur V, 662
Burk, William H. VI, 818
Burke, ??? III, 335
Burke, Albert IV, 184
Burke, Arthur III, 54
Burke, Arthur III, 152
Burke, Catharine III, 54
Burke, Charles VI, 628
Burke, Charles VI, 651
Burke, Charles A. IV, 184
Burke, Effie M. IV, 1247
Burke, Eliz. III, 181
Burke, Elizabeth III, 54
Burke, Elizabeth Ann III, 54
Burke, Elizabeth McDonald III, 54
Burke, Emma VI, 628
Burke, Emma VI, 651
Burke, Emma Virginia VI, 628
Burke, Emma Virginia VI, 651
Burke, Frances III, 54
Burke, Frances III, 152
Burke, Francis P. III, 54
Burke, Hannah IV, 1151
Burke, Hannah IV, 1186
Burke, Helen III, 409
Burke, Helen III, 418
Burke, Helen Hicks III, 397
Burke, James Leighton III, 397
Burke, Jas. L. III, 409
Burke, Jas. Leighton III, 418
Burke, John III, 54
Burke, Mabel VI, 748
Burke, Mary III, 54
Burke, Mary Ann III, 54
Burke, Rachel IV, 515
Burke, Thomas III, 54
Burke, W. M. IV, 1247
Burke, Willice Melon IV, 1247
Burkell, Francis II, 17
Burkell, Francis II, 23
Burket, Susanna I, 711
Burket, Susanna I, 733
Burkey, Aaron IV, 1036
Burkey, Elizabeth II, 342
Burkey, Emanuel IV, 1036
Burkey, Emanuel J. IV, 1036
Burkey, Harry J. IV, 1036
Burkey, Jane IV, 1036
Burkey, Margaret II, 342
Burkey, Margaret IV, 1036
Burkey, Wm. H. IV, 1036
Burkhard, Edgar V, 30
Burkhard, Phebe V, 30
Burkhardt, John V, 226
Burkhart, Ella IV, 570
Burkhart, Ella IV, 590
Burkhart, Mrs. E. C. IV, 746
Burkhart, Phebe Hartman V, 662
Burkhead, Jennette IV, 1309
Burkhead, Susanna IV, 515
Burkheart, Natalia IV, 184
Burkhill, John III, 54
Burkholder, James VI, 886
Burkholder, Martha VI, 886
Burkholder, Mary II, 720
Burkle, Juliet III, 54
Burks, Betsey VI, 886
Burks, Charles F. VI, 805
Burks, Charles F. VI, 867
Burks, Charles L. VI, 886
Burks, David VI, 886
Burks, Dolly W. VI, 886
Burks, E. C. VI, 995
Burks, Edward C. VI, 886
Burks, Edward C. VI, 896
Burks, Elizabeth VI, 886
Burks, Elvira Coots VI, 822
Burks, Frances Ann VI, 805
Burks, Frances E. H. VI, 802
Burks, Francis VI, 941
Burks, George VI, 886
Burks, George A. VI, 802
Burks, Henry VI, 886
Burks, Henry VI, 1005
Burks, John VI, 886
Burks, John B. VI, 886
Burks, John P. VI, 886
Burks, Joseph VI, 805
Burks, Joseph VI, 820
Burks, Joseph VI, 822
Burks, Judith VI, 886
Burks, Littleberry L. VI, 860
Burks, Louisa C. VI, 886
Burks, Louisa P. VI, 886
Burks, Louisa V. VI, 990
Burks, Martha A. VI, 886
Burks, Martin P. VI, 886
Burks, Martin P. VI, 992
Burks, Martin P. VI, 996
Burks, Mary VI, 886
Burks, Mildred E. VI, 886
Burks, Nancy VI, 879
Burks, Nathaniel D. VI, 886
Burks, Robert VI, 886
Burks, Sally VI, 886
Burks, Susan VI, 820
Burks, Temperance K. VI, 979
Burks, William VI, 979
Burks, William L. VI, 979
Burland, Jane II, 442
Burleigh, Benjamin III, 397
Burleigh, Edmond Jordan VI, 15
Burleigh, Elizabeth VI, 15
Burleigh, Hannah III, 397
Burleigh, Jane III, 397
Burleigh, Samuel VI, 15
Burleigh, Sarah III, 397
Burley, Ann III, 397
Burley, Benjamin III, 397
Burley, Elizabeth VI, 232
Burley, Elizabeth VI, 823
Burley, Garey VI, 814
Burley, Grace VI, 823
Burley, Hannah III, 397
Burley, Jane III, 397
Burley, Joseph II, 203
Burley, Mary VI, 814
Burley, Sarah III, 397
Burling, ??? III, 56
Burling, ??? III, 414
Burling, Abigail III, 42
Burling, Abigail III, 54
Burling, Abigail III, 378
Burling, Alice B. III, 56
Burling, Alice G. III, 54
Burling, Alice G. III, 265
Burling, Alice Gertrude III, 55
Burling, Alice Gertrude III, 271
Burling, Amy III, 56
Burling, Ann III, 54
Burling, Ann III, 55
Burling, Ann III, 154
Burling, Ann III, 200
Burling, Ann III, 248
Burling, Ann III, 378
Burling, Ann Louisa III, 54
Burling, Anna III, 54
Burling, Anna III, 114
Burling, Anna III, 265
Burling, Anna III, 271
Burling, Anna H. III, 55
Burling, Anne III, 54
Burling, Anne III, 55
Burling, Anne III, 102
Burling, Anne II III, 55
Burling, Benj. III, 54
Burling, Benj. III, 403
Burling, Benj. F. III, 55
Burling, Benj. F. III, 450
Burling, Benjamin III, 54
Burling, Benjamin III, 56
Burling, Benjamin F. III, 54
Burling, Benjamin S. II, 843
Burling, Benjamin S. II, 892
Burling, Caroline III, 56
Burling, Catharine II, 843
Burling, Catharine II, 892
Burling, Catharine III, 54
Burling, Catharine III, 55
Burling, Catharine III, 171
Burling, Catharine H. III, 54
Burling, De Witt Livingston III, 55
Burling, Deborah III, 54
Burling, Deborah III, 336
Burling, Ebenezer III, 54
Burling, Ebenezer III, 56
Burling, Edw. F. III, 265
Burling, Edward III, 54
Burling, Edward III, 55
Burling, Edward III, 114
Burling, Edward III, 117
Burling, Edward III, 274
Burling, Edward III, 336
Burling, Edward Carpenter III, 54
Burling, Edward F. III, 54
Burling, Elias III, 54
Burling, Eliz. III, 54
Burling, Eliz. III, 55
Burling, Elizabeth III, 42
Burling, Elizabeth III, 55
Burling, Elizabeth III, 56
Burling, Elizabeth III, 130
Burling, Elizabeth III, 378
Burling, Elizabeth III, 397
Burling, Elizabeth III, 414
Burling, Emily W. II, 843
Burling, Emily W. II, 892
Burling, George III, 55
Burling, Grace III, 54
Burling, Grace III, 89
Burling, Hannah II, 168
Burling, Hannah II, 203
Burling, Hannah II, 262
Burling, Hannah III, 54
Burling, Hannah III, 55
Burling, Hannah III, 56
Burling, Hannah III, 118
Burling, Hannah III, 120
Burling, Hannah III, 403
Burling, Hannah III, 450
Burling, Hebe III, 414
Burling, Henrietta III, 55
Burling, Henrietta III, 175
Burling, Henrietta III, 397
Burling, Henrietta III, 413
Burling, Henrietta III, 414
Burling, James III, 42
Burling, James III, 54
Burling, James III, 55
Burling, James III, 130
Burling, James III, 199
Burling, Jane II, 168
Burling, Jane II, 185
Burling, Jane II, 203
Burling, Jane II, 262
Burling, Jane III, 54
Burling, Jane III, 55
Burling, Jane III, 154
Burling, Jane III, 235
Burling, Jane III, 430
Burling, Jane Large II, 168
Burling, Jas. III, 54
Burling, John II, 203
Burling, John III, 54
Burling, John III, 55
Burling, John III, 56
Burling, John III, 102
Burling, John III, 154
Burling, John III, 200
Burling, John III, 248
Burling, John C. III, 55
Burling, John T. III, 55
Burling, Joseph III, 55
Burling, Joseph III, 56
Burling, Lancaster III, 55
Burling, Lillie III, 56
Burling, Lillie B. III, 56
Burling, Lillie P. III, 56
Burling, Lillie P. III, 253
Burling, Lillie T. III, 56
Burling, Lillie T. III, 264
Burling, Maria III, 55
Burling, Maria II III, 55
Burling, Martha III, 54
Burling, Martha III, 55
Burling, Mary II, 168
Burling, Mary II, 203
Burling, Mary II, 262
Burling, Mary III, 54
Burling, Mary III, 55
Burling, Mary III, 56
Burling, Mary III, 105
Burling, Mary III, 248
Burling, Mary III, 274
Burling, Mary III, 480
Burling, Mary III, 491
Burling, Mary F. III, 54
Burling, Mary F. III, 397
Burling, Mary F. III, 450
Burling, Peter III, 54
Burling, Peter III, 55
Burling, Phebe III, 54
Burling, Phebe III, 55
Burling, Phebe III, 117
Burling, Phebe III, 271
Burling, Phebe III, 336
Burling, Phebe H. III, 54
Burling, Phebe H. III, 55
Burling, Phebe H. III, 271
Burling, Philip III, 54
Burling, Philip III, 55
Burling, Rachel III, 55
Burling, Rachel III, 162
Burling, Rebecca III, 54
Burling, Rebecca III, 56
Burling, Rebecca III, 378
Burling, Rebecca III, 453
Burling, Rebeckah III, 55
Burling, Rebeckah III, 120
Burling, Rebekah III, 56
Burling, Richard III, 55
Burling, Sam'l III, 271
Burling, Samuel II, 168
Burling, Samuel II, 203
Burling, Samuel II, 262
Burling, Samuel III, 54
Burling, Samuel III, 55
Burling, Samuel III, 271
Burling, Sarah III, 43
Burling, Sarah III, 54
Burling, Sarah III, 55
Burling, Sarah III, 56
Burling, Sarah III, 171
Burling, Sarah III, 199
Burling, Sarah III, 343
Burling, Sarah W. III, 55
Burling, Sarah W. III, 210
Burling, Susan M. III, 346
Burling, Susan Matilda III, 54
Burling, Susanna III, 55
Burling, Thomas III, 55
Burling, Thomas III, 56
Burling, Thomas III, 175
Burling, Thomas III, 336
Burling, Thomas III, 397
Burling, Thomas III, 414
Burling, Thomas C. III, 55
Burling, Thomas H. III, 55
Burling, Thomas W. III, 55
Burling, Thos. III, 54
Burling, Thos. III, 55
Burling, Thos. III, 171
Burling, Walter III, 56
Burling, Wd. Ann III, 54
Burling, Wd. Jane II, 168
Burling, William III, 54
Burling, William III, 55
Burling, William III, 56
Burling, William III, 105
Burling, William III, 118
Burling, William III, 120
Burling, William Clinton III, 55
Burling, William Clinton III, 56
Burling, William James III, 56
Burling, William S. III, 56
Burling, William, Jr. III, 56
Burling, Wm. C. III, 56
Burling, Wm. Clinton III, 264
Burling, Wm. James III, 56
Burling, Wm. Raymond III, 56
Burling, Wm. Raymond III, 253
Burling, Wm., Jr. III, 43
Burlingame, Lucy Richardson II, 1047
Burn, Elizabeth II, 342
Burn, Josa II, 342
Burn, William II, 342
Burne, John V, 831
Burnell, Carrie IV, 1203
Burnes, Anne VI, 923
Burnes, Clause II, 342
Burnes, Dyer II, 342
Burnes, George V, 226
Burnes, Rachel II, 478
Burnet, ??? IV, 376
Burnet, Abbigal T. II, 317
Burnet, Abraham V, 31
Burnet, Alice V, 218
Burnet, Alice V, 226
Burnet, Amos V, 31
Burnet, Anabel M. V, 30
Burnet, Anabel M. V, 31
Burnet, Anabell IV, 77
Burnet, Anabella III, 378
Burnet, Anable V, 100
Burnet, Anibel IV, 184
Burnet, Ann IV, 77
Burnet, Ann IV, 87
Burnet, Ann IV, 184
Burnet, Ann IV, 376
Burnet, Ann IV, 466
Burnet, Ann IV, 515
Burnet, Ann V, 30
Burnet, Ann V, 31
Burnet, Ann V, 100
Burnet, Ann V, 145
Burnet, Anna IV, 77
Burnet, Anna IV, 184
Burnet, Anna IV, 376
Burnet, Anna V, 30
Burnet, Anna V, 31
Burnet, Anna V, 124
Burnet, Anna V, 145
Burnet, Anna V, 155
Burnet, Anna V, 156
Burnet, Annabel V, 145
Burnet, Annable IV, 77
Burnet, Annable IV, 184
Burnet, Annibal IV, 77
Burnet, Catherine IV, 77
Burnet, Charles V, 31
Burnet, Charles S. V, 31
Burnet, Christopher V, 31
Burnet, Creed VI, 886
Burnet, Daniel IV, 77
Burnet, Daniel IV, 87
Burnet, Daniel V, 30
Burnet, Daniel V, 31
Burnet, Daniel V, 100
Burnet, Daniel V, 145
Burnet, Darlington IV, 77
Burnet, David IV, 77
Burnet, David IV, 184
Burnet, David IV, 376
Burnet, David IV, 515
Burnet, David V, 31
Burnet, David V, 110
Burnet, David V, 143
Burnet, David V, 145
Burnet, David V, 155
Burnet, David V, 212
Burnet, Deborah IV, 77
Burnet, Deborah IV, 184
Burnet, Deborah IV, 376
Burnet, Deborah IV, 515
Burnet, Effie R. V, 155
Burnet, Eli V, 31
Burnet, Eli D. V, 31
Burnet, Elias IV, 466
Burnet, Eliza IV, 466
Burnet, Eliza V, 30
Burnet, Eliza V, 31

Burnet, Eliza V, 110
Burnet, Eliza V, 145
Burnet, Elizabeth V, 28
Burnet, Elizabeth V, 30
Burnet, Elizabeth V, 31
Burnet, Elizabeth V, 70
Burnet, Elizabeth V, 113
Burnet, Elizabeth V, 121
Burnet, Elizabeth V, 156
Burnet, Elizabeth V, 160
Burnet, Emma V, 31
Burnet, Emma V, 114
Burnet, Emma Matilda V, 31
Burnet, Francis Marion V, 155
Burnet, Franklin C. V, 31
Burnet, Geo. H. III, 56
Burnet, George V, 155
Burnet, Hannah V, 28
Burnet, Hannah V, 31
Burnet, Hannah V, 32
Burnet, Hannah V, 143
Burnet, Hannah V, 145
Burnet, Hannah V, 155
Burnet, Hannah V, 212
Burnet, Hannah J. V, 31
Burnet, Hannah T. V, 86
Burnet, Henry III, 378
Burnet, Jane III, 378
Burnet, Jemima V, 31
Burnet, Jesse V, 30
Burnet, Jesse V, 31
Burnet, Job Jeffries IV, 77
Burnet, John III, 56
Burnet, John IV, 77
Burnet, John IV, 184
Burnet, John IV, 376
Burnet, John IV, 466
Burnet, John IV, 515
Burnet, John V, 28
Burnet, John V, 30
Burnet, John V, 31
Burnet, John V, 70
Burnet, John V, 113
Burnet, John V, 145
Burnet, Jonathan V, 31
Burnet, Jonathan Y. V, 31
Burnet, Joseph V, 30
Burnet, Joseph H. V, 31
Burnet, Louisa G. V, 31
Burnet, Lydia IV, 376
Burnet, Lydia IV, 515
Burnet, Lydia V, 30
Burnet, Lydia V, 31
Burnet, Lydia V, 145
Burnet, Lydiaann V, 31
Burnet, Lydiann V, 31
Burnet, Lydiann V, 61
Burnet, Margaret V, 155
Burnet, Martha R. V, 31
Burnet, Mary III, 378
Burnet, Mary IV, 77
Burnet, Mary V, 30
Burnet, Mary V, 145
Burnet, Mary Ann V, 31
Burnet, Mary Ann V, 113
Burnet, Mary Ann V, 552
Burnet, Mary Ann V, 593
Burnet, Mary Ann VI, 886
Burnet, Mary Emma V, 31
Burnet, Mary L. V, 31
Burnet, Matilda V, 31
Burnet, Matilda P. V, 31
Burnet, Owen J. V, 31
Burnet, Phebe A. III, 56
Burnet, Rachel IV, 77
Burnet, Rachel IV, 184
Burnet, Rachel IV, 376
Burnet, Rachel IV, 515
Burnet, Rachel V, 30
Burnet, Rachel V, 145
Burnet, Rachel Ann V, 31
Burnet, Rebecca IV, 77
Burnet, Rebecca IV, 117
Burnet, Rebecca IV, 184
Burnet, Rebecca IV, 376
Burnet, Rebecca IV, 515
Burnet, Rebecca V, 30
Burnet, Rebecca V, 31
Burnet, Rebecca V, 118
Burnet, Rebecca V, 124
Burnet, Rebecca V, 145
Burnet, Rebecca V, 156
Burnet, Rebeckah IV, 376
Burnet, Robert IV, 77
Burnet, Robert IV, 184
Burnet, Robert IV, 376
Burnet, Robert IV, 515
Burnet, Robert V, 30
Burnet, Robert V, 31
Burnet, Robert V, 124
Burnet, Robert V, 145
Burnet, Robert V, 155
Burnet, Roy W. V, 156
Burnet, Ruth V, 30
Burnet, Samuel V, 31
Burnet, Sarah V, 31
Burnet, Sarah V, 32
Burnet, Sarah B. V, 31
Burnet, Sarah B. V, 123
Burnet, Sarah E. V, 31
Burnet, Sarah Ellen V, 31
Burnet, Seth V, 31
Burnet, Smith IV, 515
Burnet, Smith V, 30
Burnet, Smith V, 31
Burnet, Smith V, 145
Burnet, Stephen IV, 77
Burnet, Stephen IV, 184
Burnet, Stephen IV, 376
Burnet, Stephen V, 30
Burnet, Stephen V, 31
Burnet, Stephen V, 32
Burnet, Stephen V, 86
Burnet, Stephen V, 145
Burnet, Thomas III, 56
Burnet, Thomas IV, 77
Burnet, Thomas IV, 184
Burnet, Thomas IV, 376
Burnet, Thomas IV, 515
Burnet, Thomas V, 28
Burnet, Thomas V, 30
Burnet, Thomas V, 31
Burnet, Thomas V, 145
Burnet, Wd Rebecca IV, 95
Burnet, William IV, 376
Burnet, William IV, 515
Burnet, William V, 30
Burnet, William V, 31
Burnet, William V, 121
Burnet, William V, 145
Burnet, William G. V, 145
Burnett, ??? III, 56
Burnett, Abbigal T. II, 317
Burnett, Abigail II, 311
Burnett, Abigail T. II, 308
Burnett, Absalom VI, 886
Burnett, Alden M. III, 56
Burnett, Alice T. V, 453
Burnett, Ammon VI, 886
Burnett, Anabel M. V, 30
Burnett, Ann IV, 109
Burnett, Ann IV, 515
Burnett, Ann V, 30
Burnett, Ann V, 145
Burnett, Ann VI, 960
Burnett, Anna II, 311
Burnett, Anna IV, 184
Burnett, Annabel V, 145
Burnett, Annabella III, 56
Burnett, Betsy Ann VI, 1011
Burnett, Catharine M. VI, 887
Burnett, Celia A. VI, 887
Burnett, Charles V, 662
Burnett, Charles VI, 802
Burnett, Charles T. VI, 887
Burnett, Colin VI, 887
Burnett, Cora V, 662
Burnett, Creed VI, 802
Burnett, Creed VI, 886
Burnett, Daniel V, 30
Burnett, Daniel V, 145
Burnett, David IV, 184
Burnett, David IV, 515
Burnett, Deborah IV, 184
Burnett, Deborah IV, 515
Burnett, Dosiah Ann VI, 887
Burnett, Edmond VI, 873
Burnett, Edmond VI, 932
Burnett, Edmond VI, 940
Burnett, Edmond VI, 985
Burnett, Edmund VI, 869
Burnett, Eli V, 31
Burnett, Elisha VI, 881
Burnett, Elisha VI, 886
Burnett, Elisha VI, 960
Burnett, Elisha VI, 976
Burnett, Elisha VI, 1008
Burnett, Elisha VI, 1011
Burnett, Elisha C. VI, 887
Burnett, Eliza IV, 1128
Burnett, Eliza IV, 1132
Burnett, Eliza VI, 932
Burnett, Elizabeth V, 156
Burnett, Elizabeth VI, 802
Burnett, Elizabeth VI, 886
Burnett, Elizabeth VI, 935
Burnett, Elizabeth VI, 976
Burnett, Emma M. V, 31
Burnett, Emma M. V, 89
Burnett, Frances A. VI, 829
Burnett, Frances A. VI, 871
Burnett, Geo. H. III, 56
Burnett, George V, 321
Burnett, Henry III, 56
Burnett, Henry III, 146
Burnett, James III, 93
Burnett, James VI, 802
Burnett, James VI, 872
Burnett, James VI, 886
Burnett, James VI, 913
Burnett, James VI, 967
Burnett, James VI, 989
Burnett, James B. VI, 887
Burnett, James, Jr. VI, 887
Burnett, Jane III, 56
Burnett, Jane VI, 886
Burnett, Jane VI, 994
Burnett, Jefferson VI, 802
Burnett, Jemima V, 31
Burnett, Jemima V, 101
Burnett, Jesse V, 30
Burnett, Jesse VI, 802
Burnett, John III, 56
Burnett, John IV, 23
Burnett, John IV, 184
Burnett, John IV, 376
Burnett, John IV, 515
Burnett, John VI, 829
Burnett, John VI, 886
Burnett, John VI, 887
Burnett, John VI, 897
Burnett, John R. VI, 874
Burnett, John R. VI, 919
Burnett, John R. VI, 924
Burnett, John R. VI, 980
Burnett, John R. VI, 1013
Burnett, John S. VI, 886
Burnett, Jonathan V, 31
Burnett, Joseph V, 30
Burnett, Joseph VI, 886
Burnett, Joseph H. V, 31
Burnett, Joshua VI, 886
Burnett, Joshua VI, 887
Burnett, Joshua VI, 902
Burnett, Joshua VI, 908
Burnett, Joshua VI, 959
Burnett, Joshua VI, 985
Burnett, Joshua VI, 994
Burnett, Joshua VI, 1011
Burnett, Judith VI, 872
Burnett, Katherine VI, 886
Burnett, Kesia VI, 881
Burnett, Lavinia VI, 887
Burnett, Levicy VI, 875
Burnett, Locky VI, 850
Burnett, Louise V, 662
Burnett, Lucinda VI, 886
Burnett, Lucy VI, 886
Burnett, Lucy VI, 1015
Burnett, Lydia IV, 515
Burnett, Mabel VI, 935
Burnett, Mable VI, 885
Burnett, Mable VI, 886
Burnett, Mahalah VI, 985
Burnett, Malinda T. VI, 869
Burnett, Margaret VI, 802
Burnett, Margaret S. VI, 887
Burnett, Martha VI, 872
Burnett, Martha E. VI, 995
Burnett, Martha J. V, 321
Burnett, Mary III, 56
Burnett, Mary III, 146
Burnett, Mary IV, 77
Burnett, Mary V, 30
Burnett, Mary VI, 795
Burnett, Mary VI, 802
Burnett, Mary VI, 887
Burnett, Mary VI, 913
Burnett, Mary VI, 985
Burnett, Mary A. VI, 802
Burnett, Mary Ann VI, 886
Burnett, Mary J. III, 93
Burnett, Mary J. V, 31
Burnett, Mary J. V, 76
Burnett, Matilda V, 31
Burnett, Matilda V, 121
Burnett, Mollie E. I, 1149
Burnett, Nancy VI, 802
Burnett, Nancy VI, 873
Burnett, Nancy VI, 886
Burnett, Nancy VI, 967
Burnett, Nancy A. VI, 959
Burnett, Nettie V, 662
Burnett, Obadiah VI, 985
Burnett, Obediah VI, 886
Burnett, Orphey VI, 886
Burnett, Owen J. V, 31
Burnett, Phebe III, 56
Burnett, Phebe A. III, 56
Burnett, Phebe Ann III, 36
Burnett, Phebe Anna III, 56
Burnett, Polly M. VI, 886
Burnett, Rachel IV, 184
Burnett, Rachel IV, 515
Burnett, Rachel V, 52
Burnett, Rachel V, 87
Burnett, Rachel V, 145
Burnett, Rachel VI, 802
Burnett, Rachel VI, 881
Burnett, Rebecca IV, 184
Burnett, Rebecca IV, 376
Burnett, Rebecca IV, 515
Burnett, Rebecca V, 52
Burnett, Rebecca V, 156
Burnett, Rebecca V, 205
Burnett, Rebecca V, 896
Burnett, Rebecca VI, 887
Burnett, Rebeckah VI, 886
Burnett, Richard VI, 802
Burnett, Robert IV, 109
Burnett, Robert IV, 184
Burnett, Robert IV, 376
Burnett, Robert IV, 515
Burnett, Ruth V, 30
Burnett, Sabre VI, 989
Burnett, Sally VI, 886
Burnett, Sally VI, 1011
Burnett, Saml. VI, 886
Burnett, Samuel VI, 871
Burnett, Samuel VI, 886
Burnett, Samuel VI, 896
Burnett, Sarah VI, 802
Burnett, Sarah A. VI, 887
Burnett, Sarah Elizabeth VI, 887
Burnett, Sarah Ellen V, 31
Burnett, Sarah Ellen V, 98
Burnett, Smith IV, 515
Burnett, Stephen V, 30
Burnett, Stephen V, 145
Burnett, Susanna VI, 850
Burnett, Susanna VI, 1008
Burnett, Susannah VI, 802
Burnett, Thomas II, 308
Burnett, Thomas II, 317
Burnett, Thomas III, 56
Burnett, Thomas IV, 515
Burnett, Thomas V, 662
Burnett, Thomas VI, 802
Burnett, Thomas VI, 886
Burnett, William III, 36
Burnett, William III, 56
Burnett, William IV, 515
Burnett, William V, 30
Burnett, William VI, 802
Burnett, William VI, 850
Burnett, William VI, 886
Burnett, William W. VI, 887
Burnett, Williamson VI, 872
Burnett, Williamson VI, 887
Burnett, Williamson VI, 953
Burnett, Williamson VI, 989
Burnett, Willie H. III, 56
Burnette, Betsey VI, 849
Burnette, Mary VI, 862
Burnette, Nancy VI, 870
Burnette, Thomas VI, 862
Burnette, Wm. VI, 810
Burney, Don V. VI, 478
Burney, Don V. VI, 565
Burney, Elizabeth I, 376
Burney, Emma C. VI, 478
Burney, Emma C. VI, 565
Burney, Emma D. VI, 478
Burney, Emma E. VI, 478
Burney, Emma E. VI, 565
Burney, John I, 376
Burney, Levi C. VI, 478
Burney, Levi C. VI, 565
Burney, William I, 376
Burnham, Anna G. II, 843
Burnham, M. A. IV, 1309
Burnham, Ralph II, 33
Burnham, Richard II, 33
Burnham, Wd. Elizabeth II, 33
Burnit, Elizabeth VI, 816
Burnit, Mary I, 233
Burnit, Mary I, 256
Burnit, William VI, 816
Burnits, Nathan Allen II, 203
Burnits, Robert II, 191
Burnits, Robert II, 203
Burnley, Ann VI, 883
Burnley, Israel VI, 876
Burnley, Israel VI, 883
Burnley, Joel VI, 883
Burnley, Nancy VI, 814
Burnley, Susanna VI, 876
Burns, Adolph IV, 1203
Burns, Alfred IV, 1203
Burns, Artemisa IV, 427
Burns, Artilla G. I, 376
Burns, Carrie T. V, 552
Burns, Clause II, 342
Burns, Docy IV, 1203
Burns, Dolphus D. IV, 1203
Burns, Dyer II, 342
Burns, Elizabeth I, 802
Burns, Elizabeth II, 342
Burns, Elizabeth IV, 23
Burns, Elizabeth IV, 864
Burns, Elizabeth VI, 350
Burns, Ella Mary V, 552
Burns, Emelina F. VI, 802
Burns, Gabriel V, 226
Burns, George V, 226
Burns, Hannah II, 478
Burns, Hannah II, 687
Burns, Hannah Ann Lownes II, 730
Burns, Hope IV, 686
Burns, Hope IV, 771
Burns, Irene I, 927
Burns, Jane VI, 350
Burns, Jas. Warren III, 56
Burns, John I, 802
Burns, John IV, 23
Burns, John VI, 350
Burns, John VI, 802
Burns, Josa II, 342
Burns, Joshua II, 478
Burns, Josiah I, 802
Burns, Leah V, 226
Burns, Leah V, 321
Burns, Leah V, 376
Burns, Littleberry VI, 802
Burns, Lucy VI, 802
Burns, Lydia IV, 686
Burns, Lydia IV, 771
Burns, Malissa IV, 1203
Burns, Maris I, 802
Burns, Mary II, 986
Burns, Mary II, 1002
Burns, Mary III, 396
Burns, Mary IV, 23
Burns, Mary IV, 184
Burns, Mary IV, 244
Burns, Mary IV, 610
Burns, Mary IV, 613
Burns, Mary IV, 662
Burns, Mary VI, 350
Burns, Mary Elizabeth V, 552
Burns, Mary Jane IV, 23
Burns, Melissa IV, 1203
Burns, Ola IV, 1203
Burns, Phebe E. IV, 1203
Burns, Rachel I, 802
Burns, Rachel II, 478
Burns, Rachel IV, 23
Burns, Rachel IV, 613
Burns, Rachel V, 662
Burns, Rachel VI, 350
Burns, Raymond IV, 1203
Burns, Ruth Ann Winifred III, 56
Burns, Ruth Ann Winifred III, 218
Burns, Sarah I, 413
Burns, Sarah II, 730
Burns, Sarah IV, 1203
Burns, Sarah V, 226
Burns, Sarah V, 321
Burns, Timothy VI, 802
Burns, William II, 342
Burns, Wm. P. III, 56
Burns, Wm. P. III, 218
Burnside, Anna M. IV, 985
Burnside, Asa I, 803
Burnside, Asa I, 974
Burnside, Benjamin I, 376
Burnside, Elizabeth I, 803
Burnside, James I, 803
Burnside, James I, 971
Burnside, Levina I, 974
Burnside, Mary I, 803
Burnside, Mary I, 974
Burnside, Mary I, 988
Burnside, Mary V, 226
Burnside, Ruth I, 445
Burnside, Ruth Fauset I, 444
Burnside, Sarah I, 803
Burnside, Sarah I, 819
Burnside, Sunath I, 974
Burnsides, Asa I, 959
Burnsides, Asa I, 960
Burnsides, Asa I, 983
Burnsides, Asenath I, 959
Burnsides, Asenath I, 960
Burnsides, Asenath I, 983
Burnsides, Benjamin I, 376
Burnsides, Betsey VI, 887
Burnsides, Elizabeth I, 803
Burnsides, Elizabeth I, 983
Burnsides, James I, 983
Burnsides, Jeams I, 960
Burnsides, Mary I, 376
Burnsides, Mary I, 400

Burnsides, Mary I, 803
Burnsides, Mary I, 960
Burnsides, Mary I, 971
Burnsides, Mary I, 983
Burnsides, Robert I, 376
Burnsides, Robert I, 400
Burnsides, Sarah I, 803
Burnsides, William VI, 887
Burnstein, Eliza V, 31
Burny, Jane I, 376
Burny, Jane I, 428
Burnyeat, John VI, 7
Burnyeat, John VI, 40
Burr, Abigail II, 168
Burr, Abigail II, 213
Burr, Abigail Ann II, 204
Burr, Abigail Ann II, 229
Burr, Abigail Ann II, 282
Burr, Alcinda IV, 321
Burr, Alcinda IV, 322
Burr, Alexander II, 282
Burr, Amanda IV, 515
Burr, Amy H. IV, 515
Burr, Ann II, 478
Burr, Ann II, 641
Burr, Ann IV, 184
Burr, Ann IV, 240
Burr, Anna II, 282
Burr, Anna II, 290
Burr, Barzillai III, 56
Burr, Benjamin II, 342
Burr, Beulah II, 478
Burr, Beulah II, 641
Burr, Caleb II, 314
Burr, Caleb II, 843
Burr, Caroline II, 785
Burr, Caroline F. II, 843
Burr, Charles II, 282
Burr, Charles II, 731
Burr, David Thos. II, 785
Burr, Edith II, 478
Burr, Edith S. II, 806
Burr, Edith S. II, 843
Burr, Edith S. II, 891
Burr, Edmund W. II, 282
Burr, Elisabeth II, 203
Burr, Elizabeth II, 168
Burr, Elizabeth II, 189
Burr, Elizabeth II, 203
Burr, Elizabeth II, 208
Burr, Elizabeth II, 245
Burr, Elizabeth II, 273
Burr, Elizabeth II, 275
Burr, Elizabeth II, 342
Burr, Elizabeth II, 478
Burr, Elizabeth II, 700
Burr, Elizabeth II, 730
Burr, Elizabeth III, 56
Burr, Elizabeth A. II, 843
Burr, Elizabeth E. II, 282
Burr, Elizabeth H. II, 843
Burr, Floretta Fay IV, 1203
Burr, Hannah II, 168
Burr, Hannah II, 203
Burr, Hannah II, 219
Burr, Hannah II, 253
Burr, Hannah II, 817
Burr, Hannah III, 397
Burr, Hannah T. II, 843
Burr, Henry II, 168
Burr, Henry II, 189
Burr, Henry II, 203
Burr, Henry II, 204
Burr, Henry II, 227
Burr, Henry II, 229
Burr, Henry II, 275
Burr, Henry II, 342
Burr, Henry II, 843
Burr, Henry III, 56
Burr, Hudson II, 208
Burr, Hudson II, 282
Burr, Hudson II, 342
Burr, Hudson II, 478
Burr, Hudson Coe II, 168
Burr, Hudson S. II, 282
Burr, Isaiah II, 478
Burr, Isaiah II, 641
Burr, Israel II, 282
Burr, Jane II, 168
Burr, Jane II, 181
Burr, Jane II, 191
Burr, Jane II, 203
Burr, Jane II, 253
Burr, Jesse IV, 184
Burr, Jesse IV, 240
Burr, Jesse IV, 515
Burr, Jesse IV, 516
Burr, John II, 203
Burr, John II, 342
Burr, John II, 478
Burr, John II, 611
Burr, John III, 56
Burr, John III, 397
Burr, John III, 476
Burr, Joseph II, 168
Burr, Joseph II, 192
Burr, Joseph II, 203
Burr, Joseph II, 204
Burr, Joseph II, 208
Burr, Joseph II, 232
Burr, Joseph II, 253
Burr, Joseph II, 267
Burr, Joseph II, 273
Burr, Joseph II, 282
Burr, Joseph II, 342
Burr, Joseph II, 478
Burr, Joseph II, 843
Burr, Joseph II, 891
Burr, Joseph III, 397
Burr, Joseph IV, 184
Burr, Joseph, Jr. II, 203
Burr, Joshua S. II, 282
Burr, Keziah III, 56
Burr, Keziah III, 397
Burr, Keziah III, 476
Burr, Lavicy IV, 184
Burr, Leah II, 282
Burr, Louisa IV, 184
Burr, Louisa IV, 199
Burr, Marmaduke II, 342
Burr, Marmaduke II, 478
Burr, Martha II, 203
Burr, Martha II, 227
Burr, Martha II, 314
Burr, Martha II, 843
Burr, Martha IV, 184
Burr, Martha IV, 240
Burr, Martha IV, 515
Burr, Martha IV, 516
Burr, Mary II, 203
Burr, Mary II, 208
Burr, Mary II, 232
Burr, Mary II, 253
Burr, Mary II, 267
Burr, Mary II, 342
Burr, Mary II, 478
Burr, Mary II, 785
Burr, Mary II, 843
Burr, Mary IV, 185
Burr, Mary IV, 281
Burr, Mary H. II, 843
Burr, Mary H. II, 891
Burr, Mary T. II, 843
Burr, Mary T. II, 883
Burr, Mercy II, 192
Burr, Mercy II, 203
Burr, Mercy Ann II, 282
Burr, Mercy Ann II, 725
Burr, Mercy Ann II, 731
Burr, Mercy Ann II, 830
Burr, Mercy Ann II, 843
Burr, Merriah IV, 322
Burr, Merrick IV, 184
Burr, Merrick IV, 185
Burr, Merrick B. IV, 322
Burr, Merrick S. IV, 185
Burr, Milton IV, 184
Burr, Milton IV, 185
Burr, Milton IV, 322
Burr, Milton J. IV, 185
Burr, Milton J. IV, 322
Burr, Miriam II, 820
Burr, Orlando V, 831
Burr, Orlando R. V, 831
Burr, Pastremo R. II, 282
Burr, Phebe II, 168
Burr, Phebe II, 204
Burr, Phebe II, 229
Burr, Phebe II, 478
Burr, Phebe II, 582
Burr, Rachel II, 168
Burr, Rachel II, 191
Burr, Rachel II, 203
Burr, Rachel II, 208
Burr, Rachel II, 232
Burr, Rachel II, 314
Burr, Rachel L. IV, 515
Burr, Rebecca II, 138
Burr, Rebecca II, 203
Burr, Rebecca II, 207
Burr, Rebecca II, 230
Burr, Rebecca S. IV, 515
Burr, Rebecca W. II, 282
Burr, Rebecca W. II, 290
Burr, Richard II, 168
Burr, Richard II, 208
Burr, Ridgway II, 267
Burr, Robert II, 192
Burr, Robert II, 203
Burr, Robert II, 267
Burr, Robert II, 273
Burr, Robert Coe II, 203
Burr, Rowland II, 342
Burr, Ruthann IV, 322
Burr, Ruthanna IV, 184
Burr, Ruthanna IV, 185
Burr, Sarah II, 203
Burr, Sarah II, 227
Burr, Sarah IV, 184
Burr, Sarah IV, 185
Burr, Sarah IV, 240
Burr, Sarah IV, 322
Burr, Sarah IV, 352
Burr, Sarah Ann IV, 515
Burr, Sarah Ann IV, 516
Burr, Sarah, Jr. IV, 185
Burr, Sarah, Jr. IV, 322
Burr, Solomon II, 203
Burr, Sophia II, 203
Burr, Sophia II, 478
Burr, Susannah II, 342
Burr, Susannah II, 478
Burr, Susannah II, 693
Burr, Tylee W. II, 204
Burr, Tylee W. II, 229
Burr, Tylee W. II, 282
Burr, Vicey IV, 184
Burr, Vicey IV, 290
Burr, Wd. Susanna II, 478
Burr, Wd. Susanna II, 611
Burr, William II, 203
Burr, William II, 230
Burr, William II, 282
Burr, William II, 342
Burr, William IV, 184
Burr, William IV, 185
Burr, William IV, 322
Burr, William IV, 352
Burr, William H. II, 282
Burr, William H. II, 290
Burr, William R. II, 282
Burr, William R. II, 290
Burr, Wm. II, 478
Burr, Wm. IV, 184
Burr, Wm. IV, 240
Burr, Wm. IV, 352
Burr, Wm. H. II, 731
Burr, Wm., Jr. IV, 185
Burradail, Sarah II, 199
Burradail, William II, 199
Burrage, David II, 342
Burras, Cathron G. VI, 887
Burras, Charles VI, 887
Burras, Elizabeth VI, 821
Burras, Elizabeth VI, 887
Burras, Lydia II, 986
Burras, Polly VI, 980
Burras, Rebeckah I, 529
Burras, Rebeckah I, 575
Burras, Thomas VI, 887
Burrell, George IV, 686
Burrell, James VI, 161
Burrell, James VI, 232
Burrell, Margaret IV, 686
Burrell, Mary IV, 686
Burrell, William III, 56
Burres, Barclay V, 226
Burres, John C. V, 226
Burres, Josiah IV, 1273
Burres, Mary IV, 466
Burres, William I, 960
Burress, Ann VI, 926
Burress, Esther IV, 185
Burress, Frances VI, 941
Burrett, James I, 1026
Burridge, Adelaide IV, 1309
Burrier, Bertha IV, 686
Burrier, George IV, 686
Burrier, Nettie IV, 686
Burrier, Oscar E. IV, 686
Burrier, Virginia IV, 686
Burrill, Dorcas II, 59
Burrill, Elizabeth II, 475
Burrill, Elizabeth II, 478
Burrill, Florence J. II, 843
Burrill, Florence J. II, 881
Burrill, Mary IV, 686
Burrill, Moses II, 59
Burrill, Moses II, 99
Burrill, Wd. Dorcas II, 99
Burris, Amanda V, 614
Burris, Ann V, 614
Burris, Anna H. I, 376
Burris, Barclay V, 226
Burris, Bartley V, 299
Burris, Betsy V, 31
Burris, Betty I, 955
Burris, Betty V, 226
Burris, Bowater I, 493
Burris, Bowater I, 961
Burris, Carrie V, 552
Burris, Christie V, 304
Burris, Christine V, 299
Burris, Daniel I, 529
Burris, Daniel I, 955
Burris, Daniel I, 960
Burris, Daniel I, 961
Burris, Daniel V, 31
Burris, Daniel V, 156
Burris, Daniel V, 226
Burris, Daniel V, 299
Burris, Daniel, Jr. V, 299
Burris, Deborah I, 960
Burris, Deborough V, 226
Burris, Elizabeth V, 614
Burris, Elizabeth E. V, 614
Burris, Ella I, 1149
Burris, Emma V, 614
Burris, Esther I, 493
Burris, Esther I, 955
Burris, Esther I, 960
Burris, Esther V, 31
Burris, Frances I, 955
Burris, Frances I, 959
Burris, Frances I, 960
Burris, Frances V, 226
Burris, Frances V, 299
Burris, Francis V, 31
Burris, James V, 614
Burris, John I, 493
Burris, John I, 529
Burris, John I, 955
Burris, John I, 959
Burris, John I, 960
Burris, John V, 31
Burris, John V, 226
Burris, John V, 299
Burris, John C. V, 226
Burris, John C. V, 299
Burris, John L. V, 614
Burris, John, Jr. I, 953
Burris, John, Jr. I, 961
Burris, John, Jr. V, 31
Burris, John, Jr. V, 614
Burris, John, Sr. I, 953
Burris, John, Sr. I, 960
Burris, Joseph I, 493
Burris, Joseph I, 529
Burris, Joseph I, 960
Burris, Joseph V, 299
Burris, Luke V, 299
Burris, Mahala V, 226
Burris, Mahala V, 299
Burris, Mary V, 299
Burris, Mary J. I, 631
Burris, Miles I, 493
Burris, Miles I, 960
Burris, Milla I, 955
Burris, Milley V, 226
Burris, Milley V, 298
Burris, Milley V, 299
Burris, Milly V, 31
Burris, Moses I, 529
Burris, Moses I, 960
Burris, Nancy V, 226
Burris, Nettie V, 988
Burris, Nova I, 1149
Burris, Ollie V, 988
Burris, Rachel I, 529
Burris, Rachel I, 960
Burris, Rebecca V, 31
Burris, Rebecca V, 226
Burris, Rebeckah I, 529
Burris, Rebekah I, 955
Burris, Stephen V, 299
Burris, Susannah V, 226
Burris, Tabitha V, 226
Burris, Tabitha V, 281
Burris, Tabitha V, 299
Burris, William I, 529
Burris, William I, 960
Burris, Wm. V, 614
Burriss, Daniel V, 226
Burrough, Anna G. II, 130
Burrough, Annie G. II, 146
Burrough, Casandra V, 959
Burrough, Elizabeth II, 59
Burrough, Elizabeth II, 130
Burrough, Elizabeth II, 956
Burrough, Elizabeth II, 986
Burrough, Elizabeth II, 1031
Burrough, Hannah II, 700
Burrough, Hannah II, 731
Burrough, Hannah II, 956
Burrough, Henry II, 956
Burrough, Hester II, 956
Burrough, Jacob II, 130
Burrough, Jacob II, 843
Burrough, Jacob V, 959
Burrough, John II, 956
Burrough, John II, 1031
Burrough, John Lancaster II, 506
Burrough, John, Jr. II, 478
Burrough, Josiah II, 59
Burrough, Levi II, 798
Burrough, Lydia II, 956
Burrough, Margaret II, 956
Burrough, Mickle II, 317
Burrough, Patience V, 959
Burrough, Rachel II, 956
Burrough, Samuel II, 956
Burrough, Samuel G. II, 843
Burrough, Sarah II, 59
Burrough, Sarah II, 956
Burrough, Tacy II, 798
Burroughs, Abigail II, 478
Burroughs, Abigail II, 591
Burroughs, Ann II, 986
Burroughs, Ann II, 1019
Burroughs, Ann II, 1047
Burroughs, Ann M. VI, 887
Burroughs, Anna III, 56
Burroughs, Barbara II, 478
Burroughs, Barbara II, 526
Burroughs, Barbara II, 528
Burroughs, Blanch IV, 865
Burroughs, Cathron G. VI, 887
Burroughs, Charles III, 56
Burroughs, Charles VI, 887
Burroughs, Clark IV, 865
Burroughs, Edmund, Jr. VI, 887
Burroughs, Elizabeth II, 986
Burroughs, Elizabeth III, 56
Burroughs, Elizabeth VI, 887
Burroughs, Elizabeth W. VI, 887
Burroughs, Esther II, 986
Burroughs, Esther II, 995
Burroughs, Ethel IV, 865
Burroughs, Georgia A. IV, 185
Burroughs, Hannah II, 204
Burroughs, Hannah II, 986
Burroughs, Hannah II, 1033
Burroughs, Hazel IV, 865
Burroughs, Henry II, 986
Burroughs, Henry II, 1019
Burroughs, Jacob VI, 887
Burroughs, James VI, 887
Burroughs, James VI, 942
Burroughs, James B. VI, 887
Burroughs, Jas. VI, 874
Burroughs, John II, 478
Burroughs, John II, 526
Burroughs, John II, 528
Burroughs, John II, 986
Burroughs, John II, 995
Burroughs, John VI, 887
Burroughs, John, Jr. II, 478
Burroughs, Joseph VI, 933
Burroughs, Joseph N. VI, 887
Burroughs, Josiah II, 59
Burroughs, Laurence IV, 865
Burroughs, Lydia II, 986
Burroughs, Margaret II, 986
Burroughs, Mary II, 478
Burroughs, Mary II, 986
Burroughs, Mary H. VI, 874
Burroughs, Matilda A. VI, 887
Burroughs, Penelope III, 56
Burroughs, Rachel II, 986
Burroughs, Rhoda VI, 887
Burroughs, Robert VI, 887
Burroughs, Sally A. VI, 887
Burroughs, Samuel II, 986
Burroughs, Sarah II, 59
Burroughs, Sarah II, 802
Burroughs, Sarah II, 986
Burroughs, Sarah A. VI, 887
Burroughs, Sarah F. VI, 887
Burroughs, Sarah R. VI, 942
Burroughs, Thomas VI, 887
Burroughs, William IV, 865
Burrous, Elizabeth W. VI, 887
Burrous, James VI, 887
Burrow, Elizabeth II, 59
Burrow, John II, 983
Burrow, Mary II, 991
Burrow, Nancy I, 711
Burrow, Nancy I, 735
Burrow, Philip VI, 202
Burrow, Philip VI, 210
Burrow, Philiph VI, 161
Burrow, Sarah II, 983
Burrow, Sarah II, 986
Burrowes, Hannah II, 342
Burrows, Blanche Beatrice IV, 1309
Burrows, David II, 601
Burrows, Deborah II, 342
Burrows, Ellen IV, 1309
Burrows, Florence Sybelia IV, 1309
Burrows, Hannah II, 204
Burrows, Hannah II, 342
Burrows, Isaac II, 342
Burrows, Martin II, 342

Burrows, Mary II, 478
Burrows, Mary II, 601
Burrows, Mary II, 986
Burrows, Rachel II, 978
Burrows, Rachel II, 986
Burrows, Samuel II, 342
Burrus, Huldah Victoria I, 613
Burrus, James Gatewood VI, 232
Burrus, John VI, 232
Burrus, Mary Jane I, 613
Burrus, Mollie I, 613
Burrus, William Thomas I, 613
Burruss, Catharine VI, 802
Burruss, Charles VI, 887
Burruss, Edmund VI, 887
Burruss, Edmund VI, 980
Burruss, Edmund VI, 1001
Burruss, Edmund, Jr. VI, 887
Burruss, Elizabeth VI, 887
Burruss, Jacob VI, 887
Burruss, John P. VI, 802
Burruss, Martha VI, 1001
Burruss, Mildred H. VI, 903
Burruss, Missouri VI, 802
Burruss, Polly VI, 980
Burruss, Rhoda VI, 887
Burruss, Sally A. VI, 887
Burruss, Thomas G. VI, 801
Burruss, Thomas J. VI, 861
Burruss, Thos. G. VI, 802
Bursch, Ann VI, 735
Bursch, Ann VI, 738
Bursch, Frederick C. VI, 735
Bursch, Frederick C. VI, 738
Burse, Mary S. VI, 846
Bursen, Evelina II, 785
Bursen, John W. II, 785
Bursen, Mary II, 785
Burson, ??? IV, 185
Burson, ??? IV, 795
Burson, Aaron VI, 478
Burson, Aaron VI, 628
Burson, Abigail IV, 613
Burson, Abigail VI, 629
Burson, Abigail VI, 631
Burson, Abraham IV, 23
Burson, Ann IV, 185
Burson, Ann IV, 805
Burson, Ann V, 299
Burson, Ann V, 311
Burson, Ann VI, 478
Burson, Ann VI, 498
Burson, Ann VI, 553
Burson, Ann VI, 572
Burson, Ann VI, 587
Burson, Ann VI, 628
Burson, Ann Elizabeth V, 31
Burson, Anna IV, 185
Burson, Anne IV, 613
Burson, Anne VI, 629
Burson, Benjamin II, 478
Burson, Benjamin VI, 478
Burson, Benjamin VI, 553
Burson, Benjamin VI, 586
Burson, Benjamin VI, 587
Burson, Benjamin VI, 628
Burson, Benjamin VI, 724
Burson, Catharine IV, 613
Burson, Catharine VI, 629
Burson, Catherine IV, 805
Burson, Catherine VI, 478
Burson, David IV, 23
Burson, David IV, 185
Burson, David IV, 804
Burson, David IV, 805
Burson, David IV, 852
Burson, David V, 31
Burson, David L. V, 31
Burson, David S. IV, 805
Burson, David S. V, 31
Burson, David S. V, 52
Burson, Deborah VI, 478
Burson, Deborah VI, 526
Burson, Edith G. VI, 628
Burson, Edith G. VI, 646
Burson, Edward IV, 23
Burson, Edward V, 31
Burson, Edward V, 479
Burson, Edward V, 968
Burson, Edward Thomas V, 31
Burson, Eleanor VI, 478
Burson, Eleanor VI, 628
Burson, Elizabeth IV, 23
Burson, Elizabeth IV, 68
Burson, Elizabeth IV, 686
Burson, Elizabeth IV, 744
Burson, Elizabeth IV, 805
Burson, Elizabeth VI, 374
Burson, Esther VI, 478
Burson, Esther VI, 628
Burson, Esther VI, 691
Burson, Eveline II, 843
Burson, Garrett VI, 887
Burson, Garrett VI, 919
Burson, George VI, 478
Burson, George VI, 586
Burson, George VI, 587
Burson, George VI, 628
Burson, George VI, 724
Burson, Hannah IV, 23
Burson, Hannah IV, 185
Burson, Hannah IV, 805
Burson, Hannah VI, 478
Burson, Hannah VI, 586
Burson, Hannah VI, 587
Burson, Hannah VI, 628
Burson, Hannah VI, 707
Burson, Hannah VI, 724
Burson, Hannah VI, 975
Burson, Hannah Wells V, 31
Burson, Harriet IV, 613
Burson, Harriet IV, 653
Burson, Isaac IV, 23
Burson, Isaiah IV, 857
Burson, Isaiah VI, 478
Burson, Isaiah VI, 628
Burson, James IV, 23
Burson, James VI, 478
Burson, James VI, 484
Burson, James VI, 629
Burson, James VI, 716
Burson, Jane IV, 23
Burson, Jane IV, 185
Burson, Jane IV, 804
Burson, Jane IV, 852
Burson, Jemima V, 31
Burson, Jemima V, 479
Burson, Jemima V, 968
Burson, Jesse VI, 628
Burson, Jesse VI, 646
Burson, John IV, 686
Burson, John IV, 805
Burson, John V, 831
Burson, John VI, 628
Burson, John VI, 629
Burson, John N. V, 968
Burson, John R. VI, 887
Burson, John W. V, 479
Burson, John W. V, 968
Burson, Jonathan V, 831
Burson, Jonathan VI, 478
Burson, Jonathan VI, 629
Burson, Joseph IV, 23
Burson, Joseph IV, 805
Burson, Joseph VI, 478
Burson, Joseph VI, 526
Burson, Joseph VI, 629
Burson, Joseph VI, 631
Burson, Joseph, Jr. VI, 478
Burson, Joseph, Sr. VI, 478
Burson, Julia B. VI, 887
Burson, Laney Ann IV, 805
Burson, Laney Ann IV, 821
Burson, Levi IV, 23
Burson, Levi IV, 857
Burson, Levi VI, 629
Burson, Lydia V, 31
Burson, Lydia V, 84
Burson, Lydia V, 479
Burson, Lydia V, 506
Burson, Lydia V, 968
Burson, Lydia VI, 624
Burson, Lydia VI, 629
Burson, Lydia Ann V, 31
Burson, Margaret IV, 23
Burson, Margaret IV, 805
Burson, Margaret IV, 832
Burson, Margaret V, 31
Burson, Margaret V, 52
Burson, Marget VI, 919
Burson, Maria IV, 185
Burson, Maria IV, 311
Burson, Maria IV, 313
Burson, Martha VI, 624
Burson, Martha VI, 628
Burson, Martha VI, 629
Burson, Martha VI, 646
Burson, Mary IV, 613
Burson, Mary IV, 805
Burson, Mary V, 881
Burson, Mary VI, 478
Burson, Mary VI, 479
Burson, Mary VI, 629
Burson, Mary VI, 671
Burson, Mary VI, 716
Burson, Mary VI, 887
Burson, Mary P. VI, 987
Burson, Moses VI, 478
Burson, Moses VI, 629
Burson, Nancy VI, 934
Burson, Nathan VI, 887
Burson, Nathan VI, 919
Burson, Nathan VI, 934
Burson, Nathan VI, 954
Burson, Nathan VI, 975
Burson, Rachel II, 478
Burson, Rachel II, 627
Burson, Rachel IV, 185
Burson, Rachel IV, 237
Burson, Rachel VI, 479
Burson, Rachel VI, 629
Burson, Rachel VI, 954
Burson, Rachel Haskett V, 31
Burson, Reason G. VI, 887
Burson, Rebecca IV, 799
Burson, Rebecca IV, 805
Burson, Rebecca V, 831
Burson, Rebecca VI, 479
Burson, Rebecca VI, 502
Burson, Rebekah V, 831
Burson, Rebekah VI, 478
Burson, Rebekah VI, 479
Burson, Rebekah VI, 629
Burson, Rebekah VI, 716
Burson, Ruth VI, 478
Burson, Ruth VI, 479
Burson, Ruth VI, 629
Burson, Ruth VI, 635
Burson, Sally VI, 887
Burson, Sarah II, 986
Burson, Sarah IV, 23
Burson, Sarah IV, 42
Burson, Sarah IV, 613
Burson, Sarah IV, 805
Burson, Sarah IV, 840
Burson, Sarah VI, 475
Burson, Sarah VI, 476
Burson, Sarah VI, 478
Burson, Sarah VI, 479
Burson, Sarah VI, 583
Burson, Sarah VI, 586
Burson, Sarah VI, 587
Burson, Sarah VI, 624
Burson, Sarah VI, 628
Burson, Sarah VI, 629
Burson, Sarah VI, 700
Burson, Sarah VI, 723
Burson, Sarah VI, 724
Burson, Sarah Ann VI, 884
Burson, Silas IV, 23
Burson, Silas IV, 805
Burson, Silas VI, 478
Burson, Silas VI, 628
Burson, Sina IV, 805
Burson, Sinah IV, 805
Burson, Sinah IV, 823
Burson, Solomon VI, 478
Burson, Solomon VI, 629
Burson, Susanna VI, 479
Burson, Susanna VI, 545
Burson, Susanna VI, 629
Burson, Susannah IV, 613
Burson, Susannah VI, 478
Burson, Thirza IV, 185
Burson, Thomas IV, 23
Burson, Thomas G. VI, 884
Burson, Thomas G. VI, 955
Burson, Thomas G. VI, 987
Burson, Wd. Ann VI, 478
Burson, William II, 342
Burt, Ann III, 397
Burt, Anna III, 56
Burt, Anna III, 397
Burt, Anna III, 415
Burt, Charles III, 56
Burt, Charles III, 397
Burt, Charles III, 415
Burt, Daniel IV, 185
Burt, Daniel IV, 516
Burt, Edith IV, 1090
Burt, John III, 56
Burt, John III, 153
Burt, Margaret A. III, 56
Burt, Margaret A. III, 153
Burt, Mary III, 56
Burt, Mary J. III, 56
Burt, Mary J. III, 153
Burt, Nettie M. IV, 628
Burt, Nettie M. IV, 960
Burt, Pearl IV, 1036
Burt, Penelope III, 56
Burt, Penelope III, 158
Burt, Sarah IV, 185
Burt, Sarah IV, 322
Burten, Malinda I, 873
Burten, Malinda I, 895
Burten, Tacy IV, 127
Burtes, Elizabeth II, 59
Burtes, Elizabeth II, 69
Burtes, Jesse V, 896
Burtes, Susanna II, 59
Burtes, Susanna II, 69
Burtis, ??? III, 56
Burtis, Ann II, 204
Burtis, Cornelia M. III, 397
Burtis, Elias III, 397
Burtis, Elias III, 420
Burtis, Elisabeth II, 219
Burtis, Elizabeth II, 204
Burtis, George W. III, 397
Burtis, Hannah III, 397
Burtis, Hannah III, 420
Burtis, Jesse III, 56
Burtis, Jno. Henry III, 397
Burtis, John Henry III, 429
Burtis, Lucretia III, 397
Burtis, Lucretia III, 429
Burtis, M. Pauline III, 397
Burtis, Sarah III, 397
Burtis, Sarah III, 420
Burtis, Susannah II, 204
Burtis, Susannah II, 219
Burtis, William III, 56
Burtler, Edward I, 1149
Burtner, Lellia Hooks I, 613
Burtner, Lillie I, 631
Burtner, Lillie I, 635
Burtner, Rene L. I, 631
Burtner, Rene L. I, 635
Burton, ??? V, 662
Burton, ??? V, 722
Burton, A. Russell II, 1065
Burton, A. Russell II, 1070
Burton, Addison VI, 887
Burton, Addison VI, 958
Burton, Addison VI, 966
Burton, Agnes II, 956
Burton, Agnes II, 957
Burton, Agnes II, 1044
Burton, Agnes II, 1047
Burton, Alex VI, 867
Burton, Alexander VI, 887
Burton, Alexr. VI, 887
Burton, Alexr. VI, 980
Burton, Amos II, 843
Burton, Amos II, 986
Burton, Amos II, 1047
Burton, Amos II, 1070
Burton, Angeline VI, 980
Burton, Ann II, 956
Burton, Ann II, 957
Burton, Ann II, 986
Burton, Ann II, 1015
Burton, Ann II, 1070
Burton, Ann P. II, 701
Burton, Ann P. II, 986
Burton, Ann P. II, 1047
Burton, Ann P. II, 1048
Burton, Anna I, 939
Burton, Anna I, 945
Burton, Anna II, 813
Burton, Anna II, 1065
Burton, Anna II, 1070
Burton, Anna II, 1077
Burton, Anna V, 662
Burton, Anna E. II, 843
Burton, Anna R. II, 1070
Burton, Anna R. II, 1079
Burton, Anna Wilson I, 929
Burton, Annes V, 662
Burton, Annes V, 722
Burton, Anthony II, 442
Burton, Anthony II, 813
Burton, Anthony II, 985
Burton, Anthony II, 986
Burton, Anthony II, 1001
Burton, Anthony II, 1036
Burton, Anthony II, 1047
Burton, Anthony II, 1065
Burton, Anthony II, 1070
Burton, Anthony II, 1076
Burton, Anthony, Jr. II, 986
Burton, Anthony, Jr. II, 1047
Burton, Anthony, Jr. II, 1070
Burton, Anthony, Sr. II, 1070
Burton, Anthony, Sr. II, 1079
Burton, Arthur H. II, 957
Burton, Arthur H. II, 1047
Burton, Avaline VI, 887
Burton, Ballard V, 321
Burton, Benjamin II, 956
Burton, Benjamin II, 986
Burton, Benjamin II, 1070
Burton, Betsy VI, 802
Burton, C. C. VI, 985
Burton, Caroline II, 1070
Burton, Caroline II, 1076
Burton, Charles II, 701
Burton, Charles II, 843
Burton, Charles II, 956
Burton, Charles II, 957
Burton, Charles II, 986
Burton, Charles II, 1044
Burton, Charles II, 1047
Burton, Charles II, 1048
Burton, Charles II, 1070
Burton, Charles VI, 887
Burton, Charles VI, 1021
Burton, Charles, Jr. II, 986
Burton, Charles, Jr. II, 1047
Burton, Chas. II, 785
Burton, Clarence V, 479
Burton, Clementina VI, 207
Burton, Cornelia VI, 805
Burton, Cynthia P. VI, 1003
Burton, David VI, 887
Burton, David L. V, 226
Burton, Davis S. V, 226
Burton, Deborah II, 986
Burton, Deborah II, 1036
Burton, Deborah II, 1047
Burton, Deborah II, 1070
Burton, Deborah II, 1075
Burton, Demaris VI, 887
Burton, Edis VI, 887
Burton, Edmund VI, 887
Burton, Edmund VI, 1003
Burton, Edward J. VI, 802
Burton, Edwin J. II, 843
Burton, Edwin J. II, 1070
Burton, Edwin Jonah II, 785
Burton, Eleanor S. VI, 887
Burton, Elizabeth II, 342
Burton, Elizabeth II, 699
Burton, Elizabeth II, 785
Burton, Elizabeth II, 843
Burton, Elizabeth II, 883
Burton, Elizabeth II, 956
Burton, Elizabeth II, 986
Burton, Elizabeth II, 1047
Burton, Elizabeth IV, 686
Burton, Elizabeth IV, 805
Burton, Elizabeth VI, 799
Burton, Elizabeth VI, 802
Burton, Elizabeth VI, 887
Burton, Elizabeth VI, 932
Burton, Elizabeth VI, 985
Burton, Elizabeth C. VI, 802
Burton, Elizabeth H. II, 478
Burton, Elizabeth H. II, 731
Burton, Elizabeth H. II, 843
Burton, Elizabeth H. II, 986
Burton, Elizabeth H. II, 1065
Burton, Elizabeth H. II, 1070
Burton, Elizabeth Jane VI, 887
Burton, Ellen Elizabeth I, 928
Burton, Elva Rebecca V, 226
Burton, Elwood II, 1065
Burton, Elwood II, 1070
Burton, Emily W. VI, 802
Burton, Emma II, 1070
Burton, Emma W. II, 957
Burton, Emma W. II, 1047
Burton, Emmet V, 662
Burton, Estelle II, 1065
Burton, Florence II, 1065
Burton, Frances VI, 1007
Burton, George III, 56
Burton, George John III, 56
Burton, Giles S. II, 785
Burton, Giles S. II, 843
Burton, Giles S. II, 1070
Burton, Gillie Ann VI, 1003
Burton, Glenn Addison V, 479
Burton, Gustavus VI, 887
Burton, Gustavus A. VI, 887
Burton, Gustavus A. VI, 1016
Burton, Hannah II, 956
Burton, Hannah II, 986
Burton, Hannah II, 1001
Burton, Hannah II, 1015
Burton, Hannah II, 1035
Burton, Hannah II, 1044
Burton, Hannah II, 1047
Burton, Hannah II, 1065
Burton, Hannah B. II, 843
Burton, Hannah C. II, 1065
Burton, Hannah G. II, 1070
Burton, Hannah L. II, 478
Burton, Hannah L. II, 557
Burton, Hannah L. II, 843
Burton, Hannah Logan II, 478
Burton, Hannah W. II, 956
Burton, Hannah W. II, 1047
Burton, Hannah W. II, 1061
Burton, Harriet VI, 1014
Burton, Hazel V, 662
Burton, Henry II, 1070
Burton, Henry A. I, 613
Burton, Henry A. II, 1070
Burton, Herbert I, 939
Burton, J. W. I, 928
Burton, J. W. I, 939
Burton, J. Walter II, 957
Burton, J. Walter II, 1047

Burton, Jacob VI, 887
Burton, Jacob VI, 932
Burton, Jacob VI, 993
Burton, James II, 442
Burton, James VI, 887
Burton, James S. VI, 886
Burton, Jane II, 478
Burton, Jane II, 731
Burton, Jane II, 843
Burton, Jane II, 986
Burton, Jane II, 1036
Burton, Jane II, 1047
Burton, Jane II, 1070
Burton, Jane III, 56
Burton, Jane D. VI, 887
Burton, Jane H. II, 731
Burton, Jesse II, 478
Burton, Jesse II, 479
Burton, Jesse VI, 802
Burton, Jesse VI, 887
Burton, Jesse A. VI, 887
Burton, Jno. VI, 805
Burton, John II, 17
Burton, John II, 45
Burton, John II, 478
Burton, John II, 843
Burton, John II, 956
Burton, John II, 985
Burton, John II, 986
Burton, John II, 1001
Burton, John II, 1015
Burton, John II, 1044
Burton, John II, 1047
Burton, John II, 1065
Burton, John II, 1070
Burton, John III, 56
Burton, John V, 479
Burton, John VI, 828
Burton, John VI, 867
Burton, John VI, 887
Burton, John G. II, 986
Burton, John G. II, 1047
Burton, John G. II, 1065
Burton, John G. II, 1070
Burton, John H. II, 1065
Burton, John Sibby I, 939
Burton, John W. I, 929
Burton, John W. V, 156
Burton, John W. VI, 886
Burton, John W. VI, 958
Burton, John Wilson I, 939
Burton, John, Jr. II, 986
Burton, Jonathan II, 986
Burton, Jonathan II, 1047
Burton, Jonathan II, 1065
Burton, Jonathan II, 1070
Burton, Jonathan Prescott II, 785
Burton, Joseph, Jr. II, 785
Burton, Joshua V, 156
Burton, Judah VI, 993
Burton, K. M. I, 931
Burton, Latitia II, 1047
Burton, Lavina V. V, 614
Burton, Lena V, 479
Burton, Letitia II, 986
Burton, Lillian I, 630
Burton, Lillian I, 631
Burton, Lucy II, 956
Burton, Lucy II, 957
Burton, Lucy II, 1047
Burton, Lucy II, 1048
Burton, Lucy VI, 887
Burton, Lucy VI, 993
Burton, Lydia II, 986
Burton, Lydia II, 1047
Burton, Lydia II, 1065
Burton, Maggie V, 662
Burton, Mahlon II, 957
Burton, Margaret II, 1047
Burton, Margaret II, 1065
Burton, Margaret II, 1070
Burton, Maria A. III, 186
Burton, Marian S. II, 1070
Burton, Marion II, 1065
Burton, Marion S. II, 1065
Burton, Martha V, 226
Burton, Martha A. VI, 862
Burton, Martha A. VI, 886
Burton, Martha M. V, 226
Burton, Martha R. III, 56
Burton, Martha R. VI, 887
Burton, Mary II, 813
Burton, Mary II, 956
Burton, Mary II, 957
Burton, Mary II, 985
Burton, Mary II, 986
Burton, Mary II, 1001
Burton, Mary II, 1047
Burton, Mary II, 1070
Burton, Mary II, 1076
Burton, Mary IV, 1036
Burton, Mary VI, 887
Burton, Mary A. V, 226
Burton, Mary Ann II, 1047
Burton, Mary Ann II, 1048
Burton, Mary Ann III, 56
Burton, Mary Ann VI, 944
Burton, Mary B. II, 764
Burton, Mary B. II, 843
Burton, Mary B. II, 917
Burton, Mary B. II, 1070
Burton, Mary B. II, 1079
Burton, Mary B. Satterthwaite II, 731
Burton, Mary E. V, 479
Burton, Mary J. I, 939
Burton, Mary J. II, 1047
Burton, Mary J. II, 1053
Burton, Mary K. II, 843
Burton, Mary K. II, 1070
Burton, Mary R. VI, 802
Burton, Mary S. II, 731
Burton, Mary S. II, 843
Burton, Mary S. II, 986
Burton, Mary S. L. II, 478
Burton, Mary W. II, 701
Burton, Mary W. II, 956
Burton, Mary W. II, 1047
Burton, Mary W. II, 1048
Burton, Matilda VI, 943
Burton, Maud V, 226
Burton, Nancy VI, 867
Burton, Nancy VI, 887
Burton, Nancy VI, 928
Burton, Narcissa I, 920
Burton, Nellie I, 613
Burton, Nowell VI, 161
Burton, Nowell VI, 204
Burton, Patrick P. VI, 802
Burton, Patsey VI, 828
Burton, Payton V, 226
Burton, Peggy VI, 887
Burton, Peter II, 986
Burton, Peyton V, 226
Burton, Phebe II, 986
Burton, Phebe II, 1047
Burton, Pyyton V, 226
Burton, R. VI, 944
Burton, R. VI, 1014
Burton, Rachel II, 986
Burton, Rachel II, 1015
Burton, Rachel II, 1039
Burton, Rachel V, 320
Burton, Rachel V, 321
Burton, Rebecca II, 956
Burton, Rebecca II, 1070
Burton, Rebecca V, 479
Burton, Rebecca B. II, 843
Burton, Rebecca, Jr. II, 986
Burton, Rebecca, Jr. II, 1047
Burton, Rebeckah II, 985
Burton, Rebeckah II, 986
Burton, Reuben Bigelow III, 186
Burton, Richard V, 662
Burton, Ro. VI, 985
Burton, Robert II, 956
Burton, Robert II, 957
Burton, Robert II, 1047
Burton, Robert II, 1048
Burton, Robert VI, 802
Burton, Robert VI, 887
Burton, Rosa B. V, 226
Burton, Sally VI, 802
Burton, Sally VI, 823
Burton, Samira I, 928
Burton, Samuel II, 1070
Burton, Samuel V, 479
Burton, Samuel B. II, 785
Burton, Samuel B. II, 1065
Burton, Samuel B. II, 1070
Burton, Sarah II, 984
Burton, Sarah II, 986
Burton, Sarah VI, 802
Burton, Sarah Adaline VI, 887
Burton, Sarah M. V, 226
Burton, Semira I, 929
Burton, Susan D. II, 843
Burton, Susan H. II, 843
Burton, Susan H. II, 1070
Burton, Susanna II, 986
Burton, Susanna VI, 887
Burton, Susanna H. II, 478
Burton, Susanna H. II, 731
Burton, Susannah II, 785
Burton, Susannah H. II, 843
Burton, Susannah H. II, 986
Burton, Susannah K. II, 986
Burton, Tacy IV, 122
Burton, Thomas VI, 802
Burton, Wd. Mary II, 1065
Burton, Wd. Mary Kirk II, 785
Burton, Wilbur VI, 844
Burton, Willard II, 1048
Burton, Willard Ray V, 479
Burton, William II, 204
Burton, William II, 785
Burton, William V, 479
Burton, William VI, 161
Burton, William VI, 201
Burton, William VI, 823
Burton, William VI, 887
Burton, William VI, 983
Burton, William C. VI, 802
Burton, Wiltshire VI, 887
Burton, Winfield Scott V, 226
Burton, Wm. I, 630
Burton, Wm. II, 478
Burton, Wm. II, 731
Burton, Wm. II, 843
Burton, Wm. II, 986
Burton, Wm. II, 1070
Burton, Wm. W. I, 631
Burton, Woodson VI, 802
Burton, Woodson A. VI, 878
Burton, Woodson A. VI, 944
Burton, Woodson A. VI, 1011
Burtos, Richard II, 479
Burtt, Anne III, 267
Burtt, Henrietta III, 267
Burtt, Henrietta Mary III, 267
Burtt, Henry III, 267
Burwell, Dorcas II, 24
Burwell, Frances C. VI, 887
Burwell, G. VI, 983
Burwell, Hannah IV, 77
Burwell, Hannah IV, 105
Burwell, Moses II, 24
Burwell, Noah VI, 991
Burwell, Robert VI, 871
Burwell, Robert VI, 895
Burwell, Robert VI, 935
Burwell, Robert VI, 949
Burwell, Robert VI, 991
Burwell, William M. VI, 887
Burwon, Daniel IV, 466
Burwon, David IV, 466
Burwon, Jane IV, 466
Busbey, Ann II, 59
Busby, Adelaide II, 168
Busby, Amos II, 317
Busby, Amos, Jr. II, 283
Busby, Ann II, 479
Busby, Ann II, 582
Busby, Augusta C. II, 283
Busby, Benjamin II, 343
Busby, Benjamin II, 479
Busby, Benjamin C. II, 343
Busby, Beulah II, 168
Busby, Deborah W. II, 281
Busby, Edith II, 205
Busby, Elizabeth II, 204
Busby, Elizabeth II, 205
Busby, Elizabeth II, 228
Busby, Elizabeth Ann II, 844
Busby, Esther VI, 374
Busby, Esther VI, 443
Busby, Frances II, 479
Busby, Frances W. II, 343
Busby, Grace II, 204
Busby, Hannah II, 116
Busby, Hannah II, 168
Busby, Hannah II, 204
Busby, Hannah II, 205
Busby, Hannah II, 212
Busby, Hannah II, 222
Busby, Hannah II, 281
Busby, Hannah II, 283
Busby, Hannah II, 306
Busby, Hannah H. II, 146
Busby, Hannah H. II, 157
Busby, Hannah S. II, 731
Busby, Hudson II, 205
Busby, Hudson II, 281
Busby, Ida R. II, 283
Busby, Isaac L. II, 283
Busby, Jane II, 203
Busby, Jane II, 204
Busby, Jane II, 503
Busby, John II, 204
Busby, John II, 212
Busby, John II, 343
Busby, John II, 479
Busby, John II, 664
Busby, Joseph II, 168
Busby, Joseph II, 204
Busby, Joseph II, 968
Busby, Lidy II, 204
Busby, Lidy II, 241
Busby, Margaretta II, 205
Busby, Margaretta II, 968
Busby, Mary II, 169
Busby, Mary II, 204
Busby, Mary II, 222
Busby, Mary II, 273
Busby, Mary II, 317
Busby, Mary II, 343
Busby, Mary II, 479
Busby, Mary II, 664
Busby, Mary Ann II, 168
Busby, Mary Ann II, 205
Busby, Mary H. II, 843
Busby, Mary H. II, 874
Busby, Mary-Jane II, 317
Busby, Nathan II, 116
Busby, Nicholas II, 168
Busby, Nicholas II, 204
Busby, Nicholas II, 222
Busby, Nicholas II, 283
Busby, Nicholas II, 306
Busby, Nicholus II, 204
Busby, Nicholus II, 273
Busby, Patience II, 317
Busby, Rachel II, 205
Busby, Rachel II, 281
Busby, Rebecca II, 146
Busby, Rebecca II, 283
Busby, Rebecca II, 306
Busby, Rebecca D. II, 317
Busby, Rebecca E. II, 283
Busby, Rebecca M. II, 146
Busby, Richard II, 168
Busby, Richard II, 204
Busby, Richard II, 222
Busby, Richard II, 281
Busby, Ruth II, 116
Busby, Samuel II, 204
Busby, Susan II, 968
Busby, Susannah II, 169
Busby, Thomas T. II, 169
Busby, Thomas, Jr. II, 204
Busby, Thomas, Jr. II, 205
Busby, William II, 169
Busby, William II, 204
Busby, William II, 228
Busby, Wm. II, 273
Buschlen, Tillie IV, 1309
Buschler, Christian IV, 1327
Buschler, Lillie B. IV, 1327
Buschler, Mary IV, 1327
Bush, ??? III, 57
Bush, Aletha May IV, 1247
Bush, Amanda V, 614
Bush, Ann II, 479
Bush, Ann II, 591
Bush, Anna Priscilla IV, 932
Bush, Anna Priscilla IV, 956
Bush, Annie IV, 686
Bush, Betsey VI, 887
Bush, Betty VI, 907
Bush, Carrie IV, 1247
Bush, Charles IV, 1247
Bush, Charles VI, 888
Bush, Deborah IV, 172
Bush, Deborah IV, 185
Bush, Dorothea III, 57
Bush, Elizabeth VI, 888
Bush, Etta I, 631
Bush, Etta I, 637
Bush, George M. IV, 686
Bush, Grace Kahl IV, 1309
Bush, Hannah V, 614
Bush, Harvey IV, 686
Bush, Henry VI, 888
Bush, James IV, 686
Bush, John Thomas III, 57
Bush, Jonas III, 57
Bush, Lucy V, 614
Bush, Martha VI, 912
Bush, Mary IV, 1355
Bush, Mary VI, 912
Bush, Matilda IV, 1273
Bush, Owen V, 614
Bush, Owen F. V, 614
Bush, Patty VI, 907
Bush, Philip VI, 887
Bush, Polly VI, 888
Bush, Sarah VI, 888
Bush, Thomas VI, 888
Bush, William VI, 888
Bush, William Walton VI, 888
Bush, Wm. V, 988
Bushby, Dinah II, 479
Bushel, John II, 479
Bushel, Joseph II, 479
Bushell, Joseph II, 479
Bushong, Anna III, 57
Bushong, Anna III, 189
Bushong, Charles III, 57
Bushong, Charles H. III, 57
Bushong, Dr. Charles H. III, 57
Bushong, Dr. Charles H. III, 189
Bushong, Edith K. III, 57
Bushong, Gilbert III, 57
Bushong, Nora E. III, 57
Bushong, Nora E. III, 189
Busick, Catherine V, 988
Busick, Wm. V, 988
Buskin, ??? VI, 39
Buskin, Levin VI, 28
Buskler, Joanna V, 479
Busse, Margaret II, 32
Bussell, Anna Maria III, 220
Bussell, Eliz. III, 368
Bussell, Elizabeth III, 220
Bussell, George III, 220
Bussell, George III, 368
Bussell, Samuel Daw III, 235
Bussell, Sarah Eliza III, 235
Bussell, Sophia Jane III, 368
Busselle, Agnes III, 57
Busselle, Agnes III, 151
Busselle, Alfred III, 57
Busselle, Alfred III, 238
Busselle, Alfred, Jr. III, 57
Busselle, Ann III, 57
Busselle, Ann Maria III, 57
Busselle, Anna Maria III, 57
Busselle, Charles III, 57
Busselle, Eliz. III, 57
Busselle, Elizabeth III, 57
Busselle, Francis III, 57
Busselle, Geo. III, 57
Busselle, George III, 57
Busselle, Harriet III, 57
Busselle, Harriet C. III, 57
Busselle, Harriet C. III, 238
Busselle, John Hare III, 57
Busselle, Margaret III, 57
Busselle, Richard III, 57
Busselle, Robert Murray III, 57
Busselle, S. Marshall III, 57
Busselle, S. Marshall III, 151
Busselle, Samuel D. III, 57
Busselle, Samuel Daw III, 57
Busselle, Samuel Marshall III, 57
Busselle, Samuel Marshall, Jr. III, 57
Busselle, Sarah III, 57
Busselle, Sarah E. III, 57
Busselle, Sarah Eliza III, 57
Busselle, Sophia Jane III, 57
Bussey, Elizabeth V, 453
Bussey, Emma V, 299
Bussey, Emma V, 453
Bussey, Emma L. V, 453
Bussey, George V, 453
Bussey, George V, 662
Bussey, George A. V, 453
Bussey, Homer V, 662
Bussey, James V, 453
Bussey, James H. V, 453
Bussey, Lorella V, 453
Bussey, Nannie V, 662
Bussey, Sarah V, 299
Bussey, Wm. V, 453
Bussey, Wm. H. V, 453
Busson, William II, 342
Bussy, Emma L. V, 453
Bussy, Wm. V, 453
Bustill, Mary II, 204
Bustill, Mary II, 215
Butcher, Abigail II, 283
Butcher, Abigail Brick II, 817
Butcher, Achsah II, 204
Butcher, Adella V, 156
Butcher, Amos II, 342
Butcher, Amos W. II, 479
Butcher, Ann II, 59
Butcher, Ann II, 168
Butcher, Ann II, 196
Butcher, Ann II, 204
Butcher, Ann II, 342
Butcher, Ann II, 479
Butcher, Ann II, 628
Butcher, Ann II, 816
Butcher, Ann II, 986
Butcher, Ann VI, 374
Butcher, Ann VI, 479
Butcher, Ann VI, 735
Butcher, Ann R. II, 283
Butcher, Annie II, 817
Butcher, Annis S. IV, 185
Butcher, Benajah II, 283
Butcher, Benajah II, 817
Butcher, Caroline W. II, 283
Butcher, Catherine Ann VI, 735
Butcher, Charlotte II, 204
Butcher, Damarus II, 204
Butcher, Damarus II, 277
Butcher, David P. IV, 185
Butcher, Eleanor II, 342
Butcher, Eleanor II, 731
Butcher, Elizabeth II, 59

Butcher, Elizabeth II, 64
Butcher, Elizabeth II, 127
Butcher, Elizabeth II, 204
Butcher, Elizabeth II, 230
Butcher, Elizabeth II, 249
Butcher, Elizabeth Newell II, 788
Butcher, Ellen II, 283
Butcher, Ellen IV, 185
Butcher, Ellinor II, 168
Butcher, Ephraim IV, 729
Butcher, Ephraim Garner II, 59
Butcher, Esther II, 168
Butcher, Faith II, 204
Butcher, Frances II, 192
Butcher, Frances II, 204
Butcher, Franklin II, 342
Butcher, Franklin II, 700
Butcher, Hannah II, 59
Butcher, Hannah II, 64
Butcher, Hannah II, 101
Butcher, Hannah II, 479
Butcher, Hannah IV, 729
Butcher, Hannah W. II, 479
Butcher, Helen J. IV, 185
Butcher, Hester II, 192
Butcher, Hester II, 204
Butcher, James II, 24
Butcher, James II, 59
Butcher, James II, 127
Butcher, Jane II, 24
Butcher, Jean II, 59
Butcher, Jean II, 64
Butcher, Jean II, 92
Butcher, Job II, 24
Butcher, Job II, 59
Butcher, Job II, 204
Butcher, Job II, 342
Butcher, Job II, 479
Butcher, Job II, 680
Butcher, John II, 24
Butcher, John II, 59
Butcher, John II, 64
Butcher, John II, 196
Butcher, John II, 204
Butcher, John II, 230
Butcher, John II, 245
Butcher, John II, 342
Butcher, John II, 479
Butcher, John II, 680
Butcher, John II, 731
Butcher, John VI, 464
Butcher, John VI, 479
Butcher, John VI, 725
Butcher, John VI, 735
Butcher, John E. IV, 185
Butcher, Jonathan II, 204
Butcher, Jonathan II, 479
Butcher, Jonathan II, 986
Butcher, Jonathan VI, 374
Butcher, Jonathan VI, 440
Butcher, Jonathan VI, 479
Butcher, Jonathan VI, 725
Butcher, Jonathan VI, 735
Butcher, Jonathan III VI, 735
Butcher, Jonathan, Jr. VI, 735
Butcher, Jonathan, Jr. VI, 774
Butcher, Jonathan, Jr. VI, 775
Butcher, Joseph II, 59
Butcher, Joseph II, 204
Butcher, Joseph II, 283
Butcher, Joshua II, 247
Butcher, Katharine II, 204
Butcher, Katharine II, 245
Butcher, Lodinia IV, 185
Butcher, Lucy D. IV, 185
Butcher, Lydia II, 127
Butcher, Margaret II, 196
Butcher, Margaret II, 204
Butcher, Margarett II, 230
Butcher, Martha II, 168
Butcher, Martha II, 283
Butcher, Mary II, 24
Butcher, Mary II, 59
Butcher, Mary II, 103
Butcher, Mary II, 168
Butcher, Mary II, 204
Butcher, Mary II, 230
Butcher, Mary II, 246
Butcher, Mary II, 256
Butcher, Mary II, 266
Butcher, Mary II, 283
Butcher, Mary II, 342
Butcher, Mary II, 479
Butcher, Mary II, 661
Butcher, Mary II, 680
Butcher, Mary II, 986
Butcher, Mary II, 1043
Butcher, Mary V, 19
Butcher, Mary V, 31
Butcher, Mary E. IV, 185
Butcher, Morris II, 283
Butcher, Olive IV, 729
Butcher, Patience II, 204
Butcher, Phebe II, 204
Butcher, Phebe VI, 374
Butcher, Phebe VI, 440
Butcher, Phebe VI, 735
Butcher, Phebe VI, 774
Butcher, Prudence II, 59
Butcher, Prudence II, 247
Butcher, Rachel II, 24
Butcher, Rachel II, 57
Butcher, Rachel II, 59
Butcher, Rachel II, 76
Butcher, Rebecca II, 204
Butcher, Rebecca II, 253
Butcher, Rebecca II, 479
Butcher, Rebecca II, 728
Butcher, Rebecca II, 731
Butcher, Rebecca VI, 735
Butcher, Rebecca VI, 770
Butcher, Rebecca P. II, 283
Butcher, Rebecca P. II, 306
Butcher, Rebeckah II, 204
Butcher, Rebeckah II, 233
Butcher, Rebeckah II, 1043
Butcher, Robert Hume VI, 735
Butcher, Rowland II, 247
Butcher, Rowlin II, 247
Butcher, Samuel II, 59
Butcher, Samuel II, 168
Butcher, Samuel II, 192
Butcher, Samuel II, 199
Butcher, Samuel II, 204
Butcher, Samuel II, 246
Butcher, Samuel II, 283
Butcher, Samuel, Jr. II, 204
Butcher, Sarah II, 196
Butcher, Sarah II, 204
Butcher, Sarah II, 253
Butcher, Sarah II, 342
Butcher, Sarah II, 731
Butcher, Sarah II, 773
Butcher, Sarah VI, 374
Butcher, Sarah VI, 379
Butcher, Sarah E. II, 700
Butcher, Sarah R. II, 283
Butcher, Silence II, 204
Butcher, Susanah II, 199
Butcher, Susanah II, 204
Butcher, Susanna II, 342
Butcher, Susanna II, 479
Butcher, Susanna II, 700
Butcher, Thomas II, 59
Butcher, Thomas II, 168
Butcher, Thomas II, 196
Butcher, Thomas II, 204
Butcher, Thomas II, 230
Butcher, Thomas J. IV, 185
Butcher, Thomas Tyson II, 479
Butcher, Thomas Tyson II, 731
Butcher, Thos. II, 24
Butcher, Thos. II, 57
Butcher, Thos. II, 59
Butcher, Washington II, 342
Butcher, Washington II, 731
Butcher, Wd. Ann II, 1043
Butcher, Wd. Anne II, 204
Butcher, Wd. Margarett II, 204
Butcher, Wd. Mary II, 479
Butcher, Wd. Mary II, 680
Butcher, William II, 204
Butcher, William B. IV, 185
Butcher, William R. II, 283
Butcher, Wm. M. V, 156
Butlar, Deborah VI, 70
Butlar, James S. VI, 70
Butlar, Martha VI, 70
Butlar, Mary V, 564
Butlar, Rhoda I, 529
Butler, ??? IV, 376
Butler, ??? VI, 95
Butler, Abraham VI, 103
Butler, Achsa II, 168
Butler, Agatha V, 226
Butler, Agatha V, 227
Butler, Alfred V, 893
Butler, Alfred V, 897
Butler, Alfred VI, 56
Butler, Alfred VI, 301
Butler, Alfred VI, 302
Butler, Alice VI, 771
Butler, Allen I, 1149
Butler, Alonzo IV, 1273
Butler, Amos V, 32
Butler, Amy T. VI, 864
Butler, Ann II, 479
Butler, Ann II, 615
Butler, Ann II, 731
Butler, Ann II, 785
Butler, Ann II, 843
Butler, Ann II, 986
Butler, Ann IV, 686
Butler, Ann IV, 709
Butler, Ann IV, 923
Butler, Ann IV, 932
Butler, Ann IV, 933
Butler, Ann IV, 943
Butler, Ann IV, 949
Butler, Ann IV, 993
Butler, Ann V, 31
Butler, Ann V, 226
Butler, Ann V, 968
Butler, Ann V, 972
Butler, Ann V, 979
Butler, Ann VI, 56
Butler, Ann VI, 87
Butler, Ann VI, 102
Butler, Ann VI, 103
Butler, Ann VI, 104
Butler, Ann VI, 111
Butler, Ann VI, 117
Butler, Ann VI, 122
Butler, Ann VI, 132
Butler, Ann VI, 133
Butler, Ann VI, 161
Butler, Ann VI, 162
Butler, Ann VI, 301
Butler, Ann Eliz. VI, 92
Butler, Ann J. VI, 56
Butler, Ann Johnson VI, 56
Butler, Ann Johnson VI, 301
Butler, Ann Johnson VI, 302
Butler, Ann V. IV, 805
Butler, Anna VI, 161
Butler, Anna VI, 162
Butler, Anna VI, 201
Butler, Anna VI, 865
Butler, Anna T. IV, 933
Butler, Anna T. IV, 934
Butler, Anne VI, 42
Butler, Ansalem B. VI, 56
Butler, Anselem V, 968
Butler, Anselm V, 968
Butler, Anselm VI, 301
Butler, Anselm VI, 302
Butler, Anselm J. V, 979
Butler, Anslem B. V, 949
Butler, Anslem B. V, 968
Butler, Asaph IV, 570
Butler, Asenath IV, 932
Butler, Asenath IV, 933
Butler, Asenath IV, 984
Butler, Asenath IV, 1051
Butler, Asenath IV, 1052
Butler, Aseph IV, 377
Butler, Attie IV, 1273
Butler, Bailey IV, 1051
Butler, Bales I, 529
Butler, Bales I, 1016
Butler, Bales V, 729
Butler, Barak IV, 185
Butler, Barak IV, 1151
Butler, Benj. IV, 933
Butler, Benjamin IV, 686
Butler, Benjamin IV, 701
Butler, Benjamin IV, 709
Butler, Benjamin IV, 805
Butler, Benjamin IV, 904
Butler, Benjamin IV, 930
Butler, Benjamin IV, 932
Butler, Benjamin IV, 933
Butler, Benjamin IV, 952
Butler, Benjamin IV, 998
Butler, Benjamin IV, 1005
Butler, Benjamin IV, 1203
Butler, Benjamin V, 32
Butler, Benjamin V, 226
Butler, Benjamin VI, 56
Butler, Benjamin VI, 132
Butler, Benjamin VI, 292
Butler, Benjamin VI, 302
Butler, Benjamin P. VI, 56
Butler, Benjamin, Sr. IV, 919
Butler, Bert V, 988
Butler, Bertha V, 988
Butler, Betsy VI, 888
Butler, Beulah IV, 932
Butler, Billy VI, 802
Butler, Branch VI, 888
Butler, C. W. IV, 1309
Butler, Caleb IV, 365
Butler, Caleb IV, 377
Butler, Caleb IV, 1051
Butler, Calvin IV, 933
Butler, Caroline S. V, 893
Butler, Caroline S. V, 897
Butler, Carrie S. V, 897
Butler, Catherine VI, 56
Butler, Catherine VI, 92
Butler, Ceiley VI, 102
Butler, Ceiley VI, 108
Butler, Celia IV, 1309
Butler, Cely VI, 103
Butler, Chappel VI, 56
Butler, Charles V, 156
Butler, Charlotte II, 342
Butler, Charlotte A. VI, 56
Butler, Charlotte Ann VI, 130
Butler, Charlotte Ann VI, 132
Butler, Chas. H. V, 156
Butler, Copeland VI, 56
Butler, Copeland VI, 102
Butler, Cory IV, 1234
Butler, Daniel IV, 932
Butler, Daniel V, 32
Butler, Daniel V, 226
Butler, Daniel V, 227
Butler, Daniel VI, 56
Butler, Daniel VI, 84
Butler, Daniel VI, 102
Butler, Daniel VI, 103
Butler, Daniel VI, 104
Butler, Daniel VI, 124
Butler, Daniel VI, 132
Butler, Daniel C. VI, 133
Butler, David IV, 185
Butler, David IV, 311
Butler, David IV, 1151
Butler, David V, 32
Butler, David V, 479
Butler, David VI, 102
Butler, Deborah II, 342
Butler, Deborah II, 343
Butler, Deborah II, 479
Butler, Deborah II, 528
Butler, Deborah IV, 185
Butler, Deborah IV, 311
Butler, Deborah IV, 1151
Butler, Deborah IV, 1192
Butler, Deborah V, 897
Butler, Deborah VI, 56
Butler, Deborah VI, 133
Butler, Deborah VI, 301
Butler, Deborah VI, 302
Butler, Deborah VI, 319
Butler, Deborah VI, 327
Butler, Deborah Johnson VI, 308
Butler, Delcina I, 1149
Butler, Delila VI, 832
Butler, Dick VI, 103
Butler, Dosha VI, 802
Butler, Drusilla IV, 686
Butler, Drusilla IV, 703
Butler, Drusilla IV, 932
Butler, Drusilla IV, 933
Butler, Drusilla IV, 1203
Butler, Durham VI, 133
Butler, Edith II, 283
Butler, Edith II, 785
Butler, Edith II, 843
Butler, Edmonson I, 1149
Butler, Edna V, 479
Butler, Edna V, 541
Butler, Edna V, 552
Butler, Edna V, 605
Butler, Edna VI, 102
Butler, Edna VI, 301
Butler, Edna VI, 302
Butler, Edward I, 1149
Butler, Edward V, 479
Butler, Edward VI, 56
Butler, Edward VI, 102
Butler, Edward VI, 104
Butler, Edward VI, 132
Butler, Edward VI, 302
Butler, Edward VI, 799
Butler, Edward VI, 802
Butler, Edward VI, 846
Butler, Edward VI, 847
Butler, Edward VI, 864
Butler, Edward VI, 920
Butler, Edward Morris IV, 185
Butler, Edward Morris IV, 311
Butler, Edward Robert VI, 301
Butler, Edward T. V, 968
Butler, Edward Thos. V, 968
Butler, Edwin V, 479
Butler, Eleanor IV, 686
Butler, Eleanor IV, 932
Butler, Eli IV, 1051
Butler, Elisabeth I, 134
Butler, Elisabeth IV, 377
Butler, Elisabeth VI, 102
Butler, Elisha IV, 1234
Butler, Elisha V, 321
Butler, Elisha V, 662
Butler, Elisha VI, 56
Butler, Elisha VI, 479
Butler, Elisha M. V, 321
Butler, Elisha M. V, 662
Butler, Elizabeth II, 59
Butler, Elizabeth II, 91
Butler, Elizabeth IV, 141
Butler, Elizabeth IV, 185
Butler, Elizabeth IV, 365
Butler, Elizabeth IV, 377
Butler, Elizabeth IV, 565
Butler, Elizabeth IV, 570
Butler, Elizabeth IV, 928
Butler, Elizabeth IV, 932
Butler, Elizabeth IV, 933
Butler, Elizabeth IV, 969
Butler, Elizabeth IV, 976
Butler, Elizabeth IV, 978
Butler, Elizabeth IV, 979
Butler, Elizabeth IV, 1006
Butler, Elizabeth V, 32
Butler, Elizabeth V, 156
Butler, Elizabeth V, 227
Butler, Elizabeth V, 321
Butler, Elizabeth V, 479
Butler, Elizabeth VI, 56
Butler, Elizabeth VI, 102
Butler, Elizabeth VI, 103
Butler, Elizabeth VI, 104
Butler, Elizabeth VI, 107
Butler, Elizabeth VI, 111
Butler, Elizabeth VI, 113
Butler, Elizabeth VI, 122
Butler, Elizabeth VI, 129
Butler, Elizabeth VI, 131
Butler, Elizabeth VI, 132
Butler, Elizabeth VI, 161
Butler, Elizabeth VI, 162
Butler, Elizabeth VI, 190
Butler, Elizabeth VI, 193
Butler, Elizabeth VI, 374
Butler, Elizabeth VI, 455
Butler, Elizabeth VI, 802
Butler, Elizabeth VI, 829
Butler, Elizabeth E. VI, 802
Butler, Elizabeth P. V, 226
Butler, Elizabeth R. IV, 805
Butler, Elizabeth T. IV, 932
Butler, Elizabeth T. IV, 933
Butler, Elizabeth T. IV, 978
Butler, Ella V, 156
Butler, Ellen IV, 687
Butler, Ellen IV, 933
Butler, Emily IV, 613
Butler, Emily IV, 654
Butler, Emily IV, 933
Butler, Emily IV, 990
Butler, Emily V, 972
Butler, Emily Jane IV, 933
Butler, Emily Jane IV, 998
Butler, Emily S. IV, 613
Butler, Emily S. IV, 933
Butler, Emma C. IV, 933
Butler, Emma C. IV, 934
Butler, Emma J. IV, 993
Butler, Emma Jane IV, 933
Butler, Emma L. IV, 933
Butler, Esther IV, 932
Butler, Esther IV, 933
Butler, Esther V, 226
Butler, Esther V, 227
Butler, Esther V, 257
Butler, Esther V, 479
Butler, Esther VI, 629
Butler, Ethel B. II, 308
Butler, Eugenia VI, 56
Butler, Eugenia VI, 60
Butler, Eunice IV, 932
Butler, Eunice IV, 933
Butler, Eunice IV, 999
Butler, Eveline M. V, 897
Butler, F. O. IV, 1273
Butler, Faith II, 168
Butler, Faith VI, 102
Butler, Faith VI, 103
Butler, Faith VI, 104
Butler, Faith VI, 109
Butler, Faith VI, 122
Butler, Fam V, 479
Butler, Fillis VI, 103
Butler, Franklin J. IV, 933
Butler, Geo. D. V, 552
Butler, George IV, 932
Butler, George VI, 161
Butler, George VI, 162
Butler, George VI, 201
Butler, George B. White V, 479
Butler, Griffin VI, 888
Butler, Gulia Ann V, 968
Butler, Gulia M. VI, 56
Butler, Gulian V, 968
Butler, Gulielma M. VI, 132
Butler, Hannah III, 404
Butler, Hannah IV, 185
Butler, Hannah IV, 254
Butler, Hannah IV, 311
Butler, Hannah IV, 686
Butler, Hannah IV, 701

Butler, Hannah IV, 709
Butler, Hannah IV, 805
Butler, Hannah IV, 904
Butler, Hannah IV, 932
Butler, Hannah IV, 933
Butler, Hannah IV, 952
Butler, Hannah IV, 957
Butler, Hannah IV, 998
Butler, Hannah IV, 1005
Butler, Hannah IV, 1006
Butler, Hannah IV, 1151
Butler, Hannah VI, 920
Butler, Hannah Jane IV, 185
Butler, Hannah Jane IV, 311
Butler, Hannah P. IV, 933
Butler, Hannah P. IV, 1203
Butler, Hannah Pauline IV, 930
Butler, Hannah Pauline IV, 933
Butler, Hannah W. IV, 185
Butler, Hannah W. IV, 242
Butler, Hannah W. IV, 933
Butler, Hannah W. IV, 976
Butler, Harriet II, 774
Butler, Harriet III, 57
Butler, Harvey V, 988
Butler, Henrietta VI, 162
Butler, Henrietta M. VI, 157
Butler, Henrietta M. VI, 162
Butler, Henrietta Maria VI, 132
Butler, Henrietta Maria VI, 155
Butler, Henrietta Maria VI, 156
Butler, Henrietta Maria VI, 161
Butler, Henrietta Maria VI, 162
Butler, Henriette Maria VI, 130
Butler, Henry II, 986
Butler, Henry IV, 185
Butler, Henry IV, 377
Butler, Henry VI, 102
Butler, Henry Briggs VI, 56
Butler, Huldah VI, 102
Butler, Huldah VI, 301
Butler, Huldah VI, 339
Butler, Huldah VI, 340
Butler, Irena M. IV, 949
Butler, Irena Mary IV, 933
Butler, Irene M. IV, 949
Butler, Isaac Lloyd IV, 185
Butler, Israel II, 168
Butler, J. Ella IV, 934
Butler, J. S. VI, 56
Butler, James II, 342
Butler, James II, 731
Butler, James II, 843
Butler, James IV, 377
Butler, James IV, 1247
Butler, James V, 32
Butler, James V, 226
Butler, James V, 479
Butler, James VI, 56
Butler, James VI, 60
Butler, James VI, 102
Butler, James VI, 104
Butler, James VI, 110
Butler, James VI, 132
Butler, James VI, 161
Butler, James VI, 301
Butler, James VI, 339
Butler, James VI, 802
Butler, James VI, 850
Butler, James C. VI, 56
Butler, James Edward VI, 301
Butler, James Edward VI, 302
Butler, James L. II, 774
Butler, James L. VI, 301
Butler, James S. VI, 56
Butler, James S. VI, 301
Butler, James S. VI, 302
Butler, James S. VI, 832
Butler, James Stanton VI, 102
Butler, James Stanton VI, 301
Butler, James, Jr. VI, 56
Butler, James, Jr. VI, 87
Butler, James, Jr. VI, 301
Butler, James, Jr. VI, 307
Butler, James, Sr. VI, 102
Butler, James, Sr. VI, 104
Butler, James, Sr. VI, 301
Butler, James, Sr. VI, 307
Butler, Jane IV, 185
Butler, Jane IV, 233
Butler, Jane IV, 377
Butler, Jane IV, 1151
Butler, Jane VI, 132
Butler, Jane VI, 133
Butler, Jane VI, 134
Butler, Jared IV, 141
Butler, Jared IV, 365
Butler, Jared IV, 376
Butler, Jared IV, 377
Butler, Jared IV, 565
Butler, Jared IV, 570
Butler, Jas. VI, 103
Butler, Jehu IV, 932
Butler, Jehu IV, 933
Butler, Jemmy VI, 103
Butler, Jenny VI, 103
Butler, Jenny VI, 938
Butler, Jesse IV, 933
Butler, Jesse IV, 934
Butler, Jesse IV, 1000
Butler, Jesse V, 479
Butler, Joel Caleb IV, 1051
Butler, John I, 1047
Butler, John II, 342
Butler, John II, 343
Butler, John II, 986
Butler, John III, 57
Butler, John III, 397
Butler, John III, 404
Butler, John IV, 233
Butler, John IV, 377
Butler, John IV, 686
Butler, John IV, 703
Butler, John IV, 923
Butler, John IV, 932
Butler, John IV, 933
Butler, John IV, 949
Butler, John IV, 969
Butler, John IV, 976
Butler, John IV, 978
Butler, John IV, 993
Butler, John IV, 1006
Butler, John IV, 1051
Butler, John IV, 1203
Butler, John IV, 1234
Butler, John V, 968
Butler, John V, 988
Butler, John VI, 15
Butler, John VI, 56
Butler, John VI, 102
Butler, John VI, 104
Butler, John VI, 108
Butler, John VI, 111
Butler, John VI, 122
Butler, John VI, 132
Butler, John VI, 133
Butler, John VI, 144
Butler, John VI, 161
Butler, John VI, 162
Butler, John VI, 190
Butler, John VI, 193
Butler, John VI, 374
Butler, John VI, 675
Butler, John L. IV, 932
Butler, John L. IV, 933
Butler, John L. IV, 955
Butler, John Pearson V, 979
Butler, John, Jr. II, 59
Butler, John, Jr. IV, 933
Butler, Johnston VI, 302
Butler, Jonathan IV, 185
Butler, Jonathan IV, 311
Butler, Jonathan IV, 1151
Butler, Jonathan V, 479
Butler, Jonathan VI, 56
Butler, Jonathan VI, 102
Butler, Jonathan VI, 132
Butler, Jonathan VI, 133
Butler, Jonathan VI, 155
Butler, Jonathan VI, 156
Butler, Jonathan VI, 157
Butler, Jonathan VI, 161
Butler, Jonathan VI, 162
Butler, Jonathan VI, 301
Butler, Jonathan VI, 302
Butler, Jonathan VI, 802
Butler, Jonathan VI, 817
Butler, Jonathan VI, 829
Butler, Jonathan VI, 832
Butler, Jonothan V, 32
Butler, Jos. VI, 103
Butler, Joseph I, 233
Butler, Joseph I, 529
Butler, Joseph I, 803
Butler, Joseph II, 342
Butler, Joseph II, 986
Butler, Joseph IV, 805
Butler, Joseph IV, 932
Butler, Joseph IV, 933
Butler, Joseph IV, 998
Butler, Joseph IV, 1273
Butler, Joseph V, 226
Butler, Joseph V, 479
Butler, Joseph VI, 56
Butler, Joseph VI, 97
Butler, Joseph VI, 102
Butler, Joseph VI, 111
Butler, Joseph VI, 117
Butler, Joseph VI, 130
Butler, Joseph VI, 132
Butler, Joseph VI, 133
Butler, Joseph VI, 161
Butler, Joseph VI, 162
Butler, Joseph VI, 232
Butler, Joseph VI, 301
Butler, Joseph VI, 302
Butler, Joseph H. VI, 132
Butler, Joseph M. III, 57
Butler, Joseph S. VI, 87
Butler, Joseph W. VI, 735
Butler, Joseph W. VI, 759
Butler, Joseph, Jr. VI, 132
Butler, Joshua Asborn V, 968
Butler, Joshua O. V, 897
Butler, Joshua O. V, 968
Butler, Josiah IV, 928
Butler, Josiah IV, 932
Butler, Josiah IV, 933
Butler, Josiah VI, 102
Butler, Judith V, 32
Butler, Judith Ella IV, 933
Butler, Judy VI, 103
Butler, Julia VI, 133
Butler, Julie VI, 133
Butler, Julie VI, 144
Butler, Keziah III, 397
Butler, Keziah V, 321
Butler, Keziah D. V, 321
Butler, Keziah D. V, 662
Butler, L. R. V, 988
Butler, Lawrence IV, 857
Butler, Lawrence L. V, 988
Butler, Lawrence W. IV, 613
Butler, Lawrence W. IV, 686
Butler, Lawrence W. IV, 805
Butler, Lawrence W. IV, 850
Butler, Lawrence W. IV, 900
Butler, Lawrence W. IV, 932
Butler, Lawrence W. IV, 933
Butler, Lawrence W. IV, 999
Butler, Lawrence W. IV, 1004
Butler, Lawrence W. IV, 1006
Butler, Lazarus VI, 102
Butler, Lemuel V, 479
Butler, Lemuel VI, 132
Butler, Lemuel VI, 133
Butler, Lemuel VI, 134
Butler, Lenel VI, 132
Butler, Leuba IV, 1036
Butler, Levi R. V, 988
Butler, Lewis IV, 805
Butler, Lewis IV, 932
Butler, Lewis IV, 933
Butler, Lindley S. IV, 933
Butler, Louis IV, 805
Butler, Louisa VI, 296
Butler, Louisa VI, 301
Butler, Louisa VI, 302
Butler, Lucinda Birdson VI, 56
Butler, Lucy IV, 570
Butler, Lucy V, 32
Butler, Lucy V, 226
Butler, Lucy V, 271
Butler, Lucy VI, 102
Butler, Lydia III, 57
Butler, Lydia III, 236
Butler, Lydia IV, 686
Butler, Lydia IV, 932
Butler, Lydia IV, 934
Butler, Lydia V, 32
Butler, Lydia V, 226
Butler, Lydia V, 479
Butler, Lydia VI, 102
Butler, Lydia VI, 104
Butler, Lydia VI, 122
Butler, Malard VI, 133
Butler, Malinda VI, 802
Butler, Margaret V, 897
Butler, Margaret V, 931
Butler, Margaret VI, 102
Butler, Margaret VI, 132
Butler, Margaretta T. II, 479
Butler, Margaretta T. II, 731
Butler, Margaretta T. II, 773
Butler, Margaretta T. II, 774
Butler, Maria V, 23
Butler, Maria V, 32
Butler, Maria V, 968
Butler, Maria VI, 130
Butler, Maria VI, 132
Butler, Maria VI, 302
Butler, Maria Frances V, 968
Butler, Martha III, 397
Butler, Martha III, 404
Butler, Martha IV, 377
Butler, Martha V, 32
Butler, Martha VI, 56
Butler, Martha VI, 60
Butler, Martha VI, 102
Butler, Martha VI, 103
Butler, Martha VI, 104
Butler, Martha VI, 107
Butler, Martha VI, 133
Butler, Martha VI, 301
Butler, Martha VI, 302
Butler, Martha VI, 832
Butler, Martha Ellen VI, 735
Butler, Martha Ellen VI, 747
Butler, Martha Ellen VI, 759
Butler, Martha L. VI, 799
Butler, Mary I, 376
Butler, Mary I, 377
Butler, Mary I, 529
Butler, Mary I, 1016
Butler, Mary II, 204
Butler, Mary II, 232
Butler, Mary II, 442
Butler, Mary II, 731
Butler, Mary II, 773
Butler, Mary IV, 185
Butler, Mary IV, 365
Butler, Mary IV, 377
Butler, Mary IV, 443
Butler, Mary IV, 805
Butler, Mary IV, 932
Butler, Mary IV, 933
Butler, Mary IV, 972
Butler, Mary IV, 1004
Butler, Mary IV, 1051
Butler, Mary V, 32
Butler, Mary V, 479
Butler, Mary V, 552
Butler, Mary V, 567
Butler, Mary V, 897
Butler, Mary VI, 15
Butler, Mary VI, 56
Butler, Mary VI, 84
Butler, Mary VI, 102
Butler, Mary VI, 103
Butler, Mary VI, 104
Butler, Mary VI, 110
Butler, Mary VI, 111
Butler, Mary VI, 132
Butler, Mary VI, 133
Butler, Mary VI, 299
Butler, Mary VI, 301
Butler, Mary VI, 302
Butler, Mary VI, 846
Butler, Mary VI, 888
Butler, Mary Ann V, 756
Butler, Mary E. IV, 710
Butler, Mary E. IV, 933
Butler, Mary E. V, 968
Butler, Mary Elizabeth VI, 302
Butler, Mary Emily V, 968
Butler, Mary Emily V, 972
Butler, Mary Emily V, 979
Butler, Mary F. V, 967
Butler, Mary F. V, 968
Butler, Mary F. VI, 802
Butler, Mary M. IV, 185
Butler, Mary Rawls VI, 56
Butler, Mary Susanna V, 226
Butler, Mary, Jr. IV, 1051
Butler, Mary, Jr. VI, 104
Butler, Matilda VI, 301
Butler, Matilda VI, 302
Butler, Matilda VI, 326
Butler, Matilda Ann VI, 301
Butler, Matilda Ann VI, 302
Butler, Matthew VI, 301
Butler, May V, 156
Butler, Melissa IV, 1273
Butler, Meribah IV, 686
Butler, Meribah IV, 932
Butler, Meribah IV, 952
Butler, Meriboh IV, 904
Butler, Merihab IV, 932
Butler, Merihab J. IV, 933
Butler, Micajah V, 31
Butler, Micajah V, 968
Butler, Micajah V, 972
Butler, Micajah V, 979
Butler, Micajah VI, 15
Butler, Micajah VI, 56
Butler, Micajah VI, 102
Butler, Micajah VI, 132
Butler, Micajah VI, 133
Butler, Micajah VI, 137
Butler, Micajah D. IV, 933
Butler, Micajah D. IV, 934
Butler, Michael V, 32
Butler, Michal V, 479
Butler, Milly VI, 948
Butler, Mira IV, 934
Butler, Miriam V, 226
Butler, Miriam VI, 97
Butler, Miriam VI, 102
Butler, Miriam VI, 104
Butler, Miriam VI, 111
Butler, Miriam VI, 132
Butler, Moriah V, 979
Butler, Moses N. IV, 933
Butler, Moses N. IV, 990
Butler, Moses V. IV, 613
Butler, Moses V. IV, 654
Butler, Moses V. IV, 805
Butler, Moses V. IV, 932
Butler, Moses V. IV, 933
Butler, Mourning V, 32
Butler, Mourning V, 226
Butler, Mourning V, 227
Butler, Mourning V, 293
Butler, Mourning VI, 102
Butler, Mrs. ??? IV, 1247
Butler, Mrs. Selma IV, 1309
Butler, Myra IV, 933
Butler, Nancy IV, 1234
Butler, Nancy V, 32
Butler, Nancy V, 896
Butler, Nancy VI, 102
Butler, Nancy VI, 301
Butler, Nancy VI, 302
Butler, Nancy VI, 317
Butler, Nancy VI, 319
Butler, Nancy VI, 325
Butler, Nancy VI, 802
Butler, Nancy VI, 828
Butler, Nancy VI, 832
Butler, Nathan V, 32
Butler, Nathan V, 226
Butler, Nathan V, 227
Butler, Nathan VI, 102
Butler, Nathaniel VI, 132
Butler, Nathaniel VI, 910
Butler, Nathl. VI, 910
Butler, Nedd VI, 103
Butler, Nethaniel VI, 938
Butler, Olive IV, 933
Butler, Oliver VI, 56
Butler, Oscar IV, 1273
Butler, Paschal VI, 888
Butler, Peggy VI, 910
Butler, Penninah VI, 102
Butler, Permelia IV, 566
Butler, Permelia IV, 570
Butler, Pharaby IV, 185
Butler, Phariba IV, 377
Butler, Phariba IV, 427
Butler, Phebe I, 1149
Butler, Pheriba IV, 377
Butler, Philip John III, 57
Butler, Phillipa III, 57
Butler, Pleasant VI, 133
Butler, Polly VI, 888
Butler, Pressa VI, 103
Butler, Prince George V, 227
Butler, Priscilla V, 479
Butler, Priscilla VI, 56
Butler, Priscilla VI, 87
Butler, Priscilla VI, 102
Butler, Priscilla VI, 104
Butler, Priscilla VI, 111
Butler, Priscilla VI, 132
Butler, Priscilla VI, 301
Butler, Priscilla VI, 307
Butler, Prisy VI, 56
Butler, Prisy VI, 87
Butler, R. Elizabeth IV, 933
Butler, Ray IV, 1036
Butler, Rebecca IV, 364
Butler, Rebeckah Jane VI, 56
Butler, Rhoda I, 529
Butler, Rhoda I, 530
Butler, Rhoda I, 564
Butler, Rhoda V, 31
Butler, Rhoda V, 83
Butler, Rhoda V, 968
Butler, Rhoda A. V, 32
Butler, Rhoda A. V, 973
Butler, Rhoda Ann V, 31
Butler, Rhoda Ann V, 101
Butler, Rhoda Ann V, 968
Butler, Rhoda J. V, 32
Butler, Rhoda J. V, 968
Butler, Rhoda J. V, 979
Butler, Rhoda T. V, 31
Butler, Richard IV, 932
Butler, Richard VI, 821
Butler, Robert I, 529
Butler, Robert I, 803
Butler, Robert IV, 377
Butler, Robert V, 968
Butler, Robert VI, 102
Butler, Robert VI, 103
Butler, Robert VI, 104
Butler, Robert VI, 130
Butler, Robert VI, 132
Butler, Robert VI, 302
Butler, Robert Binford VI, 56
Butler, Robert H. VI, 132
Butler, Robert Hunnicutt VI, 102
Butler, Robert I. VI, 56
Butler, Robert II VI, 102
Butler, Robert J. VI, 56

Butler, Rodah Nixon I, 803
Butler, Rutha VI, 888
Butler, Ruthetta IV, 923
Butler, Ruthetta IV, 933
Butler, Sabilla IV, 364
Butler, Sabilla IV, 377
Butler, Sabilla IV, 438
Butler, Sabilla Smith IV, 377
Butler, Sadie IV, 1273
Butler, Salley VI, 339
Butler, Sally VI, 301
Butler, Sally VI, 340
Butler, Sam VI, 103
Butler, Samantha IV, 933
Butler, Samantha IV, 1000
Butler, Samuel I, 529
Butler, Samuel I, 1016
Butler, Samuel II, 479
Butler, Samuel V, 32
Butler, Samuel V, 226
Butler, Samuel V, 271
Butler, Samuel VI, 102
Butler, Samuel VI, 104
Butler, Samuel VI, 114
Butler, Samuel VI, 132
Butler, Samuel Elliott II, 731
Butler, Samuel Elliott II, 773
Butler, Samuel Nixon I, 803
Butler, Sarah II, 986
Butler, Sarah II, 994
Butler, Sarah IV, 185
Butler, Sarah IV, 233
Butler, Sarah IV, 613
Butler, Sarah IV, 686
Butler, Sarah IV, 687
Butler, Sarah IV, 769
Butler, Sarah IV, 805
Butler, Sarah IV, 850
Butler, Sarah IV, 900
Butler, Sarah IV, 932
Butler, Sarah IV, 933
Butler, Sarah IV, 955
Butler, Sarah IV, 999
Butler, Sarah IV, 1004
Butler, Sarah IV, 1005
Butler, Sarah IV, 1006
Butler, Sarah IV, 1008
Butler, Sarah IV, 1273
Butler, Sarah V, 32
Butler, Sarah V, 226
Butler, Sarah V, 479
Butler, Sarah VI, 97
Butler, Sarah VI, 102
Butler, Sarah VI, 103
Butler, Sarah VI, 104
Butler, Sarah VI, 124
Butler, Sarah VI, 132
Butler, Sarah VI, 161
Butler, Sarah VI, 301
Butler, Sarah VI, 802
Butler, Sarah VI, 847
Butler, Sarah VI, 849
Butler, Sarah Amanda VI, 735
Butler, Sarah Amanda VI, 759
Butler, Sarah Ann IV, 365
Butler, Sarah Ann IV, 377
Butler, Sarah Ann V, 32
Butler, Sarah Ann V, 227
Butler, Sarah Louisa IV, 933
Butler, Sarah Rufina V, 552
Butler, Sarahan V, 226
Butler, Sary VI, 797
Butler, Simmons V, 226
Butler, Simmons V, 227
Butler, Simmons F. V, 32
Butler, Simons VI, 102
Butler, Solomon VI, 971
Butler, Solomon VI, 1016
Butler, Stanton VI, 104
Butler, Stanton VI, 131
Butler, Stanton VI, 132
Butler, Staunton VI, 56
Butler, Stephen II, 774
Butler, Stephen V, 897
Butler, Stephen VI, 15
Butler, Stephen VI, 102
Butler, Stephen VI, 103
Butler, Stephen VI, 111
Butler, Stephen VI, 292
Butler, Stephen VI, 296
Butler, Stephen VI, 301
Butler, Stephen VI, 302
Butler, Stephen VI, 339
Butler, Stephen VI, 340
Butler, Stephen, Jr. VI, 301
Butler, Stephen, Jr. VI, 302
Butler, Stephen, Jr. VI, 326
Butler, Susan I, 803
Butler, Susan I, 832
Butler, Susanna I, 529
Butler, Susanna I, 1016
Butler, Susanna IV, 922
Butler, Susanna IV, 933
Butler, Susanna V, 226
Butler, Susanna VI, 102
Butler, Susanna VI, 132
Butler, Susanna VI, 301
Butler, Susannah I, 529
Butler, Susannah V, 32
Butler, Susannah V, 227
Butler, Susannah V, 321
Butler, Susannah VI, 117
Butler, Sylvester IV, 1273
Butler, T. VI, 87
Butler, Tabitha IV, 185
Butler, Tabitha IV, 377
Butler, Tabitha V, 32
Butler, Tabitha V, 226
Butler, Tabitha VI, 42
Butler, Tabitha VI, 102
Butler, Tabitha VI, 104
Butler, Tabitha VI, 301
Butler, Tabitha VI, 304
Butler, Tacy VI, 133
Butler, Thirza VI, 802
Butler, Thomas II, 343
Butler, Thomas II, 442
Butler, Thomas II, 986
Butler, Thomas IV, 933
Butler, Thomas VI, 133
Butler, Thomas VI, 802
Butler, Thomas VI, 847
Butler, Tillman VI, 102
Butler, Tilmon VI, 103
Butler, Toby VI, 804
Butler, Tony VI, 103
Butler, Uree IV, 933
Butler, Ursala V, 226
Butler, Ursala V, 227
Butler, Ursala V, 266
Butler, Ursly V, 227
Butler, Ursly VI, 102
Butler, Ursly VI, 104
Butler, Ursly VI, 114
Butler, Ursula V, 32
Butler, Ursula V, 227
Butler, Ursula V, 321
Butler, Usala V, 271
Butler, Verda IV, 1036
Butler, Virginia VI, 232
Butler, Walter E. IV, 933
Butler, Walter E. IV, 934
Butler, Wd. ??? VI, 161
Butler, Wd. Ann VI, 870
Butler, Wellington II, 308
Butler, Wike H. V, 968
Butler, Wilder I, 1149
Butler, Will VI, 103
Butler, William I, 529
Butler, William I, 1016
Butler, William I, 1149
Butler, William II, 343
Butler, William IV, 364
Butler, William IV, 377
Butler, William IV, 438
Butler, William IV, 932
Butler, William V, 32
Butler, William V, 226
Butler, William V, 257
Butler, William V, 469
Butler, William V, 479
Butler, William V, 897
Butler, William VI, 15
Butler, William VI, 56
Butler, William VI, 102
Butler, William VI, 104
Butler, William VI, 107
Butler, William VI, 122
Butler, William VI, 132
Butler, William VI, 161
Butler, William VI, 162
Butler, William VI, 301
Butler, William VI, 302
Butler, William VI, 308
Butler, William VI, 319
Butler, William VI, 325
Butler, William VI, 327
Butler, William VI, 799
Butler, William VI, 802
Butler, William VI, 888
Butler, William B. II, 308
Butler, William E. V, 31
Butler, William E. V, 83
Butler, William E. V, 101
Butler, William E. VI, 56
Butler, William Exum VI, 301
Butler, William Exum VI, 302
Butler, William H. IV, 933
Butler, William H. VI, 133
Butler, William H. VI, 302
Butler, Willis IV, 933
Butler, Wm. IV, 570
Butler, Wm. IV, 686
Butler, Wm. V, 896
Butler, Wm. V, 931
Butler, Wm. VI, 102
Butler, Wm. VI, 103
Butler, Wm. VI, 317
Butler, Wm. VI, 849
Butler, Wm. E. V, 968
Butler, Wm. E. V, 973
Butler, Wm. E. V, 979
Butler, Wm. H. IV, 933
Butler, Wyke VI, 56
Butler, Wyke H. V, 979
Butler, Wyke H. VI, 133
Butner, Emily L. I, 529
Butner, Ida V, 988
Butner, N. C. I, 530
Butner, Thaddeus M. I, 529
Butt, Margaret I, 134
Butt, Margaret I, 156
Butt., Sarah VI, 876
Butterfield, Hannah VI, 374
Butterfield, Hannah VI, 393
Butterfield, James VI, 375
Butterfield, John VI, 359
Butterfield, John VI, 374
Butterfield, John VI, 393
Butterfield, Mary VI, 374
Butterfield, Mary VI, 375
Butterfield, Mary VI, 409
Butterfield, Mary VI, 414
Butterfield, Mertie May II, 837
Butterfield, Mertie May II, 843
Butterfield, Rachel VI, 374
Butterfield, Rachel VI, 375
Butterfield, Rachel VI, 593
Butterfield, Ruth VI, 374
Butterfield, Ruth VI, 375
Butterfield, Ruth VI, 393
Butterfield, Sarah VI, 551
Butterfield, Thomas VI, 374
Butterfield, Thomas VI, 375
Butterworth, Abigail II, 283
Butterworth, Abigale V, 32
Butterworth, Amanda VI, 888
Butterworth, Amos H. V, 32
Butterworth, Ann II, 283
Butterworth, Ann V, 32
Butterworth, Ann V, 33
Butterworth, Ann V, 130
Butterworth, Arthur IV, 1309
Butterworth, Arthur V, 662
Butterworth, Averilla V, 32
Butterworth, Benj. VI, 302
Butterworth, Benj. VI, 829
Butterworth, Benjamin V, 32
Butterworth, Benjamin V, 33
Butterworth, Benjamin V, 117
Butterworth, Benjamin VI, 297
Butterworth, Benjamin VI, 302
Butterworth, Benjamin VI, 319
Butterworth, Benjamin VI, 326
Butterworth, Benjamin VI, 802
Butterworth, Benjamin VI, 806
Butterworth, Benjamin VI, 862
Butterworth, Benjamin T. V, 32
Butterworth, Benjamin T. V, 33
Butterworth, Benjamin, Jr. V, 32
Butterworth, Benjamin, Jr. V, 33
Butterworth, Betsy V, 32
Butterworth, Betsy V, 83
Butterworth, Betsy VI, 297
Butterworth, Betsy VI, 302
Butterworth, Betsy VI, 319
Butterworth, Betsy VI, 857
Butterworth, Bluford VI, 888
Butterworth, Buckley VI, 802
Butterworth, Caroline V, 32
Butterworth, Catharine II, 283
Butterworth, Charles V, 662
Butterworth, Charlie IV, 1309
Butterworth, Chas. C. V, 662
Butterworth, Clarkson V, 32
Butterworth, Clarkson V, 33
Butterworth, Dashia VI, 802
Butterworth, Edith V, 32
Butterworth, Edith V, 33
Butterworth, Edith V, 60
Butterworth, Edith P. V, 33
Butterworth, Edward V, 32
Butterworth, Edward B. V, 32
Butterworth, Edward W. V, 115
Butterworth, Elijah VI, 326
Butterworth, Elizabeth V, 32
Butterworth, Elizabeth V, 33
Butterworth, Elizabeth V, 479
Butterworth, Elizabeth V, 510
Butterworth, Elizabeth VI, 297
Butterworth, Elizabeth VI, 302
Butterworth, Elizabeth VI, 319
Butterworth, Elizabeth VI, 802
Butterworth, Elizabeth VI, 803
Butterworth, Ellen V, 32
Butterworth, Ellen V, 33
Butterworth, Ellen V, 317
Butterworth, Ellen V, 38
Butterworth, Elwood V, 33
Butterworth, Emma III, 212
Butterworth, Emma V, 32
Butterworth, Emma V, 45
Butterworth, Emma B. V, 33
Butterworth, Emma B. V, 45
Butterworth, Ernest V, 32
Butterworth, Esther II, 204
Butterworth, Esther II, 265
Butterworth, Esther II, 283
Butterworth, Esther V, 662
Butterworth, Etta V, 321
Butterworth, Etta V, 662
Butterworth, Ettie V, 662
Butterworth, Fanny V, 32
Butterworth, Fanny V, 33
Butterworth, Fanny V, 122
Butterworth, Hannah V, 32
Butterworth, Hannah V, 33
Butterworth, Hannah V, 115
Butterworth, Hannah V, 479
Butterworth, Hannah L. V, 479
Butterworth, Henry T. V, 32
Butterworth, Henry T. V, 33
Butterworth, Henry T. V, 136
Butterworth, Henry Thomas V, 32
Butterworth, Henry Thomas V, 33
Butterworth, Henry Thomas VI, 302
Butterworth, I. H. VI, 834
Butterworth, Isaac V, 32
Butterworth, Isaac V, 33
Butterworth, Isaac VI, 302
Butterworth, Isaac VI, 802
Butterworth, Isaac VI, 803
Butterworth, Isaac VI, 833
Butterworth, Isaac VI, 834
Butterworth, Isaac VI, 865
Butterworth, Isaac W. V, 32
Butterworth, Isaac W. V, 33
Butterworth, Isaac W. V, 897
Butterworth, Israel V, 32
Butterworth, Jane V, 32
Butterworth, Jane V, 33
Butterworth, Jane V, 55
Butterworth, Jane VI, 806
Butterworth, Jane VI, 823
Butterworth, Jane W. V, 55
Butterworth, Jesse V, 33
Butterworth, Jesse VI, 857
Butterworth, Jesse T. V, 32
Butterworth, Jesse T. V, 33
Butterworth, John Ogborn V, 32
Butterworth, Joseph II, 204
Butterworth, Joseph VI, 802
Butterworth, Josiah V, 32
Butterworth, Judith V, 32
Butterworth, Judith V, 33
Butterworth, Judith V, 139
Butterworth, Kalista V, 32
Butterworth, Lockey Ann VI, 888
Butterworth, Louisa V, 32
Butterworth, Martha V, 32
Butterworth, Martha V, 33
Butterworth, Mary II, 283
Butterworth, Mary II, 291
Butterworth, Mary V, 32
Butterworth, Mary VI, 834
Butterworth, Mary B. V, 33
Butterworth, Mary B. V, 93
Butterworth, Mary E. V, 32
Butterworth, Mary E. VI, 1017
Butterworth, Mary Eliza V, 32
Butterworth, Mary Eliza V, 33
Butterworth, Mary Eliza V, 56
Butterworth, Mary M. V, 32
Butterworth, Mary M. V, 33
Butterworth, Matilda VI, 833
Butterworth, Miley VI, 302
Butterworth, Milley VI, 302
Butterworth, Milly V, 32
Butterworth, Milly VI, 308
Butterworth, Milly VI, 309
Butterworth, Moorman V, 32
Butterworth, Moorman V, 122
Butterworth, Moorman VI, 302
Butterworth, Morman V, 33
Butterworth, Moses V, 33
Butterworth, Moses E. V, 32
Butterworth, Nancy V, 32
Butterworth, Nancy V, 33
Butterworth, Nancy V, 136
Butterworth, Nancy VI, 297
Butterworth, Nancy VI, 302
Butterworth, Nancy VI, 802
Butterworth, Nancy VI, 865
Butterworth, Naomi V, 32
Butterworth, Nathan V, 32
Butterworth, Paulina V, 32
Butterworth, Polly V, 32
Butterworth, Polly V, 83
Butterworth, Polly VI, 302
Butterworth, Polly VI, 326
Butterworth, Polly VI, 327
Butterworth, Polly VI, 829
Butterworth, Priscilla V, 33
Butterworth, Priscilla A. V, 32
Butterworth, Rachel V, 32
Butterworth, Rachel V, 33
Butterworth, Rachel V, 63
Butterworth, Rachel V, 117
Butterworth, Rachel VI, 297
Butterworth, Rachel VI, 302
Butterworth, Rachel VI, 306
Butterworth, Rachel VI, 319
Butterworth, Rachel VI, 333
Butterworth, Rachel VI, 802
Butterworth, Rachel B. V, 24
Butterworth, Rachel B. V, 33
Butterworth, Rachel B. V, 71
Butterworth, Rachel M. V, 32
Butterworth, Rachel M. V, 117
Butterworth, Rachel, Jr. V, 33
Butterworth, Ruth C. V, 32
Butterworth, Ruth Caroline V, 33
Butterworth, Ruth E. V, 32
Butterworth, Ruth E. V, 33
Butterworth, Ruthanna V, 32
Butterworth, Ruthanna V, 33
Butterworth, Ruthanna V, 143
Butterworth, Sally VI, 802
Butterworth, Samuel V, 31
Butterworth, Samuel V, 32
Butterworth, Samuel V, 33
Butterworth, Samuel V, 479
Butterworth, Samuel VI, 302
Butterworth, Samuel G. V, 32
Butterworth, Sarah II, 283
Butterworth, Sarah II, 343
Butterworth, Sarah V, 32
Butterworth, Sarah VI, 857
Butterworth, Sarah E. V, 31
Butterworth, Sarah E. V, 32
Butterworth, Sarah E. V, 33
Butterworth, Sarah E. V, 895
Butterworth, Sarah Jane V, 32
Butterworth, Stella H. V, 32
Butterworth, Stephen VI, 888
Butterworth, Stephen VI, 964
Butterworth, Stephen VI, 1006
Butterworth, Stephen VI, 1017
Butterworth, Steven VI, 802
Butterworth, Susan II, 811
Butterworth, Susan V, 32
Butterworth, Susan V, 33
Butterworth, Susan V, 104
Butterworth, Thomas V, 32
Butterworth, Turner W. V, 32
Butterworth, Walter Weyner IV, 1309
Butterworth, William V, 33
Butterworth, William V, 133
Butterworth, William V, 479
Butterworth, William V, 510
Butterworth, William VI, 302
Butterworth, William B. V, 33
Butterworth, William H. V, 33
Butterworth, William W. V, 32
Butterworth, Zachariah V, 83
Buttery, Frank IV, 1309
Buttery, Frank P. IV, 1309
Buttlar, Sarah IV, 1273
Buttler, John I, 1047
Buttler, Samuel II, 479
Button, Alva III, 271
Button, Deborah IV, 722
Button, Rhoda I, 529
Button, Rhoda I, 530
Button, Rhoda I, 564
Butts, Carl V, 729
Butts, Daniel C. VI, 134
Butts, Daniel C. VI, 135
Butts, Dora V, 729
Butts, Dorothy V, 729
Butts, Edward VI, 56
Butts, Edward VI, 67
Butts, Edward VI, 74
Butts, Edward VI, 80
Butts, Elizabeth III, 82
Butts, Elizabeth III, 164
Butts, Flora M. V, 729
Butts, Geo. L. V, 729
Butts, George V, 729
Butts, George E. V, 729
Butts, George W. VI, 888
Butts, Gertrude V, 729

Butts, Gladys V, 729
Butts, Grant V, 729
Butts, Henry V, 729
Butts, James S. V, 729
Butts, Joseph M. V, 729
Butts, Mabel V, 729
Butts, Mark V, 729
Butts, Mary V, 729
Butts, Mary M. V, 729
Butts, Mary R. V, 729
Butts, Mr. George V, 729
Butts, Mrs. ??? V, 729
Butts, Neddie V, 729
Butts, Nellie R. V, 729
Butts, Paul V, 729
Butts, Sarah F. VI, 888
Butts, Una V, 729
Butts, William A. V, 729
Buttweworth, Hannah L. V, 533
Buttweworth, Samuel V, 533
Butz, Elizabeth IV, 805
Buxby, Joseph E. II, 844
Buxton, Joseph II, 343
Buybey, Joseph VI, 850
Buybey, Susan VI, 850
Buyram, Isaac I, 39
Buyram, Isaac I, 50
Buyram, Sarah I, 39
Buyram, Sarah I, 50
Buyrum, James I, 39
Buzbee, Hannah II, 205
Buzbee, Hannah II, 231
Buzby, ??? II, 785
Buzby, Abel II, 168
Buzby, Abel II, 169
Buzby, Abel II, 283
Buzby, Abel II, 731
Buzby, Abigail H. II, 867
Buzby, Adelaide II, 168
Buzby, Adelaide II, 283
Buzby, Adelaide II, 299
Buzby, Alice C. II, 831
Buzby, Alice C. II, 844
Buzby, Alice E. II, 844
Buzby, Alice E. III, 57
Buzby, Amanda I. II, 785
Buzby, Amos II, 59
Buzby, Amos II, 60
Buzby, Amos II, 168
Buzby, Amos II, 169
Buzby, Amos II, 204
Buzby, Amos II, 205
Buzby, Amos II, 231
Buzby, Amos II, 232
Buzby, Amos II, 242
Buzby, Amos II, 275
Buzby, Amos II, 276
Buzby, Amos II, 283
Buzby, Amos II, 308
Buzby, Amos II, 317
Buzby, Amos II, 343
Buzby, Amos II, 785
Buzby, Amos III, 57
Buzby, Amos H. II, 169
Buzby, Amos, Jr. II, 205
Buzby, Amos, Jr. II, 283
Buzby, Ann II, 59
Buzby, Ann II, 60
Buzby, Ann II, 169
Buzby, Ann II, 204
Buzby, Ann II, 205
Buzby, Ann II, 479
Buzby, Ann F. II, 60
Buzby, Ann F. II, 169
Buzby, Ann F. II, 479
Buzby, Ann Folwell II, 479
Buzby, Anna R. II, 146
Buzby, Anna Rebecca II, 130
Buzby, Anna Rebecca II, 146
Buzby, Anna Rebecca II, 157
Buzby, Anna W. II, 844
Buzby, Anna W. III, 57
Buzby, Anna Wilson II, 785
Buzby, Aron II, 169
Buzby, Asher II, 59
Buzby, Asher II, 60
Buzby, Asher II, 113
Buzby, Asher II, 116
Buzby, Asher II, 130
Buzby, Asher II, 131
Buzby, Asher II, 146
Buzby, Asher II, 148
Buzby, Asher II, 168
Buzby, Asher II, 205
Buzby, Ashur II, 59
Buzby, Augusta C. II, 283
Buzby, Augustus C. II, 283
Buzby, Benjamin II, 168
Buzby, Benjamin II, 169
Buzby, Benjamin II, 343
Buzby, Benjamin II, 479
Buzby, Benjamin C. II, 343
Buzby, Benjamin C. II, 479
Buzby, Benjamin M. II, 168
Buzby, Beulah II, 59
Buzby, Beulah II, 60
Buzby, Beulah II, 113
Buzby, Beulah II, 130
Buzby, Beulah II, 148
Buzby, Beulah II, 168
Buzby, Beulah II, 169
Buzby, Beulah II, 205
Buzby, Beulah II, 275
Buzby, Beulah A. II, 146
Buzby, Beulah A. II, 148
Buzby, Beulah Ann II, 60
Buzby, Beulah Ann II, 116
Buzby, Beulah Ann II, 130
Buzby, Beulah Ann II, 131
Buzby, Beulah Ann II, 148
Buzby, Caroline II, 785
Buzby, Caroline II, 843
Buzby, Caroline II, 867
Buzby, Charles C. II, 148
Buzby, Chas. II, 785
Buzby, Chas. II, 867
Buzby, Daniel II, 168
Buzby, Daniel II, 205
Buzby, Deborah W. II, 283
Buzby, Dinah II, 479
Buzby, Dorothy L. II, 308
Buzby, Edith II, 169
Buzby, Edith II, 205
Buzby, Edith II, 283
Buzby, Edith II, 287
Buzby, Edward P. II, 844
Buzby, Edward P. III, 57
Buzby, Eleanor III, 57
Buzby, Eleanor III, 111
Buzby, Eleanor E. II, 844
Buzby, Eleanor Edwards II, 785
Buzby, Eleanor Scattergood II, 785
Buzby, Elgar L. II, 308
Buzby, Elgar Leeds II, 308
Buzby, Elias II, 130
Buzby, Elias II, 146
Buzby, Elias II, 157
Buzby, Elias II, 317
Buzby, Elias II, 844
Buzby, Elias S. II, 146
Buzby, Elias S. II, 308
Buzby, Elias S. II, 317
Buzby, Eliza Adah II, 785
Buzby, Eliza Ann II, 169
Buzby, Eliza Ann II, 283
Buzby, Eliza S. II, 130
Buzby, Eliza S. II, 146
Buzby, Eliza S. II, 308
Buzby, Eliza S. II, 317
Buzby, Eliza S. II, 844
Buzby, Eliza. Ann III, 57
Buzby, Elizabeth II, 168
Buzby, Elizabeth II, 169
Buzby, Elizabeth II, 204
Buzby, Elizabeth II, 205
Buzby, Elizabeth II, 227
Buzby, Elizabeth II, 308
Buzby, Elizabeth II, 479
Buzby, Elizabeth II, 986
Buzby, Elizabeth II, 1017
Buzby, Elizabeth Ann II, 844
Buzby, Elizabeth Ann III, 57
Buzby, Elizabeth Anne II, 785
Buzby, Elizabeth H. II, 479
Buzby, Elizabeth L. II, 317
Buzby, Elizabeth L. II, 321
Buzby, Ella II, 785
Buzby, Ellen II, 731
Buzby, Ellen E. II, 844
Buzby, Ellen E. II, 874
Buzby, Emily W. II, 281
Buzby, Emily W. II, 283
Buzby, Ephraim Haines II, 205
Buzby, Esther II, 168
Buzby, Esther II, 283
Buzby, Evan II, 205
Buzby, Frances II, 479
Buzby, Frances Ann II, 479
Buzby, Frances W. II, 343
Buzby, Frances W. II, 479
Buzby, George II, 168
Buzby, George II, 169
Buzby, George II, 283
Buzby, George II, 844
Buzby, George D. II, 872
Buzby, George W. II, 867
Buzby, Grace II, 204
Buzby, Granville II, 308
Buzby, Granville W. II, 168
Buzby, Granville W. II, 205
Buzby, Granville W. II, 283
Buzby, Grenville W. II, 283
Buzby, Hannah II, 60
Buzby, Hannah II, 116
Buzby, Hannah II, 168
Buzby, Hannah II, 169
Buzby, Hannah II, 204
Buzby, Hannah II, 205
Buzby, Hannah II, 222
Buzby, Hannah II, 228
Buzby, Hannah II, 231
Buzby, Hannah II, 283
Buzby, Hannah II, 305
Buzby, Hannah II, 479
Buzby, Hannah II, 819
Buzby, Hannah H. II, 146
Buzby, Hannah H. II, 157
Buzby, Hannah J. II, 844
Buzby, Hannah J. II, 872
Buzby, Hannah M. II, 168
Buzby, Hannah M. II, 283
Buzby, Hannah P. II, 130
Buzby, Hannah P. II, 139
Buzby, Hannah P. II, 146
Buzby, Hannah S. II, 731
Buzby, Hannah W. II, 60
Buzby, Hannah W. II, 169
Buzby, Hannah W. II, 283
Buzby, Hannah W. II, 479
Buzby, Hannah Wills II, 479
Buzby, Helen Wilson II, 308
Buzby, Henry II, 785
Buzby, Henry II, 844
Buzby, Henry C. II, 844
Buzby, Henry C. II, 874
Buzby, Henry C. III, 57
Buzby, Howard II, 130
Buzby, Howard II, 146
Buzby, Howard II, 308
Buzby, Howard II, 317
Buzby, Howard II, 844
Buzby, Hudson II, 168
Buzby, Hudson II, 169
Buzby, Hudson II, 186
Buzby, Hudson II, 205
Buzby, Hudson II, 276
Buzby, Hudson II, 283
Buzby, Hudson II, 287
Buzby, Hudson II, 290
Buzby, Hudson II, 298
Buzby, Hudson II, 303
Buzby, Ida II, 844
Buzby, Ida II, 908
Buzby, Ida P. II, 844
Buzby, Ida R. II, 283
Buzby, Idella II, 785
Buzby, Idella Haines II, 844
Buzby, Isaac II, 130
Buzby, Isaac II, 139
Buzby, Isaac II, 146
Buzby, Isaac II, 168
Buzby, Isaac II, 169
Buzby, Isaac II, 204
Buzby, Isaac II, 205
Buzby, Isaac II, 317
Buzby, Isaac L. II, 168
Buzby, Isaac L. II, 283
Buzby, Isabella II, 148
Buzby, Isabella P. II, 148
Buzby, Jabez II, 204
Buzby, James S. II, 867
Buzby, James W. II, 479
Buzby, Jane II, 204
Buzby, Jane Elizabeth II, 308
Buzby, Jesse Milton II, 785
Buzby, John II, 168
Buzby, John II, 169
Buzby, John II, 204
Buzby, John II, 343
Buzby, John II, 479
Buzby, John William II, 205
Buzby, Jonathan II, 169
Buzby, Joseph II, 59
Buzby, Joseph II, 60
Buzby, Joseph II, 113
Buzby, Joseph II, 130
Buzby, Joseph II, 146
Buzby, Joseph II, 168
Buzby, Joseph II, 169
Buzby, Joseph II, 204
Buzby, Joseph II, 205
Buzby, Joseph II, 275
Buzby, Joseph II, 317
Buzby, Joseph E. II, 844
Buzby, Joseph E. III, 57
Buzby, Joseph S. II, 146
Buzby, Joseph S. II, 157
Buzby, Joseph W. II, 59
Buzby, Joseph W. II, 60
Buzby, Joseph W. II, 205
Buzby, Joseph W. II, 785
Buzby, Joseph, Jr. II, 205
Buzby, Josephine II, 130
Buzby, Josephine II, 308
Buzby, Josephine II, 317
Buzby, Lidy II, 204
Buzby, Louisa M. II, 844
Buzby, Louisa M. II, 874
Buzby, Lucy II, 130
Buzby, Lucy II, 146
Buzby, Lucy W. II, 146
Buzby, Lucy W. II, 148
Buzby, Lucy W. II, 844
Buzby, Luke S. II, 130
Buzby, Luke Smith II, 146
Buzby, Margaret II, 168
Buzby, Margaret II, 204
Buzby, Margaret II, 205
Buzby, Margaret II, 227
Buzby, Margaret II, 232
Buzby, Margaret II, 783
Buzby, Margaretta II, 205
Buzby, Maria II, 169
Buzby, Maria II, 785
Buzby, Maria T. II, 844
Buzby, Maria W. II, 283
Buzby, Mark H. II, 168
Buzby, Mark H. II, 281
Buzby, Mark H. II, 283
Buzby, Martha II, 168
Buzby, Martha II, 169
Buzby, Martha II, 186
Buzby, Martha II, 205
Buzby, Martha II, 283
Buzby, Martha II, 303
Buzby, Martha T. II, 169
Buzby, Martha T. II, 283
Buzby, Martha T. II, 287
Buzby, Mary II, 116
Buzby, Mary II, 168
Buzby, Mary II, 169
Buzby, Mary II, 204
Buzby, Mary II, 205
Buzby, Mary II, 212
Buzby, Mary II, 242
Buzby, Mary II, 285
Buzby, Mary II, 308
Buzby, Mary II, 317
Buzby, Mary II, 343
Buzby, Mary II, 479
Buzby, Mary II, 512
Buzby, Mary II, 785
Buzby, Mary Ann II, 168
Buzby, Mary Ann II, 169
Buzby, Mary Ann II, 205
Buzby, Mary Ann II, 283
Buzby, Mary Ann II, 287
Buzby, Mary Ann II, 298
Buzby, Mary Ann II, 299
Buzby, Mary Ann II, 303
Buzby, Mary Ann II, 308
Buzby, Mary B. II, 148
Buzby, Mary H. II, 205
Buzby, Mary H. II, 843
Buzby, Mary Jane II, 308
Buzby, Mary L. II, 479
Buzby, Mary W. II, 60
Buzby, Mary W. II, 130
Buzby, Mary W. II, 146
Buzby, Mary W. II, 202
Buzby, Mary W. II, 205
Buzby, Mary W. II, 308
Buzby, Mary W. II, 309
Buzby, Mary W. II, 317
Buzby, Mary W. II, 844
Buzby, Mary-Jane II, 317
Buzby, Matilday II, 315
Buzby, Milicent II, 130
Buzby, Milicent II, 139
Buzby, Millicent II, 24
Buzby, Millicent II, 780
Buzby, Millicent II, 797
Buzby, Milton W. II, 146
Buzby, Milton W. II, 844
Buzby, Milton Wright II, 785
Buzby, Miriam II, 283
Buzby, Miriam C. II, 168
Buzby, Miriam C. II, 169
Buzby, Miriam E. II, 169
Buzby, Miriam E. II, 283
Buzby, Miriam E. II, 306
Buzby, Mitton II, 130
Buzby, Mordecai II, 205
Buzby, Mordecai II, 785
Buzby, Mordecai II, 844
Buzby, Mordecai II, 874
Buzby, Mordecai III, 57
Buzby, Mordecai III, 111
Buzby, Mordecai III, 213
Buzby, Nathan II, 60
Buzby, Nathan II, 116
Buzby, Nathan B. II, 148
Buzby, Nathan H. II, 168
Buzby, Nathan H. II, 205
Buzby, Nathan H. II, 283
Buzby, Nathan W. II, 130
Buzby, Nathan W. II, 146
Buzby, Nathan W. II, 148
Buzby, Nathan W. II, 844
Buzby, Nathan W. II, 908
Buzby, Nathaniel II, 130
Buzby, Nathaniel II, 780
Buzby, Nathaniel II, 797
Buzby, Nellie II, 308
Buzby, Nicholas II, 168
Buzby, Nicholas II, 169
Buzby, Nicholas II, 188
Buzby, Nicholas II, 204
Buzby, Nicholas II, 205
Buzby, Nicholas II, 283
Buzby, Nicholas II, 731
Buzby, Nicholus II, 204
Buzby, Patience II, 59
Buzby, Patience II, 60
Buzby, Patience II, 168
Buzby, Patience II, 169
Buzby, Patience II, 204
Buzby, Patience II, 205
Buzby, Patience II, 231
Buzby, Patience II, 232
Buzby, Patience II, 242
Buzby, Patience II, 275
Buzby, Patience II, 276
Buzby, Patience II, 283
Buzby, Patience II, 307
Buzby, Patience II, 308
Buzby, Patience II, 317
Buzby, Patience M. II, 169
Buzby, Patience S. II, 308
Buzby, Patience S. II, 317
Buzby, Patience S. II, 322
Buzby, Patience W. II, 819
Buzby, Paul II, 205
Buzby, Paul W. II, 169
Buzby, Phebe W. II, 308
Buzby, Phebe W. II, 317
Buzby, Phebe W. II, 327
Buzby, Phinehas II, 169
Buzby, Rachael II, 205
Buzby, Rachel II, 59
Buzby, Rachel II, 60
Buzby, Rachel II, 168
Buzby, Rachel II, 169
Buzby, Rachel II, 186
Buzby, Rachel II, 205
Buzby, Rachel II, 276
Buzby, Rachel II, 283
Buzby, Rachel II, 287
Buzby, Rachel II, 290
Buzby, Rachel II, 298
Buzby, Rachel II, 303
Buzby, Rachel II, 310
Buzby, Rachel W. II, 169
Buzby, Rachel W. II, 205
Buzby, Rachel W. II, 283
Buzby, Rachel W. II, 700
Buzby, Rachel W. II, 731
Buzby, Rebecca II, 146
Buzby, Rebecca II, 168
Buzby, Rebecca II, 169
Buzby, Rebecca II, 188
Buzby, Rebecca II, 205
Buzby, Rebecca II, 283
Buzby, Rebecca II, 706
Buzby, Rebecca II, 785
Buzby, Rebecca III, 57
Buzby, Rebecca A. II, 146
Buzby, Rebecca D. II, 308
Buzby, Rebecca D. II, 317
Buzby, Rebecca D. II, 318
Buzby, Rebecca E. II, 283
Buzby, Rebecca M. II, 146
Buzby, Rebecca M. II, 283
Buzby, Rebecca S. II, 283
Buzby, Rebecca S. II, 290
Buzby, Richard II, 168
Buzby, Richard II, 169
Buzby, Richard II, 204
Buzby, Richard II, 205
Buzby, Richard II, 283
Buzby, Richard II, 287
Buzby, Richard II, 299
Buzby, Richard II, 303
Buzby, Richard II, 308
Buzby, Robert C. II, 205
Buzby, Robert C. II, 283
Buzby, Robert Coe II, 168
Buzby, Robert Coe II, 205
Buzby, Robert Coes II, 317
Buzby, Robert E. II, 844
Buzby, Robert E. III, 57
Buzby, Robert Evans II, 785
Buzby, Robt. C. II, 168
Buzby, Ruth II, 60

Buzby, Ruth II, 113
Buzby, Ruth II, 116
Buzby, Ruth II, 130
Buzby, Ruth II, 131
Buzby, Ruth II, 146
Buzby, Ruth II, 148
Buzby, Ruth II, 205
Buzby, Ruth Anna II, 148
Buzby, Ruth Anna II, 169
Buzby, Ruth Anna II, 283
Buzby, Ruth Anna II, 284
Buzby, Samuel II, 59
Buzby, Samuel II, 60
Buzby, Samuel II, 169
Buzby, Samuel II, 204
Buzby, Samuel II, 205
Buzby, Samuel II, 785
Buzby, Samuel W. II, 168
Buzby, Samuel W. II, 283
Buzby, Sarah II, 283
Buzby, Sarah II, 305
Buzby, Sarah II, 797
Buzby, Sarah D. II, 281
Buzby, Sarah D. II, 283
Buzby, Sarah P. II, 169
Buzby, Sarah P. II, 283
Buzby, Stacy M. II, 205
Buzby, Stacy M. II, 283
Buzby, Susan II, 130
Buzby, Susan II, 308
Buzby, Susan II, 1047
Buzby, Susan II, 1059
Buzby, Susan A. II, 146
Buzby, Susan A. II, 308
Buzby, Susan A. II, 317
Buzby, Susan S. II, 146
Buzby, Susan S. II, 157
Buzby, Susanna II, 205
Buzby, Susanna II, 214
Buzby, Susanna D. II, 731
Buzby, Susannah II, 169
Buzby, Susannah II, 202
Buzby, Susannah II, 227
Buzby, Susannah II, 283
Buzby, Susannah D. II, 169
Buzby, Tabitha II, 169
Buzby, Tabitha II, 204
Buzby, Thomas II, 168
Buzby, Thomas II, 204
Buzby, Thomas II, 205
Buzby, Thomas II, 227
Buzby, Thomas II, 228
Buzby, Thomas II, 308
Buzby, Thomas II, 479
Buzby, Thomas II, 512
Buzby, Thomas Harvey II, 308
Buzby, Thomas T. II, 169
Buzby, Thomas T. II, 283
Buzby, Thomas, Jr. II, 204
Buzby, Thomas, Jr. II, 205
Buzby, Walter II, 281
Buzby, Walter J. II, 283
Buzby, Walter S. II, 169
Buzby, Wd. Rebecca Dallas II, 780
Buzby, William II, 168
Buzby, William II, 169
Buzby, William II, 202
Buzby, William II, 204
Buzby, William II, 205
Buzby, William II, 214
Buzby, William II, 227
Buzby, William II, 283
Buzby, William J. III, 57
Buzby, William L. II, 169
Buzby, William M. II, 168
Buzby, William M. II, 283
Buzby, William M. III, 57
Buzby, William N. II, 146
Buzby, William P. II, 283
Buzby, William Paul II, 283
Buzby, William, Jr. II, 205
Buzby, Wm. II, 479
Buzby, Wm. II, 867
Buzby, Wm. A. II, 60
Buzby, Wm. M. II, 844
Buzby, Wm. N. II, 59
Buzby, Wm. N. II, 843
Buzby, Wm. N. II, 867
Buzby, Wm. P. II, 731
Buzby, Wm. Paul II, 731
Buzby, Wm. Shultz, Jr. II, 908
Buzby, Wm. W. II, 843
Buzeby, Ann II, 59
Buzeby, Ann II, 77
Buzzard, Frank V, 227
Buzzard, Louella V, 453
Buzzard, Luella V, 453
Buzzard, Mary Ann V, 224
Buzzard, Mary Ann V, 227
Buzzard, Sarah V, 453
Buzzard, Selemma V, 245
Buzzard, Silemma V, 227
Buzzard, Wm. V, 453
Byar, Jane I, 39
Byar, Jane I, 61
Byard, Charles V, 664
Byard, Clyde V, 662
Byard, Elizabeth V, 479
Byard, Lenna V, 664
Byard, Nancy V, 376
Byard, Nancy V, 662
Bybee, Ann VI, 798
Bybee, Benjamin VI, 802
Bybee, Dorothy VI, 798
Bybee, Edw. VI, 831
Bybee, Edward VI, 798
Bybee, Edward VI, 808
Bybee, Edward VI, 827
Bybee, Elizabeth VI, 802
Bybee, Judith VI, 808
Bybee, Patsey VI, 802
Bybee, Sally VI, 827
Bybee, William VI, 802
Bybee, William VI, 850
Bye, ??? IV, 377
Bye, Abel IV, 1115
Bye, Abel W. IV, 516
Bye, Abel W. IV, 1088
Bye, Abel W. IV, 1090
Bye, Abraham Brown II, 986
Bye, Adaline IV, 822
Bye, Adaline IV, 841
Bye, Adaline M. IV, 692
Bye, Adaline M. IV, 757
Bye, Alva May II, 785
Bye, Amy IV, 1090
Bye, Amy Elizabeth IV, 1090
Bye, Amy Elizabeth IV, 1115
Bye, Amy Elizabeth IV, 1116
Bye, Andrew M. II, 844
Bye, Andrew Moore II, 785
Bye, Andrew Moore II, 844
Bye, Ann IV, 805
Bye, Ann IV, 827
Bye, Ann IV, 841
Bye, Anna M. IV, 1090
Bye, Anne II, 955
Bye, Anne II, 982
Bye, Arthur Edwin II, 785
Bye, Caroline II, 785
Bye, Caroline II, 844
Bye, Caroline II, 925
Bye, Catharine IV, 377
Bye, Deborah II, 957
Bye, E. Mortimer II, 844
Bye, Edith Lewis II, 785
Bye, Edith Lewis II, 844
Bye, Edith Lewis II, 913
Bye, Edward IV, 516
Bye, Edward IV, 1090
Bye, Edward IV, 1115
Bye, Edward Samuel IV, 1090
Bye, Elisha IV, 516
Bye, Elisha IV, 1090
Bye, Elisha Elizabeth Lewis IV, 1090
Bye, Elisha J. I, 233
Bye, Elisha J. IV, 1090
Bye, Eliza IV, 1090
Bye, Elizabeth II, 957
Bye, Elizabeth II, 979
Bye, Elizabeth IV, 516
Bye, Elizabeth IV, 797
Bye, Elizabeth IV, 805
Bye, Elizabeth IV, 1090
Bye, Elizabeth V, 892
Bye, Elizabeth, Jr. II, 986
Bye, Elizabeth, Jr. II, 1004
Bye, Ella Taylor II, 785
Bye, Ellen B. V, 396
Bye, Emily IV, 1090
Bye, Emily IV, 1117
Bye, Emily H. IV, 1090
Bye, Emily T. IV, 1090
Bye, Enoch Morton II, 844
Bye, Enoch Morton II, 925
Bye, Eva D. I, 233
Bye, Helen May II, 785
Bye, Hezekiah II, 957
Bye, Hezekiah IV, 841
Bye, Hugh V, 892
Bye, John II, 205
Bye, John II, 479
Bye, John II, 957
Bye, John II, 986
Bye, John II, 1021
Bye, John IV, 516
Bye, Jonas IV, 185
Bye, Jonas IV, 516
Bye, Jonas IV, 1090
Bye, Jonas IV, 1097
Bye, Jonathan IV, 185
Bye, Jonathan IV, 231
Bye, Jonathan IV, 322
Bye, Jonathan IV, 377
Bye, Jonathan IV, 516
Bye, Jonathan, Jr. IV, 185
Bye, Jonathan, Jr. IV, 226
Bye, Joseph IV, 1090
Bye, Joseph Addison IV, 1090
Bye, Joshua IV, 322
Bye, Joshua IV, 377
Bye, Lewis IV, 516
Bye, Lewis W. IV, 557
Bye, Lewis W. IV, 1090
Bye, Lewis W. IV, 1121
Bye, Louis IV, 1090
Bye, Lydia Jane IV, 1088
Bye, Lydia Jane IV, 1090
Bye, Lydia Jane IV, 1115
Bye, Mahlon Jenkinson II, 785
Bye, Margaret II, 479
Bye, Marguerette Taylor II, 785
Bye, Mariah IV, 377
Bye, Martha II, 957
Bye, Martha II, 971
Bye, Martha II, 986
Bye, Martha II, 1021
Bye, Martha IV, 516
Bye, Martha IV, 519
Bye, Martha IV, 1090
Bye, Martha IV, 1097
Bye, Mary II, 957
Bye, Mary IV, 185
Bye, Mary IV, 223
Bye, Mary IV, 226
Bye, Mary IV, 231
Bye, Mary IV, 322
Bye, Mary IV, 377
Bye, Mary IV, 414
Bye, Mary IV, 512
Bye, Mary IV, 513
Bye, Mary IV, 516
Bye, Mary IV, 1090
Bye, Mary IV, 1097
Bye, Mary Eliza IV, 1090
Bye, Mary R. IV, 516
Bye, Mary R. IV, 535
Bye, Mary R. H. IV, 516
Bye, Mary T. IV, 1090
Bye, Mary T. IV, 1115
Bye, May L. II, 844
Bye, Mercy II, 955
Bye, Phebe II, 844
Bye, Phebe IV, 377
Bye, Phebe IV, 1090
Bye, Phebe H. IV, 516
Bye, Phebe H. IV, 557
Bye, Phebe H. IV, 1090
Bye, Phebe H. IV, 1121
Bye, Philis P. II, 844
Bye, Philis P. II, 925
Bye, Pusey P. II, 844
Bye, Pusey P. II, 925
Bye, Pusey Passmore II, 785
Bye, Pusey Passmore II, 844
Bye, Rachel IV, 377
Bye, Raymond Taylor II, 785
Bye, Reading V, 396
Bye, Rebecca Louisa IV, 1090
Bye, Samuel II, 957
Bye, Samuel IV, 185
Bye, Samuel IV, 516
Bye, Samuel IV, 1090
Bye, Samuel IV, 1117
Bye, Samuel K. IV, 1090
Bye, Sarah II, 479
Bye, Sarah II, 684
Bye, Sarah II, 957
Bye, Sarah II, 986
Bye, Sarah II, 1021
Bye, Sarah IV, 516
Bye, Sarah IV, 520
Bye, Sarah IV, 613
Bye, Sarah IV, 805
Bye, Sarah V, 397
Bye, Sarah V, 892
Bye, Susanna II, 684
Bye, Susanna IV, 185
Bye, Susanna IV, 231
Bye, Susanna IV, 377
Bye, Susanna IV, 516
Bye, Thomas II, 479
Bye, Thomas II, 684
Bye, Thomas II, 955
Bye, Thomas II, 986
Bye, Thomas II, 1021
Bye, Walter E. IV, 1090
Bye, William IV, 516
Bye, William S. IV, 516
Bye, William S. IV, 1090
Bye, Wm. IV, 1090
Bye, Wm. S. IV, 1090
Byerly, Darby II, 785
Byerly, David B. III, 57
Byerly, David D. II, 844
Byerly, David D. III, 57
Byerly, David D. III, 109
Byerly, David Davis II, 785
Byerly, David Davis II, 844
Byerly, David Davis II, 937
Byerly, David Davis III, 57
Byerly, David Homer II, 785
Byerly, David Homer III, 57
Byerly, Davis Homer II, 844
Byerly, Dr. Wm. Elwood III, 58
Byerly, Elizabeth Julia II, 731
Byerly, Elizabeth Julia II, 844
Byerly, Elizabeth W. II, 840
Byerly, Elizabeth W. II, 844
Byerly, Elizabeth Wayne III, 57
Byerly, Ellwood II, 731
Byerly, Ellwood II, 785
Byerly, Ellwood II, 844
Byerly, Ellwood III, 57
Byerly, Ellwood III, 58
Byerly, Elwood II, 731
Byerly, Elwood II, 844
Byerly, Frances Rebecca II, 844
Byerly, Hannah B. II, 844
Byerly, Hannah Bunting II, 785
Byerly, James II, 731
Byerly, James V, 897
Byerly, James D. II, 731
Byerly, James D. II, 844
Byerly, Julia Elizabeth II, 785
Byerly, Martha III, 57
Byerly, Martha G. II, 844
Byerly, Martha G. III, 57
Byerly, Martha P. II, 844
Byerly, Rebecca II, 785
Byerly, Rebecca II, 844
Byerly, Rebecca II, 937
Byerly, Rebecca III, 57
Byerly, Rebecca F. III, 109
Byerly, Rebecca Frances II, 785
Byerly, Rebecca Frances III, 57
Byerly, Rebecca P. II, 844
Byerly, Rebecca P. III, 57
Byerly, Rebecca P. III, 58
Byerly, Rebecca Potts II, 785
Byerly, Sarah III, 57
Byerly, Sarah III, 109
Byerly, Sarah A. III, 57
Byerly, Sarah Ann II, 731
Byerly, Sarah Ann II, 773
Byerly, Sarah Ann II, 785
Byerly, Sarah Ann II, 844
Byerly, Sarah Ann II, 937
Byerly, Sarah Ann III, 57
Byerly, Stephen II, 731
Byerly, Stephen II, 785
Byerly, Stephen II, 844
Byerly, Stephen II, 937
Byerly, William E. III, 57
Byerly, Wm. E. III, 57
Byerly, Wm. Ellwood II, 844
Byerly, Wm. Elwood II, 785
Byers, Alice G. VI, 459
Byers, Alice G. White VI, 375
Byers, Alice G. White VI, 460
Byers, Beatrice V, 838
Byers, Ben VI, 375
Byers, Ben VI, 459
Byers, Ben VI, 460
Byers, Drucilla V, 949
Byers, Drusilla V, 950
Byers, Ona Mae IV, 989
Byfield, Ann II, 442
Byfield, Thomas II, 442
Byler, Paul IV, 865
Byllynge, Edward II, 17
Byllynge, Edward II, 163
Bylser, Robert II, 442
Byram, Alfred I, 39
Byram, Augustus I, 39
Byram, Bryan I, 39
Byram, Bryant I, 39
Byram, Cader I, 39
Byram, Caleb I, 39
Byram, Christian I, 39
Byram, Edwin I, 39
Byram, Eli I, 39
Byram, Exum I, 39
Byram, Isaac I, 39
Byram, James I, 39
Byram, Jemima I, 39
Byram, Jemmima I, 39
Byram, Joel I, 39
Byram, John I, 39
Byram, Kader I, 39
Byram, Lydia I, 39
Byram, Lydia I, 50
Byram, Lydia I, 53
Byram, Miriam I, 39
Byram, Moses I, 39
Byram, Nathan I, 39
Byram, Orpah I, 39
Byram, Robert I, 39
Byram, Sarah I, 39
Byram, Sibba I, 39
Byram, William I, 39
Byrd, ??? III, 58
Byrd, ??? VI, 149
Byrd, Alice VI, 57
Byrd, Alice VI, 59
Byrd, Amy III, 58
Byrd, Amy III, 334
Byrd, Ann III, 58
Byrd, Annie Melissa I, 212
Byrd, Betsy Ann III, 34
Byrd, Box Elder VI, 57
Byrd, Catherine G. III, 34
Byrd, Col. William VI, 23
Byrd, Daisy I. III, 34
Byrd, Dr. Orphens III, 34
Byrd, Eliza III, 34
Byrd, Elizabeth III, 58
Byrd, Elizabeth III, 250
Byrd, Elizabeth III, 378
Byrd, Elizabeth III, 388
Byrd, Elizabeth III, 389
Byrd, Elizabeth VI, 802
Byrd, Elizabeth R. III, 378
Byrd, Elizabeth R. VI, 375
Byrd, Ella IV, 1273
Byrd, Ella Leslie II, 785
Byrd, Ella Leslie II, 844
Byrd, Ella R. III, 58
Byrd, Ella R. III, 263
Byrd, Elvy VI, 56
Byrd, Elvy VI, 57
Byrd, Elvy VI, 78
Byrd, Evelyn III, 58
Byrd, Evelyn III, 334
Byrd, Frances Emma III, 34
Byrd, Geo. Radcliffe III, 58
Byrd, Geo. Radcliffe III, 334
Byrd, George V, 156
Byrd, George VI, 802
Byrd, Hannah III, 58
Byrd, Henry L. III, 34
Byrd, Howard VI, 57
Byrd, Howard E. VI, 57
Byrd, Irma Alice VI, 57
Byrd, James III, 58
Byrd, James III, 250
Byrd, James III, 378
Byrd, James III, 388
Byrd, James III, 389
Byrd, James Clark IV, 1273
Byrd, Joseph III, 58
Byrd, Josephus VI, 56
Byrd, Josephus VI, 57
Byrd, Josephus VI, 59
Byrd, Leonard J. VI, 57
Byrd, Levi I, 212
Byrd, Lois M. VI, 57
Byrd, Lucilla K. III, 34
Byrd, Margaret III, 58
Byrd, Margaret III, 263
Byrd, Margaret VI, 693
Byrd, Marrietta III, 34
Byrd, Mary III, 370
Byrd, Mary III, 378
Byrd, Mary VI, 91
Byrd, Mary Ann I, 212
Byrd, Mary B. III, 388
Byrd, Mary J. VI, 56
Byrd, Mary J. VI, 57
Byrd, Mary J. VI, 78
Byrd, Mathew III, 34
Byrd, Matthew III, 34
Byrd, Miriam C. VI, 57
Byrd, Phebe III, 378
Byrd, Phebe III, 389
Byrd, Philip G. II, 844
Byrd, Philip G. III, 58
Byrd, Philip G. III, 263
Byrd, Phillip Glenn II, 785
Byrd, Polly VI, 802
Byrd, Richard III, 58
Byrd, Sarah III, 34
Byrd, Sarah M. III, 34
Byrd, Susannah IV, 1273
Byrd, Thomas III, 58
Byrd, Thomas G. III, 378
Byrd, Thomas McArthur V, 479
Byrd, William VI, 148
Byrd, Wm. III, 34
Byrens, James VI, 939
Byries, Ruby V, 729
Byrkett, Sarah V, 743
Byrn, Carrie T. V, 552

Byrn, Ella Mary V, 552
Byrn, Mary V, 552
Byrn, Mary Elizabeth V, 552
Byrne, ??? III, 58
Byrne, Carrie T. V, 662
Byrne, Ella M. V, 662
Byrne, J. P. III, 210
Byrne, James II, 479
Byrne, John III, 58
Byrne, John III, 351
Byrne, Mary III, 58
Byrne, Mary III, 210
Byrne, Mary V, 662
Byrne, R. J. V, 662
Byrne, Ruth II, 479
Byrne, Samuel II, 479
Byrne, Sarah II, 479
Byrne, Selena III, 58
Byrne, Selena Grace III, 58
Byrne, Selena Grace III, 351
Byrnes, ??? II, 479
Byrnes, ??? III, 58
Byrnes, ??? III, 335
Byrnes, Ann P. III, 58
Byrnes, Caroline III, 58
Byrnes, Daniel II, 479
Byrnes, Daniel III, 58
Byrnes, Daniel III, 397
Byrnes, Dinah III, 58
Byrnes, Dinah III, 397
Byrnes, Eleanor III, 58
Byrnes, Elizabeth III, 58
Byrnes, Esther III, 58
Byrnes, Hannah II, 60
Byrnes, Hannah II, 112
Byrnes, Jacob F. II, 844
Byrnes, Jacob F. II, 941
Byrnes, Jacob F. III, 58
Byrnes, James II, 479
Byrnes, James IV, 642
Byrnes, John III, 58
Byrnes, Jonathan III, 58
Byrnes, Joseph III, 58
Byrnes, Joseph III, 71
Byrnes, Joshua II, 479
Byrnes, Lydia II, 408
Byrnes, Lydia III, 58
Byrnes, Mary II, 844
Byrnes, Mary II, 941
Byrnes, Mary III, 58
Byrnes, Mary III, 335
Byrnes, Mary IV, 642
Byrnes, Mary Ann III, 209
Byrnes, Rachel II, 479
Byrnes, Rachel IV, 613
Byrnes, Rachel IV, 642
Byrnes, Rebecca III, 58
Byrnes, Rebecca P. III, 58
Byrnes, Rebecca P. III, 71
Byrnes, Robert Ralston III, 58
Byrnes, Ruth II, 479
Byrnes, Samuel II, 60
Byrnes, Samuel II, 112
Byrnes, Samuel II, 479
Byrnes, Sarah II, 479
Byrnes, Sarah III, 397
Byrnes, Sarah III, 457
Byrnes, Sarah Palmer II, 844
Byrnes, Selena III, 58
Byrnes, Selena Grace III, 58
Byrnes, Thomas S. III, 58
Byrnes, Walter III, 58
Byrnes, Walter F. III, 58
Byrnes, William III, 397
Byrnes, William III, 457
Byrns, Daniel II, 479
Byrns, Jane IV, 864
Byrns, Jane IV, 865
Byrns, John IV, 865
Byrns, Mary IV, 865
Byrns, Mary VI, 302
Byrns, Milicent I, 711
Byrns, Milicent I, 721
Byrns, Millicent I, 697
Byrns, Millicent I, 702
Byron, ??? III, 246
Byron, Ada III, 121
Byron, Ada III, 246
Byron, Enos V, 988
Byron, Sally III, 58
Byron, Seth III, 58
Byron, Wd. Ada III, 58
Byron, Wd. Ada III, 120
Byrum, Annie I, 613
Byrum, Annie Leonard I, 631
Byrum, Benjamin F. V, 827
Byrum, Christian I, 39
Byrum, Eli V, 827
Byrum, Isaac I, 39
Byrum, Jemima I, 39
Byrum, Jemima I, 48
Byrum, Joel I, 39
Byrum, Lydia I, 39
Byrum, Lydia I, 87
Byrum, Nathan I, 39
Byrum, Nathan I, 48
Byrum, Orpah I, 39
Byrum, R. W. I, 613
Byrum, Robert V, 827
Byrum, William I, 39
Byrum, William I, 87
Byrum, William, Jr. V, 827
Byshop, Elizabeth I, 1027
Byshop, Elizabeth I, 1029
Byshop, Thomas I, 1027
Byxbe, Geo. E. III, 112

C???, Bertha III, 71
Cabel, George VI, 820
Cabell, Alice VI, 802
Cabell, Alice W. VI, 804
Cabell, Ann E. VI, 802
Cabell, Betsey VI, 888
Cabell, Elizabeth VI, 802
Cabell, Elizabeth L. VI, 802
Cabell, Frederic VI, 802
Cabell, George VI, 802
Cabell, George VI, 804
Cabell, George VI, 824
Cabell, Harrian VI, 888
Cabell, James VI, 802
Cabell, James Branch VI, 25
Cabell, John VI, 802
Cabell, John VI, 888
Cabell, Joseph VI, 802
Cabell, Mary B. VI, 888
Cabell, Mays VI, 814
Cabell, Nannie B. VI, 852
Cabell, Paul C. VI, 888
Cabell, Pauline J. VI, 824
Cabell, Robert J. VI, 888
Cabell, Sarah VI, 802
Cabell, William VI, 802
Cable, Alice I, 865
Cable, Ann I, 376
Cable, Eunice V, 798
Cable, Hiram I, 376
Cable, John R. I, 376
Cable, Mary F. I, 376
Cable, Phebe I, 376
Cable, William I, 376
Cacker, D. C. IV, 1151
Cacker, David IV, 1151
Cackler, David IV, 1151
Cacy, Levina V, 156
Cacy, Levina V, 730
Cadamy, James V, 227
Cadamy, John V, 227
Cadbury, Anna K. II, 701
Cadbury, Benjamin II, 701
Cadbury, Caroline W. V, 897
Cadbury, Emma II, 701
Cadbury, Joel II, 479
Cadbury, Joel II, 701
Cadbury, John W. II, 701
Cadbury, William II, 701
Cadden, Edna V, 662
Cadden, Edna V, 663
Cadden, James J. V, 662
Cadden, James J. V, 663
Caddick, Mrs. Hallie IV, 1309
Caddick, Thos. Henry IV, 1309
Caddick, Walter G. IV, 1309
Cade, Adaline V, 321
Cade, Addie V, 321
Cade, Adeline V, 321
Cade, Arthur V, 321
Cade, Elta V, 321
Cade, Etta V, 321
Cade, Frances White V, 321
Cade, Francis V, 321
Cade, Harry V, 321
Cade, Henry V, 321
Cade, Mary II, 53
Cade, Mary II, 60
Cade, Sarah V, 321
Cade, Thomas V, 321
Cade, Thomas E. V, 321
Cademy, Anta May V, 227
Cademy, Carrie V, 321
Cademy, Cora V, 227
Cademy, Cora B. V, 227
Cademy, Effie Pearl Walen V, 227
Cademy, James V, 227
Cademy, John V, 227
Cademy, Joseph V, 227
Cademy, Laura V, 227
Cadlawader, Leah V, 479
Cadle, Lavina IV, 567
Cadle, Lavina IV, 570
Cadness, Martha III, 388
Cadwalader, ??? IV, 377
Cadwalader, ??? IV, 687
Cadwalader, ??? VI, 348
Cadwalader, Aaron V, 33
Cadwalader, Aaron V, 988
Cadwalader, Abby IV, 186
Cadwalader, Abby IV, 930
Cadwalader, Abby IV, 934
Cadwalader, Abigail IV, 185
Cadwalader, Abner V, 34
Cadwalader, Abner V, 376
Cadwalader, Abner VI, 350
Cadwalader, Abram IV, 52
Cadwalader, Achilles V, 34
Cadwalader, Achilles V, 968
Cadwalader, Achilles D. V, 33
Cadwalader, Achsar IV, 516
Cadwalader, Ada B. V, 34
Cadwalader, Adah B. V, 34
Cadwalader, Agness IV, 52
Cadwalader, Albert D. V, 34
Cadwalader, Albert D. V, 479
Cadwalader, Alfred IV, 78
Cadwalader, Alfred IV, 323
Cadwalader, Alfred IV, 377
Cadwalader, Allan Jonah IV, 614
Cadwalader, Allen IV, 77
Cadwalader, Allen IV, 78
Cadwalader, Allen J. IV, 614
Cadwalader, Allen J. IV, 649
Cadwalader, Amasa IV, 186
Cadwalader, Amasa IV, 516
Cadwalader, Amos I, 961
Cadwalader, Amos I, 1003
Cadwalader, Amos VI, 350
Cadwalader, Amy IV, 77
Cadwalader, Amy IV, 108
Cadwalader, Amy IV, 655
Cadwalader, Amy V, 321
Cadwalader, Amy VI, 303
Cadwalader, Amy VI, 350
Cadwalader, Andrew V, 33
Cadwalader, Andrew V, 34
Cadwalader, Andrew V, 524
Cadwalader, Andrew W. V, 34
Cadwalader, Andrew W. V, 35
Cadwalader, Andrew W. V, 111
Cadwalader, Ann II, 987
Cadwalader, Ann II, 1029
Cadwalader, Ann II, 1031
Cadwalader, Ann II, 1047
Cadwalader, Ann IV, 77
Cadwalader, Ann IV, 86
Cadwalader, Ann IV, 322
Cadwalader, Ann IV, 516
Cadwalader, Ann IV, 613
Cadwalader, Ann IV, 667
Cadwalader, Ann IV, 687
Cadwalader, Ann IV, 787
Cadwalader, Ann Eliza V, 33
Cadwalader, Anna IV, 77
Cadwalader, Anna IV, 536
Cadwalader, Anna IV, 687
Cadwalader, Anna Hannah IV, 614
Cadwalader, Anna Howard IV, 516
Cadwalader, Anne IV, 186
Cadwalader, Annie IV, 612
Cadwalader, Annie H. IV, 667
Cadwalader, Annie H. IV, 687
Cadwalader, Aquilla V, 33
Cadwalader, Aquilla V, 34
Cadwalader, Asa IV, 71
Cadwalader, Asa IV, 77
Cadwalader, Asa IV, 185
Cadwalader, Asa IV, 930
Cadwalader, Belinda IV, 510
Cadwalader, Belinda IV, 516
Cadwalader, Belle V, 552
Cadwalader, Benjamin II, 987
Cadwalader, Benjamin II, 1047
Cadwalader, Benjamin V, 33
Cadwalader, Betsy V, 34
Cadwalader, Betsy V, 321
Cadwalader, Betsy VI, 303
Cadwalader, Birone V, 34
Cadwalader, Byram V, 299
Cadwalader, Byrom I, 961
Cadwalader, Byrom I, 1003
Cadwalader, Byrom VI, 350
Cadwalader, Caleb VI, 479
Cadwalader, Caroline IV, 516
Cadwalader, Caroline IV, 520
Cadwalader, Catharine IV, 613
Cadwalader, Catharine IV, 614
Cadwalader, Catharine V, 321
Cadwalader, Catharine V, 326
Cadwalader, Catherine V, 34
Cadwalader, Celesta M. IV, 614
Cadwalader, Celesta M. IV, 665
Cadwalader, Charles II, 987
Cadwalader, Charles V, 34
Cadwalader, Charles V, 968
Cadwalader, Charles Edward V, 33
Cadwalader, Charles T. V, 33
Cadwalader, Christena IV, 185
Cadwalader, Christena IV, 212
Cadwalader, Christian IV, 323
Cadwalader, Christian IV, 334
Cadwalader, Christiana IV, 186
Cadwalader, Christiana IV, 516
Cadwalader, Christina IV, 323
Cadwalader, Christopher IV, 516
Cadwalader, Clarkson V, 33
Cadwalader, Clarkson V, 34
Cadwalader, Clinton V, 552
Cadwalader, Clinton H. V, 34
Cadwalader, Cyrus II, 987
Cadwalader, Cyrus II, 1025
Cadwalader, Cyrus II, 1031
Cadwalader, Cyrus II, 1032
Cadwalader, Cyrus II, 1047
Cadwalader, Cyrus II, 1070
Cadwalader, Dallas P. IV, 614
Cadwalader, Dallas P. IV, 649
Cadwalader, Daniel IV, 667
Cadwalader, David II, 987
Cadwalader, David IV, 78
Cadwalader, David IV, 192
Cadwalader, David IV, 310
Cadwalader, David IV, 323
Cadwalader, David IV, 340
Cadwalader, David IV, 516
Cadwalader, David V, 33
Cadwalader, David V, 34
Cadwalader, Deborah IV, 613
Cadwalader, Deborah IV, 614
Cadwalader, Deborah IV, 687
Cadwalader, Deborah V, 33
Cadwalader, Deborah V, 34
Cadwalader, Deborah V, 54
Cadwalader, Deborah V, 968
Cadwalader, Dillon IV, 78
Cadwalader, Dillon IV, 323
Cadwalader, Dora P. V, 34
Cadwalader, Dorah Priscilla V, 34
Cadwalader, Dorothy Cheyney V, 35
Cadwalader, Dr. Jonah C. V, 35
Cadwalader, Edgar IV, 934
Cadwalader, Edgar M. IV, 614
Cadwalader, Edgar M. IV, 934
Cadwalader, Edith IV, 77
Cadwalader, Edith IV, 78
Cadwalader, Edith IV, 185
Cadwalader, Edith IV, 186
Cadwalader, Edith IV, 192
Cadwalader, Edith IV, 377
Cadwalader, Edith IV, 516
Cadwalader, Edith IV, 572
Cadwalader, Edith IV, 687
Cadwalader, Edith IV, 787
Cadwalader, Edith T. IV, 1051
Cadwalader, Edith T. IV, 1090
Cadwalader, Edith T. IV, 1113
Cadwalader, Edward II, 480
Cadwalader, Edward II, 600
Cadwalader, Edwin IV, 377
Cadwalader, Edwin IV, 687
Cadwalader, Edwin C. IV, 687
Cadwalader, Edwin F. Holloway IV, 516
Cadwalader, Eleanor I, 1003
Cadwalader, Eleanor I, 1008
Cadwalader, Eleanor I, 1011
Cadwalader, Eleanor IV, 614
Cadwalader, Eleanor IV, 655
Cadwalader, Eleanor VI, 350
Cadwalader, Elen IV, 614
Cadwalader, Elenor VI, 350
Cadwalader, Eli IV, 77
Cadwalader, Eli IV, 613
Cadwalader, Eli IV, 614
Cadwalader, Eli IV, 631
Cadwalader, Eli V, 33
Cadwalader, Eli V, 34
Cadwalader, Elinor VI, 350
Cadwalader, Elisa IV, 614
Cadwalader, Eliza IV, 185
Cadwalader, Eliza IV, 186
Cadwalader, Eliza IV, 239
Cadwalader, Eliza IV, 516
Cadwalader, Eliza IV, 613
Cadwalader, Eliza IV, 660
Cadwalader, Eliza V, 376
Cadwalader, Eliza V, 552
Cadwalader, Eliza Jane V, 662
Cadwalader, Elizabeth I, 1003
Cadwalader, Elizabeth II, 987
Cadwalader, Elizabeth II, 1025
Cadwalader, Elizabeth II, 1047
Cadwalader, Elizabeth IV, 77
Cadwalader, Elizabeth IV, 78
Cadwalader, Elizabeth IV, 141
Cadwalader, Elizabeth IV, 186
Cadwalader, Elizabeth IV, 239
Cadwalader, Elizabeth IV, 266
Cadwalader, Elizabeth IV, 322
Cadwalader, Elizabeth IV, 516
Cadwalader, Elizabeth IV, 613
Cadwalader, Elizabeth IV, 631
Cadwalader, Elizabeth IV, 667
Cadwalader, Elizabeth V, 33
Cadwalader, Elizabeth V, 34
Cadwalader, Elizabeth V, 60
Cadwalader, Elizabeth V, 149
Cadwalader, Elizabeth V, 156
Cadwalader, Elizabeth V, 968
Cadwalader, Elizabeth VI, 303
Cadwalader, Elizabeth VI, 350
Cadwalader, Elizabeth VI, 353
Cadwalader, Elizabeth A. V, 34
Cadwalader, Elizabeth Ann V, 33
Cadwalader, Elizabeth G. V, 34
Cadwalader, Ellen IV, 613
Cadwalader, Ellen C. IV, 614
Cadwalader, Ellen C. IV, 637
Cadwalader, Ellen T. IV, 613
Cadwalader, Ellin T. IV, 614
Cadwalader, Elma IV, 77
Cadwalader, Elma IV, 78
Cadwalader, Elma IV, 687
Cadwalader, Elma IV, 725
Cadwalader, Elma D. IV, 614
Cadwalader, Elma D. IV, 619
Cadwalader, Emlin IV, 78
Cadwalader, Emlin IV, 377
Cadwalader, Emma W. IV, 1273
Cadwalader, Enos V, 33
Cadwalader, Enos V, 34
Cadwalader, Esther IV, 606
Cadwalader, Esther IV, 612
Cadwalader, Esther IV, 613
Cadwalader, Esther IV, 687
Cadwalader, Esther V, 33
Cadwalader, Esther V, 34
Cadwalader, Esther V, 74
Cadwalader, Esther V, 401
Cadwalader, Esther V, 524
Cadwalader, Esther VI, 350
Cadwalader, Esther W. V, 34
Cadwalader, Esther W. V, 111
Cadwalader, Evalen IV, 77
Cadwalader, Eximina IV, 614
Cadwalader, Ezra V, 33
Cadwalader, Ezra V, 34
Cadwalader, Ezra V, 376
Cadwalader, Frank V, 552
Cadwalader, Frank V, 662
Cadwalader, Frank W. V, 34
Cadwalader, Hallie A. V, 34
Cadwalader, Hannah IV, 78
Cadwalader, Hannah IV, 83
Cadwalader, Hannah IV, 94
Cadwalader, Hannah IV, 323
Cadwalader, Hannah V, 74
Cadwalader, Hannah D. IV, 377
Cadwalader, Hannah S. V, 33
Cadwalader, Harmon IV, 77
Cadwalader, Harmon IV, 185
Cadwalader, Harmon IV, 186
Cadwalader, Harmon IV, 934
Cadwalader, Hester V, 34
Cadwalader, Hester V, 479
Cadwalader, Horace V, 34
Cadwalader, Howard IV, 377
Cadwalader, Howard IV, 687
Cadwalader, Howard IV, 828
Cadwalader, Howard IV, 934
Cadwalader, Isaac IV, 77
Cadwalader, Isaac IV, 78
Cadwalader, Isaac IV, 141
Cadwalader, Isaac IV, 239
Cadwalader, Isaac IV, 266
Cadwalader, Isaac IV, 322
Cadwalader, Isaac IV, 516
Cadwalader, Isaac IV, 613
Cadwalader, Isaac V, 321
Cadwalader, Isaac VI, 303
Cadwalader, Isaac VI, 593
Cadwalader, Isaac D. IV, 377
Cadwalader, Isaac D. IV, 687
Cadwalader, Isaac D. IV, 1051
Cadwalader, Isaac D. IV, 1091
Cadwalader, Isaac Dallas IV, 614
Cadwalader, Isaac H. V, 34
Cadwalader, Isaac H. V, 479
Cadwalader, Isaac L. IV, 687
Cadwalader, Isaac S. IV, 606
Cadwalader, Isaac S. IV, 612

Cadwalader, Isaac S. IV, 613
Cadwalader, Isaac S. IV, 614
Cadwalader, Isaac S. IV, 687
Cadwalader, Israel VI, 350
Cadwalader, Jacob II, 987
Cadwalader, Jacob II, 1029
Cadwalader, Jacob II, 1031
Cadwalader, Jacob II, 1032
Cadwalader, Jacob IV, 185
Cadwalader, Jacob IV, 186
Cadwalader, Jacob, Jr. II, 987
Cadwalader, James VI, 479
Cadwalader, James D. IV, 613
Cadwalader, James J. IV, 614
Cadwalader, Jane IV, 77
Cadwalader, Jane IV, 185
Cadwalader, Jane IV, 667
Cadwalader, Jane IV, 930
Cadwalader, Jane V, 20
Cadwalader, Jane V, 33
Cadwalader, Jane V, 34
Cadwalader, Jane V, 74
Cadwalader, Jane V, 131
Cadwalader, Jane V, 401
Cadwalader, Jane V, 479
Cadwalader, Jane V, 489
Cadwalader, Jane V, 552
Cadwalader, Jane V, 968
Cadwalader, Jane V, 977
Cadwalader, Jane VI, 303
Cadwalader, Jane VI, 350
Cadwalader, Jane VI, 353
Cadwalader, Jane N. V, 479
Cadwalader, Jesse V, 321
Cadwalader, Jesse VI, 303
Cadwalader, Jesse VI, 350
Cadwalader, Jesse K. IV, 516
Cadwalader, Jesse Kersey IV, 516
Cadwalader, Jno. IV, 323
Cadwalader, John II, 343
Cadwalader, John II, 505
Cadwalader, John II, 987
Cadwalader, John IV, 77
Cadwalader, John IV, 78
Cadwalader, John IV, 83
Cadwalader, John IV, 185
Cadwalader, John IV, 322
Cadwalader, John IV, 510
Cadwalader, John IV, 516
Cadwalader, John IV, 613
Cadwalader, John V, 34
Cadwalader, John V, 321
Cadwalader, John V, 479
Cadwalader, John V, 489
Cadwalader, John V, 968
Cadwalader, John VI, 303
Cadwalader, John VI, 593
Cadwalader, John F. V, 34
Cadwalader, John F. V, 479
Cadwalader, John H. IV, 687
Cadwalader, John J. IV, 375
Cadwalader, John J. IV, 377
Cadwalader, John J. IV, 613
Cadwalader, John J. IV, 614
Cadwalader, John J. IV, 617
Cadwalader, John J. IV, 687
Cadwalader, John J. IV, 934
Cadwalader, John T. V, 33
Cadwalader, John T. V, 34
Cadwalader, John T. V, 479
Cadwalader, John Thos. V, 968
Cadwalader, John, Jr. IV, 77
Cadwalader, John, Jr. IV, 186
Cadwalader, Jona V, 34
Cadwalader, Jonah IV, 77
Cadwalader, Jonah IV, 78
Cadwalader, Jonah IV, 185
Cadwalader, Jonah IV, 186
Cadwalader, Jonah IV, 613
Cadwalader, Jonah IV, 614
Cadwalader, Jonah IV, 687
Cadwalader, Jonah V, 33
Cadwalader, Jonah V, 34
Cadwalader, Jonah V, 62
Cadwalader, Jonah V, 321
Cadwalader, Jonah VI, 303
Cadwalader, Jonah VI, 350
Cadwalader, Jonah C. V, 34
Cadwalader, Jonah, Jr. IV, 77
Cadwalader, Jonah, Sr. IV, 77
Cadwalader, Jonas IV, 787
Cadwalader, Jonas V, 33
Cadwalader, Jones II, 480
Cadwalader, Jones II, 600
Cadwalader, Joseph I, 1003
Cadwalader, Joseph IV, 77
Cadwalader, Joseph IV, 78
Cadwalader, Joseph IV, 185
Cadwalader, Joseph IV, 186
Cadwalader, Joseph IV, 212
Cadwalader, Joseph IV, 323
Cadwalader, Joseph IV, 334
Cadwalader, Joseph IV, 516
Cadwalader, Joseph IV, 614
Cadwalader, Joseph IV, 667
Cadwalader, Joseph IV, 1090
Cadwalader, Joseph IV, 1091
Cadwalader, Joseph V, 34
Cadwalader, Joseph V, 54
Cadwalader, Joseph V, 321
Cadwalader, Joseph V, 326
Cadwalader, Joseph V, 376
Cadwalader, Joseph V, 552
Cadwalader, Joseph V, 662
Cadwalader, Joseph VI, 350
Cadwalader, Joseph VI, 375
Cadwalader, Josephl, Jr. IV, 667
Cadwalader, Judah II, 987
Cadwalader, Judah V, 34
Cadwalader, Judith I, 1003
Cadwalader, Judith V, 34
Cadwalader, Judith V, 64
Cadwalader, Judith V, 156
Cadwalader, Judith V, 185
Cadwalader, Judith V, 968
Cadwalader, Julia V, 988
Cadwalader, Lea IV, 77
Cadwalader, Leah V, 33
Cadwalader, Leah V, 34
Cadwalader, Leah V, 539
Cadwalader, Lena V, 34
Cadwalader, Lena V, 134
Cadwalader, Letitia II, 343
Cadwalader, Letitia II, 987
Cadwalader, Levi IV, 613
Cadwalader, Levi IV, 687
Cadwalader, Lina V, 34
Cadwalader, Lizzie T. IV, 1273
Cadwalader, Lloyd D. IV, 687
Cadwalader, Lloyd D. IV, 1091
Cadwalader, Loyd IV, 377
Cadwalader, Loyd IV, 687
Cadwalader, Loyd D. IV, 377
Cadwalader, Loyd D. IV, 1051
Cadwalader, Lydia IV, 77
Cadwalader, Lydia IV, 78
Cadwalader, Lydia IV, 94
Cadwalader, Lydia IV, 613
Cadwalader, Lydia IV, 614
Cadwalader, Lydia IV, 638
Cadwalader, Mahlon V, 33
Cadwalader, Mahlon V, 321
Cadwalader, Mahlon VI, 303
Cadwalader, Mahlon VI, 350
Cadwalader, Malon V, 34
Cadwalader, Margaret IV, 687
Cadwalader, Margaret IV, 828
Cadwalader, Marrah VI, 593
Cadwalader, Martha II, 343
Cadwalader, Martha IV, 516
Cadwalader, Martha V, 34
Cadwalader, Martha VI, 593
Cadwalader, Mary I, 1003
Cadwalader, Mary II, 480
Cadwalader, Mary II, 505
Cadwalader, Mary II, 987
Cadwalader, Mary II, 1025
Cadwalader, Mary II, 1031
Cadwalader, Mary II, 1032
Cadwalader, Mary II, 1047
Cadwalader, Mary II, 1070
Cadwalader, Mary IV, 77
Cadwalader, Mary IV, 185
Cadwalader, Mary IV, 186
Cadwalader, Mary IV, 311
Cadwalader, Mary IV, 314
Cadwalader, Mary IV, 516
Cadwalader, Mary IV, 535
Cadwalader, Mary IV, 613
Cadwalader, Mary IV, 614
Cadwalader, Mary IV, 934
Cadwalader, Mary V, 33
Cadwalader, Mary V, 34
Cadwalader, Mary V, 131
Cadwalader, Mary V, 185
Cadwalader, Mary V, 321
Cadwalader, Mary V, 662
Cadwalader, Mary VI, 296
Cadwalader, Mary VI, 303
Cadwalader, Mary VI, 350
Cadwalader, Mary VI, 479
Cadwalader, Mary VI, 593
Cadwalader, Mary A. IV, 934
Cadwalader, Mary Ann IV, 614
Cadwalader, Mary Ann IV, 617
Cadwalader, Mary E. V, 34
Cadwalader, Mary L. V, 968
Cadwalader, Mary L. V, 977
Cadwalader, Mary Louisa IV, 667
Cadwalader, Mary Margaret V, 33
Cadwalader, Mary P. IV, 377
Cadwalader, Mary P. IV, 687
Cadwalader, Mayland VI, 840
Cadwalader, Mercer IV, 613
Cadwalader, Mifflin IV, 77
Cadwalader, Mifflin IV, 78
Cadwalader, Mifflin IV, 377
Cadwalader, Mifflin IV, 613
Cadwalader, Mifflin IV, 614
Cadwalader, Mifflin IV, 639
Cadwalader, Mifflin IV, 667
Cadwalader, Mifflin IV, 687
Cadwalader, Mifflin IV, 934
Cadwalader, Mildred V, 34
Cadwalader, Mildred V, 968
Cadwalader, Mildred I. V, 33
Cadwalader, Mildred Jean V, 662
Cadwalader, Mildred T. V, 34
Cadwalader, Mildred T. V, 140
Cadwalader, Miriam V, 34
Cadwalader, Morris W. IV, 1273
Cadwalader, Moses I, 961
Cadwalader, Moses I, 1003
Cadwalader, Moses V, 185
Cadwalader, Moses V, 321
Cadwalader, Moses VI, 350
Cadwalader, Moses D. IV, 377
Cadwalader, Moses Dillon IV, 377
Cadwalader, Moses, Jr. VI, 303
Cadwalader, Moses, Jr. VI, 350
Cadwalader, Moses, Jur. VI, 296
Cadwalader, Naomi V, 33
Cadwalader, Naomi V, 34
Cadwalader, Naomi V, 131
Cadwalader, Naomi VI, 350
Cadwalader, Nathan IV, 185
Cadwalader, Nathan IV, 516
Cadwalader, Noah V, 33
Cadwalader, Noah V, 34
Cadwalader, Noah V, 60
Cadwalader, Oliver II, 987
Cadwalader, Oner IV, 52
Cadwalader, Patience V, 33
Cadwalader, Patience W. V, 33
Cadwalader, Patience W. V, 62
Cadwalader, Phebe II, 987
Cadwalader, Phebe II, 1003
Cadwalader, Phebe II, 1018
Cadwalader, Phebe II, 1032
Cadwalader, Phebe IV, 667
Cadwalader, Phebe V, 34
Cadwalader, Pierce J. V, 34
Cadwalader, Pierce J. V, 897
Cadwalader, Priscilla V, 33
Cadwalader, Priscilla V, 34
Cadwalader, Priscilla V, 62
Cadwalader, Rachel II, 987
Cadwalader, Rachel II, 990
Cadwalader, Rachel IV, 77
Cadwalader, Rachel IV, 113
Cadwalader, Rachel V, 33
Cadwalader, Rachel V, 34
Cadwalader, Rachel V, 54
Cadwalader, Rachel V, 479
Cadwalader, Rachel V, 489
Cadwalader, Rachel Ann IV, 516
Cadwalader, Rayburn IV, 1151
Cadwalader, Rayburn IV, 1194
Cadwalader, Rayburn V, 662
Cadwalader, Rebecca II, 480
Cadwalader, Rebecca II, 600
Cadwalader, Rebecca IV, 377
Cadwalader, Rebecca IV, 614
Cadwalader, Rebecca H. IV, 375
Cadwalader, Rebecca H. IV, 377
Cadwalader, Rebecca H. IV, 613
Cadwalader, Rebecca H. IV, 614
Cadwalader, Rebecca H. IV, 687
Cadwalader, Rebeckah II, 480
Cadwalader, Rebeckah II, 600
Cadwalader, Reece IV, 77
Cadwalader, Reece IV, 377
Cadwalader, Reece IV, 687
Cadwalader, Reece IV, 1051
Cadwalader, Rees IV, 77
Cadwalader, Rees IV, 78
Cadwalader, Rees IV, 83
Cadwalader, Rees IV, 95
Cadwalader, Rees IV, 185
Cadwalader, Rees IV, 186
Cadwalader, Rees IV, 311
Cadwalader, Rees IV, 314
Cadwalader, Rees IV, 323
Cadwalader, Rees IV, 377
Cadwalader, Rees IV, 516
Cadwalader, Rees IV, 614
Cadwalader, Rees IV, 687
Cadwalader, Rees IV, 828
Cadwalader, Rees VI, 375
Cadwalader, Rees VI, 428
Cadwalader, Rees J. IV, 687
Cadwalader, Reese IV, 377
Cadwalader, Reese IV, 1091
Cadwalader, Reese D. IV, 687
Cadwalader, Robert V, 33
Cadwalader, Ruth IV, 77
Cadwalader, Ruth IV, 83
Cadwalader, Ruth IV, 95
Cadwalader, Ruth IV, 186
Cadwalader, Ruth IV, 322
Cadwalader, Ruth IV, 516
Cadwalader, Ruth IV, 1194
Cadwalader, Ruth V, 662
Cadwalader, Ruth VI, 350
Cadwalader, Ruth VI, 353
Cadwalader, Ruth VI, 375
Cadwalader, Ruth VI, 428
Cadwalader, Ruth VI, 593
Cadwalader, Ruth VI, 965
Cadwalader, Ruth Windsor IV, 1151
Cadwalader, Sabina IV, 516
Cadwalader, Samuel IV, 77
Cadwalader, Samuel IV, 614
Cadwalader, Sarah II, 987
Cadwalader, Sarah IV, 77
Cadwalader, Sarah IV, 78
Cadwalader, Sarah IV, 83
Cadwalader, Sarah IV, 108
Cadwalader, Sarah IV, 185
Cadwalader, Sarah IV, 186
Cadwalader, Sarah IV, 192
Cadwalader, Sarah IV, 266
Cadwalader, Sarah IV, 310
Cadwalader, Sarah IV, 322
Cadwalader, Sarah IV, 323
Cadwalader, Sarah IV, 340
Cadwalader, Sarah IV, 377
Cadwalader, Sarah IV, 516
Cadwalader, Sarah IV, 613
Cadwalader, Sarah IV, 614
Cadwalader, Sarah IV, 639
Cadwalader, Sarah IV, 660
Cadwalader, Sarah IV, 667
Cadwalader, Sarah IV, 687
Cadwalader, Sarah IV, 828
Cadwalader, Sarah IV, 1051
Cadwalader, Sarah IV, 1090
Cadwalader, Sarah IV, 1091
Cadwalader, Sarah V, 473
Cadwalader, Sarah V, 479
Cadwalader, Sarah VI, 593
Cadwalader, Sarah Ann IV, 186
Cadwalader, Sarah Ann IV, 1090
Cadwalader, Sarah Ann IV, 1091
Cadwalader, Sarah Ann IV, 1109
Cadwalader, Sarah J. IV, 377
Cadwalader, Sarah J. IV, 613
Cadwalader, Sarah J. IV, 614
Cadwalader, Sarah J. IV, 687
Cadwalader, Sarah J. IV, 934
Cadwalader, Sarah James IV, 614
Cadwalader, Sarah Jane V, 21
Cadwalader, Sarah Jane V, 34
Cadwalader, Septamus IV, 614
Cadwalader, Septimus IV, 77
Cadwalader, Septimus IV, 108
Cadwalader, Septimus IV, 613
Cadwalader, Septimus IV, 660
Cadwalader, Silas V, 321
Cadwalader, Silas VI, 303
Cadwalader, Susan IV, 185
Cadwalader, Susan IV, 186
Cadwalader, Susanna II, 1047
Cadwalader, Susannah II, 987
Cadwalader, Susannah II, 1029
Cadwalader, Tamer V, 321
Cadwalader, Thomas IV, 613
Cadwalader, Thomas IV, 667
Cadwalader, Thomas IV, 687
Cadwalader, Thomas V, 33
Cadwalader, Thomas V, 34
Cadwalader, Thomas V, 74
Cadwalader, Thomas V, 131
Cadwalader, Thomas V, 401
Cadwalader, Thomas VI, 303
Cadwalader, Thomas VI, 350
Cadwalader, Thomas VI, 353
Cadwalader, Thomas VI, 946
Cadwalader, Thomas M. IV, 614
Cadwalader, Thomas, Jr. V, 34
Cadwalader, Thos. V, 33
Cadwalader, Timothy II, 987
Cadwalader, Vashti V, 33
Cadwalader, Vashti V, 34
Cadwalader, Vashti V, 131
Cadwalader, Wd Elizabeth IV, 614
Cadwalader, William IV, 77
Cadwalader, William IV, 185
Cadwalader, William IV, 186
Cadwalader, William IV, 667
Cadwalader, William IV, 934
Cadwalader, William V, 33
Cadwalader, William V, 34
Cadwalader, William C. V, 552
Cadwalader, William C. V, 662
Cadwalader, Wm. II, 987
Cadwalader, Wm. II, 1029
Cadwalader, Wm. IV, 613
Cadwalader, Wm. V, 968
Cadwalader, Wm. V, 977
Cadwalader, Wm. F. IV, 1273
Cadwalader, Wm. J. IV, 1273
Cadwaledar, Asa VI, 375
Cadwaledar, Ediath VI, 375
Cadwaledar, Mary VI, 375
Cadwaledar, Rees VI, 375
Cadwaledar, Ruth VI, 375
Cadwaleder, Mary VI, 479
Cadwaleder, Reese VI, 375
Cadwaleder, Ruth VI, 375
Cadwaleder, Ruth VI, 428
Cadwalender, Elizabeth VI, 888
Cadwalender, John VI, 888
Cadwalender, Nancy VI, 888
Cadwalender, William VI, 888
Cadwallader, ??? IV, 603
Cadwallader, Abigail VI, 479
Cadwallader, Abner V, 34
Cadwallader, Abner VI, 303
Cadwallader, Achilles V, 34
Cadwallader, Achilles V, 798
Cadwallader, Achilles VI, 303
Cadwallader, Achsah Ann II, 1047
Cadwallader, Addalena V, 729
Cadwallader, Affinity VI, 530
Cadwallader, Agnes IV, 24
Cadwallader, Agness IV, 24
Cadwallader, Aljurna II, 1047
Cadwallader, Allen J. II, 701
Cadwallader, Almeda V, 729
Cadwallader, Amasa IV, 516
Cadwallader, Amy IV, 77
Cadwallader, Amy VI, 303
Cadwallader, Amy VI, 350
Cadwallader, Amy VI, 629
Cadwallader, Andrew V, 48
Cadwallader, Andrew V, 58
Cadwallader, Andrew W. V, 58
Cadwallader, Ann II, 343
Cadwallader, Ann II, 1047
Cadwallader, Ann IV, 77
Cadwallader, Ann IV, 78
Cadwallader, Ann IV, 466
Cadwallader, Ann IV, 687
Cadwallader, Anna IV, 681
Cadwallader, Anna B. II, 957
Cadwallader, Anna B. II, 1085
Cadwallader, Annie H. IV, 667
Cadwallader, Annie H. IV, 682
Cadwallader, Annie H. IV, 687
Cadwallader, Annie M. II, 844
Cadwallader, Annie M. II, 914
Cadwallader, Aquilla V, 138
Cadwallader, Asa IV, 24
Cadwallader, Asa IV, 47
Cadwallader, Asa VI, 375
Cadwallader, Asa VI, 480
Cadwallader, Benjamin II, 957
Cadwallader, Benjamin II, 969
Cadwallader, Benjamin II, 987
Cadwallader, Benjamin II, 990
Cadwallader, Benjamin II, 1047
Cadwallader, Benjamin II, 1048
Cadwallader, Benjamin II, 1049
Cadwallader, Benjamin II, 1059
Cadwallader, Benjamin II, 1085
Cadwallader, Betsy V, 34
Cadwallader, Betsy VI, 303
Cadwallader, Birone V, 34
Cadwallader, C??? II, 343
Cadwallader, Caleb VI, 479
Cadwallader, Catharine V, 321
Cadwallader, Catherine V, 34
Cadwallader, Catherine VI, 479
Cadwallader, Charles II, 987
Cadwallader, Charles II, 1048
Cadwallader, Charles II, 1085
Cadwallader, Charles II, 1087
Cadwallader, Charles V, 34
Cadwallader, Charles VI, 303
Cadwallader, Charles B. II, 957
Cadwallader, Chas. H. II, 844
Cadwallader, Chas. H. II, 914
Cadwallader, Christiana II, 1070
Cadwallader, Christianna II, 1047
Cadwallader, Christianna II, 1058
Cadwallader, Christianna II, 1070

Cadwallader, Christianna II, 1078
Cadwallader, Cyrus II, 954
Cadwallader, Cyrus II, 957
Cadwallader, Cyrus II, 958
Cadwallader, Cyrus II, 959
Cadwallader, Cyrus II, 976
Cadwallader, Cyrus II, 987
Cadwallader, Cyrus II, 990
Cadwallader, Cyrus II, 1047
Cadwallader, Cyrus II, 1050
Cadwallader, Cyrus, Jr. II, 1047
Cadwallader, Daniel VI, 303
Cadwallader, David IV, 516
Cadwallader, David V, 21
Cadwallader, David VI, 479
Cadwallader, Deborah II, 1047
Cadwallader, Deborah IV, 609
Cadwallader, Deborah IV, 614
Cadwallader, Deborah V, 34
Cadwallader, Deborah V, 968
Cadwallader, Deborah VI, 303
Cadwallader, Dora V, 58
Cadwallader, Dr. Jonah C. V, 35
Cadwallader, Edgar IV, 934
Cadwallader, Ediath VI, 375
Cadwallader, Edith IV, 24
Cadwallader, Edith IV, 63
Cadwallader, Edith IV, 516
Cadwallader, Edith IV, 570
Cadwallader, Edith IV, 1092
Cadwallader, Edith VI, 375
Cadwallader, Edith VI, 480
Cadwallader, Edward II, 343
Cadwallader, Edward II, 480
Cadwallader, Elinor VI, 353
Cadwallader, Elizabeth II, 343
Cadwallader, Elizabeth II, 819
Cadwallader, Elizabeth II, 957
Cadwallader, Elizabeth II, 987
Cadwallader, Elizabeth II, 1047
Cadwallader, Elizabeth II, 1049
Cadwallader, Elizabeth IV, 23
Cadwallader, Elizabeth IV, 24
Cadwallader, Elizabeth IV, 57
Cadwallader, Elizabeth IV, 71
Cadwallader, Elizabeth IV, 77
Cadwallader, Elizabeth IV, 83
Cadwallader, Elizabeth V, 33
Cadwallader, Elizabeth V, 34
Cadwallader, Elizabeth VI, 303
Cadwallader, Elizabeth VI, 308
Cadwallader, Elizabeth VI, 375
Cadwallader, Elizabeth VI, 459
Cadwallader, Elizabeth VI, 479
Cadwallader, Elizabeth VI, 485
Cadwallader, Elizabeth VI, 514
Cadwallader, Elizabeth VI, 530
Cadwallader, Elizabeth VI, 629
Cadwallader, Elizabeth VI, 633
Cadwallader, Elizabeth VI, 675
Cadwallader, Elizabeth C. II, 791
Cadwallader, Ellen IV, 649
Cadwallader, Ellen T. IV, 655
Cadwallader, Esther II, 701
Cadwallader, Esther IV, 681
Cadwallader, Esther V, 48
Cadwallader, Esther V, 58
Cadwallader, Esther VI, 303
Cadwallader, Evans IV, 167
Cadwallader, Francis W. III, 393
Cadwallader, Francis W. III, 397
Cadwallader, George Warner, Jr. II, 1070
Cadwallader, Hannah II, 343
Cadwallader, Hannah II, 480
Cadwallader, Hannah II, 602
Cadwallader, Hannah VI, 479
Cadwallader, Harriet III, 393
Cadwallader, Harriet III, 397
Cadwallader, Howard IV, 805
Cadwallader, Howard IV, 934
Cadwallader, Isaac IV, 77
Cadwallader, Isaac IV, 83
Cadwallader, Isaac IV, 466
Cadwallader, Isaac IV, 516
Cadwallader, Isaac V, 897
Cadwallader, Isaac VI, 303
Cadwallader, Isaac VI, 375
Cadwallader, Isaac VI, 479
Cadwallader, Isaac D. IV, 466
Cadwallader, Isaac S. II, 701
Cadwallader, Isaac S. IV, 681
Cadwallader, Israel VI, 303
Cadwallader, Israel D. IV, 466
Cadwallader, Jacob II, 987
Cadwallader, Jacob II, 1047
Cadwallader, Jacob, Jr. II, 1047
Cadwallader, James VI, 479
Cadwallader, Jane IV, 24
Cadwallader, Jane IV, 47
Cadwallader, Jane V, 20
Cadwallader, Jane V, 34
Cadwallader, Jane VI, 303
Cadwallader, Jane VI, 485
Cadwallader, Jane VI, 629
Cadwallader, Jane VI, 633
Cadwallader, Jane Daniel VI, 303
Cadwallader, Jesse VI, 303
Cadwallader, Jesse VI, 350
Cadwallader, Jesse VI, 375
Cadwallader, Jesse VI, 629
Cadwallader, Jesse Townsend IV, 24
Cadwallader, John II, 343
Cadwallader, John II, 480
Cadwallader, John II, 602
Cadwallader, John IV, 17
Cadwallader, John IV, 22
Cadwallader, John IV, 71
Cadwallader, John IV, 75
Cadwallader, John IV, 77
Cadwallader, John IV, 167
Cadwallader, John IV, 466
Cadwallader, John VI, 303
Cadwallader, John VI, 375
Cadwallader, John VI, 479
Cadwallader, John VI, 530
Cadwallader, John VI, 586
Cadwallader, John VI, 629
Cadwallader, John VI, 675
Cadwallader, John F. V, 34
Cadwallader, John T. V, 34
Cadwallader, John Thomas VI, 303
Cadwallader, John, Jr. VI, 479
Cadwallader, Jona V, 34
Cadwallader, Jonah IV, 77
Cadwallader, Jonah IV, 78
Cadwallader, Jonah IV, 687
Cadwallader, Jonah V, 34
Cadwallader, Jonah V, 140
Cadwallader, Jonah VI, 303
Cadwallader, Jonah VI, 375
Cadwallader, Jones II, 480
Cadwallader, Joseph IV, 62
Cadwallader, Joseph IV, 507
Cadwallader, Joseph IV, 516
Cadwallader, Joseph IV, 614
Cadwallader, Joseph V, 34
Cadwallader, Joseph V, 321
Cadwallader, Joseph VI, 303
Cadwallader, Joseph VI, 375
Cadwallader, Joseph VI, 479
Cadwallader, Joseph VI, 542
Cadwallader, Joseph VI, 629
Cadwallader, Judah V, 34
Cadwallader, Judith V, 34
Cadwallader, Judith VI, 303
Cadwallader, Latitia II, 954
Cadwallader, Latitia II, 965
Cadwallader, Latitia II, 1047
Cadwallader, Laura V, 729
Cadwallader, Leah E. V, 138
Cadwallader, Letitia II, 343
Cadwallader, Letitia II, 953
Cadwallader, Letitia II, 976
Cadwallader, Letitia II, 987
Cadwallader, Lucy II, 957
Cadwallader, Lucy II, 1047
Cadwallader, Lucy II, 1048
Cadwallader, Lucy II, 1085
Cadwallader, Lydia VI, 479
Cadwallader, Lydia J. II, 1070
Cadwallader, Lydia J. II, 1082
Cadwallader, Lydia Yardley II, 825
Cadwallader, Mahlon V, 33
Cadwallader, Mahlon VI, 303
Cadwallader, Mahlon VI, 308
Cadwallader, Malon V, 34
Cadwallader, Marah IV, 23
Cadwallader, Marah IV, 24
Cadwallader, Marah IV, 62
Cadwallader, Marah VI, 479
Cadwallader, Margaret IV, 805
Cadwallader, Margarett II, 343
Cadwallader, Marianna II, 863
Cadwallader, Marrah VI, 375
Cadwallader, Martha II, 343
Cadwallader, Martha II, 480
Cadwallader, Martha II, 602
Cadwallader, Martha IV, 24
Cadwallader, Martha IV, 67
Cadwallader, Martha V, 138
Cadwallader, Mary I, 1001
Cadwallader, Mary II, 480
Cadwallader, Mary II, 954
Cadwallader, Mary II, 957
Cadwallader, Mary II, 958
Cadwallader, Mary II, 959
Cadwallader, Mary II, 969
Cadwallader, Mary II, 976
Cadwallader, Mary II, 987
Cadwallader, Mary II, 990
Cadwallader, Mary II, 1047
Cadwallader, Mary II, 1050
Cadwallader, Mary II, 1059
Cadwallader, Mary IV, 22
Cadwallader, Mary IV, 23
Cadwallader, Mary IV, 51
Cadwallader, Mary IV, 62
Cadwallader, Mary IV, 77
Cadwallader, Mary IV, 614
Cadwallader, Mary IV, 635
Cadwallader, Mary IV, 654
Cadwallader, Mary V, 33
Cadwallader, Mary V, 140
Cadwallader, Mary V, 321
Cadwallader, Mary VI, 297
Cadwallader, Mary VI, 303
Cadwallader, Mary VI, 375
Cadwallader, Mary VI, 479
Cadwallader, Mary VI, 561
Cadwallader, Mary VI, 678
Cadwallader, Mary VI, 705
Cadwallader, Mary Anna II, 785
Cadwallader, Mary C. V, 48
Cadwallader, Mary L. III, 393
Cadwallader, Mary L. III, 397
Cadwallader, Mary L. V, 19
Cadwallader, Mary L. V, 34
Cadwallader, Mary S. V, 124
Cadwallader, Mercy II, 1047
Cadwallader, Mercy II, 1054
Cadwallader, Mifflin IV, 609
Cadwallader, Mifflin IV, 614
Cadwallader, Mifflin IV, 635
Cadwallader, Mifflin IV, 655
Cadwallader, Mifflin IV, 687
Cadwallader, Mifflin IV, 727
Cadwallader, Mildred V, 34
Cadwallader, Mildred VI, 303
Cadwallader, Miriam V, 34
Cadwallader, Moses II, 957
Cadwallader, Moses II, 1047
Cadwallader, Moses II, 1048
Cadwallader, Moses II, 1085
Cadwallader, Moses V, 321
Cadwallader, Moses VI, 297
Cadwallader, Moses VI, 303
Cadwallader, Moses VI, 355
Cadwallader, Moses VI, 479
Cadwallader, Moses VI, 485
Cadwallader, Moses VI, 514
Cadwallader, Moses VI, 530
Cadwallader, Moses VI, 629
Cadwallader, Moses VI, 633
Cadwallader, Moses VI, 675
Cadwallader, Moses, Jr. VI, 303
Cadwallader, Moses, Jr. VI, 480
Cadwallader, Moses, Jr. VI, 629
Cadwallader, Moses, Sr. VI, 629
Cadwallader, Naomi VI, 303
Cadwallader, Oliver II, 987
Cadwallader, Oliver II, 1047
Cadwallader, Patience V, 140
Cadwallader, Phebe II, 987
Cadwallader, Phebe II, 1022
Cadwallader, Phebe V, 34
Cadwallader, Phebe V, 54
Cadwallader, Pierce J. V, 34
Cadwallader, Pierce J. V, 897
Cadwallader, Priscilla V, 34
Cadwallader, Priscilla V, 140
Cadwallader, Rachel II, 957
Cadwallader, Rachel II, 958
Cadwallader, Rachel II, 987
Cadwallader, Rachel V, 21
Cadwallader, Rachel VI, 375
Cadwallader, Rachel C. II, 954
Cadwallader, Rebecca II, 343
Cadwallader, Rebecca II, 480
Cadwallader, Rebecca II, 602
Cadwallader, Rebecka II, 343
Cadwallader, Rebeckah II, 480
Cadwallader, Rees IV, 17
Cadwallader, Rees IV, 23
Cadwallader, Rees IV, 24
Cadwallader, Rees IV, 71
Cadwallader, Rees IV, 77
Cadwallader, Rees IV, 805
Cadwallader, Rees VI, 375
Cadwallader, Reese VI, 375
Cadwallader, Reese VI, 479
Cadwallader, Reese VI, 480
Cadwallader, Reese VI, 542
Cadwallader, Ress IV, 57
Cadwallader, Ruth IV, 17
Cadwallader, Ruth IV, 24
Cadwallader, Ruth IV, 34
Cadwallader, Ruth IV, 75
Cadwallader, Ruth IV, 77
Cadwallader, Ruth IV, 466
Cadwallader, Ruth VI, 303
Cadwallader, Ruth VI, 350
Cadwallader, Ruth VI, 375
Cadwallader, Ruth VI, 479
Cadwallader, Ruth VI, 480
Cadwallader, Ruth VI, 542
Cadwallader, Ruth VI, 629
Cadwallader, Samuel II, 1047
Cadwallader, Sarah II, 957
Cadwallader, Sarah II, 959
Cadwallader, Sarah II, 965
Cadwallader, Sarah II, 969
Cadwallader, Sarah II, 987
Cadwallader, Sarah II, 990
Cadwallader, Sarah II, 1047
Cadwallader, Sarah II, 1048
Cadwallader, Sarah II, 1049
Cadwallader, Sarah II, 1050
Cadwallader, Sarah II, 1059
Cadwallader, Sarah II, 1085
Cadwallader, Sarah IV, 17
Cadwallader, Sarah IV, 22
Cadwallader, Sarah IV, 24
Cadwallader, Sarah IV, 71
Cadwallader, Sarah IV, 77
Cadwallader, Sarah IV, 322
Cadwallader, Sarah IV, 466
Cadwallader, Sarah IV, 516
Cadwallader, Sarah IV, 609
Cadwallader, Sarah IV, 687
Cadwallader, Sarah IV, 727
Cadwallader, Sarah IV, 805
Cadwallader, Sarah VI, 479
Cadwallader, Sarah VI, 480
Cadwallader, Sarah VI, 514
Cadwallader, Sarah VI, 629
Cadwallader, Sarah J. IV, 635
Cadwallader, Sarah M. II, 957
Cadwallader, Septimus IV, 17
Cadwallader, Septimus IV, 71
Cadwallader, Septimus VI, 479
Cadwallader, Septimus VI, 480
Cadwallader, Silas VI, 303
Cadwallader, Susan J. II, 731
Cadwallader, Susan J. II, 777
Cadwallader, Susanna II, 1047
Cadwallader, Susanna II, 1070
Cadwallader, Susanna II, 1078
Cadwallader, Thomas II, 343
Cadwallader, Thomas II, 1047
Cadwallader, Thomas II, 1070
Cadwallader, Thomas II, 1078
Cadwallader, Thomas V, 34
Cadwallader, Thomas V, 54
Cadwallader, Thomas VI, 303
Cadwallader, Thomas VI, 485
Cadwallader, Thomas VI, 629
Cadwallader, Thomas VI, 633
Cadwallader, Thomas, Jr. V, 34
Cadwallader, Thomas, Jr. VI, 303
Cadwallader, Timothy II, 1047
Cadwallader, Wd. Hannah II, 343
Cadwallader, William II, 785
Cadwallader, William V, 33
Cadwallader, William V, 124
Cadwallader, William VI, 303
Cadwallader, Wm. II, 1047
Cadwallader, Wm. II, 1070
Cadwallader, Wm. II, 1078
Cadwallader, Wm. F. II, 844
Cadwallader, Wm. F. II, 914
Cadwallader, Wm. Feaster II, 785
Cadwallender, Elizabeth VI, 888
Cadwallender, John VI, 888
Cadwallender, Juliann VI, 1008
Cadwallender, Mary VI, 888
Cadwallender, Nancy VI, 888
Cadwallender, Phebe B. VI, 888
Cadwallender, William VI, 888
Cadwaller, Marrah VI, 375
Cadwallett, Edward II, 343
Cadwallett, Hannah II, 343
Cadwallett, John II, 343
Cadwallett, Martha II, 343
Cadwallett, Rebecka II, 343
Cadwalliter, Rebecca II, 343
Cadwell, Mariam IV, 934
Cadwell, Mariam IV, 948
Cadwellender, Betsey VI, 1008
Cadwiler, Rebecca IV, 377
Cadwiler, Rebecca IV, 385
Cadwill, William II, 343
Caesars, Leason I, 901
Caffery, Charles VI, 883
Caffery, Charles VI, 885
Caffery, Charles VI, 888
Caffery, Charles VI, 890
Caffery, Charles VI, 910
Caffery, Charles VI, 932
Caffery, Charles VI, 1014
Caffery, Chas. VI, 971
Caffery, Elizabeth VI, 949
Caffery, Frances VI, 943
Caffery, John VI, 845
Caffery, John VI, 944
Caffery, Juliet VI, 932
Caffery, Moses VI, 890
Caffery, Nancy VI, 911
Caffery, Rebecca VI, 911
Caffery, Rebecca VI, 949
Caffery, Rebeckah VI, 888
Caffery, Winifred VI, 1014
Caffey, John II, 801
Caffey, Sarah Smith II, 801
Caffey, Susan II, 801
Caffrey, Elizabeth VI, 303
Caffrey, Narcissa VI, 911
Caffrey, Rebecca VI, 990
Cafrey, Charlotte VI, 990
Cage, Ann A. VI, 802
Cage, John VI, 802
Cagel, Catherine II, 442
Cagel, Mary VI, 910
Caggins, Edward H. II, 844
Caggins, Ruth Ann II, 844
Cagle, Carrett I, 922
Cagle, Henrietta I, 935
Cagle, Rebecca I, 922
Cahaley, ??? III, 58
Cahaley, ??? III, 174
Cahaley, Mabel III, 58
Cahaley, Mabel M. III, 58
Cahaley, Mabel M. III, 174
Cahill, Hiram V, 988
Cahill, J. E. IV, 1274
Cahill, Joshua IV, 1273
Cahill, Joshua IV, 1274
Cahill, Sarah V, 988
Cahoon, Charles, Jr. VI, 888
Cahoon, Elizabeth Frances VI, 888
Cahoon, John VI, 888
Cahoon, John C. VI, 57
Cahoon, John C. VI, 73
Cahoon, Matilda III, 236
Cahoon, Rachel VI, 888
Cahoon, Samuel J. VI, 888
Cahoon, Sarah Ann VI, 888
Cail, Joseph I, 39
Cain, Abigail I, 530
Cain, Abigail I, 542
Cain, Amanda Elvina II, 818
Cain, Andrew I, 605
Cain, Caroline V, 948
Cain, Caroline V, 949
Cain, Elizabeth II, 205
Cain, Elizabeth II, 231
Cain, Hannah I, 803
Cain, Hannah I, 838
Cain, Jane V, 949
Cain, John I, 592
Cain, John II, 205
Cain, John II, 231
Cain, Joshua II, 1001
Cain, Leah I, 605
Cain, Lovel VI, 888
Cain, Loving H. VI, 888
Cain, Martha Ann VI, 936
Cain, Mary I, 530
Cain, Mary I, 592
Cain, Mary V, 299
Cain, Mary VI, 871
Cain, Mary B. V, 299
Cain, Mary Jane V, 299
Cain, Mary Jane V, 949
Cain, Matthias VI, 888
Cain, Micager VI, 909
Cain, Nathan I, 592
Cain, Newel I, 592
Cain, Oney VI, 888
Cain, Priscilla II, 205
Cain, Rachel I, 592
Cain, Rachel I, 803
Cain, Rachel I, 806
Cain, Rebekah I, 803
Cain, Rebekah I, 838
Cain, Rhody VI, 888
Cain, Sally VI, 888
Cain, Saly VI, 871
Cain, Sarah I, 605
Cain, Sarah II, 987
Cain, Sarah II, 1001
Cain, Sarah VI, 936
Cain, Thomas I, 530
Cain, Thomas V, 949
Cain, Thomas VI, 888
Cain, Thornton V, 299
Cain, Thornton V, 949
Cain, William V, 299
Cain, Wm. V, 299

Cain, Wm. V, 948
Cain, Wm. V, 949
Cain, Wyatt I, 592
Caine, John II, 343
Caine, Sarah II, 343
Caine, Sarah B. III, 245
Caine, Sarah E. III, 120
Cairy, Thomas V, 157
Caisa, Meranda I, 188
Caisa, Meranda I, 190
Caise, Catharine II, 1048
Caison, Fannie I, 530
Caity, John C. IV, 1151
Calahan, Pheby. VI, 819
Calahan, Susan VI, 819
Calcup, Elizabeth II, 343
Caldhoun, Elizabeth V, 35
Caldhoun, Mary V, 35
Caldhoun, William V, 35
Caldwallader, Cyrus II, 1070
Caldwallader, Mary II, 1070
Caldwell, ??? VI, 293
Caldwell, Abigail I, 530
Caldwell, Alexander I Sup 1, 10
Caldwell, Alexander VI, 802
Caldwell, Ann II, 480
Caldwell, Ann II, 676
Caldwell, Anne VI, 802
Caldwell, Benjamin VI, 803
Caldwell, Catherine VI, 797
Caldwell, Chancellor P. V, 376
Caldwell, Daniel VI, 797
Caldwell, David V, 453
Caldwell, David VI, 931
Caldwell, Eliza VI, 981
Caldwell, Elizabeth II, 343
Caldwell, Elizabeth IV, 614
Caldwell, Elizabeth IV, 626
Caldwell, Elizabeth VI, 805
Caldwell, Emma V, 453
Caldwell, Geo. VI, 1013
Caldwell, George VI, 984
Caldwell, Henry VI, 888
Caldwell, Ione V, 453
Caldwell, Isabella VI, 802
Caldwell, J. M. V, 453
Caldwell, James V, 881
Caldwell, James E. D. VI, 805
Caldwell, Jane III, 58
Caldwell, Jno. VI, 805
Caldwell, Jno. VI, 806
Caldwell, John I Sup 1, 10
Caldwell, John II, 343
Caldwell, John VI, 303
Caldwell, John VI, 797
Caldwell, John VI, 802
Caldwell, John VI, 847
Caldwell, Judith VI, 803
Caldwell, Margaret II, 343
Caldwell, Margaret VI, 984
Caldwell, Margaret VI, 1013
Caldwell, Margaret J. VI, 854
Caldwell, Mary V, 453
Caldwell, Mary VI, 480
Caldwell, Mary VI, 511
Caldwell, Mary VI, 802
Caldwell, Mary VI, 843
Caldwell, Mary VI, 847
Caldwell, Mary VI, 853
Caldwell, Mourning VI, 888
Caldwell, Nancy VI, 834
Caldwell, Nancy VI, 853
Caldwell, Oliver VI, 802
Caldwell, Patsy VI, 802
Caldwell, Peggy VI, 981
Caldwell, Polly VI, 806
Caldwell, Sally Ann VI, 853
Caldwell, Samuel VI, 307
Caldwell, Samuel VI, 802
Caldwell, Samuel VI, 803
Caldwell, Samuel VI, 810
Caldwell, Samuel VI, 840
Caldwell, Samuel VI, 847
Caldwell, Sarah II, 343
Caldwell, Sarah IV, 614
Caldwell, Sarah IV, 643
Caldwell, Sarah A. VI, 803
Caldwell, Sophia VI, 836
Caldwell, Thomas I Sup 1, 10
Caldwell, Thurston VI, 854
Caldwell, Vincent II, 480
Caldwell, Watson VI, 803
Caleb, Malinda VI, 858
Caleb, Thomas M. VI, 858
Calen, ??? III, 58
Calen, Susan III, 58
Calender, Mary W. IV, 687
Calender, Mary W. IV, 723
Calendine, Edna V, 988
Calendine, J. H. V, 988
Calendine, Laurence V, 988
Calendine, Sarah V, 988
Calentine, Tivilie IV, 1247
Calentine, Tivilla IV, 1247
Caley, Ann II, 792
Caley, Ann II, 844
Caley, Ann II, 857
Caley, Ann II, 867
Caley, Anna II, 796
Caley, Annie II, 792
Caley, Annie II, 844
Caley, Annie II, 857
Caley, Hannah II, 796
Caley, Hannah II, 917
Caley, Hannah R. II, 844
Caley, Joseph G. II, 844
Caley, Joseph G. II, 917
Caley, Mary II, 785
Caley, Mary II, 917
Caley, Mary L. II, 844
Caley, Mary L. II, 870
Caley, Melson L. II, 917
Caley, Melson L. Rowland II, 844
Caley, Nelson VI, 888
Caley, Samuel II, 785
Caley, Samuel II, 792
Caley, Samuel II, 796
Caley, Samuel II, 844
Caley, Samuel II, 857
Caley, Samuel II, 867
Caley, Samuel II, 870
Caley, Samuel II, 917
Caley, Sarah II, 844
Caley, Sarah II, 867
Caley, Sarah G. II, 844
Caley, Sarah Grubb II, 795
Caley, Susannah VI, 888
Caley, Wm. R. II, 845
Calfbower, Mary J. V, 988
Calfer, Mrs. Celia E. IV, 186
Calflesh, Elizabeth II, 480
Calflesh, Elizabeth II, 502
Calhoon, Elizabeth IV, 377
Calhoon, Elizabeth IV, 421
Calhoon, Elizabeth V, 156
Calhoon, Hannah I, 605
Calhoon, John IV, 377
Calhoon, John IV, 421
Calhoon, John V, 156
Calhoon, John F. I, 530
Calhoon, Mary IV, 377
Calhoon, Mary V, 156
Calhoon, William V, 156
Calhoon, Wm. IV, 377
Calhoon, Wm. V, 156
Calhoun, Agnes II, 845
Calhoun, Agnes II, 859
Calhoun, Alfred I, 922
Calhoun, Charles VI, 888
Calhoun, Eliza N. Brown VI, 513
Calhoun, Elizabeth IV, 377
Calhoun, Elizabeth V, 968
Calhoun, Emma I, 922
Calhoun, Emma I, 939
Calhoun, John IV, 377
Calhoun, John VI, 888
Calhoun, John C. VI, 513
Calhoun, Mary IV, 377
Calhoun, Mary V, 968
Calhoun, Mary V, 970
Calhoun, Newton J. V, 614
Calhoun, Sarah I, 922
Calhoun, Teressa W. VI, 888
Calhoun, William IV, 377
Calhoun, Wm. IV, 377
Calhoun, Wm. V, 968
Caliham, Mary VI, 823
Calken, Almeron B. IV, 1355
Calken, Asa K. IV, 1355
Calken, Ashley R. IV, 1355
Calken, Jared IV, 1355
Calken, Minerva P. IV, 1355
Calken, Sabrina R. IV, 1355
Calken, Susannah IV, 1355
Calken, William A. IV, 1355
Calkin, Almeron B. IV, 1355
Calkin, Asa K. IV, 1355
Calkin, Ashley R. IV, 1355
Calkin, Darius C. IV, 1355
Calkin, Jared IV, 1355
Calkin, Minerva P. IV, 1355
Calkin, Sabrina R. IV, 1355
Calkin, Susannah IV, 1355
Calkin, William A. IV, 1355
Call, Ann VI, 162
Call, James IV, 186
Call, Mattie I, 1149
Call, Sarah II, 343
Call, Sarah IV, 24
Call, Sarah IV, 39
Callace, Benjamin H. V, 552
Callace, Cynthia V, 552
Callace, Elmer M. V, 552
Callace, Jane V, 552
Callace, Tillia A. V, 552
Callaham, Abner VI, 803
Callaham, Abner VI, 888
Callaham, Achiles VI, 803
Callaham, Ann VI, 803
Callaham, Catharine VI, 803
Callaham, Catharine VI, 851
Callaham, David VI, 803
Callaham, David VI, 840
Callaham, David VI, 854
Callaham, David, Jr. VI, 803
Callaham, Dolly VI, 840
Callaham, Doshia VI, 888
Callaham, Edmund H. VI, 803
Callaham, Elisha VI, 803
Callaham, Elizabeth VI, 803
Callaham, Elizabeth VI, 838
Callaham, Elizabeth VI, 839
Callaham, Elizabeth VI, 844
Callaham, Elizabeth VI, 853
Callaham, Elizabeth VI, 888
Callaham, Elizabeth Callaham VI, 803
Callaham, Febey VI, 888
Callaham, Frances VI, 803
Callaham, Frances M. VI, 803
Callaham, Jane VI, 803
Callaham, John VI, 803
Callaham, John VI, 839
Callaham, John VI, 888
Callaham, John W. VI, 803
Callaham, Judy VI, 803
Callaham, Kisiah VI, 803
Callaham, Lella VI, 803
Callaham, Martha VI, 854
Callaham, Martha D. VI, 838
Callaham, Martha I. VI, 803
Callaham, Martin VI, 803
Callaham, Mary VI, 803
Callaham, Mary A. VI, 803
Callaham, Mary W. VI, 803
Callaham, Nancy VI, 802
Callaham, Nancy VI, 803
Callaham, Pamelia VI, 803
Callaham, Phiby VI, 803
Callaham, Ralph S. VI, 888
Callaham, Richard VI, 803
Callaham, Richard VI, 851
Callaham, Richard M. VI, 803
Callaham, Robert F. VI, 803
Callaham, Sallie A. VI, 834
Callaham, Sally VI, 802
Callaham, Sally VI, 888
Callaham, Stephen VI, 802
Callaham, Stephen VI, 803
Callaham, Stephen VI, 844
Callaham, Stephen VI, 853
Callaham, Stephen VI, 888
Callaham, Tire VI, 803
Callaham, Viney VI, 803
Callaham, William VI, 803
Callahan, Abner VI, 888
Callahan, David VI, 809
Callahan, David VI, 816
Callahan, Dennis IV, 934
Callahan, Doshia VI, 888
Callahan, Edwin II, 146
Callahan, Elizabeth VI, 860
Callahan, Elnore VI, 816
Callahan, James Wilson IV, 1309
Callahan, James Wilson IV, 1323
Callahan, Jemima VI, 809
Callahan, Marianna II, 146
Callahan, Mary E. II, 144
Callahan, Mary E. II, 146
Callahan, Phebee VI, 964
Callahan, Rose Elizabeth IV, 1309
Callahan, Rose Elizabeth IV, 1323
Callahan, Rose Keetch IV, 1309
Callahan, Sarah Ann VI, 964
Callahan, Stephen VI, 964
Calland, Elizabeth VI, 949
Callard, Johnson VI, 1011
Callard, Lucinda C. VI, 1011
Callaway, Abner E. VI, 803
Callaway, Addisonia E. D. VI, 889
Callaway, Ann VI, 889
Callaway, Ann Booker VI, 943
Callaway, Betsy VI, 803
Callaway, Caleb VI, 803
Callaway, Cena VI, 980
Callaway, Chesley VI, 888
Callaway, Christiana VI, 888
Callaway, Dashia VI, 803
Callaway, Dosha VI, 802
Callaway, Dudley VI, 821
Callaway, Dudley VI, 888
Callaway, Eliza VI, 803
Callaway, Elizabeth VI, 876
Callaway, Elizabeth VI, 939
Callaway, Elizabeth VI, 975
Callaway, Elizabeth VI, 1004
Callaway, Elizabeth C. VI, 884
Callaway, Fanny VI, 998
Callaway, Frances VI, 808
Callaway, Frances VI, 841
Callaway, Francis VI, 803
Callaway, Francis VI, 885
Callaway, Francis A. VI, 815
Callaway, Francis T. VI, 889
Callaway, George VI, 916
Callaway, Henry VI, 803
Callaway, Henry VI, 821
Callaway, Henry VI, 889
Callaway, J. VI, 943
Callaway, James VI, 870
Callaway, James VI, 876
Callaway, James VI, 888
Callaway, James VI, 939
Callaway, James VI, 967
Callaway, James VI, 1001
Callaway, James VI, 1004
Callaway, James F. VI, 817
Callaway, James, Jr. VI, 925
Callaway, Joel VI, 889
Callaway, John VI, 795
Callaway, John VI, 803
Callaway, John VI, 884
Callaway, John VI, 889
Callaway, John W. VI, 848
Callaway, Joseph VI, 815
Callaway, Joseph VI, 841
Callaway, Josiah C. VI, 841
Callaway, Lucinda VI, 803
Callaway, Lucinda VI, 889
Callaway, Lucy VI, 889
Callaway, Mary VI, 925
Callaway, Mary E. VI, 808
Callaway, Matilda VI, 949
Callaway, Nancy VI, 889
Callaway, Palina VI, 889
Callaway, Patty VI, 888
Callaway, Paul C. VI, 889
Callaway, Polly VI, 803
Callaway, Polly VI, 815
Callaway, Polly VI, 883
Callaway, Polly VI, 970
Callaway, Richard VI, 977
Callaway, Sally VI, 870
Callaway, Sally VI, 967
Callaway, Sarah VI, 795
Callaway, Sarah VI, 821
Callaway, Sarah VI, 824
Callaway, Sarah VI, 888
Callaway, Sarah VI, 977
Callaway, Susan VI, 967
Callaway, Susan E. VI, 803
Callaway, Susanna VI, 932
Callaway, Susannah VI, 888
Callaway, Thomas VI, 803
Callaway, William VI, 803
Callaway, William VI, 889
Callaway, William VI, 943
Callaway, William VI, 949
Callaway, William VI, 980
Callaway, Wm. VI, 975
Callaway, Wm., Sr. VI, 998
Callaway, Zach. VI, 962
Calledonia, Callie D. I, 450
Calleham, Catharine VI, 814
Calleham, David VI, 797
Calleham, David VI, 840
Calleham, Edmund H. VI, 814
Calleham, Elisha VI, 814
Calleham, Elisha VI, 819
Calleham, Elisha VI, 858
Calleham, Elisha VI, 859
Calleham, Elizabeth VI, 803
Calleham, Gabriella VI, 859
Calleham, John VI, 803
Calleham, Kisiah VI, 803
Calleham, Margaret VI, 863
Calleham, Mary VI, 819
Calleham, Polly VI, 797
Calleham, Polly VI, 840
Calleham, Richard VI, 803
Calleham, Stephen VI, 803
Calleham, Stephen VI, 814
Calleham, Stephen VI, 840
Calleham, William VI, 863
Callendar, Hannah II, 642
Callendar, Katharine II, 205
Callender, ??? II, 440
Callender, Ann II, 816
Callender, Benjamin II, 480
Callender, Catherine II, 205
Callender, Catherine II, 440
Callender, Catherine II, 480
Callender, Dora III, 190
Callender, Hannah II, 416
Callender, Hannah II, 480
Callender, Katharine II, 205
Callender, Katherine II, 169
Callender, Katherine II, 480
Callender, Margaret II, 343
Callender, Richard II, 205
Callender, Richard II, 283
Callender, William II, 205
Callender, William II, 283
Callender, William, Jr. II, 205
Callender, Wm. II, 440
Callender, Wm., Jr. II, 480
Calley, Andrew J. II, 698
Calley, Mary J. II, 698
Calley, Sarah II, 698
Callflower, Florence V, 988
Callflower, Mary J. V, 988
Callihan, Dennis IV, 934
Callin, Albert C. III, 58
Callin, Eugene Walker III, 58
Callin, Eugene Walker III, 226
Callin, Louise III, 58
Callin, Louise III, 226
Callin, Mary III, 58
Callison, James II, 206
Callister, Constance III, 58
Callister, J. Henry III, 58
Callister, Jennie C. III, 58
Callister, Kenneth III, 58
Callonder, Katharine II, 261
Callonder, William II, 205
Callonder, William II, 261
Callow, John II, 442
Calloway, Caleb VI, 856
Calloway, Charlotte VI, 798
Calloway, David VI, 856
Calloway, Elizabeth VI, 827
Calloway, Elizabeth VI, 856
Calloway, Frances VI, 798
Calloway, Frances VI, 815
Calloway, Frances VI, 818
Calloway, John VI, 845
Calloway, Joseph VI, 815
Calloway, Joseph VI, 819
Calloway, Joseph VI, 827
Calloway, Margaret VI, 845
Calloway, Nancy VI, 819
Calloway, Richard VI, 925
Calloway, Robert F. VI, 798
Calloway, Robert F. VI, 815
Calloway, Sarah VI, 797
Calloway, Susanna VI, 815
Calloway, Thomas VI, 797
Calloway, William VI, 837
Callway, Charles VI, 888
Callway, James VI, 888
Callway, John VI, 888
Callway, Judith VI, 888
Callway, Susanna VI, 888
Callway, Tabitha VI, 888
Callway, Zachariah VI, 888
Calver, Elizabeth II, 831
Calver, Elizabeth II, 845
Calver, Jacob V, 227
Calver, Nancy V, 227
Calver, Sarah Goldson II, 779
Calver, Sarah Goldson II, 831
Calver, Sarah Goldson II, 845
Calver, Wm. C. II, 831
Calver, Wm. G. II, 845
Calvert, Adeline F. VI, 940
Calvert, Ann II, 480
Calvert, Ann W. II, 480
Calvert, Ann W. II, 594
Calvert, Anna Maria II, 701
Calvert, Betsey VI, 889
Calvert, Betsy Rose VI, 889
Calvert, Catherine Emeline VI, 889
Calvert, Charles H. VI, 889
Calvert, Elizabeth II, 480
Calvert, Elizabeth II, 536
Calvert, Elizabeth VI, 889
Calvert, Elizabeth VI, 995
Calvert, Emeline VI, 889
Calvert, Francis VI, 889
Calvert, Francis VI, 987
Calvert, George II, 480
Calvert, George II, 636
Calvert, George II, 688
Calvert, Gov. ??? VI, 11
Calvert, Hannah II, 480
Calvert, Hannah II, 594
Calvert, Hannah II, 827
Calvert, Hannah II, 845
Calvert, Hannah V, 897
Calvert, John II, 343
Calvert, John II, 442

Calvert, John VI, 357
Calvert, Joseph VI, 889
Calvert, Kennet II, 480
Calvert, Louiza II, 343
Calvert, Maria II, 343
Calvert, Martha II, 194
Calvert, Martha II, 206
Calvert, Mary II, 343
Calvert, Mary II, 480
Calvert, Mary II, 636
Calvert, Mary II, 688
Calvert, Mary Ann IV, 1051
Calvert, Mary Ann IV, 1074
Calvert, Mary F. VI, 995
Calvert, Rebecca II, 480
Calvert, Robert VI, 889
Calvert, Sally VI, 889
Calvert, Samuel VI, 57
Calvert, Samuel VI, 61
Calvert, Samuel VI, 83
Calvert, Thomas II, 343
Calvert, Thomas II, 480
Calvert, Thomas II, 594
Calvert, Thomas H. II, 701
Calvert, Thomas Pretlow VI, 57
Calvert, William II, 194
Calvert, William II, 206
Calvert, William VI, 889
Calvert, Wm. II, 480
Calvin, Edith V, 453
Calwell, James VI, 795
Calwell, Jane VI, 843
Cam, Mabel II, 60
Cam, Mabel II, 90
Camack, Mary I, 1027
Camack, Mary I, 1030
Camack, Mary V, 321
Camack, Mary V, 355
Cambbel, John I, 1017
Cambbel, Ralph I, 1017
Cambel, Hannah II, 987
Cambel, Hannah II, 1011
Cambell, Anna V, 988
Cambell, Isabel V, 794
Cambell, John VI, 889
Cambell, Lucinda VI, 889
Cambell, Lucy Wood VI, 889
Cambell, Mary I, 1035
Cambell, Widow Mary I, 1027
Cambell, William VI, 889
Camberlain, Endora M. I, 301
Camble, Alexander I, 347
Camble, Chas. I, 347
Camble, Elender I, 347
Camble, Eli I, 347
Camble, Elic I, 347
Camble, Elizabeth I, 347
Camble, Hannah I, 444
Camble, Levi I, 347
Camble, Margaret I, 347
Camble, Margret I, 347
Camble, Mary I, 347
Camble, Nancey I, 347
Camble, Owen I, 347
Camble, Rachel I, 347
Camble, Reachel I, 347
Camble, William I, 347
Camble, Wm. I, 347
Camblos, Effie II, 818
Camblos, Euphemia II, 818
Cambron, Abigail IV, 1355
Cambron, Esther IV, 1355
Cambron, Esther IV, 1367
Cambron, Hannah IV, 1355
Cambron, William IV, 1355
Camden, Maria II, 845
Camel, William VI, 8
Cameron, Abigail V, 944
Cameron, Albert IV, 687
Cameron, Albert IV, 804
Cameron, Albert IV, 805
Cameron, Albert H. IV, 183
Cameron, Albert H. IV, 186
Cameron, Alexander IV, 614
Cameron, Alexander IV, 805
Cameron, Alice IV, 687
Cameron, Angus II, 480
Cameron, Ann II, 480
Cameron, Ann II, 731
Cameron, Ann IV, 805
Cameron, Ann IV, 811
Cameron, Anna V. IV, 813
Cameron, Anna V. IV, 934
Cameron, Anna V. IV, 949
Cameron, Anna Viola IV, 934
Cameron, Arwilda IV, 966
Cameron, Barclay S. Hall IV, 186
Cameron, Beulah IV, 757
Cameron, Beulah IV, 805
Cameron, Beulah IV, 813
Cameron, Beulah IV, 819
Cameron, Beulah IV, 934
Cameron, Beulah IV, 949
Cameron, Beulah IV, 960
Cameron, Bula IV, 805
Cameron, Bula IV, 815
Cameron, Bulah IV, 934
Cameron, Clara B. IV, 687
Cameron, Clara Elizabeth IV, 805
Cameron, Daisy V, 156
Cameron, Dougal II, 206
Cameron, Edith M. IV, 934
Cameron, Edith M. IV, 962
Cameron, Edward IV, 805
Cameron, Effie IV, 687
Cameron, Elizabeth IV, 687
Cameron, Elizabeth D. IV, 183
Cameron, Elizabeth D. IV, 186
Cameron, Elizabeth D. IV, 687
Cameron, Elizabeth D. IV, 804
Cameron, Elizabeth D. IV, 805
Cameron, Emma V, 156
Cameron, Grace V, 156
Cameron, Hannah IV, 186
Cameron, Hannah IV, 614
Cameron, Hannah IV, 644
Cameron, Hannah IV, 687
Cameron, Hannah IV, 805
Cameron, Hiram IV, 805
Cameron, Hirum IV, 805
Cameron, Holland IV, 805
Cameron, Holland W. IV, 687
Cameron, Jane IV, 614
Cameron, Jane IV, 805
Cameron, Josiah IV, 186
Cameron, Josiah IV, 614
Cameron, Josiah IV, 644
Cameron, Josiah IV, 687
Cameron, Josiah IV, 805
Cameron, Josiah IV, 833
Cameron, Leonard IV, 966
Cameron, Louisa IV, 805
Cameron, Louisa IV, 840
Cameron, Louiza IV, 805
Cameron, Lydia Ann IV, 805
Cameron, Mabel IV, 805
Cameron, Mabel IV, 934
Cameron, Mabel IV, 940
Cameron, Mabel H. IV, 687
Cameron, Mabel H. IV, 758
Cameron, Mabel H. IV, 934
Cameron, Mabel H. IV, 990
Cameron, Mable IV, 805
Cameron, Mable C. IV, 757
Cameron, Mary IV, 186
Cameron, Mary IV, 215
Cameron, Mary IV, 216
Cameron, Mary IV, 819
Cameron, Mary IV, 934
Cameron, Mary IV, 960
Cameron, Mary IV, 961
Cameron, Mary E. IV, 934
Cameron, Milton IV, 757
Cameron, Milton IV, 805
Cameron, Milton IV, 813
Cameron, Milton IV, 815
Cameron, Milton IV, 819
Cameron, Milton IV, 934
Cameron, Milton IV, 949
Cameron, Milton IV, 960
Cameron, Rachel V, 897
Cameron, Rosetta K. IV, 971
Cameron, Ruth Anna L. II, 845
Cameron, Sarah Jane IV, 805
Cameron, Sarah Jane IV, 828
Cameron, William M. IV, 805
Camil, Marion I, 1149
Camlin, ??? III, 58
Camlin, Louisa III, 58
Camm, John II, 480
Camm, Mary II, 480
Camm, Olivia VI, 803
Camm, Robert VI, 803
Cammac, James I, 1027
Cammac, John V, 35
Cammach, Joanna I, 1017
Cammack, Amos I, 1017
Cammack, Amos V, 35
Cammack, Ann I, 1017
Cammack, Anna V, 662
Cammack, Charity V, 74
Cammack, Charles V, 614
Cammack, Charles V, 662
Cammack, Charlie H. V, 614
Cammack, Chas. V, 662
Cammack, Cornelia V, 614
Cammack, Cornelia C. V, 614
Cammack, Elizabeth V, 35
Cammack, Elizabeth V, 553
Cammack, Elizabeth V, 567
Cammack, Ervin V, 321
Cammack, George W. V, 321
Cammack, Hannah V, 35
Cammack, Hannah V, 74
Cammack, Irvin H. V, 321
Cammack, Ivan Oglesbee V, 662
Cammack, James I, 1017
Cammack, James I, 1027
Cammack, James V, 35
Cammack, James V, 553
Cammack, James V, 779
Cammack, Jane V, 35
Cammack, Jane V, 74
Cammack, Jane V, 567
Cammack, Joann V, 35
Cammack, Joanna I, 1017
Cammack, John I, 1017
Cammack, John V, 35
Cammack, John V, 74
Cammack, John W. V, 614
Cammack, Margaret I, 1017
Cammack, Margaret I, 1027
Cammack, Mary I, 1017
Cammack, Mary I, 1027
Cammack, Mary V, 321
Cammack, Michael V, 321
Cammack, Nellie V, 614
Cammack, Rachel I, 1017
Cammack, Rachel I, 1027
Cammack, Rachel V, 35
Cammack, Sallie V, 35
Cammack, Sallie V, 126
Cammack, Samuel I, 1017
Cammack, Samuel V, 35
Cammack, Samuel V, 74
Cammack, William I, 1017
Cammack, William V, 35
Cammack, Willie V, 321
Cammack, Willie V, 614
Cammel, Elizabeth I, 301
Cammel, Hannah I, 756
Cammel, Mary II, 60
Cammel, Mary II, 68
Cammell, Elizabeth II, 60
Cammell, Elizabeth II, 66
Cammell, John II, 442
Cammpbell, Sibyl VI, 930
Camp, Abigail IV, 891
Camp, Abigail IV, 892
Camp, Alice V, 663
Camp, Anna Belle V, 663
Camp, Bell V, 553
Camp, Benjamin V, 988
Camp, Clark V, 553
Camp, Clark V, 662
Camp, Effa May V, 662
Camp, Effie May V, 553
Camp, Eli D. V, 881
Camp, Elizabeth V, 662
Camp, Elizabeth V, 663
Camp, Elizabeth VI, 966
Camp, Emily V, 897
Camp, Emma V, 988
Camp, Florra V, 662
Camp, Frances VI, 807
Camp, Frank Brannon V, 663
Camp, Hazel Brannon V, 663
Camp, Isabele V, 553
Camp, Isabella V, 662
Camp, John V, 988
Camp, John E. VI, 807
Camp, John W. V, 988
Camp, John Wm. V, 988
Camp, Joseph Henry V, 662
Camp, Lydia IV, 1309
Camp, Lydia D. V, 880
Camp, Martha V, 988
Camp, Mary D. III, 58
Camp, Mary J. V, 662
Camp, Mary Jane V, 553
Camp, Mellie V, 897
Camp, Phebe IV, 816
Camp, Phebe Jane IV, 805
Camp, Richard D. VI, 800
Camp, Richard D. VI, 827
Camp, Ruth IV, 1203
Camp, Ruth IV, 1217
Camp, Ruth Ann V, 553
Camp, Sarah IV, 1151
Camp, Sarah IV, 1184
Camp, Susan V, 988
Camp, Ulysses V, 663
Camp, Ulysses Grant V, 663
Camp, Wm. T. V, 897
Campbel, Hannah I, 475
Campbel, Isabel V, 794
Campbel, Josiah I, 444
Campbel, Malinda V, 35
Campbel, Malinda V, 120
Campbel, Maria IV, 1355
Campbel, Rebecca V, 794
Campbel, Sarah V, 794
Campbell, ??? III, 58
Campbell, A. H. III, 58
Campbell, Aaron VI, 889
Campbell, Abel IV, 24
Campbell, Abel IV, 29
Campbell, Abel IV, 78
Campbell, Abel, Jr. IV, 78
Campbell, Ada M. III, 58
Campbell, Adelia IV, 1309
Campbell, Alex I, 347
Campbell, Alex H. III, 59
Campbell, Alex. H. III, 351
Campbell, Alexander I, 347
Campbell, Alexander I, 376
Campbell, Alexander I, 1104
Campbell, Alexander I, 1116
Campbell, Alexander IV, 78
Campbell, Alexander VI, 803
Campbell, Alexander M. VI, 874
Campbell, Alexander M. VI, 889
Campbell, Alexander W. VI, 889
Campbell, Alexander W. VI, 917
Campbell, Alexander W. VI, 989
Campbell, Alexander, Sr. I, 1116
Campbell, Alice II, 343
Campbell, Alice II, 465
Campbell, Alice II, 480
Campbell, Alice V, 988
Campbell, Allan R. III, 106
Campbell, Allen R. III, 58
Campbell, Amanda V, 897
Campbell, Amanda K. V, 897
Campbell, Ann III, 58
Campbell, Ann III, 397
Campbell, Ann III, 431
Campbell, Ann Henry VI, 889
Campbell, Ann Miller VI, 890
Campbell, Anna V, 988
Campbell, Anny VI, 875
Campbell, Anselm VI, 889
Campbell, Anthony VI, 882
Campbell, Anthony VI, 889
Campbell, Anthony VI, 896
Campbell, Anthony Cammil VI, 883
Campbell, Aram VI, 1016
Campbell, Archibald III, 58
Campbell, Archibald VI, 822
Campbell, Archibald VI, 837
Campbell, Benjamin IV, 24
Campbell, Benjamin IV, 122
Campbell, Benjamin V, 227
Campbell, Betsy VI, 883
Campbell, C. B. VI, 880
Campbell, C. R. VI, 880
Campbell, C. W. IV, 1151
Campbell, Caleb IV, 78
Campbell, Caleb IV, 122
Campbell, Capt. James VI, 908
Campbell, Catharine C. I, 628
Campbell, Catharine E. VI, 890
Campbell, Catherine V, 663
Campbell, Charity VI, 961
Campbell, Chas. IV, 1309
Campbell, Chas. V, 988
Campbell, Clark IV, 78
Campbell, Clark IV, 687
Campbell, Clark Priscilla IV, 687
Campbell, Clark R. VI, 917
Campbell, Deborah III, 310
Campbell, Deborah IV, 24
Campbell, Deborah IV, 73
Campbell, Deborah IV, 78
Campbell, Demartha VI, 889
Campbell, Dicey VI, 865
Campbell, Dora Parker V, 988
Campbell, Dugal IV, 24
Campbell, Duncan III, 310
Campbell, Edward Wilson II, 845
Campbell, Eleanor IV, 377
Campbell, Eleanor IV, 408
Campbell, Elender I, 347
Campbell, Elexander I, 1116
Campbell, Eli I, 1104
Campbell, Elic I, 347
Campbell, Eliza Ann IV, 78
Campbell, Eliza Ann IV, 121
Campbell, Eliza Ann IV, 122
Campbell, Eliza Jane VI, 944
Campbell, Elizabeth I, 347
Campbell, Elizabeth I, 376
Campbell, Elizabeth I, 1060
Campbell, Elizabeth I, 1062
Campbell, Elizabeth I, 1116
Campbell, Elizabeth I, 1117
Campbell, Elizabeth II, 60
Campbell, Elizabeth III, 201
Campbell, Elizabeth IV, 24
Campbell, Elizabeth IV, 71
Campbell, Elizabeth IV, 78
Campbell, Elizabeth IV, 82
Campbell, Elizabeth IV, 102
Campbell, Elizabeth IV, 122
Campbell, Elizabeth IV, 687
Campbell, Elizabeth IV, 697
Campbell, Elizabeth VI, 470
Campbell, Elizabeth VI, 480
Campbell, Elizabeth VI, 803
Campbell, Elizabeth VI, 822
Campbell, Elizabeth VI, 859
Campbell, Elizabeth VI, 889
Campbell, Elizabeth VI, 913
Campbell, Elizabeth VI, 998
Campbell, Ella V, 227
Campbell, Ellis IV, 78
Campbell, Elsbeth I, 1104
Campbell, Elvira VI, 983
Campbell, Ephraim IV, 24
Campbell, Esther I, 1060
Campbell, Esther IV, 24
Campbell, Esther V, 196
Campbell, Eva V, 453
Campbell, Eva V, 663
Campbell, Evelyn V, 663
Campbell, Fay V, 227
Campbell, Frances V, 663
Campbell, Frances VI, 889
Campbell, Francis V, 663
Campbell, Fred V, 798
Campbell, Fred V, 988
Campbell, George VI, 889
Campbell, Gertrude III, 58
Campbell, Gertrude III, 106
Campbell, Gertrude V, 663
Campbell, Gertrude V, 698
Campbell, Gladys V, 729
Campbell, Gracey VI, 889
Campbell, Gustavus VI, 863
Campbell, Hannah I, 376
Campbell, Hannah I, 444
Campbell, Hannah I, 675
Campbell, Hannah I, 756
Campbell, Helen III, 58
Campbell, Henry VI, 889
Campbell, Henry VI, 961
Campbell, Henry VI, 1016
Campbell, Henry T. VI, 889
Campbell, Henry T. VI, 944
Campbell, Ida I, 628
Campbell, Isaiah I, 444
Campbell, J. III, 431
Campbell, James II, 343
Campbell, James IV, 24
Campbell, James IV, 78
Campbell, James VI, 803
Campbell, James VI, 837
Campbell, James VI, 889
Campbell, James VI, 913
Campbell, James VI, 917
Campbell, James VI, 952
Campbell, James VI, 963
Campbell, James VI, 972
Campbell, James H. I, 628
Campbell, James W. VI, 890
Campbell, Jane VI, 803
Campbell, Jane VI, 837
Campbell, Jas. S. VI, 934
Campbell, Jehoakim III, 58
Campbell, Jehoiakiam III, 431
Campbell, Jehoiakim III, 397
Campbell, Jennet VI, 803
Campbell, Jenny VI, 837
Campbell, Jenny VI, 889
Campbell, Jenny VI, 1016
Campbell, Jessee A. V, 729
Campbell, John I, 922
Campbell, John I, 1027
Campbell, John I, 1035
Campbell, John IV, 24
Campbell, John IV, 1309
Campbell, John V, 729
Campbell, John V, 988
Campbell, John VI, 802
Campbell, John VI, 803
Campbell, John VI, 889
Campbell, John VI, 1006
Campbell, John B. VI, 803
Campbell, John B. VI, 859
Campbell, John B. VI, 889
Campbell, John B. VI, 1019
Campbell, John D. VI, 843
Campbell, John K. VI, 803
Campbell, Joseph IV, 78
Campbell, Joseph IV, 122
Campbell, Joseph VI, 889
Campbell, Joseph VI, 890
Campbell, Joseph VI, 929
Campbell, Joseph M. IV, 78
Campbell, Joshua VI, 803
Campbell, Josiah I, 444
Campbell, Judith VI, 889
Campbell, Judy F. VI, 889

Campbell, Julia Ann VI, 890
Campbell, Leah VI, 361
Campbell, Leah VI, 375
Campbell, Lemuel VI, 889
Campbell, Lemuel A. VI, 915
Campbell, Levi I, 1104
Campbell, Lewis IV, 24
Campbell, Lewis IV, 73
Campbell, Lewis IV, 78
Campbell, Lewis VI, 930
Campbell, Libbie V, 988
Campbell, Liza VI, 882
Campbell, Lucinda VI, 889
Campbell, Lucinda Ann VI, 930
Campbell, Lucy IV, 688
Campbell, Lucy Ann IV, 687
Campbell, Lucy Ann IV, 774
Campbell, Lucy Wood VI, 889
Campbell, Lula E. V, 663
Campbell, Luraney VI, 803
Campbell, Malinda V, 35
Campbell, Malinda V, 553
Campbell, Margaret I, 347
Campbell, Margaret I, 376
Campbell, Margaret I, 429
Campbell, Margaret I, 1102
Campbell, Margaret I, 1116
Campbell, Margaret IV, 24
Campbell, Margaret IV, 71
Campbell, Margaret V, 729
Campbell, Margaret V, 735
Campbell, Margaret VI, 803
Campbell, Margaret VI, 917
Campbell, Margreat I, 347
Campbell, Margreat I, 1104
Campbell, Maria IV, 1355
Campbell, Martha IV, 78
Campbell, Martha IV, 80
Campbell, Martha V, 35
Campbell, Martha VI, 803
Campbell, Martha VI, 889
Campbell, Martha VI, 1002
Campbell, Martha A. B. VI, 930
Campbell, Martha C. VI, 890
Campbell, Martha E. I, 922
Campbell, Martha G. VI, 803
Campbell, Martha Jane V, 35
Campbell, Mary I, 444
Campbell, Mary I, 922
Campbell, Mary I, 1104
Campbell, Mary I, 1116
Campbell, Mary I, 1117
Campbell, Mary II, 60
Campbell, Mary II, 343
Campbell, Mary II, 845
Campbell, Mary III, 214
Campbell, Mary IV, 24
Campbell, Mary IV, 74
Campbell, Mary IV, 78
Campbell, Mary IV, 106
Campbell, Mary IV, 117
Campbell, Mary IV, 122
Campbell, Mary IV, 135
Campbell, Mary IV, 687
Campbell, Mary IV, 688
Campbell, Mary VI, 803
Campbell, Mary VI, 816
Campbell, Mary VI, 889
Campbell, Mary Ann II, 845
Campbell, Mary Ann IV, 78
Campbell, Mary Ann IV, 92
Campbell, Mary Belle IV, 1309
Campbell, Mary C. VI, 803
Campbell, Mary Jane VI, 1017
Campbell, Mary M. IV, 122
Campbell, Mary M. IV, 687
Campbell, Mary M. VI, 889
Campbell, Mary M. VI, 908
Campbell, Mary Margaret IV, 78
Campbell, Mary McCraw VI, 889
Campbell, Mary S. VI, 874
Campbell, Mattie V, 729
Campbell, Maud V, 988
Campbell, Mayland Cuthbert II, 845
Campbell, Melina VI, 889
Campbell, Mildred S. VI, 889
Campbell, Milton IV, 78
Campbell, Miriam I, 530
Campbell, Miriam I, 559
Campbell, Modesta Marguerite V, 897
Campbell, Molly Patterson VI, 889
Campbell, Morgan IV, 78
Campbell, Morgan IV, 122
Campbell, Morgan IV, 132
Campbell, Morgan IV, 687
Campbell, Morgin IV, 122
Campbell, Moses VI, 889
Campbell, Moses VI, 907
Campbell, Moses VI, 913
Campbell, Nancey I, 1104
Campbell, Nancy I, 1116
Campbell, Nancy VI, 803
Campbell, Nancy VI, 884
Campbell, Nancy VI, 889
Campbell, Nat H. VI, 803
Campbell, Nathl. H. VI, 923
Campbell, Orville O. V, 663
Campbell, Owen I, 347
Campbell, Parker VI, 889
Campbell, Parker VI, 942
Campbell, Patience II, 343
Campbell, Patrick III, 59
Campbell, Patrick III, 251
Campbell, Patrick Pearsall III, 59
Campbell, Polly VI, 889
Campbell, Polly VI, 924
Campbell, Pricella IV, 687
Campbell, Priscilla IV, 78
Campbell, Priscilla H. IV, 122
Campbell, Priscilla H. IV, 132
Campbell, Rachel I, 347
Campbell, Rachel I, 1116
Campbell, Rachel I, 1131
Campbell, Rachel II, 60
Campbell, Rachel II, 110
Campbell, Rachel IV, 24
Campbell, Ralph I, 1027
Campbell, Ralph I, 1035
Campbell, Reachel I, 1104
Campbell, Rebecca IV, 687
Campbell, Rebeckah IV, 614
Campbell, Rebeckah VI, 924
Campbell, Rebekah I, 1060
Campbell, Rebekah I, 1062
Campbell, Reuben IV, 122
Campbell, Reuben Bailey IV, 122
Campbell, Rexford V, 988
Campbell, Richard VI, 934
Campbell, Robert IV, 78
Campbell, Robert IV, 122
Campbell, Robert VI, 889
Campbell, Robert VI, 1017
Campbell, Roy V, 988
Campbell, Ruth IV, 24
Campbell, Ruth IV, 27
Campbell, Ruth IV, 78
Campbell, Ruth IV, 122
Campbell, Ruth IV, 687
Campbell, Ruth IV, 688
Campbell, Ruth Ann IV, 78
Campbell, Ruth Ann IV, 122
Campbell, Ruth C. IV, 688
Campbell, Ruth C. IV, 720
Campbell, Ruthanna IV, 687
Campbell, Sally VI, 889
Campbell, Sally VI, 896
Campbell, Sally VI, 1018
Campbell, Samuel I, 1027
Campbell, Samuel IV, 78
Campbell, Samuel IV, 122
Campbell, Samuel VI, 803
Campbell, Samuel VI, 837
Campbell, Sanford P. II, 845
Campbell, Sarah I, 530
Campbell, Sarah I, 1016
Campbell, Sarah I, 1027
Campbell, Sarah I, 1030
Campbell, Sarah II, 343
Campbell, Sarah III, 59
Campbell, Sarah III, 251
Campbell, Sibyl VI, 983
Campbell, Silas IV, 1355
Campbell, Susan IV, 78
Campbell, Susan IV, 89
Campbell, Susan H. III, 351
Campbell, Susan W. III, 59
Campbell, Susanna IV, 24
Campbell, Susanna IV, 29
Campbell, Susanna IV, 78
Campbell, Susanna VI, 889
Campbell, Susanna VI, 934
Campbell, Susanna, Jr. IV, 78
Campbell, Susannah IV, 78
Campbell, Susannah VI, 889
Campbell, Tabitha II, 343
Campbell, Tempe VI, 889
Campbell, Thomas II, 343
Campbell, Thomas VI, 889
Campbell, Thomas VI, 890
Campbell, Thomas VI, 924
Campbell, Thomas S. VI, 803
Campbell, Victor V, 729
Campbell, Walter L. III, 58
Campbell, Widow Mary I, 1027
Campbell, Willard T. V, 897
Campbell, William I, 1116
Campbell, William IV, 24
Campbell, William IV, 27
Campbell, William IV, 74
Campbell, William IV, 78
Campbell, William IV, 117
Campbell, William IV, 122
Campbell, William IV, 186
Campbell, William V, 227
Campbell, William VI, 803
Campbell, William VI, 859
Campbell, William VI, 889
Campbell, William VI, 924
Campbell, William VI, 1002
Campbell, William B. IV, 122
Campbell, William L. VI, 1016
Campbell, William P. I, 376
Campbell, Wm. I, 1104
Campbell, Wm. IV, 78
Campbell, Wm. IV, 122
Campbell, Wm. IV, 687
Campbell, Wm. V, 988
Campbell, Wm. T. V, 897
Campbell, Wm. T. VI, 954
Camper, Elizabeth Ann VI, 890
Camper, Harrison VI, 890
Camper, James VI, 909
Camper, Jane VI, 890
Camper, Nancy VI, 890
Camper, Patsey VI, 890
Camper, Sharred VI, 890
Camper, Valentine VI, 890
Camperson, Ruthanna II, 801
Campf, Carl IV, 687
Campfield, Armelia IV, 1151
Campfield, Armelia IV, 1158
Campion, Ann II, 480
Campion, Ann II, 731
Campion, Ann II, 845
Campion, Anna Maria II, 786
Campion, Anna W. II, 845
Campion, Charles II, 731
Campion, Charlotte III, 72
Campion, Chas. II, 845
Campion, Elizabeth Yardley II, 731
Campion, Ellen Field II, 731
Campion, Francis II, 480
Campion, Francis II, 701
Campion, Francis II, 731
Campion, Harrison II, 786
Campion, Harrison II, 845
Campion, John II, 169
Campion, John II, 207
Campion, John Willetts II, 786
Campion, Joseph II, 731
Campion, Joseph, Jr. II, 283
Campion, Keturah II, 283
Campion, Keturah II, 293
Campion, Lucy Ann II, 701
Campion, Lucy Ann II, 731
Campion, Margaret II, 701
Campion, Margaret II, 731
Campion, Maria II, 845
Campion, Mary II, 207
Campion, Mary Vinicomb II, 731
Campion, Nathan Field II, 731
Campion, Sara VI, 28
Campion, Sarah II, 169
Campion, Sarah VI, 27
Campion, Sarah Abbott II, 731
Campion, Stacy B. II, 283
Campion, Stacy B. II, 845
Campion, Stacy B., Jr. II, 845
Campion, Wm. III, 72
Campion, Wm. Francis II, 731
Campion, Wm. Henry II, 845
Camplon, Anna W. II, 940
Camplon, Camden II, 940
Camplon, Harrison II, 940
Camplon, Maria II, 940
Camplon, Stacy B. II, 940
Campp, Alice IV, 1028
Campton, Catharine V, 160
Campton, John R. IV, 1151
Campton, Maria IV, 1151
Campton, Samuel, Jr. I, 1027
Camron, Albert IV, 687
Camron, Elizabeth I, 376
Camron, Elizabeth I, 427
Canada, Charles VI, 480
Canada, Charles VI, 569
Canada, Elizabeth V, 780
Canada, Esther V, 780
Canada, Geo. VI, 965
Canada, Hannah I, 675
Canada, John I, 530
Canada, John V, 780
Canada, Joseph I, 873
Canada, Julius Allen I, 873
Canada, Lydia I, 675
Canada, Mary I, 675
Canada, Mary Kesiah I, 873
Canada, Oliver Amanuel I, 873
Canada, Rebecca IV, 78
Canada, Rebecca IV, 105
Canada, Ruth I, 530
Canada, Sally VI, 965
Canada, Walter I, 530
Canada, Walter I, 675
Canada, Wd. Phebe VI, 480
Canada, Wd. Phebe VI, 569
Canaday, Abigail I, 530
Canaday, Abigail I, 601
Canaday, Abigail I, 605
Canaday, Amy I, 1116
Canaday, Ann I, 530
Canaday, Ann I, 600
Canaday, Ann I, 601
Canaday, Ann I, 605
Canaday, Ann I, 1116
Canaday, Ann V, 322
Canaday, Anna I, 1104
Canaday, Anna I, 1116
Canaday, Anna I, 1121
Canaday, Anna Jane I, 601
Canaday, Anna, Jr. V, 300
Canaday, Asa I, 601
Canaday, Barton I, 1116
Canaday, Ben VI, 1012
Canaday, Benjamin I, 1104
Canaday, Benjamin I, 1116
Canaday, Betsey VI, 926
Canaday, Boater I, 1104
Canaday, Boater I, 1116
Canaday, Bowater I, 493
Canaday, Bowater I, 1116
Canaday, Bowater V, 300
Canaday, Charity I, 1104
Canaday, Charity I, 1121
Canaday, Charity V, 553
Canaday, Charity V, 586
Canaday, Charles I, 493
Canaday, Charles I, 530
Canaday, Charles I, 1101
Canaday, Charles I, 1104
Canaday, Charles I, 1116
Canaday, Charles I, 1137
Canaday, Charles, Jr. I, 530
Canaday, Chearls I, 493
Canaday, Christopher V, 299
Canaday, Drucilla V, 300
Canaday, Drucilla V, 322
Canaday, Drucilla V, 341
Canaday, Drusilla V, 299
Canaday, Elihu I, 1104
Canaday, Frederick I, 1104
Canaday, Hannah I, 1116
Canaday, Harmon I, 605
Canaday, Harmon I, 1116
Canaday, Henry I, 493
Canaday, Henry I, 530
Canaday, Henry I, 1104
Canaday, Henry I, 1116
Canaday, Henry V, 299
Canaday, Henry V, 322
Canaday, Henry V, 341
Canaday, Herman I, 601
Canaday, Hermon I, 1104
Canaday, Hugh II, 480
Canaday, Jane I, 1104
Canaday, Jane I, 1149
Canaday, John I, 493
Canaday, John I, 530
Canaday, John I, 1101
Canaday, John I, 1104
Canaday, John I, 1116
Canaday, John V, 299
Canaday, John, Jr. I, 1104
Canaday, John, Jr. I, 1116
Canaday, Jonathan I, 1104
Canaday, Joshua I, 1116
Canaday, Julitha I, 1104
Canaday, Lartha I, 1116
Canaday, Latha I, 1104
Canaday, Latha I, 1116
Canaday, Letha I, 605
Canaday, Madison V, 322
Canaday, Margaret I, 493
Canaday, Margaret I, 530
Canaday, Margaret I, 1101
Canaday, Margaret I, 1104
Canaday, Margaret I, 1116
Canaday, Margaret II, 480
Canaday, Margaret V, 299
Canaday, Margaret V, 307
Canaday, Margery I, 530
Canaday, Mary I, 530
Canaday, Mary I, 1104
Canaday, Mary I, 1116
Canaday, Mary I, 1121
Canaday, Mary V, 298
Canaday, Mary V, 299
Canaday, Matilda I, 530
Canaday, Matilda I, 1104
Canaday, Matilda I, 1116
Canaday, Matison V, 300
Canaday, Minor I, 1116
Canaday, Nahan I, 530
Canaday, Nathan I, 600
Canaday, Nathan I, 601
Canaday, Nathan I, 605
Canaday, Nathan I, 1104
Canaday, Nathan V, 299
Canaday, Nathan V, 300
Canaday, Nathan V, 322
Canaday, Nathan H. I, 605
Canaday, Phebe I, 493
Canaday, Phebe I, 530
Canaday, Phebe I, 1104
Canaday, Pleasant VI, 890
Canaday, Rebekah I, 1104
Canaday, Robert I, 493
Canaday, Robert I, 1116
Canaday, Russell I, 1104
Canaday, Ruth I, 530
Canaday, Sally VI, 890
Canaday, Sarah I, 1104
Canaday, Sarah I, 1116
Canaday, Sarah V, 663
Canaday, Walter I, 493
Canaday, Walter I, 530
Canaday, Walter I, 1104
Canaday, Walter I, 1116
Canaday, Walter I, 1137
Canaday, Walter V, 215
Canaday, Walter V, 300
Canaday, Walter V, 322
Canaday, Widow Phebe I, 517
Canaday, William I, 530
Canaday, William I, 600
Canaday, William I, 601
Canaday, William I, 605
Canaday, William I, 1104
Canaday, William I, 1116
Canaday, Wm. Riley V, 300
Canaday, Wm. Riley V, 322
Canaday, Wm. Riley Madison V, 300
Canade, Salley I, 873
Canady, ??? I, 889
Canady, Abigail I, 517
Canady, Abigail I, 530
Canady, Abigail I, 564
Canady, Bowater I, 517
Canady, Caroline I, 873
Canady, Caroline I, 901
Canady, Charles I, 517
Canady, Drucilla V, 305
Canady, Easter I, 268
Canady, Elizabeth I, 873
Canady, Elizabeth VI, 948
Canady, Hannah I, 517
Canady, Henry I, 530
Canady, Henry V, 35
Canady, Henry V, 305
Canady, Jane I, 874
Canady, John V, 35
Canady, Joseph I, 517
Canady, Joseph I, 873
Canady, Joshua I, 517
Canady, Julius Allen I, 873
Canady, Mary I, 530
Canady, Mary V, 35
Canady, Mary Kesiah I, 873
Canady, Miriam I, 873
Canady, Nancy V, 35
Canady, Nathan V, 35
Canady, Oliver Amanuel I, 873
Canady, Pleasant VI, 822
Canady, Pleasant VI, 895
Canady, Pleasant VI, 923
Canady, Pleasant VI, 948
Canady, Prudence I, 517
Canady, Rachel E. I, 873
Canady, Salley I, 873
Canady, Sarah I, 517
Canady, Sarah I, 873
Canady, Sarah P. I, 873
Canady, Sophia A. VI, 895
Canady, Thomas I, 517
Canady, Walter V, 35
Canady, Walter V, 295
Canady, William I, 517
Canaida, William I, 530
Canary, Sarah IV, 186
Canary, Sarah IV, 214
Canbury, Anna Kaighn II, 731
Canbury, Benjamin II, 731
Canbury, Elizabeth Bartram II, 731
Canbury, Emma II, 731
Canbury, Joel II, 731
Canbury, John Warder II, 731
Canbury, Wm. Warder II, 731
Canby, Adelia II, 786

Canby, Amos VI, 510
Canby, Amos G. VI, 735
Canby, Andrew V, 156
Canby, Andrew E. V, 35
Canby, Ann II, 206
Canby, Ann II, 284
Canby, Ann II, 343
Canby, Ann II, 480
Canby, Ann II, 682
Canby, Ann II, 987
Canby, Ann II, 1027
Canby, Ann V, 35
Canby, Ann V, 90
Canby, Ann VI, 480
Canby, Ann VI, 510
Canby, Ann VI, 630
Canby, Ann VI, 735
Canby, Anna II, 820
Canby, Anne II, 957
Canby, Anne II, 987
Canby, Benjamin II, 480
Canby, Benjamin II, 682
Canby, Benjamin II, 957
Canby, Benjamin II, 987
Canby, Benjamin II, 1031
Canby, Benjamin II, 1042
Canby, Benjamin H. VI, 480
Canby, Benjamin Hough VI, 480
Canby, Benjamin Hough VI, 572
Canby, Beulah II, 957
Canby, Beulah II, 987
Canby, Beulah VI, 735
Canby, Caleb II, 343
Canby, Caleb II, 701
Canby, Caleb II, 731
Canby, Caleb H. II, 481
Canby, Caleb H. II, 487
Canby, Caleb H. II, 701
Canby, Caleb H. II, 702
Canby, Caleb H. II, 726
Canby, Caleb H. II, 731
Canby, Cath. Ann III, 132
Canby, Catharine II, 343
Canby, Catherine II, 481
Canby, Catherine II, 487
Canby, Catherine II, 726
Canby, Catherine II, 731
Canby, Charles II, 343
Canby, Charles II, 701
Canby, Charles II, 731
Canby, Charles II, 759
Canby, Charles II, 987
Canby, Edward II, 786
Canby, Edward II, 845
Canby, Eli II, 480
Canby, Eliza II, 786
Canby, Eliza II, 845
Canby, Eliza II, 846
Canby, Eliza VI, 735
Canby, Eliza T. VI, 508
Canby, Eliza T. VI, 509
Canby, Eliza T. VI, 629
Canby, Eliza T. VI, 656
Canby, Eliza T. VI, 657
Canby, Elizabeth II, 343
Canby, Elizabeth II, 481
Canby, Elizabeth II, 637
Canby, Elizabeth II, 731
Canby, Elizabeth II, 985
Canby, Elizabeth II, 987
Canby, Elizabeth II, 1041
Canby, Elizabeth V, 35
Canby, Elizabeth V, 71
Canby, Elizabeth V, 156
Canby, Elizabeth V, 178
Canby, Elizabeth VI, 480
Canby, Elizabeth VI, 510
Canby, Elizabeth VI, 572
Canby, Elizabeth VI, 735
Canby, Elizabeth A. II, 759
Canby, Elizabeth M. V, 35
Canby, Esther V, 35
Canby, Esther V, 156
Canby, Evan V, 156
Canby, Evan T. V, 35
Canby, Florence G. II, 786
Canby, Frances II, 869
Canby, Francis II, 481
Canby, Francis II, 637
Canby, Franklin H. II, 845
Canby, Franklin Howard II, 786
Canby, George II, 701
Canby, George II, 731
Canby, Hanameel II, 957
Canby, Hannah V, 35
Canby, Hannah VI, 375
Canby, Hannah VI, 509
Canby, Hannah VI, 629
Canby, Hannah VI, 657
Canby, Hannahmeal II, 987
Canby, Hannameel II, 1058
Canby, Henry II, 987
Canby, Hester II, 987
Canby, Hester II, 1029
Canby, Hester V, 35
Canby, Hester B. V, 35
Canby, Israel V, 35
Canby, Israel VI, 629
Canby, Israel H. VI, 480
Canby, James II, 481
Canby, James II, 637
Canby, Jane II, 343
Canby, Jane II, 481
Canby, Jane II, 487
Canby, Jane II, 701
Canby, Jane II, 702
Canby, Jane II, 726
Canby, Jane II, 731
Canby, John II, 343
Canby, John II, 731
Canby, John II, 759
Canby, John VI, 510
Canby, Jonas II, 845
Canby, Jonas II, 936
Canby, Joseph II, 480
Canby, Joseph II, 481
Canby, Joseph II, 786
Canby, Joseph II, 845
Canby, Joseph II, 846
Canby, Joseph II, 987
Canby, Joseph V, 35
Canby, Joseph V, 109
Canby, Joseph VI, 162
Canby, Joseph VI, 375
Canby, Joseph VI, 630
Canby, Joseph VI, 659
Canby, Joseph VI, 735
Canby, Joseph P. II, 786
Canby, Joseph P. II, 845
Canby, Joshua II, 1004
Canby, Joshua V, 35
Canby, Joshua V, 156
Canby, Joshua Canby II, 987
Canby, Joshua Cary II, 957
Canby, Kennett II, 480
Canby, Latitia II, 987
Canby, Latitia V, 156
Canby, Letitia II, 987
Canby, Letitia H. V, 35
Canby, Louisa V, 897
Canby, Louisa VI, 480
Canby, Lydia II, 480
Canby, Lydia II, 987
Canby, Lydia V, 35
Canby, Lydia V, 109
Canby, Lydia VI, 510
Canby, Lydia VI, 616
Canby, Lydia VI, 630
Canby, Margaret V, 897
Canby, Margaret V, 908
Canby, Martha II, 782
Canby, Martha II, 987
Canby, Martha II, 1013
Canby, Martha II, 1031
Canby, Martha VI, 630
Canby, Martha VI, 658
Canby, Martha VI, 659
Canby, Martha VI, 663
Canby, Martha VI, 666
Canby, Martha VI, 685
Canby, Mary II, 701
Canby, Mary II, 702
Canby, Mary II, 782
Canby, Mary II, 783
Canby, Mary II, 957
Canby, Mary II, 987
Canby, Mary V, 35
Canby, Mary VI, 375
Canby, Mary VI, 616
Canby, Mary VI, 618
Canby, Mary VI, 630
Canby, Mary VI, 659
Canby, Mary VI, 735
Canby, Mary C. II, 731
Canby, Mary C. II, 735
Canby, Mary Pearson II, 731
Canby, Mary, Jr. II, 987
Canby, Mary, Jr. II, 1019
Canby, Maryann V, 156
Canby, Merrit II, 481
Canby, Merritt II, 481
Canby, Mzry A. II, 759
Canby, Oliver II, 987
Canby, Phebe II, 987
Canby, Phebe II, 1027
Canby, Rachel II, 343
Canby, Rachel II, 480
Canby, Rachel II, 987
Canby, Richard S. V, 35
Canby, Richard Sprigg V, 35
Canby, Ruth Janney VI, 375
Canby, Sally II, 845
Canby, Sally II, 936
Canby, Sally III, 59
Canby, Samuel II, 481
Canby, Samuel II, 637
Canby, Samuel II, 957
Canby, Samuel II, 987
Canby, Samuel II, 1041
Canby, Samuel V, 35
Canby, Samuel V, 897
Canby, Samuel VI, 480
Canby, Samuel VI, 510
Canby, Samuel VI, 572
Canby, Samuel VI, 630
Canby, Samuel VI, 735
Canby, Samuel C. II, 845
Canby, Samuel Cassidy II, 786
Canby, Samuel F. V, 949
Canby, Samuel T. II, 845
Canby, Samuel Thomas II, 786
Canby, Samuel, Jr. II, 481
Canby, Samuel, Jr. VI, 735
Canby, Sarah II, 480
Canby, Sarah II, 565
Canby, Sarah II, 936
Canby, Sarah II, 957
Canby, Sarah II, 987
Canby, Sarah II, 1002
Canby, Sarah II, 1042
Canby, Sarah IV, 1274
Canby, Sarah IV, 1286
Canby, Sarah VI, 162
Canby, Sarah VI, 480
Canby, Sarah VI, 572
Canby, Sarah VI, 630
Canby, Sarah VI, 735
Canby, Sarah VI, 758
Canby, Susan V, 35
Canby, Susan V, 62
Canby, Susan V, 156
Canby, Susan D. V, 35
Canby, Susan D. V, 62
Canby, Susan D. V, 156
Canby, Susan D. V, 172
Canby, Susannah II, 787
Canby, Susannah II, 804
Canby, Thomas II, 480
Canby, Thomas II, 481
Canby, Thomas II, 487
Canby, Thomas II, 565
Canby, Thomas II, 957
Canby, Thomas II, 987
Canby, Thomas II, 1002
Canby, Thomas II, 1019
Canby, Thomas II, 1027
Canby, Thomas II, 1041
Canby, Thomas VI, 480
Canby, Thomas VI, 735
Canby, Thomas Y. VI, 735
Canby, Thomas Yardley II, 957
Canby, Thomas Yardley II, 987
Canby, Thomas, Jr. II, 343
Canby, Thomas, Jr. II, 480
Canby, Thomas, Jr. II, 987
Canby, Whitson II, 987
Canby, Whitson VI, 616
Canby, Whitson VI, 630
Canby, Whitson VI, 659
Canby, Whitson VI, 735
Canby, William V, 35
Canby, William VI, 162
Canby, William VI, 630
Canby, William VI, 657
Canby, William VI, 735
Canby, William Canby II, 782
Canby, William H. V, 35
Canby, William Jackson II, 343
Canby, Wm. II, 480
Canby, Wm. II, 782
Canby, Wm. II, 987
Canby, Wm. II, 1013
Canby, Wm. VI, 509
Canby, Wm. VI, 629
Canby, Wm. VI, 630
Canby, Wm. Hulme II, 987
Canby, Wm. Lownes, Jr. II, 987
Canby, Yardley VI, 735
Canda, George VI, 926
Canday, Elizabeth VI, 890
Canday, John L. VI, 890
Candill, Anna V, 156
Candill, Mark V, 156
Candle, Mary Glass V, 663
Candler, ??? VI, 293
Candler, ??? VI, 303
Candler, Abraham VI, 825
Candler, Agathay VI, 303
Candler, Agnes VI, 232
Candler, Agnes VI, 252
Candler, Agnes VI, 255
Candler, Agnes VI, 304
Candler, Agness VI, 232
Candler, Anna VI, 304
Candler, Anna VI, 333
Candler, Daniel VI, 232
Candler, Daniel VI, 291
Candler, Daniel VI, 298
Candler, Daniel VI, 303
Candler, Daniel VI, 304
Candler, Daniel VI, 798
Candler, Daniel VI, 803
Candler, Dorothy VI, 803
Candler, Eleanor VI, 297
Candler, Eleanor VI, 304
Candler, Elennor VI, 232
Candler, Elizabeth VI, 303
Candler, Elizabeth VI, 304
Candler, Elizabeth VI, 803
Candler, Elizabeth VI, 985
Candler, Francis VI, 803
Candler, Hannah VI, 939
Candler, Henry VI, 303
Candler, Henry VI, 803
Candler, Henry VI, 840
Candler, Henry VI, 856
Candler, Henry VI, 867
Candler, Henry J. VI, 835
Candler, James VI, 232
Candler, James VI, 252
Candler, James VI, 255
Candler, James VI, 298
Candler, James VI, 303
Candler, James VI, 798
Candler, James VI, 803
Candler, James VI, 840
Candler, James VI, 847
Candler, James D. VI, 799
Candler, James D. VI, 803
Candler, James G. VI, 851
Candler, James, Jr. VI, 304
Candler, Jane VI, 803
Candler, Jane VI, 825
Candler, John VI, 232
Candler, John VI, 303
Candler, John VI, 304
Candler, John VI, 803
Candler, John VI, 878
Candler, John VI, 939
Candler, John, Jr. VI, 304
Candler, Johnson VI, 303
Candler, Johnson VI, 304
Candler, Lucy VI, 298
Candler, Lucy VI, 303
Candler, Lucy VI, 304
Candler, Lucy VI, 798
Candler, Mahaly VI, 900
Candler, Martha VI, 803
Candler, Mary VI, 803
Candler, Mary A. C. VI, 803
Candler, Mildred VI, 304
Candler, Mildred VI, 803
Candler, Nancy VI, 977
Candler, Penelope VI, 799
Candler, Penelope VI, 803
Candler, Phebe VI, 803
Candler, Polly VI, 806
Candler, Rachel VI, 890
Candler, Rachel VI, 895
Candler, Robert VI, 232
Candler, Sally VI, 1021
Candler, Susan J. IV, 186
Candler, Susanna VI, 304
Candler, William VI, 232
Candler, William VI, 303
Candler, William VI, 304
Candler, William VI, 803
Candler, Wm. VI, 304
Candler, Wm. VI, 799
Candler, Wm. VI, 806
Candler, Zachariah VI, 890
Candler, Zebedee VI, 985
Candler, Zedekeah VI, 895
Candler, Zedekiah VI, 890
Candler, Zedekiah VI, 977
Candler, Zedekiah VI, 1021
Candry, Bartholomew II, 343
Candy, David V, 453
Candy, Mary V, 453
Candy, Milton V, 453
Candy, Newton V, 453
Candy, Samuel V, 453
Cane, Ann IV, 466
Cane, Dinah I, 587
Cane, Edward Clark II, 786
Cane, Elizabeth I, 803
Cane, Elizabeth I, 820
Cane, Hannah I, 803
Cane, Jane I, 803
Cane, Josie V, 156
Cane, Mary I, 587
Cane, Matthias VI, 888
Cane, Priscilla II, 205
Cane, Prisilla II, 235
Cane, Rachel I, 592
Cane, Rachel I, 803
Cane, Rebekah I, 803
Cane, Rhody VI, 888
Cane, Simon V, 553
Cane, Thomas I, 587
Canedy, Walter I, 756
Canida, Sarah I, 873
Canifax, Rhoda VI, 864
Canler, Elennor VI, 232
Cannada, Connie E. I, 621
Cannada, Crete VI, 890
Cannada, Elizabeth VI, 890
Cannada, Geo. VI, 972
Cannada, George VI, 890
Cannada, John L. VI, 890
Cannada, Pleasant VI, 890
Cannada, Sally VI, 890
Cannada, Walter I, 530
Cannaday, Abigail I, 493
Cannaday, Abigail I, 530
Cannaday, Abigail I, 540
Cannaday, Charles I, 493
Cannaday, Charles I, 530
Cannaday, Charles I, 540
Cannaday, Custy VI, 1001
Cannaday, Dempsey I, 268
Cannaday, Dinah I, 493
Cannaday, Easter I, 268
Cannaday, Esther I, 493
Cannaday, Hannah I, 493
Cannaday, John I, 493
Cannaday, John I, 530
Cannaday, John I, 577
Cannaday, John I, 1108
Cannaday, Margaret I, 493
Cannaday, Margaret I, 577
Cannaday, Margaret I, 1108
Cannaday, Margery I, 493
Cannaday, Mary I, 493
Cannaday, Nathan I, 493
Cannaday, Phebe I, 1108
Cannaday, William I, 493
Cannady, George VI, 1012
Cannady, Nancy VI, 1012
Cannady, Peggy VI, 972
Cannady, Permelia VI, 974
Cannady, Phebe I, 530
Cannady, Phebe I, 561
Cannady, Pleasant VI, 974
Cannady, Sally VI, 936
Cannady, Sarah VI, 974
Cannady, Sarah F. VI, 974
Cannafax, Ann VI, 865
Cannan, Charles II, 481
Cannan, Edward II, 481
Cannan, James II, 481
Cannan, Mary II, 481
Cannan, Sarah II, 481
Cannida, Rachel I, 1060
Cannida, Rachel I, 1062
Cannidy, Mary V, 479
Cannifax, Ann VI, 804
Cannifax, Ann T. VI, 843
Cannifax, Anne VI, 813
Cannifax, Benj. VI, 804
Cannifax, Benjamin VI, 798
Cannifax, Benjamin VI, 803
Cannifax, Benjamin VI, 845
Cannifax, Chesley VI, 804
Cannifax, Chesley VI, 843
Cannifax, Edward VI, 804
Cannifax, Eliza B. VI, 804
Cannifax, Isabella VI, 804
Cannifax, John VI, 813
Cannifax, John VI, 843
Cannifax, John VI, 850
Cannifax, John VI, 863
Cannifax, John A. VI, 804
Cannifax, Martha VI, 804
Cannifax, Martha J. VI, 804
Cannifax, Nancy VI, 803
Cannifax, Nancy VI, 804
Cannifax, Polly VI, 804
Cannifax, Radford VI, 802
Cannifax, Radford VI, 804
Cannifax, Radford VI, 813
Cannifax, Rebecca VI, 863
Cannifax, Rebeckah VI, 850
Cannifax, Rhoda VI, 799
Cannifax, Susannah VI, 813
Cannifax, William VI, 799
Cannifax, William VI, 804
Cannifax, William W. VI, 804
Cannifax, Wm. VI, 850
Cannon, ??? III, 59
Cannon, Abigail III, 59
Cannon, Abigail III, 195
Cannon, Betty I, 39
Cannon, Betty I, 76
Cannon, Carlton I, 3

Cannon, Carlton I, 39
Cannon, Charles II, 343
Cannon, Charles II, 481
Cannon, Clarissa VI, 969
Cannon, Edward II, 343
Cannon, Edward II, 481
Cannon, Elisabeth I, 3
Cannon, Elisabeth I, 39
Cannon, Elisabeth I, 74
Cannon, Elisha Bales I, 530
Cannon, Elizabeth II, 343
Cannon, George Anna I, 3
Cannon, Georgianna I, 40
Cannon, Georgianna I, 42
Cannon, Gulah I, 530
Cannon, Henry I, 3
Cannon, Henry I, 39
Cannon, Horace F. I, 530
Cannon, Horise F. I, 530
Cannon, Horris F. I, 530
Cannon, Jacob I, 3
Cannon, Jacob I, 39
Cannon, Jacob I, 63
Cannon, Jacob E. I, 3
Cannon, James I, 28
Cannon, James II, 481
Cannon, Jemima I, 3
Cannon, Jemima I, 39
Cannon, Jemima I, 63
Cannon, Jeremiah I, 39
Cannon, Jeremiah I, 66
Cannon, Jeremiah I, 74
Cannon, John I, 3
Cannon, John II, 343
Cannon, Joseph I, 3
Cannon, Joseph I, 39
Cannon, Joseph I, 76
Cannon, Julia I, 530
Cannon, Margaret I, 3
Cannon, Margaret Ann I, 3
Cannon, Martha I, 3
Cannon, Martha I, 39
Cannon, Mary I, 3
Cannon, Mary I, 39
Cannon, Mary I, 66
Cannon, Mary II, 343
Cannon, Mary II, 481
Cannon, Mary II, 535
Cannon, Mary E. I, 28
Cannon, Mary E. I, 39
Cannon, Mary E. I, 73
Cannon, Mary Eliza I, 3
Cannon, Sarah I, 35
Cannon, Sarah I, 39
Cannon, Sarah I, 76
Cannon, Sarah I, 93
Cannon, Sarah II, 343
Cannon, Sarah II, 481
Cannon, Sarah II, 608
Cannon, Sarah III, 59
Cannon, Sarah F. I, 32
Cannon, Sarah F. I, 39
Cannon, Sarah F. I, 89
Cannon, Sarah Francis I, 3
Cannon, Sophia I, 3
Cannon, Sophia I, 39
Cannon, Thomas II, 343
Cannon, Thomas II, 481
Cannon, Vallie I, 939
Cannon, Widow Jemima I, 39
Cannon, Widow Jemima I, 87
Cannon, Widow Rachel I, 39
Cannon, Widow Rachel I, 74
Cannon, William II, 343
Cannon, William VI, 969
Cannon, William Henry I, 3
Cannon, Wm. II, 481
Cannons, Elizabeth II, 343
Cannons, Mary II, 343
Cannons, Thomas II, 343
Canon, Elisha Bales I, 530
Canon, Guly Elma I, 756
Canon, Guly Elma I, 764
Canon, Horise F. I, 530
Canon, Horris F. I, 530
Canoy, John I, 888
Cansler, Louisa C. II, 284
Cansler, William W. II, 284
Canter, David V, 227
Canter, David H. V, 227
Canter, John W. V, 227
Canter, Nancy V, 227
Canterman, Elizabeth VI, 942
Canterman, Margarata VI, 942
Cantleberry, Harry IV, 186
Cantley, Adda V, 323
Cantley, Albert V, 323
Cantley, Alice V, 322
Cantley, Alonzo M. V, 323
Cantley, Amos H. V, 322
Cantley, Amos H. V, 323
Cantley, Anna V, 323
Cantley, Anna E. V, 323
Cantley, Anna J. V, 322
Cantley, Bertha L. V, 323
Cantley, Charles E. V, 323
Cantley, Clifton O. V, 323
Cantley, David E. V, 323
Cantley, Elizabeth M. V, 323
Cantley, Florence B. V, 323
Cantley, Frank V, 323
Cantley, George V, 322
Cantley, George M. V, 322
Cantley, Hattie C. V, 323
Cantley, Ida V, 323
Cantley, James V, 323
Cantley, Luena A. V, 323
Cantley, Maggie V, 323
Cantley, Mary Ann V, 323
Cantley, Mary Ellen V, 323
Cantley, Melissa V, 323
Cantley, Olga Kezia V, 323
Cantley, Pearl V, 323
Cantley, Ruth V, 323
Cantley, Ruth A. V, 323
Cantley, Samuel A. V, 323
Cantley, Thomas L. V, 322
Cantley, Thomas L. V, 323
Cantley, Thos. L. V, 323
Cantley, Walter V, 322
Cantley, Walter V, 323
Cantley, Walter Homer V, 323
Cantrell, Alcinda V, 322
Cantrell, Blanche V, 663
Cantrell, Charles V, 322
Cantrell, Chas. V, 322
Cantrell, Clayton V, 322
Cantrell, Guy E. V, 663
Cantrell, James V, 322
Cantrell, James M. V, 322
Cantrell, Robert Elmo V, 663
Cantril, Dorothy II, 442
Cantril, Mary II, 442
Cantril, Richard II, 442
Cantrill, Blanch V, 663
Cantrill, Blanche V, 663
Cantrill, Charles V, 322
Cantrill, Guy E. V, 663
Cantrill, Robert Elmo V, 663
Capanana, Ema V, 988
Capbell, Jeane VI, 961
Cape, Andrew II, 349
Cape, John VI, 890
Cape, Mary II, 349
Cape, Mary VI, 890
Cape, Peter II, 349
Cape, Sarah II, 349
Cape, Susanna II, 349
Capehart, Julia C. I, 984
Capeheart, Julia A. I, 530
Capel, Gabrel I, 190
Capel, George IV, 688
Capel, George IV, 775
Capel, Kate IV, 688
Capel, Lavern C. IV, 775
Capel, Margaret IV, 688
Capel, Mrs. ??? IV, 696
Caperoff, Doris IV, 1247
Capes, Peter II, 349
Capes, Sarah II, 349
Cappell, Curtis I, 42
Cappock, Aaron V, 804
Cappock, Abigail V, 804
Cappock, Abraham V, 804
Cappock, Abraham V, 805
Cappock, Adela V, 804
Cappock, Ahigah W. V, 804
Cappock, Aldey L. V, 804
Cappock, Alice V, 804
Cappock, Almeda V, 804
Cappock, Anabel V, 804
Cappock, Ann V, 804
Cappock, Anne V, 804
Cappock, Bailes V, 804
Cappock, Betty V, 804
Cappock, Calvin V, 804
Cappock, Charity V, 804
Cappock, Corrilla V, 804
Cappock, Cynthia V, 805
Cappock, David J. V, 804
Cappock, David M. V, 804
Cappock, Deborah V, 804
Cappock, Dianna V, 804
Cappock, Dorcas V, 804
Cappock, Elenor V, 804
Cappock, Eli V, 804
Cappock, Elijah V, 804
Cappock, Elijah V, 805
Cappock, Elisha V, 804
Cappock, Elisha V, 805
Cappock, Ellwood C. V, 804
Cappock, Eunice V, 804
Cappock, Eunice Coate V, 805
Cappock, Furnace Jay V, 804
Cappock, Herbert V, 804
Cappock, Horace V, 804
Cappock, James V, 804
Cappock, James Ellis V, 804
Cappock, Jane V, 804
Cappock, Jane H. IV, 469
Cappock, Jesse V, 804
Cappock, John V, 805
Cappock, John M. V, 804
Cappock, Lambert V, 804
Cappock, Layton V, 804
Cappock, Lorettie V, 804
Cappock, Lydia V, 804
Cappock, Lydia V, 805
Cappock, Lydia J. V, 804
Cappock, Margaret V, 804
Cappock, Margaret V, 805
Cappock, Martha V, 804
Cappock, Mary V, 804
Cappock, Mary V, 805
Cappock, Mary Ann V, 804
Cappock, Mary E. V, 804
Cappock, Maudine May V, 804
Cappock, Moses V, 804
Cappock, Orley E. V, 804
Cappock, Rachel V, 804
Cappock, Sarah V, 804
Cappock, Sarah J. V, 804
Cappock, Seth V, 804
Cappock, Susannah V, 804
Cappock, Westley V, 804
Cappock, Wm. V, 804
Cappock, Wm. V, 805
Cappock, Wm. P. V, 804
Cappock, Wright V, 804
Capps, Calvin I, 530
Capps, Elizabeth I, 530
Capps, Henry I, 530
Capps, Sarah I, 711
Capps, Sarah V, 35
Capron, ??? III, 59
Capron, Allen Newman III, 59
Capron, Edward B. III, 59
Capron, Elizabeth B. III, 59
Capron, George Truman III, 59
Capron, Grace A. III, 59
Capron, Grace A. III, 157
Capron, Jacob III, 24
Capron, Jacob III, 59
Capron, Jacob III, 157
Capron, Jane III, 59
Capron, Jane E. III, 59
Capron, Jane E. III, 157
Capron, Jane Eliz. III, 59
Capron, Jane Elizabeth III, 24
Capron, Metcalf V, 729
Capron, Oliver V, 729
Capron, Orion III, 59
Capron, Rosalinda III, 59
Capron, Sarah V, 729
Capron, Willet S. III, 59
Capron, Wm. Orion III, 59
Caps, Esther I, 377
Caps, Esther I, 419
Caps, Rachel I, 377
Caps, Sarah I, 134
Caps, Sarah I, 377
Caps, Sarah I, 418
Caps, Sarah V, 227
Capstack, Sarah III, 59
Caragun, Elizabeth II, 193
Caragun, Elizabeth II, 206
Carary, Christopher II, 24
Carary, Elizabeth II, 24
Carary, Margaret II, 24
Carary, Mary II, 24
Carary, Rachel II, 24
Carary, Roger II, 24
Carback, ??? V, 156
Carback, Elizabeth V, 156
Carback, Elizabeth A. V, 156
Carback, Elizabeth Ann V, 156
Carback, Emma J. V, 156
Carback, Emma Jane V, 156
Carback, James V, 156
Carback, James Thomas V, 156
Carback, Laura A. V, 156
Carback, Laura Alice V, 156
Carback, Martha Jane V, 156
Carback, Mary C. V, 156
Carback, Mary Catharine V, 156
Carback, Mary Elizabeth V, 156
Carback, Samuel V, 156
Carback, Thomas V, 156
Carbaugh, Mary V, 988
Card, Almira IV, 949
Card, Elmira IV, 966
Card, Miriam I, 869
Card, Miriam I, 874
Carden, Amanda J. I, 1149
Carden, Elizabeth VI, 849
Carden, James W. VI, 813
Carden, Leonard I, 1149
Carden, Lillie I, 1149
Carden, Thomas B. I, 1149
Carder, Ambrose V, 553
Carder, Anna V, 35
Carder, Clarence V, 35
Carder, Eberle V, 553
Carder, Ebler V, 553
Carder, Elizabeth V, 35
Carder, Emerson C. V, 553
Carder, Emmerson V, 553
Carder, Frederick V, 553
Carder, Hannah V, 553
Carder, Itha V, 553
Carder, Iva V, 553
Carder, Jas. M. VI, 950
Carder, Mirwama V, 553
Cardon, Leonard I, 1149
Cardwell, Charles W. VI, 839
Cardwell, Ednery A. VI, 804
Cardwell, Elizabeth VI, 804
Cardwell, Elizabeth VI, 841
Cardwell, Gabriella VI, 827
Cardwell, James VI, 804
Cardwell, James D. VI, 796
Cardwell, James D. VI, 798
Cardwell, James D. VI, 804
Cardwell, James D. VI, 827
Cardwell, James E. D. VI, 804
Cardwell, Jas. D. VI, 842
Cardwell, John VI, 804
Cardwell, Judith VI, 804
Cardwell, Mary J. VI, 804
Cardwell, May VI, 804
Cardwell, Milly VI, 841
Cardwell, Nancy VI, 804
Cardwell, Nancy VI, 866
Cardwell, Phebe VI, 804
Cardwell, Polly VI, 804
Cardwell, Rebecca VI, 735
Cardwell, Rebecca VI, 738
Cardwell, Robert VI, 804
Cardwell, Robert VI, 821
Cardwell, Robert VI, 838
Cardwell, Robert VI, 841
Cardwell, Sally VI, 838
Cardwell, Sarah VI, 804
Cardwell, Sarah A. VI, 842
Cardwell, Thomas VI, 841
Cardwell, Thomas D. VI, 838
Cardwell, Thos. D. VI, 804
Cardwell, William VI, 804
Cardwell, William VI, 841
Cardwell, William I. VI, 804
Care, ??? II, 343
Care, Ann II, 481
Care, Ann II, 799
Care, Hannah II, 343
Care, Hannah II, 481
Care, Hannah II, 615
Care, Jesse II, 343
Care, Jesse II, 481
Care, Jesse II, 596
Care, Jesse II, 799
Care, John II, 343
Care, John II, 481
Care, John II, 561
Care, John II, 596
Care, John II, 615
Care, John II, 786
Care, Lydia II, 481
Care, Lydia II, 561
Care, Mary II, 481
Care, Mary II, 561
Care, Mary II, 596
Care, Mary II, 615
Care, Mary II, 786
Care, Mary II, 845
Care, Mary, Sr. II, 786
Care, Mary, Sr. II, 845
Care, Philip II, 343
Care, Rachel II, 481
Care, Rachel II, 596
Care, Rachel II, 701
Care, Rachel II, 799
Care, Thomas II, 343
Care, Wm. II, 481
Careader, John II, 442
Carel, Elizabeth II, 60
Carel, Sarah II, 60
Carell, Henry N. VI, 977
Carell, Martha VI, 977
Caren, Elias V, 479
Caren, Elizabeth V, 479
Caren, Hannah V, 479
Caren, Jane V, 479
Caren, Martha Emily V, 479
Caren, Mary V, 479
Caren, Sarah Margaret V, 479
Carethers, Rhoda IV, 186
Carethers, Rhoda IV, 259
Carey, ??? II, 343
Carey, Aaron IV, 466
Carey, Aaron IV, 1151
Carey, Abel IV, 78
Carey, Abel IV, 101
Carey, Abel IV, 466
Carey, Abel IV, 688
Carey, Abel IV, 1151
Carey, Abel IV, 1204
Carey, Abigail III, 59
Carey, Abigail V, 322
Carey, Abigail V, 365
Carey, Abigail V, 377
Carey, Abigail V, 438
Carey, Abigail J. V, 322
Carey, Abigail Jane V, 322
Carey, Agnes IV, 865
Carey, Agnes IV, 1151
Carey, Albert V, 663
Carey, Alice IV, 680
Carey, Alice IV, 688
Carey, Alice IV, 1274
Carey, Alice V, 322
Carey, Alice V, 323
Carey, Alice V, 663
Carey, Almira V, 35
Carey, Almira V, 41
Carey, Almira V, 322
Carey, Alonzo V, 322
Carey, Alonzo V, 377
Carey, Alpheus V, 377
Carey, Alpheus V, 378
Carey, Altha V, 378
Carey, Amos V, 553
Carey, Ann V, 322
Carey, Ann V, 344
Carey, Ann V, 377
Carey, Ann V, 437
Carey, Ann E. V, 378
Carey, Ann Elizabeth V, 377
Carey, Ann O. VI, 804
Carey, Anna V, 227
Carey, Anna V, 322
Carey, Anna V, 365
Carey, Anna V, 376
Carey, Anna V, 377
Carey, Anna V, 378
Carey, Anna V, 408
Carey, Anna V, 424
Carey, Anna V, 553
Carey, Anna Barlow V, 663
Carey, Anna E. V, 377
Carey, Anna Elizabeth V, 376
Carey, Anna Head VI, 735
Carey, Anna Head VI, 752
Carey, Anna M. V, 322
Carey, Anna M. V, 330
Carey, Anna M. Farr V, 323
Carey, Anne I, 1003
Carey, Anne I, 1008
Carey, Anne I, 1011
Carey, Anne V, 322
Carey, Anne V, 324
Carey, Anne V, 332
Carey, Anne V, 388
Carey, Annie V, 897
Carey, Annie E. V, 227
Carey, Arena V, 377
Carey, Arthur L. V, 322
Carey, Arthur L. V, 330
Carey, Ashbel IV, 688
Carey, Barclay IV, 688
Carey, Barclay IV, 1151
Carey, Benjamin I, 1003
Carey, Benjamin IV, 1151
Carey, Benjamin V, 173
Carey, Benjamin V, 227
Carey, Benjamin V, 263
Carey, Benjamin V, 445
Carey, Benjamin V, 553
Carey, Benjamin C. V, 322
Carey, Benjamin L. IV, 1151
Carey, Benjamin L. IV, 1204
Carey, Bertha L. V, 663
Carey, Beula V, 481
Carey, Beulah II, 1048
Carey, Beulah V, 663
Carey, Beulah McElwee V, 614
Carey, Bulah V, 663
Carey, C. D. V, 377
Carey, Catharine V, 897
Carey, Charles IV, 688
Carey, Charles IV, 1274
Carey, Charles A. V, 377
Carey, Charles E. V, 322
Carey, Charles Enoch V, 663
Carey, Charles J. V, 553
Carey, Charles M. IV, 688

Carey, Charlotte I, 1003
Carey, Charlotte V, 227
Carey, Charlotte V, 271
Carey, Chas. V, 381
Carey, Chas. E. III, 59
Carey, Chas. M. IV, 688
Carey, Clifton O. V, 663
Carey, Clyde N. V, 729
Carey, Colleen IV, 186
Carey, Cora V, 323
Carey, Cora McPherson V, 323
Carey, Cordelia Bays V, 227
Carey, Cynthia V, 377
Carey, Cyrus V, 227
Carey, Dallas V, 663
Carey, Dallas J. V, 481
Carey, Dallis V, 663
Carey, Daniel I, 1003
Carey, Daniel V, 227
Carey, Daniel V, 322
Carey, Daniel V, 324
Carey, Daniel V, 376
Carey, Daniel V, 377
Carey, Daniel M. V, 322
Carey, Daniel M. V, 897
Carey, Daten I, 1003
Carey, David IV, 688
Carey, David V, 322
Carey, David V, 376
Carey, David V, 377
Carey, David V, 378
Carey, David E. V, 663
Carey, David M. V, 322
Carey, David M. V, 336
Carey, David M. V, 377
Carey, David M. V, 394
Carey, Dean V, 663
Carey, Deborah II, 988
Carey, Deborah II, 1048
Carey, Dora V, 378
Carey, Dr. Wm. III, 485
Carey, Edgar V, 377
Carey, Edgar V, 378
Carey, Edmond IV, 466
Carey, Edmund IV, 466
Carey, Edmund IV, 688
Carey, Edmund IV, 934
Carey, Edmund IV, 1151
Carey, Edna E. IV, 614
Carey, Edna E. IV, 618
Carey, Edna Marie V, 553
Carey, Eleanor V, 323
Carey, Eleanor V, 663
Carey, Eli V, 227
Carey, Elias I, 961
Carey, Elias I, 1004
Carey, Elias V, 183
Carey, Elias V, 227
Carey, Elias V, 322
Carey, Elias V, 376
Carey, Elias V, 377
Carey, Elias V, 378
Carey, Elias V, 397
Carey, Elias V, 412
Carey, Elias V, 416
Carey, Elias V, 897
Carey, Elias, Jr. V, 322
Carey, Eliza V, 322
Carey, Eliza V, 350
Carey, Eliza V, 376
Carey, Eliza V, 416
Carey, Eliza M. V, 418
Carey, Eliza M. VI, 827
Carey, Eliza R. V, 322
Carey, Elizabeth I, 1003
Carey, Elizabeth II, 481
Carey, Elizabeth V, 227
Carey, Elizabeth V, 263
Carey, Elizabeth V, 322
Carey, Elizabeth V, 344
Carey, Elizabeth V, 350
Carey, Elizabeth V, 377
Carey, Elizabeth V, 389
Carey, Elizabeth V, 408
Carey, Elizabeth V, 409
Carey, Elizabeth V, 512
Carey, Elizabeth V, 553
Carey, Elizabeth V, 663
Carey, Elizabeth B. V, 831
Carey, Elizabeth M. V, 663
Carey, Elizabeth Nelson V, 663
Carey, Elizabeth, Jr. V, 378
Carey, Elizabeth, Jr. V, 411
Carey, Ellen H. III, 59
Carey, Elva Jane V, 376
Carey, Elva Jane V, 378
Carey, Elwood V, 323
Carey, Emily V, 322
Carey, Emily V, 897
Carey, Enoch V, 576
Carey, Enoch L. V, 377
Carey, Enoch L. V, 378
Carey, Esther V, 481
Carey, Esther V, 576
Carey, Etta V, 173
Carey, Eva V, 377
Carey, Eva V, 378
Carey, Ferris A. III, 59
Carey, Ferris A. III, 63
Carey, Florence IV, 1274
Carey, Frances Ellen III, 59
Carey, Frank V, 323
Carey, Frank V, 553
Carey, Franklin IV, 1151
Carey, George IV, 466
Carey, George IV, 1151
Carey, Gurney B. V, 322
Carey, Hannah II, 988
Carey, Hannah IV, 607
Carey, Hannah IV, 614
Carey, Hannah V, 376
Carey, Hannah V, 377
Carey, Hannah V, 389
Carey, Hannah V, 441
Carey, Hannah M. V, 377
Carey, Hannah M. V, 378
Carey, Hannah M. V, 412
Carey, Harley V, 323
Carey, Harley V, 663
Carey, Harold V, 663
Carey, Harold Nevin V, 663
Carey, Helen V, 323
Carey, Helen V, 663
Carey, Henrietta E. III, 59
Carey, Henrietta E. III, 66
Carey, Herbert V, 323
Carey, Howard L. III, 59
Carey, Howard L. III, 66
Carey, Hulda V, 227
Carey, Huldah V, 227
Carey, Ida V, 377
Carey, Ida V, 553
Carey, Ida M. V, 378
Carey, Irena V, 377
Carey, Irena V, 378
Carey, Irena V, 897
Carey, Irvin V, 323
Carey, Isaac V, 227
Carey, Isaac V, 241
Carey, Isaac V, 322
Carey, Isaac V, 350
Carey, Isaac V, 376
Carey, Isaac V, 377
Carey, Isaac Milton V, 378
Carey, Isaac Milton V, 897
Carey, Isabella IV, 466
Carey, Isabella IV, 688
Carey, Isabella IV, 1151
Carey, Isabella IV, 1204
Carey, Isabelle IV, 466
Carey, James VI, 735
Carey, James R. IV, 688
Carey, James Walter V, 377
Carey, James Walter V, 897
Carey, Jane V, 183
Carey, Jane V, 376
Carey, Jane V, 377
Carey, Jane V, 378
Carey, Jane V, 397
Carey, Jane V, 412
Carey, Jane V, 416
Carey, Jane V, 897
Carey, Jane M. V, 576
Carey, Jennie IV, 1274
Carey, Jennie P. V, 553
Carey, Jesse V, 322
Carey, Jesse V, 663
Carey, Jesse Franklin V, 376
Carey, Jesse Franklin V, 378
Carey, Jesse G. V, 322
Carey, Jesse H. V, 323
Carey, Joel V, 271
Carey, John I, 961
Carey, John I, 1003
Carey, John I, 1008
Carey, John I, 1009
Carey, John III, 59
Carey, John V, 271
Carey, John V, 322
Carey, John V, 323
Carey, John V, 348
Carey, John V, 363
Carey, John V, 364
Carey, John V, 365
Carey, John V, 376
Carey, John V, 377
Carey, John V, 378
Carey, John V, 401
Carey, John V, 411
Carey, John V, 416
Carey, John V, 437
Carey, John V, 480
Carey, John V, 481
Carey, John V, 512
Carey, John V, 553
Carey, John V, 663
Carey, John VI, 735
Carey, John VI, 827
Carey, John Ellicott VI, 752
Carey, John F. V, 227
Carey, John F. V, 553
Carey, John H. V, 322
Carey, John Henry V, 377
Carey, John Henry V, 378
Carey, John Henry V, 897
Carey, John, Jr. V, 322
Carey, John, Jr. V, 350
Carey, Jonathan I, 961
Carey, Jonathan I, 1003
Carey, Jonathan I, 1007
Carey, Jonathan I, 1008
Carey, Jonathan V, 227
Carey, Jonathan V, 271
Carey, Jonathan V, 322
Carey, Jonathan V, 377
Carey, Jonathan V, 445
Carey, Jonathan, Jr. I, 1003
Carey, Joseph V, 376
Carey, Joseph V, 377
Carey, Joseph V, 663
Carey, Joseph V, 831
Carey, Joseph M. V, 376
Carey, Joseph M. V, 663
Carey, Joshua II, 988
Carey, Katharine A. V, 322
Carey, Kenneth IV, 865
Carey, Kenneth IV, 1151
Carey, Kenneth IV, 1274
Carey, Kezia III, 485
Carey, Lemuel V, 376
Carey, Lenna Alice V, 322
Carey, Levina V, 729
Carey, Lewella V, 377
Carey, Lewis IV, 78
Carey, Lewis IV, 466
Carey, Lewis IV, 688
Carey, Lewis IV, 1151
Carey, Lewis IV, 1204
Carey, Lewis V, 376
Carey, Lindley V, 729
Carey, Lizzie V, 381
Carey, Louis B. V, 553
Carey, Louise B. V, 481
Carey, Luella V, 378
Carey, Lydia V, 227
Carey, Lydia V, 377
Carey, Lydia V, 378
Carey, Lydia V, 401
Carey, Lydia V, 420
Carey, Lydia V, 445
Carey, Lydia V, 446
Carey, Lydia Margaret V, 377
Carey, Lydia N. V, 376
Carey, Lydia N. V, 378
Carey, Madira V, 377
Carey, Maplet H. III, 59
Carey, Maplet H. III, 63
Carey, Margaret I, 1003
Carey, Margaret I, 1008
Carey, Margaret I, 1009
Carey, Margaret IV, 1274
Carey, Margaret V, 322
Carey, Margaret V, 348
Carey, Margaret V, 363
Carey, Margaret V, 364
Carey, Margaret V, 365
Carey, Margaret V, 376
Carey, Margaret V, 377
Carey, Margaret V, 378
Carey, Margaret V, 420
Carey, Margaret V, 437
Carey, Margaret G. V, 322
Carey, Margaret G. V, 376
Carey, Margaret G. V, 377
Carey, Margaret H. V, 322
Carey, Margaret Jane V, 322
Carey, Maria IV, 688
Carey, Maria Melissa V, 227
Carey, Maria P. IV, 78
Carey, Maria P. IV, 101
Carey, Maria P. IV, 688
Carey, Mariah IV, 688
Carey, Marie Malissa V, 227
Carey, Marie Malissa V, 378
Carey, Marjorie V, 663
Carey, Martha IV, 1151
Carey, Martha IV, 1201
Carey, Martha IV, 1204
Carey, Martha V, 271
Carey, Martha V, 897
Carey, Martha VI, 735
Carey, Martha E. V, 378
Carey, Martha Emily V, 377
Carey, Martha Emily V, 378
Carey, Martha Emily V, 944
Carey, Martin V, 271
Carey, Marvin IV, 1274
Carey, Mary I, 1003
Carey, Mary II, 1048
Carey, Mary V, 227
Carey, Mary V, 271
Carey, Mary V, 322
Carey, Mary V, 364
Carey, Mary V, 377
Carey, Mary V, 378
Carey, Mary V, 438
Carey, Mary V, 663
Carey, Mary V, 696
Carey, Mary Ann V, 322
Carey, Mary Ann V, 377
Carey, Mary Charlotte V, 227
Carey, Mary Charlotte V, 445
Carey, Mary E. V, 183
Carey, Mary E. V, 322
Carey, Mary Elizabeth II, 1062
Carey, Mary Elizabeth V, 376
Carey, Mary Elizabeth V, 377
Carey, Mary Ellen V, 663
Carey, Mary Emily V, 378
Carey, Mary Emily V, 388
Carey, Mary J. V, 663
Carey, Mary J. VI, 860
Carey, Mary M. V, 663
Carey, May V, 553
Carey, Melissa V, 377
Carey, Melissa V, 378
Carey, Melvin Donald III, 59
Carey, Merium V, 271
Carey, Miles VI, 827
Carey, Miles VI, 831
Carey, Miles VI, 855
Carey, Milford IV, 1274
Carey, Miriam V, 663
Carey, Myron IV, 1151
Carey, Myron Leslie IV, 1151
Carey, Nancy IV, 1151
Carey, Nancy Jane V, 378
Carey, Naomi V, 377
Carey, Nathan V, 481
Carey, Nathan H. V, 377
Carey, Nathan H. V, 378
Carey, Neal V, 323
Carey, Neal V, 663
Carey, Nelson VI, 804
Carey, Orba V, 323
Carey, Orba V, 663
Carey, Pearl V, 553
Carey, Penina V, 322
Carey, Peninah V, 322
Carey, Peninah V, 376
Carey, Penninah V, 322
Carey, Penninah V, 363
Carey, Penninah V, 377
Carey, Pleasant V, 377
Carey, Priscilla V, 322
Carey, Priscilla V, 376
Carey, Priscilla V, 377
Carey, Priscilla V, 420
Carey, Rachel I, 1003
Carey, Rachel I, 1008
Carey, Rachel IV, 78
Carey, Rachel IV, 466
Carey, Rachel IV, 1151
Carey, Rachel V, 227
Carey, Rachel V, 322
Carey, Rachel V, 376
Carey, Rachel V, 377
Carey, Rachel V, 381
Carey, Rachel V, 397
Carey, Rachel V, 897
Carey, Rachel Anna V, 378
Carey, Rachel D. V, 365
Carey, Rachel D. V, 393
Carey, Rachel D. V, 437
Carey, Rachel D. V, 438
Carey, Rachel D. V, 831
Carey, Rachel G. V, 227
Carey, Rachel J. V, 227
Carey, Rachel J. V, 241
Carey, Rachel, Jr. I, 1008
Carey, Rachel, Jr. I, 1009
Carey, Raymond V, 323
Carey, Rebecca V, 322
Carey, Rebecca V, 336
Carey, Rebecca V, 377
Carey, Rebecca V, 394
Carey, Rebecca Jane V, 377
Carey, Rebecca Jane V, 378
Carey, Rev. Chas. J. IV, 1274
Carey, Rhoda V, 322
Carey, Rhoda V, 332
Carey, Rhoda V, 388
Carey, Rhoda V, 831
Carey, Richard I, 961
Carey, Richard VI, 860
Carey, Robert I, 1003
Carey, Robert V, 322
Carey, Robert V, 323
Carey, Robert V, 350
Carey, Robert V, 376
Carey, Robert V, 377
Carey, Robert V, 418
Carey, Robert V, 663
Carey, Robert Charles III, 59
Carey, Rosella V, 729
Carey, Ruth I, 1003
Carey, Ruth I, 1007
Carey, Ruth I, 1008
Carey, Ruth V, 173
Carey, Ruth V, 227
Carey, Ruth V, 262
Carey, Ruth V, 271
Carey, Ruth V, 322
Carey, Ruth V, 334
Carey, Ruth V, 348
Carey, Ruth V, 376
Carey, Ruth V, 445
Carey, Ruth V, 663
Carey, Ruth Anna V, 322
Carey, Ruth B. V, 227
Carey, Ruth B. V, 553
Carey, Ruth Woodard V, 323
Carey, Sampson II, 343
Carey, Sampson II, 481
Carey, Samson II, 988
Carey, Samuel I, 961
Carey, Samuel I, 1003
Carey, Samuel I, 1008
Carey, Samuel I, 1011
Carey, Samuel II, 988
Carey, Samuel V, 227
Carey, Samuel V, 322
Carey, Samuel V, 332
Carey, Samuel V, 344
Carey, Samuel V, 365
Carey, Samuel V, 376
Carey, Samuel V, 377
Carey, Samuel V, 378
Carey, Samuel V, 388
Carey, Samuel V, 408
Carey, Samuel V, 437
Carey, Samuel V, 445
Carey, Samuel V, 447
Carey, Samuel V, 553
Carey, Samuel VI, 304
Carey, Samuel Albert V, 663
Carey, Samuel F. V, 377
Carey, Samuel F. V, 378
Carey, Samuel Lewis V, 378
Carey, Samuel, Jr. V, 227
Carey, Samuel, Jr. V, 322
Carey, Samuel, Sr. I, 1008
Carey, Samuel, Sr. V, 227
Carey, Sarah I, 1008
Carey, Sarah I, 1010
Carey, Sarah IV, 466
Carey, Sarah IV, 1151
Carey, Sarah IV, 1204
Carey, Sarah V, 445
Carey, Sarah V, 447
Carey, Sarah V, 553
Carey, Sarah VI, 480
Carey, Sarah Ann IV, 1151
Carey, Sarah Ann IV, 1169
Carey, Sarah Ann V, 323
Carey, Sarah Ann V, 376
Carey, Sarah Ann V, 377
Carey, Sarah Anne V, 322
Carey, Sarah Ellen V, 322
Carey, Sarah Emeline V, 897
Carey, Sarah Lemert V, 322
Carey, Sarah M. V, 377
Carey, Sarah Margaret V, 377
Carey, Silas V, 377
Carey, Susan IV, 466
Carey, Susan IV, 1151
Carey, Susanna IV, 1151
Carey, Susanna V, 376
Carey, Susanna V, 377
Carey, Susannah IV, 466
Carey, Susannah IV, 1151
Carey, Susannah IV, 1169
Carey, Susannah IV, 1204
Carey, Susannah V, 322
Carey, Susannah V, 350
Carey, Susannah V, 377
Carey, Susannah V, 418
Carey, Sylvanus I, 1003
Carey, Sylvanus V, 227
Carey, Sylvanus V, 445
Carey, Sylvester V, 227
Carey, Thadeus V, 323
Carey, Thadeus V, 663
Carey, Thomas I, 961
Carey, Thomas I, 1004

Carey, Thomas V, 227
Carey, Thomas V, 322
Carey, Thomas V, 831
Carey, Thomas E. V, 377
Carey, Thomas E. V, 378
Carey, Thomas Elwood V, 322
Carey, Thomas Elwood V, 376
Carey, Thomas Elwood V, 377
Carey, Thomas L. V, 377
Carey, Thomas L. V, 378
Carey, Velma V, 323
Carey, Velma V, 663
Carey, Virginia V, 323
Carey, Virginia VI, 831
Carey, Walter V, 227
Carey, Walter V, 378
Carey, Wilford IV, 186
Carey, William II, 343
Carey, William IV, 466
Carey, William IV, 1151
Carey, William V, 322
Carey, William B. IV, 688
Carey, Wm. V, 323
Carey, Wm. M. V, 322
Carey, Zenas I, 1003
Carey, Zenas V, 227
Carey, Zenas V, 445
Carey, Zenas V, 446
Carfer, Jacob IV, 1274
Carfield, Drucilla I, 929
Carfield, John I, 929
Carfield, Martha I, 933
Carfield, Mary Elizabeth I, 929
Cargall, Cornelius VI, 162
Cargill, Nathaniel VI, 133
Cargill, Rev. John VI, 94
Carhart, Benjamin III, 59
Carhart, Benjamin I. III, 59
Carhart, Edwin M. III, 59
Carhart, Eliz. III, 480
Carhart, Elizabeth III, 59
Carhart, Elizabeth III, 378
Carhart, Elizabeth III, 480
Carhart, Elizabeth III, 482
Carhart, Emily Jane III, 59
Carhart, Helen III, 398
Carhart, Hendrick III, 59
Carhart, Hendrick W. III, 480
Carhart, Hendrick Wright III, 480
Carhart, James III, 378
Carhart, James III, 480
Carhart, James III, 482
Carhart, John III, 398
Carhart, John III, 438
Carhart, Joshua III, 398
Carhart, Joshua III, 440
Carhart, Phebe III, 398
Carhart, Phebe III, 440
Carhart, Rachel III, 398
Carhart, Rachel III, 438
Carhart, Sarah III, 398
Carhart, Sarah III, 440
Carhartt, Hendrick III, 59
Caridi, Maria III, 94
Carinthus, Rachel II, 988
Cark, Aseanath I, 804
Cark, Emily I, 804
Cark, Julia I, 804
Cark, Mary I, 804
Carkfield, Alexander II, 442
Carl, Alva V, 156
Carl, Catharine II, 481
Carl, Clarence V, 156
Carl, Clarence Walton V, 156
Carl, Deborah V, 156
Carl, Elizabeth I, 1027
Carl, Hannah II, 481
Carl, Louisa V, 97
Carl, Margaret IV, 1247
Carl, Margaret E. IV, 1247
Carl, Rosalee M. IV, 1247
Carl, Rosetta IV, 1247
Carl, Sarah I, 1047
Carl, Solon V, 156
Carl, Thomas II, 481
Carl, Warren V, 156
Carl, William V, 156
Carl, Willie Hayes V, 156
Carle, Amy III, 139
Carle, Ann III, 59
Carle, Ann III, 398
Carle, Benjamin II, 343
Carle, Catharine II, 471
Carle, Catharine II, 481
Carle, Catharine IV, 688
Carle, Cornelia III, 59
Carle, Cornelia III, 398
Carle, Cornelia III, 467
Carle, Cornelia P. III, 59
Carle, Cornelia R. III, 109
Carle, Cornelia W. III, 353
Carle, Daniel IV, 688
Carle, Edward III, 59
Carle, Edward III, 398
Carle, Edward H. III, 314
Carle, Edward Hicks III, 59
Carle, Edward Hicks III, 314
Carle, Elizabeth I, 874
Carle, Elizabeth I, 1016
Carle, Elizabeth III, 59
Carle, Elizabeth III, 398
Carle, Elizabeth III, 472
Carle, Elizabeth IV, 690
Carle, Gadron III, 398
Carle, Gadron III, 472
Carle, Geo. IV, 690
Carle, Hannah Mary V, 611
Carle, Harriet J. IV, 690
Carle, Jacob III, 59
Carle, Jacob III, 398
Carle, Jacob III, 454
Carle, John III, 40
Carle, John III, 59
Carle, John III, 398
Carle, John III, 419
Carle, John III, 451
Carle, John III, 467
Carle, John J. III, 59
Carle, John J. III, 109
Carle, John J. III, 353
Carle, John, Jr. III, 59
Carle, John, Jr. III, 396
Carle, John, Jr. III, 398
Carle, John, Jr. III, 419
Carle, Lydia III, 314
Carle, Margaret Hayes III, 59
Carle, Margaret Hayes III, 314
Carle, Mary III, 59
Carle, Mary III, 112
Carle, Mary III, 289
Carle, Mary III, 398
Carle, Mary III, 451
Carle, Mary E. III, 398
Carle, Mary Elizabeth III, 59
Carle, Mary Elizabeth III, 398
Carle, Mary Etta V, 988
Carle, Phebe III, 59
Carle, Phebe III, 398
Carle, Phebe III, 419
Carle, Phebe III, 451
Carle, Phebe III, 454
Carle, Phebe Ann III, 59
Carle, Phebe Ann III, 398
Carle, Robert W. III, 59
Carle, Samuel II, 343
Carle, Sarah II, 343
Carle, Sarah III, 396
Carle, Sarah III, 398
Carle, Sarah H. III, 40
Carle, Sarah H. III, 59
Carle, Sidney IV, 688
Carle, Silas III, 59
Carle, Silas III, 398
Carle, Silas J. III, 59
Carle, Silas J. III, 398
Carle, Susan III, 396
Carle, Susan III, 398
Carle, Susan III, 419
Carle, Susan H. III, 40
Carle, Susan H. III, 59
Carle, Susan W. III, 59
Carle, Susan W. III, 109
Carle, Thomas II, 471
Carle, Thomas II, 481
Carle, Thomas III, 59
Carle, Thomas III, 139
Carleill, Abraham II, 481
Carleill, Abraham II, 571
Carleill, Mary II, 481
Carleill, Mary II, 571
Carleton, Abner IV, 323
Carleton, Beulah IV, 326
Carleton, Beulah IV, 332
Carleton, Bukk G. III, 60
Carleton, Bukk Griffith III, 60
Carleton, Bukk Griffith III, 373
Carleton, Bulah IV, 323
Carleton, Clarice E. III, 60
Carleton, Edward Ash III, 60
Carleton, Hannah IV, 323
Carleton, Hannah IV, 332
Carleton, Mark II, 481
Carleton, Mark IV, 323
Carleton, Mark IV, 326
Carleton, Mark IV, 332
Carleton, Mary III, 60
Carleton, Mary III, 373
Carleton, Mary IV, 24
Carleton, Mary IV, 28
Carleton, Mary IV, 323
Carleton, Mary IV, 326
Carleton, Nathan Crawford IV, 24
Carlick, Nancy I, 874
Carlie, Elizabeth K. II, 1048
Carlies, Elizabeth II, 832
Carlies, Henry P. II, 832
Carlies, Sarah A. II, 832
Carlile, Abraham II, 206
Carlile, Abraham II, 473
Carlile, Abraham II, 481
Carlile, Abraham II, 786
Carlile, Abraham II, 790
Carlile, Abraham II, 1048
Carlile, Abraham II, 1054
Carlile, Amos II, 988
Carlile, Amos II, 1025
Carlile, Ann II, 206
Carlile, Ann II, 261
Carlile, Ann II, 473
Carlile, Ann II, 481
Carlile, Ann II, 786
Carlile, Ann II, 845
Carlile, Benjamin II, 988
Carlile, Daniel II, 987
Carlile, David II, 988
Carlile, Elizabeth II, 987
Carlile, Elizabeth II, 988
Carlile, Elizabeth II, 1023
Carlile, Elizabeth II, 1025
Carlile, Elizabeth II, 1048
Carlile, Elizabeth II, 1054
Carlile, Emily II, 845
Carlile, George V, 440
Carlile, Hannah II, 981
Carlile, Hannah II, 988
Carlile, Isaac Pearson II, 206
Carlile, John II, 206
Carlile, John II, 225
Carlile, John II, 261
Carlile, John II, 473
Carlile, John II, 481
Carlile, John II, 987
Carlile, Jonathan II, 981
Carlile, Jonathan II, 987
Carlile, Jonathan II, 988
Carlile, Jonathan, Jr. II, 988
Carlile, Joseph II, 206
Carlile, Joseph II, 1023
Carlile, Joseph I. II, 1048
Carlile, Joseph I. II, 1054
Carlile, Langston II, 206
Carlile, Langston II, 249
Carlile, Langstone II, 206
Carlile, Marcy II, 981
Carlile, Marcy II, 987
Carlile, Margrett II, 442
Carlile, Mary II, 206
Carlile, Mary II, 225
Carlile, Mary II, 481
Carlile, Mary V, 440
Carlile, Mercy II, 790
Carlile, Mercy II, 988
Carlile, Mercy II, 1048
Carlile, Mercy II, 1054
Carlile, Rebecca II, 206
Carlile, Rebecca II, 249
Carlile, Rebecca II, 256
Carlile, Rebecca II, 988
Carlile, Rebecca V, 440
Carlile, Sarah II, 206
Carlile, Sarah II, 481
Carlile, Sarah II, 1023
Carlile, Sarah III, 288
Carlile, Sarah III, 289
Carlile, Wd. Rebecca II, 790
Carline, ??? II, 343
Carline, Hannah II, 343
Carlisle, Abraham II, 343
Carlisle, Abraham II, 481
Carlisle, Abraham II, 1048
Carlisle, Ann II, 481
Carlisle, Anna II, 169
Carlisle, Charlotta IV, 1247
Carlisle, Charlotte IV, 1247
Carlisle, Elizabeth II, 981
Carlisle, Elizabeth II, 987
Carlisle, Elizabeth II, 988
Carlisle, Elizabeth II, 1048
Carlisle, Hannah II, 481
Carlisle, Hannah II, 631
Carlisle, John II, 343
Carlisle, John II, 481
Carlisle, John II, 987
Carlisle, Jonathan II, 988
Carlisle, Joseph I. II, 1048
Carlisle, Langston II, 206
Carlisle, Langston II, 481
Carlisle, Langstone II, 206
Carlisle, Leah IV, 377
Carlisle, Mary II, 343
Carlisle, Mary II, 481
Carlisle, Mercy II, 1048
Carlisle, Rebecca II, 169
Carlisle, Rebecca II, 206
Carlisle, Rebecca II, 988
Carlisle, Sarah II, 481
Carlisle, Sarah II, 604
Carll, Albert G. III, 480
Carll, Grace II, 129
Carll, Joel B. III, 480
Carll, John III, 398
Carll, John Sidney III, 480
Carll, Katharine A. III, 480
Carll, Phebe III, 398
Carll, Sally B. III, 480
Carll, Selah S. III, 480
Carll, Thos. J. III, 480
Carlson, Benjamin IV, 934
Carlson, Martha IV, 934
Carlson, Sarah Jane IV, 934
Carlton, Abner IV, 323
Carlton, Bulah IV, 323
Carlton, Buley IV, 377
Carlton, Edward Ash III, 60
Carlton, Margaret II, 343
Carlton, Mark II, 481
Carlton, Mark IV, 323
Carlton, Mark IV, 377
Carlton, Mary IV, 323
Carlton, Sarah II, 481
Carlton, Susanna II, 612
Carlton, Susannah II, 481
Carlton, William II, 343
Carlyle, Elizabeth II, 988
Carlyle, Elizabeth II, 1038
Carlyle, Jonathan II, 988
Carlyle, Jonathan II, 1038
Carlyle, Mercy II, 988
Carlyle, Mercy II, 1038
Carmack, Mary II, 343
Carmalt, Caleb II, 343
Carmalt, Caleb II, 344
Carmalt, Caleb II, 481
Carmalt, Caleb II, 482
Carmalt, Caleb II, 732
Carmalt, Caleb II, 786
Carmalt, Caleb II, 845
Carmalt, Caleb III, 60
Carmalt, Elizabeth II, 481
Carmalt, Elizabeth II, 501
Carmalt, Esther II, 482
Carmalt, Hannah II, 343
Carmalt, Hannah II, 344
Carmalt, Hannah II, 481
Carmalt, Hannah II, 482
Carmalt, Hannah II, 548
Carmalt, Hannah II, 556
Carmalt, Hannah II, 786
Carmalt, Hannah II, 845
Carmalt, Isaac II, 482
Carmalt, James II, 344
Carmalt, James II, 481
Carmalt, James II, 644
Carmalt, John II, 344
Carmalt, John II, 481
Carmalt, Jonathan II, 344
Carmalt, Jonathan II, 481
Carmalt, Jonathan II, 482
Carmalt, Jonathan II, 548
Carmalt, Jonathan II, 556
Carmalt, Jonathan II, 644
Carmalt, Jonathan II, 786
Carmalt, Jonathan II, 845
Carmalt, Jonathan, Jr. II, 482
Carmalt, Laura III, 60
Carmalt, Mary II, 344
Carmalt, Mary II, 481
Carmalt, Mary II, 556
Carmalt, Mary Ann II, 827
Carmalt, Rebecca II, 344
Carmalt, Rebecca II, 482
Carmalt, Samuel Fisher II, 786
Carmalt, Samuel Fisher II, 845
Carmalt, Sarah II, 343
Carmalt, Sarah II, 482
Carmalt, Sarah II, 732
Carmalt, Sarah II, 786
Carmalt, Sarah II, 845
Carmalt, Sarah III, 60
Carmalt, Sibbilla II, 344
Carmalt, Sibilla II, 845
Carmalt, Susanna II, 481
Carmalt, Susanna II, 482
Carmalt, Susanna II, 581
Carmalt, Susanna II, 644
Carmalt, Susannah II, 481
Carmalt, Sybilla II, 732
Carmalt, William II, 344
Carmalt, William H. III, 60
Carman, ??? III, 60
Carman, Abigail III, 398
Carman, Abigail III, 404
Carman, Anna III, 60
Carman, Charles II, 482
Carman, David P. III, 60
Carman, Edna F. IV, 186
Carman, Edward II, 482
Carman, Edward Martindale III, 60
Carman, Elizabeth II, 870
Carman, Henrietta III, 60
Carman, Henrietta III, 290
Carman, James II, 344
Carman, James II, 482
Carman, James III, 398
Carman, James S. III, 60
Carman, James S. III, 261
Carman, Julia D. III, 261
Carman, Julia S. III, 60
Carman, Levine III, 400
Carman, Lydia P. IV, 688
Carman, Lydia P. IV, 710
Carman, Martha II, 344
Carman, Martha III, 398
Carman, Mary II, 482
Carman, Mary P. III, 398
Carman, Millard V, 479
Carman, Millard H. V, 479
Carman, Rosa IV, 186
Carman, Rosa L. IV, 186
Carman, Ruth III, 398
Carman, Ruth III, 437
Carman, Ruth V, 35
Carman, Ruth V, 479
Carman, Ruth VI, 375
Carman, Samuel R. III, 60
Carman, Samuel R. III, 353
Carman, Sarah II, 482
Carman, Sarah A. III, 60
Carman, Sarah A. III, 353
Carman, Sarah F. III, 60
Carman, Sarah F. III, 353
Carman, Sarah, Sr. II, 482
Carman, Sarah, Sr. II, 558
Carman, Susanna II, 344
Carman, Susannah III, 398
Carman, Susannah III, 404
Carman, Thomas III, 398
Carman, Thomas III, 404
Carman, Thomas III, 437
Carman, Wd. Rachel III, 408
Carman, Wd. Sarah II, 812
Carman, William II, 344
Carmean, Bert V, 227
Carmean, Blanche V, 453
Carmean, Elizabeth V, 227
Carmean, Floyd V, 453
Carmean, George V, 227
Carmean, George V, 453
Carmean, Harry V, 453
Carmean, John V, 453
Carmean, Johnny V, 453
Carmean, Olive V, 227
Carmean, Sadie V, 453
Carmean, Thomas V, 227
Carmean, Wayne V, 453
Carmean, Willie V, 453
Carmean, Wm. J. V, 453
Carmeans, Elizabeth V, 227
Carmeans, Olive V, 227
Carmen, Araminta IV, 906
Carmen, John IV, 906
Carmen, Sarah J. IV, 906
Carmerly, John I, 1149
Carmerly, Thena I, 1149
Carmerly, Thena??? I, 1149
Carmichael, Alice III, 60
Carmichael, Alice III, 111
Carmichael, D. F. III, 60
Carmichael, D. F. III, 111
Carmine, Ashford V, 453
Carmine, Clara E. V, 453
Carmine, Thomas V, 227
Carmoday, Cornelius III, 60
Carmon, Rosa L. IV, 186
Carmon, Rosa L. IV, 207
Carmon, Ruth V, 35
Carmony, Callie I, 1150
Carmony, John W. I, 1150
Carmony, Margaret J. I, 1150
Carn, Magdalene VI, 959
Carn, Michael VI, 959
Carnaghan, Abigail II, 482
Carnaghan, Deborah II, 482
Carnaham, Deborah Shaw II, 790
Carnaham, Ruth II, 790
Carnaham, Samuel II, 790
Carnahan, Abigail II, 482
Carnahan, Abigail II, 684
Carnahan, Deborah II, 482
Carnahan, Imogene Dolph V, 378
Carnahan, Lucy II, 344

Carnahan, Samuel II, 482
Carnahan, Samuel, Jr. II, 482
Carncross, Elizabeth W. II, 845
Carncross, Elizabeth Wooley II, 786
Carncross, Jacob II, 786
Carncross, Jacob Augustus II, 786
Carncross, Ruth Anna L. II, 845
Carncross, Wd. Ruth Anna II, 786
Carne, Mary Ann IV, 934
Carne, Mary Ann IV, 976
Carnean, John V, 453
Carnean, Wm. J. V, 453
Carnefix, Alexander D. VI, 864
Carnefix, Edward M. VI, 890
Carnefix, Mary J. VI, 890
Carnegie, Elizabeth P. IV, 1309
Carnegie, George IV, 1309
Carnegie, Janet IV, 1309
Carnel, Diana McCauley IV, 1355
Carnel, Elizabeth McCauley IV, 1355
Carnel, Jemimah McCauley IV, 1355
Carnel, Mariah IV, 1355
Carner, Allen VI, 973
Carner, Berlinda W. VI, 878
Carner, Daniel VI, 890
Carner, David VI, 890
Carner, David VI, 1012
Carner, Elias VI, 890
Carner, Elias VI, 988
Carner, Elijah VI, 890
Carner, Elijah VI, 1010
Carner, Elizabeth VI, 890
Carner, Elizabeth VI, 954
Carner, Frankey VI, 954
Carner, George G. VI, 849
Carner, Henry VI, 890
Carner, Janetta VI, 890
Carner, John VI, 906
Carner, John VI, 954
Carner, John H. VI, 876
Carner, John H. VI, 878
Carner, John H. VI, 969
Carner, John. H. VI, 890
Carner, Judith VI, 871
Carner, Lucy Ann VI, 1012
Carner, Marinda E. VI, 890
Carner, Martha VI, 1010
Carner, Mary J. VI, 890
Carner, Nancy VI, 890
Carner, Nancy VI, 933
Carner, Sarah VI, 890
Carner, Susan Benson VI, 890
Carner, William H. VI, 890
Carnerfax, Alexander VI, 848
Carnerfix, John VI, 865
Carnes, Adam VI, 890
Carnes, Albert IV, 1151
Carnes, Albert I. IV, 1151
Carnes, Cora J. IV, 1151
Carnes, Effie IV, 1151
Carnes, Elizabeth III, 60
Carnes, Flora IV, 1151
Carnes, Harley F. IV, 1151
Carnes, Jennie IV, 1151
Carnes, Lenna IV, 1151
Carnes, Luella IV, 1151
Carnes, Luella IV, 1184
Carnes, Luella Mae IV, 1151
Carnes, Mary VI, 890
Carnes, Mary C. IV, 1151
Carnes, Miachael VI, 890
Carnes, Michael VI, 983
Carnes, Michael Kern VI, 890
Carnes, Monroe IV, 1151
Carnes, Polly VI, 890
Carnes, Sylvester Monroe IV, 1151
Carney, Abraham VI, 890
Carney, Andrew IV, 1247
Carney, Andrew N. IV, 1247
Carney, John B. VI, 1017
Carney, John W. IV, 186
Carney, Margaret E. IV, 1247
Carney, Marguerite IV, 1247
Carney, Nancy VI, 890
Carney, S. VI, 923
Carns, Elizabeth VI, 1011
Carns, George VI, 935
Carns, George VI, 992
Carns, George VI, 1011
Carns, George VI, 1016
Carns, George VI, 1017
Carns, Lidia VI, 1017
Carns, Miachael VI, 890
Carns, Polly VI, 890
Carns, Thomas VI, 1012
Carnut, Ludia I, 980
Carnut, Lydia I, 983
Carol, Wellery I, 939
Carol, Willis I, 939
Caroline, ??? VI, 174
Carothers, Charles IV, 186
Carothers, Clark IV, 186
Carothers, Ellen V, 990
Carothers, Esther IV, 186
Carothers, H. W. V, 990
Carothers, Jay IV, 186
Carothers, John IV, 186
Carothers, John W. IV, 186
Carothers, L. C. V, 990
Carothers, Phillip C. V, 990
Carothers, Rhoda IV, 186
Carothers, Samuel IV, 186
Carpenter, ??? III, 61
Carpenter, ??? III, 62
Carpenter, ??? III, 63
Carpenter, ??? III, 64
Carpenter, ??? III, 90
Carpenter, ??? III, 144
Carpenter, ??? III, 399
Carpenter, A. Lincoln III, 60
Carpenter, Aaron III, 60
Carpenter, Aaron III, 61
Carpenter, Aaron III, 62
Carpenter, Aaron III, 345
Carpenter, Aaron IV, 1152
Carpenter, Aaron B. III, 63
Carpenter, Aaron B. III, 209
Carpenter, Abby III, 61
Carpenter, Abby Jane III, 60
Carpenter, Abby Jane III, 216
Carpenter, Abby S. III, 61
Carpenter, Abby S. III, 62
Carpenter, Abby S. III, 63
Carpenter, Abby S. III, 64
Carpenter, Abby S. III, 315
Carpenter, Abel III, 398
Carpenter, Abm. Lincoln III, 63
Carpenter, Abraham II, 344
Carpenter, Abraham II, 442
Carpenter, Abraham III, 60
Carpenter, Abraham III, 61
Carpenter, Abraham V, 479
Carpenter, Abraham V, 480
Carpenter, Abraham Clock III, 60
Carpenter, Abraham Clock III, 65
Carpenter, Ada III, 61
Carpenter, Ada C. III, 64
Carpenter, Adaline III, 60
Carpenter, Adaline III, 300
Carpenter, Adelbert B. II, 732
Carpenter, Adelbert B. II, 778
Carpenter, Adelia III, 209
Carpenter, Adelia A. III, 63
Carpenter, Adelia A. III, 209
Carpenter, Adelia A. III, 325
Carpenter, Adelia Augusta III, 60
Carpenter, Adelia Augusta III, 64
Carpenter, Adeline III, 62
Carpenter, Adny IV, 1151
Carpenter, Albert F. V, 553
Carpenter, Albert Hinman III, 62
Carpenter, Albina II, 473
Carpenter, Albina II, 482
Carpenter, Alex. H. III, 213
Carpenter, Alice II, 135
Carpenter, Alice III, 60
Carpenter, Alice III, 62
Carpenter, Alice III, 64
Carpenter, Alice III, 168
Carpenter, Alice III, 398
Carpenter, Alice III, 439
Carpenter, Alice V, 897
Carpenter, Alice V, 898
Carpenter, Alice V, 920
Carpenter, Alice M. V, 898
Carpenter, Alpheus III, 60
Carpenter, Alpheus III, 62
Carpenter, Alsop III, 398
Carpenter, Amanda M. III, 60
Carpenter, Amanda M. III, 325
Carpenter, Amelia III, 60
Carpenter, Amelia III, 64
Carpenter, Amelia III, 199
Carpenter, Amelia Augusta III, 60
Carpenter, Amelia Augusta III, 64
Carpenter, Amelia C. III, 61
Carpenter, Amelia C. III, 62
Carpenter, Amos III, 60
Carpenter, Amos III, 65
Carpenter, Amully III, 62
Carpenter, Amy III, 480
Carpenter, Amy IV, 186
Carpenter, Amy T. III, 61
Carpenter, Amy T. III, 63
Carpenter, Amy T. III, 64
Carpenter, Amy T. III, 134
Carpenter, Amy T. III, 139
Carpenter, Amy T. III, 344
Carpenter, An II, 344
Carpenter, Andrew III, 398
Carpenter, Andrew IV, 186
Carpenter, Andy IV, 186
Carpenter, Ann II, 344
Carpenter, Ann III, 63
Carpenter, Ann III, 398
Carpenter, Ann III, 460
Carpenter, Ann III, 467
Carpenter, Ann IV, 1355
Carpenter, Ann B. II, 730
Carpenter, Ann B. II, 732
Carpenter, Ann E. III, 95
Carpenter, Ann Eliza III, 60
Carpenter, Ann Eliza III, 64
Carpenter, Ann Eliza III, 95
Carpenter, Ann Eliza III, 96
Carpenter, Ann L. III, 60
Carpenter, Ann Maria III, 65
Carpenter, Ann Maria V, 898
Carpenter, Anna III, 60
Carpenter, Anna III, 61
Carpenter, Anna IV, 1355
Carpenter, Anna V, 480
Carpenter, Anna V, 553
Carpenter, Anna V, 897
Carpenter, Anna V, 898
Carpenter, Anna B. III, 211
Carpenter, Anna E. III, 60
Carpenter, Anna E. III, 175
Carpenter, Anna H. III, 61
Carpenter, Anna H. III, 62
Carpenter, Anna H. IV, 688
Carpenter, Anna Lily III, 60
Carpenter, Anna Lily III, 64
Carpenter, Anna M. II, 130
Carpenter, Anna M. II, 146
Carpenter, Anna T. III, 63
Carpenter, Anna T. III, 211
Carpenter, Anna Therese III, 61
Carpenter, Anna Therese III, 265
Carpenter, Anne II, 130
Carpenter, Anne II, 482
Carpenter, Anne II, 554
Carpenter, Anne III, 398
Carpenter, Artemus III, 60
Carpenter, Arthur III, 60
Carpenter, Arthur McDowell III, 64
Carpenter, Arthur McDowell III, 105
Carpenter, Asa III, 60
Carpenter, Atlantic IV, 323
Carpenter, Atlantic IV, 329
Carpenter, Augustus Henry III, 60
Carpenter, Azariah III, 60
Carpenter, Azariah III, 61
Carpenter, Azariah III, 63
Carpenter, Barbara III, 398
Carpenter, Barbara III, 465
Carpenter, Barbara Ann II, 130
Carpenter, Beatrice J. III, 60
Carpenter, Beatrice J. III, 64
Carpenter, Beatrice J. III, 140
Carpenter, Benedict III, 398
Carpenter, Benj. III, 61
Carpenter, Benj. III, 63
Carpenter, Benj. III, 64
Carpenter, Benjamin III, 60
Carpenter, Benjamin III, 62
Carpenter, Benjamin A. II, 130
Carpenter, Caleb P. III, 61
Carpenter, Caleb P. III, 62
Carpenter, Caleb P. III, 64
Carpenter, Caleb P. III, 257
Carpenter, Caleb Pierce III, 60
Carpenter, Caleb Pierce III, 199
Carpenter, Calvin V, 479
Carpenter, Calvin V, 480
Carpenter, Calvin V, 897
Carpenter, Calvin V, 898
Carpenter, Caroline III, 60
Carpenter, Caroline III, 61
Carpenter, Caroline III, 63
Carpenter, Caroline III, 216
Carpenter, Caroline III, 358
Carpenter, Caroline V, 553
Carpenter, Caroline V, 898
Carpenter, Caroline E. V, 553
Carpenter, Caroline Esther III, 64
Carpenter, Catharine III, 61
Carpenter, Catharine III, 62
Carpenter, Catharine III, 63
Carpenter, Catharine V, 480
Carpenter, Catharine V, 897
Carpenter, Catharine V, 913
Carpenter, Catharine B. III, 61
Carpenter, Catharine B. III, 62
Carpenter, Catharine H. III, 62
Carpenter, Catherine V, 35
Carpenter, Catherine V, 85
Carpenter, Cecelia III, 62
Carpenter, Charity III, 398
Carpenter, Charity III, 476
Carpenter, Charles III, 63
Carpenter, Charles V, 480
Carpenter, Charles B. III, 60
Carpenter, Charles B. III, 61
Carpenter, Charles B. III, 265
Carpenter, Charles G. IV, 466
Carpenter, Charles G. V, 553
Carpenter, Charles Gray V, 553
Carpenter, Charles Grey V, 480
Carpenter, Charles M. III, 61
Carpenter, Charles M. III, 62
Carpenter, Charles M. III, 64
Carpenter, Charles M. III, 297
Carpenter, Charles M. III, 326
Carpenter, Charlotte III, 60
Carpenter, Charlotte III, 61
Carpenter, Charlotte III, 62
Carpenter, Charlotte III, 64
Carpenter, Charlotte III, 154
Carpenter, Charlotte III, 326
Carpenter, Charlotte M. III, 61
Carpenter, Charlotte May II, 732
Carpenter, Charlotte May II, 778
Carpenter, Chas. V, 898
Carpenter, Chas. B. III, 63
Carpenter, Chas. B. III, 211
Carpenter, Chas. G. IV, 489
Carpenter, Chas. L. IV, 1309
Carpenter, Chas. M. III, 60
Carpenter, Claretta III, 65
Carpenter, Clariss III, 65
Carpenter, Clarissa III, 61
Carpenter, Clifford H. V, 897
Carpenter, Clifford H. V, 898
Carpenter, Clinton C. V, 897
Carpenter, Cornelia III, 61
Carpenter, Cynthia III, 61
Carpenter, Daniel III, 61
Carpenter, Daniel III, 65
Carpenter, Daniel V, 898
Carpenter, Daniel F. III, 61
Carpenter, Daniel H. III, 61
Carpenter, Daniel H. V, 898
Carpenter, Daniel J. III, 61
Carpenter, Daniel J. III, 115
Carpenter, David III, 61
Carpenter, David III, 63
Carpenter, David III, 141
Carpenter, David IV, 1151
Carpenter, David IV, 1152
Carpenter, David L. III, 60
Carpenter, David L. III, 61
Carpenter, David L. III, 64
Carpenter, David L. III, 325
Carpenter, David R. III, 61
Carpenter, David R. III, 64
Carpenter, Dean III, 62
Carpenter, Deborah III, 62
Carpenter, Deborah III, 64
Carpenter, Deborah Ann IV, 1152
Carpenter, Deborah Ann IV, 1234
Carpenter, Dinah III, 398
Carpenter, Dinah III, 400
Carpenter, Dinah III, 403
Carpenter, Dora III, 60
Carpenter, Dora III, 105
Carpenter, Dorothy III, 61
Carpenter, Dorothy III, 322
Carpenter, Dorothy E. III, 62
Carpenter, Dorothy E. III, 106
Carpenter, Duanesburgh V, 480
Carpenter, Edith III, 61
Carpenter, Edith III, 63
Carpenter, Edith III, 217
Carpenter, Edith III, 344
Carpenter, Edith H. III, 61
Carpenter, Edith H. IV, 688
Carpenter, Edith H. IV, 730
Carpenter, Edmund III, 61
Carpenter, Edmund M. III, 61
Carpenter, Edmund M. III, 62
Carpenter, Edmund M. IV, 688
Carpenter, Edmund T. III, 61
Carpenter, Edna Wallace III, 64
Carpenter, Edna Wallace III, 143
Carpenter, Edward III, 61
Carpenter, Edward III, 63
Carpenter, Edward V, 479
Carpenter, Edward V, 480
Carpenter, Edward H. III, 61
Carpenter, Edward H. III, 62
Carpenter, Edwin V, 480
Carpenter, Edwin V, 553
Carpenter, Edwin V, 570
Carpenter, Edwin V, 897
Carpenter, Edwin V, 898
Carpenter, Eleanor II, 479
Carpenter, Eleanor II, 680
Carpenter, Eleanor III, 62
Carpenter, Eliakim III, 61
Carpenter, Elihu IV, 1355
Carpenter, Elisha III, 61
Carpenter, Elisha III, 398
Carpenter, Elisha III, 443
Carpenter, Eliz. H. III, 61
Carpenter, Eliz. H. III, 64
Carpenter, Eliza I, 931
Carpenter, Eliza III, 61
Carpenter, Eliza III, 63
Carpenter, Eliza III, 64
Carpenter, Eliza IV, 1152
Carpenter, Eliza V, 487
Carpenter, Eliza Ann IV, 1152
Carpenter, Eliza Ann IV, 1198
Carpenter, Eliza B. III, 141
Carpenter, Eliza D. V, 480
Carpenter, Eliza D. V, 487
Carpenter, Eliza H. III, 62
Carpenter, Eliza Mary V, 480
Carpenter, Elizabeth II, 24
Carpenter, Elizabeth II, 60
Carpenter, Elizabeth II, 69
Carpenter, Elizabeth II, 109
Carpenter, Elizabeth II, 113
Carpenter, Elizabeth II, 130
Carpenter, Elizabeth II, 139
Carpenter, Elizabeth II, 344
Carpenter, Elizabeth III, 64
Carpenter, Elizabeth III, 65
Carpenter, Elizabeth III, 141
Carpenter, Elizabeth III, 154
Carpenter, Elizabeth III, 256
Carpenter, Elizabeth III, 399
Carpenter, Elizabeth III, 401
Carpenter, Elizabeth IV, 1152
Carpenter, Elizabeth IV, 1231
Carpenter, Elizabeth IV, 1234
Carpenter, Elizabeth V, 479
Carpenter, Elizabeth V, 480
Carpenter, Elizabeth V, 553
Carpenter, Elizabeth V, 897
Carpenter, Elizabeth A. IV, 466
Carpenter, Elizabeth H. III, 209
Carpenter, Elizabeth H. V, 897
Carpenter, Elizabeth P. III, 61
Carpenter, Elizabeth P. III, 64
Carpenter, Elizabeth S. II, 130
Carpenter, Ella Cottrell IV, 1309
Carpenter, Ellen III, 65
Carpenter, Ellwood III, 61
Carpenter, Ellwood III, 62
Carpenter, Ellwood III, 63
Carpenter, Elmira IV, 1355
Carpenter, Elmira IV, 1375
Carpenter, Elmyra IV, 1355
Carpenter, Elnathan III, 61
Carpenter, Elsie III, 61
Carpenter, Elsie III, 62
Carpenter, Emeline III, 61
Carpenter, Emily III, 61
Carpenter, Emily III, 62
Carpenter, Emily III, 64
Carpenter, Emily III, 108
Carpenter, Emily III, 371
Carpenter, Emily Eliza III, 60
Carpenter, Emily Eliza III, 61
Carpenter, Emily J. III, 62
Carpenter, Emma III, 61
Carpenter, Emma III, 64
Carpenter, Emma III, 115
Carpenter, Emma IV, 688
Carpenter, Emma Jane III, 61
Carpenter, Emma Jane III, 345
Carpenter, Enoch III, 61
Carpenter, Enoch III, 95
Carpenter, Enock III, 60
Carpenter, Enock III, 96
Carpenter, Esther III, 61
Carpenter, Esther III, 64
Carpenter, Esther III, 65
Carpenter, Esther IV, 186
Carpenter, Esther V, 479
Carpenter, Esther V, 480
Carpenter, Esther V, 507
Carpenter, Esther G. III, 480
Carpenter, Esther G. III, 495
Carpenter, Esther Jane III, 63
Carpenter, Esther Jane III, 305
Carpenter, Eugene F. III, 496
Carpenter, Eveline III, 63
Carpenter, Ezra III, 61
Carpenter, Ezra V, 479
Carpenter, Ezra V, 480

Carpenter, Ezra V, 897
Carpenter, Fannie II, 133
Carpenter, Fanny P. II, 146
Carpenter, Fanny Pease II, 150
Carpenter, Ferris III, 480
Carpenter, Ferris III, 495
Carpenter, Florence III, 398
Carpenter, Florence III, 426
Carpenter, Florence III, 465
Carpenter, Florence Amelia III, 398
Carpenter, Florence Amelia III, 415
Carpenter, Florence L. II, 701
Carpenter, Florence Louella II, 732
Carpenter, Florence Louella II, 778
Carpenter, Francis III, 64
Carpenter, Francis III, 398
Carpenter, Francis W. III, 61
Carpenter, Francis W. III, 64
Carpenter, Franklin III, 61
Carpenter, Franklin T. III, 61
Carpenter, Franklin T. III, 62
Carpenter, Franklin T. III, 64
Carpenter, Frederick J. III, 60
Carpenter, Frederick J. III, 62
Carpenter, Frederick W. III, 106
Carpenter, Frederick Walton III, 61
Carpenter, Frederick Walton III, 62
Carpenter, Geo. III, 480
Carpenter, Geo. W. III, 62
Carpenter, Geo. W. IV, 1355
Carpenter, George III, 65
Carpenter, George Alexander III, 213
Carpenter, George W. III, 60
Carpenter, George W. III, 61
Carpenter, George W. III, 62
Carpenter, George W. IV, 1355
Carpenter, George W. IV, 1364
Carpenter, Grey V, 898
Carpenter, H. M. III, 216
Carpenter, Hannah II, 20
Carpenter, Hannah II, 24
Carpenter, Hannah II, 37
Carpenter, Hannah II, 38
Carpenter, Hannah II, 47
Carpenter, Hannah II, 60
Carpenter, Hannah II, 86
Carpenter, Hannah II, 93
Carpenter, Hannah II, 99
Carpenter, Hannah II, 114
Carpenter, Hannah II, 116
Carpenter, Hannah II, 344
Carpenter, Hannah II, 482
Carpenter, Hannah II, 541
Carpenter, Hannah II, 626
Carpenter, Hannah II, 649
Carpenter, Hannah II, 683
Carpenter, Hannah III, 60
Carpenter, Hannah III, 61
Carpenter, Hannah III, 62
Carpenter, Hannah III, 63
Carpenter, Hannah III, 64
Carpenter, Hannah III, 96
Carpenter, Hannah III, 153
Carpenter, Hannah III, 189
Carpenter, Hannah III, 213
Carpenter, Hannah III, 228
Carpenter, Hannah III, 230
Carpenter, Hannah III, 353
Carpenter, Hannah III, 394
Carpenter, Hannah III, 398
Carpenter, Hannah III, 480
Carpenter, Hannah III, 506
Carpenter, Hannah A. II, 116
Carpenter, Hannah A. II, 123
Carpenter, Hannah F. III, 61
Carpenter, Hannah Field III, 62
Carpenter, Hannah H. III, 61
Carpenter, Hannah H. III, 62
Carpenter, Hannah Hall II, 24
Carpenter, Hannah S. III, 496
Carpenter, Hannah T. III, 264
Carpenter, Hannah W. II, 116
Carpenter, Hannah W. II, 122
Carpenter, Hannah W. III, 60
Carpenter, Hannah W. III, 61
Carpenter, Hannah W. III, 63
Carpenter, Hannah W. III, 480
Carpenter, Hannah W. III, 493
Carpenter, Hannah, Jr. II, 482
Carpenter, Hannah, Jr. II, 523
Carpenter, Harriet III, 131
Carpenter, Harriet III, 496
Carpenter, Harriet L. III, 69
Carpenter, Harriet S. II, 786
Carpenter, Harry S. III, 62
Carpenter, Harry S. III, 98
Carpenter, Hattie A. III, 61
Carpenter, Hattie A. III, 62
Carpenter, Henrietta III, 63
Carpenter, Henry III, 62
Carpenter, Henry IV, 1151
Carpenter, Henry IV, 1152
Carpenter, Henry H. III, 62
Carpenter, Henry H. III, 193
Carpenter, Henry M. III, 60
Carpenter, Henry M. III, 62
Carpenter, Henry M. III, 63
Carpenter, Henry M. III, 64
Carpenter, Henry M. III, 216
Carpenter, Horace III, 62
Carpenter, Horace III, 96
Carpenter, Horace V, 897
Carpenter, Horace E. V, 897
Carpenter, Howard IV, 186
Carpenter, Howard H. IV, 186
Carpenter, Howard Irving III, 62
Carpenter, Isaac III, 60
Carpenter, Isaac III, 62
Carpenter, Isaac III, 63
Carpenter, Isaac III, 64
Carpenter, Isaac III, 151
Carpenter, Isaac III, 179
Carpenter, Isaac III, 257
Carpenter, Isaac III, 315
Carpenter, Isaac III, 398
Carpenter, Isaac IV, 1152
Carpenter, Isaac V, 479
Carpenter, Isaac Burling III, 62
Carpenter, Isaac T. III, 64
Carpenter, Isaac W. III, 62
Carpenter, Isaac Warner III, 62
Carpenter, Isaac, Jr. III, 61
Carpenter, Isaac, Jr. III, 62
Carpenter, Isaac, Jr. III, 64
Carpenter, Isaiah IV, 1355
Carpenter, Israel III, 62
Carpenter, Israel III, 63
Carpenter, J. Searing III, 483
Carpenter, Jacob III, 62
Carpenter, Jacob III, 398
Carpenter, Jacob III, 475
Carpenter, Jacob V, 479
Carpenter, Jacob V, 480
Carpenter, Jacob V, 897
Carpenter, Jacob A. III, 61
Carpenter, Jacob B. III, 63
Carpenter, Jacob Willetts III, 61
Carpenter, James III, 61
Carpenter, James III, 62
Carpenter, James III, 63
Carpenter, James III, 64
Carpenter, James III, 231
Carpenter, James III, 358
Carpenter, James III, 398
Carpenter, James III, 400
Carpenter, James III, 403
Carpenter, James IV, 1274
Carpenter, James E. III, 213
Carpenter, James G. III, 62
Carpenter, James S. III, 62
Carpenter, James S. III, 64
Carpenter, James T. III, 213
Carpenter, Jane III, 62
Carpenter, Jane III, 64
Carpenter, Jane III, 213
Carpenter, Jane III, 327
Carpenter, Jane Louisa III, 61
Carpenter, Jane Louisa III, 62
Carpenter, Jane Louise III, 21
Carpenter, Jane S. III, 60
Carpenter, Jane S. III, 61
Carpenter, Jane S. III, 62
Carpenter, Jane S. III, 345
Carpenter, Jane W. III, 61
Carpenter, Jane W. III, 62
Carpenter, Jane W. III, 64
Carpenter, Jas. E. III, 63
Carpenter, Jemima III, 64
Carpenter, Jemima III, 206
Carpenter, Jemina III, 63
Carpenter, Jesse G. III, 62
Carpenter, John II, 24
Carpenter, John II, 344
Carpenter, John II, 442
Carpenter, John II, 482
Carpenter, John II, 554
Carpenter, John II, 595
Carpenter, John II, 683
Carpenter, John III, 62
Carpenter, John III, 116
Carpenter, John III, 398
Carpenter, John III, 410
Carpenter, John III, 421
Carpenter, John III, 476
Carpenter, John IV, 186
Carpenter, John E. III, 61
Carpenter, John E. IV, 186
Carpenter, John H. III, 61
Carpenter, John R. II, 24
Carpenter, John R. II, 60
Carpenter, John R. II, 116
Carpenter, John R. II, 482
Carpenter, John Redman II, 24
Carpenter, John S. II, 130
Carpenter, John S., Jr. II, 130
Carpenter, John T. III, 60
Carpenter, John T. III, 62
Carpenter, John T. III, 63
Carpenter, John T. III, 64
Carpenter, John T. III, 179
Carpenter, John T. III, 186
Carpenter, John T. III, 300
Carpenter, Jos. III, 398
Carpenter, Joseph II, 344
Carpenter, Joseph III, 63
Carpenter, Joseph III, 64
Carpenter, Joseph III, 154
Carpenter, Joseph III, 398
Carpenter, Joseph III, 460
Carpenter, Joseph III, 467
Carpenter, Joseph T. III, 60
Carpenter, Joseph T. III, 62
Carpenter, Joseph T. III, 63
Carpenter, Joseph, Jr. III, 398
Carpenter, Josephine III, 62
Carpenter, Josephine E. III, 61
Carpenter, Josephine E. III, 217
Carpenter, Joshua II, 344
Carpenter, Joshuoah II, 344
Carpenter, Josiah III, 61
Carpenter, Josiah III, 62
Carpenter, Josiah III, 64
Carpenter, Julia III, 480
Carpenter, Julia III, 495
Carpenter, Julia III, 496
Carpenter, Julia Ann IV, 1355
Carpenter, Julianna IV, 1355
Carpenter, Katherine III, 61
Carpenter, Katherine III, 297
Carpenter, Laura III, 62
Carpenter, Laura III, 193
Carpenter, Laura A. V, 553
Carpenter, Laura E. III, 63
Carpenter, Laura Eliz. III, 281
Carpenter, Leonard J. III, 61
Carpenter, Letitia III, 61
Carpenter, Letitia M. III, 443
Carpenter, Lida IV, 186
Carpenter, Lincoln III, 175
Carpenter, Lizzie May IV, 186
Carpenter, Louisa II, 787
Carpenter, Louisa V, 553
Carpenter, Louisa V, 570
Carpenter, Lovinah III, 63
Carpenter, Lucretia III, 61
Carpenter, Lucy II, 130
Carpenter, Lucy II, 146
Carpenter, Lucy IV, 1355
Carpenter, Lyde IV, 186
Carpenter, Lydia III, 60
Carpenter, Lydia III, 62
Carpenter, Lydia III, 64
Carpenter, Lydia III, 327
Carpenter, Lydia V, 479
Carpenter, Lydia V, 480
Carpenter, Lydia V, 489
Carpenter, Lydia V, 553
Carpenter, Lydia V, 560
Carpenter, Mae III, 64
Carpenter, Mae III, 262
Carpenter, Malvinia IV, 1355
Carpenter, Maplet H. III, 59
Carpenter, Maplet H. III, 63
Carpenter, Margaret II, 47
Carpenter, Margaret II, 60
Carpenter, Margaret II, 112
Carpenter, Margaret II, 482
Carpenter, Margary IV, 186
Carpenter, Margery IV, 186
Carpenter, Maria III, 61
Carpenter, Maria III, 63
Carpenter, Maria V, 897
Carpenter, Maria Louisa III, 62
Carpenter, Maria Louisa III, 63
Carpenter, Maria Louisa III, 64
Carpenter, Maria Louisa III, 305
Carpenter, Martha II, 60
Carpenter, Martha II, 94
Carpenter, Martha II, 103
Carpenter, Martha II, 116
Carpenter, Martha II, 118
Carpenter, Martha II, 130
Carpenter, Martha II, 134
Carpenter, Martha II, 137
Carpenter, Martha II, 146
Carpenter, Martha II, 148
Carpenter, Martha II, 154
Carpenter, Martha II, 482
Carpenter, Martha II, 595
Carpenter, Martha III, 62
Carpenter, Martha III, 63
Carpenter, Martha III, 116
Carpenter, Martha III, 398
Carpenter, Martha III, 399
Carpenter, Martha III, 410
Carpenter, Martin Frances II, 778
Carpenter, Martin Francis II, 701
Carpenter, Martin Francis II, 732
Carpenter, Mary II, 24
Carpenter, Mary II, 60
Carpenter, Mary II, 81
Carpenter, Mary II, 86
Carpenter, Mary II, 93
Carpenter, Mary II, 97
Carpenter, Mary II, 107
Carpenter, Mary II, 114
Carpenter, Mary II, 116
Carpenter, Mary II, 130
Carpenter, Mary II, 344
Carpenter, Mary II, 482
Carpenter, Mary II, 488
Carpenter, Mary III, 61
Carpenter, Mary III, 62
Carpenter, Mary III, 63
Carpenter, Mary III, 64
Carpenter, Mary III, 98
Carpenter, Mary III, 119
Carpenter, Mary III, 141
Carpenter, Mary III, 211
Carpenter, Mary III, 294
Carpenter, Mary III, 296
Carpenter, Mary III, 358
Carpenter, Mary III, 398
Carpenter, Mary III, 412
Carpenter, Mary III, 460
Carpenter, Mary III, 475
Carpenter, Mary III, 496
Carpenter, Mary IV, 1152
Carpenter, Mary IV, 1355
Carpenter, Mary V, 35
Carpenter, Mary V, 480
Carpenter, Mary V, 553
Carpenter, Mary V, 898
Carpenter, Mary A. III, 64
Carpenter, Mary A. III, 231
Carpenter, Mary C. III, 60
Carpenter, Mary C. III, 61
Carpenter, Mary C. IV, 1355
Carpenter, Mary C. IV, 1364
Carpenter, Mary D. III, 213
Carpenter, Mary E. II, 116
Carpenter, Mary E. II, 130
Carpenter, Mary E. II, 134
Carpenter, Mary E. III, 61
Carpenter, Mary E. III, 62
Carpenter, Mary E. III, 63
Carpenter, Mary E. III, 64
Carpenter, Mary E. III, 206
Carpenter, Mary Eleanor IV, 186
Carpenter, Mary Elizabeth II, 146
Carpenter, Mary Elizabeth II, 152
Carpenter, Mary Elizabeth III, 62
Carpenter, Mary Elizabeth III, 63
Carpenter, Mary Elizabeth III, 209
Carpenter, Mary Emma III, 61
Carpenter, Mary Emma IV, 688
Carpenter, Mary Emma IV, 790
Carpenter, Mary Frances III, 184
Carpenter, Mary Frances III, 185
Carpenter, Mary H. III, 63
Carpenter, Mary H. IV, 186
Carpenter, Mary P. III, 398
Carpenter, Mary R. II, 24
Carpenter, Mary R. II, 37
Carpenter, Mary R. II, 116
Carpenter, Mary R. II, 123
Carpenter, Mary R. II, 130
Carpenter, Mary R. II, 732
Carpenter, Mary T. III, 62
Carpenter, Mary T. III, 63
Carpenter, Mary T. III, 96
Carpenter, Mary T. V, 480
Carpenter, Mary T. V, 553
Carpenter, Mary T. V, 594
Carpenter, Mary T. V, 897
Carpenter, Mary W. III, 453
Carpenter, Mary W. V, 478
Carpenter, Mary W. V, 480
Carpenter, Mary Wyatt II, 24
Carpenter, Mary Wyatt II, 795
Carpenter, Matt III, 63
Carpenter, Matthew V, 480
Carpenter, Matthew F. III, 496
Carpenter, May V, 663
Carpenter, Mercy V, 479
Carpenter, Merrill E. III, 65
Carpenter, Mildred II, 130
Carpenter, Miles B. III, 61
Carpenter, Miles B. III, 217
Carpenter, Myrtle L. III, 64
Carpenter, Myrtle L. III, 357
Carpenter, Nancy II, 133
Carpenter, Nancy IV, 1355
Carpenter, Nancy A. II, 150
Carpenter, Nathaniel III, 63
Carpenter, Nathaniel V, 480
Carpenter, Nathaniel V, 553
Carpenter, Nathaniel V, 897
Carpenter, Nathaniel V, 913
Carpenter, Nathaniel, Jr. III, 63
Carpenter, Ophelia III, 62
Carpenter, Ophelia III, 63
Carpenter, Ophelia III, 313
Carpenter, Ophelia III, 315
Carpenter, Patience III, 60
Carpenter, Patience III, 63
Carpenter, Patience III, 151
Carpenter, Patience III, 179
Carpenter, Patience III, 257
Carpenter, Peter J. III, 63
Carpenter, Peter J. III, 178
Carpenter, Phebe III, 60
Carpenter, Phebe III, 61
Carpenter, Phebe III, 62
Carpenter, Phebe III, 63
Carpenter, Phebe III, 64
Carpenter, Phebe III, 65
Carpenter, Phebe III, 325
Carpenter, Phebe III, 327
Carpenter, Phebe III, 330
Carpenter, Phebe III, 371
Carpenter, Phebe III, 398
Carpenter, Phebe III, 399
Carpenter, Phebe III, 454
Carpenter, Phebe III, 467
Carpenter, Phebe III, 470
Carpenter, Phebe III, 480
Carpenter, Phebe III, 489
Carpenter, Phebe IV, 1152
Carpenter, Phebe IV, 1166
Carpenter, Phebe IV, 1355
Carpenter, Phebe Anna III, 61
Carpenter, Phebe C. II, 116
Carpenter, Phebe C. III, 63
Carpenter, Phebe C. III, 144
Carpenter, Phebe F. III, 61
Carpenter, Phebe H. III, 62
Carpenter, Phebe H. III, 63
Carpenter, Phebe H. III, 64
Carpenter, Phebe H. III, 178
Carpenter, Phebe Jane III, 60
Carpenter, Phebe Jane III, 62
Carpenter, Phebe Jane III, 63
Carpenter, Phebe Jane III, 186
Carpenter, Phebe K. III, 63
Carpenter, Phebe S. III, 63
Carpenter, Phebe S. III, 64
Carpenter, Phebe S. III, 65
Carpenter, Phebe S. III, 346
Carpenter, Phebe W. III, 398
Carpenter, Preston II, 20
Carpenter, Preston II, 24
Carpenter, Preston II, 47
Carpenter, Preston II, 60
Carpenter, Preston II, 86
Carpenter, Preston II, 93
Carpenter, Preston II, 99
Carpenter, Preston II, 137
Carpenter, Preston II, 344
Carpenter, Preston II, 482
Carpenter, Priscilla III, 62
Carpenter, Priscilla H. III, 62
Carpenter, Rachel II, 24
Carpenter, Rachel II, 60
Carpenter, Rachel II, 68
Carpenter, Rachel III, 63
Carpenter, Rachel III, 65
Carpenter, Rachel D. III, 63
Carpenter, Rachel M. III, 114
Carpenter, Rachel R. II, 60
Carpenter, Rachel R. II, 97
Carpenter, Rachel R. II, 718
Carpenter, Rebecca II, 130
Carpenter, Rebecca II, 144
Carpenter, Rebecca II, 146
Carpenter, Rebecca II, 344
Carpenter, Rebecca III, 60
Carpenter, Rebecca III, 63
Carpenter, Rebecca III, 399
Carpenter, Rebecca III, 429
Carpenter, Rebecca B. II, 130
Carpenter, Rebecca C. III, 60

Carpenter, Rebecca C. III, 62
Carpenter, Rebecca M. III, 63
Carpenter, Rebecca W. III, 63
Carpenter, Rebecca W. III, 114
Carpenter, Rebecka II, 344
Carpenter, Rees III, 63
Carpenter, Rich. E. III, 398
Carpenter, Rich. E. III, 465
Carpenter, Richard III, 63
Carpenter, Richard E. III, 63
Carpenter, Richard E. III, 398
Carpenter, Richard E. III, 415
Carpenter, Richard E. III, 426
Carpenter, Richard E. III, 453
Carpenter, Richard E., Jr. III, 398
Carpenter, Richard E., Jr. III, 439
Carpenter, Richard Earle, Jr. III, 398
Carpenter, Richard W. III, 63
Carpenter, Riley IV, 1234
Carpenter, Robert III, 63
Carpenter, Robert III, 144
Carpenter, Robert IV, 1152
Carpenter, Robert IV, 1234
Carpenter, Robert H. III, 61
Carpenter, Robert H. III, 63
Carpenter, Robert H. III, 134
Carpenter, Robert H. III, 139
Carpenter, Robert R. III, 60
Carpenter, Robert R. III, 61
Carpenter, Robert R. III, 63
Carpenter, Robert R. III, 480
Carpenter, Robert R. III, 493
Carpenter, Robt. H. III, 64
Carpenter, Robt. H. III, 344
Carpenter, Ruth III, 61
Carpenter, Ruth III, 398
Carpenter, Ruth III, 426
Carpenter, Ruth IV, 1234
Carpenter, Ruth O. IV, 1234
Carpenter, S. Preston II, 130
Carpenter, Samuel II, 37
Carpenter, Samuel II, 344
Carpenter, Samuel II, 442
Carpenter, Samuel II, 482
Carpenter, Samuel II, 541
Carpenter, Samuel II, 554
Carpenter, Samuel II, 583
Carpenter, Samuel II, 608
Carpenter, Samuel II, 649
Carpenter, Samuel III, 63
Carpenter, Samuel III, 114
Carpenter, Samuel III, 398
Carpenter, Samuel III, 480
Carpenter, Samuel III, 489
Carpenter, Samuel III, 496
Carpenter, Samuel V, 988
Carpenter, Samuel P. II, 38
Carpenter, Samuel P. II, 116
Carpenter, Samuel P. II, 122
Carpenter, Samuel P. II, 123
Carpenter, Samuel Preston II, 24
Carpenter, Samuel Preston II, 114
Carpenter, Samuel Preston II, 116
Carpenter, Samuel Preston, Jr. II, 116
Carpenter, Samuel, Jr. II, 482
Carpenter, Samuel, Jr. II, 626
Carpenter, Sarah II, 24
Carpenter, Sarah II, 38
Carpenter, Sarah II, 116
Carpenter, Sarah II, 123
Carpenter, Sarah II, 344
Carpenter, Sarah II, 442
Carpenter, Sarah II, 701
Carpenter, Sarah III, 59
Carpenter, Sarah III, 60
Carpenter, Sarah III, 61
Carpenter, Sarah III, 62
Carpenter, Sarah III, 63
Carpenter, Sarah III, 64
Carpenter, Sarah III, 65
Carpenter, Sarah III, 87
Carpenter, Sarah III, 134
Carpenter, Sarah III, 179
Carpenter, Sarah III, 213
Carpenter, Sarah III, 300
Carpenter, Sarah III, 345
Carpenter, Sarah III, 398
Carpenter, Sarah III, 399
Carpenter, Sarah III, 401
Carpenter, Sarah III, 421
Carpenter, Sarah III, 483
Carpenter, Sarah IV, 1151
Carpenter, Sarah IV, 1152
Carpenter, Sarah IV, 1167
Carpenter, Sarah V, 479
Carpenter, Sarah VI, 496
Carpenter, Sarah VI, 642
Carpenter, Sarah VI, 661
Carpenter, Sarah VI, 664
Carpenter, Sarah VI, 744
Carpenter, Sarah VI, 754
Carpenter, Sarah A. III, 64
Carpenter, Sarah A. III, 154
Carpenter, Sarah Ann III, 62
Carpenter, Sarah Ann III, 64
Carpenter, Sarah Ann III, 65
Carpenter, Sarah Ann III, 179
Carpenter, Sarah E. III, 65
Carpenter, Sarah E. III, 496
Carpenter, Sarah F. III, 60
Carpenter, Sarah F. III, 61
Carpenter, Sarah F. III, 64
Carpenter, Sarah F. III, 141
Carpenter, Sarah Frances III, 64
Carpenter, Sarah Frances III, 177
Carpenter, Sarah W. II, 24
Carpenter, Sarah W. III, 61
Carpenter, Sarah W. III, 63
Carpenter, Sarah W. III, 64
Carpenter, Sarah Wyatt II, 116
Carpenter, Sarah Wyatt II, 122
Carpenter, Serena III, 231
Carpenter, Serena A. III, 64
Carpenter, Serena A. III, 231
Carpenter, Serena A. III, 319
Carpenter, Sidney H. III, 64
Carpenter, Sidney H. III, 143
Carpenter, Silas I, 268
Carpenter, Silas III, 61
Carpenter, Silas III, 64
Carpenter, Silas S. III, 64
Carpenter, Sophia III, 60
Carpenter, Sophia III, 61
Carpenter, Sophia III, 64
Carpenter, Sophia III, 95
Carpenter, Sophia III, 96
Carpenter, Sophia IV, 1152
Carpenter, Sophia IV, 1189
Carpenter, Sophice III, 62
Carpenter, Stephen II, 680
Carpenter, Stephen IV, 1355
Carpenter, Stephen G. III, 63
Carpenter, Stephen G. III, 64
Carpenter, Stephen G. III, 262
Carpenter, Stephen J. IV, 1355
Carpenter, Susan V, 480
Carpenter, Susan V, 515
Carpenter, Susan V, 897
Carpenter, Susan M. IV, 466
Carpenter, Susan M. V, 480
Carpenter, Susan M. V, 553
Carpenter, Susan M. V, 897
Carpenter, Susan M. V, 898
Carpenter, Susannah IV, 323
Carpenter, Susannah IV, 329
Carpenter, Thomas II, 60
Carpenter, Thomas II, 344
Carpenter, Thomas II, 442
Carpenter, Thomas II, 482
Carpenter, Thomas III, 62
Carpenter, Thomas III, 63
Carpenter, Thomas III, 64
Carpenter, Thomas III, 327
Carpenter, Thomas III, 330
Carpenter, Thomas III, 394
Carpenter, Thomas III, 398
Carpenter, Thomas V, 479
Carpenter, Thomas C. V, 479
Carpenter, Thomas, Jr. III, 64
Carpenter, Thos. III, 59
Carpenter, Thos. III, 61
Carpenter, Thos. III, 63
Carpenter, Thos. III, 345
Carpenter, Thos. III, 371
Carpenter, Thos. III, 398
Carpenter, Tiddeman III, 177
Carpenter, Timothy III, 63
Carpenter, Timothy III, 64
Carpenter, Timothy III, 206
Carpenter, Townsend III, 60
Carpenter, Townsend III, 64
Carpenter, Townsend III, 325
Carpenter, Uriah F. III, 64
Carpenter, Valentine III, 496
Carpenter, Walter III, 64
Carpenter, Walter III, 496
Carpenter, Walter V, 479
Carpenter, Walter V, 480
Carpenter, Walter V, 897
Carpenter, Walter T. III, 61
Carpenter, Walter T. IV, 466
Carpenter, Walter T. V, 480
Carpenter, Walter T. V, 515
Carpenter, Walter T. V, 553
Carpenter, Walter T. V, 897
Carpenter, Walter T. V, 898
Carpenter, Walton III, 62
Carpenter, Walton III, 64
Carpenter, Wd. Esther T. III, 61
Carpenter, Wd. Hannah II, 344
Carpenter, Wd. Hannah III, 476
Carpenter, Wd. Sarah III, 398
Carpenter, Willets III, 64
Carpenter, Willets III, 168
Carpenter, William III, 60
Carpenter, William III, 64
Carpenter, William III, 65
Carpenter, William III, 399
Carpenter, William IV, 1355
Carpenter, William V, 480
Carpenter, William Comstock V, 480
Carpenter, William E. III, 64
Carpenter, William H. III, 62
Carpenter, William H. III, 64
Carpenter, William Henry III, 60
Carpenter, William Henry III, 61
Carpenter, William S. III, 64
Carpenter, William S. III, 209
Carpenter, William T. III, 64
Carpenter, William T. III, 65
Carpenter, William T. III, 346
Carpenter, Willit III, 398
Carpenter, Winola D. III, 137
Carpenter, Winola Dorothy III, 64
Carpenter, Winola Dorothy III, 65
Carpenter, Wm. II, 24
Carpenter, Wm. II, 60
Carpenter, Wm. II, 93
Carpenter, Wm. II, 97
Carpenter, Wm. II, 113
Carpenter, Wm. II, 114
Carpenter, Wm. II, 116
Carpenter, Wm. II, 123
Carpenter, Wm. II, 130
Carpenter, Wm. II, 139
Carpenter, Wm. B. II, 133
Carpenter, Wm. B. II, 134
Carpenter, Wm. B. II, 146
Carpenter, Wm. B. II, 150
Carpenter, Wm. H. III, 60
Carpenter, Wm. H. III, 61
Carpenter, Wm. H. III, 64
Carpenter, Wm. H. III, 65
Carpenter, Wm. H. III, 141
Carpenter, Wm. H. III, 357
Carpenter, Wm. Harold III, 64
Carpenter, Wm. Harold III, 357
Carpenter, Wm. Henry III, 60
Carpenter, Wm. Henry III, 64
Carpenter, Wm. Henry III, 177
Carpenter, Wm. S. III, 61
Carpenter, Wm. Seal II, 845
Carpenter, Wm. T. III, 63
Carpenter, Wm. T. III, 305
Carpenter, Wm., Jr. II, 24
Carpenter, Wm., Jr. II, 60
Carpenter, Wm., Jr. II, 116
Carpenter, Wm., Jr. III, 401
Carpenter, Wright III, 62
Carpenter, Wright III, 63
Carpenter, Wright III, 64
Carpenter, Wright III, 213
Carpenter, Wright III, 480
Carpenter, Zeno III, 60
Carpenter, Zeno III, 63
Carpenter, Zeno III, 64
Carpenter, Zeno III, 65
Carpenter, Zeno, Jr. III, 65
Carpenter, Zeriah V, 480
Carpenter, Zeruiah V, 553
Carpenter, Zeruiah V, 897
Carpenter, Zeruiah V, 898
Carpenter, Zeruiah V, 913
Carpenter, Zerviah III, 63
Carpenter, Zophen III, 65
Carpentyer, Martha III, 399
Carpentyer, Thomas III, 399
Carper, Cornelia A. Merriman VI, 890
Carper, Jacob IV, 1274
Carper, Jacob VI, 904
Carper, Jacob VI, 945
Carper, Jacob VI, 952
Carper, Jacob VI, 980
Carper, Jacob VI, 988
Carper, Jacoby, Sr. IV, 1274
Carper, John C. VI, 890
Carpinter, Silas I, 268
Carr, Aaron V, 228
Carr, Addison IV, 466
Carr, Aletta IV, 24
Carr, Aletta IV, 141
Carr, Aletta IV, 186
Carr, Aletta IV, 466
Carr, Aletta IV, 467
Carr, Aletta IV, 485
Carr, Alice I, 530
Carr, Alice D. I, 631
Carr, Alice Deborah I, 613
Carr, Alice E. IV, 186
Carr, Alice R. I, 929
Carr, Amos V, 228
Carr, Andrew V, 228
Carr, Ann II, 206
Carr, Ann II, 212
Carr, Ann II, 284
Carr, Ann II, 302
Carr, Ann IV, 24
Carr, Ann IV, 141
Carr, Ann IV, 186
Carr, Ann IV, 466
Carr, Ann IV, 506
Carr, Ann IV, 688
Carr, Ann IV, 934
Carr, Ann VI, 510
Carr, Ann VI, 750
Carr, Anna IV, 467
Carr, Anna IV, 688
Carr, Anne IV, 141
Carr, Annie IV, 688
Carr, Anthony VI, 57
Carr, Aquila IV, 186
Carr, Aquilla IV, 466
Carr, Aquilla IV, 467
Carr, Aquilla IV, 490
Carr, Aquilla IV, 688
Carr, Aquilla VI, 531
Carr, Benj. I, 493
Carr, Benjamin I, 377
Carr, Benjamin I, 525
Carr, Benjamin I, 530
Carr, Benjamin I, 953
Carr, Benjamin I, 961
Carr, Benjamin V, 35
Carr, Benjamin V, 100
Carr, Benjamin V, 227
Carr, Benjamin V, 228
Carr, Benjamin V, 445
Carr, Benjamin W. V, 228
Carr, Bidell V, 227
Carr, Bulah V, 227
Carr, Caleb II, 169
Carr, Caleb II, 197
Carr, Caleb II, 206
Carr, Caleb II, 284
Carr, Caleb II, 302
Carr, Caleb IV, 78
Carr, Caleb IV, 934
Carr, Caroline M. III, 65
Carr, Cassandra T. II, 845
Carr, Cassandra T. II, 937
Carr, Cassandra Turner II, 786
Carr, Catharine IV, 141
Carr, Catharine IV, 466
Carr, Catharine IV, 480
Carr, Catherine IV, 24
Carr, Catherine V, 35
Carr, Charles Matlack Hatfield II, 309
Carr, Charles Matlack Hatfield II, 317
Carr, Cyrus V, 228
Carr, David IV, 934
Carr, David VI, 510
Carr, David VI, 587
Carr, David VI, 750
Carr, Eliza V, 228
Carr, Eliza V, 280
Carr, Elizabeth II, 482
Carr, Elizabeth IV, 24
Carr, Elizabeth IV, 141
Carr, Elizabeth IV, 181
Carr, Elizabeth IV, 186
Carr, Elizabeth IV, 466
Carr, Elizabeth IV, 467
Carr, Elizabeth IV, 480
Carr, Elizabeth IV, 485
Carr, Elizabeth IV, 487
Carr, Elizabeth IV, 506
Carr, Elizabeth IV, 688
Carr, Elizabeth IV, 1356
Carr, Elizabeth V, 35
Carr, Elizabeth V, 100
Carr, Elizabeth V, 227
Carr, Elizabeth V, 228
Carr, Elizabeth VI, 475
Carr, Elizabeth VI, 480
Carr, Elizabeth VI, 890
Carr, Elizabeth Ann IV, 934
Carr, Elles V, 228
Carr, Elmer O. V, 228
Carr, Elsie V, 156
Carr, Emma E. V, 228
Carr, Emma Rose II, 786
Carr, Esther IV, 466
Carr, Esther IV, 501
Carr, Esther IV, 934
Carr, Esther V, 227
Carr, Esther V, 228
Carr, Evan V, 228
Carr, Fannie III, 65
Carr, Fannie III, 167
Carr, Francis IV, 935
Carr, Francis D. IV, 934
Carr, Francis Dean IV, 934
Carr, Geo. L. I, 631
Carr, George IV, 688
Carr, George IV, 934
Carr, George IV, 935
Carr, George Lyman I, 613
Carr, Gideon Lupton IV, 186
Carr, Goldie M. I, 631
Carr, Goldie Marrillo I, 613
Carr, Guy C. V, 36
Carr, Hannah I, 961
Carr, Hannah I, 983
Carr, Hannah II, 713
Carr, Hannah II, 808
Carr, Hannah III, 65
Carr, Hannah III, 399
Carr, Hannah III, 436
Carr, Hannah III, 439
Carr, Hannah III, 495
Carr, Hannah IV, 929
Carr, Hannah IV, 934
Carr, Hannah V, 35
Carr, Hannah V, 36
Carr, Hannah Cordelia V, 228
Carr, Hannah W. II, 308
Carr, Hannah W. II, 317
Carr, Hannah W. V, 968
Carr, Harrison V, 156
Carr, Harrison M. V, 156
Carr, Henry R. IV, 688
Carr, Henry Reaves II, 284
Carr, Hezekiah V, 35
Carr, Hezekiah V, 227
Carr, Hezekiah V, 228
Carr, Hezekiah A. V, 228
Carr, Hugh VI, 890
Carr, Iredel V, 228
Carr, Iredell V, 228
Carr, Isaac II, 206
Carr, Isaac II, 212
Carr, Isaac IV, 688
Carr, Isaac IV, 934
Carr, Isaac IV, 935
Carr, Isaac IV, 946
Carr, Isaac IV, 1018
Carr, Isaac R. IV, 934
Carr, Isaac Ridgeway IV, 688
Carr, Isabella IV, 934
Carr, Isabella IV, 935
Carr, Isabella IV, 946
Carr, Jacob I, 493
Carr, James IV, 24
Carr, James IV, 141
Carr, James IV, 186
Carr, James IV, 466
Carr, James IV, 467
Carr, James IV, 473
Carr, James IV, 506
Carr, James IV, 1355
Carr, James IV, 1356
Carr, James IV, 1384
Carr, James Wesley V, 228
Carr, Jane II, 284
Carr, Jane IV, 935
Carr, Jane V, 480
Carr, Jas. IV, 466
Carr, Jas. IV, 480
Carr, Jas. IV, 485
Carr, Jemima V, 227
Carr, Jemima V, 228
Carr, Jemima V, 280
Carr, Jeremiah III, 399
Carr, Jesse IV, 24
Carr, Jesse IV, 141
Carr, Jesse IV, 466
Carr, Joab Mason II, 317
Carr, Job II, 206
Carr, Job II, 308
Carr, Job II, 317
Carr, Job III, 436
Carr, Job III, 439
Carr, Job V, 35
Carr, Job V, 36
Carr, Job V, 96
Carr, Job Mason II, 309
Carr, Job Mason II, 317
Carr, Joel IV, 466
Carr, Joel H. IV, 467
Carr, John V, 35
Carr, John V, 156
Carr, John M. III, 65

Carr, John M. V, 968
Carr, John Mason V, 35
Carr, Jonathan II, 786
Carr, Joseph IV, 934
Carr, Joseph IV, 935
Carr, Joseph M. IV, 935
Carr, Joshua IV, 24
Carr, Joshua IV, 141
Carr, Joshua IV, 466
Carr, Joshua IV, 1355
Carr, Juliatha I, 343
Carr, Juliatha I, 377
Carr, Juliatha I, 530
Carr, Juliathae I, 377
Carr, Jurdenette III, 65
Carr, Jurdenette III, 167
Carr, Kinsey IV, 24
Carr, Kinsey IV, 141
Carr, Kinsey IV, 186
Carr, Kinsey IV, 466
Carr, Kinsey IV, 496
Carr, Kittie B. IV, 688
Carr, La Rue V, 36
Carr, LaRue V, 663
Carr, LaRue V, 691
Carr, Lenora V, 988
Carr, Lizzie G. IV, 186
Carr, Louisa V, 156
Carr, Louisa V, 227
Carr, Louise V, 156
Carr, Lydia IV, 467
Carr, Lydia IV, 493
Carr, Lydia IV, 934
Carr, Lydia IV, 935
Carr, Lydia IV, 987
Carr, Lydia IV, 1356
Carr, Lymon W. I, 613
Carr, Macre Worthington II, 786
Carr, Maggie I, 613
Carr, Maggie I, 631
Carr, Margaret I, 530
Carr, Margaret II, 786
Carr, Margaret B. II, 845
Carr, Margaret B. II, 937
Carr, Martha I, 613
Carr, Martha II, 982
Carr, Martha II, 988
Carr, Mary II, 284
Carr, Mary II, 302
Carr, Mary II, 988
Carr, Mary II, 989
Carr, Mary IV, 466
Carr, Mary IV, 467
Carr, Mary IV, 473
Carr, Mary IV, 479
Carr, Mary IV, 688
Carr, Mary VI, 531
Carr, Mary VI, 977
Carr, Mary Ann II, 309
Carr, Mary Ann II, 317
Carr, Mary Ann V, 35
Carr, Mary Ann V, 36
Carr, Mary Ann V, 51
Carr, Mary Ann V, 968
Carr, Mary B. IV, 466
Carr, Mary B. IV, 490
Carr, Mary Baker V, 663
Carr, Mary Baker V, 691
Carr, Mary C. IV, 1356
Carr, Mary Esther V, 156
Carr, Mary G. IV, 466
Carr, Mary G. IV, 467
Carr, Mary H. IV, 186
Carr, Mary Jane V, 228
Carr, Mary Laticia II, 317
Carr, Mary Linton V, 663
Carr, Meriam I, 377
Carr, Meriam I, 401
Carr, Meriam V, 35
Carr, Miriam I, 377
Carr, Miriam I, 530
Carr, Miriam I, 535
Carr, Nancy IV, 466
Carr, Nathan V, 228
Carr, Nory A. V, 378
Carr, Oliver K. III, 65
Carr, Orpah IV, 501
Carr, Orpha IV, 186
Carr, Orpha IV, 466
Carr, Orpha IV, 570
Carr, Orpha IV, 935
Carr, Orpha IV, 1051
Carr, Orphia IV, 466
Carr, Pamela V, 445
Carr, Pamelia V, 228
Carr, Parmelia V, 445
Carr, Patience I, 493
Carr, Patience I, 525
Carr, Patience I, 530
Carr, Patience IV, 688
Carr, Patience IV, 777
Carr, Patience IV, 934
Carr, Patience V, 35
Carr, Patience V, 100
Carr, Patience V, 215
Carr, Patience V, 227
Carr, Patience V, 228
Carr, Patrick VI, 966
Carr, Permelia V, 228
Carr, Permely V, 228
Carr, Phebe IV, 1355
Carr, Phebe IV, 1356
Carr, Phebe IV, 1384
Carr, Priscilla IV, 24
Carr, Priscilla IV, 186
Carr, Priscilla IV, 466
Carr, Priscilla IV, 497
Carr, Priscilla IV, 688
Carr, Priscilla IV, 706
Carr, Prisilla IV, 466
Carr, Rachel I, 961
Carr, Rachel IV, 186
Carr, Rachel IV, 466
Carr, Rachel IV, 496
Carr, Rachel VI, 982
Carr, Rachel Ann V, 228
Carr, Rachel Hulda V, 228
Carr, Rachel T. III, 65
Carr, Reba V, 36
Carr, Rebecca II, 197
Carr, Rebecca II, 206
Carr, Rebecca IV, 935
Carr, Rebecca IV, 1018
Carr, Richard VI, 57
Carr, Robert F. IV, 934
Carr, Robert F. IV, 935
Carr, Roy V, 156
Carr, Ruth II, 308
Carr, Ruth II, 317
Carr, Ruth V, 35
Carr, Ruth V, 96
Carr, Ruth V, 968
Carr, Ruth Anna III, 65
Carr, Samuel II, 169
Carr, Samuel II, 206
Carr, Samuel II, 212
Carr, Samuel II, 284
Carr, Samuel II, 302
Carr, Samuel IV, 24
Carr, Samuel IV, 141
Carr, Samuel IV, 186
Carr, Samuel IV, 466
Carr, Samuel IV, 479
Carr, Samuel IV, 688
Carr, Samuel IV, 934
Carr, Samuel IV, 935
Carr, Samuel B. II, 845
Carr, Samuel B. II, 937
Carr, Samuel Buckman II, 786
Carr, Sarah II, 482
Carr, Sarah II, 525
Carr, Sarah II, 965
Carr, Sarah II, 988
Carr, Sarah II, 1009
Carr, Sarah IV, 24
Carr, Sarah IV, 141
Carr, Sarah IV, 466
Carr, Sarah IV, 467
Carr, Sarah IV, 484
Carr, Sarah IV, 497
Carr, Sarah IV, 498
Carr, Sarah IV, 935
Carr, Sarah IV, 966
Carr, Sarah IV, 1355
Carr, Sarah IV, 1356
Carr, Sarah IV, 1386
Carr, Stanley IV, 688
Carr, Susan VI, 587
Carr, Susan B. VI, 510
Carr, Susan B. VI, 746
Carr, Susanna IV, 24
Carr, Susanna IV, 186
Carr, Susanna IV, 244
Carr, Susanna IV, 466
Carr, Susanna IV, 484
Carr, Susannah IV, 141
Carr, Susannah VI, 531
Carr, Susannah B. VI, 750
Carr, Thomas I, 343
Carr, Thomas I, 377
Carr, Thomas I, 401
Carr, Thomas I, 530
Carr, Thomas I, 961
Carr, Thomas IV, 24
Carr, Thomas IV, 141
Carr, Thomas IV, 186
Carr, Thomas IV, 466
Carr, Thomas V, 35
Carr, Thomas V, 227
Carr, Thomas V, 228
Carr, Thomas V, 280
Carr, Thomas W. IV, 934
Carr, Thomas W. IV, 935
Carr, Thos. I, 377
Carr, Thos. IV, 501
Carr, Vincent L. II, 309
Carr, Vincent L. II, 317
Carr, Vincin L. II, 317
Carr, Walter S. IV, 186
Carr, Wd. Ann II, 169
Carr, Wd. Mary II, 169
Carr, Wd. Susannah B. VI, 735
Carr, Widow Susannah B. VI, 511
Carr, William III, 65
Carr, William IV, 24
Carr, William IV, 137
Carr, William IV, 141
Carr, William IV, 186
Carr, William IV, 466
Carr, William IV, 467
Carr, William IV, 493
Carr, William IV, 934
Carr, William IV, 987
Carr, William IV, 1355
Carr, William IV, 1356
Carr, William V, 227
Carr, William V, 228
Carr, William VI, 57
Carr, William H. II, 309
Carr, William Howard II, 317
Carr, Wm. IV, 181
Carr, Wm. IV, 466
Carr, Wm. IV, 484
Carr, Wm. IV, 497
Carr, Wm. W. II, 845
Carr, Wm. W. II, 937
Carr, Wm. Worthington II, 786
Carragey, Maria II, 142
Carragey, Maria II, 146
Carrel, Mary I, 475
Carrel, Sarah IV, 24
Carrel, Sarah IV, 467
Carrel, Susannah IV, 122
Carrel, Susannah IV, 123
Carrell, Hannah II, 344
Carrell, James II, 344
Carrell, Laura I, 631
Carrell, Thomas B. I, 631
Carrey, William II, 343
Carrie, Caroline VI, 85
Carrier, Bertha IV, 1036
Carrier, Florence IV, 1036
Carrier, Jacob IV, 1036
Carrier, Janet IV, 1036
Carrier, Myrtle IV, 1036
Carriger, Mary I, 1090
Carriger, Mary I, 1098
Carriger, Michael I, 1090
Carrington, ??? IV, 935
Carrington, Alice V, 36
Carrington, Alice W. VI, 804
Carrington, Charity VI, 481
Carrington, Charity VI, 577
Carrington, Fannie V, 36
Carrington, John VI, 804
Carrington, Keziah IV, 935
Carrington, Kitty VI, 804
Carrington, Mariah L. VI, 804
Carrington, Martha IV, 935
Carrington, Martin VI, 804
Carrington, Mary II, 482
Carrington, Mary II, 642
Carrington, Mary IV, 935
Carrington, Sarah II, 482
Carrington, Sarah II, 642
Carrington, Thomas II, 482
Carrington, Thomas II, 642
Carrington, Thomas IV, 935
Carrington, Walter C. VI, 804
Carrington, Wm. C. VI, 804
Carrol, Amy V, 729
Carrol, Ann IV, 323
Carrol, Celia V, 730
Carrol, David V, 480
Carrol, Deborah IV, 24
Carrol, Edward IV, 24
Carrol, Edward IV, 614
Carrol, Edward V, 300
Carrol, Edward, Jr. IV, 614
Carrol, Elizabeth IV, 24
Carrol, Elizabeth IV, 614
Carrol, Elizabeth V, 300
Carrol, Elizanna V, 300
Carrol, Emmet V, 300
Carrol, Enos V, 300
Carrol, Harley V, 729
Carrol, Isaac IV, 24
Carrol, Jesse B. VI, 890
Carrol, John V, 300
Carrol, Joseph IV, 24
Carrol, Joseph IV, 614
Carrol, Joseph V, 300
Carrol, Laura A. IV, 323
Carrol, Margery IV, 24
Carrol, Mary V, 300
Carrol, Mrs. Amy V, 729
Carrol, Phebe I, 377
Carrol, Ray J. V, 729
Carrol, Rebecca H. V, 300
Carrol, Rhoda VI, 890
Carrol, Robert IV, 323
Carrol, Rolon V, 300
Carrol, Sarah IV, 24
Carrol, Sarah V, 300
Carrol, Susanna IV, 24
Carrol, Susannah IV, 123
Carrol, Tabitha VI, 301
Carrol, Tabitha VI, 304
Carrol, Thomas IV, 24
Carrol, Thomas IV, 323
Carrol, William Foster IV, 323
Carroll, Abi V, 36
Carroll, Abi V, 37
Carroll, Aby V, 36
Carroll, Albert V, 36
Carroll, Amy III, 65
Carroll, Amy III, 157
Carroll, Ann III, 65
Carroll, Ann IV, 323
Carroll, Ann IV, 377
Carroll, Ann IV, 805
Carroll, Ann IV, 806
Carroll, Ann IV, 865
Carroll, Ann IV, 884
Carroll, Ann V, 898
Carroll, Ann L. IV, 323
Carroll, Anna B. II, 845
Carroll, Anna B. V, 36
Carroll, Anne V, 36
Carroll, Beulah II, 845
Carroll, Beulah V, 898
Carroll, Beulah A. II, 845
Carroll, Beulah A. IV, 187
Carroll, Cammie V, 36
Carroll, Cammie V, 378
Carroll, Cammie M. V, 378
Carroll, Charles D. II, 845
Carroll, Chas. D. II, 845
Carroll, Daniel J. III, 65
Carroll, Daniel J. III, 136
Carroll, David V, 480
Carroll, Debby IV, 805
Carroll, Deborah IV, 806
Carroll, Deborah IV, 840
Carroll, Deborah V, 614
Carroll, Dellila VI, 325
Carroll, Dellila VI, 829
Carroll, Dr. Thomas V, 36
Carroll, Dr. Thomas V, 898
Carroll, Earnest E. I, 939
Carroll, Edith V, 663
Carroll, Edith V, 700
Carroll, Edna V, 662
Carroll, Edna V, 663
Carroll, Edward II, 786
Carroll, Edward II, 845
Carroll, Edward III, 65
Carroll, Edward IV, 614
Carroll, Edward IV, 629
Carroll, Edward IV, 688
Carroll, Edward IV, 805
Carroll, Edward IV, 806
Carroll, Edward IV, 900
Carroll, Edward V, 300
Carroll, Edward V, 898
Carroll, Edward G. V, 477
Carroll, Edward G. V, 480
Carroll, Edward, Jr. IV, 614
Carroll, Edward, Jr. IV, 805
Carroll, Edward, Jr. IV, 806
Carroll, Eli V, 36
Carroll, Eli S. V, 36
Carroll, Eliza IV, 805
Carroll, Eliza IV, 806
Carroll, Eliza IV, 865
Carroll, Eliza A. V, 36
Carroll, Eliza A. V, 80
Carroll, Eliza Ann V, 480
Carroll, Elizabeth IV, 323
Carroll, Elizabeth IV, 614
Carroll, Elizabeth IV, 805
Carroll, Elizabeth IV, 806
Carroll, Elizabeth IV, 814
Carroll, Elizabeth IV, 865
Carroll, Elizabeth IV, 900
Carroll, Elizabeth V, 36
Carroll, Elizabeth V, 300
Carroll, Elizabeth V, 480
Carroll, Elizabeth V, 798
Carroll, Elizabeth, Jr. IV, 806
Carroll, Elizanna V, 300
Carroll, Ella II, 786
Carroll, Ella II, 845
Carroll, Ella II, 926
Carroll, Emma V, 156
Carroll, Emma C. V, 36
Carroll, Emma Mae Clement V, 36
Carroll, Emmet IV, 806
Carroll, Emmet V, 300
Carroll, Enos IV, 806
Carroll, Enos IV, 900
Carroll, Enos V, 36
Carroll, Enos V, 37
Carroll, Enos V, 300
Carroll, Enos V, 311
Carroll, Ester V, 36
Carroll, Esther V, 378
Carroll, Etheldred VI, 804
Carroll, Eva Snead V, 663
Carroll, Fidella I, 939
Carroll, Foster V, 36
Carroll, Foster V, 898
Carroll, Foster W. IV, 323
Carroll, Foster W. V, 898
Carroll, George V, 378
Carroll, George E. V, 36
Carroll, George E. V, 378
Carroll, George E. V, 614
Carroll, Hannah M. V, 614
Carroll, Hannah Mary V, 36
Carroll, Hannah Mary V, 614
Carroll, Ilo V, 663
Carroll, Ilo V, 710
Carroll, Inea V, 36
Carroll, Inez V, 378
Carroll, Isaac III, 65
Carroll, Jane V, 614
Carroll, Jane V, 663
Carroll, Jessie Anna V, 663
Carroll, John IV, 806
Carroll, John V, 300
Carroll, John V, 480
Carroll, John V, 614
Carroll, John Q. V, 36
Carroll, John Quincy V, 36
Carroll, Joseph III, 65
Carroll, Joseph IV, 323
Carroll, Joseph IV, 614
Carroll, Joseph IV, 805
Carroll, Joseph IV, 806
Carroll, Joseph IV, 814
Carroll, Joseph IV, 900
Carroll, Joseph V, 36
Carroll, Joseph V, 300
Carroll, Joseph V, 480
Carroll, Joseph C. V, 36
Carroll, Joseph F. III, 157
Carroll, Joseph Fisher III, 65
Carroll, Laura V, 36
Carroll, Laura A. IV, 323
Carroll, Laura A. V, 898
Carroll, Levina V, 300
Carroll, Levinia V, 477
Carroll, Levinia V, 480
Carroll, Marcia B. III, 65
Carroll, Marcia B. III, 136
Carroll, Marean V, 36
Carroll, Margary IV, 805
Carroll, Margary IV, 853
Carroll, Margery IV, 614
Carroll, Margory IV, 805
Carroll, Marian V, 36
Carroll, Marry V, 36
Carroll, Mary I, 475
Carroll, Mary III, 65
Carroll, Mary IV, 806
Carroll, Mary IV, 843
Carroll, Mary V, 300
Carroll, Mary V, 310
Carroll, Mary V, 378
Carroll, Mary V, 663
Carroll, Mary Ann IV, 688
Carroll, Mary Ann IV, 806
Carroll, Mary Ann IV, 865
Carroll, Mary Ann V, 36
Carroll, Mary Ann V, 37
Carroll, Mary Ann V, 300
Carroll, Mary Ann V, 311
Carroll, Mary Ann V, 894
Carroll, Mary Ann V, 898
Carroll, Mary C. V, 36
Carroll, Mary C. V, 62
Carroll, Mary T. III, 65
Carroll, Minerva IV, 995
Carroll, Olive B. V, 614
Carroll, Olive B. V, 663
Carroll, Phebe IV, 806
Carroll, Purdy H. I, 939
Carroll, Rachel IV, 614
Carroll, Rachel IV, 629
Carroll, Rachel IV, 805
Carroll, Rachel IV, 806
Carroll, Rachel IV, 865
Carroll, Rebecca V, 36

Carroll, Rebecca H. V, 36
Carroll, Rebecca H. V, 104
Carroll, Rebecca H. V, 300
Carroll, Rebecca H. V, 480
Carroll, Richard II, 786
Carroll, Robert IV, 323
Carroll, Robert W. IV, 323
Carroll, Robert W. V, 36
Carroll, Robert W. V, 898
Carroll, Rolon V, 300
Carroll, Rosa L. V, 36
Carroll, S. Wellens I, 922
Carroll, Sally IV, 614
Carroll, Sally IV, 805
Carroll, Sally IV, 853
Carroll, Samuel M. III, 65
Carroll, Sarah V, 36
Carroll, Sarah V, 300
Carroll, Sarah V, 480
Carroll, Soleon V, 663
Carroll, Solon V, 36
Carroll, Solon V, 156
Carroll, Solon V, 480
Carroll, Solon V, 614
Carroll, Solon V, 663
Carroll, Susan II, 786
Carroll, Susan II, 845
Carroll, Susan M. V, 614
Carroll, Susanna IV, 935
Carroll, Susannah IV, 806
Carroll, Thomas IV, 187
Carroll, Thomas IV, 323
Carroll, Thomas IV, 377
Carroll, Thomas IV, 805
Carroll, Thomas IV, 806
Carroll, Thomas B. I, 631
Carroll, Thos. I, 631
Carroll, Thos. V, 898
Carroll, Toby VI, 804
Carroll, Virginia V, 949
Carroll, Wd. Beulah Ann II, 786
Carroll, Wellery I, 939
Carroll, William I, 939
Carroll, William IV, 865
Carroll, William Foster IV, 323
Carroll, William Jesse Anna V, 378
Carroll, William Roberts II, 786
Carroll, Willis I, 939
Carroll, Wm. IV, 806
Carroll, Wm. IV, 935
Carroll, Wm. V, 663
Carroll, Wm. V, 898
Carroll, Wm. R. II, 845
Carroll, Wm. Roberts II, 845
Carroll, Wm. Roberts II, 926
Carroll, Wm. W. V, 898
Carrothers, Alice V, 156
Carruthers, John IV, 186
Carry, Abel IV, 688
Carry, Alice IV, 688
Carry, Charles IV, 688
Carry, David IV, 688
Carry, James R. IV, 688
Carry, Maria IV, 688
Carry, Sampson II, 481
Carry, William B. IV, 688
Carsey, Elizabeth I, 134
Carsey, Elizabeth I, 159
Carsleek, David II, 206
Carsleek, Mary II, 206
Carslike, David II, 206
Carslike, Mary II, 206
Carson, Abigail I, 961
Carson, Abigail I, 969
Carson, Achsah V, 378
Carson, Adaline IV, 935
Carson, Adam VI, 890
Carson, Adeline IV, 935
Carson, Adeline IV, 995
Carson, Alfred IV, 688
Carson, Alfred IV, 935
Carson, Almira IV, 935
Carson, Almira IV, 942
Carson, Amy IV, 323
Carson, Amy IV, 467
Carson, Andrew IV, 323
Carson, Andrew IV, 467
Carson, Andrew IV, 516
Carson, Ann V, 298
Carson, Ann V, 300
Carson, Anne II, 130
Carson, Benjamin IV, 935
Carson, Benjamin IV, 1017
Carson, Benjamin F. IV, 935
Carson, Benjamin Franklin IV, 935
Carson, Benjamin Y. IV, 935
Carson, Benjamin Yates IV, 688
Carson, Betsy VI, 847
Carson, Bowater I, 493
Carson, Bowater I, 961
Carson, Bowater V, 300
Carson, Bridget E. VI, 804
Carson, Caleb I, 961
Carson, Catharine IV, 323
Carson, Catharine IV, 516
Carson, Catherine IV, 467
Carson, Celia VI, 804
Carson, Charlotte IV, 935
Carson, Clementine V, 300
Carson, Clementine V, 309
Carson, Clemma V, 300
Carson, Cyrus W. V, 228
Carson, Dinah V, 378
Carson, Dinah VI, 525
Carson, Dinah VI, 580
Carson, Eli I, 956
Carson, Eli I, 983
Carson, Elizabeth II, 482
Carson, Elizabeth II, 564
Carson, Elizabeth IV, 935
Carson, Elizabeth IV, 981
Carson, Elizabeth VI, 804
Carson, Elizabeth VI, 815
Carson, Elizabeth VI, 820
Carson, Elizabeth VI, 849
Carson, Elizabeth VI, 975
Carson, Ella IV, 935
Carson, Ellba V, 453
Carson, Ellen V, 453
Carson, Elmira IV, 935
Carson, Esther I, 377
Carson, Esther V, 298
Carson, Esther V, 300
Carson, Esther V, 373
Carson, Esther V, 378
Carson, Frank IV, 1247
Carson, Geo. IV, 309
Carson, George IV, 187
Carson, Hannah I, 961
Carson, Harden I, 983
Carson, Isabel IV, 323
Carson, Isabel IV, 467
Carson, Isabel IV, 516
Carson, Isabella IV, 467
Carson, Jacob I, 493
Carson, Jacob I, 955
Carson, Jacob I, 956
Carson, Jacob I, 961
Carson, Jacob I, 964
Carson, Jacob I, 983
Carson, Jacob V, 300
Carson, Jacob V, 373
Carson, Jacob V, 378
Carson, Jacob, Jr. I, 956
Carson, Jacob, Jr. I, 961
Carson, Jacob, Jr. V, 298
Carson, Jacob, Jr. V, 300
Carson, James VI, 833
Carson, James VI, 847
Carson, James VI, 975
Carson, James W. VI, 807
Carson, Jane VI, 804
Carson, Jane E. VI, 846
Carson, Jemima IV, 688
Carson, Jemima IV, 806
Carson, Jemima IV, 935
Carson, Jemimah IV, 1011
Carson, Jeremiah IV, 323
Carson, Jeremiah IV, 467
Carson, Jeremiah IV, 516
Carson, Jno. VI, 847
Carson, John I, 493
Carson, John I, 953
Carson, John I, 961
Carson, John I, 969
Carson, John IV, 323
Carson, John IV, 467
Carson, John IV, 516
Carson, John IV, 688
Carson, John IV, 919
Carson, John IV, 935
Carson, John IV, 1011
Carson, John VI, 796
Carson, John VI, 802
Carson, John VI, 804
Carson, John VI, 849
Carson, John VI, 993
Carson, John D. VI, 865
Carson, John H. I, 983
Carson, John L. IV, 935
Carson, John M. V, 614
Carson, John M. V, 663
Carson, John T. IV, 688
Carson, John T. IV, 935
Carson, John T. IV, 976
Carson, John, Jr. I, 1047
Carson, John, Jr. I Sup 1, 11
Carson, Joseph VI, 890
Carson, Joseph V. I, 983
Carson, Josiah I, 956
Carson, Josiah V, 298
Carson, Josiah V, 300
Carson, Judith VI, 890
Carson, Julia IV, 935
Carson, Lizzie IV, 1234
Carson, Lucy VI, 804
Carson, Lucy B. VI, 804
Carson, Luster IV, 935
Carson, Lydia IV, 141
Carson, Lydia IV, 187
Carson, Lydia IV, 309
Carson, Lydia A. V, 228
Carson, Madison M. V, 228
Carson, Maggie IV, 1234
Carson, Martha I, 377
Carson, Martha I, 955
Carson, Martha I, 956
Carson, Martha I, 961
Carson, Martha I, 964
Carson, Martha IV, 935
Carson, Martha IV, 976
Carson, Martha IV, 1017
Carson, Martha V, 378
Carson, Martha J. VI, 804
Carson, Martha L. IV, 935
Carson, Martin L. IV, 935
Carson, Mary I, 377
Carson, Mary I, 380
Carson, Mary I, 493
Carson, Mary I, 575
Carson, Mary I, 955
Carson, Mary I, 956
Carson, Mary I, 961
Carson, Mary IV, 24
Carson, Mary IV, 46
Carson, Mary IV, 516
Carson, Mary IV, 539
Carson, Mary VI, 804
Carson, Mary VI, 833
Carson, Mary VI, 847
Carson, Mary VI, 849
Carson, Mary Ann IV, 935
Carson, Mary Ann V, 300
Carson, Mary E. V, 228
Carson, Mary M. VI, 811
Carson, McClan V, 453
Carson, Minnie IV, 1234
Carson, Morris IV, 935
Carson, Moses H. VI, 804
Carson, Moses H. VI, 811
Carson, Nancy V, 453
Carson, Nancy VI, 802
Carson, Nancy M. VI, 834
Carson, Naomi IV, 516
Carson, Naomi IV, 540
Carson, Nathan Hunt I, 956
Carson, Paul VI, 890
Carson, Peggy VI, 829
Carson, Peggy VI, 833
Carson, Peggy VI, 890
Carson, Phebe IV, 141
Carson, Phebe IV, 187
Carson, Phebe IV, 309
Carson, Phebe IV, 688
Carson, Phebe IV, 935
Carson, Phebe V, 300
Carson, Phebe V, 302
Carson, Rachel IV, 323
Carson, Rachel IV, 467
Carson, Rachel IV, 516
Carson, Rachel IV, 517
Carson, Rachel IV, 537
Carson, Rachel V, 228
Carson, Rachel V, 255
Carson, Rachel M. V, 228
Carson, Robert IV, 323
Carson, Robert IV, 467
Carson, Robert IV, 516
Carson, Robert VI, 890
Carson, Robert J. VI, 884
Carson, Robert W. VI, 834
Carson, Rosetta V, 453
Carson, Ruth I, 493
Carson, Ruth I, 961
Carson, Ruth I, 963
Carson, Ruth V, 614
Carson, Ruth V, 663
Carson, Ruth H. V, 949
Carson, Ruth H. V, 959
Carson, Salley V, 300
Carson, Sally V, 300
Carson, Sally V, 302
Carson, Sarah I, 493
Carson, Sarah I, 959
Carson, Sarah I, 961
Carson, Sarah I, 983
Carson, Sarah I, 986
Carson, Sarah IV, 688
Carson, Sarah IV, 935
Carson, Sarah IV, 1011
Carson, Sarah V, 228
Carson, Sarah V, 300
Carson, Sarah VI, 847
Carson, Sarah Jane IV, 935
Carson, Sarah Jane IV, 936
Carson, Silas I, 956
Carson, Silas V, 300
Carson, Thomas I, 1047
Carson, Thomas VI, 804
Carson, Thomas VI, 811
Carson, Thomas VI, 847
Carson, Thos. VI, 847
Carson, Uriah I, 493
Carson, Uriah I, 530
Carson, Uriah I, 956
Carson, Uriah I, 961
Carson, Uriah V, 300
Carson, Uriah V, 302
Carson, Uryah I, 955
Carson, Uryah I, 961
Carson, Widow Mary I, 530
Carson, William IV, 467
Carson, William IV, 516
Carson, William IV, 688
Carson, William IV, 935
Carson, William VI, 804
Carson, William VI, 820
Carson, William VI, 829
Carson, William VI, 833
Carson, William VI, 834
Carson, William VI, 849
Carson, William VI, 850
Carson, William VI, 993
Carson, Wm. IV, 688
Carson, Wm. IV, 981
Carson, Wm. VI, 804
Carson, Wm., Jr. VI, 804
Carstaphan, Catherine VI, 88
Carstaphen, Catherine VI, 57
Carstaphen, Catherine Carr VI, 57
Carstaphen, Catherine Carr Stephen VI, 57
Carswell, Harriet T. III, 214
Carswell, John N. III, 214
Carswell, Susan III, 214
Cart, Benjamin II, 344
Cart, Jane II, 482
Cart, Jane II, 584
Cart, Joseph II, 344
Cart, Joshua II, 482
Cart, Samuel II, 344
Cart, Samuel II, 482
Cart, Samuel II, 534
Cart, Samuel II, 584
Cart, Sarah II, 344
Cart, Sarah II, 482
Cart, Sarah II, 534
Carter, ??? II, 802
Carter, ??? III, 291
Carter, Abigail V, 615
Carter, Abigail V, 616
Carter, Abigail V, 640
Carter, Abraham II, 455
Carter, Abraham II, 482
Carter, Abraham II, 483
Carter, Abraham II, 786
Carter, Abraham II, 845
Carter, Abraham III, 65
Carter, Achsa I, 902
Carter, Achsah I, 530
Carter, Achsah I, 851
Carter, Achsah I, 855
Carter, Achsah I, 867
Carter, Achsah I, 874
Carter, Achsah I, 926
Carter, Achsah I, 936
Carter, Achsah Ann I, 851
Carter, Achsah C. I, 851
Carter, Achsah C. I, 874
Carter, Achsah C. I, 883
Carter, Achsah Catharine I, 926
Carter, Adaliza I, 851
Carter, Adaliza I, 874
Carter, Adaliza I, 877
Carter, Adalize I, 903
Carter, Adolphus V, 554
Carter, Adolphus A. V, 553
Carter, Agnes VI, 375
Carter, Albert VI, 891
Carter, Aldin W. IV, 1203
Carter, Aldon W. IV, 1203
Carter, Alfred R. IV, 615
Carter, Alice V, 379
Carter, Alice V, 989
Carter, Alice VI, 481
Carter, Alice VI, 586
Carter, Alice D. V, 378
Carter, Alice D. V, 379
Carter, Alice D. V, 480
Carter, Alice Edna IV, 378
Carter, Alice H. II, 732
Carter, Allen E. IV, 187
Carter, Allie V, 633
Carter, Allie V, 989
Carter, Alma I, 922
Carter, Alma V, 624
Carter, Almina V, 157
Carter, Almina V, 453
Carter, Almina H. V, 157
Carter, Almira E. V, 616
Carter, Almon V, 663
Carter, Almon V, 688
Carter, Almon E. V, 554
Carter, Almond IV, 1309
Carter, Almond V, 663
Carter, Alonzo V, 554
Carter, Alonzo Clinton V, 615
Carter, Alson I, 675
Carter, Alva VI, 630
Carter, Amelia V, 554
Carter, Ann I, 347
Carter, Ann I, 353
Carter, Ann I, 377
Carter, Ann I, 423
Carter, Ann I, 431
Carter, Ann I, 434
Carter, Ann I, 444
Carter, Ann I, 445
Carter, Ann I, 675
Carter, Ann I, 851
Carter, Ann I, 852
Carter, Ann I, 874
Carter, Ann I, 885
Carter, Ann II, 206
Carter, Ann II, 258
Carter, Ann V, 480
Carter, Ann V, 553
Carter, Ann V, 554
Carter, Ann V, 572
Carter, Ann V, 576
Carter, Ann V, 615
Carter, Ann VI, 890
Carter, Ann Edwards I, 444
Carter, Ann M. VI, 804
Carter, Ann Maria V, 615
Carter, Ann, Sr. I, 444
Carter, Anna I, 1008
Carter, Anna V, 378
Carter, Anna M. V, 615
Carter, Anna Mariah V, 615
Carter, Anne I, 347
Carter, Anne I, 1004
Carter, Anne I, 1008
Carter, Anne VI, 890
Carter, Annetta IV, 1203
Carter, Artemas M. V, 616
Carter, Artemas N. V, 615
Carter, Artemas N. V, 629
Carter, Asa V, 554
Carter, Asenath I, 851
Carter, Asenath I, 874
Carter, Asenath I, 889
Carter, Augustine VI, 890
Carter, Aurelies N. I, 874
Carter, Aurelius I, 803
Carter, Aurelius N. I, 851
Carter, Aurelius W. I, 803
Carter, Austin VI, 869
Carter, Belinda I, 1004
Carter, Benjamin II, 24
Carter, Benjamin II, 60
Carter, Benjamin II, 206
Carter, Benjamin II, 258
Carter, Benjamin II, 846
Carter, Benjamin IV, 378
Carter, Benjamin V, 615
Carter, Benjamin Carroll II, 846
Carter, Benjamin F. VI, 891
Carter, Benjamin F. VI, 937
Carter, Benjamin, Jr. II, 206
Carter, Berry L. VI, 891
Carter, Beryl V, 228
Carter, Betsy M. VI, 804
Carter, Beulah I, 874
Carter, Beulah IV, 378
Carter, Beulah IV, 574
Carter, Beulah M. I, 851
Carter, Beulah R. IV, 378
Carter, Blanch V, 228
Carter, Blanch V, 663
Carter, Blanche V, 663
Carter, Blanche V, 989
Carter, Braxton VI, 891
Carter, Braxton VI, 896
Carter, Brice I, 444
Carter, Callie V, 616
Carter, Catharine I, 444
Carter, Catharine I, 448
Carter, Catharine I, 756
Carter, Catharine I, 855
Carter, Catharine I, 926
Carter, Catharine II, 482

Carter, Catharine II, 672
Carter, Catharine III, 65
Carter, Catharine III, 291
Carter, Catherine II, 442
Carter, Catherine II, 482
Carter, Catherine II, 672
Carter, Celia Shulte IV, 1309
Carter, Chalkley T. IV, 865
Carter, Charles V, 157
Carter, Charles V, 228
Carter, Charles VI, 890
Carter, Charles Foster V, 157
Carter, Charlie V, 663
Carter, Charlotte VI, 891
Carter, Charlotte VI, 924
Carter, Charlotte VI, 998
Carter, Chas. V, 663
Carter, Chas. S. IV, 614
Carter, Chester V, 157
Carter, Clarence V, 378
Carter, Clarence V, 989
Carter, Clinton V, 616
Carter, Collin B. IV, 865
Carter, Cornelius I, 803
Carter, Cornelius I, 874
Carter, Cornelius N. I, 803
Carter, Cornelius N. I, 851
Carter, Cornelius N. I, 874
Carter, Cynthia VI, 630
Carter, Cynthia VI, 687
Carter, Cyrus V, 480
Carter, Cyrus V, 553
Carter, Cyrus V, 554
Carter, Cyrus V, 615
Carter, Cyrus V, 616
Carter, Cyrus B. V, 616
Carter, Cyrus E. I, 874
Carter, Cyrus E. V, 378
Carter, Cyrus E. V, 379
Carter, Cyrus E. V, 554
Carter, Cyrus E. V, 615
Carter, Cyrus E. V, 640
Carter, Cyrus F. V, 615
Carter, Cyrus S. I, 803
Carter, Cyrus S. I, 851
Carter, Cyrus S. I, 874
Carter, Daniel I, 377
Carter, Daniel II, 344
Carter, Daniel IV, 323
Carter, David I, 377
Carter, David V, 553
Carter, David V, 554
Carter, David VI, 890
Carter, David VI, 943
Carter, David E. I, 675
Carter, David Elmore V, 615
Carter, David F. V, 554
Carter, David T. VI, 891
Carter, Deborah VI, 630
Carter, Deborah VI, 678
Carter, Delila V, 554
Carter, Delilah V, 378
Carter, Delilah V, 553
Carter, Delilah V, 554
Carter, Dianna I, 675
Carter, Dina I, 444
Carter, Dinah I, 444
Carter, Dinah I, 475
Carter, Dinah I, 675
Carter, Dinah VI, 890
Carter, Dortha B. IV, 1091
Carter, Dortha B. IV, 1110
Carter, Dortha Beulah IV, 1109
Carter, E. C. L. VI, 884
Carter, Edith I, 377
Carter, Edith I, 412
Carter, Edith II, 988
Carter, Edith II, 1001
Carter, Edith IV, 570
Carter, Edith VI, 470
Carter, Edith VI, 481
Carter, Edith R. IV, 183
Carter, Edith R. IV, 570
Carter, Edith R. IV, 574
Carter, Edmund II, 988
Carter, Edna V, 36
Carter, Edward I, 377
Carter, Edward VI, 804
Carter, Edward VI, 858
Carter, Edward VI, 891
Carter, Edward Turner II, 482
Carter, Eli I, 530
Carter, Eli I, 874
Carter, Elias V, 378
Carter, Elihu V, 615
Carter, Elihu V, 616
Carter, Elihu V, 640
Carter, Elisabeth I, 134
Carter, Elisabeth II, 206
Carter, Elisabeth II, 235
Carter, Eliz. III, 216
Carter, Eliza IV, 377
Carter, Eliza VI, 891
Carter, Eliza Ann V, 553
Carter, Eliza Ann V, 554
Carter, Elizabeth I, 97
Carter, Elizabeth I, 347
Carter, Elizabeth I, 353
Carter, Elizabeth I, 377
Carter, Elizabeth I, 406
Carter, Elizabeth I, 426
Carter, Elizabeth I, 851
Carter, Elizabeth I, 874
Carter, Elizabeth I, 894
Carter, Elizabeth II, 24
Carter, Elizabeth II, 60
Carter, Elizabeth II, 344
Carter, Elizabeth II, 482
Carter, Elizabeth II, 483
Carter, Elizabeth II, 732
Carter, Elizabeth II, 845
Carter, Elizabeth III, 65
Carter, Elizabeth IV, 378
Carter, Elizabeth IV, 424
Carter, Elizabeth V, 378
Carter, Elizabeth V, 379
Carter, Elizabeth V, 410
Carter, Elizabeth V, 480
Carter, Elizabeth V, 490
Carter, Elizabeth V, 496
Carter, Elizabeth V, 553
Carter, Elizabeth V, 554
Carter, Elizabeth V, 561
Carter, Elizabeth V, 611
Carter, Elizabeth V, 615
Carter, Elizabeth V, 616
Carter, Elizabeth V, 630
Carter, Elizabeth V, 663
Carter, Elizabeth V, 670
Carter, Elizabeth V, 988
Carter, Elizabeth V, 989
Carter, Elizabeth VI, 375
Carter, Elizabeth VI, 383
Carter, Elizabeth VI, 417
Carter, Elizabeth VI, 630
Carter, Elizabeth VI, 634
Carter, Elizabeth VI, 891
Carter, Elizabeth VI, 918
Carter, Elizabeth VI, 943
Carter, Elizabeth VI, 953
Carter, Elizabeth VI, 1004
Carter, Elizabeth A. VI, 833
Carter, Elizabeth Ann VI, 943
Carter, Elizabeth C. IV, 474
Carter, Elizabeth E. V, 615
Carter, Elizabeth J. V, 378
Carter, Elizabeth Jane V, 553
Carter, Elizabeth Jane V, 554
Carter, Elizabeth M. I, 874
Carter, Ella V, 730
Carter, Ellis T. IV, 378
Carter, Ellis Tucker IV, 378
Carter, Elma B. IV, 615
Carter, Elma L. IV, 378
Carter, Elma L. IV, 402
Carter, Elmer J. V, 554
Carter, Elmore V, 615
Carter, Elton V, 378
Carter, Elton C. IV, 378
Carter, Elton C. IV, 1152
Carter, Emily V, 615
Carter, Emily Ann I, 851
Carter, Emily Ann I, 874
Carter, Emily Ann I, 883
Carter, Emily Jame VI, 891
Carter, Emily Malinda V, 616
Carter, Emily W. III, 378
Carter, Emma V, 379
Carter, Enoch I, 347
Carter, Enoch I, 434
Carter, Enoch I, 444
Carter, Enoch I, 530
Carter, Enoch I, 851
Carter, Enoch I, 874
Carter, Enoch I, 889
Carter, Enoch V, 378
Carter, Enoch V, 379
Carter, Enoch V, 480
Carter, Enoch V, 490
Carter, Enoch V, 553
Carter, Enoch V, 554
Carter, Enoch V, 561
Carter, Esther II, 60
Carter, Esther B. V, 615
Carter, Ethel IV, 1088
Carter, Ethel IV, 1091
Carter, Ethel F. V, 730
Carter, Eunice IV, 517
Carter, Eva V, 323
Carter, Eva V, 379
Carter, Eva V, 554
Carter, Eva V, 663
Carter, Eva D. V, 554
Carter, Eva D. V, 570
Carter, Evalina E. VI, 891
Carter, Fannie V, 157
Carter, Fidelia V, 615
Carter, Fidelia V, 629
Carter, Fleming VI, 891
Carter, Flora I, 867
Carter, Flora I, 936
Carter, Flora M. I, 874
Carter, Flora M. I, 906
Carter, Flora Mariah I, 851
Carter, Frances II, 442
Carter, Frances VI, 993
Carter, Frances Ann VI, 891
Carter, G. H. V, 616
Carter, G. Hamilton V, 616
Carter, Geo. V, 614
Carter, Geo. M. V, 616
Carter, George I, 347
Carter, George I, 434
Carter, George I, 675
Carter, George I, 692
Carter, George V, 480
Carter, George V, 496
Carter, George V, 553
Carter, George V, 554
Carter, George D. V, 480
Carter, George D. V, 496
Carter, George Hamilton V, 615
Carter, George L. V, 157
Carter, George L. V, 616
Carter, George Lewis V, 615
Carter, George M. V, 378
Carter, Grace II, 988
Carter, Hannah I, 347
Carter, Hannah I, 377
Carter, Hannah I, 395
Carter, Hannah I, 444
Carter, Hannah I, 449
Carter, Hannah I, 451
Carter, Hannah II, 455
Carter, Hannah II, 482
Carter, Hannah II, 483
Carter, Hannah II, 732
Carter, Hannah II, 845
Carter, Hannah II, 846
Carter, Hannah II, 918
Carter, Hannah IV, 319
Carter, Hannah IV, 574
Carter, Hannah V, 554
Carter, Hannah V, 586
Carter, Hannah V, 615
Carter, Hannah V, 649
Carter, Hannah VI, 481
Carter, Hannah VI, 488
Carter, Hannah Ann IV, 378
Carter, Hannah Ann IV, 402
Carter, Hannah B. II, 846
Carter, Hannah B. V, 616
Carter, Hannah Camble I, 444
Carter, Hannah F. II, 732
Carter, Hannah Louisa V, 615
Carter, Hannah Pemelia V, 615
Carter, Hannah R. IV, 378
Carter, Hannah R. IV, 570
Carter, Hannah R. IV, 614
Carter, Harold Robert IV, 378
Carter, Harpless H. IV, 865
Carter, Harris, John D. VI, 928
Carter, Harry Edgar V, 615
Carter, Harvey V, 989
Carter, Harvey T. V, 157
Carter, Henley I, 922
Carter, Henry I, 444
Carter, Henry II, 344
Carter, Henry II, 482
Carter, Henry II, 483
Carter, Henry II, 491
Carter, Henry IV, 1152
Carter, Henry IV, 1203
Carter, Henry VI, 375
Carter, Henry VI, 481
Carter, Hester II, 60
Carter, Hesther II, 24
Carter, Hiram V, 553
Carter, Howard V, 228
Carter, Howard V, 663
Carter, Ibba VI, 1011
Carter, Ida Bell V, 553
Carter, Ida Bell V, 554
Carter, Ida Belle V, 554
Carter, Irena V, 378
Carter, Isaac I, 675
Carter, Isaac I, 851
Carter, Isaac I, 852
Carter, Isaac I, 874
Carter, Isaac I, 894
Carter, Isaac II, 483
Carter, Isaac II, 786
Carter, Isaac II, 845
Carter, Isaac V, 378
Carter, Isaac V, 615
Carter, Isaac V, 730
Carter, Isabell I, 347
Carter, J. W. IV, 474
Carter, J. W. V, 730
Carter, Jackson V, 554
Carter, Jacob I, 851
Carter, Jacob I, 852
Carter, Jacob I, 874
Carter, Jacob II, 483
Carter, Jacob II, 732
Carter, Jacob II, 845
Carter, Jacob II, 846
Carter, James I, 444
Carter, James I, 448
Carter, James I, 675
Carter, James I, 935
Carter, James I, 1004
Carter, James II, 344
Carter, James IV, 24
Carter, James IV, 78
Carter, James IV, 369
Carter, James IV, 377
Carter, James IV, 378
Carter, James IV, 865
Carter, James IV, 1152
Carter, James IV, 1203
Carter, James V, 36
Carter, James V, 615
Carter, James VI, 162
Carter, James VI, 183
Carter, James VI, 203
Carter, James VI, 481
Carter, James VI, 488
Carter, James Allen V, 615
Carter, James Edgar IV, 1203
Carter, James M. VI, 891
Carter, James Madison VI, 891
Carter, James T. II, 786
Carter, James W. VI, 891
Carter, James Walter V, 378
Carter, James, Jr. VI, 981
Carter, Jane I, 375
Carter, Jane I, 377
Carter, Jane I, 434
Carter, Jane I, 444
Carter, Jane I, 675
Carter, Jane I, 756
Carter, Jane I, 803
Carter, Jane I, 874
Carter, Jane I, 982
Carter, Jane I, 983
Carter, Jane II, 786
Carter, Jane V, 228
Carter, Jane V, 378
Carter, Jane V, 480
Carter, Jane V, 553
Carter, Jane V, 554
Carter, Jane V, 562
Carter, Jane V, 663
Carter, Jane VI, 856
Carter, Jane E. I, 675
Carter, Jane L. II, 707
Carter, Jane, II I, 347
Carter, Jas. M. VI, 954
Carter, Jean I, 347
Carter, Jefferson VI, 891
Carter, Jehu I, 377
Carter, Jehu I, 444
Carter, Jehu I, 454
Carter, Jehu I, 874
Carter, Jehu C. I, 675
Carter, Jennie V, 663
Carter, Jenny VI, 890
Carter, Jesse I, 434
Carter, Jesse I, 530
Carter, Jesse I, 851
Carter, Jesse I, 874
Carter, Jesse I, 889
Carter, Jesse V, 157
Carter, Jesse V, 480
Carter, Jesse V, 553
Carter, Jesse V, 554
Carter, Jesse V, 614
Carter, Jesse V, 616
Carter, Jesse V, 619
Carter, Jesse W. V, 615
Carter, Jno. I, 434
Carter, Joel IV, 377
Carter, Joel IV, 1203
Carter, Joel B. IV, 378
Carter, Joel B. IV, 1152
Carter, Joel D. IV, 378
Carter, Joel K. IV, 187
Carter, John I, 347
Carter, John I, 375
Carter, John I, 377
Carter, John I, 444
Carter, John I, 451
Carter, John I, 475
Carter, John I, 530
Carter, John I, 673
Carter, John I, 675
Carter, John I, 695
Carter, John I, 803
Carter, John I, 851
Carter, John I, 852
Carter, John I, 855
Carter, John I, 867
Carter, John I, 874
Carter, John I, 902
Carter, John I, 922
Carter, John I, 926
Carter, John I, 936
Carter, John I, 1004
Carter, John II, 344
Carter, John II, 442
Carter, John II, 483
Carter, John II, 701
Carter, John II, 732
Carter, John IV, 560
Carter, John V, 378
Carter, John V, 480
Carter, John V, 553
Carter, John V, 554
Carter, John V, 570
Carter, John V, 586
Carter, John V, 615
Carter, John V, 616
Carter, John V, 649
Carter, John V, 663
Carter, John V, 730
Carter, John VI, 375
Carter, John VI, 804
Carter, John VI, 888
Carter, John VI, 890
Carter, John VI, 911
Carter, John VI, 941
Carter, John VI, 1003
Carter, John B. V, 480
Carter, John B. V, 554
Carter, John B. V, 597
Carter, John B. VI, 804
Carter, John Baker V, 553
Carter, John D. VI, 862
Carter, John Henry V, 615
Carter, John L. V, 663
Carter, John L. VI, 891
Carter, John M. V, 615
Carter, John M. VI, 894
Carter, John R. I, 675
Carter, John S. IV, 378
Carter, John S. IV, 1152
Carter, John W. V, 228
Carter, John W. V, 615
Carter, John Wm. V, 616
Carter, John, Jr. I, 377
Carter, John, Jr. I, 874
Carter, John, Jr. V, 615
Carter, John, Sr. VI, 998
Carter, Jonathan B. I, 851
Carter, Jonathan B. I, 874
Carter, Joseph I, 377
Carter, Joseph II, 786
Carter, Joseph II, 846
Carter, Joseph IV, 24
Carter, Joseph IV, 1152
Carter, Joseph V, 615
Carter, Joseph VI, 383
Carter, Joseph VI, 630
Carter, Joseph VI, 634
Carter, Joseph G. V, 615
Carter, Joseph G. V, 616
Carter, Joseph G. V, 663
Carter, Joseph H. IV, 378
Carter, Joseph, Jr. IV, 24
Carter, Josephine B. II, 846
Carter, Josephine B. II, 900
Carter, Josiah VI, 871
Carter, Josiah VI, 890
Carter, Josiah VI, 916
Carter, Josiah VI, 945
Carter, Josiah VI, 1019
Carter, Josiah, Jr. VI, 896
Carter, Juda VI, 943
Carter, Judith V, 615
Carter, Judith V, 630
Carter, Judith F. V, 474
Carter, Judith F. V, 480
Carter, Judith F. V, 549
Carter, Judith F. V, 554
Carter, Judith F. V, 615
Carter, Judith F. V, 632
Carter, Judith T. V, 554
Carter, Julia IV, 369
Carter, Julia IV, 377
Carter, Julia IV, 378
Carter, Julia IV, 1152
Carter, Julia A. I, 209
Carter, Julia A. I, 213
Carter, Julia A. V, 323

Carter, Julia Ann VI, 928
Carter, Kate III, 65
Carter, Kate III, 216
Carter, Katharine I, 925
Carter, L. Sibyl V, 616
Carter, Latitia II, 988
Carter, Latitia II, 1019
Carter, Laura IV, 1203
Carter, Laura V, 554
Carter, Laura V, 616
Carter, Laura E. V, 616
Carter, Laura M. V, 553
Carter, Laura May V, 554
Carter, Lauretta V, 554
Carter, Lavinia II, 786
Carter, Lelia Belle I, 935
Carter, Lena V, 157
Carter, Lena May V, 157
Carter, Lena Nelson II, 893
Carter, Leonard V, 323
Carter, Leonard V, 553
Carter, Leonard V, 554
Carter, Leonard V, 663
Carter, Leonard J. V, 554
Carter, Levi IV, 378
Carter, Levi IV, 574
Carter, Levi IV, 615
Carter, Levi S. IV, 378
Carter, Levi S. IV, 1152
Carter, Little Berry VI, 943
Carter, Little Berry VI, 1012
Carter, Little Burry VI, 891
Carter, Littleberry VI, 880
Carter, Littleberry VI, 943
Carter, Littleberry VI, 987
Carter, Littleburry VI, 891
Carter, Lizzie V, 663
Carter, Louis VI, 891
Carter, Louisa V, 554
Carter, Louisa V, 593
Carter, Louisa V, 615
Carter, Louisa V, 649
Carter, Louise V, 593
Carter, Louiza V, 553
Carter, Lucile V, 157
Carter, Lucile H. V, 36
Carter, Lucile H. V, 157
Carter, Lucy VI, 874
Carter, Lucy VI, 891
Carter, Ludia V, 379
Carter, Lula VI, 630
Carter, Lydia I, 377
Carter, Lydia I, 444
Carter, Lydia I, 454
Carter, Lydia I, 530
Carter, Lydia I, 851
Carter, Lydia II, 206
Carter, Lydia II, 258
Carter, Lydia II, 483
Carter, Lydia II, 577
Carter, Lydia V, 379
Carter, Lydia V, 480
Carter, Lydia V, 896
Carter, Lydia V, 898
Carter, Lydia A. V, 480
Carter, Lydia Ann V, 157
Carter, Lydia Ann V, 372
Carter, Lydia Ann V, 378
Carter, Lydia Ann V, 480
Carter, Lydia Ann V, 554
Carter, Lydia Ann VI, 375
Carter, Lydia Ann VI, 383
Carter, Lydia Ann VI, 630
Carter, Lydia Ann VI, 634
Carter, Lydia B. I, 874
Carter, Lydia B. V, 378
Carter, Lydia B. V, 615
Carter, Lydia B. V, 616
Carter, Lydia B. V, 640
Carter, Lydia M. V, 598
Carter, Lydia M. V, 710
Carter, Lydya I, 444
Carter, Mae V, 323
Carter, Magdalena VI, 890
Carter, Malinda IV, 378
Carter, Malinda IV, 406
Carter, Malinda V, 157
Carter, Malinda V, 615
Carter, Malinda V, 616
Carter, Malinda V, 619
Carter, Mansel Levi IV, 378
Carter, Marcelius V. I, 803
Carter, Marcellius V. I, 874
Carter, Marcellus I, 803
Carter, Marcellus V. I, 851
Carter, Marcius I, 803
Carter, Marcius J. I, 851
Carter, Marcius J. I, 874
Carter, Marco B. VI, 894
Carter, Margaret I, 377
Carter, Margaret I, 530
Carter, Margaret I, 874
Carter, Margaret I, 901
Carter, Margaret II, 344
Carter, Margaret II, 732
Carter, Margaret IV, 377
Carter, Margaret V, 554
Carter, Margaret V, 663
Carter, Margaret J. V, 323
Carter, Margery IV, 323
Carter, Maria II, 60
Carter, Maria S. IV, 615
Carter, Mariah II, 24
Carter, Mariam V, 615
Carter, Marion V, 228
Carter, Marion V, 663
Carter, Martain II, 482
Carter, Martha I, 444
Carter, Martha I, 448
Carter, Martha I, 756
Carter, Martha I, 803
Carter, Martha IV, 371
Carter, Martha IV, 378
Carter, Martha VI, 891
Carter, Martha A. VI, 814
Carter, Martha Ann VI, 911
Carter, Martha B. VI, 894
Carter, Martha Beulah IV, 378
Carter, Martha W. VI, 804
Carter, Marticia V, 615
Carter, Martin II, 786
Carter, Martitia V, 615
Carter, Mary I, 347
Carter, Mary I, 376
Carter, Mary I, 377
Carter, Mary I, 403
Carter, Mary I, 444
Carter, Mary I, 455
Carter, Mary I, 617
Carter, Mary I, 673
Carter, Mary I, 675
Carter, Mary I, 692
Carter, Mary I, 852
Carter, Mary I, 874
Carter, Mary I, 894
Carter, Mary I, 929
Carter, Mary I, 935
Carter, Mary I, 1004
Carter, Mary I, 1008
Carter, Mary II, 206
Carter, Mary II, 344
Carter, Mary II, 482
Carter, Mary II, 483
Carter, Mary II, 662
Carter, Mary II, 732
Carter, Mary II, 845
Carter, Mary II, 846
Carter, Mary II, 933
Carter, Mary IV, 24
Carter, Mary IV, 61
Carter, Mary IV, 78
Carter, Mary IV, 187
Carter, Mary IV, 323
Carter, Mary IV, 329
Carter, Mary IV, 378
Carter, Mary IV, 467
Carter, Mary IV, 474
Carter, Mary IV, 517
Carter, Mary IV, 570
Carter, Mary IV, 865
Carter, Mary IV, 1091
Carter, Mary IV, 1116
Carter, Mary V, 553
Carter, Mary V, 554
Carter, Mary V, 663
Carter, Mary VI, 619
Carter, Mary VI, 630
Carter, Mary VI, 689
Carter, Mary VI, 714
Carter, Mary VI, 860
Carter, Mary VI, 869
Carter, Mary VI, 880
Carter, Mary VI, 890
Carter, Mary VI, 891
Carter, Mary VI, 962
Carter, Mary A. V, 663
Carter, Mary Alice IV, 378
Carter, Mary Ann V, 554
Carter, Mary Ann V, 570
Carter, Mary Ann V, 606
Carter, Mary Ann V, 616
Carter, Mary Ann Margaret VI, 896
Carter, Mary E. III, 65
Carter, Mary E. V, 323
Carter, Mary E. V, 379
Carter, Mary E. V, 480
Carter, Mary Elma IV, 370
Carter, Mary Elma IV, 378
Carter, Mary Elma IV, 611
Carter, Mary Elma IV, 614
Carter, Mary Emily V, 323
Carter, Mary Emily V, 378
Carter, Mary Emily V, 379
Carter, Mary Emily V, 480
Carter, Mary Etta IV, 574
Carter, Mary Hannah I, 444
Carter, Mary J. IV, 378
Carter, Mary J. IV, 387
Carter, Mary J. VI, 891
Carter, Mary Jane IV, 377
Carter, Mary Jane IV, 378
Carter, Mary Jane IV, 386
Carter, Mary M. I, 675
Carter, Mary S. V, 832
Carter, Mary Susan V, 831
Carter, Masie V, 663
Carter, Masie V, 688
Carter, May IV, 1247
Carter, May V, 323
Carter, McKinley V, 989
Carter, Meary VI, 869
Carter, Melinda IV, 187
Carter, Meriam I, 444
Carter, Meriam V, 480
Carter, Meribah II, 701
Carter, Merry VI, 888
Carter, Merry VI, 918
Carter, Merry VI, 993
Carter, Milicent B. V, 615
Carter, Millicent V, 615
Carter, Milten V, 989
Carter, Milton I, 851
Carter, Milton V, 378
Carter, Milton V, 989
Carter, Milton P. IV, 865
Carter, Mima VI, 890
Carter, Miriam I, 434
Carter, Miriam I, 675
Carter, Miriam I, 692
Carter, Miriam I, 803
Carter, Miriam V, 480
Carter, Miriam V, 553
Carter, Miriam V, 614
Carter, Miriam V, 615
Carter, Miriam V, 619
Carter, Miriam Elizabeth I, 803
Carter, Mordeca I, 347
Carter, Mordecai I, 377
Carter, Mordecai V, 36
Carter, Mordica I, 377
Carter, Mordicai V, 831
Carter, Nancy I, 851
Carter, Nancy I, 874
Carter, Nancy I, 889
Carter, Nancy I, 1008
Carter, Nancy V, 378
Carter, Nancy V, 400
Carter, Nancy V, 480
Carter, Nancy V, 553
Carter, Nancy VI, 890
Carter, Nancy VI, 958
Carter, Nancy VI, 978
Carter, Nancy VI, 1019
Carter, Nancy Jane I, 851
Carter, Nathan II, 206
Carter, Nathanie V, 378
Carter, Nathaniel I, 347
Carter, Nathaniel I, 353
Carter, Nathaniel I, 434
Carter, Nathaniel I, 444
Carter, Nathaniel I, 1004
Carter, Nathaniel I, 1008
Carter, Nathaniel V, 400
Carter, Nathaniel V, 480
Carter, Nathaniel V, 553
Carter, Nathaniel V, 554
Carter, Nellie I, 939
Carter, Nellie IV, 187
Carter, Nellie C. I, 922
Carter, Nereus M. I, 851
Carter, Nerrius I, 874
Carter, Nicholas I, 347
Carter, Nicholas I, 851
Carter, Nicholas I, 852
Carter, Nicholas I, 874
Carter, Nicholas I, 903
Carter, Ocie V, 228
Carter, Oliver S. III, 216
Carter, Olivia IV, 865
Carter, Omer D. IV, 865
Carter, Opal V, 616
Carter, Orpha V, 228
Carter, Pamelia IV, 467
Carter, Pamelia IV, 471
Carter, Pamilia VI, 957
Carter, Parthena J. I, 851
Carter, Parthena J. I, 874
Carter, Patsey VI, 943
Carter, Penelope Ann VI, 928
Carter, Perry V, 554
Carter, Perry J. V, 553
Carter, Peter V, 554
Carter, Phebe I, 97
Carter, Phebe I, 134
Carter, Phebe IV, 377
Carter, Phebe V, 615
Carter, Phebe V, 632
Carter, Phebe Ann V, 553
Carter, Phebe Ann V, 554
Carter, Phebe E. IV, 378
Carter, Phebe E. IV, 407
Carter, Phebe Eliza IV, 187
Carter, Philip IV, 378
Carter, Philip IV, 574
Carter, Philip IV, 614
Carter, Phillip IV, 570
Carter, Pledge VI, 804
Carter, Polly VI, 804
Carter, Polly VI, 891
Carter, Polly VI, 896
Carter, Polly VI, 941
Carter, Polly VI, 951
Carter, Polly VI, 981
Carter, Pulley VI, 890
Carter, Rachel I, 377
Carter, Rachel I, 402
Carter, Rachel I, 851
Carter, Rachel I, 852
Carter, Rachel I, 869
Carter, Rachel I, 874
Carter, Rachel I, 919
Carter, Rachel II, 988
Carter, Rachel II, 1014
Carter, Rachel V, 378
Carter, Rachel V, 553
Carter, Rachel V, 734
Carter, Rachel E. V, 157
Carter, Rachel E. V, 379
Carter, Rachel Eva V, 323
Carter, Rachel M. V, 157
Carter, Rachel M. V, 167
Carter, Rachel M. V, 615
Carter, Rachel M. V, 620
Carter, Rebecah I, 444
Carter, Rebecca I, 347
Carter, Rebecca I, 377
Carter, Rebecca I, 403
Carter, Rebecca I, 628
Carter, Rebecca I, 741
Carter, Rebecca II, 24
Carter, Rebecca II, 60
Carter, Rebecca II, 344
Carter, Rebecca II, 483
Carter, Rebecca II, 524
Carter, Rebecca V, 580
Carter, Rebecca V, 615
Carter, Rebecca VI, 945
Carter, Rebeckah I, 444
Carter, Rebeckah I, 455
Carter, Rebeckah VI, 888
Carter, Rebekah I, 377
Carter, Restore II, 24
Carter, Restore II, 60
Carter, Restore II, 701
Carter, Richard IV, 24
Carter, Richard IV, 141
Carter, Richard IV, 187
Carter, Richard IV, 323
Carter, Richard IV, 329
Carter, Richard IV, 570
Carter, Richard IV, 1052
Carter, Richard IV, 1091
Carter, Richard Lee III, 65
Carter, Robert I, 347
Carter, Robert I, 377
Carter, Robert VI, 630
Carter, Robert VI, 891
Carter, Rufus V, 616
Carter, Rufus M. V, 615
Carter, Russel Stephen IV, 378
Carter, Ruth I, 377
Carter, Ruth I, 444
Carter, Ruth I, 451
Carter, Ruth I, 457
Carter, Ruth I, 851
Carter, Ruth I, 852
Carter, Ruth I, 874
Carter, Ruth I, 892
Carter, Ruth I, 930
Carter, Ruth I, 935
Carter, Ruth V, 616
Carter, Ruth Ann IV, 467
Carter, Ruth Ann IV, 481
Carter, Ruth C. I, 851
Carter, Ruth C. I, 874
Carter, Ruth C. I, 894
Carter, Ruth E. V, 157
Carter, Ruth May V, 616
Carter, Sabro Ramsey I, 1008
Carter, Sally VI, 804
Carter, Sally VI, 891
Carter, Sally W. VI, 880
Carter, Samuel I, 347
Carter, Samuel I, 377
Carter, Samuel I, 402
Carter, Samuel I, 412
Carter, Samuel I, 851
Carter, Samuel I, 852
Carter, Samuel I, 874
Carter, Samuel I, 892
Carter, Samuel I, 907
Carter, Samuel IV, 370
Carter, Samuel IV, 377
Carter, Samuel IV, 378
Carter, Samuel IV, 386
Carter, Samuel IV, 394
Carter, Samuel IV, 611
Carter, Samuel IV, 615
Carter, Samuel V, 323
Carter, Samuel V, 378
Carter, Samuel V, 379
Carter, Samuel V, 480
Carter, Samuel V, 553
Carter, Samuel V, 554
Carter, Samuel V, 615
Carter, Samuel VI, 804
Carter, Samuel A. VI, 891
Carter, Samuel C. IV, 614
Carter, Samuel C. V, 616
Carter, Samuel N. I, 851
Carter, Sarah I, 444
Carter, Sarah I, 455
Carter, Sarah I, 530
Carter, Sarah I, 600
Carter, Sarah I, 673
Carter, Sarah I, 675
Carter, Sarah I, 756
Carter, Sarah I, 851
Carter, Sarah I, 874
Carter, Sarah II, 482
Carter, Sarah II, 483
Carter, Sarah II, 805
Carter, Sarah II, 846
Carter, Sarah IV, 187
Carter, Sarah IV, 377
Carter, Sarah IV, 378
Carter, Sarah IV, 387
Carter, Sarah IV, 394
Carter, Sarah IV, 467
Carter, Sarah IV, 470
Carter, Sarah V, 553
Carter, Sarah V, 554
Carter, Sarah V, 597
Carter, Sarah V, 988
Carter, Sarah VI, 891
Carter, Sarah VI, 987
Carter, Sarah Ann II, 786
Carter, Sarah Ann VI, 880
Carter, Sarah Doudna IV, 400
Carter, Sarah Ellen IV, 378
Carter, Sarah Ellen IV, 394
Carter, Sarah Emily V, 554
Carter, Sarah M. V, 615
Carter, Sarah M. V, 616
Carter, Sarah S. II, 732
Carter, Sarah William I, 444
Carter, Sharon II, 483
Carter, Sharon II, 732
Carter, Sharon II, 786
Carter, Sharon II, 845
Carter, Shedrack VI, 856
Carter, Sibby I, 1004
Carter, Sibyl V, 616
Carter, Solomon VI, 890
Carter, Stella IV, 865
Carter, Stephen I, 675
Carter, Stephen I, 692
Carter, Stuart II, 786
Carter, Susan VI, 804
Carter, Susan VI, 891
Carter, Susan Alice V, 615
Carter, Susan F. V, 615
Carter, Susana M. VI, 891
Carter, Susanah II, 482
Carter, Susanah II, 491
Carter, Susanna I, 377
Carter, Susanna I, 398
Carter, Susanna I, 530
Carter, Susanna I, 874
Carter, Susanna I, 892
Carter, Susanna II, 197
Carter, Susanna II, 206
Carter, Susanna IV, 187
Carter, Susanna IV, 386
Carter, Susanna V, 553
Carter, Susanna D. V, 554
Carter, Susanna E. V, 554
Carter, Susannah I, 874
Carter, Susannah IV, 311
Carter, Susannah IV, 314
Carter, Susannah V, 480
Carter, Susannah V, 554
Carter, Susannah V, 563
Carter, Susannah V, 615

Carter, Susannah V, 640
Carter, Susannah V, 675
Carter, Susannah VI, 375
Carter, Susannah VI, 385
Carter, Susannah Delilah V, 553
Carter, Susannah F. V, 615
Carter, Susannah F. V, 616
Carter, Susannah L. V, 378
Carter, Susannah P. V, 616
Carter, Sybil J. V, 615
Carter, T. Elwood I, 851
Carter, Tabitha VI, 891
Carter, Thomas II, 24
Carter, Thomas II, 60
Carter, Thomas II, 344
Carter, Thomas II, 483
Carter, Thomas V, 615
Carter, Thomas VI, 375
Carter, Thomas C. V, 157
Carter, Thomas C. V, 453
Carter, Thomas I. VI, 804
Carter, Thos. C. V, 167
Carter, Thos. C. V, 615
Carter, Thos. C. V, 620
Carter, Velna C. I, 803
Carter, Velna C. I, 851
Carter, Velna C. I, 874
Carter, Veturia M. I, 851
Carter, Veturia M. I, 874
Carter, Walter V, 616
Carter, Walter Everett V, 616
Carter, Wd. Elizabeth Hutchins II, 786
Carter, Wd. Hannah B. II, 846
Carter, William I, 97
Carter, William I, 134
Carter, William I, 377
Carter, William I, 444
Carter, William I, 448
Carter, William I, 675
Carter, William I, 756
Carter, William I, 803
Carter, William I, 874
Carter, William II, 344
Carter, William II, 442
Carter, William II, 1014
Carter, William V, 228
Carter, William V, 480
Carter, William V, 553
Carter, William V, 554
Carter, William V, 615
Carter, William VI, 874
Carter, William VI, 890
Carter, William VI, 896
Carter, William VI, 924
Carter, William VI, 928
Carter, William VI, 953
Carter, William VI, 1004
Carter, William VI, 1011
Carter, William A. I, 675
Carter, William B. V, 554
Carter, William B. V, 615
Carter, William C. V, 480
Carter, William P. V, 615
Carter, William P. VI, 891
Carter, William S. VI, 891
Carter, William S. VI, 987
Carter, William Sutton I, 97
Carter, William T. I, 851
Carter, William T. I, 874
Carter, William, Sr. I, 444
Carter, Willie V, 663
Carter, Wilma Alberta IV, 378
Carter, Wilson V, 474
Carter, Wilson V, 549
Carter, Wilson V, 553
Carter, Wilson V, 554
Carter, Wilson V, 615
Carter, Wilson V, 630
Carter, Wilson E. V, 616
Carter, Winnifred V, 616
Carter, Wm. II, 455
Carter, Wm. II, 482
Carter, Wm. II, 662
Carter, Wm. II, 988
Carter, Wm. V, 616
Carter, Wm. V, 632
Carter, Wm. V, 640
Carter, Wm. V, 663
Carter, Wm. V, 989
Carter, Wm. VI, 943
Carter, Wm. B. V, 615
Carter, Wm. C. V, 379
Carter, Wm. P. V, 616
Carter, Wm. Smart III, 65
Carter, Zelda IV, 865
Carter, Zephaniah V, 36
Carter, Zimri I, 377
Carter, Zimri H. V, 615
Cartland, Abbie I, 874
Cartland, Abbie F. I, 803
Cartland, Alfred III, 65
Cartland, Alfred L. III, 65
Cartland, Alfred L. III, 207
Cartland, Alfred Lindley I, 803
Cartland, Alfred Lindley III, 65
Cartland, Alice I, 636
Cartland, Alice Farr III, 65
Cartland, Bessie I, 613
Cartland, Bessie Meader I, 874
Cartland, Edith Furnum I, 803
Cartland, Edith Hulda III, 65
Cartland, Edwin I, 530
Cartland, Elijah I, 613
Cartland, Elijah P. I, 803
Cartland, Elijah P. I, 874
Cartland, Elijah Wilbert I, 803
Cartland, Elisabeth I, 618
Cartland, Elisabeth White I, 613
Cartland, Elizabeth I, 530
Cartland, Ethel I, 874
Cartland, Ezra I, 530
Cartland, Fernando I, 803
Cartland, Fernando C. I, 803
Cartland, Fernando G. I, 874
Cartland, Francis Murrey I, 803
Cartland, Frank I, 874
Cartland, George Edward III, 65
Cartland, George L. III, 65
Cartland, George Lindley III, 65
Cartland, Helen I, 613
Cartland, Helen I, 626
Cartland, Helen I, 631
Cartland, Helen I, 641
Cartland, Herbert I, 631
Cartland, Herbert I, 874
Cartland, Herbert E. I, 613
Cartland, Herbert E. I, 631
Cartland, Herbert E. I, 874
Cartland, Herbert E. I, 939
Cartland, Herbert Elwood I, 560
Cartland, Herbert H. I, 803
Cartland, J. E. I, 631
Cartland, J. L. I, 618
Cartland, J. Leslie I, 40
Cartland, J. Leslie I, 613
Cartland, J. Leslie I, 631
Cartland, James E. I, 530
Cartland, James E. I, 560
Cartland, James E. I, 613
Cartland, James E. I, 620
Cartland, James E. I, 631
Cartland, James E. I, 803
Cartland, James E. I, 874
Cartland, James E. I, 939
Cartland, James Edwin I, 40
Cartland, Jane I, 874
Cartland, Jas. E. I, 631
Cartland, Jennie III, 65
Cartland, Jennie Brownell I, 803
Cartland, Jennie M. III, 65
Cartland, Jennie M. III, 207
Cartland, Joseph Leslie I, 40
Cartland, Joseph Leslie I, 84
Cartland, Joseph Leslie I, 613
Cartland, Lena III, 65
Cartland, Leslie I, 530
Cartland, Leslie I, 560
Cartland, Leslie I, 631
Cartland, Leslie I, 874
Cartland, Lestie I, 626
Cartland, Lydia I, 84
Cartland, Lydia I, 613
Cartland, Lydia I, 618
Cartland, Lydia I, 626
Cartland, Lydia N. I, 631
Cartland, Lydia N. W. I, 40
Cartland, Lydia N. W. I, 631
Cartland, Lydia Nicholson I, 40
Cartland, Lydia Wilson I, 613
Cartland, Lynn I, 803
Cartland, M. Alice I, 631
Cartland, Margarite W. I, 631
Cartland, Marguerite I, 613
Cartland, Marguerite I, 620
Cartland, Mary I, 620
Cartland, Mary Alice I, 613
Cartland, Mary Alice I, 620
Cartland, Mary Alice I, 631
Cartland, Mary E. I, 40
Cartland, Mary E. I, 530
Cartland, Mary E. I, 613
Cartland, Mary E. I, 620
Cartland, Mary E. I, 631
Cartland, Mary E. I, 939
Cartland, Melville Pierpont III, 65
Cartland, Ruth III, 65
Cartland, Ruth Eleanor III, 65
Cartland, Ruth Eleanor III, 207
Cartland, Sarah I, 613
Cartland, Sarah B. I, 803
Cartland, Sarah B. I, 874
Cartland, Widow Mary E. I, 560
Cartright, Edward IV, 1248
Cartright, Elisabeth I, 131
Cartright, Hannah B. IV, 1247
Cartright, Harley IV, 1309
Cartright, Jesse IV, 1247
Cartright, Jonathan IV, 1247
Cartright, Mary I, 131
Cartright, Mary I, 134
Cartright, Mary IV, 1247
Cartright, Murray IV, 1248
Cartright, Penninah I, 134
Cartrite, Catharine I, 273
Cartrite, Robert I, 273
Cartwright, ??? VI, 736
Cartwright, ??? VI, 779
Cartwright, Ahaz I, 134
Cartwright, Alexandria V, 36
Cartwright, Ann I, 134
Cartwright, Catharine I, 268
Cartwright, Cathern I, 134
Cartwright, Elizabeth I, 134
Cartwright, Ezekiel I, 268
Cartwright, Grace I, 134
Cartwright, Hezekiah I, 134
Cartwright, Isaac I, 134
Cartwright, Jehu I, 134
Cartwright, Jehue I, 134
Cartwright, John I, 134
Cartwright, Joseph I, 134
Cartwright, Josiah I, 134
Cartwright, Lemuel I, 265
Cartwright, Lemuel I, 268
Cartwright, Lemuel I, 272
Cartwright, Louisa Burnett V, 663
Cartwright, Marshall V, 323
Cartwright, Mary I, 134
Cartwright, Mary I, 166
Cartwright, Miriam I, 134
Cartwright, Penninah I, 134
Cartwright, Robert I, 265
Cartwright, Robert I, 268
Cartwright, Sarah I, 265
Cartwright, Sarah I, 268
Cartwright, Sarah I, 272
Cartwright, Sarah V, 36
Cartwright, Sarah VI, 779
Cartwright, Sarah Sinclair VI, 735
Cartwright, Seth V, 36
Cartwright, Tamer I, 268
Cartwright, Thomas I, 91
Cartwright, Thomas I, 92
Cartwright, Thomas I, 134
Cartwright, Thomas, Jr. I, 134
Cartwright, Thomas, Jr. I, 166
Carty, Daniel II, 344
Carty, Elizabeth VI, 803
Carty, John IV, 1152
Carty, Patrick VI, 803
Caruthers, ??? I, 7
Caruthers, Barnabus I, 3
Caruthers, Barnabus I, 4
Caruthers, Elisha W. I, 7
Caruthers, Elva I, 3
Caruthers, James II, 988
Caruthers, James VI, 481
Caruthers, James VI, 542
Caruthers, James VI, 572
Caruthers, Mourning A. I, 3
Caruthers, Mourning A. I, 4
Caruthers, Rachel II, 988
Caruthers, Rachel VI, 481
Caruthers, Wd. Rachel VI, 481
Caruthers, Widow Rachel VI, 572
Caruthus, James II, 988
Carver, ??? I, 29
Carver, Abigail IV, 19
Carver, Abigail IV, 24
Carver, Abigail IV, 49
Carver, Abigail IV, 323
Carver, Abigail IV, 343
Carver, Abigail IV, 517
Carver, Abner IV, 142
Carver, Abner IV, 517
Carver, Ada Muriel I, 29
Carver, Agnes IV, 688
Carver, Agnes V, 36
Carver, Alexander IV, 517
Carver, Alonzo T. IV, 688
Carver, Ann II, 483
Carver, Ann IV, 142
Carver, Ann IV, 517
Carver, Ann IV, 545
Carver, Ann V, 36
Carver, Ann V, 480
Carver, Anna IV, 517
Carver, Anna IV, 552
Carver, Anna B. VI, 792
Carver, Anna Bailey VI, 736
Carver, Anna Bailey VI, 792
Carver, Anna M. VI, 736
Carver, Anna M. VI, 792
Carver, Anne IV, 517
Carver, Betsy Ann IV, 24
Carver, Betsy Ann IV, 517
Carver, Caroline II, 786
Carver, Carolyn II, 846
Carver, Carolyn II, 899
Carver, Carolyn A. III, 65
Carver, Carolyn A. III, 228
Carver, Charity II, 786
Carver, Charles Ann V, 480
Carver, Charles H. VI, 736
Carver, Charles H. VI, 792
Carver, Charles R. V, 36
Carver, Cora II, 846
Carver, Cora III, 65
Carver, Cora III, 153
Carver, Cornelius VI, 804
Carver, D. Frederick II, 899
Carver, D. Frederick III, 65
Carver, D. Frederick III, 228
Carver, Dan'l I, 30
Carver, David II, 786
Carver, David II, 846
Carver, David III, 65
Carver, David Frederick II, 846
Carver, Dimsdill IV, 517
Carver, Edwin V, 36
Carver, Eli II, 786
Carver, Eli II, 846
Carver, Eli V, 36
Carver, Eli V, 480
Carver, Elijah IV, 517
Carver, Elisabeth I, 34
Carver, Elisabeth I, 40
Carver, Elisabeth I, 60
Carver, Elisabeth IV, 142
Carver, Eliz. III, 65
Carver, Eliz. III, 93
Carver, Elizabeth I, 40
Carver, Elizabeth I, 134
Carver, Elizabeth I, 144
Carver, Elizabeth II, 823
Carver, Elizabeth IV, 323
Carver, Elizabeth IV, 325
Carver, Elizabeth IV, 517
Carver, George V, 36
Carver, George V, 480
Carver, Grace II, 988
Carver, Hannah II, 344
Carver, Hannah II, 483
Carver, Hannah II, 686
Carver, Henry I, 268
Carver, Henry IV, 24
Carver, Henry IV, 78
Carver, Henry IV, 142
Carver, Henry IV, 187
Carver, Henry IV, 354
Carver, Henry IV, 517
Carver, Henry IV, 552
Carver, Henry V, 228
Carver, Henry M. IV, 517
Carver, Henry, Jr. IV, 507
Carver, Isabel II, 483
Carver, Isabell II, 681
Carver, Isabella II, 344
Carver, Isabella II, 483
Carver, Israel II, 786
Carver, Jacob II, 344
Carver, Jacob II, 821
Carver, Jacob VI, 841
Carver, Jacob M. V, 36
Carver, Jacob M. V, 480
Carver, James IV, 24
Carver, James IV, 142
Carver, James IV, 517
Carver, James IV, 525
Carver, James V, 228
Carver, James V, 238
Carver, James VI, 819
Carver, James Millison IV, 517
Carver, Job I, 134
Carver, John II, 344
Carver, John II, 483
Carver, John II, 681
Carver, John III, 65
Carver, John IV, 24
Carver, John IV, 49
Carver, John IV, 142
Carver, John IV, 323
Carver, John IV, 343
Carver, John IV, 517
Carver, John L. II, 846
Carver, John L. III, 153
Carver, John Linton II, 846
Carver, John Linton III, 65
Carver, Mabel III, 65
Carver, Mabel III, 93
Carver, Margaret I, 40
Carver, Margaret I, 89
Carver, Margaret C. I, 30
Carver, Martha J. V, 36
Carver, Martha Jane V, 36
Carver, Martha Jane V, 480
Carver, Martha P. II, 846
Carver, Mary I, 40
Carver, Mary I, 88
Carver, Mary II, 344
Carver, Mary IV, 517
Carver, Mary V, 228
Carver, Mary V, 238
Carver, Mary H. V, 36
Carver, Mary H. V, 480
Carver, Mary H. V, 484
Carver, Mary Hannah V, 36
Carver, Mary Hannah V, 480
Carver, Maud E. V, 663
Carver, Millison IV, 24
Carver, Mr. Wm. VI, 9
Carver, Phebe A. III, 65
Carver, Priscilla J. IV, 187
Carver, Rachel II, 344
Carver, Rachel V, 480
Carver, Rachel V, 524
Carver, Rachel H. II, 828
Carver, Rachel Smith II, 796
Carver, Rebecca IV, 142
Carver, Rebecca IV, 187
Carver, Rebecca IV, 292
Carver, Rebecca IV, 517
Carver, Rebekah IV, 323
Carver, Rebekah IV, 354
Carver, Richard II, 344
Carver, Richard II, 483
Carver, Ruth IV, 517
Carver, Ruth Ann V, 36
Carver, Ruth Ann V, 82
Carver, Ruth Anna V, 36
Carver, Ruth Anna V, 83
Carver, Sallie VI, 804
Carver, Samuel II, 344
Carver, Samuel Millhouse I, 40
Carver, Sarah II, 344
Carver, Sarah II, 483
Carver, Sarah II, 821
Carver, Sarah M. II, 786
Carver, Sarah M. II, 846
Carver, Sarah M. III, 65
Carver, Tabitha IV, 24
Carver, Tabitha V, 228
Carver, Talitha IV, 142
Carver, Talitha IV, 354
Carver, Talitha IV, 517
Carver, Thomas IV, 517
Carver, Thomas VI, 916
Carver, Wd. Hannah II, 821
Carver, Wd. Martha Parry II, 786
Carver, William T. IV, 517
Carver, Wilmer V, 36
Carver, Wm. II, 988
Carver, Wm. A. III, 65
Carver, Wm. A. III, 93
Carver, Wm. Williams II, 483
Carvier, Sarah Ann II, 784
Carvor, Grace II, 988
Carvor, William II, 988
Carwile, Blanch C. VI, 804
Carwile, David VI, 804
Carwile, David VI, 830
Carwile, Jacob VI, 804
Carwile, Jacob VI, 836
Carwile, Jacob VI, 862
Carwile, Joanoh VI, 804
Carwile, John VI, 804
Carwile, Judith VI, 804
Carwile, Martha VI, 804
Carwile, Martha VI, 836
Carwile, Mary VI, 804
Carwile, Matthew VI, 804
Carwile, Matthew S. VI, 804
Carwile, Nancy VI, 809
Carwile, Sarah W. VI, 804
Carwile, Thomas D. VI, 838
Carwile, Wm. VI, 804
Carwiles, Jacob VI, 860
Carwiles, John VI, 860
Carwiles, Mary VI, 808
Carwiles, Peggy VI, 860
Carwiles, Sarah W. VI, 804
Carwiles, William VI, 804
Carwiles, Wm. VI, 804
Cary, Abel IV, 688
Cary, Abigail III, 59
Cary, Alice L. III, 65
Cary, Alice L. III, 279
Cary, Amos H. V, 367
Cary, Ann II, 1048
Cary, Anna V, 227
Cary, Anna V, 322

Cary, Anna Elizabeth V, 376
Cary, Anne V, 367
Cary, Avis V, 989
Cary, Benjamin V, 227
Cary, Beula V, 481
Cary, Beulah II, 988
Cary, Beulah II, 1048
Cary, Beulah III, 66
Cary, Beulah III, 108
Cary, Bula McElwee V, 481
Cary, Charles Newton V, 367
Cary, Charles W. III, 66
Cary, Chas. E. III, 59
Cary, Cinthia VI, 481
Cary, Cordelia Bays V, 227
Cary, Cordelia Bays Green V, 242
Cary, Cynthia VI, 299
Cary, Cynthia VI, 304
Cary, Cynthia VI, 630
Cary, Cynthia VI, 631
Cary, Dallas J. V, 480
Cary, Dallas J. V, 481
Cary, Daniel V, 227
Cary, Daniel V, 322
Cary, David V, 367
Cary, David F. V, 367
Cary, Deborah II, 988
Cary, Deborah II, 1032
Cary, Deborah II, 1048
Cary, Ebenezer III, 480
Cary, Edith S. II, 734
Cary, Edmund IV, 688
Cary, Egbert II, 279
Cary, Egbert Snell II, 279
Cary, Egbert Snell II, 284
Cary, Elias V, 227
Cary, Elias V, 322
Cary, Elias V, 480
Cary, Elias VI, 304
Cary, Eliza V, 322
Cary, Eliza E. III, 66
Cary, Elizabeth II, 823
Cary, Elizabeth II, 1048
Cary, Elizabeth V, 157
Cary, Elizabeth V, 227
Cary, Elizabeth V, 416
Cary, Elizabeth V, 453
Cary, Elizabeth V, 480
Cary, Elizabeth V, 481
Cary, Elizabeth VI, 631
Cary, Elizabeth B. V, 831
Cary, Elizabeth Milton II, 279
Cary, Elizabeth Milton II, 284
Cary, Ellen H. III, 59
Cary, Elmer V, 453
Cary, Elwood O. V, 367
Cary, Enoch L. V, 480
Cary, Esther V, 481
Cary, Ferris A. III, 59
Cary, Frances Ellen III, 59
Cary, Hannah II, 988
Cary, Hannah V, 480
Cary, Hannah M. V, 481
Cary, Harold V, 481
Cary, Harriet E. V, 367
Cary, Harry V, 989
Cary, Helen II, 1070
Cary, Helen II, 1083
Cary, Henrietta E. III, 59
Cary, Hephzibah II, 988
Cary, Howard L. III, 59
Cary, Isaac V, 376
Cary, Isaac V, 416
Cary, Isabel B. II, 1070
Cary, Isabella II, 1070
Cary, Isabella IV, 466
Cary, Isabella IV, 497
Cary, James Edgar V, 367
Cary, Jane V, 376
Cary, Jane V, 480
Cary, Jervis III, 65
Cary, Jervis III, 279
Cary, Jesse Logan III, 66
Cary, Jesse Logan III, 108
Cary, John I, 1008
Cary, John III, 59
Cary, John V, 322
Cary, John V, 376
Cary, John V, 480
Cary, John V, 481
Cary, John VI, 304
Cary, John VI, 481
Cary, John VI, 630
Cary, John VI, 631
Cary, John VI, 855
Cary, John Milton III, 66
Cary, Jonathan V, 227
Cary, Jonathan VI, 304
Cary, Jonathan VI, 481
Cary, Jonathan VI, 630
Cary, Jonathan VI, 631
Cary, Joseph II, 823
Cary, Joseph II, 1048
Cary, Joseph III, 66
Cary, Joseph V, 831
Cary, Joseph M. V, 376
Cary, Joshua II, 988
Cary, Joshua II, 1048
Cary, Joshua Alban Cope II, 732
Cary, Kezia III, 480
Cary, Kezia III, 486
Cary, Louise B. V, 481
Cary, Lucinda V, 989
Cary, Lydia III, 66
Cary, Maplet H. III, 59
Cary, Margaret II, 988
Cary, Margaret II, 1032
Cary, Margaret V, 376
Cary, Margaret G. V, 322
Cary, Maria III, 66
Cary, Maria P. IV, 688
Cary, Martha II, 279
Cary, Martha II, 284
Cary, Martha Emily V, 481
Cary, Martha Eunty V, 480
Cary, Mary II, 828
Cary, Mary II, 988
Cary, Mary II, 1048
Cary, Mary III, 480
Cary, Mary V, 227
Cary, Mary V, 480
Cary, Mary VI, 399
Cary, Mary Ann V, 879
Cary, Mary Ann V, 881
Cary, Mary Charlotte V, 227
Cary, Mary E. V, 480
Cary, Mary Elizabeth II, 791
Cary, Mary Elizabeth II, 1048
Cary, Mary Elizabeth V, 480
Cary, Matthew V, 367
Cary, Melvin Donald III, 59
Cary, Miles VI, 13
Cary, Miles VI, 843
Cary, Minervia V, 367
Cary, Nathan V, 481
Cary, Nathan H. V, 480
Cary, Penninah V, 322
Cary, Penninah V, 367
Cary, Rachel V, 227
Cary, Rachel V, 322
Cary, Rachel V, 376
Cary, Rachel VI, 304
Cary, Rachel VI, 481
Cary, Rachel VI, 630
Cary, Rachel VI, 631
Cary, Rachel D. V, 367
Cary, Rachel D. V, 831
Cary, Rachel G. V, 227
Cary, Rachel G. V, 242
Cary, Rebecca V, 367
Cary, Rebecca V, 474
Cary, Rebecca V, 480
Cary, Rhoda V, 157
Cary, Rhoda V, 480
Cary, Rhoda V, 831
Cary, Robert V, 376
Cary, Robert V, 416
Cary, Robert Charles III, 59
Cary, Robert D. II, 1048
Cary, Rose III, 66
Cary, Rose III, 108
Cary, Ruth V, 376
Cary, Samson II, 483
Cary, Samson II, 988
Cary, Samson II, 1032
Cary, Samuel II, 988
Cary, Samuel II, 1032
Cary, Samuel II, 1048
Cary, Samuel V, 227
Cary, Samuel V, 322
Cary, Samuel V, 376
Cary, Samuel VI, 299
Cary, Samuel VI, 304
Cary, Samuel VI, 481
Cary, Samuel VI, 630
Cary, Samuel VI, 631
Cary, Samuel Albert V, 367
Cary, Samuel F. V, 480
Cary, Samuel, Jr. V, 227
Cary, Samuel, Jr. V, 322
Cary, Samuel, Jr. VI, 631
Cary, Samuel, Sr. V, 227
Cary, Sarah II, 1048
Cary, Sarah III, 65
Cary, Sarah III, 279
Cary, Sarah IV, 1204
Cary, Sarah VI, 104
Cary, Sarah VI, 109
Cary, Sarah VI, 304
Cary, Sarah VI, 481
Cary, Sarah VI, 630
Cary, Sarah VI, 631
Cary, Sarah VI, 843
Cary, Sarah Margaret V, 480
Cary, Sarah Margaret V, 481
Cary, Silas II, 1048
Cary, Susan IV, 1151
Cary, Susan IV, 1173
Cary, Susanna V, 376
Cary, Susanna V, 416
Cary, Susannah IV, 1204
Cary, Sylvanus V, 227
Cary, Thadeus L. V, 367
Cary, Thomas V, 157
Cary, Thomas V, 227
Cary, Thomas V, 322
Cary, Thomas V, 474
Cary, Thomas V, 480
Cary, Thomas V, 831
Cary, Thomas VI, 13
Cary, Thomas VI, 304
Cary, Thomas VI, 631
Cary, Thomas Canby II, 988
Cary, Thomas Lindley V, 367
Cary, Wd. Mary Elizabeth II, 823
Cary, William III, 480
Cary, William III, 486
Cary, Zenas V, 227
Casaway, David II, 202
Casaway, David II, 206
Casaway, John II, 206
Casaway, Mary II, 202
Casaway, Mary II, 206
Casaway, Thomas II, 206
Casaway, William II, 206
Casdorp, Herman II, 483
Casdorp, Herman II, 692
Casdorp, Mary II, 483
Casdorp, Wd. Mary II, 692
Casdrop, Elizabeth II, 483
Casdrop, Harman II, 344
Casdrop, Harmon II, 344
Casdrop, Herman II, 483
Casdrop, Mary II, 344
Casdrop, Mary II, 483
Casdrope, Harman II, 344
Casdrope, Mary II, 344
Case, A. J. IV, 1152
Case, Alice IV, 187
Case, Alice C. IV, 187
Case, Anna II, 1048
Case, Anna II, 1051
Case, Annie A. VI, 631
Case, Annie A. VI, 651
Case, Arthur B. III, 342
Case, Catharine II, 1048
Case, Catharine A. IV, 187
Case, Charles IV, 1152
Case, Charles G. IV, 467
Case, Eleanor Frost III, 378
Case, Eleanor Frost III, 384
Case, Elizabeth A. III, 66
Case, Emma IV, 187
Case, Etta IV, 1152
Case, Frances L. III, 66
Case, Frances L. III, 342
Case, Frances W. III, 66
Case, Frank Edw. III, 378
Case, G. W. IV, 1152
Case, Gulielma Maria Springett II, 1048
Case, Isaiah IV, 688
Case, J. Johnson IV, 187
Case, Jacob IV, 187
Case, James III, 66
Case, Jennie E. IV, 187
Case, John II, 1048
Case, Johnson IV, 187
Case, Joseph IV, 187
Case, Lydia VI, 375
Case, Lydia VI, 416
Case, Margaret I, 530
Case, Margaret IV, 688
Case, Margaret P. IV, 689
Case, Martha II, 1070
Case, Martha II, 1078
Case, Mary VI, 375
Case, Mary VI, 416
Case, Matilda M. III, 378
Case, Oliver C. IV, 187
Case, Paul Edward III, 378
Case, Paul Edward III, 384
Case, Philip II, 1048
Case, Reuben VI, 375
Case, Reuben VI, 416
Case, Robt. L., Jr. III, 66
Case, Sarah II, 1048
Case, Sarah IV, 1152
Case, Thos. III, 254
Case, Ureann IV, 688
Case, Wm. F. III, 66
Caseby, Edward II, 56
Caseby, Edward II, 82
Caseby, Elizabeth II, 56
Caseby, Elizabeth II, 82
Casey, Levina V, 156
Casey, Levina V, 730
Casey, Mary I, 930
Casey, Mary A. V, 832
Casey, Neoma VI, 958
Casey, William VI, 958
Cash, Eunice IV, 319
Cash, Eunice IV, 323
Cash, Frances H. VI, 994
Casham, Abraham VI, 891
Casham, Zilpha VI, 891
Cashart, Benjamin I. III, 248
Cashart, Elizabeth III, 248
Cashat, Ann I, 377
Cashat, Ann I, 416
Cashat, Ann V, 379
Cashat, David V, 379
Cashat, Dorcas I, 377
Cashat, Dorcas I, 402
Cashat, Eleanor I, 377
Cashat, Eleanor V, 379
Cashat, John I, 377
Cashat, Margaret I, 377
Cashat, Mary I, 417
Cashat, Rachel I, 377
Cashat, Rachel I, 416
Cashat, Sarah I, 377
Cashat, Sarah I, 416
Cashat, Thomas I, 377
Cashat, Thomas I, 416
Cashat, Thomas V, 379
Cashat, Welmet I, 378
Cashat, Welmett I, 377
Cashatt, Ann V, 228
Cashatt, Ann V, 323
Cashatt, Ann V, 379
Cashatt, David V, 228
Cashatt, David V, 323
Cashatt, David V, 379
Cashatt, Elanor V, 379
Cashatt, Eleanor I, 377
Cashatt, Eleanor I, 416
Cashatt, Eleanor V, 323
Cashatt, Eleanor V, 379
Cashatt, Eleanor V, 392
Cashatt, John I, 377
Cashatt, John I, 402
Cashatt, John V, 228
Cashatt, John V, 323
Cashatt, Joseph V, 228
Cashatt, Joseph V, 323
Cashatt, Margaret I, 377
Cashatt, Margaret V, 228
Cashatt, Margaret V, 323
Cashatt, Margaret V, 357
Cashatt, Maria V, 379
Cashatt, Maria Sarah V, 379
Cashatt, Mariah V, 323
Cashatt, Mary I, 377
Cashatt, Rachel I, 377
Cashatt, Rachel V, 228
Cashatt, Rachel V, 323
Cashatt, Rachel V, 357
Cashatt, Sarah I, 377
Cashatt, Sarah V, 323
Cashatt, Sarah V, 379
Cashatt, Sarah V, 429
Cashatt, Thomas V, 228
Cashatt, Thomas V, 323
Cashatt, Thomas V, 379
Cashatt, Welmett I, 377
Cashatt, Welmett I, 402
Cashet, Margaret I, 377
Cashet, Rachel I, 377
Cashet, Rachel I, 406
Cashett, Rachel V, 323
Cashman, Mary VI, 948
Cashner, David V, 730
Cashner, Eva V, 730
Cashner, Frank V, 730
Cashner, Harry V, 730
Cashner, John V, 989
Cashner, Lizzie V, 730
Cashow, Ellen III, 399
Cashow, Helena III, 399
Caskey, Charles IV, 806
Caskey, Chas. IV, 806
Caskey, Christina IV, 960
Caskey, Harriet IV, 806
Caskey, Hollis IV, 806
Caskey, Ida May IV, 1204
Caskey, James R. IV, 806
Caskey, John IV, 806
Caskey, John F. IV, 1204
Caskey, Mattie Pearl IV, 1204
Caskey, Vesta IV, 806
Casperson, Ann II, 116
Casperson, Ann II, 120
Casperson, Ann II, 146
Casperson, Ann II, 152
Cass, Benjamin V, 228
Cass, Burch V, 453
Cass, Cynthia A. V, 228
Cass, Jacob V, 228
Cass, Lydia V, 228
Cass, Mary Ann IV, 806
Cass, Mary Ann IV, 825
Cass, Phebe V, 228
Cassaday, Hannah E. IV, 1036
Cassaday, Jane II, 60
Cassady, Anna IV, 935
Cassady, Anna IV, 952
Cassall, Nicholas II, 483
Cassaway, David II, 206
Cassaway, John II, 206
Cassaway, Mary II, 206
Cassaway, Thomas II, 206
Cassaway, William II, 206
Cassel, Arnold II, 483
Cassel, Arnold II, 526
Cassel, Arnold II, 536
Cassel, Daniel II, 483
Cassel, Elizabeth II, 469
Cassel, Elizabeth II, 483
Cassel, Hannah II, 483
Cassel, James II, 344
Cassel, Johannes II, 344
Cassel, Lydia II, 453
Cassel, Lydia II, 483
Cassel, Lydia II, 517
Cassel, Lydia II, 526
Cassel, Mary II, 483
Cassel, Mary II, 495
Cassel, Nicholas II, 483
Cassel, Rebecca II, 483
Cassel, Rebecca II, 642
Cassel, Susanna II, 483
Cassel, Susannah II, 483
Cassel, Susannah II, 536
Cassel, Veronica II, 483
Cassel, Veronica II, 677
Cassell, Arnold II, 206
Cassell, Arnold II, 256
Cassell, Arnold II, 344
Cassell, Arnold II, 345
Cassell, Arnold II, 456
Cassell, Arnold II, 483
Cassell, Arnold II, 504
Cassell, Benjamin II, 344
Cassell, Daniel II, 344
Cassell, Daniel II, 483
Cassell, Deborah II, 206
Cassell, Deborah II, 256
Cassell, Deborah II, 344
Cassell, Elizabeth II, 344
Cassell, Elizabeth II, 483
Cassell, George II, 344
Cassell, Hannah II, 344
Cassell, Hannah II, 483
Cassell, Israel II, 456
Cassell, Israel II, 483
Cassell, James II, 344
Cassell, James II, 345
Cassell, James II, 483
Cassell, Johannes II, 344
Cassell, Johannis II, 344
Cassell, John II, 344
Cassell, John II, 483
Cassell, Lydia II, 344
Cassell, Lydia II, 483
Cassell, Margaret V, 730
Cassell, Mary II, 344
Cassell, Mary II, 482
Cassell, Nicholas II, 206
Cassell, Nicholas II, 256
Cassell, Nicholas II, 344
Cassell, Nicholas II, 483
Cassell, Peter II, 344
Cassell, Phebe II, 345
Cassell, Rebecca II, 456
Cassell, Rebecca II, 483
Cassell, Sarah II, 344
Cassell, Sarah II, 345
Cassell, Sarah II, 469
Cassell, Sarah II, 483
Cassell, Susanna II, 344
Cassell, Susanna II, 483
Cassell, Susanna II, 504
Cassell, Susannah II, 483
Cassell, Susannah II, 508
Cassell, Veronica II, 344
Cassell, Veronica II, 483
Cassell, Wd. ??? II, 483
Cassell, Wd. Susanna II, 345
Cassey, Elizabeth I, 134
Cassey, Elizabeth I, 159
Cassey, Emma I, 335
Cassidy, Ann IV, 935
Cassidy, Anna IV, 935
Cassidy, Eliza II, 786

assidy, Eliza II, 845
assidy, Eliza II, 846
assidy, Jane II, 53
assidy, Samuel II, 786
assidy, Samuel II, 796
assidy, Sarah II, 786
assidy, Sarah II, 796
assidy, Wd. Hannah Wood II, 796
assile, Sarah II, 483
assin, Charles L. II, 846
assin, Chas. Luke II, 786
assin, Emily II, 786
assin, Emma L. II, 786
assin, Isaac S. II, 846
assin, Isaac Sharpless II, 786
assin, Rachel II, 786
assin, Rebecca II, 786
assin, Ruthanna II, 786
assin, Susanna L. II, 846
assin, Susannah Shober II, 786
assin, Thos. II, 786
assin, Thos. W. II, 786
assin, Thos. Worrall II, 786
assle, Arnold II, 344
assle, Arnold II, 345
assle, John II, 344
assle, Wd. Susanna II, 345
asson, Curtis III, 66
asswell, Israel II, 345
asswell, John II, 345
ast, Ellen V, 554
ast, Ellen Hooten V, 664
ast, Irene V, 664
ast, Ollie V, 664
ast, Walter V, 36
aster, Elizabeth II, 345
aster, John II, 345
aster, Rachel II, 345
astle, Arnold III, 66
astle, Israel II, 345
astle, Julia M. IV, 187
astle, Peter II, 345
astle, Susannah II, 483
astle, William II, 345
astle, Wm. V, 989
astleman, Sarah E. IV, 187
asto, Hazel IV, 1204
asto, Nella IV, 1204
asto, William IV, 1204
asto, Wm. IV, 1204
astough, B. F. IV, 806
astrop, Elizabeth II, 483
asy, John V, 859
asy, Mary Alma V, 859
ate, Robert VI, 162
atell, Albert IV, 936
atell, Albert R. IV, 936
atell, Almina M. C. IV, 936
atell, Alzada IV, 936
atell, Ann IV, 936
atell, Arvine IV, 936
atell, Binford T. IV, 936
atell, Charles IV, 936
atell, Clara H. IV, 936
atell, Clark IV, 936
atell, David IV, 936
atell, Deborah IV, 936
atell, Edward IV, 936
atell, Eleanor IV, 936
atell, Elizabeth IV, 936
atell, Elizabeth C. IV, 936
atell, Elmina M. IV, 936
atell, Elmira IV, 936
atell, Emaline IV, 936
atell, Esthar Beulah IV, 936
atell, Esther IV, 936
atell, Ezra IV, 936
atell, Ezraetta IV, 936
atell, Fayetta IV, 936
atell, Hannah IV, 936
atell, Hannah W. IV, 936
atell, Henrietta IV, 936
atell, Isaac IV, 936
atell, James, Jr. IV, 936
atell, Jonathan W. IV, 936
atell, Julia Ann IV, 936
atell, Julian IV, 936
atell, Lanora B. IV, 936
atell, Lavina IV, 936
atell, Lewis IV, 936
atell, Lydia IV, 936
atell, Margaret IV, 936
atell, Martha IV, 936
atell, Mary IV, 936
atell, Mary Leota IV, 936
atell, Orlando J. IV, 936
atell, Orlando Mary Leota IV, 936
atell, Rebecca IV, 936
atell, Rebecca A. IV, 936
Catell, Sarah IV, 936
Catell, Sarah Elizabeth IV, 936
Catell, Sarah Jane IV, 935
Catell, Sarah Jane IV, 936
Catell, Thomas S. IV, 936
Catell, Uree E. IV, 936
Catell, Wm. IV, 936
Cater, Margaret I, 422
Cateright, Grace I, 141
Cateright, Thomas I, 134
Cateright, Thomas I, 141
Cates, Elizabeth I, 1116
Cates, Mary N. I, 925
Cates, Minerva Evelin I, 1116
Cates, Rachel I, 1116
Cates, Rachel I, 1131
Cathcart, Allen II, 345
Cathcart, Allen II, 483
Cathcart, Lydia II, 483
Cathcart, Martha II, 345
Cathcart, Mary II, 483
Cathcart, Mary II, 682
Cathcart, Sarah II, 345
Cathcart, Sarah II, 483
Cathcart, Sarah II, 597
Cathcart, Stephen II, 483
Cathcart, William II, 345
Cathcart, Wm. II, 483
Cather, Adeliah VI, 691
Cather, Ann VI, 691
Cather, Hannah E. VI, 375
Cather, Hannah Ellen VI, 438
Cather, Helen VI, 376
Cather, Helen G. VI, 375
Cather, James VI, 691
Cather, James L. VI, 375
Cather, Mabel VI, 375
Cather, Mabel VI, 376
Cather, Mabel VI, 439
Cather, Mary E. VI, 375
Cather, Mary Gail VI, 375
Cather, Mary Gail VI, 376
Cather, Millard F. VI, 375
Cather, Sarah G. VI, 375
Cather, Wilber E. VI, 376
Cather, Wilber Earl VI, 375
Cather, Wilber Earl VI, 439
Cather, Wilbur Earl VI, 376
Catheral, Rachel II, 211
Cathon, Jesse VI, 57
Cathon, John VI, 57
Cathon, Josiah West IV, 689
Cathrall, Benjamin II, 206
Cathrall, Benjamin II, 345
Cathrall, Edward II, 169
Cathrall, Edward II, 206
Cathrall, Edward II, 345
Cathrall, Edward II, 483
Cathrall, Hannah II, 206
Cathrall, Hannah II, 345
Cathrall, Hannah II, 483
Cathrall, Isaac II, 345
Cathrall, Mary II, 206
Cathrall, Mary II, 209
Cathrall, Mary II, 345
Cathrall, Rachel II, 169
Cathrall, Rachel II, 206
Cathrall, Rachel II, 211
Cathrall, Rachel II, 345
Cathrall, Sarah II, 206
Cathrall, Sarah II, 211
Cathrall, Sarah II, 345
Cathrell, Benjamin II, 345
Cathrell, Edward II, 345
Cathrell, Edward II, 483
Cathrell, Edward II, 490
Cathrell, Edward II, 548
Cathrell, Hannah II, 345
Cathrell, Hannah II, 483
Cathrell, Hannah II, 490
Cathrell, Isaac II, 345
Cathrell, Isaac II, 483
Cathrell, Isaac II, 490
Cathrell, Mary II, 345
Cathrell, Rachel II, 345
Cathrell, Rachel II, 483
Cathrell, Rachel II, 548
Cathrell, Sarah II, 345
Cathrill, Edward II, 345
Cathrill, Mary II, 345
Cathrill, Rachel II, 345
Catlett, Elizabeth VI, 988
Cato, Martha I, 299
Cato, Martha I, 301
Cato, Mary IV, 567
Cato, Mary IV, 570
Caton, Ann II, 345
Caton, Florence IV, 1204
Caton, Jacomiah III, 66
Caton, Lydia IV, 1356
Caton, Margaret IV, 1356
Caton, Mary F. II, 846
Caton, Nehemiah Colvin IV, 1356
Caton, Thomas Baker IV, 1356
Catrite, Robert I, 268
Catt, Ella IV, 1152
Catt, George IV, 1152
Cattall, Deborah IV, 759
Cattall, Hannah IV, 759
Cattall, James IV, 759
Cattel, Deborah II, 169
Cattel, Elijah II, 60
Cattel, Emeline IV, 936
Cattel, Hannah II, 169
Cattel, James II, 169
Cattel, Lydia IV, 1204
Cattel, Lydia IV, 1224
Cattel, Mary II, 60
Cattel, Wm. II, 60
Cattell, Albert IV, 79
Cattell, Albert IV, 123
Cattell, Albert R. IV, 1036
Cattell, Allen IV, 689
Cattell, Almina M. C. IV, 1003
Cattell, Almira IV, 123
Cattell, Amy T. IV, 936
Cattell, Amy T. IV, 973
Cattell, Ann II, 24
Cattell, Ann IV, 24
Cattell, Ann IV, 77
Cattell, Ann IV, 78
Cattell, Ann IV, 79
Cattell, Ann IV, 689
Cattell, Ann IV, 738
Cattell, Ann IV, 935
Cattell, Ann IV, 1036
Cattell, Ann D. IV, 79
Cattell, Ann D. IV, 689
Cattell, Anna IV, 82
Cattell, Anna May IV, 1036
Cattell, Annar IV, 936
Cattell, Annar IV, 992
Cattell, Anner IV, 939
Cattell, Beulah IV, 79
Cattell, Beulah IV, 84
Cattell, Beulah IV, 187
Cattell, Binford IV, 1014
Cattell, Caroline E. IV, 187
Cattell, Catharine IV, 1309
Cattell, Catharine V, 554
Cattell, Catherine DeVol IV, 1152
Cattell, Charity II, 169
Cattell, Charity II, 206
Cattell, Charles B. IV, 1036
Cattell, Chas. IV, 1036
Cattell, Clara IV, 993
Cattell, Clara H. IV, 993
Cattell, Cornelia IV, 187
Cattell, David IV, 24
Cattell, David IV, 78
Cattell, David IV, 79
Cattell, David IV, 84
Cattell, David IV, 87
Cattell, David IV, 187
Cattell, David IV, 241
Cattell, David IV, 1309
Cattell, David VI, 376
Cattell, David VI, 460
Cattell, David DeVol V, 554
Cattell, David M. IV, 187
Cattell, Deborah II, 169
Cattell, Deborah IV, 79
Cattell, Deborah IV, 684
Cattell, Deborah IV, 689
Cattell, Deborah IV, 701
Cattell, Deborah IV, 738
Cattell, Deborah IV, 765
Cattell, Deborah IV, 935
Cattell, Deborah IV, 936
Cattell, Deborah IV, 950
Cattell, Deborah IV, 992
Cattell, Deborah IV, 998
Cattell, Deborah IV, 1228
Cattell, Edith IV, 187
Cattell, Edith IV, 241
Cattell, Edith IV, 973
Cattell, Edith B. IV, 187
Cattell, Edith Elma IV, 187
Cattell, Edward IV, 187
Cattell, Edward D. IV, 187
Cattell, Eleanor IV, 806
Cattell, Eleanor IV, 931
Cattell, Eleanor IV, 1036
Cattell, Elijah II, 24
Cattell, Elijah II, 60
Cattell, Eliza B. IV, 187
Cattell, Elizabeth IV, 24
Cattell, Elizabeth IV, 71
Cattell, Elizabeth IV, 77
Cattell, Elizabeth IV, 78
Cattell, Elizabeth IV, 79
Cattell, Elizabeth IV, 82
Cattell, Elizabeth IV, 86
Cattell, Elizabeth IV, 689
Cattell, Elizabeth IV, 701
Cattell, Elizabeth IV, 927
Cattell, Elizabeth IV, 935
Cattell, Elizabeth IV, 993
Cattell, Elizabeth IV, 1036
Cattell, Elizabeth VI, 376
Cattell, Elizabeth C. IV, 930
Cattell, Elma IV, 79
Cattell, Elma IV, 187
Cattell, Elmar IV, 187
Cattell, Elmina IV, 79
Cattell, Elmina IV, 941
Cattell, Elmina IV, 999
Cattell, Elmina IV, 1003
Cattell, Emaline IV, 939
Cattell, Emeline J. IV, 187
Cattell, Emma L. IV, 187
Cattell, Enoch IV, 24
Cattell, Enoch IV, 29
Cattell, Enoch IV, 79
Cattell, Enoch IV, 83
Cattell, Enoch IV, 689
Cattell, Erce Etta IV, 1036
Cattell, Esther IV, 24
Cattell, Esther IV, 78
Cattell, Esther IV, 79
Cattell, Esther IV, 86
Cattell, Esther IV, 187
Cattell, Esther IV, 689
Cattell, Esther IV, 935
Cattell, Esther IV, 940
Cattell, Esther IV, 992
Cattell, Esther B. IV, 123
Cattell, Esther Beulah IV, 79
Cattell, Euphemia IV, 1036
Cattell, Everett V, 554
Cattell, Everett L. IV, 1309
Cattell, Everett L. V, 554
Cattell, Ezra IV, 78
Cattell, Ezra IV, 79
Cattell, Ezra IV, 104
Cattell, Ezra IV, 187
Cattell, Ezra IV, 260
Cattell, Ezra IV, 689
Cattell, Ezra IV, 935
Cattell, Ezra IV, 973
Cattell, Ezra IV, 997
Cattell, Ezra IV, 1036
Cattell, Ezra Brenaman IV, 187
Cattell, Fazetta IV, 950
Cattell, Florence Amy IV, 1036
Cattell, Frank C. IV, 1036
Cattell, Geo. IV, 187
Cattell, Geo. IV, 188
Cattell, Geo. IV, 260
Cattell, George IV, 79
Cattell, George IV, 104
Cattell, George IV, 187
Cattell, George IV, 267
Cattell, Gertrude H. IV, 806
Cattell, Hannah II, 169
Cattell, Hannah IV, 24
Cattell, Hannah IV, 78
Cattell, Hannah IV, 117
Cattell, Hannah IV, 689
Cattell, Hannah IV, 935
Cattell, Hannah W. IV, 79
Cattell, Hannah Wright IV, 78
Cattell, Harvey B. IV, 187
Cattell, Harvey G. IV, 187
Cattell, Henrietta IV, 997
Cattell, Herman IV, 1036
Cattell, Herman Clifford IV, 1036
Cattell, Homer IV, 1036
Cattell, Homer E. IV, 1036
Cattell, Hope II, 169
Cattell, Hope II, 206
Cattell, Horace IV, 187
Cattell, Horace M. IV, 187
Cattell, Howard IV, 1036
Cattell, Howard B. IV, 1036
Cattell, Huldah IV, 187
Cattell, Ida M. IV, 1014
Cattell, Ida May IV, 1036
Cattell, Isaac IV, 689
Cattell, Isaac IV, 935
Cattell, Isaac IV, 1036
Cattell, James II, 169
Cattell, James II, 206
Cattell, James IV, 79
Cattell, James IV, 82
Cattell, James IV, 684
Cattell, James IV, 689
Cattell, James IV, 701
Cattell, James IV, 738
Cattell, James IV, 765
Cattell, James IV, 919
Cattell, James IV, 935
Cattell, James IV, 936
Cattell, James IV, 992
Cattell, James IV, 998
Cattell, James IV, 1228
Cattell, James, Jr. II, 169
Cattell, James, Jr. IV, 79
Cattell, James, Jr. IV, 947
Cattell, Jane II, 169
Cattell, Jane H. IV, 79
Cattell, Jane H. IV, 104
Cattell, Jane H. IV, 187
Cattell, Jane H. IV, 188
Cattell, Jane H. IV, 260
Cattell, Janet G. IV, 1036
Cattell, Jonas II, 206
Cattell, Jonas II, 249
Cattell, Jonas IV, 24
Cattell, Jonas IV, 77
Cattell, Jonas IV, 78
Cattell, Jonas IV, 79
Cattell, Jonas IV, 82
Cattell, Jonas IV, 86
Cattell, Jonas IV, 935
Cattell, Jonas VI, 376
Cattell, Jonas D. IV, 689
Cattell, Jonas, Jr. IV, 79
Cattell, Jonathan IV, 950
Cattell, Jonathan W. IV, 79
Cattell, Jonathan Wright IV, 78
Cattell, Jones D. IV, 689
Cattell, Joseph II, 206
Cattell, Joseph IV, 689
Cattell, Joseph IV, 806
Cattell, Joseph IV, 931
Cattell, Joseph IV, 935
Cattell, Joseph IV, 936
Cattell, Joseph IV, 939
Cattell, Joseph IV, 992
Cattell, Joseph IV, 1036
Cattell, Josiah II, 169
Cattell, Julia Ann IV, 689
Cattell, Juliann IV, 689
Cattell, Katie May IV, 1036
Cattell, Leota IV, 1036
Cattell, Levi IV, 973
Cattell, Lewis IV, 187
Cattell, Lewis IV, 1036
Cattell, Lewis E. IV, 187
Cattell, Lois IV, 1036
Cattell, Lonora B. IV, 993
Cattell, Lurena P. IV, 187
Cattell, Lydia IV, 689
Cattell, Lydia IV, 935
Cattell, Lydia IV, 998
Cattell, Lydia IV, 1204
Cattell, Lydia H. P. IV, 187
Cattell, Lydia H. P. IV, 467
Cattell, Lydia H. P. IV, 936
Cattell, Margaret IV, 78
Cattell, Margaret IV, 79
Cattell, Margaret IV, 84
Cattell, Margaret IV, 87
Cattell, Margaret IV, 187
Cattell, Margaret IV, 241
Cattell, Margaret VI, 376
Cattell, Margaret VI, 460
Cattell, Marianna IV, 79
Cattell, Marianna IV, 187
Cattell, Marjorie IV, 187
Cattell, Marjorie IV, 188
Cattell, Martha IV, 24
Cattell, Martha IV, 29
Cattell, Martha IV, 79
Cattell, Martha IV, 689
Cattell, Martha IV, 935
Cattell, Martha Jr IV, 79
Cattell, Martha P. IV, 187
Cattell, Martha, Jr. IV, 83
Cattell, Mary II, 24
Cattell, Mary II, 169
Cattell, Mary II, 206
Cattell, Mary II, 249
Cattell, Mary IV, 25
Cattell, Mary IV, 79
Cattell, Mary IV, 84
Cattell, Mary IV, 123
Cattell, Mary IV, 187
Cattell, Mary IV, 689
Cattell, Mary IV, 935
Cattell, Mary IV, 950
Cattell, Mary IV, 999
Cattell, Mary IV, 1204
Cattell, Mary IV, 1228
Cattell, Mary B. IV, 187
Cattell, Mary B. IV, 267
Cattell, Maryanna IV, 187
Cattell, Maryanne IV, 79
Cattell, Mathew P. IV, 187
Cattell, Mays IV, 1036
Cattell, Mira J. IV, 188
Cattell, Myra IV, 78
Cattell, Myra IV, 79

Cattell, Myra IV, 87
Cattell, Myra G. IV, 187
Cattell, Myra J. IV, 187
Cattell, Oliver IV, 187
Cattell, Orlando IV, 689
Cattell, Rachel IV, 24
Cattell, Rachel IV, 71
Cattell, Rachel IV, 78
Cattell, Rachel IV, 82
Cattell, Rebecca A. IV, 936
Cattell, Rebecca C. IV, 1036
Cattell, Richard Bartley Channing IV, 187
Cattell, Ruthan P. IV, 188
Cattell, Ruthanna IV, 79
Cattell, Ruthanna IV, 104
Cattell, Ruthanna IV, 187
Cattell, Ruthanna IV, 260
Cattell, Ruthanna IV, 936
Cattell, Ruthanna P. IV, 79
Cattell, Ruthanna P. IV, 187
Cattell, Sarah IV, 689
Cattell, Sarah IV, 765
Cattell, Sarah IV, 935
Cattell, Sarah VI, 376
Cattell, Sarah Elizabeth IV, 79
Cattell, Sarah J. IV, 1014
Cattell, Sarah J. IV, 1036
Cattell, Sarah Lela IV, 1036
Cattell, Stephenson IV, 187
Cattell, Tazetta C. IV, 978
Cattell, Thomas IV, 993
Cattell, Thos. IV, 993
Cattell, Thos. S. IV, 927
Cattell, Thos. S. IV, 1036
Cattell, Urie Etta IV, 1036
Cattell, William II, 169
Cattell, William IV, 24
Cattell, William IV, 79
Cattell, William IV, 84
Cattell, William M. IV, 187
Cattell, William Maurice IV, 187
Cattell, William, Jr. IV, 187
Cattell, Winifred IV, 1309
Cattell, Wm. II, 24
Cattell, Wm. IV, 79
Cattell, Wm. IV, 123
Cattell, Wm. IV, 950
Cattell, Wm. IV, 999
Cattle, Ann II, 206
Cattle, Charity II, 206
Cattle, Deborah II, 206
Cattle, Elizabeth II, 206
Cattle, Hannah II, 206
Cattle, Hope II, 206
Cattle, Hope II, 237
Cattle, James II, 206
Cattle, James, Jr. II, 206
Cattle, Jane II, 206
Cattle, Jane II, 240
Cattle, Jonas II, 206
Cattle, Joseph II, 206
Cattle, Josiah II, 206
Cattle, Mary II, 206
Cattle, Rachel II, 206
Cattle, Ruthanna P. IV, 187
Cattle, Sarah VI, 376
Cattle, William II, 206
Catton, Josiah VI, 57
Cattreke, Mary I, 134
Cattreke, Mary I, 166
Cattreke, Thomas, Jr. I, 134
Cattreke, Thomas, Jr. I, 166
Cattrell, Elizabeth IV, 1036
Cattrell, Isaac IV, 1036
Cattrell, Rebecca C. IV, 1036
Cattrell, Thos. S. IV, 1036
Caudle, Elizabeth I, 984
Caudle, Jemima I, 756
Caudle, Jemima I, 760
Caudle, Lydea I, 803
Caudle, Vallie I, 939
Cauley, Berry VI, 891
Cauley, Rhoda VI, 891
Caulk, Lydia II, 484
Caulk, Lydia II, 498
Caulk, Oliver II, 484
Caulk, Oliver II, 498
Caulk, Phebe II, 484
Caulk, Phebe II, 498
Caulley, Jonathan II, 60
Caulley, Margaret II, 345
Caully, Hannah II, 60
Causey, C. L. I, 939
Causey, Chester Roy I, 939
Causey, Ila I, 922
Causey, Rebecca J. I, 803
Causey, Rebecca J. I, 839
Causey, Wm. Garlin I, 939
Causler, Louisa C. II, 294
Caustin, Martha III, 66
Cavan, Dora J. IV, 1309
Cavan, Jordan IV, 1309
Cavan, Sarah VI, 467
Cavan, Sarah VI, 481
Cavanagh, ??? III, 66
Cave, Boyd V, 989
Cave, J. IV, 1274
Cave, John V, 989
Cave, Joseph IV, 1274
Cave, Mary Jane IV, 1274
Caven, Ann E. V, 898
Caven, Mary E. V, 898
Cavender, Abraham V, 898
Cavender, Abram V, 898
Cavender, Amos V, 898
Cavender, Andrew L. V, 898
Cavender, Anthony V, 898
Cavender, Anthony T. V, 898
Cavender, Elizabeth II, 813
Cavender, Elizabeth II, 846
Cavender, Elizabeth II, 901
Cavender, Elizabeth M. II, 846
Cavender, Elizabeth M. II, 906
Cavender, Fanny II, 813
Cavender, Fanny II, 846
Cavender, Fanny II, 906
Cavender, Hannah II, 846
Cavender, Hannah II, 901
Cavender, Hannah V, 898
Cavender, Harriett V, 898
Cavender, Ida V, 616
Cavender, John H. II, 846
Cavender, John H. II, 901
Cavender, Martha V, 798
Cavender, Mrs. ??? V, 616
Cavender, Rebecca V, 898
Cavender, Thomas S. II, 846
Cavender, Thos. II, 846
Cavender, Thos. II, 901
Cavender, Thos. S. II, 906
Cavender, Thos. Shoemaker II, 813
Cavender, Wm. V, 898
Caveny, Mary II, 988
Caves, J. IV, 1274
Cavin, Sarah VI, 481
Cavin, Sarah VI, 586
Cavin, Sarah VI, 736
Cavin, Sarah VI, 793
Caviness, Isaac I, 378
Caviness, Mary I, 378
Caviness, Mary A. I, 378
Cavis, Joseph IV, 1274
Cawl, ??? III, 67
Cawl, Abbie III, 66
Cawl, Abbie III, 259
Cawl, Eliza III, 66
Cawl, Eliza III, 67
Cawl, Florence III, 17
Cawl, Florence III, 66
Cawl, Florence A. III, 59
Cawl, Florence A. III, 66
Cawl, Florence A. III, 100
Cawl, Franklin R. III, 66
Cawl, Franklin R. III, 259
Cawl, Henrietta E. III, 59
Cawl, Henrietta E. III, 66
Cawl, Henrietta Estelle III, 66
Cawl, Hugh III, 66
Cawl, Mary E. III, 66
Cawl, Melvin Allen III, 66
Cawl, Robert III, 66
Cawl, Robert C. III, 66
Cawl, Robert C. III, 100
Cawl, Robert Cone III, 66
Cawl, Robert E. III, 59
Cawl, Robt. Cone III, 17
Cawl, Robt. E. III, 66
Cawl, Ruth F. III, 100
Cawl, Ruth Florence III, 66
Cawl, Stephen III, 66
Cawley, Allen VI, 891
Cawley, Amy II, 24
Cawley, Amy II, 55
Cawley, Amy II, 60
Cawley, Amy II, 116
Cawley, Amy II, 120
Cawley, Amy II, 130
Cawley, Amy B. II, 147
Cawley, Elizabeth B. II, 144
Cawley, Elizabeth B. II, 151
Cawley, Hannah II, 24
Cawley, Hannah II, 55
Cawley, Hannah II, 60
Cawley, Hannah II, 130
Cawley, James VI, 891
Cawley, Jeremiah VI, 924
Cawley, Jeremiah VI, 947
Cawley, Jonathan II, 24
Cawley, Jonathan II, 55
Cawley, Jonathan II, 60
Cawley, Jonathan II, 130
Cawley, Mary VI, 891
Cawley, Polly VI, 891
Cawley, Samuel II, 24
Cawley, Samuel II, 55
Cawley, Samuel II, 60
Cawley, Wm. A. II, 144
Cawley, Wm. A. II, 151
Cawthorn, Eliza A. VI, 804
Cawthorn, Wm. B. VI, 804
Cay, Ann O. VI, 804
Cay, Nelson VI, 804
Cayle, Henrietta I, 611
Cayton, Mary F. II, 846
Cayton, Mary F. II, 930
Cazzins, Eleanor II, 496
Cazzins, George II, 496
Cearl, Elizabeth II, 60
Ceas, Lenora IV, 1274
Ceas, Louis IV, 1274
Cecal, Lydia Elizabeth I, 874
Cecal, Lydia Elizabeth I, 895
Cecherst, Ella I, 900
Cecil, Alfred III, 66
Cecil, Alfred III, 268
Cecil, Allen Brown I, 922
Cecil, Ardella V, 798
Cecil, Aurelia Lualta I, 922
Cecil, Berdie IV, 1204
Cecil, Bernice I, 939
Cecil, Carl Myron I, 922
Cecil, Correl M. I, 939
Cecil, D. Loretta I, 611
Cecil, Daisy IV, 1204
Cecil, David I, 939
Cecil, David Allen I, 922
Cecil, David Myers I, 922
Cecil, David O. I, 611
Cecil, David O. I, 922
Cecil, David O. I, 939
Cecil, Diana Luatta I, 922
Cecil, Dianna L. I, 939
Cecil, Eliza I, 936
Cecil, Ella V, 323
Cecil, Ella L. III, 66
Cecil, Ella L. III, 267
Cecil, Ella L. III, 268
Cecil, Esther IV, 1152
Cecil, Esther IV, 1204
Cecil, Esther Ann IV, 1204
Cecil, Esther Bernice I, 922
Cecil, George Donovan I, 922
Cecil, Gurney I, 631
Cecil, Harley J. V, 798
Cecil, Helen Elizabeth I, 922
Cecil, Helen Elizabeth I, 939
Cecil, Jesse Elisabeth I, 611
Cecil, Jesse Elizabeth I, 922
Cecil, Jesse Elizabeth I, 937
Cecil, Jesse W. I, 922
Cecil, Jessie Elizabeth I, 631
Cecil, Jessie Elizabeth I, 939
Cecil, Joseph Gilbert I, 922
Cecil, L. Elizabeth I, 922
Cecil, Lillie Lee I, 922
Cecil, Luetta I, 922
Cecil, Lydia E. I, 852
Cecil, Mabel Florence V, 798
Cecil, Margaret III, 66
Cecil, Margaret III, 268
Cecil, Mary IV, 1204
Cecil, Mary V, 228
Cecil, Mary V, 255
Cecil, Mollie IV, 1152
Cecil, Mollie IV, 1204
Cecil, Naomi IV, 1152
Cecil, Naomi IV, 1204
Cecil, Russell Teague V, 798
Cecil, Susan Elisabeth I, 615
Cecil, William IV, 1204
Cecil, William E. I, 939
Cecil, William Evan I, 922
Cecil, Willie IV, 1204
Cecille, Mary IV, 378
Cecille, Mary IV, 517
Cell, Sarah I, 418
Cellem, Elizabeth IV, 467
Cells, Charles V, 554
Cells, Lucie V, 554
Cells, Susie V, 554
Cemery, Miriam W. IV, 615
Cemery, Miriam W. IV, 665
Cemmack, James I, 1027
Cemmack, Margaret I, 1027
Cemmack, Mary I, 1027
Cemonas, Nancy VI, 953
Cemonas, Stephen VI, 953
Cents, Catharine VI, 908
Cerline, John II, 442
Cernea, Anna T. II, 846
Cernea, William T. III, 66
Cernea, Wm. T. II, 846
Cerres, Sarah II, 345
Certain, Duncan V, 664
Certain, Duncan M. V, 664
Certain, Matilda J. V, 664
Certain, Sarah A. V, 664
Cese, Charlotte III, 168
Cese, Charlotte III, 267
Cessn, Stephen I, 530
Cessna, Stephen I, 530
Cester, Martha I, 531
Cester, Martha I, 572
Cester, William I, 531
Cester, William I, 572
Cetey, Mary VI, 900
Cetey, Sam VI, 900
Cetty, Christian VI, 900
Chace, Abby L. II, 1087
Chace, Abby L. II, 1089
Chace, Anna H. II, 957
Chace, Hannah II, 1048
Chace, Harvey II, 1048
Chace, Jane II, 957
Chace, Jane C. II, 1048
Chace, Jonathan II, 957
Chace, Jonathan II, 1048
Chace, Marcia III, 66
Chace, Marcia III, 257
Chace, Marcia R. III, 66
Chace, Mary Ann II, 284
Chace, Sarah P. VI, 741
Chace, William Beverly II, 284
Chace, Wm. Henry III, 66
Chace, Wm. Henry III, 257
Chadawick, Margret I, 803
Chadewick, Anna I, 530
Chads, Ann II, 345
Chadwalader, Isaac VI, 593
Chadwalader, John VI, 593
Chadwalader, Marrah VI, 593
Chadwalader, Martha VI, 593
Chadwalader, Mary VI, 593
Chadwalader, Ruth VI, 593
Chadwalader, Sarah VI, 593
Chadwell, Emily IV, 467
Chadwell, Emily IV, 491
Chadwick, ??? III, 359
Chadwick, Aaron III, 66
Chadwick, Anna I, 530
Chadwick, Anna V, 300
Chadwick, Annie H. III, 66
Chadwick, Asenath I, 923
Chadwick, Clarence W. III, 66
Chadwick, Daniel III, 66
Chadwick, Daniel III, 150
Chadwick, Elisa V, 895
Chadwick, Elisa V, 898
Chadwick, Elisabeth II, 484
Chadwick, Eliza III, 44
Chadwick, Eliza V, 36
Chadwick, Elizabeth I, 778
Chadwick, Elizabeth I, 923
Chadwick, Elizabeth II, 484
Chadwick, Elizabeth II, 555
Chadwick, Emma W. III, 66
Chadwick, Eunice V, 36
Chadwick, Eunice V, 898
Chadwick, Eunice V, 924
Chadwick, Florence III, 20
Chadwick, Florence III, 66
Chadwick, Hepseba V, 895
Chadwick, Hepsibah V, 36
Chadwick, Hepsibah V, 37
Chadwick, Jane II, 207
Chadwick, Jane II, 233
Chadwick, Jane II, 980
Chadwick, Jane II, 988
Chadwick, John I, 778
Chadwick, John I, 803
Chadwick, John I, 923
Chadwick, John II, 484
Chadwick, John L. III, 66
Chadwick, John R. III, 66
Chadwick, Joshua I, 778
Chadwick, Joshua I, 803
Chadwick, Joshua, Jr. I, 803
Chadwick, Leah I, 778
Chadwick, Margaret I, 778
Chadwick, Margarett I, 803
Chadwick, Margret I, 803
Chadwick, Mary I, 778
Chadwick, Mary I, 803
Chadwick, Mary III, 66
Chadwick, Mary III, 150
Chadwick, Mary III, 359
Chadwick, Miriam I, 778
Chadwick, Miriam I, 803
Chadwick, Mittie I, 268
Chadwick, Mitty I, 268
Chadwick, Mitty IV, 25
Chadwick, Paul III, 66
Chadwick, Paul A. III, 66
Chadwick, Phebe III, 66
Chadwick, Phebe III, 150
Chadwick, Phebe V, 898
Chadwick, Phebe V, 925
Chadwick, Rhoda V, 925
Chadwick, Richard V, 925
Chadwick, Stanley H. III, 20
Chadwick, Stanley H. III, 66
Chadwick, Thadeus V, 895
Chadwick, William II, 207
Chadwick, William II, 233
Chadwick, Wm. II, 980
Chadwick, Wm. II, 988
Chadwicks, Mitty IV, 25
Chaffant, Aaron V, 323
Chaffant, Abner V, 37
Chaffant, Abner V, 323
Chaffant, Bulah V, 323
Chaffant, Esther V, 323
Chaffant, Jacob V, 323
Chaffant, Jonathan B. V, 323
Chaffant, Margaret V, 323
Chaffant, Mary V, 323
Chaffant, Nathan H. V, 323
Chaffant, Priscilla V, 323
Chaffant, Ruth V, 315
Chaffant, Ruth V, 323
Chaffant, Sarah V, 323
Chaffant, William V, 323
Chaffee, Caroline II, 717
Chaffin, A. IV, 1248
Chaffin, A. M. IV, 1248
Chaffin, Ananias IV, 123
Chaffin, Catharine VI, 891
Chaffin, E. J. IV, 1248
Chaffin, Edward VI, 891
Chaffin, James IV, 188
Chaffin, Jane VI, 891
Chaffin, John VI, 891
Chaffin, Joseph VI, 891
Chaffin, Joseph VI, 938
Chaffin, Joshua VI, 891
Chaffin, Josiah VI, 937
Chaffin, Lurena Margaret VI, 891
Chaffin, Lydia IV, 1309
Chaffin, Martha Ann VI, 891
Chaffin, Mary III, 335
Chaffin, Mary III, 347
Chaffin, Mary VI, 891
Chaffin, Nancy D. VI, 891
Chaffin, Polly VI, 938
Chaffin, Rebecca VI, 869
Chaffin, Rhoda VI, 937
Chaffin, Stephen VI, 869
Chaffin, Stephen VI, 891
Chaffin, Stephen VI, 938
Chaffin, Wm. IV, 1309
Chafin, Edward VI, 891
Chafin, John II, 169
Chafin, Mary VI, 891
Chaimbers, Sarah I, 431
Chain, Anna IV, 615
Chain, Anna IV, 631
Chain, Macre II, 846
Chain, Macre W. II, 786
Chaldwell, Sarah IV, 643
Chalender, Chas. V, 323
Chalender, Jaeson V, 229
Chalfan, Aaron IV, 188
Chalfan, James IV, 188
Chalfan, James IV, 292
Chalfan, Margaret IV, 188
Chalfan, Ruth IV, 188
Chalfan, Ruth IV, 292
Chalfant, Aaron V, 319
Chalfant, Aaron V, 323
Chalfant, Abel IV, 79
Chalfant, Abel IV, 103
Chalfant, Abel IV, 323
Chalfant, Abel V, 949
Chalfant, Able IV, 79
Chalfant, Abner V, 300
Chalfant, Abner V, 323
Chalfant, Amos IV, 79
Chalfant, Ann IV, 79
Chalfant, Ann IV, 123
Chalfant, Ann IV, 378
Chalfant, Ann IV, 452
Chalfant, Ann IV, 689
Chalfant, Ann IV, 936
Chalfant, Annanias IV, 79
Chalfant, Asa L. V, 300
Chalfant, Asa L. V, 323
Chalfant, Beulah V, 323
Chalfant, Bulah V, 323
Chalfant, Edwin V, 300
Chalfant, Edwin V, 323
Chalfant, Eli IV, 79
Chalfant, Eliza IV, 79

Chalfant, Eliza Ann IV, 79
Chalfant, Eliza Ann IV, 103
Chalfant, Eliza Ann IV, 123
Chalfant, Elizabeth IV, 79
Chalfant, Elizabeth IV, 108
Chalfant, Elizabeth IV, 323
Chalfant, Elizabeth IV, 378
Chalfant, Elizabeth V, 319
Chalfant, Elizabeth V, 323
Chalfant, Ephraim IV, 323
Chalfant, Esther V, 323
Chalfant, Evan IV, 79
Chalfant, Evan, Jr. IV, 79
Chalfant, Ezekiel IV, 323
Chalfant, Ezekiel IV, 378
Chalfant, Gauis IV, 689
Chalfant, Hannah IV, 79
Chalfant, Hannah IV, 103
Chalfant, Hannah IV, 323
Chalfant, Hannah V, 949
Chalfant, Jacob V, 323
Chalfant, Jesse IV, 323
Chalfant, Jesse IV, 378
Chalfant, Jesse IV, 452
Chalfant, Jesse IV, 455
Chalfant, Joel IV, 323
Chalfant, Joel IV, 378
Chalfant, Jonathan V, 323
Chalfant, Jonathan B. V, 323
Chalfant, Joseph Negus IV, 123
Chalfant, Joshua IV, 79
Chalfant, Lydia IV, 79
Chalfant, Lydia IV, 323
Chalfant, Lydia IV, 341
Chalfant, Lydia IV, 378
Chalfant, Lydia IV, 455
Chalfant, Margaret V, 300
Chalfant, Margaret V, 323
Chalfant, Mary II, 801
Chalfant, Mary IV, 79
Chalfant, Mary IV, 96
Chalfant, Mary IV, 323
Chalfant, Mary V, 323
Chalfant, Miller IV, 323
Chalfant, Millera IV, 323
Chalfant, Milton IV, 323
Chalfant, Nathan V, 323
Chalfant, Nathan H. V, 323
Chalfant, Phebe II, 801
Chalfant, Phebe IV, 323
Chalfant, Phebe IV, 350
Chalfant, Priscilla V, 323
Chalfant, Rachel IV, 79
Chalfant, Rachel IV, 323
Chalfant, Rachel IV, 378
Chalfant, Rachel IV, 455
Chalfant, Rachel N. IV, 323
Chalfant, Rachel N. IV, 352
Chalfant, Robert IV, 323
Chalfant, Robert IV, 378
Chalfant, Ruth IV, 79
Chalfant, Ruth V, 300
Chalfant, Ruth V, 323
Chalfant, Sarah IV, 79
Chalfant, Sarah IV, 105
Chalfant, Sarah V, 300
Chalfant, Sarah V, 323
Chalfant, Thomas IV, 79
Chalfant, Thos. II, 801
Chalfant, William V, 323
Chalfant, William P. V, 300
Chalfant, Wm. V, 323
Chalfin, Ann IV, 378
Chalfin, Jesse IV, 378
Chalfinch, Aaron V, 228
Chalfinch, Abner V, 228
Chalfinch, Beulah V, 228
Chalfinch, Esther V, 228
Chalfinch, Jacob V, 228
Chalfinch, Jonathan V, 228
Chalfinch, Mary V, 228
Chalfinch, Nathan V, 228
Chalfinch, Priscilla V, 228
Chalfinch, Ruth V, 228
Chalfinch, William V, 228
Chalfond, Aaron V, 228
Chalfont, Aaron V, 228
Chalfont, Abner V, 228
Chalfont, Abner V, 260
Chalfont, Abner V, 300
Chalfont, Abner V, 323
Chalfont, Ada V, 229
Chalfont, Adaline V, 229
Chalfont, Asa L. V, 300
Chalfont, Asa L. V, 323
Chalfont, Beulah V, 228
Chalfont, Bulah M. V, 228
Chalfont, Bulah M. V, 257
Chalfont, Edwin V, 300
Chalfont, Edwin V, 323
Chalfont, Eliza Ann IV, 123
Chalfont, Eliza Ann IV, 131
Chalfont, Elizabeth V, 228
Chalfont, Elizabeth V, 229
Chalfont, Esther V, 227
Chalfont, Esther V, 228
Chalfont, Glenn V, 229
Chalfont, Hester Leuie V, 229
Chalfont, Jacob V, 228
Chalfont, Jacob V, 229
Chalfont, Jonathan V, 228
Chalfont, Jonathan V, 229
Chalfont, Lydia IV, 79
Chalfont, Lydia IV, 95
Chalfont, Margaret V, 228
Chalfont, Margaret V, 300
Chalfont, Margaret V, 323
Chalfont, Martha V, 300
Chalfont, Martha V, 309
Chalfont, Mary V, 228
Chalfont, Nathan V, 228
Chalfont, Nathan V, 229
Chalfont, Ortla Glenford V, 229
Chalfont, Priscilla V, 228
Chalfont, Priscilla V, 267
Chalfont, Priscilla V, 379
Chalfont, Priscilla V, 423
Chalfont, Ruth I, 1008
Chalfont, Ruth V, 227
Chalfont, Ruth V, 228
Chalfont, Ruth V, 229
Chalfont, Ruth V, 257
Chalfont, Ruth V, 260
Chalfont, Ruth V, 267
Chalfont, Ruth V, 300
Chalfont, Ruth V, 323
Chalfont, Sarah V, 228
Chalfont, Sarah V, 300
Chalfont, Sarah V, 323
Chalfont, William V, 227
Chalfont, William V, 228
Chalfont, William V, 229
Chalfont, William V, 267
Chalfont, William V, 323
Chalfont, William P. V, 300
Chalfont, Williamd, Jr. V, 228
Chalfont, Wm. V, 228
Chalfont, Wm. V, 257
Chalfont, Wm., Jr. V, 300
Chaliner, Elizabeth II, 207
Chalkley, Abigail II, 345
Chalkley, Ann II, 484
Chalkley, George II, 345
Chalkley, Martha II, 345
Chalkley, Martha II, 473
Chalkley, Martha II, 484
Chalkley, Rebecca II, 345
Chalkley, Rebecca II, 484
Chalkley, Rebecca II, 563
Chalkley, Robert II, 345
Chalkley, Robert II, 484
Chalkley, Thomas II, 345
Chalkley, Thomas II, 473
Chalkley, Thomas II, 484
Chalkley, Thomas II, 521
Chalkley, Thomas II, 522
Chalkley, Thomas II, 563
Chalkley, Thos. II, 345
Challender, Andrew V, 229
Challender, Charles A. V, 323
Challender, Chas. V, 323
Challender, Henry V, 229
Challender, Jaeson V, 229
Challender, Martha J. V, 323
Challender, Mary Jane V, 323
Chalmers, Everett III, 66
Chalmers, Gordon Keith III, 66
Chalmers, Gordon Keith III, 307
Chalmers, Mary Ann VI, 473
Chalmers, Mary Ann VI, 481
Chalmers, Mary Ann VI, 492
Chalmers, Mary Ann VI, 509
Chalmers, Mary Ann VI, 510
Chalmers, Mary Ann VI, 512
Chalmers, Mary Ann VI, 513
Chalmers, Mary Ann VI, 542
Chalmers, Mary Ann VI, 543
Chalmers, Maryc Ann VI, 511
Chalmers, Roberta T. III, 66
Chalmers, Roberta T. III, 307
Chalmers, Sarah III, 66
Chalmers, Wm. VI, 481
Chalnoer, Daniel VI, 162
Chaloner, Daniel II, 484
Chamberlain, Abel II, 484
Chamberlain, Abigail VI, 376
Chamberlain, Achsah II, 988
Chamberlain, Acsah II, 988
Chamberlain, Acsah II, 990
Chamberlain, Ann IV, 323
Chamberlain, Benjamin II, 345
Chamberlain, Benjamin II, 484
Chamberlain, Benjamin II, 793
Chamberlain, Catharine Ann III, 66
Chamberlain, Catharine Ann III, 148
Chamberlain, Cora IV, 1274
Chamberlain, Edith B. VI, 532
Chamberlain, Edw VI, 186
Chamberlain, Edward VI, 162
Chamberlain, Edward VI, 174
Chamberlain, Edward VI, 186
Chamberlain, Eleanor III, 66
Chamberlain, Eleanor III, 148
Chamberlain, Elija VI, 376
Chamberlain, Eliza IV, 615
Chamberlain, Eliza IV, 630
Chamberlain, Elizabeth IV, 323
Chamberlain, Elizabeth VI, 376
Chamberlain, Endora M. I, 301
Chamberlain, Esther VI, 532
Chamberlain, Etta Belle V, 379
Chamberlain, Francis VI, 532
Chamberlain, George IV, 1274
Chamberlain, George VI, 532
Chamberlain, Gersham VI, 376
Chamberlain, Gilbert III, 66
Chamberlain, Gilbert III, 148
Chamberlain, Hannah IV, 323
Chamberlain, Hannah IV, 331
Chamberlain, Jacob V, 379
Chamberlain, James II, 846
Chamberlain, James IV, 323
Chamberlain, James V, 989
Chamberlain, James D. V, 989
Chamberlain, Jane I, 378
Chamberlain, Jean VI, 376
Chamberlain, Jennie IV, 1274
Chamberlain, John II, 345
Chamberlain, John II, 988
Chamberlain, John II, 990
Chamberlain, John IV, 323
Chamberlain, John VI, 376
Chamberlain, John VI, 481
Chamberlain, Jonas VI, 376
Chamberlain, Lucinda III, 242
Chamberlain, Lucinda III, 357
Chamberlain, Mary II, 793
Chamberlain, Mary IV, 323
Chamberlain, Mary IV, 358
Chamberlain, Mary IV, 615
Chamberlain, Mary IV, 637
Chamberlain, Mary VI, 376
Chamberlain, Mary F. IV, 188
Chamberlain, Mina E. IV, 1309
Chamberlain, Mollie W. I, 301
Chamberlain, Oliver VI, 532
Chamberlain, Phebe II, 988
Chamberlain, Phebe Taylor II, 990
Chamberlain, Rebecca IV, 188
Chamberlain, Rebecca IV, 300
Chamberlain, Robert II, 484
Chamberlain, S. Elliott VI, 532
Chamberlain, Sarah II, 194
Chamberlain, Sarah II, 207
Chamberlain, Wd. Mary Ann II, 793
Chamberlain, William IV, 323
Chamberlain, Zillah VI, 376
Chamberlaine, Robert II, 484
Chamberlin, Abigail VI, 376
Chamberlin, Abigail VI, 386
Chamberlin, Edith D. VI, 481
Chamberlin, Edith D. VI, 531
Chamberlin, Elija VI, 376
Chamberlin, Elijah VI, 376
Chamberlin, Elijah VI, 421
Chamberlin, Elizabeth VI, 376
Chamberlin, Gersham VI, 376
Chamberlin, James II, 846
Chamberlin, Jean VI, 376
Chamberlin, Jean VI, 421
Chamberlin, John VI, 376
Chamberlin, John VI, 481
Chamberlin, Jonas VI, 376
Chamberlin, Joseph VI, 376
Chamberlin, Mary VI, 376
Chamberlin, Mary VI, 421
Chamberlin, Mary VI, 424
Chamberlin, Zillah VI, 376
Chambers, ??? IV, 378
Chambers, ??? IV, 901
Chambers, Abbie V, 989
Chambers, Abigail IV, 378
Chambers, Abigail IV, 452
Chambers, Abigail IV, 806
Chambers, Abigail IV, 901
Chambers, Agness VI, 940
Chambers, Alice P. II, 786
Chambers, Amy I, 378
Chambers, Amy I, 404
Chambers, Amy Hadley II, 786
Chambers, Amy T. II, 846
Chambers, Amy T. II, 924
Chambers, Ann III, 66
Chambers, Ann IV, 188
Chambers, Ann IV, 324
Chambers, Ann IV, 378
Chambers, Ann IV, 517
Chambers, Ann IV, 806
Chambers, Ann IV, 900
Chambers, Ann IV, 901
Chambers, Ann IV, 907
Chambers, Ann IV, 908
Chambers, Ann IV, 913
Chambers, Ann IV, 917
Chambers, Ann IV, 918
Chambers, Ann IV, 937
Chambers, Ann IV, 998
Chambers, Ann IV, 1152
Chambers, Ann Eliza IV, 1152
Chambers, Ann Eliza IV, 1174
Chambers, Anne J. II, 846
Chambers, Anne Jane II, 786
Chambers, Arthur L. II, 846
Chambers, Augusta IV, 900
Chambers, Barnard II, 841
Chambers, Beatrice Myrtle IV, 937
Chambers, Benj. II, 345
Chambers, Benjamin II, 345
Chambers, Benjamin II, 484
Chambers, Benjamin II, 653
Chambers, Benjamin IV, 188
Chambers, Benjamin IV, 324
Chambers, Benjamin IV, 517
Chambers, Benjamin IV, 689
Chambers, Benjamin IV, 901
Chambers, Benjamin I. III, 66
Chambers, Benjamin S. IV, 806
Chambers, Binford Vincent IV, 937
Chambers, C. Robert V, 664
Chambers, Calvin VI, 57
Chambers, Caroline VI, 57
Chambers, Caroline W. II, 846
Chambers, Carrie II, 846
Chambers, Carrie Luanna IV, 937
Chambers, Catharine II, 484
Chambers, Catharine II, 732
Chambers, Charles IV, 452
Chambers, Charlotte III, 66
Chambers, Charlotte H. III, 66
Chambers, Chas. Theodore IV, 378
Chambers, Cloyde C. IV, 937
Chambers, Cloyde Clever IV, 937
Chambers, Curtis Allen IV, 937
Chambers, Cyrus II, 846
Chambers, Cyrus, Jr. II, 786
Chambers, Cyrus, Jr. II, 846
Chambers, Cyrus, Jr. II, 851
Chambers, Cyrus, Jr. II, 913
Chambers, David IV, 188
Chambers, David IV, 1152
Chambers, David M. II, 732
Chambers, Deborah IV, 324
Chambers, Deborah IV, 325
Chambers, Deborah IV, 340
Chambers, Deborah IV, 378
Chambers, Deborah IV, 399
Chambers, Deborah IV, 452
Chambers, Deborah IV, 517
Chambers, Deborah IV, 570
Chambers, Deborah IV, 806
Chambers, Deborah IV, 1152
Chambers, Deborah IV, 1197
Chambers, Deborah IV, 1198
Chambers, Earl V, 989
Chambers, Edith IV, 378
Chambers, Edith Graham II, 786
Chambers, Edmund H. II, 732
Chambers, Edwin II, 786
Chambers, Edwin II, 787
Chambers, Edwin II, 846
Chambers, Eleanor IV, 900
Chambers, Eleanor IV, 901
Chambers, Eleanor IV, 937
Chambers, Elener I, 444
Chambers, Elenor I, 444
Chambers, Elenor I, 449
Chambers, Elihu IV, 1152
Chambers, Eliner I, 348
Chambers, Eliza IV, 689
Chambers, Eliza IV, 901
Chambers, Eliza IV, 917
Chambers, Eliza H. VI, 1011
Chambers, Elizabeth I, 348
Chambers, Elizabeth I, 378
Chambers, Elizabeth I, 418
Chambers, Elizabeth II, 484
Chambers, Elizabeth II, 664
Chambers, Elizabeth II, 786
Chambers, Elizabeth II, 846
Chambers, Elizabeth IV, 324
Chambers, Elizabeth IV, 900
Chambers, Elizabeth IV, 901
Chambers, Elizabeth A. IV, 1091
Chambers, Elizabeth A. IV, 1104
Chambers, Elizabeth S. IV, 901
Chambers, Ellen IV, 324
Chambers, Ellenor IV, 937
Chambers, Elma Cailetta IV, 378
Chambers, Elmore L. IV, 1152
Chambers, Emey I, 348
Chambers, Emma IV, 1248
Chambers, Emma S. II, 732
Chambers, Ethel IV, 1248
Chambers, Eunace IV, 1152
Chambers, Eunice IV, 1152
Chambers, Floyd V, 989
Chambers, Frances Canby II, 786
Chambers, Frances Canby II, 846
Chambers, Frances Canby II, 924
Chambers, Frances J. III, 66
Chambers, Frances Jane III, 66
Chambers, Fred V, 989
Chambers, Frederick IV, 937
Chambers, Frederick James IV, 937
Chambers, George R. II, 1048
Chambers, George R. II, 1060
Chambers, Grace I, 348
Chambers, Grace I, 444
Chambers, Grace I, 449
Chambers, Hannah I, 348
Chambers, Hannah II, 345
Chambers, Hannah II, 484
Chambers, Hannah II, 653
Chambers, Hannah II, 701
Chambers, Hannah II, 786
Chambers, Hannah II, 846
Chambers, Hannah II, 1048
Chambers, Hannah II, 1054
Chambers, Hannah T. II, 786
Chambers, Hannah T. II, 790
Chambers, Helen II, 846
Chambers, Helen II, 851
Chambers, Helen Pyle II, 786
Chambers, Isabella II, 786
Chambers, J. III, 66
Chambers, J. Howard II, 846
Chambers, J. N. IV, 806
Chambers, J. Paul II, 846
Chambers, James I, 348
Chambers, James II, 846
Chambers, James II, 924
Chambers, James IV, 188
Chambers, James IV, 324
Chambers, James IV, 378
Chambers, James IV, 570
Chambers, James IV, 596
Chambers, James IV, 806
Chambers, James IV, 857
Chambers, James IV, 897
Chambers, James IV, 900
Chambers, James IV, 901
Chambers, James IV, 907
Chambers, James IV, 917
Chambers, James IV, 937
Chambers, James IV, 1152
Chambers, James C. IV, 452
Chambers, James H. IV, 901
Chambers, James H. IV, 913
Chambers, James H. IV, 918
Chambers, James H. IV, 937
Chambers, James H. IV, 998
Chambers, James Howard II, 786
Chambers, James Howard II, 846
Chambers, James Howard II, 924
Chambers, James N. IV, 689
Chambers, James N. IV, 806
Chambers, James N. IV, 901
Chambers, James N. IV, 937
Chambers, Jane IV, 188
Chambers, Jane IV, 806
Chambers, Jane IV, 900
Chambers, Jane IV, 1152
Chambers, Jane W. IV, 1152
Chambers, Jane W. IV, 1171
Chambers, Jas. IV, 901
Chambers, Jennie Ida Emma IV, 378
Chambers, Joel VI, 891
Chambers, John II, 484
Chambers, John IV, 324
Chambers, John IV, 325
Chambers, John IV, 806
Chambers, John IV, 901
Chambers, John IV, 1152
Chambers, John IV, 1171
Chambers, John VI, 57

Chambers, John C. IV, 1152
Chambers, John C. IV, 1171
Chambers, John C. IV, 1248
Chambers, John P. II, 786
Chambers, John P. II, 846
Chambers, John P. II, 913
Chambers, John Paul II, 846
Chambers, John W. II, 1048
Chambers, John W. II, 1060
Chambers, Josiah VI, 858
Chambers, Kennett Square II, 787
Chambers, Laura May IV, 806
Chambers, Laura May IV, 901
Chambers, Laura May IV, 937
Chambers, Levi IV, 324
Chambers, Levi IV, 517
Chambers, Lewis V, 989
Chambers, Lewis D. IV, 1152
Chambers, Lindley IV, 452
Chambers, Lorena IV, 918
Chambers, Luceny III, 66
Chambers, Lucy A. II, 701
Chambers, Luke IV, 1152
Chambers, Lydia Ann IV, 452
Chambers, Margaret IV, 324
Chambers, Margaret IV, 325
Chambers, Margaret IV, 378
Chambers, Margaret IV, 517
Chambers, Margaret IV, 806
Chambers, Margaret IV, 937
Chambers, Margaret IV, 1152
Chambers, Margaret E. IV, 937
Chambers, Maria II, 846
Chambers, Mark II, 732
Chambers, Martha II, 786
Chambers, Martha B. II, 846
Chambers, Mary I, 348
Chambers, Mary II, 1048
Chambers, Mary II, 1060
Chambers, Mary III, 67
Chambers, Mary IV, 324
Chambers, Mary IV, 340
Chambers, Mary IV, 378
Chambers, Mary IV, 452
Chambers, Mary IV, 517
Chambers, Mary IV, 570
Chambers, Mary IV, 596
Chambers, Mary IV, 806
Chambers, Mary IV, 900
Chambers, Mary IV, 901
Chambers, Mary IV, 907
Chambers, Mary IV, 937
Chambers, Mary IV, 1052
Chambers, Mary IV, 1066
Chambers, Mary IV, 1152
Chambers, Mary A. II, 846
Chambers, Mary A. II, 913
Chambers, Mary A. Pyle II, 786
Chambers, Mary Ann IV, 324
Chambers, Mary Ann IV, 325
Chambers, Mary Ann IV, 1152
Chambers, Mary B. II, 846
Chambers, Mary B. II, 851
Chambers, Mary Brosius II, 787
Chambers, Mary C. II, 937
Chambers, Mary Ellen IV, 1152
Chambers, Mary J. IV, 865
Chambers, Mary J. IV, 880
Chambers, Mary Jane IV, 188
Chambers, Mary Jane IV, 227
Chambers, Mary Jane IV, 901
Chambers, Mary M. II, 913
Chambers, Mary P. II, 787
Chambers, Mary P. II, 841
Chambers, Mary P. II, 846
Chambers, Mary T. IV, 378
Chambers, Mary W. II, 846
Chambers, Miles III, 66
Chambers, Minnie IV, 245
Chambers, Mira J. IV, 187
Chambers, Mira J. IV, 188
Chambers, Moses VI, 902
Chambers, Nancy I, 444
Chambers, Nancy IV, 188
Chambers, Nora IV, 937
Chambers, Nora Alice IV, 937
Chambers, Norman Barnard II, 787
Chambers, Paul Brosius II, 787
Chambers, Priscilla E. IV, 1152
Chambers, Priscilla Elma IV, 1152
Chambers, Rachel W. IV, 1152
Chambers, Rachel W. IV, 1171
Chambers, Raymond V, 989
Chambers, Rhoda VI, 891
Chambers, Rhoda S. II, 1048
Chambers, Rhoda S. II, 1060
Chambers, Richard I, 348
Chambers, Richard II, 732
Chambers, Richard IV, 937
Chambers, Richard Vincent IV, 937
Chambers, Robert IV, 324
Chambers, Robert IV, 806
Chambers, Robert V, 664
Chambers, Robert Elwood IV, 1152
Chambers, Robert W. IV, 188
Chambers, Robt. W. IV, 187
Chambers, Ruth Anna H. V, 664
Chambers, Ruth Anna Hare V, 664
Chambers, Ruthan P. IV, 188
Chambers, Ruthanna Hare V, 616
Chambers, S. Barnard II, 846
Chambers, Sam'l D. VI, 804
Chambers, Saml I, 348
Chambers, Samuel I, 348
Chambers, Samuel I, 378
Chambers, Samuel I, 444
Chambers, Samuel I, 449
Chambers, Samuel IV, 324
Chambers, Samuel IV, 325
Chambers, Samuel IV, 340
Chambers, Samuel IV, 378
Chambers, Samuel IV, 452
Chambers, Samuel IV, 517
Chambers, Samuel IV, 570
Chambers, Samuel IV, 806
Chambers, Samuel IV, 901
Chambers, Samuel IV, 918
Chambers, Samuel IV, 1152
Chambers, Samuel, Jr. IV, 378
Chambers, Samuel, Sr. I, 434
Chambers, Sarah I, 348
Chambers, Sarah I, 378
Chambers, Sarah I, 444
Chambers, Sarah I, 446
Chambers, Sarah II, 345
Chambers, Sarah II, 825
Chambers, Sarah D. II, 846
Chambers, Sarah E. VI, 804
Chambers, Sarah Jane IV, 452
Chambers, Sarah Jane IV, 1152
Chambers, Simon Barnard II, 787
Chambers, Simon Barnard II, 846
Chambers, Sina Ann IV, 901
Chambers, Sina Ann IV, 913
Chambers, Sorena IV, 901
Chambers, Stacy IV, 806
Chambers, Susanna II, 846
Chambers, Susanna IV, 806
Chambers, Susanna IV, 937
Chambers, Susanna P. II, 846
Chambers, Susannah II, 846
Chambers, T. Susanna IV, 806
Chambers, T. Susanna IV, 937
Chambers, Tamar IV, 324
Chambers, Tamar IV, 901
Chambers, Tamar IV, 918
Chambers, Tamar S. IV, 901
Chambers, Tamer IV, 324
Chambers, Tamer IV, 378
Chambers, Tamer IV, 517
Chambers, Tamer IV, 1152
Chambers, Theodore Marriott II, 786
Chambers, Thomas IV, 324
Chambers, Thomas IV, 517
Chambers, Thomas IV, 900
Chambers, Thomas IV, 901
Chambers, Thos. IV, 900
Chambers, Valentine IV, 689
Chambers, Valentine IV, 937
Chambers, Voluntine M. IV, 937
Chambers, William II, 786
Chambers, William IV, 324
Chambers, William IV, 901
Chambers, William Canby II, 786
Chambers, William R. IV, 937
Chambers, William T. IV, 1152
Chambers, Winnie A. V, 989
Chambers, Wm. II, 484
Chambers, Wm. II, 701
Chambers, Wm. II, 846
Chambers, Wm. IV, 517
Chambers, Wm. IV, 937
Chambers, Wm. J. IV, 1248
Chambers, Wm. Llewelyn IV, 1052
Chambles, Alia V, 157
Chambles, Alie V, 157
Chambles, B. D. V, 157
Chambles, Elsie V, 157
Chambles, Flora V, 157
Chambles, Frank V, 157
Chambles, Hannah II, 61
Chambles, Jettie V, 157
Chambles, Rebecka II, 61
Chambles, Sarah II, 61
Chambles, Sarah E. V, 157
Chambles, Sarah Ellen V, 157
Chambless, Frank V, 157
Chambless, James II, 138
Chambless, Jettie V, 157
Chambless, Mary II, 484
Chambless, Sarah II, 138
Chambless, Sarah Ellen V, 157
Chamblis, Alie V, 157
Chamblis, Elinor II, 345
Chamblis, Elonar II, 61
Chamblis, James II, 61
Chamblis, James II, 76
Chamblis, Sarah II, 61
Chamblis, Sarah II, 76
Chamblis, Susanah II, 61
Chaming, Jamima VI, 233
Chamless, James II, 41
Chamless, Sarah II, 41
Chamlis, Elizabeth II, 60
Chamlis, Elizabeth II, 105
Chamlis, James II, 49
Chamlis, James II, 61
Chamlis, Margaret II, 49
Chamlis, Margaret II, 61
Chamnes, Elenor II, 24
Chamnes, James II, 24
Chamnes, Mary II, 24
Chamnes, Mary II, 61
Chamnes, Mary II, 484
Chamnes, Nathaniel II, 24
Chamnes, Nathaniel II, 60
Chamnes, Nathaniel II, 112
Chamnes, Rebeka II, 60
Chamnes, Rebeka II, 112
Chamness, Abigail I, 378
Chamness, Abigail I, 397
Chamness, Abigail I, 650
Chamness, Abigail I, 675
Chamness, Abigail I, 676
Chamness, Abigail I, 756
Chamness, Abigail Hannah I, 756
Chamness, Allen Jay I, 650
Chamness, Aluce I, 650
Chamness, Amy I, 378
Chamness, Amy I, 423
Chamness, Amy I, 650
Chamness, Amy I, 651
Chamness, Amy I, 675
Chamness, Amy I, 676
Chamness, Amy I, 687
Chamness, Amy I, 688
Chamness, Ann I, 348
Chamness, Ann I, 378
Chamness, Ann I, 380
Chamness, Ann I, 650
Chamness, Ann I, 675
Chamness, Ann I, 683
Chamness, Anthony I, 343
Chamness, Anthony I, 348
Chamness, Anthony I, 349
Chamness, Anthony I, 366
Chamness, Anthony I, 378
Chamness, Anthony I, 429
Chamness, Anthony I, 531
Chamness, Anthony I, 544
Chamness, Anthony I, 650
Chamness, Anthony I, 675
Chamness, Anthony I, 676
Chamness, Anthony I, 687
Chamness, Anthony I, 692
Chamness, Anthony I, 803
Chamness, Anthony VI, 481
Chamness, Anthony, Jr. I, 378
Chamness, Anthony, Sr. I, 676
Chamness, Arlando I, 676
Chamness, Arlendo G. I, 676
Chamness, Armella I, 650
Chamness, Caleb I, 378
Chamness, Charity I, 378
Chamness, Charity I, 410
Chamness, Charity I, 531
Chamness, Charity I, 874
Chamness, Charity I, 875
Chamness, David I, 650
Chamness, David I, 651
Chamness, David S. I, 415
Chamness, David S. I, 651
Chamness, David S. I, 676
Chamness, Davis S. I, 378
Chamness, Dun I, 651
Chamness, Dun I, 675
Chamness, Dun I, 676
Chamness, Dun L. I, 756
Chamness, Dun L. I, 766
Chamness, Dunn L. I, 756
Chamness, Edeth I, 651
Chamness, Edith I, 651
Chamness, Edith I, 675
Chamness, Edith I, 683
Chamness, Edith I, 756
Chamness, Edward I, 444
Chamness, Edward I, 455
Chamness, Edward I, 650
Chamness, Edward I, 651
Chamness, Edward I, 675
Chamness, Edward II, 60
Chamness, Eleanor I, 675
Chamness, Elenor II, 24
Chamness, Elinor I, 650
Chamness, Eliza I, 651
Chamness, Eliza J. I, 676
Chamness, Eliza Jane I, 651
Chamness, Eliza Jane I, 676
Chamness, Eliza Jane I, 756
Chamness, Eliza Jane I, 763
Chamness, Elizabeth I, 348
Chamness, Elizabeth I, 378
Chamness, Elizabeth I, 401
Chamness, Elizabeth I, 430
Chamness, Elizabeth I, 651
Chamness, Elizabeth I, 675
Chamness, Elizabeth I, 686
Chamness, Elizabeth II, 24
Chamness, Elizabeth II, 60
Chamness, Elizabeth VI, 481
Chamness, Elizabeth D. I, 378
Chamness, Elizabeth D. I, 415
Chamness, Elizabeth D. I, 650
Chamness, Elizabeth D. I, 676
Chamness, Elma I, 650
Chamness, Elma I, 676
Chamness, Elma I, 689
Chamness, Elonar II, 61
Chamness, Emily I, 614
Chamness, Emily I, 650
Chamness, Emily I, 675
Chamness, Emily I, 676
Chamness, Emily I, 677
Chamness, Emily Eliza I, 650
Chamness, Emily Eliza I, 676
Chamness, Eunice I, 675
Chamness, George I, 378
Chamness, George W. I, 378
Chamness, H. C. I, 651
Chamness, Hannah I, 378
Chamness, Hannah I, 444
Chamness, Hannah I, 449
Chamness, Hannah I, 455
Chamness, Hannah I, 650
Chamness, Hannah I, 651
Chamness, Hannah I, 666
Chamness, Hannah I, 675
Chamness, Hannah I, 676
Chamness, Hannah I, 683
Chamness, Hannah I, 799
Chamness, Hannah I, 803
Chamness, Hannah II, 24
Chamness, Hannah II, 61
Chamness, Hannah II, 77
Chamness, Hannah E. I, 651
Chamness, Hannah Emeline I, 676
Chamness, Isaac I, 592
Chamness, Isaac I, 597
Chamness, Isaac I, 651
Chamness, Isabel I, 378
Chamness, Isabel I, 592
Chamness, Isabel I, 651
Chamness, Isabel I, 674
Chamness, Isabel I, 675
Chamness, Isabel I, 756
Chamness, Isabella I, 756
Chamness, Isabelle I, 676
Chamness, Israel I, 378
Chamness, James II, 24
Chamness, James II, 60
Chamness, James II, 61
Chamness, Jane I, 378
Chamness, Jane I, 420
Chamness, Jane I, 650
Chamness, Jane I, 675
Chamness, Jane C. I, 676
Chamness, Jane C. I, 692
Chamness, Jean I, 348
Chamness, Jesse I, 430
Chamness, Jesse I, 651
Chamness, Jesse I, 675
Chamness, Joel I, 711
Chamness, John I, 348
Chamness, John I, 378
Chamness, Joseph I, 348
Chamness, Joseph I, 378
Chamness, Joseph I, 412
Chamness, Joseph I, 430
Chamness, Joseph I, 444
Chamness, Joseph I, 450
Chamness, Joseph I, 531
Chamness, Joseph I, 645
Chamness, Joseph I, 651
Chamness, Joseph I, 666
Chamness, Joseph I, 675
Chamness, Joseph I, 687
Chamness, Joseph I, 711
Chamness, Joseph I, 799
Chamness, Joseph I, 803
Chamness, Joseph VI, 481
Chamness, Joshua I, 348
Chamness, Joshua I, 378
Chamness, Joshua I, 651
Chamness, Joshua I, 675
Chamness, Joshua I, 680
Chamness, Joshua I, 741
Chamness, Joshua, Jr. I, 378
Chamness, Lorenzo I, 676
Chamness, Lorenzo L. I, 651
Chamness, Lorenzo S. I, 676
Chamness, Lydia I, 348
Chamness, Lydia I, 378
Chamness, Lydia I, 384
Chamness, Lydia I, 426
Chamness, Lydia I, 651
Chamness, Lydia I, 675
Chamness, Lydia I, 680
Chamness, Malinda I, 348
Chamness, Margaret I, 378
Chamness, Margaret I, 412
Chamness, Margaret I, 429
Chamness, Margaret I, 444
Chamness, Margaret I, 651
Chamness, Margaret I, 675
Chamness, Margaret I, 677
Chamness, Margaret I, 687
Chamness, Margaret II, 24
Chamness, Margaret II, 61
Chamness, Margret I, 348
Chamness, Margret I, 378
Chamness, Margret I, 411
Chamness, Marth I, 675
Chamness, Martha I, 348
Chamness, Martha I, 378
Chamness, Martha I, 400
Chamness, Martha I, 651
Chamness, Martha I, 675
Chamness, Martha I, 685
Chamness, Martha I, 874
Chamness, Martha I, 875
Chamness, Martha VI, 481
Chamness, Mary I, 348
Chamness, Mary I, 349
Chamness, Mary I, 378
Chamness, Mary I, 384
Chamness, Mary I, 650
Chamness, Mary I, 675
Chamness, Mary I, 676
Chamness, Mary I, 678
Chamness, Mary I, 684
Chamness, Mary I, 756
Chamness, Mary I, 766
Chamness, Mary II, 24
Chamness, Mary II, 60
Chamness, Mary II, 61
Chamness, Mary II, 99
Chamness, Mary II, 484
Chamness, Mary V, 27
Chamness, Mary V, 37
Chamness, Mary VI, 481
Chamness, Mary VI, 485
Chamness, Mary Ellen I, 650
Chamness, Miles I, 650
Chamness, Miles I, 651
Chamness, Miles I, 676
Chamness, Milo I, 651
Chamness, Milo I, 676
Chamness, Milton I, 651
Chamness, Milton I, 676
Chamness, Morning I, 711
Chamness, Mourning I, 651
Chamness, Mourning I, 675
Chamness, Mourning I, 685
Chamness, Nathan I, 651
Chamness, Nathan I, 675
Chamness, Nathan I, 756
Chamness, Nathan I, 766
Chamness, Nathaniel II, 24
Chamness, Nathaniel II, 60
Chamness, Nathaniel, Jr. II, 61
Chamness, Nereus I, 650
Chamness, Nereus Barzilla I, 756
Chamness, Orlando G. I, 651
Chamness, Owen I, 650
Chamness, Rachel I, 348
Chamness, Rachel I, 378
Chamness, Rachel I, 394
Chamness, Rachel I, 429
Chamness, Rachel I, 531
Chamness, Rachel I, 544
Chamness, Rachel I, 675

Chamness, Rachel Haworth I, 378
Chamness, Rebecah I, 592
Chamness, Rebecca I, 592
Chamness, Rebecca I, 597
Chamness, Rebecca I, 675
Chamness, Rebecca I, 676
Chamness, Rebecca I, 756
Chamness, Rebecca I, 766
Chamness, Rebecka II, 61
Chamness, Rebeckah II, 24
Chamness, Rebeka II, 60
Chamness, Ruth I, 378
Chamness, Ruth I, 444
Chamness, Ruth I, 450
Chamness, Ruth I, 651
Chamness, Ruth I, 675
Chamness, Ruth I, 711
Chamness, Sally I, 348
Chamness, Sally I, 378
Chamness, Sally I, 423
Chamness, Samuel I, 444
Chamness, Samuel I, 651
Chamness, Samuel I, 711
Chamness, Sarah I, 343
Chamness, Sarah I, 348
Chamness, Sarah I, 349
Chamness, Sarah I, 366
Chamness, Sarah I, 378
Chamness, Sarah I, 425
Chamness, Sarah I, 444
Chamness, Sarah I, 675
Chamness, Sarah I, 678
Chamness, Sarah I, 803
Chamness, Sarah II, 61
Chamness, Sarah VI, 481
Chamness, Sarah Welmett I, 378
Chamness, Susanah II, 61
Chamness, Susanna I, 378
Chamness, Susanna I, 417
Chamness, Susanna I, 651
Chamness, Susanna I, 675
Chamness, Susanna I, 687
Chamness, Susannah II, 24
Chamness, Susannah II, 61
Chamness, Susannah VI, 481
Chamness, Sushanna I, 348
Chamness, Widow Susanna I, 666
Chamness, William I, 348
Chamness, William I, 378
Chamness, William I, 423
Chamness, William I, 592
Chamness, William I, 650
Chamness, William I, 651
Chamness, William I, 674
Chamness, William I, 675
Chamness, William I, 683
Chamness, William I, 756
Chamness, William, Jr. I, 378
Chamness, William, Sr. I, 675
Chamness, Wm. I, 378
Chamney, Charity I, 531
Chamney, Joseph I, 531
Chamney, Rachel I, 531
Chamneys, Nathaniel II, 24
Chamneys, Susannah II, 24
Chamnis, Edward II, 60
Chamnis, James II, 60
Chamnis, James II, 95
Chamnis, Mary II, 60
Chamnis, Mary II, 95
Champ, John H. IV, 188
Champ, John Henry IV, 188
Champion, Ann II, 480
Champion, Ann II, 787
Champion, Ann II, 845
Champion, Chas. II, 787
Champion, Chas. II, 845
Champion, Edgar R. IV, 689
Champion, Elizabeth VI, 736
Champion, Francis II, 207
Champion, Francis II, 480
Champion, Hannah II, 779
Champion, John II, 207
Champion, John II, 345
Champion, John III, 399
Champion, John III, 422
Champion, Joseph II, 207
Champion, Joseph II, 269
Champion, Katheren II, 197
Champion, Katheren II, 207
Champion, Margaret II, 731
Champion, Mary II, 207
Champion, Mary II, 269
Champion, Mary II, 988
Champion, Mary III, 67
Champion, Mary III, 186
Champion, Mary III, 399
Champion, Mary III, 422
Champion, Matthew II, 169
Champion, Matthew II, 197
Champion, Matthew II, 207
Champion, Nathaniel II, 988
Champion, Nathaniel II, 990
Champion, Newton II, 787
Champion, Newton W. II, 787
Champion, Rachel II, 787
Champion, Rebecca L. III, 67
Champion, Sarah III, 399
Champion, Sarah III, 422
Champlis, Mary II, 61
Champnes, Edward II, 17
Champnes, Elizabeth II, 24
Champnes, Elizabeth II, 30
Champnes, Hannah II, 49
Champnes, Hannah II, 61
Champnes, Hannah II, 92
Champnes, Hannah II, 97
Champnes, James II, 24
Champnes, James II, 61
Champnes, John II, 97
Champnes, Margaret II, 24
Champnes, Mary II, 30
Champnes, Nathaniel, Jr. II, 17
Champnes, Nathaniel, Jr. II, 61
Champnes, Nathaniel, Jr. II, 90
Champnes, Nathaniel, Sr. II, 17
Champnes, Nathaniel, Sr. II, 30
Champnes, Susannah II, 61
Champnes, Susannah II, 90
Champney, Edna Alice VI, 622
Champney, Edna Alice VI, 627
Champney, Edna Alice VI, 631
Champney, Lyman VI, 622
Champney, Lyman VI, 627
Champney, Lyman VI, 631
Champneys, Nethaniel II, 45
Champneys, Nethaniel, Jr. II, 45
Champneys, Sarah II, 61
Champneys, Sarah II, 99
Chance, Adda Jane V, 229
Chance, Ann V, 229
Chance, Ann V, 243
Chance, Asa V, 229
Chance, Atwell V, 229
Chance, Bertha V, 664
Chance, Bertha May V, 664
Chance, Charles V, 664
Chance, Chas. H. V, 664
Chance, Chas. Wm. V, 664
Chance, Cyrus V, 664
Chance, David V, 229
Chance, Elizabeth I, 1008
Chance, Elizabeth I, 1011
Chance, Elizabeth J. V, 229
Chance, Emma V, 229
Chance, Harry V, 157
Chance, Iarrot V, 229
Chance, Isaac V, 229
Chance, Isaac V, 323
Chance, Isaac V, 324
Chance, Isaac, Jr. V, 229
Chance, Levi V, 229
Chance, Lola V, 832
Chance, Margaret V, 664
Chance, Mary E. V, 229
Chance, Maude V, 157
Chance, Nancy V, 229
Chance, Nancy V, 244
Chance, O. E. V, 832
Chance, Orville V, 832
Chance, Parrot V, 229
Chance, Reuben V, 323
Chance, Rosanna V, 323
Chance, Samuel I, 378
Chance, Samuel I, 711
Chance, Samuel I, 803
Chance, Samuel I, 1066
Chance, Sarah V, 229
Chance, Tilghman V, 229
Chance, Tilghman V, 243
Chance, Tilman V, 229
Chance, Tilmon V, 949
Chance, Vilee IV, 188
Chance, Vilee IV, 283
Chance, William V, 229
Chance, Zella V, 664
Chance, Zella Jane V, 664
Chanceler, Rebecka II, 442
Chanceler, William II, 442
Chancellor, Alfred IV, 1204
Chancellor, Dr. William II, 345
Chancellor, John II, 345
Chancellor, Samuel II, 345
Chancellor, William II, 345
Chancellor, William, Jr. II, 345
Chancellor, Wm. IV, 1204
Chancey, Amee I, 135
Chancey, Amee I, 157
Chancey, Ann I, 135
Chancey, Ann I, 364
Chancey, Ann I, 365
Chancey, Ann I, 378
Chancey, Ann I, 379
Chancey, Daniel I, 135
Chancey, Daniel I, 364
Chancey, Daniel I, 365
Chancey, Daniel I, 379
Chancey, Daniel I Sup 1, 3
Chancey, David I, 135
Chancey, David I, 157
Chancey, Deborah I, 97
Chancey, Deborah I, 134
Chancey, Deborah I, 166
Chancey, Edmund I, 134
Chancey, Edmund I, 135
Chancey, Edmund, Jr. I, 135
Chancey, Edward I, 92
Chancey, Edward I, 135
Chancey, Elisabeth I, 135
Chancey, Elisabeth I, 166
Chancey, Jacob I, 135
Chancey, Jacob I, 136
Chancey, Mary I, 135
Chancey, Mary I, 136
Chancey, Mary I, 379
Chancey, Mary I, 400
Chancey, Pleasant I, 364
Chancey, Pleasant I, 379
Chancey, Pleasant I, 419
Chancey, Rachel I, 365
Chancey, Rachel I, 379
Chancey, Ruth I, 135
Chancey, Sarah I, 97
Chancey, Sarah I, 135
Chancey, William I, 97
Chancey, William I, 134
Chancey, William I, 135
Chancey, William I, 166
Chancey, William, Jr. I, 97
Chancey, William, Sr. I, 97
Chancey, Zachariah I Sup 1, 6
Chancy, Ann I, 97
Chancy, Ann I, 378
Chancy, Deborah I, 97
Chancy, Elizabeth I, 97
Chancy, Hannah I, 97
Chancy, Jeremiah I, 97
Chancy, Mary I, 97
Chancy, Mary I, 379
Chancy, Pleasant I, 379
Chancy, Rachel I, 379
Chancy, Rachel I, 420
Chancy, Sarah I, 97
Chancy, William I, 97
Chancy, Zach. I Sup 1, 7
Chander, Frances II, 442
Chander, Mary II, 496
Chander, Sarah II, 61
Chander, Thomas II, 442
Chanders, Edward II, 485
Chanders, Elizabeth II, 345
Chanders, Frances II, 468
Chanders, Frances II, 485
Chanders, Francis II, 345
Chanders, Joseph II, 345
Chanders, Paul II, 345
Chanders, Thomas II, 345
Chanders, Thomas II, 442
Chanders, William II, 345
Chandlee, Albert VI, 369
Chandlee, Albert VI, 376
Chandlee, Ann VI, 376
Chandlee, Ann VI, 455
Chandlee, Anna II, 847
Chandlee, Benjamin II, 484
Chandlee, Benjamin II, 495
Chandlee, Benjamin V, 37
Chandlee, Benjamin VI, 376
Chandlee, Benjamin L. V, 37
Chandlee, Benjamin, Jr. II, 484
Chandlee, Brooke VI, 482
Chandlee, Catharine VI, 376
Chandlee, Catharine France VI, 376
Chandlee, Deborah VI, 474
Chandlee, Deborah VI, 481
Chandlee, Edward II, 787
Chandlee, Edward VI, 482
Chandlee, Edward Walker VI, 376
Chandlee, Edwin II, 787
Chandlee, Elizabeth VI, 376
Chandlee, Emily III, 432
Chandlee, Emily J. III, 399
Chandlee, Eunice VI, 361
Chandlee, Eunice VI, 440
Chandlee, Gainer II, 787
Chandlee, Gainer II, 846
Chandlee, Gainer II, 914
Chandlee, Gainer VI, 481
Chandlee, Gainor VI, 481
Chandlee, George II, 787
Chandlee, George II, 818
Chandlee, George II, 845
Chandlee, George II, 846
Chandlee, George II, 847
Chandlee, George II, 914
Chandlee, George II, 922
Chandlee, George II, 936
Chandlee, George VI, 474
Chandlee, George VI, 481
Chandlee, George, Jr. VI, 482
Chandlee, George, Sr. II, 787
Chandlee, Goldsmith VI, 361
Chandlee, Goldsmith VI, 376
Chandlee, Goldsmith VI, 440
Chandlee, Goldsmith VI, 455
Chandlee, Goldsmith VI, 593
Chandlee, Goldsmith VI, 595
Chandlee, Goldsmith VI, 599
Chandlee, Goldsmith VI, 600
Chandlee, Goldsmith VI, 603
Chandlee, Goldsmith, Jr. VI, 376
Chandlee, Goldsmith, Jr. VI, 462
Chandlee, Goodsmith VI, 604
Chandlee, Hannah II, 846
Chandlee, Hannah II, 847
Chandlee, Hannah II, 914
Chandlee, Hannah II, 922
Chandlee, Hannah VI, 376
Chandlee, Hannah VI, 482
Chandlee, Hannah VI, 592
Chandlee, Hannah VI, 593
Chandlee, Hannah R. II, 847
Chandlee, Hannah R. II, 922
Chandlee, Hannah Townsend II, 787
Chandlee, Hannah Townsend II, 818
Chandlee, Janney VI, 482
Chandlee, John VI, 376
Chandlee, John G. V, 968
Chandlee, Jonathan Wright VI, 376
Chandlee, Mahlon VI, 376
Chandlee, Mahlon VI, 482
Chandlee, Mary VI, 376
Chandlee, Mary VI, 474
Chandlee, Mary VI, 481
Chandlee, Mary VI, 593
Chandlee, Mary VI, 594
Chandlee, Mary VI, 606
Chandlee, Mary Ann II, 847
Chandlee, Mary Elizabeth V, 968
Chandlee, Mary R. II, 847
Chandlee, Mary R. II, 922
Chandlee, Mary Richards II, 787
Chandlee, Mary Richards II, 818
Chandlee, Nathan VI, 482
Chandlee, Phebe VI, 376
Chandlee, Phebe VI, 462
Chandlee, Phebe N. V, 37
Chandlee, Ruth III, 399
Chandlee, Ruth III, 432
Chandlee, Samuel P. II, 847
Chandlee, Sarah II, 484
Chandlee, Sarah II, 495
Chandlee, Sarah VI, 376
Chandlee, Sarah VI, 770
Chandlee, Sarah Ann VI, 369
Chandlee, Sarah Ann VI, 376
Chandlee, Sarah M. VI, 376
Chandlee, Sarah M. VI, 431
Chandlee, Webster III, 399
Chandlee, Webster III, 432
Chandlee, Wm. II, 484
Chandlee, Wm. VI, 474
Chandlee, Wm. VI, 481
Chandler, ??? II, 787
Chandler, ??? V, 965
Chandler, Aaron IV, 80
Chandler, Aaron V, 36
Chandler, Aaron V, 37
Chandler, Aaron V, 137
Chandler, Aaron B. V, 37
Chandler, Abagail II, 61
Chandler, Abagail II, 86
Chandler, Abi V, 36
Chandler, Abi V, 37
Chandler, Alexander M. II, 847
Chandler, Alfred E. V, 37
Chandler, Alisabeth I, 1017
Chandler, Almira T. II, 847
Chandler, Alonzo D. III, 399
Chandler, Ann I, 1017
Chandler, Ann I, 1027
Chandler, Ann II, 484
Chandler, Ann II, 615
Chandler, Ann IV, 25
Chandler, Ann IV, 79
Chandler, Ann IV, 80
Chandler, Ann IV, 117
Chandler, Ann V, 37
Chandler, Ann VI, 376
Chandler, Ann VI, 449
Chandler, Ann H. III, 325
Chandler, Anna M. II, 847
Chandler, Anne IV, 517
Chandler, Aquilla V, 37
Chandler, Aquilla Goldsmith V, 37
Chandler, Asa V, 37
Chandler, Asa V, 38
Chandler, Asahel V, 37
Chandler, Benjamin V, 37
Chandler, Benjamin V, 140
Chandler, Benjamin L. V, 37
Chandler, Benjamin Lewis V, 37
Chandler, Bennett IV, 517
Chandler, Bennett V, 229
Chandler, Calvin V, 481
Chandler, Calvin B. V, 481
Chandler, Catharine IV, 517
Chandler, Catharine VI, 431
Chandler, Catherine II, 345
Chandler, Catherine V, 229
Chandler, D. Webster II, 847
Chandler, D. Webster II, 939
Chandler, Daniel VI, 303
Chandler, Daniel VI, 304
Chandler, Daniel Webster II, 787
Chandler, Daniel Webster II, 847
Chandler, David I, 1017
Chandler, David III, 399
Chandler, David IV, 80
Chandler, David V, 37
Chandler, David V, 62
Chandler, Deborah III, 399
Chandler, Edwin V, 37
Chandler, Eleanor VI, 297
Chandler, Eleanor VI, 304
Chandler, Eli IV, 25
Chandler, Eli IV, 80
Chandler, Eli IV, 324
Chandler, Eli IV, 517
Chandler, Eli V, 37
Chandler, Eli V, 220
Chandler, Eli V, 229
Chandler, Elisha IV, 517
Chandler, Elisha V, 229
Chandler, Elisha V, 324
Chandler, Elisha M. IV, 517
Chandler, Elisha M. V, 229
Chandler, Eliza II, 787
Chandler, Elizabeth I, 1027
Chandler, Elizabeth I, 1034
Chandler, Elizabeth II, 61
Chandler, Elizabeth II, 90
Chandler, Elizabeth II, 345
Chandler, Elizabeth II, 484
Chandler, Elizabeth II, 593
Chandler, Elizabeth II, 632
Chandler, Elizabeth V, 37
Chandler, Elizabeth V, 815
Chandler, Elizabeth Ann IV, 517
Chandler, Elizabeth Ann V, 229
Chandler, Elizabeth Margaret II, 484
Chandler, Ella B. V, 38
Chandler, Ella S. II, 847
Chandler, Ellen V, 33
Chandler, Ellen V, 38
Chandler, Ellwood V, 37
Chandler, Elwood V, 37
Chandler, Elwood V, 38
Chandler, Emily C. II, 948
Chandler, Emily J. III, 399
Chandler, Emma B. M. II, 847
Chandler, Emma F. II, 787
Chandler, Enoch IV, 25
Chandler, Enoch IV, 71
Chandler, Enoch IV, 79
Chandler, Enoch IV, 80
Chandler, Enoch IV, 101
Chandler, Enoch IV, 167
Chandler, Enoch IV, 324
Chandler, Enoch IV, 517
Chandler, Enoch V, 229
Chandler, Enoch, Jr. IV, 25
Chandler, Enoch, Jr. IV, 80
Chandler, Enoch, Jr. IV, 324
Chandler, Enoch, Jr. IV, 517
Chandler, Ester II, 61
Chandler, Esther II, 61
Chandler, Esther II, 77
Chandler, Esther IV, 25
Chandler, Esther IV, 79
Chandler, Esther IV, 80
Chandler, Esther IV, 89
Chandler, Esther IV, 517
Chandler, Esther V, 37
Chandler, Esther C. II, 847
Chandler, Esther L. II, 847

Chandler, Esther L. II, 939
Chandler, Eunice Ann V, 968
Chandler, Eunice Ann V, 974
Chandler, Frances II, 61
Chandler, Frances II, 72
Chandler, Gabriel I, 1017
Chandler, George II, 345
Chandler, George II, 484
Chandler, George II, 593
Chandler, George II, 847
Chandler, George III, 67
Chandler, Goldsmith V, 37
Chandler, Goldsmith V, 968
Chandler, Goldsmith VI, 373
Chandler, Goldsmith, Jr. V, 37
Chandler, Hannah I, 611
Chandler, Hannah II, 51
Chandler, Hannah II, 61
Chandler, Hannah II, 78
Chandler, Hannah II, 108
Chandler, Hannah II, 484
Chandler, Hannah II, 519
Chandler, Hannah IV, 25
Chandler, Hannah IV, 49
Chandler, Hannah IV, 68
Chandler, Hannah IV, 79
Chandler, Hannah IV, 80
Chandler, Hannah IV, 101
Chandler, Hannah IV, 324
Chandler, Hannah IV, 517
Chandler, Hannah V, 37
Chandler, Hannah V, 137
Chandler, Hannah V, 220
Chandler, Hannah V, 229
Chandler, Hannah Ann V, 28
Chandler, Hannah Ann V, 29
Chandler, Hannah Ann V, 37
Chandler, Hannah S. V. II, 732
Chandler, Hannah S. V. II, 772
Chandler, Isaac IV, 25
Chandler, Isaac IV, 517
Chandler, Isaac V, 37
Chandler, Israel I, 1017
Chandler, Israel I, 1027
Chandler, Jacob I, 961
Chandler, Jacob I, 1015
Chandler, Jacob I, 1017
Chandler, Jacob I, 1027
Chandler, Jacob VI, 376
Chandler, Jacob VI, 449
Chandler, Jane IV, 80
Chandler, Jane IV, 517
Chandler, Jane IV, 520
Chandler, Jason IV, 80
Chandler, Jason IV, 517
Chandler, Jesse II, 787
Chandler, John I, 961
Chandler, John II, 51
Chandler, John II, 61
Chandler, John II, 66
Chandler, John II, 90
Chandler, John II, 345
Chandler, John II, 442
Chandler, John II, 484
Chandler, John II, 593
Chandler, John II, 787
Chandler, John II, 847
Chandler, John II, 939
Chandler, John IV, 517
Chandler, John V, 229
Chandler, John VI, 303
Chandler, John VI, 304
Chandler, John VI, 319
Chandler, John C. IV, 517
Chandler, John C. V, 229
Chandler, John F. V, 38
Chandler, John G. V, 968
Chandler, John T. V, 37
Chandler, John W. II, 847
Chandler, John, Jr. II, 24
Chandler, Jonathan I, 1017
Chandler, Jonathan I, 1027
Chandler, Jonathan IV, 25
Chandler, Jonathan IV, 27
Chandler, Jonathan IV, 80
Chandler, Jonathan Goldsmith V, 37
Chandler, Joseph I, 961
Chandler, Joseph V, 37
Chandler, Joseph V, 38
Chandler, Joshua IV, 25
Chandler, Joshua IV, 79
Chandler, Joshua IV, 80
Chandler, Josiah II, 24
Chandler, Judith D. IV, 188
Chandler, Katherine II, 442
Chandler, Laura C. II, 847
Chandler, Levi I, 961
Chandler, Lewis W. V, 37
Chandler, Louisa II, 787
Chandler, Lucy Long IV, 1309
Chandler, Lydia V, 37
Chandler, Lydia V, 141
Chandler, Lydia Ann V, 37
Chandler, Mahlon VI, 431
Chandler, Margaret II, 345
Chandler, Margaret II, 484
Chandler, Margaret II, 519
Chandler, Margaret II, 654
Chandler, Margaret IV, 25
Chandler, Margaret IV, 79
Chandler, Margaret IV, 80
Chandler, Margaret IV, 110
Chandler, Margaretta V, 37
Chandler, Maria IV, 517
Chandler, Maria V, 37
Chandler, Maria V, 137
Chandler, Maria F. IV, 517
Chandler, Maria Jane II, 787
Chandler, Maria Jane II, 847
Chandler, Maria Jane II, 939
Chandler, Maria P. V, 229
Chandler, Marianna V, 37
Chandler, Marie P. V, 229
Chandler, Martha IV, 25
Chandler, Martha IV, 27
Chandler, Martha IV, 79
Chandler, Martha IV, 80
Chandler, Martha IV, 95
Chandler, Martha IV, 517
Chandler, Martha V, 37
Chandler, Martha V, 52
Chandler, Mary II, 61
Chandler, Mary II, 66
Chandler, Mary II, 96
Chandler, Mary II, 484
Chandler, Mary II, 658
Chandler, Mary IV, 79
Chandler, Mary IV, 80
Chandler, Mary IV, 324
Chandler, Mary IV, 517
Chandler, Mary IV, 523
Chandler, Mary IV, 543
Chandler, Mary IV, 558
Chandler, Mary IV, 1091
Chandler, Mary IV, 1121
Chandler, Mary V, 37
Chandler, Mary V, 220
Chandler, Mary V, 229
Chandler, Mary VI, 320
Chandler, Mary A. II, 814
Chandler, Mary Ann II, 847
Chandler, Mary Ann V, 37
Chandler, Mary Elizabeth V, 37
Chandler, Mary Elizabeth V, 968
Chandler, Mary L. II, 847
Chandler, Mary P. IV, 517
Chandler, Matilda IV, 1309
Chandler, Matilda B. IV, 517
Chandler, Matilda B. V, 229
Chandler, Merriam V, 37
Chandler, Milton V, 37
Chandler, Miriam IV, 80
Chandler, Miriam V, 37
Chandler, Miriam V, 111
Chandler, Pall II, 61
Chandler, Patience II, 442
Chandler, Percy M. II, 847
Chandler, Phebe II, 169
Chandler, Phebe II, 207
Chandler, Phebe II, 484
Chandler, Phebe IV, 25
Chandler, Phebe IV, 79
Chandler, Phebe IV, 80
Chandler, Phebe IV, 89
Chandler, Phebe V, 37
Chandler, Phebe V, 968
Chandler, Phebe E. II, 847
Chandler, Phebe N. V, 37
Chandler, Rache IV, 25
Chandler, Rachel II, 787
Chandler, Rachel IV, 25
Chandler, Rachel IV, 39
Chandler, Rachel IV, 79
Chandler, Rachel IV, 80
Chandler, Rachel IV, 517
Chandler, Rachel IV, 541
Chandler, Rachel Alma Daniel V, 37
Chandler, Rachel H. S. IV, 1356
Chandler, Rebecca II, 787
Chandler, Rebecca V, 37
Chandler, Rebecca V, 140
Chandler, Rebecca V, 222
Chandler, Rebecca V, 229
Chandler, Rebecca P. V, 37
Chandler, Rebecca W. IV, 517
Chandler, Rebecca W. IV, 522
Chandler, Rebeckah W. IV, 517
Chandler, Rowland C. II, 847
Chandler, Ruth III, 399
Chandler, Ruthanna V, 37
Chandler, Samuel II, 442
Chandler, Samuel II, 484
Chandler, Samuel II, 615
Chandler, Samuel II, 632
Chandler, Sarah II, 61
Chandler, Sarah IV, 25
Chandler, Sarah IV, 79
Chandler, Sarah IV, 80
Chandler, Sarah IV, 89
Chandler, Sarah IV, 517
Chandler, Sarah IV, 523
Chandler, Sarah IV, 560
Chandler, Sarah Ann IV, 517
Chandler, Sarah Jane IV, 324
Chandler, Sarah Jane IV, 336
Chandler, Sarah Jane V, 37
Chandler, Sarah Jane V, 62
Chandler, Sarah M. VI, 431
Chandler, Sidney J. V, 37
Chandler, Sidney Jane V, 37
Chandler, Spencer IV, 80
Chandler, Sue V, 989
Chandler, Susan J. IV, 230
Chandler, Susanna VI, 304
Chandler, Susannah II, 484
Chandler, Swithen IV, 80
Chandler, Swithen IV, 517
Chandler, Swithen IV, 523
Chandler, Swithen VI, 376
Chandler, Swithin IV, 25
Chandler, Swithin IV, 39
Chandler, Swithin IV, 80
Chandler, Tabitha IV, 80
Chandler, Tabitha IV, 104
Chandler, Thomas II, 345
Chandler, Thomas II, 484
Chandler, Thomas II, 519
Chandler, Thomas A. II, 847
Chandler, Thomas Allen II, 787
Chandler, Thomas C. II, 847
Chandler, Thomas H. II, 847
Chandler, Thomas, Jr. II, 484
Chandler, Thos. Allen II, 847
Chandler, Thos. Chalkley II, 787
Chandler, Thos. H. II, 847
Chandler, Walter D. V, 37
Chandler, Warren V, 37
Chandler, Wd. Elizabeth II, 345
Chandler, Wd. Esther Lloyd Thomas II, 787
Chandler, Webster III, 399
Chandler, William IV, 25
Chandler, William IV, 68
Chandler, William V, 229
Chandler, William VI, 303
Chandler, William VI, 304
Chandler, William VI, 319
Chandler, William VI, 330
Chandler, William VI, 348
Chandler, William Allen II, 787
Chandler, William F. V, 37
Chandler, William Guest II, 345
Chandler, William, Jr. IV, 25
Chandler, Willis I, 961
Chandler, Wm. II, 61
Chandler, Wm. II, 86
Chandler, Wm. VI, 304
Chandler, Wm. VI, 335
Chandler, Wm. A. II, 847
Chandler, Wm. Guest II, 484
Chandler, Wm. R. II, 847
Chandler, Zed VI, 900
Chandles, Aaron V, 111
Chandles, Hannah V, 111
Chandles, Miriam V, 37
Chandles, Miriam V, 111
Chaney, Bell V, 324
Chaney, Belle V, 324
Chaney, Charles V, 664
Chaney, Charles Robinson VI, 733
Chaney, Cora V, 324
Chaney, Cyrus IV, 1248
Chaney, Cyrus C. IV, 1248
Chaney, Elizabeth V, 358
Chaney, Elizabeth VI, 733
Chaney, Hannah VI, 733
Chaney, Harriett P. V, 324
Chaney, Harriett P. V, 325
Chaney, Hattie V, 324
Chaney, Hattie V, 664
Chaney, Herman IV, 1248
Chaney, Hermon IV, 1248
Chaney, Homer V, 324
Chaney, Ida IV, 1248
Chaney, Inez IV, 1248
Chaney, J. W. V, 664
Chaney, Jacob V, 324
Chaney, James Wesley V, 324
Chaney, John I, 40
Chaney, John I, 68
Chaney, Maggie Alice IV, 1248
Chaney, Margaret IV, 1248
Chaney, Mary I. VI, 805
Chaney, Miriam I, 40
Chaney, Miriam I, 68
Chaney, Rebecca I Sup 1, 7
Chaney, Sarah V, 229
Chaney, Sarah V, 252
Chaney, Thos. P. VI, 805
Chaney, W. T. IV, 1248
Chaney, Wm. V, 324
Chaney, Zach. I Sup 1, 7
Chang, Charles C. III, 67
Chanlen, Peyton VI, 865
Chanler, Aquilla G. V, 37
Chanler, Benj. Lewis V, 37
Chanler, Ellen Jane V, 37
Chanler, Marietta V, 37
Chanler, Phebe N. V, 37
Chanler, Ruthanna V, 37
Channders, Paul II, 345
Channel, Billy V, 664
Channel, Edith T. V, 664
Channel, Walter F. V, 664
Channell, Esther II, 345
Channell, Esther II, 484
Channer, Alice I, 335
Channey, Ida IV, 1248
Channey, W. T. IV, 1248
Chansey, Sarah I, 135
Chantler, David III, 67
Chantry, Eusebius Read II, 732
Chantry, Eusebius Reed II; 732
Chantry, Thomas IV, 80
Chanty, Eliza May II, 732
Chany, Absalom IV, 1062
Chany, Mary IV, 1052
Chany, Mary IV, 1062
Chany, Tacy IV, 80
Chany, Tacy IV, 89
Chany, Thirza IV, 80
Chany, Thirza IV, 90
Chapel, Emily I, 135
Chapel, Jesse VI, 805
Chapel, Jesse A. I, 233
Chapel, Lyda I, 190
Chapel, Lyda I, 194
Chapel, Lydia I, 135
Chapel, Lydia I, 190
Chapel, Margaret VI, 180
Chapel, Martha VI, 805
Chapel, Mary I, 190
Chapel, Mary Ann I, 233
Chapel, Matilda IV, 1197
Chapel, Mourning I, 40
Chapel, Peninah I, 190
Chapel, Pharaby I, 40
Chapel, Pharaby I, 135
Chapel, Phareby I, 190
Chapel, Rachel I, 40
Chapel, William VI, 57
Chapell, Ann VI, 161
Chapell, Hana VI, 162
Chapell, Margaret VI, 180
Chapell, Margaret VI, 183
Chapell, Rebeckah VI, 158
Chapell, Thomas VI, 183
Chapell, Thomas, Jr. VI, 183
Chapens, Silas V, 832
Chapin, ??? III, 67
Chapin, Carrie III, 67
Chapin, Ethel E. III, 67
Chapin, Hiram I, 379
Chapin, Hiram C. I, 379
Chapin, Inez III, 67
Chapin, Josiah II, 484
Chapin, Lydia H. III, 67
Chapin, Lydia Underhill III, 67
Chapin, William C. III, 67
Chaplin, Ada V, 324
Chaplin, Adda V, 324
Chaplin, Effie Elliott V, 453
Chaplin, Elizabeth VI, 805
Chaplin, Frances IV, 1356
Chaplin, Francis A. IV, 1356
Chaplin, George V, 38
Chaplin, Wm. R. VI, 805
Chapline, Elizabeth IV, 142
Chapline, Elizabeth IV, 146
Chapline, Margaret S. IV, 324
Chapline, Margaret S. IV, 353
Chaplun, Harry V, 300
Chapman, ??? VI, 39
Chapman, A. Wright III, 67
Chapman, A. Wright III, 300
Chapman, A. Wright III, 396
Chapman, A. Wright III, 399
Chapman, A. Wright III, 424
Chapman, A. Wright V, 898
Chapman, Aaron IV, 467
Chapman, Aaron IV, 476
Chapman, Aaron IV, 689
Chapman, Aaron IV, 727
Chapman, Aaron IV, 925
Chapman, Aaron IV, 937
Chapman, Aaron IV, 1146
Chapman, Aaron IV, 1152
Chapman, Albert III, 67
Chapman, Albert T. III, 67
Chapman, Alice I, 379
Chapman, Alice I, 385
Chapman, Alse I, 379
Chapman, Ann I, 360
Chapman, Ann I, 379
Chapman, Ann I, 407
Chapman, Ann I, 1108
Chapman, Ann II, 732
Chapman, Ann II, 787
Chapman, Ann II, 847
Chapman, Ann II, 978
Chapman, Ann II, 988
Chapman, Ann II, 1012
Chapman, Ann II, 1017
Chapman, Ann IV, 188
Chapman, Ann IV, 615
Chapman, Ann V, 38
Chapman, Ann Eliza II, 732
Chapman, Ann Eliza II, 847
Chapman, Anna I, 379
Chapman, Anna III, 67
Chapman, Anna IV, 188
Chapman, Anna IV, 615
Chapman, Anna Eliza II, 787
Chapman, Anne I, 379
Chapman, Anne S. III, 396
Chapman, Anne S. III, 399
Chapman, Asahel I, 1116
Chapman, Baldwin II, 732
Chapman, Baldwin III, 67
Chapman, Beatrix V, 898
Chapman, Ben VI, 28
Chapman, Benj. VI, 805
Chapman, Benjamin II, 485
Chapman, Benjamin V, 28
Chapman, Benjamin V, 38
Chapman, Catharine VI, 805
Chapman, Charles A. V, 898
Chapman, Charles B. V, 38
Chapman, Charles F. V, 38
Chapman, Charles F. V, 107
Chapman, Charles F. V, 124
Chapman, Charles F. V, 968
Chapman, Charles H. III, 67
Chapman, Charles H. III, 255
Chapman, Charlotte III, 67
Chapman, Charlotte III, 458
Chapman, Charlotte V, 38
Chapman, Charlotte V, 63
Chapman, Charlotte V, 898
Chapman, Charlotte H. III, 67
Chapman, Charlotte H. III, 323
Chapman, Charlotte H. V, 38
Chapman, Charlotte H. V, 898
Chapman, Charlotte H. V, 968
Chapman, Chas. V, 898
Chapman, Chas. F. V, 976
Chapman, Chas. H. III, 67
Chapman, Chas. H. III, 137
Chapman, Chas. H. V, 898
Chapman, Christian II, 202
Chapman, Christian II, 207
Chapman, David III, 67
Chapman, Dillwyn Parrish II, 787
Chapman, Doshia VI, 876
Chapman, Edward II, 732
Chapman, Edward II, 847
Chapman, Edward III, 67
Chapman, Edward B. II, 847
Chapman, Edward Danforth III, 67
Chapman, Eliza III, 66
Chapman, Eliza III, 67
Chapman, Elizabeth I, 379
Chapman, Elizabeth III, 378
Chapman, Elizabeth III, 389
Chapman, Elizabeth V, 898
Chapman, Elizabeth VI, 963
Chapman, Elizabeth Foulke III, 67
Chapman, Elizabeth M. V, 38
Chapman, Elizabeth M. V, 124
Chapman, Elizabeth M. V, 968
Chapman, Elizabeth M. V, 976
Chapman, Elizabeth S. VI, 905
Chapman, Ellen II, 345
Chapman, Ellin II, 484
Chapman, Ellwood II, 732
Chapman, Ellwood IV, 1204
Chapman, Elwood II, 847
Chapman, Elwood IV, 188
Chapman, Elwood IV, 305

Chapman, Elwood IV, 615
Chapman, Elwood IV, 666
Chapman, Emily VI, 783
Chapman, Esther III, 67
Chapman, Frances IV, 1356
Chapman, Francis A. IV, 1356
Chapman, Frank V, 453
Chapman, Gertrude V, 379
Chapman, Gertrude V, 440
Chapman, Giles VI, 357
Chapman, Giles, Jr. I, 1027
Chapman, Grace III, 399
Chapman, Grace III, 424
Chapman, Grace S. III, 396
Chapman, Grace S. III, 399
Chapman, Grace W. III, 67
Chapman, Grace W. III, 300
Chapman, Grace W. III, 399
Chapman, Grace W. III, 424
Chapman, Hannah II, 207
Chapman, Hannah II, 988
Chapman, Henry H. VI, 891
Chapman, Howard III, 28
Chapman, Howard III, 67
Chapman, Howard V, 898
Chapman, Isaac II, 484
Chapman, Isaac II, 592
Chapman, Isaac II, 988
Chapman, Isaac II, 1017
Chapman, Isaac III, 67
Chapman, J. Frank I, 1149
Chapman, James II, 203
Chapman, James II, 207
Chapman, James II, 345
Chapman, James II, 484
Chapman, James II, 485
Chapman, James Albert V, 38
Chapman, James H. V, 38
Chapman, James Wright III, 67
Chapman, Jane II, 345
Chapman, Jane II, 484
Chapman, Jane II, 485
Chapman, Jane II, 632
Chapman, Jane II, 741
Chapman, Jane II, 787
Chapman, Jane II, 847
Chapman, Jane V, 898
Chapman, Jane VI, 886
Chapman, Jane P. IV, 615
Chapman, Jane P. IV, 1204
Chapman, Jane Phemer IV, 615
Chapman, John II, 484
Chapman, John II, 485
Chapman, John II, 497
Chapman, John II, 732
Chapman, John II, 787
Chapman, John II, 847
Chapman, John II, 988
Chapman, John IV, 188
Chapman, John IV, 615
Chapman, John IV, 1204
Chapman, John VI, 481
Chapman, John Barton III, 67
Chapman, John C. II, 484
Chapman, John, Jr. II, 484
Chapman, Jonathan II, 345
Chapman, Jos. B. III, 67
Chapman, Joseph II, 787
Chapman, Joseph II, 847
Chapman, Joseph II, 978
Chapman, Joseph II, 988
Chapman, Joseph II, 1017
Chapman, Joseph V, 38
Chapman, Joseph B. V, 38
Chapman, Joseph B. V, 63
Chapman, Joseph B. V, 968
Chapman, Joseph, Jr. II, 787
Chapman, Josephine A. III, 67
Chapman, Josiah II, 485
Chapman, Josiah II, 732
Chapman, Josiah II, 787
Chapman, Josiah II, 847
Chapman, Josiah III, 67
Chapman, Keturah II, 787
Chapman, Keturah II, 847
Chapman, Lucy III, 28
Chapman, Lucy III, 67
Chapman, Lucy V, 379
Chapman, Lydia I, 379
Chapman, Lydia II, 847
Chapman, Lydia IV, 188
Chapman, Lydia IV, 615
Chapman, Lydia VI, 963
Chapman, Lydia H. II, 847
Chapman, M. Josephine I, 1149
Chapman, Maggie C. V, 898
Chapman, Margaret I, 360
Chapman, Margaret I, 379
Chapman, Margaret I, 531
Chapman, Margaret I, 1101
Chapman, Margaret I, 1108
Chapman, Margaret V, 898
Chapman, Margaret V, 901
Chapman, Margaret C. V, 38
Chapman, Margaret C. V, 898
Chapman, Margaretta V, 38
Chapman, Margery II, 988
Chapman, Margery II, 1004
Chapman, Mariana III, 67
Chapman, Mariana W. III, 67
Chapman, Marianna W. III, 323
Chapman, Marianna W. V, 898
Chapman, Marina III, 137
Chapman, Martha II, 345
Chapman, Martha II, 484
Chapman, Martha II, 485
Chapman, Martha IV, 925
Chapman, Martha IV, 937
Chapman, Martha IV, 1146
Chapman, Martha IV, 1152
Chapman, Martha IV, 1197
Chapman, Martha P. III, 67
Chapman, Mary I, 379
Chapman, Mary I, 425
Chapman, Mary II, 345
Chapman, Mary II, 484
Chapman, Mary II, 485
Chapman, Mary II, 592
Chapman, Mary II, 688
Chapman, Mary II, 732
Chapman, Mary II, 787
Chapman, Mary II, 847
Chapman, Mary II, 988
Chapman, Mary II, 1017
Chapman, Mary III, 67
Chapman, Mary III, 255
Chapman, Mary III, 454
Chapman, Mary IV, 467
Chapman, Mary IV, 476
Chapman, Mary IV, 689
Chapman, Mary IV, 727
Chapman, Mary IV, 1152
Chapman, Mary IV, 1204
Chapman, Mary V, 28
Chapman, Mary V, 38
Chapman, Mary V, 898
Chapman, Mary VI, 28
Chapman, Mary VI, 481
Chapman, Mary VI, 593
Chapman, Mary VI, 969
Chapman, Mary Ann II, 972
Chapman, Mary Ann Jones VI, 912
Chapman, Mary Anna V, 898
Chapman, Mary B. V, 38
Chapman, Mary Ellen III, 67
Chapman, Mary F. II, 847
Chapman, Mary Hutchinson II, 988
Chapman, Mary J. IV, 1152
Chapman, Mary P. III, 67
Chapman, Mary P. III, 137
Chapman, Mary W. IV, 615
Chapman, Mary W. IV, 1204
Chapman, Mary W. V, 898
Chapman, Mercy II, 485
Chapman, Mercy II, 497
Chapman, Mercy V, 38
Chapman, Mercy G. II, 485
Chapman, Miami V, 38
Chapman, Micall II, 202
Chapman, Micall II, 207
Chapman, Miles I, 379
Chapman, Miles I, 531
Chapman, Miles I, 961
Chapman, Miles I, 1101
Chapman, Miles I, 1116
Chapman, Minerva Coleman VI, 805
Chapman, Nancy VI, 891
Chapman, Nathan VI, 805
Chapman, Nathan VI, 912
Chapman, Nathan VI, 969
Chapman, Nathaniel VI, 905
Chapman, Nathaniel VI, 963
Chapman, Noah III, 67
Chapman, Noah V, 898
Chapman, Noah H. III, 67
Chapman, Noah H. III, 323
Chapman, Noah H. V, 38
Chapman, Noah H. V, 898
Chapman, Norton C. IV, 1152
Chapman, Norton D. IV, 1152
Chapman, Orpha IV, 615
Chapman, Rachel II, 732
Chapman, Rachel II, 847
Chapman, Rachel II, 978
Chapman, Rachel II, 988
Chapman, Rachel H. II, 732
Chapman, Rachel H. II, 766
Chapman, Rachel H. II, 847
Chapman, Rachel H. II, 919
Chapman, Rebecca II, 203
Chapman, Rebecca II, 207
Chapman, Robert IV, 1309
Chapman, Robert A. IV, 1309
Chapman, Robert D. V, 38
Chapman, Robert M. V, 898
Chapman, Sally Ann IV, 615
Chapman, Samuel I, 379
Chapman, Samuel I, 1015
Chapman, Samuel I, 1027
Chapman, Samuel I Sup 1, 10
Chapman, Samuel II, 345
Chapman, Samuel II, 484
Chapman, Samuel B. II, 787
Chapman, Samuel B. II, 847
Chapman, Samuel B. III, 67
Chapman, Samuel Baldwin II, 847
Chapman, Samuel Baldwin III, 67
Chapman, Sarah I, 343
Chapman, Sarah I, 379
Chapman, Sarah II, 484
Chapman, Sarah II, 485
Chapman, Sarah II, 549
Chapman, Sarah V, 28
Chapman, Sarah V, 38
Chapman, Sarah VI, 481
Chapman, Sarah VI, 489
Chapman, Sarah A. IV, 188
Chapman, Sarah A. IV, 305
Chapman, Sarah Ann IV, 188
Chapman, Sarah Ann IV, 615
Chapman, Sarah Ann IV, 666
Chapman, Sarah Ann IV, 1204
Chapman, Sarah Glover II, 787
Chapman, Sarah H. II, 847
Chapman, Sarah Harvey II, 787
Chapman, Sarah P. II, 787
Chapman, Sarah P. II, 847
Chapman, Sarah, Jr. II, 485
Chapman, Seely Ann IV, 615
Chapman, Seth II, 847
Chapman, Seth III, 399
Chapman, Seth Baldwin II, 847
Chapman, Silas V, 379
Chapman, Susan VI, 947
Chapman, Thomas I, 379
Chapman, Thomas I, 531
Chapman, Thomas I, 961
Chapman, Thomas I, 1101
Chapman, Thomas I, 1108
Chapman, Thomas I Sup 1, 8
Chapman, Thomas II, 978
Chapman, Thomas II, 988
Chapman, Thomas Ellwood II, 732
Chapman, Thomas Ellwood II, 787
Chapman, Thomas Ellwood II, 847
Chapman, Thos. I, 360
Chapman, Thos. Ellwood II, 847
Chapman, Thos. Elwood II, 847
Chapman, Virginia III, 67
Chapman, Virginia W. III, 67
Chapman, Wd. Mary II, 787
Chapman, Wd. Mary Frances Adams II, 787
Chapman, William I, 1027
Chapman, William I Sup 1, 10
Chapman, William II, 345
Chapman, William III, 67
Chapman, William E. III, 67
Chapman, William Edward III, 67
Chapman, Wilmina IV, 1309
Chapman, Wm. V, 898
Chapman, Wm. B. V, 898
Chapman, Wm. Edward III, 67
Chapman, Zeny VI, 876
Chapmean, Elizabeth VI, 805
Chapmean, Phillip VI, 805
Chappel, Abigale I, 40
Chappel, Abigale I, 57
Chappel, Agnes VI, 104
Chappel, Agness VI, 111
Chappel, Albertson I, 182
Chappel, Albertson I, 190
Chappel, Alice II, 714
Chappel, Amos I, 5
Chappel, Amos I, 40
Chappel, Ann I, 5
Chappel, Caleb I, 40
Chappel, Caleb I, 41
Chappel, Christian Ann I, 41
Chappel, Christiana I, 5
Chappel, Creesey I, 37
Chappel, Creesey I, 41
Chappel, Curtis I, 42
Chappel, Dorcas I, 40
Chappel, Elisabeth I, 4
Chappel, Elisabeth I, 5
Chappel, Elisabeth I, 41
Chappel, Elisabeth I, 135
Chappel, Elisabeth I, 159
Chappel, Eliza Ann I, 41
Chappel, Elizabeth I, 182
Chappel, Elizabeth VI, 118
Chappel, Elmira I, 5
Chappel, Emily I, 40
Chappel, Emily I, 135
Chappel, Esther I, 40
Chappel, Esther I, 69
Chappel, Esther P. I, 5
Chappel, Gabrel I, 190
Chappel, Gabriel I, 135
Chappel, Gabriel I, 182
Chappel, Gabriel I, 184
Chappel, Gabriel I, 190
Chappel, Gideon I, 4
Chappel, Gideon I, 40
Chappel, Gulielma I, 41
Chappel, Gulielma I, 58
Chappel, Gulielma J. I, 5
Chappel, Helana I, 40
Chappel, Henry I, 40
Chappel, Henry I, 41
Chappel, Henry I, 69
Chappel, Henry R. I, 5
Chappel, Huldah I, 40
Chappel, Huldah I, 41
Chappel, Isaac I, 5
Chappel, Isaac I, 41
Chappel, Isaac I, 135
Chappel, Isaac I, 159
Chappel, Isaac V, 832
Chappel, Isaiah I, 190
Chappel, Jacob I, 40
Chappel, Jacob H. I, 190
Chappel, Jacob Harvah I, 182
Chappel, James I, 41
Chappel, James C. I, 5
Chappel, James C. I, 41
Chappel, James Thomas II, 714
Chappel, Jane VI, 106
Chappel, Jeptha W. I, 5
Chappel, Jeremiah VI, 57
Chappel, Jesse I, 40
Chappel, Jesse A. I, 5
Chappel, Jesse A. I, 41
Chappel, Jesse P. I, 3
Chappel, Jesse P. I, 41
Chappel, Joab I, 40
Chappel, Job I, 40
Chappel, Job I, 190
Chappel, John I, 5
Chappel, John I, 40
Chappel, John I, 52
Chappel, John III, 67
Chappel, John III, 252
Chappel, Jonathan I, 5
Chappel, Jonathan I, 40
Chappel, Joseph I, 5
Chappel, Joseph I, 40
Chappel, Joseph I, 75
Chappel, Joseph I, 135
Chappel, Joseph I, 166
Chappel, Joseph John I, 4
Chappel, Joseph John I, 41
Chappel, Josiah I, 190
Chappel, Keziah I, 5
Chappel, Keziah I, 41
Chappel, Leora A. C. II, 714
Chappel, Lyda I, 190
Chappel, Lydia I, 135
Chappel, Lydia I, 182
Chappel, Lydia I, 184
Chappel, Lydia I, 190
Chappel, Lydia I, 198
Chappel, Malachi I, 40
Chappel, Margaret VI, 162
Chappel, Margaret Ann I, 5
Chappel, Mark I, 5
Chappel, Mark I, 40
Chappel, Mark I, 85
Chappel, Martha I, 5
Chappel, Martha I, 40
Chappel, Martha I, 41
Chappel, Martha I, 135
Chappel, Martha I, 159
Chappel, Martha VI, 57
Chappel, Mary I, 4
Chappel, Mary I, 5
Chappel, Mary I, 40
Chappel, Mary I, 41
Chappel, Mary I, 52
Chappel, Mary I, 182
Chappel, Mary I, 190
Chappel, Mary A. I, 5
Chappel, Mary Ann I, 41
Chappel, Milicent I, 41
Chappel, Miriam I, 5
Chappel, Miriam I, 40
Chappel, Moses I, 190
Chappel, Nancy I, 5
Chappel, Nathan I, 40
Chappel, Palen I, 40
Chappel, Peggy VI, 57
Chappel, Peninah I, 190
Chappel, Peninu I, 5
Chappel, Pharaby I, 40
Chappel, Pharaby I, 135
Chappel, Phareby I, 190
Chappel, Rachel I, 5
Chappel, Rachel I, 40
Chappel, Rachel I, 80
Chappel, Rachel I, 85
Chappel, Raner I, 40
Chappel, Rebeckah VI, 162
Chappel, Reuben I, 5
Chappel, Reuben I, 37
Chappel, Reuben I, 41
Chappel, Reuben Perry I, 5
Chappel, Rhoda I, 40
Chappel, Rhoda I, 86
Chappel, Rhody I, 40
Chappel, Ruben I, 182
Chappel, Rueben I, 190
Chappel, Ruth I, 40
Chappel, Ruth I, 69
Chappel, Sally Ann I, 5
Chappel, Samuel I, 5
Chappel, Samuel I, 40
Chappel, Sarah I, 3
Chappel, Sarah I, 5
Chappel, Sarah I, 40
Chappel, Sarah I, 41
Chappel, Sarah I, 58
Chappel, Sarah I, 69
Chappel, Sarah I, 75
Chappel, Sarah I, 135
Chappel, Sarah I, 166
Chappel, Sarah III, 67
Chappel, Sarah III, 252
Chappel, Sarah A. E. I, 5
Chappel, Sarah Squires I, 40
Chappel, Sibia I, 4
Chappel, Silas I, 5
Chappel, Silas S. I, 5
Chappel, Silas W. I, 5
Chappel, Squires I, 5
Chappel, Squires I, 40
Chappel, Squires I, 57
Chappel, Thomas VI, 57
Chappel, Thomas F. I, 5
Chappel, William I, 40
Chappel, William I, 41
Chappel, William I, 190
Chappel, William VI, 57
Chappel, William, Sr. I, 190
Chappell, ??? I, 7
Chappell, ??? I, 10
Chappell, ??? VI, 95
Chappell, Abbie S. II, 732
Chappell, Abby II, 700
Chappell, Abby S. II, 701
Chappell, Abby S. II, 729
Chappell, Abby S. II, 732
Chappell, Abigail I, 10
Chappell, Abigail I, 32
Chappell, Abigale I, 40
Chappell, Agnes VI, 104
Chappell, Agnes VI, 158
Chappell, Agnes VI, 159
Chappell, Agnes VI, 162
Chappell, Agnes VI, 304
Chappell, Agnes VI, 340
Chappell, Agness VI, 104
Chappell, Agness VI, 133
Chappell, Agness VI, 141
Chappell, Agness VI, 162
Chappell, Albert I, 17
Chappell, Alethia I, 42
Chappell, Alethia A. I, 6
Chappell, Alice I, 42
Chappell, Alice II, 701
Chappell, Alice II, 732
Chappell, Alice II, 757
Chappell, Alice C. II, 705
Chappell, Alice D. I, 6
Chappell, Alice D. I, 42
Chappell, Alice J. I, 41
Chappell, Alice P. I, 5
Chappell, Ambrose H. I, 5
Chappell, Ambrose H. I, 42
Chappell, Amos I, 40
Chappell, Ann I, 42
Chappell, Ann I, 228
Chappell, Ann VI, 132
Chappell, Ann VI, 133
Chappell, Ann VI, 135
Chappell, Ann VI, 162

Chappell, Ann VI, 212
Chappell, Ann B. VI, 133
Chappell, Ann B. VI, 142
Chappell, Anna I, 4
Chappell, Anna Sophronia I, 41
Chappell, Anne VI, 177
Chappell, Anne VI, 211
Chappell, Beatrice Newby I, 3
Chappell, Benjamin VI, 104
Chappell, Benjamin VI, 133
Chappell, Benjamin VI, 135
Chappell, Benjamin VI, 141
Chappell, Benjamin VI, 158
Chappell, Benjamin VI, 159
Chappell, Benjamin VI, 162
Chappell, Betsey Ann I, 4
Chappell, Betsey Ann I, 6
Chappell, Betsy Ann I, 6
Chappell, Burley VI, 304
Chappell, Caleb I, 3
Chappell, Caleb I, 4
Chappell, Caleb I, 12
Chappell, Caleb I, 40
Chappell, Caleb I, 41
Chappell, Caleb I, 42
Chappell, Charles C. I, 41
Chappell, Charles F. I, 41
Chappell, Charlotte I, 42
Chappell, Charlotte Abigail I, 6
Chappell, Charlotte C. I, 228
Chappell, Chrissie I, 4
Chappell, Chrissie I, 42
Chappell, Christian I, 6
Chappell, Christian Ann I, 41
Chappell, Christian G. I, 6
Chappell, Christopher C. I, 41
Chappell, Clarence C. I, 4
Chappell, Clinton Caspren I, 3
Chappell, Creesey I, 41
Chappell, Crissie G. I, 42
Chappell, Curtis S. I, 5
Chappell, Cynthia Ann IV, 1152
Chappell, Cynthia Ann IV, 1153
Chappell, Cyrus G. I, 6
Chappell, Cyrus G. I, 42
Chappell, D. L. I, 4
Chappell, Dorcas I, 4
Chappell, Dorcas I, 40
Chappell, Earl E. I, 42
Chappell, Earle E. I, 5
Chappell, Edmund I, 234
Chappell, Edward I, 8
Chappell, Edward L. I, 3
Chappell, Edward L. I, 12
Chappell, Edward L. I, 42
Chappell, Edward L. I, 59
Chappell, Edward Leyden I, 5
Chappell, Edward Robert I, 3
Chappell, Elenora I, 41
Chappell, Eli P. I, 41
Chappell, Elias E. I, 41
Chappell, Elias Edwin I, 4
Chappell, Elias J. I, 5
Chappell, Elihu I, 3
Chappell, Elihu I, 4
Chappell, Elihu I, 209
Chappell, Elijah R. I, 4
Chappell, Elijah Rix I, 41
Chappell, Elisabeth I, 4
Chappell, Elisabeth I, 5
Chappell, Elisabeth I, 8
Chappell, Elisabeth I, 11
Chappell, Elisabeth I, 27
Chappell, Elisabeth I, 40
Chappell, Elisabeth I, 41
Chappell, Elisabeth I, 43
Chappell, Elisabeth A. I, 42
Chappell, Elisabeth Ann I, 4
Chappell, Elisabeth Ann I, 6
Chappell, Elisabeth Ann I, 41
Chappell, Elisabeth Ann I, 42
Chappell, Elisabeth Ann I, 44
Chappell, Elisabeth Deans I, 5
Chappell, Eliza VI, 133
Chappell, Eliza VI, 136
Chappell, Eliza A. I, 17
Chappell, Eliza Ann I, 41
Chappell, Eliza Ann I, 72
Chappell, Eliza Deans I, 4
Chappell, Eliza Deans I, 20
Chappell, Eliza Deans I, 41
Chappell, Elizabeth I, 4
Chappell, Elizabeth I, 6
Chappell, Elizabeth I, 19
Chappell, Elizabeth I, 233
Chappell, Elizabeth VI, 104
Chappell, Elizabeth VI, 935
Chappell, Elizabeth Alice I, 5
Chappell, Elizabeth Anne II, 705
Chappell, Ella N. I, 42
Chappell, Ellen Basset I, 6
Chappell, Ellen Bassett I, 42
Chappell, Ellen R. I, 42
Chappell, Elma N. I, 6
Chappell, Elma N. I, 42
Chappell, Elmira I, 3
Chappell, Elmira I, 5
Chappell, Elmira I, 12
Chappell, Elmira I, 41
Chappell, Elmira J. I, 42
Chappell, Elmire J. I, 42
Chappell, Emily I, 40
Chappell, Emma Elisabeth I, 4
Chappell, Ernest I, 42
Chappell, Esther I, 4
Chappell, Esther I, 6
Chappell, Esther I, 7
Chappell, Esther I, 40
Chappell, Esther P. I, 27
Chappell, Esther P. I, 41
Chappell, Esther P. I, 88
Chappell, Exum I, 3
Chappell, Exum I, 4
Chappell, Exum I, 20
Chappell, Exum I, 41
Chappell, Gabriel I, 190
Chappell, George A. I, 41
Chappell, Gideon I, 4
Chappell, Gideon I, 19
Chappell, Gideon I, 40
Chappell, Gideon I, 41
Chappell, Gidion I, 40
Chappell, Gidion I, 75
Chappell, Gilbert I, 5
Chappell, Grace Lee I, 3
Chappell, Gulielma I, 41
Chappell, Gurney D. I, 4
Chappell, Gurnie I, 42
Chappell, Hana VI, 162
Chappell, Hariet A. I, 4
Chappell, Harriett Ann I, 209
Chappell, Harvey Roundtree I, 5
Chappell, Hattie A. I, 209
Chappell, Hattie J. I, 4
Chappell, Helana I, 40
Chappell, Henry I, 4
Chappell, Henry I, 6
Chappell, Henry I, 7
Chappell, Henry I, 40
Chappell, Henry I, 41
Chappell, Henry C. I, 6
Chappell, Henry G. I, 6
Chappell, Henry Lane I, 3
Chappell, Henry N. IV, 1152
Chappell, Henry R. I, 4
Chappell, Henry Thomas I, 5
Chappell, Howard Wilson I, 3
Chappell, Huldah I, 4
Chappell, Huldah I, 40
Chappell, Huldah I, 41
Chappell, Huldah I, 58
Chappell, Ira A. I, 209
Chappell, Irma Marie I, 3
Chappell, Isaac I, 5
Chappell, Isaac I, 40
Chappell, Isaac I, 41
Chappell, Isabella I, 5
Chappell, Israel I, 3
Chappell, Israel I, 4
Chappell, Israel I, 5
Chappell, Israel I, 41
Chappell, Israel Malica I, 41
Chappell, J. Edgar I, 209
Chappell, J. Herman I, 209
Chappell, J. Mahlon I, 42
Chappell, J. Thomas I, 5
Chappell, Jacob I, 40
Chappell, James I, 40
Chappell, James I, 41
Chappell, James II, 700
Chappell, James C. I, 4
Chappell, James C. I, 5
Chappell, James C. I, 41
Chappell, James C. I, 42
Chappell, James C. II, 701
Chappell, James Christopher I, 4
Chappell, James Douglas IV, 1152
Chappell, James Douglas IV, 1153
Chappell, James E. I, 209
Chappell, James H. I, 41
Chappell, James H. I, 42
Chappell, James H. II, 701
Chappell, James H. II, 729
Chappell, James H. II, 732
Chappell, James Henry I, 209
Chappell, James R. I, 42
Chappell, James S. I, 41
Chappell, James S. I, 209
Chappell, James S. I, 233
Chappell, James Thomas I, 4
Chappell, James Thomas I, 41
Chappell, James Thomas II, 701
Chappell, James Thomas II, 732
Chappell, James Thomas II, 757
Chappell, Jane VI, 104
Chappell, Jane VI, 119
Chappell, Jane A. I, 41
Chappell, Jane Ellen I, 4
Chappell, Jane Rebecca I, 31
Chappell, Jane S. I, 6
Chappell, Jas. T. I, 42
Chappell, Jeptha I, 41
Chappell, Jeptha W. I, 4
Chappell, Jeremiah VI, 57
Chappell, Jesse I, 4
Chappell, Jesse I, 12
Chappell, Jesse I, 40
Chappell, Jesse I, 41
Chappell, Jesse I, 209
Chappell, Jesse A. I, 3
Chappell, Jesse A. I, 4
Chappell, Jesse A. I, 6
Chappell, Jesse A. I, 41
Chappell, Jesse A. I, 233
Chappell, Jesse A. I, 234
Chappell, Jesse B. I, 5
Chappell, Jesse Mahlon I, 41
Chappell, Jesse Mahlon I, 209
Chappell, Jesse P. I, 4
Chappell, Jesse P. I, 5
Chappell, Jesse P. I, 41
Chappell, Jesse T. I, 42
Chappell, Jesse T. E. I, 6
Chappell, Jessie H. I, 209
Chappell, Jethro I, 41
Chappell, Joab I, 40
Chappell, Job I, 5
Chappell, Job I, 40
Chappell, John I, 40
Chappell, John II, 701
Chappell, John VI, 104
Chappell, John VI, 162
Chappell, John VI, 177
Chappell, John VI, 211
Chappell, John VI, 212
Chappell, John C. I, 41
Chappell, John R. I, 41
Chappell, John R. I, 42
Chappell, John S. I, 3
Chappell, John S. I, 42
Chappell, John T. I, 5
Chappell, John T. II, 732
Chappell, John W. I, 4
Chappell, John William I, 42
Chappell, John, Jr. I, 40
Chappell, Jonathan I, 40
Chappell, Jonathan I, 41
Chappell, Joseph I, 40
Chappell, Joseph J. I, 41
Chappell, Joseph John I, 41
Chappell, Julia I, 41
Chappell, Julia I, 50
Chappell, Julia I, 676
Chappell, Julia Ann I, 41
Chappell, Julia Anna I, 5
Chappell, Julianna I, 12
Chappell, Julianna I, 42
Chappell, Julianna I, 59
Chappell, Julianna E. I, 5
Chappell, Julianna E. I, 12
Chappell, Keziah I, 40
Chappell, Keziah I, 41
Chappell, Keziah I, 64
Chappell, Laura I, 4
Chappell, Laura Ann I, 41
Chappell, Laura Anna I, 5
Chappell, Leah I, 40
Chappell, Lee Burton I, 4
Chappell, Leora A. II, 701
Chappell, Leora A. II, 732
Chappell, Leora Alice II, 732
Chappell, Leora Alice II, 757
Chappell, Leora C. I, 5
Chappell, Lucinda I, 3
Chappell, Lucy M. I, 4
Chappell, Lyddia I, 40
Chappell, Lydia I, 5
Chappell, Lydia I, 6
Chappell, Lydia I, 7
Chappell, Lydia I, 41
Chappell, Lydia I, 43
Chappell, Lydia I, 190
Chappell, Lydia E. I, 42
Chappell, Lydia P. I, 6
Chappell, Lydia V. I, 6
Chappell, Lydia V. I, 42
Chappell, Mable Leora I, 4
Chappell, Malachi I, 40
Chappell, Malichi I, 41
Chappell, Mamie L. I, 209
Chappell, Margaret I, 41
Chappell, Margaret VI, 162
Chappell, Margaret S. I, 19
Chappell, Maria VI, 104
Chappell, Maria VI, 137
Chappell, Mark I, 40
Chappell, Martha I, 3
Chappell, Martha I, 4
Chappell, Martha I, 5
Chappell, Martha I, 40
Chappell, Martha I, 41
Chappell, Martha I, 209
Chappell, Martha I, 233
Chappell, Martha I, 234
Chappell, Martha VI, 158
Chappell, Martha VI, 159
Chappell, Martha VI, 162
Chappell, Martha VI, 183
Chappell, Martha B. I, 4
Chappell, Martha P. I, 12
Chappell, Martha P. I, 41
Chappell, Martha P. I, 59
Chappell, Martha R. I, 5
Chappell, Mary I, 3
Chappell, Mary I, 4
Chappell, Mary I, 5
Chappell, Mary I, 12
Chappell, Mary I, 40
Chappell, Mary I, 41
Chappell, Mary I, 75
Chappell, Mary VI, 100
Chappell, Mary VI, 101
Chappell, Mary VI, 104
Chappell, Mary A. I, 4
Chappell, Mary A. I, 5
Chappell, Mary A. I, 6
Chappell, Mary A. I, 41
Chappell, Mary A. I, 42
Chappell, Mary A. I, 58
Chappell, Mary Ann I, 4
Chappell, Mary Ann I, 41
Chappell, Mary Ann I, 209
Chappell, Mary Ann I, 233
Chappell, Mary Ann II, 701
Chappell, Mary Ann Elisabeth I, 12
Chappell, Mary C. I, 3
Chappell, Mary C. I, 4
Chappell, Mary E. I, 3
Chappell, Mary E. I, 4
Chappell, Mary E. I, 42
Chappell, Mary E. I, 59
Chappell, Mary E. II, 701
Chappell, Mary E. W. II, 732
Chappell, Mary Elisabeth I, 4
Chappell, Mary F. I, 41
Chappell, Mary Isabella I, 5
Chappell, Matilda IV, 1152
Chappell, Matilda B. IV, 1152
Chappell, Mazy A. I, 41
Chappell, Merritt Brown IV, 1152
Chappell, Merritt Brown IV, 1153
Chappell, Milicent I, 4
Chappell, Milicent I, 12
Chappell, Milicent I, 41
Chappell, Millicent I, 41
Chappell, Minerva I, 5
Chappell, Minerva E. I, 41
Chappell, Miriam I, 40
Chappell, Missouri I, 42
Chappell, Missouri C. I, 41
Chappell, Missouri M. I, 8
Chappell, Mourning I, 20
Chappell, Mourning I, 40
Chappell, Mourning A. I, 3
Chappell, Mourning A. I, 4
Chappell, Mourning A. I, 41
Chappell, Myra Emily I, 3
Chappell, Nathan I, 40
Chappell, Neally M. I, 6
Chappell, Neally M. I, 42
Chappell, Nellie G. I, 42
Chappell, Nellie J. I, 6
Chappell, Nereus I, 5
Chappell, Nereus W. I, 6
Chappell, Nereus W. I, 42
Chappell, Obed I, 4
Chappell, Obed I, 5
Chappell, Obed I, 6
Chappell, Obed I, 31
Chappell, Obed I, 41
Chappell, Obed I, 42
Chappell, Obed E. I, 4
Chappell, Obed Elsberry I, 41
Chappell, Ora L. I, 209
Chappell, Palen I, 40
Chappell, Patsey I, 4
Chappell, Patsy Ann I, 41
Chappell, Peggy VI, 57
Chappell, Pharaby I, 40
Chappell, Purvis I, 5
Chappell, Rachel I, 40
Chappell, Randolph H. I, 42
Chappell, Randolph H. II, 701
Chappell, Randolph H. II, 732
Chappell, Randolph Henry I, 4
Chappell, Raner I, 40
Chappell, Ray Winslow I, 3
Chappell, Rebecca I, 4
Chappell, Rebecca I, 5
Chappell, Rebecca I, 6
Chappell, Rebecca I, 31
Chappell, Rebecca I, 42
Chappell, Rebeckah VI, 159
Chappell, Rebeckah VI, 162
Chappell, Reuben I, 4
Chappell, Reuben I, 6
Chappell, Reuben I, 41
Chappell, Rhoda I, 40
Chappell, Rhody I, 40
Chappell, Robert I, 41
Chappell, Robert VI, 130
Chappell, Robert VI, 132
Chappell, Robert VI, 133
Chappell, Robert VI, 141
Chappell, Rolland I, 209
Chappell, Rufus I, 4
Chappell, Rufus Edwin I, 41
Chappell, Ruth I, 40
Chappell, Ruth Anna I, 5
Chappell, Ruthanna I, 5
Chappell, Sallie I, 233
Chappell, Sallie Ann I, 12
Chappell, Samuel I, 5
Chappell, Samuel I, 40
Chappell, Sarah I, 4
Chappell, Sarah I, 5
Chappell, Sarah I, 39
Chappell, Sarah I, 40
Chappell, Sarah I, 41
Chappell, Sarah A. E. I, 11
Chappell, Sarah B. I, 41
Chappell, Sarah E. I, 209
Chappell, Sarah Elisabeth I, 6
Chappell, Sarah Elisabeth I, 42
Chappell, Sarah F. II, 729
Chappell, Sarah F. II, 732
Chappell, Sarah Jane IV, 1152
Chappell, Sarah Jane IV, 1153
Chappell, Sarah L. I, 41
Chappell, Sarah Mae I, 3
Chappell, Sarah Squires I, 40
Chappell, Sarah W. II, 700
Chappell, Sarah W. II, 701
Chappell, Sibia I, 4
Chappell, Sibia Ann I, 41
Chappell, Silas I, 4
Chappell, Silas I, 5
Chappell, Silas I, 6
Chappell, Silas I, 8
Chappell, Silas I, 11
Chappell, Silas I, 27
Chappell, Silas I, 40
Chappell, Silas I, 41
Chappell, Silas I, 43
Chappell, Silas I, 233
Chappell, Silas S. I, 6
Chappell, Silas S. I, 42
Chappell, Silas W. I, 3
Chappell, Silas W. I, 12
Chappell, Silas W. I, 41
Chappell, Silas W. I, 42
Chappell, Silas W. II, 705
Chappell, Sophronia A. I, 42
Chappell, Squires I, 4
Chappell, Squires I, 12
Chappell, Squires I, 40
Chappell, Susanna I, 3
Chappell, Susanna I, 41
Chappell, Susanna I, 42
Chappell, Sybie Ann I, 41
Chappell, Sybie Ann I, 42
Chappell, Temperance E. I, 5
Chappell, Thomas I, 6
Chappell, Thomas I, 41
Chappell, Thomas I, 228
Chappell, Thomas VI, 104
Chappell, Thomas VI, 119
Chappell, Thomas VI, 158
Chappell, Thomas VI, 162
Chappell, Thomas F. I, 6
Chappell, Thomas F. I, 42
Chappell, Thomas S. I, 42
Chappell, Timothy I, 4
Chappell, Townsend I, 6
Chappell, Townsend I, 42
Chappell, Townsend I, 58
Chappell, Victoria I, 42
Chappell, Victoria A. I, 6
Chappell, Wd. Anne VI, 162
Chappell, William I, 5
Chappell, William I, 6
Chappell, William I, 40

Chappell, William I, 41
Chappell, William VI, 935
Chappell, William H. I, 41
Chappell, William H. I, 42
Chappell, William T. I, 5
Chappell, William T. I, 42
Chappell, William W. I, 6
Chappell, William W. I, 41
Chapple, Elisabeth I, 4
Chapple, Healy I, 4
Chapple, Isaac I, 4
Chapple, John III, 67
Chapple, Leah I, 40
Chapple, Mary I, 4
Chapple, Miriam I, 4
Chapple, Palin I, 4
Chapple, Penina I, 4
Chapple, Rachall I, 4
Chapple, Roda I, 4
Chapple, Sarah III, 67
Charathers, Philip C. V, 990
Charek, Emma IV, 1309
Charek, Rose IV, 1309
Charles, Abigail I, 35
Charles, Abigail I, 42
Charles, Abigail I, 135
Charles, Abigail I, 182
Charles, Abigail I, 190
Charles, Abigail I, 697
Charles, Abigail I, 875
Charles, Abigail, II I, 697
Charles, Abram V, 730
Charles, Ann I, 42
Charles, Ann I, 300
Charles, Ann I, 301
Charles, Anna I, 875
Charles, Anne I, 852
Charles, Anne I, 875
Charles, Benjamin I, 42
Charles, Benjamin I, 55
Charles, Benjamin I, 182
Charles, Caroline D. I, 676
Charles, Charlotte V, 300
Charles, Charlotte V, 305
Charles, Daniel I, 697
Charles, Edith I, 803
Charles, Edith I, 821
Charles, Elienor II, 345
Charles, Elisabeath I, 135
Charles, Elisabeath I, 151
Charles, Elisabeth I, 42
Charles, Elisabeth I, 64
Charles, Elisabeth I, 70
Charles, Elisabeth I, 71
Charles, Eliza D. V, 481
Charles, Elizabeth I, 90
Charles, Elizabeth I, 282
Charles, Elizabeth I, 697
Charles, Elizabeth I, 711
Charles, Elizabeth I, 731
Charles, Elizabeth I Sup 1, 3
Charles, Elizabeth I Sup 1, 4
Charles, Elizabeth I Sup 1, 7
Charles, Elizabeth VI, 163
Charles, Elizabeth VI, 178
Charles, Elizabeth VI, 179
Charles, Elvy I, 711
Charles, Elvy I, 730
Charles, Eva C. V, 324
Charles, Eva C. V, 616
Charles, Gulielma I, 42
Charles, Gulielma I, 71
Charles, Gulielma I, 695
Charles, Gulielma I, 697
Charles, Gulielma I, 711
Charles, Gulielma I, 718
Charles, Hannah I, 379
Charles, Hannah I, 592
Charles, Hannah I Sup 1, 3
Charles, Hannah C. V, 324
Charles, Hannah E. V, 324
Charles, Hannah E. V, 616
Charles, Henry VI, 163
Charles, Jane I, 34
Charles, Jane I, 42
Charles, Jean I, 97
Charles, John I, 42
Charles, John I, 71
Charles, John I, 282
Charles, John I, 299
Charles, John I, 301
Charles, John I, 697
Charles, John I, 711
Charles, John I, 730
Charles, John I Sup 1, 7
Charles, John V, 730
Charles, John VI, 788
Charles, Joseph I, 42
Charles, Joseph I, 182
Charles, Joseph I, 190
Charles, Joseph I, 697
Charles, Joseph I, 711
Charles, Joshua I, 282
Charles, Joshua I, 301
Charles, Leah I, 847
Charles, Leah I, 852
Charles, Leah I, 875
Charles, Leaha I, 875
Charles, Lee P. V, 324
Charles, Lee P. V, 616
Charles, Lenora IV, 1356
Charles, Lydia VI, 163
Charles, Lydia VI, 182
Charles, Lydia VI, 190
Charles, Lydia VI, 193
Charles, Margaret I, 42
Charles, Margaret I, 77
Charles, Margaret I, 301
Charles, Margaret I, 311
Charles, Martha VI, 163
Charles, Martha VI, 182
Charles, Mary I, 42
Charles, Mary I, 135
Charles, Mary I, 168
Charles, Mary I, 282
Charles, Mary I, 301
Charles, Mary I, 306
Charles, Mary I, 852
Charles, Mary I, 875
Charles, Mary I, 1070
Charles, Mary VI, 163
Charles, Matthew V, 481
Charles, Nathan I, 697
Charles, Richard I Sup 1, 3
Charles, Rufus O. V, 324
Charles, Rufus O. V, 616
Charles, Ruth I, 282
Charles, Ruth I, 299
Charles, Ruth I, 300
Charles, Ruth I, 301
Charles, Samuel I, 35
Charles, Samuel I, 42
Charles, Samuel I, 71
Charles, Samuel I, 92
Charles, Samuel I, 135
Charles, Samuel I, 151
Charles, Samuel I, 182
Charles, Samuel I, 190
Charles, Samuel I, 695
Charles, Samuel I, 697
Charles, Samuel I, 711
Charles, Samuel V, 730
Charles, Samuel, Jr. I Sup 1, 3
Charles, Samuell I, 97
Charles, Samuell I, 135
Charles, Sarah I, 42
Charles, Sarah I, 55
Charles, Sarah I, 86
Charles, Sarah I, 125
Charles, Sarah I, 135
Charles, Sarah I, 176
Charles, Sarah I, 182
Charles, Sarah I, 190
Charles, Sarah I, 201
Charles, Sarah I, 282
Charles, Sarah I, 301
Charles, Sarah I, 306
Charles, Sarah I, 697
Charles, Sarah I, 711
Charles, Sarah I, 852
Charles, Sarah I, 875
Charles, Sarah I Sup 1, 3
Charles, Sarah Ann I, 135
Charles, Sarah Ann I, 151
Charles, Sary I, 135
Charles, Silvanus I, 135
Charles, Solomon I, 852
Charles, Sylvanus I, 42
Charles, Thomas V, 300
Charles, Thomas V, 305
Charles, Thomas VI, 163
Charles, Thomas VI, 178
Charles, Thomas VI, 182
Charles, Thos. VI, 190
Charles, William I, 34
Charles, William I, 42
Charles, William I, 135
Charles, William I, 182
Charles, William I, 190
Charles, William I, 301
Charles, William I, 852
Charles, William I, 875
Charles, William I Sup 1, 3
Charles, William I Sup 1, 4
Charles, William H. IV, 1356
Charles, William R. V, 324
Charles, Wm. I, 847
Charles, Wm. R. V, 324
Charles, Wm. R. V, 616
Charlesbury, Nancy I, 191
Charlesbury, Nancy I, 195
Charleston, John VI, 818
Charlesworth, Geo. Ridout I, 617
Charlesworth, Hannah I, 617
Charlesworth, Martha C. I, 617
Charleton, Benjamin III, 67
Charleton, Edward Ash III, 67
Charleton, James Hale III, 67
Charleton, Margery III, 67
Charlick, Henry III, 67
Charlick, Henry III, 294
Charlick, Mary III, 67
Charlick, Mary III, 294
Charls, Anne I, 875
Charls, Gulielma I, 651
Charls, Leah I, 873
Charls, Leah I, 875
Charls, Martha II, 207
Charls, Martha II, 214
Charls, Samuel I, 651
Charls, Sarah I, 651
Charlton, ??? V, 157
Charlton, Albert B. VI, 805
Charlton, Alice V, 157
Charlton, Anna II, 899
Charlton, Benjamin III, 67
Charlton, Charles L. V, 157
Charlton, Chester Carter V, 157
Charlton, Clara V, 157
Charlton, Elizabeth IV, 806
Charlton, Elizabeth IV, 825
Charlton, Elizabeth VI, 866
Charlton, Elmer V, 157
Charlton, Elvan V, 157
Charlton, Elvin V, 157
Charlton, Fred V, 157
Charlton, James VI, 805
Charlton, John V, 157
Charlton, Lucretia VI, 805
Charlton, Lydia A. V, 157
Charlton, Margery III, 67
Charlton, Mary Elizabeth V, 157
Charlton, Nancy VI, 805
Charlton, Nancy VI, 815
Charlton, Nellie R. V, 157
Charlton, Rachel M. V, 152
Charlton, Rachel M. V, 157
Charlton, Susan B. V, 157
Charlton, Susannah C. V, 157
Charlton, Wilson V, 157
Charnock, Elizabeth Ann IV, 517
Charnock, Elizabeth Ann IV, 542
Charrington, Margaret VI, 376
Chasby, Chas. V, 898
Chasby, Elizabeth V, 898
Chasby, Lydia B. V, 898
Chase, Abigail IV, 25
Chase, Abner IV, 25
Chase, Alice III, 68
Chase, Alice U. III, 68
Chase, Alice U. III, 91
Chase, Allice IV, 1356
Chase, Amanda II, 847
Chase, Amanda M. II, 847
Chase, Amazia IV, 1356
Chase, Anna IV, 1356
Chase, Anna IV, 1386
Chase, Anthony III, 68
Chase, Artemas IV, 1356
Chase, Benjamin IV, 1153
Chase, Borden II, 732
Chase, Borden III, 67
Chase, Borden III, 68
Chase, Borden III, 124
Chase, Caroline III, 67
Chase, Caroline III, 68
Chase, Charles IV, 1153
Chase, Chas. II, 847
Chase, Cynthia Chase IV, 1356
Chase, Daniel H. IV, 1356
Chase, Daniel M. V, 730
Chase, Dinah I, 531
Chase, Dinah I, 586
Chase, Dinah I, 587
Chase, Dinah I, 803
Chase, Ebenezer IV, 1356
Chase, Edith II, 284
Chase, Edith L. II, 284
Chase, Edith L. II, 732
Chase, Edith Laurie II, 732
Chase, Edith Lawrie II, 284
Chase, Edith Lawrie II, 701
Chase, Edward III, 68
Chase, Edward Oliver II, 732
Chase, Elisabeth IV, 1356
Chase, Eliza III, 67
Chase, Eliza IV, 1153
Chase, Eliza IV, 1356
Chase, Eliza B. III, 68
Chase, Eliza Brown II, 732
Chase, Eliza Brown III, 67
Chase, Elizabeth A. III, 68
Chase, Elizabeth B. II, 732
Chase, Emelia IV, 1356
Chase, Estelle IV, 1309
Chase, Geo. IV, 1153
Chase, George H. II, 847
Chase, Hannah II, 1048
Chase, Hannah IV, 1153
Chase, Hannah IV, 1356
Chase, Harriet III, 68
Chase, Harriet A. III, 68
Chase, Harriet K. II, 732
Chase, Harvey II, 1048
Chase, Hepzibah V, 898
Chase, Hepzibah V, 932
Chase, Ichabod IV, 1356
Chase, James I, 531
Chase, James B. III, 68
Chase, Jane C. II, 1048
Chase, Jane C. II, 1056
Chase, Jas. B. III, 68
Chase, Jonathan II, 1048
Chase, Jonathan II, 1056
Chase, Joseph IV, 1153
Chase, Joseph W. III, 68
Chase, Josiah D. III, 68
Chase, Laura IV, 1356
Chase, Laura H. IV, 1356
Chase, Levi H. IV, 1356
Chase, Lydia III, 66
Chase, Lydia III, 138
Chase, Lydia III, 259
Chase, Lydia E. III, 68
Chase, Maria B. II, 732
Chase, Mariann II, 732
Chase, Mary III, 68
Chase, Mary IV, 1153
Chase, Mary Ann II, 284
Chase, Mary Ann II, 701
Chase, Mary Ann II, 732
Chase, Mary B. III, 68
Chase, Mary F. II, 847
Chase, Mary Jane IV, 1356
Chase, Mary L. III, 68
Chase, Mary L. IV, 188
Chase, Mary L. IV, 190
Chase, Nathan IV, 1356
Chase, Nathan IV, 1368
Chase, Nehemiah IV, 1153
Chase, Peter IV, 1356
Chase, Phebe IV, 1356
Chase, Phebe G. III, 68
Chase, Richard Wyatt II, 284
Chase, Richard Wyatt II, 701
Chase, Richard Wyatt II, 732
Chase, Ruth III, 68
Chase, Ruth B. II, 732
Chase, Ruth B. III, 67
Chase, Ruth B. III, 124
Chase, Sallann IV, 1356
Chase, Sally Ann IV, 1356
Chase, Sarah IV, 1356
Chase, Sarah IV, 1368
Chase, Sarah Folger III, 67
Chase, Thomas III, 68
Chase, Thomas III, 91
Chase, Thomas IV, 1153
Chase, Thomas C. IV, 1356
Chase, Thomas H. III, 68
Chase, Thomas Herbert III, 68
Chase, Wd. Frances II, 847
Chase, Wd. Mary Frances Adams II, 787
Chase, Willard III, 68
Chase, William B. II, 284
Chase, William B. II, 701
Chase, William B. III, 67
Chase, William B. III, 68
Chase, William Beverly II, 284
Chase, William Cromwell III, 68
Chase, Wing IV, 1356
Chase, Witham Beverly II, 701
Chase, Wm. IV, 1153
Chase, Wm. B. II, 732
Chase, Wm. Beverly II, 732
Chase, Wm. Bunker II, 732
Chase, Zimri I, 531
Chase, Zimri I, 586
Chase, Zimri I, 587
Chase, Zimri I, 592
Chase, Zimri I, 803
Chase, Zimri I, 907
Chason, Elizabeth I, 379
Chason, Hannah I, 379
Chason, Hannah I, 401
Chastain, John VI, 1006
Chastain, Lewis VI, 945
Chastain, William VI, 908
Chasteen, Elizabeth VI, 891
Chasteen, John VI, 891
Chasteen, Stephen VI, 899
Chastin, Lydda VI, 891
Chastin, William VI, 891
Chastings, Mary A. VI, 57
Chastings, Mary A. VI, 87
Chatham, Sidna II, 345
Chatin, Sarah II, 485
Chatten, ??? III, 68
Chatten, Elizabeth II, 284
Chatten, Elizabeth II, 732
Chatten, Stephen J. III, 68
Chatterton, Joan III, 68
Chattin, Abraham II, 485
Chattin, Abraham II, 496
Chattin, Anna II, 61
Chattin, Anna II, 79
Chattin, Edmund Evans II, 784
Chattin, Elizabeth II, 284
Chattin, Elizabeth II, 732
Chattin, Hannah II, 485
Chattin, Hannah II, 635
Chattin, James II, 485
Chattin, James II, 496
Chattin, John II, 784
Chattin, Judson Hutchinson II, 784
Chattin, Mary II, 485
Chattin, Nixson II, 485
Chattin, Rachel II, 485
Chattin, Rachel II, 784
Chattin, Rachel Ann II, 784
Chattin, Rebecca II, 485
Chattin, Rebecca II, 665
Chattin, Sarah II, 485
Chattin, Wd. Sarah II, 496
Chattle, Jonas IV, 71
Chauncey, Arline III, 68
Chauncey, Daniel III, 68
Chauncey, Kate III, 68
Chaunders, ??? II, 566
Chaunders, Edward II, 485
Chaunders, Elizabeth II, 485
Chaunders, Elizabeth II, 600
Chaunders, Frances II, 485
Chaunders, Hannah II, 566
Chaunders, Jane II, 485
Chaunders, Joseph II, 566
Chaunders, Lydia II, 566
Chaunders, Mary II, 566
Chaunders, Nathaniel II, 566
Chaunders, Paul II, 485
Chaunders, Paul II, 566
Chaunders, Paul II, 600
Chaunders, Wd. Jane II, 566
Chaunders, Wd. Johnson II, 566
Chaunders, Wm. II, 566
Chawner, Alice I, 335
Chawner, John S. I, 182
Chawner, John S. I, 191
Chawner, John Squire I, 188
Chawner, John Squire I, 191
Chawner, Mary I, 191
Chawner, Sarah I, 182
Chawner, Sarah I, 188
Chawner, Sarah I, 191
Chawner, Thomas I, 182
Chawner, Thomas I, 191
Cheade, J. S. VI, 805
Cheade, Judith M. VI, 805
Cheadle, Anne VI, 232
Cheadle, Anne VI, 233
Cheadle, Elizabeth VI, 45
Cheadle, Elizabeth VI, 232
Cheadle, Elizabeth VI, 234
Cheadle, George VI, 232
Cheadle, George VI, 233
Cheadle, Jacob VI, 233
Cheadle, James VI, 250
Cheadle, John VI, 45
Cheadle, John VI, 163
Cheadle, John VI, 227
Cheadle, John VI, 232
Cheadle, John VI, 233
Cheadle, John VI, 243
Cheadle, John VI, 244
Cheadle, John VI, 249
Cheadle, John VI, 285
Cheadle, John R. VI, 250
Cheadle, Judith VI, 163
Cheadle, Judith VI, 218
Cheadle, Judith VI, 219
Cheadle, Judith VI, 232
Cheadle, Judith VI, 233
Cheadle, Lucy VI, 233
Cheadle, Manoah VI, 232
Cheadle, Martha VI, 232
Cheadle, Martha VI, 244
Cheadle, Mary VI, 232
Cheadle, Mary VI, 233
Cheadle, Mary VI, 243
Cheadle, Mary VI, 246
Cheadle, Mary VI, 247
Cheadle, Mary VI, 285
Cheadle, Millicent VI, 232

Cheadle, Molly VI, 232
Cheadle, Sarah VI, 233
Cheadle, Susan VI, 250
Cheadle, Susan R. VI, 250
Cheadle, Susannah VI, 250
Cheadle, Thomas VI, 163
Cheadle, Thomas VI, 218
Cheadle, Thomas VI, 219
Cheadle, Thomas VI, 232
Cheadle, Thomas VI, 233
Cheadle, Thomas VI, 244
Cheadle, Thomas VI, 246
Cheadle, Thomas VI, 275
Cheadle, Unity VI, 250
Cheadle, Ursla VI, 233
Cheadles, Elizabeth Hargrave VI, 45
Cheadles, John VI, 45
Cheak, Ann I, 379
Cheak, Dudley VI, 891
Cheak, John VI, 892
Cheak, Susanna VI, 891
Cheak, Susanna VI, 892
Cheak, Willis I, 531
Cheaston, Elizabeth I, 357
Cheaston, Hannah I, 357
Cheaston, Richard I, 357
Cheatam, Ann II, 345
Cheatam, Ann II, 485
Cheatam, Elizabeth II, 345
Cheatam, Elizabeth II, 485
Cheatam, Hannah II, 455
Cheatam, Hannah II, 485
Cheatam, James II, 345
Cheatam, John II, 345
Cheatam, John II, 485
Cheatam, Joseph II, 345
Cheatam, Joseph II, 485
Cheatam, Sidna II, 345
Cheatam, Wd. An II, 345
Cheatham, Avis R. VI, 859
Cheatham, Bernard VI, 823
Cheatham, Carline VI, 805
Cheatham, Catharine VI, 805
Cheatham, Cynthia VI, 795
Cheatham, Eleazer VI, 804
Cheatham, Eleazer VI, 848
Cheatham, Elizabeth VI, 805
Cheatham, Isabel VI, 805
Cheatham, Isham VI, 805
Cheatham, Lucy VI, 805
Cheatham, Martha VI, 805
Cheatham, Mary II, 485
Cheatham, Mary II, 498
Cheatham, Mary VI, 818
Cheatham, Mary A. VI, 848
Cheatham, Mathew VI, 805
Cheatham, Matilda J. VI, 818
Cheatham, May C. VI, 803
Cheatham, Peter VI, 795
Cheatham, Peter VI, 804
Cheatham, Peter VI, 859
Cheatham, Phebe VI, 804
Cheatham, Phebe E. P. VI, 820
Cheatham, Robert E. VI, 803
Cheatham, Robert E. VI, 805
Cheatham, Robertson B. VI, 805
Cheatham, Robinson VI, 848
Cheatham, Sally VI, 859
Cheatham, Samuel R. VI, 819
Cheatham, Samuel R. VI, 823
Cheatham, Sarah VI, 859
Cheatham, Tabitha VI, 848
Cheatham, Thomas O. VI, 864
Cheatham, Thos. I. M. VI, 805
Cheatham, Ward VI, 805
Cheatham, Ward VI, 859
Cheatham, William A. VI, 859
Cheatham, Wm. H. VI, 805
Cheatham, Z. E. VI, 812
Cheatham, Z. E. VI, 820
Cheatham, Zaccheus VI, 805
Cheatham, Zacheus E. VI, 796
Cheatman, Martha VI, 816
Cheatman, Robertson VI, 816
Cheatom, John II, 345
Cheatom, Wd. An II, 345
Cheatum, John II, 345
Cheatwood, Ann E. VI, 992
Cheatwood, Celia VI, 909
Cheatwood, Daniel B. VI, 891
Cheatwood, Dolly W. VI, 886
Cheatwood, Evalina E. VI, 891
Cheatwood, Harriett VI, 891
Cheatwood, Hiram VI, 886
Cheatwood, Hiram VI, 891
Cheatwood, John VI, 891
Cheatwood, John VI, 923
Cheatwood, Louisa P. VI, 886
Cheatwood, Lucy E. VI, 935
Cheatwood, Nancy VI, 891
Cheatwood, Nancy VI, 909
Cheatwood, Sally P. VI, 891
Cheband, John II, 346
Chedle, John VI, 163
Chedle, Judith VI, 163
Chedle, Thomas VI, 163
Chedwick, Mittie I, 268
Chedwick, Mittie I, 270
Chee, Cherry III, 68
Chee, Loy Ding Chu III, 68
Cheek, Ann I, 379
Cheek, Dudley VI, 891
Cheek, Ellis I, 1027
Cheek, Ellis I Sup 1, 10
Cheek, Henry VI, 891
Cheek, James I, 379
Cheek, James I, 1027
Cheek, James I Sup 1, 10
Cheek, Jane I, 444
Cheek, Jenny VI, 891
Cheek, John VI, 892
Cheek, Lydia S. VI, 892
Cheek, Martha VI, 854
Cheek, Mary I, 444
Cheek, Mary T. VI, 909
Cheek, Nancy D. VI, 891
Cheek, Pasty VI, 892
Cheek, Robert I, 379
Cheek, Sarah Ann VI, 933
Cheek, Stelley VI, 1009
Cheek, Susan Frances VI, 892
Cheek, Susanna VI, 891
Cheek, Susanna VI, 892
Cheek, Susannah VI, 1012
Cheek, Thomas J. VI, 892
Cheek, William I, 961
Cheek, William H. VI, 892
Cheek, William H. VI, 1017
Cheek, William N. I, 444
Cheek, William P. VI, 891
Cheek, William P. VI, 899
Cheek, Wm. P. VI, 909
Cheek, Wm. P. VI, 933
Cheek, Wm. P. VI, 1012
Cheeke, Henry VI, 891
Cheeke, Jenny VI, 891
Cheeseman, ??? III, 68
Cheeseman, Alexander III, 68
Cheeseman, Ann III, 68
Cheeseman, Ann III, 238
Cheeseman, Benjamin III, 68
Cheeseman, Benjamin F. III, 68
Cheeseman, Edward III, 68
Cheeseman, Eliza III, 68
Cheeseman, Eliza III, 238
Cheeseman, Forman III, 68
Cheeseman, Forman III, 238
Cheeseman, H. III, 68
Cheeseman, Jacob III, 68
Cheeseman, James III, 68
Cheeseman, John III, 68
Cheeseman, John C. III, 68
Cheeseman, John C. III, 164
Cheeseman, John C., Jr. III, 68
Cheeseman, Lindley III, 68
Cheeseman, Margaret III, 68
Cheeseman, Martha III, 68
Cheeseman, Martha M. III, 68
Cheeseman, Martha M. III, 164
Cheeseman, Mary III, 68
Cheeseman, Timothy M. III, 68
Cheeseman, Timothy Matlack III, 68
Cheeseman, Willet Hicks III, 68
Cheeseman, William III, 68
Cheesman, Alfred W. III, 399
Cheesman, Annie E. III, 399
Cheesman, J. L. III, 415
Cheesman, John L. III, 399
Cheesman, John L. III, 415
Cheesman, Mary E. III, 399
Cheesman, Phebe A. III, 399
Cheesman, Phebe A. III, 415
Cheetam, Ann II, 485
Cheetam, Anne II, 511
Cheetam, John II, 485
Cheetam, John II, 511
Cheever, Etta IV, 1274
Cheever, Ettie IV, 1274
Cheever, Henry IV, 1274
Cheever, John II, 485
Cheever, John VI, 57
Chegel, John VI, 163
Chellis, Charles V, 730
Chellis, Freda IV, 689
Chellis, Freida IV, 689
Chellis, George W. IV, 1248
Chellis, Rachel V, 730
Chelton, Anne II, 511
Chelton, John II, 511
Chenault, Elizabeth VI, 805
Chenault, Louisa VI, 824
Chenault, William VI, 805
Chenault, William VI, 824
Chenaworth, John V, 157
Chenaworth, Wilson V, 157
Chendley, Goldsmith VI, 725
Cheneworth, John V, 157
Cheney, Ada III, 458
Cheney, Anna B. II, 847
Cheney, Charles Robinson VI, 733
Cheney, Edw. J. III, 68
Cheney, Eliz. III, 68
Cheney, Elizabeth VI, 733
Cheney, Eugene Price III, 458
Cheney, Florence III, 68
Cheney, Florence Annabel III, 94
Cheney, Florence M. III, 68
Cheney, Hannah VI, 733
Cheney, Mary VI, 736
Cheney, Mary VI, 737
Cheney, Moses E. III, 94
Cheney, Moses Edward III, 68
Cheney, Mr. ??? III, 68
Cheney, Mrs. ??? III, 68
Chenoweth, Caroline V, 38
Chenoweth, Francis IV, 1309
Chenoweth, Howard V, 38
Chenoweth, John V, 989
Chenoweth, Mary IV, 1309
Chenoweth, Mr. ??? V, 229
Chenoweth, Mrs. ??? V, 229
Chenoweth, Reece V, 229
Chenoweth, Rosa V, 229
Cheny, Isah IV, 1274
Cherington, Abigail IV, 689
Cherington, Anna IV, 142
Cherington, Anne IV, 146
Cherington, Emily IV, 689
Cherington, Rachel IV, 146
Cherington, Thomas IV, 146
Cherrington, Anna IV, 142
Cherrington, Rachel IV, 258
Cherry, Agnes IV, 188
Cherry, Arthur Lee V, 229
Cherry, Caroline IV, 188
Cherry, Corey Maud V, 229
Cherry, E. Ellen V, 229
Cherry, Eliza E. V, 229
Cherry, Elizabeth Ellen V, 229
Cherry, Elizabeth Ellen V, 243
Cherry, Gulielma V, 229
Cherry, Hazael D. V, 241
Cherry, Hazel D. V, 229
Cherry, J. A. V, 229
Cherry, James Pursey V, 229
Cherry, Julielma M. V, 219
Cherry, Julielma M. V, 229
Cherry, Martha V, 229
Cherry, Martha V, 324
Cherry, May Belle IV, 1310
Cherry, Milly V, 229
Cherry, Milly M. V, 229
Cherry, Milly M. V, 241
Cherry, Ralph Elroy V, 229
Cherry, Richard V, 229
Cherry, Sarah IV, 188
Cherry, Walter Ray V, 229
Cherry, William V, 229
Cherry, William V, 243
Chesher, Joel VI, 376
Cheshire, Joel II, 988
Chesley, Doctor John II, 345
Chesley, Hannah B. II, 847
Chesley, John II, 787
Chesley, Wd. Hannah II, 787
Chesseman, Margaret III, 307
Chessington, Abigail IV, 689
Chessington, Emly IV, 689
Chessman, Deborah II, 957
Chessman, Joshua II, 957
Chessman, Joshua II, 988
Chessman, Joshua II, 1027
Chessman, Mary II, 957
Chessman, Ruth II, 957
Chessman, Ruth II, 988
Chessman, Ruth II, 1027
Chester, John I, 531
Chester, Martha I, 531
Chester, Richard I, 268
Chester, Samuel II, 61
Chester, Samuel II, 485
Chester, William I, 531
Chesterman, Frank II, 787
Chesterman, Frank E. II, 787
Chesterman, Mary Elizabeth II, 787
Chestman, Joshua II, 988
Cheston, Ann I, 6
Cheston, Ann I Sup 1, 3
Cheston, Daniel I, 6
Cheston, Elisabeth I Sup 1, 3
Cheston, Elizabeth I Sup 1, 3
Cheston, Hannah I Sup 1, 3
Cheston, Joseph I Sup 1, 3
Cheston, Mary I Sup 1, 3
Cheston, Rachel I Sup 1, 3
Cheston, Rahcel I Sup 1, 4
Cheston, Richard I, 6
Cheston, Richard I Sup 1, 3
Cheston, Richard I Sup 1, 4
Cheston, Richard, Jr. I Sup 1, 3
Cheston, Sarah I, 6
Chesum, Benjamin VI, 963
Chetham, Elizabeth II, 345
Chetham, Elizabeth II, 485
Chetham, Elizabeth II, 636
Chetham, James II, 345
Chetham, John II, 485
Chetham, John II, 636
Chetham, Joseph II, 345
Chetham, Joseph II, 485
Chetham, Joseph II, 636
Chetham, Robinson VI, 814
Chevalier, Olive E. III, 68
Chevee, Etta IV, 1274
Chew, ??? II, 426
Chew, Abigail I, 961
Chew, Abigail I, 1001
Chew, Abigail I, 1004
Chew, Abigail I, 1008
Chew, Abigail V, 379
Chew, Abigail V, 481
Chew, Abigail VI, 593
Chew, Abigail VI, 596
Chew, Alice I, 961
Chew, Alice I, 1004
Chew, Alice V, 481
Chew, Alice V, 554
Chew, Alice V, 573
Chew, Alice VI, 593
Chew, Angeline V, 38
Chew, Angeline V, 554
Chew, Ann V, 38
Chew, Benjamin, Jr. II, 485
Chew, Dr. Samuel II, 426
Chew, Elizabeth II, 207
Chew, Emily V, 38
Chew, Emily V, 554
Chew, Ephraem I, 1008
Chew, Ephraim V, 379
Chew, Ephraim V, 481
Chew, Ephriam I, 1004
Chew, Eva V, 229
Chew, Eva V, 453
Chew, Evi I, 1004
Chew, Hannah V, 379
Chew, Isaac I, 1004
Chew, Isaac V, 379
Chew, Isaac V, 481
Chew, Israel I, 961
Chew, Israel I, 1004
Chew, Israel VI, 593
Chew, John I, 1004
Chew, John V, 379
Chew, John V, 481
Chew, John M. V, 379
Chew, Joseph V, 379
Chew, Joseph M. V, 379
Chew, Julia Ann V, 229
Chew, Julia Ann V, 453
Chew, Julia Ann V, 664
Chew, Julianna V, 453
Chew, Keziah II, 61
Chew, L. Louisa V, 229
Chew, Louisa V, 453
Chew, Lydia V, 379
Chew, Malinda V, 38
Chew, Malinda V, 67
Chew, Malinda V, 554
Chew, Martha V, 481
Chew, Martha V, 554
Chew, Mary I, 1004
Chew, Mary II, 485
Chew, Mary II, 500
Chew, Mary V, 38
Chew, Mary V, 51
Chew, Mary V, 379
Chew, Mary V, 409
Chew, Mary V, 481
Chew, Mary V, 554
Chew, Mary V, 584
Chew, Matilda V, 453
Chew, Miles V, 554
Chew, Milton V, 379
Chew, Minerva A. V, 453
Chew, Minerva Adelaid V, 229
Chew, N. Sarah V, 229
Chew, Nathan V, 379
Chew, R. Matilda V, 229
Chew, Rachel I, 531
Chew, Rachel I, 1008
Chew, Rachel V, 379
Chew, Rachel V, 481
Chew, Rebecca V, 38
Chew, Rebecca V, 554
Chew, Rebecca V, 584
Chew, Rebecca VI, 376
Chew, Rebecca VI, 436
Chew, Rees V, 229
Chew, Rees E. V, 453
Chew, Reuben I, 1004
Chew, Reuben V, 38
Chew, Reuben V, 554
Chew, Reuben V, 584
Chew, Rueben V, 481
Chew, Ruth I, 1004
Chew, Ruth V, 38
Chew, Ruth V, 66
Chew, Ruth V, 481
Chew, Ruth V, 554
Chew, Ruth V, 573
Chew, Samuel I, 961
Chew, Samuel I, 1004
Chew, Samuel II, 485
Chew, Samuel V, 481
Chew, Samuel VI, 376
Chew, Samuel VI, 593
Chew, Samuel VI, 596
Chew, Sarah V, 453
Chew, William V, 229
Chew, William V, 379
Chew, William V, 453
Chew, William V, 481
Chew, William V, 664
Chew, Wm. V, 453
Chewing, Elizabeth VI, 805
Chewing, Harden VI, 805
Chewning, Achilles VI, 874
Chewning, Achilles VI, 892
Chewning, Burwell VI, 892
Chewning, Callohill D. VI, 892
Chewning, Calohill D. VI, 936
Chewning, Catharine VI, 892
Chewning, Dicy VI, 892
Chewning, Eliza J. VI, 892
Chewning, Elizabeth VI, 874
Chewning, Harding VI, 817
Chewning, Jameme VI, 233
Chewning, James VI, 892
Chewning, Jemima VI, 233
Chewning, John VI, 892
Chewning, Kellis VI, 936
Chewning, Kellis VI, 964
Chewning, Kellis VI, 980
Chewning, Killes VI, 892
Chewning, Lucy VI, 892
Chewning, Mary S. H. VI, 892
Chewning, Minerva S. VI, 892
Chewning, Polly VI, 964
Chewning, Sally VI, 892
Chewning, Sarah VI, 936
Chewning, Walter VI, 892
Cheyne, Elizabeth II, 485
Cheyney, Ada U. III, 399
Cheyney, Anna B. II, 847
Cheyney, Edith S. VI, 57
Cheyney, Edith S. VI, 82
Cheyney, Edith S. VI, 83
Cheyney, Elizabeth II, 566
Cheyney, Ellen VI, 57
Cheyney, Ellen VI, 82
Cheyney, Ellen M. II, 732
Cheyney, Ellen M. II, 745
Cheyney, Eugene Price III, 399
Cheyney, Eugene Price III, 449
Cheyney, George VI, 82
Cheyney, George S. III, 399
Cheyney, Jesse S. II, 732
Cheyney, Jesse S. II, 745
Cheyney, Jessee VI, 57
Cheyney, Jessee VI, 82
Cheyney, Joseph W. II, 701
Cheyney, Joseph Walker II, 732
Cheyney, Joseph Walker II, 745
Cheyney, Lydia II, 701
Cheyney, Lydia Hartz II, 732
Cheyney, Mary P. III, 399
Cheyney, Sarah E. II, 701
Cheyney, Sarah Elizabeth II, 732
Cheyney, Sarah Elizabeth II, 745
Cheyney, Sarah H. II, 732
Cheyney, Walker C. VI, 82
Cheyney, William Walker II, 701
Cheyney, Wm. Walker II, 732
Chichester, ??? III, 272
Chichester, Mary III, 480
Chichester, Mary III, 491
Chichester, Mrs. ??? VI, 11
Chichester, Sarah E. III, 68
Chichester, Sarah E. III, 272
Chichester, William VI, 11
Chick, Anderson VI, 805

hick, Anderson VI, 847
hick, Betsy VI, 892
hick, Corbin VI, 892
hick, Damaris II, 442
hick, Dudley VI, 805
hick, Hannah II, 442
hick, Henry VI, 805
hick, James II, 442
hick, James II, 485
hick, Lucy VI, 805
hick, Margaret VI, 805
hick, Mary B. VI, 808
hick, Milly VI, 808
hick, Rachel II, 345
hick, William VI, 860
hicken, Anne IV, 518
hicken, Daniel IV, 324
hicken, Daniel IV, 518
hicken, Daniel David IV, 518
hicken, David IV, 324
hicken, Elenor IV, 324
hicken, Eleonor IV, 515
hicken, Eleonor IV, 518
hicken, Henry Farson IV, 518
hicken, John IV, 324
hicken, John IV, 518
hicken, Mary IV, 324
hicken, Mary IV, 518
hicken, Mary IV, 527
hicken, Mary IV, 528
hicken, Mary IV, 560
hicken, Mary IV, 561
hickston, Eviline V, 379
hickston, Eviline V, 394
hickyter, Tom VI, 12
hilcot, Mary VI, 376
hilcote, Charles IV, 1204
hilcote, Charley IV, 1204
hilcote, Denton IV, 1204
hilcote, Donald IV, 1204
hilcote, Dorothy IV, 1204
hilcote, Dorothy IV, 1310
hilcote, Laurie IV, 1204
hilcote, Luella IV, 1204
hilcote, Mattie IV, 1204
hilcote, Morgan IV, 1204
hilcote, Morgan T. IV, 1204
hilcote, Myrtle IV, 1204
hilcote, Roy IV, 1204
hilcote, Ruth IV, 1204
hilcote, Susan IV, 1204
hilcote, Viola IV, 1204
hilcote, Voy IV, 1204
hilcote, Wm. B. IV, 1204
hild, Aaron II, 988
hild, Agnetus III, 68
hild, Agnetus III, 217
hild, Amee II, 207
hild, Amy II, 988
hild, Amy II, 1029
hild, Anna III, 69
hild, Anna III, 285
hild, Anne II, 207
hild, Cadwalader II, 988
hild, Cassie L. II, 847
hild, Cassie L. II, 894
hild, Cephus II, 985
hild, Cephus II, 988
hild, Daniel II, 988
hild, Daniel II, 989
hild, Edward Stanton II, 988
hild, Elizabeth II, 988
hild, Elizabeth N. II, 847
hild, Emma S. II, 894
hild, Hannah II, 965
hild, Hannah II, 985
hild, Hannah II, 988
hild, Hannah III, 99
hild, Hannah B. II, 967
hild, Hannah B. II, 1048
hild, Hannah B. II, 1058
hild, Hector C. Ivins II, 1070
hild, Henry T. II, 847
hild, Henry T. II, 894
hild, Jno. II, 207
hild, John II, 317
hild, John II, 894
hild, John II, 1070
hild, John M. II, 847
hild, John M. II, 894
hild, John Mason II, 847
hild, John Mason III, 68
hild, Joseph II, 985
hild, Joseph II, 988
hild, Joseph, Jr. II, 989
hild, Josephine III, 68
hild, Josephine F. III, 217
hild, Josephine H. III, 217
hild, Justies VI, 163
hild, Lucy B. II, 701
hild, Lucy B. II, 732
Child, Mahlon II, 701
Child, Mahlon II, 957
Child, Mahlon M. II, 1047
Child, Mahlon M. II, 1048
Child, Mary II, 207
Child, Mary II, 957
Child, Mary III, 46
Child, Mary T. II, 1070
Child, Mary T. II, 1074
Child, Mary W. II, 701
Child, Mary W. II, 732
Child, Mary W. II, 733
Child, Mary W. II, 1047
Child, Mary W. II, 1048
Child, Moses II, 967
Child, Moses II, 988
Child, Moses II, 1047
Child, Moses II, 1048
Child, Nancy II, 967
Child, Nancy II, 1047
Child, Nancy II, 1048
Child, Naylor II, 988
Child, Oliver II, 988
Child, Percilla II, 985
Child, Percilla II, 988
Child, Rachel II, 1070
Child, Samuel II, 988
Child, Samuel II, 989
Child, Sarah A. II, 847
Child, Sarah A. II, 894
Child, Sarah Louise III, 285
Child, William L. II, 701
Child, Wm. III, 69
Child, Wm. III, 285
Child, Wm. L. II, 733
Childers, Esther V, 730
Childers, Mary A. IV, 188
Childers, Noah VI, 163
Childers, Orvy D. IV, 188
Childra, Martha IV, 142
Childra, Martha IV, 378
Childra, Phebe IV, 378
Childra, Sally IV, 378
Childras, Jenny VI, 809
Childre, Martha IV, 378
Childre, Phebe IV, 378
Childre, Sally IV, 378
Childres, Esty V, 730
Childres, Mary V, 730
Childress, Cynthia Alice VI, 376
Childress, Elizabeth I, 920
Childress, Elizabeth VI, 376
Childress, Elizabeth VI, 405
Childress, Elizabeth VI, 892
Childress, Elizabeth VI, 987
Childress, ELizabeth E. VI, 805
Childress, Esther V, 730
Childress, Esty V, 730
Childress, Fleming VI, 805
Childress, Jenny VI, 807
Childress, Joel J. VI, 376
Childress, John B. VI, 805
Childress, John Walter VI, 376
Childress, John Walter VI, 405
Childress, Mary V, 730
Childress, Mary V, 771
Childress, Nancy VI, 805
Childress, Nancy VI, 892
Childress, Obediah VI, 804
Childress, Patty VI, 987
Childress, Polly VI, 843
Childress, Polly A. VI, 805
Childress, Royal VI, 892
Childress, Samuel VI, 807
Childress, Thomas VI, 892
Childress, Vaulton VI, 805
Childs, Alselea V, 730
Childs, Daniel II, 988
Childs, Elbert E. IV, 1310
Childs, Grace Evelyn VI, 377
Childs, Grace Evolyn VI, 377
Childs, Griffin VI, 377
Childs, Griffith VI, 377
Childs, Hannah II, 970
Childs, Hannah II, 988
Childs, Harry B. VI, 377
Childs, Harry Boley VI, 377
Childs, J. M. V, 730
Childs, J. W. V, 730
Childs, John II, 309
Childs, John A. VI, 377
Childs, Joseph II, 988
Childs, Mamie H. VI, 377
Childs, Mary II, 284
Childs, Mary II, 309
Childs, Mary VI, 377
Childs, Mary C. VI, 377
Childs, Mary Hannah VI, 377
Childs, Moses II, 988
Childs, Naylor II, 988
Childs, Phoebe IV, 1310
Childs, Rebecca V, 898
Childs, Rebecca V, 899
Childs, Richard VI, 481
Childs, Samuel II, 988
Childs, Sarah Louise III, 153
Childs, Susan S. VI, 377
Childs, V. S. A. V, 730
Chiles, Agnes VI, 233
Chiles, Agnes VI, 249
Chiles, Agnes VI, 285
Chiles, Agnes VI, 286
Chiles, Agness VI, 233
Chiles, Ann VI, 233
Chiles, Ann VI, 246
Chiles, Ann VI, 259
Chiles, Ann VI, 269
Chiles, Ann VI, 940
Chiles, Anne VI, 233
Chiles, Boling VI, 233
Chiles, Elizabeth VI, 920
Chiles, Henry VI, 233
Chiles, John VI, 280
Chiles, John VI, 920
Chiles, John VI, 940
Chiles, Lucy VI, 233
Chiles, Manoah VI, 232
Chiles, Manoah VI, 233
Chiles, Manoah, Jr. VI, 233
Chiles, Mary VI, 233
Chiles, Mary VI, 259
Chiles, Mary VI, 280
Chiles, Menoah VI, 233
Chiles, Menoah VI, 246
Chiles, Menoah VI, 249
Chiles, Patte VI, 233
Chiles, Patte VI, 251
Chiles, Patty VI, 233
Chiles, Samuel VI, 233
Chiles, Sarah VI, 233
Chiles, Susanna VI, 332
Chiles, Susannah VI, 233
Chiles, Susannah VI, 260
Chillis, George W. IV, 1248
Chillman, Emma Adele II, 808
Chilson, Anna W. IV, 937
Chilson, Arthur IV, 1310
Chilson, Arthur B. IV, 1310
Chilston, Bridget II, 485
Chilston, Bridget II, 534
Chilton, Adaline VI, 805
Chilton, Andrew I, 875
Chilton, Ann S. VI, 842
Chilton, Catharine VI, 805
Chilton, Effa Ann I, 875
Chilton, Eleanor VI, 481
Chilton, Eleanor VI, 512
Chilton, Elizabeth VI, 892
Chilton, Elizabeth Ann VI, 890
Chilton, Emeline S. VI, 892
Chilton, Emily M. VI, 913
Chilton, Everett A. I, 875
Chilton, George N. VI, 892
Chilton, George N. VI, 913
Chilton, Henry I, 875
Chilton, Henry VI, 838
Chilton, Henry VI, 890
Chilton, Henry VI, 909
Chilton, Henry VI, 911
Chilton, Henry A. I, 875
Chilton, Henry H. VI, 892
Chilton, Ira I, 875
Chilton, James T. VI, 890
Chilton, James T. VI, 892
Chilton, Jas. VI, 912
Chilton, John VI, 805
Chilton, John M. I, 875
Chilton, John P. VI, 805
Chilton, John P. VI, 892
Chilton, John P. VI, 938
Chilton, John P. VI, 978
Chilton, Joseph VI, 805
Chilton, Joseph VI, 846
Chilton, Joseph VI, 848
Chilton, Judith VI, 847
Chilton, Martha I, 875
Chilton, Martha J. VI, 892
Chilton, Mary I, 875
Chilton, Mary Ann VI, 892
Chilton, Mary Jane VI, 892
Chilton, Nancy VI, 913
Chilton, Peggy VI, 805
Chilton, Polly J. VI, 909
Chilton, Raleigh VI, 805
Chilton, Rawleigh VI, 892
Chilton, Richard VI, 512
Chilton, Richard VI, 827
Chilton, Richard VI, 842
Chilton, Richard VI, 847
Chilton, Richard L. VI, 840
Chilton, Richard L. VI, 854
Chilton, Richard, Jr. VI, 827
Chilton, Robert S. VI, 805
Chilton, Samira E. I, 875
Chilton, Sarah E. VI, 892
Chilton, Stephen A. I, 875
Chilton, William N. I, 875
Chilton, William W. VI, 892
Chinetwith, Mr. ??? V, 229
Chinetwith, Mrs. ??? V, 229
Chinewith, Rebecca IV, 615
Chinewith, Rebecca IV, 653
Chineworth, Susannah C. V, 157
Chinsley, Edith III, 69
Chinsley, Edith B. III, 303
Chinsley, Elwood A. III, 69
Chinsley, Elwood A. III, 303
Chinsley, Ethel III, 69
Chinsley, Leonard III, 69
Chipman, Elisabeth I, 840
Chipman, Elizabeth I, 778
Chipman, Elizabeth I, 803
Chipman, Elizabeth I, 836
Chipman, Luiza I, 803
Chipman, Luzena I, 531
Chipman, Luzena I, 803
Chipman, Martha I, 778
Chipman, Martha I, 803
Chipman, Mary I, 803
Chipman, Mary I, 813
Chipman, Mary II, 207
Chipman, Mary II, 239
Chipman, Molly I, 803
Chipman, Parris I, 803
Chipman, Sarah I, 803
Chippendale, Sarah V, 898
Chism, Elizabeth V, 664
Chism, Martin VI, 805
Chism, Matilda V, 664
Chism, Sarah V, 664
Chism, Susan VI, 805
Chittum, Benjamin V, 157
Chittum, Cora V, 157
Chittum, James VI, 881
Choate, Calvin IV, 1310
Choate, Calvin R. IV, 1310
Choate, Louie Haladay IV, 1310
Chogwell, Mary IV, 1091
Chogwell, Mary IV, 1101
Cholerton, Mary II, 721
Cholie, Lucy VI, 892
Cholie, William A. VI, 892
Chopourian, Angel Agnes III, 103
Chopson, Mary A. V, 713
Chouning, Jemimah VI, 233
Chounings, Jameme VI, 233
Chounings, Jamima VI, 233
Chounings, Jemima VI, 233
Chounings, Jemimah VI, 233
Chounings, Joseph VI, 233
Chrisco, J. C. I, 939
Chrisco, James C. I, 922
Chrisco, John C. I, 939
Chrisco, Martha I, 939
Chrisco, Martha E. I, 922
Chrisco, S. E. I, 922
Chrisco, W. C. I, 922
Chrisman, Amanda V, 453
Chrisman, Carl V, 453
Chrisman, Carl O. V, 453
Chrisman, Carrie V, 453
Chrisman, Clarence V, 300
Chrisman, Dena V, 300
Chrisman, Emma V, 453
Chrisman, Estella V, 453
Chrisman, Grace V, 453
Chrisman, Hannah II, 710
Chrisman, Isaac II, 710
Chrisman, John V, 453
Chrisman, Josephine V, 453
Chrisman, Margaret L. II, 710
Chrisman, Margery V, 453
Chrisman, Mary IV, 671
Chrisman, Mary IV, 696
Chrisman, Mary V, 453
Chrisman, Wendell L. V, 453
Chrisman, Wilber L. V, 453
Chrisman, Wilbur V, 453
Chrisman, Wilma Jean V, 300
Chrisman, Wm. V, 300
Chrisman, Wm. V, 453
Chrispin, Ann II, 212
Christ, Joseph W. V, 979
Christ, Phebe V, 835
Christ, Rebecca Ann V, 979
Christ, Ruthanna V, 979
Christ, Thirza IV, 80
Christ, William P. V, 979
Christ, William R. V, 979
Christen, Mabel IV, 937
Christenberry, Harry V, 324
Christenburg, ??? I, 711
Christenburg, J. A. I, 711
Christenburg, Joseph I, 711
Christenbury, ??? I, 711
Christenbury, J. A. I, 711
Christenbury, Joseph I, 711
Christian, Abner VI, 892
Christian, Abner VI, 958
Christian, Alma IV, 689
Christian, Anthony VI, 821
Christian, Anthony VI, 892
Christian, Anthony VI, 1011
Christian, Billy VI, 163
Christian, Billy VI, 171
Christian, Charles A. I, 875
Christian, Charles M. VI, 886
Christian, Chas. L. VI, 1000
Christian, Chas. M. VI, 805
Christian, Cornelia VI, 805
Christian, David IV, 689
Christian, Edith V, 324
Christian, Edward D. VI, 801
Christian, Edward D. VI, 805
Christian, Eliza VI, 892
Christian, Frances VI, 892
Christian, Frances Ann VI, 805
Christian, H. A. VI, 804
Christian, John L. VI, 163
Christian, Julia VI, 914
Christian, Lucy VI, 805
Christian, Magdaline VI, 892
Christian, Martha VI, 849
Christian, Mary VI, 986
Christian, Mary Ann VI, 892
Christian, Patrick G. VI, 890
Christian, Patrick H. VI, 892
Christian, Patrick H. VI, 962
Christian, Sally VI, 892
Christian, Thomas VI, 163
Christian, Thomas C. VI, 892
Christian, W. H. B. VI, 849
Christian, Walter VI, 892
Christian, Wm. IV, 1310
Christian, Wm. D. VI, 805
Christie, John Luckey III, 69
Christie, Martha II, 346
Christie, Mary II, 486
Christie, Mary II, 533
Christie, Mary Margaret III, 79
Christman, Ella L. II, 713
Christman, Isaac F. II, 713
Christman, Rebecca II, 713
Christon, ??? III, 91
Christon, Ann III, 91
Christon, Rebecca VI, 834
Christopher, Aristobulus II, 442
Christopher, Blanch V, 379
Christopher, Henry II, 442
Christopher, Henry Aristobulus II, 442
Christopher, John II, 442
Christopher, Judah II, 442
Christopher, Mary II, 346
Christopher, Mary II, 442
Christopher, Nathaniel II, 442
Christopher, Phebe II, 442
Christy, Bella III, 49
Christy, Elijah VI, 805
Christy, Elijah VI, 837
Christy, Hannah III, 69
Christy, John Luckey III, 69
Christy, Mary II, 486
Christy, Mary A. VI, 837
Christy, Mary Ann V, 324
Christy, Mary Ann V, 352
Christy, Mary C. III, 31
Christy, Mary C. III, 39
Christy, Mary Margaret III, 69
Christy, Polly VI, 805
Christy, Sarah II, 485
Christy, Sarah II, 669
Christy, Sarah Jane IV, 324
Christy, Sarah Jane IV, 347
Christy, Thomas II, 485
Christy, Thomas II, 669
Chuband, Ann II, 346
Chuband, John II, 346
Chubb, Nanna V, 989
Chubb, Richard II, 486
Chubb, Sarah II, 346
Chubb, Susanna VI, 892
Chubb, Thomas VI, 892
Chubb, Violl II, 346
Chuldrios, Nancy VI, 892
Chuldrios, Thomas VI, 892
Chuning, Jemima VI, 163
Chuning, Jemima VI, 185
Chuning, Jemima VI, 186
Chuning, Joseph VI, 163
Chuning, Joseph VI, 185
Chuning, Joseph VI, 186
Chuning, Joseph VI, 233
Church, Ann II, 989

Church, Anna B. III, 69
Church, Austin III, 69
Church, Austin Harris III, 69
Church, Austin Harris III, 247
Church, Benjamin III, 69
Church, Delphina I, 875
Church, Delphina I, 882
Church, Edward II, 989
Church, Elizabeth II, 46
Church, Elizabeth VI, 30
Church, Ella III, 229
Church, Florence I, 922
Church, Florence White I, 939
Church, Harriet L. III, 69
Church, Isaac II, 207
Church, Isaac Monroe III, 69
Church, Jane II, 207
Church, Joseph II, 989
Church, Joseph, Jr. II, 989
Church, M. E. I, 942
Church, M. E. VI, 617
Church, M. E. VI, 667
Church, Mary VI, 889
Church, Mary A. III, 69
Church, Matty VI, 892
Church, Rachel II, 825
Church, Rebecca II, 989
Church, Rebeckah II, 989
Church, Rebekah II, 1043
Church, Robert VI, 889
Church, Robert VI, 892
Church, Ruth III, 69
Church, Ruth III, 247
Church, Samuel II, 825
Church, Samuel II, 1043
Church, Sarah II, 207
Church, Sarah II, 989
Church, Sarah II, 1043
Church, Stephen III, 69
Church, Stephen H. III, 69
Church, Stephen K. III, 69
Church, Wd. Sarah II, 825
Church, Wm. Wyatt I, 939
Churchill, Ann Maria III, 69
Churchill, Bertha IV, 1310
Churchill, Bertha Emma IV, 1310
Churchill, Eva IV, 1310
Churchill, Eva Anna IV, 1310
Churchill, John IV, 1310
Churchill, Lillian IV, 1310
Churchill, Lillie IV, 1310
Churchill, Lucetta I, 853
Churchill, Mrs. A. M. IV, 1310
Churchill, Mrs. John IV, 1310
Churchman, Alfred III, 69
Churchman, Ann VI, 706
Churchman, Ann E. II, 207
Churchman, Anne II, 207
Churchman, Anne II, 486
Churchman, Anne VI, 631
Churchman, Anne VI, 706
Churchman, Caleb D. III, 254
Churchman, Caroline III, 69
Churchman, Edw. III, 69
Churchman, Edward II, 346
Churchman, Edward VI, 631
Churchman, Edward VI, 706
Churchman, Eliza III, 69
Churchman, Emily II, 317
Churchman, Emily II, 847
Churchman, Emily II, 900
Churchman, Emily III, 69
Churchman, Gainer II, 787
Churchman, Gainer VI, 481
Churchman, Gainor VI, 481
Churchman, George VI, 481
Churchman, Hannah II, 207
Churchman, Hannah II, 787
Churchman, Hannah II, 795
Churchman, Hannah III, 69
Churchman, Hannah III, 255
Churchman, Hannah VI, 481
Churchman, Hannah James VI, 736
Churchman, Isabel III, 69
Churchman, James II, 207
Churchman, John II, 207
Churchman, John II, 317
Churchman, Joseph II, 207
Churchman, Joseph II, 787
Churchman, Joseph III, 69
Churchman, Joseph III, 255
Churchman, Mary II, 346
Churchman, Mary II, 486
Churchman, Mary III, 69
Churchman, Mary III, 270
Churchman, Mary H. II, 804
Churchman, Micajah III, 69
Churchman, Owen II, 346
Churchman, Owen II, 486
Churchman, Owen III, 69
Churchman, Owen III, 130
Churchman, Owen III, 270
Churchman, Pennell II, 346
Churchman, Pennell III, 69
Churchman, Phebe II, 207
Churchman, Phebe III, 69
Churchman, Phebe III, 255
Churchman, Reb. III, 69
Churchman, Reb. III, 130
Churchman, Reb. III, 163
Churchman, Rebecca VI, 631
Churchman, Rebecca VI, 706
Churchman, Rebecca C. III, 69
Churchman, Samuel II, 207
Churchman, Samuel II, 787
Churchman, Samuel III, 69
Churchman, Samuel III, 254
Churchman, Sarah II, 317
Churchman, Sarah II, 787
Churchman, Sarah II, 847
Churchman, Sarah III, 69
Churchman, Sarah Ann III, 69
Churchman, Sarah Ann III, 270
Churchman, Sarah Anna III, 49
Churchman, Sinclair III, 69
Churchman, William H. III, 69
Churchman, William M. II, 346
Churchman, William M. III, 69
Churchman, Wm. H. II, 847
Churchman, Wm. H. III, 69
Cicinese, John IV, 1310
Cilley, Sherberne A. III, 69
Cinard, Elizabeth IV, 378
Citi, Jacob VI, 998
Citty, John VI, 892
Citty, Mary VI, 892
City, Abraham VI, 1019
City, Catherine VI, 1019
City, Elizabeth VI, 963
City, Jacob VI, 886
City, Jacob VI, 963
City, Jacob VI, 1019
City, Nancy VI, 998
City, Polly VI, 1019
City, Sally VI, 886
Clabaugh, Jane V, 616
Clabaugh, Ruth V, 616
Clabey, Mary VI, 805
Clabey, William VI, 805
Clabough, Jane V, 616
Clagg, James VI, 892
Clagg, James B. VI, 892
Clagg, Judith VI, 892
Clagg, Martha D. VI, 892
Claiborn, Anna III, 237
Claiborne, Anna III, 308
Claibourn, Richard C. VI, 139
Claibourne, Richard C. VI, 133
Claire, Mary I Sup 1, 3
Claire, Timothy I Sup 1, 3
Clairwater, Hannah V, 230
Clairwater, Hannah V, 445
Clairy, Elisabeth I, 135
Claiton, Marian I, 804
Claiton, Miriam I, 804
Clampet, Mary I, 799
Clampet, Mary I, 803
Clampfer, Mary II, 486
Clampfer, Mary II, 573
Clampit, Ruth I, 911
Clampit, Ruth I, 914
Clampitt, Eliza IV, 500
Clampitt, Eliza IV, 1008
Clampitt, Emily J. IV, 1008
Clampitt, Jennie E. IV, 500
Clampitt, Joel IV, 500
Clampitt, Joel K. IV, 1008
Clanshaid, Ephraim I, 120
Clanshaid, Millicent I, 120
Clanther, Mary II, 61
Clanther, Mary II, 76
Clanther, Philop II, 61
Clanther, Philop II, 76
Clap, Anna II, 574
Clap, John III, 413
Clap, Phebe III, 413
Clapp, Allan II, 701
Clapp, Allen III, 69
Clapp, Ann Eliza III, 70
Clapp, Anna III, 70
Clapp, Anna W. III, 69
Clapp, Arrelia G. I, 939
Clapp, Arrelia G. I, 941
Clapp, Arthur III, 70
Clapp, Barbie I, 614
Clapp, Belle S. III, 69
Clapp, Benjamin III, 69
Clapp, Benjamin III, 295
Clapp, Catharine IV, 467
Clapp, Catharine IV, 494
Clapp, Deborah IV, 467
Clapp, Deborah IV, 494
Clapp, Edmee III, 180
Clapp, Eliza IV, 467
Clapp, Eliza IV, 486
Clapp, Eliza A. II, 823
Clapp, Eliza Jane I, 932
Clapp, Elizabeth II, 802
Clapp, Elizabeth III, 70
Clapp, Elizabeth A. III, 70
Clapp, Elizabeth, Jr. III, 69
Clapp, Emma I, 932
Clapp, Emma I, 939
Clapp, Enoch II, 848
Clapp, Enoch II, 892
Clapp, George Fitch III, 179
Clapp, George Frederick III, 179
Clapp, Henrietta Emaline I, 614
Clapp, Henry I, 932
Clapp, Henry Frost III, 69
Clapp, Herbert W. III, 69
Clapp, Herbert W. III, 108
Clapp, Hugh Van I, 614
Clapp, Isaac H. III, 69
Clapp, James IV, 467
Clapp, Jas. IV, 494
Clapp, John III, 69
Clapp, John III, 70
Clapp, John III, 179
Clapp, John III, 311
Clapp, John III, 399
Clapp, John III, 419
Clapp, John A. III, 70
Clapp, John Clapp III, 179
Clapp, John F. I, 631
Clapp, John Rye III, 69
Clapp, John U. III, 180
Clapp, John W. I, 631
Clapp, John William I, 614
Clapp, John Wm. I, 627
Clapp, Katharine M. III, 179
Clapp, Laura Jane I, 614
Clapp, Laura Jane I, 627
Clapp, Margaret III, 69
Clapp, Margaret III, 70
Clapp, Margaret III, 179
Clapp, Margaret III, 180
Clapp, Margaret C. III, 179
Clapp, Maria III, 70
Clapp, Maria A. III, 70
Clapp, Mary II, 848
Clapp, Mary II, 892
Clapp, Mary III, 69
Clapp, Mary III, 179
Clapp, Mary M. III, 69
Clapp, Mary M. III, 108
Clapp, Mary T. II, 848
Clapp, Mary T. II, 892
Clapp, Mary Tyson II, 806
Clapp, Phebe III, 70
Clapp, Phebe III, 311
Clapp, Phebe III, 399
Clapp, Phebe III, 419
Clapp, Phebe C. III, 179
Clapp, Phebe H. III, 69
Clapp, Phebe H. III, 70
Clapp, Phebe H. III, 179
Clapp, Phebe H. III, 311
Clapp, Phebe M. III, 70
Clapp, Phebe M. III, 192
Clapp, Phoebe III, 69
Clapp, Sam'l III, 69
Clapp, Samuel III, 399
Clapp, Samuel H. III, 69
Clapp, Samuel H. III, 70
Clapp, Samuel H. III, 192
Clapp, Samuel H., Jr. III, 70
Clapp, Sarah III, 69
Clapp, Sarah III, 295
Clapp, Sarah III, 378
Clapp, Sidney I, 756
Clapp, Silas III, 70
Clapp, Silas III, 378
Clapp, Thomas III, 378
Clapp, William Alson I, 614
Clapp, William M. I, 939
Clapp, William R. III, 70
Clapp, William, Jr. III, 70
Clapper, Emmanuel V, 989
Clapper, Raymond V, 989
Clapps, Emma I, 939
Clapsadle, Harry IV, 1274
Clapsadle, Jesse IV, 1274
Clapsadle, Nellie IV, 1274
Clar, Robert, Sr. VI, 889
Clarbour, Tabitha II, 824
Clarby, Lydia R. V, 898
Clarck, Mahala I, 528
Clarck, Mahala I, 532
Clare, Ann I, 6
Clare, Benjamin II, 346
Clare, Elisa I, 6
Clare, Elizabeth I, 379
Clare, Elizabeth I Sup 1, 3
Clare, Elizabeth I Sup 1, 6
Clare, Elizabeth II, 346
Clare, Esther I Sup 1, 6
Clare, Esther II, 346
Clare, Esther II, 486
Clare, Esther II, 487
Clare, George II, 346
Clare, George II, 486
Clare, George W. V, 554
Clare, Hannah I, 6
Clare, Hannah I Sup 1, 3
Clare, Hannah I Sup 1, 6
Clare, Hepsabeth I, 6
Clare, Hester II, 346
Clare, Jane I, 6
Clare, Jane I Sup 1, 5
Clare, Janne I Sup 1, 8
Clare, John II, 346
Clare, John II, 486
Clare, Josephine V, 554
Clare, Mary I, 6
Clare, Mary I, 108
Clare, Mary I Sup 1, 3
Clare, Mary I Sup 1, 4
Clare, Mary II, 346
Clare, Mary Josephine V, 554
Clare, Mary Newby I, 102
Clare, Sarah I, 6
Clare, Sarah I, 90
Clare, Sarah I Sup 1, 3
Clare, Sarah I Sup 1, 6
Clare, Timothy I, 1
Clare, Timothy I, 6
Clare, Timothy I, 90
Clare, Timothy I, 92
Clare, Timothy I, 102
Clare, Timothy I, 108
Clare, Timothy I Sup 1, 3
Clare, Timothy I Sup 1, 4
Clare, Timothy I Sup 1, 6
Clare, Timothy I Sup 1, 8
Clare, William II, 346
Clare, Wm. II, 486
Clarey, Barns VI, 45
Clarey, Mary VI, 45
Clarida, Beulah T. I, 631
Clarida, Bulah I, 614
Clarida, Franklin W. I, 614
Clarida, John W. I, 631
Clarida, John William I, 614
Clarida, Mary Jane I, 614
Clarida, Mary Jane I, 631
Clarida, Mattie I, 614
Clark, ??? III, 114
Clark, ??? III, 174
Clark, ??? III, 185
Clark, ??? V, 870
Clark, ??? VI, 293
Clark, A. Bertie IV, 1310
Clark, A. T. V, 379
Clark, Aaron V, 871
Clark, Abel Thomas IV, 25
Clark, Abigail I, 531
Clark, Abigail I, 605
Clark, Abigail I, 676
Clark, Abigail I, 804
Clark, Abigail I, 828
Clark, Abigail II, 346
Clark, Abigail III, 70
Clark, Abigail III, 197
Clark, Abigail V, 871
Clark, Abigail VI, 163
Clark, Abigail G. V, 555
Clark, Abigail G. V, 567
Clark, Abigail J. V, 676
Clark, Abigail Jemima I, 676
Clark, Abishai II, 787
Clark, Abraham IV, 570
Clark, Absalom II, 486
Clark, Absalom II, 487
Clark, Achsa II, 129
Clark, Achsah II, 207
Clark, Achsah P. II, 848
Clark, Ada III, 71
Clark, Adwin VI, 806
Clark, Agnes III, 293
Clark, Agnes III, 322
Clark, Agnes VI, 305
Clark, Agness I, 379
Clark, Agness I, 397
Clark, Agness I, 743
Clark, Alexander I, 379
Clark, Alexander I, 711
Clark, Alexander I, 743
Clark, Alexander I, 756
Clark, Alexander I, 757
Clark, Alexander C. I, 711
Clark, Alfred I, 697
Clark, Alfred I, 711
Clark, Alfred III, 70
Clark, Alfred Clark III, 70
Clark, Alibeth I, 1017
Clark, Alice IV, 188
Clark, Alice VI, 482
Clark, Alonzo A. V, 616
Clark, Alta V, 664
Clark, Alvin V, 555
Clark, Alvin V, 591
Clark, Alvin Dewitt V, 664
Clark, Amanda K. III, 228
Clark, Amanda K. III, 229
Clark, Amanda Kellogg III, 71
Clark, Amanda T. I, 1149
Clark, Amasa III, 70
Clark, Amasa III, 122
Clark, Amelia III, 399
Clark, Amelia III, 416
Clark, Amelia III, 421
Clark, Amy III, 70
Clark, Amy III, 71
Clark, Amy III, 106
Clark, Amy IV, 570
Clark, Amy IV, 592
Clark, Amy Jane III, 71
Clark, Amza IV, 865
Clark, Andrew H. III, 70
Clark, Angeline V, 616
Clark, Ann I, 348
Clark, Ann I, 359
Clark, Ann I, 379
Clark, Ann I, 394
Clark, Ann I, 410
Clark, Ann I, 711
Clark, Ann I, 803
Clark, Ann II, 116
Clark, Ann II, 207
Clark, Ann II, 487
Clark, Ann II, 522
Clark, Ann II, 981
Clark, Ann II, 989
Clark, Ann II, 1025
Clark, Ann IV, 379
Clark, Ann IV, 570
Clark, Ann IV, 599
Clark, Ann IV, 1274
Clark, Ann V, 591
Clark, Ann VI, 234
Clark, Ann VI, 285
Clark, Ann VI, 482
Clark, Ann Louise III, 70
Clark, Ann Louise III, 180
Clark, Ann Roth II, 486
Clark, Ann S. III, 70
Clark, Anna I, 379
Clark, Anna I, 493
Clark, Anna I, 605
Clark, Anna I, 697
Clark, Anna I, 711
Clark, Anna II, 147
Clark, Anna II, 848
Clark, Anna II, 870
Clark, Anna V, 989
Clark, Anna Brace V, 38
Clark, Anna Brace V, 157
Clark, Anna Mabel IV, 188
Clark, Anna Maria IV, 80
Clark, Anne VI, 234
Clark, Annie I, 617
Clark, Annie J. V, 591
Clark, Annie M. III, 70
Clark, Arther B. VI, 893
Clark, Arthur V, 664
Clark, Aseanath I, 804
Clark, Asenath I, 493
Clark, Asenath I, 531
Clark, Asenath I, 532
Clark, Asenath I, 676
Clark, Asenath I, 743
Clark, Asenath I, 756
Clark, Asenath I, 757
Clark, Asenath I, 804
Clark, Asenath I, 875
Clark, Asenath I, 886
Clark, Asenath IV, 1051
Clark, Asenath IV, 1052
Clark, Asenath VI, 234
Clark, At. T. V, 379
Clark, Atwood V, 664
Clark, B. Franklin III, 70
Clark, Bailing VI, 285
Clark, Barzella Worth I, 757
Clark, Barzilla I, 743
Clark, Bathsheba II, 129
Clark, Bathsheba II, 169
Clark, Bathsheba II, 207
Clark, Bathsheba II, 217
Clark, Bathsheba II, 346
Clark, Bathsheba II, 468
Clark, Bathsheba II, 487
Clark, Bathsheba II, 747

Clark, Bell V, 555
Clark, Belle V, 664
Clark, Benj. I, 493
Clark, Benj. II, 468
Clark, Benj. II, 487
Clark, Benj. II, 747
Clark, Benj. III, 71
Clark, Benj. III, 125
Clark, Benjamin I, 343
Clark, Benjamin I, 379
Clark, Benjamin I, 531
Clark, Benjamin I, 601
Clark, Benjamin I, 605
Clark, Benjamin II, 129
Clark, Benjamin II, 169
Clark, Benjamin II, 207
Clark, Benjamin II, 217
Clark, Benjamin II, 346
Clark, Benjamin II, 486
Clark, Benjamin II, 1048
Clark, Benjamin III, 70
Clark, Benjamin III, 126
Clark, Benjamin VI, 234
Clark, Benjamin VI, 265
Clark, Benjamin VI, 285
Clark, Benjamin F. V, 898
Clark, Benjamin Franklin III, 70
Clark, Benjamin T. III, 70
Clark, Bennett VI, 805
Clark, Bernard II, 1048
Clark, Bernice IV, 1248
Clark, Betsey III, 71
Clark, Betsey III, 313
Clark, Betsy I, 605
Clark, Betsy Ann II, 1048
Clark, Betty VI, 234
Clark, Betty VI, 285
Clark, Beulah II, 207
Clark, Beulah II, 346
Clark, Beulah II, 486
Clark, Beulah II, 489
Clark, Beulah II, 559
Clark, Beulah II, 848
Clark, Beulah A. II, 848
Clark, Beulah Ann V, 871
Clark, Binjamin I, 379
Clark, Bolin I, 531
Clark, Boling VI, 234
Clark, Boling VI, 283
Clark, Boling VI, 304
Clark, Boling VI, 305
Clark, Bolling VI, 234
Clark, Bolling VI, 285
Clark, Bowlen VI, 234
Clark, Bowling VI, 163
Clark, Bowling VI, 839
Clark, Bowling VI, 845
Clark, Bowling VI, 866
Clark, C. P. V, 989
Clark, Caldwell I, 711
Clark, Caleb I, 493
Clark, Caleb I, 531
Clark, Caleb I, 532
Clark, Caleb I, 601
Clark, Caleb I, 605
Clark, Caleb III, 70
Clark, Caleb V, 871
Clark, Caleph I, 493
Clark, Camp V, 555
Clark, Caroline I, 711
Clark, Caroline I, 715
Clark, Caroline A. IV, 1356
Clark, Caroline A. IV, 1368
Clark, Caroline H. II, 701
Clark, Caroline H. II, 733
Clark, Caroline H. II, 741
Clark, Cassius V, 555
Clark, Cassius V, 664
Clark, Cassius Clark V, 555
Clark, Cassius Clark V, 591
Clark, Catharine III, 71
Clark, Catharine III, 175
Clark, Catharine IV, 80
Clark, Catharine IV, 85
Clark, Catharine IV, 188
Clark, Catharine IV, 1310
Clark, Catharine VI, 854
Clark, Catharine VI, 957
Clark, Catharine M. IV, 1310
Clark, Catherine IV, 80
Clark, Catherine VI, 844
Clark, Charles I, 601
Clark, Charles I, 605
Clark, Charles II, 207
Clark, Charles II, 989
Clark, Charles II, 1013
Clark, Charles II, 1033
Clark, Charles V, 664
Clark, Charles VI, 285
Clark, Charles Burley IV, 188
Clark, Charles E. IV, 580
Clark, Charles Lynch VI, 305
Clark, Charles Neal VI, 305
Clark, Charles S. IV, 1153
Clark, Charlotte H. VI, 990
Clark, Chas. IV, 1310
Clark, Chas. T. IV, 570
Clark, Chrisr VI, 163
Clark, Christian I, 379
Clark, Christian I, 531
Clark, Christian VI, 234
Clark, Christiana I, 493
Clark, Christiana II, 61
Clark, Christiana II, 93
Clark, Christiana VI, 285
Clark, Christianna I, 531
Clark, Christianna I, 804
Clark, Christianna I, 827
Clark, Christinia I, 804
Clark, Christopher I, 379
Clark, Christopher VI, 234
Clark, Christopher VI, 273
Clark, Christopher VI, 274
Clark, Christopher VI, 275
Clark, Christopher VI, 283
Clark, Christopher VI, 285
Clark, Christopher VI, 805
Clark, Christopher VI, 824
Clark, Christopher VI, 828
Clark, Christopher VI, 834
Clark, Christopher VI, 854
Clark, Christopher VI, 861
Clark, Christopher VI, 990
Clark, Christopher Terrell VI, 233
Clark, Christopher, Jr. VI, 285
Clark, Christopher, Jr. VI, 999
Clark, Clara IV, 689
Clark, Clara H. IV, 1036
Clark, Clara Paddock V, 898
Clark, Clement VI, 806
Clark, Clement VI, 840
Clark, Clestea B. V, 555
Clark, Clinton B., Jr. VI, 235
Clark, Colville III, 70
Clark, Constant VI, 884
Clark, Cora I, 631
Clark, Cordelia VI, 196
Clark, Cornelius II, 61
Clark, Cornelius V, 157
Clark, Curtis IV, 378
Clark, Curtis IV, 1274
Clark, Cynthia Ann I, 676
Clark, Cyrus B. III, 70
Clark, Cyrus B. III, 219
Clark, Dabney VI, 805
Clark, Daniel I, 676
Clark, Daniel I, 697
Clark, Daniel I, 711
Clark, Daniel I, 803
Clark, Daniel I, 804
Clark, Daniel I, 836
Clark, Daniel III, 70
Clark, Daniel V, 656
Clark, Daniel V, 664
Clark, Daniel VI, 234
Clark, Daniel VI, 235
Clark, Daniel VI, 482
Clark, Daniel VI, 631
Clark, Daniel Candler VI, 305
Clark, Daniel J. V, 664
Clark, Dannie V, 664
Clark, David I, 531
Clark, David I Sup 1, 9
Clark, David II, 207
Clark, David II, 217
Clark, David II, 346
Clark, David II, 486
Clark, David II, 511
Clark, David III, 70
Clark, David V, 871
Clark, David VI, 805
Clark, David VI, 842
Clark, David VI, 892
Clark, Deborah II, 207
Clark, Deborah II, 522
Clark, Deborah III, 70
Clark, Deborah III, 71
Clark, Deborah IV, 378
Clark, Deborah IV, 1274
Clark, Deborah E. II, 207
Clark, Deborah E. II, 848
Clark, Deborah K. II, 207
Clark, Deborah M. III, 70
Clark, Deborah M. III, 125
Clark, Deborah M. III, 126
Clark, Dora J. VI, 57
Clark, Dorcas III, 70
Clark, Dorcas III, 71
Clark, Dorcas III, 348
Clark, Dorothy III, 70
Clark, Dorothy III, 132
Clark, Dosha VI, 872
Clark, Doshia VI, 871
Clark, Doshia VI, 893
Clark, Dougan I, 379
Clark, Dougan I, 493
Clark, Dougan I, 531
Clark, Dougan I, 532
Clark, Dougan I, 711
Clark, Dougan I, 741
Clark, Dougan I, 743
Clark, Dougan I, 756
Clark, Dougan I, 757
Clark, Dougan I, 804
Clark, Dougan I, 875
Clark, Dougan I, 886
Clark, Dougan I Sup 1, 10
Clark, Dougan C. I, 379
Clark, Dougan, Jr. I, 531
Clark, Dougan, Jr. VI, 234
Clark, Dougan, Sr. I, 531
Clark, Dougan, Sr. I, 532
Clark, Dougan, Sr. VI, 234
Clark, Dugan I, 457
Clark, Dugan, Jr. VI, 229
Clark, Dugan, Jr. VI, 235
Clark, E. Josephine IV, 1310
Clark, Ebeneezer II, 346
Clark, Ebenezer II, 169
Clark, Ebenezer II, 207
Clark, Ebenezer II, 486
Clark, Ebenezer II, 487
Clark, Edgar V, 616
Clark, Edith II, 346
Clark, Edith II, 486
Clark, Edith IV, 570
Clark, Edith IV, 1248
Clark, Edith V, 664
Clark, Edith G. IV, 570
Clark, Edith G. IV, 580
Clark, Edmond I, 743
Clark, Edmond VI, 234
Clark, Edmund I, 531
Clark, Edmund I, 756
Clark, Edward VI, 163
Clark, Edward VI, 234
Clark, Edward VI, 285
Clark, Edward VI, 304
Clark, Edward VI, 305
Clark, Edward VI, 321
Clark, Edward B. VI, 805
Clark, Edwin I, 756
Clark, Effie May V, 555
Clark, Elam I, 605
Clark, Eleanor I, 711
Clark, Eleanor I, 756
Clark, Eleanor III, 71
Clark, Eleanor S. IV, 1310
Clark, Elenor I, 756
Clark, Elgie M. IV, 1310
Clark, Eli I, 601
Clark, Eli I, 605
Clark, Elias C. A. I, 494
Clark, Elihu Pedrick II, 487
Clark, Elijah II, 207
Clark, Eliner I, 875
Clark, Elinor S. IV, 1310
Clark, Elisabeth I, 614
Clark, Elisabeth II, 486
Clark, Elisabeth II, 511
Clark, Elisabeth II, 633
Clark, Elisabeth Swain I, 627
Clark, Elisha II, 487
Clark, Eliz. III, 71
Clark, Eliza I, 565
Clark, Eliza II, 207
Clark, Eliza V, 899
Clark, Eliza V, 905
Clark, Eliza VI, 866
Clark, Eliza E. III, 71
Clark, Eliza Wincy I, 676
Clark, Elizabeth I, 493
Clark, Elizabeth I, 601
Clark, Elizabeth I, 711
Clark, Elizabeth I, 739
Clark, Elizabeth I, 1017
Clark, Elizabeth II, 169
Clark, Elizabeth II, 207
Clark, Elizabeth II, 256
Clark, Elizabeth II, 346
Clark, Elizabeth II, 486
Clark, Elizabeth II, 487
Clark, Elizabeth II, 572
Clark, Elizabeth II, 621
Clark, Elizabeth II, 669
Clark, Elizabeth II, 787
Clark, Elizabeth II, 989
Clark, Elizabeth II, 1033
Clark, Elizabeth II, 1048
Clark, Elizabeth III, 70
Clark, Elizabeth III, 71
Clark, Elizabeth IV, 324
Clark, Elizabeth IV, 338
Clark, Elizabeth IV, 379
Clark, Elizabeth IV, 865
Clark, Elizabeth IV, 1274
Clark, Elizabeth IV, 1297
Clark, Elizabeth V, 150
Clark, Elizabeth V, 157
Clark, Elizabeth V, 616
Clark, Elizabeth V, 832
Clark, Elizabeth V, 854
Clark, Elizabeth V, 899
Clark, Elizabeth V, 925
Clark, Elizabeth V, 949
Clark, Elizabeth VI, 163
Clark, Elizabeth VI, 234
Clark, Elizabeth VI, 265
Clark, Elizabeth VI, 273
Clark, Elizabeth VI, 285
Clark, Elizabeth VI, 799
Clark, Elizabeth VI, 805
Clark, Elizabeth VI, 824
Clark, Elizabeth VI, 838
Clark, Elizabeth VI, 848
Clark, Elizabeth VI, 892
Clark, Elizabeth VI, 1006
Clark, Elizabeth Ann IV, 865
Clark, Elizabeth Ann IV, 879
Clark, Elizabeth C. VI, 866
Clark, Elizabeth C. C. VI, 842
Clark, Elizabeth G. II, 61
Clark, Elizabeth Stanton V, 898
Clark, Elizabeth Storey III, 70
Clark, Elizabeth Storey III, 185
Clark, Elizabeth Story III, 71
Clark, Elizabeth V. H. II, 720
Clark, Elizabeth W. II, 848
Clark, Elizabeth W. IV, 324
Clark, Ella V, 664
Clark, Ella T. IV, 188
Clark, Ellen V, 554
Clark, Ellen V, 555
Clark, Ellen V, 568
Clark, Ellen White I, 631
Clark, Ellsworth V, 379
Clark, Elma Carlotta IV, 379
Clark, Elma Charlotta IV, 570
Clark, Elmer IV, 1310
Clark, Elmore V, 379
Clark, Elwood V, 554
Clark, Elwood V, 555
Clark, Elwood V, 591
Clark, Elwood V, 664
Clark, Elwworth V, 379
Clark, Emily I, 532
Clark, Emily I, 676
Clark, Emily I, 756
Clark, Emily I, 804
Clark, Emily B. VI, 795
Clark, Emma III, 70
Clark, Emma III, 106
Clark, Emma IV, 188
Clark, Emma V, 121
Clark, Emma G. V, 38
Clark, Emy C. I, 804
Clark, Ephraim I, 135
Clark, Erbin I, 756
Clark, Erbin Cooper I, 756
Clark, Estella A. IV, 689
Clark, Estella M. V, 555
Clark, Ester I, 1060
Clark, Ester I, 1062
Clark, Esther II, 346
Clark, Esther III, 70
Clark, Esther III, 71
Clark, Esther III, 199
Clark, Esther V, 949
Clark, Esther A. III, 70
Clark, Esther A. III, 122
Clark, Ethel IV, 1248
Clark, Eunas I, 494
Clark, Eunice I, 743
Clark, Eunice III, 70
Clark, Eunice III, 71
Clark, Eunice A. I, 605
Clark, Eunice A. I, 711
Clark, Eunice A. I, 720
Clark, Eva D. V, 554
Clark, Ezra IV, 865
Clark, Fam IV, 1274
Clark, Fanny B. VI, 980
Clark, Flora V, 555
Clark, Florence P. IV, 1310
Clark, Floyd C. IV, 1248
Clark, Frances II, 169
Clark, Frances Ann VI, 937
Clark, Francis I, 379
Clark, Francis I, 493
Clark, Francis I, 531
Clark, Francis I, 804
Clark, Francis IV, 188
Clark, Francis IV, 689
Clark, Francis VI, 163
Clark, Francis VI, 196
Clark, Francis VI, 234
Clark, Francis VI, 285
Clark, Francis VI, 803
Clark, Francis E. IV, 689
Clark, Francis, Jr. VI, 234
Clark, Francis, Jr. VI, 285
Clark, Frank VI, 196
Clark, Frank H. I, 939
Clark, Frank W. IV, 188
Clark, Frank Ward IV, 188
Clark, Frederick III, 70
Clark, Freeman IV, 1234
Clark, G. Fisher III, 70
Clark, G. Whitefield III, 70
Clark, Geo. IV, 1310
Clark, Geo. V, 989
Clark, Geo. P. III, 399
Clark, Geo. P. IV, 142
Clark, Geo. W. IV, 1310
Clark, George III, 399
Clark, George III, 416
Clark, George III, 421
Clark, George IV, 188
Clark, George IV, 324
Clark, George V, 121
Clark, George VI, 893
Clark, George E. I, 743
Clark, George E. V, 38
Clark, George M. V, 38
Clark, George P. IV, 188
Clark, George P. IV, 311
Clark, George P. IV, 314
Clark, Gertrude IV, 1204
Clark, Gideon III, 71
Clark, Gideon W. III, 70
Clark, Gilbert V, 616
Clark, Glenn W. IV, 1310
Clark, Grace V, 656
Clark, Grace V, 664
Clark, Grace Fulton IV, 1310
Clark, Gulielma V, 664
Clark, H. D. IV, 1248
Clark, Hannah I, 379
Clark, Hannah I, 493
Clark, Hannah I, 531
Clark, Hannah I, 601
Clark, Hannah I, 605
Clark, Hannah I, 711
Clark, Hannah I, 756
Clark, Hannah I, 804
Clark, Hannah I, 843
Clark, Hannah II, 61
Clark, Hannah II, 129
Clark, Hannah II, 207
Clark, Hannah II, 346
Clark, Hannah II, 468
Clark, Hannah II, 486
Clark, Hannah II, 487
Clark, Hannah II, 522
Clark, Hannah II, 634
Clark, Hannah II, 782
Clark, Hannah II, 788
Clark, Hannah II, 806
Clark, Hannah II, 848
Clark, Hannah II, 872
Clark, Hannah II, 989
Clark, Hannah III, 70
Clark, Hannah IV, 188
Clark, Hannah IV, 251
Clark, Hannah IV, 378
Clark, Hannah IV, 518
Clark, Hannah V, 38
Clark, Hannah V, 142
Clark, Hannah V, 229
Clark, Hannah V, 230
Clark, Hannah V, 871
Clark, Hannah VI, 163
Clark, Hannah A. II, 61
Clark, Hannah E. I, 804
Clark, Hannah Hewlings II, 169
Clark, Hannah M. IV, 188
Clark, Hannah M. IV, 518
Clark, Hariot V, 794
Clark, Harmon I, 493
Clark, Harry IV, 1248
Clark, Helen L. III, 71
Clark, Helen L. III, 174
Clark, Henrietta IV, 806
Clark, Henry I, 1017
Clark, Henry II, 207
Clark, Henry II, 787
Clark, Henry II, 848
Clark, Henry IV, 689
Clark, Henry IV, 806
Clark, Henry IV, 901
Clark, Henry V, 157
Clark, Henry V, 230
Clark, Henry V, 324
Clark, Henry V, 871

Clark, Henry VI, 163
Clark, Henry VI, 164
Clark, Henry VI, 377
Clark, Henry VI, 796
Clark, Henry VI, 805
Clark, Henry VI, 835
Clark, Henry VI, 848
Clark, Henry J. V, 230
Clark, Henry M. III, 70
Clark, Henry Neal V, 38
Clark, Henry T. I, 493
Clark, Henry T. III, 70
Clark, Henry T. III, 180
Clark, Henry, Jr. V, 157
Clark, Hester I, 1017
Clark, Hezekiah I, 531
Clark, Hezekiah I, 676
Clark, Hezekiah I, 804
Clark, Hezekiah IV, 1356
Clark, Hezekiah IV, 1368
Clark, Hezekiah P. I, 804
Clark, Hezekiah S. I, 531
Clark, Hezekiah S. I, 804
Clark, Hezekiah S. I, 828
Clark, Holdridge IV, 865
Clark, Honor II, 61
Clark, Horace B. IV, 188
Clark, Hugh P. IV, 324
Clark, Hugh P. IV, 329
Clark, Hull III, 71
Clark, Hyram T. I, 1149
Clark, Ida Ellen IV, 1310
Clark, Ira VI, 893
Clark, Ira VI, 957
Clark, Ira E. VI, 812
Clark, Ira E. VI, 892
Clark, Ira E. VI, 937
Clark, Irene M. III, 70
Clark, Irene M. III, 132
Clark, Isaac I, 493
Clark, Isaac I, 531
Clark, Isaac I, 532
Clark, Isaac I, 601
Clark, Isaac I, 605
Clark, Isaac V, 871
Clark, Isaac VI, 234
Clark, Isaac N. IV, 324
Clark, Isaac N. IV, 338
Clark, Isaac Thornton II, 989
Clark, Isaac, Jr. II, 522
Clark, Isabel V, 555
Clark, Isabel Reeder III, 70
Clark, Isabel Reeder III, 233
Clark, Isabella III, 70
Clark, Isabella Amanda K. III, 70
Clark, Isaiah III, 70
Clark, Isham VI, 893
Clark, Isham VI, 905
Clark, Isham VI, 945
Clark, Jacob III, 70
Clark, Jacob III, 71
Clark, Jacob B. III, 201
Clark, James I, 493
Clark, James I, 531
Clark, James I, 601
Clark, James I, 605
Clark, James I, 711
Clark, James II, 346
Clark, James VI, 377
Clark, James VI, 378
Clark, James VI, 805
Clark, James VI, 825
Clark, James N. I, 605
Clark, James R. IV, 1310
Clark, Jane I, 875
Clark, Jane II, 243
Clark, Jane II, 346
Clark, Jane II, 468
Clark, Jane II, 486
Clark, Jane II, 487
Clark, Jane II, 733
Clark, Jane II, 848
Clark, Jane II, 989
Clark, Jane III, 70
Clark, Jane IV, 188
Clark, Jane IV, 324
Clark, Jane IV, 350
Clark, Jane IV, 901
Clark, Jane IV, 1248
Clark, Jane V, 38
Clark, Jane V, 832
Clark, Jane V, 899
Clark, Jane V, 938
Clark, Jane VI, 806
Clark, Jane A. E. VI, 885
Clark, Jane Elizabeth IV, 188
Clark, Jediah I, 711
Clark, Jedidah I, 697
Clark, Jehu I, 493
Clark, Jemima V, 555
Clark, Jemima V, 591
Clark, Jemima V, 664
Clark, Jemima B. V, 664
Clark, Jemima Clark Osborn V, 555
Clark, Jemima Osborn V, 555
Clark, Jemimah V, 591
Clark, Jemimah V, 668
Clark, Jennie V, 616
Clark, Jennie Ida Emma IV, 379
Clark, Jennie Ida Emma IV, 570
Clark, Jeremiah V, 616
Clark, Jesse I, 493
Clark, Jesse I, 531
Clark, Jesse I, 743
Clark, Jesse I, 756
Clark, Jesse I, 804
Clark, Jesse I, 843
Clark, Jesse IV, 379
Clark, Jesse V, 664
Clark, Jesse V, 832
Clark, Jesse V, 854
Clark, Jesse VI, 377
Clark, Jesse VI, 892
Clark, Jesse C. V, 664
Clark, Jessee I, 531
Clark, Jno. VI, 482
Clark, Jno. VI, 805
Clark, Joel V, 871
Clark, Joel C. V, 871
Clark, John I, 359
Clark, John I, 379
Clark, John I, 493
Clark, John I, 531
Clark, John I, 554
Clark, John I, 578
Clark, John I, 600
Clark, John I, 601
Clark, John I, 605
Clark, John I, 697
Clark, John I, 711
Clark, John I, 722
Clark, John I, 756
Clark, John I, 803
Clark, John I, 804
Clark, John I, 875
Clark, John I, 1017
Clark, John I, 1027
Clark, John I, 1035
Clark, John I, 1070
Clark, John II, 346
Clark, John II, 442
Clark, John II, 486
Clark, John II, 487
Clark, John II, 848
Clark, John III, 70
Clark, John III, 71
Clark, John III, 181
Clark, John IV, 188
Clark, John IV, 806
Clark, John IV, 901
Clark, John IV, 1248
Clark, John IV, 1310
Clark, John IV, 1356
Clark, John V, 157
Clark, John V, 324
Clark, John V, 616
Clark, John V, 730
Clark, John V, 832
Clark, John V, 841
Clark, John V, 871
Clark, John VI, 163
Clark, John VI, 233
Clark, John VI, 234
Clark, John VI, 285
Clark, John VI, 377
Clark, John VI, 482
Clark, John VI, 805
Clark, John VI, 839
Clark, John VI, 842
Clark, John VI, 844
Clark, John VI, 852
Clark, John VI, 867
Clark, John VI, 892
Clark, John VI, 893
Clark, John A. I, 804
Clark, John A. V, 157
Clark, John Anson I, 531
Clark, John D. III, 480
Clark, John F. I, 601
Clark, John G. I, 493
Clark, John G. I, 494
Clark, John H. I, 601
Clark, John H. II, 701
Clark, John H. V, 324
Clark, John Hull III, 71
Clark, John J. II, 848
Clark, John Joshua II, 787
Clark, John Joshua II, 848
Clark, John M. I, 493
Clark, John M. I, 605
Clark, John M. I, 711
Clark, John M. I, 720
Clark, John M. I, 743
Clark, John M. VI, 806
Clark, John P. VI, 806
Clark, John P. VI, 832
Clark, John Wesley I, 1149
Clark, John, Jr. I, 379
Clark, John, Jr. I, 531
Clark, John, Jr. VI, 482
Clark, John, Sr. I, 379
Clark, Jonathan I, 493
Clark, Jonathan I, 531
Clark, Jonathan I, 600
Clark, Jonathan I, 601
Clark, Jonathan I, 605
Clark, Jonathan I, 711
Clark, Jonathan I, 1017
Clark, Jonathan I, 1070
Clark, Jonathan I, 1071
Clark, Jonathan I Sup 1, 9
Clark, Jonathan III, 70
Clark, Jonathan V, 157
Clark, Jonathan V, 481
Clark, Jonathan V, 899
Clark, Jonathan B. I, 743
Clark, Jonathan Backhouse I, 757
Clark, Jonothan V, 38
Clark, Joseph I, 379
Clark, Joseph I, 743
Clark, Joseph I, 756
Clark, Joseph II, 61
Clark, Joseph II, 169
Clark, Joseph II, 207
Clark, Joseph II, 486
Clark, Joseph II, 487
Clark, Joseph II, 669
Clark, Joseph II, 701
Clark, Joseph II, 848
Clark, Joseph II, 989
Clark, Joseph III, 71
Clark, Joseph IV, 378
Clark, Joseph IV, 570
Clark, Joseph IV, 1274
Clark, Joseph VI, 234
Clark, Joseph VI, 273
Clark, Joseph VI, 795
Clark, Joseph VI, 892
Clark, Joseph VI, 893
Clark, Joseph VI, 905
Clark, Joseph A. I, 743
Clark, Joseph Addison I, 757
Clark, Joseph B. V, 379
Clark, Joseph Boyd V, 379
Clark, Joseph Oldden II, 487
Clark, Joseph Olden II, 487
Clark, Joseph P. III, 181
Clark, Joseph Pierce III, 181
Clark, Joseph Sill III, 70
Clark, Joseph Sill III, 71
Clark, Joseph W. IV, 689
Clark, Joseph Warner II, 787
Clark, Joseph, Jr. II, 486
Clark, Josiah III, 71
Clark, Josiah B. III, 71
Clark, Josiah G. III, 71
Clark, Josiah Henry H. III, 71
Clark, Judiah I, 711
Clark, Judith VI, 233
Clark, Judith VI, 234
Clark, Judith VI, 285
Clark, Judith VI, 842
Clark, Judith VI, 889
Clark, Judith M. VI, 805
Clark, Julia I, 756
Clark, Julia I, 804
Clark, Julia III, 71
Clark, Julia K. II, 169
Clark, Julia K. II, 284
Clark, Katharine I, 631
Clark, Katharine VI, 945
Clark, Katherine T. III, 149
Clark, Kelita I, 493
Clark, Kenneth E. IV, 1248
Clark, Laura IV, 1204
Clark, Laura A. IV, 140
Clark, Laura A. IV, 142
Clark, Laura S. IV, 188
Clark, Laurey Samaria IV, 188
Clark, Lavina E. I, 605
Clark, Leah I, 601
Clark, Lena V, 664
Clark, Lena M. V, 664
Clark, Lenna V, 658
Clark, Lenna V, 664
Clark, Leona IV, 689
Clark, Lester W. III, 70
Clark, Lester W. III, 132
Clark, Leuisa I, 601
Clark, Lewis V, 871
Clark, Lewis Chester I, 939
Clark, Lewis Latham I, 531
Clark, Libbie IV, 1248
Clark, Lillian H. IV, 806
Clark, Lillian H. IV, 1036
Clark, Lillie May V, 616
Clark, Lindley V, 379
Clark, Lindley V, 555
Clark, Lindley V, 591
Clark, Lindley V, 664
Clark, Lindley D. VI, 57
Clark, Lizzie IV, 1310
Clark, Lloyd J. IV, 1248
Clark, Louisa I, 676
Clark, Louisa I, 743
Clark, Louisa I, 756
Clark, Louisa I, 757
Clark, Louise Francis III, 71
Clark, Louise Francis III, 313
Clark, Lucile V, 989
Clark, Lucinda I, 1149
Clark, Lucy VI, 234
Clark, Lucy VI, 273
Clark, Lucy VI, 839
Clark, Lucy VI, 892
Clark, Luis Latham I, 531
Clark, Luiza I, 494
Clark, Luzena I, 493
Clark, Luzena I, 531
Clark, Luzena I, 601
Clark, Luzena M. I, 531
Clark, Luzena M. I, 605
Clark, Lydia I, 1117
Clark, Lydia Ann IV, 324
Clark, Lydia Ann IV, 329
Clark, Mabel Frances III, 70
Clark, Mabel Frances III, 219
Clark, Mable IV, 137
Clark, Maggie A. V, 664
Clark, Mahala I, 532
Clark, Mahala I, 601
Clark, Mahalah I, 605
Clark, Makey VI, 892
Clark, Malinda I, 605
Clark, Malinda III, 71
Clark, Malinda III, 134
Clark, Margaret I, 493
Clark, Margaret I, 531
Clark, Margaret I, 554
Clark, Margaret I, 601
Clark, Margaret I, 605
Clark, Margaret I, 711
Clark, Margaret I, 718
Clark, Margaret I, 804
Clark, Margaret I, 875
Clark, Margaret I, 1070
Clark, Margaret II, 462
Clark, Margaret II, 486
Clark, Margaret II, 989
Clark, Margaret IV, 188
Clark, Margaret IV, 324
Clark, Margaret V, 664
Clark, Margaret V, 832
Clark, Margaret V, 871
Clark, Margaret VI, 805
Clark, Margaret A. I, 601
Clark, Margaret Ann IV, 324
Clark, Margaret Ann IV, 350
Clark, Margaret Ann IV, 689
Clark, Margaret Ann IV, 758
Clark, Margaret C. IV, 188
Clark, Margaret Sabina IV, 188
Clark, Margret I, 601
Clark, Maria II, 487
Clark, Maria IV, 689
Clark, Maria V, 38
Clark, Maria B. V, 38
Clark, Maria Louisa III, 71
Clark, Maria Louisa III, 237
Clark, Maria T. III, 70
Clark, Maria T. III, 71
Clark, Maria T. III, 125
Clark, Mariah VI, 893
Clark, Marianna III, 498
Clark, Marianna W. V, 38
Clark, Marjorie IV, 1248
Clark, Mark I, 135
Clark, Mark I, 711
Clark, Marris V, 555
Clark, Martha I, 135
Clark, Martha I, 459
Clark, Martha I, 493
Clark, Martha I, 531
Clark, Martha I, 673
Clark, Martha I, 676
Clark, Martha I, 711
Clark, Martha I, 875
Clark, Martha II, 284
Clark, Martha II, 302
Clark, Martha II, 317
Clark, Martha II, 325
Clark, Martha II, 486
Clark, Martha II, 848
Clark, Martha II, 989
Clark, Martha II, 998
Clark, Martha III, 70
Clark, Martha IV, 806
Clark, Martha IV, 901
Clark, Martha V, 38
Clark, Martha V, 300
Clark, Martha V, 871
Clark, Martha VI, 805
Clark, Martha A. VI, 806
Clark, Martha M. III, 70
Clark, Martha P. V, 701
Clark, Martha R. I, 1149
Clark, Martha W. II, 317
Clark, Mary I, 92
Clark, Mary I, 135
Clark, Mary I, 140
Clark, Mary I, 359
Clark, Mary I, 379
Clark, Mary I, 419
Clark, Mary I, 494
Clark, Mary I, 531
Clark, Mary I, 593
Clark, Mary I, 601
Clark, Mary I, 626
Clark, Mary I, 676
Clark, Mary I, 711
Clark, Mary I, 722
Clark, Mary I, 723
Clark, Mary I, 756
Clark, Mary I, 803
Clark, Mary I, 804
Clark, Mary I, 836
Clark, Mary I, 875
Clark, Mary I, 1017
Clark, Mary I, 1060
Clark, Mary II, 61
Clark, Mary II, 207
Clark, Mary II, 486
Clark, Mary II, 487
Clark, Mary II, 522
Clark, Mary II, 701
Clark, Mary II, 713
Clark, Mary II, 720
Clark, Mary II, 787
Clark, Mary II, 848
Clark, Mary II, 989
Clark, Mary II, 1015
Clark, Mary III, 71
Clark, Mary III, 161
Clark, Mary III, 181
Clark, Mary III, 361
Clark, Mary IV, 188
Clark, Mary IV, 379
Clark, Mary IV, 570
Clark, Mary IV, 865
Clark, Mary V, 38
Clark, Mary V, 899
Clark, Mary V, 932
Clark, Mary V, 949
Clark, Mary VI, 233
Clark, Mary VI, 321
Clark, Mary VI, 377
Clark, Mary VI, 482
Clark, Mary VI, 528
Clark, Mary VI, 672
Clark, Mary VI, 805
Clark, Mary VI, 814
Clark, Mary VI, 892
Clark, Mary VI, 893
Clark, Mary A. VI, 805
Clark, Mary A. T. VI, 839
Clark, Mary Alice IV, 188
Clark, Mary Ann III, 71
Clark, Mary Ann IV, 923
Clark, Mary Ann IV, 937
Clark, Mary Ann V, 871
Clark, Mary Ann VI, 956
Clark, Mary Anna II, 848
Clark, Mary Anna III, 70
Clark, Mary Anne III, 114
Clark, Mary B. I, 1149
Clark, Mary B. II, 129
Clark, Mary C. III, 71
Clark, Mary E. IV, 1310
Clark, Mary E. IV, 1325
Clark, Mary E. V, 616
Clark, Mary Elizabeth VI, 377
Clark, Mary Elizabeth VI, 378
Clark, Mary H. VI, 826
Clark, Mary J. I, 601
Clark, Mary J. IV, 1234
Clark, Mary J. V, 555
Clark, Mary M. I, 531
Clark, Mary M. I, 743
Clark, Mary M. II, 848
Clark, Mary P. III, 35
Clark, Mary P. III, 71
Clark, Mary P. III, 161
Clark, Mary T. VI, 893

Clark, Mary W. I, 711
Clark, Mary W. V, 899
Clark, Mary, Jr. II, 1013
Clark, Matilda IV, 1128
Clark, Matilda IV, 1140
Clark, Matilda VI, 806
Clark, Matilda VI, 892
Clark, Maud IV, 1310
Clark, Maud V, 664
Clark, Maud E. V, 663
Clark, Melinda I, 601
Clark, Melinda III, 71
Clark, Melinda VI, 893
Clark, Meribah II, 346
Clark, Meribah II, 486
Clark, Meribah II, 634
Clark, Micajah I, 135
Clark, Micajah VI, 233
Clark, Micajah VI, 285
Clark, Micajah VI, 305
Clark, Micajah VI, 320
Clark, Micajah VI, 805
Clark, Micajah VI, 806
Clark, Micajah VI, 892
Clark, Mildred IV, 188
Clark, Mildred V, 989
Clark, Mildred VI, 233
Clark, Mildred VI, 234
Clark, Mill VI, 233
Clark, Milla VI, 234
Clark, Milla VI, 274
Clark, Milla VI, 275
Clark, Milley VI, 234
Clark, Milly VI, 805
Clark, Milly VI, 863
Clark, Milton I, 493
Clark, Milton I, 601
Clark, Minnie III, 17
Clark, Minnie IV, 1248
Clark, Mirium A. I, 743
Clark, Molly I, 379
Clark, Molly I, 423
Clark, Molly VI, 234
Clark, Molly VI, 285
Clark, Morris III, 70
Clark, Morris III, 71
Clark, Morris W. V, 664
Clark, Mourning VI, 233
Clark, Mourning VI, 285
Clark, Mrs. Eleanor IV, 1320
Clark, Mrs. May IV, 1310
Clark, Nancy I, 379
Clark, Nancy I, 697
Clark, Nancy I, 711
Clark, Nancy I, 722
Clark, Nancy I, 756
Clark, Nancy III, 70
Clark, Nancy III, 122
Clark, Nancy IV, 1248
Clark, Nancy IV, 1356
Clark, Nancy V, 379
Clark, Nancy VI, 805
Clark, Nancy VI, 814
Clark, Nancy VI, 836
Clark, Nancy VI, 839
Clark, Nancy VI, 892
Clark, Nancy VI, 1009
Clark, Nancy Arabella III, 71
Clark, Nancy E. IV, 1248
Clark, Nancy I. I, 743
Clark, Nancy Jane I, 757
Clark, Nancy P. VI, 806
Clark, Nancy S. VI, 892
Clark, Naomi I, 605
Clark, Naomi Farquhar V, 664
Clark, Nathan I, 494
Clark, Nathan I, 531
Clark, Nathan I, 532
Clark, Nathan I, 601
Clark, Nathan I, 605
Clark, Nathan I, 743
Clark, Nathan I, 756
Clark, Nathan II, 989
Clark, Nathan III, 35
Clark, Nathan III, 71
Clark, Nathan III, 161
Clark, Nathan H. I, 531
Clark, Nathan H. I, 532
Clark, Nathan H. I, 804
Clark, Nathan H. I, 829
Clark, Nathaniel III, 70
Clark, Nathaniel III, 71
Clark, Nellie V, 324
Clark, Nellie B. IV, 1248
Clark, Nettie IV, 1310
Clark, Nicholas I, 379
Clark, Nicholas I, 493
Clark, Nicholas I, 531
Clark, Nicholas I, 804
Clark, Nicholas I, 1066
Clark, Nicholas VI, 234
Clark, Nicholas VI, 285
Clark, Nicholas, Jr. I, 1070
Clark, Norman III, 70
Clark, Norrey VI, 893
Clark, Novry VI, 939
Clark, O. C. VI, 841
Clark, Olen IV, 1310
Clark, Orran IV, 1274
Clark, Orthodox C. VI, 826
Clark, Orthodox C. VI, 854
Clark, Oscar V, 157
Clark, Owen S. III, 71
Clark, Patricia III, 70
Clark, Patty VI, 805
Clark, Paulet VI, 827
Clark, Paulet VI, 839
Clark, Paulett VI, 805
Clark, Paulett VI, 807
Clark, Paulett VI, 854
Clark, Pearly May V, 664
Clark, Peggy VI, 991
Clark, Penelope VI, 234
Clark, Phariba I, 233
Clark, Phariba I, 238
Clark, Phebe I, 379
Clark, Phebe I, 430
Clark, Phebe V, 616
Clark, Phebe VI, 163
Clark, Phebe L. V, 379
Clark, Plesent VI, 806
Clark, Polly VI, 852
Clark, Polly VI, 955
Clark, Rachel I, 711
Clark, Rachel I, 756
Clark, Rachel I, 1017
Clark, Rachel I, 1060
Clark, Rachel I, 1061
Clark, Rachel II, 61
Clark, Rachel II, 93
Clark, Rachel II, 207
Clark, Rachel II, 346
Clark, Rachel II, 989
Clark, Rachel III, 71
Clark, Rachel IV, 806
Clark, Rachel IV, 901
Clark, Rachel VI, 305
Clark, Rachel E. II, 848
Clark, Rachel R. II, 733
Clark, Rebecah VI, 482
Clark, Rebecca II, 486
Clark, Rebecca II, 487
Clark, Rebecca II, 518
Clark, Rebecca II, 747
Clark, Rebecca II, 787
Clark, Rebecca II, 848
Clark, Rebecca III, 71
Clark, Rebecca IV, 592
Clark, Rebecca IV, 806
Clark, Rebecca IV, 901
Clark, Rebecca IV, 908
Clark, Rebecca V, 38
Clark, Rebecca V, 469
Clark, Rebecca V, 481
Clark, Rebecca V, 532
Clark, Rebecca VI, 163
Clark, Rebecca Ann I, 493
Clark, Rebecca E. V, 379
Clark, Rebecca P. III, 71
Clark, Rebecka II, 346
Clark, Rebeckah II, 207
Clark, Rebeckah VI, 158
Clark, Rebeckah VI, 163
Clark, Rebeckah VI, 482
Clark, Rebeckah S. VI, 163
Clark, Rebekah II, 486
Clark, Rebekah II, 500
Clark, Rebekah VI, 482
Clark, Reuben III, 71
Clark, Reuben B. III, 71
Clark, Rhoda V, 949
Clark, Rhoda R. I, 743
Clark, Richard II, 989
Clark, Richard III, 71
Clark, Richard VI, 805
Clark, Richard VI, 825
Clark, Richard VI, 867
Clark, Richard G. II, 61
Clark, Richard L. II, 720
Clark, Richmond II, 848
Clark, Robert I, 711
Clark, Robert IV, 188
Clark, Robert IV, 324
Clark, Robert IV, 350
Clark, Robert IV, 689
Clark, Robert IV, 806
Clark, Robert IV, 1274
Clark, Robert IV, 1297
Clark, Robert V, 949
Clark, Robert VI, 233
Clark, Robert VI, 285
Clark, Robert VI, 330
Clark, Robert VI, 805
Clark, Robert VI, 863
Clark, Robert VI, 864
Clark, Robert VI, 892
Clark, Robert VI, 895
Clark, Robert VI, 952
Clark, Robert VI, 988
Clark, Rosa IV, 806
Clark, Rosa V, 551
Clark, Rufus III, 70
Clark, Rufus III, 71
Clark, Rufus III, 228
Clark, Rufus III, 237
Clark, Runame IV, 560
Clark, Ruth I, 493
Clark, Ruth I, 531
Clark, Ruth I, 600
Clark, Ruth I, 605
Clark, Ruth I, 711
Clark, Ruth I, 721
Clark, Ruth I, 1070
Clark, Ruth I, 1071
Clark, Ruth IV, 25
Clark, Ruth IV, 80
Clark, Ruth A. V, 555
Clark, Sallie I, 711
Clark, Sally VI, 805
Clark, Sally VI, 930
Clark, Samantha V, 664
Clark, Samaria IV, 142
Clark, Samaria IV, 188
Clark, Samaria I. IV, 311
Clark, Samaria I. IV, 314
Clark, Samaria J. III, 399
Clark, Samaria J. IV, 188
Clark, Samuel I, 676
Clark, Samuel I, 711
Clark, Samuel I, 722
Clark, Samuel I, 756
Clark, Samuel I, 804
Clark, Samuel II, 169
Clark, Samuel II, 346
Clark, Samuel II, 468
Clark, Samuel II, 486
Clark, Samuel II, 634
Clark, Samuel II, 787
Clark, Samuel III, 71
Clark, Samuel IV, 25
Clark, Samuel IV, 80
Clark, Samuel IV, 188
Clark, Samuel IV, 251
Clark, Samuel IV, 518
Clark, Samuel VI, 892
Clark, Samuel Peterson II, 787
Clark, Samyra H. I, 804
Clark, Sarah I, 135
Clark, Sarah I, 379
Clark, Sarah I, 391
Clark, Sarah I, 444
Clark, Sarah I, 452
Clark, Sarah II, 61
Clark, Sarah II, 169
Clark, Sarah II, 207
Clark, Sarah II, 346
Clark, Sarah II, 486
Clark, Sarah II, 487
Clark, Sarah II, 559
Clark, Sarah III, 70
Clark, Sarah III, 71
Clark, Sarah III, 237
Clark, Sarah III, 298
Clark, Sarah IV, 865
Clark, Sarah IV, 1356
Clark, Sarah IV, 1373
Clark, Sarah V, 481
Clark, Sarah V, 499
Clark, Sarah V, 564
Clark, Sarah V, 832
Clark, Sarah VI, 163
Clark, Sarah VI, 305
Clark, Sarah VI, 377
Clark, Sarah VI, 806
Clark, Sarah VI, 807
Clark, Sarah VI, 812
Clark, Sarah VI, 839
Clark, Sarah VI, 893
Clark, Sarah A. I, 1149
Clark, Sarah A. V, 379
Clark, Sarah Ann II, 848
Clark, Sarah Ann II, 872
Clark, Sarah Ann V, 379
Clark, Sarah Ann V, 421
Clark, Sarah Coates II, 805
Clark, Sarah E. VI, 905
Clark, Sarah F. VI, 888
Clark, Sarah Field II, 989
Clark, Sarah G. III, 70
Clark, Sarah G. III, 71
Clark, Sarah Hammond III, 70
Clark, Sarah I. VI, 229
Clark, Sarah I. VI, 234
Clark, Sarah I. VI, 235
Clark, Sarah J. V, 870
Clark, Sarah J. VI, 235
Clark, Sarah L. I, 531
Clark, Sarah R. III, 71
Clark, Sarah Rebecca III, 71
Clark, Sarah W. III, 181
Clark, Saryan VI, 997
Clark, Scott IV, 1248
Clark, Semira H. I, 804
Clark, Semira H. I, 829
Clark, Semira K. I, 531
Clark, Silvanus I, 135
Clark, Simeon Ray VI, 893
Clark, Solomon IV, 188
Clark, Solomon IV, 378
Clark, Solomon IV, 379
Clark, Solomon IV, 570
Clark, Solomon IV, 599
Clark, Solomon IV, 1274
Clark, Solomon VI, 885
Clark, Solomon VI, 893
Clark, Solomon VI, 955
Clark, Stacy B. II, 1048
Clark, Stacy Buckman II, 989
Clark, Stephen R. III, 399
Clark, Sucky VI, 233
Clark, Susan VI, 806
Clark, Susan VI, 893
Clark, Susanna I, 379
Clark, Susanna I, 531
Clark, Susanna II, 487
Clark, Susanna V, 871
Clark, Susannah VI, 377
Clark, Susannah VI, 805
Clark, Susannah VI, 867
Clark, Tabitha VI, 285
Clark, Tabitha VI, 286
Clark, Tabitha VI, 287
Clark, Tacy V, 664
Clark, Tacy E. III, 399
Clark, Tacy E. III, 421
Clark, Tacy Elthena IV, 188
Clark, Tacy M. V, 555
Clark, Tamar V, 379
Clark, Tamar V, 420
Clark, Theodore IV, 140
Clark, Theodore IV, 142
Clark, Theodore IV, 188
Clark, Thomas I, 711
Clark, Thomas I, 1017
Clark, Thomas II, 129
Clark, Thomas II, 346
Clark, Thomas II, 468
Clark, Thomas II, 486
Clark, Thomas II, 634
Clark, Thomas III, 71
Clark, Thomas III, 175
Clark, Thomas III, 201
Clark, Thomas IV, 806
Clark, Thomas IV, 901
Clark, Thomas VI, 234
Clark, Thomas VI, 244
Clark, Thomas VI, 285
Clark, Thomas VI, 805
Clark, Thomas VI, 955
Clark, Thomas E. I, 743
Clark, Thomas Elwood I, 757
Clark, Thomas M. VI, 805
Clark, Thomas M. VI, 835
Clark, Thomas M. VI, 856
Clark, Thomas N. VI, 842
Clark, Thomas P. II, 207
Clark, Thomas P. II, 487
Clark, Thomas S. II, 522
Clark, Thomas Shreve II, 522
Clark, Thomas, Jr. III, 71
Clark, Thomas, Sr. VI, 234
Clark, Thos. II, 61
Clark, Thos. II, 93
Clark, Thos. II, 848
Clark, Thos. II, 872
Clark, Thos. M. VI, 842
Clark, Unice I, 531
Clark, Urlean I, 743
Clark, Ursula VI, 234
Clark, Velma V, 989
Clark, Vera IV, 1248
Clark, Verona V, 379
Clark, Verona V, 899
Clark, W. D. IV, 1248
Clark, Walter IV, 1310
Clark, Walter V, 989
Clark, Walter C. III, 70
Clark, Wd. Alida C. V, 832
Clark, Wd. Alida C. V, 841
Clark, Wd. Elizabeth II, 169
Clark, Wd. Jane II, 701
Clark, Wd. Jane II, 787
Clark, Wd. Mary II, 346
Clark, Wd. Meribah II, 486
Clark, Wd. Sarah III, 71
Clark, Wesley H. I, 1149
Clark, Wheeler II, 989
Clark, Widow Martha I, 578
Clark, William I, 379
Clark, William I, 614
Clark, William I, 627
Clark, William I, 711
Clark, William I, 743
Clark, William I, 756
Clark, William I, 757
Clark, William I, 875
Clark, William I, 1027
Clark, William I Sup 1, 10
Clark, William II, 169
Clark, William II, 207
Clark, William II, 346
Clark, William II, 486
Clark, William II, 500
Clark, William IV, 806
Clark, William IV, 901
Clark, William IV, 1234
Clark, William V, 871
Clark, William V, 898
Clark, William VI, 41
Clark, William VI, 163
Clark, William VI, 234
Clark, William VI, 377
Clark, William VI, 799
Clark, William VI, 803
Clark, William VI, 829
Clark, William VI, 836
Clark, William VI, 838
Clark, William Brown II, 487
Clark, William C. I, 493
Clark, William C. I, 601
Clark, William D. I, 743
Clark, William David III, 71
Clark, William Elery IV, 188
Clark, William J. VI, 164
Clark, William Johnson VI, 305
Clark, William, Jr. I, 756
Clark, Wilson IV, 806
Clark, Winaford I, 531
Clark, Wineford VI, 234
Clark, Winiford VI, 305
Clark, Winifred VI, 234
Clark, Wm. II, 61
Clark, Wm. II, 486
Clark, Wm. II, 518
Clark, Wm. II, 522
Clark, Wm. II, 559
Clark, Wm. II, 989
Clark, Wm. II, 1033
Clark, Wm. IV, 689
Clark, Wm. IV, 901
Clark, Wm. IV, 1310
Clark, Wm. A. II, 522
Clark, Wm. Brown II, 733
Clark, Wm. E. II, 848
Clark, Wm. Edward II, 787
Clark, Wm. G. III, 71
Clark, Wm. G. III, 313
Clark, Wm. G. VI, 805
Clark, Wm. Guy V, 379
Clark, Wm. H. IV, 1310
Clark, Wm. Lawrie II, 486
Clark, Wm. M. IV, 1248
Clark, Wm. Mark IV, 1248
Clark, Wm. R. IV, 188
Clark, Wm. Robinson IV, 188
Clark, Wm., Jr. II, 486
Clark, Yancy I, 804
Clark, Zachariah I, 493
Clark, Zodoc I, 135
Clarke, Abigail VI, 163
Clarke, Abigail VI, 164
Clarke, Absalom II, 486
Clarke, Agnes VI, 251
Clarke, Amy III, 71
Clarke, Ann II, 456
Clarke, Ann II, 641
Clarke, Ann Roth II, 486
Clarke, Anna Maria IV, 80
Clarke, Annie M. III, 70
Clarke, Benj. II, 442
Clarke, Benjamin II, 1048
Clarke, Benjamin III, 70
Clarke, Benjamin VI, 285
Clarke, Bernard II, 1048
Clarke, Beulah A. II, 848
Clarke, Beulah A. II, 937
Clarke, Bowling VI, 158
Clarke, Bowling VI, 163
Clarke, Bowling VI, 291
Clarke, Captain Christopher VI, 290
Clarke, Catharine III, 71
Clarke, Catherine IV, 80
Clarke, Charles II, 207
Clarke, Christian VI, 273

Clarke, Cora V, 344
Clarke, David II, 486
Clarke, Dorcas III, 71
Clarke, Elijah II, 207
Clarke, Elisha II, 456
Clarke, Elizabeth II, 346
Clarke, Elizabeth II, 989
Clarke, Elizabeth VI, 163
Clarke, Elizabeth VI, 891
Clarke, Elizabeth A. II, 784
Clarke, Ella V, 551
Clarke, Elwood V, 551
Clarke, Eunice III, 71
Clarke, Frances II, 442
Clarke, Francis II, 442
Clarke, Francis VI, 273
Clarke, Francis VI, 284
Clarke, Francis, Jr. VI, 273
Clarke, Frederick III, 70
Clarke, Gideon III, 71
Clarke, Hannah II, 486
Clarke, Hannah II, 492
Clarke, Hannah II, 898
Clarke, Hannah III, 70
Clarke, Hannah VI, 163
Clarke, Henry II, 787
Clarke, Henry II, 848
Clarke, Henry II, 898
Clarke, Henry VI, 163
Clarke, Henry VI, 164
Clarke, Henry VI, 198
Clarke, Honor II, 61
Clarke, Honor II, 80
Clarke, Isham VI, 875
Clarke, Isham VI, 956
Clarke, Isham VI, 997
Clarke, Isham VI, 1009
Clarke, Jacob III, 71
Clarke, Jacob B. III, 234
Clarke, James II, 346
Clarke, Jane III, 101
Clarke, Jane VI, 885
Clarke, John II, 486
Clarke, John II, 492
Clarke, John II, 898
Clarke, John III, 70
Clarke, John III, 71
Clarke, John III, 120
Clarke, John VI, 163
Clarke, John J. II, 848
Clarke, John Joshua II, 848
Clarke, Joseph II, 486
Clarke, Joseph II, 848
Clarke, Joseph II, 989
Clarke, Joseph III, 71
Clarke, Joseph VI, 631
Clarke, Joseph Oldden II, 487
Clarke, Joseph Olden II, 456
Clarke, Julia III, 291
Clarke, Martha II, 456
Clarke, Martha Elizabeth VI, 736
Clarke, Martha M. III, 201
Clarke, Mary II, 486
Clarke, Mary II, 787
Clarke, Mary II, 848
Clarke, Mary II, 898
Clarke, Mary III, 58
Clarke, Mary III, 71
Clarke, Mary III, 173
Clarke, Mary VI, 198
Clarke, Mary Anna II, 848
Clarke, Mary M. II, 848
Clarke, Micajah VI, 305
Clarke, Nancy VI, 1006
Clarke, Nathaniel III, 58
Clarke, Nathaniel III, 71
Clarke, Phebe VI, 163
Clarke, Phebe VI, 945
Clarke, Rachel II, 989
Clarke, Rachel E. II, 848
Clarke, Rebecca II, 848
Clarke, Rebecca III, 71
Clarke, Rebecca P. III, 58
Clarke, Rebecca P. III, 71
Clarke, Rebeckah S. VI, 163
Clarke, Rebeckah S. VI, 212
Clarke, Rosa V, 551
Clarke, Rufus III, 191
Clarke, Sarah III, 70
Clarke, Sarah III, 71
Clarke, Sarah III, 120
Clarke, Sarah VI, 290
Clarke, Sarah VI, 817
Clarke, Sarah G. III, 191
Clarke, Sarah L. I, 531
Clarke, Sarah R. III, 71
Clarke, Sarah R. III, 191
Clarke, Susan VI, 943
Clarke, Susanna II, 487
Clarke, Thomas II, 486
Clarke, Thomas III, 71
Clarke, William II, 346
Clarke, William VI, 28
Clarke, William J. VI, 164
Clarke, Wm. II, 61
Clarke, Wm. II, 80
Clarke, Wm. E. II, 848
Clarke, Wm. Lawrie II, 486
Clarkson, Ann J. VI, 826
Clarkson, Anselm VI, 326
Clarkson, Auselm VI, 814
Clarkson, Auselm VI, 826
Clarkson, Auselm VI, 829
Clarkson, Elisabeth I, 628
Clarkson, Elizabeth II, 487
Clarkson, Elizabeth II, 572
Clarkson, Elizabeth VI, 806
Clarkson, Elizabeth VI, 866
Clarkson, Elvira P. VI, 893
Clarkson, Helen III, 71
Clarkson, Helen E. III, 71
Clarkson, Helen E. III, 212
Clarkson, Helen W. III, 71
Clarkson, Helen W. III, 212
Clarkson, James F. VI, 806
Clarkson, James L. VI, 866
Clarkson, Jas. B. III, 71
Clarkson, Jas. B. III, 212
Clarkson, Jesse I, 628
Clarkson, Julius VI, 893
Clarkson, Lucy VI, 806
Clarkson, M. P. VI, 806
Clarkson, Margaret VI, 806
Clarkson, Martha D. VI, 814
Clarkson, Nelson VI, 866
Clarkson, Polly VI, 326
Clarkson, Polly VI, 829
Clarkson, Reuben VI, 806
Clarkson, Sarah P. VI, 893
Clarkson, Thomas VI, 806
Clarkson, Thomas VI, 846
Clarkson, William L. VI, 893
Clarkson, Zerilda VI, 806
Clary, ??? VI, 95
Clary, Abigail I, 191
Clary, Ann I, 191
Clary, Ann I, 532
Clary, Ann VI, 104
Clary, Ann VI, 105
Clary, Anna I, 532
Clary, Anna I, 545
Clary, Barnabas I, 875
Clary, Barner I, 532
Clary, Barnes I, 97
Clary, Barnes I, 135
Clary, Barnes I, 532
Clary, Barnes VI, 104
Clary, Barns I, 191
Clary, Barns I, 875
Clary, Barns VI, 45
Clary, Catharine I, 135
Clary, Catharine I, 191
Clary, Catharine I, 199
Clary, Catharine I, 697
Clary, Catharine I, 711
Clary, Catherine I, 182
Clary, Charles I, 42
Clary, Charles I, 182
Clary, Charles I, 191
Clary, Charles I, 532
Clary, Charles VI, 57
Clary, Charles VI, 104
Clary, Charles W. I, 191
Clary, Elisabeth I, 135
Clary, Elisabeth I, 156
Clary, Elisabeth I, 191
Clary, Elizabeth I, 97
Clary, Elizabeth I, 135
Clary, Elizabeth I, 154
Clary, Elizabeth I, 182
Clary, Elizabeth I, 532
Clary, Elizabeth I, 711
Clary, Elizabeth VI, 104
Clary, Elizabeth Jordan VI, 57
Clary, Hannah Jordan VI, 57
Clary, James I, 191
Clary, James VI, 104
Clary, James VI, 122
Clary, Jemima I, 42
Clary, Jemima I, 80
Clary, John I, 42
Clary, John I, 56
Clary, John I, 191
Clary, Jordan I, 135
Clary, Jordan I, 191
Clary, Jordan I, 711
Clary, Jordan VI, 57
Clary, Jordan VI, 101
Clary, Jordan VI, 104
Clary, Jorden I, 697
Clary, Jordon I, 182
Clary, Jordon I, 191
Clary, Jordon I, 199
Clary, Leuilla Tanly I, 182
Clary, Lucilla I, 711
Clary, Lucillar I, 135
Clary, Lucy VI, 104
Clary, Lucy VI, 109
Clary, Martha VI, 97
Clary, Martha VI, 104
Clary, Mary I, 42
Clary, Mary I, 78
Clary, Mary I, 135
Clary, Mary I, 156
Clary, Mary I, 182
Clary, Mary VI, 45
Clary, Mary VI, 99
Clary, Mary VI, 104
Clary, Mary VI, 109
Clary, Mary Ann I, 182
Clary, Mary King VI, 797
Clary, Miles VI, 797
Clary, Miriam I, 42
Clary, Miriam I, 56
Clary, Morning VI, 45
Clary, Nancy I, 97
Clary, Peninah I, 182
Clary, Peninah I, 191
Clary, Peninah I, 202
Clary, Polly VI, 104
Clary, Priscilla VI, 101
Clary, Priscilla VI, 104
Clary, Rex I, 135
Clary, Sarah I, 135
Clary, Sarah I, 182
Clary, Sarah I, 711
Clary, Sarah VI, 104
Clary, Susanna I, 191
Clary, Susanna I, 198
Clary, Thomas VI, 99
Clary, Thomas VI, 104
Clary, William I, 42
Clary, William I, 97
Clary, William I, 135
Clary, William I, 154
Clary???, Sarah VI, 109
Clasbey, Anna I, 804
Clasbey, Anna I, 825
Clasbey, Charles I, 804
Clasbey, Charles I, 983
Clasbey, Lenna I, 983
Clasby, Ann I, 773
Clasby, Anna I, 778
Clasby, Anna I, 804
Clasby, Charles I, 532
Clasby, Charles I, 773
Clasby, Charles I, 778
Clasby, Charles I, 804
Clasby, Elizabeth I, 778
Clasby, Lydia V, 893
Clasby, Lydia V, 899
Clasby, Lydia V, 905
Clasby, Mary I, 778
Clasby, Mary I, 804
Clasby, Mary I, 833
Clase, Esther II, 486
Clash, Debbie Trew II, 848
Clash, Deborah True II, 848
Clash, Elizabeth T. II, 848
Clash, Elizabeth Thomas II, 848
Clash, Garrettson II, 848
Clash, George Vickers II, 848
Clash, James B. II, 848
Clash, James Brown II, 848
Clash, Mary Rebecca II, 848
Class, Charles II, 346
Class, Esther II, 346
Class, Humphrey II, 346
Class, John II, 346
Classby, Chas. V, 905
Classby, Elizabeth V, 905
Classby, Lydia V, 905
Classe, Esther II, 487
Classon, Dominicus IV, 690
Clater, Amelia III, 72
Clater, Sophia III, 72
Clater, William III, 72
Claton, Anna I, 532
Claton, Archada I, 532
Claton, Cada I, 494
Claton, Elizabeth I, 380
Claton, Elizabeth I, 532
Claton, Evan B. I, 532
Claton, Even I, 494
Claton, John I, 494
Claton, John I, 532
Claton, John I, 804
Claton, John I, 820
Claton, Lucia I, 532
Claton, Lucy I, 494
Claton, Marian I, 804
Claton, Mary I, 494
Claton, Mary I, 532
Claton, Miriam I, 532
Claton, Miriam I, 804
Claton, Nancy I, 494
Claton, Nancy I, 532
Claton, Sarah I, 494
Claton, Sarah I, 532
Claton, Thomas B. I, 532
Claton, Tommy I, 494
Claton, Widow Miriam I, 820
Claudis, George VI, 806
Claudis, Henry T. VI, 806
Claudis, Nelly VI, 806
Clausen, Eva IV, 1310
Claussen, Charles IV, 188
Clavert, Hannah II, 787
Clavert, Samuel VI, 72
Clawson, Ann V, 555
Clawson, Ann V, 574
Clawson, Charles IV, 188
Clawson, Charles IV, 189
Clawson, Elizabeth Sears V, 616
Clawson, George IV, 189
Clawson, Josephine IV, 189
Clawson, Josiah V, 38
Clawson, Mary A. I, 875
Clawson, Mary T. IV, 189
Clawson, Rebecca V, 38
Clawson, Rebecca V, 112
Clawson, Rebeccah V, 38
Clawson, Rebekah I, 380
Clawson, Rebekah VI, 482
Clawson, Susanna W. V, 555
Clawson, Susanna W. V, 567
Clawson, Taylor IV, 189
Clawson, William V, 38
Clawson, William V, 112
Clay, Alida Alice III, 72
Clay, Alida Alice III, 170
Clay, Alide Alice III, 72
Clay, Ann II, 442
Clay, Ann C. E. VI, 893
Clay, C. VI, 883
Clay, C. VI, 890
Clay, C. VI, 892
Clay, C. VI, 894
Clay, C. VI, 900
Clay, C. VI, 903
Clay, C. VI, 910
Clay, C. VI, 918
Clay, C. VI, 919
Clay, C. VI, 921
Clay, C. VI, 928
Clay, C. VI, 956
Clay, C. VI, 963
Clay, C. VI, 977
Clay, C. VI, 990
Clay, C. VI, 992
Clay, C. VI, 997
Clay, C. VI, 1005
Clay, C. VI, 1014
Clay, C. VI, 1015
Clay, C. VI, 1020
Clay, Catharine IV, 518
Clay, Catharine IV, 552
Clay, Catharine VI, 806
Clay, Charles VI, 882
Clay, Charles VI, 893
Clay, Charles VI, 915
Clay, Charles VI, 985
Clay, Charles VI, 994
Clay, David VI, 980
Clay, Dewitt C. VI, 893
Clay, Editha VI, 893
Clay, Elizabeth VI, 806
Clay, Elizabeth VI, 893
Clay, Elizabeth E. VI, 802
Clay, Elizabeth N. VI, 893
Clay, Geo. Harry III, 72
Clay, Henry VI, 727
Clay, Henry W. VI, 806
Clay, James A. VI, 893
Clay, Jane IV, 865
Clay, Jane IV, 867
Clay, Jean III, 72
Clay, John III, 72
Clay, John Henry V, 379
Clay, Junius A. VI, 840
Clay, Junius A. VI, 893
Clay, Lois Marie III, 72
Clay, Madge V, 453
Clay, Marston VI, 795
Clay, Marston VI, 818
Clay, Marstone VI, 806
Clay, Martha J. VI, 806
Clay, Mary IV, 689
Clay, Mary IV, 749
Clay, Mary V, 880
Clay, Mary V, 881
Clay, Mary Ann VI, 824
Clay, Mary C. E. VI, 893
Clay, Mary Eleanor III, 72
Clay, O. G. VI, 818
Clay, Odin G. VI, 893
Clay, Odin G. VI, 949
Clay, Paul VI, 795
Clay, Paul VI, 893
Clay, Paul A. VI, 893
Clay, Paul A. VI, 903
Clay, Paul A. VI, 961
Clay, Robert II, 442
Clay, Sally VI, 806
Clay, Sarah Ann VI, 893
Clay, Stephen VI, 802
Clay, Stephen VI, 806
Clay, Stephen VI, 824
Clay, Stephen VI, 834
Clay, Susanna VI, 795
Clay, Theodore III, 170
Clay, Theodore Wm. III, 72
Clayborne, George V, 230
Claybrook, Patsey H. VI, 940
Clayburn, Patsey H. VI, 940
Claypole, Jane II, 487
Claypole, Lindy IV, 1153
Claypole, Mariah V, 230
Claypole, Mark Pettet IV, 1153
Claypole, Nancy IV, 1153
Claypole, Sarah V, 230
Claypool, Jane II, 702
Claypool, Nancy V, 298
Claypool, Nancy V, 300
Claypoole, ??? II, 442
Claypoole, Abraham II, 346
Claypoole, Deborah II, 346
Claypoole, Deborah II, 487
Claypoole, Deborah II, 541
Claypoole, Edith II, 442
Claypoole, Eleanor II, 463
Claypoole, Eleanor II, 487
Claypoole, Elizabeth II, 346
Claypoole, Elizabeth II, 481
Claypoole, Elizabeth II, 643
Claypoole, Elizabeth II, 705
Claypoole, George II, 346
Claypoole, George II, 487
Claypoole, George II, 541
Claypoole, George II, 554
Claypoole, George II, 635
Claypoole, Hannah II, 346
Claypoole, Helena II, 463
Claypoole, Helena II, 487
Claypoole, Isaac II, 346
Claypoole, James II, 346
Claypoole, James II, 442
Claypoole, James II, 487
Claypoole, James II, 552
Claypoole, James II, 648
Claypoole, Jane II, 481
Claypoole, Jane II, 487
Claypoole, John II, 346
Claypoole, John II, 463
Claypoole, John II, 481
Claypoole, John II, 643
Claypoole, John II, 705
Claypoole, Joseph II, 442
Claypoole, Josiah II, 442
Claypoole, Martha II, 346
Claypoole, Martha II, 487
Claypoole, Martha II, 554
Claypoole, Mary II, 346
Claypoole, Mary II, 487
Claypoole, Mary II, 493
Claypoole, Mary II, 552
Claypoole, Nancy V, 904
Claypoole, Nathaniel II, 442
Claypoole, Nathaniel II, 487
Claypoole, Nathaniel II, 552
Claypoole, Rachel II, 487
Claypoole, Rachel II, 648
Claypoole, Rachel II, 705
Claypoole, Samuel II, 346
Claypoole, Susanna II, 487
Claypoole, Susanna II, 643
Claypoole, Susannah II, 487
Claypoole, Wd. Rose II, 463
Claypoole, William II, 346
Clayton, Ann VI, 962
Clayton, Ann P. VI, 962
Clayton, Anna I, 532
Clayton, Archada I, 532
Clayton, Arthur VI, 962
Clayton, Arthur W. VI, 893
Clayton, Arthur W. VI, 962
Clayton, Belle V, 555
Clayton, Benoni I, 532
Clayton, Carah I, 712
Clayton, Catharine II, 848
Clayton, Catharine VI, 962
Clayton, Clarissa VI, 893
Clayton, Clarissa VI, 921
Clayton, Content II, 207
Clayton, David II, 487

Clayton, Deborah III, 72
Clayton, Dicy VI, 893
Clayton, Elivira VI, 1007
Clayton, Eliza VI, 893
Clayton, Eliza Ann IV, 1356
Clayton, Eliza W. VI, 1007
Clayton, Elizabeth I, 532
Clayton, Elizabeth II, 787
Clayton, Elizabeth II, 989
Clayton, Elizabeth VI, 893
Clayton, Elizabeth Catharine VI, 956
Clayton, Elizabeth Jane II, 787
Clayton, Elizabeth Jane II, 848
Clayton, Elliott I, 268
Clayton, Evan B. I, 532
Clayton, Frances VI, 893
Clayton, Frances G. VI, 935
Clayton, Frederick V, 899
Clayton, Hannah II, 810
Clayton, Hannah II, 848
Clayton, Hannah II, 851
Clayton, Hannah L. II, 848
Clayton, Hannah Littler II, 787
Clayton, Hannah Webster II, 848
Clayton, Honor II, 200
Clayton, Honor II, 207
Clayton, Jacob II, 848
Clayton, Jacob B. II, 810
Clayton, Jacob E. II, 848
Clayton, Jacob E. II, 851
Clayton, Jacob Engle II, 787
Clayton, James A. C. VI, 893
Clayton, James M. III, 72
Clayton, Jasper VI, 893
Clayton, Jasper VI, 939
Clayton, Jean VI, 482
Clayton, John I, 532
Clayton, John II, 346
Clayton, John II, 787
Clayton, John VI, 935
Clayton, John VI, 950
Clayton, John VI, 956
Clayton, John VI, 1012
Clayton, John Willis VI, 893
Clayton, Lewis VI, 893
Clayton, Lockey VI, 914
Clayton, Lucia I, 532
Clayton, Lucinda VI, 893
Clayton, Lucinda VI, 996
Clayton, Lucinda H. VI, 893
Clayton, Lucinda H. VI, 970
Clayton, Lucinday VI, 1007
Clayton, Lucy I, 532
Clayton, Lucy I, 579
Clayton, Lydia B. IV, 689
Clayton, Lydia B. IV, 732
Clayton, Maria Louisa II, 815
Clayton, Maria Louisa II, 848
Clayton, Maris L. II, 848
Clayton, Maris L. II, 910
Clayton, Martha II, 989
Clayton, Mary I, 528
Clayton, Mary I, 532
Clayton, Mary VI, 469
Clayton, Mary A. VI, 893
Clayton, Mary A. VI, 939
Clayton, Mary B. II, 848
Clayton, Mary B. II, 851
Clayton, Mary Butler II, 789
Clayton, Mary Butler II, 848
Clayton, Mary Harrison VI, 1012
Clayton, Mary L. II, 133
Clayton, Miriam I, 532
Clayton, Nancy I, 532
Clayton, Nancy I, 569
Clayton, Nancy VI, 893
Clayton, Parnal II, 207
Clayton, Pernal II, 989
Clayton, Pettus O. VI, 893
Clayton, Polly VI, 1007
Clayton, Prudence II, 163
Clayton, Prudence II, 207
Clayton, Prudence II, 252
Clayton, Prudence VI, 477
Clayton, Rachel VI, 806
Clayton, Richard II, 346
Clayton, Robert II, 346
Clayton, Samuel II, 487
Clayton, Sarah I, 532
Clayton, Sarah I, 712
Clayton, Sarah II, 848
Clayton, Sarah A. II, 848
Clayton, Sarah A. II, 899
Clayton, Sarah Anna II, 810
Clayton, Solomon VI, 806
Clayton, Susan IV, 1274
Clayton, Susanna II, 487
Clayton, Susanna C. II, 848
Clayton, Susanna P. VI, 950
Clayton, Thomas II, 207
Clayton, Thomas II, 487
Clayton, Thomas II, 733
Clayton, Thomas VI, 296
Clayton, Thomas B. I, 532
Clayton, Thomas L. VI, 893
Clayton, Thomas R. VI, 1004
Clayton, Thos. L. VI, 893
Clayton, William W. VI, 893
Clayton, Wm., Jun. II, 163
Clayton, Wm., Sr. II, 163
Claytor, Alvin VI, 893
Claytor, Alvin VI, 1000
Claytor, Ann E. VI, 964
Claytor, Arthur W. VI, 893
Claytor, Charlotte VI, 893
Claytor, Dr. John VI, 959
Claytor, Edward M. VI, 970
Claytor, Edward M. VI, 986
Claytor, Eliza VI, 893
Claytor, Eliza Jane VI, 893
Claytor, Elizabeth R. VI, 942
Claytor, Harriet H. VI, 927
Claytor, Harvey VI, 968
Claytor, Harvey VI, 980
Claytor, J. L. VI, 949
Claytor, James E. VI, 893
Claytor, James E. VI, 949
Claytor, James E. VI, 964
Claytor, James L. VI, 893
Claytor, James L. VI, 948
Claytor, Jas. H. VI, 980
Claytor, Jno. VI, 992
Claytor, Jno. C. VI, 986
Claytor, John VI, 882
Claytor, John VI, 893
Claytor, John VI, 927
Claytor, John VI, 965
Claytor, John P. VI, 893
Claytor, John W. VI, 982
Claytor, Julia VI, 893
Claytor, Julia Ann VI, 893
Claytor, Lock VI, 893
Claytor, Lockey VI, 994
Claytor, Locky VI, 893
Claytor, Lucinda VI, 996
Claytor, Margaret H. VI, 893
Claytor, Martha VI, 893
Claytor, Martha VI, 981
Claytor, Martha VI, 986
Claytor, Martha E. VI, 882
Claytor, Martha M. VI, 980
Claytor, Martha N. VI, 893
Claytor, Mary VI, 893
Claytor, Mary E. VI, 986
Claytor, Mary P. VI, 893
Claytor, Narcissa VI, 893
Claytor, Paulina C. VI, 893
Claytor, Peggy VI, 963
Claytor, Robert M. VI, 893
Claytor, Robert M. VI, 942
Claytor, S. G. VI, 925
Claytor, Sally P. VI, 950
Claytor, Saml. A. VI, 893
Claytor, Samuel VI, 882
Claytor, Samuel VI, 893
Claytor, Samuel VI, 921
Claytor, Samuel VI, 959
Claytor, Samuel VI, 963
Claytor, Samuel VI, 1000
Claytor, Samuel A. VI, 893
Claytor, Samuel G. VI, 893
Claytor, Sophia E. VI, 893
Claytor, Susan R. VI, 959
Claytor, Susana M. VI, 893
Claytor, Thomas VI, 305
Claytor, Thomas VI, 326
Claytor, Thomas L. VI, 954
Claytor, Thomas R. VI, 889
Claytor, Thomas R. VI, 893
Claytor, Thos. L. VI, 961
Claytor, Thos. R. VI, 950
Claytor, William G. VI, 893
Claytor, William P. VI, 893
Claytor, Wm. G. VI, 943
Claywell, Peter VI, 797
Claywell, Peter VI, 854
Claywell, Rachel VI, 855
Clealand, Isaac Thomas V, 481
Clealand, John William V, 481
Clealand, John Wm. V, 481
Clealand, Luther V, 481
Clealand, Marietta V, 481
Clealand, Martha Ellen V, 481
Clealand, Martin Luther V, 481
Clealand, Rebecca Jane V, 481
Clealand, Sarah Ann V, 481
Clealand, Thomas V, 481
Clealand, William V, 481
Clear, Chester G. V, 832
Clear, Esther II, 486
Clear, Joetta R. V. V, 832
Clear, Joetta V. V, 832
Clear, John II, 346
Clear, Maria H. V, 832
Clear, Warren E., Jr. V, 832
Cleark, William I, 379
Clearwater, Ann I, 1091
Clearwater, Ann I, 1099
Clearwater, Charlie V, 616
Clearwater, Chas. V, 616
Clearwater, Elizabeth I, 1091
Clearwater, Esther V, 616
Clearwater, Esther B. V, 616
Clearwater, Hannah I, 1091
Clearwater, Hannah V, 230
Clearwater, Hannah V, 616
Clearwater, Jachab V, 616
Clearwater, Jacob I, 1077
Clearwater, Jacob I, 1091
Clearwater, Jacob V, 616
Clearwater, John V, 616
Clearwater, John T. V, 616
Clearwater, Joseph V, 616
Clearwater, Joseph W. V, 616
Clearwater, Sarah Jane V, 616
Clearwater, Sarah Jane V, 642
Cleaver, Abigail IV, 25
Cleaver, Abigail V, 17
Cleaver, Abigail V, 38
Cleaver, Abigail V, 39
Cleaver, Abigail V, 46
Cleaver, Abigail V, 61
Cleaver, Abigail V, 115
Cleaver, Abigail VI, 593
Cleaver, Abigail VI, 604
Cleaver, Alice IV, 25
Cleaver, Alice IV, 26
Cleaver, Alice V, 39
Cleaver, Alice VI, 365
Cleaver, Alice VI, 377
Cleaver, Alice G. IV, 25
Cleaver, Alice G. IV, 26
Cleaver, Allen Grinnell IV, 937
Cleaver, Amelia IV, 25
Cleaver, Amos G. IV, 25
Cleaver, Amos G. IV, 26
Cleaver, Ann IV, 25
Cleaver, Ann IV, 26
Cleaver, Anna IV, 806
Cleaver, Anna IV, 820
Cleaver, Anna V, 39
Cleaver, Benjamin IV, 26
Cleaver, Bentley IV, 25
Cleaver, Betsy Ann IV, 25
Cleaver, Caroline V, 555
Cleaver, Carrie L. IV, 937
Cleaver, Carrie Louanna IV, 937
Cleaver, Carrie Luanna IV, 937
Cleaver, Carrie Marie IV, 937
Cleaver, Daniel V, 555
Cleaver, David IV, 25
Cleaver, David V, 38
Cleaver, David V, 39
Cleaver, David V, 555
Cleaver, Deborah IV, 806
Cleaver, Deborah IV, 813
Cleaver, Edward VI, 377
Cleaver, Edward B. VI, 377
Cleaver, Edward B. VI, 482
Cleaver, Eli IV, 25
Cleaver, Eli IV, 189
Cleaver, Eli T. IV, 25
Cleaver, Eli U. IV, 25
Cleaver, Eli V. IV, 26
Cleaver, Eliza IV, 25
Cleaver, Eliza IV, 33
Cleaver, Elizabeth IV, 21
Cleaver, Elizabeth IV, 25
Cleaver, Elizabeth IV, 26
Cleaver, Elizabeth IV, 865
Cleaver, Elizabeth IV, 881
Cleaver, Elizabeth V, 94
Cleaver, Elizabeth VI, 377
Cleaver, Elizabeth VI, 415
Cleaver, Elizabeth VI, 631
Cleaver, Elizabeth VI, 673
Cleaver, Evalyn IV, 937
Cleaver, Ezekial VI, 604
Cleaver, Ezekiel IV, 25
Cleaver, Ezekiel V, 17
Cleaver, Ezekiel V, 38
Cleaver, Ezekiel V, 39
Cleaver, Ezekiel V, 46
Cleaver, Ezekiel V, 49
Cleaver, Ezekiel V, 61
Cleaver, Ezekiel V, 115
Cleaver, Ezekiel V, 130
Cleaver, Ezekiel VI, 377
Cleaver, Ezekiel VI, 415
Cleaver, Ezekiel VI, 593
Cleaver, Ezekiel VI, 600
Cleaver, Ezekiel VI, 631
Cleaver, Ezekiel VI, 673
Cleaver, Ezekiel L. V, 39
Cleaver, Ezekiel L. V, 968
Cleaver, Ezekiel, Jr. V, 39
Cleaver, Fam IV, 26
Cleaver, Hiram IV, 26
Cleaver, Hiram V, 324
Cleaver, Hiram T. IV, 25
Cleaver, Hiram T. IV, 806
Cleaver, Hiram T. IV, 820
Cleaver, I. A. IV, 937
Cleaver, Isaac IV, 25
Cleaver, Isaac IV, 26
Cleaver, Isaac IV, 57
Cleaver, Isaac IV, 937
Cleaver, Isaac A. IV, 26
Cleaver, Isaac Allen IV, 937
Cleaver, Isaac Jefferson IV, 25
Cleaver, Isaac N. IV, 26
Cleaver, J. A. IV, 937
Cleaver, J. Allen IV, 937
Cleaver, Jane IV, 25
Cleaver, Jane IV, 26
Cleaver, Jane IV, 61
Cleaver, Jane C., Jr. IV, 25
Cleaver, Jane W. II, 848
Cleaver, Jane Walker II, 787
Cleaver, Jas. IV, 937
Cleaver, Jefferson IV, 26
Cleaver, Jesse V, 39
Cleaver, Jesse A. V, 39
Cleaver, John IV, 25
Cleaver, John IV, 26
Cleaver, John V, 39
Cleaver, John Ira IV, 25
Cleaver, John Ira IV, 26
Cleaver, John W. IV, 25
Cleaver, Lena M. IV, 937
Cleaver, Lesh B. IV, 26
Cleaver, Levi V, 39
Cleaver, Levi L. V, 39
Cleaver, Lewis K. IV, 25
Cleaver, Lydia V, 38
Cleaver, Lydia V, 39
Cleaver, Lydia V, 46
Cleaver, Mahlon IV, 25
Cleaver, Martha IV, 26
Cleaver, Martha V, 38
Cleaver, Martha V, 39
Cleaver, Martha V, 49
Cleaver, Martha VI, 377
Cleaver, Martha VI, 442
Cleaver, Mary II, 487
Cleaver, Mary IV, 937
Cleaver, Mary V, 38
Cleaver, Mary V, 39
Cleaver, Mary V, 49
Cleaver, Mary V, 61
Cleaver, Mary V, 130
Cleaver, Mary V, 968
Cleaver, Mary VI, 593
Cleaver, Mary VI, 631
Cleaver, Mary VI, 673
Cleaver, Mary A. VI, 494
Cleaver, Mary Ann IV, 25
Cleaver, Mary Eliza IV, 26
Cleaver, Matilda V, 555
Cleaver, Matilda V, 600
Cleaver, Nathan IV, 25
Cleaver, Nathan IV, 26
Cleaver, Nathan IV, 45
Cleaver, Nathan V, 38
Cleaver, Nathan V, 39
Cleaver, Peter IV, 25
Cleaver, Peter IV, 26
Cleaver, Peter IV, 61
Cleaver, Peter V, 38
Cleaver, Peter V, 39
Cleaver, Peter V, 44
Cleaver, Peter VI, 377
Cleaver, Peter VI, 593
Cleaver, Philena IV, 25
Cleaver, Philena IV, 26
Cleaver, Rachel Ann IV, 25
Cleaver, Rachel Ann IV, 58
Cleaver, Rebecca IV, 25
Cleaver, Rebecca Ivins II, 787
Cleaver, Rebecca J. II, 848
Cleaver, Samuel IV, 25
Cleaver, Samuel G. IV, 25
Cleaver, Sarah IV, 25
Cleaver, Sarah IV, 45
Cleaver, Sarah IV, 46
Cleaver, Sarah IV, 937
Cleaver, Sarah V, 44
Cleaver, Sarah V, 481
Cleaver, Sarah V, 555
Cleaver, Sarah H. IV, 937
Cleaver, Sarah L. IV, 26
Cleaver, Sarah L. IV, 937
Cleaver, Susanna IV, 25
Cleaver, Susanna IV, 57
Cleaver, Susanna S. IV, 26
Cleaver, Unice V, 324
Cleaver, William II, 787
Cleaver, William V, 39
Cleaver, William H. V, 39
Cleaver, William J. IV, 937
Cleaver, Wm. J. IV, 937
Cleaver, Wm. Jefferson IV, 937
Cleavers, Mary II, 487
Cleaves, Elizabeth II, 487
Cleaves, Rebecca II, 487
Cleavinger, Ann VI, 593
Cleavinger, Edith VI, 593
Cleavinger, John VI, 593
Cleavinger, Joseph VI, 593
Cleavinger, Mary VI, 378
Cleavinger, Mary VI, 445
Cleavinger, Mary VI, 593
Cleavinger, Rachel VI, 593
Cleever, Sarah V, 555
Clefton, Mary II, 61
Clegg, Christina I, 922
Clegg, Christine M. I, 939
Clegg, Thomas V, 730
Clegg, Thomas V, 798
Cleland, Carl Emmett V, 555
Cleland, Caroline V, 379
Cleland, Charles V, 555
Cleland, Clarence V, 555
Cleland, Clarence Raymond V, 555
Cleland, Cora A. V, 555
Cleland, Delila J. V, 555
Cleland, Delilah Jane V, 555
Cleland, Earl Wm. V, 555
Cleland, Elva V, 555
Cleland, Henry B. V, 379
Cleland, Ida V, 555
Cleland, Irena V, 555
Cleland, Irena Belle V, 555
Cleland, James V, 379
Cleland, James V, 555
Cleland, John V, 555
Cleland, John V, 664
Cleland, John W. V, 555
Cleland, Larkin V, 379
Cleland, Larkin V, 411
Cleland, Luther V, 555
Cleland, Luther Thos. V, 555
Cleland, Marietta V, 555
Cleland, Marten Luther V, 555
Cleland, Mary E. V, 555
Cleland, Mary Ella V, 555
Cleland, Mary Etta V, 555
Cleland, Melcena V, 379
Cleland, Melcena V, 411
Cleland, Melcina V, 379
Cleland, Nancy Jane V, 379
Cleland, Phebe V, 379
Cleland, Phebe V, 411
Cleland, Rebecca V, 555
Cleland, Rebecca V, 694
Cleland, Rebecca Daugherty V, 664
Cleland, Rebecca Jane V, 555
Cleland, Ruth Etta V, 555
Cleland, Sarah V, 555
Cleland, Sarah A. V, 555
Cleland, Sarah Ann V, 555
Cleland, Thomas V, 555
Cleland, William V, 555
Cleland, Wm. V, 555
Clelland, Caroline V, 379
Clelland, Clarence V, 555
Clelland, Irena V, 555
Clelland, Isaac Thomas V, 481
Clelland, John William V, 481
Clelland, John Wm. V, 481
Clelland, Luther V, 481
Clelland, Marietta V, 481
Clelland, Martha Ellen V, 481
Clelland, Martin Luther V, 481
Clelland, Mercy IV, 80
Clelland, Mercy IV, 116
Clelland, Rebecca Jane V, 481
Clelland, Ruth Etta V, 555
Clelland, Sarah Ann V, 481
Clelland, Thomas V, 481
Clelland, William V, 481
Clemens, C. IV, 1274
Clemens, Clare II, 487
Clemens, Clarence V, 989
Clemens, Claude V, 664
Clemens, Claude V, 989
Clemens, Claudie V, 989
Clemens, Elizabeth VI, 978
Clemens, Ella V, 380
Clemens, Ella V, 664
Clemens, Ella Murphy V, 989
Clemens, Ellen V, 989

Clemens, John V, 989
Clemens, John C. V, 989
Clemens, L. S. V, 989
Clemens, Leroy V, 664
Clemens, Leroy V, 989
Clemens, Leroy F. V, 664
Clemens, Leroy S. V, 324
Clemens, Leroy S. V, 989
Clemens, Martha III, 399
Clemens, Pamelia VI, 894
Clemens, Samuel VI, 894
Clemens, Samuel VI, 1001
Clemens, Sarah V, 324
Clemens, Sarah L. V, 324
Clemens, Thos. V, 989
Clement, Aaron II, 733
Clement, Abigail III, 72
Clement, Adam VI, 806
Clement, Adam VI, 832
Clement, Adam VI, 841
Clement, Adam VI, 859
Clement, Adam, Jr. VI, 806
Clement, Agness VI, 813
Clement, Ann II, 58
Clement, Ann II, 61
Clement, Ann II, 207
Clement, Ann II, 274
Clement, Ann II, 487
Clement, Ann Eliza III, 72
Clement, Benj. VI, 806
Clement, Benjamin VI, 806
Clement, Betty VI, 831
Clement, Beulah II, 207
Clement, Beulah II, 274
Clement, Catharine II, 848
Clement, Catharine II, 894
Clement, Charles III, 72
Clement, Charles III, 399
Clement, Charles III, 480
Clement, Charles A. VI, 806
Clement, Daniel III, 72
Clement, Daniel III, 313
Clement, Deborah III, 43
Clement, Deborah III, 72
Clement, Eliza H. II, 488
Clement, Eliza H. II, 494
Clement, Elizabeth II, 24
Clement, Elizabeth II, 61
Clement, Elizabeth II, 207
Clement, Elizabeth II, 346
Clement, Elizabeth II, 488
Clement, Elizabeth II, 806
Clement, Elizabeth II, 848
Clement, Elizabeth II, 894
Clement, Elizabeth III, 72
Clement, Elizabeth Hudson II, 317
Clement, Elizabeth L. II, 488
Clement, Elizabeth L. II, 733
Clement, Elizabeth L. II, 750
Clement, Elizabeth S. II, 701
Clement, Elizabeth W. II, 310
Clement, Evan II, 207
Clement, Evan II, 274
Clement, Evan II, 487
Clement, Evan II, 701
Clement, Geo. W. VI, 806
Clement, George VI, 831
Clement, Hannah II, 487
Clement, Hannah II, 488
Clement, Hannah II, 682
Clement, Hannah III, 72
Clement, Hannah III, 313
Clement, Henrietta III, 378
Clement, Henry III, 72
Clement, Henry III, 362
Clement, Henry III, 378
Clement, Henry III, 389
Clement, Henry III, 480
Clement, Isaac II, 787
Clement, Isaac II, 848
Clement, Isaac II, 919
Clement, Jacob II, 207
Clement, James II, 207
Clement, James II, 487
Clement, James III, 72
Clement, James III, 114
Clement, James W. II, 487
Clement, James Willis II, 487
Clement, Jane III, 72
Clement, Jane III, 399
Clement, Jane III, 407
Clement, Jane III, 473
Clement, Jane VI, 806
Clement, Jarvis III, 399
Clement, John II, 488
Clement, John II, 733
Clement, John VI, 806
Clement, John A. II, 701
Clement, John James II, 488
Clement, John James II, 733
Clement, Johnson VI, 832
Clement, Jonathan III, 43
Clement, Jonathan III, 72
Clement, Joseph II, 58
Clement, Joseph II, 61
Clement, Joseph II, 487
Clement, Joseph II, 488
Clement, Joseph III, 72
Clement, Joseph III, 399
Clement, Joseph III, 407
Clement, Joseph III, 473
Clement, Joseph C. II, 488
Clement, Joseph E. III, 72
Clement, Joseph, Jr. III, 399
Clement, Juliet E. VI, 854
Clement, Juriah VI, 814
Clement, Juriah VI, 832
Clement, Louisa II, 488
Clement, Louisa B. II, 733
Clement, Louisa B. II, 774
Clement, Louisa J. VI, 806
Clement, Lucretia Mott II, 317
Clement, Lydia II, 487
Clement, Lydia II, 488
Clement, Mahalah Ann V, 948
Clement, Mahalah Ann V, 949
Clement, Mark II, 848
Clement, Mark II, 894
Clement, Martha III, 72
Clement, Martha III, 399
Clement, Martha VI, 806
Clement, Mary II, 488
Clement, Mary II, 787
Clement, Mary II, 848
Clement, Mary II, 919
Clement, Mary III, 72
Clement, Mary III, 399
Clement, Mary III, 474
Clement, Mary VI, 806
Clement, Mary VI, 813
Clement, Mary VI, 814
Clement, Mary A. III, 43
Clement, Mary A. III, 72
Clement, Mary E. VI, 894
Clement, Mary G. VI, 806
Clement, Mary S. II, 317
Clement, Mary S. II, 848
Clement, Mary T. II, 317
Clement, Mathew II, 346
Clement, Mercy III, 399
Clement, Mercy III, 473
Clement, Nancy VI, 806
Clement, Orenda VI, 806
Clement, Polinia I, 926
Clement, Polly VI, 806
Clement, Rachel II, 701
Clement, Robert A. VI, 894
Clement, Robert A. VI, 1022
Clement, Ruth II, 24
Clement, Ruth II, 61
Clement, Ruth III, 378
Clement, Ruth Anna II, 701
Clement, Ruth Anna II, 733
Clement, Ruth L. III, 72
Clement, Ruth L. III, 362
Clement, Ruth L. III, 389
Clement, Samuel II, 207
Clement, Samuel II, 274
Clement, Samuel II, 487
Clement, Samuel II, 848
Clement, Samuel II, 894
Clement, Samuel L. II, 488
Clement, Samuel L. II, 733
Clement, Sarah II, 346
Clement, Sarah III, 72
Clement, Sarah III, 399
Clement, Sarah III, 474
Clement, Sarah III, 480
Clement, Sarah VI, 806
Clement, Sarah VI, 841
Clement, Sarah A. II, 488
Clement, Sarah A. II, 733
Clement, Stephen III, 378
Clement, Thomas II, 61
Clement, Thomas II, 487
Clement, Thos. II, 24
Clement, Wd. Abigail III, 114
Clement, Wd. Ann II, 487
Clement, William III, 378
Clement, William VI, 806
Clement, William VI, 813
Clement, William A. VI, 802
Clement, William A. VI, 807
Clement, William A. VI, 814
Clement, William A. VI, 820
Clement, William A. VI, 826
Clement, William A. VI, 827
Clement, William A. VI, 851
Clement, William B. III, 378
Clement, William F. VI, 830
Clement, William Loyd Garrison II, 317
Clement, Wm. II, 487
Clement, Wm. II, 488
Clement, Wm. II, 919
Clement, Wm. A. VI, 806
Clement, Wm. B. III, 389
Clement, Wm. C. II, 488
Clement, Wm. C. II, 701
Clement, Wm. Lloyd Garrison II, 787
Clement, Wm. Lloyd Garrison II, 848
Clement, Zebedee II, 346
Clements, Adam VI, 846
Clements, Adam VI, 894
Clements, Angness VI, 894
Clements, Benjamin VI, 894
Clements, Charles III, 399
Clements, Charles A. VI, 806
Clements, Dorothy V, 454
Clements, Elizabeth II, 346
Clements, Elizabeth II, 989
Clements, Elizabeth II, 990
Clements, Emma V, 454
Clements, Hattie V, 454
Clements, Jane III, 72
Clements, John VI, 952
Clements, John C. V, 989
Clements, Johnson VI, 846
Clements, Joseph III, 72
Clements, Margaret V, 454
Clements, Mary E. VI, 894
Clements, Mary T. II, 316
Clements, Mathew II, 346
Clements, Pamelia VI, 894
Clements, Rachel VI, 894
Clements, Raymond V, 454
Clements, Richard P. VI, 57
Clements, Richard P. VI, 58
Clements, Robert A. VI, 894
Clements, Samuel VI, 894
Clements, Sarah III, 72
Clements, Sarah III, 105
Clements, Sarah III, 399
Clements, Susannah VI, 846
Clements, Thomas II, 487
Clements, William A. VI, 795
Clements, William A. VI, 806
Clements, Wm. A. VI, 811
Clemer, David V, 157
Clemer, David H. V, 157
Clemer, Oscar V, 157
Clemer, Osker V, 157
Clemets, Benjamin VI, 894
Clemets, Rachel VI, 894
Clemison, Wd. Elizabeth II, 488
Clemison, Wd. Elizabeth II, 562
Clemmens, Claude V, 664
Clemmens, Ella V, 664
Clemmens, Fred V, 616
Clemmens, Katie V, 616
Clemmens, Leroy V, 664
Clemment, Hannah II, 487
Clemment, James W. II, 487
Clemmer, Daisy Howell V, 481
Clemmer, David H. V, 157
Clemmer, Oscar V, 157
Clemmings, Anna I, 611
Clemmons, Comfort I, 532
Clemmons, Elizabeth I, 1007
Clemmons, Elizabeth I, 1008
Clemmons, Gaspar VI, 806
Clemmons, Peter I, 532
Clemmons, Polly I, 532
Clemmons, Polly VI, 806
Clemmons, Rebecca I, 532
Clemmons, Rebecca I, 572
Clemmons, Richard P. VI, 57
Clemmons, Richard P. VI, 58
Clemmons, Richard P. VI, 80
Clemonds, Ann II, 61
Clemons, Leroy V, 989
Clemons, Rebecca I, 532
Clemons, Sarah L. V, 324
Clempson, Alice IV, 937
Clempson, Alice IV, 938
Clempson, Alice IV, 1129
Clempson, Alice A. IV, 937
Clempson, Alice A. IV, 938
Clempson, Alice A. IV, 1013
Clempson, Ann IV, 937
Clempson, Benjamin IV, 937
Clempson, Benjamin F. IV, 938
Clempson, Clotilda IV, 937
Clempson, Francis IV, 937
Clempson, Isaac IV, 937
Clempson, Isaac IV, 938
Clempson, James IV, 937
Clempson, James IV, 938
Clempson, James C. IV, 937
Clempson, James L. IV, 937
Clempson, James L. IV, 938
Clempson, James L. IV, 1129
Clempson, James Lee IV, 937
Clempson, James Lee IV, 938
Clempson, James P. IV, 937
Clempson, Joel IV, 937
Clempson, John IV, 937
Clempson, Joseph IV, 937
Clempson, Lydia IV, 937
Clempson, Lydia Star IV, 938
Clempson, Martha E. IV, 937
Clempson, Mary IV, 938
Clempson, Mary A. IV, 937
Clempson, Mary Ann IV, 937
Clempson, Mary C. IV, 937
Clempson, Reuben IV, 901
Clempson, Reuben IV, 937
Clempson, Reuben IV, 938
Clempson, Rosco IV, 1129
Clempson, Roscoe IV, 937
Clempson, Roscoe IV, 938
Clempson, Tryphena B. IV, 937
Clempson, Tryphena B. IV, 938
Clempson, Tryphena B. IV, 1129
Clempson, Wm. P. IV, 937
Clemsen, Allice IV, 806
Clemsen, Eliza IV, 806
Clemsen, James L. IV, 806
Clemsen, James Lee IV, 806
Clemsen, Rosco IV, 806
Clemsen, Triphemia IV, 806
Clemsen, Tryphena IV, 806
Clemson, Alice IV, 937
Clemson, Alice IV, 1129
Clemson, Ann IV, 689
Clemson, Ann IV, 937
Clemson, Anna V, 454
Clemson, Benjamin IV, 937
Clemson, Francis IV, 937
Clemson, Hannah IV, 689
Clemson, Hannah IV, 901
Clemson, Hannah IV, 904
Clemson, Isaac IV, 690
Clemson, Isaac IV, 937
Clemson, Isaac IV, 938
Clemson, Isaac T. IV, 901
Clemson, James II, 346
Clemson, James II, 488
Clemson, James IV, 689
Clemson, James IV, 901
Clemson, James IV, 937
Clemson, James IV, 938
Clemson, James IV, 1036
Clemson, James L. IV, 937
Clemson, James L. IV, 1129
Clemson, James Lee IV, 690
Clemson, John IV, 690
Clemson, John IV, 937
Clemson, Joseph IV, 690
Clemson, Joseph IV, 937
Clemson, Lydia IV, 901
Clemson, Lydia IV, 937
Clemson, Lydia Starr IV, 690
Clemson, Mary IV, 938
Clemson, Mary A. IV, 901
Clemson, Mary A. IV, 937
Clemson, Mary Ann IV, 690
Clemson, Mary Ann IV, 901
Clemson, Mary Ann IV, 914
Clemson, Mary Ann IV, 937
Clemson, Mary J. IV, 1036
Clemson, Pusy IV, 690
Clemson, Reuben IV, 689
Clemson, Reuben IV, 690
Clemson, Reuben IV, 901
Clemson, Rosco IV, 1129
Clemson, Roscoe IV, 937
Clemson, Rubin IV, 690
Clemson, Tryphena B. IV, 937
Clemson, Tryphena B. IV, 1129
Clemson, Wd. Elizabeth II, 488
Clemson, Wm. P. IV, 937
Clemson, Wm. Penn IV, 689
Clenden, Isaac II, 787
Clenden, Wd. Mercy II, 787
Clendenan, Amy IV, 518
Clendenan, Benjamin IV, 518
Clendenan, Elizabeth IV, 513
Clendenan, Elizabeth IV, 518
Clendenan, Stephen IV, 513
Clendenan, Stephen IV, 518
Clendenen, Hannah IV, 189
Clendenen, Isaac IV, 1052
Clendenen, Mira II, 733
Clendenin, Elizabeth II, 488
Clendenin, Elizabeth II, 848
Clendenin, Joshua II, 848
Clendenin, Katherine Magill II, 848
Clendenin, Mercy II, 848
Clendenin, Rachel II, 848
Clendenin, Sarah II, 488
Clendening, Jesse VI, 482
Clendening, Jesse VI, 584
Clendening, Prudence VI, 482
Clendening, Prudence VI, 584
Clendening, Sarah VI, 482
Clendening, Sarah VI, 584
Clendennen, Elizabeth IV, 189
Clendennen, Hannah IV, 189
Clendennen, Jasper Seybold VI, 482
Clendennen, Jesse VI, 482
Clendennen, Matilda Jane IV, 189
Clendennen, Prudence VI, 482
Clendennen, Rebeckah VI, 485
Clendennen, Rebekah VI, 559
Clendennen, Robert VI, 559
Clendennen, Sarah IV, 189
Clendennen, Sarah VI, 482
Clendennen, Sarah Louiza IV, 189
Clendennen, Stephen IV, 189
Clendennin, Elizabeth II, 346
Clendenning, ??? VI, 584
Clendenning, Ann VI, 377
Clendenning, Ann VI, 461
Clendenning, Elizabeth IV, 379
Clendenning, James VI, 584
Clendenning, Katherine Magill II, 848
Clendenning, Rebekah VI, 633
Clendenning, Rebekah VI, 698
Clendennon, Amy IV, 379
Clendennon, Elizabeth IV, 455
Clendennon, Hannah IV, 379
Clendennon, Hannah IV, 390
Clendennon, Hannah IV, 455
Clendennon, Isaac IV, 390
Clendennon, Isaac IV, 455
Clendennon, Rebecca IV, 390
Clendenon, Amy IV, 379
Clendenon, Amy IV, 409
Clendenon, Amy IV, 438
Clendenon, Benjamin IV, 379
Clendenon, Benjamin IV, 409
Clendenon, Benjamin IV, 438
Clendenon, Benjamin E. IV, 379
Clendenon, Charles Francis IV, 1052
Clendenon, David IV, 1052
Clendenon, Eliza B. IV, 1052
Clendenon, Elizabeth II, 488
Clendenon, Elizabeth II, 848
Clendenon, Elizabeth IV, 379
Clendenon, Elizabeth IV, 797
Clendenon, Elizabeth Whiteside II, 787
Clendenon, Elizabeth, Jr. II, 488
Clendenon, Elwood II, 787
Clendenon, Esther IV, 379
Clendenon, Esther IV, 421
Clendenon, Hannah IV, 379
Clendenon, Hannah IV, 421
Clendenon, Hannah IV, 455
Clendenon, Hannah IV, 1052
Clendenon, Hannah IV, 1072
Clendenon, Isaac IV, 379
Clendenon, Isaac IV, 421
Clendenon, Isaac IV, 455
Clendenon, Isaac IV, 1052
Clendenon, Isaac IV, 1072
Clendenon, Isaac Wilson IV, 379
Clendenon, Isaac, Jr. IV, 379
Clendenon, Isaac, Jr. IV, 1052
Clendenon, Joanna IV, 379
Clendenon, Joshua II, 848
Clendenon, Kennet II, 488
Clendenon, Lydia IV, 379
Clendenon, Lydia IV, 438
Clendenon, Lydia IV, 455
Clendenon, Lydia IV, 797
Clendenon, Maria IV, 379
Clendenon, Maria IV, 1052
Clendenon, Maria IV, 1072
Clendenon, Martha J. IV, 1052
Clendenon, Martha Jane IV, 1052
Clendenon, Martha Jane IV, 1060
Clendenon, Mary IV, 1052
Clendenon, Mary H. IV, 1052
Clendenon, Matilda IV, 379
Clendenon, Matilda IV, 383
Clendenon, Matilda Jane IV, 379
Clendenon, Matilda Jane IV, 1129
Clendenon, Matilda Jane IV, 1130
Clendenon, Mercy II, 848
Clendenon, Mira II, 488
Clendenon, Mira II, 733
Clendenon, Rachel II, 208

lendenon, Rachel II, 488
lendenon, Rachel II, 733
lendenon, Rebecca IV, 379
lendenon, Rebecca IV, 1061
lendenon, Rebeckah IV, 379
lendenon, Sarah II, 488
lendenon, Sarah II, 733
lendenon, Sarah IV, 379
lendenon, Sarah Louisa IV, 379
lendenon, Stephen IV, 379
lendenon, Stephen IV, 383
lendenon, Stephen IV, 797
lendenon, Wm. IV, 379
lendenon, Wm. IV, 1052
lendenon, Wm. I. IV, 1052
lendinning, Katharine Magill II, 914
lerk, Alexander I, 401
lerk, Anna I, 401
lerk, Benjamin II, 488
lerk, Benjamin II, 566
lerk, Caleb I, 531
lerk, Christopher VI, 889
lerk, David II, 346
lerk, Edward VI, 163
lerk, Elizabeth I, 1055
lerk, Elizabeth II, 346
lerk, Ephraim I, 135
lerk, Francis I, 531
lerk, Francis VI, 163
lerk, Henry I, 1055
lerk, Isham VI, 884
lerk, James VI, 962
lerk, Jane V, 832
lerk, John I, 1055
lerk, John, Jr. I, 531
lerk, Joseph II, 346
lerk, Lewis Latham I, 531
lerk, Maria V, 38
lerk, Martha II, 488
lerk, Martha II, 566
lerk, Mary V, 38
lerk, Mary V, 93
lerk, Meribah II, 488
lerk, Micajah I, 135
lerk, Samuel II, 488
lerk, Sarah II, 61
lerk, Sarah II, 488
lerk, Thomas II, 488
lerks, Bolin VI, 291
lerkston, Ketita I, 471
leveland, Cyrus III, 72
leveland, Cyrus III, 315
leveland, Elizabeth V, 664
leveland, Elizabeth Ann V, 664
leveland, Emily P. III, 72
leveland, Emily P. III, 315
leveland, Estella V, 664
leveland, Fanny VI, 894
leveland, Huldah A. IV, 1274
leveland, Ida III, 72
leveland, Ida III, 315
leveland, Larkin VI, 894
leveland, Wm. V, 664
levenger, Ann VI, 593
levenger, Ann Elizabeth VI, 377
levenger, Ann Elizabeth VI, 378
levenger, Ann Elizabeth VI, 405
levenger, Ann Elizabeth VI, 406
levenger, B. Franklin VI, 377
levenger, B. Franklin VI, 378
levenger, B. Franklin VI, 405
levenger, B. Franklin VI, 406
levenger, Bertha B. VI, 377
levenger, Bertha B. VI, 378
levenger, Carrie A. VI, 378
levenger, Carrie Alice VI, 377
levenger, Carrie Alice VI, 378
levenger, Carroll C. VI, 377
levenger, Carroll C. VI, 378
levenger, Charles VI, 377
levenger, Charles E. VI, 377
levenger, Charles E. VI, 378
levenger, David VI, 371
levenger, David VI, 377
levenger, David VI, 438
levenger, Drury D. VI, 377
levenger, Drury D. VI, 378
levenger, Drury D. VI, 437
levenger, Edith VI, 593
levenger, Edith M. VI, 377
levenger, Edith M. VI, 378
levenger, Edith M. VI, 437
levenger, Etha B. VI, 377
levenger, Etha B. VI, 378
levenger, Etha Brown VI, 377
levenger, Etha Brown VI, 378
levenger, Etta B. VI, 378
levenger, Evangeline VI, 377
levenger, Francis V, 616
levenger, Francis E. V, 616
Clevenger, Frank M. VI, 377
Clevenger, Frank M. VI, 438
Clevenger, Frank M. VI, 439
Clevenger, Franklin B. VI, 377
Clevenger, Genevieve VI, 377
Clevenger, Genevive VI, 378
Clevenger, Grace E. VI, 377
Clevenger, Grace E. VI, 378
Clevenger, Hannah V, 39
Clevenger, Hannah VI, 371
Clevenger, Hannah VI, 377
Clevenger, Hannah VI, 378
Clevenger, Hannah VI, 438
Clevenger, Hattie VI, 376
Clevenger, Hattie VI, 377
Clevenger, Hattie VI, 378
Clevenger, Hattie VI, 405
Clevenger, Hattie VI, 415
Clevenger, James N. V, 989
Clevenger, John VI, 378
Clevenger, John VI, 593
Clevenger, Joseph VI, 593
Clevenger, Joshua II, 323
Clevenger, Lissie V, 555
Clevenger, Lydia II, 317
Clevenger, Lydia II, 323
Clevenger, M. B. IV, 1204
Clevenger, Mahlon IV, 1204
Clevenger, Martha V, 989
Clevenger, Martha VI, 377
Clevenger, Martha Louise VI, 377
Clevenger, Mary VI, 373
Clevenger, Mary VI, 377
Clevenger, Mary VI, 378
Clevenger, Mary VI, 482
Clevenger, Mary VI, 566
Clevenger, Mary VI, 593
Clevenger, Mary F. VI, 377
Clevenger, Mary Frances VI, 377
Clevenger, Mary Frances VI, 438
Clevenger, Mary Frances VI, 689
Clevenger, Mary Frances VI, 695
Clevenger, Mary H. VI, 377
Clevenger, Mary H. VI, 378
Clevenger, Mary Hannah VI, 377
Clevenger, Mary Hannah VI, 438
Clevenger, Mary Hannah VI, 439
Clevenger, Mary Jane VI, 378
Clevenger, Mary Jane VI, 438
Clevenger, Mary R. VI, 378
Clevenger, Massa V, 157
Clevenger, Massa V, 177
Clevenger, Phebe VI, 482
Clevenger, Phebe VI, 509
Clevenger, Phebe VI, 593
Clevenger, Rachel VI, 593
Clevenger, Sarah V, 616
Clevenger, Sophia B. VI, 377
Clevenger, Sophia B. VI, 438
Clevenger, Sophia B. VI, 439
Clevenger, Stanley VI, 378
Clevenger, Stanley Chas. VI, 377
Clevenger, Sue S. VI, 378
Clevenger, Susan VI, 377
Clevenger, Susan S. VI, 377
Clevenger, Washington VI, 377
Clevenger, William VI, 377
Clever, Alice VI, 377
Clever, Caroline V, 555
Clever, David V, 555
Clever, Edward VI, 377
Clever, Ezekiel V, 39
Clever, Ezekiel VI, 377
Clever, Jemimah II, 61
Clever, Jemimah II, 67
Clever, Martha VI, 377
Clever, Sarah V, 555
Clevinger, Hannah VI, 378
Clevinger, John VI, 378
Clevinger, Mary VI, 378
Clevinger, Mary VI, 448
Clewes, Joseph II, 196
Clewes, Meribah II, 488
Clewes, Patience II, 196
Clews, ??? II, 989
Clews, Hannah VI, 482
Clews, Hannah VI, 533
Clews, Joseph VI, 482
Clews, Ruth VI, 482
Clews, Ruth VI, 547
Clews, Sarah II, 978
Clews, Wd. Sarah II, 989
Clibborn, Edward V, 899
Clibborn, Frederick II, 733
Clibborn, John III, 72
Clibborn, Joshua II, 488
Clibborn, Joshua, Jr. II, 488
Clibborn, Lydia II, 488
Clibborn, Samuel III, 72
Clibborn, Wm. Cooper III, 72
Cliborn, Eligier C. VI, 884
Clibourn, Elizabeth VI, 981
Cliburn, Rhody VI, 869
Cliburn, Sary VI, 869
Clickner, Ott V, 230
Cliff, Agatha IV, 379
Cliff, Mary E. IV, 1310
Cliff, Sarah IV, 379
Cliff, Sarah IV, 413
Cliffe, Robert II, 488
Clifford, ??? III, 72
Clifford, ??? III, 262
Clifford, Amelia IV, 1310
Clifford, Ann I, 1076
Clifford, Ann II, 208
Clifford, Ann II, 226
Clifford, Ann II, 240
Clifford, Ann II, 347
Clifford, Ann II, 442
Clifford, Anna II, 208
Clifford, Anna II, 240
Clifford, Anna II, 347
Clifford, Anna II, 488
Clifford, Anna II, 532
Clifford, Anna II, 989
Clifford, Anna V, 664
Clifford, Anna V, 709
Clifford, Anna, Jr. II, 488
Clifford, Anna, Jr. II, 532
Clifford, Anne II, 488
Clifford, Anne II, 654
Clifford, Cliford II, 957
Clifford, Deborah II, 347
Clifford, Edward II, 347
Clifford, Elizabeth II, 347
Clifford, Elizabeth II, 488
Clifford, Elizabeth II, 654
Clifford, Elizabeth II, 989
Clifford, Elizabeth II, 1018
Clifford, Elizabeth III, 72
Clifford, Elizabeth E. III, 72
Clifford, Elizabeth E. III, 262
Clifford, George II, 347
Clifford, Hannah II, 208
Clifford, Hannah II, 226
Clifford, Hannah II, 240
Clifford, Hannah II, 259
Clifford, Hannah II, 989
Clifford, Hannah II, 998
Clifford, James II, 957
Clifford, John II, 347
Clifford, John II, 488
Clifford, John II, 957
Clifford, P. J. V, 664
Clifford, P. J. V, 709
Clifford, Pearl Edith IV, 1310
Clifford, Rebecca II, 347
Clifford, Rebecca II, 488
Clifford, Rebecca II, 620
Clifford, Sarah II, 347
Clifford, Sarah II, 957
Clifford, Thomas II, 208
Clifford, Thomas II, 226
Clifford, Thomas II, 259
Clifford, Thomas II, 347
Clifford, Thomas II, 442
Clifford, Thomas II, 488
Clifford, Thomas II, 532
Clifford, Thomas II, 654
Clifford, Thomas II, 957
Clifford, Thomas II, 989
Clifford, Thomas II, 991
Clifford, Thomas II, 998
Clifford, Thomas, Jr. II, 347
Clifford, Thomas, Jr. II, 488
Clifford, Thomazine II, 347
Cliffords, Anna II, 1026
Cliffords, Thomas II, 1026
Cliffton, Ann II, 488
Cliffton, Catharine II, 347
Cliffton, Elizabeth II, 488
Cliffton, Elizabeth II, 676
Cliffton, Ella V, 57
Cliffton, Hannah II, 347
Cliffton, Hannah II, 488
Cliffton, Hannah II, 632
Cliffton, Henry II, 475
Cliffton, Henry II, 488
Cliffton, Henry II, 489
Cliffton, Henry II, 495
Cliffton, Henry II, 510
Cliffton, Henry II, 632
Cliffton, Henry II, 676
Cliffton, John II, 488
Cliffton, John II, 489
Cliffton, John II, 495
Cliffton, John II, 632
Cliffton, Mary II, 475
Cliffton, Mary II, 482
Cliffton, Mary II, 488
Cliffton, Rachel II, 489
Cliffton, Rachel II, 495
Cliffton, Sarah II, 347
Cliffton, Sarah II, 489
Cliffton, Wd. Sarah II, 488
Cliffton, Wd. Sarah II, 510
Cliffton, William II, 347
Clift, Mrs. Mary IV, 1310
Clift, Samuel II, 208
Clifton, Adelaide I, 620
Clifton, Adelaide Perle I, 631
Clifton, Ann II, 488
Clifton, Anne II, 208
Clifton, Catharine II, 347
Clifton, Catherine II, 488
Clifton, Catherine II, 540
Clifton, Charles IV, 1153
Clifton, Charles K. IV, 1153
Clifton, Charles R. IV, 1153
Clifton, Deborah II, 347
Clifton, Elizabeth II, 25
Clifton, Elizabeth II, 61
Clifton, Elizabeth II, 106
Clifton, Elizabeth II, 488
Clifton, Elizabeth II, 489
Clifton, Elizabeth II, 535
Clifton, Ella III, 72
Clifton, Ella III, 130
Clifton, Ella III, 194
Clifton, Ella III, 336
Clifton, Ester II, 51
Clifton, Ester II, 61
Clifton, Frances V, 230
Clifton, Hannah II, 347
Clifton, Hannah II, 488
Clifton, Henry II, 347
Clifton, Henry II, 442
Clifton, Henry II, 488
Clifton, Henry II, 489
Clifton, Henry II, 594
Clifton, Henry III, 16
Clifton, Henry III, 72
Clifton, Hugh II, 25
Clifton, Hugh II, 51
Clifton, Hugh II, 61
Clifton, Hugh II, 106
Clifton, Joan II, 442
Clifton, Joan II, 488
Clifton, John II, 347
Clifton, John II, 464
Clifton, John II, 488
Clifton, John II, 489
Clifton, John II, 540
Clifton, John W. I, 620
Clifton, Jonathan VI, 806
Clifton, Joseph II, 25
Clifton, Joseph II, 347
Clifton, Letitia II, 347
Clifton, Louisa I, 620
Clifton, Margaret IV, 1153
Clifton, Mary II, 25
Clifton, Mary II, 61
Clifton, Mary II, 208
Clifton, Mary II, 347
Clifton, Mary II, 488
Clifton, Mary III, 72
Clifton, Rachel II, 347
Clifton, Rachel II, 464
Clifton, Rachel II, 488
Clifton, Rachel II, 489
Clifton, Rebecka II, 347
Clifton, Rebekah III, 16
Clifton, Rebekah III, 72
Clifton, Sarah II, 61
Clifton, Sarah II, 93
Clifton, Sarah II, 347
Clifton, Sarah II, 488
Clifton, Sarah II, 489
Clifton, Sarah II, 575
Clifton, Sarah III, 72
Clifton, Sarah C. V, 39
Clifton, Sarah L. III, 130
Clifton, Sarah L. V, 39
Clifton, Thomas VI, 844
Clifton, Thos. V, 616
Clifton, Usley VI, 806
Clifton, Wd. Sarah II, 488
Clifton, Wd. Sarah II, 594
Clifton, Wilbur V, 230
Clifton, William II, 25
Clifton, William II, 347
Clifton, William III, 72
Clifton, William III, 130
Clifton, Wm. II, 488
Clifton, Wm. II, 540
Clinard, Elizabeth I, 921
Clinard, Mattie I, 930
Clinard, Mrs. J. W. I, 939
Cline, Abigail V, 881
Cline, Abraham V, 881
Cline, Albert V, 555
Cline, Ambert Albert V, 555
Cline, Ambert Albert V, 664
Cline, Belva Mabel V, 555
Cline, Belva Mable V, 664
Cline, Bertha W. IV, 1310
Cline, Charles V, 380
Cline, Cora Brown V, 664
Cline, Eleanor V, 481
Cline, Eleanor V, 509
Cline, Eliza V, 664
Cline, Eliza J. V, 555
Cline, Estella V, 157
Cline, Fred V, 380
Cline, Fredy V, 380
Cline, Geo. W. V, 380
Cline, George V, 881
Cline, Harriet Ann IV, 581
Cline, Isaac II, 347
Cline, Isaac H. V, 881
Cline, Israel V, 481
Cline, Jacob II, 347
Cline, Jemima E. V, 881
Cline, Jennie V, 454
Cline, Jennie V, 664
Cline, John II, 347
Cline, John V, 555
Cline, John A. V, 664
Cline, Laura V, 157
Cline, Louella V, 664
Cline, Louisa V, 318
Cline, Louisa V, 324
Cline, Madison F. V, 555
Cline, Madison J. V, 664
Cline, Maggie M. V, 157
Cline, Martha J. V, 380
Cline, Martha Jane V, 405
Cline, Mary V, 324
Cline, Mary V, 481
Cline, Mary A. V, 555
Cline, Mary E. V, 880
Cline, Mary E. V, 881
Cline, Mary M. V, 881
Cline, Mary V. V, 664
Cline, Mattie J. V, 380
Cline, Mellie V, 157
Cline, Miss Lula F. IV, 1310
Cline, Mrs. Mary IV, 1310
Cline, Pearl V, 157
Cline, Phebe Ann V, 881
Cline, Rachel V, 481
Cline, Rachel V, 509
Cline, Sarah V, 664
Cline, Susannah V, 324
Cline, Thelma V, 664
Cline, Victoria V, 157
Cline, Wm. Oscar V, 881
Cliness, Augusta B. V, 230
Clingaman, Harry IV, 1274
Clingaman, Horatio IV, 1274
Clingaman, Lucy IV, 1274
Clingaman, William IV, 1274
Clingamon, Harry IV, 1274
Clingamon, Horatio IV, 1274
Clingenfield, Rebecca V, 730
Clinger, Ann A. II, 848
Clinger, Chas. Frederick V, 989
Clinger, Daniel C. V, 989
Clinger, Edgar II, 787
Clinger, Edgar II, 790
Clinger, Elizabeth N. II, 848
Clinger, Elizabeth N. II, 885
Clinger, Elizabeth N. II, 901
Clinger, Elizabeth Neal II, 787
Clinger, Elizabeth W. II, 848
Clinger, Gertrude V, 989
Clinger, Jane J. II, 848
Clinger, Julia V, 989
Clinger, Mary E. II, 848
Clinger, Mary E. II, 868
Clinger, Sally A. II, 848
Clinger, Sally Ann Neal II, 787
Clinger, Sarah Ann V, 989
Clinger, Stephen Cox II, 848
Clinger, Stephen P. Cox II, 848
Clinger, Wd. Elizabeth Neal II, 790
Clinger, Wm. II, 848
Clinginpeel, Ann VI, 894
Clinginpeel, J. VI, 894
Clinkenbeard, Edward VI, 894
Clinkenbeard, Elizabeth VI, 894
Clinkenbeard, Jacob VI, 894
Clinkenbeard, Lewis T. VI, 894
Clinkenbeard, Lidia VI, 894
Clinkenbeard, Nancy VI, 894
Clinness, Augusta Barrett V, 664
Clinness, Augusta Barrett V, 715
Clinness, Augusta J. V, 664
Clinton, Bertha V, 703
Clinton, Elijah J. V, 703
Clinton, Margaretta V, 703
Clinton, Mark V, 703

Clipard, Deborah V, 555
Clipard, Deborah V, 597
Clipard, James V, 598
Clipard, Lydia V, 598
Clipard, Lydia Ann V, 598
Clipard, Sarah B. V, 598
Clirk, Nancy I, 756
Clise, Lulu Barker IV, 1310
Cliver, Etta S. V, 555
Clock, Abraham III, 72
Clock, Albert V. III, 510
Clock, Asa M. III, 510
Clock, Elizabeth III, 510
Clock, Elizabeth S. III, 510
Clock, Jesse A. III, 510
Clock, Jesse M. III, 510
Clock, Jetlie Pierce III, 510
Clock, Wd. Elizabeth III, 72
Clodd, Katherine II, 489
Clode, Joseph II, 489
Clode, Wd. Hannah II, 489
Clodfelder, Flora Jane I, 922
Clodfelter, Flora I, 937
Clodfelter, Flora I, 939
Clodfelter, Flora A. I, 939
Clodfelter, Manilla Crocker I, 939
Clodhopper, Daniel VI, 850
Clodhopper, Polly VI, 850
Clopton, Abner W. VI, 806
Clopton, Sally B. VI, 806
Closan, Cornelius II, 442
Close, Ann III, 72
Close, Charlotte III, 47
Close, Charlotte III, 72
Close, Ethel III, 72
Close, Ethel B. III, 47
Close, Ethel B. III, 72
Close, Ethel Brooks III, 72
Close, Harriet A. II, 805
Close, James III, 47
Close, James III, 72
Close, Mary IV, 324
Close, Mary IV, 352
Close, Robt. W. III, 72
Close, Thelma IV, 1036
Closs, Mary E. VI, 894
Closs, Morgan VI, 894
Closs, Morgan VI, 936
Closs, Wm. VI, 968
Clossen, Dominicus IV, 690
Clossen, Elizabeth II, 1048
Clossen, Mary II, 1048
Clossen, Mordecai II, 1048
Clossen, Sarah II, 733
Clossman, Mary III, 481
Closson, Elizabeth II, 1048
Closson, John II, 1048
Closson, Mary II, 1048
Closson, Mordecai II, 1048
Closson, Rebecca II, 1048
Closson, Sarah II, 489
Closson, Sarah II, 701
Closson, Sarah II, 733
Clothier, Abigal II, 208
Clothier, Abugal II, 253
Clothier, Adeline II, 934
Clothier, Albert Hallowell II, 788
Clothier, Anna II, 284
Clothier, Anna B. II, 788
Clothier, Anna Mary II, 790
Clothier, Anne II, 208
Clothier, Anne Bartram II, 788
Clothier, Anne S. II, 792
Clothier, Anne S. II, 849
Clothier, Anne S. II, 879
Clothier, Anne Smith II, 788
Clothier, Caleb II, 169
Clothier, Caleb II, 787
Clothier, Caleb II, 788
Clothier, Caleb II, 842
Clothier, Caleb II, 848
Clothier, Caleb II, 878
Clothier, Caleb II, 879
Clothier, Caleb II, 934
Clothier, Caleb III, 72
Clothier, Caleb, Jr. II, 788
Clothier, Caroline II, 788
Clothier, Catharine II, 790
Clothier, Catharine II, 848
Clothier, Catharine II, 878
Clothier, Catherine II, 788
Clothier, Clarkson II, 788
Clothier, Clarkson II, 849
Clothier, Elizabeth II, 169
Clothier, Elizabeth II, 284
Clothier, Elizabeth II, 489
Clothier, Elizabeth II, 654
Clothier, Elizabeth II, 787
Clothier, Elizabeth II, 788
Clothier, Elizabeth II, 848
Clothier, Elizabeth II, 878
Clothier, Elizabeth II, 879
Clothier, Elizabeth II, 917
Clothier, Elizabeth II, 934
Clothier, Elizabeth H. II, 842
Clothier, Elizabeth H. II, 849
Clothier, Elizabeth Hallowell II, 784
Clothier, Elizabeth Hallowell II, 787
Clothier, Elizabeth Jackson II, 788
Clothier, Elizabeth Jackson II, 849
Clothier, Elizabeth Jackson II, 917
Clothier, Franklin II, 788
Clothier, Hannah F. II, 842
Clothier, Hannah F. II, 848
Clothier, Hannah F. II, 849
Clothier, Hannah F. III, 72
Clothier, Hannah Fletcher II, 787
Clothier, Hannah Fletcher II, 788
Clothier, Hannah Hallowell II, 788
Clothier, Hannah Hallowell II, 849
Clothier, Hannah Hollowell II, 879
Clothier, Henry II, 208
Clothier, Henry II, 253
Clothier, Henry II, 788
Clothier, Isaac H. II, 849
Clothier, Isaac H. II, 875
Clothier, Isaac H. II, 879
Clothier, Isaac H. II, 917
Clothier, Isaac H. III, 72
Clothier, Isaac H. III, 223
Clothier, Isaac Hallowell II, 787
Clothier, Isaac Hallowell II, 788
Clothier, Jacob Worrell II, 788
Clothier, James II, 208
Clothier, James II, 284
Clothier, James II, 489
Clothier, James II, 848
Clothier, James II, 934
Clothier, Jane II, 208
Clothier, Jane II, 489
Clothier, Jane II, 593
Clothier, Jane H. III, 72
Clothier, Jane H. III, 106
Clothier, John II, 208
Clothier, John II, 347
Clothier, John II, 489
Clothier, John II, 790
Clothier, John W. II, 284
Clothier, John W. II, 309
Clothier, John W. II, 317
Clothier, John W. II, 848
Clothier, John W. II, 849
Clothier, John W. II, 878
Clothier, John Warrington II, 788
Clothier, Lucretia Mott II, 787
Clothier, Lydia III, 72
Clothier, Lydia III, 223
Clothier, Lydia Biddle II, 788
Clothier, Mary II, 169
Clothier, Mary II, 192
Clothier, Mary II, 208
Clothier, Mary II, 788
Clothier, Mary II, 974
Clothier, Mary II, 989
Clothier, Mary C. II, 849
Clothier, Mary C. II, 875
Clothier, Mary C. II, 879
Clothier, Mary C. II, 917
Clothier, Mary C. III, 72
Clothier, Mary C. III, 223
Clothier, Mary Clapp II, 788
Clothier, Mary Jackson II, 788
Clothier, Mary Jackson II, 849
Clothier, Mary Jackson II, 875
Clothier, Morris Lewis II, 788
Clothier, Rebecca II, 788
Clothier, Sally Ann II, 788
Clothier, Samuel II, 489
Clothier, Walter II, 788
Clothier, William II, 208
Clothier, William II, 284
Clothier, William Jackson II, 788
Clothier, William Penn II, 788
Clothier, Wm. II, 489
Clothier, Wm. P. III, 72
Clothier, Wm. P. III, 106
Clothier, Wm. Penn II, 849
Clothier, Wm., Jr. II, 489
Cloud, ??? V, 147
Cloud, Abigail I, 348
Cloud, Abigail I, 380
Cloud, Abigail I, 676
Cloud, Abigail V, 39
Cloud, Abigail V, 157
Cloud, Abigail V, 193
Cloud, Abner I, 348
Cloud, Abner I, 380
Cloud, Ann I, 380
Cloud, Ann I, 410
Cloud, Ann I, 412
Cloud, Ann I, 1043
Cloud, Ann I, 1117
Cloud, Ann V, 39
Cloud, Anna V, 39
Cloud, Anna V, 105
Cloud, Anna Mary II, 788
Cloud, Anna Mary II, 849
Cloud, Anna Wood II, 849
Cloud, Anne I, 348
Cloud, Annie VI, 378
Cloud, Benjamin II, 116
Cloud, Benjamin II, 124
Cloud, Charles R. II, 170
Cloud, Charles R. II, 284
Cloud, Chas. II, 788
Cloud, Chas. II, 849
Cloud, Cornelius V, 39
Cloud, Cornelius H. V, 39
Cloud, Cynthia M. V, 39
Cloud, Cynthia Marlissa V, 39
Cloud, Daniel I, 348
Cloud, Daniel I, 380
Cloud, Daniel I, 445
Cloud, Elizabeth I, 380
Cloud, Elizabeth I, 1116
Cloud, Elizabeth I, 1117
Cloud, Elizabeth V, 39
Cloud, Enoch W. II, 788
Cloud, Enoch W. II, 849
Cloud, Enoch Wickersham II, 788
Cloud, Esther I, 1043
Cloud, Esther II, 116
Cloud, Esther II, 124
Cloud, Flora II, 788
Cloud, Flora M. II, 849
Cloud, Frank J. II, 849
Cloud, Hannah I, 380
Cloud, Hannah I, 651
Cloud, Hannah I, 676
Cloud, Hannah I, 680
Cloud, Hannah I, 1043
Cloud, Hannah I, 1047
Cloud, Hannah II, 489
Cloud, Hannah II, 788
Cloud, Hannah V, 39
Cloud, Hannah V, 157
Cloud, Hannah V, 164
Cloud, Henry Clay II, 788
Cloud, Herbert S. II, 849
Cloud, Herbert Scull II, 849
Cloud, J. Cooper II, 849
Cloud, Jacob I, 348
Cloud, Jacob I, 380
Cloud, James I, 380
Cloud, Jane II, 826
Cloud, Jane V, 39
Cloud, Jesse II, 788
Cloud, Jesse II, 849
Cloud, Joel I, 348
Cloud, Joel I, 380
Cloud, Joel I, 445
Cloud, Joel I, 1041
Cloud, Joel I, 1043
Cloud, Joel I, 1047
Cloud, Joel V, 39
Cloud, Joel V, 157
Cloud, Joel V, 164
Cloud, Joel, Jr. I, 1043
Cloud, John I, 445
Cloud, John II, 347
Cloud, Jonathan I, 348
Cloud, Jonathan I, 380
Cloud, Jonathan I, 1117
Cloud, Jonathan V, 39
Cloud, Jonathan Milton V, 39
Cloud, Joseph I, 348
Cloud, Joseph I, 380
Cloud, Joseph I, 651
Cloud, Joseph I, 676
Cloud, Joseph I, 680
Cloud, Joseph I, 1041
Cloud, Joseph II, 489
Cloud, Joseph V, 39
Cloud, Joseph V, 157
Cloud, Joseph V, 469
Cloud, Joseph V, 481
Cloud, Joseph V, 504
Cloud, Joseph Cooper II, 788
Cloud, Joseph Cooper II, 849
Cloud, Joseph Howard II, 849
Cloud, Lydea I, 1043
Cloud, Lydia Ann II, 788
Cloud, Lydia Ann II, 849
Cloud, Martha I, 380
Cloud, Martha I, 403
Cloud, Martha I, 443
Cloud, Martha I, 445
Cloud, Mary I, 348
Cloud, Mary I, 380
Cloud, Mary I, 443
Cloud, Mary I, 445
Cloud, Mary I, 1043
Cloud, Mary I, 1117
Cloud, Mary II, 788
Cloud, Mary V, 39
Cloud, Mary V, 79
Cloud, Mary V, 157
Cloud, Mary V, 481
Cloud, Mary V, 504
Cloud, Mary VI, 378
Cloud, Mary VI, 446
Cloud, Mary Earl I, 348
Cloud, Mary Earl V, 39
Cloud, Mary P. II, 849
Cloud, Mary S. II, 849
Cloud, Mordaecai I, 348
Cloud, Mordecai I, 348
Cloud, Mordicai I, 676
Cloud, Phebe II, 826
Cloud, Rebekah I, 1043
Cloud, Sallie French II, 788
Cloud, Samuel I, 348
Cloud, Samuel I, 380
Cloud, Sarah I, 445
Cloud, Sarah I, 448
Cloud, Sarah I, 452
Cloud, Sarah I, 1043
Cloud, Tamar V, 39
Cloud, Thomas V, 39
Cloud, Wd. Hannah II, 489
Cloud, William V, 39
Cloud, Wm. A. II, 788
Cloud, Wm. I. II, 826
Cloud, Wm. Wood II, 849
Cloudis, Frances VI, 848
Cloudis, George W. VI, 848
Cloudis, Mary VI, 848
Cloudis, Rebecca VI, 806
Cloudis, William VI, 806
Cloudy, Mary II, 489
Cloudy, Mary II, 675
Clough, Alice H. III, 73
Clough, Alice H. III, 345
Clough, Anna Josephine III, 73
Clough, Anna Josephine III, 238
Clough, Anne II, 130
Clough, Annie III, 73
Clough, Arthur Dana III, 73
Clough, Arthur Dana III, 238
Clough, Clarence A. III, 73
Clough, Clarence A. III, 193
Clough, Dana B. III, 73
Clough, Dana B. III, 109
Clough, Dana B. III, 345
Clough, Emma J. III, 193
Clough, Ethel III, 73
Clough, George II, 957
Clough, George II, 989
Clough, George II, 1000
Clough, Hannah III, 73
Clough, Jane II, 130
Clough, Jonathan III, 73
Clough, Lucinda III, 73
Clough, Lucinda E. III, 73
Clough, Lucinda E. III, 109
Clough, Lucinda E. III, 345
Clough, Marion IV, 1310
Clough, Mary II, 957
Clough, Mary II, 989
Clough, Mary II, 1000
Clough, Mary II, 1026
Clough, Pleasant II, 989
Clough, Richard M. III, 73
Clough, Richard M. III, 238
Clough, Richard Munier III, 73
Clough, Roy G. II, 130
Clough, Thomas II, 130
Clousen, Eva IV, 1310
Clouser, A. IV, 1248
Clover, Elizabeth IV, 865
Clover, Elizabeth IV, 881
Clow, Belle IV, 1274
Clow, E. N. IV, 1274
Clowdis, David F. VI, 814
Clowdis, Henry G. VI, 894
Clowdis, Martha Ann VI, 894
Clowes, ??? II, 989
Clowes, Christian II, 989
Clowes, Edith VI, 622
Clowes, Edith VI, 631
Clowes, Elizabeth II, 989
Clowes, Elizabeth VI, 482
Clowes, Elizabeth VI, 494
Clowes, John II, 989
Clowes, John, Jr. II, 989
Clowes, Joseph II, 62
Clowes, Joseph II, 989
Clowes, Joseph II, 1022
Clowes, Margery II, 989
Clowes, Margery II, 1002
Clowes, Margery, Jr. II, 989
Clowes, Mary II, 989
Clowes, Mary VI, 482
Clowes, Mary VI, 529
Clowes, Meribah II, 488
Clowes, Meribah II, 989
Clowes, Rebeckah II, 989
Clowes, Sarah II, 975
Clowes, Sarah II, 989
Clowes, Sarah VI, 482
Clowes, Sarah VI, 494
Clowes, Thomas II, 989
Clowes, Wd. Sarah II, 989
Clowes, Wm. II, 989
Clowes, Wm. II, 1029
Clows, Christian II, 989
Clows, Christian II, 1018
Clows, John II, 957
Clows, John II, 988
Clows, John II, 989
Clows, Joseph II, 208
Clows, Mary II, 957
Clows, Mary II, 988
Clows, Mary II, 989
Clows, Meribah II, 957
Clows, Meribah II, 989
Clows, Patience II, 208
Clows, Rebeckah II, 989
Clows, Rebeckah II, 1009
Clows, Sarah II, 989
Clows, Thomas II, 989
Clows, Thomas II, 1018
Cloyd, Bessie III, 73
Cloyd, Dolly VI, 894
Cloyd, Edwin C. III, 21
Cloyd, Edwin C. III, 73
Cloyd, Joseph, Jr. VI, 894
Cloyd, Joseph, Sr. VI, 894
Cloyd, Josephine III, 21
Cloyd, Josephine III, 73
Cloyd, Mary Jane III, 73
Cloyd, Wm. III, 73
Cluff, Elizabeth V, 230
Cluff, Margery V, 230
Cluff, Marjorie V, 230
Cluff, Marjory V, 230
Cluff, Toby II, 442
Clun, Capt. ??? II, 442
Clun, Mary II, 442
Clunkan, Edward II, 986
Clunn, Adrian P. II, 130
Clunn, Hannah P. II, 130
Clutch, ??? V, 39
Clutch, Elizabeth V, 39
Clutch, Lydia V, 39
Clutch, Lydia V, 71
Clutch, Lydia E. V, 39
Clutch, Rachel V, 21
Clutch, Rachel V, 39
Clutch, Rachel A. V, 39
Clutter, Andrew J. V, 989
Clutter, John V, 989
Clutter, Mary V, 989
Cluxton, Carey V, 380
Cluxton, Chloe V, 380
Cluxton, Clara V, 380
Cluxton, Clayton V, 380
Cluxton, Evelyn V, 39
Cluxton, Evelyn V, 72
Cluxton, Evelyn V, 380
Cluxton, Halcy V, 380
Cluxton, Margaret V, 404
Cluxton, Richard V, 380
Cluxton, Sarah R. V, 404
Cluxton, Wm. V, 404
Clybourne, Elizabeth VI, 894
Clybourne, Leonard VI, 894
Clyburn, Anna VI, 894
Clyburn, Daniel VI, 894
Clyburn, Elizabeth VI, 894
Clyburn, Leonard VI, 894
Clyda, Lewis I, 335
Clyde, Hiram V, 230
Clymer, Christopher II, 347
Clymer, Deborah II, 347
Clymer, Deborah II, 489
Clymer, Deborah II, 524
Clymer, Elizabeth II, 347
Clymer, Elizabeth II, 489
Clymer, Elizabeth II, 595
Clymer, Elizabeth II, 804
Clymer, Elizabeth II, 812
Clymer, William II, 347
Coad, Elizabeth R. II, 733
Coad, Elizabeth R. II, 767
Coad, Elsie A. III, 73
Coaker, Alice III, 73

oaker, Brian VI, 171
oaker, Dorcas III, 73
oaker, Dorcas III, 188
oaker, Nicholas III, 73
oaker, Nicholas III, 188
oaker, Rachel Handley VI, 171
oaksby, Wm. II, 62
oaksley, William II, 208
oal, Anna I, 757
oal, Anna I, 762
oal, Charles IV, 615
oal, Elizabeth I, 1004
oal, Joseph II, 62
oal, Joseph IV, 615
oal, Joseph B. IV, 615
oal, Lucinda V, 454
oal, Mary Townsend IV, 615
oal, Susannah IV, 615
oale, Amelia VI, 482
oale, Amelia VI, 483
oale, Amelia VI, 509
oale, Amelia VI, 649
oale, Amelia VI, 736
oale, Amelia VI, 750
oale, Amelia R. II, 849
oale, Anna VI, 569
oale, Anna VI, 570
oale, Anna L. II, 849
oale, Benjamin S. IV, 615
oale, Benjamin T. IV, 615
oale, Cecilia H. V, 899
oale, Charles IV, 615
oale, Cornelia S. II, 849
oale, Edith II, 788
oale, Eleanor V, 230
oale, Eliza II, 785
oale, Eliza II, 816
oale, Elizabeth II, 628
oale, Elizabeth S. II, 849
oale, Elizabeth Sutton II, 815
oale, Elizabeth Sutton II, 849
oale, Elizabeth Sutton II, 910
oale, Ellis V, 893
oale, Hannah II, 199
oale, Hannah II, 208
oale, Harriett H. VI, 483
oale, Harriett H. VI, 649
oale, Hetty Jane II, 788
oale, Hetty S. II, 849
oale, Hetty S. II, 910
oale, Isaac II, 849
oale, James S. II, 849
oale, James S. II, 905
oale, Joseph IV, 615
oale, Joseph B. IV, 615
oale, Lewis VI, 482
oale, Lewis VI, 509
oale, Lewis VI, 554
oale, Lewis VI, 565
oale, Lewis VI, 567
oale, Lewis VI, 649
oale, Lewis VI, 736
oale, Lewis VI, 750
oale, Lydia VI, 482
oale, Lydia VI, 483
oale, Lydia VI, 509
oale, Lydia VI, 554
oale, Lydia VI, 565
oale, Lydia VI, 567
oale, Lydia VI, 736
oale, Margaret VI, 483
oale, Mary II, 409
oale, Mary II, 849
oale, Mary Anna IV, 615
oale, Mary B. IV, 615
oale, Mary Ella V, 899
oale, Mary Ellen V, 893
oale, Mary Ellen V, 899
oale, Mary Iddings II, 905
oale, Mary Townsend IV, 615
oale, Mary W. II, 849
oale, Phebe V, 899
oale, Phebe VI, 482
oale, Phebe VI, 565
oale, Phebe VI, 567
oale, Philip II, 491
oale, Robinson S. VI, 483
oale, S. Robinson II, 788
oale, S. Robinson II, 849
oale, S. Robinson II, 910
oale, Sallie E. II, 849
oale, Samuel VI, 482
oale, Samuel VI, 483
oale, Samuel VI, 509
oale, Samuel VI, 554
oale, Samuel VI, 565
oale, Samuel VI, 567
oale, Samuel VI, 736
oale, Sarah IV, 615
oale, Sarah V, 230
oale, Sarah B. IV, 615
Coale, Sarah P. IV, 615
Coale, Sarah W. IV, 615
Coale, Shipwith III, 73
Coale, Skipwith VI, 483
Coale, Susan J. II, 849
Coale, Susanna IV, 615
Coale, Susannah IV, 615
Coale, Susannah VI, 482
Coale, Susannah VI, 554
Coale, Thos. E. V, 899
Coale, Thos. H. II, 849
Coale, W. L. Garrison IV, 615
Coale, Wd Sarah IV, 615
Coale, Wm. VI, 569
Coale, Wm. VI, 570
Coale, Wm. Ellis V, 899
Coales, Amelia VI, 750
Coales, Amelis VI, 511
Coales, Charles Cyrenius V, 832
Coales, Deborah V, 832
Coales, Elizabeth V, 832
Coales, Lewis VI, 511
Coales, Lewis VI, 750
Coales, Lydiann V, 832
Coales, Margaret V, 832
Coales, Mary V, 832
Coales, Pierson V, 832
Coales, Sarah M. V, 832
Coalman, Grace II, 990
Coals, Ann Margaret IV, 380
Coals, Charles IV, 379
Coals, Charles Cyrenus IV, 380
Coals, Deborah IV, 380
Coals, Elizabeth IV, 380
Coals, Lydia Ann IV, 380
Coals, Mary IV, 380
Coals, Paerson IV, 380
Coals, Sarah M. IV, 380
Coalson, Caleb II, 62
Coalson, Sarah II, 62
Coarse, David II, 489
Coarse, Isaac II, 489
Coat, Barzilla II, 208
Coat, Charlotte V, 157
Coat, Charlotte V, 213
Coat, Chas. V, 158
Coat, Edith II, 208
Coat, Edith II, 244
Coat, Elizabeth I, 1027
Coat, Elizabeth I, 1028
Coat, Elizabeth II, 208
Coat, Henry I, 1027
Coat, Henry I, 1030
Coat, Henry V, 39
Coat, Isaac V, 39
Coat, John I, 1027
Coat, John V, 482
Coat, Lydia V, 39
Coat, Margaret I, 1027
Coat, Margaret I, 1028
Coat, Marmaduk II, 208
Coat, Marmaduke I, 1027
Coat, Martha V, 482
Coat, Mary I, 1027
Coat, Mary I, 1030
Coat, Mary I, 1036
Coat, Mary V, 39
Coat, Moses I, 1027
Coat, Moses I, 1028
Coat, Rebecca V, 482
Coat, Rebecca V, 484
Coat, Rhoda V, 39
Coat, Samuel I, 1027
Coat, Samuel I, 1028
Coat, Samuel V, 39
Coat, Sarah L. V, 380
Coat, William I, 1027
Coate, ??? V, 800
Coate, ??? V, 801
Coate, A. C. V, 731
Coate, Abiather D. V, 801
Coate, Abiather Davis V, 802
Coate, Abiather Davis V, 822
Coate, Abigail V, 779
Coate, Abigail V, 801
Coate, Abigail V, 819
Coate, Abijah V, 731
Coate, Abijah V, 799
Coate, Abijah V, 800
Coate, Abijah J. V, 730
Coate, Abijah J. V, 801
Coate, Abijah J. V, 802
Coate, Abijah J. V, 804
Coate, Adila V, 730
Coate, Adila V, 779
Coate, Adila V, 786
Coate, Adila V, 800
Coate, Adila V, 801
Coate, Adila V, 802
Coate, Adila V, 812
Coate, Adilah V, 801
Coate, Agnes V, 482
Coate, Agnes V, 611
Coate, Agnes V, 616
Coate, Agnes V, 665
Coate, Agnes V, 797
Coate, Agnes V, 801
Coate, Aldes V, 802
Coate, Alex V, 801
Coate, Alfred V, 799
Coate, Alice S. V, 481
Coate, Alice S. V, 482
Coate, Allen V, 801
Coate, Allen V, 802
Coate, Almeda V, 801
Coate, Almeda V, 804
Coate, Alva V, 800
Coate, Alvah V, 730
Coate, Alvah V, 731
Coate, Alvin P. V, 481
Coate, Alvine V, 730
Coate, Ambrose B. V, 801
Coate, Ann V, 799
Coate, Anna V, 731
Coate, Anna V, 801
Coate, Anna D. V, 665
Coate, Anna Elizabeth V, 730
Coate, Anna Jane V, 800
Coate, Anna Maud V, 665
Coate, Anne II, 170
Coate, Anne V, 802
Coate, Anne V, 814
Coate, Annie D. V, 665
Coate, Annie Maud V, 665
Coate, Aquilla V, 482
Coate, B. W. IV, 1248
Coate, Barzilla II, 208
Coate, Barzillai II, 208
Coate, Belle V, 731
Coate, Benj. C. V, 802
Coate, Benj. J. V, 801
Coate, Benjamin IV, 1248
Coate, Benjamin V, 481
Coate, Benjamin V, 798
Coate, Benjamin V, 801
Coate, Benjamin V, 813
Coate, Benjamin V, 819
Coate, Benjamin V, 822
Coate, Benjamin C. V, 799
Coate, Benjamin J. V, 799
Coate, Benjamin Johnson V, 800
Coate, Benjamin, Jr. V, 802
Coate, Bertha M. V, 802
Coate, Bethany V, 801
Coate, Betsy Ann II, 284
Coate, Betsy Ann II, 305
Coate, Beulah II, 208
Coate, Caleb V, 730
Coate, Caleb V, 731
Coate, Caleb V, 798
Coate, Caleb V, 800
Coate, Caleb V, 801
Coate, Caleb V, 802
Coate, Calvin V, 800
Coate, Calvin V, 801
Coate, Calvin W. V, 802
Coate, Candace V, 802
Coate, Candas V, 802
Coate, Carl E. V, 731
Coate, Carlton V, 802
Coate, Casper V, 731
Coate, Catherine V, 800
Coate, Catherine V, 802
Coate, Cathern V, 801
Coate, Cecil V, 731
Coate, Celestia V, 800
Coate, Charity V, 800
Coate, Charley V, 801
Coate, Clara V, 800
Coate, Clara Almeda V, 801
Coate, Clara Almeida V, 731
Coate, Clarkson V, 730
Coate, Clarkson V, 800
Coate, Cyrus V, 481
Coate, Cyrus V, 482
Coate, Cyrus V, 556
Coate, D. M. V, 731
Coate, David V, 800
Coate, David H. V, 799
Coate, David J. V, 799
Coate, David J. V, 800
Coate, David J. V, 802
Coate, David M. V, 730
Coate, David M. V, 731
Coate, David M. V, 798
Coate, David M. V, 800
Coate, David M. V, 802
Coate, David M., Jr. V, 731
Coate, David Orland V, 731
Coate, David Orland V, 801
Coate, David Wm. V, 801
Coate, Delila V, 797
Coate, Delila V, 801
Coate, Delila V, 802
Coate, Delila V, 822
Coate, Delilah V, 556
Coate, Delilah V, 665
Coate, Donald William V, 665
Coate, Dorcas V, 800
Coate, Drusila V, 813
Coate, Drusilla V, 813
Coate, Eddie V, 731
Coate, Edgar V, 731
Coate, Edith II, 208
Coate, Eleanor V, 799
Coate, Eleanor V, 803
Coate, Elen V, 800
Coate, Elijah V, 481
Coate, Elijah V, 482
Coate, Elijah V, 665
Coate, Elijah V, 730
Coate, Elijah V, 736
Coate, Elijah V, 799
Coate, Elijah V, 801
Coate, Elijah V, 802
Coate, Elijah V, 803
Coate, Elijah S. V, 482
Coate, Elijah Smith V, 481
Coate, Eliza V, 730
Coate, Eliza V, 800
Coate, Eliza V, 802
Coate, Elizabeth I, 1027
Coate, Elizabeth I, 1034
Coate, Elizabeth II, 208
Coate, Elizabeth II, 911
Coate, Elizabeth V, 40
Coate, Elizabeth V, 482
Coate, Elizabeth V, 556
Coate, Elizabeth V, 570
Coate, Elizabeth V, 730
Coate, Elizabeth V, 731
Coate, Elizabeth V, 798
Coate, Elizabeth V, 799
Coate, Elizabeth V, 800
Coate, Elizabeth V, 801
Coate, Elizabeth V, 802
Coate, Elizabeth V, 809
Coate, Elizabeth V, 810
Coate, Elizabeth V, 811
Coate, Elizabeth V, 814
Coate, Elizabeth V, 815
Coate, Elizabeth V, 819
Coate, Elizabeth B. V, 482
Coate, Elizabeth B. V, 679
Coate, Elizabeth C. V, 800
Coate, Elizabeth C. V, 803
Coate, Elizabeth P. V, 482
Coate, Elizabeth P. V, 509
Coate, Elizabeth Painter V, 481
Coate, Ellen V, 802
Coate, Ellen V, 809
Coate, Ellwood V, 731
Coate, Ellwood V, 802
Coate, Elvina V, 801
Coate, Elwood V, 800
Coate, Emeline V, 730
Coate, Emma V, 736
Coate, Emma Anna E. V, 731
Coate, Emmeline John V, 800
Coate, Ernest V, 802
Coate, Esther I, 1018
Coate, Esther V, 39
Coate, Esther V, 481
Coate, Esther V, 482
Coate, Esther V, 495
Coate, Esther V, 556
Coate, Esther V, 567
Coate, Esther V, 616
Coate, Esther V, 730
Coate, Esther V, 748
Coate, Esther V, 766
Coate, Esther V, 798
Coate, Esther V, 799
Coate, Esther V, 800
Coate, Esther V, 801
Coate, Esther V, 802
Coate, Esther V, 813
Coate, Esther V, 815
Coate, Esther T. V, 736
Coate, Ethel C. V, 802
Coate, Eunice V, 799
Coate, Eunice V, 803
Coate, Ezra V, 730
Coate, F. J. V, 801
Coate, Fannie J. V, 801
Coate, Flora V, 570
Coate, Flora V, 665
Coate, Florence V, 731
Coate, Florence Eveline V, 800
Coate, Florence Eveline V, 801
Coate, Gula V, 989
Coate, Gula May V, 989
Coate, H. A. V, 570
Coate, Hannah II, 208
Coate, Hannah II, 210
Coate, Hannah II, 270
Coate, Hannah V, 731
Coate, Hannah V, 800
Coate, Hannah C. V, 730
Coate, Hannah C. V, 801
Coate, Hannah C. V, 820
Coate, Harriet V, 725
Coate, Harriet V, 730
Coate, Harriet V, 731
Coate, Harriet V, 797
Coate, Harriet V, 802
Coate, Harriet Anthony V, 801
Coate, Harriett V, 801
Coate, Harris V, 731
Coate, Harry R. V, 731
Coate, Harvey V, 799
Coate, Henry I, 1018
Coate, Henry I, 1027
Coate, Henry V, 39
Coate, Henry V, 40
Coate, Henry V, 143
Coate, Henry V, 723
Coate, Henry V, 730
Coate, Henry V, 734
Coate, Henry V, 798
Coate, Henry V, 801
Coate, Henry V, 802
Coate, Henry V, 807
Coate, Henry V, 811
Coate, Henry V, 814
Coate, Henry V, 815
Coate, Henry V, 819
Coate, Henry W. V, 730
Coate, Henry W. V, 731
Coate, Henry W. V, 798
Coate, Henry W. V, 800
Coate, Henry W. V, 801
Coate, Henry W. V, 805
Coate, Henry W. V, 816
Coate, Henry W. V, 820
Coate, Henry, Jr. V, 802
Coate, Henry, Jr. V, 808
Coate, Hepsibah V, 813
Coate, Hershel H. V, 665
Coate, Hester V, 40
Coate, Hiram V, 481
Coate, Hiram V, 482
Coate, Hiram V, 665
Coate, Hiram V, 799
Coate, Hiram Alvin V, 482
Coate, Hiram Alvin V, 665
Coate, Hiram W. V, 665
Coate, Hugh V, 731
Coate, Hugh V, 802
Coate, Humphrey V, 481
Coate, Hyram V, 800
Coate, Ida V, 731
Coate, Idella V, 730
Coate, Ira V, 800
Coate, Isaac V, 39
Coate, Isaac V, 40
Coate, Isaac V, 731
Coate, Isaac V, 798
Coate, Isaac V, 801
Coate, Isaac V, 802
Coate, Isaac V, 813
Coate, Isaac Lewis V, 482
Coate, J. C. F. V, 801
Coate, James I, 1018
Coate, James I, 1027
Coate, James I, 1034
Coate, James II, 256
Coate, James II, 489
Coate, James II, 679
Coate, James V, 39
Coate, James V, 730
Coate, James V, 766
Coate, James V, 779
Coate, James V, 798
Coate, James V, 799
Coate, James V, 800
Coate, James V, 802
Coate, James V, 804
Coate, James V, 813
Coate, James, Jr. V, 802
Coate, Jane V, 39
Coate, Jane V, 731
Coate, Jane V, 798
Coate, Jane V, 799
Coate, Jane V, 801
Coate, Jane V, 811
Coate, Jane V, 816
Coate, Jean V, 799
Coate, Jean V, 815
Coate, Jemima V, 731
Coate, Jemima V, 989
Coate, Jemima J. V, 800
Coate, Jemima J. V, 801
Coate, Jemima P. IV, 1248

Coate, Jesse I, 1018
Coate, Jesse V, 39
Coate, Jesse V, 731
Coate, Jesse V, 798
Coate, Jesse V, 799
Coate, Jesse V, 800
Coate, Jesse V, 801
Coate, Jesse V, 802
Coate, Jesse V, 803
Coate, Jesse V, 804
Coate, Jesse V, 816
Coate, Jesse G. V, 800
Coate, Jesse M. V, 800
Coate, Jesse M. V, 801
Coate, Jesse M. V, 802
Coate, John I, 1018
Coate, John I, 1027
Coate, John II, 208
Coate, John V, 39
Coate, John V, 481
Coate, John V, 482
Coate, John V, 505
Coate, John V, 556
Coate, John V, 616
Coate, John V, 630
Coate, John V, 730
Coate, John V, 731
Coate, John V, 734
Coate, John V, 766
Coate, John V, 795
Coate, John V, 798
Coate, John V, 799
Coate, John V, 800
Coate, John V, 802
Coate, John V, 804
Coate, John V, 813
Coate, John V, 816
Coate, John B. V, 665
Coate, John H. V, 731
Coate, John H. V, 798
Coate, John H. V, 801
Coate, John J. V, 731
Coate, John J. V, 802
Coate, John L. V, 800
Coate, John, Jr. V, 482
Coate, John, Jr. V, 802
Coate, Jonathan V, 732
Coate, Jonathan V, 779
Coate, Jonathan V, 786
Coate, Jonathan V, 800
Coate, Jonathan V, 801
Coate, Jonathan C. V, 730
Coate, Jonathan C. V, 799
Coate, Jonathan C. V, 800
Coate, Jonathan C. V, 802
Coate, Jonathan C. V, 811
Coate, Jones V, 801
Coate, Joseph II, 168
Coate, Joseph V, 39
Coate, Joseph V, 481
Coate, Joseph V, 482
Coate, Joseph V, 730
Coate, Joseph V, 735
Coate, Joseph V, 798
Coate, Joseph V, 806
Coate, Joseph L. V, 797
Coate, Joseph L. V, 801
Coate, Joseph T. V, 482
Coate, Joseph T. V, 611
Coate, Joseph T. V, 616
Coate, Joseph T. V, 665
Coate, Joseph T. V, 799
Coate, Josephine II, 808
Coate, Joshua V, 730
Coate, Joshua V, 779
Coate, Joshua V, 786
Coate, Joshua V, 801
Coate, Joshua V, 802
Coate, Joshua V, 812
Coate, Josiah V, 801
Coate, Josias V, 730
Coate, Josias V, 799
Coate, Josias V, 800
Coate, Juli Ann J. V, 799
Coate, Juliann V, 801
Coate, Juliann V, 816
Coate, Kittie E. V, 731
Coate, L. Maurice V, 802
Coate, Laura Alice V, 802
Coate, Leo Guy V, 665
Coate, Leonard B. V, 731
Coate, Leonard J. V, 802
Coate, Lester Hershel V, 665
Coate, Lewis Johnson V, 482
Coate, Lewis Johnson V, 616
Coate, Lewis Johnson V, 801
Coate, Lincoln V, 665
Coate, Lindley Elwood V, 800
Coate, Lindley M. V, 481
Coate, Lindley M. V, 482
Coate, Lindley M. V, 799
Coate, Lindley M. V, 800
Coate, Lindley M. V, 802
Coate, Loran V, 665
Coate, Loren A. V, 665
Coate, Loren M. V, 801
Coate, Loretta V, 731
Coate, Lorettie V, 801
Coate, Lucian Clare V, 482
Coate, Lucinda V, 731
Coate, Lucinda S. V, 731
Coate, Lucy V, 481
Coate, Lucy A. V, 802
Coate, Lucy Cote V, 482
Coate, Lurana V, 730
Coate, Lurana V, 799
Coate, Lurana V, 800
Coate, Lurana V, 813
Coate, Luranah V, 730
Coate, Luranah V, 766
Coate, Luranah V, 779
Coate, Luranah V, 799
Coate, Luranah V, 804
Coate, Luraneh V, 795
Coate, Lurena V, 779
Coate, Lydia V, 39
Coate, Lydia V, 730
Coate, Lydia V, 731
Coate, Lydia V, 734
Coate, Lydia V, 735
Coate, Lydia V, 798
Coate, Lydia V, 800
Coate, Lydia V, 802
Coate, Lydia V, 806
Coate, Lydia V, 822
Coate, Lydia A. V, 731
Coate, Lydia Alice V, 800
Coate, Lydia Davis V, 801
Coate, Lydia Jane V, 800
Coate, Lydia Jane V, 801
Coate, Mabel V, 731
Coate, Marcus V, 731
Coate, Margaret I, 1027
Coate, Margaret V, 39
Coate, Margaret V, 730
Coate, Margaret V, 731
Coate, Margaret V, 733
Coate, Margaret V, 798
Coate, Margaret V, 799
Coate, Margaret V, 800
Coate, Margaret V, 801
Coate, Margaret V, 804
Coate, Margaret V, 810
Coate, Margaret V, 811
Coate, Margaret V, 815
Coate, Mark V, 731
Coate, Marmaduk II, 170
Coate, Marmaduk II, 208
Coate, Marmaduk II, 251
Coate, Marmaduke I, 1018
Coate, Marmaduke I, 1027
Coate, Marmaduke II, 170
Coate, Marmaduke II, 208
Coate, Marmaduke V, 39
Coate, Marmaduke V, 616
Coate, Marmaduke V, 730
Coate, Marmaduke V, 798
Coate, Marmaduke V, 799
Coate, Martha V, 40
Coate, Martha V, 93
Coate, Martha V, 481
Coate, Martha V, 482
Coate, Martha V, 511
Coate, Martha V, 591
Coate, Martha V, 701
Coate, Martha V, 730
Coate, Martha V, 731
Coate, Martha V, 732
Coate, Martha V, 799
Coate, Martha V, 802
Coate, Martha C. V, 731
Coate, Martha C. V, 802
Coate, Martha E. V, 800
Coate, Martha Emaline V, 800
Coate, Martha F. V, 800
Coate, Mary I, 1018
Coate, Mary I, 1027
Coate, Mary I, 1034
Coate, Mary II, 168
Coate, Mary II, 208
Coate, Mary II, 251
Coate, Mary II, 256
Coate, Mary II, 489
Coate, Mary II, 679
Coate, Mary V, 39
Coate, Mary V, 40
Coate, Mary V, 481
Coate, Mary V, 482
Coate, Mary V, 616
Coate, Mary V, 630
Coate, Mary V, 730
Coate, Mary V, 731
Coate, Mary V, 734
Coate, Mary V, 770
Coate, Mary V, 779
Coate, Mary V, 790
Coate, Mary V, 791
Coate, Mary V, 798
Coate, Mary V, 799
Coate, Mary V, 800
Coate, Mary V, 801
Coate, Mary V, 802
Coate, Mary V, 803
Coate, Mary V, 804
Coate, Mary V, 811
Coate, Mary V, 813
Coate, Mary V, 814
Coate, Mary V, 815
Coate, Mary V, 816
Coate, Mary V, 819
Coate, Mary A. V, 800
Coate, Mary Agnes V, 665
Coate, Mary Ann V, 799
Coate, Mary B. V, 482
Coate, Mary B. V, 556
Coate, Mary B. V, 800
Coate, Mary B. V, 801
Coate, Mary B. V, 813
Coate, Mary C. V, 731
Coate, Mary E. V, 482
Coate, Mary E. V, 665
Coate, Mary Elma V, 801
Coate, Mary Emily V, 801
Coate, Mary J. V, 801
Coate, Mary J. V, 802
Coate, Mary Johnson V, 801
Coate, Mary L. V, 800
Coate, Mary M. V, 730
Coate, Mary M. V, 731
Coate, Mary M. V, 800
Coate, Mary T. V, 730
Coate, Mary Tucker V, 802
Coate, Mattie A. V, 801
Coate, Maurice V, 802
Coate, Melissa V, 730
Coate, Melissa V, 731
Coate, Menalcas Crew V, 731
Coate, Mercie A. V, 482
Coate, Mercie A. V, 551
Coate, Mercie A. V, 556
Coate, Mercy Ann V, 481
Coate, Merie V, 556
Coate, Merrick V, 665
Coate, Milly V, 730
Coate, Mima V, 989
Coate, Mina V, 731
Coate, Moses I, 1018
Coate, Moses I, 1027
Coate, Moses V, 39
Coate, Moses V, 730
Coate, Moses V, 798
Coate, Moses V, 801
Coate, Moses V, 802
Coate, Moses V, 810
Coate, Moses V, 815
Coate, Moses V, 819
Coate, Moses, Jr. V, 801
Coate, Mrs. Mamie V, 753
Coate, N. C. V, 731
Coate, Nancy V, 482
Coate, Nancy V, 665
Coate, Nancy V, 730
Coate, Nancy V, 731
Coate, Nancy V, 734
Coate, Nancy V, 799
Coate, Nancy V, 800
Coate, Nancy V, 801
Coate, Nancy V, 802
Coate, Naomi V, 731
Coate, Naomi V, 801
Coate, Naomi Ann V, 797
Coate, Naomi Ann V, 802
Coate, Ned Cecil V, 731
Coate, Nellie V, 731
Coate, Ophelia V, 698
Coate, Ophelia Adelaide D. V, 481
Coate, Orlistis V, 665
Coate, Orlistus V, 801
Coate, Orlistus L. V, 665
Coate, Orlistus S. V, 665
Coate, Orrin V, 730
Coate, Orrin V, 731
Coate, Orrin S. V, 731
Coate, Oscar Elmer V, 801
Coate, Phebe V, 799
Coate, Phebe V, 800
Coate, Phebe V, 801
Coate, Phebe V, 804
Coate, Phebe V, 805
Coate, Phebe V, 807
Coate, Phebe V, 816
Coate, Prudence V, 799
Coate, Prudence V, 801
Coate, R. Harris V, 801
Coate, Rachel II, 168
Coate, Rachel II, 208
Coate, Rachel V, 40
Coate, Rachel V, 481
Coate, Rachel V, 482
Coate, Rachel V, 768
Coate, Rachel V, 779
Coate, Rachel V, 786
Coate, Rachel V, 798
Coate, Rachel V, 799
Coate, Rachel V, 800
Coate, Rachel V, 801
Coate, Rachel V, 802
Coate, Rachel V, 819
Coate, Rachel Emma V, 800
Coate, Rachel W. V, 482
Coate, Rachel W. V, 665
Coate, Rachel, Jr. V, 800
Coate, Rebecca II, 208
Coate, Rebecca II, 239
Coate, Rebecca V, 481
Coate, Rebecca V, 482
Coate, Rebecca V, 555
Coate, Rebecca V, 557
Coate, Rebecca V, 667
Coate, Rebecca V, 730
Coate, Rebecca V, 798
Coate, Rebecca V, 799
Coate, Rebecca V, 800
Coate, Rebecca V, 801
Coate, Rebecca V, 802
Coate, Rebecca V, 803
Coate, Rebecca C. V, 736
Coate, Rebecca D. V, 800
Coate, Rebecca D. V, 816
Coate, Rebecca Mary V, 481
Coate, Rebecca Mary V, 482
Coate, Rebecca Mary V, 665
Coate, Rebekah V, 39
Coate, Rebekah V, 143
Coate, Rhoda V, 39
Coate, Rhoda V, 40
Coate, Rhoda V, 799
Coate, Rhoda V, 800
Coate, Rhoda V, 801
Coate, Rhoda V, 813
Coate, Rhosa V, 798
Coate, Robert V, 731
Coate, Robert V, 798
Coate, Robert V, 799
Coate, Robert V, 800
Coate, Robert V, 801
Coate, Robert V, 802
Coate, Robert V, 989
Coate, Robert H. V, 731
Coate, Robert H. V, 802
Coate, Robert W. V, 802
Coate, Robt. Harris V, 800
Coate, Rosa J. V, 731
Coate, Rosannah V, 779
Coate, Rufus V, 802
Coate, Ruth Anna II, 284
Coate, Sally V, 799
Coate, Sally V, 802
Coate, Sally V, 808
Coate, Sampson V, 799
Coate, Samuel I, 1018
Coate, Samuel I, 1027
Coate, Samuel V, 39
Coate, Samuel V, 40
Coate, Samuel V, 730
Coate, Samuel V, 795
Coate, Samuel V, 797
Coate, Samuel V, 798
Coate, Samuel V, 800
Coate, Samuel V, 801
Coate, Samuel V, 802
Coate, Samuel V, 811
Coate, Samuel V, 813
Coate, Samuel V, 815
Coate, Samuel A. II, 208
Coate, Samuel M. V, 799
Coate, Samuel M. V, 801
Coate, Samuel T. V, 725
Coate, Samuel T. V, 730
Coate, Samuel T. V, 731
Coate, Samuel T. V, 802
Coate, Sarah I, 1018
Coate, Sarah I, 1027
Coate, Sarah I, 1030
Coate, Sarah II, 284
Coate, Sarah V, 730
Coate, Sarah V, 731
Coate, Sarah V, 759
Coate, Sarah V, 798
Coate, Sarah V, 799
Coate, Sarah V, 800
Coate, Sarah V, 801
Coate, Sarah V, 802
Coate, Sarah V, 815
Coate, Sarah C. V, 800
Coate, Sarah L. V, 665
Coate, Sarah Lydia V, 665
Coate, Sarah R. V, 800
Coate, Seth V, 799
Coate, Susanna V, 802
Coate, Susanna V, 813
Coate, T. E. V, 802
Coate, T. E., Jr. V, 802
Coate, Thomas II, 284
Coate, Thomas V, 39
Coate, Thomas V, 730
Coate, Thomas V, 759
Coate, Thomas V, 798
Coate, Thomas V, 800
Coate, Thomas V, 801
Coate, Thomas C. V, 799
Coate, Thomas E. V, 802
Coate, Thomas Elleman V, 731
Coate, Thomas Elwood V, 731
Coate, Thomas Elwood V, 802
Coate, Thomas J. V, 800
Coate, Thomas J. V, 802
Coate, Thos. V, 802
Coate, Thos. Elwood V, 800
Coate, Tula May V, 801
Coate, Vashti V, 731
Coate, Vashti V, 801
Coate, Vernon L. V, 665
Coate, Wade Lorton V, 799
Coate, Walter V. V, 801
Coate, Warren V, 731
Coate, Warren V, 801
Coate, Warren C. V, 731
Coate, Warren D. V, 801
Coate, William I, 1015
Coate, William I, 1018
Coate, William I, 1027
Coate, William I, 1034
Coate, William II, 170
Coate, William II, 208
Coate, William II, 275
Coate, William V, 40
Coate, William V, 730
Coate, William V, 770
Coate, William V, 798
Coate, William V, 800
Coate, William V, 801
Coate, William J. V, 800
Coate, William K. V, 665
Coate, William Longstreet V, 4
Coate, Wm. V, 801
Coate, Wm. V, 802
Coate, Wm. V, 814
Coate, Zenas A. V, 665
Coates, Aaron II, 489
Coates, Aaron II, 989
Coates, Abigail II, 822
Coates, Albert V, 731
Coates, Alice II, 347
Coates, Alice II, 489
Coates, Alice II, 576
Coates, Alice V, 731
Coates, Alice H. V, 732
Coates, Alice M. VI, 736
Coates, Alice M. VI, 784
Coates, Amanda IV, 1248
Coates, Amos II, 490
Coates, Amy II, 489
Coates, Amy II, 554
Coates, Ann II, 347
Coates, Ann VI, 483
Coates, Ann G. IV, 891
Coates, Ann Lucretia II, 347
Coates, Ann Lucretia II, 490
Coates, Ann Lucretia II, 849
Coates, Ann Lucretia II, 916
Coates, Anna II, 788
Coates, Annice V, 731
Coates, Aquilla VI, 483
Coates, B. W. IV, 1248
Coates, Benj. II, 489
Coates, Benjamin II, 347
Coates, Benjamin II, 490
Coates, Benjamin II, 701
Coates, Benjamin IV, 1248
Coates, Benjamin C. V, 731
Coates, Benjamin H. II, 701
Coates, Benjamin H. II, 733
Coates, Benjamin Wreford V, 7
Coates, Bessie V, 731
Coates, Beulah II, 208
Coates, Beulah II, 253
Coates, Beulah II, 347
Coates, Beulah II, 402
Coates, Beulah II, 478
Coates, Beulah II, 486
Coates, Beulah II, 489
Coates, Beulah II, 701
Coates, Bula II, 348

ates, Bulah II, 348
ates, Caleb II, 347
ates, Caleb II, 490
ates, Caleb II, 788
ates, Caleb II, 849
ates, Cecil V, 731
ates, Chalkley II, 788
ates, Chalkley II, 824
ates, Chalkley II, 849
ates, Chalkley II, 931
ates, Chalkley II, 932
ates, Charles V, 158
ates, Charles Stow II, 788
ates, Chas. Stow II, 849
ates, Christopher Columbus IV, 1248
ates, Deborah II, 849
ates, Deborah V, 899
ates, Edwin II, 858
ates, Edwin H. II, 347
ates, Edwin H. II, 849
ates, Edwin Howard II, 849
ates, Eleanor Ethel II, 788
ates, Eliz. III, 182
ates, Eliz. III, 347
ates, Eliza VI, 378
ates, Eliza VI, 380
ates, Eliza VI, 736
ates, Elizabeth II, 347
ates, Elizabeth II, 489
ates, Elizabeth II, 490
ates, Elizabeth II, 615
ates, Elizabeth II, 788
ates, Elizabeth II, 849
ates, Elizabeth II, 850
ates, Elizabeth II, 866
ates, Elizabeth III, 100
ates, Elizabeth L. II, 849
ates, Elizabeth Truman II, 788
ates, Elmer Ruan II, 788
ates, Elmer Ruan II, 849
ates, Enoch II, 347
ates, Enoch II, 489
ates, Enoch II, 668
ates, Enock II, 348
ates, Esther II, 489
ates, Esther II, 490
ates, Esther II, 686
ates, Esther II, 790
ates, Esther II, 794
ates, Esther II, 808
ates, Esther II, 817
ates, Esther V, 731
ates, Esther R. IV, 891
ates, Esther R. IV, 894
ates, Esther S. II, 490
ates, Esther Virginia II, 809
ates, Esther Virginia II, 849
ates, Ethel V, 759
ates, Ethel Moore II, 788
ates, Ethel Moore II, 850
ates, Evangeline II, 849
ates, Evangeline II, 901
ates, Evangiline II, 849
ates, G. L. V, 732
ates, George II, 347
ates, George II, 489
ates, George II, 656
ates, George M. II, 347
ates, George M. II, 489
ates, George M. II, 490
ates, George M. II, 701
ates, George Morrison II, 733
ates, Georgiana H. M. II, 866
ates, Grace II, 347
ates, Grace II, 489
ates, Grace II, 656
ates, Gracie V, 731
ates, Gurney Leroy V, 732
ates, H. Leota V, 732
ates, Hannah II, 347
ates, Hannah II, 849
ates, Hartt G. VI, 736
ates, Henry II, 347
ates, Henry II, 490
ates, Henry V, 40
ates, Henry V, 732
ates, Hester V, 40
ates, Howard VI, 736
ates, Howard VI, 784
ates, Ida Mary II, 849
ates, Idella V, 731
ates, Irene II, 824
ates, Irene II, 849
ates, Irene II, 931
ates, Isaac II, 347
ates, Isaac II, 490
ates, Isaac II, 661
ates, Isaac II, 733
ates, Isaac II, 849
ates, Isaac IV, 894
Coates, Isaac V, 40
Coates, James II, 347
Coates, James II, 442
Coates, James II, 489
Coates, James VI, 554
Coates, Jemima J. IV, 1248
Coates, Jemima P. IV, 1248
Coates, Jesse II, 490
Coates, John II, 208
Coates, John II, 347
Coates, John II, 489
Coates, John G. II, 849
Coates, John Gilbert II, 849
Coates, John Langdale, Jr. II, 489
Coates, John R. II, 347
Coates, John R. II, 489
Coates, John R. II, 490
Coates, John R. II, 701
Coates, John R. II, 733
Coates, John R. III, 73
Coates, Jos. Hartshorne II, 347
Coates, Joseph II, 490
Coates, Joseph III, 73
Coates, Joseph Hartshorne II, 490
Coates, Joseph P. II, 733
Coates, Joseph P. Horner II, 347
Coates, Joseph Ridgway II, 489
Coates, Joseph S. II, 347
Coates, Joseph S. II, 490
Coates, Joseph S. III, 73
Coates, Joseph S. III, 272
Coates, Josiah II, 347
Coates, Josiah II, 348
Coates, Josiah II, 489
Coates, Josiah II, 603
Coates, Josiah L. II, 489
Coates, Josiah Langdale II, 347
Coates, Josiah Langdale II, 489
Coates, Josiah Langdale II, 554
Coates, Langdale II, 347
Coates, Lewis Montgomery II, 788
Coates, Loretta V, 731
Coates, Louis M. II, 849
Coates, Lydia II, 347
Coates, Lydia II, 489
Coates, Lydia II, 490
Coates, Lydia II, 643
Coates, Lydia II, 849
Coates, Lydia III, 73
Coates, Lydia V, 922
Coates, Lydien II, 849
Coates, Margaret II, 347
Coates, Margaret IV, 891
Coates, Margaret IV, 892
Coates, Margaretta III, 310
Coates, Marguerite V, 731
Coates, Martha V, 324
Coates, Mary II, 208
Coates, Mary II, 253
Coates, Mary II, 347
Coates, Mary II, 489
Coates, Mary II, 490
Coates, Mary II, 554
Coates, Mary II, 576
Coates, Mary II, 603
Coates, Mary II, 604
Coates, Mary II, 607
Coates, Mary II, 643
Coates, Mary II, 653
Coates, Mary II, 661
Coates, Mary II, 701
Coates, Mary II, 733
Coates, Mary II, 788
Coates, Mary II, 817
Coates, Mary II, 849
Coates, Mary II, 931
Coates, Mary IV, 894
Coates, Mary V, 40
Coates, Mary VI, 483
Coates, Mary VI, 553
Coates, Mary VI, 554
Coates, Mary A. V, 158
Coates, Mary Ann II, 788
Coates, Mary Ann II, 824
Coates, Mary Ann II, 849
Coates, Mary B. S. IV, 1248
Coates, Mary H. II, 788
Coates, Mary S. IV, 1248
Coates, Mary Shoemaker II, 661
Coates, Mercy II, 489
Coates, Morton II, 347
Coates, Morton II, 489
Coates, Morton II, 490
Coates, Morton II, 733
Coates, Moses II, 788
Coates, Moses II, 817
Coates, Mrs. W. H. V, 732
Coates, Omar C. V, 732
Coates, Oscar W. II, 909
Coates, Oscar W. II, 939
Coates, Paty V, 732
Coates, Pauline II, 781
Coates, Phares V, 732
Coates, Phebe V, 732
Coates, Phebe R. II, 849
Coates, Priscilla II, 489
Coates, Rachel II, 849
Coates, Rachel IV, 891
Coates, Rachel IV, 895
Coates, Rachel V, 40
Coates, Rachel C. V, 732
Coates, Rebecca II, 347
Coates, Rebecca II, 489
Coates, Rebecca II, 490
Coates, Rebecca II, 849
Coates, Rebecca V, 899
Coates, Rebecca B. III, 73
Coates, Rebecca H. III, 31
Coates, Reynell II, 347
Coates, Rhoda V, 40
Coates, Ridgeway VI, 483
Coates, Robert II, 849
Coates, Robert Livezey II, 788
Coates, Robert Livezey II, 850
Coates, Robert Livezey II, 866
Coates, Rose II, 347
Coates, Rose II, 348
Coates, Rose II, 489
Coates, Rose II, 668
Coates, Ruth Anna II, 169
Coates, Samuel II, 347
Coates, Samuel II, 348
Coates, Samuel II, 478
Coates, Samuel II, 489
Coates, Samuel II, 554
Coates, Samuel II, 576
Coates, Samuel II, 603
Coates, Samuel II, 643
Coates, Samuel II, 701
Coates, Samuel III, 73
Coates, Samuel V, 40
Coates, Sarah II, 347
Coates, Sarah II, 348
Coates, Sarah II, 489
Coates, Sarah II, 490
Coates, Sarah II, 649
Coates, Sarah II, 701
Coates, Sarah II, 733
Coates, Sarah II, 849
Coates, Sarah II, 858
Coates, Sarah III, 73
Coates, Sarah III, 272
Coates, Sarah Ann II, 849
Coates, Sarah B. IV, 690
Coates, Sarah B. IV, 777
Coates, Sarah M. III, 73
Coates, Sarah N. II, 733
Coates, Sarah R. II, 347
Coates, Sarah R. II, 490
Coates, Saunders II, 347
Coates, Saunders II, 490
Coates, Saunders III, 31
Coates, Saunders III, 73
Coates, Sidney II, 489
Coates, Sidney II, 733
Coates, Stalker II, 788
Coates, Susanna II, 348
Coates, Susannah II, 489
Coates, Thomas II, 347
Coates, Thomas II, 348
Coates, Thomas II, 489
Coates, Thomas II, 563
Coates, Thomas, Jr. II, 348
Coates, Virginia V, 731
Coates, Wd. Mary II, 489
Coates, William II, 347
Coates, William II, 348
Coates, William H. V, 732
Coates, Wm. II, 489
Coates, Wm. II, 653
Coates, Wm. II, 788
Coates, Wm. II, 849
Coates, Wm. II, 850
Coates, Wm. II, 866
Coates, Wm. Bailey II, 788
Coates, Wm. Bailey II, 849
Coates, Wm. Bailey II, 850
Coates, Wreford V, 731
Coats, Aaron II, 489
Coats, Aaron II, 989
Coats, Agnes V, 556
Coats, Agness V, 556
Coats, Alice II, 489
Coats, Alice II, 576
Coats, Alice S. V, 556
Coats, Amanda IV, 1248
Coats, Amelia Baker IV, 1153
Coats, Ann II, 347
Coats, Ann G. IV, 895
Coats, Anna D. V, 555
Coats, Annie D. V, 556
Coats, Annie Maud V, 556
Coats, Aquila IV, 112
Coats, Aquila IV, 117
Coats, Aquila VI, 378
Coats, Aquila VI, 431
Coats, Aquilla V, 324
Coats, Aquilla V, 482
Coats, Aquilla VI, 378
Coats, Aquilla VI, 483
Coats, Benjamin F. V, 324
Coats, Betsey VI, 942
Coats, Beulah II, 347
Coats, Beulah V, 891
Coats, Beulah V, 899
Coats, Caleb II, 849
Coats, Charles V, 158
Coats, Charlotte V, 157
Coats, Chas. V, 158
Coats, Christopher Columbus IV, 1248
Coats, Cyrus V, 556
Coats, David Curl V, 555
Coats, Deborah II, 849
Coats, Deborah IV, 1153
Coats, Deborah IV, 1173
Coats, Deborah V, 899
Coats, Deborah V, 950
Coats, Delilah V, 556
Coats, Delilah B. V, 555
Coats, Donald Wm. V, 555
Coats, Edwin Hadley V, 556
Coats, Elijah V, 158
Coats, Elijah V, 555
Coats, Elijah S. V, 556
Coats, Eliza VI, 378
Coats, Elizabeth II, 347
Coats, Elizabeth II, 489
Coats, Elizabeth II, 849
Coats, Elizabeth II, 850
Coats, Elizabeth V, 40
Coats, Elizabeth B. V, 556
Coats, Esther V, 556
Coats, Esther Virginia II, 849
Coats, Flora V, 555
Coats, Flora V, 556
Coats, George II, 347
Coats, Grace II, 347
Coats, Gula V, 989
Coats, H. A. V, 556
Coats, Hannah II, 849
Coats, Hannah IV, 142
Coats, Hannah IV, 1153
Coats, Hannah V, 324
Coats, Hannah V, 326
Coats, Hannah VI, 378
Coats, Hannah S. IV, 80
Coats, Hannah S. IV, 112
Coats, Hannah S. IV, 117
Coats, Henry I, 532
Coats, Hiram V, 158
Coats, Hiram V, 482
Coats, Hiram V, 522
Coats, Hiram V, 555
Coats, Hiram V, 556
Coats, Hiram Alvin V, 555
Coats, Hiram Alvin V, 556
Coats, Isaac IV, 895
Coats, Isaac IV, 1153
Coats, Isaac V, 324
Coats, Isaac Lewis VI, 378
Coats, Isaac Preston IV, 1153
Coats, James I, 532
Coats, James II, 347
Coats, James II, 442
Coats, James V, 39
Coats, James A. V, 324
Coats, James Seamore IV, 1153
Coats, John II, 347
Coats, John II, 442
Coats, John II, 489
Coats, John V, 556
Coats, John VI, 378
Coats, John B. V, 555
Coats, John, Jr. V, 556
Coats, Joseph T. V, 556
Coats, Joseph William V, 555
Coats, Joshua V, 810
Coats, Joshua Richards IV, 1153
Coats, Josiah T. V, 556
Coats, Kenneth V, 555
Coats, Leo Guy V, 556
Coats, Lester V, 556
Coats, Lester Hershel V, 555
Coats, Lincoln V, 555
Coats, Loran V, 556
Coats, Loran Alphonso V, 556
Coats, Lorin Alphonso V, 556
Coats, Lovesa May V, 555
Coats, Lydia IV, 142
Coats, Lydia IV, 1153
Coats, Lydia IV, 1173
Coats, Lydia Ann IV, 142
Coats, Lydien IV, 1153
Coats, Marmaduke I, 532
Coats, Martha V, 324
Coats, Martha V, 556
Coats, Martha V, 810
Coats, Martha E. V, 324
Coats, Martha Jane V, 158
Coats, Mary I, 532
Coats, Mary I, 1117
Coats, Mary I, 1121
Coats, Mary II, 347
Coats, Mary II, 442
Coats, Mary II, 489
Coats, Mary IV, 80
Coats, Mary IV, 117
Coats, Mary IV, 895
Coats, Mary V, 40
Coats, Mary V, 950
Coats, Mary A. V, 158
Coats, Mary Agness V, 555
Coats, Mary Ann IV, 1153
Coats, Mary Ann IV, 1161
Coats, Mary B. V, 556
Coats, Mary E. V, 555
Coats, Mary E. V, 556
Coats, Mary Elizabeth V, 555
Coats, Merie V, 556
Coats, Merrick V, 555
Coats, Merrick D. V, 556
Coats, Mima V, 989
Coats, Moses II, 989
Coats, Moses II, 1004
Coats, Moses IV, 117
Coats, Moses VI, 380
Coats, Nancy V, 556
Coats, Orlestus V, 556
Coats, Orlistes V, 556
Coats, Orlistus V, 555
Coats, Phebe IV, 1153
Coats, Phebe R. IV, 1153
Coats, Preston IV, 1153
Coats, Priscilla II, 489
Coats, Priscilla II, 614
Coats, Priscilla II, 989
Coats, Priscilla II, 1004
Coats, Rachel I, 532
Coats, Rachel I, 1016
Coats, Rachel II, 203
Coats, Rachel II, 208
Coats, Rachel II, 849
Coats, Rachel IV, 80
Coats, Rachel IV, 1153
Coats, Rachel V, 555
Coats, Rachel VI, 378
Coats, Rachel VI, 431
Coats, Rachel W. V, 482
Coats, Rachel W. V, 522
Coats, Rachel W. V, 556
Coats, Rebecca IV, 1153
Coats, Rebecca V, 158
Coats, Rebecca V, 555
Coats, Rebecca V, 898
Coats, Rebecca V, 899
Coats, Rebecca Mary V, 556
Coats, Rebecka II, 442
Coats, Ridgeway VI, 483
Coats, Robert V, 989
Coats, Rosannah V, 792
Coats, Rose II, 347
Coats, Ruth Anna II, 283
Coats, Ruth Anna II, 284
Coats, Ruth Eva V, 555
Coats, Samuel II, 347
Coats, Samuel II, 489
Coats, Samuel II, 989
Coats, Samuel II, 1024
Coats, Sarah II, 348
Coats, Sarah Ann IV, 1153
Coats, Sarah Ann V, 950
Coats, Sarah Jane IV, 891
Coats, Sarah Jane IV, 895
Coats, Seymour IV, 1173
Coats, Sidney IV, 80
Coats, Thomas II, 284
Coats, Thomas II, 347
Coats, Thomas II, 348
Coats, Thomas II, 442
Coats, William II, 347
Coats, William II, 348
Coats, William V, 40
Coats, Wm. II, 489
Coats, Wm. II, 614
Coats, Wm. Kirk V, 555
Coatsutton, Isabel II, 62
Cobb, Agathy IV, 379
Cobb, Agathy IV, 458
Cobb, Albert IV, 939
Cobb, Alfred VI, 58

Cobb, Alice VI, 55
Cobb, Alice VI, 58
Cobb, Amos IV, 940
Cobb, Amy IV, 694
Cobb, Anna M. VI, 58
Cobb, Anna W. IV, 939
Cobb, Ansalem IV, 940
Cobb, Ansalem IV, 968
Cobb, Ansalem L. IV, 939
Cobb, Artelia Jennie I, 621
Cobb, Benj. VI, 53
Cobb, Benj. Evans VI, 56
Cobb, Benjamin VI, 58
Cobb, Benjamin VI, 74
Cobb, Benjamin VI, 90
Cobb, Benjamin E. VI, 58
Cobb, Bertha L. IV, 1037
Cobb, Cora IV, 939
Cobb, David Albert IV, 939
Cobb, Edith VI, 53
Cobb, Edy VI, 58
Cobb, Edy VI, 90
Cobb, Effie J. VI, 58
Cobb, Effie J. VI, 74
Cobb, Eli Haines IV, 80
Cobb, Elihu IV, 1037
Cobb, Elizabeth IV, 1024
Cobb, Elizabeth IV, 1025
Cobb, Elizabeth VI, 1005
Cobb, Elizabeth P. IV, 940
Cobb, Elizabeth P. IV, 975
Cobb, Ervine IV, 939
Cobb, Esther IV, 939
Cobb, Esther V, 158
Cobb, Franklin VI, 58
Cobb, George VI, 58
Cobb, Grace IV, 940
Cobb, Grace IV, 968
Cobb, Hannah C. IV, 938
Cobb, Hannah M. IV, 939
Cobb, Isidore IV, 939
Cobb, James, Jr. IV, 1234
Cobb, Jane VI, 56
Cobb, Jane VI, 58
Cobb, Jane VI, 74
Cobb, John VI, 843
Cobb, John Emerson IV, 939
Cobb, Joseph VI, 91
Cobb, Leslie R. IV, 1037
Cobb, Letitia IV, 1025
Cobb, Letitia IV, 1026
Cobb, Levi IV, 1023
Cobb, Levi IV, 1024
Cobb, Lida IV, 939
Cobb, Lucy Jane IV, 1204
Cobb, Lucy Jane IV, 1222
Cobb, Lynch IV, 939
Cobb, Mabel IV, 690
Cobb, Margaret IV, 938
Cobb, Margaret IV, 1024
Cobb, Martha VI, 53
Cobb, Martha VI, 58
Cobb, Martha VI, 64
Cobb, Martha VI, 88
Cobb, Martha C. VI, 58
Cobb, Martha J. VI, 58
Cobb, Martha J. VI, 64
Cobb, Mary IV, 80
Cobb, Mary IV, 940
Cobb, Mary VI, 91
Cobb, Mary VI, 275
Cobb, Mary Alice VI, 58
Cobb, Mary Ann IV, 1037
Cobb, Mattie E. VI, 91
Cobb, Myrtle M. IV, 1037
Cobb, Nancy VI, 53
Cobb, Nancy VI, 58
Cobb, Nancy VI, 843
Cobb, Nancy A. VI, 58
Cobb, Nancy Alice VI, 55
Cobb, Nancy J. VI, 91
Cobb, Newit VI, 58
Cobb, Newit VI, 64
Cobb, Newitt VI, 53
Cobb, Newitt VI, 55
Cobb, Newitt VI, 58
Cobb, Newitt VI, 88
Cobb, Nicholas H. VI, 927
Cobb, Phebe IV, 80
Cobb, Phebe IV, 91
Cobb, Phebe IV, 765
Cobb, Pleasant IV, 694
Cobb, Rachel IV, 1023
Cobb, Rachel IV, 1025
Cobb, Robert IV, 940
Cobb, Robert IV, 975
Cobb, Robert VI, 275
Cobb, Roenna VI, 58
Cobb, Roenna VI, 90
Cobb, Rosa VI, 53
Cobb, Rosa VI, 58
Cobb, Rosa J. IV, 1037
Cobb, Rose IV, 690
Cobb, Rowena VI, 91
Cobb, Sarah VI, 58
Cobb, Sarah Ellen IV, 939
Cobb, Simeon R. IV, 940
Cobb, Thomas W. IV, 938
Cobb, Unity IV, 939
Cobb, Waddy IV, 938
Cobb, Waddy IV, 1024
Cobb, William IV, 80
Cobb, William IV, 690
Cobb, William VI, 58
Cobb, Wm. IV, 80
Cobb, Wm. H. IV, 1036
Cobbett, Samuel II, 442
Cobbett, William II, 442
Cobbitt, Samuel II, 442
Cobbs, ??? IV, 938
Cobbs, ??? VI, 806
Cobbs, ??? VI, 894
Cobbs, A. J. IV, 690
Cobbs, Abigail IV, 690
Cobbs, Abigail IV, 764
Cobbs, Abigail IV, 938
Cobbs, Abigail IV, 939
Cobbs, Abigail VI, 235
Cobbs, Abraham IV, 1212
Cobbs, Ada IV, 941
Cobbs, Ada B. IV, 939
Cobbs, Ada B. IV, 941
Cobbs, Agatha IV, 379
Cobbs, Agatha IV, 690
Cobbs, Agatha IV, 938
Cobbs, Agatha IV, 939
Cobbs, Agatha IV, 940
Cobbs, Agatha VI, 235
Cobbs, Agniss VI, 994
Cobbs, Albert IV, 690
Cobbs, Albert IV, 939
Cobbs, Albert IV, 940
Cobbs, Albert IV, 941
Cobbs, Albert IV, 986
Cobbs, Alice IV, 939
Cobbs, Alva J. IV, 941
Cobbs, Alvay J. IV, 939
Cobbs, Amasa IV, 938
Cobbs, Amos IV, 940
Cobbs, Amos England IV, 938
Cobbs, Amy IV, 690
Cobbs, Amy IV, 694
Cobbs, Amy IV, 764
Cobbs, Amy IV, 765
Cobbs, Amy IV, 781
Cobbs, Amy IV, 938
Cobbs, Amy IV, 940
Cobbs, Amy IV, 941
Cobbs, Amy IV, 969
Cobbs, Amy IV, 988
Cobbs, Amy VI, 235
Cobbs, Amy VI, 276
Cobbs, Ann IV, 189
Cobbs, Ann IV, 690
Cobbs, Ann IV, 789
Cobbs, Ann IV, 806
Cobbs, Ann IV, 808
Cobbs, Ann IV, 938
Cobbs, Ann IV, 939
Cobbs, Ann IV, 940
Cobbs, Ann IV, 982
Cobbs, Ann IV, 989
Cobbs, Ann IV, 999
Cobbs, Ann VI, 894
Cobbs, Ann VI, 903
Cobbs, Ann L. IV, 940
Cobbs, Ann L. VI, 894
Cobbs, Ann M. L. VI, 806
Cobbs, Ann P. VI, 806
Cobbs, Ann Stanard VI, 896
Cobbs, Anna IV, 189
Cobbs, Anna IV, 236
Cobbs, Anna IV, 938
Cobbs, Anna IV, 939
Cobbs, Anna E. IV, 939
Cobbs, Anna S. IV, 939
Cobbs, Anna W. IV, 939
Cobbs, Anna W. IV, 940
Cobbs, Annar IV, 939
Cobbs, Anne IV, 939
Cobbs, Anne U. IV, 940
Cobbs, Anne U. IV, 974
Cobbs, Anner IV, 940
Cobbs, Annie L. IV, 940
Cobbs, Annie S. IV, 189
Cobbs, Ansalem IV, 189
Cobbs, Ansalem IV, 690
Cobbs, Ansalem IV, 806
Cobbs, Ansalem IV, 808
Cobbs, Ansalem IV, 858
Cobbs, Ansalem IV, 938
Cobbs, Ansalem IV, 939
Cobbs, Ansalem IV, 940
Cobbs, Ansalem IV, 999
Cobbs, Ansalem Ervin IV, 939
Cobbs, Ansalem L. IV, 939
Cobbs, Ansalem L. IV, 940
Cobbs, Ansalem L. IV, 999
Cobbs, Ansalem Lynch IV, 938
Cobbs, Ansalm IV, 989
Cobbs, Ansalm IV, 1204
Cobbs, Ansalm IV, 1212
Cobbs, Anselm IV, 690
Cobbs, Anselm VI, 235
Cobbs, Anslem IV, 940
Cobbs, Anslem E. IV, 940
Cobbs, Anslum IV, 940
Cobbs, Balinda T. IV, 1204
Cobbs, Balinda T. IV, 1212
Cobbs, Bedford VI, 235
Cobbs, Belinda T. IV, 1204
Cobbs, Benjamin VI, 235
Cobbs, Benjamin F. VI, 930
Cobbs, Benjamin F. VI, 984
Cobbs, Bertha L. IV, 1037
Cobbs, Betty VI, 806
Cobbs, Caleb VI, 806
Cobbs, Carl Thomas IV, 939
Cobbs, Carl Thomas IV, 940
Cobbs, Caroline IV, 939
Cobbs, Caroline IV, 940
Cobbs, Caspar IV, 938
Cobbs, Caspar IV, 940
Cobbs, Cassandra E. VI, 894
Cobbs, Catherine IV, 939
Cobbs, Catherine IV, 940
Cobbs, Charles IV, 938
Cobbs, Charles IV, 940
Cobbs, Charles VI, 806
Cobbs, Charles VI, 828
Cobbs, Charles VI, 894
Cobbs, Charles G. VI, 894
Cobbs, Charles L. VI, 806
Cobbs, Charles L. VI, 880
Cobbs, Charles L. VI, 896
Cobbs, Charles R. VI, 797
Cobbs, Charles R. VI, 806
Cobbs, Charles R. VI, 827
Cobbs, Charles R. VI, 848
Cobbs, Charlotte Eleanor VI, 971
Cobbs, Chas. VI, 894
Cobbs, Chas. G. VI, 912
Cobbs, Christina VI, 806
Cobbs, Cidna C. IV, 940
Cobbs, Cidna C. IV, 966
Cobbs, Clara IV, 939
Cobbs, Clara IV, 940
Cobbs, Clara IV, 1013
Cobbs, Clark Edgar IV, 939
Cobbs, Clotilda Jane IV, 939
Cobbs, Cora IV, 939
Cobbs, Cynthia IV, 1204
Cobbs, David VI, 235
Cobbs, David Albert IV, 939
Cobbs, Demaris VI, 887
Cobbs, Dolly VI, 830
Cobbs, Edmund VI, 830
Cobbs, Edmund VI, 894
Cobbs, Edmund VI, 903
Cobbs, Edmund VI, 971
Cobbs, Edmund VI, 997
Cobbs, Edmund VI, 1005
Cobbs, Edna IV, 938
Cobbs, Edna IV, 940
Cobbs, Edna IV, 1001
Cobbs, Eli IV, 938
Cobbs, Eli IV, 940
Cobbs, Elihu IV, 939
Cobbs, Elihu IV, 940
Cobbs, Elihu IV, 999
Cobbs, Elihu IV, 1037
Cobbs, Elijah IV, 938
Cobbs, Elinor B. IV, 939
Cobbs, Eliza IV, 324
Cobbs, Eliza IV, 690
Cobbs, Eliza IV, 939
Cobbs, Eliza VI, 235
Cobbs, Eliza VI, 806
Cobbs, Eliza F. P. VI, 976
Cobbs, Elizabeth IV, 690
Cobbs, Elizabeth IV, 764
Cobbs, Elizabeth IV, 938
Cobbs, Elizabeth IV, 940
Cobbs, Elizabeth IV, 975
Cobbs, Elizabeth IV, 997
Cobbs, Elizabeth VI, 235
Cobbs, Elizabeth VI, 256
Cobbs, Elizabeth VI, 838
Cobbs, Elizabeth VI, 893
Cobbs, Elizabeth VI, 894
Cobbs, Elizabeth VI, 998
Cobbs, Elizabeth A. VI, 843
Cobbs, Elizabeth A. VI, 894
Cobbs, Elizabeth Ann IV, 940
Cobbs, Elizabeth Ann IV, 999
Cobbs, Elizabeth P. IV, 938
Cobbs, Elizabeth P. IV, 940
Cobbs, Elizabeth P. IV, 1036
Cobbs, Ella IV, 940
Cobbs, Ella B. IV, 939
Cobbs, Ellen IV, 925
Cobbs, Ellen IV, 939
Cobbs, Ellen IV, 940
Cobbs, Ellen IV, 941
Cobbs, Emaline IV, 939
Cobbs, Emaline IV, 940
Cobbs, Emeline IV, 936
Cobbs, Emily IV, 940
Cobbs, Emily IV, 946
Cobbs, Emily VI, 933
Cobbs, Emily W. IV, 939
Cobbs, Emma W. VI, 939
Cobbs, Emmeline IV, 940
Cobbs, Emmor IV, 938
Cobbs, Emmor IV, 940
Cobbs, Ervine IV, 939
Cobbs, Esther IV, 936
Cobbs, Esther IV, 939
Cobbs, Esther IV, 940
Cobbs, Esther IV, 986
Cobbs, Evalina P. VI, 988
Cobbs, Frances VI, 806
Cobbs, Frances VI, 841
Cobbs, Frances VI, 849
Cobbs, Frances L. VI, 806
Cobbs, Francis VI, 841
Cobbs, George IV, 927
Cobbs, George IV, 938
Cobbs, George IV, 939
Cobbs, George IV, 940
Cobbs, Gideon IV, 938
Cobbs, Gideon IV, 940
Cobbs, Ginerva IV, 939
Cobbs, Ginerva IV, 975
Cobbs, Grace IV, 938
Cobbs, Grace IV, 940
Cobbs, Grace IV, 1204
Cobbs, Grace IV, 1212
Cobbs, Hannah IV, 938
Cobbs, Hannah IV, 986
Cobbs, Hannah IV, 1204
Cobbs, Hannah IV, 1206
Cobbs, Hannah C. IV, 677
Cobbs, Hannah C. IV, 690
Cobbs, Hannah C. IV, 938
Cobbs, Hannah C. IV, 939
Cobbs, Hannah C. IV, 940
Cobbs, Hannah M. IV, 939
Cobbs, Henry IV, 938
Cobbs, Henry IV, 940
Cobbs, Henry P. IV, 189
Cobbs, Henry P. IV, 236
Cobbs, Henry P. IV, 939
Cobbs, Henry P. IV, 940
Cobbs, Henry P. IV, 974
Cobbs, Henry W. IV, 938
Cobbs, Herbert L. IV, 940
Cobbs, Herbert S. IV, 939
Cobbs, Homer IV, 939
Cobbs, Homer IV, 940
Cobbs, Homer IV, 941
Cobbs, Hudson L. VI, 894
Cobbs, Irven IV, 941
Cobbs, Irven T. IV, 939
Cobbs, Isaac I. IV, 939
Cobbs, Isaac J. IV, 940
Cobbs, Isabella IV, 939
Cobbs, Isabella IV, 940
Cobbs, Isabella Emily IV, 927
Cobbs, Isabella Emily IV, 940
Cobbs, Isidore IV, 939
Cobbs, J. B. VI, 833
Cobbs, James VI, 806
Cobbs, James VI, 894
Cobbs, James H. VI, 806
Cobbs, James M. VI, 806
Cobbs, James V. VI, 894
Cobbs, James V. VI, 1005
Cobbs, Jane VI, 806
Cobbs, Jane VI, 894
Cobbs, Jeffery VI, 894
Cobbs, Jehu IV, 938
Cobbs, Jehu IV, 940
Cobbs, Jennet IV, 924
Cobbs, Jennet IV, 940
Cobbs, Jennett IV, 938
Cobbs, Jenny VI, 894
Cobbs, Jesse IV, 690
Cobbs, Jesse IV, 938
Cobbs, Jesse IV, 940
Cobbs, Jesse IV, 1204
Cobbs, Jesse VI, 836
Cobbs, Jesse VI, 894
Cobbs, Joanna IV, 690
Cobbs, Joanna IV, 938
Cobbs, Joanna IV, 969
Cobbs, Joanna VI, 235
Cobbs, Joel IV, 1037
Cobbs, Joel A. IV, 939
Cobbs, John IV, 690
Cobbs, John IV, 938
Cobbs, John IV, 940
Cobbs, John VI, 806
Cobbs, John VI, 812
Cobbs, John VI, 829
Cobbs, John VI, 838
Cobbs, John VI, 839
Cobbs, John VI, 841
Cobbs, John VI, 848
Cobbs, John VI, 894
Cobbs, John VI, 982
Cobbs, John VI, 988
Cobbs, John B. VI, 806
Cobbs, John B. VI, 867
Cobbs, John C. VI, 883
Cobbs, John C. VI, 894
Cobbs, John C. VI, 971
Cobbs, John E. IV, 939
Cobbs, John E. IV, 1005
Cobbs, John Emerson IV, 939
Cobbs, John L. VI, 893
Cobbs, John L. VI, 894
Cobbs, John L. VI, 903
Cobbs, John L. VI, 923
Cobbs, John L. VI, 980
Cobbs, John L. VI, 994
Cobbs, John M. VI, 903
Cobbs, John S. VI, 887
Cobbs, John T. IV, 939
Cobbs, John T. IV, 940
Cobbs, John T. IV, 999
Cobbs, Jonathan IV, 938
Cobbs, Jonathan IV, 940
Cobbs, Joseph IV, 690
Cobbs, Joseph IV, 783
Cobbs, Joseph IV, 921
Cobbs, Joseph IV, 938
Cobbs, Joseph IV, 939
Cobbs, Joseph IV, 998
Cobbs, Joseph VI, 235
Cobbs, Joseph T. IV, 938
Cobbs, Joseph T. IV, 940
Cobbs, Joshua IV, 938
Cobbs, Joshua IV, 939
Cobbs, Joshua IV, 940
Cobbs, Josiah IV, 927
Cobbs, Josiah IV, 938
Cobbs, Josiah IV, 939
Cobbs, Josiah IV, 940
Cobbs, Josiah IV, 1204
Cobbs, Judith VI, 235
Cobbs, Judith VI, 997
Cobbs, Judith Ann IV, 939
Cobbs, Judith S. VI, 894
Cobbs, Julia C. IV, 939
Cobbs, Kenneth Wade IV, 939
Cobbs, Laura C. IV, 939
Cobbs, Laura May IV, 939
Cobbs, Lavina IV, 939
Cobbs, Lavina IV, 940
Cobbs, Leslie R. IV, 1037
Cobbs, Letitia IV, 1024
Cobbs, Levinia VI, 848
Cobbs, Lewis VI, 235
Cobbs, Lida IV, 939
Cobbs, Lida IV, 1005
Cobbs, Lindsey IV, 690
Cobbs, Lindsey IV, 789
Cobbs, Lindsey IV, 938
Cobbs, Lindsey IV, 940
Cobbs, Linsey IV, 690
Cobbs, Linsey IV, 939
Cobbs, Littleberry VI, 235
Cobbs, Living VI, 894
Cobbs, Lois Jane IV, 939
Cobbs, Lucinda IV, 690
Cobbs, Lucinda IV, 938
Cobbs, Lucinda IV, 939
Cobbs, Lucinda IV, 940
Cobbs, Lucinde IV, 928
Cobbs, Lucinde IV, 940
Cobbs, Lucy IV, 938
Cobbs, Lucy E. IV, 926
Cobbs, Lucy E. IV, 940
Cobbs, Lucy Henry VI, 894
Cobbs, Lucy Jane IV, 938
Cobbs, Lucy Jane IV, 939
Cobbs, Lucy Jane IV, 989
Cobbs, Lydia IV, 938
Cobbs, Lydia IV, 940
Cobbs, Lydia IV, 974
Cobbs, Lydia Ann IV, 921
Cobbs, Lydia Ann IV, 938
Cobbs, Lydia Ann IV, 939
Cobbs, Lydia Ann IV, 999

obbs, Lynch IV, 939
obbs, Lynch IV, 975
obbs, Lynch IV, 991
obbs, Mabel IV, 690
obbs, Mabel IV, 939
obbs, Mabel IV, 940
obbs, Malinda VI, 839
obbs, Margaret IV, 690
obbs, Margaret IV, 938
obbs, Margaret IV, 970
obbs, Margaret IV, 997
obbs, Margaret Anna IV, 975
obbs, Margaret Annah IV, 939
obbs, Margaretta IV, 931
obbs, Margaretta IV, 938
obbs, Margaretta IV, 940
obbs, Maria Louisa VI, 994
obbs, Marial L. VI, 806
obbs, Marietta A. IV, 939
obbs, Marietta A. IV, 991
obbs, Martha IV, 690
obbs, Martha IV, 938
obbs, Martha VI, 235
obbs, Martha VI, 269
obbs, Martha VI, 272
obbs, Martha VI, 806
obbs, Martha VI, 829
obbs, Martha VI, 903
obbs, Martha B. VI, 894
obbs, Martin IV, 939
obbs, Martin IV, 940
obbs, Mary IV, 690
obbs, Mary IV, 765
obbs, Mary IV, 927
obbs, Mary IV, 938
obbs, Mary IV, 939
obbs, Mary IV, 940
obbs, Mary IV, 1010
obbs, Mary IV, 1212
obbs, Mary VI, 235
obbs, Mary VI, 274
obbs, Mary VI, 795
obbs, Mary VI, 799
obbs, Mary VI, 806
obbs, Mary VI, 848
obbs, Mary A. IV, 938
obbs, Mary A. IV, 970
obbs, Mary A. VI, 895
obbs, Mary A. VI, 903
obbs, Mary Ann IV, 690
obbs, Mary Ann IV, 938
obbs, Mary Ann IV, 939
obbs, Mary Ann IV, 940
obbs, Mary Ann IV, 984
obbs, Mary Ann IV, 999
obbs, Mary Ann IV, 1037
obbs, Mary Annah IV, 939
obbs, Mary E. IV, 939
obbs, Mary E. IV, 940
obbs, Mary Epps VI, 961
obbs, Mary Etta IV, 925
obbs, Mary J. VI, 973
obbs, Mary Jane IV, 938
obbs, Mary Lewis VI, 796
obbs, Mary M. VI, 797
obbs, Mary S. IV, 940
obbs, Mary, Jr. IV, 940
obbs, Maryanna IV, 940
obbs, May IV, 1037
obbs, Mildred VI, 806
obbs, Mina A. VI, 806
obbs, Minnie IV, 940
obbs, Minnie V. IV, 939
obbs, Minnie V. IV, 948
obbs, Myrtle M. IV, 1037
obbs, N. H. VI, 879
obbs, N. H. VI, 880
obbs, N. H. VI, 889
obbs, N. H. VI, 908
obbs, N. H. VI, 920
obbs, N. H. VI, 938
obbs, N. H. VI, 942
obbs, N. H. VI, 951
obbs, N. H. VI, 956
obbs, N. H. VI, 968
obbs, N. H. VI, 971
obbs, N. H. VI, 978
obbs, N. H. VI, 980
obbs, N. H. VI, 986
obbs, N. H. VI, 987
obbs, N. H. VI, 995
obbs, N. H. VI, 1018
obbs, Nancy VI, 854
obbs, Nancy VI, 894
obbs, Nich. H. VI, 971
obbs, Nicholas VI, 903
obbs, Nicholas A. VI, 922
obbs, Nicholas A. VI, 1012
obbs, Nicholas H. VI, 883
obbs, Nicholas H. VI, 887
obbs, Nicholas H. VI, 889
Cobbs, Nicholas H. VI, 894
Cobbs, Nicholas H. VI, 898
Cobbs, Nicholas H. VI, 899
Cobbs, Nicholas H. VI, 903
Cobbs, Nicholas H. VI, 919
Cobbs, Nicholas H. VI, 927
Cobbs, Nicholas H. VI, 928
Cobbs, Nicholas H. VI, 933
Cobbs, Nicholas H. VI, 942
Cobbs, Nicholas H. VI, 949
Cobbs, Nicholas H. VI, 951
Cobbs, Nicholas H. VI, 955
Cobbs, Nicholas H. VI, 956
Cobbs, Nicholas H. VI, 965
Cobbs, Nicholas H. VI, 977
Cobbs, Nicholas H. VI, 983
Cobbs, Nicholas H. VI, 984
Cobbs, Nicholas H. VI, 990
Cobbs, Nicholas H. VI, 994
Cobbs, Nicholas H. VI, 995
Cobbs, Nicholas H. VI, 996
Cobbs, Nicholas H. VI, 998
Cobbs, Nicholas H. VI, 1001
Cobbs, Nicholas H. VI, 1007
Cobbs, Nicholas H. VI, 1017
Cobbs, Olmy IV, 1204
Cobbs, Peggy VI, 894
Cobbs, Pleasant IV, 690
Cobbs, Pleasant IV, 694
Cobbs, Pleasant IV, 764
Cobbs, Pleasant IV, 765
Cobbs, Pleasant IV, 919
Cobbs, Pleasant IV, 938
Cobbs, Pleasant IV, 969
Cobbs, Pleasant IV, 1204
Cobbs, Pleasant VI, 276
Cobbs, Pleasant, Jr. IV, 938
Cobbs, Pleasant, Jr. IV, 940
Cobbs, Pleasants VI, 235
Cobbs, Polly VI, 806
Cobbs, Polly VI, 894
Cobbs, Polly C. VI, 912
Cobbs, Rachel IV, 940
Cobbs, Rachel A. IV, 939
Cobbs, Rachel A. IV, 940
Cobbs, Rebecca IV, 690
Cobbs, Rebecca IV, 694
Cobbs, Rebecca IV, 938
Cobbs, Rebecca IV, 939
Cobbs, Rebecca VI, 235
Cobbs, Rhoda IV, 690
Cobbs, Rhoda IV, 764
Cobbs, Rhoda IV, 938
Cobbs, Rhoda VI, 235
Cobbs, Robert IV, 938
Cobbs, Robert IV, 939
Cobbs, Robert IV, 940
Cobbs, Robert IV, 1010
Cobbs, Robert VI, 235
Cobbs, Robert VI, 274
Cobbs, Robert VI, 796
Cobbs, Robert VI, 810
Cobbs, Robert VI, 835
Cobbs, Robert VI, 843
Cobbs, Robert Vencnor IV, 938
Cobbs, Robert Venenor IV, 690
Cobbs, Robert Vincnor VI, 235
Cobbs, Rosa J. IV, 1037
Cobbs, Rose IV, 690
Cobbs, Ruth IV, 927
Cobbs, Ruth IV, 939
Cobbs, Ruth IV, 940
Cobbs, Ruth IV, 1204
Cobbs, Ruthanna IV, 938
Cobbs, Ruthanna IV, 939
Cobbs, Ruthanna IV, 940
Cobbs, Ruthanna IV, 1008
Cobbs, Sally VI, 806
Cobbs, Sally VI, 841
Cobbs, Sally VI, 894
Cobbs, Sally VI, 942
Cobbs, Sally L. VI, 870
Cobbs, Samuel VI, 806
Cobbs, Samuel VI, 827
Cobbs, Samuel VI, 894
Cobbs, Samuel D. VI, 854
Cobbs, Sarah IV, 938
Cobbs, Sarah IV, 940
Cobbs, Sarah IV, 1204
Cobbs, Sarah VI, 795
Cobbs, Sarah VI, 827
Cobbs, Sarah VI, 835
Cobbs, Sarah VI, 894
Cobbs, Sarah Ann IV, 938
Cobbs, Sarah Ann IV, 939
Cobbs, Sarah Ann IV, 940
Cobbs, Sarah Ann IV, 981
Cobbs, Sarah Ann IV, 1204
Cobbs, Sarah E. IV, 939
Cobbs, Sarah Ellen IV, 939
Cobbs, Sarah Ellen IV, 940
Cobbs, Sarah Ellen IV, 1005
Cobbs, Sarah J. VI, 894
Cobbs, Sarahann IV, 1204
Cobbs, Sarahann IV, 1206
Cobbs, Sarahann IV, 1212
Cobbs, Selina E. IV, 1024
Cobbs, Sibyl IV, 931
Cobbs, Sibyl IV, 940
Cobbs, Sidney IV, 938
Cobbs, Sidney IV, 940
Cobbs, Sidney IV, 941
Cobbs, Silas IV, 939
Cobbs, Silas IV, 940
Cobbs, Simeon IV, 938
Cobbs, Simeon IV, 939
Cobbs, Simeon R. IV, 939
Cobbs, Simeon R. IV, 940
Cobbs, Simon VI, 806
Cobbs, Sophia W. VI, 990
Cobbs, Susanna VI, 812
Cobbs, Susanna VI, 828
Cobbs, Susannah VI, 806
Cobbs, Sybil IV, 938
Cobbs, Tacy IV, 690
Cobbs, Tacy IV, 783
Cobbs, Tacy IV, 921
Cobbs, Tacy IV, 938
Cobbs, Tacy IV, 939
Cobbs, Tacy IV, 940
Cobbs, Tacy IV, 998
Cobbs, Tandy P. VI, 806
Cobbs, Tazwell VI, 894
Cobbs, Terrel IV, 938
Cobbs, Thomas IV, 1204
Cobbs, Thomas IV, 1206
Cobbs, Thomas VI, 235
Cobbs, Thomas VI, 256
Cobbs, Thomas VI, 269
Cobbs, Thomas VI, 272
Cobbs, Thomas VI, 795
Cobbs, Thomas VI, 806
Cobbs, Thomas VI, 812
Cobbs, Thomas VI, 847
Cobbs, Thomas A. IV, 940
Cobbs, Thomas A. VI, 806
Cobbs, Thomas A. VI, 841
Cobbs, Thomas A. VI, 864
Cobbs, Thomas C. IV, 1204
Cobbs, Thomas Ferrell IV, 938
Cobbs, Thomas J. IV, 939
Cobbs, Thomas J. VI, 820
Cobbs, Thomas Jefferson IV, 939
Cobbs, Thomas L. IV, 938
Cobbs, Thomas L. IV, 939
Cobbs, Thomas L. IV, 940
Cobbs, Thomas T. IV, 690
Cobbs, Thomas T. IV, 938
Cobbs, Thomas T. IV, 940
Cobbs, Thomas T. IV, 1204
Cobbs, Thomas Terrell IV, 690
Cobbs, Thomas W. IV, 938
Cobbs, Thomas W. IV, 939
Cobbs, Thomas W. IV, 940
Cobbs, Thos. L. IV, 940
Cobbs, Thos. T. IV, 981
Cobbs, Thos. Terrell IV, 690
Cobbs, Tilghman VI, 806
Cobbs, Tilghman A. VI, 990
Cobbs, Tilghman A. VI, 998
Cobbs, Timothy IV, 936
Cobbs, Timothy IV, 938
Cobbs, Timothy IV, 939
Cobbs, Timothy IV, 940
Cobbs, Unity IV, 939
Cobbs, Unity IV, 940
Cobbs, Unity IV, 975
Cobbs, Unity IV, 991
Cobbs, Unity IV, 999
Cobbs, Ura IV, 690
Cobbs, Uree IV, 938
Cobbs, Uree IV, 939
Cobbs, Uree IV, 998
Cobbs, Uree Ella IV, 939
Cobbs, Verla Lucile IV, 939
Cobbs, Verla Lucile IV, 941
Cobbs, Virgil Lee IV, 939
Cobbs, Virginia L. VI, 980
Cobbs, Waddy IV, 690
Cobbs, Waddy IV, 938
Cobbs, Waddy IV, 970
Cobbs, Waddy IV, 997
Cobbs, Waddy VI, 870
Cobbs, Waddy VI, 894
Cobbs, Waddy VI, 912
Cobbs, Waddy VI, 976
Cobbs, Warmer VI, 894
Cobbs, Watson B. VI, 833
Cobbs, William IV, 690
Cobbs, William VI, 795
Cobbs, William VI, 843
Cobbs, William VI, 894
Cobbs, William VI, 954
Cobbs, William VI, 997
Cobbs, William Henry IV, 939
Cobbs, William J. IV, 939
Cobbs, William T. VI, 806
Cobbs, Wm. H. IV, 940
Cobbs, Wm. H. IV, 1036
Cobbs, Wm. Henry IV, 939
Cobbs, Wm. Henry IV, 940
Cobbs, Wm. J. IV, 940
Cobbs, Wm. Y. IV, 1037
Cobbw, John L. VI, 893
Cobern, James VI, 378
Cobern, Robert VI, 378
Cobert, Sarah II, 490
Cobert, Sarah II, 686
Cobes, William II, 348
Coble, Alice I, 642
Coble, Alice Tomlinson I, 631
Coble, Ann I, 424
Coble, Bessie I, 623
Coble, Bessie I, 631
Coble, Bessie I, 638
Coble, Eliza IV, 324
Coble, Eliza IV, 341
Coble, Epsie I, 614
Coble, Margaret I, 614
Coble, Margaret I, 631
Coble, Margaret I, 643
Coble, Margaret I, 933
Coble, Mary I, 623
Coble, Mrs. Epsie I, 631
Coble, Noah I, 623
Coble, Sarah V, 779
Coble, Sarah V, 794
Coble, William Conrad I, 614
Coblert, Sarah VI, 894
Coborn, Sabina IV, 690
Coborn, Sarah IV, 901
Cobourn, Abigail IV, 690
Cobourn, Abigail IV, 901
Cobourn, Abigail IV, 941
Cobourn, Abigail IV, 997
Cobourn, Abigail Jr. IV, 899
Cobourn, Abigail Jr. IV, 901
Cobourn, Agnes III, 73
Cobourn, Annie R. IV, 690
Cobourn, Benjamin IV, 690
Cobourn, Benjamin IV, 901
Cobourn, Benjamin IV, 941
Cobourn, Benjamin IV, 997
Cobourn, Curtis L. IV, 690
Cobourn, Elizabeth II, 490
Cobourn, Elizabeth IV, 901
Cobourn, Elizabeth IV, 941
Cobourn, Ella IV, 807
Cobourn, Ella IV, 901
Cobourn, Ella Ida IV, 690
Cobourn, Ellen IV, 941
Cobourn, Ellen IV, 943
Cobourn, Ezra IV, 690
Cobourn, Ezra IV, 901
Cobourn, Harriet J. IV, 690
Cobourn, Harriett IV, 901
Cobourn, Harvy Fowler IV, 901
Cobourn, J. George IV, 901
Cobourn, Jacob IV, 941
Cobourn, Jacob IV, 943
Cobourn, Jacob IV, 972
Cobourn, John IV, 690
Cobourn, John IV, 901
Cobourn, John IV, 908
Cobourn, John A. IV, 690
Cobourn, John Alexander IV, 690
Cobourn, John Alexander IV, 901
Cobourn, John G. IV, 690
Cobourn, John George IV, 690
Cobourn, Joseph IV, 690
Cobourn, Joseph IV, 901
Cobourn, Joseph L. IV, 690
Cobourn, Joseph Laron IV, 901
Cobourn, Joseph Lawrence IV, 690
Cobourn, Kurtis S. IV, 690
Cobourn, Martha Jane IV, 941
Cobourn, Martha Jane IV, 972
Cobourn, Mary E. IV, 690
Cobourn, Nathan IV, 690
Cobourn, Nathan IV, 901
Cobourn, Prudence II, 490
Cobourn, Rachel IV, 901
Cobourn, Sabina IV, 690
Cobourn, Sarah IV, 690
Cobourn, Sarah IV, 901
Cobourn, Sarah IV, 912
Cobourn, Sarah Elizabeth IV, 901
Cobourn, Sarah Jr. IV, 908
Cobourn, Sarah L. IV, 690
Cobourn, Sarah Lenora IV, 690
Cobourn, Thirza IV, 690
Cobourn, Thirza IV, 901
Cobourn, William Franklin IV, 690
Cobourn, Wm. F. IV, 690
Cobron, Martha II, 490
Cobron, Martha II, 635
Coburn, Abigail IV, 806
Coburn, Abigail IV, 941
Coburn, Abigail IV, 997
Coburn, Abigail, Jr. IV, 806
Coburn, Alfaretta K. IV, 941
Coburn, Benjamin IV, 806
Coburn, Benjamin IV, 941
Coburn, Benjamin IV, 997
Coburn, Carrie III, 108
Coburn, Chas. W. IV, 941
Coburn, David IV, 807
Coburn, David IV, 858
Coburn, Elizabeth II, 490
Coburn, Elizabeth IV, 806
Coburn, Elizabeth IV, 941
Coburn, Elizabeth IV, 997
Coburn, Ella IV, 807
Coburn, Ellen IV, 921
Coburn, Ellen IV, 941
Coburn, George IV, 807
Coburn, Hannah IV, 806
Coburn, Jacob IV, 806
Coburn, Jacob IV, 921
Coburn, Jacob IV, 941
Coburn, James VI, 378
Coburn, John IV, 807
Coburn, Joseph II, 490
Coburn, Judith Ann IV, 921
Coburn, Judith Ann IV, 941
Coburn, Martha II, 490
Coburn, Martha II, 635
Coburn, Martha J. IV, 941
Coburn, Martha Jane IV, 941
Coburn, Phebe VI, 378
Coburn, Prudence II, 490
Coburn, Robert VI, 378
Coburn, Robert VI, 461
Coburn, Robt. VI, 483
Coburn, Sarah IV, 806
Coburn, Thomas II, 490
Coburn, Unity IV, 941
Coch, Elisabeth I, 137
Coch, Elisabeth I, 155
Coche, Miriam II, 208
Cochin, Edney VI, 807
Cochin, Jacob VI, 807
Cochran, ??? III, 73
Cochran, Alexander VI, 805
Cochran, Ann VI, 378
Cochran, Ann Elizabeth VI, 378
Cochran, Anna VI, 378
Cochran, Anna VI, 459
Cochran, Anna VI, 460
Cochran, Carrie A. VI, 378
Cochran, Carrie Alice VI, 378
Cochran, Dr. Frederick VI, 378
Cochran, Dr. Hiram W. VI, 378
Cochran, Emma A. III, 73
Cochran, Etha VI, 378
Cochran, Etha B. VI, 377
Cochran, Etha B. VI, 378
Cochran, Etha Brown VI, 377
Cochran, Etta B. VI, 378
Cochran, Fred A. VI, 366
Cochran, Frederick A. VI, 377
Cochran, Frederick A. VI, 378
Cochran, Frederick A. VI, 460
Cochran, Frederick A., Jr. VI, 377
Cochran, Frederick A., Jr. VI, 378
Cochran, Frederick Augustus, Sr. VI, 378
Cochran, Gladys Virginia VI, 378
Cochran, Henry Firter III, 73
Cochran, Hiram VI, 378
Cochran, Hiram VI, 460
Cochran, Hiran W. VI, 378
Cochran, Hollis IV, 1274
Cochran, Jane H. F. III, 73
Cochran, John A. IV, 189
Cochran, Lucy IV, 189
Cochran, Lucy May VI, 631
Cochran, Lucy May VI, 712
Cochran, Mary VI, 378
Cochran, Mary Elizabeth IV, 1037
Cochran, Mary Elizabeth VI, 377
Cochran, Mary Elizabeth VI, 378
Cochran, Mary L. IV, 189
Cochran, Mary S. VI, 378
Cochran, Mary Susan VI, 378
Cochran, Mary Susan VI, 460
Cochran, Maud IV, 941
Cochran, Susie IV, 1037
Cochran, Wallace L. III, 73
Cochran, Willard IV, 941
Cochran, Wm. H. III, 73

Cochrane, ??? III, 73
Cochrane, Ella Victoria III, 73
Cochrane, Emma A. III, 73
Cochrane, Florence L. III, 73
Cochrane, Florence Louise III, 73
Cochrane, Gladys III, 73
Cochrane, Henry Firter III, 73
Cochrane, Ira Lee III, 73
Cochrane, Jane H. F. III, 73
Cochrane, Vincent III, 73
Cochrane, Wallace L. III, 73
Cochrane, Wm. H. III, 73
Cochrel, Benjamin D. IV, 1248
Cochrel, John IV, 1248
Cochrel, Rose IV, 1248
Cochrine, Cornelius VI, 357
Cock, ??? III, 74
Cock, Abigail III, 401
Cock, Abigail III, 402
Cock, Abigail III, 403
Cock, Abigail III, 458
Cock, Abraham III, 74
Cock, Abraham III, 117
Cock, Abraham III, 292
Cock, Abraham III, 378
Cock, Abraham III, 379
Cock, Abraham III, 380
Cock, Abraham III, 385
Cock, Abraham III, 388
Cock, Abraham III, 401
Cock, Abram III, 400
Cock, Ada IV, 80
Cock, Ada B. II, 850
Cock, Ada B. II, 873
Cock, Adam III, 74
Cock, Adonijah III, 73
Cock, Albert L. III, 403
Cock, Alexander W. III, 378
Cock, Alfred III, 399
Cock, Alfred III, 457
Cock, Alfred III, 459
Cock, Alice III, 73
Cock, Alice III, 74
Cock, Alice III, 112
Cock, Allen S. III, 402
Cock, Alonzo VI, 797
Cock, Alva IV, 581
Cock, Amanda VI, 631
Cock, Ambrose III, 73
Cock, Ambrose III, 400
Cock, Amelia III, 402
Cock, Amelia III, 403
Cock, Amey III, 74
Cock, Amey III, 399
Cock, Amos III, 402
Cock, Amy III, 73
Cock, Amy III, 74
Cock, Amy III, 75
Cock, Amy III, 378
Cock, Amy III, 384
Cock, Amy III, 401
Cock, Amy III, 456
Cock, Andrew III, 73
Cock, Andrew III, 75
Cock, Andrew III, 76
Cock, Andrew III, 318
Cock, Andrew III, 340
Cock, Andrew III, 378
Cock, Andrew III, 379
Cock, Andrew III, 399
Cock, Andrew III, 452
Cock, Andrew III, 453
Cock, Andrew L. III, 74
Cock, Ann III, 74
Cock, Ann III, 75
Cock, Ann III, 399
Cock, Ann III, 400
Cock, Ann III, 401
Cock, Ann III, 402
Cock, Ann III, 452
Cock, Ann III, 453
Cock, Ann III, 465
Cock, Ann Augusta III, 74
Cock, Ann Augusta III, 75
Cock, Ann Augusta III, 358
Cock, Ann Elizabeth III, 400
Cock, Anna III, 74
Cock, Anna III, 76
Cock, Anna III, 399
Cock, Anna III, 403
Cock, Anne III, 73
Cock, Anne III, 398
Cock, Anne III, 400
Cock, Anne III, 401
Cock, Anne III, 402
Cock, Anne III, 403
Cock, Anne III, 404
Cock, Anne III, 410
Cock, Anne III, 413
Cock, Anne III, 435
Cock, Archiblad VI, 807
Cock, Arthur M. III, 74
Cock, Arthur M. III, 75
Cock, Aug C. III, 455
Cock, Augustus G. III, 399
Cock, Benj. Embree Hicks III, 74
Cock, Benjamin III, 74
Cock, Benjamin III, 378
Cock, Benjamin III, 379
Cock, Benjamin III, 384
Cock, Benjamin III, 399
Cock, Benjamin III, 400
Cock, Benjamin III, 401
Cock, Benjamin III, 402
Cock, Benjamin III, 412
Cock, Benjamin III, 423
Cock, Benjamin III, 438
Cock, Benjamin III, 461
Cock, Benjamin E. III, 400
Cock, Benjamin F. III, 400
Cock, Benjamin H. III, 74
Cock, Benjamin Hicks III, 74
Cock, Benjamin T. III, 459
Cock, Benson IV, 80
Cock, Boler VI, 802
Cock, Boler VI, 807
Cock, Boler VI, 824
Cock, Caroline R. III, 403
Cock, Catharine III, 400
Cock, Catharine III, 461
Cock, Catharine VI, 799
Cock, Catharine VI, 807
Cock, Catharine H. VI, 807
Cock, Charity III, 74
Cock, Charity III, 75
Cock, Charles III, 74
Cock, Charles III, 75
Cock, Charles W. III, 378
Cock, Charles W. III, 379
Cock, Charlotte III, 73
Cock, Charlotte III, 75
Cock, Charlotte III, 178
Cock, Charlotte VI, 797
Cock, Chastain VI, 807
Cock, Clark III, 400
Cock, Clark III, 402
Cock, Clarke III, 432
Cock, Clemence III, 403
Cock, Clemence III, 410
Cock, Coleman B. VI, 807
Cock, Coles Feke III, 401
Cock, Daniel III, 74
Cock, Daniel III, 75
Cock, Daniel III, 399
Cock, Daniel III, 400
Cock, Daniel III, 401
Cock, Daniel III, 402
Cock, Daniel III, 403
Cock, Daniel III, 404
Cock, Daniel III, 441
Cock, Daniel III, 449
Cock, Daniel III, 456
Cock, Daniel III, 457
Cock, Daniel III, 461
Cock, Daniel D. III, 401
Cock, Daniel F. III, 75
Cock, Daniel F. III, 400
Cock, Daniel F. III, 426
Cock, Daniel T. III, 73
Cock, David III, 75
Cock, David III, 400
Cock, David III, 401
Cock, David III, 402
Cock, David III, 453
Cock, Deborah III, 74
Cock, Deborah III, 400
Cock, Deborah III, 401
Cock, Deborah III, 402
Cock, Deborah III, 405
Cock, Deliverance III, 74
Cock, Della III, 74
Cock, Dinah III, 398
Cock, Dinah III, 399
Cock, Dinah III, 400
Cock, Dinah III, 401
Cock, Dinah III, 402
Cock, Dinah III, 403
Cock, Dinah III, 411
Cock, Dinah III, 420
Cock, Dorothy III, 75
Cock, Dorothy III, 400
Cock, Dorothy III, 401
Cock, Dorothy III, 402
Cock, Dorothy III, 414
Cock, Dr. Thomas III, 75
Cock, Drury VI, 807
Cock, Edmund III, 74
Cock, Edward III, 73
Cock, Edward McD. III, 400
Cock, Effingham III, 73
Cock, Effingham III, 74
Cock, Effingham III, 75
Cock, Effingham III, 112
Cock, Effingham III, 239
Cock, Effingham III, 378
Cock, Effingham Moses III, 74
Cock, Elijah III, 74
Cock, Elijah III, 321
Cock, Elijah III, 401
Cock, Elisha IV, 482
Cock, Eliz. III, 74
Cock, Eliz. III, 248
Cock, Eliz. F. III, 358
Cock, Eliz. T. III, 42
Cock, Eliza III, 74
Cock, Eliza VI, 807
Cock, Eliza H. III, 75
Cock, Eliza T. III, 248
Cock, Elizabeth III, 31
Cock, Elizabeth III, 74
Cock, Elizabeth III, 75
Cock, Elizabeth III, 76
Cock, Elizabeth III, 147
Cock, Elizabeth III, 400
Cock, Elizabeth III, 401
Cock, Elizabeth III, 402
Cock, Elizabeth III, 403
Cock, Elizabeth III, 405
Cock, Elizabeth III, 410
Cock, Elizabeth III, 432
Cock, Elizabeth III, 433
Cock, Elizabeth III, 439
Cock, Elizabeth III, 440
Cock, Elizabeth III, 443
Cock, Elizabeth III, 449
Cock, Elizabeth III, 451
Cock, Elizabeth III, 455
Cock, Elizabeth III, 456
Cock, Elizabeth III, 457
Cock, Elizabeth IV, 80
Cock, Elizabeth IV, 102
Cock, Elizabeth VI, 164
Cock, Elizabeth VI, 828
Cock, Elizabeth VI, 1001
Cock, Elizabeth C. III, 402
Cock, Elizabeth H. III, 76
Cock, Elizabeth H. III, 401
Cock, Elizabeth H. III, 403
Cock, Elizabeth L. III, 74
Cock, Elizabeth M. III, 74
Cock, Elizabeth M. III, 300
Cock, Elizabeth M. III, 400
Cock, Elizabeth M. VI, 807
Cock, Elizabeth T. III, 75
Cock, Elizabeth T. III, 378
Cock, Elizabeth T. III, 385
Cock, Ellen M. III, 403
Cock, Emeliza III, 400
Cock, Emeliza III, 458
Cock, Emiline I. VI, 856
Cock, Emily III, 75
Cock, Emily L. III, 42
Cock, Emily L. III, 74
Cock, Emmor VI, 631
Cock, Esther III, 75
Cock, Esther III, 76
Cock, Esther III, 400
Cock, Esther III, 411
Cock, Esther III, 417
Cock, Esther C. III, 75
Cock, Esther E. III, 284
Cock, Eugenie P. III, 400
Cock, Eugenie P. III, 458
Cock, Fannie III, 399
Cock, Fanny III, 400
Cock, Fanny III, 401
Cock, Fanny III, 402
Cock, Florence Eliz. III, 401
Cock, Frances VI, 807
Cock, Frances E. H. VI, 802
Cock, Frances S. III, 400
Cock, Frederick III, 417
Cock, Frederick E. III, 74
Cock, Frederick E. III, 400
Cock, Frederick H. III, 401
Cock, Freelove III, 75
Cock, Freelove III, 400
Cock, Freelove III, 402
Cock, G. Embree Hicks III, 74
Cock, Geo. E. III, 74
Cock, Geo. E. III, 300
Cock, Geo. Wm. III, 400
Cock, George III, 74
Cock, George III, 378
Cock, George III, 401
Cock, George VI, 817
Cock, George VI, 828
Cock, George VI, 833
Cock, George VI, 920
Cock, George VI, 945
Cock, George B. II, 850
Cock, George D. IV, 80
Cock, George E. III, 74
Cock, George E. III, 378
Cock, George E. III, 400
Cock, George E. III, 419
Cock, George Embree III, 400
Cock, George Embree Hicks III, 74
Cock, George H. III, 74
Cock, George H. III, 164
Cock, George Hicks III, 74
Cock, George Townsend III, 76
Cock, George W. VI, 797
Cock, George W. VI, 807
Cock, Goerge VI, 1001
Cock, Hallie Olive IV, 581
Cock, Hannah III, 74
Cock, Hannah III, 75
Cock, Hannah III, 76
Cock, Hannah III, 99
Cock, Hannah III, 116
Cock, Hannah III, 378
Cock, Hannah III, 384
Cock, Hannah III, 400
Cock, Hannah III, 401
Cock, Hannah III, 402
Cock, Hannah III, 403
Cock, Hannah III, 404
Cock, Hannah III, 410
Cock, Hannah III, 423
Cock, Hannah III, 438
Cock, Hannah III, 439
Cock, Hannah III, 440
Cock, Hannah III, 461
Cock, Harriet III, 73
Cock, Harriet III, 74
Cock, Harriet III, 112
Cock, Harriet H. III, 239
Cock, Henry III, 73
Cock, Henry III, 74
Cock, Henry III, 75
Cock, Henry III, 76
Cock, Henry III, 116
Cock, Henry III, 288
Cock, Henry III, 395
Cock, Henry III, 396
Cock, Henry III, 399
Cock, Henry III, 400
Cock, Henry III, 401
Cock, Henry III, 402
Cock, Henry III, 403
Cock, Henry III, 410
Cock, Henry III, 432
Cock, Henry III, 439
Cock, Henry III, 440
Cock, Henry III, 456
Cock, Henry III, 457
Cock, Henry A. III, 400
Cock, Hezekiah III, 75
Cock, Hezekiah III, 400
Cock, Hezekiah III, 401
Cock, Ida III, 403
Cock, Ida E. III, 403
Cock, Isaac III, 74
Cock, Isaac III, 75
Cock, Isaac III, 76
Cock, Isaac III, 378
Cock, Isaac III, 400
Cock, Isaac III, 401
Cock, Isaac III, 402
Cock, Isaac III, 443
Cock, Isaac H. III, 401
Cock, Isaac H. III, 403
Cock, Isaac H. III, 417
Cock, Isaac Hicks III, 401
Cock, Isaac Hicks III, 403
Cock, Isaac S. III, 458
Cock, Israel III, 75
Cock, Israel III, 402
Cock, Jacob III, 74
Cock, Jacob III, 401
Cock, James III, 75
Cock, James III, 99
Cock, James III, 116
Cock, James III, 126
Cock, James III, 400
Cock, James III, 401
Cock, James III, 402
Cock, James III, 410
Cock, James III, 414
Cock, James III, 450
Cock, James IV, 80
Cock, Jane III, 75
Cock, Jane III, 400
Cock, Jane III, 426
Cock, Jane VI, 807
Cock, Jane M. III, 74
Cock, Jane M. III, 75
Cock, Janette III, 75
Cock, Jannette III, 400
Cock, Jemima III, 400
Cock, Jemima III, 402
Cock, Jemima III, 433
Cock, Jemima S. III, 402
Cock, Jemimah VI, 920
Cock, Jerusha S. III, 402
Cock, Jesse III, 75
Cock, Jessie F. III, 403
Cock, Jessie W. III, 401
Cock, Job III, 402
Cock, John III, 73
Cock, John III, 74
Cock, John III, 75
Cock, John III, 400
Cock, John III, 401
Cock, John III, 402
Cock, John III, 440
Cock, John III, 459
Cock, John IV, 79
Cock, John IV, 80
Cock, John VI, 807
Cock, John VI, 830
Cock, John VI, 945
Cock, John L. III, 73
Cock, John L. III, 75
Cock, John, Jr. IV, 80
Cock, Jordan W. III, 378
Cock, Joseph III, 74
Cock, Joseph S. III, 75
Cock, Joseph W. VI, 802
Cock, Joshua III, 75
Cock, Joshua III, 147
Cock, Joshua III, 400
Cock, Joshua III, 402
Cock, Joshua III, 410
Cock, Josiah III, 75
Cock, Josiah III, 401
Cock, Josiah III, 412
Cock, Lanah III, 400
Cock, Lanah III, 402
Cock, Lanah III, 412
Cock, Lanah III, 423
Cock, Lanah III, 461
Cock, Laviner IV, 80
Cock, Lettie VI, 807
Cock, Levine III, 400
Cock, Loretta III, 400
Cock, Loretta III, 401
Cock, Loretta III, 405
Cock, Lydia III, 75
Cock, Lydia III, 400
Cock, Lydia III, 401
Cock, Lydia III, 402
Cock, Lydia III, 453
Cock, Margaret III, 75
Cock, Margaret III, 76
Cock, Margaret III, 402
Cock, Margaret III, 410
Cock, Margaret IV, 80
Cock, Margaret T. III, 400
Cock, Margaretta III, 75
Cock, Maria IV, 80
Cock, Maria IV, 116
Cock, Maria M. III, 74
Cock, Maria M. III, 76
Cock, Maria Margaretta III, 75
Cock, Marianna III, 400
Cock, Marianna III, 459
Cock, Marie Louise III, 401
Cock, Marmaduke Eale Phiany III, 449
Cock, Martha III, 74
Cock, Martha III, 75
Cock, Martha III, 147
Cock, Martha III, 260
Cock, Martha III, 340
Cock, Martha III, 379
Cock, Martha III, 399
Cock, Martha III, 400
Cock, Martha III, 402
Cock, Martha III, 412
Cock, Martha III, 432
Cock, Martha III, 438
Cock, Martha III, 452
Cock, Martha VI, 806
Cock, Martha VI, 807
Cock, Martha T. III, 75
Cock, Martha T. III, 340
Cock, Mary III, 41
Cock, Mary III, 73
Cock, Mary III, 74
Cock, Mary III, 75
Cock, Mary III, 116
Cock, Mary III, 129
Cock, Mary III, 163
Cock, Mary III, 318
Cock, Mary III, 340
Cock, Mary III, 378
Cock, Mary III, 395
Cock, Mary III, 396
Cock, Mary III, 399
Cock, Mary III, 400
Cock, Mary III, 401
Cock, Mary III, 402

ock, Mary III, 403
ock, Mary III, 410
ock, Mary III, 417
ock, Mary III, 440
ock, Mary III, 447
ock, Mary III, 449
ock, Mary III, 450
ock, Mary III, 452
ock, Mary III, 453
ock, Mary III, 456
ock, Mary III, 457
ock, Mary III, 459
ock, Mary III, 461
ock, Mary IV, 80
ock, Mary VI, 807
ock, Mary VI, 851
ock, Mary VI, 945
ock, Mary A. R. VI, 807
ock, Mary Ann III, 400
ock, Mary Ann IV, 482
ock, Mary Augusta III, 378
ock, Mary C. III, 379
ock, Mary C. III, 461
ock, Mary C. IV, 73
ock, Mary C. IV, 80
ock, Mary E. III, 31
ock, Mary E. III, 74
ock, Mary E. III, 378
ock, Mary E. III, 381
ock, Mary Elizabeth III, 401
ock, Mary F. VI, 807
ock, Mary H. III, 74
ck, Mary H. III, 400
ock, Mary H. III, 403
ock, Mary L. III, 401
ock, Mary M. II, 850
ck, Mary M. III, 74
ock, Mary M. III, 75
ock, Mary M. III, 300
ock, Mary M. III, 400
ock, Mary M. III, 419
ck, Mary T. III, 401
ock, Mary W. III, 403
ock, Mary W. III, 417
ock, Matilda K. III, 400
ock, Meriba III, 75
ock, Miriam II, 211
ock, Miriam II, 240
ock, Nancy VI, 831
ock, Noah III, 402
ock, Penelope III, 402
ock, Peter III, 400
ock, Phebe III, 73
ock, Phebe III, 74
ock, Phebe III, 75
ock, Phebe III, 76
ock, Phebe III, 178
ock, Phebe III, 378
ck, Phebe III, 399
ck, Phebe III, 400
ck, Phebe III, 401
ck, Phebe III, 402
ck, Phebe III, 450
ck, Phebe III, 456
ck, Phebe Ann III, 399
ck, Phebe Anna III, 74
ck, Phebe Anna III, 75
ck, Phebe Anna III, 238
ock, Phebe Anna III, 239
ck, Phebe T. III, 402
ck, Phiany III, 402
ock, Polly VI, 807
ck, Rachel III, 73
ck, Rachel III, 74
ck, Rachel III, 399
ock, Rachel IV, 79
ock, Rachel IV, 80
ock, Rebecca III, 401
ck, Rebecca III, 402
ck, Rebecca III, 403
ck, Rebecca III, 412
ck, Rebecca III, 459
ock, Rebecca VI, 833
ck, Rebeckah VI, 838
ck, Rees III, 73
ck, Rees III, 401
ck, Rees III, 402
ock, Rees III, 439
ck, Rhoda III, 401
ck, Richard III, 75
ck, Richard III, 401
ck, Richard III, 402
ck, Richard III, 403
ck, Richard III, 458
ck, Richard III, 459
ck, Richard VI, 807
ck, Richard, Sr. VI, 807
ock, Robert III, 402
ock, Robert IV, 80
ck, Robert E. III, 378
ck, Robert W. III, 456
Cock, Rosanna III, 75
Cock, Rosannah III, 75
Cock, Rosannah III, 400
Cock, Rosannah III, 401
Cock, Roseannah III, 400
Cock, Roseannah III, 402
Cock, Roseannah III, 403
Cock, Roseannah III, 449
Cock, Roseannah III, 457
Cock, Sally VI, 802
Cock, Samuel III, 75
Cock, Samuel III, 260
Cock, Samuel III, 399
Cock, Samuel III, 400
Cock, Samuel III, 401
Cock, Samuel III, 402
Cock, Samuel III, 403
Cock, Samuel III, 404
Cock, Samuel III, 405
Cock, Samuel III, 433
Cock, Samuel III, 438
Cock, Samuel III, 449
Cock, Samuel III, 451
Cock, Samuel III, 452
Cock, Samuel Cock III, 402
Cock, Sarah III, 73
Cock, Sarah III, 74
Cock, Sarah III, 75
Cock, Sarah III, 76
Cock, Sarah III, 99
Cock, Sarah III, 117
Cock, Sarah III, 126
Cock, Sarah III, 288
Cock, Sarah III, 317
Cock, Sarah III, 378
Cock, Sarah III, 379
Cock, Sarah III, 380
Cock, Sarah III, 389
Cock, Sarah III, 400
Cock, Sarah III, 401
Cock, Sarah III, 402
Cock, Sarah III, 403
Cock, Sarah III, 404
Cock, Sarah III, 406
Cock, Sarah III, 414
Cock, Sarah III, 416
Cock, Sarah III, 427
Cock, Sarah III, 440
Cock, Sarah III, 441
Cock, Sarah III, 459
Cock, Sarah VI, 830
Cock, Sarah Ann III, 75
Cock, Sarah Ann IV, 80
Cock, Sarah Emma III, 378
Cock, Sarah Frances III, 178
Cock, Silas III, 400
Cock, Silas III, 402
Cock, Stephen III, 73
Cock, Stephen III, 74
Cock, Stephen III, 75
Cock, Stephen III, 178
Cock, Stephen III, 411
Cock, Stephen III, 412
Cock, Stone III, 402
Cock, Susan III, 117
Cock, Susan III, 292
Cock, Susan III, 378
Cock, Susan III, 379
Cock, Susan III, 380
Cock, Susan III, 385
Cock, Susan III, 388
Cock, Susan III, 401
Cock, Susan III, 402
Cock, Susan W. III, 378
Cock, Susan W. III, 389
Cock, Susan W. IV, 80
Cock, Susanna VI, 807
Cock, Susannah III, 400
Cock, Susannah W. VI, 797
Cock, Tabitha VI, 807
Cock, Temperance III, 74
Cock, Temperance III, 321
Cock, Thomas III, 74
Cock, Thomas III, 75
Cock, Thomas III, 76
Cock, Thomas III, 248
Cock, Thomas III, 284
Cock, Thomas III, 401
Cock, Thomas III, 402
Cock, Thomas III, 447
Cock, Thomas VI, 797
Cock, Thomas VI, 799
Cock, Thomas VI, 807
Cock, Thomas VI, 810
Cock, Thomas VI, 831
Cock, Thomas C. VI, 848
Cock, Thomas T. III, 75
Cock, Thomas T. III, 76
Cock, Thomas, Jr. III, 75
Cock, Thos. III, 42
Cock, Thos. III, 74
Cock, Thos. III, 358
Cock, Thos. VI, 799
Cock, Thos., Jr. VI, 806
Cock, Thos., Sr. VI, 807
Cock, Townsend III, 76
Cock, Townsend III, 402
Cock, Townsend III, 410
Cock, Uriah III, 402
Cock, Uriah III, 450
Cock, Wd. Elizabeth III, 399
Cock, Wd. Elizabeth III, 403
Cock, Wd. Rachel III, 75
Cock, William III, 73
Cock, William III, 74
Cock, William III, 76
Cock, William III, 378
Cock, William III, 398
Cock, William III, 399
Cock, William III, 400
Cock, William III, 401
Cock, William III, 402
Cock, William III, 410
Cock, William III, 411
Cock, William III, 420
Cock, William IV, 80
Cock, William VI, 797
Cock, William VI, 802
Cock, William VI, 807
Cock, William VI, 817
Cock, William VI, 830
Cock, William VI, 838
Cock, William E. III, 74
Cock, William E. III, 76
Cock, William E. III, 378
Cock, William E. III, 381
Cock, William E. III, 403
Cock, William E., Jr. III, 378
Cock, William Henry III, 378
Cock, William Howard III, 74
Cock, William J. VI, 807
Cock, William R. III, 75
Cock, William R. III, 76
Cock, William T. III, 401
Cock, William T. III, 402
Cock, William T. III, 403
Cock, William W. III, 401
Cock, William W. III, 403
Cock, William Willets III, 403
Cock, Wm. III, 31
Cock, Wm. III, 420
Cock, Wm. Burling III, 403
Cock, Wm. E. III, 381
Cock, Wm. E. III, 389
Cock, Wm. Embree III, 74
Cock, Wm. W. III, 401
Cock, Zoar III, 399
Cock, Zoar III, 465
Cockayne, Elizabeth IV, 379
Cockburn, James II, 788
Cockburn, James II, 850
Cockburn, Rebecca II, 850
Cockburn, Sarah IV, 121
Cockburn, Sarah IV, 123
Cocke, Amanda VI, 647
Cocke, Drury W. VI, 844
Cocke, John VI, 945
Cocke, Richard VI, 164
Cocke, Thomas VI, 133
Cocke, Thomas VI, 138
Cocke, Thomas VI, 815
Cocke, William VI, 858
Cockerall, Elizabeth VI, 1017
Cockerall, James V, 454
Cockerel, Benjamin D. IV, 1248
Cockerel, John IV, 1248
Cockerel, Rose IV, 1248
Cockerel, Roulber N. IV, 1248
Cockerell, Ina H. V, 665
Cockerell, Ina Hadley V, 665
Cockerell, James V, 454
Cockerell, James V, 665
Cockerell, Mary V. V, 230
Cockerell, Nellie V, 454
Cockerell, Nellie V, 665
Cockerell, Nellie S. V, 665
Cockerell, Phebe V, 230
Cockerell, Phebe V, 265
Cockerham, Huldah Victoria I, 613
Cockerham, Milley VI, 1016
Cockerham, Susanna VI, 1016
Cockerile, Nellie S. V, 695
Cockerill, Ina V, 454
Cockerill, Ina B. V, 454
Cockerill, Ina H. V, 665
Cockerill, James V, 454
Cockerill, Mary V, 454
Cockerill, Mary V. V, 230
Cockerill, Mary V. V, 243
Cockerill, Nellie V, 454
Cockerill, Sarah V, 454
Cockerill, Walter V, 454
Cockfeld, Elizabeth II, 490
Cockfield, Elizabeth II, 348
Cockfield, Elizabeth II, 490
Cockfield, Hannah II, 348
Cockfield, Hannah II, 490
Cockfield, Hannah II, 599
Cockfield, Joshua II, 348
Cockfield, Joshua II, 490
Cockfield, Joshua II, 599
Cockfield, Mary II, 348
Cocking, Mary II, 490
Cocking, Mary II, 657
Cockitt, Richard II, 442
Cockran, Elizabeth VI, 903
Cockran, Samuel VI, 903
Cockrane, Janet VI, 902
Cockrane, Mary VI, 902
Cockrane, Samuel VI, 902
Cockrell, Jesse VI, 736
Cockrell, Jesse VI, 745
Cockrell, Kezia VI, 631
Cockrell, Kezia VI, 657
Cockrell, Margaret VI, 631
Cockrell, Mary Elizabeth VI, 736
Cockrell, Mary Elizabeth VI, 745
Cockrell, Mary Estella VI, 736
Cockrell, Mary Estella VI, 745
Cockrell, Phebe V, 230
Cockrill, Daniel VI, 610
Cockrill, James V, 454
Cockrill, Nellie V, 454
Cockrill, Walter V, 454
Cockrille, Margaret VI, 622
Cockrille, Margaret VI, 628
Cockrille, Margaret VI, 631
Cockrom, Samuel II, 348
Cocks, Abigail III, 401
Cocks, Abraham II, 989
Cocks, Abraham II, 1040
Cocks, Armenia III, 76
Cocks, Armenia III, 154
Cocks, Caroline R. III, 417
Cocks, David III, 464
Cocks, Eliz. H. III, 449
Cocks, Elizabeth I, 1028
Cocks, Elizabeth I, 1038
Cocks, Elizabeth III, 76
Cocks, Elizabeth III, 347
Cocks, Elizabeth H. III, 449
Cocks, Florence Eliz. III, 401
Cocks, Florence Elizabeth III, 468
Cocks, Florence Elizabeth III, 469
Cocks, Frances S. III, 404
Cocks, G. W. III, 423
Cocks, Geo. III, 404
Cocks, George III, 347
Cocks, George H. III, 48
Cocks, George H. III, 76
Cocks, George W. III, 391
Cocks, Harriet III, 76
Cocks, Isaac I, 535
Cocks, Isaac III, 401
Cocks, Isaac III, 450
Cocks, Isaac H. III, 449
Cocks, Isaac H. III, 469
Cocks, Isaac H. III, 470
Cocks, Isaac H. III, 472
Cocks, Isaac Hicks III, 401
Cocks, Isaac Hicks III, 468
Cocks, Jehu I, 535
Cocks, Jemima I, 45
Cocks, Jemima I, 50
Cocks, Jemima I, 97
Cocks, Jeremiah I, 97
Cocks, Jessie F. III, 475
Cocks, Jessie W. III, 401
Cocks, John I, 45
Cocks, John I, 50
Cocks, John I, 97
Cocks, John III, 76
Cocks, John III, 154
Cocks, Joseph I, 97
Cocks, Josiah I, 137
Cocks, Lydia III, 464
Cocks, Mary II, 350
Cocks, Mary III, 48
Cocks, Mary III, 76
Cocks, Mary Eliz. III, 450
Cocks, Mary Elizabeth III, 401
Cocks, Mary M. III, 347
Cocks, Mary T. III, 470
Cocks, Mary T. III, 472
Cocks, Mary W. III, 76
Cocks, Mary W. III, 418
Cocks, Mary W. III, 449
Cocks, Matilda K. III, 404
Cocks, Miriam I, 97
Cocks, Miriam I, 137
Cocks, Phebe III, 76
Cocks, Phebe C. III, 76
Cocks, Phebe C. III, 154
Cocks, Phebe T. III, 464
Cocks, Richard II, 350
Cocks, Richard III, 401
Cocks, Robert III, 76
Cocks, Rowland III, 76
Cocks, Rowland III, 347
Cocks, Sarah I, 137
Cocks, Sarah III, 44
Cocks, Sarah III, 76
Cocks, Thomas II, 350
Cocks, Townsend III, 76
Cocks, William III, 44
Cocks, William III, 76
Cocks, William Willets III, 417
Cocks, William Willets III, 475
Cocks, Wm. W. III, 401
Cockshall, Jonathan II, 574
Cockshall, Martha II, 574
Cockshaw, Jonathan II, 348
Cockshaw, Martha II, 348
Coddington, ??? III, 75
Coddington, ??? III, 92
Coddington, Margaret III, 75
Coddington, Margaret III, 76
Coddington, Margaret III, 92
Coddington, Mary II, 348
Coddington, Mary III, 76
Coddington, Rich'd III, 76
Coddington, Thomas II, 348
Coddington, William II, 348
Codwise, Mildred VI, 417
Coe, Amelia II, 117
Coe, Amelia II, 348
Coe, Amelia II, 490
Coe, Ann II, 170
Coe, Anna II, 117
Coe, Anna II, 121
Coe, Anna II, 348
Coe, Anna II, 490
Coe, Anna II, 538
Coe, Celeste IV, 1310
Coe, Elizabeth II, 203
Coe, Elizabeth II, 208
Coe, Elizabeth II, 348
Coe, Elizabeth II, 490
Coe, Esther II, 170
Coe, Esther II, 208
Coe, Esther II, 490
Coe, Hannah II, 208
Coe, Hannah II, 251
Coe, Hannah II, 490
Coe, Isabella IV, 962
Coe, James Guest II, 348
Coe, James Guest II, 490
Coe, Jane II, 170
Coe, Jane II, 203
Coe, Jane II, 208
Coe, Jane II, 236
Coe, Jane II, 251
Coe, Jane II, 267
Coe, Jane II, 490
Coe, Jane II, 538
Coe, Jean II, 348
Coe, Joseph II, 208
Coe, Joseph II, 490
Coe, Lydia P. I, 328
Coe, Lydia P. I, 329
Coe, Mary II, 208
Coe, Mary II, 236
Coe, Mary II, 348
Coe, Mary II, 490
Coe, Rebecca II, 117
Coe, Rebecca II, 124
Coe, Rebecca II, 208
Coe, Rebecca II, 348
Coe, Rebecca II, 490
Coe, Richard II, 348
Coe, Richard II, 490
Coe, Robert II, 170
Coe, Robert II, 203
Coe, Robert II, 208
Coe, Robert II, 236
Coe, Robert II, 251
Coe, Robert II, 267
Coe, Robert II, 348
Coe, Robert II, 490
Coe, Robert II, 538
Coe, Robert, Jr. II, 490
Coe, Robert, Jr. II, 538
Coe, Samuel II, 208
Coe, Samuel II, 490
Coe, Samuel C. II, 490
Coe, Samuel E. II, 208
Coe, Samuel E. II, 490
Coe, Samuel E. II, 733
Coe, Samuel Emlen II, 701
Coe, Timothy VI, 11
Coe, Wd. Jane II, 170

Coe, Wd. Sara VI, 11
Coe, William II, 208
Coe, Wm. II, 490
Coeburn, Joseph II, 490
Coeburn, Prudence II, 490
Coep, Joshua IV, 153
Coep, Rebecca IV, 153
Coer, Bertha III, 501
Cofee, Alice IV, 352
Cofee, John IV, 352
Cofee, Mary IV, 352
Cofeild, Martha VI, 45
Cofer, Abraham VI, 895
Cofer, Amanda H. VI, 948
Cofer, Ann Eliza VI, 895
Cofer, Barshaba VI, 895
Cofer, Catharine L. VI, 990
Cofer, Elizabeth VI, 900
Cofer, Elizabeth VI, 1017
Cofer, Frances VI, 894
Cofer, George VI, 876
Cofer, George VI, 894
Cofer, George VI, 895
Cofer, George VI, 990
Cofer, Hope VI, 894
Cofer, J. M. VI, 872
Cofer, J. M. VI, 915
Cofer, Jacob VI, 894
Cofer, Jacob VI, 895
Cofer, Jacob VI, 941
Cofer, Jacob VI, 1017
Cofer, James M. VI, 947
Cofer, James M. VI, 988
Cofer, Jenny VI, 894
Cofer, Jesse VI, 894
Cofer, Jesse VI, 900
Cofer, Jesse VI, 987
Cofer, John VI, 895
Cofer, John VI, 909
Cofer, John C. VI, 895
Cofer, John C. VI, 914
Cofer, Joseph VI, 894
Cofer, Joseph VI, 903
Cofer, Joseph VI, 907
Cofer, Josiah H. VI, 941
Cofer, Julia VI, 58
Cofer, Julia VI, 68
Cofer, Lucreti E. VI, 895
Cofer, Lucy H. VI, 914
Cofer, Mary VI, 941
Cofer, Mary A. VI, 895
Cofer, Mary S. VI, 987
Cofer, Nancy VI, 895
Cofer, Pleasant D. VI, 876
Cofer, Pleasant D. VI, 895
Cofer, Sarah VI, 894
Cofer, Sarah A. VI, 876
Cofer, Sarah B. VI, 895
Cofer, Sophia A. VI, 895
Cofer, Thomas VI, 895
Cofer, Thos. VI, 903
Cofere, J. M. VI, 876
Coffe, Tacy IV, 1025
Coffe, Tacy H. IV, 1025
Coffee, ??? VI, 348
Coffee, Abner VI, 816
Coffee, Abner VI, 961
Coffee, Abner VI, 1005
Coffee, Alice IV, 324
Coffee, Alice IV, 332
Coffee, Alice IV, 379
Coffee, Amelia A. VI, 894
Coffee, Ann IV, 325
Coffee, Ann VI, 378
Coffee, Anne VI, 455
Coffee, Banister VI, 816
Coffee, Banister VI, 894
Coffee, Betsey IV, 324
Coffee, Betsey IV, 352
Coffee, Betsey V, 40
Coffee, Betsy IV, 379
Coffee, Betsy IV, 690
Coffee, Betsy IV, 691
Coffee, Betty IV, 325
Coffee, Celina E. VI, 1005
Coffee, Charles IV, 142
Coffee, Charles IV, 691
Coffee, Charles VI, 350
Coffee, Charles W. IV, 325
Coffee, Charles W. IV, 691
Coffee, Charles W. V, 40
Coffee, Charles William V, 40
Coffee, Delaney VI, 961
Coffee, Eliza IV, 325
Coffee, Eliza IV, 379
Coffee, Eliza Ann VI, 894
Coffee, Elizabeth V, 40
Coffee, Elizabeth VI, 305
Coffee, Elizabeth VI, 894
Coffee, Elizabeth F. II, 850
Coffee, George F. II, 850
Coffee, George F. III, 76
Coffee, Grace II, 490
Coffee, Grace II, 505
Coffee, Grace II, 850
Coffee, Grace II, 855
Coffee, Grace III, 76
Coffee, Holcomb L. VI, 894
Coffee, Holcombe L. VI, 919
Coffee, Holcombe L. VI, 961
Coffee, Holcum L. VI, 1005
Coffee, Isaac IV, 142
Coffee, Isaac IV, 324
Coffee, Isaac IV, 325
Coffee, Isaac IV, 352
Coffee, Isaac IV, 379
Coffee, Isaac IV, 690
Coffee, Isaac IV, 691
Coffee, Isaac V, 40
Coffee, Isaac VI, 350
Coffee, James II, 348
Coffee, James II, 490
Coffee, Jesse VI, 894
Coffee, John IV, 142
Coffee, John IV, 324
Coffee, John IV, 332
Coffee, John IV, 334
Coffee, John IV, 379
Coffee, John IV, 433
Coffee, John IV, 627
Coffee, John IV, 691
Coffee, John VI, 305
Coffee, John VI, 309
Coffee, John VI, 350
Coffee, John VI, 355
Coffee, John VI, 378
Coffee, John VI, 483
Coffee, John VI, 490
Coffee, John S. IV, 325
Coffee, John S. IV, 379
Coffee, John, Jr. VI, 483
Coffee, John, Jr. VI, 544
Coffee, Jonathan II, 850
Coffee, Jonathan IV, 325
Coffee, Jonathan IV, 691
Coffee, Jonathan IV, 725
Coffee, Jonathan W. IV, 691
Coffee, Joseph IV, 142
Coffee, Joseph IV, 324
Coffee, Joseph VI, 305
Coffee, Joseph VI, 350
Coffee, Joshua H. VI, 885
Coffee, Legan L. VI, 988
Coffee, Lemuel VI, 874
Coffee, Lemuel VI, 900
Coffee, Lenis VI, 816
Coffee, Lewis Fussell II, 850
Coffee, Lydia S. IV, 324
Coffee, Lydia S. IV, 332
Coffee, Lydia S. IV, 379
Coffee, Mareb IV, 142
Coffee, Mareb IV, 627
Coffee, Mary II, 348
Coffee, Mary IV, 142
Coffee, Mary IV, 324
Coffee, Mary VI, 305
Coffee, Mary VI, 350
Coffee, Mary Ann IV, 325
Coffee, Mary Ann IV, 379
Coffee, Mary Atmore II, 850
Coffee, Mary Attmore II, 850
Coffee, Mary J. VI, 885
Coffee, Merab IV, 212
Coffee, Merab IV, 324
Coffee, Merab IV, 334
Coffee, Merab VI, 350
Coffee, Polly VI, 894
Coffee, Priscilla IV, 691
Coffee, Priscilla W. IV, 725
Coffee, Purnell W. VI, 894
Coffee, Rachel IV, 142
Coffee, Rachel IV, 324
Coffee, Rachel IV, 325
Coffee, Rachel IV, 334
Coffee, Rachel IV, 433
Coffee, Rachel IV, 531
Coffee, Rachel IV, 533
Coffee, Rachel IV, 627
Coffee, Rachel IV, 691
Coffee, Rachel VI, 305
Coffee, Rachel VI, 350
Coffee, Rachel VI, 378
Coffee, Rachel VI, 483
Coffee, Rachel A. IV, 379
Coffee, Rachel Ann IV, 691
Coffee, Rachel Ann V, 40
Coffee, Rachel, Jr. VI, 544
Coffee, Ruth IV, 142
Coffee, Ruth IV, 379
Coffee, Ruth IV, 433
Coffee, Ruth IV, 841
Coffee, Ruth VI, 350
Coffee, Ruthy VI, 894
Coffee, Tacy IV, 1025
Coffee, Tacy IV, 1027
Coffee, Thomas III, 76
Coffee, Thomas A. III, 76
Coffee, Thomas Elwood IV, 325
Coffee, Thomas Elwood IV, 379
Coffee, Thos. Atmore II, 850
Coffee, Thos. Attmore II, 850
Coffee, William IV, 324
Coffee, William IV, 325
Coffee, William IV, 379
Coffee, William VI, 305
Coffee, William VI, 350
Coffee, William VI, 378
Coffee, William VI, 455
Coffee, William VI, 483
Coffee, William H. II, 701
Coffee, Wm. II, 850
Coffee, Wm. IV, 142
Coffelt, Addie V, 158
Coffelt, Charles W. V, 158
Coffelt, Chas. W. V, 158
Coffelt, Cora May V, 158
Coffelt, Elizabeth A. V, 158
Coffelt, Floy E. V, 158
Coffelt, Frances L. V, 158
Coffelt, Frank V, 158
Coffelt, George V, 158
Coffelt, John V, 158
Coffelt, John Freeman V, 158
Coffelt, Julia A. V, 158
Coffelt, Julia Ann V, 158
Coffen, Mary II, 490
Coffen, Mary II, 675
Coffer, George VI, 886
Coffer, Josiah VI, 886
Coffer, Susanna VI, 886
Coffery, Charles VI, 820
Coffery, Sarah VI, 827
Coffett, Charles W. V, 158
Coffey, John IV, 336
Coffey, Rachel IV, 324
Coffey, Rachel IV, 336
Coffey, William VI, 305
Coffield, ??? I, 3
Coffield, George Anna I, 3
Coffield, H. Irvin I, 922
Coffield, Mildred I, 922
Coffield, Mildred I, 939
Coffin, ??? V, 315
Coffin, A. V. I, 533
Coffin, Aaron I, 586
Coffin, Aaron I, 587
Coffin, Aaron I, 593
Coffin, Aaron I, 651
Coffin, Aaron I, 676
Coffin, Aaron I, 778
Coffin, Aaron I, 797
Coffin, Aaron I, 804
Coffin, Aaron I, 805
Coffin, Aaron I, 907
Coffin, Aaron I, 911
Coffin, Abel I, 778
Coffin, Abel I, 804
Coffin, Abel I, 805
Coffin, Abel I, 810
Coffin, Abel I, 816
Coffin, Abel I, 907
Coffin, Abel, Jr. I, 805
Coffin, Abigail I, 494
Coffin, Abigail I, 533
Coffin, Abigail I, 588
Coffin, Abigail I, 712
Coffin, Abigail I, 721
Coffin, Abigail I, 741
Coffin, Abigail I, 743
Coffin, Abigail I, 757
Coffin, Abigail I, 778
Coffin, Abigail I, 779
Coffin, Abigail I, 804
Coffin, Abigail I, 805
Coffin, Abigail I, 814
Coffin, Abigail I, 819
Coffin, Abigail I, 826
Coffin, Abigail I, 961
Coffin, Abigail V, 920
Coffin, Abijah I, 494
Coffin, Abijah I, 532
Coffin, Abijah I, 569
Coffin, Abijah I, 778
Coffin, Abijah I, 971
Coffin, Abner I, 533
Coffin, Achsah I, 494
Coffin, Achsah I, 533
Coffin, Achsah I, 549
Coffin, Adaline V, 380
Coffin, Adam I, 797
Coffin, Adam I, 804
Coffin, Adam I, 971
Coffin, Adam I, 983
Coffin, Adam V, 731
Coffin, Adam V, 794
Coffin, Adam V, 899
Coffin, Adam V, 905
Coffin, Addison I, 533
Coffin, Adele III, 76
Coffin, Albert I, 533
Coffin, Albert IV, 189
Coffin, Albert IV, 467
Coffin, Albert IV, 691
Coffin, Albert IV, 807
Coffin, Albert M. IV, 467
Coffin, Albert M. IV, 471
Coffin, Albert M. IV, 500
Coffin, Albert M. IV, 615
Coffin, Albert M. IV, 661
Coffin, Albert M. IV, 691
Coffin, Alberta M. IV, 467
Coffin, Aletha I, 533
Coffin, Aletha I, 676
Coffin, Alex. J. III, 76
Coffin, Alexander J. III, 76
Coffin, Alexander J. III, 77
Coffin, Alexander J. III, 303
Coffin, Alfred I, 494
Coffin, Alfred I, 588
Coffin, Alfred I, 779
Coffin, Alfred I, 805
Coffin, Alfred V. I, 533
Coffin, Alice II, 822
Coffin, Allen I, 587
Coffin, Allen I, 983
Coffin, Alpheus I, 778
Coffin, Alpheus I, 806
Coffin, Alpheus V, 380
Coffin, And. G. III, 354
Coffin, Andrew III, 77
Coffin, Andrew G. III, 76
Coffin, Andrew G. III, 286
Coffin, Andrew G. III, 403
Coffin, Anid I, 983
Coffin, Ann I, 494
Coffin, Ann I, 533
Coffin, Ann I, 555
Coffin, Ann I, 804
Coffin, Ann I, 815
Coffin, Ann III, 77
Coffin, Ann V, 731
Coffin, Anna I, 587
Coffin, Anna I, 588
Coffin, Anna I, 676
Coffin, Anna I, 690
Coffin, Anna I, 797
Coffin, Anna I, 804
Coffin, Anna I, 805
Coffin, Anna I, 911
Coffin, Anna I, 983
Coffin, Anna II, 490
Coffin, Anna II, 788
Coffin, Anna II, 811
Coffin, Anna II, 850
Coffin, Anna III, 76
Coffin, Anna IV, 691
Coffin, Anna IV, 1310
Coffin, Anna V, 324
Coffin, Anna Haldy IV, 1248
Coffin, Annaliza I, 588
Coffin, Anne I, 778
Coffin, Anne V, 322
Coffin, Anne V, 324
Coffin, Aron I, 533
Coffin, Aron I, 552
Coffin, Arthur III, 76
Coffin, Arthur III, 133
Coffin, Avis Anna III, 76
Coffin, Barnabas I, 494
Coffin, Barnabas I, 532
Coffin, Barnabas I, 773
Coffin, Barnabas I, 778
Coffin, Barnabas I, 804
Coffin, Barnabas I, 805
Coffin, Barnabas I, 843
Coffin, Barnabas I, 971
Coffin, Barnabas I, 1016
Coffin, Barnabas I, 1053
Coffin, Barnabas, Jr. I, 778
Coffin, Benj. I, 651
Coffin, Benjamin I, 587
Coffin, Benjamin I, 593
Coffin, Benjamin I, 651
Coffin, Benjamin I, 676
Coffin, Benjamin I, 804
Coffin, Benjamin I, 805
Coffin, Benjamin I, 983
Coffin, Benjamin III, 77
Coffin, Benjamin IV, 471
Coffin, Benjamin V, 40
Coffin, Benjamin V, 731
Coffin, Benjamin V, 899
Coffin, Benjamin Franklin V, 899
Coffin, Bethuel I, 494
Coffin, Bethuel I, 532
Coffin, Bethuel I, 533
Coffin, Bethuel I, 536
Coffin, Bethuel I, 559
Coffin, Bethuel I, 804
Coffin, Beulah I, 494
Coffin, Beulah I, 533
Coffin, Beulah I, 568
Coffin, Beulah I, 805
Coffin, Beulah T. IV, 471
Coffin, Binjamin I, 651
Coffin, Caleb III, 76
Coffin, Caleb III, 202
Coffin, Calvin I, 587
Coffin, Calvin I, 983
Coffin, Caroline V, 380
Coffin, Caroline E. IV, 483
Coffin, Caroline E. V, 899
Coffin, Carrie B. III, 76
Coffin, Carrie B. III, 362
Coffin, Catharine I, 533
Coffin, Catharine I, 559
Coffin, Catharine I, 605
Coffin, Catharine I, 778
Coffin, Catharine I, 805
Coffin, Catharine I, 983
Coffin, Catharine V, 731
Coffin, Catharine V, 899
Coffin, Charles III, 76
Coffin, Charles IV, 189
Coffin, Charles IV, 467
Coffin, Charles IV, 615
Coffin, Charles IV, 807
Coffin, Charles IV, 858
Coffin, Charles B. IV, 467
Coffin, Charles C. IV, 471
Coffin, Charles C. V, 380
Coffin, Charles F. V, 40
Coffin, Charles F. V, 83
Coffin, Charles F. V, 899
Coffin, Charlotte III, 76
Coffin, Chas. IV, 189
Coffin, Chas. IV, 467
Coffin, Chas. IV, 471
Coffin, Chas. IV, 476
Coffin, Chas. V, 899
Coffin, Chas. F. V, 899
Coffin, Christopher V, 899
Coffin, Christopher V, 920
Coffin, Christopher Colger V, 40
Coffin, Clarissa VI, 631
Coffin, Clarissa VI, 666
Coffin, Clarissa VI, 693
Coffin, Cyrene I, 494
Coffin, Cyrene I, 779
Coffin, Cyrene I, 802
Coffin, Cyrene I, 805
Coffin, Cyrus I, 533
Coffin, Cyrus V, 899
Coffin, Cyrus J. III, 76
Coffin, Daniel V, 324
Coffin, Daniel V, 342
Coffin, Daniel V, 380
Coffin, Daniel V, 406
Coffin, Daniel V, 407
Coffin, David I, 779
Coffin, David I, 805
Coffin, David V, 230
Coffin, David V, 256
Coffin, David V, 322
Coffin, David V, 324
Coffin, David V, 350
Coffin, David V, 380
Coffin, David N. Kembel I, 757
Coffin, Deborah I, 494
Coffin, Deborah I, 533
Coffin, Deborah I, 779
Coffin, Deborah I, 804
Coffin, Deborah I, 839
Coffin, Deborah I, 852
Coffin, Deborah I, 875
Coffin, Deborah I, 905
Coffin, Deborah IV, 467
Coffin, Deborah V, 482
Coffin, Deborah V, 505
Coffin, Dinah V, 230
Coffin, Dinah V, 256
Coffin, Dinah V, 324
Coffin, Dinah V, 325
Coffin, Dinah V, 342
Coffin, Dinah V, 365
Coffin, Dinah V, 454
Coffin, Dinah V, 459
Coffin, Duncan C. I, 533
Coffin, Edwin V, 380
Coffin, Eliab III, 76
Coffin, Eliab III, 77
Coffin, Elihu I, 445
Coffin, Elihu I, 494
Coffin, Elihu I, 533
Coffin, Elihu I, 588

offin, Elihu I, 779
offin, Elihu I, 801
offin, Elihu I, 805
offin, Elihue I, 494
offin, Elijah I, 494
offin, Elijah I, 533
offin, Elijah I, 546
offin, Elijah I, 605
offin, Elijah V, 40
offin, Elijah V, 899
offin, Elijah V, 927
offin, Elijah VI, 408
offin, Elisabeth I, 804
offin, Elisabeth I, 820
offin, Elisha I, 494
offin, Elisha I, 532
offin, Elisha I, 533
offin, Elisha I, 743
offin, Elisha I, 757
offin, Eliz. S. III, 354
offin, Eliza I, 983
offin, Eliza I, 997
offin, Eliza III, 120
offin, Eliza V, 40
offin, Eliza V, 324
offin, Eliza V, 380
offin, Eliza V, 407
offin, Eliza V, 899
offin, Eliza V, 906
offin, Eliza V, 939
offin, Eliza VI, 758
offin, Eliza Caroline V, 380
offin, Eliza F. III, 183
offin, Eliza F. VI, 631
offin, Eliza F. VI, 666
offin, Eliza F. VI, 668
offin, Eliza F. VI, 693
offin, Eliza. S. III, 76
offin, Elizabeth I, 375
offin, Elizabeth I, 380
offin, Elizabeth I, 426
offin, Elizabeth I, 494
offin, Elizabeth I, 532
offin, Elizabeth I, 533
offin, Elizabeth I, 569
offin, Elizabeth I, 651
offin, Elizabeth I, 673
offin, Elizabeth I, 676
offin, Elizabeth I, 684
offin, Elizabeth I, 712
offin, Elizabeth I, 715
offin, Elizabeth I, 778
offin, Elizabeth I, 779
offin, Elizabeth I, 804
offin, Elizabeth I, 805
offin, Elizabeth I, 825
offin, Elizabeth I, 852
offin, Elizabeth I, 875
offin, Elizabeth I, 885
offin, Elizabeth I, 889
offin, Elizabeth I, 1001
offin, Elizabeth I, 1008
offin, Elizabeth I, 1010
offin, Elizabeth II, 490
offin, Elizabeth III, 77
offin, Elizabeth III, 286
offin, Elizabeth III, 403
offin, Elizabeth IV, 467
offin, Elizabeth IV, 471
offin, Elizabeth V, 380
offin, Elizabeth V, 439
offin, Elizabeth V, 482
offin, Elizabeth V, 541
offin, Elizabeth V, 731
offin, Elizabeth V, 899
offin, Elizabeth V, 920
offin, Elizabeth E. I, 806
offin, Elizabeth Hosier I, 1008
offin, Elizabeth M. III, 76
offin, Elizabeth M. III, 286
offin, Elizabeth R. III, 76
offin, Elizabeth W. I, 533
offin, Elizabeth W. I, 544
offin, Ella III, 77
offin, Elmina IV, 615
offin, Elmina IV, 661
offin, Elmina H. I, 533
offin, Elmina H. I, 540
offin, Elmira IV, 467
offin, Elmira IV, 500
offin, Elmira T. IV, 467
offin, Embree I, 533
offin, Embree I, 540
offin, Emily V, 380
offin, Emily V, 407
offin, Emily B. III, 76
offin, Emma L. III, 76
offin, Emry I, 533
offin, Emy I, 533
offin, Enoch I, 587
offin, Enoch I, 983
Coffin, Esther I, 494
Coffin, Esther I, 532
Coffin, Esther I, 533
Coffin, Esther I, 550
Coffin, Esther I, 574
Coffin, Esther III, 76
Coffin, Esther III, 77
Coffin, Esther III, 202
Coffin, Eugene IV, 1310
Coffin, Eunice I, 587
Coffin, Eunice I, 875
Coffin, Eunice I, 983
Coffin, Eunice III, 52
Coffin, Eunice III, 76
Coffin, Eunice III, 77
Coffin, Eunice C. III, 53
Coffin, Eunice W. I, 743
Coffin, Eunice W. I, 757
Coffin, Eva III, 76
Coffin, Eva III, 133
Coffin, Eva V, 380
Coffin, Francis V, 731
Coffin, Francis W. III, 76
Coffin, Francis W. III, 362
Coffin, Frank III, 76
Coffin, Frank W. III, 76
Coffin, Franklin I, 587
Coffin, Frederick L. III, 76
Coffin, George I, 911
Coffin, George III, 77
Coffin, George Fox I, 778
Coffin, George Mitchell III, 77
Coffin, Grace I, 779
Coffin, Grace I, 852
Coffin, Grace I, 875
Coffin, Grace I, 882
Coffin, Grace II, 490
Coffin, Hannah I, 494
Coffin, Hannah I, 532
Coffin, Hannah I, 533
Coffin, Hannah I, 536
Coffin, Hannah I, 561
Coffin, Hannah I, 587
Coffin, Hannah I, 773
Coffin, Hannah I, 778
Coffin, Hannah I, 779
Coffin, Hannah I, 804
Coffin, Hannah I, 805
Coffin, Hannah I, 821
Coffin, Hannah I, 852
Coffin, Hannah I, 875
Coffin, Hannah I, 983
Coffin, Hannah II, 348
Coffin, Hannah II, 490
Coffin, Hannah IV, 189
Coffin, Hannah IV, 467
Coffin, Hannah IV, 471
Coffin, Hannah V, 324
Coffin, Hannah V, 366
Coffin, Hannah Amelia V, 899
Coffin, Hannah Amelia V, 941
Coffin, Harriet M. III, 76
Coffin, Harvey I, 494
Coffin, Harvey I, 805
Coffin, Hazadiah III, 76
Coffin, Hebsebeth I, 804
Coffin, Henry III, 76
Coffin, Henry III, 112
Coffin, Henry III, 286
Coffin, Henry III, 403
Coffin, Henry V, 40
Coffin, Henry C. V, 899
Coffin, Henry W. V, 899
Coffin, Hephsel I, 1008
Coffin, Hephsibeth I, 1008
Coffin, Hepsebah V, 899
Coffin, Hepsebah V, 906
Coffin, Hepshibah I, 1008
Coffin, Hepsibah I, 533
Coffin, Hepzabah I, 804
Coffin, Hepzabeth I, 804
Coffin, Hepzibah I, 778
Coffin, Hepzibah V, 40
Coffin, Hervey I, 588
Coffin, Hervey I, 779
Coffin, Hervey I, 805
Coffin, Hervey I, 830
Coffin, Hezediah III, 76
Coffin, Hezekiah III, 76
Coffin, Homer III, 76
Coffin, Homer T. III, 76
Coffin, Howard II, 442
Coffin, Howard E. V, 731
Coffin, Hudson III, 76
Coffin, Huldah I, 778
Coffin, Huldah I, 804
Coffin, Huldah I, 805
Coffin, Huldah I, 828
Coffin, Huldah I, 838
Coffin, I. Sherwood III, 76
Coffin, I. Sherwood III, 403
Coffin, I. Sherwood III, 468
Coffin, Ida III, 76
Coffin, Ida III, 354
Coffin, Ida III, 469
Coffin, Ida E. III, 468
Coffin, Irena I, 588
Coffin, Isaac I, 778
Coffin, Isaiah V, 899
Coffin, Isaiah V, 906
Coffin, J. Sherwood III, 354
Coffin, Jacob II, 348
Coffin, Jacob II, 442
Coffin, Jacob II, 490
Coffin, Jacob II, 629
Coffin, Jacob, Jr. II, 490
Coffin, James I, 779
Coffin, James I, 804
Coffin, James I, 839
Coffin, James I, 852
Coffin, James I, 875
Coffin, James II, 348
Coffin, Jane I, 445
Coffin, Jane I, 533
Coffin, Jane I, 574
Coffin, Jedidah I, 651
Coffin, Jemima I, 870
Coffin, Jemima I, 875
Coffin, Jemima V, 731
Coffin, Jemima VI, 305
Coffin, Jemima O. I, 875
Coffin, Jeremiah I, 778
Coffin, Jesse I, 778
Coffin, Jesse V, 324
Coffin, Jesse V, 380
Coffin, Jesse V, 407
Coffin, Jesse V, 439
Coffin, Jesse V, 482
Coffin, Jesse V, 541
Coffin, Jethro I, 779
Coffin, Jethro I, 805
Coffin, Job I, 494
Coffin, John I, 494
Coffin, John I, 533
Coffin, John I, 588
Coffin, John I, 651
Coffin, John I, 712
Coffin, John I, 721
Coffin, John I, 741
Coffin, John I, 743
Coffin, John I, 757
Coffin, John I, 764
Coffin, John I, 778
Coffin, John I, 779
Coffin, John I, 805
Coffin, John VI, 631
Coffin, John VI, 666
Coffin, John VI, 693
Coffin, John M. I, 743
Coffin, John M. I, 757
Coffin, Jonathan I, 533
Coffin, Jonathan I, 778
Coffin, Jonathan I, 779
Coffin, Jonathan I, 805
Coffin, Jorham III, 76
Coffin, Joseph I, 532
Coffin, Joseph I, 533
Coffin, Joseph I, 778
Coffin, Joseph I, 804
Coffin, Joseph I, 805
Coffin, Joseph I, 826
Coffin, Joseph III, 77
Coffin, Joseph IV, 467
Coffin, Joseph VI, 305
Coffin, Joseph B. I, 533
Coffin, Joseph E. I, 588
Coffin, Joseph Elwood I, 983
Coffin, Joseph J. I, 805
Coffin, Joseph J. III, 76
Coffin, Joseph Paddock, Jr. V, 40
Coffin, Joseph T. I, 533
Coffin, Joseph, Jr. I, 805
Coffin, Judith III, 77
Coffin, Judith V, 899
Coffin, Katharine I, 605
Coffin, Katharine I, 608
Coffin, Katharine Ellouise IV, 691
Coffin, Laban VI, 305
Coffin, Laura Ann I, 494
Coffin, Leatha I, 533
Coffin, Lena III, 76
Coffin, Lena III, 347
Coffin, Leuzena I, 983
Coffin, Levi I, 494
Coffin, Levi I, 532
Coffin, Levi I, 582
Coffin, Levi I, 605
Coffin, Levi I, 608
Coffin, Levi I, 778
Coffin, Levi I, 805
Coffin, Levi V, 899
Coffin, Levi, Jr. I, 533
Coffin, Levi, Sr. I, 533
Coffin, Levina V, 324
Coffin, Levina V, 365
Coffin, Libni I, 488
Coffin, Libni I, 494
Coffin, Libni I, 532
Coffin, Libni I, 533
Coffin, Libni I, 773
Coffin, Libni I, 778
Coffin, Libni I, 804
Coffin, Libni I, 825
Coffin, Libni I, 961
Coffin, Libni I, 1008
Coffin, Libni, Jr. I, 804
Coffin, Libni, Sr. I, 532
Coffin, Lora V, 380
Coffin, Louis Haldy IV, 691
Coffin, Louisa I, 805
Coffin, Louzena I, 995
Coffin, Lucretia II, 490
Coffin, Lucretia II, 801
Coffin, Lucretia II, 811
Coffin, Luzena I, 588
Coffin, Lydia I, 587
Coffin, Lydia I, 651
Coffin, Lydia I, 773
Coffin, Lydia I, 779
Coffin, Lydia I, 852
Coffin, Lydia I, 875
Coffin, Lydia I, 884
Coffin, Lydia I, 983
Coffin, Lydia III, 76
Coffin, Lydia III, 77
Coffin, Lydia III, 303
Coffin, Lydia V, 300
Coffin, Lydia V, 301
Coffin, Lydia V, 324
Coffin, Lydia V, 325
Coffin, Lydia V, 454
Coffin, Lydia B. III, 77
Coffin, Lydia C. III, 52
Coffin, Lydia M. I, 588
Coffin, Macrina I, 778
Coffin, Mahetable I, 532
Coffin, Mahitable I, 804
Coffin, Margaret V, 899
Coffin, Margaret V, 905
Coffin, Maria I, 588
Coffin, Maria I, 779
Coffin, Maria I, 805
Coffin, Maria I, 807
Coffin, Mariam A. V, 899
Coffin, Mark III, 77
Coffin, Marmaduke I, 852
Coffin, Martha I, 778
Coffin, Martha I, 805
Coffin, Martha II, 490
Coffin, Martha II, 619
Coffin, Mary I, 494
Coffin, Mary I, 533
Coffin, Mary I, 581
Coffin, Mary I, 587
Coffin, Mary I, 588
Coffin, Mary I, 651
Coffin, Mary I, 676
Coffin, Mary I, 743
Coffin, Mary I, 757
Coffin, Mary I, 773
Coffin, Mary I, 778
Coffin, Mary I, 779
Coffin, Mary I, 797
Coffin, Mary I, 804
Coffin, Mary I, 805
Coffin, Mary I, 825
Coffin, Mary I, 839
Coffin, Mary I, 983
Coffin, Mary I, 992
Coffin, Mary II, 490
Coffin, Mary III, 76
Coffin, Mary III, 77
Coffin, Mary IV, 26
Coffin, Mary IV, 467
Coffin, Mary IV, 471
Coffin, Mary IV, 615
Coffin, Mary IV, 807
Coffin, Mary V, 40
Coffin, Mary V, 85
Coffin, Mary V, 230
Coffin, Mary V, 255
Coffin, Mary V, 256
Coffin, Mary V, 322
Coffin, Mary V, 324
Coffin, Mary V, 342
Coffin, Mary V, 350
Coffin, Mary V, 380
Coffin, Mary V, 445
Coffin, Mary V, 459
Coffin, Mary V, 899
Coffin, Mary V, 921
Coffin, Mary A. I, 445
Coffin, Mary A. I, 452
Coffin, Mary Ann I, 445
Coffin, Mary Ann I, 533
Coffin, Mary C. III, 76
Coffin, Mary C. IV, 471
Coffin, Mary F. V, 899
Coffin, Mary S. III, 76
Coffin, Mary W. I, 533
Coffin, Mary W. I, 557
Coffin, Mary W. I, 620
Coffin, Mary White I, 533
Coffin, Matthew I, 494
Coffin, Matthew I, 532
Coffin, Matthew I, 533
Coffin, Matthew I, 558
Coffin, Matthew I, 561
Coffin, Matthew I, 779
Coffin, Matthew I, 804
Coffin, Matthew I, 805
Coffin, Matthew I, 847
Coffin, Matthew I, 852
Coffin, Matthew I, 875
Coffin, Matthew, Jr. I, 852
Coffin, Matthew, Jr. I, 875
Coffin, Mehetable I, 778
Coffin, Mehitable I, 533
Coffin, Mehitable I, 536
Coffin, Merab III, 77
Coffin, Merrill IV, 1310
Coffin, Merrill M. IV, 691
Coffin, Milicent I, 805
Coffin, Milicent I, 828
Coffin, Milly I, 778
Coffin, Miriam I, 532
Coffin, Miriam I, 676
Coffin, Miriam I, 693
Coffin, Miriam I, 743
Coffin, Miriam I, 757
Coffin, Miriam I, 778
Coffin, Miriam V, 899
Coffin, Miriam Allinson V, 927
Coffin, Mornen I, 757
Coffin, Mornen I, 763
Coffin, Moses I, 651
Coffin, Moses I, 805
Coffin, Moses I, 907
Coffin, Moses I, 911
Coffin, Moses V, 731
Coffin, Moses V, 899
Coffin, Mournen I, 743
Coffin, Mournin I, 651
Coffin, Nancy B. V, 899
Coffin, Naomi I, 600
Coffin, Naomi I, 628
Coffin, Naomi V, 40
Coffin, Naomi V, 899
Coffin, Naomi V, 927
Coffin, Naomi P. I, 524
Coffin, Naomi P. I, 533
Coffin, Naomy I, 533
Coffin, Naomy I, 546
Coffin, Nathan I, 375
Coffin, Nathan I, 380
Coffin, Nathan I, 494
Coffin, Nathan I, 533
Coffin, Nathan Dicks I, 779
Coffin, Nathan Dix I, 805
Coffin, Nathan H. I, 533
Coffin, Nathaniel I, 778
Coffin, Nathaniel I, 804
Coffin, Nathaniel I, 961
Coffin, Nathaniel M. III, 77
Coffin, Obed I, 778
Coffin, Obed IV, 467
Coffin, Olive V, 230
Coffin, Olive V, 300
Coffin, Oliver I, 805
Coffin, Oliver V, 921
Coffin, Oliver, Sr. V, 920
Coffin, Olover G. I, 778
Coffin, Oscar V, 380
Coffin, Patience V, 324
Coffin, Patience V, 342
Coffin, Patience V, 380
Coffin, Patience V, 406
Coffin, Patience V, 407
Coffin, Paul I, 494
Coffin, Paul I, 533
Coffin, Paul I, 805
Coffin, Peter I, 532
Coffin, Peter I, 533
Coffin, Peter I, 804
Coffin, Phebe I, 494
Coffin, Phebe I, 533
Coffin, Phebe I, 574
Coffin, Phebe I, 588
Coffin, Phebe I, 593
Coffin, Phebe I, 651
Coffin, Phebe I, 673
Coffin, Phebe I, 676
Coffin, Phebe I, 778

Coffin, Phebe I, 779
Coffin, Phebe I, 794
Coffin, Phebe I, 804
Coffin, Phebe I, 805
Coffin, Phebe I, 828
Coffin, Phebe I, 844
Coffin, Phebe I, 911
Coffin, Phebe IV, 807
Coffin, Phebe IV, 1356
Coffin, Phebe V, 324
Coffin, Phebe V, 355
Coffin, Pricilla I, 875
Coffin, Prisalah I, 712
Coffin, Prisalah I, 721
Coffin, Priscilla I, 380
Coffin, Priscilla I, 494
Coffin, Priscilla I, 532
Coffin, Priscilla I, 533
Coffin, Priscilla I, 550
Coffin, Priscilla I, 565
Coffin, Priscilla I, 651
Coffin, Priscilla I, 712
Coffin, Priscilla I, 743
Coffin, Priscilla I, 778
Coffin, Priscilla I, 779
Coffin, Priscilla I, 804
Coffin, Priscilla I, 805
Coffin, Priscilla I, 828
Coffin, Priscilla I, 852
Coffin, Priscilla I, 875
Coffin, Priscilla I, 886
Coffin, Priscilla I, 1008
Coffin, Priscilla I, 1010
Coffin, Priscilla II, 348
Coffin, Priscilla V, 324
Coffin, Priscilla V, 350
Coffin, Priscilla V, 380
Coffin, Priscilla V, 419
Coffin, Prudence I, 494
Coffin, Prudence I, 532
Coffin, Prudence I, 533
Coffin, Prudence I, 582
Coffin, Prudence I, 605
Coffin, Rachel I, 533
Coffin, Rachel I, 651
Coffin, Rachel I, 778
Coffin, Rachel I, 805
Coffin, Rachel I, 830
Coffin, Rachel II, 490
Coffin, Rachel II, 629
Coffin, Rachel IV, 467
Coffin, Rachel IV, 479
Coffin, Rebeca I, 494
Coffin, Rebecca I, 805
Coffin, Rebecca I, 828
Coffin, Rebecca IV, 189
Coffin, Rebecca IV, 467
Coffin, Rebecca IV, 476
Coffin, Rebecca V, 731
Coffin, Rebecca M. III, 76
Coffin, Rebeckah I, 778
Coffin, Reuben V, 40
Coffin, Reubin VI, 58
Coffin, Rhoda I, 777
Coffin, Rhoda I, 778
Coffin, Rhoda I, 802
Coffin, Rhoda I, 804
Coffin, Rhoda I, 805
Coffin, Rhoda I, 810
Coffin, Rhoda I, 836
Coffin, Rhoda A. II, 284
Coffin, Rhoda M. V, 40
Coffin, Rhoda M. V, 83
Coffin, Robert III, 52
Coffin, Robert III, 76
Coffin, Robert III, 77
Coffin, Robt. III, 76
Coffin, Roda I, 804
Coffin, Rollin J. III, 77
Coffin, Roxana I, 612
Coffin, Rufus V, 380
Coffin, Ruth I, 588
Coffin, Ruth I, 651
Coffin, Ruth I, 778
Coffin, Ruth I, 804
Coffin, Ruth I, 805
Coffin, Ruth I, 911
Coffin, Ruth I, 983
Coffin, Ruth I, 998
Coffin, Ruth I, 1007
Coffin, Ruth I, 1008
Coffin, Ruth III, 76
Coffin, Ruth H. I, 805
Coffin, Ruth H. I, 839
Coffin, Salley I, 743
Coffin, Salley I, 804
Coffin, Salley I, 839
Coffin, Sally I, 804
Coffin, Sally I, 875
Coffin, Sally III, 76
Coffin, Salmon III, 76
Coffin, Salmon III, 77
Coffin, Samuel I, 494
Coffin, Samuel I, 532
Coffin, Samuel I, 651
Coffin, Samuel I, 676
Coffin, Samuel I, 712
Coffin, Samuel I, 743
Coffin, Samuel I, 757
Coffin, Samuel I, 773
Coffin, Samuel I, 778
Coffin, Samuel I, 779
Coffin, Samuel I, 804
Coffin, Samuel I, 825
Coffin, Samuel I Sup 1, 9
Coffin, Samuel V, 40
Coffin, Samuel V, 215
Coffin, Samuel V, 230
Coffin, Samuel V, 256
Coffin, Samuel V, 324
Coffin, Samuel V, 325
Coffin, Samuel V, 342
Coffin, Samuel V, 365
Coffin, Samuel V, 366
Coffin, Samuel V, 454
Coffin, Samuel V, 459
Coffin, Samuel D. I, 445
Coffin, Samuel D. I, 452
Coffin, Samuel D. I, 533
Coffin, Sarah I, 494
Coffin, Sarah I, 533
Coffin, Sarah I, 552
Coffin, Sarah I, 778
Coffin, Sarah I, 801
Coffin, Sarah I, 804
Coffin, Sarah I, 805
Coffin, Sarah I, 840
Coffin, Sarah I, 843
Coffin, Sarah I, 907
Coffin, Sarah I, 911
Coffin, Sarah II, 348
Coffin, Sarah II, 442
Coffin, Sarah II, 490
Coffin, Sarah III, 76
Coffin, Sarah V, 40
Coffin, Sarah V, 899
Coffin, Sarah V, 906
Coffin, Sarah V, 922
Coffin, Sarah A. I, 533
Coffin, Sarah A. I, 579
Coffin, Sarah A. I, 806
Coffin, Sarah A. I, 840
Coffin, Sarah Barnard V, 40
Coffin, Sarah E. V, 731
Coffin, Sarah Emeline V, 899
Coffin, Sarah L. III, 76
Coffin, Sarah M. V, 920
Coffin, Semira I, 533
Coffin, Serena I, 588
Coffin, Seth I, 532
Coffin, Seth I, 773
Coffin, Seth I, 804
Coffin, Seth I, 847
Coffin, Seth I, 971
Coffin, Seth I Sup 1, 10
Coffin, Shubal I, 805
Coffin, Shubal G. I, 778
Coffin, Shubal G. I, 875
Coffin, Sirena I, 805
Coffin, Solomon V, 899
Coffin, Stephen I, 587
Coffin, Stephen I, 778
Coffin, Stephen I, 805
Coffin, Stephen I, 983
Coffin, Stillborn III, 76
Coffin, Susan V, 380
Coffin, Susanna I, 533
Coffin, Susanna I, 605
Coffin, Susanna I, 805
Coffin, Susannah V. III, 76
Coffin, Susannah V. III, 112
Coffin, T. Homer III, 347
Coffin, Temperance I, 983
Coffin, Thomas I, 676
Coffin, Thomas I, 693
Coffin, Thomas I, 779
Coffin, Thomas I, 805
Coffin, Thomas II, 348
Coffin, Thomas II, 490
Coffin, Thomas B. I, 533
Coffin, Thomas C. I, 588
Coffin, Thomas Clarkson I, 983
Coffin, Thomas E. I, 778
Coffin, Thomas Eugene IV, 691
Coffin, Thomas M. II, 490
Coffin, Thomas M. II, 733
Coffin, Thomas Mayhew II, 490
Coffin, Thos. II, 788
Coffin, Thos. II, 811
Coffin, Thos. M. II, 788
Coffin, Thos. M. II, 850
Coffin, Vestal I, 494
Coffin, Vestal I, 533
Coffin, Walter II, 348
Coffin, Warner M. I, 533
Coffin, Wd. Anna II, 788
Coffin, Wd. Sarah V, 920
Coffin, Widow Eliza F. VI, 693
Coffin, Widow Elizabeth I, 676
Coffin, Widow Hannah I, 558
Coffin, Widow Martha I, 816
Coffin, Wilbur III, 76
Coffin, William I, 380
Coffin, William I, 494
Coffin, William I, 532
Coffin, William I, 533
Coffin, William I, 550
Coffin, William I, 565
Coffin, William I, 587
Coffin, William I, 588
Coffin, William I, 593
Coffin, William I, 651
Coffin, William I, 676
Coffin, William I, 778
Coffin, William I, 779
Coffin, William I, 804
Coffin, William I, 805
Coffin, William I, 821
Coffin, William I, 911
Coffin, William I, 983
Coffin, William I Sup 1, 9
Coffin, William IV, 691
Coffin, William V, 380
Coffin, William G. I, 533
Coffin, William G. V, 899
Coffin, William H. V, 899
Coffin, William Henry III, 76
Coffin, William, Jr. I, 532
Coffin, William, Jr. I, 593
Coffin, Wilson V, 380
Coffin, Wm. I, 380
Coffin, Wm. I, 426
Coffin, Wm. I, 690
Coffin, Wm. H. V, 899
Coffin, Zachariah I, 586
Coffin, Zachariah I, 593
Coffin, Zachariah I, 794
Coffin, Zachariah I, 805
Coffin, Zacharias I, 494
Coffin, Zacharias I, 533
Coffin, Zacharias I, 574
Coffin, Zacharias I, 588
Coffin, Zacharias I, 779
Coffin, Zacharias I, 805
Coffin, Zacharius I, 805
Coffin, Zephaniah III, 76
Coffington, Elizabeth IV, 323
Coffington, Elizabeth IV, 325
Coffins, Hannah I, 571
Coffman, Abie V, 40
Coffman, Anna IV, 189
Coffman, Arch. W. V, 158
Coffman, Charles W. IV, 189
Coffman, Edith IV, 189
Coffman, Effie V, 158
Coffman, Eunice Mary IV, 189
Coffman, George IV, 189
Coffman, James IV, 813
Coffman, Jane IV, 813
Coffman, Lillian May IV, 189
Coffman, Mellie V, 158
Coffman, Minerva E. IV, 379
Coffman, Minerva E. IV, 389
Coffman, Minerva E. IV, 807
Coffman, Minerva E. IV, 813
Coffman, Mrs. Earle IV, 189
Coffman, Muriel M. IV, 1310
Coffman, Nellie E. IV, 971
Coffman, Robert M. II, 788
Coffrey, Charles VI, 807
Coffrey, Charles VI, 810
Coffrey, Elizabeth VI, 807
Coffrey, John VI, 807
Coffrey, Nancy VI, 807
Coffrey, Polly VI, 810
Coffyn, Guilelema III, 307
Cofield, Dorcas VI, 104
Cofield, Dorcas VI, 106
Cofield, Georgianna I, 40
Cofield, Georgianna I, 42
Cofield, Sarah VI, 45
Cofinder, John VI, 895
Cofinder, Sina VI, 895
Cofing, Hannah II, 483
Cofing, Hannah II, 490
Cofing, Jacob II, 483
Cofing, Jacob II, 490
Coflin, Elizabeth IV, 189
Cogal, Betsey IV, 325
Cogal, Isaac IV, 325
Cogal, Ralph IV, 325
Cogal, Sarah IV, 325
Cogel, Isaac IV, 26
Cogel, Isaac VI, 632
Cogel, Sarah IV, 26
Cogel, Sarah VI, 632
Cogell, Catherine VI, 380
Cogell, Dinah VI, 380
Cogell, John VI, 380
Coggans, Ann II, 348
Coggans, Katherine II, 490
Coggeshall, Anna III, 77
Coggeshall, Anna III, 340
Coggeshall, Anna P. II, 834
Coggeshall, Anna P. II, 850
Coggeshall, Annuel Harvey V, 832
Coggeshall, Caleb I, 806
Coggeshall, Caleb III, 77
Coggeshall, Caleb III, 340
Coggeshall, Caleb VI, 350
Coggeshall, Charles Thompson III, 77
Coggeshall, Deborah I, 534
Coggeshall, Deborah I, 559
Coggeshall, Deborah II, 834
Coggeshall, Deborah II, 850
Coggeshall, Deborah III, 77
Coggeshall, Deborah III, 147
Coggeshall, Deborah III, 340
Coggeshall, Deborah V, 779
Coggeshall, Edward IV, 941
Coggeshall, Edward VI, 350
Coggeshall, Edwin W. III, 77
Coggeshall, Edwin W. III, 340
Coggeshall, Eliz. III, 77
Coggeshall, Eliz. III, 340
Coggeshall, Elizabeth I, 534
Coggeshall, Elizabeth I, 541
Coggeshall, Elizabeth I, 983
Coggeshall, Elizabeth III, 77
Coggeshall, Elizabeth V, 616
Coggeshall, Elizabeth M. III, 77
Coggeshall, Elwood II, 834
Coggeshall, Elwood W. II, 850
Coggeshall, Emily Jane V, 832
Coggeshall, Emma III, 77
Coggeshall, Emma III, 126
Coggeshall, Florence III, 77
Coggeshall, Frances III, 77
Coggeshall, Frederick L. III, 77
Coggeshall, Geo D. II, 850
Coggeshall, Geo. D. II, 834
Coggeshall, Geo. D. III, 77
Coggeshall, Geo. Dillwyn III, 77
Coggeshall, George D. II, 850
Coggeshall, George D. III, 77
Coggeshall, Giles III, 77
Coggeshall, Giles H. II, 491
Coggeshall, Giles H. II, 802
Coggeshall, Giles H. III, 77
Coggeshall, Giles H. III, 126
Coggeshall, Hannah V, 832
Coggeshall, Harriet T. III, 77
Coggeshall, Harriet T. III, 90
Coggeshall, Harvey V, 832
Coggeshall, Job I, 533
Coggeshall, Job I, 534
Coggeshall, Job I, 806
Coggeshall, Job I, 825
Coggeshall, Job III, 77
Coggeshall, Job V, 779
Coggeshall, Job VI, 350
Coggeshall, John V, 611
Coggeshall, John V, 616
Coggeshall, Jonathan II, 490
Coggeshall, Lindley V, 832
Coggeshall, Lindly V, 832
Coggeshall, Lucy VI, 350
Coggeshall, Marianna III, 77
Coggeshall, Marianna III, 126
Coggeshall, Marianna III, 183
Coggeshall, Martha II, 490
Coggeshall, Mary I, 806
Coggeshall, Mary VI, 350
Coggeshall, Mary Anna II, 802
Coggeshall, Mary R. II, 802
Coggeshall, Mary R. III, 77
Coggeshall, Mary R. III, 183
Coggeshall, Mary Rhoades III, 77
Coggeshall, Milicent I, 712
Coggeshall, Milicent I, 728
Coggeshall, Miriam I, 806
Coggeshall, Miriam I, 825
Coggeshall, Morton C. III, 77
Coggeshall, Morton C. III, 90
Coggeshall, Nancy V, 611
Coggeshall, Nancy V, 616
Coggeshall, Pemele I, 712
Coggeshall, Peter I, 534
Coggeshall, Peter I, 712
Coggeshall, Sarah IV, 931
Coggeshall, Sarah IV, 941
Coggeshall, Sarah B. IV, 941
Coggeshall, Sarah Emily III, 77
Coggeshall, Sarah Emily III, 16
Coggeshall, Sarah Walter III, 7
Coggeshall, Sophia IV, 941
Coggeshall, Tristam VI, 305
Coggeshall, Tristram I, 533
Coggeshall, Tristram I, 593
Coggeshall, Tristram IV, 931
Coggeshall, Tristram IV, 941
Coggeshall, Tristram V, 616
Coggeshall, Tristram VI, 350
Coggeshall, Tristrim I, 983
Coggeshall, Trustom I, 712
Coggeshall, Trustom I, 728
Coggeshall, Trustram I, 534
Coggeshall, Trustram I, 541
Coggeshall, Walter III, 77
Coggeshall, Walter III, 160
Coggeshall, William Albert V, 8
Coggeshall, William V. V, 832
Coggeshall, William W. III, 77
Coggin, Thomas C. VI, 873
Coggins, Edward Heston II, 788
Coggins, Jane I, 676
Coggins, Ruth Anna II, 850
Coggins, Ruthann II, 788
Coggshall, Caleb I, 42
Coggshall, Caleb I, 534
Coggshall, Caleb I, 806
Coggshall, Caleb I, 983
Coggshall, Deborah I, 533
Coggshall, Deborah I, 534
Coggshall, Deborah I, 806
Coggshall, Deborah I Sup 1, 9
Coggshall, Edward I, 983
Coggshall, Elizabeth I, 534
Coggshall, Elizabeth I, 983
Coggshall, Elizabeth I, 984
Coggshall, Elizabeth I, 992
Coggshall, Eunice I, 712
Coggshall, Eunice Worth I, 697
Coggshall, Eunice Worth I, 712
Coggshall, Gayer I, 983
Coggshall, Geyer I, 984
Coggshall, Ghiles I, 983
Coggshall, Hannah V, 832
Coggshall, Jane VI, 341
Coggshall, Job I, 533
Coggshall, Job I, 534
Coggshall, Job I, 806
Coggshall, Job I, 907
Coggshall, Job I, 983
Coggshall, John Milton I, 697
Coggshall, John Milton I, 712
Coggshall, Jonathan I, 983
Coggshall, Jonathan I, 984
Coggshall, Lettice I, 984
Coggshall, Lidia I, 983
Coggshall, Lindly V, 832
Coggshall, Lucy I, 983
Coggshall, Lucy VI, 305
Coggshall, Lucy VI, 341
Coggshall, Lydia I, 983
Coggshall, Mary I, 534
Coggshall, Mary I, 567
Coggshall, Mary I, 806
Coggshall, Mary I, 983
Coggshall, Milicent I, 712
Coggshall, Milisent I, 712
Coggshall, Millicent I, 697
Coggshall, Miriam I, 806
Coggshall, N. C. I, 534
Coggshall, Pamelia I, 534
Coggshall, Parmelia I, 534
Coggshall, Parmelia I, 574
Coggshall, Parmelia I, 983
Coggshall, Pemele I, 712
Coggshall, Permela I, 983
Coggshall, Permelia I, 983
Coggshall, Peter I, 534
Coggshall, Peter I, 712
Coggshall, Peter I, 806
Coggshall, Peter I, 983
Coggshall, Rachel I, 983
Coggshall, Rachel I, 984
Coggshall, Sarah I, 806
Coggshall, Sarah B. IV, 941
Coggshall, Sarah Newby I, 712
Coggshall, Thomas Ellwood I, 697
Coggshall, Thomas Elwood I, 71
Coggshall, Trestram I, 983
Coggshall, Tristam VI, 305
Coggshall, Tristram I, 533
Coggshall, Tristram I, 697
Coggshall, Tristram I, 712
Coggshall, Tristram I, 806
Coggshall, Tristram I, 983
Coggshall, Tristram VI, 305
Coggshall, Tristram VI, 341
Coggshall, Tristrim I, 983

ggshall, Trustom I, 712
ggshall, Trustram I, 534
ggshall, Trustram I, 983
ggshell, Meribah IV, 1356
ggshell, Rachel I, 992
gill, Abraham IV, 143
gill, Ekiza VI, 380
gill, Hannah VI, 380
gill, Isaac IV, 143
gill, Ralph II, 210
gill, William VI, 380
gins, Katherine II, 490
gne, Anna III, 133
gsale, Milla I, 757
gshall, Caleb I, 494
gshall, Caleb I, 534
gshall, David, Jr. VI, 342
gshall, Deborah I, 534
gshall, Gayer I, 494
gshall, Gayer I, 983
gshall, Ghiles I, 983
gshall, Giles H. II, 491
gshall, Jane VI, 342
gshall, Job I, 494
gshall, Jonathan I, 494
gshall, Jonathan II, 490
gshall, Jonathan II, 574
gshall, Lucy VI, 342
gshall, Lydia I, 494
gshall, Martha II, 490
gshall, Martha II, 574
gshall, Micajah, Jr. VI, 342
gshall, Milla I, 757
gshall, N. C. I, 534
gshall, Pamela I, 494
gshall, Patty VI, 342
gshall, Peter I, 494
gshall, Peter I, 983
gshall, Rachel I, 494
gshall, Tristam VI, 342
gshall, Tristram I, 494
gshall, Tristram I, 533
gshall, Tristram I, 806
gshall, Tristrem I, 757
gshall, Trustrem I, 757
gshell, Geyer I, 984
gshell, Lettice I, 984
gshell, Lettice I, 995
gshell, Lucy I, 983
gshell, Mary I, 983
gswell, Abby S. III, 78
gwell, Joseph VI, 944
harn, James VI, 807
harn, Mary VI, 807
harn, Obedience VI, 807
harn, Thomas VI, 807
hen, Mary Ann II, 1047
hen, Mary Ann II, 1048
hn, Ann S. II, 850
hn, Ann S. II, 940
hn, Elizabeth J. II, 850
hn, Elizabeth J. II, 940
hn, Elizabeth Jane II, 850
hn, Joseph S. II, 850
hn, Joseph S. II, 940
hn, Lizzie T. III, 277
hn, Lydia III, 175
hn, Peter II, 850
hn, Peter II, 940
hns, Joel IV, 691
hns, Mary IV, 691
hoe, Mary J. IV, 964
hoe, Mary J. IV, 987
hu, Aaron B. III, 78
hu, Aaron B. III, 320
hu, Anna Louise III, 78
hu, Anna Louise III, 191
hu, Anna S. III, 78
hu, Annabel III, 323
hu, Annabell III, 78
hu, Eliz. I. III, 177
hu, Eliz. J. III, 78
hu, Elizabeth III, 78
hu, Elizabeth J. III, 78
hu, Elizabeth J. III, 357
hu, Elizabeth W. III, 78
hu, Eugenie Lecordier III, 78
hu, Eugenie Lecordier III, 320
hu, Harriet III, 78
hu, Henry M. III, 78
hu, Henry M. III, 323
hu, Henry S. III, 78
hu, Henry Wallace III, 78
hu, J. S. III, 177
hu, Joseph III, 78
hu, Joseph S. III, 78
hu, Joseph S. III, 177
hu, Joseph S. III, 357
hu, Julia III, 78
hu, La Motte III, 78
hu, Lizzie T. III, 175
Cohu, Lydia E. III, 177
Cohu, Lydia L. III, 78
Cohu, Lydia L. III, 176
Cohu, Peter III, 78
Cohu, Rachel III, 210
Cohu, Rachel H. III, 78
Cohu, Rachel H. III, 210
Cohu, William III, 78
Cohu, William III, 210
Cohu, Wm. McC III, 78
Coil, Ann V, 40
Coil, Ann V, 122
Coil, Emma V, 665
Coil, Jesse V, 989
Coil, Jessie V, 989
Coil, Joseph V, 989
Coil, Urban V, 665
Coit, Sarah III, 480
Coit, Sarah M. III, 483
Coke, Amanda VI, 647
Cokeley, Jacob IV, 189
Coker, Alice III, 73
Coker, Diza VI, 104
Coker, Dorcas III, 73
Coker, Jonathan VI, 104
Coker, Lucy VI, 104
Coker, Lucy VI, 124
Coker, Nicholas III, 73
Coknour, Mary E. V, 989
Coks, Peter I, 535
Colbert, Alexander VI, 895
Colbert, Lemuel VI, 807
Colbert, Nancy VI, 895
Colbert, Phebe VI, 807
Colbert, Thirsah VI, 379
Colbert, Thirsah VI, 458
Colbourn, Allie I, 622
Colbourne, William VI, 11
Colburn, Abigail IV, 941
Colburn, Benjamin IV, 941
Colburn, Emily E. IV, 379
Colburn, Emily E. IV, 402
Colburn, George IV, 807
Colburn, Ida E. IV, 807
Colburn, Jacob IV, 941
Colburn, John VI, 945
Colburn, Rebecca VI, 657
Colburn, Sally VI, 945
Colburn, Sarah IV, 941
Colby, Ella H. V, 731
Colby, Myrta IV, 807
Colby, Ray F. IV, 807
Colclaser, Abigail IV, 26
Colclaser, Abigail IV, 29
Colclaser, Eleanor IV, 26
Colclaser, Eleanor IV, 29
Colclaser, Rachel May IV, 29
Coldburn, Elizabeth VI, 895
Coldburn, John VI, 895
Coldburn, Margaret VI, 895
Coldburn, William VI, 895
Colden, Ann III, 78
Colden, Mary Ann III, 78
Coldren, Hannah IV, 545
Coldren, Jesse IV, 123
Coldren, Martha IV, 78
Coldren, Martha IV, 80
Coldron, Jesse IV, 119
Coldwell, James V, 40
Coldwell, James V, 133
Coldwell, John V, 40
Coldwell, Joseph V, 40
Coldwell, Margaret V, 40
Coldwell, Martha V, 40
Coldwell, Martha V, 133
Coldwell, Mary V, 40
Coldwell, Miriam V, 40
Cole, ??? V, 158
Cole, A. F. IV, 1248
Cole, Achsa R. IV, 467
Cole, Achsah IV, 467
Cole, Adelaide I, 623
Cole, Amelia VI, 379
Cole, Ann II, 460
Cole, Ann II, 491
Cole, Ann II, 649
Cole, Ann IV, 26
Cole, Ann Margaret V, 881
Cole, Anna I, 757
Cole, Annie V, 423
Cole, Bertie I, 627
Cole, Bonnie Raper I, 939
Cole, Byron F. IV, 1248
Cole, Catharine VI, 807
Cole, Charles II, 62
Cole, Charles II, 491
Cole, Charles V, 881
Cole, Charles Bell I, 623
Cole, Charles C. III, 382
Cole, Clara III, 78
Cole, Clara III, 155
Cole, Damaris II, 208
Cole, Damaris II, 248
Cole, Daniel II, 491
Cole, Darius IV, 1357
Cole, Darius, Jr. IV, 1357
Cole, Deborah II, 491
Cole, E. B. I, 627
Cole, Efphama A. V, 950
Cole, Eglentine VI, 895
Cole, Elender VI, 946
Cole, Elijah IV, 467
Cole, Eliza I, 614
Cole, Eliza Ann II, 799
Cole, Elizabeth II, 62
Cole, Elizabeth II, 92
Cole, Elizabeth II, 477
Cole, Elizabeth II, 491
Cole, Elizabeth V, 881
Cole, Elizabeth V, 989
Cole, Elizabeth VI, 981
Cole, Emily IV, 1274
Cole, Emily IV, 1296
Cole, Francis VI, 946
Cole, Francis VI, 981
Cole, Francis VI, 1009
Cole, Frank Wm. III, 78
Cole, Frank Wm. III, 155
Cole, George II, 477
Cole, George II, 491
Cole, Hannah I, 1027
Cole, Hannah II, 208
Cole, Hannah V, 380
Cole, Harry B. V, 950
Cole, Ira Lee V, 665
Cole, Isaiah I, 614
Cole, J. L. V, 454
Cole, James I, 935
Cole, James V, 158
Cole, James VI, 895
Cole, Jane IV, 957
Cole, Jemima VI, 882
Cole, Jennie IV, 1248
Cole, Jeremiah V, 665
Cole, John II, 491
Cole, John II, 631
Cole, John II, 632
Cole, John IV, 467
Cole, John V, 380
Cole, John V, 950
Cole, John A. IV, 1274
Cole, John B. VI, 132
Cole, John B. VI, 133
Cole, John Godwin II, 477
Cole, John Godwin II, 491
Cole, John S. II, 491
Cole, Joseph I, 348
Cole, Joseph IV, 467
Cole, Joseph B. III, 78
Cole, Josiah VI, 5
Cole, Josiah VI, 6
Cole, Josiah VI, 40
Cole, Kate I, 627
Cole, Kate I, 642
Cole, Kitty VI, 1009
Cole, L. D. I, 631
Cole, Lee Reese I, 614
Cole, Leena I, 614
Cole, Leo Benson I, 614
Cole, Lewis V, 158
Cole, Lewis VI, 379
Cole, Lottie W. IV, 957
Cole, Louis J. V, 158
Cole, Louisa IV, 1274
Cole, Louiza IV, 1274
Cole, Lucinda V, 579
Cole, Lydia Ann V, 881
Cole, M. IV, 467
Cole, M. Laura III, 78
Cole, M. Laura III, 155
Cole, Mahala IV, 467
Cole, Mahala IV, 499
Cole, Margaret II, 460
Cole, Margaret II, 491
Cole, Margaret IV, 467
Cole, Margaret Jewel I, 614
Cole, Marian Frances I, 623
Cole, Martha II, 491
Cole, Martha C. II, 477
Cole, Martha C. II, 491
Cole, Martha C. III, 78
Cole, Mary I, 935
Cole, Mary I, 1008
Cole, Mary I, 1010
Cole, Mary II, 348
Cole, Mary II, 491
Cole, Mary IV, 518
Cole, Mary IV, 544
Cole, Mary IV, 941
Cole, Mary IV, 1052
Cole, Mary V, 158
Cole, Mary V, 881
Cole, Mary V, 968
Cole, Mary V, 979
Cole, Mary VI, 788
Cole, Mary VI, 946
Cole, Mary Ann IV, 1357
Cole, Mary B. IV, 1052
Cole, Mary B. IV, 1066
Cole, Mary B. IV, 1071
Cole, Mary E. V, 158
Cole, Mary Ella V. IV, 467
Cole, Minna V, 158
Cole, Minnie V, 158
Cole, Moses II, 491
Cole, Nancy J. V, 665
Cole, Pearson V, 881
Cole, Phebe V, 899
Cole, Philip II, 491
Cole, Philip C. V, 380
Cole, Phillip G. V, 380
Cole, Rachel I, 695
Cole, Rachel I, 712
Cole, Rachel I, 736
Cole, Rachel IV, 1052
Cole, Rachel IV, 1071
Cole, Rachel V, 482
Cole, Raymond IV, 467
Cole, Richard IV, 1052
Cole, Richard IV, 1071
Cole, Richard M. IV, 1052
Cole, Robert T. V, 665
Cole, Roland IV, 467
Cole, Rolen IV, 467
Cole, Rolland IV, 467
Cole, Ruth I, 928
Cole, Ruth Evans I, 935
Cole, Sallie I, 380
Cole, Samuel VI, 807
Cole, Sarah I, 348
Cole, Sarah I, 380
Cole, Sarah IV, 467
Cole, Sarah IV, 615
Cole, Sarah V, 230
Cole, Sarah V, 244
Cole, Sarah VI, 481
Cole, Sarah B. IV, 615
Cole, Sarah M. V, 881
Cole, Sarah S. IV, 1052
Cole, Sarah S. IV, 1071
Cole, Silas VI, 913
Cole, Susan J. II, 849
Cole, Susan J. II, 941
Cole, Sushannah I, 348
Cole, Viola IV, 467
Cole, Viola T. IV, 467
Cole, William IV, 467
Cole, William VI, 736
Cole, Wm. II, 460
Cole, Wm. II, 491
Cole, Wm. B. IV, 1052
Cole, Wm. B. IV, 1071
Cole, Wm. Llewelyn IV, 1052
Cole, Wm. W. IV, 957
Coleburn, John VI, 909
Coleburn, Rebecca VI, 909
Colegate, Edward II, 348
Coleman, ??? III, 79
Coleman, ??? III, 103
Coleman, ??? III, 222
Coleman, Abigail I, 282
Coleman, Abigail I, 301
Coleman, Abigail I, 306
Coleman, Abraham III, 78
Coleman, Abraham B. III, 78
Coleman, Abraham B. III, 79
Coleman, Acsah II, 988
Coleman, Acsah II, 990
Coleman, Addison VI, 892
Coleman, Addison VI, 895
Coleman, Alexandria III, 79
Coleman, Almira B. III, 78
Coleman, Alvis I, 338
Coleman, Ann II, 491
Coleman, Ann II, 678
Coleman, Ann VI, 501
Coleman, Ann VI, 807
Coleman, Ann B. II, 491
Coleman, Ann B. II, 701
Coleman, Ann B. VI, 895
Coleman, Ann W. VI, 865
Coleman, Anna V, 146
Coleman, Anna E. III, 78
Coleman, Anna E. III, 181
Coleman, Anna M. III, 78
Coleman, Anna M. III, 103
Coleman, Annie III, 78
Coleman, Annie Claire III, 242
Coleman, Archibald III, 78
Coleman, Archibald III, 79
Coleman, Archibald III, 242
Coleman, Avis I, 282
Coleman, Avis I, 301
Coleman, Avis I, 311
Coleman, Avis III, 78
Coleman, Avis B. III, 78
Coleman, Avis B. III, 122
Coleman, Bartlett B. VI, 807
Coleman, Benjamin II, 1070
Coleman, Benjamin III, 78
Coleman, Benjamin W. II, 1070
Coleman, Bennett I, 301
Coleman, Bessie T. IV, 189
Coleman, Bethia Y. III, 20
Coleman, Bethia Y. III, 78
Coleman, Bethiah V, 788
Coleman, Betsey VI, 895
Coleman, Betsy VI, 807
Coleman, Burnett B. I, 282
Coleman, Carline VI, 805
Coleman, Caroline III, 78
Coleman, Caroline III, 253
Coleman, Caroline VI, 859
Coleman, Caroline M. VI, 895
Coleman, Caroline M. VI, 1003
Coleman, Catharine VI, 811
Coleman, Catharine VI, 970
Coleman, Catharine Deyerle VI, 808
Coleman, Cephalonia VI, 895
Coleman, Charles III, 78
Coleman, Charles A. IV, 189
Coleman, Charles S. III, 20
Coleman, Charles S. III, 78
Coleman, Charles S. III, 79
Coleman, Charles W. V, 899
Coleman, Chas. IV, 1310
Coleman, Chas. I. III, 78
Coleman, Clarissa III, 78
Coleman, Clarissa III, 122
Coleman, Daniel VI, 235
Coleman, David II, 988
Coleman, David II, 989
Coleman, David II, 990
Coleman, David II, 1036
Coleman, David II, 1048
Coleman, David III, 78
Coleman, David III, 122
Coleman, David VI, 807
Coleman, David VI, 820
Coleman, Deborah III, 78
Coleman, Deborah III, 79
Coleman, Donald Whitaker III, 78
Coleman, Easter VI, 895
Coleman, Edith J. I, 282
Coleman, Edward B. III, 78
Coleman, Edward B. III, 79
Coleman, Elias I, 282
Coleman, Elias I, 301
Coleman, Elias I, 315
Coleman, Elijah I, 264
Coleman, Elijah I, 282
Coleman, Elijah I, 301
Coleman, Elijah I, 303
Coleman, Elijah I, 305
Coleman, Elijah I, 314
Coleman, Elijah I, 328
Coleman, Elijah I, 338
Coleman, Elisabeth Rosa I, 614
Coleman, Eliza III, 78
Coleman, Eliza III, 79
Coleman, Eliza III, 181
Coleman, Eliza VI, 895
Coleman, Eliza S. W. VI, 807
Coleman, Elizabeth I, 282
Coleman, Elizabeth I, 301
Coleman, Elizabeth I, 305
Coleman, Elizabeth I, 309
Coleman, Elizabeth II, 170
Coleman, Elizabeth II, 208
Coleman, Elizabeth II, 239
Coleman, Elizabeth II, 245
Coleman, Elizabeth II, 348
Coleman, Elizabeth II, 491
Coleman, Elizabeth II, 516
Coleman, Elizabeth II, 645
Coleman, Elizabeth II, 964
Coleman, Elizabeth II, 1070
Coleman, Elizabeth IV, 615
Coleman, Elizabeth IV, 679
Coleman, Elizabeth IV, 735
Coleman, Elizabeth IV, 746
Coleman, Elizabeth IV, 836
Coleman, Elizabeth VI, 805
Coleman, Elizabeth VI, 862
Coleman, Elizabeth VI, 865
Coleman, Elizabeth VI, 953
Coleman, Elizabeth VI, 1000
Coleman, Ellis II, 348
Coleman, Elsie Bertha IV, 1310
Coleman, Emily III, 78
Coleman, Emily III, 222
Coleman, Emily M. III, 90

Coleman, Emily Montgomery III, 78
Coleman, Emily Montgomery III, 79
Coleman, Esther II, 348
Coleman, Esther VI, 895
Coleman, Eugene IV, 1310
Coleman, Eunice V, 788
Coleman, Ferdinand T. III, 78
Coleman, Flora B. III, 79
Coleman, Francis III, 79
Coleman, Francis B. Troy III, 78
Coleman, Frank V, 146
Coleman, Frank V, 158
Coleman, Frank J. V, 158
Coleman, Frederick William III, 79
Coleman, Geo. III, 20
Coleman, Geo. III, 78
Coleman, Geo. III, 79
Coleman, George III, 78
Coleman, George III, 79
Coleman, George III, 181
Coleman, George M. V, 899
Coleman, Grace II, 989
Coleman, Grace II, 990
Coleman, Grace II, 1036
Coleman, Hannah II, 170
Coleman, Hannah II, 208
Coleman, Hannah II, 245
Coleman, Hannah II, 348
Coleman, Hannah II, 463
Coleman, Hannah II, 491
Coleman, Hannah II, 524
Coleman, Harriett L. I, 282
Coleman, Isaac P. II, 284
Coleman, Isaac Pearson II, 208
Coleman, Isabella G. VI, 895
Coleman, James II, 348
Coleman, James II, 733
Coleman, James II, 850
Coleman, James IV, 189
Coleman, James VI, 805
Coleman, James VI, 811
Coleman, James VI, 888
Coleman, James VI, 892
Coleman, James VI, 895
Coleman, James VI, 981
Coleman, James B. VI, 807
Coleman, James Macy III, 78
Coleman, James Macy III, 79
Coleman, James Macy III, 321
Coleman, Jane II, 1070
Coleman, Jane VI, 807
Coleman, Jane B. II, 1070
Coleman, Jared III, 79
Coleman, Jeesey VI, 961
Coleman, Jesse I, 282
Coleman, Jesse I, 301
Coleman, Jesse I, 315
Coleman, Jesse I, 656
Coleman, Jesse VI, 895
Coleman, Jesse VI, 905
Coleman, John I, 627
Coleman, John II, 988
Coleman, John II, 989
Coleman, John II, 990
Coleman, John II, 1036
Coleman, John III, 78
Coleman, John III, 79
Coleman, John V, 788
Coleman, John V, 989
Coleman, John VI, 483
Coleman, John VI, 501
Coleman, John VI, 886
Coleman, John VI, 895
Coleman, John VI, 970
Coleman, John VI, 1011
Coleman, John J. IV, 1310
Coleman, John Miller V, 989
Coleman, John S. I, 282
Coleman, Jordan VI, 905
Coleman, Joseph II, 348
Coleman, Joseph II, 463
Coleman, Joseph II, 491
Coleman, Katie I, 627
Coleman, Leighton P. III, 79
Coleman, Leroy VI, 892
Coleman, Leroy VI, 895
Coleman, Leroy VI, 978
Coleman, Leroy VI, 1011
Coleman, Lindsay VI, 807
Coleman, Lindsay VI, 895
Coleman, Louisa III, 216
Coleman, Louisa VI, 826
Coleman, Louisa VI, 1011
Coleman, Louisa Y. III, 78
Coleman, Louisa Y. III, 79
Coleman, Lucy M. VI, 895
Coleman, Lydia H. V, 899
Coleman, M. E. III, 78
Coleman, M. Elizabeth IV, 612
Coleman, Mabel III, 79
Coleman, Malvena IV, 189
Coleman, Margaret II, 491
Coleman, Maria III, 79
Coleman, Maria III, 335
Coleman, Maria B. III, 78
Coleman, Mariah VI, 895
Coleman, Martha V, 146
Coleman, Martha A. VI, 819
Coleman, Martha J. VI, 892
Coleman, Mary I, 282
Coleman, Mary I, 301
Coleman, Mary I, 313
Coleman, Mary I, 314
Coleman, Mary II, 348
Coleman, Mary II, 463
Coleman, Mary II, 491
Coleman, Mary II, 645
Coleman, Mary V, 899
Coleman, Mary VI, 859
Coleman, Mary VI, 887
Coleman, Mary VI, 895
Coleman, Mary A. E. VI, 820
Coleman, Mary C. IV, 189
Coleman, Mary Eliz. III, 78
Coleman, Mary Elma III, 78
Coleman, Mary Elma III, 321
Coleman, Mary J. I, 282
Coleman, Mary Margaret III, 69
Coleman, Mary Margaret III, 79
Coleman, Mary W. III, 79
Coleman, Mary W. III, 222
Coleman, Mary W. VI, 736
Coleman, Mary W. VI, 765
Coleman, Milton IV, 1310
Coleman, Minnie V, 146
Coleman, Minnie V, 158
Coleman, Minnie M. V, 158
Coleman, Minnie May V, 146
Coleman, Mollie T. IV, 189
Coleman, Mordecai II, 348
Coleman, Naomi J. V, 989
Coleman, Nathan I, 282
Coleman, Nathan I, 301
Coleman, Nathan III, 78
Coleman, Nathan III, 79
Coleman, Nathan VI, 736
Coleman, Nathaniel II, 170
Coleman, Nathaniel II, 208
Coleman, Nathaniel II, 239
Coleman, Nathaniel II, 245
Coleman, Nicholas VI, 1011
Coleman, Obed V, 899
Coleman, Obed B. V, 899
Coleman, Pasty VI, 892
Coleman, Patrick H. VI, 808
Coleman, Patrick H. VI, 819
Coleman, Pauline VI, 807
Coleman, Peninah D. I, 282
Coleman, Penninah D. I, 301
Coleman, Penninah D. I, 328
Coleman, Permelia VI, 895
Coleman, Pharibe I, 328
Coleman, Phebe I, 806
Coleman, Phebe I, 807
Coleman, Phebe II, 170
Coleman, Phebe III, 78
Coleman, Phebe III, 79
Coleman, Phebe IV, 189
Coleman, Phebe VI, 379
Coleman, Phebe VI, 459
Coleman, Phebe VI, 736
Coleman, Pherabe I, 282
Coleman, Pheriba I, 301
Coleman, Pheriba I, 315
Coleman, Pheriba I, 656
Coleman, Phinehas I, 301
Coleman, Phinihas I, 282
Coleman, Pinninah D. I, 328
Coleman, Pinninah D. I, 330
Coleman, Polly VI, 966
Coleman, Polly VI, 981
Coleman, Prudence II, 491
Coleman, Rachel I, 282
Coleman, Rachel I, 301
Coleman, Rachel I, 303
Coleman, Rachel I, 328
Coleman, Rachel I, 338
Coleman, Rachel II, 491
Coleman, Rachel II, 645
Coleman, Rachel VI, 895
Coleman, Rebecca II, 348
Coleman, Rebecca B. III, 78
Coleman, Rebecca B. III, 90
Coleman, Rebecca Fitzhugh III, 79
Coleman, Rebecka II, 348
Coleman, Rebeckah II, 442
Coleman, Richard V, 899
Coleman, Robert B. III, 79
Coleman, Robert B. A. III, 79
Coleman, Robert H. III, 79
Coleman, Robert H. VI, 808
Coleman, Robert L. VI, 819
Coleman, Robert L. VI, 895
Coleman, Robert S. VI, 808
Coleman, Robt. III, 79
Coleman, Roch. III, 79
Coleman, Rosa I, 627
Coleman, Rosalie III, 79
Coleman, Rosalie H. III, 79
Coleman, Ruth I, 627
Coleman, Ruth II, 988
Coleman, Ruth II, 989
Coleman, Ruth II, 990
Coleman, Ruth II, 1036
Coleman, S. P. VI, 805
Coleman, Sallie I, 656
Coleman, Sally I, 282
Coleman, Sally I, 301
Coleman, Sally I, 303
Coleman, Sally I, 315
Coleman, Sally V, 899
Coleman, Sally VI, 888
Coleman, Sally VI, 895
Coleman, Sam'l S. III, 79
Coleman, Samuel II, 348
Coleman, Samuel II, 1070
Coleman, Samuel III, 79
Coleman, Samuel IV, 679
Coleman, Samuel VI, 895
Coleman, Samuel Bettle II, 491
Coleman, Samuel M. III, 79
Coleman, Samuel Matlack VI, 736
Coleman, Samuel S. III, 79
Coleman, Samuel S. III, 222
Coleman, Samuel S. VI, 736
Coleman, Samuel S. VI, 765
Coleman, Samuel, Jr. II, 284
Coleman, Samuel, Jr. II, 491
Coleman, Sarah II, 348
Coleman, Sarah II, 491
Coleman, Sarah II, 510
Coleman, Sarah II, 523
Coleman, Sarah II, 552
Coleman, Sarah IV, 679
Coleman, Sarah E. VI, 807
Coleman, Sarah E. VI, 892
Coleman, Sarah M. III, 79
Coleman, Saul S. III, 79
Coleman, Silas III, 78
Coleman, Silas B. III, 78
Coleman, Silas B. III, 79
Coleman, Silas B. III, 90
Coleman, Sophia VI, 978
Coleman, Sophia B. III, 20
Coleman, Sophia B. III, 78
Coleman, Sophronia M. I, 282
Coleman, Spilsby VI, 807
Coleman, Stephen II, 348
Coleman, Stephen II, 491
Coleman, Susan III, 79
Coleman, Susan M. III, 79
Coleman, Susan Mary III, 79
Coleman, Susanna V, 899
Coleman, Susanna VI, 892
Coleman, Susannah V, 899
Coleman, Susannah VI, 953
Coleman, Sylvanus V, 899
Coleman, Thadeus V, 899
Coleman, Theophilas I, 301
Coleman, Thomas II, 208
Coleman, Thomas II, 348
Coleman, Thomas II, 491
Coleman, Viola May IV, 1310
Coleman, Washington III, 79
Coleman, Washington VI, 736
Coleman, Wd. Anna III, 78
Coleman, Wd. Elizabeth II, 170
Coleman, Wiatt VI, 895
Coleman, William II, 348
Coleman, William II, 442
Coleman, William VI, 895
Coleman, William B. III, 78
Coleman, William B. III, 79
Coleman, William E. VI, 807
Coleman, William E. VI, 820
Coleman, Wm. II, 442
Coleman, Wm. II, 463
Coleman, Wm. II, 516
Coleman, Wm. II, 523
Coleman, Wm. II, 524
Coleman, Wm. B. III, 69
Coleman, Wyatt VI, 895
Coleman, Zilpha I, 301
Coleman, Zilpha I, 314
Coles, Abigail III, 398
Coles, Abigail III, 404
Coles, Abigail P. III, 404
Coles, Agnes III, 79
Coles, Alan Marple III, 79
Coles, Albert III, 403
Coles, Albert III, 423
Coles, Alexander Youngs III, 404
Coles, Alice III, 79
Coles, Amelia III, 403
Coles, Amelia III, 404
Coles, Amelia III, 416
Coles, Amelia III, 417
Coles, Amelia III, 460
Coles, Amelia III, 461
Coles, Amelia III, 475
Coles, Amelia III, 480
Coles, Amelia III, 487
Coles, Amos, Jr. II, 310
Coles, Amy III, 406
Coles, Ann III, 403
Coles, Ann III, 404
Coles, Ann III, 416
Coles, Ann III, 423
Coles, Ann III, 430
Coles, Ann III, 460
Coles, Ann III, 480
Coles, Ann III, 487
Coles, Ann C. III, 404
Coles, Ann Margaret IV, 379
Coles, Ann Margaret IV, 380
Coles, Ann Margaret V, 881
Coles, Anna III, 79
Coles, Anna III, 399
Coles, Anna III, 403
Coles, Anna III, 404
Coles, Anna III, 416
Coles, Anna IV, 189
Coles, Anna Adelia III, 404
Coles, Anna Adelia III, 420
Coles, Anne III, 403
Coles, Anne III, 404
Coles, Anne III, 423
Coles, Annie III, 393
Coles, Annie H. III, 393
Coles, Annie H. III, 403
Coles, Annie H. III, 404
Coles, Benjamin III, 403
Coles, Benjamin III, 404
Coles, C. H. IV, 189
Coles, Caleb III, 79
Coles, Caroline III, 403
Coles, Caroline Sarah III, 403
Coles, Caroline Sarah III, 439
Coles, Charles II, 62
Coles, Charles III, 481
Coles, Charles III, 502
Coles, Charles IV, 379
Coles, Charles V, 881
Coles, Charles Cyrenius IV, 379
Coles, Charles Cyrenus IV, 380
Coles, Chas. III, 404
Coles, Chas. Cyrenius IV, 379
Coles, Daniel II, 491
Coles, Daniel III, 404
Coles, Daniel III, 422
Coles, Daniel III, 423
Coles, Daniel III, 480
Coles, Daniel III, 487
Coles, Daniel C. III, 403
Coles, David II, 25
Coles, David R. III, 79
Coles, Debora IV, 379
Coles, Deborah II, 491
Coles, Deborah IV, 379
Coles, Deborah IV, 380
Coles, Deborah V, 879
Coles, Deborah V, 881
Coles, Divine H. III, 404
Coles, Divine Hewlett III, 403
Coles, Divine Hewlett III, 407
Coles, Edward Frost III, 403
Coles, Eleanor III, 403
Coles, Eliz. III, 461
Coles, Eliza III, 79
Coles, Eliza IV, 380
Coles, Eliza IV, 418
Coles, Elizabeth II, 62
Coles, Elizabeth II, 170
Coles, Elizabeth III, 401
Coles, Elizabeth III, 403
Coles, Elizabeth III, 404
Coles, Elizabeth III, 450
Coles, Elizabeth IV, 379
Coles, Elizabeth IV, 380
Coles, Elizabeth V, 881
Coles, Elizabeth B. III, 404
Coles, Elizabeth F. III, 408
Coles, Elizabeth H. III, 403
Coles, Elizabeth H. III, 404
Coles, Elizabeth H. III, 461
Coles, Ellen Gardner III, 79
Coles, Ellen Gardner III, 86
Coles, Frances S. III, 400
Coles, Frances S. III, 404
Coles, Frank IV, 189
Coles, Franklin Albert III, 403
Coles, Franklin Albert III, 439
Coles, Hanna III, 403
Coles, Hannah II, 25
Coles, Hannah II, 62
Coles, Hannah III, 79
Coles, Hannah III, 260
Coles, Hannah III, 313
Coles, Hannah III, 403
Coles, Hannah III, 404
Coles, Hannah III, 405
Coles, Hannah III, 450
Coles, Henry III, 403
Coles, Henry III, 404
Coles, Henry III, 412
Coles, Henry W. III, 404
Coles, Henry Whitson III, 403
Coles, Isaac II, 849
Coles, Isaac II, 905
Coles, Isaac III, 399
Coles, Isaac III, 403
Coles, Isaac III, 404
Coles, Isaac III, 466
Coles, Isaac III, 470
Coles, Isaac C. III, 403
Coles, Isaac R. III, 400
Coles, Isaac R. III, 403
Coles, Isaac R. III, 404
Coles, Jacob II, 25
Coles, Jacob III, 79
Coles, Jacob III, 400
Coles, Jacob III, 402
Coles, Jacob III, 403
Coles, Jacob III, 404
Coles, Jacob III, 416
Coles, Jacob III, 417
Coles, Jacob III, 430
Coles, Jacob III, 452
Coles, James T. VI, 995
Coles, James W. III, 79
Coles, Jane III, 404
Coles, Jane III, 430
Coles, Jarvis III, 398
Coles, Jarvis III, 404
Coles, Jemima III, 460
Coles, John III, 79
Coles, John III, 86
Coles, John III, 476
Coles, John VI, 807
Coles, John Hewlett III, 404
Coles, John S. II, 25
Coles, Jordan III, 79
Coles, Jordan III, 378
Coles, Jos. III, 450
Coles, Joseph II, 25
Coles, Joseph II, 62
Coles, Joseph III, 74
Coles, Joseph III, 79
Coles, Joseph III, 260
Coles, Joseph III, 314
Coles, Joseph III, 403
Coles, Joseph III, 404
Coles, Joseph III, 405
Coles, Joseph III, 438
Coles, Julia II, 310
Coles, Kezia III, 403
Coles, Kezia III, 480
Coles, Kezia III, 502
Coles, Kezia W. III, 460
Coles, Keziah III, 397
Coles, Keziah III, 403
Coles, Keziah III, 404
Coles, Keziah III, 466
Coles, Lavinia III, 403
Coles, Lavinia III, 408
Coles, Leonard III, 403
Coles, Leonard F. III, 396
Coles, Leonard F. III, 404
Coles, Little Tommy III, 404
Coles, Lorette III, 404
Coles, Louisa W. VI, 807
Coles, Lydia II, 310
Coles, Lydia A. III, 403
Coles, Lydia A. III, 407
Coles, Lydia Ann IV, 379
Coles, Lydia Ann IV, 380
Coles, Lydia Ann V, 881
Coles, Lydia H. II, 284
Coles, Lydia H. II, 290
Coles, Margaret III, 79
Coles, Margaret III, 175
Coles, Maria A. III, 404
Coles, Maria A. III, 431
Coles, Mariah A. III, 393
Coles, Mariah O. III, 403
Coles, Marion III, 79
Coles, Marion III, 175
Coles, Martha II, 25
Coles, Martha III, 403
Coles, Martha III, 404

les, Martha III, 412
les, Martha III, 416
les, Martha T. III, 404
les, Mary II, 25
les, Mary II, 491
les, Mary III, 79
les, Mary III, 378
les, Mary III, 403
les, Mary III, 404
les, Mary III, 470
les, Mary III, 481
les, Mary III, 502
les, Mary IV, 379
les, Mary IV, 380
les, Mary IV, 443
les, Mary V, 881
les, Mary A. III, 404
les, Mary A. III, 409
les, Mary Amelia III, 403
les, Mary Ann II, 284
les, Mary Ann III, 79
les, Mary Parwina IV, 379
les, Mary W. II, 849
les, Mary W. II, 905
les, Mary W. III, 403
les, May Gertrude III, 404
les, May Gertrude III, 407
les, Nathaniel III, 397
les, Nathaniel III, 403
les, Nathaniel III, 404
les, Nathaniel III, 450
les, Oscar L. III, 404
les, Paerson IV, 380
les, Pamelia III, 480
les, Pamelia III, 502
les, Pearson V, 881
les, Penelope III, 79
les, Penelope III, 314
les, Penelope III, 404
les, Penelope III, 450
les, Phebe III, 404
les, Phebe III, 457
les, Rhuben B. II, 310
les, Richard II, 25
les, Richard II, 62
les, Richard M. II, 25
les, Richard S. II, 62
les, Robert III, 79
les, Robert III, 313
les, Robert Reed III, 403
les, Robert, Jr. III, 470
les, Sallie III, 431
les, Sallie E. II, 849
les, Sallie E. II, 905
les, Sallie P. III, 404
les, Sallie P. III, 407
les, Samuel II, 25
les, Samuel II, 170
les, Samuel III, 79
les, Samuel III, 403
les, Samuel III, 408
les, Sarah II, 62
les, Sarah II, 138
les, Sarah III, 79
les, Sarah III, 86
les, Sarah III, 400
les, Sarah III, 402
les, Sarah III, 403
les, Sarah III, 404
les, Sarah III, 416
les, Sarah III, 417
les, Sarah III, 451
les, Sarah III, 452
les, Sarah III, 476
les, Sarah III, 481
les, Sarah III, 502
les, Sarah Amelia III, 404
les, Sarah Amelia III, 409
les, Sarah Amelia III, 475
les, Sarah H. III, 404
les, Sarah M. IV, 379
les, Sarah M. IV, 380
les, Sarah M. V, 881
les, Sarah S. II, 25
les, Sarah W. IV, 615
les, Solomon III, 404
les, Solomon III, 457
les, Susan III, 396
les, Susan III, 404
les, Temperance III, 403
les, Temperance III, 404
les, Thomas III, 403
les, Thomas III, 404
les, Thomas III, 416
les, Thomas III, 460
les, Thomas III, 461
les, Thomas III, 475
les, Thomas III, 480
les, Thomas III, 502
les, Thomas A. III, 404
les, Thomas H. III, 403
Coles, Thomas H. III, 404
Coles, Thomas H. III, 420
Coles, Thomas H. III, 431
Coles, Thos. III, 403
Coles, Thos. III, 404
Coles, Thos. III, 416
Coles, Thos. H. II, 849
Coles, Thos. H. II, 905
Coles, Thos. H. III, 404
Coles, Thos. H. III, 407
Coles, Wd. Amelia III, 422
Coles, Wd. Amelia III, 423
Coles, Wd. Anne III, 403
Coles, Wd. Hannah III, 438
Coles, William III, 79
Coles, William III, 175
Coles, William C. III, 404
Coles, William C. III, 460
Coles, William H. III, 404
Coles, William H., Jr. III, 404
Coles, Wm. II, 62
Coles, Wm. H. III, 393
Coles, Wm. H. III, 403
Coles, Wm. H. III, 404
Coles, Wm. H. III, 409
Coles, Wm. H. III, 431
Coles, Wm. N. II, 62
Coles, Wm. S. II, 25
Coleson, Ann II, 492
Coleson, Caleb II, 25
Coleson, Mary II, 54
Coleson, Naomi II, 62
Coleson, Naomi II, 80
Coleson, Rebecca I, 42
Coleson, Rebecca I, 86
Coleson, Rebecca Ann II, 25
Coleson, Rebecca Ann II, 62
Coleson, Sarah II, 25
Coleson, Sarah II, 62
Coleson, Sarah II, 492
Coleson, Uriah VI, 379
Coleson, Wm. II, 54
Coleston, Margaret II, 492
Coletrane, Adaliza C. I, 743
Coletrane, Allen Baily I, 743
Coletrane, Branson I, 743
Coletrane, David Childs I, 743
Coletrane, Deborah Ellen I, 744
Coletrane, Elizabeth Allace I, 744
Coletrane, Elizabeth P. I, 743
Coletrane, Elizabeth Roella I, 744
Coletrane, Ewdoxia Jane I, 743
Coletrane, Hannah I, 744
Coletrane, Hannah Conela I, 744
Coletrane, Hannah Jane I, 744
Coletrane, Jacob I, 744
Coletrane, Jesse Franklin I, 744
Coletrane, John Calvin I, 744
Coletrane, John Madison I, 743
Coletrane, Joseph W. I, 743
Coletrane, Martha I, 743
Coletrane, Martha Ann I, 744
Coletrane, Mary I, 744
Coletrane, Mary J. I, 743
Coletrane, Mary Jane I, 744
Coletrane, Rachel Maria I, 744
Coletrane, Rachel Roxana I, 744
Coletrane, Reuben I, 744
Coletrane, Semira I, 744
Coletrane, William I, 744
Coletrane, William Anderson I, 744
Coley, Emily I, 925
Coley, Henrietta I, 614
Coley, Henrietta I, 624
Coley, J. D. I, 614
Coley, J. D. I, 616
Coley, J. D. I, 624
Coley, Rachel I, 301
Coley, Rachel I, 314
Coley, Widow Henrietta I, 616
Colflesh, Emma IV, 1153
Colflesh, J. C. IV, 1153
Colflesh, James IV, 1153
Colflesh, Samuel IV, 1153
Colhoun, Margaret II, 788
Coliar, Mariam I, 301
Coliar, Mariam I, 307
Colier, Amos IV, 1248
Colier, Elizabeth A. IV, 1248
Colier, Samuel I, 233
Colier, Smith I, 302
Colier, Temperance I, 301
Colier, Temperance I, 302
Coline, John II, 442
Colket, Carl III, 79
Colket, Eliz. Paxson III, 242
Colket, Elizabeth III, 79
Colket, Elizabeth P. III, 79
Colket, Elizabeth P. III, 361
Colket, Ethel II, 850
Colket, Ethel II, 907
Colket, Ethel III, 79
Colket, Ethel III, 361
Colket, Ethel P. III, 242
Colket, J. Hamilton III, 79
Colket, J. Hamilton III, 361
Colket, James Hamilton II, 850
Colket, James Hamilton II, 907
Colket, James Hamilton III, 79
Colket, Jane H. III, 79
Colket, Jas. H. III, 242
Colket, Jennie H. II, 850
Colket, Jennie H. II, 907
Colket, Wm. W. II, 850
Colket, Wm. W. II, 907
Colket, Wm. Walker III, 79
Colladay, Amanda M. II, 852
Colladay, Amanda M. II, 919
Colladay, Anna III, 79
Colladay, Anna III, 80
Colladay, Anna III, 123
Colladay, Elizabeth F. III, 80
Colladay, Henry S. III, 79
Colladay, Henry S. III, 80
Colladay, Henry S. III, 123
Colladay, Jacob M. III, 79
Colladay, Julia III, 79
Collar, Sarah IV, 1357
Collar, Sarah IV, 1361
Collens, Daniel IV, 189
Collens, Earnest IV, 189
Collens, Elizabeth IV, 189
Collens, Mahlon I, 961
Coller, Rachel V, 40
Coller, Rachel V, 122
Coller, Thomas VI, 235
Collers, Elizabeth V, 989
Collerson, Ruth I, 1117
Collerson, Ruth I, 1122
Collet, Mary V, 146
Collet, Mary VI, 396
Collet, Rebecca V, 64
Collet, Rebecca V, 146
Collett, Alice V, 482
Collett, Alice V, 486
Collett, Annie B. V, 158
Collett, Charity VI, 379
Collett, Charity VI, 396
Collett, Daniel VI, 379
Collett, Dr. Fred III, 80
Collett, Mary III, 80
Collett, Mary III, 274
Collett, Mary VI, 379
Collett, Mary I. III, 80
Collett, Rebecca V, 158
Collett, Rebecca V, 482
Collett, Rebekah VI, 379
Collett, Rebekah VI, 397
Collett, Sarah V, 158
Collett, Sarah V, 187
Collett, Virginia V, 158
Collett, Virginia V, 187
Collett, Wm. R. V, 989
Colley, Amy II, 209
Colley, Frances VI, 867
Colley, Jane III, 318
Colley, Jane III, 379
Colley, Jane III, 385
Colley, John II, 442
Colley, John II, 482
Colley, John II, 491
Colley, Martha II, 442
Colley, Samuel II, 209
Colley, Susanah II, 482
Colley, Susanah II, 491
Collice, Benna H. V, 556
Collice, Cynthia V, 556
Collice, Elmer M. V, 556
Collice, Jane E. V, 556
Collice, Lillie V, 556
Collier, Asa I, 302
Collier, Benjamin II, 62
Collier, Benjamin II, 74
Collier, Bessie I, 335
Collier, Catharine I, 335
Collier, Drucilla I, 929
Collier, Elisabeth I, 135
Collier, Elisabeth I, 136
Collier, Elisabeth I, 161
Collier, Elisabeth I, 233
Collier, Elizabeth II, 62
Collier, Elizabeth II, 74
Collier, George I, 335
Collier, George W. I, 335
Collier, Hannah E. V, 230
Collier, Isabell II, 62
Collier, John M. E. I, 302
Collier, Jonathan V, 324
Collier, Jonathan V, 325
Collier, Joseph I, 282
Collier, Josiah I, 282
Collier, Julia I, 335
Collier, Louise I, 921
Collier, Mahala J. V, 230
Collier, Margaret I, 301
Collier, Margaret I, 335
Collier, Margaret V, 230
Collier, Margaret V, 324
Collier, Margaret V, 325
Collier, Margarit II, 163
Collier, Marris I, 301
Collier, Martha I, 301
Collier, Martha I, 317
Collier, Mary I, 301
Collier, Mary I, 875
Collier, Mary I, 905
Collier, Mary V, 230
Collier, Mary V, 324
Collier, Mary V, 325
Collier, Matilda I, 302
Collier, Millie R. I, 302
Collier, Miriam I, 301
Collier, Miriam V, 230
Collier, Miriam V, 324
Collier, Miriam V, 325
Collier, Revel I, 335
Collier, Rhoda I, 301
Collier, Robert S. I, 335
Collier, Ruth I, 921
Collier, Samuel I, 135
Collier, Samuel I, 136
Collier, Samuel I, 161
Collier, Samuel I, 233
Collier, Samuel I, 282
Collier, Samuel V, 230
Collier, Samuel V, 324
Collier, Samuel V, 325
Collier, Sarah IV, 1357
Collier, Sarah IV, 1361
Collier, W. G. I, 302
Collier, William I, 335
Collier, William V, 230
Collier, William H. I, 921
Collignow, John B. V, 325
Collignow, Joseph V, 325
Collin, Matthew I, 152
Colling, Daniel IV, 1052
Colling, David IV, 1052
Colling, Elizabeth IV, 1052
Colling, Ernest IV, 1052
Colling, Francis II, 225
Colling, John IV, 1052
Colling, Mary IV, 1052
Collingnow, Joseph V, 325
Collings, Earnest IV, 189
Collings, Elizabeth IV, 189
Collings, Francis II, 209
Collings, James II, 442
Collings, John VI, 27
Collings, John VI, 28
Collings, John VI, 37
Collings, Joseph II, 209
Collings, Margaret II, 491
Collings, Mary II, 699
Collings, Mary VI, 28
Collings, Mary VI, 37
Collings, Rebecca II, 200
Collings, Rebecca II, 209
Collings, Rebecca II, 491
Collins, ??? III, 43
Collins, ??? III, 81
Collins, ??? V, 556
Collins, ??? V, 899
Collins, ??? VI, 293
Collins, Aaron II, 348
Collins, Abel C. III, 80
Collins, Abel C. III, 308
Collins, Abel T. III, 80
Collins, Abigail II, 591
Collins, Abraham II, 170
Collins, Abram, Jr. IV, 1153
Collins, Agnes V, 990
Collins, Albert II, 170
Collins, Albert II, 284
Collins, Alfred III, 80
Collins, Alice B. II, 147
Collins, Alice B. II, 156
Collins, Allen II, 130
Collins, Almasin V, 900
Collins, Almerin V, 230
Collins, Amelia Jane III, 81
Collins, Amirca I, 301
Collins, Amirica I, 301
Collins, Amy IV, 1353
Collins, Amy R. IV, 1357
Collins, Amy R. IV, 1361
Collins, Andrew V, 989
Collins, Andrew V, 990
Collins, Andrew VI, 820
Collins, Andrew VI, 842
Collins, Andrew VI, 854
Collins, Andrew J. VI, 816
Collins, Ann II, 170
Collins, Ann II, 209
Collins, Ann II, 284
Collins, Ann II, 348
Collins, Ann II, 491
Collins, Ann II, 492
Collins, Ann II, 614
Collins, Ann II, 687
Collins, Ann III, 81
Collins, Ann III, 139
Collins, Ann IV, 81
Collins, Ann VI, 593
Collins, Ann VI, 599
Collins, Ann VI, 736
Collins, Ann VI, 769
Collins, Ann VI, 807
Collins, Ann Dudley III, 81
Collins, Ann Elizabeth VI, 1006
Collins, Ann Say III, 80
Collins, Ann W. II, 170
Collins, Ann W. II, 284
Collins, Ann W. II, 292
Collins, Anna III, 80
Collins, Anna III, 81
Collins, Anna III, 308
Collins, Anna III, 336
Collins, Anna B. II, 170
Collins, Anna B. II, 307
Collins, Anna B. III, 80
Collins, Anna C. II, 1048
Collins, Anna L. II, 209
Collins, Anna Say II, 170
Collins, Anna V. II, 284
Collins, Annie III, 80
Collins, Annie V, 989
Collins, Arthur II, 209
Collins, Arthur II, 284
Collins, Arthur II, 1048
Collins, Arthur III, 81
Collins, Augustus II, 701
Collins, Benj. S. III, 81
Collins, Benj. S. III, 309
Collins, Benjamin II, 209
Collins, Benjamin II, 701
Collins, Benjamin II, 989
Collins, Benjamin II, 990
Collins, Benjamin III, 80
Collins, Benjamin IV, 189
Collins, Benjamin IV, 1153
Collins, Benjamin VI, 305
Collins, Benjamin S. III, 40
Collins, Benjamin S. III, 80
Collins, Benjamin Say II, 170
Collins, Benjamin Say III, 80
Collins, Byron C. IV, 1310
Collins, Byron C. IV, 1336
Collins, Calvin VI, 895
Collins, Caroline II, 170
Collins, Caroline II, 279
Collins, Caroline II, 284
Collins, Caroline III, 80
Collins, Caroline III, 81
Collins, Catherine II, 348
Collins, Cathrine VI, 895
Collins, Chalkley II, 348
Collins, Chalkley III, 80
Collins, Charles I, 534
Collins, Charles II, 170
Collins, Charles II, 209
Collins, Charles II, 263
Collins, Charles II, 476
Collins, Charles II, 491
Collins, Charles II, 701
Collins, Charles II, 1048
Collins, Charles III, 80
Collins, Charles III, 81
Collins, Charles B. II, 701
Collins, Charles Ward V, 556
Collins, Christopher S. VI, 801
Collins, Clarkson T. III, 80
Collins, Content III, 80
Collins, Cornelia III, 80
Collins, Cornelia III, 81
Collins, D. III, 81
Collins, Daniel W. V, 989
Collins, David VI, 807
Collins, Deborah III, 80
Collins, Deborah III, 81
Collins, Edith II, 1048
Collins, Edith III, 80
Collins, Edward II, 348
Collins, Edward III, 80
Collins, Edward III, 81
Collins, Edward D. III, 81
Collins, Edward S. III, 81
Collins, Eleanor V, 230
Collins, Eleanor V, 900
Collins, Elenor F. VI, 807
Collins, Eli IV, 1357
Collins, Eliz III, 35

Collins, Eliz. III, 80
Collins, Elizabeth II, 170
Collins, Elizabeth II, 209
Collins, Elizabeth II, 284
Collins, Elizabeth II, 491
Collins, Elizabeth II, 578
Collins, Elizabeth II, 605
Collins, Elizabeth II, 850
Collins, Elizabeth II, 888
Collins, Elizabeth II, 989
Collins, Elizabeth II, 990
Collins, Elizabeth II, 1018
Collins, Elizabeth III, 80
Collins, Elizabeth III, 250
Collins, Elizabeth V, 325
Collins, Elizabeth A. II, 284
Collins, Elizabeth B. III, 80
Collins, Elizabeth B. III, 81
Collins, Elizabeth C. II, 733
Collins, Elizabeth C. II, 734
Collins, Elizabeth C. III, 80
Collins, Elizabeth C. III, 130
Collins, Ella IV, 1248
Collins, Ellen III, 80
Collins, Ellen V, 325
Collins, Ellen J. V, 325
Collins, Ellenor V, 899
Collins, Ellie B. V, 230
Collins, Elma IV, 1274
Collins, Elmer V, 990
Collins, Elva E. V, 556
Collins, Elvira III, 81
Collins, Emeline III, 35
Collins, Emeline III, 80
Collins, Emily B. III, 81
Collins, Emma III, 81
Collins, Emma III, 158
Collins, Emma V, 989
Collins, Emma D. III, 81
Collins, Emmeline III, 80
Collins, Esther IV, 81
Collins, Esther IV, 117
Collins, Ethel Warner VI, 757
Collins, Etta V, 990
Collins, Eunice III, 80
Collins, Eunice III, 81
Collins, Eunice III, 130
Collins, Euphemia II, 348
Collins, Eva V, 230
Collins, Ezra III, 80
Collins, Ezra III, 81
Collins, Ezra III, 130
Collins, F. M. V, 325
Collins, Fannie B. II, 170
Collins, Florence V, 990
Collins, Floyd L. V, 990
Collins, Frances B. II, 170
Collins, Francis II, 170
Collins, Francis II, 209
Collins, Francis II, 263
Collins, Francis II, 284
Collins, Francis II, 1048
Collins, Francis IV, 81
Collins, Franklin V, 989
Collins, Frederick III, 80
Collins, George III, 80
Collins, George V, 325
Collins, George VI, 807
Collins, George B. III, 80
Collins, George F. VI, 816
Collins, Gertrude III, 81
Collins, Gibson V, 989
Collins, Grandison VI, 895
Collins, Gulielma Maria III, 80
Collins, Gurney L. I, 939
Collins, Hannah II, 62
Collins, Hannah II, 130
Collins, Hannah II, 284
Collins, Hannah II, 292
Collins, Hannah III, 40
Collins, Hannah III, 80
Collins, Hannah III, 81
Collins, Hannah III, 97
Collins, Hannah III, 244
Collins, Hannah III, 309
Collins, Hannah Elma III, 81
Collins, Hannah W. II, 733
Collins, Hannah W. II, 748
Collins, Hannah W. III, 81
Collins, Hannah W. III, 368
Collins, Harold David II, 147
Collins, Harold David II, 156
Collins, Harriet VI, 895
Collins, Harry E. V, 556
Collins, Hazel V, 665
Collins, Henderson I, 301
Collins, Henry Albert II, 284
Collins, Henry F. VI, 807
Collins, Henry F. VI, 895
Collins, Henry H. III, 81
Collins, Henry Hill III, 80
Collins, Hollis Lloyd II, 170
Collins, Homer IV, 1248
Collins, Isaac I, 301
Collins, Isaac II, 170
Collins, Isaac II, 174
Collins, Isaac II, 209
Collins, Isaac II, 243
Collins, Isaac II, 263
Collins, Isaac II, 476
Collins, Isaac II, 491
Collins, Isaac II, 733
Collins, Isaac II, 734
Collins, Isaac II, 748
Collins, Isaac III, 80
Collins, Isaac III, 81
Collins, Isaac III, 139
Collins, Isaac III, 250
Collins, Isaac III, 308
Collins, Isaac III, 341
Collins, Isaac IV, 1357
Collins, Isaac VI, 164
Collins, Isaac B. III, 80
Collins, Isaac N. V, 989
Collins, Isaac, Jr. II, 209
Collins, Jacob P. II, 147
Collins, Jacob P. II, 156
Collins, James II, 850
Collins, James II, 888
Collins, James III, 80
Collins, James IV, 1353
Collins, James IV, 1357
Collins, James IV, 1361
Collins, James IV, 1368
Collins, James V, 556
Collins, James VI, 807
Collins, James B. VI, 807
Collins, James P. IV, 1357
Collins, Jane V, 556
Collins, Jane V, 597
Collins, Jane Lydia VI, 736
Collins, Jane M. III, 81
Collins, Jasper V, 989
Collins, Job III, 80
Collins, Job III, 346
Collins, Job III, 481
Collins, John II, 170
Collins, John II, 209
Collins, John II, 284
Collins, John II, 292
Collins, John II, 307
Collins, John II, 850
Collins, John II, 916
Collins, John III, 35
Collins, John III, 80
Collins, John III, 81
Collins, John IV, 81
Collins, John IV, 117
Collins, John V, 230
Collins, John V, 455
Collins, John V, 989
Collins, John VI, 807
Collins, John E. V, 325
Collins, John Eli V, 325
Collins, Joseph II, 170
Collins, Joseph II, 209
Collins, Joseph III, 80
Collins, Joseph III, 81
Collins, Joseph III, 158
Collins, Joseph III, 309
Collins, Joseph IV, 1248
Collins, Joseph IV, 1357
Collins, Joseph VI, 305
Collins, Joseph B. II, 209
Collins, Joseph B. III, 81
Collins, Joseph H. III, 81
Collins, Joseph L. V, 556
Collins, Joseph W. III, 80
Collins, Joseph W. III, 81
Collins, Joshua II, 348
Collins, Joshua II, 463
Collins, Joshua II, 491
Collins, Joshua III, 28
Collins, Josiah Southwick II, 209
Collins, Josie V, 990
Collins, Julian VI, 807
Collins, Karrick Pelouza VI, 757
Collins, Laura V, 556
Collins, Laura Beard V, 380
Collins, Laura May V, 556
Collins, Lavine V, 989
Collins, Leo IV, 865
Collins, Levi V, 556
Collins, Lewis V, 380
Collins, Lewis G. V, 556
Collins, Lindley M. III, 81
Collins, Lockey VI, 807
Collins, Louisa V, 989
Collins, Louisa VI, 842
Collins, Lucinda G. V, 325
Collins, Lucy III, 81
Collins, Lucy Ann IV, 1357
Collins, Lucy Ann IV, 1363
Collins, Lufern IV, 1248
Collins, Lydia II, 209
Collins, Lydia II, 711
Collins, Lynn II, 491
Collins, Mable V, 665
Collins, Maggie V, 230
Collins, Maggie V, 900
Collins, Maggie L. V, 899
Collins, Maggie L. V, 900
Collins, Mahala V, 230
Collins, Mahlon I, 806
Collins, Mahlon I, 961
Collins, Mahlon D. III, 81
Collins, Manson V, 665
Collins, Margaret II, 209
Collins, Margaret II, 243
Collins, Margaret II, 491
Collins, Margaret III, 80
Collins, Margaret V, 230
Collins, Margaret C. III, 238
Collins, Margaret M. II, 209
Collins, Margaret M. II, 733
Collins, Margaret M. II, 734
Collins, Margaret M. III, 80
Collins, Margaretta III, 80
Collins, Margaretta III, 81
Collins, Margaretta C. III, 81
Collins, Margrett II, 348
Collins, Maria III, 28
Collins, Maria III, 81
Collins, Maria W. III, 81
Collins, Marian V, 325
Collins, Mark II, 170
Collins, Mark II, 284
Collins, Mark II, 292
Collins, Martha II, 348
Collins, Martha II, 491
Collins, Martha IV, 1357
Collins, Martha V, 556
Collins, Martha V, 914
Collins, Martha A. V, 900
Collins, Martha Isabella IV, 925
Collins, Martha Lawrie III, 80
Collins, Martha Lipponcott IV, 841
Collins, Martha Louise VI, 377
Collins, Mary II, 170
Collins, Mary II, 209
Collins, Mary II, 239
Collins, Mary II, 348
Collins, Mary II, 491
Collins, Mary II, 591
Collins, Mary II, 614
Collins, Mary III, 80
Collins, Mary IV, 865
Collins, Mary IV, 1357
Collins, Mary V, 556
Collins, Mary VI, 303
Collins, Mary VI, 888
Collins, Mary Anna II, 170
Collins, Mary C. III, 308
Collins, Mary D. III, 81
Collins, Mary E. III, 81
Collins, Mary E. III, 106
Collins, Mary E. V, 989
Collins, Mary Emma III, 81
Collins, Mary Foster III, 81
Collins, Mary G. III, 83
Collins, Mary L. II, 284
Collins, Mary L. II, 307
Collins, Mary Louise V, 665
Collins, Mary O. III, 80
Collins, Mary S. III, 81
Collins, Mary Taber III, 81
Collins, Mary Taber III, 309
Collins, Mary V. VI, 807
Collins, Mason V, 665
Collins, May Amelia V, 556
Collins, Melva D. V, 556
Collins, Melvina IV, 1248
Collins, Micajah II, 348
Collins, Micajah III, 80
Collins, Minda V, 990
Collins, Murray H. V, 899
Collins, Murray H. V, 900
Collins, Nancy V, 380
Collins, Nancy V, 455
Collins, Nancy VI, 854
Collins, Narcissa IV, 925
Collins, Nathan K. V, 556
Collins, Nellie V, 990
Collins, Nora V, 990
Collins, Paul V, 665
Collins, Peninah IV, 385
Collins, Perry V, 989
Collins, Peter III, 80
Collins, Peter III, 81
Collins, Peter VI, 807
Collins, Peter VI, 833
Collins, Phebe III, 80
Collins, Phebe III, 346
Collins, Phebe B. III, 81
Collins, Phebe B. III, 309
Collins, Phebe W. III, 81
Collins, Polley VI, 895
Collins, Presley VI, 895
Collins, Priscilla I, 136
Collins, Rachel II, 170
Collins, Rachel II, 209
Collins, Rachel II, 243
Collins, Rachel II, 263
Collins, Rachel II, 476
Collins, Rachel II, 491
Collins, Rachel II, 733
Collins, Rachel II, 748
Collins, Rachel III, 80
Collins, Rachel III, 81
Collins, Rachel III, 139
Collins, Rachel III, 250
Collins, Rachel IV, 1357
Collins, Rachel IV, 1368
Collins, Rachel VI, 736
Collins, Rachel Hunt IV, 81
Collins, Rachel Minnie V, 899
Collins, Rachel Minnie V, 900
Collins, Ranso IV, 1248
Collins, Ransom IV, 1248
Collins, Ranson I, 301
Collins, Rebecca II, 170
Collins, Rebecca II, 209
Collins, Rebecca II, 491
Collins, Rebecca III, 80
Collins, Rebecca III, 81
Collins, Rebecca III, 139
Collins, Rebecca III, 308
Collins, Rebecca III, 309
Collins, Rebecca III, 341
Collins, Rebecca IV, 467
Collins, Rebecca V, 325
Collins, Rebecca E. V, 325
Collins, Richard II, 209
Collins, Richard VI, 1006
Collins, Richard S. III, 28
Collins, Richard S. III, 80
Collins, Richard S. III, 81
Collins, Richard S. III, 355
Collins, Richard S. III, 360
Collins, Robert B. III, 80
Collins, Robert B. III, 81
Collins, Robert B. III, 238
Collins, Robt. B. III, 80
Collins, Robt. B. III, 81
Collins, Ruby V, 990
Collins, Ruth C. IV, 1310
Collins, Ruth C. IV, 1336
Collins, Ruth Russell IV, 1310
Collins, S. C. I, 534
Collins, Sallie II, 284
Collins, Sallie II, 850
Collins, Sallie L. II, 916
Collins, Samuel II, 130
Collins, Samuel IV, 1357
Collins, Samuel B. III, 80
Collins, Samuel B. III, 81
Collins, Samuel C. I, 534
Collins, Samuel C. II, 1048
Collins, Samuel C. VI, 736
Collins, Sarah II, 170
Collins, Sarah II, 209
Collins, Sarah II, 263
Collins, Sarah II, 348
Collins, Sarah II, 491
Collins, Sarah II, 492
Collins, Sarah II, 1065
Collins, Sarah II, 1070
Collins, Sarah II, 1074
Collins, Sarah III, 28
Collins, Sarah III, 80
Collins, Sarah III, 81
Collins, Sarah III, 355
Collins, Sarah III, 368
Collins, Sarah VI, 303
Collins, Sarah Ann II, 348
Collins, Sarah Ann II, 491
Collins, Sarah Ann II, 591
Collins, Sarah C. III, 158
Collins, Sarah C. V, 665
Collins, Sarah D. V, 556
Collins, Sarah H. VI, 807
Collins, Sarah S. II, 147
Collins, Sarah S. II, 156
Collins, Sarah T. III, 360
Collins, Sary Elisha VI, 888
Collins, Sidney II, 850
Collins, Sidney H. II, 850
Collins, Sophia IV, 1353
Collins, Sophia IV, 1357
Collins, Sophia IV, 1361
Collins, Sophia IV, 1368
Collins, Sophia V, 989
Collins, Stacy II, 209
Collins, Stacy III, 80
Collins, Stacy B. II, 733
Collins, Stacy B. II, 748
Collins, Stacy B. III, 80
Collins, Stacy B. III, 81
Collins, Stacy B. III, 106
Collins, Stacy B., Jr. III, 81
Collins, Stacy Budd II, 170
Collins, Stephen II, 348
Collins, Stephen II, 491
Collins, Stephen II, 591
Collins, Stephen II, 614
Collins, Stephen IV, 925
Collins, Susan V, 455
Collins, Susan E. V, 556
Collins, Susan H. II, 850
Collins, Susan H. II, 916
Collins, Susanna II, 442
Collins, Susanna III, 80
Collins, Susannah II, 170
Collins, Susannah II, 209
Collins, Susannah II, 263
Collins, Susannah Ann II, 209
Collins, Sussannah VI, 807
Collins, Sydney Hoopes II, 850
Collins, Theodore III, 80
Collins, Theodore III, 81
Collins, Thomas II, 170
Collins, Thomas II, 209
Collins, Thomas II, 348
Collins, Thomas III, 80
Collins, Thomas III, 81
Collins, Thomas V, 40
Collins, Thomas V, 325
Collins, Thomas A. II, 170
Collins, Thomas Elwood III, 81
Collins, Walter V, 665
Collins, Walter V, 990
Collins, Walter D. V, 990
Collins, Walter, Jr. V, 665
Collins, Wd Esther IV, 81
Collins, Wd. Deborah II, 170
Collins, Wd. Rebecca II, 174
Collins, William II, 170
Collins, William II, 348
Collins, William III, 80
Collins, William III, 81
Collins, William V, 325
Collins, William V, 556
Collins, William Albert II, 170
Collins, William B. III, 80
Collins, William B. III, 81
Collins, William H. III, 81
Collins, William M. III, 80
Collins, William P. III, 81
Collins, Willis I. V, 989
Collins, Wm. A. V, 556
Collins, Wm. B. III, 81
Collins, Wm. B. III, 139
Collins, Wm. Dennis VI, 736
Collins, Wm. M. II, 733
Collins, Wm. M. II, 734
Collins, Wm. Morris III, 80
Collins, Zaccheus II, 701
Collins, Zacheus II, 348
Collins, Zacheus II, 491
Collins, Zacheus II, 591
Collins, Zacheus II, 614
Collior, Margaret II, 209
Collior, Margaret II, 238
Collison, Ruth I, 1117
Colloway, Elizabeth E. VI, 815
Collum, Luella V, 832
Collum, Robert V, 835
Collum, Sarah Luella V, 834
Colly, John II, 348
Colly, John II, 442
Colly, Susannah II, 348
Collyer, Benejah V, 40
Collyer, Benjamin II, 25
Collyer, Elizabeth I, 301
Collyer, Elizabeth II, 25
Collyer, Elizabeth IV, 380
Collyer, Elizabeth V, 40
Collyer, Isabel II, 25
Collyer, John II, 25
Collyer, John IV, 380
Collyer, John V, 40
Collyer, Jonothan V, 40
Collyer, Martha II, 25
Collyer, Mary IV, 380
Collyer, Mary V, 40
Collyer, Miriam I, 301
Collyer, Percillah II, 25
Collyer, Rachel V, 40
Collyer, Rhoda IV, 380
Collyer, Rhoda V, 40
Collyer, Samuel I, 136
Collyer, Samuel II, 25
Collyer, Sarah II, 25
Collyer, William II, 25

Colman, ??? III, 365
Colman, Abigail I, 282
Colman, Betsey I, 282
Colman, Celia I, 282
Colman, Elijah I, 282
Colman, Ezekiel I, 282
Colman, Jesse I, 282
Colman, Martha V, 146
Colman, Mary I, 282
Colman, Mary Elma III, 365
Colman, Pheriba I, 282
Colman, Sally I, 282
Colman, Willis I, 282
Colons, Margaret III, 81
Colons, Margaret III, 83
Colons, Margaret III, 243
Colons, Margaret III, 302
Colpitt, Mary IV, 376
Colpitt, Mary IV, 380
Colsen, Mary P. IV, 561
Colson, Ann II, 492
Colson, Anna R. II, 134
Colson, Asa II, 25
Colson, Asa L. II, 134
Colson, Azuba II, 62
Colson, Azuba II, 85
Colson, Azubah II, 62
Colson, Caleb II, 25
Colson, Caleb II, 57
Colson, Caleb II, 62
Colson, David II, 25
Colson, David II, 53
Colson, David II, 62
Colson, David II, 85
Colson, David II, 117
Colson, Deborah II, 62
Colson, Deborah II, 492
Colson, Deborah II, 733
Colson, Elizabeth II, 25
Colson, Elizabeth II, 62
Colson, Elizabeth II, 85
Colson, Esther VI, 379
Colson, George II, 25
Colson, George II, 62
Colson, George II, 70
Colson, George II, 85
Colson, Hannah II, 62
Colson, Helen II, 134
Colson, Helen II, 152
Colson, Hephzibah II, 53
Colson, Hephzibah II, 62
Colson, Hepzibah II, 25
Colson, Jonathan II, 25
Colson, Joshua II, 492
Colson, Mary II, 25
Colson, Mary II, 62
Colson, Mary II, 70
Colson, Naomi II, 62
Colson, Rebecca Ann II, 25
Colson, Rebecca Ann II, 62
Colson, Rebecca Ann II, 701
Colson, Rebeckah I, 42
Colson, Sarah II, 25
Colson, Sarah II, 57
Colson, Sarah II, 62
Colson, Sarah II, 90
Colson, Sarah II, 492
Colson, Sarah VI, 379
Colson, Silvia II, 62
Colson, Silvia II, 98
Colson, Sylvia II, 57
Colson, Sylvia II, 62
Colson, Sylvia II, 348
Colson, Sylvia Spicer II, 492
Colson, Tamer I, 1091
Colson, Tamer I, 1092
Colson, Tamer VI, 379
Colson, Tamor VI, 379
Colson, Uriah VI, 379
Colson, Wd. Mary II, 62
Colson, Wm. II, 57
Colson, Wm. II, 62
Colston, Tamer I, 534
Colston, Tamer VI, 593
Colston, Thomas IV, 82
Colter, Lydia V, 158
Colter, Lydia V, 183
Colton, Abigail III, 81
Colton, Abigail VI, 164
Colton, Ann III, 192
Colton, Ann K. III, 81
Colton, John Bowne III, 81
Colton, Reuben III, 81
Colton, S. I. H. III, 192
Colton, Samuel Horton III, 81
Colton, Samuel Horton III, 192
Coltrain, Abigail I, 779
Coltrain, Charles C. I, 779
Coltrain, Elma Jane I, 779
Coltrain, Hannah I, 757
Coltrain, Hannah I, 769
Coltrain, Jane I, 757
Coltrain, Jesse I, 779
Coltrain, Jesse I, 806
Coltrain, Margaret A. I, 233
Coltrain, Mary E. I, 233
Coltrain, Mary M. I, 779
Coltrain, Phariba I, 233
Coltrain, Ruth A. I, 779
Coltrain, Sarah E. I, 233
Coltrain, Tamer I, 939
Coltrain, William A. I, 233
Coltrain, William P. I, 779
Coltraine, Phariba I, 233
Coltrane, Abigail I, 806
Coltrane, Abigail I, 839
Coltrane, Abigail I, 875
Coltrane, Adela Catharine I, 751
Coltrane, Adeliza I, 923
Coltrane, Albert C. I, 676
Coltrane, Albert L. I, 676
Coltrane, Alexander Smith I, 651
Coltrane, Alice I, 744
Coltrane, Alice I, 875
Coltrane, Alice Luetta I, 875
Coltrane, Allen J. I, 697
Coltrane, Allen Jay I, 744
Coltrane, Allen Jay I, 757
Coltrane, Anna I, 697
Coltrane, Anna I, 757
Coltrane, Anna E. I, 744
Coltrane, Anna M. I, 712
Coltrane, Anna M. I, 736
Coltrane, Anna M. I, 744
Coltrane, Anna M. I, 757
Coltrane, Anna M. I, 771
Coltrane, Branson I, 757
Coltrane, Caroline I, 757
Coltrane, Caroline I, 761
Coltrane, Caroline Elizabeth I, 757
Coltrane, Catharine I, 712
Coltrane, Catharine Adela I, 757
Coltrane, Catherine I, 722
Coltrane, D. Franklin I, 712
Coltrane, David I, 852
Coltrane, David A. I, 757
Coltrane, David Alexander I, 744
Coltrane, David C. I, 757
Coltrane, Deborah Newlin I, 757
Coltrane, Deida I, 852
Coltrane, Didah I, 875
Coltrane, Eleanor I, 921
Coltrane, Eliza Cleopatra I, 757
Coltrane, Eliza Jane I, 751
Coltrane, Eliza Jane I, 757
Coltrane, Eliza Jane I, 767
Coltrane, Elizabeth I, 744
Coltrane, Elizabeth I, 747
Coltrane, Elizabeth I, 757
Coltrane, Elizabeth I, 761
Coltrane, Elizabeth I, 772
Coltrane, Elizabeth C. I, 744
Coltrane, Elizabeth Jane I, 744
Coltrane, Elizabeth Newlin I, 757
Coltrane, Elizabeth Patience I, 757
Coltrane, Ella J. I, 852
Coltrane, Ellen I, 625
Coltrane, Emma I, 651
Coltrane, Emma A. I, 676
Coltrane, Endoxia Jane I, 757
Coltrane, Esther J. I, 676
Coltrane, Esther J. I, 681
Coltrane, Esther Jane I, 676
Coltrane, Eunice L. I, 676
Coltrane, Flora I, 712
Coltrane, George F. I, 697
Coltrane, George F. I, 744
Coltrane, George Fox I, 757
Coltrane, Hannah I, 757
Coltrane, Isaac I, 757
Coltrane, Jacob I, 743
Coltrane, Jacob I, 744
Coltrane, Jacob I, 757
Coltrane, Jacob I, 869
Coltrane, Jacob I, 875
Coltrane, Jacob, Jr. I, 757
Coltrane, James I, 697
Coltrane, James I, 712
Coltrane, James I, 757
Coltrane, James A. I, 712
Coltrane, James A. I, 744
Coltrane, James A. I, 757
Coltrane, James A. I, 771
Coltrane, James Addison I, 744
Coltrane, James R. I, 875
Coltrane, James Ruffin I, 852
Coltrane, James Ruffin I, 875
Coltrane, Jane I, 743
Coltrane, Jane I, 744
Coltrane, Jane I, 757
Coltrane, Jane I, 761
Coltrane, Jesse I, 744
Coltrane, Jesse I, 757
Coltrane, Jesse I, 806
Coltrane, Jesse I, 839
Coltrane, John Addison I, 875
Coltrane, John C. I, 697
Coltrane, John C. I, 744
Coltrane, John M. I, 757
Coltrane, Jonathan W. I, 676
Coltrane, Joseph W. I, 757
Coltrane, Lemuel I, 852
Coltrane, Lemuel I, 875
Coltrane, Lewis I, 875
Coltrane, Lindsay I, 676
Coltrane, Lindsey I, 651
Coltrane, Lydia Ann I, 744
Coltrane, Margaret I, 651
Coltrane, Margaret I, 676
Coltrane, Martha I, 757
Coltrane, Martha I, 766
Coltrane, Martha I, 852
Coltrane, Martha E. I, 676
Coltrane, Martha P. I, 209
Coltrane, Mary I, 744
Coltrane, Mary I, 757
Coltrane, Mary I, 758
Coltrane, Mary I, 806
Coltrane, Mary I, 869
Coltrane, Mary I, 875
Coltrane, Mary I, 926
Coltrane, Mary A. I, 712
Coltrane, Mary A. I, 757
Coltrane, Mary Ann I, 676
Coltrane, Mary E. I, 209
Coltrane, Mary Josephine I, 757
Coltrane, Mary Roella I, 875
Coltrane, Minnie J. I, 852
Coltrane, Miriam E. I, 676
Coltrane, Miriam E. I, 685
Coltrane, Nancy I, 757
Coltrane, Nancy I, 759
Coltrane, Nancy I, 928
Coltrane, Nancy Lorena I, 875
Coltrane, Nannie I, 875
Coltrane, Nathan I, 757
Coltrane, Nathan Adolphus I, 744
Coltrane, Nathan N. I, 744
Coltrane, Nelson I, 744
Coltrane, Nelson I, 757
Coltrane, Rachel I, 757
Coltrane, Rachel I, 759
Coltrane, Rachel Abigail I, 757
Coltrane, Rachel Mary Ann I, 676
Coltrane, Rachel Mary Ann I, 686
Coltrane, Reuben I, 744
Coltrane, Reuben I, 757
Coltrane, Roella I, 875
Coltrane, Rufus Eugene I, 875
Coltrane, Sally Margaret I, 757
Coltrane, Sally Margaret I, 761
Coltrane, Sarah I, 757
Coltrane, Sarah I, 760
Coltrane, Sarah E. I, 209
Coltrane, Sarah T. I, 676
Coltrane, Shubel G. I, 676
Coltrane, Solomon I, 651
Coltrane, Solomon H. I, 651
Coltrane, Solomon H. I, 676
Coltrane, Sonisa I, 676
Coltrane, Sonisa I, 689
Coltrane, Spencer A. I, 712
Coltrane, Spencer A. I, 722
Coltrane, Spencer A. I, 757
Coltrane, Spencer Allen I, 744
Coltrane, Susan I, 852
Coltrane, Tamer I, 757
Coltrane, Tamer I, 922
Coltrane, William I, 651
Coltrane, William I, 676
Coltrane, William I, 744
Coltrane, William I, 757
Coltrane, William I, 758
Coltrane, William I, 806
Coltrane, William I, 875
Coltrane, William A. I, 209
Coltrane, William L. I, 697
Coltrane, William L. I, 744
Coltson, George II, 62
Coltson, Hannah II, 62
Coltson, Hannah II, 90
Colver, Jenny VI, 807
Colver, Joseph VI, 807
Colvert, Alex VI, 895
Colvert, Eliza II, 348
Colvert, George II, 348
Colvert, Mary II, 348
Colvert, Nancey VI, 895
Colvert, Thomas II, 348
Colvin, Alice III, 82
Colvin, Alice III, 152
Colvin, Amaziah V, 380
Colvin, Amy III, 82
Colvin, Amy Mary III, 166
Colvin, Caroline C. IV, 1357
Colvin, Caroline M. C. IV, 691
Colvin, Caroline S. IV, 691
Colvin, Caroline S. IV, 1351
Colvin, Elisabeth W. IV, 1357
Colvin, George IV, 1234
Colvin, Hannah V, 158
Colvin, Hannah V, 482
Colvin, Henry III, 82
Colvin, Henry III, 152
Colvin, Henry III, 166
Colvin, Isaac IV, 1357
Colvin, Jane III, 82
Colvin, John III, 82
Colvin, Lucy A. VI, 807
Colvin, Lydia IV, 691
Colvin, Lydia IV, 1351
Colvin, Lydia IV, 1357
Colvin, M. Pearl V, 158
Colvin, Margaret Caton IV, 1357
Colvin, Mina IV, 1234
Colvin, Nehemiah IV, 691
Colvin, Nehemiah IV, 1351
Colvin, Nehemiah IV, 1357
Colvin, Phebe IV, 1357
Colvin, Phebe V, 158
Colvin, Phebe V, 169
Colvin, Phila IV, 1357
Colvin, Pricilla V, 380
Colvin, Priscilla V, 380
Colvin, Rebecca V, 158
Colvin, Rebecca V, 192
Colvin, Robert VI, 807
Colvin, Sarah IV, 26
Colvin, Sarah IV, 58
Colvin, Thomas Baker IV, 1357
Colvin, Thomas L. Baker IV, 691
Colvin, Thomas L. Baker IV, 1357
Colvin, Thomas S. Baker IV, 691
Colvin, Thomas S. Baker IV, 1351
Colvin, Thomas S. Baker IV, 1357
Colwell, James V, 40
Colwell, John VI, 305
Colwell, Joseph V, 832
Colwell, Marium V, 832
Colyar, Benajah IV, 142
Colyar, Elizabeth I, 209
Colyar, James I, 210
Colyar, James IV, 142
Colyar, John I, 210
Colyar, John IV, 142
Colyar, Mariam I, 210
Colyar, Mary IV, 142
Colyar, Rhody IV, 142
Colyar, Sam I, 209
Colyar, Samuel I, 210
Colyar, Zachariah I, 210
Colyer, Achsah I, 282
Colyer, Ann I, 283
Colyer, Ann I, 301
Colyer, Ann I, 305
Colyer, Anna I, 283
Colyer, Asa I, 302
Colyer, Asa B. I, 283
Colyer, Asa B. I, 302
Colyer, Benajah IV, 142
Colyer, Caroline E. III, 481
Colyer, Clarence S. III, 481
Colyer, Doctor M. S. D. I, 283
Colyer, Doctor M. S. D. I, 302
Colyer, Edward I, 301
Colyer, Edward F. I, 283
Colyer, Elizabeth I, 97
Colyer, Elizabeth I, 283
Colyer, Elizabeth I, 301
Colyer, Elizabeth III, 481
Colyer, Elizabeth IV, 380
Colyer, Elwood I, 283
Colyer, Elwood I, 301
Colyer, Elwood I, 302
Colyer, George F. III, 481
Colyer, Henrietta M. I, 283
Colyer, Henrietta M. I, 302
Colyer, Isabell II, 62
Colyer, Isabell II, 64
Colyer, Isaiah I, 302
Colyer, Jacob III, 481
Colyer, James I, 283
Colyer, James I, 301
Colyer, James IV, 142
Colyer, John I, 301
Colyer, John I, 315
Colyer, John IV, 142
Colyer, John M. I, 283
Colyer, John M. I, 302
Colyer, John M. E. I, 302
Colyer, Joseph I, 302
Colyer, Joseph IV, 142
Colyer, Joseph W. I, 283
Colyer, Margaret I, 301
Colyer, Margaret I, 315
Colyer, Marris I, 301
Colyer, Martha I, 283
Colyer, Martha I, 301
Colyer, Mary I, 301
Colyer, Mary IV, 142
Colyer, Mary IV, 380
Colyer, Matilda I, 302
Colyer, Micajah I, 283
Colyer, Millie R. I, 302
Colyer, Miriam I, 301
Colyer, Miriam IV, 1274
Colyer, Miriam IV, 1286
Colyer, Naamon I, 301
Colyer, Naman I, 301
Colyer, Namon I, 282
Colyer, Namon I, 283
Colyer, Nancy M. I, 283
Colyer, Otheniah I, 301
Colyer, Othneil I, 283
Colyer, Patience I, 283
Colyer, Patience I, 302
Colyer, Phebe I, 283
Colyer, Piety I, 282
Colyer, Ramsom G. I, 283
Colyer, Rhoda I, 301
Colyer, Rhoda I, 315
Colyer, Rhoda IV, 380
Colyer, Rhody IV, 142
Colyer, Richard I, 283
Colyer, Richard I, 301
Colyer, Rufus C. I, 283
Colyer, Rufus D. I, 302
Colyer, Samuel I, 97
Colyer, Samuel I, 283
Colyer, Samuel I, 301
Colyer, Samuel I, 302
Colyer, Samuel I, 315
Colyer, Sarah I, 283
Colyer, Sarah I, 301
Colyer, Sarah I, 306
Colyer, Sarah III, 504
Colyer, Silas E. I, 282
Colyer, Silas E. I, 301
Colyer, Smith I, 302
Colyer, Smitha J. I, 283
Colyer, Temperance I, 283
Colyer, Temperance I, 301
Colyer, Temperance I, 302
Colyer, Temperance I, 306
Colyer, W. G. I, 302
Colyer, Widow Temperence I, 283
Colyer, William I, 283
Colyer, William I, 301
Colyer, William I, 306
Colyer, William G. I, 283
Colyer, William G. I, 302
Colyer, William Penn I, 301
Colyer, Zachariah I, 97
Colyer, Zachariah I, 283
Colyer, Zachariah I, 301
Colyer, Zachariah I, 305
Colyier, Naamon I, 301
Comander, Joseph I, 97
Comb, John I, 256
Comb, Rebecca II, 348
Comb, Samuel II, 348
Comb, Winnifred I, 256
Comba, Benjamin IV, 1153
Comba, Benjamin, Jr. IV, 1153
Comba, Charity IV, 1153
Comba, Rebecca IV, 1153
Comba, Rebecca R. IV, 1153
Comba, Samuel C. IV, 1153
Combe, Benjamin II, 990
Combe, Hannah II, 957
Combe, Mary II, 988
Combe, Mary II, 990
Combe, Samuel II, 492
Combe, Samuel II, 957
Comber, Ann I, 380
Comber, Ann I, 382
Comber, Deborah V, 832
Comber, Deborah V, 833
Comber, Elizabeth I, 380
Comber, Lydia I, 380
Comber, Lydia I, 382
Comber, Lydia I, 399
Comber, Mary I, 380
Comber, Mordecai I, 380
Comber, Rebeccah V, 833
Comber, Rebekah I, 380
Comber, Rebekah I, 390

Comber, Sarah I, 380
Comber, Sarah I, 425
Comber, Susanna I, 380
Comber, Tamer I, 380
Comber, Tamer I, 403
Comber, Tamer Kinworthy I, 380
Combes, Frank C. III, 82
Combes, Frank C., Jr. III, 82
Combes, Mary III, 82
Combs, Abigail II, 990
Combs, Abigail III, 100
Combs, Albert H. III, 82
Combs, Albert H. III, 164
Combs, Almyra V, 40
Combs, Almyra V, 125
Combs, Amos III, 82
Combs, Ann III, 82
Combs, Ann IV, 324
Combs, Benj. IV, 324
Combs, Benjamin II, 209
Combs, Benjamin II, 990
Combs, Benjamin IV, 325
Combs, Charity II, 209
Combs, Charity IV, 324
Combs, Charity IV, 325
Combs, Charity V, 950
Combs, Daniel D. III, 404
Combs, Deborah IV, 325
Combs, Deborah IV, 327
Combs, Deborah Ann III, 404
Combs, Dorinda III, 82
Combs, Dorinda III, 100
Combs, Elias III, 404
Combs, Elias H. III, 481
Combs, Elizabeth II, 788
Combs, Elizabeth II, 990
Combs, Elizabeth II, 1071
Combs, Elizabeth Newell II, 788
Combs, Ezecal, Jr. II, 1071
Combs, Ezekel II, 990
Combs, Ezekial II, 1071
Combs, Ezekial, Jr. II, 1071
Combs, Ezekiel II, 788
Combs, Ezekiel II, 990
Combs, Ezical, Jr. II, 1071
Combs, Frank C. III, 82
Combs, Frank C., Jr. III, 82
Combs, George IV, 325
Combs, Hannah II, 990
Combs, Henrietta III, 82
Combs, Hulda II, 990
Combs, Huldah II, 990
Combs, Jamima V, 298
Combs, Jamima V, 300
Combs, John III, 481
Combs, John W. III, 82
Combs, Martin III, 100
Combs, Martin H. III, 82
Combs, Mary II, 492
Combs, Mary II, 543
Combs, Mary II, 990
Combs, Mary III, 82
Combs, Mary III, 126
Combs, Mary III, 404
Combs, Mary Ann II, 209
Combs, Mary Ann IV, 325
Combs, Mary C. III, 164
Combs, Mary E. III, 82
Combs, Rebecca II, 990
Combs, Rebecca IV, 325
Combs, Rebecca, Jr. II, 990
Combs, Rebeckah II, 492
Combs, Samuel II, 492
Combs, Samuel II, 990
Combs, Samuel II, 995
Combs, Samuel IV, 325
Combs, Sarah II, 209
Combs, Sarah II, 492
Combs, Sarah II, 587
Combs, Sarah II, 1048
Combs, Sarah II, 1049
Combs, Sarah II, 1071
Combs, Sarah VI, 483
Combs, Sarah VI, 552
Combs, Sarah W. II, 1071
Combs, Stephen II, 990
Combs, T. Ellwood II, 850
Combs, Thos. Elwood II, 788
Combs, Wd. Hannah II, 995
Combs, William II, 990
Combs, Winney I, 233
Combs, Winnifred I, 233
Combs, Wm. II, 586
Comegys, Ann II, 348
Comegys, Ann II, 492
Comegys, Anna III, 110
Comegys, Cornelius II, 348
Comely, Abigail II, 990
Comely, Abigail II, 992
Comely, Abraham II, 492
Comely, Abraham II, 990
Comely, Abraham II, 999
Comely, Agnes II, 990
Comely, Alice IV, 26
Comely, Alice G. IV, 26
Comely, Ann II, 492
Comely, Ann II, 990
Comely, Ann II, 999
Comely, Benjamin II, 990
Comely, Ezra IV, 26
Comely, Hannah II, 990
Comely, Isaac II, 990
Comely, Isaac IV, 26
Comely, Isaac W. IV, 26
Comely, Jacob II, 990
Comely, John II, 492
Comely, John II, 990
Comely, John II, 992
Comely, John II, 999
Comely, Lydia IV, 26
Comely, Mary II, 990
Comely, Mary V, 482
Comely, Phebe IV, 26
Comely, Samuel IV, 26
Comely, Susanna IV, 26
Comely, Susannah II, 990
Comely, William IV, 189
Comer, ??? V, 823
Comer, Aaron I, 461
Comer, Aaron I, 475
Comer, Amos I, 380
Comer, Amos I, 457
Comer, Amos I, 461
Comer, Amos I, 475
Comer, Amos I, 481
Comer, Amos I, 1055
Comer, Amos V, 40
Comer, Amos V, 158
Comer, Ann I, 348
Comer, Ann I, 378
Comer, Ann I, 380
Comer, Ann I, 461
Comer, Ann I, 1055
Comer, Ann V, 158
Comer, Anna V, 40
Comer, Anna V, 82
Comer, Anne I, 1060
Comer, Anne I, 1061
Comer, Clara V, 40
Comer, Deborah V, 832
Comer, Elisabeth I, 481
Comer, Eliza Jane V, 665
Comer, Elizabeth I, 348
Comer, Elizabeth I, 380
Comer, Elizabeth I, 461
Comer, Elizabeth I, 475
Comer, Elizabeth I, 1027
Comer, Elizabeth I, 1053
Comer, Elizabeth I, 1055
Comer, Elizabeth I, 1060
Comer, Elizabeth I, 1063
Comer, Elizabeth V, 40
Comer, Henry I, 475
Comer, Hester V, 158
Comer, Hester V, 159
Comer, Hester Compton V, 158
Comer, James I, 1055
Comer, James V, 158
Comer, Jesse I, 348
Comer, Jesse I, 378
Comer, Jesse I, 380
Comer, John I, 348
Comer, John I, 380
Comer, John I, 961
Comer, John I, 1055
Comer, John V, 158
Comer, Joseph I, 348
Comer, Joseph I, 380
Comer, Joseph I, 1027
Comer, Joseph I, 1055
Comer, Joseph I, 1060
Comer, Joseph V, 40
Comer, Joseph V, 158
Comer, Joseph V, 159
Comer, Joseph V, 731
Comer, Lyda I, 348
Comer, Lydia I, 348
Comer, Lydia I, 380
Comer, Lydia I, 1061
Comer, Margaretta VI, 837
Comer, Margrett II, 348
Comer, Martha I, 380
Comer, Martha I, 1055
Comer, Martha I, 1060
Comer, Martha I, 1061
Comer, Martha V, 40
Comer, Martha V, 158
Comer, Mary I, 348
Comer, Mary I, 380
Comer, Mary I, 1055
Comer, Mary I, 1060
Comer, Mary V, 40
Comer, Mary V, 158
Comer, Mordecai I, 380
Comer, Nancy I, 461
Comer, Nancy I, 475
Comer, Phebe I, 380
Comer, Phebe I, 382
Comer, Phebe V, 230
Comer, Rebecca I, 348
Comer, Rebecca I, 380
Comer, Rebecca I, 457
Comer, Rebecca I, 461
Comer, Rebecca V, 832
Comer, Rebeccah V, 40
Comer, Rebekah I, 348
Comer, Rebekah I, 380
Comer, Rebekah I, 1060
Comer, Rebekah V, 832
Comer, Robert I, 348
Comer, Robert I, 380
Comer, Robert I, 461
Comer, Robert I, 1027
Comer, Robert I, 1055
Comer, Robert I, 1060
Comer, Robert I, 1061
Comer, Robert V, 40
Comer, Robert V, 158
Comer, Sarah I, 348
Comer, Sarah I, 380
Comer, Silas I, 461
Comer, Silas I, 475
Comer, Stephen I, 348
Comer, Stephen I, 380
Comer, Stephen I, 1027
Comer, Stephen I, 1055
Comer, Stephen I, 1060
Comer, Stephen I, 1061
Comer, Stephen V, 158
Comer, Susanah I, 961
Comer, Susanna I, 380
Comer, Susannah I, 963
Comer, Tamar I, 1055
Comer, Tamer I, 348
Comer, Tamer I, 380
Comer, Tamer Kinworthy I, 380
Comer, Thomas I, 380
Comer, Thomas I, 961
Comer, Thomas VI, 130
Comer, Thomas VI, 133
Comer, William I, 380
Comer, William I, 461
Comer, William I, 475
Comers, Robert I, 380
Comfort, Aaron II, 957
Comfort, Aaron II, 958
Comfort, Aaron II, 1041
Comfort, Aaron II, 1049
Comfort, Aaron II, 1071
Comfort, Aaron IV, 1357
Comfort, Aaron IV, 1358
Comfort, Aaron IV, 1378
Comfort, Aaron IV, 1381
Comfort, Aaron I. II, 1071
Comfort, Aaron Ivens II, 850
Comfort, Aaron Ivins II, 850
Comfort, Aaron J. II, 317
Comfort, Aaron J. II, 850
Comfort, Aaron, Jr. II, 1048
Comfort, Adrian IV, 1357
Comfort, Albert II, 957
Comfort, Albert II, 958
Comfort, Albert II, 1045
Comfort, Albert II, 1048
Comfort, Albert II, 1049
Comfort, Albert D. II, 1087
Comfort, Ann II, 209
Comfort, Ann II, 946
Comfort, Ann II, 957
Comfort, Ann II, 958
Comfort, Ann II, 972
Comfort, Ann II, 990
Comfort, Ann II, 995
Comfort, Ann II, 1005
Comfort, Ann II, 1032
Comfort, Ann II, 1039
Comfort, Ann II, 1048
Comfort, Ann II, 1049
Comfort, Ann II, 1051
Comfort, Ann II, 1071
Comfort, Ann II, 1080
Comfort, Ann IV, 1357
Comfort, Ann IV, 1378
Comfort, Ann IV, 1380
Comfort, Ann IV, 1381
Comfort, Ann C. II, 972
Comfort, Ann Elizabeth II, 957
Comfort, Ann Elizabeth II, 958
Comfort, Ann Elizabeth II, 1049
Comfort, Ann G. II, 1071
Comfort, Ann G. II, 1073
Comfort, Ann I. II, 1071
Comfort, Ann I. II, 1082
Comfort, Ann T. II, 1048
Comfort, Anna Elizabeth II, 957
Comfort, Anna S. II, 1085
Comfort, Annie II, 1065
Comfort, Annie II, 1071
Comfort, Annie II, 1079
Comfort, Annie S. II, 1087
Comfort, Beulah II, 701
Comfort, Beulah II, 990
Comfort, Beulah II, 1048
Comfort, Beulah C. II, 1071
Comfort, Beulah C. II, 1073
Comfort, Caroline II, 1071
Comfort, Charles B. II, 957
Comfort, Charles B. II, 1049
Comfort, Charles B. II, 1085
Comfort, Charles B. II, 1087
Comfort, Charles B., Jr. II, 1087
Comfort, Charlotte II, 1065
Comfort, Charlotte II, 1071
Comfort, Cyrus E. II, 958
Comfort, David II, 701
Comfort, David II, 990
Comfort, Dorcas IV, 1153
Comfort, Dorcas IV, 1157
Comfort, Edith Decou II, 1049
Comfort, Edmund II, 701
Comfort, Edward C. II, 957
Comfort, Edwin M. IV, 1153
Comfort, Edwin W. IV, 1153
Comfort, Effie IV, 1153
Comfort, Effie Arms IV, 865
Comfort, Eliza II, 1049
Comfort, Eliza W. II, 990
Comfort, Eliza W. II, 1032
Comfort, Elizabeth II, 286
Comfort, Elizabeth II, 291
Comfort, Elizabeth II, 957
Comfort, Elizabeth II, 958
Comfort, Elizabeth II, 959
Comfort, Elizabeth II, 987
Comfort, Elizabeth II, 990
Comfort, Elizabeth II, 1007
Comfort, Elizabeth II, 1047
Comfort, Elizabeth II, 1049
Comfort, Elizabeth II, 1050
Comfort, Elizabeth II, 1063
Comfort, Elizabeth II, 1071
Comfort, Elizabeth C. II, 946
Comfort, Elizabeth C. II, 959
Comfort, Elizabeth M. II, 957
Comfort, Elizabeth M. II, 1049
Comfort, Elizabeth M. IV, 1357
Comfort, Elizabeth M. IV, 1378
Comfort, Elizabeth P. IV, 1357
Comfort, Elizabeth P. IV, 1378
Comfort, Elizabeth R. IV, 1357
Comfort, Elizabeth R. IV, 1358
Comfort, Elizabeth, Jr. II, 1071
Comfort, Ellis II, 209
Comfort, Ellis II, 492
Comfort, Ellis II, 958
Comfort, Ellis II, 990
Comfort, Ellis II, 1005
Comfort, Ellis II, 1048
Comfort, Ellis II, 1071
Comfort, Ellis W. II, 1065
Comfort, Ellis W. II, 1071
Comfort, Elvira II, 1071
Comfort, Elwood II, 957
Comfort, Elwood II, 1049
Comfort, Elwood IV, 1357
Comfort, Elwood IV, 1358
Comfort, Elwood IV, 1378
Comfort, Emma II, 1071
Comfort, Ezra II, 958
Comfort, Ezra II, 990
Comfort, Ezra II, 1047
Comfort, Ezra IV, 1153
Comfort, Ezra Margaret II, 1049
Comfort, Ezrah II, 1049
Comfort, Fred IV, 865
Comfort, Fred IV, 1153
Comfort, George II, 1049
Comfort, George II, 1065
Comfort, George II, 1071
Comfort, George II, 1075
Comfort, George II, 1077
Comfort, George II, 1079
Comfort, George I. II, 1065
Comfort, George I. II, 1071
Comfort, George M. II, 957
Comfort, George M. II, 1049
Comfort, Georgianna II, 1071
Comfort, Georgianna II, 1079
Comfort, Grace II, 958
Comfort, Harry B. II, 1065
Comfort, Henry B. II, 1071
Comfort, Henry W. II, 957
Comfort, Henry W. II, 958
Comfort, Henry W. II, 990
Comfort, Henry W. II, 1049
Comfort, Ira II, 958
Comfort, Ira II, 990
Comfort, James C. II, 957
Comfort, James H. IV, 1153
Comfort, Jane II, 957
Comfort, Jane II, 1049
Comfort, Jane IV, 1148
Comfort, Jane IV, 1153
Comfort, Jane IV, 1357
Comfort, Jane IV, 1378
Comfort, Jane C. II, 958
Comfort, Jane C. II, 1049
Comfort, Jeremiah II, 957
Comfort, Jeremiah II, 958
Comfort, Jeremiah II, 990
Comfort, Jeremiah II, 991
Comfort, Jeremiah II, 1047
Comfort, Jeremiah II, 1049
Comfort, Jesse II, 1049
Comfort, Jno. II, 209
Comfort, John II, 275
Comfort, John II, 946
Comfort, John II, 957
Comfort, John II, 958
Comfort, John II, 972
Comfort, John II, 990
Comfort, John II, 995
Comfort, John II, 1005
Comfort, John II, 1017
Comfort, John II, 1032
Comfort, John II, 1039
Comfort, John II, 1071
Comfort, John III, 82
Comfort, John S. II, 957
Comfort, John S. II, 958
Comfort, John S. II, 1049
Comfort, John W. II, 1048
Comfort, John Woolman II, 1071
Comfort, John, Jr. II, 1049
Comfort, Jonathan II, 958
Comfort, Jonathan J. II, 957
Comfort, Jonathan J. II, 1049
Comfort, Jonathan J. IV, 1357
Comfort, Joseph II, 958
Comfort, Joseph II, 990
Comfort, Joseph E. IV, 1357
Comfort, Josiah II, 954
Comfort, Josiah II, 957
Comfort, Josiah II, 958
Comfort, Josiah II, 987
Comfort, Josiah II, 1045
Comfort, Josiah II, 1048
Comfort, Josiah II, 1049
Comfort, Lydia II, 284
Comfort, Lydia II, 701
Comfort, Lydia II, 733
Comfort, Lydia II, 850
Comfort, Lydia II, 957
Comfort, Lydia II, 990
Comfort, Lydia II, 1049
Comfort, Lydia I. II, 850
Comfort, Lydia I. II, 990
Comfort, Lydia I. II, 1071
Comfort, Lydia J. II, 209
Comfort, Lydia P. II, 958
Comfort, Lydia P. II, 1049
Comfort, Lydia W. II, 1045
Comfort, Lydia W. II, 1049
Comfort, Lydia W. II, 1085
Comfort, Marcy II, 958
Comfort, Margaret II, 958
Comfort, Margaret II, 1047
Comfort, Margaret II, 1049
Comfort, Martha II, 990
Comfort, Martha II, 1041
Comfort, Martha V. IV, 1358
Comfort, Mary II, 209
Comfort, Mary II, 275
Comfort, Mary II, 957
Comfort, Mary II, 958
Comfort, Mary II, 962
Comfort, Mary II, 990
Comfort, Mary II, 993
Comfort, Mary II, 1005
Comfort, Mary II, 1007
Comfort, Mary II, 1017
Comfort, Mary II, 1032
Comfort, Mary II, 1039
Comfort, Mary II, 1048
Comfort, Mary II, 1049
Comfort, Mary II, 1068
Comfort, Mary II, 1071
Comfort, Mary II, 1082
Comfort, Mary IV, 1153
Comfort, Mary IV, 1357
Comfort, Mary IV, 1381
Comfort, Mary Ann II, 958
Comfort, Mary Anna Vansant II, 1071
Comfort, Mary B. II, 1071

mfort, Mary E. II, 209
mfort, Mary E. II, 990
mfort, Mary Ellis II, 209
mfort, Mary G. Stout IV, 1357
mfort, Mary Ivins II, 780
mfort, Mary T. II, 954
mfort, Mary T. II, 958
mfort, Mary T. II, 1045
mfort, Mary T. II, 1048
mfort, Mary T. II, 1049
mfort, Mary W. II, 1068
mfort, Mercy II, 957
mfort, Mercy II, 958
mfort, Mercy II, 990
mfort, Mercy II, 995
mfort, Mercy II, 1048
mfort, Mercy II, 1049
mfort, Mercy Taylor II, 1071
mfort, Merriam II, 147
nfort, Merriam II, 1071
mfort, Miriam II, 147
mfort, Miriam II, 209
mfort, Miriam II, 990
mfort, Miriam II, 1049
mfort, Moses II, 957
mfort, Moses II, 958
mfort, Moses II, 987
mfort, Moses II, 990
mfort, Moses II, 1007
mfort, Moses II, 1048
mfort, Moses II, 1049
nfort, Moses II, 1071
nfort, Moses IV, 1357
nfort, Moses IV, 1374
nfort, Moses, Jr. II, 1048
nfort, Moses, Jr. II, 1071
nfort, Olivia C. IV, 1357
nfort, Olivia C. IV, 1382
nfort, Phebe II, 990
nfort, Phebe IV, 1153
nfort, Phebe IV, 1177
nfort, Phebe IV, 1197
nfort, Rachel II, 946
nfort, Rachel II, 957
nfort, Rachel II, 958
nfort, Rachel II, 987
nfort, Rachel II, 990
nfort, Rachel II, 1045
nfort, Rachel II, 1048
nfort, Rachel II, 1049
nfort, Rachel C. II, 954
nfort, Ralph Harold IV, 865
nfort, Rebecca II, 990
nfort, Rebecca II, 1041
nfort, Rebecca II, 1044
nfort, Rebecca II, 1048
nfort, Rebecca II, 1049
nfort, Rebecca II, 1068
nfort, Rebecca II, 1071
nfort, Rebecca II, 1075
nfort, Rebecca II, 1077
nfort, Rebeckah II, 958
nfort, Rebeckah II, 990
nfort, Rebeckah II, 1017
nfort, Rebekah II, 1049
nfort, Rebekah II, 1071
nfort, Rebekah II, 1075
nfort, Rebekah II, 1080
nfort, Rhoda IV, 1153
nfort, Robert II, 990
nfort, Robert II, 1071
nfort, Robert IV, 1147
nfort, Robert IV, 1153
nfort, Robert P. II, 1071
nfort, Robert P. IV, 1153
nfort, Robert, Jr. IV, 1153
nfort, Robert, Sr. IV, 1153
nfort, Ruth IV, 1147
nfort, Ruth IV, 1153
nfort, Ruth IV, 1177
nfort, S. Emlen IV, 1357
nfort, S. Emlen IV, 1382
nfort, Samuel II, 957
nfort, Samuel II, 959
nfort, Samuel II, 990
nfort, Samuel II, 1017
nfort, Samuel II, 1041
fort, Samuel II, 1048
fort, Samuel II, 1049
fort, Samuel II, 1065
fort, Samuel II, 1071
fort, Samuel II, 1075
fort, Samuel II, 1079
fort, Samuel II, 1080
fort, Samuel II, 1084
fort, Samuel C. II, 957
fort, Sarah II, 209
fort, Sarah II, 264
fort, Sarah II, 706
fort, Sarah II, 718
fort, Sarah II, 957
Comfort, Sarah II, 958
Comfort, Sarah II, 969
Comfort, Sarah II, 987
Comfort, Sarah II, 990
Comfort, Sarah II, 991
Comfort, Sarah II, 1032
Comfort, Sarah II, 1048
Comfort, Sarah II, 1049
Comfort, Sarah II, 1071
Comfort, Sarah IV, 1153
Comfort, Sarah IV, 1197
Comfort, Sarah IV, 1357
Comfort, Sarah IV, 1374
Comfort, Sarah Jane IV, 1153
Comfort, Sarah T. II, 1048
Comfort, Sarah W. II, 1071
Comfort, Sophia T. II, 957
Comfort, Stephen II, 209
Comfort, Stephen II, 264
Comfort, Stephen II, 957
Comfort, Stephen II, 958
Comfort, Stephen II, 990
Comfort, Stephen II, 991
Comfort, Stephen II, 995
Comfort, Stephen II, 1048
Comfort, Stephen II, 1068
Comfort, Stephen II, 1071
Comfort, Stephen IV, 1153
Comfort, Stephen C. II, 1071
Comfort, Stephen D. IV, 1153
Comfort, Stephen, Jr. II, 492
Comfort, Susan II, 1071
Comfort, Susan II, 1077
Comfort, Susan II, 1079
Comfort, Susan Elizabeth II, 1071
Comfort, Susan Elizabeth II, 1073
Comfort, Susan L. II, 1065
Comfort, Susan, Jr. II, 1071
Comfort, Susan, Jr. II, 1075
Comfort, William II, 958
Comfort, William II, 1065
Comfort, William IV, 1153
Comfort, William S. II, 957
Comfort, William W. II, 209
Comfort, Wm. II, 990
Comfort, Wm. II, 1071
Comfort, Wm. IV, 1177
Comfort, Wm. W. II, 990
Comfort, Wolston IV, 1358
Comfort, Woolston II, 957
Comfort, Woolston II, 1049
Comfort, Woolston IV, 1357
Coming, Daniel I, 1075
Coming, Elizabeth I, 1075
Coming, Joan I, 1075
Coming, John I, 1075
Coming, Sarah I, 1075
Comings, Ann II, 352
Comings, John II, 352
Comins, Mary IV, 1274
Comley, Abigail II, 492
Comley, Abigail II, 990
Comley, Abraham II, 990
Comley, Agnes II, 990
Comley, Alice IV, 26
Comley, Benjamin IV, 189
Comley, Charles II, 492
Comley, Chas. II, 850
Comley, Chas. II, 915
Comley, David IV, 189
Comley, David B. IV, 189
Comley, David, Jr. IV, 189
Comley, Eliza Jane IV, 189
Comley, Eliza Jane IV, 223
Comley, Emma II, 850
Comley, Emma II, 915
Comley, Emma R. II, 733
Comley, Emma R. II, 850
Comley, Hannah II, 990
Comley, Helen II, 846
Comley, Helen II, 851
Comley, Helen Atkinson II, 833
Comley, Helen Atkinson II, 851
Comley, Isaac II, 990
Comley, Isaac IV, 26
Comley, Jacob II, 990
Comley, James IV, 189
Comley, John II, 349
Comley, John II, 990
Comley, John IV, 189
Comley, Julia E. V, 900
Comley, Lester II, 846
Comley, Lester II, 851
Comley, Lydia IV, 26
Comley, Lydia T. II, 833
Comley, Mary II, 492
Comley, Mary II, 990
Comley, Mary B. II, 846
Comley, Mary B. II, 851
Comley, Phebe IV, 26
Comley, Robert II, 833
Comley, Robert II, 851
Comley, Rowland II, 846
Comley, Rowland II, 851
Comley, Samuel IV, 26
Comley, Sarah II, 349
Comley, Sarah IV, 189
Comley, Sarah IV, 222
Comley, Sarah W. II, 850
Comley, Sarah W. II, 915
Comley, Seth II, 850
Comley, Seth J. II, 850
Comley, Seth J. II, 915
Comley, Susanna IV, 26
Comley, Susannah II, 492
Comley, Susannah II, 990
Comley, Wd. Hannah II, 492
Comley, William IV, 189
Comly, Aaron W. II, 788
Comly, Aaron W. II, 850
Comly, Aaron W. II, 915
Comly, Abigail II, 492
Comly, Abraham II, 349
Comly, Abraham II, 492
Comly, Alice II, 788
Comly, Alice B. II, 851
Comly, Alice G. IV, 25
Comly, Alice G. IV, 26
Comly, Ann II, 492
Comly, Ann II, 794
Comly, Anna Miller II, 788
Comly, Benjamin IV, 189
Comly, Caroline F. II, 851
Comly, Caroline Ridgway II, 788
Comly, Caroline S. II, 850
Comly, Charles II, 349
Comly, Charles II, 492
Comly, Charles Allen II, 349
Comly, Charles Allen II, 492
Comly, Chas. II, 850
Comly, Chas. II, 915
Comly, Chas. Francis II, 789
Comly, David, Jr. IV, 189
Comly, Deborah II, 850
Comly, Eliza Jane IV, 189
Comly, Elizabeth II, 349
Comly, Elizabeth II, 492
Comly, Elizabeth II, 788
Comly, Elizabeth II, 850
Comly, Elizabeth II, 915
Comly, Elizabeth N. II, 851
Comly, Elizabeth Newbold II, 788
Comly, Elizabeth Oliver II, 788
Comly, Elizabeth P. II, 850
Comly, Elizabeth R. II, 850
Comly, Emily C. II, 851
Comly, Emma II, 788
Comly, Emma II, 850
Comly, Emma R. II, 850
Comly, Emma Ridgway II, 788
Comly, Emmor II, 850
Comly, Ethan II, 788
Comly, Ezra II, 788
Comly, Ezra IV, 25
Comly, Ezra IV, 26
Comly, Fanny II, 850
Comly, Frances B. V, 900
Comly, Frances B. V, 926
Comly, George Norwood II, 851
Comly, Hannah II, 668
Comly, Hannah II, 851
Comly, Hannah C. II, 851
Comly, Hannah R. II, 850
Comly, Helen II, 851
Comly, Helen A. II, 850
Comly, Helen Atkinson II, 851
Comly, Helen Trump II, 789
Comly, Helen Trump II, 827
Comly, Henry Budd II, 788
Comly, Isaac II, 492
Comly, Isaac II, 850
Comly, Isaac, Jr. II, 209
Comly, J. IV, 1026
Comly, Jacob II, 492
Comly, Jacob II, 668
Comly, John II, 349
Comly, John II, 492
Comly, John II, 668
Comly, John II, 851
Comly, John IV, 189
Comly, John Norris II, 789
Comly, Joseph Pancoast II, 788
Comly, Joshua W. II, 349
Comly, Joshua W. II, 492
Comly, Joshua Wright II, 492
Comly, Joshua Wright II, 788
Comly, Julia V, 900
Comly, Julia E. V, 900
Comly, Lester II, 788
Comly, Lester II, 851
Comly, Lillie II, 788
Comly, Lucy II, 492
Comly, Lucy W. II, 492
Comly, Lucy Wright II, 349
Comly, Lydia T. II, 788
Comly, Lydia T. II, 850
Comly, Lydia T. II, 851
Comly, Marion S. II, 788
Comly, Martha W. IV, 1026
Comly, Mary II, 492
Comly, Mary II, 824
Comly, Mary V, 900
Comly, Mary V, 924
Comly, Mary B. II, 851
Comly, Mary K. II, 788
Comly, Mary Mott II, 788
Comly, Mary W. II, 117
Comly, Mary W. II, 122
Comly, Rachel II, 819
Comly, Rebecca II, 851
Comly, Rebecca B. II, 850
Comly, Rebecca Budd II, 851
Comly, Robert II, 788
Comly, Robert II, 850
Comly, Robert II, 851
Comly, Rowland II, 851
Comly, Samuel IV, 26
Comly, Sarah II, 349
Comly, Sarah II, 492
Comly, Sarah II, 668
Comly, Sarah II, 788
Comly, Sarah II, 824
Comly, Sarah IV, 189
Comly, Sarah IV, 807
Comly, Sarah IV, 853
Comly, Sarah V, 900
Comly, Sarah R. V, 900
Comly, Sarah R. V, 914
Comly, Sarah Ridgway II, 788
Comly, Sarah W. II, 492
Comly, Sarah W. II, 850
Comly, Sarah Waln II, 788
Comly, Seth II, 492
Comly, Seth II, 850
Comly, Seth Iredell II, 788
Comly, Seth J. II, 850
Comly, Susan R. II, 788
Comly, Susanna IV, 26
Comly, Susannah II, 492
Comly, Thos. Ridgway II, 788
Comly, Timothy II, 492
Comly, Wd. Hannah II, 492
Comly, Wd. Rebecca A. II, 788
Comly, William II, 349
Comly, William IV, 189
Commack, James I, 1027
Commack, James V, 35
Commack, Rachel I, 1027
Commander, Hannah I, 136
Commander, Hannah I, 139
Commander, Sarah I, 136
Commander, Sarah I, 157
Commegys, Ann II, 492
Commer, John I, 961
Commin, David II, 213
Commin, Richard II, 213
Common, Sarah I, 375
Common, Sarah I, 380
Common, William I, 380
Common, William VI, 379
Common, William, Jr. I, 380
Common, Wm. I, 375
Common, Wm. I, 380
Commons, Cassie V, 832
Commons, Clinton V, 832
Commons, David V, 732
Commons, David V, 756
Commons, Elizabeth V, 732
Commons, Elizabeth V, 746
Commons, Elizabeth V, 756
Commons, Elizabeth V, 757
Commons, Eva A. III, 82
Commons, Eva A. III, 308
Commons, Evelyn Alice III, 82
Commons, Evelyn Alice III, 308
Commons, Hannah I, 1008
Commons, Isaac I, 744
Commons, Isaac I, 757
Commons, Isaac I, 961
Commons, Isaac V, 732
Commons, Isaac V, 832
Commons, Isaac, Jr. V, 832
Commons, Isacc, Jr. V, 864
Commons, J. Clinton V, 832
Commons, Jacob I, 757
Commons, Jacob I, 758
Commons, Joel I, 757
Commons, John I, 961
Commons, John V, 732
Commons, John V, 746
Commons, John V, 756
Commons, John V, 757
Commons, Joseph I, 757
Commons, Keziah V, 832
Commons, Keziah V, 864
Commons, Keziah S. V, 832
Commons, Lydda I, 961
Commons, Lydia I, 1008
Commons, Mary V, 832
Commons, Phebe I, 961
Commons, Phebe I, 1007
Commons, Phebe I, 1008
Commons, Rachel V, 732
Commons, Rachel V, 746
Commons, Rachel V, 756
Commons, Rachel V, 779
Commons, Robert I, 534
Commons, Robert I, 961
Commons, Robert I, 1008
Commons, Robert V, 732
Commons, Ruth I, 961
Commons, Ruth I, 1001
Commons, Ruth I, 1008
Commons, Ruth V, 732
Commons, Sarah I, 380
Commons, Sarah I, 744
Commons, Thomas V, 900
Commons, Walter III, 82
Commons, Walter III, 308
Commons, Wayne V, 732
Commons, William I, 744
Commons, William I, 961
Commons, William IV, 26
Commons, William, Jr. I, 757
Compher, Mary VI, 631
Compher, Mary VI, 642
Compher, Mary VI, 643
Compher, Wm. VI, 631
Compher, Wm. VI, 643
Compton, ??? V, 160
Compton, Ada V, 41
Compton, Adaline E. V, 160
Compton, Adeline V, 206
Compton, Albert E. V, 41
Compton, Albert E. V, 161
Compton, Alice V, 159
Compton, Ally I, 1055
Compton, Ally V, 159
Compton, Ally V, 160
Compton, Ally V, 191
Compton, Ally C. V, 556
Compton, Ally C. V, 665
Compton, Alta B. V, 161
Compton, Alta B. V, 556
Compton, Alta B. V, 665
Compton, Amos I, 1018
Compton, Amos I, 1027
Compton, Amos I, 1055
Compton, Amos I, 1056
Compton, Amos I, 1058
Compton, Amos I, 1060
Compton, Amos V, 40
Compton, Amos V, 158
Compton, Amos V, 159
Compton, Amos V, 160
Compton, Amos V, 161
Compton, Amos V, 167
Compton, Amos V, 173
Compton, Amos V, 181
Compton, Amos V, 189
Compton, Amos V, 191
Compton, Amos V, 950
Compton, Amos E. V, 160
Compton, Amos L. V, 159
Compton, Amos S. V, 160
Compton, Amos S. V, 161
Compton, Ann I, 1055
Compton, Ann V, 40
Compton, Ann V, 41
Compton, Ann V, 147
Compton, Ann V, 155
Compton, Ann V, 158
Compton, Ann V, 159
Compton, Ann V, 160
Compton, Ann V, 162
Compton, Ann V, 173
Compton, Ann V, 189
Compton, Ann V, 206
Compton, Ann V, 482
Compton, Ann R. V, 160
Compton, Ann R. V, 161
Compton, Ann W. V, 230
Compton, Anna V, 159
Compton, Anna V, 161
Compton, Anna V, 230
Compton, Anna Mary V, 732
Compton, Annie R. V, 160
Compton, Arrena V, 160
Compton, Augustus M. V, 161
Compton, Benjamin V, 159
Compton, Benjamin V, 161
Compton, Benjamin V, 616

Compton, Benjamin V, 649
Compton, Betty I, 1055
Compton, Betty V, 40
Compton, Betty V, 158
Compton, Betty V, 159
Compton, Betty V, 191
Compton, Betty V, 482
Compton, Blanch V, 665
Compton, C. H. IV, 1248
Compton, Catharine V, 159
Compton, Catharine V, 779
Compton, Catherine V, 159
Compton, Catherine V, 161
Compton, Catherine V, 189
Compton, Catherine V, 194
Compton, Catherine V, 779
Compton, Catherine M. V, 160
Compton, Cena VI, 905
Compton, Charity V, 159
Compton, Charles V, 41
Compton, Charles V, 161
Compton, Charles Weldon V, 161
Compton, Christian V, 176
Compton, Christiana V, 159
Compton, Christiana V, 171
Compton, Christiana V, 194
Compton, Christiana V, 728
Compton, Christiana V, 732
Compton, Christianna V, 40
Compton, Christianna V, 171
Compton, Christianna V, 732
Compton, Christopher V, 161
Compton, Clara V, 160
Compton, Clarissa V, 159
Compton, Cleo Fife V, 665
Compton, Daniel V, 41
Compton, Deborah V, 159
Compton, Deborah V, 160
Compton, Deborah V, 181
Compton, Delitha V, 616
Compton, Delitha Ann V, 616
Compton, Delitha Ann V, 732
Compton, Delithia V, 610
Compton, Dinah I, 1056
Compton, Dinah I, 1058
Compton, Dinah I, 1060
Compton, Dinah I, 1062
Compton, Dinah V, 40
Compton, Dinah V, 158
Compton, Dinah V, 159
Compton, Dinah V, 160
Compton, Dinah V, 161
Compton, Dinah V, 179
Compton, Dinah V, 191
Compton, Dinah T. V, 163
Compton, E. V, 41
Compton, Edith V, 151
Compton, Edith V, 161
Compton, Edith V, 474
Compton, Edith V, 482
Compton, Edith A. V, 160
Compton, Edward VI, 164
Compton, Eli I, 1055
Compton, Eli V, 158
Compton, Eli V, 159
Compton, Eli V, 160
Compton, Eli V, 177
Compton, Eli V, 181
Compton, Eli V, 194
Compton, Eli V, 209
Compton, Elijah V, 41
Compton, Elijah V, 159
Compton, Elijah V, 161
Compton, Elizabeth I, 1018
Compton, Elizabeth I, 1027
Compton, Elizabeth I, 1055
Compton, Elizabeth I, 1058
Compton, Elizabeth I, 1060
Compton, Elizabeth IV, 1310
Compton, Elizabeth V, 40
Compton, Elizabeth V, 77
Compton, Elizabeth V, 156
Compton, Elizabeth V, 158
Compton, Elizabeth V, 159
Compton, Elizabeth V, 160
Compton, Elizabeth V, 161
Compton, Elizabeth V, 173
Compton, Elizabeth V, 186
Compton, Elizabeth V, 195
Compton, Elizabeth V, 779
Compton, Elizabeth VI, 881
Compton, Elizabeth Alice V, 160
Compton, Elizabeth Ann V, 161
Compton, Elizabeth Ann V, 482
Compton, Elizabeth Ann V, 483
Compton, Elizabeth Ann V, 516
Compton, Elizabeth Ann V, 535
Compton, Elizabeth Hurley V, 161
Compton, Elizabeth Hurley V, 483
Compton, Elizabeth Mather IV, 1310
Compton, Elizabeth Mather IV, 1328
Compton, Ella V, 160
Compton, Ella V, 161
Compton, Ella V, 173
Compton, Ella C. V, 160
Compton, Ella S. V, 160
Compton, Elmer J. V, 160
Compton, Emily VI, 895
Compton, Emily Alice V, 160
Compton, Esther V, 160
Compton, Esther V, 161
Compton, Esther V, 196
Compton, Esther V, 204
Compton, Esther V, 482
Compton, Ethel V, 161
Compton, Ethel V, 192
Compton, Ethel F. V, 160
Compton, Ethel Sanders V, 161
Compton, Eunice I, 1055
Compton, Eunice V, 159
Compton, Eunice V, 160
Compton, Eunice V, 177
Compton, Eunice V, 181
Compton, Eunice V, 189
Compton, Eunice V, 192
Compton, Eunice V, 194
Compton, Eunice V, 209
Compton, Eva N. V, 160
Compton, Fannie V, 161
Compton, Florence V, 832
Compton, Florence V, 835
Compton, Forest D. V, 41
Compton, Forest D. V, 160
Compton, Frances VI, 936
Compton, Francis V, 779
Compton, Hannah I, 1056
Compton, Hannah V, 158
Compton, Hannah V, 159
Compton, Hannah V, 161
Compton, Hannah V, 162
Compton, Hannah V, 177
Compton, Hannah Ann V, 161
Compton, Hannah Ann V, 482
Compton, Hannah Ann V, 483
Compton, Henry I, 1056
Compton, Henry V, 40
Compton, Henry V, 158
Compton, Henry V, 159
Compton, Henry V, 160
Compton, Henry V, 161
Compton, Henry V, 171
Compton, Henry V, 189
Compton, Henry V, 616
Compton, Henry V, 730
Compton, Henry V, 731
Compton, Henry V, 732
Compton, Henry V, 754
Compton, Henry V, 800
Compton, Henry Allen V, 732
Compton, Hester V, 158
Compton, Hester V, 159
Compton, Hettie Phebe V, 160
Compton, Horace V, 154
Compton, Horace F. V, 160
Compton, Horace Forest D. V, 161
Compton, Horace Foster V, 160
Compton, Ina M. V, 160
Compton, Ina May V, 154
Compton, Irvin IV, 1248
Compton, Isaac V, 732
Compton, Isaac P. V, 40
Compton, Isaac P. V, 41
Compton, Isaac P. V, 161
Compton, Isaac Pedric V, 159
Compton, Isaac Pedrick V, 40
Compton, Isaiah VI, 895
Compton, Israel V, 159
Compton, Israel V, 161
Compton, James V, 159
Compton, James V, 161
Compton, James V, 482
Compton, James V, 483
Compton, James O. V, 160
Compton, James Orville V, 160
Compton, Jane I, 1055
Compton, Jane V, 159
Compton, Jane V, 161
Compton, Jane V, 168
Compton, Jane V, 482
Compton, Jennie V, 160
Compton, Jesse V, 41
Compton, Jesse V, 159
Compton, Jesse V, 160
Compton, Jesse V, 161
Compton, Jesse V, 204
Compton, Jesse C. V, 161
Compton, Jesse M. V, 41
Compton, Jesse M. V, 161
Compton, Joab VI, 895
Compton, Joal VI, 936
Compton, Joel V, 159
Compton, Joel V, 161
Compton, Joel VI, 895
Compton, Joel VI, 918
Compton, Joel T. V, 160
Compton, John I, 1018
Compton, John I, 1027
Compton, John I, 1055
Compton, John I, 1056
Compton, John II, 492
Compton, John V, 40
Compton, John V, 41
Compton, John V, 125
Compton, John V, 155
Compton, John V, 158
Compton, John V, 159
Compton, John V, 161
Compton, John V, 162
Compton, John V, 168
Compton, John V, 189
Compton, John V, 196
Compton, John V, 206
Compton, John V, 482
Compton, John V, 665
Compton, John VI, 895
Compton, John L. V, 160
Compton, John L. V, 665
Compton, John L. V, 709
Compton, John M. V, 159
Compton, John S. V, 160
Compton, John W. V, 556
Compton, John W. V, 665
Compton, Joseph I, 1018
Compton, Joseph V, 40
Compton, Joseph V, 159
Compton, Joseph V, 161
Compton, Joseph V, 171
Compton, Joseph V, 176
Compton, Joseph V, 732
Compton, Joseph V, 779
Compton, Joseph Edward V, 160
Compton, Josephine V, 160
Compton, Josephine V, 161
Compton, Josephine V, 556
Compton, Josephine V, 665
Compton, Josephine V, 721
Compton, Josephine Starbuck V, 665
Compton, Joshua I, 1018
Compton, Joshua I, 1027
Compton, Joshua I, 1055
Compton, Joshua I, 1057
Compton, Joshua I, 1060
Compton, Joshua I, 1061
Compton, Joshua V, 40
Compton, Joshua V, 151
Compton, Joshua V, 158
Compton, Joshua V, 159
Compton, Joshua V, 160
Compton, Joshua V, 161
Compton, Joshua V, 474
Compton, Joshua V, 482
Compton, Joshua E. V, 482
Compton, Judith V, 159
Compton, Judith V, 161
Compton, Judith V, 482
Compton, Judith Ann V, 161
Compton, Judith Ann V, 483
Compton, Judith Ann V, 516
Compton, Julia VI, 895
Compton, Lester M. V, 160
Compton, Lester M. V, 161
Compton, Leta M. V, 665
Compton, Leta M. V, 709
Compton, Lidia V, 880
Compton, Lidia V, 881
Compton, Lillie V, 160
Compton, Lillie M. V, 161
Compton, Lindley Murray V, 732
Compton, Lizzie V, 161
Compton, Lorena A. V, 160
Compton, Lorena A. V, 161
Compton, Louisa Jane V, 160
Compton, Lucetta V, 161
Compton, Lucetta V, 482
Compton, Lucy V, 154
Compton, Lucy A. V, 160
Compton, Lucy Ann V, 160
Compton, Lydia I, 1055
Compton, Lydia V, 40
Compton, Lydia V, 41
Compton, Lydia V, 155
Compton, Lydia V, 158
Compton, Lydia V, 159
Compton, Lydia V, 160
Compton, Lydia V, 181
Compton, Lydia V, 191
Compton, Lydia V, 482
Compton, Lydia V, 732
Compton, Lydia VI, 895
Compton, Lydia Ellen V, 732
Compton, Lydia Jane V, 160
Compton, Mabel V, 41
Compton, Mabel V, 665
Compton, Mabel V, 669
Compton, Margaret V, 161
Compton, Margaret V, 616
Compton, Margaret V, 649
Compton, Maria V, 159
Compton, Maria V, 194
Compton, Marianna V, 154
Compton, Marianna V, 160
Compton, Marianne V, 154
Compton, Marianne V, 160
Compton, Martha V, 41
Compton, Martha V, 159
Compton, Martha V, 160
Compton, Martha V, 482
Compton, Martha V, 730
Compton, Martha V, 731
Compton, Martha V, 732
Compton, Martha V, 800
Compton, Martha V, 802
Compton, Martha Ellen V, 159
Compton, Martha F. V, 41
Compton, Martha J. V, 170
Compton, Martha Jane V, 159
Compton, Martha R. V, 160
Compton, Martha R. V, 183
Compton, Mary I, 1055
Compton, Mary II, 206
Compton, Mary II, 209
Compton, Mary II, 492
Compton, Mary V, 40
Compton, Mary V, 158
Compton, Mary V, 159
Compton, Mary V, 160
Compton, Mary V, 161
Compton, Mary V, 178
Compton, Mary V, 201
Compton, Mary V, 616
Compton, Mary V, 732
Compton, Mary Ann V, 41
Compton, Mary Ann V, 125
Compton, Mary Ann V, 126
Compton, Mary Ann V, 159
Compton, Mary Ann V, 160
Compton, Mary Ann V, 161
Compton, Mary Ann V, 206
Compton, Mary Anna V, 41
Compton, Mary C. V, 482
Compton, Mary E. V, 160
Compton, Mary E. V, 161
Compton, Mary Eliza V, 161
Compton, Mary Elizabeth V, 160
Compton, Mary Elizabeth V, 161
Compton, Mary Ellen V, 160
Compton, Mary M. V, 482
Compton, Mathew V, 158
Compton, Mathew V, 161
Compton, Mathew V, 196
Compton, Matilda I, 1057
Compton, Matilda V, 159
Compton, Matilda V, 161
Compton, Matilda V, 171
Compton, Matthew I, 1018
Compton, Matthew I, 1027
Compton, Matthew I, 1055
Compton, Matthew V, 40
Compton, Matthew V, 482
Compton, Matthew VI, 895
Compton, Meredith VI, 895
Compton, Meredith VI, 905
Compton, Meredith VI, 959
Compton, Meredith VI, 1014
Compton, Minnie F. V, 160
Compton, Minnie May V, 160
Compton, Minnie May V, 161
Compton, Miriam V, 160
Compton, Miriam Minerva V, 161
Compton, Miriam N. V, 161
Compton, Miriam W. V, 160
Compton, Nancy I, 1056
Compton, Nancy V, 158
Compton, Nancy V, 159
Compton, Nancy V, 161
Compton, Nancy V, 163
Compton, Nancy V, 170
Compton, Nancy V, 482
Compton, Nancy V, 535
Compton, Nancy Ann V, 159
Compton, Nancy Ann V, 732
Compton, Nancy D. V, 160
Compton, Nathan I, 1055
Compton, Nathan V, 40
Compton, Nathan V, 158
Compton, Nathan V, 482
Compton, Neal V, 161
Compton, Neil V, 161
Compton, Nellie May V, 161
Compton, Obadiah V, 161
Compton, Orilla E. V, 773
Compton, Oritla V, 732
Compton, Patty I, 1057
Compton, Patty V, 159
Compton, Patty V, 161
Compton, Patty V, 176
Compton, Patty V, 732
Compton, Phares V, 159
Compton, Phares V, 161
Compton, Phares V, 163
Compton, Phares V, 170
Compton, Phares V, 732
Compton, Pharos V, 610
Compton, Pharos V, 616
Compton, Phebe I, 1055
Compton, Phebe V, 155
Compton, Phebe V, 158
Compton, Phebe V, 159
Compton, Phebe V, 161
Compton, Phebe V, 211
Compton, Phebe V, 482
Compton, Phebe V, 537
Compton, Phebe V, 732
Compton, Phebe A. V, 616
Compton, Phebe A. V, 625
Compton, Phebe Ann V, 159
Compton, Phebe Ann V, 160
Compton, Phebe Ann V, 177
Compton, Phebe E. V, 161
Compton, Polly VI, 895
Compton, Polly VI, 959
Compton, Priscilla V, 161
Compton, Priscilla S. V, 41
Compton, R. L. V, 665
Compton, Rachel I, 1017
Compton, Rachel I, 1018
Compton, Rachel I, 1027
Compton, Rachel I, 1055
Compton, Rachel V, 158
Compton, Rachel V, 159
Compton, Rachel V, 160
Compton, Rachel V, 161
Compton, Rachel V, 189
Compton, Rachel V, 196
Compton, Rachel V, 482
Compton, Rachel V, 616
Compton, Rachel V, 728
Compton, Rachel V, 730
Compton, Rachel V, 731
Compton, Rachel V, 732
Compton, Rachel V, 754
Compton, Rachel V, 800
Compton, Rachel V, 802
Compton, Rachel C. V, 732
Compton, Rachel Emma V, 732
Compton, Ralph G. V, 161
Compton, Ralph J. V, 160
Compton, Ramuel V, 159
Compton, Rebecca I, 1055
Compton, Rebecca I, 1056
Compton, Rebecca I, 1057
Compton, Rebecca I, 1058
Compton, Rebecca V, 40
Compton, Rebecca V, 41
Compton, Rebecca V, 125
Compton, Rebecca V, 158
Compton, Rebecca V, 159
Compton, Rebecca V, 161
Compton, Rebecca V, 167
Compton, Rebecca V, 171
Compton, Rebecca V, 181
Compton, Rebecca V, 189
Compton, Rebecca V, 191
Compton, Rebecca V, 194
Compton, Rebecca V, 469
Compton, Rebecca J. V, 159
Compton, Rebecca J. V, 160
Compton, Rebecca Jane V, 482
Compton, Rebecca Millhouse I, 1056
Compton, Rebeckah V, 159
Compton, Rebeckah V, 160
Compton, Rebeckah V, 196
Compton, Rebeckah V, 482
Compton, Rebekah I, 1055
Compton, Rebekah I, 1060
Compton, Rebekah I, 1061
Compton, Rebekah I, 1062
Compton, Rebekah V, 40
Compton, Rebekah V, 158
Compton, Rees A. V, 159
Compton, Rhesa A. V, 160
Compton, Richard V, 155
Compton, Ruth I, 1055
Compton, Ruth V, 160
Compton, Ruth V, 161
Compton, Ruth V, 176
Compton, Ruth Edna V, 160
Compton, Ruth Edna V, 161

ompton, Sally I, 1018
ompton, Sally I, 1055
ompton, Sally I, 1056
ompton, Sally V, 40
ompton, Sally V, 77
ompton, Sally V, 158
ompton, Sally V, 159
ompton, Sally V, 179
ompton, Sally Nelson I, 1027
ompton, Sally Nelson I, 1058
ompton, Samantha V, 161
ompton, Samantha V, 732
ompton, Saml. I, 1058
ompton, Samuel I, 1018
ompton, Samuel I, 1027
ompton, Samuel I, 1055
ompton, Samuel I, 1056
ompton, Samuel I, 1059
ompton, Samuel I, 1060
ompton, Samuel V, 40
ompton, Samuel V, 155
ompton, Samuel V, 158
ompton, Samuel V, 159
ompton, Samuel V, 160
ompton, Samuel V, 161
ompton, Samuel V, 191
ompton, Samuel V, 211
ompton, Samuel V, 212
ompton, Samuel V, 482
ompton, Samuel V, 721
ompton, Samuel V, 732
ompton, Samuel VI, 895
ompton, Samuel B. V, 160
ompton, Samuel B. V, 161
ompton, Samuel T. V, 159
ompton, Samuel T. V, 160
ompton, Samuel T. V, 161
ompton, Samuel T. V, 556
ompton, Samuel T. V, 665
ompton, Samuel, Jr. I, 1027
ompton, Samuel, Sr. V, 158
ompton, Sarah I, 1027
ompton, Sarah I, 1055
ompton, Sarah I, 1058
ompton, Sarah V, 155
ompton, Sarah V, 158
ompton, Sarah V, 159
ompton, Sarah V, 160
ompton, Sarah V, 192
ompton, Sarah V, 206
ompton, Sarah V, 482
ompton, Sarah V, 483
ompton, Sarah V, 773
ompton, Sarah VI, 895
ompton, Sarah J. V, 160
ompton, Sarah J. V, 732
ompton, Sarah J. V, 745
ompton, Sarah Jane V, 159
ompton, Seth I, 1055
ompton, Seth V, 158
ompton, Seth V, 160
ompton, Seth V, 161
ompton, Seth V, 176
ompton, Seth V, 616
ompton, Seth Wm. V, 161
ompton, Stephen I, 1018
ompton, Stephen I, 1027
ompton, Stephen I, 1055
ompton, Stephen I, 1056
ompton, Stephen I, 1058
ompton, Stephen I, 1060
ompton, Stephen I, 1062
ompton, Stephen V, 40
ompton, Stephen V, 158
ompton, Stephen V, 159
ompton, Stephen V, 161
ompton, Stephen V, 179
ompton, Stephen V, 191
ompton, Stephen V, 469
ompton, Susanna V, 161
ompton, Susanna D. V, 160
ompton, Susannah V, 41
ompton, Susannah E. V, 41
ompton, Susannah E. V, 45
ompton, Sylvia Jane V, 732
ompton, Tamar I, 1056
ompton, Tamar I, 1059
ompton, Tamar V, 159
ompton, Tamar V, 161
ompton, Tamar V, 212
ompton, Tamar Owen I, 1056
ompton, Theo Christine V, 832
ompton, Theo Christine V, 835
ompton, Thomas W. V, 161
ompton, Thomas Walter V, 161
ompton, Uriah V, 160
ompton, Uriah V, 161
ompton, Walton V, 160
ompton, Walton V, 161
ompton, Warren V, 155
ompton, Wayne V, 206
Compton, Westley G. V, 160
Compton, Widow Elizabeth I, 1055
Compton, William I, 1018
Compton, William I, 1027
Compton, William I, 1055
Compton, William I, 1056
Compton, William II, 206
Compton, William II, 209
Compton, William V, 158
Compton, William V, 732
Compton, William V, 745
Compton, William V, 773
Compton, William E. V, 160
Compton, William F. V, 159
Compton, William F. V, 161
Compton, William Forsle V, 159
Compton, Wm. II, 492
Compton, Wm. V, 161
Compton, Wm. V, 192
Compton, Wm. V, 194
Compton, Wm. V, 206
Compton, Wm. E. V, 160
Comstock, ??? III, 82
Comstock, Aaron IV, 1359
Comstock, Abigail IV, 1358
Comstock, Abigail IV, 1359
Comstock, Albert III, 82
Comstock, Albert V. IV, 1359
Comstock, Alma J. IV, 1358
Comstock, Almy Jane IV, 1359
Comstock, Almy Jane IV, 1361
Comstock, Andrew II, 492
Comstock, Andrew II, 733
Comstock, Andrew IV, 1310
Comstock, Andrew J. IV, 1310
Comstock, Angeline M. IV, 1358
Comstock, Ann III, 82
Comstock, Ann III, 232
Comstock, Ann IV, 1358
Comstock, Ann E. III, 82
Comstock, Anna IV, 1358
Comstock, Anna V, 483
Comstock, Anna V, 900
Comstock, Anna P. IV, 1358
Comstock, Anne III, 225
Comstock, Anne III, 243
Comstock, Caleb IV, 1359
Comstock, Caleb O. IV, 1358
Comstock, Caroline IV, 1358
Comstock, Caroline A. IV, 1358
Comstock, Caroline Agnes III, 82
Comstock, Catharine IV, 1358
Comstock, Catharine IV, 1359
Comstock, Catharine IV, 1380
Comstock, Catherine IV, 1359
Comstock, Charlotte III, 82
Comstock, Charlotte F. IV, 1359
Comstock, Charlotte H. III, 38
Comstock, Charlotte H. III, 82
Comstock, Charlotte H. III, 91
Comstock, Chloe IV, 1358
Comstock, Daniel J. IV, 1358
Comstock, Darius IV, 1358
Comstock, Derius IV, 1359
Comstock, Ebenezar V, 483
Comstock, Edny IV, 1358
Comstock, Edwin IV, 1358
Comstock, Elisabeth IV, 1358
Comstock, Eliz. III, 82
Comstock, Eliz. III, 156
Comstock, Eliza IV, 1310
Comstock, Eliza. III, 82
Comstock, Elizabeth III, 82
Comstock, Elizabeth III, 154
Comstock, Elizabeth IV, 1310
Comstock, Elizabeth IV, 1358
Comstock, Elizabeth IV, 1380
Comstock, Elizabeth V, 483
Comstock, Elizabeth V, 900
Comstock, Elizabeth V, 919
Comstock, Elizabeth Ann III, 82
Comstock, Elsie III, 38
Comstock, Elsie III, 82
Comstock, Emeline V, 483
Comstock, Emeline V, 900
Comstock, Emmeline V, 900
Comstock, Esther IV, 1358
Comstock, George III, 82
Comstock, Harriet T. III, 82
Comstock, Harriet T. III, 293
Comstock, Huldah IV, 1376
Comstock, Huldah Ann IV, 1358
Comstock, Isaac IV, 1358
Comstock, Isaac Hathaway IV, 1358
Comstock, Jacob Carpenter V, 483
Comstock, Jacob Carpenter V, 900
Comstock, James M. IV, 1358
Comstock, Jared IV, 1358
Comstock, Jared IV, 1359
Comstock, Jared IV, 1380
Comstock, Job S. III, 82
Comstock, John M. III, 82
Comstock, John T. IV, 1358
Comstock, John T. IV, 1359
Comstock, Joseph Elliot IV, 1358
Comstock, Joseph H. IV, 1358
Comstock, Joseph O. IV, 1359
Comstock, Joseph Otis IV, 1358
Comstock, Louisa M. III, 82
Comstock, Lucy III, 82
Comstock, Lucy III, 156
Comstock, Lydia IV, 1358
Comstock, Lydia IV, 1359
Comstock, Martha III, 82
Comstock, Martha III, 171
Comstock, Mary IV, 1358
Comstock, Mary V, 483
Comstock, Mary V, 900
Comstock, Mary Gray IV, 1358
Comstock, Mary J. III, 82
Comstock, Mary J. III, 243
Comstock, Mary S. IV, 1358
Comstock, Mary S. IV, 1359
Comstock, Matthew V, 483
Comstock, Matthew V, 900
Comstock, Milo IV, 1358
Comstock, Minerva IV, 1358
Comstock, Nathan III, 38
Comstock, Nathan III, 82
Comstock, Nathan III, 91
Comstock, Nathan III, 156
Comstock, Nathan III, 225
Comstock, Nathan III, 232
Comstock, Nathan III, 243
Comstock, Nathan IV, 1358
Comstock, Nathan IV, 1359
Comstock, Nathan F. IV, 1358
Comstock, Nathan L. IV, 1358
Comstock, Nathan P. IV, 1359
Comstock, Nathan, Jr. III, 82
Comstock, Otis IV, 1376
Comstock, Patience IV, 1358
Comstock, Patience IV, 1376
Comstock, Peace IV, 1358
Comstock, Perry J. IV, 1359
Comstock, Phebe III, 82
Comstock, Phebe IV, 1358
Comstock, Phebe Ann IV, 1358
Comstock, Phebe Ann IV, 1359
Comstock, Phebe Ann IV, 1360
Comstock, Phebe Bailey IV, 1358
Comstock, Phebe Maria IV, 1358
Comstock, Philip III, 82
Comstock, Philip III, 293
Comstock, Rhoene IV, 1359
Comstock, Roby IV, 1358
Comstock, Roena IV, 1359
Comstock, Roena C. IV, 1358
Comstock, Roena C. IV, 1359
Comstock, Roene C. IV, 1359
Comstock, Rowena IV, 1358
Comstock, Rowena B. IV, 1359
Comstock, Rowena C. IV, 1359
Comstock, Rowene IV, 1358
Comstock, Sally IV, 1358
Comstock, Sally IV, 1359
Comstock, Samuel III, 82
Comstock, Samuel IV, 1358
Comstock, Samuel F. IV, 1310
Comstock, Sarah V, 483
Comstock, Sarah V, 900
Comstock, Sarah M. III, 82
Comstock, Sarah M. III, 232
Comstock, Sidney IV, 1358
Comstock, Stephen B. IV, 1358
Comstock, Susan V, 483
Comstock, Susan V, 900
Comstock, Susannah IV, 1358
Comstock, Sydney P. IV, 1358
Comstock, Thomas III, 82
Comstock, Thomas III, 154
Comstock, Thomas, Jr. III, 82
Comstock, Wd. Elizabeth III, 82
Comstock, William III, 82
Comstock, William V, 483
Comstock, William W. IV, 1358
Comstock, Wm. V, 900
Comstock, Wm. J. IV, 1358
Comstock, Zeno IV, 1359
Comton, Ann V, 40
Comton, Ann V, 109
Comton, Ann V, 141
Comton, Christianna V, 40
Comton, Christianna V, 125
Comton, Delitha Ann V, 616
Comton, Elizabeth V, 40
Comton, John V, 40
Comton, John V, 109
Comton, Joseph V, 40
Comton, Joseph V, 125
Comton, Nathan V, 141
Comton, Rebekah V, 40
Comton, Rebekah V, 141
Comton, Samuel V, 40
Con, Patience IV, 691
Conant, Doris IV, 1204
Conant, Frances IV, 1204
Conant, Lindora IV, 1204
Conant, Marian U. IV, 1204
Conant, Virgie Marie IV, 1204
Conard, A. J. V, 293
Conard, Abigail VI, 629
Conard, Abigail VI, 631
Conard, Alfred V, 325
Conard, Alfred F. II, 789
Conard, Alfred F. II, 851
Conard, Alice V, 41
Conard, Alice V, 85
Conard, Alice R. V, 41
Conard, Alice R. V, 300
Conard, Almira V, 41
Conard, Almira V, 300
Conard, Amea V, 325
Conard, Ann II, 851
Conard, Ann II, 921
Conard, Anna II, 851
Conard, Anna V, 230
Conard, Anna V, 325
Conard, Anna Clark II, 789
Conard, Anna S. II, 789
Conard, Anthony II, 147
Conard, Anthony II, 157
Conard, Benjamin V, 41
Conard, Benjamin V, 300
Conard, Bertha V, 325
Conard, Calvin II, 789
Conard, Calvin II, 851
Conard, Carnelius V, 41
Conard, Caroline Clayton II, 789
Conard, Carrie V, 665
Conard, Carrie Emily II, 851
Conard, Charles V, 41
Conard, Charles V, 300
Conard, Charles V, 325
Conard, Chas. II, 851
Conard, Chas. W. V, 325
Conard, Cornelius II, 851
Conard, Cornelius V, 41
Conard, Cornelius V, 300
Conard, Daniel II, 130
Conard, David II, 789
Conard, David II, 851
Conard, Dora V, 325
Conard, Dr. Robert V, 41
Conard, Edith V, 325
Conard, Edith M. V, 325
Conard, Eliza II, 130
Conard, Eliza V, 300
Conard, Eliza B. II, 147
Conard, Elizabeth II, 733
Conard, Elizabeth Letitia II, 1049
Conard, Elizabeth Letitia II, 1056
Conard, Ellen II, 851
Conard, Elma E. V, 41
Conard, Elwood V, 41
Conard, Elwood H. V, 41
Conard, Elwood H. V, 300
Conard, Emily V, 325
Conard, Emma J. V, 325
Conard, Enos V, 230
Conard, Enos V, 325
Conard, Esther V, 41
Conard, Esther VI, 379
Conard, Evans V, 41
Conard, Francis P. II, 851
Conard, Francis Paxson II, 789
Conard, Frank V, 325
Conard, Franklin V, 41
Conard, Franklin V, 300
Conard, George B. V, 41
Conard, George R. V, 41
Conard, George R. V, 300
Conard, Hannah E. II, 157
Conard, Harriet P. V, 325
Conard, Harriett P. V, 324
Conard, Harriett P. V, 325
Conard, Harvey E. V, 41
Conard, Hattie E. V, 293
Conard, Helen C. II, 851
Conard, Helen Clayton II, 789
Conard, Helen G. V, 41
Conard, Henry II, 851
Conard, Henry N. II, 851
Conard, Henry Norman II, 789
Conard, Henry Shoemaker II, 1049
Conard, Henry Shoemaker II, 1056
Conard, Homer V, 325
Conard, James V, 325
Conard, James VI, 379
Conard, James VI, 484
Conard, James VI, 580
Conard, James VI, 582
Conard, James, Jr. VI, 379
Conard, James, Sr. VI, 379
Conard, Jane II, 851
Conard, Jane II, 914
Conard, Jane VI, 546
Conard, Jean VI, 379
Conard, Jesse II, 851
Conard, Jesse II, 921
Conard, John VI, 546
Conard, John P. II, 851
Conard, John R. II, 851
Conard, John Roberts II, 789
Conard, John S. II, 851
Conard, Jonathan VI, 546
Conard, Jonathan Lukens II, 851
Conard, Joseph II, 789
Conard, Joseph II, 851
Conard, Joseph V, 41
Conard, Joseph V, 300
Conard, Joseph V, 325
Conard, Joseph V, 352
Conard, Joseph Ambler II, 851
Conard, Joseph W. V, 325
Conard, Judith VI, 632
Conard, Laura Owens II, 789
Conard, Lenna May V, 325
Conard, Lewis II, 851
Conard, Lewis V, 41
Conard, Lewis V, 300
Conard, Lewis V, 325
Conard, Lewis V, 380
Conard, Lucretia II, 851
Conard, Lucretia C., Jr. II, 851
Conard, Lucretia Crispin II, 789
Conard, Lucy Corse II, 789
Conard, Lydia V, 41
Conard, Lydia V, 325
Conard, Lydia Ann V, 41
Conard, Lydia Ann V, 325
Conard, Lydia W. V, 321
Conard, Margaret II, 349
Conard, Margaret II, 492
Conard, Margaret II, 575
Conard, Maria II, 789
Conard, Maria II, 851
Conard, Maria V, 230
Conard, Maria V, 325
Conard, Maris II, 851
Conard, Maris V, 41
Conard, Martha II, 477
Conard, Martha II, 628
Conard, Martha V, 41
Conard, Martha V, 300
Conard, Martha V, 325
Conard, Martha VI, 485
Conard, Mary V, 41
Conard, Mary V, 325
Conard, Mary B. II, 848
Conard, Mary B. II, 851
Conard, Mary B. C. II, 851
Conard, Mary Butler II, 789
Conard, Mary F. L. II, 851
Conard, Mary H. II, 851
Conard, Mary Jane V, 293
Conard, Mary Lukens II, 789
Conard, Mathew II, 349
Conard, Matilda V, 325
Conard, Milton II, 851
Conard, Milton II, 921
Conard, Nathan II, 130
Conard, Nathan II, 147
Conard, Osborn II, 733
Conard, Phebe V, 230
Conard, Phebe V, 325
Conard, Phoebe V, 325
Conard, Rachel II, 147
Conard, Rachel II, 157
Conard, Rachel II, 851
Conard, Rachel II, 921
Conard, Rachel IV, 570
Conard, Rachel A. II, 147
Conard, Rachel A. II, 157
Conard, Rachel Ann II, 780
Conard, Rachel K. II, 789
Conard, Rachel K. IV, 570
Conard, Rachel P. II, 848
Conard, Rachel P. II, 851
Conard, Rachel Paxson II, 789
Conard, Rachel S. II, 851
Conard, Rebecca II, 789
Conard, Rebecca II, 851
Conard, Rebecca II, 921
Conard, Rebecca V, 41
Conard, Rebecca V, 300
Conard, Rebecca V, 325
Conard, Rebecca V, 352

Conard, Rebecca S. II, 851
Conard, Rebecca S. II, 1049
Conard, Rebecca S. II, 1056
Conard, Robert V, 665
Conard, Robert Corse II, 789
Conard, Robert R. V, 41
Conard, Samuel II, 349
Conard, Samuel II, 789
Conard, Samuel II, 848
Conard, Samuel II, 851
Conard, Sarah II, 130
Conard, Sarah II, 851
Conard, Sarah IV, 142
Conard, Sarah IV, 154
Conard, Sarah V, 41
Conard, Sarah V, 300
Conard, Sarah V, 325
Conard, Sarah V, 352
Conard, Sarah VI, 374
Conard, Sarah VI, 379
Conard, Sarah VI, 546
Conard, Sarah C. IV, 691
Conard, Sarah C. IV, 757
Conard, Sarah E. II, 851
Conard, Sarah E. V, 325
Conard, Sarah R. II, 851
Conard, Sinah IV, 518
Conard, Sinai IV, 518
Conard, Sinai IV, 539
Conard, Stella V, 325
Conard, Stella V, 665
Conard, Susanna V, 300
Conard, Susannah V, 41
Conard, Susannah V, 325
Conard, Susannah L. V, 325
Conard, Thomas Pennington II, 1049
Conard, Thomas Pennington II, 1056
Conard, Thos. II, 789
Conard, Thos. II, 851
Conard, Thos. II, 921
Conard, Thos. C. II, 851
Conard, Thos. Judson Whitney II, 851
Conard, Walter V, 325
Conard, Walter M. II, 789
Conard, Walter V. V, 230
Conard, Walter V. V, 665
Conard, Wd. Elizabeth VI, 580
Conard, William V, 41
Conard, William W. V, 41
Conard, Wm. II, 147
Conard, Wm. II, 157
Conard, Wm. II, 789
Conard, Wm. II, 848
Conard, Wm. II, 851
Conard, Wm. V, 300
Conard, Wm. VI, 580
Conaro, Mary II, 192
Conaro, Thomas II, 192
Conaroe, Elizabeth V, 833
Conaroe, Elizabeth V, 873
Conaroe, Harriet V, 833
Conaroe, Harriet V, 868
Conaroe, John V, 833
Conaroe, Patience II, 209
Conarro, Andrew II, 192
Conarro, Atkinson II, 209
Conarro, Caleb II, 209
Conarro, Jane II, 192
Conarro, Mary II, 209
Conarro, Patience II, 209
Conarro, Patience II, 229
Conarroe, Aaron V, 832
Conarroe, Alice V, 832
Conarroe, Alice V, 833
Conarroe, Alice J. V, 833
Conarroe, Amy Ann V, 832
Conarroe, Anna V, 848
Conarroe, Clayton V, 833
Conarroe, Clayton V, 848
Conarroe, Clayton F. V, 833
Conarroe, Clayton T. V, 832
Conarroe, Clayton T. V, 833
Conarroe, Dora A. V, 833
Conarroe, Earl V, 833
Conarroe, Edgar V, 833
Conarroe, Edgar A. V, 833
Conarroe, Elanora V, 833
Conarroe, Elda V, 833
Conarroe, Elda Orcilla V, 833
Conarroe, Elizabeth V, 832
Conarroe, Elizabeth V, 833
Conarroe, Elizabeth V, 852
Conarroe, Elizabeth A. V, 833
Conarroe, Elizabeth C. V, 852
Conarroe, Elnora V, 833
Conarroe, Elnora V, 848
Conarroe, Fanny V, 833
Conarroe, Flora M. V, 833
Conarroe, Frances J. V, 833
Conarroe, Gabriel V, 833
Conarroe, Gabriel S. V, 832
Conarroe, Gabriel S. V, 833
Conarroe, Harriet V, 832
Conarroe, Harriet V, 833
Conarroe, Harriet D. V, 833
Conarroe, Harriett V, 852
Conarroe, Harriett V, 865
Conarroe, Ivea L. V, 833
Conarroe, Ivea Leona V, 833
Conarroe, Joel V, 833
Conarroe, Joel Ellis V, 832
Conarroe, John V, 832
Conarroe, John V, 833
Conarroe, John V, 852
Conarroe, John V, 865
Conarroe, John E. V, 833
Conarroe, John W. V, 833
Conarroe, Julia M. V, 833
Conarroe, Katie J. V, 833
Conarroe, Katie Jane V, 833
Conarroe, Laurence V, 833
Conarroe, Lawrence V, 833
Conarroe, Leroy V, 833
Conarroe, Leroy A. V, 833
Conarroe, Martha V, 832
Conarroe, Martha V, 833
Conarroe, Martha V, 834
Conarroe, Mary V, 833
Conarroe, Mary V, 865
Conarroe, Mary Anna V, 833
Conarroe, Mary B. V, 833
Conarroe, Mary Belle V, 833
Conarroe, Mary Belle V, 856
Conarroe, Mary S. V, 832
Conarroe, Reading A. V, 832
Conarroe, Reading A. V, 833
Conarroe, Sarah V, 833
Conarroe, Sarah L. V, 833
Conarroe, William V, 833
Conarroe, William B. V, 832
Conarroe, William B. V, 833
Conarroe, William E. V, 833
Conarroe, Willie V, 833
Conarrow, Thomas II, 209
Conaway, Aaron V, 793
Conaway, Abigail V, 779
Conaway, Abigail V, 802
Conaway, Ann II, 852
Conaway, Eli V, 779
Conaway, Eli V, 802
Conaway, Elizabeth V, 779
Conaway, Elizabeth V, 793
Conaway, Elizabeth V, 802
Conaway, Elizabeth V, 803
Conaway, James II, 789
Conaway, James V, 779
Conaway, James V, 802
Conaway, James D. V, 779
Conaway, Lydia V, 793
Conaway, Lydia V, 802
Conaway, Mary VI, 379
Conaway, Rebecca V, 780
Conaway, Rebecca V, 793
Conaway, Rebecca V, 802
Conaway, Samuel V, 779
Conaway, Samuel V, 802
Conaway, Wd. Ann II, 789
Concklin, Erwin III, 142
Concklin, Erwin R. III, 83
Concklin, Erwin Raymond III, 83
Concklin, Joseph III, 83
Concklin, Josiah III, 83
Concklin, Leah III, 83
Concklin, Leah H. III, 143
Concklin, Martha III, 83
Concklin, Mary L. III, 83
Concklin, Mildred Laura III, 83
Concklin, Mildred Laura III, 142
Conckling, Martha III, 405
Condell, Elizabeth II, 349
Condell, Lydia II, 349
Condell, William II, 349
Conden, Wm. T. V, 665
Conder, Elizabeth VI, 380
Conder, Margaret VI, 380
Condon, Mary II, 62
Condon, Mary II, 105
Condray, Prudence VI, 799
Condrey, Caleb VI, 807
Condrey, Lucy J. VI, 807
Condrey, Patience VI, 817
Condrey, Susannah VI, 807
Condrey, William VI, 807
Condrey, William VI, 817
Cone, Alice IV, 1359
Cone, Birthday IV, 1154
Conely, Caty VI, 832
Conero, Thomas II, 209
Cones, Lillie V, 990
Cones, Phebe V, 990
Cones, Wm. V, 990
Coney, Aden S. IV, 1154
Coney, Benedict IV, 1154
Coney, Harvey IV, 1154
Coney, James VI, 895
Coney, Lavina IV, 1154
Coney, Lovina B. IV, 1154
Coney, Nancy VI, 305
Coney, Nancy VI, 326
Coney, Nancy VI, 895
Coney, Phebe II, 62
Coney, Phebey II, 62
Coney, Phebey II, 85
Coney, Sarah Evaline IV, 1154
Coney, Susan IV, 1148
Coney, Susan IV, 1154
Coney, Susan A. IV, 1205
Coney, Susan Adelaide IV, 1154
Confer, Johanna V, 161
Congdon, Charles III, 82
Congdon, Elizabeth VI, 235
Congdon, Elizabeth A. VI, 235
Congdon, Elizabeth A. VI, 237
Congdon, Elizabeth Ann VI, 236
Congdon, Ellen L. III, 82
Congdon, Emma III, 132
Congdon, Emma III, 363
Congdon, Emma III, 364
Congdon, Emma III, 365
Congdon, Emma III, 366
Congdon, Emma C. III, 366
Congdon, Eunice I, 534
Congdon, Eunice I, 537
Congdon, Gilbert VI, 235
Congdon, Gilbert VI, 236
Congdon, Gilbert VI, 237
Congdon, Jonathan VI, 235
Congdon, Lydia I, 534
Congdon, William I, 534
Conger, Charley V, 483
Conger, Eliza V, 230
Conger, Eri V, 483
Conger, George V, 483
Conger, Gertrude V, 617
Conger, Ira V, 483
Conger, Irena V, 483
Conger, Joseph V, 483
Conger, Lena V, 483
Conger, Lettie O. IV, 1248
Conger, Missouri Etta V, 483
Conger, Nora M. V, 483
Conger, Oliver V, 483
Conger, Orange V, 483
Conger, Sarah V, 483
Conger, Sarah Ann V, 483
Conger, Vena Viola V, 483
Congers, Arline III, 82
Congers, Arline III, 334
Conggshall, Lettice I, 992
Coning, George III, 83
Coning, Mary Adline I, 1153
Coning, William I, 1149
Coning, William I, 1153
Conkle, Beulah IV, 865
Conkle, Beulah IV, 885
Conkle, Elizabeth II, 851
Conkle, Henry II, 492
Conkle, Rebecca II, 702
Conkle, Susanna II, 702
Conklin, Amy III, 228
Conklin, Anna B. III, 37
Conklin, Anna H. III, 83
Conklin, Armenia III, 76
Conklin, Armenia III, 154
Conklin, C. Leslie IV, 1310
Conklin, Charles IV, 1205
Conklin, Charles IV, 1234
Conklin, David III, 83
Conklin, David P. III, 83
Conklin, Deborah III, 404
Conklin, Dora E. V, 617
Conklin, Edward B. III, 404
Conklin, Edward Boote III, 83
Conklin, Eleanor III, 83
Conklin, Eliz. III, 83
Conklin, Elizabeth III, 83
Conklin, Elizabeth III, 404
Conklin, Elizabeth III, 451
Conklin, Elizabeth IV, 1234
Conklin, Elizabeth R. III, 83
Conklin, Elizabeth T. III, 83
Conklin, Ellen III, 404
Conklin, Ellen C. III, 83
Conklin, Ellen C. III, 196
Conklin, Elmer J. V, 617
Conklin, Elsie IV, 1205
Conklin, Enoch III, 83
Conklin, Erwin III, 83
Conklin, Erwin R. III, 83
Conklin, Erwin Raymond III, 83
Conklin, Frank Henry III, 83
Conklin, Hannah III, 318
Conklin, Hannah III, 319
Conklin, Henrietta III, 405
Conklin, Iona E. V, 617
Conklin, Isaac III, 83
Conklin, Isabella Leah III, 83
Conklin, Jacob III, 83
Conklin, Jacob III, 228
Conklin, Jacob III, 393
Conklin, Jacob III, 404
Conklin, Jacob III, 451
Conklin, Jacob III, 453
Conklin, Jacob III, 459
Conklin, James III, 83
Conklin, James III, 404
Conklin, James Arthur III, 83
Conklin, James W. III, 404
Conklin, Jean III, 83
Conklin, John III, 83
Conklin, John V, 556
Conklin, John W. V, 556
Conklin, Joseph III, 83
Conklin, Josiah III, 83
Conklin, Josiah III, 243
Conklin, Josiah Raymond III, 83
Conklin, Katherine III, 83
Conklin, Leah III, 83
Conklin, Leah H. III, 83
Conklin, Margaret III, 83
Conklin, Margaret III, 243
Conklin, Margaret Elizabeth III, 83
Conklin, Maria IV, 1205
Conklin, Martha III, 83
Conklin, Martha III, 405
Conklin, Martha III, 481
Conklin, Martha III, 495
Conklin, Mary III, 393
Conklin, Mary III, 404
Conklin, Mary III, 453
Conklin, Mary III, 459
Conklin, Mary A. III, 83
Conklin, Mary L. III, 83
Conklin, Mildred Laura III, 83
Conklin, Mrs. Leslie IV, 1310
Conklin, Phebe III, 83
Conklin, Phebe III, 404
Conklin, Phebe III, 481
Conklin, Phebe Martha III, 495
Conklin, Rachel III, 83
Conklin, Stephen III, 481
Conklin, Stephen III, 495
Conklin, William III, 83
Conklin, William III, 196
Conklin, Wm. III, 83
Conklin, Wm. III, 404
Conkling, Phebe R. V, 935
Conley, Charles C. IV, 1311
Conley, Chas. C. IV, 1248
Conley, Chas. C. IV, 1311
Conley, Irene IV, 1311
Conley, Jeanette IV, 1248
Conley, Mary V, 732
Conley, Miriam Barlow V, 665
Conley, Mrs. C. C. IV, 1248
Conley, Paul Jones IV, 1248
Conley, Thomas V, 732
Conlin, Hannah IV, 1205
Conlin, Hannah IV, 1213
Conly, Kisla VI, 807
Conly, Ruth V, 161
Conly, Ruth V, 173
Conly, Sarah VI, 807
Conn, Dinah Ann IV, 691
Conn, Dinah Ann IV, 786
Conn, Esther II, 209
Conn, Esther IV, 691
Conn, Eunice Celeste III, 405
Conn, Grace K. III, 405
Conn, Naomi IV, 1052
Conn, Naomi IV, 1068
Conn, Patience IV, 691
Conn, Phebe III, 405
Conn, Phebe Ann III, 483
Conn, Richard III, 483
Conn, Richard D. III, 405
Conn, Sarah III, 405
Conn, Sibelia VI, 235
Conn, Sibelia A. VI, 235
Conn, Sibelia A. VI, 257
Connad, Sinah IV, 518
Connal, Olive V, 325
Connally, Alis VI, 810
Connally, Patrick VI, 810
Connally, William VI, 810
Connar, Susan V, 556
Connard, Almira V, 35
Connard, Almira V, 41
Connard, Carrie V, 665
Connard, Carrie Emily II, 851
Connard, Carrie Emily II, 884
Connard, Elwood V, 41
Connard, Franklin V, 41
Connard, James VI, 546
Connard, James, Jr. VI, 379
Connard, James, Sr. VI, 379
Connard, John H. IV, 380
Connard, John P. II, 851
Connard, John P. II, 884
Connard, John P. II, 899
Connard, Jonathan Lukens II, 851
Connard, Jonathan Lukens II, 899
Connard, Joseph Ambler II, 851
Connard, Joseph Ambler II, 884
Connard, Lewis V, 325
Connard, Lydia V, 41
Connard, Lydia V, 325
Connard, Lydia Ann V, 325
Connard, Maria V, 325
Connard, Maris V, 41
Connard, Martha V, 41
Connard, Mary F. L. II, 851
Connard, Mary F. L. II, 884
Connard, Mary F. L. II, 899
Connard, Mary H. II, 851
Connard, Mary H. II, 899
Connard, Phebe V, 325
Connard, Rachel IV, 189
Connard, Rachel K. IV, 570
Connard, Rachel K. IV, 586
Connard, Rebecca V, 325
Connard, Sarah V, 41
Connard, Sarah V, 325
Connard, Thos. Judson Whitney II, 851
Connard, William IV, 189
Connaro, Thomas II, 209
Connaroe, Elnora V, 833
Connaroe, Frances J. V, 833
Connaroe, Gabriel S. V, 833
Connaroe, Ivea L. V, 833
Connaroe, John W. V, 833
Connaroe, Julia M. V, 833
Connaroe, Katie J. V, 833
Connarro, Antrim II, 209
Connarro, Elinor II, 209
Connarro, Elinor II, 277
Connarro, Isaac II, 209
Connarro, Isaac II, 277
Connarro, Mary II, 209
Connarro, Rebecca II, 209
Connarro, Thomas II, 209
Connaway, John II, 442
Connaway, Polly VI, 881
Connel, Lucinda V, 380
Connel, Lucinda V, 617
Connell, Alice V, 325
Connell, Alice V, 346
Connell, Catharine V, 325
Connell, Catharine V, 346
Connell, Frank Leslie V, 660
Connell, Frank Leslie V, 665
Connell, Fred IV, 1311
Connell, Glenn V, 325
Connell, Lucinda V, 644
Connell, Mae V, 732
Connell, Maggie M. V, 732
Connell, Olive V, 325
Connell, Olive V, 660
Connell, Olive V, 665
Connelly, Clara VI, 669
Connelly, Clara VI, 758
Connelly, Clara C. VI, 631
Conner, ??? V, 162
Conner, Ann V, 162
Conner, Anna I, 1056
Conner, Anna V, 162
Conner, Annie V, 41
Conner, Cader I, 136
Conner, Catharine I, 1043
Conner, Catharine I, 1056
Conner, Catharine V, 162
Conner, Catherine V, 41
Conner, Catherine V, 161
Conner, Catherine V, 483
Conner, Clara V, 41
Conner, David Mills V, 162
Conner, Demsey I, 136
Conner, Demsey I, 160
Conner, Elisabeth I, 136
Conner, Elisabeth I, 165
Conner, Elizabeth I, 136
Conner, Elizabeth IV, 26
Conner, Elizabeth IV, 32
Conner, Elizabeth IV, 81
Conner, Ellen Sherwood V, 41
Conner, Emma V, 617
Conner, Esther V, 162
Conner, Esther V, 191

Conner, Hannah V, 162
Conner, Helen Stratton V, 665
Conner, Isaac I, 1056
Conner, Isaac V, 41
Conner, Isaac V, 162
Conner, Jesse I, 1043
Conner, Jesse I, 1056
Conner, Jesse V, 41
Conner, Jesse V, 161
Conner, Jesse V, 162
Conner, Jesse V, 191
Conner, Jesse V, 483
Conner, Jesse V, 732
Conner, John I, 136
Conner, John I, 165
Conner, John I, 1027
Conner, John I, 1041
Conner, John I, 1043
Conner, John I, 1047
Conner, John I, 1056
Conner, John V, 41
Conner, John V, 161
Conner, John V, 162
Conner, John V, 483
Conner, John V, 732
Conner, John VI, 379
Conner, John Morgan VI, 362
Conner, Joseph V, 41
Conner, Leila III, 89
Conner, Lewis R. III, 89
Conner, Lile V, 617
Conner, Martha VI, 362
Conner, Martha VI, 379
Conner, Martha H. V, 162
Conner, Mary I, 121
Conner, Mary I, 135
Conner, Mary I, 136
Conner, Mary I, 160
Conner, Mary I, 169
Conner, Mary I, 1041
Conner, Mary I, 1043
Conner, Mary I, 1056
Conner, Mary V, 41
Conner, Mary V, 162
Conner, Mary V, 222
Conner, Mary V, 230
Conner, Mary VI, 362
Conner, Mary VI, 379
Conner, Mary VI, 925
Conner, Mary Connor V, 162
Conner, Mrs. ??? IV, 1274
Conner, Nancy V, 483
Conner, Phebe IV, 81
Conner, Phebe IV, 105
Conner, Rachel I, 1041
Conner, Rachel I, 1043
Conner, Rachel I, 1056
Conner, Rachel V, 41
Conner, Rachel V, 161
Conner, Rachel V, 162
Conner, Rachel V, 483
Conner, Rebecca I, 1056
Conner, Rebecca V, 162
Conner, Rev. ??? IV, 1274
Conner, Ruth I, 136
Conner, Sylvia M. V, 162
Conner, Thomas I, 1043
Conner, Thomas I, 1056
Conner, Thomas V, 41
Conner, Thomas V, 162
Conner, Thomas V, 483
Conner, Virginia R. IV, 276
Conner, Wallace L. III, 83
Conner, William I, 1043
Conner, William I, 1056
Conner, William IV, 81
Conner, William V, 41
Conner, William V, 161
Conner, William V, 162
Conner, William H. H. I, 758
Conner, Wm. IV, 81
Conner, Wm. V, 162
Conner, Wm. V, 483
Conner, Wm. B. VI, 947
Conners, A. B. III, 83
Conners, Bessie III, 83
Conners, Cath. B. III, 83
Conners, Chas. H. III, 83
Conners, Edward V, 915
Conners, Eurity V, 915
Conners, Gertrude III, 83
Conners, Leila III, 83
Conners, Lewis A. III, 83
Conners, Mary A. III, 83
Conners, Wallace L. III, 83
Conney, James VI, 798
Conney, John VI, 798
Conning, George III, 83
Conning, Harold J. IV, 1205
Conning, Joseph I, 1149
Conning, Margret I, 1149
Conning, Mary Addaline I, 1149
Conning, Mary Adline I, 1149
Conning, William I, 1149
Connolly, Clara C. VI, 668
Connoly, Eunice II, 493
Connoly, Joseph II, 349
Connoly, Sarah II, 349
Connor, ??? V, 147
Connor, A. B. III, 153
Connor, Anna V, 162
Connor, Archie I, 209
Connor, Catharine V, 162
Connor, Catherine V, 41
Connor, Catherine V, 98
Connor, Cora V, 419
Connor, David Mills V, 162
Connor, Demsey I, 136
Connor, Esther V, 162
Connor, Ethel V, 419
Connor, Gertrude III, 153
Connor, Hannah V, 162
Connor, Hattie A. I, 209
Connor, Isaac V, 41
Connor, Isaac V, 162
Connor, Jesse V, 162
Connor, John V, 41
Connor, John V, 162
Connor, Mary Connor V, 162
Connor, Rachel V, 41
Connor, Rachel V, 162
Connor, Rebecca V, 162
Connor, Taylor V, 419
Connor, William V, 162
Connor, Wm. V, 162
Connoway, John VI, 895
Connoway, Milly VI, 895
Conolee, Joseph II, 349
Conorow, Caleb II, 194
Conorow, Caleb II, 209
Conorow, Patience II, 194
Conorow, Patience II, 209
Conover, ??? III, 149
Conover, ??? III, 301
Conover, Angelina III, 149
Conover, Corinthe V, 380
Conover, Fremont IV, 1274
Conover, Hannah V, 41
Conover, Hannah V, 53
Conover, Hester V, 666
Conover, Kathelene IV, 1274
Conover, Margaret IV, 1274
Conover, Mary III, 83
Conover, Mary III, 301
Conover, Mary V, 41
Conover, Mary S. V, 900
Conover, Rachel II, 799
Conover, Rachel II, 1049
Conover, Rachel II, 1051
Conover, Rachel II, 1071
Conover, Rachel II, 1073
Conover, Rena V, 666
Conover, Sarah S. II, 799
Conover, Theodore II, 799
Conoway, Elizabeth V, 41
Conoway, Elizabeth V, 779
Conoway, James V, 41
Conoway, Lydia V, 41
Conoway, Samuel V, 41
Conquest, Mr. ??? VI, 9
Conquest, Mr. Richard VI, 9
Conrad, Abraham II, 493
Conrad, Albert Ely II, 789
Conrad, Alfred Marple II, 789
Conrad, Amelia III, 212
Conrad, Ann II, 820
Conrad, Ann II, 851
Conrad, Ann II, 924
Conrad, Ann Thompson II, 789
Conrad, Anna II, 349
Conrad, Anna II, 733
Conrad, Anna II, 746
Conrad, Carrie IV, 1248
Conrad, Charles II, 349
Conrad, Charles II, 493
Conrad, Charles II, 702
Conrad, Charles II, 733
Conrad, Charles II, 734
Conrad, Clarence IV, 1248
Conrad, Curboy IV, 1248
Conrad, Edna Garrett II, 789
Conrad, Elijah II, 349
Conrad, Elijah II, 493
Conrad, Elizabeth II, 349
Conrad, Elizabeth II, 493
Conrad, Elizabeth II, 598
Conrad, Elizabeth II, 702
Conrad, Elizabeth VI, 379
Conrad, Elizabeth VI, 546
Conrad, Elizabeth C. II, 733
Conrad, Elizabeth C. II, 754
Conrad, Ellen II, 820
Conrad, Ellen II, 851
Conrad, Ellen II, 924
Conrad, Ellen III, 344
Conrad, Ellwood B. IV, 615
Conrad, Ellwood B. IV, 941
Conrad, Elma IV, 726
Conrad, Elma G. IV, 691
Conrad, Elma G. IV, 941
Conrad, Elma G. IV, 967
Conrad, Elwood IV, 807
Conrad, Elwood B. II, 130
Conrad, Elwood B. II, 147
Conrad, Elwood B. IV, 691
Conrad, Elwood B. IV, 807
Conrad, Elwood B. IV, 811
Conrad, Elwood B. IV, 989
Conrad, Emerson IV, 615
Conrad, Emerson IV, 648
Conrad, Emerson IV, 691
Conrad, Emerson IV, 745
Conrad, Emerson IV, 941
Conrad, Emmerson IV, 691
Conrad, Emmerson IV, 941
Conrad, Esther V, 881
Conrad, Esther VI, 379
Conrad, Esther VI, 478
Conrad, Esther, Jr. V, 881
Conrad, Eunice IV, 941
Conrad, Eunice IV, 989
Conrad, Eunice H. IV, 807
Conrad, Eunice H. IV, 941
Conrad, Eunice H. IV, 989
Conrad, Eva M. IV, 615
Conrad, Eva M. IV, 648
Conrad, Eva M. IV, 691
Conrad, Eva M. IV, 745
Conrad, Eva N. IV, 615
Conrad, Eva N. IV, 941
Conrad, Eva W. IV, 941
Conrad, Florence II, 851
Conrad, Florence E. II, 789
Conrad, Florence E. II, 851
Conrad, Florence E. II, 865
Conrad, Florence L. II, 851
Conrad, Florence L. II, 870
Conrad, Frances IV, 948
Conrad, Frederick IV, 691
Conrad, George VI, 379
Conrad, Goldie IV, 1248
Conrad, Hannah IV, 142
Conrad, Hannah IV, 189
Conrad, Hannah VI, 379
Conrad, Harold IV, 1248
Conrad, Harold H. II, 789
Conrad, Harry IV, 1248
Conrad, Herbert Styer II, 789
Conrad, Hilda May IV, 1248
Conrad, Horace G. II, 789
Conrad, Horace G. II, 851
Conrad, Horace G. II, 929
Conrad, Isaac II, 851
Conrad, Isaac II, 865
Conrad, Isaac II, 870
Conrad, James V, 881
Conrad, James VI, 379
Conrad, James Linton II, 493
Conrad, James Sinton II, 702
Conrad, James Sinton II, 733
Conrad, James Sinton II, 734
Conrad, James, Jr. V, 833
Conrad, James, Jr. V, 881
Conrad, James, Jr. VI, 379
Conrad, Jane VI, 379
Conrad, Job II, 789
Conrad, Job II, 820
Conrad, Job II, 851
Conrad, Job II, 924
Conrad, John II, 349
Conrad, John II, 733
Conrad, John S. II, 851
Conrad, John S. II, 865
Conrad, John Scotton II, 789
Conrad, John Styer II, 789
Conrad, Jonathan II, 493
Conrad, Joseph II, 702
Conrad, Joseph IV, 807
Conrad, Joseph IV, 941
Conrad, Joseph V, 881
Conrad, Joseph VI, 379
Conrad, Joseph L. IV, 691
Conrad, Joseph L. IV, 726
Conrad, Joseph L. IV, 941
Conrad, Joseph L. IV, 967
Conrad, Joseph Lewis IV, 691
Conrad, Joyce II, 702
Conrad, Lewis IV, 691
Conrad, Lewis IV, 807
Conrad, Lillian II, 789
Conrad, Lucie L. B. II, 851
Conrad, Lucy II, 349
Conrad, Lucy II, 733
Conrad, Lucy II, 757
Conrad, Marian II, 789
Conrad, Mary IV, 142
Conrad, Mary IV, 189
Conrad, Mary IV, 691
Conrad, Mary IV, 941
Conrad, Mary E. IV, 691
Conrad, Mary Elizabeth IV, 941
Conrad, Mary R. I, 922
Conrad, Meriam II, 621
Conrad, Miriam II, 493
Conrad, Myrtle IV, 1248
Conrad, Nathan VI, 379
Conrad, Nelson J. IV, 941
Conrad, Orabel IV, 1248
Conrad, Osborn II, 734
Conrad, Pamelia H. II, 789
Conrad, Parmelia H. II, 851
Conrad, Parmelia Henly II, 851
Conrad, Parmelia Henly II, 929
Conrad, Phebe IV, 691
Conrad, Phebe IV, 811
Conrad, Phebe IV, 941
Conrad, Phebe B. IV, 807
Conrad, Phebe W. IV, 615
Conrad, Phebe W. IV, 691
Conrad, Phebe W. IV, 941
Conrad, Phebe W. IV, 948
Conrad, Phebe W. IV, 989
Conrad, Rachel V, 881
Conrad, Rachel VI, 379
Conrad, Rachel R. II, 851
Conrad, Rachel R. II, 865
Conrad, Rachel R. II, 870
Conrad, Rachel S. II, 851
Conrad, Rebecca IV, 807
Conrad, Rebecca Adamson IV, 691
Conrad, Rebecca C. IV, 941
Conrad, Rebecca C. IV, 948
Conrad, Rebecca E. IV, 941
Conrad, Ruth V, 881
Conrad, Ruth VI, 379
Conrad, Sally Ann II, 493
Conrad, Sally Ann II, 702
Conrad, Sally Ann II, 733
Conrad, Samuel I, 922
Conrad, Samuel IV, 691
Conrad, Samuel IV, 941
Conrad, Samuel E. IV, 691
Conrad, Sarah II, 349
Conrad, Sarah II, 734
Conrad, Sarah IV, 142
Conrad, Sarah IV, 189
Conrad, Sarah VI, 379
Conrad, Sarah VI, 430
Conrad, Solomon II, 349
Conrad, Solomon II, 493
Conrad, Solomon II, 733
Conrad, Solomon W. II, 493
Conrad, Solomon W. II, 702
Conrad, Stella IV, 1248
Conrad, Susan II, 349
Conrad, Susan II, 725
Conrad, Susan II, 733
Conrad, Thomas II, 851
Conrad, Thomas IV, 142
Conrad, Thos. C. II, 851
Conrad, Timothy A. II, 733
Conrad, Timothy Abbott II, 349
Conrad, Virginia May IV, 941
Conrad, Wauneta IV, 941
Conrad, William II, 349
Conrad, William IV, 142
Conrad, William B. II, 702
Conrad, Wm. B. II, 734
Conro, Andrew II, 209
Conro, Eleanor II, 209
Conro, Jane II, 209
Conro, Rebecca II, 209
Conroe, Darwin IV, 167
Conroe, Grace II, 209
Conroe, Grace II, 228
Conrow, A. Engle II, 309
Conrow, A. Engle, Jr. II, 309
Conrow, Abraham II, 309
Conrow, Aguilla IV, 518
Conrow, Albert IV, 518
Conrow, Alfred E. IV, 519
Conrow, Alfred Edward IV, 518
Conrow, Alfred Edward IV, 519
Conrow, Alma E. III, 83
Conrow, Alma E. III, 249
Conrow, Andrew II, 209
Conrow, Andrew, Jr. II, 209
Conrow, Anna IV, 189
Conrow, Anna IV, 243
Conrow, Anna IV, 380
Conrow, Anna IV, 518
Conrow, Anna IV, 522
Conrow, Anna IV, 528
Conrow, Anna IV, 570
Conrow, Anna Alida II, 805
Conrow, Anna Alida II, 889
Conrow, Anna Beeson II, 309
Conrow, Anna Edgerton IV, 576
Conrow, Anna L. III, 83
Conrow, Anna L. III, 149
Conrow, Anna M. IV, 212
Conrow, Anne IV, 189
Conrow, Anne IV, 518
Conrow, Annie IV, 518
Conrow, Antrim II, 209
Conrow, Antrim II, 493
Conrow, Atkinson II, 62
Conrow, Atkinson II, 72
Conrow, Atkinson II, 209
Conrow, Barbara Dutton III, 83
Conrow, Caleb II, 62
Conrow, Caleb II, 209
Conrow, Caleb II, 349
Conrow, Caleb, Jr. II, 62
Conrow, Carlton H. IV, 518
Conrow, Caroline D. II, 309
Conrow, Caroline D. II, 317
Conrow, Caroline D. II, 798
Conrow, Caroline D. II, 851
Conrow, Caroline D. II, 852
Conrow, Caroline D. II, 872
Conrow, Carroll M. VI, 580
Conrow, Charles D. IV, 518
Conrow, Charlotte Biddle II, 789
Conrow, Chas. D. IV, 518
Conrow, Chas. D. IV, 529
Conrow, Chas. D. IV, 691
Conrow, Chas. D. IV, 718
Conrow, Clayton III, 83
Conrow, Clayton VI, 483
Conrow, Clayton VI, 580
Conrow, Clayton VI, 581
Conrow, Darling II, 201
Conrow, Darling II, 209
Conrow, Darling II, 789
Conrow, Darling IV, 142
Conrow, Darling IV, 189
Conrow, Darling IV, 380
Conrow, Darling IV, 518
Conrow, Darling IV, 522
Conrow, Darling IV, 570
Conrow, Darling IV, 576
Conrow, Darling VI, 593
Conrow, Darling VI, 594
Conrow, Darling VI, 595
Conrow, Darling, Jr. IV, 518
Conrow, David IV, 189
Conrow, David IV, 212
Conrow, David IV, 243
Conrow, David IV, 518
Conrow, David IV, 528
Conrow, David J. IV, 518
Conrow, Deborah IV, 518
Conrow, Deborah F. IV, 518
Conrow, Deborah F. IV, 529
Conrow, Deborah F. IV, 691
Conrow, Deborah F. IV, 718
Conrow, Deborah Hayes IV, 691
Conrow, E. Spencer II, 852
Conrow, Edith IV, 570
Conrow, Edith IV, 577
Conrow, Edith A. IV, 518
Conrow, Edith A. IV, 519
Conrow, Edith Anna IV, 518
Conrow, Edith Anna IV, 522
Conrow, Edith M. IV, 518
Conrow, Edmund H. IV, 518
Conrow, Edmund H. IV, 547
Conrow, Edward H. IV, 518
Conrow, Edward H. IV, 519
Conrow, Eleanor II, 209
Conrow, Eleanor Hite III, 83
Conrow, Elinor II, 209
Conrow, Eliza III, 83
Conrow, Elizabeth II, 201
Conrow, Elizabeth II, 209
Conrow, Elizabeth II, 781
Conrow, Elizabeth II, 789
Conrow, Elizabeth II, 838
Conrow, Elizabeth II, 852
Conrow, Elizabeth IV, 519
Conrow, Elizabeth E. II, 789
Conrow, Elizabeth E. II, 838
Conrow, Elizabeth E. II, 852
Conrow, Elizabeth Ruth IV, 518
Conrow, Elsie I, 225
Conrow, Emma II, 789
Conrow, Emma H. III, 83
Conrow, Emma S. III, 83
Conrow, Emma S. III, 180
Conrow, Eunice IV, 142
Conrow, Eunice IV, 570
Conrow, Eunice VI, 593
Conrow, Florence L. II, 852

Conrow, Frances II, 991
Conrow, Francis IV, 518
Conrow, George E. B. II, 851
Conrow, George E. B. II, 852
Conrow, George Elkinton Barber II, 789
Conrow, Gertrude E. IV, 519
Conrow, Gertrude Ellen IV, 518
Conrow, Grace II, 209
Conrow, Hannah VI, 483
Conrow, Hannah VI, 580
Conrow, Hannah VI, 581
Conrow, Hannah VI, 582
Conrow, Harvey R. IV, 519
Conrow, Harvey Rockwell IV, 518
Conrow, Harvey Rockwell IV, 519
Conrow, Herman III, 83
Conrow, Herman III, 180
Conrow, Howard II, 852
Conrow, Howard F. II, 838
Conrow, Howard F. II, 851
Conrow, Howard F. II, 852
Conrow, Howard F. III, 83
Conrow, Howard Fairfax II, 789
Conrow, Howard Paxson III, 83
Conrow, Isaac II, 209
Conrow, Jacob IV, 142
Conrow, Jacob IV, 518
Conrow, Jacob IV, 570
Conrow, Jacob VI, 593
Conrow, Jacob VI, 594
Conrow, Jane II, 209
Conrow, Jonathan IV, 243
Conrow, Jonathan H. III, 83
Conrow, Jonathan H. III, 149
Conrow, Jonathan Hutchinson III, 83
Conrow, Joseph II, 317
Conrow, Joseph IV, 518
Conrow, Joseph B. II, 309
Conrow, Joseph B. II, 317
Conrow, Joseph B. II, 851
Conrow, Joseph B. II, 852
Conrow, Joseph B. II, 872
Conrow, Joseph B. II, 886
Conrow, Joseph Brown II, 789
Conrow, Joseph D. II, 309
Conrow, Joseph D. II, 317
Conrow, Joseph D. II, 851
Conrow, Joseph D. II, 852
Conrow, Joseph D. II, 872
Conrow, Joseph Wallace III, 83
Conrow, Joseph Wallace III, 249
Conrow, Josiah IV, 518
Conrow, Lavinia R. II, 852
Conrow, Lewis IV, 518
Conrow, Lydia IV, 518
Conrow, Martha IV, 518
Conrow, Martha M. IV, 518
Conrow, Martha M. IV, 547
Conrow, Martha R. IV, 518
Conrow, Martha R. IV, 519
Conrow, Mary II, 62
Conrow, Mary II, 209
Conrow, Mary II, 493
Conrow, Mary IV, 518
Conrow, Mary IV, 1129
Conrow, Mary VI, 580
Conrow, Mary VI, 581
Conrow, Mary G. III, 83
Conrow, Mary H. II, 309
Conrow, Mary H. II, 317
Conrow, Mary H. II, 851
Conrow, Mary H. II, 852
Conrow, Mary H. II, 886
Conrow, Mary J. IV, 518
Conrow, Mary J. IV, 522
Conrow, Mary J. IV, 691
Conrow, Mary J. IV, 1091
Conrow, Mary J. IV, 1101
Conrow, Mary M. IV, 519
Conrow, Mary S. VI, 483
Conrow, Mary S. VI, 581
Conrow, Maud M. II, 852
Conrow, Minnie II, 309
Conrow, Morris W. II, 852
Conrow, Patience II, 62
Conrow, Patience II, 209
Conrow, Prudence II, 62
Conrow, Prudence II, 72
Conrow, Prudence II, 130
Conrow, Prudence II, 147
Conrow, Rachel IV, 142
Conrow, Rachel IV, 189
Conrow, Rachel IV, 243
Conrow, Rachel IV, 518
Conrow, Rachel VI, 593
Conrow, Rachel VI, 594
Conrow, Rachel VI, 595
Conrow, Rebecca II, 209
Conrow, Rebecca II, 493
Conrow, Rebecca IV, 142
Conrow, Rebecca IV, 518
Conrow, Rebeckah VI, 594
Conrow, Roger Hunt III, 83
Conrow, Ruth IV, 189
Conrow, Ruth IV, 243
Conrow, Ruth IV, 518
Conrow, Ruth IV, 539
Conrow, Sarah II, 201
Conrow, Sarah II, 209
Conrow, Sarah III, 481
Conrow, Sarah VI, 789
Conrow, Sarah VI, 793
Conrow, Sarah B. II, 309
Conrow, Sarah B. II, 317
Conrow, Sarah B. II, 851
Conrow, Sarah B. II, 852
Conrow, Sarah B. II, 872
Conrow, Sarah B. II, 886
Conrow, Sarah Bartlett II, 789
Conrow, Sarah E. VI, 736
Conrow, Sarah E. VI, 793
Conrow, Stacy II, 284
Conrow, Stacy II, 285
Conrow, Susanna II, 309
Conrow, T. Rollin IV, 518
Conrow, Thomas II, 209
Conrow, Thomas II, 493
Conrow, Thomas IV, 142
Conrow, Thomas IV, 189
Conrow, Thomas IV, 518
Conrow, Thomas IV, 539
Conrow, Thomas VI, 594
Conrow, Thomas H. IV, 518
Conrow, Thomas H. IV, 522
Conrow, Thomas W. IV, 1091
Conrow, Thomas W. IV, 1101
Conrow, Thornton Spencer II, 309
Conrow, Thos. IV, 243
Conrow, Thos. IV, 518
Conrow, Thos. H. IV, 518
Conrow, Thos. H. IV, 691
Conrow, Unice VI, 594
Conrow, Wilbur Biddle II, 789
Conrow, William R. Lippincott II, 309
Consolver, Celia VI, 998
Consolver, John VI, 1020
Consolver, Jonathan VI, 895
Consolver, Jonathan VI, 998
Consolver, Milley VI, 895
Constable, Dorothy V, 391
Constable, John V, 391
Constable, Martha V, 391
Constant, Benona IV, 1154
Constant, Bert V, 617
Constant, Charles IV, 1154
Constant, Edgar IV, 1154
Constant, Edna V, 617
Constant, Gertrude Conger V, 617
Constant, Ione V, 617
Constant, Jonathan IV, 1154
Constant, Lydia IV, 1154
Constant, Samuel IV, 1154
Constant, Zephaniah IV, 1154
Constantian, Avedis III, 103
Constantian, Joseph J. III, 83
Constantian, Virginia A. III, 103
Contant, ??? III, 117
Contant, Mary II, 720
Contant, Sarah L. III, 117
Converse, Fred S. IV, 1311
Converse, Fred Sumner IV, 1311
Converse, Hattie IV, 1311
Converse, Hattie M. IV, 1311
Conway, Ann II, 789
Conway, Ann II, 852
Conway, Anna Mary II, 801
Conway, Beulah Ann VI, 736
Conway, Elizabeth V, 41
Conway, Elizabeth V, 162
Conway, James II, 789
Conway, James V, 41
Conway, James V, 162
Conway, James VI, 895
Conway, John V, 325
Conway, John VI, 895
Conway, Joseph V, 41
Conway, Lydia V, 41
Conway, Lydia V, 162
Conway, Mary VI, 379
Conway, Mary VI, 397
Conway, Mary Belinda II, 801
Conway, Rebecca VI, 444
Conway, Samuel V, 41
Conway, Samuel V, 162
Conway, Wd. Ann II, 789
Conway, Willy VI, 895
Conwell, Clyde Walter V, 990
Conwell, Elmer V, 990
Conwell, Mary E. I, 233
Conwell, Ora Isaac V, 990
Cony, Phebe II, 62
Cooder, Clarissa V, 41
Cooder, Clarissa V, 47
Cooe, Mary VI, 483
Cooe, Mary VI, 508
Cooe, Mary VI, 519
Cooe, Mary VI, 521
Cooe, Mary VI, 661
Cooe, Mary VI, 673
Cooe, Wm. Holmes VI, 483
Cook, ??? III, 83
Cook, ??? III, 84
Cook, ??? III, 194
Cook, ??? III, 294
Cook, ??? V, 147
Cook, ??? V, 823
Cook, Abbie H. IV, 190
Cook, Abbie H. IV, 692
Cook, Abbie Louesa IV, 468
Cook, Abigail H. IV, 692
Cook, Abraham I, 487
Cook, Abraham I, 494
Cook, Abraham I, 495
Cook, Abraham I, 524
Cook, Abraham I, 534
Cook, Abraham I, 562
Cook, Abraham I, 779
Cook, Abraham I, 806
Cook, Abraham I, 961
Cook, Abraham I, 1056
Cook, Abraham I, 1057
Cook, Abraham IV, 26
Cook, Abraham V, 42
Cook, Abraham V, 43
Cook, Abraham V, 117
Cook, Abraham V, 140
Cook, Abraham V, 162
Cook, Abraham V, 175
Cook, Abram I, 534
Cook, Ada V, 325
Cook, Adala Ann II, 734
Cook, Adala Ann II, 747
Cook, Addie V, 325
Cook, Aemos II, 349
Cook, Albert IV, 941
Cook, Albert IV, 1311
Cook, Alexander W. IV, 692
Cook, Alfred I, 876
Cook, Alice V, 990
Cook, Aljeline I, 875
Cook, Allen I, 534
Cook, Allen IV, 26
Cook, Allen IV, 142
Cook, Almira V, 454
Cook, Almira Carey V, 325
Cook, Alva G. IV, 570
Cook, Alva G. IV, 571
Cook, Amanda A. VI, 896
Cook, Amanda Jane I, 876
Cook, Ambrose V, 380
Cook, Amelia III, 83
Cook, Amelia E. V, 163
Cook, Amos I, 1018
Cook, Amos I, 1027
Cook, Amos I, 1038
Cook, Amos I, 1056
Cook, Amos I, 1060
Cook, Amos IV, 26
Cook, Amos V, 17
Cook, Amos V, 41
Cook, Amos V, 42
Cook, Amos V, 43
Cook, Amos V, 130
Cook, Amos V, 162
Cook, Amos V, 163
Cook, Amos V, 164
Cook, Amos V, 166
Cook, Amos V, 171
Cook, Amos V, 209
Cook, Amos V, 325
Cook, Amos V, 328
Cook, Amos V, 483
Cook, Amos V, 523
Cook, Amos V, 541
Cook, Amos V, 833
Cook, Amos V, 834
Cook, Amos V, 900
Cook, Amos Cook IV, 26
Cook, Amy V, 230
Cook, Amy V, 290
Cook, Andrew M. V, 42
Cook, Andrew M. V, 900
Cook, Angelina I, 852
Cook, Ann I, 806
Cook, Ann I, 837
Cook, Ann I, 875
Cook, Ann I, 1018
Cook, Ann I, 1027
Cook, Ann I, 1028
Cook, Ann I, 1031
Cook, Ann I, 1056
Cook, Ann I, 1057
Cook, Ann I, 1060
Cook, Ann I, 1061
Cook, Ann I, 1062
Cook, Ann III, 84
Cook, Ann IV, 26
Cook, Ann IV, 75
Cook, Ann IV, 117
Cook, Ann IV, 190
Cook, Ann IV, 557
Cook, Ann IV, 941
Cook, Ann IV, 980
Cook, Ann IV, 1024
Cook, Ann V, 42
Cook, Ann V, 69
Cook, Ann V, 140
Cook, Ann V, 146
Cook, Ann V, 162
Cook, Ann V, 163
Cook, Ann V, 230
Cook, Ann V, 246
Cook, Ann V, 483
Cook, Ann E. III, 84
Cook, Ann E. IV, 692
Cook, Ann E. IV, 740
Cook, Ann Eliza II, 852
Cook, Ann Elizabeth V, 900
Cook, Ann H. IV, 81
Cook, Ann H. IV, 190
Cook, Ann H. IV, 927
Cook, Ann H. IV, 941
Cook, Ann P. V, 163
Cook, Ann P. V, 192
Cook, Anna I, 495
Cook, Anna I, 526
Cook, Anna I, 534
Cook, Anna I, 779
Cook, Anna I, 806
Cook, Anna I, 875
Cook, Anna II, 969
Cook, Anna III, 83
Cook, Anna III, 322
Cook, Anna IV, 123
Cook, Anna V, 42
Cook, Anna V, 900
Cook, Anna C. IV, 1091
Cook, Anna C. IV, 1104
Cook, Anne I, 852
Cook, Anne I, 875
Cook, Arthur II, 349
Cook, Axey V, 171
Cook, Barton II, 349
Cook, Barton II, 734
Cook, Bathsheba V, 780
Cook, Bathsheba V, 786
Cook, Bathsheba J. V, 780
Cook, Benjamin II, 349
Cook, Benjamin IV, 468
Cook, Benjamin V, 43
Cook, Benjamin VI, 807
Cook, Benjamin Hawkins V, 42
Cook, Benjamin L. IV, 189
Cook, Benjamin L. IV, 468
Cook, Bertha IV, 570
Cook, Bertha IV, 1311
Cook, Bertha H. IV, 1311
Cook, Besse A. V, 43
Cook, Bessie V, 164
Cook, Bessie Ione V, 300
Cook, Betsy I, 779
Cook, Betsy I, 806
Cook, Betsy I, 838
Cook, Betty IV, 26
Cook, Betty V, 42
Cook, Betty V, 146
Cook, Betty VI, 105
Cook, C. Alex. III, 84
Cook, Caleb II, 493
Cook, Caleb IV, 692
Cook, Caleb IV, 710
Cook, Caleb IV, 1029
Cook, Caleb C. I, 779
Cook, Caleb C. III, 83
Cook, Caleb Edwin III, 84
Cook, Carl Alva IV, 570
Cook, Caroline III, 51
Cook, Caroline III, 83
Cook, Caroline L. III, 83
Cook, Carrie III, 51
Cook, Carrie E. III, 51
Cook, Carrie E. III, 83
Cook, Carrie E. III, 135
Cook, Catharine II, 349
Cook, Catherine II, 349
Cook, Charity I, 779
Cook, Charity I, 1018
Cook, Charity I, 1026
Cook, Charity I, 1028
Cook, Charity V, 42
Cook, Charity V, 162
Cook, Charity V, 163
Cook, Charity V, 185
Cook, Charity V, 191
Cook, Charity V, 230
Cook, Charity V, 469
Cook, Charity V, 833
Cook, Charity V, 834
Cook, Charity V, 840
Cook, Charles II, 349
Cook, Charles II, 734
Cook, Charles Gilpin III, 83
Cook, Charles Gilpin III, 322
Cook, Charles L. IV, 692
Cook, Charles L. IV, 792
Cook, Chas. II, 852
Cook, Clarkey I, 302
Cook, Clarkey I, 312
Cook, Clarkson F. V, 780
Cook, Clarkson F. V, 786
Cook, Clarkson J. I, 876
Cook, Cora IV, 941
Cook, Cora IV, 1311
Cook, Cora M. IV, 1309
Cook, Cora M. IV, 1311
Cook, Cornelia M. III, 84
Cook, Cornelius III, 51
Cook, Cornelius III, 83
Cook, Cornelius W. III, 84
Cook, Cynthia IV, 1359
Cook, Cynthia A. I, 936
Cook, Daniel II, 442
Cook, Daniel II, 789
Cook, Deborah V, 832
Cook, Deborah V, 833
Cook, Deborah VI, 58
Cook, Deborah VI, 235
Cook, Deborah VI, 246
Cook, Deborah VI, 248
Cook, Delilah V, 833
Cook, Delilah V, 851
Cook, Della IV, 807
Cook, Della Haven IV, 692
Cook, Dennis M. V, 325
Cook, Dianah I, 1018
Cook, Dinah I, 1056
Cook, Dinah I, 1057
Cook, Dinah I, 1058
Cook, Dinah I, 1059
Cook, Dinah I, 1060
Cook, Dinah I, 1062
Cook, Dinah IV, 26
Cook, Dinah V, 28
Cook, Dinah V, 42
Cook, Dinah V, 43
Cook, Dinah V, 124
Cook, Dinah V, 160
Cook, Dinah V, 162
Cook, Dinah V, 163
Cook, Dinah V, 191
Cook, Dinah V, 209
Cook, Dinah V, 666
Cook, Dinah T. V, 163
Cook, Dinah T. V, 164
Cook, Donald Cecil IV, 570
Cook, Dorothy S. III, 84
Cook, Drusilla IV, 692
Cook, Drusilla IV, 791
Cook, Ebenezer III, 83
Cook, Ebenezer III, 84
Cook, Edith IV, 692
Cook, Edith Ann IV, 692
Cook, Edward I, 43
Cook, Edward B. IV, 468
Cook, Edwin IV, 692
Cook, Eleanor IV, 468
Cook, Eleanor IV, 615
Cook, Eleanor IV, 648
Cook, Eleanor V, 833
Cook, Eleanor V, 836
Cook, Elenor IV, 615
Cook, Elenor V, 42
Cook, Elenor V, 96
Cook, Eli I, 495
Cook, Eli I, 534
Cook, Eli I, 1015
Cook, Eli I, 1018
Cook, Eli I, 1027
Cook, Eli I, 1031
Cook, Eli I, 1056
Cook, Eli I, 1060
Cook, Eli V, 42
Cook, Eli V, 162
Cook, Eli V, 833
Cook, Eli V, 834
Cook, Eli V, 836
Cook, Eli, Jr. V, 833
Cook, Elias IV, 468
Cook, Elihu V, 834
Cook, Elijah V, 42

Cook, Elijah VI, 58
Cook, Elinor II, 349
Cook, Elis IV, 468
Cook, Elisabeth V, 483
Cook, Elisha II, 493
Cook, Elisha IV, 117
Cook, Elisha IV, 189
Cook, Elisha IV, 190
Cook, Elisha IV, 468
Cook, Elisha IV, 941
Cook, Elisha V, 42
Cook, Elisha, Jr. IV, 468
Cook, Eliza V, 454
Cook, Eliza V, 881
Cook, Eliza V, 888
Cook, Eliza A., Sr. I, 876
Cook, Eliza Ann II, 789
Cook, Eliza Anne I, 876
Cook, Eliza J. V, 300
Cook, Eliza Jane IV, 1129
Cook, Eliza Jane IV, 1137
Cook, Eliza M. IV, 1024
Cook, Eliza M. V, 950
Cook, Eliza W. V, 949
Cook, Eliza W. V, 950
Cook, Elizabeth I, 302
Cook, Elizabeth I, 308
Cook, Elizabeth I, 314
Cook, Elizabeth I, 524
Cook, Elizabeth I, 528
Cook, Elizabeth I, 534
Cook, Elizabeth I, 779
Cook, Elizabeth I, 806
Cook, Elizabeth I, 1018
Cook, Elizabeth I, 1027
Cook, Elizabeth I, 1038
Cook, Elizabeth I, 1053
Cook, Elizabeth I, 1056
Cook, Elizabeth I, 1060
Cook, Elizabeth II, 349
Cook, Elizabeth II, 442
Cook, Elizabeth II, 709
Cook, Elizabeth II, 722
Cook, Elizabeth II, 734
Cook, Elizabeth II, 749
Cook, Elizabeth II, 789
Cook, Elizabeth II, 852
Cook, Elizabeth III, 84
Cook, Elizabeth III, 197
Cook, Elizabeth IV, 26
Cook, Elizabeth IV, 123
Cook, Elizabeth IV, 127
Cook, Elizabeth IV, 190
Cook, Elizabeth IV, 193
Cook, Elizabeth IV, 468
Cook, Elizabeth IV, 519
Cook, Elizabeth IV, 530
Cook, Elizabeth IV, 648
Cook, Elizabeth IV, 692
Cook, Elizabeth V, 17
Cook, Elizabeth V, 41
Cook, Elizabeth V, 42
Cook, Elizabeth V, 43
Cook, Elizabeth V, 52
Cook, Elizabeth V, 72
Cook, Elizabeth V, 162
Cook, Elizabeth V, 163
Cook, Elizabeth V, 191
Cook, Elizabeth V, 214
Cook, Elizabeth V, 230
Cook, Elizabeth V, 264
Cook, Elizabeth V, 483
Cook, Elizabeth V, 833
Cook, Elizabeth V, 834
Cook, Elizabeth V, 836
Cook, Elizabeth V, 848
Cook, Elizabeth V, 900
Cook, Elizabeth V, 921
Cook, Elizabeth V, 950
Cook, Elizabeth VI, 53
Cook, Elizabeth VI, 58
Cook, Elizabeth VI, 133
Cook, Elizabeth VI, 915
Cook, Elizabeth VI, 923
Cook, Elizabeth Brazleton I, 534
Cook, Elizabeth D. VI, 736
Cook, Elizabeth F. III, 84
Cook, Elizabeth F. III, 194
Cook, Elizabeth H. IV, 519
Cook, Elizabeth L. IV, 189
Cook, Elizabeth L. IV, 468
Cook, Elizabeth L. IV, 470
Cook, Elizabeth P. V, 900
Cook, Ella V, 43
Cook, Ella V, 230
Cook, Ella V, 231
Cook, Ella V, 454
Cook, Ella V, 834
Cook, Ella Lillian IV, 692
Cook, Ella Lillian IV, 807
Cook, Ellen IV, 1154
Cook, Ellen V, 26
Cook, Ellen V, 42
Cook, Ellen V, 122
Cook, Ellis IV, 26
Cook, Ellis IV, 142
Cook, Ellis IV, 648
Cook, Ellis V, 231
Cook, Ellis V, 325
Cook, Ellis T. IV, 1311
Cook, Elma V, 325
Cook, Elma V, 328
Cook, Elma C. V, 164
Cook, Elma C. V, 166
Cook, Elma C. V, 325
Cook, Elma D. V, 43
Cook, Elmer V, 230
Cook, Elmer V, 231
Cook, Elmer V, 300
Cook, Elmer V, 454
Cook, Elmore IV, 1234
Cook, Emily IV, 865
Cook, Emily IV, 870
Cook, Emily H. IV, 865
Cook, Emma V, 231
Cook, Emma V, 325
Cook, Emma V, 900
Cook, Emma B. V, 950
Cook, Emma J. V, 950
Cook, Enos IV, 692
Cook, Enos IV, 740
Cook, Enos IV, 1024
Cook, Ephraim IV, 557
Cook, Ernest E. V, 43
Cook, Esther I, 1058
Cook, Esther IV, 941
Cook, Esther V, 617
Cook, Esther Jane V, 42
Cook, Eunice V, 163
Cook, Eunice V, 171
Cook, Fern Bishop IV, 1311
Cook, Flora V, 325
Cook, Florence J. IV, 570
Cook, Florence P. IV, 468
Cook, Francis II, 442
Cook, Francis II, 487
Cook, Francis II, 493
Cook, Francis II, 969
Cook, Fransena IV, 692
Cook, Fransina IV, 1024
Cook, Fransina IV, 1028
Cook, Geo. W. V, 990
Cook, George II, 852
Cook, George IV, 190
Cook, George IV, 468
Cook, George V, 162
Cook, George VI, 856
Cook, George W. VI, 896
Cook, Gertrude IV, 1311
Cook, Grace III, 84
Cook, Gulielma M. II, 709
Cook, Gulielma M. II, 734
Cook, Gulielma M. S. P. II, 749
Cook, Gulielma Maria II, 734
Cook, H. IV, 556
Cook, Hallie Olive IV, 570
Cook, Hanah V, 163
Cook, Hannah I, 495
Cook, Hannah I, 534
Cook, Hannah I, 538
Cook, Hannah I, 779
Cook, Hannah I, 806
Cook, Hannah I, 961
Cook, Hannah I, 964
Cook, Hannah I, 966
Cook, Hannah II, 349
Cook, Hannah III, 244
Cook, Hannah III, 405
Cook, Hannah IV, 26
Cook, Hannah IV, 142
Cook, Hannah IV, 151
Cook, Hannah IV, 380
Cook, Hannah IV, 556
Cook, Hannah IV, 692
Cook, Hannah IV, 710
Cook, Hannah IV, 1029
Cook, Hannah IV, 1234
Cook, Hannah V, 159
Cook, Hannah V, 162
Cook, Hannah V, 163
Cook, Hannah V, 171
Cook, Hannah V, 191
Cook, Hannah V, 192
Cook, Hannah V, 209
Cook, Hannah V, 325
Cook, Hannah V, 666
Cook, Hannah V, 788
Cook, Hannah V, 833
Cook, Hannah V, 834
Cook, Hannah V, 968
Cook, Hannah V, 971
Cook, Hannah B. V, 42
Cook, Hannah B. V, 43
Cook, Hannah B. V, 47
Cook, Hannah F. IV, 325
Cook, Hannah Francena IV, 519
Cook, Hannah Francena IV, 557
Cook, Hannah J. V, 43
Cook, Hannah J. V, 163
Cook, Hannah J. V, 164
Cook, Hannah Josephine V, 163
Cook, Hannah Josephine V, 164
Cook, Hannah Josephine V, 188
Cook, Hannah K. IV, 347
Cook, Hannah Kemp IV, 1029
Cook, Hannah M. IV, 941
Cook, Hannah Maria V, 666
Cook, Hannah Mariah V, 164
Cook, Harbert I, 1018
Cook, Harmon VI, 896
Cook, Harriet B. V, 141
Cook, Harriett E. V, 43
Cook, Harry II, 969
Cook, Harry P. III, 84
Cook, Hattie IV, 1234
Cook, Helen I, 262
Cook, Helen Elizabeth III, 84
Cook, Henrietta II, 349
Cook, Henry I, 961
Cook, Henry IV, 1234
Cook, Henry V, 833
Cook, Henry V, 834
Cook, Henry F. V, 192
Cook, Hiram V, 42
Cook, Howard B. IV, 1024
Cook, Isaac I, 302
Cook, Isaac I, 495
Cook, Isaac I, 534
Cook, Isaac I, 779
Cook, Isaac I, 806
Cook, Isaac I, 1015
Cook, Isaac I, 1018
Cook, Isaac I, 1027
Cook, Isaac I, 1028
Cook, Isaac I, 1056
Cook, Isaac I, 1057
Cook, Isaac I, 1058
Cook, Isaac I, 1059
Cook, Isaac I, 1060
Cook, Isaac I, 1062
Cook, Isaac III, 84
Cook, Isaac IV, 26
Cook, Isaac IV, 615
Cook, Isaac V, 42
Cook, Isaac V, 146
Cook, Isaac V, 162
Cook, Isaac V, 170
Cook, Isaac V, 178
Cook, Isaac V, 185
Cook, Isaac V, 198
Cook, Isaac V, 230
Cook, Isaac V, 469
Cook, Isaac V, 833
Cook, Isaac V, 834
Cook, Isaac H. IV, 615
Cook, Isaac H. IV, 691
Cook, Isaac H. IV, 692
Cook, Isaac Newton V, 834
Cook, Isaac W. I, 302
Cook, Isaac W. V, 950
Cook, Isaac Warner V, 950
Cook, Isaac, Jr. I, 1028
Cook, Isaac, Jr. V, 163
Cook, Isaac, Sr. I, 1056
Cook, Isabella VI, 802
Cook, Isidore E. IV, 941
Cook, Jacob I, 495
Cook, Jacob I, 779
Cook, Jacob I, 806
Cook, Jacob I, 1018
Cook, Jacob II, 349
Cook, Jacob V, 42
Cook, Jacob V, 163
Cook, Jacob V, 900
Cook, James I, 876
Cook, James I, 1056
Cook, James II, 493
Cook, James IV, 468
Cook, James IV, 692
Cook, James V, 42
Cook, James V, 96
Cook, James V, 162
Cook, James V, 833
Cook, James V, 836
Cook, James V, 990
Cook, James VI, 58
Cook, James VI, 69
Cook, James D. IV, 190
Cook, James D. IV, 468
Cook, James E. I, 876
Cook, James H. IV, 692
Cook, James T. I, 1149
Cook, James Welcher I, 876
Cook, James, Jr. V, 834
Cook, Jane II, 209
Cook, Jane II, 214
Cook, Jane II, 349
Cook, Jane IV, 557
Cook, Jane V, 900
Cook, Jas. M. V, 900
Cook, Jason V, 42
Cook, Jay Russel V, 834
Cook, Jean I, 1060
Cook, Jehu I, 779
Cook, Jemima I, 806
Cook, Jemimah I, 534
Cook, Jennette IV, 1154
Cook, Jeremiah IV, 26
Cook, Jeremiah IV, 142
Cook, Jeremiah IV, 380
Cook, Jeremiah IV, 403
Cook, Jesse I, 302
Cook, Jesse I, 961
Cook, Jesse I, 966
Cook, Jesse V, 833
Cook, Jesse V, 900
Cook, Jesse V, 950
Cook, Jesse W. I, 779
Cook, Jesse W. V, 42
Cook, Jesse W. V, 900
Cook, Jesse W. V, 950
Cook, Job W. III, 84
Cook, Joel III, 83
Cook, Joel V, 833
Cook, Joel VI, 58
Cook, Joel VI, 105
Cook, Joel VI, 235
Cook, Joel VI, 246
Cook, Joel VI, 248
Cook, Joel VI, 279
Cook, John I, 495
Cook, John I, 534
Cook, John I, 779
Cook, John I, 806
Cook, John I, 961
Cook, John I, 1018
Cook, John I, 1028
Cook, John I, 1057
Cook, John I, 1060
Cook, John I, 1063
Cook, John II, 349
Cook, John II, 493
Cook, John II, 734
Cook, John II, 789
Cook, John II, 852
Cook, John II, 991
Cook, John II, 1026
Cook, John IV, 26
Cook, John IV, 81
Cook, John V, 42
Cook, John V, 124
Cook, John V, 146
Cook, John V, 162
Cook, John V, 163
Cook, John V, 170
Cook, John V, 181
Cook, John V, 191
Cook, John V, 209
Cook, John V, 380
Cook, John V, 483
Cook, John V, 556
Cook, John V, 666
Cook, John V, 788
Cook, John V, 794
Cook, John V, 833
Cook, John V, 840
Cook, John V, 843
Cook, John VI, 58
Cook, John VI, 105
Cook, John VI, 379
Cook, John VI, 896
Cook, John A. III, 84
Cook, John C. V, 160
Cook, John C. V, 163
Cook, John C. V, 164
Cook, John Cook V, 42
Cook, John Edgar V, 164
Cook, John Edgar V, 666
Cook, John G. III, 84
Cook, John Gamble III, 84
Cook, John K. V, 380
Cook, John W. III, 84
Cook, John, Jr. V, 163
Cook, John, Jr. V, 171
Cook, Jonathan I, 495
Cook, Jonathan I, 534
Cook, Jonathan I, 1018
Cook, Jonathan V, 163
Cook, Jonathan V, 833
Cook, Jonathan V, 834
Cook, Jonathan M. V, 163
Cook, Joseph I, 779
Cook, Joseph I, 806
Cook, Joseph I, 844
Cook, Joseph I, 1018
Cook, Joseph I, 1028
Cook, Joseph II, 442
Cook, Joseph V, 42
Cook, Joseph V, 147
Cook, Joseph V, 162
Cook, Joseph V, 230
Cook, Joseph V, 264
Cook, Joseph V, 483
Cook, Joseph V, 833
Cook, Joseph V, 900
Cook, Joseph Alexander III, 84
Cook, Joseph Alexander III, 111
Cook, Joseph H. III, 84
Cook, Joseph K. V, 900
Cook, Joseph R. V, 42
Cook, Joseph, Jr. V, 163
Cook, Joseph, Sr. V, 163
Cook, Joshua V, 163
Cook, Josiah VI, 58
Cook, Josiah VI, 104
Cook, Josiah VI, 105
Cook, Josiah VI, 133
Cook, Josiah VI, 235
Cook, Josiah D. V, 163
Cook, Josiah D. V, 380
Cook, Judith I, 806
Cook, Judith I, 813
Cook, Judith V, 42
Cook, Julia Ann VI, 927
Cook, Julius N. I, 876
Cook, Kate IV, 1234
Cook, Katharine Elizabeth III, 83
Cook, Kezia I, 1028
Cook, Kezia I, 1031
Cook, Keziah V, 42
Cook, Laura J. III, 84
Cook, Laura J. III, 197
Cook, Laura J. III, 206
Cook, Laura J. III, 344
Cook, Laura J. VI, 736
Cook, Laura J. VI, 790
Cook, Lavina V, 990
Cook, Lazarus Johnson VI, 58
Cook, Leander IV, 1024
Cook, Lemuel II, 349
Cook, Lettie I, 932
Cook, Levi I, 961
Cook, Levi I, 964
Cook, Levi I, 1018
Cook, Levi I, 1056
Cook, Levi I, 1060
Cook, Levi I, 1061
Cook, Levi IV, 26
Cook, Levi V, 26
Cook, Levi V, 42
Cook, Levi V, 69
Cook, Levi V, 122
Cook, Levi V, 146
Cook, Levi V, 162
Cook, Levi V, 833
Cook, Levina V, 990
Cook, Lewis V, 833
Cook, Lewis P. III, 84
Cook, Lewis P. III, 197
Cook, Lewis P. VI, 736
Cook, Lewis P. VI, 790
Cook, Lillie M. V, 43
Cook, Lizzie S. V, 163
Cook, Louella D. V, 163
Cook, Louella D. V, 666
Cook, Louise V, 834
Cook, Louise C. III, 84
Cook, Lovetta V, 666
Cook, Lovice IV, 380
Cook, Lovice IV, 403
Cook, Lovisa IV, 380
Cook, Lovise IV, 380
Cook, Luella D. V, 164
Cook, Lyda I, 806
Cook, Lydea I, 1060
Cook, Lydia I, 534
Cook, Lydia I, 552
Cook, Lydia I, 779
Cook, Lydia I, 806
Cook, Lydia I, 844
Cook, Lydia I, 961
Cook, Lydia II, 349
Cook, Lydia II, 493
Cook, Lydia II, 734
Cook, Lydia II, 852
Cook, Lydia IV, 117
Cook, Lydia IV, 123
Cook, Lydia IV, 190
Cook, Lydia IV, 468
Cook, Lydia IV, 692
Cook, Lydia IV, 792
Cook, Lydia V, 42
Cook, Lydia V, 117
Cook, Lydia V, 163
Cook, Lydia V, 177

Cook, Lydia V, 780
Cook, Lydia VI, 104
Cook, Lydia VI, 105
Cook, Lydia VI, 109
Cook, Lydia VI, 235
Cook, Lydia Ann V, 163
Cook, Lydia Ann V, 181
Cook, Lydia B. II, 734
Cook, Lydia B. II, 852
Cook, Lydia Barton II, 789
Cook, Lydia R. IV, 380
Cook, Lydia R. IV, 421
Cook, Lysandra I, 557
Cook, Lysandra Lindley I, 534
Cook, M. A. VI, 896
Cook, Mabel J. IV, 1311
Cook, Mabel J. T. IV, 1311
Cook, Mahala I, 779
Cook, Mahala I, 798
Cook, Mahala I, 806
Cook, Mahlon V, 42
Cook, Major William VI, 890
Cook, Malinda J. V, 617
Cook, Mannah Maria V, 163
Cook, Marcellious V, 141
Cook, Marcellius V, 900
Cook, Marcellius S. V, 42
Cook, Marcellius S. V, 900
Cook, Marcellius S. V, 949
Cook, Marcellius S. V, 950
Cook, Marcellous V, 42
Cook, Margaret I, 534
Cook, Margaret I, 554
Cook, Margaret VI, 305
Cook, Margaret Anna V, 43
Cook, Margaret B. IV, 190
Cook, Margaret I. III, 84
Cook, Margrett II, 442
Cook, Maria V, 163
Cook, Marion F. III, 84
Cook, Marion Fenimore III, 84
Cook, Marion Fennimore III, 111
Cook, Marion Louise III, 84
Cook, Martha I, 1018
Cook, Martha I, 1027
Cook, Martha I, 1031
Cook, Martha I, 1053
Cook, Martha I, 1056
Cook, Martha I, 1060
Cook, Martha III, 322
Cook, Martha III, 405
Cook, Martha IV, 691
Cook, Martha IV, 692
Cook, Martha IV, 773
Cook, Martha V, 42
Cook, Martha V, 162
Cook, Martha V, 163
Cook, Martha V, 164
Cook, Martha V, 181
Cook, Martha V, 833
Cook, Martha V, 851
Cook, Martha VI, 817
Cook, Martha C. IV, 175
Cook, Martha C. IV, 190
Cook, Martha G. III, 83
Cook, Martha J. IV, 807
Cook, Martha J. V, 164
Cook, Martha Jr. IV, 692
Cook, Martha P. III, 84
Cook, Martha P. III, 322
Cook, Martha, Jr. IV, 692
Cook, Martha, Jr. V, 833
Cook, Mary I, 377
Cook, Mary I, 380
Cook, Mary I, 494
Cook, Mary I, 534
Cook, Mary I, 562
Cook, Mary I, 575
Cook, Mary I, 580
Cook, Mary I, 773
Cook, Mary I, 779
Cook, Mary I, 806
Cook, Mary I, 833
Cook, Mary I, 875
Cook, Mary I, 961
Cook, Mary I, 1018
Cook, Mary I, 1026
Cook, Mary I, 1027
Cook, Mary I, 1028
Cook, Mary I, 1038
Cook, Mary I, 1053
Cook, Mary I, 1056
Cook, Mary I, 1057
Cook, Mary I, 1058
Cook, Mary I, 1060
Cook, Mary I, 1061
Cook, Mary I, 1062
Cook, Mary II, 285
Cook, Mary II, 296
Cook, Mary II, 317
Cook, Mary II, 322
Cook, Mary II, 349
Cook, Mary II, 493
Cook, Mary II, 991
Cook, Mary II, 1026
Cook, Mary III, 294
Cook, Mary IV, 26
Cook, Mary IV, 81
Cook, Mary IV, 98
Cook, Mary IV, 142
Cook, Mary IV, 380
Cook, Mary IV, 468
Cook, Mary V, 40
Cook, Mary V, 42
Cook, Mary V, 43
Cook, Mary V, 70
Cook, Mary V, 130
Cook, Mary V, 136
Cook, Mary V, 162
Cook, Mary V, 163
Cook, Mary V, 164
Cook, Mary V, 170
Cook, Mary V, 209
Cook, Mary V, 214
Cook, Mary V, 380
Cook, Mary V, 483
Cook, Mary V, 502
Cook, Mary V, 541
Cook, Mary V, 833
Cook, Mary V, 834
Cook, Mary V, 843
Cook, Mary VI, 53
Cook, Mary VI, 58
Cook, Mary VI, 69
Cook, Mary VI, 91
Cook, Mary VI, 105
Cook, Mary VI, 235
Cook, Mary VI, 896
Cook, Mary Ann IV, 26
Cook, Mary Ann IV, 57
Cook, Mary Ann IV, 189
Cook, Mary Ann IV, 190
Cook, Mary Ann IV, 468
Cook, Mary Ann IV, 519
Cook, Mary Ann IV, 530
Cook, Mary Ann IV, 692
Cook, Mary Ann V, 834
Cook, Mary Annie V, 163
Cook, Mary Binford VI, 133
Cook, Mary C. VI, 922
Cook, Mary Catharine I, 876
Cook, Mary Eliza I, 876
Cook, Mary Elizabeth II, 493
Cook, Mary Elizabeth V, 163
Cook, Mary Eva IV, 468
Cook, Mary Gilpin III, 83
Cook, Mary H. IV, 692
Cook, Mary J. VI, 58
Cook, Mary J. VI, 235
Cook, Mary Jane I, 621
Cook, Mary Jane IV, 190
Cook, Mary Jane IV, 263
Cook, Mary Jane IV, 468
Cook, Mary Jane IV, 692
Cook, Mary Jane VI, 235
Cook, Mary Jane VI, 279
Cook, Mary L. IV, 188
Cook, Mary L. IV, 190
Cook, Mary L. V, 43
Cook, Mary L. V, 164
Cook, Mary Louisa IV, 190
Cook, Mary M. I, 876
Cook, Mary S. V, 163
Cook, Mary S. V, 198
Cook, Mary W. V, 43
Cook, Mary W. V, 950
Cook, Mary Wilkinson I, 1056
Cook, Matilda II, 789
Cook, Mattie V, 325
Cook, Mattie J. IV, 807
Cook, Maurice V, 43
Cook, Maynard V, 666
Cook, Melvina H. III, 125
Cook, Milton I, 852
Cook, Miriam I, 300
Cook, Miriam I, 302
Cook, Moses I, 495
Cook, Myrtle IV, 570
Cook, Nancy IV, 123
Cook, Nancy IV, 128
Cook, Nancy V, 780
Cook, Nancy VI, 856
Cook, Narcissa V, 380
Cook, Nathan I, 302
Cook, Nathan I, 495
Cook, Nathan I, 534
Cook, Nathan I, 538
Cook, Nathan I, 779
Cook, Nathan I, 806
Cook, Nathan I, 961
Cook, Nathan I, 1056
Cook, Nathan IV, 75
Cook, Nathan IV, 117
Cook, Nathan IV, 190
Cook, Nathan IV, 927
Cook, Nathan IV, 941
Cook, Nathan V, 42
Cook, Nathan V, 162
Cook, Nathan V, 832
Cook, Nathan V, 833
Cook, Nathan V, 834
Cook, Nathan V, 836
Cook, Nathan V, 851
Cook, Nathan, Jr. I, 806
Cook, Nathaniel V, 42
Cook, Nellie V, 325
Cook, Nellie V, 345
Cook, Noah V, 42
Cook, Noah V, 900
Cook, Noah V, 990
Cook, Obadiah V, 833
Cook, Obediah V, 834
Cook, Olive I, 1018
Cook, Olive I, 1060
Cook, Olive I, 1061
Cook, Olive I, 1063
Cook, Olive V, 42
Cook, Olive V, 162
Cook, Olive V, 163
Cook, Olive V, 178
Cook, Olive V, 833
Cook, Olive V, 834
Cook, Olive V, 840
Cook, Olive V, 843
Cook, Oliver M. IV, 468
Cook, Orville V, 192
Cook, Oxley II, 349
Cook, Patience I, 961
Cook, Patience I, 966
Cook, Patience II, 973
Cook, Peggy VI, 896
Cook, Perry P. IV, 1309
Cook, Perry P. IV, 1311
Cook, Peter I, 1018
Cook, Peter V, 42
Cook, Peter V, 162
Cook, Peter V, 483
Cook, Phebe I, 494
Cook, Phebe I, 495
Cook, Phebe I, 534
Cook, Phebe I, 562
Cook, Phebe I, 779
Cook, Phebe I, 1056
Cook, Phebe V, 42
Cook, Phebe V, 162
Cook, Phebe V, 163
Cook, Phebe V, 170
Cook, Phebe V, 483
Cook, Phebe V, 833
Cook, Phebe Ann V, 192
Cook, Phineas V, 43
Cook, Phineas W. V, 42
Cook, Plesent I, 534
Cook, Priscilla I, 625
Cook, Priscilla II, 442
Cook, Priscilla VI, 58
Cook, Priscilla VI, 104
Cook, Rachel I, 494
Cook, Rachel I, 495
Cook, Rachel I, 534
Cook, Rachel I, 553
Cook, Rachel I, 779
Cook, Rachel I, 803
Cook, Rachel I, 806
Cook, Rachel I, 1018
Cook, Rachel I, 1028
Cook, Rachel I, 1034
Cook, Rachel I, 1060
Cook, Rachel I, 1062
Cook, Rachel II, 493
Cook, Rachel II, 734
Cook, Rachel IV, 26
Cook, Rachel IV, 123
Cook, Rachel IV, 130
Cook, Rachel IV, 142
Cook, Rachel IV, 380
Cook, Rachel V, 833
Cook, Rachel W. II, 711
Cook, Rachel, Jr. I, 534
Cook, Rebeca I, 1028
Cook, Rebecca I, 1036
Cook, Rebecca I, 1058
Cook, Rebecca IV, 26
Cook, Rebecca IV, 81
Cook, Rebecca V, 42
Cook, Rebecca V, 162
Cook, Rebecca V, 170
Cook, Rebecca V, 380
Cook, Rebeckah I, 1018
Cook, Rebekah I, 1056
Cook, Rebekah I, 1060
Cook, Rebekah I, 1062
Cook, Rebekah V, 42
Cook, Rebekah VI, 379
Cook, Richard II, 493
Cook, Richard II, 709
Cook, Richard II, 734
Cook, Richard II, 749
Cook, Richard II, 789
Cook, Richard V, 230
Cook, Robert I, 1056
Cook, Robert V, 162
Cook, Robert V, 483
Cook, Robert V, 502
Cook, Roxollie D. V, 231
Cook, Rufus I, 876
Cook, Ruth I, 495
Cook, Ruth I, 534
Cook, Ruth I, 556
Cook, Ruth I, 1018
Cook, Ruth I, 1028
Cook, Ruth I, 1030
Cook, Ruth I, 1056
Cook, Ruth I, 1057
Cook, Ruth IV, 26
Cook, Ruth IV, 122
Cook, Ruth IV, 123
Cook, Ruth V, 42
Cook, Ruth V, 117
Cook, Ruth V, 122
Cook, Ruth V, 140
Cook, Ruth V, 162
Cook, Ruth V, 163
Cook, Ruth V, 175
Cook, Ruth Emma V, 43
Cook, Ruth Hannah V, 42
Cook, Saaah V, 42
Cook, Sallie I, 876
Cook, Sally I, 534
Cook, Sally I, 551
Cook, Sally V, 162
Cook, Sally VI, 807
Cook, Sally VI, 896
Cook, Samuel II, 349
Cook, Samuel III, 405
Cook, Samuel V, 159
Cook, Samuel V, 162
Cook, Samuel V, 163
Cook, Samuel V, 191
Cook, Samuel V, 192
Cook, Samuel V, 325
Cook, Samuel VI, 896
Cook, Samuel B. V, 42
Cook, Samuel B. V, 43
Cook, Samuel M. V, 900
Cook, Samuel S. VI, 896
Cook, Samuel W. V, 163
Cook, Samuel W. V, 164
Cook, Samuel W. V, 181
Cook, Sandia I, 621
Cook, Sandy I, 876
Cook, Sanford I, 876
Cook, Sarah I, 136
Cook, Sarah I, 174
Cook, Sarah I, 302
Cook, Sarah I, 307
Cook, Sarah I, 312
Cook, Sarah I, 495
Cook, Sarah I, 528
Cook, Sarah I, 534
Cook, Sarah I, 779
Cook, Sarah I, 806
Cook, Sarah I, 839
Cook, Sarah I, 1018
Cook, Sarah I, 1028
Cook, Sarah I, 1030
Cook, Sarah I, 1056
Cook, Sarah I, 1058
Cook, Sarah I, 1060
Cook, Sarah I, 1061
Cook, Sarah I, 1062
Cook, Sarah I, 1117
Cook, Sarah I, 1128
Cook, Sarah I, 1149
Cook, Sarah III, 83
Cook, Sarah IV, 26
Cook, Sarah IV, 81
Cook, Sarah IV, 110
Cook, Sarah IV, 142
Cook, Sarah IV, 380
Cook, Sarah IV, 455
Cook, Sarah IV, 692
Cook, Sarah V, 42
Cook, Sarah V, 43
Cook, Sarah V, 118
Cook, Sarah V, 162
Cook, Sarah V, 163
Cook, Sarah V, 170
Cook, Sarah V, 177
Cook, Sarah V, 178
Cook, Sarah V, 556
Cook, Sarah V, 803
Cook, Sarah V, 833
Cook, Sarah V, 834
Cook, Sarah V, 836
Cook, Sarah V, 900
Cook, Sarah VI, 58
Cook, Sarah VI, 70
Cook, Sarah VI, 896
Cook, Sarah A. V, 962
Cook, Sarah A. Cook V, 950
Cook, Sarah Ann V, 950
Cook, Sarah B. L. III, 84
Cook, Sarah C. IV, 692
Cook, Sarah C. IV, 705
Cook, Sarah E. VI, 890
Cook, Sarah I. IV, 692
Cook, Sarah I. IV, 710
Cook, Sarah Pennel IV, 26
Cook, Sarah T. III, 84
Cook, Sarah T. V, 164
Cook, Sarah T. V, 181
Cook, Seth I, 1056
Cook, Seth V, 42
Cook, Seth V, 43
Cook, Seth V, 162
Cook, Seth V, 163
Cook, Seth C. V, 164
Cook, Sidney IV, 940
Cook, Sidney IV, 941
Cook, Stacey IV, 773
Cook, Stacy IV, 691
Cook, Stacy IV, 692
Cook, Stacy, Jr. IV, 692
Cook, Stephen I, 961
Cook, Stephen I, 966
Cook, Stephen I, 1056
Cook, Stephen IV, 26
Cook, Stephen IV, 380
Cook, Stephen V, 41
Cook, Stephen V, 42
Cook, Stephen V, 43
Cook, Stephen V, 52
Cook, Stephen V, 72
Cook, Stephen V, 136
Cook, Stephen V, 162
Cook, Susan B. P. III, 33
Cook, Susan B. P. III, 349
Cook, Susan G. V, 950
Cook, Susanna IV, 81
Cook, Susanna IV, 108
Cook, Susanna V, 42
Cook, Susanna V, 834
Cook, Susannah I, 1018
Cook, Susannah I, 1028
Cook, Susannah I, 1034
Cook, Susannah V, 42
Cook, Susannah V, 72
Cook, Susannah V, 483
Cook, Susannah V, 523
Cook, Susannah V, 833
Cook, Susannah VI, 379
Cook, Susannah VI, 380
Cook, Sylvanua H. I, 876
Cook, T. IV, 556
Cook, Tamar V, 163
Cook, Tamar V, 380
Cook, Tamer V, 163
Cook, Theadore V, 900
Cook, Theodor V, 42
Cook, Theodore M. V, 900
Cook, Thomas I, 302
Cook, Thomas I, 380
Cook, Thomas I, 534
Cook, Thomas I, 621
Cook, Thomas I, 773
Cook, Thomas I, 779
Cook, Thomas I, 806
Cook, Thomas I, 875
Cook, Thomas I, 1018
Cook, Thomas I, 1028
Cook, Thomas I, 1031
Cook, Thomas I, 1066
Cook, Thomas I, 1070
Cook, Thomas II, 442
Cook, Thomas III, 84
Cook, Thomas IV, 17
Cook, Thomas IV, 26
Cook, Thomas IV, 123
Cook, Thomas IV, 519
Cook, Thomas V, 42
Cook, Thomas V, 162
Cook, Thomas V, 325
Cook, Thomas VI, 379
Cook, Thomas VI, 380
Cook, Thomas VI, 896
Cook, Thomas W. V, 42
Cook, Thomas Wistar II, 493
Cook, Thomas, Jr. I, 806
Cook, Thomas, Jr. IV, 123
Cook, Thomas, Jr. V, 163
Cook, Thos. I, 562
Cook, Thos. V, 214
Cook, Thos. W. V, 900
Cook, Thos., Sr. I, 779

Cook, Uriah I, 1018
Cook, Uriah IV, 123
Cook, Uriah V, 42
Cook, Uriah V, 162
Cook, Uriah V, 483
Cook, Wd. Elizabeth D. VI, 736
Cook, Wd. Elizabeth Newton II, 789
Cook, Wd. Jane III, 84
Cook, Wd. Margarett II, 349
Cook, Welcher I, 876
Cook, Widow Mary I, 534
Cook, Widow Mary I, 806
Cook, Wilcher I, 876
Cook, William I, 534
Cook, William I, 779
Cook, William I, 806
Cook, William I, 852
Cook, William I, 875
Cook, William I, 1018
Cook, William I, 1060
Cook, William I, 1061
Cook, William IV, 692
Cook, William V, 42
Cook, William V, 163
Cook, William V, 833
Cook, William V, 834
Cook, William VI, 28
Cook, William VI, 105
Cook, William VI, 896
Cook, William H. IV, 692
Cook, William H. VI, 896
Cook, William Hasket V, 42
Cook, William M. IV, 190
Cook, William M. IV, 468
Cook, William Mode IV, 468
Cook, William P. V, 43
Cook, William W. I, 534
Cook, Willis I, 302
Cook, Willis P. V, 834
Cook, Winifred Harvey V, 556
Cook, Wm. II, 789
Cook, Wm. IV, 570
Cook, Wm. IV, 692
Cook, Wm. V, 164
Cook, Wm. V, 300
Cook, Wm. V, 454
Cook, Wm. H. V, 617
Cook, Wm. Henry IV, 692
Cook, Wm. T. V, 900
Cook, Wm. Wilbur James III, 84
Cook, Wright I, 1018
Cook, Wright I, 1028
Cook, Wright I, 1036
Cook, Wright V, 42
Cook, Wright V, 162
Cook, Wright V, 230
Cook, Wright V, 246
Cook, Wright V, 380
Cook, Wright V, 483
Cook, Zachariah V, 162
Cook, Zebulon S. I, 1149
Cook, Zilpha I, 302
Cook, Zilpha I, 312
Cook, Zimri I, 806
Cook, Zimri V, 42
Cook, Zimri V, 780
Cook, Zimry I, 779
Cook, Zuni VI, 58
Cooke, Archibald IV, 845
Cooke, Archibald G. IV, 771
Cooke, Arthur II, 643
Cooke, Arthur II, 691
Cooke, Barton II, 734
Cooke, Bessie IV, 771
Cooke, Bessie IV, 845
Cooke, Caleb II, 493
Cooke, Catherine II, 349
Cooke, Charles II, 734
Cooke, Chas. II, 852
Cooke, Edwin IV, 692
Cooke, Edwin IV, 718
Cooke, Elisha II, 493
Cooke, Elizabeth VI, 495
Cooke, Elizabeth VI, 496
Cooke, Ella IV, 772
Cooke, Ella Lillian IV, 692
Cooke, Ella Lillian IV, 771
Cooke, Ella Lillian IV, 807
Cooke, Ella Lillian IV, 845
Cooke, Ella Lillian IV, 846
Cooke, Ellen II, 170
Cooke, Enoch II, 170
Cooke, Francis II, 493
Cooke, Isaac W. I, 283
Cooke, Jane III, 182
Cooke, John II, 170
Cooke, John II, 349
Cooke, John II, 585
Cooke, John II, 702
Cooke, John II, 734
Cooke, John II, 789
Cooke, John II, 852
Cooke, John II, 898
Cooke, Joseph II, 442
Cooke, Joshua II, 170
Cooke, Lydia II, 349
Cooke, Lydia II, 585
Cooke, Lydia II, 702
Cooke, Lydia II, 734
Cooke, Lydia II, 852
Cooke, Lydia II, 898
Cooke, Lydia B. II, 734
Cooke, Lydia B. II, 852
Cooke, Lydia B. II, 898
Cooke, Lydia Barton II, 789
Cooke, Martha IV, 691
Cooke, Martha IV, 692
Cooke, Martha IV, 728
Cooke, Mary II, 170
Cooke, Mary II, 442
Cooke, Mary IV, 718
Cooke, Mary Elizabeth II, 493
Cooke, Mary Elizabeth II, 585
Cooke, Mary H. IV, 692
Cooke, Stacy IV, 691
Cooke, Stacy IV, 692
Cooke, Stacy, Jr. IV, 692
Cooke, Stacy, Jr. IV, 728
Cooke, Temperance I, 283
Cooke, Wd. Jane III, 84
Cooke, William VI, 28
Cooke, William H. IV, 692
Cooke, Wm. Wilbur James III, 84
Cooke, Wm. Wilbur James III, 182
Cooke, Wm. Wilbur James III, 206
Cooke, Wodard I, 283
Cooker, Abigail I, 920
Cooker, Lindsay I, 920
Cooker, Martha III, 405
Cooker, Mary III, 405
Cooker, Simon III, 405
Cooker, Winnie I, 920
Cooks, Elizabeth IV, 1024
Cooks, Elizabeth IV, 1025
Cooksey, Anne VI, 990
Cooksey, Carrie V, 990
Cooksey, Clara V, 990
Cooksey, Hobart IV, 1274
Cooksey, Lamester VI, 990
Cooksey, Martha IV, 1274
Cooksey, Obediah V, 990
Cookson, G. B. IV, 1311
Cookson, Mrs. Irene IV, 1311
Cookson, Samuel VI, 483
Cookus, Lydia VI, 631
Cookus, Lydia VI, 644
Coole, Helen C. V, 666
Coole, Martha V, 740
Cooledge, ??? III, 98
Cooledge, ??? III, 184
Cooledge, Caroline III, 98
Cooledge, Caroline III, 184
Cooledge, Daniel III, 84
Cooledge, George F. III, 84
Cooledge, Phebe H. III, 84
Cooledge, Ruth III, 84
Cooledge, Ruth III, 228
Cooledge, William Penn III, 84
Cooley, Catharine III, 84
Cooley, Clementine B. IV, 1311
Cooley, Eleanor III, 84
Cooley, Eleanor III, 184
Cooley, Eleanor III, 234
Cooley, Eliz. III, 216
Cooley, Justus H. III, 84
Cooley, Justus H. III, 184
Cooley, Keziah III, 155
Cooley, Keziah III, 176
Cooley, Maggie III, 84
Cooley, Marjorie III, 405
Cooley, Marjorie III, 418
Cooley, Mary III, 153
Cooley, Mary III, 340
Cooley, Mary H. III, 84
Cooley, Mary H. III, 184
Cooley, Samuel H. III, 84
Coolidge, Carrie Louisa III, 84
Coolidge, Carrie Louisa III, 369
Coolidge, Daniel III, 84
Coolidge, George F. III, 84
Coolidge, Helen III, 15
Coolidge, Henry III, 84
Coolidge, Henry III, 369
Coolidge, Phebe III, 84
Coolidge, Phebe H. III, 84
Coolidge, Ruth III, 84
Coolidge, William Penn III, 84
Coombe, Rebeckah II, 492
Coombe, Rebeckah II, 607
Coombe, Samuel II, 492
Coombe, Samuel II, 607
Coombs, Ann IV, 142
Coombs, Benjamin IV, 142
Coombs, Charity IV, 142
Coombs, Deborah IV, 142
Coombs, George IV, 142
Coombs, Hannah II, 486
Coombs, John II, 467
Coombs, John II, 486
Coombs, John II, 492
Coombs, John IV, 142
Coombs, Mary II, 492
Coombs, Mary IV, 142
Coombs, Ruth II, 62
Coombs, Ruth II, 87
Coombs, Sarah II, 492
Coomer, Edward IV, 1154
Coomer, Elbert IV, 1154
Coomer, Emma IV, 1154
Cooms, John II, 349
Cooms, Martha II, 349
Coon, Anna Jane II, 829
Coon, Austin V, 990
Coon, Dinah V, 212
Coon, Elizabeth VI, 896
Coon, Harriet V, 990
Coon, Jacob VI, 896
Coon, Jesse V, 990
Coon, John H. V, 990
Coon, Lillie V, 990
Coon, Phebe V, 990
Coon, Wm. V, 990
Coone, John H. V, 990
Cooney, Bettie Lillie I, 614
Cooney, Betty Lillie I, 631
Cooney, Eugene F. I, 614
Cooney, James VI, 798
Cooney, James VI, 896
Cooney, Mary Ann VI, 798
Cooney, Nancy VI, 896
Coons, A. G. W. V, 381
Coons, Abigaail V, 751
Coons, Abigail I, 712
Coons, Abigail I, 731
Coons, Abraham G. W. V, 380
Coons, Abraham G. W. V, 381
Coons, Charles Martin V, 381
Coons, Davolt I, 712
Coons, Davoull I, 712
Coons, Gasper I, 712
Coons, George I, 712
Coons, Hannah I, 712
Coons, Hannah V, 751
Coons, Jasper I, 712
Coons, Jasper I, 731
Coons, John I, 712
Coons, John H. V, 381
Coons, John Henry V, 380
Coons, Joseph Davis V, 381
Coons, Maria V, 381
Coons, Maria D. V, 381
Coons, Mariah D. V, 381
Coons, Martha I, 708
Coons, Martha I, 712
Coons, Mary I, 712
Coons, Mary V, 380
Coons, Mary A. IV, 1274
Coons, Massa I, 712
Coons, Sarah V, 381
Coons, Sarah Ellen V, 380
Coons, Thomas S. V, 381
Coons, Thomas Sherman V, 381
Coonse, Abigail I, 712
Coonse, Hannah I, 712
Coope, Elizabeth IV, 26
Coope, Isaac IV, 43
Coope, Jesse IV, 26
Coope, Jesse IV, 29
Coope, John IV, 17
Coope, John IV, 26
Coope, John IV, 69
Coope, John IV, 71
Coope, Margaret IV, 26
Coope, Margaret IV, 29
Coope, Mary IV, 17
Coope, Mary IV, 26
Coope, Ruth IV, 26
Coope, Ruth IV, 69
Coope, Samuel IV, 71
Coope, Samuel IV, 81
Coope, Samuel IV, 115
Coope, Sarah IV, 43
Coope, Sarah IV, 115
Cooper, ??? III, 89
Cooper, ??? III, 206
Cooper, ??? III, 249
Cooper, Abigail I, 1117
Cooper, Abigail I, 1133
Cooper, Abigail II, 493
Cooper, Abigail II, 523
Cooper, Abigail V, 43
Cooper, Abigail V, 732
Cooper, Abigail M. II, 724
Cooper, Abijah V, 780
Cooper, Absolom I, 1117
Cooper, Absolom V, 732
Cooper, Ada Narcissa II, 789
Cooper, Adam VI, 896
Cooper, Adam VI, 929
Cooper, Adam VI, 934
Cooper, Alan Wood II, 789
Cooper, Albert IV, 380
Cooper, Albert IV, 902
Cooper, Albert IV, 1052
Cooper, Alfred V, 43
Cooper, Alfred H. II, 494
Cooper, Alfred H. II, 734
Cooper, Alfred H. II, 852
Cooper, Alfred H. II, 920
Cooper, Alfred H. II, 930
Cooper, Alice III, 85
Cooper, Alice IV, 692
Cooper, Alice IV, 693
Cooper, Alice V, 231
Cooper, Alice E. III, 84
Cooper, Alice E. III, 85
Cooper, Allen V, 780
Cooper, Alson H. I, 712
Cooper, Alvin V, 231
Cooper, Amos V, 43
Cooper, Amos V, 301
Cooper, Amos V, 308
Cooper, Amy V, 231
Cooper, Amy V, 256
Cooper, Amy V, 454
Cooper, Amy Ann V, 825
Cooper, Amy Ann V, 832
Cooper, Amy Ann V, 834
Cooper, Ann II, 25
Cooper, Ann II, 62
Cooper, Ann II, 63
Cooper, Ann II, 87
Cooper, Ann II, 117
Cooper, Ann II, 125
Cooper, Ann II, 210
Cooper, Ann II, 349
Cooper, Ann II, 493
Cooper, Ann II, 494
Cooper, Ann II, 815
Cooper, Ann II, 991
Cooper, Ann II, 1021
Cooper, Ann IV, 380
Cooper, Ann IV, 410
Cooper, Ann IV, 519
Cooper, Ann IV, 539
Cooper, Ann IV, 712
Cooper, Ann IV, 807
Cooper, Ann IV, 901
Cooper, Ann IV, 914
Cooper, Ann IV, 1025
Cooper, Ann V, 301
Cooper, Ann T. III, 84
Cooper, Anna II, 789
Cooper, Anna II, 852
Cooper, Anna II, 854
Cooper, Anna III, 309
Cooper, Anna IV, 866
Cooper, Anna VI, 896
Cooper, Anna B. IV, 615
Cooper, Anna C. II, 852
Cooper, Anna Jane III, 84
Cooper, Anna M. II, 130
Cooper, Anna M. II, 147
Cooper, Anna P. IV, 611
Cooper, Anne II, 494
Cooper, Anne C. II, 852
Cooper, Anne T. III, 85
Cooper, Annie II, 852
Cooper, Annie II, 891
Cooper, Annie IV, 1025
Cooper, Annie Roberts II, 789
Cooper, Annie Roberts II, 852
Cooper, Annie Rulon II, 789
Cooper, Ardelia IV, 1248
Cooper, Arthur VI, 956
Cooper, Asenath II, 822
Cooper, Asenath A. IV, 692
Cooper, Augusta V, 666
Cooper, Bartlow VI, 483
Cooper, Benjamin I, 712
Cooper, Benjamin I, 1028
Cooper, Benjamin I, 1043
Cooper, Benjamin I, 1047
Cooper, Benjamin I, 1117
Cooper, Benjamin II, 62
Cooper, Benjamin II, 63
Cooper, Benjamin II, 88
Cooper, Benjamin II, 493
Cooper, Benjamin II, 494
Cooper, Benjamin II, 991
Cooper, Benjamin V, 732
Cooper, Benjamin C. II, 494
Cooper, Benjamin C. II, 734
Cooper, Benjamin Clark II, 25
Cooper, Benjamin Clark II, 494
Cooper, Benjamin D. II, 63
Cooper, Benjamin Franklin IV, 914
Cooper, Benjamin, Jr. I, 1117
Cooper, Benjamin, Jr. V, 732
Cooper, Bertha A. IV, 615
Cooper, Bertha A. IV, 616
Cooper, Bertha A. IV, 692
Cooper, Betsy VI, 896
Cooper, Binjamin I, 1050
Cooper, C. D. IV, 1274
Cooper, Caleb II, 494
Cooper, Calvin II, 822
Cooper, Calvin IV, 865
Cooper, Calvin IV, 873
Cooper, Calvin IV, 901
Cooper, Calvin IV, 914
Cooper, Carl V, 556
Cooper, Carl Thadeous V, 990
Cooper, Caroline III, 176
Cooper, Carrie Laota IV, 1248
Cooper, Catharine II, 62
Cooper, Catharine II, 98
Cooper, Cedora V, 231
Cooper, Chalkley IV, 902
Cooper, Charity I, 1028
Cooper, Charles I, 43
Cooper, Charles V, 454
Cooper, Charles VI, 984
Cooper, Charles E. IV, 692
Cooper, Charles H. IV, 693
Cooper, Charles Haines II, 494
Cooper, Charles M. II, 1046
Cooper, Charles M. II, 1049
Cooper, Charles P. II, 1071
Cooper, Charley IV, 692
Cooper, Charlotte III, 84
Cooper, Charlotte III, 85
Cooper, Charlotte H. II, 852
Cooper, Charlotte H. II, 928
Cooper, Charlotte Louisa II, 494
Cooper, Charlotte Louisa II, 734
Cooper, Chas. Cooper V, 454
Cooper, Chas. Eli IV, 942
Cooper, Chas. H. IV, 692
Cooper, Chilion II, 1049
Cooper, Christena V, 834
Cooper, Christina V, 834
Cooper, Cora V, 231
Cooper, Courtland II, 130
Cooper, Cyrus IV, 615
Cooper, Cyrus IV, 616
Cooper, Cyrus IV, 692
Cooper, D. IV, 914
Cooper, Dabney VI, 956
Cooper, Daniel II, 493
Cooper, Daniel II, 682
Cooper, David II, 25
Cooper, David II, 63
Cooper, David II, 130
Cooper, David II, 147
Cooper, David II, 493
Cooper, David II, 593
Cooper, David II, 734
Cooper, David II, 806
Cooper, David II, 852
Cooper, David II, 854
Cooper, David V, 834
Cooper, David B. II, 789
Cooper, David B. II, 852
Cooper, David P. II, 1057
Cooper, David S. III, 31
Cooper, David S. III, 84
Cooper, David, Jr. II, 789
Cooper, David, Jr. II, 852
Cooper, David, Jr. II, 919
Cooper, Deborah II, 25
Cooper, Deborah II, 63
Cooper, Deborah II, 349
Cooper, Deborah II, 493
Cooper, Dorothea Anna Nathalia VI, 631
Cooper, Dorothy IV, 866
Cooper, Dr. Simon III, 405
Cooper, E. Cortland II, 852
Cooper, Earnest V, 454
Cooper, Edith G. IV, 692
Cooper, Edward II, 143
Cooper, Edward II, 147
Cooper, Edward II, 1049
Cooper, Edward IV, 1025
Cooper, Edward C. II, 852
Cooper, Edward Courtland II, 147
Cooper, Edward P. II, 130
Cooper, Edward P. II, 147
Cooper, Edward P. II, 789

Cooper, Edward P. II, 852
Cooper, Edward P. II, 919
Cooper, Edward Pancoast II, 789
Cooper, Edwin K. II, 734
Cooper, Effie IV, 1248
Cooper, Eleanor V, 301
Cooper, Eleanor V, 309
Cooper, Eleanor H. III, 84
Cooper, Elenor V, 43
Cooper, Eli IV, 560
Cooper, Eli V, 231
Cooper, Eli V, 454
Cooper, Eli B. IV, 519
Cooper, Elias Paxson Lownes II, 1049
Cooper, Elijah V, 832
Cooper, Elijah V, 834
Cooper, Eliz III, 489
Cooper, Eliz. D. III, 85
Cooper, Eliza II, 852
Cooper, Eliza II, 930
Cooper, Eliza Ann III, 31
Cooper, Eliza Ann III, 84
Cooper, Eliza H. II, 488
Cooper, Eliza H. II, 494
Cooper, Elizabeth I, 1060
Cooper, Elizabeth I, 1063
Cooper, Elizabeth II, 115
Cooper, Elizabeth II, 117
Cooper, Elizabeth II, 493
Cooper, Elizabeth II, 495
Cooper, Elizabeth II, 544
Cooper, Elizabeth II, 789
Cooper, Elizabeth II, 822
Cooper, Elizabeth IV, 519
Cooper, Elizabeth IV, 522
Cooper, Elizabeth IV, 807
Cooper, Elizabeth IV, 866
Cooper, Elizabeth IV, 873
Cooper, Elizabeth IV, 901
Cooper, Elizabeth IV, 902
Cooper, Elizabeth IV, 914
Cooper, Elizabeth V, 43
Cooper, Elizabeth V, 47
Cooper, Elizabeth V, 556
Cooper, Elizabeth V, 732
Cooper, Elizabeth V, 780
Cooper, Elizabeth V, 784
Cooper, Elizabeth V, 793
Cooper, Elizabeth V, 794
Cooper, Elizabeth V, 834
Cooper, Elizabeth V, 839
Cooper, Elizabeth V, 849
Cooper, Elizabeth C. IV, 692
Cooper, Elizabeth C. IV, 693
Cooper, Elizabeth D. II, 494
Cooper, Elizabeth D. II, 734
Cooper, Elizabeth D. II, 852
Cooper, Elizabeth Dawson II, 789
Cooper, Elizabeth M. II, 789
Cooper, Elizabeth M. II, 852
Cooper, Elizabeth M. II, 891
Cooper, Elizabeth M. II, 934
Cooper, Elizabeth Proctor III, 84
Cooper, Elizabeth R. II, 852
Cooper, Elizabeth W. V, 43
Cooper, Elizabeth Y. II, 852
Cooper, Elizabeth, Sr. V, 834
Cooper, Ella IV, 692
Cooper, Ella IV, 780
Cooper, Elleanor II, 793
Cooper, Ellen II, 702
Cooper, Ellen II, 734
Cooper, Ellen III, 84
Cooper, Ellwood II, 702
Cooper, Ellwood II, 734
Cooper, Ellwood III, 84
Cooper, Ellwood III, 163
Cooper, Elma IV, 190
Cooper, Elma IV, 311
Cooper, Elma IV, 312
Cooper, Elma V, 43
Cooper, Elma V, 301
Cooper, Elma V, 303
Cooper, Elmer IV, 1248
Cooper, Elwood II, 702
Cooper, Elwood II, 734
Cooper, Elwood II, 756
Cooper, Elwood III, 84
Cooper, Elwood V, 43
Cooper, Ely IV, 560
Cooper, Emma II, 147
Cooper, Emma II, 153
Cooper, Emma II, 852
Cooper, Emma II, 894
Cooper, Emma C. II, 135
Cooper, Emma T. II, 130
Cooper, Emma T. II, 147
Cooper, Esther II, 34
Cooper, Esther II, 35
Cooper, Esther II, 493
Cooper, Esther II, 561
Cooper, Esther II, 958
Cooper, Esther IV, 519
Cooper, Esther IV, 525
Cooper, Esther V, 834
Cooper, Esther V, 839
Cooper, Eva IV, 866
Cooper, Eva Lucile V, 556
Cooper, Evan IV, 380
Cooper, Evan IV, 807
Cooper, Evan IV, 901
Cooper, Evan IV, 902
Cooper, Evan IV, 910
Cooper, Evan IV, 914
Cooper, Evan IV, 942
Cooper, Everett V, 556
Cooper, Ewing V, 454
Cooper, Fannie III, 84
Cooper, Fannie III, 163
Cooper, Fanny H. L. VI, 896
Cooper, Felix V, 834
Cooper, Ferebe I, 1117
Cooper, Ferraba V, 732
Cooper, Ferrebee I, 1047
Cooper, Ferrebee I, 1050
Cooper, Florence IV, 1234
Cooper, Forest IV, 866
Cooper, Frances IV, 628
Cooper, Frances IV, 763
Cooper, Frances C. IV, 741
Cooper, Frances S. VI, 934
Cooper, Gainer IV, 901
Cooper, Geo. IV, 865
Cooper, Geo. IV, 901
Cooper, George V, 834
Cooper, George Willard V, 556
Cooper, Guli Elma IV, 519
Cooper, Gulielma IV, 519
Cooper, Gulielma IV, 560
Cooper, Hannah II, 25
Cooper, Hannah II, 63
Cooper, Hannah II, 130
Cooper, Hannah II, 170
Cooper, Hannah II, 208
Cooper, Hannah II, 210
Cooper, Hannah II, 274
Cooper, Hannah II, 276
Cooper, Hannah II, 285
Cooper, Hannah II, 493
Cooper, Hannah II, 494
Cooper, Hannah II, 504
Cooper, Hannah II, 806
Cooper, Hannah II, 852
Cooper, Hannah II, 854
Cooper, Hannah II, 991
Cooper, Hannah II, 1012
Cooper, Hannah II, 1049
Cooper, Hannah II, 1057
Cooper, Hannah III, 31
Cooper, Hannah III, 38
Cooper, Hannah III, 84
Cooper, Hannah III, 206
Cooper, Hannah IV, 1025
Cooper, Hannah V, 826
Cooper, Hannah V, 834
Cooper, Hannah V, 836
Cooper, Hannah V, 849
Cooper, Hannah V, 900
Cooper, Hannah B. II, 1049
Cooper, Hannah Booth III, 31
Cooper, Hannah C. II, 852
Cooper, Hannah C. II, 932
Cooper, Hannah G. III, 84
Cooper, Hannah G. III, 85
Cooper, Hannah Gillam Albertson II, 830
Cooper, Hannah H. II, 1046
Cooper, Hannah R. II, 143
Cooper, Hannah R. II, 147
Cooper, Hannah W. II, 1046
Cooper, Hannah W. II, 1049
Cooper, Harriet IV, 1234
Cooper, Harriett IV, 1234
Cooper, Harry IV, 866
Cooper, Harry E. IV, 692
Cooper, Harry E. IV, 693
Cooper, Harry E. IV, 807
Cooper, Harry E. IV, 842
Cooper, Harry J. IV, 692
Cooper, Harry J. IV, 942
Cooper, Helen Juanita V, 556
Cooper, Henry II, 702
Cooper, Henry II, 734
Cooper, Henry II, 1049
Cooper, Henry III, 84
Cooper, Henry IV, 1025
Cooper, Henry VI, 908
Cooper, Henry C. II, 143
Cooper, Henry C. II, 147
Cooper, Henry R. II, 852
Cooper, Henry Richardson III, 84
Cooper, Hester II, 349
Cooper, Hinchman IV, 380
Cooper, Hinchman IV, 902
Cooper, Howard II, 702
Cooper, Howard M. II, 852
Cooper, Howard M. II, 924
Cooper, Hugh L. VI, 896
Cooper, Hulda V, 834
Cooper, Ida Adella IV, 1052
Cooper, Irene Rebecca V, 556
Cooper, Isaac I, 1028
Cooper, Isaac I, 1041
Cooper, Isaac I, 1043
Cooper, Isaac I, 1047
Cooper, Isaac I, 1117
Cooper, Isaac II, 210
Cooper, Isaac II, 494
Cooper, Isaac V, 43
Cooper, Isaac V, 732
Cooper, Isaac V, 780
Cooper, Isaac V, 784
Cooper, Isaac V, 793
Cooper, Isaac Mickle II, 494
Cooper, Jacob I, 1028
Cooper, Jacob II, 349
Cooper, Jacob II, 493
Cooper, Jacob II, 495
Cooper, Jacob V, 43
Cooper, Jacob V, 834
Cooper, Jacob V, 839
Cooper, Jacob V, 849
Cooper, Jacob, Jr. V, 834
Cooper, James II, 25
Cooper, James II, 62
Cooper, James II, 87
Cooper, James II, 115
Cooper, James II, 117
Cooper, James II, 349
Cooper, James II, 493
Cooper, James II, 557
Cooper, James II, 561
Cooper, James II, 986
Cooper, James II, 991
Cooper, James IV, 1025
Cooper, James IV, 1248
Cooper, James C. II, 991
Cooper, James F. IV, 1248
Cooper, James R. IV, 615
Cooper, James W. V, 43
Cooper, Jane I, 448
Cooper, Jane II, 958
Cooper, Jane II, 990
Cooper, Jane II, 991
Cooper, Jane II, 1071
Cooper, Jane IV, 807
Cooper, Jane IV, 901
Cooper, Jane IV, 902
Cooper, Jane IV, 912
Cooper, Jane V, 301
Cooper, Jane V, 308
Cooper, Jane V, 834
Cooper, Jeremiah V, 834
Cooper, Jeremiah VI, 379
Cooper, Jesse V, 43
Cooper, Jesse V, 301
Cooper, Jesse V, 309
Cooper, Jessie II, 852
Cooper, Joanna I, 1060
Cooper, Joanna I, 1061
Cooper, Joanna Elizabet VI, 929
Cooper, Joel I, 1117
Cooper, Joel V, 732
Cooper, Joel Atkinson II, 494
Cooper, John I, 380
Cooper, John I, 1075
Cooper, John I, 1117
Cooper, John II, 494
Cooper, John II, 593
Cooper, John II, 734
Cooper, John II, 789
Cooper, John II, 852
Cooper, John II, 894
Cooper, John II, 924
Cooper, John II, 958
Cooper, John II, 991
Cooper, John II, 1049
Cooper, John III, 84
Cooper, John IV, 311
Cooper, John IV, 312
Cooper, John V, 43
Cooper, John V, 301
Cooper, John V, 303
Cooper, John V, 732
Cooper, John VI, 896
Cooper, John VI, 961
Cooper, John B. II, 62
Cooper, John Borton II, 63
Cooper, John Elias V, 834
Cooper, John H. II, 852
Cooper, John Haldeman II, 789
Cooper, John Lister III, 31
Cooper, John Lister III, 38
Cooper, John Lister III, 84
Cooper, John R. V, 43
Cooper, John W. II, 991
Cooper, John W. V, 900
Cooper, Jonathan V, 834
Cooper, Jonathan V, 839
Cooper, Jonathan, Jr. V, 834
Cooper, Joseph I, 1028
Cooper, Joseph I, 1047
Cooper, Joseph I, 1117
Cooper, Joseph II, 63
Cooper, Joseph II, 181
Cooper, Joseph II, 210
Cooper, Joseph II, 252
Cooper, Joseph II, 274
Cooper, Joseph II, 349
Cooper, Joseph II, 493
Cooper, Joseph II, 504
Cooper, Joseph II, 558
Cooper, Joseph II, 958
Cooper, Joseph III, 85
Cooper, Joseph III, 481
Cooper, Joseph V, 43
Cooper, Joseph V, 732
Cooper, Joseph V, 780
Cooper, Joseph VI, 807
Cooper, Joseph VI, 816
Cooper, Joseph B. II, 210
Cooper, Joseph B. II, 274
Cooper, Joseph B. II, 1046
Cooper, Joseph Bacon II, 62
Cooper, Joseph Bacon II, 105
Cooper, Joseph Barclay IV, 615
Cooper, Joseph Brown II, 494
Cooper, Joseph C. II, 130
Cooper, Joseph C. II, 147
Cooper, Joseph C. V, 43
Cooper, Joseph C. V, 52
Cooper, Joseph C. V, 780
Cooper, Joseph C. V, 781
Cooper, Joseph Ellis II, 789
Cooper, Joseph Ellis II, 852
Cooper, Joseph Lownes II, 1049
Cooper, Joseph Morgan II, 789
Cooper, Joseph Morgan II, 852
Cooper, Joseph P. III, 84
Cooper, Joseph P. III, 85
Cooper, Joseph Phipps III, 84
Cooper, Joseph Phipps III, 85
Cooper, Joseph, Jr. II, 493
Cooper, Joseph, Jr. II, 558
Cooper, Joshua IV, 807
Cooper, Katie IV, 1234
Cooper, Kitty VI, 976
Cooper, Leah V, 301
Cooper, Leah V, 308
Cooper, Leatitia II, 1014
Cooper, Lettie V, 454
Cooper, Lewis II, 494
Cooper, Lewis II, 734
Cooper, Lewis A. Woolman IV, 942
Cooper, Louise H. V, 556
Cooper, Lucy II, 852
Cooper, Lucy II, 924
Cooper, Lucy II, 934
Cooper, Lucy VI, 717
Cooper, Lucy Pearl II, 789
Cooper, Lucy S. II, 852
Cooper, Lydea I, 1060
Cooper, Lydia II, 181
Cooper, Lydia II, 210
Cooper, Lydia II, 252
Cooper, Lydia II, 349
Cooper, Lydia II, 494
Cooper, Lydia II, 782
Cooper, Lydia V, 43
Cooper, Lydia V, 52
Cooper, Lydia V, 780
Cooper, Lydia V, 781
Cooper, Lydia V, 834
Cooper, Lydia V, 839
Cooper, Lydia V, 874
Cooper, Lydia V, 881
Cooper, Lydia A. IV, 692
Cooper, Lydia A. IV, 789
Cooper, Lydia A. IV, 942
Cooper, Lydia A. IV, 1017
Cooper, Lydia A. IV, 1018
Cooper, Lydia B. II, 147
Cooper, Lydia E. V, 43
Cooper, Lydia F. II, 143
Cooper, Lydia F. II, 147
Cooper, Mabel IV, 1248
Cooper, Mackaria VI, 896
Cooper, Magdalen III, 85
Cooper, Mahlon II, 1049
Cooper, Mahlon IV, 1025
Cooper, Margaret II, 494
Cooper, Margaret IV, 519
Cooper, Margaret IV, 539
Cooper, Margaret IV, 560
Cooper, Margaret C. II, 1049
Cooper, Margaret C. II, 1058
Cooper, Margaret E. V, 43
Cooper, Margaret Ellen V, 43
Cooper, Maria II, 852
Cooper, Maria II, 1049
Cooper, Marmaduke II, 493
Cooper, Marmaduke II, 494
Cooper, Martha II, 185
Cooper, Martha II, 473
Cooper, Martha II, 493
Cooper, Martha III, 85
Cooper, Martha III, 405
Cooper, Martha IV, 380
Cooper, Martha IV, 519
Cooper, Martha IV, 902
Cooper, Martha IV, 942
Cooper, Martha A. J. VI, 941
Cooper, Martha D. Stevens IV, 692
Cooper, Mary I, 534
Cooper, Mary I, 1028
Cooper, Mary I, 1032
Cooper, Mary I, 1061
Cooper, Mary II, 25
Cooper, Mary II, 38
Cooper, Mary II, 56
Cooper, Mary II, 62
Cooper, Mary II, 63
Cooper, Mary II, 82
Cooper, Mary II, 87
Cooper, Mary II, 349
Cooper, Mary II, 493
Cooper, Mary II, 494
Cooper, Mary II, 558
Cooper, Mary II, 588
Cooper, Mary II, 630
Cooper, Mary II, 682
Cooper, Mary II, 689
Cooper, Mary II, 702
Cooper, Mary II, 708
Cooper, Mary II, 724
Cooper, Mary II, 804
Cooper, Mary II, 852
Cooper, Mary II, 986
Cooper, Mary II, 991
Cooper, Mary II, 1014
Cooper, Mary II, 1049
Cooper, Mary III, 85
Cooper, Mary III, 349
Cooper, Mary III, 405
Cooper, Mary III, 424
Cooper, Mary III, 458
Cooper, Mary IV, 380
Cooper, Mary IV, 902
Cooper, Mary IV, 910
Cooper, Mary IV, 942
Cooper, Mary IV, 1025
Cooper, Mary V, 43
Cooper, Mary V, 138
Cooper, Mary V, 139
Cooper, Mary V, 780
Cooper, Mary V, 794
Cooper, Mary V, 826
Cooper, Mary V, 834
Cooper, Mary V, 855
Cooper, Mary VI, 736
Cooper, Mary VI, 772
Cooper, Mary Ann II, 789
Cooper, Mary Ann IV, 807
Cooper, Mary Ann IV, 1129
Cooper, Mary Ann IV, 1133
Cooper, Mary Ann V, 43
Cooper, Mary Anne II, 852
Cooper, Mary Anne II, 920
Cooper, Mary Cooper II, 804
Cooper, Mary D. III, 85
Cooper, Mary D. III, 249
Cooper, Mary E. IV, 692
Cooper, Mary E. IV, 693
Cooper, Mary E. IV, 941
Cooper, Mary E. IV, 942
Cooper, Mary E. IV, 1004
Cooper, Mary E. V, 43
Cooper, Mary E. V, 900
Cooper, Mary E. V, 937
Cooper, Mary E. VI, 904
Cooper, Mary E. Cooper IV, 692
Cooper, Mary Elizabeth IV, 942
Cooper, Mary Elizabeth IV, 1004
Cooper, Mary Ellen V, 454
Cooper, Mary H. II, 63
Cooper, Mary H. IV, 692
Cooper, Mary H. Smith IV, 741
Cooper, Mary J. V, 43
Cooper, Mary J. V, 78
Cooper, Mary Jane V, 43
Cooper, Mary L. II, 852
Cooper, Mary L. II, 860

Cooper, Mary M. II, 852
Cooper, Mary M. II, 924
Cooper, Mary Mickle II, 894
Cooper, Mary W. II, 38
Cooper, Maryann IV, 902
Cooper, Maryann V, 732
Cooper, Mercy II, 801
Cooper, Mifflin II, 702
Cooper, Mordecai I, 1117
Cooper, Mordecai V, 732
Cooper, Mordecai Stokes II, 494
Cooper, Morris II, 734
Cooper, Morris II, 756
Cooper, Morris V, 231
Cooper, Moses C. Stevens IV, 692
Cooper, Mrs. J. W. V, 617
Cooper, Mrs. Mason I, 631
Cooper, Nancy VI, 858
Cooper, Nathan I, 1028
Cooper, Nelson VI, 896
Cooper, Nicholas IV, 325
Cooper, Nicholas IV, 519
Cooper, Nicholas IV, 526
Cooper, Nicholas IV, 560
Cooper, Paul II, 62
Cooper, Paul II, 98
Cooper, Peggy VI, 924
Cooper, Pharoba I, 1028
Cooper, Phebe I, 1060
Cooper, Phebe II, 734
Cooper, Phebe II, 756
Cooper, Phebe IV, 807
Cooper, Phebe IV, 901
Cooper, Phebe IV, 902
Cooper, Phebe IV, 906
Cooper, Phebe E. V, 900
Cooper, Phebe Jane V, 301
Cooper, Phebe Jane V, 308
Cooper, Phebe W. II, 852
Cooper, Pherraba V, 732
Cooper, Phoebe P. II, 702
Cooper, Pine II, 56
Cooper, Polly VI, 979
Cooper, Priscilla II, 21
Cooper, Priscilla II, 62
Cooper, Priscilla II, 115
Cooper, Priscilla II, 117
Cooper, Priscilla II, 130
Cooper, Priscilla II, 135
Cooper, Priscilla II, 147
Cooper, Priscilla IV, 519
Cooper, Priscilla IV, 522
Cooper, Prudence I, 1043
Cooper, Prudence I, 1053
Cooper, Prudence I, 1060
Cooper, Prudence II, 37
Cooper, Prudence V, 732
Cooper, Prudence V, 780
Cooper, Prudence V, 793
Cooper, Prudence V, 794
Cooper, Prudence V, 803
Cooper, Rachel II, 62
Cooper, Rachel II, 105
Cooper, Rachel II, 983
Cooper, Rachel II, 991
Cooper, Rachel II, 1049
Cooper, Rachel IV, 123
Cooper, Rachel IV, 124
Cooper, Rachel IV, 902
Cooper, Rachel IV, 1025
Cooper, Rachel V, 834
Cooper, Rachel V, 850
Cooper, Rachel VI, 631
Cooper, Rachel VI, 636
Cooper, Rachel VI, 667
Cooper, Rachel VI, 701
Cooper, Rachel VI, 703
Cooper, Rachel VI, 705
Cooper, Rachel VI, 706
Cooper, Rachel VI, 708
Cooper, Rachel VI, 896
Cooper, Rachel Paxson II, 789
Cooper, Ralph V, 43
Cooper, Ralph V, 834
Cooper, Rebecah II, 493
Cooper, Rebecca II, 349
Cooper, Rebecca II, 493
Cooper, Rebecca II, 519
Cooper, Rebecca Ann II, 702
Cooper, Rebeccah II, 557
Cooper, Redman II, 734
Cooper, Redman II, 789
Cooper, Redman II, 852
Cooper, Redman II, 854
Cooper, Reeder, Alice Malone IV, 914
Cooper, Rhoda I, 380
Cooper, Rhoda I, 398
Cooper, Rhoda V, 780
Cooper, Rhoda V, 784
Cooper, Rhoda V, 794
Cooper, Richard M. II, 724
Cooper, Robert III, 85
Cooper, Robert Barclay IV, 741
Cooper, Ruth IV, 26
Cooper, Ruth IV, 34
Cooper, Ruth IV, 1025
Cooper, Ruth C. IV, 692
Cooper, Ruth C. IV, 693
Cooper, Ruth C. IV, 807
Cooper, Ruth C. IV, 842
Cooper, Sallie V, 454
Cooper, Sallie Kaighn II, 803
Cooper, Sally VI, 807
Cooper, Samuel I, 1028
Cooper, Samuel I, 1061
Cooper, Samuel I Sup 1, 10
Cooper, Samuel II, 25
Cooper, Samuel II, 349
Cooper, Samuel II, 456
Cooper, Samuel II, 494
Cooper, Samuel II, 539
Cooper, Samuel III, 85
Cooper, Samuel IV, 519
Cooper, Samuel IV, 615
Cooper, Samuel IV, 616
Cooper, Samuel IV, 692
Cooper, Samuel IV, 741
Cooper, Samuel IV, 789
Cooper, Samuel IV, 941
Cooper, Samuel IV, 1017
Cooper, Samuel C. II, 734
Cooper, Samuel C. II, 852
Cooper, Samuel Clark II, 789
Cooper, Samuel J. V, 454
Cooper, Samuel Lewis II, 852
Cooper, Samuel R. Colloday II, 852
Cooper, Sarah I, 625
Cooper, Sarah I, 1028
Cooper, Sarah I, 1060
Cooper, Sarah I, 1117
Cooper, Sarah II, 25
Cooper, Sarah II, 181
Cooper, Sarah II, 210
Cooper, Sarah II, 220
Cooper, Sarah II, 252
Cooper, Sarah II, 274
Cooper, Sarah II, 702
Cooper, Sarah II, 712
Cooper, Sarah II, 804
Cooper, Sarah II, 852
Cooper, Sarah II, 957
Cooper, Sarah II, 958
Cooper, Sarah II, 990
Cooper, Sarah II, 991
Cooper, Sarah II, 1049
Cooper, Sarah III, 84
Cooper, Sarah III, 163
Cooper, Sarah IV, 380
Cooper, Sarah IV, 519
Cooper, Sarah IV, 526
Cooper, Sarah IV, 541
Cooper, Sarah IV, 560
Cooper, Sarah IV, 571
Cooper, Sarah IV, 578
Cooper, Sarah IV, 615
Cooper, Sarah IV, 692
Cooper, Sarah IV, 741
Cooper, Sarah IV, 769
Cooper, Sarah IV, 902
Cooper, Sarah IV, 941
Cooper, Sarah IV, 1017
Cooper, Sarah V, 231
Cooper, Sarah V, 732
Cooper, Sarah V, 834
Cooper, Sarah VI, 896
Cooper, Sarah VI, 941
Cooper, Sarah VI, 956
Cooper, Sarah Ann II, 1049
Cooper, Sarah Ann II, 1055
Cooper, Sarah Ann V, 834
Cooper, Sarah Ann V, 869
Cooper, Sarah B. II, 130
Cooper, Sarah B. II, 147
Cooper, Sarah B. II, 852
Cooper, Sarah B. II, 919
Cooper, Sarah Bassett II, 789
Cooper, Sarah E. V, 950
Cooper, Sarah Elizabeth IV, 615
Cooper, Sarah Esther V, 950
Cooper, Sarah Esther V, 958
Cooper, Sarah Jr. IV, 519
Cooper, Sarah M. IV, 692
Cooper, Sarah Mickle II, 806
Cooper, Sarah P. II, 494
Cooper, Sarah P. II, 702
Cooper, Sarah P. II, 734
Cooper, Sarah P. II, 756
Cooper, Sarah P. III, 29
Cooper, Sarah P. III, 84
Cooper, Sarah P. IV, 693
Cooper, Sarah P. IV, 789
Cooper, Sarah, Sr. IV, 519
Cooper, Sibil V, 231
Cooper, Sibil J. V, 231
Cooper, Simon III, 85
Cooper, Simon III, 349
Cooper, Simon III, 405
Cooper, Simon III, 458
Cooper, Sina Ellen IV, 1052
Cooper, Sina Ellen IV, 1062
Cooper, Susan IV, 519
Cooper, Susan IV, 520
Cooper, Susan B. II, 789
Cooper, Susan C. II, 789
Cooper, Susan C. II, 852
Cooper, Susan C. II, 919
Cooper, Susan P. II, 852
Cooper, Susanna IV, 807
Cooper, Susanna IV, 839
Cooper, Susannah IV, 807
Cooper, Susannah IV, 865
Cooper, Susannah IV, 901
Cooper, Sybell II, 493
Cooper, Sybil II, 493
Cooper, Sybil II, 593
Cooper, Sylvia J. I, 380
Cooper, Thelma Louise V, 556
Cooper, Thomas II, 473
Cooper, Thomas II, 494
Cooper, Thomas II, 990
Cooper, Thomas II, 991
Cooper, Thomas V, 43
Cooper, Thomas VI, 896
Cooper, Thomas A. II, 702
Cooper, Thos. Charles IV, 615
Cooper, Vernon VI, 631
Cooper, Vernon VI, 636
Cooper, W. IV, 914
Cooper, Walter M. IV, 611
Cooper, Walter M. IV, 615
Cooper, Walter M. IV, 616
Cooper, Warner II, 63
Cooper, Wayne II, 991
Cooper, Wd. Asenath II, 822
Cooper, Wd. Jane II, 991
Cooper, Wd. Mary II, 493
Cooper, Wd. Phebe II, 789
Cooper, Welmet I, 1117
Cooper, Welmet V, 43
Cooper, Welmet V, 732
Cooper, William I, 1015
Cooper, William I, 1028
Cooper, William I, 1032
Cooper, William I, 1117
Cooper, William II, 25
Cooper, William II, 130
Cooper, William II, 210
Cooper, William II, 276
Cooper, William II, 349
Cooper, William II, 958
Cooper, William III, 85
Cooper, William IV, 81
Cooper, William IV, 519
Cooper, William IV, 902
Cooper, William IV, 914
Cooper, William IV, 1234
Cooper, William V, 43
Cooper, William V, 556
Cooper, William V, 732
Cooper, William V, 834
Cooper, William VI, 896
Cooper, William VI, 924
Cooper, William VI, 976
Cooper, William VI, 979
Cooper, William Alfred II, 789
Cooper, William E. II, 789
Cooper, William E. VI, 904
Cooper, William T. III, 85
Cooper, William W. II, 789
Cooper, William W. II, 991
Cooper, William, Jr. V, 834
Cooper, Wilmer A. IV, 616
Cooper, Wm. II, 25
Cooper, Wm. II, 56
Cooper, Wm. II, 62
Cooper, Wm. II, 63
Cooper, Wm. II, 87
Cooper, Wm. II, 135
Cooper, Wm. II, 523
Cooper, Wm. II, 588
Cooper, Wm. II, 630
Cooper, Wm. II, 804
Cooper, Wm. II, 852
Cooper, Wm. II, 891
Cooper, Wm. II, 991
Cooper, Wm. IV, 1234
Cooper, Wm. Alfred II, 852
Cooper, Wm. Chalkley IV, 942
Cooper, Wm. E. II, 852
Cooper, Wm. E. II, 934
Cooper, Wm. Edward III, 84
Cooper, Wm. Edward III, 85
Cooper, Wm. J. II, 852
Cooper, Wm. Joseph II, 852
Cooper, Wm. Joseph II, 894
Cooper, Wm. P. II, 789
Cooper, Wm. T. II, 147
Cooper, Wm. W. II, 147
Cooper, Wm. W. II, 852
Cooper, Wm. W. V, 900
Cooper, Wm., Jr. II, 25
Cooper, Wm., Jr. II, 493
Cooper, Yarnel V, 301
Coover, Dora IV, 1275
Coover, Elizabeth IV, 1274
Coover, Elizabeth D. IV, 1274
Coover, Elizabeth D. IV, 1298
Coover, Maryvalen IV, 1274
Coover, Melvin IV, 1275
Coover, Melvin L. IV, 1275
Coover, Wm. IV, 1274
Coover, Wm. B. IV, 1275
Cope, ??? IV, 190
Cope, ??? IV, 693
Cope, ??? IV, 1125
Cope, A. L. IV, 807
Cope, A. L. IV, 845
Cope, Aaron Vansciock IV, 27
Cope, Abigail IV, 142
Cope, Abigail IV, 149
Cope, Abigail IV, 163
Cope, Abigail IV, 190
Cope, Abigail IV, 191
Cope, Abigail IV, 311
Cope, Abigail IV, 902
Cope, Abigail IV, 1052
Cope, Abigail VI, 379
Cope, Abigail VI, 380
Cope, Abigail VI, 447
Cope, Abigail Ann II, 494
Cope, Achsah IV, 125
Cope, Achsah IV, 135
Cope, Achsah IV, 617
Cope, Achsah IV, 618
Cope, Achsah IV, 942
Cope, Achsah IV, 951
Cope, Achsah H. IV, 125
Cope, Achsah H. IV, 942
Cope, Achsia H. IV, 124
Cope, Ada B. IV, 902
Cope, Adah B. IV, 902
Cope, Adah B. IV, 918
Cope, Adah B. IV, 942
Cope, Albert IV, 81
Cope, Albert IV, 123
Cope, Albert IV, 401
Cope, Albert IV, 693
Cope, Albert IV, 800
Cope, Albert B. IV, 694
Cope, Albert M. IV, 608
Cope, Albert M. IV, 617
Cope, Albert M. IV, 678
Cope, Albert M. IV, 693
Cope, Albert M. IV, 694
Cope, Albert M. IV, 715
Cope, Albert M. IV, 730
Cope, Albert M. IV, 797
Cope, Albert M. IV, 807
Cope, Albert N. IV, 639
Cope, Albertha IV, 694
Cope, Alexander Logan IV, 807
Cope, Alexia Thomas II, 702
Cope, Alexis T. II, 734
Cope, Alfred II, 349
Cope, Alfred II, 734
Cope, Alfred II, 948
Cope, Alfred IV, 142
Cope, Alfred Lewis IV, 694
Cope, Alfred Louis IV, 617
Cope, Alfred Louis IV, 618
Cope, Alfred Louis IV, 693
Cope, Alice IV, 26
Cope, Alice IV, 32
Cope, Alice IV, 69
Cope, Alice IV, 81
Cope, Alice IV, 85
Cope, Alice IV, 121
Cope, Alice IV, 122
Cope, Alice IV, 123
Cope, Alice IV, 124
Cope, Alice IV, 126
Cope, Alice IV, 817
Cope, Alice IV, 978
Cope, Alice C. IV, 639
Cope, Alice G. IV, 135
Cope, Alice G. IV, 802
Cope, Alice G. IV, 807
Cope, Alice M. IV, 468
Cope, Allen IV, 81
Cope, Allen IV, 123
Cope, Allen IV, 616
Cope, Allen IV, 617
Cope, Allen IV, 693
Cope, Allen B. IV, 618
Cope, Allen Bennett IV, 616
Cope, Alliance O. IV, 469
Cope, Allison IV, 27
Cope, Almira IV, 81
Cope, Almira IV, 123
Cope, Almira IV, 693
Cope, Almira IV, 935
Cope, Almira IV, 942
Cope, Alta E. IV, 808
Cope, Alta E. IV, 845
Cope, Alta E. IV, 846
Cope, Alta Elizabeth IV, 807
Cope, Alvah IV, 942
Cope, Alverda IV, 1154
Cope, Amelia IV, 468
Cope, Amos IV, 81
Cope, Amos IV, 123
Cope, Amos IV, 124
Cope, Amos IV, 135
Cope, Amos IV, 190
Cope, Amos IV, 191
Cope, Amos IV, 519
Cope, Amos IV, 614
Cope, Amos IV, 616
Cope, Amos IV, 618
Cope, Amos IV, 622
Cope, Amos IV, 934
Cope, Amos A. IV, 191
Cope, Amos L. IV, 190
Cope, Amos L. IV, 289
Cope, Amy IV, 26
Cope, Amy IV, 29
Cope, Amy IV, 81
Cope, Amy IV, 84
Cope, Amy IV, 191
Cope, Amy IV, 617
Cope, Amy A. IV, 190
Cope, Amy Jane IV, 693
Cope, Andrew II, 349
Cope, Ann II, 349
Cope, Ann IV, 123
Cope, Ann IV, 124
Cope, Ann IV, 141
Cope, Ann IV, 142
Cope, Ann IV, 183
Cope, Ann IV, 190
Cope, Ann IV, 191
Cope, Ann IV, 616
Cope, Ann IV, 617
Cope, Ann IV, 618
Cope, Ann IV, 658
Cope, Ann IV, 803
Cope, Ann IV, 807
Cope, Ann IV, 866
Cope, Ann IV, 879
Cope, Ann IV, 915
Cope, Ann D. II, 946
Cope, Ann D. IV, 190
Cope, Ann E. IV, 191
Cope, Ann E. IV, 311
Cope, Ann E. IV, 313
Cope, Anna II, 349
Cope, Anna II, 1087
Cope, Anna II, 1089
Cope, Anna IV, 81
Cope, Anna IV, 124
Cope, Anna IV, 135
Cope, Anna IV, 807
Cope, Anna IV, 809
Cope, Anna IV, 819
Cope, Anna IV, 845
Cope, Anna IV, 945
Cope, Anna C. IV, 802
Cope, Anna C. IV, 819
Cope, Anna Ellora III, 85
Cope, Anna Ellora III, 298
Cope, Anna F. IV, 694
Cope, Anna Florence IV, 401
Cope, Anna Florence IV, 693
Cope, Anna Florence IV, 715
Cope, Anna H. II, 702
Cope, Anna Mary IV, 902
Cope, Anna Mary IV, 918
Cope, Anna S. II, 730
Cope, Anna S. II, 734
Cope, Anna S. II, 948
Cope, Anna S. II, 1085
Cope, Anna S. II, 1087
Cope, Anne IV, 123
Cope, Anne IV, 124
Cope, Annette II, 734
Cope, Arthur L. IV, 468
Cope, Arthur Morris IV, 617
Cope, Barak A. IV, 693
Cope, Barak A. IV, 694
Cope, Benj. H. IV, 211
Cope, Benj. H. IV, 280
Cope, Benjamin IV, 123
Cope, Benjamin IV, 124

Cope, Benjamin IV, 190
Cope, Benjamin IV, 191
Cope, Benjamin IV, 468
Cope, Benjamin IV, 617
Cope, Benjamin IV, 693
Cope, Benjamin IV, 807
Cope, Benjamin H. II, 948
Cope, Benjamin H. IV, 190
Cope, Benjamin H. IV, 191
Cope, Benjamin T. IV, 191
Cope, Benjamin W. IV, 468
Cope, Bernard IV, 694
Cope, Buton H. IV, 468
Cope, Byron IV, 191
Cope, Byron H. IV, 190
Cope, Byron H. IV, 807
Cope, Byron H. IV, 813
Cope, Caleb II, 210
Cope, Caleb II, 494
Cope, Caleb II, 509
Cope, Caleb IV, 26
Cope, Caleb IV, 29
Cope, Caleb IV, 81
Cope, Caleb IV, 84
Cope, Caleb IV, 123
Cope, Caleb IV, 142
Cope, Caleb IV, 191
Cope, Caleb IV, 616
Cope, Caleb IV, 658
Cope, Caleb VI, 379
Cope, Caleb B. II, 946
Cope, Caleb B. II, 1087
Cope, Caleb B. II, 1089
Cope, Caleb D. II, 946
Cope, Caleb, Jr. IV, 617
Cope, Calvin IV, 81
Cope, Calvin IV, 124
Cope, Calvin IV, 135
Cope, Calvin IV, 618
Cope, Calvin IV, 915
Cope, Calvin C. IV, 618
Cope, Caroline II, 494
Cope, Caroline II, 717
Cope, Caroline IV, 81
Cope, Caroline IV, 123
Cope, Caroline IV, 190
Cope, Caroline IV, 191
Cope, Caroline IV, 693
Cope, Caroline IV, 942
Cope, Caroline Annette II, 702
Cope, Caroline Elizabeth II, 702
Cope, Caroline R. II, 734
Cope, Caroline R. II, 777
Cope, Celia IV, 617
Cope, Celia IV, 618
Cope, Celia IV, 651
Cope, Chalkley B. IV, 190
Cope, Chalkley B. IV, 191
Cope, Charles IV, 123
Cope, Charles IV, 124
Cope, Charles IV, 135
Cope, Charles IV, 142
Cope, Charles IV, 190
Cope, Charles IV, 191
Cope, Charles IV, 412
Cope, Charles IV, 468
Cope, Charles IV, 807
Cope, Charles IV, 813
Cope, Charles Binns IV, 27
Cope, Charles Binns IV, 124
Cope, Charles C. IV, 468
Cope, Charles Showmaker II, 494
Cope, Charlotte IV, 191
Cope, Chas. IV, 819
Cope, Chas. B. IV, 125
Cope, Chas. L. IV, 616
Cope, Chester A. IV, 618
Cope, Chester A. IV, 694
Cope, Chester Albert IV, 617
Cope, Chester Albert IV, 693
Cope, Clarence IV, 808
Cope, Clarkson IV, 124
Cope, Clementine II, 702
Cope, Clementine II, 734
Cope, Cornelius IV, 468
Cope, Cornelius IV, 1037
Cope, Cornelius Crew IV, 468
Cope, Cyrus IV, 942
Cope, Darlington II, 946
Cope, Darlington IV, 190
Cope, Darlington IV, 191
Cope, David II, 717
Cope, David IV, 142
Cope, David Ellyson IV, 942
Cope, Dawsey IV, 27
Cope, Dawsey IV, 122
Cope, Dawsey IV, 123
Cope, Dawsey IV, 124
Cope, Dawsey IV, 715
Cope, Dawsy IV, 132
Cope, Dawsy IV, 780
Cope, Deborah II, 820
Cope, Deborah II, 821
Cope, Deby II, 717
Cope, Demsey IV, 81
Cope, Drusilla IV, 942
Cope, Earl IV, 808
Cope, Earnest IV, 1311
Cope, Edeny Emily IV, 124
Cope, Edgar II, 702
Cope, Edgar II, 734
Cope, Edith IV, 123
Cope, Edith IV, 124
Cope, Edith IV, 616
Cope, Edith IV, 693
Cope, Edith IV, 866
Cope, Edith IV, 942
Cope, Edith IV, 978
Cope, Edith E. IV, 694
Cope, Edith G. IV, 124
Cope, Edith G. IV, 692
Cope, Edith G. IV, 693
Cope, Edith G. IV, 694
Cope, Edith Mary IV, 380
Cope, Edith Mary IV, 442
Cope, Edith S. II, 734
Cope, Edna IV, 135
Cope, Edna E. IV, 135
Cope, Edna E. IV, 519
Cope, Edna E. IV, 614
Cope, Edna E. IV, 617
Cope, Edna E. IV, 618
Cope, Edna Emily IV, 124
Cope, Edna Emily IV, 135
Cope, Edna L. IV, 124
Cope, Edward IV, 124
Cope, Edward IV, 126
Cope, Edward IV, 142
Cope, Edward IV, 191
Cope, Edward J. IV, 807
Cope, Edward Y. IV, 124
Cope, Edward Y. IV, 135
Cope, Edward Y. IV, 802
Cope, Edward Y. IV, 807
Cope, Edwin IV, 942
Cope, Elbert L. IV, 609
Cope, Elbert L. IV, 617
Cope, Elbert L. IV, 618
Cope, Elbert L. IV, 694
Cope, Elbert Lorain IV, 693
Cope, Elbert Lorain IV, 807
Cope, Elbert Loren IV, 652
Cope, Elbert Lorin IV, 807
Cope, Eleanor II, 349
Cope, Elener T. Coper II, 702
Cope, Elenor II, 734
Cope, Elenor II, 772
Cope, Eli IV, 617
Cope, Elias IV, 142
Cope, Elihu IV, 27
Cope, Elihu IV, 123
Cope, Elihu IV, 124
Cope, Elipha IV, 693
Cope, Eliphas IV, 694
Cope, Eliphas IV, 866
Cope, Eliphus IV, 616
Cope, Eliphus IV, 618
Cope, Elisabeth IV, 617
Cope, Elisabeth IV, 643
Cope, Elisha IV, 124
Cope, Eliz. III, 446
Cope, Eliza IV, 81
Cope, Eliza IV, 124
Cope, Eliza IV, 126
Cope, Eliza IV, 135
Cope, Eliza IV, 136
Cope, Eliza IV, 616
Cope, Eliza IV, 617
Cope, Eliza IV, 622
Cope, Eliza IV, 637
Cope, Eliza IV, 693
Cope, Eliza IV, 866
Cope, Eliza A. IV, 1205
Cope, Eliza Ann IV, 694
Cope, Eliza Ann IV, 1205
Cope, Elizabeth II, 700
Cope, Elizabeth IV, 26
Cope, Elizabeth IV, 27
Cope, Elizabeth IV, 81
Cope, Elizabeth IV, 83
Cope, Elizabeth IV, 85
Cope, Elizabeth IV, 121
Cope, Elizabeth IV, 122
Cope, Elizabeth IV, 123
Cope, Elizabeth IV, 124
Cope, Elizabeth IV, 125
Cope, Elizabeth IV, 129
Cope, Elizabeth IV, 130
Cope, Elizabeth IV, 190
Cope, Elizabeth IV, 289
Cope, Elizabeth IV, 468
Cope, Elizabeth IV, 519
Cope, Elizabeth IV, 529
Cope, Elizabeth IV, 606
Cope, Elizabeth IV, 616
Cope, Elizabeth IV, 617
Cope, Elizabeth IV, 620
Cope, Elizabeth IV, 634
Cope, Elizabeth IV, 693
Cope, Elizabeth IV, 694
Cope, Elizabeth IV, 716
Cope, Elizabeth IV, 807
Cope, Elizabeth IV, 863
Cope, Elizabeth IV, 866
Cope, Elizabeth IV, 877
Cope, Elizabeth IV, 879
Cope, Elizabeth IV, 899
Cope, Elizabeth IV, 1004
Cope, Elizabeth IV, 1037
Cope, Elizabeth VI, 379
Cope, Elizabeth A. IV, 468
Cope, Elizabeth Alice IV, 618
Cope, Elizabeth Alice IV, 640
Cope, Elizabeth Alice IV, 693
Cope, Elizabeth Alice IV, 730
Cope, Elizabeth C. II, 733
Cope, Elizabeth C. II, 734
Cope, Elizabeth Cooper II, 349
Cope, Elizabeth D. IV, 617
Cope, Elizabeth D. IV, 866
Cope, Elizabeth Dixon IV, 616
Cope, Elizabeth H. IV, 468
Cope, Elizabeth H. IV, 845
Cope, Elizabeth L. II, 702
Cope, Elizabeth L. IV, 191
Cope, Elizabeth M. IV, 611
Cope, Elizabeth M. IV, 617
Cope, Elizabeth M. IV, 618
Cope, Elizabeth M. IV, 942
Cope, Elizabeth W. II, 702
Cope, Elizabeth W. II, 734
Cope, Elizabeth W. IV, 468
Cope, Elizabeth W. IV, 693
Cope, Ella L. IV, 618
Cope, Ella L. IV, 644
Cope, Ella Lavina IV, 617
Cope, Ella Lavina IV, 866
Cope, Ellen IV, 124
Cope, Ellen B. IV, 617
Cope, Ellen B. IV, 618
Cope, Ellen B. IV, 942
Cope, Ellen C. IV, 412
Cope, Ellen P. IV, 190
Cope, Ellen P. IV, 191
Cope, Ellen P. IV, 617
Cope, Ellen S. IV, 380
Cope, Ellen S. IV, 413
Cope, Ellen S. IV, 807
Cope, Ellen S. IV, 826
Cope, Ellis IV, 191
Cope, Ellis IV, 325
Cope, Ellis IV, 519
Cope, Ellis IV, 560
Cope, Ellis IV, 616
Cope, Ellis IV, 617
Cope, Elma IV, 81
Cope, Elma IV, 123
Cope, Elma IV, 124
Cope, Elma IV, 134
Cope, Elma IV, 678
Cope, Elma IV, 693
Cope, Elma IV, 694
Cope, Elma IV, 707
Cope, Elma IV, 845
Cope, Elma C. IV, 707
Cope, Elmer Dean IV, 617
Cope, Elmira IV, 27
Cope, Elmira IV, 124
Cope, Elmira IV, 127
Cope, Elmira IV, 693
Cope, Elmire IV, 27
Cope, Emaline IV, 942
Cope, Emeline II, 349
Cope, Emeline II, 702
Cope, Emeline IV, 608
Cope, Emeline IV, 617
Cope, Emeline IV, 942
Cope, Emily IV, 81
Cope, Emily IV, 123
Cope, Emily IV, 143
Cope, Emily IV, 153
Cope, Emily IV, 693
Cope, Emily IV, 942
Cope, Emily C. II, 948
Cope, Emily Edna IV, 124
Cope, Emily Edna IV, 622
Cope, Emma II, 494
Cope, Emma IV, 693
Cope, Emma IV, 694
Cope, Emmer IV, 123
Cope, Emmor IV, 81
Cope, Emmor IV, 124
Cope, Emmor IV, 618
Cope, Emor IV, 616
Cope, Emor IV, 866
Cope, Enos II, 1085
Cope, Ernest F. IV, 468
Cope, Ernest Luther IV, 617
Cope, Esther H. IV, 845
Cope, Etta V. IV, 468
Cope, Etta V. IV, 469
Cope, Etta V. IV, 807
Cope, Etta V. IV, 1249
Cope, Eva May IV, 1205
Cope, Evan IV, 81
Cope, Evan IV, 124
Cope, Ezra IV, 693
Cope, F. J. IV, 468
Cope, F. Wood IV, 1037
Cope, Florence IV, 693
Cope, Florence N. IV, 124
Cope, Florence N. IV, 694
Cope, Florence N. IV, 731
Cope, Florence S. IV, 468
Cope, Frances II, 494
Cope, Francis IV, 124
Cope, Francis IV, 618
Cope, Francis M. IV, 468
Cope, Francis R. II, 730
Cope, Francis R. II, 734
Cope, Francis R. IV, 135
Cope, Francis R. IV, 617
Cope, Francis R. IV, 618
Cope, Franklin M. IV, 468
Cope, Franklin Samuel IV, 616
Cope, Fred J. IV, 1249
Cope, Frederic J. IV, 468
Cope, Frederick A. IV, 807
Cope, Frederick J. IV, 468
Cope, Frederick J. IV, 469
Cope, Frederick J. IV, 807
Cope, Frederick J. IV, 1249
Cope, Geo. IV, 124
Cope, Geo. IV, 127
Cope, Geo. IV, 142
Cope, Geo. IV, 158
Cope, George IV, 27
Cope, George IV, 123
Cope, George IV, 124
Cope, George IV, 141
Cope, George IV, 142
Cope, George IV, 161
Cope, George IV, 163
Cope, George IV, 190
Cope, George IV, 191
Cope, George IV, 693
Cope, George VI, 379
Cope, George VI, 380
Cope, George VI, 447
Cope, George, Jr. IV, 191
Cope, Gibson Binns IV, 191
Cope, Grace IV, 123
Cope, Grace IV, 190
Cope, Grace IV, 191
Cope, Grace IV, 311
Cope, Grace VI, 379
Cope, Grace VI, 380
Cope, Grace VI, 448
Cope, Hanna M. IV, 190
Cope, Hanna M. IV, 211
Cope, Hannah II, 210
Cope, Hannah IV, 81
Cope, Hannah IV, 121
Cope, Hannah IV, 123
Cope, Hannah IV, 124
Cope, Hannah IV, 125
Cope, Hannah IV, 126
Cope, Hannah IV, 519
Cope, Hannah IV, 544
Cope, Hannah IV, 560
Cope, Hannah IV, 562
Cope, Hannah IV, 616
Cope, Hannah IV, 617
Cope, Hannah IV, 693
Cope, Hannah IV, 709
Cope, Hannah IV, 817
Cope, Hannah F. II, 948
Cope, Hannah K. IV, 693
Cope, Hannah M. IV, 190
Cope, Hannah R. IV, 693
Cope, Hannah R. IV, 716
Cope, Hannah S. II, 1087
Cope, Hannah S. II, 1089
Cope, Hannah T. II, 948
Cope, Hannah Y. IV, 135
Cope, Hannah Y. IV, 635
Cope, Hannah Y. IV, 667
Cope, Hannah Y. IV, 692
Cope, Hannah Y. IV, 693
Cope, Hannah Y. IV, 707
Cope, Hannah Y. IV, 713
Cope, Hannah Y. IV, 731
Cope, Harmon J. IV, 608
Cope, Harold IV, 468
Cope, Harvey IV, 618
Cope, Harvey Cleaver IV, 616
Cope, Harvey Cleaver IV, 866
Cope, Harvey D. IV, 616
Cope, Harvey D. IV, 866
Cope, Helen P. IV, 617
Cope, Helen P. IV, 652
Cope, Helen P. IV, 808
Cope, Helen P. IV, 839
Cope, Helen Phebe IV, 617
Cope, Helena IV, 190
Cope, Henry II, 494
Cope, Henry II, 730
Cope, Henry II, 734
Cope, Henry IV, 26
Cope, Henry IV, 27
Cope, Henry IV, 34
Cope, Henry IV, 81
Cope, Henry IV, 123
Cope, Henry IV, 124
Cope, Henry IV, 617
Cope, Henry IV, 693
Cope, Herman V, 900
Cope, Herman U. V, 900
Cope, Hiram IV, 81
Cope, Hiram IV, 124
Cope, Hiram IV, 190
Cope, Hiram IV, 289
Cope, Hiram IV, 616
Cope, Hiram IV, 942
Cope, Howard IV, 468
Cope, Howard IV, 469
Cope, Howard H. IV, 618
Cope, Howard H. IV, 694
Cope, Howard Herman IV, 617
Cope, Howard Herman IV, 693
Cope, I. E. IV, 468
Cope, Ida M. IV, 468
Cope, Inez IV, 469
Cope, Inez IV, 1249
Cope, Inez A. IV, 468
Cope, Inez A. IV, 807
Cope, Inez A. IV, 1249
Cope, Isaac IV, 26
Cope, Isaac IV, 81
Cope, Isaac IV, 106
Cope, Isaac IV, 123
Cope, Isaac IV, 124
Cope, Isaac IV, 126
Cope, Isaac IV, 129
Cope, Isaac IV, 131
Cope, Isaac IV, 134
Cope, Isaac IV, 190
Cope, Isaac IV, 191
Cope, Isaac IV, 608
Cope, Isaac IV, 616
Cope, Isaac IV, 623
Cope, Isaac IV, 902
Cope, Isaac IV, 942
Cope, Isaac VI, 379
Cope, Isaac G. IV, 1004
Cope, Isaac P. IV, 27
Cope, Isaac Perkins IV, 27
Cope, Isaac Perkins IV, 124
Cope, Israel II, 349
Cope, Israel II, 494
Cope, Israel II, 702
Cope, Israel II, 733
Cope, Israel II, 734
Cope, Israel IV, 81
Cope, Israel IV, 606
Cope, Israel IV, 616
Cope, Israel IV, 620
Cope, Israel IV, 693
Cope, Israel IV, 863
Cope, Israel IV, 866
Cope, Israel IV, 877
Cope, Israel IV, 879
Cope, Israel IV, 899
Cope, Israel VI, 379
Cope, Israel, Jr. IV, 617
Cope, Israel, Jr. IV, 866
Cope, J. Alban II, 734
Cope, J. H. IV, 468
Cope, Jacob IV, 167
Cope, Jacob IV, 190
Cope, Jacob IV, 191
Cope, Jacob IV, 325
Cope, Jacob IV, 519
Cope, Jacob IV, 560
Cope, James IV, 142
Cope, James IV, 157
Cope, James IV, 190
Cope, James IV, 191
Cope, James IV, 311
Cope, James IV, 313
Cope, James IV, 616
Cope, James IV, 618
Cope, James IV, 693
Cope, James IV, 694
Cope, James IV, 866

Cope, James VI, 379
Cope, James VI, 380
Cope, James A. IV, 123
Cope, James A. IV, 124
Cope, James A. IV, 125
Cope, James A. IV, 135
Cope, James A. IV, 617
Cope, James A. IV, 618
Cope, James A. IV, 942
Cope, James A. IV, 951
Cope, James Byron IV, 616
Cope, James Byron IV, 617
Cope, James Byron IV, 693
Cope, James D. IV, 81
Cope, Jane IV, 142
Cope, Jane IV, 190
Cope, Jane IV, 191
Cope, Jane IV, 616
Cope, Jane IV, 618
Cope, Jane IV, 693
Cope, Jane IV, 866
Cope, Jane IV, 873
Cope, Jane VI, 380
Cope, Jane A. IV, 81
Cope, Jane H. IV, 617
Cope, Jane H. IV, 866
Cope, Jane L. IV, 468
Cope, Jane L. IV, 505
Cope, Jane L. IV, 693
Cope, Jane Sarah IV, 191
Cope, Jaspar II, 494
Cope, Jasper II, 349
Cope, Jasper II, 494
Cope, Jasper IV, 123
Cope, Jasper IV, 693
Cope, Jasper IV, 694
Cope, Jennie L. IV, 468
Cope, Jesse IV, 26
Cope, Jesse IV, 27
Cope, Jesse IV, 81
Cope, Jesse IV, 84
Cope, Jesse IV, 121
Cope, Jesse IV, 122
Cope, Jesse IV, 123
Cope, Jesse IV, 129
Cope, Jesse IV, 135
Cope, Jesse IV, 616
Cope, Jesse IV, 617
Cope, Jesse IV, 659
Cope, Jesse IV, 693
Cope, Jesse IV, 716
Cope, Jesse IV, 942
Cope, Jesse VI, 379
Cope, John II, 349
Cope, John II, 494
Cope, John II, 702
Cope, John IV, 26
Cope, John IV, 27
Cope, John IV, 44
Cope, John IV, 59
Cope, John IV, 69
Cope, John IV, 81
Cope, John IV, 121
Cope, John IV, 123
Cope, John IV, 124
Cope, John IV, 125
Cope, John IV, 190
Cope, John IV, 191
Cope, John IV, 311
Cope, John IV, 313
Cope, John IV, 616
Cope, John IV, 617
Cope, John IV, 658
Cope, John IV, 1129
Cope, John VI, 379
Cope, John A. IV, 902
Cope, John A. IV, 918
Cope, John A. IV, 942
Cope, John Cousins IV, 27
Cope, John Cousins IV, 124
Cope, John Cozens IV, 27
Cope, John D. IV, 616
Cope, John D. IV, 617
Cope, John D. IV, 618
Cope, John Dixon IV, 616
Cope, John F. IV, 124
Cope, John F. IV, 617
Cope, John F. IV, 866
Cope, John F. IV, 942
Cope, John F. IV, 1091
Cope, John Henry IV, 942
Cope, John Negus IV, 124
Cope, John P. IV, 519
Cope, John Raley IV, 27
Cope, John S. IV, 190
Cope, John S. IV, 191
Cope, John Smith IV, 123
Cope, John, Jr. IV, 81
Cope, Jonathan II, 946
Cope, Jonathan II, 948
Cope, Jos. H. IV, 468
Cope, Joseph IV, 26
Cope, Joseph IV, 27
Cope, Joseph IV, 81
Cope, Joseph IV, 83
Cope, Joseph IV, 85
Cope, Joseph IV, 123
Cope, Joseph IV, 124
Cope, Joseph IV, 126
Cope, Joseph IV, 130
Cope, Joseph IV, 132
Cope, Joseph IV, 190
Cope, Joseph IV, 191
Cope, Joseph IV, 468
Cope, Joseph IV, 616
Cope, Joseph IV, 617
Cope, Joseph IV, 634
Cope, Joseph IV, 637
Cope, Joseph IV, 693
Cope, Joseph IV, 807
Cope, Joseph IV, 866
Cope, Joseph IV, 873
Cope, Joseph VI, 379
Cope, Joseph Cope IV, 617
Cope, Joseph H. IV, 124
Cope, Joseph H. IV, 142
Cope, Joseph H. IV, 154
Cope, Joseph H. IV, 191
Cope, Joseph H. IV, 468
Cope, Joseph Shreve IV, 124
Cope, Joseph W. IV, 618
Cope, Joseph W. IV, 942
Cope, Joseph Warren IV, 616
Cope, Joseph, Jr. IV, 616
Cope, Joshua IV, 32
Cope, Joshua IV, 69
Cope, Joshua IV, 81
Cope, Joshua IV, 85
Cope, Joshua IV, 121
Cope, Joshua IV, 122
Cope, Joshua IV, 123
Cope, Joshua IV, 124
Cope, Joshua IV, 126
Cope, Joshua IV, 135
Cope, Joshua IV, 136
Cope, Joshua IV, 142
Cope, Joshua IV, 191
Cope, Joshua IV, 693
Cope, Joshua IV, 817
Cope, Joshua IV, 978
Cope, Joshua VI, 379
Cope, Joshua VI, 380
Cope, Joshua Alban II, 702
Cope, Joshua Alban II, 734
Cope, Joshua S. II, 948
Cope, Joshua S. II, 1085
Cope, Joshua S. II, 1087
Cope, Joshua S. II, 1089
Cope, Judith IV, 81
Cope, Judith IV, 123
Cope, Judith IV, 131
Cope, Judith IV, 132
Cope, Juli Ann IV, 161
Cope, Julia IV, 142
Cope, Julia IV, 158
Cope, Julia Ann IV, 158
Cope, Julia Ann IV, 191
Cope, Julia Ann IV, 571
Cope, Julia Ann IV, 597
Cope, Juliann IV, 142
Cope, Juliann IV, 203
Cope, June IV, 468
Cope, June IV, 469
Cope, Laycurgas IV, 693
Cope, Leedom Sharp IV, 807
Cope, Lemuel IV, 190
Cope, Lester IV, 807
Cope, Lester IV, 808
Cope, Lewis IV, 81
Cope, Lewis IV, 123
Cope, Lewis J. IV, 468
Cope, Licurgus IV, 694
Cope, Lindley IV, 190
Cope, Lindley IV, 468
Cope, Lindley M. IV, 191
Cope, Lizza S. IV, 190
Cope, Lizzie S. IV, 169
Cope, Lizzie S. IV, 191
Cope, Lois IV, 469
Cope, Lois IV, 808
Cope, Lois M. IV, 1249
Cope, Louis IV, 124
Cope, Louis IV, 125
Cope, Louis IV, 635
Cope, Louis IV, 667
Cope, Louis IV, 692
Cope, Louis IV, 693
Cope, Louis IV, 707
Cope, Louis IV, 713
Cope, Louis IV, 731
Cope, Louis M. IV, 1249
Cope, Louis P. IV, 135
Cope, Louis T. IV, 468
Cope, Louis, Jr. IV, 135
Cope, Louisa L. IV, 617
Cope, Louisa L. IV, 627
Cope, Louiza IV, 616
Cope, Lucina IV, 616
Cope, Lucina IV, 866
Cope, Lucinda IV, 81
Cope, Lucinda IV, 124
Cope, Lucinda IV, 135
Cope, Lucinda IV, 618
Cope, Lucinda IV, 693
Cope, Lucinda IV, 694
Cope, Lucinda IV, 923
Cope, Lucinda IV, 942
Cope, Lucy B. IV, 468
Cope, Lulu IV, 468
Cope, Lycurgas IV, 616
Cope, Lycurgas IV, 617
Cope, Lycurgas IV, 618
Cope, Lycurgus IV, 694
Cope, Lycurgus IV, 866
Cope, Lycurgus IV, 1205
Cope, Lydia II, 349
Cope, Lydia IV, 81
Cope, Lydia IV, 123
Cope, Lydia IV, 126
Cope, Lydia IV, 616
Cope, Lydia IV, 693
Cope, Lydia IV, 712
Cope, Lydia IV, 866
Cope, Lydia IV, 877
Cope, Lydia IV, 942
Cope, M. A. IV, 468
Cope, Maey II, 777
Cope, Malinda IV, 609
Cope, Malinda A. IV, 617
Cope, Malinda E. IV, 617
Cope, Malinda E. IV, 618
Cope, Malinda E. IV, 693
Cope, Malinda E. IV, 694
Cope, Malinda P. IV, 652
Cope, Margaret II, 349
Cope, Margaret II, 494
Cope, Margaret II, 733
Cope, Margaret II, 734
Cope, Margaret IV, 26
Cope, Margaret IV, 81
Cope, Margaret IV, 84
Cope, Margaret IV, 124
Cope, Margaret IV, 135
Cope, Margaret IV, 191
Cope, Margaret IV, 325
Cope, Margaret IV, 519
Cope, Margaret IV, 560
Cope, Margaret IV, 562
Cope, Margaret IV, 616
Cope, Margaret IV, 617
Cope, Margaret IV, 618
Cope, Margaret IV, 622
Cope, Margaret IV, 659
Cope, Margaret IV, 942
Cope, Margaret IV, 950
Cope, Margaret IV, 951
Cope, Margaret Ann IV, 845
Cope, Margaret C. II, 702
Cope, Maria IV, 519
Cope, Maria IV, 557
Cope, Maria IV, 558
Cope, Maria IV, 618
Cope, Maria IV, 666
Cope, Maria Elma IV, 616
Cope, Maria Elma IV, 618
Cope, Maria Elma IV, 658
Cope, Mariah Elma IV, 693
Cope, Mariah Elma IV, 866
Cope, Marietta IV, 190
Cope, Marietta IV, 211
Cope, Marietta IV, 280
Cope, Marietta IV, 469
Cope, Marietta IV, 942
Cope, Marietta S. IV, 191
Cope, Marietta V. IV, 1249
Cope, Marmaduke C. II, 349
Cope, Marmaduke C. II, 702
Cope, Martha IV, 81
Cope, Martha IV, 122
Cope, Martha IV, 123
Cope, Martha IV, 124
Cope, Martha IV, 190
Cope, Martha IV, 191
Cope, Martha IV, 289
Cope, Martha IV, 468
Cope, Martha IV, 505
Cope, Martha IV, 516
Cope, Martha IV, 519
Cope, Martha IV, 693
Cope, Martha IV, 707
Cope, Martha Ann IV, 190
Cope, Martha C. IV, 694
Cope, Martha C. IV, 707
Cope, Martha J. IV, 468
Cope, Martha K. II, 1087
Cope, Martha M. IV, 468
Cope, Martha V. IV, 121
Cope, Martha V. IV, 124
Cope, Martha V. IV, 177
Cope, Martha V. IV, 191
Cope, Martha W. IV, 468
Cope, Mary II, 349
Cope, Mary II, 494
Cope, Mary II, 509
Cope, Mary II, 702
Cope, Mary II, 704
Cope, Mary II, 734
Cope, Mary II, 772
Cope, Mary II, 959
Cope, Mary IV, 26
Cope, Mary IV, 69
Cope, Mary IV, 71
Cope, Mary IV, 81
Cope, Mary IV, 106
Cope, Mary IV, 123
Cope, Mary IV, 124
Cope, Mary IV, 129
Cope, Mary IV, 142
Cope, Mary IV, 163
Cope, Mary IV, 190
Cope, Mary IV, 191
Cope, Mary IV, 302
Cope, Mary IV, 311
Cope, Mary IV, 313
Cope, Mary IV, 325
Cope, Mary IV, 519
Cope, Mary IV, 612
Cope, Mary IV, 616
Cope, Mary IV, 617
Cope, Mary IV, 618
Cope, Mary IV, 659
Cope, Mary IV, 693
Cope, Mary IV, 694
Cope, Mary IV, 866
Cope, Mary IV, 879
Cope, Mary VI, 379
Cope, Mary VI, 380
Cope, Mary A. IV, 469
Cope, Mary A. IV, 934
Cope, Mary Ann II, 349
Cope, Mary Ann II, 494
Cope, Mary Ann II, 713
Cope, Mary Ann II, 734
Cope, Mary Ann IV, 27
Cope, Mary Ann IV, 40
Cope, Mary Ann IV, 81
Cope, Mary Ann IV, 123
Cope, Mary Ann IV, 124
Cope, Mary Ann IV, 135
Cope, Mary Ann IV, 468
Cope, Mary Ann IV, 614
Cope, Mary Ann IV, 617
Cope, Mary Ann IV, 693
Cope, Mary Ann IV, 1025
Cope, Mary C. IV, 618
Cope, Mary C. IV, 654
Cope, Mary E. IV, 191
Cope, Mary E. IV, 468
Cope, Mary E. IV, 641
Cope, Mary E. IV, 678
Cope, Mary E. IV, 693
Cope, Mary E. IV, 800
Cope, Mary E. IV, 831
Cope, Mary Elizabeth IV, 616
Cope, Mary Elizabeth IV, 618
Cope, Mary Elizabeth IV, 651
Cope, Mary Ella IV, 380
Cope, Mary Ella IV, 519
Cope, Mary Ellen IV, 380
Cope, Mary Ellen IV, 693
Cope, Mary Etta V. IV, 468
Cope, Mary H. IV, 27
Cope, Mary H. IV, 617
Cope, Mary Isabel IV, 190
Cope, Mary Isabella IV, 191
Cope, Mary J. IV, 380
Cope, Mary J. IV, 519
Cope, Mary J. IV, 552
Cope, Mary Jane IV, 380
Cope, Mary M. IV, 135
Cope, Mary M. IV, 380
Cope, Mary M. IV, 449
Cope, Mary M. IV, 693
Cope, Mary M. IV, 780
Cope, Mary Marsh IV, 617
Cope, Mary Marsh IV, 866
Cope, Mary N. IV, 616
Cope, Mary N. IV, 634
Cope, Mary S. II, 948
Cope, Mary S. II, 1087
Cope, Mary V. IV, 866
Cope, Mary V. IV, 873
Cope, Maryann IV, 124
Cope, Matilda Ann IV, 693
Cope, Mattie IV, 468
Cope, Mattie M. IV, 468
Cope, Melinda IV, 616
Cope, Melissa IV, 81
Cope, Melissa IV, 124
Cope, Melissa IV, 618
Cope, Melissa IV, 628
Cope, Melissa IV, 693
Cope, Melissa IV, 715
Cope, Melisse IV, 135
Cope, Mercey IV, 693
Cope, Mercy IV, 81
Cope, Mercy IV, 121
Cope, Mercy IV, 123
Cope, Mercy IV, 124
Cope, Mercy IV, 134
Cope, Mercy IV, 667
Cope, Mercy IV, 693
Cope, Mercy IV, 942
Cope, Moses IV, 142
Cope, Nathan IV, 142
Cope, Nathan IV, 519
Cope, Nathan IV, 616
Cope, Nathan IV, 617
Cope, Nathan IV, 693
Cope, Nathan IV, 866
Cope, Nathan IV, 873
Cope, Nathan VI, 594
Cope, Oliver II, 349
Cope, Oliver II, 494
Cope, Oliver IV, 27
Cope, Oliver IV, 123
Cope, Oliver IV, 124
Cope, Oliver IV, 190
Cope, Oliver IV, 616
Cope, Oliver IV, 618
Cope, Oliver IV, 693
Cope, Oliver IV, 709
Cope, Oliver IV, 807
Cope, Oliver IV, 866
Cope, Oliver E. IV, 693
Cope, Oliver P. IV, 190
Cope, Oliver P. IV, 191
Cope, Oliver W. II, 948
Cope, Oliver Wilson II, 702
Cope, Opkia IV, 190
Cope, Otis M. III, 85
Cope, Otis M. III, 298
Cope, Owen Stratton IV, 617
Cope, Paul S. IV, 694
Cope, Pearson IV, 190
Cope, Pearson L. IV, 191
Cope, Perkins IV, 123
Cope, Peter II, 349
Cope, Phebe IV, 142
Cope, Phebe IV, 157
Cope, Phebe IV, 191
Cope, Phebe IV, 401
Cope, Phebe IV, 608
Cope, Phebe IV, 616
Cope, Phebe IV, 618
Cope, Phebe IV, 693
Cope, Phebe IV, 715
Cope, Phebe IV, 800
Cope, Phebe IV, 866
Cope, Phebe IV, 873
Cope, Phebe A. II, 946
Cope, Phebe Y. IV, 617
Cope, Phebe Y. IV, 639
Cope, Phebe Y. IV, 678
Cope, Phebe Y. IV, 693
Cope, Phebe Y. IV, 730
Cope, Phebe Y. IV, 797
Cope, Phebe Y. IV, 807
Cope, Price IV, 694
Cope, Priscilla IV, 124
Cope, Priscilla IV, 693
Cope, Priscilla IV, 713
Cope, Priscilla C. IV, 694
Cope, Priscilla C. IV, 713
Cope, R. M. IV, 468
Cope, Rachel II, 738
Cope, Rachel II, 739
Cope, Rachel IV, 81
Cope, Rachel IV, 123
Cope, Rachel IV, 124
Cope, Rachel IV, 135
Cope, Rachel IV, 142
Cope, Rachel IV, 190
Cope, Rachel IV, 191
Cope, Rachel IV, 242
Cope, Rachel IV, 325
Cope, Rachel IV, 412
Cope, Rachel IV, 519
Cope, Rachel IV, 544
Cope, Rachel IV, 608
Cope, Rachel IV, 614
Cope, Rachel IV, 616
Cope, Rachel IV, 617
Cope, Rachel IV, 618
Cope, Rachel IV, 623

Cope, Rachel IV, 637
Cope, Rachel IV, 652
Cope, Rachel IV, 807
Cope, Rachel IV, 813
Cope, Rachel IV, 902
Cope, Rachel IV, 934
Cope, Rachel IV, 942
Cope, Rachel E. IV, 190
Cope, Rachel E. IV, 807
Cope, Rachel E. IV, 819
Cope, Rachel Elizabeth IV, 845
Cope, Rachel G. IV, 807
Cope, Rachel G. IV, 809
Cope, Rachel G. IV, 845
Cope, Rachel H. IV, 616
Cope, Rachel P. II, 730
Cope, Rachel P. II, 734
Cope, Rachel Tacy IV, 617
Cope, Rachel Tacy IV, 618
Cope, Rachel Tacy IV, 693
Cope, Rachel Tacy IV, 694
Cope, Rachel Tacy IV, 744
Cope, Rachel W. IV, 81
Cope, Rachel W. IV, 123
Cope, Rachel W. IV, 124
Cope, Rachel W. IV, 125
Cope, Rachel W. IV, 132
Cope, Rachel W. IV, 135
Cope, Rachel W. IV, 618
Cope, Raily IV, 123
Cope, Reason IV, 616
Cope, Rebecca II, 349
Cope, Rebecca II, 494
Cope, Rebecca II, 820
Cope, Rebecca IV, 81
Cope, Rebecca IV, 124
Cope, Rebecca IV, 142
Cope, Rebecca IV, 154
Cope, Rebecca IV, 190
Cope, Rebecca IV, 191
Cope, Rebecca IV, 468
Cope, Rebecca IV, 611
Cope, Rebecca IV, 616
Cope, Rebecca IV, 617
Cope, Rebecca IV, 658
Cope, Rebecca IV, 679
Cope, Rebecca IV, 863
Cope, Rebecca IV, 866
Cope, Rebecca IV, 899
Cope, Rebecca M. IV, 121
Cope, Rebecca M. IV, 123
Cope, Rebecca M. IV, 468
Cope, Reno Jane IV, 608
Cope, Robert IV, 617
Cope, Robert J. IV, 124
Cope, Robert J. IV, 135
Cope, Robert J. IV, 618
Cope, Robert J. IV, 942
Cope, Robert Jr IV, 617
Cope, Ruth IV, 26
Cope, Ruth IV, 27
Cope, Ruth IV, 44
Cope, Ruth IV, 64
Cope, Ruth IV, 81
Cope, Ruth IV, 123
Cope, Ruth IV, 124
Cope, Ruth IV, 125
Cope, Ruth IV, 126
Cope, Ruth IV, 134
Cope, Ruth IV, 190
Cope, Ruth IV, 191
Cope, Ruth IV, 610
Cope, Ruth IV, 616
Cope, Ruth IV, 617
Cope, Ruth IV, 866
Cope, Ruth IV, 1052
Cope, Ruth IV, 1082
Cope, Ruth Ann IV, 190
Cope, Ruth Griffith IV, 190
Cope, Ruthanna IV, 191
Cope, Ruthanna IV, 273
Cope, S. J. IV, 1311
Cope, Sallie C. II, 948
Cope, Sallie C. II, 949
Cope, Samuel IV, 26
Cope, Samuel IV, 81
Cope, Samuel IV, 121
Cope, Samuel IV, 123
Cope, Samuel IV, 124
Cope, Samuel IV, 126
Cope, Samuel IV, 142
Cope, Samuel IV, 190
Cope, Samuel IV, 468
Cope, Samuel IV, 505
Cope, Samuel IV, 616
Cope, Samuel IV, 617
Cope, Samuel IV, 667
Cope, Samuel IV, 712
Cope, Samuel IV, 866
Cope, Samuel VI, 379
Cope, Samuel D. IV, 617
Cope, Samuel Franklin IV, 618
Cope, Samuel Neill IV, 866
Cope, Samuel W. IV, 135
Cope, Samuel W. IV, 693
Cope, Samuel, Jr. IV, 123
Cope, Samuel, Jr. IV, 134
Cope, Samuel, Jr. IV, 693
Cope, Sara Mildred IV, 1004
Cope, Sarah II, 349
Cope, Sarah II, 702
Cope, Sarah IV, 26
Cope, Sarah IV, 27
Cope, Sarah IV, 34
Cope, Sarah IV, 55
Cope, Sarah IV, 59
Cope, Sarah IV, 81
Cope, Sarah IV, 106
Cope, Sarah IV, 121
Cope, Sarah IV, 123
Cope, Sarah IV, 124
Cope, Sarah IV, 126
Cope, Sarah IV, 131
Cope, Sarah IV, 132
Cope, Sarah IV, 134
Cope, Sarah IV, 142
Cope, Sarah IV, 190
Cope, Sarah IV, 191
Cope, Sarah IV, 311
Cope, Sarah IV, 468
Cope, Sarah IV, 616
Cope, Sarah IV, 693
Cope, Sarah IV, 712
Cope, Sarah IV, 715
Cope, Sarah IV, 807
Cope, Sarah IV, 813
Cope, Sarah IV, 866
Cope, Sarah IV, 942
Cope, Sarah IV, 989
Cope, Sarah VI, 379
Cope, Sarah VI, 448
Cope, Sarah A. IV, 942
Cope, Sarah Ann IV, 81
Cope, Sarah Ann IV, 122
Cope, Sarah Ann IV, 123
Cope, Sarah Ann IV, 124
Cope, Sarah Ann IV, 132
Cope, Sarah Ann IV, 135
Cope, Sarah Ann IV, 183
Cope, Sarah Ann IV, 190
Cope, Sarah Ann IV, 191
Cope, Sarah Ann IV, 210
Cope, Sarah Ann IV, 311
Cope, Sarah Ann IV, 312
Cope, Sarah Ann IV, 616
Cope, Sarah Ann IV, 618
Cope, Sarah Ann IV, 687
Cope, Sarah Ann IV, 693
Cope, Sarah Ann IV, 694
Cope, Sarah Ann IV, 780
Cope, Sarah B. II, 494
Cope, Sarah B. II, 702
Cope, Sarah C. IV, 191
Cope, Sarah Emily IV, 616
Cope, Sarah Emily IV, 866
Cope, Sarah Emma IV, 616
Cope, Sarah Emma IV, 618
Cope, Sarah G. IV, 27
Cope, Sarah Jane IV, 27
Cope, Sarah Jane IV, 46
Cope, Sarah Jane IV, 123
Cope, Sarah Jane IV, 124
Cope, Sarah L. IV, 124
Cope, Sarah M. III, 85
Cope, Sarah M. III, 298
Cope, Sarah M. IV, 807
Cope, Sarah M. IV, 808
Cope, Sarah R. IV, 124
Cope, Sarah R. IV, 130
Cope, Sarah R. IV, 571
Cope, Sarah R. IV, 589
Cope, Sarah Raley IV, 124
Cope, Sarah S. IV, 27
Cope, Sarah S. IV, 44
Cope, Sarah S. IV, 124
Cope, Sarah T. IV, 190
Cope, Sarah W. II, 734
Cope, Sarah W. IV, 304
Cope, Seward Burton IV, 807
Cope, Sherman B. IV, 694
Cope, Simon IV, 81
Cope, Simon IV, 616
Cope, Simon IV, 617
Cope, Simon IV, 693
Cope, Sophia IV, 191
Cope, Sophia IV, 325
Cope, Sophia IV, 519
Cope, Sophia IV, 544
Cope, Stanley IV, 1154
Cope, Stanley IV, 1311
Cope, Susan IV, 617
Cope, Susan L. II, 702
Cope, Susan L. II, 1049
Cope, Susanah D. IV, 694
Cope, Susanna II, 349
Cope, Susanna IV, 866
Cope, Susannah IV, 142
Cope, Susannah IV, 616
Cope, Susannah IV, 617
Cope, Susannah IV, 915
Cope, Susannah H. IV, 606
Cope, Susannah H. IV, 616
Cope, T. W. IV, 468
Cope, Thomas II, 349
Cope, Thomas IV, 519
Cope, Thomas IV, 557
Cope, Thomas C. IV, 135
Cope, Thomas C. IV, 380
Cope, Thomas C. IV, 519
Cope, Thomas C. IV, 552
Cope, Thomas C. IV, 618
Cope, Thomas C. IV, 666
Cope, Thomas Clarkson IV, 124
Cope, Thomas P. II, 349
Cope, Thomas P. II, 494
Cope, Thomas P. II, 702
Cope, Thomas P. II, 734
Cope, Thomas P. II, 772
Cope, Thomas P. II, 777
Cope, Thomas Pim II, 494
Cope, Thomas Pim II, 509
Cope, Thomas W. IV, 468
Cope, Thomas White IV, 191
Cope, Thos. IV, 124
Cope, Thos. IV, 468
Cope, Thos. C. IV, 558
Cope, Uriah IV, 27
Cope, Uriah IV, 124
Cope, W. D. II, 702
Cope, Walter C. IV, 519
Cope, Walter T. IV, 468
Cope, Wiletts IV, 190
Cope, Willets IV, 123
Cope, Willets IV, 124
Cope, Willets IV, 191
Cope, Willets IV, 468
Cope, Willett IV, 468
Cope, William IV, 124
Cope, William IV, 190
Cope, William IV, 191
Cope, William IV, 618
Cope, William Albert IV, 190
Cope, William Albert IV, 191
Cope, William D. II, 702
Cope, William G. IV, 694
Cope, William J. IV, 845
Cope, William L. IV, 618
Cope, William L. IV, 651
Cope, William L. IV, 694
Cope, William L. IV, 744
Cope, William Loren IV, 694
Cope, William Lorin IV, 618
Cope, William M. IV, 190
Cope, William M. IV, 191
Cope, William M. IV, 468
Cope, Willis IV, 81
Cope, Willis IV, 124
Cope, Willits IV, 468
Cope, Willits IV, 505
Cope, Wilmer II, 948
Cope, Wm. II, 494
Cope, Wm. II, 1049
Cope, Wm. IV, 124
Cope, Wm. IV, 135
Cope, Wm. IV, 616
Cope, Wm. IV, 617
Cope, Wm. B. IV, 693
Cope, Wm. D. II, 702
Cope, Wm. D. II, 734
Cope, Wm. David IV, 617
Cope, Wm. L. IV, 617
Cope, Wm. Logan IV, 617
Cope, Wm. Logan IV, 693
Cope, Wm. Logan, Jr. IV, 693
Cope, Wm. Loren IV, 617
Cope, Wood IV, 468
Cope, Zillah M. II, 948
Cope, Zillah M. II, 949
Copehart, Ira IV, 694
Copeland, ??? I, 7
Copeland, ??? I, 16
Copeland, ??? I, 279
Copeland, ??? III, 85
Copeland, ??? VI, 24
Copeland, ??? VI, 39
Copeland, ??? VI, 48
Copeland, A. Rebecca I, 235
Copeland, A. Rebecca I, 239
Copeland, Abigail I, 6
Copeland, Achsah I, 229
Copeland, Achsah I, 233
Copeland, Ada M. III, 373
Copeland, Adelia V, 454
Copeland, Albert V, 900
Copeland, Albert L. V, 900
Copeland, Albert Luther V, 900
Copeland, Alexander I, 210
Copeland, Alfred I, 210
Copeland, Alfred E. I, 44
Copeland, Alfred E. I, 59
Copeland, Alfred E. I, 235
Copeland, Alfred Elwood I, 210
Copeland, Alfred Elwood I, 211
Copeland, Alice I, 44
Copeland, Alice I, 59
Copeland, Alice I, 214
Copeland, Alice V, 900
Copeland, Alice VI, 57
Copeland, Alice VI, 59
Copeland, Alice H. V, 900
Copeland, Alice V. I, 211
Copeland, Alvin L. I, 210
Copeland, Ambrose III, 373
Copeland, Ammalisia I, 235
Copeland, Amy Rebecca I, 212
Copeland, Amy Rebecca I, 214
Copeland, Angelina I, 234
Copeland, Angeline I, 44
Copeland, Angeline I, 210
Copeland, Angeline I, 211
Copeland, Angeline I, 214
Copeland, Angeline I, 227
Copeland, Angeline I, 235
Copeland, Angeline I, 240
Copeland, Angie I, 207
Copeland, Ann I, 5
Copeland, Ann I, 206
Copeland, Ann I, 208
Copeland, Ann I, 210
Copeland, Ann I, 212
Copeland, Ann I, 233
Copeland, Ann I, 234
Copeland, Ann I, 235
Copeland, Ann I, 248
Copeland, Ann II, 494
Copeland, Ann III, 150
Copeland, Ann III, 373
Copeland, Ann IV, 27
Copeland, Ann IV, 28
Copeland, Ann IV, 191
Copeland, Ann IV, 380
Copeland, Ann IV, 571
Copeland, Ann VI, 59
Copeland, Ann Eliza IV, 50
Copeland, Anna I, 233
Copeland, Anna E. I, 235
Copeland, Anna E. I, 236
Copeland, Anna E. I, 239
Copeland, Anna Ethell I, 212
Copeland, Anne I, 43
Copeland, Anne I, 73
Copeland, Annie III, 405
Copeland, Annie Jane I, 210
Copeland, Annie Melissa I, 212
Copeland, Aron I, 235
Copeland, Arretta J. I, 44
Copeland, Arthur F. I, 236
Copeland, Asenath I, 44
Copeland, Asenath H. I, 6
Copeland, Asenath H. I, 44
Copeland, Axcy I, 210
Copeland, Benj. T. I, 210
Copeland, Benj. T. I, 211
Copeland, Benja. T. I, 210
Copeland, Benjamin I, 43
Copeland, Benjamin I, 210
Copeland, Benjamin I, 211
Copeland, Benjamin I, 231
Copeland, Benjamin I, 233
Copeland, Benjamin I, 234
Copeland, Benjamin I, 240
Copeland, Benjamin I, 251
Copeland, Benjamin I, 876
Copeland, Benjamin VI, 59
Copeland, Benjamin VI, 133
Copeland, Benjamin D. I, 7
Copeland, Benjamin D. I, 43
Copeland, Benjamin F. I, 234
Copeland, Benjamin F. I, 235
Copeland, Benjamin F. I, 236
Copeland, Benjamin Franklin I, 210
Copeland, Benjamin Jordan VI, 59
Copeland, Benjamin Porter I, 210
Copeland, Benjamin T. I, 210
Copeland, Benjamin T. I, 211
Copeland, Benjamin T. I, 235
Copeland, Benjamin T. I, 239
Copeland, Benjamin T. I, 258
Copeland, Benjamine T. I, 211
Copeland, Bertha Gertrude I, 212
Copeland, Bertha M. I, 212
Copeland, Betcy I, 233
Copeland, Betsey I, 6
Copeland, Betsey I, 210
Copeland, Betsey I, 233
Copeland, Betsey Ann I, 6
Copeland, Betsy I, 8
Copeland, Betsy Ann I, 6
Copeland, Betsy Ann I, 43
Copeland, Bonsel IV, 191
Copeland, Bonsel IV, 571
Copeland, Caleb I, 44
Copeland, Caleb II, 494
Copeland, Caleb Francis I, 7
Copeland, Carrie H. I, 7
Copeland, Catharin I, 208
Copeland, Catharine I, 43
Copeland, Catharine I, 88
Copeland, Catharine I, 231
Copeland, Catharine I, 235
Copeland, Catharine F. I, 211
Copeland, Catherine I, 7
Copeland, Catherine I, 26
Copeland, Charity I, 43
Copeland, Charity I, 87
Copeland, Charles I, 43
Copeland, Charles I, 44
Copeland, Charles D. I, 8
Copeland, Charles F. I, 302
Copeland, Charles Fox I, 210
Copeland, Charles Fox I, 283
Copeland, Charles R. I, 59
Copeland, Charles T. I, 212
Copeland, Christian I, 210
Copeland, Clementina I, 210
Copeland, Clementina I, 235
Copeland, Cora B. I, 235
Copeland, Cora E. I, 235
Copeland, Cora Emma I, 211
Copeland, Cora Isabella I, 210
Copeland, Cordie V, 454
Copeland, Cornelia I, 44
Copeland, Cornelius I, 235
Copeland, Cornelius A. I, 210
Copeland, Cornelius A. I, 211
Copeland, Cornelius A. I, 235
Copeland, Cowperthwaite III, 373
Copeland, Cynthia I, 984
Copeland, Cynthia I, 997
Copeland, Daniel L. I, 44
Copeland, Daniel Loring I, 8
Copeland, David I, 44
Copeland, David I, 210
Copeland, David I, 212
Copeland, David I, 231
Copeland, David I, 233
Copeland, David I, 234
Copeland, David I, 235
Copeland, David II, 210
Copeland, David IV, 380
Copeland, David IV, 571
Copeland, David V, 900
Copeland, David J. V, 900
Copeland, David Josiah III, 373
Copeland, David Josiah V, 900
Copeland, David Lindley I, 7
Copeland, Deborah III, 373
Copeland, Delfira I, 212
Copeland, Delia V, 454
Copeland, Delphina M. I, 6
Copeland, Delphina M. I, 44
Copeland, Delphina M. I, 54
Copeland, Dempsey I, 6
Copeland, Dempsey I, 43
Copeland, Dempsey I, 76
Copeland, Dempsey I, 233
Copeland, Dempsey L. I, 5
Copeland, Dempsey L. I, 6
Copeland, Dempsey L. I, 44
Copeland, Dempsey L. I, 54
Copeland, Dempsey, Jr. I, 44
Copeland, Demsey I, 6
Copeland, Demsey I, 8
Copeland, Demsey I, 43
Copeland, Demsey I, 210
Copeland, Demsey L. I, 6
Copeland, Demsy I, 233
Copeland, Demsy I, 234
Copeland, Demsy I, 244
Copeland, Doratha I, 191
Copeland, Doratha I, 199
Copeland, Dorotha I, 191
Copeland, Dorotha I, 234
Copeland, Dorothy I, 43
Copeland, Dorothy I, 211
Copeland, Dorothy I, 234
Copeland, Dorothy I, 235
Copeland, Dorothy I, 283
Copeland, Dorothy I, 302
Copeland, Dorothy I, 928
Copeland, Dorothy I, 984
Copeland, Dorothy Delphina I, 21

eland, Dorothy J. I, 235
eland, Dorothy J. I, 249
eland, Dorothy Jane I, 212
eland, Dorthea I, 234
eland, E. G. I, 302
eland, Edith I, 235
eland, Edith Hubbard I, 235
eland, Edmon I, 210
eland, Edmon P. I, 212
eland, Edmond P. I, 210
eland, Edmund I, 234
eland, Edmund P. I, 235
eland, Edwin I, 43
eland, Edwin G. I, 210
eland, Edwin G. I, 234
eland, Edwin G. I, 283
eland, Edwin G. I, 302
eland, Edwin G. I, 315
eland, Edwin G. I, 984
eland, Edwin G. I, 990
eland, Edwin Griffith I, 234
eland, Edwin Hadley I, 283
eland, Eleanor D. I, 7
eland, Eli I, 210
eland, Eli I, 211
eland, Eli I, 212
eland, Eli I, 221
eland, Eli I, 222
eland, Eli I, 233
eland, Eli I, 234
eland, Eli I, 235
eland, Eli I, 249
eland, Eli I, 259
eland, Eli I, 876
eland, Eli I, 888
eland, Eli C. I, 208
eland, Eli C. I, 211
eland, Eli C. I, 234
eland, Eli C. I, 235
eland, Eli Macy I, 211
eland, Eli P. I, 235
eland, Elihu I, 6
eland, Elihu I, 7
eland, Elihu I, 43
eland, Elihu I, 44
eland, Elihu I, 212
eland, Elihu I, 235
eland, Elisabeth I, 5
eland, Elisabeth I, 7
eland, Elisabeth I, 8
eland, Elisabeth I, 40
eland, Elisabeth I, 43
eland, Elisabeth I, 44
eland, Elisabeth I, 57
eland, Elisabeth I, 64
eland, Elisabeth I, 85
eland, Elisabeth I, 191
eland, Elisabeth I, 198
eland, Elisabeth I, 234
eland, Elisabeth A. I, 7
eland, Elisabeth Ann I, 6
eland, Elisabeth Ann I, 41
eland, Elisabeth Ann I, 44
eland, Elisabeth G. I, 8
eland, Elisabeth H. I, 235
eland, Elisabeth H. I, 257
eland, Elisabeth J. I, 7
eland, Elisabeth Louvina I, 7
eland, Elisha I, 7
eland, Elisha I, 8
eland, Elisha I, 26
eland, Elisha I, 43
eland, Elisha I, 88
eland, Elisha I, 233
eland, Elisha I, 234
eland, Elisha VI, 48
eland, Elisha VI, 59
eland, Elisha N. I, 235
eland, Elisha W. I, 7
eland, Eliza III, 182
eland, Eliza III, 245
eland, Eliza IV, 469
eland, Eliza Ann I, 211
eland, Eliza Isabella I, 212
eland, Eliza Jane I, 211
eland, Elizabeth I, 7
eland, Elizabeth I, 210
eland, Elizabeth I, 211
eland, Elizabeth I, 234
eland, Elizabeth I, 235
eland, Elizabeth I, 241
eland, Elizabeth I, 927
eland, Elizabeth VI, 59
eland, Elizabeth VI, 60
eland, Elizabeth VI, 66
eland, Elizabeth VI, 86
eland, Elizabeth Anne II, 705
eland, Elizabeth C. I, 928
eland, Elizabeth H. I, 227
eland, Elizabeth Harriett
I, 211
Copeland, Ella G. I, 211
Copeland, Ella G. I, 217
Copeland, Ella G. I, 235
Copeland, Ella G. I, 242
Copeland, Ellanora D. I, 212
Copeland, Ellen I, 210
Copeland, Ellen I, 235
Copeland, Ellen Frances I, 44
Copeland, Ellen Wrenshall I, 283
Copeland, Elnore D. I, 44
Copeland, Elton G. I, 210
Copeland, Elwood I, 212
Copeland, Elwood I, 234
Copeland, Ely I, 233
Copeland, Ely I, 258
Copeland, Emily I, 44
Copeland, Emily I, 59
Copeland, Emily I, 210
Copeland, Emily L. I, 210
Copeland, Emily L. I, 235
Copeland, Emily S. I, 44
Copeland, Emily S. I, 59
Copeland, Emma I, 235
Copeland, Ernest H. I, 210
Copeland, Ernest H. I, 235
Copeland, Ernest H. I, 236
Copeland, Essie I, 235
Copeland, Ester I, 211
Copeland, Esther I, 6
Copeland, Esther I, 7
Copeland, Esther I, 8
Copeland, Esther I, 43
Copeland, Esther I, 44
Copeland, Esther I, 51
Copeland, Esther I, 87
Copeland, Esther Ann I, 6
Copeland, Esther Ann I, 44
Copeland, Esther Ann I, 89
Copeland, Esther J. I, 208
Copeland, Esther J. I, 211
Copeland, Esther P. I, 7
Copeland, Esther P. I, 43
Copeland, Esther P. I, 234
Copeland, Ethel M. I, 236
Copeland, Ethel Marie I, 211
Copeland, Eva Elma I, 212
Copeland, Exum I, 212
Copeland, Exum VI, 71
Copeland, F. Rebecca I, 211
Copeland, F. Rebecca I, 236
Copeland, Foster Harvey I, 211
Copeland, Frances I, 235
Copeland, Frances I, 252
Copeland, Frances R. I, 229
Copeland, Frances R. I, 234
Copeland, Frances R. I, 235
Copeland, Frances Rebecca I, 207
Copeland, Frances Rebecca I, 212
Copeland, Francis Eli I, 211
Copeland, Francis Rebecca I, 235
Copeland, Genette I, 235
Copeland, George B. V, 164
Copeland, George W. III, 373
Copeland, Gilbert I, 7
Copeland, Gilbert L. I, 6
Copeland, Gilbert L. I, 44
Copeland, Grace II, 349
Copeland, Grace II, 494
Copeland, Grace B. I, 211
Copeland, Griffith I, 43
Copeland, Gulia I, 44
Copeland, Gulia J. I, 44
Copeland, Gulielma I, 5
Copeland, Gulielma I, 6
Copeland, Gulielma I, 7
Copeland, Gulielma I, 8
Copeland, Gulielma I, 43
Copeland, Gulielma I, 44
Copeland, Gulielma I, 51
Copeland, Gulielma I, 58
Copeland, Gulielma A. I, 7
Copeland, Gulielma J. I, 5
Copeland, Gulielma J. I, 44
Copeland, Gurny I, 235
Copeland, H. Isabella I, 7
Copeland, H. T. I, 235
Copeland, Hannah I, 43
Copeland, Hannah I, 876
Copeland, Hannah I, 888
Copeland, Hannah VI, 7
Copeland, Hannah VI, 33
Copeland, Hannah J. I, 208
Copeland, Hannah J. I, 211
Copeland, Hannah J. I, 234
Copeland, Hannah S. I, 7
Copeland, Harmon Hair VI, 59
Copeland, Harriet Francis I, 210
Copeland, Harriet Isabella I, 7
Copeland, Harriett Ellen I, 6
Copeland, Harriett I. I, 6
Copeland, Hattie E. I, 44
Copeland, Hattie E. I, 75
Copeland, Helen M. III, 373
Copeland, Henodorus I, 7
Copeland, Henry I, 7
Copeland, Henry I, 8
Copeland, Henry I, 43
Copeland, Henry I, 87
Copeland, Henry I, 191
Copeland, Henry I, 198
Copeland, Henry I, 199
Copeland, Henry I, 206
Copeland, Henry I, 211
Copeland, Henry I, 234
Copeland, Henry I, 235
Copeland, Henry I, 283
Copeland, Henry I, 302
Copeland, Henry I, 928
Copeland, Henry I, 984
Copeland, Henry Lazarus I, 283
Copeland, Henry, Jr. I, 43
Copeland, Henry, Sr. I, 211
Copeland, Herbert I, 7
Copeland, Herman I, 7
Copeland, Hollowell I, 233
Copeland, Hugh I, 44
Copeland, Ida Leanora I, 7
Copeland, Isabella I, 16
Copeland, Isabella I, 234
Copeland, Isabella II, 494
Copeland, Isabella II, 683
Copeland, J. Rufus I, 235
Copeland, J. Rufus I, 262
Copeland, J. T. I, 236
Copeland, J. Thomas I, 211
Copeland, J. Thomas I, 235
Copeland, J. U. I, 235
Copeland, Jacob I, 7
Copeland, Jacob I, 8
Copeland, Jacob I, 27
Copeland, Jacob I, 43
Copeland, Jacob I, 74
Copeland, Jacob I, 88
Copeland, James I, 6
Copeland, James I, 7
Copeland, James I, 8
Copeland, James I, 43
Copeland, James I, 73
Copeland, James I, 210
Copeland, James I, 211
Copeland, James IV, 191
Copeland, James IV, 571
Copeland, James VI, 45
Copeland, James VI, 59
Copeland, James VI, 78
Copeland, James B. IV, 571
Copeland, James Bonsall IV, 191
Copeland, James E. I, 212
Copeland, James Elwood I, 212
Copeland, James Elwood I, 235
Copeland, James H. I, 44
Copeland, James H. I, 59
Copeland, James H. I, 234
Copeland, James Henry I, 6
Copeland, James Henry I, 7
Copeland, James Henry I, 43
Copeland, James Henry I, 44
Copeland, James Henry I, 210
Copeland, James Henry I, 211
Copeland, James Thomas I, 44
Copeland, James V. I, 235
Copeland, James W. I, 211
Copeland, James W. I, 217
Copeland, James W. I, 218
Copeland, James W. I, 226
Copeland, James W. I, 234
Copeland, James W. I, 235
Copeland, James W. I, 255
Copeland, James W. I, 534
Copeland, James W. I, 571
Copeland, James Wilfred I, 212
Copeland, James William I, 211
Copeland, James Winslow I, 234
Copeland, James, Jr. VI, 59
Copeland, Jane I, 6
Copeland, Jane I, 7
Copeland, Jane I, 210
Copeland, Jane I, 212
Copeland, Jane I, 231
Copeland, Jane I, 233
Copeland, Jane I, 234
Copeland, Jane IV, 28
Copeland, Jane VI, 279
Copeland, Jane E. I, 208
Copeland, Jane E. I, 214
Copeland, Jane E. I, 232
Copeland, Jane E. I, 235
Copeland, Jane E. I, 239
Copeland, Jane Eliza I, 211
Copeland, Jas. W. I, 235
Copeland, Jeanetta S. I, 212
Copeland, Jemima I, 233
Copeland, Jemimah I, 302
Copeland, Jemimah I, 712
Copeland, Jeptha Thomas I, 212
Copeland, Jesse I, 7
Copeland, Jesse I, 12
Copeland, Jesse I, 35
Copeland, Jesse I, 43
Copeland, Jesse I, 44
Copeland, Jesse I, 64
Copeland, Jesse I, 207
Copeland, Jesse I, 210
Copeland, Jesse I, 211
Copeland, Jesse I, 212
Copeland, Jesse I, 214
Copeland, Jesse I, 227
Copeland, Jesse I, 233
Copeland, Jesse I, 234
Copeland, Jesse I, 235
Copeland, Jesse I, 248
Copeland, Jesse I, 534
Copeland, Jesse VI, 58
Copeland, Jesse VI, 59
Copeland, Jesse VI, 66
Copeland, Jesse VI, 71
Copeland, Jesse B. I, 211
Copeland, Jesse Baum I, 212
Copeland, Jesse Mahlon I, 44
Copeland, Jesse R. I, 7
Copeland, Jesse R. I, 44
Copeland, Jesse T. I, 212
Copeland, Jesse Thomas I, 211
Copeland, Joanna I, 210
Copeland, John I, 8
Copeland, John I, 43
Copeland, John I, 206
Copeland, John I, 211
Copeland, John I, 212
Copeland, John I, 233
Copeland, John I, 234
Copeland, John I, 283
Copeland, John I, 302
Copeland, John I, 316
Copeland, John I, 712
Copeland, John III, 405
Copeland, John IV, 28
Copeland, John IV, 191
Copeland, John IV, 571
Copeland, John VI, 22
Copeland, John VI, 24
Copeland, John VI, 31
Copeland, John VI, 59
Copeland, John VI, 60
Copeland, John Elisha I, 44
Copeland, John Ernest I, 212
Copeland, John G. I, 212
Copeland, John M. IV, 469
Copeland, John O. I, 234
Copeland, John O. I, 235
Copeland, John Oliver I, 210
Copeland, John Porter VI, 59
Copeland, John R. I, 44
Copeland, John R. I, 235
Copeland, John R. I, 249
Copeland, John Randolph I, 211
Copeland, John Rufus I, 7
Copeland, John Rufus I, 211
Copeland, John Ruphus I, 212
Copeland, John, Jr. I, 235
Copeland, Jonathan I, 4
Copeland, Jonathan I, 208
Copeland, Jonathan I, 212
Copeland, Jonathan I, 233
Copeland, Jonathan I, 234
Copeland, Jonathan I, 248
Copeland, Jonathan I, 283
Copeland, Jonathan I, 712
Copeland, Jonathan II, 494
Copeland, Jonathan A. I, 212
Copeland, Jonathan Alexander
I, 212
Copeland, Joseph I, 6
Copeland, Joseph I, 7
Copeland, Joseph I, 8
Copeland, Joseph I, 9
Copeland, Joseph I, 10
Copeland, Joseph I, 40
Copeland, Joseph I, 43
Copeland, Joseph I, 212
Copeland, Joseph I, 234
Copeland, Joseph IV, 191
Copeland, Joseph IV, 571
Copeland, Joseph VI, 24
Copeland, Joseph C. I, 44
Copeland, Joseph D. I, 7
Copeland, Joseph E. I, 211
Copeland, Joseph G. I, 7
Copeland, Joseph G. I, 8
Copeland, Joseph G. I, 43
Copeland, Joseph G. I, 44
Copeland, Joseph H. I, 235
Copeland, Joseph Henry I, 211
Copeland, Joseph J. I, 211
Copeland, Joseph J. V, 900
Copeland, Joseph John V, 900
Copeland, Joseph Y. I, 212
Copeland, Joseph, Jr. I, 43
Copeland, Josephas I, 234
Copeland, Josephine I, 210
Copeland, Josephine I, 234
Copeland, Josephine E. Futrell
I, 236
Copeland, Josephus I, 43
Copeland, Josephus I. I, 212
Copeland, Josephus J. I, 7
Copeland, Joshua I, 7
Copeland, Joshua I, 43
Copeland, Joshua I, 136
Copeland, Joshua I, 161
Copeland, Joshua I, 234
Copeland, Joshua I, 302
Copeland, Joshua T. I, 212
Copeland, Joshua Thomas I, 210
Copeland, Josiah I, 6
Copeland, Josiah I, 7
Copeland, Josiah I, 8
Copeland, Josiah I, 43
Copeland, Josiah I, 44
Copeland, Josiah I, 51
Copeland, Josiah I, 207
Copeland, Josiah I, 210
Copeland, Josiah I, 211
Copeland, Josiah I, 212
Copeland, Josiah I, 214
Copeland, Josiah I, 226
Copeland, Josiah I, 229
Copeland, Josiah I, 234
Copeland, Josiah I, 235
Copeland, Josiah I, 239
Copeland, Josiah Foster I, 8
Copeland, Josiah R. I, 6
Copeland, Josiah R. I, 8
Copeland, Josiah R. I, 43
Copeland, Josiah R. I, 44
Copeland, Josiah R. I, 231
Copeland, Josiah R. I, 234
Copeland, Jshua I, 712
Copeland, Judith I, 212
Copeland, Judith I, 233
Copeland, Judith I, 234
Copeland, Judith I, 250
Copeland, Judith I, 251
Copeland, Judith Ann I, 211
Copeland, Judith Ann I, 214
Copeland, Julia Edna I, 210
Copeland, Julia Elizabeth I, 283
Copeland, Julia Elma I, 8
Copeland, Julia Emma I, 44
Copeland, Julia Wheeler I, 211
Copeland, Julianna I, 59
Copeland, Karan I, 6
Copeland, Kezia I, 211
Copeland, Kezia I, 235
Copeland, Keziah I, 44
Copeland, Keziah I, 210
Copeland, Keziah I, 212
Copeland, Keziah I, 217
Copeland, Keziah I, 218
Copeland, Keziah E. I, 234
Copeland, Keziah E. I, 235
Copeland, Keziah E. I, 534
Copeland, Keziah E. I, 571
Copeland, Laura Folger I, 283
Copeland, Laura W. I, 7
Copeland, Leah I, 302
Copeland, Lear I, 302
Copeland, Lee V, 454
Copeland, Lelia I, 212
Copeland, Lindley M. I, 235
Copeland, Linley M. I, 212
Copeland, Lucius I. I, 43
Copeland, Lucius J. I, 7
Copeland, Lucius J. I, 44
Copeland, Lucretia III, 405
Copeland, Luther Clifton I, 212
Copeland, Lyddia I, 40
Copeland, Lydia I, 6
Copeland, Lydia I, 7
Copeland, Lydia I, 9
Copeland, Lydia I, 10
Copeland, Lydia I, 43
Copeland, Lydia IV, 571
Copeland, Lydia V, 900
Copeland, Lydia E. I, 210
Copeland, Lydia E. I, 235
Copeland, Lydia E. I, 239
Copeland, Lydia E. Futrell I, 258
Copeland, Lydia L. I, 7
Copeland, Lydia L. I, 9
Copeland, Lydia L. I, 44
Copeland, Lydia Parthena I, 7
Copeland, M. Rebecca I, 211
Copeland, Maggie M. I, 876

Copeland, Maggie P. I, 16
Copeland, Margaret I, 11
Copeland, Margaret I, 210
Copeland, Margaret I, 235
Copeland, Margaret II, 494
Copeland, Margaret A. I, 234
Copeland, Margaret A. I, 249
Copeland, Margaret Ann I, 43
Copeland, Margaret Ann I, 234
Copeland, Margaret Deborah I, 210
Copeland, Margaret J. I, 11
Copeland, Margra VI, 59
Copeland, Margra VI, 65
Copeland, Margra VI, 66
Copeland, Maria J. I, 234
Copeland, Maria J. I, 235
Copeland, Maria J. I, 249
Copeland, Maria Jane I, 211
Copeland, Maria Jane I, 221
Copeland, Mariah I, 208
Copeland, Mariah I, 210
Copeland, Mariah I, 212
Copeland, Mariah I, 235
Copeland, Mariah J. I, 208
Copeland, Mariah J. I, 211
Copeland, Mariah J. I, 235
Copeland, Mariam I, 210
Copeland, Mark I, 210
Copeland, Martha I, 4
Copeland, Martha I, 5
Copeland, Martha I, 7
Copeland, Martha I, 43
Copeland, Martha I, 44
Copeland, Martha I, 74
Copeland, Martha I, 88
Copeland, Martha I, 210
Copeland, Martha I, 211
Copeland, Martha I, 212
Copeland, Martha I, 231
Copeland, Martha I, 233
Copeland, Martha I, 234
Copeland, Martha I, 235
Copeland, Martha I, 242
Copeland, Martha I, 248
Copeland, Martha VI, 45
Copeland, Martha A. I, 212
Copeland, Martha Ann I, 234
Copeland, Martha Ann I, 240
Copeland, Martha C. I, 7
Copeland, Martha Elisabeth I, 43
Copeland, Martha Elisabeth I, 44
Copeland, Martha Elisabeth I, 88
Copeland, Martha Eliza I, 210
Copeland, Martha Fariba I, 234
Copeland, Martha Jane I, 211
Copeland, Martha Louisa I, 7
Copeland, Martha Pheriba I, 210
Copeland, Martha R. I, 226
Copeland, Martha R. I, 234
Copeland, Martha R. I, 248
Copeland, Martha Roberts I, 212
Copeland, Martha Rogerson I, 234
Copeland, Martha S. I, 7
Copeland, Martha S. I, 27
Copeland, Martha S. I, 227
Copeland, Martha Sarah I, 211
Copeland, Mary I, 7
Copeland, Mary I, 8
Copeland, Mary I, 206
Copeland, Mary I, 210
Copeland, Mary I, 211
Copeland, Mary I, 212
Copeland, Mary I, 233
Copeland, Mary I, 234
Copeland, Mary I, 235
Copeland, Mary I, 236
Copeland, Mary I, 244
Copeland, Mary I, 257
Copeland, Mary I, 262
Copeland, Mary I, 302
Copeland, Mary I, 712
Copeland, Mary I, 716
Copeland, Mary II, 494
Copeland, Mary IV, 380
Copeland, Mary IV, 469
Copeland, Mary IV, 571
Copeland, Mary VI, 45
Copeland, Mary VI, 59
Copeland, Mary VI, 60
Copeland, Mary VI, 66
Copeland, Mary VI, 86
Copeland, Mary VI, 91
Copeland, Mary VI, 133
Copeland, Mary VI, 138
Copeland, Mary VI, 821
Copeland, Mary VI, 861
Copeland, Mary Abigail I, 212
Copeland, Mary Ann I, 7
Copeland, Mary Ann I, 43
Copeland, Mary Ann I, 61
Copeland, Mary Ann I, 211
Copeland, Mary Ann I, 234
Copeland, Mary Ann I, 252
Copeland, Mary Ann II, 559
Copeland, Mary Ariedna I, 210
Copeland, Mary E. I, 26
Copeland, Mary E. I, 44
Copeland, Mary E. I, 83
Copeland, Mary E. I, 207
Copeland, Mary Edna I, 211
Copeland, Mary Eliza I, 7
Copeland, Mary Ellen I, 210
Copeland, Mary Elma I, 7
Copeland, Mary F. I, 218
Copeland, Mary F. I, 235
Copeland, Mary F. I, 249
Copeland, Mary Florence I, 211
Copeland, Mary H. I, 211
Copeland, Mary H. I, 212
Copeland, Mary H. I, 234
Copeland, Mary I. I, 984
Copeland, Mary Isabella I, 44
Copeland, Mary J. I, 44
Copeland, Mary J. I, 234
Copeland, Mary J. I, 984
Copeland, Mary J. I, 990
Copeland, Mary J. II, 709
Copeland, Mary J. VI, 60
Copeland, Mary Jane I, 7
Copeland, Mary Jane I, 43
Copeland, Mary Jane I, 44
Copeland, Mary Jane I, 210
Copeland, Mary Jane I, 232
Copeland, Mary Jane I, 234
Copeland, Mary Rebecca I, 210
Copeland, Mary S. VI, 59
Copeland, Mary S. VI, 86
Copeland, Mattie R. I, 235
Copeland, Mattie R. I, 256
Copeland, Maud I, 212
Copeland, McChesney I, 7
Copeland, McChesney I, 44
Copeland, Meriam I, 233
Copeland, Meriam I, 712
Copeland, Milercent I, 212
Copeland, Milicent I, 234
Copeland, Milisent I, 233
Copeland, Milisent I, 245
Copeland, Milisent I, 248
Copeland, Millie I, 44
Copeland, Millie I, 59
Copeland, Minnie Bell I, 211
Copeland, Minnie Belle I, 235
Copeland, Minnie E. I, 235
Copeland, Miriam I, 7
Copeland, Miriam I, 43
Copeland, Miriam I, 57
Copeland, Miriam I, 210
Copeland, Miriam I, 302
Copeland, Miriam I, 712
Copeland, Miriam I, 727
Copeland, Miriam C. I, 12
Copeland, Miriam R. I, 235
Copeland, Miriam R. I, 245
Copeland, Miriam Rebecca I, 211
Copeland, Missouri M. I, 8
Copeland, Mylercent I, 234
Copeland, Mylercent I, 245
Copeland, Nancy I, 210
Copeland, Nancy I, 233
Copeland, Nancy I, 258
Copeland, Nathan IV, 469
Copeland, Nathan Gurny I, 211
Copeland, Nellie I, 12
Copeland, Nicholas Scott I, 8
Copeland, Nora I, 212
Copeland, Oliff I, 210
Copeland, Oliff I, 233
Copeland, Oliff I, 241
Copeland, Oliver Randolph I, 7
Copeland, Ora I, 44
Copeland, Peggy VI, 59
Copeland, Penninah I, 35
Copeland, Penninah I, 43
Copeland, Penninah I, 63
Copeland, Pharaba I, 233
Copeland, Pharaba I, 240
Copeland, Pherby I, 212
Copeland, Philip V, 900
Copeland, Philip VI, 816
Copeland, Phineas T. I, 8
Copeland, Phinehas I, 43
Copeland, Pleasant I, 7
Copeland, Pleasant I, 27
Copeland, Pleasant I, 43
Copeland, Pleasant I, 82
Copeland, Pleasant I, 88
Copeland, Polly VI, 59
Copeland, Polly VI, 65
Copeland, Polly VI, 71
Copeland, Pricila I, 210
Copeland, Priscilla I, 43
Copeland, Priscilla I, 73
Copeland, Priscilla I, 231
Copeland, Priscilla I, 233
Copeland, Rachel I, 43
Copeland, Rachel I, 51
Copeland, Rachel I, 65
Copeland, Rachel I, 212
Copeland, Rachel I, 233
Copeland, Rachel I, 234
Copeland, Rachel VI, 59
Copeland, Rachel VI, 867
Copeland, Rachell I, 233
Copeland, Rachell I, 261
Copeland, Rebeca VI, 59
Copeland, Rebecca I, 11
Copeland, Rebecca I, 43
Copeland, Rebecca I, 76
Copeland, Rebecca I, 210
Copeland, Rebecca I, 211
Copeland, Rebecca I, 214
Copeland, Rebecca I, 226
Copeland, Rebecca I, 233
Copeland, Rebecca I, 234
Copeland, Rebecca I, 235
Copeland, Rebecca I, 251
Copeland, Rebecca IV, 618
Copeland, Rebecca IV, 621
Copeland, Rebecca J. I, 43
Copeland, Rebecca Jane I, 8
Copeland, Rebecca Jane I, 234
Copeland, Rebekah I, 876
Copeland, Rebekah Jane I, 210
Copeland, Reuben Perry I, 6
Copeland, Robert I, 43
Copeland, Robert VI, 59
Copeland, Rodema Elen I, 211
Copeland, Rosella VI, 59
Copeland, Rosella VI, 66
Copeland, Roxana I, 235
Copeland, Roxanna Rebecca I, 212
Copeland, Roxie I, 212
Copeland, Roy V, 454
Copeland, Ruth VI, 59
Copeland, Ruth VI, 66
Copeland, Ruth W. I, 210
Copeland, Sallie A. I, 234
Copeland, Sallie A. I, 283
Copeland, Sallie A. I, 302
Copeland, Sallie J. I, 235
Copeland, Sallie S. I, 44
Copeland, Sallie S. I, 56
Copeland, Sally I, 235
Copeland, Sally A. P. I, 210
Copeland, Sally W. I, 211
Copeland, Samariah I, 208
Copeland, Samira I, 212
Copeland, Samuel I, 43
Copeland, Samuel I, 302
Copeland, Samuel V, 454
Copeland, Samuel VI, 59
Copeland, Samuel VI, 66
Copeland, Samuel VI, 80
Copeland, Samuel VI, 86
Copeland, Sarah I, 7
Copeland, Sarah I, 8
Copeland, Sarah I, 35
Copeland, Sarah I, 43
Copeland, Sarah I, 48
Copeland, Sarah I, 50
Copeland, Sarah I, 210
Copeland, Sarah I, 211
Copeland, Sarah I, 212
Copeland, Sarah I, 214
Copeland, Sarah I, 233
Copeland, Sarah I, 234
Copeland, Sarah I, 240
Copeland, Sarah I, 248
Copeland, Sarah I, 249
Copeland, Sarah I, 259
Copeland, Sarah I, 261
Copeland, Sarah I, 302
Copeland, Sarah I, 534
Copeland, Sarah I, 712
Copeland, Sarah II, 494
Copeland, Sarah II, 614
Copeland, Sarah IV, 571
Copeland, Sarah VI, 59
Copeland, Sarah VI, 78
Copeland, Sarah A. I, 54
Copeland, Sarah A. I, 235
Copeland, Sarah A. I, 302
Copeland, Sarah A. I, 315
Copeland, Sarah A. IV, 571
Copeland, Sarah Abigail I, 6
Copeland, Sarah Ann IV, 380
Copeland, Sarah Ann IV, 571
Copeland, Sarah C. I, 211
Copeland, Sarah E. I, 59
Copeland, Sarah Edna I, 210
Copeland, Sarah Hannah I, 210
Copeland, Sarah J. I, 44
Copeland, Sarah J. I, 210
Copeland, Sarah J. I, 212
Copeland, Sarah J. I, 235
Copeland, Sarah J. I, 236
Copeland, Sarah J. I, 255
Copeland, Sarah J., Sr. I, 235
Copeland, Sarah Jane I, 8
Copeland, Sarah Jane I, 43
Copeland, Sarah Jane I, 44
Copeland, Sarah Jane I, 211
Copeland, Sarah Jane I, 226
Copeland, Sarah Jane I, 231
Copeland, Sarah Jane I, 234
Copeland, Sarah Rachel I, 7
Copeland, Sarah S. I, 7
Copeland, Sarah S. I, 10
Copeland, Silas VI, 59
Copeland, Silas Benjamin Lamb I, 44
Copeland, Stella V, 454
Copeland, Susan Alice Lamb I, 44
Copeland, Susanah I, 210
Copeland, Susanah I, 712
Copeland, Susanna I, 283
Copeland, Susanna I, 302
Copeland, Susanna I, 311
Copeland, Susanna I, 316
Copeland, Susanna I, 712
Copeland, Susannah I, 43
Copeland, Susannah I, 136
Copeland, Susannah I, 161
Copeland, Susannah I, 302
Copeland, Susannah I, 712
Copeland, Susie I, 211
Copeland, Tamer I, 43
Copeland, Tamer I, 88
Copeland, Temperance I, 44
Copeland, Temperance M. I, 6
Copeland, Thamer I, 8
Copeland, Thomas I, 5
Copeland, Thomas I, 7
Copeland, Thomas I, 8
Copeland, Thomas I, 43
Copeland, Thomas I, 51
Copeland, Thomas I, 57
Copeland, Thomas I, 210
Copeland, Thomas I, 233
Copeland, Thomas VI, 45
Copeland, Thomas VI, 59
Copeland, Thomas VI, 65
Copeland, Thomas VI, 86
Copeland, Thomas E. I, 235
Copeland, Thomas F. I, 44
Copeland, Thomas J. I, 7
Copeland, Thomas J. I, 43
Copeland, Thomas J. I, 44
Copeland, Thomas J. I, 212
Copeland, Thomas J. I, 235
Copeland, Thomas, Jr. I, 8
Copeland, Walter Jay I, 283
Copeland, Widow Penninah I, 43
Copeland, Widow Pleasant Winslow I, 43
Copeland, William I, 43
Copeland, William I, 73
Copeland, William I, 210
Copeland, William I, 212
Copeland, William I, 233
Copeland, William I, 234
Copeland, William I, 250
Copeland, William VI, 48
Copeland, William VI, 59
Copeland, William H. I, 210
Copeland, William H. I, 212
Copeland, William Henby I, 59
Copeland, William L. I, 211
Copeland, William L. I, 212
Copeland, William L. I, 235
Copeland, William Luther I, 26
Copeland, William Walter I, 44
Copeland, William, Jr. VI, 59
Copeland, Winneford I, 283
Copeland, Winneford I, 302
Copeland, Winneford I, 712
Copeland, Wm. VI, 54
Copeland, Wm. L. I, 211
Copeland, Wm. W. I, 211
Copeland, Zac. I, 191
Copeland, Zachariah VI, 59
Copeland, Zachariah VI, 78
Copeland, Zachariah VI, 133
Copeland, Zenophen I, 44
Copeland, Zenophen E. I, 7
Copelin, Dorotha I, 191
Copelin, Elizabeth VI, 804
Copeling, Anney VI, 807
Copeling, Thomas VI, 807
Copeman, Emma V, 990
Coper, Elizabeth P. II, 757
Coper, Israel II, 756
Coper, Margaret II, 756
Coper, Mary Ann II, 756
Coperthwait, Elizabeth II, 496
Coperthwaite, Hugh II, 194
Coperthwaite, Kesiah II, 194
Copic, Aaron I, 1081
Copic, Aaron, Jr. I, 1081
Copic, Abigail I, 1081
Copic, Abigail I, 1091
Copic, Abigail IV, 902
Copic, Abraham I, 1081
Copic, Elijah I, 1081
Copic, Elizabeth I, 1081
Copic, John I, 1081
Copic, Josiah I, 1081
Copic, Margaret I, 1081
Copic, Samuel I, 1091
Copic, Wm. G. IV, 902
Copick, Jonathan IV, 1091
Copick, Mary IV, 1091
Copland, ??? I, 11
Copland, Dempsey I, 43
Copland, Elisha VI, 59
Copland, Isabella I, 5
Copland, James VI, 45
Copland, James VI, 59
Copland, James, Jr. VI, 59
Copland, John VI, 28
Copland, John VI, 59
Copland, Joseph VI, 28
Copland, Maggie M. I, 876
Copland, Martha I, 43
Copland, Martha VI, 45
Copland, Mary VI, 28
Copland, Mary VI, 60
Copland, Pleasant I, 7
Copland, Sarah I, 11
Copland, Sarah Jane I, 43
Copland, Silas VI, 59
Copland, Zachariah VI, 59
Coplin, Joshua C. I, 97
Coplin, Susanna I, 97
Copline, Miriam I, 302
Copner, Joseph II, 25
Copner, Joseph II, 63
Copner, Sinnick Sinnickson II,
Copock, Abigail IV, 902
Copock, Barton D. IV, 902
Copock, Elizabeth Jane IV, 90
Copock, Harlem L. IV, 902
Copock, William G. IV, 902
Coppage, Thomas VI, 235
Coppage, Thomas VI, 236
Coppcock, Ellen IV, 941
Coppcock, Jehu IV, 941
Coppcock, Judith IV, 941
Coppcok, Sarah IV, 797
Coppeck, Ellen IV, 694
Coppeck, Jane II, 611
Coppeck, Jehu IV, 694
Copper, Mary Ann V, 107
Copperas, Alice P. V, 666
Copperthwait, Elizabeth II, 34
Copperthwait, Grace II, 991
Copperthwait, John II, 63
Copperthwait, Joseph II, 991
Copperthwait, Mark II, 63
Copperthwait, Mary II, 63
Copperthwait, Mary II, 111
Copperthwait, Samuel II, 63
Copperthwait, Samuel II, 991
Copperthwait, Sarah II, 63
Copperthwait, Thomas II, 63
Copperthwait, Thomas Shreve 496
Copperthwait, Thomas, Jr. II,
Copperthwait, Thos. II, 63
Copperthwait, Thos. II, 111
Copperthwaite, Elizabeth II, 4
Copperthwaite, Hannah II, 23
Copperthwaite, Hope II, 239
Copperthwaite, Joseph II, 496
Copperthwaite, Joseph II, 991
Copperthwaite, Samuel II, 49
Copperthwaite, Sarah II, 87
Copperthwaite, Thomas, Jr. II, 63
Copperthwate, William, Jr. II, 285
Copperthwite, John II, 63
Copperthwite, Sarah II, 63
Copperthwite, Thomas II, 63
Coppic, Timothy IV, 1154
Coppick, Aaron I, 1091
Coppick, Abigail IV, 903
Coppick, Edwin IV, 669
Coppick, Lydia Ann IV, 967
Coppick, Prudence I, 1091

oppick, Wm. G. IV, 903
oppoc, Catharine IV, 1129
oppock, ??? V, 803
oppock, Aaron I, 1018
oppock, Aaron I, 1028
oppock, Aaron I, 1077
oppock, Aaron I, 1091
oppock, Aaron I, 1099
oppock, Aaron I, 1149
oppock, Aaron I, 1150
oppock, Aaron IV, 191
oppock, Aaron IV, 690
oppock, Aaron IV, 694
oppock, Aaron IV, 942
oppock, Aaron IV, 943
oppock, Aaron IV, 999
oppock, Aaron V, 43
oppock, Aaron V, 164
oppock, Aaron V, 170
oppock, Aaron V, 800
oppock, Aaron V, 803
oppock, Aaron V, 804
oppock, Aaron J. V, 803
oppock, Abigail I, 1018
oppock, Abigail I, 1028
oppock, Abigail I, 1039
oppock, Abigail I, 1081
oppock, Abigail I, 1091
oppock, Abigail IV, 694
oppock, Abigail IV, 808
oppock, Abigail IV, 811
oppock, Abigail IV, 902
oppock, Abigail IV, 942
oppock, Abigail IV, 943
oppock, Abigail IV, 993
oppock, Abigail D. IV, 694
oppock, Abigail D. IV, 809
oppock, Abraham I, 1150
oppock, Abram I, 1149
oppock, Addie V, 805
oppock, Albert IV, 808
oppock, Albert IV, 809
oppock, Albert N. V, 733
oppock, Albert Newton V, 733
oppock, Alexander V, 799
oppock, Allen V, 804
oppock, Allen V, 805
oppock, Allen, Jr. V, 805
oppock, Almeda V, 381
oppock, Almeda V, 801
oppock, Almeda V, 804
oppock, Amy IV, 690
oppock, Amy IV, 694
oppock, Amy IV, 942
oppock, Amy IV, 943
oppock, Amy IV, 999
oppock, Amzi V, 804
oppock, Amzi V, 805
oppock, Ann I, 1018
oppock, Ann I, 1028
oppock, Ann IV, 191
oppock, Ann IV, 694
oppock, Ann IV, 695
oppock, Ann IV, 806
oppock, Ann IV, 808
oppock, Ann IV, 933
oppock, Ann IV, 942
oppock, Ann IV, 943
oppock, Ann IV, 949
oppock, Ann IV, 955
oppock, Ann IV, 977
oppock, Ann V, 43
oppock, Ann V, 733
oppock, Ann V, 805
oppock, Ann L. IV, 695
oppock, Ann Samuel IV, 694
oppock, Anna IV, 943
oppock, Anna V, 164
oppock, Anna V, 381
oppock, Anna V, 803
oppock, Anna V, 805
oppock, Anna V, 821
oppock, Anne I, 1032
oppock, Anne V, 761
oppock, Anne V, 795
oppock, Anne V, 797
oppock, Anne V, 803
oppock, Anne Jay I, 1028
oppock, Anny V, 803
oppock, Anson V, 804
oppock, Anson V, 805
oppock, Barbara V, 733
oppock, Barbara V, 772
oppock, Barclay IV, 694
oppock, Barclay IV, 695
oppock, Barclay IV, 943
oppock, Bartholomew II, 494
oppock, Barton IV, 694
oppock, Barton D. IV, 902
oppock, Benj. V, 811
oppock, Benj. H. IV, 694
Coppock, Benjamin I, 1018
Coppock, Benjamin I, 1028
Coppock, Benjamin I, 1032
Coppock, Benjamin IV, 808
Coppock, Benjamin IV, 856
Coppock, Benjamin IV, 902
Coppock, Benjamin IV, 918
Coppock, Benjamin IV, 943
Coppock, Benjamin IV, 1091
Coppock, Benjamin V, 733
Coppock, Benjamin V, 736
Coppock, Benjamin V, 795
Coppock, Benjamin V, 799
Coppock, Benjamin V, 801
Coppock, Benjamin V, 803
Coppock, Benjamin V, 804
Coppock, Benjamin V, 807
Coppock, Benjamin V, 816
Coppock, Benjamin A. IV, 809
Coppock, Benjamin C. V, 803
Coppock, Benjamin H. IV, 695
Coppock, Benjamin H. IV, 808
Coppock, Benjamin N. IV, 808
Coppock, Benjamin S. IV, 943
Coppock, Calvin V, 805
Coppock, Catharine IV, 82
Coppock, Catharine IV, 143
Coppock, Catharine IV, 191
Coppock, Catharine IV, 469
Coppock, Catharine IV, 618
Coppock, Catharine IV, 694
Coppock, Catharine IV, 943
Coppock, Catharine IV, 1091
Coppock, Catharine IV, 1129
Coppock, Catherine IV, 81
Coppock, Catherine IV, 808
Coppock, Charity V, 733
Coppock, Charity V, 803
Coppock, Charity V, 804
Coppock, Charity V, 810
Coppock, Charles H. V, 733
Coppock, Charles M. V, 733
Coppock, Clarence A. V, 381
Coppock, Cora IV, 1037
Coppock, Corilla A. V, 733
Coppock, Corilla Ann V, 733
Coppock, Corilla Ann V, 805
Coppock, Cynthy V, 803
Coppock, Cynthy V, 805
Coppock, Cynthy V, 809
Coppock, David IV, 808
Coppock, David IV, 847
Coppock, David V, 733
Coppock, David V, 799
Coppock, David V, 805
Coppock, David J. V, 731
Coppock, David J. V, 733
Coppock, David J. V, 801
Coppock, David M. V, 804
Coppock, David M. V, 805
Coppock, David M. V, 812
Coppock, Dayton V, 733
Coppock, Delilah V, 803
Coppock, Della P. V, 381
Coppock, Diannah V, 819
Coppock, Edith IV, 808
Coppock, Edith IV, 809
Coppock, Edwin IV, 943
Coppock, Eleanor IV, 694
Coppock, Eleanor IV, 730
Coppock, Eleanor V, 799
Coppock, Eleanor V, 803
Coppock, Eleanor V, 805
Coppock, Eleanor V, 807
Coppock, Eleanor B. V, 803
Coppock, Eleanor H. V, 733
Coppock, Eleanor H. V, 803
Coppock, Eleanor Harriet V, 805
Coppock, Elen IV, 694
Coppock, Eli IV, 942
Coppock, Eli V, 803
Coppock, Elijah I, 1149
Coppock, Elijah V, 733
Coppock, Elijah V, 803
Coppock, Elisha I, 1149
Coppock, Eliza Ann IV, 943
Coppock, Eliza Ann IV, 1007
Coppock, Elizabeth I, 1018
Coppock, Elizabeth I, 1027
Coppock, Elizabeth I, 1028
Coppock, Elizabeth I, 1117
Coppock, Elizabeth I, 1140
Coppock, Elizabeth IV, 808
Coppock, Elizabeth V, 381
Coppock, Elizabeth V, 733
Coppock, Elizabeth V, 737
Coppock, Elizabeth V, 780
Coppock, Elizabeth V, 799
Coppock, Elizabeth V, 803
Coppock, Elizabeth V, 805
Coppock, Elizabeth V, 807
Coppock, Elizabeth C. V, 800
Coppock, Elizabeth C. V, 803
Coppock, Elizabeth C. V, 805
Coppock, Elizabeth C. V, 817
Coppock, Elizabeth E. V, 736
Coppock, Elizabeth E. V, 803
Coppock, Elizabeth J. IV, 809
Coppock, Elizabeth Jane IV, 694
Coppock, Elizabeth Jane IV, 902
Coppock, Elizabeth N. V, 803
Coppock, Ella IV, 809
Coppock, Ella IV, 1311
Coppock, Ella Florence IV, 809
Coppock, Ella M. IV, 809
Coppock, Ella M. IV, 1311
Coppock, Ellen IV, 143
Coppock, Ellen IV, 694
Coppock, Ellen IV, 743
Coppock, Ellen IV, 765
Coppock, Ellen IV, 942
Coppock, Ellen IV, 943
Coppock, Ellin IV, 191
Coppock, Ellwood V, 805
Coppock, Elmer IV, 809
Coppock, Elmer B. IV, 694
Coppock, Elmer B. IV, 695
Coppock, Elmer B. IV, 808
Coppock, Elnor V, 381
Coppock, Elwood V, 804
Coppock, Emily V, 805
Coppock, Emma V, 381
Coppock, Enoch IV, 808
Coppock, Enos IV, 943
Coppock, Ephraim V, 801
Coppock, Ephraim V, 803
Coppock, Ephraim V, 805
Coppock, Esther IV, 808
Coppock, Esther IV, 809
Coppock, Esther IV, 856
Coppock, Esther IV, 902
Coppock, Esther IV, 918
Coppock, Esther V, 733
Coppock, Esther V, 799
Coppock, Esther V, 801
Coppock, Esther V, 803
Coppock, Esther V, 804
Coppock, Esther V, 805
Coppock, Esther V, 807
Coppock, Esther V, 816
Coppock, Esther W. IV, 694
Coppock, Esther W. IV, 695
Coppock, Esther W. IV, 808
Coppock, Esther W. IV, 902
Coppock, Eunice V, 43
Coppock, Eunice V, 733
Coppock, Eunice V, 761
Coppock, Eunice V, 799
Coppock, Eunice V, 803
Coppock, Eunice V, 805
Coppock, Eunice V, 820
Coppock, Eunice Anna V, 821
Coppock, Ezra IV, 695
Coppock, Ezra IV, 808
Coppock, Ezra IV, 815
Coppock, Ezra IV, 943
Coppock, Ezra IV, 955
Coppock, Fannie V, 733
Coppock, Frank V, 733
Coppock, Frank V, 805
Coppock, Freddie D. V, 805
Coppock, Geo V, 733
Coppock, Hannah IV, 804
Coppock, Hannah IV, 808
Coppock, Hannah IV, 809
Coppock, Hannah IV, 851
Coppock, Hannah IV, 985
Coppock, Hannah IV, 1013
Coppock, Hannah V, 43
Coppock, Hannah V, 733
Coppock, Hannah V, 780
Coppock, Hannah V, 784
Coppock, Hannah V, 791
Coppock, Hannah V, 794
Coppock, Hannah C. IV, 1012
Coppock, Hannah E. IV, 943
Coppock, Hannah E. IV, 976
Coppock, Hannah E. B. IV, 943
Coppock, Hannah Elizabeth IV, 943
Coppock, Hannah Lavina IV, 695
Coppock, Hannah Levina IV, 808
Coppock, Harlan L. IV, 809
Coppock, Harlem L. IV, 902
Coppock, Harlen IV, 694
Coppock, Harvey V, 804
Coppock, Harvey V, 805
Coppock, Harvy V, 805
Coppock, Henry IV, 943
Coppock, Henry V, 799
Coppock, Henry V, 803
Coppock, Henry V, 804
Coppock, Henry V, 805
Coppock, Henry Harvey V, 805
Coppock, Hester V, 799
Coppock, Homer J. IV, 809
Coppock, Ida S. IV, 809
Coppock, Isaac I, 1018
Coppock, Isaac I, 1028
Coppock, Isaac IV, 143
Coppock, Isaac IV, 152
Coppock, Isaac IV, 191
Coppock, Isaac IV, 380
Coppock, Isaac IV, 694
Coppock, Isaac IV, 730
Coppock, Isaac IV, 748
Coppock, Isaac IV, 942
Coppock, Isaac IV, 943
Coppock, Isaac V, 43
Coppock, Isaac V, 800
Coppock, Isaac V, 803
Coppock, Isaac V, 805
Coppock, Isaac C. V, 733
Coppock, Isaac C. V, 803
Coppock, Isaac C. V, 805
Coppock, Isaac T. IV, 808
Coppock, Isaac T. IV, 809
Coppock, Isaac T. IV, 943
Coppock, Isaac T. IV, 944
Coppock, Isabel V, 733
Coppock, Jacob I, 1104
Coppock, Jacob IV, 943
Coppock, James I, 1028
Coppock, James IV, 694
Coppock, James IV, 942
Coppock, James IV, 943
Coppock, James V, 43
Coppock, James V, 733
Coppock, James V, 746
Coppock, James V, 780
Coppock, James V, 784
Coppock, James V, 803
Coppock, James V, 805
Coppock, James V, 812
Coppock, James W. V, 805
Coppock, James, Jr. V, 805
Coppock, Jane I, 1018
Coppock, Jane I, 1028
Coppock, Jane I, 1104
Coppock, Jane II, 494
Coppock, Jane IV, 469
Coppock, Jane IV, 478
Coppock, Jane IV, 797
Coppock, Jane IV, 807
Coppock, Jane IV, 808
Coppock, Jane IV, 856
Coppock, Jane IV, 902
Coppock, Jane IV, 943
Coppock, Jane IV, 1012
Coppock, Jane IV, 1016
Coppock, Jane V, 43
Coppock, Jane V, 723
Coppock, Jane V, 730
Coppock, Jane V, 733
Coppock, Jane V, 780
Coppock, Jane V, 792
Coppock, Jane V, 798
Coppock, Jane V, 799
Coppock, Jane V, 801
Coppock, Jane V, 803
Coppock, Jane V, 805
Coppock, Jane V, 810
Coppock, Jane V, 811
Coppock, Jane V, 812
Coppock, Jane V, 820
Coppock, Jane H. IV, 808
Coppock, Jane J. V, 805
Coppock, Jane, Sr. V, 733
Coppock, Jas. V, 784
Coppock, Jeddie Carlton V, 805
Coppock, Jehu IV, 694
Coppock, Jehu IV, 765
Coppock, Jehu IV, 933
Coppock, Jehu IV, 942
Coppock, Jehu IV, 993
Coppock, Jehu IV, 997
Coppock, Jehu IV, 1011
Coppock, Jeremiah IV, 618
Coppock, Jeremiah IV, 656
Coppock, Jeremiah IV, 804
Coppock, Jeremiah IV, 808
Coppock, Jeremiah IV, 810
Coppock, Jesse V, 43
Coppock, Jesse V, 803
Coppock, Jesse V, 805
Coppock, Jesse C. V, 804
Coppock, Jesse L. V, 381
Coppock, Jesse Lucell V, 381
Coppock, Job Warren IV, 943
Coppock, Joe F. V, 805
Coppock, Joel I, 1104
Coppock, John I, 1018
Coppock, John I, 1028
Coppock, John I, 1032
Coppock, John I, 1091
Coppock, John I, 1149
Coppock, John I, 1150
Coppock, John IV, 81
Coppock, John IV, 82
Coppock, John IV, 143
Coppock, John IV, 191
Coppock, John IV, 469
Coppock, John IV, 618
Coppock, John IV, 694
Coppock, John IV, 808
Coppock, John IV, 943
Coppock, John V, 43
Coppock, John V, 164
Coppock, John V, 723
Coppock, John V, 733
Coppock, John V, 761
Coppock, John V, 780
Coppock, John V, 799
Coppock, John V, 810
Coppock, John V, 821
Coppock, John J. V, 780
Coppock, John James I, 1104
Coppock, John Mc V, 733
Coppock, John S. IV, 808
Coppock, John W. V, 733
Coppock, John, Sr. I, 1028
Coppock, Jonathan II, 494
Coppock, Jonathan IV, 808
Coppock, Jonathan IV, 810
Coppock, Jonathan IV, 842
Coppock, Jonathan IV, 943
Coppock, Jonathan IV, 1091
Coppock, Jos. J. IV, 191
Coppock, Joseph I, 1018
Coppock, Joseph I, 1028
Coppock, Joseph IV, 808
Coppock, Joseph IV, 942
Coppock, Joseph IV, 943
Coppock, Joseph V, 733
Coppock, Joseph V, 780
Coppock, Joseph V, 798
Coppock, Joseph V, 801
Coppock, Joseph V, 803
Coppock, Joseph V, 804
Coppock, Joseph V, 805
Coppock, Joseph V, 810
Coppock, Joseph V, 811
Coppock, Joseph C. V, 805
Coppock, Joseph J. IV, 809
Coppock, Joseph J. IV, 814
Coppock, Joseph J. IV, 943
Coppock, Joseph J. IV, 944
Coppock, Joseph L. IV, 808
Coppock, Joseph L. IV, 943
Coppock, Joseph, Jr. I, 1028
Coppock, Joshua IV, 469
Coppock, Joshua IV, 478
Coppock, Joshua IV, 743
Coppock, Joshua IV, 797
Coppock, Joshua IV, 807
Coppock, Joshua IV, 808
Coppock, Joshua IV, 856
Coppock, Joshua IV, 902
Coppock, Joshua IV, 943
Coppock, Joshua IV, 1012
Coppock, Joshua IV, 1016
Coppock, Josiah I, 1149
Coppock, Josiah I, 1150
Coppock, Josiah V, 819
Coppock, Judith IV, 694
Coppock, Judith IV, 765
Coppock, Judith IV, 933
Coppock, Judith IV, 942
Coppock, Judith IV, 944
Coppock, Judith IV, 993
Coppock, Judith IV, 997
Coppock, Judith IV, 1011
Coppock, June V, 805
Coppock, Laura IV, 943
Coppock, Laura IV, 944
Coppock, Laura IV, 975
Coppock, Laura H. IV, 944
Coppock, Layton V, 381
Coppock, Layton V, 799
Coppock, Layton V, 803
Coppock, Layton V, 805
Coppock, Levi IV, 694
Coppock, Levi IV, 695
Coppock, Levi IV, 943
Coppock, Levi IV, 1205
Coppock, Lewis V, 381
Coppock, Lindley V, 381
Coppock, Lindley V, 441
Coppock, Lindsey IV, 942
Coppock, Lindsey IV, 943
Coppock, Louisa V, 780
Coppock, Louisa V, 792
Coppock, Louisa V, 804
Coppock, Louisa V, 819

Coppock, Lucinda IV, 809
Coppock, Lucinda V, 805
Coppock, Lucy IV, 809
Coppock, Lucy IV, 942
Coppock, Lydda Ann IV, 808
Coppock, Lyddaann IV, 809
Coppock, Lydia IV, 808
Coppock, Lydia IV, 822
Coppock, Lydia IV, 943
Coppock, Lydia V, 164
Coppock, Lydia V, 733
Coppock, Lydia V, 745
Coppock, Lydia V, 780
Coppock, Lydia V, 791
Coppock, Lydia V, 792
Coppock, Lydia V, 803
Coppock, Lydia Anna IV, 943
Coppock, Lydia E. IV, 943
Coppock, Lydia E. IV, 976
Coppock, Lydia J. V, 803
Coppock, Lydianna IV, 943
Coppock, Lyndley V, 381
Coppock, Mabel IV, 943
Coppock, Mahetable IV, 808
Coppock, Mahitable J. IV, 695
Coppock, Margaret I, 1027
Coppock, Margaret I, 1028
Coppock, Margaret I, 1091
Coppock, Margaret I, 1099
Coppock, Margaret I, 1117
Coppock, Margaret IV, 943
Coppock, Margaret V, 731
Coppock, Margaret V, 733
Coppock, Margaret V, 798
Coppock, Margaret V, 799
Coppock, Margaret V, 800
Coppock, Margaret V, 801
Coppock, Margaret V, 803
Coppock, Margaret V, 815
Coppock, Margaret Ann I, 1104
Coppock, Margaret Ellen IV, 808
Coppock, Margaret Ellen IV, 809
Coppock, Margarett I, 1018
Coppock, Marget I, 1018
Coppock, Maria IV, 694
Coppock, Maria IV, 943
Coppock, Maria V, 733
Coppock, Maria B. IV, 695
Coppock, Maria E. V, 805
Coppock, Mariah V, 805
Coppock, Mariba V, 43
Coppock, Marmaduke V, 799
Coppock, Martha I, 1117
Coppock, Martha V, 43
Coppock, Martha V, 381
Coppock, Martha V, 441
Coppock, Martha V, 784
Coppock, Martha V, 794
Coppock, Martha V, 811
Coppock, Martha E. V, 733
Coppock, Martha Ellen V, 733
Coppock, Marther I, 1028
Coppock, Marther I, 1038
Coppock, Mary I, 1018
Coppock, Mary I, 1028
Coppock, Mary I, 1032
Coppock, Mary IV, 143
Coppock, Mary IV, 152
Coppock, Mary IV, 380
Coppock, Mary IV, 571
Coppock, Mary IV, 808
Coppock, Mary IV, 814
Coppock, Mary IV, 842
Coppock, Mary IV, 943
Coppock, Mary IV, 1052
Coppock, Mary IV, 1091
Coppock, Mary V, 164
Coppock, Mary V, 170
Coppock, Mary V, 733
Coppock, Mary V, 758
Coppock, Mary V, 780
Coppock, Mary V, 781
Coppock, Mary V, 799
Coppock, Mary V, 800
Coppock, Mary V, 801
Coppock, Mary V, 803
Coppock, Mary V, 804
Coppock, Mary V, 807
Coppock, Mary A. V, 805
Coppock, Mary A. V, 810
Coppock, Mary Ann V, 803
Coppock, Mary Ann V, 804
Coppock, Mary Ann V, 805
Coppock, Mary C. V, 804
Coppock, Mary E. IV, 276
Coppock, Mary E. V, 381
Coppock, Mary E. V, 733
Coppock, Mary Elizabeth V, 804
Coppock, Mary Elizabeth V, 805
Coppock, Mary Emma IV, 191
Coppock, Mary Ethel V, 805
Coppock, Mary H. V, 805
Coppock, Mary K. V, 805
Coppock, Mary Louisa IV, 943
Coppock, Mary Louisa IV, 975
Coppock, Mary Viola IV, 943
Coppock, Maryann V, 780
Coppock, Maryann V, 783
Coppock, Maryann V, 810
Coppock, Maud V, 733
Coppock, Mehetable IV, 808
Coppock, Mehetable IV, 827
Coppock, Mehetable J. IV, 694
Coppock, Mehetable J. IV, 743
Coppock, Mehitable J. IV, 1205
Coppock, Mehitable J. IV, 1217
Coppock, Mildred IV, 943
Coppock, Mildred IV, 944
Coppock, Milley IV, 808
Coppock, Milley IV, 810
Coppock, Moriah V, 804
Coppock, Moses I, 1028
Coppock, Moses V, 43
Coppock, Moses V, 733
Coppock, Moses V, 745
Coppock, Moses V, 780
Coppock, Moses V, 781
Coppock, Moses V, 791
Coppock, Moses V, 792
Coppock, Moses V, 803
Coppock, Moses V, 805
Coppock, Moses V, 807
Coppock, Moses V, 820
Coppock, Mrs. Lucinda IV, 809
Coppock, Nellie IV, 748
Coppock, Nellie V, 805
Coppock, Nora V, 805
Coppock, Oscar V, 733
Coppock, Phebe IV, 748
Coppock, Phebe IV, 809
Coppock, Phebe A. IV, 943
Coppock, Phebe A. IV, 944
Coppock, Phebe Laura IV, 943
Coppock, Pleasant IV, 694
Coppock, Pleasant IV, 942
Coppock, Pleasant IV, 943
Coppock, Pleasant IV, 976
Coppock, Pleasant IV, 1007
Coppock, Prudence I, 1091
Coppock, Prudence I, 1092
Coppock, Rachel IV, 694
Coppock, Rachel IV, 743
Coppock, Rachel IV, 808
Coppock, Rachel V, 780
Coppock, Rachel V, 801
Coppock, Rachel V, 803
Coppock, Rachel V, 804
Coppock, Rachel V, 810
Coppock, Rachel G. IV, 807
Coppock, Rachel G. IV, 809
Coppock, Rachel G. IV, 845
Coppock, Ralph IV, 809
Coppock, Ralph IV, 944
Coppock, Ralph S. IV, 809
Coppock, Ralph S. IV, 943
Coppock, Ralph S. IV, 944
Coppock, Rebecca IV, 191
Coppock, Rebecca IV, 618
Coppock, Rebecca IV, 656
Coppock, Rebecca IV, 690
Coppock, Rebecca IV, 694
Coppock, Rebecca IV, 730
Coppock, Rebecca IV, 808
Coppock, Rebecca IV, 809
Coppock, Rebecca IV, 814
Coppock, Rebecca IV, 847
Coppock, Rebecca IV, 851
Coppock, Rebecca IV, 942
Coppock, Rebecca IV, 943
Coppock, Rebecca IV, 999
Coppock, Rebecca IV, 1012
Coppock, Rebecca V, 799
Coppock, Rebecca V, 803
Coppock, Rebecca E. IV, 191
Coppock, Rebecca E. IV, 944
Coppock, Rebeckah V, 780
Coppock, Rhoda IV, 694
Coppock, Rhoda IV, 942
Coppock, Rileigh G. V, 381
Coppock, Riley G. V, 381
Coppock, Robert E. IV, 191
Coppock, Robert E. IV, 276
Coppock, Ruth II, 720
Coppock, Ruth IV, 191
Coppock, Ruth IV, 694
Coppock, Ruth IV, 765
Coppock, Ruth IV, 942
Coppock, Ruth IV, 943
Coppock, Ruth IV, 1011
Coppock, Ruth V, 164
Coppock, Ruth Ann IV, 808
Coppock, Ruth Ann IV, 815
Coppock, Ruth Ann IV, 1091
Coppock, Ruth Anna IV, 808
Coppock, Ruth Anna IV, 809
Coppock, Ruth Anna IV, 810
Coppock, Ruth Anna IV, 856
Coppock, Ruth Anna IV, 1016
Coppock, Ruthanna IV, 808
Coppock, Ruthanna IV, 856
Coppock, Ruthanna IV, 943
Coppock, Ruthanna IV, 1091
Coppock, Ruthanna IV, 1129
Coppock, Sally V, 799
Coppock, Sally V, 803
Coppock, Sampson V, 733
Coppock, Sampson V, 803
Coppock, Samson V, 805
Coppock, Samson V, 810
Coppock, Samuel I, 1018
Coppock, Samuel I, 1091
Coppock, Samuel IV, 143
Coppock, Samuel IV, 191
Coppock, Samuel IV, 690
Coppock, Samuel IV, 694
Coppock, Samuel IV, 743
Coppock, Samuel IV, 765
Coppock, Samuel IV, 808
Coppock, Samuel IV, 942
Coppock, Samuel IV, 943
Coppock, Samuel IV, 977
Coppock, Samuel V, 733
Coppock, Samuel V, 780
Coppock, Samuel V, 783
Coppock, Samuel V, 803
Coppock, Samuel V, 805
Coppock, Samuel Jones IV, 808
Coppock, Samuel R. IV, 942
Coppock, Samuel Robert IV, 694
Coppock, Samuel, Jr. IV, 191
Coppock, Samuel, Jr. IV, 694
Coppock, Samuel, Jr. IV, 943
Coppock, Samuel, Sr. IV, 694
Coppock, Sarah II, 494
Coppock, Sarah IV, 191
Coppock, Sarah IV, 567
Coppock, Sarah IV, 571
Coppock, Sarah IV, 808
Coppock, Sarah IV, 810
Coppock, Sarah IV, 943
Coppock, Sarah IV, 1091
Coppock, Sarah V, 805
Coppock, Sarah V, 808
Coppock, Sarah E. IV, 960
Coppock, Sarah Elmy IV, 943
Coppock, Sarah F. V, 803
Coppock, Sarah F. V, 811
Coppock, Sarah J. V, 805
Coppock, Sarah W. V, 804
Coppock, Sibyl IV, 743
Coppock, Sophia IV, 943
Coppock, Susana V, 812
Coppock, Susanna V, 43
Coppock, Susanna V, 113
Coppock, Susanna V, 803
Coppock, Susanna V, 804
Coppock, Susanna V, 805
Coppock, Susanna V, 807
Coppock, Susanna I. V, 805
Coppock, Susannah I, 1018
Coppock, Susannah I, 1028
Coppock, Susannah I, 1029
Coppock, Susannah I, 1032
Coppock, Susannah V, 43
Coppock, Susannah V, 733
Coppock, Susannah V, 736
Coppock, Susannah V, 746
Coppock, Susannah V, 780
Coppock, Susannah V, 799
Coppock, Susannah V, 803
Coppock, Susannah V, 804
Coppock, Susannah V, 805
Coppock, Susannah V, 807
Coppock, Susannah V, 810
Coppock, Thomas I, 1018
Coppock, Thomas I, 1028
Coppock, Thomas IV, 694
Coppock, Thomas IV, 808
Coppock, Thomas IV, 942
Coppock, Thomas IV, 943
Coppock, Thomas V, 799
Coppock, Thomas V, 803
Coppock, Thomas V, 805
Coppock, Timothy IV, 191
Coppock, Timothy IV, 694
Coppock, Timothy IV, 808
Coppock, Timothy IV, 827
Coppock, Timothy IV, 1154
Coppock, Ulipsus V, 733
Coppock, Ulysses G. V, 733
Coppock, Unity IV, 694
Coppock, Unity IV, 942
Coppock, Unity IV, 943
Coppock, Unity IV, 997
Coppock, Walter V, 733
Coppock, Wesley V, 381
Coppock, Wesley V, 780
Coppock, Wesley V, 805
Coppock, Westley V, 805
Coppock, William I, 1018
Coppock, William I, 1150
Coppock, William V, 43
Coppock, William V, 733
Coppock, William V, 799
Coppock, William V, 803
Coppock, William C. V, 804
Coppock, William Ewing I, 1117
Coppock, William F. V, 381
Coppock, William G. IV, 808
Coppock, William G. IV, 809
Coppock, William G. IV, 902
Coppock, William L. V, 381
Coppock, William Layton V, 381
Coppock, William P. V, 733
Coppock, Wm. V, 733
Coppock, Wm. V, 804
Coppock, Wm. V, 810
Coppock, Wm. G. IV, 694
Coppock, Wm. G. IV, 808
Coppock, Wm. G. IV, 902
Coppock, Wm. I. I, 1104
Coppock, Wm. J. V, 805
Coppock, Wm. J. V, 900
Coppock, Wm. P. V, 733
Coppock, Wm. W. IV, 811
Coppock, Zimri V, 803
Coppock, Zimri V, 804
Coppuck, Elizabeth I, 1117
Coppuck, Margaret I, 1117
Copsey, Arch V, 164
Copsey, Archibald V, 164
Copsey, Bernice V, 164
Copsey, Bertina V, 164
Copsey, Carl V, 164
Copsey, Eliza V, 164
Copsey, Harry V, 164
Copsey, Kate V, 164
Copsey, Laura V, 164
Copsey, Laura M. V, 164
Copsey, Mary V, 164
Copsey, Mertie V, 164
Copsey, Nellie M. V, 164
Copsey, Nina V, 164
Copsey, Philip V, 164
Copsey, Rosa V, 164
Copsey, Vernon V, 164
Copsey, Walter V, 164
Copsey, William V, 164
Coram, Arthur B. IV, 1275
Coram, Ellen IV, 1275
Coram, John J. IV, 1275
Coram, John James IV, 1275
Coram, Mary IV, 1275
Coram, Nellie IV, 1275
Coram, Olive C. IV, 1275
Coran, Ellen IV, 1273
Coran, Ellen IV, 1275
Coran, John J. IV, 1273
Coran, John J. IV, 1275
Corathers, C. P. V, 990
Corathers, Delilah V, 990
Corathers, Edward V, 990
Corathers, Ellen V, 990
Corathers, H. W. V, 990
Corathers, Harley V, 990
Corathers, Hattie V, 990
Corathers, J. L. V, 990
Corathers, John L. V, 990
Corathers, Julia V, 990
Corathers, L. C. V, 990
Corathers, Lemuel V, 990
Corathers, Mary V, 990
Corathers, Orlie V, 990
Corathers, Philip C. V, 990
Corathers, Phillip C. V, 990
Corathers, Wilbert R. V, 990
Corbean, Samuel V, 666
Corbean, William V, 666
Corbean, Wm. V, 666
Corben, Norah B. IV, 1249
Corbet, Ann II, 495
Corbet, Dora IV, 1275
Corbet, Elizabeth II, 495
Corbet, Emma II, 734
Corbet, Henry II, 495
Corbet, Henry II, 734
Corbet, Joseph II, 495
Corbet, Mary II, 494
Corbet, Mary II, 554
Corbett, Anna III, 290
Corbett, Joseph II, 495
Corbett, Lydia II, 495
Corbett, Martha VI, 737
Corbett, Mary I, 302
Corbett, Mary I, 306
Corbett, Mary VI, 736
Corbett, Mary VI, 737
Corbett, Peninah I, 302
Corbett, Sarah VI, 737
Corbett, Zilpha I, 932
Corbin, ??? III, 85
Corbin, Anna V, 900
Corbin, Anna V, 938
Corbin, Betty Ilene IV, 1154
Corbin, Bruce IV, 1249
Corbin, Bryce T. IV, 1249
Corbin, Clara B. III, 373
Corbin, Earl IV, 1249
Corbin, Earl T. IV, 1249
Corbin, Ellen IV, 1249
Corbin, Ellen N. IV, 1249
Corbin, Ellen Rhoda IV, 1154
Corbin, Grover D. IV, 1154
Corbin, Jerome IV, 1249
Corbin, Lafayette IV, 1249
Corbin, Ludlow Vincent IV, 1154
Corbin, Mary VI, 45
Corbin, Norah B. IV, 1249
Corbin, Paul IV, 1311
Corbin, Rebecca Ann II, 494
Corbin, Rebecca Ann II, 644
Corbin, Samuel V, 666
Corbin, Thomas N. IV, 1249
Corbin, Warren III, 373
Corbin, Wm. V, 666
Corbint, Charles II, 853
Corbit, Ann II, 349
Corbit, Ann II, 495
Corbit, Ann II, 807
Corbit, Caroline II, 853
Corbit, Caroline R. II, 349
Corbit, Caroline R. II, 734
Corbit, Caroline R. II, 814
Corbit, Caroline R. II, 853
Corbit, Caroline R. II, 909
Corbit, Charles II, 789
Corbit, Chas. II, 853
Corbit, Cowgill II, 495
Corbit, Daniel II, 494
Corbit, Daniel II, 495
Corbit, Edward Stabler II, 789
Corbit, Elizabeth II, 349
Corbit, Elizabeth II, 468
Corbit, Elizabeth II, 494
Corbit, Elizabeth II, 495
Corbit, Elizabeth II, 791
Corbit, Elizabeth II, 853
Corbit, Elizabeth II, 855
Corbit, Elizabeth II, 882
Corbit, Emma II, 702
Corbit, Emma II, 734
Corbit, Emma II, 789
Corbit, Emma II, 811
Corbit, Emma II, 853
Corbit, Emma II, 904
Corbit, Helen II, 789
Corbit, Henry II, 494
Corbit, Henry II, 495
Corbit, Henry II, 734
Corbit, Henry C. II, 349
Corbit, Henry C. II, 468
Corbit, Henry C. II, 495
Corbit, Henry C. II, 702
Corbit, Henry C. II, 734
Corbit, Henry C. II, 853
Corbit, Henry C. II, 855
Corbit, Henry C. II, 904
Corbit, Henry C. II, 909
Corbit, Henry Cowgill II, 349
Corbit, Jonas Preston II, 349
Corbit, Jonathan II, 495
Corbit, Joseph II, 349
Corbit, Joseph II, 468
Corbit, Joseph II, 494
Corbit, Joseph II, 495
Corbit, Joseph II, 789
Corbit, Joseph II, 791
Corbit, Joseph II, 853
Corbit, Joseph II, 855
Corbit, Lydia II, 494
Corbit, Lydia II, 495
Corbit, Lydia C. II, 853
Corbit, Lydia C. II, 855
Corbit, Lydia Cowgill II, 791
Corbit, Lydia Cowgill II, 853
Corbit, Mary II, 494
Corbit, Peninah I, 302
Corbit, Peninah I, 306
Corbit, Sarah II, 349
Corbit, Sarah II, 468
Corbit, Sarah II, 495
Corbit, Sarah II, 702
Corbit, Sarah II, 734
Corbit, Sarah B. II, 853
Corbit, Sarah B. II, 904

orbit, Sarah B. II, 909
orbit, Thomas II, 349
orbit, Thomas II, 495
orbit, Wd. Elizabeth II, 789
orbit, Wm. II, 494
orbit, Wm. Francis II, 789
orbitt, Chas. II, 853
orbitt, Daniel II, 494
orbitt, Wm. II, 494
orby, Mary II, 210
orcoren, Charlotte II, 495
orcoren, Charlotte II, 565
orde, Bardey III, 204
orde, Mary E. III, 204
ordel, Elizabeth I, 984
ordel, Lucy A. P. VI, 807
ordel, Paschal VI, 807
ordell, Geo. W. V, 990
orden, Elizabeth I, 1008
orden, Elizabeth I, 1009
orden, Lillie I, 1149
order, Elizabeth I, 1008
order, Elizabeth I, 1009
order, Elizabeth V, 371
order, Elizabeth V, 381
order, Elizabeth VI, 369
order, Leola V, 43
ordery, Esther II, 495
ordery, Esther II, 596
ordery, Mary II, 495
ordery, Mary II, 578
ordle, Abbigail I, 980
ordle, Abbigail I, 984
ordle, Elen I, 984
ordle, Elizabeth I, 984
ordle, Rebecca I, 984
ordon, Rachel V, 483
ordon, Rachel V, 504
ordray, Emma IV, 695
ordray, Ethel S. IV, 695
ordry, Deborah II, 349
ordry, Deborah II, 495
ordry, Esther II, 495
ordry, Hugh II, 349
ordry, Hugh II, 495
ordry, Mary II, 495
ordwell, Vincent II, 495
ore, Emily V, 43
ore, Emily V, 58
ore, Enoch II, 210
ore, Louisa I, 302
ore, Louisa I, 303
ore, Mary II, 210
ore, Mary II, 216
ore, Seth W. V, 43
ore???, Louisa I, 302
ore???, Louisa I, 303
oresdale, Emma V, 484
oresdale, Lydia V, 484
orey, Bula McElwee V, 481
orey, Dorcas V, 666
orey, Dorcas V, 703
orey, Joseph M. V, 666
orey, Joseph M. V, 703
orey, Nicy Lavina IV, 1154
ork, Isaiah V, 990
orkall, Elizabeth VI, 1017
orker, Elizabeth II, 493
orker, Elizabeth II, 495
orker, John Large II, 495
orker, Mary II, 442
orker, Mary II, 495
orker, Mary II, 523
orker, Rebecca II, 349
orker, Rebecca II, 495
orker, Sarah II, 495
orker, Sarah II, 576
orker, Sarah II, 991
orker, Sarah II, 1009
orker, Wd. Mary II, 495
orker, Wd. Mary II, 670
orker, William II, 349
orker, Wm. II, 442
orker, Wm. II, 495
orker, Wm. II, 523
orleis, Clara W. III, 15
orless, ??? III, 85
orless, Bernard III, 373
orless, Joseph II, 137
orless, Mary II, 137
orlett, Lillian S. IV, 1311
orlette, Claribel IV, 1311
orlette, Hariet M. IV, 1311
orlette, Harriett IV, 1311
orlette, Jessie IV, 1311
orlette, Lillian S. IV, 1311
orlette, Martha IV, 1311
orlette, Mary L. IV, 1311
orlette, Mary M. IV, 1311
orlette, Mina C. IV, 1311
orlette, Mona IV, 1311
Corlette, Mrs. Mary IV, 1311
Corley, Berry VI, 896
Corley, Beverley VI, 896
Corley, Bevly. VI, 875
Corley, Caniel VI, 896
Corley, Elizabeth VI, 896
Corley, James VI, 869
Corley, James VI, 896
Corley, Jeremiah VI, 896
Corley, John VI, 984
Corley, John W. VI, 988
Corley, Judith VI, 875
Corley, Judith VI, 896
Corley, Lucy VI, 993
Corley, Milley VI, 896
Corley, Nancy VI, 896
Corley, Phebe VI, 869
Corley, Rhoda VI, 896
Corley, Sarah VI, 896
Corley, Tamsey VI, 896
Corley, William VI, 896
Corley, William VI, 938
Corley, William VI, 993
Corlies, ??? III, 79
Corlies, ??? III, 85
Corlies, ??? III, 350
Corlies, Albert III, 85
Corlies, Albert III, 86
Corlies, Alfred III, 86
Corlies, Alfred W. III, 86
Corlies, Amelia III, 86
Corlies, Amelia III, 373
Corlies, Amos III, 373
Corlies, Ann II, 853
Corlies, Ann II, 939
Corlies, Ann III, 373
Corlies, Annie W. III, 99
Corlies, Annie W. III, 373
Corlies, Annie Wright III, 85
Corlies, Benj. III, 85
Corlies, Benj. III, 86
Corlies, Benj. III, 298
Corlies, Benjamin II, 734
Corlies, Benjamin III, 27
Corlies, Benjamin III, 86
Corlies, Benjamin III, 215
Corlies, Briton II, 350
Corlies, Briton II, 495
Corlies, Briton III, 86
Corlies, Briton III, 379
Corlies, Britton II, 495
Corlies, Britton II, 853
Corlies, Britton II, 863
Corlies, Caroline II, 790
Corlies, Caroline II, 833
Corlies, Caroline A. II, 833
Corlies, Caroline A. II, 853
Corlies, Caroline C. III, 85
Corlies, Caroline H. II, 853
Corlies, Caroline H. II, 901
Corlies, Clara II, 790
Corlies, Clara II, 853
Corlies, Clara II, 899
Corlies, Clara W. III, 85
Corlies, Cornelia L. III, 86
Corlies, Deborah III, 85
Corlies, Edith A. II, 853
Corlies, Edith Atlee II, 790
Corlies, Edith W. III, 85
Corlies, Edith W. III, 144
Corlies, Edmee III, 180
Corlies, Edmee Alcine III, 85
Corlies, Edmund W. III, 144
Corlies, Edna III, 86
Corlies, Edward Alex. III, 85
Corlies, Edward Alexander III, 85
Corlies, Edward Garrigues III, 85
Corlies, Edward L. III, 85
Corlies, Edward L. III, 86
Corlies, Edwin II, 853
Corlies, Edwin III, 85
Corlies, Eleanor W. III, 85
Corlies, Eliz. III, 219
Corlies, Elizabeth II, 350
Corlies, Elizabeth II, 827
Corlies, Elizabeth II, 853
Corlies, Elizabeth II, 939
Corlies, Elizabeth III, 85
Corlies, Elizabeth III, 86
Corlies, Elizabeth A. II, 495
Corlies, Elizabeth T. III, 86
Corlies, Elizabeth W. II, 832
Corlies, Elizabeth W. II, 853
Corlies, Elizabeth W. III, 85
Corlies, Ellen III, 85
Corlies, Ellen Gardner III, 79
Corlies, Ellen Gardner III, 86
Corlies, Emily III, 85
Corlies, Emily III, 86
Corlies, Emily III, 265
Corlies, Esther III, 86
Corlies, Esther III, 203
Corlies, Esther L. III, 86
Corlies, F. Haines III, 85
Corlies, Florence II, 790
Corlies, Frederick Joseph III, 86
Corlies, George III, 85
Corlies, George W. III, 85
Corlies, George, Jr. III, 85
Corlies, Hannah III, 85
Corlies, Hannah III, 86
Corlies, Hannah III, 159
Corlies, Henry De Witt III, 85
Corlies, Henry P. II, 789
Corlies, Henry P. II, 853
Corlies, Henry P. II, 939
Corlies, Henry P. III, 85
Corlies, Hester III, 86
Corlies, Howard W. III, 85
Corlies, J. Edgar III, 15
Corlies, J. Edgar III, 370
Corlies, Jabez II, 833
Corlies, Jacob III, 85
Corlies, Jacob III, 144
Corlies, Jacob III, 159
Corlies, Jacob W. II, 495
Corlies, Jacob W. II, 853
Corlies, Jacob W. II, 863
Corlies, Jacob Wooley II, 790
Corlies, Jno. Edgar III, 85
Corlies, Jno. Edgar III, 179
Corlies, John III, 85
Corlies, John III, 86
Corlies, John III, 219
Corlies, John E. III, 86
Corlies, John Edgar III, 85
Corlies, John Edgar III, 99
Corlies, John Edgar III, 180
Corlies, John Edgar III, 373
Corlies, John W. III, 85
Corlies, John W. III, 86
Corlies, John W. III, 373
Corlies, Joseph II, 495
Corlies, Joseph II, 1065
Corlies, Joseph II, 1071
Corlies, Joseph III, 86
Corlies, Joseph N. III, 86
Corlies, Joseph W. III, 85
Corlies, Joseph W. III, 86
Corlies, Joseph W. III, 265
Corlies, Joseph W. III, 379
Corlies, Joseph W. III, 385
Corlies, Joseph William III, 86
Corlies, Joseph Wm. III, 86
Corlies, Lydia III, 85
Corlies, Lydia III, 108
Corlies, Lydia L. III, 85
Corlies, Lydia L. III, 86
Corlies, Lydia L. III, 265
Corlies, Lydia L. III, 379
Corlies, Lydia L. III, 385
Corlies, Margaret II, 817
Corlies, Margaret III, 85
Corlies, Margaret III, 298
Corlies, Margaret G. III, 85
Corlies, Margaret H. III, 86
Corlies, Margaret Longstreth II, 790
Corlies, Margaret N. III, 86
Corlies, Margaret N. III, 298
Corlies, Margaret S. III, 144
Corlies, Mary III, 86
Corlies, Mary III, 316
Corlies, Mary B. III, 15
Corlies, Mary B. III, 85
Corlies, Mary B. III, 99
Corlies, Mary B. III, 179
Corlies, Mary B. III, 180
Corlies, Mary B. III, 370
Corlies, Mary B. III, 373
Corlies, Mary M. II, 833
Corlies, Mary N. III, 27
Corlies, Mary N. III, 86
Corlies, Mary W. II, 853
Corlies, Mary Wilson II, 790
Corlies, Newtown III, 85
Corlies, Octaire Emile II, 790
Corlies, Patience III, 85
Corlies, Patience C. III, 86
Corlies, Patience Caroline III, 159
Corlies, Phebe III, 27
Corlies, Phebe III, 85
Corlies, Phebe III, 86
Corlies, Phebe III, 170
Corlies, Phebe III, 215
Corlies, Phebe III, 298
Corlies, Phebe III, 373
Corlies, Richard Stanton III, 86
Corlies, S. Fisher II, 833
Corlies, S. Fisher II, 853
Corlies, S. Fisher II, 901
Corlies, Samuel F. II, 853
Corlies, Samuel Fisher II, 790
Corlies, Samuel Fisher II, 853
Corlies, Samuel G. III, 86
Corlies, Sarah II, 790
Corlies, Sarah II, 799
Corlies, Sarah II, 853
Corlies, Sarah II, 863
Corlies, Sarah III, 86
Corlies, Sarah III, 350
Corlies, Sarah III, 379
Corlies, Sarah A. II, 853
Corlies, Sarah Allinson II, 780
Corlies, Sarah Allinson III, 85
Corlies, Sarah F. II, 853
Corlies, Sarah F. II, 901
Corlies, Sarah Fisher II, 790
Corlies, Sarah Fisher II, 853
Corlies, Sarah L. III, 86
Corlies, Sarah L. III, 203
Corlies, Sarah L. III, 215
Corlies, Sarah W. III, 86
Corlies, Sarah W. III, 219
Corlies, Thomas II, 350
Corlies, Thomas II, 495
Corlies, Thomas II, 853
Corlies, Thos. II, 853
Corlies, Walter III, 86
Corlies, Wd. Elizabeth II, 789
Corlies, Wd. Sarah III, 219
Corlies, Wd. Sarah W. III, 86
Corlies, William III, 86
Corlies, William Henry III, 85
Corlies, William Moore II, 790
Corlies, William S. III, 86
Corlies, William W. III, 86
Corlies, Wm. II, 853
Corlies, Wm. II, 939
Corlies, Wm. H. II, 853
Corlies, Wm. H. II, 899
Corlies, Wm. Henry II, 853
Corlies, Wm. M. II, 853
Corlies, Wm. Moore II, 853
Corliss, Jacob W. II, 853
Corlitt, Claribel IV, 1311
Corlitt, Harriett IV, 1311
Corlitt, Lillian S. IV, 1311
Corlitt, Mrs. Mary IV, 1311
Corman, Mary II, 483
Corman, Mary II, 495
Cormaney, Callie I, 1150
Cormell, Frank V, 325
Cormell, Kate V, 325
Cormell, Lewis V, 325
Cormell, Moletus Elbert V, 325
Cormell, Oscar B. V, 325
Cormer, Wm. B. VI, 977
Cormn, Ellen IV, 1275
Cornal, Lydia V, 900
Corne, Jane II, 350
Corne, John II, 350
Cornean, Rebecca V, 900
Cornean, Rebecca H. V, 900
Corneau, Charles II, 853
Corneau, Chas. II, 853
Corneau, Chas. C. II, 915
Corneau, Chas. Sharpless II, 790
Corneau, Elizabeth II, 853
Corneau, Elizabeth C. II, 853
Corneau, Elizabeth C. II, 857
Corneau, Elizabeth C. II, 915
Corneau, Elizabeth Coates II, 790
Corneau, Elizabeth R. II, 853
Corneau, Helen II, 853
Corneau, Helen C. II, 853
Corneau, Helen C. II, 915
Corneau, Henry Charles II, 790
Corneau, Henry Charles II, 853
Cornegys, Ann II, 495
Cornegys, Ann II, 616
Corneilson, Eleanor III, 86
Corneilson, Eleanor Linnie III, 86
Corneilson, Janice III, 86
Corneilson, Thomas R. III, 86
Cornel, Catharine I, 534
Cornel, Catherine I, 534
Corneles, Peter II, 17
Cornelius, Ann III, 464
Cornelius, Ann M. VI, 896
Cornelius, Anna III, 464
Cornelius, Anne III, 405
Cornelius, Antoinette III, 510
Cornelius, Cynthia T. IV, 1359
Cornelius, Edward IV, 1359
Cornelius, Edwin C. VI, 808
Cornelius, Elizabeth B. III, 510
Cornelius, Hannah I, 1008
Cornelius, Henry III, 510
Cornelius, Henry S. III, 510
Cornelius, Jane III, 510
Cornelius, Jemima III, 405
Cornelius, John III, 405
Cornelius, John III, 426
Cornelius, John III, 481
Cornelius, John III, 490
Cornelius, Jonathan III, 405
Cornelius, Jonathan III, 464
Cornelius, Lot III, 461
Cornelius, Lott III, 405
Cornelius, Mary III, 405
Cornelius, Mary III, 426
Cornelius, Mary III, 481
Cornelius, Mary III, 490
Cornelius, Mary VI, 808
Cornelius, Mary C. III, 405
Cornelius, Mary C. III, 461
Cornelius, Mary J. III, 510
Cornelius, Phebe A. IV, 1359
Cornelius, Samuel III, 405
Cornelius, Samuel III, 510
Cornelius, Sarah III, 405
Cornelius, Sarah III, 435
Cornelius, Sarah III, 464
Cornelius, William C. VI, 896
Cornelius, William H. IV, 1359
Cornell, ??? III, 87
Cornell, ??? III, 88
Cornell, ??? III, 178
Cornell, ??? III, 405
Cornell, ??? III, 413
Cornell, ??? VI, 380
Cornell, ??? VI, 406
Cornell, Abigail III, 86
Cornell, Adine V, 666
Cornell, Adrien III, 87
Cornell, Albert III, 87
Cornell, Albert III, 88
Cornell, Alfred IV, 1311
Cornell, Alice III, 86
Cornell, Alice III, 88
Cornell, Alletta K. III, 87
Cornell, Amy III, 87
Cornell, Amy VI, 751
Cornell, Anna III, 87
Cornell, Anna III, 88
Cornell, Anna III, 208
Cornell, Anna III, 290
Cornell, Anna IV, 1359
Cornell, Anna Maria III, 88
Cornell, Anne III, 86
Cornell, Anne III, 87
Cornell, Annie III, 99
Cornell, Asa IV, 1359
Cornell, Benj. III, 87
Cornell, Benj. III, 88
Cornell, Benjamin III, 86
Cornell, Benjamin III, 115
Cornell, Benjamin III, 373
Cornell, Benjamin IV, 1359
Cornell, Benjamin, Jr. III, 86
Cornell, Blanche V, 381
Cornell, Caleb III, 144
Cornell, Caleb III, 405
Cornell, Caroline III, 86
Cornell, Catharine III, 87
Cornell, Catharine III, 405
Cornell, Catherine III, 36
Cornell, Catherine Mailor III, 34
Cornell, Charles III, 86
Cornell, Charles III, 87
Cornell, Charles G. III, 86
Cornell, Charles G. III, 99
Cornell, Charles Henry III, 87
Cornell, Charles P. III, 373
Cornell, Charles W. III, 87
Cornell, Charles W., Jr. III, 87
Cornell, Comfort III, 86
Cornell, Daniel IV, 1359
Cornell, Daniel, Jr. IV, 1359
Cornell, David III, 87
Cornell, David VI, 380
Cornell, David W. III, 87
Cornell, Deborah III, 43
Cornell, Deborah III, 87
Cornell, Deborah III, 126
Cornell, Deborah III, 379
Cornell, Dorcas III, 141
Cornell, Edgar V. III, 87
Cornell, Edw. III, 87
Cornell, Edward III, 87
Cornell, Edward III, 154
Cornell, Edward III, 298
Cornell, Edward, Jr. III, 87
Cornell, Elijah III, 87
Cornell, Eliz. III, 86
Cornell, Eliz. III, 88
Cornell, Eliz. III, 104
Cornell, Eliza P. III, 87
Cornell, Eliza P. III, 291

Cornell, Elizabeth III, 87
Cornell, Elizabeth III, 373
Cornell, Elizabeth V, 381
Cornell, Elizabeth V, 666
Cornell, Elizabeth H. III, 36
Cornell, Embley Pidcock II, 1070
Cornell, Embley Pidcock II, 1071
Cornell, Esther III, 87
Cornell, Esther III, 154
Cornell, Esther III, 298
Cornell, Esther IV, 1359
Cornell, Esther S. III, 87
Cornell, Fanny Emily III, 87
Cornell, Ferris III, 86
Cornell, Ferris III, 87
Cornell, Ferris III, 88
Cornell, Flushing III, 88
Cornell, Franklin III, 87
Cornell, Franklin III, 243
Cornell, Franklin III, 301
Cornell, Franklin M. III, 87
Cornell, Freelove III, 405
Cornell, Geo. Davidson III, 87
Cornell, George III, 373
Cornell, George R. V, 901
Cornell, George T. IV, 695
Cornell, Hannah III, 87
Cornell, Hannah III, 88
Cornell, Hannah III, 146
Cornell, Hannah III, 313
Cornell, Hannah III, 405
Cornell, Hannah III, 439
Cornell, Hannah III, 442
Cornell, Hannah III, 449
Cornell, Harold Barclay III, 87
Cornell, Hempsted III, 86
Cornell, Henry De Witt III, 373
Cornell, Hetty III, 373
Cornell, Isabella IV, 944
Cornell, Jacob IV, 1359
Cornell, James B. III, 88
Cornell, James C. III, 87
Cornell, James Lovett III, 87
Cornell, James Mott III, 379
Cornell, Jesse III, 88
Cornell, Job IV, 1359
Cornell, John III, 405
Cornell, John V, 381
Cornell, John V, 901
Cornell, John Edgar III, 87
Cornell, John F. III, 87
Cornell, John J. VI, 737
Cornell, John S. III, 87
Cornell, John, Jr. III, 88
Cornell, Joseph III, 87
Cornell, Joseph III, 373
Cornell, Joseph N. III, 373
Cornell, Joshua III, 87
Cornell, Joshua III, 146
Cornell, Joshua III, 313
Cornell, Josiah III, 36
Cornell, Josiah III, 87
Cornell, Josiah III, 208
Cornell, Josiah D. III, 86
Cornell, Julien Davies III, 87
Cornell, Julien Davies III, 303
Cornell, Julien Martin III, 87
Cornell, Katherine III, 87
Cornell, Katherine III, 298
Cornell, Lee V, 164
Cornell, Letitia II, 1070
Cornell, Letitia II, 1071
Cornell, Lizzie V, 381
Cornell, Lucretia II, 1071
Cornell, Lydia IV, 1359
Cornell, Lydia V, 901
Cornell, Lydia Ann IV, 1359
Cornell, Lydia P. III, 88
Cornell, Margaret IV, 695
Cornell, Margaret N. III, 373
Cornell, Marion H. III, 87
Cornell, Marion H. III, 243
Cornell, Mark III, 87
Cornell, Mark III, 88
Cornell, Mark III, 290
Cornell, Mark S. III, 87
Cornell, Martha C. III, 87
Cornell, Martha C. III, 301
Cornell, Martha W. III, 87
Cornell, Mary III, 86
Cornell, Mary III, 87
Cornell, Mary III, 88
Cornell, Mary III, 178
Cornell, Mary III, 208
Cornell, Mary III, 252
Cornell, Mary III, 359
Cornell, Mary III, 373
Cornell, Mary III, 405
Cornell, Mary III, 442
Cornell, Mary V, 901
Cornell, Mary A. III, 87
Cornell, Mary Ann III, 267
Cornell, Mary Ann III, 268
Cornell, Mary Annette III, 87
Cornell, Mary Annette III, 291
Cornell, Mary B. III, 86
Cornell, Mary B. III, 87
Cornell, Mary D. VI, 380
Cornell, Mary Elizabeth V, 381
Cornell, Mary H. III, 86
Cornell, Mary H. III, 87
Cornell, Mary L. VI, 380
Cornell, Mary L. VI, 407
Cornell, Mary N. III, 87
Cornell, Mary N. III, 373
Cornell, Mary P. II, 1070
Cornell, Mary P. II, 1071
Cornell, Mary U. IV, 1359
Cornell, Permelia III, 86
Cornell, Permelia III, 115
Cornell, Peter III, 87
Cornell, Phebe III, 86
Cornell, Phebe III, 87
Cornell, Phebe III, 105
Cornell, Phebe III, 146
Cornell, Phebe III, 251
Cornell, Phebe III, 373
Cornell, Phebe III, 405
Cornell, Phebe III, 413
Cornell, Phebe III, 481
Cornell, Phebe IV, 1359
Cornell, Phebe IV, 1375
Cornell, Phebe A. T. III, 87
Cornell, Phebe C. III, 87
Cornell, Phebe F. III, 88
Cornell, Phebe R. III, 87
Cornell, Rebecca III, 87
Cornell, Rev. Ferris D. III, 379
Cornell, Reynolds III, 87
Cornell, Rich. III, 87
Cornell, Rich. III, 291
Cornell, Richard III, 86
Cornell, Richard III, 87
Cornell, Richard III, 88
Cornell, Richard III, 105
Cornell, Richard III, 126
Cornell, Richard III, 251
Cornell, Richard III, 313
Cornell, Richard III, 405
Cornell, Richard III, 442
Cornell, Richard III, 449
Cornell, Richard Mott III, 379
Cornell, Richardson III, 87
Cornell, Robert III, 87
Cornell, Robert III, 88
Cornell, Robert C. III, 87
Cornell, Samuel III, 88
Cornell, Samuel IV, 1359
Cornell, Samuel N. IV, 1359
Cornell, Sarah III, 88
Cornell, Sarah III, 161
Cornell, Sarah III, 237
Cornell, Sarah III, 268
Cornell, Sarah III, 313
Cornell, Sarah IV, 1359
Cornell, Sarah IV, 1375
Cornell, Sarah Ann III, 88
Cornell, Sarah L. III, 373
Cornell, Sarah M. III, 379
Cornell, Sarah R. III, 87
Cornell, Sarah R. III, 243
Cornell, Sarah R. III, 301
Cornell, Sarah T. III, 86
Cornell, Sarah T. III, 87
Cornell, Sarah U. III, 88
Cornell, Silas III, 88
Cornell, Silas III, 237
Cornell, Silas III, 379
Cornell, Stephen III, 87
Cornell, Stephen III, 88
Cornell, Stephen IV, 1359
Cornell, Stephen B. IV, 1359
Cornell, Stephen S. III, 88
Cornell, Susan A. III, 87
Cornell, Susan M. V, 901
Cornell, Swarthmore III, 87
Cornell, Theodore III, 88
Cornell, Thomas III, 88
Cornell, Thomas C. III, 88
Cornell, Virginia III, 87
Cornell, Virginia III, 303
Cornell, Walter III, 87
Cornell, Walter III, 373
Cornell, Wd. Annie W. III, 86
Cornell, Wd. Mary III, 87
Cornell, Wd. Mary D. VI, 406
Cornell, Wd. Phebe III, 86
Cornell, Wd. Phebe III, 144
Cornell, Willard Haviland III, 87
Cornell, William V, 901
Cornell, William C. III, 88
Cornell, William H. V, 901
Cornell, William T. III, 88
Cornell, William, Jr. V, 901
Cornell, Wm. V, 901
Cornhill, Deborah III, 126
Cornhill, Richard III, 126
Corning, Allen III, 405
Corning, Aug. III, 393
Corning, Augustus III, 394
Corning, Augustus III, 405
Corning, Sarah III, 393
Corning, Sarah III, 394
Corning, Sarah Allen III, 405
Cornliff, Alice IV, 191
Cornliki, Alice IV, 191
Cornthwait, Alisanna IV, 618
Cornthwait, C. W. IV, 618
Cornthwait, Elizabeth II, 958
Cornthwait, Elizabeth II, 991
Cornthwait, Elizabeth, Jr. II, 991
Cornthwait, John II, 958
Cornthwait, John II, 991
Cornthwait, John VI, 532
Cornthwait, Mary VI, 532
Cornthwait, Phebe II, 958
Cornthwait, Phebe II, 991
Cornthwait, Robert II, 958
Cornthwait, Robert II, 991
Cornthwait, Robert IV, 618
Cornthwait, Ruth II, 958
Cornthwait, Ruth II, 991
Cornthwait, Thomas II, 958
Cornthwait, Thomas II, 991
Cornthwait, William Peck IV, 618
Cornthwaite, Elizabeth II, 991
Cornthwaite, John II, 495
Cornthwaite, John II, 991
Cornthwaite, Robert II, 991
Cornthwaite, Thomas II, 991
Cornthwate, William Peck IV, 618
Cornthwite, John II, 1014
Cornthwite, Ruth II, 991
Cornthwite, Ruth II, 1014
Cornwall, ??? III, 88
Cornwall, Aspinwall III, 405
Cornwall, Aspinwall III, 427
Cornwall, Elizabeth III, 405
Cornwall, Francis II, 583
Cornwall, Francis II, 626
Cornwall, Jane III, 405
Cornwall, Jerusha III, 405
Cornwall, John II, 442
Cornwall, John E. III, 405
Cornwall, Lydia I, 44
Cornwall, Mary III, 427
Cornwall, Phebe III, 405
Cornwall, Priscilla III, 405
Cornwall, Priscilla III, 427
Cornwall, Samuel VI, 8
Cornwall, Samuel VI, 42
Cornwall, Samuel VI, 93
Cornwall, Willis III, 405
Cornwell, ??? III, 101
Cornwell, ??? VI, 95
Cornwell, Aaron I, 44
Cornwell, Aaron I, 191
Cornwell, Aaron VI, 105
Cornwell, Ann I, 44
Cornwell, Ann VI, 104
Cornwell, Ann VI, 105
Cornwell, Ann VI, 124
Cornwell, Anne I, 189
Cornwell, Aron VI, 104
Cornwell, Aron VI, 105
Cornwell, Benjamin VI, 124
Cornwell, Clothildah VI, 124
Cornwell, Dozae VI, 124
Cornwell, Elisabeth I, 44
Cornwell, Elizabeth I, 191
Cornwell, Elizabeth I, 196
Cornwell, Elizabeth III, 405
Cornwell, Elizabeth VI, 42
Cornwell, Elizabeth VI, 60
Cornwell, Elizabeth VI, 105
Cornwell, Elizabeth VI, 119
Cornwell, Elizabeth VI, 124
Cornwell, Elizabeth VI, 164
Cornwell, Elizabeth VI, 165
Cornwell, Francis VI, 124
Cornwell, Jacob I, 44
Cornwell, Jacob VI, 95
Cornwell, Jacob VI, 105
Cornwell, Jacob VI, 124
Cornwell, Jacob VI, 164
Cornwell, Jacob VI, 165
Cornwell, Jacob VI, 167
Cornwell, Jerusha III, 405
Cornwell, Joel VI, 98
Cornwell, John I, 22
Cornwell, John I, 44
Cornwell, John I, 79
Cornwell, John VI, 94
Cornwell, John VI, 105
Cornwell, John E. III, 405
Cornwell, John, Jr. VI, 105
Cornwell, Joseph VI, 105
Cornwell, Lemuel VI, 124
Cornwell, Lucy VI, 124
Cornwell, Lydia I, 22
Cornwell, Lydia I, 44
Cornwell, Margaret VI, 60
Cornwell, Mary I, 136
Cornwell, Mary I, 167
Cornwell, Mary VI, 45
Cornwell, Mary VI, 46
Cornwell, Mary VI, 60
Cornwell, Mary VI, 105
Cornwell, Mary VI, 116
Cornwell, Mary VI, 124
Cornwell, Mary Ann III, 88
Cornwell, Mary Ann III, 101
Cornwell, Moses I, 44
Cornwell, Moses I, 191
Cornwell, Moses VI, 105
Cornwell, Mourning I, 22
Cornwell, Mourning VI, 105
Cornwell, Mourning VI, 124
Cornwell, Nancy VI, 60
Cornwell, Phanakey VI, 124
Cornwell, Phebe III, 405
Cornwell, Samuel I, 136
Cornwell, Samuel I, 167
Cornwell, Samuel VI, 93
Cornwell, Samuel VI, 98
Cornwell, Samuel VI, 105
Cornwell, Samuel VI, 124
Cornwell, Samuel, Jr. VI, 60
Cornwell, Samuel, Jr. VI, 98
Cornwell, Samuel, Sr. VI, 105
Cornwell, Sarah VI, 52
Cornwell, Sarah VI, 60
Cornwell, Sarah VI, 98
Cornwell, Sarah VI, 105
Cornwell, Sarah VI, 124
Cornwell, Stephen III, 88
Cornwell, Walter V, 990
Cornwell, Widow Anne I, 191
Cornwell, Widow Lydia I, 79
Cornwell, William I, 44
Cornwell, William VI, 105
Cornwell, William VI, 116
Cornwell, Willis III, 405
Corpuck, Martha I, 1117
Correy, Leota DeEtta V, 805
Corry, Joice II, 350
Corry, Sarah II, 350
Corry, Thomas II, 350
Corry, William II, 350
Corsa, Bennington III, 481
Corsa, Frankie W. III, 481
Corsa, George W. III, 481
Corsa, Isaac V. III, 481
Corsa, Minnie III, 481
Corsa, Sarah III, 88
Corsa, Sarah III, 379
Corsa, Sarah III, 481
Corsand, Hannah I, 136
Corse, Abigail III, 88
Corse, Abigail III, 104
Corse, Albert IV, 955
Corse, Albert E. IV, 955
Corse, Anna IV, 955
Corse, Anna Clark II, 789
Corse, Barney III, 88
Corse, Barney III, 278
Corse, Barney III, 379
Corse, Benjamin II, 799
Corse, Caroline III, 88
Corse, Cornelia III, 88
Corse, David III, 88
Corse, Deborah III, 88
Corse, Eliza L. III, 88
Corse, Elizabeth III, 88
Corse, Elizabeth IV, 944
Corse, Elizabeth IV, 955
Corse, Elizabeth M. IV, 944
Corse, Elizabeth M. IV, 954
Corse, Esther S. III, 88
Corse, Frankford III, 88
Corse, Frederick Aug. III, 88
Corse, Frederick Augustus III, 88
Corse, George F. III, 88
Corse, Israel III, 86
Corse, Israel III, 88
Corse, Israel III, 104
Corse, Israel III, 313
Corse, Israel III, 336
Corse, James IV, 954
Corse, James M. II, 702
Corse, James M. II, 734
Corse, James R. II, 702
Corse, Jane P. II, 702
Corse, John B. III, 88
Corse, Josephine III, 88
Corse, Laura III, 88
Corse, Laura P. III, 88
Corse, Lucy Campbell II, 782
Corse, Lydia III, 88
Corse, Lydia III, 313
Corse, Lydia Ann III, 88
Corse, Lydia Ann III, 313
Corse, Margaretta II, 702
Corse, Mary III, 88
Corse, Mary III, 278
Corse, Mary E. III, 88
Corse, Mary E. III, 252
Corse, Mary E. III, 379
Corse, Mary Lydia III, 88
Corse, Mary W. III, 88
Corse, Rebecca II, 702
Corse, Rebecca II, 799
Corse, Rebecca IV, 954
Corse, Rebecca IV, 955
Corse, Robert III, 88
Corse, Robert Sinclair III, 88
Corse, Sally II, 799
Corse, Samuel Leggett III, 88
Corse, Susan III, 88
Corse, William III, 88
Corse, William Henry IV, 955
Corse, William J. D. III, 88
Corse, William L. III, 88
Corsen, Ella IV, 1249
Corsen, Frank IV, 1249
Corsey, Phebe I, 876
Corsey, Phebe I, 880
Corslie, Mary I, 936
Corson, Elizabeth A. S. II, 853
Corson, Hannah II, 991
Corson, Hannah II, 1038
Corson, Sarah D. II, 807
Cort, Cressie Mildred Hooten V, 556
Cort, Hannah L. V, 556
Cort, Margaret V, 576
Cort, Margaret Hooten V, 556
Cortelyon, ??? III, 455
Cortelyon, Adrienne III, 405
Corties, Elihu II, 210
Cortland, Abbie III, 338
Cortlette, Mamie L. IV, 1311
Cortney, Israel IV, 695
Cortney, Susan IV, 695
Cortney, William V, 454
Corum, John J. IV, 1275
Corwan, John V, 231
Corwin, Charlie IV, 1275
Corwin, Cornie IV, 1275
Corwin, Dora IV, 1275
Corwin, Emline IV, 1275
Corwin, Guy IV, 1275
Corwin, James IV, 1205
Corwin, Jane III, 476
Corwin, Jane IV, 1275
Corwin, John IV, 1275
Corwin, John V, 231
Corwin, Lida IV, 1275
Corwin, Mahala C. V, 43
Corwin, Mahala C. V, 85
Corwin, Mamie IV, 1205
Corwin, Mariana V, 43
Corwin, Marianna V, 43
Corwin, Nancy IV, 1275
Corwin, Rollie IV, 1275
Corwin, Samuel V, 231
Corwin, Samuel, Jr. V, 231
Corwin, Sarah V, 43
Corwin, Sarah V, 116
Cory, Henry V, 990
Cory, Joice II, 350
Cory, Lucinda V, 990
Cory, Mary V, 231
Cory, Mary V, 480
Cory, William II, 350
Cosan, Sarah I, 136
Cosand, ??? I, 13
Cosand, Aaron I, 8
Cosand, Aaron I, 45
Cosand, Aaron I, 70
Cosand, Aaron I, 136
Cosand, Aaron I, 155
Cosand, Aaron I, 182
Cosand, Aaron I, 191
Cosand, Aaron I, 194
Cosand, Aaron I, 697
Cosand, Aaron I, 712
Cosand, Abigail I, 44
Cosand, Abigail I, 136
Cosand, Abigail I, 166
Cosand, Abigail I, 191
Cosand, Abigail I, 705
Cosand, Angelina I, 697
Cosand, Angelina I, 712

osand, Angelina I, 732
osand, Ann I, 191
osand, Ann I, 194
osand, Anna I, 191
osand, Aron I, 45
osand, Aron I, 136
osand, Benjamin I, 97
osand, Benjamin I, 136
osand, Benjamin I, 140
osand, Benjamin I, 144
osand, Benjamin I, 163
osand, Benjamin I, 182
osand, Benjamin I, 191
osand, Benjamin I, 196
osand, Benjamin I, 712
osand, Benjamin P. I, 1150
osand, Benjamin, Jr. I, 191
osand, Charles I, 136
osand, Charles I, 182
osand, Charles I, 191
osand, Charles I, 202
osand, Charles I, 779
osand, Charles I, 806
osand, Charles F. I, 779
osand, Clarence IV, 944
osand, Edmund I, 183
osand, Edmund I, 779
osand, Edmund I, 806
osand, Edwin I, 697
osand, Edwin D. I, 712
osand, Elizabeth I, 806
osand, Elma IV, 944
osand, Elvey I, 779
osand, Elvy I, 136
osand, Elvy I, 182
osand, Elvy I, 191
osand, Elvy I, 202
osand, Elvy I, 806
osand, Emely I, 779
osand, Emely I, 806
osand, Emily I, 136
osand, Emily I, 183
osand, Emily I, 806
osand, Emily I, 844
osand, Evelyn Lorene IV, 944
osand, Gabriel I, 44
osand, Gabriel I, 45
osand, Gabriel I, 136
osand, Gabriel I, 153
osand, Gabriel I, 182
osand, Gabriel I, 183
osand, Gabriel I, 191
osand, Gabriel I, 705
osand, Gabriel I, 712
osand, Gabril I, 97
osand, Gabril I, 136
osand, Hannah I, 45
osand, Hannah I, 136
osand, Hannah I, 191
osand, Hannah I, 712
osand, Hannah, Jr. I, 136
osand, Hannah, Jr. I, 155
osand, James I, 191
osand, James W. I, 182
osand, John I, 45
osand, John I, 136
osand, John I, 147
osand, John I, 180
osand, John I, 183
osand, John I, 191
osand, John I, 779
osand, John IV, 944
osand, John, Jr. I, 191
osand, Jordon I, 182
osand, Joseph I, 136
osand, Joseph I, 183
osand, Joseph I, 191
osand, Joseph I, 697
osand, Joseph I, 705
osand, Joseph I, 712
osand, Joseph I, 729
osand, Joseph I, 779
osand, Joseph I, 806
osand, Joseph I, 876
osand, Maggie IV, 944
osand, Maggie Vietta IV, 944
osand, Margaret I, 97
osand, Margaret I, 136
osand, Martha I, 136
osand, Martha I, 182
osand, Martha I, 191
osand, Mary I, 97
osand, Mary I, 136
osand, Mary I, 140
osand, Mary I, 144
osand, Mary I, 182
osand, Mary I, 191
osand, Mary I, 196
osand, Mary I, 697
osand, Mary I, 712
osand, Mary I, 729
Cosand, Mary IV, 1245
Cosand, Mary V, 150
Cosand, Mary Ann I, 183
Cosand, Mary Ann I, 779
Cosand, Mary Ann I, 806
Cosand, Mary R. I, 697
Cosand, Merriam I, 191
Cosand, Morgan I, 183
Cosand, Morgan I, 191
Cosand, Nathan I, 97
Cosand, Nathan I, 136
Cosand, Nathan I, 183
Cosand, Nathan I, 191
Cosand, Peninah I, 136
Cosand, Peninah I, 146
Cosand, Peninah I, 191
Cosand, Penninah I, 136
Cosand, Penninah I, 163
Cosand, Phineas N. I, 697
Cosand, Phineas N. I, 712
Cosand, Rendel Loren IV, 944
Cosand, Ruth I, 712
Cosand, Samuel I, 182
Cosand, Samuel I, 191
Cosand, Samuel I, 712
Cosand, Sarah I, 8
Cosand, Sarah I, 13
Cosand, Sarah I, 45
Cosand, Sarah I, 97
Cosand, Sarah I, 136
Cosand, Sarah I, 147
Cosand, Sarah I, 153
Cosand, Sarah I, 176
Cosand, Sarah I, 180
Cosand, Sarah I, 182
Cosand, Sarah I, 183
Cosand, Sarah I, 191
Cosand, Sarah I, 201
Cosand, Sarah I, 712
Cosand, Sarah I, 779
Cosand, Sarah I, 1150
Cosand, Sarah M. I, 697
Cosand, Theda Louise IV, 944
Cosand, Thomas I, 97
Cosand, Thomas I, 183
Cosand, Thomas I, 697
Cosand, Thomas I, 712
Cosand, Thomas Jordon I, 182
Cosand, Widow Sarah I, 45
Cosand, Widow Sarah I, 70
Cosand, William I, 182
Cosand, William I, 191
Cosand, William I, 712
Cosby, Frances VI, 967
Cosby, Margaret I, 381
Cosby, Ruth I, 381
Cosdaile, Ann II, 210
Coshet, Mary II, 495
Cosins, John II, 496
Cosman, Eliza III, 88
Cosner, Abigail I, 806
Cosner, Abigail I, 834
Cosner, Abigail I, 911
Cosner, John I, 911
Coss, Benjamin V, 483
Coss, Benjamin V, 666
Coss, Eunice V, 666
Coss, Jacob V, 666
Coss, Minnie V, 666
Coss, Phebe V, 483
Coss, Phebe V, 666
Coss, Virgil V, 666
Cossan, Abigail I, 34
Cossan, Abigail I, 44
Cossan, Gabriel I, 34
Cossan, Gabriel I, 44
Cossand, Aaron I, 136
Cossand, Charles I, 136
Cosse, Mary II, 495
Cosse, Mary II, 500
Costard, Rachel II, 350
Costard, Samuel II, 350
Coster, Arnold II, 350
Coster, Arnold II, 489
Coster, Arnold II, 495
Coster, John II, 350
Coster, Joseph II, 350
Coster, Rachel II, 350
Coster, Rachel II, 489
Coster, Rachel II, 495
Coster, Samuel II, 350
Coster, William II, 350
Costil, Ann II, 170
Costil, Hannah II, 63
Costil, Hannah II, 170
Costil, Joseph II, 170
Costil, Josiah II, 170
Costil, Mary II, 170
Costil, Uriah II, 170
Costile, Ann II, 210
Costile, Joseph II, 210
Costill, Ann II, 210
Costill, Esther II, 63
Costill, Esther II, 94
Costill, Hannah II, 63
Costill, Hannah II, 94
Costill, Hannah II, 210
Costill, Hannah R. II, 63
Costill, Joseph II, 63
Costill, Joseph II, 94
Costill, Joseph II, 210
Costill, Josiah II, 63
Costill, Josiah II, 94
Costill, Josiah II, 210
Costill, Josiah R. II, 63
Costill, Josiah, Jr. II, 117
Costill, Mary II, 210
Costill, Mary L. II, 317
Costill, Uriah II, 210
Costill, Uriah II, 285
Costin, Sarah II, 495
Coston, Addie B. III, 83
Coston, Addie B. III, 89
Coston, Herbert H. III, 83
Coston, Herbert H. III, 89
Coston, Jane Fearlam II, 991
Coston, Leila III, 83
Coston, Leila III, 89
Coston, Wm. Hudd II, 995
Costord, John II, 350
Costord, Joseph II, 350
Cotant, Ann Malinda IV, 1234
Cotant, Ann Matilda IV, 1154
Cotant, Benona IV, 1154
Cotant, Benona IV, 1234
Cotant, Benona L. IV, 1234
Cotant, Benona, Jr. IV, 1154
Cotant, Benoni IV, 1205
Cotant, Benoni IV, 1234
Cotant, Benoni L. IV, 1205
Cotant, Benoni L. IV, 1234
Cotant, Benoni Leander IV, 1205
Cotant, Charles IV, 1154
Cotant, Charles IV, 1234
Cotant, Charles Chester IV, 1205
Cotant, Charles Chester IV, 1234
Cotant, Charles E. IV, 1234
Cotant, Charles S. IV, 1154
Cotant, Clara Mariah IV, 1234
Cotant, Clarence IV, 1234
Cotant, Edgar IV, 1154
Cotant, Edgar IV, 1234
Cotant, Edward H. IV, 1234
Cotant, Edwin IV, 1205
Cotant, Edwin S. IV, 1205
Cotant, Edwin S. IV, 1211
Cotant, Eliza IV, 191
Cotant, Eliza IV, 248
Cotant, Eliza IV, 1205
Cotant, Eliza IV, 1234
Cotant, Ella G. IV, 1234
Cotant, Elwel S. IV, 1205
Cotant, Elwin S. IV, 1205
Cotant, Elwin S. IV, 1234
Cotant, Fam IV, 1234
Cotant, George W. IV, 1205
Cotant, George W. IV, 1234
Cotant, Gideon IV, 1205
Cotant, Gideon B. IV, 1154
Cotant, Gideon B. IV, 1205
Cotant, Hannah IV, 1234
Cotant, Isaac W. IV, 1234
Cotant, Jonathan IV, 1154
Cotant, Jonathan IV, 1234
Cotant, Joseph IV, 1154
Cotant, Joseph IV, 1205
Cotant, Joseph H. IV, 1154
Cotant, Joseph H. IV, 1234
Cotant, Josephine L. IV, 1234
Cotant, Louisa IV, 1205
Cotant, Louisa IV, 1211
Cotant, Louisa H. IV, 1205
Cotant, Lydia IV, 1154
Cotant, Lydia IV, 1205
Cotant, Lydia IV, 1234
Cotant, Mary IV, 1234
Cotant, Mary E. IV, 1234
Cotant, Mary E. IV, 1237
Cotant, Mary Elizabeth IV, 1234
Cotant, Mary J. IV, 1234
Cotant, Mary Jane IV, 1234
Cotant, Matilda A. IV, 1234
Cotant, Mercy A. IV, 1234
Cotant, Mercy Ann IV, 1234
Cotant, Phebe IV, 1234
Cotant, Purdy H. IV, 1154
Cotant, Purdy H. IV, 1234
Cotant, Rachel IV, 1205
Cotant, Rachel H. IV, 1205
Cotant, Rachel H. IV, 1227
Cotant, Rachel H. IV, 1234
Cotant, Samuel IV, 1154
Cotant, Samuel IV, 1234
Cotant, Zehainah B. IV, 1234
Cotant, Zehamiah B. IV, 1205
Cotant, Zephamiah IV, 1227
Cotant, Zephamiah B. IV, 1205
Cotant, Zephamiah B. IV, 1234
Cotant, Zephaniah IV, 1154
Cotant, Zephaniah IV, 1205
Cotant, Zephaniah IV, 1234
Cotant, Zephaniah B. IV, 1205
Cotching, Elizabeth VI, 28
Cotching, Elizabeth VI, 30
Cotching, Thomas VI, 30
Cote, Agnes V, 482
Cote, Elizabeth V, 482
Cote, Esther V, 506
Cote, Hiram V, 506
Cote, John V, 482
Cote, John V, 506
Cote, Joseph T. V, 482
Cote, Lewis Johnson V, 506
Cote, Lindley M. V, 506
Cote, Lucy V, 506
Cote, Martha V, 506
Cote, Mary V, 506
Cote, Rebecca V, 506
Coterell, Lyddia VI, 953
Cothran, Alex. V, 803
Cothran, Alexander V, 803
Cothran, Alexander V, 805
Cothran, Alexander V, 813
Cothran, Anna V, 803
Cothran, Anna V, 805
Cothran, Eliza VI, 808
Cothran, Eunice V, 803
Cothran, Hannah V, 800
Cothran, Hannah V, 805
Cothran, Hester V, 799
Cothran, Hester V, 803
Cothran, Hester V, 805
Cothran, Hester V, 813
Cothran, James V, 806
Cothran, Jane V, 805
Cothran, Jane V, 813
Cothran, Jesse V, 800
Cothran, Mary V, 806
Cothran, Mary T. VI, 808
Cothran, Phebe V, 800
Cothran, Phebe V, 805
Cothran, William H. VI, 808
Cothren, Alexander V, 813
Cothren, Hannah II, 350
Cothren, Hester V, 813
Cothren, Jane V, 813
Cothron, Ann V, 733
Cothron, David V, 733
Cothron, Elizabeth VI, 305
Cothron, Esther V, 733
Cothron, Hannah V, 733
Cothron, Jane Esther V, 733
Cothron, Mark V, 733
Cotner, Mary Jane I, 381
Cotner, Owen I, 381
Cotral, Sally VI, 896
Cotral, Thomas VI, 896
Cotrell, James VI, 896
Cotrell, James VI, 953
Cotrell, Martha Jane VI, 896
Cotrell, Polly VI, 896
Cotrell, Susannah VI, 896
Cotrell, Thomas J. VI, 896
Cotrill, Mary A. VI, 893
Cott, ??? III, 89
Cott, Peter III, 394
Cott, Sarah III, 89
Cotter, Josiah I, 136
Cotter, Josiah I, 170
Cotter, Peggy I, 136
Cotter, Sarah I, 136
Cotter, Sarah I, 170
Cotteral, Ephraim V, 733
Cotteral, Lucinda V, 733
Cotteral, Martin V, 733
Cotterall, Anna VI, 945
Cotterall, Betsy VI, 953
Cotterall, Thomas VI, 945
Cotterall, Thomas VI, 953
Cottereill, Grace V, 990
Cotterell, Anna VI, 913
Cotterell, Stephen VI, 946
Cotterill, Ann VI, 941
Cottern, Hannah V, 805
Cottery, Abel II, 495
Cottery, Mary II, 495
Cottery, Sarah II, 495
Cottey, Abel II, 350
Cottey, Abel II, 484
Cottey, Abell II, 350
Cottey, Benjamin II, 350
Cottey, Sarah II, 484
Cottey, Sarah II, 495
Cottom, Katy VI, 896
Cottom, Thomas VI, 896
Cotton, ??? III, 138
Cotton, Ann V, 483
Cotton, Caroline III, 138
Cotton, Jane II, 722
Cotton, Rachel II, 313
Cotton, Richard V, 483
Cottrell, Edith VI, 957
Cottrell, Ellce IV, 1311
Cottrell, Emma IV, 1311
Cottrell, James VI, 896
Cottrell, John VI, 941
Cottrell, Josephine IV, 1311
Cottrell, Lydia VI, 1020
Cottrell, Martha Jane VI, 896
Cottrell, Mary Ann Margaret VI, 896
Cottrell, Mrs. Mary IV, 1311
Cottrell, Polly VI, 896
Cottrell, Sally VI, 896
Cottrell, Sally VI, 946
Cottrell, Sarah VI, 896
Cottrell, Stella IV, 1311
Cottrell, Susannah VI, 896
Cottrell, Thomas VI, 896
Cottrell, Thomas J. VI, 896
Cotty, Abell II, 350
Cotty, Benjamin II, 350
Couborn, Nathan IV, 690
Coubourn, John IV, 901
Coubourn, Sarah IV, 901
Couburn, Phebe VI, 380
Couburn, Robert VI, 380
Couch, Ann VI, 153
Couch, Ann VI, 164
Couch, Ann VI, 210
Couch, Ann VI, 236
Couch, Ann B. VI, 895
Couch, Ann W. VI, 164
Couch, Ann Watson VI, 164
Couch, Ann Wolston VI, 236
Couch, Anna VI, 153
Couch, Anna VI, 164
Couch, Anna M. I, 535
Couch, Anna M. I, 806
Couch, Anne VI, 236
Couch, Burton L. IV, 1311
Couch, Daniel VI, 164
Couch, Daniel VI, 236
Couch, David I, 535
Couch, David I, 806
Couch, Deborah VI, 164
Couch, Deborah VI, 236
Couch, Doshia VI, 896
Couch, Elizabeth I, 806
Couch, Elizabeth I, 830
Couch, Eunice I, 806
Couch, Eunice I, 810
Couch, Infant VI, 164
Couch, James VI, 164
Couch, James VI, 236
Couch, Jesse E. VI, 896
Couch, John Oliver I, 535
Couch, Luticie I, 535
Couch, Lydia I, 535
Couch, Margaret VI, 164
Couch, Margaret VI, 236
Couch, Maria VI, 1003
Couch, Martitia I, 626
Couch, Martitia I, 628
Couch, Mary I, 806
Couch, Mary I, 834
Couch, Mary VI, 164
Couch, Mary VI, 236
Couch, Mary M. VI, 1003
Couch, Mary Y. VI, 164
Couch, Mary Younghusband VI, 236
Couch, Mesheck I, 806
Couch, Mildred VI, 899
Couch, Mrs. Doshia VI, 895
Couch, Rebecca VI, 164
Couch, Rebecca VI, 236
Couch, Rebeckah VI, 164
Couch, Ruffin I, 535
Couch, Samuel I, 495
Couch, Samuel I, 535
Couch, Samuel VI, 153
Couch, Samuel VI, 164
Couch, Samuel VI, 236
Couch, Samuel VI, 350
Couch, Samuel, Jr. VI, 164
Couch, Samuel, Jr. VI, 236
Couch, Samuel, Jr. VI, 350
Couch, Sarah Jane I, 535
Couch, William VI, 899
Cougal, Amos V, 483
Cougal, Ann V, 483
Cougal, Asa V, 483
Cougal, Bennet V, 483

Cougal, Cyrus V, 483
Cougal, Edith V, 483
Cougal, Edwin V, 483
Cougal, Elisha V, 483
Cougal, Gulielma V, 483
Cougal, Hannah V, 483
Cougal, James V, 483
Cougal, John V, 483
Cougal, Margaret V, 483
Cougal, Rebecca V, 483
Cougal, Septima II, 984
Cougal, Septima II, 991
Cougal, Susannah V, 483
Cougel, Henery VI, 380
Cougel, Isaac VI, 380
Cougel, James VI, 380
Cougel, Mary VI, 380
Cougel, Rachel VI, 380
Cougel, Ruth VI, 380
Coughlin, Dennis IV, 191
Coughlin, Eliza IV, 380
Coughlin, Eliza IV, 404
Coughlin, Esther IV, 191
Cougle, Hannah V, 43
Cougle, Hannah V, 93
Cougle, William V, 43
Couley, Francis III, 89
Coulsin, Samuel VI, 392
Coulsin, Tamer VI, 392
Coulsom, John I, 1091
Coulson, Abigail IV, 902
Coulson, Abigail IV, 903
Coulson, Ada Jane IV, 866
Coulson, Ada Lane IV, 867
Coulson, Allen IV, 695
Coulson, Allen IV, 902
Coulson, Amos IV, 82
Coulson, Amos IV, 618
Coulson, Amy IV, 902
Coulson, Amy IV, 903
Coulson, Amy IV, 918
Coulson, Ann IV, 618
Coulson, Ann IV, 809
Coulson, Ann IV, 856
Coulson, Ann IV, 866
Coulson, Ann IV, 902
Coulson, Ann IV, 903
Coulson, Anna IV, 902
Coulson, Azubah II, 62
Coulson, Benjamin IV, 866
Coulson, Benjamin IV, 902
Coulson, Benjamin IV, 903
Coulson, Caleb II, 62
Coulson, Caroline IV, 866
Coulson, Catharine IV, 618
Coulson, Catharine IV, 902
Coulson, Catherine Harvey IV, 82
Coulson, David II, 62
Coulson, David IV, 82
Coulson, David IV, 324
Coulson, David IV, 325
Coulson, David IV, 618
Coulson, David IV, 695
Coulson, David IV, 809
Coulson, David IV, 840
Coulson, David IV, 866
Coulson, David IV, 902
Coulson, David IV, 903
Coulson, David IV, 914
Coulson, David IV, 923
Coulson, David IV, 944
Coulson, Deborah II, 52
Coulson, Deborah II, 62
Coulson, Deborah II, 734
Coulson, Della IV, 695
Coulson, Dorothy Jane IV, 695
Coulson, Edith IV, 695
Coulson, Elizabeth I, 1117
Coulson, Elizabeth II, 54
Coulson, Elizabeth II, 62
Coulson, Elizabeth IV, 695
Coulson, Elizabeth IV, 840
Coulson, Elizabeth IV, 902
Coulson, Elizabeth IV, 914
Coulson, Elizabeth A. IV, 695
Coulson, Elwood IV, 866
Coulson, Esther VI, 380
Coulson, Esther VI, 385
Coulson, Fanny IV, 902
Coulson, Frank IV, 695
Coulson, Frank C. IV, 902
Coulson, Frank H. IV, 695
Coulson, George II, 54
Coulson, George II, 62
Coulson, Hannah II, 62
Coulson, Hannah II, 83
Coulson, Hannah IV, 903
Coulson, Hannah C. IV, 914
Coulson, Harvey IV, 618
Coulson, Ida M. IV, 907
Coulson, Jabez I, 1081
Coulson, Jabez I, 1150
Coulson, Jabez IV, 27
Coulson, Jabez IV, 82
Coulson, Jabez IV, 618
Coulson, Jabez IV, 809
Coulson, Jabez IV, 838
Coulson, Jabez IV, 902
Coulson, Jabez IV, 903
Coulson, Jane IV, 27
Coulson, Jane IV, 37
Coulson, Jane IV, 82
Coulson, Jane IV, 325
Coulson, Jane IV, 618
Coulson, Jane IV, 809
Coulson, Jane IV, 866
Coulson, Jane IV, 886
Coulson, Jane IV, 902
Coulson, Jane IV, 903
Coulson, Jane IV, 910
Coulson, Jane IV, 944
Coulson, Jehu IV, 27
Coulson, Jehu IV, 37
Coulson, Jehu IV, 82
Coulson, Jehu IV, 325
Coulson, Jehu IV, 618
Coulson, Jehu IV, 809
Coulson, Jehu IV, 866
Coulson, Jehu IV, 886
Coulson, Jehu IV, 902
Coulson, Jehu IV, 903
Coulson, Jehu IV, 944
Coulson, Jehu, Jr. IV, 809
Coulson, Jehue IV, 618
Coulson, Jesse IV, 82
Coulson, Jesse IV, 618
Coulson, Jesse IV, 809
Coulson, Jesse IV, 866
Coulson, Jesse IV, 886
Coulson, Jesse IV, 902
Coulson, Jesse IV, 923
Coulson, Jesse IV, 944
Coulson, Jesse Craddick I, 1091
Coulson, Job IV, 902
Coulson, Job IV, 903
Coulson, Job IV, 918
Coulson, John I, 1081
Coulson, John I, 1091
Coulson, John I, 1092
Coulson, John I, 1095
Coulson, John I, 1096
Coulson, John I, 1150
Coulson, John IV, 695
Coulson, John IV, 809
Coulson, John IV, 902
Coulson, John, Jr. I, 1091
Coulson, John, Jr. I, 1150
Coulson, Joseph IV, 902
Coulson, Laura IV, 695
Coulson, Laura V. IV, 695
Coulson, Laura V. IV, 902
Coulson, Lewis IV, 907
Coulson, Lizzie A. IV, 902
Coulson, Lydia IV, 695
Coulson, Lydia IV, 902
Coulson, Lydia IV, 903
Coulson, Mahlon IV, 902
Coulson, Margaret I, 1140
Coulson, Margaret IV, 324
Coulson, Margaret IV, 325
Coulson, Margaret IV, 695
Coulson, Margaret IV, 903
Coulson, Margaret IV, 1129
Coulson, Mariah IV, 907
Coulson, Martha IV, 25
Coulson, Martha IV, 27
Coulson, Martha Rose IV, 695
Coulson, Mary IV, 866
Coulson, Mary IV, 886
Coulson, Mary IV, 923
Coulson, Mary IV, 944
Coulson, Mary L. IV, 902
Coulson, Pim IV, 902
Coulson, Rachel I, 1140
Coulson, Rachel IV, 82
Coulson, Rachel IV, 618
Coulson, Rachel IV, 695
Coulson, Rachel IV, 809
Coulson, Rachel IV, 866
Coulson, Rachel IV, 886
Coulson, Rachel IV, 902
Coulson, Rachel IV, 923
Coulson, Rachel IV, 944
Coulson, Ruth IV, 902
Coulson, Ruth IV, 903
Coulson, Ruth IV, 918
Coulson, Ruth May IV, 695
Coulson, Samuel IV, 25
Coulson, Samuel IV, 27
Coulson, Samuel VI, 380
Coulson, Samuel VI, 385
Coulson, Samuel VI, 483
Coulson, Samuel VI, 644
Coulson, Sarah II, 62
Coulson, Sarah IV, 866
Coulson, Sarah IV, 902
Coulson, Sarah VI, 379
Coulson, Sarah VI, 380
Coulson, Sarah VI, 392
Coulson, Sarah VI, 483
Coulson, Sarah VI, 498
Coulson, Sarah VI, 644
Coulson, Seth IV, 618
Coulson, Seth IV, 866
Coulson, Seth IV, 903
Coulson, Sewel IV, 866
Coulson, Sewell IV, 866
Coulson, Susan IV, 867
Coulson, Susanna IV, 866
Coulson, Tamar IV, 25
Coulson, Tamar IV, 27
Coulson, Tamer I, 1091
Coulson, Tamer VI, 379
Coulson, Tamer VI, 380
Coulson, Tamer VI, 385
Coulson, Tamer VI, 483
Coulson, Tamer VI, 498
Coulson, Thomas IV, 27
Coulson, Thomas IV, 82
Coulson, Uriah IV, 82
Coulson, Uriah IV, 618
Coulson, Uriah IV, 809
Coulson, Uriah IV, 856
Coulson, Uriah IV, 866
Coulson, Wd. Sarah IV, 809
Coulson, Wd. Sarah IV, 838
Coulson, William I, 1150
Coulson, William IV, 866
Coulson, William IV, 902
Coulson, Wm. II, 52
Coulson, Wm. II, 62
Coulson, Wm. IV, 866
Coulter, Asa V, 164
Coulter, Barney I, 922
Coulter, Geo. U. I, 922
Coulter, Geo. U. I, 923
Coulter, George N. I, 939
Coulter, George N. I, 944
Coulter, Lillian I, 922
Coulter, Lillian I, 923
Coulter, Lillian I, 939
Coulter, Lillian I, 944
Coulter, Lucetta I, 922
Coulter, Lydia V, 149
Coulter, Lydia V, 164
Coulter, Lydia V, 167
Coulter, Martha A. V, 164
Coulter, Martha A. V, 210
Coulter, Martha A. R. V, 164
Coulter, Martha Ann Rebecca V, 164
Coulter, Mary E. V, 164
Coulter, Mary E. V, 183
Coulter, Mary J. E. V, 164
Coulter, Mary Jane Elizabeth V, 164
Coulton, Sarah II, 495
Coultrain, Abigail I, 875
Coultrain, Martha I, 757
Coultrain, Mary I, 875
Coultran, Didah I, 875
Coultran, Didah I, 904
Coultrane, Mary I, 757
Councellar, John II, 147
Council, Annie VI, 60
Council, Annie VI, 75
Council, Burnetta VI, 60
Council, Iva G. I, 228
Council, James VI, 60
Council, James VI, 61
Council, James VI, 85
Council, James VI, 91
Council, James J. VI, 60
Council, Joel VI, 60
Council, John A. VI, 60
Council, John R. VI, 60
Council, John R. VI, 75
Council, Joseph VI, 60
Council, Joseph L. VI, 60
Council, Louisa VI, 60
Council, Louisa VI, 85
Council, Mary VI, 60
Council, Mattie VI, 60
Council, Mattie E. VI, 60
Council, Mattie E. VI, 61
Council, Mattie E. VI, 91
Council, Paul I, 228
Council, Paul VI, 60
Council, Pauline VI, 60
Council, Robert VI, 60
Council, Sarah VI, 60
Council, Sarah E. VI, 60
Council, Sarah E. VI, 85
Council, Treasy VI, 60
Council, Viola VI, 60
Council, Viola VI, 61
Council, Virginia VI, 60
Council, Virginia A. VI, 60
Council, Virginia A. VI, 85
Councill, Mattie VI, 91
Councill, Trecy VI, 91
Councilman, Elizabeth I, 381
Councilman, Ella I, 381
Councilman, George I, 381
Councilman, John I, 381
Councilman, Martha J. I, 381
Councilman, Milo I, 381
Counseller, Frank V, 990
Counselman, John II, 958
Counselman, John II, 1071
Counselman, Phebe II, 991
Counselman, Phebe II, 1026
Counselman, Rebecca II, 958
Counselman, Rebecca II, 991
Counselman, Rebecca II, 1071
Counselor, Frank V, 990
Counterman, James IV, 1154
Counterman, William H. IV, 1154
Counterman, Wm. IV, 1154
Counts, Mary A. V, 806
Couper, Charles II, 350
Couper, Elizabeth II, 350
Couper, Elizabeth II, 495
Couper, Ester II, 350
Couper, Jacob II, 442
Couper, James II, 350
Couper, John II, 350
Couper, Joseph II, 350
Couper, Mary II, 350
Couper, Rachel II, 350
Couper, Rebecka II, 350
Couper, Samuel II, 350
Couper, Samuel II, 442
Couper, Sarah II, 350
Couper, Sarah II, 442
Couper, Wm. II, 991
Coupland, Mary I, 302
Coupland, Rachel I, 43
Couplin, Ann IV, 571
Couplin, David IV, 571
Couplin, James IV, 571
Couplin, Leah I, 302
Couplin, Leah I, 311
Couplin, Lydia IV, 571
Couplin, Lydia IV, 587
Couplin, Mary IV, 571
Couplin, Mary IV, 584
Couplin, Sarah Ann IV, 567
Couplin, Sarah Ann IV, 571
Course, Isaac II, 350
Course, Peter II, 350
Courson, Anna II, 784
Courtenay, James Gibbons III, 89
Courtney, Addison IV, 647
Courtney, Alonzo IV, 695
Courtney, Alpha Nettie IV, 944
Courtney, Alpha Nettie IV, 1037
Courtney, Ann IV, 648
Courtney, Ann IV, 695
Courtney, Ann IV, 809
Courtney, Ann IV, 858
Courtney, Ann IV, 944
Courtney, Ann IV, 961
Courtney, Ann IV, 1025
Courtney, Ann Neill IV, 618
Courtney, Anna IV, 944
Courtney, Anne IV, 695
Courtney, Calvin V, 231
Courtney, Daniel II, 350
Courtney, Dozier IV, 695
Courtney, Dozier IV, 809
Courtney, Edward IV, 695
Courtney, Edward IV, 781
Courtney, Edward IV, 809
Courtney, Edward IV, 944
Courtney, Edward IV, 1021
Courtney, Edward IV, 1025
Courtney, Ella IV, 1037
Courtney, Emaline IV, 695
Courtney, Emeline IV, 1025
Courtney, Emeline IV, 1029
Courtney, Emily IV, 944
Courtney, Emily IV, 1007
Courtney, Emily R. IV, 944
Courtney, Emly Jane IV, 944
Courtney, Etta IV, 1037
Courtney, Eva D. IV, 618
Courtney, Eva D. IV, 647
Courtney, Eva D. IV, 648
Courtney, Eva D. IV, 742
Courtney, Fred IV, 1037
Courtney, Hannah IV, 695
Courtney, Hannah IV, 809
Courtney, Hercules II, 350
Courtney, Homer IV, 944
Courtney, Isaac IV, 695
Courtney, Isaac IV, 944
Courtney, Isaac IV, 1025
Courtney, Israel IV, 695
Courtney, Israel IV, 719
Courtney, Israel IV, 809
Courtney, Israel IV, 1025
Courtney, J. M. IV, 695
Courtney, J. M. IV, 1037
Courtney, James I, 381
Courtney, James IV, 695
Courtney, James IV, 809
Courtney, James M. IV, 695
Courtney, James Monroe IV, 94
Courtney, Jane Ann IV, 1025
Courtney, Jeduthan IV, 1025
Courtney, John IV, 695
Courtney, John IV, 944
Courtney, John IV, 1025
Courtney, Joseph I, 381
Courtney, Joseph IV, 647
Courtney, Joseph A. IV, 742
Courtney, Judith IV, 695
Courtney, Laura IV, 944
Courtney, Laura IV, 1037
Courtney, Margaret IV, 944
Courtney, Margaret IV, 977
Courtney, Martha IV, 27
Courtney, Martha IV, 695
Courtney, Martha IV, 809
Courtney, Mary I, 381
Courtney, Mary II, 495
Courtney, Mary II, 651
Courtney, Mary IV, 944
Courtney, Mary IV, 1025
Courtney, Mary IV, 1029
Courtney, Mary Ann IV, 695
Courtney, Mary Ann IV, 809
Courtney, Mary J. IV, 742
Courtney, Mary V. IV, 695
Courtney, Monroe IV, 944
Courtney, Morton IV, 618
Courtney, Moses IV, 695
Courtney, Moses IV, 809
Courtney, Moses IV, 858
Courtney, Nathan IV, 695
Courtney, Nettie IV, 695
Courtney, Nettie IV, 944
Courtney, Orlan IV, 695
Courtney, Orlar James IV, 103
Courtney, Phebe IV, 695
Courtney, Phebe IV, 1021
Courtney, Phebe IV, 1025
Courtney, Phebe C. IV, 695
Courtney, Phebe C. IV, 1025
Courtney, Phebe G. IV, 695
Courtney, Phebe G. IV, 781
Courtney, Phebe Y. IV, 809
Courtney, Phebe Y. IV, 944
Courtney, Pilema Pearl IV, 10
Courtney, Rebecca Emily IV, 6
Courtney, Rebecca Emily IV, 1007
Courtney, Ruth II, 495
Courtney, Ruth B. IV, 1025
Courtney, Sarah IV, 695
Courtney, Sarah IV, 944
Courtney, Sarah IV, 1025
Courtney, Sarah IV, 1028
Courtney, Susan IV, 695
Courtney, Susan IV, 719
Courtney, Susan IV, 1025
Courtney, Thomas M. IV, 695
Courtney, Thomas M. IV, 1025
Courtney, Voluntine IV, 944
Courtney, William V, 454
Courtney, William H. IV, 1025
Courtney, William M. IV, 695
Courtney, Wm. IV, 695
Courtney, Wm. IV, 944
Courtney, Wm. IV, 1037
Courtney, Wm. V, 454
Courtney, Wm. H. IV, 695
Courtney, Wm. M. IV, 944
Courto, Frances M. V, 381
Courto, Lizzie V, 381
Courto, Mary V, 381
Courto, Victoria V, 381
Courtright, Alice III, 333
Courtright, Amos IV, 1154
Courtright, Maggie IV, 1154
Courts, Elizabeth V, 381
Courts, Francis M. V, 381
Courts, Mary V, 381
Courts, Victory V, 381
Couse, Clem E. IV, 1311
Couse, Crew IV, 1311
Couse, Elsie IV, 1311
Couse, Esther IV, 1311
Couse, Glenn E. IV, 1311

use, Lillian IV, 1311
use, Lois R. IV, 1037
use, Louisa IV, 1037
use, Louisa IV, 1043
use, Marie IV, 1311
use, Mrs. ??? IV, 1311
use, Walter IV, 1311
usins, Ann VI, 380
usins, Benjamin IV, 325
usins, Bessie V, 733
usins, Elizabeth VI, 380
usins, Harrison V, 733
usins, Henry VI, 133
usins, Henry VI, 137
usins, Hester VI, 380
usins, Jas. IV, 891
usins, John VI, 380
usins, Mary VI, 380
usins, Mary VI, 808
usins, Mary Ann IV, 891
usins, Sarah VI, 380
usins, Susanna VI, 380
usins, Susannah VI, 380
usins, Thomas B. VI, 808
usins, Wendell V, 733
utant, Benona L. IV, 1234
utant, Benoni L. IV, 1234
utant, Charles IV, 1234
utant, Charles Chester IV, 1234
utant, Clarence IV, 1234
utant, Edward H. IV, 1234
utant, Edwin IV, 1205
utant, Eliza IV, 1234
utant, Ella G. IV, 1234
utant, Elwin S. IV, 1234
utant, George W. IV, 1234
utant, Gilbert III, 89
utant, Gilbert III, 116
utant, Grace D. III, 89
utant, Grace D. III, 330
utant, Henry III, 89
utant, Joseph IV, 1205
utant, Joseph H. IV, 1234
utant, Julia R. III, 89
utant, Julia S. III, 330
utant, Lawrence B. III, 89
utant, Lawrence B. III, 330
utant, Louisa IV, 1205
utant, Mary E. IV, 1234
utant, Mary Elizabeth IV, 1234
utant, Mary J. IV, 1234
utant, Mary Jane IV, 1234
utant, Mary V. III, 89
utant, Mary V. III, 116
utant, Matilda A. IV, 1242
utant, Peter III, 89
utant, Peter III, 158
utant, Peter J. III, 89
utant, Rachel H. IV, 1234
utant, Samuel IV, 1234
utant, Sarah L. III, 89
utant, Sarah P. III, 89
utant, Sarah P. III, 158
utant, Susannah III, 89
utant, Zehainah B. IV, 1234
utant, Zephamiah B. IV, 1234
utney, Hercules II, 350
uts, Elizabeth V, 381
uts, Frances V, 381
uts, Frances M. V, 381
uts, Francis M. V, 381
uts, Lizzie V, 381
uts, Mary V, 381
uts, Mary Lizzie V, 381
uts, Victoria V, 381
uts, Victory V, 381
uzens, Ann IV, 27
uzens, Ann IV, 62
uzens, Hannah IV, 27
uzens, Hannah IV, 59
uzens, John IV, 17
uzens, John IV, 27
uzens, John IV, 59
uzens, John IV, 62
uzens, John VI, 379
uzens, John VI, 380
uzens, Mary IV, 27
uzens, Mary IV, 39
uzens, Sarah IV, 17
uzens, Sarah IV, 27
uzens, Sarah IV, 59
uzens, Sarah IV, 62
uzens, Sarah VI, 379
uzens, Sarah VI, 380
uzens, Susannah VI, 379
uzens, Susannah VI, 380
van, Mattie V, 231
ve, Aveline VI, 808
ve, Elizabeth II, 350
Cove, George W. VI, 808
Covel, Micajah IV, 191
Coventon, Fanny I, 381
Coventon, Fanny I, 410
Coventry, Asenath P. IV, 380
Coventry, Asenath P. IV, 453
Coventry, Sarah IV, 571
Coventry, Sarah IV, 575
Coventry, Susanna IV, 519
Coventry, Susanna IV, 556
Coverdale, Ann III, 72
Coverdale, Grace V, 666
Coverdale, Grace V, 704
Coverdale, Hattie V, 381
Coverdale, Mary N. V, 990
Coverdale, Nancy V, 990
Coverdale, Nannie V, 990
Coverdale, Sally V, 666
Covert, ??? III, 89
Covert, Adolph III, 405
Covert, Caleb III, 400
Covert, Caleb III, 405
Covert, David M. IV, 1311
Covert, Deborah III, 400
Covert, Deborah III, 405
Covert, Edmund II, 350
Covert, Elizabeth III, 89
Covert, Elizabeth III, 103
Covert, Elizabeth III, 405
Covert, Hannah III, 405
Covert, Isaac II, 350
Covert, Isaac III, 401
Covert, Isaac III, 405
Covert, Isabella II, 350
Covert, Jacob III, 89
Covert, Jacob F. III, 405
Covert, James IV, 1311
Covert, Leonard III, 89
Covert, Leonard III, 103
Covert, Loretta III, 401
Covert, Loretta III, 405
Covert, Margaret II, 350
Covert, Marmaduke III, 405
Covert, Martin IV, 1311
Covert, Mary II, 350
Covert, Mary III, 400
Covert, Minnie IV, 1311
Covert, Phebe III, 405
Covert, Theirlove A. III, 89
Covert, Thomas L. III, 89
Covey, Catharine Deyerle VI, 808
Covey, Samuel VI, 808
Covil, Hannah IV, 1154
Covil, Micajah IV, 1154
Covill, Hannah IV, 1154
Covill, Micajah IV, 1154
Covington, Elizabeth IV, 323
Covington, Elizabeth IV, 325
Covington, Elizabeth IV, 519
Covington, George VI, 826
Covington, George VI, 837
Covington, George VI, 860
Covington, Henry VI, 808
Covington, Henry VI, 836
Covington, James VI, 866
Covington, John VI, 847
Covington, John VI, 866
Covington, Malenda VI, 865
Covington, Martin VI, 844
Covington, Mary VI, 808
Covington, Rebecca VI, 847
Covington, Sarah VI, 866
Covington, Susan VI, 837
Covolt, Clara V, 164
Cowan, Andrew VI, 896
Cowan, Elizabeth VI, 896
Cowan, Ernest I, 620
Cowan, Ida V, 164
Cowan, Maria M. V, 43
Cowan, Myrtle Effie I, 620
Cowan, Peggy VI, 977
Cowan, Rebeckah VI, 896
Cowan, Robert VI, 896
Cowan, Robert VI, 946
Cowan, Robert VI, 966
Cowan, Robt. VI, 961
Cowan, Robt. VI, 977
Cowan, Sophia V, 901
Cowan, Susannah II, 478
Cowan, Susannah Burden II, 495
Cowan, Wm. IV, 1275
Coward, Elizabeth VI, 892
Coward, Reuben VI, 892
Cowarden, Susanna VI, 380
Cowarden, Susannah VI, 384
Cowden, Blanch L. V, 556
Cowden, Penninah IV, 380
Cowder, Blanch L. V, 666
Cowder, Donald H. V, 666
Cowder, Wm. T. V, 666
Cowdry, Henrietta III, 89
Cowdry, Henrietta III, 175
Cowdry, Samuel III, 89
Cowdry, Samuel III, 175
Cowen, Mary I, 1116
Cowen, Mary I, 1117
Cowen, Myrtle E. I, 631
Cowen, Myrtle E. I, 636
Cowen, Susannah II, 495
Cowen, Susannah II, 574
Cowen, Susannah Burden II, 495
Cowes, George II, 63
Cowgall, Caleb VI, 380
Cowgall, Clayton II, 495
Cowgall, Haenry VI, 380
Cowgall, Isaac VI, 380
Cowgall, John VI, 380
Cowgall, Ruth VI, 380
Cowgall, Sarah VI, 380
Cowgall, Thomas II, 495
Cowgall, Thomas VI, 380
Cowgell, Elizabeth II, 63
Cowgil, Ann IV, 695
Cowgil, Asa V, 231
Cowgil, Charlotte IV, 695
Cowgil, Ellen V, 231
Cowgil, Hannah L. V, 582
Cowgil, John V, 231
Cowgil, Jonathan V, 231
Cowgil, Joseph IV, 695
Cowgil, Lucinda IV, 695
Cowgil, Margarett V, 231
Cowgil, Sarah IV, 695
Cowgill, ??? V, 381
Cowgill, Aaron IV, 380
Cowgill, Aaron IV, 1154
Cowgill, Abarilla IV, 1154
Cowgill, Abarilla IV, 1234
Cowgill, Abbarilla IV, 1205
Cowgill, Abi V, 381
Cowgill, Abigail IV, 619
Cowgill, Abigail IV, 867
Cowgill, Abigail IV, 882
Cowgill, Abigail V, 270
Cowgill, Abigail VI, 236
Cowgill, Aborilla IV, 1154
Cowgill, Abraham IV, 143
Cowgill, Abraham IV, 325
Cowgill, Abraham IV, 352
Cowgill, Abraham IV, 380
Cowgill, Adaline IV, 325
Cowgill, Agnes Jane IV, 867
Cowgill, Albert G. V, 454
Cowgill, Alice V, 666
Cowgill, Alice V, 712
Cowgill, Alice Amelia IV, 1154
Cowgill, Allen IV, 1275
Cowgill, Alma V, 381
Cowgill, Alverda IV, 1154
Cowgill, Amos V, 325
Cowgill, Amos V, 326
Cowgill, Amos V, 381
Cowgill, Amos V, 483
Cowgill, Amos V, 516
Cowgill, Angelica II, 853
Cowgill, Angelica II, 910
Cowgill, Angelina IV, 1275
Cowgill, Ann II, 790
Cowgill, Ann IV, 380
Cowgill, Ann IV, 618
Cowgill, Ann IV, 619
Cowgill, Ann IV, 695
Cowgill, Ann IV, 1275
Cowgill, Ann V, 325
Cowgill, Ann V, 381
Cowgill, Ann V, 483
Cowgill, Ann VI, 380
Cowgill, Ann S. IV, 325
Cowgill, Ann S. IV, 350
Cowgill, Anna II, 989
Cowgill, Anna IV, 619
Cowgill, Anna IV, 1275
Cowgill, Anna IV, 1286
Cowgill, Anna Lea II, 790
Cowgill, Anna Lee II, 853
Cowgill, Anne V, 325
Cowgill, Anne V, 335
Cowgill, Armina Jane IV, 903
Cowgill, Asa V, 231
Cowgill, Asa V, 260
Cowgill, Asa V, 301
Cowgill, Asa V, 325
Cowgill, Asa V, 326
Cowgill, Asa V, 483
Cowgill, Asa M. IV, 1275
Cowgill, Avarilla IV, 1205
Cowgill, Benj. V, 301
Cowgill, Benjamin V, 231
Cowgill, Benjamin V, 253
Cowgill, Benjamin V, 454
Cowgill, Benjamin VI, 380
Cowgill, Benjamin F. V, 231
Cowgill, Benjamin F. V, 326
Cowgill, Benjamin Franklin V, 301
Cowgill, Bennet V, 381
Cowgill, Bennet V, 483
Cowgill, Bennett V, 231
Cowgill, Bennett V, 381
Cowgill, Bennett V, 556
Cowgill, Berch M. V, 454
Cowgill, Bertha Frances V, 381
Cowgill, Betsey IV, 325
Cowgill, Betsy IV, 192
Cowgill, Betsy IV, 325
Cowgill, Betsy IV, 350
Cowgill, Betsy IV, 352
Cowgill, Betsy IV, 380
Cowgill, Birch V, 454
Cowgill, Burch M. V, 454
Cowgill, Caleb IV, 619
Cowgill, Caleb IV, 649
Cowgill, Caleb IV, 867
Cowgill, Caleb VI, 380
Cowgill, Calvin V, 381
Cowgill, Calvin P. II, 853
Cowgill, Calvin Philips II, 790
Cowgill, Carl V, 666
Cowgill, Carolina V, 263
Cowgill, Caroline IV, 1275
Cowgill, Caroline V, 231
Cowgill, Caroline D. IV, 1154
Cowgill, Caroline M. V, 231
Cowgill, Carrie V, 301
Cowgill, Carrie V, 454
Cowgill, Carrie V, 666
Cowgill, Carrie E. IV, 1275
Cowgill, Catharine V, 325
Cowgill, Catharine VI, 380
Cowgill, Catharine Ann VI, 380
Cowgill, Catherine V, 231
Cowgill, Catherine V, 325
Cowgill, Catherine V, 381
Cowgill, Catherine VI, 380
Cowgill, Charles II, 853
Cowgill, Charles G. V, 231
Cowgill, Charles G. V, 454
Cowgill, Charlotte IV, 619
Cowgill, Charlotte IV, 657
Cowgill, Charlotte IV, 695
Cowgill, Charlotte IV, 867
Cowgill, Charlotte IV, 882
Cowgill, Charlotte VI, 236
Cowgill, Charlotte VI, 594
Cowgill, Charlotte VI, 598
Cowgill, Charlottee IV, 619
Cowgill, Chas. II, 790
Cowgill, Chas. II, 853
Cowgill, Chas. II, 910
Cowgill, Chloe V, 454
Cowgill, Clara II, 853
Cowgill, Clarence V, 666
Cowgill, Clarence O. V, 454
Cowgill, Clayton II, 495
Cowgill, Cynthia IV, 1275
Cowgill, Cyrus V, 381
Cowgill, Cyrus V, 483
Cowgill, Cyrus V, 556
Cowgill, Daniel IV, 619
Cowgill, Daniel C. II, 853
Cowgill, Daniel C. II, 892
Cowgill, David IV, 867
Cowgill, David V, 454
Cowgill, Dinah VI, 380
Cowgill, Dinah K. V, 231
Cowgill, Dinah K. V, 286
Cowgill, Direxa H. IV, 1154
Cowgill, Don V, 666
Cowgill, Earnest V, 454
Cowgill, Edith V, 381
Cowgill, Edith V, 483
Cowgill, Edith V, 516
Cowgill, Edith E. IV, 657
Cowgill, Edman II, 210
Cowgill, Edman II, 246
Cowgill, Edmond II, 194
Cowgill, Edmond II, 210
Cowgill, Edmond II, 991
Cowgill, Edmund II, 202
Cowgill, Edmund II, 210
Cowgill, Edwin V, 231
Cowgill, Edwin V, 483
Cowgill, Edwin V, 556
Cowgill, Ekiza VI, 380
Cowgill, Eleanor V, 301
Cowgill, Eleanor V, 454
Cowgill, Eleanor VI, 362
Cowgill, Eleanor VI, 380
Cowgill, Eleanor H. IV, 469
Cowgill, Eleanor H. IV, 1275
Cowgill, Electa IV, 1275
Cowgill, Elenor IV, 1249
Cowgill, Elenor V, 325
Cowgill, Eli IV, 1234
Cowgill, Eli IV, 1275
Cowgill, Elias B. IV, 192
Cowgill, Elias B. IV, 325
Cowgill, Elisha V, 231
Cowgill, Elisha V, 270
Cowgill, Elisha V, 325
Cowgill, Elisha V, 381
Cowgill, Elisha V, 483
Cowgill, Elisha V, 556
Cowgill, Eliza IV, 864
Cowgill, Eliza IV, 867
Cowgill, Eliza IV, 944
Cowgill, Eliza IV, 1091
Cowgill, Eliza IV, 1275
Cowgill, Eliza VI, 378
Cowgill, Eliza VI, 380
Cowgill, Elizabeth II, 63
Cowgill, Elizabeth II, 210
Cowgill, Elizabeth II, 789
Cowgill, Elizabeth II, 791
Cowgill, Elizabeth IV, 380
Cowgill, Elizabeth IV, 867
Cowgill, Elizabeth V, 243
Cowgill, Elizabeth V, 270
Cowgill, Ellen V, 231
Cowgill, Ellen V, 301
Cowgill, Ellen V, 454
Cowgill, Ellen V, 566
Cowgill, Ellen V, 666
Cowgill, Ellen V, 677
Cowgill, Ellen C. V, 231
Cowgill, Ellen M. V, 557
Cowgill, Ellen P. IV, 380
Cowgill, Ellen P. IV, 440
Cowgill, Ellen W. V, 231
Cowgill, Ellen W. V, 557
Cowgill, Ellen W. V, 568
Cowgill, Elma IV, 325
Cowgill, Eloner VI, 380
Cowgill, Esther IV, 192
Cowgill, Esther IV, 325
Cowgill, Esther IV, 349
Cowgill, Esther IV, 380
Cowgill, Esther IV, 1147
Cowgill, Esther IV, 1154
Cowgill, Esther IV, 1275
Cowgill, Esther V, 270
Cowgill, Ethel V, 454
Cowgill, Evan IV, 867
Cowgill, Evan Thomas IV, 867
Cowgill, Ezekiel III, 89
Cowgill, Frank V, 454
Cowgill, Frank V, 666
Cowgill, Frank Roderick V, 301
Cowgill, Frederick V, 243
Cowgill, Geo. V, 381
Cowgill, Gershom V, 270
Cowgill, Guli Elma Hannah V, 556
Cowgill, Guli-elma V, 556
Cowgill, Gulielma V, 231
Cowgill, Gulielma V, 381
Cowgill, Gulielma V, 483
Cowgill, Gulielma V, 556
Cowgill, Gulielma Perdue V, 231
Cowgill, Haenry VI, 380
Cowgill, Hannah V, 231
Cowgill, Hannah V, 270
Cowgill, Hannah V, 324
Cowgill, Hannah V, 326
Cowgill, Hannah V, 381
Cowgill, Hannah V, 483
Cowgill, Hannah V, 556
Cowgill, Hannah VI, 380
Cowgill, Hannah Coats V, 231
Cowgill, Harry V, 301
Cowgill, Harry V, 454
Cowgill, Harry V, 666
Cowgill, Harry H. V, 666
Cowgill, Henery VI, 380
Cowgill, Henry II, 198
Cowgill, Henry II, 210
Cowgill, Henry II, 789
Cowgill, Henry II, 853
Cowgill, Henry II, 910
Cowgill, Henry IV, 325
Cowgill, Henry IV, 618
Cowgill, Henry IV, 619
Cowgill, Henry IV, 867
Cowgill, Henry IV, 1275
Cowgill, Henry IV, 1286
Cowgill, Henry V, 231
Cowgill, Henry V, 301
Cowgill, Henry V, 325
Cowgill, Henry V, 454
Cowgill, Henry VI, 362
Cowgill, Henry VI, 380
Cowgill, Henry VI, 594
Cowgill, Henry Cowgill II, 789
Cowgill, Henry, Jr. VI, 380

Cowgill, Hester IV, 1275
Cowgill, Hiram V, 381
Cowgill, Ida V, 666
Cowgill, Ida S. V, 666
Cowgill, Imo V, 454
Cowgill, Isaac II, 210
Cowgill, Isaac IV, 143
Cowgill, Isaac IV, 192
Cowgill, Isaac IV, 325
Cowgill, Isaac IV, 330
Cowgill, Isaac IV, 349
Cowgill, Isaac IV, 352
Cowgill, Isaac IV, 380
Cowgill, Isaac V, 270
Cowgill, Isaac VI, 380
Cowgill, Isaac VI, 483
Cowgill, Isaac VI, 492
Cowgill, Isaac VI, 594
Cowgill, Isaac VI, 632
Cowgill, Isaac VI, 638
Cowgill, Isaac, Jr. IV, 325
Cowgill, Israel IV, 619
Cowgill, Israel IV, 867
Cowgill, J. B. V, 301
Cowgill, Jacob V, 270
Cowgill, James IV, 619
Cowgill, James IV, 657
Cowgill, James IV, 695
Cowgill, James IV, 867
Cowgill, James IV, 868
Cowgill, James IV, 882
Cowgill, James IV, 944
Cowgill, James IV, 1091
Cowgill, James V, 325
Cowgill, James V, 483
Cowgill, James VI, 236
Cowgill, James VI, 380
Cowgill, James VI, 594
Cowgill, James VI, 598
Cowgill, James S. IV, 944
Cowgill, James S. IV, 1091
Cowgill, James Simpson IV, 695
Cowgill, James Simpson IV, 867
Cowgill, James Simpson IV, 944
Cowgill, James Simpson IV, 1091
Cowgill, James Stanley, Jr. IV, 695
Cowgill, James Williamson IV, 867
Cowgill, Jane IV, 325
Cowgill, Jane IV, 330
Cowgill, Jane IV, 380
Cowgill, Jane IV, 944
Cowgill, Jemima V, 231
Cowgill, Jemima V, 253
Cowgill, Jemima V, 271
Cowgill, Jemima I. V, 381
Cowgill, Jennet II, 194
Cowgill, Jennet II, 210
Cowgill, Jennitt II, 210
Cowgill, Jennitt II, 237
Cowgill, Jephthah IV, 325
Cowgill, Jeptha IV, 380
Cowgill, Jesse V, 231
Cowgill, Jessie V, 231
Cowgill, Jno. II, 210
Cowgill, Joel IV, 619
Cowgill, Joel IV, 695
Cowgill, Joel IV, 867
Cowgill, Joel IV, 903
Cowgill, Joel VI, 236
Cowgill, John II, 210
Cowgill, John II, 790
Cowgill, John II, 984
Cowgill, John II, 991
Cowgill, John IV, 469
Cowgill, John IV, 619
Cowgill, John IV, 867
Cowgill, John IV, 882
Cowgill, John IV, 1249
Cowgill, John IV, 1275
Cowgill, John V, 43
Cowgill, John V, 231
Cowgill, John V, 300
Cowgill, John V, 301
Cowgill, John V, 324
Cowgill, John V, 325
Cowgill, John V, 454
Cowgill, John V, 483
Cowgill, John V, 666
Cowgill, John VI, 236
Cowgill, John VI, 380
Cowgill, John VI, 448
Cowgill, John B. V, 231
Cowgill, John B. V, 666
Cowgill, John Bernard V, 301
Cowgill, John Frederic V, 381
Cowgill, John Lea II, 790
Cowgill, John Lee II, 853
Cowgill, John Parker V, 301
Cowgill, John, Jr. V, 325
Cowgill, John, Jr. VI, 380
Cowgill, Johnson IV, 944
Cowgill, Jonathan II, 63
Cowgill, Jonathan IV, 325
Cowgill, Jonathan IV, 350
Cowgill, Jonathan IV, 380
Cowgill, Jonathan IV, 657
Cowgill, Jonathan IV, 867
Cowgill, Jonathan V, 231
Cowgill, Jonathan V, 301
Cowgill, Jonathan B. V, 231
Cowgill, Jonathan B. V, 243
Cowgill, Jonathan B. V, 454
Cowgill, Jonathan B. V, 557
Cowgill, Jonathan B. V, 580
Cowgill, Joseph II, 789
Cowgill, Joseph II, 991
Cowgill, Joseph IV, 192
Cowgill, Joseph IV, 380
Cowgill, Joseph IV, 438
Cowgill, Joseph IV, 619
Cowgill, Joseph IV, 695
Cowgill, Joseph IV, 867
Cowgill, Joseph IV, 903
Cowgill, Joseph IV, 944
Cowgill, Joseph IV, 1275
Cowgill, Joseph S. IV, 1275
Cowgill, Joseph S. IV, 1281
Cowgill, Josephine IV, 1249
Cowgill, Josephine V, 231
Cowgill, Joshua IV, 944
Cowgill, Josiah IV, 944
Cowgill, Josiah Joshua IV, 1091
Cowgill, Joyce II, 210
Cowgill, Joyce II, 261
Cowgill, Kate V, 573
Cowgill, Kate V, 666
Cowgill, Katharine VI, 380
Cowgill, Katie V, 231
Cowgill, Katie V, 557
Cowgill, Latham T. IV, 867
Cowgill, Lemuel Crene IV, 867
Cowgill, Lemuel Crew IV, 619
Cowgill, Lemuel Crew IV, 867
Cowgill, Leslie W. V, 326
Cowgill, Levi IV, 619
Cowgill, Levi IV, 1147
Cowgill, Levi IV, 1154
Cowgill, Levi IV, 1275
Cowgill, Levi, Jr. IV, 1154
Cowgill, Lewis IV, 867
Cowgill, Lewis IV, 871
Cowgill, Lidya II, 63
Cowgill, Lidya II, 65
Cowgill, Lilly D. V, 381
Cowgill, Louisa V, 557
Cowgill, Louisa V, 580
Cowgill, Lucinda IV, 695
Cowgill, Lucinda V, 231
Cowgill, Lucinda V, 243
Cowgill, Lucinda V, 301
Cowgill, Lucinda V, 557
Cowgill, Lucinda V, 568
Cowgill, Lucretia M. II, 790
Cowgill, Lucretia M. II, 853
Cowgill, Lucretia M. II, 910
Cowgill, Lucy IV, 695
Cowgill, Lucy IV, 944
Cowgill, Lucy IV, 1091
Cowgill, Luzena T. V, 454
Cowgill, Lydia II, 495
Cowgill, Lydia IV, 619
Cowgill, Lydia IV, 642
Cowgill, Lydia IV, 695
Cowgill, Lydia IV, 736
Cowgill, Lydia IV, 867
Cowgill, Lydia IV, 1275
Cowgill, Lydia V, 300
Cowgill, Lydia V, 301
Cowgill, Lydia V, 313
Cowgill, Lydia V, 324
Cowgill, Lydia V, 325
Cowgill, Lydia V, 326
Cowgill, Lydia V, 367
Cowgill, Lydia V, 381
Cowgill, Lydia V, 454
Cowgill, Lydia VI, 380
Cowgill, Lydia VI, 429
Cowgill, Lydia Ann IV, 325
Cowgill, Lydia Ann IV, 352
Cowgill, Lydia M. V, 454
Cowgill, Lydia P. II, 853
Cowgill, Lydia Pusey II, 790
Cowgill, Lydia S. V, 454
Cowgill, Margaret II, 202
Cowgill, Margaret II, 210
Cowgill, Margaret IV, 619
Cowgill, Margaret IV, 867
Cowgill, Margaret IV, 886
Cowgill, Margaret V, 231
Cowgill, Margaret V, 260
Cowgill, Margaret V, 301
Cowgill, Margaret V, 381
Cowgill, Margaret V, 483
Cowgill, Margarett V, 231
Cowgill, Mariam IV, 867
Cowgill, Maris V, 381
Cowgill, Maris M. V, 381
Cowgill, Martha IV, 1275
Cowgill, Martha IV, 1287
Cowgill, Martha Ann IV, 1275
Cowgill, Martha B. V, 454
Cowgill, Marthy IV, 1275
Cowgill, Mary II, 170
Cowgill, Mary II, 198
Cowgill, Mary II, 210
Cowgill, Mary II, 285
Cowgill, Mary II, 495
Cowgill, Mary II, 702
Cowgill, Mary IV, 657
Cowgill, Mary IV, 903
Cowgill, Mary IV, 944
Cowgill, Mary VI, 380
Cowgill, Mary VI, 409
Cowgill, Mary Alma V, 381
Cowgill, Mary Alma V, 433
Cowgill, Mary Ann IV, 1275
Cowgill, Mary Ann IV, 1281
Cowgill, Mary Armina IV, 944
Cowgill, Mary B. II, 892
Cowgill, Mary Barrett II, 807
Cowgill, Mary E. IV, 1275
Cowgill, Mary E. V, 454
Cowgill, Mary E. V, 557
Cowgill, Mary E. V, 666
Cowgill, Mary Elizabeth IV, 867
Cowgill, Mary H. IV, 657
Cowgill, Mary Jane IV, 1275
Cowgill, Mary Jane V, 381
Cowgill, Mary Jane V, 414
Cowgill, Mary Jean V, 301
Cowgill, Mary S. II, 853
Cowgill, Matilda IV, 1091
Cowgill, Matilda IV, 1275
Cowgill, Menton Pimm V, 270
Cowgill, Micajah C. V, 557
Cowgill, Millie E. V, 666
Cowgill, Milton V, 231
Cowgill, Milton V, 301
Cowgill, Miriam IV, 867
Cowgill, Miriam IV, 871
Cowgill, Mollie V, 231
Cowgill, Mollie V, 557
Cowgill, Nathan V, 381
Cowgill, Nathaniel E. II, 853
Cowgill, Nathaniel N. II, 853
Cowgill, Nehemiah II, 210
Cowgill, Nehemiah II, 261
Cowgill, Obedience IV, 1275
Cowgill, Olive Ann V, 381
Cowgill, Oscar V, 231
Cowgill, Oscar V, 301
Cowgill, Paul Raymond V, 301
Cowgill, Phineas IV, 192
Cowgill, Phineas IV, 325
Cowgill, Phinehas IV, 180
Cowgill, Phinehas IV, 192
Cowgill, Phinehas IV, 325
Cowgill, Phinneas IV, 380
Cowgill, R. Henry IV, 192
Cowgill, Rachel II, 210
Cowgill, Rachel IV, 619
Cowgill, Rachel IV, 649
Cowgill, Rachel IV, 657
Cowgill, Rachel IV, 695
Cowgill, Rachel IV, 766
Cowgill, Rachel IV, 867
Cowgill, Rachel V, 231
Cowgill, Rachel V, 301
Cowgill, Rachel V, 454
Cowgill, Rachel VI, 236
Cowgill, Rachel VI, 380
Cowgill, Rachel VI, 594
Cowgill, Ralph II, 210
Cowgill, Ralph II, 247
Cowgill, Ralph II, 261
Cowgill, Ralph II, 991
Cowgill, Ralph IV, 143
Cowgill, Ralph IV, 192
Cowgill, Ralph IV, 325
Cowgill, Ralph IV, 350
Cowgill, Ralph IV, 352
Cowgill, Ralph IV, 380
Cowgill, Rebecca IV, 325
Cowgill, Rebecca IV, 350
Cowgill, Rebecca IV, 380
Cowgill, Rebecca IV, 438
Cowgill, Rebecca IV, 867
Cowgill, Rebecca IV, 869
Cowgill, Rebecca IV, 903
Cowgill, Rebecca IV, 944
Cowgill, Rebecca IV, 1001
Cowgill, Rebecca IV, 1091
Cowgill, Rebecca V, 231
Cowgill, Rebecca V, 325
Cowgill, Rebecca V, 326
Cowgill, Rebecca V, 381
Cowgill, Rebecca V, 483
Cowgill, Rebecca V, 556
Cowgill, Robert W. IV, 1275
Cowgill, Roderick V, 454
Cowgill, Roderick V, 666
Cowgill, Roscoe L. IV, 1154
Cowgill, Roy IV, 1154
Cowgill, Ruth IV, 619
Cowgill, Ruth IV, 903
Cowgill, Ruth IV, 944
Cowgill, Ruth VI, 380
Cowgill, Ruth A. IV, 657
Cowgill, Ruthanna IV, 1154
Cowgill, Ruthanna V, 666
Cowgill, Ruthanna V, 698
Cowgill, S. Macy V, 454
Cowgill, Samira V, 231
Cowgill, Samira V, 326
Cowgill, Samuel IV, 619
Cowgill, Samuel IV, 1275
Cowgill, Samuel C. V, 231
Cowgill, Samuel C. V, 263
Cowgill, Samuel S. V, 454
Cowgill, Sarah II, 789
Cowgill, Sarah IV, 192
Cowgill, Sarah IV, 325
Cowgill, Sarah IV, 352
Cowgill, Sarah IV, 380
Cowgill, Sarah IV, 469
Cowgill, Sarah IV, 618
Cowgill, Sarah IV, 619
Cowgill, Sarah IV, 695
Cowgill, Sarah IV, 867
Cowgill, Sarah IV, 868
Cowgill, Sarah IV, 871
Cowgill, Sarah IV, 882
Cowgill, Sarah IV, 904
Cowgill, Sarah IV, 1154
Cowgill, Sarah IV, 1275
Cowgill, Sarah V, 301
Cowgill, Sarah V, 308
Cowgill, Sarah V, 381
Cowgill, Sarah V, 666
Cowgill, Sarah VI, 380
Cowgill, Sarah VI, 483
Cowgill, Sarah VI, 492
Cowgill, Sarah VI, 594
Cowgill, Sarah VI, 632
Cowgill, Sarah VI, 638
Cowgill, Sarah A. IV, 180
Cowgill, Sarah Ann IV, 192
Cowgill, Sarah Ann IV, 325
Cowgill, Sarah Ann IV, 1275
Cowgill, Sarah E. V, 454
Cowgill, Sarah Ellen V, 301
Cowgill, Sarah Ellen V, 454
Cowgill, Sarah Ellen V, 666
Cowgill, Sarah F. IV, 380
Cowgill, Sarah F. IV, 451
Cowgill, Sarah Jane V, 217
Cowgill, Sarah Jane V, 231
Cowgill, Sarah Jane V, 301
Cowgill, Sarah Jr. IV, 867
Cowgill, Sarah Jr. IV, 882
Cowgill, Sarah, Jr. II, 989
Cowgill, Sarah, Jr. II, 991
Cowgill, Septeme II, 202
Cowgill, Septeme II, 210
Cowgill, Sidney VI, 380
Cowgill, Simpson IV, 619
Cowgill, Simpson VI, 236
Cowgill, Sina E. IV, 657
Cowgill, Susan S. II, 853
Cowgill, Susan S. II, 892
Cowgill, Susanna IV, 619
Cowgill, Susanna IV, 1275
Cowgill, Susanna VI, 380
Cowgill, Susanna VI, 448
Cowgill, Susannah II, 210
Cowgill, Susannah II, 247
Cowgill, Susannah II, 991
Cowgill, Susannah IV, 619
Cowgill, Susannah IV, 1275
Cowgill, Susannah V, 325
Cowgill, Susannah V, 483
Cowgill, Susannah VI, 380
Cowgill, T. Roy V, 454
Cowgill, Thomas II, 495
Cowgill, Thomas II, 991
Cowgill, Thomas IV, 619
Cowgill, Thomas IV, 657
Cowgill, Thomas IV, 1154
Cowgill, Thomas IV, 1275
Cowgill, Thomas V, 666
Cowgill, Thomas VI, 380
Cowgill, Thos. IV, 469
Cowgill, Thos. IV, 618
Cowgill, Thos. IV, 619
Cowgill, Unity IV, 657
Cowgill, V. Irene IV, 1154
Cowgill, Vira Emely V, 381
Cowgill, Wd Esther IV, 1154
Cowgill, Wd. Ann P. II, 790
Cowgill, Wd. Elizabeth II, 789
Cowgill, William IV, 325
Cowgill, William IV, 380
Cowgill, William V, 325
Cowgill, William V, 326
Cowgill, William VI, 380
Cowgill, William B. V, 454
Cowgill, William H. IV, 867
Cowgle, Isaac VI, 594
Cowhard, Aggy VI, 965
Cowhard, John VI, 885
Cowhard, John VI, 896
Cowhard, Ransemon VI, 899
Cowhard, Reuben VI, 885
Cowhard, Reuben VI, 899
Cowhard, Reuben VI, 965
Cowhard, Sally VI, 896
Cowhard, Sarah VI, 885
Cowin, Jane II, 991
Cowin, Jane II, 1002
Cowins, Wm. IV, 1275
Cowl, Mary B. IV, 615
Cowl, Mary B. IV, 661
Cowles, H. B. VI, 880
Cowles, Mary IV, 1311
Cowley, Hannah A. II, 114
Cowligg, Mary VI, 390
Cowling, Martha F. VI, 846
Cowling, Susanna II, 703
Cowling, Susanna II, 722
Cowman, Attwood II, 496
Cowman, Daniel V, 454
Cowman, Edward V, 968
Cowman, Edward V, 969
Cowman, Elizabeth V, 968
Cowman, Elizabeth V, 969
Cowman, Inez V, 454
Cowman, James V, 969
Cowman, Jennette V, 454
Cowman, John V, 454
Cowman, John VI, 726
Cowman, John, Jr. VI, 737
Cowman, Joseph VI, 726
Cowman, Laura V, 454
Cowman, Mary II, 495
Cowman, Mary II, 496
Cowman, Mary II, 607
Cowman, Mary II, 651
Cowman, Mathew II, 495
Cowman, Mathew II, 651
Cowman, Nathan II, 495
Cowman, Nathan II, 651
Cowman, Ruth V, 454
Cowmans, Inez V, 454
Cowmen, Tacy Jenet V, 231
Cowmen, Tacy Jenet V, 280
Cowne, Reuben V, 454
Cowper, ??? III, 89
Cowper, Ann II, 350
Cowper, Elizabeth II, 651
Cowper, Hannah G. III, 85
Cowper, Joseph P. III, 85
Cowper, Magdalen III, 85
Cowper, Magdalene II, 63
Cowper, Mary II, 63
Cowper, Mary II, 496
Cowper, Mary III, 85
Cowper, Thomas S. II, 210
Cowper, William II, 350
Cowper, William II, 496
Cowper, William III, 85
Cowper, William T. III, 85
Cowper, Wm. II, 63
Cowper, Wm. Edward III, 85
Cowperthwait, Alfred II, 854
Cowperthwait, Anna II, 852
Cowperthwait, Anna II, 854
Cowperthwait, Elizabeth III, 89
Cowperthwait, Elizabeth III, 28
Cowperthwait, Ella IV, 380
Cowperthwait, Grace III, 89
Cowperthwait, Hope II, 170
Cowperthwait, Hugh III, 89
Cowperthwait, John II, 170
Cowperthwait, John III, 16
Cowperthwait, John III, 89
Cowperthwait, John III, 287
Cowperthwait, Joseph II, 170
Cowperthwait, Joseph II, 790
Cowperthwait, Joseph II, 852
Cowperthwait, Joseph II, 854
Cowperthwait, Levi R. IV, 380
Cowperthwait, Mark II, 63
Cowperthwait, Mary M. IV, 381

›wperthwait, Mary M. IV, 438
›wperthwait, Rebecca II, 170
›wperthwait, Rebecca II, 852
›wperthwait, Rebecca II, 854
›wperthwait, Samuel II, 63
›wperthwait, Sarah III, 16
›wperthwait, Sarah III, 89
›wperthwait, Thomas II, 63
›wperthwait, Thomas S. II, 496
›wperthwait, Thomas Shreve II, 210
›wperthwait, Thomas Shreve II, 211
›wperthwait, Wd. Grace III, 42
›wperthwait, Wd. Grace III, 89
›wperthwait, Wd. Rebecca II, 790
›wperthwait, William II, 170
›wperthwait, William II, 211
›wperthwait, William C. IV, 380
›wperthwait, William, Jr. II, 210
›wperthwait, Wm. C. IV, 438
›wperthwaite, Alfred II, 854
›wperthwaite, Ambrose II, 496
›wperthwaite, Anna II, 789
›wperthwaite, Anna II, 854
›wperthwaite, Cornelia F. II, 854
›wperthwaite, Edwin II, 853
›wperthwaite, Edwin II, 854
›wperthwaite, Elizabeth II, 496
›wperthwaite, Elizabeth II, 509
›wperthwaite, Henry II, 854
›wperthwaite, Hope II, 210
›wperthwaite, Hugh II, 210
›wperthwaite, Jacob II, 496
›wperthwaite, John II, 210
›wperthwaite, John II, 496
›wperthwaite, Joseph II, 496
›wperthwaite, Joseph II, 702
›wperthwaite, Joseph II, 854
›wperthwaite, Joseph, Jr. II, 854
›wperthwaite, Kesiah II, 210
›wperthwaite, Levi R. II, 734
›wperthwaite, Mary II, 210
›wperthwaite, Mary II, 246
›wperthwaite, Rebecca II, 854
›wperthwaite, Rebecca Lippincott II, 210
›wperthwaite, Ruth C. II, 734
›wperthwaite, Samuel II, 210
›wperthwaite, Samuel II, 496
›wperthwaite, Sarah II, 210
›wperthwaite, Shreeve II, 210
›wperthwaite, Stacy II, 210
›wperthwaite, Stacy II, 496
›wperthwaite, Thomas S. II, 496
›wperthwaite, Thomas Shreve II, 210
›wperthwaite, Thomas Shreve II, 211
›wperthwaite, Thomas Shreve II, 496
›wperthwaite, William II, 210
›wperthwaite, William II, 211
›wperthwaite, William II, 285
›wperthwaite, William, Jr. II, 210
›wperthwaite, William, Jr. II, 285
›wperthwaite, Wm. II, 702
›wperthwaite, Wm., Jr. II, 496
›wpland, Ann II, 63
›wpland, Anna II, 350
›wpland, Cadwallader II, 63
›wpland, Caleb II, 63
›wpland, Caleb II, 350
›wpland, Caleb II, 494
›wpland, Caleb II, 607
›wpland, David II, 350
›wpland, David Chew II, 63
›wpland, Isabella II, 494
›wpland, John II, 350
›wpland, Jonathan II, 350
›wpland, Jonathan II, 607
›wpland, Joshua II, 63
wpland, Joshua II, 350
›wpland, Margaret II, 494
›wpland, Martha II, 350
›wpland, Mary II, 494
wpland, Mary II, 535
›wpland, Mary II, 607
›wpland, Samuel II, 350
›wpland, Sarah II, 63
x, ??? I, 279
›x, ??? III, 63
›x, ??? III, 90
›x, ??? III, 330
Cox, ??? V, 315
Cox, A. M. V, 232
Cox, Aaron I, 137
Cox, Aaron I, 191
Cox, Aaron I, 265
Cox, Aaron I, 284
Cox, Aaron I, 466
Cox, Aaron I, 476
Cox, Aaron V, 44
Cox, Aaron V, 318
Cox, Aaron V, 326
Cox, Abba I, 283
Cox, Abba I, 1070
Cox, Abba I, 1071
Cox, Abby Ann III, 89
Cox, Abby Jane III, 89
Cox, Abel I, 284
Cox, Abel I, 382
Cox, Abel I, 461
Cox, Abel I, 462
Cox, Abel I, 464
Cox, Abel I, 475
Cox, Abel I, 476
Cox, Abel III, 89
Cox, Abigail I, 464
Cox, Abigail I, 477
Cox, Abigail I, 478
Cox, Abigail I, 481
Cox, Abigail II, 211
Cox, Abigail II, 215
Cox, Abijah I, 677
Cox, Able I, 383
Cox, Abner I, 284
Cox, Abner II, 496
Cox, Abraham II, 350
Cox, Abraham II, 496
Cox, Abraham II, 583
Cox, Abraham II, 607
Cox, Abraham III, 379
Cox, Abraham V, 232
Cox, Abraham VI, 880
Cox, Abraham VI, 1000
Cox, Abraham L. II, 496
Cox, Abraham L. III, 89
Cox, Abraham Liddon II, 496
Cox, Absalm VI, 808
Cox, Absilet I, 328
Cox, Absilla I, 323
Cox, Absilla I, 328
Cox, Absilla I, 807
Cox, Absillia I, 323
Cox, Absolom I, 535
Cox, Achcha I, 323
Cox, Achcha I, 328
Cox, Acheha R. I, 324
Cox, Achsah I, 284
Cox, Achsah I, 285
Cox, Achsah I, 303
Cox, Achsah I, 624
Cox, Achsah A. I, 323
Cox, Achsah A. I, 328
Cox, Achsah A. I, 331
Cox, Achsah A. I, 441
Cox, Achsah R. I, 323
Cox, Achsah R. I, 652
Cox, Achsah R. I, 677
Cox, Achsha I, 328
Cox, Ada V, 834
Cox, Ada C. I, 463
Cox, Ada C. I, 466
Cox, Ada G. I, 478
Cox, Adaline V, 326
Cox, Adam I, 383
Cox, Addi Milton I, 462
Cox, Adonijah III, 90
Cox, Agnes I, 631
Cox, Agnes V, 44
Cox, Agnes Lee I, 614
Cox, Albert V, 326
Cox, Aletha R. I, 466
Cox, Alexander M. I, 614
Cox, Alexander M. I, 631
Cox, Alfred V, 232
Cox, Alfred F. I, 383
Cox, Alfred Franklin I, 383
Cox, Alfred Isham I, 383
Cox, Alfred J. V, 232
Cox, Alice I, 461
Cox, Alice I, 477
Cox, Alice I, 713
Cox, Alice I, 717
Cox, Alice V, 44
Cox, Alice J. IV, 1205
Cox, Alma I, 213
Cox, Alonzo J. V, 382
Cox, Alpheus Milican I, 463
Cox, Alta I, 612
Cox, Alta I, 630
Cox, Alvira IV, 469
Cox, Alvira E. IV, 469
Cox, Amelia D. I, 466
Cox, Amey I, 382
Cox, Amey I, 383
Cox, Amey I, 462
Cox, Amey I, 465
Cox, Amey I, 475
Cox, Amey I, 535
Cox, Amey I, 1047
Cox, Amey I, 1050
Cox, Amos I, 462
Cox, Amy I, 373
Cox, Amy I, 382
Cox, Amy I, 383
Cox, Amy I, 457
Cox, Amy I, 463
Cox, Amy I, 464
Cox, Amy I, 466
Cox, Amy I, 475
Cox, Amy I, 476
Cox, Amy I, 477
Cox, Amy I, 481
Cox, Amy I, 484
Cox, Amy I, 652
Cox, Amy I, 676
Cox, Amy V, 484
Cox, Amy VI, 350
Cox, Amy VI, 480
Cox, Amy VI, 629
Cox, Amy E. I, 677
Cox, Anabel B. III, 68
Cox, Andrew V, 232
Cox, Andrew M. V, 232
Cox, Angie Latona IV, 1154
Cox, Ann I, 130
Cox, Ann I, 136
Cox, Ann I, 137
Cox, Ann I, 192
Cox, Ann I, 380
Cox, Ann I, 382
Cox, Ann I, 383
Cox, Ann I, 462
Cox, Ann I, 476
Cox, Ann I, 477
Cox, Ann I, 535
Cox, Ann I, 676
Cox, Ann I, 688
Cox, Ann I, 1015
Cox, Ann I, 1028
Cox, Ann I, 1031
Cox, Ann I, 1047
Cox, Ann I, 1048
Cox, Ann I, 1104
Cox, Ann I, 1117
Cox, Ann II, 170
Cox, Ann II, 180
Cox, Ann II, 211
Cox, Ann II, 215
Cox, Ann II, 248
Cox, Ann II, 350
Cox, Ann II, 496
Cox, Ann II, 813
Cox, Ann III, 89
Cox, Ann V, 43
Cox, Ann V, 44
Cox, Ann V, 164
Cox, Ann V, 301
Cox, Ann V, 767
Cox, Ann A. II, 854
Cox, Ann E. I, 465
Cox, Ann Freyser I, 382
Cox, Ann Mariah I, 323
Cox, Ann Stanard VI, 896
Cox, Anna I, 283
Cox, Anna I, 284
Cox, Anna I, 299
Cox, Anna I, 302
Cox, Anna I, 462
Cox, Anna I, 463
Cox, Anna I, 465
Cox, Anna I, 474
Cox, Anna I, 476
Cox, Anna I, 477
Cox, Anna I, 605
Cox, Anna I, 713
Cox, Anna I, 758
Cox, Anna I, 1018
Cox, Anna II, 403
Cox, Anna III, 89
Cox, Anna IV, 381
Cox, Anna IV, 408
Cox, Anna V, 164
Cox, Anna V, 188
Cox, Anna A. II, 833
Cox, Anna A. II, 854
Cox, Anna C. III, 336
Cox, Anna E. I, 479
Cox, Anna Mae V, 232
Cox, Anna Mariah I, 328
Cox, Anna Mary I, 335
Cox, Anna Mary IV, 981
Cox, Annabel III, 94
Cox, Annabel B. III, 89
Cox, Annabel B. III, 94
Cox, Anne I, 183
Cox, Anne I, 284
Cox, Anne I, 303
Cox, Anne I, 313
Cox, Anne I, 315
Cox, Anne I, 460
Cox, Anne I, 465
Cox, Anne IV, 143
Cox, Annie I, 617
Cox, Annie B. I, 614
Cox, Anny I, 303
Cox, Anny I, 310
Cox, Anson I, 462
Cox, Anson I, 478
Cox, Aprilla I, 213
Cox, Apsilla I, 323
Cox, Arlando I, 462
Cox, Arlen W. I, 652
Cox, Arlendo I, 807
Cox, Armenia III, 89
Cox, Armenia III, 336
Cox, Artemis Harmony I, 923
Cox, Artemus H. I, 939
Cox, Arthur W. I, 466
Cox, Arthur W. I, 478
Cox, Artilla A. I, 461
Cox, Artilla A. I, 465
Cox, Artilla Ann I, 478
Cox, Artina I, 619
Cox, Asenath I, 462
Cox, Asenath I, 463
Cox, Asenath I, 465
Cox, Asenath I, 474
Cox, Asenath I, 477
Cox, Asenath I, 478
Cox, Asenath I, 481
Cox, Asenath I, 677
Cox, Asenath I, 679
Cox, Asenath I, 806
Cox, Asenath B. I, 478
Cox, Asenath B. I, 807
Cox, Asenath J. I, 383
Cox, Asenath J. I, 398
Cox, Asenath L. I, 479
Cox, Austin VI, 808
Cox, Avis I, 284
Cox, Avis I, 303
Cox, Avis I, 320
Cox, Axcy I, 236
Cox, Baines II, 350
Cox, Bains II, 496
Cox, Barna I, 328
Cox, Barnabas I, 303
Cox, Barnabass I, 303
Cox, Barnaby I, 323
Cox, Barney I, 284
Cox, Barney I, 323
Cox, Barney B. I, 328
Cox, Bedford Elijah I, 236
Cox, Belle IV, 1155
Cox, Benj. I, 349
Cox, Benjamin I, 375
Cox, Benjamin I, 381
Cox, Benjamin I, 382
Cox, Benjamin I, 383
Cox, Benjamin I, 445
Cox, Benjamin I, 457
Cox, Benjamin I, 461
Cox, Benjamin I, 462
Cox, Benjamin I, 464
Cox, Benjamin I, 466
Cox, Benjamin I, 475
Cox, Benjamin I, 476
Cox, Benjamin I, 477
Cox, Benjamin I, 535
Cox, Benjamin I, 676
Cox, Benjamin I, 1104
Cox, Benjamin I, 1117
Cox, Benjamin II, 211
Cox, Benjamin II, 496
Cox, Benjamin II, 790
Cox, Benjamin II, 854
Cox, Benjamin III, 89
Cox, Benjamin III, 379
Cox, Benjamin III, 382
Cox, Benjamin IV, 619
Cox, Benjamin V, 44
Cox, Benjamin V, 301
Cox, Benjamin V, 733
Cox, Benjamin VI, 827
Cox, Benjamin VI, 846
Cox, Benjamin D. IV, 619
Cox, Benjamin F. I, 478
Cox, Benjamin G. I, 478
Cox, Bennet IV, 381
Cox, Bennet IV, 571
Cox, Benoist James III, 89
Cox, Benoist James III, 94
Cox, Benoni Simon I, 462
Cox, Bertha I, 939
Cox, Bertha V, 382
Cox, Bertha C. I, 933
Cox, Bertha E. I, 652
Cox, Bertha Emily I, 923
Cox, Bertha J. V, 382
Cox, Bessie M. I, 933
Cox, Bessie M. I, 939
Cox, Bessie M. I, 940
Cox, Bessie M. I, 948
Cox, Bessie Mary I, 923
Cox, Betsey I, 1104
Cox, Betsy Ann V, 326
Cox, Bettie I, 303
Cox, Betty I, 283
Cox, Betty I, 303
Cox, Binjamin I, 382
Cox, Binjamin I, 676
Cox, Binjamin I, 687
Cox, Blanche G. IV, 1311
Cox, Brackenridge VI, 862
Cox, Branson I, 462
Cox, Breckenridge VI, 896
Cox, Brian I, 303
Cox, C. J. I, 614
Cox, C. J. I, 617
Cox, Caleb I, 137
Cox, Caleb I, 183
Cox, Caleb I, 191
Cox, Caleb V, 810
Cox, Calvin I, 303
Cox, Calvin I, 464
Cox, Calvin I, 477
Cox, Calvin I, 479
Cox, Calvin I, 614
Cox, Carl I, 614
Cox, Carl M. I, 631
Cox, Carl Miller I, 383
Cox, Caroline I, 462
Cox, Caroline H. III, 89
Cox, Carrie Troy I, 383
Cox, Carson W. IV, 1311
Cox, Caspar IV, 192
Cox, Casper IV, 192
Cox, Casper Tison I, 713
Cox, Catharine I, 348
Cox, Catharine I, 381
Cox, Catharine I, 382
Cox, Catharine I, 383
Cox, Catharine I, 400
Cox, Catharine I, 409
Cox, Catharine I, 445
Cox, Catharine I, 451
Cox, Catharine I, 461
Cox, Catharine I, 463
Cox, Catharine I, 464
Cox, Catharine I, 465
Cox, Catharine I, 466
Cox, Catharine I, 472
Cox, Catharine I, 474
Cox, Catharine I, 475
Cox, Catharine I, 476
Cox, Catharine I, 477
Cox, Catharine I, 485
Cox, Catharine I, 535
Cox, Catharine I, 549
Cox, Catharine I, 652
Cox, Catharine I, 676
Cox, Catharine I, 677
Cox, Catharine I, 679
Cox, Catharine I, 984
Cox, Catharine I, 992
Cox, Catharine II, 350
Cox, Catharine V, 44
Cox, Catharine V, 321
Cox, Catharine V, 326
Cox, Catharine V, 765
Cox, Catharine S. I, 335
Cox, Catherine I, 343
Cox, Catherine I, 344
Cox, Catherine I, 1104
Cox, Catherine I, 1117
Cox, Catherine V, 34
Cox, Catherine V, 733
Cox, Catherine V, 969
Cox, Catherine C. VI, 896
Cox, Celia I, 283
Cox, Celia I, 303
Cox, Celia I, 312
Cox, Celia V, 164
Cox, Celia V, 990
Cox, Charity I, 283
Cox, Charity I, 303
Cox, Charity V, 44
Cox, Charity V, 232
Cox, Charity V, 255
Cox, Charity V, 794
Cox, Charles I, 373
Cox, Charles I, 382
Cox, Charles I, 383
Cox, Charles I, 462
Cox, Charles I, 463

Cox, Charles I, 466
Cox, Charles I, 472
Cox, Charles I, 475
Cox, Charles I, 476
Cox, Charles I, 477
Cox, Charles I, 478
Cox, Charles I, 479
Cox, Charles I, 605
Cox, Charles II, 350
Cox, Charles VI, 808
Cox, Charles Herbert I, 923
Cox, Charles M. I, 323
Cox, Charles M. I, 328
Cox, Charles Micajah I, 45
Cox, Charles S. I, 465
Cox, Charles T. I, 464
Cox, Charles W. III, 379
Cox, Charles, Jr. I, 463
Cox, Charlotte I, 303
Cox, Chella I, 323
Cox, Chelly I, 303
Cox, Chelly I, 308
Cox, Chester V, 483
Cox, Cheston E. I, 652
Cox, Chloe Gilbert V, 232
Cox, Christiana Hughes VI, 737
Cox, Christina Hughes VI, 734
Cox, Christina Hughes VI, 737
Cox, Christopher I, 535
Cox, Clara V, 232
Cox, Clara I. I, 940
Cox, Clara Ione I, 923
Cox, Clarance I, 631
Cox, Clarce I, 323
Cox, Clarence Joseph I, 614
Cox, Clarkson J. I, 479
Cox, Clarkson J. I, 758
Cox, Clarkson J. I, 770
Cox, Clarkston J. I, 464
Cox, Conelia A. I, 465
Cox, Connie Bell I, 236
Cox, Cora I, 619
Cox, Cora I, 635
Cox, Cora E. I, 631
Cox, Cora E. I, 677
Cox, Cora Jackson I, 631
Cox, Cordelia I, 328
Cox, Cordelia A. I, 323
Cox, Cordelia A. I, 807
Cox, Cordelia E. I, 466
Cox, Cordelia E. I, 467
Cox, Cordilla A. I, 807
Cox, Cynthia I, 478
Cox, Cynthia N. I, 463
Cox, Cyrus I, 939
Cox, Cyrus E. I, 677
Cox, Cyrus Enoch I, 652
Cox, Cyrus N. I, 465
Cox, Daniel I, 284
Cox, Daniel I, 303
Cox, Daniel I, 382
Cox, Daniel I, 457
Cox, Daniel I, 462
Cox, Daniel I, 466
Cox, Daniel I, 477
Cox, Daniel I, 478
Cox, Daniel I, 677
Cox, Daniel B. I, 465
Cox, Daniel D. III, 451
Cox, David I, 183
Cox, David I, 382
Cox, David I, 462
Cox, David I, 463
Cox, David I, 477
Cox, David I, 481
Cox, David I, 535
Cox, David I, 1015
Cox, David I, 1028
Cox, David I, 1104
Cox, David V, 44
Cox, David V, 164
Cox, David V, 733
Cox, David V, 734
Cox, David V, 766
Cox, David V, 767
Cox, David Carroll I, 236
Cox, Dawson I, 476
Cox, Deborah I, 383
Cox, Deborah I, 391
Cox, Deborah I, 462
Cox, Deborah I, 463
Cox, Deborah I, 1041
Cox, Deborah I, 1117
Cox, Deborah III, 90
Cox, Deborah IV, 381
Cox, Deborah IV, 455
Cox, Deborah V, 483
Cox, Deborah V, 484
Cox, Delfina I, 465
Cox, Delilah I, 477
Cox, Delilah I, 482
Cox, Della Jane I, 713
Cox, Delphina I, 478
Cox, Dennis I, 477
Cox, Dinah I, 381
Cox, Dinah I, 383
Cox, Dinah I, 676
Cox, Dinah I, 688
Cox, Dolly VI, 846
Cox, Doris V, 232
Cox, Dougan C. I, 383
Cox, Dougan Clark I, 614
Cox, Dr. Jos. R. II, 180
Cox, Drusilla IV, 381
Cox, Drusilla IV, 571
Cox, E. L. Nathan I, 464
Cox, E. Milton I, 479
Cox, Easter I, 302
Cox, Easter I, 307
Cox, Edgar J. I, 323
Cox, Edith I, 614
Cox, Edith V, 484
Cox, Edith V, 514
Cox, Edith W. V, 483
Cox, Edmond I, 283
Cox, Edmund I, 303
Cox, Edmund I, 1070
Cox, Edna I, 478
Cox, Edna I, 614
Cox, Edna V, 232
Cox, Edna V, 255
Cox, Edney I, 463
Cox, Edny I, 463
Cox, Edom I, 495
Cox, Edward I, 713
Cox, Edward C. II, 790
Cox, Edward C. II, 854
Cox, Edward P. II, 350
Cox, Effie I, 383
Cox, Effie May I, 923
Cox, Effie May I, 939
Cox, Egbert G. III, 213
Cox, Eleanor IV, 192
Cox, Eleazar I, 462
Cox, Eleazar I, 478
Cox, Eli I, 349
Cox, Eli I, 376
Cox, Eli I, 382
Cox, Eli I, 383
Cox, Eli I, 464
Cox, Eli I, 478
Cox, Eli I, 923
Cox, Eli I, 933
Cox, Eli V, 164
Cox, Eli VI, 896
Cox, Eli A. I, 713
Cox, Eli C. I, 462
Cox, Elihu I, 462
Cox, Elihu I, 652
Cox, Elihu I, 676
Cox, Elihu I, 677
Cox, Elihu I, 688
Cox, Elihu I, 1150
Cox, Elija I, 382
Cox, Elijah V, 44
Cox, Elisabeth I, 137
Cox, Elisabeth I, 155
Cox, Elisabeth I, 613
Cox, Elisabeth II, 790
Cox, Elisabeth A. I, 236
Cox, Elisabeth Ann I, 236
Cox, Elisabith I, 303
Cox, Elisha I, 382
Cox, Elisha I, 405
Cox, Elisha I, 462
Cox, Elisha I, 463
Cox, Elisha I, 465
Cox, Elisha I, 476
Cox, Elisha I, 477
Cox, Elisha V, 382
Cox, Elisha M. I, 462
Cox, Elisha M. I, 478
Cox, Elisha M. I, 479
Cox, Elisha M. I, 484
Cox, Elisha Milton I, 465
Cox, Eliz. N. III, 89
Cox, Eliz. N. III, 274
Cox, Eliza I, 462
Cox, Eliza V, 382
Cox, Eliza An I, 464
Cox, Eliza Ann I, 283
Cox, Eliza J. III, 89
Cox, Eliza J. III, 177
Cox, Eliza Jane I, 652
Cox, Elizabeth I, 283
Cox, Elizabeth I, 284
Cox, Elizabeth I, 299
Cox, Elizabeth I, 302
Cox, Elizabeth I, 303
Cox, Elizabeth I, 307
Cox, Elizabeth I, 308
Cox, Elizabeth I, 312
Cox, Elizabeth I, 328
Cox, Elizabeth I, 349
Cox, Elizabeth I, 358
Cox, Elizabeth I, 381
Cox, Elizabeth I, 382
Cox, Elizabeth I, 383
Cox, Elizabeth I, 390
Cox, Elizabeth I, 400
Cox, Elizabeth I, 409
Cox, Elizabeth I, 462
Cox, Elizabeth I, 465
Cox, Elizabeth I, 466
Cox, Elizabeth I, 476
Cox, Elizabeth I, 477
Cox, Elizabeth I, 481
Cox, Elizabeth I, 535
Cox, Elizabeth I, 688
Cox, Elizabeth I, 758
Cox, Elizabeth I, 768
Cox, Elizabeth I, 923
Cox, Elizabeth I, 984
Cox, Elizabeth I, 1028
Cox, Elizabeth II, 496
Cox, Elizabeth II, 627
Cox, Elizabeth II, 648
Cox, Elizabeth II, 734
Cox, Elizabeth II, 803
Cox, Elizabeth II, 854
Cox, Elizabeth II, 1071
Cox, Elizabeth IV, 143
Cox, Elizabeth IV, 192
Cox, Elizabeth IV, 381
Cox, Elizabeth IV, 446
Cox, Elizabeth IV, 571
Cox, Elizabeth IV, 576
Cox, Elizabeth V, 44
Cox, Elizabeth V, 326
Cox, Elizabeth V, 484
Cox, Elizabeth V, 527
Cox, Elizabeth V, 733
Cox, Elizabeth V, 767
Cox, Elizabeth V, 768
Cox, Elizabeth VI, 60
Cox, Elizabeth VI, 164
Cox, Elizabeth VI, 350
Cox, Elizabeth VI, 737
Cox, Elizabeth VI, 808
Cox, Elizabeth VI, 896
Cox, Elizabeth VI, 904
Cox, Elizabeth VI, 986
Cox, Elizabeth A. I, 652
Cox, Elizabeth A. I, 677
Cox, Elizabeth A. I, 680
Cox, Elizabeth A. I, 876
Cox, Elizabeth Amy I, 652
Cox, Elizabeth Ann I, 212
Cox, Elizabeth Ann I, 535
Cox, Elizabeth Ann VI, 60
Cox, Elizabeth Avis I, 323
Cox, Elizabeth J. II, 734
Cox, Elizabeth N. II, 854
Cox, Elizabeth W. II, 826
Cox, Elizabeth W. II, 854
Cox, Elizabeth W. II, 876
Cox, Elizabeth Walton II, 800
Cox, Elizanna I, 303
Cox, Ella M. I, 677
Cox, Ellen M. III, 424
Cox, Elminia Ellen I, 464
Cox, Elmira I, 464
Cox, Elmira I, 478
Cox, Elnathan I, 477
Cox, Elsie IV, 1154
Cox, Elsie IV, 1155
Cox, Elva F. I, 466
Cox, Elvirah IV, 469
Cox, Elwood I, 464
Cox, Elwood I, 478
Cox, Elwood I, 535
Cox, Elwood Mahlon I, 464
Cox, Emeline I, 478
Cox, Emeline D. I, 462
Cox, Emery I, 465
Cox, Emery W. I, 631
Cox, Emey I, 345
Cox, Emey I, 381
Cox, Emey I, 383
Cox, Emey I, 462
Cox, Emily I, 464
Cox, Emily I, 478
Cox, Emily I, 614
Cox, Emily I, 652
Cox, Emily I, 676
Cox, Emily I, 677
Cox, Emily VI, 934
Cox, Emily Hannah I, 464
Cox, Emma I, 923
Cox, Emma I, 933
Cox, Emma V, 44
Cox, Emma VI, 737
Cox, Emma VI, 768
Cox, Emma Agnes I, 614
Cox, Emma B. I, 939
Cox, Emma D. IV, 1154
Cox, Emma D. IV, 1155
Cox, Emma Gertrude I, 213
Cox, Emma Gertrude I, 236
Cox, Emma Gertrude I, 323
Cox, Emma H. I, 631
Cox, Emma J. V, 617
Cox, Emoline D. I, 465
Cox, Enoch I, 381
Cox, Enoch I, 382
Cox, Enoch I, 441
Cox, Enoch I, 462
Cox, Enoch I, 466
Cox, Enoch I, 475
Cox, Enoch I, 477
Cox, Enoch I, 652
Cox, Enoch I, 655
Cox, Enoch I, 676
Cox, Enoch I, 677
Cox, Enoch V, 44
Cox, Enoch V, 231
Cox, Enoch V, 232
Cox, Enoch V, 245
Cox, Enoch V, 250
Cox, Enoch L. I, 479
Cox, Enoch L. I, 614
Cox, Enoch L. I, 652
Cox, Enoch L. I, 677
Cox, Enoch L. E. I, 462
Cox, Enoch R. II, 854
Cox, Enoch Roberts II, 790
Cox, Enoch, Jr. V, 232
Cox, Enock I, 478
Cox, Enos I, 465
Cox, Enos I, 984
Cox, Enos I, 998
Cox, Esther I, 462
Cox, Esther I, 463
Cox, Esther I, 495
Cox, Esther I, 535
Cox, Esther I, 575
Cox, Esther V, 232
Cox, Esther V, 326
Cox, Esther Ann V, 734
Cox, Eula Lata I, 383
Cox, Eunice I, 463
Cox, Eunice I, 464
Cox, Eunice I, 466
Cox, Eunice I, 476
Cox, Eunice I, 478
Cox, Evan I, 1104
Cox, Evan I, 1117
Cox, Exum I, 303
Cox, Exum I, 312
Cox, Exum Thomas I, 283
Cox, Ezekiel Stanton I, 323
Cox, Ezra I, 383
Cox, Ezra I, 462
Cox, Fannie Luisa V, 834
Cox, Fannie Peel I, 335
Cox, Fellow I, 303
Cox, Flora Agnes I, 323
Cox, Flora Edna I, 463
Cox, Francelia III, 89
Cox, Francelia III, 94
Cox, Frances VI, 808
Cox, Frances Marien I, 465
Cox, Francisco I, 466
Cox, Francisco T. I, 478
Cox, Franklin N. V, 617
Cox, Frederick I, 1104
Cox, Gertrude I, 381
Cox, Gertrude I, 382
Cox, Gertrude V, 44
Cox, Gertrude V, 231
Cox, Gertrude V, 232
Cox, Gertrude V, 245
Cox, Gertrude V, 250
Cox, Gideon I, 462
Cox, Gideon I, 463
Cox, Gideon I, 466
Cox, Gideon I, 474
Cox, Gideon I, 477
Cox, Gideon I, 478
Cox, Gideon I, 483
Cox, Gideon I, 806
Cox, Gideon I, 807
Cox, Gidion I, 478
Cox, Guelma I, 463
Cox, Guli Elma I, 465
Cox, Gurney L. I, 677
Cox, Hannah I, 348
Cox, Hannah I, 349
Cox, Hannah I, 358
Cox, Hannah I, 370
Cox, Hannah I, 372
Cox, Hannah I, 381
Cox, Hannah I, 382
Cox, Hannah I, 383
Cox, Hannah I, 409
Cox, Hannah I, 417
Cox, Hannah I, 457
Cox, Hannah I, 462
Cox, Hannah I, 463
Cox, Hannah I, 465
Cox, Hannah I, 475
Cox, Hannah I, 476
Cox, Hannah I, 477
Cox, Hannah I, 478
Cox, Hannah I, 652
Cox, Hannah I, 676
Cox, Hannah I, 677
Cox, Hannah I, 1117
Cox, Hannah I, 1131
Cox, Hannah II, 170
Cox, Hannah II, 211
Cox, Hannah II, 350
Cox, Hannah II, 790
Cox, Hannah II, 823
Cox, Hannah III, 90
Cox, Hannah IV, 27
Cox, Hannah V, 43
Cox, Hannah V, 44
Cox, Hannah V, 157
Cox, Hannah V, 164
Cox, Hannah V, 205
Cox, Hannah V, 231
Cox, Hannah V, 733
Cox, Hannah E. V, 326
Cox, Hannah Gillingham VI, 73
Cox, Hannah L. I, 479
Cox, Hannah Lavina I, 464
Cox, Hannah Louania I, 465
Cox, Hannah S. I, 479
Cox, Hannah Smith II, 211
Cox, Hannah Smith II, 213
Cox, Hannah W. VI, 737
Cox, Hannah W. VI, 742
Cox, Harman I, 381
Cox, Harman I, 382
Cox, Harmon I, 382
Cox, Harmon I, 383
Cox, Harmon I, 463
Cox, Harmon I, 464
Cox, Harmon I, 465
Cox, Harmon I, 466
Cox, Harmon I, 477
Cox, Harmon I, 478
Cox, Harmon V, 232
Cox, Harmon VI, 483
Cox, Harmon VI, 523
Cox, Harmon T. I, 464
Cox, Harmon T. I, 478
Cox, Harriet Pauline V, 232
Cox, Harriet S. II, 790
Cox, Harriet Stockton II, 790
Cox, Harriett III, 89
Cox, Harriett III, 213
Cox, Henry I, 335
Cox, Henry I, 382
Cox, Henry I, 465
Cox, Henry I, 466
Cox, Henry I, 478
Cox, Henry I, 612
Cox, Henry I, 713
Cox, Henry I, 1117
Cox, Henry III, 89
Cox, Henry III, 90
Cox, Henry V, 164
Cox, Henry V, 617
Cox, Henry Davis I, 323
Cox, Henry E. I, 324
Cox, Henry H. III, 89
Cox, Henry H. III, 329
Cox, Herbert I, 939
Cox, Herbert I, 940
Cox, Herbert Micajah I, 236
Cox, Herbert P. I, 466
Cox, Herbert W. I, 323
Cox, Herman I, 348
Cox, Herman I, 381
Cox, Herman I, 383
Cox, Herman V, 44
Cox, Herman VI, 464
Cox, Hermon I, 381
Cox, Hermon VI, 380
Cox, Hester V, 231
Cox, Hinsey I, 284
Cox, Homer L. IV, 1311
Cox, Homer, Jr. IV, 1311
Cox, Hope III, 89
Cox, Hope III, 90
Cox, Hope III, 203
Cox, Hubert Micajah I, 213
Cox, Hugh V, 232
Cox, Huldah I, 462
Cox, Huldah I, 463
Cox, Huldah I, 477
Cox, Huldah I, 478
Cox, Huldah I, 483

, Huldah E. I, 463
, Ila I, 938
, Ira I, 335
, Irene I, 478
, Irene Emeline Hannah I, 477
, Irvin W. I, 236
, Isaac I, 283
, Isaac I, 284
, Isaac I, 303
, Isaac I, 314
, Isaac I, 323
, Isaac I, 370
, Isaac I, 381
, Isaac I, 382
, Isaac I, 462
, Isaac I, 463
, Isaac I, 466
, Isaac I, 476
, Isaac I, 478
, Isaac I, 485
, Isaac I, 487
, Isaac I, 535
, Isaac I, 605
, Isaac I, 607
, Isaac I, 807
, Isaac I, 1015
, Isaac II, 496
, Isaac II, 648
, Isaac II, 650
, Isaac II, 790
, Isaac III, 89
, Isaac III, 90
, Isaac V, 164
, Isaac V, 734
, Isaac VI, 60
, Isaac VI, 89
, Isaac VI, 350
, Isaac Elihu I, 463
, Isaac H. I, 323
, Isaac H. I, 328
, Isaac H. I, 331
, Isaac N. IV, 1154
, Isaac P., Jr. IV, 619
, Isaac Parker I, 303
, Isaac Powel IV, 619
, Isaac W. IV, 1154
, Isabella I, 323
, Isaiah I, 652
, Isaiah I, 676
, Isaiah I, 677
, Isaiah V, 301
, Isaiah V, 767
, Isaiah F. I, 466
, Isham I, 383
, Isham VI, 808
, Isham VI, 852
, Isom I, 383
, Isom I, 466
x, Israel II, 496
x, Israel II, 627
x, Ivon N. I, 236
x, J. B. IV, 1249
x, J. Elwood I, 876
x, J. Elwood I, 939
x, J. Elwood, Jr. I, 923
x, J. Gurney I, 923
x, J. Gurney I, 939
x, J. J. I, 535
x, J. J. I, 939
x, J. T. I, 479
x, J. William I, 475
x, Jacob I, 137
x, Jacob I, 191
x, Jacob I, 265
x, Jacob I, 268
x, Jacob I, 382
x, Jacob I, 409
x, Jacob I, 475
x, Jacob I, 876
x, Jacob II, 350
x, Jacob IV, 27
x, Jacob IV, 82
x, Jacob V, 232
x, Jacob, Jr. I, 476
x, Jahu I, 495
x, Jalie I, 939
x, James I, 283
x, James I, 284
x, James I, 303
x, James I, 312
x, James I, 323
x, James I, 328
x, James II, 350
x, James II, 496
x, James II, 648
x, James II, 790
x, James II, 854
x, James IV, 469
x, James V, 43
x, James V, 44
Cox, James V, 164
Cox, James V, 382
Cox, James V, 733
Cox, James VI, 808
Cox, James VI, 896
Cox, James A. I, 713
Cox, James Stanton I, 284
Cox, James Thomas I, 323
Cox, James W. IV, 469
Cox, Jane I, 348
Cox, Jane I, 374
Cox, Jane I, 381
Cox, Jane I, 382
Cox, Jane I, 383
Cox, Jane I, 417
Cox, Jane I, 463
Cox, Jane I, 464
Cox, Jane I, 465
Cox, Jane I, 466
Cox, Jane I, 467
Cox, Jane I, 476
Cox, Jane I, 477
Cox, Jane I, 480
Cox, Jane I, 481
Cox, Jane I, 677
Cox, Jane I, 680
Cox, Jane II, 211
Cox, Jane II, 285
Cox, Jane II, 734
Cox, Jane III, 89
Cox, Jane IV, 240
Cox, Jane IV, 469
Cox, Jane V, 44
Cox, Jane V, 164
Cox, Jane V, 232
Cox, Jane V, 301
Cox, Jane V, 309
Cox, Jane V, 766
Cox, Jane V, 767
Cox, Jane V, 806
Cox, Jane V, 969
Cox, Jane V, 973
Cox, Jane VI, 483
Cox, Jane VI, 986
Cox, Jane J. II, 854
Cox, Jane J. III, 274
Cox, Jane M. V, 810
Cox, Jane M. V, 969
Cox, Jane P. II, 735
Cox, Jane T. II, 916
Cox, Jannette I, 466
Cox, Jared IV, 571
Cox, Jean I, 382
Cox, Jean I, 393
Cox, Jehu I, 495
Cox, Jehu I, 535
Cox, Jehu I, 575
Cox, Jehu V, 231
Cox, Jehue V, 232
Cox, Jemima I, 45
Cox, Jemima I, 97
Cox, Jemima I, 136
Cox, Jemima I, 375
Cox, Jemima I, 383
Cox, Jemima I, 461
Cox, Jemima I, 462
Cox, Jemima I, 476
Cox, Jemima I, 477
Cox, Jemima I, 1028
Cox, Jemima V, 44
Cox, Jemima V, 733
Cox, Jemima V, 734
Cox, Jeremiah I, 97
Cox, Jeremiah I, 137
Cox, Jeremiah I, 265
Cox, Jeremiah I, 268
Cox, Jeremiah I, 349
Cox, Jeremiah I, 381
Cox, Jeremiah I, 382
Cox, Jeremiah I, 414
Cox, Jeremiah I, 445
Cox, Jeremiah I, 451
Cox, Jeremiah I, 463
Cox, Jeremiah I, 477
Cox, Jeremiah V, 44
Cox, Jeremiah V, 232
Cox, Jeremiah V, 301
Cox, Jeremiah V, 969
Cox, Jeremiah S. I, 465
Cox, Jeremiah S. I, 479
Cox, Jeremiah S. I, 619
Cox, Jeremiah S. I, 677
Cox, Jeremiah Simon I, 465
Cox, Jesse I, 328
Cox, Jesse I, 381
Cox, Jesse I, 382
Cox, Jesse I, 383
Cox, Jesse I, 406
Cox, Jesse I, 457
Cox, Jesse I, 462
Cox, Jesse I, 463
Cox, Jesse I, 476
Cox, Jesse I, 477
Cox, Jesse I, 478
Cox, Jesse I, 652
Cox, Jesse III, 89
Cox, Jesse V, 382
Cox, Jesse Franklin I, 652
Cox, Jesse Franklin I, 677
Cox, Jesse J. I, 323
Cox, Jesse J. I, 652
Cox, Jesse J. I, 677
Cox, Jesse James I, 323
Cox, Jesse W. V, 382
Cox, Jewell Frances I, 614
Cox, Joab I, 213
Cox, Job I, 1104
Cox, Joe V, 232
Cox, Joel I, 349
Cox, Joel I, 382
Cox, Joel IV, 143
Cox, Joel IV, 571
Cox, Joel VI, 896
Cox, Joel VI, 952
Cox, Joel VI, 954
Cox, Joel M. IV, 381
Cox, John I, 45
Cox, John I, 97
Cox, John I, 136
Cox, John I, 137
Cox, John I, 149
Cox, John I, 183
Cox, John I, 191
Cox, John I, 192
Cox, John I, 265
Cox, John I, 268
Cox, John I, 269
Cox, John I, 283
Cox, John I, 284
Cox, John I, 303
Cox, John I, 310
Cox, John I, 349
Cox, John I, 381
Cox, John I, 382
Cox, John I, 414
Cox, John I, 464
Cox, John I, 465
Cox, John I, 476
Cox, John I, 477
Cox, John I, 535
Cox, John I, 652
Cox, John I, 923
Cox, John I, 1015
Cox, John I, 1028
Cox, John I, 1075
Cox, John II, 170
Cox, John II, 211
Cox, John II, 248
Cox, John II, 350
Cox, John II, 496
Cox, John II, 583
Cox, John II, 735
Cox, John II, 813
Cox, John III, 89
Cox, John III, 90
Cox, John III, 203
Cox, John III, 336
Cox, John IV, 27
Cox, John IV, 82
Cox, John IV, 143
Cox, John IV, 381
Cox, John IV, 403
Cox, John IV, 455
Cox, John IV, 469
Cox, John V, 43
Cox, John V, 44
Cox, John V, 149
Cox, John V, 164
Cox, John V, 301
Cox, John V, 484
Cox, John V, 524
Cox, John V, 733
Cox, John V, 734
Cox, John V, 767
Cox, John V, 780
Cox, John V, 806
Cox, John V, 834
Cox, John V, 969
Cox, John V, 973
Cox, John VI, 824
Cox, John VI, 844
Cox, John VI, 859
Cox, John VI, 862
Cox, John Bryant I, 324
Cox, John C. I, 807
Cox, John C. II, 496
Cox, John Calvin IV, 1205
Cox, John E. I, 323
Cox, John E. I, 328
Cox, John E. I, 807
Cox, John Exum I, 323
Cox, John M. I, 478
Cox, John M. I, 744
Cox, John M. I, 758
Cox, John Milton I, 464
Cox, John Riley I, 478
Cox, John Scarlet I, 465
Cox, John Scarlot I, 477
Cox, John Sherman V, 834
Cox, John T. I, 465
Cox, John W. I, 328
Cox, John W. H. V, 617
Cox, John William I, 351
Cox, John William I, 382
Cox, John William I, 405
Cox, John William I, 463
Cox, John William I, 465
Cox, John William I, 475
Cox, John, Jr. I, 381
Cox, John, Jr. II, 211
Cox, John, Jr. II, 215
Cox, John, Jr. III, 90
Cox, John, Jr. IV, 381
Cox, John, Sr. I, 381
Cox, John, Sr. V, 733
Cox, Jonathan I, 137
Cox, Jonathan I, 183
Cox, Jonathan I, 192
Cox, Jonathan I, 284
Cox, Jonathan I, 303
Cox, Jonathan I, 463
Cox, Jonathan I, 464
Cox, Jonathan I, 466
Cox, Jonathan I, 475
Cox, Jonathan I, 477
Cox, Jonathan I, 478
Cox, Jonathan I, 535
Cox, Jonathan I, 713
Cox, Jonathan I, 923
Cox, Jonathan I, 1028
Cox, Jonathan V, 43
Cox, Jonathan V, 44
Cox, Jonathan V, 734
Cox, Jonathan V, 794
Cox, Jonathan E. I, 137
Cox, Jonathan E. I, 212
Cox, Jonathan E. I, 213
Cox, Jonathan E. I, 214
Cox, Jonathan E. I, 236
Cox, Jonathan E. I, 535
Cox, Jonathan E. I, 613
Cox, Jonathan E. I, 876
Cox, Jonathan E. VI, 60
Cox, Jonathan Elwood I, 213
Cox, Jonathan Elwood I, 236
Cox, Jonathan Elwood I, 535
Cox, Jonathan Elwood I, 923
Cox, Jonathan Elwood VI, 60
Cox, Jonathan S. I, 236
Cox, Jonathan, Jr. V, 43
Cox, Jordon I, 183
Cox, Joseph I, 45
Cox, Joseph I, 97
Cox, Joseph I, 137
Cox, Joseph I, 183
Cox, Joseph I, 191
Cox, Joseph I, 192
Cox, Joseph I, 265
Cox, Joseph I, 268
Cox, Joseph I, 303
Cox, Joseph I, 312
Cox, Joseph I, 358
Cox, Joseph I, 381
Cox, Joseph I, 383
Cox, Joseph I, 463
Cox, Joseph I, 464
Cox, Joseph I, 465
Cox, Joseph I, 466
Cox, Joseph I, 476
Cox, Joseph I, 676
Cox, Joseph I, 688
Cox, Joseph I, 713
Cox, Joseph I, 1117
Cox, Joseph II, 211
Cox, Joseph II, 496
Cox, Joseph II, 790
Cox, Joseph III, 90
Cox, Joseph IV, 143
Cox, Joseph IV, 192
Cox, Joseph IV, 381
Cox, Joseph IV, 469
Cox, Joseph IV, 571
Cox, Joseph IV, 576
Cox, Joseph V, 44
Cox, Joseph V, 232
Cox, Joseph V, 326
Cox, Joseph VI, 477
Cox, Joseph VI, 483
Cox, Joseph B. IV, 1249
Cox, Joseph Cadwallader V, 44
Cox, Joseph D. I, 535
Cox, Joseph D. I, 876
Cox, Joseph Dundas I, 923
Cox, Joseph G. II, 790
Cox, Joseph G. II, 854
Cox, Joseph G., Jr. II, 854
Cox, Joseph J. I, 236
Cox, Joseph J. I, 323
Cox, Joseph J. I, 328
Cox, Joseph J. I, 329
Cox, Joseph J. I, 535
Cox, Joseph J. I, 876
Cox, Joseph J. I, 923
Cox, Joseph J. Gurney I, 462
Cox, Joseph Jesse I, 462
Cox, Joseph John I, 212
Cox, Joseph John I, 535
Cox, Joseph John I, 923
Cox, Joseph John VI, 60
Cox, Joseph John Mary E. VI, 60
Cox, Joseph M. I, 137
Cox, Joseph M. IV, 192
Cox, Joseph M. IV, 288
Cox, Joseph P. I, 477
Cox, Joseph W. V, 326
Cox, Joseph W. VI, 734
Cox, Joseph W. VI, 737
Cox, Joseph Warington VI, 748
Cox, Joseph Warrington VI, 734
Cox, Joseph Warrington VI, 737
Cox, Joseph, Jr. II, 318
Cox, Joseph, Jr. II, 325
Cox, Josephine II, 854
Cox, Joshua I, 381
Cox, Joshua I, 382
Cox, Joshua I, 383
Cox, Joshua I, 457
Cox, Joshua I, 462
Cox, Joshua I, 463
Cox, Joshua I, 475
Cox, Joshua I, 476
Cox, Joshua I, 477
Cox, Joshua II, 350
Cox, Joshua V, 44
Cox, Joshua V, 231
Cox, Joshua V, 301
Cox, Josiah I, 137
Cox, Josiah I, 183
Cox, Josiah I, 191
Cox, Josiah I, 236
Cox, Josiah I, 254
Cox, Josiah I, 265
Cox, Josiah I, 283
Cox, Josiah I, 284
Cox, Josiah I, 302
Cox, Josiah I, 315
Cox, Josiah I, 466
Cox, Josiah I, 1070
Cox, Josiah V, 44
Cox, Judah I, 1070
Cox, Judeth I, 303
Cox, Judeth I, 1070
Cox, Judith I, 236
Cox, Judith I, 254
Cox, Judith I, 283
Cox, Judith I, 302
Cox, Judith I, 303
Cox, Judith I, 315
Cox, Judith VI, 164
Cox, Judith VI, 808
Cox, Judith W. VI, 808
Cox, Julia I, 465
Cox, Julia I, 478
Cox, Julia Ann IV, 985
Cox, Julia E. I, 465
Cox, Julia Roberta I, 323
Cox, Juliatha I, 381
Cox, Juliatha I, 535
Cox, Julitha I, 1104
Cox, Julither I, 1104
Cox, Julius C. I, 479
Cox, Julius C. I, 482
Cox, Julius Clarkson I, 465
Cox, Junius Thomas I, 464
Cox, Juretta I, 758
Cox, Juretta I, 763
Cox, Jurita I, 467
Cox, K. Elma I, 479
Cox, K. Elma I, 483
Cox, Katharine I, 349
Cox, Katharine I, 381
Cox, Katharine I, 466
Cox, Katharine V, 231
Cox, Katie Mable I, 383
Cox, Kezia I, 351
Cox, Kezia I, 383
Cox, Kezia I, 386
Cox, Kezia I, 463
Cox, Kezia E. I, 478
Cox, Kezia Elma I, 463
Cox, L. H. I, 614
Cox, L. L. I, 335
Cox, L. Lillie I, 335
Cox, Larkan I, 463

Cox, Larken I, 462
Cox, Larkin I, 478
Cox, Lattice I, 382
Cox, Laura I, 328
Cox, Laura I, 807
Cox, Laura Adella I, 323
Cox, Lavina I, 383
Cox, Lavina I, 477
Cox, Lavina I, 478
Cox, Lawrence P. IV, 1205
Cox, Leah Catharine I, 463
Cox, Leah Catharine I, 464
Cox, Leanna L. I, 383
Cox, Leanna L. I, 430
Cox, Lena IV, 469
Cox, Lena May IV, 469
Cox, Lenley B. IV, 981
Cox, Leo I, 631
Cox, Leo Millikan I, 614
Cox, Leslie Franklin I, 323
Cox, Lester IV, 192
Cox, Letchworth II, 211
Cox, Letitia V, 44
Cox, Letitia Luezer I, 984
Cox, Levi I, 283
Cox, Levi I, 323
Cox, Levi I, 463
Cox, Levi I, 466
Cox, Levi I, 477
Cox, Levi I, 478
Cox, Levi I, 479
Cox, Levi I, 483
Cox, Levi I, 613
Cox, Levi IV, 143
Cox, Levi IV, 381
Cox, Levi IV, 1311
Cox, Levi F. IV, 1311
Cox, Levisa I, 758
Cox, Lewis Elijah I, 477
Cox, Lidia I, 302
Cox, Lillian H. I, 614
Cox, Lillian H. I, 631
Cox, Lillie I, 335
Cox, Lillie I, 923
Cox, Lillie I, 930
Cox, Lillie I, 940
Cox, Lillie Donna I, 713
Cox, Lindley Elbert I, 213
Cox, Lindley Elbert I, 236
Cox, Lindley Hoag I, 323
Cox, Littleberry VI, 808
Cox, Lizzie V, 834
Cox, Lorenzo I, 303
Cox, Losada I, 465
Cox, Losada I, 477
Cox, Lou E. I, 303
Cox, Louetta I, 466
Cox, Louisa I, 283
Cox, Louisa I, 284
Cox, Louisa I, 302
Cox, Louisa I, 303
Cox, Louisa I, 923
Cox, Louisa S. III, 89
Cox, Louisa S. III, 329
Cox, Louise R. V, 326
Cox, Lourie I, 302
Cox, Lourie I, 310
Cox, Love E. I, 323
Cox, Lucinda VI, 852
Cox, Lucy VI, 808
Cox, Lucy VI, 941
Cox, Lucy Lee I, 335
Cox, Luelva L. I, 466
Cox, Luetta VI, 737
Cox, Luize I, 465
Cox, Luna I, 939
Cox, Luna Ellen I, 923
Cox, Lura I, 383
Cox, Lydia I, 236
Cox, Lydia I, 251
Cox, Lydia I, 269
Cox, Lydia I, 284
Cox, Lydia I, 302
Cox, Lydia I, 303
Cox, Lydia I, 312
Cox, Lydia I, 328
Cox, Lydia I, 349
Cox, Lydia I, 351
Cox, Lydia I, 375
Cox, Lydia I, 380
Cox, Lydia I, 381
Cox, Lydia I, 382
Cox, Lydia I, 383
Cox, Lydia I, 391
Cox, Lydia I, 405
Cox, Lydia I, 445
Cox, Lydia I, 457
Cox, Lydia I, 463
Cox, Lydia I, 464
Cox, Lydia I, 465
Cox, Lydia I, 466
Cox, Lydia I, 475
Cox, Lydia I, 476
Cox, Lydia I, 477
Cox, Lydia I, 478
Cox, Lydia I, 479
Cox, Lydia I, 482
Cox, Lydia I, 713
Cox, Lydia I, 758
Cox, Lydia I, 1104
Cox, Lydia I, 1117
Cox, Lydia II, 735
Cox, Lydia V, 232
Cox, Lydia V, 301
Cox, Lydia V, 309
Cox, Lydia VI, 880
Cox, Lydia E. I, 807
Cox, Lydia J. II, 965
Cox, Lydia Jane I, 463
Cox, Lydia Jane I, 465
Cox, Lydia Leanna I, 383
Cox, Lydia M. IV, 192
Cox, Lydia P. IV, 192
Cox, Mabel I, 213
Cox, Macajah I, 213
Cox, Macajah I, 236
Cox, Maggie Belfour I, 383
Cox, Mahala I, 463
Cox, Mahala I, 465
Cox, Mahala I, 478
Cox, Mahetabel I, 323
Cox, Mahetta A. I, 328
Cox, Mahetta A. I, 329
Cox, Mahitabel I, 303
Cox, Mahitabel I, 304
Cox, Mahitabel I, 323
Cox, Mahittabel Frances I, 323
Cox, Mahlon I, 383
Cox, Mahlon I, 457
Cox, Mahlon I, 463
Cox, Mahlon I, 464
Cox, Mahlon I, 465
Cox, Mahlon I, 466
Cox, Mahlon I, 475
Cox, Mahlon I, 476
Cox, Mahlon I, 477
Cox, Mahlon I, 984
Cox, Mahlon H. I, 652
Cox, Mahlon H. I, 677
Cox, Mahlon N. I, 465
Cox, Malissa J. I, 462
Cox, Mamie Clark I, 383
Cox, Manley M. I, 807
Cox, Manly M. I, 462
Cox, Manly M. I, 478
Cox, Manly M. I, 807
Cox, Margaret I, 183
Cox, Margaret I, 191
Cox, Margaret I, 192
Cox, Margaret I, 213
Cox, Margaret I, 214
Cox, Margaret I, 376
Cox, Margaret I, 381
Cox, Margaret I, 382
Cox, Margaret I, 419
Cox, Margaret I, 441
Cox, Margaret I, 461
Cox, Margaret I, 464
Cox, Margaret I, 474
Cox, Margaret I, 476
Cox, Margaret I, 619
Cox, Margaret I, 631
Cox, Margaret I, 652
Cox, Margaret I, 676
Cox, Margaret I, 677
Cox, Margaret I, 692
Cox, Margaret I, 920
Cox, Margaret I, 1026
Cox, Margaret I, 1028
Cox, Margaret I, 1104
Cox, Margaret I, 1117
Cox, Margaret I, 1125
Cox, Margaret I Sup 1, 11
Cox, Margaret V, 44
Cox, Margaret VI, 734
Cox, Margaret VI, 737
Cox, Margaret VI, 748
Cox, Margaret D. I, 465
Cox, Margaret D. I, 478
Cox, Margaret D. I, 479
Cox, Margaret D. I, 631
Cox, Margaret D. I, 675
Cox, Margaret D. I, 677
Cox, Margaret E. I, 535
Cox, Margaret E. I, 566
Cox, Margaret Edna I, 212
Cox, Margaret Elma I, 535
Cox, Margaret Louise I, 614
Cox, Margarett Ann I, 323
Cox, Margera I, 984
Cox, Margery I, 349
Cox, Margery I, 382
Cox, Margery I, 465
Cox, Margery I, 477
Cox, Margery I, 485
Cox, Margery I, 984
Cox, Margery V, 44
Cox, Margery V, 301
Cox, Margery C. IV, 1012
Cox, Marguerite Kathleen I, 923
Cox, Maria IV, 571
Cox, Maria V, 326
Cox, Maria V, 364
Cox, Maria Louise III, 451
Cox, Mariah IV, 381
Cox, Mariah IV, 571
Cox, Mariah Elizabeth I, 713
Cox, Mariam I, 137
Cox, Mariam I, 268
Cox, Mariam I, 269
Cox, Marie I, 923
Cox, Marie I, 930
Cox, Marie Louise III, 401
Cox, Marion Sims I, 323
Cox, Marmaduke IV, 381
Cox, Martha I, 134
Cox, Martha I, 137
Cox, Martha I, 345
Cox, Martha I, 349
Cox, Martha I, 370
Cox, Martha I, 375
Cox, Martha I, 381
Cox, Martha I, 382
Cox, Martha I, 383
Cox, Martha I, 399
Cox, Martha I, 429
Cox, Martha I, 445
Cox, Martha I, 459
Cox, Martha I, 462
Cox, Martha I, 463
Cox, Martha I, 464
Cox, Martha I, 466
Cox, Martha I, 478
Cox, Martha I, 535
Cox, Martha I, 676
Cox, Martha I, 876
Cox, Martha II, 350
Cox, Martha II, 496
Cox, Martha II, 583
Cox, Martha II, 607
Cox, Martha II, 636
Cox, Martha III, 90
Cox, Martha III, 379
Cox, Martha III, 382
Cox, Martha V, 43
Cox, Martha V, 44
Cox, Martha V, 124
Cox, Martha V, 326
Cox, Martha V, 337
Cox, Martha V, 833
Cox, Martha V, 834
Cox, Martha VI, 808
Cox, Martha VI, 859
Cox, Martha Ann V, 44
Cox, Martha Ann V, 83
Cox, Martha E. III, 322
Cox, Martha Edna I, 463
Cox, Martha Edney I, 463
Cox, Martha H. VI, 737
Cox, Martha Jane I, 464
Cox, Martha Jane I, 465
Cox, Martha Jane IV, 192
Cox, Martin M. II, 790
Cox, Mary I, 183
Cox, Mary I, 191
Cox, Mary I, 265
Cox, Mary I, 280
Cox, Mary I, 283
Cox, Mary I, 284
Cox, Mary I, 299
Cox, Mary I, 302
Cox, Mary I, 303
Cox, Mary I, 307
Cox, Mary I, 310
Cox, Mary I, 312
Cox, Mary I, 323
Cox, Mary I, 349
Cox, Mary I, 375
Cox, Mary I, 381
Cox, Mary I, 382
Cox, Mary I, 383
Cox, Mary I, 402
Cox, Mary I, 403
Cox, Mary I, 405
Cox, Mary I, 406
Cox, Mary I, 409
Cox, Mary I, 419
Cox, Mary I, 441
Cox, Mary I, 457
Cox, Mary I, 461
Cox, Mary I, 462
Cox, Mary I, 463
Cox, Mary I, 464
Cox, Mary I, 465
Cox, Mary I, 466
Cox, Mary I, 470
Cox, Mary I, 472
Cox, Mary I, 475
Cox, Mary I, 476
Cox, Mary I, 477
Cox, Mary I, 478
Cox, Mary I, 479
Cox, Mary I, 485
Cox, Mary I, 535
Cox, Mary I, 620
Cox, Mary I, 652
Cox, Mary I, 655
Cox, Mary I, 676
Cox, Mary I, 677
Cox, Mary I, 923
Cox, Mary I, 939
Cox, Mary I, 948
Cox, Mary I, 1018
Cox, Mary I, 1019
Cox, Mary I, 1028
Cox, Mary I, 1047
Cox, Mary I, 1056
Cox, Mary I, 1059
Cox, Mary I, 1060
Cox, Mary I, 1061
Cox, Mary I, 1063
Cox, Mary I, 1117
Cox, Mary I, 1150
Cox, Mary II, 211
Cox, Mary II, 350
Cox, Mary II, 496
Cox, Mary II, 574
Cox, Mary III, 90
Cox, Mary III, 229
Cox, Mary IV, 143
Cox, Mary IV, 381
Cox, Mary IV, 423
Cox, Mary IV, 1249
Cox, Mary V, 43
Cox, Mary V, 44
Cox, Mary V, 164
Cox, Mary V, 205
Cox, Mary V, 231
Cox, Mary V, 232
Cox, Mary V, 244
Cox, Mary V, 250
Cox, Mary V, 301
Cox, Mary V, 318
Cox, Mary V, 326
Cox, Mary V, 483
Cox, Mary V, 484
Cox, Mary V, 514
Cox, Mary V, 733
Cox, Mary V, 767
Cox, Mary VI, 60
Cox, Mary VI, 89
Cox, Mary A. I, 465
Cox, Mary A. I, 652
Cox, Mary A. I, 677
Cox, Mary A. I, 684
Cox, Mary Abygill I, 323
Cox, Mary Alice III, 90
Cox, Mary Ann I, 478
Cox, Mary Ann I, 479
Cox, Mary Ann I, 486
Cox, Mary Ann I, 713
Cox, Mary Ann I, 984
Cox, Mary Ann I, 987
Cox, Mary Ann I, 998
Cox, Mary Ann VI, 862
Cox, Mary C. I, 323
Cox, Mary C. III, 379
Cox, Mary C. VI, 737
Cox, Mary D. I, 535
Cox, Mary D. I, 876
Cox, Mary D. I, 923
Cox, Mary D. I, 939
Cox, Mary E. I, 236
Cox, Mary E. I, 255
Cox, Mary E. I, 323
Cox, Mary E. I, 324
Cox, Mary E. I, 328
Cox, Mary E. I, 329
Cox, Mary E. I, 330
Cox, Mary E. I, 337
Cox, Mary E. I, 383
Cox, Mary E. I, 479
Cox, Mary E. I, 482
Cox, Mary E. I, 535
Cox, Mary E. I, 560
Cox, Mary E. I, 613
Cox, Mary E. I, 619
Cox, Mary E. I, 620
Cox, Mary E. I, 652
Cox, Mary E. I, 677
Cox, Mary E. I, 688
Cox, Mary E. I, 936
Cox, Mary E. III, 213
Cox, Mary E. Clinger II, 854
Cox, Mary E. M. I, 303
Cox, Mary E. M. I, 323
Cox, Mary E. M. I, 335
Cox, Mary Elisabeth I, 614
Cox, Mary Eliza I, 212
Cox, Mary Eliza I, 535
Cox, Mary Eliza VI, 60
Cox, Mary Ellen I, 925
Cox, Mary Emoline I, 465
Cox, Mary Etta II, 285
Cox, Mary F. I, 466
Cox, Mary F. I, 478
Cox, Mary F. I, 483
Cox, Mary Gulielma I, 383
Cox, Mary Jane I, 463
Cox, Mary Jane I, 465
Cox, Mary Jane V, 326
Cox, Mary L. II, 496
Cox, Mary L. II, 854
Cox, Mary L. III, 451
Cox, Mary Liddon II, 496
Cox, Mary Martha V, 231
Cox, Mary N. III, 89
Cox, Mary N. III, 203
Cox, Mary Newbold III, 89
Cox, Mary Nicholas IV, 1311
Cox, Mary R. Minty I, 744
Cox, Mary S. I, 940
Cox, Mary W. I, 923
Cox, Mary W. VI, 737
Cox, Mary Walton I, 923
Cox, Mascilda VI, 808
Cox, Maude I, 213
Cox, Mehetabel I, 213
Cox, Mehetable I, 228
Cox, Mehettabel Avis I, 323
Cox, Mehitabel I, 236
Cox, Melissa Jane I, 464
Cox, Melva Amy V, 834
Cox, Melvina I, 323
Cox, Merlin IV, 1155
Cox, Merlin Lee IV, 1154
Cox, Micajah I, 27
Cox, Micajah I, 228
Cox, Micajah I, 236
Cox, Micajah I, 251
Cox, Micajah I, 264
Cox, Micajah I, 283
Cox, Micajah I, 284
Cox, Micajah I, 285
Cox, Micajah I, 302
Cox, Micajah I, 303
Cox, Micajah I, 310
Cox, Micajah I, 321
Cox, Micajah I, 323
Cox, Micajah I, 328
Cox, Micajah I, 329
Cox, Micajah T. I, 335
Cox, Micajah Thomas I, 324
Cox, Micajah Thomas I, 335
Cox, Michael I, 459
Cox, Michael I, 464
Cox, Michael I, 478
Cox, Michal I, 284
Cox, Micheel I, 303
Cox, Micheel I, 309
Cox, Mildred I, 284
Cox, Mildred I, 303
Cox, Mildred I, 309
Cox, Mildred I, 325
Cox, Mildred VI, 808
Cox, Mildred E. I, 325
Cox, Mildred Jennett I, 213
Cox, Millicent I, 283
Cox, Millicent I, 303
Cox, Millicent I, 314
Cox, Milton V, 326
Cox, Milton V, 382
Cox, Mina V, 834
Cox, Mincher I, 463
Cox, Mincher I, 475
Cox, Miriam I, 97
Cox, Miriam I, 137
Cox, Miriam I, 149
Cox, Miriam I, 183
Cox, Miriam I, 192
Cox, Miriam I, 265
Cox, Miriam I, 267
Cox, Miriam I, 268
Cox, Miriam I, 284
Cox, Miriam I, 285
Cox, Miriam I, 302
Cox, Miriam I, 303
Cox, Miriam I, 317
Cox, Miriam I, 321
Cox, Miriam I, 325
Cox, Miriam I, 328
Cox, Miriam I, 476
Cox, Miriam I, 713
Cox, Miriam I, 738
Cox, Miriam II, 211

x, Miriam V, 382
x, Mittie I, 213
x, Molly VI, 824
x, Molsey Emmer I, 479
x, Moorman V, 231
x, Moriah IV, 381
x, Moses II, 350
x, Moses II, 496
x, Moses II, 627
x, Myrta V, 454
x, N. B. I, 328
x, Nancy I, 335
x, Nancy I, 445
x, Nancy I, 452
x, Nancy I, 463
x, Nancy I, 465
x, Nancy I, 466
x, Nancy I, 477
x, Nancy I, 478
x, Nancy I, 940
x, Nancy V, 733
x, Nancy VI, 844
x, Nancy VI, 1011
x, Nancy A. I, 466
x, Nancy Ann I, 467
x, Nancy C. I, 478
x, Nancy J. I, 464
x, Nancy Jane I, 652
x, Nancy Jane I, 677
x, Nancy V. I, 745
x, Naomi I, 463
x, Naomi I, 475
x, Naomi I, 476
x, Naomi I, 477
x, Naomia I, 478
x, Naomy I, 475
x, Naomy I, 476
x, Narcissa Clementine I, 465
x, Nathan I, 183
x, Nathan I, 284
x, Nathan I, 323
x, Nathan I, 382
x, Nathan I, 383
x, Nathan I, 409
x, Nathan I, 457
x, Nathan I, 462
x, Nathan I, 463
x, Nathan I, 464
x, Nathan I, 466
x, Nathan I, 475
x, Nathan I, 476
x, Nathan I, 477
x, Nathan I, 478
x, Nathan I, 485
x, Nathan I, 713
x, Nathan I, 717
x, Nathan I, 1150
x, Nathan V, 232
x, Nathan V, 301
x, Nathan B. I, 45
x, Nathan B. I, 284
x, Nathan B. I, 323
x, Nathan B. I, 328
x, Nathan B. I, 331
x, Nathan Emery I, 479
x, Nathan Emery I, 614
x, Nathan Emory I, 614
ox, Nathan Eugene I, 335
ox, Nathan M. I, 476
x, Nathan R. I, 464
x, Nathan T. I, 328
x, Nathan Thomas I, 323
ox, Nathan W. I, 462
x, Nathan W. I, 464
x, Nathan W. I, 478
ox, Nathaniel I, 349
ox, Nathaniel I, 381
ox, Nathaniel I, 382
ox, Nathaniel I, 461
ox, Nathaniel I, 464
ox, Nathaniel I, 465
ox, Nathaniel I, 476
ox, Nathaniel I, 477
ox, Nathaniel I, 478
ox, Nathaniel I, 482
ox, Nathaniel I, 676
ox, Nathaniel I, 758
ox, Needham I, 303
ox, Nehemiah V, 733
ox, Nehemiah V, 734
ox, Neri I, 464
ox, Neri I, 477
ox, Neri I, 478
ox, Neri I, 481
ox, Nicholas I, 381
ox, Nicholas I, 463
ox, Nicholas I, 464
ox, Nicholas I, 465
ox, Nicholas I, 477
ox, Nicholas I, 478
ox, Nicholas I, 481

Cox, Noel P. IV, 619
Cox, Norine Virginia I, 940
Cox, Nowel IV, 619
Cox, Obed I, 464
Cox, Obed I, 465
Cox, Obed I, 477
Cox, Obed I, 478
Cox, Obed I, 485
Cox, Obed T. I, 465
Cox, Obert Ceroby I, 713
Cox, Olive I, 923
Cox, Olive Spencer I, 939
Cox, Oliver I, 383
Cox, Oliver I, 923
Cox, Oliver I, 930
Cox, Oliver G. I, 462
Cox, Oliver G. I, 478
Cox, Oliver G. I, 807
Cox, Oliver L. I, 713
Cox, Oliver S. I, 807
Cox, Oliver Wendal I, 713
Cox, Ora May I, 383
Cox, Orlando I, 478
Cox, Orlando I, 807
Cox, Orpha I, 303
Cox, Oscar I, 631
Cox, Oscar L. I, 614
Cox, Oscar L. I, 631
Cox, Oscar L. I, 652
Cox, Owen Dudley I, 465
Cox, Ozias I, 465
Cox, P. V, 232
Cox, Paris I, 462
Cox, Paris I, 478
Cox, Parris Jay I, 652
Cox, Parris Jay I, 677
Cox, Patience I, 349
Cox, Patience I, 381
Cox, Patience I, 382
Cox, Patience I, 414
Cox, Patience I, 463
Cox, Patience I, 478
Cox, Patience I, 479
Cox, Patience I, 613
Cox, Patience V, 44
Cox, Patience V, 301
Cox, Patience V, 307
Cox, Paul I, 335
Cox, Peggy M. VI, 896
Cox, Penelipe I, 323
Cox, Penelope L. I, 478
Cox, Peninah I, 283
Cox, Peninah I, 284
Cox, Peninah I, 303
Cox, Peninah I, 463
Cox, Peninah I, 477
Cox, Peninah I, 485
Cox, Penninah I, 228
Cox, Penninah Terretta I, 213
Cox, Penninah Terretta I, 323
Cox, Penope R. I, 465
Cox, Perry I, 303
Cox, Peter I, 535
Cox, Peter I, 1015
Cox, Peter I, 1041
Cox, Peter I, 1104
Cox, Peter I, 1117
Cox, Peter I, 1125
Cox, Peter I Sup 1, 11
Cox, Peter V, 164
Cox, Pharaba I, 323
Cox, Pharibe I, 328
Cox, Pheba I, 1071
Cox, Pheba Abbe I, 303
Cox, Phebe I, 280
Cox, Phebe I, 283
Cox, Phebe I, 284
Cox, Phebe I, 302
Cox, Phebe I, 303
Cox, Phebe I, 306
Cox, Phebe I, 308
Cox, Phebe I, 370
Cox, Phebe I, 380
Cox, Phebe I, 381
Cox, Phebe I, 382
Cox, Phebe I, 383
Cox, Phebe I, 457
Cox, Phebe I, 462
Cox, Phebe I, 465
Cox, Phebe I, 475
Cox, Phebe I, 476
Cox, Phebe I, 1070
Cox, Phebe II, 211
Cox, Phebe III, 89
Cox, Phebe III, 90
Cox, Phebe III, 229
Cox, Phebe V, 44
Cox, Phebe V, 129
Cox, Phebe V, 231
Cox, Phebe V, 232
Cox, Phebe V, 246

Cox, Phebe V, 766
Cox, Phebe V, 810
Cox, Phebe VI, 350
Cox, Phebe VI, 913
Cox, Phebe H. III, 63
Cox, Phebe H. III, 90
Cox, Pheriba I, 284
Cox, Philip VI, 942
Cox, Phineas I, 465
Cox, Phineas I, 477
Cox, Phinehas I, 479
Cox, Phinelias I, 383
Cox, Phoebe V, 734
Cox, Polley I, 323
Cox, Polly I, 183
Cox, Powel IV, 619
Cox, Priscella I, 462
Cox, Priscilla IV, 381
Cox, Priscilla IV, 571
Cox, Priscilla V, 733
Cox, Priscilla VI, 663
Cox, R. Paten IV, 1205
Cox, Rachel I, 284
Cox, Rachel I, 301
Cox, Rachel I, 303
Cox, Rachel I, 338
Cox, Rachel I, 383
Cox, Rachel I, 457
Cox, Rachel I, 461
Cox, Rachel I, 462
Cox, Rachel I, 464
Cox, Rachel I, 475
Cox, Rachel I, 476
Cox, Rachel I, 480
Cox, Rachel I, 605
Cox, Rachel I, 607
Cox, Rachel I, 676
Cox, Rachel I, 687
Cox, Rachel II, 211
Cox, Rachel II, 262
Cox, Rachel II, 803
Cox, Rachel III, 89
Cox, Rachel IV, 27
Cox, Rachel IV, 82
Cox, Rachel IV, 143
Cox, Rachel IV, 381
Cox, Rachel IV, 403
Cox, Rachel IV, 455
Cox, Rachel IV, 571
Cox, Rachel V, 326
Cox, Rachel V, 337
Cox, Rachel C. I, 464
Cox, Rachel French II, 790
Cox, Rachel M. IV, 192
Cox, Rachel M. IV, 288
Cox, Raiford Artemis I, 923
Cox, Rebeca I, 382
Cox, Rebecah I, 465
Cox, Rebecca I, 381
Cox, Rebecca I, 461
Cox, Rebecca I, 462
Cox, Rebecca I, 463
Cox, Rebecca I, 464
Cox, Rebecca I, 465
Cox, Rebecca I, 466
Cox, Rebecca I, 475
Cox, Rebecca I, 476
Cox, Rebecca I, 477
Cox, Rebecca I, 478
Cox, Rebecca I, 484
Cox, Rebecca I, 655
Cox, Rebecca I, 676
Cox, Rebecca I, 677
Cox, Rebecca I, 680
Cox, Rebecca I, 984
Cox, Rebecca II, 496
Cox, Rebecca II, 650
Cox, Rebecca II, 702
Cox, Rebecca IV, 27
Cox, Rebecca IV, 82
Cox, Rebecca IV, 381
Cox, Rebecca IV, 389
Cox, Rebecca IV, 571
Cox, Rebecca IV, 576
Cox, Rebecca V, 617
Cox, Rebecca V, 733
Cox, Rebecca VI, 1000
Cox, Rebecca A. II, 734
Cox, Rebecca Allen II, 735
Cox, Rebecca C. I, 383
Cox, Rebecca C. I, 415
Cox, Rebecca Caroline I, 383
Cox, Rebecca Elnor I, 984
Cox, Rebeccah I, 466
Cox, Rebeckah I, 535
Cox, Rebeckah I, 1015
Cox, Rebeckah I, 1018
Cox, Rebekah I, 381
Cox, Rebekah I, 382
Cox, Rebekah I, 395
Cox, Rebekah I, 984

Cox, Redford Elijah I, 213
Cox, Reece I, 934
Cox, Reuben I, 464
Cox, Reuben I, 478
Cox, Reuben D. I, 744
Cox, Reuben G. I, 478
Cox, Reuben J. I, 463
Cox, Reuben J. I, 465
Cox, Reuben J. I, 478
Cox, Reuben J. I, 486
Cox, Rheuben I, 478
Cox, Rhoda I, 459
Cox, Rhoda I, 464
Cox, Rhoda I, 477
Cox, Rhoda I, 478
Cox, Rhodema E. I, 478
Cox, Richard I, 279
Cox, Richard I, 284
Cox, Richard I, 302
Cox, Richard I, 303
Cox, Richard I, 304
Cox, Richard I, 307
Cox, Richard I, 308
Cox, Richard I, 310
Cox, Richard I, 312
Cox, Richard I, 313
Cox, Richard I, 535
Cox, Richard I, 631
Cox, Richard I, 1015
Cox, Richard I, 1018
Cox, Richard I, 1028
Cox, Richard I, 1047
Cox, Richard I, 1048
Cox, Richard II, 350
Cox, Richard V, 44
Cox, Richard V, 164
Cox, Richard VI, 164
Cox, Richard A. I, 283
Cox, Richard Albertson I, 303
Cox, Richard Clarkson I, 614
Cox, Richard T. I, 323
Cox, Richard, Jr. I, 303
Cox, Robert I, 284
Cox, Robert I, 302
Cox, Robert I, 303
Cox, Robert I, 311
Cox, Robert I, 463
Cox, Robert I, 467
Cox, Robert I, 476
Cox, Robert I, 478
Cox, Robert III, 90
Cox, Robert III, 229
Cox, Robert IV, 27
Cox, Robert IV, 82
Cox, Robert V, 454
Cox, Robert V, 617
Cox, Robert H. VI, 808
Cox, Robert H. VI, 896
Cox, Roberta Jane I, 324
Cox, Roger Minter VI, 737
Cox, Roland VI, 737
Cox, Rosco Lavigia I, 323
Cox, Roscoe Lavidga I, 213
Cox, Roscoe Lavigia I, 236
Cox, Roxanah I, 462
Cox, Roxannah M. I, 478
Cox, Roxie Mildred I, 213
Cox, Roxie Mildred I, 323
Cox, Roxie Milford I, 236
Cox, Ruth I, 284
Cox, Ruth I, 325
Cox, Ruth I, 381
Cox, Ruth I, 382
Cox, Ruth I, 417
Cox, Ruth I, 457
Cox, Ruth I, 461
Cox, Ruth I, 462
Cox, Ruth I, 463
Cox, Ruth I, 464
Cox, Ruth I, 465
Cox, Ruth I, 466
Cox, Ruth I, 473
Cox, Ruth I, 475
Cox, Ruth I, 476
Cox, Ruth I, 477
Cox, Ruth I, 478
Cox, Ruth I, 479
Cox, Ruth I, 484
Cox, Ruth I, 612
Cox, Ruth I, 652
Cox, Ruth I, 676
Cox, Ruth I, 677
Cox, Ruth II, 350
Cox, Ruth II, 496
Cox, Ruth II, 583
Cox, Ruth IV, 192
Cox, Ruth V, 44
Cox, Ruth V, 149
Cox, Ruth V, 164
Cox, Ruth V, 301
Cox, Ruth Ellen I, 465

Cox, S. E. V, 232
Cox, S. J. I, 335
Cox, S. Louisa III, 90
Cox, S. Louisa III, 330
Cox, Sabina I, 467
Cox, Sabina I, 477
Cox, Sabina Emerella V, 232
Cox, Sabra I, 677
Cox, Sabra R. I, 479
Cox, Sabra R. I, 677
Cox, Sabra R. I, 680
Cox, Salley I, 323
Cox, Sallie I, 335
Cox, Sallie I, 614
Cox, Sallie I, 624
Cox, Sallie I, 652
Cox, Sallie V, 326
Cox, Sallie P. V, 232
Cox, Sallie W. I, 616
Cox, Sallie Woodard I, 303
Cox, Sallie Woodard I, 316
Cox, Sally I, 264
Cox, Sally I, 284
Cox, Sally I, 301
Cox, Sally I, 302
Cox, Sally I, 303
Cox, Sally I, 311
Cox, Sally I, 323
Cox, Sally I, 328
Cox, Sally I, 329
Cox, Sally A. II, 854
Cox, Sally Hockett I, 677
Cox, Sally W. I, 296
Cox, Sally W. I, 328
Cox, Sally W. I, 330
Cox, Sally Woodard I, 284
Cox, Samila W. I, 744
Cox, Samira I, 383
Cox, Samira IV, 841
Cox, Samira A. I, 383
Cox, Samuel I, 348
Cox, Samuel I, 381
Cox, Samuel I, 382
Cox, Samuel I, 391
Cox, Samuel I, 462
Cox, Samuel I, 463
Cox, Samuel I, 465
Cox, Samuel I, 476
Cox, Samuel I, 477
Cox, Samuel I, 478
Cox, Samuel II, 350
Cox, Samuel II, 442
Cox, Samuel II, 496
Cox, Samuel III, 90
Cox, Samuel IV, 240
Cox, Samuel V, 232
Cox, Samuel V, 483
Cox, Samuel V, 484
Cox, Samuel V, 514
Cox, Samuel J. I, 303
Cox, Samuel J. I, 323
Cox, Samuel L. I, 335
Cox, Samuel M. I, 465
Cox, Samuel Mincher I, 465
Cox, Sanders I, 284
Cox, Sanford Charles I, 463
Cox, Sarah I, 27
Cox, Sarah I, 137
Cox, Sarah I, 236
Cox, Sarah I, 268
Cox, Sarah I, 269
Cox, Sarah I, 283
Cox, Sarah I, 284
Cox, Sarah I, 296
Cox, Sarah I, 297
Cox, Sarah I, 302
Cox, Sarah I, 303
Cox, Sarah I, 304
Cox, Sarah I, 309
Cox, Sarah I, 310
Cox, Sarah I, 316
Cox, Sarah I, 317
Cox, Sarah I, 320
Cox, Sarah I, 323
Cox, Sarah I, 328
Cox, Sarah I, 331
Cox, Sarah I, 376
Cox, Sarah I, 381
Cox, Sarah I, 382
Cox, Sarah I, 383
Cox, Sarah I, 384
Cox, Sarah I, 393
Cox, Sarah I, 400
Cox, Sarah I, 461
Cox, Sarah I, 462
Cox, Sarah I, 463
Cox, Sarah I, 464
Cox, Sarah I, 465
Cox, Sarah I, 466
Cox, Sarah I, 473
Cox, Sarah I, 475

Cox, Sarah I, 476
Cox, Sarah I, 477
Cox, Sarah I, 478
Cox, Sarah I, 479
Cox, Sarah I, 619
Cox, Sarah I, 623
Cox, Sarah I, 713
Cox, Sarah I, 717
Cox, Sarah I, 876
Cox, Sarah I, 1028
Cox, Sarah I, 1031
Cox, Sarah I, 1060
Cox, Sarah I, 1063
Cox, Sarah II, 211
Cox, Sarah II, 309
Cox, Sarah II, 318
Cox, Sarah II, 325
Cox, Sarah II, 350
Cox, Sarah II, 485
Cox, Sarah II, 496
Cox, Sarah II, 583
Cox, Sarah II, 607
Cox, Sarah II, 793
Cox, Sarah III, 89
Cox, Sarah III, 90
Cox, Sarah III, 213
Cox, Sarah IV, 27
Cox, Sarah IV, 82
Cox, Sarah IV, 192
Cox, Sarah IV, 240
Cox, Sarah IV, 325
Cox, Sarah IV, 381
Cox, Sarah IV, 519
Cox, Sarah IV, 576
Cox, Sarah IV, 696
Cox, Sarah V, 43
Cox, Sarah V, 44
Cox, Sarah V, 164
Cox, Sarah V, 231
Cox, Sarah V, 232
Cox, Sarah V, 321
Cox, Sarah V, 326
Cox, Sarah V, 337
Cox, Sarah V, 454
Cox, Sarah V, 733
Cox, Sarah V, 766
Cox, Sarah V, 834
Cox, Sarah VI, 164
Cox, Sarah VI, 206
Cox, Sarah VI, 305
Cox, Sarah VI, 350
Cox, Sarah VI, 475
Cox, Sarah VI, 477
Cox, Sarah VI, 483
Cox, Sarah VI, 548
Cox, Sarah VI, 572
Cox, Sarah VI, 622
Cox, Sarah VI, 714
Cox, Sarah VI, 824
Cox, Sarah A. I, 478
Cox, Sarah A. VI, 808
Cox, Sarah Adeline I, 479
Cox, Sarah Ann II, 734
Cox, Sarah Ann II, 735
Cox, Sarah Cumi I, 284
Cox, Sarah Cuony I, 324
Cox, Sarah E. I, 328
Cox, Sarah E. I, 329
Cox, Sarah E. I, 463
Cox, Sarah E. I, 478
Cox, Sarah E. VI, 737
Cox, Sarah Elizabeth I, 323
Cox, Sarah Elizabeth I, 613
Cox, Sarah Elizabeth V, 834
Cox, Sarah Emeline I, 464
Cox, Sarah F. I, 472
Cox, Sarah J. I, 462
Cox, Sarah J. I, 466
Cox, Sarah J. I, 478
Cox, Sarah J. I, 479
Cox, Sarah J. I, 484
Cox, Sarah M. I, 465
Cox, Sarah M. V, 382
Cox, Sarah W. I, 45
Cox, Sarah W. I, 323
Cox, Sarah W. I, 328
Cox, Sarah W. I, 331
Cox, Sarah Woodard I, 323
Cox, Selah I, 303
Cox, Selah V, 43
Cox, Selah V, 44
Cox, Selina III, 107
Cox, Selina III, 291
Cox, Sen. William I, 457
Cox, Seth I, 465
Cox, Seth I, 477
Cox, Seth I, 479
Cox, Seth IV, 381
Cox, Seth IV, 571
Cox, Silas I, 383
Cox, Silas I, 652
Cox, Silas I, 676
Cox, Silas I, 677
Cox, Silas I, 679
Cox, Silas D. I, 462
Cox, Silas Woodard I, 323
Cox, Simeon I, 462
Cox, Simon I, 462
Cox, Simon I, 464
Cox, Simon I, 465
Cox, Simon I, 473
Cox, Simon I, 476
Cox, Simon I, 478
Cox, Simon V, 44
Cox, Simon Allen I, 464
Cox, Simpsom V, 734
Cox, Simpson V, 733
Cox, Smithson I, 284
Cox, Smithson I, 302
Cox, Smithson I, 310
Cox, Smytha Augusta I, 613
Cox, Solomon I, 349
Cox, Solomon I, 380
Cox, Solomon I, 381
Cox, Solomon I, 382
Cox, Solomon I, 383
Cox, Solomon I, 457
Cox, Solomon I, 465
Cox, Solomon I, 466
Cox, Solomon I, 475
Cox, Solomon I, 476
Cox, Solomon I, 477
Cox, Solomon I, 478
Cox, Solomon I, 535
Cox, Solomon I, 1117
Cox, Solomon I Sup 1, 8
Cox, Sophronia I, 323
Cox, Sophronia I, 758
Cox, Sophronia I, 770
Cox, Sophronia I, 924
Cox, Sophronia P. I, 323
Cox, Sophronia P. I, 328
Cox, Sophronia P. I, 652
Cox, Sophronia P. I, 677
Cox, Sophronia P. I, 686
Cox, Spencer Raymond I, 923
Cox, Spotswood H. VI, 896
Cox, Stanton I, 284
Cox, Stanton I, 296
Cox, Stanton I, 301
Cox, Stanton I, 303
Cox, Stanton I, 320
Cox, Stanton I, 321
Cox, Stanton I, 323
Cox, Stanton I, 328
Cox, Stanton I, 652
Cox, Stanton William I, 323
Cox, Stephen I, 382
Cox, Stephen I, 457
Cox, Stephen I, 462
Cox, Stephen I, 464
Cox, Stephen I, 465
Cox, Stephen I, 476
Cox, Stephen I, 477
Cox, Stephen I, 478
Cox, Stephen I, 535
Cox, Stephen II, 790
Cox, Stephen II, 854
Cox, Stephen III, 89
Cox, Stephen III, 90
Cox, Stephen III, 274
Cox, Stephen IV, 143
Cox, Stephen IV, 381
Cox, Stephen IV, 571
Cox, Stephen V, 44
Cox, Stephen V, 231
Cox, Stephen V, 326
Cox, Stephen VI, 164
Cox, Stephen Clarkson I, 479
Cox, Stephen H. I, 464
Cox, Stephen M. I, 479
Cox, Stephen P. II, 854
Cox, Stephen Sidney I, 463
Cox, Stephen Sidny I, 463
Cox, Steuben D. IV, 192
Cox, Susan II, 496
Cox, Susan III, 379
Cox, Susan V, 484
Cox, Susan C. VI, 896
Cox, Susan F. II, 790
Cox, Susan F. II, 854
Cox, Susan H. II, 854
Cox, Susan S. II, 854
Cox, Susana I, 284
Cox, Susanna I, 495
Cox, Susanna I, 535
Cox, Susanna I, 560
Cox, Susanna II, 170
Cox, Susanna II, 496
Cox, Susanna II, 648
Cox, Susanna V, 44
Cox, Susanna V, 164
Cox, Susanna VI, 807
Cox, Susanna H. II, 496
Cox, Susannah I, 302
Cox, Susannah I, 303
Cox, Susannah I, 310
Cox, Susannah I, 316
Cox, Susannah II, 211
Cox, Susannah II, 248
Cox, Susannah II, 496
Cox, Susannah II, 650
Cox, Susannah II, 812
Cox, Susannah II, 813
Cox, Susannah V, 43
Cox, Susannah V, 483
Cox, Susannah V, 484
Cox, Susannah V, 514
Cox, Susannah V, 728
Cox, Susannah V, 733
Cox, Susannah V, 734
Cox, Sybril Losada I, 465
Cox, Tabitha I, 323
Cox, Tabitha A. I, 328
Cox, Tabitha A. I, 329
Cox, Tacey I, 459
Cox, Tacy I, 464
Cox, Tacy I, 478
Cox, Talitha I, 323
Cox, Talton D. I, 923
Cox, Talton D. I, 940
Cox, Tamar I, 1053
Cox, Tamar I, 1056
Cox, Tamar I, 1059
Cox, Tamar I, 1060
Cox, Tamar V, 157
Cox, Tamar V, 164
Cox, Tamer I, 381
Cox, Tamer I, 382
Cox, Tamer I, 466
Cox, Tamer I, 475
Cox, Tamer I, 476
Cox, Tamer I, 1018
Cox, Tamer IV, 27
Cox, Tamsen R. V, 617
Cox, Tempy Caroline I, 479
Cox, Thamer I, 381
Cox, Thamer I, 384
Cox, Thomas I, 236
Cox, Thomas I, 267
Cox, Thomas I, 268
Cox, Thomas I, 279
Cox, Thomas I, 283
Cox, Thomas I, 284
Cox, Thomas I, 302
Cox, Thomas I, 303
Cox, Thomas I, 306
Cox, Thomas I, 307
Cox, Thomas I, 325
Cox, Thomas I, 370
Cox, Thomas I, 381
Cox, Thomas I, 382
Cox, Thomas I, 383
Cox, Thomas I, 384
Cox, Thomas I, 400
Cox, Thomas I, 445
Cox, Thomas I, 452
Cox, Thomas I, 463
Cox, Thomas I, 464
Cox, Thomas I, 465
Cox, Thomas I, 466
Cox, Thomas I, 473
Cox, Thomas I, 475
Cox, Thomas I, 476
Cox, Thomas I, 477
Cox, Thomas I, 478
Cox, Thomas I, 535
Cox, Thomas I, 695
Cox, Thomas I, 1018
Cox, Thomas I, 1019
Cox, Thomas I, 1028
Cox, Thomas I, 1047
Cox, Thomas I, 1056
Cox, Thomas I, 1059
Cox, Thomas I, 1060
Cox, Thomas II, 350
Cox, Thomas II, 496
Cox, Thomas IV, 27
Cox, Thomas IV, 82
Cox, Thomas IV, 143
Cox, Thomas IV, 381
Cox, Thomas IV, 696
Cox, Thomas IV, 944
Cox, Thomas V, 147
Cox, Thomas V, 157
Cox, Thomas V, 164
Cox, Thomas V, 231
Cox, Thomas V, 321
Cox, Thomas V, 326
Cox, Thomas V, 337
Cox, Thomas V, 469
Cox, Thomas V, 483
Cox, Thomas V, 484
Cox, Thomas V, 514
Cox, Thomas VI, 737
Cox, Thomas VI, 984
Cox, Thomas B. I, 303
Cox, Thomas B. I, 304
Cox, Thomas B. I, 323
Cox, Thomas Elwood I, 323
Cox, Thomas Jones I, 614
Cox, Thomas M. V, 483
Cox, Thomas M. V, 484
Cox, Thomas William I, 236
Cox, Thomas, Jr. I, 382
Cox, Thomas, Jr. V, 44
Cox, Thomas, Jr. V, 231
Cox, Thomas, Jr. V, 326
Cox, Thomas, Jr. V, 337
Cox, Thomas, Sr. I, 382
Cox, Thomas, Sr. V, 44
Cox, Thomas, Sr. V, 231
Cox, Thos. I, 345
Cox, Thos. B. I, 321
Cox, Timothey I, 483
Cox, Timothy I, 464
Cox, Timothy I, 466
Cox, Timothy I, 478
Cox, Timothy I, 713
Cox, Timothy III, 90
Cox, Tomas I, 1060
Cox, Ulysses Hadley I, 323
Cox, Velma Lee I, 614
Cox, Vercia Pitts IV, 1311
Cox, Vida I, 614
Cox, Vida I, 631
Cox, Vida M. I, 617
Cox, Vincent V, 326
Cox, Viola Hicks I, 940
Cox, Virgil H. IV, 1205
Cox, Virginia Dare I, 614
Cox, Voluntine VI, 941
Cox, W. M. I, 614
Cox, Walter I, 284
Cox, Walter I, 303
Cox, Walter I, 323
Cox, Walter IV, 469
Cox, Walter V, 990
Cox, Walter A. I, 713
Cox, Walter H. VI, 737
Cox, Walter H. VI, 742
Cox, Warner L. I, 463
Cox, Wd. Elizabeth II, 496
Cox, Wd. Elizabeth Neal II, 790
Cox, Wd. Josephine A. II, 790
Cox, Wd. Sarah II, 496
Cox, Widow Elizabeth I, 744
Cox, Widow Ruth I, 465
Cox, Widow Sally I, 303
Cox, Widow Sally I, 311
Cox, Wiley I, 466
Cox, Wiley I, 476
Cox, Wilie I, 303
Cox, William I, 213
Cox, William I, 236
Cox, William I, 283
Cox, William I, 297
Cox, William I, 303
Cox, William I, 316
Cox, William I, 323
Cox, William I, 328
Cox, William I, 330
Cox, William I, 343
Cox, William I, 349
Cox, William I, 381
Cox, William I, 382
Cox, William I, 383
Cox, William I, 445
Cox, William I, 457
Cox, William I, 461
Cox, William I, 462
Cox, William I, 463
Cox, William I, 464
Cox, William I, 466
Cox, William I, 475
Cox, William I, 476
Cox, William I, 477
Cox, William I, 478
Cox, William I, 535
Cox, William I, 713
Cox, William I, 738
Cox, William I, 806
Cox, William I, 1015
Cox, William I, 1028
Cox, William I, 1104
Cox, William I, 1117
Cox, William II, 211
Cox, William II, 350
Cox, William III, 90
Cox, William IV, 381
Cox, William IV, 469
Cox, William IV, 571
Cox, William V, 44
Cox, William V, 164
Cox, William V, 326
Cox, William V, 382
Cox, William V, 617
Cox, William VI, 808
Cox, William VI, 889
Cox, William C. I, 478
Cox, William C. VI, 808
Cox, William Carlyle I, 614
Cox, William H. I, 463
Cox, William H. I, 478
Cox, William H. II, 790
Cox, William H. III, 90
Cox, William Henry I, 212
Cox, William Henry I, 479
Cox, William J. V, 834
Cox, William L. VI, 808
Cox, William McKinley I, 614
Cox, William Orlando I, 479
Cox, William R. I, 323
Cox, William T. I, 284
Cox, William T. I, 323
Cox, William T. I, 328
Cox, William T. I, 335
Cox, William Thomas I, 236
Cox, William Thomas I, 255
Cox, William W. I, 323
Cox, William Wilson I, 45
Cox, William, Jr. I, 328
Cox, William, Jr. I, 381
Cox, William, Jr. I, 476
Cox, William, Sr. I, 303
Cox, William, Sr. I, 321
Cox, William, Sr. I, 323
Cox, William, Sr. I, 476
Cox, Winey I, 324
Cox, Winnie I, 303
Cox, Winnie I, 307
Cox, Wistar I, 631
Cox, Wm. I, 349
Cox, Wm. I, 375
Cox, Wm. I, 383
Cox, Wm. I, 402
Cox, Wm. II, 496
Cox, Wm. II, 583
Cox, Wm. II, 854
Cox, Wm. V, 301
Cox, Wm. V, 326
Cox, Wm. V, 382
Cox, Wm. E. III, 424
Cox, Wm. G. III, 89
Cox, Wm. G. III, 213
Cox, Wm. H. II, 854
Cox, Wm. McKinley I, 631
Cox, Wm. Neall II, 790
Cox, Wm. P. V, 617
Cox, Yancey H. I, 466
Cox, Yancy H. I, 467
Cox, Yancy H. I, 478
Cox, Zeno I, 462
Cox, Zeno Jeremiah I, 462
Cox, Zilpa I, 323
Cox, Zilpha I, 303
Cox, Zilpha I, 310
Cox, Zilpha I, 311
Cox, Zilpha I, 338
Cox, Zilphia I, 283
Cox, Zimri I, 462
Cox, Zimri I, 477
Coxe, Anne IV, 143
Coxe, John IV, 143
Coxe, Levi IV, 143
Coxe, Mary II, 484
Coxe, Mary II, 496
Coxe, Mary IV, 143
Coxe, Rachel IV, 143
Coxe, Stephen IV, 143
Coxe, Thomas II, 484
Coxe, Thomas II, 496
Coxe, Thomas IV, 143
Coy, Henry IV, 1234
Coy, Mabel IV, 767
Coy, Mabel Anna IV, 1000
Coy, Mable A. IV, 696
Coy, Mary V, 382
Coy, Mary A. V, 382
Coy, Mattie V, 165
Coy, Simon P. V, 165
Coy, Simon Peter V, 164
Coy, Simon Peter V, 165
Coykendall, ??? III, 319
Coykendall, Ann III, 90
Coykendall, Sarah C. III, 319
Coykendall, Sarah O. III, 90
Coykendall, Sarah O. III, 319
Coykendall, Wm. L. III, 90
Coyle, Earle V, 165
Coyle, Emma V, 666
Coyle, Florence V, 165
Coyle, Jeanie Maury VI, 770
Coyle, Lee V, 165
Coyle, Mary Maud IV, 1311

oyle, Patrick VI, 896
oyle, Sarah Florence V, 165
oyle, Susannah VI, 896
oyle, Urban V, 666
oyle, Wm. Lee V, 165
oyne, Anna III, 317
ozadd, James V, 557
ozadd, Kittie V, 557
ozen, Josa., Jr. II, 496
ozens, Benjamin II, 496
ozens, Eleanor II, 496
ozens, Elizabeth Crippen II, 854
ozens, Elizabeth Crippen II, 866
ozens, George II, 496
ozens, John II, 496
ozens, John IV, 192
ozens, Josa., Jr. II, 496
ozens, Joshua II, 496
ozens, Rebecca II, 702
ozens, Sarah IV, 192
ozens, Susanna II, 702
ozine, Catharine III, 90
ozine, Catharine III, 303
ozine, Florence III, 90
ozine, Florence III, 303
ozine, Joseph III, 90
ozine, Joseph III, 303
ozins, Benjamin II, 496
ozins, Benjamin IV, 325
rab, Mary II, 496
rab, Wm. II, 63
rab, Wm. II, 496
rabb, Alice II, 669
rabb, Alice III, 90
rabb, Mary II, 496
rabb, Mary II, 668
rabb, Richard III, 90
rabb, Wm. II, 63
rabbe, Alvion Abram IV, 944
rabbe, Martha IV, 944
rabbs, Albion IV, 944
rabbs, Alvion Abram IV, 944
rabbs, Anna IV, 944
rabbs, Martha IV, 944
raber, Alice VI, 60
raber, Alice VI, 82
raber, Fannie VI, 60
raber, Fannie VI, 82
raber, John VI, 60
raber, John VI, 82
rabough, Daniel IV, 1312
rabtree, Alice F. V, 990
rabtree, Emily III, 90
rabtree, Emily M. III, 90
rabtree, Emily Montgomery III, 78
rabtree, Hattie V, 990
rabtree, Howard A. V, 990
rabtree, Jerry V, 990
rabtree, Lottie V, 990
rabtree, William Alonzo III, 90
rabtree, Wm. Alonzo III, 78
rachel, Jane V, 974
rachet, Jane V, 968
raddick, Jesse I, 1091
raddock, Ann VI, 801
raddock, Betsy VI, 808
raddock, David VI, 808
raddock, David VI, 897
raddock, David VI, 980
raddock, Elizabeth VI, 808
raddock, Emily VI, 829
raddock, James VI, 819
raddock, John VI, 808
raddock, John VI, 829
raddock, John C. VI, 808
raddock, Keturah VI, 860
raddock, Martha Jane VI, 980
raddock, Mary VI, 839
raddock, Mary E. VI, 808
raddock, Mary T. VI, 897
raddock, Michel VI, 848
raddock, Moses VI, 826
raddock, Sarah A. VI, 826
rady, ??? III, 428
rady, Gulielma M. III, 428
rafford, Elizabeth IV, 28
rafford, Eva I, 383
rafford, Frances IV, 28
rafford, James I, 652
rafford, John IV, 28
rafford, Lucy I, 383
rafford, Lucy I, 410
rafford, Mary I, 383
rafford, Mary I, 401
rafford, Susanna IV, 27
rafford, Susanna IV, 52
rafford, William IV, 28
raford, Cathron I, 368
Craford, Eave I, 368
Craford, James I, 368
Craft, ??? III, 90
Craft, Abel II, 170
Craft, Abel II, 212
Craft, Abigail III, 406
Craft, Abraham III, 406
Craft, Achsah III, 406
Craft, Aden II, 170
Craft, Aden II, 211
Craft, Aden Gibbs II, 991
Craft, Aiden II, 211
Craft, Amy II, 170
Craft, Amy II, 212
Craft, Amy II, 229
Craft, Amy II, 310
Craft, Amy Ann IV, 1359
Craft, Ann II, 206
Craft, Ann II, 211
Craft, Ann II, 212
Craft, Ann II, 496
Craft, Ann II, 616
Craft, Ann III, 405
Craft, Ann III, 406
Craft, Ann III, 439
Craft, Ann IV, 192
Craft, Ann IV, 325
Craft, Ann IV, 326
Craft, Ann IV, 381
Craft, Ann IV, 567
Craft, Ann IV, 571
Craft, Ann IV, 1052
Craft, Ann IV, 1091
Craft, Ann IV, 1100
Craft, Ann IV, 1129
Craft, Ann IV, 1359
Craft, Asa II, 170
Craft, Asa II, 212
Craft, Asa IV, 192
Craft, Asa IV, 381
Craft, Asa IV, 399
Craft, Asa IV, 400
Craft, Asa IV, 571
Craft, Barney II, 496
Craft, Barney II, 616
Craft, Benj. III, 406
Craft, Benjamin II, 171
Craft, Benjamin W. III, 397
Craft, Benjamin W. III, 405
Craft, Beulah II, 170
Craft, Beulah II, 211
Craft, Beulah II, 991
Craft, Capt. Dan. III, 406
Craft, Charity II, 211
Craft, Charlotte IV, 1359
Craft, Coles III, 406
Craft, Deborah II, 211
Craft, Deborah II, 285
Craft, Derick III, 406
Craft, Derick III, 420
Craft, Edith II, 170
Craft, Edward III, 406
Craft, Edward E. III, 405
Craft, Edward E. III, 406
Craft, Edward E. III, 464
Craft, Eli IV, 1359
Craft, Eliza II, 170
Craft, Elizabeth II, 170
Craft, Elizabeth II, 175
Craft, Elizabeth II, 206
Craft, Elizabeth II, 211
Craft, Elizabeth II, 212
Craft, Elizabeth II, 229
Craft, Elizabeth II, 285
Craft, Elizabeth II, 302
Craft, Elizabeth II, 310
Craft, Elizabeth IV, 319
Craft, Elizabeth IV, 325
Craft, Elizabeth IV, 1359
Craft, Ellen III, 399
Craft, Ellen V, 384
Craft, Emlen II, 170
Craft, Emlen II, 285
Craft, Ephraim IV, 192
Craft, Ephraim IV, 381
Craft, Esther II, 211
Craft, Esther III, 90
Craft, Esther III, 266
Craft, Esther III, 406
Craft, Esther III, 451
Craft, Esther M. IV, 1359
Craft, Esther M. IV, 1363
Craft, Evaline IV, 192
Craft, Evaline IV, 381
Craft, Evaline IV, 400
Craft, Eveline IV, 381
Craft, Eveline IV, 402
Craft, Evelyn III, 464
Craft, Evelyn T. III, 406
Craft, Fannie III, 406
Craft, Fanny III, 406
Craft, Fleming Lockard VI, 897
Craft, Frances III, 406
Craft, Frederick M. III, 405
Craft, Freelove III, 406
Craft, Freelove III, 461
Craft, George II, 115
Craft, George II, 117
Craft, George II, 143
Craft, George II, 147
Craft, George II, 170
Craft, George II, 175
Craft, George II, 206
Craft, George II, 211
Craft, George II, 212
Craft, George II, 217
Craft, George II, 225
Craft, George II, 229
Craft, George II, 269
Craft, George II, 285
Craft, George II, 302
Craft, George II, 309
Craft, George II, 310
Craft, George II, 318
Craft, George II, 823
Craft, George II, 991
Craft, George II, 1035
Craft, George, Jr. II, 147
Craft, George, Jr. II, 170
Craft, George, Jr. II, 211
Craft, George, Jr. II, 991
Craft, Gershom II, 211
Craft, Grace II, 211
Craft, Hannah II, 211
Craft, Hannah II, 259
Craft, Hannah II, 959
Craft, Hannah II, 960
Craft, Hannah III, 90
Craft, Hannah III, 266
Craft, Hannah III, 405
Craft, Hannah III, 406
Craft, Hannah III, 407
Craft, Hannah III, 410
Craft, Hannah III, 411
Craft, Hannah III, 412
Craft, Hannah III, 439
Craft, Hannah III, 461
Craft, Hannah IV, 1129
Craft, Helena III, 406
Craft, Ida III, 94
Craft, Ida Beauvais III, 94
Craft, Isaac III, 406
Craft, Isaac IV, 192
Craft, James II, 170
Craft, James II, 171
Craft, James II, 206
Craft, James II, 211
Craft, James II, 212
Craft, James II, 991
Craft, James II, 1035
Craft, James III, 90
Craft, James III, 266
Craft, James III, 405
Craft, James III, 406
Craft, James III, 407
Craft, James III, 412
Craft, James III, 439
Craft, James IV, 192
Craft, James IV, 381
Craft, James IV, 571
Craft, James IV, 1052
Craft, James IV, 1091
Craft, James L. IV, 571
Craft, James L. VI, 897
Craft, James, Jr. II, 170
Craft, Jane II, 965
Craft, Jane II, 966
Craft, Jane II, 1049
Craft, Jane II, 1056
Craft, Jennie B. III, 405
Craft, Jesse II, 211
Craft, Jesse IV, 381
Craft, Jesse IV, 571
Craft, Jesse IV, 1052
Craft, Jesse IV, 1080
Craft, Jesse IV, 1091
Craft, Jesse IV, 1129
Craft, Job II, 211
Craft, Job IV, 1359
Craft, John II, 25
Craft, John II, 170
Craft, John II, 211
Craft, John II, 496
Craft, John II, 616
Craft, John IV, 325
Craft, John IV, 381
Craft, John IV, 571
Craft, John IV, 944
Craft, John IV, 1091
Craft, John IV, 1359
Craft, John V, 384
Craft, John A. IV, 1359
Craft, John A. IV, 1363
Craft, John Rachel IV, 1091
Craft, John T. III, 405
Craft, John W. IV, 571
Craft, Joseph II, 211
Craft, Joseph IV, 192
Craft, Joseph IV, 381
Craft, Joseph L. IV, 381
Craft, Joseph Osborn II, 211
Craft, Judith III, 406
Craft, Judith III, 465
Craft, Lindley IV, 192
Craft, Lindley IV, 381
Craft, Lydia II, 170
Craft, Lydia II, 211
Craft, Lydia II, 991
Craft, Lydia IV, 320
Craft, Lydia IV, 326
Craft, Lydia IV, 381
Craft, Lydia IV, 567
Craft, Lydia IV, 571
Craft, Lydia Ann IV, 1359
Craft, Margaret II, 170
Craft, Margaret II, 171
Craft, Margaret II, 211
Craft, Margaret II, 212
Craft, Margaret IV, 325
Craft, Margaret IV, 326
Craft, Margaret IV, 571
Craft, Margaret IV, 944
Craft, Marsey II, 211
Craft, Marsey II, 217
Craft, Martha II, 170
Craft, Martha II, 212
Craft, Martha II, 233
Craft, Martha II, 234
Craft, Martha III, 90
Craft, Martha III, 397
Craft, Martha III, 405
Craft, Martha III, 406
Craft, Martha IV, 571
Craft, Martha VI, 897
Craft, Mary II, 25
Craft, Mary II, 63
Craft, Mary II, 115
Craft, Mary II, 117
Craft, Mary II, 143
Craft, Mary II, 147
Craft, Mary II, 170
Craft, Mary II, 211
Craft, Mary II, 212
Craft, Mary II, 217
Craft, Mary II, 225
Craft, Mary II, 269
Craft, Mary II, 285
Craft, Mary II, 302
Craft, Mary II, 991
Craft, Mary II, 1035
Craft, Mary III, 90
Craft, Mary III, 266
Craft, Mary III, 406
Craft, Mary IV, 326
Craft, Mary IV, 381
Craft, Mary IV, 571
Craft, Mary IV, 1052
Craft, Mary IV, 1080
Craft, Mary IV, 1081
Craft, Mary IV, 1129
Craft, Mary IV, 1139
Craft, Mary V, 44
Craft, Mary VI, 929
Craft, Mary B. II, 147
Craft, Mary J. VI, 897
Craft, Mary V. IV, 1091
Craft, Mercy II, 211
Craft, Millie IV, 192
Craft, Millie IV, 381
Craft, Millie IV, 388
Craft, Millisent IV, 381
Craft, Oliver III, 406
Craft, Oliver III, 451
Craft, Orin IV, 1359
Craft, Penina IV, 400
Craft, Peninah IV, 192
Craft, Peninah IV, 381
Craft, Peninah IV, 399
Craft, Peter III, 399
Craft, Peter III, 406
Craft, Phebe III, 406
Craft, Phebe III, 412
Craft, Phoebe VI, 897
Craft, Rachel II, 170
Craft, Rachel II, 211
Craft, Rachel III, 406
Craft, Rachel IV, 192
Craft, Rachel IV, 325
Craft, Rachel IV, 326
Craft, Rachel IV, 352
Craft, Rachel V, 384
Craft, Rachel B. IV, 571
Craft, Rachel B. IV, 1091
Craft, Rachel B. IV, 1100
Craft, Rebecca II, 143
Craft, Rebecca II, 147
Craft, Rebecca II, 170
Craft, Rebecca II, 211
Craft, Rebecca II, 225
Craft, Rebecca II, 823
Craft, Rebecca II, 991
Craft, Rebecca IV, 326
Craft, Rebecca IV, 381
Craft, Rebecca IV, 404
Craft, Rhoda Ann Vernon IV, 1129
Craft, Richard III, 406
Craft, Richard III, 410
Craft, Ridgeway IV, 325
Craft, Ridgway II, 211
Craft, Samuel II, 170
Craft, Samuel II, 211
Craft, Samuel II, 212
Craft, Samuel II, 259
Craft, Samuel II, 285
Craft, Samuel II, 302
Craft, Samuel II, 965
Craft, Samuel IV, 192
Craft, Samuel IV, 320
Craft, Samuel IV, 325
Craft, Samuel IV, 326
Craft, Samuel IV, 567
Craft, Samuel IV, 571
Craft, Samuel IV, 1052
Craft, Samuel IV, 1053
Craft, Samuel IV, 1091
Craft, Samuel IV, 1100
Craft, Samuel IV, 1129
Craft, Samuel IV, 1130
Craft, Samuel IV, 1359
Craft, Samuel, Jr. II, 211
Craft, Samuel, Jr. IV, 325
Craft, Sarah II, 170
Craft, Sarah II, 171
Craft, Sarah II, 206
Craft, Sarah II, 211
Craft, Sarah II, 496
Craft, Sarah II, 616
Craft, Sarah III, 90
Craft, Sarah III, 406
Craft, Sarah IV, 571
Craft, Sarah IV, 944
Craft, Sarah IV, 945
Craft, Sarah IV, 1052
Craft, Sarah IV, 1053
Craft, Sarah IV, 1129
Craft, Sarah IV, 1130
Craft, Sarah V, 44
Craft, Sarah V, 137
Craft, Sarah J. IV, 1002
Craft, Simon III, 405
Craft, Solomon III, 406
Craft, Stacey II, 211
Craft, Stacey IV, 325
Craft, Stacy II, 170
Craft, Stacy IV, 325
Craft, Stephen III, 406
Craft, Stephen III, 411
Craft, Stephen III, 461
Craft, Sterling R. III, 94
Craft, Susan VI, 897
Craft, Susan R. IV, 696
Craft, Susan R. IV, 751
Craft, Susanna II, 212
Craft, Tacy II, 170
Craft, Tacy II, 212
Craft, Temperance III, 405
Craft, Temperance III, 406
Craft, Temperance III, 420
Craft, Thomas II, 211
Craft, Thomas III, 406
Craft, Thomas VI, 897
Craft, Thomas VI, 929
Craft, Thomas VI, 933
Craft, Thomas VI, 1002
Craft, Thos. III, 406
Craft, Washington VI, 897
Craft, Watson II, 170
Craft, Watson II, 212
Craft, Wd. Amy II, 175
Craft, Wd. Elizabeth II, 170
Craft, Wd. Mary II, 171
Craft, William II, 170
Craft, William II, 211
Craft, William IV, 325
Craft, William IV, 381
Craft, William IV, 571
Craft, Wilmot III, 406
Craft, Wm. IV, 325
Craft, Wm. IV, 352
Craft, Wm. IV, 567
Craft, Wm. IV, 571
Craft, Wm. IV, 1091
Craft, Wm. Elisha IV, 1129

Craft, Wright III, 406
Craft, Wright III, 465
Craft, Zilpha IV, 1129
Craft, Zilpha E. IV, 1091
Craft, Zipha Eliza IV, 192
Craftos, Christopher II, 40
Craftos, Martha II, 40
Cragg, Eleanor III, 90
Cragg, Eleonor III, 170
Cragg, Wd. Eleanor III, 129
Cragg, William III, 90
Craghead, Betsy L. VI, 886
Craghead, Betsy Robinson VI, 897
Craghead, Cathrine VI, 897
Craghead, Charles VI, 897
Craghead, Charles P. VI, 926
Craghead, Elizabeth VI, 881
Craghead, Elizabeth F. VI, 897
Craghead, Femenine VI, 897
Craghead, John VI, 897
Craghead, John VI, 946
Craghead, Josiah VI, 897
Craghead, Julia Ann VI, 897
Craghead, Lucy VI, 912
Craghead, Mary VI, 870
Craghead, Mary VI, 897
Craghead, Mary F. VI, 926
Craghead, Nancy VI, 897
Craghead, Robert VI, 897
Craghead, Robert VI, 945
Craghead, Robert A. VI, 897
Craghead, Sally VI, 897
Craghead, Suckey VI, 946
Craghead, Thomas J. VI, 1003
Craghead, Thomas R. VI, 897
Craghead, Townsend VI, 897
Craghead, William VI, 897
Craghill, Aaron H. VI, 394
Craghill, Alice B. VI, 394
Craghill, Amy VI, 394
Craghill, Anna J. VI, 394
Craghill, David L. VI, 394
Craghill, Elizabeth B. VI, 394
Craghill, Hannah P. VI, 394
Craghill, Hannah S. VI, 394
Craghill, James H. VI, 394
Craghill, James R. VI, 394
Craghill, Jane R. VI, 394
Craghill, John VI, 394
Craghill, John M. VI, 394
Craghill, John W. VI, 394
Craghill, John, Jr. VI, 394
Craghill, John, Sr. VI, 394
Craghill, Jonas Janney, Jr. VI, 394
Craghill, Joseph Clarkson VI, 394
Craghill, Joseph H. VI, 394
Craghill, Kezia T. VI, 394
Craghill, Lydia H. VI, 394
Craghill, Martha Ann VI, 394
Craghill, Mary VI, 380
Craghill, Mary VI, 393
Craghill, Mary VI, 394
Craghill, Mary P. VI, 394
Craghill, Mary, Sr. VI, 394
Craghill, Rachel VI, 394
Craghill, Rachel Anna VI, 394
Craghill, Richard S. VI, 394
Craghill, Robert D. VI, 394
Craghill, Seth Smith VI, 394
Craghill, Virginia A. VI, 394
Craghill, William P. VI, 394
Craig, Absalom IV, 809
Craig, Absolom IV, 809
Craig, Absolom VI, 632
Craig, Adam VI, 897
Craig, Adam VI, 997
Craig, Addison V, 557
Craig, Alfred B. V, 734
Craig, Alfred M. VI, 897
Craig, Alonzo V, 666
Craig, Alonzo V, 675
Craig, Amy Ether V, 165
Craig, Andrew II, 171
Craig, Andrew II, 212
Craig, Andrew II, 497
Craig, Andrew VI, 897
Craig, Ann II, 25
Craig, Ann II, 63
Craig, Ann II, 88
Craig, Ann VI, 1003
Craig, Anna II, 497
Craig, Anne II, 640
Craig, Archibald VI, 897
Craig, Archibald G. VI, 897
Craig, Archibald G. VI, 976
Craig, Barsheba VI, 897
Craig, Catharine II, 882
Craig, Catharine H. II, 854
Craig, Catharine H. II, 882
Craig, Charity V, 165
Craig, Charity V, 557
Craig, Charity V, 666
Craig, Charity S. V, 557
Craig, Charles V, 165
Craig, Charles VI, 828
Craig, Charles VI, 876
Craig, Charles VI, 897
Craig, Charles VI, 916
Craig, Charles VI, 976
Craig, Charles VI, 1013
Craig, Chas. V, 165
Craig, Daniel Pierce VI, 897
Craig, Deborah IV, 607
Craig, Deborah IV, 608
Craig, Deborah IV, 619
Craig, Deborah IV, 696
Craig, Deborah IV, 797
Craig, Deborah IV, 809
Craig, Deborah IV, 858
Craig, Deborah VI, 483
Craig, Deborah VI, 508
Craig, Deborah VI, 632
Craig, Dollie V, 666
Craig, Dollie V, 675
Craig, Dortha V, 557
Craig, Ebenezer II, 350
Craig, Ebenezer II, 497
Craig, Eleanor IV, 619
Craig, Eleanor Wilson II, 803
Craig, Elenor IV, 619
Craig, Elinor W. II, 854
Craig, Elinor Wilson II, 854
Craig, Elinor Wilson II, 882
Craig, Elizabeth II, 212
Craig, Elizabeth II, 350
Craig, Elizabeth II, 497
Craig, Elizabeth II, 640
Craig, Elizabeth IV, 607
Craig, Elizabeth IV, 619
Craig, Elizabeth IV, 809
Craig, Elizabeth VI, 632
Craig, Elizabeth VI, 897
Craig, Elizabeth VI, 988
Craig, Elizabeth VI, 1003
Craig, Elizabeth Ann VI, 897
Craig, Elizabeth R. VI, 897
Craig, Elizabeth, Jr. II, 497
Craig, Elizabeth, Jr. II, 640
Craig, Eloner IV, 809
Craig, Emelina IV, 902
Craig, Emeline IV, 918
Craig, Emmor K. II, 854
Craig, Florence V, 990
Craig, Francis V, 165
Craig, Frank IV, 1234
Craig, Frank IV, 1312
Craig, Frank V, 990
Craig, Franklin V, 990
Craig, Geo. Andrew II, 854
Craig, George Andrew II, 790
Craig, George, Jr. II, 854
Craig, George, Jr. II, 857
Craig, Grace II, 350
Craig, Henrietta VI, 897
Craig, Henry VI, 897
Craig, Isabelle V, 990
Craig, Jacob II, 25
Craig, Jacob II, 63
Craig, Jacob V, 44
Craig, James IV, 696
Craig, James IV, 754
Craig, James IV, 809
Craig, James IV, 858
Craig, James IV, 860
Craig, James V, 165
Craig, James V, 326
Craig, James V, 557
Craig, James V, 666
Craig, James V, 990
Craig, James VI, 632
Craig, James VI, 897
Craig, James A. V, 165
Craig, James A. V, 557
Craig, James A. V, 666
Craig, James F. I, 445
Craig, James H. VI, 897
Craig, James M. V, 326
Craig, James S. VI, 897
Craig, Jane IV, 809
Craig, Jane IV, 833
Craig, Jane VI, 897
Craig, Jenny VI, 922
Craig, Jerome V, 990
Craig, John II, 212
Craig, John II, 854
Craig, John II, 882
Craig, John III, 90
Craig, John VI, 897
Craig, John C. II, 790
Craig, John C. II, 854
Craig, John C. II, 857
Craig, Jonathan IV, 809
Craig, Jonathan VI, 632
Craig, Jos. V, 990
Craig, Joseph V, 990
Craig, Kitturah VI, 897
Craig, Laetitia II, 63
Craig, Lambert II, 640
Craig, Leatitia II, 25
Craig, Leatitia II, 63
Craig, Leatitia II, 88
Craig, Leatitia II, 90
Craig, Letitia II, 63
Craig, Letitia V, 44
Craig, Letitia V, 89
Craig, Letitia V, 580
Craig, Lettitia II, 25
Craig, Lititia V, 557
Craig, Lovy VI, 897
Craig, Lucinda VI, 897
Craig, Lydia IV, 608
Craig, Lydia IV, 619
Craig, Lydia IV, 620
Craig, Lydia IV, 809
Craig, Lydia VI, 632
Craig, Maggie V, 990
Craig, Margaret V, 990
Craig, Margaret A. V, 990
Craig, Martha II, 25
Craig, Martha II, 63
Craig, Martha V, 28
Craig, Martha V, 44
Craig, Martha V, 89
Craig, Martha V, 106
Craig, Mary II, 212
Craig, Mary II, 497
Craig, Mary II, 566
Craig, Mary IV, 754
Craig, Mary IV, 809
Craig, Mary Agnes II, 790
Craig, Mary Agnes II, 854
Craig, Mary Ann V, 880
Craig, Mary Ann V, 881
Craig, Mary C. II, 854
Craig, Mary Jr. IV, 696
Craig, Mary R. II, 854
Craig, Mary R. II, 857
Craig, Mary Rebecca II, 790
Craig, Mary Rebecca II, 854
Craig, Mary, Jr. VI, 632
Craig, Maryann V, 28
Craig, Maryann V, 44
Craig, Mildred V, 734
Craig, Milly VI, 897
Craig, Nancy V, 165
Craig, Nancy VI, 997
Craig, Polly VI, 897
Craig, Rebecca IV, 858
Craig, Rebecca IV, 860
Craig, Rebecca M. V, 326
Craig, Rhoda VI, 897
Craig, Richard VI, 897
Craig, Robert VI, 897
Craig, Robert VI, 988
Craig, Robert L. VI, 897
Craig, Rome V, 990
Craig, Rome C. V, 990
Craig, Samuel II, 25
Craig, Samuel II, 63
Craig, Samuel V, 28
Craig, Samuel V, 89
Craig, Sarah II, 25
Craig, Sarah II, 63
Craig, Sarah II, 857
Craig, Sarah VI, 897
Craig, Sarah VI, 976
Craig, Sarah Frances V, 165
Craig, Theodicia II, 497
Craig, Theodosia II, 212
Craig, Theodosia II, 497
Craig, Thomas Rogers II, 497
Craig, Thos. Janney II, 854
Craig, Walter V, 990
Craig, Wd Deborah IV, 797
Craig, Wd. Joicey VI, 897
Craig, Wd. Lettitia II, 35
Craig, William II, 35
Craig, William IV, 809
Craig, William VI, 632
Craig, William VI, 944
Craig, William VI, 1003
Craig, Wm. II, 25
Craig, Wm. II, 63
Craig, Wm. II, 497
Craig, Wm. IV, 607
Craig, Wm. IV, 696
Craig, Wm. IV, 809
Craig, Wm. V, 990
Craig, Wm. VI, 483
Craig, Wm. VI, 508
Craig, Wm. Craig VI, 632
Craig, Wm. Wells II, 497
Craig, Wm., Jr. II, 63
Craige, Andrew II, 212
Craige, Anna II, 497
Craige, Ebenezer II, 350
Craige, John II, 212
Craige, Rittur VI, 1014
Craige, Theodosia II, 212
Craigg, Archibald VI, 920
Craigg, Charles VI, 897
Craigg, Daniel Pierce VI, 897
Craigg, Elizabeth VI, 1003
Craigg, Henry VI, 897
Craigg, Isaac V, 969
Craigg, James H. VI, 869
Craigg, James H. VI, 897
Craigg, James H. VI, 902
Craigg, James S. VI, 897
Craigg, Kitturian VI, 994
Craigg, Kiturah VI, 920
Craigg, Lucinda VI, 897
Craigg, Martha E. VI, 869
Craigg, Mary VI, 876
Craigg, Mary VI, 887
Craigg, Mary VI, 937
Craigg, Milly VI, 897
Craigg, Patsey VI, 1014
Craigg, Rhoda VI, 897
Craigg, Richard VI, 897
Craigg, Robert VI, 994
Craigg, Sarah VI, 897
Craigg, Sarah VI, 944
Craigg, Skitturian VI, 994
Craigg, Sophia VI, 920
Craigg, Sophia VI, 921
Craigg, Wd. Joicey VI, 897
Craigg, Wm. II, 497
Craighead, Elizabeth B. V, 901
Craighead, Elizabeth Griffith V, 901
Craighead, Robert V, 734
Craighead, Robert Murnan V, 901
Craighead, Sarah V, 301
Craighead, Sarah V, 308
Craighead, Thos. J. V, 901
Craighead, Thos. Jas. V, 901
Craik, James VI, 754
Craik, Rebecca Jane Walker VI, 754
Crain, James VI, 864
Crain, James VI, 897
Crain, James VI, 923
Crain, John VI, 923
Crain, Joseph VI, 891
Crain, Ketura VI, 923
Crain, Massey VI, 897
Crain, Polly VI, 923
Craine, James VI, 802
Craine, John VI, 891
Craine, John VI, 910
Craine, Joseph VI, 897
Craine, Lucy H. VI, 910
Craine, Mary VI, 802
Craine, Nancy VI, 897
Craine, Polly VI, 923
Craine, Polly VI, 985
Craine, Susanna VI, 891
Cralle, Aphfera VI, 851
Cralle, Calista VI, 834
Cralle, Elizabeth VI, 851
Cralle, Fanny VI, 851
Cralle, Leroy VI, 808
Cralle, Lindsay VI, 808
Cralle, Maria VI, 834
Cralle, Martha E. VI, 808
Cralle, Mary VI, 808
Cralle, Mary C. VI, 803
Cralle, Nancy VI, 808
Cralle, Nancy VI, 834
Cralle, William VI, 808
Cramblet, William IV, 381
Cramblett, Elizabeth IV, 381
Cramblett, Elizabeth IV, 401
Cramblett, William IV, 381
Cramer, Andrew VI, 483
Cramer, Andrew VI, 484
Cramer, Asuba II, 212
Cramer, Elizabeth II, 212
Cramer, Hannah VI, 483
Cramer, Hannah VI, 484
Cramer, Jane L. I, 923
Cramer, Lucius V, 557
Cramer, Lucy M. V, 557
Cramer, Lydia V, 617
Cramer, Lydia V, 630
Cramer, Mary II, 212
Cramer, Mary II, 257
Cramer, Ruth II, 212
Cramer, Ruth II, 263
Cramer, Stephen II, 212
Cramer, William II, 212
Cramer, William II, 263
Cramer, Wilson IV, 1155
Cramford, Josiah IV, 867
Cramlet, Elizabeth IV, 381
Crammer, Asuba II, 212
Crammer, Asuba II, 274
Crammer, Eliza V, 907
Crammer, Sarah II, 497
Crammer, Sarah II, 585
Cramp, Alice Mary V, 940
Cramp, Alice White V, 901
Cramp, Emma V, 901
Cramp, Jacob G. V, 901
Cramp, Mary V, 901
Cramp, Theodore Wm. V, 901
Cramp, Theodore Wm. V, 940
Crampacker, John VI, 1004
Crampton, Casandra M. V, 44
Crampton, Cassandra M. V, 44
Crampton, Cleo V, 382
Crampton, Cleo Fife V, 382
Crampton, Earl V, 382
Crampton, Earl V, 734
Crampton, Earl Hudley V, 382
Crampton, Elizabeth V, 44
Crampton, Elizabeth VI, 380
Crampton, Elizabeth Neil V, 44
Crampton, George V, 734
Crampton, Grace V, 734
Crampton, Ira Hundley V, 666
Crampton, Ira Hundley V, 672
Crampton, Jeremiah V, 44
Crampton, Jeremiah VI, 380
Crampton, Jeremiah Cooper V, 44
Crampton, Jonathan V, 44
Crampton, Jonothan V, 44
Crampton, Joshua V, 44
Crampton, Joshua VI, 380
Crampton, Joshua Johnson V, 4
Crampton, L. N. V, 734
Crampton, Mary V, 44
Crampton, Mary V, 65
Crampton, Mary VI, 380
Crampton, Mary Cooper V, 44
Crampton, Merrick V, 44
Crampton, Merrick VI, 380
Crampton, Merrick Star V, 44
Crampton, Merrick Starr V, 44
Crampton, Osella L. V, 734
Crampton, Rachel V, 44
Crampton, Rachel V, 65
Crampton, Rachel VI, 380
Crampton, Rachel Miller V, 44
Crampton, Ruth Haines V, 44
Crampton, Ruthanna V, 382
Crampton, Samuel V, 44
Crampton, Samuel V, 65
Crampton, Samuel VI, 380
Cramton, Cleo V, 382
Cramton, Earl V, 382
Cramton, Emily VI, 897
Cramton, Joab VI, 897
Cramton, Jonathan V, 44
Cramton, Ruthanna V, 382
Crandell, Dorothy III, 90
Crandell, Dorothy III, 240
Crandell, Harriett III, 90
Crandell, Harriett III, 240
Crandell, Lewis III, 90
Crandell, Lewis III, 240
Crane, Adrian III, 90
Crane, Amos IV, 1360
Crane, Amos R. III, 90
Crane, Amos R. IV, 1359
Crane, Amos R. IV, 1360
Crane, Amos R. IV, 1363
Crane, Angeline VI, 897
Crane, Ann Eliza IV, 1359
Crane, Ann Eliza IV, 1368
Crane, Aramintha III, 77
Crane, Aramintha III, 90
Crane, Armistead D. VI, 897
Crane, Audrey IV, 1312
Crane, Benjamin L. IV, 1359
Crane, Benjamin L. IV, 1360
Crane, Benjamin L. IV, 1368
Crane, Calvin IV, 1359
Crane, Calvin B. IV, 1360
Crane, Charity IV, 1359
Crane, Charity IV, 1360
Crane, Charles Henry IV, 1360
Crane, Charrity IV, 1359
Crane, Clarissa IV, 1360
Crane, Clarissa P. IV, 1359
Crane, Cram VI, 897
Crane, Deborah R. III, 90
Crane, Deborah R. IV, 1359
Crane, Deborah R. IV, 1360

Crane, Deborah R. IV, 1364
Crane, Dorcas Jane IV, 1360
Crane, Elgin IV, 1312
Crane, Elijah III, 90
Crane, Elijah IV, 1359
Crane, Elijah IV, 1360
Crane, Elijah IV, 1364
Crane, Elizabeth II, 958
Crane, Elizabeth VI, 897
Crane, Emma V, 666
Crane, Frances J. VI, 897
Crane, Fred V, 666
Crane, George IV, 1359
Crane, George IV, 1360
Crane, George L. IV, 1359
Crane, George, Jr. IV, 1360
Crane, H. D. IV, 1312
Crane, Harriet T. III, 77
Crane, Harriet T. III, 90
Crane, Herbert D. IV, 1312
Crane, Irene VI, 798
Crane, Iyla G. IV, 1312
Crane, James VI, 798
Crane, James VI, 897
Crane, James, Jr. VI, 897
Crane, James, Sr. VI, 897
Crane, Jane IV, 1359
Crane, Jane IV, 1363
Crane, Jane D. IV, 1360
Crane, Jason III, 77
Crane, Jason III, 90
Crane, John VI, 897
Crane, Joseph VI, 897
Crane, Joseph U. II, 958
Crane, Josiah III, 90
Crane, Leah IV, 1360
Crane, Lucy IV, 1359
Crane, Lucy VI, 802
Crane, Martha W. VI, 897
Crane, Mary II, 205
Crane, Mary II, 212
Crane, Mary II, 285
Crane, Mary III, 90
Crane, Mary IV, 1359
Crane, Mary IV, 1360
Crane, Mary IV, 1364
Crane, Mary VI, 897
Crane, Mary Ann VI, 897
Crane, Mary M. IV, 615
Crane, Massey VI, 897
Crane, Matthew F. III, 90
Crane, Matthew T. III, 90
Crane, Moming VI, 897
Crane, Mourning VI, 897
Crane, Nancy VI, 897
Crane, Nathan IV, 1360
Crane, Nathan S. III, 90
Crane, Nathan S. IV, 1360
Crane, Nathan Selleck III, 90
Crane, Polly VI, 897
Crane, Robert V, 666
Crane, Sally VI, 897
Crane, Sarah V, 901
Crane, Sarah V, 906
Crane, Sarah VI, 897
Crane, Shadrack VI, 866
Crane, Shadrack VI, 899
Crane, Shadrack M. VI, 897
Crane, Wiatt VI, 884
Crane, Wiatt VI, 897
Crane, William III, 90
Crane, William E. III, 90
Crane, William E. IV, 1360
Crane, William W. VI, 897
Crane, Wm. E. IV, 1360
Crane, Wm. Elijah III, 90
Cranfield, Hannah Ann I, 981
Cranfield, Hannah Ann I, 984
Cranford, Charles V, 232
Cranford, Ettie I, 713
Cranford, Henry Samuel I, 713
Cranford, John I, 713
Cranford, John C. I, 713
Cranford, Nancy M. I, 677
Cranford, Nancy M. I, 680
Cranford, Robertie I, 713
Cranford, Sophronia I, 713
Cranford, Sophronia I, 725
Crank, Albert VI, 923
Crank, Albert G. VI, 898
Crank, Alexander VI, 880
Crank, Alexander VI, 897
Crank, Alexander VI, 900
Crank, Alexander M. VI, 897
Crank, Elizabeth S. VI, 898
Crank, Gabarilla E. VI, 880
Crank, James L. VI, 898
Crank, John D. VI, 898
Crank, Julianna VI, 897
Crank, Mary V, 981
Crank, Mary L. VI, 808
Crank, Nancy VI, 849
Crank, Permelia VI, 898
Crank, Robert P. VI, 808
Crank, Salinia VI, 897
Crank, Sejus VI, 898
Crank, Susan L. VI, 898
Crank, William J. VI, 898
Cranmer, Abraham VI, 484
Cranmer, Andrew VI, 484
Cranmer, Andrew VI, 559
Cranmer, Eliza V, 901
Cranmer, Hannah VI, 484
Cranmer, Hannah VI, 559
Cranmer, Hannah VI, 698
Cranmer, Mary VI, 484
Cranmer, Sarah VI, 484
Crannmer, Andrew VI, 483
Crannmer, Hannah VI, 483
Cranston, Alfred B. VI, 236
Cranston, Alfred Henry VI, 236
Cranston, Charles VI, 236
Cranston, Edith S. II, 854
Cranston, Edith S. II, 944
Cranston, Elizabeth Bernard II, 854
Cranston, Elizabeth Hicks II, 790
Cranston, Evanna II, 854
Cranston, Evanna II, 913
Cranston, Hannah II, 790
Cranston, Hannah VI, 236
Cranston, Hannah A. VI, 236
Cranston, J. Barnard II, 790
Cranston, Joseph II, 790
Cranston, Joseph M. II, 854
Cranston, Martha S. II, 854
Cranston, Martha S. II, 944
Cranston, Mary II, 130
Cranston, Mary II, 790
Cranston, Mary Barnard II, 790
Cranston, Nancy A. V, 990
Cranston, Samuel II, 790
Cranston, Samuel II, 854
Cranston, Samuel II, 944
Cranston, Samuel P. II, 854
Cranston, Simon II, 790
Cranston, William VI, 236
Crantz, Ardenia VI, 898
Crantz, Mary VI, 1016
Crantz, Michael VI, 898
Crantz, Michael VI, 1016
Crapp, John II, 442
Crapp, Joseph II, 442
Crapp, Mary II, 442
Crapp, Mary II, 497
Crapp, Mary II, 525
Crapp, Priscilla II, 442
Crapp, Susannah II, 442
Crary, John VI, 898
Crary, Rebeca II, 104
Crary, Rebecca II, 63
Crary, Susan VI, 898
Crary, Thomas II, 63
Crary, Thomas II, 104
Crary, Thomas Thompson II, 63
Crashaw, Dorothy II, 212
Crashaw, Samuel R. V, 950
Crassman, Jane V, 898
Crasto, Rachel III, 430
Crater, Clementine I, 614
Crater, Dorothy I, 940
Crater, J. W. I, 614
Crater, James Williamson I, 614
Crater, Mary Arlene I, 614
Crater, Mary Crater I, 614
Crater, Merlin I, 614
Crater, Mrs. Ruth I, 940
Crater, Nellie Isabel I, 614
Crater, Ruth I, 940
Crater, William Newlin I, 614
Crates, Clifford V, 991
Crates, Deck V, 990
Craton, Miriam VI, 133
Craton, Miriam VI, 140
Cratty, Bertie V, 734
Cratty, Eliza H. V, 734
Cratty, Hannah IV, 1155
Cratty, James H. V, 734
Cratty, James M. V, 734
Cratty, Margaret V, 734
Cratty, Sarah Jane IV, 1155
Crauge, Elizabeth II, 212
Crauge, Elizabeth II, 248
Crauge, John II, 212
Crauge, John II, 248
Crause, Alpha V, 991
Crause, Mary V, 991
Crause, Mate IV, 1312
Craven, Abigail VI, 632
Craven, Abigail VI, 652
Craven, Albina VI, 626
Craven, Albina VI, 719
Craven, Albinah VI, 632
Craven, Albinah VI, 719
Craven, Alfred A. I, 614
Craven, Almeda C. I, 479
Craven, Almira I, 466
Craven, Almira I, 479
Craven, Amellia I, 479
Craven, Amy C. I, 479
Craven, Ann II, 497
Craven, Ann II, 677
Craven, Bessie I, 923
Craven, Charles I, 923
Craven, Charles V, 232
Craven, Charles V, 326
Craven, Charles F. I, 940
Craven, Charley V, 326
Craven, Delilah I, 466
Craven, Delilah I, 479
Craven, Duval I, 614
Craven, E. S. I, 631
Craven, Edwin Ashbury I, 614
Craven, Eli A. I, 383
Craven, Eli A. I, 614
Craven, Eli F. I, 631
Craven, Eli Franklin I, 614
Craven, Elisabeth I, 468
Craven, Eliza Jane I, 614
Craven, Enoch S. I, 614
Craven, Ernest V, 326
Craven, Evelyn C. III, 90
Craven, Evelyn C. III, 275
Craven, Frances I, 479
Craven, Francis Keziah I, 466
Craven, Gracetta VI, 652
Craven, Guilford VI, 652
Craven, Guilford G. VI, 632
Craven, Hannah I, 382
Craven, Hannah I, 383
Craven, Hannah I, 479
Craven, Hannah IV, 192
Craven, Hannah Craven IV, 298
Craven, Henrietta I, 614
Craven, Henrietta Peeler I, 631
Craven, Huldah I, 479
Craven, Irvin I, 940
Craven, Ishi III, 90
Craven, Ishi III, 275
Craven, J. H. I, 479
Craven, Jacob Holt I, 479
Craven, James I, 923
Craven, James Irvin I, 923
Craven, James Irvin I, 940
Craven, John Stalker I, 466
Craven, Joseph I, 614
Craven, Keziah I, 466
Craven, Keziah I, 479
Craven, Keziah I, 758
Craven, Lansing V, 326
Craven, Lansing F. V, 232
Craven, Lansing F. V, 326
Craven, Lewis I, 479
Craven, Lewis I, 758
Craven, Louise I, 614
Craven, Lucy J. I, 468
Craven, Margaret I, 383
Craven, Margaret VI, 652
Craven, Margaret Ann I, 614
Craven, Martha I, 479
Craven, Martha J. I, 614
Craven, Mary II, 63
Craven, Mary II, 96
Craven, Mary IV, 1052
Craven, Mary Bunting III, 90
Craven, Mary Bunting III, 275
Craven, Mary J. I, 614
Craven, Mary J. I, 631
Craven, Minnie I, 614
Craven, Minnie V, 991
Craven, Mrs. E. F. I, 631
Craven, Nancy V, 326
Craven, Nancy Jane V, 232
Craven, Nancy Jane V, 326
Craven, Nathan I, 466
Craven, Nathan I, 479
Craven, Oliver I, 466
Craven, Oliver I, 479
Craven, Phebe I, 479
Craven, Rachell II, 63
Craven, Rachell II, 112
Craven, Roger VI, 632
Craven, Ross C. VI, 632
Craven, Ross C. VI, 652
Craven, Ross C. VI, 653
Craven, Ross C. VI, 685
Craven, Rufus C. I, 479
Craven, Ruth I, 940
Craven, Samuel I, 466
Craven, Sanson V, 232
Craven, Sarah E. I, 479
Craven, Sarah Elisabeth I, 614
Craven, Thomas II, 63
Craven, Thomas W. V, 232
Craven, Thompson IV, 1052
Craven, Wd. Ann II, 55
Craven, Wd. Ann II, 63
Craven, Widow Grace VI, 632
Craven, Widow Grace VI, 652
Craven, Widow Grace VI, 685
Craven, Wm. I, 468
Cravens, Melville IV, 1155
Cravin, Sanson V, 232
Crawford, Abel VI, 381
Crawford, Abel Lee IV, 82
Crawford, Abel Lee IV, 867
Crawford, Able IV, 82
Crawford, Ada IV, 1004
Crawford, Alace A. IV, 803
Crawford, Albert I. IV, 809
Crawford, Alfred T. IV, 945
Crawford, Alfred Thomas IV, 945
Crawford, Alice IV, 802
Crawford, Alice IV, 803
Crawford, Alice IV, 809
Crawford, Alice IV, 929
Crawford, Alice IV, 945
Crawford, Alice V, 382
Crawford, Alice A. IV, 809
Crawford, Alice A. IV, 929
Crawford, Alice A. IV, 945
Crawford, Alice M. V, 382
Crawford, Alice R. II, 702
Crawford, Alice R. II, 735
Crawford, Alice R. IV, 192
Crawford, Alice R. IV, 282
Crawford, Alice R. S. II, 735
Crawford, Alice R. S. IV, 192
Crawford, Amelia M. V, 991
Crawford, Ann IV, 27
Crawford, Ann IV, 28
Crawford, Ann IV, 32
Crawford, Ann IV, 57
Crawford, Anna V, 382
Crawford, Arthur IV, 945
Crawford, Arthur B. IV, 809
Crawford, Arthur B. IV, 945
Crawford, Atlantic V, 232
Crawford, Benedick VI, 381
Crawford, Benjamin IV, 28
Crawford, Beulah IV, 19
Crawford, Beulah IV, 28
Crawford, Cassandra IV, 82
Crawford, Cassandra VI, 381
Crawford, Charles V, 232
Crawford, Charles E. IV, 809
Crawford, Charles E. IV, 929
Crawford, Charles E. IV, 945
Crawford, Charles Edward IV, 945
Crawford, Charles Edwin IV, 809
Crawford, Charles H. IV, 696
Crawford, Charlotte VI, 898
Crawford, Chas. E. IV, 945
Crawford, Chas. Edward IV, 809
Crawford, Christiana IV, 82
Crawford, Christianna IV, 82
Crawford, Christine IV, 82
Crawford, Cyril III, 90
Crawford, Cyril III, 330
Crawford, Deborah IV, 192
Crawford, Deborah IV, 302
Crawford, Deborah IV, 945
Crawford, Deborah IV, 1014
Crawford, Dorothy Ellen II, 702
Crawford, Dorothy Ellen II, 735
Crawford, Dorothy Ellen IV, 192
Crawford, Dr. George B. V, 484
Crawford, Edith Melvina IV, 783
Crawford, Edward IV, 803
Crawford, Effie Wiggins I, 335
Crawford, Elijah IV, 82
Crawford, Elijah VI, 381
Crawford, Elizabeth I, 632
Crawford, Elizabeth IV, 27
Crawford, Elizabeth IV, 28
Crawford, Elizabeth IV, 47
Crawford, Elizabeth IV, 78
Crawford, Elizabeth IV, 82
Crawford, Elizabeth V, 382
Crawford, Elizabeth V, 398
Crawford, Elizabeth V, 437
Crawford, Elizabeth A. IV, 125
Crawford, Ella IV, 941
Crawford, Ephraim IV, 27
Crawford, Ephraim IV, 52
Crawford, Ephraim IV, 82
Crawford, Ephraim IV, 104
Crawford, Ephraim VI, 381
Crawford, Ephraim, Jr. IV, 82
Crawford, Eva I, 383
Crawford, Eve I, 383
Crawford, Florence V, 382
Crawford, Florence Emma V, 382
Crawford, Frances IV, 22
Crawford, Frances IV, 27
Crawford, Frances IV, 28
Crawford, Frances IV, 47
Crawford, Frances IV, 56
Crawford, Frances IV, 69
Crawford, Frances IV, 76
Crawford, Frances IV, 82
Crawford, Frances IV, 326
Crawford, Francis V, 991
Crawford, George V, 382
Crawford, George V, 666
Crawford, George VI, 928
Crawford, George C. V, 382
Crawford, George S. V, 382
Crawford, George W. V, 382
Crawford, George Webster V, 382
Crawford, Grace IV, 929
Crawford, Grace IV, 945
Crawford, Grace C. IV, 802
Crawford, Hannah IV, 27
Crawford, Hannah IV, 28
Crawford, Hannah IV, 35
Crawford, Hannah IV, 954
Crawford, Harriett VI, 662
Crawford, Harriett VI, 737
Crawford, Harriett VI, 757
Crawford, Harriett Isabelle VI, 737
Crawford, Harriett Isabelle VI, 753
Crawford, Harriett Isabelle VI, 757
Crawford, Henry M. IV, 28
Crawford, Hulda I, 303
Crawford, Huldah I, 303
Crawford, Israel IV, 28
Crawford, J. H. I, 303
Crawford, Jacob IV, 82
Crawford, James I, 284
Crawford, James I, 383
Crawford, James I, 677
Crawford, James II, 463
Crawford, James II, 497
Crawford, James IV, 17
Crawford, James IV, 24
Crawford, James IV, 27
Crawford, James IV, 82
Crawford, James VI, 381
Crawford, James Robinet IV, 28
Crawford, James Sidwill IV, 82
Crawford, Jane IV, 865
Crawford, Jane IV, 867
Crawford, Jane IV, 877
Crawford, Jennie V, 484
Crawford, Jesse Leah IV, 945
Crawford, Jessie Leah IV, 809
Crawford, Jessie Leah IV, 844
Crawford, Jessie Leah IV, 945
Crawford, Jessie Leah IV, 1004
Crawford, Jessie Leah C. IV, 255
Crawford, John IV, 27
Crawford, John IV, 28
Crawford, John V, 382
Crawford, John V, 437
Crawford, John V, 666
Crawford, John VI, 381
Crawford, John B. II, 702
Crawford, John B. II, 735
Crawford, John B. IV, 192
Crawford, John B. IV, 282
Crawford, John B. IV, 945
Crawford, John H. I, 284
Crawford, John H. I, 303
Crawford, John M. V, 991
Crawford, John Warren VI, 737
Crawford, John Warren VI, 757
Crawford, Jonas V, 382
Crawford, Joseph IV, 27
Crawford, Joseph IV, 82
Crawford, Joseph V, 262
Crawford, Joseph VI, 381
Crawford, Josia VI, 381
Crawford, Josiah IV, 17
Crawford, Josiah IV, 71
Crawford, Josiah IV, 82
Crawford, Josiah IV, 867
Crawford, Josiah VI, 381
Crawford, Josiah, Jr. IV, 27
Crawford, Katharine I, 383
Crawford, Leona V, 666
Crawford, Levania T. I, 284
Crawford, Levi IV, 82
Crawford, Levi VI, 381
Crawford, Lottie IV, 783
Crawford, Lucie M. VI, 964
Crawford, Lucy I, 383
Crawford, Lydia IV, 28
Crawford, Lydia IV, 902
Crawford, Margaret IV, 20
Crawford, Margaret IV, 24

Crawford, Margaret IV, 27
Crawford, Margaret IV, 28
Crawford, Margaret IV, 82
Crawford, Margaret IV, 945
Crawford, Margaret IV, 982
Crawford, Margaret V, 262
Crawford, Margaret VI, 380
Crawford, Margaret VI, 381
Crawford, Margaret, Jr. IV, 28
Crawford, Mark IV, 28
Crawford, Mark IV, 82
Crawford, Martha I, 303
Crawford, Mary I, 303
Crawford, Mary I, 316
Crawford, Mary I, 383
Crawford, Mary IV, 22
Crawford, Mary IV, 28
Crawford, Mary IV, 32
Crawford, Mary IV, 125
Crawford, Mary IV, 129
Crawford, Mary IV, 323
Crawford, Mary IV, 326
Crawford, Mary IV, 1360
Crawford, Mary VI, 381
Crawford, Mary VI, 398
Crawford, Mary Isabel IV, 913
Crawford, Meribe V, 44
Crawford, Meribe V, 118
Crawford, Michael I, 303
Crawford, Mrs. Jessie IV, 672
Crawford, Nancy I, 284
Crawford, Nathan IV, 28
Crawford, Nathan IV, 323
Crawford, Nathan IV, 326
Crawford, Nathan IV, 902
Crawford, Nathan, Jr. IV, 28
Crawford, Orrenia I, 284
Crawford, Priscilla IV, 22
Crawford, Priscilla IV, 28
Crawford, Priscilla IV, 56
Crawford, Priscilla IV, 69
Crawford, Priscilla W. IV, 125
Crawford, Rachel VI, 381
Crawford, Rachel VI, 423
Crawford, Rebecca Jane V, 262
Crawford, Reuben VI, 949
Crawford, Richard IV, 22
Crawford, Richard IV, 28
Crawford, Richard IV, 56
Crawford, Richard IV, 69
Crawford, Richard I. IV, 125
Crawford, Richard, Jr. IV, 28
Crawford, Robert W. IV, 809
Crawford, Robert W. IV, 945
Crawford, Ruth III, 90
Crawford, Ruth IV, 24
Crawford, Ruth IV, 27
Crawford, Ruth IV, 82
Crawford, Ruth IV, 108
Crawford, Ruth VI, 381
Crawford, Ruth M. III, 330
Crawford, Saml. L. VI, 964
Crawford, Samuel V, 232
Crawford, Samuel H. V, 232
Crawford, Samuel L. VI, 898
Crawford, Sara IV, 255
Crawford, Sara IV, 302
Crawford, Sara IV, 802
Crawford, Sara IV, 809
Crawford, Sara IV, 844
Crawford, Sarah I, 383
Crawford, Sarah II, 463
Crawford, Sarah II, 497
Crawford, Sarah II, 702
Crawford, Sarah IV, 27
Crawford, Sarah IV, 28
Crawford, Sarah IV, 33
Crawford, Sarah IV, 56
Crawford, Sarah IV, 125
Crawford, Sarah IV, 127
Crawford, Sarah IV, 929
Crawford, Sarah IV, 945
Crawford, Sarah IV, 982
Crawford, Sarah IV, 1014
Crawford, Sarah VI, 381
Crawford, Sarah B. IV, 192
Crawford, Sarah B. IV, 945
Crawford, Sarah E. V, 382
Crawford, Sarah Frances IV, 28
Crawford, Sarah Frances IV, 57
Crawford, Seaborn IV, 28
Crawford, Seaborn IV, 47
Crawford, Seaborn IV, 56
Crawford, Seaborn IV, 69
Crawford, Seaborn IV, 82
Crawford, Seaborn IV, 326
Crawford, Susanna IV, 27
Crawford, Susanna IV, 52
Crawford, Susanna IV, 82
Crawford, Susanna IV, 104
Crawford, Thomas IV, 69
Crawford, Thomas IV, 255
Crawford, Thomas IV, 945
Crawford, Thomas A. II, 702
Crawford, Thomas A. IV, 802
Crawford, Thomas A. IV, 809
Crawford, Thomas A. IV, 844
Crawford, Thomas A. IV, 929
Crawford, Thomas A. IV, 945
Crawford, Thomas A. IV, 982
Crawford, Thomas F. IV, 28
Crawford, Thomas M. IV, 867
Crawford, Thos. IV, 802
Crawford, Thos. A. IV, 192
Crawford, Thos. A. IV, 1014
Crawford, Tobias J. IV, 902
Crawford, Trawyer Hermon I, 284
Crawford, Troy I, 303
Crawford, Troy H. I, 303
Crawford, Troyer I, 303
Crawford, William I, 284
Crawford, William IV, 27
Crawford, William IV, 28
Crawford, William IV, 35
Crawford, William VI, 381
Crawford, Wm. IV, 783
Crawley, Adan VI, 808
Crawley, Beverly VI, 808
Crawley, Beverly VI, 851
Crawley, Charles VI, 808
Crawley, Elizabeth VI, 820
Crawley, James VI, 808
Crawley, Jane VI, 808
Crawley, Jefferson VI, 808
Crawley, Jno. VI, 808
Crawley, John VI, 820
Crawley, Mary II, 63
Crawley, Mary B. VI, 808
Crawley, Mary E. VI, 808
Crawley, Mary E. VI, 853
Crawley, Milly VI, 808
Crawley, Nancy VI, 808
Crawley, Peggy VI, 808
Crawley, Polly VI, 808
Crawley, Ralph VI, 808
Crawley, Thomas II, 497
Creacy, Elizabeth VI, 898
Creacy, John VI, 898
Creacy, William VI, 898
Creager, Catherine II, 350
Creager, Pearl V, 202
Creaghead, Elizabeth V, 901
Creaghead, Elizabeth B. V, 901
Creaghead, Elizabeth Griffith V, 901
Creaghead, Elizabeth Griffith V, 944
Creaghead, Robert M. V, 901
Creaghead, Robert Murnan V, 901
Creaghead, Samuel V, 901
Creaghead, Susan M. V, 901
Creaghead, Thos. J. V, 901
Creaghead, Thos. James V, 901
Creaghead, Thos. James V, 944
Creaghead, Thos. Jas. V, 901
Creamer, Andrew II, 350
Creamer, Beach V, 617
Creamer, Frank V, 617
Creamer, Lydia V, 617
Creamer, Olive V, 617
Creamer, Ollie V, 454
Creasey, Archibald VI, 897
Creasey, Bethani VI, 1018
Creasey, Betsey VI, 898
Creasey, Caroline F. VI, 1008
Creasey, Charles VI, 898
Creasey, David H. VI, 900
Creasey, David H. VI, 909
Creasey, David H. VI, 972
Creasey, David H. VI, 998
Creasey, David H. VI, 1012
Creasey, David H. VI, 1019
Creasey, Drusilla VI, 898
Creasey, Edmund VI, 813
Creasey, Elias VI, 885
Creasey, Elizabeth VI, 898
Creasey, Elizabeth VI, 908
Creasey, Elizabeth VI, 1008
Creasey, Eunice VI, 903
Creasey, Fleming VI, 866
Creasey, Franklin VI, 898
Creasey, Franklin VI, 942
Creasey, Franklin VI, 968
Creasey, George VI, 898
Creasey, Henry W. VI, 1020
Creasey, Jesse VI, 898
Creasey, John VI, 898
Creasey, John VI, 908
Creasey, Jubal VI, 808
Creasey, Judith VI, 898
Creasey, Jurah VI, 813
Creasey, Kitturah VI, 898
Creasey, Levina VI, 898
Creasey, Lockey VI, 808
Creasey, Lucy VI, 968
Creasey, Mary VI, 898
Creasey, Mary VI, 972
Creasey, Mary VI, 1012
Creasey, Patsy VI, 967
Creasey, Pleasant VI, 898
Creasey, Polly VI, 898
Creasey, Polly VI, 999
Creasey, Roger W. VI, 920
Creasey, Samuel VI, 973
Creasey, Sindey VI, 898
Creasey, Susan VI, 808
Creasey, Susanna VI, 812
Creasey, Susanna VI, 887
Creasey, Thomas VI, 887
Creasey, Thomas VI, 898
Creasey, Thomas VI, 903
Creasey, Thomas VI, 972
Creasey, Thomas VI, 1018
Creasey, Thos. VI, 968
Creasey, Wiatt VI, 898
Creasey, Will. John VI, 1009
Creasey, William VI, 898
Creasey, William VI, 952
Creasey, Wyatt VI, 808
Creasy, A. VI, 899
Creasy, Ann VI, 898
Creasy, Archibald VI, 898
Creasy, Barshaba VI, 898
Creasy, Benjamin VI, 898
Creasy, Betsey VI, 898
Creasy, Bird VI, 898
Creasy, Bird VI, 968
Creasy, Casann B. VI, 920
Creasy, Cathanders VI, 899
Creasy, Charles VI, 873
Creasy, Charles VI, 898
Creasy, Charles VI, 1020
Creasy, Charlotte VI, 899
Creasy, Claiborn VI, 999
Creasy, Claiborne VI, 898
Creasy, Claiborne VI, 900
Creasy, Claiborne VI, 913
Creasy, Claiborne VI, 933
Creasy, Claiborne, Jr. VI, 999
Creasy, Claiborne, Jr. VI, 1008
Creasy, Claibourn VI, 898
Creasy, Claibourn VI, 999
Creasy, Daniel O. VI, 899
Creasy, David VI, 898
Creasy, David H. VI, 891
Creasy, David H. VI, 899
Creasy, David H. VI, 901
Creasy, David H. VI, 990
Creasy, David H. VI, 999
Creasy, Demandy VI, 899
Creasy, Dianah VI, 898
Creasy, Drusilla VI, 898
Creasy, Elias M. VI, 899
Creasy, Elizabeth VI, 898
Creasy, Elizabeth VI, 899
Creasy, Elizabeth VI, 990
Creasy, Elizabeth Ann VI, 898
Creasy, Elizabeth B. VI, 999
Creasy, Elizabeth Jane VI, 899
Creasy, Elmary VI, 1019
Creasy, Elusty VI, 898
Creasy, Emily VI, 1020
Creasy, Fleming VI, 808
Creasy, Fleming VI, 984
Creasy, Franklin VI, 898
Creasy, George VI, 898
Creasy, George A. VI, 808
Creasy, Harriett C. VI, 899
Creasy, James VI, 898
Creasy, Jane VI, 898
Creasy, Jane Emeline VI, 1001
Creasy, Jefferson VI, 898
Creasy, Jesse VI, 898
Creasy, Jesse VI, 1012
Creasy, Johanna D. VI, 1012
Creasy, John VI, 898
Creasy, John VI, 999
Creasy, John VI, 1019
Creasy, John P. VI, 899
Creasy, John T. VI, 898
Creasy, John T. VI, 968
Creasy, Jubal VI, 898
Creasy, Judith VI, 898
Creasy, Judith VI, 999
Creasy, Kalista VI, 985
Creasy, Kitturah VI, 898
Creasy, Leonard S. VI, 899
Creasy, Levina VI, 898
Creasy, Lockey VI, 808
Creasy, Louisa VI, 898
Creasy, Lucinda VI, 898
Creasy, Lucinda VI, 900
Creasy, Lucinda VI, 999
Creasy, Lydia E. VI, 936
Creasy, Malinda VI, 898
Creasy, Malissa Ann VI, 899
Creasy, Margaret VI, 899
Creasy, Margaret VI, 999
Creasy, Mark VI, 899
Creasy, Martha Jane VI, 899
Creasy, Mary VI, 898
Creasy, Mary VI, 968
Creasy, Mary VI, 972
Creasy, Mary VI, 1007
Creasy, Mary T. VI, 808
Creasy, Melinda VI, 898
Creasy, Meredith L. VI, 999
Creasy, Nancy VI, 873
Creasy, Nancy VI, 1001
Creasy, Nimrod VI, 899
Creasy, Obadiah VI, 898
Creasy, Parthena VI, 1008
Creasy, Paulina J. VI, 899
Creasy, Peter VI, 898
Creasy, Pleasant VI, 808
Creasy, Pleasant VI, 898
Creasy, Polly VI, 898
Creasy, Polly P. VI, 968
Creasy, Rebecca VI, 917
Creasy, Roger W. VI, 898
Creasy, Roger W. VI, 1012
Creasy, Sally VI, 898
Creasy, Samuel VI, 1020
Creasy, Samuel H. VI, 899
Creasy, Sarah VI, 898
Creasy, Sarah A. VI, 808
Creasy, Sarah Jane VI, 899
Creasy, Savana H. VI, 990
Creasy, Sindey VI, 898
Creasy, Siner VI, 898
Creasy, Suckey VI, 898
Creasy, Susan VI, 808
Creasy, Susanna G. VI, 898
Creasy, Susannah VI, 898
Creasy, Thomas VI, 898
Creasy, Thomas VI, 967
Creasy, Thomas VI, 968
Creasy, Thomas VI, 1007
Creasy, Thomas F. VI, 920
Creasy, Thomas F. VI, 985
Creasy, Thomas, Jr. VI, 1007
Creasy, Washington VI, 899
Creasy, Wiatt VI, 898
Creasy, William VI, 898
Creasy, William VI, 899
Creasy, William A. VI, 899
Creasy, William A. VI, 999
Creasy, William H. VI, 898
Creasy, William H. VI, 1001
Creasy, William J. VI, 899
Creasy, William J. VI, 933
Creasy, William J. VI, 1001
Creasy, Wilmouth VI, 898
Creasy, Wyatt VI, 808
Creaton, Margret II, 991
Creaton, Margret II, 994
Crecy, Sarah VI, 909
Credell, Mildred VI, 830
Credell, Nancy VI, 830
Creecy, Clabourn VI, 1008
Creed, Augustine VI, 899
Creed, Ransemon VI, 899
Creeden, Hiram V, 617
Creeden, John V, 617
Creeden, Manerva V, 617
Creeden, Minerva V, 617
Creeden, William V, 617
Creeden, Wm. V, 617
Creek, Caesars V, 155
Creek, Charity V, 155
Creek, Symons I, 92
Creek, William I, 91
Creell, William M. V, 232
Creesey, Avey VI, 933
Creesey, Bird VI, 898
Creesey, David VI, 898
Creesey, Jubal VI, 898
Creesey, Lucy VI, 926
Creesey, Lucy VI, 1020
Creesey, Pleasant VI, 926
Creesey, Polly VI, 898
Creesey, Siner VI, 898
Creesey, Susannah VI, 898
Creesey, Thomas VI, 1020
Creesey, William VI, 1012
Creesey, Wm. VI, 966
Creesy, Bird VI, 892
Creesy, Charles VI, 1020
Creesy, Elizabeth VI, 898
Creesy, Franklin VI, 898
Creesy, Lucy VI, 1020
Creesy, Mary VI, 918
Creesy, Nancy D. VI, 891
Creesy, Sally VI, 898
Creesy, Thomas VI, 898
Creesy, Thomas VI, 917
Creesy, Thomas F. VI, 937
Creesy, William VI, 918
Cregg, Hannah V, 834
Cregg, Hannah V, 873
Cregging, Mary II, 497
Cregging, Mary II, 583
Creighton, Charles V, 165
Creighton, Chas. V, 165
Creighton, Dr. Hamilton V, 165
Creighton, Fannie V, 99
Creighton, Fanny C. V, 979
Creighton, Florence E. IV, 192
Creighton, Florence E. IV, 229
Creighton, Frank C. V, 979
Creighton, Hamilton V, 165
Creighton, Jenette V, 165
Creighton, John B. V, 969
Creighton, John Benj. V, 969
Creighton, Mary V, 969
Creighton, Mary V, 976
Creighton, Mary V, 979
Creighton, Mary Ann V, 979
Creighton, Nettie V, 165
Creighton, S. Emma Guard V, 165
Creighton, Samuel V, 969
Creighton, Samuel Thos. V, 969
Creighton, William V, 979
Creighton, Wm. V, 969
Crenshaw, Achilles D. VI, 237
Crenshaw, Allen VI, 899
Crenshaw, Ann VI, 236
Crenshaw, Ann C. VI, 79
Crenshaw, Ann C. VI, 237
Crenshaw, Ann D. VI, 235
Crenshaw, Anne C. VI, 237
Crenshaw, Belle VI, 237
Crenshaw, Cornelius VI, 808
Crenshaw, Cornelius VI, 864
Crenshaw, David VI, 894
Crenshaw, David VI, 959
Crenshaw, Deborah VI, 237
Crenshaw, Deborah VI, 381
Crenshaw, Deborah Ann VI, 236
Crenshaw, Deborah Ann VI, 237
Crenshaw, Deborah Ann VI, 258
Crenshaw, Deborah D. VI, 236
Crenshaw, Edmund VI, 237
Crenshaw, Edmund A. II, 735
Crenshaw, Edmund Austin VI, 236
Crenshaw, Eliza VI, 236
Crenshaw, Eliza VI, 237
Crenshaw, Eliza C. VI, 237
Crenshaw, Eliza C. VI, 265
Crenshaw, Eliza Catharine VI, 236
Crenshaw, Eliza Catherine VI, 266
Crenshaw, Eliza H. VI, 237
Crenshaw, Eliza Kate VI, 237
Crenshaw, Eliza Kate VI, 266
Crenshaw, Eliza Susan VI, 954
Crenshaw, Elizabeth VI, 935
Crenshaw, Elizabeth A. VI, 235
Crenshaw, Elizabeth A. VI, 237
Crenshaw, Elizabeth Ann VI, 236
Crenshaw, Harriet Elizabeth VI, 975
Crenshaw, Henry Pleasants VI, 237
Crenshaw, Infant VI, 237
Crenshaw, James VI, 263
Crenshaw, James H. VI, 237
Crenshaw, James H. VI, 238
Crenshaw, James H. VI, 265
Crenshaw, James Hoge VI, 236
Crenshaw, James Hoge VI, 237
Crenshaw, James Hoge, Jr. VI, 237
Crenshaw, Jno. VI, 899
Crenshaw, Jno. VI, 975
Crenshaw, Jno. VI, 987
Crenshaw, John VI, 818
Crenshaw, John VI, 899
Crenshaw, John Austin VI, 236
Crenshaw, John B. VI, 226
Crenshaw, John B. VI, 236
Crenshaw, John B. VI, 237
Crenshaw, John B. VI, 238
Crenshaw, John B. VI, 248
Crenshaw, John B. VI, 249
Crenshaw, John B. VI, 258
Crenshaw, John B. VI, 266
Crenshaw, John B. VI, 273
Crenshaw, John B. VI, 381
Crenshaw, John B. VI, 401

renshaw, John Bacon VI, 164
renshaw, John Bacon VI, 236
renshaw, John Bacon VI, 381
renshaw, John Balderston VI, 249
renshaw, John Chapman VI, 236
renshaw, John P. VI, 381
renshaw, Joseph VI, 237
renshaw, Joseph P. VI, 237
renshaw, Judith VI, 237
renshaw, Judith A. VI, 237
renshaw, Judith A. VI, 238
renshaw, Judith A. VI, 248
renshaw, Judith A. VI, 273
renshaw, Judith Ann VI, 236
renshaw, Judith Ann VI, 237
renshaw, Judith Isabella VI, 236
renshaw, Judith Isabella VI, 237
renshaw, Judith Isabella VI, 273
renshaw, Louisa VI, 808
renshaw, Lucie Ann VI, 943
renshaw, Lucy VI, 899
renshaw, Lucy VI, 903
renshaw, M. Belle VI, 237
renshaw, M. Belle VI, 265
renshaw, M. E. VI, 238
renshaw, Margaret E. VI, 237
renshaw, Margaret Elizabeth VI, 236
renshaw, Mariah Frances VI, 939
renshaw, Martha Ann VI, 899
renshaw, Martha C. VI, 890
renshaw, Martha Isabella VI, 237
renshaw, Mary VI, 816
renshaw, Mary B. VI, 249
renshaw, Mary F. VI, 237
renshaw, Mary Frances VI, 236
renshaw, Mary J. D. VI, 60
renshaw, Mary J. D. VI, 79
renshaw, Mary J. D. VI, 80
renshaw, Mary Jane VI, 92
renshaw, Mary Jane VI, 236
renshaw, Mary Jane VI, 237
renshaw, Mary Jane VI, 265
renshaw, Mary Winston VI, 959
renshaw, Mary Y. VI, 164
renshaw, Mary Y. VI, 236
renshaw, Mary Y. VI, 237
renshaw, Nathan C. VI, 164
renshaw, Nathan C. Crenshaw VI, 381
renshaw, Nathaniel VI, 226
renshaw, Nathaniel VI, 236
renshaw, Nathaniel VI, 381
renshaw, Nathaniel B. VI, 237
renshaw, Nathaniel Bacon VI, 236
renshaw, Nathaniel Bacon VI, 237
renshaw, Nathaniel C. VI, 60
renshaw, Nathaniel C. VI, 79
renshaw, Nathaniel C. VI, 164
renshaw, Nathaniel C. VI, 235
renshaw, Nathaniel C. VI, 236
renshaw, Nathaniel C. VI, 237
renshaw, Nathaniel C. VI, 238
renshaw, Pleasants VI, 238
renshaw, Priscilla VI, 899
renshaw, Rachel VI, 236
renshaw, Rachel VI, 237
renshaw, Rachel VI, 381
renshaw, Rachel VI, 401
renshaw, Rachel Frances VI, 236
renshaw, Rachel H. VI, 258
renshaw, Rachel H. VI, 266
renshaw, Richard VI, 899
renshaw, Richard VI, 954
renshaw, Ro. W. VI, 1010
renshaw, Samuel VI, 899
renshaw, Samuel H. VI, 890
renshaw, Samuel H. VI, 939
renshaw, Samuel H. VI, 954
renshaw, Sara VI, 249
renshaw, Sara W. VI, 237
renshaw, Sara Willets VI, 237
renshaw, Sara Willets VI, 248
renshaw, Sarah VI, 249
renshaw, Sarah VI, 894
renshaw, Sarah W. VI, 249
renshaw, Sarah W. VI, 899
renshaw, Sarah Willits VI, 237
renshaw, Susannah VI, 980
renshaw, Walter Crew VI, 237
Crenshaw, William Pleasants VI, 237
Crenshaw, Willitts Bassett VI, 236
Crepon, James III, 91
Crepps, Elizabeth IV, 1234
Crepps, Jenet IV, 1234
Crepps, Jennet IV, 1234
Crepps, Michael IV, 1234
Crepps, Moses W. IV, 1234
Crepps, Orpha IV, 1234
Cresey, Sarah I, 45
Cresey, Sarah I, 73
Creson, Abigail M. V, 881
Creson, Abigail M. V, 882
Crespin, Mathias V, 211
Crespin, Sarah V, 211
Cress, Cora V, 734
Cress, Dessie V, 734
Cress, Glenn V, 734
Cress, Janie V, 734
Cress, Lenna V, 734
Cress, Treva V, 734
Cressin, Emlen II, 735
Cressin, John H. II, 735
Cressin, Rachel II, 735
Cressin, Sarah H. II, 735
Cressin, Walter II, 735
Cressin, Wm. II, 735
Cresson, Ann II, 351
Cresson, Ann II, 498
Cresson, Ann H. II, 498
Cresson, Ann H. II, 673
Cresson, Anna II, 350
Cresson, Anna II, 351
Cresson, Anna II, 497
Cresson, Anna II, 679
Cresson, Annabella II, 350
Cresson, Annabella II, 351
Cresson, Annabella II, 497
Cresson, Annabella II, 498
Cresson, Annabella II, 514
Cresson, Annabella II, 516
Cresson, Annabella E. II, 735
Cresson, Annabella E. II, 776
Cresson, Anne II, 351
Cresson, Benjamin II, 350
Cresson, Benjamin II, 351
Cresson, Benjamin II, 497
Cresson, Benjamin II, 622
Cresson, Caleb II, 350
Cresson, Caleb II, 351
Cresson, Caleb II, 497
Cresson, Caleb II, 514
Cresson, Caleb II, 516
Cresson, Caleb II, 735
Cresson, Caleb II, 767
Cresson, Caleb II, 776
Cresson, Caleb, Jr. II, 497
Cresson, Caleb, Jr. II, 498
Cresson, Caleb, Jr. II, 516
Cresson, Charles II, 351
Cresson, Charles II, 735
Cresson, Charles C. II, 735
Cresson, Clement II, 351
Cresson, Clement II, 498
Cresson, Deborah II, 350
Cresson, Deborah II, 497
Cresson, Deborah II, 622
Cresson, Deborah Ann II, 351
Cresson, Deborah Ann II, 498
Cresson, Deborah P. II, 350
Cresson, Ebenezer II, 351
Cresson, Ebenezer II, 497
Cresson, Edmond II, 351
Cresson, Edmund II, 351
Cresson, Eleanor II, 351
Cresson, Eliza II, 351
Cresson, Elizabeth II, 351
Cresson, Elizabeth II, 498
Cresson, Elizabeth II, 592
Cresson, Elizabeth II, 641
Cresson, Elizabeth H. II, 735
Cresson, Elizabeth H. II, 764
Cresson, Elizabeth Hooten II, 498
Cresson, Elliott II, 351
Cresson, Elliott II, 497
Cresson, Elliott II, 498
Cresson, Emlen II, 351
Cresson, Emlen II, 497
Cresson, Emlen II, 735
Cresson, George II, 351
Cresson, Hannah II, 351
Cresson, Hannah II, 497
Cresson, Hannah II, 560
Cresson, Hannah II, 594
Cresson, Hannah II, 634
Cresson, Hannah II, 673
Cresson, Hannah II, 735
Cresson, Hannah II, 854
Cresson, Hannah H. II, 854
Cresson, Hannah Humphreys II, 498
Cresson, Humphreys II, 498
Cresson, James II, 350
Cresson, James II, 351
Cresson, James II, 485
Cresson, James II, 497
Cresson, James II, 498
Cresson, James II, 514
Cresson, James II, 516
Cresson, James II, 529
Cresson, James II, 552
Cresson, James II, 560
Cresson, James II, 592
Cresson, James II, 622
Cresson, James II, 673
Cresson, James II, 735
Cresson, James II, 854
Cresson, James H. III, 91
Cresson, James, Jr. II, 735
Cresson, Jane II, 351
Cresson, Jane Chapman II, 351
Cresson, Jane Chapman II, 498
Cresson, Jane Chapman II, 735
Cresson, Jeremiah II, 351
Cresson, Jeremiah II, 497
Cresson, Jeremiah II, 594
Cresson, Jeremiah II, 634
Cresson, John II, 350
Cresson, John II, 351
Cresson, John II, 497
Cresson, John II, 552
Cresson, John A. II, 497
Cresson, John Armitt II, 351
Cresson, John C. II, 498
Cresson, John Chapman II, 351
Cresson, John Chapman II, 498
Cresson, John Elliott II, 350
Cresson, John Elliott II, 351
Cresson, John Elliott II, 497
Cresson, John Elliott II, 498
Cresson, John H. II, 350
Cresson, John H. II, 351
Cresson, John H. II, 498
Cresson, John H. II, 641
Cresson, John H. II, 644
Cresson, John H. II, 735
Cresson, John H. II, 736
Cresson, John H. II, 764
Cresson, Joseph II, 351
Cresson, Joseph II, 485
Cresson, Joseph II, 498
Cresson, Joseph II, 702
Cresson, Joseph, Jr. II, 702
Cresson, Joshua II, 350
Cresson, Joshua II, 351
Cresson, Joshua II, 497
Cresson, Joshua II, 498
Cresson, Liddie II, 351
Cresson, Martha II, 351
Cresson, Martha II, 991
Cresson, Martha II, 1023
Cresson, Martha Warner II, 498
Cresson, Mary II, 350
Cresson, Mary II, 351
Cresson, Mary II, 497
Cresson, Mary II, 498
Cresson, Mary II, 634
Cresson, Mary Ann II, 498
Cresson, Mary E. II, 497
Cresson, Mary Emlen II, 351
Cresson, Mary Emlen II, 735
Cresson, Mary Emlen II, 767
Cresson, Mary W. II, 735
Cresson, Mary W. II, 736
Cresson, Mercy II, 485
Cresson, Mercy II, 497
Cresson, Mercy II, 498
Cresson, Mercy II, 702
Cresson, Mercy Ann II, 702
Cresson, Mercy Anna II, 351
Cresson, Mercy Anna II, 702
Cresson, Rachel II, 351
Cresson, Rachel II, 497
Cresson, Rachel II, 498
Cresson, Rachel II, 641
Cresson, Rachel II, 644
Cresson, Rachel II, 735
Cresson, Rachel II, 736
Cresson, Rachel II, 764
Cresson, Rebecca II, 350
Cresson, Rebecca II, 351
Cresson, Rebecca II, 497
Cresson, Rebecca II, 529
Cresson, Rebecca II, 552
Cresson, Rebecca II, 641
Cresson, Rebecca G. II, 351
Cresson, Rebecca G. II, 702
Cresson, Rebecca W. II, 498
Cresson, Rebecca W. II, 644
Cresson, Rebecca Walter II, 498
Cresson, Rebekah II, 497
Cresson, Rebekah II, 584
Cresson, Samuel II, 351
Cresson, Samuel II, 702
Cresson, Sarah II, 350
Cresson, Sarah II, 351
Cresson, Sarah II, 485
Cresson, Sarah II, 497
Cresson, Sarah II, 498
Cresson, Sarah II, 514
Cresson, Sarah II, 516
Cresson, Sarah II, 529
Cresson, Sarah II, 552
Cresson, Sarah II, 560
Cresson, Sarah II, 592
Cresson, Sarah II, 622
Cresson, Sarah II, 735
Cresson, Sarah II, 741
Cresson, Sarah E. II, 497
Cresson, Sarah E. II, 735
Cresson, Sarah E. II, 767
Cresson, Sarah E. II, 776
Cresson, Sarah Emlen II, 351
Cresson, Sarah Emlen II, 498
Cresson, Sarah H. II, 350
Cresson, Sarah H. II, 735
Cresson, Sarah P. II, 498
Cresson, Sarah P. II, 735
Cresson, Sarah P. II, 854
Cresson, Sarah, Jr. II, 498
Cresson, Solomon II, 350
Cresson, Solomon II, 351
Cresson, Solomon II, 497
Cresson, Solomon II, 516
Cresson, Solomon II, 584
Cresson, Solomon II, 679
Cresson, Susan V. II, 735
Cresson, Susan V. II, 772
Cresson, Susanna II, 350
Cresson, Tacy II, 351
Cresson, Tacy II, 498
Cresson, Tacy II, 729
Cresson, Tacy II, 735
Cresson, Tacy II, 854
Cresson, Thomas Walter II, 351
Cresson, Walter II, 351
Cresson, Walter II, 498
Cresson, Walter II, 641
Cresson, Walter II, 735
Cresson, Warder II, 351
Cresson, Warder II, 498
Cresson, Wd. ??? II, 351
Cresson, Wd. Sarah II, 351
Cresson, William II, 351
Cresson, Wm. II, 498
Cresson, Wm. II, 641
Cresson, Wm. II, 735
Cresson, Wm. P. II, 735
Creswell, Cynthia A. V, 484
Creswell, John V, 484
Creswell, Keziah V, 484
Creswell, Louetta A. V, 484
Creswell, Sarah A. V, 484
Cresy, Jubal VI, 866
Cresy, Lyndney J. VI, 866
Cresy, Mary VI, 967
Cresy, Nimrod VI, 866
Cresy, Pleasant, Jr. VI, 917
Cretty, Charles III, 91
Cretty, Elizabeth B. III, 91
Cretty, Leslie III, 91
Cretty, Leslie A. III, 91
Cretty, Virginia III, 91
Creviston, Emma IV, 1275
Creviston, Esther A. IV, 1275
Creviston, Eveline IV, 1275
Creviston, Huldah IV, 1275
Creviston, Joseph IV, 1275
Creviston, Larkin IV, 1275
Creviston, Rufus IV, 1275
Creviston, Sarah IV, 1275
Crew, ??? IV, 795
Crew, ??? IV, 946
Crew, ??? IV, 1125
Crew, Abigail IV, 810
Crew, Abigail IV, 1092
Crew, Abigail VI, 167
Crew, Abigail F. IV, 566
Crew, Abigail F. IV, 572
Crew, Abigail F. IV, 1092
Crew, Abner IV, 193
Crew, Abner IV, 382
Crew, Abner IV, 600
Crew, Abner IV, 1092
Crew, Abner F. IV, 382
Crew, Abraham IV, 810
Crew, Abraham IV, 830
Crew, Abraham IV, 853
Crew, Abraham S. IV, 946
Crew, Abram IV, 810
Crew, Abram IV, 946
Crew, Abram L. IV, 946
Crew, Acenath IV, 567
Crew, Acenath IV, 572
Crew, Agatha VI, 164
Crew, Agatha VI, 168
Crew, Agatha VI, 172
Crew, Agatha VI, 182
Crew, Agathy VI, 15
Crew, Agathy VI, 165
Crew, Agathy VI, 167
Crew, Agathy VI, 185
Crew, Agathy VI, 186
Crew, Agga VI, 239
Crew, Aggea VI, 239
Crew, Aggy VI, 238
Crew, Agnes I, 356
Crew, Agnes I, 383
Crew, Agnes I, 807
Crew, Agnes VI, 238
Crew, Agnes VI, 239
Crew, Agnes VI, 273
Crew, Agness I, 383
Crew, Agness VI, 239
Crew, Agness VI, 273
Crew, Albert IV, 708
Crew, Albert E. IV, 708
Crew, Alfeus V, 484
Crew, Alfred IV, 945
Crew, Allard H. IV, 946
Crew, Almedia IV, 382
Crew, Almedia IV, 458
Crew, Almedia IV, 571
Crew, Almedia IV, 572
Crew, Almedia IV, 601
Crew, Almedia IV, 1092
Crew, Amos IV, 1091
Crew, Amos IV, 1092
Crew, Amy B. IV, 794
Crew, Andrew I, 213
Crew, Andrew I, 236
Crew, Andrew VI, 105
Crew, Andrew VI, 149
Crew, Andrew VI, 158
Crew, Andrew VI, 164
Crew, Andrew VI, 165
Crew, Andrew VI, 166
Crew, Andrew VI, 167
Crew, Andrew VI, 169
Crew, Andrew VI, 170
Crew, Andrew VI, 172
Crew, Andrew VI, 173
Crew, Andrew VI, 174
Crew, Andrew VI, 185
Crew, Andrew VI, 212
Crew, Andrew VI, 213
Crew, Andrew VI, 215
Crew, Andrew VI, 238
Crew, Andrew VI, 239
Crew, Andrew Binford I, 213
Crew, Andrew Binford I, 236
Crew, Andrew, Jr. VI, 158
Crew, Andrew, Jr. VI, 160
Crew, Andrew, Jr. VI, 165
Crew, Andrew, Jr. VI, 167
Crew, Andrew, Jr. VI, 168
Crew, Andrew, Jr. VI, 169
Crew, Andrew, Jr. VI, 174
Crew, Andrew, Jr. VI, 189
Crew, Andrew, Senior VI, 165
Crew, Andrew, Sr. VI, 167
Crew, Ann I, 213
Crew, Ann I, 236
Crew, Ann IV, 192
Crew, Ann IV, 193
Crew, Ann IV, 374
Crew, Ann IV, 375
Crew, Ann IV, 381
Crew, Ann IV, 382
Crew, Ann IV, 386
Crew, Ann IV, 572
Crew, Ann IV, 922
Crew, Ann IV, 946
Crew, Ann IV, 1091
Crew, Ann IV, 1092
Crew, Ann IV, 1094
Crew, Ann V, 44
Crew, Ann VI, 101
Crew, Ann VI, 165
Crew, Ann VI, 167
Crew, Ann VI, 168
Crew, Ann VI, 178
Crew, Ann VI, 179
Crew, Ann VI, 209
Crew, Ann VI, 240
Crew, Ann Eliza IV, 193
Crew, Ann Eliza IV, 381
Crew, Ann Eliza IV, 382
Crew, Ann Eliza IV, 432
Crew, Ann Eliza VI, 238
Crew, Anna IV, 192

Crew, Anna IV, 382
Crew, Anna IV, 431
Crew, Anna IV, 469
Crew, Anna IV, 492
Crew, Anna IV, 573
Crew, Anna IV, 708
Crew, Anna IV, 1092
Crew, Anna IV, 1106
Crew, Anna VI, 105
Crew, Anna VI, 106
Crew, Anna VI, 166
Crew, Anna VI, 170
Crew, Anna VI, 238
Crew, Anna VI, 240
Crew, Anna E. IV, 193
Crew, Anna E. IV, 223
Crew, Anna E. IV, 946
Crew, Anna E. IV, 965
Crew, Anna M. IV, 902
Crew, Anna M. IV, 947
Crew, Anna M. IV, 1091
Crew, Anne IV, 1052
Crew, Anne VI, 105
Crew, Anne VI, 164
Crew, Anne VI, 167
Crew, Anne VI, 196
Crew, Anne E. VI, 240
Crew, Annie M. IV, 968
Crew, Annie M. IV, 1000
Crew, Annie Margery IV, 1000
Crew, Aquilla IV, 193
Crew, Aquilla IV, 381
Crew, Aquilla IV, 391
Crew, Aquilla IV, 572
Crew, Aquilla VI, 101
Crew, Armisby VI, 238
Crew, Armsbee VI, 239
Crew, Armsberry I, 1066
Crew, Armsby I, 383
Crew, Armsby I, 807
Crew, Armsby VI, 239
Crew, Armsley I, 713
Crew, Armsley I, 1066
Crew, Arthur VI, 166
Crew, Arthur Fleming IV, 1091
Crew, Asenath IV, 193
Crew, Asenath IV, 375
Crew, Asenath IV, 381
Crew, Asenath IV, 382
Crew, Asenath IV, 510
Crew, Asenath IV, 519
Crew, Ashely Johnson VI, 240
Crew, Audra V, 165
Crew, Bana VI, 165
Crew, Barclay IV, 193
Crew, Barclay IV, 381
Crew, Barclay IV, 382
Crew, Barzilla IV, 708
Crew, Ben VI, 168
Crew, Benj. IV, 490
Crew, Benj. VI, 166
Crew, Benjamin I, 236
Crew, Benjamin IV, 192
Crew, Benjamin IV, 465
Crew, Benjamin IV, 469
Crew, Benjamin IV, 696
Crew, Benjamin IV, 809
Crew, Benjamin IV, 810
Crew, Benjamin IV, 945
Crew, Benjamin V, 731
Crew, Benjamin V, 734
Crew, Benjamin VI, 105
Crew, Benjamin VI, 110
Crew, Benjamin VI, 111
Crew, Benjamin VI, 133
Crew, Benjamin VI, 165
Crew, Benjamin VI, 166
Crew, Benjamin VI, 168
Crew, Benjamin VI, 169
Crew, Benjamin VI, 170
Crew, Benjamin VI, 191
Crew, Benjamin VI, 194
Crew, Benjamin VI, 220
Crew, Benjamin VI, 221
Crew, Benjamin VI, 238
Crew, Benjamin VI, 240
Crew, Benjamin VI, 265
Crew, Benjamin Hawkins VI, 306
Crew, Benjamin L. IV, 469
Crew, Benjamin, Jr. VI, 169
Crew, Benjamin, Jr. VI, 170
Crew, Caleb I, 213
Crew, Caleb I, 961
Crew, Caleb VI, 105
Crew, Caleb VI, 106
Crew, Caleb VI, 168
Crew, Caroline IV, 696
Crew, Caroline IV, 945
Crew, Caroline IV, 946
Crew, Caroline IV, 1018
Crew, Caroline IV, 1091
Crew, Caroline VI, 239
Crew, Caroline L. IV, 469
Crew, Caroline L. V, 666
Crew, Caroline Ladd V, 666
Crew, Carrol M. IV, 946
Crew, Carroll IV, 947
Crew, Caspar W. V, 734
Crew, Casper W. V, 734
Crew, Catherine VI, 166
Crew, Catherine VI, 170
Crew, Catherine VI, 191
Crew, Catherine VI, 195
Crew, Chalkley IV, 193
Crew, Chalkley IV, 572
Crew, Chapell VI, 165
Crew, Chappell VI, 101
Crew, Charles I, 213
Crew, Charles I, 961
Crew, Charles IV, 946
Crew, Charles IV, 947
Crew, Charles IV, 974
Crew, Charles IV, 1091
Crew, Charles IV, 1092
Crew, Charles IV, 1129
Crew, Charles VI, 105
Crew, Charles VI, 106
Crew, Charles VI, 238
Crew, Charles Corwin IV, 946
Crew, Charles E. IV, 1092
Crew, Charles Evans IV, 1091
Crew, Charles H. IV, 469
Crew, Charles Henry IV, 1092
Crew, Charles Lewis IV, 1052
Crew, Charlie IV, 572
Crew, Cherrie IV, 974
Crew, Chlotilda IV, 946
Crew, Chlotilda IV, 1011
Crew, Clara Alma IV, 946
Crew, Clara Crew IV, 947
Crew, Clarey VI, 165
Crew, Clark IV, 945
Crew, Clary VI, 170
Crew, Clary VI, 180
Crew, Clotilda IV, 696
Crew, Clotilda IV, 945
Crew, Collin I, 236
Crew, Cora Cobb IV, 946
Crew, Cornelius VI, 165
Crew, Cornelius VI, 170
Crew, Daniel VI, 165
Crew, Daniel VI, 170
Crew, David I, 779
Crew, David I, 807
Crew, David IV, 810
Crew, David IV, 1091
Crew, David IV, 1092
Crew, David VI, 164
Crew, David VI, 165
Crew, David VI, 167
Crew, David VI, 168
Crew, David VI, 170
Crew, David VI, 197
Crew, David VI, 213
Crew, David VI, 238
Crew, David W. IV, 1092
Crew, Dawcella VI, 306
Crew, Deborah IV, 192
Crew, Deborah IV, 469
Crew, Deborah VI, 238
Crew, Deborah VI, 240
Crew, Deborah A. IV, 469
Crew, Deborah A. IV, 1275
Crew, Deborah A. V, 666
Crew, Deborah Ann IV, 193
Crew, Deborah Ann IV, 217
Crew, Deborah D. IV, 192
Crew, Deborah D. VI, 240
Crew, Deborah Tace VI, 238
Crew, Delitha IV, 572
Crew, Delitha IV, 1052
Crew, Delitha IV, 1092
Crew, Delitha IV, 1096
Crew, Dorothy VI, 238
Crew, Dorothy VI, 239
Crew, Dorothy VI, 252
Crew, Dorothy VI, 256
Crew, Dr. Benj. V, 734
Crew, Drewscilla VI, 305
Crew, Drewzilla VI, 239
Crew, Drucilla IV, 572
Crew, Drucilly VI, 306
Crew, Drusilla IV, 193
Crew, Drusilla VI, 306
Crew, Edith IV, 185
Crew, Edith IV, 192
Crew, Edith IV, 570
Crew, Edith IV, 572
Crew, Edith IV, 1091
Crew, Edith IV, 1092
Crew, Edna IV, 571
Crew, Edna IV, 572
Crew, Edna VI, 153
Crew, Edna VI, 166
Crew, Edna VI, 169
Crew, Edna VI, 170
Crew, Edward VI, 166
Crew, Edward B. IV, 192
Crew, Edwin IV, 381
Crew, Edwin IV, 571
Crew, Edwin IV, 1050
Crew, Edwin IV, 1052
Crew, Edwin IV, 1055
Crew, Edwin IV, 1092
Crew, Edwin A. IV, 946
Crew, Edwin A. IV, 947
Crew, Effie M. V, 165
Crew, Eleanor IV, 469
Crew, Eleanor IV, 519
Crew, Eleanor H. IV, 469
Crew, Eleanor H. IV, 1275
Crew, Eleazer VI, 133
Crew, Eleazer VI, 166
Crew, Eleazer VI, 169
Crew, Eleazer VI, 170
Crew, Eli IV, 193
Crew, Eli IV, 381
Crew, Eli IV, 571
Crew, Eli IV, 572
Crew, Eli V, 45
Crew, Elias IV, 572
Crew, Elias IV, 808
Crew, Elias IV, 810
Crew, Elias IV, 1052
Crew, Elias IV, 1129
Crew, Elija VI, 171
Crew, Elijah IV, 193
Crew, Elijah IV, 571
Crew, Elijah IV, 572
Crew, Elisa Ann IV, 696
Crew, Elisabeth I, 236
Crew, Elisha I, 213
Crew, Elisha I, 236
Crew, Eliza Ann IV, 696
Crew, Eliza Ann IV, 784
Crew, Eliza Ann IV, 945
Crew, Eliza Ann IV, 946
Crew, Eliza Ann IV, 953
Crew, Eliza Ann VI, 239
Crew, Eliza B. IV, 370
Crew, Eliza B. IV, 382
Crew, Eliza B. IV, 1049
Crew, Eliza B. IV, 1052
Crew, Eliza Blanche IV, 370
Crew, Eliza Jane IV, 469
Crew, Eliza Jane IV, 536
Crew, Eliza Jane VI, 166
Crew, Eliza P. VI, 170
Crew, Elizabeth I, 807
Crew, Elizabeth I, 834
Crew, Elizabeth IV, 192
Crew, Elizabeth IV, 193
Crew, Elizabeth IV, 223
Crew, Elizabeth IV, 469
Crew, Elizabeth IV, 492
Crew, Elizabeth IV, 505
Crew, Elizabeth IV, 519
Crew, Elizabeth IV, 572
Crew, Elizabeth IV, 579
Crew, Elizabeth IV, 696
Crew, Elizabeth IV, 945
Crew, Elizabeth IV, 947
Crew, Elizabeth IV, 971
Crew, Elizabeth IV, 1129
Crew, Elizabeth V, 44
Crew, Elizabeth V, 45
Crew, Elizabeth V, 232
Crew, Elizabeth V, 326
Crew, Elizabeth V, 382
Crew, Elizabeth V, 428
Crew, Elizabeth VI, 106
Crew, Elizabeth VI, 160
Crew, Elizabeth VI, 164
Crew, Elizabeth VI, 165
Crew, Elizabeth VI, 166
Crew, Elizabeth VI, 167
Crew, Elizabeth VI, 168
Crew, Elizabeth VI, 169
Crew, Elizabeth VI, 170
Crew, Elizabeth VI, 172
Crew, Elizabeth VI, 173
Crew, Elizabeth VI, 191
Crew, Elizabeth VI, 194
Crew, Elizabeth VI, 196
Crew, Elizabeth VI, 197
Crew, Elizabeth VI, 198
Crew, Elizabeth VI, 213
Crew, Elizabeth VI, 238
Crew, Elizabeth VI, 240
Crew, Elizabeth A. IV, 469
Crew, Elizabeth A. IV, 505
Crew, Elizabeth Ann IV, 469
Crew, Elizabeth Ann IV, 505
Crew, Elizabeth Ann IV, 947
Crew, Elizabeth Ann IV, 993
Crew, Elizabeth Ann VI, 170
Crew, Elizabeth Anna IV, 1013
Crew, Elizabeth Annar IV, 946
Crew, Elizabeth H. IV, 192
Crew, Elizabeth H. IV, 228
Crew, Elizabeth H. IV, 946
Crew, Elizabeth Ladd VI, 238
Crew, Elizabeth M. IV, 708
Crew, Elizabeth M. VI, 166
Crew, Elizabeth M. VI, 201
Crew, Ellison I, 236
Crew, Ellwood IV, 1092
Crew, Ellyson I, 236
Crew, Ellyson VI, 100
Crew, Ellyson VI, 105
Crew, Ellyson VI, 158
Crew, Ellyson VI, 164
Crew, Ellyson VI, 165
Crew, Ellyson VI, 167
Crew, Ellyson VI, 168
Crew, Ellyson VI, 169
Crew, Ellyson VI, 192
Crew, Elwood IV, 1091
Crew, Emily IV, 572
Crew, Emily IV, 940
Crew, Emily IV, 945
Crew, Emily IV, 946
Crew, Emily F. IV, 902
Crew, Emily Jane IV, 945
Crew, Emma IV, 810
Crew, Emma IV, 1092
Crew, Emmor IV, 945
Crew, Emmor IV, 946
Crew, Emmor IV, 947
Crew, Esther IV, 572
Crew, Esther IV, 696
Crew, Esther IV, 945
Crew, Esther IV, 946
Crew, Esther IV, 955
Crew, Esther IV, 960
Crew, Esther IV, 993
Crew, Esther IV, 1005
Crew, Esther IV, 1017
Crew, Esther IV, 1092
Crew, Ethel Francine IV, 974
Crew, Eva IV, 947
Crew, Eva IV, 1092
Crew, Eva C. IV, 946
Crew, Eva C. IV, 947
Crew, Exum VI, 165
Crew, Exum S. VI, 169
Crew, Ezra IV, 1091
Crew, Ezra IV, 1129
Crew, Ezra VI, 165
Crew, Fannie VI, 239
Crew, Fanny I, 383
Crew, Fanny I, 385
Crew, Faris VI, 165
Crew, Faris VI, 170
Crew, Farmer IV, 193
Crew, Farmer IV, 572
Crew, Fleming IV, 696
Crew, Fleming IV, 945
Crew, Fleming IV, 946
Crew, Fleming IV, 985
Crew, Fleming IV, 1052
Crew, Fleming IV, 1068
Crew, Fleming IV, 1091
Crew, Fleming IV, 1092
Crew, Fleming IV, 1109
Crew, Fleming VI, 238
Crew, Frances I, 383
Crew, Frances VI, 239
Crew, Francis I, 383
Crew, Galley VI, 168
Crew, Gallin VI, 167
Crew, Galtry VI, 165
Crew, Garland IV, 696
Crew, Gatley VI, 149
Crew, Gatley VI, 165
Crew, Gatley VI, 166
Crew, Gatley VI, 167
Crew, Gatley VI, 168
Crew, Gatley VI, 169
Crew, Gatley VI, 197
Crew, George IV, 571
Crew, George Lupton IV, 192
Crew, George M. IV, 1091
Crew, George M. IV, 1092
Crew, Gideon IV, 929
Crew, Gideon IV, 945
Crew, Gideon IV, 946
Crew, Gideon IV, 947
Crew, Gideon VI, 168
Crew, Hannah IV, 465
Crew, Hannah IV, 469
Crew, Hannah IV, 514
Crew, Hannah IV, 519
Crew, Hannah IV, 809
Crew, Hannah IV, 946
Crew, Hannah IV, 947
Crew, Hannah V, 39
Crew, Hannah V, 44
Crew, Hannah V, 45
Crew, Hannah V, 730
Crew, Hannah VI, 105
Crew, Hannah VI, 106
Crew, Hannah VI, 113
Crew, Hannah VI, 158
Crew, Hannah VI, 160
Crew, Hannah VI, 164
Crew, Hannah VI, 165
Crew, Hannah VI, 166
Crew, Hannah VI, 167
Crew, Hannah VI, 168
Crew, Hannah VI, 169
Crew, Hannah VI, 170
Crew, Hannah VI, 172
Crew, Hannah VI, 211
Crew, Hannah VI, 215
Crew, Hannah VI, 216
Crew, Hardaman VI, 133
Crew, Hardamon VI, 133
Crew, Hardiman VI, 133
Crew, Hardy VI, 105
Crew, Harriet IV, 946
Crew, Helen C. V, 666
Crew, Henrico VI, 239
Crew, Henrietta IV, 192
Crew, Henrietta VI, 240
Crew, Henry I, 213
Crew, Henry I, 236
Crew, Henry IV, 171
Crew, Henry IV, 185
Crew, Henry IV, 192
Crew, Henry IV, 381
Crew, Henry IV, 463
Crew, Henry IV, 469
Crew, Henry IV, 570
Crew, Henry IV, 572
Crew, Henry IV, 696
Crew, Henry IV, 946
Crew, Henry IV, 947
Crew, Henry IV, 1052
Crew, Henry IV, 1091
Crew, Henry IV, 1092
Crew, Henry V, 165
Crew, Henry V, 666
Crew, Henry VI, 165
Crew, Henry VI, 169
Crew, Henry Carton IV, 1091
Crew, Hiram V, 39
Crew, Hiram V, 44
Crew, Hosea IV, 571
Crew, Hosea IV, 572
Crew, Howard J. IV, 974
Crew, Hulda Jane IV, 798
Crew, Hulda Jane IV, 810
Crew, Huldah IV, 696
Crew, Huldah VI, 169
Crew, Huldah VI, 239
Crew, Huldah VI, 240
Crew, Huldah VI, 271
Crew, Huldah Jane IV, 810
Crew, Ida M. IV, 966
Crew, Ida M. IV, 973
Crew, Ida Mary IV, 946
Crew, Ida Mary IV, 947
Crew, Ida May IV, 193
Crew, Idella IV, 946
Crew, Idella IV, 947
Crew, Idella D. IV, 947
Crew, Idella S. IV, 946
Crew, Idella S. IV, 951
Crew, Isaac I, 213
Crew, Isaac I, 236
Crew, Isaac IV, 193
Crew, Isaac IV, 381
Crew, Isaac IV, 565
Crew, Isaac IV, 571
Crew, Isaac IV, 572
Crew, Isaac IV, 579
Crew, Isaac VI, 99
Crew, Isaac VI, 106
Crew, Isaac VI, 165
Crew, Isaac VI, 170
Crew, Isabell IV, 945
Crew, Isabella IV, 696
Crew, Isabella IV, 934
Crew, Isabella IV, 946
Crew, J. Antram IV, 1006
Crew, Jacob I, 213
Crew, Jacob I, 236
Crew, Jacob IV, 192
Crew, Jacob IV, 374
Crew, Jacob IV, 381
Crew, Jacob IV, 426
Crew, Jacob IV, 469
Crew, Jacob IV, 475
Crew, Jacob IV, 492

Crew, Jacob IV, 505
Crew, Jacob IV, 519
Crew, Jacob IV, 571
Crew, Jacob IV, 572
Crew, Jacob IV, 600
Crew, Jacob IV, 946
Crew, Jacob IV, 1092
Crew, Jacob VI, 98
Crew, Jacob VI, 99
Crew, Jacob VI, 105
Crew, Jacob VI, 106
Crew, Jacob VI, 165
Crew, Jacob VI, 166
Crew, Jacob VI, 167
Crew, Jacob VI, 169
Crew, Jacob VI, 196
Crew, James I, 213
Crew, James I, 236
Crew, James IV, 193
Crew, James IV, 469
Crew, James IV, 567
Crew, James IV, 571
Crew, James IV, 572
Crew, James IV, 595
Crew, James IV, 601
Crew, James IV, 696
Crew, James IV, 809
Crew, James IV, 810
Crew, James IV, 1013
Crew, James IV, 1052
Crew, James IV, 1092
Crew, James V, 484
Crew, James V, 901
Crew, James VI, 101
Crew, James VI, 105
Crew, James VI, 165
Crew, James VI, 166
Crew, James VI, 167
Crew, James VI, 168
Crew, James VI, 169
Crew, James VI, 170
Crew, James VI, 181
Crew, James VI, 198
Crew, James VI, 238
Crew, James VI, 239
Crew, James VI, 240
Crew, James VI, 245
Crew, James VI, 246
Crew, James VI, 252
Crew, James VI, 262
Crew, James VI, 268
Crew, James VI, 269
Crew, James VI, 270
Crew, James VI, 276
Crew, James VI, 291
Crew, James Butler VI, 306
Crew, James H. IV, 946
Crew, James H. IV, 947
Crew, James R. IV, 945
Crew, Jane IV, 810
Crew, Jane IV, 830
Crew, Jane IV, 853
Crew, Jane IV, 946
Crew, Jane VI, 164
Crew, Jane VI, 166
Crew, Jane VI, 211
Crew, Jane VI, 240
Crew, Jane VI, 1004
Crew, Jane T. VI, 240
Crew, Jane Temperance VI, 238
Crew, Jephtha IV, 193
Crew, Jephtha IV, 1092
Crew, Jepthah IV, 571
Crew, Jesse IV, 223
Crew, Jesse IV, 696
Crew, Jesse IV, 1091
Crew, Jesse IV, 1129
Crew, Jesse VI, 101
Crew, Jesse VI, 165
Crew, Jesse VI, 166
Crew, Jesse VI, 169
Crew, Jesse VI, 191
Crew, Jesse VI, 194
Crew, Jesse VI, 216
Crew, Jesse VI, 238
Crew, Jesse VI, 239
Crew, Jesse VI, 240
Crew, Jesse B. IV, 192
Crew, Jesse B. IV, 228
Crew, Jesse B. IV, 946
Crew, Jesse B. VI, 170
Crew, Jesse Milton VI, 166
Crew, Joanna V, 484
Crew, Joel VI, 165
Crew, John I, 213
Crew, John I, 236
Crew, John I, 961
Crew, John I, 1008
Crew, John II, 351
Crew, John II, 498
Crew, John IV, 193
Crew, John IV, 375
Crew, John IV, 381
Crew, John IV, 382
Crew, John IV, 386
Crew, John IV, 431
Crew, John IV, 510
Crew, John IV, 519
Crew, John IV, 567
Crew, John IV, 571
Crew, John IV, 572
Crew, John IV, 696
Crew, John IV, 701
Crew, John IV, 809
Crew, John IV, 902
Crew, John IV, 945
Crew, John IV, 946
Crew, John IV, 953
Crew, John IV, 960
Crew, John IV, 1091
Crew, John IV, 1092
Crew, John IV, 1094
Crew, John V, 44
Crew, John V, 232
Crew, John V, 382
Crew, John V, 484
Crew, John VI, 15
Crew, John VI, 105
Crew, John VI, 106
Crew, John VI, 148
Crew, John VI, 149
Crew, John VI, 153
Crew, John VI, 164
Crew, John VI, 165
Crew, John VI, 166
Crew, John VI, 167
Crew, John VI, 168
Crew, John VI, 169
Crew, John VI, 172
Crew, John VI, 182
Crew, John VI, 186
Crew, John VI, 189
Crew, John VI, 196
Crew, John VI, 209
Crew, John VI, 211
Crew, John VI, 213
Crew, John VI, 291
Crew, John VI, 306
Crew, John A. V, 484
Crew, John C. IV, 193
Crew, John C. IV, 572
Crew, John Ellison V, 44
Crew, John Ellison VI, 105
Crew, John Fleming IV, 1091
Crew, John Fleming IV, 1092
Crew, John H. IV, 1052
Crew, John H. V, 45
Crew, John Hunnicutt VI, 166
Crew, John P. IV, 945
Crew, John P. IV, 946
Crew, John, Jr. VI, 167
Crew, John, Jr. VI, 169
Crew, John, Jr. VI, 172
Crew, John, Jr. VI, 173
Crew, John, Jr. VI, 174
Crew, John, Jr. VI, 238
Crew, John, Sr. VI, 166
Crew, John, Sr. VI, 167
Crew, John, Sr. VI, 168
Crew, Johua IV, 1091
Crew, Jonathan I, 213
Crew, Jonathan I, 236
Crew, Jonathan IV, 696
Crew, Jonathan IV, 810
Crew, Jonathan IV, 945
Crew, Jonathan IV, 946
Crew, Jonathan IV, 1017
Crew, Jonathan Antrim IV, 947
Crew, Jonathan Clarance IV, 1129
Crew, Jonathan Clarence IV, 1129
Crew, Jons. VI, 1004
Crew, Joseph I, 356
Crew, Joseph I, 383
Crew, Joseph I, 593
Crew, Joseph I, 807
Crew, Joseph IV, 381
Crew, Joseph IV, 572
Crew, Joseph IV, 810
Crew, Joseph IV, 947
Crew, Joseph IV, 955
Crew, Joseph IV, 1091
Crew, Joseph IV, 1092
Crew, Joseph VI, 164
Crew, Joseph VI, 165
Crew, Joseph VI, 167
Crew, Joseph VI, 168
Crew, Joseph VI, 169
Crew, Joseph VI, 176
Crew, Joseph VI, 185
Crew, Joseph VI, 198
Crew, Joseph VI, 238
Crew, Joseph VI, 239
Crew, Joseph VI, 273
Crew, Joseph B. IV, 946
Crew, Joseph Leander IV, 572
Crew, Joseph Leander IV, 946
Crew, Joseph, Jr. VI, 167
Crew, Joseph, Jr. VI, 173
Crew, Joshua I, 213
Crew, Joshua I, 961
Crew, Joshua IV, 696
Crew, Joshua IV, 764
Crew, Joshua IV, 945
Crew, Joshua IV, 946
Crew, Joshua IV, 997
Crew, Joshua IV, 1018
Crew, Joshua IV, 1052
Crew, Joshua IV, 1091
Crew, Joshua IV, 1092
Crew, Joshua V, 44
Crew, Joshua V, 232
Crew, Joshua V, 382
Crew, Joshua VI, 105
Crew, Joshua VI, 106
Crew, Joshua VI, 165
Crew, Joshua VI, 239
Crew, Joshua VI, 240
Crew, Joshua F. IV, 1092
Crew, Joshua II VI, 105
Crew, Josiah I, 236
Crew, Josiah IV, 193
Crew, Josiah IV, 381
Crew, Josiah VI, 167
Crew, Josiah VI, 168
Crew, Josiah VI, 169
Crew, Josiah VI, 200
Crew, Josiah W. V, 45
Crew, Judith I, 213
Crew, Judith I, 236
Crew, Judith I, 1008
Crew, Judith IV, 381
Crew, Judith IV, 382
Crew, Judith IV, 565
Crew, Judith IV, 571
Crew, Judith IV, 593
Crew, Judith IV, 696
Crew, Judith IV, 707
Crew, Judith IV, 809
Crew, Judith IV, 810
Crew, Judith IV, 945
Crew, Judith IV, 946
Crew, Judith V, 44
Crew, Judith V, 232
Crew, Judith V, 382
Crew, Judith VI, 99
Crew, Judith VI, 105
Crew, Judith VI, 106
Crew, Judith VI, 165
Crew, Judith VI, 167
Crew, Judith VI, 168
Crew, Judith VI, 169
Crew, Judith VI, 182
Crew, Judith VI, 238
Crew, Judith VI, 239
Crew, Judith VI, 240
Crew, Judith VI, 245
Crew, Judith VI, 246
Crew, Judith VI, 268
Crew, Judith Ann IV, 946
Crew, Judith Terrell VI, 241
Crew, Kate IV, 572
Crew, Lancelot VI, 170
Crew, Lancelot VI, 238
Crew, Lancelot VI, 240
Crew, Laura IV, 978
Crew, Laura IV, 1006
Crew, Laura Jane IV, 946
Crew, Lauretta C. IV, 902
Crew, Lavina V, 44
Crew, Lavina V, 45
Crew, Lavina V, 92
Crew, Lemuel IV, 192
Crew, Lemuel IV, 696
Crew, Lemuel VI, 166
Crew, Lemuel VI, 170
Crew, Lemuel VI, 178
Crew, Lemuel VI, 179
Crew, Lemuel VI, 240
Crew, Lemuel VI, 272
Crew, Lemuel Hargaves VI, 238
Crew, Leon Mahlon IV, 974
Crew, Letilberry I, 1047
Crew, Lewindy IV, 810
Crew, Linwood David IV, 946
Crew, Littleberry I, 876
Crew, Littleberry I, 1047
Crew, Littleberry IV, 696
Crew, Littleberry IV, 809
Crew, Littleberry V, 734
Crew, Littleberry VI, 238
Crew, Littleberry VI, 240
Crew, Littleberry VI, 269
Crew, Littlebery IV, 696
Crew, Littlebery IV, 858
Crew, Littlebury VI, 238
Crew, Littlebury VI, 239
Crew, Littlebury VI, 271
Crew, Louisa VI, 241
Crew, Lucinda IV, 810
Crew, Lucinda IV, 825
Crew, Lucy I, 383
Crew, Lucy I, 807
Crew, Lucy IV, 565
Crew, Lucy IV, 571
Crew, Lucy IV, 572
Crew, Lucy IV, 590
Crew, Lucy VI, 239
Crew, Lucy B. VI, 240
Crew, Lucy Bell VI, 238
Crew, Lucy E. IV, 1091
Crew, Lucy E. IV, 1092
Crew, Lydia IV, 193
Crew, Lydia IV, 572
Crew, Lydia IV, 851
Crew, Lydia IV, 945
Crew, Lydia IV, 1012
Crew, Lydia IV, 1013
Crew, Lydia IV, 1092
Crew, Lydia VI, 165
Crew, Lydia VI, 167
Crew, Lydia VI, 169
Crew, Lydia VI, 192
Crew, Lydia S. IV, 1092
Crew, Lydia S. IV, 1115
Crew, Mahlon IV, 810
Crew, Mahlon IV, 946
Crew, Mahlon IV, 947
Crew, Mahlon IV, 973
Crew, Malcohm IV, 810
Crew, Malcom IV, 810
Crew, Malcom IV, 853
Crew, Margaret IV, 171
Crew, Margaret IV, 192
Crew, Margaret IV, 193
Crew, Margaret IV, 463
Crew, Margaret IV, 469
Crew, Margaret IV, 696
Crew, Margaret IV, 800
Crew, Margaret IV, 810
Crew, Margaret IV, 917
Crew, Margaret IV, 927
Crew, Margaret IV, 946
Crew, Margaret IV, 1007
Crew, Margaret VI, 105
Crew, Margaret VI, 110
Crew, Margaret VI, 111
Crew, Margaret VI, 165
Crew, Margaret VI, 166
Crew, Margaret VI, 168
Crew, Margaret VI, 169
Crew, Margaret VI, 190
Crew, Margaret VI, 193
Crew, Margaret VI, 201
Crew, Margaret VI, 228
Crew, Margaret VI, 238
Crew, Margaret VI, 239
Crew, Margaret VI, 240
Crew, Margaret VI, 265
Crew, Margaret E. IV, 192
Crew, Margaret E. V, 484
Crew, Margaret E. VI, 240
Crew, Margaret Owen VI, 166
Crew, Margaret T. VI, 240
Crew, Margaret Talitha VI, 238
Crew, Margery IV, 696
Crew, Margery IV, 701
Crew, Margery IV, 902
Crew, Margery IV, 945
Crew, Margery IV, 946
Crew, Margery IV, 947
Crew, Margery IV, 953
Crew, Margery IV, 960
Crew, Mariam IV, 381
Crew, Mariam IV, 431
Crew, Mariam IV, 572
Crew, Martha I, 213
Crew, Martha I, 236
Crew, Martha IV, 193
Crew, Martha IV, 382
Crew, Martha IV, 410
Crew, Martha IV, 810
Crew, Martha IV, 853
Crew, Martha IV, 1092
Crew, Martha IV, 1094
Crew, Martha V, 44
Crew, Martha V, 110
Crew, Martha VI, 101
Crew, Martha VI, 105
Crew, Martha VI, 106
Crew, Martha VI, 166
Crew, Martha VI, 167
Crew, Martha VI, 168
Crew, Martha VI, 240
Crew, Martha Louis VI, 238
Crew, Martin IV, 1129
Crew, Mary I, 213
Crew, Mary I, 236
Crew, Mary I, 252
Crew, Mary I, 383
Crew, Mary I, 397
Crew, Mary I, 535
Crew, Mary IV, 193
Crew, Mary IV, 365
Crew, Mary IV, 381
Crew, Mary IV, 382
Crew, Mary IV, 469
Crew, Mary IV, 475
Crew, Mary IV, 566
Crew, Mary IV, 571
Crew, Mary IV, 572
Crew, Mary IV, 573
Crew, Mary IV, 696
Crew, Mary IV, 707
Crew, Mary IV, 743
Crew, Mary IV, 784
Crew, Mary IV, 902
Crew, Mary IV, 927
Crew, Mary IV, 934
Crew, Mary IV, 945
Crew, Mary IV, 946
Crew, Mary IV, 947
Crew, Mary IV, 993
Crew, Mary IV, 1000
Crew, Mary IV, 1005
Crew, Mary IV, 1011
Crew, Mary IV, 1017
Crew, Mary IV, 1052
Crew, Mary IV, 1091
Crew, Mary IV, 1096
Crew, Mary IV, 1129
Crew, Mary IV, 1130
Crew, Mary V, 67
Crew, Mary V, 484
Crew, Mary V, 514
Crew, Mary VI, 27
Crew, Mary VI, 28
Crew, Mary VI, 37
Crew, Mary VI, 101
Crew, Mary VI, 158
Crew, Mary VI, 160
Crew, Mary VI, 164
Crew, Mary VI, 165
Crew, Mary VI, 166
Crew, Mary VI, 167
Crew, Mary VI, 168
Crew, Mary VI, 169
Crew, Mary VI, 170
Crew, Mary VI, 173
Crew, Mary VI, 176
Crew, Mary VI, 181
Crew, Mary VI, 189
Crew, Mary VI, 191
Crew, Mary VI, 194
Crew, Mary VI, 197
Crew, Mary VI, 198
Crew, Mary VI, 200
Crew, Mary VI, 213
Crew, Mary VI, 238
Crew, Mary VI, 239
Crew, Mary VI, 240
Crew, Mary VI, 262
Crew, Mary VI, 269
Crew, Mary VI, 271
Crew, Mary A. IV, 381
Crew, Mary A. IV, 382
Crew, Mary Ann IV, 600
Crew, Mary B. IV, 572
Crew, Mary B. IV, 1050
Crew, Mary B. IV, 1052
Crew, Mary B. IV, 1055
Crew, Mary B. IV, 1092
Crew, Mary C. IV, 1052
Crew, Mary C. IV, 1068
Crew, Mary Catharine IV, 946
Crew, Mary Ellen IV, 902
Crew, Mary Ellen IV, 1000
Crew, Mary H. IV, 469
Crew, Mary H. IV, 519
Crew, Mary H. IV, 902
Crew, Mary H. IV, 1249
Crew, Mary H. IV, 1275
Crew, Mary L. IV, 1052
Crew, Mary L. IV, 1091
Crew, Mary L. IV, 1092
Crew, Mary L. IV, 1102
Crew, Mary Maria IV, 946
Crew, Mary R. VI, 240
Crew, Mary Rice VI, 238
Crew, Massey VI, 164
Crew, Massey VI, 166
Crew, Massey VI, 185
Crew, Matilda IV, 1052
Crew, Matilda V, 382

Crew, Matilda M. IV, 810
Crew, Matilda M. IV, 828
Crew, Matilda P. IV, 810
Crew, Menalcas V, 734
Crew, Menalcas Stanley V, 734
Crew, Menalcus S. V, 734
Crew, Meriam VI, 170
Crew, Merriam IV, 946
Crew, Micajah IV, 192
Crew, Micajah VI, 165
Crew, Micajah VI, 166
Crew, Micajah VI, 168
Crew, Micajah VI, 190
Crew, Micajah VI, 193
Crew, Micajah VI, 228
Crew, Micajah VI, 238
Crew, Micajah VI, 239
Crew, Micajah VI, 240
Crew, Micajah VI, 247
Crew, Micajah VI, 262
Crew, Micajah VI, 276
Crew, Micajah VI, 306
Crew, Micajah VI, 333
Crew, Micajah L. VI, 240
Crew, Micajah Lemuel VI, 238
Crew, Micajah, Jr. VI, 239
Crew, Micajah, Jr. VI, 306
Crew, Mildred IV, 696
Crew, Mildred VI, 240
Crew, Milley IV, 808
Crew, Milley IV, 809
Crew, Milley IV, 810
Crew, Milley IV, 945
Crew, Milley IV, 1052
Crew, Milley IV, 1091
Crew, Milley VI, 238
Crew, Millie IV, 1018
Crew, Milly IV, 696
Crew, Milly IV, 764
Crew, Milly IV, 946
Crew, Milly IV, 997
Crew, Milton IV, 572
Crew, Miriam IV, 193
Crew, Miriam IV, 375
Crew, Miriam IV, 382
Crew, Miriam IV, 945
Crew, Miriam IV, 1091
Crew, Miriam IV, 1092
Crew, Miriam VI, 133
Crew, Miriam VI, 153
Crew, Miriam VI, 165
Crew, Miriam VI, 166
Crew, Miriam VI, 169
Crew, Miriam H. VI, 131
Crew, Miriam H. VI, 134
Crew, Miriam, Jr. VI, 170
Crew, Molley VI, 165
Crew, Molly VI, 169
Crew, Molly VI, 216
Crew, Mourning VI, 15
Crew, Mourning VI, 166
Crew, Mourning VI, 168
Crew, Nancy IV, 192
Crew, Nancy IV, 259
Crew, Nancy IV, 696
Crew, Nancy IV, 766
Crew, Nancy IV, 810
Crew, Nancy IV, 945
Crew, Nancy IV, 946
Crew, Nancy IV, 997
Crew, Nancy V, 730
Crew, Nancy V, 731
Crew, Nancy V, 734
Crew, Nancy V, 800
Crew, Nancy VI, 165
Crew, Nancy VI, 166
Crew, Nancy VI, 169
Crew, Nancy VI, 170
Crew, Nancy VI, 191
Crew, Nancy VI, 209
Crew, Nancy VI, 238
Crew, Nancy VI, 239
Crew, Nancy VI, 274
Crew, Nancy VI, 276
Crew, Nancy C. IV, 830
Crew, Nancy T. IV, 192
Crew, Nancy T. IV, 259
Crew, Nancy T. VI, 170
Crew, Narcissa IV, 469
Crew, Narcissa IV, 490
Crew, Narcissa VI, 133
Crew, Narcissa VI, 166
Crew, Narcissa VI, 170
Crew, Nathaniel E. VI, 240
Crew, Nathaniel Edmund VI, 238
Crew, Nathaniel Jarrett IV, 696
Crew, Nellie IV, 810
Crew, Nicholas VI, 238
Crew, Nicholas VI, 240
Crew, Nicholas VI, 305
Crew, Nicholas VI, 306
Crew, Obadiah IV, 696
Crew, Obadiah IV, 927
Crew, Obadiah IV, 934
Crew, Obadiah IV, 945
Crew, Obadiah IV, 947
Crew, Obadiah IV, 1000
Crew, Obadiah IV, 1005
Crew, Obadiah IV, 1011
Crew, Obadiah VI, 238
Crew, Obadiah VI, 239
Crew, Obadiah VI, 262
Crew, Obediah IV, 707
Crew, Obediah IV, 743
Crew, Obediah IV, 784
Crew, Obediah IV, 902
Crew, Obediah VI, 170
Crew, Obediah VI, 238
Crew, Obediah VI, 240
Crew, Oliver IV, 193
Crew, Oliver IV, 572
Crew, Oris D. IV, 947
Crew, Orris D. IV, 946
Crew, Orris D. IV, 947
Crew, Orris David IV, 946
Crew, Osborn IV, 572
Crew, Osborn IV, 1092
Crew, Owen Milton VI, 166
Crew, Owen Milton VI, 238
Crew, Owen Milton VI, 240
Crew, Peggy VI, 166
Crew, Peggy VI, 169
Crew, Peggy VI, 191
Crew, Peggy VI, 194
Crew, Peggy VI, 240
Crew, Peggy VI, 257
Crew, Peter VI, 101
Crew, Peter VI, 169
Crew, Phariba IV, 572
Crew, Phariba IV, 1052
Crew, Phebe I, 807
Crew, Phebe IV, 810
Crew, Phebe IV, 849
Crew, Phebe IV, 946
Crew, Phebe IV, 947
Crew, Phebe IV, 973
Crew, Phebe IV, 1129
Crew, Phebe V, 45
Crew, Phebe Ann IV, 946
Crew, Phebe Ann IV, 947
Crew, Phebe Ann IV, 967
Crew, Phebe Jane IV, 696
Crew, Phebe Jane IV, 780
Crew, Pheriba IV, 1091
Crew, Pleasant V, 666
Crew, Pleasant VI, 166
Crew, Priscilla IV, 381
Crew, Priscilla IV, 382
Crew, Rachel I, 236
Crew, Rachel I, 535
Crew, Rachel IV, 192
Crew, Rachel IV, 193
Crew, Rachel IV, 374
Crew, Rachel IV, 375
Crew, Rachel IV, 381
Crew, Rachel IV, 382
Crew, Rachel IV, 391
Crew, Rachel IV, 426
Crew, Rachel IV, 456
Crew, Rachel IV, 465
Crew, Rachel IV, 519
Crew, Rachel IV, 571
Crew, Rachel IV, 572
Crew, Rachel IV, 600
Crew, Rachel IV, 696
Crew, Rachel IV, 708
Crew, Rachel IV, 945
Crew, Rachel IV, 946
Crew, Rachel IV, 1091
Crew, Rachel IV, 1129
Crew, Rachel IV, 1130
Crew, Rachel V, 45
Crew, Rachel VI, 98
Crew, Rachel VI, 99
Crew, Rachel VI, 105
Crew, Rachel VI, 106
Crew, Rachel VI, 166
Crew, Rachel VI, 170
Crew, Rachel VI, 209
Crew, Rachel VI, 210
Crew, Rachel VI, 306
Crew, Rachel A. IV, 1006
Crew, Rachel B. IV, 1088
Crew, Rachel B. IV, 1092
Crew, Rachel F. IV, 382
Crew, Rachel F. IV, 572
Crew, Rana VI, 165
Crew, Raney VI, 170
Crew, Rebecca IV, 193
Crew, Rebecca IV, 381
Crew, Rebecca IV, 382
Crew, Rebecca IV, 426
Crew, Rebecca IV, 427
Crew, Rebecca IV, 571
Crew, Rebecca IV, 572
Crew, Rebecca IV, 573
Crew, Rebecca IV, 590
Crew, Rebecca IV, 591
Crew, Rebecca IV, 593
Crew, Rebecca IV, 595
Crew, Rebecca IV, 696
Crew, Rebecca IV, 708
Crew, Rebecca IV, 810
Crew, Rebecca IV, 853
Crew, Rebecca IV, 927
Crew, Rebecca IV, 929
Crew, Rebecca IV, 945
Crew, Rebecca IV, 946
Crew, Rebecca IV, 947
Crew, Rebecca IV, 1091
Crew, Rebecca IV, 1092
Crew, Rebecca V, 44
Crew, Rebecca V, 45
Crew, Rebecca J. IV, 1129
Crew, Rebecca J. IV, 1134
Crew, Rebecca W. IV, 382
Crew, Rebeckah VI, 165
Crew, Rebeckah VI, 170
Crew, Rhoda I, 535
Crew, Robert I, 236
Crew, Robert I, 247
Crew, Robert IV, 192
Crew, Robert IV, 193
Crew, Robert IV, 259
Crew, Robert IV, 571
Crew, Robert IV, 800
Crew, Robert IV, 810
Crew, Robert IV, 917
Crew, Robert IV, 927
Crew, Robert IV, 946
Crew, Robert IV, 993
Crew, Robert IV, 1007
Crew, Robert IV, 1092
Crew, Robert V, 730
Crew, Robert VI, 15
Crew, Robert VI, 149
Crew, Robert VI, 164
Crew, Robert VI, 165
Crew, Robert VI, 166
Crew, Robert VI, 167
Crew, Robert VI, 168
Crew, Robert VI, 169
Crew, Robert VI, 170
Crew, Robert VI, 171
Crew, Robert VI, 172
Crew, Robert VI, 188
Crew, Robert VI, 191
Crew, Robert VI, 209
Crew, Robert VI, 238
Crew, Robert VI, 274
Crew, Robert VI, 276
Crew, Robert C. VI, 181
Crew, Robert F. IV, 193
Crew, Robert Hunnicutt VI, 165
Crew, Robert T. IV, 193
Crew, Robert T. IV, 223
Crew, Robert T. IV, 946
Crew, Robert T. IV, 965
Crew, Robert Terrill IV, 192
Crew, Robt. VI, 188
Crew, Ruth IV, 810
Crew, Ruth IV, 835
Crew, Ruth VI, 158
Crew, Ruth VI, 160
Crew, Ruth VI, 165
Crew, Ruth VI, 168
Crew, Ruth Ann IV, 810
Crew, Ruth Anna IV, 192
Crew, Ruth Anna IV, 808
Crew, Ruth Anna IV, 810
Crew, Ruthanna IV, 193
Crew, Ruthanna IV, 223
Crew, Ruthanna IV, 1129
Crew, Salley Leadbetter VI, 165
Crew, Samuel IV, 193
Crew, Samuel VI, 169
Crew, Samuel H. IV, 192
Crew, Samuel H. VI, 240
Crew, Samuel I. VI, 240
Crew, Samuel Izard VI, 238
Crew, Sarah I, 236
Crew, Sarah I, 593
Crew, Sarah I, 779
Crew, Sarah I, 807
Crew, Sarah I, 829
Crew, Sarah IV, 193
Crew, Sarah IV, 465
Crew, Sarah IV, 469
Crew, Sarah IV, 490
Crew, Sarah IV, 567
Crew, Sarah IV, 571
Crew, Sarah IV, 572
Crew, Sarah IV, 595
Crew, Sarah IV, 601
Crew, Sarah IV, 696
Crew, Sarah IV, 743
Crew, Sarah IV, 808
Crew, Sarah IV, 810
Crew, Sarah IV, 850
Crew, Sarah IV, 945
Crew, Sarah IV, 1052
Crew, Sarah IV, 1091
Crew, Sarah IV, 1092
Crew, Sarah IV, 1119
Crew, Sarah V, 44
Crew, Sarah V, 45
Crew, Sarah VI, 106
Crew, Sarah VI, 133
Crew, Sarah VI, 137
Crew, Sarah VI, 153
Crew, Sarah VI, 164
Crew, Sarah VI, 165
Crew, Sarah VI, 166
Crew, Sarah VI, 167
Crew, Sarah VI, 168
Crew, Sarah VI, 169
Crew, Sarah VI, 170
Crew, Sarah VI, 171
Crew, Sarah VI, 172
Crew, Sarah VI, 173
Crew, Sarah VI, 185
Crew, Sarah VI, 189
Crew, Sarah VI, 213
Crew, Sarah VI, 214
Crew, Sarah VI, 220
Crew, Sarah VI, 221
Crew, Sarah VI, 238
Crew, Sarah VI, 239
Crew, Sarah VI, 240
Crew, Sarah VI, 256
Crew, Sarah Ann IV, 192
Crew, Sarah Ann IV, 244
Crew, Sarah Ann IV, 469
Crew, Sarah Ann IV, 484
Crew, Sarah Ann IV, 946
Crew, Sarah Ann IV, 985
Crew, Sarah Ann IV, 1091
Crew, Sarah Ann IV, 1109
Crew, Sarah Ann V, 484
Crew, Sarah Ann VI, 133
Crew, Sarah Ann VI, 170
Crew, Sarah B. VI, 238
Crew, Sarah B. VI, 240
Crew, Sarah Bacon VI, 238
Crew, Sarah Crispe VI, 181
Crew, Sarah D. IV, 572
Crew, Sarah E. IV, 1091
Crew, Sarah E. IV, 1092
Crew, Sarah J. IV, 917
Crew, Sarah Jane IV, 946
Crew, Sarah Jane IV, 1007
Crew, Sarah Jane IV, 1129
Crew, Sarah L. IV, 1092
Crew, Sarah L. IV, 1119
Crew, Sarah Ladd V, 44
Crew, Sarah Ladd VI, 105
Crew, Sarah Lizzie IV, 572
Crew, Sibyl E. IV, 974
Crew, Sucai VI, 239
Crew, Sucky VI, 238
Crew, Susan U. VI, 240
Crew, Susan Unity VI, 238
Crew, Susanna I, 231
Crew, Susanna I, 236
Crew, Susanna I, 383
Crew, Susanna I, 410
Crew, Susanna IV, 810
Crew, Susanna IV, 853
Crew, Susanna IV, 1092
Crew, Susanna IV, 1101
Crew, Susanna VI, 154
Crew, Susanna VI, 170
Crew, Susanna VI, 238
Crew, Susanna VI, 240
Crew, Susannah IV, 1092
Crew, Susannah VI, 165
Crew, Tabitha IV, 193
Crew, Tabitha IV, 572
Crew, Tabitha VI, 240
Crew, Tace VI, 228
Crew, Tace VI, 229
Crew, Tace VI, 238
Crew, Tace VI, 239
Crew, Tace D. VI, 240
Crew, Tallitha VI, 238
Crew, Tarleton IV, 192
Crew, Tarlton VI, 240
Crew, Terrell IV, 1091
Crew, Terrell IV, 1092
Crew, Terrell VI, 165
Crew, Terrell VI, 170
Crew, Theopilus IV, 192
Crew, Theresa Mary IV, 946
Crew, Thomas IV, 572
Crew, Thomas IV, 696
Crew, Thomas IV, 810
Crew, Thomas IV, 945
Crew, Thomas IV, 946
Crew, Thomas IV, 1091
Crew, Thomas IV, 1092
Crew, Thomas VI, 101
Crew, Thomas VI, 166
Crew, Thomas VI, 168
Crew, Thomas VI, 201
Crew, Thomas C. V, 484
Crew, Thomas Elwood IV, 1091
Crew, Thomas F. VI, 240
Crew, Thomas Joseph IV, 193
Crew, Thomas, Sr. VI, 101
Crew, ThomasL, Jr. VI, 101
Crew, Thos. IV, 922
Crew, Thos. F. V, 901
Crew, Thressa M. IV, 1013
Crew, Unity IV, 696
Crew, Unity IV, 770
Crew, Unity IV, 945
Crew, Unity IV, 1005
Crew, Unity VI, 228
Crew, Unity VI, 229
Crew, Unity VI, 238
Crew, Unity VI, 239
Crew, Unity VI, 268
Crew, Unity VI, 271
Crew, Unity VI, 731
Crew, Unity VI, 737
Crew, Vera Viola IV, 974
Crew, Walter IV, 192
Crew, Walter VI, 238
Crew, Walter VI, 240
Crew, Walter F. VI, 240
Crew, Walter Fleming VI, 238
Crew, Wd. Elizabeth VI, 174
Crew, Wd. lizabeth VI, 189
Crew, Wd. Mary VI, 197
Crew, Will VI, 167
Crew, William IV, 192
Crew, William IV, 193
Crew, William IV, 365
Crew, William IV, 381
Crew, William IV, 572
Crew, William IV, 810
Crew, William IV, 1091
Crew, William IV, 1129
Crew, William VI, 164
Crew, William VI, 166
Crew, William VI, 167
Crew, William VI, 168
Crew, William VI, 170
Crew, William VI, 211
Crew, William VI, 238
Crew, William VI, 239
Crew, William VI, 240
Crew, William VI, 241
Crew, William Allison IV, 1129
Crew, William B. IV, 1091
Crew, William H. IV, 469
Crew, William Henry IV, 469
Crew, William Lane VI, 167
Crew, William R. VI, 240
Crew, William Rice VI, 240
Crew, William T. IV, 600
Crew, Wilson IV, 946
Crew, Winna I, 236
Crew, Winne I, 236
Crew, Winney I, 236
Crew, Winney I, 247
Crew, Winona V, 666
Crew, Winona B. IV, 469
Crew, Winona B. V, 666
Crew, Wm. IV, 192
Crew, Wm. IV, 566
Crew, Wm. IV, 593
Crew, Wm. IV, 1052
Crew, Wm. IV, 1096
Crew, Wm. IV, 1130
Crew, Wm. B. IV, 1092
Crew, Wm. H. IV, 946
Crew, Wm. Henry IV, 708
Crew, Wm. Henry IV, 946
Crew, Wm. Henry V, 666
Crew, Wrenny VI, 856
Crew, Zachariah E. IV, 945
Crew, Zechariah E. IV, 946
Crewdson, Mary Eleanor III, 218
Crews, Agness VI, 810
Crews, Alfeus V, 484
Crews, Amy VI, 924
Crews, Andrew VI, 105
Crews, Ann V, 44
Crews, Ann VI, 808
Crews, Anna V, 22
Crews, Asa VI, 899
Crews, Benjamin VI, 105
Crews, Carriline VI, 931
Crews, Catharine VI, 983

Crews, Charlotte VI, 864
Crews, Clary VI, 899
Crews, David I, 911
Crews, David VI, 899
Crews, David M. V, 534
Crews, David P. M. VI, 808
Crews, Dawcella VI, 808
Crews, Dr. J. VI, 841
Crews, Edward VI, 899
Crews, Elesebeth VI, 819
Crews, Elizabeth I, 807
Crews, Elizabeth V, 45
Crews, Elizabeth V, 143
Crews, Elizabeth VI, 808
Crews, Ellyson VI, 105
Crews, Gideon VI, 808
Crews, Gideon VI, 899
Crews, Gideon VI, 946
Crews, Hannah I, 535
Crews, Hannah I, 579
Crews, Hannah V, 484
Crews, Hannah V, 557
Crews, Huldah I, 445
Crews, Isaac VI, 808
Crews, Isaac VI, 810
Crews, Isaac VI, 811
Crews, Israel V, 534
Crews, Jacob V, 534
Crews, James V, 484
Crews, James VI, 808
Crews, James VI, 811
Crews, James P. VI, 808
Crews, Jesse VI, 339
Crews, Jesse VI, 882
Crews, Jesse VI, 883
Crews, Jesse VI, 899
Crews, Jesse VI, 924
Crews, Jesse VI, 997
Crews, Jesse Frank V, 534
Crews, Joanna V, 484
Crews, John V, 484
Crews, John VI, 803
Crews, John VI, 808
Crews, John VI, 899
Crews, John A. V, 484
Crews, John H. V, 45
Crews, Joseph I, 593
Crews, Joseph I, 907
Crews, Joseph VI, 808
Crews, Joseph VI, 899
Crews, Joseph VI, 921
Crews, Joseph VI, 931
Crews, Joseph VI, 989
Crews, Josiah VI, 808
Crews, Josiah VI, 819
Crews, Josiah VI, 862
Crews, Josiah VI, 864
Crews, Judith VI, 808
Crews, Lauraina VI, 899
Crews, Letilberry I, 1047
Crews, Liddy VI, 899
Crews, Lindsay VI, 899
Crews, Littleberry VI, 808
Crews, Lucy VI, 899
Crews, Margaret VI, 105
Crews, Margaret VI, 862
Crews, Margaret E. V, 484
Crews, Martha VI, 841
Crews, Martha VI, 919
Crews, Martha Ann VI, 946
Crews, Martha B. VI, 899
Crews, Martha J. VI, 989
Crews, Martha W. VI, 822
Crews, Mary I, 535
Crews, Mary V, 484
Crews, Mary V, 557
Crews, Mary V, 573
Crews, Mary VI, 339
Crews, Mary VI, 808
Crews, Mary VI, 997
Crews, Mary Ann VI, 808
Crews, Mary F. VI, 921
Crews, Mary I. VI, 808
Crews, Mary J. VI, 808
Crews, Mary Jane VI, 899
Crews, Nancy VI, 819
Crews, Nancy VI, 899
Crews, Nancy VI, 983
Crews, Nicholas VI, 808
Crews, Obediah VI, 808
Crews, Patsy VI, 811
Crews, Phebe I, 806
Crews, Phebe I, 807
Crews, Phebe V, 45
Crews, Polly VI, 803
Crews, Polly VI, 899
Crews, Polly VI, 991
Crews, Polly M. VI, 808
Crews, Rachal VI, 882
Crews, Rachel I, 535
Crews, Rachel VI, 808
Crews, Rebecca V, 45
Crews, Rebecca V, 557
Crews, Rhoda I, 535
Crews, Ruth V, 557
Crews, Ruth V, 600
Crews, Sarah I, 807
Crews, Sarah I, 907
Crews, Sarah I, 911
Crews, Sarah V, 45
Crews, Sarah V, 144
Crews, Sarah V, 484
Crews, Sarah V, 534
Crews, Sarah Ann V, 484
Crews, Sarah E. V, 534
Crews, Sena VI, 899
Crews, Susannah V, 484
Crews, Susannah V, 533
Crews, Thomas C. V, 484
Crews, William VI, 803
Crews, William VI, 808
Crews, William VI, 819
Crews, Wrenny VI, 810
Criddle, Finch VI, 984
Criddle, Franky VI, 874
Criddle, James VI, 809
Criddle, Jemima VI, 809
Criddle, Keziah VI, 828
Criddlebow, Minnie I, 920
Criddlebow, Mrs. Minnie I, 937
Criddlebow, Mrs. Minnie I, 940
Crider, Fred IV, 1312
Crider, Fred C. IV, 1312
Crider, Henry VI, 809
Crider, John V, 991
Crider, John F. V, 991
Crider, Joseph M. V, 991
Crider, Mary L. V, 991
Crider, Pamelia VI, 809
Crim, Garfield VI, 484
Crim, James II, 212
Crim, James II, 285
Crim, James II, 854
Crim, James II, 879
Crim, John I. VI, 484
Crim, Julia VI, 484
Crim, Mary II, 171
Crim, Mary II, 212
Crim, Mary II, 285
Crim, Mary II, 735
Crim, Mary II, 854
Crim, Mary II, 879
Crim, Mary S. II, 854
Crim, Mary S. II, 879
Crinshaw, Ann C. VI, 60
Crinshaw, Ann C. VI, 80
Crinshaw, Mary J. D. VI, 60
Crinshaw, Nathaniel C. VI, 60
Crinshaw, Nathaniel C. Crinshaw VI, 80
Cripo, Jacob VI, 900
Cripo, Sally VI, 900
Crippen, Catharine IV, 469
Crippen, Henry IV, 469
Crippen, Ora IV, 469
Crippen, Robert IV, 469
Crippen, Sarah IV, 469
Crippen, William IV, 469
Crippin, Catharine IV, 469
Crippin, Henry IV, 469
Crippin, Sarah IV, 469
Crippin, William IV, 469
Cripps, Ann II, 553
Cripps, Anne II, 212
Cripps, Benjamin II, 63
Cripps, Benjamin II, 64
Cripps, Benjamin II, 212
Cripps, Benjamin II, 233
Cripps, Elizabeth II, 64
Cripps, Hannah II, 63
Cripps, Hannah II, 86
Cripps, Hannah II, 204
Cripps, Hannah II, 212
Cripps, Hannah II, 237
Cripps, Hannah II, 498
Cripps, Hannah II, 552
Cripps, John II, 64
Cripps, John II, 163
Cripps, John II, 212
Cripps, Martha II, 64
Cripps, Martha II, 80
Cripps, Martha II, 212
Cripps, Mary II, 51
Cripps, Mary II, 63
Cripps, Mary II, 163
Cripps, Mary II, 212
Cripps, Mary II, 233
Cripps, Mary Andrews II, 64
Cripps, Nathaniel II, 63
Cripps, Nathaniel II, 212
Cripps, Samuel II, 212
Cripps, Samuel II, 237
Cripps, Samuel II, 498
Cripps, Samuel II, 552
Cripps, Virgin II, 212
Cripps, Virgin II, 243
Cripps, Virgin II, 250
Cripps, Whitton II, 64
Cripps, Whitton II, 80
Crips, Ann II, 270
Crips, Ann II, 553
Crips, Benjamin II, 63
Crips, Hannah II, 212
Crips, John II, 171
Crips, Martha II, 20
Crips, Martha II, 127
Crips, Martha II, 212
Crips, Mary II, 20
Crips, Mary II, 63
Crips, Mary II, 127
Crips, Mary II, 171
Crips, Mary II, 212
Crips, Nathaniel II, 171
Crips, Nathaniel II, 212
Crips, Samuel II, 212
Crips, Theophila II, 171
Crips, Whitton II, 20
Crips, Whitton II, 127
Cripsol, Jacob VI, 899
Cripsol, Sally VI, 899
Crisco, Armelia I, 876
Crisco, Armelia I, 885
Crisco, Asenath I, 876
Crisco, Asenath I, 904
Crisco, Enoch I, 876
Crisco, Hannah M. I, 758
Crisco, Ida I, 876
Crisco, Ida I, 895
Crisco, John I, 876
Crisco, John H. I, 852
Crisco, Joseph A. I, 744
Crisco, Martha I, 939
Crisco, Sybil C. I, 876
Crisco, William P. I, 876
Criscow, Addison I, 758
Criscow, Hannah M. I, 758
Criscow, John I, 758
Criscow, John C. I, 758
Criscow, Joseph A. I, 758
Crisinbery, Floyd V, 557
Crisinbery, Floyd Vernon V, 557
Crisinbery, Grace V, 557
Crisinbery, Mildred V, 557
Crisinbery, Mildred Elizabeth V, 557
Crisinbery, Nancy V, 557
Crisinbery, P. V. V, 557
Crisinbery, Peter V. V, 557
Crisinbery, Wm. V, 557
Crisman, Catherine II, 351
Crisman, Mary H. IV, 696
Crisp, Sarah VI, 170
Crispe, Elizabeth VI, 155
Crispe, Elizabeth VI, 171
Crispe, Mary VI, 164
Crispe, Sarah VI, 164
Crispe, Sarah VI, 166
Crispe, Sarah VI, 170
Crispe, Sarah VI, 171
Crispe, Thomas VI, 171
Crispen, ??? III, 91
Crispen, David V, 445
Crispen, Elizabeth V, 45
Crispen, Hannah IV, 945
Crispen, Hews II, 128
Crispen, Jeremiah III, 91
Crispen, John V, 445
Crispen, Margaret II, 128
Crispen, Mary II, 128
Crispen, Mary V, 45
Crispen, Mary V, 138
Crispen, Phebe V, 445
Crispen, Rachel V, 445
Crispen, Sarah V, 165
Crispen, Silus II, 528
Crispen, Susanna II, 528
Crispen, Thomas II, 498
Crispen, Thomas II, 528
Crispin, ??? V, 443
Crispin, Abraham V, 950
Crispin, Ann II, 212
Crispin, Ann V, 232
Crispin, Benjamin II, 212
Crispin, Benjamin II, 246
Crispin, Benjamin V, 232
Crispin, Caleb II, 212
Crispin, Charles V, 232
Crispin, Charlotte IV, 930
Crispin, David V, 232
Crispin, David V, 447
Crispin, Davis V, 232
Crispin, Davis V, 272
Crispin, Drucilla V, 949
Crispin, Drusilla V, 950
Crispin, Eliza II, 789
Crispin, Elizabeth II, 64
Crispin, Elizabeth II, 147
Crispin, Elizabeth II, 157
Crispin, Elizabeth II, 212
Crispin, Elizabeth II, 268
Crispin, Elizabeth V, 45
Crispin, Elizabeth V, 76
Crispin, Elizabeth V, 165
Crispin, Elizabeth V, 232
Crispin, Elizabeth V, 290
Crispin, Elizabeth V, 901
Crispin, Francis V, 165
Crispin, Hannah II, 212
Crispin, Hannah IV, 696
Crispin, Hannah IV, 945
Crispin, Hannah V, 950
Crispin, Hannah V, 955
Crispin, Hetty II, 702
Crispin, Hetty II, 735
Crispin, Hews II, 144
Crispin, Hews II, 147
Crispin, Hezekiah II, 64
Crispin, Isaac V, 950
Crispin, Isaac Postgait V, 232
Crispin, Isaac Ward V, 901
Crispin, John V, 232
Crispin, John V, 272
Crispin, John, Jr. V, 232
Crispin, Jonathan II, 64
Crispin, Jonathan II, 117
Crispin, Jonathan II, 147
Crispin, Jonathan II, 157
Crispin, Jonathan V, 45
Crispin, Jonathan V, 76
Crispin, Jonathan V, 901
Crispin, Joseph II, 64
Crispin, Joseph II, 147
Crispin, Joseph II, 157
Crispin, Joseph V, 45
Crispin, Joseph V, 901
Crispin, Joseph, Jr. II, 64
Crispin, Joshua II, 212
Crispin, Joshua V, 232
Crispin, Josiah II, 117
Crispin, Levy II, 64
Crispin, Lucy II, 352
Crispin, Maggie B. II, 144
Crispin, Maggie B. II, 147
Crispin, Margaret II, 64
Crispin, Margaret II, 212
Crispin, Margaret II, 246
Crispin, Martha II, 147
Crispin, Martha II, 157
Crispin, Martha II, 212
Crispin, Martha A. II, 147
Crispin, Mary II, 212
Crispin, Mary II, 250
Crispin, Mary II, 252
Crispin, Mary II, 261
Crispin, Mary II, 268
Crispin, Mary II, 352
Crispin, Mary II, 498
Crispin, Mary II, 539
Crispin, Mary II, 585
Crispin, Mary V, 45
Crispin, Mary V, 165
Crispin, Mary V, 232
Crispin, Mary Augusta II, 144
Crispin, Mary Augusta II, 147
Crispin, Mary Postgate V, 232
Crispin, Mary W. V, 45
Crispin, Mary W. V, 76
Crispin, Mary Ward V, 45
Crispin, Mary Ward V, 901
Crispin, Mathias V, 165
Crispin, Mathias V, 232
Crispin, Mathias V, 950
Crispin, Matthias V, 950
Crispin, Matthias V, 962
Crispin, Page II, 117
Crispin, Patience II, 212
Crispin, Patience II, 227
Crispin, Phebe VI, 368
Crispin, Phebe VI, 381
Crispin, Pilesgrove II, 157
Crispin, Prudence II, 64
Crispin, Rachel II, 498
Crispin, Rachel II, 683
Crispin, Rachel V, 232
Crispin, Rachel V, 272
Crispin, Rachel V, 447
Crispin, Rebecca II, 212
Crispin, Rebecca V, 45
Crispin, Rebecca V, 901
Crispin, Rebecca E. V, 19
Crispin, Rebecca E. V, 45
Crispin, Roland II, 64
Crispin, Rowland V, 45
Crispin, Rowland Owen V, 45
Crispin, Rowland Owen V, 901
Crispin, Samuel II, 117
Crispin, Samuel II, 352
Crispin, Sarah II, 212
Crispin, Sarah II, 352
Crispin, Sarah II, 498
Crispin, Sarah II, 569
Crispin, Sarah II, 579
Crispin, Sarah V, 165
Crispin, Sarah V, 950
Crispin, Sarah V, 962
Crispin, Seth II, 212
Crispin, Silas II, 212
Crispin, Silas II, 227
Crispin, Silas II, 352
Crispin, Silas II, 498
Crispin, Silas II, 569
Crispin, Silas II, 683
Crispin, Silas, Jr. II, 212
Crispin, Silus II, 498
Crispin, Susanna II, 498
Crispin, Szmuel II, 498
Crispin, Thomas II, 352
Crispin, Thomas II, 498
Crispin, Thomas V, 232
Crispin, William II, 352
Crispin, Wm. II, 212
Crispin, Wm. II, 498
Crispin, Wm. II, 683
Criss, Cora V, 734
Criss, Virgin II, 212
Crissenberry, Annie V, 617
Crisso, Jacob VI, 900
Crisso, Jacob VI, 930
Crisso, Sally VI, 900
Crisson, Ann III, 91
Crisson, Jeremiah III, 91
Crist, Allison V, 835
Crist, Allison B. V, 834
Crist, Allison B. V, 835
Crist, Elbert M. V, 835
Crist, Elnora V, 835
Crist, Elnora V, 852
Crist, Elwood V, 835
Crist, Elwood O. V, 835
Crist, Emma V, 835
Crist, Eva V, 835
Crist, Eva V, 843
Crist, Florence V, 832
Crist, Florence V, 835
Crist, Francis M. V, 835
Crist, Frank V, 852
Crist, Grace Irene V, 835
Crist, Grace Irene V, 838
Crist, Gracie Irene V, 835
Crist, Homer R. V, 835
Crist, Homer Raymond V, 835
Crist, John V, 834
Crist, John V, 835
Crist, Loretta V, 835
Crist, Margaret Ann V, 835
Crist, Martha V, 835
Crist, Pearl V, 835
Crist, Phebe V, 834
Crist, Phebe V, 835
Crist, Sarah Luella V, 834
Crist, Theo Christine V, 835
Criswell, John V, 484
Criswell, Keziah V, 484
Criswell, Lou Esther V, 666
Criswell, Louetta A. V, 484
Criswell, Marion V, 666
Criswell, Sarah A. V, 484
Criswell, Ursul V, 666
Criswell, Ursula V, 666
Crite, Elizabeth A. V, 382
Crite, George V, 382
Crite, Gracie C. V, 382
Crites, ??? V, 165
Crites, Ann V, 566
Crites, Anna V, 557
Crites, Anna Ethel V, 566
Crites, Anna Peelle V, 667
Crites, Charles V, 165
Crites, Charles W. V, 165
Crites, Edith V, 165
Crites, Edith V, 617
Crites, Edith M. V, 557
Crites, Elmina V, 165
Crites, Elmina J. V, 165
Crites, Francis H. IV, 1249
Crites, James V, 165
Crites, James M. V, 165
Crites, Jane V, 165
Crites, Jesse V, 557
Crites, Jesse W. V, 165
Crites, John V, 165
Crites, John V, 566
Crites, John V, 617
Crites, John C. V, 165
Crites, John C. V, 557

Crites, Judith V, 667
Crites, Malinda V, 165
Crites, Marjean V, 667
Crites, Pauline V, 667
Crites, Pauline V, 688
Crites, Phebe Malinda V, 165
Crites, Ruth Anna V, 617
Crites, Ruthanna V, 165
Crites, Sarah V, 947
Crites, Sarah V, 950
Crites, Wendell S. V, 557
Crites, Willis V, 667
Crites, Willis V, 688
Critten, Albert E. V, 734
Critten, Eva J. V, 734
Critten, James F. V, 734
Critten, Louise V, 734
Crittenden, Mary A. VI, 809
Crittenden, William VI, 809
Crittenton, Mary VI, 840
Crittenton, Richard VI, 840
Crittenton, Wm. VI, 840
Croaker, Brian VI, 171
Croaker, Rachel VI, 171
Croaker, Rachel Handley VI, 171
Croan, Honour II, 442
Croan, Nicholas II, 442
Croasdale, Achsah II, 825
Croasdale, Agnes II, 991
Croasdale, Agnes II, 1002
Croasdale, Alice II, 498
Croasdale, Alice II, 624
Croasdale, Amos V, 484
Croasdale, Anna II, 810
Croasdale, Anna II, 854
Croasdale, Anna II, 900
Croasdale, Anna E. II, 1065
Croasdale, Benjamin Rowland II, 854
Croasdale, Catharine M. II, 855
Croasdale, Catharine M. II, 932
Croasdale, Catherine M. II, 790
Croasdale, Catherine M. II, 810
Croasdale, Charles II, 790
Croasdale, Charles Edward Amos T. V, 45
Croasdale, Edward II, 790
Croasdale, Edward II, 854
Croasdale, Edward II, 1065
Croasdale, Edward II, 1072
Croasdale, Edward H. II, 1065
Croasdale, Edward H. II, 1071
Croasdale, Edward H. II, 1073
Croasdale, Elizabeth II, 790
Croasdale, Elizabeth II, 854
Croasdale, Elizabeth II, 1072
Croasdale, Elizabeth Coombs II, 790
Croasdale, Elizabeth P. II, 800
Croasdale, Elizabeth P. II, 803
Croasdale, Emily V, 484
Croasdale, Emma V, 484
Croasdale, Ethel A. II, 1072
Croasdale, Ethel Anna II, 1065
Croasdale, Ethel Anna II, 1072
Croasdale, Ethel Anna II, 1078
Croasdale, Franklin B. II, 1065
Croasdale, Franklin B. II, 1072
Croasdale, Franklin B. II, 1073
Croasdale, Grace VI, 484
Croasdale, Hannah B. II, 854
Croasdale, Hannah T. II, 790
Croasdale, Hannah T. II, 855
Croasdale, Hannah T. II, 932
Croasdale, Helen II, 790
Croasdale, Jacob C. II, 1065
Croasdale, Jacob C. II, 1071
Croasdale, Jacob C. II, 1072
Croasdale, James P. II, 803
Croasdale, Jane II, 790
Croasdale, Jane VI, 632
Croasdale, Jane VI, 701
Croasdale, Jane VI, 709
Croasdale, Jeremiah II, 790
Croasdale, Jeremiah II, 854
Croasdale, Jeremiah II, 855
Croasdale, Jeremiah II, 932
Croasdale, Jeremiah VI, 484
Croasdale, John P. II, 790
Croasdale, John P. II, 855
Croasdale, Joseph II, 790
Croasdale, Joseph V, 45
Croasdale, Joseph C. IV, 28
Croasdale, Joseph S. IV, 28
Croasdale, Joseph, Jr. V, 45
Croasdale, Laura P. II, 854
Croasdale, Laura P. II, 883
Croasdale, Laura Paxson II, 803
Croasdale, Lydia II, 790
Croasdale, Lydia V, 45
Croasdale, Lydia V, 484
Croasdale, Marion L. II, 1072
Croasdale, Marion L. II, 1081
Croasdale, Marion S. II, 1072
Croasdale, Martha R. III, 91
Croasdale, Mary VI, 632
Croasdale, Mary D. VI, 615
Croasdale, Mary D. VI, 632
Croasdale, Mary H. V, 480
Croasdale, Mary H. V, 484
Croasdale, Mary Martha II, 1065
Croasdale, Mary Martha II, 1071
Croasdale, Mary Martha II, 1072
Croasdale, Mary Martha II, 1073
Croasdale, Mary R. II, 854
Croasdale, Mary R. II, 900
Croasdale, Mercy II, 958
Croasdale, Mercy II, 1065
Croasdale, Mercy H. II, 1072
Croasdale, Mercy M. II, 1071
Croasdale, Mercy M. II, 1072
Croasdale, Mercy M. II, 1073
Croasdale, Mercy M. II, 1075
Croasdale, Miriam II, 854
Croasdale, Miriam T. II, 831
Croasdale, Miriam T. II, 855
Croasdale, Miriam Tilton II, 790
Croasdale, Phebe II, 790
Croasdale, Rachel II, 1071
Croasdale, Rachel II, 1075
Croasdale, Rachel H. II, 1072
Croasdale, Rachel H. II, 1073
Croasdale, Robert II, 790
Croasdale, Robert II, 831
Croasdale, Robert II, 854
Croasdale, Robert II, 855
Croasdale, Robert II, 900
Croasdale, Robert II, 1071
Croasdale, Robert Allen II, 790
Croasdale, Robert Lucas II, 991
Croasdale, Robert M. II, 1065
Croasdale, Robert M. II, 1071
Croasdale, Robert M. II, 1072
Croasdale, Robert M. II, 1073
Croasdale, Robert M. II, 1075
Croasdale, Sarah II, 991
Croasdale, Sarah Cary VI, 484
Croasdale, Sarah Jane II, 1071
Croasdale, Sarah Jane II, 1083
Croasdale, Sarah P. VI, 632
Croasdale, Sarah P. VI, 635
Croasdale, Sarah P. VI, 672
Croasdale, Stevenson III, 91
Croasdale, William II, 958
Croasdale, William II, 991
Croasdale, William A. VI, 632
Croasdale, William T. III, 91
Croasdale, Willis VI, 615
Croasdale, Willis VI, 632
Croasdall, Grace VI, 246
Croasdell, Sarah II, 958
Croasdell, Thomas II, 352
Croasdell, William II, 958
Croat, Mary II, 212
Crobough, Chester IV, 1312
Crobough, Chester IV, 1328
Crobough, Jean IV, 1312
Crobough, Margaret IV, 1312
Crobough, Margaret IV, 1328
Crobough, S. Chester IV, 1312
Crobough, S. Chester, Jr. IV, 1312
Crobough, Samuel Chester IV, 1312
Crochet, Mary IV, 867
Crock, Austie Stephens V, 454
Crocker, Abbey III, 253
Crocker, Gladys T. III, 91
Crocker, Gladys T. III, 311
Crocker, James I, 296
Crocker, Louisa IV, 74
Crocker, Louisa IV, 82
Crocker, Louiza IV, 74
Crocker, Lucinda E. I, 296
Crocker, Ruth I, 296
Crocket, Mary IV, 877
Crockett, A. C. IV, 1312
Crockett, Archie IV, 1276
Crockett, Edith D. IV, 1312
Crockett, Gladys IV, 1312
Crockett, Hugh VI, 899
Crockett, James V, 382
Crockett, James V, 484
Crockett, Jane IV, 1312
Crockett, John VI, 849
Crockett, Joseph VI, 899
Crockett, Joseph VI, 945
Crockett, Lucy VI, 899
Crockett, Mary VI, 945
Crockett, Mildred Blackburn VI, 899
Crockett, Mr. ??? IV, 1276
Crockett, Mrs. ??? IV, 1276
Crockett, Rebecca VI, 642
Crockett, Rebecca VI, 656
Crockett, Ruth IV, 1276
Crockett, Ruth IV, 1312
Crockett, Walter IV, 1312
Crockham, Deborah II, 498
Crockham, John II, 498
Crockham, Mary II, 498
Crockham, Wm. II, 498
Crockson, Abraham II, 484
Crockson, Abraham II, 498
Crockson, Esther II, 484
Crockson, Esther II, 498
Crockson, Lydia II, 484
Crockson, Lydia II, 498
Crockson, Oliver Caulk II, 498
Croe, Abigail I, 713
Croe, Abigail I, 716
Crofford, Eva I, 383
Crofford, Katharine I, 383
Crofford, Katharine I, 429
Crofford, Katherine VI, 582
Crofford, Sarah I, 383
Croft, Elizabeth IV, 143
Croft, Jesse IV, 143
Croft, Job IV, 1360
Croft, John IV, 143
Croft, Joseph IV, 143
Croft, Ridgway IV, 143
Croft, Samuel IV, 143
Croggs, Cinthe I, 997
Croggs, Cinthe I, 999
Croker, Abigail Jane I, 923
Croker, Albert Lindsey I, 923
Croker, Annie I, 923
Croker, David S. I, 923
Croker, David S. I, 940
Croker, Dorothy C. I, 923
Croker, Dorothy Gavelle I, 940
Croker, Fletcher I, 940
Croker, Henry Fletcher I, 923
Croker, Mable M. I, 923
Croker, Marilla Mable I, 940
Croker, Mrs. D. S. I, 940
Croker, Winnie I, 940
Croker, Winnie Estus I, 923
Croker, Zebedee I, 923
Crokum, Susanna II, 352
Croley, Angelina B. VI, 809
Croley, Jemima VI, 809
Croley, John VI, 809
Croley, John VI, 834
Croley, Permelia VI, 834
Croley, Tyree VI, 809
Crom, Gilbert VI, 879
Crom, Gilbert VI, 964
Cromain, Ruth V, 734
Cromell, Bessie IV, 1312
Cromwell, ??? III, 28
Cromwell, ??? III, 92
Cromwell, ??? III, 93
Cromwell, Alice U. III, 68
Cromwell, Alice U. III, 91
Cromwell, Alice U. III, 93
Cromwell, Ann III, 55
Cromwell, Ann III, 91
Cromwell, Ann III, 318
Cromwell, Ann III, 319
Cromwell, Anna III, 28
Cromwell, Anna III, 91
Cromwell, Anna III, 92
Cromwell, Anna III, 93
Cromwell, Anna III, 95
Cromwell, Anna III, 118
Cromwell, Anna III, 120
Cromwell, Anna III, 481
Cromwell, Anna IV, 1249
Cromwell, Anna B. III, 92
Cromwell, Anna C. III, 118
Cromwell, Anne III, 92
Cromwell, Avis Leggett III, 283
Cromwell, Benjamin III, 283
Cromwell, Caroline III, 68
Cromwell, Caroline III, 91
Cromwell, Caroline III, 92
Cromwell, Caroline III, 93
Cromwell, Caroline III, 326
Cromwell, Caroline Ann III, 91
Cromwell, Caroline Ann III, 93
Cromwell, Caroline H. III, 32
Cromwell, Caroline H. III, 283
Cromwell, Charles III, 91
Cromwell, Charles III, 92
Cromwell, Charles III, 93
Cromwell, Charles E. III, 92
Cromwell, Charlotte III, 91
Cromwell, Charlotte III, 92
Cromwell, Charlotte III, 93
Cromwell, Charlotte III, 283
Cromwell, Charlotte III, 406
Cromwell, Charlotte H. III, 82
Cromwell, Charlotte H. III, 91
Cromwell, Chas. III, 92
Cromwell, Cornelia III, 92
Cromwell, Daniel III, 91
Cromwell, Daniel III, 367
Cromwell, Daniel J. III, 91
Cromwell, Daniel, Jr. III, 91
Cromwell, David III, 91
Cromwell, David III, 92
Cromwell, David III, 93
Cromwell, David III, 118
Cromwell, David III, 283
Cromwell, Dr. William III, 283
Cromwell, Dr. William F. III, 283
Cromwell, Edward III, 35
Cromwell, Edward III, 91
Cromwell, Edward III, 92
Cromwell, Edward III, 93
Cromwell, Edward M. III, 92
Cromwell, Edwin H. III, 283
Cromwell, Eliz S. III, 148
Cromwell, Eliz. III, 91
Cromwell, Eliz. III, 266
Cromwell, Eliz. III, 367
Cromwell, Eliza U. III, 93
Cromwell, Elizabeth III, 91
Cromwell, Elizabeth III, 92
Cromwell, Elizabeth III, 93
Cromwell, Elizabeth III, 148
Cromwell, Elizabeth III, 283
Cromwell, Elizabeth III, 367
Cromwell, Elizabeth H. III, 283
Cromwell, Elizabeth R. III, 92
Cromwell, Elizabeth R. III, 341
Cromwell, Ellison III, 428
Cromwell, Emily III, 91
Cromwell, Emily III, 92
Cromwell, Emily C. III, 283
Cromwell, Everett Ernest III, 91
Cromwell, Fannie III, 92
Cromwell, Francis III, 92
Cromwell, Frank III, 92
Cromwell, Franklin III, 283
Cromwell, Fred'k III, 283
Cromwell, Frederick C. III, 283
Cromwell, Geo. III, 93
Cromwell, George III, 91
Cromwell, George III, 92
Cromwell, George W. III, 92
Cromwell, Gertrude III, 91
Cromwell, Gertrude III, 92
Cromwell, Governor Oliver VI, 39
Cromwell, Gulielma III, 283
Cromwell, Gulielma Matilda III, 283
Cromwell, Hannah III, 92
Cromwell, Hannah III, 93
Cromwell, Hannah III, 345
Cromwell, Hannah C. III, 92
Cromwell, Hannah H. III, 283
Cromwell, Hannah W. III, 92
Cromwell, Hannah W. III, 135
Cromwell, Helen III, 92
Cromwell, Helen III, 285
Cromwell, Henry III, 43
Cromwell, Henry III, 91
Cromwell, Henry III, 92
Cromwell, Henry III, 285
Cromwell, Henry B. III, 91
Cromwell, Henry B. III, 92
Cromwell, Henry B. III, 282
Cromwell, Henry B. III, 283
Cromwell, Henry B., Jr. III, 92
Cromwell, Henry Jenkins III, 283
Cromwell, Howard III, 283
Cromwell, Isabella III, 91
Cromwell, Isabella III, 93
Cromwell, Israel A. III, 92
Cromwell, Israel A. III, 93
Cromwell, Israel Anderson III, 91
Cromwell, James III, 91
Cromwell, James III, 92
Cromwell, James III, 93
Cromwell, James III, 283
Cromwell, James III, 406
Cromwell, James M. III, 92
Cromwell, James William III, 93
Cromwell, James Wm. III, 92
Cromwell, Jane R. III, 406
Cromwell, Jas. III, 406
Cromwell, John III, 91
Cromwell, John III, 92
Cromwell, John III, 93
Cromwell, John III, 95
Cromwell, John III, 135
Cromwell, John III, 227
Cromwell, John III, 345
Cromwell, John III, 406
Cromwell, John III, 466
Cromwell, John III, 481
Cromwell, John III, 504
Cromwell, John J. III, 91
Cromwell, John J. III, 92
Cromwell, John, Jr. III, 92
Cromwell, Joseph II, 442
Cromwell, Joseph H. III, 283
Cromwell, Joshua T. III, 91
Cromwell, Joshua T. III, 148
Cromwell, Letitia III, 92
Cromwell, Louise III, 135
Cromwell, Louise B. III, 92
Cromwell, Louise C. III, 92
Cromwell, Lydia B. III, 91
Cromwell, Lydia B. III, 92
Cromwell, Margaret III, 92
Cromwell, Maria III, 92
Cromwell, Martha III, 91
Cromwell, Martha III, 92
Cromwell, Martha III, 93
Cromwell, Martha III, 283
Cromwell, Martha W. III, 35
Cromwell, Martha W. III, 91
Cromwell, Mary III, 76
Cromwell, Mary III, 92
Cromwell, Mary III, 283
Cromwell, Mary III, 346
Cromwell, Mary III, 353
Cromwell, Mary III, 406
Cromwell, Mary III, 467
Cromwell, Mary III, 468
Cromwell, Mary Eliza. III, 93
Cromwell, Mary J. III, 283
Cromwell, Mary M. III, 92
Cromwell, Mary, Jr. III, 283
Cromwell, Mollie A. III, 93
Cromwell, Molllie A. III, 294
Cromwell, Oliver III, 82
Cromwell, Oliver III, 91
Cromwell, Oliver III, 92
Cromwell, Oliver III, 406
Cromwell, Oliver III, 455
Cromwell, Oliver III, 468
Cromwell, Oliver VI, 6
Cromwell, Oliver VI, 41
Cromwell, Phebe III, 91
Cromwell, Phebe III, 92
Cromwell, Phebe III, 93
Cromwell, Phebe III, 406
Cromwell, Phebe III, 466
Cromwell, Phebe III, 481
Cromwell, Phebe III, 504
Cromwell, Phebe Jane III, 92
Cromwell, Phebe Jane III, 93
Cromwell, Rachel III, 92
Cromwell, Rachel III, 283
Cromwell, Rachel M. III, 91
Cromwell, Rebecca III, 91
Cromwell, Rebecca III, 92
Cromwell, Rebecca III, 93
Cromwell, Rebecca III, 118
Cromwell, Rebecca III, 281
Cromwell, Rebecca III, 283
Cromwell, Rich. III, 92
Cromwell, Richard III, 92
Cromwell, Richard III, 341
Cromwell, Richard, Jr. III, 92
Cromwell, Robert III, 91
Cromwell, Robert III, 92
Cromwell, Robert III, 93
Cromwell, Robert III, 294
Cromwell, Robert H. III, 92
Cromwell, Robert H. III, 93
Cromwell, Ruth III, 93
Cromwell, Samuel III, 283
Cromwell, Samuel K. III, 91
Cromwell, Samuel K. III, 92
Cromwell, Samuel K. III, 93
Cromwell, Sarah III, 82
Cromwell, Sarah III, 91
Cromwell, Sarah III, 92
Cromwell, Sarah III, 93
Cromwell, Sarah III, 227
Cromwell, Sarah III, 283
Cromwell, Sarah III, 406
Cromwell, Sarah III, 455
Cromwell, Sarah III, 468
Cromwell, Sarah A. III, 91
Cromwell, Sarah Ann III, 93
Cromwell, Sarah B. III, 294
Cromwell, Sarah B. III, 295
Cromwell, Sarah H. III, 283
Cromwell, Sarah M. III, 91
Cromwell, Sarah M. III, 92
Cromwell, Sarah M. III, 93
Cromwell, Sarah M. III, 95
Cromwell, Sarah M. III, 285
Cromwell, Sarah W. III, 43
Cromwell, Sidney III, 93
Cromwell, Solomon H. III, 93
Cromwell, Thomas III, 93

Cromwell, Valentine H. III, 283
Cromwell, Wait B. III, 283
Cromwell, Walter III, 92
Cromwell, Walter III, 283
Cromwell, Wd. Sarah III, 32
Cromwell, Willet III, 283
Cromwell, Willet H. III, 283
Cromwell, Willet, Jr. III, 283
Cromwell, William III, 91
Cromwell, William III, 92
Cromwell, William III, 93
Cromwell, William III, 283
Cromwell, William III, 326
Cromwell, William A. III, 93
Cromwell, William B. III, 91
Cromwell, William B. III, 93
Cromwell, William D. III, 93
Cromwell, William F. III, 283
Cromwell, William K. III, 283
Cromwell, Wm. III, 32
Cromwell, Wm. III, 68
Cromwell, Wm. III, 91
Cromwell, Wm. III, 92
Cromwell, Wm. Valentine III, 283
Cron, Ida IV, 193
Crone, Eliza V, 991
Crone, John A. III, 20
Crone, John A. III, 93
Crone, Peter V, 991
Crone, Sarah III, 20
Crone, Sarah A. III, 93
Crone, Wm. V, 991
Cronk, Jackson V, 981
Croo, Rachel V, 45
Crook, Caroline III, 25
Crook, Jno VI, 28
Crook, John VI, 28
Crook, Mary I, 713
Crook, Mary I, 724
Crook, Mary Elizabeth IV, 1155
Crook, Mina Davis IV, 1205
Crooke, Mary II, 485
Crooke, Mary II, 498
Crooker, ??? III, 406
Crooker, ??? III, 464
Crooker, Anne III, 406
Crooker, Daniel III, 406
Crooker, Eliz. III, 406
Crooker, Elizabeth III, 93
Crooker, Elizabeth III, 406
Crooker, Elizabeth III, 464
Crooker, Esther III, 406
Crooker, Esther III, 451
Crooker, Fannie III, 406
Crooker, Isaac III, 406
Crooker, Jacob III, 406
Crooker, Jacob III, 459
Crooker, Jacob III, 481
Crooker, Jarvis III, 406
Crooker, John III, 406
Crooker, John T. III, 406
Crooker, Mary III, 404
Crooker, Mary III, 406
Crooker, Phebe III, 406
Crooker, Phebe III, 459
Crooker, Phebe III, 481
Crooker, Phebe A. III, 406
Crooker, Ruth III, 406
Crooker, Ruth III, 451
Crooker, Samson III, 406
Crooker, Simeon III, 93
Crooker, Wd. Phebe III, 406
Crooker, William III, 406
Crooker, William III, 451
Crooker, Wm. III, 406
Crookham, Mary II, 352
Crookham, Robert II, 352
Crookham, Susanna II, 352
Crookham, William II, 352
Crooks, Anna M. IV, 1249
Crooks, Caroline II, 799
Crooks, Laura B. IV, 696
Crooks, Laura B. IV, 1312
Crooks, Margaret II, 460
Crooks, Margaret II, 463
Crooks, Margaret II, 498
Crooks, Margaret II, 735
Crooks, Mary II, 498
Crookshanks, Cicely II, 499
Crookshanks, Cicely II, 664
Crookshanks, Rebekah II, 499
Croom, Noami I, 335
Croper, Eliz III, 489
Cropff, Barbara VI, 809
Cropff, Henry VI, 809
Cropper, Albert V, 454
Cropper, Etta V, 454
Cropper, Lowell V, 454
Cropper, Mary J. V, 454
Crosbie, Isabella II, 707
Crosby, Ann III, 27
Crosby, Ann III, 93
Crosby, Charles J. III, 93
Crosby, Elizabeth II, 213
Crosby, Elizabeth II, 272
Crosby, Ellen III, 93
Crosby, John II, 212
Crosby, John II, 213
Crosby, John II, 223
Crosby, John II, 258
Crosby, John II, 272
Crosby, Joshua II, 352
Crosby, Joshua II, 498
Crosby, Lucretia M. II, 862
Crosby, Lydia V, 967
Crosby, Lydia V, 969
Crosby, Marie Haliday IV, 1312
Crosby, Mary II, 212
Crosby, Mary II, 220
Crosby, Mary II, 258
Crosby, Mary J. III, 27
Crosby, Mary J. III, 93
Crosby, Rebecca II, 213
Crosby, Rebecca II, 223
Crosby, Richard II, 862
Crosby, Robert III, 27
Crosby, Robert III, 93
Crosby, Sarah II, 241
Crosby, Thomas II, 498
Crosdale, Sarah II, 1012
Crosdell, Wm. II, 1039
Croshaw, Jane D. II, 1072
Croshaw, Samuel R. V, 950
Croshaw, Thomas V, 950
Croshaw, Thomas S. V, 950
Crosher, John, Jr. II, 213
Crosier, Ann IV, 326
Crosier, Ann IV, 333
Crosier, Judah IV, 333
Crosier, Margaret B. II, 1072
Crosier, Mercy II, 1072
Crosier, Sarah IV, 333
Crosier, Wm. II, 1072
Crosley, Elizabeth IV, 520
Crosley, Emily IV, 696
Crosley, Emma IV, 696
Crosley, Flora IV, 696
Crosley, Hannah IV, 520
Crosley, Hester IV, 520
Crosley, John IV, 519
Crosley, Martha IV, 520
Crosley, Martha IV, 548
Crosley, Mary IV, 520
Crosley, Moses IV, 520
Crosley, Rachel IV, 519
Crosley, Rebecca IV, 520
Crosley, Rebecca IV, 555
Crosley, Samuel IV, 519
Crosley, Sarah IV, 143
Crosley, Sarah IV, 519
Crosley, Tamor IV, 143
Crosley, Thamar IV, 519
Crosman, Alfred B. III, 93
Crosman, Charles S. III, 93
Crosman, Charles S. III, 130
Crosman, Cornelia A. III, 93
Crosman, Elizabeth III, 93
Crosman, Elizabeth III, 277
Crosman, Mary H. III, 93
Crosman, Sarah III, 93
Crosman, Sarah III, 130
Cross, Abbie Willard V, 45
Cross, Alice IV, 1312
Cross, Alice E. IV, 1312
Cross, Alonzo IV, 968
Cross, Ann II, 352
Cross, Ann II, 498
Cross, Ann II, 735
Cross, Ann II, 790
Cross, Ann II, 855
Cross, Anna II, 991
Cross, Anna II, 1034
Cross, Annie I, 614
Cross, Elizabeth IV, 469
Cross, Emma V, 617
Cross, Geo. T. V, 617
Cross, Hannah IV, 28
Cross, Hannah IV, 37
Cross, John II, 498
Cross, John II, 991
Cross, John II, 1034
Cross, John VI, 149
Cross, Joseph II, 352
Cross, Joseph II, 991
Cross, Joseph II, 1034
Cross, Lillian IV, 968
Cross, Mary II, 64
Cross, Mary II, 111
Cross, Maude IV, 968
Cross, Mollie IV, 1276
Cross, Mrs. C. W. IV, 1312
Cross, Rachel II, 991
Cross, Rachel II, 1018
Cross, Roby I, 615
Cross, Ruth IV, 720
Cross, Samuel Alexander I, 615
Cross, Samuel Henley I, 615
Cross, Sarah Ellen I, 615
Cross, Susan Elisabeth I, 615
Cross, Susan Lillian I, 615
Cross, Thomas II, 352
Cross, Thomas Eugene I, 615
Cross, Thomas L. V, 617
Cross, Thos. L. V, 617
Crossan, Thomas II, 352
Crossby, Lydia II, 790
Crosse, Elizabeth III, 53
Crosse, Elizabeth III, 93
Crossen, Bess IV, 1249
Crossen, Deane IV, 1249
Crossley, Ada B. IV, 939
Crossley, Amy IV, 193
Crossley, Amy IV, 300
Crossley, Amy IV, 520
Crossley, Carl IV, 193
Crossley, Caroline IV, 382
Crossley, Caroline IV, 516
Crossley, Caroline IV, 520
Crossley, Earnest IV, 193
Crossley, Eliza IV, 520
Crossley, Eliza IV, 939
Crossley, Elizabeth IV, 143
Crossley, Elizabeth IV, 193
Crossley, Elizabeth IV, 520
Crossley, Elizabeth IV, 532
Crossley, Elsey A. IV, 193
Crossley, Emily IV, 696
Crossley, Emily IV, 701
Crossley, Emma IV, 696
Crossley, Esther IV, 143
Crossley, Esther IV, 193
Crossley, Esther IV, 520
Crossley, Flora IV, 696
Crossley, George IV, 520
Crossley, Hannah IV, 143
Crossley, Hannah IV, 193
Crossley, Hannah IV, 520
Crossley, Hester IV, 520
Crossley, James IV, 193
Crossley, James IV, 520
Crossley, Jane IV, 193
Crossley, Jane IV, 382
Crossley, Jane IV, 467
Crossley, Jane IV, 517
Crossley, Jane IV, 520
Crossley, Jessie IV, 469
Crossley, John IV, 143
Crossley, John IV, 148
Crossley, John IV, 193
Crossley, John IV, 326
Crossley, John IV, 347
Crossley, John IV, 382
Crossley, John IV, 519
Crossley, John IV, 520
Crossley, John IV, 532
Crossley, Jonathan IV, 143
Crossley, Jonathan IV, 193
Crossley, Jonathan IV, 326
Crossley, Jonathan IV, 382
Crossley, Jonathan IV, 520
Crossley, Jonathan V, 901
Crossley, Jordon IV, 520
Crossley, Jos. IV, 520
Crossley, Joseph IV, 520
Crossley, Leana IV, 382
Crossley, Leana IV, 520
Crossley, Leannah IV, 520
Crossley, Louise C. VI, 899
Crossley, Lydia IV, 520
Crossley, Martha IV, 520
Crossley, Mary IV, 143
Crossley, Mary IV, 193
Crossley, Mary IV, 520
Crossley, Mary V, 901
Crossley, Mary Jane IV, 193
Crossley, Mary Jane IV, 233
Crossley, Moses IV, 143
Crossley, Moses IV, 193
Crossley, Moses IV, 382
Crossley, Moses IV, 517
Crossley, Moses IV, 520
Crossley, Ora IV, 193
Crossley, Phebe IV, 193
Crossley, Phebe IV, 326
Crossley, Phebe IV, 351
Crossley, Phebe IV, 520
Crossley, Plummer IV, 469
Crossley, Rachel IV, 143
Crossley, Rachel IV, 148
Crossley, Rachel IV, 173
Crossley, Rachel IV, 193
Crossley, Rachel IV, 519
Crossley, Rachel Ann IV, 193
Crossley, Rebecca IV, 193
Crossley, Rebecca IV, 293
Crossley, Rebecca IV, 520
Crossley, Roscoe S. IV, 939
Crossley, Samuel IV, 143
Crossley, Samuel IV, 193
Crossley, Samuel IV, 326
Crossley, Samuel IV, 351
Crossley, Samuel IV, 519
Crossley, Samuel IV, 520
Crossley, Samuel C. IV, 520
Crossley, Sarah IV, 143
Crossley, Sarah IV, 326
Crossley, Sarah IV, 347
Crossley, Sarah IV, 519
Crossley, Simeon IV, 520
Crossley, Simeon V, 901
Crossley, Tamar IV, 193
Crossley, Tamar IV, 347
Crossley, Tamar IV, 532
Crossley, Tamer IV, 148
Crossley, Tamer IV, 326
Crossley, Tamor IV, 143
Crossley, Thamar IV, 519
Crossley, William R. VI, 899
Crossly, Amy IV, 520
Crossly, Caroline IV, 520
Crossly, George IV, 520
Crossly, James IV, 520
Crossly, Jane IV, 520
Crossly, John IV, 520
Crossly, Jonathan IV, 520
Crossly, Leannah IV, 520
Crossly, Lydia IV, 520
Crossly, Martha IV, 520
Crossly, Mary V, 901
Crossly, Phebe IV, 520
Crossly, Rebecca IV, 520
Crossly, Samuel C. IV, 520
Crossly, Simeon IV, 520
Crossly, Simeon V, 901
Crossman, ??? III, 496
Crossman, Alfred B. III, 353
Crossman, Cornelia A. III, 353
Crossman, Daniel V, 901
Crossman, Elizabeth V, 901
Crossman, Elizabeth V, 920
Crossman, Hannah V, 901
Crossman, Hannah V, 924
Crossman, Hannah S. V, 901
Crossman, Jane V, 901
Crossman, Jane V, 920
Crossman, Jane N. V, 901
Crossman, Margaret V, 898
Crossman, Margaret V, 901
Crossman, Martha V, 895
Crossman, Martha V, 901
Crossman, Mary III, 481
Crossman, Mary III, 496
Crossman, Mary R. III, 353
Crossman, Peleg V, 901
Crossman, Sarah W. V, 901
Crossman, William V, 901
Crossman, William F. V, 901
Crossman, William H. V, 901
Crossman, Wm. V, 901
Croswell, Rosana III, 59
Croswell, Rosanna III, 248
Crothers, Adaline IV, 193
Crothers, Adeline A. IV, 193
Crothers, C. P. V, 990
Crothers, Charles H. IV, 193
Crothers, Edward V, 990
Crothers, George IV, 193
Crothers, George H. IV, 193
Crothers, John L. V, 990
Crothers, John W. IV, 193
Crothers, Julia V, 990
Crothers, Orlie V, 990
Crothers, Rachel B. IV, 1129
Crothers, Samuel J. IV, 193
Crothers, Samuel L. IV, 193
Crothers, Sarah M. IV, 193
Crothers, Sarah R. IV, 193
Crothers, Thomas IV, 193
Crothers, Thomas W. IV, 193
Crothers, William IV, 193
Crotts, Henry I, 923
Crotts, Henry I, 940
Crotts, Matilda I, 940
Crotts, Matilda C. I, 923
Crotty, Aney VI, 899
Crotty, Anny VI, 899
Crotty, Eliza VI, 899
Crotty, John J. VI, 899
Crotty, Michael VI, 899
Crouch, Abraham VI, 809
Crouch, Achilles VI, 900
Crouch, Achilles VI, 940
Crouch, Alexander Wilson III, 65
Crouch, Alexander Wilson III, 93
Crouch, Barsheba VI, 899
Crouch, Beatrice I, 940
Crouch, Benjamin VI, 900
Crouch, Cana VI, 899
Crouch, Charity VI, 1008
Crouch, Charles VI, 864
Crouch, Charles VI, 900
Crouch, Charles VI, 909
Crouch, Charlotte VI, 877
Crouch, Charlotte VI, 966
Crouch, Dennis VI, 900
Crouch, Elizabeth VI, 864
Crouch, Elizabeth VI, 897
Crouch, Elizabeth VI, 900
Crouch, Emmet I, 940
Crouch, Emmett L. I, 923
Crouch, Emmett L. I, 940
Crouch, Eunice VI, 972
Crouch, Fanney VI, 933
Crouch, Frances VI, 900
Crouch, George VI, 809
Crouch, Green VI, 877
Crouch, Green VI, 899
Crouch, Jabez W. VI, 963
Crouch, Jacob VI, 900
Crouch, Jacob VI, 1019
Crouch, Jane I, 923
Crouch, Jane VI, 900
Crouch, Jane T. VI, 975
Crouch, Jenny VI, 899
Crouch, John VI, 899
Crouch, John VI, 917
Crouch, John VI, 972
Crouch, Joicy VI, 900
Crouch, Joseph VI, 899
Crouch, Joseph VI, 947
Crouch, Joseph VI, 966
Crouch, Joseph VI, 1008
Crouch, Joseph VI, 1015
Crouch, Joseph VI, 1018
Crouch, Joshua VI, 900
Crouch, Josiah VI, 900
Crouch, Josiah VI, 1008
Crouch, Josiah VI, 1018
Crouch, Lewis VI, 864
Crouch, Lewis VI, 865
Crouch, Lewis VI, 899
Crouch, Lewis VI, 933
Crouch, Lewis O. VI, 900
Crouch, Locky VI, 900
Crouch, Louis O. VI, 900
Crouch, Lucinda VI, 933
Crouch, Mabel III, 65
Crouch, Mabel III, 93
Crouch, March E. VI, 963
Crouch, Margaret VI, 877
Crouch, Martha VI, 917
Crouch, Mary VI, 865
Crouch, Mary A. VI, 900
Crouch, Mary Ann VI, 899
Crouch, Mary Ann VI, 900
Crouch, Mary P. VI, 809
Crouch, Matilda VI, 899
Crouch, Mildred VI, 899
Crouch, Mildred B. I, 940
Crouch, Mildred Marceila I, 923
Crouch, Millissa C. VI, 900
Crouch, Minnie I, 940
Crouch, Nancy VI, 900
Crouch, Nancy VI, 901
Crouch, Nancy VI, 909
Crouch, Peter VI, 900
Crouch, Peter VI, 933
Crouch, Polley VI, 1019
Crouch, Polly VI, 899
Crouch, Polly VI, 900
Crouch, Polly VI, 947
Crouch, Polly VI, 972
Crouch, Priscilla IV, 28
Crouch, Priscilla IV, 57
Crouch, Richard I, 923
Crouch, Rolley VI, 899
Crouch, Rolly VI, 877
Crouch, Rolly VI, 899
Crouch, Rolly VI, 900
Crouch, Rolly VI, 901
Crouch, Rolly VI, 909
Crouch, Rolly VI, 972
Crouch, Sally VI, 899
Crouch, Saluda Ann VI, 1018
Crouch, Sarah VI, 899
Crouch, Sarah A. VI, 809
Crouch, Sarah B. VI, 963
Crouch, Sophira VI, 900
Crouch, Tabitha VI, 940
Crouch, Thomas VI, 900
Crouch, V. F. I, 940
Crouch, Violet VI, 1019
Crouch, William VI, 897
Crouch, William VI, 899

Crouch, William VI, 963
Crouch, William VI, 975
Crouch, William D. VI, 900
Crouch, William E. VI, 972
Crouch, William H. VI, 865
Croucher, Jesse Elma V, 326
Croucher, Margaret Ann V, 326
Croucher, Mary Caroline V, 326
Croucher, Rebecca V, 326
Crouise, Stephen VI, 842
Crouse, Adeline V, 667
Crouse, Alpha V, 991
Crouse, Cora V, 667
Crouse, Ellen II, 707
Crouse, Elon F. II, 702
Crouse, Emma T. V, 667
Crouse, Frank II, 702
Crouse, Fransena V, 667
Crouse, Geo. E. V, 667
Crouse, Helen II, 702
Crouse, Ida May V, 667
Crouse, Iva Lou V, 667
Crouse, Ivolen V, 667
Crouse, Lola V, 991
Crouse, Melvina V, 667
Crouse, Minervia V, 667
Crouse, Nancy II, 706
Crouse, Patricia Ann V, 991
Crouse, Susan F. V, 667
Crouse, Uree IV, 927
Crouse, Uree IV, 945
Crouse, Wm. V, 667
Crouse, Wm. H. V, 667
Crow, Abigail I, 383
Crow, Abigail I, 384
Crow, Abigail I, 404
Crow, Abigail I, 713
Crow, Aleenda VI, 809
Crow, Alunda VI, 810
Crow, Bertha A. V, 991
Crow, Bertha Morrison V, 991
Crow, C. VI, 809
Crow, Chester Arthur V, 991
Crow, Cora V, 991
Crow, Daisy Vinetia I, 335
Crow, Ellen V, 991
Crow, Enola V, 991
Crow, Franklin Pierce V, 991
Crow, Garner V, 991
Crow, Grace I, 384
Crow, Grace I, 713
Crow, Hannah I, 384
Crow, Hannah I, 713
Crow, Huldah V, 991
Crow, James I, 713
Crow, James V, 991
Crow, Julia V, 991
Crow, Maggie I, 335
Crow, Manirva V, 991
Crow, Needham I, 335
Crow, Needham C. I, 335
Crow, Rachel I, 384
Crow, Rachel I, 710
Crow, Rachel I, 713
Crow, Reuben I, 384
Crow, Reuben I, 695
Crow, Ruben I, 713
Crow, Ruth I, 384
Crow, Ruth I, 713
Crow, Ruth I, 722
Crow, Sarah V, 991
Crow, Sarah Lou Ellen I, 335
Crow, Thomas Clement I, 335
Crowder, Abner V, 165
Crowder, Abner W. V, 165
Crowder, Charles IV, 1276
Crowder, Cora IV, 1276
Crowder, Elizabeth F. VI, 900
Crowder, Elizabeth Frances VI, 900
Crowder, James V, 991
Crowder, John V, 991
Crowder, John H. VI, 900
Crowder, Joseph VI, 900
Crowder, Louie IV, 1276
Crowder, Mahaly VI, 900
Crowder, Mary IV, 1276
Crowder, Samuel R. III, 93
Crowder, Samuel R. III, 222
Crowder, Sarah VI, 969
Crowder, Teressa III, 93
Crowder, Teressa Roberta III, 222
Crowder, William VI, 900
Crowder, William VI, 1021
Crowell, Agnes V, 835
Crowell, Arnold IV, 1312
Crowell, Bessie IV, 1312
Crowell, Cassinda V, 835
Crowell, Daniel IV, 1312
Crowell, Elizabeth IV, 1312
Crowell, Elvira IV, 1312
Crowell, Emma Gertrude V, 835
Crowell, Erving IV, 1312
Crowell, Frances III, 53
Crowell, Frances III, 276
Crowell, James IV, 1312
Crowell, John IV, 1312
Crowell, Milton V, 835
Crowell, Percy IV, 1312
Crowell, Susan V, 835
Crowell, Susannah I, 713
Crowell, Susannah I, 738
Crowell, Verlinda V, 835
Crowell, Walter IV, 1312
Crowley, Betsey VI, 852
Crowley, Elizabeth VI, 830
Crowley, James VI, 852
Crowley, John VI, 809
Crowley, John VI, 835
Crowley, Lucy VI, 809
Crowley, Mary VI, 830
Crowley, Polly VI, 835
Crowley, Ralph VI, 802
Crowley, Ralph VI, 809
Crowley, Thomas VI, 830
Crowley, Wm. R. VI, 803
Crown, Anna Mary IV, 278
Crown, Clara Bell IV, 278
Crown, Forrest E. IV, 278
Crown, Foust IV, 278
Crown, Jesse VI, 932
Crown, John C. IV, 278
Crown, Lizzie IV, 278
Crown, Mollie IV, 278
Crown, Oda IV, 278
Crown, Ruth D. IV, 278
Crown, S. V. IV, 278
Crown, Saml. B. IV, 278
Crown, Samuel Vincent IV, 278
Crown, Sara E. IV, 278
Crowsdale, Amos V, 484
Crowsdale, Emily V, 484
Crowsdale, Lydia V, 484
Crowshaw, Jane D. II, 1072
Crowshaw, Jane D. II, 1078
Crowshaw, John II, 1072
Crowshaw, John II, 1078
Crowshaw, Mary II, 1072
Crowshaw, Mary II, 1078
Crowshaw, Samuel II, 1072
Crowshaw, Samuel II, 1078
Crowthers, Adeline A. IV, 193
Crowthers, Thomas W. IV, 193
Croxin, Lydia II, 484
Croxin, Lydia II, 498
Croxton, Arthur I, 45
Croxton, Elisabeth I, 45
Croxton, Elisabeth I, 67
Croxton, John II, 498
Croxton, Sarah I, 45
Croxton, Sarah I, 46
Croy, Ann IV, 143
Croy, Ann IV, 382
Croy, Ann IV, 451
Croy, Binford IV, 572
Croy, Elizabeth IV, 572
Croy, Elizabeth IV, 590
Croy, Jacob IV, 139
Croy, Jacob IV, 143
Croy, John IV, 143
Croy, John IV, 382
Croy, Judith IV, 572
Croy, Margaret IV, 143
Croy, Margaret IV, 382
Croy, Mathias IV, 143
Croy, Mathias IV, 382
Croy, Rebecca IV, 143
Croy, Rebecca IV, 363
Croy, Rebecca IV, 382
Croy, Rebecca IV, 572
Croy, Rebecca IV, 590
Croy, Richard IV, 143
Croy, Richard IV, 382
Croy, Susannah IV, 572
Croy, Suzannah IV, 139
Croy, Suzannah IV, 143
Croy, William IV, 572
Croyter, Rebecca Lea II, 499
Croyter, Rebecca Lea II, 575
Crozer, Amelia II, 992
Crozer, Amelia II, 994
Crozer, Ann IV, 326
Crozer, Ann IV, 330
Crozer, Ann IV, 520
Crozer, Anne IV, 520
Crozer, Charles IV, 619
Crozer, Elener IV, 326
Crozer, Elenor IV, 651
Crozer, Elisabeth IV, 619
Crozer, Elizabeth IV, 619
Crozer, Elizabeth IV, 867
Crozer, Elizabeth IV, 871
Crozer, Henry IV, 867
Crozer, James IV, 326
Crozer, James IV, 330
Crozer, James IV, 346
Crozer, James IV, 359
Crozer, James IV, 520
Crozer, James IV, 619
Crozer, James IV, 867
Crozer, Jesse Leroy IV, 867
Crozer, John IV, 326
Crozer, John IV, 651
Crozer, Jonathan IV, 619
Crozer, Jonathan IV, 867
Crozer, Jonathan IV, 874
Crozer, Joshua W. IV, 520
Crozer, Joshua W. V, 301
Crozer, Margaret B. II, 1072
Crozer, Martha IV, 619
Crozer, Martha IV, 867
Crozer, Martha H. IV, 867
Crozer, Mary IV, 326
Crozer, Mary IV, 346
Crozer, Mary IV, 520
Crozer, Mary IV, 619
Crozer, Mary IV, 867
Crozer, Mary B. IV, 867
Crozer, Mercy II, 958
Crozer, Mercy II, 992
Crozer, Phebe II, 992
Crozer, Phebe II, 1015
Crozer, Phebe S. IV, 867
Crozer, Phebe S. IV, 874
Crozer, Rachel IV, 359
Crozer, Rachel IV, 520
Crozer, Reasin IV, 619
Crozer, Reason IV, 619
Crozer, Reason IV, 867
Crozer, Samuel IV, 382
Crozer, Samuel IV, 520
Crozer, Samuel IV, 619
Crozer, Sarah II, 992
Crozer, Sarah II, 994
Crozer, Sarah IV, 210
Crozer, Sarah IV, 382
Crozer, Sarah IV, 516
Crozer, Sarah IV, 520
Crozer, Sarah IV, 619
Crozer, Sarah IV, 867
Crozer, Sarah IV, 871
Crozer, Susanna P. IV, 867
Crozer, Susannah IV, 619
Crozer, Susannah IV, 651
Crozer, Susannah IV, 867
Crozer, Thomas II, 992
Crozer, Thomas II, 994
Crozer, Thomas IV, 520
Crozer, Thomas IV, 619
Crozer, Thomas IV, 867
Crozer, Thomas IV, 871
Crozer, Thomas IV, 902
Crozer, Thos. IV, 520
Crozer, Thos. IV, 619
Crozer, Thos. IV, 867
Crozer, William II, 958
Crozer, Wm. II, 992
Crozier, Ann IV, 326
Crozier, Delia III, 48
Crozier, Delia III, 93
Crozier, Elener IV, 326
Crozier, Eva Jennie III, 48
Crozier, Eva Jennie III, 93
Crozier, Helen IV, 947
Crozier, Hiram B. III, 48
Crozier, Hiram B. III, 93
Crozier, James IV, 326
Crozier, James IV, 902
Crozier, John IV, 326
Crozier, Lillian IV, 947
Crozier, Lillian Madeline IV, 947
Crozier, Mary IV, 193
Crozier, Mary IV, 210
Crozier, Mary IV, 326
Crozier, Mercy II, 1072
Crozier, Rachel IV, 326
Crozier, Ray IV, 947
Crozier, Sarah II, 992
Crozier, Sarah IV, 193
Crozier, Sarah IV, 301
Crozier, Sarah IV, 326
Crozier, Sarah IV, 382
Crozier, Sarah IV, 902
Crozier, Susannah IV, 326
Crozier, Susannah IV, 346
Crozier, Thomas IV, 326
Crozier, Thomas IV, 902
Crozier, Wm. II, 992
Cruch, Edith II, 352
Cruck, Mary II, 352
Cruckshank, Alexander II, 352
Cruckshank, Barbara II, 499
Cruckshank, Barbara II, 515
Cruckshank, Barbra II, 499
Cruckshank, Barbra II, 518
Cruckshank, Cisley II, 499
Cruckshank, Elizabeth II, 352
Cruckshank, Elizabeth II, 519
Cruckshank, George II, 499
Cruckshank, George II, 518
Cruckshank, James II, 352
Cruckshank, John II, 352
Cruckshank, Joseph II, 352
Cruckshank, Joseph, Jr. II, 352
Cruckshank, Mary II, 352
Cruckshank, Mary II, 519
Cruckshank, Mary II, 709
Cruckshank, Mary II, 712
Cruckshank, Maurice II, 352
Cruckshank, Rachel II, 499
Cruckshank, Samuel II, 519
Cruckshank, Susanna II, 352
Cruckshank, Susanna II, 499
Cruckshank, Susannah II, 352
Cruckshanks, Alexander II, 352
Cruckshanks, Elizabeth II, 499
Cruckshanks, Joseph II, 352
Cruckshanks, Joseph II, 499
Cruckshanks, Joseph, Jr. II, 352
Cruckshanks, Rachel II, 352
Cruckshanks, Rachel II, 499
Cruckshanks, Susannah II, 352
Cruckshanks, Susannah II, 499
Cruder, Hallie V, 617
Cruea, Allie V, 734
Cruea, Austin V, 734
Cruea, John V, 734
Cruea, Mayme V, 734
Crues, Sarah I, 773
Cruickshank, Barbara II, 499
Cruickshank, Barbra II, 499
Cruickshank, Catherine Taylor II, 499
Cruickshank, Cicely II, 499
Cruickshank, Cisley II, 499
Cruickshank, Cissley II, 499
Cruickshank, Elizabeth II, 499
Cruickshank, George II, 499
Cruickshank, James II, 499
Cruickshank, John II, 499
Cruickshank, Joseph II, 499
Cruickshank, Margaret II, 499
Cruickshank, Margaret Elmslie II, 499
Cruickshank, Mary II, 499
Cruickshank, Rachel II, 499
Cruickshank, Rebekah II, 499
Cruickshank, Susanna II, 499
Cruickshank, Susannah II, 499
Cruickshanks, Elizabeth II, 558
Cruickshanks, Nellie May IV, 1155
Cruise, Joshua V, 232
Cruise, Pleasant V, 667
Cruit, Elizabeth V, 382
Cruit, Elizabeth V, 617
Cruit, George V, 382
Cruit, George A. V, 382
Cruit, George E. V, 382
Cruit, George E. V, 617
Cruit, Grace C. V, 617
Cruit, Gracie C. V, 382
Cruit, Gracy V, 382
Cruit, Lizzie V, 382
Cruit, Lizzie V, 702
Crukshank, Cissley II, 472
Crukshank, Cissley II, 499
Crukshank, James II, 499
Crukshank, John II, 684
Crukshank, Joseph II, 499
Crukshank, Joseph II, 591
Crukshank, Joseph II, 684
Crukshank, Joseph II, 702
Crukshank, Mary II, 499
Crukshank, Mary II, 591
Crukshank, Mary II, 684
Crukshank, Rachel II, 702
Crukshank, Susanna II, 684
Crum, ??? IV, 947
Crum, Agness VI, 900
Crum, Alfaretta IV, 947
Crum, Almira IV, 947
Crum, Almira B. IV, 947
Crum, Alpharetta IV, 947
Crum, Alton W. IV, 947
Crum, Asenath Lorane IV, 947
Crum, Asenath Lorena IV, 947
Crum, Daisy IV, 947
Crum, Daisy J. IV, 947
Crum, Elizabeth VI, 484
Crum, Elmira IV, 947
Crum, Gibson IV, 947
Crum, Gilbert VI, 873
Crum, Gilbert VI, 906
Crum, Gilbert VI, 935
Crum, Gilbert VI, 1005
Crum, Gilbert VI, 1015
Crum, Gilson IV, 947
Crum, Isaac VI, 900
Crum, Laura IV, 979
Crum, Lorena IV, 947
Crum, Mary C. IV, 947
Crum, Mary Catharine IV, 947
Crum, William Alton IV, 947
Crum, Wm. Alton IV, 947
Crum., Elizabeth VI, 946
Crumb, Elizabeth VI, 1015
Crumb, Gilbert VI, 872
Crumb, Gilbert VI, 901
Crumb, Gilbert VI, 906
Crumb, Gilbert VI, 925
Crumb, Gilbert VI, 1015
Crumbly, Abraham I, 1081
Crumbly, Abraham I, 1091
Crumbly, Abraham I, 1095
Crumbly, Anne I, 1081
Crumbly, Asa I, 1081
Crumbly, Elizabeth I, 1081
Crumbly, Elizabeth I, 1091
Crumbly, Elizabeth I, 1095
Crumbly, Isaac H. I, 1081
Crumbly, Martha I, 1081
Crumbly, Mary I, 1081
Crumbly, Samuel M. I, 1081
Crumbly, William I, 1091
Crumby, Abraham I, 1091
Crumine, Ruth V, 734
Crumine, Ruth V, 806
Crumley, Aaron H. I, 1150
Crumley, Abraham I, 1091
Crumley, Abraham I, 1150
Crumley, Blanch V, 382
Crumley, Blanch V, 667
Crumley, Charles V, 382
Crumley, Charles, Sr. V, 382
Crumley, Clark V, 667
Crumley, Elizabeth I, 1091
Crumley, Elizabeth I, 1150
Crumley, Elizabeth C. I, 1140
Crumley, Esther V, 382
Crumley, Henry V, 382
Crumley, Henry B. V, 667
Crumley, Jane V, 165
Crumley, Jane V, 205
Crumley, Jennie V, 667
Crumley, Laura V, 667
Crumley, Martha I, 1091
Crumley, Martha I, 1150
Crumley, Martha I, 1155
Crumley, Mary I, 1091
Crumley, Mary VI, 381
Crumley, Mary VI, 436
Crumley, Mary E. V, 382
Crumley, Mary E. V, 667
Crumley, Mollie V, 382
Crumley, Mollie V, 667
Crumley, Rhoda I, 1150
Crumley, Rosalta V, 667
Crumley, Rosanna V, 667
Crumley, Samuel M. I, 1091
Crumley, William I, 1091
Crumley, William I, 1150
Crumly, Aaron H. I, 1081
Crumly, Aaron Hammer I, 1140
Crumly, Abraham I, 1081
Crumly, Abraham I, 1091
Crumly, Abraham I, 1150
Crumly, Aritha I, 1140
Crumly, Elizabeth I, 1091
Crumly, Elizabeth Chloe I, 1081
Crumly, Henry B. V, 667
Crumly, James Jones I, 1081
Crumly, Jane I, 1081
Crumly, Mary I, 1091
Crumly, Mary I, 1095
Crumly, Mary V, 484
Crumly, Mary V, 487
Crumly, Rhoda I, 1081
Crumly, Rhoda I, 1140
Crumly, Rita??? I, 1081
Crumly, Sarah VI, 381
Crumly, Sarah VI, 384
Crumly, William I, 1081
Crumly, William I, 1140
Crumly, Writty I, 1081
Crumm, Gilbert VI, 898
Crump, Beverley VI, 900
Crump, Charles VI, 873
Crump, Charles VI, 900
Crump, Chas. VI, 924
Crump, Daniel VI, 881
Crump, Elizabeth VI, 889
Crump, Elizabeth VI, 900
Crump, Fendall VI, 904

Crump, Fendall VI, 907
Crump, Fendall VI, 948
Crump, Frances M. VI, 900
Crump, George VI, 900
Crump, Gilbert VI, 900
Crump, Letty VI, 900
Crump, Mary VI, 900
Crump, Mary W. VI, 924
Crump, Nancy VI, 925
Crump, P. VI, 900
Crump, Pamelia VI, 809
Crump, Pamelia VI, 966
Crump, Permelia VI, 900
Crump, Polly VI, 935
Crump, Rhoda VI, 900
Crump, Richard VI, 889
Crump, Sally VI, 883
Crump, Sophia VI, 881
Crump, Susanna VI, 900
Crump, Susanna VI, 948
Crump, Susannah VI, 924
Crump, Thomas VI, 809
Crump, Thomas VI, 881
Crump, Thomas VI, 900
Crump, Wilkerson VI, 900
Crump, William VI, 900
Crump, William P. VI, 900
Crumpacker, Angeline L. VI, 979
Crumpacker, Charlotte VI, 900
Crumpacker, Constance VI, 900
Crumpacker, Dandridge VI, 900
Crumpacker, Edward VI, 900
Crumpacker, Elizabeth VI, 898
Crumpacker, Elizal VI, 900
Crumpacker, Elvira VI, 913
Crumpacker, Hannah VI, 900
Crumpacker, Jacob VI, 900
Crumpacker, Joel VI, 900
Crumpacker, Joel VI, 913
Crumpacker, Joel VI, 920
Crumpacker, Joel VI, 935
Crumpacker, John VI, 900
Crumpacker, Judith VI, 900
Crumpacker, Lucinda VI, 900
Crumpacker, Mary VI, 900
Crumpacker, Mary VI, 1004
Crumpacker, Mary S. VI, 900
Crumpacker, Mildred S. VI, 900
Crumpacker, Owen VI, 900
Crumpacker, Peter VI, 898
Crumpacker, Peter VI, 900
Crumpacker, Polly VI, 901
Crumpacker, Richard VI, 900
Crumpecker, Abram VI, 871
Crumpecker, Charlotte VI, 902
Crumpecker, Constance VI, 900
Crumpecker, D. VI, 971
Crumpecker, Dandridge VI, 900
Crumpecker, Elizabeth VI, 809
Crumpecker, Frances VI, 871
Crumpecker, Joel VI, 818
Crumpecker, Joel VI, 900
Crumpecker, John VI, 809
Crumpecker, Lucinda VI, 900
Crumpecker, Martha VI, 1008
Crumpecker, Owen VI, 935
Crumpecker, Owen VI, 1008
Crumpecker, Peter VI, 871
Crumpecker, Peter VI, 902
Crumpecker, Richard VI, 902
Crumpler, Mary VI, 60
Crumply, Mary VI, 381
Crumpt, Margariet P. VI, 903
Crumpt, Thomas VI, 905
Crumpt., Margaret P. VI, 905
Crumpton, Angelina VI, 809
Crumpton, Angelina VI, 818
Crumpton, Archibald VI, 809
Crumpton, David VI, 923
Crumpton, David VI, 995
Crumpton, Elizabeth VI, 484
Crumpton, Emily VI, 900
Crumpton, Fanny VI, 923
Crumpton, Henry VI, 809
Crumpton, Jacob VI, 900
Crumpton, John VI, 484
Crumpton, John VI, 812
Crumpton, John Bartholomew VI, 484
Crumpton, Mary VI, 381
Crumpton, Peggy VI, 995
Crumpton, Polly VI, 809
Crumpton, Sarah VI, 900
Crumpton, Sidney VI, 363
Crumpton, Sidney VI, 381
Crumpton, William VI, 900
Crumrine, Ema IV, 1276
Crumton, Sidney VI, 381
Crunkilton, Margaret Anita IV, 1312
Cruse, Agness G. VI, 837
Cruse, James II, 442
Cruse, John II, 442
Cruse, Joseph II, 442
Cruse, Judy VI, 850
Cruse, Magdalen II, 442
Cruse, Magdeline II, 442
Cruse, Mary II, 442
Cruse, Mary VI, 837
Cruse, Matilda V, 382
Cruse, Matilda V, 411
Cruse, Ruth II, 442
Cruse, Sarah V, 484
Cruse, William II, 442
Crusher, Ann II, 192
Crusher, Ann II, 213
Crusher, Dorothy II, 213
Crusher, George II, 213
Crusher, George II, 224
Crusher, Hannah II, 213
Crusher, Hannah II, 224
Crusher, John II, 192
Crusher, John II, 213
Crusher, John II, 247
Crusher, John, Jr. II, 213
Crusher, Mary II, 213
Crusher, Mary II, 247
Crusher, Mary VI, 541
Crusher, Rachel II, 192
Crusher, Rachel II, 213
Crusher, Sarah II, 192
Crusher, Sarah II, 213
Crussie, Charles II, 213
Crutchfield, Alfred III, 93
Crutchfield, Douglas Milton III, 93
Crutchfield, Ethel III, 93
Crutchfield, Ethel III, 343
Crutchfield, Frank III, 93
Crutchfield, Frank III, 343
Crutchfield, Philip Jerome III, 93
Crutchfield, Ruth I, 384
Crute, Clara V, 326
Crute, Elizabeth V, 667
Crute, Lizzie V, 667
Crute, Mary V, 326
Crute, Mintie V, 326
Cruthers, Wd. Rachel VI, 542
Cruthes, Lydia I, 378
Cruthes, Lydia I, 384
Cruze, Ann I, 346
Cruze, John I, 346
Cruze, Ruth I, 346
Cry, Hugh H. I, 1150
Cry, Susan Ann I, 1150
Crye, Hugh I, 1140
Cryer, Elizabeth VI, 98
Cryer, Elizabeth VI, 106
Crygier, Alice V. III, 93
Crygier, Alice V. III, 128
Crygier, Catharine A. III, 93
Crygier, Catharine A. III, 128
Crygier, James H. III, 93
Crygier, James H. III, 128
Cryso, Jacob VI, 900
Cryso, Rebecca VI, 900
Cryso, Sally VI, 900
Cubben, Edward IV, 1312
Cubberson, Sarah I, 384
Cubberson, Sarah I, 402
Cubcaub, Stalin IV, 1086
Cubit, Elizabeth IV, 1234
Cubit, Robert IV, 1234
Cuckler, Harry IV, 1312
Cuckler, Harry A. IV, 1312
Cuckler, Samuel IV, 1312
Cuckler, Samuel H. IV, 1312
Cude, Callie I, 615
Cude, Callie I, 632
Cude, Callie T. I, 632
Cude, Charles I, 632
Cude, Charles S. I, 615
Cude, Charles S. I, 632
Cude, Delphina I, 615
Cude, Eleanor I, 677
Cude, Elisabeth Stanley I, 615
Cude, Elizabeth Stanley I, 632
Cude, Marjorie Gardner I, 615
Cude, Marjorie Gardner I, 632
Cude, Martin Luther I, 615
Cude, Robert Hollingsworth I, 615
Cude, Robert Hollingsworth I, 632
Cuff, Absalom II, 352
Cuff, Ester II, 352
Cuff, Martha II, 352
Culberson, Anna E. I, 445
Culberson, Sarah I, 384
Culberson, Susanna I, 384
Culbertson, Anna C. I, 445
Culbertson, Anna E. I, 445
Culbertson, L. P. IV, 1312
Culbertson, Mildred IV, 1312
Culbertson, Mrs. ??? IV, 1312
Culbertson, Nancy V, 617
Culbertson, Robert V, 617
Culbertson, Sarah IV, 866
Culbertson, Susan IV, 867
Culin, Charles II, 352
Culin, Elizabeth A. II, 731
Culin, John II, 352
Culin, Mary II, 702
Culin, Mary A. II, 731
Culin, Mary C. II, 731
Culin, Mary C. II, 735
Culin, Mary Canby II, 735
Culin, Robert S. II, 702
Culin, Robert Stewart II, 702
Culin, Susanna II, 499
Culin, Susanna II, 702
Culin, Susanna S. II, 702
Culin, Wm. J. II, 731
Cull, Lucy IV, 810
Cullars, Andrew V, 734
Cullars, Maggie V, 734
Cullenberger, Hazel R. IV, 696
Cullenberger, Hazel Ruby IV, 696
Cullenberger, Mr. Geo. IV, 696
Cullenberger, Mrs. ??? IV, 696
Culler, Byron IV, 696
Culler, Hadie IV, 696
Culler, Haidee IV, 696
Culler, Kenneth IV, 696
Cullers, Andrew V, 734
Cullers, Maggie V, 734
Cullers, Margaret V, 734
Cully, Lillian Gambier IV, 1312
Culpeper, Lord ??? VI, 146
Culpeper, Sarah I, 137
Culpeper, Sarah I, 162
Culpeper, Susanna VI, 231
Culpin, Elizabeth II, 499
Culver, Amy III, 93
Culver, James W. III, 93
Culver, Jenny VI, 809
Culver, Joseph VI, 809
Culver, Martha IV, 1234
Culver, Martha V, 806
Culver, Martha W. IV, 1234
Culver, Mary III, 93
Cumbee, Charles VI, 809
Cumbee, Emanuel VI, 809
Cumbee, Emmanuel VI, 846
Cumbee, Levicy VI, 809
Cumbee, Margaret VI, 847
Cumbee, Molly VI, 809
Cumbee, Morgan VI, 809
Cumbee, Nancy VI, 809
Cumbee, Nancy VI, 817
Cumbee, Peter VI, 809
Cumbee, Susannah VI, 846
Cumbee, Thomas VI, 847
Cumberlidge, Rachel II, 466
Cumberlidge, Rachel II, 499
Cumbridge, Giles II, 442
Cumbridge, Wauke II, 442
Cumby, Catharine VI, 801
Cumby, Emanuel VI, 809
Cumby, Kitty VI, 800
Cumby, Levicy VI, 809
Cumby, Molly VI, 809
Cumby, Morgan VI, 809
Cumby, Peter VI, 860
Cumby, Peter W. VI, 854
Cumby, Rebeckah VI, 860
Cumby, Sarah VI, 860
Cumby, Simeon VI, 801
Cumby, Simeon VI, 860
Cumby, Suannoe VI, 860
Cumerine, Susanna B. V, 950
Cumerine, Susanna B. V, 956
Cumfort, Jeremiah II, 990
Cumfort, Jeremiah II, 1037
Cumins, Harper H. I, 535
Cumins, Sarah V, 950
Cumins, Sarah V, 961
Cumley, Abigail II, 499
Cumley, Abraham II, 499
Cumley, Ann II, 499
Cumley, Hannah II, 499
Cumley, Isaac II, 499
Cumley, John II, 499
Cumley, John IV, 469
Cumley, Mary II, 499
Cumley, Priscilla IV, 469
Cumley, Susanna II, 499
Cumly, Abigail II, 990
Cumly, Abigail II, 992
Cumly, Abraham II, 499
Cumly, Abraham II, 990
Cumly, Abraham II, 992
Cumly, Agnes II, 990
Cumly, Ann II, 499
Cumly, Ann II, 992
Cumly, Benjamin II, 992
Cumly, Hannah II, 990
Cumly, Isaac II, 990
Cumly, Jacob II, 990
Cumly, John II, 990
Cumly, John II, 992
Cumly, Mary II, 499
Cumly, Mary II, 990
Cumly, Mary II, 992
Cumly, Susannah II, 990
Cummer, Harry III, 93
Cummer, Harry III, 363
Cummer, Mildred III, 93
Cummer, Mildred III, 363
Cummin, Carrie III, 94
Cummin, Carrie III, 267
Cummin, Carrie C. III, 94
Cummin, Eleanor Claire III, 94
Cummin, Ida Beauvais III, 94
Cummin, J. Louise III, 94
Cummin, Jean III, 94
Cummin, Jos. H. III, 94
Cummin, Jos. W. III, 94
Cummin, Joseph W. III, 94
Cummin, Joseph W. III, 267
Cummin, Marian III, 94
Cummin, Marian III, 334
Cummin, Marian Louise III, 94
Cummin, Melville P. III, 94
Cummin, Melville P. III, 334
Cummin, Melville Porter III, 94
Cummin, Walter Edwin III, 94
Cumming, Asher II, 499
Cumming, David II, 499
Cumming, David II, 506
Cumming, David II, 553
Cumming, David B. II, 500
Cumming, George M. II, 499
Cumming, George M. II, 500
Cumming, George M. II, 506
Cumming, Grace II, 850
Cumming, Grace II, 855
Cumming, Hannah II, 499
Cumming, Hannah II, 506
Cumming, John II, 735
Cumming, Lydia Ann II, 735
Cumming, Martha II, 499
Cumming, Martha II, 735
Cumming, Rachel II, 506
Cumming, Rachel II, 679
Cumming, Rebecca II, 499
Cumming, Rebecca II, 553
Cumming, Samuel II, 507
Cumming, Sarah II, 499
Cumming, Sarah II, 553
Cumming, Solomon II, 499
Cumming, Solomon II, 735
Cumming, Wm. II, 499
Cummings, Alice I, 632
Cummings, Alice C. I, 535
Cummings, Alice Della I, 615
Cummings, Ann II, 352
Cummings, Ann II, 499
Cummings, Annie I, 616
Cummings, Annie C. I, 624
Cummings, Asher II, 499
Cummings, Benjamin Wilson II, 500
Cummings, David II, 213
Cummings, David II, 352
Cummings, David II, 499
Cummings, David II, 598
Cummings, David B. II, 500
Cummings, Edward III, 94
Cummings, Eleanor II, 352
Cummings, Elizabeth I, 535
Cummings, Elizabeth I, 583
Cummings, Elizabeth II, 352
Cummings, Elizabeth II, 499
Cummings, Elizabeth IV, 687
Cummings, Elizabeth IV, 697
Cummings, Ella G. I, 527
Cummings, Ella G. I, 535
Cummings, Elma D. IV, 614
Cummings, Elma D. IV, 619
Cummings, Emeline I, 535
Cummings, Emeline I, 615
Cummings, Emeline I, 622
Cummings, Emeline I, 624
Cummings, Emily II, 500
Cummings, Emma I, 622
Cummings, Enos I, 535
Cummings, Enos I, 622
Cummings, Enos I, 624
Cummings, Enos F. I, 615
Cummings, Ethel M. IV, 619
Cummings, Ethel M. IV, 621
Cummings, Ethel Margaret IV, 619
Cummings, Flora V, 667
Cummings, George II, 352
Cummings, George II, 499
Cummings, George M. II, 499
Cummings, George M. II, 500
Cummings, Hannah II, 352
Cummings, Hannah II, 499
Cummings, Hannah II, 500
Cummings, Hannah II, 631
Cummings, Harper H. I, 535
Cummings, Harriott II, 499
Cummings, Jane II, 352
Cummings, Jane II, 499
Cummings, Jennie I, 626
Cummings, Jennie I, 628
Cummings, John II, 352
Cummings, John II, 499
Cummings, John II, 735
Cummings, John S. II, 735
Cummings, Julianna II, 499
Cummings, Julius I, 535
Cummings, Lee I, 535
Cummings, Lee G. I, 626
Cummings, Lee G. I, 628
Cummings, Lydia Ann II, 735
Cummings, Lydia Ann II, 743
Cummings, Margaret II, 499
Cummings, Maria II, 499
Cummings, Martha II, 499
Cummings, Martha II, 735
Cummings, Martha L. VI, 632
Cummings, Martha T. II, 735
Cummings, Martitia I, 626
Cummings, Martitia I, 628
Cummings, Mary II, 171
Cummings, Mary II, 213
Cummings, Mary II, 352
Cummings, Mary II, 499
Cummings, Nora I, 535
Cummings, Rachel II, 499
Cummings, Rachel II, 598
Cummings, Rebecca II, 499
Cummings, Richard II, 213
Cummings, Samuel II, 352
Cummings, Samuel II, 499
Cummings, Sarah II, 352
Cummings, Sarah II, 499
Cummings, Solomon II, 499
Cummings, Solomon II, 735
Cummings, Thomas II, 171
Cummings, Thomas II, 213
Cummings, Thomas II, 499
Cummings, Thomas, Jr. II, 499
Cummings, Wm. II, 499
Cummings, Wm. C. II, 499
Cummington, Anna IV, 1312
Cummins, ??? VI, 674
Cummins, Alexr. VI, 903
Cummins, Alice IV, 1312
Cummins, Blanchie V, 617
Cummins, Edwin IV, 1312
Cummins, Eleanor II, 352
Cummins, Elizabeth IV, 28
Cummins, Elizabeth IV, 32
Cummins, Emma V, 617
Cummins, Fannie IV, 1312
Cummins, Flora M. V, 617
Cummins, Frances IV, 1205
Cummins, Frances F. IV, 1205
Cummins, Francis J. V, 617
Cummins, Horace D. V, 617
Cummins, Jane II, 499
Cummins, John II, 352
Cummins, Joseph Lawrence II, 790
Cummins, Lana IV, 572
Cummins, Lana IV, 581
Cummins, Lizzie A. II, 815
Cummins, Martha V, 617
Cummins, Martha L. VI, 674
Cummins, Mary IV, 1276
Cummins, Mary A. I, 929
Cummins, Mary Mattis II, 790
Cummins, Robert IV, 1312
Cummins, Robert V, 617
Cummins, Robert G. V, 617
Cummins, Ruth IV, 28
Cummins, Ruth IV, 32
Cummins, Sallie I, 929
Cummins, Susanna IV, 581
Cummins, Thos. V, 901
Cummins, Townsend M. V, 617
Cummins, W. T. IV, 1205
Cummins, Walkup Nimrod V, 617
Cummins, Warren I, 929
Cummins, Wm. II, 499
Cummins, Worthie L. V, 617
Cumpton, Amos I, 1027
Cumpton, Anna V, 230
Cumpton, Anna V, 262
Cumpton, Isacah VI, 905

Cumpton, John VI, 895
Cumpton, Josiah VI, 900
Cumpton, Jules VI, 900
Cumpton, Lydia VI, 895
Cumpton, Martha VI, 966
Cumpton, Sarah VI, 966
Cunard, Abigail VI, 632
Cunard, Ann VI, 485
Cunard, Ann VI, 632
Cunard, Edward VI, 485
Cunard, Edward VI, 632
Cunard, Edward, Jr. VI, 485
Cunard, Elizabeth IV, 193
Cunard, Gerrard VI, 484
Cunard, Henry VI, 485
Cunard, Henry VI, 632
Cunard, Jarret VI, 485
Cunard, Jarret VI, 632
Cunard, John VI, 485
Cunard, John VI, 632
Cunard, Judith VI, 485
Cunard, Judith VI, 632
Cunard, Pamela VI, 485
Cunard, Pamela VI, 632
Cunard, Sarah VI, 485
Cunard, Sarah VI, 632
Cuncan, Edmond II, 994
Cunch, James VI, 236
Cundell, William II, 352
Cunderton, Ann II, 442
Cundiff, Betsey VI, 901
Cundiff, Charlotte VI, 1013
Cundiff, Chesley VI, 901
Cundiff, Christopher VI, 901
Cundiff, Christopher VI, 911
Cundiff, Christopher VI, 944
Cundiff, Christopher VI, 1015
Cundiff, Christopher C. VI, 901
Cundiff, Eleanor VI, 901
Cundiff, Eli VI, 901
Cundiff, Elijah VI, 809
Cundiff, Elijah VI, 901
Cundiff, Elijah VI, 922
Cundiff, Elijah VI, 948
Cundiff, Elijah C. VI, 874
Cundiff, Elijah C. VI, 901
Cundiff, Elijah C. VI, 918
Cundiff, Elijah C. VI, 923
Cundiff, Elijah C. VI, 947
Cundiff, Elijah C. VI, 1012
Cundiff, Elijah E. VI, 901
Cundiff, Elijah E. VI, 960
Cundiff, Elisha VI, 303
Cundiff, Elisha VI, 901
Cundiff, Elisha VI, 908
Cundiff, Elisha VI, 1013
Cundiff, Elizabeth VI, 900
Cundiff, Elizabeth VI, 901
Cundiff, Elizabeth VI, 908
Cundiff, Elizabeth VI, 922
Cundiff, Elizabeth Frances VI, 888
Cundiff, Frances VI, 809
Cundiff, George W. VI, 901
Cundiff, Gorgg T. VI, 925
Cundiff, Grigg T. VI, 901
Cundiff, Henry B. VI, 901
Cundiff, Henry B. VI, 922
Cundiff, Henry B. VI, 962
Cundiff, Isaac VI, 900
Cundiff, Isaac VI, 901
Cundiff, Isaac VI, 911
Cundiff, Isaac VI, 922
Cundiff, Isaac VI, 942
Cundiff, Isaac VI, 964
Cundiff, Isaac VI, 1013
Cundiff, Isham VI, 901
Cundiff, James VI, 809
Cundiff, James VI, 900
Cundiff, James VI, 901
Cundiff, James VI, 904
Cundiff, James VI, 975
Cundiff, James VI, 997
Cundiff, James VI, 1007
Cundiff, Jane VI, 901
Cundiff, Jemima VI, 922
Cundiff, Jenny VI, 901
Cundiff, Jeremiah VI, 901
Cundiff, Jesse VI, 901
Cundiff, Jesse VI, 947
Cundiff, Jimmy VI, 901
Cundiff, John VI, 874
Cundiff, John VI, 897
Cundiff, John VI, 901
Cundiff, John VI, 967
Cundiff, John VI, 972
Cundiff, Joice VI, 901
Cundiff, Joice VI, 980
Cundiff, Jonathan VI, 901
Cundiff, Jonathan VI, 959
Cundiff, Jonathan E. VI, 901
Cundiff, Jubal VI, 863
Cundiff, Jubal VI, 901
Cundiff, Levice VI, 901
Cundiff, Lewis VI, 895
Cundiff, Lewis VI, 900
Cundiff, Lewis VI, 901
Cundiff, Lucinda Jane VI, 922
Cundiff, Lucy VI, 901
Cundiff, Lucy VI, 922
Cundiff, Lucy VI, 947
Cundiff, Mariah F. VI, 947
Cundiff, Marion M. VI, 944
Cundiff, Mary VI, 900
Cundiff, Mary VI, 901
Cundiff, Mary VI, 916
Cundiff, Mary VI, 966
Cundiff, Mary VI, 980
Cundiff, Mary VI, 997
Cundiff, Mary VI, 1013
Cundiff, Mary Ann Amanda VI, 901
Cundiff, Mary Jane VI, 948
Cundiff, Mary M. VI, 901
Cundiff, Mary S. VI, 966
Cundiff, Milley VI, 922
Cundiff, Milly VI, 922
Cundiff, Nancy VI, 901
Cundiff, Pamelia VI, 908
Cundiff, Peggy VI, 916
Cundiff, Permelia VI, 964
Cundiff, Polly VI, 901
Cundiff, Polly VI, 916
Cundiff, Rebecca VI, 901
Cundiff, Rebecca V. VI, 1015
Cundiff, Rhoda VI, 911
Cundiff, Richard VI, 874
Cundiff, Richard VI, 901
Cundiff, Salley VI, 901
Cundiff, Sally VI, 809
Cundiff, Sally VI, 901
Cundiff, Sally T. VI, 901
Cundiff, Sarah VI, 901
Cundiff, Sarah E. VI, 901
Cundiff, Sarah Jane VI, 901
Cundiff, Sary Elisha VI, 888
Cundiff, Shadrack VI, 901
Cundiff, Spicer VI, 901
Cundiff, Thomas VI, 880
Cundiff, Thomas VI, 901
Cundiff, Uriah VI, 901
Cundiff, Uriah H. VI, 901
Cundiff, Wd. Joicey VI, 897
Cundiff, William VI, 901
Cundiff, William B. VI, 901
Cundiff, Willis VI, 901
Cundiff, Winefred VI, 902
Cundill, Wm. II, 500
Cuningham, Rachel II, 992
Cuningham, Rachel II, 1032
Cuningham, Rebeckah II, 64
Cunnard, Abigail VI, 631
Cunnard, Ann VI, 470
Cunnard, Ann VI, 484
Cunnard, Ann VI, 485
Cunnard, Ann VI, 539
Cunnard, Edward VI, 484
Cunnard, Edward VI, 485
Cunnard, Edward, Jr. VI, 485
Cunnard, Elizabeth VI, 484
Cunnard, Gerrard VI, 484
Cunnard, Henry VI, 484
Cunnard, Henry VI, 485
Cunnard, James VI, 484
Cunnard, Jane VI, 484
Cunnard, Jarret VI, 485
Cunnard, John VI, 485
Cunnard, John, Jr. VI, 485
Cunnard, Jonathan VI, 484
Cunnard, Judith VI, 484
Cunnard, Judith VI, 485
Cunnard, Martha VI, 485
Cunnard, Nathan VI, 485
Cunnard, Pamela VI, 485
Cunnard, Sarah VI, 484
Cunnard, Sarah VI, 485
Cunnard, Thomas VI, 485
Cunnard???, Abigail VI, 629
Cunningham, ??? III, 94
Cunningham, Abner III, 94
Cunningham, Alexander I, 713
Cunningham, Ann I, 713
Cunningham, Ann II, 500
Cunningham, Anna I, 713
Cunningham, Anna III, 94
Cunningham, Anna VI, 828
Cunningham, Caroline VI, 381
Cunningham, Charles V, 382
Cunningham, Charles J. V, 382
Cunningham, Dalton V, 382
Cunningham, Dalton H. V, 382
Cunningham, David III, 94
Cunningham, E. Caroline VI, 369
Cunningham, E. Caroline VI, 370
Cunningham, E. Caroline VI, 383
Cunningham, Edward VI, 381
Cunningham, Edward L. VI, 369
Cunningham, Eliza III, 94
Cunningham, Eliza VI, 817
Cunningham, Elizabeth II, 352
Cunningham, Elizabeth II, 500
Cunningham, Elizabeth III, 94
Cunningham, Elizabeth IV, 190
Cunningham, Elizabeth IV, 193
Cunningham, Elizabeth V, 382
Cunningham, Elizabeth V, 901
Cunningham, Elizabeth VI, 381
Cunningham, Elizabeth VI, 809
Cunningham, Elizabeth VI, 901
Cunningham, Elizabeth A. V, 382
Cunningham, ELizabeth H. VI, 369
Cunningham, Elizabeth L. IV, 468
Cunningham, Elizabeth L. IV, 470
Cunningham, Finley IV, 193
Cunningham, Frank V, 382
Cunningham, George H. VI, 901
Cunningham, George H. VI, 949
Cunningham, Girl III, 94
Cunningham, Hannah VI, 901
Cunningham, Harriett IV, 1155
Cunningham, Hattie IV, 193
Cunningham, Hattie IV, 196
Cunningham, Ida V, 232
Cunningham, James III, 94
Cunningham, James IV, 196
Cunningham, James VI, 901
Cunningham, James C. VI, 901
Cunningham, James L. IV, 193
Cunningham, James M. V, 399
Cunningham, John VI, 948
Cunningham, John A. VI, 901
Cunningham, John P. VI, 809
Cunningham, John P. VI, 814
Cunningham, Judith I, 1007
Cunningham, Judith I, 1008
Cunningham, Judith VI, 901
Cunningham, Kate III, 68
Cunningham, Lauderwick P. VI, 989
Cunningham, Lavina S. VI, 901
Cunningham, Leana I, 612
Cunningham, Lizzie V, 382
Cunningham, Lodowick P. VI, 901
Cunningham, Louisa W. VI, 901
Cunningham, Lucy VI, 805
Cunningham, Lulu IV, 196
Cunningham, Margaret IV, 193
Cunningham, Martha Jane VI, 989
Cunningham, Martha P. VI, 901
Cunningham, Mary II, 500
Cunningham, Mary II, 1072
Cunningham, Mary II, 1074
Cunningham, Mary III, 90
Cunningham, Mary E. VI, 849
Cunningham, Mary J. C. VI, 809
Cunningham, Mary M. VI, 901
Cunningham, Mary P. VI, 814
Cunningham, Murrell VI, 800
Cunningham, Nancy VI, 857
Cunningham, Polly VI, 901
Cunningham, Rachel II, 992
Cunningham, Rachel II, 1049
Cunningham, Randolph VI, 901
Cunningham, Randolph VI, 989
Cunningham, Rebecca II, 64
Cunningham, Rebecca II, 109
Cunningham, Rebeckah II, 64
Cunningham, Rhoda VI, 850
Cunningham, Richard VI, 805
Cunningham, Richard VI, 817
Cunningham, Richard VI, 857
Cunningham, Robert Nicholas IV, 193
Cunningham, Samuel VI, 849
Cunningham, Samuel F. VI, 901
Cunningham, Samuel H. VI, 814
Cunningham, Sarah V, 399
Cunningham, Sarah VI, 800
Cunningham, Susanna VI, 874
Cunningham, Susanna VI, 942
Cunningham, Susannah VI, 901
Cunningham, Susie E. V, 901
Cunningham, Susie E. V, 904
Cunningham, Viola Belle IV, 193
Cunningham, William VI, 809
Cunningham, William VI, 828
Cunningham, William VI, 882
Cunningham, William VI, 901
Cunningham, William H. VI, 901
Cunningham, William H. VI, 902
Cunnington, Anna IV, 1312
Cunnington, Joseph IV, 1312
Cunrad, Abraham II, 493
Cunrod, Elizabeth VI, 379
Cunrod, Elizabeth VI, 408
Cunrod, James VI, 379
Cunrod, James VI, 408
Cunrod, Jane VI, 379
Cunrod, Jane VI, 408
Cuomo, Maria III, 94
Cuomo, Pietro III, 94
Cuomo, Taddeo III, 94
Cupp, Manda V, 991
Curbit, Mary II, 213
Curborough, Hannah II, 500
Curcuit, Hannah II, 213
Curcuit, Hannah II, 273
Curd, Charlotte V, 396
Curel, Margery I, 384
Curits, Catharine III, 290
Curits, Lewis B. III, 290
Curl, ??? V, 557
Curl, Alma IV, 1205
Curl, Alonzo V, 45
Curl, Alonzo V, 558
Curl, Alonzo S. V, 617
Curl, Alvin IV, 1276
Curl, Amos IV, 1276
Curl, Amos V, 950
Curl, Amos P. IV, 1276
Curl, Amos P. IV, 1282
Curl, Amy V, 484
Curl, Amy VI, 306
Curl, Amy VI, 340
Curl, Amy VI, 381
Curl, Amy VI, 485
Curl, Ann IV, 1276
Curl, Anna V, 557
Curl, Anna V, 573
Curl, Anna VI, 341
Curl, Anthony V, 617
Curl, Archibald VI, 809
Curl, Archibald VI, 902
Curl, Asenath I, 434
Curl, Asenath I, 445
Curl, Benjamin IV, 697
Curl, Benjamin V, 484
Curl, Benjamin VI, 341
Curl, C. Davis I, 615
Curl, Caleb Stratton IV, 697
Curl, Catharine IV, 1276
Curl, Catharine V, 484
Curl, Catharine V, 969
Curl, Catharine V, 974
Curl, Catherine V, 484
Curl, Caty V, 950
Curl, Channing V, 558
Curl, Channing David V, 557
Curl, Charles VI, 381
Curl, Charles VI, 485
Curl, Chas. V, 667
Curl, Clifford I, 236
Curl, Clifford D. I, 630
Curl, Clifford D. I, 632
Curl, Curl IV, 1155
Curl, Daniel Stacy V, 557
Curl, Daniel Stacy V, 558
Curl, Darby IV, 697
Curl, David V, 482
Curl, David V, 484
Curl, David V, 557
Curl, David V, 667
Curl, David A. IV, 1276
Curl, David Channing V, 558
Curl, Edward D. IV, 1276
Curl, Elias IV, 697
Curl, Elias V, 484
Curl, Elias V, 485
Curl, Elias V, 557
Curl, Elias F. V, 557
Curl, Elias F. V, 570
Curl, Elias Fisher V, 557
Curl, Elihu IV, 1276
Curl, Eliza IV, 1276
Curl, Eliza IV, 1282
Curl, Eliza V, 484
Curl, Eliza V, 517
Curl, Eliza V, 557
Curl, Eliza V, 969
Curl, Eliza V, 973
Curl, Eliza VI, 902
Curl, Eliza A. V, 667
Curl, Eliza Ann V, 557
Curl, Eliza Ann V, 667
Curl, Eliza J. IV, 1276
Curl, Elizabeth I, 535
Curl, Elizabeth I, 1016
Curl, Elizabeth IV, 28
Curl, Elizabeth IV, 46
Curl, Elizabeth V, 484
Curl, Elizabeth V, 557
Curl, Elizabeth VI, 381
Curl, Elizabeth VI, 485
Curl, Elvis J. I, 615
Curl, Elwood V, 557
Curl, Emily E. IV, 1276
Curl, Emma V, 617
Curl, Enoch V, 45
Curl, Enoch VI, 350
Curl, Esther V, 557
Curl, Esther V, 667
Curl, F. M. IV, 1205
Curl, Flora V, 557
Curl, Flora V, 583
Curl, Flora E. V, 667
Curl, Frank V, 557
Curl, Frank V, 558
Curl, Frank V, 667
Curl, Frank M. V, 667
Curl, George I, 434
Curl, George I, 445
Curl, George G. VI, 809
Curl, Gilielma Maria V, 484
Curl, Gulielma Mariah V, 484
Curl, Hadley V, 45
Curl, Hadly VI, 350
Curl, Hannah V, 45
Curl, Hannah VI, 350
Curl, Hannah VI, 381
Curl, Hannah VI, 485
Curl, Hannah P. V, 667
Curl, Henry V, 667
Curl, Henry H. V, 557
Curl, Hiram V, 557
Curl, Hiram V, 558
Curl, Hiram V, 667
Curl, Jacob V, 484
Curl, Jacob VI, 341
Curl, Jacob P. V, 484
Curl, James IV, 697
Curl, James V, 45
Curl, James V, 484
Curl, James VI, 350
Curl, James VI, 381
Curl, James VI, 485
Curl, James VI, 550
Curl, James VI, 632
Curl, James VI, 693
Curl, Jane VI, 809
Curl, Jemima V, 484
Curl, Jeremiah I, 434
Curl, Jeremiah I, 445
Curl, Joel IV, 697
Curl, Joel V, 484
Curl, Joel V, 485
Curl, John IV, 697
Curl, John V, 45
Curl, John V, 484
Curl, John VI, 350
Curl, John G. IV, 470
Curl, Joseph IV, 697
Curl, Joseph IV, 1269
Curl, Joseph IV, 1276
Curl, Joseph V, 45
Curl, Joseph V, 484
Curl, Joseph V, 950
Curl, Joseph VI, 341
Curl, Joseph VI, 350
Curl, Joseph VI, 485
Curl, Joseph VI, 809
Curl, Joseph F. V, 484
Curl, Judith V, 473
Curl, Judith V, 484
Curl, Kate I, 615
Curl, Kate I, 630
Curl, Kate I, 632
Curl, Kathrine II, 992
Curl, Katie V, 557
Curl, Lena V, 617
Curl, Lena V, 667
Curl, Levi VI, 341
Curl, Louisa IV, 1276
Curl, Louisa IV, 1286
Curl, Louisa A. V, 97
Curl, Louiza IV, 1276
Curl, Lydia V, 557
Curl, Lydia V, 583
Curl, Lydia V, 667
Curl, Mahlon I, 434
Curl, Mahlon VI, 341
Curl, Margery I, 384
Curl, Margery I, 434
Curl, Margery I, 445
Curl, Marietta IV, 1276
Curl, Martha V, 484
Curl, Martha H. V, 557
Curl, Martha H. V, 667
Curl, Mary I, 434
Curl, Mary I, 443
Curl, Mary I, 445

Curl, Mary V, 473
Curl, Mary V, 484
Curl, Mary V, 485
Curl, Mary VI, 485
Curl, Mary E. IV, 1276
Curl, Mary E. V, 617
Curl, Mattie H. V, 674
Curl, Mina IV, 1205
Curl, Morris IV, 1276
Curl, Morris A. IV, 1276
Curl, Nancy V, 484
Curl, Nancy E. IV, 1249
Curl, Naome VI, 341
Curl, Naomi IV, 697
Curl, Naomi V, 391
Curl, Naomi V, 484
Curl, Naomi P. V, 557
Curl, Olive V, 45
Curl, Olive V, 558
Curl, Olive V, 667
Curl, Olive M. V, 558
Curl, Oliver V, 557
Curl, Ora IV, 1205
Curl, Orville V, 617
Curl, Oscar B. IV, 1276
Curl, Otis IV, 1276
Curl, Otis W. IV, 1276
Curl, Ova IV, 1155
Curl, Ova IV, 1205
Curl, Pearl IV, 1282
Curl, Rachel IV, 1276
Curl, Rachel V, 484
Curl, Rachel V, 557
Curl, Rachel VI, 350
Curl, Rebecca V, 482
Curl, Rebecca V, 484
Curl, Rebecca V, 557
Curl, Rebecca V, 586
Curl, Rebecca V, 667
Curl, Rebecca V, 969
Curl, Rebecca V, 973
Curl, Rebeccah VI, 381
Curl, Rebeckah VI, 306
Curl, Rebeckah VI, 341
Curl, Rebekah VI, 485
Curl, Rhoda M. V, 557
Curl, Rhoda M. V, 667
Curl, Ruth I, 434
Curl, Ruth I, 445
Curl, Ruth V, 45
Curl, Ruth VI, 350
Curl, Ruth VI, 485
Curl, Ruth VI, 550
Curl, Ruth VI, 632
Curl, Ruth VI, 693
Curl, Salathiel P. V, 617
Curl, Sally VI, 341
Curl, Samuel IV, 28
Curl, Samuel IV, 619
Curl, Samuel IV, 697
Curl, Samuel V, 45
Curl, Samuel V, 326
Curl, Samuel V, 557
Curl, Samuel V, 583
Curl, Samuel V, 667
Curl, Samuel VI, 350
Curl, Samuel, Jr. IV, 619
Curl, Sarah I, 384
Curl, Sarah I, 434
Curl, Sarah I, 445
Curl, Sarah I, 535
Curl, Sarah I, 1016
Curl, Sarah IV, 28
Curl, Sarah IV, 697
Curl, Sarah V, 45
Curl, Sarah V, 484
Curl, Sarah V, 557
Curl, Sarah V, 667
Curl, Sarah VI, 341
Curl, Sarah VI, 809
Curl, Sarah E. V, 557
Curl, Sarah E. V, 617
Curl, Sarah E. V, 667
Curl, Sarah Elizabeth V, 557
Curl, Sarah Elizabeth V, 570
Curl, Sarah May I, 615
Curl, Sarah Melissa V, 667
Curl, Susan VI, 809
Curl, Susan M. V, 617
Curl, Susanna IV, 28
Curl, Susannah IV, 697
Curl, Susannah VI, 381
Curl, Susannah VI, 485
Curl, Viola V, 557
Curl, W. H. IV, 1155
Curl, William I, 434
Curl, William I, 445
Curl, Willie IV, 1205
Curl, Wm. IV, 1205
Curl, Wm. H. IV, 1205
Curl, Wm., Jr. IV, 1205
Curle, ??? VI, 306
Curle, Amy VI, 306
Curle, Amy VI, 341
Curle, Charles VI, 306
Curle, Elias VI, 306
Curle, Elizabeth VI, 306
Curle, Emma VI, 306
Curle, Hannah VI, 306
Curle, Hannah VI, 311
Curle, James VI, 306
Curle, James VI, 381
Curle, Joel V, 484
Curle, Jos. VI, 306
Curle, Jos. VI, 311
Curle, Joseph IV, 697
Curle, Joseph IV, 707
Curle, Joseph VI, 306
Curle, Joseph VI, 341
Curle, Joseph VI, 809
Curle, Mary VI, 485
Curle, Mary VI, 496
Curle, Polly VI, 989
Curle, Rebecca IV, 707
Curle, Rebeckah VI, 306
Curle, Rebeckah VI, 311
Curle, Rebeckah VI, 341
Curle, Ruth VI, 306
Curle, Samuel VI, 306
Curle, Sarah I, 1041
Curle, Sarah VI, 306
Curle, Sarah VI, 809
Curle, Susanna VI, 306
Curle, Susannah IV, 697
Curle, Susannah IV, 707
Curle, Susannah VI, 485
Curle, Susannah VI, 496
Curle, Susannah VI, 498
Curles, ??? VI, 293
Curlett, Lillian V, 165
Curley, Lydia I, 580
Curlis, Margaret II, 828
Curll, Dan'l B. III, 94
Curll, Daniel B., Jr. III, 263
Curll, Daniel Bernard, Jr. III, 94
Curll, Lillian III, 94
Curll, Priscilla III, 94
Curll, Priscilla A. III, 263
Curn, Patrick V, 45
Curn, Patrick Francis V, 45
Curran, Patrick V, 45
Curran, Patrick Francis V, 45
Curren, Charles IV, 1155
Curren, Nancy IV, 1155
Currey, Elizabeth II, 443
Currey, Herbert II, 443
Currey, John II, 443
Currie, ??? IV, 1312
Currie, Alice IV, 1312
Currie, Chas. Campbell IV, 1312
Currie, Chas. F. IV, 1312
Currie, James A. IV, 1312
Currie, Mary II, 352
Currie, Mary IV, 1312
Currie, Maud IV, 1312
Currie, Robert IV, 1312
Currie, Ruth Lois IV, 1312
Currie, Sarah II, 500
Currier, Catherin II, 64
Currier, Catherin II, 65
Currier, Elizabeth II, 55
Currier, Elizabeth II, 64
Currier, Harriett IV, 1234
Currier, Precepta IV, 1234
Currin, Susannah IV, 1360
Currin, Susannah IV, 1385
Curry, Abbie V, 485
Curry, Abraham II, 117
Curry, Ann I. II, 117
Curry, Anna III, 16
Curry, Anna III, 94
Curry, Anna M. V, 485
Curry, Bertha III, 486
Curry, Bertha III, 508
Curry, Chester V, 485
Curry, Cornelius IV, 751
Curry, Elizabeth II, 442
Curry, Elizabeth II, 443
Curry, Elmer V, 485
Curry, Emma IV, 751
Curry, Emma C. IV, 697
Curry, Hannah II, 115
Curry, Hannah II, 117
Curry, Hannah IV, 751
Curry, Herbert II, 442
Curry, Herbert II, 443
Curry, Isaac II, 117
Curry, James II, 442
Curry, John III, 16
Curry, John III, 94
Curry, Jonathan II, 443
Curry, Mary II, 64
Curry, Mary II, 117
Curry, Mary II, 352
Curry, Mary II, 495
Curry, Mary II, 500
Curry, Mary J. III, 264
Curry, Mary J. III, 369
Curry, Mary Jane III, 16
Curry, Mary Jane III, 94
Curry, Meribah II, 64
Curry, Sarah II, 352
Curry, Sarah II, 500
Curry, Sarah II, 590
Curry, Viola V, 485
Curry, William II, 352
Curry, William H. V, 485
Curry, Wm. II, 117
Curshal, Maria V, 379
Curshal, Maria V, 388
Curtain, Margaret V, 454
Curtis, ??? II, 443
Curtis, ??? III, 94
Curtis, ??? III, 300
Curtis, Abbie H. V, 326
Curtis, Abigail II, 213
Curtis, Achsah II, 213
Curtis, Achsah II, 735
Curtis, Albin III, 94
Curtis, Alice V, 558
Curtis, Andrew V, 734
Curtis, Andrew V, 735
Curtis, Andrew V, 780
Curtis, Ann IV, 1234
Curtis, Ann V, 901
Curtis, Anna III, 300
Curtis, Anna IV, 143
Curtis, Anna IV, 146
Curtis, Anna V, 667
Curtis, Anna Louise III, 94
Curtis, Arthur M. III, 94
Curtis, Asa II, 352
Curtis, Azariah V, 667
Curtis, Belle V, 558
Curtis, Bertsell V, 558
Curtis, Betsy VI, 819
Curtis, Carl V, 485
Curtis, Caroline V, 667
Curtis, Carrie V, 326
Curtis, Catharine III, 94
Curtis, Catharine V, 326
Curtis, Catharine V, 734
Curtis, Catharine V, 780
Curtis, Catharine V, 816
Curtis, Catherine V, 780
Curtis, Charles II, 352
Curtis, Charles II, 735
Curtis, Charles III, 94
Curtis, Charles V, 326
Curtis, Charles V, 667
Curtis, Charles VI, 721
Curtis, Chas. E. V, 326
Curtis, Christian VI, 968
Curtis, Christopher VI, 902
Curtis, Clement II, 213
Curtis, Crisley VI, 943
Curtis, Daniel V, 780
Curtis, David VI, 902
Curtis, David T. V, 326
Curtis, Davis V, 780
Curtis, Dovie V, 326
Curtis, E. H. IV, 1205
Curtis, E. Lewis B. III, 94
Curtis, Earl Wilson V, 485
Curtis, Edith G. III, 94
Curtis, Edward A. V, 326
Curtis, Effie I, 923
Curtis, Effie V, 667
Curtis, Elam V, 780
Curtis, Elihu II, 213
Curtis, Elihu II, 352
Curtis, Elihu II, 500
Curtis, Elisha II, 352
Curtis, Eliz. III, 53
Curtis, Eliza V, 991
Curtis, Elizabeth II, 213
Curtis, Elizabeth II, 217
Curtis, Elizabeth II, 352
Curtis, Elizabeth II, 962
Curtis, Elizabeth II, 992
Curtis, Elizabeth II, 1008
Curtis, Elizabeth III, 94
Curtis, Elizabeth III, 182
Curtis, Elizabeth IV, 1205
Curtis, Elizabeth V, 667
Curtis, Elizabeth VI, 943
Curtis, Elizabeth A. V, 667
Curtis, Ella I, 615
Curtis, Ella V, 752
Curtis, Ella Bernard V, 326
Curtis, Ella Sluder I, 632
Curtis, Emmet IV, 1205
Curtis, Ephraim P. III, 94
Curtis, Ercil V, 667
Curtis, Ercil V, 672
Curtis, Estella V, 327
Curtis, Estella T. V, 326
Curtis, Esther III, 94
Curtis, Esther V, 752
Curtis, Ethel V, 327
Curtis, Eva H. VI, 721
Curtis, Florence Gertrude IV, 1205
Curtis, Frank V, 326
Curtis, Frank V, 558
Curtis, Frank V, 667
Curtis, Fronia V, 326
Curtis, Geo. D. III, 94
Curtis, Grace V, 667
Curtis, Harrison V, 667
Curtis, Harvey V, 667
Curtis, Helen V, 667
Curtis, Henry V, 780
Curtis, Hester V, 667
Curtis, Hester V, 672
Curtis, Isaac I, 615
Curtis, Ithiel V, 780
Curtis, Ivy V, 667
Curtis, James V, 780
Curtis, James V, 991
Curtis, James C. V, 326
Curtis, Jane II, 171
Curtis, Jennie V, 326
Curtis, Jennie V, 667
Curtis, Jesse V, 780
Curtis, Jessie V, 326
Curtis, John II, 213
Curtis, John III, 94
Curtis, John V, 734
Curtis, John V, 752
Curtis, John V, 780
Curtis, John V, 789
Curtis, John V, 816
Curtis, John V, 901
Curtis, John E. I, 615
Curtis, John E. I, 620
Curtis, John H. V, 780
Curtis, Jonathan II, 64
Curtis, Jonathan II, 213
Curtis, Jonathan II, 500
Curtis, Joseph II, 352
Curtis, Joseph II, 735
Curtis, Joseph III, 94
Curtis, Josephine II, 702
Curtis, Kate V, 667
Curtis, Katharine V, 789
Curtis, Katherine V, 752
Curtis, Lillian III, 94
Curtis, Lillian V, 667
Curtis, Lucinda V, 326
Curtis, Lucinda V, 558
Curtis, Lucy V, 326
Curtis, Lucy V, 558
Curtis, Lucy V, 734
Curtis, M. E. IV, 1205
Curtis, Margaret II, 352
Curtis, Margaret II, 500
Curtis, Margaret II, 702
Curtis, Maria V, 326
Curtis, Marmaduke II, 500
Curtis, Martha I, 613
Curtis, Martha V, 558
Curtis, Mary II, 171
Curtis, Mary II, 443
Curtis, Mary II, 485
Curtis, Mary II, 500
Curtis, Mary V, 734
Curtis, Mary V, 735
Curtis, Mary V, 780
Curtis, Mary V, 781
Curtis, Mary V, 782
Curtis, Mary VI, 968
Curtis, Mary A. III, 94
Curtis, Mary Ann I, 1150
Curtis, Mary C. I, 1150
Curtis, Mary E. V, 326
Curtis, Mary L. V, 901
Curtis, Mary P. III, 94
Curtis, Mercy II, 213
Curtis, Mordecai II, 797
Curtis, Nancy V, 780
Curtis, Nancy V, 789
Curtis, Nancy V, 806
Curtis, Nancy V, 816
Curtis, Nancy V, 817
Curtis, Nancy M. V, 326
Curtis, Opal V, 558
Curtis, Phariba I, 615
Curtis, R. V. I, 923
Curtis, Rebecca II, 797
Curtis, Rebecca III, 94
Curtis, Rebecca III, 182
Curtis, Rebecca V, 780
Curtis, Rebeckah V, 780
Curtis, Rebekah II, 486
Curtis, Rebekah II, 500
Curtis, Richard II, 443
Curtis, Richard Bruce V, 667
Curtis, Robert II, 213
Curtis, Rose V, 485
Curtis, Sally VI, 902
Curtis, Samuel III, 94
Curtis, Samuel V, 780
Curtis, Sanford V, 667
Curtis, Sarah II, 213
Curtis, Sarah II, 735
Curtis, Sarah V, 752
Curtis, Sarah V, 780
Curtis, Stephen III, 94
Curtis, Stephen III, 182
Curtis, Stephen V, 326
Curtis, Stephen C. V, 326
Curtis, Thomas II, 171
Curtis, Thomas II, 213
Curtis, Thomas II, 217
Curtis, Thomas II, 352
Curtis, Thomas II, 443
Curtis, Thomas II, 735
Curtis, Thomas III, 94
Curtis, Thomas V, 326
Curtis, Thomas V, 327
Curtis, Thomas VI, 357
Curtis, Tilton II, 213
Curtis, Virgil V, 485
Curtis, William V, 326
Curtis, Wm. Ercil V, 667
Curtis, Wm. H. V, 667
Curtiss, Elizabeth II, 194
Curtiss, Elizabeth II, 213
Curtiss, Margrett II, 443
Curtiss, Thomas II, 194
Curtiss, Thomas II, 213
Curtiss, Thomas II, 443
Curts, Sanford V, 667
Cushman, Bertha H. V, 548
Cushman, Sarah V, 835
Cushman, Sarah V, 860
Cushman, Sarah E. V, 548
Cusick, Dora E. IV, 193
Cusick, Elizabeth IV, 193
Cusick, Emily F. IV, 193
Cusick, James IV, 193
Cusick, James C. IV, 193
Cusick, John IV, 193
Cusick, John A. IV, 193
Cusick, Ona IV, 193
Cusick, Oswell H. IV, 193
Cusick, Sarah M. IV, 193
Cusick, William H. IV, 193
Cussins, Harrison V, 733
Custard, Arnold II, 350
Custard, Hannah IV, 28
Custard, Hannah IV, 41
Custard, J. W. IV, 1249
Custard, Rachel II, 500
Custard, William II, 350
Custeard, J. W. IV, 1249
Custer, Ida V, 991
Custis, Anna V, 667
Custis, Azariah V, 667
Custis, Caroline V, 667
Custis, Charles V, 667
Custis, Effie V, 667
Custis, Elizabeth V, 667
Custis, Elizabeth A. V, 667
Custis, Elon V, 667
Custis, Frank V, 667
Custis, Grace V, 667
Custis, Harrison V, 667
Custis, Jennie V, 667
Custis, Kate V, 667
Custis, Wm. H. V, 667
Customs, Mary II, 213
Customs, Mary II, 238
Custor, Dieney VI, 873
Cuthbert, Mary II, 500
Cuthbert, Mary II, 609
Cuthbertson, Alexander IV, 1312
Cuthbertson, Alice IV, 1249
Cuthbertson, Jennie IV, 1312
Cutken, Sarah III, 191
Cutlar, Benjamin II, 992
Cutlar, Benjamin II, 1036
Cutlar, Mary II, 992
Cutlar, Mary II, 1036
Cutler, Ann II, 992
Cutler, Anna III, 431
Cutler, Benjamin II, 981
Cutler, Benjamin II, 992
Cutler, David II, 992
Cutler, Deborah II, 992
Cutler, Eleanor II, 213
Cutler, Hannah II, 981
Cutler, Hannah II, 992
Cutler, Joshua II, 992

Cutler, Lawrence II, 992
Cutler, Lydia IV, 1276
Cutler, Marcy II, 992
Cutler, Margaret II, 500
Cutler, Margaret II, 674
Cutler, Mary II, 992
Cutler, Mary II, 1018
Cutler, Sarah II, 213
Cutler, Sarah II, 958
Cutler, Sarah II, 992
Cutrell, Elijah I, 236
Cutrell, Elisabeth I, 236
Cutrell, Elisabeth I, 249
Cutrell, Evelyn Frances I, 236
Cutrell, Lewis I, 236
Cutrell, Louis I, 213
Cutrell, Louis I, 236
Cutrell, Louis I, 247
Cutrell, Maria F. I, 236
Cutrell, Maria F. I, 247
Cutrell, Mariah I, 213
Cutrell, Mariah F. I, 236
Cutrell, Mariah F. I, 247
Cutrell, Mary I, 236
Cutten, ??? III, 94
Cutten, Mary Frances III, 94
Cuzens, John VI, 380
Cuzens, John VI, 457
Cuzzins, Eleanor II, 496
Cuzzins, George II, 496
Cypert, Charity I, 360
Cypert, Charity I, 384
Cypert, Francis I, 360
Cypert, Francis I, 384
Cypert, Larrance I, 365
Cypert, Margaret I, 360
Cypert, Margaret I, 365
Cypert, Margaret I, 384
Cypert, Margaret I, 407
Cyphers, Margaret I, 384
Cyrus, Bartholomew VI, 809
Cyrus, Bartholomew VI, 860
Cyrus, Claiborn VI, 809
Cyrus, Claiborn VI, 841
Cyrus, Claiborne VI, 809
Cyrus, Elizabeth VI, 841
Cyrus, Elizabeth VI, 846
Cyrus, Frances VI, 809
Cyrus, Jane VI, 809
Cyrus, Keziah VI, 809
Cyrus, Lucy VI, 809
Cyrus, Nicholas VI, 809
Cyrus, Phebe VI, 809
Cyrus, Solomon VI, 809
Cyrus, William VI, 809

D'Camp, Ann V, 883
D'Camp, Anna V, 881
D'Camp, John M. V, 836
D, Mary F. VI, 566
D???, Catharine T. III, 125
Dabbs, Mary VI, 876
Dabe, Donald Carl V, 721
Dabe, Frank V, 667
Dabe, Frank V, 721
Dabe, Freda V, 711
Dabe, Freda Louise V, 667
Dabe, Freda Louise V, 711
Dabe, Josephine V, 667
Dabe, Louise V, 667
Dabe, Louise V, 721
Dabe, Verna V, 667
Dabe, Verna V, 687
Dabe, Verna Marie V, 667
Dabney, Agness VI, 945
Dabney, Albert V, 969
Dabney, Ann VI, 902
Dabney, Anney VI, 955
Dabney, Arna VI, 956
Dabney, Betsey VI, 902
Dabney, Caroline V, 969
Dabney, Caroline V, 970
Dabney, Charles VI, 902
Dabney, Cornelius VI, 947
Dabney, Cornelius VI, 972
Dabney, Cornelius VI, 979
Dabney, Cornelius VI, 996
Dabney, Edna V, 969
Dabney, Fanny VI, 939
Dabney, George VI, 902
Dabney, George VI, 972
Dabney, George VI, 985
Dabney, George William VI, 805
Dabney, George William VI, 811
Dabney, George William VI, 845
Dabney, George William VI, 854
Dabney, Jenny VI, 902
Dabney, Jno. VI, 842
Dabney, John VI, 809
Dabney, John VI, 832
Dabney, John B. VI, 854
Dabney, John B. VI, 858
Dabney, John Q. VI, 822
Dabney, John Q. VI, 854
Dabney, John William VI, 843
Dabney, Judge ??? VI, 292
Dabney, Julieta Pretlow V, 969
Dabney, Lucy VI, 854
Dabney, Lucy VI, 956
Dabney, Lusanny VI, 902
Dabney, Mariah L. VI, 804
Dabney, Mary VI, 955
Dabney, Milly VI, 809
Dabney, Molley VI, 945
Dabney, Nancy VI, 947
Dabney, Nancy VI, 972
Dabney, Nathan VI, 902
Dabney, Rachel VI, 939
Dabney, Salley VI, 979
Dabney, Susan M. VI, 858
Dabney, William VI, 911
Daboy, Caroline V, 969
Daboy, Edna V, 969
Dachis, Samuel I, 876
Dacon, David VI, 873
Dacon, Frances VI, 873
Dacon, Nancy VI, 873
Dacon, Nancy VI, 1001
Dacon, Permelia VI, 915
Dadney, Becky VI, 902
Dadney, William VI, 902
Dager, Calisty V, 991
Dager, Frederick V, 991
Dagger, John II, 24
Dague, Lester IV, 1249
Dague, Samuel V, 991
Dahl, Anabel B. III, 68
Dahl, Anna C. E. III, 94
Dahl, Anna C. E. III, 149
Dahl, Annabel III, 94
Dahl, Annabel B. III, 94
Dahl, Annabel B. C. III, 342
Dahl, Catharine III, 94
Dahl, Catherine III, 228
Dahl, Eliz. Bancker III, 342
Dahl, Elizabeth B. III, 94
Dahl, Elizabeth Bancher III, 94
Dahl, Florence III, 68
Dahl, Florence Annabel III, 94
Dahl, Geo. W. III, 342
Dahl, Geo. Wash. III, 94
Dahl, Geo. Washington III, 94
Dahl, Geo. Work. III, 94
Dahl, George W. III, 68
Dahl, Gustava S. III, 94
Dahl, Harold A. III, 94
Dahl, Harold A. C. III, 94
Dahl, Harold A. C. III, 149
Dahl, Harold Arrid Cox III, 94
Dahl, Inez H. III, 94
Dahl, Inez H. III, 149
Dahl, James Benoist III, 94
Dahl, John C. III, 94
Dahl, John C. III, 228
Dail, Esther A. I, 45
Dail, Harriett E. I, 45
Dail, John M. I, 45
Dail, William I, 45
Daile, Peter II, 443
Dailey, Eva IV, 1037
Dailey, Eva V, 667
Dailey, Eva V, 720
Dailey, John VI, 291
Dailey, Matilda V, 550
Dailey, Milo V, 667
Dailey, Morris V, 667
Dailey, Morris V, 720
Dailey, Zarilda Jesse V, 667
Daily, Anna I, 621
Daily, Annie H. I, 615
Daily, Annie Hunter I, 615
Daily, Edmond I, 615
Daily, Elisabeth IV, 1360
Daily, Eliza I, 615
Daily, Eliza A. V, 232
Daily, Margaret Ann I, 615
Daily, Matilda Black V, 558
Daily, Milo V, 667
Daily, Myra IV, 1235
Daily, Pritchard B. I, 632
Daily, Pritchet Benton I, 621
Daily, W. H., Sr. I, 632
Daily, William Henry I, 615
Daily, Wm. Henry I, 621
Daisley, Alice III, 95
Daisley, Alice III, 338
Daisley, Frank III, 95
Daken, Elias V, 485
Daken, James V, 485
Dakin, Ada V, 45
Dakin, Ann V, 573
Dakin, Annie Knee V, 165
Dakin, Aus V, 558
Dakin, Cassie V, 165
Dakin, Catherine V, 134
Dakin, Deborah V, 45
Dakin, Deborah V, 70
Dakin, Deborah V, 573
Dakin, Elias V, 485
Dakin, Emma V, 45
Dakin, Eva M. V, 45
Dakin, Frank M. V, 45
Dakin, George V, 573
Dakin, George Dakin, Sr. V, 45
Dakin, George W. V, 45
Dakin, George, Jr. V, 45
Dakin, Hamelton Dakin V, 45
Dakin, Hamilton V, 165
Dakin, Ida May V, 45
Dakin, James V, 45
Dakin, James V, 118
Dakin, James V, 485
Dakin, James V. V, 485
Dakin, Jehiel V, 45
Dakin, Jonathan VI, 915
Dakin, Jonathan VI, 917
Dakin, Jonathan VI, 957
Dakin, Jonathan, Sr. VI, 917
Dakin, Joseph D. V, 573
Dakin, Lydia E. V, 45
Dakin, Lydia E. V, 87
Dakin, Maria V, 139
Dakin, Mariah V, 573
Dakin, Martha V, 573
Dakin, Martha A. V, 45
Dakin, Mary V, 558
Dakin, Mary V, 573
Dakin, Nancy V, 45
Dakin, Nancy V, 114
Dakin, Nancy V, 118
Dakin, Nancy VI, 957
Dakin, Nancy VI, 1001
Dakin, Nancy Ann V, 45
Dakin, Nancy Ann V, 114
Dakin, Nary V, 558
Dakin, Nellie R. V, 165
Dakin, Nellie Rebecca V, 45
Dakin, Philip V, 485
Dakin, Preserved V, 558
Dakin, Prudie V, 45
Dakin, Rachel III, 130
Dakin, Rachel L. V, 485
Dakin, Rockyfellar V, 485
Dakin, Rockyfeller V, 485
Dakin, Rockyfeller V, 950
Dakin, Sally VI, 917
Dakin, Sarah V, 165
Dakin, Sarah V, 184
Dakin, Sarah A. V, 45
Dakin, Sarah A. V, 165
Dakin, Sarah J. V, 45
Dakin, Sarah J. V, 118
Dakin, Sarah Jane V, 45
Dakin, Sarah L. V, 485
Dakin, Simon D. V, 573
Dakin, Susannah E. V, 41
Dakin, Susannah E. V, 45
Dakin, Thankful V, 485
Dakin, William Henry III, 95
Dakin, William Henry V, 485
Dakin, Zebulon B. V, 485
Dalbey, Abner II, 814
Dalbey, Sarah II, 814
Dalby, Elizabeth VI, 381
Dalby, Elizabeth VI, 446
Dalby, Mary VI, 381
Dalby, Mary VI, 443
Dalby, Tacy S. VI, 381
Dale, Ann I, 384
Dale, Betsey VI, 958
Dale, Christopher II, 285
Dale, Deborah I, 372
Dale, Deborah I, 384
Dale, Elizabeth VI, 801
Dale, Esther I, 45
Dale, Esther A. I, 45
Dale, Gertrude V, 165
Dale, Hannah I, 384
Dale, Harriet E. I, 45
Dale, Harriett E. I, 45
Dale, Henry I, 384
Dale, Isaac I, 349
Dale, Isaac I, 372
Dale, Isaac I, 384
Dale, Jemima VI, 902
Dale, John VI, 801
Dale, John VI, 829
Dale, John M. I, 45
Dale, Joshua II, 980
Dale, Margaret I, 384
Dale, Margaret I, 394
Dale, Mary II, 500
Dale, Mary VI, 902
Dale, Mary VI, 958
Dale, Mary VI, 982
Dale, Mary VI, 1006
Dale, Mary Elisabeth I, 45
Dale, Mary Elisabeth I, 83
Dale, Mary, Jr. II, 500
Dale, Perry V, 382
Dale, Rebecca M. VI, 381
Dale, Richard VI, 902
Dale, Richard VI, 944
Dale, Richard VI, 958
Dale, Richard VI, 1006
Dale, Sally VI, 982
Dale, Verna V, 165
Dale, William I, 45
Dale, William VI, 902
Dalkhe, Rose IV, 947
Dall, Emma Elizabeth IV, 1312
Dall, Robert IV, 1205
Dallace, Diana VI, 1019
Dallas, Anne VI, 1015
Dallas, Caroline VI, 902
Dallas, Elizabeth VI, 816
Dallas, Elizabeth VI, 936
Dallas, Eunice V, 863
Dallas, Hannah VI, 902
Dallas, James J. VI, 902
Dallas, Jno. C. VI, 872
Dallas, John VI, 902
Dallas, John VI, 1015
Dallas, John, Jr. VI, 902
Dallas, Joshua VI, 902
Dallas, Jubal VI, 902
Dallas, Mary B. II, 38
Dallas, Millicent II, 780
Dallas, Millicent II, 797
Dallas, Nancy VI, 902
Dallas, Pamelia VI, 1006
Dallas, Permelia VI, 1006
Dallas, Rebecca V, 863
Dallas, Salley VI, 902
Dallas, Suttle VI, 902
Dallas, William V, 863
Dallas, Winefred VI, 902
Dallice, Hannah VI, 902
Dallice, John VI, 902
Dallice, Jubal VI, 902
Dallice, Marmaduke VI, 1016
Dallice, Salley VI, 902
Dallice, Salley VI, 1016
Dalling, William VI, 381
Dallis, Agnes VI, 965
Dallis, Betsey VI, 1004
Dallis, Elizabeth VI, 809
Dallis, Elizabeth VI, 998
Dallis, John VI, 901
Dallis, John VI, 902
Dallis, John VI, 1004
Dallis, John VI, 1013
Dallis, Lucy VI, 901
Dallis, Lucy A. VI, 950
Dallis, Marmaduke VI, 809
Dallis, Marmaduke VI, 966
Dallis, Marmaduke VI, 998
Dallis, Polly VI, 966
Dallis, Winefred VI, 902
Dallis, Winney VI, 1004
Dallon, Thos. V, 991
Dalsin, Frank V, 45
Dalton, Adam V, 165
Dalton, Charles V, 617
Dalton, Dennis V, 667
Dalton, Dennis V, 668
Dalton, Earl V, 617
Dalton, Edith Louise V, 667
Dalton, Edith Louise V, 668
Dalton, Elizabeth VI, 872
Dalton, Elon V, 667
Dalton, Elon V, 668
Dalton, Estella V, 327
Dalton, Estella V, 667
Dalton, Helen Myrtle V, 658
Dalton, Helen Myrtle V, 667
Dalton, Henry V, 658
Dalton, Henry V, 667
Dalton, James VI, 902
Dalton, James VI, 967
Dalton, Lee Anna V, 667
Dalton, Lee Anna H. V, 667
Dalton, Margaret II, 992
Dalton, Margaret II, 1024
Dalton, Nancy VI, 809
Dalton, Naomi V, 668
Dalton, Nellie V, 667
Dalton, Nellie F. V, 667
Dalton, Polly VI, 902
Dalton, Pomp V, 668
Dalton, Pomp A. V, 667
Dalton, Pomp A. V, 668
Dalton, Reuben VI, 809
Dalton, Robert VI, 902
Dalton, Sarah VI, 902
Dalton, Tabitha VI, 902
Dalton, Timothe VI, 872
Daly, Dennis II, 64
Daly, Mary III, 95
Daly, Sarah H. III, 95
Daly, Thomas T. III, 95
Dalzell, Alfaretta IV, 947
Dalzell, Alfretta IV, 959
Dalzell, Alpharetta IV, 947
Dalzell, Elizabeth II, 500
Dalzell, George IV, 947
Dalzell, George B. IV, 947
Dalzell, Harry IV, 947
Dalzell, Harry Leo IV, 947
Dalzell, Hazel IV, 947
Dalzell, Hazel IV, 959
Dalzell, Isadora Pearl IV, 947
Dalzell, James II, 500
Dalzell, Otley V. IV, 947
Dalzell, Otley V. IV, 959
Dalzell, Sarah Jane IV, 1155
Dalzelle, George IV, 1235
Dalzelle, Ransom IV, 1235
Dalzelle, Sarah Jane IV, 1235
Damartharay, ??? III, 106
Damartharay, Rebecca III, 106
Dame, Amy Ann III, 95
Dame, Amy Anna III, 95
Dame, John E. II, 735
Dame, John E. III, 95
Dame, John Ellison III, 95
Dame, John Ellison III, 230
Dame, Jonathan III, 95
Dame, Mary III, 95
Dame, Moses II, 735
Dame, Moses III, 95
Dame, Owen III, 95
Dame, Rebecca III, 95
Dame, Rebecca III, 230
Dame, Sarah U. III, 95
Dame, Wm. Birdsall III, 95
Damel, Lydie V, 558
Damel, Martha V, 558
Damel, Martha Jane V, 558
Damel, Rebecca V, 558
Damel, Robert V, 558
Damel, Robert Bond V, 558
Damel, William V, 558
Damer, Aleenda VI, 809
Damer, Thomas VI, 809
Dameron, Eleanor S. VI, 887
Dameron, Phebe VI, 887
Dameron, William VI, 910
Dameron, William VI, 983
Dameron, William VI, 994
Damron, Angeline VI, 902
Damron, Elizabeth VI, 931
Damron, Jane VI, 923
Damron, John VI, 809
Damron, Malachi VI, 902
Damron, Margaret VI, 902
Damron, Phebe VI, 923
Damron, Phebe VI, 931
Damron, Sarah VI, 809
Damron, Zachariah VI, 902
Damson, Melvina IV, 619
Damson, Melvina IV, 625
Danail, Rebeck II, 64
Danala, Elizabeth IV, 1312
Danbert, Wm. V, 991
Danby, Amy III, 95
Danby, Amy III, 111
Danby, Robert III, 95
Danby, Robert III, 111
Dance, Sarah II, 735
Dance, Sarah IV, 1053
Dando, Beulah P. II, 735
Dando, Beulah P. II, 758
Dandridge, Alex VI, 809
Dandridge, Susan VI, 809
Dane, ??? III, 95
Dane, Charlotte VI, 902
Dane, John VI, 171
Dane, John VI, 902
Dane, John, Jr. VI, 171
Dane, Mary II, 500
Dane, Pleasants VI, 171
Dane, Richard VI, 171
Dane, Richard VI, 205
Dane, Richard VI, 219
Dane, Samuel III, 343
Dane, Sarah III, 343
Dane, Stephen Woodson VI, 171
Danel, Rebecca II, 64
Danford, James II, 500
Danford, Ruth II, 992
Danford, Ruth II, 1025
Danforth, Carrie V, 45
Danforth, Effie V, 45

anforth, Effie V, 46
anforth, Effie L. III, 212
anforth, Emma III, 212
anforth, Emma V, 45
anforth, Emma V, 46
anforth, Emma B. V, 33
anforth, Emma B. V, 45
anforth, Emma B. V, 46
anforth, Henry V, 46
anforth, Henry T. V, 46
anforth, Henry Thomas V, 45
anforth, Horace P. III, 212
anforth, Horace P. V, 45
anforth, Horace P. V, 46
anforth, Robert V, 46
anforth, Robert Southgate V, 45
ange, Ida IV, 193
anhert, Elizabeth E. V, 991
anhert, Wm. V, 991
aniel, ??? V, 46
aniel, ??? VI, 348
aniel, Aaron II, 25
aniel, Aaron II, 64
aniel, Aaron II, 104
aniel, Abijah VI, 381
aniel, Agness VI, 810
aniel, Alexander VI, 809
aniel, Alice V, 485
aniel, Andrew VI, 381
aniel, Anie VI, 633
aniel, Ann VI, 633
aniel, Ann VI, 696
aniel, Annie I, 335
aniel, Barney I, 335
aniel, Benj. VI, 931
aniel, Benjamin V, 46
aniel, Benjamin VI, 485
aniel, Benjamin VI, 633
aniel, Benjamin VI, 638
aniel, Betsy A. VI, 858
aniel, Daniel VI, 485
aniel, David II, 25
aniel, David Chandler V, 46
aniel, Dorothea III, 95
aniel, Dorothea III, 334
aniel, Edith VI, 809
aniel, Edmond II, 25
aniel, Edmund II, 25
aniel, Edmund VI, 810
aniel, Edward H. VI, 633
aniel, Elisha V, 485
aniel, Elizabeth II, 25
aniel, Elizabeth II, 53
aniel, Elizabeth II, 64
aniel, Elizabeth II, 108
aniel, Elizabeth II, 443
aniel, Elizabeth VI, 802
aniel, Elizabeth VI, 810
aniel, Elizabeth VI, 858
aniel, Elizabeth VI, 902
aniel, Elsie Fern I, 940
aniel, Elvira A. S. VI, 814
aniel, Esther IV, 653
aniel, Esther VI, 381
aniel, Esther VI, 437
aniel, Esther VI, 480
aniel, Esther VI, 485
aniel, Esther VI, 559
aniel, Esther VI, 562
aniel, Esther VI, 613
aniel, Esther VI, 629
aniel, Esther VI, 633
aniel, Esther VI, 671
aniel, Esther VI, 695
aniel, Esther VI, 698
aniel, Esther, Jr. VI, 633
aniel, Esther, Jr. VI, 695
aniel, Frederick VI, 633
aniel, George I, 303
aniel, George II, 64
aniel, Gilbert Pearson I, 335
aniel, Hannah II, 64
aniel, Hannah IV, 28
aniel, Hannah IV, 619
aniel, Hannah IV, 656
aniel, Hannah IV, 657
aniel, Hannah VI, 306
aniel, Hannah VI, 350
aniel, Hannah VI, 381
aniel, Hannah VI, 485
aniel, Hannah VI, 559
aniel, Hannah VI, 633
aniel, Hannah VI, 698
aniel, Henry II, 25
aniel, Henry III, 95
aniel, Henry III, 334
aniel, Isabel II, 25
aniel, Isabel II, 64
aniel, Isabel II, 500
aniel, Isabel, Sr. II, 64
aniel, Isabel, Sr. II, 89
Daniel, Isabell II, 62
Daniel, Isabell II, 64
Daniel, Jael II, 25
Daniel, James II, 25
Daniel, James II, 53
Daniel, James II, 62
Daniel, James II, 64
Daniel, James II, 96
Daniel, James II, 443
Daniel, James IV, 28
Daniel, James IV, 619
Daniel, James IV, 656
Daniel, James VI, 306
Daniel, James VI, 350
Daniel, James VI, 485
Daniel, James VI, 559
Daniel, James VI, 633
Daniel, James VI, 698
Daniel, James VI, 810
Daniel, James VI, 858
Daniel, James VI, 902
Daniel, Jane II, 25
Daniel, Jane VI, 480
Daniel, Jane VI, 485
Daniel, Jane VI, 528
Daniel, Jane VI, 629
Daniel, Jane VI, 633
Daniel, Jane VI, 810
Daniel, Jasper IV, 28
Daniel, Jasper VI, 306
Daniel, Jayn II, 64
Daniel, Jean II, 64
Daniel, Jemima VI, 825
Daniel, Jesper IV, 619
Daniel, Jesper VI, 350
Daniel, John I, 303
Daniel, John II, 25
Daniel, John II, 64
Daniel, John IV, 28
Daniel, John IV, 619
Daniel, John V, 46
Daniel, John VI, 350
Daniel, John VI, 810
Daniel, John VI, 860
Daniel, John VI, 902
Daniel, John VI, 996
Daniel, John F. V, 46
Daniel, John M. VI, 830
Daniel, Jonathan IV, 28
Daniel, Joseph II, 25
Daniel, Joseph II, 500
Daniel, Joseph VI, 381
Daniel, Joseph VI, 382
Daniel, Joseph VI, 485
Daniel, Joseph VI, 633
Daniel, Joseph H. VI, 381
Daniel, Joseph M. VI, 830
Daniel, Josiah VI, 809
Daniel, Josiah VI, 810
Daniel, Josiah VI, 858
Daniel, Katy VI, 996
Daniel, Kezih VI, 810
Daniel, Levi VI, 810
Daniel, Leviney VI, 858
Daniel, Lucy VI, 810
Daniel, Lucy Ann VI, 853
Daniel, Lydia II, 64
Daniel, Lydia II, 76
Daniel, Lydia V, 485
Daniel, Lydia VI, 381
Daniel, Lydia E. V, 46
Daniel, Lydia E. V, 485
Daniel, Lydia E. VI, 381
Daniel, Major ??? I, 303
Daniel, Mannerva V, 485
Daniel, Margaret VI, 381
Daniel, Margaret VI, 810
Daniel, Martha IV, 697
Daniel, Martha IV, 770
Daniel, Martha V, 46
Daniel, Martha V, 485
Daniel, Martha VI, 381
Daniel, Martha VI, 382
Daniel, Martha VI, 485
Daniel, Martha VI, 633
Daniel, Martha VI, 695
Daniel, Martha VI, 810
Daniel, Martha J. V, 46
Daniel, Martha J. V, 78
Daniel, Martha Jane V, 485
Daniel, Martha Jane V, 503
Daniel, Martha Jane VI, 381
Daniel, Martha S. VI, 913
Daniel, Mary II, 25
Daniel, Mary IV, 28
Daniel, Mary IV, 619
Daniel, Mary IV, 646
Daniel, Mary IV, 697
Daniel, Mary VI, 306
Daniel, Mary VI, 350
Daniel, Mary VI, 485
Daniel, Mary VI, 562
Daniel, Mary VI, 804
Daniel, Mary VI, 809
Daniel, Mary VI, 825
Daniel, Mary Ann VI, 381
Daniel, Mary Belle V, 46
Daniel, Mary Ellen I, 335
Daniel, Maryann VI, 381
Daniel, Milley VI, 902
Daniel, Minor VI, 810
Daniel, Nancy VI, 809
Daniel, Nancy VI, 810
Daniel, Neall II, 64
Daniel, Patsy VI, 810
Daniel, Peter VI, 804
Daniel, Peter VI, 809
Daniel, Peter VI, 810
Daniel, Peter VI, 858
Daniel, Peter, Jr. VI, 825
Daniel, Peter, Sr. VI, 809
Daniel, Phebe V, 485
Daniel, Phebe Ann IV, 143
Daniel, Phebe Ann IV, 157
Daniel, Polly I, 303
Daniel, Polly VI, 809
Daniel, Polly VI, 839
Daniel, Polly VI, 1006
Daniel, Priscilla VI, 809
Daniel, R. Alma V, 46
Daniel, Rachel II, 52
Daniel, Rachel II, 59
Daniel, Rachel II, 64
Daniel, Rachel IV, 697
Daniel, Rachel V, 46
Daniel, Rachel V, 485
Daniel, Rachel VI, 381
Daniel, Rachel VI, 633
Daniel, Rachel VI, 701
Daniel, Rachel Alma V, 46
Daniel, Rebecca II, 64
Daniel, Rebecca IV, 28
Daniel, Rebecca IV, 619
Daniel, Rebecca IV, 656
Daniel, Rebecca V, 46
Daniel, Rebecca V, 485
Daniel, Rebecca VI, 381
Daniel, Rebecca VI, 485
Daniel, Rebecca A. V, 46
Daniel, Rebecca Ann VI, 381
Daniel, Rebeccah Ann V, 485
Daniel, Rebeck II, 64
Daniel, Rebeckah II, 25
Daniel, Rebeckah II, 64
Daniel, Rebeckah II, 103
Daniel, Rebeckah II, 108
Daniel, Rebeckah VI, 306
Daniel, Rebeckah VI, 350
Daniel, Rebekah II, 64
Daniel, Rebekah II, 104
Daniel, Rebekah VI, 381
Daniel, Rebekah VI, 385
Daniel, Rebekah VI, 633
Daniel, Rhoda VI, 797
Daniel, Richard VI, 802
Daniel, Richard VI, 858
Daniel, Robert V, 46
Daniel, Robert V, 485
Daniel, Robert VI, 381
Daniel, Robert VI, 382
Daniel, Robert VI, 804
Daniel, Robert VI, 809
Daniel, Robert VI, 810
Daniel, Robert B. V, 46
Daniel, Robert B. V, 485
Daniel, Robert B. VI, 381
Daniel, Robert Bond V, 485
Daniel, Robert Bond VI, 381
Daniel, Robert P. VI, 810
Daniel, Rosa I, 335
Daniel, Rosalia I, 335
Daniel, Ruth II, 64
Daniel, Ruth II, 96
Daniel, Ruth V, 46
Daniel, Ruth VI, 381
Daniel, Ruth Wright VI, 633
Daniel, Salley VI, 927
Daniel, Sally VI, 810
Daniel, Samuel II, 25
Daniel, Samuel VI, 633
Daniel, Sarah II, 25
Daniel, Sarah II, 56
Daniel, Sarah II, 64
Daniel, Sarah VI, 485
Daniel, Sarah VI, 613
Daniel, Sarah VI, 633
Daniel, Sarah VI, 671
Daniel, Sarah VI, 809
Daniel, Sarah VI, 810
Daniel, Sarah J. V, 46
Daniel, Sarah Jane V, 46
Daniel, Sarah Jane V, 62
Daniel, Sarah Jane VI, 381
Daniel, Sarah Jane VI, 633
Daniel, Seemie I, 303
Daniel, Sidney V, 46
Daniel, Sidney VI, 381
Daniel, Sidney VI, 389
Daniel, Sidney VI, 633
Daniel, Sidney VI, 638
Daniel, Sidny VI, 381
Daniel, Spenser V, 485
Daniel, Susanna VI, 836
Daniel, Susannah VI, 633
Daniel, Susannah VI, 810
Daniel, Sydney V, 46
Daniel, Tace IV, 619
Daniel, Tace IV, 625
Daniel, Tace VI, 350
Daniel, Tacy IV, 28
Daniel, Tacy VI, 350
Daniel, Thomas II, 25
Daniel, Thomas II, 64
Daniel, Thomas II, 500
Daniel, Thomas VI, 809
Daniel, Thomas VI, 810
Daniel, Thos. II, 25
Daniel, W. H. I, 303
Daniel, William I, 335
Daniel, William II, 25
Daniel, William IV, 28
Daniel, William IV, 619
Daniel, William IV, 697
Daniel, William V, 46
Daniel, William V, 485
Daniel, William VI, 306
Daniel, William VI, 350
Daniel, William VI, 381
Daniel, William VI, 480
Daniel, William VI, 485
Daniel, William VI, 559
Daniel, William VI, 562
Daniel, William VI, 613
Daniel, William VI, 633
Daniel, William VI, 671
Daniel, William VI, 695
Daniel, William VI, 698
Daniel, William VI, 809
Daniel, William VI, 810
Daniel, William VI, 814
Daniel, William VI, 839
Daniel, William F. V, 46
Daniel, William F. V, 485
Daniel, William F. VI, 381
Daniel, William, Jr. VI, 485
Daniel, Wm. II, 25
Daniel, Wm. II, 52
Daniel, Wm. II, 59
Daniel, Wm. II, 64
Daniel, Wm. II, 108
Daniel, Wm. II, 500
Daniel, Wm. IV, 653
Daniel, Wm. IV, 697
Daniel, Wm. IV, 770
Daniel, Wm. VI, 629
Daniel, Wm. VI, 633
Daniel, Wm. Waightman II, 64
Danield, Martha IV, 385
Daniell, Elizabeth II, 64
Daniell, Elizabeth II, 76
Daniell, Hannah II, 59
Daniell, Jean II, 59
Daniell, Neall II, 64
Daniell, Neall II, 76
Daniell, Thomas II, 59
Daniels, Alice V, 485
Daniels, Amanda IV, 1155
Daniels, Anna IV, 1147
Daniels, Anna IV, 1155
Daniels, Anna IV, 1205
Daniels, Annie M. II, 855
Daniels, Asenath I, 923
Daniels, Ebeneezar C. IV, 1155
Daniels, Ebeneezer C. IV, 1174
Daniels, Ebenezer IV, 1155
Daniels, Ebenezer IV, 1205
Daniels, Ebenezer C. IV, 1205
Daniels, Elisha V, 485
Daniels, Gilbert Pearson I, 335
Daniels, John IV, 619
Daniels, John V, 46
Daniels, John B. V, 165
Daniels, John Chapman IV, 1155
Daniels, John F. V, 46
Daniels, Lindley IV, 1205
Daniels, Louie IV, 1235
Daniels, Lucy Farnum IV, 1312
Daniels, Lydia Ann IV, 143
Daniels, Lydia Ann IV, 326
Daniels, Lydiann IV, 143
Daniels, Mannerva V, 485
Daniels, Maria IV, 1155
Daniels, Maria IV, 1205
Daniels, Martha V, 485
Daniels, Martha VI, 695
Daniels, Mary E. IV, 1235
Daniels, Phebe V, 485
Daniels, Phebe Ann IV, 143
Daniels, Rachel V, 46
Daniels, Rachel V, 54
Daniels, Rachel V, 485
Daniels, Rachel V, 536
Daniels, Rebecca V, 485
Daniels, Ruth V, 46
Daniels, Ruth V, 110
Daniels, Sarah IV, 1155
Daniels, Sarah IV, 1174
Daniels, Sarah IV, 1205
Daniels, Sarah V, 401
Daniels, Sarah O. V, 382
Daniels, Sidny VI, 381
Daniels, Spenser V, 485
Daniels, William IV, 697
Daniels, William IV, 1155
Dankert, Elizabeth E. V, 991
Dankin, Amos V, 46
Dankin, Isaac V, 46
Dankin, Mary V, 46
Dankin, Rachel V, 46
Dankin, Samuel V, 46
Dankin, Sarah V, 46
Danly, Stacy I, 984
Dann, Jane VI, 816
Dann, Margit VI, 816
Dannat, Julia III, 95
Dannat, Susan III, 95
Dannat, William III, 95
Dannel, James II, 64
Dannel, James II, 91
Dannel, Jayn II, 64
Dannel, Jayn II, 91
Dannel, Thomas VI, 134
Dannel, Thomas VI, 144
Danner, Frank V, 991
Danner, Mamie V, 991
Danner, Rose V, 991
Danner, Russel V, 991
Danniel, Margaret VI, 381
Danniell, Elizabeth II, 64
Danniell, Elizabeth II, 86
Danniell, Richard II, 64
Danning, Frank V, 991
Danning, Rose V, 991
Danning, Russel V, 991
Dannison, Sam V, 991
Dannols, Isabel II, 64
Dannot, Julia III, 156
Dannot, Susan III, 156
Dannot, William III, 156
Dansel, Annie V, 991
Dansey, Esther II, 504
Dansey, Esther II, 535
Danson, John II, 500
Danson, Patience I, 304
Daragh, Ann II, 500
Daragh, Charles II, 500
Daragh, Susanna II, 500
Darbeshire, Sarah V, 668
Darbey, Samuel V, 558
Darbeyshare, Lucy V, 668
Darbeyshare, Maggie V, 668
Darbeyshire, Emma V, 668
Darbeyshire, James V, 668
Darbeyshire, John V, 668
Darbeyshire, John A. V, 668
Darbeyshire, John N. V, 668
Darbeyshire, Lucy V, 668
Darbeyshire, Maggie V, 668
Darbeyshire, Oliver N. V, 668
Darbeyshire, Rhoda C. W. V, 668
Darbeyshire, Sarah V, 668
Darbeyshire, Sarah Ann V, 668
Darby, Anne III, 95
Darby, Anne III, 481
Darby, Elizabeth II, 958
Darby, Elizabeth II, 992
Darby, Elizabeth II, 1007
Darby, Hannah I, 372
Darby, Hannah I, 384
Darby, Hannah V, 218
Darby, Hannah V, 232
Darby, John II, 958
Darby, John III, 95
Darby, John III, 481
Darby, John III, 494
Darby, Kezia III, 95
Darby, Kezia III, 481
Darby, Kezia III, 494
Darby, Mary III, 95
Darby, Milley VI, 965
Darby, Phebe III, 95
Darby, Rachel IV, 370
Darby, Rachel IV, 382
Darby, Rebecca II, 443

Darby, Sally VI, 902
Darby, Samuel III, 95
Darby, Sarah II, 992
Darby, Sarah II, 1004
Darby, Stephen VI, 902
Darby, Thomas VI, 965
Darby, Wd. Elizabeth II, 992
Darby, William II, 443
Darby, William II, 958
Darby, William II, 992
Darby, Wm. II, 992
Darbyshare, John V, 668
Darbyshare, John, Jr. II, 993
Darbyshare, Sarah Ann V, 668
Darbyshire, Emma V, 668
Darbyshire, Jennie V, 327
Darbyshire, Jennie S. V, 327
Darden, Elisabeth I, 236
Darden, Elizabeth Gertrude I, 623
Darden, Eunice I, 45
Darden, Eunice I, 60
Darden, Eunice I, 632
Darden, Eunice M. I, 45
Darden, Eunice M. I, 632
Darden, Gertrude I, 14
Darden, J. R. I, 15
Darden, J. Robert I, 8
Darden, Martha J. I, 45
Darden, Martha J. I, 83
Darden, Martha Jane I, 8
Darden, Ruth Anna I, 15
Darden, William VI, 70
Dardin, J. Robert I, 22
Dardin, Martha Jane I, 22
Dare, Ann Elizabeth II, 147
Dare, Ann Elizabeth II, 159
Dare, Anna E. II, 855
Dare, Catherine VI, 382
Dare, Elizabeth VI, 382
Dare, Elonar II, 51
Dare, Elonar II, 64
Dare, Franklin II, 147
Dare, Gideon VI, 382
Dare, Gideon VI, 400
Dare, Gideon George VI, 382
Dare, Gideon George VI, 400
Dare, Henry VI, 382
Dare, James Walter II, 790
Dare, James Walter II, 855
Dare, Lydia M. VI, 382
Dare, Lydia M. VI, 400
Dare, Mark R. II, 790
Dare, Mary B. II, 790
Dare, Sarah Jane VI, 382
Dare, Sarah Jane VI, 400
Darick, John V, 327
Darick, Rachel V, 327
Darin, Lewis VI, 902
Darin, Obedience VI, 902
Daring, Martin V, 991
Daring, Tilman V, 991
Dark, Anne II, 992
Dark, John II, 992
Dark, Samuel II, 992
Dark, Samuel II, 1041
Dark, William II, 952
Darke, Ann II, 958
Darke, Samuel II, 958
Darke, Thomas II, 958
Darkin, Ann II, 25
Darkin, Ann II, 64
Darkin, Elizabeth II, 59
Darkin, Elizabeth II, 64
Darkin, Hannah II, 25
Darkin, Hannah II, 64
Darkin, Hannah II, 80
Darkin, Hannah II, 89
Darkin, Hannah II, 104
Darkin, Jale II, 25
Darkin, John II, 25
Darkin, John II, 59
Darkin, John II, 64
Darkin, Joseph II, 25
Darkin, Joseph II, 64
Darkin, Richard II, 25
Darkin, Sarah II, 25
Darkin, Sarah II, 64
Darkin, Sarah II, 112
Darkins, Ann II, 64
Darkins, Ann II, 86
Darkins, Hannah II, 49
Darkins, Hannah II, 64
Darkins, John II, 64
Darkins, John II, 88
Darkins, Joseph II, 49
Darkins, Joseph II, 64
Darkins, Joseph II, 86
Darkins, Sarah II, 64
Darkins, Sarah II, 88
Darley, Mary III, 95
Darley, Sarah H. III, 95
Darley, Thos. T. III, 95
Darling, Elizabeth II, 978
Darling, Elizabeth II, 992
Darling, Hamilton III, 95
Darling, Isaac III, 95
Darling, Jane III, 95
Darling, Kezia III, 481
Darling, Rebecca IV, 1155
Darling, Rebecca IV, 1174
Darling, Sarah III, 481
Darling, Walter V, 46
Darlington Peirce, Cosmelia VI, 750
Darlington Peirce, Wm. VI, 750
Darlington, Ann IV, 79
Darlington, Ann IV, 82
Darlington, Ann IV, 697
Darlington, Ann IV, 936
Darlington, Ann IV, 1360
Darlington, Ann VI, 382
Darlington, Ann VI, 419
Darlington, Ann Darlington IV, 947
Darlington, Anna IV, 82
Darlington, Anna IV, 1360
Darlington, Anna IV, 1373
Darlington, Anna V, 301
Darlington, Anna V, 327
Darlington, Anna VI, 382
Darlington, Benjamin II, 500
Darlington, Benjamin V, 969
Darlington, Brinton IV, 82
Darlington, Brinton IV, 697
Darlington, Brinton IV, 777
Darlington, Catharine IV, 125
Darlington, Catharine IV, 697
Darlington, Catharine IV, 787
Darlington, Catharine VI, 419
Darlington, Catharine W. IV, 82
Darlington, Catharine W. IV, 697
Darlington, Catherine IV, 82
Darlington, Catherine IV, 116
Darlington, Catherine VI, 382
Darlington, Edith II, 855
Darlington, Elizabeth II, 855
Darlington, Elizabeth H. II, 855
Darlington, Elizabeth Smedley II, 855
Darlington, Elma C. IV, 82
Darlington, Elma C. IV, 697
Darlington, Emanuel II, 781
Darlington, Esther IV, 697
Darlington, Esther IV, 725
Darlington, Hannah IV, 82
Darlington, Hannah IV, 125
Darlington, Hannah IV, 697
Darlington, Isabel II, 855
Darlington, Isabella II, 855
Darlington, Israel IV, 82
Darlington, Israel IV, 1360
Darlington, Israel IV, 1373
Darlington, James, Jr. IV, 947
Darlington, Jane Catharine W. IV, 697
Darlington, Jess IV, 82
Darlington, Jesse IV, 82
Darlington, Jesse IV, 1360
Darlington, Jesse IV, 1381
Darlington, Jesse D. II, 855
Darlington, Jesse, Jr. V, 969
Darlington, John IV, 697
Darlington, Leslie V, 687
Darlington, Luzerne IV, 1360
Darlington, Martha II, 781
Darlington, Martha IV, 82
Darlington, Martha IV, 697
Darlington, Martha IV, 777
Darlington, Mary II, 855
Darlington, Mary IV, 82
Darlington, Mary IV, 697
Darlington, Mary Baker II, 855
Darlington, Mary E. II, 855
Darlington, Maud M. II, 855
Darlington, Maude Mary II, 855
Darlington, Rachel IV, 78
Darlington, Rachel IV, 79
Darlington, Rachel IV, 82
Darlington, Rachel IV, 697
Darlington, Rachel IV, 1360
Darlington, Richard V, 969
Darlington, Sarah II, 781
Darlington, Sarah V, 969
Darlington, Sarah V, 978
Darlington, Smedley II, 855
Darlington, Stephen IV, 78
Darlington, Stephen IV, 79
Darlington, Stephen IV, 82
Darlington, Stephen IV, 697
Darlington, Stephen IV, 1360
Darlington, Susannah IV, 1360
Darlington, Susannah IV, 1373
Darlington, Susannah IV, 1381
Darlington, Thomas IV, 82
Darlington, Thomas IV, 697
Darlington, Thomas IV, 725
Darlington, William IV, 82
Darlington, William IV, 116
Darlington, William IV, 697
Darlington, William T. IV, 82
Darlington, Wm. IV, 125
Darlington, Wm. IV, 697
Darlington, Wm. IV, 787
Darlington, Wm. Sanford IV, 697
Darlington, Wm. T. IV, 82
Darlington, Wm. T. IV, 697
Darlington, Wm. T. V, 901
Darly, ??? III, 346
Darly, Mary III, 95
Darly, Phebe III, 95
Darly, Sarah H. III, 95
Darly, Sarah H. III, 346
Darly, Thos. T. III, 95
Darmon, Bessie P. II, 855
Darmon, Bessie P. II, 920
Darmon, Beulah R. II, 855
Darmon, Beulah R. II, 920
Darmon, Elizabeth P. II, 855
Darmon, Samuel S. II, 855
Darmon, Samuel S. II, 916
Darmon, Samuel S. II, 920
Darmon, Wm. II, 855
Darmon, Wm. II, 920
Darnald, Susannah IV, 520
Darnall, Sarah Bartlett II, 789
Darnel, Aaron II, 213
Darnel, Ann VI, 633
Darnel, Ann VI, 687
Darnel, Deborah II, 213
Darnel, Deborah II, 264
Darnel, Edward II, 213
Darnel, Edward II, 264
Darnel, Jane II, 213
Darnel, Jane II, 264
Darnel, Pharaba IV, 1053
Darnel, Phariby IV, 1053
Darnel, Phariby IV, 1058
Darnel, Samuel II, 213
Darnel, Samuel II, 264
Darnell, Aaron II, 213
Darnell, Alice C. III, 406
Darnell, Ann II, 64
Darnell, Anna J. II, 855
Darnell, Anna Mary II, 790
Darnell, Anna Mary III, 406
Darnell, Caleb II, 285
Darnell, Charles II, 285
Darnell, Elizabeth II, 64
Darnell, Elizabeth II, 86
Darnell, Elnathan H. II, 855
Darnell, Emily A. II, 285
Darnell, Geo. Wm. II, 855
Darnell, George Wm. II, 855
Darnell, Hannah S. II, 285
Darnell, James F. VI, 940
Darnell, James, Jr. VI, 902
Darnell, John II, 64
Darnell, Joseph H. II, 285
Darnell, Lydia II, 285
Darnell, Martha VI, 902
Darnell, Martha Ann VI, 940
Darnell, Mary V, 881
Darnell, Mary V, 888
Darnell, Mary Ella II, 855
Darnell, Mary Ella II, 862
Darnell, Mary Ellen II, 855
Darnell, Nathan Howard II, 855
Darnell, Sarah Bartlett II, 789
Darnell, Sarah P. II, 285
Darnell, Valentine VI, 940
Darnell, Warrington II, 790
Darnell, Warrington III, 406
Darnell, William I, 535
Darnelle, Ann II, 64
Darnelly, Ann II, 56
Darnelly, Ann II, 64
Darner, Alunda VI, 810
Darner, Thomas VI, 810
Darragh, Ann II, 500
Darragh, Charles II, 500
Darragh, Lydia II, 352
Darragh, Lydia II, 500
Darragh, Margaret II, 352
Darragh, Susanna II, 452
Darragh, Susanna II, 500
Darrah, Margaret II, 352
Darrough, Susanna II, 500
Darrow, Mary V, 327
Darrow, Mary V, 352
Dart, ??? III, 95
Dart, Edna III, 95
Dart, Edna III, 97
Dart, Edward III, 95
Dart, Edward III, 97
Dart, Edward III, 361
Dart, Elizabeth III, 95
Dart, Elizabeth Starr III, 95
Dart, Hester III, 95
Dart, Hester III, 97
Dart, Hester M. III, 361
Dart, Hester M. W. III, 95
Daryman, Charles IV, 1037
Daryman, Lydia IV, 1037
Daskin, Laura B. V, 617
Dasson, Ann I, 807
Date, Rebecca II, 500
Date, Rebecca II, 621
Daubin, Griffin VI, 591
Daubins, A. F. IV, 193
Daubins, M. P. IV, 193
Dauble, Agnes Schissel III, 95
Dauble, Agnes V. III, 95
Daublin, Catherine VI, 382
Daublin, Elizabeth VI, 382
Daublin, Griffith VI, 382
Daublin, Joseph VI, 382
Daublin, Maryann VI, 382
Daublin, Sarah VI, 382
Daublin, Thomas VI, 382
Daudle, Joseph IV, 193
Daugherday, Susanna II, 508
Daugherty, Aaron C. VI, 937
Daugherty, Alfred V, 382
Daugherty, Arda IV, 1249
Daugherty, Benjamin V, 558
Daugherty, Elizabeth VI, 961
Daugherty, Frances V, 558
Daugherty, Frank V, 558
Daugherty, Frank V, 668
Daugherty, Frank V, 672
Daugherty, Isabella E. VI, 937
Daugherty, James V, 382
Daugherty, James VI, 902
Daugherty, James VI, 983
Daugherty, James VI, 1017
Daugherty, James C. V, 617
Daugherty, Jessie IV, 1249
Daugherty, Juda VI, 937
Daugherty, Judith VI, 902
Daugherty, Lawrence V, 617
Daugherty, Marie V, 668
Daugherty, Marie V, 672
Daugherty, Mary Ann V, 382
Daugherty, Mary Jane V, 382
Daugherty, Mary R. VI, 1017
Daugherty, Mildred VI, 902
Daugherty, Patria VI, 983
Daugherty, Sally VI, 986
Daugherty, Sarah II, 508
Daugherty, Sarah IV, 470
Daugherty, Sarah IV, 502
Daugherty, Sarah VI, 902
Daugherty, Stephen VI, 986
Daugherty, Susan V, 617
Daugherty, Thomas VI, 877
Daugherty, Thomas VI, 902
Daugherty, William V, 558
Daugherty, William VI, 986
Daugherty, Willis S. VI, 896
Daugherty, Willis S. VI, 902
Daughtry, Elijah I, 237
Daughtry, Elizabeth I, 237
Daughtry, Elizabeth I, 254
Daugler, James C. V, 991
Daukirt, Elizabeth V, 991
Daukirt, John V, 991
Daunce, Sarah II, 500
Dauphin, Jane II, 786
Dauphin, John II, 786
Dauphin, Sarah Ann II, 786
Daurytierty, Polly VI, 922
Dauson, John II, 992
Davees, Anna IV, 770
Davees, Louisa IV, 770
Davees, Louiza IV, 697
Davees, Wm. IV, 770
Daveis, Anna IV, 765
Daveis, Martha IV, 765
Daveis, Wm. IV, 765
Davenport, ??? III, 45
Davenport, Almira Jane IV, 697
Davenport, Almira Jane IV, 777
Davenport, Amelia IV, 1249
Davenport, Ameret Jane VI, 865
Davenport, Andrew O. III, 96
Davenport, Ann E. III, 95
Davenport, Ann E. III, 96
Davenport, Ann Eliza III, 60
Davenport, Ann Eliza III, 95
Davenport, Ann Eliza III, 96
Davenport, Ann P. VI, 806
Davenport, Ann P. VI, 810
Davenport, Anna III, 91
Davenport, Anna III, 95
Davenport, Anna IV, 1249
Davenport, Armeda IV, 1249
Davenport, Benjamin II, 500
Davenport, Celain VI, 839
Davenport, Celia VI, 880
Davenport, Charles IV, 1249
Davenport, Charles VI, 839
Davenport, Charles VI, 865
Davenport, Charles B. III, 95
Davenport, Charles B. III, 96
Davenport, Charles B. III, 255
Davenport, Charles E. III, 95
Davenport, Charles E. III, 370
Davenport, Charles Emery III, 96
Davenport, Chas. VI, 858
Davenport, Chas. B. III, 95
Davenport, Chas. E. III, 91
Davenport, Chas. E. III, 95
Davenport, Chris. VI, 839
Davenport, Christopher VI, 902
Davenport, Clark IV, 1249
Davenport, David III, 95
Davenport, David M. III, 95
Davenport, David M. III, 96
Davenport, Dudley III, 95
Davenport, Dudley III, 364
Davenport, Eliz. D. III, 95
Davenport, Eliza II, 500
Davenport, Elizabeth II, 213
Davenport, Elizabeth II, 500
Davenport, Elizabeth VI, 860
Davenport, Elizabeth VI, 864
Davenport, Elizabeth VI, 981
Davenport, Enoch Franklin III, 95
Davenport, Enoch Franklin III, 96
Davenport, Enoch Franklin III, 212
Davenport, Esther III, 96
Davenport, Francis II, 213
Davenport, Francis II, 214
Davenport, George C. III, 95
Davenport, Glover VI, 801
Davenport, Glover VI, 810
Davenport, Hannah III, 45
Davenport, Hannah III, 95
Davenport, Hannah III, 96
Davenport, Hughston VI, 810
Davenport, Ira M. III, 60
Davenport, Ira M. III, 95
Davenport, Ira M. III, 96
Davenport, Irene B. III, 95
Davenport, Irene B. III, 364
Davenport, Isaac II, 352
Davenport, Isaac II, 500
Davenport, Joel VI, 902
Davenport, Joel VI, 995
Davenport, Joseph II, 352
Davenport, Joseph VI, 902
Davenport, Julia C. III, 96
Davenport, Julia C. III, 348
Davenport, Leah III, 95
Davenport, Leah III, 370
Davenport, Lucy IV, 1249
Davenport, Lydia B. III, 96
Davenport, Lydia B. III, 233
Davenport, Marget VI, 902
Davenport, Marie Louise III, 96
Davenport, Marie Louise III, 27?
Davenport, Martha VI, 810
Davenport, Martin W. VI, 860
Davenport, Mary VI, 902
Davenport, Mary VI, 962
Davenport, Mary VI, 995
Davenport, Mary L. VI, 839
Davenport, Mary T. III, 62
Davenport, Mary T. III, 96
Davenport, Minerva VI, 902
Davenport, Miriam K. III, 95
Davenport, Miriam K. III, 212
Davenport, Mourning VI, 995
Davenport, Nancy I, 758
Davenport, Nancy VI, 902
Davenport, Phebe III, 96
Davenport, Phebe B. III, 95
Davenport, Phebe C. III, 62
Davenport, Phebe C. III, 95
Davenport, Phebe C. III, 96
Davenport, Phebe C. III, 229
Davenport, Phebe C. III, 326
Davenport, Priscilla VI, 984
Davenport, Rebecca II, 213
Davenport, Rebecca II, 214
Davenport, Retta III, 95
Davenport, Retta III, 255
Davenport, Reuben B. III, 95
Davenport, Reuben B. III, 96
Davenport, Reuben B. III, 279

avenport, Sarah A. VI, 858
avenport, Sarah N. III, 96
avenport, Stephen III, 95
avenport, Stephen III, 96
avenport, Susan H. VI, 832
avenport, Susanna VI, 902
avenport, Theodore III, 95
avenport, Wiley E. I, 744
avenport, Wiley E. I, 758
avenport, Will IV, 1249
avenport, William VI, 880
avenport, William VI, 902
avenport, William VI, 962
avenport, William F. III, 95
avenport, William Francis III, 96
avenport, William Francis III, 348
avenport, William H. III, 96
avenport, Wilson VI, 802
avenport, Wilson VI, 857
avenport, Wm. IV, 1249
avenport, Wm. D. III, 62
avenport, Wm. D. III, 95
avenport, Wm. D. III, 96
averson, Jane VI, 809
aves, Agnes II, 502
aves, Daniel I, 961
aves, Sarah II, 502
avice, Abiather V, 730
avice, Adella I, 887
avice, Bartlett J. I, 876
avice, Bartlett J. I, 887
avice, Betsy Ann I, 601
avice, Cornelia I, 876
avice, David I, 876
avice, David I, 895
avice, Israel Agnes I, 601
avice, Jessee I, 601
avice, Joel I, 601
avice, Josiah VI, 106
avice, Julia I, 601
avice, Lydia I, 895
avice, Lydia V, 730
avice, Lydia V, 735
avice, Lydia V, 835
avice, Miriam I, 328
avice, Nancy I, 601
avice, Richard II, 117
avice, Sarah V, 835
avice, Sophia I, 443
avice, Sopia I, 445
avice, William I, 961
avice, William E. I, 328
avid, ??? VI, 348
avid, ??? VI, 969
avid, Abram VI, 902
avid, Ann II, 450
avid, Ann II, 501
avid, Ann II, 855
avid, Ann IV, 339
avid, Ann VI, 114
avid, Daniel IV, 339
avid, Davis VI, 114
avid, Dr. ??? I, 671
avid, Eleanor VI, 858
avid, Elizabeth II, 501
avid, Eunice I, 671
avid, Evan II, 450
avid, Evan II, 501
avid, Isaac VI, 902
avid, James VI, 114
avid, John VI, 858
avid, Lewis II, 501
avid, Lydia IV, 641
avid, Malinda VI, 902
avid, Mary VI, 185
avid, Matthew VI, 114
avid, Micajah VI, 185
avid, Nancy V, 451
avid, Rachel VI, 902
avid, Robert VI, 1006
avid, Ruth IV, 326
avid, Ruth IV, 327
avid, Ruth IV, 520
avid, Sarah II, 501
avid, Sarah II, 536
avid, Sarah IV, 326
avid, Sarah IV, 339
avids, ??? III, 96
avids, Ann II, 501
avids, Benj. II, 501
avids, Benjamin II, 501
avids, Benjamin III, 96
avids, Casper M. III, 96
avids, Christian II, 501
avids, Elizabeth II, 501
avids, Evan II, 501
avids, Hannah II, 501
avids, Hugh II, 501
avids, Lewis II, 501
Davids, Margaret II, 501
Davids, Margaret II, 553
Davids, Rees II, 501
Davids, Sarah II, 501
Davids, Sarah II, 536
Davids, Tacy II, 501
Davidson, Abner VI, 810
Davidson, Achsah I, 744
Davidson, Agness VI, 810
Davidson, Ahimaaz I, 744
Davidson, Ahimaaze I, 758
Davidson, Alex VI, 804
Davidson, Alex VI, 811
Davidson, Alexander I, 350
Davidson, Alexander I, 1091
Davidson, Alexander I, 1105
Davidson, Alexander I, 1117
Davidson, Alexander VI, 810
Davidson, Andrew III, 96
Davidson, Andrew III, 174
Davidson, Andrew J. III, 96
Davidson, Ann VI, 903
Davidson, Baker VI, 903
Davidson, Bellinda I, 744
Davidson, Beryl V, 455
Davidson, Betty Manley IV, 697
Davidson, Carolyn VI, 810
Davidson, Catharine VI, 864
Davidson, Catherine I, 1117
Davidson, Catherine I, 1126
Davidson, Charlotte IV, 194
Davidson, Charlotte IV, 1155
Davidson, Clara V, 455
Davidson, David VI, 810
Davidson, David VI, 903
Davidson, E. F. VI, 976
Davidson, Edmund F. VI, 883
Davidson, Edmund F. VI, 903
Davidson, Edmund F. VI, 980
Davidson, Edward VI, 903
Davidson, Elender VI, 810
Davidson, Eliza VI, 810
Davidson, Elizabeth I, 350
Davidson, Elizabeth I, 1105
Davidson, Elizabeth I, 1117
Davidson, Elizabeth I, 1122
Davidson, Elizabeth VI, 797
Davidson, Elizabeth VI, 804
Davidson, Elizabeth VI, 807
Davidson, Elizabeth VI, 810
Davidson, Elizabeth VI, 811
Davidson, Elizabeth VI, 859
Davidson, Elizabeth VI, 903
Davidson, Ella V, 301
Davidson, Elvira VI, 827
Davidson, Emery IV, 1155
Davidson, Ethel IV, 1249
Davidson, Eunice VI, 903
Davidson, Eunice VI, 936
Davidson, Evry IV, 194
Davidson, Fannie I, 876
Davidson, Fanny I, 876
Davidson, Fanny I, 893
Davidson, Frances I, 1105
Davidson, Frances VI, 810
Davidson, George I, 744
Davidson, George I, 758
Davidson, George I, 876
Davidson, George I, 892
Davidson, George IV, 194
Davidson, George IV, 1155
Davidson, George VI, 810
Davidson, George VI, 903
Davidson, Gretta III, 96
Davidson, Gretta III, 174
Davidson, Hannah I, 758
Davidson, Hannah I, 1105
Davidson, Hannah I, 1117
Davidson, Hannah I, 1119
Davidson, Hannah IV, 194
Davidson, Hannah IV, 1155
Davidson, Harriet L. II, 132
Davidson, Hiram IV, 1249
Davidson, Irena I, 758
Davidson, Isabella VI, 804
Davidson, Isaiah I, 758
Davidson, Jacob I, 350
Davidson, Jacob I, 1091
Davidson, Jacob I, 1105
Davidson, Jacob I, 1117
Davidson, James I, 677
Davidson, James I, 688
Davidson, James I, 744
Davidson, James I, 758
Davidson, James I, 876
Davidson, James I, 1091
Davidson, James I, 1105
Davidson, James I, 1117
Davidson, James IV, 470
Davidson, James VI, 807
Davidson, James VI, 810
Davidson, James, Jr. I, 744
Davidson, James, Jr. I, 758
Davidson, James, Junr. VI, 902
Davidson, James, Sr. VI, 902
Davidson, Jane I, 744
Davidson, Jane VI, 810
Davidson, Janet VI, 902
Davidson, Jesse VI, 811
Davidson, John I, 744
Davidson, John VI, 807
Davidson, John VI, 810
Davidson, John VI, 858
Davidson, John Wesley V, 734
Davidson, Joseph I, 350
Davidson, Joseph I, 758
Davidson, Joseph I, 1091
Davidson, Joseph I, 1105
Davidson, Joseph I, 1117
Davidson, Joseph VI, 800
Davidson, Joseph VI, 810
Davidson, Joseph VI, 864
Davidson, Joseph S. VI, 808
Davidson, Josiah I, 744
Davidson, Leroy VI, 867
Davidson, Lillian R. II, 132
Davidson, Loatta III, 96
Davidson, Loatta III, 225
Davidson, Loranee I, 677
Davidson, Loranee I, 744
Davidson, Lowrena I, 876
Davidson, Luella IV, 470
Davidson, Lurana I, 744
Davidson, Lyda I, 350
Davidson, Lydia I, 744
Davidson, Lydia I, 758
Davidson, Lydia I, 876
Davidson, Lydia I, 892
Davidson, Lydia I, 1105
Davidson, Mack IV, 1249
Davidson, Malinda VI, 810
Davidson, Margaret VI, 820
Davidson, Marjarah I, 744
Davidson, Martha I, 677
Davidson, Martha I, 688
Davidson, Martha I, 744
Davidson, Martha I, 758
Davidson, Martha IV, 1249
Davidson, Martha VI, 810
Davidson, Martha VI, 851
Davidson, Martha A. VI, 800
Davidson, Martha S. I, 758
Davidson, Martitia I, 744
Davidson, Martitia I, 876
Davidson, Mary I, 744
Davidson, Mary I, 758
Davidson, Mary VI, 810
Davidson, Mary VI, 832
Davidson, Mary VI, 903
Davidson, Mary I. VI, 798
Davidson, Meredith VI, 936
Davidson, Mordecai I, 744
Davidson, Mordecai I, 758
Davidson, Nancy VI, 807
Davidson, Nancy VI, 810
Davidson, Nancy VI, 832
Davidson, Nancy VI, 903
Davidson, Nathan I, 744
Davidson, Ora Lee V, 301
Davidson, Parker IV, 194
Davidson, Parker IV, 1155
Davidson, Paulina A. VI, 811
Davidson, Polly VI, 810
Davidson, Polly VI, 861
Davidson, Rachel I, 744
Davidson, Rachel VI, 808
Davidson, Rebecca II, 702
Davidson, Reece IV, 194
Davidson, Reece IV, 1155
Davidson, Richard I, 350
Davidson, Richard I, 1091
Davidson, Richard I, 1105
Davidson, Richard I, 1117
Davidson, Ruth I, 1077
Davidson, Ruth I, 1091
Davidson, Ruth II, 136
Davidson, Ruth Marie III, 96
Davidson, Samuel VI, 797
Davidson, Samuel VI, 798
Davidson, Samuel VI, 801
Davidson, Samuel VI, 808
Davidson, Samuel VI, 810
Davidson, Samuel VI, 811
Davidson, Samuel VI, 828
Davidson, Samuel VI, 903
Davidson, Sarah VI, 855
Davidson, Sarah Ann IV, 194
Davidson, Sarah Ann IV, 1155
Davidson, Susanna VI, 811
Davidson, Susannah I, 744
Davidson, Thomas I, 1091
Davidson, Thomas II, 501
Davidson, Thomas VI, 810
Davidson, Thomas VI, 903
Davidson, Tishie I, 876
Davidson, Tishie I, 900
Davidson, William I, 350
Davidson, William I, 744
Davidson, William I, 1091
Davidson, William I, 1105
Davidson, William I, 1117
Davidson, William VI, 810
Davidson, William VI, 903
Davidson, William W. VI, 810
Davidson, Wm. L. II, 132
Davidson, Young VI, 810
Davie, Mary II, 51
Davie, Mary II, 65
Davies, Abiathar I, 1043
Davies, Abiathar V, 46
Davies, Abiather V, 835
Davies, Abigail I, 384
Davies, Abigail I, 412
Davies, Abigail V, 735
Davies, Alfred B. III, 96
Davies, Allen V, 735
Davies, Amos I, 1043
Davies, Ann I, 384
Davies, Ann I, 407
Davies, Ann IV, 27
Davies, Ann IV, 28
Davies, Ann V, 735
Davies, Ann C. E. VI, 893
Davies, Ann Eliza IV, 27
Davies, Ann F. VI, 984
Davies, Benjamin I, 1043
Davies, Benjamin V, 46
Davies, Benjamin V, 735
Davies, Benjamin V, 835
Davies, Benjamin T. VI, 984
Davies, Benjn. T. VI, 921
Davies, Catahrine V, 735
Davies, Charles I, 343
Davies, Charles I, 349
Davies, Charles I, 384
Davies, Charles VI, 382
Davies, Charlotte T. V, 735
Davies, Chas. I, 349
Davies, Editha VI, 893
Davies, Eleanor C. V, 735
Davies, Elizabeth I, 373
Davies, Elizabeth I, 384
Davies, Elizabeth I, 425
Davies, Elizabeth Ann VI, 1009
Davies, Evan II, 462
Davies, Evan II, 501
Davies, Ezra V, 735
Davies, Hannah I, 343
Davies, Hannah I, 349
Davies, Hannah I, 384
Davies, Hannah I, 387
Davies, Hannah I, 529
Davies, Hannah I, 535
Davies, Hannah II, 352
Davies, Hannah VI, 382
Davies, Henry V, 735
Davies, Henry VI, 991
Davies, Henry G. III, 96
Davies, Henry Landon VI, 893
Davies, Isaac V, 735
Davies, Issachar II, 501
Davies, Iva V, 735
Davies, Iva I. V, 735
Davies, James II, 501
Davies, Jane IV, 28
Davies, Jane V, 881
Davies, Jesse I, 713
Davies, John I, 349
Davies, John I, 373
Davies, John I, 384
Davies, John I, 695
Davies, John I, 1043
Davies, John V, 46
Davies, John R. V, 735
Davies, John, Jr. I, 384
Davies, Jonathan V, 735
Davies, Joseph I, 384
Davies, Joseph I, 387
Davies, Joseph II, 502
Davies, Joseph, Jr. I, 984
Davies, Joshua I, 236
Davies, Joshua IV, 28
Davies, Lindley V, 735
Davies, Lucy VI, 991
Davies, Lucy W. VI, 895
Davies, Luella Toms V, 735
Davies, Lydia I, 1043
Davies, Lydia V, 46
Davies, Lydia V, 735
Davies, Martha IV, 697
Davies, Mary I, 349
Davies, Mary I, 373
Davies, Mary I, 384
Davies, Mary I, 1043
Davies, Mary II, 462
Davies, Mary II, 501
Davies, Mary II, 502
Davies, Mary V, 46
Davies, Mary V, 735
Davies, Mary A. V, 735
Davies, Mary Elizabeth VI, 921
Davies, Maye VI, 984
Davies, Mayo VI, 921
Davies, Micajah I, 713
Davies, Miles IV, 27
Davies, Miles IV, 28
Davies, Mrs. Mary V, 735
Davies, Rachel I, 1043
Davies, Rachel II, 609
Davies, Rachel V, 46
Davies, Rachel V, 735
Davies, Rachel VI, 382
Davies, Rayborn H. V, 735
Davies, Rhoda I, 1043
Davies, Riley V, 735
Davies, Ruth I, 373
Davies, Ruth I, 384
Davies, Ruth I, 1007
Davies, Ruth I, 1008
Davies, Sabilla V, 46
Davies, Sam B. VI, 893
Davies, Samantha V, 735
Davies, Samuel I, 1043
Davies, Samuel V, 46
Davies, Samuel VI, 223
Davies, Samuel, Jr. V, 735
Davies, Sarah I, 384
Davies, Sarah I, 414
Davies, Sarah I, 1043
Davies, Sarah II, 501
Davies, Sarah IV, 382
Davies, Sarah V, 46
Davies, Sibilla I, 1043
Davies, Simon V, 735
Davies, Thomas I, 384
Davies, Thomas I, 535
Davies, Wd. Rachel II, 501
Davies, Willa V, 735
Davies, William I, 384
Davies, William I, 407
Davies, William T. VI, 964
Davis, ??? I, 32
Davis, ??? II, 791
Davis, ??? III, 96
Davis, ??? III, 97
Davis, ??? IV, 795
Davis, ??? VI, 348
Davis, A. J. V, 232
Davis, A. J. V, 233
Davis, A. J. V, 328
Davis, Aaron I, 713
Davis, Aaron I, 876
Davis, Abbie E. I, 237
Davis, Abiathar I, 1047
Davis, Abiathar I, 1048
Davis, Abiathar V, 46
Davis, Abiathar D. V, 734
Davis, Abiathar, Sr. V, 735
Davis, Abiather I, 1047
Davis, Abiather IV, 382
Davis, Abiather V, 46
Davis, Abiather V, 723
Davis, Abiather V, 734
Davis, Abiather V, 735
Davis, Abiather V, 745
Davis, Abiather V, 806
Davis, Abiather V, 835
Davis, Abiather VI, 486
Davis, Abigail I, 265
Davis, Abigail I, 269
Davis, Abigail I, 276
Davis, Abigail I, 384
Davis, Abigail I, 662
Davis, Abigail II, 26
Davis, Abigail II, 65
Davis, Abigail II, 147
Davis, Abigail II, 157
Davis, Abigail II, 213
Davis, Abigail II, 790
Davis, Abigail V, 735
Davis, Abigail C. I, 807
Davis, Abigail Cornelia I, 758
Davis, Abigail E. I, 745
Davis, Abigail R. I, 779
Davis, Abigail, Jr. II, 53
Davis, Abigail, Jr. II, 65
Davis, Abner I, 467
Davis, Abraham IV, 28
Davis, Abraham IV, 82
Davis, Abraham IV, 620
Davis, Abraham IV, 698
Davis, Abraham VI, 485
Davis, Abraham VI, 486
Davis, Abraham Barker III, 96

Davis, Abram IV, 470
Davis, Absalet I, 285
Davis, Absalet I, 304
Davis, Absella I, 304
Davis, Absellit I, 304
Davis, Absellit I, 320
Davis, Absillet I, 284
Davis, Absillet I, 328
Davis, Achsa I, 698
Davis, Achsa I, 985
Davis, Achsa I, 999
Davis, Achsah R. I, 677
Davis, Achsah R. I, 714
Davis, Ada V, 383
Davis, Adam I, 652
Davis, Adam I, 1008
Davis, Adela I, 713
Davis, Adela I, 876
Davis, Adela H. I, 779
Davis, Adela H. I, 807
Davis, Adella I, 807
Davis, Adella I, 876
Davis, Adella M. V, 485
Davis, Agnes II, 502
Davis, Agnes V, 835
Davis, Ailce I, 56
Davis, Ailse I, 758
Davis, Albert II, 147
Davis, Albert IV, 903
Davis, Albert Arthur IV, 1092
Davis, Albert Franklin V, 835
Davis, Alce V, 46
Davis, Aldas V, 806
Davis, Alec I, 45
Davis, Alexander III, 30
Davis, Alexander III, 97
Davis, Alfred II, 791
Davis, Alic I, 269
Davis, Alice I, 45
Davis, Alice I, 269
Davis, Alice I, 652
Davis, Alice I, 679
Davis, Alice I, 744
Davis, Alice I, 758
Davis, Alice I, 807
Davis, Alice I, 837
Davis, Alice IV, 697
Davis, Alice IV, 698
Davis, Alice IV, 1092
Davis, Alice IV, 1113
Davis, Alice IV, 1129
Davis, Alice V, 558
Davis, Alice V, 780
Davis, Alice V, 969
Davis, Alice V, 991
Davis, Alice VI, 706
Davis, Alice Jane V, 47
Davis, Alice Jane V, 618
Davis, Alice M. V, 233
Davis, Alice M. V, 242
Davis, Allen II, 352
Davis, Allen V, 46
Davis, Allen V, 485
Davis, Allen V, 558
Davis, Allen V, 734
Davis, Allen V, 735
Davis, Allen W. I, 697
Davis, Allen W. I, 714
Davis, Allen Winslow I, 714
Davis, Almina I, 876
Davis, Almina I, 894
Davis, Alse I, 758
Davis, Alton Kenneth VI, 737
Davis, Alton Kenneth, Jr. VI, 737
Davis, Amanda II, 132
Davis, Amaziah I, 1004
Davis, Amie II, 65
Davis, Amie II, 72
Davis, Amor I, 744
Davis, Amor I, 807
Davis, Amor I, 837
Davis, Amos I, 1028
Davis, Amos IV, 382
Davis, Amos IV, 409
Davis, Amos IV, 810
Davis, Amos V, 46
Davis, Amos V, 485
Davis, Amos V, 734
Davis, Amos V, 835
Davis, Amos J. V, 328
Davis, Ana I, 779
Davis, Andrew McF. III, 96
Davis, Andria III, 97
Davis, Angelina V, 835
Davis, Angelina V, 870
Davis, Angelina E. I, 714
Davis, Angeline V, 871
Davis, Ann I, 350
Davis, Ann I, 384
Davis, Ann I, 713
Davis, Ann I, 719
Davis, Ann I, 807
Davis, Ann I, 845
Davis, Ann I, 974
Davis, Ann I, 975
Davis, Ann I, 984
Davis, Ann I, 1008
Davis, Ann II, 147
Davis, Ann II, 213
Davis, Ann II, 269
Davis, Ann II, 443
Davis, Ann II, 501
Davis, Ann II, 683
Davis, Ann II, 826
Davis, Ann II, 855
Davis, Ann III, 96
Davis, Ann III, 304
Davis, Ann IV, 28
Davis, Ann IV, 143
Davis, Ann IV, 365
Davis, Ann IV, 382
Davis, Ann IV, 399
Davis, Ann IV, 408
Davis, Ann IV, 415
Davis, Ann IV, 470
Davis, Ann IV, 495
Davis, Ann IV, 520
Davis, Ann IV, 528
Davis, Ann IV, 558
Davis, Ann IV, 573
Davis, Ann IV, 583
Davis, Ann IV, 810
Davis, Ann IV, 1092
Davis, Ann V, 327
Davis, Ann V, 335
Davis, Ann V, 485
Davis, Ann V, 618
Davis, Ann V, 735
Davis, Ann V, 749
Davis, Ann V, 813
Davis, Ann VI, 106
Davis, Ann VI, 810
Davis, Ann B. II, 814
Davis, Ann Eliza IV, 520
Davis, Ann G. VI, 810
Davis, Ann N. III, 148
Davis, Anna I, 265
Davis, Anna I, 269
Davis, Anna I, 495
Davis, Anna I, 536
Davis, Anna I, 713
Davis, Anna I, 807
Davis, Anna I, 956
Davis, Anna I, 984
Davis, Anna III, 96
Davis, Anna III, 279
Davis, Anna IV, 697
Davis, Anna IV, 698
Davis, Anna IV, 703
Davis, Anna IV, 810
Davis, Anna IV, 947
Davis, Anna V, 47
Davis, Anna V, 165
Davis, Anna V, 455
Davis, Anna V, 793
Davis, Anna V, 794
Davis, Anna B. V, 806
Davis, Anna Bella V, 165
Davis, Anna C. II, 790
Davis, Anna C. II, 855
Davis, Anna C. II, 871
Davis, Anna Coffin II, 798
Davis, Anna E. VI, 782
Davis, Anna Laura II, 791
Davis, Anna Laura II, 856
Davis, Anna M. III, 96
Davis, Anna M. III, 182
Davis, Anna M. V, 735
Davis, Anna Maria V, 46
Davis, Anna Maria V, 112
Davis, Anna Maria V, 902
Davis, Anna Maria V, 927
Davis, Anna Maria VI, 351
Davis, Anna Mariah VI, 307
Davis, Anna N. III, 49
Davis, Anna N. III, 96
Davis, Anna N. III, 256
Davis, Annalyle I, 940
Davis, Annanias C. V, 47
Davis, Annas I, 677
Davis, Annas I, 683
Davis, Anne I, 269
Davis, Anne I, 975
Davis, Anne II, 501
Davis, Anne IV, 382
Davis, Anne IV, 520
Davis, Anne B. II, 855
Davis, Anne B. II, 908
Davis, Annie I, 223
Davis, Annie I, 807
Davis, Annie IV, 382
Davis, Annie VI, 633
Davis, Annie VI, 649
Davis, Annie Lyle I, 924
Davis, Annis V, 902
Davis, Annis VI, 171
Davis, Annis VI, 306
Davis, Annis VI, 307
Davis, Annis VI, 350
Davis, Annis E. VI, 980
Davis, Armanis C. V, 46
Davis, Arnold VI, 633
Davis, Arnold VI, 703
Davis, Arnold Boone VI, 649
Davis, Arnold Boone VI, 706
Davis, Arnold Boone VI, 737
Davis, Arnold Boone VI, 738
Davis, Arthur V, 327
Davis, Arthur B. VI, 903
Davis, Arthur E. II, 791
Davis, Arthur F. IV, 1092
Davis, Arthur T. IV, 1129
Davis, Asa Elkinton II, 502
Davis, Asariah VI, 810
Davis, Asenath I, 285
Davis, Asenath I, 304
Davis, Asenath I, 314
Davis, Asenath I, 495
Davis, Asenath IV, 143
Davis, Asenath IV, 573
Davis, Asenath IV, 599
Davis, Axum I, 714
Davis, Azor I, 975
Davis, Azula I, 1150
Davis, B. M. I, 615
Davis, B. M. I, 632
Davis, B. M. I, 641
Davis, Banner I, 940
Davis, Barbara V, 383
Davis, Barlet Y. I, 779
Davis, Bartlett A. I, 713
Davis, Bartlett J. I, 876
Davis, Bartlett Y. I, 714
Davis, Bartlett Y. I, 807
Davis, Bayard I, 335
Davis, Bell V, 668
Davis, Beniah I, 876
Davis, Beniamin I, 269
Davis, Benj. I, 349
Davis, Benj. IV, 620
Davis, Benj. V, 734
Davis, Benjamin I, 137
Davis, Benjamin I, 265
Davis, Benjamin I, 269
Davis, Benjamin I, 479
Davis, Benjamin I, 876
Davis, Benjamin II, 309
Davis, Benjamin II, 352
Davis, Benjamin II, 353
Davis, Benjamin II, 501
Davis, Benjamin II, 502
Davis, Benjamin II, 703
Davis, Benjamin II, 736
Davis, Benjamin IV, 620
Davis, Benjamin IV, 698
Davis, Benjamin IV, 810
Davis, Benjamin IV, 892
Davis, Benjamin IV, 895
Davis, Benjamin V, 46
Davis, Benjamin V, 735
Davis, Benjamin V, 835
Davis, Benjamin VI, 306
Davis, Benjamin VI, 351
Davis, Benjamin VI, 486
Davis, Benjamin VI, 810
Davis, Benjamin A. R. I, 714
Davis, Benjamin B. IV, 697
Davis, Benjamin B. IV, 698
Davis, Benjamin B. IV, 810
Davis, Benjamin B. IV, 826
Davis, Benjm. I, 473
Davis, Benjm. I, 479
Davis, Benoni I, 876
Davis, Bertha V, 668
Davis, Bertha D. V, 668
Davis, Berthenia V, 485
Davis, Berthenia O. V, 618
Davis, Betcey Ann I, 698
Davis, Betsey V, 327
Davis, Betsey V, 814
Davis, Betsy V, 327
Davis, Betsy V, 735
Davis, Betsy V, 749
Davis, Betsy V, 806
Davis, Betsy V, 807
Davis, Betsy VI, 256
Davis, Betsy VI, 810
Davis, Betsy Ann I, 495
Davis, Betsy Ann I, 605
Davis, Bettie VI, 721
Davis, Bettie VI, 738
Davis, Betty I, 285
Davis, Betty II, 819
Davis, Betty VI, 634
Davis, Betty VI, 810
Davis, Betty VI, 854
Davis, Birchie S. V, 233
Davis, Birchie S. V, 328
Davis, Birta IV, 1249
Davis, Blanch V, 552
Davis, Blanch E. V, 558
Davis, Bridget I, 974
Davis, Bridget I, 984
Davis, Bridget I, 985
Davis, Bridget I, 987
Davis, Bridget E. VI, 851
Davis, Burthenia O. V, 485
Davis, Burthernia O. V, 522
Davis, Caleb I, 45
Davis, Caleb I, 98
Davis, Caleb I, 137
Davis, Caleb IV, 698
Davis, Caleb V, 46
Davis, Caleb V, 460
Davis, Caleb V, 474
Davis, Calvin V, 485
Davis, Calvin Hiram V, 618
Davis, Calvin W. V, 486
Davis, Carl I, 940
Davis, Carl Roscoe I, 923
Davis, Caroline I, 713
Davis, Caroline I, 714
Davis, Caroline I, 737
Davis, Caroline I, 738
Davis, Caroline I, 745
Davis, Caroline I, 758
Davis, Caroline I, 876
Davis, Caroline II, 309
Davis, Caroline V, 233
Davis, Caroline V, 618
Davis, Caroline V, 902
Davis, Caroline E. I, 745
Davis, Carrie V, 558
Davis, Carrie B. V, 558
Davis, Cassandra IV, 82
Davis, Catahrine V, 735
Davis, Catharine I, 984
Davis, Catharine I, 997
Davis, Catharine II, 502
Davis, Catharine IV, 83
Davis, Catharine IV, 113
Davis, Catharine IV, 520
Davis, Catharine IV, 558
Davis, Catharine IV, 804
Davis, Catharine IV, 811
Davis, Catharine IV, 892
Davis, Catharine IV, 895
Davis, Catharine IV, 947
Davis, Catharine V, 794
Davis, Catharine VI, 475
Davis, Catharine VI, 485
Davis, Catharine VI, 621
Davis, Catharine VI, 737
Davis, Catharine A. VI, 938
Davis, Catherine IV, 810
Davis, Catherine VI, 633
Davis, Celia I, 285
Davis, Celia I, 304
Davis, Celia I, 311
Davis, Charity I, 285
Davis, Charity I, 304
Davis, Charity I, 313
Davis, Charity I, 328
Davis, Charity II, 26
Davis, Charity IV, 143
Davis, Charity IV, 365
Davis, Charity IV, 382
Davis, Charity F. I, 285
Davis, Charles I, 344
Davis, Charles I, 346
Davis, Charles I, 349
Davis, Charles I, 366
Davis, Charles I, 384
Davis, Charles I, 414
Davis, Charles I, 457
Davis, Charles I, 460
Davis, Charles I, 466
Davis, Charles I, 467
Davis, Charles I, 468
Davis, Charles I, 471
Davis, Charles I, 479
Davis, Charles I, 495
Davis, Charles I, 530
Davis, Charles I, 535
Davis, Charles I, 662
Davis, Charles I, 667
Davis, Charles I, 876
Davis, Charles I, 974
Davis, Charles I, 984
Davis, Charles I, 1008
Davis, Charles II, 26
Davis, Charles II, 309
Davis, Charles II, 352
Davis, Charles II, 353
Davis, Charles II, 502
Davis, Charles II, 819
Davis, Charles III, 96
Davis, Charles V, 455
Davis, Charles V, 485
Davis, Charles V, 486
Davis, Charles VI, 382
Davis, Charles VI, 485
Davis, Charles B. V, 46
Davis, Charles B. V, 47
Davis, Charles B. V, 486
Davis, Charles E. IV, 1092
Davis, Charles E. IV, 1129
Davis, Charles Gideon VI, 633
Davis, Charles Gideon VI, 634
Davis, Charles Gideon VI, 677
Davis, Charles Gideon VI, 738
Davis, Charles H. II, 791
Davis, Charles Henry I, 8
Davis, Charles Henry I, 45
Davis, Charles Henry V, 902
Davis, Charles James II, 791
Davis, Charles P. II, 309
Davis, Charles W. VI, 60
Davis, Charlotte V, 46
Davis, Charlotte V, 835
Davis, Charlotte V, 844
Davis, Charlotte V, 902
Davis, Charlotte VI, 308
Davis, Charlotte VI, 351
Davis, Charlotte E. V, 835
Davis, Charlotte T. V, 735
Davis, Charyty I, 956
Davis, Chas. II, 26
Davis, Chas. II, 65
Davis, Chas. II, 66
Davis, Chas. II, 803
Davis, Chas. V, 558
Davis, Chas. V, 991
Davis, Chas. Alfred II, 791
Davis, Chas. E. IV, 1092
Davis, Chas. H. V, 902
Davis, Chas. Merlin V, 328
Davis, Chauncey Woodhill II, 70
Davis, Chrissie I, 923
Davis, Christian II, 352
Davis, Christian II, 353
Davis, Christian II, 651
Davis, Christopher Harmon V, 327
Davis, Christy III, 96
Davis, Cinderella I, 923
Davis, Cinderella K. I, 759
Davis, Cinthia Horton IV, 28
Davis, Clara Ellen V, 383
Davis, Clarence IV, 1129
Davis, Clarence V, 835
Davis, Clarissa I, 269
Davis, Clement VI, 903
Davis, Clementine III, 96
Davis, Clementine III, 233
Davis, Clifford V, 618
Davis, Clifton C. I, 237
Davis, Connie I, 615
Davis, Connie J. I, 632
Davis, Connie J. I, 641
Davis, Cora I, 626
Davis, Cora G. V, 165
Davis, Cordelia A. I, 807
Davis, Cordelia Ann I, 779
Davis, Cornelia I, 876
Davis, Correla I, 8
Davis, Cynderella K. I, 237
Davis, Cynderilla I, 237
Davis, Cynthia IV, 224
Davis, Cynthia IV, 337
Davis, Cynthia Horton IV, 40
Davis, Cynthia Horton IV, 193
Davis, Cynthia Horton IV, 311
Davis, Cynthia Horton IV, 312
Davis, Cynthia Horton IV, 326
Davis, Cynthia Horton IV, 892
Davis, Cynthia Horton IV, 893
Davis, Cyrus I, 237
Davis, Cyrus I, 495
Davis, Cyrus I, 923
Davis, Cyrus S. I, 745
Davis, Cyrus S. I, 759
Davis, Dabney W. VI, 903
Davis, Dadney W. VI, 903
Davis, Dale V, 668
Davis, Dan V, 233
Davis, Daniel I, 349
Davis, Daniel I, 495
Davis, Daniel I, 961
Davis, Daniel I, 974
Davis, Daniel I, 984
Davis, Daniel I, 985
Davis, Daniel III, 96
Davis, Daniel IV, 28
Davis, Daniel IV, 82

Davis, Daniel IV, 740
Davis, Daniel IV, 1092
Davis, Daniel V, 233
Davis, Daniel V, 327
Davis, Daniel V, 335
Davis, Daniel V, 485
Davis, Daniel C. IV, 1092
Davis, Daniel N. IV, 1092
Davis, Daniel N. IV, 1129
Davis, David I, 652
Davis, David I, 713
Davis, David I, 738
Davis, David I, 745
Davis, David I, 758
Davis, David I, 759
Davis, David I, 876
Davis, David I, 985
Davis, David I, 1004
Davis, David II, 26
Davis, David II, 65
Davis, David II, 131
Davis, David II, 132
Davis, David II, 147
Davis, David II, 157
Davis, David II, 213
Davis, David II, 309
Davis, David II, 352
Davis, David II, 501
Davis, David II, 785
Davis, David II, 790
Davis, David II, 791
Davis, David II, 793
Davis, David II, 855
Davis, David II, 856
Davis, David II, 861
Davis, David II, 912
Davis, David IV, 697
Davis, David IV, 810
Davis, David IV, 827
Davis, David IV, 903
Davis, David IV, 913
Davis, David V, 735
Davis, David VI, 106
Davis, David VI, 171
Davis, David VI, 306
Davis, David VI, 307
Davis, David VI, 475
Davis, David VI, 815
Davis, David A. I, 745
Davis, David Allen V, 233
Davis, David Allen V, 328
Davis, David C. II, 138
Davis, David Davis II, 785
Davis, David E. II, 131
Davis, David E. II, 147
Davis, David F. I, 745
Davis, David G. I, 745
Davis, David H. II, 502
Davis, David H. II, 855
Davis, David H. III, 96
Davis, David H. III, 182
Davis, David J. I, 876
Davis, David Jones II, 502
Davis, David L. I, 698
Davis, David L. I, 714
Davis, David L. I, 807
Davis, David L. I, 876
Davis, David L. I, 883
Davis, David L. IV, 947
Davis, David M. I, 745
Davis, David M. II, 117
Davis, David M. II, 147
Davis, David M. II, 157
Davis, David M. II, 856
Davis, David M. II, 890
Davis, David Matlack II, 790
Davis, David S. I, 745
Davis, David S. I, 759
Davis, David W. I, 758
Davis, David W. I, 807
Davis, David, Jr. II, 117
Davis, Davis W. I, 807
Davis, Deborah I, 495
Davis, Deborah I, 536
Davis, Deborah I, 541
Davis, Deborah II, 992
Davis, Deborah IV, 364
Davis, Deborah IV, 384
Davis, Deborah IV, 399
Davis, Deborah IV, 520
Davis, Deborah IV, 528
Davis, Deborah VI, 306
Davis, Deborah H. III, 96
Davis, Deborah L. II, 855
Davis, Deborah S. II, 706
Davis, Deborah S. IV, 193
Davis, Deborah S. IV, 214
Davis, Deborah S. IV, 423
Davis, Deborah S. IV, 673
Davis, Delila V, 328
Davis, Delila V, 349
Davis, Delilah I, 677
Davis, Delilah I, 681
Davis, Delilah J. I, 677
Davis, Dellie V. V, 806
Davis, Delora IV, 438
Davis, Delphina I, 876
Davis, Delphina I, 884
Davis, Dianna I, 758
Davis, Dina I, 667
Davis, Dinah I, 349
Davis, Dinah I, 466
Davis, Dinah I, 479
Davis, Dinah I, 484
Davis, Dinah I, 974
Davis, Dinah I, 984
Davis, Dinah I, 986
Davis, Dinah II, 501
Davis, Dora I, 922
Davis, Dora V, 233
Davis, Doratha II, 26
Davis, Doratha Wills VI, 911
Davis, Dorathy II, 502
Davis, Dorcas V, 734
Davis, Dorcas V, 735
Davis, Dorcas V, 835
Davis, Dorkis V, 46
Davis, Dorkis V, 86
Davis, Dorothy II, 26
Davis, Dorothy VI, 45
Davis, E. Columbus IV, 1276
Davis, Earl I, 335
Davis, Ebeneezer V, 383
Davis, Edgar III, 481
Davis, Edgar III, 499
Davis, Edith I, 304
Davis, Edith I, 314
Davis, Edith I, 652
Davis, Edith I, 677
Davis, Edith I, 682
Davis, Edith I, 698
Davis, Edith I, 713
Davis, Edith I, 721
Davis, Edith I, 985
Davis, Edith IV, 573
Davis, Edith IV, 620
Davis, Edith IV, 653
Davis, Edith IV, 810
Davis, Edith IV, 903
Davis, Edith Bogan V, 558
Davis, Edith J. II, 139
Davis, Edith Mosher V, 47
Davis, Edith S. III, 97
Davis, Edna III, 95
Davis, Edna III, 97
Davis, Edna V, 233
Davis, Edna V, 328
Davis, Edward II, 147
Davis, Edward II, 856
Davis, Edward II, 901
Davis, Edward IV, 28
Davis, Edward IV, 82
Davis, Edward IV, 193
Davis, Edward VI, 357
Davis, Edward VI, 485
Davis, Edward VI, 738
Davis, Edward VI, 810
Davis, Edward H. II, 147
Davis, Edward H. VI, 634
Davis, Edward M. II, 736
Davis, Edward M. II, 790
Davis, Edward M. II, 855
Davis, Edward M. II, 856
Davis, Edward M. II, 871
Davis, Edward M. III, 96
Davis, Edward M., Jr. II, 791
Davis, Edward M., Jr. II, 856
Davis, Edward Morris II, 791
Davis, Edward West II, 791
Davis, Effa Z. V, 383
Davis, Effie IV, 1276
Davis, Effie Z. V, 383
Davis, Eldena V, 618
Davis, Eleanor II, 501
Davis, Eleanor III, 96
Davis, Eleanor IV, 810
Davis, Eleanor IV, 900
Davis, Eleanor IV, 903
Davis, Eleanor VI, 475
Davis, Eleanor C. V, 735
Davis, Eleanor C. V, 750
Davis, Eleanor C. V, 806
Davis, Eleanor H. V, 902
Davis, Eleazar W. I, 758
Davis, Eleazar W. I, 767
Davis, Eleazer I, 745
Davis, Elenor II, 26
Davis, Elezabeath I, 137
Davis, Elezabeath I, 172
Davis, Eli IV, 698
Davis, Elihu I, 1118
Davis, Elihu V, 301
Davis, Elihu V, 835
Davis, Elihu John William V, 301
Davis, Elijah I, 285
Davis, Elijah I, 796
Davis, Elijah I, 807
Davis, Elijah I, 1004
Davis, Elisabeth I, 45
Davis, Elisabeth I, 56
Davis, Elisabeth I, 137
Davis, Elisabeth I, 140
Davis, Elisabeth I, 152
Davis, Elisabeth II, 501
Davis, Elisabeth II, 554
Davis, Elisabeth II, 605
Davis, Elisabeth IV, 697
Davis, Elisha II, 65
Davis, Elisha II, 791
Davis, Elisha V, 46
Davis, Elisha V, 969
Davis, Elisha L. IV, 697
Davis, Eliz. III, 96
Davis, Eliz. III, 219
Davis, Eliza I, 985
Davis, Eliza I, 995
Davis, Eliza IV, 520
Davis, Eliza Ann I, 479
Davis, Eliza E. I, 745
Davis, Eliza J. III, 102
Davis, Eliza Jane I, 8
Davis, Eliza Jane V, 485
Davis, Eliza L. III, 97
Davis, Elizabeth I, 98
Davis, Elizabeth I, 172
Davis, Elizabeth I, 269
Davis, Elizabeth I, 285
Davis, Elizabeth I, 304
Davis, Elizabeth I, 312
Davis, Elizabeth I, 338
Davis, Elizabeth I, 349
Davis, Elizabeth I, 366
Davis, Elizabeth I, 384
Davis, Elizabeth I, 460
Davis, Elizabeth I, 466
Davis, Elizabeth I, 467
Davis, Elizabeth I, 495
Davis, Elizabeth I, 652
Davis, Elizabeth I, 655
Davis, Elizabeth I, 677
Davis, Elizabeth I, 687
Davis, Elizabeth I, 698
Davis, Elizabeth I, 713
Davis, Elizabeth I, 745
Davis, Elizabeth I, 758
Davis, Elizabeth I, 768
Davis, Elizabeth I, 807
Davis, Elizabeth I, 956
Davis, Elizabeth I, 958
Davis, Elizabeth I, 961
Davis, Elizabeth I, 969
Davis, Elizabeth I, 984
Davis, Elizabeth I, 985
Davis, Elizabeth I, 988
Davis, Elizabeth I, 1000
Davis, Elizabeth I, 1004
Davis, Elizabeth I, 1007
Davis, Elizabeth I, 1008
Davis, Elizabeth I, 1009
Davis, Elizabeth I, 1011
Davis, Elizabeth I, 1012
Davis, Elizabeth I, 1013
Davis, Elizabeth I, 1114
Davis, Elizabeth I, 1118
Davis, Elizabeth II, 26
Davis, Elizabeth II, 65
Davis, Elizabeth II, 73
Davis, Elizabeth II, 111
Davis, Elizabeth II, 117
Davis, Elizabeth II, 121
Davis, Elizabeth II, 352
Davis, Elizabeth II, 353
Davis, Elizabeth II, 443
Davis, Elizabeth II, 480
Davis, Elizabeth II, 481
Davis, Elizabeth II, 501
Davis, Elizabeth II, 502
Davis, Elizabeth II, 637
Davis, Elizabeth II, 683
Davis, Elizabeth II, 736
Davis, Elizabeth II, 791
Davis, Elizabeth II, 793
Davis, Elizabeth II, 803
Davis, Elizabeth II, 832
Davis, Elizabeth II, 853
Davis, Elizabeth II, 855
Davis, Elizabeth II, 856
Davis, Elizabeth II, 901
Davis, Elizabeth II, 992
Davis, Elizabeth II, 1035
Davis, Elizabeth III, 96
Davis, Elizabeth III, 97
Davis, Elizabeth III, 304
Davis, Elizabeth III, 398
Davis, Elizabeth III, 472
Davis, Elizabeth IV, 83
Davis, Elizabeth IV, 143
Davis, Elizabeth IV, 382
Davis, Elizabeth IV, 408
Davis, Elizabeth IV, 619
Davis, Elizabeth IV, 697
Davis, Elizabeth IV, 698
Davis, Elizabeth IV, 785
Davis, Elizabeth IV, 810
Davis, Elizabeth IV, 885
Davis, Elizabeth V, 46
Davis, Elizabeth V, 233
Davis, Elizabeth V, 327
Davis, Elizabeth V, 382
Davis, Elizabeth V, 383
Davis, Elizabeth V, 389
Davis, Elizabeth V, 485
Davis, Elizabeth V, 617
Davis, Elizabeth V, 618
Davis, Elizabeth V, 644
Davis, Elizabeth V, 668
Davis, Elizabeth V, 735
Davis, Elizabeth V, 806
Davis, Elizabeth VI, 256
Davis, Elizabeth VI, 306
Davis, Elizabeth VI, 351
Davis, Elizabeth VI, 382
Davis, Elizabeth VI, 485
Davis, Elizabeth VI, 619
Davis, Elizabeth VI, 633
Davis, Elizabeth VI, 677
Davis, Elizabeth VI, 721
Davis, Elizabeth VI, 732
Davis, Elizabeth VI, 737
Davis, Elizabeth VI, 738
Davis, Elizabeth VI, 881
Davis, Elizabeth VI, 903
Davis, Elizabeth VI, 921
Davis, Elizabeth VI, 1001
Davis, Elizabeth A. II, 855
Davis, Elizabeth A. V, 46
Davis, Elizabeth A. V, 485
Davis, Elizabeth Alice V, 46
Davis, Elizabeth Alice V, 80
Davis, Elizabeth Ann I, 466
Davis, Elizabeth Ann II, 793
Davis, Elizabeth Ann II, 855
Davis, Elizabeth Ann II, 861
Davis, Elizabeth Ann III, 96
Davis, Elizabeth Ann III, 97
Davis, Elizabeth Ann III, 305
Davis, Elizabeth Ann V, 46
Davis, Elizabeth Ann V, 98
Davis, Elizabeth B. VI, 334
Davis, Elizabeth B. VI, 842
Davis, Elizabeth C. II, 791
Davis, Elizabeth C. II, 855
Davis, Elizabeth C. II, 871
Davis, Elizabeth Corbit II, 798
Davis, Elizabeth F. I, 985
Davis, Elizabeth Gibbs VI, 911
Davis, Elizabeth H. II, 736
Davis, Elizabeth H. II, 739
Davis, Elizabeth J. I, 759
Davis, Elizabeth J. V, 668
Davis, Elizabeth K. II, 139
Davis, Elizabeth L. II, 117
Davis, Elizabeth L. IV, 810
Davis, Elizabeth L. IV, 839
Davis, Elizabeth M. I, 714
Davis, Elizabeth M. II, 791
Davis, Elizabeth M. II, 855
Davis, Elizabeth, Jr. I, 1008
Davis, Elizabeth, Sr. I, 876
Davis, Ella V, 991
Davis, Ella VI, 633
Davis, Ella VI, 634
Davis, Ella VI, 677
Davis, Ella VI, 738
Davis, Ellen I, 677
Davis, Ellen I, 683
Davis, Ellen III, 96
Davis, Ellen H. V, 902
Davis, Ellis I, 940
Davis, Ellis IV, 28
Davis, Ellis IV, 82
Davis, Ellis IV, 470
Davis, Ellis IV, 495
Davis, Ellis IV, 698
Davis, Ellis IV, 810
Davis, Ellis IV, 833
Davis, Ellis V, 617
Davis, Ellis VI, 485
Davis, Ellwood II, 736
Davis, Ellwood B. II, 736
Davis, Elma IV, 697
Davis, Elma M. I, 714
Davis, Elmy Ann IV, 383
Davis, Elmy Ann IV, 432
Davis, Elnathan VI, 903
Davis, Elonar II, 65
Davis, Eloner II, 65
Davis, Else I, 758
Davis, Elsie VI, 60
Davis, Elsie A. I, 923
Davis, Elsie Morgan VI, 634
Davis, Elva IV, 383
Davis, Elva IV, 458
Davis, Elva E. I, 237
Davis, Elwood II, 139
Davis, Elwood II, 736
Davis, Elwood II, 785
Davis, Elwood V, 835
Davis, Elzena I, 984
Davis, Emily I, 698
Davis, Emily II, 791
Davis, Emily II, 856
Davis, Emily II, 933
Davis, Emily V, 233
Davis, Emily V, 327
Davis, Emily V, 618
Davis, Emily VI, 903
Davis, Emily F. I, 714
Davis, Emily F. I, 738
Davis, Emily F. I, 807
Davis, Emily Louise III, 97
Davis, Emma IV, 1092
Davis, Emma V, 455
Davis, Emma Alderson V, 902
Davis, Enoch I, 265
Davis, Enoch I, 269
Davis, Enoch I, 349
Davis, Enoch I, 466
Davis, Enoch I, 467
Davis, Enoch I, 479
Davis, Enoch I, 626
Davis, Enoch H. I, 467
Davis, Enos I, 974
Davis, Enos IV, 892
Davis, Enos IV, 914
Davis, Epsie I, 614
Davis, Ermina V, 233
Davis, Eslie A. V, 485
Davis, Ester II, 65
Davis, Esther I, 265
Davis, Esther I, 269
Davis, Esther II, 26
Davis, Esther II, 501
Davis, Esther II, 502
Davis, Esther II, 611
Davis, Esther II, 735
Davis, Esther II, 791
Davis, Esther II, 855
Davis, Esther II, 908
Davis, Esther IV, 697
Davis, Esther IV, 698
Davis, Esther IV, 727
Davis, Esther IV, 947
Davis, Esther V, 262
Davis, Esther F. III, 49
Davis, Esther F. III, 96
Davis, Esther Osborn V, 327
Davis, Esther S. II, 855
Davis, Esther Scott II, 791
Davis, Esther T. II, 791
Davis, Esther, Jr. II, 117
Davis, Ethel S. I, 237
Davis, Ethith V, 47
Davis, Ettie V, 233
Davis, Eugenia VI, 56
Davis, Eugenia VI, 60
Davis, Eugenia VI, 61
Davis, Eunice IV, 382
Davis, Eunice IV, 698
Davis, Eunice IV, 786
Davis, Eunice IV, 947
Davis, Eunice V, 618
Davis, Eunice V, 668
Davis, Eva V, 47
Davis, Eva D. IV, 1092
Davis, Eva Emeline V, 991
Davis, Eva Irene IV, 1129
Davis, Eva L. IV, 1129
Davis, Eva Lurena IV, 1092
Davis, Evaline I, 1004
Davis, Evan II, 501
Davis, Evan II, 791
Davis, Evan II, 803
Davis, Evan II, 853
Davis, Evan II, 855
Davis, Evan II, 901
Davis, Evangeline V, 233
Davis, Eve I, 677
Davis, Eve I, 689
Davis, Eveline I, 985
Davis, Eveline I, 996
Davis, Eveline V, 618
Davis, Evlyn Stoneman I, 985
Davis, Exum I, 304
Davis, Exum I, 698

Davis, Exum O. I, 304
Davis, Exum Outland I, 285
Davis, Ezekial I, 304
Davis, Ezekial I, 314
Davis, Ezekial I, 320
Davis, Ezekiel I, 284
Davis, Ezekiel I, 285
Davis, Ezekiel I, 304
Davis, Ezekiel I, 328
Davis, Ezekiel M. I, 285
Davis, Ezekiel T. I, 285
Davis, Ezra I, 984
Davis, Ezra V, 735
Davis, Ezra V, 780
Davis, F. V, 806
Davis, Fanny V, 233
Davis, Flora IV, 1249
Davis, Floyd V, 991
Davis, Frances III, 406
Davis, Frances III, 426
Davis, Frances IV, 520
Davis, Frances Eleanor II, 703
Davis, Francis I, 611
Davis, Francis III, 96
Davis, Francis IV, 193
Davis, Francis IV, 382
Davis, Francis IV, 383
Davis, Francis IV, 441
Davis, Francis IV, 520
Davis, Francis IV, 550
Davis, Francis Edgar IV, 382
Davis, Francis Edgar IV, 383
Davis, Francis M. I, 269
Davis, Francis M. I, 745
Davis, Francis M. I, 758
Davis, Francis M. I, 759
Davis, Francis S. I, 652
Davis, Francis S. I, 677
Davis, Frank V, 806
Davis, Frank M. I, 237
Davis, Franklin I, 697
Davis, Franklin I, 713
Davis, Franklin I, 714
Davis, Franklin I, 758
Davis, Franklin I, 807
Davis, Franklin V, 991
Davis, Fred V, 991
Davis, Fred L. V, 233
Davis, Frederick VI, 633
Davis, Frederick VI, 649
Davis, Frederick L. V, 233
Davis, Frederick L. V, 328
Davis, G. B. V, 668
Davis, Gabriel II, 26
Davis, Gabriel II, 65
Davis, Gabriel II, 87
Davis, Geo. V, 991
Davis, Geo. B. V, 618
Davis, Geo. B. V, 668
Davis, Geo. W. V, 991
Davis, George I, 974
Davis, George I, 984
Davis, George II, 213
Davis, George II, 352
Davis, George II, 502
Davis, George V, 991
Davis, George B. I, 269
Davis, George B. V, 618
Davis, George M. II, 502
Davis, George R. IV, 1276
Davis, George W. I, 759
Davis, Gideon IV, 326
Davis, Gideon VI, 619
Davis, Gideon VI, 659
Davis, Gideon VI, 737
Davis, Gideon VI, 738
Davis, Gideon VI, 748
Davis, Glen IV, 1205
Davis, Glenn IV, 1205
Davis, Grace Ann III, 96
Davis, Gulielma VI, 470
Davis, Gulielma VI, 486
Davis, H. Cornelia I, 883
Davis, H. E. V, 233
Davis, Haisley I, 876
Davis, Hallowell III, 17
Davis, Hallowell III, 49
Davis, Hallowell III, 96
Davis, Haly I, 713
Davis, Handy T. V, 328
Davis, Handy T. V, 668
Davis, Hannah I, 269
Davis, Hannah I, 344
Davis, Hannah I, 346
Davis, Hannah I, 349
Davis, Hannah I, 362
Davis, Hannah I, 366
Davis, Hannah I, 373
Davis, Hannah I, 384
Davis, Hannah I, 414
Davis, Hannah I, 460
Davis, Hannah I, 466
Davis, Hannah I, 467
Davis, Hannah I, 468
Davis, Hannah I, 471
Davis, Hannah I, 479
Davis, Hannah I, 481
Davis, Hannah I, 485
Davis, Hannah I, 495
Davis, Hannah I, 535
Davis, Hannah I, 626
Davis, Hannah I, 652
Davis, Hannah I, 662
Davis, Hannah I, 667
Davis, Hannah I, 758
Davis, Hannah I, 764
Davis, Hannah I, 770
Davis, Hannah I, 800
Davis, Hannah I, 807
Davis, Hannah I, 961
Davis, Hannah I, 966
Davis, Hannah I, 971
Davis, Hannah I, 974
Davis, Hannah I, 984
Davis, Hannah I, 1008
Davis, Hannah I, 1009
Davis, Hannah I, 1060
Davis, Hannah I, 1062
Davis, Hannah I, 1091
Davis, Hannah I, 1094
Davis, Hannah I Sup 1, 3
Davis, Hannah II, 26
Davis, Hannah II, 65
Davis, Hannah II, 77
Davis, Hannah II, 100
Davis, Hannah II, 112
Davis, Hannah II, 213
Davis, Hannah II, 352
Davis, Hannah II, 501
Davis, Hannah II, 502
Davis, Hannah II, 992
Davis, Hannah II, 1034
Davis, Hannah III, 97
Davis, Hannah IV, 28
Davis, Hannah IV, 50
Davis, Hannah IV, 55
Davis, Hannah IV, 82
Davis, Hannah IV, 143
Davis, Hannah IV, 371
Davis, Hannah IV, 382
Davis, Hannah IV, 415
Davis, Hannah IV, 470
Davis, Hannah IV, 573
Davis, Hannah IV, 620
Davis, Hannah IV, 698
Davis, Hannah IV, 810
Davis, Hannah IV, 892
Davis, Hannah IV, 903
Davis, Hannah IV, 904
Davis, Hannah IV, 913
Davis, Hannah IV, 914
Davis, Hannah V, 46
Davis, Hannah V, 383
Davis, Hannah V, 409
Davis, Hannah V, 485
Davis, Hannah V, 486
Davis, Hannah V, 902
Davis, Hannah V, 927
Davis, Hannah V, 932
Davis, Hannah V, 938
Davis, Hannah VI, 350
Davis, Hannah VI, 351
Davis, Hannah VI, 352
Davis, Hannah VI, 382
Davis, Hannah VI, 485
Davis, Hannah A. V, 486
Davis, Hannah B. I, 269
Davis, Hannah B. V, 43
Davis, Hannah B. V, 47
Davis, Hannah C. II, 791
Davis, Hannah C. II, 856
Davis, Hannah D. I, 655
Davis, Hannah D. IV, 810
Davis, Hannah G. II, 702
Davis, Hannah Galaspie II, 502
Davis, Hannah Gilespey II, 736
Davis, Hannah J. V, 902
Davis, Hannah Kester V, 485
Davis, Hannah L. I, 745
Davis, Hannah L. IV, 947
Davis, Hannah N. III, 96
Davis, Hannah P. II, 502
Davis, Hannah P. II, 855
Davis, Hannah P. II, 856
Davis, Hannah P. II, 918
Davis, Hannah S. II, 117
Davis, Hannah S. II, 124
Davis, Hannah S. II, 128
Davis, Hannah S. II, 145
Davis, Hannah S. IV, 947
Davis, Hannah Smith II, 211
Davis, Hannah Smith II, 213
Davis, Hannah V. II, 856
Davis, Hannah V. II, 921
Davis, Hannah Vashti II, 855
Davis, Hardin VI, 903
Davis, Harley V, 455
Davis, Harmon I, 495
Davis, Harmon I, 1004
Davis, Harmon IV, 143
Davis, Harmon IV, 371
Davis, Harmon IV, 382
Davis, Harmon IV, 415
Davis, Harmon V, 233
Davis, Harmon V, 327
Davis, Harmon V, 335
Davis, Harmon V, 445
Davis, Harmon Kester V, 485
Davis, Harold Bennett V, 668
Davis, Harrian VI, 888
Davis, Harriet E. V, 328
Davis, Harriett E. V, 233
Davis, Harrison F. III, 97
Davis, Harry I, 807
Davis, Harry C. V, 991
Davis, Harry M. III, 96
Davis, Harry W. V, 328
Davis, Harry Wilber V, 233
Davis, Harvey C. I, 237
Davis, Harvey J. I, 237
Davis, Hattie V, 829
Davis, Hattie E. V, 232
Davis, Hattie E. V, 233
Davis, Hattie E. V, 328
Davis, Helen II, 791
Davis, Helene VI, 737
Davis, Henrietta P. H. III, 96
Davis, Henry I, 8
Davis, Henry I, 18
Davis, Henry I, 45
Davis, Henry I, 98
Davis, Henry I, 285
Davis, Henry I, 304
Davis, Henry I, 495
Davis, Henry I, 536
Davis, Henry I, 559
Davis, Henry I, 713
Davis, Henry I, 719
Davis, Henry I, 779
Davis, Henry I, 807
Davis, Henry I, 923
Davis, Henry III, 96
Davis, Henry V, 233
Davis, Henry V, 455
Davis, Henry V, 558
Davis, Henry V, 735
Davis, Henry V, 806
Davis, Henry V, 969
Davis, Henry VI, 306
Davis, Henry VI, 307
Davis, Henry VI, 349
Davis, Henry VI, 350
Davis, Henry VI, 351
Davis, Henry VI, 706
Davis, Henry VI, 902
Davis, Henry VI, 903
Davis, Henry Ann VI, 862
Davis, Henry Ann VI, 903
Davis, Henry C. II, 856
Davis, Henry C. III, 96
Davis, Henry C. III, 202
Davis, Henry C. III, 224
Davis, Henry Clinton IV, 382
Davis, Henry Corbit II, 790
Davis, Henry Corbit II, 791
Davis, Henry Davis I, 269
Davis, Henry Franklin VI, 634
Davis, Henry Franklin VI, 738
Davis, Henry K. B. II, 791
Davis, Henry K. B. II, 856
Davis, Henry L. VI, 807
Davis, Henry L. VI, 888
Davis, Henry L. VI, 903
Davis, Henry M. III, 97
Davis, Henry M. V, 735
Davis, Henry Munson III, 96
Davis, Henry T. V, 545
Davis, Henry T. V, 558
Davis, Henry Wilkins II, 791
Davis, Hephsibah I, 677
Davis, Hepzibah I, 495
Davis, Hepzibah I, 536
Davis, Hepzibeth I, 495
Davis, Hepzibeth I, 535
Davis, Herbert V, 165
Davis, Herbert E. I, 807
Davis, Herbert L. I, 698
Davis, Herbert L. I, 714
Davis, Herbert L. I, 807
Davis, Herephila VI, 737
Davis, Hermon I, 961
Davis, Hermon I, 966
Davis, Herophila IV, 810
Davis, Herophila IV, 811
Davis, Herophila IV, 814
Davis, Hester II, 26
Davis, Hester V, 301
Davis, Hester V, 313
Davis, Hettie C. II, 117
Davis, Hetty C. II, 117
Davis, Hetty C. II, 121
Davis, Hezekiah I, 1004
Davis, Hiram IV, 382
Davis, Hiram V, 558
Davis, Hiram V, 617
Davis, Hiram V, 618
Davis, Hiram V, 644
Davis, Hiram V, 735
Davis, Hiram C. IV, 28
Davis, Hiram E. IV, 326
Davis, Hiram E. IV, 382
Davis, Hiram E. IV, 1155
Davis, Hope I, 1008
Davis, Horace A. III, 49
Davis, Horace A. III, 96
Davis, Horace A. III, 148
Davis, Horace A. III, 256
Davis, Horace Andrew III, 96
Davis, Horace Bancroft III, 275
Davis, Howel VI, 961
Davis, Hugh II, 502
Davis, Huldah I, 45
Davis, Huldah I, 78
Davis, Huldah I, 237
Davis, Huldah I, 280
Davis, Huldah I, 285
Davis, Huldah I, 495
Davis, Huldah I, 536
Davis, Huldah I, 559
Davis, Huldah Elizabeth IV, 698
Davis, Huldah Ellen V, 835
Davis, Icy May V, 233
Davis, Ida V, 233
Davis, Ida V, 991
Davis, Irene I, 940
Davis, Irene Miriam I, 940
Davis, Isaac I, 758
Davis, Isaac I, 974
Davis, Isaac I, 984
Davis, Isaac II, 65
Davis, Isaac II, 111
Davis, Isaac II, 502
Davis, Isaac II, 702
Davis, Isaac II, 736
Davis, Isaac II, 739
Davis, Isaac III, 96
Davis, Isaac III, 97
Davis, Isaac III, 304
Davis, Isaac IV, 143
Davis, Isaac IV, 382
Davis, Isaac IV, 698
Davis, Isaac IV, 904
Davis, Isaac V, 735
Davis, Isaac V, 780
Davis, Isaac V, 806
Davis, Isaac VI, 306
Davis, Isaac VI, 307
Davis, Isaac VI, 351
Davis, Isaac VI, 382
Davis, Isaac VI, 594
Davis, Isaac L. V, 485
Davis, Isaac P. I, 759
Davis, Isaac R. II, 853
Davis, Isaac R. II, 855
Davis, Isaac R. II, 871
Davis, Isaac Roberts II, 502
Davis, Isaac Roberts II, 735
Davis, Isaac Roberts II, 791
Davis, Isaac Roberts II, 855
Davis, Isaac S. V, 485
Davis, Isaachar II, 501
Davis, Isabelle I, 616
Davis, Isachar II, 352
Davis, Isham VI, 903
Davis, Israel V, 327
Davis, Issachar II, 501
Davis, Iva V, 735
Davis, Iva I. V, 735
Davis, J. E. V, 232
Davis, J. Franklin I, 807
Davis, J. Franklin I, 829
Davis, J. H. I, 876
Davis, J. H. I, 923
Davis, J. Harvey V, 455
Davis, J. Henry I, 698
Davis, J. K. IV, 698
Davis, J. O. V, 560
Davis, J. Orland V, 328
Davis, Jacob I, 265
Davis, Jacob I, 269
Davis, Jacob I, 276
Davis, Jacob I, 350
Davis, Jacob I, 807
Davis, Jacob I, 975
Davis, Jacob I, 984
Davis, Jacob I Sup 1, 10
Davis, Jacob II, 26
Davis, Jacob II, 65
Davis, Jacob II, 102
Davis, Jacob II, 117
Davis, Jacob II, 131
Davis, Jacob IV, 28
Davis, Jacob IV, 82
Davis, Jacob V, 233
Davis, Jacob V, 445
Davis, Jacob V, 780
Davis, Jacob V, 791
Davis, Jacob V, 991
Davis, James I, 45
Davis, James I, 92
Davis, James I, 98
Davis, James I, 132
Davis, James I, 137
Davis, James I, 265
Davis, James I, 269
Davis, James I, 652
Davis, James I, 677
Davis, James I, 713
Davis, James I, 714
Davis, James I, 737
Davis, James I, 876
Davis, James II, 26
Davis, James II, 352
Davis, James II, 353
Davis, James II, 463
Davis, James II, 501
Davis, James II, 502
Davis, James II, 636
Davis, James III, 97
Davis, James IV, 810
Davis, James V, 618
Davis, James V, 749
Davis, James V, 813
Davis, James V, 902
Davis, James V, 991
Davis, James VI, 357
Davis, James VI, 382
Davis, James VI, 810
Davis, James VI, 921
Davis, James Arthur V, 902
Davis, James B. I, 335
Davis, James B. V, 991
Davis, James Davis II, 785
Davis, James E. V, 328
Davis, James F. I, 779
Davis, James Franklin I, 807
Davis, James H. I, 614
Davis, James H. I, 677
Davis, James Henry I, 615
Davis, James Henry I, 617
Davis, James Henry I, 618
Davis, James L. VI, 60
Davis, James M. I, 745
Davis, James M. I, 756
Davis, James M. I, 758
Davis, James M. I, 779
Davis, James M. I, 807
Davis, James Madison I, 807
Davis, James Monroe I, 467
Davis, James N. I, 758
Davis, James Orland V, 328
Davis, James P. V, 618
Davis, James S. I, 269
Davis, James S. II, 855
Davis, James S. III, 97
Davis, James S. IV, 520
Davis, Jane I, 45
Davis, Jane I, 75
Davis, Jane I, 536
Davis, Jane I, 677
Davis, Jane I, 685
Davis, Jane I, 758
Davis, Jane I, 759
Davis, Jane I, 807
Davis, Jane I, 925
Davis, Jane I, 1118
Davis, Jane II, 128
Davis, Jane II, 501
Davis, Jane II, 719
Davis, Jane II, 1049
Davis, Jane III, 97
Davis, Jane IV, 28
Davis, Jane IV, 82
Davis, Jane IV, 193
Davis, Jane IV, 382
Davis, Jane IV, 441
Davis, Jane IV, 903
Davis, Jane IV, 904
Davis, Jane IV, 1276
Davis, Jane V, 232
Davis, Jane V, 233
Davis, Jane V, 283
Davis, Jane V, 301
Davis, Jane V, 327
Davis, Jane V, 881

Davis, Jane VI, 810
Davis, Jane VI, 895
Davis, Jane E. I, 18
Davis, Jane Eliza V, 485
Davis, Jane S. IV, 383
Davis, Jane S. IV, 520
Davis, Jay V, 233
Davis, Jay V, 328
Davis, Jeams I, 98
Davis, Jeams I, 137
Davis, Jeams I, 172
Davis, Jehu IV, 382
Davis, Jehu IV, 1092
Davis, Jehu IV, 1101
Davis, Jehu IV, 1129
Davis, Jehu IV, 1133
Davis, Jehu V, 327
Davis, Jehu H. IV, 1129
Davis, Jemima I, 677
Davis, Jemima IV, 143
Davis, Jemima IV, 573
Davis, Jemima IV, 583
Davis, Jeneal S. I, 495
Davis, Jenette E. V, 668
Davis, Jennie III, 133
Davis, Jennie III, 298
Davis, Jennie V, 455
Davis, Jennie Mary V, 806
Davis, Jennie Morris II, 791
Davis, Jennis M. II, 856
Davis, Jesse I, 45
Davis, Jesse I, 137
Davis, Jesse I, 265
Davis, Jesse I, 269
Davis, Jesse I, 335
Davis, Jesse I, 495
Davis, Jesse I, 605
Davis, Jesse I, 652
Davis, Jesse I, 655
Davis, Jesse I, 677
Davis, Jesse I, 687
Davis, Jesse I, 698
Davis, Jesse I, 713
Davis, Jesse I, 741
Davis, Jesse I, 745
Davis, Jesse I, 758
Davis, Jesse I, 805
Davis, Jesse I, 807
Davis, Jesse I, 984
Davis, Jesse I, 1004
Davis, Jesse I, 1008
Davis, Jesse V, 233
Davis, Jesse V, 780
Davis, Jesse VI, 486
Davis, Jesse L. V, 233
Davis, Jesse L. V, 328
Davis, Jesse W. I, 745
Davis, Jesse W. I, 779
Davis, Jno IV, 520
Davis, Joanna II, 785
Davis, Joanna II, 793
Davis, Joanna II, 855
Davis, Joanna II, 861
Davis, Joanna H. II, 855
Davis, Joanna H. II, 912
Davis, Job I, 744
Davis, Job I, 758
Davis, Joel I, 140
Davis, Joel I, 495
Davis, Joel I, 536
Davis, Joel I, 605
Davis, Joel I, 652
Davis, Joel I, 697
Davis, Joel I, 698
Davis, Joel I, 713
Davis, Joel, Jr. I, 698
Davis, Joel, Jr. I, 713
Davis, John I, 98
Davis, John I, 137
Davis, John I, 237
Davis, John I, 285
Davis, John I, 304
Davis, John I, 313
Davis, John I, 319
Davis, John I, 328
Davis, John I, 349
Davis, John I, 350
Davis, John I, 363
Davis, John I, 378
Davis, John I, 384
Davis, John I, 467
Davis, John I, 479
Davis, John I, 495
Davis, John I, 535
Davis, John I, 536
Davis, John I, 677
Davis, John I, 685
Davis, John I, 713
Davis, John I, 807
Davis, John I, 876
Davis, John I, 960
Davis, John I, 961
Davis, John I, 974
Davis, John I, 975
Davis, John I, 984
Davis, John I, 989
Davis, John I, 1004
Davis, John I, 1009
Davis, John I, 1118
Davis, John II, 26
Davis, John II, 65
Davis, John II, 73
Davis, John II, 98
Davis, John II, 352
Davis, John II, 353
Davis, John II, 443
Davis, John II, 469
Davis, John II, 501
Davis, John II, 855
Davis, John II, 992
Davis, John IV, 326
Davis, John IV, 382
Davis, John IV, 810
Davis, John IV, 892
Davis, John IV, 903
Davis, John IV, 1092
Davis, John V, 46
Davis, John V, 233
Davis, John V, 301
Davis, John V, 327
Davis, John V, 485
Davis, John V, 486
Davis, John V, 618
Davis, John V, 730
Davis, John V, 735
Davis, John V, 744
Davis, John V, 794
Davis, John V, 806
Davis, John V, 807
Davis, John V, 835
Davis, John V, 902
Davis, John V, 927
Davis, John V, 932
Davis, John V, 938
Davis, John VI, 171
Davis, John VI, 285
Davis, John VI, 306
Davis, John VI, 307
Davis, John VI, 327
Davis, John VI, 350
Davis, John VI, 351
Davis, John VI, 352
Davis, John VI, 485
Davis, John VI, 795
Davis, John VI, 803
Davis, John VI, 810
Davis, John VI, 817
Davis, John VI, 851
Davis, John A. I, 612
Davis, John A. I, 921
Davis, John Albert V, 618
Davis, John B. I, 807
Davis, John C. III, 96
Davis, John C. III, 97
Davis, John C. III, 305
Davis, John C. VI, 737
Davis, John Calvin V, 485
Davis, John Coate V, 734
Davis, John David VI, 795
Davis, John David Dews VI, 803
Davis, John F. I, 495
Davis, John F. IV, 193
Davis, John F. IV, 382
Davis, John F. IV, 383
Davis, John F. IV, 399
Davis, John F. IV, 441
Davis, John F. IV, 520
Davis, John F. IV, 528
Davis, John H. I, 940
Davis, John H. III, 97
Davis, John H. III, 102
Davis, John H. IV, 947
Davis, John Horton IV, 28
Davis, John Horton IV, 311
Davis, John I. V, 668
Davis, John J. VI, 999
Davis, John M. V, 735
Davis, John Morgan VI, 721
Davis, John Morgan VI, 738
Davis, John R. I, 269
Davis, John R. I, 285
Davis, John R. I, 758
Davis, John R. V, 735
Davis, John Richardson I, 269
Davis, John T. VI, 903
Davis, John T. VI, 970
Davis, John T. VI, 980
Davis, John Thomas I, 467
Davis, John Thos. V, 617
Davis, John Uriah V, 835
Davis, John W. III, 96
Davis, John Wistar II, 703
Davis, John, Jr. I, 304
Davis, John, Jr. I, 384
Davis, John, Jr. I, 984
Davis, John, Jr. V, 301
Davis, John, Jr. V, 902
Davis, John, Sr. I, 984
Davis, Jonas M. I, 269
Davis, Jonathan I, 758
Davis, Jonathan I, 984
Davis, Jonathan II, 353
Davis, Jonathan II, 1049
Davis, Jonathan III, 97
Davis, Jonathan IV, 948
Davis, Jonathan V, 735
Davis, Jonathan V, 806
Davis, Jonathan Pickering VI, 389
Davis, Jordan V, 233
Davis, Jordan V, 241
Davis, Jordan V, 243
Davis, Jordan V, 262
Davis, Jordan V, 284
Davis, Jorden V, 327
Davis, Jorden R. I, 985
Davis, Jordon V, 327
Davis, Jose I, 807
Davis, Jose I, 1004
Davis, Josee V, 233
Davis, Joseph I, 265
Davis, Joseph I, 269
Davis, Joseph I, 349
Davis, Joseph I, 350
Davis, Joseph I, 362
Davis, Joseph I, 384
Davis, Joseph I, 495
Davis, Joseph I, 536
Davis, Joseph I, 559
Davis, Joseph I, 652
Davis, Joseph I, 807
Davis, Joseph I, 971
Davis, Joseph I, 974
Davis, Joseph I, 975
Davis, Joseph I, 984
Davis, Joseph II, 65
Davis, Joseph II, 353
Davis, Joseph II, 501
Davis, Joseph II, 502
Davis, Joseph II, 791
Davis, Joseph III, 97
Davis, Joseph IV, 143
Davis, Joseph IV, 365
Davis, Joseph IV, 382
Davis, Joseph IV, 573
Davis, Joseph IV, 697
Davis, Joseph IV, 698
Davis, Joseph V, 233
Davis, Joseph V, 328
Davis, Joseph V, 455
Davis, Joseph V, 485
Davis, Joseph V, 618
Davis, Joseph V, 780
Davis, Joseph VI, 382
Davis, Joseph VI, 486
Davis, Joseph C. V, 455
Davis, Joseph E. V, 485
Davis, Joseph E. V, 496
Davis, Joseph H. V, 233
Davis, Joseph L. V, 485
Davis, Joseph L. V, 496
Davis, Joseph M. V, 735
Davis, Joseph P. II, 502
Davis, Joseph P. II, 736
Davis, Joseph Parry II, 502
Davis, Joseph T. V, 327
Davis, Joseph Townsend II, 791
Davis, Joseph W. I, 269
Davis, Joseph W. I, 758
Davis, Joseph Wesley V, 618
Davis, Joseph Wicker I, 269
Davis, Joseph, Jr. I, 269
Davis, Joseph, Jr. I, 984
Davis, Joseph, Sr. I, 984
Davis, Joshua I, 45
Davis, Joshua I, 78
Davis, Joshua I, 236
Davis, Joshua I, 237
Davis, Joshua I, 285
Davis, Joshua I, 304
Davis, Joshua I, 312
Davis, Joshua I, 698
Davis, Joshua I, 713
Davis, Joshua I, 974
Davis, Joshua I, 1004
Davis, Joshua IV, 28
Davis, Joshua IV, 82
Davis, Joshua IV, 83
Davis, Joshua IV, 382
Davis, Joshua IV, 619
Davis, Joshua IV, 620
Davis, Joshua IV, 697
Davis, Joshua IV, 698
Davis, Joshua IV, 740
Davis, Joshua IV, 867
Davis, Joshua V, 327
Davis, Joshua V, 383
Davis, Joshua V, 617
Davis, Joshua F. V, 327
Davis, Joshua F. V, 382
Davis, Joshua F. V, 383
Davis, Joshua N. I, 714
Davis, Joshua, Jr. IV, 28
Davis, Joshua, Jr. IV, 82
Davis, Josiah I, 466
Davis, Josiah I, 479
Davis, Josiah II, 26
Davis, Josiah II, 855
Davis, Josiah II, 908
Davis, Josiah IV, 382
Davis, Josiah IV, 383
Davis, Josiah IV, 520
Davis, Josiah VI, 106
Davis, Josiah R. I, 304
Davis, Josias IV, 82
Davis, Jourdon I, 1004
Davis, Judah VI, 903
Davis, Judith I, 536
Davis, Judith I, 559
Davis, Judith II, 502
Davis, Julia I, 605
Davis, Julia I, 698
Davis, Julia Alice II, 791
Davis, Julia E. III, 97
Davis, Julia R. I, 807
Davis, Julia R. I, 843
Davis, Julius L. I, 759
Davis, Julius R. I, 923
Davis, Julius Robert I, 924
Davis, July I, 495
Davis, Kathleen V, 328
Davis, Kelly I, 807
Davis, Kelly W. I, 758
Davis, Kelly W. I, 759
Davis, Kelly W. I, 807
Davis, Kenderdine II, 352
Davis, Kennie IV, 948
Davis, Kesiah I, 445
Davis, Kezia I, 807
Davis, Kezia I, 818
Davis, Kezia I, 1004
Davis, Kezia I, 1008
Davis, Kezia I, 1011
Davis, Keziah I, 434
Davis, Keziah I, 445
Davis, Keziah I, 470
Davis, Keziah I, 536
Davis, Keziah IV, 326
Davis, Keziah IV, 353
Davis, Keziah V, 734
Davis, Kittie V, 835
Davis, L. A. VI, 933
Davis, L. Ray I, 923
Davis, Laura I, 807
Davis, Laura Ann V, 835
Davis, Laura Ann V, 867
Davis, Laura B. V, 328
Davis, Lavena V, 618
Davis, Lawrence Alexander I, 615
Davis, Leander I, 714
Davis, Leetitia II, 502
Davis, Lella VI, 803
Davis, Leon I, 335
Davis, Leroy V, 618
Davis, Leroy S. V, 47
Davis, Leroy S. V, 558
Davis, Leta V, 253
Davis, Leta E. V, 233
Davis, Letitia II, 65
Davis, Letitia II, 104
Davis, Letitia II, 501
Davis, Letitia II, 502
Davis, Letitia II, 627
Davis, Letta V, 328
Davis, Letta E. V, 233
Davis, Lettie Ray I, 924
Davis, Leuisa I, 1004
Davis, Leuzena I, 1004
Davis, Levi V, 233
Davis, Levi VI, 737
Davis, Lewella V, 383
Davis, Lewis V, 618
Davis, Lewis VI, 903
Davis, Lewis E. V, 328
Davis, Lewis M. IV, 1276
Davis, Lewis W. V, 618
Davis, Libbie V, 991
Davis, Liddea I, 98
Davis, Liddia I, 137
Davis, Liddia I, 140
Davis, Lidia V, 485
Davis, Lidia V, 515
Davis, Lieuella V, 327
Davis, Lillian III, 96
Davis, Lillian III, 219
Davis, Lillian IV, 698
Davis, Lillian IV, 811
Davis, Lillian IV, 948
Davis, Lillian VI, 633
Davis, Lindley IV, 382
Davis, Lindley IV, 383
Davis, Lindley IV, 520
Davis, Lindley V, 734
Davis, Lindley V, 735
Davis, Lindley H. I, 467
Davis, Littleton VI, 60
Davis, Lizzie VI, 60
Davis, Lizzie C. I, 698
Davis, Lizzie C. I, 714
Davis, Lizzie C. I, 807
Davis, Lorena V, 343
Davis, Lorena H. V, 328
Davis, Lorena Hinman V, 327
Davis, Lorenzo V, 328
Davis, Louella V, 668
Davis, Louella H. V, 486
Davis, Louella H. V, 668
Davis, Louie Palmer V, 618
Davis, Louisa IV, 845
Davis, Louisa IV, 947
Davis, Louisa VI, 306
Davis, Louisa VI, 307
Davis, Louisa VI, 350
Davis, Louisa VI, 351
Davis, Louise III, 97
Davis, Louise III, 298
Davis, Louiza IV, 697
Davis, Louiza IV, 698
Davis, Louzena I, 985
Davis, Louzena I, 988
Davis, Love I, 495
Davis, Love I, 536
Davis, Love V, 301
Davis, Lucinda I, 758
Davis, Lucinda IV, 697
Davis, Lucinda IV, 698
Davis, Lucinda IV, 1128
Davis, Lucinda IV, 1129
Davis, Lucinda VI, 810
Davis, Lucinda M. IV, 1092
Davis, Lucinda M. IV, 1129
Davis, Lucretia M. V, 859
Davis, Lucy II, 502
Davis, Lucy II, 791
Davis, Lucy II, 856
Davis, Lucy III, 96
Davis, Lucy III, 97
Davis, Lucy V, 896
Davis, Lucy VI, 865
Davis, Lucy VI, 903
Davis, Lucy A. V, 991
Davis, Luella V, 327
Davis, Luella V, 383
Davis, Luella H. V, 485
Davis, Luella Toms V, 735
Davis, Lulu V, 991
Davis, Lusena C. I, 495
Davis, Luvena V, 383
Davis, Luvenia V, 383
Davis, Lydda I, 98
Davis, Lydda I, 961
Davis, Lyddia I, 137
Davis, Lyddia I, 149
Davis, Lyddia I, 167
Davis, Lydia I, 103
Davis, Lydia I, 149
Davis, Lydia I, 459
Davis, Lydia I, 467
Davis, Lydia I, 473
Davis, Lydia I, 479
Davis, Lydia I, 495
Davis, Lydia I, 528
Davis, Lydia I, 535
Davis, Lydia I, 536
Davis, Lydia I, 559
Davis, Lydia I, 565
Davis, Lydia I, 807
Davis, Lydia I, 876
Davis, Lydia I, 960
Davis, Lydia I, 1004
Davis, Lydia I, 1008
Davis, Lydia I, 1009
Davis, Lydia I, 1013
Davis, Lydia I, 1047
Davis, Lydia I, 1048
Davis, Lydia II, 352
Davis, Lydia II, 501
Davis, Lydia II, 502
Davis, Lydia II, 626
Davis, Lydia II, 657
Davis, Lydia II, 678
Davis, Lydia II, 1049
Davis, Lydia IV, 382
Davis, Lydia IV, 619

Davis, Lydia IV, 620
Davis, Lydia IV, 635
Davis, Lydia IV, 698
Davis, Lydia IV, 724
Davis, Lydia IV, 810
Davis, Lydia IV, 903
Davis, Lydia IV, 914
Davis, Lydia IV, 947
Davis, Lydia V, 39
Davis, Lydia V, 46
Davis, Lydia V, 47
Davis, Lydia V, 133
Davis, Lydia V, 233
Davis, Lydia V, 243
Davis, Lydia V, 327
Davis, Lydia V, 361
Davis, Lydia V, 486
Davis, Lydia V, 730
Davis, Lydia V, 734
Davis, Lydia V, 735
Davis, Lydia V, 744
Davis, Lydia V, 745
Davis, Lydia V, 806
Davis, Lydia V, 835
Davis, Lydia VI, 106
Davis, Lydia VI, 382
Davis, Lydia A. V, 47
Davis, Lydia Alice V, 46
Davis, Lydia Alice V, 47
Davis, Lydia C. II, 853
Davis, Lydia C. II, 855
Davis, Lydia C. II, 871
Davis, Lydia Cowgill II, 791
Davis, Lydia D. I, 984
Davis, Lydia Ellen V, 233
Davis, Lydia M. V, 485
Davis, Lydia Margaret V, 327
Davis, Lydia May II, 309
Davis, Lydia, Jr. I, 137
Davis, Lydia, Jr. I, 149
Davis, Mae V, 233
Davis, Mahala C. V, 806
Davis, Mahitabel I, 303
Davis, Mahitabel I, 304
Davis, Mahlon I, 984
Davis, Mahlon V, 327
Davis, Malinda I, 985
Davis, Malon Cox I, 479
Davis, Mar V, 243
Davis, Marcy II, 26
Davis, Margaret I, 45
Davis, Margaret I, 98
Davis, Margaret I, 137
Davis, Margaret I, 139
Davis, Margaret I, 269
Davis, Margaret I, 304
Davis, Margaret I, 619
Davis, Margaret I, 713
Davis, Margaret I, 714
Davis, Margaret I, 720
Davis, Margaret I, 779
Davis, Margaret I, 796
Davis, Margaret I, 807
Davis, Margaret I, 984
Davis, Margaret II, 213
Davis, Margaret II, 501
Davis, Margaret II, 502
Davis, Margaret II, 613
Davis, Margaret III, 30
Davis, Margaret III, 97
Davis, Margaret IV, 193
Davis, Margaret IV, 326
Davis, Margaret V, 328
Davis, Margaret V, 485
Davis, Margaret V, 668
Davis, Margaret V, 734
Davis, Margaret V, 735
Davis, Margaret VI, 382
Davis, Margaret VI, 524
Davis, Margaret VI, 903
Davis, Margaret E. VI, 924
Davis, Margaret Stevens II, 703
Davis, Margaret Stoop V, 668
Davis, Margaret, Sr. I, 1004
Davis, Margarett VI, 486
Davis, Margery I, 349
Davis, Margret I, 807
Davis, Margrett II, 352
Davis, Maria I, 805
Davis, Maria I, 807
Davis, Maria II, 790
Davis, Maria II, 855
Davis, Maria II, 901
Davis, Maria III, 96
Davis, Maria L. IV, 697
Davis, Maria M. II, 855
Davis, Maria M. II, 856
Davis, Maria M. II, 871
Davis, Mariah I, 714
Davis, Mariah V, 558
Davis, Mariam I, 479
Davis, Marian III, 275
Davis, Marion I, 876
Davis, Mark I, 974
Davis, Mark I, 975
Davis, Mark I, 984
Davis, Mark V, 46
Davis, Mark V, 47
Davis, Mark V, 780
Davis, Martha I, 269
Davis, Martha I, 612
Davis, Martha I, 618
Davis, Martha I, 628
Davis, Martha I, 632
Davis, Martha I, 634
Davis, Martha I, 714
Davis, Martha I, 807
Davis, Martha I, 876
Davis, Martha I, 887
Davis, Martha I, 904
Davis, Martha I, 934
Davis, Martha I, 1008
Davis, Martha I, 1011
Davis, Martha II, 65
Davis, Martha II, 117
Davis, Martha II, 120
Davis, Martha II, 132
Davis, Martha II, 352
Davis, Martha II, 353
Davis, Martha II, 501
Davis, Martha II, 502
Davis, Martha II, 667
Davis, Martha II, 791
Davis, Martha II, 824
Davis, Martha II, 856
Davis, Martha III, 96
Davis, Martha III, 224
Davis, Martha IV, 383
Davis, Martha IV, 439
Davis, Martha IV, 697
Davis, Martha IV, 698
Davis, Martha IV, 892
Davis, Martha IV, 947
Davis, Martha IV, 1092
Davis, Martha IV, 1104
Davis, Martha V, 46
Davis, Martha V, 118
Davis, Martha V, 233
Davis, Martha V, 327
Davis, Martha V, 335
Davis, Martha V, 361
Davis, Martha V, 618
Davis, Martha VI, 171
Davis, Martha VI, 240
Davis, Martha VI, 306
Davis, Martha VI, 486
Davis, Martha VI, 706
Davis, Martha VI, 730
Davis, Martha VI, 737
Davis, Martha VI, 767
Davis, Martha VI, 788
Davis, Martha VI, 903
Davis, Martha A. I, 779
Davis, Martha A. V, 835
Davis, Martha A. V, 856
Davis, Martha Almira I, 807
Davis, Martha Ann I, 759
Davis, Martha Ann V, 327
Davis, Martha Ann VI, 738
Davis, Martha C. I, 677
Davis, Martha C. I, 689
Davis, Martha C. I, 745
Davis, Martha C. I, 759
Davis, Martha C. I, 769
Davis, Martha Davis II, 791
Davis, Martha Delilah I, 615
Davis, Martha Delilah I, 632
Davis, Martha E. I, 612
Davis, Martha Elizabeth I, 921
Davis, Martha Esther V, 233
Davis, Martha I. I, 745
Davis, Martha M. I, 714
Davis, Martha M. I, 876
Davis, Martha M. II, 856
Davis, Marthy I, 304
Davis, Marthy I, 319
Davis, Martin I, 1004
Davis, Martin V, 233
Davis, Martin V, 327
Davis, Mary I, 45
Davis, Mary I, 50
Davis, Mary I, 98
Davis, Mary I, 137
Davis, Mary I, 158
Davis, Mary I, 265
Davis, Mary I, 269
Davis, Mary I, 275
Davis, Mary I, 276
Davis, Mary I, 285
Davis, Mary I, 304
Davis, Mary I, 311
Davis, Mary I, 315
Davis, Mary I, 319
Davis, Mary I, 349
Davis, Mary I, 350
Davis, Mary I, 363
Davis, Mary I, 378
Davis, Mary I, 384
Davis, Mary I, 396
Davis, Mary I, 409
Davis, Mary I, 418
Davis, Mary I, 445
Davis, Mary I, 452
Davis, Mary I, 457
Davis, Mary I, 467
Davis, Mary I, 468
Davis, Mary I, 470
Davis, Mary I, 495
Davis, Mary I, 535
Davis, Mary I, 536
Davis, Mary I, 557
Davis, Mary I, 582
Davis, Mary I, 612
Davis, Mary I, 614
Davis, Mary I, 652
Davis, Mary I, 713
Davis, Mary I, 723
Davis, Mary I, 741
Davis, Mary I, 757
Davis, Mary I, 758
Davis, Mary I, 807
Davis, Mary I, 921
Davis, Mary I, 974
Davis, Mary I, 975
Davis, Mary I, 984
Davis, Mary I, 989
Davis, Mary I, 996
Davis, Mary I, 1004
Davis, Mary I, 1008
Davis, Mary I, 1047
Davis, Mary I, 1091
Davis, Mary I, 1118
Davis, Mary I, 1126
Davis, Mary II, 26
Davis, Mary II, 65
Davis, Mary II, 102
Davis, Mary II, 111
Davis, Mary II, 131
Davis, Mary II, 132
Davis, Mary II, 138
Davis, Mary II, 352
Davis, Mary II, 353
Davis, Mary II, 464
Davis, Mary II, 501
Davis, Mary II, 502
Davis, Mary II, 544
Davis, Mary II, 582
Davis, Mary II, 655
Davis, Mary II, 703
Davis, Mary II, 736
Davis, Mary II, 824
Davis, Mary II, 958
Davis, Mary II, 992
Davis, Mary II, 1015
Davis, Mary II, 1025
Davis, Mary II, 1035
Davis, Mary IV, 28
Davis, Mary IV, 83
Davis, Mary IV, 193
Davis, Mary IV, 326
Davis, Mary IV, 382
Davis, Mary IV, 383
Davis, Mary IV, 441
Davis, Mary IV, 520
Davis, Mary IV, 550
Davis, Mary IV, 573
Davis, Mary IV, 597
Davis, Mary IV, 619
Davis, Mary IV, 697
Davis, Mary IV, 698
Davis, Mary IV, 718
Davis, Mary IV, 758
Davis, Mary IV, 778
Davis, Mary IV, 785
Davis, Mary IV, 810
Davis, Mary IV, 826
Davis, Mary IV, 840
Davis, Mary IV, 858
Davis, Mary IV, 892
Davis, Mary IV, 903
Davis, Mary IV, 904
Davis, Mary IV, 914
Davis, Mary IV, 947
Davis, Mary IV, 1155
Davis, Mary IV, 1176
Davis, Mary V, 46
Davis, Mary V, 140
Davis, Mary V, 162
Davis, Mary V, 165
Davis, Mary V, 214
Davis, Mary V, 232
Davis, Mary V, 233
Davis, Mary V, 327
Davis, Mary V, 328
Davis, Mary V, 335
Davis, Mary V, 383
Davis, Mary V, 394
Davis, Mary V, 445
Davis, Mary V, 455
Davis, Mary V, 485
Davis, Mary V, 507
Davis, Mary V, 519
Davis, Mary V, 558
Davis, Mary V, 560
Davis, Mary V, 618
Davis, Mary V, 734
Davis, Mary V, 735
Davis, Mary V, 744
Davis, Mary V, 745
Davis, Mary V, 780
Davis, Mary V, 781
Davis, Mary V, 794
Davis, Mary V, 806
Davis, Mary VI, 171
Davis, Mary VI, 187
Davis, Mary VI, 240
Davis, Mary VI, 306
Davis, Mary VI, 313
Davis, Mary VI, 350
Davis, Mary VI, 351
Davis, Mary VI, 382
Davis, Mary VI, 456
Davis, Mary VI, 485
Davis, Mary VI, 486
Davis, Mary VI, 903
Davis, Mary A. I, 759
Davis, Mary A. I, 761
Davis, Mary A. III, 97
Davis, Mary A. V, 232
Davis, Mary A. V, 284
Davis, Mary A. V, 735
Davis, Mary A. V, 859
Davis, Mary A. VI, 307
Davis, Mary A. VI, 339
Davis, Mary A. VI, 903
Davis, Mary A. E. V, 232
Davis, Mary Ann I, 745
Davis, Mary Ann II, 828
Davis, Mary Ann II, 855
Davis, Mary Ann II, 941
Davis, Mary Ann IV, 810
Davis, Mary Ann IV, 903
Davis, Mary Ann IV, 917
Davis, Mary Ann V, 46
Davis, Mary Ann V, 47
Davis, Mary Ann V, 233
Davis, Mary Ann V, 549
Davis, Mary Ann V, 558
Davis, Mary Ann V, 617
Davis, Mary Ann V, 618
Davis, Mary Ann V, 644
Davis, Mary Ann VI, 308
Davis, Mary Ann VI, 339
Davis, Mary Ann VI, 999
Davis, Mary Annie VI, 737
Davis, Mary Annie VI, 746
Davis, Mary Annie VI, 781
Davis, Mary Annie VI, 782
Davis, Mary B. IV, 697
Davis, Mary B. IV, 698
Davis, Mary B. IV, 810
Davis, Mary B. IV, 826
Davis, Mary B. IV, 1205
Davis, Mary Bunting III, 90
Davis, Mary Bunting III, 275
Davis, Mary C. II, 138
Davis, Mary C. E. VI, 893
Davis, Mary Catharine Jones II, 703
Davis, Mary Catherine II, 703
Davis, Mary E. I, 745
Davis, Mary E. I, 779
Davis, Mary E. I, 807
Davis, Mary E. I, 829
Davis, Mary E. II, 117
Davis, Mary E. II, 791
Davis, Mary E. III, 96
Davis, Mary E. III, 97
Davis, Mary E. III, 102
Davis, Mary E. IV, 1129
Davis, Mary E. V, 455
Davis, Mary Elizabeth I, 758
Davis, Mary Elizabeth IV, 1092
Davis, Mary Elizabeth V, 668
Davis, Mary Elizabeth V, 902
Davis, Mary G. VI, 810
Davis, Mary H. II, 856
Davis, Mary H. II, 890
Davis, Mary H. V, 328
Davis, Mary H. V, 969
Davis, Mary H. V, 976
Davis, Mary J. I, 677
Davis, Mary J. I, 681
Davis, Mary J. I, 745
Davis, Mary J. IV, 193
Davis, Mary J. VI, 903
Davis, Mary Jane I, 269
Davis, Mary Jane I, 479
Davis, Mary Jane I, 615
Davis, Mary Jane I, 617
Davis, Mary Jane I, 618
Davis, Mary Jane I, 758
Davis, Mary Jane I, 759
Davis, Mary Jane V, 327
Davis, Mary Jane V, 991
Davis, Mary Jordan V, 902
Davis, Mary Jordan VI, 351
Davis, Mary Jordan Samuel V, 4
Davis, Mary Jordon V, 938
Davis, Mary Jurdan VI, 307
Davis, Mary L. V, 233
Davis, Mary L. V, 328
Davis, Mary M. IV, 697
Davis, Mary Martitia I, 467
Davis, Mary S. IV, 520
Davis, Mary W. II, 502
Davis, Mary W. II, 703
Davis, Mary W. II, 736
Davis, Mary W. II, 739
Davis, Mary, II, 561
Davis, Mary, Jr. VI, 307
Davis, Mathias III, 406
Davis, Mathias III, 426
Davis, Matilda I, 714
Davis, Matilda I, 985
Davis, Matilda I, 1000
Davis, Matilda Ann IV, 383
Davis, Matilda Ann IV, 432
Davis, Mattie L. V, 233
Davis, Maurice Evans III, 95
Davis, Maurice Evans III, 97
Davis, May V, 991
Davis, Mehitabel I, 284
Davis, Mehitabel I, 495
Davis, Mehitable I, 285
Davis, Mehitable I, 533
Davis, Mehitable I, 536
Davis, Melvina IV, 382
Davis, Mercy II, 65
Davis, Mercy II, 80
Davis, Mercy II, 93
Davis, Merium I, 466
Davis, Merium I, 467
Davis, Merlin V, 328
Davis, Micajah I, 698
Davis, Micajah I, 713
Davis, Micajah I, 714
Davis, Micajah I, 1091
Davis, Micajah VI, 171
Davis, Micajah VI, 187
Davis, Micajah VI, 240
Davis, Micajah VI, 301
Davis, Micajah VI, 306
Davis, Micajah VI, 307
Davis, Micajah VI, 340
Davis, Micajah VI, 351
Davis, Micajah VI, 843
Davis, Micajah VI, 935
Davis, Micajah VI, 944
Davis, Micajah VI, 1010
Davis, Micajah, Jr. VI, 903
Davis, Michael IV, 573
Davis, Michal I, 285
Davis, Michal I, 304
Davis, Michal I, 319
Davis, Michale IV, 382
Davis, Michel IV, 365
Davis, Michel IV, 382
Davis, Mildred E. V, 668
Davis, Mildred H. VI, 903
Davis, Miles IV, 28
Davis, Miles IV, 82
Davis, Miles IV, 326
Davis, Miles IV, 382
Davis, Miles V, 780
Davis, Miller I, 652
Davis, Miller I, 713
Davis, Miller I, 721
Davis, Miller I, 741
Davis, Miller I, 758
Davis, Milly I, 677
Davis, Milly I, 682
Davis, Milton I, 714
Davis, Milton C. II, 703
Davis, Milton Cornwell II, 736
Davis, Mina IV, 1205
Davis, Minerva V, 327
Davis, Minerva V, 460
Davis, Minerva V, 474
Davis, Minerva V, 485
Davis, Minnie Luella V, 806
Davis, Miraum I, 745
Davis, Miriam I, 34
Davis, Miriam I, 45
Davis, Miriam I, 47

Davis, Miriam I, 137
Davis, Miriam I, 164
Davis, Miriam I, 285
Davis, Miriam I, 328
Davis, Miriam I, 479
Davis, Miriam I, 495
Davis, Miriam I, 530
Davis, Miriam I, 535
Davis, Miriam I, 605
Davis, Mirium I, 467
Davis, Mordacai I, 479
Davis, Mordecai I, 466
Davis, Mordecai I, 479
Davis, Morgan VI, 737
Davis, Morning VI, 810
Davis, Morris I, 349
Davis, Morris I, 495
Davis, Morris I, 961
Davis, Morris I, 1004
Davis, Morris II, 791
Davis, Morris II, 855
Davis, Morris II, 856
Davis, Morris II, 918
Davis, Morris V, 383
Davis, Morris, Jr. I, 1004
Davis, Morris, Sr. I, 985
Davis, Morriss II, 1049
Davis, Moses I, 495
Davis, Moses I, 807
Davis, Moses I, 845
Davis, Moses I, 956
Davis, Moses I, 961
Davis, Moses I, 1008
Davis, Moses IV, 143
Davis, Moses IV, 365
Davis, Moses IV, 408
Davis, Moses IV, 573
Davis, Moses IV, 583
Davis, Mrs. Mary V, 735
Davis, Mrs. Rebecca Hildebrand V, 991
Davis, Murray Willis V, 806
Davis, Nancey I, 698
Davis, Nancy I, 445
Davis, Nancy I, 466
Davis, Nancy I, 467
Davis, Nancy I, 495
Davis, Nancy I, 605
Davis, Nancy I, 698
Davis, Nancy I, 713
Davis, Nancy I, 720
Davis, Nancy I, 745
Davis, Nancy I, 757
Davis, Nancy I, 759
Davis, Nancy I, 985
Davis, Nancy I, 1004
Davis, Nancy V, 233
Davis, Nancy V, 455
Davis, Nancy V, 734
Davis, Nancy V, 781
Davis, Nancy VI, 171
Davis, Nancy VI, 306
Davis, Nancy VI, 307
Davis, Nancy VI, 308
Davis, Nancy VI, 351
Davis, Nancy VI, 619
Davis, Nancy VI, 659
Davis, Nancy VI, 737
Davis, Nancy VI, 738
Davis, Nancy VI, 748
Davis, Nancy VI, 795
Davis, Nancy VI, 810
Davis, Nancy VI, 851
Davis, Nancy B. III, 406
Davis, Nancy B. III, 426
Davis, Nancy G. VI, 810
Davis, Nancy Jane I, 758
Davis, Nancy Jane I, 759
Davis, Nancy S. I, 269
Davis, Nancy V. I, 745
Davis, Naomi II, 791
Davis, Naomi III, 96
Davis, Naomi III, 202
Davis, Naomi L. III, 202
Davis, Nathan I, 98
Davis, Nathan I, 137
Davis, Nathan I, 304
Davis, Nathan I, 698
Davis, Nathan I, 713
Davis, Nathan I, 745
Davis, Nathan I, 757
Davis, Nathan I, 758
Davis, Nathan I, 759
Davis, Nathan I, 769
Davis, Nathan I, 807
Davis, Nathan I, 961
Davis, Nathan I, 974
Davis, Nathan I, 984
Davis, Nathan II, 65
Davis, Nathan II, 111
Davis, Nathan II, 703
Davis, Nathan V, 39
Davis, Nathan V, 46
Davis, Nathan V, 969
Davis, Nathan V, 976
Davis, Nathan David I, 714
Davis, Nathan E. I, 759
Davis, Nathan H. I, 495
Davis, Nathan H. V, 859
Davis, Nathaniel VI, 903
Davis, Nehemiah IV, 326
Davis, Nell Herring I, 335
Davis, Nellie M. I, 807
Davis, Nelly V, 806
Davis, Nelson H. IV, 810
Davis, Neziah I, 984
Davis, Neziah I, 1004
Davis, Ola V, 558
Davis, Ola Chamberlain V, 558
Davis, Olive IV, 740
Davis, Olive V, 991
Davis, Olive Ellen V, 46
Davis, Olive Ellen V, 47
Davis, Oliver VI, 634
Davis, Oliver VI, 738
Davis, Olivia E. V, 47
Davis, Omal V, 668
Davis, Onal V, 668
Davis, Ora E. V, 383
Davis, Orland V, 668
Davis, Orpha I, 304
Davis, Orra E. V, 383
Davis, Patia A. I, 807
Davis, Patia Ann I, 758
Davis, Patience I, 652
Davis, Patience I, 677
Davis, Pattie VI, 60
Davis, Paul Estel V, 232
Davis, Pauline III, 17
Davis, Paune III, 96
Davis, Penelope I, 923
Davis, Penelope II, 443
Davis, Penington V, 485
Davis, Penninah I, 697
Davis, Penninah I, 698
Davis, Penninah I, 713
Davis, Pennington V, 485
Davis, Perkins II, 309
Davis, Peter I, 495
Davis, Peter I, 533
Davis, Peter I, 536
Davis, Peter I, 713
Davis, Peter I, 876
Davis, Peter III, 97
Davis, Peter V, 233
Davis, Peter V, 445
Davis, Phariba IV, 573
Davis, Phebe I, 495
Davis, Phebe I, 876
Davis, Phebe II, 26
Davis, Phebe III, 481
Davis, Phebe IV, 28
Davis, Phebe IV, 83
Davis, Phebe IV, 193
Davis, Phebe IV, 620
Davis, Phebe IV, 810
Davis, Phebe IV, 854
Davis, Phebe IV, 855
Davis, Phebe V, 241
Davis, Phebe V, 243
Davis, Phebe V, 262
Davis, Phebe V, 284
Davis, Phebe V, 460
Davis, Phebe V, 485
Davis, Phebe V, 496
Davis, Phebe V, 735
Davis, Phebe VI, 485
Davis, Phebe Belinda I, 876
Davis, Phebe D. III, 499
Davis, Phebe E. IV, 1129
Davis, Phebe Elizabeth V, 233
Davis, Phebe Emma IV, 1092
Davis, Phebe H. V, 485
Davis, Phebe J. I, 940
Davis, Phebe Jane I, 924
Davis, Phebe S. II, 855
Davis, Phebe Shotwell II, 791
Davis, Pinninah I, 713
Davis, Pinninah I, 727
Davis, Plato M. I, 237
Davis, Pleasant V, 780
Davis, Pleasant V, 781
Davis, Polly VI, 306
Davis, Polly VI, 307
Davis, Polly VI, 335
Davis, Polly VI, 351
Davis, Polly VI, 810
Davis, Polly VI, 939
Davis, Polly C. VI, 903
Davis, Polly Henry VI, 903
Davis, Priscilla I, 495
Davis, Priscilla I, 536
Davis, Priscilla I, 542
Davis, Priscilla II, 855
Davis, Priscilla II, 860
Davis, Priscilla IV, 1053
Davis, Priscilla V, 991
Davis, Rachel I, 304
Davis, Rachel I, 313
Davis, Rachel I, 349
Davis, Rachel I, 384
Davis, Rachel I, 415
Davis, Rachel I, 457
Davis, Rachel I, 471
Davis, Rachel I, 479
Davis, Rachel I, 484
Davis, Rachel I, 677
Davis, Rachel I, 687
Davis, Rachel I, 713
Davis, Rachel I, 721
Davis, Rachel I, 745
Davis, Rachel I, 757
Davis, Rachel I, 758
Davis, Rachel I, 759
Davis, Rachel I, 876
Davis, Rachel I, 878
Davis, Rachel I, 894
Davis, Rachel I, 959
Davis, Rachel I, 961
Davis, Rachel I, 975
Davis, Rachel I, 981
Davis, Rachel I, 984
Davis, Rachel I, 1004
Davis, Rachel II, 26
Davis, Rachel II, 65
Davis, Rachel II, 66
Davis, Rachel II, 352
Davis, Rachel II, 353
Davis, Rachel II, 501
Davis, Rachel II, 502
Davis, Rachel II, 508
Davis, Rachel II, 636
Davis, Rachel II, 791
Davis, Rachel IV, 28
Davis, Rachel IV, 82
Davis, Rachel IV, 83
Davis, Rachel IV, 143
Davis, Rachel IV, 311
Davis, Rachel IV, 371
Davis, Rachel IV, 382
Davis, Rachel IV, 619
Davis, Rachel IV, 697
Davis, Rachel IV, 698
Davis, Rachel IV, 740
Davis, Rachel IV, 778
Davis, Rachel IV, 810
Davis, Rachel IV, 827
Davis, Rachel IV, 892
Davis, Rachel IV, 903
Davis, Rachel IV, 913
Davis, Rachel V, 46
Davis, Rachel V, 485
Davis, Rachel V, 723
Davis, Rachel V, 734
Davis, Rachel V, 735
Davis, Rachel V, 753
Davis, Rachel V, 806
Davis, Rachel V, 835
Davis, Rachel V, 851
Davis, Rachel VI, 382
Davis, Rachel VI, 390
Davis, Rachel VI, 903
Davis, Rachel A. I, 759
Davis, Rachel Almeda V, 233
Davis, Rachel Almedia V, 618
Davis, Rachel Almina I, 876
Davis, Rachel E. I, 745
Davis, Rachel Horton IV, 326
Davis, Rachel L. I, 745
Davis, Rachel Minerva V, 24
Davis, Rachel Minerva V, 46
Davis, Rachel Minerva V, 47
Davis, Rachel R. I, 745
Davis, Ralph Waldo V, 232
Davis, Ratchel I, 984
Davis, Ray I, 940
Davis, Rayborn H. V, 735
Davis, Raymond I, 335
Davis, Rebeca IV, 1054
Davis, Rebecah V, 301
Davis, Rebecca I, 479
Davis, Rebecca I, 495
Davis, Rebecca I, 536
Davis, Rebecca I, 714
Davis, Rebecca I, 758
Davis, Rebecca I, 759
Davis, Rebecca I, 763
Davis, Rebecca I, 767
Davis, Rebecca I, 974
Davis, Rebecca I, 975
Davis, Rebecca I, 984
Davis, Rebecca II, 353
Davis, Rebecca II, 501
Davis, Rebecca II, 703
Davis, Rebecca II, 785
Davis, Rebecca II, 820
Davis, Rebecca IV, 28
Davis, Rebecca IV, 83
Davis, Rebecca IV, 697
Davis, Rebecca IV, 758
Davis, Rebecca IV, 947
Davis, Rebecca IV, 1053
Davis, Rebecca V, 301
Davis, Rebecca V, 485
Davis, Rebecca V, 516
Davis, Rebecca V, 618
Davis, Rebecca V, 780
Davis, Rebecca V, 791
Davis, Rebecca V, 835
Davis, Rebecca V, 870
Davis, Rebecca VI, 106
Davis, Rebecca B. V, 835
Davis, Rebecca E. I, 714
Davis, Rebecca H. VI, 903
Davis, Rebecca J. I, 745
Davis, Rebecca Jane V, 617
Davis, Rebecca T. IV, 697
Davis, Rebecca T. IV, 698
Davis, Rebeccah I, 535
Davis, Rebecka V, 311
Davis, Rebeckah I, 529
Davis, Rebeckah I, 535
Davis, Rebeckah I, 980
Davis, Rebeckah I, 984
Davis, Rebeckah II, 65
Davis, Rebeckah II, 98
Davis, Rebeckar I, 137
Davis, Rebekah I, 137
Davis, Rebekah I, 177
Davis, Rebekah I, 677
Davis, Rebekah I, 679
Davis, Rebekah I, 984
Davis, Rebekah I, 1008
Davis, Rebekah IV, 620
Davis, Rebekah VI, 486
Davis, Rebekah VI, 574
Davis, Rena I, 924
Davis, Reuben I, 137
Davis, Reuben I, 745
Davis, Reuben I, 757
Davis, Reuben I, 758
Davis, Reuben I, 759
Davis, Reuben C. I, 745
Davis, Reuben L. I, 745
Davis, Rhoda I, 265
Davis, Rhoda I, 269
Davis, Rhoda I, 273
Davis, Rhoda I, 1004
Davis, Rhoda I, 1008
Davis, Rhoda I, 1013
Davis, Rhoda V, 734
Davis, Rhoda R. I, 237
Davis, Rhoda T. V, 735
Davis, Rich I, 713
Davis, Rich I, 876
Davis, Richard I, 285
Davis, Richard I, 304
Davis, Richard I, 311
Davis, Richard I, 319
Davis, Richard I Sup 1, 3
Davis, Richard II, 117
Davis, Richard II, 352
Davis, Richard II, 353
Davis, Richard II, 501
Davis, Richard II, 855
Davis, Richard VI, 171
Davis, Richard VI, 285
Davis, Richard VI, 307
Davis, Richard VI, 382
Davis, Richard VI, 903
Davis, Richard VI, 987
Davis, Richard VI, 988
Davis, Richard L. I, 269
Davis, Richard L. I, 304
Davis, Richard M. I, 285
Davis, Richard W. II, 703
Davis, Richard Wistar III, 97
Davis, Richardson VI, 307
Davis, Riley V, 734
Davis, Riley V, 735
Davis, Riley V, 753
Davis, Riley V, 835
Davis, Riley V, 844
Davis, Riley V, 851
Davis, Robert I, 45
Davis, Robert I, 98
Davis, Robert I, 137
Davis, Robert I, 138
Davis, Robert I, 139
Davis, Robert I, 285
Davis, Robert I, 714
Davis, Robert I, 924
Davis, Robert I, 985
Davis, Robert IV, 810
Davis, Robert IV, 903
Davis, Robert V, 232
Davis, Robert V, 233
Davis, Robert V, 558
Davis, Robert V, 835
Davis, Robert VI, 285
Davis, Robert VI, 903
Davis, Robert Dobbin II, 791
Davis, Robert Milton I, 807
Davis, Robert Pleasants VI, 171
Davis, Robert Pleasants VI, 307
Davis, Robert Yancey I, 677
Davis, Robert Yancy I, 677
Davis, Roberta Jane V, 233
Davis, Rodney VI, 382
Davis, Rodney VI, 619
Davis, Rodney VI, 633
Davis, Rodney VI, 677
Davis, Rodney VI, 721
Davis, Rodney VI, 732
Davis, Rodney VI, 737
Davis, Rodney VI, 738
Davis, Rollah V, 618
Davis, Rollin V, 735
Davis, Royal J. III, 97
Davis, Royal J. III, 298
Davis, Royal Stanton III, 97
Davis, Ruben I, 652
Davis, Ruby Herring I, 335
Davis, Rufus Banner I, 924
Davis, Rufus K. I, 758
Davis, Rufus R. I, 807
Davis, Rufus W. I, 269
Davis, Rumford II, 353
Davis, Russel V, 233
Davis, Russel V, 486
Davis, Russell V, 232
Davis, Ruth I, 132
Davis, Ruth I, 137
Davis, Ruth I, 269
Davis, Ruth I, 346
Davis, Ruth I, 349
Davis, Ruth I, 362
Davis, Ruth I, 384
Davis, Ruth I, 466
Davis, Ruth I, 473
Davis, Ruth I, 479
Davis, Ruth I, 652
Davis, Ruth I, 677
Davis, Ruth I, 713
Davis, Ruth I, 807
Davis, Ruth I, 876
Davis, Ruth I, 974
Davis, Ruth I, 984
Davis, Ruth I, 995
Davis, Ruth I, 1008
Davis, Ruth I, 1009
Davis, Ruth II, 147
Davis, Ruth II, 718
Davis, Ruth II, 908
Davis, Ruth IV, 1129
Davis, Ruth IV, 1133
Davis, Ruth V, 47
Davis, Ruth V, 80
Davis, Ruth V, 327
Davis, Ruth V, 330
Davis, Ruth V, 558
Davis, Ruth V, 618
Davis, Ruth VI, 486
Davis, Ruth VI, 666
Davis, Ruth A. I, 237
Davis, Ruth B. II, 855
Davis, Ruth E. II, 147
Davis, Ruth Hannah VI, 633
Davis, Ruth M. I, 714
Davis, Ruth M. I, 807
Davis, Ruth P. IV, 1092
Davis, Ruth P. IV, 1101
Davis, Ruth P. IV, 1129
Davis, Ruthanna II, 309
Davis, S. H. VI, 924
Davis, S. H. VI, 982
Davis, Sabilla V, 46
Davis, Sadie V, 328
Davis, Sadie V, 668
Davis, Sadie M. V, 232
Davis, Sadie M. V, 241
Davis, Salina F. I, 1150
Davis, Sally I, 1008
Davis, Sally I, 1011
Davis, Sally VI, 817
Davis, Samantha V, 735
Davis, Samira I, 697
Davis, Samira I, 714
Davis, Samira I, 807
Davis, Samira I, 876
Davis, Samira I, 903
Davis, Samira A. I, 714
Davis, Sampson II, 501
Davis, Samson II, 501
Davis, Samson II, 651

Davis, Samuel I, 677
Davis, Samuel I, 1004
Davis, Samuel I, 1091
Davis, Samuel I, 1094
Davis, Samuel II, 352
Davis, Samuel II, 353
Davis, Samuel II, 501
Davis, Samuel II, 502
Davis, Samuel II, 636
Davis, Samuel III, 97
Davis, Samuel IV, 28
Davis, Samuel IV, 83
Davis, Samuel IV, 697
Davis, Samuel IV, 698
Davis, Samuel IV, 718
Davis, Samuel IV, 758
Davis, Samuel IV, 778
Davis, Samuel IV, 785
Davis, Samuel IV, 810
Davis, Samuel IV, 903
Davis, Samuel IV, 947
Davis, Samuel V, 46
Davis, Samuel V, 86
Davis, Samuel V, 233
Davis, Samuel V, 328
Davis, Samuel V, 734
Davis, Samuel V, 735
Davis, Samuel V, 835
Davis, Samuel V, 902
Davis, Samuel V, 991
Davis, Samuel VI, 15
Davis, Samuel VI, 171
Davis, Samuel VI, 306
Davis, Samuel VI, 307
Davis, Samuel VI, 350
Davis, Samuel VI, 351
Davis, Samuel VI, 486
Davis, Samuel VI, 738
Davis, Samuel Anthony VI, 307
Davis, Samuel B. I, 745
Davis, Samuel B. VI, 634
Davis, Samuel Coles II, 65
Davis, Samuel E. V, 233
Davis, Samuel E. V, 328
Davis, Samuel Griscom II, 353
Davis, Samuel H. I, 779
Davis, Samuel H. I, 807
Davis, Samuel Jones V, 734
Davis, Samuel P. II, 855
Davis, Samuel P. II, 856
Davis, Samuel T. VI, 634
Davis, Samuel T. VI, 680
Davis, Samuel T. VI, 684
Davis, Samuel V. V, 46
Davis, Samuel, Jr. V, 735
Davis, Samuel, Jr. VI, 486
Davis, Samyra I, 807
Davis, Santford L. I, 923
Davis, Sarah I, 45
Davis, Sarah I, 46
Davis, Sarah I, 98
Davis, Sarah I, 137
Davis, Sarah I, 138
Davis, Sarah I, 147
Davis, Sarah I, 161
Davis, Sarah I, 237
Davis, Sarah I, 265
Davis, Sarah I, 285
Davis, Sarah I, 304
Davis, Sarah I, 307
Davis, Sarah I, 318
Davis, Sarah I, 349
Davis, Sarah I, 363
Davis, Sarah I, 381
Davis, Sarah I, 384
Davis, Sarah I, 428
Davis, Sarah I, 495
Davis, Sarah I, 536
Davis, Sarah I, 617
Davis, Sarah I, 760
Davis, Sarah I, 1008
Davis, Sarah I, 1011
Davis, Sarah I, 1118
Davis, Sarah I Sup 1, 3
Davis, Sarah II, 65
Davis, Sarah II, 73
Davis, Sarah II, 87
Davis, Sarah II, 117
Davis, Sarah II, 131
Davis, Sarah II, 285
Davis, Sarah II, 300
Davis, Sarah II, 309
Davis, Sarah II, 352
Davis, Sarah II, 353
Davis, Sarah II, 463
Davis, Sarah II, 501
Davis, Sarah II, 502
Davis, Sarah II, 506
Davis, Sarah II, 703
Davis, Sarah II, 736
Davis, Sarah II, 791
Davis, Sarah II, 958
Davis, Sarah II, 1049
Davis, Sarah IV, 326
Davis, Sarah IV, 382
Davis, Sarah IV, 409
Davis, Sarah IV, 573
Davis, Sarah IV, 698
Davis, Sarah IV, 740
Davis, Sarah IV, 762
Davis, Sarah IV, 810
Davis, Sarah IV, 833
Davis, Sarah IV, 947
Davis, Sarah IV, 994
Davis, Sarah V, 46
Davis, Sarah V, 233
Davis, Sarah V, 282
Davis, Sarah V, 327
Davis, Sarah V, 734
Davis, Sarah V, 735
Davis, Sarah V, 835
Davis, Sarah V, 902
Davis, Sarah VI, 307
Davis, Sarah VI, 349
Davis, Sarah VI, 350
Davis, Sarah VI, 351
Davis, Sarah VI, 382
Davis, Sarah VI, 388
Davis, Sarah VI, 419
Davis, Sarah VI, 475
Davis, Sarah VI, 486
Davis, Sarah A. V, 902
Davis, Sarah A. V, 932
Davis, Sarah A. VI, 903
Davis, Sarah Ann II, 147
Davis, Sarah Ann II, 157
Davis, Sarah Ann II, 790
Davis, Sarah Ann II, 824
Davis, Sarah Ann II, 855
Davis, Sarah Ann II, 856
Davis, Sarah Ann II, 890
Davis, Sarah Ann II, 931
Davis, Sarah Ann V, 233
Davis, Sarah Ann V, 485
Davis, Sarah B. III, 97
Davis, Sarah B. III, 244
Davis, Sarah Catharine V, 233
Davis, Sarah Christian I, 615
Davis, Sarah Christian I, 632
Davis, Sarah D. II, 855
Davis, Sarah D. V, 383
Davis, Sarah E. V, 735
Davis, Sarah E. G. IV, 383
Davis, Sarah E. R. I, 32
Davis, Sarah Eleanor IV, 382
Davis, Sarah Elizabeth V, 327
Davis, Sarah F. IV, 810
Davis, Sarah Florence V, 835
Davis, Sarah H. III, 97
Davis, Sarah H. III, 256
Davis, Sarah Haydock III, 97
Davis, Sarah I. I, 714
Davis, Sarah Lydia V, 327
Davis, Sarah Lydia V, 383
Davis, Sarah M. V, 328
Davis, Sarah M. V, 493
Davis, Sarah Maria V, 233
Davis, Sarah Merrit V, 902
Davis, Sarah W. I, 304
Davis, Sarah W. I, 316
Davis, Sarah W. V, 383
Davis, Sarah Zalinda VI, 782
Davis, Sary I, 91
Davis, Seha V, 734
Davis, Selah I, 304
Davis, Selah I, 1008
Davis, Selah I, 1011
Davis, Semira I, 713
Davis, Seth II, 1049
Davis, Sewell F. I, 758
Davis, Sherman S. V, 991
Davis, Sidney IV, 1205
Davis, Sidney Clapp I, 758
Davis, Sidney G. IV, 1205
Davis, Silas I, 961
Davis, Silas I, 1004
Davis, Silas V, 47
Davis, Silas V, 558
Davis, Silas V, 618
Davis, Simoh V, 780
Davis, Simon I, 974
Davis, Simon I, 975
Davis, Simon I, 984
Davis, Simon V, 735
Davis, Simon V, 780
Davis, Simon V, 781
Davis, Smith IV, 193
Davis, Smith IV, 382
Davis, Smith IV, 383
Davis, Smith IV, 520
Davis, Solomon IV, 740
Davis, Sophia I, 445
Davis, Sophia IV, 697
Davis, Sophia H. VI, 903
Davis, Sophia Susanna VI, 634
Davis, Sophia Susanna VI, 680
Davis, Sophia Susanna VI, 684
Davis, Sophronia I, 335
Davis, Sophronia P. I, 467
Davis, Sophronia P. I, 479
Davis, Sopia I, 445
Davis, Spencer V, 46
Davis, Spencer V, 47
Davis, Spenser V, 46
Davis, States V, 618
Davis, Stella V, 383
Davis, Stephen V, 835
Davis, Stephen H. I, 779
Davis, Stephen H. I, 807
Davis, Stephen H. I, 843
Davis, Sue W. V, 47
Davis, Susan IV, 928
Davis, Susan E. II, 819
Davis, Susan M. II, 855
Davis, Susan M. II, 912
Davis, Susan M. III, 96
Davis, Susan M. III, 97
Davis, Susan M. III, 182
Davis, Susan T. IV, 697
Davis, Susanna I, 265
Davis, Susanna I, 269
Davis, Susanna I, 495
Davis, Susanna I, 758
Davis, Susanna II, 353
Davis, Susanna II, 502
Davis, Susanna VI, 171
Davis, Susanna VI, 307
Davis, Susanna VI, 633
Davis, Susanna VI, 634
Davis, Susanna VI, 706
Davis, Susanna Luesor Mary Delila I, 758
Davis, Susanna Martha VI, 307
Davis, Susannah I, 269
Davis, Susannah II, 213
Davis, Susannah II, 224
Davis, Susannah V, 383
Davis, Susannah VI, 240
Davis, Susannah VI, 306
Davis, Susannah VI, 351
Davis, Susannah VI, 649
Davis, Susannah VI, 703
Davis, Susannah VI, 738
Davis, Susannah Elizabeth VI, 634
Davis, Susannah Elizabeth VI, 738
Davis, Sybel J. I, 755
Davis, Sybel M. I, 745
Davis, Syble J. I, 759
Davis, T. E. V, 835
Davis, Tabitha IV, 382
Davis, Tabitha IV, 383
Davis, Tabitha IV, 441
Davis, Tacy IV, 28
Davis, Tacy VI, 485
Davis, Tacy VI, 486
Davis, Tacy VI, 529
Davis, Tacy A. IV, 1101
Davis, Tacy Ann IV, 1092
Davis, Tacy Ann IV, 1129
Davis, Tacy Ann IV, 1133
Davis, Tacy S. II, 791
Davis, Tacy S. II, 855
Davis, Tacy S. II, 856
Davis, Tacy S. II, 918
Davis, Talitha Ann I, 269
Davis, Talitha E. I, 335
Davis, Tallitha I, 269
Davis, Tallitha I, 271
Davis, Tamar I, 349
Davis, Tamar I, 961
Davis, Tamar I, 969
Davis, Tamar I, 1004
Davis, Tamar E. I, 745
Davis, Tamer I, 349
Davis, Tamer I, 384
Davis, Tamer I, 416
Davis, Tamer I, 460
Davis, Tamer I, 495
Davis, Tamer I, 958
Davis, Tamer I, 1008
Davis, Tamer I, 1013
Davis, Tamer V, 320
Davis, Tamer V, 327
Davis, Tamerlane VI, 810
Davis, Thamer I, 373
Davis, Thamer I, 381
Davis, Thamer I, 384
Davis, Theodoshey VI, 903
Davis, Theodosia VI, 921
Davis, Thomas I, 45
Davis, Thomas I, 56
Davis, Thomas I, 98
Davis, Thomas I, 137
Davis, Thomas I, 140
Davis, Thomas I, 177
Davis, Thomas I, 269
Davis, Thomas I, 271
Davis, Thomas I, 349
Davis, Thomas I, 384
Davis, Thomas I, 434
Davis, Thomas I, 445
Davis, Thomas I, 467
Davis, Thomas I, 479
Davis, Thomas I, 495
Davis, Thomas I, 529
Davis, Thomas I, 535
Davis, Thomas I, 536
Davis, Thomas I, 557
Davis, Thomas I, 677
Davis, Thomas I, 807
Davis, Thomas I, 953
Davis, Thomas I, 958
Davis, Thomas I, 961
Davis, Thomas I, 974
Davis, Thomas I, 984
Davis, Thomas I, 1004
Davis, Thomas I, 1011
Davis, Thomas I, 1118
Davis, Thomas II, 26
Davis, Thomas II, 65
Davis, Thomas II, 352
Davis, Thomas II, 353
Davis, Thomas II, 501
Davis, Thomas II, 506
Davis, Thomas II, 582
Davis, Thomas II, 791
Davis, Thomas II, 992
Davis, Thomas II, 1035
Davis, Thomas III, 305
Davis, Thomas IV, 382
Davis, Thomas V, 46
Davis, Thomas V, 233
Davis, Thomas V, 301
Davis, Thomas V, 327
Davis, Thomas V, 455
Davis, Thomas V, 485
Davis, Thomas VI, 306
Davis, Thomas VI, 351
Davis, Thomas VI, 485
Davis, Thomas VI, 738
Davis, Thomas VI, 782
Davis, Thomas VI, 810
Davis, Thomas VI, 851
Davis, Thomas VI, 890
Davis, Thomas VI, 903
Davis, Thomas VI, 980
Davis, Thomas A. V, 327
Davis, Thomas C. I, 495
Davis, Thomas C. V, 835
Davis, Thomas E. I, 758
Davis, Thomas E. I, 759
Davis, Thomas Elwood V, 835
Davis, Thomas F. V, 455
Davis, Thomas J. V, 233
Davis, Thomas J. V, 328
Davis, Thomas John V, 445
Davis, Thomas L. I, 285
Davis, Thomas L. V, 233
Davis, Thomas L. V, 328
Davis, Thomas Lorenzo V, 233
Davis, Thomas M. I, 237
Davis, Thomas M. I, 269
Davis, Thomas M. V, 327
Davis, Thomas T. V, 233
Davis, Thomas T. V, 455
Davis, Thomas, Jr. I, 953
Davis, Thomas, Jr. I, 1008
Davis, Thomas, Jr. VI, 706
Davis, Thomas, Sr. I, 1008
Davis, Thos. I, 470
Davis, Thos. II, 26
Davis, Thos. II, 791
Davis, Thos. E. V, 327
Davis, Thos. J. V, 328
Davis, Thos. M. V, 327
Davis, Thos. W. II, 855
Davis, Thos. Wilkins II, 791
Davis, Timothy V, 383
Davis, Trecinda I, 304
Davis, Tristram I, 495
Davis, Tristram I, 535
Davis, Tristram I, 536
Davis, Tristram V, 233
Davis, Tristram V, 301
Davis, Tristram, Jr. I, 536
Davis, Tristrum I, 536
Davis, Tristrum V, 301
Davis, Trustram I, 536
Davis, Uriah V, 835
Davis, V. Pearl VI, 60
Davis, Valentine V, 327
Davis, Valentine V, 383
Davis, Veo V, 47
Davis, Victoria Titala V, 327
Davis, Victoria V. V, 618
Davis, W. Banne I, 923
Davis, Walter V, 165
Davis, Warner I, 652
Davis, Warner I, 677
Davis, Warner I, 682
Davis, Warner I, 713
Davis, Warwick I, 758
Davis, Wd Hannah IV, 797
Davis, Wd. Ann II, 213
Davis, Wd. Betsy V, 813
Davis, Wd. Elizabeth P. III, 305
Davis, Wd. Esther II, 352
Davis, Wd. Jane II, 502
Davis, Wd. Joanna H. II, 791
Davis, Wd. Lucy II, 502
Davis, Wd. Lucy II, 513
Davis, Wd. Mary II, 501
Davis, Wd. Rachel II, 501
Davis, Welmet V, 233
Davis, Welmet V, 301
Davis, Wenlock Reynolds I, 479
Davis, Wesley T. V, 328
Davis, Wesley Taylor V, 327
Davis, Westminister I, 807
Davis, Widow Ann I, 744
Davis, Widow Rebecca I, 989
Davis, Wiley J. M. I, 714
Davis, Willa V, 735
Davis, William I, 91
Davis, William I, 98
Davis, William I, 137
Davis, William I, 167
Davis, William I, 269
Davis, William I, 285
Davis, William I, 304
Davis, William I, 349
Davis, William I, 350
Davis, William I, 384
Davis, William I, 495
Davis, William I, 713
Davis, William I, 807
Davis, William I, 876
Davis, William I, 961
Davis, William I, 974
Davis, William I, 975
Davis, William I, 984
Davis, William I, 985
Davis, William I, 988
Davis, William I, 1004
Davis, William I, 1008
Davis, William I, 1118
Davis, William II, 213
Davis, William II, 269
Davis, William II, 352
Davis, William II, 353
Davis, William II, 703
Davis, William II, 958
Davis, William III, 97
Davis, William IV, 82
Davis, William IV, 83
Davis, William IV, 619
Davis, William IV, 947
Davis, William V, 46
Davis, William V, 617
Davis, William V, 835
Davis, William V, 902
Davis, William VI, 56
Davis, William VI, 60
Davis, William VI, 159
Davis, William VI, 163
Davis, William VI, 171
Davis, William VI, 292
Davis, William VI, 306
Davis, William VI, 307
Davis, William VI, 308
Davis, William VI, 329
Davis, William VI, 350
Davis, William VI, 351
Davis, William VI, 382
Davis, William VI, 634
Davis, William VI, 738
Davis, William VI, 806
Davis, William VI, 810
Davis, William A. I, 758
Davis, William A. I, 807
Davis, William Banner I, 924
Davis, William C. I, 304
Davis, William C. IV, 382
Davis, William C. IV, 383
Davis, William C. IV, 1092
Davis, William Davis VI, 782
Davis, William E. I, 285
Davis, William E. I, 304
Davis, William E. I, 328
Davis, William E. I, 745
Davis, William F. VI, 382
Davis, William H. V, 835
Davis, William H. VI, 810

avis, William J. I, 285
avis, William J. I, 698
avis, William J. I, 714
avis, William J. I, 738
avis, William J. I, 807
avis, William John Thomas VI, 307
avis, William L. VI, 903
avis, William M. V, 870
avis, William S. I, 269
avis, William S. V, 485
avis, William S. V, 902
avis, William S. VI, 633
avis, William T. VI, 60
avis, William T. VI, 903
avis, William Wills III, 97
avis, William, Jr. I, 984
avis, William, Jr. VI, 307
avis, William, Jr. VI, 308
avis, William, Jr. VI, 311
avis, William, Jr. VI, 330
avis, William, Jr. VI, 339
avis, William, Jr. VI, 351
avis, William, Sr. I, 807
avis, William, Sr. VI, 307
avis, Williard L. V, 486
avis, Willis L. I, 269
avis, Willis Spencer I, 940
avis, Wilmer W. II, 791
avis, Wilmer W. II, 856
avis, Wilson IV, 520
avis, Wilson W. I, 745
avis, Winslow I, 698
avis, Winslow I, 713
avis, Winslow I, 720
avis, Winslow I, 779
avis, Winslow I, 807
avis, Winslow H. I, 495
avis, Wm. I, 961
avis, Wm. II, 128
avis, Wm. II, 501
avis, Wm. II, 856
avis, Wm. III, 96
avis, Wm. III, 219
avis, Wm. IV, 697
avis, Wm. IV, 703
avis, Wm. IV, 892
avis, Wm. V, 301
avis, Wm. V, 991
avis, Wm. VI, 60
avis, Wm. A. II, 855
avis, Wm. Augustus II, 791
avis, Wm. C. IV, 1092
avis, Wm. C. IV, 1129
avis, Wm. E. V, 991
avis, Wm. G. II, 147
avis, Wm. H. V, 991
avis, Wm. J. V, 455
avis, Wm. L. V, 618
avis, Wm. L. V, 806
avis, Wm. M. II, 855
avis, Wm. Morris II, 791
avis, Wm. Morris II, 855
avis, Wm. Morris, Jr. II, 791
avis, Wm. Morris, Jr. II, 856
avis, Wm. N. II, 131
avis, Wm. N. II, 147
avis, Wm. P. II, 791
avis, Wm. P. II, 856
avis, Wm. Penrose II, 791
avis, Wm. S. V, 618
avis, Wm., Jr. VI, 737
avis, Wm., Jr. VI, 782
avis, Wm., Sr. I, 876
avis, Young VI, 843
avis, Zachariah I, 285
avis, Zachariah I, 304
avis, Zachariah VI, 946
avis, Zackry VI, 903
avis, Zalinda VI, 307
avis, Zalinda VI, 308
avis, Zalinda VI, 329
avis, Zalinda VI, 330
avis, Zalinda VI, 339
avis, Zalinda VI, 351
avis, Zalinda VI, 737
avis, Zalinda VI, 782
avis, Zilpha I, 328
avis-Moon, Martha VI, 767
avise, Beaty I, 98
avise, Hannah II, 501
avise, Hannah II, 609
avise, James I, 98
avise, Jeams I, 98
avise, Joshua I, 98
avise, Mary I, 98
avise, Robert I, 98
avise, Ruth I, 98
avise, Thomas I, 98
avison, Ann IV, 194
avison, Benjamin VI, 810
Davison, Benjamin VI, 903
Davison, Charlotte IV, 194
Davison, David Lindley I, 698
Davison, Eliza IV, 720
Davison, Elizabeth I, 350
Davison, Elizabeth IV, 83
Davison, Elizabeth IV, 100
Davison, Emery L. IV, 194
Davison, Eunice VI, 903
Davison, Evry IV, 194
Davison, Geo. IV, 219
Davison, George I, 350
Davison, George IV, 194
Davison, George VI, 903
Davison, Hannah I, 350
Davison, Hannah I, 384
Davison, Hannah I, 385
Davison, Hannah I, 536
Davison, Hannah I, 571
Davison, Hannah IV, 194
Davison, Hannah IV, 219
Davison, Isaiah I, 350
Davison, James I, 263
Davison, James I, 269
Davison, James I, 350
Davison, James I, 366
Davison, James I, 384
Davison, James I, 385
Davison, James I, 536
Davison, James I, 571
Davison, James I, 698
Davison, James VI, 903
Davison, Jamima IV, 799
Davison, Jamima IV, 811
Davison, John I, 350
Davison, John I, 373
Davison, John I, 384
Davison, John I, 385
Davison, Joseph I, 1117
Davison, Josiah William I, 698
Davison, Loranah I, 350
Davison, Lorance I, 536
Davison, Lowrana I, 385
Davison, Lurance I, 536
Davison, Lurena I, 385
Davison, Lydia I, 350
Davison, Lydia I, 366
Davison, Lydia I, 384
Davison, Lydia I, 422
Davison, Lydia I, 1117
Davison, Margaret I, 385
Davison, Margaret I, 415
Davison, Margaret VI, 859
Davison, Mary I, 350
Davison, Mary I, 366
Davison, Mary I, 384
Davison, Mary I, 385
Davison, Mary I, 415
Davison, Mary V, 558
Davison, Mary VI, 903
Davison, Moses I, 350
Davison, Mosses I, 385
Davison, Parker IV, 194
Davison, Penina IV, 573
Davison, Peninah IV, 569
Davison, Rachel I, 350
Davison, Rachel I, 373
Davison, Rachel I, 384
Davison, Rachel I, 385
Davison, Rebecca VI, 810
Davison, Reece IV, 194
Davison, Rees IV, 194
Davison, Ruth I, 384
Davison, Ruth I, 385
Davison, Ruth I, 536
Davison, Ruth I, 571
Davison, Ruth I, 698
Davison, Samuel I, 350
Davison, Samuel I, 385
Davison, Samuel VI, 859
Davison, Samuel VI, 903
Davison, Sarah I, 350
Davison, Sarah I, 385
Davison, Sarah I, 412
Davison, Sarah Ann IV, 194
Davison, Susanna I, 350
Davison, Susanna I, 385
Davison, Susanna I, 415
Davison, William I, 269
Davison, William I, 350
Davison, William I, 384
Davison, William I, 385
Davison, William I, 536
Davison, William I, 571
Davison, William I, 1117
Daviss, Elizabeth II, 443
Daviss, George II, 352
Daviss, John II, 352
Daviss, John II, 440
Daviss, John II, 443
Daviss, Mary II, 352
Daviss, William II, 443
Davisson, James I, 384
Davisson, James I, 385
Davisson, Joseph VI, 810
Davisson, Mosses I, 385
Davisson, Polly VI, 810
Davisson, Samuel I, 385
Davisson, William I, 269
Davisson, William I, 384
Davisson, William I, 385
Davitt, Elisha VI, 903
Davitt, Margariet P. VI, 903
Dawes, Abijah II, 502
Dawes, Abijah II, 503
Dawes, Abraham II, 353
Dawes, Abraham II, 502
Dawes, Abraham II, 503
Dawes, Ann II, 353
Dawes, Ann II, 502
Dawes, Ann II, 503
Dawes, Ann II, 598
Dawes, Anna II, 791
Dawes, Anna II, 856
Dawes, Benj. II, 443
Dawes, Cephas II, 353
Dawes, Cephas II, 502
Dawes, Charles II, 503
Dawes, Deborah II, 503
Dawes, Deborah II, 696
Dawes, Deborah II, 703
Dawes, Edward II, 353
Dawes, Edward II, 502
Dawes, Edward II, 503
Dawes, Edward II, 535
Dawes, Edward II, 598
Dawes, Elizabeth II, 503
Dawes, Elizabeth II, 592
Dawes, George II, 502
Dawes, George II, 535
Dawes, Hannah II, 502
Dawes, Hannah II, 535
Dawes, Jonathan II, 353
Dawes, Jonathan II, 502
Dawes, Jonathan II, 503
Dawes, Jonathan II, 598
Dawes, Josiah II, 502
Dawes, Judith II, 502
Dawes, Marcy II, 502
Dawes, Martha II, 502
Dawes, Mary II, 353
Dawes, Mary II, 443
Dawes, Mary II, 502
Dawes, Mary II, 503
Dawes, Mary II, 557
Dawes, Mary II, 598
Dawes, Mary II, 1049
Dawes, Mary Whitlock II, 503
Dawes, Mary Whitlock II, 557
Dawes, Mercy II, 502
Dawes, Mercy II, 535
Dawes, Rumford II, 353
Dawes, Rumford II, 502
Dawes, Rumford II, 503
Dawes, Rumford II, 557
Dawes, Samuel II, 443
Dawes, Samuel Gray II, 502
Dawes, Samuel Gray II, 535
Dawes, Sarah II, 502
Dawes, Sarah II, 535
Dawes, Sibyl II, 353
Dawes, Sibyl II, 503
Dawn, Alis VI, 810
Dawn, Edmund VI, 810
Dawn, Edmund VI, 829
Dawn, Edward VI, 855
Dawn, Fanny VI, 810
Dawn, Lewsey VI, 800
Dawn, Margaret VI, 800
Dawn, Margate VI, 855
Dawn, Meraler VI, 855
Dawn, William VI, 810
Dawnib, Isabel II, 443
Daws, Charlie V, 455
Daws, Henry V, 455
Daws, Margaret V, 455
Daws, Mary V, 455
Daws, Plympton V, 455
Dawsey, John VI, 810
Dawsey, Sally VI, 810
Dawson, Aaron II, 65
Dawson, Abraham VI, 974
Dawson, Agness VI, 903
Dawson, Alvin J. IV, 375
Dawson, Amos VI, 903
Dawson, Ann I, 807
Dawson, Ann I, 1067
Dawson, Ann I, 1070
Dawson, Ann II, 65
Dawson, Ann II, 503
Dawson, Ann VI, 486
Dawson, Ann VI, 501
Dawson, Ann Eliza VI, 895
Dawson, Ann Powel II, 353
Dawson, Anna II, 65
Dawson, Anna II, 91
Dawson, Anna II, 503
Dawson, Anna IV, 383
Dawson, Anna S. IV, 374
Dawson, Anna S. IV, 383
Dawson, Anna Sarah III, 97
Dawson, Anne II, 353
Dawson, Anne II, 503
Dawson, Anne II, 640
Dawson, Annie IV, 194
Dawson, Arthur K. I, 632
Dawson, Benj. R. VI, 803
Dawson, Benjamin II, 503
Dawson, Benjamin II, 526
Dawson, Benjamin II, 528
Dawson, Benjamin IV, 83
Dawson, Benjamin R. VI, 919
Dawson, Benjamin R. VI, 962
Dawson, Benjamin R. VI, 966
Dawson, Benjamin R. VI, 995
Dawson, Benjamin Swett II, 214
Dawson, Betsey VI, 921
Dawson, Blanch I, 638
Dawson, Blanch Moore I, 632
Dawson, Braxton VI, 895
Dawson, Braxton L. VI, 903
Dawson, Caleb IV, 383
Dawson, Catharine VI, 903
Dawson, Catherine II, 353
Dawson, Chalkley IV, 194
Dawson, Chalkley IV, 371
Dawson, Chalkley IV, 383
Dawson, Chalkley IV, 394
Dawson, Chalkley IV, 513
Dawson, Chalkley IV, 520
Dawson, Chalkley IV, 1092
Dawson, Clara Leanna IV, 375
Dawson, Clary IV, 383
Dawson, Clement Laws II, 791
Dawson, Clinton Ellsworth IV, 383
Dawson, Clinton Elsworth IV, 194
Dawson, Clinton Elsworth IV, 383
Dawson, Clinton Elsworth IV, 573
Dawson, Cordie B. IV, 1276
Dawson, Cyrena I, 677
Dawson, Cyrena I, 686
Dawson, Daniel I, 1067
Dawson, Daniel I, 1070
Dawson, Daniel II, 353
Dawson, Daniel II, 503
Dawson, Daniel II, 667
Dawson, Deborah II, 353
Dawson, Deborah II, 503
Dawson, Dorcas II, 65
Dawson, Dorcas II, 92
Dawson, Dorothy II, 503
Dawson, Elener VI, 903
Dawson, Eli IV, 194
Dawson, Eli IV, 383
Dawson, Eli B. IV, 573
Dawson, Eli B. IV, 597
Dawson, Elias II, 353
Dawson, Elias II, 503
Dawson, Elias II, 652
Dawson, Elisabeth II, 503
Dawson, Elisabeth II, 528
Dawson, Elisha II, 791
Dawson, Elizabeth II, 353
Dawson, Elizabeth II, 371
Dawson, Elizabeth II, 503
Dawson, Elizabeth II, 526
Dawson, Elizabeth II, 543
Dawson, Elizabeth II, 640
Dawson, Elizabeth II, 652
Dawson, Elizabeth II, 662
Dawson, Elizabeth II, 703
Dawson, Elizabeth II, 736
Dawson, Elizabeth II, 992
Dawson, Elizabeth II, 993
Dawson, Elizabeth IV, 77
Dawson, Elizabeth IV, 83
Dawson, Elizabeth IV, 143
Dawson, Elizabeth IV, 144
Dawson, Elizabeth IV, 372
Dawson, Elizabeth IV, 383
Dawson, Elizabeth IV, 573
Dawson, Elizabeth VI, 974
Dawson, Elizabeth A. VI, 964
Dawson, Elizabeth Ann VI, 964
Dawson, Elizabeth W. II, 703
Dawson, Elizabeth W. II, 736
Dawson, Ella C. IV, 470
Dawson, Ellen III, 97
Dawson, Ellen III, 271
Dawson, Ellen M. III, 406
Dawson, Ellen M. III, 439
Dawson, Elmira IV, 194
Dawson, Elvira IV, 383
Dawson, Emanuel II, 443
Dawson, Esther II, 503
Dawson, Esther II, 513
Dawson, Esther IV, 383
Dawson, Esther IV, 573
Dawson, Esther W. IV, 383
Dawson, Esther W. IV, 573
Dawson, Esther W. IV, 597
Dawson, Frances VI, 894
Dawson, Francis II, 65
Dawson, Francis II, 213
Dawson, Francis II, 214
Dawson, Francis II, 235
Dawson, Francis II, 263
Dawson, Geo. W. III, 406
Dawson, Geo. W. III, 439
Dawson, Geo. W. VI, 898
Dawson, George II, 353
Dawson, George IV, 83
Dawson, George IV, 1276
Dawson, George VI, 903
Dawson, George W. VI, 885
Dawson, George W. VI, 964
Dawson, George W. VI, 1005
Dawson, Hannah IV, 509
Dawson, Hannah IV, 520
Dawson, Helen D. III, 406
Dawson, Helen D. III, 439
Dawson, Heneriter I, 1067
Dawson, Henrietta III, 191
Dawson, Henry IV, 194
Dawson, Henry IV, 383
Dawson, Henry V, 328
Dawson, Herbert Henry III, 97
Dawson, Herbert Henry III, 271
Dawson, Isaac I, 927
Dawson, Isaac II, 353
Dawson, Isaac II, 440
Dawson, Isaac II, 503
Dawson, Isaac II, 646
Dawson, Isaac II, 856
Dawson, Isaac IV, 83
Dawson, Isaac IV, 326
Dawson, Isaac IV, 520
Dawson, Isaac V, 165
Dawson, Isaac, Jr. II, 856
Dawson, Isaack V, 969
Dawson, Jacob VI, 903
Dawson, James IV, 1276
Dawson, James Poultney II, 703
Dawson, Jane II, 214
Dawson, Jane II, 353
Dawson, Jane II, 440
Dawson, Jane II, 503
Dawson, Jane II, 693
Dawson, Jane IV, 383
Dawson, Jane VI, 803
Dawson, Jane Vernon IV, 372
Dawson, Jedediah II, 65
Dawson, Jemima VI, 903
Dawson, Jemima VI, 1001
Dawson, Jemima VI, 1005
Dawson, Jeremiah VI, 903
Dawson, Jeremiah VI, 1005
Dawson, Jesse IV, 143
Dawson, Jesse IV, 144
Dawson, Jesse IV, 372
Dawson, Jesse IV, 383
Dawson, Jesse IV, 573
Dawson, Jesse, Jr. IV, 383
Dawson, Joel IV, 373
Dawson, Joel IV, 374
Dawson, Joel IV, 375
Dawson, Joel IV, 379
Dawson, Joel IV, 383
Dawson, Joel IV, 441
Dawson, Joel IV, 520
Dawson, Joel IV, 573
Dawson, Joel IV, 1092
Dawson, John I, 1067
Dawson, John I, 1070
Dawson, John II, 353
Dawson, John II, 443
Dawson, John II, 503
Dawson, John II, 526
Dawson, John II, 992
Dawson, John IV, 322
Dawson, John IV, 1249
Dawson, John V, 328
Dawson, John VI, 903
Dawson, John VI, 915
Dawson, John VI, 917
Dawson, John VI, 1000
Dawson, John VI, 1006
Dawson, John Dosin VI, 953
Dawson, John P. VI, 895
Dawson, Joseph IV, 143

Dawson, Joseph IV, 383
Dawson, Josiah II, 503
Dawson, Leroy F. VI, 861
Dawson, Letitia II, 736
Dawson, Letitia Poultney II, 353
Dawson, Lewis VI, 903
Dawson, Lidia II, 65
Dawson, Lidya II, 63
Dawson, Lidya II, 65
Dawson, Lilley I, 1067
Dawson, Lilly I, 1070
Dawson, Lilly I, 1072
Dawson, Luanna VI, 863
Dawson, Lucy T. VI, 903
Dawson, Lydia II, 65
Dawson, Lydia II, 214
Dawson, Lydia II, 260
Dawson, Lydia IV, 83
Dawson, Lydia IV, 326
Dawson, Lydia IV, 327
Dawson, M. A. VI, 896
Dawson, Malinda IV, 383
Dawson, Manuell II, 353
Dawson, Marie IV, 1249
Dawson, Martha I, 927
Dawson, Martha IV, 194
Dawson, Martha IV, 383
Dawson, Martha IV, 394
Dawson, Martha IV, 425
Dawson, Martha IV, 573
Dawson, Martha S. IV, 383
Dawson, Martin VI, 921
Dawson, Mary I, 714
Dawson, Mary II, 214
Dawson, Mary II, 353
Dawson, Mary II, 440
Dawson, Mary II, 503
Dawson, Mary II, 646
Dawson, Mary II, 652
Dawson, Mary II, 667
Dawson, Mary II, 856
Dawson, Mary IV, 194
Dawson, Mary IV, 374
Dawson, Mary IV, 375
Dawson, Mary IV, 383
Dawson, Mary V, 328
Dawson, Mary VI, 903
Dawson, Mary VI, 953
Dawson, Mary A. Blanche I, 622
Dawson, Mary Elizabeth I, 927
Dawson, Mary L. VI, 1005
Dawson, Mary Lightfoot VI, 903
Dawson, Mary M. IV, 383
Dawson, Mary Matilda IV, 194
Dawson, Mary Matilda IV, 383
Dawson, Mary P. IV, 383
Dawson, Mary P. IV, 441
Dawson, Matilda IV, 379
Dawson, Matilda IV, 383
Dawson, Matilda IV, 1092
Dawson, Melvina IV, 383
Dawson, Melvina IV, 394
Dawson, Milley I, 1067
Dawson, Minnie Dell IV, 1276
Dawson, Mira IV, 383
Dawson, Mordecai II, 353
Dawson, Mordecai II, 503
Dawson, Mordecai L. II, 503
Dawson, Mordecai L. II, 703
Dawson, Mordecai L. II, 736
Dawson, Moses II, 65
Dawson, Myra IV, 375
Dawson, Myra IV, 383
Dawson, Nancy VI, 915
Dawson, Nathan IV, 372
Dawson, Nathan IV, 383
Dawson, Nathan IV, 569
Dawson, Nathan IV, 573
Dawson, Noah I, 1067
Dawson, Patience I, 285
Dawson, Patience IV, 143
Dawson, Patience IV, 383
Dawson, Patience IV, 437
Dawson, Patsey VI, 1006
Dawson, Paulina J. VI, 899
Dawson, Peninah IV, 372
Dawson, Peninah IV, 383
Dawson, Pleasant VI, 903
Dawson, Pleasant VI, 988
Dawson, Polly VI, 903
Dawson, Rachel II, 213
Dawson, Rachel II, 214
Dawson, Rachel II, 235
Dawson, Rachel II, 263
Dawson, Rachel II, 503
Dawson, Rachel II, 703
Dawson, Rachel II, 736
Dawson, Rachel II, 992
Dawson, Rachel II, 993
Dawson, Randall IV, 375
Dawson, Rebecca II, 503
Dawson, Rebecca II, 703
Dawson, Rebecca IV, 383
Dawson, Rebecca Ann IV, 371
Dawson, Rebecca Ann IV, 383
Dawson, Rebecca Ann IV, 520
Dawson, Rebecca Anna IV, 383
Dawson, Rebecca Anna IV, 513
Dawson, Rebecca Anna IV, 520
Dawson, Rhoda VI, 988
Dawson, Richard II, 65
Dawson, Richard II, 213
Dawson, Richard II, 214
Dawson, Richard II, 235
Dawson, Richard II, 260
Dawson, Richard Blackham II, 503
Dawson, Richard Blackham II, 693
Dawson, Robert II, 353
Dawson, Robert II, 503
Dawson, Robert II, 513
Dawson, Robert II, 662
Dawson, Robert VI, 903
Dawson, Robert B. VI, 899
Dawson, Robert D. VI, 894
Dawson, Robert Dudley VI, 903
Dawson, Roderick D. VI, 903
Dawson, Rose II, 503
Dawson, Rose II, 535
Dawson, Ruth IV, 77
Dawson, Ruth IV, 83
Dawson, Ruth IV, 322
Dawson, Ruth IV, 326
Dawson, Sarah II, 214
Dawson, Sarah II, 263
Dawson, Sarah II, 353
Dawson, Sarah IV, 77
Dawson, Sarah IV, 194
Dawson, Sarah IV, 322
Dawson, Sarah IV, 372
Dawson, Sarah IV, 373
Dawson, Sarah IV, 379
Dawson, Sarah IV, 383
Dawson, Sarah IV, 394
Dawson, Sarah IV, 520
Dawson, Sarah IV, 569
Dawson, Sarah IV, 573
Dawson, Sarah IV, 598
Dawson, Sarah IV, 1092
Dawson, Sarah VI, 903
Dawson, Sarah VI, 917
Dawson, Sarah VI, 1000
Dawson, Sarah K. IV, 1276
Dawson, Sina IV, 326
Dawson, Sina IV, 383
Dawson, Sinah IV, 83
Dawson, Sinah IV, 515
Dawson, Sinah IV, 520
Dawson, Solomon II, 503
Dawson, Susan II, 803
Dawson, Susan IV, 83
Dawson, Susan IV, 326
Dawson, Susan IV, 519
Dawson, Susan IV, 520
Dawson, Susan VI, 861
Dawson, Susan C. IV, 470
Dawson, Susan C. VI, 1001
Dawson, Susanna VI, 1006
Dawson, Susannah VI, 1000
Dawson, Tacy VI, 903
Dawson, Tamar IV, 409
Dawson, Tamer J. IV, 383
Dawson, Tamor IV, 383
Dawson, Thomas II, 353
Dawson, Thomas II, 503
Dawson, Thomas VI, 357
Dawson, Warner II, 353
Dawson, Wd. Jane II, 503
Dawson, Wd. Mary Laws II, 791
Dawson, Willets IV, 194
Dawson, William II, 353
Dawson, William II, 703
Dawson, William IV, 77
Dawson, William IV, 83
Dawson, William VI, 803
Dawson, William E. IV, 470
Dawson, Willis IV, 383
Dawson, Wm. II, 503
Dawson, Wm. II, 640
Dawson, Wm. II, 662
Dawson, Wm., Jr. II, 503
Dawson, Zachariah II, 992
Dawson, Zachariah II, 993
Day, ??? III, 97
Day, ??? III, 242
Day, ??? III, 328
Day, Agnes IV, 948
Day, Amanda V, 165
Day, Ann I, 852
Day, Ann I, 877
Day, Ann II, 353
Day, Ann IV, 572
Day, Anna IV, 573
Day, Anna Braithwaite III, 97
Day, Annie L. IV, 383
Day, Annie L. IV, 454
Day, Benjamin F. V, 165
Day, Bessie V, 165
Day, Catharine I, 873
Day, Catharine I, 877
Day, Catharine II, 504
Day, Catherine I, 877
Day, Catherine II, 503
Day, Catherine II, 695
Day, Catherine VI, 382
Day, Charles Roswell IV, 1206
Day, Clarence Willard IV, 1206
Day, Daniel I, 877
Day, Daniel VI, 810
Day, Deborah I, 852
Day, Deborah I, 877
Day, Deborah I, 881
Day, Deborah, Jr. I, 877
Day, Edward II, 353
Day, Edward E. IV, 1249
Day, Edward Munson III, 97
Day, Eliza II, 856
Day, Eliza II, 943
Day, Elizabeth II, 171
Day, Elizabeth VI, 903
Day, Elizabeth VI, 980
Day, Evan VI, 382
Day, Ezekiel VI, 903
Day, George VI, 382
Day, Grace II, 503
Day, Grace II, 623
Day, Grace III, 97
Day, Hannah I, 852
Day, Hannah I, 877
Day, Hannah I, 889
Day, Hannah II, 353
Day, Hannah V, 165
Day, Hannah VI, 810
Day, Henry VI, 810
Day, Jane IV, 515
Day, Jane IV, 521
Day, Jane R. III, 97
Day, Jane R. III, 315
Day, John I, 852
Day, John I, 1047
Day, John II, 171
Day, John II, 353
Day, John II, 503
Day, John II, 510
Day, John II, 623
Day, John II, 695
Day, John IV, 1205
Day, John Mahlon IV, 1205
Day, Joseph II, 503
Day, Joseph II, 504
Day, Joseph II, 695
Day, Joseph V, 165
Day, Joseph VI, 382
Day, Joseph, Jr. VI, 382
Day, Josephine III, 97
Day, Josephine III, 242
Day, Josie V, 165
Day, Katharine VI, 382
Day, Leroy V, 165
Day, Lydia VI, 382
Day, Lydia VI, 412
Day, Maggie V, 165
Day, Mahlon III, 97
Day, Mahlon III, 315
Day, Mahlon IV, 948
Day, Mahlon IV, 1206
Day, Margaret I, 385
Day, Margret I, 1047
Day, Martha I, 852
Day, Martha I, 877
Day, Mary I, 877
Day, Mary II, 171
Day, Mary III, 97
Day, Mary III, 315
Day, Mary IV, 194
Day, Mary IV, 234
Day, Mary IV, 572
Day, Mary IV, 573
Day, Mary VI, 810
Day, Mary Jane IV, 521
Day, Mary Jane IV, 551
Day, Mary Kerr III, 97
Day, Mary, Jr. I, 877
Day, Minnie V, 165
Day, Mordecai II, 503
Day, Mountier I, 877
Day, Nancy V, 981
Day, Nancy VI, 810
Day, Nathan I, 852
Day, Peter VI, 903
Day, Polly VI, 903
Day, Priscilla I, 877
Day, Priscilla I, 902
Day, Rebecca IV, 572
Day, Rebecca IV, 573
Day, Rhode I, 877
Day, Richard I, 852
Day, Richard I, 877
Day, Richard, Jr. I, 877
Day, Richard, Jr. I, 889
Day, Ruth III, 97
Day, Ruth III, 154
Day, Ruth IV, 948
Day, Ruth C. IV, 1312
Day, Samuel M. II, 703
Day, Samuel M. II, 736
Day, Sarah I, 877
Day, Sarah II, 171
Day, Sarah II, 196
Day, Sarah II, 214
Day, Sarah II, 353
Day, Sarah II, 503
Day, Sarah II, 510
Day, Sarah II, 703
Day, Sarah IV, 383
Day, Sarah IV, 426
Day, Sarah V, 165
Day, Sarah Ann III, 97
Day, Sarah Gould III, 97
Day, Sherman V, 165
Day, Sophia W. VI, 903
Day, Stephen VI, 903
Day, Stephen VI, 930
Day, Stephen M. II, 703
Day, Stephen Munson II, 214
Day, Steven Mason II, 214
Day, Susan II, 700
Day, Susan III, 97
Day, Susan B. III, 97
Day, Tempe VI, 990
Day, Therman V, 165
Day, Thomas I, 852
Day, Thomas VI, 810
Day, Thomas VI, 903
Day, Viola V, 165
Day, W. E. IV, 948
Day, Walter E. IV, 948
Day, William I, 852
Day, William I, 877
Day, William VI, 903
Day, William H. V, 165
Day, Wm. VI, 954
Day, Zephel Marie IV, 1205
Daybill, Alfred III, 97
Daybill, Alfred III, 363
Daybill, Baby III, 97
Daybill, Elizabeth III, 97
Daybill, Elizabeth III, 363
Daybill, Fred III, 363
Daybill, Lilian Edna III, 97
Daybill, Mabelle J. III, 97
Daybill, Mabelle J. III, 183
Daybill, Susie III, 97
Daybill, William III, 97
Daybill, William R. III, 97
Daybill, William R. III, 183
Daybill, Wm. III, 363
Daye, Joseph II, 503
Dayly, Dennis II, 64
Daymude, Cora IV, 1249
Daynes, Mr. Wm. VI, 9
Dayorman, William IV, 194
Dayorman, William C. IV, 194
Days, Margaret I, 385
Dayton, Sarah III, 108
De Bost, ??? III, 98
De Bost, John III, 98
De Cost, Caroline III, 98
De Cost, Franklin III, 98
De Cost, Hannah III, 98
De Cost, Silvanus III, 98
De Cou, Samuel E. II, 957
De Cou, Sarah B. II, 957
De Cou, Sophia T. II, 957
De Cow, Martha II, 214
De Graff, Alice III, 98
De Graff, Alice III, 114
De Graff, Levvineus III, 114
De Graff, Livineus III, 98
De Grauw, Sarah T. III, 99
De Haven, Ann II, 805
De Laplaine, Elizabeth III, 99
De Laplaine, Joseph III, 99
De Lashure, Hope III, 99
De Long, ??? III, 310
De Long, Marion H. III, 99
De Long, Marion H. III, 310
De Montaloo, Evaristo III, 99
De Montaloo, Louise III, 99
De Montaloo, Marie III, 99
De Montalvo, Evaristo III, 238
De Montalvo, Louise III, 238
De Mott, Charles Fowler III, 407
De Mott, Davis III, 407
De Mott, Sarah Ann III, 407
De Rosa, Francesco III, 100
De Rosa, Raffaela III, 100
De Rosa, Ulysses III, 100
De St Croix, Euphemia III, 100
De Veze, Bessie M. III, 30
De Veze, Bessie M. III, 100
De Veze, Camille III, 27
De Veze, Camille III, 30
De Veze, Camille III, 100
De Voe, Eleanor III, 100
De Voe, Elizabeth A. III, 100
De Voe, Hannah Augusta III, 10
De Voe, Isaac B. III, 100
De Voe, Moses III, 100
De Voe, Susan III, 100
De Vol, Amanda B. III, 100
De Vol, Amanda B. III, 151
De Vol, Amanda B. III, 162
De Vol, Catharine V, 554
De Vol, Isaac B. III, 21
De Vol, Katharien D. III, 162
De Vol, Katie A. III, 100
De Vol, Katie A. III, 151
De Vol, Rowland G. III, 100
De Vol, Rowland G. III, 151
De Vol, Rowland G. III, 162
Deacly, Jemimah V, 668
Deacon, Achsah II, 214
Deacon, Amos II, 309
Deacon, Ann II, 171
Deacon, Ann II, 214
Deacon, Ann II, 215
Deacon, Ann II, 285
Deacon, Ann II, 306
Deacon, Anna II, 171
Deacon, Anna C. II, 856
Deacon, Anna Cary II, 791
Deacon, Anna H. II, 285
Deacon, Anna M. II, 171
Deacon, Anna M. II, 285
Deacon, Anna M. II, 292
Deacon, Anne II, 214
Deacon, Anne II, 228
Deacon, Annie S. II, 318
Deacon, Annie S. II, 327
Deacon, Barzilla II, 214
Deacon, Barzillai II, 214
Deacon, Benj. II, 171
Deacon, Benj. II, 285
Deacon, Benj. Franklin II, 171
Deacon, Benjamin II, 171
Deacon, Benjamin II, 214
Deacon, Benjamin II, 285
Deacon, Benjamin II, 306
Deacon, Benjamin E. II, 171
Deacon, Benjamin F. II, 285
Deacon, Benjamin H. II, 285
Deacon, Beulah II, 285
Deacon, Caroline II, 171
Deacon, Catharine L. II, 856
Deacon, Catharine L. II, 873
Deacon, Charles II, 171
Deacon, Charles F. II, 171
Deacon, Charles R. II, 171
Deacon, Charles R. II, 285
Deacon, Charles T. II, 285
Deacon, Edmund II, 171
Deacon, Edmund II, 285
Deacon, Edmund II, 791
Deacon, Edmund II, 856
Deacon, Edmund II, 873
Deacon, Elizabeth II, 171
Deacon, Elizabeth II, 178
Deacon, Elizabeth II, 285
Deacon, Elizabeth II, 302
Deacon, Elizabeth II, 307
Deacon, Elizabeth B. II, 318
Deacon, Elizabeth B. II, 325
Deacon, Elizabeth W. II, 171
Deacon, Elizabeth W. II, 285
Deacon, Elizabeth W. II, 292
Deacon, Elizabeth W. II, 306
Deacon, Ellen II, 171
Deacon, Ellen II, 285
Deacon, Emma L. II, 831
Deacon, Emma L. II, 856
Deacon, Eva B. II, 286
Deacon, Eva B. II, 290
Deacon, Frances VI, 873
Deacon, Francess II, 26
Deacon, Franciss II, 26
Deacon, Frederick H. II, 285
Deacon, Frederick Howard II, 171
Deacon, George II, 17
Deacon, George II, 26
Deacon, George II, 51
Deacon, George II, 65
Deacon, George II, 171

con, George II, 178
con, George II, 207
con, George II, 214
con, George II, 245
con, George II, 259
con, George II, 261
con, George B. II, 171
con, George B. II, 182
con, George B. II, 285
con, George B. II, 299
con, George Burr II, 171
con, George E. II, 285
con, George Edmund II, 171
con, George Sydney II, 171
con, Hannah II, 171
con, Hannah II, 214
con, Hannah II, 245
con, Hannah II, 285
con, Hannah II, 299
con, Hannah II, 306
con, Hannah II, 307
con, Hannah II, 791
con, Hester II, 214
con, Hester II, 273
con, Howard II, 171
con, Howard R. II, 856
con, Howard Ridgway II, 791
con, Isaac II, 171
con, Isaac II, 214
con, Israel II, 214
con, Israel II, 286
con, Israel II, 290
con, James II, 171
con, James II, 214
con, James W. II, 285
con, Jane II, 171
con, Jane II, 209
con, Jane II, 214
con, Jno. C. II, 285
con, John II, 171
con, John II, 214
con, John II, 273
con, John II, 285
con, John II, 299
con, John II, 307
con, John II, 791
con, John B. II, 285
con, John C. II, 171
con, John C. II, 285
con, John E. II, 171
con, John E. II, 285
con, John L. II, 171
con, John L. II, 285
con, John, Jr. II, 214
con, Joseph II, 214
con, Joseph H. II, 171
con, Joseph H. II, 285
con, Joseph Herbert II, 171
con, Joseph Herbert II, 285
con, Josephine II, 791
con, Kesiah II, 171
con, Keturah II, 171
con, Keziah II, 171
con, Lewis J. II, 856
con, Louis II, 856
con, Louis Joseph II, 856
con, Louis Joseph II, 867
con, Lydia M. II, 171
con, Mahitabel II, 214
con, Margaret II, 65
con, Margret II, 65
con, Maria W. II, 171
con, Maria W. II, 285
con, Marie B. II, 285
con, Marie B. II, 306
con, Martha II, 171
con, Martha II, 214
con, Martha II, 259
con, Martha R. II, 171
con, Martha R. II, 285
con, Mary II, 171
con, Mary II, 182
con, Mary II, 214
con, Mary II, 261
con, Mary II, 285
con, Mary II, 299
con, Mary B. II, 171
con, Mary B. II, 285
con, Mary B. II, 306
con, Mary R. II, 171
con, Mary W. II, 309
con, Mary Wildman II, 856
con, Mehetabel II, 214
con, Mehetible II, 171
con, Mehitible II, 214
con, Mehittible II, 214
con, Miriam II, 171
con, Miriam II, 214
con, Miriam II, 229
con, Naomi II, 171
con, Peter II, 214
Deacon, Rachel II, 171
Deacon, Rachel E. II, 856
Deacon, Rachel Evans II, 791
Deacon, Rebecca II, 171
Deacon, Rebecca II, 309
Deacon, Rebecca D. II, 317
Deacon, Rebecca D. II, 318
Deacon, Rebecca W. II, 286
Deacon, Rebecca W. II, 290
Deacon, Robert II, 214
Deacon, Samuel II, 171
Deacon, Samuel II, 214
Deacon, Samuel G. II, 171
Deacon, Samuel, Jr. II, 214
Deacon, Sarah H. II, 171
Deacon, Sarah H. II, 285
Deacon, Susanna II, 205
Deacon, Susanna II, 214
Deacon, Susannah II, 51
Deacon, Susannah II, 65
Deacon, Susannah II, 171
Deacon, Susannah II, 214
Deacon, Susannah II, 245
Deacon, Theodocia II, 171
Deacon, Thomas II, 214
Deacon, Thomas E. II, 171
Deacon, Thomas E. II, 214
Deacon, Thomas E. II, 285
Deacon, Thomas E. II, 292
Deacon, Thomas E. II, 307
Deacon, Thomas Eyre II, 171
Deacon, Thomas W. II, 285
Deacon, Thomas W. II, 292
Deacon, Uriah W. II, 171
Deacon, Wd. Achsah D. II, 171
Deacon, Wd. Catherine L. II, 791
Deacon, Wd. Maria W. II, 171
Deacon, William II, 214
Deacon, William R. II, 171
Deacon, William R. II, 285
Deadman, Bertha III, 98
Deadman, Bertha Margaret III, 98
Deadman, Bertha Margaret III, 237
Deadman, Clara Victoria III, 98
Deadman, Edith III, 98
Deadman, Harold III, 98
Deadman, Harold A. III, 98
Deadman, Harold A. III, 237
Deadman, Horace A. III, 98
Deadman, Sarah III, 98
Deadmons, Elizabeth VI, 903
Deadmons, Thomas VI, 903
Deakin, James V, 435
Deakin, Jane I, 1150
Deakin, Maria V, 668
Deakin, Samantha M. V, 435
Deakin, Susan V, 435
Deakins, Jane I, 1150
Deakins, Robert I, 1150
Deakins, Robert T. I, 1150
Deakins, Wm. B. I, 1150
Deal, ??? III, 346
Deal, Elizabeth II, 722
Deal, John IV, 1276
Deal, Mary II, 504
Deal, Mary, Jr. II, 504
Deal, Nancy VI, 923
Deal, Peninah III, 98
Deal, Peninah III, 346
Deal, Samuel II, 504
Deal, Sarah III, 98
Deal, Sarah Parker VI, 923
Deal, William I, 45
Deal, William Taylor I, 45
Deale, Mary II, 353
Deale, Mary II, 504
Dealey, Fay Virra V, 991
Dealey, Junita V, 991
Dealey, Kermit V, 991
Dealey, Lenore V, 991
Deall, Mary II, 474
Deall, Mary II, 504
Deall, Samuel II, 474
Deall, Samuel II, 504
Deam, Bertha Ruth V, 558
Deam, Chas. E. V, 558
Deam, Mrs. Ruth V, 558
Deam, Roger Francis V, 558
Deam, Ruth V, 558
Deams, Sarah Elizabeth IV, 1129
Deams, Sarah Elizabeth IV, 1137
Dean, ??? III, 95
Dean, ??? III, 245
Dean, ??? IV, 1125
Dean, Abigail IV, 698
Dean, Abigail IV, 811
Dean, Abigail IV, 902
Dean, Abigail IV, 903
Dean, Abigail M. IV, 1360
Dean, Addie IV, 1249
Dean, Agnes III, 15
Dean, Agnes III, 46
Dean, Agnes III, 54
Dean, Agnes III, 98
Dean, Agnes III, 228
Dean, Alexander II, 504
Dean, Alexander II, 992
Dean, Alice J. IV, 811
Dean, Almeda IV, 1130
Dean, Almeda B. IV, 1129
Dean, Almeda B. IV, 1130
Dean, Amos IV, 698
Dean, Amos IV, 903
Dean, Amy III, 98
Dean, Amy IV, 584
Dean, Amy IV, 811
Dean, Amy IV, 903
Dean, Amy IV, 1092
Dean, Amy IV, 1093
Dean, Amy IV, 1103
Dean, Ann II, 700
Dean, Ann II, 720
Dean, Ann II, 982
Dean, Ann II, 992
Dean, Ann IV, 698
Dean, Ann IV, 802
Dean, Ann IV, 811
Dean, Ann IV, 845
Dean, Ann IV, 903
Dean, Ann VI, 931
Dean, Anna III, 98
Dean, Anna B. V, 941
Dean, Anna Elliott V, 902
Dean, Anne III, 403
Dean, Annie Delphina I, 632
Dean, Archer B. V, 902
Dean, Archer Griffin V, 902
Dean, Artemas IV, 1360
Dean, Artemas I. IV, 1360
Dean, Arthur III, 98
Dean, Barten IV, 1129
Dean, Barton IV, 698
Dean, Barton IV, 770
Dean, Barton IV, 802
Dean, Barton IV, 811
Dean, Barton IV, 827
Dean, Barton IV, 858
Dean, Barton IV, 902
Dean, Barton IV, 903
Dean, Bessie I, 632
Dean, Caroline IV, 811
Dean, Caroline IV, 1129
Dean, Caroline IV, 1130
Dean, Caroline S. IV, 903
Dean, Caroline S. IV, 904
Dean, Caroline S. IV, 913
Dean, Carrie Bell I, 632
Dean, Catherin II, 65
Dean, Charity II, 786
Dean, Conelia I, 919
Dean, Cornelia III, 46
Dean, Cornelia III, 98
Dean, Dane III, 98
Dean, Daniel III, 98
Dean, Daniel S. II, 504
Dean, Daniel S. III, 98
Dean, David II, 65
Dean, David II, 504
Dean, David IV, 698
Dean, Davis IV, 903
Dean, Deborah II, 353
Dean, Deborah L. V, 486
Dean, Deborah L. V, 530
Dean, Dianna V, 437
Dean, Edith IV, 698
Dean, Edith IV, 748
Dean, Edith IV, 811
Dean, Edith IV, 903
Dean, Edna IV, 1092
Dean, Edna IV, 1110
Dean, Edna P. IV, 1093
Dean, Edward III, 98
Dean, Edward IV, 811
Dean, Edward IV, 1130
Dean, Eleanor IV, 698
Dean, Eleanor IV, 748
Dean, Eleanor IV, 811
Dean, Eleanor IV, 856
Dean, Eleanor IV, 903
Dean, Elisabeth II, 504
Dean, Eliza III, 98
Dean, Eliza Barton IV, 811
Dean, Elizaann IV, 903
Dean, Elizabeth I, 536
Dean, Elizabeth I, 586
Dean, Elizabeth I, 588
Dean, Elizabeth I, 593
Dean, Elizabeth II, 353
Dean, Elizabeth III, 98
Dean, Elizabeth III, 245
Dean, Elizabeth III, 314
Dean, Elizabeth IV, 691
Dean, Elizabeth IV, 698
Dean, Elizabeth IV, 770
Dean, Elizabeth IV, 801
Dean, Elizabeth IV, 802
Dean, Elizabeth IV, 807
Dean, Elizabeth IV, 811
Dean, Elizabeth IV, 815
Dean, Elizabeth IV, 857
Dean, Elizabeth IV, 902
Dean, Elizabeth IV, 903
Dean, Elizabeth IV, 904
Dean, Elizabeth IV, 948
Dean, Elizabeth IV, 1092
Dean, Elizabeth IV, 1093
Dean, Elizabeth IV, 1129
Dean, Elizabeth IV, 1130
Dean, Elizabeth IV, 1133
Dean, Elizabeth V, 902
Dean, Elizabeth Ann IV, 897
Dean, Elizabeth B. IV, 903
Dean, Elizabeth B. IV, 1131
Dean, Elizabeth D. IV, 811
Dean, Elizabeth L. V, 902
Dean, Elizabeth L. V, 938
Dean, Elizann IV, 911
Dean, Ellwood IV, 1092
Dean, Ellwood IV, 1093
Dean, Elwood IV, 903
Dean, Elwood IV, 904
Dean, Elwood IV, 1092
Dean, Elwood IV, 1093
Dean, Elwood IV, 1130
Dean, Ephraim IV, 698
Dean, Ephraim IV, 811
Dean, Ephraim IV, 903
Dean, Ephraim IV, 1130
Dean, Evaretta IV, 1130
Dean, Evaretta L. IV, 811
Dean, Evaretta Lydia IV, 1130
Dean, Francis IV, 811
Dean, Francis IV, 824
Dean, Francis IV, 903
Dean, Francis IV, 948
Dean, Francis IV, 1129
Dean, Francis IV, 1130
Dean, Francis IV, 1134
Dean, Garwood III, 98
Dean, Geo. B. V, 902
Dean, Geo. H. V, 902
Dean, Geo. H. V, 938
Dean, George III, 98
Dean, George B. V, 902
Dean, George H. V, 902
Dean, Georgia May I, 632
Dean, Gilbert III, 98
Dean, Gulielma I, 588
Dean, Gulielma I, 593
Dean, Hannah III, 98
Dean, Hannah IV, 698
Dean, Hannah IV, 802
Dean, Hannah IV, 811
Dean, Hannah IV, 827
Dean, Hannah IV, 853
Dean, Hannah IV, 903
Dean, Hannah IV, 904
Dean, Hannah IV, 913
Dean, Hannah IV, 1092
Dean, Hannah IV, 1093
Dean, Hannah IV, 1103
Dean, Hannah IV, 1130
Dean, Hannah IV, 1206
Dean, Hannah C. IV, 811
Dean, Hannah C. IV, 815
Dean, Hannah C. IV, 1130
Dean, Hannah C. IV, 1131
Dean, Henry II, 504
Dean, Henry III, 98
Dean, Henry IV, 811
Dean, Henry Loyd III, 98
Dean, Ida J. IV, 1129
Dean, Ida J. IV, 1130
Dean, Isaac I, 536
Dean, Isaac I, 588
Dean, Isaac III, 98
Dean, Isaac IV, 698
Dean, Isaac IV, 811
Dean, Israel III, 15
Dean, Israel III, 46
Dean, Israel III, 98
Dean, J. Earl IV, 1313
Dean, James IV, 802
Dean, James IV, 811
Dean, James H. IV, 811
Dean, James Harvey IV, 748
Dean, James Harvey IV, 856
Dean, James Hervey IV, 698
Dean, James Hervey IV, 811
Dean, James Hervey IV, 903
Dean, James Hervy IV, 903
Dean, Jericho III, 98
Dean, John III, 98
Dean, John III, 178
Dean, John IV, 1360
Dean, John S. IV, 1129
Dean, John S. IV, 1133
Dean, Jonathan IV, 691
Dean, Jonathan IV, 698
Dean, Jonathan IV, 801
Dean, Jonathan IV, 807
Dean, Jonathan IV, 811
Dean, Jonathan IV, 815
Dean, Jonathan IV, 857
Dean, Jonathan IV, 903
Dean, Jonathan IV, 904
Dean, Jonathan IV, 913
Dean, Jonathan IV, 948
Dean, Jonathan IV, 1103
Dean, Jonathan IV, 1129
Dean, Jonathan IV, 1130
Dean, Jonathan IV, 1131
Dean, Jonathan IV, 1133
Dean, Jonathan V, 902
Dean, Jonathan R. IV, 698
Dean, Jonathan R. IV, 811
Dean, Jonathan R. IV, 858
Dean, Jonathan R. IV, 897
Dean, Jonathan R. IV, 1092
Dean, Jonathan R. IV, 1103
Dean, Joseph II, 504
Dean, Joseph III, 98
Dean, Joseph III, 406
Dean, Joseph III, 475
Dean, Joseph A. III, 98
Dean, Joseph Abbott III, 98
Dean, Joseph B. IV, 811
Dean, Joshua IV, 811
Dean, Joshua S. IV, 698
Dean, Joshua S. IV, 811
Dean, Joshua S. IV, 903
Dean, Joshua S. IV, 907
Dean, Joshua S. IV, 1130
Dean, L. Earl IV, 1313
Dean, L. Earle IV, 1313
Dean, L. Marion IV, 1313
Dean, Lavina IV, 903
Dean, Lavina IV, 1053
Dean, Lavina IV, 1064
Dean, Lavina IV, 1092
Dean, Lavina IV, 1093
Dean, Lavina IV, 1103
Dean, Lavina IV, 1206
Dean, Leaha II, 65
Dean, Leal II, 65
Dean, Lydia I, 536
Dean, Lydia I, 593
Dean, Lydia III, 98
Dean, Lydia IV, 811
Dean, Lydia IV, 1130
Dean, Lydia B. IV, 811
Dean, Mable Ruth I, 632
Dean, Mamie C. IV, 1313
Dean, Margret II, 65
Dean, Maria I, 588
Dean, Maria I, 593
Dean, Martha IV, 811
Dean, Martha IV, 844
Dean, Martha IV, 857
Dean, Martha IV, 1130
Dean, Mary II, 353
Dean, Mary II, 504
Dean, Mary III, 62
Dean, Mary III, 98
Dean, Mary III, 403
Dean, Mary III, 406
Dean, Mary III, 475
Dean, Mary IV, 1360
Dean, Mary V, 902
Dean, Mary A. IV, 811
Dean, Mary Ann III, 98
Dean, Mary Ann IV, 811
Dean, Mary Ann IV, 847
Dean, Mary Ann IV, 903
Dean, Mary Ann IV, 907
Dean, Mary Ann IV, 915
Dean, Mary Ann IV, 1129
Dean, Mary Ann IV, 1130
Dean, Mary Ann IV, 1133
Dean, Mary B. IV, 811
Dean, Mary Olivia V, 757
Dean, Maryann IV, 811
Dean, Michael King IV, 1053
Dean, Milton IV, 470
Dean, Milton IV, 811
Dean, Milton IV, 903
Dean, Minnie C. IV, 1313
Dean, Miriam III, 98
Dean, Morris B. V, 902
Dean, Morris Burgess V, 902
Dean, Mrs. N. A. I, 632
Dean, N. A. I, 632

Dean, Nathan Horace I, 632
Dean, Nathaniel II, 353
Dean, Nicholas II, 214
Dean, Penina IV, 811
Dean, Penina IV, 824
Dean, Penina IV, 1129
Dean, Penina IV, 1130
Dean, Penina IV, 1134
Dean, Penina H. IV, 1130
Dean, Phebe IV, 691
Dean, Phebe IV, 811
Dean, Phebe IV, 941
Dean, Phebe Ann IV, 1359
Dean, Phebe Ann IV, 1360
Dean, Phebe B. IV, 807
Dean, Phebe E. IV, 698
Dean, Phebe E. IV, 748
Dean, Phebe W. IV, 811
Dean, Phebe W. IV, 941
Dean, Phebe W. IV, 989
Dean, Polly IV, 811
Dean, Polly IV, 859
Dean, Rachel IV, 811
Dean, Rachel IV, 844
Dean, Rachel S. IV, 801
Dean, Rachel S. IV, 811
Dean, Rachel S. IV, 903
Dean, Rebecca III, 98
Dean, Rhoda I, 714
Dean, Rhoda I, 985
Dean, Rhoda I, 992
Dean, Rhoda IV, 811
Dean, Rhoda IV, 903
Dean, Richard II, 65
Dean, Richard II, 353
Dean, Robert III, 98
Dean, Robert A. III, 98
Dean, Robert B. III, 98
Dean, Roland IV, 1093
Dean, Rowland IV, 1093
Dean, Rowland IV, 1206
Dean, Sally I, 593
Dean, Samuel III, 98
Dean, Samuel III, 314
Dean, Samuel III, 343
Dean, Sarah III, 98
Dean, Sarah III, 314
Dean, Sarah III, 343
Dean, Sarah III, 368
Dean, Sarah A. IV, 1130
Dean, Sarah A. IV, 1133
Dean, Sarah Ann IV, 811
Dean, Sarah Ann IV, 1130
Dean, Sarah B. V, 902
Dean, Sarah Jane I, 632
Dean, Sarah L. IV, 811
Dean, Stephen III, 98
Dean, Stephen IV, 194
Dean, Stephen IV, 470
Dean, Stephen IV, 698
Dean, Stephen IV, 748
Dean, Stephen IV, 811
Dean, Stephen IV, 903
Dean, Stephen B. III, 98
Dean, Susan J. V, 950
Dean, Tazetta E. IV, 811
Dean, Thomas III, 98
Dean, Thomas III, 403
Dean, Uriah I, 588
Dean, Uriah I, 593
Dean, Valeria III, 98
Dean, Walter Hampton I, 632
Dean, Wd. Anne III, 403
Dean, Widow Katharine II, 353
Dean, William III, 98
Dean, William III, 403
Dean, William III, 423
Dean, William IV, 1360
Dean, William W. IV, 811
Dean, William W. IV, 903
Dean, Wm. IV, 1360
Dean, Wm. H. IV, 1313
Deane, Alexander II, 504
Deane, Allen Griswold II, 703
Deane, Angeline VI, 828
Deane, Catherin II, 64
Deane, Catherin II, 65
Deane, Elizabeth III, 98
Deane, James II, 703
Deane, James VI, 828
Deane, Joseph II, 504
Deane, Mamie C. IV, 1313
Deane, Martha Elizabeth II, 703
Deane, Richard II, 64
Deane, Richard II, 65
Deane, Samuel III, 98
Deane, Silas VI, 438
Deane, William VI, 828
Deaner, Elizabeth VI, 810
Deaner, George VI, 810
Deaner, George VI, 847
Deaner, Jathina VI, 847
Deaner, Sarah VI, 810
Deanor, George VI, 817
Deanor, George VI, 846
Deanor, Martha VI, 817
Deanor, Mary VI, 846
Deans, Annie I, 335
Deans, Bessie I, 632
Deans, Bessie I, 643
Deans, Bessie Wilson I, 628
Deans, Charlie I, 335
Deans, Charlie I, 336
Deans, Decia I, 628
Deans, Lizzie I, 336
Deans, Phebe A. I, 304
Deans, Phebe E. I, 304
Deans, Phebe E. I, 305
Deans, Richard II, 677
Deans, Woodard I, 628
Dear, Cloe I, 677
Dear, Cloe I, 681
Deardoff, Abraham VI, 904
Deardoff, Anna VI, 904
Deardoff, Anne VI, 870
Deardoff, Charles H. VI, 904
Deardoff, Charles H. VI, 957
Deardoff, Edna VI, 904
Deardoff, Elizabeth VI, 904
Deardoff, Emily J. VI, 904
Deardoff, Henry VI, 904
Deardoff, Jacob VI, 904
Deardoff, John H. VI, 904
Deardoff, Margarett VI, 904
Deardoff, Mary E. VI, 904
Deardoff, Nancy VI, 904
Deardoff, Peter VI, 904
Deardoff, Peter VI, 923
Deardoff, Peter VI, 957
Deardoff, Peter, Jr. VI, 870
Deardoff, Peter, Sr. VI, 870
Deardoff, Sally L. VI, 904
Deardoff, Samuel VI, 904
Deardoff, Samuel VI, 961
Deardoff, Susan J. VI, 957
Deardorf, Henry VI, 904
Deardorf, Henry VI, 987
Deardorf, Lydia V, 47
Deardorf, Lydia V, 49
Deardorf, Margarett VI, 904
Deardorf, Polly VI, 946
Deardorf, Susanna VI, 987
Deardorff, Apharacia V, 618
Deardorff, Charles H. VI, 957
Deardorff, Christina VI, 946
Deardorff, Henry VI, 946
Deardorff, Olivia A. VI, 957
Deardorff, Peter VI, 896
Deardorff, Peter VI, 957
Dearduff, Abraham VI, 904
Dearduff, Apharacia V, 486
Dearduff, Apharacia V, 505
Dearen, Betsey VI, 996
Dearen, Celia Ann VI, 904
Dearen, Edward W. VI, 904
Dearen, Elizabeth VI, 904
Dearen, Elizabeth VI, 944
Dearen, Elizabeth VI, 951
Dearen, Frances VI, 944
Dearen, Frances E. VI, 904
Dearen, Green VI, 904
Dearen, Jabez VI, 904
Dearen, Jabez VI, 944
Dearen, Jane VI, 934
Dearen, Jemimah VI, 904
Dearen, Joel VI, 904
Dearen, John VI, 904
Dearen, John VI, 915
Dearen, John VI, 964
Dearen, John VI, 996
Dearen, John, Jr. VI, 904
Dearen, Lewis VI, 904
Dearen, Lockey VI, 951
Dearen, Lucinda VI, 904
Dearen, Nancy VI, 904
Dearen, Obedience VI, 904
Dearen, Patsey VI, 904
Dearen, Patty VI, 964
Dearen, Polly VI, 904
Dearen, Rhoda VI, 904
Dearen, Richard VI, 904
Dearen, Richd. VI, 911
Dearen, Silas VI, 904
Dearen, Silas Deeren VI, 904
Dearen, Stephen VI, 904
Dearen, William VI, 904
Dearin, Green VI, 904
Dearin, Green VI, 917
Dearin, Jabez VI, 887
Dearin, Jabez VI, 904
Dearin, Jamimah VI, 869
Dearin, John, Jr. VI, 904
Dearin, Lucinda VI, 904
Dearin, Lucy VI, 869
Dearin, Matilda VI, 915
Dearin, Nancy VI, 904
Dearin, Polly VI, 904
Dearin, Rhoda VI, 904
Dearin, Richard VI, 915
Dearin, Richard VI, 943
Dearin, Richard VI, 1015
Dearin, Silas VI, 904
Dearin, Silas Deeren VI, 904
Dearing, Catharine VI, 960
Dearing, Catharine VI, 1008
Dearing, Celia Ann VI, 904
Dearing, Edward W. VI, 881
Dearing, Edward W. VI, 904
Dearing, Elizabeth VI, 798
Dearing, Elizabeth VI, 810
Dearing, Elizabeth VI, 873
Dearing, Elizabeth VI, 960
Dearing, Elizabeth VI, 971
Dearing, Frances E. VI, 904
Dearing, Gracy VI, 940
Dearing, Jabez VI, 957
Dearing, James VI, 810
Dearing, James G. VI, 795
Dearing, Jamima VI, 940
Dearing, Margaret VI, 799
Dearing, Martha Ann VI, 878
Dearing, Mary J. VI, 957
Dearing, Mason VI, 940
Dearing, Mildred A. VI, 883
Dearing, Nancy VI, 873
Dearing, Nancy VI, 904
Dearing, Polly J. VI, 938
Dearing, Richard VI, 904
Dearing, Richard VI, 958
Dearing, Richard VI, 960
Dearing, Rosamond VI, 798
Dearing, Sally VI, 971
Dearing, Sarah Jane VI, 1022
Dearing, Silas VI, 878
Dearing, Silas VI, 888
Dearing, Silas VI, 995
Dearing, William VI, 904
Dearing, William VI, 938
Dearren, Jamimah VI, 991
Dearren, Joel VI, 991
Dearren, John VI, 904
Dearren, Parkey VI, 991
Dearren, Polly VI, 904
Dearth, Alexander V, 735
Dearth, Barbara V, 735
Dearth, Keturah V, 47
Dearth, Keturah V, 133
Dearth, Orion F. V, 735
Dearth, Susan V, 991
Dearth, Susan V, 992
Death, Mary VI, 382
Death, Mary VI, 462
Deaton, Angelet E. I, 385
Deaton, Camilla F. I, 922
Deaton, Camilla F. I, 931
Deaton, Ila I, 931
Deaton, John A. I, 931
Deaton, Sallie I, 385
Deaton, Sarah I, 385
Deaver, Abraham VI, 486
Deaver, Basel VI, 486
Deaver, Chew VI, 486
Deaver, Jonah VI, 486
Deaver, Margaret VI, 486
Deaver, Mary VI, 486
Deaver, Misael VI, 486
Deaver, Misal VI, 486
Deaver, Sophia VI, 486
Deaves, Isabell II, 65
Deaves, Issabel II, 65
DeB Roop, Mary II, 752
Debo, Daniel P. VI, 936
Debo, Elizabeth VI, 879
Debo, Elizabeth VI, 904
Debo, Henry VI, 904
Debo, Jane VI, 904
Debo, John VI, 904
Debo, Lucy VI, 904
Debo, Malinda H. VI, 925
Debo, Mary VI, 936
Debo, Mary Ann VI, 904
Debo, Michael VI, 879
Debo, Michael, Jr. VI, 904
Debo, Michael, Jr. VI, 995
Debo, Michael, Jr. VI, 1001
Debo, Samuel VI, 904
Debo, Valentine VI, 904
Debo, Wilmoth VI, 904
Deboard, Anna V, 558
Deboard, Clifford V, 558
Deboard, Isaac V, 558
Deboard, Ivy V, 558
Deboard, James V, 558
Deboard, James Marion V, 558
Deboard, Leroy V, 558
Deboard, Maggie V, 558
Deboard, Myrtle V, 558
Deboard, Ottie V, 558
Deboard, Roy V, 558
Deboard, Will V, 558
Deboard, William V, 558
Debooe, Susan III, 195
Deboor, Polly VI, 921
DeBrahm, John Wm. II, 504
Decamp, Anna V, 835
Decamp, Anna V, 836
Decamp, Anna V, 881
DeCamp, Charles V, 668
DeCamp, Chas. V, 668
Decamp, Eli V, 835
Decamp, Eli V, 836
Decamp, Eliza Ann V, 881
Decamp, Hannah V, 835
Decamp, Hannah V, 836
Decamp, Hannah V, 881
Decamp, Hannah D. V, 835
Decamp, Jane V, 835
Decamp, Jane V, 836
Decamp, Jane V, 881
Decamp, John A. V, 881
Decamp, John M. V, 835
Decamp, John M. V, 836
Decamp, John M. V, 881
Decamp, John W. V, 836
DeCamp, Lambert V, 668
Decamp, Lissie V, 992
Decamp, Lydia V, 830
Decamp, Lydia V, 835
Decamp, Lydia V, 836
Decamp, Lydia V, 881
DeCamp, Mary E. V, 668
DeCamp, Mary Edith V, 668
DeCamp, Mary Elizabeth V, 668
DeCamp, Matilda V, 668
DeCamp, Matilda L. V, 668
DeCamp, Matilda Louisa V, 668
Decamp, William V, 836
DeCamp, William E. V, 668
Decamp, Wm. V, 881
Decamp, Wm. V, 992
DeCamp, Wm. E. V, 668
DeCaw, Joseph IV, 1360
Deck, Chloe V, 564
Deck, George V, 564
Deck, J. V. V, 558
Deck, Joe V. V, 558
Deck, Martha V, 558
Decka, John II, 214
Decka, Mary II, 214
Decker, Albert V, 233
Decker, Alice IV, 1313
Decker, Alpharetta V, 233
Decker, Amanda V, 992
Decker, Edith V, 233
Decker, Ellen V, 233
Decker, Henry V, 992
Decker, Ida V, 992
Decker, Levina V, 233
Decker, Louie V, 233
Decker, Lydia V, 233
Decker, Lydia A. V, 233
Decker, Maggie V, 233
Decker, Malissa V, 233
Decker, Mary V, 233
Decker, Mary E. V, 233
Decker, Melissa V, 233
Decker, Rachel V, 233
Decker, Richard C. V, 992
Decker, Sarah M. I, 1150
Decker, Sylvester V, 233
Decker, Webster V, 233
Decker, Willia A. V, 992
Decker, Wm. V, 992
Decker, Wm. E. V, 992
Decks, Achilles V, 47
Decks, Agatha V, 47
Decon, John II, 353
Decon, Mary II, 214
Decost, Caroline III, 184
Decost, Franklin III, 184
Decou, Isaac II, 318
Decou, Joseph IV, 1360
DeCou, Ruth Anna II, 856
DeCou, Wm. II, 856
DeCoursey, Sarah Jane II, 813
Decow, Abraham II, 353
Decow, Amelia II, 214
Decow, Amelia II, 267
Decow, Ann II, 214
Decow, Ann II, 246
Decow, Ann Lowrie II, 201
Decow, Charles S. II, 214
Decow, Hannah II, 171
Decow, Hannah II, 178
Decow, Hannah II, 214
Decow, Hannah II, 237
Decow, Hannah II, 245
Decow, Hannah II, 353
Decow, Hannah II, 504
Decow, Hannah II, 516
Decow, Hannah, Jr. II, 214
Decow, Isaac II, 171
Decow, Isaac II, 214
Decow, Isaac II, 245
Decow, Jacob II, 353
Decow, John II, 193
Decow, John II, 214
Decow, John, Jr. II, 65
Decow, John, Jr. II, 214
Decow, Joseph II, 214
Decow, Martha II, 214
Decow, Mary II, 65
Decow, Mary II, 201
Decow, Mary II, 214
Decow, Mary II, 215
Decow, Mary II, 267
Decow, Rebecca II, 213
Decow, Rebecca II, 214
Decow, Robert II, 215
Decow, Robert Thomas II, 215
Decow, Samuel II, 214
Decow, Samuel II, 267
Decow, Sarah II, 193
Decow, Sarah II, 214
Decow, Thomas II, 201
Decow, Thomas II, 214
Decow, William III, 98
Dederick, Thomas V, 165
Dedmond, Thomas VI, 908
Dedric, Alece V. V, 486
Dedric, Mary V, 486
Dedrick, Alice V, 482
Dedrick, Alice V, 486
Dedrick, Anna L. V, 558
Dedrick, Ella V, 166
Dedrick, Eva V, 166
Dedrick, Thomas V, 165
Deeble, Elisabeth II, 504
Deeble, Elisabeth II, 579
Deeble, Elisabeth II, 646
Deeble, Elizabeth II, 504
Deeble, George II, 504
Deeble, Richard II, 504
Deeds, Pearl VI, 382
Deeds, Teresa III, 349
Deem, Abigail IV, 808
Deem, Catharine VI, 811
Deem, John VI, 811
Deems, Ann IV, 28
Deems, Ann IV, 54
Deems, Eliza P. IV, 1249
Deems, Elizabeth IV, 28
Deems, Mark IV, 28
Deems, Mark IV, 54
Deen, Elizabeth I, 536
Deen, Elizabeth I, 911
Deen, Guli Elma I, 911
Deen, Gulielma I, 911
Deen, Isaac I, 911
Deen, Isaac I, 914
Deen, Leaha II, 65
Deen, Leal II, 65
Deen, Lydia I, 593
Deen, Margret II, 49
Deen, Margret II, 65
Deen, Stephen IV, 470
Deen, Uriah I, 593
Deen, Widow Elizabeth I, 911
Deen, Widow Elizabeth I, 914
Deene, Alice I, 1118
Deene, Alice I, 1135
Deener, Dezena VI, 800
Deener, Jacob VI, 811
Deener, Sally VI, 811
Deering, Celissa V, 992
Deering, Clara S. V, 992
Deering, Elizabeth VI, 806
Deering, James VI, 806
Deering, James VI, 821
Deering, James VI, 864
Deering, Lucius V, 992
Deering, Milly VI, 821
Deering, Nancy VI, 864
Deering, Sally VI, 806
Deetrick, Olive E. V, 735
Deetrick, Olive E. V, 737
Defebaugh, Ann V, 618
Defebaugh, Ann V, 622
Defenbaugh, Ray G. IV, 698
Deffebaugh, Ann V, 618
Deffield, Wilma V, 992
Defoe, Mary VI, 904
Defoe, Zacharkah VI, 904
Deford, Esther I, 1150
Deford, James Henry I, 1150

Deford, Mary L. R. I, 1150
Defrance, Mary IV, 194
Defrance, Mary IV, 269
Degarma, Dorothy IV, 194
Degarma, Maud IV, 194
Degarma, Mildred IV, 194
Degarma, Ola IV, 194
Degarmo, Ola May IV, 470
DeGarmore, Ella IV, 194
DeGarmore, Iva IV, 194
DeGarmore, Rachel IV, 194
Degood, Elizabeth IV, 1155
Degrauw, Jennie III, 424
Degroat, Emily V, 618
Degroat, Emily V, 635
Degroot, Sarah III, 49
Degroot, Sarah III, 99
Dehaven, Albert V, 166
Dehaven, Amos W. V, 166
Dehaven, Bertha E. V, 166
Dehaven, Emeline V, 166
Dehaven, Emma V, 166
Dehaven, Isaac VI, 904
DeHaven, Mary C. II, 856
Dehaven, Peter V, 166
Dehaven, Prudence VI, 904
Deilks, Jerusha V, 418
Deilks, John V, 418
Deilks, Mary Edith V, 418
Deirns, Timothy VI, 813
Deison, Charles VI, 811
Deison, Paulina VI, 824
Deison, Sally M. VI, 811
Deison, Sarah VI, 824
Deitchel, Carl IV, 1249
Deitchel, Clarence IV, 1249
Deitchle, Carl IV, 1249
Deitchle, Clarence IV, 1249
Deitchle, Lula IV, 1249
DeJarnett, John VI, 811
DeJarnett, John M. VI, 811
DeJarnett, Judith VI, 811
DeJarnett, Nancy VI, 811
DeJarnett, Walker VI, 811
DeJarnette, Betsey VI, 801
DeJarnette, Daniel VI, 861
DeJarnette, James VI, 801
DeJarnette, Walter VI, 863
DeKoning, Blanche R. IV, 1313
DeKoning, Jacob IV, 1313
Delamater, Ruth S. III, 99
Delancy, Calvin IV, 1235
Delancy, Lucy IV, 1235
Delancy, Lucy A. IV, 1235
Delaney, Bessie IV, 194
Delaney, Dessie IV, 194
Delaney, Hannah II, 65
Delaney, Margaret II, 504
Delaney, Margaret II, 639
Delano, Amasa I, 138
Delano, Anne I, 121
Delano, Eliza Howland III, 99
Delano, Mary H. III, 99
Delanoy, Annie III, 99
Delanoy, Annie W. III, 99
Delanoy, Annie W. III, 373
Delanoy, Emma III, 99
Delanoy, John A. III, 99
Delanoy, Wd. Annie W. III, 86
Delanoy, William C. III, 99
Delanoy, Wm. C. III, 373
Delanoy, Wm. P. III, 86
Delantes, Laura IV, 992
Delany, Bessie V, 1014
Delany, Hannah II, 96
Delany, Martha VI, 310
Delany, Martha VI, 904
Delany, Mary II, 353
Delany, Thomas VI, 310
Delany, Thomas VI, 904
Delaphane, Carrie V, 668
Delaphane, Gibson V, 668
Delaphane, Martha V, 668
Delaphane, Wm. V, 668
Delaplain, Christian II, 458
Delaplain, Christian II, 504
Delaplain, Elizabeth II, 504
Delaplain, Eve II, 458
Delaplain, Eve II, 504
Delaplain, James II, 504
Delaplain, Judith II, 504
Delaplain, Mary II, 504
Delaplain, Nicholas II, 504
Delaplain, Susanna II, 483
Delaplain, Susanna II, 504
Delaplaine, ??? III, 99
Delaplaine, Abigail II, 215
Delaplaine, Abigail II, 219
Delaplaine, Abigail III, 99
Delaplaine, Charlotte III, 99
Delaplaine, Collin R. III, 99
Delaplaine, Collins III, 99
Delaplaine, Easter III, 407
Delaplaine, Easter III, 476
Delaplaine, Elias III, 99
Delaplaine, Elizabeth III, 99
Delaplaine, Elizabeth III, 168
DeLaplaine, Elizabeth III, 221
Delaplaine, Esther III, 99
Delaplaine, Esther III, 192
Delaplaine, Esther III, 197
Delaplaine, Euphemia III, 99
Delaplaine, Hannah III, 68
Delaplaine, Hannah III, 74
Delaplaine, Hannah III, 99
Delaplaine, Isaac III, 99
Delaplaine, James III, 74
Delaplaine, James III, 99
Delaplaine, Joseph II, 215
Delaplaine, Joseph II, 219
Delaplaine, Joseph III, 68
Delaplaine, Joseph III, 99
DeLaplaine, Joseph III, 221
Delaplaine, Joseph, Jr. III, 406
Delaplaine, Joshua II, 215
Delaplaine, Joshua III, 99
Delaplaine, Joshua III, 197
Delaplaine, Joshua III, 407
Delaplaine, Joshua III, 476
Delaplaine, Joshua, Jr. III, 99
Delaplaine, Margaret III, 99
Delaplaine, Mary II, 215
Delaplaine, Mary III, 99
Delaplaine, Nicholas III, 99
Delaplaine, Nicholas III, 168
Delaplaine, Phebe III, 99
Delaplaine, Phebe III, 113
Delaplaine, Philadelphia III, 99
Delaplaine, Philadelphia III, 406
Delaplaine, Philadelphia III, 444
Delaplaine, Philah III, 99
Delaplaine, Samuel III, 99
Delaplaine, Sarah III, 99
Delaplane, Joshua II, 204
Delaplane, Judith II, 504
Delaplane, Lewis V, 618
Delaplane, Mary II, 204
Delaplane, Mary II, 215
Delaplane, Wm. E. V, 618
Delaplayne, Elizabeth II, 504
Delaplayne, Elizabeth II, 551
Delaplayne, Nicholas II, 504
Delaplayne, Nicholas II, 551
Delatush, Elizabeth II, 215
Delaval, Lydia A. III, 403
Delaval, Lydia A. III, 407
Delavall, Hannah II, 353
Delavall, Hannah II, 504
Delavall, Hannah II, 549
Delavall, Hannah II, 583
Delavall, Hannah III, 99
Delavall, Hannah III, 211
Delavall, John II, 353
Delavall, John II, 504
Delavall, John II, 583
Delavall, John III, 99
Delavall, John III, 211
Delavall, Mary II, 353
Delavall, Mary III, 99
Delavall, Thomas III, 99
Delbon, Ange III, 407
Delbon, Ange III, 430
Delbon, Argia D. III, 430
Delbon, Argie D. III, 407
Delbon, Melisande III, 430
Delbon, Mesalinda III, 407
Delbridge, Milley VI, 904
Delbridge, Robert VI, 904
Deleany, Callie May V, 558
Deleplane, Carrie V, 618
Deleplane, Guy E. V, 618
Deleplane, Lewis V, 618
Deleplane, Lewis R. V, 618
Deleplane, Martha V, 668
Deleplane, William V, 166
Deleplane, Wm. V, 618
Deleplane, Wm. E. V, 618
Deliplane, William V, 166
Deliplane, Wm. E. V, 166
Dell, Flora V, 985
Dell, Robert II, 443
Dell-Doing, Florence VI, 771
Dellaplane, Wm. V, 618
Dellefosse, Hope II, 215
Dellice, John VI, 904
Dellice, Salley VI, 904
Dellis, Brintha J. VI, 950
Dellis, Carline VI, 932
Dellis, Caroline VI, 904
Dellis, Hannah VI, 950
Dellis, John VI, 904
Dellis, John R. VI, 932
Dellis, John, Jr. VI, 904
Dellis, Joseph J. VI, 904
Dellis, Ludy Ann VI, 904
Dellis, Phebe VI, 904
Dellis, Robert VI, 904
Dellis, Salley VI, 904
Delliss, John R. VI, 969
Delmuth, Garnet IV, 182
Delmuth, Garnet Brown IV, 194
Delmuth, Lizzie IV, 182
Delmuth, Mabel Hawthorn IV, 182
Delon, Ann I, 98
Delon, Ann I, 137
Delon, Caroline I, 138
Delon, Caroline I, 172
Delon, David I, 98
Delon, Hannah I, 98
Delon, Hannah I, 137
Delon, Henry I, 98
Delon, Henry I, 133
Delon, Henry I, 137
Delon, Henry I, 138
Delon, Henry I, 147
Delon, Isaiah I, 138
Delon, Jesse I, 98
Delon, Jesse I, 137
Delon, Jonathan I, 98
Delon, Jonathan I, 138
Delon, Joseph I, 138
Delon, Josiah I, 98
Delon, Margaret I, 98
Delon, Margaret I, 138
Delon, Mark I, 98
Delon, Mark I, 137
Delon, Mark A. I, 98
Delon, Mark A. I, 138
Delon, Mark Anthony I, 137
Delon, Mark Anthony I, 163
Delon, Mary I, 98
Delon, Mary I, 133
Delon, Mary I, 137
Delon, Mary I, 163
Delon, Miriam I, 98
Delon, Miriam I, 137
Delon, Miriam I, 877
Delon, Nancy I, 98
Delon, Nancy I, 134
Delon, Nancy I, 137
Delon, Nancy I, 138
Delon, Nancy I, 143
Delon, Nathan I, 98
Delon, Nathan I, 134
Delon, Nathan I, 137
Delon, Penelope I, 98
Delon, Peniah I, 808
Delon, Peninah I, 98
Delon, Peninah I, 137
Delon, Penniah I, 808
Delon, Penninah I, 133
Delon, Penninah I, 137
Delon, Penninah I, 138
Delon, Penninah I, 147
Delon, Reuben I, 98
Delon, Samuel I, 98
Delon, Samuel I, 808
Delon, Sarah I, 98
Delon, Sarah I, 131
Delon, Sarah I, 137
Delon, Simeon I, 98
Delon, Simeon I, 137
Delon, William I, 137
Delon, William I, 138
Delon, Williams I, 98
Delong, Bert V, 992
Delong, Chora IV, 1276
Delong, Cora IV, 1276
Delong, Henry VI, 904
Delong, Nancy VI, 904
Delong, William IV, 1276
Delong, Wm. IV, 1276
DeLottee, Minnie V, 735
Delp, Adalaide Fenimore II, 856
Delp, Adalaide Fenimore II, 860
Delp, Adelaide II, 856
Delp, Anna P. II, 856
Delp, Anna P. II, 860
Delp, Wm. II, 856
Delp, Wm. M. II, 860
Delplaine, Joseph, Jr. III, 444
Delsomme, Anna Frances III, 339
Delworth, Jonathan II, 353
Delworth, Thomas II, 353
Delzell, Alfretta IV, 964
Delzell, Alpharetta IV, 947
Delzell, George IV, 947
Delzell, Harry IV, 947
Delzell, Hazel IV, 947
Delzell, Isadore Pearl IV, 964
Delzell, Otley V. IV, 964
Delzell, Phebe IV, 698
Demaine, Lydia Emily IV, 194
Deman, Nancy J. V, 992
Demans, Phebe I, 1028
Demans, Phebe I, 1035
Demarest, Rebecca III, 28
DeMaret, Catharine IV, 1313
Demark, Bethany Eliza I, 340
Demby, Pauline IV, 194
Demford, Samuel II, 992
DeMilt, ??? III, 407
Demilt, Benjamin III, 99
Demilt, Elizabeth III, 99
DeMilt, Mary III, 407
DeMilt, Obadiah III, 407
Demilt, Peter III, 99
Demilt, Samuel III, 99
Demilt, Thomas III, 99
Deming, Margaret IV, 194
Deming, Margaret IV, 249
Demint, Clara V, 992
Demint, Clarence V, 992
Demint, Drusella V, 992
Demint, Drusilla J. V, 992
Demint, Emma V, 992
Demint, Frank V, 992
DeMint, Frank V, 992
Demint, Frank V, 992
Demint, Golda V, 992
Demint, Jesse V, 992
Demint, John V, 992
Demint, John A. V, 992
Demint, Lucy V, 992
Demint, Lydian V, 992
Demint, Martha V, 992
Demint, Marthie V, 992
Demint, Merlle V, 992
Demint, Sherman V, 992
Demint, Susan V, 992
Demmon, Delilah V, 992
Demmon, Jane V, 992
Demmon, Wm. V, 992
Demoss, Ann VI, 904
Demoss, Delilah V, 992
Demoss, James I, 495
Demoss, James VI, 904
Demoss, Joanna I, 536
Demoss, Joanna I, 1028
Demoss, Joanna I, 1038
Demoss, Phebe I, 495
Demoss, Thomas VI, 904
Demoss, Wm. W. V, 992
Demoss, Zana VI, 904
Dempsey, Aneliza IV, 1276
Dempsey, John V, 383
Dempsey, John Wesley V, 992
Dempsey, Joseph IV, 407
Dempsey, Rachel D. II, 318
Dempsey, Rachel D. II, 323
Dempter, Ruth H. IV, 194
Demsey, Sarah IV, 29
Demspter, Joseph S. IV, 194
Demspter, Ruth H. IV, 194
Den, Anna II, 26
Den, David II, 26
Den, Elizabeth II, 26
Den, John II, 26
Den, John, Jr. II, 26
Den, Mary II, 26
Den, Rachel II, 26
Den, Rebecca II, 26
Den, Rhoda II, 26
Den, Richard II, 26
Den, Sarah II, 26
Den, Susannah II, 26
Den, Wm. II, 26
Denavant, Eldridge VI, 852
Denavant, Francis VI, 852
Denby, Thomas I, 138
Dendelsbeck, Elizabeth Ann II, 117
Dendelsbeck, Elizabeth Ann II, 120
Dendinger, Dr. W. C. I, 632
Dendinger, Dr. W. C. I, 636
Dendinger, Eunice I, 615
Dendinger, Eunice I, 632
Dendinger, Eunice I, 636
Dendinger, Walter Clark I, 615
Denel, Sarah III, 106
Dener, Elizabeth VI, 811
Dener, George VI, 847
Dener, John VI, 811
Dener, Mary M. VI, 811
Dener, Sarah VI, 847
Dener, William VI, 811
Denes, Grass II, 66
Denham, Anna IV, 1313
Denham, Mabel IV, 1313
Denham, Thomas II, 353
Denham, Thomas II, 504
Denhouse, Lewis, Jr. IV, 811
Denice, Anne II, 66
Denice, Anne II, 96
Denier, George VI, 824
Denis, Absolem I, 745
Denis, Branson I, 745
Denis, Cyntha I, 745
Denis, Delilah I, 745
Denis, Elisha I, 745
Denis, Elizabeth I, 745
Denis, Fanny I, 745
Denis, Jesse I, 536
Denis, Jesse I, 745
Denis, Joseph I, 745
Denis, Lucinda I, 745
Denis, Mahlon I, 745
Denis, Margaret I, 745
Denis, Mary I, 745
Denis, Mary IV, 107
Denis, Nathan I, 745
Denis, Thomas I, 745
Denis, William I, 745
Denis, William IV, 1276
Denis, Wilson I, 745
Denise, Cornelius II, 504
Denise, Cornelius II, 510
Denise, Mary II, 504
Denise, Mary II, 510
Denison, Catharine V, 992
Denkhaus, Ella IV, 811
Denkhaus, Lewis IV, 811
Denkhaus, Lewis, Jr. IV, 811
Denkhaus, Vesta IV, 811
Denkhous, Ella IV, 760
Denkhous, Grace IV, 760
Denkhous, Louis IV, 760
Denlinger, Dorothy III, 100
Denlinger, Henry K. III, 100
Denlinger, Janet III, 100
Denlinger, Rebecca V, 47
Denlinger, Rebecca V, 64
Denman, Chas. W. IV, 1276
Denman, Enola IV, 1206
Denman, Monroe IV, 1206
Denman, Sarah IV, 1206
Denn, Amos II, 26
Denn, Ann II, 26
Denn, Ann II, 29
Denn, Ann II, 66
Denn, Anna II, 26
Denn, Anna II, 28
Denn, Anna H. II, 856
Denn, Anne II, 117
Denn, Anne II, 118
Denn, Daniel II, 26
Denn, David II, 26
Denn, Elizabeth II, 26
Denn, Elizabeth II, 29
Denn, Elizabeth II, 34
Denn, Elizabeth II, 51
Denn, Elizabeth II, 59
Denn, Elizabeth II, 65
Denn, Elizabeth II, 66
Denn, Elizabeth II, 83
Denn, Elizabeth II, 85
Denn, Elizabeth II, 93
Denn, Elizabeth II, 110
Denn, Elizabeth II, 504
Denn, Elizabeth II, 664
Denn, Elizabeth, Jr. II, 66
Denn, Hannah II, 815
Denn, James II, 26
Denn, James II, 34
Denn, James II, 65
Denn, James II, 66
Denn, James II, 83
Denn, James II, 85
Denn, John II, 26
Denn, John II, 28
Denn, John II, 29
Denn, John II, 51
Denn, John II, 65
Denn, John II, 66
Denn, John II, 97
Denn, John II, 117
Denn, John II, 118
Denn, John II, 504
Denn, John Maddock II, 26
Denn, John Madox II, 59
Denn, John Madox II, 65
Denn, John, Jr. II, 26
Denn, John, Jr. II, 66
Denn, John, Jr. II, 97
Denn, John, Jr. II, 117
Denn, John, Jr. II, 118
Denn, Leah II, 26
Denn, Leah II, 66
Denn, Leah II, 90
Denn, Lydia II, 66
Denn, Lydia II, 101
Denn, Lydia II, 102
Denn, Marcy II, 26

Denn, Margaret II, 26
Denn, Margaret II, 65
Denn, Margaret II, 66
Denn, Margaret II, 75
Denn, Margaret II, 131
Denn, Margret II, 65
Denn, Mary II, 26
Denn, Mary II, 65
Denn, Mary II, 90
Denn, Mercy II, 65
Denn, Mercy II, 107
Denn, Naomi II, 65
Denn, Naomi II, 107
Denn, Naomy II, 26
Denn, Oscar R. II, 131
Denn, Paul II, 26
Denn, Paul II, 66
Denn, Paul II, 101
Denn, Rachel II, 26
Denn, Rachel II, 29
Denn, Rachel II, 66
Denn, Rachel II, 73
Denn, Rachel II, 117
Denn, Rachel II, 118
Denn, Rachel J. II, 29
Denn, Rebecca II, 26
Denn, Rhoda II, 26
Denn, Rhoda II, 28
Denn, Rhoda II, 29
Denn, Rhoda II, 66
Denn, Rhoda II, 97
Denn, Rhoda II, 117
Denn, Rhoda II, 118
Denn, Richard II, 26
Denn, Samuel II, 29
Denn, Samuel II, 504
Denn, Sarah II, 26
Denn, Susannah II, 26
Denn, Susannah II, 66
Denn, Susannah II, 97
Denn, Winifred II, 131
Denn, Wm. II, 26
Denn, Wm. II, 28
Dennam, Anna IV, 1313
Denney, Azariah I, 962
Denney, Azariah V, 836
Denney, David V, 836
Denney, David B. V, 836
Denney, Eli V, 836
Denney, Elizabeth I, 1009
Denney, Elizabeth V, 836
Denney, Esther V, 836
Denney, Francis V, 836
Denney, Henry V, 836
Denney, Huldah Ann V, 836
Denney, James V, 836
Denney, Joel V, 836
Denney, John I, 962
Denney, John V, 836
Denney, Jonathan V, 836
Denney, Jordan V, 836
Denney, Jorden I, 962
Denney, Jorden V, 836
Denney, Jordon V, 836
Denney, Joseph V, 836
Denney, Keziah V, 836
Denney, Lazarus I, 962
Denney, Lazarus I, 1009
Denney, Lazarus V, 826
Denney, Lazarus V, 836
Denney, Lazerus I, 962
Denney, Lazzirous I, 1009
Denney, Mahlon V, 836
Denney, Margaret V, 836
Denney, Martha Jane Eeks V, 836
Denney, Mary V, 826
Denney, Mary V, 836
Denney, Michael V, 836
Denney, Michel V, 836
Denney, Rebecca V, 836
Denney, Reuben V, 836
Denney, Ruben V, 836
Denney, Sarah I, 1009
Denney, Sarah V, 836
Denney, Shubal V, 836
Denney, Shubeal V, 836
Denney, Shubel I, 962
Denney, Shubel V, 836
Denney, Susana V, 836
Denney, Susanna I, 1009
Denney, Susanna V, 836
Denney, Susannah V, 836
Denney, Wd. Rebecca V, 836
Denney, William I, 962
Denney, William V, 836
Dennie, Joseph III, 100
Dennie, Mary III, 100
Dennie, Sarah III, 347
Dennie, Sarah L. III, 100
Dennie, Thomas III, 100
Dennie, Thomas III, 347
Dennin, Andrew VI, 382
Dennin, Anthony VI, 382
Dennin, Eleanor VI, 382
Dennin, John VI, 382
Dennin, Joseph VI, 382
Dennin, Rachel VI, 382
Dennin, Susannah VI, 382
Dennin, William VI, 382
Denning, John II, 856
Denning, John IV, 620
Denning, Margaret IV, 194
Dennis, Aaron IV, 83
Dennis, Aaron IV, 125
Dennis, Aaron IV, 470
Dennis, Aaron IV, 521
Dennis, Abraham II, 992
Dennis, Abram II, 992
Dennis, Absalom I, 652
Dennis, Absalom I, 678
Dennis, Absalom I, 689
Dennis, Absalom I, 759
Dennis, Absolam I, 759
Dennis, Albert V, 735
Dennis, Albert H. V, 735
Dennis, Alfred III, 100
Dennis, Alfred III, 300
Dennis, Alice J. IV, 194
Dennis, Amy II, 291
Dennis, Ann I, 496
Dennis, Ann I, 536
Dennis, Ann II, 26
Dennis, Ann II, 66
Dennis, Ann II, 504
Dennis, Ann VI, 735
Dennis, Ann VI, 738
Dennis, Ann VI, 946
Dennis, Anna Irene I, 759
Dennis, Anne II, 66
Dennis, Arad IV, 1155
Dennis, Arad P. IV, 1155
Dennis, Asenath IV, 83
Dennis, Asenith IV, 83
Dennis, Asenith IV, 106
Dennis, Benjamin II, 353
Dennis, Benjamin II, 992
Dennis, Caroline F. VI, 735
Dennis, Caroline F. VI, 738
Dennis, Ceasar VI, 888
Dennis, Ceaser VI, 992
Dennis, Charles IV, 698
Dennis, Charles C. VI, 735
Dennis, Charles C. VI, 738
Dennis, Clara V, 735
Dennis, Cornelius II, 504
Dennis, David W. V, 668
Dennis, David Worth V, 668
Dennis, Deborah IV, 83
Dennis, Deborah IV, 125
Dennis, Delila I, 677
Dennis, Delilah I, 605
Dennis, Delilah I, 652
Dennis, Delilah I, 677
Dennis, Delilah I, 678
Dennis, Delilah I, 680
Dennis, Delilah I, 741
Dennis, Delilah I, 759
Dennis, Delilah I, 929
Dennis, Delilah Maria I, 759
Dennis, Dorcas II, 26
Dennis, Ebenezer II, 1072
Dennis, Edith IV, 83
Dennis, Edith S. V, 47
Dennis, Edward II, 26
Dennis, Edward G. II, 215
Dennis, Edward G. II, 286
Dennis, Elisha I, 605
Dennis, Elisha I, 607
Dennis, Elisha I, 652
Dennis, Elisha I, 675
Dennis, Elisha I, 677
Dennis, Elisha I, 759
Dennis, Elisha VI, 946
Dennis, Eliza II, 1072
Dennis, Eliza II, 1074
Dennis, Eliza III, 31
Dennis, Eliza III, 100
Dennis, Elizabeth I, 385
Dennis, Elizabeth I, 495
Dennis, Elizabeth I, 496
Dennis, Elizabeth I, 652
Dennis, Elizabeth I, 677
Dennis, Elizabeth I, 692
Dennis, Elizabeth I, 741
Dennis, Elizabeth II, 26
Dennis, Elizabeth II, 64
Dennis, Elizabeth II, 66
Dennis, Elizabeth II, 80
Dennis, Elizabeth II, 134
Dennis, Elizabeth II, 286
Dennis, Elizabeth II, 291
Dennis, Elizabeth V, 618
Dennis, Elizabeth VI, 861
Dennis, Elizabeth VI, 904
Dennis, Elizabeth VI, 946
Dennis, Emily V, 618
Dennis, Emily V, 639
Dennis, Esther II, 992
Dennis, Esther IV, 698
Dennis, Eunice I, 678
Dennis, Eunice I, 689
Dennis, Eunice I, 759
Dennis, Fauney I, 652
Dennis, Flavia Sarah I, 759
Dennis, Flora IV, 1155
Dennis, Forrest V, 735
Dennis, Frances III, 100
Dennis, Frances III, 300
Dennis, Frances IV, 1360
Dennis, Frank IV, 1155
Dennis, George II, 1072
Dennis, Glenn V, 735
Dennis, Grace II, 26
Dennis, Grace II, 51
Dennis, Grace II, 56
Dennis, Grace II, 66
Dennis, Grace II, 353
Dennis, Grace IV, 1053
Dennis, Grace IV, 1093
Dennis, Grass II, 66
Dennis, Hannah II, 26
Dennis, Hannah II, 66
Dennis, Hannah II, 105
Dennis, Hannah II, 286
Dennis, Hannah II, 504
Dennis, Hannah II, 992
Dennis, Hannah II, 1052
Dennis, Hannah II, 1072
Dennis, Hannah II, 1076
Dennis, Hannah III, 100
Dennis, Hannah, Jr. II, 1072
Dennis, Hattie IV, 1155
Dennis, Henry II, 26
Dennis, Henry II, 51
Dennis, Henry II, 66
Dennis, Henry II, 134
Dennis, Henry II, 291
Dennis, Henry II, 353
Dennis, Henry II, 504
Dennis, Henry II, 588
Dennis, Henry G. II, 215
Dennis, Henry G. II, 286
Dennis, Hezekiah IV, 384
Dennis, Howard V, 735
Dennis, Increase IV, 384
Dennis, Increase IV, 447
Dennis, Increase W. IV, 384
Dennis, Isaac H. VI, 861
Dennis, Jacob IV, 1360
Dennis, James II, 66
Dennis, James VI, 904
Dennis, James VI, 910
Dennis, Jane II, 504
Dennis, Jane IV, 698
Dennis, Jesse I, 536
Dennis, Jesse I, 573
Dennis, Jesse I, 652
Dennis, Jesse I, 759
Dennis, Jesse I, 808
Dennis, Jesse II, 291
Dennis, John II, 26
Dennis, John II, 66
Dennis, John II, 100
Dennis, John II, 353
Dennis, John II, 504
Dennis, John IV, 83
Dennis, John IV, 447
Dennis, John Speakman II, 992
Dennis, John, Jr. IV, 83
Dennis, Jonathan II, 26
Dennis, Jonathan II, 58
Dennis, Jonathan II, 66
Dennis, Jonathan II, 286
Dennis, Jonathan II, 353
Dennis, Jonathan II, 504
Dennis, Jonathan II, 992
Dennis, Joseph I, 496
Dennis, Joseph I, 536
Dennis, Joseph II, 26
Dennis, Joseph II, 66
Dennis, Joseph II, 992
Dennis, Kesiah IV, 83
Dennis, Kezia II, 992
Dennis, Keziah IV, 83
Dennis, L. Helen II, 286
Dennis, L. Helen II, 290
Dennis, L. R. VI, 241
Dennis, Lane IV, 1037
Dennis, Lizzie IV, 1037
Dennis, Lizzie IV, 1313
Dennis, Lizzie M. IV, 1313
Dennis, Lottie IV, 1155
Dennis, Louisa Martha II, 286
Dennis, Louise II, 286
Dennis, Louise II, 290
Dennis, Louise Martha II, 290
Dennis, Luce II, 51
Dennis, Luce II, 66
Dennis, Lucy II, 26
Dennis, Lucy II, 40
Dennis, Lucy Ann V, 618
Dennis, Lucy Ann V, 639
Dennis, Luisa Betsey I, 536
Dennis, Lusena I, 536
Dennis, Lydia II, 992
Dennis, Mahlon I, 759
Dennis, Malen I, 652
Dennis, Margaret I, 675
Dennis, Margaret I, 677
Dennis, Margaret I, 759
Dennis, Martha II, 26
Dennis, Martha II, 504
Dennis, Martha II, 588
Dennis, Martha IV, 125
Dennis, Mary I, 652
Dennis, Mary II, 26
Dennis, Mary II, 66
Dennis, Mary II, 100
Dennis, Mary II, 102
Dennis, Mary II, 134
Dennis, Mary II, 353
Dennis, Mary II, 504
Dennis, Mary II, 992
Dennis, Mary IV, 83
Dennis, Mary IV, 194
Dennis, Mary IV, 220
Dennis, Mary IV, 1053
Dennis, Mary IV, 1056
Dennis, Mary IV, 1276
Dennis, Mary V, 486
Dennis, Mary VI, 910
Dennis, Mary W. II, 291
Dennis, Miriam IV, 1088
Dennis, Miriam IV, 1093
Dennis, Miriam A. IV, 1093
Dennis, Naomi II, 66
Dennis, Naomi II, 100
Dennis, Naomy II, 58
Dennis, Naomy II, 66
Dennis, Nathan I, 652
Dennis, Nathan V, 486
Dennis, Phebe IV, 447
Dennis, Philip II, 26
Dennis, Philip II, 40
Dennis, Philip II, 51
Dennis, Philip II, 66
Dennis, Philip, Jr. II, 26
Dennis, Philip, Jr. II, 66
Dennis, Philip, Jr. II, 105
Dennis, Philip, Jr. II, 992
Dennis, Phillip II, 992
Dennis, Prudence II, 26
Dennis, Rachel II, 26
Dennis, Rachel II, 40
Dennis, Rachel II, 65
Dennis, Rachel II, 66
Dennis, Rachel II, 99
Dennis, Rachel II, 353
Dennis, Rachel IV, 83
Dennis, Rebeca I, 759
Dennis, Rebecca I, 677
Dennis, Rebecca I, 678
Dennis, Rebecca I, 759
Dennis, Rebecca II, 353
Dennis, Ruth I, 605
Dennis, Ruth I, 607
Dennis, Ruth I, 759
Dennis, Samuel II, 26
Dennis, Samuel II, 66
Dennis, Samuel II, 80
Dennis, Samuel II, 102
Dennis, Samuel II, 504
Dennis, Samuel II, 533
Dennis, Samuel II, 992
Dennis, Samuel D. II, 286
Dennis, Sarah I, 495
Dennis, Sarah I, 536
Dennis, Sarah II, 26
Dennis, Sarah II, 66
Dennis, Sarah II, 87
Dennis, Sarah II, 89
Dennis, Sarah II, 992
Dennis, Sarah II, 993
Dennis, Sarah IV, 1155
Dennis, Susan B. II, 215
Dennis, Susan B. II, 286
Dennis, Susan B. II, 289
Dennis, Thomas I, 495
Dennis, Thomas I, 496
Dennis, Thomas I, 536
Dennis, Thomas I, 652
Dennis, Thomas I, 677
Dennis, Thomas I, 692
Dennis, Thomas I, 759
Dennis, Thomas II, 353
Dennis, Thomas II, 504
Dennis, Thomas V, 618
Dennis, Thomas, Jr. I, 645
Dennis, Thos. V, 639
Dennis, Townsend II, 992
Dennis, Unity I, 536
Dennis, Unity I, 573
Dennis, Unity I, 759
Dennis, William I, 496
Dennis, William I, 605
Dennis, William I, 652
Dennis, William I, 677
Dennis, William I, 678
Dennis, William I, 680
Dennis, William I, 741
Dennis, William I, 759
Dennis, William II, 215
Dennis, William II, 286
Dennis, William II, 289
Dennis, William IV, 1276
Dennis, William Brown II, 286
Dennis, William Brown II, 290
Dennis, William Harvey II, 286
Dennis, William Harvey II, 290
Dennis, William, Jr. I, 759
Dennis, Wilmet III, 481
Dennis, Wilmot III, 100
Dennis, Wilmot III, 379
Dennis, Winifred M. III, 100
Dennis, Winifred M. III, 300
Dennison, Charles IV, 1249
Dennison, Ellen C. II, 791
Dennison, Goldie IV, 1249
Dennison, Jane Parrish II, 791
Dennison, Laura IV, 1249
Dennison, Maria IV, 1249
Dennison, Maris IV, 1249
Denniss, Ann II, 504
Denniss, Benjamin II, 353
Denniss, Elizabeth I, 385
Denniss, Jane II, 504
Denniss, Johanniss II, 443
Denniss, John II, 443
Denniss, Thomas II, 504
Dennon, Alda W. V, 233
Dennon, Hiram V, 233
Dennon, Jimmy J. V, 233
Dennon, Mary Ann V, 233
Dennon, Rachel E. V, 233
Denny, ??? III, 100
Denny, Azariah V, 836
Denny, Azariah V, 868
Denny, David V, 836
Denny, David B. V, 836
Denny, Dillty I, 536
Denny, Eli V, 836
Denny, Elizabeth I, 985
Denny, Elizabeth V, 833
Denny, Elizabeth V, 836
Denny, Emery Loring V, 558
Denny, Francis V, 836
Denny, Henry V, 836
Denny, Henry H. V, 558
Denny, Iva M. IV, 971
Denny, James V, 836
Denny, Jane VI, 382
Denny, Jane VI, 433
Denny, Joel V, 836
Denny, John III, 100
Denny, John V, 833
Denny, John V, 836
Denny, John W. V, 558
Denny, Jordan V, 836
Denny, Jordon V, 836
Denny, Joseph V, 836
Denny, Josie Beryl V, 558
Denny, Julia V, 328
Denny, Keziah V, 836
Denny, Keziah V, 848
Denny, Lazarus I, 962
Denny, Lazarus V, 833
Denny, Lazarus V, 836
Denny, Lazarus V, 848
Denny, Lelia I, 940
Denny, Lelia I, 943
Denny, Levi Milton V, 558
Denny, Mahlon V, 836
Denny, Margaret V, 836
Denny, Martin V. V, 558
Denny, Mary V, 836
Denny, Mary V, 837
Denny, Michael V, 836
Denny, Michael V, 862
Denny, Michael W. IV, 971
Denny, Olive IV, 928
Denny, Permela V, 558
Denny, Permelia V, 558
Denny, Rebecca V, 836
Denny, Rebecca V, 868

Denny, Reuben V, 836
Denny, Robert V, 328
Denny, Rosetta K. IV, 971
Denny, Sarah III, 100
Denny, Sarah IV, 620
Denny, Sarah IV, 654
Denny, Sarah V, 833
Denny, Sarah V, 836
Denny, Sarah V, 848
Denny, Shubal V, 836
Denny, Shubeal V, 836
Denny, Susan Frances V, 558
Denny, Susanna I, 1009
Denny, Susanna V, 833
Denny, Susanna V, 836
Denny, Susannah V, 836
Denny, Walter VI, 382
Denny, Walter VI, 433
Denny, William V, 836
Denny, Wm. S. II, 856
Densel, Cyrus V, 992
Densel, Edward V, 992
Densel, Nettie V, 992
Densel, Wesley V, 992
Densey, Ann II, 353
Densey, Esther II, 504
Densey, Esther II, 535
Densey, John II, 353
Densey, John II, 354
Densey, John II, 504
Densey, John II, 551
Densey, John II, 599
Densey, Sarah II, 353
Densey, Sarah II, 354
Densey, Sarah II, 504
Densey, Sarah II, 599
Densey, Thomas II, 354
Densil, Cyrus V, 992
Densmore, Abial IV, 1360
Densmore, Abigail IV, 1360
Densmore, Caroline T. IV, 1360
Densmore, Charles K. IV, 1360
Densmore, Content K. IV, 1355
Densmore, Content K. IV, 1360
Densmore, Harriet F. IV, 1360
Densmore, John W. IV, 1360
Densmore, Joshua D. IV, 1360
Densmore, Josiah F. IV, 1360
Densmore, Moses F. IV, 1360
Densmore, Uriah H. IV, 1360
Denson, ??? VI, 39
Denson, ??? VI, 48
Denson, ??? VI, 95
Denson, Amay VI, 28
Denson, Amy VI, 36
Denson, Ann I, 237
Denson, Ann I, 304
Denson, Ann I, 317
Denson, Ann VI, 45
Denson, Ann VI, 46
Denson, Ann VI, 61
Denson, Ann VI, 88
Denson, Ann VI, 236
Denson, Benj. VI, 46
Denson, Benjamin I, 237
Denson, Benjamin I, 256
Denson, Benjamin VI, 45
Denson, Benjamin VI, 61
Denson, Benjamin VI, 62
Denson, Benjamin, Jr. I, 237
Denson, Betsy VI, 61
Denson, Betsy VI, 62
Denson, Betty VI, 45
Denson, Betty VI, 46
Denson, Christian VI, 45
Denson, David VI, 61
Denson, Demsey VI, 61
Denson, Demsey Johnson VI, 61
Denson, Dorothy VI, 61
Denson, Elisabeth I, 138
Denson, Elizabeth I, 115
Denson, Elizabeth I, 237
Denson, Elizabeth I, 304
Denson, Elizabeth I, 319
Denson, Elizabeth VI, 45
Denson, Elizabeth VI, 61
Denson, Elizabeth VI, 106
Denson, Elizabeth Miller VI, 905
Denson, Erwin VI, 905
Denson, Fannie L. VI, 61
Denson, Ffrances VI, 48
Denson, Frances VI, 28
Denson, Francis VI, 28
Denson, Francis VI, 61
Denson, Hollowell VI, 45
Denson, Hulda I, 237
Denson, Isabell VI, 61
Denson, James I, 138
Denson, James I, 162
Denson, James VI, 28
Denson, James VI, 48
Denson, James VI, 61
Denson, James VI, 106
Denson, Jane VI, 106
Denson, Jane W. VI, 61
Denson, Jane Watson VI, 79
Denson, Jesse I, 237
Denson, Jethrough VI, 61
Denson, John I, 213
Denson, John I, 237
Denson, John VI, 27
Denson, John VI, 28
Denson, John VI, 47
Denson, John VI, 48
Denson, John VI, 61
Denson, Jordan VI, 15
Denson, Jordan VI, 61
Denson, Joseph I, 213
Denson, Joseph I, 237
Denson, Joseph I, 259
Denson, Joseph VI, 28
Denson, Joseph VI, 45
Denson, Joseph VI, 59
Denson, Joseph VI, 61
Denson, Joseph VI, 62
Denson, Joseph VI, 63
Denson, Joseph VI, 106
Denson, Katheren VI, 28
Denson, Levi W. VI, 61
Denson, Levy W. VI, 61
Denson, Martha VI, 45
Denson, Martha VI, 61
Denson, Martha VI, 87
Denson, Mary I, 213
Denson, Mary I, 237
Denson, Mary I, 256
Denson, Mary I, 259
Denson, Mary VI, 15
Denson, Mary VI, 17
Denson, Mary VI, 27
Denson, Mary VI, 28
Denson, Mary VI, 45
Denson, Mary VI, 46
Denson, Mary VI, 61
Denson, Mary VI, 67
Denson, Mary Reakes I, 237
Denson, Molly I, 237
Denson, Patience I, 304
Denson, Patience VI, 45
Denson, Rhoda I, 213
Denson, Samuel VI, 61
Denson, Sara VI, 28
Denson, Sara VI, 32
Denson, Sarah VI, 28
Denson, Thomas VI, 106
Denson, Tooke VI, 61
Denson, Tuke VI, 61
Denson, Wd. Frances VI, 28
Denson, Widow Elisabeth I, 138
Denson, Widow Elisabeth I, 162
Denson, William VI, 7
Denson, William VI, 22
Denson, William VI, 28
Denson, William VI, 40
Denson, William VI, 45
Denson, William VI, 106
Denson, Wm. VI, 7
Denson, Wm. VI, 36
Denson, Wm. VI, 46
Densons, ??? VI, 23
Densy, John II, 353
Densy, Sarah II, 353
Dent, Amanda VI, 962
Dent, Betsy McManama VI, 905
Dent, Chilnesse VI, 940
Dent, Doshia VI, 990
Dent, Elizabeth VI, 960
Dent, Esther Board VI, 905
Dent, Hannah II, 493
Dent, Hannah II, 504
Dent, Isaac Gilpin VI, 905
Dent, Jabez VI, 888
Dent, Jabez B. VI, 905
Dent, John VI, 943
Dent, John VI, 960
Dent, John VI, 962
Dent, John VI, 990
Dent, John I. VI, 951
Dent, John J. VI, 905
Dent, John J. VI, 940
Dent, John J. VI, 960
Dent, John, Jr. VI, 944
Dent, Joseph II, 736
Dent, Joseph W. II, 791
Dent, Joseph W. II, 856
Dent, Liddy VI, 944
Dent, Lydia VI, 943
Dent, Margaret II, 354
Dent, Mary VI, 905
Dent, Milley Dollard VI, 905
Dent, Nancy VI, 943
Dent, Peter VI, 882
Dent, Peter VI, 905
Dent, Peter VI, 940
Dent, Peter L. VI, 962
Dent, Pincy W. VI, 905
Dent, Robert II, 493
Dent, Robert II, 504
Dent, Sally Ann VI, 936
Dent, Sarah Ann VI, 888
Dent, William VI, 905
Dent, William VI, 943
Denton, ??? III, 407
Denton, Albert IV, 1155
Denton, Ana Caroline IV, 1004
Denton, Caroline IV, 1004
Denton, Eliz. III, 474
Denton, Geo. A. IV, 1004
Denton, Herricks III, 407
Denton, James III, 407
Denton, James III, 451
Denton, James VI, 811
Denton, Jane III, 407
Denton, Jane III, 451
Denton, John I, 1075
Denton, John III, 407
Denton, John III, 409
Denton, Mary II, 354
Denton, Mercy II, 505
Denton, Mercy II, 636
Denton, Patsy VI, 811
Denton, Ruth III, 407
Denton, Ruth III, 409
Denwicks, Katherine II, 505
Denwood, Levin VI, 11
Denwood, Mary VI, 11
Denwood, Susanna VI, 11
Deny, Mary V, 836
Denzer, Margaret IV, 1206
Deonteroche, Abigail III, 100
Dephenport, Rebeckah I, 714
Dephenport, Rebeckah I, 715
Deplone, Anthony II, 354
Deplone, John II, 354
Deplone, Waneky II, 354
Deplovy, John II, 443
Depray, Kezia I, 237
Depray, Kezia I, 246
Depriest, Austin VI, 859
DePriest, Calista VI, 834
DePriest, Calistia VI, 852
DePriest, Cassandria VI, 811
Depriest, Charles VI, 806
Depriest, Charles VI, 831
DePriest, Christiana VI, 846
DePriest, Christina VI, 846
DePriest, Eliza VI, 834
DePriest, Frances VI, 811
DePriest, Horatio VI, 811
Depriest, Horatio VI, 832
Depriest, Horatio VI, 833
DePriest, Horatio VI, 834
DePriest, Jno. VI, 808
DePriest, Jno., Jr. VI, 846
DePriest, John VI, 806
DePriest, John VI, 829
DePriest, John VI, 852
Depriest, John R. VI, 849
DePriest, John, Jr. VI, 811
DePriest, John, Jr. VI, 852
DePriest, Louisa VI, 808
Depriest, Lucy VI, 859
DePriest, Martha VI, 811
DePriest, Martha VI, 834
DePriest, Mary VI, 806
DePriest, Nancy L. VI, 811
DePriest, Sarah VI, 806
DePriest, Sarah VI, 829
DePriest, Turpan VI, 811
DePriest, William H. VI, 811
DePrior, Delila VI, 91
Depue, Margaret IV, 384
Depue, Margaret IV, 455
Deputy, Caroline I, 1150
Deputy, Charles I, 1150
Deputy, David III, 82
Deputy, David III, 100
Deputy, Emerson E. I, 1150
Deputy, Henrietta III, 82
Deputy, Henrietta C. III, 100
Deputy, John I, 1150
Deputy, King I, 1150
Deputy, Sarah E. I, 1150
Derbert, John H. IV, 1206
Derbishare, Thomas II, 993
Derbishire, Mary II, 993
Derborow, Mary II, 510
Derborow, Mary II, 668
Derby, Anna IV, 1313
Derby, William II, 443
Derbyshire, Aaron IV, 1361
Derbyshire, Ann II, 958
Derbyshire, Ann II, 993
Derbyshire, Caroline II, 800
Derbyshire, Cynthia IV, 1360
Derbyshire, David IV, 1361
Derbyshire, David S. IV, 1360
Derbyshire, Gurney G. IV, 1313
Derbyshire, Isaac IV, 1360
Derbyshire, Isaac IV, 1361
Derbyshire, John II, 354
Derbyshire, John II, 993
Derbyshire, John, Jr. II, 993
Derbyshire, Joseph IV, 1361
Derbyshire, Lydia IV, 1360
Derbyshire, Lydia S. IV, 1361
Derbyshire, Mary II, 958
Derbyshire, Mary II, 993
Derbyshire, Mary II, 1072
Derbyshire, Mary Jane IV, 1360
Derbyshire, Mary Jane IV, 1361
Derbyshire, Rhoda C. W. V, 668
Derbyshire, Rosanna IV, 1361
Derbyshire, Rosanna IV, 1382
Derbyshire, Sarah II, 958
Derbyshire, Sarah II, 993
Derbyshire, Sarah II, 1072
Derbyshire, Thomas II, 505
Derbyshire, Thomas II, 993
Derbyshire, Zachariah IV, 1360
Derbyshire, Zechariah IV, 1360
Derefill, Anne VI, 890
Deremus, Emma V, 618
Derflinger, Alex IV, 1276
Derflinger, Anna V, 992
Derflinger, Mattie IV, 1276
Derflinger, Wm. IV, 1276
Derham, Matilda I, 371
Derham, Matilda I, 388
Derina, Sarah I, 765
Derk, Hannah V, 234
Derk, Hannah V, 445
Derkinderen, James II, 505
Dermin, Andrew VI, 382
Dermin, Anthony VI, 382
Dermin, Eleanor VI, 382
Dermin, John VI, 382
Dermin, Joseph VI, 382
Dermin, Rachel VI, 382
Dermin, Susannah VI, 382
Dermin, William VI, 382
Dernel, Ida Belle V, 234
Derossett, Polly VI, 811
Derossett, Samuel VI, 811
DeRouse, Laura II, 856
Derr, Ann IV, 805
Derr, Ann IV, 811
Derr, Edgar IV, 698
Derr, Edgar IV, 754
Derr, Edgar IV, 812
Derr, Edgar IV, 948
Derr, Edgar D. IV, 948
Derr, Eliza IV, 948
Derr, Isabel IV, 754
Derr, Isabella IV, 698
Derr, Isabella IV, 812
Derr, James IV, 698
Derr, James IV, 812
Derr, James IV, 948
Derr, James D. IV, 811
Derr, Lamoine IV, 812
Derr, Lemoine IV, 698
Derr, Leroy IV, 1037
Derr, Lilian IV, 812
Derr, Lilian D. IV, 812
Derr, Lillian IV, 698
Derr, Lillian IV, 754
Derr, Lillian IV, 948
Derr, Lillian D. IV, 948
Derr, Lydia A. IV, 811
Derr, Lydia Ann IV, 698
Derr, M. F. IV, 812
Derr, Margaret F. IV, 812
Derr, Mary IV, 1037
Derr, Mary E. IV, 1037
Derr, Maud IV, 811
Derr, Naomi IV, 698
Derr, Naomi IV, 714
Derr, Naomi IV, 812
Derr, Naomi D. IV, 948
Derr, Naomi Delight IV, 948
Derree, Anne II, 172
Derrick, Robert IV, 1313
Derrick, Robert IV, 1325
Derrick, Robert E. IV, 1325
Derrick, Robert Lincoln IV, 1313
Derrick, Ruth IV, 1313
Derrick, Ruth IV, 1325
Derry, Bethia IV, 521
Derry, Bethia IV, 556
Derryfield, Ann Jurden VI, 905
Derryfield, William VI, 905
Des Jardine, Chas. B. III, 433
Des Jardine, Eliz. C. III, 433
Des Jardine, Katharine Valine III, 433
Des Jardins, Chas B. III, 433
Des Jardins, Eliz. C. III, 433
Des Jardins, Katharine V. III, 433
Deselmes, C. IV, 521
Deselmes, Jesse IV, 521
Deselmes, Phebe IV, 521
Deselms, Ann IV, 143
Deselms, Benjamin IV, 143
Deselms, Benjamin IV, 521
Deselms, David IV, 143
Deselms, David IV, 521
Deselms, Eleanor IV, 143
Deselms, Elizabeth IV, 143
Deselms, Elizabeth IV, 326
Deselms, Elizabeth IV, 331
Deselms, Elizabeth IV, 521
Deselms, Elizabeth VI, 382
Deselms, Elizabeth VI, 430
Deselms, Hannah IV, 143
Deselms, Hannah IV, 326
Deselms, Hannah IV, 331
Deselms, Jacob IV, 143
Deselms, Jacob IV, 326
Deselms, Jacob IV, 346
Deselms, Jacob IV, 521
Deselms, Jesse IV, 143
Deselms, Jesse IV, 326
Deselms, Jesse IV, 331
Deselms, Jonas IV, 521
Deselms, Jonathan IV, 143
Deselms, Jonathan IV, 521
Deselms, Joseph IV, 143
Deselms, Joseph IV, 326
Deselms, Joseph IV, 521
Deselms, Lydia IV, 521
Deselms, Rhoda IV, 143
Deselms, Rhoda IV, 326
Deselms, Rhoda IV, 346
Deselms, Rhoda IV, 521
Deselms, Ruthanna IV, 521
Deselms, Ruthanna IV, 537
Deshler, Catharine II, 505
Deshler, Catharine II, 637
Deshler, David II, 354
Deshler, David II, 505
Deshler, David II, 580
Deshler, David II, 604
Deshler, David II, 637
Deshler, Esther II, 505
Deshler, Esther II, 604
Deshler, Geo. A. IV, 1249
Deshler, George IV, 1249
Deshler, Helen IV, 1249
Deshler, Isaac II, 354
Deshler, Mary II, 354
Deshler, Mary II, 505
Deshler, Mary II, 580
Deshler, Mary II, 637
Deshler, Samuel II, 354
Deshler, Sarah II, 354
DeSimoni, Louis IV, 1313
Despard, Cornelia III, 100
Despard, Cornelia III, 349
Despard, Marie Corlies III, 100
Despard, Walter Douglas III, 100
Despard, Walter Douglas III, 349
Desselms, Eleanor IV, 521
Desselms, Elizabeth IV, 521
Desselms, Jacob IV, 521
Desselms, Rhoda IV, 521
Detchean, Arthur IV, 1037
Detchean, Louisa IV, 1037
Dettworth, Joseph II, 354
Dettworth, William II, 354
Detvick, Emma V, 735
Detwiler, Eliz. III, 109
Detzell, Phebe IV, 607
Detzell, Phebe IV, 620
Deuel, Sarah III, 181
Deuell, Agnes III, 135
Deuell, Agnes G. III, 100
Deuell, Geo. H. III, 100
Deuell, George H. III, 135
Deulea, Rebecca IV, 30
Deuly, Lydia IV, 84
Deuro, James H. V, 233
DeVechary, Vera Frew IV, 1313
Deveney, Rebeck II, 66
Devenny, Eliza IV, 867
Devenny, Mary II, 66
Devenny, Rebeck II, 66
Devenny, Rebeckah II, 66
Devenport, Wiley E. I, 758
Dever, Abraham VI, 486
Dever, Alice II, 505
Dever, Alice II, 736
Dever, Alice II, 756
Dever, Benjamin II, 354

Dever, Margaret IV, 1276
Dever, Margaret IV, 1285
Deverell, Abigail III, 100
Deverell, Anthony II, 856
Deverell, Anthony II, 864
Deverell, Deborah R. II, 856
Deverell, Deborah R. II, 864
Deverell, Hannah III, 100
Deverell, Hannah III, 163
Deverell, Margaret II, 856
Deverell, Margaret II, 864
Devers, Elizabeth IV, 143
Devers, Elizabeth IV, 151
Devert, Fred E. IV, 1313
Devert, Frederick IV, 1313
Devert, Lottie IV, 1313
Devert, Lottie F. IV, 1313
DeVie, Jessie IV, 1313
Devine, Caroline IV, 1276
Deviney, Rebeckah II, 26
Devinney, Mary II, 66
Devinney, Mary II, 107
Devinny, Mary II, 66
Devinny, Mary II, 107
Devis, Mathew II, 354
Devit, Angeline F. V, 47
Devo, Charles V, 233
Devo, Charles Frederick V, 233
Devo, Mary J. V, 233
Devo, Miriam VI, 382
Devo, Miriam VI, 435
Devoe, Eliz. A. III, 333
Devoe, Isaac B. III, 333
DeVoe, Isaac B. III, 333
Devoe, Mary V, 992
Devoe, Robert V, 486
DeVoe, Susan III, 195
Devol, Catharine IV, 948
Devol, Catharine Isabella IV, 948
DeVol, Catherine IV, 1155
Devol, Charles IV, 948
DeVol, Charles IV, 1155
DeVol, Charles IV, 1190
Devol, Charles Edward IV, 948
Devol, Ezra IV, 948
DeVol, Ezra IV, 1155
Devol, George IV, 948
DeVol, George IV, 1155
DeVol, Isabella IV, 1155
DeVol, Leona IV, 1155
DeVol, Leora IV, 1155
DeVol, Leora IV, 1190
DeVol, Margaret Ruth IV, 1155
Devol, Mary Elizabeth IV, 948
Devol, Mary Isabella IV, 948
Devol, William Ezra IV, 948
Devon, Addie IV, 1249
Devon, Frank M. V, 455
Devonshire, Alice II, 354
Devonshire, Alice II, 505
Devos, Bertha E. V, 455
Devos, Clara G. V, 455
Devos, David J. V, 455
Devos, Nancy V, 455
Devos, Samuel V, 455
Devoss, Bertha E. V, 455
Devoss, Clara G. V, 455
Devoss, David J. V, 455
Devoss, Margaret V, 233
DeVoss, Margaret V, 233
Devoss, Nancy V, 455
Devoss, Samuel V, 233
Devoss, Samuel V, 455
DeVoy, Sarah W. V, 902
DeVoy, Sarah W. V, 919
Devult, Martha IV, 143
Devult, Martha IV, 163
Dew, Abigail I, 265
Dew, Abigail IV, 29
Dew, Abigail IV, 194
Dew, Abigail IV, 308
Dew, Albert IV, 194
Dew, Albert IV, 326
Dew, Albert IV, 560
Dew, Alen IV, 194
Dew, Allen IV, 194
Dew, Allen IV, 326
Dew, Allen IV, 560
Dew, Arthur Walter IV, 771
Dew, Cherry I, 265
Dew, Cherry I, 269
Dew, Cherry IV, 29
Dew, Cherry IV, 143
Dew, Cherry IV, 150
Dew, Clara May IV, 698
Dew, Clyde Allen IV, 698
Dew, Delany I, 269
Dew, Eleanor IV, 771
Dew, Elias I, 265
Dew, Elias I, 269
Dew, Elias IV, 29
Dew, Elias IV, 194
Dew, Elias IV, 246
Dew, Elias IV, 311
Dew, Elias IV, 326
Dew, Elias IV, 521
Dew, Elias IV, 560
Dew, Ester IV, 311
Dew, Ester IV, 313
Dew, Esther IV, 194
Dew, Ezekiel IV, 194
Dew, Fam IV, 560
Dew, Fannah IV, 194
Dew, Fannah IV, 218
Dew, John IV, 194
Dew, John IV, 326
Dew, John IV, 521
Dew, Joseph I, 265
Dew, Joseph I, 269
Dew, Joseph IV, 29
Dew, Joseph IV, 137
Dew, Joseph IV, 150
Dew, Joseph IV, 194
Dew, Joseph IV, 218
Dew, Joseph IV, 308
Dew, Joseph IV, 521
Dew, Lany I, 265
Dew, Lany I, 269
Dew, Lany I, 270
Dew, Levinah I, 265
Dew, Levinah I, 269
Dew, Levinah I, 270
Dew, Liverman IV, 194
Dew, M. Eleanor IV, 699
Dew, Maria IV, 194
Dew, Maria IV, 326
Dew, Mary I, 265
Dew, Mary I, 269
Dew, Mary I, 272
Dew, Mary IV, 194
Dew, Mary IV, 521
Dew, Mary Eleanor IV, 698
Dew, Mary Eleanor IV, 699
Dew, Ruth IV, 194
Dew, Ruth IV, 311
Dew, Ruth IV, 326
Dew, Ruth IV, 521
Dew, Salem IV, 698
Dew, Sarah I, 265
Dew, Sarah I, 269
Dew, Sarah I, 277
Dew, Sarah IV, 194
Dew, Sarah IV, 226
Dew, Sarah IV, 246
Dew, Sarah IV, 326
Dew, Sarah IV, 521
Dew, Sarah IV, 568
Dew, Sarah IV, 573
Dew, Susanna I, 265
Dew, Susanna IV, 29
Dew, Susanna IV, 143
Dew, Susanna IV, 194
Dew, Susanna IV, 521
Dew, Susanna IV, 540
Dew, Susannah I, 269
Dew, Susannah IV, 150
Dew, Thomas IV, 194
Dew, Thomas Roderick IV, 699
Dew, Veilee I, 269
Dew, Vialey I, 269
Dew, Vila IV, 194
Dew, Vila IV, 226
Dew, Vilee IV, 308
Dew, Viley I, 265
Dew, Viley I, 269
Dew, Viley IV, 29
Dew, Viley IV, 150
Dew, Viley IV, 194
Dew, Vylee I, 269
Dew, Walter A. IV, 699
Dew, Walter Arthur IV, 698
Dew, Walter Arthur IV, 699
Dewalt, Anna IV, 195
Dewalt, Anna Lora IV, 195
Dewalt, Jennie IV, 195
Dewalt, Lavinia IV, 195
Dewalt, Leroy IV, 195
Dewalt, Maggie May IV, 195
Dewalt, Mahlon IV, 195
Dewalt, Peter IV, 195
Dewalt, Samuel IV, 195
Dewault, Mahlon IV, 195
Dewberry, Jacob II, 505
Dewberry, Mary II, 354
Dewees, ??? IV, 1093
Dewees, Aaron IV, 384
Dewees, Aaron IV, 573
Dewees, Aaron IV, 579
Dewees, Aaron IV, 1053
Dewees, Aaron IV, 1054
Dewees, Aaron IV, 1093
Dewees, Aaron P. II, 703
Dewees, Aaron P. II, 736
Dewees, Aaron P. IV, 1054
Dewees, Aaron, Jr. IV, 1054
Dewees, Alfred H. II, 703
Dewees, Alfred H. II, 736
Dewees, Almeda IV, 1054
Dewees, Almedia IV, 1054
Dewees, Almedia IV, 1066
Dewees, Amy F. II, 736
Dewees, Amy F. IV, 1054
Dewees, Amy J. II, 703
Dewees, Amy T. IV, 1053
Dewees, Amy T. IV, 1093
Dewees, Amy T. IV, 1094
Dewees, Amy, Jr. II, 736
Dewees, Ann II, 828
Dewees, Ann IV, 573
Dewees, Ann IV, 1053
Dewees, Ann IV, 1054
Dewees, Ann IV, 1066
Dewees, Ann IV, 1122
Dewees, Ann Hunter II, 828
Dewees, Ann M. IV, 195
Dewees, Ann M. IV, 1053
Dewees, Anna IV, 276
Dewees, Anna IV, 384
Dewees, Anna IV, 389
Dewees, Anna IV, 1053
Dewees, Anna IV, 1054
Dewees, Anna IV, 1061
Dewees, Anna IV, 1093
Dewees, Anna IV, 1095
Dewees, Anna Harmer IV, 1093
Dewees, Arthur IV, 195
Dewees, Barak IV, 1054
Dewees, Baruch IV, 1054
Dewees, Beason T. IV, 1053
Dewees, Benjamin IV, 1122
Dewees, Beulah Emily IV, 144
Dewees, Beulah Emily IV, 1054
Dewees, Beulah Emily IV, 1061
Dewees, Bula Elma IV, 195
Dewees, Bula Emily IV, 1053
Dewees, Bulaelma B. IV, 195
Dewees, Bulielma IV, 195
Dewees, Bulielma IV, 326
Dewees, Bulyelma IV, 195
Dewees, Caleb IV, 1053
Dewees, Charles IV, 948
Dewees, Charles B. IV, 195
Dewees, Charles B. IV, 1053
Dewees, Charles B. IV, 1054
Dewees, Charles B. IV, 1093
Dewees, Charles W. IV, 699
Dewees, Charles W. IV, 812
Dewees, Charles W. IV, 948
Dewees, Charles W. IV, 1093
Dewees, Chas. W. IV, 699
Dewees, Chas. W. IV, 1094
Dewees, Clara R. IV, 195
Dewees, Clara R. IV, 699
Dewees, Clara Rosella IV, 699
Dewees, Clarissa IV, 1093
Dewees, Clarissa R. IV, 1093
Dewees, Clarissa R. IV, 1116
Dewees, Clifton E. IV, 573
Dewees, Cornelius II, 828
Dewees, Cornelius IV, 319
Dewees, Cornelius IV, 326
Dewees, Cornelius IV, 1053
Dewees, Cornelius IV, 1087
Dewees, Cornelius IV, 1093
Dewees, David IV, 144
Dewees, David IV, 195
Dewees, David IV, 326
Dewees, David IV, 1093
Dewees, David V, 836
Dewees, David B. IV, 195
Dewees, David B. IV, 470
Dewees, David B. IV, 481
Dewees, David B. IV, 1053
Dewees, David B. V, 836
Dewees, Debbie IV, 1053
Dewees, Debby IV, 125
Dewees, Debby IV, 326
Dewees, Debby IV, 384
Dewees, Debby IV, 812
Dewees, Debby IV, 1053
Dewees, Debby IV, 1093
Dewees, Debby IV, 1094
Dewees, Debby IV, 1099
Dewees, Debe IV, 1055
Dewees, Deborah IV, 125
Dewees, Deborah IV, 135
Dewees, Deborah IV, 699
Dewees, Deborah IV, 1053
Dewees, Deborah IV, 1093
Dewees, Dorathy M. II, 703
Dewees, Dorothy M. II, 736
Dewees, Edith IV, 1053
Dewees, Edith IV, 1094
Dewees, Elis IV, 144
Dewees, Elizabeth II, 699
Dewees, Elizabeth IV, 1053
Dewees, Elizabeth IV, 1054
Dewees, Elizabeth IV, 1055
Dewees, Elizabeth IV, 1093
Dewees, Elizabeth IV, 1122
Dewees, Ellis IV, 195
Dewees, Ellis IV, 326
Dewees, Ellis IV, 384
Dewees, Ellis IV, 1053
Dewees, Ellis IV, 1054
Dewees, Ellis Lee IV, 195
Dewees, Elwood IV, 573
Dewees, Emma J. II, 703
Dewees, Emma J. II, 736
Dewees, Emma J. IV, 513
Dewees, Emma J. IV, 521
Dewees, Emma Jane IV, 513
Dewees, Ernest Joseph III, 100
Dewees, Esther IV, 143
Dewees, Esther IV, 144
Dewees, Esther IV, 155
Dewees, Eunice II, 703
Dewees, Eunice II, 736
Dewees, Eunice IV, 1053
Dewees, Eunice IV, 1054
Dewees, Ezra IV, 195
Dewees, Ezra IV, 1054
Dewees, Ezra IV, 1094
Dewees, Florence Martha IV, 195
Dewees, Florence Martha IV, 699
Dewees, George M. IV, 1053
Dewees, George M. IV, 1054
Dewees, George M. IV, 1093
Dewees, Greenberry IV, 1093
Dewees, Greenberry P. IV, 195
Dewees, Greenberry P. IV, 1053
Dewees, Greenberry P. IV, 1054
Dewees, Greenbury P. IV, 195
Dewees, Greenbury P. IV, 1053
Dewees, Greenbury P. IV, 1093
Dewees, Griffith IV, 699
Dewees, Griffith IV, 812
Dewees, Griffith IV, 948
Dewees, Griffith IV, 1053
Dewees, Griffith IV, 1093
Dewees, Griffith IV, 1106
Dewees, Gula Elma IV, 195
Dewees, Guli Elma IV, 1053
Dewees, Guli Elma IV, 1066
Dewees, Gulielma IV, 195
Dewees, Gulielma IV, 326
Dewees, Guliema IV, 144
Dewees, Hanna H. II, 736
Dewees, Hannah IV, 139
Dewees, Hannah IV, 143
Dewees, Hannah IV, 144
Dewees, Hannah IV, 147
Dewees, Hannah IV, 195
Dewees, Hannah IV, 326
Dewees, Hannah IV, 384
Dewees, Hannah IV, 470
Dewees, Hannah IV, 1052
Dewees, Hannah IV, 1053
Dewees, Hannah IV, 1093
Dewees, Hannah V, 834
Dewees, Hannah V, 836
Dewees, Hannah A. IV, 1093
Dewees, Hannah F. V, 836
Dewees, Hannah H. IV, 1053
Dewees, Hannah H. IV, 1054
Dewees, Hannah Maria IV, 195
Dewees, Hannah Maria IV, 1053
Dewees, Hannah Maria IV, 1054
Dewees, Hannah Maria IV, 1081
Dewees, Harvey II, 736
Dewees, Hendrycus II, 443
Dewees, Isaac IV, 125
Dewees, Isaac IV, 129
Dewees, Isaac IV, 1053
Dewees, Isaac IV, 1054
Dewees, Isaac IV, 1093
Dewees, Isaac V, 836
Dewees, Isaac E. IV, 699
Dewees, Isaac E. IV, 948
Dewees, Isaac E. IV, 1093
Dewees, Isaac Edwin IV, 699
Dewees, Isaac Edwin IV, 948
Dewees, Isaiah IV, 1053
Dewees, Isaiah F. IV, 195
Dewees, Isaiah F. IV, 1053
Dewees, Isaiah F. IV, 1054
Dewees, J. Hervey II, 703
Dewees, James IV, 125
Dewees, James IV, 135
Dewees, James IV, 144
Dewees, James IV, 195
Dewees, James IV, 384
Dewees, James IV, 573
Dewees, James IV, 1053
Dewees, James IV, 1054
Dewees, James IV, 1088
Dewees, James IV, 1093
Dewees, James E. IV, 195
Dewees, James E. IV, 276
Dewees, James E. IV, 699
Dewees, James E. IV, 1053
Dewees, James E. IV, 1054
Dewees, James E. IV, 1093
Dewees, James Henry IV, 521
Dewees, James Hervey IV, 513
Dewees, James W. IV, 1053
Dewees, James, Jr. IV, 1054
Dewees, James, Jr. IV, 1093
Dewees, Jane II, 703
Dewees, Jane IV, 384
Dewees, Jane IV, 573
Dewees, Jane IV, 1053
Dewees, Jas. Henry IV, 513
Dewees, Jesse II, 703
Dewees, Jesse IV, 195
Dewees, Jesse IV, 384
Dewees, Jesse IV, 573
Dewees, Jesse IV, 699
Dewees, Jesse IV, 1053
Dewees, Jesse IV, 1054
Dewees, Jesse IV, 1060
Dewees, Jesse IV, 1093
Dewees, Jesse IV, 1094
Dewees, Jesse H. IV, 176
Dewees, Jesse H. IV, 195
Dewees, Jesse H. IV, 369
Dewees, Jesse H. IV, 699
Dewees, Jesse H. IV, 1054
Dewees, Jesse, Jr. IV, 1054
Dewees, Joanna IV, 143
Dewees, Joanna IV, 144
Dewees, John IV, 384
Dewees, John IV, 521
Dewees, John E. IV, 1061
Dewees, Jonathan IV, 1054
Dewees, Jonathan F. IV, 195
Dewees, Jonathan F. IV, 1053
Dewees, Jos. Howard IV, 195
Dewees, Jos. N. III, 100
Dewees, Joseph IV, 384
Dewees, Joseph IV, 573
Dewees, Joseph IV, 1053
Dewees, Joseph Howard IV, 195
Dewees, Joseph Howard IV, 699
Dewees, Joshua IV, 176
Dewees, Joshua IV, 567
Dewees, Joshua IV, 573
Dewees, Joshua IV, 579
Dewees, Joshua IV, 1053
Dewees, Joshua IV, 1054
Dewees, Lemuel F. IV, 1053
Dewees, Lewis IV, 144
Dewees, Lewis M. IV, 1053
Dewees, Lewis M. IV, 1054
Dewees, Lewis M. IV, 1093
Dewees, Lewis W. IV, 195
Dewees, Louisa IV, 1093
Dewees, Louise IV, 812
Dewees, Loyd N. IV, 1053
Dewees, Lucetta V. III, 100
Dewees, Lydia IV, 1053
Dewees, Maranda IV, 573
Dewees, Maranda IV, 579
Dewees, Maranda IV, 1054
Dewees, Margaret IV, 144
Dewees, Margaret IV, 1053
Dewees, Margaret H. IV, 195
Dewees, Margaret H. IV, 699
Dewees, Margaret Jane IV, 1053
Dewees, Margaret Jane IV, 1054
Dewees, Margaret Jane IV, 1057
Dewees, Maria II, 703
Dewees, Maria IV, 521
Dewees, Maria IV, 1053
Dewees, Maria IV, 1054
Dewees, Maria IV, 1056
Dewees, Maria IV, 1093
Dewees, Mariah IV, 195
Dewees, Mariam P. IV, 384
Dewees, Mariam P. IV, 1094
Dewees, Mariana IV, 176
Dewees, Mariana IV, 177
Dewees, Mariana IV, 195
Dewees, Mariana IV, 567
Dewees, Mariana IV, 573
Dewees, Marion B. II, 703
Dewees, Marion B. II, 736
Dewees, Martha IV, 176
Dewees, Martha IV, 567
Dewees, Martha IV, 573
Dewees, Martha IV, 579
Dewees, Martha IV, 699
Dewees, Martha IV, 948
Dewees, Martha IV, 1053
Dewees, Martha IV, 1093

ewees, Martha H. IV, 195
ewees, Martha H. IV, 213
ewees, Martha R. IV, 948
ewees, Martha R. IV, 949
ewees, Martha Ruth IV, 948
ewees, Martha W. IV, 195
ewees, Martha W. IV, 384
ewees, Martha W. IV, 699
ewees, Martha W. IV, 1054
ewees, Martha W. IV, 1060
ewees, Martha W. IV, 1093
ewees, Mary IV, 125
ewees, Mary IV, 143
ewees, Mary IV, 144
ewees, Mary IV, 155
ewees, Mary IV, 164
ewees, Mary IV, 195
ewees, Mary IV, 384
ewees, Mary IV, 521
ewees, Mary IV, 528
ewees, Mary IV, 573
ewees, Mary IV, 699
ewees, Mary IV, 710
ewees, Mary IV, 948
ewees, Mary IV, 1053
ewees, Mary IV, 1054
ewees, Mary IV, 1093
ewees, Mary IV, 1099
ewees, Mary IV, 1106
ewees, Mary A. IV, 573
ewees, Mary Ann IV, 195
ewees, Mary Ann IV, 1054
ewees, Mary Ann IV, 1066
ewees, Mary C. IV, 176
ewees, Mary C. IV, 195
ewees, Mary C. IV, 369
ewees, Mary C. IV, 699
ewees, Mary C. IV, 789
ewees, Mary C. IV, 790
ewees, Mary Dewees IV, 699
ewees, Mary E. IV, 384
ewees, Mary E. IV, 1054
ewees, Mary Emma IV, 1053
ewees, Mary Emma IV, 1054
ewees, Mary G. IV, 699
ewees, Mary G. IV, 948
ewees, Mary H. IV, 1053
ewees, Mary H. IV, 1093
ewees, Mary H. IV, 1098
ewees, Mary L. IV, 195
ewees, Mary L. IV, 1054
ewees, Mary L. IV, 1061
ewees, Mary R. IV, 812
ewees, Mary R. IV, 948
ewees, Mary S. IV, 1053
ewees, Mary, Jr. IV, 144
ewees, Maryanna IV, 1053
ewees, Mathew W. IV, 1054
ewees, Matilda IV, 1093
ewees, Mildred Rebecca IV, 195
ewees, Mildred Rebecca IV, 699
ewees, Milicent IV, 1054
ewees, Milicent IV, 1088
ewees, Milicent IV, 1093
ewees, Miranda IV, 573
ewees, Miranda IV, 1054
ewees, Miranda G. IV, 573
ewees, Miranda J. IV, 1054
ewees, Miriam P. IV, 384
ewees, Miriam P. IV, 1054
ewees, Miriam P. IV, 1060
ewees, Nancy IV, 1052
ewees, Naomi IV, 812
ewees, Naomi IV, 1093
ewees, Naomi B. IV, 1093
ewees, Nathan II, 703
ewees, Nathan II, 736
ewees, Nathan IV, 1053
ewees, Nathan IV, 1054
ewees, Nathan IV, 1063
ewees, Nathan IV, 1093
ewees, Nathan IV, 1103
ewees, Owen IV, 143
ewees, Owen IV, 144
ewees, Owen IV, 155
ewees, Owen IV, 164
ewees, Owen IV, 195
ewees, Owen IV, 326
ewees, Penina E. IV, 573
ewees, Penina E. IV, 579
ewees, Penina E. G. IV, 573
ewees, Peninah IV, 1122
ewees, Rachel IV, 276
ewees, Rachel IV, 384
ewees, Rachel IV, 470
ewees, Rachel IV, 481
ewees, Rachel IV, 553
ewees, Rachel IV, 1053
ewees, Rachel IV, 1054
ewees, Rachel IV, 1094
ewees, Rachel IV, 1115
Dewees, Rachel IV, 1116
Dewees, Rachel M. IV, 1053
Dewees, Rebeca IV, 1054
Dewees, Rebecca II, 703
Dewees, Rebecca IV, 125
Dewees, Rebecca IV, 129
Dewees, Rebecca IV, 130
Dewees, Rebecca IV, 195
Dewees, Rebecca IV, 384
Dewees, Rebecca IV, 573
Dewees, Rebecca IV, 699
Dewees, Rebecca IV, 1053
Dewees, Rebecca IV, 1054
Dewees, Rebecca IV, 1063
Dewees, Rebecca IV, 1093
Dewees, Rebecca IV, 1103
Dewees, Rebecca V, 836
Dewees, Rebecca H. II, 736
Dewees, Rebecca H. IV, 1053
Dewees, Rebecca H. IV, 1054
Dewees, Rebecca H. IV, 1093
Dewees, Rebecca Huestis II, 736
Dewees, Rebecca W. IV, 319
Dewees, Rebecca W. IV, 326
Dewees, Rebecca W. IV, 1087
Dewees, Rebecca W. IV, 1093
Dewees, Rezin Thomas IV, 1093
Dewees, Rezin Thompson IV, 1054
Dewees, Rhoda Ann IV, 1052
Dewees, Richard S. IV, 1054
Dewees, Richard Stanton IV, 1053
Dewees, Robert H. IV, 1093
Dewees, Roy H. IV, 1053
Dewees, Roy H. IV, 1054
Dewees, Roy H. IV, 1093
Dewees, Ruth Anna IV, 699
Dewees, Ruth Anna IV, 812
Dewees, Ruth F. III, 100
Dewees, Ruth F. Smith IV, 1122
Dewees, Ruthann IV, 1093
Dewees, Ruthann IV, 1106
Dewees, Ruthanna IV, 812
Dewees, Ruthanna IV, 948
Dewees, Ruthanna IV, 1054
Dewees, Ruthanna IV, 1093
Dewees, Samuel IV, 139
Dewees, Samuel IV, 143
Dewees, Samuel IV, 144
Dewees, Samuel IV, 195
Dewees, Samuel IV, 326
Dewees, Samuel IV, 470
Dewees, Samuel IV, 1053
Dewees, Sarah II, 828
Dewees, Sarah IV, 195
Dewees, Sarah IV, 384
Dewees, Sarah IV, 573
Dewees, Sarah IV, 594
Dewees, Sarah IV, 1052
Dewees, Sarah IV, 1053
Dewees, Sarah IV, 1054
Dewees, Sarah IV, 1055
Dewees, Sarah IV, 1088
Dewees, Sarah IV, 1093
Dewees, Sarah IV, 1103
Dewees, Sarah IV, 1122
Dewees, Sarah IV, 1129
Dewees, Sarah IV, 1130
Dewees, Sarah Ann IV, 1053
Dewees, Sarah Ann IV, 1054
Dewees, Sarah Ann IV, 1093
Dewees, Sarah Ann IV, 1102
Dewees, Sarah H. II, 703
Dewees, Sarah H. II, 736
Dewees, Sarah M. IV, 1053
Dewees, Sarah M. IV, 1054
Dewees, Sarah M. IV, 1093
Dewees, Smith IV, 1053
Dewees, Smith IV, 1054
Dewees, Tabitha IV, 213
Dewees, Thomas II, 703
Dewees, Thomas IV, 144
Dewees, Thomas IV, 195
Dewees, Thomas IV, 384
Dewees, Thomas IV, 573
Dewees, Thomas IV, 699
Dewees, Thomas IV, 1052
Dewees, Thomas IV, 1053
Dewees, Thomas IV, 1060
Dewees, Thomas IV, 1093
Dewees, Thomas V, 836
Dewees, Thomas Arthur IV, 195
Dewees, Thomas Arthur IV, 699
Dewees, Thomas K. IV, 1053
Dewees, Thomas L. IV, 195
Dewees, Thomas L. IV, 1053
Dewees, Thomas L. IV, 1054
Dewees, Thomas Lee IV, 195
Dewees, Thomas Lee IV, 1053
Dewees, Thomas Lee IV, 1054
Dewees, Thomas T. IV, 195
Dewees, Thomas, Jr. IV, 195
Dewees, Thos. IV, 195
Dewees, Thos. IV, 213
Dewees, Thos. L. IV, 1054
Dewees, Watson IV, 1054
Dewees, Watson W. IV, 1054
Dewees, William IV, 125
Dewees, William IV, 384
Dewees, William IV, 389
Dewees, William IV, 573
Dewees, William IV, 594
Dewees, William IV, 1053
Dewees, William IV, 1093
Dewees, William V, 836
Dewees, William H. IV, 195
Dewees, William H. IV, 1053
Dewees, William N. IV, 573
Dewees, William P. II, 703
Dewees, William, Sr. IV, 1093
Dewees, Wm. IV, 125
Dewees, Wm. IV, 326
Dewees, Wm. IV, 573
Dewees, Wm. IV, 812
Dewees, Wm. IV, 1053
Dewees, Wm. IV, 1054
Dewees, Wm. IV, 1055
Dewees, Wm. IV, 1056
Dewees, Wm. IV, 1093
Dewees, Wm. IV, 1094
Dewees, Wm. IV, 1099
Dewees, Wm. IV, 1122
Dewees, Wm. H. IV, 1053
Dewees, Wm. H. IV, 1054
Dewees, Wm. H. IV, 1093
Dewees, Wm. P. IV, 521
Dewees, Wm., Jr. IV, 384
Dewees, Wm., Jr. IV, 573
Dewees, Zebulon IV, 1093
Deweese, ??? IV, 1085
Deweese, Aaron IV, 384
Deweese, Aaron IV, 458
Deweese, Aaron IV, 573
Deweese, Almedia IV, 384
Deweese, Anna IV, 384
Deweese, Bulielma IV, 326
Deweese, Buly Elma IV, 384
Deweese, Buly Emly IV, 326
Deweese, Charles W. IV, 812
Deweese, Chas. W. IV, 699
Deweese, Cornelius IV, 326
Deweese, Cornelius IV, 384
Deweese, David IV, 326
Deweese, David V, 836
Deweese, David B. V, 836
Deweese, Debby IV, 326
Deweese, Debby IV, 384
Deweese, Debby IV, 812
Deweese, Deborah IV, 384
Deweese, Ellis IV, 326
Deweese, Ellis IV, 384
Deweese, Ellis Lee IV, 384
Deweese, Florence Martha IV, 812
Deweese, Griffith IV, 384
Deweese, Griffith IV, 699
Deweese, Griffith IV, 812
Deweese, Gulielma IV, 326
Deweese, Gulielma IV, 384
Deweese, Hannah IV, 326
Deweese, Hannah IV, 384
Deweese, Hannah V, 836
Deweese, Hannah Mariah IV, 384
Deweese, Isaac IV, 384
Deweese, Isaac V, 836
Deweese, Isaac E. IV, 812
Deweese, Isaac Edwin IV, 812
Deweese, James IV, 384
Deweese, James E. IV, 384
Deweese, James Ezra IV, 812
Deweese, Jane IV, 384
Deweese, Jane IV, 459
Deweese, Jane, Jr. IV, 384
Deweese, Jesse IV, 384
Deweese, Jesse IV, 400
Deweese, Jesse IV, 573
Deweese, Jesse IV, 576
Deweese, Jesse IV, 812
Deweese, Jesse H. IV, 384
Deweese, Jesse H. IV, 812
Deweese, Jesse Hall IV, 812
Deweese, Joanna IV, 144
Deweese, John IV, 384
Deweese, Joseph IV, 384
Deweese, Joseph Howard IV, 812
Deweese, Jospeh H. IV, 812
Deweese, Louisa IV, 812
Deweese, Louisa IV, 822
Deweese, Louisa M. IV, 812
Deweese, Louise IV, 812
Deweese, Lulu V, 668
Deweese, Margaret IV, 144
Deweese, Margaret Hannah IV, 812
Deweese, Margaret Jane IV, 384
Deweese, Maria IV, 384
Deweese, Maria IV, 431
Deweese, Mariam P. IV, 384
Deweese, Mariam P. IV, 400
Deweese, Marry C. IV, 812
Deweese, Martha Ruth IV, 812
Deweese, Martha W. IV, 384
Deweese, Mary IV, 384
Deweese, Mary IV, 431
Deweese, Mary IV, 458
Deweese, Mary IV, 573
Deweese, Mary IV, 699
Deweese, Mary Ann IV, 384
Deweese, Mary C. IV, 812
Deweese, Mary C. IV, 856
Deweese, Mary C. Woolman IV, 812
Deweese, Mary E. IV, 384
Deweese, Mary Emma IV, 384
Deweese, Mary G. IV, 812
Deweese, Mary R. IV, 384
Deweese, Mary R. IV, 431
Deweese, Mary R. IV, 812
Deweese, Matthew W. IV, 384
Deweese, Mildred H. IV, 812
Deweese, Miriam P. IV, 384
Deweese, Naomi IV, 812
Deweese, Nellie V, 668
Deweese, Owen IV, 144
Deweese, Owen IV, 326
Deweese, Rachel IV, 384
Deweese, Rachel IV, 1053
Deweese, Rebecca IV, 384
Deweese, Rebecca IV, 576
Deweese, Rebecca V, 836
Deweese, Rebecca W. IV, 326
Deweese, Rebecca W. IV, 327
Deweese, Ruth Anna IV, 699
Deweese, Ruth Anna IV, 812
Deweese, Ruthanna IV, 812
Deweese, Samuel IV, 326
Deweese, Samuel IV, 384
Deweese, Sarah IV, 195
Deweese, Sarah IV, 384
Deweese, Sarah IV, 387
Deweese, Sarah IV, 459
Deweese, Thomas IV, 384
Deweese, Thomas IV, 459
Deweese, Thomas V, 836
Deweese, Thomas L. IV, 326
Deweese, Thomas L. IV, 1054
Deweese, Thomas Lee IV, 384
Deweese, Thomas, Jr. IV, 384
Deweese, Watson IV, 384
Deweese, William IV, 384
Deweese, William V, 836
Deweese, William, Jr. IV, 384
Deweese, Wm. IV, 326
Deweese, Wm. IV, 431
Deweese, Wm. IV, 812
Deweese, Wm., Jr. IV, 384
Deweesee, Chas. W. IV, 816
Deweesee, Mary R. IV, 816
Dewel, Hannah II, 215
Dewel, John II, 215
Dewel, Mary II, 67
Dewer, Ann II, 505
Dewer, Ann II, 633
Dewer, Mary II, 505
Dewer, Sarah II, 505
Dewer, Thomas II, 978
Dewers, Anna IV, 1067
Dewers, Griffith IV, 1067
Dewes, Col. Thomas VI, 22
Dewess, Mariam P. IV, 384
Dewey, John T. I, 927
Dewey, Leffie B. V, 992
Dewey, Lelia I, 927
Dewey, Margaret VI, 616
Dewey, Margaret VI, 702
Dewey, Mariah IV, 1361
Dewey, Mariah IV, 1379
Dewey, Sarah I, 927
Dewil, Elizabeth II, 67
Dewire, Jane II, 856
Dewire, Jane II, 876
Dewit, Rachel V, 208
Dewit, Rebecca V, 207
Dewit, Rebecca V, 208
Dewit, Thomas V, 208
Dewit, Wm. V, 208
DeWitt, Aaron VI, 846
Dewitt, Aaron VI, 905
DeWitt, Aaron VI, 986
Dewitt, Aaron VI, 1001
Dewitt, Abigal VI, 905
Dewitt, Alanson VI, 905
Dewitt, Ann VI, 986
Dewitt, Betsy VI, 1001
Dewitt, Caleb VI, 895
Dewitt, Caleb VI, 905
Dewitt, Cassandra E. VI, 894
DeWitt, Catharine M. VI, 887
Dewitt, Chas. K. IV, 1276
Dewitt, Clarence V, 306
DeWitt, Dorcas VI, 887
Dewitt, Dorcas VI, 905
Dewitt, Elisha VI, 905
Dewitt, Elisha VI, 943
DeWitt, Elisha VI, 956
Dewitt, Elisha D. VI, 905
Dewitt, Elisha D. VI, 971
Dewitt, Elizabeth VI, 905
DeWitt, Elizabeth VI, 915
Dewitt, Elizabeth F. VI, 905
Dewitt, Elizabtth Baughn VI, 905
DeWitt, Everett III, 276
Dewitt, Frankie IV, 1276
DeWitt, Gloria IV, 1313
Dewitt, Harry V, 306
DeWitt, Henry VI, 915
Dewitt, Henry Ann VI, 905
DeWitt, James VI, 887
Dewitt, James VI, 905
Dewitt, James VI, 971
DeWitt, James VI, 974
DeWitt, James VI, 976
DeWitt, James VI, 1015
Dewitt, James VI, 1020
Dewitt, James M. VI, 905
Dewitt, James, Jr. VI, 992
Dewitt, James, Senr. VI, 905
Dewitt, James, Sr. VI, 992
Dewitt, Jeremiah VI, 905
Dewitt, Jeremiah T. VI, 894
Dewitt, Jeremiah T. VI, 932
DeWitt, Jesse VI, 895
Dewitt, Jesse VI, 905
Dewitt, John VI, 905
Dewitt, John A. VI, 905
Dewitt, John Ross VI, 1003
Dewitt, Julia Ann VI, 905
Dewitt, Louisa A. VI, 905
DeWitt, Malinda VI, 1015
Dewitt, Margaret P. VI, 905
Dewitt, Marselles IV, 1276
DeWitt, Mary VI, 915
Dewitt, Mary VI, 1003
Dewitt, Mary F. VI, 971
DeWitt, Mary R. VI, 986
Dewitt, Mary Read VI, 905
Dewitt, Mary Whorley VI, 905
Dewitt, Milley VI, 1020
Dewitt, Myrtle V, 306
Dewitt, Nancy Ann VI, 932
Dewitt, Nancy Coleman VI, 905
Dewitt, Nelson C. VI, 905
Dewitt, Pamela VI, 992
DeWitt, Pamelia A. VI, 976
Dewitt, Paulina A. VI, 1004
Dewitt, Polly VI, 1020
Dewitt, Rebecca V, 166
Dewitt, Rhoda Coleman VI, 905
Dewitt, Robert V, 993
Dewitt, Salley Baughon VI, 905
Dewitt, Sarah E. VI, 905
Dewitt, Solomon VI, 901
Dewitt, Susanna Coleman VI, 905
Dewitt, Thomas VI, 905
Dewitt, William VI, 905
Dewitt, William H. VI, 905
DeWitt, Wm. H. VI, 976
DeWitt, Zacharian N. VI, 887
DeWitte, William V, 486
Dewley, Dawson IV, 522
Dewley, Eliza Annah IV, 522
Dewley, Lydia IV, 522
Dewley, Maxon IV, 522
Dewley, Ruthanne IV, 522
Dewley, Sinah Jane IV, 522
Dewley, Susanna IV, 522
Dewley, Thomas Elwood IV, 522
Dewley, William IV, 522
Dewly, Avis IV, 125
Dewly, Joshua IV, 125
Dewly, Maxen IV, 125
Dewrey, William VI, 909
Dews, Elcy VI, 844
Dews, Elizabeth VI, 811
Dews, Elizabeth A. VI, 844
Dews, Frances VI, 808
Dews, Lucy VI, 811
Dews, Mary Ann II, 736
Dews, Reuben VI, 811
Dews, Sally VI, 811
Dews, Samuel VI, 811

Dews, Sarah Powers II, 736
Dews, Thomas I, 698
Dews, Thomas I, 714
Dewsbury, Joan III, 107
Dewsbury, John III, 107
Dewstoe, Sophia III, 309
Dexson, Clement II, 993
Dexson, Emma V, 487
Dexson, Lennie V, 487
Dexson, Thomas V, 487
Dexson, Wilson V, 487
Dexter, Christiana IV, 1206
Dexter, Elijah IV, 1206
Dexter, Elisa C. IV, 1206
Dexter, Elisa C. IV, 1209
Dexter, Eliza C. IV, 1206
Dexter, Lova V, 735
Dexter, Wm. L. IV, 1206
Dexter, Wm. L. IV, 1209
Deyarle, Bowman VI, 811
Deyarle, Catharine VI, 811
Deyerle, Elizabeth S. VI, 905
Deyerle, John VI, 905
Deyerle, Permelia VI, 905
Deyo, ??? III, 185
Deyo, Aletta III, 185
Deyo, Amanda III, 100
Deyo, Amanda III, 303
Deyo, Charles III, 100
Deyo, Charles III, 303
Deyo, Eleanor III, 100
Deyo, Eleanor III, 303
Deyo, Eleanor III, 407
Deyo, Eleanor III, 448
Deyo, Ewing III, 185
Deyo, Seth Smith III, 185
Dezell, Alice III, 100
Dezell, Alice III, 183
Dezell, Egbert G. III, 100
Dezell, Franc III, 100
Dezell, Franc III, 183
Dezell, John T. III, 100
Dezell, John T. III, 183
Dezelms, Ann IV, 143
Dezelms, Benjamin IV, 143
Dezelms, David IV, 143
Dezelms, Eleanor IV, 143
Dezelms, Elizabeth IV, 143
Dezelms, Hannah IV, 143
Dezelms, Jacob IV, 143
Dezelms, Jesse IV, 143
Dezelms, Jonathan IV, 143
Dezelms, Joseph IV, 143
Dezelms, Rhoda IV, 143
Diament, Albert L. II, 857
Diament, Christiana Cadwallader II, 819
Diament, Elizabeth II, 819
Diament, Elizabeth II, 857
Diament, Elizabeth C. II, 791
Diament, Elizabeth C. II, 835
Diament, Elizabeth C. II, 857
Diament, Elizabeth C. II, 921
Diament, Francis II, 791
Diament, Francis II, 819
Diament, Francis S. II, 831
Diament, Francis S. II, 845
Diament, Ida M. II, 857
Diament, Mary Frances L. II, 857
Diament, Mary Frances Lightfoot II, 791
Diament, Melosina H. II, 857
Diamond, Edith V, 166
Diamond, Emma V, 166
Diamond, Harriett V, 166
Diamond, Helen V, 166
Diamond, John V, 166
Diamond, Mary Belle V, 166
Diamond, Robert V, 488
Diamond, Robert C. V, 166
Dibble, Catharine V, 957
Dibble, Catherine Dibble V, 950
Dibble, Elisabeth II, 504
Dibble, Eunice V, 902
Dibble, Sarah Ostrone V, 950
Dibol, Conklin V, 668
Dibra, Daniel V, 809
Dibra, Daniel V, 816
Dibra, Elizabeth V, 806
Dibra, Elizabeth V, 809
Dibra, Elizabeth V, 816
Dibra, Rebecca V, 806
Dibra, Samuel V, 806
Dibra, Susannah V, 806
Dibra, Susannah V, 816
Dibrell, Charles VI, 811
Dibrell, Lucy VI, 811
Dibrell, Wilmuth VI, 819
Dibrell, Wilmuth W. VI, 819
Dicas, Mary II, 354
Dick, Achilles V, 902
Dick, Elisha C. VI, 738
Dick, Martha I, 618
Dick, Minnie I, 618
Dick, Patience VI, 365
Dick, Patience VI, 383
Dickasan, Margaret V, 902
Dickens, Cornelia I, 935
Dickens, Cornelia I, 940
Dickens, Cornelia Annie I, 924
Dickens, Ella I, 935
Dickens, Ella I, 940
Dickens, John I, 924
Dickens, John I, 935
Dickens, Mary Ella I, 924
Dickens, Violet I, 924
Dickensheet, Alonzo V, 992
Dickensheet, Freeman V, 992
Dickensheet, Valley V, 992
Dickensheet, Voley V, 992
Dickenson, Abigail II, 505
Dickenson, Ann II, 505
Dickenson, Ann II, 506
Dickenson, Ann II, 637
Dickenson, Asa D. VI, 811
Dickenson, Austin VI, 811
Dickenson, Cadwallader II, 506
Dickenson, Charity I, 45
Dickenson, Charity I, 67
Dickenson, Charles V, 455
Dickenson, Chas. V, 455
Dickenson, Clara V, 668
Dickenson, Clara O. V, 668
Dickenson, Daniel II, 505
Dickenson, Daniel VI, 594
Dickenson, Deborah IV, 948
Dickenson, Deborah IV, 1001
Dickenson, Elizabeth II, 505
Dickenson, Elizabeth II, 736
Dickenson, Elizabeth III, 134
Dickenson, Elizabeth IV, 1280
Dickenson, Emma P. III, 212
Dickenson, Fanney VI, 905
Dickenson, Francis VI, 905
Dickenson, Hannah II, 66
Dickenson, Hannah III, 101
Dickenson, Hannah III, 134
Dickenson, Hannah W. II, 506
Dickenson, James II, 505
Dickenson, Jemima VI, 594
Dickenson, John II, 505
Dickenson, John II, 506
Dickenson, John III, 134
Dickenson, Jonathan III, 101
Dickenson, Jonathan V, 668
Dickenson, Joseph VI, 594
Dickenson, Joseph R. III, 212
Dickenson, Judah VI, 811
Dickenson, Lydia IV, 1295
Dickenson, Maria II, 505
Dickenson, Marianna V, 668
Dickenson, Marianne V, 668
Dickenson, Mary II, 505
Dickenson, Mary II, 608
Dickenson, Mary III, 105
Dickenson, Mary VI, 594
Dickenson, Merchant III, 101
Dickenson, Ola V, 455
Dickenson, Oren V, 668
Dickenson, Phebe II, 215
Dickenson, Ray C. V, 455
Dickenson, Rebeckah VI, 594
Dickenson, Richard II, 505
Dickenson, Roy C. V, 455
Dickenson, Sally II, 505
Dickenson, Sally VI, 811
Dickenson, Samuel II, 505
Dickenson, Sarah II, 505
Dickenson, Sarah II, 506
Dickenson, Sarah Norris II, 505
Dickenson, Solomon II, 506
Dickenson, Susanna II, 354
Dickenson, Valentine III, 212
Dickenson, Wm. J. VI, 905
Dickenson, Zebulon III, 105
Dicker, Easter II, 27
Dicker, Elizabeth II, 27
Dicker, Esther II, 26
Dicker, Esther II, 27
Dicker, Esther II, 66
Dicker, Esther II, 77
Dicker, Hannah II, 26
Dicker, Hannah II, 66
Dicker, Hannah II, 67
Dicker, Hester II, 27
Dicker, Lydia II, 27
Dicker, Richard II, 26
Dicker, Richard II, 27
Dicker, Richard II, 66
Dicker, Richard II, 77
Dicker, Rudick II, 66
Dickerson, Agnis. VI, 973
Dickerson, Bartlet VI, 962
Dickerson, Bartlett VI, 905
Dickerson, Booker VI, 881
Dickerson, Celia VI, 932
Dickerson, Cena VI, 905
Dickerson, Clement VI, 932
Dickerson, Clements VI, 905
Dickerson, Clemmont VI, 949
Dickerson, Delpha VI, 973
Dickerson, Dolly G. VI, 962
Dickerson, Edney VI, 1000
Dickerson, Eli V, 440
Dickerson, Eliza V, 383
Dickerson, Eliza V, 440
Dickerson, Elizabeth I, 304
Dickerson, Elizabeth I, 314
Dickerson, Elizabeth VI, 972
Dickerson, Elizabeth VI, 985
Dickerson, Emma V, 440
Dickerson, Emma P. III, 100
Dickerson, Emme V, 440
Dickerson, Evelina VI, 905
Dickerson, Fanny VI, 905
Dickerson, Francis VI, 941
Dickerson, Frankey Mays VI, 905
Dickerson, Genevra IV, 195
Dickerson, Hattie V, 440
Dickerson, Hezekiah VI, 905
Dickerson, Ida V, 383
Dickerson, Ida Belle V, 383
Dickerson, James VI, 905
Dickerson, James VI, 927
Dickerson, James W. VI, 905
Dickerson, John V, 440
Dickerson, John G. VI, 905
Dickerson, John S. VI, 888
Dickerson, Joseph VI, 985
Dickerson, Joseph VI, 1000
Dickerson, Joseph R. III, 100
Dickerson, Lizzie V, 440
Dickerson, Louisa V, 440
Dickerson, Mariah V, 440
Dickerson, Mary I, 304
Dickerson, Mary III, 100
Dickerson, Mary VI, 905
Dickerson, Mina V, 440
Dickerson, Minna V, 440
Dickerson, Nancy VI, 985
Dickerson, Nancy VI, 995
Dickerson, Nettie V, 440
Dickerson, Patsy VI, 881
Dickerson, Patsy Jane VI, 905
Dickerson, Pincy W. VI, 905
Dickerson, Polly VI, 905
Dickerson, Polly VI, 949
Dickerson, Rebecca V, 383
Dickerson, Rebecca E. V, 383
Dickerson, Ro. N. VI, 903
Dickerson, Roseanna VI, 905
Dickerson, Sally VI, 905
Dickerson, Sally VI, 941
Dickerson, Sally VI, 993
Dickerson, Sally VI, 995
Dickerson, Valentine III, 100
Dickerson, Wd. Ann III, 100
Dickerson, William V, 383
Dickerson, William VI, 889
Dickerson, William VI, 905
Dickerson, William VI, 910
Dickerson, William VI, 972
Dickerson, William J. VI, 905
Dickerson, William J. VI, 975
Dickerson, William, Jr. VI, 905
Dickerson, William, Jr. VI, 975
Dickerson, Wm. VI, 973
Dickerson, Wm. J. VI, 995
Dickeson, Anne E. II, 131
Dickeson, Auxencio M. P. V. H. II, 131
Dickeson, Mary Jane II, 131
Dickeson, Mary S. II, 131
Dickeson, Sarah II, 993
Dickeson, Wilbur S. II, 131
Dickey, Ann V, 328
Dickey, Ann V, 383
Dickey, Ann V, 428
Dickey, Ann VI, 838
Dickey, Anna V, 383
Dickey, Asenath V, 383
Dickey, Aseneth V, 328
Dickey, Asenith V, 328
Dickey, Asenith V, 383
Dickey, Benjamin IV, 195
Dickey, Benjamin H. IV, 195
Dickey, Charity V, 328
Dickey, Charity V, 383
Dickey, Edmund VI, 838
Dickey, Edward VI, 819
Dickey, Edward VI, 838
Dickey, Elizabeth V, 328
Dickey, Elizabeth V, 383
Dickey, Elizabeth VI, 858
Dickey, Elizabeth Charity V, 383
Dickey, Elwood B. IV, 948
Dickey, Horace G. IV, 195
Dickey, James IV, 699
Dickey, James V, 328
Dickey, James V, 383
Dickey, James VI, 811
Dickey, James VI, 830
Dickey, James VI, 838
Dickey, Jane V, 47
Dickey, Jane V, 61
Dickey, Jane V, 328
Dickey, Jane V, 383
Dickey, Jane V, 836
Dickey, Jean VI, 838
Dickey, Jno. VI, 838
Dickey, John VI, 804
Dickey, John VI, 808
Dickey, John VI, 811
Dickey, John VI, 819
Dickey, John VI, 838
Dickey, John VI, 858
Dickey, L??? IV, 195
Dickey, Laura M. IV, 195
Dickey, Leanah IV, 195
Dickey, Leanna IV, 195
Dickey, Leanna IV, 300
Dickey, Lucinda V, 328
Dickey, Lucinda V, 383
Dickey, Lucinda V, 404
Dickey, Margaret VI, 800
Dickey, Margaret VI, 811
Dickey, Mary Ann V, 328
Dickey, Mary Ann V, 383
Dickey, Mary E. III, 481
Dickey, Mary W. VI, 830
Dickey, Matilda V, 328
Dickey, Matilda V, 383
Dickey, Matilda V, 427
Dickey, Nancy E. VI, 838
Dickey, Nimrod V, 328
Dickey, Nimrod V, 383
Dickey, Nimrod V, 428
Dickey, Pamelia VI, 858
Dickey, Phebe V, 328
Dickey, Phebe Jane V, 328
Dickey, Phebe Jane V, 383
Dickey, Phebe W. IV, 948
Dickey, Phineas IV, 195
Dickey, Phinius IV, 195
Dickey, Rebecca IV, 699
Dickey, Rebecca IV, 948
Dickey, Rebecca C. IV, 941
Dickey, Rebecca C. IV, 948
Dickey, Robert H. VI, 811
Dickey, Robert H. VI, 830
Dickey, Samuel VI, 800
Dickey, Samuel VI, 811
Dickey, Sarah V, 383
Dickey, Sarah V, 428
Dickey, Sarah VI, 811
Dickey, Sarah VI, 819
Dickey, Sarah Ann V, 383
Dickey, Sarah Phebe V, 383
Dickey, Susan VI, 811
Dickey, Susanna VI, 811
Dickienson, Hannah III, 273
Dickienson, Jonathan III, 273
Dickinson, ??? II, 354
Dickinson, ??? III, 101
Dickinson, ??? III, 165
Dickinson, Abigail II, 505
Dickinson, Abigail II, 694
Dickinson, Abigail II, 698
Dickinson, Achsah Ann III, 339
Dickinson, Alice Mary III, 101
Dickinson, Andrew IV, 1276
Dickinson, Ann II, 453
Dickinson, Ann II, 505
Dickinson, Ann III, 379
Dickinson, Ann Eliza II, 857
Dickinson, Ann Eliza V, 902
Dickinson, Anna III, 101
Dickinson, Anna III, 407
Dickinson, Anna IV, 1276
Dickinson, Anna W. III, 101
Dickinson, Anna W. III, 407
Dickinson, Anna W. III, 447
Dickinson, Anne III, 407
Dickinson, Anne III, 458
Dickinson, Asa D. VI, 811
Dickinson, Bartlet VI, 939
Dickinson, Bartlett VI, 939
Dickinson, Benjamin II, 505
Dickinson, Benjamin II, 510
Dickinson, Cadwalader II, 505
Dickinson, Cadwalader II, 506
Dickinson, Cadwalader II, 551
Dickinson, Cadwalader IV, 83
Dickinson, Cadwallader II, 215
Dickinson, Cadwallader II, 243
Dickinson, Cadwallader II, 354
Dickinson, Cadwallader II, 505
Dickinson, Cadwallader II, 506
Dickinson, Cadwallader II, 521
Dickinson, Carson III, 100
Dickinson, Celia I, 285
Dickinson, Charles III, 101
Dickinson, Charles A. II, 506
Dickinson, Charles G. III, 100
Dickinson, Charles W. I, 262
Dickinson, Clara V, 486
Dickinson, Clement VI, 905
Dickinson, Daniel I, 285
Dickinson, Daniel II, 354
Dickinson, Daniel II, 505
Dickinson, Daniel II, 506
Dickinson, David III, 100
Dickinson, David III, 101
Dickinson, David III, 407
Dickinson, David VI, 905
Dickinson, Deborah II, 505
Dickinson, Duncan M. IV, 1276
Dickinson, Edmund II, 506
Dickinson, Edmund III, 100
Dickinson, Edwin II, 703
Dickinson, Edwin II, 736
Dickinson, Eleanor III, 100
Dickinson, Eleanor Jane III, 348
Dickinson, Elenor III, 348
Dickinson, Eliz. III, 100
Dickinson, Eliza III, 379
Dickinson, Eliza IV, 1276
Dickinson, Eliza Ann V, 902
Dickinson, Elizabeth I, 285
Dickinson, Elizabeth II, 459
Dickinson, Elizabeth II, 505
Dickinson, Elizabeth II, 506
Dickinson, Elizabeth II, 510
Dickinson, Elizabeth II, 551
Dickinson, Elizabeth II, 736
Dickinson, Elizabeth III, 101
Dickinson, Elizabeth IV, 83
Dickinson, Elizabeth IV, 107
Dickinson, Elizabeth IV, 1276
Dickinson, Emily L. V, 902
Dickinson, Emily S. V, 902
Dickinson, Emma D. III, 165
Dickinson, Emma M. III, 100
Dickinson, Emma Mary III, 100
Dickinson, Emma Mary III, 165
Dickinson, Fanney VI, 905
Dickinson, Frances III, 101
Dickinson, Frances VI, 882
Dickinson, Francis II, 354
Dickinson, Francis VI, 905
Dickinson, Gains IV, 83
Dickinson, Gardner L. IV, 1276
Dickinson, Grace II, 354
Dickinson, Grace II, 490
Dickinson, Grace II, 505
Dickinson, Grace III, 100
Dickinson, Grace III, 101
Dickinson, Grace III, 110
Dickinson, Grace III, 165
Dickinson, Hannah II, 66
Dickinson, Hannah II, 505
Dickinson, Hannah II, 593
Dickinson, Hannah II, 798
Dickinson, Hannah III, 100
Dickinson, Hannah III, 101
Dickinson, Hannah IV, 83
Dickinson, Hannah IV, 1276
Dickinson, Hannah W. II, 453
Dickinson, Hannah W. II, 506
Dickinson, Henry II, 506
Dickinson, Henry III, 100
Dickinson, Henry III, 101
Dickinson, Henry III, 110
Dickinson, Henry III, 165
Dickinson, Henry III, 407
Dickinson, Isaac II, 354
Dickinson, Isaac III, 100
Dickinson, Isaac III, 407
Dickinson, Isaac J. III, 407
Dickinson, Isabella III, 101
Dickinson, Jamaica II, 505
Dickinson, James I, 285
Dickinson, James I, 304
Dickinson, James II, 354
Dickinson, James II, 490
Dickinson, James II, 505
Dickinson, James V, 902
Dickinson, James VI, 147
Dickinson, James Hunt III, 101
Dickinson, Jane III, 101
Dickinson, Jane III, 399
Dickinson, Jane III, 407
Dickinson, Jane V, 902
Dickinson, Jane VI, 934

Dickinson, Jane Clark II, 215
Dickinson, Jane Clark II, 505
Dickinson, Jas. III, 407
Dickinson, Jeannie III, 100
Dickinson, Jeannie III, 101
Dickinson, Jesse IV, 29
Dickinson, John I, 285
Dickinson, John II, 215
Dickinson, John II, 354
Dickinson, John II, 453
Dickinson, John II, 505
Dickinson, John II, 703
Dickinson, John II, 736
Dickinson, John III, 100
Dickinson, John III, 101
Dickinson, John III, 345
Dickinson, John III, 379
Dickinson, John V, 902
Dickinson, John V, 903
Dickinson, John V, 920
Dickinson, John M. III, 101
Dickinson, Jonathan II, 354
Dickinson, Jonathan II, 505
Dickinson, Jonathan III, 101
Dickinson, Jonathan III, 399
Dickinson, Jonathan III, 407
Dickinson, Jonathan III, 447
Dickinson, Jonathan V, 486
Dickinson, Joseph II, 354
Dickinson, Joseph II, 510
Dickinson, Joseph III, 101
Dickinson, Joseph III, 407
Dickinson, Joseph III, 414
Dickinson, Joseph IV, 83
Dickinson, Joseph IV, 1269
Dickinson, Joseph VI, 993
Dickinson, Joseph N. IV, 1276
Dickinson, Joseph, Jr. IV, 83
Dickinson, Joshua M. IV, 1276
Dickinson, Leonard K. III, 101
Dickinson, Lucinda VI, 1013
Dickinson, Lydia II, 710
Dickinson, Lydia II, 717
Dickinson, Lydia III, 101
Dickinson, Lydia III, 379
Dickinson, Lydia IV, 1276
Dickinson, Lydia V, 902
Dickinson, Lydia V, 920
Dickinson, Margaret II, 800
Dickinson, Margaret II, 857
Dickinson, Margaret III, 101
Dickinson, Margaret III, 379
Dickinson, Margaret V, 902
Dickinson, Margaret M. IV, 1276
Dickinson, Maria II, 354
Dickinson, Maria II, 505
Dickinson, Maria III, 101
Dickinson, Mariah IV, 1276
Dickinson, Marian III, 101
Dickinson, Marianna III, 407
Dickinson, Marianna V, 486
Dickinson, Marianne V, 668
Dickinson, Marianne V, 702
Dickinson, Martha Ann VI, 894
Dickinson, Martin M. IV, 1276
Dickinson, Mary I, 304
Dickinson, Mary II, 61
Dickinson, Mary II, 66
Dickinson, Mary II, 354
Dickinson, Mary II, 480
Dickinson, Mary II, 505
Dickinson, Mary II, 510
Dickinson, Mary II, 521
Dickinson, Mary II, 551
Dickinson, Mary III, 101
Dickinson, Mary III, 345
Dickinson, Mary III, 379
Dickinson, Mary III, 407
Dickinson, Mary V, 902
Dickinson, Mary V, 903
Dickinson, Mary Ann III, 88
Dickinson, Mary Ann III, 101
Dickinson, Mary Ann Noble VI, 905
Dickinson, Mary E. II, 703
Dickinson, Mary E. II, 736
Dickinson, Mary Jane II, 712
Dickinson, Mary T. VI, 1018
Dickinson, Mary W. II, 946
Dickinson, Matilda IV, 1276
Dickinson, Matilda IV, 1277
Dickinson, Matthew Reid III, 407
Dickinson, Merchant III, 101
Dickinson, Miriam I, 304
Dickinson, Miriam I, 315
Dickinson, Morris II, 505
Dickinson, Morris II, 551
Dickinson, Mrs. Mary VI, 934
Dickinson, N. L. VI, 886
Dickinson, Narcissa VI, 939
Dickinson, Nathaniel III, 407
Dickinson, Nuzum IV, 83
Dickinson, Oren V, 486
Dickinson, Pamelia III, 407
Dickinson, Patsy IV, 1276
Dickinson, Patsy Bouthe VI, 894
Dickinson, Penelliphy I, 304
Dickinson, Penelope I, 285
Dickinson, Pennelliphy I, 318
Dickinson, Phebe II, 215
Dickinson, Phebe III, 395
Dickinson, Phebe III, 407
Dickinson, Phebe Anna II, 717
Dickinson, Polley VI, 975
Dickinson, Polly I, 285
Dickinson, Rachel II, 505
Dickinson, Rachel II, 521
Dickinson, Rebecca IV, 83
Dickinson, Reuben III, 101
Dickinson, Reuben L. III, 101
Dickinson, Rhoda VI, 905
Dickinson, Richard II, 215
Dickinson, Richard II, 505
Dickinson, Richard IV, 83
Dickinson, Robert IV, 1276
Dickinson, Roger II, 505
Dickinson, Rose III, 407
Dickinson, Roxey III, 101
Dickinson, Ruth A. III, 407
Dickinson, Sally II, 505
Dickinson, Sally II, 506
Dickinson, Sally VI, 811
Dickinson, Sally Morris II, 354
Dickinson, Sally N. II, 736
Dickinson, Samuel II, 480
Dickinson, Samuel II, 505
Dickinson, Samuel III, 100
Dickinson, Samuel III, 101
Dickinson, Samuel III, 407
Dickinson, Sarah II, 354
Dickinson, Sarah II, 505
Dickinson, Sarah II, 506
Dickinson, Sarah III, 101
Dickinson, Sarah III, 407
Dickinson, Sarah III, 414
Dickinson, Sarah F. VI, 953
Dickinson, Sarah L. III, 407
Dickinson, Sarah Norris II, 505
Dickinson, Shrewbury III, 101
Dickinson, Solomon II, 453
Dickinson, Solomon II, 505
Dickinson, Sophie G. V, 47
Dickinson, Susan III, 379
Dickinson, Susan III, 407
Dickinson, Susanna II, 354
Dickinson, Susanna II, 736
Dickinson, Susanna III, 101
Dickinson, Susanna III, 379
Dickinson, Susanna IV, 1276
Dickinson, Susannah II, 505
Dickinson, Susannah II, 506
Dickinson, Susannah II, 517
Dickinson, Susannah V, 902
Dickinson, Susannah V, 903
Dickinson, Susannah V, 920
Dickinson, Thomas IV, 83
Dickinson, Thomas IV, 1276
Dickinson, Townsend III, 101
Dickinson, Townsend III, 407
Dickinson, Townsend III, 458
Dickinson, Wd. Phebe III, 407
Dickinson, Wd. Sarah III, 407
Dickinson, William I, 285
Dickinson, William I, 304
Dickinson, William I, 315
Dickinson, William I, 318
Dickinson, William VI, 953
Dickinson, William W. VI, 800
Dickinson, Wm. II, 505
Dickinson, Wm. II, 510
Dickinson, Wm. VI, 916
Dickinson, Wm. J. VI, 882
Dickinson, Zebulon III, 101
Dickinson, Zebulun III, 407
Dickison, Jane Clark II, 215
Dicks, ??? I, 385
Dicks, Accalus I, 537
Dicks, Acellus I, 496
Dicks, Achilles V, 47
Dicks, Achilles V, 486
Dicks, Achilles V, 558
Dicks, Achilles V, 902
Dicks, Achilles VI, 308
Dicks, Achilles D. V, 47
Dicks, Achilles D. V, 558
Dicks, Ackelles I, 536
Dicks, Agatha I, 496
Dicks, Agatha I, 536
Dicks, Agatha I, 537
Dicks, Agatha I, 577
Dicks, Agatha V, 47
Dicks, Agatha V, 233
Dicks, Agatha V, 902
Dicks, Agatha V, 909
Dicks, Agatha VI, 308
Dicks, Agnes I, 554
Dicks, Alfred M. I, 678
Dicks, Amy I, 678
Dicks, Ann I, 496
Dicks, Ann I, 554
Dicks, Ann I, 678
Dicks, Ann I, 681
Dicks, Ann I, 714
Dicks, Ann I, 759
Dicks, Ann V, 837
Dicks, Ann V, 844
Dicks, Ann T. V, 837
Dicks, Ann T. V, 863
Dicks, Ann, Jr. I, 537
Dicks, Ann, Jr. I, 553
Dicks, Anna I, 554
Dicks, Archibald I, 714
Dicks, Archibald M. I, 714
Dicks, Aris I, 554
Dicks, Barthen I, 554
Dicks, Caleb I, 554
Dicks, Caleb, Sr. I, 554
Dicks, Calvin V, 47
Dicks, Calvin Yancy I, 554
Dicks, Cornelius I, 678
Dicks, Cornelius T. I, 652
Dicks, Cornelius T. I, 678
Dicks, Deborah I, 358
Dicks, Deborah I, 434
Dicks, Deborah I, 496
Dicks, Deborah I, 554
Dicks, Deborah I, 652
Dicks, Deborah I, 653
Dicks, Deborah I, 657
Dicks, Dr. ??? VI, 727
Dicks, Edith I, 554
Dicks, Eleanor I, 652
Dicks, Elias I, 554
Dicks, Elijah J. V, 47
Dicks, Elizabeth I, 434
Dicks, Elizabeth I, 496
Dicks, Elizabeth I, 523
Dicks, Elizabeth I, 536
Dicks, Elizabeth I, 537
Dicks, Elizabeth I, 551
Dicks, Elizabeth I, 554
Dicks, Elizabeth I, 572
Dicks, Elizabeth I, 652
Dicks, Elizabeth I, 653
Dicks, Elizabeth I, 674
Dicks, Elizabeth I, 678
Dicks, Elizabeth V, 47
Dicks, Elizabeth V, 486
Dicks, Elizabeth V, 537
Dicks, Elizabeth W. V, 43
Dicks, Elizabeth W. V, 47
Dicks, Elizabeth, Jr. I, 537
Dicks, Elizabeth, Sr. I, 537
Dicks, Enoch I, 554
Dicks, Enoch V, 837
Dicks, Enoch V, 844
Dicks, Enoch S. V, 837
Dicks, Enock S. V, 836
Dicks, Esther I, 496
Dicks, Esther I, 536
Dicks, Esther I, 582
Dicks, Esther I, 653
Dicks, Esther I, 678
Dicks, Eunice V, 826
Dicks, Eunice V, 837
Dicks, Eunice Margaret I, 652
Dicks, Evan I, 554
Dicks, Evan IV, 521
Dicks, Grace I, 496
Dicks, Grace I, 536
Dicks, Grace I, 540
Dicks, Hannah I, 496
Dicks, Hannah I, 532
Dicks, Hannah I, 536
Dicks, Hannah I, 537
Dicks, Hannah I, 554
Dicks, Hannah I, 581
Dicks, Hannah V, 47
Dicks, Hannah V, 558
Dicks, Hannah V, 836
Dicks, Hannah V, 837
Dicks, Harland IV, 327
Dicks, Hester II, 443
Dicks, Hezekiah I, 554
Dicks, Hope I, 554
Dicks, Isaac H. V, 837
Dicks, Isabella II, 443
Dicks, Jacob I, 554
Dicks, James I, 536
Dicks, James I, 652
Dicks, James I, 657
Dicks, James I, 658
Dicks, James I, 678
Dicks, James I, 759
Dicks, James IV, 327
Dicks, James IV, 521
Dicks, James B. V, 47
Dicks, Jane II, 814
Dicks, Jemima I, 554
Dicks, Jesse I, 496
Dicks, Job I, 496
Dicks, Job I, 537
Dicks, Job I, 581
Dicks, John I, 554
Dicks, John II, 443
Dicks, John IV, 327
Dicks, John IV, 521
Dicks, John G. V, 836
Dicks, John G. V, 837
Dicks, Jonathan I, 385
Dicks, Jonathan I, 554
Dicks, Jonathan II, 506
Dicks, Jonathan V, 836
Dicks, Jonathan V, 837
Dicks, Joseph I, 554
Dicks, Joseph IV, 327
Dicks, Joshua I, 496
Dicks, Joshua I, 523
Dicks, Joshua I, 536
Dicks, Joshua I, 537
Dicks, Joshua V, 47
Dicks, Josiah I, 554
Dicks, Keziah V, 836
Dicks, Keziah V, 837
Dicks, Levi V, 47
Dicks, Levi V, 559
Dicks, Levi L. I, 554
Dicks, Lida I, 434
Dicks, Lydia I, 385
Dicks, Lydia I, 393
Dicks, Lydia I, 496
Dicks, Lydia I, 554
Dicks, Margaret I, 385
Dicks, Margaret I, 427
Dicks, Margaret I, 678
Dicks, Martha I, 496
Dicks, Martha I. V, 47
Dicks, Mary I, 375
Dicks, Mary I, 385
Dicks, Mary I, 431
Dicks, Mary I, 434
Dicks, Mary I, 445
Dicks, Mary I, 496
Dicks, Mary I, 524
Dicks, Mary I, 536
Dicks, Mary I, 537
Dicks, Mary I, 550
Dicks, Mary I, 554
Dicks, Mary I, 678
Dicks, Mary II, 506
Dicks, Mary V, 47
Dicks, Mary VI, 468
Dicks, Merab I, 759
Dicks, Micajah I, 496
Dicks, Micajah I, 536
Dicks, Micajah V, 909
Dicks, Micajah VI, 308
Dicks, Naomy I, 496
Dicks, Nathan I, 375
Dicks, Nathan I, 385
Dicks, Nathan I, 434
Dicks, Nathan I, 445
Dicks, Nathan I, 487
Dicks, Nathan I, 496
Dicks, Nathan I, 524
Dicks, Nathan I, 536
Dicks, Nathan I, 537
Dicks, Nathan I, 554
Dicks, Nathan I, 652
Dicks, Nathan I, 653
Dicks, Nathan I, 678
Dicks, Nathan II, 354
Dicks, Nathan V, 47
Dicks, Nathan V, 233
Dicks, Nathan V, 253
Dicks, Nathan V, 486
Dicks, Nathan V, 558
Dicks, Nathan V, 902
Dicks, Nathan VI, 308
Dicks, Nathan VI, 468
Dicks, Ormelia J. I, 554
Dicks, Peter I, 385
Dicks, Peter I, 457
Dicks, Peter I, 487
Dicks, Peter I, 496
Dicks, Peter I, 536
Dicks, Peter I, 645
Dicks, Peter I, 648
Dicks, Peter I, 652
Dicks, Peter I, 653
Dicks, Peter I, 678
Dicks, Peter I, 681
Dicks, Peter I, 714
Dicks, Peter I, 741
Dicks, Peter I, 759
Dicks, Peter II, 354
Dicks, Peter IV, 327
Dicks, Peter IV, 521
Dicks, Peter V, 486
Dicks, Peter V, 537
Dicks, Polly I, 554
Dicks, Pratt I, 554
Dicks, Rachel I, 434
Dicks, Rachel I, 457
Dicks, Rachel I, 536
Dicks, Rachel I, 554
Dicks, Rachel I, 652
Dicks, Rachel I, 657
Dicks, Rachel I, 658
Dicks, Rachel I, 678
Dicks, Rachel I, 684
Dicks, Rebeca I, 554
Dicks, Rebecca II, 506
Dicks, Rebecca V, 220
Dicks, Rebekah I, 496
Dicks, Rhoda I, 496
Dicks, Rhoda I, 537
Dicks, Rhoda I, 546
Dicks, Ruth I, 358
Dicks, Ruth I, 385
Dicks, Ruth I, 434
Dicks, Ruth I, 445
Dicks, Ruth I, 496
Dicks, Ruth I, 536
Dicks, Ruth I, 544
Dicks, Ruth I, 652
Dicks, Ruth I, 678
Dicks, Ruth I, 681
Dicks, Ruth I, 759
Dicks, Ruth V, 735
Dicks, Sally I, 537
Dicks, Sally I, 551
Dicks, Sally I, 554
Dicks, Sally V, 47
Dicks, Sally V, 233
Dicks, Sally V, 253
Dicks, Samuel S. V, 837
Dicks, Sarah I, 434
Dicks, Sarah I, 443
Dicks, Sarah I, 445
Dicks, Sarah I, 496
Dicks, Sarah I, 525
Dicks, Sarah I, 536
Dicks, Sarah I, 537
Dicks, Sarah I, 554
Dicks, Sarah I, 559
Dicks, Sarah I, 648
Dicks, Sarah I, 678
Dicks, Sarah I, 759
Dicks, Sarah IV, 327
Dicks, Sarah V, 96
Dicks, Sarah V, 909
Dicks, Sarah VI, 308
Dicks, Sarah M. V, 47
Dicks, Seth I, 496
Dicks, Seth I, 537
Dicks, Seth I, 551
Dicks, Solomon I, 554
Dicks, Surry I, 554
Dicks, Susan I, 714
Dicks, Tamar I, 652
Dicks, Tamar I, 678
Dicks, Tamar I, 681
Dicks, Tamer I, 658
Dicks, Thomas I, 554
Dicks, Timothy I, 554
Dicks, William I, 496
Dicks, William I, 536
Dicks, William I, 537
Dicks, William I, 553
Dicks, William I, 554
Dicks, William I, 577
Dicks, William I, 582
Dicks, William I, 652
Dicks, William I, 653
Dicks, William I, 759
Dicks, William V, 47
Dicks, William V, 233
Dicks, William VI, 308
Dicks, William C. I, 678
Dicks, William Clarkson I, 678
Dicks, William, Jr. I, 554
Dicks, Wm. I, 496
Dicks, Wm. Calvin V, 559
Dicks, Zachariah I, 536
Dicks, Zachariah I, 540
Dicks, Zachariah V, 486
Dicks, Zacharias I, 358
Dicks, Zacharias I, 385
Dicks, Zacharias I, 434
Dicks, Zacharias I, 487
Dicks, Zacharias I, 496
Dicks, Zacharias I, 536
Dicks, Zacharias I, 544
Dicks, Zacharias I, 695

Dicks, Zacharias V, 735
Dickson, Ann Carson VI, 906
Dickson, Dinah VI, 383
Dickson, Elizabeth II, 354
Dickson, George VI, 903
Dickson, George VI, 975
Dickson, James VI, 821
Dickson, Jas. III, 407
Dickson, John IV, 699
Dickson, Jonathan II, 215
Dickson, Joseph V, 992
Dickson, Joseph VI, 906
Dickson, Joseph VI, 927
Dickson, Joshua VI, 383
Dickson, Martha II, 215
Dickson, Martha Arthur VI, 906
Dickson, Mary VI, 975
Dickson, Matthew Reid III, 407
Dickson, Matthew Reid III, 459
Dickson, Pamelia III, 407
Dickson, Phebe III, 407
Dickson, Phebe III, 459
Dickson, Philipiney I, 873
Dickson, Philipiney I, 877
Dickson, Ruth I, 445
Dickson, Sarah V, 806
Dickson, Sarah VI, 872
Dickson, Thomas VI, 811
Dickson, Thomas VI, 906
Dicky, Jane V, 836
Diday, Pearl IV, 994
Didon, John Frederick II, 354
Die, Solomon IV, 1361
Diehl, Adam II, 130
Diehl, Adam II, 145
Diehl, Adam II, 147
Diehl, Elizabeth II, 130
Diehl, Elizabeth II, 145
Diehl, Elizabeth II, 147
Diehl, Martha II, 130
Diehl, Martha II, 145
Diehl, Martha II, 147
Diehl, Mary II, 803
Dieka, Mary II, 214
Dieker, ??? III, 101
Dieker, Elmira III, 101
Dieker, Henry III, 101
Diem, J. Martin III, 101
Diener, Sarah VI, 839
Dier, Mary I, 537
Dieter, Louisa Maria III, 122
Dietrich, Elizabeth III, 101
Dietrich, John III, 101
Dietrich, John III, 197
Dietrich, Margaret III, 197
Dietrich, Margaret B. III, 101
Dietrich, Margaret B. III, 197
Dietrick, John III, 150
Dietrick, Margaret B. III, 150
Diffee, Alfred M. I, 935
Diffee, Ethel D. I, 935
Diffee, Louie I, 935
Diffee, Prim L. I, 617
Diffendale, ??? III, 70
Diffendale, Jane III, 70
Diffendale, Jane III, 101
Difford, Alfred IV, 1313
Difford, Mary IV, 1313
Difford, Mary A. IV, 470
Difford, Mary A. IV, 1313
Difford, William B. IV, 470
Difford, Wm. IV, 1313
Difford, Wm. B. IV, 1313
Diggs, Agnes VI, 241
Diggs, Agness I, 385
Diggs, Agness I, 388
Diggs, Armsby I, 808
Diggs, Armsley I, 714
Diggs, Arnesbee I, 714
Diggs, Benjamin I, 714
Diggs, Caroline I, 714
Diggs, Fanny I, 383
Diggs, Fanny I, 385
Diggs, Fanny I, 714
Diggs, Fanny I, 808
Diggs, Fanny I, 1070
Diggs, Fany I, 714
Diggs, Hannah I, 714
Diggs, John I, 714
Diggs, John I, 808
Diggs, John I, 1070
Diggs, Judith I, 385
Diggs, Judith I, 808
Diggs, Judith VI, 241
Diggs, Judith VI, 243
Diggs, Judith VI, 244
Diggs, Little Berry I, 1070
Diggs, Little Berry I, 1072
Diggs, Littleberry I, 808
Diggs, Littlebury I, 714
Diggs, Littleton I, 714
Diggs, Lucy I, 714
Diggs, Lydia I, 714
Diggs, Lydia I, 1070
Diggs, Lydia I, 1072
Diggs, Margery I, 385
Diggs, Margery I, 714
Diggs, Margery I, 808
Diggs, Mark I, 714
Diggs, Mark I, 808
Diggs, Marshal I, 385
Diggs, Marshall VI, 241
Diggs, Mary I, 714
Diggs, Pleasant I, 385
Diggs, Pleasant VI, 241
Diggs, Rebeckah VI, 241
Diggs, Rebekah I, 385
Diggs, Rebekah I, 410
Diggs, Sarah I, 385
Diggs, Sarah I, 416
Diggs, Sarah VI, 241
Diggs, William I, 385
Diggs, William I, 714
Diggs, William I, 808
Diggs, William I, 1070
Diggs, William VI, 241
Diggs, William VI, 244
Diggs, Wm. I, 385
Diggs, Wm. VI, 243
Digs, Armsley I, 714
Digs, Benjamin I, 714
Digs, Benjamin I, 1066
Digs, Caroline I, 714
Digs, Caroline I, 1066
Digs, Fanny I, 714
Digs, Fanny I, 1066
Digs, Fany I, 714
Digs, Fany I, 1066
Digs, Hannah I, 714
Digs, Hannah I, 1066
Digs, John I, 714
Digs, John I, 1066
Digs, Littleton I, 714
Digs, Littleton I, 1066
Digs, Lucy I, 714
Digs, Lucy I, 1066
Digs, Lydia I, 714
Digs, Lydia I, 1066
Digs, Margery I, 714
Digs, Margery I, 1066
Digs, Mark I, 714
Digs, Mark I, 1066
Digs, Mary I, 714
Digs, Mary I, 717
Digs, William I, 714
Digs, William I, 1066
Digs, William Armsley I, 1066
Dildy, Mary I, 208
Dileno, Ann I, 45
Dileno, Ann I, 76
Dilhorn, George II, 506
Dilhorn, George IV, 83
Dilhorn, Mary IV, 83
Dilhorn, Milnor IV, 83
Dilhorn, Nathaniel II, 354
Dilhorn, Nathaniel II, 506
Dilhorn, Nathaniel IV, 29
Dilhorn, Nathaniel IV, 83
Dilhorn, Robert IV, 83
Dilhorn, Robert Milnor IV, 83
Dilks, Anna V, 383
Dilks, Anna V, 421
Dilks, Beulah II, 131
Dilks, Clark T. II, 147
Dilks, Clark Thompson II, 131
Dilks, John I. V, 383
Dilks, Thomas II, 131
Dill, Anna V, 837
Dill, Anna A. V, 455
Dill, Charles V, 166
Dill, Eliza V, 455
Dill, Elizabeth J. V, 455
Dill, James V, 455
Dill, John VI, 811
Dill, John VI, 823
Dill, Matilda II, 789
Dill, Phebe V, 47
Dill, Venia VI, 811
Dillard, Ann VI, 810
Dillard, Ann VI, 811
Dillard, Benjamin VI, 811
Dillard, Ediah VI, 905
Dillard, James VI, 811
Dillard, James VI, 905
Dillard, James VI, 1021
Dillard, James M. VI, 840
Dillard, Jno. VI, 1003
Dillard, John VI, 811
Dillard, John VI, 850
Dillard, John VI, 853
Dillard, John VI, 905
Dillard, John VI, 963
Dillard, Lucinda VI, 810
Dillard, Lucy VI, 811
Dillard, Lucy M. VI, 963
Dillard, Lynch VI, 852
Dillard, Martha A. VI, 1002
Dillard, Nancy E. VI, 811
Dillard, Ora Moore I, 632
Dillard, Sally P. Moore VI, 905
Dille, Cyrus IV, 1276
Dillen, Abigail V, 486
Dillen, Ann V, 476
Dillen, Ann V, 486
Dillen, Anna V, 293
Dillen, Charity V, 544
Dillen, Elizabeth IV, 620
Dillen, Hannah V, 486
Dillen, James IV, 620
Dillen, Jesse V, 486
Dillen, Luke V, 486
Dillen, Luke V, 544
Dillen, Rachel IV, 327
Diller, Elizabeth C. II, 853
Diller, Elizabeth C. II, 857
Diller, Esther C. II, 857
Diller, Esther C. II, 915
Diller, Esther R. II, 857
Diller, Rowland W. II, 857
Diller, Rowland W. II, 915
Dillhorn, Ann II, 354
Dillhorn, Ann II, 506
Dillhorn, George II, 354
Dillhorn, George II, 506
Dillhorn, George VI, 594
Dillhorn, Mary VI, 594
Dillhorn, Nathaniel II, 354
Dillhorn, Nathaniel II, 506
Dillhorn, Nathaniel IV, 29
Dillhorne, Ann II, 463
Dillhorne, Ann II, 506
Dillhorne, George II, 463
Dillhorne, George II, 506
Dillin, Hannah IV, 83
Dillin, Isaac IV, 83
Dillin, John IV, 83
Dillin, Martha IV, 83
Dillin, Mary IV, 83
Dillin, Mercy II, 506
Dillin, Moses IV, 83
Dillin, Rebekah IV, 83
Dillin, Wm. II, 736
Dillingham, ??? IV, 1141
Dillingham, Abigail IV, 195
Dillingham, Abigail IV, 241
Dillingham, Abigail IV, 1155
Dillingham, Abigail IV, 1156
Dillingham, Alfred IV, 1155
Dillingham, Alfred IV, 1156
Dillingham, Allen IV, 1361
Dillingham, Amy IV, 1357
Dillingham, Amy IV, 1361
Dillingham, Amy Bowerman IV, 1361
Dillingham, Amy R. IV, 1357
Dillingham, Amy R. IV, 1361
Dillingham, Annie I, 208
Dillingham, Cemantha Adelia IV, 1156
Dillingham, Cementha Adelia IV, 1156
Dillingham, Clifton V, 486
Dillingham, Deborah IV, 1155
Dillingham, Degorah V, 934
Dillingham, Edith IV, 195
Dillingham, Edith IV, 242
Dillingham, Edith IV, 1155
Dillingham, Edith IV, 1156
Dillingham, Eliza IV, 1156
Dillingham, Eliza IV, 1194
Dillingham, Elizabeth IV, 241
Dillingham, Elizabeth IV, 1155
Dillingham, Elizabeth IV, 1156
Dillingham, Elizabeth IV, 1167
Dillingham, Elizabeth IV, 1361
Dillingham, Elizabeth Johnson IV, 1156
Dillingham, Elwood IV, 1155
Dillingham, Elwood IV, 1276
Dillingham, Hannah IV, 195
Dillingham, Hannah IV, 1155
Dillingham, Hannah IV, 1156
Dillingham, Hannah IV, 1186
Dillingham, Hiram IV, 195
Dillingham, Hiram IV, 1155
Dillingham, Hiram IV, 1156
Dillingham, Ignatius V, 934
Dillingham, James IV, 195
Dillingham, James IV, 1155
Dillingham, James IV, 1156
Dillingham, James Albert IV, 1361
Dillingham, Jane IV, 1155
Dillingham, Jane IV, 1156
Dillingham, Jane IV, 1159
Dillingham, Jesse Lloyd, Jr. IV, 195
Dillingham, John IV, 195
Dillingham, John IV, 1155
Dillingham, John IV, 1156
Dillingham, Joseph IV, 1357
Dillingham, Joseph IV, 1361
Dillingham, Joseph W. IV, 1361
Dillingham, Mary III, 101
Dillingham, Mary III, 109
Dillingham, Mary IV, 195
Dillingham, Mary IV, 1155
Dillingham, Mary IV, 1361
Dillingham, Mary J. IV, 1156
Dillingham, Meribah IV, 1361
Dillingham, Micajah IV, 195
Dillingham, Micajah IV, 241
Dillingham, Micajah IV, 1155
Dillingham, Micajah IV, 1194
Dillingham, Michael VI, 872
Dillingham, Mira IV, 195
Dillingham, Mira IV, 1150
Dillingham, Mira IV, 1155
Dillingham, Mira IV, 1156
Dillingham, Nancy IV, 1145
Dillingham, Nancy IV, 1155
Dillingham, Nancy IV, 1156
Dillingham, Oliver D. IV, 1156
Dillingham, Philip IV, 1361
Dillingham, Richard IV, 1155
Dillingham, Richard IV, 1167
Dillingham, Ruth V, 934
Dillingham, Sarah IV, 195
Dillingham, Sarah IV, 1155
Dillingham, Sarah IV, 1156
Dillingham, Sarah IV, 1167
Dillingham, Sarah IV, 1169
Dillingham, Sarah IV, 1357
Dillingham, Sarah IV, 1361
Dillingham, Sarah W. IV, 1155
Dillingham, Silvanus IV, 1155
Dillingham, Silvanus IV, 1361
Dillingham, Sylvanus IV, 195
Dillingham, Sylvanus IV, 1156
Dillingham, Wilmie Abigail IV, 1156
Dillion, Abdon VI, 630
Dillion, Ann VI, 630
Dillion, Isaac VI, 630
Dillion, Lydia Ann VI, 630
Dillistin, Ann III, 45
Dillistin, Hazel B. III, 44
Dillistin, Helen B. III, 101
Dillistin, Helen B. III, 186
Dillistin, Howard P. III, 44
Dillistin, Howard P. III, 101
Dillistin, Howard P. III, 186
Dillistin, Jennie B. III, 44
Dillistin, Jennie B. III, 101
Dillistin, Jinnie B. W. III, 186
Dillistin, Laura III, 45
Dilliston, Hazel III, 101
Dilliston, Helen B. III, 101
Dilliston, Howard P. III, 101
Dilliston, Jennie B. III, 101
Dillman, Hannah Ann V, 881
Dillon, ??? VI, 634
Dillon, Abdon VI, 383
Dillon, Abdon VI, 616
Dillon, Abdon VI, 634
Dillon, Abdon VI, 685
Dillon, Abdon VI, 686
Dillon, Abigail I, 496
Dillon, Abigail V, 486
Dillon, Abigail V, 544
Dillon, Absalom V, 486
Dillon, Absalom V, 559
Dillon, Absolom I, 537
Dillon, Achsah I, 496
Dillon, Achsah I, 537
Dillon, Achsah I, 547
Dillon, Agnes V, 486
Dillon, Agnes VI, 486
Dillon, Agness I, 537
Dillon, Agness I, 572
Dillon, Agness IV, 29
Dillon, Agness V, 166
Dillon, Agness VI, 634
Dillon, Agness VI, 675
Dillon, Albert V, 486
Dillon, Allen V, 486
Dillon, Ann I, 537
Dillon, Ann I, 1106
Dillon, Ann IV, 29
Dillon, Ann IV, 76
Dillon, Ann IV, 83
Dillon, Ann IV, 385
Dillon, Ann IV, 419
Dillon, Ann V, 486
Dillon, Ann V, 618
Dillon, Ann V, 648
Dillon, Ann VI, 383
Dillon, Ann VI, 433
Dillon, Ann VI, 486
Dillon, Ann VI, 503
Dillon, Ann VI, 616
Dillon, Ann VI, 634
Dillon, Ann VI, 686
Dillon, Ann Elizabeth VI, 634
Dillon, Anna V, 233
Dillon, Anna V, 234
Dillon, Anna V, 293
Dillon, Anna V, 294
Dillon, Anna VI, 685
Dillon, Arabelle V, 294
Dillon, Asahel IV, 385
Dillon, Aseneth I, 808
Dillon, Aseneth I, 815
Dillon, Bertha IV, 385
Dillon, Bertha IV, 403
Dillon, Betsey I, 1082
Dillon, Betty V, 486
Dillon, Betty V, 543
Dillon, Betty V, 618
Dillon, Calvin V, 486
Dillon, Calvin V, 487
Dillon, Charity I, 537
Dillon, Charity I, 562
Dillon, Charity V, 486
Dillon, Charity V, 618
Dillon, Charity VI, 383
Dillon, Charity VI, 435
Dillon, Daniel I, 343
Dillon, Daniel I, 385
Dillon, Daniel I, 487
Dillon, Daniel I, 496
Dillon, Daniel I, 537
Dillon, Daniel I, 547
Dillon, Daniel I, 808
Dillon, Daniel I, 1070
Dillon, Daniel I, 1082
Dillon, Daniel I, 1091
Dillon, Daniel V, 618
Dillon, Daniel VI, 383
Dillon, Daniel, Jr. I, 537
Dillon, Daniel, Sr. V, 618
Dillon, Deborah VI, 486
Dillon, Deborah VI, 616
Dillon, Deborah VI, 634
Dillon, Edith IV, 327
Dillon, Edith IV, 384
Dillon, Edith IV, 385
Dillon, Elisabeth IV, 620
Dillon, Elizabeth I, 496
Dillon, Elizabeth I, 537
Dillon, Elizabeth I, 544
Dillon, Elizabeth I, 956
Dillon, Elizabeth I, 1082
Dillon, Elizabeth I, 1091
Dillon, Elizabeth IV, 327
Dillon, Elizabeth IV, 385
Dillon, Elizabeth IV, 457
Dillon, Elizabeth IV, 620
Dillon, Elizabeth IV, 662
Dillon, Elizabeth IV, 868
Dillon, Elizabeth V, 486
Dillon, Elizabeth V, 537
Dillon, Elizabeth Ann IV, 29
Dillon, Elizabeth D. IV, 892
Dillon, Elizabeth D. IV, 893
Dillon, Elizabeth L. V, 486
Dillon, Ellen V, 234
Dillon, Emily J. V, 992
Dillon, Esther Sophia I, 1082
Dillon, Ettie May V, 234
Dillon, Ezra VI, 634
Dillon, Garret I, 956
Dillon, Garret I, 1091
Dillon, Garret I, 1092
Dillon, Garret I, 1097
Dillon, Garrett I, 1082
Dillon, Garrett I, 1091
Dillon, Garrit I, 1082
Dillon, Gulielma V, 559
Dillon, Hannah I, 496
Dillon, Hannah I, 537
Dillon, Hannah I, 569
Dillon, Hannah I, 808
Dillon, Hannah I, 877
Dillon, Hannah IV, 78
Dillon, Hannah IV, 83
Dillon, Hannah IV, 327
Dillon, Hannah IV, 384
Dillon, Hannah IV, 385
Dillon, Hannah IV, 422
Dillon, Hannah V, 445
Dillon, Hannah V, 486
Dillon, Hannah V, 544
Dillon, Hannah V, 618
Dillon, Hannah VI, 383

llon, Hannah VI, 460
llon, Hannah VI, 486
llon, Hannah VI, 634
llon, Hannah VI, 651
llon, Henry VI, 807
llon, Henry VI, 833
llon, Hur I, 547
llon, Isaac I, 496
llon, Isaac I, 537
llon, Isaac IV, 83
llon, Isaac IV, 327
llon, Isaac IV, 384
llon, Isaac IV, 385
llon, Isaac V, 486
llon, Isaac VI, 375
llon, Isaac VI, 383
llon, Isaac VI, 634
llon, Isaac E. I, 1082
llon, Isac I, 1091
llon, Isaiah I, 808
llon, James I, 496
llon, James I, 956
llon, James I, 1081
llon, James I, 1082
llon, James I, 1090
llon, James I, 1091
llon, James IV, 29
llon, James IV, 620
llon, James IV, 662
llon, James IV, 868
llon, James IV, 894
llon, James V, 618
llon, James VI, 383
llon, James VI, 486
llon, James VI, 503
llon, James VI, 634
llon, James VI, 686
llon, James VI, 704
llon, James Alexander I, 1082
llon, James W. V, 618
llon, James, Jr. VI, 383
llon, James, Sr. VI, 634
llon, James, Sr. VI, 704
llon, Jane I, 537
llon, Jane V, 486
llon, Jane V, 491
llon, Jas. VI, 486
llon, Jemima I, 1082
llon, Jemima I, 1091
llon, Jemima I, 1098
llon, Jemimah I, 956
llon, Jemimah I, 1082
llon, Jess V, 618
llon, Jesse I, 496
llon, Jesse I, 537
llon, Jesse I, 569
llon, Jesse V, 166
llon, Jesse V, 175
llon, Jesse V, 486
llon, Jesse V, 544
llon, Jesse, Jr. I, 537
llon, John I, 1091
llon, John IV, 29
llon, John IV, 83
llon, John IV, 384
llon, John V, 618
llon, John VI, 383
llon, John VI, 386
llon, John VI, 486
llon, John VI, 634
llon, John VI, 807
llon, John VI, 833
llon, John Columbus I, 1082
llon, John James VI, 634
llon, John, Jr. VI, 486
llon, Jonah William VI, 634
llon, Jonathan I, 496
llon, Jonathan I, 537
llon, Jonathan I, 572
llon, Jonathan I, 808
llon, Jonathan V, 166
llon, Jonathan V, 486
llon, Jonathan V, 618
llon, Jonathan P. I, 808
llon, Joseph V, 486
llon, Joseph V, 487
llon, Joseph V, 618
llon, Joseph VI, 634
llon, Joseph Abdon VI, 634
llon, Joshua I, 808
llon, Joshua I, 1070
llon, Josiah VI, 486
llon, Josiah VI, 634
llon, Keziah IV, 327
llon, Keziah IV, 385
llon, Keziah IV, 392
llon, Laban I, 1082
llon, Laban I, 1091
llon, Leah I, 808
llon, Lida I, 1082
llon, Lidy I, 956
Dillon, Lloyd IV, 83
Dillon, Lloyd IV, 327
Dillon, Lloyd IV, 385
Dillon, Loyd IV, 384
Dillon, Lucy VI, 833
Dillon, Luke I, 496
Dillon, Luke V, 486
Dillon, Luke V, 618
Dillon, Lydia I, 496
Dillon, Lydia I, 537
Dillon, Lydia I, 547
Dillon, Lydia I, 1082
Dillon, Lydia V, 293
Dillon, Lydia VI, 362
Dillon, Lydia VI, 383
Dillon, Lydia VI, 386
Dillon, Lydia Ann VI, 375
Dillon, Lydia Ann VI, 383
Dillon, Lydia Ann VI, 634
Dillon, Lydia Ann VI, 691
Dillon, Lydia Arabel V, 234
Dillon, Margaret I, 1082
Dillon, Margaret I, 1091
Dillon, Margaret I, 1092
Dillon, Margaret I, 1097
Dillon, Margaret IV, 327
Dillon, Margaret IV, 385
Dillon, Martha I, 496
Dillon, Martha I, 537
Dillon, Martha I, 539
Dillon, Martha I, 1082
Dillon, Martha IV, 83
Dillon, Martha IV, 363
Dillon, Martha IV, 385
Dillon, Martha IV, 470
Dillon, Martha V, 234
Dillon, Martha V, 668
Dillon, Martha Ellen V, 293
Dillon, Mary I, 537
Dillon, Mary I, 1082
Dillon, Mary IV, 83
Dillon, Mary IV, 327
Dillon, Mary V, 47
Dillon, Mary V, 81
Dillon, Mary V, 166
Dillon, Mary V, 175
Dillon, Mary V, 233
Dillon, Mary V, 486
Dillon, Mary V, 503
Dillon, Mary VI, 370
Dillon, Mary VI, 383
Dillon, Mary VI, 430
Dillon, Mary VI, 634
Dillon, Mary VI, 704
Dillon, Mary Elvina I, 1082
Dillon, Mary Jane I, 1082
Dillon, Mary Jane I, 1091
Dillon, Mary Jane V, 234
Dillon, Mary Jane V, 293
Dillon, Mary Jane V, 486
Dillon, Mary M. VI, 901
Dillon, Miriam I, 808
Dillon, Miriam I, 812
Dillon, Miriam I, 877
Dillon, Moses IV, 83
Dillon, Moses IV, 327
Dillon, Moses IV, 363
Dillon, Moses IV, 384
Dillon, Moses VI, 486
Dillon, Mrs. Bell V, 992
Dillon, Nancy VI, 634
Dillon, Nancy VI, 662
Dillon, Nancy VI, 678
Dillon, Nancy VI, 680
Dillon, Nancy VI, 685
Dillon, Naomi V, 618
Dillon, Nathan I, 496
Dillon, Nathan I, 537
Dillon, Nathan V, 233
Dillon, Nathan V, 486
Dillon, Nathan V, 503
Dillon, Neal Frazer I, 1082
Dillon, Noah IV, 385
Dillon, Patience I, 496
Dillon, Patience I, 537
Dillon, Patience I, 546
Dillon, Patrick H. VI, 998
Dillon, Peniah I, 808
Dillon, Penniah I, 808
Dillon, Peter I, 343
Dillon, Peter I, 385
Dillon, Peter I, 496
Dillon, Peter I, 537
Dillon, Peter I, 544
Dillon, Peter I, 562
Dillon, Peter I, 956
Dillon, Peter I, 1077
Dillon, Peter I, 1082
Dillon, Peter I, 1091
Dillon, Peter I, 1092
Dillon, Peter I, 1095
Dillon, Peter I, 1096
Dillon, Peter VI, 383
Dillon, Peter, Jr. I, 537
Dillon, Peter, Jr. I, 1082
Dillon, Peter, Jr. I, 1091
Dillon, Peter, Sr. I, 1082
Dillon, Phebe I, 956
Dillon, Phebe I, 1082
Dillon, Phebe I, 1091
Dillon, Phebe I, 1097
Dillon, Phebe VI, 383
Dillon, Phebe VI, 386
Dillon, Rachel I, 1082
Dillon, Rachel I, 1091
Dillon, Rachel I, 1093
Dillon, Rachel IV, 29
Dillon, Rachel IV, 144
Dillon, Rachel IV, 327
Dillon, Rachel IV, 385
Dillon, Rachel IV, 434
Dillon, Rachel VI, 486
Dillon, Rachel VI, 490
Dillon, Rebecca IV, 83
Dillon, Rebecca IV, 327
Dillon, Rebecca IV, 620
Dillon, Rebecca VI, 486
Dillon, Rebecca VI, 686
Dillon, Rebeckah VI, 634
Dillon, Rebekah IV, 83
Dillon, Rebekah VI, 486
Dillon, Rhoda IV, 327
Dillon, Rhoda IV, 332
Dillon, Richard H. V, 486
Dillon, Richard H. V, 537
Dillon, Richard Henry V, 486
Dillon, Ruth I, 1082
Dillon, Ruth I, 1090
Dillon, Ruth I, 1091
Dillon, Ruth V, 233
Dillon, Ruth V, 249
Dillon, Ruth V, 486
Dillon, Ruth V, 618
Dillon, Ruth VI, 616
Dillon, Samuel I, 808
Dillon, Samuel V, 486
Dillon, Samuel V, 487
Dillon, Samuel B. I, 1082
Dillon, Samuel B. I, 1091
Dillon, Samuel B. I, 1093
Dillon, Sarah I, 496
Dillon, Sarah I, 537
Dillon, Sarah I, 956
Dillon, Sarah I, 1082
Dillon, Sarah IV, 327
Dillon, Sarah IV, 385
Dillon, Sarah V, 486
Dillon, Sarah V, 618
Dillon, Sarah VI, 383
Dillon, Sarah VI, 486
Dillon, Sarah Ann V, 486
Dillon, Solomon I, 1082
Dillon, Susanna I, 496
Dillon, Susanna I, 537
Dillon, Susanna I, 574
Dillon, Susanna VI, 383
Dillon, Susanna Jane I, 1082
Dillon, Susannah I, 496
Dillon, Susannah I, 956
Dillon, Susannah I, 1082
Dillon, Susannah I, 1091
Dillon, Susannah I, 1092
Dillon, Susannah VI, 486
Dillon, Susannah VI, 539
Dillon, Sussannah VI, 807
Dillon, Thamasin VI, 634
Dillon, Thomas IV, 620
Dillon, Thomas V, 486
Dillon, Thomas Holton I, 1082
Dillon, Vashti IV, 371
Dillon, Vashti IV, 385
Dillon, Walter I, 537
Dillon, Walter V, 486
Dillon, William I, 496
Dillon, William I, 537
Dillon, William I, 808
Dillon, William I, 956
Dillon, William I, 1070
Dillon, William I, 1082
Dillon, William I, 1091
Dillon, William I, 1092
Dillon, William IV, 29
Dillon, William IV, 144
Dillon, William V, 294
Dillon, William V, 486
Dillon, William V, 618
Dillon, William VI, 634
Dillon, William Alvin V, 234
Dillon, William Anderson I, 1082
Dillon, Wm. V, 618
Dillon, Wm. VI, 486
Dillon, Wm., Jr. VI, 486
Dillone, Mrs. Bell V, 992
Dills, Mary IV, 1235
Dillwin, Ann II, 211
Dillwin, Ann II, 215
Dillwin, John II, 211
Dillwin, Marcy II, 354
Dillwin, Susanna II, 354
Dillwin, Susannah II, 211
Dillworth, Ann II, 354
Dillworth, Catherine II, 354
Dillworth, Charles M. IV, 196
Dillworth, Edith II, 823
Dillworth, John II, 354
Dillworth, Mary II, 354
Dillworth, Samuel II, 506
Dillworth, Sarah II, 354
Dillworth, Sarah II, 506
Dillworth, Susanna II, 354
Dillworth, Thomas II, 354
Dillworth, William II, 215
Dillworth, William II, 354
Dillworth, Wm. II, 506
Dillworth, Wm. II, 993
Dillwyn, Ann II, 215
Dillwyn, Ann II, 813
Dillwyn, George II, 172
Dillwyn, George II, 215
Dillwyn, George II, 506
Dillwyn, George II, 549
Dillwyn, George III, 381
Dillwyn, George Painter II, 693
Dillwyn, John II, 215
Dillwyn, John II, 262
Dillwyn, John II, 354
Dillwyn, John II, 506
Dillwyn, John II, 549
Dillwyn, John II, 612
Dillwyn, John II, 618
Dillwyn, Logan II, 215
Dillwyn, Lydia II, 354
Dillwyn, Marcey II, 506
Dillwyn, Marcey II, 618
Dillwyn, Peter Worrall II, 215
Dillwyn, Peter Worrall II, 506
Dillwyn, Sarah II, 215
Dillwyn, Sarah II, 217
Dillwyn, Sarah II, 506
Dillwyn, Sarah II, 549
Dillwyn, Sarah Logan II, 172
Dillwyn, Sarah Logan II, 262
Dillwyn, Susanna II, 192
Dillwyn, Susanna II, 215
Dillwyn, Susanna II, 217
Dillwyn, Susanna II, 506
Dillwyn, Susanna II, 612
Dillwyn, Susanna II, 693
Dillwyn, Susannah II, 172
Dillwyn, Susannah II, 215
Dillwyn, Wd. Sarah II, 172
Dillwyn, Wd. Susannah II, 506
Dillwyn, William II, 215
Dillwyn, William II, 217
Dillwyn, William II, 262
Dillwyn, Wm. II, 506
Dillwyn, Wm. II, 618
Dillwynn, George II, 506
Dillwynn, Sarah II, 506
Dilon, William I, 137
Dilton, Mary VI, 677
Dilwin, Elizabeth II, 354
Dilwin, John II, 354
Dilwin, Lydia II, 354
Dilwin, Marcy II, 354
Dilwin, Sarah II, 354
Dilwin, Susanna II, 354
Dilwin, Susannah II, 354
Dilwin, William II, 354
Dilworth, Abigail IV, 196
Dilworth, Abigail V, 902
Dilworth, Abigail P. IV, 196
Dilworth, Abigail R. IV, 311
Dilworth, Abigail R. IV, 314
Dilworth, Abigail R. V, 902
Dilworth, Abraham IV, 144
Dilworth, Abraham IV, 196
Dilworth, Abraham R. IV, 195
Dilworth, Abraham R. IV, 196
Dilworth, Abraham R. IV, 231
Dilworth, Abram IV, 195
Dilworth, Ann II, 506
Dilworth, Ann II, 691
Dilworth, Ann IV, 195
Dilworth, Ann IV, 196
Dilworth, Ann IV, 327
Dilworth, Anne VI, 106
Dilworth, Arrington I, 927
Dilworth, Caleb IV, 195
Dilworth, Caleb IV, 196
Dilworth, Caleb IV, 327
Dilworth, Caleb D. IV, 196
Dilworth, Caleb J. V, 902
Dilworth, Camie I, 931
Dilworth, Charles II, 477
Dilworth, Charles II, 506
Dilworth, Charles M. IV, 196
Dilworth, Charlotte IV, 195
Dilworth, Charlotte IV, 196
Dilworth, Edith II, 821
Dilworth, Eleanor IV, 521
Dilworth, Elizabeth IV, 195
Dilworth, Elizabeth IV, 196
Dilworth, Elizabeth IV, 521
Dilworth, Hanna IV, 196
Dilworth, Hannah II, 499
Dilworth, Hannah II, 506
Dilworth, Hannah IV, 196
Dilworth, James II, 506
Dilworth, James II, 691
Dilworth, James IV, 521
Dilworth, Jane IV, 144
Dilworth, Jane IV, 195
Dilworth, Jane IV, 196
Dilworth, Jane IV, 271
Dilworth, Jane D. IV, 311
Dilworth, Jane D. IV, 314
Dilworth, John IV, 521
Dilworth, John P. II, 958
Dilworth, John R. IV, 195
Dilworth, John R. IV, 196
Dilworth, Jonathan II, 506
Dilworth, Joseph II, 477
Dilworth, Joseph II, 506
Dilworth, Joseph II, 958
Dilworth, Lydia IV, 196
Dilworth, Martha II, 958
Dilworth, Martha IV, 195
Dilworth, Martha IV, 196
Dilworth, Martha IV, 199
Dilworth, Martha IV, 231
Dilworth, Martha V, 902
Dilworth, Mary II, 477
Dilworth, Mary II, 506
Dilworth, Mary IV, 171
Dilworth, Mary IV, 195
Dilworth, Mary IV, 196
Dilworth, Mary IV, 521
Dilworth, Mary IV, 560
Dilworth, Nicholas II, 499
Dilworth, Nicholas II, 506
Dilworth, Rachel II, 477
Dilworth, Rachel II, 506
Dilworth, Rankin IV, 196
Dilworth, Rankin V, 902
Dilworth, Rebecca IV, 144
Dilworth, Rebecca IV, 195
Dilworth, Rebecca IV, 196
Dilworth, Rebecca IV, 202
Dilworth, Rebecca IV, 327
Dilworth, Rebecca IV, 330
Dilworth, Rebecca Ann IV, 196
Dilworth, Rebecca Ann V, 902
Dilworth, Rebecca F. IV, 196
Dilworth, Rhoads R. IV, 327
Dilworth, Rhoads R. IV, 330
Dilworth, Rhodes IV, 144
Dilworth, Rhodes IV, 196
Dilworth, Rhodes IV, 202
Dilworth, Rhodes R. IV, 195
Dilworth, Richard II, 506
Dilworth, Samuel II, 506
Dilworth, Samuel II, 703
Dilworth, Sarah I, 613
Dilworth, Sarah I, 927
Dilworth, Sarah II, 354
Dilworth, Sarah II, 461
Dilworth, Sarah II, 506
Dilworth, Sarah IV, 144
Dilworth, Sarah IV, 196
Dilworth, Sarah IV, 249
Dilworth, Sarah Caroline I, 618
Dilworth, Sarah Caroline I, 927
Dilworth, Sarah Dilworth V, 902
Dilworth, Sarah E. IV, 195
Dilworth, Sarah M. V, 902
Dilworth, Sona Caroline I, 623
Dilworth, Susanna II, 499
Dilworth, Susanna II, 506
Dilworth, Thomas II, 354
Dilworth, Thomas II, 506
Dilworth, William IV, 195
Dilworth, William IV, 196
Dilworth, William IV, 521
Dilworth, William IV, 560
Dilworth, Wm. II, 506
Dilworth, Wm. II, 691
Dilworth, Wm. IV, 171
Dilworth, Wm. Henry Evans V, 902
Dilwyn, John II, 354
Dilwyn, Margaret II, 443
Dilwyn, Sarah II, 506
Dilwyn, Sarah II, 528

Dilwyn, Wm. II, 506
Dilwyn, Wm. II, 528
Dilyer, Letitia II, 507
Dimary, C. H. IV, 1276
Dimary, Watson IV, 1276
Dimeck, Sarah II, 507
Dimery, C. H. IV, 1276
Dimery, Micajah IV, 1276
Dimery, Watson IV, 1276
Dimmick, Sydney IV, 1313
Dimmit, Alice I, 385
Dimmit, Alice I, 1118
Dimmitt, Alice I, 379
Dimmitt, Alice I, 385
Dimmitt, Alice I, 1102
Dimmitt, Alice I, 1118
Dimmitt, Diana I, 1118
Dimmitt, Dianna I, 1118
Dimmoiks, Sarah II, 993
Dimney, Edward VI, 811
Dimney, Luckey VI, 811
Dimock, Ella M. III, 462
Dimock, Sarah II, 507
Dimock, Sarah II, 993
Dimock, Tobias II, 507
Dimock, Tobias II, 958
Dimock, Tobias II, 993
Dimork, Sarah II, 507
Dimork, Sarah II, 541
Dimork, Tobias II, 507
Dimork, Tobias II, 541
Dimsdale, William II, 354
Dimsdale, Wm. II, 507
Dinegar, Adelaide W. III, 101
Dinegar, Hannah III, 101
Dinegar, Hannah III, 114
Dinegar, Hannah III, 166
Dinegar, Jonas III, 101
Dinegar, Jonas III, 166
Dinegar, Wd. Adelaide W. III, 166
Dinge, Mary IV, 692
Dingee, Adaline IV, 29
Dingee, Adaline IV, 125
Dingee, Adaline IV, 620
Dingee, Adaline IV, 868
Dingee, Adaline IV, 948
Dingee, Adaline V, 47
Dingee, Adaline V, 48
Dingee, Agnes Grisselle VI, 383
Dingee, Ann IV, 29
Dingee, Ann IV, 31
Dingee, Ann VI, 383
Dingee, Anna V, 47
Dingee, Anna V, 65
Dingee, Arthur III, 481
Dingee, Arthur III, 496
Dingee, Barshaba IV, 196
Dingee, Bathsheba IV, 29
Dingee, Bathsheba IV, 196
Dingee, Bathsheba IV, 812
Dingee, Bathsheba IV, 851
Dingee, Bathsheba IV, 858
Dingee, Bathsheba V, 487
Dingee, Bethsheba IV, 620
Dingee, Bethsheba V, 487
Dingee, Bethshebe V, 487
Dingee, Charles II, 507
Dingee, Charles IV, 20
Dingee, Charles IV, 24
Dingee, Charles IV, 29
Dingee, Charles IV, 31
Dingee, Charles IV, 38
Dingee, Charles IV, 39
Dingee, Charles IV, 196
Dingee, Charles IV, 620
Dingee, Charles IV, 689
Dingee, Charles IV, 868
Dingee, Charles V, 47
Dingee, Charles V, 301
Dingee, Charles V, 487
Dingee, Charles VI, 383
Dingee, Charles H. IV, 83
Dingee, Charles Hillis IV, 83
Dingee, Christopher II, 507
Dingee, Clarissa V, 41
Dingee, Clarissa V, 47
Dingee, David IV, 29
Dingee, David IV, 868
Dingee, Elizabeth IV, 620
Dingee, Elizabeth B. IV, 620
Dingee, Emma I. II, 857
Dingee, Emma I. II, 880
Dingee, Esther III, 481
Dingee, Esther III, 496
Dingee, Hannah IV, 29
Dingee, Hannah IV, 39
Dingee, Hannah IV, 868
Dingee, Hannah V, 47
Dingee, Hannah V, 301
Dingee, Hannah V, 305
Dingee, Hannah VI, 383
Dingee, Jacob II, 703
Dingee, Jacob II, 707
Dingee, Jacob IV, 620
Dingee, Jacob IV, 630
Dingee, Jane II, 703
Dingee, Jane II, 707
Dingee, John IV, 29
Dingee, John IV, 196
Dingee, John IV, 620
Dingee, John IV, 812
Dingee, John IV, 851
Dingee, John IV, 858
Dingee, John IV, 868
Dingee, John V, 487
Dingee, John VI, 383
Dingee, John Milton V, 487
Dingee, John T. IV, 868
Dingee, Lydia V, 47
Dingee, Marcus V, 47
Dingee, Margaretta P. II, 703
Dingee, Margaretta P. II, 736
Dingee, Martha IV, 24
Dingee, Martha IV, 29
Dingee, Martha IV, 31
Dingee, Martha IV, 38
Dingee, Martha IV, 39
Dingee, Martha IV, 56
Dingee, Martha IV, 620
Dingee, Martha IV, 689
Dingee, Martha V, 487
Dingee, Martha VI, 383
Dingee, Martha Jr IV, 79
Dingee, Martha Nathan IV, 196
Dingee, Martha, Jr. IV, 83
Dingee, Mary II, 703
Dingee, Mary II, 736
Dingee, Mary IV, 20
Dingee, Mary IV, 29
Dingee, Mary IV, 196
Dingee, Mary IV, 868
Dingee, Mary D. II, 707
Dingee, Mary D. II, 736
Dingee, Mary D. II, 746
Dingee, Nathan IV, 29
Dingee, Patience III, 101
Dingee, Rachel IV, 29
Dingee, Rachel IV, 38
Dingee, Rachel VI, 383
Dingee, Rebecca IV, 620
Dingee, Rebecca IV, 630
Dingee, Rebecca A. IV, 630
Dingee, Richard IV, 868
Dingee, Ruth IV, 29
Dingee, Ruth IV, 196
Dingee, Ruth IV, 620
Dingee, Ruth V, 47
Dingee, Ruth V, 487
Dingee, Ruth Martha IV, 196
Dingee, Samuel IV, 29
Dingee, Samuel IV, 868
Dingee, Sarah II, 507
Dingee, Sarah IV, 29
Dingee, Sarah VI, 383
Dingee, Talbot IV, 868
Dingee, Uriah IV, 29
Dingee, William IV, 29
Dingee, William IV, 868
Dingey, Bethshebe V, 487
Dingey, Charles V, 487
Dingey, Christopher II, 354
Dingey, John V, 487
Dingy, Adaline IV, 948
Dingy, Ann V, 383
Dingy, Bethsheba V, 487
Dingy, Charles V, 301
Dingy, Charles V, 487
Dingy, Charles Hillis IV, 83
Dingy, Christopher II, 354
Dingy, Hannah V, 47
Dingy, Hannah V, 383
Dingy, Hannah V, 406
Dingy, James II, 354
Dingy, John IV, 948
Dingy, John V, 487
Dingy, John Milton V, 487
Dingy, Lydia V, 383
Dingy, Mary II, 354
Dinkins, Elizabeth I, 985
Dinkins, Elizabeth I, 1009
Dinkins, Elizabeth I, 1013
Dinnen, Abigail IV, 26
Dinnen, Abigail IV, 29
Dinnen, Andrew IV, 29
Dinnen, Anthony IV, 29
Dinnen, Eleanor IV, 26
Dinnen, Eleanor IV, 29
Dinnen, John IV, 29
Dinnen, Joseph IV, 29
Dinnen, Rachel IV, 29
Dinnen, Rachel IV, 48
Dinnen, Rachel May IV, 29
Dinnen, Susanna IV, 29
Dinnen, William IV, 29
Dinnis, Jonathan II, 504
Dinoil, Anne II, 66
Dinwiddie, Ann VI, 865
Dinwiddie, Anne VI, 817
Dinwiddie, Catharine VI, 811
Dinwiddie, Celina VI, 862
Dinwiddie, Edward W. VI, 906
Dinwiddie, Elizabeth VI, 828
Dinwiddie, Elizabeth VI, 849
Dinwiddie, Ellis VI, 811
Dinwiddie, Frances VI, 801
Dinwiddie, Frances VI, 817
Dinwiddie, James VI, 804
Dinwiddie, James VI, 811
Dinwiddie, James VI, 849
Dinwiddie, James VI, 865
Dinwiddie, James VI, 905
Dinwiddie, James VI, 1008
Dinwiddie, Jane VI, 811
Dinwiddie, Joel W. VI, 811
Dinwiddie, John VI, 803
Dinwiddie, John VI, 812
Dinwiddie, Joseph VI, 804
Dinwiddie, Joseph VI, 828
Dinwiddie, Joseph VI, 829
Dinwiddie, Joseph VI, 862
Dinwiddie, Lucinda L. VI, 906
Dinwiddie, Martha VI, 803
Dinwiddie, Mary VI, 804
Dinwiddie, Mary VI, 905
Dinwiddie, Mary M. VI, 811
Dinwiddie, Nancy VI, 812
Dinwiddie, Nancy Bryan VI, 811
Dinwiddie, Rebecca V, 21
Dinwiddie, S. A. Holland VI, 905
Dinwiddie, W. M. VI, 801
Dinwiddie, William VI, 812
Dinwiddie, William VI, 847
Dinwiddie, William W. VI, 862
Dinwiddie, Wm. W. VI, 801
Dinwiddle, Joseph VI, 811
Dinwiddle, Mary VI, 811
Dinwiddle, Polly VI, 811
Dinwiddle, Rebecca V, 48
Dinwiddle, William VI, 811
Dionne, Lewis V, 559
Dipery, Louesa V, 992
Dippery, A. C. V, 992
Dippery, Anna V, 992
Dippery, Daniel V, 992
Dippery, Louesa V, 992
Dippery, Mary V, 992
Dippery, Sarah V, 992
Dipra, Louesa V, 992
Dirk, Hannah V, 234
Dirk, Hannah VI, 383
Dirk, Hannah VI, 431
Dirkey, Rachel V, 234
Dirkin, Alexander II, 736
Dirkin, Alexander II, 769
Dirkin, Deborah II, 736
Dirkin, Mary II, 736
Dirkin, Mary II, 769
Dirkin, Walter II, 736
Dirkin, Walter II, 769
Dirkin, Wd. Deborah II, 736
Dirkin, Wd. Deborah II, 769
Dirks, Mildred VI, 770
Dirvall, Rebekah II, 443
Dirvall, William II, 443
Disbro, Gertrude V, 166
Disbro, Jennie V, 166
Disbrough, Joseph V, 48
Disbrow, Alice Jane V, 559
Disbrow, Alice Jane V, 584
Disbrow, Levi III, 101
Disbrow, Mary III, 101
Diselm, Elizabeth IV, 143
Diselms, Joseph IV, 521
Dishan, Dinah V, 48
Dishbrough, Charles Edwin V, 166
Dishbrough, Gertrude V, 166
Dishbrough, Ida May V, 166
Dishbrough, Jennie V, 166
Dishbrough, Joseph V, 166
Dishbrough, Mary Dorothy V, 166
Dishman, Jeremiah VI, 906
Dishman, Jeremiah VI, 962
Dishman, Nancy Miller VI, 906
Dishman, Sally VI, 906
Dishman, Sally VI, 962
Dishman, William VI, 906
Dishon, Dinah V, 48
Dishong, Emma V, 992
Dishong, Sarah A. V, 992
Disselmes, Benjamin IV, 521
Disselmes, C. IV, 521
Disselmes, David IV, 521
Disselmes, Eleanor IV, 521
Disselmes, Elizabeth IV, 521
Disselmes, Jacob IV, 521
Disselmes, Jacob Hannah IV, 521
Disselmes, Jesse IV, 521
Disselmes, Jonas IV, 521
Disselmes, Jonathan IV, 521
Disselmes, Joseph IV, 521
Disselmes, Lydia IV, 521
Disselmes, Mary IV, 521
Disselmes, Phebe IV, 521
Disselmes, Polly IV, 521
Disselmes, Rhoda IV, 521
Disselmes, Ruthanna IV, 521
Disturnell, Anna C. III, 102
Disturnell, Charles III, 102
Disturnell, Elizabeth III, 102
Disturnell, Frances III, 102
Disturnell, Frances III, 186
Disturnell, Frances D. III, 102
Disturnell, George William III, 102
Disturnell, Jane III, 102
Disturnell, Jane III, 186
Disturnell, Jane III, 357
Disturnell, Jane W. III, 102
Disturnell, Jennie III, 102
Disturnell, Jennie D. III, 304
Disturnell, Mary G. III, 102
Disturnell, Mary G. III, 274
Disturnell, Matilda R. III, 102
Disturnell, Thomas W. III, 102
Disturnell, William III, 102
Disturnell, William III, 357
Disturnell, Wm. III, 102
Disturnell, Wm. III, 186
Dithridge, Ed. IV, 948
Dithridge, Minnie IV, 948
Dithridge, Minnie V. IV, 948
Ditto, Lucy VI, 811
Ditto, Peter VI, 811
Ditto, Peter VI, 842
Diuguid, Augustus VI, 855
Diuguid, Credylla VI, 848
Diuguid, Elizabeth S. VI, 837
Diuguid, George VI, 807
Diuguid, George A. VI, 801
Diuguid, George A. VI, 811
Diuguid, J. S. VI, 837
Diuguid, Jas. H. VI, 869
Diuguid, Jemima VI, 855
Diuguid, Jesse T. VI, 848
Diuguid, Jesse T. VI, 854
Diuguid, Martha B. VI, 811
Diuguid, Mary A. VI, 845
Diuguid, Nancy S. VI, 854
Diuguid, Paulina A. VI, 811
Diuguid, Sampson VI, 811
Diuguid, Sampson VI, 817
Diuguid, Stephen S. VI, 805
Diuguid, William VI, 855
Diuguid, William S. VI, 848
Diuguid, Wm. VI, 854
Diuguid, Wm. S. VI, 837
Diven, Catharine V, 455
Diven, Catherine V, 312
Diven, Charles V, 455
Diven, Elsie Barrett V, 455
Diven, Frank V, 455
Diven, Inez Elsie V, 455
Diven, James V, 312
Diven, James V, 455
Diven, Mary V, 455
Diven, Mary J. V, 312
Diven, Sarah V, 455
Divens, Elsie Barrett V, 455
Divens, Inez Elsie V, 455
Diver, Elizabeth III, 102
Diver, Elizabeth III, 276
Diver, Helen IV, 1037
Diver, Richard III, 102
Diver, Richard III, 276
Divers, Bess M. IV, 1313
Divers, Frances Powell VI, 906
Divers, William VI, 906
Divind, Deborah V, 806
Divind, Michael V, 806
Divine, Joseph V, 234
Divine, Margaret II, 864
Divine, Martha II, 52
Divine, Martha II, 66
Dix, ??? I, 385
Dix, Achilles VI, 308
Dix, Achilles D. V, 47
Dix, Agatha I, 877
Dix, Agatha VI, 308
Dix, Ann I, 496
Dix, Ann I, 741
Dix, Ann I, 759
Dix, Calvin V, 47
Dix, Cornelius I, 678
Dix, David V, 992
Dix, Deborah I, 385
Dix, Deborah I, 404
Dix, Deborah Lindly I, 385
Dix, Eli I, 496
Dix, Elizabeth I, 385
Dix, Elizabeth I, 678
Dix, Elizabeth V, 486
Dix, Hannah I, 537
Dix, Hannah V, 837
Dix, Hannah V, 839
Dix, Isaac H. V, 837
Dix, James I, 445
Dix, James III, 102
Dix, James IV, 521
Dix, Jemima III, 102
Dix, Jonathan I, 385
Dix, Jonathan V, 837
Dix, Laurie P. V, 992
Dix, Lydia I, 385
Dix, Margaret I, 385
Dix, Martha I, 385
Dix, Mary I, 385
Dix, Mary I, 399
Dix, Mary I, 402
Dix, Mary I, 404
Dix, Mary I, 445
Dix, Micajah I, 877
Dix, Nathan I, 385
Dix, Nathan I, 445
Dix, Nathan I, 877
Dix, Nathan V, 47
Dix, Nathan V, 486
Dix, Nathan VI, 106
Dix, Nathan VI, 308
Dix, Peter I, 385
Dix, Rachel I, 870
Dix, Rachel I, 877
Dix, Ruth I, 385
Dix, Ruth I, 408
Dix, Ruth I, 445
Dix, Ruth I, 628
Dix, Ruth I, 741
Dix, Samuel S. V, 837
Dix, Sarah I, 445
Dix, Sarah I, 678
Dix, Sarah I, 877
Dix, Susan I, 714
Dix, Susan I, 723
Dix, William I, 385
Dix, William I, 496
Dix, William I, 877
Dix, William V, 47
Dix, William VI, 308
Dix, Zachariah I, 385
Dix, Zachariah V, 486
Dix, Zacharias I, 385
Dixan, Jane VI, 806
Dixe, Elinor II, 443
Dixen, Hannah IV, 84
Dixen, Samuel IV, 84
Dixen, Samuel IV, 91
Dixen, Thomas IV, 84
Dixey, Charles II, 354
Dixey, Hannah C. II, 915
Dixey, Hannah C. II, 942
Dixey, Harriet II, 793
Dixey, Thomas II, 354
Dixey, Thos. II, 915
Dixey, Thos. II, 942
Dixon, ??? II, 791
Dixon, ??? IV, 603
Dixon, ??? IV, 620
Dixon, ??? VI, 495
Dixon, Abel I, 351
Dixon, Abigail I, 345
Dixon, Abigail I, 350
Dixon, Abigail I, 386
Dixon, Abigail I, 421
Dixon, Abigail I, 423
Dixon, Adam VI, 906
Dixon, Ambrose VI, 11
Dixon, Amy IV, 26
Dixon, Amy IV, 81
Dixon, Amy IV, 84
Dixon, Andrew II, 354
Dixon, Ann I, 386
Dixon, Ann I, 537
Dixon, Ann I, 1048
Dixon, Ann II, 507
Dixon, Ann II, 703
Dixon, Ann II, 736
Dixon, Ann II, 791
Dixon, Ann IV, 29
Dixon, Ann IV, 55
Dixon, Ann V, 48
Dixon, Ann VI, 495
Dixon, Ann VI, 496
Dixon, Ann Carson VI, 906
Dixon, Ann T. II, 736

Dixon, Anna II, 355
Dixon, Anna II, 507
Dixon, Anna VI, 635
Dixon, Anne I, 350
Dixon, Anne VI, 1003
Dixon, Annie D. I, 286
Dixon, Annie D. I, 386
Dixon, Annie D. I, 388
Dixon, Anthony II, 60
Dixon, Anthony II, 66
Dixon, Arthur VI, 872
Dixon, Asenath E. I, 386
Dixon, Benj. I, 350
Dixon, Benj. I, 358
Dixon, Benj. I, 407
Dixon, Benjamin I, 386
Dixon, Benjamin F. I, 386
Dixon, Bertha IV, 1313
Dixon, Bertha P. IV, 1313
Dixon, Bessie Marie IV, 1250
Dixon, Betsy VI, 816
Dixon, Caleb I, 350
Dixon, Caleb I, 386
Dixon, Caleb II, 791
Dixon, Caleb I. II, 736
Dixon, Caleb Iddings II, 791
Dixon, Caleb J. II, 857
Dixon, Caleb T. II, 736
Dixon, Carington I, 759
Dixon, Carrington I, 759
Dixon, Catharine I, 350
Dixon, Catharine I, 386
Dixon, Catharine I, 423
Dixon, Catharine I, 445
Dixon, Catharine I, 446
Dixon, Catherine I, 285
Dixon, Catherine I, 352
Dixon, Catherine I, 386
Dixon, Catherine V, 234
Dixon, Charity I, 350
Dixon, Charity I, 371
Dixon, Charity I, 386
Dixon, Charity IV, 621
Dixon, Charity IV, 699
Dixon, Charles A. II, 791
Dixon, Charles A. II, 857
Dixon, Charles C. V, 234
Dixon, Chas. A. II, 791
Dixon, Chas. A. II, 842
Dixon, Chas. A. II, 857
Dixon, Cicero I, 387
Dixon, Clara III, 102
Dixon, Clara III, 239
Dixon, Cleopatra I, 386
Dixon, Cleopatra I, 430
Dixon, Cora V, 487
Dixon, Cordelia I, 632
Dixon, Cornelia I, 632
Dixon, Cornelia Frances I, 615
Dixon, Cynthia V, 487
Dixon, Cynthia Middleton V, 487
Dixon, Cyrus IV, 196
Dixon, Cyrus IV, 289
Dixon, Cyrus IV, 621
Dixon, Cyrus IV, 699
Dixon, Cyrus IV, 868
Dixon, Cyrus IV, 871
Dixon, David I, 350
Dixon, David I, 386
Dixon, Dinah IV, 17
Dixon, Dinah IV, 620
Dixon, Dinah IV, 621
Dixon, Dinah IV, 667
Dixon, Dinah VI, 496
Dixon, Edgar Austin II, 791
Dixon, Edith I, 386
Dixon, Edith IV, 29
Dixon, Edith IV, 84
Dixon, Edith IV, 105
Dixon, Edna IV, 196
Dixon, Edna IV, 289
Dixon, Edward C. II, 791
Dixon, Edward Caleb II, 791
Dixon, Edward Caleb II, 842
Dixon, Edward Caleb II, 857
Dixon, Eleanor I, 351
Dixon, Eli I, 351
Dixon, Eli I, 1048
Dixon, Eli VI, 635
Dixon, Elisha I, 351
Dixon, Eliza IV, 83
Dixon, Eliza IV, 84
Dixon, Eliza IV, 620
Dixon, Eliza IV, 699
Dixon, Eliza A. V, 668
Dixon, Eliza Ann IV, 620
Dixon, Eliza Ann IV, 621
Dixon, Eliza Ann IV, 655
Dixon, Eliza Ann IV, 892
Dixon, Eliza Ann IV, 894
Dixon, Eliza Ann V, 668
Dixon, Eliza Ann S. IV, 621
Dixon, Eliza Ann S. IV, 892
Dixon, Elizabeth I, 304
Dixon, Elizabeth I, 308
Dixon, Elizabeth I, 345
Dixon, Elizabeth I, 350
Dixon, Elizabeth I, 351
Dixon, Elizabeth I, 358
Dixon, Elizabeth I, 370
Dixon, Elizabeth I, 386
Dixon, Elizabeth I, 402
Dixon, Elizabeth II, 60
Dixon, Elizabeth II, 66
Dixon, Elizabeth II, 354
Dixon, Elizabeth II, 355
Dixon, Elizabeth IV, 17
Dixon, Elizabeth IV, 29
Dixon, Elizabeth IV, 81
Dixon, Elizabeth IV, 83
Dixon, Elizabeth IV, 84
Dixon, Elizabeth IV, 196
Dixon, Elizabeth IV, 521
Dixon, Elizabeth IV, 539
Dixon, Elizabeth IV, 616
Dixon, Elizabeth IV, 620
Dixon, Elizabeth IV, 621
Dixon, Elizabeth IV, 661
Dixon, Elizabeth IV, 699
Dixon, Elizabeth IV, 751
Dixon, Elizabeth IV, 866
Dixon, Elizabeth IV, 868
Dixon, Elizabeth IV, 871
Dixon, Elizabeth V, 234
Dixon, Elizabeth VI, 486
Dixon, Elizabeth VI, 497
Dixon, Elizabeth VI, 796
Dixon, Elizabeth VI, 968
Dixon, Elizabeth VI, 1005
Dixon, Elizabeth A. II, 801
Dixon, Elizabeth V. I, 285
Dixon, Ella V, 234
Dixon, Ellen I, 387
Dixon, Emanuel IV, 29
Dixon, Emanuel IV, 620
Dixon, Emma V, 487
Dixon, Eula L. I, 387
Dixon, Eunice I, 534
Dixon, Eunice I, 537
Dixon, Eunice VI, 241
Dixon, Finley V, 234
Dixon, Flora I, 386
Dixon, Flora I, 397
Dixon, Flora C. I, 285
Dixon, Frances I, 620
Dixon, Frances IV, 948
Dixon, Francis IV, 948
Dixon, Francis H. I, 285
Dixon, Franklin M. II, 736
Dixon, George I, 386
Dixon, George I, 534
Dixon, George I, 537
Dixon, George I, 615
Dixon, George VI, 241
Dixon, George VI, 1003
Dixon, George A. V, 234
Dixon, George Washington II, 791
Dixon, George, Jr. I, 386
Dixon, George, Jr. VI, 906
Dixon, Gurney J. I, 387
Dixon, H IV, 948
Dixon, H. M. I, 386
Dixon, H??? IV, 948
Dixon, Hannah I, 350
Dixon, Hannah I, 351
Dixon, Hannah I, 370
Dixon, Hannah I, 386
Dixon, Hannah I, 400
Dixon, Hannah I, 421
Dixon, Hannah II, 66
Dixon, Hannah II, 791
Dixon, Hannah IV, 29
Dixon, Hannah IV, 53
Dixon, Hannah IV, 83
Dixon, Hannah IV, 84
Dixon, Hannah IV, 196
Dixon, Hannah IV, 327
Dixon, Hannah IV, 610
Dixon, Hannah IV, 620
Dixon, Hannah IV, 621
Dixon, Hannah IV, 629
Dixon, Hannah IV, 630
Dixon, Hannah IV, 650
Dixon, Hannah IV, 664
Dixon, Hannah IV, 667
Dixon, Hannah IV, 699
Dixon, Hannah IV, 892
Dixon, Hannah IV, 948
Dixon, Hannah IV, 1054
Dixon, Hannah VI, 906
Dixon, Henrietta T. II, 857
Dixon, Henrietta Troth II, 791
Dixon, Henry I, 1048
Dixon, Henry II, 507
Dixon, Henry IV, 17
Dixon, Henry IV, 26
Dixon, Henry IV, 29
Dixon, Henry IV, 70
Dixon, Henry IV, 616
Dixon, Henry IV, 620
Dixon, Henry IV, 699
Dixon, Henry VI, 171
Dixon, Henry VI, 495
Dixon, Henry VI, 496
Dixon, Henry VI, 635
Dixon, Henry P. II, 857
Dixon, Henry T. II, 736
Dixon, Henry T. II, 791
Dixon, Henry, Jr. IV, 29
Dixon, Henry, Jr. IV, 620
Dixon, Hiram V, 234
Dixon, Hiram P. V, 234
Dixon, Homer V, 668
Dixon, Hugh I, 351
Dixon, Hugh W. I, 386
Dixon, Ida III, 265
Dixon, Immanuel IV, 29
Dixon, Ina V, 992
Dixon, Isaac IV, 83
Dixon, Isaac IV, 84
Dixon, Isaac IV, 92
Dixon, Isaac IV, 620
Dixon, Isaac IV, 633
Dixon, Isaac IV, 699
Dixon, Isaac S. II, 507
Dixon, Isaac S. II, 736
Dixon, Isabella IV, 84
Dixon, Isabella IV, 699
Dixon, Izora I, 387
Dixon, James I, 351
Dixon, James II, 507
Dixon, James II, 736
Dixon, James II, 791
Dixon, James IV, 699
Dixon, James VI, 487
Dixon, James VI, 497
Dixon, James VI, 635
Dixon, James VI, 811
Dixon, James VI, 816
Dixon, James VI, 865
Dixon, James VI, 872
Dixon, James VI, 906
Dixon, James VI, 926
Dixon, James A. I, 386
Dixon, James M. VI, 795
Dixon, James Norris II, 507
Dixon, James S. IV, 699
Dixon, Jane IV, 83
Dixon, Jane IV, 84
Dixon, Jane IV, 103
Dixon, Jane IV, 106
Dixon, Jane IV, 196
Dixon, Jane IV, 327
Dixon, Jane IV, 521
Dixon, Jane IV, 620
Dixon, Jane IV, 621
Dixon, Jane IV, 633
Dixon, Jane IV, 699
Dixon, Jane V, 234
Dixon, Jane VI, 906
Dixon, Jenny VI, 872
Dixon, Jesse I, 285
Dixon, Jesse I, 350
Dixon, Jesse I, 352
Dixon, Jesse I, 386
Dixon, Joel I, 386
Dixon, Joel I, 412
Dixon, John I, 286
Dixon, John I, 350
Dixon, John I, 386
Dixon, John I, 421
Dixon, John I, 759
Dixon, John I, 1048
Dixon, John II, 354
Dixon, John II, 355
Dixon, John II, 507
Dixon, John II, 565
Dixon, John II, 634
Dixon, John II, 791
Dixon, John II, 857
Dixon, John IV, 29
Dixon, John IV, 81
Dixon, John IV, 83
Dixon, John IV, 84
Dixon, John IV, 92
Dixon, John IV, 610
Dixon, John IV, 620
Dixon, John IV, 621
Dixon, John IV, 629
Dixon, John IV, 632
Dixon, John IV, 667
Dixon, John IV, 699
Dixon, John IV, 892
Dixon, John VI, 486
Dixon, John VI, 487
Dixon, John VI, 497
Dixon, John VI, 635
Dixon, John VI, 833
Dixon, John VI, 865
Dixon, John VI, 866
Dixon, John VI, 872
Dixon, John VI, 906
Dixon, John VI, 968
Dixon, John A. VI, 872
Dixon, John A. VI, 906
Dixon, John C. I, 387
Dixon, John George VI, 806
Dixon, John N. IV, 621
Dixon, John P. IV, 699
Dixon, John Petit IV, 699
Dixon, John Pettit IV, 621
Dixon, John W. II, 735
Dixon, John W. II, 736
Dixon, John Walker II, 355
Dixon, John, Jr. IV, 84
Dixon, John, Jr. IV, 621
Dixon, John, Jr. VI, 812
Dixon, Jonathan I, 350
Dixon, Jonathan II, 215
Dixon, Jonathan II, 507
Dixon, Jos Edwards II, 355
Dixon, Joseph I, 350
Dixon, Joseph I, 351
Dixon, Joseph I, 386
Dixon, Joseph I, 430
Dixon, Joseph I, 1048
Dixon, Joseph II, 354
Dixon, Joseph II, 355
Dixon, Joseph II, 507
Dixon, Joseph II, 565
Dixon, Joseph II, 735
Dixon, Joseph II, 736
Dixon, Joseph IV, 29
Dixon, Joseph IV, 84
Dixon, Joseph IV, 521
Dixon, Joseph V, 234
Dixon, Joseph V, 992
Dixon, Joseph VI, 906
Dixon, Joseph Edward II, 507
Dixon, Joseph John Gurney I, 351
Dixon, Joseph M. I, 386
Dixon, Joshua I, 285
Dixon, Joshua I, 304
Dixon, Joshua I, 350
Dixon, Joshua I, 386
Dixon, Joshua I, 387
Dixon, Joshua IV, 29
Dixon, Joshua IV, 620
Dixon, Joshua IV, 621
Dixon, Joshua IV, 667
Dixon, Joshua IV, 699
Dixon, Joshua, Jr. IV, 621
Dixon, Josiah IV, 17
Dixon, Jubal VI, 1007
Dixon, Julia I, 350
Dixon, Julia I, 386
Dixon, Julia I, 406
Dixon, Julia I, 615
Dixon, Julia A. I, 386
Dixon, Julia A. I, 387
Dixon, Julia Ann V, 234
Dixon, Katharine I, 350
Dixon, Katharine I, 386
Dixon, Kezia I, 351
Dixon, Kezia I, 383
Dixon, Kezia I, 386
Dixon, Kezia VI, 906
Dixon, Keziah I, 386
Dixon, Larkin I, 632
Dixon, Larkin Lafayette I, 615
Dixon, Lennie V, 487
Dixon, Lester V, 668
Dixon, Letty VI, 900
Dixon, Levi IV, 620
Dixon, Lillie Bell I, 8
Dixon, Lizzie J. I, 386
Dixon, Locky VI, 872
Dixon, Lot IV, 620
Dixon, Lucena IV, 620
Dixon, Lucinda I, 351
Dixon, Lucretia IV, 620
Dixon, Lucretia IV, 621
Dixon, Lucretia IV, 651
Dixon, Lucretia IV, 699
Dixon, Lucy VI, 964
Dixon, Lula II, 791
Dixon, Lula II, 842
Dixon, Lula II, 857
Dixon, Lydia I, 351
Dixon, Lydia I, 371
Dixon, Lydia I, 386
Dixon, Lydia I, 625
Dixon, Lydia IV, 83
Dixon, Lydia IV, 84
Dixon, Lydia IV, 620
Dixon, Lydia IV, 621
Dixon, Lydia IV, 699
Dixon, Lydia IV, 785
Dixon, Lydia IV, 948
Dixon, Lydia V, 301
Dixon, Lydia V, 668
Dixon, Lydia Ann IV, 621
Dixon, Lydia Ann IV, 636
Dixon, Lydiann IV, 620
Dixon, Mahlon I, 350
Dixon, Mahlon I, 386
Dixon, Margaret IV, 26
Dixon, Margaret IV, 29
Dixon, Margaret IV, 81
Dixon, Margaret IV, 84
Dixon, Margaret VI, 906
Dixon, Margaret Worth II, 791
Dixon, Margrett II, 354
Dixon, Maria IV, 650
Dixon, Maria V, 234
Dixon, Mariam I, 759
Dixon, Mariam I, 771
Dixon, Marie I, 386
Dixon, Marie I, 394
Dixon, Marietta I, 627
Dixon, Martha II, 215
Dixon, Martha II, 238
Dixon, Martha II, 261
Dixon, Martha IV, 621
Dixon, Martha VI, 906
Dixon, Martha Arthur VI, 906
Dixon, Martha Jane I, 285
Dixon, Martha, Senr. VI, 906
Dixon, Mary I, 350
Dixon, Mary I, 351
Dixon, Mary I, 386
Dixon, Mary I, 408
Dixon, Mary I, 409
Dixon, Mary I, 412
Dixon, Mary I, 415
Dixon, Mary I, 417
Dixon, Mary I, 430
Dixon, Mary II, 354
Dixon, Mary II, 355
Dixon, Mary II, 507
Dixon, Mary II, 565
Dixon, Mary II, 634
Dixon, Mary IV, 29
Dixon, Mary IV, 81
Dixon, Mary IV, 83
Dixon, Mary IV, 84
Dixon, Mary IV, 91
Dixon, Mary IV, 92
Dixon, Mary IV, 607
Dixon, Mary IV, 620
Dixon, Mary IV, 664
Dixon, Mary IV, 717
Dixon, Mary IV, 868
Dixon, Mary IV, 871
Dixon, Mary IV, 948
Dixon, Mary IV, 1013
Dixon, Mary VI, 812
Dixon, Mary VI, 968
Dixon, Mary A. I, 386
Dixon, Mary Ann II, 507
Dixon, Mary Ann II, 729
Dixon, Mary Ann II, 736
Dixon, Mary Ann IV, 621
Dixon, Mary Ann V, 234
Dixon, Mary Anna II, 791
Dixon, Mary Anna II, 842
Dixon, Mary Anna II, 857
Dixon, Mary J. II, 791
Dixon, Mary J. II, 857
Dixon, Mary J. II, 918
Dixon, Mary Jane IV, 699
Dixon, Mary McClard VI, 906
Dixon, Mary W. II, 735
Dixon, Mary W. II, 736
Dixon, Mary Walker II, 355
Dixon, Mary Walker II, 507
Dixon, Mary Wilson VI, 906
Dixon, Mary-Ann II, 507
Dixon, Matilda IV, 621
Dixon, Meredith VI, 825
Dixon, Meredith VI, 906
Dixon, Michael I, 770
Dixon, Milo I, 387
Dixon, Miriam I, 386
Dixon, Miriam I, 417
Dixon, Miriam I, 759
Dixon, Moses H. VI, 837
Dixon, Nahunta I, 387
Dixon, Nancy VI, 812
Dixon, Nancy VI, 926
Dixon, Nathan I, 350
Dixon, Nathan I, 351
Dixon, Nathan I, 386

Dixon, Nathan I, 429
Dixon, Nathan I, 457
Dixon, Nathan IV, 83
Dixon, Nathan IV, 84
Dixon, Nathan IV, 620
Dixon, Nathan IV, 621
Dixon, Nathan IV, 699
Dixon, Nathan IV, 812
Dixon, Nathan V, 234
Dixon, Nathan Warrington IV, 948
Dixon, Nellie V, 668
Dixon, Newton IV, 620
Dixon, Newton IV, 621
Dixon, Newton IV, 655
Dixon, Newton IV, 892
Dixon, Newton IV, 894
Dixon, Olive I, 351
Dixon, Onedas V, 234
Dixon, Pamelia VI, 906
Dixon, Pamelia L. VI, 909
Dixon, Patience I, 350
Dixon, Patience I, 386
Dixon, Patience I, 415
Dixon, Patience I, 759
Dixon, Permelia V, 234
Dixon, Peter I, 350
Dixon, Phebe I, 350
Dixon, Polly VI, 812
Dixon, Polly VI, 865
Dixon, Polly Mitchell VI, 906
Dixon, Purley V, 234
Dixon, Rachel II, 735
Dixon, Rachel IV, 620
Dixon, Rachel VI, 812
Dixon, Rachel VI, 903
Dixon, Ralph I, 537
Dixon, Rebecca I, 351
Dixon, Rebecca I, 386
Dixon, Rebecca II, 355
Dixon, Rebecca II, 507
Dixon, Rebecca IV, 24
Dixon, Rebecca IV, 29
Dixon, Rebecca IV, 70
Dixon, Rebecca IV, 83
Dixon, Rebecca IV, 84
Dixon, Rebecca IV, 618
Dixon, Rebecca IV, 620
Dixon, Rebecca IV, 621
Dixon, Rebecca IV, 699
Dixon, Rebecca IV, 702
Dixon, Rebecca A. IV, 620
Dixon, Rebecca A. IV, 629
Dixon, Rebecca E. V, 234
Dixon, Rebecca M. I, 386
Dixon, Rebecca, Jr. IV, 83
Dixon, Rebeccah I, 1108
Dixon, Rebeckah IV, 71
Dixon, Rebekah IV, 84
Dixon, Robert II, 507
Dixon, Robert II, 824
Dixon, Robert Russell VI, 906
Dixon, Rosana I, 387
Dixon, Rosanna V. I, 387
Dixon, Rosannah I, 387
Dixon, Roxanna I, 386
Dixon, Roxie I, 387
Dixon, Roxie I, 428
Dixon, Ruth I, 350
Dixon, Ruth I, 351
Dixon, Ruth I, 358
Dixon, Ruth I, 386
Dixon, Ruth I, 387
Dixon, Ruth I, 394
Dixon, Ruth I, 407
Dixon, Ruth I, 416
Dixon, Ruth I, 423
Dixon, Ruth I, 445
Dixon, Ruth I, 759
Dixon, Ruth I, 769
Dixon, Ruth II, 507
Dixon, Ruth II, 565
Dixon, Ruth II, 735
Dixon, Ruth IV, 26
Dixon, Ruth IV, 69
Dixon, Ruth IV, 83
Dixon, Ruth IV, 84
Dixon, Ruth IV, 92
Dixon, Ruth IV, 95
Dixon, Ruth IV, 616
Dixon, Ruth IV, 621
Dixon, Ruth IV, 632
Dixon, Ruth IV, 699
Dixon, Ruth V, 234
Dixon, Ruth VI, 487
Dixon, Ruth VI, 635
Dixon, Ruth J. II, 355
Dixon, Ruth J. II, 507
Dixon, Ruth J. II, 736
Dixon, Sallie I, 286
Dixon, Sallie H. I, 387
Dixon, Sally VI, 833
Dixon, Sally VI, 837
Dixon, Sam V, 48
Dixon, Samuel I, 386
Dixon, Samuel IV, 29
Dixon, Samuel IV, 83
Dixon, Samuel IV, 84
Dixon, Samuel IV, 196
Dixon, Samuel IV, 327
Dixon, Samuel IV, 521
Dixon, Samuel IV, 621
Dixon, Samuel IV, 630
Dixon, Samuel IV, 650
Dixon, Samuel IV, 664
Dixon, Samuel IV, 699
Dixon, Samuel IV, 948
Dixon, Samuel IV, 1054
Dixon, Samuel VI, 635
Dixon, Samuel B. IV, 620
Dixon, Samuel Hadley II, 791
Dixon, Sarah I, 350
Dixon, Sarah I, 351
Dixon, Sarah I, 369
Dixon, Sarah I, 386
Dixon, Sarah I, 406
Dixon, Sarah I, 421
Dixon, Sarah I, 428
Dixon, Sarah I, 429
Dixon, Sarah I, 741
Dixon, Sarah II, 791
Dixon, Sarah IV, 83
Dixon, Sarah IV, 84
Dixon, Sarah IV, 95
Dixon, Sarah IV, 196
Dixon, Sarah IV, 327
Dixon, Sarah IV, 521
Dixon, Sarah IV, 621
Dixon, Sarah V, 806
Dixon, Sarah VI, 486
Dixon, Sarah VI, 487
Dixon, Sarah VI, 497
Dixon, Sarah VI, 635
Dixon, Sarah Ann IV, 620
Dixon, Sarah Ann IV, 650
Dixon, Sarah C. I, 386
Dixon, Sarah E. I, 386
Dixon, Serentha J. V, 234
Dixon, Signy Wilson VI, 906
Dixon, Silas I, 386
Dixon, Silas V, 234
Dixon, Simion I, 386
Dixon, Simon I, 343
Dixon, Simon I, 350
Dixon, Simon I, 351
Dixon, Simon I, 386
Dixon, Simon IV, 29
Dixon, Simon IV, 196
Dixon, Simon IV, 620
Dixon, Simon IV, 621
Dixon, Simon IV, 699
Dixon, Simon IV, 751
Dixon, Simon V, 234
Dixon, Simon E. V, 234
Dixon, Simon M. I, 386
Dixon, Simon M. I, 421
Dixon, Solomon I, 350
Dixon, Solomon I, 351
Dixon, Solomon I, 386
Dixon, Solomon I, 406
Dixon, Solomon I, 1048
Dixon, Solomon VI, 464
Dixon, Solomon VI, 487
Dixon, Solomon VI, 635
Dixon, Solomon VI, 670
Dixon, Sophia I, 386
Dixon, Sophia I, 430
Dixon, Stephen I, 351
Dixon, Stephen I, 1048
Dixon, Susanna I, 759
Dixon, Susanna IV, 24
Dixon, Susanna IV, 29
Dixon, Susanna IV, 83
Dixon, Susanna IV, 84
Dixon, Susanna IV, 196
Dixon, Susanna VI, 906
Dixon, Susanna Radey VI, 906
Dixon, Susannah IV, 84
Dixon, Susannah IV, 327
Dixon, Susannah IV, 511
Dixon, Susannah IV, 521
Dixon, Susannah IV, 633
Dixon, Susannah VI, 486
Dixon, Susannah VI, 497
Dixon, Susannah VI, 796
Dixon, Susannah Hancock II, 791
Dixon, Tamer V, 234
Dixon, Thomas I, 350
Dixon, Thomas I, 351
Dixon, Thomas I, 386
Dixon, Thomas I, 421
Dixon, Thomas IV, 83
Dixon, Thomas IV, 84
Dixon, Thomas IV, 620
Dixon, Thomas IV, 621
Dixon, Thomas V, 487
Dixon, Thomas VI, 812
Dixon, Thomas VI, 872
Dixon, Thomas VI, 900
Dixon, Thomas VI, 906
Dixon, Thomas VI, 941
Dixon, Thomas VI, 974
Dixon, Thomas VI, 1005
Dixon, Thomas J. I, 387
Dixon, Thomas W. I, 386
Dixon, Thomas, Senr. VI, 906
Dixon, Thos. I, 345
Dixon, Thos. I, 350
Dixon, Thos. I, 364
Dixon, Tubal VI, 906
Dixon, Tubal VI, 926
Dixon, Unity VI, 906
Dixon, W. J. IV, 1249
Dixon, W. T. IV, 1249
Dixon, Wd. Ann II, 824
Dixon, Wd. Susannah VI, 487
Dixon, Widow Anna VI, 670
Dixon, William I, 350
Dixon, William I, 940
Dixon, William II, 355
Dixon, William IV, 24
Dixon, William IV, 29
Dixon, William IV, 71
Dixon, William IV, 83
Dixon, William IV, 84
Dixon, William IV, 103
Dixon, William IV, 196
Dixon, William IV, 327
Dixon, William IV, 521
Dixon, William V, 234
Dixon, William V, 668
Dixon, William VI, 906
Dixon, William E. VI, 812
Dixon, William Jesse I, 285
Dixon, William M. I, 940
Dixon, William, Jr. IV, 84
Dixon, Wilson V, 487
Dixon, Winnie V, 234
Dixon, Winny VI, 906
Dixon, Wm. IV, 83
Dixon, Wm. IV, 84
Dixon, Wm. V, 668
Dixon, Wm. Austin II, 791
Dixon, Wm. B. II, 736
Dixon, Zelinda B. I, 386
Dixon, Zeno I, 386
Dixon, Zeno H. I, 387
Dixon, Zeno H. I, 1150
Dixon, Zimri I, 383
Dixon, Zimri I, 386
Dixson, ??? IV, 620
Dixson, Abel I, 351
Dixson, Abigail I, 386
Dixson, Ann IV, 868
Dixson, Caleb J. II, 857
Dixson, Cyrus IV, 868
Dixson, Dinah IV, 629
Dixson, Dinah IV, 660
Dixson, Dinah IV, 667
Dixson, Edith I, 351
Dixson, Eliza IV, 620
Dixson, Elizabeth IV, 26
Dixson, Elizabeth IV, 616
Dixson, Elizabeth IV, 620
Dixson, Elizabeth IV, 630
Dixson, Elizabeth IV, 638
Dixson, Elizabeth IV, 651
Dixson, Elizabeth IV, 660
Dixson, Elizabeth IV, 868
Dixson, Elizabeth VI, 383
Dixson, Emanuel IV, 620
Dixson, Emy VI, 383
Dixson, Hannah I, 360
Dixson, Hannah I, 1108
Dixson, Hannah IV, 620
Dixson, Hannah IV, 667
Dixson, Henrietta T. II, 833
Dixson, Henrietta T. II, 857
Dixson, Henry IV, 616
Dixson, Henry IV, 620
Dixson, Henry IV, 630
Dixson, Henry VI, 383
Dixson, Henry, Jr. IV, 620
Dixson, James VI, 487
Dixson, Joel I, 351
Dixson, John I, 351
Dixson, John II, 354
Dixson, John II, 355
Dixson, John II, 507
Dixson, John IV, 92
Dixson, John IV, 620
Dixson, John IV, 667
Dixson, John IV, 868
Dixson, John VI, 968
Dixson, Joseph I, 351
Dixson, Joseph II, 354
Dixson, Joshua IV, 620
Dixson, Joshua IV, 629
Dixson, Joshua IV, 660
Dixson, Joshua IV, 667
Dixson, Joshua IV, 868
Dixson, Joshua, Jr. IV, 621
Dixson, Laura VI, 684
Dixson, Lot IV, 620
Dixson, Lucena IV, 620
Dixson, Lucretia IV, 868
Dixson, Lydia IV, 621
Dixson, Lydia IV, 657
Dixson, Lydiann IV, 620
Dixson, Martha IV, 868
Dixson, Mary I, 351
Dixson, Mary I, 360
Dixson, Mary II, 355
Dixson, Mary IV, 92
Dixson, Mary IV, 620
Dixson, Mary IV, 630
Dixson, Mary IV, 868
Dixson, Mary VI, 968
Dixson, Mary Ann IV, 868
Dixson, Miriam I, 351
Dixson, Nathan I, 351
Dixson, Nathan IV, 620
Dixson, Nathan IV, 621
Dixson, Nathan IV, 868
Dixson, Newton IV, 620
Dixson, Rachel IV, 620
Dixson, Rachel IV, 629
Dixson, Rachel VI, 646
Dixson, Rachel VI, 683
Dixson, Rebecca I, 360
Dixson, Rebecca IV, 83
Dixson, Rebecca IV, 620
Dixson, Rebecca VI, 383
Dixson, Rebecca, Jr. IV, 83
Dixson, Rebeccah I, 1108
Dixson, Ruth I, 351
Dixson, Ruth II, 507
Dixson, Ruth IV, 621
Dixson, Ruth IV, 632
Dixson, Ruth VI, 383
Dixson, Ruth VI, 487
Dixson, Samuel B. IV, 620
Dixson, Sarah I, 351
Dixson, Sarah VI, 487
Dixson, Silas I, 351
Dixson, Simon IV, 620
Dixson, Simon IV, 621
Dixson, Simon IV, 638
Dixson, Simon IV, 651
Dixson, Solomon VI, 487
Dixson, Sophia I, 351
Dixson, Stephen I, 351
Dixson, Susanna IV, 92
Dixson, Thomas I, 360
Dixson, Thomas I, 386
Dixson, Thomas I, 1108
Dixson, Thomas IV, 621
Dixson, William II, 355
Dixson, Zimri I, 351
Doak, Clara V, 668
Doak, Clara H. V, 668
Doak, James Herbert V, 668
Doak, Joseph V, 668
Doak, Marianna V, 668
Doak, Verna V, 687
Doan, ??? R. V, 669
Doan, A. N. V, 559
Doan, Abigail II, 993
Doan, Absolam V, 487
Doan, Adaline V, 618
Doan, Adaline V, 638
Doan, Agnes V, 383
Doan, Albert I, 237
Doan, Albert V, 48
Doan, Albert V, 487
Doan, Albert V, 669
Doan, Albert W. V, 669
Doan, Alice Rebecca V, 669
Doan, Alma V, 669
Doan, Amanda V, 487
Doan, Amanda V, 533
Doan, Ann I, 351
Doan, Ann I, 387
Doan, Ann V, 559
Doan, Ann V, 574
Doan, Ann H. V, 559
Doan, Anna V, 669
Doan, Anna Margaret I, 714
Doan, Anna Margaret I, 1105
Doan, Annie V, 669
Doan, Annie L. V, 669
Doan, Asariah V, 487
Doan, Asenath I, 698
Doan, Asenath I, 714
Doan, Asenath I, 1105
Doan, Asenath IV, 1055
Doan, Asenath IV, 1060
Doan, Azariah V, 487
Doan, Azariah W. V, 668
Doan, Bertha V, 669
Doan, Betsey V, 487
Doan, Betsy V, 487
Doan, Betsy V, 488
Doan, Burrett L. V, 669
Doan, Burritt T. V, 669
Doan, Calvin V, 487
Doan, Calvin V, 559
Doan, Calvin V, 669
Doan, Calvin B. V, 559
Doan, Charles V, 383
Doan, Charles V, 669
Doan, Charles V, 699
Doan, Charles A. V, 487
Doan, Chas. V, 669
Doan, Clarinda V, 559
Doan, Clarinda V, 576
Doan, Clinton M. V, 487
Doan, Clinton M. V, 669
Doan, Corwin V, 669
Doan, Corwin F. V, 669
Doan, Daniel II, 993
Doan, Daniel IV, 1054
Doan, David I, 1092
Doan, David I, 1105
Doan, David I, 1150
Doan, David IV, 196
Doan, David V, 487
Doan, David V, 669
Doan, David W. V, 669
Doan, Deborah IV, 385
Doan, Deborah IV, 1055
Doan, Deborah V, 487
Doan, Deborah E. V, 488
Doan, Deborah E. V, 534
Doan, Dorothy V, 48
Doan, E. V, 559
Doan, Earl Chas. V, 383
Doan, Ebanezar I, 351
Doan, Ebanezar I, 387
Doan, Ebanezar I, 678
Doan, Ebenezar I, 351
Doan, Ebenezar I, 387
Doan, Ebenezer I, 420
Doan, Eddie V, 669
Doan, Edith Jessie V, 559
Doan, Edward V, 487
Doan, Elebeth I, 1105
Doan, Eli V, 559
Doan, Elisabeth I, 351
Doan, Elisha V, 487
Doan, Eliza V, 487
Doan, Eliza V, 488
Doan, Eliza V, 669
Doan, Eliza D. V, 480
Doan, Eliza D. V, 487
Doan, Eliza E. V, 669
Doan, Elizabeth I, 351
Doan, Elizabeth I, 387
Doan, Elizabeth I, 420
Doan, Elizabeth I, 421
Doan, Elizabeth I, 678
Doan, Elizabeth I, 1108
Doan, Elizabeth IV, 196
Doan, Elizabeth V, 48
Doan, Elizabeth V, 487
Doan, Elizabeth V, 488
Doan, Elizabeth V, 496
Doan, Ella M. V, 404
Doan, Ellwood I, 698
Doan, Ellwood I, 975
Doan, Elma V, 669
Doan, Elwood I, 714
Doan, Emma V, 559
Doan, Emma V, 669
Doan, Enos V, 30
Doan, Enos V, 48
Doan, Enos Albert I, 237
Doan, Ephraim I, 351
Doan, Ephraim I, 387
Doan, Ephraim I, 396
Doan, Ephraim I, 420
Doan, Ephraim V, 559
Doan, Ephraim V, 568
Doan, Ephraim V, 574
Doan, Ephraim, Jr. I, 387
Doan, Esther V, 669
Doan, Esther V, 712
Doan, Esther Ann I, 237
Doan, Esther Ann V, 48
Doan, Eunice V, 48
Doan, Eunice V, 559
Doan, Eunice V, 669
Doan, Eva V, 669
Doan, Eva Arometta V, 487
Doan, Evaline V, 669

Doan, Everett V, 669
Doan, Fannie V, 693
Doan, Florence V, 669
Doan, Florence Holbrook V, 48
Doan, Frances V, 669
Doan, Francis V, 487
Doan, Francis M. V, 669
Doan, Francis N. V, 669
Doan, Frank L. V, 669
Doan, George B. V, 669
Doan, George C. V, 669
Doan, Grace I, 387
Doan, Grace I, 429
Doan, Hannah I, 351
Doan, Hannah I, 384
Doan, Hannah I, 387
Doan, Hannah I, 396
Doan, Hannah V, 48
Doan, Hannah V, 128
Doan, Hannah V, 487
Doan, Hannah V, 533
Doan, Hannah VI, 487
Doan, Hannah Davis I, 387
Doan, Hannah P. V, 669
Doan, Harrison J. V, 487
Doan, Hazel V, 669
Doan, Hazel V, 695
Doan, Hazel V, 699
Doan, Henrietta V, 669
Doan, Henry V, 383
Doan, Isaac V, 487
Doan, Isaac V, 488
Doan, Isaac V, 559
Doan, Israel V, 487
Doan, Jacob I, 351
Doan, Jacob I, 387
Doan, Jacob I Sup 1, 9
Doan, Jacob V, 48
Doan, Jacob V, 128
Doan, Jacob V, 487
Doan, Jacob V, 533
Doan, James V, 559
Doan, Jane V, 559
Doan, Jane W. VI, 584
Doan, Jane Walker VI, 487
Doan, Jane Walker VI, 584
Doan, Jemima I, 351
Doan, Jemima I, 387
Doan, Jemima I, 425
Doan, Jemima V, 48
Doan, Jemima V, 63
Doan, Jemima V, 487
Doan, Jemima V, 488
Doan, Jemima V, 495
Doan, Jemima V, 559
Doan, Jemima V, 567
Doan, Jesse I, 351
Doan, Jesse I, 387
Doan, Jesse I, 698
Doan, Jesse I, 714
Doan, Jesse I, 975
Doan, Jesse I, 1105
Doan, Jesse V, 48
Doan, Jesse V, 474
Doan, Jesse V, 487
Doan, Jesse V, 669
Doan, Jesse E. V, 669
Doan, Joe T. V, 669
Doan, John I, 237
Doan, John I, 343
Doan, John I, 351
Doan, John I, 359
Doan, John I, 386
Doan, John I, 387
Doan, John I, 421
Doan, John I, 678
Doan, John I, 698
Doan, John I, 714
Doan, John I, 975
Doan, John I, 1105
Doan, John I, 1108
Doan, John IV, 1055
Doan, John V, 48
Doan, John V, 487
Doan, John V, 528
Doan, John V, 559
Doan, John V, 618
Doan, John V, 644
Doan, John V, 669
Doan, John E. I, 237
Doan, Jonathan I, 351
Doan, Jonathan I, 387
Doan, Jonathan I, 1105
Doan, Jonathan I, 1150
Doan, Jonathan V, 48
Doan, Jonathan V, 487
Doan, Jonathan V, 538
Doan, Jonathan V, 618
Doan, Jonathan V, 669
Doan, Jonathan, Sr. V, 669
Doan, Joseph I, 343
Doan, Joseph I, 351
Doan, Joseph I, 387
Doan, Joseph I, 425
Doan, Joseph I, 1105
Doan, Joseph V, 48
Doan, Joseph V, 487
Doan, Joseph V, 488
Doan, Joseph L. V, 669
Doan, Joseph T. V, 669
Doan, Joseph W. V, 487
Doan, Joseph W. V, 618
Doan, Joseph William V, 488
Doan, Joseph, Jr. I, 387
Doan, Joseph, Jr. V, 480
Doan, Joseph, Jr. V, 487
Doan, Joseph, Jr. V, 488
Doan, Joseph, Jr. V, 534
Doan, Joseph, Sr. V, 487
Doan, Lewis V, 669
Doan, Lina V, 669
Doan, Lizzie V, 669
Doan, Lizzie M. V, 669
Doan, Louisa V, 669
Doan, Louisa N. V, 669
Doan, Lucinda V, 487
Doan, Lucinda C. V, 669
Doan, Lydia IV, 1094
Doan, Lydia IV, 1108
Doan, Lydia V, 48
Doan, Lydia V, 474
Doan, Lydia V, 487
Doan, Lydia M. IV, 1094
Doan, Mabel V, 383
Doan, Mabel V, 665
Doan, Mabel V, 669
Doan, Mahlon I, 351
Doan, Mahlon I, 387
Doan, Marcia Sibyl V, 48
Doan, Maria V, 487
Doan, Maria V, 669
Doan, Maria E. V, 487
Doan, Maria E. V, 488
Doan, Maria E. V, 539
Doan, Maria Fannie V, 669
Doan, Maria M. V, 488
Doan, Maria M. V, 514
Doan, Marion E. V, 488
Doan, Marion E. V, 539
Doan, Martha I, 351
Doan, Martha I, 387
Doan, Martha I, 407
Doan, Martha I, 698
Doan, Martha I, 714
Doan, Martha I, 1105
Doan, Martha V, 48
Doan, Martha V, 669
Doan, Martha A. I, 237
Doan, Martha Ann V, 30
Doan, Martha Ann V, 48
Doan, Martha Ann Anderson I, 237
Doan, Martha E. V, 559
Doan, Martha Emma V, 559
Doan, Martha G. V, 668
Doan, Martha M. V, 669
Doan, Mary I, 351
Doan, Mary II, 990
Doan, Mary II, 993
Doan, Mary IV, 385
Doan, Mary IV, 1054
Doan, Mary IV, 1055
Doan, Mary V, 404
Doan, Mary V, 484
Doan, Mary V, 487
Doan, Mary V, 488
Doan, Mary Ann V, 48
Doan, Mary Ann V, 106
Doan, Mary E. V, 669
Doan, Mary Ellen V, 487
Doan, Mary Emily V, 48
Doan, Mary Jane V, 487
Doan, Mary Jane V, 528
Doan, Mary Sharden I, 387
Doan, Mercy II, 809
Doan, Myra V, 48
Doan, Naomi V, 487
Doan, Nathan I, 351
Doan, Nathan I, 387
Doan, Nathan V, 487
Doan, Nelson V, 383
Doan, Norman V, 669
Doan, Norman H. V, 669
Doan, Phebe V, 328
Doan, Phebe V, 363
Doan, Phebe V, 487
Doan, Phebe V, 535
Doan, Phebe V, 538
Doan, Phebe V, 618
Doan, Phebe E. V, 669
Doan, Polley I, 698
Doan, Polly I, 714
Doan, Polly I, 1105
Doan, Rachel I, 351
Doan, Rachel I, 387
Doan, Rachel II, 993
Doan, Rachel V, 48
Doan, Rachel V, 487
Doan, Rachel V, 501
Doan, Reachel I, 1105
Doan, Rebecca V, 48
Doan, Rebecca F. V, 487
Doan, Rebecca Jane V, 487
Doan, Robert I, 698
Doan, Robert I, 714
Doan, Robert I, 1105
Doan, Robert E. V, 487
Doan, Robert E. V, 488
Doan, Robert E. V, 669
Doan, Robert R. V, 665
Doan, Robert R. V, 669
Doan, Ruth I, 351
Doan, Ruth I, 359
Doan, Ruth I, 386
Doan, Ruth I, 387
Doan, Ruth I, 407
Doan, Ruth I, 1108
Doan, Ruth V, 48
Doan, Ruth V, 469
Doan, Ruth V, 487
Doan, Ruth V, 496
Doan, Salathiel I, 698
Doan, Salathiel I, 975
Doan, Salithiel I, 714
Doan, Salley I, 698
Doan, Sally I, 714
Doan, Sally I, 1105
Doan, Samuel II, 993
Doan, Sant V, 383
Doan, Sarah I, 351
Doan, Sarah I, 387
Doan, Sarah I, 420
Doan, Sarah I, 698
Doan, Sarah I, 714
Doan, Sarah I, 975
Doan, Sarah I, 1105
Doan, Sarah II, 993
Doan, Sarah V, 559
Doan, Sarah J. V, 669
Doan, Sarah Jane V, 487
Doan, Sarah Jane V, 618
Doan, Sarah Jane V, 644
Doan, Saray I, 1105
Doan, Spencer V, 487
Doan, Susanna II, 507
Doan, Susanna II, 537
Doan, Sylvia V, 383
Doan, Sylvia V, 405
Doan, Thomas I, 351
Doan, Thomas I, 387
Doan, Thomas I, 714
Doan, Thomas V, 487
Doan, Thomas W. I, 698
Doan, Thos. W. I, 1105
Doan, Ulissas V, 487
Doan, Ulyses G. V, 669
Doan, Ulysses V, 669
Doan, Walker V, 669
Doan, Wendell P. V, 487
Doan, William I, 351
Doan, William I, 387
Doan, William IV, 385
Doan, William IV, 1054
Doan, William IV, 1055
Doan, William V, 48
Doan, William V, 487
Doan, William V, 488
Doan, William V, 669
Doan, William A. V, 669
Doan, William H. V, 559
Doan, William Penn I, 1105
Doan, Wilson V, 48
Doan, Wilson Spray V, 48
Doan, Wm. IV, 1055
Doan, Wm. IV, 1060
Doan, Wm. V, 383
Doan, Wm. V, 669
Doan, Wm. H. V, 559
Doane, Alice III, 102
Doane, Alice H. III, 325
Doane, Alice Howes III, 102
Doane, Alice Mary III, 102
Doane, Alice Mary III, 202
Doane, Anna I, 1118
Doane, Asenath I, 1118
Doane, Benj. III, 102
Doane, Benjamin III, 102
Doane, Benjamin III, 202
Doane, Benjamin D. III, 102
Doane, Benjamin H. III, 97
Doane, Benjamin H. III, 102
Doane, Benjamin H. III, 325
Doane, Benjamin Hervey III, 102
Doane, Daniel II, 993
Doane, Diadema III, 17
Doane, Elizabeth I, 349
Doane, Elizabeth I, 373
Doane, Elizabeth I, 387
Doane, Hannah I, 349
Doane, Hannah Davis I, 387
Doane, Jane W. II, 857
Doane, Jesse I, 387
Doane, John I, 349
Doane, John I, 387
Doane, Margaret I, 1118
Doane, Maria III, 102
Doane, Martha I, 387
Doane, Martha I, 397
Doane, Martha I, 1118
Doane, Martha Ann V, 48
Doane, Mary I, 418
Doane, Mary I, 1118
Doane, Mary III, 102
Doane, Mary III, 202
Doane, Mary E. III, 97
Doane, Mary E. III, 102
Doane, Mary Sharden I, 387
Doane, Mrs. ??? III, 68
Doane, Polly I, 1118
Doane, Rachel I, 387
Doane, Rachel I, 429
Doane, Ruth I, 349
Doane, Sarah I, 1118
Doane, Sarah II, 985
Doane, Sarah II, 993
Doangworth, Dorothy II, 172
Doangworth, Richard II, 172
Doano, Hannah I, 384
Dobbins, ??? VI, 348
Dobbins, Abner VI, 308
Dobbins, Alexander VI, 979
Dobbins, Alexander VI, 982
Dobbins, Alexr. VI, 906
Dobbins, Ann I, 351
Dobbins, Ann I, 387
Dobbins, Ann I, 808
Dobbins, Ann I, 971
Dobbins, Ann I, 975
Dobbins, Ann I, 985
Dobbins, Catherine VI, 308
Dobbins, Caty VI, 308
Dobbins, Daniel I, 985
Dobbins, Edith IV, 327
Dobbins, Edith IV, 332
Dobbins, Eli I, 993
Dobbins, Elizabeth VI, 308
Dobbins, Elizabeth VI, 351
Dobbins, Elizabeth VI, 353
Dobbins, Griffin VI, 308
Dobbins, Jacob I, 351
Dobbins, Jacob I, 387
Dobbins, Jacob I, 808
Dobbins, Jacob I, 971
Dobbins, Jacob I, 985
Dobbins, Jacob, Jr. I, 975
Dobbins, Jacob, Sr. I, 975
Dobbins, James II, 443
Dobbins, Jemima I, 975
Dobbins, John I, 351
Dobbins, John I, 808
Dobbins, John I, 975
Dobbins, John I, 985
Dobbins, John VI, 308
Dobbins, John VI, 906
Dobbins, Jonah VI, 308
Dobbins, Joseph VI, 308
Dobbins, Joshua I, 351
Dobbins, Joshua I, 975
Dobbins, Joshua I, 985
Dobbins, Lydia VI, 308
Dobbins, Margaret VI, 308
Dobbins, Martha I, 985
Dobbins, Mary I, 351
Dobbins, Mary I, 387
Dobbins, Mary I, 808
Dobbins, Mary I, 975
Dobbins, Mary I, 985
Dobbins, Mary II, 443
Dobbins, Mary IV, 327
Dobbins, Mary IV, 332
Dobbins, Mary Ann I, 624
Dobbins, Mary Ann I, 932
Dobbins, Mary Ann I, 985
Dobbins, Mary Ann I, 996
Dobbins, Mary Mills I, 988
Dobbins, Maryann VI, 308
Dobbins, Rebecca I, 351
Dobbins, Rebecca I, 975
Dobbins, Rebecca I, 985
Dobbins, Rebeckah I, 985
Dobbins, Rebeckah I, 993
Dobbins, Rebekah I, 387
Dobbins, Rebekah I, 808
Dobbins, Ruth I, 351
Dobbins, Ruth I, 387
Dobbins, Ruth I, 808
Dobbins, Ruth I, 975
Dobbins, Ruth I, 985
Dobbins, Ruth I, 991
Dobbins, Ruth I, 996
Dobbins, Sarah I, 351
Dobbins, Sarah I, 808
Dobbins, Sarah I, 975
Dobbins, Sarah VI, 591
Dobbins, Susanna I, 985
Dobbins, Susanna IV, 327
Dobbins, Susanna IV, 332
Dobbins, Susannah I, 985
Dobbins, Suzan I, 985
Dobbins, Theodotia VI, 906
Dobbins, Thomas I, 351
Dobbins, Thomas I, 975
Dobbins, Thomas I, 985
Dobbins, Thomas VI, 308
Dobbins, William I, 351
Dobbins, William I, 808
Dobbins, William I, 975
Dobbins, William I, 985
Dobbins, William I, 988
Dobbins, William, Jr. I, 985
Dobbins, William, Sr. I, 985
Dobbs, William II, 443
Dobens, Suzan I, 985
Dobin, Abner VI, 594
Dobin, Catharine VI, 594
Dobin, Elizabeth VI, 594
Dobin, Griffin VI, 594
Dobin, John VI, 594
Dobin, Jonah VI, 594
Dobin, Joseph VI, 594
Dobin, Lydia VI, 594
Dobin, Mary Ann VI, 594
Dobin, Thomas VI, 594
Dobins, Jacob I, 985
Dobins, Jonah VI, 859
Dobins, Susannah I, 985
Dobord, Anna V, 558
Dobord, Isaac V, 558
Dobord, Ivy V, 558
Dobord, Leroy V, 558
Dobs, Mary II, 443
Dobs, William II, 443
Dobson, ??? III, 102
Dobson, Aleda III, 102
Dobson, Ann III, 102
Dobson, Ann VI, 879
Dobson, Anna IV, 812
Dobson, Anna IV, 849
Dobson, Anne III, 55
Dobson, Anne III, 102
Dobson, Catharine III, 102
Dobson, Elizabeth II, 507
Dobson, Elizabeth III, 40
Dobson, Elizabeth III, 102
Dobson, Elizabeth III, 251
Dobson, Elizabeth VI, 812
Dobson, Esther III, 102
Dobson, Ethel IV, 1206
Dobson, Geo. L. VI, 804
Dobson, Hannah III, 102
Dobson, Joseph Dobson III, 288
Dobson, Joyce III, 102
Dobson, Lydia VI, 832
Dobson, Margaret II, 507
Dobson, Margaret II, 606
Dobson, Margaret III, 102
Dobson, Margaret III, 285
Dobson, Margaret III, 288
Dobson, Margret II, 507
Dobson, Mary III, 102
Dobson, Nancy VI, 821
Dobson, Peter III, 102
Dobson, Polly VI, 821
Dobson, Samuel II, 791
Dobson, Samuel II, 857
Dobson, Sarah I, 615
Dobson, Sarah I, 623
Dobson, Sarah II, 466
Dobson, Sarah II, 507
Dobson, Sarah III, 102
Dobson, Sarah III, 288
Dobson, Sarah Jane I, 985
Dobson, Sarah, Jr. II, 507
Dobson, Susannah III, 102
Dobson, Thomas II, 507
Dobson, Thomas II, 606
Dobson, Thomas III, 40
Dobson, Thomas III, 55
Dobson, Thomas III, 102
Dobson, Thomas III, 251
Dobson, Thos. III, 102
Dobson, Thos. III, 285
Dobson, Thos. III, 288
Dobson, William VI, 806
Dobson, William VI, 821

Dobson, William VI, 832
Dobson, William C. VI, 812
Dobson, Wm. C. VI, 879
Dobson, Wm. O. VI, 804
Dobuert, Carlene A. III, 145
Dobuest, Carline A. III, 343
Dobyne, Abner VI, 594
Dobyne, Catharine VI, 594
Dobyne, Elizabeth VI, 594
Dobyne, Griffin VI, 594
Dobyne, Griffith VI, 594
Dobyne, John VI, 594
Dobyne, Jonah VI, 594
Dobyne, Joseph VI, 594
Dobyne, Lydia VI, 594
Dobyne, Mary Ann VI, 594
Dobyne, Sarah VI, 591
Dobyne, Sarah VI, 594
Dobyne, Thomas VI, 594
Dobyns, Abner VI, 351
Dobyns, Abner VI, 906
Dobyns, Abner VI, 929
Dobyns, Abner VI, 1015
Dobyns, Albert VI, 906
Dobyns, Albert VI, 948
Dobyns, Albert VI, 998
Dobyns, Albert VI, 1008
Dobyns, Artheme VI, 1008
Dobyns, Catherine VI, 318
Dobyns, Catherine VI, 909
Dobyns, Caty VI, 308
Dobyns, Caty VI, 318
Dobyns, Caty VI, 326
Dobyns, Caty VI, 351
Dobyns, Caty VI, 352
Dobyns, Charlotte VI, 948
Dobyns, Deborah W. VI, 906
Dobyns, Eliza VI, 906
Dobyns, Eliza S. VI, 906
Dobyns, Elizabeth VI, 351
Dobyns, Elizabeth VI, 873
Dobyns, Elizabeth VI, 906
Dobyns, Elizabeth VI, 957
Dobyns, Elizabeth W. VI, 1009
Dobyns, Elizabeth Wilks VI, 906
Dobyns, Grace VI, 1008
Dobyns, Grace Woodford VI, 906
Dobyns, Gracy VI, 990
Dobyns, Griffin VI, 351
Dobyns, Griffin VI, 906
Dobyns, Griffin A. VI, 906
Dobyns, Henry D. VI, 990
Dobyns, Henry T. VI, 906
Dobyns, Jane VI, 906
Dobyns, John VI, 870
Dobyns, John VI, 906
Dobyns, John VI, 913
Dobyns, Jonah VI, 351
Dobyns, Jonah VI, 899
Dobyns, Jonah VI, 906
Dobyns, Joseph VI, 351
Dobyns, Joseph VI, 906
Dobyns, Joseph VI, 1019
Dobyns, Josiah VI, 940
Dobyns, Judy Ann E. VI, 906
Dobyns, Lucy VI, 1015
Dobyns, Mrs. Salley VI, 898
Dobyns, Nancy VI, 351
Dobyns, Nancy C. VI, 990
Dobyns, Nancy McGlothlan VI, 906
Dobyns, Patty Travis VI, 906
Dobyns, Polly VI, 938
Dobyns, Sally VI, 898
Dobyns, Sally Woodford VI, 906
Dobyns, Samuel VI, 938
Dobyns, Sarah VI, 909
Dobyns, Sarah VI, 1015
Dobyns, Sophia VI, 906
Dobyns, Sophia VI, 948
Dobyns, Sophia VI, 958
Dobyns, Theodotia VI, 906
Dobyns, Thomas VI, 351
Dobyns, Thomas VI, 906
Dobyns, Thomas G. VI, 840
Dobyns, Thomas G. VI, 948
Dobyns, William VI, 958
Dobyns, William N. VI, 906
Dockery, ??? I, 921
Dockery, Hazel Briggs I, 940
Dockery, Mary Hazel I, 921
Dockton, Judah I Sup 1, 3
Dockton, Judah I Sup 1, 6
Dockton, Thomas I Sup 1, 3
Dockton, Thomas I Sup 1, 6
Dod, Aaron I, 299
Dod, Aaron I, 304
Dod, Aaron I, 714
Dod, Albanah VI, 383
Dod, Albanah VI, 451
Dod, Daniel I, 714
Dod, Edward VI, 383
Dod, Edward VI, 451
Dod, Jacob I, 714
Dod, Joseph I, 714
Dod, Mary VI, 451
Dod, Nathan I, 714
Dod, Rebecca I, 299
Dod, Rebecca I, 304
Dod, William I, 714
Dodd, Aaron I, 285
Dodd, Aaron I, 304
Dodd, Aaron I, 714
Dodd, Aaron IV, 144
Dodd, Aaron IV, 385
Dodd, Aaron IV, 456
Dodd, Aaron IV, 574
Dodd, Albanah VI, 383
Dodd, Albenah VI, 383
Dodd, Ann V, 302
Dodd, Ann VI, 487
Dodd, Anna IV, 385
Dodd, Anna IV, 398
Dodd, Anna IV, 574
Dodd, Anna IV, 1094
Dodd, Anne IV, 1094
Dodd, Anne W. IV, 591
Dodd, Anne Williams IV, 574
Dodd, Arnold IV, 574
Dodd, Arthur IV, 196
Dodd, Beatrice IV, 196
Dodd, Bertha V, 328
Dodd, Carl V, 488
Dodd, Catherine VI, 487
Dodd, Catherine VI, 551
Dodd, Celah IV, 385
Dodd, Celia IV, 574
Dodd, Celia IV, 595
Dodd, Charles V, 488
Dodd, Charles T. III, 102
Dodd, Clarence V, 488
Dodd, Daniel I, 285
Dodd, Daniel I, 714
Dodd, Daniel IV, 144
Dodd, David V, 166
Dodd, David V, 669
Dodd, Dessie V, 328
Dodd, Edward VI, 383
Dodd, Edward VI, 487
Dodd, Elizabeth I, 285
Dodd, Elizabeth I, 304
Dodd, Elizabeth IV, 144
Dodd, Elizabeth IV, 327
Dodd, Elizabeth IV, 358
Dodd, Elizabeth IV, 385
Dodd, Elizabeth IV, 456
Dodd, Elizabeth V, 328
Dodd, Emma V, 328
Dodd, Eunice IV, 574
Dodd, Eunice IV, 1094
Dodd, Felix IV, 196
Dodd, Goldie V, 488
Dodd, Howard IV, 196
Dodd, Isaac Wilson, Jr. IV, 327
Dodd, Jacob I, 285
Dodd, Jacob I, 714
Dodd, James Hadly Arnold IV, 385
Dodd, Jane VI, 487
Dodd, Jane VI, 494
Dodd, Jean VI, 494
Dodd, Jean Gore VI, 539
Dodd, Jesse VI, 487
Dodd, John I, 1028
Dodd, John I Sup 1, 10
Dodd, John VI, 171
Dodd, John VI, 487
Dodd, Joseph I, 285
Dodd, Joseph I, 714
Dodd, Joseph IV, 144
Dodd, Joseph IV, 385
Dodd, Joseph IV, 398
Dodd, Joseph IV, 574
Dodd, Joseph V, 302
Dodd, Joseph Patterson IV, 574
Dodd, Joseph Patterson IV, 1094
Dodd, Josie V, 488
Dodd, Lenna V, 618
Dodd, Leslie V, 328
Dodd, Lulu IV, 196
Dodd, Lydia VI, 487
Dodd, Margaret VI, 487
Dodd, Margaret VI, 494
Dodd, Margaret VI, 539
Dodd, Marion E. III, 102
Dodd, Mary I, 285
Dodd, Mary I, 304
Dodd, Mary I, 714
Dodd, Mary IV, 144
Dodd, Mary IV, 385
Dodd, Mary V, 328
Dodd, Mary V, 618
Dodd, Mary VI, 383
Dodd, Mary VI, 487
Dodd, Nathan I, 285
Dodd, Nathan I, 714
Dodd, Nathan IV, 144
Dodd, Nathan IV, 365
Dodd, Nathan IV, 385
Dodd, Nathan IV, 574
Dodd, Nathan IV, 591
Dodd, Nathan IV, 1094
Dodd, Ollie V, 488
Dodd, Orpah IV, 385
Dodd, Orpha IV, 574
Dodd, Peninah I, 285
Dodd, Peninah I, 304
Dodd, Peninah IV, 385
Dodd, Peninnah IV, 144
Dodd, Piety I, 285
Dodd, Piety I, 304
Dodd, Piety IV, 144
Dodd, Piety IV, 385
Dodd, Rachel IV, 385
Dodd, Rachel IV, 574
Dodd, Rachel IV, 594
Dodd, Rachel VI, 383
Dodd, Rebecah I, 304
Dodd, Rebecca I, 285
Dodd, Rebecca I, 304
Dodd, Rebecca I, 714
Dodd, Rebecca IV, 144
Dodd, Rebecca IV, 377
Dodd, Rebecca IV, 385
Dodd, Rebecca IV, 393
Dodd, Rebecca IV, 574
Dodd, Rebecca M. III, 102
Dodd, Rebeckah I, 304
Dodd, Rebeckah IV, 144
Dodd, Rebeckah IV, 456
Dodd, Rhodas IV, 196
Dodd, Ruth I, 285
Dodd, Ruth I, 304
Dodd, Ruth IV, 144
Dodd, Ruth IV, 363
Dodd, Ruth IV, 365
Dodd, Ruth IV, 385
Dodd, Ruth IV, 412
Dodd, Ruth IV, 574
Dodd, Ruth IV, 1094
Dodd, Sarah I, 285
Dodd, Sarah I, 304
Dodd, Sarah I, 714
Dodd, Sarah I, 1062
Dodd, Sarah IV, 144
Dodd, Sarah IV, 385
Dodd, Sarah IV, 453
Dodd, Sarah V, 166
Dodd, Sarah V, 383
Dodd, Sarah V, 438
Dodd, Sarah VI, 487
Dodd, Sarah VI, 554
Dodd, Sarah, Jr. I, 1060
Dodd, Susanna VI, 812
Dodd, Thermon V, 166
Dodd, Thomas I, 1060
Dodd, Thomas VI, 487
Dodd, Thomas VI, 554
Dodd, Thomas VI, 812
Dodd, Thurman V, 166
Dodd, Thurman V, 669
Dodd, Vergil V, 488
Dodd, Virgil V, 618
Dodd, Walter IV, 196
Dodd, Widow Sarah I, 1060
Dodd, William I, 285
Dodd, William I, 714
Dodd, William I, 1028
Dodd, William I Sup 1, 10
Dodd, William IV, 385
Dodd, William V, 488
Dodd, William VI, 487
Dodd, Wm. IV, 144
Dodd, Wm. VI, 487
Dodd, Zilpha I, 304
Dodd, Zilpha IV, 144
Dodd, Zilphia I, 285
Dodds, Anna Louisa V, 902
Dodds, Anna Louisa V, 911
Dodds, Annetta V, 28
Dodds, Annetta B. V, 48
Dodds, Carl V, 48
Dodds, Carl W. V, 48
Dodds, Carrie V, 455
Dodds, Goldie L. V, 48
Dodds, Isaac V, 455
Dodds, Isaiah L. V, 48
Dodds, J. Emerson V, 28
Dodds, J. Emerson V, 48
Dodds, Joseph V, 455
Dodds, Josephine V, 48
Dodds, Josephine A. V, 48
Dodds, Leslie V, 455
Dodds, Margaery L. V, 455
Dodds, Mary V, 455
Dodds, Mary E. V, 455
Dodds, Mary R. V, 48
Dodds, Ollie V, 455
Dodds, Otto V, 455
Dodds, Ray V, 455
Dodds, Samantha V, 455
Dodds, Wilbur V, 455
Dodds, William V, 488
Dodds, Wm. C. V, 48
Dodds, Zilla V, 455
Dodge, ??? III, 479
Dodge, Abigail III, 433
Dodge, Abigail III, 479
Dodge, Abigail III, 481
Dodge, Adam III, 407
Dodge, Amelia III, 305
Dodge, Amy III, 34
Dodge, Amy III, 123
Dodge, Amy Anna III, 102
Dodge, Benj. III, 470
Dodge, Benjamin III, 407
Dodge, Beth. III, 481
Dodge, Catharine C. III, 407
Dodge, Edward III, 102
Dodge, Elizabeth III, 394
Dodge, Elizabeth III, 407
Dodge, Elizabeth III, 481
Dodge, Elizabeth III, 492
Dodge, Hannah III, 481
Dodge, Hannah III, 492
Dodge, Isaac III, 102
Dodge, Isaac H. III, 407
Dodge, James III, 29
Dodge, James C. III, 102
Dodge, Jane III, 407
Dodge, Jeremiah III, 407
Dodge, John III, 394
Dodge, John III, 407
Dodge, John III, 433
Dodge, John III, 481
Dodge, John III, 492
Dodge, Jos. C. III, 102
Dodge, Joseph III, 407
Dodge, Joseph C. III, 102
Dodge, Joseph C. III, 103
Dodge, Joseph C. III, 300
Dodge, Judith IV, 1156
Dodge, Judith IV, 1206
Dodge, Kezia III, 103
Dodge, Margaret III, 256
Dodge, Margaret III, 305
Dodge, Maria III, 102
Dodge, Maria III, 103
Dodge, Martha III, 102
Dodge, Martha III, 103
Dodge, Martha III, 300
Dodge, Martha III, 470
Dodge, Mary III, 394
Dodge, Mary III, 407
Dodge, Mary III, 481
Dodge, Phebe III, 102
Dodge, Phebe III, 407
Dodge, Phebe III, 470
Dodge, Phebe III, 476
Dodge, Phebe W. III, 102
Dodge, Phebe W. III, 103
Dodge, Rebecca II, 507
Dodge, Rebecca II, 552
Dodge, Rebekah II, 355
Dodge, Rosanna III, 29
Dodge, Rosanna B. III, 102
Dodge, Rosannah III, 102
Dodge, Sarah III, 407
Dodge, Sarah Elizabeth III, 102
Dodge, Thos. III, 103
Dodge, Tristram III, 407
Dodge, Tristram III, 476
Dodge, Wd. Abigail III, 407
Dodge, Wd. Abigail III, 433
Dodge, Wd. Phebe III, 407
Dodgson, Charles F. III, 236
Dodgson, Elizabeth III, 89
Dodgson, Elizabeth III, 103
Dodgson, John III, 89
Dodgson, John III, 103
Dodgson, John III, 236
Dodgson, Lydia III, 89
Dodgson, Lydia III, 103
Dodgson, Lydia III, 168
Dodgson, Lydia III, 236
Dodgson, Lydia S. III, 103
Dodgson, Sara. III, 236
Dodman, Clara III, 78
Dodman, Clara III, 155
Dodson, Charles P. III, 103
Dodson, Clara V, 669
Dodson, Clara V, 903
Dodson, Des demona III, 103
Dodson, Emala IV, 29
Dodson, Emala IV, 45
Dodson, Judith VI, 804
Dodson, Mary F. III, 103
Dodson, Tabitha V, 992
Dodson, Tebitha V, 992
Dodson, Wesley III, 103
Dodson, William Howard II, 703
Dodsworth, John III, 103
Dodzweit, Siegfried IV, 1313
Doe, Henrietta M. V, 669
Doe, Mary II, 355
Doe, Mary II, 507
Doe, Mary II, 613
Doeg, ??? III, 103
Doer, Mary II, 1049
Doer, Mary II, 1056
Dogde, Martha III, 34
Doggett, Milly V, 328
Doggett, Milly V, 358
Doggett, Richard VI, 906
Doggett, Wd. Rhoda Evans VI, 906
Dogue, Ida IV, 196
Doherty, Harriett Alida III, 103
Doherty, Harriett Alida III, 243
Doherty, Harriett M. III, 103
Doherty, Harriett M. III, 243
Doherty, John III, 103
Doherty, John III, 243
Dohety, Hannah V, 48
Dohety, Hannah V, 102
Dohner, Ella V, 736
Dohner, Emma V, 736
Dohrman, Mabel IV, 1313
Doile, Ambrose II, 355
Doing, Charles H. VI, 369
Doing, Charles H. VI, 383
Doing, Charles H. VI, 732
Doing, Florence Dell III, 409
Doing, Florence Dell VI, 369
Doing, Florence Dell VI, 383
Doing, Florence Dell VI, 732
Doing, Florence Dell VI, 739
Doing, Florence Dell VI, 747
Doing, James Herald VI, 369
Doing, James Herald VI, 383
Doing, Lilliam Elizbeth VI, 383
Doing, Rosa VI, 369
Doing, Rosa VI, 732
Doing, Rosa H. VI, 383
Doing, Rosa Herald VI, 383
Doing, Tacy VI, 369
Doing, Tacy VI, 383
Dokeridge, Polly VI, 863
Dokes, Nancy VI, 812
Dokes, Samuel VI, 812
Dolby, Eliza Ann II, 803
Dolby, Eliza Ann II, 811
Dolby, Elizabeth II, 507
Dolby, Elizabeth II, 736
Dolby, Elizabeth II, 771
Dolby, Isaac II, 507
Dolby, James II, 736
Dolby, James B. II, 507
Dolby, James B. II, 736
Dolby, John II, 803
Dolby, Mary II, 507
Dolby, Mary II, 703
Dolby, Mary II, 736
Dolby, Phebe Anne II, 857
Dolby, Sarah II, 803
Dolby, Sarah Eliza II, 857
Dolby, Tacy S. VI, 381
Dolby, Tacy S. VI, 383
Dolby, Tacy S. VI, 400
Dolby, Virginia II, 857
Dolby, Virginia L. II, 857
Dolby, Virginia L. II, 904
Dolby, Wm., Jr. II, 507
Dolder, Bertha IV, 1250
Dolder, Bessie IV, 1250
Dolder, Emily II, 1059
Dolder, Emily II, 1061
Dolder, Lillie IV, 1250
Dolder, Rolland Miller IV, 1250
Dolder, Ruth Eldora IV, 1250
Dolder, Will IV, 1250
Dolder, Willie IV, 1250
Dolder, Wm. IV, 1250
Dolder, Wm. A. IV, 1250
Dole, Ann IV, 774
Dole, Daniel IV, 699
Dole, Elisabeth IV, 699
Dole, Elizabeth IV, 699
Dole, James Langstaff IV, 699
Dole, Jericho John III, 186
Dole, John III, 103
Dole, John III, 407
Dole, Mark IV, 699
Dole, Mary III, 103
Dole, Mary III, 407

ole, Michael IV, 699
ole, Peter II, 66
ole, Robert Lewis V, 903
ole, Russel V, 903
ole, Russel V, 918
ole, Ruth V, 903
ole, Ruth V, 918
ole, Sarah II, 507
ole, Sarah II, 537
ole, Sarah IV, 699
ole, Sarah IV, 747
ole, Wd. Mary III, 103
ole, Wd. Mary III, 186
oll, Amelia II, 318
oll, Amelia II, 324
oll, Charles IV, 196
oll, Geo. Dewie IV, 196
oll, Geo., Jr. IV, 196
ollar, Eunice V, 863
ollar, Rebecca V, 863
ollar, Robert VI, 971
ollar, William V, 863
ollard, Agness VI, 903
ollard, Betsy VI, 876
ollard, Betsy VI, 896
ollard, Elizabeth VI, 986
ollard, Mary VI, 932
ollard, Nancy Carner VI, 906
ollard, Reuben VI, 932
ollard, Rhuben VI, 920
ollard, Sarah VI, 987
ollard, Susannah VI, 987
ollard, William VI, 896
ollard, William VI, 906
ollard, William) VI, 876
olliver, Eliza J. V, 166
olliver, James J. V, 166
olliver, Maryelle V, 151
olliver, Maryelle V, 166
olliver, R. H. V, 151
olliver, R. H. V, 166
olman, Catharine IV, 1313
olmen, John IV, 196
olmen, Joseph IV, 196
olph, Catherine V, 383
olph, Ernest V, 383
olph, Imogene V, 383
olph, Jessie V, 383
olph, Ora V, 383
olton, Andrew VI, 906
olton, Lucy Ann Brooke VI, 906
olton, Seneth Pullin VI, 906
olton, Wilston VI, 906
oman, Catharine IV, 1313
ominy, Mary V, 992
ominy, Mary Margaret V, 992
omire, Christopher VI, 905
onahea, Charles VI, 812
onahea, Sally VI, 812
onald, Benjamin A. VI, 907
onald, James VI, 907
onald, James VI, 934
onald, Martha Hughes VI, 907
onald, Robert VI, 922
onald, Sally VI, 810
onald, Sally Cann VI, 907
onalds, Sarah M. V, 559
onalds, Sarah M. V, 601
onaldson, ??? III, 143
onaldson, Alice IV, 1130
onaldson, Alice IV, 1136
onaldson, Arthur II, 215
onaldson, Arthur II, 507
onaldson, Deborah III, 103
onaldson, Deborah III, 143
onaldson, Elisabeth II, 507
onaldson, Elisabeth VI, 510
onaldson, Elizabeth II, 215
onaldson, Elizabeth II, 507
onaldson, Elizabeth II, 616
onaldson, Elizabeth V, 903
onaldson, Elizabeth V, 931
onaldson, Elizabeth VI, 487
onaldson, Gertrude C. III, 407
onaldson, Glendora B. V, 618
onaldson, Henrietta L. III, 103
onaldson, Henrietta L. III, 143
onaldson, Isaac II, 507
onaldson, Isaac II, 791
onaldson, Isaac III, 103
onaldson, Jane II, 703
onaldson, Jane II, 857
onaldson, Mary Ann V, 903
onaldson, May Gertrude III, 404
onaldson, May Gertrude III, 407
onaldson, Nora V, 669
onaldson, Sarah II, 507
onaldson, Sarah II, 537
onaldson, Stanley Justus III, 404
Donaldson, Stanley Justus III, 407
Donaldson, T. F. I, 1150
Donaldson, W. G. IV, 1250
Donaldson, Wd. Jane II, 791
Donaldson, Wenona V, 618
Donally, James II, 507
Donally, John II, 507
Donally, John III, 103
Donally, Mary II, 507
Donally, Mary III, 103
Donally, Mary III, 213
Donally, Mary IV, 812
Donally, Wd. Mary II, 588
Donard, Mary IV, 196
Donard, William IV, 196
Donaway, Kathrine VI, 979
Donchian, Angel Agnes III, 103
Donchian, Bessie III, 103
Donchian, Bessie III, 373
Donchian, Daniel Dikran III, 103
Donchian, Dikran III, 103
Donchian, Dikran B. III, 103
Donchian, Eugenie III, 103
Donchian, Levon Peter III, 103
Donchian, Levon Peter III, 344
Donchian, Levorn Peter III, 103
Donchian, Paul D. III, 373
Donchian, Paul Dikran III, 103
Donchian, Suzanne III, 103
Donchian, Suzanne III, 344
Donchian, Virginia III, 103
Donchian, Virginia A. III, 103
Donchian, Virginia Christine III, 103
Done, Abigail II, 993
Done, Elwood I, 714
Done, Ephraim II, 355
Done, Hannah I, 387
Done, Jesse I, 714
Done, Jesse I, 985
Done, John I, 714
Done, Mary II, 993
Done, Robert I, 714
Done, Salathiel I, 985
Done, Salithiel I, 714
Done, Sarah I, 714
Done, Sarah I, 985
Done, Sarah I, 1118
Done, Sarah II, 993
Done, Susanna II, 355
Donehue, Jane V, 992
Donehue, Pattie V, 992
Donelly, Edna IV, 700
Doner, Belle V, 992
Doner, Lolie V, 992
Doner, Orva Leroy V, 993
Doner, Thomas V, 992
Doniphan, Alex VI, 890
Doniphan, Alexander VI, 836
Donlevy, ??? III, 162
Donlevy, Alice III, 103
Donlevy, Alice III, 162
Donlevy, Intaglio III, 103
Donlevy, John III, 103
Donley, Edna IV, 812
Donley, George W. V, 383
Donley, Howard IV, 812
Donley, J. Walter V, 383
Donley, John W. V, 383
Donley, Jonathan IV, 1250
Donley, Mary IV, 812
Donley, Mary M. V, 383
Donley, Nancy V, 383
Donley, Riie Ann V, 383
Donley, Wilsher L. V, 383
Donnahue, Mary II, 507
Donnahue, Mary II, 585
Donnal, James F. VI, 940
Donnal, Lucy Jane VI, 940
Donnal, Volentine VI, 940
Donnaldson, Arthur II, 507
Donnaldson, Elizabeth II, 507
Donnalley, Laura Edith IV, 948
Donnally, Augustus V, 48
Donnally, Cadwallader V, 48
Donnally, Elizabeth V, 48
Donnally, Laura Edith IV, 948
Donnally, Lewis V, 34
Donnally, Lewis V, 48
Donnally, Mary V, 34
Donnally, Mary C. V, 48
Donnan, Anna IV, 1156
Donnan, Annie IV, 1156
Donnan, Bessie Pearl IV, 1156
Donnan, John IV, 1156
Donnan, John W. IV, 1156
Donnan, Milo Clark IV, 1156
Donnehow, Mary II, 507
Donnehow, Mary II, 576
Donnelly, James II, 507
Donnelly, John II, 507
Donnelly, John II, 696
Donnelly, Mary II, 507
Donnelly, Mary II, 696
Donnelly, Mary R. IV, 1250
Donnen, Annie IV, 1156
Donnen, John IV, 1156
Donnen, John W. IV, 1156
Donnigan, Mattie IV, 1250
Donoho, Charles VI, 881
Donoho, Charles VI, 907
Donoho, Edward VI, 907
Donoho, Elizabeth Lowry VI, 907
Donoho, James VI, 907
Donoho, Q. C. V, 383
Donoho, Rachel McDonald VI, 907
Donoho, Robert VI, 1008
Donoho, Sally VI, 907
Donohoe, Abigail V, 383
Donohoe, John V, 383
Donohoe, Mary V, 383
Donohoe, Q. C. V, 383
Donohoe, Quincy Clay V, 383
Donohoe, Quinn C. V, 383
Donohue, Rachel McDonald V, 669
Donohue, Rachel McDonald V, 721
Donolly, John II, 507
Donothan, Rachel Wood VI, 920
Donvin, Phebe III, 407
Dooley, Aaron VI, 907
Dooley, Alexander J. VI, 908
Dooley, Alfred VI, 908
Dooley, Amily Callaway VI, 907
Dooley, Angeline M. Taylor VI, 908
Dooley, Ann VI, 878
Dooley, Ann Eliza VI, 908
Dooley, Ann Erwin VI, 907
Dooley, Ann L. VI, 908
Dooley, Anna Gilpin VI, 907
Dooley, Anne VI, 991
Dooley, Betsey VI, 907
Dooley, Betty VI, 907
Dooley, Caleb VI, 908
Dooley, Caroline Ann VI, 908
Dooley, Cata VI, 907
Dooley, Caty VI, 907
Dooley, Clarissa VI, 918
Dooley, David, Sr. VI, 991
Dooley, Eliza VI, 907
Dooley, Eliza Powell VI, 908
Dooley, Elizabeth II, 443
Dooley, Elizabeth VI, 878
Dooley, Elizabeth VI, 908
Dooley, Elizabeth VI, 909
Dooley, Elizabeth VI, 920
Dooley, Elizabeth VI, 946
Dooley, Elizabeth VI, 999
Dooley, Elizabeth VI, 1013
Dooley, Elizabeth VI, 1016
Dooley, Elizabeth Birks VI, 907
Dooley, Elizabeth Gilpin VI, 908
Dooley, Emeline P. VI, 940
Dooley, Ephraim VI, 907
Dooley, Frances VI, 908
Dooley, Frances Crump VI, 907
Dooley, George VI, 889
Dooley, George VI, 907
Dooley, George VI, 991
Dooley, Harmony VI, 908
Dooley, Harriett Estes VI, 908
Dooley, Henry VI, 907
Dooley, Henry VI, 1016
Dooley, Hulda Sharp VI, 907
Dooley, Jabez VI, 908
Dooley, Jacob VI, 907
Dooley, Jacob VI, 912
Dooley, James VI, 907
Dooley, James B. VI, 940
Dooley, Jane VI, 918
Dooley, Jane VI, 1012
Dooley, Janny Vaughan VI, 907
Dooley, Jenny VI, 991
Dooley, Jesse VI, 907
Dooley, John II, 443
Dooley, John VI, 907
Dooley, John VI, 908
Dooley, John VI, 946
Dooley, John VI, 962
Dooley, John VI, 999
Dooley, John VI, 1019
Dooley, Joshua IV, 84
Dooley, Joshua VI, 816
Dooley, Joshua VI, 908
Dooley, Josiah Wood VI, 907
Dooley, Katy VI, 907
Dooley, Katy VI, 944
Dooley, Martha VI, 927
Dooley, Mary VI, 889
Dooley, Mary VI, 907
Dooley, Mary VI, 952
Dooley, Mary VI, 1019
Dooley, Mary N. Feather VI, 908
Dooley, Matilda Bush VI, 907
Dooley, Micajah VI, 908
Dooley, Milly VI, 884
Dooley, Molley VI, 907
Dooley, Molly VI, 907
Dooley, Molly Squires VI, 907
Dooley, Moses VI, 879
Dooley, Moses VI, 907
Dooley, Moses VI, 961
Dooley, Moses VI, 1012
Dooley, Nancy VI, 991
Dooley, Nancy VI, 998
Dooley, Nancy VI, 999
Dooley, Obadiah VI, 907
Dooley, Patsey VI, 991
Dooley, Permelia VI, 951
Dooley, Peter Fitzhugh VI, 907
Dooley, Polly Wood VI, 907
Dooley, Rachel VI, 991
Dooley, Rachell VI, 907
Dooley, Rebeckah VI, 920
Dooley, Rebeckah VI, 927
Dooley, Rhoda VI, 877
Dooley, Robert VI, 909
Dooley, Sally VI, 907
Dooley, Sally Hanks VI, 908
Dooley, Sarah VI, 950
Dooley, Sarah Jones VI, 908
Dooley, Sarah Williams VI, 907
Dooley, Sede Wood VI, 907
Dooley, Sedy Smith VI, 907
Dooley, Sharp Noah VI, 991
Dooley, Stephen VI, 907
Dooley, Stephen VI, 909
Dooley, Stephen VI, 927
Dooley, Stephen VI, 962
Dooley, Susan VI, 950
Dooley, Susan Jane VI, 962
Dooley, Thomas VI, 907
Dooley, Thomas VI, 908
Dooley, Thomas VI, 944
Dooley, Thomas VI, 995
Dooley, Thomas VI, 999
Dooley, Thomas VI, 1016
Dooley, Thomas, Jr. VI, 998
Dooley, Thomas, Senr. VI, 907
Dooley, Thos. VI, 908
Dooley, Tilman J. VI, 940
Dooley, William VI, 908
Dooley, William VI, 962
Dooley, William VI, 967
Dooley, William VI, 968
Dooley, William B. VI, 908
Dooling, Rachel VI, 909
Doolittle, Sylvia Ann IV, 1235
Doolittle, Sylvia Ann IV, 1236
Dooly, Elizabeth Birks VI, 907
Dooly, Henry VI, 907
Dooly, John VI, 907
Dooly, Lydia IV, 326
Dooly, Lydia IV, 327
Dooly, Maxin IV, 327
Dooly, Maxon IV, 327
Dooly, Molly VI, 907
Dooly, Stephen VI, 907
Dooney, James II, 993
Dora, Margaret I, 685
Doran, Caroline II, 791
Doran, Caroline II, 857
Doran, Francis II, 147
Doran, Francis II, 792
Doran, Francis II, 857
Doran, Francis W. II, 147
Doran, James V, 234
Doran, James V, 455
Doran, William V, 234
Doran, Wm. V, 455
Doran, Wm. W. II, 147
Doran, Wm. Warren II, 791
Doras, Doras V, 915
Doras, Sarah V, 915
Dore, Margaret III, 94
Dore, Margaret III, 289
Dorey, Benjamin II, 355
Dorham, Matthew II, 215
Dority, Turisse V, 383
Dorlan, May IV, 1344
Dorland, ??? III, 78
Dorland, Andrew II, 845
Dorland, Andrew II, 857
Dorland, Andrew III, 103
Dorland, Andrew III, 264
Dorland, Andrew VI, 738
Dorland, Anna III, 103
Dorland, Anna III, 279
Dorland, Anna M. III, 78
Dorland, Anna M. III, 103
Dorland, Annie II, 792
Dorland, Annie II, 857
Dorland, Annie III, 103
Dorland, Annie Rebecca VI, 738
Dorland, Carlotta III, 103
Dorland, Claudia M. V, 903
Dorland, Edward H. II, 792
Dorland, Edward H. II, 845
Dorland, Edward H. II, 857
Dorland, Edward H. III, 103
Dorland, Edward H. VI, 738
Dorland, Elizabeth III, 103
Dorland, Gulielma D. Warder V, 903
Dorland, Gulielma M. V, 903
Dorland, Gulielma M. V, 940
Dorland, Henry E. VI, 738
Dorland, Jonathan III, 103
Dorland, Maria L. III, 263
Dorland, Maria L. III, 264
Dorland, Mary Elizabeth VI, 738
Dorland, Mary Elizabeth VI, 787
Dorland, Philip III, 103
Dorland, Rebecca II, 845
Dorland, Rebecca II, 857
Dorland, Rebecca III, 103
Dorland, Rebecca L. VI, 738
Dorland, Sarah III, 396
Dorland, Sarah III, 407
Dorland, Sarah E. III, 103
Dorland, Thomas G. III, 103
Dorland, Walter V, 48
Dorland, Walter E. V, 48
Dorland, William L. VI, 738
Dorland, William L. VI, 787
Dorland, Wm. L. VI, 738
Dorman, Ann I Sup 1, 3
Dorman, Elizabeth V, 806
Dorman, Elsie V, 166
Dorman, Hannah I Sup 1, 4
Dorman, Hannah I Sup 1, 7
Dorman, Richard I Sup 1, 3
Dormer, Elizabeth P. II, 857
Dormer, Elizabeth P. II, 920
Dormire, Anna Ewing VI, 908
Dormire, Christopher VI, 908
Dornin, Elizabeth Ann III, 103
Dornin, Oscar III, 103
Dorothy, Mary I, 678
Dorr, M. F. IV, 812
Dorrance, Elvira II, 1072
Dorrance, Elvira II, 1081
Dorrely, Ada IV, 1250
Dorsett, Amanda I, 924
Dorsett, Amanda I, 929
Dorsett, Amanda I, 940
Dorsett, Elizabeth I, 479
Dorsett, Elizabeth I, 924
Dorsett, Emily J. I, 479
Dorsett, Eva I, 479
Dorsett, Hattie Corilla I, 926
Dorsett, Hezekiah I, 924
Dorsett, Lilian Flora I, 479
Dorsett, Lou I, 926
Dorsett, Lula I, 940
Dorsett, Lula S. I, 924
Dorsett, Merab I, 759
Dorsett, Sarah J. I, 625
Dorsett, W. L. I, 926
Dorsey, Abigail II, 355
Dorsey, Abigail II, 508
Dorsey, Abigail II, 603
Dorsey, Benedict II, 355
Dorsey, Benedict II, 508
Dorsey, Benedict II, 591
Dorsey, Benedict II, 598
Dorsey, Benedict II, 603
Dorsey, Benedict II, 658
Dorsey, Benedict II, 792
Dorsey, Benedict II, 857
Dorsey, Benedict II, 874
Dorsey, Benedict II, 933
Dorsey, Benedict, Jr. II, 508
Dorsey, Daniel II, 355
Dorsey, Elizabeth II, 792
Dorsey, Elizabeth K. II, 857
Dorsey, Greenberry II, 598
Dorsey, Hannah II, 508
Dorsey, Hannah II, 601
Dorsey, John II, 355
Dorsey, John M. II, 355
Dorsey, Leonard II, 355
Dorsey, Loyd VI, 908
Dorsey, Margaret II, 857
Dorsey, Margaret II, 933
Dorsey, Martha II, 508
Dorsey, Martha II, 598
Dorsey, Mary II, 355
Dorsey, Mary II, 508
Dorsey, Mary II, 591

Dorsey, Mary II, 598
Dorsey, Mary II, 792
Dorsey, Mary II, 857
Dorsey, Mary II, 874
Dorsey, Mary II, 883
Dorsey, Mary II, 933
Dorsey, Mary Knight II, 792
Dorsey, Mary M. VI, 908
Dorsey, Rebekah II, 355
Dorsey, Sarah II, 355
Dorsey, Sarah II, 508
Dorsey, Sarah II, 591
Dorsey, Sarah II, 603
Dorsey, Sarah II, 658
Dorsey, Sarah II, 792
Dorsey, Sarah II, 857
Dorsey, Sarah H. II, 857
Dorsey, Sarah Stanton II, 857
Dorsey, Stanton II, 355
Dorsey, Stanton II, 508
Dorsey, Stanton II, 857
Dorsey, Stanton II, 933
Dorsey, Susannah II, 857
Dorsey, Susannah II, 874
Dorsey, Thomas II, 508
Dorsey, Vincent II, 355
Dorsey, William II, 355
Dorsey, William II, 792
Dorsey, Wm. II, 857
Dorsey, Wm. II, 874
Dortin, Nancy VI, 812
Dortin, Reubin VI, 812
Dos Santos, Antonio Elias Borges III, 38
Dos Santos, Antonio Elias Borges III, 103
Dos Santos, Charlotte III, 103
Dos Santos, Charlotte R. III, 38
Dos Santos, Feliciano E. III, 103
Dos Santos, Secrinka III, 103
Doss, Aaron VI, 908
Doss, Agness VI, 867
Doss, Ann VI, 908
Doss, Anne VI, 867
Doss, Azariah VI, 869
Doss, Azariah VI, 938
Doss, Azariah VI, 1007
Doss, Azariah, Jr. VI, 869
Doss, Edward VI, 795
Doss, Edward VI, 808
Doss, Eliza VI, 849
Doss, Elizabeth VI, 797
Doss, Elizabeth VI, 812
Doss, Elizabeth VI, 850
Doss, Elizabeth VI, 1007
Doss, Emily F. VI, 866
Doss, H. M. VI, 866
Doss, Hannah VI, 938
Doss, Hartwell VI, 812
Doss, Hartwell VI, 825
Doss, Hartwell M. VI, 818
Doss, Hartwell M. VI, 856
Doss, Hartwell M. VI, 861
Doss, Hartwell M. VI, 862
Doss, James VI, 837
Doss, Jane VI, 812
Doss, Joel VI, 908
Doss, John VI, 832
Doss, Liddy VI, 869
Doss, Littleberry VI, 850
Doss, Lucinda P. VI, 861
Doss, Lydia L. VI, 812
Doss, Mary VI, 813
Doss, Mary VI, 931
Doss, Mary Ann VI, 846
Doss, Mary C. VI, 859
Doss, Mary J. VI, 855
Doss, Mary Swain VI, 908
Doss, Micajah VI, 908
Doss, Milly Cundiff VI, 908
Doss, Minerva C. VI, 818
Doss, Mocha VI, 812
Doss, Overstreet VI, 812
Doss, Overstreet VI, 849
Doss, Overstreet VI, 859
Doss, Pamelia VI, 908
Doss, Parker S. VI, 812
Doss, Parkey VI, 812
Doss, Patsy VI, 812
Doss, Phillip VI, 812
Doss, Polly Truman VI, 908
Doss, Robert VI, 908
Doss, Robert O. VI, 849
Doss, Scytha VI, 859
Doss, Stephen VI, 908
Doss, Susan VI, 825
Doss, Tabby VI, 989
Doss, Thomas VI, 812
Doss, William VI, 855
Doss, William I. VI, 812
Doss, Wm. J. VI, 804
Doster, Bell V, 618
Doster, Catherine V, 234
Doster, Catherine V, 265
Doster, Clara V, 234
Doster, Clara W. V, 328
Doster, Clarissa N. V, 234
Doster, Ella V, 234
Doster, Elma V, 325
Doster, Elma V, 328
Doster, Elma C. V, 164
Doster, Elma C. V, 166
Doster, Elma C. V, 328
Doster, Elma H. V, 234
Doster, Grace III, 104
Doster, Grace III, 176
Doster, Harriett V, 234
Doster, Harriett V, 237
Doster, John V, 234
Doster, John V, 325
Doster, John V, 456
Doster, John V, 466
Doster, John B. III, 104
Doster, John B. III, 176
Doster, John Q. V, 234
Doster, Lewis V, 455
Doster, Lydia V, 466
Doster, Maria V, 456
Doster, Martha V, 234
Doster, Mary V, 234
Doster, Mary V, 265
Doster, Mary V, 325
Doster, Mary V, 328
Doster, Mary Catharine III, 104
Doster, Mary Catharine III, 176
Doster, Mary M. V, 234
Doster, Mary Matilda V, 328
Doster, Matilda V, 234
Doster, Miller C. V, 328
Doster, Rebecca V, 466
Doster, Savilla V, 234
Dotson, Elizabeth VI, 818
Dotson, Ellen May IV, 363
Dotson, Ellen May IV, 385
Dotson, Nacy Chitten VI, 818
Dotten, Louisa III, 120
Dotten, Louisa III, 167
Doty, ??? III, 86
Doty, ??? III, 328
Doty, Abigail III, 86
Doty, Abigail III, 88
Doty, Abigail III, 104
Doty, Amy IV, 1361
Doty, Amy IV, 1371
Doty, Anne III, 408
Doty, Anne III, 450
Doty, Celinda IV, 1361
Doty, Charity III, 407
Doty, Charity E. III, 104
Doty, Charles III, 407
Doty, Charles III, 408
Doty, Charles III, 451
Doty, Comfort III, 88
Doty, Comfort III, 104
Doty, Daniel III, 408
Doty, David IV, 1361
Doty, Elias IV, 1206
Doty, Elias W. IV, 1206
Doty, Eliz. III, 88
Doty, Eliz. III, 104
Doty, Elizabeth III, 104
Doty, Elizabeth III, 407
Doty, Elizabeth III, 408
Doty, Elizabeth III, 451
Doty, Elizabeth III, 472
Doty, Enos IV, 1361
Doty, George III, 407
Doty, Hannah III, 406
Doty, Hannah III, 407
Doty, Hannah III, 408
Doty, Isaac III, 104
Doty, Isaac III, 407
Doty, Isaac III, 408
Doty, Isaac III, 451
Doty, Isaac III, 452
Doty, Isaac III, 472
Doty, Isaac, Jr. III, 450
Doty, Jacob III, 104
Doty, Jacob T. III, 104
Doty, John III, 408
Doty, John IV, 1156
Doty, John IV, 1361
Doty, John Jay IV, 1361
Doty, John Jay IV, 1371
Doty, John S. IV, 1361
Doty, Joseph IV, 1250
Doty, Joseph A. IV, 1250
Doty, Kezia III, 448
Doty, Keziah III, 408
Doty, Lydia IV, 1361
Doty, Mabel IV, 1250
Doty, Margaret III, 408
Doty, Margaret III, 453
Doty, Mary III, 408
Doty, Mary III, 457
Doty, Mary IV, 1361
Doty, Maud IV, 1250
Doty, Maude IV, 1250
Doty, Mollie IV, 1250
Doty, Moses M. III, 379
Doty, Phebe III, 104
Doty, Phebe III, 214
Doty, Phebe III, 408
Doty, Phebe III, 481
Doty, Phebe A. IV, 1148
Doty, Phebe A. IV, 1156
Doty, Richard III, 408
Doty, Richard III, 453
Doty, Samuel III, 407
Doty, Samuel III, 408
Doty, Sarah III, 104
Doty, Sarah III, 451
Doty, Sarah III, 452
Doty, Sarah IV, 1361
Doty, Selinda IV, 1361
Doty, Silas IV, 1361
Doty, Susie IV, 1206
Doty, Thomas IV, 1156
Doty, Thomas O. IV, 1156
Doty, Wd. Sarah III, 408
Doty, Willet R. III, 104
Doty, Willie IV, 1206
Doud, Mary I, 387
Doud, Mary I, 390
Doude, Rebekah I, 373
Doude, Rebekah I, 387
Doudle, Alice IV, 197
Doudna, ??? I, 279
Doudna, ??? IV, 1085
Doudna, A. M. IV, 280
Doudna, Abbie IV, 569
Doudna, Abbie IV, 574
Doudna, Abigail IV, 196
Doudna, Abigail IV, 386
Doudna, Abigail IV, 387
Doudna, Abigail IV, 575
Doudna, Abner Fawcett IV, 948
Doudna, Achsah I, 285
Doudna, Achsah I, 304
Doudna, Achsah IV, 569
Doudna, Achsah IV, 574
Doudna, Achsah IV, 582
Doudna, Agnes H. IV, 386
Doudna, Albert H. IV, 387
Doudna, Albert H. IV, 388
Doudna, Albert H. IV, 400
Doudna, Alfred M. IV, 196
Doudna, Alfred M. IV, 574
Doudna, Alfred M. IV, 575
Doudna, Alice IV, 388
Doudna, Alice B. IV, 196
Doudna, Alice B. IV, 280
Doudna, Alice B. IV, 575
Doudna, Alice Bertha IV, 575
Doudna, Alonzo IV, 386
Doudna, Amy IV, 794
Doudna, Amy IV, 1094
Doudna, Amy B. IV, 794
Doudna, Ann IV, 144
Doudna, Ann IV, 196
Doudna, Ann IV, 381
Doudna, Ann IV, 386
Doudna, Ann IV, 405
Doudna, Ann IV, 551
Doudna, Ann IV, 574
Doudna, Ann IV, 575
Doudna, Ann IV, 589
Doudna, Ann IV, 768
Doudna, Ann IV, 1094
Doudna, Ann B. IV, 387
Doudna, Ann Eliza IV, 387
Doudna, Ann Eliza IV, 404
Doudna, Ann Eliza IV, 457
Doudna, Ann Eliza IV, 1094
Doudna, Ann Eliza W. IV, 388
Doudna, Ann R. IV, 521
Doudna, Anna I, 285
Doudna, Anna I, 304
Doudna, Anna IV, 144
Doudna, Anna IV, 385
Doudna, Anna IV, 387
Doudna, Anna IV, 421
Doudna, Anna IV, 431
Doudna, Anna IV, 435
Doudna, Anna IV, 438
Doudna, Anna IV, 551
Doudna, Anna IV, 585
Doudna, Anna IV, 591
Doudna, Anna IV, 735
Doudna, Anna B. IV, 387
Doudna, Anna B. IV, 401
Doudna, Anna B. IV, 521
Doudna, Anna D. IV, 762
Doudna, Anne I, 304
Doudna, Anne IV, 385
Doudna, Anne IV, 590
Doudna, Asenath I, 285
Doudna, Asenath I, 304
Doudna, Asenath IV, 144
Doudna, Asenath IV, 196
Doudna, Asenath IV, 371
Doudna, Asenath IV, 374
Doudna, Asenath IV, 375
Doudna, Asenath IV, 385
Doudna, Asenath IV, 386
Doudna, Asenath IV, 387
Doudna, Asenath IV, 568
Doudna, Asenath IV, 574
Doudna, Asenath IV, 578
Doudna, Asenath IV, 614
Doudna, Asenath IV, 687
Doudna, Asenath E. IV, 574
Doudna, Asenath Elma IV, 510
Doudna, Asenath Elma IV, 521
Doudna, Asenath Elma IV, 522
Doudna, Asenath Elma IV, 566
Doudna, Asenath Elma IV, 575
Doudna, Balinda IV, 574
Doudna, Barnwell P. IV, 574
Doudna, Belinda IV, 196
Doudna, Belinda IV, 387
Doudna, Belinda IV, 521
Doudna, Belinda IV, 575
Doudna, Belinda A. IV, 521
Doudna, Belinda A. IV, 531
Doudna, Bellinda IV, 411
Doudna, Benjamin IV, 196
Doudna, Benjamin IV, 386
Doudna, Benjamin IV, 574
Doudna, Bertha L. IV, 575
Doudna, Bertha L. IV, 578
Doudna, Beulah M. IV, 574
Doudna, Blance D. IV, 400
Doudna, Blanche IV, 388
Doudna, Blanche D. IV, 387
Doudna, Burwell P. IV, 574
Doudna, Charity I, 285
Doudna, Charity I, 304
Doudna, Charity II, 959
Doudna, Charity IV, 144
Doudna, Charity IV, 385
Doudna, Charity IV, 566
Doudna, Charity IV, 576
Doudna, Charity IV, 596
Doudna, Charity IV, 949
Doudna, Charles IV, 386
Doudna, Charles IV, 387
Doudna, Charles IV, 521
Doudna, Charles IV, 1094
Doudna, Charles A. IV, 521
Doudna, Chester IV, 575
Doudna, Chester E. IV, 387
Doudna, Chester E. IV, 401
Doudna, Chester E. IV, 574
Doudna, Chester E. IV, 575
Doudna, Chester E. IV, 582
Doudna, Clarissa IV, 387
Doudna, Clarissa IV, 388
Doudna, Clarissa IV, 1094
Doudna, Claud IV, 387
Doudna, Cynah IV, 385
Doudna, David IV, 385
Doudna, David IV, 387
Doudna, Debby IV, 1094
Doudna, Deborah IV, 574
Doudna, Deborah IV, 575
Doudna, Deborah IV, 1055
Doudna, Deborah IV, 1094
Doudna, Deborah E. IV, 575
Doudna, Deborah E. IV, 587
Doudna, Delbert H. IV, 574
Doudna, Dillwun IV, 570
Doudna, Dillwyn IV, 592
Doudna, Dillwyn W. IV, 183
Doudna, Dillwyn W. IV, 569
Doudna, Dillwyn W. IV, 574
Doudna, Dilwyn IV, 574
Doudna, Eddie IV, 386
Doudna, Edgar S. IV, 574
Doudna, Edith IV, 570
Doudna, Edith R. IV, 183
Doudna, Edith R. IV, 569
Doudna, Edith R. IV, 574
Doudna, Edith R. IV, 592
Doudna, Edward B. IV, 388
Doudna, Edwin IV, 196
Doudna, Edwin IV, 387
Doudna, Edwin IV, 574
Doudna, Edwin IV, 575
Doudna, Edwin IV, 794
Doudna, Edwin IV, 1094
Doudna, Edwin Crew IV, 575
Doudna, Edwin J. IV, 794
Doudna, Eli IV, 387
Doudna, Eli B. IV, 387
Doudna, Eli B. IV, 1094
Doudna, Elisha IV, 196
Doudna, Elisha IV, 385
Doudna, Elisha IV, 386
Doudna, Elisha IV, 387
Doudna, Elisha IV, 569
Doudna, Elisha IV, 575
Doudna, Elisha IV, 587
Doudna, Elisha IV, 592
Doudna, Elisha IV, 1055
Doudna, Elisha IV, 1073
Doudna, Eliza Ann IV, 1094
Doudna, Elizabeth I, 304
Doudna, Elizabeth IV, 143
Doudna, Elizabeth IV, 144
Doudna, Elizabeth IV, 383
Doudna, Elizabeth IV, 385
Doudna, Elizabeth IV, 446
Doudna, Elizabeth IV, 574
Doudna, Elizabeth C. IV, 388
Doudna, Elizabeth C. IV, 407
Doudna, Elizabeth C. IV, 575
Doudna, Elizabeth C. IV, 583
Doudna, Elma May IV, 574
Doudna, Elwood IV, 386
Doudna, Elwood IV, 387
Doudna, Elwood IV, 521
Doudna, Elwood T. IV, 521
Doudna, Ema IV, 526
Doudna, Ephraim IV, 386
Doudna, Ephraim IV, 387
Doudna, Erma L. IV, 387
Doudna, Erma L. IV, 401
Doudna, Ernest J. IV, 388
Doudna, Esther IV, 374
Doudna, Esther IV, 386
Doudna, Esther IV, 387
Doudna, Esther IV, 1094
Doudna, Ethelyn IV, 388
Doudna, Ethelyn IV, 403
Doudna, Eunice IV, 196
Doudna, Eunice IV, 386
Doudna, Eunice IV, 574
Doudna, Eva IV, 1094
Doudna, Evaline IV, 1094
Doudna, Ezra IV, 1094
Doudna, Flanner IV, 196
Doudna, Frances IV, 366
Doudna, Frances P. IV, 387
Doudna, Frank E. IV, 574
Doudna, George IV, 386
Doudna, Hannah IV, 144
Doudna, Hannah IV, 163
Doudna, Hannah IV, 196
Doudna, Hannah IV, 385
Doudna, Hannah IV, 387
Doudna, Hannah IV, 574
Doudna, Hannah IV, 575
Doudna, Hannah IV, 586
Doudna, Hannah IV, 599
Doudna, Hannah Ann IV, 196
Doudna, Hannah Ann IV, 387
Doudna, Hannah Ann IV, 402
Doudna, Hannah Anne IV, 386
Doudna, Hannah E. IV, 196
Doudna, Hannah E. IV, 575
Doudna, Hannah W. IV, 1055
Doudna, Harold Edmund IV, 575
Doudna, Henry IV, 177
Doudna, Henry IV, 196
Doudna, Henry IV, 365
Doudna, Henry IV, 370
Doudna, Henry IV, 373
Doudna, Henry IV, 385
Doudna, Henry IV, 386
Doudna, Henry IV, 387
Doudna, Henry IV, 396
Doudna, Henry IV, 430
Doudna, Henry IV, 455
Doudna, Henry IV, 1055
Doudna, Henry IV, 1092
Doudna, Henry IV, 1094
Doudna, Henry IV, 1096
Doudna, Henry, Jr. IV, 196
Doudna, Henry, Jr. IV, 387
Doudna, Hetty IV, 386
Doudna, Hosea I, 285
Doudna, Hosea IV, 144
Doudna, Hosea IV, 381
Doudna, Hosea IV, 385
Doudna, Hosea IV, 387
Doudna, Hosea IV, 391
Doudna, Hosea IV, 431
Doudna, Hosea IV, 521
Doudna, Hosea B. IV, 521
Doudna, Hosea, Jr. IV, 196
Doudna, Isaac IV, 196
Doudna, Isaac IV, 386
Doudna, Isaac IV, 428
Doudna, Isaac IV, 574

Doudna, Isaac IV, 575
Doudna, Isaac IV, 592
Doudna, Isaac IV, 1055
Doudna, Isaac H. IV, 574
Doudna, Isaac, Jr. IV, 575
Doudna, James IV, 384
Doudna, James IV, 385
Doudna, James IV, 387
Doudna, James IV, 794
Doudna, James IV, 1053
Doudna, James IV, 1055
Doudna, James IV, 1094
Doudna, James IV, 1118
Doudna, Jasin IV, 521
Doudna, Jason IV, 368
Doudna, Jason IV, 386
Doudna, Jason IV, 387
Doudna, Jason IV, 521
Doudna, Jephtha IV, 1094
Doudna, Jeptha IV, 386
Doudna, Jeptha IV, 387
Doudna, Jeptha IV, 1055
Doudna, Jesse IV, 196
Doudna, Jesse IV, 385
Doudna, Jesse IV, 387
Doudna, Jesse IV, 574
Doudna, Jesse IV, 575
Doudna, Jesse IV, 591
Doudna, Jesse IV, 1055
Doudna, Jesse I. IV, 386
Doudna, Jesse I. IV, 388
Doudna, Jesse I. IV, 459
Doudna, Jesse I. IV, 575
Doudna, Jesse I. IV, 1055
Doudna, Joel I, 285
Doudna, Joel IV, 144
Doudna, Joel IV, 196
Doudna, Joel IV, 374
Doudna, Joel IV, 386
Doudna, Joel IV, 409
Doudna, Joel J. IV, 521
Doudna, Joel, Jr. IV, 196
Doudna, John I, 285
Doudna, John I, 304
Doudna, John I, 307
Doudna, John IV, 143
Doudna, John IV, 144
Doudna, John IV, 160
Doudna, John IV, 196
Doudna, John IV, 371
Doudna, John IV, 374
Doudna, John IV, 377
Doudna, John IV, 385
Doudna, John IV, 387
Doudna, John IV, 388
Doudna, John IV, 400
Doudna, John IV, 417
Doudna, John IV, 426
Doudna, John IV, 435
Doudna, John IV, 521
Doudna, John IV, 569
Doudna, John IV, 574
Doudna, John IV, 575
Doudna, John IV, 595
Doudna, John IV, 1094
Doudna, John A. IV, 574
Doudna, John A. IV, 575
Doudna, John C. IV, 1055
Doudna, John E. IV, 387
Doudna, John E. IV, 388
Doudna, John E. IV, 401
Doudna, John E. IV, 521
Doudna, John Elwood IV, 386
Doudna, John M. IV, 575
Doudna, John S. IV, 196
Doudna, John S. IV, 387
Doudna, John S. IV, 448
Doudna, John S. IV, 575
Doudna, John S. IV, 596
Doudna, John S. IV, 1094
Doudna, John V. IV, 1094
Doudna, John, Jr. IV, 574
Doudna, John, Jr. IV, 578
Doudna, Joseph II, 946
Doudna, Joseph IV, 196
Doudna, Joseph IV, 385
Doudna, Joseph IV, 386
Doudna, Joseph IV, 387
Doudna, Joseph IV, 400
Doudna, Joseph IV, 411
Doudna, Joseph IV, 438
Doudna, Joseph IV, 450
Doudna, Joseph IV, 521
Doudna, Joseph IV, 531
Doudna, Joseph IV, 575
Doudna, Joseph IV, 794
Doudna, Joseph IV, 1055
Doudna, Joseph IV, 1094
Doudna, Joseph Ellmer IV, 574
Doudna, Joseph Elmer IV, 575
Doudna, Joseph F. IV, 387
Doudna, Joseph F. IV, 388
Doudna, Joseph F. IV, 457
Doudna, Joseph H. IV, 387
Doudna, Joseph H. IV, 406
Doudna, Joseph H. IV, 574
Doudna, Joseph H. IV, 575
Doudna, Joseph H. IV, 583
Doudna, Joseph Sylvester IV, 574
Doudna, Joseph T. IV, 387
Doudna, Joseph W. IV, 566
Doudna, Joseph W. IV, 574
Doudna, Joseph W. IV, 575
Doudna, Joseph W. IV, 583
Doudna, Joseph W. IV, 586
Doudna, Joseph W. IV, 1094
Doudna, Joshua IV, 387
Doudna, Joshua IV, 575
Doudna, Joshua IV, 1055
Doudna, Joshua IV, 1094
Doudna, Josiah IV, 196
Doudna, Josiah IV, 365
Doudna, Josiah IV, 387
Doudna, Josiah IV, 521
Doudna, Josiah IV, 575
Doudna, Josiah W. IV, 366
Doudna, Josiah W. IV, 387
Doudna, Josiah W. IV, 388
Doudna, Kenneth L. IV, 575
Doudna, Knois IV, 144
Doudna, Knois IV, 163
Doudna, Knowas IV, 144
Doudna, Knowes IV, 385
Doudna, Knowis IV, 387
Doudna, Knowis IV, 574
Doudna, Knowles IV, 386
Doudna, Laura A. IV, 369
Doudna, Laura A. IV, 387
Doudna, Laura A. IV, 388
Doudna, Lillian IV, 365
Doudna, Lillian IV, 366
Doudna, Lillian M. IV, 366
Doudna, Lindley IV, 1094
Doudna, Louisa IV, 386
Doudna, Louisa IV, 388
Doudna, Louisa IV, 459
Doudna, Louisa IV, 574
Doudna, Louisa IV, 575
Doudna, Louisa IV, 591
Doudna, Louisa IV, 794
Doudna, Louisa IV, 1055
Doudna, Louisa M. IV, 1094
Doudna, Louisa M. IV, 1118
Doudna, Louisa P. IV, 1055
Doudna, Louiza IV, 575
Doudna, Louiza M. IV, 1094
Doudna, Louiza P. IV, 575
Doudna, Lydia IV, 365
Doudna, Lydia IV, 386
Doudna, Lydia IV, 387
Doudna, Lydia IV, 566
Doudna, Lydia IV, 575
Doudna, Lydia IV, 1094
Doudna, Lydia IV, 1122
Doudna, Lydia Jane IV, 386
Doudna, M. Ethel IV, 459
Doudna, M. J. IV, 400
Doudna, Margaret IV, 365
Doudna, Margaret IV, 385
Doudna, Margaret IV, 387
Doudna, Margaret IV, 584
Doudna, Margaret IV, 591
Doudna, Margaret IV, 595
Doudna, Margaret IV, 819
Doudna, Margery H. IV, 574
Doudna, Margery H. IV, 575
Doudna, Margery H. IV, 592
Doudna, Mariah IV, 575
Doudna, Mariam IV, 567
Doudna, Mariam IV, 575
Doudna, Marian Ethelyn IV, 575
Doudna, Marian Ethelyn IV, 582
Doudna, Marian Ethlyn IV, 575
Doudna, Marion Ethlyn IV, 387
Doudna, Marion Ethlyn IV, 401
Doudna, Martha IV, 196
Doudna, Martha IV, 365
Doudna, Martha IV, 373
Doudna, Martha IV, 385
Doudna, Martha IV, 386
Doudna, Martha IV, 387
Doudna, Martha IV, 392
Doudna, Martha IV, 396
Doudna, Martha IV, 428
Doudna, Martha IV, 430
Doudna, Martha IV, 455
Doudna, Martha IV, 574
Doudna, Martha IV, 575
Doudna, Martha IV, 592
Doudna, Martha IV, 948
Doudna, Martha IV, 952
Doudna, Martha IV, 1055
Doudna, Martha IV, 1092
Doudna, Martha IV, 1094
Doudna, Martha IV, 1096
Doudna, Martha IV, 1097
Doudna, Martha E. IV, 387
Doudna, Martha E. IV, 400
Doudna, Martha E. IV, 574
Doudna, Martha Ellen IV, 196
Doudna, Martha Ellen IV, 386
Doudna, Martha Jr. IV, 1094
Doudna, Martha W. M. IV, 574
Doudna, Martha, Jr. IV, 387
Doudna, Martha, Jr. IV, 1055
Doudna, Martha, Jr. IV, 1096
Doudna, Mary I, 304
Doudna, Mary I, 307
Doudna, Mary II, 946
Doudna, Mary IV, 144
Doudna, Mary IV, 160
Doudna, Mary IV, 196
Doudna, Mary IV, 368
Doudna, Mary IV, 374
Doudna, Mary IV, 381
Doudna, Mary IV, 385
Doudna, Mary IV, 386
Doudna, Mary IV, 387
Doudna, Mary IV, 391
Doudna, Mary IV, 397
Doudna, Mary IV, 398
Doudna, Mary IV, 405
Doudna, Mary IV, 430
Doudna, Mary IV, 431
Doudna, Mary IV, 450
Doudna, Mary IV, 521
Doudna, Mary IV, 569
Doudna, Mary IV, 574
Doudna, Mary IV, 575
Doudna, Mary IV, 595
Doudna, Mary IV, 1055
Doudna, Mary IV, 1073
Doudna, Mary B. IV, 387
Doudna, Mary B. IV, 572
Doudna, Mary B. IV, 575
Doudna, Mary B. IV, 1052
Doudna, Mary B. IV, 1055
Doudna, Mary B. IV, 1092
Doudna, Mary B. IV, 1094
Doudna, Mary D. IV, 375
Doudna, Mary D. IV, 387
Doudna, Mary E. IV, 575
Doudna, Mary E. IV, 1055
Doudna, Mary Ethel IV, 388
Doudna, Mary Ethel IV, 575
Doudna, Mary Etta IV, 574
Doudna, Mary Etta IV, 575
Doudna, Mary H. IV, 387
Doudna, Mary H. IV, 411
Doudna, Mary H. IV, 521
Doudna, Mary H. IV, 1094
Doudna, Mary J. IV, 378
Doudna, Mary J. IV, 387
Doudna, Mary Jane IV, 196
Doudna, Mary Jane IV, 377
Doudna, Mary Jane IV, 386
Doudna, Mary Jane IV, 388
Doudna, Mary Jane IV, 400
Doudna, Mary Melissa IV, 1094
Doudna, Mary P. IV, 196
Doudna, Mary P. IV, 387
Doudna, Mary P. IV, 1055
Doudna, Mary V. IV, 794
Doudna, Mary V. IV, 1094
Doudna, Matilda IV, 177
Doudna, Matilda IV, 196
Doudna, Matilda IV, 370
Doudna, Matilda IV, 386
Doudna, Matilda IV, 387
Doudna, Matilda IV, 575
Doudna, Matilda IV, 584
Doudna, Matilda IV, 1055
Doudna, Matilda IV, 1092
Doudna, Maud IV, 387
Doudna, Milesent IV, 385
Doudna, Milicent IV, 387
Doudna, Milicent IV, 396
Doudna, Milisent IV, 386
Doudna, Miriam I, 285
Doudna, Miriam I, 304
Doudna, Miriam I, 307
Doudna, Miriam IV, 144
Doudna, Miriam IV, 196
Doudna, Miriam IV, 385
Doudna, Miriam IV, 426
Doudna, Miriam IV, 569
Doudna, Miriam IV, 574
Doudna, Miriam IV, 575
Doudna, Miriam IV, 1055
Doudna, Nathan IV, 196
Doudna, Nathan IV, 575
Doudna, Nathan M. IV, 386
Doudna, Nathan W. IV, 575
Doudna, Nora IV, 196
Doudna, Nora IV, 575
Doudna, Nora IV, 583
Doudna, Nora E. IV, 387
Doudna, Nora E. IV, 388
Doudna, Nora E. IV, 406
Doudna, Nora E. IV, 575
Doudna, Nora Elma IV, 574
Doudna, Nora Elma IV, 575
Doudna, Norah E. IV, 387
Doudna, Nowis IV, 574
Doudna, O. IV, 576
Doudna, Patty IV, 387
Doudna, Peninah I, 285
Doudna, Peninah IV, 144
Doudna, Peninnah IV, 385
Doudna, Peninnah IV, 417
Doudna, Penninah I, 304
Doudna, Phebe IV, 196
Doudna, Phebe IV, 386
Doudna, Phebe IV, 387
Doudna, Phebe IV, 438
Doudna, Phebe IV, 574
Doudna, Phebe IV, 575
Doudna, Phebe Anna IV, 574
Doudna, Phebe Anna IV, 575
Doudna, Phebe Anna IV, 598
Doudna, Rachel IV, 375
Doudna, Rachel IV, 386
Doudna, Rachel IV, 387
Doudna, Rachel IV, 438
Doudna, Rachel IV, 458
Doudna, Rachel IV, 521
Doudna, Rachel IV, 558
Doudna, Rachel IV, 762
Doudna, Rachel Ann IV, 387
Doudna, Rachel Ann IV, 574
Doudna, Rachel Ann IV, 575
Doudna, Rachel Ann IV, 587
Doudna, Rachel L. IV, 369
Doudna, Rachel L. IV, 387
Doudna, Rachel W. IV, 387
Doudna, Rachel W. IV, 521
Doudna, Rebecca IV, 196
Doudna, Rebecca IV, 370
Doudna, Rebecca IV, 374
Doudna, Rebecca IV, 386
Doudna, Rebecca IV, 387
Doudna, Rebecca IV, 409
Doudna, Rebecca IV, 1094
Doudna, Rebecca W. IV, 517
Doudna, Rebecca W. IV, 522
Doudna, Rebecca, Jr. IV, 196
Doudna, Rebeckah IV, 385
Doudna, Richard Gene IV, 575
Doudna, Robert IV, 386
Doudna, Robert IV, 1094
Doudna, Robert Gene IV, 575
Doudna, Robert H. IV, 374
Doudna, Robert H. IV, 386
Doudna, Robert H. IV, 387
Doudna, Robert H. IV, 1094
Doudna, Rosa IV, 387
Doudna, Rosetta IV, 387
Doudna, Rosetta IV, 400
Doudna, Rosetta IV, 566
Doudna, Rosetta IV, 574
Doudna, Rosetta IV, 575
Doudna, Rosetta IV, 583
Doudna, Rosetta IV, 586
Doudna, Rosetta B. IV, 575
Doudna, Rosetta B. IV, 586
Doudna, Rosetta H. IV, 574
Doudna, Russel J. IV, 388
Doudna, Russel J. IV, 575
Doudna, Russell J. IV, 574
Doudna, Russell J. IV, 575
Doudna, Russell J. IV, 578
Doudna, Ruth IV, 366
Doudna, Ruth IV, 375
Doudna, Ruth IV, 387
Doudna, Ruth IV, 574
Doudna, Ruth IV, 575
Doudna, Ruth B. IV, 366
Doudna, Ruth B. IV, 387
Doudna, Ruth S. IV, 387
Doudna, Ruth S. IV, 388
Doudna, Ruth S. IV, 408
Doudna, Ruth Virginia IV, 574
Doudna, Sally IV, 385
Doudna, Sally IV, 387
Doudna, Samuel IV, 386
Doudna, Samuel IV, 387
Doudna, Samuel IV, 1055
Doudna, Samuel IV, 1094
Doudna, Samuel C. IV, 196
Doudna, Samuel C. IV, 386
Doudna, Samuel C. IV, 388
Doudna, Sara IV, 574
Doudna, Sara IV, 596
Doudna, Sarah I, 285
Doudna, Sarah I, 304
Doudna, Sarah IV, 143
Doudna, Sarah IV, 144
Doudna, Sarah IV, 196
Doudna, Sarah IV, 371
Doudna, Sarah IV, 373
Doudna, Sarah IV, 374
Doudna, Sarah IV, 375
Doudna, Sarah IV, 377
Doudna, Sarah IV, 378
Doudna, Sarah IV, 385
Doudna, Sarah IV, 386
Doudna, Sarah IV, 387
Doudna, Sarah IV, 388
Doudna, Sarah IV, 394
Doudna, Sarah IV, 404
Doudna, Sarah IV, 406
Doudna, Sarah IV, 417
Doudna, Sarah IV, 421
Doudna, Sarah IV, 435
Doudna, Sarah IV, 441
Doudna, Sarah IV, 448
Doudna, Sarah IV, 571
Doudna, Sarah IV, 574
Doudna, Sarah IV, 575
Doudna, Sarah IV, 1053
Doudna, Sarah IV, 1055
Doudna, Sarah IV, 1094
Doudna, Sarah F. IV, 575
Doudna, Sarah Knowles IV, 385
Doudna, Sarah Rebecca IV, 1094
Doudna, Sarah, Jr. I, 304
Doudna, Sina IV, 196
Doudna, Smith IV, 574
Doudna, Smith IV, 575
Doudna, Stanley J. IV, 575
Doudna, Stephen IV, 386
Doudna, Stephen IV, 1094
Doudna, Suphemia IV, 196
Doudna, Tabitha IV, 374
Doudna, Tabitha IV, 386
Doudna, Tabitha C. IV, 196
Doudna, Tabitha C. IV, 369
Doudna, Tabitha C. IV, 386
Doudna, Tabitha C. IV, 387
Doudna, Temperance IV, 385
Doudna, Temperance IV, 387
Doudna, Temperance IV, 455
Doudna, Thomas IV, 196
Doudna, Thomas IV, 375
Doudna, Thomas IV, 386
Doudna, Thomas IV, 387
Doudna, Thomas IV, 438
Doudna, Thomas IV, 458
Doudna, Thomas IV, 521
Doudna, Thomas IV, 558
Doudna, Thomas IV, 574
Doudna, Thomas IV, 575
Doudna, Thomas IV, 762
Doudna, Thomas E. IV, 794
Doudna, Thomas E. IV, 1094
Doudna, Thomas Exum IV, 794
Doudna, Thomas P. IV, 386
Doudna, Wallace IV, 388
Doudna, Walter IV, 387
Doudna, Walter IV, 1094
Doudna, Waneta M. IV, 387
Doudna, Wauneta IV, 575
Doudna, Wauneta R. IV, 183
Doudna, Wauneta R. IV, 574
Doudna, Wauneta Rosetta IV, 184
Doudna, Wauneta Rosetta IV, 196
Doudna, Wauneta Rosetta IV, 569
Doudna, William IV, 386
Doudna, William IV, 387
Doudna, William IV, 388
Doudna, William F. IV, 574
Doudna, William W. IV, 574
Doudna, Willis E. IV, 386
Doudna, Willoughby IV, 386
Doudna, Willoughby IV, 387
Doudna, Wm. IV, 365
Doudna, Wm. IV, 566
Doudna, Wm. IV, 575
Doudna, Wm. IV, 1094
Doudna, Wm. D. IV, 575
Doudna, Wm. W. IV, 575
Doudna, Wm. W. IV, 1055
Doudna, Wm. Wallace IV, 575
Doudna, Zilpah IV, 385
Doudna, Zilpah IV, 388
Doudna, Zilpha I, 304
Doudna, Zilpha IV, 144
Doudna, Zilphia I, 285
Doudne, Sarah I, 304
Doudny, Charity IV, 388
Doudny, John IV, 388
Doudny, Miriam IV, 388

Doudy, Joseph II, 792
Doudy, Wd. Phebe II, 792
Dougal, Cora V, 993
Dougal, E. B. V, 993
Dougal, Eva V, 993
Dougal, Nora V, 993
Dougal, Samuel V, 993
Dougal, Wm. V, 993
Dougan, Rebecca I, 714
Dougan, Rebecca I, 718
Dougherty, Alexander III, 104
Dougherty, Alfred V, 383
Dougherty, Annie J. VI, 383
Dougherty, Annie J. VI, 411
Dougherty, Betsy V, 25
Dougherty, Betsy V, 48
Dougherty, Dicey VI, 812
Dougherty, Eda Ann VI, 913
Dougherty, Eliza V, 234
Dougherty, Eliza F. V, 234
Dougherty, Elizabeth V, 488
Dougherty, Elizabeth V, 537
Dougherty, Elizabeth VI, 812
Dougherty, Florence B. V, 559
Dougherty, Garret VI, 323
Dougherty, Garret VI, 859
Dougherty, Gerrard VI, 812
Dougherty, Hannah V, 48
Dougherty, Henrietta V, 455
Dougherty, Ida Maxine V, 559
Dougherty, James VI, 913
Dougherty, Jane I, 1029
Dougherty, Jared VI, 824
Dougherty, John V, 234
Dougherty, John VI, 812
Dougherty, Letice VI, 812
Dougherty, Mary II, 508
Dougherty, Mary II, 792
Dougherty, Mary II, 803
Dougherty, Mary Jane V, 383
Dougherty, Robert II, 508
Dougherty, Sarah II, 508
Dougherty, Sarah II, 648
Dougherty, Sarah VI, 902
Dougherty, Sarah VI, 1005
Dougherty, Susanna II, 508
Dougherty, Susannah II, 508
Dougherty, Thomas VI, 902
Dougherty, Turisse V, 383
Dougherty, William VI, 812
Dougherty, Willis S. VI, 913
Dougherty, Wm. V, 559
Dougherty, Wm. Joseph V, 559
Doughman, John VI, 908
Doughman, Matilda V, 48
Doughman, Matilda V, 123
Doughman, Matilda S. V, 48
Doughman, Molly VI, 908
Doughtman, Matilda V, 48
Doughtman, Matilda V, 93
Doughtry, Abigail I, 237
Doughtry, Abigail I, 248
Doughtry, Bathsheba I, 237
Doughtry, Bersheba I, 206
Doughtry, Bryan I, 45
Doughtry, Bryan I, 237
Doughtry, Bryan I, 239
Doughtry, Elijah I, 237
Doughtry, Elizabeth I, 237
Doughtry, Enos I, 237
Doughtry, Jesse I, 237
Doughtry, Josiah I, 237
Doughtry, Lillie I, 237
Doughtry, Lillie I, 243
Doughtry, Lillie E. I, 237
Doughtry, Rachel I, 206
Doughtry, Rachel I, 237
Doughtry, Rachel I, 239
Doughtry, Ruth I, 237
Doughtry, Ruth I, 257
Doughtry, Tinsie I, 237
Doughtry, Tinsie I, 243
Doughtry, Tinsie D. I, 237
Doughty, ??? III, 379
Doughty, Abigail III, 104
Doughty, Abigail III, 105
Doughty, Abigail III, 164
Doughty, Abigail III, 418
Doughty, Ame III, 104
Doughty, Amy III, 104
Doughty, Ann III, 104
Doughty, Ann III, 105
Doughty, Anne III, 408
Doughty, Benj. III, 105
Doughty, Benj. III, 165
Doughty, Benj. III, 321
Doughty, Benj. III, 408
Doughty, Benj. III, 457
Doughty, Benjamin III, 104
Doughty, Benjamin III, 105
Doughty, Benjamin III, 321
Doughty, Benjamin III, 379
Doughty, Benjamin III, 407
Doughty, Benjamin III, 408
Doughty, Benjamin III, 472
Doughty, Benjamin III, 481
Doughty, Capt. James I, 1075
Doughty, Charity III, 104
Doughty, Charity III, 110
Doughty, Charity III, 407
Doughty, Charles III, 87
Doughty, Charles III, 101
Doughty, Charles III, 104
Doughty, Charles III, 105
Doughty, Charles III, 193
Doughty, Charles III, 379
Doughty, Charles III, 407
Doughty, Charles III, 408
Doughty, Chas. III, 104
Doughty, Chas. III, 105
Doughty, Chas. III, 408
Doughty, Christopher III, 104
Doughty, Daniel III, 104
Doughty, Daniel III, 408
Doughty, Deborah III, 104
Doughty, Deborah III, 105
Doughty, Deborah III, 199
Doughty, Donald Morgan III, 407
Doughty, Donald Morgan III, 448
Doughty, Edward II, 355
Doughty, Elener III, 104
Doughty, Elias III, 104
Doughty, Elias, Jr. III, 104
Doughty, Elias, Jr. III, 108
Doughty, Eliz. III, 104
Doughty, Eliz. III, 408
Doughty, Eliz. III, 457
Doughty, Elizabeth III, 104
Doughty, Elizabeth III, 321
Doughty, Elizabeth III, 407
Doughty, Elizabeth III, 408
Doughty, Elizabeth III, 443
Doughty, Esther III, 104
Doughty, Esther III, 105
Doughty, Esther III, 377
Doughty, Esther III, 379
Doughty, Evelyn III, 407
Doughty, Frances III, 104
Doughty, Francis III, 56
Doughty, Francis III, 104
Doughty, Francis III, 105
Doughty, George III, 407
Doughty, George M. III, 379
Doughty, George Masters III, 105
Doughty, George Masters III, 379
Doughty, Hannah III, 104
Doughty, Hannah III, 165
Doughty, Hannah III, 379
Doughty, Hannah III, 407
Doughty, Hannah III, 408
Doughty, Hannah III, 447
Doughty, Hannah III, 457
Doughty, Hannah III, 472
Doughty, Harriet III, 407
Doughty, Isaac III, 407
Doughty, Isaac III, 408
Doughty, Isaac III, 443
Doughty, Isaac T. III, 104
Doughty, Jacob III, 104
Doughty, James III, 104
Doughty, John III, 104
Doughty, John III, 105
Doughty, John III, 164
Doughty, John III, 408
Doughty, John III, 418
Doughty, John III, 447
Doughty, Joseph III, 105
Doughty, Keziah III, 408
Doughty, Lydia III, 407
Doughty, Lydia III, 448
Doughty, Margaret III, 104
Doughty, Margaret III, 200
Doughty, Margaret III, 379
Doughty, Margaret III, 408
Doughty, Margaret Ann III, 379
Doughty, Martha III, 314
Doughty, Martha III, 408
Doughty, Mary II, 451
Doughty, Mary II, 508
Doughty, Mary III, 56
Doughty, Mary III, 101
Doughty, Mary III, 104
Doughty, Mary III, 105
Doughty, Mary III, 108
Doughty, Mary III, 193
Doughty, Mary III, 379
Doughty, Mary III, 408
Doughty, Mary III, 443
Doughty, Mary III, 472
Doughty, Mary E. III, 408
Doughty, Mary E. III, 414
Doughty, Moses M. III, 379
Doughty, Nellie V, 736
Doughty, Obadiah III, 104
Doughty, Obadiah III, 105
Doughty, Palmer III, 104
Doughty, Paulin V, 736
Doughty, Peggy Ann III, 379
Doughty, Phebe III, 87
Doughty, Phebe III, 104
Doughty, Phebe III, 105
Doughty, Phebe III, 408
Doughty, Phebe III, 481
Doughty, Philadelphia III, 105
Doughty, Philadelphia III, 321
Doughty, Philadelphia III, 408
Doughty, Philadelphia III, 457
Doughty, Rebecca III, 104
Doughty, Rebecca III, 105
Doughty, Richard III, 408
Doughty, Robert II, 508
Doughty, Robert III, 105
Doughty, Roslyn III, 407
Doughty, Samuel III, 105
Doughty, Samuel III, 199
Doughty, Samuel III, 353
Doughty, Samuel III, 379
Doughty, Samuel III, 407
Doughty, Samuel III, 408
Doughty, Samuel C. III, 379
Doughty, Samuel, Jr. III, 105
Doughty, Sarah II, 215
Doughty, Sarah II, 234
Doughty, Sarah II, 508
Doughty, Sarah II, 648
Doughty, Sarah III, 72
Doughty, Sarah III, 104
Doughty, Sarah III, 105
Doughty, Sarah III, 164
Doughty, Sarah III, 193
Doughty, Sarah III, 379
Doughty, Sarah III, 408
Doughty, Sarah III, 418
Doughty, Sarah III, 419
Doughty, Thomas III, 408
Doughty, W. C. V, 736
Doughty, Wd. Deborah III, 353
Doughty, Wd. Sarah III, 408
Doughty, William III, 105
Doughty, William III, 379
Doughty, William III, 408
Doughty, William III, 472
Doughty, Wm. III, 379
Doughty, Wm. E. III, 407
Douglas, Achilles VI, 303
Douglas, Achilles VI, 308
Douglas, Achilles VI, 312
Douglas, Achilles VI, 319
Douglas, Achilles VI, 327
Douglas, Achilles VI, 330
Douglas, Achilles VI, 799
Douglas, Achilles VI, 812
Douglas, Achilles Moorman VI, 308
Douglas, Agatha VI, 308
Douglas, Ann VI, 16
Douglas, Ann L. VI, 812
Douglas, Anna V, 328
Douglas, Anna V, 670
Douglas, Anna B. V, 328
Douglas, Anna Bell V, 669
Douglas, Anne VI, 285
Douglas, Annie B. V, 669
Douglas, Benjamin III, 105
Douglas, Benjamin D. III, 105
Douglas, Betsy VI, 241
Douglas, Charles VI, 285
Douglas, Charles B. V, 736
Douglas, Charles Terrell VI, 308
Douglas, Charles, Jr. VI, 241
Douglas, Charlie V, 670
Douglas, Chas. A. V, 559
Douglas, Chas. A. V, 598
Douglas, Chas. Baily V, 669
Douglas, Chloe V, 328
Douglas, Chloe V, 619
Douglas, Chloe V, 669
Douglas, Chloe V, 670
Douglas, Chloe Ann V, 619
Douglas, Chloe Anna V, 328
Douglas, Chloe Anna V, 619
Douglas, Chloe Anna V, 669
Douglas, Christine V, 328
Douglas, Christine V, 669
Douglas, Christine A. V, 670
Douglas, Cornelius V, 559
Douglas, Cornelius V, 619
Douglas, Cornelius V, 669
Douglas, Cyrus IV, 1277
Douglas, David V, 384
Douglas, David V, 619
Douglas, David V, 736
Douglas, David VI, 1021
Douglas, David F. V, 328
Douglas, David F. V, 619
Douglas, David F. V, 736
Douglas, David Franklin V, 328
Douglas, David Franklin V, 619
Douglas, David Franklin V, 669
Douglas, David Franklin V, 670
Douglas, David Franklin V, 736
Douglas, Deborah VI, 303
Douglas, Deborah VI, 308
Douglas, Deborah VI, 319
Douglas, Deborah VI, 326
Douglas, Deborah Johnson VI, 308
Douglas, Demsey VI, 63
Douglas, Demsey VI, 73
Douglas, Demsey VI, 87
Douglas, Editha VI, 933
Douglas, Edward V, 736
Douglas, Edward VI, 812
Douglas, Edward VI, 853
Douglas, Edward S. V, 559
Douglas, Edward S. V, 598
Douglas, Effie V, 736
Douglas, Effie J. V, 736
Douglas, Elaine V, 736
Douglas, Eliza IV, 730
Douglas, Elizabeth II, 785
Douglas, Elizabeth IV, 1340
Douglas, Elizabeth V, 559
Douglas, Elizabeth V, 598
Douglas, Elizabeth V, 619
Douglas, Elizabeth V, 633
Douglas, Elizabeth VI, 301
Douglas, Elizabeth VI, 303
Douglas, Elizabeth VI, 308
Douglas, Elizabeth VI, 319
Douglas, Elizabeth VI, 327
Douglas, Elsie V, 736
Douglas, Emma L. V, 736
Douglas, Emma R. V, 234
Douglas, Emma R. V, 736
Douglas, Emma T. V, 736
Douglas, Ester V, 736
Douglas, Frank H. III, 105
Douglas, Franklin V, 669
Douglas, Geo. Gifford V, 619
Douglas, Geo. W. V, 328
Douglas, George G. V, 669
Douglas, George Gifford V, 328
Douglas, George Gifford V, 619
Douglas, George Gifford V, 669
Douglas, George W. III, 105
Douglas, Gifford T. V, 736
Douglas, Grace C. III, 105
Douglas, Harriet E. V, 559
Douglas, Harriet E. V, 598
Douglas, Henry V, 669
Douglas, James VI, 806
Douglas, James VI, 812
Douglas, James VI, 853
Douglas, Jane VI, 804
Douglas, Jesse C. V, 328
Douglas, Jesse C. V, 619
Douglas, Jesse C. V, 670
Douglas, Jesse Carter V, 328
Douglas, Jesse Carter V, 619
Douglas, Jesse Carter V, 669
Douglas, John IV, 730
Douglas, John V, 619
Douglas, John V, 669
Douglas, John VI, 16
Douglas, John H. V, 619
Douglas, John Henry V, 328
Douglas, John Henry V, 619
Douglas, John Henry V, 669
Douglas, John Henry V, 670
Douglas, John Henry, Jr. V, 328
Douglas, John Henry, Jr. V, 619
Douglas, John L. VI, 308
Douglas, John Lynch VI, 308
Douglas, John N. V, 559
Douglas, John N. V, 613
Douglas, John N. V, 619
Douglas, Judith VI, 16
Douglas, Judith VI, 308
Douglas, Judith VI, 319
Douglas, Judith VI, 325
Douglas, Judith VI, 327
Douglas, Laura A. IV, 1156
Douglas, Laura A. IV, 1182
Douglas, Lucy George VI, 799
Douglas, Lydia V, 736
Douglas, Lydia E. V, 619
Douglas, Lydia M. V, 384
Douglas, Margaret IV, 1340
Douglas, Margaret V, 669
Douglas, Margaret V, 736
Douglas, Margaret A. V, 328
Douglas, Margaret A. V, 619
Douglas, Margaret Ann V, 669
Douglas, Maria V, 559
Douglas, Maria V, 619
Douglas, Maria V, 629
Douglas, Mariah V, 619
Douglas, Marium V, 619
Douglas, Mary III, 105
Douglas, Mary IV, 730
Douglas, Mary V, 559
Douglas, Mary V, 611
Douglas, Mary V, 619
Douglas, Mary V, 620
Douglas, Mary V, 642
Douglas, Mary VI, 308
Douglas, Mary VI, 750
Douglas, Mary Ann VI, 812
Douglas, Mary Belle IV, 400
Douglas, Mary Elsie V, 736
Douglas, Mary Leckey V, 328
Douglas, Mary Lecky V, 669
Douglas, Mary Narcissa V, 619
Douglas, Matthew IV, 1340
Douglas, Mellie V, 670
Douglas, Merium V, 619
Douglas, Milley VI, 308
Douglas, Milly VI, 308
Douglas, Miriam V, 328
Douglas, Miriam V, 619
Douglas, Miriam V, 669
Douglas, Miriam C. V, 328
Douglas, Miriam C. V, 619
Douglas, Miriam C. V, 669
Douglas, Miriam C. V, 670
Douglas, Mirium V, 619
Douglas, Phebe V, 669
Douglas, Phebe Ann V, 619
Douglas, Phebe N. V, 559
Douglas, Phebe N. V, 619
Douglas, Polly VI, 806
Douglas, R. W. V, 736
Douglas, Robert VI, 804
Douglas, Robert Terrell VI, 308
Douglas, Robert W. V, 328
Douglas, Robert W. V, 619
Douglas, Robert W. V, 669
Douglas, Robert W. V, 670
Douglas, Robert W. V, 736
Douglas, Robert Walter V, 619
Douglas, Robert, Jr. V, 736
Douglas, Sarah V, 559
Douglas, Sarah V, 619
Douglas, Sarah VI, 308
Douglas, Sarah VI, 319
Douglas, Sarah VI, 324
Douglas, Sarah VI, 853
Douglas, Sarah T. V, 613
Douglas, Sarah T. V, 619
Douglas, Smith V, 598
Douglas, Susan IV, 1277
Douglas, Thomas VI, 241
Douglas, Thomas J. V, 559
Douglas, Thomas J. V, 598
Douglas, Winnifred E. V, 736
Douglas, Wm. II, 993
Douglass, ??? VI, 283
Douglass, Abigah VI, 907
Douglass, Abijah VI, 908
Douglass, Achilis VI, 241
Douglass, Achilles VI, 285
Douglass, Achilles VI, 308
Douglass, Achilles VI, 344
Douglass, Achillis VI, 276
Douglass, Alfred VI, 907
Douglass, Alfred VI, 908
Douglass, Anne VI, 241
Douglass, Anne VI, 285
Douglass, Archilles VI, 861
Douglass, Betsy VI, 241
Douglass, Catharine VI, 908
Douglass, Charles VI, 240
Douglass, Charles VI, 241
Douglass, Charles VI, 285
Douglass, Charles, Jr. VI, 241
Douglass, Chloe V, 619
Douglass, Chloe Ann V, 619
Douglass, Chloe Anna V, 619
Douglass, David V, 384
Douglass, David V, 619
Douglass, David VI, 908
Douglass, David VI, 929
Douglass, David VI, 951
Douglass, David VI, 994
Douglass, David VI, 1006
Douglass, David F. V, 736
Douglass, Dorcas VI, 241
Douglass, Dorcas VI, 285
Douglass, Edward H. VI, 903
Douglass, Edward H. VI, 908
Douglass, Edward H. VI, 929
Douglass, Effie J. V, 736
Douglass, Elizabeth VI, 241
Douglass, Elizabeth VI, 276

uglass, Elizabeth VI, 285
uglass, Elizabeth VI, 308
uglass, Elizabeth VI, 337
uglass, Elizabeth VI, 849
uglass, Elizabeth VI, 926
uglass, Elizabeth VI, 951
uglass, Emma L. V, 736
uglass, Emma T. V, 736
uglass, Frances S. VI, 908
uglass, Geo. VI, 947
uglass, George VI, 875
uglass, George VI, 896
uglass, James VI, 806
uglass, Jesse Carter V, 619
uglass, John VI, 241
uglass, John VI, 285
uglass, John VI, 806
uglass, John VI, 908
uglass, John B. VI, 973
uglass, John H. V, 615
uglass, John H. V, 619
uglass, John Henry V, 619
uglass, John Henry, Jr. V, 619
uglass, John, Jr. VI, 241
uglass, Judith VI, 241
uglass, Judith VI, 285
uglass, Kitty Gissag VI, 908
uglass, Louisa J. VI, 929
uglass, Lucinda VI, 893
uglass, Lucy Spriggs VI, 907
uglass, Lydia M. V, 384
uglass, Marium V, 619
uglass, Mary J. VI, 908
uglass, Merium V, 619
uglass, Micajah VI, 241
uglass, Mildred VI, 344
uglass, Mildred VI, 861
uglass, Milly VI, 308
uglass, Milly VI, 344
uglass, Milly Whalar VI, 907
uglass, Milly Wheeler VI, 908
uglass, Miriam V, 615
uglass, Miriam V, 619
uglass, Mirium V, 619
uglass, Murphy VI, 896
uglass, Murphy VI, 908
uglass, Nancy VI, 908
uglass, Nancy VI, 926
uglass, Nancy VI, 994
uglass, Nancy A. VI, 908
uglass, Polly VI, 241
uglass, Polly VI, 285
uglass, Polly VI, 875
uglass, Robert VI, 241
uglass, Robert D. VI, 933
uglass, Robert H. VI, 908
uglass, Robert H. VI, 931
uglass, Robert H. VI, 994
uglass, Sally VI, 896
uglass, Sally VI, 908
uglass, Sarah VI, 908
uglass, Sarah L. VI, 796
uglass, Susannah VI, 947
uglass, Thomas VI, 241
uglass, Thomas VI, 285
uglass, William VI, 908
uglass, Wm. II, 993
uglass, Wm. VI, 961
uiphan, Alex. VI, 981
ulde, Lydia IV, 522
ulde, Maxon IV, 522
ulde, Ruthanna IV, 522
ulde, Sinai Jane IV, 522
ulde, Susanna IV, 522
ulde, William D. IV, 522
ove, Alice V, 384
ove, Alice May V, 328
ove, Alice May V, 384
ove, B. F. V, 384
ove, Belteshazzer V, 384
ove, Belteshazzer G. V, 384
ove, Beltesshazzar V, 328
ove, Beltshazzer V, 384
ove, Edith L. VI, 738
ove, Edith L. VI, 762
ove, Elizabeth V, 384
ove, Emeline V, 384
ove, Emiline V, 384
ove, Jacob V, 328
ove, Lanford VI, 907
ove, Lizzie M. V, 328
ove, Martha V, 328
ove, Martha V, 384
ove, Mary C. V, 328
ove, Mary Jane V, 328
ove, Mattie V, 384
ove, Milla V, 328
ove, Mirtilla V, 384
ove, Myrtle V, 328
ove, Myrtle V, 384
ove, Nancy VI, 996
Dove, Nancy Emeline V, 328
Dove, Nancy Emeline V, 384
Dove, Nancy Emiline V, 384
Dove, Nancy Toler VI, 907
Dove, Netta V, 328
Dove, Nettie V, 328
Dove, Riley G. V, 328
Dove, Stephen C. V, 328
Dove, Wilber V, 328
Dove, Wilbur V, 384
Dove, Wilbur A. V, 384
Dove, William V, 328
Dovener, William IV, 197
Dovener, William N. IV, 197
Dovener, William W. IV, 197
Dow, Catharine VI, 908
Dow, Elijah II, 508
Dow, Josephine IV, 1037
Dow, Lorenzo VI, 908
Dowdell, Alice IV, 197
Dowdell, Joseph IV, 197
Dowdey, Elijah VI, 921
Dowdle, Alice IV, 197
Dowdle, Amanda IV, 197
Dowdle, Charles IV, 197
Dowdle, Elmer IV, 197
Dowdle, George IV, 197
Dowdle, Jane II, 508
Dowdle, Jonas IV, 197
Dowdle, Joseph IV, 197
Dowdle, Mary II, 355
Dowdle, Sarah II, 355
Dowdle, Sarah IV, 197
Dowdle, Silas IV, 197
Dowdle, Walter R. IV, 197
Dowdle, William H. IV, 197
Dowdna, John A. IV, 575
Dowdna, Mary Etta IV, 575
Dowdney, Elizabeth II, 993
Dowdney, Elizabeth II, 995
Dowdney, John II, 993
Dowdney, Mary II, 993
Dowdney, Mary II, 1030
Dowdney, Sarah II, 993
Dowdney, Sarah II, 1014
Dowdney, Sarah II, 1016
Dowdney, Thomas II, 993
Dowdney, Thomas II, 1016
Dowdney, Wm. II, 993
Dowdney, Wm. II, 995
Dowdy, Allen G. VI, 812
Dowdy, Allen G. VI, 841
Dowdy, Allen G. VI, 860
Dowdy, Allen G. VI, 865
Dowdy, Aney VI, 899
Dowdy, Ann VI, 812
Dowdy, Ann VI, 860
Dowdy, Anne VI, 1013
Dowdy, Anny VI, 899
Dowdy, Anny VI, 909
Dowdy, Betsy VI, 992
Dowdy, Carie A. VI, 909
Dowdy, Catharine VI, 891
Dowdy, Celia VI, 909
Dowdy, Charlotte VI, 1016
Dowdy, Charlotte Mayse VI, 909
Dowdy, Claborn VI, 810
Dowdy, Claborn VI, 812
Dowdy, Claiborne VI, 812
Dowdy, Claibourne VI, 860
Dowdy, Crete VI, 890
Dowdy, David VI, 909
Dowdy, Drusilla VI, 898
Dowdy, Edward VI, 812
Dowdy, Edward H. VI, 818
Dowdy, Eleanor Creasey VI, 908
Dowdy, Elijah VI, 860
Dowdy, Elijah VI, 908
Dowdy, Elijah VI, 909
Dowdy, Elijah VI, 916
Dowdy, Elijah VI, 921
Dowdy, Elijah VI, 954
Dowdy, Elizabeth VI, 908
Dowdy, Elvira VI, 909
Dowdy, Emeline VI, 919
Dowdy, Foster VI, 909
Dowdy, Henry VI, 909
Dowdy, Hundley VI, 881
Dowdy, Hundley VI, 890
Dowdy, Hundley VI, 901
Dowdy, Hundley VI, 908
Dowdy, Hundley VI, 909
Dowdy, Hundley VI, 971
Dowdy, Hundley VI, 992
Dowdy, Hundly VI, 936
Dowdy, Hundly VI, 1007
Dowdy, Hundly, Sr. VI, 939
Dowdy, Jaine VI, 909
Dowdy, Jane VI, 882
Dowdy, Jane VI, 908
Dowdy, Jane F. VI, 812
Dowdy, Jesse VI, 909
Dowdy, Jno VI, 812
Dowdy, Johan VI, 985
Dowdy, John VI, 812
Dowdy, John VI, 862
Dowdy, John VI, 891
Dowdy, John VI, 897
Dowdy, John VI, 907
Dowdy, John VI, 909
Dowdy, John VI, 918
Dowdy, John VI, 1013
Dowdy, John C. VI, 972
Dowdy, John Foster VI, 909
Dowdy, John, Jr. VI, 908
Dowdy, Judith VI, 898
Dowdy, Judith VI, 909
Dowdy, Judy F. VI, 971
Dowdy, Julia Ann VI, 985
Dowdy, Lavina S. VI, 901
Dowdy, Lewis VI, 909
Dowdy, Lewis C. VI, 812
Dowdy, Locky L. VI, 939
Dowdy, Lucinda VI, 862
Dowdy, Lucinda VI, 898
Dowdy, Lucinda VI, 904
Dowdy, Lucinda VI, 908
Dowdy, Lucinda VI, 909
Dowdy, Lucy VI, 972
Dowdy, Mare VI, 1013
Dowdy, Martha VI, 954
Dowdy, Martha Ann VI, 943
Dowdy, Martha J. VI, 812
Dowdy, Martha J. Holt VI, 909
Dowdy, Mary VI, 795
Dowdy, Mary VI, 860
Dowdy, Mary VI, 908
Dowdy, Mary VI, 978
Dowdy, Mary VI, 985
Dowdy, Mary Ann VI, 909
Dowdy, Mary Ann VI, 921
Dowdy, Mary Foster VI, 907
Dowdy, Mary J. VI, 865
Dowdy, Mary T. VI, 909
Dowdy, Mildred VI, 812
Dowdy, Mildred VI, 860
Dowdy, Mildred VI, 904
Dowdy, Mildred VI, 909
Dowdy, Mildred VI, 919
Dowdy, Mildred VI, 943
Dowdy, Mildred VI, 985
Dowdy, Milly VI, 909
Dowdy, Nancy VI, 812
Dowdy, Nancy VI, 897
Dowdy, Nancy VI, 909
Dowdy, Nancy VI, 918
Dowdy, Patsy VI, 844
Dowdy, Patsy VI, 916
Dowdy, Patsy Ann VI, 909
Dowdy, Phebe VI, 908
Dowdy, Phoebe VI, 909
Dowdy, Polly VI, 812
Dowdy, Polly VI, 898
Dowdy, Richard VI, 909
Dowdy, Robina VI, 799
Dowdy, Sally VI, 1007
Dowdy, Sarah VI, 810
Dowdy, Sarah VI, 812
Dowdy, Sarah VI, 909
Dowdy, Sarah J. VI, 818
Dowdy, Susan E. VI, 909
Dowdy, Tabithy VI, 973
Dowdy, W. M. VI, 909
Dowdy, Walter B. VI, 909
Dowdy, Walter B. VI, 939
Dowdy, Wiatt VI, 908
Dowdy, Wiatt VI, 909
Dowdy, Wiatt VI, 916
Dowdy, William VI, 812
Dowdy, William VI, 898
Dowdy, William VI, 899
Dowdy, William VI, 908
Dowdy, William VI, 909
Dowdy, William VI, 966
Dowdy, William VI, 998
Dowdy, William VI, 1001
Dowdy, William VI, 1015
Dowdy, William S. VI, 909
Dowdy, Willy VI, 916
Dowdy, Wm. VI, 909
Dowdy, Woodson VI, 909
Dowdy, Wyatt VI, 812
Dowdy, Zekill VI, 909
Dowdy, Zilly VI, 998
Dowel, Almarinda V, 455
Dowel, Ann II, 214
Dowel, Ann II, 215
Dowel, Foster VI, 801
Dowel, Phebe II, 215
Dowel, Phebe II, 267
Dowel, Phebe II, 286
Dowell, Almarinda V, 234
Dowell, Almarinda V, 455
Dowell, Ann II, 172
Dowell, Ann II, 215
Dowell, Catherine VI, 909
Dowell, David P. V, 462
Dowell, Dicey V, 462
Dowell, Elijah VI, 812
Dowell, Elijah VI, 943
Dowell, Elisha VI, 907
Dowell, Eliza V, 462
Dowell, Elizabeth VI, 812
Dowell, Elizabeth VI, 943
Dowell, Fanny VI, 909
Dowell, Foster VI, 812
Dowell, Francis VI, 909
Dowell, Francis VI, 969
Dowell, Geo. V, 455
Dowell, James VI, 909
Dowell, Jemima Board VI, 907
Dowell, John VI, 909
Dowell, Letitia W. VI, 812
Dowell, Lydia VI, 812
Dowell, Mary Caine VI, 909
Dowell, Micajah VI, 909
Dowell, Micajah VI, 940
Dowell, Micajah VI, 954
Dowell, Micajah VI, 959
Dowell, Nancy VI, 997
Dowell, Nehemiah VI, 895
Dowell, Nehemiah VI, 997
Dowell, Peggy VI, 895
Dowell, Pleasant VI, 812
Dowell, Polly VI, 940
Dowell, Sally VI, 812
Dowell, William II, 355
Dowell, William VI, 13
Dowen, Gertie IV, 1313
Dowen, Mrs. Gertrude Modros IV, 1313
Dowey, Elender VI, 983
Dowles, Adaline V, 47
Dowles, Adaline V, 48
Down, Ann IV, 84
Down, Sarah V, 559
Down, William V, 559
Downard, Clara V, 559
Downard, Clara Leona IV, 197
Downard, Eliza IV, 84
Downard, Eliza IV, 115
Downard, Lizzie V, 559
Downard, Mary C. IV, 197
Downard, W. H. IV, 197
Downard, William IV, 197
Downard, William V, 559
Downard, Wm. H. IV, 197
Downe, Jane V, 234
Downe, Mary II, 508
Downer, Andrew O. III, 105
Downer, Ernest Page III, 379
Downer, Ernest Page III, 381
Downer, Esther III, 105
Downer, Helen May III, 379
Downer, Helen May III, 381
Downer, Mary C. IV, 197
Downes, Anna IV, 812
Downes, Elizabeth IV, 519
Downes, Elizabeth IV, 522
Downes, Elizabeth V, 48
Downes, Elizabeth C. V, 48
Downes, Jane G. V, 950
Downes, Jane G. V, 957
Downey, Hannah II, 958
Downey, Hannah II, 993
Downey, Hannah II, 995
Downey, James II, 958
Downey, James II, 993
Downey, James II, 995
Downey, James, Jr. II, 993
Downey, Mary II, 958
Downey, Mary II, 993
Downey, Mary II, 1014
Downey, Sarah II, 958
Downey, Sarah II, 993
Downhour, Carle V, 993
Downie, Jane V, 234
Downing, ??? III, 105
Downing, ??? III, 260
Downing, ??? III, 503
Downing, Abigail VI, 383
Downing, Abigail VI, 456
Downing, Abraham III, 105
Downing, Ada Irene V, 49
Downing, Adella M. V, 49
Downing, Alfred III, 408
Downing, Almina J. V, 49
Downing, Almina J. V, 124
Downing, Amey III, 423
Downing, Amy III, 408
Downing, Amy III, 467
Downing, Ananias III, 481
Downing, Ananias III, 482
Downing, Ann II, 993
Downing, Ann II, 1033
Downing, Ann III, 406
Downing, Ann T. II, 993
Downing, Anna III, 482
Downing, Anna V, 993
Downing, Anne III, 423
Downing, Anne III, 424
Downing, Anne III, 481
Downing, Asa III, 408
Downing, Asa III, 462
Downing, Benj. III, 408
Downing, Benj. III, 467
Downing, Benj. III, 473
Downing, Benjamin III, 105
Downing, Benjamin III, 408
Downing, Benjamin III, 473
Downing, Benjamin III, 482
Downing, Benjamin III, 506
Downing, Beulah IV, 621
Downing, Beulah IV, 868
Downing, Calvin IV, 1277
Downing, Carl V, 670
Downing, Carl V, 694
Downing, Catherine V, 234
Downing, Charity III, 408
Downing, Charles II, 993
Downing, Charles II, 1033
Downing, Coe III, 481
Downing, Cornelia III, 408
Downing, Cornelia III, 449
Downing, Daniel III, 105
Downing, Daniel III, 481
Downing, Daniel III, 482
Downing, Daniel III, 495
Downing, Daniel IV, 621
Downing, Daniel IV, 868
Downing, David II, 993
Downing, Deborah III, 481
Downing, Deborah III, 482
Downing, Dora III, 60
Downing, Dora III, 105
Downing, Edward V, 993
Downing, Eleanor VI, 383
Downing, Eli V, 993
Downing, Eliza II, 508
Downing, Eliza II, 647
Downing, Eliza III, 105
Downing, Eliza III, 408
Downing, Eliza A. III, 105
Downing, Eliza J. V, 993
Downing, Elizabeth II, 508
Downing, Elizabeth II, 993
Downing, Elizabeth III, 396
Downing, Elizabeth III, 397
Downing, Elizabeth III, 403
Downing, Elizabeth III, 408
Downing, Elizabeth III, 449
Downing, Elizabeth III, 481
Downing, Elizabeth III, 482
Downing, Elizabeth III, 499
Downing, Elizabeth F. III, 408
Downing, Ellen VI, 383
Downing, Ellen VI, 435
Downing, Ezekiel VI, 909
Downing, Gabriel V, 993
Downing, George III, 105
Downing, George III, 408
Downing, George III, 423
Downing, George III, 482
Downing, George S. III, 105
Downing, Hannah C. II, 719
Downing, Hannah M. V, 48
Downing, Hannah M. V, 49
Downing, Helen III, 450
Downing, Henry II, 508
Downing, Henry III, 481
Downing, Henry III, 482
Downing, Henry, Jr. III, 481
Downing, Isaac III, 105
Downing, Isaac III, 408
Downing, Isaac III, 475
Downing, Isaac P. III, 409
Downing, Israel W. II, 857
Downing, Israel W. II, 888
Downing, Jacob II, 508
Downing, Jacob II, 647
Downing, Jacob II, 993
Downing, Jacob III, 105
Downing, Jacob III, 482
Downing, Jacob III, 499
Downing, Jacob V, 48
Downing, Jacob V, 135
Downing, James III, 60
Downing, James III, 105
Downing, James III, 396
Downing, James III, 408
Downing, James III, 481
Downing, James III, 482
Downing, James V, 234
Downing, Jane IV, 342

Downing, Jane V, 135
Downing, Jane VI, 384
Downing, Jane P. II, 857
Downing, Jane P. II, 888
Downing, Jane U. V, 49
Downing, Jane W. V, 48
Downing, Jemima III, 481
Downing, Jemima III, 482
Downing, John III, 105
Downing, John IV, 621
Downing, John IV, 868
Downing, John IV, 1156
Downing, John IV, 1206
Downing, John VI, 383
Downing, John VI, 907
Downing, John VI, 909
Downing, John VI, 954
Downing, Jordan II, 508
Downing, Joseph II, 993
Downing, Joseph V, 49
Downing, Joseph J. V, 49
Downing, Joseph J. V, 124
Downing, Joseph M. II, 993
Downing, Joseph M. II, 1035
Downing, Joseph R. II, 993
Downing, Joseph R. II, 1033
Downing, Julia III, 60
Downing, Julia III, 105
Downing, L. Ruble V, 559
Downing, Latitia III, 475
Downing, Latitia W. III, 408
Downing, Lax III, 408
Downing, Letitia III, 408
Downing, Luther Ruble V, 559
Downing, Lydia A. II, 857
Downing, Lydia A. II, 888
Downing, Margaret III, 481
Downing, Margaret III, 482
Downing, Margaret III, 503
Downing, Margaret VI, 954
Downing, Maria V, 49
Downing, Maria V, 116
Downing, Maria M. V, 48
Downing, Maria M. V, 49
Downing, Martha II, 993
Downing, Martha II, 1015
Downing, Martha II, 1035
Downing, Martha III, 408
Downing, Martha III, 467
Downing, Martha III, 470
Downing, Martha III, 481
Downing, Martha III, 482
Downing, Martha III, 495
Downing, Martha III, 506
Downing, Martha V, 993
Downing, Martha B. II, 857
Downing, Mary II, 508
Downing, Mary III, 105
Downing, Mary VI, 366
Downing, Mary VI, 383
Downing, Mary Ann II, 993
Downing, Mary Ann II, 1035
Downing, Mary Ann III, 260
Downing, Mary C. III, 408
Downing, Mary W. III, 408
Downing, Mary W. III, 409
Downing, Matilda V, 135
Downing, Matilda J. V, 49
Downing, Matilda Jane V, 49
Downing, Miller VI, 738
Downing, Moses III, 408
Downing, Olivia V, 670
Downing, Olivia V, 694
Downing, Phebe III, 407
Downing, Phebe III, 408
Downing, Phebe III, 409
Downing, Phebe III, 441
Downing, Phebe III, 464
Downing, Phebe III, 473
Downing, Phebe III, 482
Downing, Phebe III, 506
Downing, Phebe V, 302
Downing, Phebe VI, 369
Downing, Phebe VI, 383
Downing, Phebe VI, 435
Downing, Phebe VI, 442
Downing, Phebe R. III, 408
Downing, Phebe W. III, 105
Downing, Rachel VI, 909
Downing, Rebecca IV, 621
Downing, Rebecca IV, 868
Downing, Rebecca V, 56
Downing, Rebecca V, 98
Downing, Rebecca M. II, 857
Downing, Rebecca Malin II, 857
Downing, Reuben W. V, 993
Downing, Richard II, 888
Downing, Richard II, 993
Downing, Richard III, 105
Downing, Richard H. II, 857
Downing, Richard, Jr. II, 993
Downing, Richard, Jr. III, 482
Downing, Rosannah III, 408
Downing, Rosannah III, 467
Downing, Rosetta K. III, 105
Downing, Ruth III, 482
Downing, Ruth VI, 369
Downing, Ruth VI, 383
Downing, Samuel II, 993
Downing, Samuel II, 1015
Downing, Samuel II, 1035
Downing, Samuel III, 105
Downing, Samuel VI, 383
Downing, Samuel VI, 384
Downing, Samuel B. III, 105
Downing, Samuel, Jr. VI, 384
Downing, Sandwith II, 508
Downing, Sarah II, 508
Downing, Sarah II, 647
Downing, Sarah III, 105
Downing, Sarah III, 409
Downing, Sarah III, 421
Downing, Sarah VI, 383
Downing, Sarah E. II, 993
Downing, Sarah R. III, 105
Downing, Sarah R. III, 408
Downing, Sarah R. III, 464
Downing, Sarah T. III, 482
Downing, Silas III, 105
Downing, Silas III, 397
Downing, Silas III, 403
Downing, Silas III, 408
Downing, Silas III, 421
Downing, Silas III, 441
Downing, Silas III, 449
Downing, Silas III, 453
Downing, Silas III, 455
Downing, Silas III, 464
Downing, Silas F. III, 408
Downing, Stephen III, 105
Downing, Stephen III, 408
Downing, Susan III, 482
Downing, Susanna IV, 1156
Downing, Susanna IV, 1181
Downing, Theodosia III, 408
Downing, Theodosia III, 462
Downing, Theodosia III, 475
Downing, Thomas II, 993
Downing, Thomas III, 105
Downing, Thomas III, 467
Downing, Thomas R. III, 409
Downing, Thos. III, 408
Downing, Trenton II, 993
Downing, Tristram III, 407
Downing, Tristram III, 408
Downing, Wd. Elizabeth III, 467
Downing, Wd. Martha III, 481
Downing, Wd. Rachel III, 408
Downing, Wd. Sarah III, 408
Downing, Wilbur Sherman V, 559
Downing, William III, 105
Downing, William IV, 621
Downing, William IV, 868
Downing, William VI, 369
Downing, William VI, 383
Downing, William VI, 435
Downing, William VI, 952
Downing, William M. II, 993
Downing, Wm. IV, 1156
Downing, Wm. V, 302
Downs, Ann IV, 84
Downs, Anna IV, 327
Downs, Anna IV, 522
Downs, Catharine W. II, 1087
Downs, Elizabeth IV, 327
Downs, Elizabeth IV, 522
Downs, Esther IV, 1277
Downs, Esther V, 950
Downs, Jane G. V, 950
Downs, Jeremiah IV, 84
Downs, Jeremiah IV, 327
Downs, Jeremiah IV, 522
Downs, John IV, 948
Downs, Lydia IV, 84
Downs, Mariam IV, 934
Downs, Mariam IV, 948
Downs, Mary IV, 84
Downs, Mary IV, 101
Downs, Miriam IV, 948
Downs, Samuel IV, 948
Downs, Sarah IV, 327
Downs, Sarah IV, 522
Downs, Thomas IV, 327
Downs, Thomas IV, 522
Downs, William IV, 327
Downs, William IV, 522
Downs, Wm. IV, 522
Downy, Margaret VI, 812
Downy, Patsy VI, 936
Downy, Watt VI, 812
Dowty, Amy II, 355
Doxey, Elizabeth III, 105
Doxey, Emily III, 409
Doxey, Margaret III, 409
Doxey, Mary G. III, 482
Doxey, Samuel III, 409
Doxey, Sarah III, 409
Doxey, William F. III, 482
Doxsey, Elizabeth III, 105
Doxy, Elizabeth III, 105
Doyel, Hannah IV, 121
Doyel, Hannah IV, 125
Doyle, Bessie IV, 1250
Doyle, Edward IV, 1250
Doyle, Elizabeth II, 993
Doyle, Elizabeth II, 995
Doyle, Jessie IV, 1239
Doyle, Joseph II, 993
Doyle, Margaret VI, 61
Doyle, Margaret VI, 909
Doyle, Mary VI, 61
Doyle, Mary VI, 67
Doyle, Mary VI, 91
Doyle, Mary J. V, 234
Doyle, Nathan VI, 61
Doyle, Philip VI, 61
Doyle, Rhoda VI, 61
Doyle, Sarah II, 508
Doyle, Susan B. III, 105
Doyle, Thomas III, 105
Doyle, Wd. Sarah II, 508
Doyle, William VI, 61
Doyle, William VI, 909
Doyle, William VI, 920
Doyle, William H. VI, 61
Doyle, Zachariah VI, 61
Doyle, Zachariah VI, 67
Drace, Margaret V, 455
Draegert, George III, 409
Draegert, George C. III, 404
Draegert, Sarah Amelia III, 404
Draegert, Sarah Amelia III, 409
Drake, ??? III, 105
Drake, A. J. V, 559
Drake, Abraham VI, 909
Drake, Abram VI, 909
Drake, Allen VI, 909
Drake, Allen VI, 1019
Drake, Alse IV, 1055
Drake, Alse IV, 1062
Drake, Andrew V, 559
Drake, Andrew V, 993
Drake, Andrew VI, 909
Drake, Ann V, 49
Drake, Ann V, 64
Drake, Ann V, 670
Drake, Anne VI, 962
Drake, Annie V, 670
Drake, Arra Anne VI, 61
Drake, Augustus III, 105
Drake, Betsy VI, 77
Drake, Betsy VI, 909
Drake, Cad VI, 909
Drake, Cad VI, 932
Drake, Catherine III, 105
Drake, Catherine V, 869
Drake, Celia III, 105
Drake, Charles III, 105
Drake, Claton VI, 907
Drake, Delilah VI, 61
Drake, Delilah VI, 63
Drake, Dollie E. C. VI, 61
Drake, Eliza V, 328
Drake, Eliza J. V, 328
Drake, Elizabeth II, 823
Drake, Elizabeth II, 1049
Drake, Elizabeth VI, 909
Drake, Ellen VI, 52
Drake, Ellen VI, 61
Drake, Emily E. III, 105
Drake, Emma Dall IV, 1313
Drake, Eva IV, 1277
Drake, Ezra VI, 61
Drake, George VI, 60
Drake, George VI, 61
Drake, Hallock III, 105
Drake, Harriet J. VI, 909
Drake, Herbert L. VI, 61
Drake, Ida V, 559
Drake, Israel VI, 487
Drake, James III, 105
Drake, James VI, 77
Drake, James VI, 909
Drake, Jane VI, 487
Drake, Jemimah VI, 909
Drake, John III, 105
Drake, John IV, 1277
Drake, John V, 384
Drake, John W. V, 559
Drake, Junius VI, 61
Drake, Junius Fenton VI, 61
Drake, Junius W. VI, 52
Drake, Junius W. VI, 61
Drake, Lawrence V, 670
Drake, Lawrence V, 690
Drake, Leonard C. V, 559
Drake, Lida IV, 1277
Drake, Louie Belle V, 559
Drake, Lucy VI, 61
Drake, Lucy VI, 77
Drake, Lucy VI, 91
Drake, Mark VI, 61
Drake, Mary III, 105
Drake, Mary V, 559
Drake, Mary VI, 61
Drake, Mary F. III, 105
Drake, Mary Jane V, 384
Drake, Mary Jane V, 387
Drake, Mary Turner VI, 909
Drake, Nancy VI, 909
Drake, Nellie J. VI, 61
Drake, Opal V, 670
Drake, Opal V, 690
Drake, Owen VI, 909
Drake, Pamelia L. VI, 909
Drake, Phebe B. III, 105
Drake, Pheby VI, 61
Drake, Polly Graham VI, 907
Drake, Rachel II, 215
Drake, Rachel II, 992
Drake, Rachel II, 993
Drake, Rebecca III, 105
Drake, Robert II, 992
Drake, Robert II, 993
Drake, Rosa VI, 61
Drake, Rosa VI, 91
Drake, Sally VI, 909
Drake, Sarah II, 56
Drake, Sarah II, 67
Drake, Sarah III, 276
Drake, Sarah VI, 61
Drake, Sary Meador VI, 907
Drake, Susan S. III, 105
Drake, Susie VI, 61
Drake, Sylvia M. V, 384
Drake, Tabitha III, 105
Drake, Thomas III, 105
Drake, Thomas VI, 61
Drake, Turner VI, 907
Drake, Viola VI, 60
Drake, Viola VI, 61
Drake, Virginia V, 328
Drake, William VI, 61
Drake, William VI, 77
Drake, William VI, 909
Drake, William VI, 962
Drandt, Ella W. III, 106
Drandt, Ella W. III, 362
Drandt, Otto A. III, 106
Drandt, Otto A. III, 362
Draper, ??? VI, 39
Draper, ??? VI, 48
Draper, Aaron VI, 62
Draper, Achsah I, 183
Draper, Amey II, 508
Draper, Amey II, 686
Draper, Amy II, 27
Draper, Asa I, 192
Draper, Benjamin I, 183
Draper, Benjamin I, 192
Draper, Benjamin I, 808
Draper, Betsy VI, 61
Draper, Betsy VI, 62
Draper, Chalkley I, 192
Draper, Chalkley I, 202
Draper, Chas. H. V, 993
Draper, Chas. Henry V, 993
Draper, Delphina I, 877
Draper, Delphina I, 883
Draper, Denson VI, 62
Draper, Edith II, 508
Draper, Edith II, 529
Draper, Edward II, 27
Draper, Edward II, 53
Draper, Edward II, 66
Draper, Edward II, 67
Draper, Elisabeth I, 192
Draper, Elizabeth I, 183
Draper, Elizabeth I, 714
Draper, Elizabeth V, 302
Draper, Elizabeth V, 311
Draper, Elizabeth VI, 62
Draper, Elizabeth, Jr. IV, 327
Draper, Elizabeth, Jr. VI, 62
Draper, Elizabeth, Sr. IV, 327
Draper, Elizabeth, Sr. VI, 62
Draper, Emma II, 796
Draper, Exum I, 192
Draper, Gulaelma I, 183
Draper, Hannah I, 183
Draper, Hannah II, 27
Draper, Hannah II, 66
Draper, Hannah II, 67
Draper, Isaac I, 183
Draper, Jackson VI, 909
Draper, Jael II, 27
Draper, James II, 355
Draper, James II, 508
Draper, James II, 736
Draper, James Jordan Scott VI, 62
Draper, Jemima I, 183
Draper, Jemima II, 27
Draper, Jemima V, 234
Draper, Jemima V, 292
Draper, Jemima V, 302
Draper, Jemima V, 313
Draper, Jemimah II, 61
Draper, Jemimah II, 67
Draper, Jeremiah V, 993
Draper, Jeremiah VI, 62
Draper, Jesey VI, 62
Draper, Jesse I, 46
Draper, Jesse I, 183
Draper, Jesse I, 192
Draper, Jesse I, 714
Draper, Jesse I, 808
Draper, Jesse V, 302
Draper, Jesse VI, 62
Draper, John I, 183
Draper, John I, 192
Draper, John I, 714
Draper, John V, 302
Draper, John VI, 61
Draper, John VI, 62
Draper, Jonathan II, 355
Draper, Jonathan II, 508
Draper, Joseph I, 36
Draper, Joseph I, 45
Draper, Joseph I, 183
Draper, Joseph I, 190
Draper, Joseph I, 192
Draper, Joseph I, 714
Draper, Joseph V, 234
Draper, Joseph V, 302
Draper, Joseph VI, 62
Draper, Joshua I, 192
Draper, Joshua I, 714
Draper, Joshua IV, 868
Draper, Joshua V, 302
Draper, Josiah I, 45
Draper, Josiah I, 63
Draper, Josiah I, 192
Draper, Josiah I, 714
Draper, Josiah V, 234
Draper, Josiah V, 292
Draper, Josiah V, 302
Draper, Josiah V, 313
Draper, Lam I, 208
Draper, Lydda I, 38
Draper, Lydda I, 45
Draper, Lydda I, 714
Draper, Lydia I, 36
Draper, Lydia I, 45
Draper, Lydia I, 183
Draper, Lydia I, 192
Draper, Lydia V, 234
Draper, Margaret VI, 91
Draper, Mariam I, 192
Draper, Mariam I, 714
Draper, Martin I, 192
Draper, Martin V, 993
Draper, Mary I, 34
Draper, Mary I, 45
Draper, Mary I, 46
Draper, Mary I, 63
Draper, Mary I, 138
Draper, Mary I, 148
Draper, Mary I, 183
Draper, Mary I, 192
Draper, Mary II, 27
Draper, Mary II, 53
Draper, Mary II, 67
Draper, Mary V, 993
Draper, Mary VI, 362
Draper, Mary VI, 384
Draper, Mary Powel VI, 62
Draper, Mary, Jr. I, 138
Draper, Mary, Jr. I, 148
Draper, Maryann V, 302
Draper, Meriam I, 714
Draper, Milicent I, 104
Draper, Milicent I, 138
Draper, Milicent I, 148
Draper, Miliscent I, 45
Draper, Miliscent I, 61
Draper, Miriam I, 45
Draper, Miriam I, 63
Draper, Miriam I, 714
Draper, Miriam V, 302
Draper, Miriam VI, 62
Draper, Nancy I, 192
Draper, Nathan I, 192
Draper, Nathan I, 714
Draper, Oswin John VI, 62

per, Patience II, 355
per, Patience II, 508
per, Patience II, 661
per, Patience VI, 45
per, Peninah I, 183
per, Peninah I, 190
per, Peninah I, 192
per, Peter I, 45
per, Peter I, 138
per, Peter I, 192
per, Philip I, 237
per, Polly J. VI, 909
per, Rachall I, 10
per, Rachel I, 45
per, Rachel I, 54
per, Rachel II, 355
per, Rachel II, 502
per, Rachel II, 508
per, Rebecah I, 192
per, Rebecca II, 67
per, Rebeckah II, 27
per, Rebeckah II, 736
per, Rhoda I, 192
per, Rhoda I, 202
per, Rhoda I, 237
per, Rhoda I, 250
per, S??? I, 192
per, Samuel I, 34
per, Samuel I, 46
per, Samuel I, 192
per, Sarah I, 138
per, Sarah I, 150
per, Sarah I, 183
per, Sarah I, 192
per, Sarah II, 508
per, Sarah II, 624
per, Sarah VI, 62
per, Sarah VI, 73
per, Silas I, 8
per, Silas I, 45
per, Silas I, 46
per, Silas I, 138
per, Silas I, 148
per, Silas I, 192
per, Silas VI, 62
per, Silas VI, 91
per, Susan V, 993
per, Thomas I, 38
per, Thomas I, 45
per, Thomas I, 63
per, Thomas I, 138
per, Thomas I, 180
per, Thomas I, 183
per, Thomas I, 192
per, Thomas II, 27
per, Thomas II, 67
per, Thomas II, 355
per, Thomas VI, 45
per, Thomas VI, 62
per, Thomas Ricks VI, 62
per, Thomas, Jr. VI, 62
per, Thos. II, 27
per, Widow Sallie Ann I, 208
per, William I, 183
per, William I, 192
per, William VI, 62
pper, Ozella I, 227
ughn, Elmer E. I, 940
whon, Anna I, 537
whorn, Ann I, 537
whorn, Anna I, 537
y, Hattie IV, 1156
y, Hattie IV, 1206
yson, Sarah II, 508
yson, Sarah II, 626
man, Caroline IV, 1313
man, Edward W. IV, 1313
sler, Dorothy E. III, 62
sler, Dorothy E. III, 106
sler, John H. III, 62
sler, John H. III, 106
sler, Sophia F. III, 62
sler, Sophia F. III, 106
w, Benjamin VI, 58
w, Benjamin VI, 62
w, Caleb III, 73
w, Drew III, 73
w, Hannah III, 73
w, Hannah Fletcher III, 73
w, Isaac H. III, 73
w, Jane III, 73
w, Jane H. III, 72
w, Jane H. III, 106
w, Susan III, 73
w, Susan III, 106
w, Wm. III, 72
w, Wm. III, 106
w, Wm. P. III, 73
w, Wm. Penn III, 73
wett, George VI, 11
wry, Amarilla F. VI, 1020
Drewry, Andrew P. VI, 909
Drewry, Charlotte E. VI, 1001
Drewry, Daniel VI, 1020
Drewry, Frances VI, 909
Drewry, J. VI, 910
Drewry, James VI, 909
Drewry, John VI, 909
Drewry, John VI, 1001
Drewry, Joseph C. VI, 910
Drewry, Judy Ann VI, 909
Drewry, Mary L. F. VI, 910
Drewry, Tabitha I. VI, 910
Drewry, William G. VI, 910
Drewry, William G. VI, 1020
Drews, Gus IV, 1313
Drews, Mrs. Gus IV, 1313
Drexter, Matilda III, 183
Drey, Hattie IV, 1206
Driggs, Lavina IV, 1127
Driggs, Lavina IV, 1130
Drinkard, Archibald VI, 833
Drinkard, Duncy VI, 812
Drinkard, Elizabeth VI, 812
Drinkard, Elizabeth VI, 833
Drinkard, James VI, 833
Drinker, ??? VI, 738
Drinker, Abigail II, 355
Drinker, Abigail II, 509
Drinker, Abigail B. II, 509
Drinker, Abigail B. II, 655
Drinker, Adino II, 687
Drinker, Ann II, 355
Drinker, Ann II, 687
Drinker, Ann Morgan II, 355
Drinker, Ann Morgan II, 509
Drinker, Anna M. III, 106
Drinker, Catherine II, 687
Drinker, Charles II, 172
Drinker, Charles II, 215
Drinker, Charles II, 355
Drinker, Charles II, 509
Drinker, Charles II, 994
Drinker, Daniel II, 172
Drinker, Daniel II, 215
Drinker, Daniel II, 355
Drinker, Daniel II, 508
Drinker, Daniel II, 509
Drinker, Daniel II, 543
Drinker, Deborah Cole II, 687
Drinker, Dinah II, 687
Drinker, Edward II, 355
Drinker, Edward III, 106
Drinker, Eliza II, 355
Drinker, Eliza II, 509
Drinker, Eliza II, 601
Drinker, Elizabeth II, 196
Drinker, Elizabeth II, 215
Drinker, Elizabeth II, 355
Drinker, Elizabeth II, 508
Drinker, Elizabeth II, 509
Drinker, Elizabeth II, 543
Drinker, Elizabeth II, 617
Drinker, Elizabeth II, 642
Drinker, Elizabeth II, 655
Drinker, Elizabeth II, 687
Drinker, Elizabeth II, 994
Drinker, Elizabeth VI, 487
Drinker, Elizabeth VI, 738
Drinker, Elizabeth Kinsey VI, 738
Drinker, Esther II, 215
Drinker, Esther II, 509
Drinker, Esther II, 736
Drinker, Esther II, 994
Drinker, Esther D. II, 737
Drinker, Esther D. II, 760
Drinker, Frances II, 355
Drinker, George II, 355
Drinker, George II, 509
Drinker, George VI, 487
Drinker, George VI, 535
Drinker, George VI, 738
Drinker, George VI, 766
Drinker, George VI, 779
Drinker, Hannah II, 172
Drinker, Hannah II, 215
Drinker, Hannah II, 355
Drinker, Hannah II, 508
Drinker, Hannah II, 509
Drinker, Hannah II, 543
Drinker, Hannah II, 564
Drinker, Hannah II, 617
Drinker, Hannah II, 655
Drinker, Hannah II, 666
Drinker, Hannah II, 687
Drinker, Hannah II, 736
Drinker, Hannah II, 993
Drinker, Hannah II, 994
Drinker, Hannah VI, 171
Drinker, Hannah VI, 212
Drinker, Hannah VI, 487
Drinker, Hannah VI, 535
Drinker, Hannah VI, 738
Drinker, Hannah VI, 766
Drinker, Hannah VI, 779
Drinker, Hannah S. II, 172
Drinker, Henry II, 172
Drinker, Henry II, 215
Drinker, Henry II, 355
Drinker, Henry II, 508
Drinker, Henry II, 509
Drinker, Henry II, 543
Drinker, Henry II, 601
Drinker, Henry II, 632
Drinker, Henry II, 642
Drinker, Henry II, 655
Drinker, Henry II, 656
Drinker, Henry II, 994
Drinker, Henry S. II, 215
Drinker, Henry S. II, 355
Drinker, Henry S. II, 509
Drinker, Henry S. II, 617
Drinker, Henry S. II, 655
Drinker, Henry S. II, 993
Drinker, Henry W. II, 509
Drinker, Henry, Jr. II, 508
Drinker, Henry, Jr. II, 509
Drinker, Henry, Jr. II, 556
Drinker, Hester II, 215
Drinker, Hezekiah II, 687
Drinker, Isaac II, 687
Drinker, James II, 355
Drinker, Joanna III, 106
Drinker, John II, 355
Drinker, John II, 451
Drinker, John II, 494
Drinker, John II, 508
Drinker, John II, 509
Drinker, John II, 601
Drinker, John II, 656
Drinker, John II, 666
Drinker, John Henry II, 355
Drinker, John Henry II, 509
Drinker, John, Jr. II, 508
Drinker, John, Jr. II, 632
Drinker, Joseph II, 355
Drinker, Joseph II, 508
Drinker, Joseph II, 543
Drinker, Joseph II, 564
Drinker, Joseph II, 687
Drinker, Joseph II, 993
Drinker, Joseph VI, 171
Drinker, Joseph VI, 487
Drinker, Joseph VI, 535
Drinker, Joseph VI, 738
Drinker, Joseph VI, 766
Drinker, Joseph D. II, 355
Drinker, Joseph D. II, 509
Drinker, Mary II, 215
Drinker, Mary II, 355
Drinker, Mary II, 494
Drinker, Mary II, 508
Drinker, Mary II, 509
Drinker, Mary II, 556
Drinker, Mary II, 564
Drinker, Mary II, 601
Drinker, Mary II, 656
Drinker, Mary II, 736
Drinker, Mary II, 994
Drinker, Priscilla II, 687
Drinker, Rachel II, 355
Drinker, Rachel II, 494
Drinker, Rachel II, 508
Drinker, Rachel II, 509
Drinker, Rachel II, 632
Drinker, Rachel II, 666
Drinker, Rachel II, 687
Drinker, Rebecca II, 443
Drinker, Rebecca II, 509
Drinker, Rebecca VI, 487
Drinker, Rebecca VI, 735
Drinker, Rebecca VI, 738
Drinker, Richard II, 509
Drinker, Ruth VI, 487
Drinker, Ruth VI, 535
Drinker, Ruth VI, 738
Drinker, Ruth VI, 759
Drinker, Ruth VI, 766
Drinker, Ruth VI, 779
Drinker, Samuel II, 355
Drinker, Samuel II, 687
Drinker, Samuel VI, 487
Drinker, Samuel VI, 738
Drinker, Sandwith II, 215
Drinker, Sandwith II, 509
Drinker, Sandwith II, 736
Drinker, Sandwith II, 994
Drinker, Sarah II, 215
Drinker, Sarah II, 509
Drinker, Sarah II, 687
Drinker, Sarah II, 728
Drinker, Sarah II, 736
Drinker, Sarah II, 994
Drinker, Susanna II, 355
Drinker, Susannah II, 451
Drinker, Susannah II, 483
Drinker, Susannah II, 508
Drinker, Susannah II, 686
Drinker, Susannah VI, 487
Drinker, Susannah VI, 738
Drinker, Tabitha II, 453
Drinker, Tabitha II, 508
Drinker, Thomas II, 355
Drinker, Thomas II, 687
Drinker, Wd. Elizabeth II, 174
Drinker, William II, 994
Drinker, William VI, 487
Drinker, William VI, 738
Drinker, William Waln III, 106
Drinker, Wm. II, 215
Drinker, Wm. II, 509
Drinker, Wm. II, 687
Drinker, Wm. II, 993
Drinker, Wm. Waln II, 736
Drinkhouse, Andrew J. II, 792
Drinkhouse, Andrew J. II, 854
Drinkhouse, Andrew J. II, 857
Drinkhouse, Henry II, 792
Drinkhouse, Mary II, 792
Drinkhouse, Mary R. II, 854
Drinkhouse, Mary R. II, 857
Drinkhouse, Mary Rebecca II, 790
Drinkhouse, Rebecca A. II, 854
Drinkhouse, Rebecca A. II, 857
Drinkhouse, Rebecca Ann II, 792
Drinkwater, Elizabeth VI, 812
Drinkwater, Emanuel VI, 812
Drinkwater, John VI, 812
Drinkwater, Katey VI, 812
Drinkwater, Mary VI, 863
Drinkwater, Nancy VI, 812
Drinkwater, Samuel VI, 812
Drinkwater, Samuel VI, 848
Drireall, John II, 443
Driscal, Anna V, 329
Driscal, Hannah V, 329
Driscal, John H. V, 329
Driscal, Simon V, 329
Driscall, Annie V, 224
Driscall, Emma V, 329
Driscall, George H. V, 329
Driscol, Anna V, 234
Driscol, Cynthia A. V, 329
Driscol, Fronia V, 670
Driscol, Harry V, 329
Driscol, Horatio V, 329
Driscol, J. W. V, 329
Driscol, Martha Ann V, 329
Driscol, Noah V, 329
Driscol, Rosa V, 329
Driscol, William V, 329
Driscoll, Anna V, 234
Driscoll, Annie V, 234
Driscoll, Bessie V, 329
Driscoll, David V, 329
Driscoll, Emma V, 329
Driscoll, Frank V, 329
Driscoll, Harry V, 234
Driscoll, Mary Wilson V, 329
Driscoll, Phebe Ann V, 329
Driscoll, Sina V, 329
Driskall, Cynthia A. V, 329
Driskall, David V, 329
Driskall, Lewis V, 329
Driskall, Lizzie V, 329
Driskall, Martha A. V, 329
Driskall, Martha E. V, 329
Driskall, Mary E. V, 329
Driskill, Adam VI, 810
Driskill, Adam VI, 812
Driskill, Adam VI, 854
Driskill, Adam VI, 855
Driskill, Adam VI, 863
Driskill, Agnes VI, 843
Driskill, Agness VI, 854
Driskill, Alexander VI, 800
Driskill, Alexander VI, 812
Driskill, Alexander VI, 818
Driskill, Alexander VI, 853
Driskill, Anna V, 329
Driskill, Anney VI, 841
Driskill, Bessie V, 329
Driskill, Cynthia A. V, 329
Driskill, Daniel VI, 812
Driskill, Daniel VI, 826
Driskill, Daniel VI, 839
Driskill, Daniel VI, 841
Driskill, Daniel VI, 863
Driskill, David V, 329
Driskill, David VI, 812
Driskill, Edward VI, 812
Driskill, Elizabeth VI, 812
Driskill, Emma V, 329
Driskill, Frank V, 329
Driskill, George V, 329
Driskill, George H. V, 329
Driskill, Hannah V, 329
Driskill, Harry V, 234
Driskill, Harry V, 329
Driskill, Horatio V, 329
Driskill, Isam V, 329
Driskill, Isom V, 329
Driskill, J. W. V, 329
Driskill, John V, 329
Driskill, John H. V, 329
Driskill, Larkin VI, 812
Driskill, Larkin VI, 813
Driskill, Lewis V, 329
Driskill, Lina V, 329
Driskill, Lizzie V, 329
Driskill, Lorenza V, 329
Driskill, Lorenzo V, 329
Driskill, Louie V, 329
Driskill, Lucinda VI, 813
Driskill, Martha A. V, 329
Driskill, Martha Ann V, 329
Driskill, Martha E. V, 329
Driskill, Mary VI, 812
Driskill, Mary E. V, 329
Driskill, Mary Wilson V, 329
Driskill, Milly VI, 812
Driskill, Milly VI, 855
Driskill, Nancy Walker VI, 812
Driskill, Noah V, 329
Driskill, Pheba A. V, 329
Driskill, Phebe Ann V, 329
Driskill, Polly VI, 800
Driskill, Polly B. VI, 812
Driskill, Polly H. VI, 812
Driskill, Richard VI, 797
Driskill, Richard VI, 812
Driskill, Richard VI, 841
Driskill, Rosa V, 329
Driskill, Sarah VI, 812
Driskill, Simon V, 329
Driskill, Sina V, 329
Driskill, Susanna VI, 812
Driskill, Susannah VI, 812
Driskill, William V, 329
Driskill, William VI, 812
Driskill, William VI, 826
Driver, Alexander W. VI, 171
Driver, Ann VI, 171
Driver, James VI, 171
Driver, John VI, 171
Driver, Lucy VI, 171
Driver, Martha VI, 171
Driver, Mary VI, 171
Driver, Richard III, 106
Driver, Sarah VI, 171
Driver, Thomas VI, 171
Drought, Mansfield IV, 700
Drought, Margaret IV, 700
Drought, Mary B. IV, 700
Drought, Mr. ??? IV, 700
Drought, Mrs. ??? IV, 700
Drought, Mrs. W. R. IV, 700
Drought, Wallace IV, 700
Drought, Wallace R. IV, 700
Drummand, Sarah IV, 355
Drummon, Margaret VI, 926
Drummon, Thomas VI, 926
Drummond, Catherine VI, 909
Drummond, John VI, 11
Drummond, Julia VI, 817
Drummond, Louvinia G. VI, 880
Drummond, Mary J. VI, 852
Drummond, Sarah IV, 327
Drummond, Thomas VI, 880
Drummond, Thomas VI, 909
Drummond, Thos. VI, 817
Drumond, Thomas VI, 852
Drury, A. P. D. VI, 907
Drury, Abigail III, 49
Drury, Andrew P. VI, 909
Drury, Anny VI, 909
Drury, Catherine VI, 909
Drury, Charlotte Grouch VI, 907
Drury, Daniel VI, 909
Drury, Daniel VI, 1009
Drury, E. VI, 907
Drury, Elijah VI, 909
Drury, Elvira VI, 909
Drury, Frances VI, 909
Drury, Gardner P. III, 49
Drury, George W. VI, 909
Drury, Isaac VI, 909
Drury, J. VI, 910
Drury, James VI, 909
Drury, Jane E. III, 49
Drury, Jno. VI, 907
Drury, John VI, 909
Drury, John VI, 1001

Drury, Joseph VI, 869
Drury, Joseph VI, 876
Drury, Joseph VI, 880
Drury, Joseph VI, 883
Drury, Joseph VI, 884
Drury, Joseph VI, 889
Drury, Joseph VI, 890
Drury, Joseph VI, 898
Drury, Joseph VI, 899
Drury, Joseph VI, 902
Drury, Joseph VI, 903
Drury, Joseph VI, 906
Drury, Joseph VI, 907
Drury, Joseph VI, 908
Drury, Joseph VI, 909
Drury, Joseph VI, 910
Drury, Joseph VI, 913
Drury, Joseph VI, 916
Drury, Joseph VI, 917
Drury, Joseph VI, 918
Drury, Joseph VI, 919
Drury, Joseph VI, 925
Drury, Joseph VI, 926
Drury, Joseph VI, 928
Drury, Joseph VI, 930
Drury, Joseph VI, 932
Drury, Joseph VI, 933
Drury, Joseph VI, 934
Drury, Joseph VI, 935
Drury, Joseph VI, 937
Drury, Joseph VI, 939
Drury, Joseph VI, 941
Drury, Joseph VI, 942
Drury, Joseph VI, 966
Drury, Joseph VI, 968
Drury, Joseph VI, 971
Drury, Joseph VI, 977
Drury, Joseph VI, 984
Drury, Joseph VI, 986
Drury, Joseph VI, 990
Drury, Joseph VI, 991
Drury, Joseph VI, 1012
Drury, Joseph VI, 1014
Drury, Joseph VI, 1017
Drury, Joseph VI, 1022
Drury, Joseph C. VI, 910
Drury, Judy Ann VI, 909
Drury, Lucinda VI, 909
Drury, Mary VI, 909
Drury, Mary VI, 913
Drury, Mary L. F. VI, 910
Drury, Nancy VI, 909
Drury, Nancy VI, 1000
Drury, Peggy VI, 880
Drury, Phoebe VI, 909
Drury, Portlock VI, 909
Drury, Priscilla VI, 909
Drury, Rebecca VI, 909
Drury, Sarah VI, 909
Drury, Tabitha I. VI, 910
Drury, Thomas VI, 909
Drury, William VI, 909
Drury, William G. VI, 910
Drury, Wm. VI, 1000
Dry, Richard II, 994
Dryden, Laura Marguerite IV, 679
Dryton, Sarah VI, 28
Du Bois, Caroline III, 309
Du Bois, Mary Ann IV, 144
Du Bois, Mary Ann IV, 146
Du Bois, Tuthill III, 309
Du Vall, Caroline E. III, 107
Du Vall, Charles E. III, 176
Du Vall, Charles Edward III, 107
Du Vall, Charles Russell III, 107
Du Vall, Chas. E. III, 107
Du Vall, Edith Eloise III, 107
Du Vall, Edith L. III, 107
Du Vall, Edward Harold III, 107
Du Vall, Edwin III, 107
Du Vall, Emeline Hanah III, 107
Du Vall, Frank Stewart III, 107
Du Vall, Frank Stuart III, 107
Du Vall, Jas. C. III, 107
Du Vall, Marguerite III, 107
Du Vall, Mary Ella III, 107
Du Vall, Mary Ella III, 176
Dual, Phebe V, 881
Duall, Lydia V, 881
Duall, Lydia V, 885
Dually, Cary A. VI, 812
Dually, Susan VI, 812
Dubel, Annie Eliza II, 318
Dubel, Annie Eliza II, 323
Dubel, Sarah L. II, 318
Duberow, Joseph II, 356
Duble, Sarah L. II, 318
Dubois, Anna III, 106
Dubois, Caroline III, 106
Dubois, Daniel P. III, 106
Dubois, Daniel P. III, 184
Dubois, Evaline P. III, 58
Dubois, Evaline P. III, 106
Dubois, Evelyn Jeanne III, 106
Dubois, Evelyn Jeanne III, 218
Dubois, Gertrude III, 58
Dubois, Gertrude III, 106
Dubois, Hannah V, 49
Dubois, Hannah V, 104
Dubois, John Coert III, 58
Dubois, John Coert III, 106
DuBois, John Joseph IV, 161
DuBois, Juliann IV, 161
Dubois, Koert III, 106
Dubois, Koert III, 181
Dubois, Lucy M. III, 106
Dubois, Lucy M. III, 205
Dubois, Lucy M. III, 218
Dubois, Mary III, 106
Dubois, Mary III, 181
DuBois, Mary Ann IV, 161
Dubois, Phebe III, 106
Dubois, Phebe Ann III, 184
DuBois, Susanna II, 153
Dubois, Thomas III, 106
Dubois, Tuthill III, 106
Dubre, Hannah II, 466
Dubre, Hannah II, 509
Dubre, Jacob II, 355
Dubre, Jacob II, 466
Dubre, Jacob II, 509
Dubre, Joseph II, 466
Dubre, Joseph II, 509
Dubre, Sarah II, 994
Dubree, Elizabeth II, 355
Dubree, Elizabeth II, 509
Dubree, Elizabeth II, 675
Dubree, George II, 355
Dubree, Hannah II, 355
Dubree, Hannah II, 463
Dubree, Hannah II, 509
Dubree, Hannah II, 671
Dubree, Hugh II, 355
Dubree, Jacob II, 355
Dubree, Jacob II, 356
Dubree, Jacob II, 509
Dubree, Jacob, Jr. II, 355
Dubree, Jacob, Jr. II, 356
Dubree, Jacob, Jr. II, 509
Dubree, James II, 355
Dubree, James II, 509
Dubree, James II, 675
Dubree, Jane II, 355
Dubree, Jane II, 356
Dubree, John II, 355
Dubree, John II, 509
Dubree, Joseph II, 355
Dubree, Joseph II, 356
Dubree, Joseph II, 463
Dubree, Joseph II, 509
Dubree, Mary II, 356
Dubree, Mary II, 509
Dubree, Mary II, 671
Dubree, Phebe II, 509
Dubree, Wm. II, 509
Dubree, Wm. II, 671
Dubrer, Nathan Evans II, 857
Dubrey, John II, 509
Dubrey, Wm. II, 509
Dubrie, Mary II, 356
Ducas, Thomas IV, 197
Ducely, Anne I, 243
Ducely, Anne I, 256
Duche, Anthony II, 356
Duche, Sarah II, 356
Duche, Sarah II, 509
Duche, Sarah II, 518
Duchee, Sarah II, 509
Duchee, Sarah II, 562
Duck, Christian VI, 62
Duck, Christian VI, 87
Duck, Joseph VI, 62
Duck, Sarah Elizabeth III, 106
Duck, Sophia Louisa III, 106
Ducker, Abner VI, 373
Ducker, Daniel VI, 373
Ducker, Elizabeth VI, 373
Ducker, Esther VI, 373
Ducker, Isaac VI, 373
Ducker, James VI, 373
Ducker, Jesse VI, 373
Ducker, Lydia VI, 373
Ducker, Mary VI, 372
Ducker, Mary VI, 384
Ducker, Oddy VI, 373
Ducker, Rebecca VI, 373
Ducker, Sarah VI, 373
Ducker, Tacy IV, 311
Ducker, Timothy VI, 373
Ducker, Timothy, Jr. VI, 373
Ducker, William VI, 373
Ducket, Dinah I, 1061
Ducket, Dinah I, 1063
Ducket, Ruth II, 509
Ducket, Sarah L. I, 1150
Ducket, Thomas II, 509
Duckett, Ruth II, 356
Duckett, Thomas II, 691
Duckitt, Ann II, 356
Duckitt, Jonathan II, 356
Duckitt, Nathaniel II, 356
Duckitt, Ruth II, 356
Duckitt, Thomas II, 356
Duckworth, Elizabeth II, 683
Duckworth, Elizabeth II, 994
Duckworth, Elizabeth II, 1034
Dudgeon, Alexander VI, 813
Dudgeon, Alexander VI, 857
Dudgeon, Elizabeth VI, 813
Dudgeon, Farthing, Thomas VI, 813
Dudgeon, James VI, 813
Dudgeon, John Patrick, Jr. VI, 795
Dudgeon, Martha VI, 813
Dudgeon, Nancy VI, 795
Dudgeon, Nancy VI, 813
Dudgeon, William VI, 813
Dudley, ??? III, 70
Dudley, Abner VI, 813
Dudley, Abrm. III, 106
Dudley, Absolem VI, 813
Dudley, Agnes Haines II, 800
Dudley, Amy III, 70
Dudley, Amy III, 106
Dudley, Ann II, 310
Dudley, Ann II, 356
Dudley, Ann II, 509
Dudley, Ann III, 106
Dudley, Ann III, 287
Dudley, Ann VI, 822
Dudley, Ann S. II, 857
Dudley, Ann S. III, 106
Dudley, Anna VI, 852
Dudley, Anne II, 509
Dudley, Armistead VI, 801
Dudley, Armistead VI, 813
Dudley, Armistead VI, 852
Dudley, Avalinda IV, 673
Dudley, Betsy VI, 808
Dudley, Betsy VI, 813
Dudley, Beulah V, 736
Dudley, Blanch V, 488
Dudley, Carey A. VI, 813
Dudley, Cary A. VI, 822
Dudley, Charles V, 736
Dudley, Charles S. V, 736
Dudley, Charlotte Hippinstall VI, 907
Dudley, Clara V, 455
Dudley, D. III, 81
Dudley, Edith Smith IV, 1156
Dudley, Edne VI, 795
Dudley, Edward II, 509
Dudley, Edward III, 70
Dudley, Edward III, 81
Dudley, Edward III, 106
Dudley, Elizabeth VI, 813
Dudley, Elton V, 49
Dudley, Emeline VI, 738
Dudley, Emma III, 70
Dudley, Emma III, 106
Dudley, Emma H. II, 824
Dudley, Esther II, 823
Dudley, Eva May V, 670
Dudley, Florence VI, 738
Dudley, Florence VI, 790
Dudley, Frances S. Kasey VI, 907
Dudley, Francis W. Hall II, 737
Dudley, Frank V, 670
Dudley, Fredda V, 736
Dudley, Freeda V, 736
Dudley, Garland V, 559
Dudley, Garland V, 670
Dudley, Guilford III, 106
Dudley, Isaac II, 318
Dudley, Isaac VI, 738
Dudley, Jemima VI, 813
Dudley, Jesse VI, 813
Dudley, John II, 509
Dudley, John III, 106
Dudley, John V, 670
Dudley, John VI, 795
Dudley, John VI, 808
Dudley, John VI, 809
Dudley, John VI, 813
Dudley, John VI, 822
Dudley, John VI, 832
Dudley, John S. VI, 813
Dudley, Joshua III, 106
Dudley, Katherine S. VI, 795
Dudley, Lucy VI, 813
Dudley, Lucy A. VI, 813
Dudley, Margaret III, 106
Dudley, Martha V, 559
Dudley, Martha V, 670
Dudley, Martha VI, 813
Dudley, Mary II, 476
Dudley, Mary II, 509
Dudley, Mary III, 81
Dudley, Mary III, 106
Dudley, Mary VI, 813
Dudley, Mary A. VI, 818
Dudley, Mary B. II, 706
Dudley, Mary B. II, 737
Dudley, Mary B. II, 744
Dudley, Mary E. III, 81
Dudley, Mary E. III, 106
Dudley, Mary H. VI, 813
Dudley, Middleton VI, 738
Dudley, Nancy V, 670
Dudley, Nancy VI, 307
Dudley, Nancy VI, 308
Dudley, Nellie V, 736
Dudley, Peter V, 670
Dudley, Phillis VI, 801
Dudley, Preston VI, 813
Dudley, Rachel VI, 813
Dudley, Richard VI, 813
Dudley, Sally VI, 829
Dudley, Samuel III, 106
Dudley, Stephen VI, 907
Dudley, Susan B. VI, 813
Dudley, Temperance Hippinstall VI, 907
Dudley, Thomas VI, 907
Dudley, Wd. Ann II, 792
Dudley, William VI, 813
Dudley, William E. III, 106
Dudley, William E. III, 287
Dudley, Wm. Edward II, 792
Dudley, Wm. F. V, 166
Dudley, Wm. R. VI, 907
Dudley, Wyley VI, 813
Dudley, Wylie VI, 850
Dudly, Charlotte Hippinstall VI, 907
Dudly, Stephen VI, 907
Duel, Abigail B. V, 881
Duel, Ann II, 117
Duel, Elizabeth II, 67
Duel, Gwin II, 67
Duel, Hannah II, 27
Duel, Hannah II, 67
Duel, Hannah II, 249
Duel, John II, 27
Duel, John II, 67
Duel, John II, 249
Duel, John V, 881
Duel, John, Jr. II, 67
Duel, Joseph II, 117
Duel, Joshua V, 881
Duel, Keziah V, 881
Duel, Lydia II, 67
Duel, Lydia V, 881
Duel, Lydia B. V, 881
Duel, Mary II, 67
Duel, Phebe II, 67
Duel, Phebe V, 881
Duel, Rachel V, 881
Duel, Sarah V, 881
Duel, Thomas II, 67
Duell, ??? III, 175
Duell, Catharine III, 106
Duell, Catharine III, 175
Duell, Elizabeth A. II, 857
Duell, Elizabeth A. II, 905
Duell, Hannah II, 67
Duell, Hannah II, 215
Duell, John II, 67
Duell, John II, 84
Duell, John II, 215
Duell, John Hull III, 106
Duell, Joseph III, 106
Duell, Lydia II, 67
Duell, Lydia II, 84
Duell, Sarah III, 106
Duell, Sarah V, 881
Duer, Abigail II, 994
Duer, Abigail Pancoast II, 994
Duer, Ann II, 958
Duer, Charles II, 1065
Duer, Charles II, 1072
Duer, Deborah II, 958
Duer, Deborah II, 994
Duer, Deborah II, 1035
Duer, Elias II, 1072
Duer, Elias C. II, 1072
Duer, Eliza II, 959
Duer, Elizabeth II, 958
Duer, Elizabeth II, 994
Duer, Ellen II, 958
Duer, Ellin II, 959
Duer, Hannah II, 959
Duer, John II, 958
Duer, John H. V, 234
Duer, Joseph II, 958
Duer, Joseph II, 959
Duer, Joseph II, 994
Duer, Joseph II, 1035
Duer, Joseph, Jr. II, 994
Duer, Mary II, 958
Duer, Mary II, 994
Duer, Mary II, 1072
Duer, Mary II, 1076
Duer, Rachel II, 994
Duer, Sarah II, 505
Duer, Sarah II, 958
Duer, Thomas II, 958
Duer, Thomas II, 977
Duer, Thomas II, 994
Duff, Ann F. IV, 197
Duff, Ann F. IV, 232
Duff, Daniel V, 302
Duff, Daniel V, 312
Duff, Elizabeth IV, 1054
Duff, Elizabeth IV, 1055
Duff, Elizabeth VI, 241
Duff, Elizabeth VI, 275
Duff, Matilda V, 234
Duff, Matilda V, 258
Duff, Nancy V, 302
Duff, Nancy V, 312
Duffield, Anna B. IV, 197
Duffield, Anna B. IV, 210
Duffield, Esther E. V, 837
Duffield, Esther Elma V, 837
Duffield, George V, 837
Duffield, Helen V, 993
Duffield, Paul V, 993
Duffield, Rebekah II, 509
Duffield, Robert V, 993
Duffy, Ann VI, 594
Duffy, Ann VI, 605
Duffy, Eliza Ann VI, 910
Duffy, Phillip VI, 910
Duffy, Sarah Ann II, 737
Duffy, Sarah Ann II, 750
Dugan, Cassie IV, 956
Dugan, Chas. M. V, 619
Dugan, Hannah IV, 29
Dugan, Harriet L. V, 619
Dugan, Sarah J. V, 619
Dugan, Sarah Jane V, 619
Dugan, Susan V, 619
Dugan, Susan Louisa III, 106
Dugan, Susan Louisa III, 367
Dugdale, Ann IV, 823
Dugdale, Ann V, 950
Dugdale, Ann Hillis IV, 812
Dugdale, Charles IV, 700
Dugdale, Charles IV, 812
Dugdale, Charles R. IV, 812
Dugdale, Charles R. V, 950
Dugdale, Chas. R. VI, 750
Dugdale, Edward II, 172
Dugdale, Edward II, 286
Dugdale, Edward II, 737
Dugdale, Edward T. II, 172
Dugdale, Edward T. II, 286
Dugdale, Elizabeth II, 215
Dugdale, Elizabeth II, 216
Dugdale, Elizabeth II, 286
Dugdale, Elizabeth II, 303
Dugdale, Elizabeth II, 737
Dugdale, Elizabeth IV, 812
Dugdale, Elizabeth V, 950
Dugdale, Emma II, 172
Dugdale, Esther E. II, 286
Dugdale, Eveline IV, 812
Dugdale, Eveline V, 950
Dugdale, George II, 286
Dugdale, George II, 737
Dugdale, George Henry II, 17
Dugdale, George Henry II, 28
Dugdale, John II, 216
Dugdale, John II, 254
Dugdale, John IV, 700
Dugdale, John IV, 812
Dugdale, John V, 950
Dugdale, Joseph II, 216
Dugdale, Joseph IV, 700
Dugdale, Joseph IV, 812
Dugdale, Joseph A. IV, 812
Dugdale, Joseph A. V, 950
Dugdale, Joseph A. VI, 384
Dugdale, Lea IV, 799
Dugdale, Lea IV, 812
Dugdale, Mary IV, 700
Dugdale, Mary IV, 799
Dugdale, Mary IV, 812
Dugdale, Mary E. V, 950
Dugdale, Mary E. V, 962
Dugdale, Mary F. IV, 799

gdale, Mary F. IV, 812
gdale, Mary Richardson VI, 750
gdale, Rachel IV, 812
gdale, Rachel E. V, 950
gdale, Ruth IV, 84
gdale, Ruth IV, 812
gdale, Ruth V, 950
gdale, Sally IV, 812
gdale, Sarah II, 215
gdale, Sarah II, 216
gdale, Sarah II, 254
gdale, Sarah IV, 700
gdale, Sarah IV, 812
gdale, Sarah A. V, 950
gdale, Sarah B. II, 216
gdale, Sarah B. IV, 700
gdale, Sarah B. IV, 812
gdale, Sarah B. V, 950
gdale, Sarah Barton II, 216
gdale, Sarah Barton II, 254
gdale, Sarah Elizabeth V, 950
gdale, Sarah M. II, 172
gdale, Sarah M. II, 286
gdale, Sarah W. II, 286
gdale, Sarah W. II, 303
gdale, Sarah W. II, 737
gdale, Thomas II, 172
gdale, Thomas II, 215
gdale, Thomas II, 216
gdale, Thomas II, 254
gdale, Thomas II, 286
gdale, Thomas II, 303
gdale, Thomas II, 703
gdale, Thomas IV, 700
gdale, Thomas IV, 812
gdale, Thomas G. IV, 812
gdale, Thomas G. V, 950
gdale, Thomas, Jr. II, 216
gdale, Thomas, Jr. II, 737
gdale, Thomas, Sr. II, 737
gdale, Wd. Sarah W. II, 172
gdale, William IV, 812
gdale, Wm. IV, 700
gdale, Wm. IV, 812
gdale, Wm. R. IV, 812
gdale, Wm. R. IV, 823
gdale, Wm. R. V, 950
glas, David Franklin V, 328
glas, George Gifford V, 328
glas, Margaret A. V, 328
glas, Robert W. V, 328
glass, Alice II, 443
glass, David VI, 1018
glass, Isabella II, 443
glass, Martha A. VI, 1018
glass, Nathaniel II, 443
glass, William II, 443
glass, Wm. A. VI, 1018
guid, Jane II, 737
guid, Jane II, 738
guid, Jane E. VI, 813
guid, Jane Isabella II, 703
guid, John II, 703
guid, John II, 737
guid, John II, 738
guid, Joseph II, 737
guid, Mary II, 703
guid, Mary Cope II, 737
guid, Mary Cope II, 738
guid, Stephen VI, 813
guid, Wm. Morrison II, 703
guid, Wm. Morrison II, 737
guid, Wm. Morrison II, 738
iguid, Jesse T. VI, 864
k, Julia I, 445
ke, ??? VI, 28
ke, A. B. VI, 864
ke, Abram VI, 62
ke, Amanda VI, 829
ke, Amy V, 993
ke, Anna V, 993
ke, Archibald B. VI, 829
ke, Caroline VI, 864
ke, Catharine I, 237
ke, Catharine I, 243
ke, David V, 993
ke, David M. V, 993
ke, Ida V, 993
ke, John I, 237
ke, John I, 260
ke, John Peele I, 213
ke, Margret VI, 28
ke, Martha V, 455
ke, Martha VI, 62
ke, Martha VI, 85
ke, Mary I, 237
ke, Mary I, 245
ke, Mary VI, 28
ke, Pharaby I, 237
ke, Pharaby I, 260
Duke, Sarah I, 46
Duke, Sarah I, 206
Duke, Sarah I, 213
Duke, Sarah I, 225
Duke, Sarah I, 237
Duke, Sarah V, 993
Duke, Sarah VI, 27
Duke, Sarah VI, 28
Duke, Thomas VI, 27
Duke, Thomas VI, 28
Duke, Thomas VI, 106
Duke, Thomas VI, 118
Duke, Thomas, Sr. VI, 28
Duke, Thos., Senior VI, 30
Dukehart, Ann IV, 621
Dukehart, Ann P. IV, 621
Dukehart, John IV, 621
Dukehart, John Peck IV, 621
Dukehart, John, Jr. IV, 621
Dukehart, Margaret Ann IV, 621
Dukehart, Sarah Jane IV, 621
Dukeher, Thomas II, 443
Dukemanneer, Ann V, 49
Dukemanneer, Isaac V, 49
Dukemineer, Ann V, 49
Dukemineer, Ann V, 110
Dukemineer, Ann V, 139
Dukemineer, Anna V, 49
Dukemineer, Elizabeth V, 49
Dukemineer, Elizabeth V, 110
Dukemineer, Hannah V, 49
Dukemineer, Hannah V, 139
Dukemineer, Isaac V, 49
Dukemineer, Isaac V, 110
Dukemineer, Isaac V, 139
Dukes, Abram VI, 62
Dukeshire, ??? III, 106
Dukeshire, Elizabeth D. III, 308
Dukeshire, Elizabeth O. III, 106
Dukminear, Ann V, 49
Dukminear, Elizabeth V, 49
Dukminear, Hannah V, 49
Dula, Lydia IV, 470
Dulaney, Daniel VI, 531
Dulea, Rebecca IV, 30
Dulell, Sarah II, 318
Dulell, Sarah II, 327
Duley, Avis IV, 125
Duley, Avis IV, 522
Duley, Dawson IV, 522
Duley, Eliza Annah IV, 522
Duley, Joshua IV, 125
Duley, Joshua IV, 522
Duley, Lydia IV, 522
Duley, Maxon IV, 522
Duley, Ruthanna IV, 522
Duley, Ruthanne IV, 522
Duley, Sinah Jane IV, 522
Duley, Sinai Jane IV, 522
Duley, Susanna IV, 522
Duley, Thomas Elwood IV, 522
Duley, William IV, 522
Duley, William D. IV, 522
Dulin, Rhoda V, 736
Dulin, Rhoda V, 754
Dulin, Ruth II, 857
Dulin, Ruth II, 858
Dulin, Ruth II, 902
Duling, Anna Johnson V, 903
Duling, Elizabeth IV, 470
Duling, Elizabeth IV, 475
Dull, Etta V, 993
Dull, Jerry W. V, 993
Dull, Sarah II, 849
Dull, Sarah II, 858
Duly, Ann IV, 84
Duly, Aves IV, 30
Duly, Avis IV, 30
Duly, John IV, 30
Duly, Joshua IV, 30
Duly, Joshua IV, 84
Duly, Lydia IV, 84
Duly, Lydia IV, 197
Duly, Maxon IV, 327
Duly, Phebe IV, 84
Duly, Phebe IV, 107
Duly, Rebecca IV, 30
Duly, Rebecca IV, 84
Duly, Rebecca Deulea IV, 30
Duly, Sarah IV, 84
Duly, Sarah IV, 114
Dumartharay, ??? III, 350
Dumartharay, Rebecca III, 350
Dumford, Elias V, 384
Dumford, Elias S. V, 384
Dumford, Emily Annetta V, 384
Dumford, Harry W. V, 384
Dumford, Harvey W. V, 384
Dumford, Olive V, 384
Dumford, Olive E. V, 384
Dumford, Sabilta V, 384
Dumford, Sarah V, 384
Dumm, Bert IV, 1250
Dumm, Etta IV, 1250
Dumont, Anne E. II, 858
Dumont, Annie A. III, 106
Dumont, Annie A. III, 369
Dumont, Annie E. II, 858
Dumont, Augustus P. II, 858
Dumont, Elizabeth M. III, 106
Dumont, Horace T. II, 858
Dumont, John B. III, 106
Dumont, John B. III, 369
Dumpson, Mary Ann III, 482
Dumum, James, Jr. VI, 905
Dun, Ann VI, 384
Dun, Ann VI, 397
Dun, James VI, 384
Dun, Rebecca VI, 384
Dun, Rebecca VI, 456
Dun, Sarah VI, 381
Dun, Sarah VI, 384
Dun, William VI, 384
Dunahew, ??? V, 993
Dunavant, Emily J. VI, 904
Dunavant, Josephus VI, 904
Dunavant, Mary VI, 966
Dunavant, William E. VI, 852
Dunaway, Anna IV, 1277
Dunaway, Charles E. IV, 1277
Dunaway, Eleanor IV, 1277
Dunaway, George Edward IV, 1277
Dunaway, Gertrude King IV, 1277
Dunaway, Martha IV, 1274
Dunbar, ??? III, 107
Dunbar, ??? III, 146
Dunbar, Anna I, 698
Dunbar, Anna I, 714
Dunbar, Anna I, 730
Dunbar, Anna I, 736
Dunbar, Beulah III, 107
Dunbar, Daniel III, 107
Dunbar, Daniel III, 291
Dunbar, Daniel III, 370
Dunbar, Elisha VI, 813
Dunbar, Eliza I, 698
Dunbar, Fanny I, 698
Dunbar, Helen IV, 1250
Dunbar, James M. I, 714
Dunbar, James M. I, 723
Dunbar, James Madison I, 698
Dunbar, John I, 698
Dunbar, John I, 714
Dunbar, Joseph John I, 698
Dunbar, Jurah VI, 813
Dunbar, Juriah VI, 1020
Dunbar, Leander H. I, 698
Dunbar, Louisa I, 714
Dunbar, Louisa E. I, 714
Dunbar, Louisa E. I, 723
Dunbar, Mariah Abigail I, 714
Dunbar, Mary I, 698
Dunbar, Mary I, 714
Dunbar, Mary I, 723
Dunbar, Mary III, 107
Dunbar, Mary III, 240
Dunbar, Mary E. I, 714
Dunbar, Mary E. I, 719
Dunbar, Mary H. III, 291
Dunbar, Naomi III, 107
Dunbar, Naomi III, 146
Dunbar, Naomi III, 291
Dunbar, Naomi III, 370
Dunbar, Rebecca III, 107
Dunbar, Rebecca III, 370
Dunbar, Sarah I, 698
Dunbar, Sarah I, 714
Dunbar, Thomas C. I, 714
Dunbar, Thomas C. I, 719
Dunbar, Thomas Clarkson I, 698
Dunbar, Wd. Naomi III, 107
Dunbaugh, Elizabeth V, 166
Dunbaugh, Ida V, 166
Duncan, Agnes III, 165
Duncan, Alice B. VI, 487
Duncan, Alice W. VI, 472
Duncan, Amelia I, 1019
Duncan, Amos V, 781
Duncan, Amos V, 794
Duncan, Ann VI, 912
Duncan, Bessie Mercer V, 329
Duncan, Dr. ??? VI, 472
Duncan, Elisha I, 1029
Duncan, Elizabeth II, 496
Duncan, Elizabeth II, 509
Duncan, Elizabeth II, 649
Duncan, Elizabeth V, 49
Duncan, Elizabeth V, 166
Duncan, Elizabeth V, 488
Duncan, Elizabeth V, 736
Duncan, Elizabeth V, 761
Duncan, Elizabeth V, 781
Duncan, Elizabeth B. II, 286
Duncan, Elizabeth B. II, 297
Duncan, Enos I, 1019
Duncan, Esther II, 509
Duncan, Esther II, 590
Duncan, Florence VI, 843
Duncan, George VI, 910
Duncan, George W. VI, 910
Duncan, Hannah II, 356
Duncan, Hercules VI, 487
Duncan, Hercules VI, 587
Duncan, James VI, 910
Duncan, James F. V, 234
Duncan, Jemima IV, 144
Duncan, Jemima N. IV, 144
Duncan, Jesse I, 1019
Duncan, Jesse V, 736
Duncan, Jesse V, 761
Duncan, John II, 356
Duncan, John II, 509
Duncan, John II, 649
Duncan, John VI, 843
Duncan, John VI, 912
Duncan, Joseph II, 356
Duncan, Joseph II, 509
Duncan, Joshua I, 1019
Duncan, Lee V, 455
Duncan, Margaret I, 877
Duncan, Margaret I, 896
Duncan, Margaret IV, 30
Duncan, Margaret VI, 487
Duncan, Margaret VI, 587
Duncan, Mary I, 1019
Duncan, Mary II, 356
Duncan, Mary IV, 144
Duncan, Mary V, 736
Duncan, Mary V, 794
Duncan, Mary VI, 626
Duncan, Mary VI, 628
Duncan, Mary VI, 635
Duncan, Mary VI, 910
Duncan, Mary Ann VI, 910
Duncan, Mary E. VI, 813
Duncan, Permelia VI, 912
Duncan, Robert II, 356
Duncan, Robert II, 509
Duncan, Robert II, 590
Duncan, Robert III, 409
Duncan, Robert VI, 813
Duncan, Samuel I, 1019
Duncan, Samuel V, 736
Duncan, Sarah II, 1049
Duncan, Sarah IV, 30
Duncan, Sarah IV, 40
Duncan, Sarah V, 736
Duncan, Sarah VI, 487
Duncan, Sarah VI, 587
Duncan, Sarah S. IV, 144
Duncan, Sary I, 1019
Duncan, Tamer Ann V, 166
Duncan, Thomas V, 329
Duncan, Thomas, Jr. II, 356
Duncan, Thos., Sr. V, 329
Duncan, William VI, 977
Dundas, Clara A. I, 612
Dundas, John I, 537
Dundas, John I, 923
Dundas, John I, 924
Dundas, Mary I, 923
Dundas, Mary D. I, 923
Dundas, Phebe Jane I, 924
Dundas, Sarah I, 923
Dundas, Sarah I, 924
Dundy, Dillwyn C. IV, 444
Dundy, Elizabeth IV, 444
Dunephant, Zadoc V, 166
Dunfee, Elizabeth II, 216
Dunfee, Thomas II, 216
Dunfee, Wd. Elizabeth II, 216
Dunfield, Dorothy II, 67
Dunfield, Dorothy II, 104
Dunfield, Dorrothy II, 67
Dunford, Elizabeth II, 443
Dunford, John II, 443
Dunford, Sarah II, 443
Dungan, Amos V, 806
Dungan, Anna V, 806
Dungan, Clyde W. V, 384
Dungan, Drusilla V, 806
Dungan, Elizabeth IV, 1004
Dungan, Elizabeth V, 806
Dungan, Hannah IV, 197
Dungan, Isaac V, 806
Dungan, Jemima N. IV, 162
Dungan, Jesse V, 806
Dungan, John H. V, 384
Dungan, Louisa V, 384
Dungan, Mary IV, 197
Dungan, Mary IV, 327
Dungan, Mary IV, 470
Dungan, Mary V, 384
Dungan, Mary V, 806
Dungan, Mary A. V, 384
Dungan, Oliver IV, 470
Dungan, Rachel V, 806
Dungan, Richard V, 806
Dungan, Richard P. V, 806
Dungan, Samuel V, 806
Dungan, Sarah S. IV, 146
Dungan, William O. IV, 470
Dungen, Mary IV, 470
Dungerfield, M. Lambeth VI, 854
Dungerfield, Susanah VI, 854
Dungworth, Elizabeth II, 356
Dungworth, Elizabeth II, 472
Dungworth, Elizabeth II, 509
Dungworth, Elizabeth II, 510
Dungworth, Emanuel II, 356
Dungworth, Emanuel II, 509
Dungworth, Emmanuel II, 356
Dungworth, Emmanuel II, 472
Dungworth, Hester II, 356
Dungworth, John II, 356
Dungworth, Manuel II, 356
Dungworth, Richard II, 356
Dungworth, Richard II, 472
Dungworth, Richard II, 509
Dunham, Addie Clifton I, 632
Dunham, Benjamin II, 356
Dunham, David II, 27
Dunham, David II, 67
Dunham, David E. V, 49
Dunham, Elizabeth II, 27
Dunham, Elizabeth II, 67
Dunham, Elizabeth II, 107
Dunham, Elizabeth II, 108
Dunham, Geo. W. V, 670
Dunham, George I, 632
Dunham, George P. V, 670
Dunham, Jemima III, 107
Dunham, Jemima III, 343
Dunham, Jessie Myrtle IV, 1313
Dunham, Job II, 27
Dunham, Job II, 67
Dunham, John II, 27
Dunham, John II, 67
Dunham, John II, 510
Dunham, Jonathan II, 356
Dunham, Mary E. II, 858
Dunham, Sarah III, 134
Dunham, Shobal II, 27
Dunham, Shubal II, 67
Dunham, Virginia II, 806
Dunham, William II, 27
Dunham, Wm. II, 27
Dunham, Wm. II, 67
Dunham, Wm. Smith II, 67
Dunham, Wm. Smith II, 107
Duning, Exum I, 207
Duning, Sarah J. I, 207
Duning, Sophronia I, 207
Dunivant, Alice V, 166
Dunivant, Zadoc V, 166
Dunivant, Zadock V, 166
Dunkan, Edmond II, 994
Dunkan, George II, 994
Dunkan, John II, 991
Dunkan, John II, 994
Dunkan, Mary II, 994
Dunkan, Sarah II, 994
Dunkan, Sarah II, 1004
Dunken, Amos V, 736
Dunken, Margaret I, 877
Dunken, Margaret I, 1016
Dunker, Jesse V, 49
Dunkin, Amos I, 1092
Dunkin, Amos V, 736
Dunkin, Amos V, 781
Dunkin, Elisha I, 1029
Dunkin, Elizabeth I, 537
Dunkin, Elizabeth IV, 197
Dunkin, Elizabeth IV, 219
Dunkin, Elizabeth V, 736
Dunkin, Elizabeth V, 781
Dunkin, Isaac I, 1092
Dunkin, Isaac V, 736
Dunkin, Isaac V, 781
Dunkin, Jesse I, 1092
Dunkin, Jesse V, 736
Dunkin, John I, 1029
Dunkin, Margaret I, 537
Dunkin, Mary I, 1029
Dunkin, Mary V, 736
Dunkin, Mary V, 781
Dunkin, Mary V, 818
Dunkin, Milcha I, 1029
Dunkin, Nelson I, 1029
Dunkin, Rachel I, 1029
Dunkin, Rachel V, 736
Dunkin, Rachel V, 818

Dunkin, Richard I, 1029
Dunkin, Samuel I, 1029
Dunkin, Samuel I, 1092
Dunkin, Samuel V, 736
Dunkin, Samuel V, 818
Dunkin, Sarah V, 736
Dunkin, Sarah V, 751
Dunkon, George II, 994
Dunkon, Mary II, 994
Dunlap, Aaron Thos. I, 1140
Dunlap, Ann VI, 488
Dunlap, Anna V, 993
Dunlap, Aritta I, 1140
Dunlap, Asa IV, 1277
Dunlap, Blanch IV, 1277
Dunlap, Cary IV, 1277
Dunlap, Charity II, 67
Dunlap, Cynthia I, 1140
Dunlap, David Huston I, 1150
Dunlap, Elizabeth II, 216
Dunlap, Elizabeth IV, 812
Dunlap, Elizabeth IV, 849
Dunlap, Elizabeth VI, 488
Dunlap, Elizabeth S. VI, 488
Dunlap, Elizabeth Schooley VI, 488
Dunlap, Ephraim Henry I, 1140
Dunlap, Ethel M. IV, 619
Dunlap, Ethel M. IV, 621
Dunlap, George IV, 1277
Dunlap, Henry I, 1150
Dunlap, I. W. I, 1150
Dunlap, Ina V, 993
Dunlap, Isaac I, 1150
Dunlap, Isaac Wilson I, 1140
Dunlap, Iva F. IV, 1277
Dunlap, James VI, 488
Dunlap, James Blain I, 1140
Dunlap, James D. I, 1140
Dunlap, James D. I, 1150
Dunlap, James Deving I, 1140
Dunlap, John IV, 700
Dunlap, John H. IV, 700
Dunlap, John Thomas I, 1140
Dunlap, Joseph VI, 488
Dunlap, Joseph M. VI, 488
Dunlap, Lawrence IV, 1277
Dunlap, Lucinda I, 1150
Dunlap, Lucinda IV, 1277
Dunlap, Martha Elizabeth I, 1140
Dunlap, Mollie I, 1150
Dunlap, Mrs. J. P. IV, 1277
Dunlap, Oliver F. IV, 1277
Dunlap, Palmira I, 1150
Dunlap, Ruth V, 559
Dunlap, Samuel I, 1140
Dunlap, Samuel I, 1150
Dunlap, Sarah I, 1150
Dunlap, Sarah Emeline I, 1140
Dunlap, Sarah M. IV, 1277
Dunlap, Stella I, 1150
Dunlap, Susan IV, 1277
Dunlap, Volantine IV, 1277
Dunlap, W. A. I, 1150
Dunlap, Wm. IV, 1277
Dunlap, Wm. Adkin I, 1140
Dunlop, Eleanor III, 107
Dunlop, James D. I, 1150
Dunn, Ada IV, 1037
Dunn, Ann I, 387
Dunn, Ann I, 401
Dunn, Ann II, 27
Dunn, Ann VI, 373
Dunn, Ann VI, 384
Dunn, Anna M. II, 147
Dunn, Anna M. II, 157
Dunn, Anna Maria II, 131
Dunn, Anna Maria II, 147
Dunn, Anne V, 559
Dunn, Benajah II, 27
Dunn, Benajah II, 67
Dunn, Benjamin I, 1041
Dunn, Blanche V, 234
Dunn, Catharine VI, 456
Dunn, Catherine VI, 384
Dunn, Charles V, 234
Dunn, Clara V, 559
Dunn, Clara V, 619
Dunn, Clara A. V, 619
Dunn, Cornelia III, 107
Dunn, Cornelia B. III, 175
Dunn, Cornelius VI, 910
Dunn, Davis Wesley V, 619
Dunn, Debby VI, 412
Dunn, Debby VI, 452
Dunn, Deborah II, 27
Dunn, Deborah II, 67
Dunn, Deborah II, 78
Dunn, Deborah II, 104
Dunn, Deborah, Jr. II, 54
Dunn, Deborah, Jr. II, 67
Dunn, Ed. V, 619
Dunn, Edward H. V, 619
Dunn, Eleanor III, 107
Dunn, Eleanor III, 148
Dunn, Elizabeth I, 387
Dunn, Elizabeth I, 417
Dunn, Elizabeth I, 1048
Dunn, Elizabeth I, 1050
Dunn, Elizabeth II, 131
Dunn, Elizabeth II, 510
Dunn, Elizabeth VI, 412
Dunn, Elizabeth VI, 910
Dunn, Elizabeth Louise II, 131
Dunn, Florence IV, 1250
Dunn, George III, 107
Dunn, George III, 175
Dunn, George D. V, 670
Dunn, Geva K. V, 619
Dunn, Gulielma II, 67
Dunn, Gulielma II, 81
Dunn, Hannah I, 372
Dunn, Hannah I, 387
Dunn, Hannah VI, 384
Dunn, Isaac II, 27
Dunn, Jacob I Sup 1, 9
Dunn, James VI, 384
Dunn, James O. V, 670
Dunn, James Oregon V, 670
Dunn, John I, 387
Dunn, John II, 27
Dunn, John II, 510
Dunn, Jonathan II, 67
Dunn, Jonathan II, 106
Dunn, Jonathan II, 131
Dunn, Joseph I, 387
Dunn, Joseph VI, 870
Dunn, Joseph VI, 910
Dunn, Joseph VI, 1000
Dunn, Joseph VI, 1013
Dunn, Josiah I, 1048
Dunn, Josiah II, 27
Dunn, Josiah III, 107
Dunn, Josiah VI, 907
Dunn, Josiah VI, 910
Dunn, Lester Harris V, 619
Dunn, Lestie Helen V, 619
Dunn, Louisa III, 107
Dunn, Lucetta IV, 1094
Dunn, Lucetta IV, 1122
Dunn, Lydia IV, 1361
Dunn, Lydia IV, 1373
Dunn, Madgalena VI, 910
Dunn, Mahlon H. III, 107
Dunn, Mahlon H. III, 148
Dunn, Mahlon H., Jr. III, 107
Dunn, Margaret Mahew VI, 907
Dunn, Mary I, 387
Dunn, Mary I, 403
Dunn, Mary I, 1047
Dunn, Mary I, 1048
Dunn, Mary II, 27
Dunn, Mary II, 216
Dunn, Mary II, 994
Dunn, Mary III, 107
Dunn, Mary VI, 412
Dunn, Mary Ann IV, 1037
Dunn, Mary Frances V, 559
Dunn, Naomi II, 27
Dunn, Naomi II, 52
Dunn, Naomi II, 67
Dunn, Nathan II, 27
Dunn, Nathan II, 67
Dunn, Nathan II, 98
Dunn, Nathan II, 510
Dunn, Nehemiah I Sup 1, 11
Dunn, Nehemieh I, 1048
Dunn, Ottis Edward V, 619
Dunn, Precilla IV, 327
Dunn, Priscilla IV, 519
Dunn, Priscilla IV, 522
Dunn, Rachel II, 27
Dunn, Rebecca II, 27
Dunn, Rebecca II, 67
Dunn, Rebecca II, 95
Dunn, Rebecca VI, 384
Dunn, Rebeckah II, 27
Dunn, Rhoda II, 27
Dunn, Rhoda II, 67
Dunn, Rhoda II, 90
Dunn, Rhoda II, 98
Dunn, Richard II, 27
Dunn, Richard II, 67
Dunn, Richard VI, 813
Dunn, Robert IV, 1037
Dunn, Robert Leslie V, 619
Dunn, Ruth I, 387
Dunn, Ruth II, 67
Dunn, Ruth II, 106
Dunn, S. Clifford III, 107
Dunn, Sally Claxon VI, 907
Dunn, Samuel I, 387
Dunn, Samuel VI, 907
Dunn, Sarah I, 373
Dunn, Sarah I, 387
Dunn, Sarah I, 1048
Dunn, Sarah II, 27
Dunn, Sarah II, 67
Dunn, Sarah II, 104
Dunn, Sarah II, 106
Dunn, Sarah II, 457
Dunn, Sarah II, 510
Dunn, Sarah II, 529
Dunn, Sarah Gibson VI, 813
Dunn, Thackery II, 147
Dunn, Thomas II, 510
Dunn, Thomas VI, 812
Dunn, Thomas VI, 849
Dunn, Wash. V, 559
Dunn, Wd. Sarah II, 488
Dunn, Wd. Sarah II, 510
Dunn, Whitfield V, 234
Dunn, William I, 387
Dunn, William I Sup 1, 9
Dunn, William II, 27
Dunn, William II, 216
Dunn, William II, 271
Dunn, William II, 356
Dunn, William V, 488
Dunn, William VI, 384
Dunn, William M. V, 488
Dunn, Wm. II, 67
Dunn, Wm. II, 510
Dunn, Wm. II, 529
Dunn, Wm. II, 994
Dunn, Zacheus II, 27
Dunn, Zacheus II, 67
Dunn, Zacheus II, 78
Dunn, Zacheus II, 104
Dunnavant, Eldridge VI, 813
Dunnavant, Elizabeth VI, 813
Dunnavant, Frances VI, 813
Dunnavant, Josepheus VI, 813
Dunnavant, Leroy C. VI, 813
Dunnavant, Lucinda VI, 813
Dunnavant, Nancy VI, 813
Dunnavant, Shadwick VI, 813
Dunnavant, William VI, 813
Dunnegan, James V, 670
Dunnevant, Zadock V, 166
Dunnigan, James V, 670
Dunning, Aaron I, 213
Dunning, Agnes Powers V, 903
Dunning, Andrew I, 213
Dunning, Exum I, 213
Dunning, Exum I, 221
Dunning, Exum E. I, 237
Dunning, Judith A. I, 213
Dunning, Sarah J. I, 213
Dunning, Sophronia I, 213
Dunning, Sophronia I, 237
Dunning, Sophronia I, 252
Dunning, Sophronia Jane I, 221
Dunnington, Henry VI, 843
Dunnington, Jane VI, 813
Dunnington, Walter VI, 813
Dunns, Mary III, 107
Dunns, Mary III, 143
Dunsley, Dorothy II, 67
Dunsley, Dorothy II, 104
Dunsley, Dorrothy II, 67
Dunsmith, Elsie V, 670
Dunsmith, Elsie V, 672
Dunsmith, Theodore V, 670
Dunsmith, Theodore V, 672
Dunwick, Catharine II, 510
Dunwoodie, John II, 443
Dupes, Alty V, 993
Dupes, Geo. V, 993
Dupes, George M. V, 993
Dupes, Sarah V, 993
Dupes, Sarah L. V, 993
Dupes, Sarah M. V, 993
Dupin, Louisa III, 107
Duplonvis, John II, 697
Duplouvis, John II, 510
Duplouvis, Whankey II, 510
Dupoy, Lillie V, 234
Dupree, Annie I, 924
Dupree, Benjamin Owen I, 228
Dupree, Lee Ora I, 228
Dupree, Lewis VI, 106
Dupree, Margaret I, 621
Dupree, Thomas I, 940
Dupree, Thomas B. I, 924
Dupree, Thomas Byrd I, 924
Duprior, Aurean VI, 62
Duprior, Delilah VI, 61
Duprior, Delilah VI, 63
Duprior, Dollie E. C. VI, 62
Duprior, Ellen VI, 62
Duprior, Franklin VI, 63
Duprior, George VI, 62
Duprior, Herbert L. VI, 62
Duprior, Junius VI, 62
Duprior, Junius F. VI, 62
Duprior, Junius Fenton VI, 62
Duprior, Junius W. VI, 62
Duprior, Lucy VI, 62
Duprior, Mark VI, 62
Duprior, Mary VI, 62
Duprior, Nancy VI, 63
Duprior, Nancy A. VI, 61
Duprior, Nellie J. VI, 62
Duprior, Peter VI, 61
Duprior, Peter VI, 63
Duprior, Pheby VI, 62
Duprior, Rosa VI, 62
Duprior, Sarah L. VI, 62
Duprior, Susie VI, 62
Duprior, Thomas VI, 62
Duprior, Viola VI, 62
Duprior, William VI, 62
Duprior, Wm. VI, 62
Dupuy, Elizabeth VI, 813
Dupuy, Harieta VI, 813
Dupuy, John B. VI, 813
Dupuy, William VI, 813
Dupvior, Delilah VI, 63
Durand, Bessie B. III, 107
Durand, Elizabeth III, 107
Durand, Elizabeth III, 257
Durand, William W. III, 107
Durant, Clara IV, 1156
Durant, L. L. IV, 1156
Durant, Mattie IV, 1156
Durban, Adda Mary V, 384
Durban, Alice IV, 297
Durban, Alice Vernon IV, 197
Durban, Artie E. V, 384
Durban, Carrie B. V, 384
Durban, Charles C. V, 384
Durban, Ellen V, 384
Durban, George B. V, 384
Durban, Josephine V, 384
Durban, Nancy V, 384
Durban, William J. V, 384
Durban, Wm. V, 384
Durban, Wm. Joseph V, 384
Durberah, Elizabeth II, 356
Durberah, Joseph II, 356
Durberow, Ann II, 356
Durberow, Daniel II, 356
Durberow, Deborah II, 356
Durberow, Elizabeth II, 356
Durberow, Hannah II, 356
Durberow, Hannah II, 451
Durberow, Hugh II, 356
Durberow, Hugh II, 451
Durberow, Hugh II, 510
Durberow, Isaac II, 356
Durberow, Jacob II, 356
Durberow, Jane II, 356
Durberow, John II, 356
Durberow, Joseph II, 356
Durberow, Josiah II, 356
Durberow, Mary II, 356
Durberow, Rebecca II, 356
Durberow, Samuel II, 356
Durberow, Sarah II, 356
Durberow, Stephen II, 356
Durberow, Wd. Hannah II, 510
Durberow, William II, 356
Durbin, Addie V, 670
Durbin, Alice IV, 197
Durbin, Alice Vernon IV, 197
Durbin, Annie IV, 197
Durbin, Carnie IV, 197
Durbin, Carrie B. V, 384
Durbin, David E. IV, 197
Durbin, Edith L. IV, 197
Durbin, George IV, 197
Durbin, Harry IV, 197
Durbin, Harry D. IV, 197
Durbin, Ida IV, 700
Durbin, Ida V, 670
Durbin, John V, 234
Durbin, Joseph S. IV, 700
Durbin, Josephine IV, 197
Durbin, Josie V, 670
Durbin, Lemuel IV, 197
Durbin, Lizzie IV, 197
Durbin, Louella V, 670
Durbin, Luella V, 670
Durbin, Maggie IV, 197
Durbin, Margaret IV, 700
Durbin, Mary Alice IV, 197
Durbin, Minnie IV, 197
Durbin, Minnie L. IV, 197
Durbin, Pearl IV, 700
Durbin, Roy IV, 197
Durbin, Sarah IV, 197
Durbin, Thomas E. IV, 700
Durbin, Walter E. IV, 197
Durbin, William IV, 197
Durborah, Elizabeth II, 356
Durborah, Hugh II, 356
Durborah, John II, 356
Durborough, Ann II, 510
Durborough, Daniel II, 510
Durborough, Elisabeth II, 467
Durborough, Elisabeth II, 510
Durborough, Jacob II, 510
Durborough, Sarah II, 510
Durborough, Sarah II, 517
Durborough, Wd. Sarah II, 510
Durborow, Ann II, 356
Durborow, Ann II, 510
Durborow, Anne II, 510
Durborow, Daniel II, 510
Durborow, Elisabeth II, 510
Durborow, Elizabeth II, 510
Durborow, Elizabeth II, 663
Durborow, Hannah II, 510
Durborow, Hannah II, 581
Durborow, Hugh II, 503
Durborow, Hugh II, 510
Durborow, Hugh II, 663
Durborow, Jacob II, 510
Durborow, Jane II, 356
Durborow, Jane II, 510
Durborow, John II, 503
Durborow, John II, 510
Durborow, John II, 546
Durborow, Joseph II, 505
Durborow, Mary II, 504
Durborow, Mary II, 505
Durborow, Mary II, 510
Durborow, Rebecca II, 510
Durborow, Rebeckah II, 546
Durborow, Samuel II, 510
Durborow, Sarah II, 503
Durborow, Sarah II, 510
Durborow, Wd. Hannah II, 510
Durborow, Wd. Sarah II, 510
Durborow, Wm. II, 510
Durborrow, Daniel II, 510
Durborrow, Elizabeth II, 510
Durborrow, Elizabeth II, 607
Durborrow, Hugh II, 510
Durborrow, Jacob II, 216
Durborrow, Mary II, 510
Durborrow, Wm. II, 510
Durburow, Anne II, 451
Durburow, Anne II, 510
Durburow, Daniel II, 510
Durburow, Daniel II, 649
Durburow, Elizabeth II, 510
Durburow, Elizabeth II, 513
Durburow, Hannah II, 451
Durburow, Hannah II, 510
Durburow, Hannah II, 649
Durburow, Hugh II, 451
Durburow, Hugh II, 510
Durburow, Hugh II, 528
Durburow, Jacob II, 356
Durburow, Jacob II, 451
Durburow, Jacob II, 510
Durburow, Jacob II, 513
Durburow, Jacob II, 671
Durburow, Jane II, 510
Durburow, Jane II, 671
Durburow, John II, 510
Durburow, John II, 668
Durburow, Joseph II, 356
Durburow, Mary II, 510
Durburow, Mary II, 668
Durburow, Samuel II, 510
Durburow, Samuel II, 671
Durburow, Sarah II, 510
Durburow, Sarah II, 528
Durburrow, Ann II, 356
Durburrow, Daniel II, 491
Durburrow, Hannah II, 356
Durburrow, Jacob II, 356
Durburrow, John II, 356
Durburrow, Rebecca II, 356
Durburrow, Samuel II, 510
Durburrow, Sarah II, 491
Durburrow, William II, 356
Dure, Abigail II, 994
Dure, Abigail Pancoast II, 994
Dure, Ann II, 994
Dure, Deborah II, 958
Dure, Deborah II, 994
Dure, Eliza II, 959
Dure, Elizabeth II, 994
Dure, Elizabeth II, 1021
Dure, Ellen II, 958
Dure, Ellin II, 959
Dure, Hannah II, 959
Dure, John II, 958
Dure, John II, 994
Dure, John II, 997

ure, Joseph II, 959
ure, Joseph II, 994
ure, Joseph II, 997
ure, Joseph, Jr. II, 994
ure, Martha II, 994
ure, Martha II, 997
ure, Mary II, 958
ure, Mary II, 985
ure, Mary II, 994
ure, Mary II, 997
ure, Rachel II, 994
ure, Sarah II, 997
ure, Thomas II, 958
ure, Thomas II, 994
ure, Thomas II, 1021
ure, Yeamans II, 997
uree, Mary Speer V, 166
urell, Ann II, 443
urell, Jonathan II, 443
urell, Lydia II, 737
rell, Moses II, 443
rfee, Anna B. III, 107
rfee, Anna B. III, 224
urfee, Bessie III, 107
urfee, Bessie III, 181
rfee, Elihu V, 903
urfee, Julia D. V, 932
urfee, Julia D. Smith V, 903
urfee, Julia P. V, 903
rfee, Maria V, 903
urfee, Wm. W. III, 107
urfey, Cornelia VI, 717
urfey, Cornelia N. VI, 635
rfey, Cornelia N. VI, 717
rfey, Cornelia Needles VI, 488
urfey, Cornelia Needles VI, 575
urfey, Cornelia Needles VI, 577
urfey, Geo. Jackson VI, 577
urfey, George J., Jr. VI, 488
urfey, George J., Jr. VI, 635
urfey, George Jackson VI, 488
urfey, George Jackson VI, 575
urfey, George Jackson VI, 635
urfey, George Jackson VI, 717
urfey, Lilia VI, 488
urfey, Lilia VI, 575
urfey, Lilia VI, 635
urfey, Lilia VI, 717
urfey, Robert W. VI, 488
urfey, Robert W. VI, 635
urfey, Zachery Goodrich VI, 488
urfey, Zachery Goodrich VI, 575
urfey, Zachery Goodrich VI, 635
urfey, Zachery Goodrich VI, 717
urflinger, Annie V, 993
urfy, Fanny VI, 813
urfy, James VI, 813
urham, ??? VI, 95
urham, Arabella I, 1118
urham, Arabella VI, 134
urham, Arrabella I, 1118
urham, Austin I, 877
urham, Betsey I, 1140
urham, Daniel I, 1118
urham, Daniel I, 1137
urham, Daniel I, 1140
urham, Daniel I, 1150
urham, Daniel I, 1151
urham, Daniel VI, 134
urham, Esther I, 1118
urham, Esther VI, 106
urham, Esther VI, 134
urham, Etta I, 388
urham, Gabriel I, 1140
urham, Gabriel I, 1150
urham, Hannah IV, 700
urham, Hannah IV, 759
urham, James B. VI, 829
urham, James B. VI, 838
urham, Jane I, 371
urham, Jane I, 388
urham, Jane I, 1140
urham, Jane VI, 132
urham, Jane VI, 134
urham, Malvina J. I, 388
urham, Martha P. VI, 90
urham, Matilda I, 388
urham, Matthew II, 994
urham, Patsey I, 1140
urham, Polly VI, 910
urham, Rosa L. I, 388
urham, Ruth I, 1118
urham, Ruth I, 1132
urham, Ruth VI, 134
urham, Salley L. I, 1140
urham, Samira I, 537
urham, Samira I, 560
urham, Sarah Jane I, 615
urham, Thomas I, 1118
urham, Thomas I, 1140
urham, Thomas I, 1150
Durham, Thomas I, 1151
Durham, Thomas VI, 89
Durham, Thomas VI, 134
Durham, William I, 1118
Durham, William I, 1137
Durham, William I, 1140
Durham, William I, 1150
Durham, William I, 1151
Durham, William VI, 910
Durham, William H. I, 1140
Durham, William Harrison I, 1150
Durkee, Stella Reid IV, 1156
Durnbaugh, Catherine V, 166
Durnbaugh, Elizabeth V, 166
Durnbaugh, Ida V, 166
Durnbaugh, Welber V, 166
Durnel, Pebe I, 1009
Durnel, Phebe I, 1009
Durnell, Cornelia V, 234
Durnell, Cornelia A. V, 234
Durnell, Harmannis V, 234
Durnell, Ida Belle V, 234
Durnell, John F. V, 234
Durnell, Mary E. V, 234
Durnell, Nora E. V, 234
Durnil, Pebe I, 1009
Durphe, Elizabeth II, 443
Durr, Leona IV, 1250
Durrance, Francis II, 994
Durrance, Francis II, 1018
Durrett, Celey VI, 910
Durrett, Elizabeth VI, 921
Durrett, Esther VI, 910
Durrett, John VI, 910
Durrett, John VI, 975
Durrett, Mary W. VI, 978
Durrett, Nancy VI, 954
Durrett, Richard VI, 875
Durrett, Richard VI, 910
Durrett, Sally VI, 975
Durrett, Sarah VI, 910
Durrett, William VI, 910
Durrett, William VI, 980
Durrett, Wm. VI, 976
Durrett, Wm. VI, 991
Durrett, Wm. VI, 1010
Durrum, John VI, 867
Durrum, Mildred VI, 867
Durrun, James B. VI, 867
Duryea, ??? III, 111
Duryea, ??? III, 409
Duryea, ??? III, 496
Duryea, Ann III, 107
Duryea, Ann III, 111
Duryea, Caroline S. III, 482
Duryea, Cornelia III, 482
Duryea, Cornelia III, 495
Duryea, Daniel III, 480
Duryea, Daniel III, 482
Duryea, Daniel III, 495
Duryea, Daniel P. III, 482
Duryea, Edgar H. III, 482
Duryea, Edgar H. III, 493
Duryea, Elizabeth III, 409
Duryea, Elizabeth III, 421
Duryea, Elizabeth III, 480
Duryea, Elizabeth III, 482
Duryea, Elizabeth III, 486
Duryea, Ethalinda III, 482
Duryea, George III, 409
Duryea, George III, 421
Duryea, George III, 486
Duryea, Henry Sands III, 482
Duryea, Jane III, 409
Duryea, Jane III, 482
Duryea, Jane III, 493
Duryea, Jemima III, 482
Duryea, Jemima III, 496
Duryea, John, Jr. III, 482
Duryea, Mary Ella III, 482
Duryea, Mary Ella III, 493
Duryea, Mary Emer III, 482
Duryea, Mary J. III, 482
Duryea, Mary J. III, 493
Duryea, Phebe III, 393
Duryea, Phebe III, 409
Duryea, Phebe III, 421
Duryea, Phebe III, 449
Duryea, Phebe III, 482
Duryea, Phebe III, 486
Duryea, Robert III, 409
Dusenbury, Abigail III, 379
Dusenbury, Abigail III, 387
Dusenbury, Benjamin III, 409
Dusenbury, Benjamin III, 445
Dusenbury, Eliz. III, 474
Dusenbury, Henry III, 107
Dusenbury, Henry III, 129
Dusenbury, Jane III, 107
Dusenbury, Jane III, 129
Dusenbury, Joan III, 107
Dusenbury, John III, 107
Dusenbury, Mary III, 107
Dusenbury, Mary III, 129
Dusenbury, Mary III, 379
Dusenbury, Peter III, 379
Dusenbury, Sarah III, 409
Dusenbury, Sarah III, 445
Dusman, Rachel, Jr. II, 356
Dussell, Rebecca II, 510
Dussum, James VI, 838
Dussum, Lucy D. VI, 838
Dutcher, ??? III, 409
Dutcher, ??? III, 467
Dutcher, ??? III, 468
Dutcher, Alice V, 993
Dutcher, Drucilla V, 993
Dutcher, Edward III, 468
Dutcher, Ertie V, 993
Dutcher, Geo. W. V, 993
Dutcher, George V, 993
Dutcher, Hannah T. III, 468
Dutcher, Helen III, 409
Dutcher, Helen T. III, 409
Dutcher, Helen T. III, 467
Dutcher, Helen T. III, 468
Dutcher, Nellie IV, 1313
Dutcher, Ralph V, 993
Dutcher, Samuel III, 467
Dutcher, Viola V, 993
Dutton, Ann Eliza IV, 1094
Dutton, Anna IV, 197
Dutton, Anna IV, 311
Dutton, Anna IV, 314
Dutton, Anna IV, 315
Dutton, Anna IV, 1009
Dutton, Anna Ellen VI, 488
Dutton, Annetta IV, 197
Dutton, Asa V, 49
Dutton, Benjamin II, 510
Dutton, Charles II, 172
Dutton, Charles II, 286
Dutton, Charles III, 107
Dutton, Charles III, 281
Dutton, Charles S. II, 946
Dutton, Charles Spencer II, 172
Dutton, Chas. IV, 1009
Dutton, Chester Smedley III, 107
Dutton, Clara E. V, 235
Dutton, Cora Maude IV, 197
Dutton, Cynthia IV, 197
Dutton, David I, 1092
Dutton, David IV, 197
Dutton, David IV, 311
Dutton, David IV, 812
Dutton, David V, 49
Dutton, David V, 235
Dutton, David V, 236
Dutton, David V, 253
Dutton, David V, 294
Dutton, David V, 947
Dutton, David VI, 384
Dutton, David Smith IV, 812
Dutton, David Smith IV, 868
Dutton, David Smith IV, 904
Dutton, Deborah IV, 806
Dutton, Deborah IV, 812
Dutton, Deborah IV, 813
Dutton, Deborah IV, 904
Dutton, Dorothy III, 107
Dutton, Dorothy Dean V, 455
Dutton, E. Eliza III, 180
Dutton, Edith Helen II, 172
Dutton, Edmund IV, 812
Dutton, Elisha IV, 812
Dutton, Elisha IV, 904
Dutton, Eliza IV, 812
Dutton, Eliza IV, 843
Dutton, Eliza IV, 904
Dutton, Elizabeth II, 172
Dutton, Elizabeth V, 235
Dutton, Elizabeth L. II, 286
Dutton, Elizabeth P. V, 257
Dutton, Elizabeth P. V, 294
Dutton, Elizabeth S. VI, 488
Dutton, Elizabeth Schooley VI, 488
Dutton, Ellen III, 107
Dutton, Ellen M. III, 281
Dutton, Elmer IV, 197
Dutton, Elmer E. IV, 197
Dutton, Emma III, 107
Dutton, Emma III, 180
Dutton, Emma VI, 488
Dutton, Emma VI, 514
Dutton, Emma VI, 524
Dutton, Emma VI, 534
Dutton, Emma VI, 555
Dutton, Emma VI, 556
Dutton, Emma VI, 565
Dutton, Emma E. IV, 813
Dutton, Emma Eliza III, 180
Dutton, Emma Eliza VI, 488
Dutton, Emma Eliza VI, 513
Dutton, Emma F. VI, 565
Dutton, Ezra IV, 197
Dutton, Ezra IV, 1025
Dutton, Francis IV, 868
Dutton, George II, 172
Dutton, Georgianna IV, 1009
Dutton, Grace III, 107
Dutton, Grace III, 281
Dutton, Hannah II, 172
Dutton, Hannah II, 286
Dutton, Hannah II, 510
Dutton, Hannah II, 674
Dutton, Hannah IV, 197
Dutton, Hannah IV, 311
Dutton, Hannah IV, 812
Dutton, Hannah IV, 823
Dutton, Hannah IV, 901
Dutton, Hannah IV, 904
Dutton, Hannah V, 235
Dutton, Hannah V, 253
Dutton, Hannah VI, 384
Dutton, Hannah A. II, 279
Dutton, Hannah A. II, 286
Dutton, Hannah E. II, 172
Dutton, Hannah E. II, 181
Dutton, Hannah E. II, 286
Dutton, Hannah E. II, 299
Dutton, Hannah H. IV, 197
Dutton, Hattie IV, 1250
Dutton, Helen E. II, 172
Dutton, Helen E. II, 286
Dutton, Henry IV, 812
Dutton, Henry IV, 868
Dutton, Henry IV, 904
Dutton, Isaac II, 510
Dutton, James V, 49
Dutton, James B. III, 107
Dutton, James B. VI, 488
Dutton, James F. B. VI, 488
Dutton, James Famandis Bicoe VI, 524
Dutton, James Famandis Biscoe VI, 488
Dutton, James V. V, 49
Dutton, Jennet IV, 1025
Dutton, Jeremiah T. V, 235
Dutton, Jeremiah Thomas V, 235
Dutton, Joanna IV, 812
Dutton, Joanna IV, 868
Dutton, Joanna IV, 883
Dutton, Joanna IV, 904
Dutton, John II, 172
Dutton, John II, 216
Dutton, John V, 38
Dutton, John V, 49
Dutton, John VI, 565
Dutton, John B. II, 737
Dutton, John B. III, 107
Dutton, John B. III, 180
Dutton, John B. VI, 488
Dutton, John B. VI, 514
Dutton, John B. VI, 556
Dutton, John Bidderson VI, 488
Dutton, John Bidderson VI, 524
Dutton, John Bidderson VI, 534
Dutton, John Bidderson VI, 555
Dutton, John Brinton II, 510
Dutton, John F. III, 107
Dutton, John F. III, 291
Dutton, John H. Mendinghall IV, 813
Dutton, John M. Mendenhall IV, 197
Dutton, John Walthon III, 107
Dutton, Jonathan V, 235
Dutton, Jonathan B. V, 235
Dutton, Jonathan E. V, 235
Dutton, Joseph IV, 311
Dutton, Joseph IV, 313
Dutton, Joseph IV, 812
Dutton, Joseph IV, 858
Dutton, Joseph IV, 868
Dutton, Joseph IV, 883
Dutton, Joseph IV, 904
Dutton, Lary Mary VI, 384
Dutton, Lauretta III, 107
Dutton, Lauretta III, 291
Dutton, Leota IV, 197
Dutton, Lewis V, 235
Dutton, Lewis V, 329
Dutton, Lewis C. V, 235
Dutton, Lewis Clarkson V, 235
Dutton, Lydia II, 510
Dutton, Lydia IV, 868
Dutton, Lydia V, 47
Dutton, Lydia V, 49
Dutton, Lydia V, 219
Dutton, Lydia V, 235
Dutton, Lydia V, 950
Dutton, Lydia V, 960
Dutton, Margaret V, 49
Dutton, Margaret V, 235
Dutton, Margaret V, 236
Dutton, Maria IV, 812
Dutton, Maria IV, 832
Dutton, Maria IV, 904
Dutton, Martha IV, 868
Dutton, Martha IV, 904
Dutton, Martha V, 38
Dutton, Martha V, 49
Dutton, Martha Ann IV, 197
Dutton, Marvin IV, 197
Dutton, Mary II, 172
Dutton, Mary II, 279
Dutton, Mary II, 286
Dutton, Mary IV, 197
Dutton, Mary IV, 904
Dutton, Mary V, 29
Dutton, Mary V, 49
Dutton, Mary V, 235
Dutton, Mary V, 947
Dutton, Mary V, 950
Dutton, Mary VI, 384
Dutton, Mary VI, 412
Dutton, Mary A. T. II, 858
Dutton, Mary F. VI, 478
Dutton, Mary F. VI, 488
Dutton, Mary F. VI, 561
Dutton, Mary F. VI, 565
Dutton, Mary F. VI, 566
Dutton, Mary F. VI, 567
Dutton, Mary F. VI, 783
Dutton, Mary Frances VI, 488
Dutton, Matilda IV, 812
Dutton, Matilda IV, 904
Dutton, Melissa M. III, 107
Dutton, Melissa Madeline III, 107
Dutton, Melissa Madeline VI, 488
Dutton, Murden IV, 197
Dutton, Nettie Blanche IV, 197
Dutton, Phebe IV, 812
Dutton, Phebe IV, 868
Dutton, Phebe IV, 904
Dutton, Phebe V, 49
Dutton, Phebe V, 235
Dutton, Phebe V, 236
Dutton, Phebe V, 253
Dutton, Phebe V, 294
Dutton, Phebe V, 947
Dutton, Phebe D. IV, 813
Dutton, Phebe D. IV, 856
Dutton, Philena IV, 1025
Dutton, Philena IV, 1026
Dutton, Rachel IV, 311
Dutton, Rachel A. V, 235
Dutton, Rachel Almeda V, 235
Dutton, Richard II, 510
Dutton, Robert IV, 197
Dutton, Robert IV, 311
Dutton, Robert IV, 315
Dutton, Rowland I. II, 286
Dutton, Rowland J. II, 172
Dutton, Rowland J. II, 286
Dutton, Ruthanna II, 786
Dutton, Sarah II, 286
Dutton, Sarah II, 299
Dutton, Sarah IV, 197
Dutton, Sarah IV, 251
Dutton, Sarah IV, 311
Dutton, Sarah IV, 313
Dutton, Sarah IV, 812
Dutton, Sarah IV, 813
Dutton, Sarah IV, 833
Dutton, Sarah IV, 852
Dutton, Sarah IV, 904
Dutton, Sarah J. II, 172
Dutton, Sarah J. II, 286
Dutton, Sarah L. VI, 524
Dutton, Sarah M. II, 792
Dutton, Sidney V, 235
Dutton, Sidney V, 258
Dutton, Sidney E. V, 235
Dutton, Silas V, 235
Dutton, Silus V, 49
Dutton, Spencer II, 286
Dutton, Susanna VI, 380
Dutton, Susannah IV, 311
Dutton, Susannah VI, 384
Dutton, Thomas I, 1092
Dutton, Thomas II, 172
Dutton, Thomas II, 279
Dutton, Thomas II, 286
Dutton, Thomas II, 299
Dutton, Thomas IV, 812
Dutton, Thomas IV, 868
Dutton, Thomas IV, 904
Dutton, Thomas V, 49

Dutton, Thomas V, 219
Dutton, Thomas V, 235
Dutton, Thomas V, 257
Dutton, Thomas V, 294
Dutton, Thomas, Jr. II, 216
Dutton, Thos. II, 181
Dutton, William R. II, 172
Dutton, William R. II, 286
Duty, Charlotte M. IV, 1313
Duty, Lydia Maxie VI, 242
Duuton, Anna Ellen VI, 534
Duval, Anna VI, 940
Duval, Elisha VI, 910
Duval, Elizabeth VI, 803
Duval, Jemima VI, 935
Duval, Katie VI, 384
Duval, Katie VI, 431
Duval, Katie VI, 739
Duval, Katie VI, 770
Duval, Keziah VI, 913
Duval, Lewis VI, 910
Duval, Lucy H. VI, 910
Duval, Nellie VI, 628
Duval, Peggy VI, 910
Duval, Phillip VI, 803
Duval, Samuel VI, 832
Duval, Skinner VI, 910
Duval, Skinner VI, 913
Duval, Skinner VI, 935
Duval, Skinner VI, 940
Duvall, Ann E. VI, 802
Duvall, Benjamin VI, 841
Duvall, Chas. E. III, 257
Duvall, Dashy VI, 813
Duvall, Edith Eloise III, 257
Duvall, Hessie VI, 813
Duvall, John VI, 813
Duvall, Lewis VI, 841
Duvall, Lewis VI, 910
Duvall, Lydia IV, 30
Duvall, Lydia IV, 49
Duvall, Marvin VI, 813
Duvall, Mary Ella III, 257
Duvall, Mereen VI, 813
Duvall, Millie IV, 381
Duvall, Millie IV, 388
Duvall, Nellie VI, 624
Duvall, Nellie VI, 635
Duvall, Peggy VI, 910
Duvall, Sally VI, 841
Duvall, Sally VI, 866
Duvall, Skinner VI, 866
Duvall, Skinner VI, 910
Duvall, Susannah VI, 813
Duwitt, Palina VI, 889
Duxton, Johnson VI, 907
Duxton, Nancy Huts VI, 907
Dwadehouse, William II, 443
Dwaryhous, Mary II, 356
Dwees, Elizabeth III, 66
Dwees, Ernest J. III, 66
Dwees, Ruth Florence III, 66
Dwiggin, Mary V, 488
Dwiggin, Sarah V, 488
Dwiggings, Mary I, 537
Dwiggins, Agnes I, 537
Dwiggins, Anna V, 619
Dwiggins, Arthur R. V, 619
Dwiggins, Charles I, 632
Dwiggins, Charles B. V, 619
Dwiggins, Charles Edwin V, 619
Dwiggins, Charles Wade I, 615
Dwiggins, Charles Wade, Jr. I, 615
Dwiggins, Chas. B. V, 619
Dwiggins, Chas. E. V, 619
Dwiggins, Clara Anna V, 619
Dwiggins, Clara E. V, 619
Dwiggins, Edith Lucile V, 619
Dwiggins, Emma V, 619
Dwiggins, Emma Ellena V, 619
Dwiggins, Eva Matilda V, 619
Dwiggins, Howard C. V, 619
Dwiggins, Jacqueline Rea I, 615
Dwiggins, James F. V, 619
Dwiggins, James Farr V, 619
Dwiggins, Julia Ballinger I, 615
Dwiggins, Juliette I, 615
Dwiggins, Juliette B. I, 632
Dwiggins, Lizzie V, 619
Dwiggins, Mabel H. IV, 388
Dwiggins, Mabel H. IV, 412
Dwiggins, Mary I, 537
Dwiggins, Mary V, 619
Dwiggins, Mary V, 670
Dwiggins, Moses F. V, 619
Dwiggins, Phebe V, 619
Dwiggins, Rebecca B. V, 619
Dwiggins, Robert J. V, 619
Dwiggins, Salley I, 537
Dwiggins, Sally V, 619
Dwiggins, Sarah I, 537
Dwiggins, Sarah V, 488
Dwiggins, Sarah V, 619
Dwiggins, Sarah May V, 619
Dwiggins, Zimri V, 619
Dwight, Mary III, 107
Dwight, William III, 107
Dwire, Elizabeth VI, 910
Dwire, Jack VI, 910
Dwyer, Hugh II, 443
Dwyer, Joseph J. V, 455
Dwyer, Mary VI, 384
Dwyer, Rob. II, 443
Dwyer, Sarah V, 455
Dwyer, Sarah Jane V, 455
Dyamond, Edith V, 166
Dyamond, Emma V, 166
Dyamond, Helen V, 166
Dyamond, John V, 166
Dyamond, Mary Belle V, 166
Dyar, Elizabeth I, 912
Dyar, Wd. Sarah II, 510
Dych, Esther II, 510
Dyche, Esther II, 458
Dye, Archie IV, 1156
Dye, Delmar IV, 1156
Dye, Edna IV, 1156
Dye, Eliz. III, 65
Dye, Eliz. III, 93
Dye, Eva IV, 1156
Dye, Eva L. IV, 1156
Dye, Lucy M. IV, 1156
Dye, Mandus V, 736
Dye, Solomon IV, 1361
Dyer, Alexander II, 510
Dyer, Amanda IV, 363
Dyer, Amanda IV, 388
Dyer, Bracket IV, 388
Dyer, Brackett IV, 1156
Dyer, Daniel M. I, 1151
Dyer, Elijah VI, 829
Dyer, Elizabeth I, 912
Dyer, Elizabeth I, 914
Dyer, Elizabeth II, 356
Dyer, Emma IV, 197
Dyer, Ethel IV, 1250
Dyer, George I, 912
Dyer, George H. I, 912
Dyer, James I, 537
Dyer, John II, 356
Dyer, John II, 994
Dyer, John VI, 309
Dyer, John VI, 813
Dyer, Josiah VI, 488
Dyer, Mahaly I, 912
Dyer, Margrett II, 443
Dyer, Mary I, 537
Dyer, Mary IV, 197
Dyer, Mary L. I, 537
Dyer, Mary L. I, 543
Dyer, Mathew II, 443
Dyer, Miley VI, 302
Dyer, Milly V, 49
Dyer, Milly VI, 308
Dyer, Milly VI, 309
Dyer, Milly Butterworth VI, 813
Dyer, Rachel II, 443
Dyer, Ruth VI, 629
Dyer, Ruth VI, 635
Dyer, Sarah II, 510
Dyer, Seina I, 537
Dyer, Wd. Sarah II, 510
Dyers, Elijah VI, 326
Dylwyn, John II, 506
Dylwyn, Sarah II, 501
Dylwyn, Sarah II, 506
Dymike, Tobias II, 958
Dymmock, Sarah II, 507
Dymmock, Wd. Sarah II, 562
Dymond, Edith V, 488
Dymond, Elizabeth V, 903
Dymond, Emma V, 488
Dymond, George F. V, 912
Dymond, Georgina III, 170
Dymond, Georgina III, 291
Dymond, Georgina V, 903
Dymond, Georgina V, 912
Dymond, Goerge F. III, 170
Dymond, Harriett V, 166
Dymond, Helen V, 488
Dymond, Jane III, 170
Dymond, Jane V, 912
Dymond, John V, 488
Dymond, Mary Bell V, 488
Dymond, Mary Georgian V, 903
Dymond, Robert V, 488
Dymond, Robert Lestlie V, 488
Dyre, Daniel M. I, 1151
Dysert, Mary M. V, 993
Dysert, W. N. V, 993
Dysert, Wm. M. V, 993
Dyson, Agnes Ann IV, 700
Dyson, Eleanor IV, 700
Dyson, Jemimah I, 445
Dyson, Jemimah I, 449
Dyson, Mason IV, 700
Dyson, Sarah Wilhelmina IV, 700
Dyson, William IV, 700

E???, Cynthia III, 345
E???, Florence III, 168
E???, Thomas II, 196
Each, Gideon II, 356
Each, Jane II, 356
Each, Mary I, 1092
Each, Phebe I, 1092
Each, Priscilla II, 356
Eaches, Ann VI, 488
Eaches, Ann VI, 739
Eaches, Homer II, 858
Eaches, Juliana V, 488
Eaches, Juliana V, 523
Eaches, Lydia M. II, 858
Eaches, Mary II, 510
Eaches, Mary V, 49
Eaches, Mary VI, 384
Eaches, Phebe V, 49
Eaches, Phebe V, 488
Eaches, Phebe VI, 384
Eaches, Phebe VI, 451
Eaches, Robert V, 488
Eachue, Mary II, 510
Eachus, Anna M. II, 858
Eachus, Anna Mary II, 792
Eachus, Bathsheba II, 792
Eachus, Betsy V, 488
Eachus, Clara F. II, 858
Eachus, Daniel I, 388
Eachus, David V, 488
Eachus, David F. V, 488
Eachus, Geo. W. II, 858
Eachus, George W. II, 858
Eachus, George Washington II, 792
Eachus, Homer II, 792
Eachus, Homer II, 858
Eachus, Homer, Jr. V, 903
Eachus, Jane II, 792
Eachus, Jane L. II, 858
Eachus, Jennie Thompson II, 802
Eachus, John Julian V, 488
Eachus, Julia Ann V, 110
Eachus, Juliana V, 488
Eachus, Lydia M. II, 858
Eachus, Mabel II, 858
Eachus, Mary V, 49
Eachus, Mary V, 90
Eachus, Mary VI, 384
Eachus, Mary E. II, 792
Eachus, Mary E. II, 858
Eachus, Phebe V, 488
Eachus, Phebe VI, 384
Eachus, Priscila V, 110
Eachus, Robert V, 488
Eachus, Virgil II, 792
Eachus, Virgil T. II, 858
Eachus, Virgil Trego II, 792
Eachus, Wd. Lydia M. II, 792
Eadens, Alexander VI, 910
Eadens, Benjamin VI, 910
Eadens, Caty Page VI, 910
Eadens, Charlotte Arthur VI, 910
Eadens, Delilah VI, 1003
Eadens, Elisha VI, 910
Eadens, Jesse VI, 910
Eadens, Jesse VI, 946
Eadens, Jesse VI, 1003
Eadens, Joel VI, 910
Eadens, Sally VI, 910
Eadens, Sophia VI, 910
Eades, Charles VI, 910
Eades, Eades, Chas. VI, 910
Eades, Edward VI, 993
Eades, Elizabeth VI, 910
Eades, Fanny Gallaway VI, 910
Eades, Joseph VI, 910
Eades, Mary VI, 993
Eades, Sarah VI, 910
Eades, William VI, 875
Eads, Andrew I, 985
Eads, Edward VI, 979
Eads, Elizabeth VI, 910
Eads, Elizabeth VI, 1008
Eads, Jenny VI, 822
Eads, Jesse VI, 822
Eads, Joseph VI, 910
Eads, Lindsey I, 985
Eads, Rachel VI, 942
Eads, Robert VI, 1008
Eads, Sarah VI, 979
Eads, Thomas I, 962
Eads, Wm. V, 993
Eagan, Lena Clark VI, 739
Eager, Sarah I, 137
Eager, Sarah I, 138
Eagg, George V, 993
Eagg, Lizzie V, 993
Eaghtin, Clarence C. IV, 700
Eagie, Jonathan V, 993
Eagin, Mary II, 1049
Eagle, Elizabeth II, 858
Eagle, Isaac V, 98
Eagle, Sarah V, 98
Eagler, James V, 993
Eagler, Louisa V, 993
Eaglesfield, Ann II, 462
Eaglesfield, Ann II, 510
Eaglesfield, Benjamin II, 443
Eaglesfield, George II, 443
Eaglesfield, William II, 443
Eagletin, Clarence C. IV, 700
Eagleton, Clarence IV, 966
Eagleton, Margaret IV, 966
Eagy, Alice M. V, 993
Eagy, Dora V, 993
Eagy, Etta V, 993
Eagy, George V, 993
Eagy, Gertie V, 993
Eagy, Jonathan V, 993
Eagy, Lizzie V, 993
Eagy, Oliver V, 993
Eagy, Sarah V, 993
Eakey, Sarah IV, 30
Eakey, Sarah IV, 46
Eakin, Aaron S. IV, 197
Eakin, Aaron S. IV, 280
Eakin, Anna M. III, 221
Eakin, Anna M. III, 223
Eakin, Annie B. IV, 197
Eakin, Elias H. IV, 197
Eakin, Eva B. IV, 197
Eakin, Eva B. IV, 280
Eakin, Nathan VI, 910
Eakin, Stephen VI, 910
Eakin, Susanna Preston VI, 910
Eakins, Catharine V, 736
Ealey, Christian VI, 45
Ealey, William VI, 47
Ealy, Mary VI, 910
Ealy, William VI, 910
Eames, Asa III, 108
Eames, Edward III, 107
Eames, Francis L. III, 108
Eames, Frank L. III, 371
Eames, Harriet III, 108
Eames, Sarah III, 108
Eames, Sarah III, 371
Eanes, Henry Walthal VI, 814
Eanes, Mary VI, 814
Eanes, William VI, 810
Eans, Elizabeth VI, 800
Eans, John VI, 800
Earhart, Bessie V, 736
Earhart, Catharine Elizabeth V, 736
Earhart, Eph. V, 736
Earhart, Lester V, 736
Earhart, Roy V, 736
Earidges, John II, 356
Earl, Aaron IV, 1156
Earl, Aaron IV, 1157
Earl, Aaron IV, 1160
Earl, Abigail II, 286
Earl, Adaline IV, 1156
Earl, Alvin IV, 1157
Earl, Alvira IV, 1157
Earl, Ann Craig II, 681
Earl, Anna IV, 1157
Earl, Anna IV, 1159
Earl, Anna Craig II, 511
Earl, Anna Maria III, 108
Earl, Anne IV, 1156
Earl, Anne Craig II, 511
Earl, Benj. IV, 1156
Earl, Benjamin IV, 1156
Earl, Benjamin IV, 1157
Earl, Carrie A. V, 329
Earl, Cassin V, 235
Earl, Charlotte II, 286
Earl, Clara IV, 1157
Earl, Clara Lillian Alberta IV, 1157
Earl, Clayton IV, 1157
Earl, Clayton Laselle IV, 1157
Earl, Dorcas III, 108
Earl, Dorcas III, 236
Earl, Dorcas IV, 1153
Earl, Dorcas IV, 1156
Earl, Dorcas IV, 1157
Earl, Edith IV, 1250
Earl, Elisabeth I, 46
Earl, Elisabeth I, 138
Earl, Elizabeth S. III, 108
Earl, Elma J. IV, 700
Earl, Elma Jessie IV, 700
Earl, Elvira IV, 1157
Earl, Esther II, 179
Earl, Esther II, 216
Earl, Frances II, 216
Earl, Francis II, 216
Earl, Franklin II, 286
Earl, Franklin IV, 1156
Earl, Franklin IV, 1157
Earl, George Delano IV, 1156
Earl, Gertrude II, 172
Earl, Gilbethorp II, 216
Earl, Hannah II, 511
Earl, Hannah II, 792
Earl, Hannah II, 858
Earl, Hannah IV, 1156
Earl, Hannah IV, 1157
Earl, Hannah IV, 1160
Earl, Hannah IV, 1180
Earl, Hannah M. IV, 700
Earl, Henrietta IV, 1156
Earl, Henrietta IV, 1157
Earl, Henry II, 858
Earl, Henry IV, 1157
Earl, Hester II, 216
Earl, John I, 46
Earl, John I, 138
Earl, John II, 216
Earl, John II, 510
Earl, John II, 511
Earl, John II, 681
Earl, John III, 108
Earl, John III, 236
Earl, Jonathan III, 108
Earl, Joseph II, 172
Earl, Joseph B. II, 172
Earl, Leno Orlando IV, 1156
Earl, Lewis IV, 1157
Earl, Lillie IV, 700
Earl, Louisa IV, 1156
Earl, Louisa H. IV, 1156
Earl, Martha II, 216
Earl, Martha II, 258
Earl, Mary II, 216
Earl, Mary II, 227
Earl, Mary II, 511
Earl, Mary D. II, 286
Earl, Mary Hannah IV, 700
Earl, Mary M. III, 69
Earl, Mary M. III, 108
Earl, Mercy IV, 1361
Earl, Mrs. ??? IV, 1250
Earl, Nancy Jane IV, 1157
Earl, Nathaniel IV, 1156
Earl, Nathaniel IV, 1157
Earl, Nettie V, 455
Earl, Oliver III, 108
Earl, Phebe II, 511
Earl, Phebe III, 108
Earl, Phebe IV, 1156
Earl, Pliny III, 108
Earl, Rebecca II, 216
Earl, Rebecca II, 286
Earl, Rebecca II, 510
Earl, Rebecca II, 681
Earl, Rebecca II, 703
Earl, Rebecca N. II, 511
Earl, Rebecca N. II, 737
Earl, Rev. Marmaduke III, 405
Earl, Richard II, 286
Earl, Richard W. II, 172
Earl, Richard W. II, 286
Earl, Robert III, 108
Earl, Sarah I, 138
Earl, Sarah II, 216
Earl, Sarah II, 286
Earl, Sarah III, 108
Earl, Sarah III, 236
Earl, Sarah IV, 1156
Earl, Sarah B. II, 172
Earl, Sary I, 138
Earl, Sidney V. IV, 700
Earl, Susan Emily IV, 700
Earl, Tantham II, 216
Earl, Tantham II, 227
Earl, Taunton II, 286
Earl, Theodosia II, 172
Earl, Theodosia II, 286
Earl, Thomas II, 510
Earl, Thomas II, 511
Earl, Thomas II, 681
Earl, Thomas III, 69
Earl, Thomas, Jr. II, 216
Earl, Tucker II, 511
Earl, William II, 216
Earl, William II, 258
Earl, William II, 709
Earl, William IV, 1156
Earl, William Gidley IV, 1156

, Wm. II, 258
, Zeno IV, 1157
e, ??? III, 409
e, ??? III, 418
e, Abigail II, 286
e, Alma IV, 1328
e, Anna Craig II, 511
e, Anna Maria III, 108
e, Anne Craig II, 511
e, Caroline II, 792
e, Caroline II, 858
e, Caroline H. III, 397
e, Carroll B. IV, 1328
e, Cassin V, 235
e, Clarence V, 993
e, Clarence B. V, 993
e, Elsina V, 993
e, Ethel E. V, 993
e, Eugene D. V, 993
e, Eugene G. V, 993
e, George H. II, 737
e, George H. II, 858
e, George Hussey II, 356
e, George Hussey II, 737
e, George Hussey II, 858
e, Granvil W. V, 993
e, Granville W. V, 993
e, Hannah II, 511
e, Hannah II, 737
e, Hannah II, 792
e, Hannah II, 858
e, Harvey V, 993
e, Hattie C. V, 993
e, Helen III, 409
e, Helen Hicks III, 397
e, Henry II, 792
e, Henry II, 858
e, Howard D. V, 993
e, Ida V, 235
e, James H. V, 993
e, John II, 510
e, John II, 511
e, John D. III, 397
e, John M. II, 858
e, Lenard V, 993
e, Leonard F. V, 993
e, Lillie IV, 700
e, Mable A. IV, 1206
e, Mable A. IV, 1218
e, Margaret V, 993
e, Marmaduke III, 405
e, Martha B. II, 858
e, Mary II, 356
e, Mary II, 511
e, Mary II, 737
e, Mary II, 792
e, Mary II, 858
e, Mary D. II, 286
e, Myrtia V, 993
e, Myrtle A. V, 993
e, Phebe II, 511
e, Phebe II, 737
e, Phebe II, 858
e, Phebe II, 867
e, Phebe III, 108
e, Phebe III, 133
e, Pliny III, 108
e, Ray V, 235
e, Rebecca II, 216
e, Rebecca II, 510
e, Rebecca N. II, 511
e, Rebecca N. II, 737
e, Rev. Marmaduke III, 400
e, Rev. Marmaduke III, 402
e, Richard II, 286
e, Robert III, 108
e, Sarah II, 286
e, Sarah II, 356
e, Sarah H. II, 858
e, Thomas II, 356
e, Thomas II, 510
e, Thomas II, 511
e, Thomas II, 737
e, Thomas II, 792
e, Thos. II, 858
e, Tucker II, 511
ey, Abner VI, 813
ey, Ann VI, 813
ey, Cora A. V, 670
ey, Edmund J. VI, 813
ey, Elizabeth VI, 796
ey, Ferdinand VI, 910
ey, Frances VI, 892
ey, Frances E. VI, 935
ey, Henry VI, 813
ey, Joshua VI, 813
ey, Margaret VI, 813
ey, Martha Jones VI, 949
ey, Mary VI, 910
ey, Mary E. VI, 813
ey, Ned VI, 813
Earley, Patsey VI, 813
Earley, Patty Jones VI, 813
Earley, Polly VI, 935
Earll, Sarah I, 138
Earll, Sarah I, 173
Earls, Elisabeth I, 138
Early, Abner VI, 796
Early, Abner VI, 815
Early, Abner VI, 910
Early, Abner VI, 971
Early, Albert V, 559
Early, Alfred V, 619
Early, Ann VI, 919
Early, Ann Dennis VI, 910
Early, Anne V, 619
Early, Artie J. IV, 1157
Early, Blanche IV, 700
Early, Catharine VI, 949
Early, Charles IV, 700
Early, Charlotte IV, 1157
Early, Charlotte VI, 910
Early, Charlotte A. VI, 958
Early, Clementine Louisa VI, 1013
Early, Doshey VI, 910
Early, Elizabeth V, 619
Early, Elizabeth VI, 910
Early, Elizabeth VI, 1000
Early, Elizabeth VI, 1003
Early, Ferdinand VI, 910
Early, Grace IV, 700
Early, Irena V, 619
Early, Jabez VI, 910
Early, Jacob VI, 910
Early, Jacob VI, 946
Early, James VI, 910
Early, James A. VI, 987
Early, Jenny VI, 965
Early, Jeremiah VI, 910
Early, Jeremiah VI, 965
Early, Jno. VI, 953
Early, Jobal VI, 892
Early, Joel VI, 895
Early, Joel VI, 919
Early, Joel VI, 935
Early, Joel VI, 1003
Early, Joel VI, 1013
Early, John IV, 1157
Early, John VI, 796
Early, John VI, 926
Early, John F. V, 619
Early, John W. VI, 945
Early, Joshua VI, 813
Early, Joshua VI, 910
Early, Joshua VI, 1000
Early, Lafayette V, 619
Early, Laura P. I, 1151
Early, Lizzie S. IV, 1037
Early, Louie V, 559
Early, Lucy S. VI, 952
Early, Marietta V, 619
Early, Martha VI, 892
Early, Martha J. VI, 919
Early, Mary IV, 1157
Early, Mary VI, 827
Early, Mary VI, 910
Early, Mary A. V, 619
Early, Mary L. F. VI, 910
Early, Mary M. V, 619
Early, Matilda VI, 796
Early, Matilda VI, 872
Early, Melceinia V, 619
Early, Michael I, 1151
Early, Mildred Marie V, 559
Early, Moses P. V, 619
Early, Mrs. ??? VI, 919
Early, Noradim D. VI, 910
Early, Orlando M. V, 619
Early, Patsey VI, 813
Early, Patsy VI, 980
Early, Patsy R. VI, 945
Early, Peletiah Jones VI, 910
Early, Permelia M. VI, 910
Early, Polley VI, 910
Early, Rosa V, 619
Early, Rosa F. V, 619
Early, Sally VI, 870
Early, Sally VI, 1020
Early, Sarah VI, 847
Early, Sarah B. VI, 895
Early, Sarah V. V, 619
Early, Silas D. VI, 988
Early, Sophia VI, 910
Early, Susan V, 619
Early, Susan J. V, 619
Early, Susan O. V, 619
Early, Susanna VI, 910
Early, Thomas VI, 910
Early, Thomas VI, 945
Early, Thomas VI, 1020
Early, Tubal VI, 910
Early, W. VI, 990
Early, William VI, 797
Early, William VI, 824
Early, William VI, 910
Early, William B. VI, 910
Early., Eliza J. VI, 946
Earnest, Ada IV, 1037
Earnest, Pearl IV, 1037
Earnshaw, Ann IV, 470
Earnshaw, Ann IV, 487
Earnshaw, Cornelia L. III, 108
Earnshaw, Elizabeth II, 699
Earnshaw, Geo. IV, 470
Earnshaw, Geo. IV, 487
Earnshaw, Geo. IV, 492
Earnshaw, George IV, 470
Earnshaw, George IV, 1206
Earnshaw, George, Jr. IV, 470
Earnshaw, George, Jr. IV, 1157
Earnshaw, George, Sr. IV, 470
Earnshaw, George, Sr. IV, 1157
Earnshaw, Hannah IV, 470
Earnshaw, Jos. W. III, 108
Earnshaw, Lydia III, 108
Earnshaw, Mary IV, 470
Earnshaw, Mary IV, 487
Earnshaw, Sarah IV, 470
Earnshaw, Sarah IV, 492
Earnshaw, Sarah IV, 1157
Earnshaw, Sarah IV, 1206
Earp, Theresa III, 108
Earsh, John IV, 388
Easborn, Hulda II, 1072
Easborn, Mariah II, 1072
Easborn, Robert R. II, 1072
Easborn, Samuel II, 1072
Easborn, Wm. E. II, 1072
Easburn, Sarah II, 1050
Easely, Daniel IV, 522
Easely, Edith IV, 522
Easely, Edith VI, 309
Easely, Stephen IV, 522
Eashus, Betsy V, 487
Eashus, Betsy V, 488
Easlack, Marmaduke V, 329
Easlack, Ruth V, 302
Easlack, Ruth V, 311
Easley, Daniel IV, 321
Easley, Daniel IV, 327
Easley, Edith IV, 321
Easley, Edith IV, 327
Easley, Edith VI, 309
Easley, Isaac IV, 327
Easley, Isaac IV, 470
Easley, John IV, 327
Easley, Mary Ann IV, 321
Easley, Mary Ann IV, 327
Easley, Richard IV, 197
Easley, Richard IV, 327
Easley, Ruth IV, 326
Easley, Ruth IV, 327
Easley, Sarah IV, 321
Easley, Sarah IV, 327
Easley, Stephen IV, 327
Easly, Barclay Ballard VI, 309
Easly, Daniel IV, 522
Easly, Daniel VI, 309
Easly, Daniel, Jr. IV, 522
Easly, Dorothy II, 216
Easly, Dorothy II, 240
Easly, Edith IV, 522
Easly, Edith VI, 309
Easly, Isaac IV, 522
Easly, Isaac VI, 309
Easly, Jane B. IV, 522
Easly, Jane D. IV, 522
Easly, John IV, 522
Easly, John IV, 537
Easly, John VI, 309
Easly, Marian VI, 309
Easly, Mary Ann VI, 309
Easly, Maryann VI, 309
Easly, Nancy IV, 522
Easly, Nancy IV, 537
Easly, Phebe IV, 522
Easly, Phebe IV, 542
Easly, Rachel IV, 522
Easly, Rachel VI, 309
Easly, Rhoda IV, 522
Easly, Richard IV, 522
Easly, Richard VI, 309
Easly, Robert Hanna VI, 309
Easly, Ruth VI, 309
Easly, Sarah VI, 309
Easly, Sarah Ann IV, 522
Easly, Stephen IV, 522
Easly, Stephen VI, 309
Eason, Anna Lee I, 46
Eason, Elisabeth I, 46
Eason, Esther E. I, 30
Eason, Flotilla I, 30
Eason, Horace I, 8
Eason, Horace I, 27
Eason, Lydia I, 8
Eason, Lydia I, 46
Eason, Lydia M. I, 8
Eason, Lydia M. I, 27
Eason, Mary Louise I, 8
Eason, Mildred Elisabeth I, 8
Eason, Reuben I, 30
Eason, William Thomas I, 8
Eason, William Thomas I, 46
East, Calphurnia VI, 864
East, Elizabeth A. VI, 860
East, Ezekiel VI, 824
East, Grief E. VI, 839
East, Joseph VI, 813
East, Mary Hundley VI, 813
East, Mildred VI, 813
East, Polly Bell VI, 813
East, Rachel I, 1009
East, Sally VI, 824
East, Shadrack VI, 813
East, Thomas VI, 813
East, Thomas VI, 824
East, William I, 1151
Eastborn, David II, 1072
Eastbourn, Beulah II, 994
Eastbourn, Ellwood II, 994
Eastbourn, Hannah, Jr. II, 994
Eastbourn, Huldah II, 994
Eastbourn, John II, 511
Eastbourn, John II, 567
Eastbourn, Jonathan II, 994
Eastbourn, Josiah II, 994
Eastbourn, Kezia II, 511
Eastbourn, Kirkbride II, 1072
Eastbourn, Lewis II, 994
Eastbourn, Margaret II, 567
Eastbourn, Samuel, Jr. II, 994
Eastbourn, Sarah II, 511
Eastbourn, Wm. II, 994
Eastbourne, George II, 511
Eastburn, Aaron II, 955
Eastburn, Aaron II, 959
Eastburn, Aaron II, 965
Eastburn, Aaron II, 1047
Eastburn, Aaron II, 1050
Eastburn, Agnes II, 511
Eastburn, Agness II, 511
Eastburn, Albert II, 1065
Eastburn, Amanda E. II, 1072
Eastburn, Amanda E. II, 1074
Eastburn, Amelia II, 1065
Eastburn, Amelia II, 1072
Eastburn, Amos II, 858
Eastburn, Amos II, 876
Eastburn, Ann II, 803
Eastburn, Ann II, 958
Eastburn, Ann II, 972
Eastburn, Ann II, 1050
Eastburn, Anna II, 959
Eastburn, Anna II, 1063
Eastburn, Anna II, 1072
Eastburn, Anna II, 1077
Eastburn, Anna P. II, 1072
Eastburn, Asenath II, 1053
Eastburn, Asenath P. II, 1050
Eastburn, Asenith II, 959
Eastburn, Benjamin II, 356
Eastburn, Benjamin II, 511
Eastburn, Benjamin II, 994
Eastburn, Beulah II, 994
Eastburn, Beulah II, 1050
Eastburn, Beulah II, 1072
Eastburn, Caroline II, 1072
Eastburn, Carrie II, 858
Eastburn, Carrie II, 867
Eastburn, Channing II, 703
Eastburn, Clara M. II, 858
Eastburn, Cyrus II, 959
Eastburn, Cyrus II, 1053
Eastburn, David II, 994
Eastburn, David II, 1050
Eastburn, David II, 1072
Eastburn, Edward II, 1072
Eastburn, Edward Ivins II, 858
Eastburn, Elisabeth II, 511
Eastburn, Elizabeth II, 511
Eastburn, Elizabeth II, 737
Eastburn, Elizabeth II, 959
Eastburn, Elizabeth II, 994
Eastburn, Elizabeth II, 1050
Eastburn, Elizabeth II, 1063
Eastburn, Elizabeth C. II, 959
Eastburn, Elizabeth K. II, 1072
Eastburn, Elizabeth M. II, 948
Eastburn, Elizabeth M. II, 949
Eastburn, Elizabeth M. II, 1050
Eastburn, Ellen II, 703
Eastburn, Ellwood II, 994
Eastburn, Elwood II, 1050
Eastburn, Elwood S. II, 994
Eastburn, Elwood S. II, 1072
Eastburn, Esther II, 356
Eastburn, Frances R. VI, 739
Eastburn, Franklin II, 954
Eastburn, Franklin II, 959
Eastburn, Franklin II, 1050
Eastburn, George II, 511
Eastburn, Grace II, 959
Eastburn, Grace II, 1050
Eastburn, Hannah II, 216
Eastburn, Hannah II, 511
Eastburn, Hannah II, 992
Eastburn, Hannah II, 994
Eastburn, Hannah II, 1050
Eastburn, Hannah II, 1072
Eastburn, Hannah II, 1074
Eastburn, Hannah III, 293
Eastburn, Hannah VI, 615
Eastburn, Hannah VI, 632
Eastburn, Hannah VI, 635
Eastburn, Hannah VI, 638
Eastburn, Hannah H. II, 959
Eastburn, Hannah H. II, 1050
Eastburn, Hannah K. II, 1072
Eastburn, Hannah, Jr. II, 994
Eastburn, Henry K. II, 858
Eastburn, Henry K. II, 867
Eastburn, Herbert M. II, 959
Eastburn, Herbert M. II, 1050
Eastburn, Howard P. II, 1050
Eastburn, Howard Percy II, 959
Eastburn, Hulda II, 1072
Eastburn, Huldah II, 994
Eastburn, Huldah II, 1040
Eastburn, Huldah II, 1050
Eastburn, Huldah II, 1072
Eastburn, Huldy II, 1072
Eastburn, Isaac S. II, 959
Eastburn, Isaac S. II, 1050
Eastburn, Isaac S. II, 1051
Eastburn, Isabella II, 1072
Eastburn, J. Albert II, 959
Eastburn, Jacob II, 858
Eastburn, Jacob II, 1072
Eastburn, Jacob II, 1077
Eastburn, John II, 511
Eastburn, John E. II, 858
Eastburn, John Palmer II, 1072
Eastburn, Jonathan II, 858
Eastburn, Jonathan II, 876
Eastburn, Jonathan II, 959
Eastburn, Jonathan II, 992
Eastburn, Jonathan II, 994
Eastburn, Jonathan II, 1049
Eastburn, Jonathan II, 1050
Eastburn, Jonathan II, 1051
Eastburn, Joseph II, 959
Eastburn, Joseph II, 994
Eastburn, Joseph II, 1050
Eastburn, Joseph II, 1063
Eastburn, Joseph M. II, 959
Eastburn, Joseph M. II, 1050
Eastburn, Josiah II, 994
Eastburn, Josiah II, 1065
Eastburn, Josiah II, 1072
Eastburn, Kezia II, 511
Eastburn, Kezia II, 703
Eastburn, Kezia II, 737
Eastburn, Kirkbride II, 994
Eastburn, Kirkbride II, 1050
Eastburn, Kirkbride II, 1072
Eastburn, Laura II, 959
Eastburn, Laura II, 1055
Eastburn, Lewis II, 994
Eastburn, Lewis II, 1072
Eastburn, Lewis Elwood II, 1050
Eastburn, Lillian II, 959
Eastburn, Lillian II, 1050
Eastburn, Lillian II, 1054
Eastburn, Lillian E. II, 959
Eastburn, Lillian H. II, 1050
Eastburn, Lillian H. II, 1053
Eastburn, Lindley H. II, 959
Eastburn, Lindley H. II, 1050
Eastburn, Macre II, 994
Eastburn, Macre II, 1050
Eastburn, Macrie II, 1072
Eastburn, Mahlon II, 994
Eastburn, Margaret II, 703
Eastburn, Maria Ann II, 994
Eastburn, Maria Ann II, 1050
Eastburn, Maria Ann II, 1072
Eastburn, Maria Ann II, 1075
Eastburn, Mariah II, 1072
Eastburn, Marianna II, 959
Eastburn, Marianna II, 1050
Eastburn, Marianna II, 1051
Eastburn, Mary II, 511
Eastburn, Mary II, 559
Eastburn, Mary II, 695

Eastburn, Mary II, 959
Eastburn, Mary II, 965
Eastburn, Mary II, 1045
Eastburn, Mary II, 1047
Eastburn, Mary II, 1050
Eastburn, Mary B. II, 959
Eastburn, Mary B. II, 1050
Eastburn, Mary C. II, 1050
Eastburn, Mary C. II, 1056
Eastburn, Mary C. II, 1087
Eastburn, Mary C. II, 1089
Eastburn, Mary E. II, 955
Eastburn, Mary Elizabeth II, 954
Eastburn, Mercy II, 955
Eastburn, Mercy II, 959
Eastburn, Mercy II, 977
Eastburn, Mercy II, 994
Eastburn, Miriam II, 858
Eastburn, Miriam I. II, 858
Eastburn, Miriam I. II, 867
Eastburn, Moses II, 994
Eastburn, Moses II, 1008
Eastburn, Rachel II, 216
Eastburn, Rachel II, 994
Eastburn, Rachel II, 1008
Eastburn, Rebecca VI, 616
Eastburn, Rebecca VI, 635
Eastburn, Rebecca VI, 671
Eastburn, Rebecca VI, 672
Eastburn, Robert II, 356
Eastburn, Robert II, 994
Eastburn, Robert II, 1008
Eastburn, Robert II, 1050
Eastburn, Robert II, 1072
Eastburn, Robert II, 1077
Eastburn, Robert K. II, 858
Eastburn, Robert K. II, 867
Eastburn, Robert K. II, 1072
Eastburn, Robert R. II, 1072
Eastburn, Robert, Jr. II, 511
Eastburn, Ruth II, 994
Eastburn, Ruth II, 1050
Eastburn, Ruth A. III, 215
Eastburn, Samuel II, 992
Eastburn, Samuel II, 994
Eastburn, Samuel II, 1049
Eastburn, Samuel II, 1050
Eastburn, Samuel II, 1065
Eastburn, Samuel II, 1072
Eastburn, Samuel II, 1074
Eastburn, Samuel A. II, 959
Eastburn, Samuel Arthur II, 1050
Eastburn, Samuel C. II, 959
Eastburn, Samuel C. II, 1050
Eastburn, Samuel, Jr. II, 994
Eastburn, Samuel, Jr. II, 1040
Eastburn, Samuel, Jr. II, 1072
Eastburn, Sarah II, 216
Eastburn, Sarah II, 356
Eastburn, Sarah II, 511
Eastburn, Sarah II, 665
Eastburn, Sarah II, 959
Eastburn, Sarah II, 965
Eastburn, Sarah II, 992
Eastburn, Sarah II, 994
Eastburn, Sarah II, 1047
Eastburn, Sarah II, 1050
Eastburn, Sarah II, 1077
Eastburn, Sarah C. II, 954
Eastburn, Sarah C. II, 1050
Eastburn, Sarah Cadwallader II, 1044
Eastburn, Sarah Cadwallader II, 1050
Eastburn, Sarah M. II, 858
Eastburn, Sarah M. II, 876
Eastburn, Sarah P. VI, 635
Eastburn, Sarah S. II, 147
Eastburn, Sarah S. II, 148
Eastburn, Sarah S. II, 157
Eastburn, Sarah T. II, 1072
Eastburn, Sarah T. II, 1077
Eastburn, Sidney II, 858
Eastburn, Sidney II, 876
Eastburn, Sidney II, 1050
Eastburn, Sidney II, 1051
Eastburn, Sidney W. II, 959
Eastburn, Sidney W. II, 1050
Eastburn, Sydney II, 959
Eastburn, Thomas II, 959
Eastburn, Thomas II, 1050
Eastburn, Thomas II, 1065
Eastburn, Thomas II, 1072
Eastburn, Thomas K. II, 1072
Eastburn, Wd. Esther II, 511
Eastburn, William E. II, 1065
Eastburn, Wm. II, 994
Eastburn, Wm. E. II, 1050
Eastburn, Wm. E. II, 1072
Eastburne, Agnes II, 511
Eastburne, Elisabeth II, 486
Eastburne, Elisabeth II, 511
Eastburne, Kezia II, 703
Eastburnn, Edward II, 1072
Eastburnn, Elwood S. II, 1072
Eastburnn, Huldy II, 1072
Eastburnn, Lewis II, 1072
Eastburnn, Maria Ann II, 1072
Eastburnn, Robert K. II, 1072
Eastburnn, Samuel II, 1072
Eastep, Molly VI, 885
Eastept, Ruth VI, 921
Easter, Amy V, 455
Easter, Ann V, 299
Easter, Ann V, 302
Easter, Anna III, 108
Easter, Anna III, 153
Easter, Anne III, 108
Easter, Blanch V, 455
Easter, Edward V, 455
Easter, Hamilton III, 108
Easter, Hamilton III, 153
Easter, Ida V, 235
Easter, Ida V, 258
Easter, John III, 108
Easter, John V, 235
Easter, John C. V, 235
Easter, John W. V, 235
Easter, Kittie V, 235
Easter, Lydia III, 108
Easter, Lydia VI, 813
Easter, Lydia A. V, 235
Easter, Lydia R. III, 108
Easter, Lydia R. III, 118
Easter, Mabel IV, 880
Easter, Marion A. V, 235
Easter, Mathew VI, 807
Easter, Mathew VI, 851
Easter, Rachel V, 455
Easter, Rosetta V, 235
Easter, Susan VI, 813
Easter, Thomas VI, 813
Easter, Viola B. V, 235
Easter, Wm. V, 455
Easter, Wm. W. VI, 813
Easterling, Ann I, 1059
Easterling, Ann V, 166
Easterling, Ann V, 212
Easterling, Anna M. IV, 948
Easterling, Anna M. IV, 953
Easterling, Caleb V, 166
Easterling, Caleb V, 171
Easterling, Eleanor V, 212
Easterling, Ellanor V, 166
Easterling, Ellanor V, 188
Easterling, Enoch V, 166
Easterling, Henry V, 212
Easterling, Horace V. IV, 948
Easterling, Horace V. IV, 953
Easterling, Martha V, 166
Easterling, Martha V, 171
Easterling, Mary I, 1057
Easterling, Mary V, 166
Easterling, Mary V, 171
Easterling, Thomas V, 166
Easterly, George I, 1151
Easterly, Martha I, 1151
Eastin, Charles VI, 309
Eastlack, Esther C. II, 737
Eastlack, George II, 737
Eastlack, Hezekiah II, 216
Eastlack, Hezekiah II, 232
Eastlack, Hezekiah II, 737
Eastlack, Israel II, 511
Eastlack, Israel II, 737
Eastlack, Israel II, 858
Eastlack, Israel II, 866
Eastlack, Louisa II, 858
Eastlack, Louisa G. II, 737
Eastlack, Louisa G. II, 742
Eastlack, Margaret II, 216
Eastlack, Margaret II, 232
Eastlack, Margaret II, 737
Eastlack, Marmaduke V, 235
Eastlack, Marmaduke V, 329
Eastlack, Marmaduke V, 445
Eastlack, Restore II, 216
Eastlack, Restore II, 232
Eastlack, Ruth V, 235
Eastlack, Sarah II, 216
Eastlack, Sarah II, 232
Eastlack, Thomas II, 172
Eastland, Ann II, 67
Eastlock, Ruth V, 49
Eastlock, Ruth V, 96
Eastlock, Ruth V, 285
Eastman, Benj. F. IV, 700
Eastman, Benjamin Franklin IV, 621
Eastman, Benjamin Franklin IV, 700
Eastman, Beulah III, 66
Eastman, Beulah III, 108
Eastman, Calista V, 49
Eastman, Caroline V. III, 451
Eastman, Carrie III, 108
Eastman, Charles Edwin IV, 700
Eastman, Chas. Edwin IV, 700
Eastman, Chas. F. III, 327
Eastman, David V, 235
Eastman, Ethel III, 327
Eastman, Ethel P. III, 108
Eastman, Ethel Wesley III, 108
Eastman, Geo. W. III, 482
Eastman, Gerard Lester III, 482
Eastman, Gerard Lester III, 490
Eastman, Harriett IV, 700
Eastman, Heneretta IV, 904
Eastman, Heneretta IV, 917
Eastman, Henrietta IV, 700
Eastman, Howard P. III, 108
Eastman, James V, 235
Eastman, James E. III, 108
Eastman, Jennie D. III, 482
Eastman, Julea IV, 700
Eastman, Julia F. IV, 906
Eastman, Julia Francis IV, 700
Eastman, Juoia Frances IV, 700
Eastman, Lavisa IV, 621
Eastman, Louie V, 993
Eastman, Lovica IV, 700
Eastman, Lovis IV, 700
Eastman, Lovisa IV, 621
Eastman, Lovisa IV, 700
Eastman, Lovisa IV, 906
Eastman, Mary III, 104
Eastman, Mary III, 108
Eastman, Mary IV, 700
Eastman, Mary V, 993
Eastman, Mrs. Mary V, 993
Eastman, Pascal IV, 700
Eastman, Pascal Morel IV, 700
Eastman, Pascal Morrell IV, 700
Eastman, Percival III, 451
Eastman, Rachel W. III, 327
Eastman, Richard IV, 700
Eastman, Richard IV, 906
Eastman, Richard V, 993
Eastman, Robert F. III, 327
Eastman, Robt. Felt. III, 108
Eastman, Roslyn III, 482
Eastman, Sarah III, 108
Eastman, Susanna V, 235
Eastman, Susannah V, 235
Eastman, Violet A. III, 482
Eastman, Violet A. III, 490
Eastman, Wesley III, 66
Easton, Charles VI, 242
Easton, Elizabeth VI, 242
Easton, Ella IV, 197
Easton, Isabell IV, 1277
Easton, Melville IV, 1277
Easton, Patience II, 356
Easton, Redwood IV, 30
Easton, Sara III, 204
Easton, Sarah E. V, 49
Eastwick, Andrew M. II, 858
Eastwick, Andrew M. II, 894
Eastwick, Andrew M., Jr. II, 858
Eastwick, Andrew M., Jr. II, 894
Eastwick, Lydia Ann II, 858
Eastwick, Lydia Ann II, 894
Eastwick, Martha II, 858
Eastwick, Martha G. II, 894
Eaton, Ann II, 67
Eaton, Ann II, 98
Eaton, Ann II, 485
Eaton, Anne II, 511
Eaton, Benjamin II, 67
Eaton, Benjamin II, 98
Eaton, Deborah IV, 325
Eaton, Deborah IV, 327
Eaton, Helen III, 409
Eaton, Helen III, 410
Eaton, Isabella IV, 1277
Eaton, James V, 329
Eaton, Jane II, 511
Eaton, Jane II, 517
Eaton, John A. IV, 1277
Eaton, John H. IV, 1277
Eaton, John W. III, 409
Eaton, John W. III, 410
Eaton, Lydia IV, 327
Eaton, Lydia IV, 328
Eaton, Mary VI, 413
Eaton, Mary A. III, 409
Eaton, Mary A. III, 410
Eaton, Melville IV, 1277
Eaton, Olive IV, 868
Eaton, Rachel IV, 576
Eaton, Rachel VI, 384
Eaton, Samuel IV, 1277
Eave, Ann II, 511
Eavens, Sarah I, 48
Eavens, Sarah I, 50
Eavenson, Alban T. II, 840
Eavenson, Alban T. II, 858
Eavenson, Alban T. II, 916
Eavenson, Alban T. II, 918
Eavenson, Alben T. II, 858
Eavenson, Alben T. II, 916
Eavenson, Alben Taylor II, 792
Eavenson, Albert Taylor II, 792
Eavenson, Emily II, 840
Eavenson, Emily II, 858
Eavenson, Emily II, 916
Eavenson, Hannah Tomlinson II, 792
Eavenson, Howard N. II, 858
Eavenson, Jones II, 858
Eavenson, Jones II, 916
Eavenson, Lewis L. II, 858
Eavenson, Lewis L. II, 918
Eavenson, Lewis Lincoln II, 792
Eavenson, Mary A. II, 858
Eavenson, Mary A. II, 916
Eavenson, Mary Ann II, 818
Eavenson, Phebe M. II, 858
Eavenson, Rachel T. II, 858
Eavenson, Rachel T. II, 918
Eavenson, Rachel Tomlinson II, 792
Eavenson, Sarah T. II, 858
Eavenson, Sarah T. II, 916
Eavenson, Susan II, 792
Eavenson, Susan B. II, 840
Eavenson, Susan B. II, 858
Eavenson, Susan B. II, 916
Eavenson, Susan B. II, 918
Eavenson, Susan Bean II, 792
Eavenson, Susan Irene II, 858
Eavenson, Thomas Scott II, 792
Eaves, John I, 588
Eaves, John I, 593
Eaves, Mary I, 588
Eaves, Mary I, 593
Eaves, Ruthanna IV, 1050
Eaves, Ruthanna IV, 1056
Eaves, Susan IV, 1056
Eaves, Susan IV, 1060
Eaves, Susanna IV, 144
Eaves, Susanna IV, 154
Eaves, William K. I, 588
Eavs, Hannah I, 537
Eavs, Hannah I, 550
Eavs, John I, 593
Eayre, Anna M. VI, 779
Eayre, Anna M. VI, 786
Eayre, Elizabet B. VI, 747
Eayre, Elizabeth B. VI, 740
Eayre, Hannah II, 791
Eayre, Hannah H. VI, 740
Eayre, Hannah H. VI, 747
Eayre, Hannah H. VI, 748
Eayre, Isaac W. VI, 740
Eayre, Isaac W. VI, 747
Eayre, Mary II, 219
Eayre, Thomas II, 173
Eayrs, Margaret II, 219
Eayrs, Margaret II, 273
Eayrs, Richard II, 219
Eayrs, Thomas II, 219
Ebaugh, Sarah Amanda VI, 735
Ebaugh, Sarah Amanda VI, 759
Eberhart, Rachel IV, 125
Eberhart, Rachel IV, 128
Ebersole, Clara A. IV, 1277
Eble, Nancy IV, 1313
Eblen, Eliza VI, 488
Eblen, Eliza VI, 489
Eblen, Elizabeth VI, 488
Eblen, Elizabeth VI, 489
Eblen, Elizah VI, 542
Eblen, Hannah VI, 488
Eblen, Hannah VI, 489
Eblen, Isaac II, 356
Eblen, Isaac VI, 488
Eblen, Isaac VI, 489
Eblen, John VI, 488
Eblen, John VI, 489
Eblen, John VI, 542
Eblen, Mary VI, 488
Eblen, Mary VI, 489
Eblen, Mary VI, 542
Eblen, Michael II, 356
Eblen, Mitchell II, 356
Eblen, Peter II, 356
Eblen, Rachel VI, 488
Eblen, Rachel VI, 489
Eblen, Rebekah VI, 635
Eblen, Rebekah VI, 687
Eblen, Samuel VI, 488
Eblen, Samuel VI, 489
Eblin, Eliza VI, 488
Eblin, Eliza VI, 489
Eblin, Elizabeth VI, 488
Eblin, Elizabeth VI, 489
Eblin, Elizah VI, 542
Eblin, Hance VI, 488
Eblin, Hannah VI, 481
Eblin, Hannah VI, 488
Eblin, Hannah VI, 489
Eblin, Isaac VI, 488
Eblin, Isaac VI, 489
Eblin, John VI, 488
Eblin, John VI, 489
Eblin, John, Jr. VI, 489
Eblin, Mary VI, 488
Eblin, Mary VI, 489
Eblin, Mary VI, 549
Eblin, Michal VI, 488
Eblin, Rachel VI, 488
Eblin, Rachel VI, 489
Eblin, Samuel VI, 488
Eblin, Samuel VI, 489
Eblin, Sarah VI, 489
Ebon, Sarah V, 559
Eccles, John VI, 290
Eccles, John Milton V, 837
Eccles, Mary IV, 1206
Eccles, Rachel V, 837
Eccles, Wm. IV, 1206
Eccleston, Daniel II, 511
Echelberger, Mary IV, 197
Echelberger, Mary IV, 219
Echels, Rachel I, 808
Echels, Rachel I, 819
Echolds, John VI, 309
Echols, ??? VI, 293
Echols, Agness VI, 813
Echols, Angelina Mary Jane VI, 919
Echols, Ann M. VI, 804
Echols, Champness VI, 813
Echols, Eleazer VI, 845
Echols, Elizabeth VI, 813
Echols, Elizabeth VI, 833
Echols, Elizabeth I. VI, 796
Echols, Isaac VI, 911
Echols, J. H. VI, 919
Echols, James VI, 796
Echols, James VI, 798
Echols, John VI, 309
Echols, Joseph VI, 813
Echols, Joseph VI, 844
Echols, Judith VI, 309
Echols, Judith VI, 328
Echols, Mary VI, 911
Echols, Mary C. VI, 798
Echols, Moses VI, 813
Echols, Sarah VI, 309
Echols, William VI, 309
Echols, William, Jr. VI, 309
Echols, William, Sr. VI, 309
Echroyd, Henry IV, 327
Echroyd, Sarah N. IV, 249
Echus, Mary VI, 384
Echus, Phebe VI, 384
Eckel, Lilla C. II, 806
Eckel, Mary W. V, 883
Eckenrode, ??? VI, 5
Eckert, Alfred W. II, 858
Eckert, Edith May II, 792
Eckert, Florence II, 858
Eckert, John II, 792
Eckert, Lilian W. II, 839
Eckert, Lillian W. II, 858
Eckert, Mary II, 792
Eckert, Mary II, 858
Eckert, May W. II, 858
Eckhert, ??? IV, 1314
Eckhert, Stella Cottrell IV, 13
Eckhoff, Nettie H. V, 903
Eckhoff, Nettie Haisley V, 903
Eckholds, John VI, 351
Eckhols, Becky VI, 902
Eckhols, Betsey VI, 902
Eckhols, Elizabeth VI, 933
Eckhols, Isaac VI, 911
Eckhols, Isaac VI, 1004
Eckhols, Jacob VI, 900
Eckhols, Jacob VI, 902
Eckhols, Jacob VI, 910
Eckhols, Jacob VI, 911
Eckhols, Jacob VI, 915
Eckhols, Jacob VI, 933
Eckhols, Jacob VI, 941
Eckhols, Jacob VI, 942
Eckhols, James VI, 891
Eckhols, James VI, 901
Eckhols, James VI, 910
Eckhols, James VI, 941
Eckhols, James H. VI, 901
Eckhols, James H. VI, 911

khols, Jane VI, 901
khols, Jenny VI, 910
khols, Jenny Hancock VI, 910
khols, John VI, 886
khols, Judith VI, 911
khols, Mary VI, 886
khols, Mary VI, 910
khols, Mary VI, 911
khols, Peregrin VI, 964
khols, Polly VI, 915
khols, Rhoda VI, 911
khols, Tabitha VI, 941
kle, Mary W. V, 881
kles, John VI, 291
kley, John II, 357
kley, Marcy II, 450
kley, Marcy II, 651
kley, Marry IV, 197
kley, Wd. Sarah II, 357
kman, Firman V, 49
koff, Nettie H. V, 903
kolls, Mary VI, 900
kols, Jacob VI, 910
kols, Jacob VI, 1001
kols, Mary VI, 910
kovey, Elizabeth VI, 884
kovey, Mathias VI, 884
kroyd, Elizabeth W. IV, 327
kroyd, Hannah IV, 327
kroyd, Henry IV, 327
kroyd, John H. IV, 327
kroyd, John Hayworth IV, 327
kroyd, Louisa IV, 327
kroyd, Martha IV, 327
kroyd, Rachel W. IV, 327
kroyd, Richard II, 511
kroyd, Sarah IV, 327
kroyd, Sarah M. IV, 327
kroyd, Sarah W. IV, 327
kstein, Erhardt III, 108
kstein, Erhardt III, 268
kstein, Johanna III, 108
kstein, Johanna III, 268
kstein, R. C. IV, 700
kstein, Wilhelmina III, 108
kstein, Wilhelmina III, 268
e, Jno. VI, 291
es, John VI, 291
es, Rachel I, 808
lls, Sarah VI, 309
lls, William, Sr. VI, 309
ls, William VI, 309
oyd, Hannah IV, 327
oyd, Henry II, 291
oyd, Henry IV, 388
oyd, John IV, 388
oyd, John H. IV, 388
oyd, Joseph II, 511
oyd, Joshua Maule IV, 197
oyd, Louisa IV, 388
oyd, Martha IV, 327
oyd, Richard II, 511
oyd, Sarah IV, 388
oyd, Sarah N. IV, 198
oyd, Sarah N. IV, 249
lie, Allen W. IV, 700
lingfield, Franklin V, 166
lings, Sarah IV, 198
lins, Clara B. III, 108
lins, Clara B. III, 270
lins, Margaret III, 108
lins, Margaret III, 270
lins, Thos. K. III, 108
lins, Thos. K. III, 270
ls, Andrew I, 962
ls, Ann VI, 804
ls, Betsy VI, 813
ls, Clarissa I, 962
ls, Deltla VI, 819
ls, Elizabeth VI, 802
ls, Elizabeth VI, 813
ls, Harriston VI, 813
ls, Huiston VI, 813
ls, J. L. VI, 819
ls, Jane VI, 832
ls, Jenney VI, 838
ls, Jesse VI, 813
ls, Jesse VI, 838
ls, John VI, 813
ls, John VI, 818
ls, John VI, 838
ls, Lindsey I, 962
ls, Lindsey I, 985
ls, Lucy VI, 813
ls, Nancy VI, 831
ls, Nevile VI, 813
ls, Polly VI, 843
ls, Sally VI, 802
ls, Sarah I, 962
ls, Sarah VI, 818
ls, Sealy I, 962
Edds, Thomas I, 962
Edds, Thomas VI, 818
Edds, Thomas VI, 843
Edds, Thos VI, 804
Eddy, Albert V, 993
Eddy, Allen IV, 1157
Eddy, Allen W. IV, 700
Eddy, Allen W. IV, 1157
Eddy, Allen W. IV, 1235
Eddy, Ann II, 511
Eddy, Ann II, 590
Eddy, Ann III, 108
Eddy, Anna VI, 739
Eddy, Anna Ashline-Eddy VI, 749
Eddy, Anna M. IV, 1157
Eddy, Anna Mary IV, 1157
Eddy, Annie IV, 1157
Eddy, Aron III, 108
Eddy, Belle VI, 739
Eddy, Belle VI, 749
Eddy, Caspar Wister II, 511
Eddy, Casper II, 511
Eddy, Casper Wistar III, 108
Eddy, Catharine V, 993
Eddy, Charles II, 511
Eddy, Charles III, 108
Eddy, Chas. V, 993
Eddy, Chas. Louis V, 993
Eddy, Daniel II, 511
Eddy, Frances II, 511
Eddy, Geo. V, 993
Eddy, George II, 511
Eddy, George H. I, 632
Eddy, Hannah II, 511
Eddy, Hannah III, 108
Eddy, Hannah III, 152
Eddy, Hannah, Jr. III, 108
Eddy, Henry II, 511
Eddy, Henry III, 108
Eddy, Henry V, 993
Eddy, Huldah IV, 1235
Eddy, Huldah IV, 1239
Eddy, Huldah R. IV, 1157
Eddy, Huldah R. IV, 1235
Eddy, Ira G. IV, 1157
Eddy, Ira G. IV, 1235
Eddy, James II, 357
Eddy, James II, 511
Eddy, James II, 590
Eddy, James III, 108
Eddy, John II, 357
Eddy, John II, 511
Eddy, John H. III, 108
Eddy, John L. IV, 1157
Eddy, John L. IV, 1235
Eddy, John R. IV, 1157
Eddy, John R. IV, 1235
Eddy, John S. IV, 1157
Eddy, John Turpin II, 511
Eddy, Joseph IV, 1157
Eddy, Joseph IV, 1235
Eddy, Laura IV, 1157
Eddy, Laura A. IV, 1157
Eddy, Laura Annette IV, 1157
Eddy, Lavina IV, 198
Eddy, Lavina IV, 214
Eddy, Lucy III, 108
Eddy, Lucy Ann IV, 1157
Eddy, Lucy Ann IV, 1235
Eddy, Lucy Ann IV, 1239
Eddy, Lucy H. III, 108
Eddy, Lucy H. III, 286
Eddy, Lydia IV, 1157
Eddy, Lydia IV, 1231
Eddy, Lydia IV, 1235
Eddy, Lydia B. IV, 1157
Eddy, Mary II, 357
Eddy, Mary II, 511
Eddy, Mary II, 561
Eddy, Mary III, 108
Eddy, Mary IV, 1206
Eddy, Mary IV, 1213
Eddy, Mary IV, 1235
Eddy, Mattie IV, 1157
Eddy, Paulina IV, 1235
Eddy, Pauline IV, 1238
Eddy, Perlina IV, 1157
Eddy, Perlina IV, 1235
Eddy, Rebecca II, 511
Eddy, Reuben IV, 1157
Eddy, Reuben IV, 1235
Eddy, Ruth IV, 1157
Eddy, Ruth IV, 1235
Eddy, Sarah II, 511
Eddy, Sarah III, 65
Eddy, Sarah III, 279
Eddy, Sarah IV, 1361
Eddy, Sarah V, 993
Eddy, Sherman G. IV, 1157
Eddy, Sherman G. IV, 1235
Eddy, Thomas II, 511
Eddy, Thomas III, 108
Eddy, Thomas III, 152
Eddy, Wd. Mary II, 511
Eddy, Willard IV, 1157
Eddy, William II, 357
Eddy, William VI, 749
Eddy, Wm. VI, 739
Edens, Doratha Wills VI, 911
Edens, Jesse VI, 911
Edens, Jesse VI, 912
Edes, Lindsey I, 962
Edewards, Mary II, 67
Edgar, ??? III, 326
Edgar, Alfred E. H. VI, 911
Edgar, Amos III, 108
Edgar, Anne VI, 915
Edgar, Betsy VI, 911
Edgar, Catharine VI, 911
Edgar, Clementin III, 108
Edgar, Clementine III, 326
Edgar, Dorcas III, 108
Edgar, Elizabeth VI, 911
Edgar, Elizabeth VI, 986
Edgar, Elizabeth P. VI, 911
Edgar, Grace II, 443
Edgar, Henry VI, 880
Edgar, Henry VI, 911
Edgar, Henry VI, 955
Edgar, James III, 108
Edgar, James III, 109
Edgar, James VI, 911
Edgar, James VI, 924
Edgar, James VI, 986
Edgar, James VI, 1010
Edgar, James VI, 1021
Edgar, Jenny VI, 927
Edgar, Jesse VI, 902
Edgar, John II, 443
Edgar, John VI, 911
Edgar, John VI, 915
Edgar, John VI, 1021
Edgar, John H. VI, 911
Edgar, Joseph II, 357
Edgar, Judah VI, 1010
Edgar, Juriah VI, 814
Edgar, Katharine Ann V, 783
Edgar, Katherine Ann V, 781
Edgar, Lewis VI, 814
Edgar, Lydia III, 108
Edgar, Margaret III, 108
Edgar, Margrett II, 357
Edgar, Nancy VI, 911
Edgar, Nancy VI, 924
Edgar, Pamelia III, 108
Edgar, Pamella VI, 911
Edgar, Phebe VI, 911
Edgar, Rebeckah VI, 911
Edgar, Richard II, 443
Edgar, Sarah II, 443
Edgar, Sarah III, 109
Edgar, Sarah VI, 1021
Edgar, Tabitha VI, 913
Edgar, Thomas VI, 911
Edgar, Thomas VI, 950
Edgar, Thomas VI, 971
Edgar, Thomas VI, 1009
Edgar, Thos. VI, 913
Edgar, William III, 108
Edgar, William III, 109
Edgar, William VI, 911
Edgcomb, Ann II, 357
Edgcomb, Joseph II, 357
Edgcomb, Nathaniel II, 357
Edgcomb, Nathaniel II, 511
Edgcomb, Sarah II, 357
Edgcomb, Sarah II, 511
Edgcomb, Symon II, 357
Edgcombe, Nathaniel II, 511
Edgcombe, Nathaniel II, 548
Edgcombe, Sarah II, 357
Edgcome, Nathaniel II, 216
Edgcome, Nathaniel II, 514
Edgcome, Sarah II, 514
Edge, Edith II, 703
Edge, Edward VI, 814
Edge, Elam VI, 797
Edge, Elam VI, 854
Edge, Jane II, 443
Edge, Joshua P. II, 703
Edge, Margaret III, 109
Edge, Margaret Janet III, 109
Edge, Mary III, 101
Edge, Mary III, 109
Edge, Nancy VI, 814
Edge, Richard II, 443
Edge, Thomas II, 512
Edge, Thomas II, 703
Edge, Walter III, 109
Edge, Walter S. III, 101
Edge, Walter S. III, 109
Edgecombe, Ann II, 357
Edgecombe, Joseph II, 357
Edgell, Elizabeth II, 357
Edgell, Hannah II, 357
Edgell, John II, 357
Edgell, Mary II, 357
Edgell, Rebecca II, 357
Edgell, Rebecka II, 357
Edgell, Rebeckah II, 357
Edgell, Rebekah II, 512
Edgell, Simon II, 357
Edgell, Wm. II, 512
Edger, Grace II, 443
Edgereton, Jas. IV, 357
Edgereton, Mary Ann IV, 357
Edgerston, William H. I, 328
Edgerton, ??? I, 279
Edgerton, ??? I, 287
Edgerton, ??? IV, 1085
Edgerton, ??? V, 877
Edgerton, Abigail IV, 327
Edgerton, Abigail IV, 355
Edgerton, Abigail IV, 576
Edgerton, Abigail IV, 598
Edgerton, Abigail IV, 1055
Edgerton, Abigail V, 837
Edgerton, Abigail V, 882
Edgerton, Abigail V, 886
Edgerton, Abigail VI, 384
Edgerton, Abigail VI, 489
Edgerton, Abigail VI, 566
Edgerton, Abigail VI, 567
Edgerton, Abijah IV, 388
Edgerton, Abijah IV, 389
Edgerton, Abijah IV, 450
Edgerton, Abijah IV, 1095
Edgerton, Absalet I, 305
Edgerton, Absalet J. I, 286
Edgerton, Absalett I, 286
Edgerton, Absalett I, 287
Edgerton, Absalett I, 294
Edgerton, Absalett I, 305
Edgerton, Absalit J. I, 286
Edgerton, Absalott I, 287
Edgerton, Absilla I, 287
Edgerton, Absilla I, 305
Edgerton, Absilla I, 316
Edgerton, Absillet I, 287
Edgerton, Absilly I, 305
Edgerton, Acenith IV, 577
Edgerton, Achsah IV, 367
Edgerton, Achsah IV, 566
Edgerton, Achsah IV, 576
Edgerton, Adaline IV, 1088
Edgerton, Adaline IV, 1095
Edgerton, Albert I, 305
Edgerton, Albert Lambert IV, 576
Edgerton, Alene Lydia II, 959
Edgerton, Alexander I, 286
Edgerton, Alexander A. I, 305
Edgerton, Alice IV, 389
Edgerton, Alice IV, 419
Edgerton, Alice IV, 654
Edgerton, Alice Caroline IV, 577
Edgerton, Alice Lydia II, 967
Edgerton, Alice Semira IV, 621
Edgerton, Aline Lydia II, 1050
Edgerton, Allen T. Lee IV, 1095
Edgerton, Almeda IV, 1095
Edgerton, Almeda IV, 1100
Edgerton, Alpheus Lelon I, 286
Edgerton, Alson R. Wall I, 287
Edgerton, Amanda M. I, 286
Edgerton, Amanda M. I, 305
Edgerton, Amanda M. I, 309
Edgerton, Amy IV, 388
Edgerton, Amy L. IV, 389
Edgerton, Amy L. IV, 413
Edgerton, Amy L. IV, 700
Edgerton, Ann I, 301
Edgerton, Ann I, 305
Edgerton, Ann IV, 198
Edgerton, Ann IV, 327
Edgerton, Ann IV, 388
Edgerton, Ann IV, 389
Edgerton, Ann IV, 573
Edgerton, Ann IV, 585
Edgerton, Anna II, 705
Edgerton, Anna II, 714
Edgerton, Anna II, 721
Edgerton, Anna IV, 198
Edgerton, Anna IV, 212
Edgerton, Anna IV, 376
Edgerton, Anna IV, 384
Edgerton, Anna IV, 388
Edgerton, Anna IV, 389
Edgerton, Anna IV, 518
Edgerton, Anna IV, 522
Edgerton, Anna IV, 570
Edgerton, Anna IV, 573
Edgerton, Anna IV, 576
Edgerton, Anna IV, 577
Edgerton, Anna IV, 591
Edgerton, Anna IV, 598
Edgerton, Anna IV, 700
Edgerton, Anna IV, 807
Edgerton, Anna IV, 949
Edgerton, Anna IV, 1093
Edgerton, Anna IV, 1095
Edgerton, Anna B. IV, 389
Edgerton, Anna B. IV, 700
Edgerton, Anna Daisy Gilmer I, 286
Edgerton, Anna E. IV, 366
Edgerton, Anna E. IV, 389
Edgerton, Anna M. IV, 198
Edgerton, Anna M. IV, 568
Edgerton, Anna M. IV, 576
Edgerton, Anna M. IV, 577
Edgerton, Anna M. IV, 803
Edgerton, Anna M. IV, 813
Edgerton, Anna Mabel IV, 198
Edgerton, Anna Mabel IV, 389
Edgerton, Anna Mabel IV, 402
Edgerton, Anna Mabel IV, 813
Edgerton, Anna Mabel IV, 819
Edgerton, Anna Mable IV, 401
Edgerton, Anna Mary IV, 577
Edgerton, Anna Mary IV, 742
Edgerton, Anna Maud I, 632
Edgerton, Anna Maude I, 632
Edgerton, Anna R. IV, 388
Edgerton, Anna R. IV, 446
Edgerton, Anna R. IV, 577
Edgerton, Anna R. IV, 595
Edgerton, Anna T. IV, 432
Edgerton, Anna V. IV, 813
Edgerton, Anna V. IV, 934
Edgerton, Anna V. IV, 949
Edgerton, Anna Viola IV, 949
Edgerton, Anne IV, 569
Edgerton, Anne IV, 576
Edgerton, Anne IV, 598
Edgerton, Anne IV, 1095
Edgerton, Annie IV, 576
Edgerton, Annie D. I, 286
Edgerton, Annie D. I, 305
Edgerton, Annie D. I, 386
Edgerton, Annie D. I, 388
Edgerton, Annie E. IV, 576
Edgerton, Annie E. IV, 577
Edgerton, Annie M. I, 287
Edgerton, Annie M. IV, 813
Edgerton, Annie Maud I, 615
Edgerton, Annie V. I, 324
Edgerton, Annie V. I, 336
Edgerton, Anthony J. IV, 621
Edgerton, Aquilla IV, 388
Edgerton, Arcada I, 286
Edgerton, Arcada I, 305
Edgerton, Arcada I, 317
Edgerton, Arlina Mable I, 336
Edgerton, Arthur IV, 813
Edgerton, Arthur H. IV, 622
Edgerton, Arthur Howell IV, 621
Edgerton, Arthur J. IV, 1095
Edgerton, Asenath IV, 388
Edgerton, Asenath IV, 389
Edgerton, Asenath IV, 409
Edgerton, Asenath IV, 576
Edgerton, Asenath IV, 577
Edgerton, Asenath IV, 1055
Edgerton, Asenath IV, 1095
Edgerton, Asenath IV, 1104
Edgerton, Avice IV, 388
Edgerton, Barney R. I, 286
Edgerton, Bathsheba IV, 327
Edgerton, Bathsheba IV, 388
Edgerton, Benajah IV, 388
Edgerton, Bertha IV, 832
Edgerton, Bertha E. I, 324
Edgerton, Bertha E. I, 336
Edgerton, Bertha Mary IV, 522
Edgerton, Bertha Mary IV, 555
Edgerton, Bertha May I, 305
Edgerton, Bertha W. IV, 522
Edgerton, Bertie H. I, 286
Edgerton, Bettie Ann I, 615
Edgerton, Beulah IV, 813
Edgerton, Beulah IV, 934
Edgerton, Beulah IV, 949
Edgerton, Carelton IV, 389
Edgerton, Carleton IV, 388
Edgerton, Caroline I, 286
Edgerton, Caroline I, 305
Edgerton, Caroline IV, 576
Edgerton, Caroline IV, 577
Edgerton, Chalkley IV, 1095
Edgerton, Charity I, 287
Edgerton, Charity II, 959
Edgerton, Charity IV, 198
Edgerton, Charity IV, 327
Edgerton, Charity IV, 385

Edgerton, Charity IV, 388
Edgerton, Charity IV, 522
Edgerton, Charity IV, 566
Edgerton, Charity IV, 576
Edgerton, Charity IV, 577
Edgerton, Charity IV, 585
Edgerton, Charity IV, 596
Edgerton, Charity IV, 621
Edgerton, Charity IV, 700
Edgerton, Charity IV, 813
Edgerton, Charity IV, 949
Edgerton, Charity D. I, 286
Edgerton, Charity D. I, 305
Edgerton, Charles IV, 198
Edgerton, Charles IV, 389
Edgerton, Charles IV, 576
Edgerton, Charles IV, 577
Edgerton, Charles S. II, 1050
Edgerton, Charles Taylor II, 959
Edgerton, Charlotte I, 285
Edgerton, Charlotte I, 286
Edgerton, Charlotte I, 287
Edgerton, Charlotte I, 289
Edgerton, Charlotte I, 305
Edgerton, Charlotte I, 317
Edgerton, Charlotte I, 328
Edgerton, Chelley I, 285
Edgerton, Chelley I, 286
Edgerton, Chelly I, 286
Edgerton, Chelly I, 287
Edgerton, Chelly I, 328
Edgerton, Chelly Effie I, 287
Edgerton, Chelly Frances I, 286
Edgerton, Chester J. IV, 621
Edgerton, Chester J. IV, 622
Edgerton, Christian I, 287
Edgerton, Christian I, 297
Edgerton, Christiana IV, 388
Edgerton, Christiana IV, 570
Edgerton, Christiana IV, 576
Edgerton, Christianna IV, 580
Edgerton, Clarkson IV, 388
Edgerton, Clarkson J. IV, 1095
Edgerton, D. H. I, 305
Edgerton, Daniel IV, 389
Edgerton, David IV, 198
Edgerton, David IV, 384
Edgerton, David IV, 388
Edgerton, David IV, 389
Edgerton, David IV, 425
Edgerton, David IV, 576
Edgerton, David IV, 577
Edgerton, David IV, 949
Edgerton, David IV, 950
Edgerton, David IV, 1055
Edgerton, David IV, 1095
Edgerton, David Silas I, 286
Edgerton, Dessie T. IV, 389
Edgerton, Dessie Terrell IV, 389
Edgerton, Dorothy II, 959
Edgerton, Dorothy IV, 605
Edgerton, Dorothy IV, 621
Edgerton, E. I, 305
Edgerton, E. E. I, 305
Edgerton, Edith IV, 522
Edgerton, Edith IV, 570
Edgerton, Edith IV, 577
Edgerton, Edith Anna IV, 518
Edgerton, Edith Anna IV, 522
Edgerton, Edna I, 287
Edgerton, Edna I, 294
Edgerton, Edna I, 305
Edgerton, Edna I, 315
Edgerton, Edward II, 967
Edgerton, Edward IV, 522
Edgerton, Edward IV, 953
Edgerton, Edward Edgerton IV, 949
Edgerton, Edward F. IV, 621
Edgerton, Edward R. IV, 1095
Edgerton, Edwin I, 305
Edgerton, Edwin D. I, 285
Edgerton, Edwin D. I, 286
Edgerton, Eleanor Sara IV, 581
Edgerton, Eli IV, 576
Edgerton, Elijah C. I, 286
Edgerton, Eliza A. V, 951
Edgerton, Eliza A. V, 957
Edgerton, Elizabeth I, 286
Edgerton, Elizabeth I, 287
Edgerton, Elizabeth I, 301
Edgerton, Elizabeth I, 305
Edgerton, Elizabeth I, 308
Edgerton, Elizabeth I, 328
Edgerton, Elizabeth I, 985
Edgerton, Elizabeth IV, 144
Edgerton, Elizabeth IV, 388
Edgerton, Elizabeth IV, 389
Edgerton, Elizabeth IV, 432
Edgerton, Elizabeth IV, 576
Edgerton, Elizabeth IV, 585
Edgerton, Elizabeth IV, 742
Edgerton, Elizabeth IV, 1055
Edgerton, Elizabeth IV, 1065
Edgerton, Elizabeth IV, 1081
Edgerton, Elizabeth IV, 1095
Edgerton, Elizabeth IV, 1119
Edgerton, Elizabeth V, 49
Edgerton, Elizabeth V, 829
Edgerton, Elizabeth V, 837
Edgerton, Elizabeth V, 839
Edgerton, Elizabeth A. I, 328
Edgerton, Elizabeth A. IV, 198
Edgerton, Elizabeth A. IV, 246
Edgerton, Elizabeth A. IV, 949
Edgerton, Elizabeth A. IV, 977
Edgerton, Elizabeth A. IV, 1019
Edgerton, Elizabeth Ann V, 837
Edgerton, Elizabeth V. I, 285
Edgerton, Ella M. IV, 1095
Edgerton, Ella M. IV, 1102
Edgerton, Ellen II, 967
Edgerton, Ellen IV, 389
Edgerton, Ellen IV, 576
Edgerton, Ellen IV, 577
Edgerton, Ellen IV, 742
Edgerton, Ellen IV, 813
Edgerton, Ellen IV, 949
Edgerton, Ellen IV, 953
Edgerton, Ellen IV, 1095
Edgerton, Ellen B. IV, 425
Edgerton, Elma IV, 1095
Edgerton, Elma IV, 1123
Edgerton, Elma B. I, 237
Edgerton, Elsie IV, 621
Edgerton, Elsie IV, 622
Edgerton, Elsie IV, 644
Edgerton, Emaline E. IV, 1095
Edgerton, Emaline E. IV, 1112
Edgerton, Emeline IV, 1095
Edgerton, Emily A. IV, 1095
Edgerton, Emily A. IV, 1110
Edgerton, Enoch H. I, 286
Edgerton, Esther I, 336
Edgerton, Esther II, 357
Edgerton, Esther IV, 198
Edgerton, Esther IV, 384
Edgerton, Esther IV, 388
Edgerton, Esther IV, 389
Edgerton, Esther IV, 413
Edgerton, Esther IV, 425
Edgerton, Esther IV, 576
Edgerton, Esther IV, 577
Edgerton, Esther IV, 949
Edgerton, Esther IV, 950
Edgerton, Esther IV, 1095
Edgerton, Esther Irene IV, 813
Edgerton, Esther Irene IV, 835
Edgerton, Ethel I, 336
Edgerton, Ethel N. Satterthwait IV, 813
Edgerton, Eunice II, 720
Edgerton, Eunice IV, 328
Edgerton, Eunice IV, 354
Edgerton, Eunice IV, 574
Edgerton, Eunice IV, 576
Edgerton, Eunice IV, 596
Edgerton, Eunice IV, 598
Edgerton, Eva S. IV, 198
Edgerton, Exum I, 305
Edgerton, Exum P. I, 286
Edgerton, Exum P. I, 305
Edgerton, Fernando Cartland I, 286
Edgerton, Flora I, 305
Edgerton, Francis T. I, 287
Edgerton, Frank IV, 1250
Edgerton, Frank A. IV, 1250
Edgerton, Franklin I, 336
Edgerton, G. G. I, 305
Edgerton, Gabriel I, 287
Edgerton, Gabriel I, 305
Edgerton, Geneva I, 305
Edgerton, George I, 336
Edgerton, George L. I, 286
Edgerton, George L. I, 305
Edgerton, George L. I, 328
Edgerton, George Whitford I, 287
Edgerton, Gilbert D. IV, 389
Edgerton, Gilbert J. IV, 813
Edgerton, Grace VI, 384
Edgerton, Grace VI, 566
Edgerton, Grace VI, 567
Edgerton, Hannah IV, 144
Edgerton, Hannah IV, 389
Edgerton, Hannah V, 49
Edgerton, Hannah V, 837
Edgerton, Hannah V, 882
Edgerton, Hannah V, 884
Edgerton, Haschell I, 305
Edgerton, Hattie Varman VI, 384
Edgerton, Henrietta M. I, 287
Edgerton, Henry Franklin I, 286
Edgerton, Henry L. I, 336
Edgerton, Henry Leslie I, 305
Edgerton, Hetta A. I, 287
Edgerton, Horace J. IV, 198
Edgerton, Horace J. IV, 813
Edgerton, Horace J. IV, 934
Edgerton, Horace J. IV, 949
Edgerton, Horace Joseph IV, 949
Edgerton, Howard IV, 605
Edgerton, Ida H. I, 286
Edgerton, Inona C. I, 324
Edgerton, Iona C. I, 336
Edgerton, Isaac IV, 576
Edgerton, Isaac Huestis IV, 1095
Edgerton, Isham C. I, 324
Edgerton, Isham C. I, 336
Edgerton, Israel IV, 1095
Edgerton, J. Clarkson IV, 366
Edgerton, J. Clarkson IV, 389
Edgerton, J. Clarkson IV, 700
Edgerton, J. Howard IV, 609
Edgerton, J. Howard IV, 621
Edgerton, J. Howard IV, 622
Edgerton, J. Howard IV, 813
Edgerton, J. Howard, Jr. IV, 621
Edgerton, J. M. I, 336
Edgerton, J. Russell II, 1050
Edgerton, J. Russell II, 1053
Edgerton, J. Russell Lowell II, 959
Edgerton, J. W. I, 286
Edgerton, James I, 286
Edgerton, James I, 287
Edgerton, James I, 302
Edgerton, James I, 304
Edgerton, James I, 305
Edgerton, James I, 985
Edgerton, James II, 714
Edgerton, James II, 721
Edgerton, James IV, 144
Edgerton, James IV, 198
Edgerton, James IV, 212
Edgerton, James IV, 327
Edgerton, James IV, 388
Edgerton, James IV, 389
Edgerton, James IV, 413
Edgerton, James IV, 423
Edgerton, James IV, 522
Edgerton, James IV, 573
Edgerton, James IV, 576
Edgerton, James IV, 585
Edgerton, James IV, 588
Edgerton, James IV, 591
Edgerton, James IV, 598
Edgerton, James IV, 600
Edgerton, James IV, 700
Edgerton, James IV, 949
Edgerton, James IV, 1055
Edgerton, James IV, 1095
Edgerton, James IV, 1119
Edgerton, James V, 951
Edgerton, James B. I, 286
Edgerton, James B. I, 305
Edgerton, James C. IV, 813
Edgerton, James C. IV, 835
Edgerton, James Charles IV, 813
Edgerton, James E. IV, 1095
Edgerton, James W. IV, 570
Edgerton, James W. IV, 576
Edgerton, James W. IV, 577
Edgerton, James Warder IV, 522
Edgerton, James, Jr. IV, 389
Edgerton, James, Jr. IV, 577
Edgerton, Jane IV, 198
Edgerton, Jane IV, 327
Edgerton, Jane IV, 388
Edgerton, Janice Mary IV, 813
Edgerton, Jannara I, 286
Edgerton, Jas. IV, 579
Edgerton, Jas. W. IV, 518
Edgerton, Jas. W. IV, 555
Edgerton, Jebtha IV, 1095
Edgerton, Jennie E. I, 336
Edgerton, Jennie E. I, 338
Edgerton, Jephthah IV, 1095
Edgerton, Jeremiah IV, 949
Edgerton, Jesse IV, 144
Edgerton, Jesse IV, 198
Edgerton, Jesse IV, 246
Edgerton, Jesse IV, 388
Edgerton, Jesse IV, 389
Edgerton, Jesse IV, 401
Edgerton, Jesse IV, 576
Edgerton, Jesse IV, 621
Edgerton, Jesse IV, 622
Edgerton, Jesse IV, 628
Edgerton, Jesse IV, 647
Edgerton, Jesse IV, 658
Edgerton, Jesse IV, 700
Edgerton, Jesse IV, 713
Edgerton, Jesse IV, 742
Edgerton, Jesse IV, 813
Edgerton, Jesse IV, 817
Edgerton, Jesse IV, 949
Edgerton, Jesse IV, 960
Edgerton, Jesse IV, 977
Edgerton, Jesse IV, 981
Edgerton, Jesse Anderson I, 286
Edgerton, Jesse Dewees IV, 1055
Edgerton, Jesse Edgerton IV, 577
Edgerton, Jesse N. IV, 198
Edgerton, Jesse N. IV, 379
Edgerton, Jesse N. IV, 389
Edgerton, Jesse N. IV, 807
Edgerton, Jesse N. IV, 813
Edgerton, Jesse N. IV, 842
Edgerton, Jesse Wilmer Hall IV, 577
Edgerton, John I, 286
Edgerton, John I, 287
Edgerton, John IV, 144
Edgerton, John IV, 385
Edgerton, John IV, 389
Edgerton, John IV, 409
Edgerton, John IV, 577
Edgerton, John IV, 1055
Edgerton, John IV, 1056
Edgerton, John IV, 1065
Edgerton, John IV, 1094
Edgerton, John IV, 1095
Edgerton, John IV, 1116
Edgerton, John IV, 1119
Edgerton, John Clarkson IV, 389
Edgerton, John Edward IV, 581
Edgerton, John H. I, 286
Edgerton, John H. I, 287
Edgerton, John H. I, 305
Edgerton, John H. I, 328
Edgerton, John H. I, 330
Edgerton, John H. I, 336
Edgerton, John H. IV, 1095
Edgerton, John Harvey IV, 1095
Edgerton, John Henry I, 324
Edgerton, John Henry I, 615
Edgerton, John M. I, 305
Edgerton, John M. I, 328
Edgerton, John T. I, 237
Edgerton, John Vernon IV, 1055
Edgerton, John, Jr. IV, 1095
Edgerton, Jonathan T. I, 286
Edgerton, Jonathan T. I, 305
Edgerton, Jos. IV, 198
Edgerton, Joseph I, 286
Edgerton, Joseph I, 287
Edgerton, Joseph I, 304
Edgerton, Joseph I, 305
Edgerton, Joseph I, 310
Edgerton, Joseph I, 715
Edgerton, Joseph I, 985
Edgerton, Joseph II, 959
Edgerton, Joseph IV, 198
Edgerton, Joseph IV, 327
Edgerton, Joseph IV, 385
Edgerton, Joseph IV, 388
Edgerton, Joseph IV, 389
Edgerton, Joseph IV, 522
Edgerton, Joseph IV, 541
Edgerton, Joseph IV, 566
Edgerton, Joseph IV, 568
Edgerton, Joseph IV, 570
Edgerton, Joseph IV, 576
Edgerton, Joseph IV, 577
Edgerton, Joseph IV, 585
Edgerton, Joseph IV, 596
Edgerton, Joseph IV, 621
Edgerton, Joseph IV, 700
Edgerton, Joseph IV, 807
Edgerton, Joseph IV, 813
Edgerton, Joseph IV, 949
Edgerton, Joseph IV, 1095
Edgerton, Joseph V, 837
Edgerton, Joseph VI, 384
Edgerton, Joseph VI, 566
Edgerton, Joseph VI, 567
Edgerton, Joseph B. IV, 621
Edgerton, Joseph B. IV, 622
Edgerton, Joseph B. IV, 644
Edgerton, Joseph E. IV, 577
Edgerton, Joseph J. II, 959
Edgerton, Joseph J. II, 1050
Edgerton, Joseph John II, 959
Edgerton, Joseph S. IV, 576
Edgerton, Joseph S. IV, 591
Edgerton, Joseph T. I, 305
Edgerton, Joseph V. IV, 1095
Edgerton, Joseph W. IV, 1095
Edgerton, Joseph, Jr. IV, 522
Edgerton, Joseph, Jr. IV, 576
Edgerton, Joseph, Jr. IV, 588
Edgerton, Joseph, Sr. II, 1050
Edgerton, Josey T. I, 286
Edgerton, Joshua Howard IV, 622
Edgerton, July V. I, 287
Edgerton, L. I, 305
Edgerton, Laura IV, 1095
Edgerton, Laura IV, 1116
Edgerton, Laura Ann Moore I, 336
Edgerton, Laura Susan IV, 621
Edgerton, Lavina IV, 605
Edgerton, Lavina H. IV, 609
Edgerton, Lavina H. IV, 621
Edgerton, Lawrence Lewis IV, 742
Edgerton, Lazarus I, 305
Edgerton, Lazarus E. I, 286
Edgerton, Lazarus E. I, 287
Edgerton, Lemuel Addison IV, 1095
Edgerton, Lena May IV, 1095
Edgerton, Lena May IV, 1101
Edgerton, Lerry I, 305
Edgerton, Lerry H. I, 324
Edgerton, Libbie I, 305
Edgerton, Lillian G. I, 336
Edgerton, Lillian Mary IV, 581
Edgerton, Lindley I, 336
Edgerton, Lindley IV, 1095
Edgerton, Lindley H. IV, 1095
Edgerton, Lindley J. I, 237
Edgerton, Lindley M. I, 328
Edgerton, Lloyd B. IV, 576
Edgerton, Lloyd B. IV, 577
Edgerton, Loretta F. IV, 576
Edgerton, Loretta F. IV, 577
Edgerton, Loretta F. IV, 591
Edgerton, Lorettie E. I, 324
Edgerton, Lotte I, 287
Edgerton, Louesa IV, 577
Edgerton, Louisa IV, 388
Edgerton, Louisa IV, 389
Edgerton, Louisa IV, 577
Edgerton, Louiza IV, 576
Edgerton, Loury Ellen I, 287
Edgerton, Lucile Mary IV, 949
Edgerton, Lucinda IV, 621
Edgerton, Lucinda IV, 1095
Edgerton, Luther M. I, 286
Edgerton, Lydia IV, 576
Edgerton, Lydia IV, 577
Edgerton, Lydia IV, 1095
Edgerton, Lydia P. IV, 522
Edgerton, Lydia P. IV, 541
Edgerton, Lydia S. II, 959
Edgerton, Lydia S. IV, 522
Edgerton, Lydia S. IV, 588
Edgerton, M. I, 305
Edgerton, M. A. I, 305
Edgerton, Mae II, 1050
Edgerton, Mae II, 1053
Edgerton, Margaret Ann Cathrine I, 286
Edgerton, Maria Annie I, 305
Edgerton, Maria Annie I, 309
Edgerton, Marianna IV, 622
Edgerton, Marry D. I, 287
Edgerton, Martha I, 287
Edgerton, Martha I, 304
Edgerton, Martha I, 305
Edgerton, Martha I, 310
Edgerton, Martha I, 715
Edgerton, Martha I, 985
Edgerton, Martha IV, 388
Edgerton, Martha IV, 389
Edgerton, Martha IV, 567
Edgerton, Martha IV, 576
Edgerton, Martha IV, 1055
Edgerton, Martha IV, 1056
Edgerton, Martha IV, 1095
Edgerton, Martha IV, 1116
Edgerton, Martha IV, 1123
Edgerton, Martha A. I, 287
Edgerton, Martha F. I, 305
Edgerton, Martha R. IV, 948
Edgerton, Martha R. IV, 949
Edgerton, Mary I, 286
Edgerton, Mary I, 287
Edgerton, Mary I, 294
Edgerton, Mary I, 295
Edgerton, Mary I, 297
Edgerton, Mary I, 305
Edgerton, Mary I, 316
Edgerton, Mary I, 985
Edgerton, Mary II, 709
Edgerton, Mary IV, 144
Edgerton, Mary IV, 198
Edgerton, Mary IV, 212
Edgerton, Mary IV, 388
Edgerton, Mary IV, 389
Edgerton, Mary IV, 394
Edgerton, Mary IV, 401

erton, Mary IV, 414
erton, Mary IV, 569
erton, Mary IV, 576
erton, Mary IV, 578
erton, Mary IV, 580
erton, Mary IV, 584
erton, Mary IV, 585
erton, Mary IV, 594
erton, Mary IV, 813
erton, Mary IV, 949
erton, Mary IV, 1094
erton, Mary IV, 1095
erton, Mary IV, 1104
erton, Mary IV, 1119
erton, Mary IV, 1277
erton, Mary V, 837
erton, Mary V, 870
erton, Mary A. I, 285
erton, Mary A. I, 305
erton, Mary A. I, 328
erton, Mary A. I, 330
erton, Mary A. IV, 577
erton, Mary A. IV, 949
erton, Mary Ann I, 287
erton, Mary Ann IV, 327
erton, Mary Ann IV, 388
erton, Mary Ann IV, 401
erton, Mary Ann IV, 576
erton, Mary Ann IV, 579
erton, Mary Ann IV, 588
erton, Mary Ann IV, 813
erton, Mary Anna IV, 401
erton, Mary Anna IV, 621
erton, Mary Anna IV, 622
erton, Mary Anna IV, 628
erton, Mary Anna IV, 813
erton, Mary Anna IV, 960
erton, Mary Anna IV, 961
erton, Mary Anne IV, 522
erton, Mary C. IV, 813
erton, Mary C. IV, 846
erton, Mary C. IV, 949
erton, Mary D. I, 324
erton, Mary D. I, 336
erton, Mary Eliza IV, 522
erton, Mary Ellen IV, 621
erton, Mary Emma IV, 388
erton, Mary Emma IV, 576
erton, Mary Emma IV, 577
gerton, Mary H. IV, 198
gerton, Mary H. IV, 581
gerton, Mary H. IV, 800
gerton, Mary H. IV, 807
gerton, Mary H. IV, 813
gerton, Mary H. IV, 819
gerton, Mary H. IV, 832
gerton, Mary J. I, 287
gerton, Mary J. I, 289
gerton, Mary J. I, 305
gerton, Mary J. I, 309
gerton, Mary J. IV, 949
gerton, Mary J. A. IV, 949
gerton, Mary J. F. IV, 949
gerton, Mary K. IV, 176
gerton, Mary K. IV, 198
gerton, Mary M. I, 305
gerton, Mary T. IV, 1095
gerton, Mary Z. IV, 1095
gerton, Mary Z. IV, 1100
gerton, Maud I, 237
gerton, Maud H. I, 237
gerton, Melva II, 1050
gerton, Melva A. IV, 949
gerton, Melva Anna IV, 581
gerton, Melva Gertrude II, 959
gerton, Melva Gertrude II, 1050
gerton, Melva Gertrude II, 1053
gerton, Mialma R. IV, 949
gerton, Michael I, 285
gerton, Michael I, 286
gerton, Michael I, 287
gerton, Michael I, 305
gerton, Michael Allen I, 286
gerton, Michael T. I, 286
gerton, Michel I, 328
gerton, Mildred IV, 581
gerton, Mildred R. IV, 198
gerton, Mildred R. IV, 813
gerton, Mildred Rachel IV, 577
gerton, Mildred Rachel IV, 582
gerton, Mildred Rachel IV, 813
gerton, Mildred Rachel IV, 819
gerton, Milford I, 286
gerton, Minerva E. IV, 379
gerton, Minerva E. IV, 389
gerton, Minerva E. IV, 807
gerton, Minerva E. IV, 813
gerton, Minnie A. I, 286
gerton, Miriam IV, 576
Edgerton, Mollie I, 286
Edgerton, Morgan IV, 1055
Edgerton, Myrtle I, 336
Edgerton, N. I, 305
Edgerton, N. A. I, 305
Edgerton, Nahunta I, 388
Edgerton, Nathan I, 286
Edgerton, Nathan I, 287
Edgerton, Nathan I, 305
Edgerton, Nathan IV, 198
Edgerton, Nathan IV, 388
Edgerton, Nathan IV, 576
Edgerton, Nathan H. II, 959
Edgerton, Nathan H. IV, 577
Edgerton, Nathan Huntley II, 1050
Edgerton, Nathan Huntley II, 1053
Edgerton, Nathan P. I, 286
Edgerton, Nathan P. I, 305
Edgerton, Nathan T. I, 287
Edgerton, Nathaniel IV, 576
Edgerton, Nellie IV, 576
Edgerton, Nelly IV, 388
Edgerton, Nelly IV, 394
Edgerton, Nona I, 305
Edgerton, Nympa J. I, 286
Edgerton, Nympha J. I, 305
Edgerton, Oliver IV, 1095
Edgerton, Orpha I, 305
Edgerton, Orpha A. I, 286
Edgerton, Owen I, 287
Edgerton, Owen I, 985
Edgerton, Owen IV, 576
Edgerton, Patience IV, 388
Edgerton, Patience IV, 403
Edgerton, Patty I, 985
Edgerton, Paul I, 336
Edgerton, Paul C. I, 615
Edgerton, Paul C. I, 632
Edgerton, Penninah A. I, 305
Edgerton, Penninah A. E. I, 286
Edgerton, Phebe I, 287
Edgerton, Phebe I, 305
Edgerton, Phebe I, 307
Edgerton, Phebe E. I, 286
Edgerton, Phebe E. I, 304
Edgerton, Phebe E. I, 305
Edgerton, Pheby I, 305
Edgerton, Pheby I, 318
Edgerton, Piety I, 287
Edgerton, Pity Jane I, 305
Edgerton, Pollie I, 286
Edgerton, Polly I, 305
Edgerton, Prudence IV, 389
Edgerton, Prudence V, 49
Edgerton, Prudence V, 837
Edgerton, Prudence V, 882
Edgerton, Prudence V, 888
Edgerton, R. Bertha IV, 813
Edgerton, Rabacah I, 985
Edgerton, Rachel I, 287
Edgerton, Rachel II, 699
Edgerton, Rachel II, 704
Edgerton, Rachel II, 711
Edgerton, Rachel IV, 198
Edgerton, Rachel IV, 388
Edgerton, Rachel IV, 389
Edgerton, Rachel IV, 412
Edgerton, Rachel IV, 427
Edgerton, Rachel IV, 576
Edgerton, Rachel IV, 577
Edgerton, Rachel IV, 591
Edgerton, Rachel IV, 813
Edgerton, Rachel V, 49
Edgerton, Rachel V, 837
Edgerton, Rachel V, 882
Edgerton, Rachel V, 888
Edgerton, Rachel E. II, 714
Edgerton, Rachel E. IV, 807
Edgerton, Raymomd Milton IV, 813
Edgerton, Raymond IV, 813
Edgerton, Raymond M. IV, 948
Edgerton, Raymond M. IV, 949
Edgerton, Raymond Milton IV, 949
Edgerton, Rebecca I, 287
Edgerton, Rebecca I, 297
Edgerton, Rebecca II, 703
Edgerton, Rebecca IV, 381
Edgerton, Rebecca IV, 389
Edgerton, Rebecca IV, 571
Edgerton, Rebecca IV, 573
Edgerton, Rebecca IV, 576
Edgerton, Rebecca IV, 579
Edgerton, Rebecca IV, 699
Edgerton, Rebecca IV, 1054
Edgerton, Rebecca IV, 1055
Edgerton, Rebecca IV, 1093
Edgerton, Rebecca B. IV, 198
Edgerton, Rebecca B. IV, 813
Edgerton, Rebecca Bertha IV, 198
Edgerton, Rebecca Bertha IV, 813
Edgerton, Rebecca Bertha IV, 832
Edgerton, Rebeckah I, 304
Edgerton, Rebeckah I, 312
Edgerton, Rebeckah I, 985
Edgerton, Rebeckah I, 994
Edgerton, Reuben I, 985
Edgerton, Reuben IV, 388
Edgerton, Reuben IV, 389
Edgerton, Reuben IV, 403
Edgerton, Rhoda IV, 388
Edgerton, Rhoda IV, 389
Edgerton, Rhoda IV, 450
Edgerton, Rhoda IV, 1095
Edgerton, Rhoda IV, 1101
Edgerton, Richard I, 286
Edgerton, Richard I, 305
Edgerton, Richard IV, 144
Edgerton, Richard IV, 198
Edgerton, Richard IV, 212
Edgerton, Richard IV, 388
Edgerton, Richard IV, 389
Edgerton, Richard IV, 394
Edgerton, Richard IV, 569
Edgerton, Richard IV, 576
Edgerton, Richard IV, 578
Edgerton, Richard IV, 580
Edgerton, Richard IV, 584
Edgerton, Richard IV, 1055
Edgerton, Richard IV, 1095
Edgerton, Richard IV, 1119
Edgerton, Richard W. I, 286
Edgerton, Richard W. I, 305
Edgerton, Robert IV, 198
Edgerton, Robert IV, 388
Edgerton, Robert IV, 576
Edgerton, Robert IV, 577
Edgerton, Robert IV, 1095
Edgerton, Robert Donald II, 959
Edgerton, Robert Donald II, 1050
Edgerton, Robert P. I, 286
Edgerton, Ruben I, 985
Edgerton, Russel J. II, 1050
Edgerton, Ruth IV, 388
Edgerton, Ruth IV, 394
Edgerton, Ruth IV, 576
Edgerton, Ruth IV, 578
Edgerton, Ruth IV, 579
Edgerton, Ruth IV, 621
Edgerton, Ruth Ann IV, 1095
Edgerton, S. Ellen IV, 981
Edgerton, Sallie I, 305
Edgerton, Sallie I, 319
Edgerton, Sallie I, 336
Edgerton, Sallie A. II, 1050
Edgerton, Sallie Manly I, 336
Edgerton, Sally I, 295
Edgerton, Sally I, 305
Edgerton, Sally I, 316
Edgerton, Samira IV, 401
Edgerton, Samira IV, 813
Edgerton, Samuel IV, 144
Edgerton, Samuel IV, 389
Edgerton, Samuel V, 49
Edgerton, Samuel V, 837
Edgerton, Samuel J. V, 829
Edgerton, Sara M. IV, 813
Edgerton, Sarah I, 237
Edgerton, Sarah I, 280
Edgerton, Sarah I, 286
Edgerton, Sarah I, 287
Edgerton, Sarah I, 294
Edgerton, Sarah I, 302
Edgerton, Sarah I, 304
Edgerton, Sarah I, 305
Edgerton, Sarah I, 308
Edgerton, Sarah I, 312
Edgerton, Sarah I, 313
Edgerton, Sarah I, 324
Edgerton, Sarah II, 703
Edgerton, Sarah IV, 144
Edgerton, Sarah IV, 198
Edgerton, Sarah IV, 327
Edgerton, Sarah IV, 330
Edgerton, Sarah IV, 388
Edgerton, Sarah IV, 389
Edgerton, Sarah IV, 393
Edgerton, Sarah IV, 423
Edgerton, Sarah IV, 451
Edgerton, Sarah IV, 576
Edgerton, Sarah IV, 577
Edgerton, Sarah IV, 584
Edgerton, Sarah IV, 589
Edgerton, Sarah IV, 807
Edgerton, Sarah IV, 813
Edgerton, Sarah IV, 1055
Edgerton, Sarah IV, 1095
Edgerton, Sarah IV, 1103
Edgerton, Sarah IV, 1119
Edgerton, Sarah V, 49
Edgerton, Sarah V, 880
Edgerton, Sarah V, 882
Edgerton, Sarah V, 951
Edgerton, Sarah A. I, 287
Edgerton, Sarah A. I, 678
Edgerton, Sarah A. I, 681
Edgerton, Sarah A. II, 959
Edgerton, Sarah A. II, 1050
Edgerton, Sarah A. II, 1053
Edgerton, Sarah Anna I, 305
Edgerton, Sarah Antram II, 959
Edgerton, Sarah E. I, 286
Edgerton, Sarah E. I, 328
Edgerton, Sarah E. I, 330
Edgerton, Sarah E. I, 336
Edgerton, Sarah E. I, 615
Edgerton, Sarah E. I, 678
Edgerton, Sarah E. I, 681
Edgerton, Sarah E. IV, 1095
Edgerton, Sarah E. IV, 1098
Edgerton, Sarah E. V, 829
Edgerton, Sarah Elizabeth IV, 522
Edgerton, Sarah J. I, 305
Edgerton, Sarah J. II, 721
Edgerton, Sarah J. IV, 576
Edgerton, Sarah J. IV, 598
Edgerton, Sarah M. IV, 198
Edgerton, Sarah M. IV, 807
Edgerton, Sarah Margaret IV, 198
Edgerton, Sarah May I, 615
Edgerton, Sarah May I, 632
Edgerton, Sarah P. IV, 1095
Edgerton, Sarah S. IV, 388
Edgerton, Sarah S. IV, 577
Edgerton, Sarah T. IV, 576
Edgerton, Sarah T. IV, 577
Edgerton, Sarah T. IV, 588
Edgerton, Sarah, Jr. IV, 389
Edgerton, Semira IV, 621
Edgerton, Semira IV, 622
Edgerton, Semira IV, 628
Edgerton, Semira IV, 647
Edgerton, Semira IV, 658
Edgerton, Semira IV, 742
Edgerton, Semira IV, 813
Edgerton, Semira IV, 960
Edgerton, Semira IV, 981
Edgerton, Semira Ellen IV, 621
Edgerton, Semira Ellen IV, 622
Edgerton, Semira Ellen IV, 647
Edgerton, Semira Ellen IV, 813
Edgerton, Silas I, 286
Edgerton, Silas I, 287
Edgerton, Silly I, 287
Edgerton, Sina IV, 577
Edgerton, Sina Branthingham IV, 813
Edgerton, Smitha Elizabeth I, 287
Edgerton, Sophronia I, 237
Edgerton, Sophronia I, 305
Edgerton, Sophronia P. I, 237
Edgerton, Stephen Arthur IV, 621
Edgerton, Stephen T. I, 305
Edgerton, Sufferance I, 286
Edgerton, Susan IV, 621
Edgerton, Susan IV, 700
Edgerton, Susan IV, 713
Edgerton, Susan IV, 813
Edgerton, Susan IV, 817
Edgerton, Susan G. IV, 389
Edgerton, Susan G. IV, 622
Edgerton, Susan G. IV, 700
Edgerton, Susan G. IV, 813
Edgerton, Susan G. IV, 949
Edgerton, Susanna G. IV, 622
Edgerton, Sybil B. IV, 949
Edgerton, Tabitha I, 305
Edgerton, Tabitha I, 311
Edgerton, Tabitha IV, 389
Edgerton, Tabitha V, 49
Edgerton, Tabitha V, 837
Edgerton, Tabitha O. I, 289
Edgerton, Tabitha Octovo I, 287
Edgerton, Tamar IV, 1095
Edgerton, Tamar IV, 1119
Edgerton, Tamor IV, 1095
Edgerton, Thomas I, 286
Edgerton, Thomas I, 287
Edgerton, Thomas I, 294
Edgerton, Thomas I, 302
Edgerton, Thomas I, 304
Edgerton, Thomas I, 305
Edgerton, Thomas I, 316
Edgerton, Thomas I, 985
Edgerton, Thomas II, 512
Edgerton, Thomas IV, 198
Edgerton, Thomas IV, 389
Edgerton, Thomas IV, 576
Edgerton, Thomas IV, 1095
Edgerton, Thomas V, 837
Edgerton, Thomas V, 870
Edgerton, Thomas D. IV, 576
Edgerton, Thomas J. IV, 1095
Edgerton, Thomas Jefferson IV, 1095
Edgerton, Thomas S. V, 837
Edgerton, Thomas, Jr. II, 512
Edgerton, Tilitha I, 287
Edgerton, Tilman P. IV, 1095
Edgerton, Virgil W. IV, 949
Edgerton, W. H. I, 305
Edgerton, W. K. I, 305
Edgerton, W. L. I, 305
Edgerton, W. R. I, 305
Edgerton, Walter IV, 176
Edgerton, Walter IV, 198
Edgerton, Walter IV, 381
Edgerton, Walter IV, 388
Edgerton, Walter IV, 389
Edgerton, Walter IV, 401
Edgerton, Walter IV, 571
Edgerton, Walter IV, 576
Edgerton, Walter IV, 577
Edgerton, Walter IV, 581
Edgerton, Walter IV, 800
Edgerton, Walter IV, 807
Edgerton, Walter IV, 813
Edgerton, Walter IV, 819
Edgerton, Walter IV, 832
Edgerton, Walter IV, 934
Edgerton, Walter IV, 949
Edgerton, Walter V, 951
Edgerton, Walter V, 957
Edgerton, Walter G. IV, 622
Edgerton, Walter G. IV, 813
Edgerton, Walter G. IV, 846
Edgerton, Walter G. IV, 949
Edgerton, Walter J. IV, 388
Edgerton, Walter J. IV, 389
Edgerton, Walter J. IV, 432
Edgerton, Walter J. IV, 446
Edgerton, Walter J. IV, 576
Edgerton, Walter J. IV, 577
Edgerton, Walter J. IV, 595
Edgerton, Walter J. IV, 949
Edgerton, Wd. Grace VI, 384
Edgerton, Wilford D. IV, 198
Edgerton, Wilford D. IV, 813
Edgerton, Wilfred IV, 813
Edgerton, Wilfred D. IV, 198
Edgerton, Willard B. IV, 389
Edgerton, William I, 285
Edgerton, William I, 286
Edgerton, William I, 287
Edgerton, William I, 289
Edgerton, William I, 295
Edgerton, William I, 297
Edgerton, William I, 305
Edgerton, William I, 316
Edgerton, William I, 328
Edgerton, William I, 985
Edgerton, William IV, 144
Edgerton, William IV, 198
Edgerton, William IV, 327
Edgerton, William IV, 388
Edgerton, William IV, 389
Edgerton, William IV, 393
Edgerton, William IV, 522
Edgerton, William IV, 576
Edgerton, William IV, 1095
Edgerton, William V, 49
Edgerton, William V, 837
Edgerton, William Benbow I, 615
Edgerton, William Benbow I, 632
Edgerton, William D. IV, 576
Edgerton, William E. I, 328
Edgerton, William E. I, 330
Edgerton, William F. I, 305
Edgerton, William F. I, 328
Edgerton, William Franklin I, 286
Edgerton, William H. I, 286
Edgerton, William H. I, 287
Edgerton, William H. I, 305
Edgerton, William H. I, 328
Edgerton, William Henry I, 286
Edgerton, William Henry I, 287
Edgerton, William I. I, 286
Edgerton, William L. I, 237
Edgerton, William R. I, 287
Edgerton, William R. I, 305
Edgerton, William R. I, 328
Edgerton, William R. I, 336
Edgerton, William T. V, 837
Edgerton, William W. I, 286
Edgerton, William W. V, 837
Edgerton, William, Sr. I, 287

Edgerton, William, Sr. I, 294
Edgerton, Willie W. I, 237
Edgerton, Wilson IV, 621
Edgerton, Wilson IV, 742
Edgerton, Wilson IV, 813
Edgerton, Wimfred Mae II, 959
Edgerton, Winifred M. II, 1050
Edgerton, Wm. IV, 144
Edgerton, Wm. IV, 330
Edgerton, Wm. IV, 394
Edgerton, Wm. IV, 576
Edgerton, Wm. V, 882
Edgerton, Wm. V, 886
Edgerton, Wm. D. IV, 388
Edgerton, Wm. D. IV, 577
Edgerton, Wm. Dewees IV, 577
Edgerton, Zeno I, 237
Edgerton, Zeno I, 305
Edgerton, Zilpah IV, 385
Edgerton, Zilpah IV, 388
Edgerton, Zilpah IV, 1095
Edgerton, Zilpah IV, 1119
Edgerton, Zilpha I, 286
Edgerton, Zilpha I, 305
Edgerton, Zilpha I, 309
Edgerton, Zilpha I, 311
Edgerton, Zilpha I, 619
Edgerton, Zilpha IV, 388
Edgerton, Zilpha IV, 389
Edgerton, Zilpha IV, 1055
Edgerton, Zilpha IV, 1065
Edgerton, Zilpha IV, 1094
Edgerton, Zilpha IV, 1095
Edgerton, Zilphia I, 287
Edgerton, Zilphia I, 622
Edget, Webster III, 109
Edgett, Rebekah II, 512
Edgett, Rebekah II, 597
Edghill, Cornelius II, 443
Edghill, Elizabeth II, 443
Edghill, Hannah II, 357
Edghill, John II, 357
Edghill, Rebecca II, 443
Edghill, Rebecka II, 357
Edghill, Rebeckah II, 357
Edghill, Simon II, 357
Edgington, Frank A. IV, 1250
Edgington, Hannah IV, 1157
Edgington, Lillie IV, 1157
Edgington, Minnie IV, 1157
Edgington, Oakley V, 488
Edinger, Margaret IV, 1037
Edinger, Park B. IV, 1037
Edingfield, Erma V, 166
Edingfield, Franklin V, 166
Edington, James VI, 814
Edington, James VI, 818
Edington, Louisa VI, 814
Edins, Benjamin VI, 309
Edkin, Ann B. IV, 677
Edkin, Ann B. IV, 700
Edkin, Joanna IV, 700
Edler, Susanna I, 894
Edminson, John I, 1151
Edmond, Annie V, 455
Edmonds, Catharine VI, 814
Edmonds, Charlotte VI, 911
Edmonds, Esmon VI, 911
Edmonds, Geo. H. VI, 814
Edmonds, Joseph VI, 911
Edmonds, Rachel VI, 902
Edmonds, Sophia Green VI, 911
Edmondson, Bertha V, 882
Edmondson, Charles D. V, 882
Edmondson, Earl V, 882
Edmondson, Edward II, 512
Edmondson, Elizabeth II, 512
Edmondson, Elizabeth II, 859
Edmondson, Esther II, 801
Edmondson, Frank V, 882
Edmondson, Hester IV, 1277
Edmondson, Hester IV, 1293
Edmondson, John I, 1118
Edmondson, John I, 1151
Edmondson, John F. II, 859
Edmondson, Joseph I, 1029
Edmondson, Lydia II, 512
Edmondson, Lydia II, 611
Edmondson, Margret I, 808
Edmondson, Mary I, 808
Edmondson, Mary IV, 198
Edmondson, Miriam V, 882
Edmondson, Rebeccah I, 1056
Edmondson, Samuel I, 808
Edmondson, Sarah I, 808
Edmondson, Solomon I, 808
Edmondson, Solomon I, 1092
Edmondson, Solomon I, 1151
Edmondson, Susanna I, 808
Edmondson, Susannah I, 808
Edmondson, Susannah I, 1091
Edmondson, Susannah I, 1092
Edmondson, Thomas I, 1118
Edmondson, Thomas I, 1151
Edmonson, Ann IV, 622
Edmonson, Ann V, 488
Edmonson, Eli IV, 622
Edmonson, Eli IV, 1055
Edmonson, Elizabeth V, 488
Edmonson, Ester V, 488
Edmonson, Esther V, 488
Edmonson, Franklin IV, 1055
Edmonson, John IV, 622
Edmonson, John IV, 1055
Edmonson, Jonathan IV, 622
Edmonson, Jonathan IV, 1055
Edmonson, Louis IV, 1055
Edmonson, Maria V, 488
Edmonson, Phebe IV, 1055
Edmonson, Ruth IV, 1055
Edmonson, Sarah IV, 622
Edmonson, Susannah I, 1092
Edmonson, Thomas I, 1092
Edmonson, Thomas I, 1118
Edmonson, Thomas V, 488
Edmonson, William V, 488
Edmunds, Mary VI, 63
Edmunds, Sarah VI, 63
Edmundson, ??? VI, 22
Edmundson, ??? VI, 41
Edmundson, ??? VI, 145
Edmundson, Abner IV, 622
Edmundson, Abner IV, 701
Edmundson, Amos IV, 868
Edmundson, Ann II, 792
Edmundson, Ann II, 858
Edmundson, Ann IV, 622
Edmundson, Ann IV, 638
Edmundson, Ann IV, 665
Edmundson, Ann IV, 868
Edmundson, Ann IV, 884
Edmundson, Ann V, 488
Edmundson, Ann V, 951
Edmundson, Cabel J. I, 1029
Edmundson, Caleb I, 1019
Edmundson, Caleb I, 1029
Edmundson, Caleb, Jr. I, 1029
Edmundson, Caleb, Sr. I, 1029
Edmundson, Edward II, 512
Edmundson, Edward V, 903
Edmundson, Ehos. V, 959
Edmundson, Eli IV, 622
Edmundson, Eli IV, 632
Edmundson, Eli IV, 665
Edmundson, Eli IV, 868
Edmundson, Eli IV, 872
Edmundson, Elisabeth II, 512
Edmundson, Eliza IV, 617
Edmundson, Eliza IV, 622
Edmundson, Elizabeth II, 512
Edmundson, Elizabeth II, 801
Edmundson, Elizabeth II, 859
Edmundson, Elizabeth V, 488
Edmundson, Elizabeth V, 951
Edmundson, Elizabeth V, 959
Edmundson, Ellen IV, 622
Edmundson, Ellen IV, 701
Edmundson, Ester V, 488
Edmundson, Esther V, 488
Edmundson, Esther V, 951
Edmundson, Esther V, 959
Edmundson, Franklin IV, 868
Edmundson, Franklin IV, 1055
Edmundson, Gulielma IV, 622
Edmundson, Gulielma IV, 638
Edmundson, Hannah IV, 622
Edmundson, Hannah IV, 701
Edmundson, Hannah VI, 490
Edmundson, Henry II, 357
Edmundson, Hester I, 1019
Edmundson, Hiram IV, 622
Edmundson, Hiram IV, 868
Edmundson, Hyram IV, 622
Edmundson, Irene IV, 368
Edmundson, Irene IV, 389
Edmundson, Isaac I, 1029
Edmundson, Isaac N. IV, 701
Edmundson, Isaac Newton IV, 622
Edmundson, Jane IV, 622
Edmundson, Jane IV, 701
Edmundson, John I, 962
Edmundson, John I, 1092
Edmundson, John II, 792
Edmundson, John II, 858
Edmundson, John II, 859
Edmundson, John IV, 622
Edmundson, John IV, 632
Edmundson, John IV, 659
Edmundson, John IV, 701
Edmundson, John IV, 868
Edmundson, John IV, 884
Edmundson, John IV, 1055
Edmundson, John V, 488
Edmundson, John V, 951
Edmundson, John F. II, 859
Edmundson, John, Jr. IV, 622
Edmundson, John, Jr. IV, 868
Edmundson, Jonathan IV, 622
Edmundson, Jonathan IV, 635
Edmundson, Jonathan IV, 701
Edmundson, Jonathan IV, 868
Edmundson, Joseph I, 1029
Edmundson, Joseph II, 801
Edmundson, Lydia II, 512
Edmundson, Lydia II, 610
Edmundson, Margaret I, 962
Edmundson, Margaret I, 1053
Edmundson, Margaret I, 1091
Edmundson, Margaret I, 1092
Edmundson, Margret I, 1061
Edmundson, Maria IV, 868
Edmundson, Maria V, 488
Edmundson, Maria V, 951
Edmundson, Mariah V, 488
Edmundson, Marian IV, 885
Edmundson, Mary I, 808
Edmundson, Mary I, 962
Edmundson, Mary IV, 622
Edmundson, Mary IV, 701
Edmundson, Mary Ellen VI, 618
Edmundson, Mary Ellen VI, 635
Edmundson, Nathan IV, 868
Edmundson, Oscar IV, 701
Edmundson, Phebe IV, 30
Edmundson, Phebe IV, 64
Edmundson, Phebe IV, 622
Edmundson, Phebe IV, 642
Edmundson, Phebe IV, 701
Edmundson, Phebe IV, 868
Edmundson, Phebe IV, 885
Edmundson, Phebe Ann IV, 622
Edmundson, Phebe Ann IV, 635
Edmundson, Priscilla II, 357
Edmundson, Ruth IV, 622
Edmundson, Ruth IV, 632
Edmundson, Ruth IV, 665
Edmundson, Ruth IV, 701
Edmundson, Ruth IV, 868
Edmundson, Ruth IV, 872
Edmundson, Ruth IV, 1055
Edmundson, Samuel I, 808
Edmundson, Samuel II, 792
Edmundson, Samuel L. IV, 622
Edmundson, Samuel L. IV, 701
Edmundson, Sarah IV, 622
Edmundson, Sarah IV, 659
Edmundson, Sarah IV, 868
Edmundson, Sarah IV, 884
Edmundson, Sina IV, 701
Edmundson, Sina Ann IV, 622
Edmundson, Solomon I, 1092
Edmundson, Susanah I, 962
Edmundson, Susannah I, 808
Edmundson, Susannah I, 1077
Edmundson, Susannah I, 1092
Edmundson, Susannah II, 792
Edmundson, Susannah II, 858
Edmundson, Thomas I, 1092
Edmundson, Thomas V, 488
Edmundson, Thomas V, 951
Edmundson, Thomas, Jr. V, 951
Edmundson, Thos. IV, 622
Edmundson, William I, 1029
Edmundson, William III, 13
Edmundson, William IV, 622
Edmundson, William V, 488
Edmundson, William VI, 13
Edmundson, William VI, 22
Edmundson, William VI, 41
Edmundson, William VI, 145
Edmundson, Wm. V, 951
Edmunson, Abner IV, 701
Edmunson, Alice IV, 389
Edmunson, Alice H. IV, 389
Edmunson, Ellen IV, 701
Edmunson, Franklin IV, 389
Edmunson, Hannah IV, 701
Edmunson, Isaac N. IV, 701
Edmunson, Jane IV, 701
Edmunson, John IV, 701
Edmunson, Jonathan IV, 701
Edmunson, Mary IV, 701
Edmunson, Mary Irene IV, 389
Edmunson, Oscar IV, 701
Edmunson, Phebe IV, 701
Edmunson, Priscilla II, 357
Edmunson, Ruth IV, 701
Edmunson, Samuel L. IV, 701
Edmunson, Sina IV, 701
Edmunson, William IV, 389
Ednew, Elizabeth II, 995
Ednew, Elizabeth II, 1018
Edny, Sampson VI, 820
Edridge, Hannah II, 513
Edridge, John II, 17
Edsal, Ruth A. IV, 701
Edsil, Ruth A. IV, 701
Edson, Sarah P. II, 859
Edson, Sarah P. VI, 739
Edson, Sarah Pancoast VI, 739
Edson, Sarah Pancoast VI, 775
Edson, Silas D. II, 792
Edson, Silas D. II, 859
Edson, Silas Dunbar II, 792
Edson, Silas Dunbar VI, 739
Edson, Silas Dunbar VI, 775
Edson, Wd. Sarah Pancoast II, 792
Edster, Elizabeth VI, 854
Edster, Mathew VI, 854
Edward, Catharine I, 538
Edward, David I, 538
Edward, David II, 512
Edward, Eliza Ann II, 464
Edward, Eliza Ann II, 512
Edward, Elizabeth II, 512
Edward, Elizabeth II, 665
Edward, Gemima I, 538
Edward, Griffith II, 464
Edward, Hannah I, 1008
Edward, Hannah I, 1009
Edward, Jemimah II, 357
Edward, John I, 538
Edward, Joseph I, 388
Edward, Joshua I, 538
Edward, Maggie IV, 768
Edward, Martha I, 570
Edward, Martha A. I, 798
Edward, Martha A. I, 808
Edward, Mary II, 117
Edward, Milton I, 593
Edward, Richard II, 665
Edward, Ruth I, 1008
Edward, Ruth I, 1009
Edward, Sarah II, 464
Edward, Solomon I, 538
Edward, Thomas II, 995
Edward, William V, 50
Edwards, ??? I, 624
Edwards, ??? III, 196
Edwards, ??? III, 206
Edwards, ??? III, 229
Edwards, Aaron II, 117
Edwards, Aaron II, 148
Edwards, Aaron II, 151
Edwards, Abigail I, 538
Edwards, Absalem I, 496
Edwards, Absolom I, 497
Edwards, Absolom I, 538
Edwards, Adaline IV, 1206
Edwards, Agnes II, 845
Edwards, Agnes II, 859
Edwards, Alexander II, 479
Edwards, Alexander II, 512
Edwards, Alexander IV, 701
Edwards, Alice II, 785
Edwards, Alice II, 792
Edwards, Alice II, 793
Edwards, Alice II, 859
Edwards, Allen V, 166
Edwards, Allen V, 167
Edwards, Allen V, 204
Edwards, Ann I, 445
Edwards, Ann I, 447
Edwards, Ann II, 117
Edwards, Ann II, 357
Edwards, Ann II, 512
Edwards, Ann II, 588
Edwards, Ann II, 642
Edwards, Ann V, 50
Edwards, Ann V, 105
Edwards, Ann V, 167
Edwards, Ann V, 560
Edwards, Ann R. II, 859
Edwards, Ann R. II, 883
Edwards, Anna V, 235
Edwards, Anna B. V, 903
Edwards, Anna M. II, 859
Edwards, Anna R. II, 737
Edwards, Annie V, 51
Edwards, Anuel I, 538
Edwards, Anuel I, 962
Edwards, Archibald I, 445
Edwards, Archibald I, 447
Edwards, Archibald V, 50
Edwards, Archibald V, 105
Edwards, Archibald V, 560
Edwards, Armely I, 540
Edwards, Armilla I, 601
Edwards, Arthur V, 670
Edwards, Asa I, 601
Edwards, Asenath I, 371
Edwards, Asenath I, 877
Edwards, Asenath V, 235
Edwards, Asenath V, 329
Edwards, Asenath V, 348
Edwards, Asenath Edwards I, 388
Edwards, Athelia V, 51
Edwards, B. Y. I, 557
Edwards, B. Y. I, 938
Edwards, Barclay II, 117
Edwards, Barna I, 305
Edwards, Bartlett Yancey I, 5
Edwards, Benjamin J. II, 737
Edwards, Benjamin Johnson II, 357
Edwards, Benjamin Johnson II, 737
Edwards, Benjamin Johnson II, 859
Edwards, Bert V, 560
Edwards, Bertha V, 235
Edwards, Bertha May V, 167
Edwards, Beulah I, 606
Edwards, Birtha V, 235
Edwards, Bonnie V, 670
Edwards, Bonnie V, 692
Edwards, Burch Carter V, 235
Edwards, Calvin I, 601
Edwards, Caroline I, 538
Edwards, Caroline I, 557
Edwards, Caroline IV, 1206
Edwards, Caroline E. III, 109
Edwards, Caroline S. II, 131
Edwards, Caroline S. II, 148
Edwards, Caroline S. II, 151
Edwards, Catharine I, 538
Edwards, Catharine I, 550
Edwards, Catharine I, 600
Edwards, Catharine I, 601
Edwards, Catherine VI, 384
Edwards, Catherine VI, 399
Edwards, Cerena I, 606
Edwards, Charity V, 167
Edwards, Charles I, 538
Edwards, Charles V, 51
Edwards, Charles V, 329
Edwards, Charles V, 736
Edwards, Charles C. II, 737
Edwards, Charles W. V, 167
Edwards, Charlotte V, 51
Edwards, Chas. Craft II, 792
Edwards, Chas. R. IV, 1314
Edwards, Christian II, 512
Edwards, Christian II, 583
Edwards, Christiana II, 357
Edwards, Christianna II, 512
Edwards, Christianna II, 549
Edwards, Christianna V, 51
Edwards, Clarissa III, 109
Edwards, Cortland IV, 1206
Edwards, Cyrena I, 538
Edwards, Cyrena I, 601
Edwards, Daniel II, 512
Edwards, Daniel V, 736
Edwards, Daniel, Jr. II, 512
Edwards, David I, 496
Edwards, David I, 497
Edwards, David I, 524
Edwards, David I, 537
Edwards, David I, 538
Edwards, David II, 357
Edwards, David II, 512
Edwards, David II, 549
Edwards, David II, 583
Edwards, David II, 589
Edwards, David V, 50
Edwards, David V, 51
Edwards, David V, 619
Edwards, David V, 620
Edwards, David V, 670
Edwards, David V, 736
Edwards, David V, 903
Edwards, David Brown I, 877
Edwards, Delilah I, 601
Edwards, Delilah I, 606
Edwards, Della A. I, 759
Edwards, Della A. I, 770
Edwards, Duncan III, 59
Edwards, Duncan III, 109
Edwards, Earl Nelson V, 670
Edwards, Ebanezar I, 538
Edwards, Ebenezar I, 497
Edwards, Ebenezar I, 538
Edwards, Edith V, 51
Edwards, Edith V, 103
Edwards, Edith V, 166
Edwards, Edith V, 175
Edwards, Edith V, 560
Edwards, Edith V, 670
Edwards, Edith Ann V, 50
Edwards, Edward Aiken V, 670
Edwards, Edward B. II, 737

Edwards, Edward, Sr. II, 807
Edwards, Edwin L. V, 51
Edwards, Eleanor I, 496
Edwards, Eleanor I, 497
Edwards, Eleanor I, 538
Edwards, Eleanor I, 575
Edwards, Eleanor II, 357
Edwards, Eleanor II, 512
Edwards, Eleanor C. V, 50
Edwards, Eleanor C. V, 134
Edwards, Eleanor C. V, 560
Edwards, Elen I, 497
Edwards, Elijah I, 619
Edwards, Elinor I, 343
Edwards, Elinor I, 388
Edwards, Elinor VI, 384
Edwards, Eliza II, 792
Edwards, Eliza II, 859
Edwards, Eliza III, 109
Edwards, Eliza IV, 1206
Edwards, Eliza V, 50
Edwards, Eliza V, 560
Edwards, Eliza Ann II, 357
Edwards, Eliza Ann II, 512
Edwards, Eliza Ann III, 27
Edwards, Eliza Ann III, 109
Edwards, Eliza B. II, 737
Edwards, Eliza E. V, 619
Edwards, Eliza E. V, 670
Edwards, Eliza E. V, 903
Edwards, Eliza H. II, 859
Edwards, Eliza H. VI, 911
Edwards, Eliza Jane V, 50
Edwards, Elizabeth I, 497
Edwards, Elizabeth I, 528
Edwards, Elizabeth I, 537
Edwards, Elizabeth I, 678
Edwards, Elizabeth II, 131
Edwards, Elizabeth II, 357
Edwards, Elizabeth II, 512
Edwards, Elizabeth II, 589
Edwards, Elizabeth II, 737
Edwards, Elizabeth IV, 84
Edwards, Elizabeth IV, 112
Edwards, Elizabeth V, 50
Edwards, Elizabeth V, 65
Edwards, Elizabeth V, 105
Edwards, Elizabeth V, 302
Edwards, Elizabeth V, 560
Edwards, Elizabeth V, 571
Edwards, Elizabeth V, 663
Edwards, Elizabeth V, 670
Edwards, Elizabeth V, 678
Edwards, Elizabeth VI, 1008
Edwards, Elizabeth Ann V, 50
Edwards, Elizabeth H. II, 737
Edwards, Elizabeth Hildeburn II, 357
Edwards, Elizabeth Hildeburn II, 737
Edwards, Elizabeth Hildeburn II, 859
Edwards, Elizabeth Margaret II, 792
Edwards, Ella V, 167
Edwards, Ellen II, 793
Edwards, Ellwood V, 51
Edwards, Elsie V, 670
Edwards, Elsie V, 678
Edwards, Elvie V, 670
Edwards, Elvira I, 538
Edwards, Elwood V, 167
Edwards, Emaline V, 167
Edwards, Emily H. V, 235
Edwards, Emma III, 109
Edwards, Emma III, 206
Edwards, Emma V, 384
Edwards, Emma C. II, 859
Edwards, Emma H. II, 737
Edwards, Emma H. V, 167
Edwards, Essie I, 336
Edwards, Eusis Helen White V, 903
Edwards, Evalina V, 51
Edwards, Ezekiel II, 357
Edwards, Fillis I, 497
Edwards, Frank V, 329
Edwards, Gairus I, 601
Edwards, Gemima I, 538
Edwards, Gemima V, 166
Edwards, George II, 458
Edwards, George II, 512
Edwards, George II, 681
Edwards, Gilbert I, 538
Edwards, Granderson V, 167
Edwards, Griffith II, 357
Edwards, Griffith II, 512
Edwards, Griffith II, 549
Edwards, Griffith II, 583
Edwards, Griffith II, 703
Edwards, Griffith II, 737
Edwards, Griffith II, 749
Edwards, Griffith II, 792
Edwards, Griffith E. II, 357
Edwards, Griffith, Jr. II, 512
Edwards, Griffith, Jr. II, 703
Edwards, Griffith, Jr. II, 737
Edwards, Griffith, Jr. II, 792
Edwards, Griffith, Jr. II, 859
Edwards, Hadley V, 50
Edwards, Hannah I, 388
Edwards, Hannah I, 496
Edwards, Hannah I, 497
Edwards, Hannah I, 524
Edwards, Hannah I, 534
Edwards, Hannah I, 537
Edwards, Hannah I, 538
Edwards, Hannah I, 543
Edwards, Hannah II, 216
Edwards, Hannah II, 357
Edwards, Hannah II, 470
Edwards, Hannah II, 512
Edwards, Hannah II, 538
Edwards, Hannah V, 50
Edwards, Hannah V, 51
Edwards, Hannah V, 71
Edwards, Hannah V, 329
Edwards, Hannah V, 337
Edwards, Hannah V, 903
Edwards, Hannah Amelia V, 903
Edwards, Hannual I, 496
Edwards, Hannuel I, 538
Edwards, Hannuel I, 550
Edwards, Hanuel I, 487
Edwards, Hanuel I, 497
Edwards, Hanuel I, 537
Edwards, Hanuel I, 538
Edwards, Hanuel I, 600
Edwards, Hanuel I, 601
Edwards, Hanuel I, 606
Edwards, Hanuel, Sr. I, 606
Edwards, Harlan V, 50
Edwards, Harlan V, 51
Edwards, Harlan E. V, 51
Edwards, Harlan H. V, 50
Edwards, Henery I, 538
Edwards, Henrietta I, 538
Edwards, Henry I, 496
Edwards, Henry I, 538
Edwards, Henry I, 962
Edwards, Henry V, 167
Edwards, Hepsibah V, 167
Edwards, Hepsibath V, 180
Edwards, Honour II, 357
Edwards, Ira VI, 601
Edwards, Ira I, 606
Edwards, Irene IV, 701
Edwards, Isaac I, 497
Edwards, Isaac I, 538
Edwards, Isaac II, 357
Edwards, Isaac II, 512
Edwards, Isaac V, 50
Edwards, Isaac V, 51
Edwards, Isaac V, 68
Edwards, Isaac V, 98
Edwards, Isaac V, 560
Edwards, Isaac V, 573
Edwards, Isaac Fisher V, 50
Edwards, Jacob II, 512
Edwards, Jain I, 445
Edwards, Jairus I, 606
Edwards, James I, 496
Edwards, James I, 497
Edwards, James I, 538
Edwards, James I, 589
Edwards, James I, 1048
Edwards, James II, 792
Edwards, James V, 235
Edwards, James V, 329
Edwards, James V, 663
Edwards, James V, 670
Edwards, James B. V, 50
Edwards, James, Jr. I, 538
Edwards, James, Jr. II, 859
Edwards, Jamima I, 497
Edwards, Jane I, 445
Edwards, Jane I, 497
Edwards, Jane I, 538
Edwards, Jane I, 555
Edwards, Jane I, 589
Edwards, Jane I, 593
Edwards, Jane I, 808
Edwards, Jane I, 1048
Edwards, Jane II, 512
Edwards, Jane II, 681
Edwards, Jane III, 109
Edwards, Jane III, 229
Edwards, Jane IV, 522
Edwards, Jane IV, 543
Edwards, Jane V, 49
Edwards, Jane V, 50
Edwards, Jane V, 79
Edwards, Jane V, 166
Edwards, Jane V, 180
Edwards, Jane V, 329
Edwards, Jane V, 341
Edwards, Jane V, 560
Edwards, Jane V, 578
Edwards, Jane V, 781
Edwards, Jane H. V, 50
Edwards, Jane H. V, 98
Edwards, Jehu V, 50
Edwards, Jemima I, 496
Edwards, Jemima I, 538
Edwards, Jemima II, 512
Edwards, Jemima II, 683
Edwards, Jemima V, 50
Edwards, Jemima V, 167
Edwards, Jemima V, 175
Edwards, Jemima V, 180
Edwards, Jemima V, 903
Edwards, Jemimah II, 357
Edwards, Jemmimah V, 175
Edwards, Jeremiah I, 497
Edwards, Jesse V, 235
Edwards, Jesse G. II, 859
Edwards, John I, 524
Edwards, John I, 538
Edwards, John I, 600
Edwards, John I, 601
Edwards, John I, 606
Edwards, John II, 216
Edwards, John II, 218
Edwards, John II, 357
Edwards, John II, 476
Edwards, John II, 512
Edwards, John II, 793
Edwards, John II, 818
Edwards, John III, 109
Edwards, John V, 50
Edwards, John V, 51
Edwards, John V, 146
Edwards, John V, 560
Edwards, John V, 994
Edwards, John VI, 12
Edwards, John VI, 1008
Edwards, John D. V, 50
Edwards, John D. V, 71
Edwards, John E. VI, 907
Edwards, John Isaac V, 560
Edwards, John, Jr. I, 606
Edwards, John, Jr. II, 512
Edwards, Johnson II, 737
Edwards, Johnson II, 859
Edwards, Jonathan I, 388
Edwards, Jonathan I, 496
Edwards, Jonathan I, 538
Edwards, Jonathan II, 512
Edwards, Jonathan V, 50
Edwards, Jonathan B. I, 678
Edwards, Jonathan Conroy V, 384
Edwards, Joseph I, 388
Edwards, Joseph II, 67
Edwards, Joseph II, 470
Edwards, Joseph II, 512
Edwards, Joseph II, 538
Edwards, Joseph II, 792
Edwards, Joseph II, 859
Edwards, Joseph J. II, 737
Edwards, Joseph J. II, 859
Edwards, Joseph Johnson II, 357
Edwards, Joseph Johnson II, 737
Edwards, Joseph Johnson II, 792
Edwards, Joseph Johnson II, 859
Edwards, Joshua I, 496
Edwards, Joshua I, 497
Edwards, Joshua I, 537
Edwards, Joshua I, 538
Edwards, Joshua I, 601
Edwards, Joshua I, 606
Edwards, Joshua V, 49
Edwards, Joshua V, 50
Edwards, Joshua V, 68
Edwards, Joshua V, 559
Edwards, Joshua V, 560
Edwards, Joshua V, 573
Edwards, Joshua H. V, 50
Edwards, Joshua, Jr. I, 538
Edwards, Julia A. I, 538
Edwards, Lawrence V, 235
Edwards, Lemuel IV, 1206
Edwards, Leonard IV, 1314
Edwards, Letitia V, 670
Edwards, Levi F. V, 670
Edwards, Levi T. V, 670
Edwards, Lewis III, 27
Edwards, Lewis III, 109
Edwards, Lewis V, 670
Edwards, Lewis V, 678
Edwards, Lewis T. V, 670
Edwards, Linda W. II, 859
Edwards, Louise I, 877
Edwards, Lydia II, 512
Edwards, Lydia IV, 459
Edwards, Lydia V, 50
Edwards, Lydia V, 51
Edwards, Lydia V, 112
Edwards, Lydia V, 115
Edwards, Lydia V, 560
Edwards, Lydia E. V, 51
Edwards, Lydia E. V, 85
Edwards, M. D. I, 305
Edwards, M. D. I, 759
Edwards, M. D. I, 770
Edwards, M. Morris V, 903
Edwards, Mack I, 305
Edwards, Mack I, 624
Edwards, Maggie IV, 701
Edwards, Mahalah I, 601
Edwards, Mahaly J. I, 538
Edwards, Mahaly J. I, 573
Edwards, Mamie I, 624
Edwards, Mammie Cox I, 619
Edwards, Mandy Jane V, 167
Edwards, Marcus I, 877
Edwards, Margaret II, 512
Edwards, Margaret II, 589
Edwards, Margaret IV, 813
Edwards, Margaret IV, 904
Edwards, Margaret V, 736
Edwards, Margaret Elizabeth II, 859
Edwards, Margaret Erma V, 51
Edwards, Mariana C. III, 109
Edwards, Mariana C. L. III, 196
Edwards, Marianna L. III, 109
Edwards, Marion V, 235
Edwards, Martha I, 388
Edwards, Martha I, 497
Edwards, Martha I, 538
Edwards, Martha V, 50
Edwards, Martha V, 903
Edwards, Martha A. I, 808
Edwards, Martha H. V, 50
Edwards, Martha J. V, 619
Edwards, Martha J. V, 670
Edwards, Martha J. V, 903
Edwards, Mary I, 336
Edwards, Mary I, 388
Edwards, Mary I, 445
Edwards, Mary I, 446
Edwards, Mary I, 497
Edwards, Mary I, 606
Edwards, Mary I, 624
Edwards, Mary I, 1057
Edwards, Mary II, 67
Edwards, Mary II, 116
Edwards, Mary II, 216
Edwards, Mary II, 218
Edwards, Mary II, 479
Edwards, Mary II, 512
Edwards, Mary II, 540
Edwards, Mary II, 640
Edwards, Mary II, 641
Edwards, Mary II, 818
Edwards, Mary III, 109
Edwards, Mary III, 206
Edwards, Mary IV, 701
Edwards, Mary IV, 949
Edwards, Mary V, 38
Edwards, Mary V, 49
Edwards, Mary V, 50
Edwards, Mary V, 51
Edwards, Mary V, 67
Edwards, Mary V, 105
Edwards, Mary V, 113
Edwards, Mary V, 166
Edwards, Mary V, 167
Edwards, Mary V, 175
Edwards, Mary V, 204
Edwards, Mary V, 560
Edwards, Mary V, 736
Edwards, Mary A. V, 670
Edwards, Mary Ann II, 357
Edwards, Mary Ann II, 737
Edwards, Mary Ann II, 749
Edwards, Mary Ann II, 792
Edwards, Mary Ann II, 859
Edwards, Mary Ann IV, 813
Edwards, Mary Ann IV, 839
Edwards, Mary Ann V, 36
Edwards, Mary Ann V, 50
Edwards, Mary Ann V, 51
Edwards, Mary Avilla V, 560
Edwards, Mary E. V, 50
Edwards, Mary E. C. V, 329
Edwards, Mary E. Carter V, 670
Edwards, Mary Edwards I, 715
Edwards, Mary Elizabeth V, 235
Edwards, Mary G. Agnes II, 859
Edwards, Mary J. V, 670
Edwards, Mary Jane V, 50
Edwards, Mary Jane V, 560
Edwards, Mary Julia A. I, 877
Edwards, Mary L. P. VI, 917
Edwards, Mary Lola I, 624
Edwards, Mary Yerkes II, 792
Edwards, Melitha I, 601
Edwards, Meribah II, 796
Edwards, Milton I, 593
Edwards, Milton V, 50
Edwards, Milton T. V, 50
Edwards, Minnie IV, 1206
Edwards, Morgan I, 388
Edwards, Morgan I, 715
Edwards, Morgan I, 1092
Edwards, Morgan I, 1118
Edwards, Nancy I, 538
Edwards, Nancy I, 600
Edwards, Nancy I, 601
Edwards, Nancy IV, 1314
Edwards, Nancy V, 50
Edwards, Nancy V, 98
Edwards, Nancy V, 167
Edwards, Nancy V, 560
Edwards, Nancy V, 573
Edwards, Nancy V, 903
Edwards, Nancy VI, 870
Edwards, Nancy VI, 938
Edwards, Nancy Harvey V, 50
Edwards, Nathan I, 496
Edwards, Nathan V, 50
Edwards, Nathaniel I, 388
Edwards, Nathaniel I, 445
Edwards, Nathaniel I, 446
Edwards, Nathaniel V, 49
Edwards, Nathaniel V, 67
Edwards, Nathaniel V, 560
Edwards, Nathaniel, Jr. V, 560
Edwards, Nettie I, 613
Edwards, Nettie V, 51
Edwards, Nettie V, 619
Edwards, Nettie V, 670
Edwards, Nettie V, 903
Edwards, Octavius IV, 1314
Edwards, Pauli IV, 949
Edwards, Pennie I, 538
Edwards, Peter I, 388
Edwards, Phebe III, 109
Edwards, Philip II, 357
Edwards, Philis I, 538
Edwards, Phillis I, 497
Edwards, Philo III, 109
Edwards, Polly V, 167
Edwards, Rachel I, 371
Edwards, Rachel I, 388
Edwards, Rachel I, 496
Edwards, Rachel I, 497
Edwards, Rachel I, 538
Edwards, Rachel I, 601
Edwards, Rachel II, 148
Edwards, Rachel II, 151
Edwards, Rachel II, 357
Edwards, Rachel II, 476
Edwards, Rachel II, 512
Edwards, Rachel II, 641
Edwards, Rachel II, 737
Edwards, Rachel II, 818
Edwards, Rachel IV, 1206
Edwards, Rachel VI, 384
Edwards, Rachel VI, 436
Edwards, Rachel Peirce II, 357
Edwards, Rebecca II, 357
Edwards, Rebecca II, 512
Edwards, Rebecca II, 792
Edwards, Rebecca II, 859
Edwards, Rebecca V, 50
Edwards, Rebecca V, 101
Edwards, Rebecca V, 670
Edwards, Rebecca VI, 384
Edwards, Rebecca VI, 399
Edwards, Rebecca Harlan H. V, 560
Edwards, Rebecca I. II, 859
Edwards, Rebecca J. II, 737
Edwards, Rebecca J. II, 859
Edwards, Rebecca Jane II, 792
Edwards, Rebecca Jane II, 859
Edwards, Rebecca Johnson II, 737
Edwards, Rebekah I, 497
Edwards, Rebekah I, 538
Edwards, Rees IV, 949
Edwards, Richard II, 357
Edwards, Richard II, 512
Edwards, Richard II, 589
Edwards, Robert III, 109
Edwards, Robert V, 235
Edwards, Robert L. III, 109
Edwards, Robert, Jr. V, 235
Edwards, Robertson I, 606
Edwards, Robinson I, 601
Edwards, Roxie I, 336
Edwards, Ruth I, 538

Edwards, Ruth I, 606
Edwards, Ruth V, 49
Edwards, Ruth V, 50
Edwards, Ruth V, 167
Edwards, Ruth V, 560
Edwards, Ruth V, 567
Edwards, Ruth E. V, 565
Edwards, Sally VI, 911
Edwards, Samuel II, 131
Edwards, Samuel H. II, 703
Edwards, Samuel H. II, 737
Edwards, Samuel Hildeburn II, 357
Edwards, Samuel Hildeburn II, 512
Edwards, Samuel Hildeburn II, 737
Edwards, Samuel M. II, 148
Edwards, Samuel M. II, 151
Edwards, Sarah I, 497
Edwards, Sarah I, 538
Edwards, Sarah I, 710
Edwards, Sarah I, 715
Edwards, Sarah II, 117
Edwards, Sarah II, 357
Edwards, Sarah II, 470
Edwards, Sarah II, 512
Edwards, Sarah II, 549
Edwards, Sarah II, 703
Edwards, Sarah II, 737
Edwards, Sarah II, 749
Edwards, Sarah II, 792
Edwards, Sarah V, 50
Edwards, Sarah V, 67
Edwards, Sarah V, 167
Edwards, Sarah V, 329
Edwards, Sarah V, 559
Edwards, Sarah V, 560
Edwards, Sarah V, 572
Edwards, Sarah V, 573
Edwards, Sarah V, 680
Edwards, Sarah V, 994
Edwards, Sarah C. III, 109
Edwards, Sarah E. I, 619
Edwards, Sarah S. V, 329
Edwards, Sarles III, 109
Edwards, Sinson A. VI, 911
Edwards, Solomon I, 538
Edwards, Solomon I, 601
Edwards, Solomon D. I, 538
Edwards, Solomon D. I, 573
Edwards, Sophia VI, 870
Edwards, Spencer V, 736
Edwards, Stanley V, 235
Edwards, Susan I, 538
Edwards, Susan IV, 1206
Edwards, Susan R. II, 737
Edwards, Susan W. III, 59
Edwards, Susan W. III, 109
Edwards, Susanna I, 877
Edwards, Susanna IV, 1206
Edwards, Susanna R. II, 737
Edwards, Susannah IV, 1206
Edwards, Susannah V, 50
Edwards, Thomas II, 26
Edwards, Thomas II, 131
Edwards, Thomas II, 479
Edwards, Thomas II, 512
Edwards, Thomas II, 995
Edwards, Thomas V, 670
Edwards, Thomas VI, 911
Edwards, Thomas Hoppin I, 877
Edwards, Thomas T. Haddock V, 50
Edwards, Thomas, Jr. II, 117
Edwards, Thursa I, 601
Edwards, Volumna IV, 1206
Edwards, Warner Tomlinson II, 67
Edwards, Wd. Alice II, 793
Edwards, Wd. Elizabeth II, 807
Edwards, Wd. Mary Austin II, 792
Edwards, Wellington IV, 1206
Edwards, Widow Abigail I, 524
Edwards, William I, 445
Edwards, William I, 496
Edwards, William I, 497
Edwards, William I, 538
Edwards, William II, 357
Edwards, William IV, 1235
Edwards, William V, 49
Edwards, William V, 50
Edwards, William V, 105
Edwards, William V, 166
Edwards, William V, 167
Edwards, William V, 175
Edwards, William Daniel V, 50
Edwards, William H. V, 50
Edwards, William H. V, 560
Edwards, William H. V, 670
Edwards, William L. II, 703
Edwards, William Lloyd II, 357
Edwards, Willis IV, 1206
Edwards, Wm. II, 512
Edwards, Wm. V, 167
Edwards, Wm. V, 180
Edwards, Wm. V, 903
Edwards, Wm. V, 994
Edwards, Wm. VI, 870
Edwards, Wm. H. III, 109
Edwards, Wm. H. V, 670
Edwards, Wm. Henry V, 50
Edwards, Wm. L. II, 737
Edwards, Yancy I, 601
Eeks, Martha Jane V, 837
Eels, R. F. III, 57
Eels, R. F. III, 109
Eels, Rebecca F. III, 109
Eels, Rebecca Frances II, 859
Eeter, Addie C. IV, 1157
Egbert, Fannie Ray III, 27
Egbert, Fannie Ray III, 109
Egbert, George F. III, 27
Egbert, George F. III, 109
Egbert, John III, 236
Egbert, Phebe III, 236
Egbert, Phebe E. III, 236
Egbert, Sarah III, 236
Egden, Esther II, 512
Egden, George II, 512
Egden, Hugh II, 512
Egden, Wd. Mary II, 512
Egge, Adam II, 443
Egge, Richard II, 443
Eggman, Abraham II, 67
Eggman, Abraham II, 68
Eggman, Bartholomew II, 67
Eggman, Bartholomew II, 68
Eggman, Elizabeth II, 67
Eggman, Sarah II, 67
Eggman, Sarah II, 68
Eggman, Sarah II, 85
Eggmon, Abraham II, 67
Eggmon, Bartholomew II, 67
Eggmon, Bartholomew II, 68
Eggmon, Elizabeth II, 67
Eggmon, Sarah II, 67
Egington, Hannah IV, 1157
Egington, Lillie IV, 1157
Eglington, John II, 68
Egly, Hannah II, 216
Egrell, William II, 357
Ehler, Mary V, 806
Ehler, Sarah V, 806
Ehmer, Anna IV, 1314
Ehmer, Christian IV, 1314
Ehmer, Fred IV, 1314
Ehmer, Martha IV, 1314
Ehmer, Mrs. Anna IV, 1314
Ehmer, Teddy IV, 1314
Ehrhardt, Sarah V, 51
Ehrhardt, Sarah V, 92
Ehrman, Artis H. III, 16
Ehrman, Artis H. III, 109
Ehrman, John III, 109
Ehrman, Mary A. III, 109
Ehrman, Mary E. III, 16
Ehrman, Mary E. III, 109
Eidds, William VI, 843
Eider, John VI, 11
Eids, Thurston VI, 819
Eids, William VI, 802
Eidson, B. A. VI, 1004
Eidson, Barnabas VI, 814
Eidson, Barnabas A. VI, 911
Eidson, Boice VI, 872
Eidson, Boyce VI, 911
Eidson, Boyce VI, 920
Eidson, Boyce VI, 930
Eidson, Boyce VI, 965
Eidson, Boyce VI, 992
Eidson, Edward VI, 911
Eidson, Elizabeth VI, 911
Eidson, F. B. A. VI, 911
Eidson, Frances VI, 885
Eidson, Frances A. VI, 992
Eidson, Hannah VI, 920
Eidson, Henry VI, 823
Eidson, Henry VI, 830
Eidson, Henry VI, 841
Eidson, Henry VI, 845
Eidson, Henry VI, 911
Eidson, Henry VI, 982
Eidson, Henry, Jr. VI, 841
Eidson, James VI, 814
Eidson, Jane VI, 845
Eidson, Jemima VI, 859
Eidson, John VI, 814
Eidson, John VI, 859
Eidson, John VI, 911
Eidson, Joseph VI, 864
Eidson, Lucinda VI, 911
Eidson, Maildred VI, 926
Eidson, Martha D. VI, 814
Eidson, Mary Moorman VI, 814
Eidson, Milly VI, 841
Eidson, Nancy VI, 814
Eidson, Nancy VI, 841
Eidson, Nancy VI, 885
Eidson, Nancy VI, 911
Eidson, Pamelia VI, 814
Eidson, Patsy VI, 911
Eidson, Penelope VI, 850
Eidson, Polly VI, 830
Eidson, Polly M. VI, 992
Eidson, Salley VI, 911
Eidson, Sally VI, 841
Eidson, Sally VI, 911
Eidson, Shelton VI, 911
Eidson, Susanna VI, 823
Eidson, William VI, 814
Eidson, William VI, 823
Eidson, William VI, 826
Eidson, William VI, 830
Eidson, William VI, 841
Eidson, William VI, 911
Eidson, William VI, 920
Eilers, Ann III, 397
Eilers, Ann III, 409
Eilers, Ann Bailey VI, 732
Eilers, Ann Bailey VI, 739
Eilers, K. Fritz III, 397
Eilers, K. Fritz III, 409
Eilers, K. Fritz VI, 732
Eilers, K. Fritz VI, 739
Eilers, Karl VI, 739
Eilers, Leonie W. VI, 739
Eilert, Eliz. III, 109
Eilert, Elizabeth III, 73
Eilert, Jos. III, 109
Eilert, Joseph III, 73
Eilert, Lucinda E. III, 73
Eilert, Lucinda E. III, 109
Eiley, Elizabeth V, 994
Eiley, Ida V, 994
Eiley, Mary II, 792
Eirey, Sarah VI, 636
Eirey, Sarah VI, 690
Eisenbrey, Henry Ebner II, 792
Eisenbrey, J. Lehman II, 851
Eisenbrey, J. Lehman II, 924
Eisenbrey, Mary Ann II, 792
Eisenbrey, Mary Ann II, 859
Eitzel, Dorothy E. II, 131
Eitzel, Edna II, 131
Eitzel, Howard S. II, 131
Ekel, Felicia H. II, 859
Elafritz, Delphina V, 736
Elam, ??? VI, 291
Elam, Catharine III, 269
Elam, Elizabeth VI, 863
Elam, Emanuel II, 513
Elam, Franky VI, 855
Elam, Gervis VI, 171
Elam, Joseph VI, 172
Elam, Joseph VI, 209
Elam, Joseph VI, 212
Elam, Joseph VI, 216
Elam, Lewallen VI, 814
Elam, Mary VI, 814
Elam, Mary VI, 841
Elam, Obedience VI, 841
Elam, Patsy VI, 812
Elam, Richard VI, 841
Elam, Richard VI, 842
Elam, Richard VI, 855
Elam, Richard VI, 944
Elam, Robert III, 109
Elam, Robert VI, 171
Elam, Samuel III, 109
Elam, Susanna VI, 812
Elam, Susanna VI, 863
Elam, Susannah VI, 841
Elamon, Enos V, 807
Elamon, Isom V, 807
Elamon, Margaret V, 807
Elams, Emanuel VI, 98
Elams, Emanuel VI, 106
Elams, Emanuel VI, 122
Elams, Samuel VI, 106
Elbeck, John Stapler II, 513
Elbeck, Martha II, 513
Elbeck, Wd. Martha II, 513
Elbeck, Wd. Martha II, 546
Elberman, Sarah II, 286
Elberman, Theophilus II, 286
Elbin, Rebecca II, 817
Elbis, Ann II, 1065
Elbon, Emma V, 51
Elbon, Frank S. V, 51
Elcock, Rebecca Ann V, 51
Elder, Alfred VI, 814
Elder, Bethia II, 722
Elder, Bethia B. II, 737
Elder, Bethia B. II, 774
Elder, Bethia Bowman II, 737
Elder, Bethis Bowman II, 703
Elder, Branson V, 994
Elder, Constantine VI, 911
Elder, David Edward V, 670
Elder, Dorothy E. V, 670
Elder, Effie A. V, 994
Elder, Elias C. I, 759
Elder, Eliza E. VI, 992
Elder, Elizabeth VI, 814
Elder, Emily IV, 701
Elder, Eparian VI, 814
Elder, Flora C. IV, 701
Elder, Gordon Richard V, 994
Elder, Graden V, 994
Elder, Harriet J. VI, 909
Elder, Helen V, 994
Elder, James II, 703
Elder, James II, 722
Elder, James II, 737
Elder, James II, 774
Elder, James VI, 814
Elder, James J. VI, 909
Elder, John I, 759
Elder, John V, 994
Elder, John, Jr. I, 759
Elder, Jordan IV, 701
Elder, Joseph V, 384
Elder, Joseph VI, 808
Elder, Louisa I, 759
Elder, Louisa I, 760
Elder, Louisa I, 853
Elder, Louise I, 616
Elder, Marie V, 994
Elder, Marium I, 759
Elder, Martha VI, 814
Elder, Martha VI, 848
Elder, Martha Yancie VI, 804
Elder, Mary Belinda I, 759
Elder, Nancy VI, 812
Elder, Nancy VI, 853
Elder, Newton V, 994
Elder, Newton W. V, 994
Elder, Oliver VI, 812
Elder, Oliver VI, 814
Elder, Oliver VI, 848
Elder, Oliver VI, 853
Elder, Patsy VI, 814
Elder, Patsy VI, 841
Elder, Patty V, 994
Elder, Polly VI, 804
Elder, Polly VI, 814
Elder, Polly M. VI, 808
Elder, Rebecca W. E. II, 737
Elder, Rebecca W. E. II, 768
Elder, Rebecca White II, 703
Elder, Rebecca White II, 737
Elder, Richard VI, 853
Elder, Robert C. VI, 814
Elder, Rosa V, 994
Elder, Sarah I, 759
Elder, Sarah A. VI, 814
Elder, Susanna I, 877
Elder, Susanna II, 703
Elder, Susanna II, 722
Elder, Susanna C. II, 737
Elder, Susanna C. II, 774
Elder, Susannah I, 877
Elder, Thomas VI, 911
Elderfield, Charles J. VI, 739
Elderfield, Eleanor C. VI, 739
Elderfield, Mary Elizabeth VI, 731
Elderfield, Mary Elizabeth VI, 739
Elderfield, Rob't Cooley VI, 731
Elderfield, Robert Cooley VI, 731
Elderfield, Robert Cooley VI, 739
Elders, Nannie I, 933
Eldrage, Jaheu II, 513
Eldred, Flora V, 670
Eldred, Flora E. V, 620
Eldred, Harry S. V, 670
Eldred, Martha III, 409
Eldred, Martha III, 421
Eldred, Martha III, 486
Eldred, Phebe III, 409
Eldred, Phebe III, 421
Eldred, Phebe III, 470
Eldred, Rebecca III, 409
Eldred, Rebecca Ann III, 409
Eldred, Richard III, 409
Eldred, Richard III, 421
Eldred, Richard III, 470
Eldredge, Elizabeth II, 510
Eldredge, Elizabeth II, 513
Eldredge, Hannah II, 525
Eldredge, Jehu II, 510
Eldredge, Jehu II, 513
Eldredge, Stacy M. III, 109
Eldredge, Wm. II, 510
Eldredge, Wm. II, 513
Eldreth, Abigail II, 619
Eldrid, Phebe IV, 1361
Eldridg, Katherine VI, 384
Eldridge, ??? II, 357
Eldridge, Abigail II, 194
Eldridge, Abigail II, 216
Eldridge, Abigail II, 228
Eldridge, Abigail II, 309
Eldridge, Amey II, 216
Eldridge, Amey II, 240
Eldridge, Anna III, 109
Eldridge, Charles II, 117
Eldridge, Cornelia II, 792
Eldridge, Cornelia W. II, 859
Eldridge, Cornelia W. II, 936
Eldridge, Deborah Malandra II, 828
Eldridge, Elizabeth II, 357
Eldridge, Elizabeth II, 513
Eldridge, Esther II, 357
Eldridge, Hannah II, 357
Eldridge, Hannah Clark II, 68
Eldridge, Hannah P. II, 513
Eldridge, Hannah Pancoast II, 794
Eldridge, Hannah Pancoast II, 810
Eldridge, Ira II, 286
Eldridge, Isaac II, 68
Eldridge, Jacob II, 357
Eldridge, Jaheu II, 513
Eldridge, James II, 357
Eldridge, James McCletche II, 216
Eldridge, Jehu II, 357
Eldridge, Jehu II, 513
Eldridge, Job II, 513
Eldridge, Job II, 792
Eldridge, Job II, 794
Eldridge, Job II, 828
Eldridge, Job II, 859
Eldridge, John II, 357
Eldridge, Jonathan II, 194
Eldridge, Jonathan II, 216
Eldridge, Jonathan II, 228
Eldridge, Jonathan II, 309
Eldridge, Jonathan II, 357
Eldridge, Jonathan II, 513
Eldridge, Jonathan II, 538
Eldridge, Jonathan II, 610
Eldridge, Joseph II, 357
Eldridge, Joseph II, 513
Eldridge, Joseph P. II, 792
Eldridge, Lydia II, 715
Eldridge, Martha III, 357
Eldridge, Mary II, 68
Eldridge, Mary II, 200
Eldridge, Mary II, 216
Eldridge, Mary II, 228
Eldridge, Mary II, 309
Eldridge, Mary II, 357
Eldridge, Mary II, 513
Eldridge, Noah II, 216
Eldridge, Obadiah II, 357
Eldridge, Obadiah II, 513
Eldridge, Obadiah II, 538
Eldridge, Obadiah II, 610
Eldridge, Obediah II, 357
Eldridge, Phebe II, 68
Eldridge, Phebe II, 357
Eldridge, Phebe II, 513
Eldridge, Phebe II, 538
Eldridge, Phebe W. II, 737
Eldridge, Phebe W. II, 775
Eldridge, Rachel IV, 701
Eldridge, Rachel IV, 726
Eldridge, Samuel II, 357
Eldridge, Samuel II, 513
Eldridge, Sarah II, 33
Eldridge, Sarah II, 357
Eldridge, Sarah II, 513
Eldridge, Sarah Ann II, 286
Eldridge, Sarah E. III, 409
Eldridge, Sarah E. III, 415
Eldridge, Simeon I, 538
Eldridge, Simeon L. III, 409
Eldridge, Simeon L. III, 415
Eldridge, Stacy M. II, 792
Eldridge, Stacy M. II, 859
Eldridge, Stacy M. III, 109
Eldridge, Tacie II, 794
Eldridge, Tacy II, 828
Eldridge, Thomas II, 357
Eldridge, Thomas II, 513
Eldridge, Thomas VI, 172
Eldridge, Thomas VI, 212
Eldridge, Wd. Mary II, 513

ldridge, Wd. Mary II, 610
ldridge, William II, 357
ldridge, William Matlack II, 357
ldridge, Wm. II, 513
ldridge, Wm. M. II, 513
ldridge, Wm. Matlack II, 513
ldrige, Ira II, 286
ldrige, Job II, 513
leman, Enos I, 1019
leman, Mary I, 1019
leot, Elizabeth I Sup 1, 3
leot, Jacob I, 90
leot, Sarah I, 90
lerman, Enos V, 821
lerman, Margaret V, 821
lerman, Mary V, 821
les, Selia I, 306
les, Selia I, 308
let, Catherine VI, 1015
lexander, Joshua V, 994
lexander, Stephen V, 994
ley, ??? VI, 48
ley, Jane VI, 134
ley, Sarah E. C. VI, 63
ley, Sarah E. C. VI, 75
ley, Sophine VI, 63
ley, Sophine VI, 67
ley, William VI, 16
ley, William VI, 47
ley, William VI, 48
ley, William VI, 63
ley, William VI, 72
leyet, Harold IV, 1278
lferey, Joseph III, 444
lferey, Rachel III, 444
lford, Byron IV, 1250
lford, Delia IV, 1250
lford, Delia IV, 1314
lford, Edgar IV, 1314
lford, Luther Edgar IV, 1250
lford, Virginia IV, 1250
lford, Virginia IV, 1314
lfre, Henry II, 358
lfre, Sarah II, 358
lfreeth, Caleb II, 474
lfreeth, Hannah II, 513
lfreeth, Hannah II, 670
lfreeth, Jeremiah II, 670
lfreeth, Jeremiah, Jr. II, 513
lfreeth, Jeremiah, Jr. II, 670
lfreeth, Martha II, 474
lfreeth, Martha II, 513
lfreth, Abigail II, 513
lfreth, Abigail II, 703
lfreth, Abigail P. II, 737
lfreth, Ann II, 703
lfreth, Ann B. II, 737
lfreth, Ann B. II, 738
lfreth, Bennington II, 738
lfreth, Caleb II, 357
lfreth, Caleb II, 513
lfreth, Elisabeth II, 513
lfreth, Elizabeth II, 357
lfreth, Elizabeth II, 452
lfreth, Elizabeth II, 513
lfreth, Elizabeth II, 546
lfreth, Elizabeth II, 592
lfreth, Elizabeth II, 995
lfreth, Esther II, 503
lfreth, Esther II, 513
lfreth, Gove II, 357
lfreth, Hannah II, 513
lfreth, Henry II, 513
lfreth, Henry II, 531
lfreth, Henry II, 546
lfreth, Henry II, 696
lfreth, Jacob R. II, 513
lfreth, Jacob R. II, 737
lfreth, James II, 703
lfreth, James II, 737
lfreth, James II, 738
lfreth, Jeremiah II, 357
lfreth, Jeremiah II, 452
lfreth, Jeremiah II, 503
lfreth, Jeremiah II, 513
lfreth, Jeremiah II, 592
lfreth, Jeremiah II, 610
lfreth, Jeremiah II, 633
lfreth, Jeremiah II, 681
lfreth, Jeremiah III, 409
lfreth, Jeremiah, Jr. II, 357
lfreth, Jeremiah, Jr. II, 513
lfreth, John II, 357
lfreth, John II, 513
lfreth, John II, 546
lfreth, John II, 737
lfreth, John II, 995
lfreth, John Bennington II, 738
lfreth, Joseph II, 357
lfreth, Kaleb II, 460
lfreth, Kaleb II, 513
Elfreth, Martha II, 357
Elfreth, Martha II, 513
Elfreth, Mary II, 20
Elfreth, Mary II, 357
Elfreth, Mary II, 513
Elfreth, Mary II, 636
Elfreth, Mary II, 681
Elfreth, Mary II, 698
Elfreth, Miriam II, 703
Elfreth, Miriam II, 738
Elfreth, Rachel II, 357
Elfreth, Rachel II, 513
Elfreth, Rachel III, 409
Elfreth, Sarah II, 357
Elfreth, Sarah II, 460
Elfreth, Sarah II, 513
Elfreth, Sarah II, 610
Elfreth, Sarah II, 696
Elfreth, Wd. Leetitia II, 633
Elfreth, Wd. Letitia II, 513
Elfreth, Wd. Mary II, 513
Elfreth, William Henry II, 703
Elfrey, Caleb II, 358
Elfrey, Elizabeth II, 357
Elfrey, Henry II, 357
Elfrey, Henry II, 358
Elfrey, Jeremiah II, 357
Elfrey, Jeremiah II, 358
Elfrey, Jeremy II, 358
Elfrey, Joseph II, 358
Elfrey, Joshua II, 358
Elfrey, Josiah II, 358
Elfrey, Letitia II, 358
Elfrey, Sarah II, 357
Elfrey, Sarah II, 358
Elfrith, Caleb II, 357
Elfrith, Elizabeth II, 357
Elfrith, Mary II, 357
Elfryth, Elizabeth II, 357
Elfryth, Jeremiah II, 357
Elfryth, John II, 357
Elfryth, Rachel II, 357
Elfryth, Sarah II, 357
Elgar, ??? VI, 726
Elgar, Ann VI, 739
Elgar, Elizabeth VI, 739
Elgar, Jos. VI, 490
Elgar, Joseph II, 358
Elgar, Joseph II, 513
Elgar, Joseph VI, 489
Elgar, Margaret II, 358
Elgar, Margaret II, 513
Elgar, Margaret VI, 739
Elgar, Margaret E. VI, 490
Elgar, Mary II, 513
Elgar, Mary VI, 359
Elgar, Mary VI, 474
Elgar, Mary VI, 481
Elgar, Mary VI, 490
Elgin, Diedamia VI, 489
Elgin, Elizabeth VI, 814
Elgin, John VI, 814
Elgin, Sarah E. VI, 636
Elgin, Sarah E. VI, 713
Elgy, Agathy I, 238
Elgy, Kezia I, 238
Eli, Henry B. VI, 816
Eli, Henry B. VI, 835
Eli, Henry B. VI, 853
Elias, Andrew Curtis IV, 701
Elias, Myra S. IV, 701
Eliman, Catharine I, 388
Eliman, David I, 1029
Eliman, Dinah I, 388
Eliman, Elizabeth I, 1029
Eliman, Esther I, 388
Eliman, Esther Pearson I, 1029
Eliman, Hannah I, 1029
Eliman, Isaac I, 1029
Eliman, Jane I, 1029
Eliman, Jas. III, 291
Eliman, John I, 388
Eliman, Martha I, 1029
Eliman, Mary I, 388
Eliman, Mary E. III, 291
Eliman, Steedham I, 1029
Eliman, William I, 1029
Elimon, John I, 388
Elinger, Florence M. IV, 1314
Eliot, Alice IV, 30
Eliot, Catharine I, 445
Eliot, Elisabeth I, 138
Eliot, Elizabeth IV, 30
Eliot, Elizabeth IV, 42
Eliot, Elviry V, 828
Eliot, Elviry V, 837
Eliot, Hannah V, 51
Eliot, Hannah V, 128
Eliot, Isaac IV, 30
Eliot, Jemima I, 47
Eliot, John I, 678
Eliot, John IV, 144
Eliot, John IV, 997
Eliot, Joseph IV, 30
Eliot, Joseph IV, 42
Eliot, Leah I, 47
Eliot, Lidia I, 138
Eliot, Mary I, 678
Eliot, Mary IV, 997
Eliot, Obadiah I, 678
Eliot, Rachel I, 138
Eliot, Rachel IV, 144
Eliot, Sarah I, 678
Eliott, Achsah I, 48
Eliott, Catherine I, 985
Eliott, Esther I, 48
Eliott, Hannah V, 837
Eliott, Huldah I, 48
Eliott, John I, 985
Eliott, John I, 996
Eliott, Lydia I, 48
Eliott, Margaret I, 48
Eliott, Mary I, 48
Eliott, Mary I, 985
Eliott, Mary I, 996
Eliott, Rhoda I, 138
Elis, Sarah II, 514
Elis, Solomon I, 1151
Elisan, Mille I, 962
Elise, Elizabeth II, 213
Elise, Elizabeth II, 217
Elison, Eunice V, 329
Elison, Eunice V, 340
Elison, John I, 809
Elison, John I, 836
Elison, Mary VI, 106
Elison, Milla I, 809
Elison, Milla I, 836
Elison, Mrs. D. V, 994
Elison, Sarah VI, 106
Elizabeth, ??? I Sup 1, 8
Elizabeth, Anna V, 660
Elizabeth, Bessie B. V, 660
Elizabeth, Betsey VI, 619
Elizabeth, Betsy VI, 317
Elizabeth, Bettie VI, 634
Elizabeth, Betty VI, 320
Elizabeth, Jane I Sup 1, 8
Elizabeth, Jonathan I Sup 1, 8
Elizabeth, Olive V, 660
Elizabeth, Virginia VI, 437
Elkenton, Abraham II, 216
Elkenton, Esther II, 68
Elkenton, Gertrue II, 68
Elkenton, Job II, 68
Elkenton, John II, 68
Elkenton, Joseph II, 68
Elkenton, Joshua II, 68
Elkenton, Mary II, 68
Elkenton, Thomas II, 68
Elketon, Elisabeth II, 192
Elketon, Elisabeth II, 216
Elketon, Elizabeth II, 195
Elketon, Elizabeth II, 216
Elketon, George II, 192
Elketon, Joseph II, 192
Elketon, Joseph II, 216
Elkington, Asa II, 513
Elkington, Charles II, 513
Elkington, George II, 513
Elkington, Joseph II, 513
Elkington, Joseph IV, 577
Elkington, Joseph IV, 591
Elkington, Joseph S. IV, 577
Elkington, Letitia II, 513
Elkington, Malinda IV, 577
Elkington, Malinda IV, 591
Elkington, Mary IV, 577
Elkington, Rebecca II, 513
Elkinson, Elizabeth II, 216
Elkinton, Abby II, 703
Elkinton, Abby II, 704
Elkinton, Abby II, 709
Elkinton, Abby IV, 389
Elkinton, Abby IV, 451
Elkinton, Abby W. II, 738
Elkinton, Abby W. II, 748
Elkinton, Abby W. IV, 389
Elkinton, Abraham II, 172
Elkinton, Abraham II, 216
Elkinton, Alfred C. II, 703
Elkinton, Alfred C. II, 704
Elkinton, Alfred C. II, 709
Elkinton, Alfred C. II, 738
Elkinton, Alfred C. II, 748
Elkinton, Alfred C. II, 768
Elkinton, Alfred C. IV, 389
Elkinton, Alfred C. IV, 451
Elkinton, Alfred W. II, 703
Elkinton, Alfred W. II, 704
Elkinton, Alfred W. II, 738
Elkinton, Alfred W. II, 771
Elkinton, Alfred Willis II, 704
Elkinton, Ann II, 44
Elkinton, Ann II, 138
Elkinton, Ann Dallas Clark II, 138
Elkinton, Anna II, 704
Elkinton, Anna II, 709
Elkinton, Anna F. II, 704
Elkinton, Anna F. II, 738
Elkinton, Anna F. II, 771
Elkinton, Anna L. II, 117
Elkinton, Anna L. II, 704
Elkinton, Anna Rhoads II, 738
Elkinton, Anna Rhoads II, 739
Elkinton, Anna S. II, 117
Elkinton, Anna S. II, 119
Elkinton, Anna Walton II, 703
Elkinton, Anna Walton II, 738
Elkinton, Anna Walton II, 748
Elkinton, Annie II, 152
Elkinton, Asa II, 68
Elkinton, Asa II, 84
Elkinton, Asa II, 216
Elkinton, Asa II, 358
Elkinton, Asa II, 502
Elkinton, Asa II, 513
Elkinton, Asa II, 514
Elkinton, Asa II, 647
Elkinton, Carol II, 704
Elkinton, Charles II, 358
Elkinton, Charles II, 513
Elkinton, Charles II, 514
Elkinton, Charles II, 738
Elkinton, Christopher II, 704
Elkinton, Dorothy II, 704
Elkinton, Edith II, 117
Elkinton, Edith II, 119
Elkinton, Edith II, 286
Elkinton, Edith II, 358
Elkinton, Edith II, 514
Elkinton, Edith II, 647
Elkinton, Edith M. II, 703
Elkinton, Eleanor II, 704
Elkinton, Eleanor II, 738
Elkinton, Eleanor Rhoads II, 738
Elkinton, Elisabeth II, 216
Elkinton, Elisabeth II, 268
Elkinton, Elizabeth II, 172
Elkinton, Elizabeth II, 216
Elkinton, Elizabeth II, 220
Elkinton, Elizabeth II, 228
Elkinton, Elizabeth II, 738
Elkinton, Elizabeth II, 797
Elkinton, Enoch II, 172
Elkinton, Enoch II, 216
Elkinton, Ernest II, 703
Elkinton, Esther II, 68
Elkinton, Frances II, 719
Elkinton, Frances D. II, 704
Elkinton, Frances D. II, 738
Elkinton, Frances D. II, 769
Elkinton, Francis II, 216
Elkinton, George II, 172
Elkinton, George II, 210
Elkinton, George II, 216
Elkinton, George II, 268
Elkinton, George II, 273
Elkinton, George II, 286
Elkinton, George II, 358
Elkinton, George II, 502
Elkinton, George II, 513
Elkinton, George II, 738
Elkinton, George M. II, 117
Elkinton, George M. II, 119
Elkinton, George M. II, 286
Elkinton, George M. II, 358
Elkinton, George M. II, 514
Elkinton, George W. II, 286
Elkinton, George W. II, 514
Elkinton, George W. II, 647
Elkinton, Gertrew II, 68
Elkinton, Gertrue II, 68
Elkinton, Hannah Gillaspy Davis II, 513
Elkinton, Hannah Gillaspy Davis II, 514
Elkinton, Helen II, 704
Elkinton, Henry T. II, 703
Elkinton, Herbert Roberts II, 704
Elkinton, Hester II, 68
Elkinton, Howard W. II, 738
Elkinton, Howard W. II, 754
Elkinton, Howard West II, 704
Elkinton, Jemima II, 216
Elkinton, Jemima II, 273
Elkinton, Jemima II, 827
Elkinton, Job II, 68
Elkinton, John II, 68
Elkinton, John II, 138
Elkinton, John II, 172
Elkinton, John II, 216
Elkinton, John A. II, 861
Elkinton, John A. II, 864
Elkinton, Jos. S. II, 703
Elkinton, Joseph II, 68
Elkinton, Joseph II, 216
Elkinton, Joseph II, 513
Elkinton, Joseph II, 514
Elkinton, Joseph II, 703
Elkinton, Joseph II, 704
Elkinton, Joseph II, 719
Elkinton, Joseph II, 730
Elkinton, Joseph II, 737
Elkinton, Joseph II, 738
Elkinton, Joseph Passmore II, 704
Elkinton, Joseph Passmore II, 730
Elkinton, Joseph Passmore II, 738
Elkinton, Joseph Pimm II, 797
Elkinton, Joseph Russell II, 738
Elkinton, Joseph S. II, 704
Elkinton, Joseph S. II, 714
Elkinton, Joseph S. II, 738
Elkinton, Joseph S. II, 757
Elkinton, Joseph S. IV, 389
Elkinton, Joshua II, 68
Elkinton, Katharine W. II, 738
Elkinton, Katharine W. II, 754
Elkinton, Katharine Wistar II, 704
Elkinton, Latitia II, 514
Elkinton, Latitia II, 647
Elkinton, Letitia II, 358
Elkinton, Letitia II, 513
Elkinton, Letticia II, 68
Elkinton, Letticia II, 84
Elkinton, Lindley M. II, 117
Elkinton, Lindley M. II, 119
Elkinton, Lois II, 704
Elkinton, Lucy II, 502
Elkinton, Lucy II, 513
Elkinton, Lucy II, 514
Elkinton, Lucy II, 738
Elkinton, Malinda II, 703
Elkinton, Malinda II, 704
Elkinton, Malinda II, 714
Elkinton, Malinda II, 738
Elkinton, Malinda II, 757
Elkinton, Malinda IV, 389
Elkinton, Margaret E. II, 703
Elkinton, Margaret E. II, 738
Elkinton, Margaret E. II, 768
Elkinton, Margaretta II, 358
Elkinton, Margaretta II, 514
Elkinton, Mary II, 60
Elkinton, Mary II, 68
Elkinton, Mary II, 98
Elkinton, Mary II, 210
Elkinton, Mary II, 216
Elkinton, Mary II, 703
Elkinton, Mary II, 704
Elkinton, Mary II, 719
Elkinton, Mary II, 738
Elkinton, Mary Cope II, 737
Elkinton, Mary Cope II, 738
Elkinton, Mary P. II, 704
Elkinton, Mary P. II, 714
Elkinton, Mary P. II, 738
Elkinton, Mary P. II, 757
Elkinton, Mary Russell II, 730
Elkinton, Peter West II, 704
Elkinton, Phebe II, 68
Elkinton, Phebe II, 84
Elkinton, Rebecca II, 286
Elkinton, Rebecca II, 513
Elkinton, Rebecca II, 514
Elkinton, Rebecca II, 704
Elkinton, Richard II, 358
Elkinton, Robert Henry II, 704
Elkinton, Ruth II, 704
Elkinton, Sarah II, 216
Elkinton, Sarah II, 502
Elkinton, Sarah II, 513
Elkinton, Sarah II, 514
Elkinton, Sarah II, 704
Elkinton, Sarah II, 719
Elkinton, Sarah II, 738
Elkinton, Sarah W. II, 703
Elkinton, Sarah W. II, 704
Elkinton, Sarah W. II, 719
Elkinton, Sarah W. II, 730
Elkinton, Sarah W. II, 737
Elkinton, Sarah W. II, 738
Elkinton, Theodora II, 704
Elkinton, Thomas II, 68
Elkinton, Thomas W. II, 704
Elkinton, Thomas W. II, 738
Elkinton, Wd. Anna Rhoda II, 797
Elkinton, Wd. Lucy II, 502

Elkinton, Wd. Lucy II, 513
Elkinton, William T. II, 704
Elkinton, Wm. T. II, 738
Elkston, George II, 216
Elkston, George II, 254
Elkston, Mary II, 216
Elkston, Mary II, 254
Ellage, Nancy VI, 959
Ellans, Joseph V, 903
Ellans, Martha V, 903
Ellans, Rachel V, 903
Ellans, Tullon V, 903
Ellbeck, Martha II, 514
Elleman, ??? V, 807
Elleman, Aldes V, 807
Elleman, Angus V, 903
Elleman, Ann V, 806
Elleman, Ann E. V, 752
Elleman, Anna V, 737
Elleman, Anna E. V, 737
Elleman, Anna Mary V, 807
Elleman, Artie V, 737
Elleman, Asa V, 737
Elleman, Aubra E. V, 737
Elleman, Aubrey V, 737
Elleman, Audrey V, 808
Elleman, Benj. Franklin V, 737
Elleman, Benjamin V, 736
Elleman, Benjamin V, 737
Elleman, Benjamin V, 807
Elleman, Benjamin V, 808
Elleman, Bertha V, 737
Elleman, Betsy V, 806
Elleman, Betsy V, 807
Elleman, Caroline V, 807
Elleman, Catharine I, 1019
Elleman, Catharine I, 1029
Elleman, Catherine V, 806
Elleman, Charles V, 737
Elleman, Clara V, 737
Elleman, Clara Hannah V, 807
Elleman, David I, 1029
Elleman, David V, 806
Elleman, David V, 807
Elleman, David V, 808
Elleman, David W. V, 736
Elleman, David W. V, 737
Elleman, David W. V, 808
Elleman, David, Jr. V, 737
Elleman, Delbert Clarkson V, 807
Elleman, Dorcas V, 736
Elleman, Dorcas V, 807
Elleman, Dorothy V, 737
Elleman, Drusilla I, 1118
Elleman, Drusilla V, 736
Elleman, Drusilla V, 761
Elleman, Drusilla V, 821
Elleman, Eber V, 737
Elleman, Elden L. V, 737
Elleman, Eldena Elda V, 807
Elleman, Elizabeth I, 1029
Elleman, Elizabeth I, 1118
Elleman, Elizabeth V, 733
Elleman, Elizabeth V, 737
Elleman, Elizabeth V, 768
Elleman, Elizabeth V, 803
Elleman, Elizabeth V, 806
Elleman, Elizabeth V, 807
Elleman, Elizabeth V, 820
Elleman, Elizabeth V, 821
Elleman, Elizabeth E. V, 736
Elleman, Emeline V, 807
Elleman, Enos I, 1015
Elleman, Enos I, 1019
Elleman, Enos I, 1029
Elleman, Enos I, 1118
Elleman, Enos V, 736
Elleman, Enos V, 806
Elleman, Enos V, 807
Elleman, Enos V, 820
Elleman, Enos Clifford V, 807
Elleman, Enos W. V, 903
Elleman, Esther V, 737
Elleman, Esther V, 804
Elleman, Esther V, 807
Elleman, Esther V, 808
Elleman, Esther Pearson I, 1029
Elleman, Esther T. V, 736
Elleman, Esther T. V, 737
Elleman, Eunice V, 903
Elleman, Faye V, 737
Elleman, Flora A. V, 737
Elleman, Frances Esty V, 808
Elleman, Hannah I, 1029
Elleman, Hannah V, 767
Elleman, Hannah V, 807
Elleman, Harold David V, 737
Elleman, Harvey V, 737
Elleman, Horace Melvin V, 808
Elleman, Horatio P. V, 736
Elleman, Horatio P. V, 737
Elleman, Irlena V, 737
Elleman, Isaac I, 1029
Elleman, Isaac V, 733
Elleman, Isaac V, 736
Elleman, Isaac V, 737
Elleman, Isaac V, 748
Elleman, Isaac V, 803
Elleman, Isaac V, 806
Elleman, Isaac V, 807
Elleman, Isaac V, 808
Elleman, Isaac V, 813
Elleman, Isaac E. V, 736
Elleman, Isaac J. V, 736
Elleman, Isaac J. V, 737
Elleman, Isaiah P. V, 768
Elleman, Isam V, 807
Elleman, Isom V, 807
Elleman, Isom V, 808
Elleman, James V, 737
Elleman, James V, 806
Elleman, James V, 807
Elleman, Jane I, 1029
Elleman, Jane V, 736
Elleman, Jane V, 737
Elleman, Jane V, 740
Elleman, Jane V, 803
Elleman, Jane V, 806
Elleman, Jane V, 807
Elleman, Jesse V, 806
Elleman, John I, 1028
Elleman, John I, 1029
Elleman, John V, 736
Elleman, John V, 737
Elleman, John V, 761
Elleman, John V, 767
Elleman, John V, 806
Elleman, John V, 807
Elleman, John V, 821
Elleman, John H. V, 807
Elleman, John, Sr. V, 737
Elleman, Jordan V, 736
Elleman, Jordan V, 807
Elleman, Jorden V, 807
Elleman, Jorden V, 808
Elleman, Jos. Aaron V, 807
Elleman, Joseph V, 807
Elleman, Joseph V, 808
Elleman, Joseph V, 903
Elleman, Joseph Alton V, 807
Elleman, Juanita V, 737
Elleman, Kenneth V, 737
Elleman, Lewis H. V, 807
Elleman, Lindley V, 736
Elleman, Lindley M. V, 737
Elleman, Lindley M. V, 808
Elleman, Lizzie V, 737
Elleman, Lizzie Kessler V, 737
Elleman, Lula V, 737
Elleman, Lydia Viola V, 807
Elleman, Maggie V, 903
Elleman, Margaret V, 736
Elleman, Margaret V, 807
Elleman, Margaret V, 808
Elleman, Margaret V, 820
Elleman, Margaret A. V, 807
Elleman, Mark V, 807
Elleman, Martha I, 1029
Elleman, Martha V, 737
Elleman, Martha C. V, 807
Elleman, Martha E. V, 812
Elleman, Mary IV, 985
Elleman, Mary V, 736
Elleman, Mary V, 737
Elleman, Mary V, 748
Elleman, Mary V, 780
Elleman, Mary V, 781
Elleman, Mary V, 803
Elleman, Mary V, 806
Elleman, Mary V, 807
Elleman, Mary V, 813
Elleman, Mary L. Dorea V, 807
Elleman, Mary Rosella V, 736
Elleman, Mary Rosella V, 737
Elleman, Mary Rozella Zelora Edgar V, 808
Elleman, Mattie V, 737
Elleman, Mattie M. V, 737
Elleman, Maxine V, 737
Elleman, Melvin V, 737
Elleman, Merrick V, 737
Elleman, Minerva V, 807
Elleman, Minnie Pearl V, 807
Elleman, Mirriam V, 737
Elleman, Mrs. Bertha V, 737
Elleman, Olive V, 737
Elleman, Olive E. V, 735
Elleman, Olive E. V, 737
Elleman, Orris Alder V, 807
Elleman, Osa V, 737
Elleman, Owen V, 736
Elleman, Owen V, 737
Elleman, Owen V, 807
Elleman, Owen V, 808
Elleman, Pearl E. V, 737
Elleman, Pearl E. V, 739
Elleman, Peasley V, 737
Elleman, Phebe V, 807
Elleman, Rachel V, 737
Elleman, Rachel V, 807
Elleman, Rachel C. V, 736
Elleman, Rachel Elleman V, 807
Elleman, Rebecca V, 807
Elleman, Rhoda V, 768
Elleman, Robert V, 737
Elleman, Robert Walter V, 807
Elleman, Rosetta Ellen V, 807
Elleman, Ruth V, 737
Elleman, Samantha Viola V, 736
Elleman, Samuel Viola V, 737
Elleman, Sarah V, 807
Elleman, Sarah A. V, 737
Elleman, Sarah Ann V, 737
Elleman, Sarah Elizabeth V, 807
Elleman, Son V, 807
Elleman, Sophia V, 808
Elleman, Steedham I, 1029
Elleman, Susanna I, 1118
Elleman, Susanna V, 51
Elleman, Susanna V, 737
Elleman, Susanna V, 767
Elleman, Susannah I, 1028
Elleman, Susannah I, 1029
Elleman, Susannah V, 758
Elleman, Susannah V, 761
Elleman, Susannah V, 807
Elleman, Susannah V, 818
Elleman, Susannah V, 821
Elleman, Tace V, 807
Elleman, Tace V, 821
Elleman, Temperance I, 1118
Elleman, Temperance V, 807
Elleman, Thomas V, 807
Elleman, Thomas V, 812
Elleman, Thomas Alva V, 807
Elleman, Vesta V, 737
Elleman, Ward V, 737
Elleman, Wiliam A. V, 737
Elleman, William I, 1029
Elleman, William V, 736
Elleman, William V, 737
Elleman, William V, 795
Elleman, William V, 806
Elleman, William V, 807
Elleman, Wm. V, 736
Elleman, Wm. V, 803
Elleman, Wm. V, 804
Elleman, Wm. V, 807
Elleman, Wm. V, 808
Elleman, Wm. Calvin V, 807
Elleman, Wm. Isaac V, 807
Elleman, Wm. J. V, 807
Elleman, Wright V, 808
Elleman, Zebora V, 737
Elleman, Zehora Edgar V, 736
Ellemon, Susannah V, 748
Ellen, Martha V, 727
Ellen, Ruth I, 427
Ellen, Ruth IV, 1073
Ellen, Sarah IV, 394
Ellenberger, Joseph V, 488
Ellenberger, Myrtle V, 488
Ellenton, Rebecca VI, 869
Elleott, Elias I, 808
Eller, Rachel V, 737
Eller, Rachel V, 758
Eller, Rosa V, 994
Ellerman, Angus V, 903
Ellerman, Enos V, 903
Ellerman, Enos W. V, 903
Ellerman, Eunice V, 903
Ellerman, Gottlieb IV, 198
Ellerman, Joseph V, 903
Ellerman, Maggie V, 903
Ellerman, Sarah II, 286
Ellerman, Sarah IV, 609
Ellerman, Sarah IV, 622
Ellerman, Sarah IV, 949
Ellerman, Theophilos IV, 609
Ellerman, Theophilos IV, 622
Ellerman, Theophilus II, 286
Ellerman, Theophilus IV, 622
Ellerman, Theophilus IV, 949
Ellerman, Theopholis IV, 622
Ellerman, Theopolis IV, 949
Ellers, Elizabeth V, 806
Ellerson, Alfonso L. I, 940
Ellerson, Mary VI, 63
Ellerton, Mary II, 514
Ellerton, Sarah IV, 949
Ellerton, Theophilus IV, 949
Elles, Wesley Merrion V, 236
Ellesdon, Dorothy II, 358
Ellesdon, Naomy II, 358
Elleson, Anna IV, 701
Elleson, Garret Robert VI, 147
Elleson, John IV, 701
Elleson, Margery IV, 701
Elleson, Mary IV, 701
Elleson, Robert IV, 701
Elleson, Wm. IV, 701
Elleson, Zachariah IV, 701
Elless, William VI, 242
Ellet, Almira IV, 949
Ellet, Charles II, 68
Ellet, Charles II, 514
Ellet, Chas. II, 27
Ellet, Chas. II, 139
Ellet, Chas., Jr. VI, 814
Ellet, Curtis IV, 949
Ellet, Curtis V, 716
Ellet, Edith I, 1118
Ellet, Effie IV, 949
Ellet, Effie IV, 986
Ellet, Elizabeth II, 27
Ellet, Elizabeth II, 68
Ellet, Elizabeth II, 84
Ellet, Elmer S. IV, 949
Ellet, Elvira A. S. VI, 814
Ellet, Esther I, 1118
Ellet, Hannah II, 27
Ellet, Hannah II, 50
Ellet, Hannah II, 68
Ellet, Hannah II, 131
Ellet, Hannah II, 139
Ellet, Hannah Carpenter II, 27
Ellet, Hannah Carpenter II, 68
Ellet, Henry VI, 814
Ellet, Irene M. IV, 949
Ellet, James VI, 839
Ellet, Jannet VI, 814
Ellet, John II, 27
Ellet, John II, 68
Ellet, John II, 100
Ellet, John II, 131
Ellet, John II, 217
Ellet, John IV, 949
Ellet, Louise V, 716
Ellet, Maria C. II, 117
Ellet, Maria C. II, 131
Ellet, Maria Chambless II, 68
Ellet, Maria Chamless II, 27
Ellet, Martin VI, 814
Ellet, Mary II, 27
Ellet, Mary II, 68
Ellet, Mary II, 75
Ellet, Mary II, 100
Ellet, Mary II, 131
Ellet, Mary VI, 814
Ellet, Nancy VI, 814
Ellet, Paulina VI, 814
Ellet, Rachel II, 27
Ellet, Rachel II, 68
Ellet, Rachel II, 139
Ellet, Robert VI, 814
Ellet, Samuel II, 27
Ellet, Sarah I, 388
Ellet, Sarah I, 414
Ellet, Sarah II, 27
Ellet, Sarah II, 55
Ellet, Sarah II, 68
Ellet, Sarah II, 217
Ellet, Sarah II, 218
Ellet, Thos. II, 27
Ellet, Welmet I, 1118
Ellet, William VI, 814
Ellet, Wm. II, 27
Ellett, Charles II, 68
Ellett, Charles II, 514
Ellett, Deborah I, 388
Ellett, Deborah I, 428
Ellett, Elmer E. IV, 949
Ellett, Elmira IV, 966
Ellett, Emma IV, 924
Ellett, Emma IV, 966
Ellett, Emma V. IV, 966
Ellett, Hannah II, 990
Ellett, John II, 68
Ellett, John IV, 966
Ellett, Louise IV, 949
Ellett, Maria C. II, 117
Ellett, Martha VI, 853
Ellett, Rachel II, 68
Ellett, Rachel II, 825
Ellett, Sarah I, 388
Ellett, Wd. Hannah II, 995
Elleyson, Gertrude IV, 993
Elleyson, Merle C. IV, 993
Ellfreth, Elisabeth II, 452
Ellfreth, Elisabeth II, 513
Ellfreth, Elisabeth II, 590
Ellfreth, Elizabeth VI, 560
Ellfreth, Mary II, 513
Ellfreth, Mary II, 651
Ellfreth, Rachel II, 513
Ellick, Catherine II, 358
Ellick, Catherine II, 514
Ellick, John II, 358
Ellicot, Wd. Mary VI, 752
Ellicott, Abijah VI, 739
Ellicott, Abijah VI, 767
Ellicott, Andrew VI, 739
Ellicott, Ann VI, 739
Ellicott, Ann VI, 746
Ellicott, Cassandra VI, 489
Ellicott, Elizabeth VI, 474
Ellicott, Elizabeth VI, 489
Ellicott, Elizabeth VI, 739
Ellicott, George VI, 474
Ellicott, Hannah VI, 489
Ellicott, Hannah VI, 530
Ellicott, Hannah VI, 739
Ellicott, John VI, 489
Ellicott, John VI, 530
Ellicott, John VI, 735
Ellicott, John A. VI, 739
Ellicott, John, Jr. VI, 662
Ellicott, John, Jr. VI, 739
Ellicott, John, Jr. VI, 752
Ellicott, John, Jr. VI, 767
Ellicott, Jonathan VI, 739
Ellicott, Joseph C. III, 109
Ellicott, Latitia II, 995
Ellicott, Leah VI, 489
Ellicott, Leah VI, 530
Ellicott, Martha VI, 735
Ellicott, Mary VI, 739
Ellicott, Mary M. III, 273
Ellicott, Nathaniel II, 995
Ellicott, Nathaniel VI, 489
Ellicott, Nathaniel VI, 739
Ellicott, Nathaniel, Jr. VI, 489
Ellicott, Rachel VI, 739
Ellicott, Rachel VI, 746
Ellicott, Thomas VI, 489
Ellicott, Wd. Mary VI, 519
Ellicott, Wd. Mary VI, 767
Ellicott, Widow Mary Mitchell VI, 662
Elliman, Catharine I, 1019
Elliman, David V, 51
Elliman, Drusilla V, 51
Elliman, Elizabeth I, 1019
Elliman, Elizabeth V, 51
Elliman, Emme I, 1019
Elliman, Enos I, 1019
Elliman, Enos V, 51
Elliman, Hannah I, 1019
Elliman, Hannah V, 51
Elliman, Isaac V, 51
Elliman, James B. III, 109
Elliman, Jane V, 51
Elliman, John I, 1019
Elliman, John I, 1029
Elliman, John, Sr. I, 1019
Elliman, Mary I, 1019
Elliman, Mary V, 51
Elliman, Mary E. III, 109
Elliman, Susanna V, 51
Elliman, Susannah I, 1029
Elliman, Susannah V, 51
Elliman, Temperance V, 51
Elliman, William I, 1019
Elliman, William I, 1029
Elliman, William V, 51
Elliman, William V, 723
Ellimore, William I, 388
Ellington, Kate I, 926
Ellington, Rebeckah VI, 983
Ellinson, Sarah II, 859
Elliot, Abraham I, 1118
Elliot, Andrew II, 995
Elliot, Andrew II, 1014
Elliot, Ann I, 1076
Elliot, Ann V, 737
Elliot, Armella I, 678
Elliot, Axsom I, 678
Elliot, Axsom I, 683
Elliot, Axum I, 653
Elliot, Axum I, 678
Elliot, Axum I, 686
Elliot, Benjamin IV, 30
Elliot, Beulah I, 1076
Elliot, Bulah I, 1076
Elliot, Catharine I, 678
Elliot, Catharine I, 682
Elliot, Charles V, 737
Elliot, Edith V, 737
Elliot, Elias I, 183
Elliot, Elisabeth II, 514
Elliot, Elizabeth IV, 622
Elliot, Esther V, 737
Elliot, Francis IV, 30
Elliot, Hannah II, 68
Elliot, Hannah IV, 622

lliot, Helana I, 102
lliot, Helena I, 138
lliot, Helena I, 145
lliot, Henry I, 183
lliot, Israel I, 1118
lliot, Israel V, 737
lliot, Jacob I, 678
lliot, Jacob I, 1118
lliot, Jacob V, 737
lliot, James I, 183
lliot, Job I, 808
lliot, Job Scott I, 183
lliot, John II, 514
lliot, Lamira IV, 1157
lliot, Lamira IV, 1193
lliot, Louella V, 737
lliot, Margaret III, 160
lliot, Martha IV, 84
lliot, Martha IV, 101
lliot, Martha J. IV, 198
lliot, Mary I, 183
lliot, Mary V, 737
lliot, Milicent IV, 1130
lliot, Milicent IV, 1132
lliot, Nixon I, 183
lliot, Obadiah I, 675
lliot, Olive V, 737
lliot, Penina I, 183
lliot, Peninah I, 35
lliot, Rhoda I, 183
lliot, Robert, Jr. VI, 805
lliot, Ruth I, 138
lliot, Sarah I, 47
lliot, Sarah I, 653
lliot, Sarah I, 675
lliot, Sarah I, 678
lliot, Sarah I, 686
lliot, Sarah Jane III, 160
lliot, Thomas I, 1076
lliot, Thomas, Jr. I, 1076
lliot, Thomas, Sen. I, 1076
lliot, Thos. VI, 805
lliot, Wilmet V, 737
lliot, Zilpha I, 678
lliott, ??? IV, 1269
lliott, A. M. I, 808
lliott, Aaron I, 8
lliott, Aaron I, 48
lliott, Aaron I, 81
lliott, Aaron I, 98
lliott, Aaron I, 99
lliott, Aaron I, 138
lliott, Aaron I, 139
lliott, Aaron I, 160
lliott, Aaron I, 593
lliott, Aaron I, 595
lliott, Aaron I, 620
lliott, Aaron I, 780
lliott, Aaron I, 808
lliott, Aaron I, 829
lliott, Aaron IV, 895
lliott, Aaron Marchel I, 808
lliott, Aaron Marshall I, 139
lliott, Aaron Marshall I, 780
lliott, Abigail I, 98
lliott, Abigail I, 99
lliott, Abigail I, 138
lliott, Abigail I, 139
lliott, Abigail I, 183
lliott, Abigail I, 189
lliott, Abigail I, 192
lliott, Abigail I, 653
lliott, Abigail I, 678
lliott, Abigail I, 688
lliott, Abigail I, 808
Elliott, Abigail VI, 951
Elliott, Abigail F. I, 877
Elliott, Abigail P. I, 139
Elliott, Abner IV, 1278
Elliott, Abraham I, 8
Elliott, Abraham I, 9
Elliott, Abraham I, 46
Elliott, Abraham I, 47
Elliott, Abraham I, 48
Elliott, Abraham I, 57
Elliott, Abraham I, 86
Elliott, Abraham I, 388
Elliott, Abraham I, 413
Elliott, Abraham I, 538
Elliott, Abraham I, 678
Elliott, Abraham I, 759
Elliott, Abraham I, 760
Elliott, Abraham I, 1118
Elliott, Abraham Lincoln IV, 1277
Elliott, Abraham S. III, 366
Elliott, Absila I, 8
Elliott, Absilla I, 48
Elliott, Absilla I, 71
Elliott, Achsa I, 214
Elliott, Achsah I, 9
Elliott, Achsah I, 48
Elliott, Achsah I, 238
Elliott, Achsah I, 253
Elliott, Acsah I, 47
Elliott, Acsah I, 71
Elliott, Ada I, 620
Elliott, Ada I, 636
Elliott, Ada Lea I, 632
Elliott, Ada Lee I, 632
Elliott, Ada Lee I, 641
Elliott, Ada M. I, 808
Elliott, Adaline IV, 1096
Elliott, Adam VI, 911
Elliott, Adam VI, 925
Elliott, Aggy VI, 814
Elliott, Agnes IV, 892
Elliott, Alacka IV, 1278
Elliott, Alexander V, 329
Elliott, Alexander V, 384
Elliott, Alexandria IV, 1157
Elliott, Alfred IV, 1277
Elliott, Alice IV, 30
Elliott, Alice IV, 46
Elliott, Allen Curtis I, 615
Elliott, Almira IV, 949
Elliott, Alpheus I, 9
Elliott, Alpheus I, 48
Elliott, Alson I, 924
Elliott, Alson E. I, 877
Elliott, Alvaretta IV, 1157
Elliott, Amasa I, 138
Elliott, Amasie I, 192
Elliott, Amos IV, 1277
Elliott, Amos VI, 911
Elliott, Amos VI, 918
Elliott, Amy Etta IV, 1206
Elliott, Amyetta IV, 1206
Elliott, Ann I, 46
Elliott, Ann I, 238
Elliott, Ann I, 1118
Elliott, Ann IV, 892
Elliott, Ann IV, 1157
Elliott, Ann IV, 1178
Elliott, Ann IV, 1277
Elliott, Ann V, 384
Elliott, Ann VI, 739
Elliott, Ann H. I, 214
Elliott, Ann H. I, 238
Elliott, Ann M. VI, 814
Elliott, Ann R. I, 139
Elliott, Ann R. I, 160
Elliott, Ann Robinson I, 98
Elliott, Anna I, 138
Elliott, Anna I, 192
Elliott, Anna VI, 636
Elliott, Anna VI, 702
Elliott, Anna T. VI, 636
Elliott, Anna T. VI, 701
Elliott, Anna T. VI, 706
Elliott, Anna Vesta IV, 1277
Elliott, Annabella II, 358
Elliott, Annabella II, 368
Elliott, Annabella II, 497
Elliott, Annabella II, 514
Elliott, Annabella II, 535
Elliott, Annabella II, 559
Elliott, Annabella II, 738
Elliott, Annabella II, 776
Elliott, Annette IV, 1277
Elliott, Annie T. VI, 615
Elliott, Annie T. VI, 636
Elliott, Annis I, 745
Elliott, Annis I, 760
Elliott, Archibald VI, 814
Elliott, Archie I, 262
Elliott, Armelia I, 760
Elliott, Armella I, 678
Elliott, Armella I, 760
Elliott, Armella I, 762
Elliott, Armilla I, 678
Elliott, Aron I, 620
Elliott, Arthur B. III, 409
Elliott, Arthur Boswell III, 409
Elliott, Axey I, 213
Elliott, Axsom I, 678
Elliott, Axum I, 678
Elliott, Axum I, 698
Elliott, Axy I, 213
Elliott, Belle I, 924
Elliott, Belle I, 940
Elliott, Ben VI, 812
Elliott, Beniamin I, 46
Elliott, Beniamin I, 78
Elliott, Benjamin I, 9
Elliott, Benjamin I, 47
Elliott, Benjamin I, 48
Elliott, Benjamin I, 192
Elliott, Benjamin IV, 30
Elliott, Benjamin IV, 895
Elliott, Benjamin V, 235
Elliott, Benjamin VI, 814
Elliott, Benjamin A. IV, 1277
Elliott, Benjamin Toms I, 183
Elliott, Betcy I, 745
Elliott, Betsy I, 678
Elliott, Betty I, 46
Elliott, Betty I, 60
Elliott, Betty I, 760
Elliott, Beulah T. VI, 615
Elliott, Beulah Thomas VI, 615
Elliott, Beulah Thomas VI, 636
Elliott, Caleb I, 8
Elliott, Caleb I, 46
Elliott, Caleb I, 47
Elliott, Caleb I, 48
Elliott, Caleb I, 56
Elliott, Caleb I, 61
Elliott, Caleb I, 63
Elliott, Caleb I, 138
Elliott, Caroline I, 8
Elliott, Caroline I, 48
Elliott, Caroline I, 877
Elliott, Caroline I, 894
Elliott, Caroline IV, 1277
Elliott, Caroline V, 949
Elliott, Caroline V, 951
Elliott, Catharine I, 9
Elliott, Catharine I, 445
Elliott, Catharine I, 678
Elliott, Catharine I, 698
Elliott, Catharine I, 715
Elliott, Catharine I, 985
Elliott, Catharine V, 329
Elliott, Catharine V, 384
Elliott, Catharine VI, 729
Elliott, Catherine I, 985
Elliott, Chalkley I, 8
Elliott, Chalkley I, 48
Elliott, Charles I, 47
Elliott, Charles I, 213
Elliott, Charles II, 68
Elliott, Charles II, 514
Elliott, Charles IV, 1278
Elliott, Charles H. VI, 911
Elliott, Charles W. I, 214
Elliott, Charles W. I, 238
Elliott, Charlotte I, 99
Elliott, Charlotte I, 138
Elliott, Chas. I, 924
Elliott, Chas. William VI, 911
Elliott, Chloe IV, 1277
Elliott, Clarence IV, 1206
Elliott, Clarence IV, 1277
Elliott, Clarence H. IV, 1206
Elliott, Cora IV, 470
Elliott, Cornelia III, 109
Elliott, Cornelia III, 366
Elliott, Cornelia W. III, 326
Elliott, Curtis IV, 949
Elliott, Curtis V, 670
Elliott, Cynthia I, 8
Elliott, Cynthia I, 48
Elliott, Cynthia I Sup 1, 7
Elliott, Cynthia V, 235
Elliott, Dabney VI, 830
Elliott, Dale Hodgin I, 615
Elliott, Dale Hodgin I, 632
Elliott, Daniel II, 358
Elliott, Daniel II, 514
Elliott, Daniel II, 738
Elliott, Daniel II, 776
Elliott, David I, 780
Elliott, David IV, 1206
Elliott, David V, 329
Elliott, David V, 330
Elliott, David S. I, 780
Elliott, David S. IV, 1204
Elliott, David W. I, 139
Elliott, David W. I, 808
Elliott, David W. I, 816
Elliott, David White I, 8
Elliott, Deborah I, 388
Elliott, Deborah I, 445
Elliott, Deidia I, 48
Elliott, Delano I, 192
Elliott, Delilah I, 36
Elliott, Delilah I, 46
Elliott, Dempsey I, 46
Elliott, Dianna I, 1118
Elliott, Dillan L. IV, 1277
Elliott, Dillard IV, 1277
Elliott, Dora III, 409
Elliott, Dora F. III, 409
Elliott, Dora F. III, 449
Elliott, Dora Flournoy III, 409
Elliott, Dorithy I, 192
Elliott, Dorothy I, 47
Elliott, Dorothy I, 138
Elliott, Doshia VI, 911
Elliott, E. W. I, 940
Elliott, Earnest V, 455
Elliott, Edath I, 653
Elliott, Edith I, 715
Elliott, Edith I, 1118
Elliott, Edith IV, 892
Elliott, Edmund III, 109
Elliott, Edna Estelle I, 615
Elliott, Edna Estelle I, 632
Elliott, Edwin V, 51
Elliott, Effie IV, 949
Elliott, Elba IV, 1277
Elliott, Elba L. IV, 1277
Elliott, Eleas S. I, 238
Elliott, Eli III, 109
Elliott, Eli III, 331
Elliott, Eli IV, 1157
Elliott, Eli IV, 1196
Elliott, Eli VI, 615
Elliott, Eli VI, 636
Elliott, Eli VI, 702
Elliott, Eli VI, 706
Elliott, Eli VI, 739
Elliott, Elias I, 43
Elliott, Elias I, 48
Elliott, Elias I, 192
Elliott, Elias I, 213
Elliott, Elias I, 227
Elliott, Elias I, 238
Elliott, Elias I, 538
Elliott, Elias I, 780
Elliott, Elias I, 808
Elliott, Elias I, 836
Elliott, Elias IV, 1206
Elliott, Elias S. I, 48
Elliott, Elias S. I, 213
Elliott, Elias S. I, 238
Elliott, Elias S. I, 262
Elliott, Elias S. I, 538
Elliott, Elias S. I, 576
Elliott, Elias T. I, 238
Elliott, Elihu Oliver I, 780
Elliott, Elijah I, 852
Elliott, Elijah I, 877
Elliott, Elijah I, 924
Elliott, Elijah I, 940
Elliott, Elijah IV, 328
Elliott, Elijah IV, 389
Elliott, Elisabeth I, 35
Elliott, Elisabeth I, 46
Elliott, Elisabeth I, 48
Elliott, Elisabeth I, 61
Elliott, Elisabeth I, 138
Elliott, Elisabeth I, 615
Elliott, Elisabeth II, 514
Elliott, Elisabeth G. I, 213
Elliott, Elisha I, 48
Elliott, Eliza I, 81
Elliott, Eliza I, 538
Elliott, Eliza Ann I, 192
Elliott, Eliza Ann IV, 1277
Elliott, Eliza Elma IV, 1157
Elliott, Eliza Elma IV, 1193
Elliott, Eliza G. I, 1151
Elliott, Eliza J. V, 329
Elliott, Eliza J. V, 384
Elliott, Elizabeth I, 8
Elliott, Elizabeth I, 47
Elliott, Elizabeth I, 48
Elliott, Elizabeth I, 54
Elliott, Elizabeth I, 138
Elliott, Elizabeth I, 157
Elliott, Elizabeth I, 214
Elliott, Elizabeth I, 388
Elliott, Elizabeth I, 538
Elliott, Elizabeth I, 653
Elliott, Elizabeth I, 678
Elliott, Elizabeth I, 691
Elliott, Elizabeth I, 715
Elliott, Elizabeth I Sup 1, 8
Elliott, Elizabeth II, 358
Elliott, Elizabeth II, 514
Elliott, Elizabeth II, 678
Elliott, Elizabeth II, 738
Elliott, Elizabeth IV, 30
Elliott, Elizabeth IV, 46
Elliott, Elizabeth IV, 69
Elliott, Elizabeth IV, 144
Elliott, Elizabeth IV, 156
Elliott, Elizabeth IV, 328
Elliott, Elizabeth IV, 346
Elliott, Elizabeth IV, 389
Elliott, Elizabeth IV, 701
Elliott, Elizabeth IV, 813
Elliott, Elizabeth IV, 868
Elliott, Elizabeth IV, 873
Elliott, Elizabeth IV, 949
Elliott, Elizabeth IV, 1149
Elliott, Elizabeth IV, 1157
Elliott, Elizabeth IV, 1160
Elliott, Elizabeth IV, 1193
Elliott, Elizabeth IV, 1206
Elliott, Elizabeth IV, 1211
Elliott, Elizabeth IV, 1273
Elliott, Elizabeth IV, 1277
Elliott, Elizabeth V, 329
Elliott, Elizabeth V, 384
Elliott, Elizabeth VI, 739
Elliott, Elizabeth VI, 814
Elliott, Elizabeth VI, 819
Elliott, Elizabeth VI, 862
Elliott, Elizabeth VI, 911
Elliott, Elizabeth Ann IV, 1277
Elliott, Elizabeth K. VI, 975
Elliott, Elizabeth T. IV, 1206
Elliott, Elizabeth T. IV, 1277
Elliott, Elizabeth T. IV, 1281
Elliott, Ella IV, 1158
Elliott, Ella IV, 1206
Elliott, Ella M. IV, 1157
Elliott, Ellen IV, 1157
Elliott, Ellen E. IV, 1277
Elliott, Ellen Elizabeth IV, 1277
Elliott, Ellie IV, 1157
Elliott, Elliott I, 9
Elliott, Ellwood I, 698
Elliott, Elmer E. IV, 949
Elliott, Elmer S. IV, 949
Elliott, Elva V, 235
Elliott, Elviry V, 837
Elliott, Elvy I, 48
Elliott, Elwood I, 985
Elliott, Emerson E. IV, 1277
Elliott, Emily I, 35
Elliott, Emily I, 48
Elliott, Ephraim I, 9
Elliott, Ephraim I, 46
Elliott, Ephraim I, 47
Elliott, Ephraim I, 76
Elliott, Ephraim I, 653
Elliott, Ephram I, 715
Elliott, Esabella I, 144
Elliott, Esterianna V, 51
Elliott, Esther I, 8
Elliott, Esther I, 48
Elliott, Esther I, 388
Elliott, Esther I, 1118
Elliott, Esther II, 358
Elliott, Esther II, 514
Elliott, Esther IV, 1278
Elliott, Ettie IV, 1157
Elliott, Eve I, 1118
Elliott, Eve I, 1131
Elliott, Ewen W. V, 235
Elliott, Exum I, 46
Elliott, Exum I, 47
Elliott, Exum I, 66
Elliott, Exum I, 138
Elliott, Exum I, 139
Elliott, Exum I, 192
Elliott, Exum I, 209
Elliott, Exum I, 213
Elliott, Exum I, 214
Elliott, Exum I, 238
Elliott, Exum I, 695
Elliott, Exum I, 715
Elliott, Exum I, 985
Elliott, Ezekiel I, 615
Elliott, Fannie V, 837
Elliott, Florence A. II, 704
Elliott, Foster I, 48
Elliott, Frances I, 238
Elliott, Frances VI, 911
Elliott, Frances A. VI, 911
Elliott, Francis I, 9
Elliott, Francis I, 47
Elliott, Francis I, 48
Elliott, Francis I, 66
Elliott, Francis I, 138
Elliott, Francis I, 214
Elliott, Francis I, 238
Elliott, Francis IV, 30
Elliott, Frank V, 670
Elliott, Frank R. V, 657
Elliott, Frank R. V, 670
Elliott, Frank Roy V, 670
Elliott, Frank, Jr. V, 670
Elliott, Franklin I, 1151
Elliott, Freda I, 940
Elliott, Freda Belle I, 924
Elliott, Fredrick I, 48
Elliott, Gabriel I, 8
Elliott, Gabriel I, 46
Elliott, Gabriel I, 47
Elliott, Gabriel I, 48
Elliott, Gabriel I, 52
Elliott, Gabriel I, 138
Elliott, Gansby I, 47
Elliott, Garland IV, 1277
Elliott, Geo. VI, 636
Elliott, George I, 139
Elliott, George I, 745
Elliott, George I, 760
Elliott, George IV, 1277
Elliott, George VI, 702
Elliott, George F. I, 213

Elliott, Gilbert Alex Boswell III, 420
Elliott, Gilbert Alex. B. III, 409
Elliott, Gilbert Alex. B. III, 449
Elliott, Gilbert Alex. Boswell III, 409
Elliott, Gilbert Alex. Boswell III, 446
Elliott, Gillice I, 8
Elliott, Grant IV, 1206
Elliott, Gulielma I, 48
Elliott, Gulielma I, 57
Elliott, Hague I, 9
Elliott, Hague I, 46
Elliott, Hamon IV, 1277
Elliott, Hannah I, 46
Elliott, Hannah I, 47
Elliott, Hannah I, 50
Elliott, Hannah I, 98
Elliott, Hannah I, 136
Elliott, Hannah I, 138
Elliott, Hannah I, 139
Elliott, Hannah I, 151
Elliott, Hannah I, 538
Elliott, Hannah I, 653
Elliott, Hannah I, 674
Elliott, Hannah I, 678
Elliott, Hannah I, 715
Elliott, Hannah II, 60
Elliott, Hannah II, 358
Elliott, Hannah II, 514
Elliott, Hannah II, 559
Elliott, Hannah IV, 608
Elliott, Hannah IV, 622
Elliott, Hannah IV, 1204
Elliott, Hannah IV, 1206
Elliott, Hannah IV, 1277
Elliott, Hannah V, 51
Elliott, Hannah V, 837
Elliott, Hannah V, 882
Elliott, Hannah B. V, 51
Elliott, Hannah C. IV, 1206
Elliott, Harold IV, 1278
Elliott, Harriet Wiseman I, 615
Elliott, Harriett I, 209
Elliott, Harriett I, 214
Elliott, Harriett I, 238
Elliott, Harriett E. I, 213
Elliott, Harriett E. I, 238
Elliott, Harriett Wiseman I, 632
Elliott, Harvey II, 358
Elliott, Harvey II, 514
Elliott, Helen I, 262
Elliott, Helena I, 138
Elliott, Hemphrey I, 47
Elliott, Henderson I, 48
Elliott, Henderson W. I, 9
Elliott, Henry I, 9
Elliott, Henry I, 47
Elliott, Henry I, 48
Elliott, Henry I, 238
Elliott, Henry I, 780
Elliott, Henry I, 808
Elliott, Henry I, 877
Elliott, Henry VI, 796
Elliott, Henry E. I, 213
Elliott, Hephsibeth I, 1075
Elliott, Hepsiba I, 759
Elliott, Hepsibeth I, 715
Elliott, Hepzibah I, 678
Elliott, Hepzibah I, 684
Elliott, Hepzibah I, 689
Elliott, Hester I, 538
Elliott, Hezekiah W. IV, 1277
Elliott, Howell I, 8
Elliott, Huldah I, 8
Elliott, Huldah I, 46
Elliott, Huldah I, 47
Elliott, Huldah I, 48
Elliott, Huldah I, 63
Elliott, Huldah I, 698
Elliott, Huldah I, 741
Elliott, Huldah I, 745
Elliott, Humphrey I, 8
Elliott, Humphrey I, 48
Elliott, Humprey I, 9
Elliott, Humprey I Sup 1, 7
Elliott, Ida V, 455
Elliott, India Marion I, 213
Elliott, Ira S. IV, 1096
Elliott, Irena M. IV, 949
Elliott, Irene Evelyn I, 213
Elliott, Irene M. IV, 949
Elliott, Isaac I, 9
Elliott, Isaac I, 46
Elliott, Isaac I, 47
Elliott, Isaac I, 48
Elliott, Isaac I, 61
Elliott, Isaac I, 138
Elliott, Isaac I, 192
Elliott, Isaac I, 698
Elliott, Isaac I, 985
Elliott, Isaac II, 358
Elliott, Isaac II, 514
Elliott, Isaac IV, 30
Elliott, Isaac IV, 46
Elliott, Isaac IV, 701
Elliott, Isaac IV, 1096
Elliott, Isaac IV, 1157
Elliott, Isaac IV, 1277
Elliott, Isaac D. IV, 1277
Elliott, Isaac H. IV, 1206
Elliott, Isaac H. IV, 1277
Elliott, Isaac Hamilton IV, 1206
Elliott, Isaac Hamilton IV, 1211
Elliott, Isaac Hamilton IV, 1277
Elliott, Isaac Hamilton IV, 1281
Elliott, Isaac J. IV, 1096
Elliott, Isaac, Jr. IV, 30
Elliott, Isabella I, 48
Elliott, Isabella I, 98
Elliott, Isabella I, 139
Elliott, Isabella I, 160
Elliott, Isabella III, 109
Elliott, Isabella P. I, 48
Elliott, Israel I, 538
Elliott, Israel I, 1101
Elliott, Israel I, 1118
Elliott, Israel W. IV, 1096
Elliott, J. Gurney I, 780
Elliott, Jacob I, 46
Elliott, Jacob I, 47
Elliott, Jacob I, 388
Elliott, Jacob I, 538
Elliott, Jacob I, 653
Elliott, Jacob I, 678
Elliott, Jacob I, 684
Elliott, Jacob I, 689
Elliott, Jacob I, 695
Elliott, Jacob I, 698
Elliott, Jacob I, 715
Elliott, Jacob I, 759
Elliott, Jacob I, 985
Elliott, Jacob I, 995
Elliott, Jacob I, 1118
Elliott, Jacob, Jr. I, 715
Elliott, James I, 46
Elliott, James I, 55
Elliott, James I, 59
Elliott, James I, 87
Elliott, James I, 138
Elliott, James I, 183
Elliott, James I, 192
Elliott, James I, 200
Elliott, James I, 715
Elliott, James I, 759
Elliott, James I, 808
Elliott, James II, 514
Elliott, James IV, 30
Elliott, James V, 455
Elliott, James VI, 814
Elliott, James VI, 911
Elliott, James Arnold I, 615
Elliott, James H. I, 877
Elliott, James H. VI, 911
Elliott, James Henry I, 924
Elliott, James M. IV, 1278
Elliott, James N. I, 780
Elliott, James R. I, 214
Elliott, James Sheldon IV, 1277
Elliott, James T. I, 238
Elliott, James T. I, 808
Elliott, James Thomas I, 139
Elliott, James Thomas I, 214
Elliott, James Thomas I, 780
Elliott, James Thomas I, 808
Elliott, James W. I, 139
Elliott, James, Jr. I, 192
Elliott, Jamima I, 63
Elliott, Jane II, 358
Elliott, Jane V, 455
Elliott, Jane VI, 814
Elliott, Jane VI, 860
Elliott, Jas. H. VI, 930
Elliott, Jean Cecilia III, 409
Elliott, Jehew IV, 1277
Elliott, Jehu IV, 1157
Elliott, Jemima I, 8
Elliott, Jemima I, 9
Elliott, Jemima I, 39
Elliott, Jemima I, 47
Elliott, Jemima I, 48
Elliott, Jemima I, 388
Elliott, Jemima I, 538
Elliott, Jemima I, 678
Elliott, Jemima I, 756
Elliott, Jemima I, 760
Elliott, Jemima VI, 814
Elliott, Jemmimah I, 745
Elliott, Jennie IV, 1158
Elliott, Jesse I, 47
Elliott, Jesse IV, 328
Elliott, Jesse V, 329
Elliott, Jesse V, 384
Elliott, Jesse V, 670
Elliott, Jesse VI, 489
Elliott, Jesse D. VI, 911
Elliott, Jesse D. VI, 974
Elliott, Jesse D. VI, 986
Elliott, Jesse D. VI, 1018
Elliott, Jesse H. IV, 328
Elliott, Jesse H. IV, 334
Elliott, Jesse H. VI, 739
Elliott, Jesse J. V, 670
Elliott, Joab I, 47
Elliott, Joab I, 72
Elliott, Joanna I, 238
Elliott, Job I, 46
Elliott, Job I, 47
Elliott, Job I, 192
Elliott, Job I, 808
Elliott, Jody V, 455
Elliott, Joel I, 653
Elliott, Joel IV, 328
Elliott, Joel IV, 389
Elliott, John I, 98
Elliott, John I, 138
Elliott, John I, 151
Elliott, John I, 238
Elliott, John I, 388
Elliott, John I, 538
Elliott, John I, 653
Elliott, John I, 678
Elliott, John I, 698
Elliott, John I, 715
Elliott, John I, 985
Elliott, John II, 358
Elliott, John II, 497
Elliott, John II, 514
Elliott, John II, 535
Elliott, John II, 559
Elliott, John II, 634
Elliott, John II, 678
Elliott, John II, 704
Elliott, John IV, 144
Elliott, John IV, 328
Elliott, John IV, 346
Elliott, John IV, 358
Elliott, John IV, 389
Elliott, John IV, 701
Elliott, John IV, 949
Elliott, John IV, 1277
Elliott, John V, 51
Elliott, John VI, 911
Elliott, John VI, 920
Elliott, John VI, 972
Elliott, John A. I, 99
Elliott, John Bidwell I, 262
Elliott, John C. VI, 814
Elliott, John D. IV, 1157
Elliott, John D. IV, 1193
Elliott, John D. IV, 1206
Elliott, John D. IV, 1277
Elliott, John Francis I, 213
Elliott, John Francis I, 238
Elliott, John Griffith II, 358
Elliott, John Griffith II, 514
Elliott, John Hadley IV, 1277
Elliott, John Henry I, 213
Elliott, John Livingston B. III, 409
Elliott, John Richard IV, 1277
Elliott, John, Jr. II, 358
Elliott, John, Jr. II, 514
Elliott, John, Jr. II, 634
Elliott, John, Jr. II, 738
Elliott, John, Sr. II, 358
Elliott, Jonathan I, 8
Elliott, Jonathan I, 48
Elliott, Jonathan Pearson I, 46
Elliott, Jos. R. I, 238
Elliott, Joseph I, 8
Elliott, Joseph I, 9
Elliott, Joseph I, 46
Elliott, Joseph I, 47
Elliott, Joseph I, 48
Elliott, Joseph I, 50
Elliott, Joseph I, 98
Elliott, Joseph I, 99
Elliott, Joseph I, 138
Elliott, Joseph I, 139
Elliott, Joseph I, 175
Elliott, Joseph I, 183
Elliott, Joseph I, 192
Elliott, Joseph I, 209
Elliott, Joseph I, 238
Elliott, Joseph I, 538
Elliott, Joseph I, 653
Elliott, Joseph I, 675
Elliott, Joseph I, 678
Elliott, Joseph I, 741
Elliott, Joseph I, 745
Elliott, Joseph I, 760
Elliott, Joseph II, 514
Elliott, Joseph III, 109
Elliott, Joseph IV, 30
Elliott, Joseph IV, 701
Elliott, Joseph IV, 949
Elliott, Joseph IV, 1277
Elliott, Joseph Barker I, 924
Elliott, Joseph C. I, 207
Elliott, Joseph C. I, 214
Elliott, Joseph C. I, 238
Elliott, Joseph Copeland I, 238
Elliott, Joseph E. I, 213
Elliott, Joseph G. I, 48
Elliott, Joseph John Gurney I, 139
Elliott, Joseph P. I, 48
Elliott, Joseph Parker I, 98
Elliott, Joseph Thomas I, 213
Elliott, Josephene I, 214
Elliott, Josephine I, 238
Elliott, Joshua I, 8
Elliott, Joshua I, 9
Elliott, Joshua I, 46
Elliott, Joshua I, 47
Elliott, Joshua I, 72
Elliott, Joshua I, 123
Elliott, Joshua I, 262
Elliott, Joshua Bidwell I, 213
Elliott, Josiah I, 46
Elliott, Josiah I, 47
Elliott, Josie A. I, 213
Elliott, Judith VI, 911
Elliott, Julany I, 47
Elliott, Julia I, 238
Elliott, Julia A. I, 209
Elliott, Julia A. I, 213
Elliott, Julia A. I, 238
Elliott, Julia A. I, 538
Elliott, Julia A. I, 576
Elliott, Julia Ann I, 213
Elliott, Julia E. I, 213
Elliott, Julianah I, 46
Elliott, Julianah I, 86
Elliott, Julianna I, 8
Elliott, Julianna I, 9
Elliott, Karen I, 38
Elliott, Karen I, 48
Elliott, Kate V, 670
Elliott, Katharine I, 445
Elliott, Katharine I, 455
Elliott, Katharine I, 760
Elliott, Kemp McCoy I, 615
Elliott, L. Thomas I, 632
Elliott, Lamira IV, 328
Elliott, Lamira IV, 358
Elliott, Lamira IV, 389
Elliott, Lamira IV, 1157
Elliott, Lavinia M. VI, 855
Elliott, Lawrence A. IV, 1157
Elliott, Leah I, 46
Elliott, Leah I, 47
Elliott, Leah I, 56
Elliott, Leah I, 74
Elliott, Leonidas V, 235
Elliott, Levi IV, 1096
Elliott, Liana IV, 1277
Elliott, Lidia I, 138
Elliott, Lilla III, 409
Elliott, Lizzie J. I, 238
Elliott, Lorena V, 657
Elliott, Lorena V, 670
Elliott, Lottie Pearl I, 213
Elliott, Louise IV, 949
Elliott, Louise V, 670
Elliott, Louise M. IV, 949
Elliott, Lucinda IV, 328
Elliott, Lucinda IV, 355
Elliott, Lurania I, 139
Elliott, Lyddia I, 66
Elliott, Lydia I, 9
Elliott, Lydia I, 47
Elliott, Lydia I, 48
Elliott, Lydia I, 73
Elliott, Lydia I, 653
Elliott, Lydia I, 759
Elliott, Lydia I, 924
Elliott, Lydia II, 358
Elliott, Lydia II, 514
Elliott, Lydia II, 649
Elliott, Lydia II, 738
Elliott, Lydia II, 776
Elliott, Lydia IV, 327
Elliott, Lydia IV, 328
Elliott, Lydia IV, 868
Elliott, Lydia IV, 876
Elliott, Lydia IV, 904
Elliott, Lydia IV, 1277
Elliott, Lydia VI, 915
Elliott, Lydia VI, 920
Elliott, Lydia M. IV, 1277
Elliott, M. Ada I, 808
Elliott, Mahlon IV, 1277
Elliott, Malenda I, 745
Elliott, Malinda I, 678
Elliott, Malinda I, 760
Elliott, Malinda V, 329
Elliott, Malinda V, 330
Elliott, Margaret I, 9
Elliott, Margaret I, 36
Elliott, Margaret I, 46
Elliott, Margaret I, 47
Elliott, Margaret I, 48
Elliott, Margaret I, 49
Elliott, Margaret I, 71
Elliott, Margaret I, 139
Elliott, Margaret I, 192
Elliott, Margaret I, 213
Elliott, Margaret I, 214
Elliott, Margaret I, 238
Elliott, Margaret I, 305
Elliott, Margaret I, 314
Elliott, Margaret I, 653
Elliott, Margaret II, 358
Elliott, Margaret II, 514
Elliott, Margaret II, 634
Elliott, Margaret II, 704
Elliott, Margaret III, 109
Elliott, Margaret IV, 1157
Elliott, Margaret IV, 1196
Elliott, Margaret VI, 739
Elliott, Margaret VI, 814
Elliott, Margaret Scott I, 138
Elliott, Margaret Scott I, 175
Elliott, Margaretta II, 514
Elliott, Margaretta II, 704
Elliott, Margret I, 306
Elliott, Maria IV, 813
Elliott, Maria IV, 822
Elliott, Mariam I, 214
Elliott, Mariam I, 615
Elliott, Mariam Tomes I, 192
Elliott, Marion I, 192
Elliott, Martha I, 46
Elliott, Martha I, 47
Elliott, Martha I, 48
Elliott, Martha I, 213
Elliott, Martha I, 238
Elliott, Martha I, 780
Elliott, Martha I, 808
Elliott, Martha I, 836
Elliott, Martha IV, 813
Elliott, Martha IV, 949
Elliott, Martha IV, 997
Elliott, Martha IV, 1206
Elliott, Martha IV, 1278
Elliott, Martha VI, 805
Elliott, Martha VI, 814
Elliott, Martha D. I, 615
Elliott, Martha D. I, 632
Elliott, Martha Fern I, 615
Elliott, Martha J. IV, 289
Elliott, Martha Jane I, 48
Elliott, Martha Jane I, 238
Elliott, Martha Nixon I, 192
Elliott, Martha R. I, 213
Elliott, Martha S. VI, 814
Elliott, Martin IV, 1157
Elliott, Martin IV, 1158
Elliott, Martin IV, 1206
Elliott, Martin William VI, 803
Elliott, Mary I, 8
Elliott, Mary I, 9
Elliott, Mary I, 46
Elliott, Mary I, 47
Elliott, Mary I, 48
Elliott, Mary I, 52
Elliott, Mary I, 55
Elliott, Mary I, 66
Elliott, Mary I, 68
Elliott, Mary I, 74
Elliott, Mary I, 78
Elliott, Mary I, 79
Elliott, Mary I, 86
Elliott, Mary I, 99
Elliott, Mary I, 138
Elliott, Mary I, 139
Elliott, Mary I, 188
Elliott, Mary I, 192
Elliott, Mary I, 214
Elliott, Mary I, 238
Elliott, Mary I, 257
Elliott, Mary I, 388
Elliott, Mary I, 623
Elliott, Mary I, 653
Elliott, Mary I, 675
Elliott, Mary I, 678
Elliott, Mary I, 715
Elliott, Mary I, 730
Elliott, Mary I, 808
Elliott, Mary I, 845
Elliott, Mary I, 924
Elliott, Mary I, 985

Elliott, Mary I, 995
Elliott, Mary II, 358
Elliott, Mary II, 514
Elliott, Mary II, 535
Elliott, Mary II, 634
Elliott, Mary II, 678
Elliott, Mary II, 704
Elliott, Mary II, 738
Elliott, Mary III, 109
Elliott, Mary IV, 701
Elliott, Mary IV, 949
Elliott, Mary IV, 1157
Elliott, Mary IV, 1277
Elliott, Mary IV, 1278
Elliott, Mary V, 737
Elliott, Mary VI, 739
Elliott, Mary VI, 814
Elliott, Mary A. I, 207
Elliott, Mary A. I, 214
Elliott, Mary A. I, 238
Elliott, Mary A. VI, 814
Elliott, Mary Ann I, 48
Elliott, Mary Ann I, 139
Elliott, Mary Ann I, 140
Elliott, Mary Ann I, 163
Elliott, Mary Ann I, 214
Elliott, Mary Ann I, 238
Elliott, Mary Ann I, 780
Elliott, Mary Ann I, 808
Elliott, Mary Ann I, 816
Elliott, Mary B. I, 213
Elliott, Mary E. V, 455
Elliott, Mary Elma I, 213
Elliott, Mary Etta I, 924
Elliott, Mary F. III, 326
Elliott, Mary F. III, 366
Elliott, Mary J. II, 859
Elliott, Mary J. C. VI, 809
Elliott, Mary Jane I, 780
Elliott, Mary Jane I, 808
Elliott, Mary P. VI, 814
Elliott, Mary Richards II, 649
Elliott, Mary Rosilla IV, 1277
Elliott, Mary S. I, 48
Elliott, Mary S. I, 213
Elliott, Mary S. I, 214
Elliott, Mary S. I, 808
Elliott, Mary Symons I, 8
Elliott, Mary Symons I, 48
Elliott, Mary Symons I, 81
Elliott, Mary T. VI, 923
Elliott, Mary Toms I, 192
Elliott, Mather IV, 1277
Elliott, Matilda IV, 328
Elliott, Matilda IV, 1276
Elliott, Matilda IV, 1277
Elliott, Matilda Ann IV, 1277
Elliott, Matthew IV, 1277
Elliott, Melina I, 760
Elliott, Meriam I, 98
Elliott, Mildred I, 877
Elliott, Mildred I, 926
Elliott, Mildred Ada I, 780
Elliott, Miles I, 46
Elliott, Miles I, 47
Elliott, Miles I, 56
Elliott, Miley I, 47
Elliott, Milton I, 877
Elliott, Milton VI, 908
Elliott, Miriam I, 8
Elliott, Miriam I, 45
Elliott, Miriam I, 46
Elliott, Miriam I, 47
Elliott, Miriam I, 57
Elliott, Miriam I, 87
Elliott, Miriam I, 138
Elliott, Miriam I, 238
Elliott, Miriam I, 615
Elliott, Miriam I, 808
Elliott, Mordecai I, 46
Elliott, Mordecai I, 47
Elliott, Mordecai I, 74
Elliott, Mordecai M. I, 98
Elliott, Mordica I, 48
Elliott, Morris II, 358
Elliott, Morris Archibald I, 213
Elliott, Moses I, 46
Elliott, Moses I, 54
Elliott, Moses I, 138
Elliott, Moses IV, 30
Elliott, Moses IV, 1277
Elliott, Mourning I, 46
Elliott, Mourning I, 47
Elliott, Mourning I, 86
Elliott, Mrs. Iva Tracy V, 994
Elliott, Nancy I, 47
Elliott, Nancy I, 48
Elliott, Nancy I, 759
Elliott, Nancy IV, 1277
Elliott, Nancy VI, 804
Elliott, Nancy VI, 814
Elliott, Nancy VI, 911
Elliott, Nancy VI, 918
Elliott, Narcissa VI, 911
Elliott, Nathan I, 46
Elliott, Nathan I, 48
Elliott, Nathan I, 99
Elliott, Nathan I, 138
Elliott, Nathan I, 139
Elliott, Nathan I, 163
Elliott, Nathan I, 445
Elliott, Nathan I, 455
Elliott, Nathan I, 653
Elliott, Nathan I, 678
Elliott, Nathan I, 715
Elliott, Nathan I, 745
Elliott, Nathan I, 759
Elliott, Nathan I, 760
Elliott, Nathan I, 768
Elliott, Nixon I, 47
Elliott, Nixon I, 73
Elliott, Nixon I, 192
Elliott, Nixon I, 808
Elliott, Obadiah I, 653
Elliott, Obadiah I, 678
Elliott, Obadiah I, 715
Elliott, Obed I, 46
Elliott, Obediah I, 445
Elliott, Obediah I, 457
Elliott, Obediah I, 678
Elliott, Obediah I, 715
Elliott, Obediah I, 759
Elliott, Obediah I, 760
Elliott, Obediah I, 762
Elliott, Olie May Jane I, 213
Elliott, Orpha I, 46
Elliott, Orpha I, 60
Elliott, Patience I, 46
Elliott, Patience I, 47
Elliott, Patience I, 56
Elliott, Penina I, 47
Elliott, Peninah I, 46
Elliott, Peninah I, 47
Elliott, Peninah I, 192
Elliott, Peninah I, 199
Elliott, Penninah I, 8
Elliott, Penninah I, 9
Elliott, Penninah I, 46
Elliott, Penninah I, 48
Elliott, Penninah I, 50
Elliott, Penninah I, 73
Elliott, Penninah I, 139
Elliott, Penninah I, 163
Elliott, Penninah I, 192
Elliott, Penninah I, 196
Elliott, Peter I, 745
Elliott, Peter I, 760
Elliott, Peter II, 514
Elliott, Pharaby I, 238
Elliott, Phariba I, 233
Elliott, Phariba I, 238
Elliott, Pharoah I, 46
Elliott, Pheba VI, 860
Elliott, Phebe IV, 30
Elliott, Phebe Ann IV, 328
Elliott, Pheraba I, 48
Elliott, Pheriba I, 47
Elliott, Pheriba I, 72
Elliott, Phiraba I, 48
Elliott, Pretlow I, 46
Elliott, Pretlow I, 47
Elliott, Pretlow I, 60
Elliott, Pretlow I, 192
Elliott, Priscilla I, 388
Elliott, Priscilla I, 538
Elliott, Priscilla Jane IV, 1277
Elliott, Pritlow I, 45
Elliott, Pritlow I, 46
Elliott, Pritlow I, 68
Elliott, Quintain I, 9
Elliott, R. Cordelia I, 627
Elliott, R. Cordelia I, 808
Elliott, R. Cordelia I, 824
Elliott, Rache I, 538
Elliott, Rachel I, 8
Elliott, Rachel I, 9
Elliott, Rachel I, 46
Elliott, Rachel I, 47
Elliott, Rachel I, 48
Elliott, Rachel I, 52
Elliott, Rachel I, 56
Elliott, Rachel I, 72
Elliott, Rachel I, 123
Elliott, Rachel I, 138
Elliott, Rachel I, 173
Elliott, Rachel I, 388
Elliott, Rachel I, 538
Elliott, Rachel I, 760
Elliott, Rachel I, 767
Elliott, Rachel I, 808
Elliott, Rachel IV, 30
Elliott, Rachel IV, 64
Elliott, Rachel IV, 144
Elliott, Rachel IV, 328
Elliott, Rachel IV, 334
Elliott, Rachel IV, 346
Elliott, Rachel IV, 358
Elliott, Rachel IV, 389
Elliott, Rachel IV, 892
Elliott, Rachel IV, 895
Elliott, Randolf I, 759
Elliott, Rebecca I, 214
Elliott, Rebecca I, 238
Elliott, Rebecca I, 715
Elliott, Rebecca I, 985
Elliott, Rebecca II, 514
Elliott, Rebecca IV, 30
Elliott, Rebecca IV, 1277
Elliott, Rebecca Ann V, 51
Elliott, Rebecca Ann V, 55
Elliott, Rebecca Deulea IV, 30
Elliott, Rebecca M. V, 51
Elliott, Rebecca Marshall II, 358
Elliott, Rebecca Marshall II, 514
Elliott, Rebecca Olive IV, 1277
Elliott, Rebecca T. II, 859
Elliott, Rebecka I, 47
Elliott, Rebeckah I, 46
Elliott, Rebeckah I, 67
Elliott, Rebeka I, 86
Elliott, Rebekah I, 698
Elliott, Resea IV, 389
Elliott, Reuben IV, 1157
Elliott, Reuben VI, 739
Elliott, Rheas IV, 328
Elliott, Rhesa IV, 328
Elliott, Rhese IV, 328
Elliott, Rhoda I, 47
Elliott, Rhoda I, 73
Elliott, Rhoda I, 138
Elliott, Rhoda I, 139
Elliott, Rhoda I, 192
Elliott, Rhoda I, 305
Elliott, Rhoda I, 306
Elliott, Rhoda I, 626
Elliott, Rhoda I, 678
Elliott, Rhoda I, 687
Elliott, Rhoda I, 780
Elliott, Rhoda I, 808
Elliott, Rhoda V, 831
Elliott, Rhoda V, 837
Elliott, Rhoda B. I, 593
Elliott, Rhoda B. I, 595
Elliott, Rhoda C. I, 139
Elliott, Rhoda C. I, 620
Elliott, Rhoda C. I, 808
Elliott, Rhoda C. I, 829
Elliott, Rhoda Coffin I, 620
Elliott, Rhoda Cordelia I, 620
Elliott, Rhoda Cordelia I, 780
Elliott, Ricks I, 238
Elliott, Rix I, 138
Elliott, Rix I, 214
Elliott, Robert II, 704
Elliott, Robert VI, 814
Elliott, Robert VI, 855
Elliott, Robert VI, 911
Elliott, Robert VI, 975
Elliott, Robert Barckley I, 780
Elliott, Robert Clark V, 670
Elliott, Robert W. VI, 814
Elliott, Robert, Jr. VI, 804
Elliott, Rose I, 262
Elliott, Roxanna I, 926
Elliott, Roxanna I, 927
Elliott, Ruth I, 46
Elliott, Ruth I, 59
Elliott, Ruth I, 138
Elliott, Ruth I, 538
Elliott, Ruth I, 678
Elliott, Ruth I, 741
Elliott, Ruth I, 745
Elliott, Ruth I, 760
Elliott, Ruth I, 1118
Elliott, Ruth I, 1133
Elliott, Ruth IV, 30
Elliott, Ruth IV, 46
Elliott, Ruth IV, 1157
Elliott, Ruth IV, 1206
Elliott, Ruth IV, 1273
Elliott, Ruth IV, 1277
Elliott, Ruth V, 235
Elliott, Ruth Sisney I, 388
Elliott, Sally VI, 812
Elliott, Samey I, 538
Elliott, Samira IV, 389
Elliott, Samira IV, 454
Elliott, Samuel I, 47
Elliott, Samuel I, 138
Elliott, Samuel I, 192
Elliott, Samuel II, 358
Elliott, Samuel II, 514
Elliott, Samuel II, 649
Elliott, Samuel II, 704
Elliott, Samuel III, 109
Elliott, Samuel IV, 289
Elliott, Samuel IV, 949
Elliott, Samuel IV, 997
Elliott, Sarah I, 43
Elliott, Sarah I, 45
Elliott, Sarah I, 46
Elliott, Sarah I, 47
Elliott, Sarah I, 48
Elliott, Sarah I, 61
Elliott, Sarah I, 67
Elliott, Sarah I, 76
Elliott, Sarah I, 78
Elliott, Sarah I, 80
Elliott, Sarah I, 99
Elliott, Sarah I, 138
Elliott, Sarah I, 139
Elliott, Sarah I, 141
Elliott, Sarah I, 147
Elliott, Sarah I, 183
Elliott, Sarah I, 192
Elliott, Sarah I, 200
Elliott, Sarah I, 213
Elliott, Sarah I, 214
Elliott, Sarah I, 238
Elliott, Sarah I, 388
Elliott, Sarah I, 445
Elliott, Sarah I, 538
Elliott, Sarah I, 653
Elliott, Sarah I, 678
Elliott, Sarah I, 688
Elliott, Sarah I, 715
Elliott, Sarah I, 745
Elliott, Sarah I, 759
Elliott, Sarah I, 760
Elliott, Sarah I, 762
Elliott, Sarah I, 768
Elliott, Sarah II, 217
Elliott, Sarah IV, 30
Elliott, Sarah IV, 289
Elliott, Sarah IV, 867
Elliott, Sarah IV, 868
Elliott, Sarah IV, 904
Elliott, Sarah IV, 949
Elliott, Sarah IV, 1157
Elliott, Sarah V, 51
Elliott, Sarah VI, 739
Elliott, Sarah VI, 911
Elliott, Sarah B. III, 109
Elliott, Sarah Catharine I, 213
Elliott, Sarah Catherine I, 213
Elliott, Sarah Catherine I, 227
Elliott, Sarah E. I, 209
Elliott, Sarah E. I, 214
Elliott, Sarah E. I, 238
Elliott, Sarah Jinnette I, 924
Elliott, Sarah Lena I, 213
Elliott, Sarah M. IV, 1157
Elliott, Sarah M. IV, 1196
Elliott, Sarah P. III, 109
Elliott, Sarah P. III, 331
Elliott, Sarah Saphronia I, 780
Elliott, Saretta V, 670
Elliott, Saretta V, 718
Elliott, Seth I, 46
Elliott, Seth I, 47
Elliott, Seth I, 78
Elliott, Seth I, 192
Elliott, Silas I, 8
Elliott, Silas I, 48
Elliott, Simeon IV, 1096
Elliott, Sitka IV, 1277
Elliott, Sitka IV, 1278
Elliott, Solomon I, 8
Elliott, Solomon I, 46
Elliott, Solomon I, 47
Elliott, Solomon I, 48
Elliott, Solomon I, 87
Elliott, Solomon I, 98
Elliott, Solomon I, 192
Elliott, Solomon Edward I, 214
Elliott, Sophronia I, 808
Elliott, Sophronia I, 835
Elliott, Stamey Lee I, 615
Elliott, Stamey Lee I, 632
Elliott, Stanton I, 9
Elliott, Stanton I, 48
Elliott, Stephen I, 46
Elliott, Stephen I, 538
Elliott, Susan V, 329
Elliott, Susan V, 384
Elliott, Susan Ann VI, 911
Elliott, Susan S. V, 882
Elliott, Susanna IV, 892
Elliott, Susanna IV, 895
Elliott, Susannah I, 139
Elliott, Susannah I, 163
Elliott, Susannah V, 384
Elliott, Tabitha VI, 830
Elliott, Tereca I, 877
Elliott, Teresa I, 852
Elliott, Thomas I, 46
Elliott, Thomas I, 47
Elliott, Thomas I, 48
Elliott, Thomas I, 61
Elliott, Thomas I, 86
Elliott, Thomas I, 98
Elliott, Thomas I, 99
Elliott, Thomas I, 138
Elliott, Thomas I, 139
Elliott, Thomas I, 175
Elliott, Thomas I, 183
Elliott, Thomas I, 189
Elliott, Thomas I, 192
Elliott, Thomas I, 199
Elliott, Thomas I, 238
Elliott, Thomas I, 262
Elliott, Thomas I, 678
Elliott, Thomas I, 808
Elliott, Thomas I, 926
Elliott, Thomas I, 1075
Elliott, Thomas II, 514
Elliott, Thomas II, 678
Elliott, Thomas IV, 1277
Elliott, Thomas VI, 804
Elliott, Thomas VI, 809
Elliott, Thomas VI, 814
Elliott, Thomas B. I, 48
Elliott, Thomas B. I, 213
Elliott, Thomas B. I, 214
Elliott, Thomas B. I, 238
Elliott, Thomas Floyd I, 615
Elliott, Thomas Floyd I, 632
Elliott, Thomas Lockey I, 615
Elliott, Thomas P. I, 214
Elliott, Thomas, Jr. I, 139
Elliott, Thomas, Sr. I, 139
Elliott, Thos. IV, 1277
Elliott, Thos. VI, 814
Elliott, Thos. Olien IV, 1277
Elliott, Thos. P. I, 214
Elliott, Toms R. I, 238
Elliott, Townsend I, 47
Elliott, Upton IV, 1157
Elliott, Upton VI, 739
Elliott, Urshla I, 985
Elliott, Usley I, 698
Elliott, Usley I, 715
Elliott, Vachal I, 48
Elliott, Vernon V, 455
Elliott, Veronica III, 409
Elliott, Veronica III, 449
Elliott, Veronica B. III, 409
Elliott, Virginia V, 670
Elliott, Virginia C. V, 670
Elliott, Wd. Dora F. III, 446
Elliott, Welmet I, 1101
Elliott, Welmet I, 1118
Elliott, Widow Charlotte I, 175
Elliott, Widow Esabella I, 139
Elliott, Widow Isabella I, 177
Elliott, Widow Martha I, 87
Elliott, Widow Sarah I, 47
Elliott, Widow Sarah I, 66
Elliott, Widow Sarah I, 413
Elliott, Wilkinson IV, 1277
Elliott, William I, 46
Elliott, William I, 47
Elliott, William I, 139
Elliott, William I, 163
Elliott, William I, 177
Elliott, William I, 388
Elliott, William I, 538
Elliott, William I, 780
Elliott, William I, 808
Elliott, William I Sup 1, 8
Elliott, William II, 358
Elliott, William V, 51
Elliott, William V, 329
Elliott, William V, 384
Elliott, William VI, 739
Elliott, William VI, 796
Elliott, William VI, 803
Elliott, William VI, 809
Elliott, William VI, 814
Elliott, William VI, 915
Elliott, William VI, 951
Elliott, William A. VI, 814
Elliott, William Anderson I, 99
Elliott, William H. I, 214
Elliott, William H. I, 238
Elliott, William H. VI, 911
Elliott, William H. VI, 920
Elliott, William H. S. III, 326
Elliott, William Harrison I, 214
Elliott, William L. I, 48
Elliott, William L. III, 326
Elliott, William Lancaster Bailey I, 98
Elliott, William Newby I, 46
Elliott, William P. VI, 814

Elliott, William Penn I, 139
Elliott, William T. I, 214
Elliott, William T. I, 238
Elliott, Willis I, 47
Elliott, Willis D. VI, 814
Elliott, Wilmington V, 51
Elliott, Winslow I, 47
Elliott, Wm. I, 413
Elliott, Wm. II, 514
Elliott, Wm. IV, 1157
Elliott, Wm. V, 384
Elliott, Wm. VI, 860
Elliott, Wm. Ennis IV, 1277
Elliott, Wm. G. IV, 1277
Elliott, Wm. H. IV, 1157
Elliott, Wm. L. III, 109
Elliott, Wyke I, 8
Elliott, Wyke I, 48
Elliott, Zachariah I, 192
Elliott, Zachariah Nixon I, 183
Elliott, Zacheus Olien IV, 1277
Elliott, Zilpha I, 678
Elliott, Zilpha I, 698
Elliott, Zilpha I, 715
Elliott, Zilpha I, 985
Elliott, Zilpha I, 995
Elliotte, Katharine I, 760
Ellis, ??? III, 225
Ellis, ??? IV, 137
Ellis, ??? V, 315
Ellis, A. J. V, 167
Ellis, Aaron II, 217
Ellis, Abel V, 456
Ellis, Abigail I, 388
Ellis, Abigail I, 1082
Ellis, Abigail IV, 523
Ellis, Abigail B. IV, 522
Ellis, Abner I, 1082
Ellis, Abner I, 1083
Ellis, Abner I, 1092
Ellis, Abner I, 1095
Ellis, Abner B. I, 1082
Ellis, Abner C. V, 167
Ellis, Abraham V, 384
Ellis, Abraham V, 385
Ellis, Acsa M. II, 859
Ellis, Acsa M. II, 864
Ellis, Ada V, 456
Ellis, Adah VI, 489
Ellis, Albert V, 237
Ellis, Alice V, 488
Ellis, Alice V, 671
Ellis, Alice Adaline V, 237
Ellis, Alice Matilda V, 237
Ellis, Alida E. II, 859
Ellis, Alida E. II, 899
Ellis, Alisha VI, 385
Ellis, Almarinda V, 455
Ellis, Almeda V, 237
Ellis, Amanda Adeline I, 1082
Ellis, Amos I, 497
Ellis, Amos II, 172
Ellis, Amos IV, 144
Ellis, Amos IV, 328
Ellis, Amos VI, 385
Ellis, Amos Coulson V, 167
Ellis, Ann V, 385
Ellis, Ann V, 419
Ellis, Ann V, 560
Ellis, Ann VI, 911
Ellis, Ann VI, 912
Ellis, Ann Eliza III, 225
Ellis, Ann I. II, 1072
Ellis, Ann I. II, 1074
Ellis, Anna I, 1083
Ellis, Anna II, 862
Ellis, Anna II, 872
Ellis, Anna IV, 1110
Ellis, Anna V, 51
Ellis, Anna V, 236
Ellis, Anna V, 265
Ellis, Anna V, 384
Ellis, Anna V, 385
Ellis, Anna V, 560
Ellis, Anna V, 969
Ellis, Anna C. V, 51
Ellis, Anna Moon V, 415
Ellis, Anne I, 1092
Ellis, Aquila V, 488
Ellis, Aquilla V, 330
Ellis, Aquilla V, 560
Ellis, Asa IV, 522
Ellis, Asa IV, 523
Ellis, Asenath I, 1083
Ellis, Asenath I, 1092
Ellis, Asenath I, 1151
Ellis, Asenath I, 1155
Ellis, Athaliah V, 236
Ellis, Athaliah V, 237
Ellis, Athaliah V, 281
Ellis, Barkley VI, 384
Ellis, Benjamin II, 189
Ellis, Benjamin II, 514
Ellis, Benjamin II, 515
Ellis, Benjamin VI, 873
Ellis, Benjamin VI, 911
Ellis, Benjamin VI, 958
Ellis, Benjamin VI, 960
Ellis, Benjamin VI, 984
Ellis, Benjamin C. VI, 912
Ellis, Benjamin M. VI, 912
Ellis, Benjamin, Sr. VI, 969
Ellis, Berkeley??? VI, 384
Ellis, Betsey VI, 1006
Ellis, Betsy VI, 911
Ellis, Beulah I, 1105
Ellis, Beulah V, 51
Ellis, Bevan IV, 523
Ellis, Bonnir V, 620
Ellis, Bulah V, 385
Ellis, Calvin V, 237
Ellis, Carey V, 384
Ellis, Caroline I, 1082
Ellis, Caroline I, 1092
Ellis, Caroline I, 1095
Ellis, Caroline V, 236
Ellis, Caroline V, 456
Ellis, Catharine IV, 522
Ellis, Catharine IV, 523
Ellis, Catharine V, 302
Ellis, Catherine IV, 1278
Ellis, Catherine VI, 172
Ellis, Chaney Field VI, 814
Ellis, Charity V, 384
Ellis, Charity VI, 385
Ellis, Charles II, 358
Ellis, Charles II, 515
Ellis, Charles II, 704
Ellis, Charles II, 738
Ellis, Charles V, 488
Ellis, Charles J. II, 859
Ellis, Charles J. II, 934
Ellis, Charles Maynard V, 560
Ellis, Charles R. II, 738
Ellis, Charty I, 1118
Ellis, Charty I, 1129
Ellis, Chas II, 515
Ellis, Chas. J. II, 792
Ellis, Chas. J. II, 859
Ellis, Chas. J. II, 864
Ellis, Chas. J. II, 899
Ellis, Chas. J. II, 925
Ellis, Chas. J. II, 942
Ellis, Christopher V, 488
Ellis, Clarence V, 671
Ellis, Clarence Homer V, 671
Ellis, Clarkson V, 167
Ellis, Clifford II, 859
Ellis, Clifford Justice II, 859
Ellis, Clifford Justice II, 899
Ellis, Conda S. V, 456
Ellis, Cordie S. V, 237
Ellis, Cynthia V, 384
Ellis, Cyrenius V, 236
Ellis, Cyrenus V, 456
Ellis, Cyrus V, 236
Ellis, Cyrus V, 237
Ellis, D. Webster V, 456
Ellis, Daniel I, 1082
Ellis, Daniel I, 1083
Ellis, Daniel V, 384
Ellis, Daniel B. I, 1082
Ellis, Daniel H. V, 384
Ellis, Daniel H. V, 385
Ellis, Daniel Webster V, 237
Ellis, David I, 1083
Ellis, David I, 1092
Ellis, David IV, 144
Ellis, David V, 235
Ellis, David V, 236
Ellis, David V, 237
Ellis, David V, 253
Ellis, David V, 288
Ellis, David V, 456
Ellis, David VI, 385
Ellis, David VI, 814
Ellis, David Barrett V, 237
Ellis, David W. V, 456
Ellis, David William V, 236
Ellis, Deborah II, 358
Ellis, Deborah II, 704
Ellis, Deborah VI, 384
Ellis, Deborah T. II, 515
Ellis, Deborah T. II, 704
Ellis, Deborah Tyson II, 738
Ellis, Delilah V, 235
Ellis, Delilah V, 236
Ellis, Delphina I, 1084
Ellis, Dicey VI, 911
Ellis, Dinah VI, 385
Ellis, Dorcas V, 384
Ellis, Dorcas V, 560
Ellis, Dorcas V, 586
Ellis, Dr. Newton C. I, 1151
Ellis, Edith U. V, 51
Ellis, Edith V. V, 51
Ellis, Edwin V, 384
Ellis, Edwin V, 385
Ellis, Edwin VI, 106
Ellis, Edwin C. V, 385
Ellis, Edwin C. V, 837
Ellis, Eleanor I, 1083
Ellis, Eleanor V, 51
Ellis, Eleanor V, 236
Ellis, Eleanor V, 278
Ellis, Eleanor VI, 384
Ellis, Eleanor VI, 385
Ellis, Eleanor VI, 398
Ellis, Eleanor VI, 412
Ellis, Eleanor VI, 958
Ellis, Elennor I, 1092
Ellis, Elenor V, 951
Ellis, Elenor VI, 489
Ellis, Eli I, 1083
Ellis, Eli V, 236
Ellis, Elijah I, 1055
Ellis, Elijah I, 1083
Ellis, Elijah V, 51
Ellis, Elijah V, 157
Ellis, Elijah V, 159
Ellis, Elijah V, 167
Ellis, Elijah V, 235
Ellis, Elijah V, 236
Ellis, Elijah V, 237
Ellis, Elijah V, 456
Ellis, Elijah Harvey V, 167
Ellis, Elijah Leroy V, 456
Ellis, Elinor VI, 384
Ellis, Elisabeth II, 217
Ellis, Elisabeth II, 234
Ellis, Elisabeth VI, 384
Ellis, Elisha I, 538
Ellis, Elisha IV, 144
Ellis, Elisha IV, 522
Ellis, Elisha IV, 523
Ellis, Elisha IV, 532
Ellis, Elisha VI, 384
Ellis, Elisha VI, 385
Ellis, Elisha VI, 440
Ellis, Elisha Ellis IV, 144
Ellis, Elisha Ellis VI, 385
Ellis, Eliza III, 109
Ellis, Eliza III, 225
Ellis, Eliza IV, 868
Ellis, Eliza IV, 880
Ellis, Eliza V, 456
Ellis, Eliza V, 560
Ellis, Eliza V, 589
Ellis, Eliza B. V, 237
Ellis, Eliza B. V, 560
Ellis, Elizabeth I, 497
Ellis, Elizabeth I, 1082
Ellis, Elizabeth I, 1083
Ellis, Elizabeth I, 1084
Ellis, Elizabeth I, 1086
Ellis, Elizabeth I, 1092
Ellis, Elizabeth I, 1099
Ellis, Elizabeth I, 1151
Ellis, Elizabeth II, 172
Ellis, Elizabeth II, 217
Ellis, Elizabeth IV, 30
Ellis, Elizabeth IV, 144
Ellis, Elizabeth IV, 523
Ellis, Elizabeth IV, 532
Ellis, Elizabeth IV, 701
Ellis, Elizabeth IV, 805
Ellis, Elizabeth IV, 814
Ellis, Elizabeth V, 167
Ellis, Elizabeth V, 235
Ellis, Elizabeth V, 236
Ellis, Elizabeth V, 237
Ellis, Elizabeth V, 288
Ellis, Elizabeth V, 330
Ellis, Elizabeth V, 384
Ellis, Elizabeth V, 385
Ellis, Elizabeth V, 671
Ellis, Elizabeth V, 808
Ellis, Elizabeth VI, 384
Ellis, Elizabeth VI, 385
Ellis, Elizabeth VI, 429
Ellis, Elizabeth VI, 430
Ellis, Elizabeth VI, 448
Ellis, Elizabeth VI, 594
Ellis, Elizabeth VI, 838
Ellis, Elizabeth VI, 894
Ellis, Elizabeth Barrett V, 237
Ellis, Elizabeth C. V, 51
Ellis, Elizabeth C. V, 167
Ellis, Elizabeth Frances VI, 912
Ellis, Elizabeth J. IV, 1130
Ellis, Elizabeth J. V, 456
Ellis, Elizabeth M. I, 1082
Ellis, Elizabeth Wooley II, 786
Ellis, Ella Everetta V, 167
Ellis, Ellen II, 514
Ellis, Ellis I, 1077
Ellis, Ellis I, 1082
Ellis, Ellis I, 1083
Ellis, Ellis I, 1091
Ellis, Ellis I, 1092
Ellis, Ellis I, 1095
Ellis, Ellis I, 1096
Ellis, Ellis I, 1151
Ellis, Ellis V, 167
Ellis, Ellis V, 808
Ellis, Ellis VI, 384
Ellis, Ellis VI, 385
Ellis, Ellis VI, 430
Ellis, Elwood V, 384
Ellis, Elwood V, 560
Ellis, Elwood O. V, 385
Ellis, Emaline I, 1090
Ellis, Emaline I, 1092
Ellis, Emely V, 951
Ellis, Emily II, 859
Ellis, Emily II, 942
Ellis, Emily V, 167
Ellis, Emily VI, 958
Ellis, Emily A. V, 167
Ellis, Emily E. V, 236
Ellis, Emily Elizabeth V, 237
Ellis, Enos I, 1082
Ellis, Enos I, 1092
Ellis, Enos I, 1140
Ellis, Enos I, 1151
Ellis, Enos IV, 30
Ellis, Enos IV, 701
Ellis, Enos IV, 814
Ellis, Enos V, 167
Ellis, Enos VI, 383
Ellis, Enos VI, 384
Ellis, Enos VI, 385
Ellis, Enos VI, 429
Ellis, Enos VI, 430
Ellis, Enos VI, 594
Ellis, Enos Jewry V, 237
Ellis, Enos, Jr. IV, 814
Ellis, Enos. IV, 622
Ellis, Esther A. II, 704
Ellis, Ethel Martin V, 620
Ellis, Etta V, 456
Ellis, Evan Tyson II, 358
Ellis, Evan Tyson II, 515
Ellis, Evan Tyson II, 738
Ellis, Fannie IV, 523
Ellis, Francis II, 217
Ellis, Francis II, 234
Ellis, Francis V, 236
Ellis, Francis V, 237
Ellis, Francis V, 560
Ellis, Francis B. I, 1140
Ellis, Franklin II, 859
Ellis, Franklin II, 934
Ellis, Gainer IV, 30
Ellis, Gainer IV, 701
Ellis, Gainer IV, 814
Ellis, Gainer VI, 385
Ellis, Gainor IV, 827
Ellis, George VI, 172
Ellis, George VI, 203
Ellis, George VI, 206
Ellis, George VI, 912
Ellis, Guli E. V, 51
Ellis, Guli E. V, 69
Ellis, Guli Elma V, 167
Ellis, Gulielma V, 51
Ellis, Gulielma V, 167
Ellis, H. B. V, 620
Ellis, Hannah I, 1082
Ellis, Hannah I, 1083
Ellis, Hannah I, 1084
Ellis, Hannah I, 1089
Ellis, Hannah I, 1092
Ellis, Hannah II, 172
Ellis, Hannah II, 792
Ellis, Hannah IV, 522
Ellis, Hannah IV, 523
Ellis, Hannah IV, 532
Ellis, Hannah V, 51
Ellis, Hannah V, 167
Ellis, Hannah V, 235
Ellis, Hannah V, 236
Ellis, Hannah V, 253
Ellis, Hannah V, 288
Ellis, Hannah V, 330
Ellis, Hannah V, 385
Ellis, Hannah V, 456
Ellis, Hannah VI, 384
Ellis, Hannah VI, 429
Ellis, Hannah Amilda V, 236
Ellis, Hannah Eliza I, 1084
Ellis, Hannah Ellen V, 236
Ellis, Hannah Ellen V, 253
Ellis, Hannah Ellin V, 236
Ellis, Hannah J. I, 1082
Ellis, Harley V, 456
Ellis, Harley G. V, 456
Ellis, Harmannus V, 237
Ellis, Harmanus V, 456
Ellis, Harriet H. VI, 385
Ellis, Harriet H. VI, 394
Ellis, Harriett V, 234
Ellis, Harriett V, 236
Ellis, Harriett V, 237
Ellis, Harvey II, 859
Ellis, Harvey G. IV, 1130
Ellis, Harvey J. IV, 1130
Ellis, Henry I, 1082
Ellis, Henry II, 172
Ellis, Henry II, 286
Ellis, Henry C. II, 859
Ellis, Henry L. I, 1083
Ellis, Hiram V, 385
Ellis, Howard V, 560
Ellis, India V, 167
Ellis, Isaac I, 1083
Ellis, Isaac II, 68
Ellis, Isaac II, 97
Ellis, Isaac IV, 1278
Ellis, Isaac V, 51
Ellis, Isaac V, 236
Ellis, Isaac V, 237
Ellis, Isaac H. I, 1083
Ellis, Isaac J. I, 1082
Ellis, Isaac Larkin V, 236
Ellis, Isaac Lewis II, 514
Ellis, Ivan V, 670
Ellis, J. P. I, 1151
Ellis, J. W. V, 167
Ellis, Jacob I, 1082
Ellis, Jacob I, 1083
Ellis, Jacob I, 1084
Ellis, Jacob I, 1086
Ellis, Jacob I, 1092
Ellis, Jacob I, 1151
Ellis, Jacob V, 167
Ellis, Jacob V, 214
Ellis, Jacob V, 236
Ellis, Jacob V, 330
Ellis, Jacob J. I, 1140
Ellis, Jacob Pheneas I, 1083
Ellis, Jah I, 1151
Ellis, James I, 1092
Ellis, James V, 51
Ellis, James V, 236
Ellis, James V, 237
Ellis, James V, 385
Ellis, James V, 417
Ellis, James V, 749
Ellis, James A. I, 1083
Ellis, James A. I, 1092
Ellis, James C. I, 1140
Ellis, James C. I, 1151
Ellis, James Ellwood V, 237
Ellis, James Elwood V, 236
Ellis, James Elwood Francis V, 560
Ellis, James H. VI, 898
Ellis, James H. VI, 997
Ellis, James M. V, 384
Ellis, James M. V, 385
Ellis, James M. V, 560
Ellis, James W. V, 236
Ellis, Jamima I, 877
Ellis, Jamima I, 897
Ellis, Jane V, 236
Ellis, Jane V, 237
Ellis, Jane V, 256
Ellis, Jane V, 456
Ellis, Jane VI, 384
Ellis, Jane VI, 385
Ellis, Jane VI, 430
Ellis, Jane VI, 456
Ellis, Jane VI, 912
Ellis, Jean VI, 384
Ellis, Jean VI, 411
Ellis, Jehu I, 962
Ellis, Jehu I, 1105
Ellis, Jehu I, 1118
Ellis, Jehu I, 1129
Ellis, Jehu V, 51
Ellis, Jehu V, 235
Ellis, Jehu V, 302
Ellis, Jehu V, 384
Ellis, Jehu V, 385
Ellis, Jehu V, 560
Ellis, Jehu V, 969
Ellis, Jehu VI, 385
Ellis, Jemima V, 620
Ellis, Jesse I, 1083
Ellis, Jesse I, 1090
Ellis, Jesse I, 1092
Ellis, Jesse H. I, 1083
Ellis, Jesse W. I, 1084
Ellis, Jesse William V, 237

Ellis, Jesse, Sr. I, 1092
Ellis, Job I, 1083
Ellis, Job I, 1092
Ellis, Job II, 217
Ellis, Job V, 51
Ellis, Job V, 236
Ellis, John I, 962
Ellis, John I, 1082
Ellis, John I, 1083
Ellis, John I, 1091
Ellis, John I, 1092
Ellis, John I, 1151
Ellis, John II, 217
Ellis, John IV, 522
Ellis, John IV, 523
Ellis, John V, 51
Ellis, John V, 167
Ellis, John V, 235
Ellis, John V, 236
Ellis, John V, 384
Ellis, John V, 456
Ellis, John VI, 172
Ellis, John VI, 384
Ellis, John VI, 873
Ellis, John VI, 912
Ellis, John A. I, 1083
Ellis, John Asbury I, 1082
Ellis, John Calvin V, 236
Ellis, John Compton V, 167
Ellis, John D. I, 1083
Ellis, John Henry IV, 1278
Ellis, John Jr. IV, 911
Ellis, John Lee VI, 385
Ellis, John W. VI, 172
Ellis, Jonathan I, 538
Ellis, Jonathan I, 1083
Ellis, Jonathan I, 1092
Ellis, Jonathan IV, 144
Ellis, Jonathan IV, 522
Ellis, Jonathan IV, 523
Ellis, Jonathan V, 236
Ellis, Jonathan V, 237
Ellis, Jonathan V, 302
Ellis, Jonathan V, 330
Ellis, Jonathan V, 363
Ellis, Jonathan V, 384
Ellis, Jonathan V, 385
Ellis, Jonathan V, 488
Ellis, Jonathan V, 560
Ellis, Jonathan VI, 385
Ellis, Jonathan VI, 594
Ellis, Jonathan M. IV, 523
Ellis, Jonathan N. V, 330
Ellis, Jonathan W. V, 330
Ellis, Jonathan W. V, 488
Ellis, Jonathan W. V, 560
Ellis, Jonathan, Jr. IV, 144
Ellis, Jonathan, Jr. IV, 523
Ellis, Jonathan, Jr. V, 302
Ellis, Jonathan, Sr. V, 330
Ellis, Joseph I, 1082
Ellis, Joseph I, 1083
Ellis, Joseph II, 217
Ellis, Joseph VI, 911
Ellis, Joseph VI, 1011
Ellis, Joseph R. V, 237
Ellis, Joseph R. V, 456
Ellis, Joseph Rees V, 236
Ellis, Joshua II, 217
Ellis, Joshua IV, 144
Ellis, Joshua IV, 513
Ellis, Joshua IV, 522
Ellis, Joshua IV, 523
Ellis, Joshua V, 330
Ellis, Josiah II, 358
Ellis, Judith VI, 816
Ellis, Julian VI, 969
Ellis, Katie A. V, 620
Ellis, Kennett VI, 385
Ellis, Keziah I, 962
Ellis, Keziah I, 1083
Ellis, Keziah I, 1092
Ellis, Keziah II, 514
Ellis, Keziah VI, 384
Ellis, Keziah VI, 385
Ellis, Keziah VI, 459
Ellis, Kittie A. M. IV, 1250
Ellis, Kitty IV, 1250
Ellis, Kiturah VI, 172
Ellis, Lafayette I, 1084
Ellis, Laura V, 671
Ellis, Lavelle V, 456
Ellis, Leah II, 172
Ellis, Leneas H. V, 237
Ellis, Leon C. V, 837
Ellis, Leon Orland V, 385
Ellis, Leon Orlando V, 837
Ellis, Leona May V, 385
Ellis, Leonadis V, 167
Ellis, Leonidas F. V, 51
Ellis, Lester V, 456
Ellis, Levi I, 1092
Ellis, Levi IV, 522
Ellis, Levi IV, 523
Ellis, Levi V, 51
Ellis, Levi V, 236
Ellis, Levi V, 455
Ellis, Levi V, 456
Ellis, Levi, Jr. V, 237
Ellis, Lewis II, 505
Ellis, Lewis IV, 523
Ellis, Lewis VI, 814
Ellis, Lillie Ross V, 237
Ellis, Linius V, 456
Ellis, Linnaeus V, 671
Ellis, Lizzie IV, 701
Ellis, Lizzie V, 456
Ellis, Lizzy V, 237
Ellis, Louella II, 934
Ellis, Louella S. II, 859
Ellis, Louisa V, 384
Ellis, Louisa V, 385
Ellis, Louisa V, 417
Ellis, Louisa V, 749
Ellis, Louiza V, 385
Ellis, Louiza Jane I, 1082
Ellis, Luci II, 217
Ellis, Lucy I, 336
Ellis, Lucy II, 217
Ellis, Lucy VI, 814
Ellis, Lucy C. VI, 912
Ellis, Lucy Maria VI, 912
Ellis, Lulu V, 167
Ellis, Lulu C. V, 167
Ellis, Lulu Pearson V, 167
Ellis, Lydia I, 1083
Ellis, Lydia I, 1084
Ellis, Lydia I, 1086
Ellis, Lydia I, 1118
Ellis, Lydia I, 1133
Ellis, Lydia IV, 144
Ellis, Lydia IV, 522
Ellis, Lydia IV, 523
Ellis, Lydia V, 51
Ellis, Lydia V, 164
Ellis, Lydia V, 167
Ellis, Lydia V, 235
Ellis, Lydia V, 236
Ellis, Lydia V, 292
Ellis, Lydia V, 330
Ellis, Lydia V, 456
Ellis, Lydia V, 560
Ellis, Lydia V, 951
Ellis, Lydia VI, 594
Ellis, Lydia Ann V, 384
Ellis, Lydia Ann V, 385
Ellis, Lydia Ann V, 560
Ellis, Lydia Ann V, 969
Ellis, Lydia Jane V, 237
Ellis, Lydia Jr. IV, 523
Ellis, Lydia Margaret V, 237
Ellis, Lydia Margaret V, 238
Ellis, Lydia Margaret V, 384
Ellis, Lydia Mary V, 330
Ellis, Lydia Mary V, 385
Ellis, Lydia Mary V, 412
Ellis, Lydia Mary V, 488
Ellis, Lydia Mary V, 515
Ellis, Lydia Mary V, 560
Ellis, Lydia, Jr. IV, 513
Ellis, M. J. I, 1084
Ellis, Magdalin VI, 385
Ellis, Magdaline I, 1083
Ellis, Malven Ursula V, 456
Ellis, Mamie V, 560
Ellis, Margaret I, 1092
Ellis, Margaret II, 358
Ellis, Margaret II, 514
Ellis, Margaret V, 235
Ellis, Margaret V, 236
Ellis, Margaret V, 292
Ellis, Margaret VI, 362
Ellis, Margaret VI, 384
Ellis, Margaret VI, 385
Ellis, Margaret VI, 423
Ellis, Margaret VI, 435
Ellis, Margaret Ann V, 951
Ellis, Margaret Balding IV, 144
Ellis, Margaret Ellen V, 236
Ellis, Margaret Ellen V, 237
Ellis, Margaret H. V, 236
Ellis, Margaret Matilda V, 237
Ellis, Margery VI, 594
Ellis, Margery VI, 602
Ellis, Maria V, 456
Ellis, Mariah V, 236
Ellis, Mariah V, 455
Ellis, Mariam IV, 522
Ellis, Marion V, 560
Ellis, Marmaduke I, 1082
Ellis, Martha I, 1082
Ellis, Martha I, 1083
Ellis, Martha I, 1086
Ellis, Martha I, 1092
Ellis, Martha I, 1096
Ellis, Martha II, 217
Ellis, Martha IV, 144
Ellis, Martha IV, 522
Ellis, Martha IV, 523
Ellis, Martha V, 51
Ellis, Martha V, 167
Ellis, Martha V, 237
Ellis, Martha V, 302
Ellis, Martha V, 456
Ellis, Martha VI, 385
Ellis, Martha Ann I, 1084
Ellis, Martha Ann IV, 523
Ellis, Martha Ann VI, 911
Ellis, Martha C. V, 620
Ellis, Martha E. V, 635
Ellis, Martha Jane V, 236
Ellis, Mary I, 301
Ellis, Mary I, 306
Ellis, Mary I, 962
Ellis, Mary I, 1082
Ellis, Mary I, 1083
Ellis, Mary I, 1084
Ellis, Mary I, 1092
Ellis, Mary I, 1118
Ellis, Mary II, 68
Ellis, Mary II, 97
Ellis, Mary II, 172
Ellis, Mary II, 286
Ellis, Mary II, 514
Ellis, Mary II, 599
Ellis, Mary IV, 30
Ellis, Mary IV, 144
Ellis, Mary IV, 198
Ellis, Mary IV, 267
Ellis, Mary IV, 328
Ellis, Mary IV, 522
Ellis, Mary IV, 523
Ellis, Mary IV, 526
Ellis, Mary IV, 577
Ellis, Mary IV, 582
Ellis, Mary IV, 622
Ellis, Mary IV, 633
Ellis, Mary IV, 701
Ellis, Mary IV, 904
Ellis, Mary IV, 1096
Ellis, Mary IV, 1100
Ellis, Mary IV, 1278
Ellis, Mary V, 167
Ellis, Mary V, 222
Ellis, Mary V, 235
Ellis, Mary V, 236
Ellis, Mary V, 237
Ellis, Mary V, 259
Ellis, Mary V, 265
Ellis, Mary V, 302
Ellis, Mary V, 330
Ellis, Mary V, 335
Ellis, Mary V, 384
Ellis, Mary V, 456
Ellis, Mary V, 488
Ellis, Mary V, 560
Ellis, Mary VI, 384
Ellis, Mary VI, 385
Ellis, Mary VI, 398
Ellis, Mary VI, 430
Ellis, Mary VI, 594
Ellis, Mary VI, 596
Ellis, Mary VI, 912
Ellis, Mary A. V, 385
Ellis, Mary Ann I, 1082
Ellis, Mary Ann V, 236
Ellis, Mary Ann V, 384
Ellis, Mary Ann V, 837
Ellis, Mary Anne IV, 522
Ellis, Mary B. VI, 957
Ellis, Mary Belle V, 51
Ellis, Mary E. V, 51
Ellis, Mary E. V, 237
Ellis, Mary E. V, 456
Ellis, Mary Elizabeth I, 1082
Ellis, Mary Elizabeth V, 237
Ellis, Mary Ellen V, 236
Ellis, Mary Ellen V, 237
Ellis, Mary Jane I, 1083
Ellis, Mary Jane I, 1092
Ellis, Mary Jane I, 1096
Ellis, Mary Jane IV, 522
Ellis, Mary Jane IV, 523
Ellis, Mary Jane IV, 550
Ellis, Mary Jane IV, 1096
Ellis, Mary Jane IV, 1110
Ellis, Mary Jane V, 51
Ellis, Mary Jane V, 236
Ellis, Mary Jane V, 237
Ellis, Mary Jane V, 255
Ellis, Mary Jane VI, 912
Ellis, Mary M. IV, 814
Ellis, Mary M. IV, 835
Ellis, Mary M. IV, 904
Ellis, Mary M. IV, 911
Ellis, Mary Malissa I, 1084
Ellis, Mary R. V, 167
Ellis, Mary Rebecca V, 167
Ellis, Mary Rebecca V, 488
Ellis, Mary Ryan VI, 912
Ellis, Mary, Jr. IV, 904
Ellis, Matilda I, 1083
Ellis, Matilda II, 792
Ellis, Matilda II, 859
Ellis, Matilda II, 925
Ellis, Matilda V, 236
Ellis, Matilda V, 237
Ellis, Matilda VI, 873
Ellis, Matilda A. II, 864
Ellis, Matilda M. V, 237
Ellis, Matilda S. II, 859
Ellis, Matilda S. II, 899
Ellis, Matilda S. II, 934
Ellis, Matilda S. II, 942
Ellis, Maynard V, 560
Ellis, Mercy IV, 814
Ellis, Mercy IV, 827
Ellis, Merriam II, 217
Ellis, Milicent V, 237
Ellis, Miriam I, 1083
Ellis, Miriam II, 172
Ellis, Miriam IV, 513
Ellis, Miriam IV, 523
Ellis, Miriam, Jr. IV, 522
Ellis, Mordecai I, 1077
Ellis, Mordecai I, 1083
Ellis, Mordecai I, 1092
Ellis, Mordecai I, 1105
Ellis, Mordecai I, 1151
Ellis, Mordecai V, 51
Ellis, Mordecai V, 219
Ellis, Mordecai V, 235
Ellis, Mordecai V, 236
Ellis, Mordecai V, 280
Ellis, Mordecai V, 330
Ellis, Mordecai V, 385
Ellis, Mordecai VI, 384
Ellis, Mordecai VI, 385
Ellis, Mordecai, Jr. V, 236
Ellis, Mordeci VI, 385
Ellis, Mordica I, 962
Ellis, Mordicai V, 215
Ellis, Mordicai VI, 384
Ellis, Mordicai VI, 398
Ellis, Morris VI, 489
Ellis, Morris VI, 586
Ellis, Morris Rees V, 235
Ellis, Morris Rees V, 237
Ellis, Morris, Sr. VI, 385
Ellis, Mourning Arthur V, 456
Ellis, Mycajah I, 1129
Ellis, Myrtie E. V, 385
Ellis, Nancy V, 969
Ellis, Nancy VI, 987
Ellis, Nancy VI, 1011
Ellis, Nancy Ann I, 1084
Ellis, Nancy Jane I, 1140
Ellis, Nancy Jane V, 384
Ellis, Nancy Jane V, 385
Ellis, Nancy Jane V, 560
Ellis, Nancy Jane V, 969
Ellis, Naomi IV, 144
Ellis, Naomi IV, 523
Ellis, Naomi IV, 537
Ellis, Naomi VI, 385
Ellis, Nathan II, 514
Ellis, Nathan W. II, 217
Ellis, Nehemiah I, 962
Ellis, Nehemiah I, 1083
Ellis, Nehemiah I, 1092
Ellis, Nehemiah I, 1101
Ellis, Nehemiah I, 1118
Ellis, Nehemiah V, 51
Ellis, Nehemiah V, 167
Ellis, Nehemiah V, 235
Ellis, Nehemiah V, 236
Ellis, Nehemiah V, 330
Ellis, Nehemiah V, 335
Ellis, Nehemiah V, 384
Ellis, Nehemiah V, 385
Ellis, Nehemiah VI, 384
Ellis, Nehemiah VI, 385
Ellis, Nehemiah VI, 451
Ellis, Nehimiah I, 1083
Ellis, Nehimiah I, 1092
Ellis, Nehimiah I, 1118
Ellis, Nehmiah I, 1118
Ellis, Orville V, 620
Ellis, Oswin W. I, 1083
Ellis, Ovan V, 671
Ellis, Patrick H. VI, 867
Ellis, Permelia VI, 912
Ellis, Peter II, 172
Ellis, Peter II, 217
Ellis, Peter IV, 523
Ellis, Peter V, 302
Ellis, Peter Marsh IV, 522
Ellis, Peter Marsh V, 302
Ellis, Phebe I, 1092
Ellis, Phebe I, 1105
Ellis, Phebe I, 1118
Ellis, Phebe I, 1129
Ellis, Phebe II, 217
Ellis, Phebe V, 51
Ellis, Phebe V, 235
Ellis, Phebe V, 384
Ellis, Phebe V, 385
Ellis, Phebe VI, 385
Ellis, Phebe J. II, 786
Ellis, Phoebe V, 369
Ellis, Pleasant VI, 967
Ellis, Polithia V, 167
Ellis, Polley VI, 984
Ellis, Polly VI, 911
Ellis, Polly VI, 957
Ellis, Polly VI, 992
Ellis, Polly Ann VI, 932
Ellis, Prudence I, 1082
Ellis, Prudence I, 1091
Ellis, Prudence I, 1092
Ellis, Prudence C. I, 1140
Ellis, Rachel I, 1083
Ellis, Rachel I, 1090
Ellis, Rachel I, 1092
Ellis, Rachel I, 1093
Ellis, Rachel IV, 144
Ellis, Rachel IV, 247
Ellis, Rachel IV, 523
Ellis, Rachel IV, 539
Ellis, Rachel V, 51
Ellis, Rachel V, 236
Ellis, Rachel V, 237
Ellis, Rachel V, 280
Ellis, Rachel VI, 411
Ellis, Rachel A. V, 385
Ellis, Rachel Ann IV, 1130
Ellis, Rachel Ann IV, 1137
Ellis, Rachel Ann V, 384
Ellis, Rachel Ann V, 385
Ellis, Rachel Jane V, 384
Ellis, Rachel M. IV, 522
Ellis, Rachel M. IV, 523
Ellis, Rachel M. IV, 526
Ellis, Rachel M. V, 157
Ellis, Rachel M. V, 167
Ellis, Rachel M. V, 615
Ellis, Rachel M. V, 620
Ellis, Rachel Maria V, 167
Ellis, Raymond II, 859
Ellis, Rebecah I, 1092
Ellis, Rebecca I, 1055
Ellis, Rebecca II, 217
Ellis, Rebecca II, 792
Ellis, Rebecca II, 859
Ellis, Rebecca II, 925
Ellis, Rebecca IV, 523
Ellis, Rebecca V, 157
Ellis, Rebecca V, 159
Ellis, Rebecca V, 167
Ellis, Rebecca V, 214
Ellis, Rebecca V, 237
Ellis, Rebecca V, 283
Ellis, Rebecca V, 330
Ellis, Rebecca V, 456
Ellis, Rebecca E. V, 236
Ellis, Rebecca G. II, 172
Ellis, Rebecca Jane IV, 1130
Ellis, Rebecca Jane IV, 1133
Ellis, Rebecca Jane V, 167
Ellis, Rebecca Jane V, 169
Ellis, Rebeccah Ellen V, 236
Ellis, Rebeckah E. I, 1083
Ellis, Rebekah VI, 381
Ellis, Rebekah VI, 384
Ellis, Rebekah VI, 385
Ellis, Rebekah VI, 430
Ellis, Rees IV, 144
Ellis, Rees V, 235
Ellis, Rees V, 236
Ellis, Rees VI, 385
Ellis, Rhoda V, 456
Ellis, Rhoda VI, 790
Ellis, Rhoda Narcissa I, 1082
Ellis, Richard V, 560
Ellis, Richard VI, 816
Ellis, Richard VI, 822
Ellis, Richard VI, 912
Ellis, Richard Dale V, 620
Ellis, Richard S. V, 488
Ellis, Richard T. V, 330
Ellis, Richard T. V, 560
Ellis, Robert I, 1083
Ellis, Robert II, 505
Ellis, Robert II, 515
Ellis, Robert II, 712

Ellis, Robert IV, 1250
Ellis, Robert V, 167
Ellis, Robert V, 236
Ellis, Robert V, 330
Ellis, Robert V, 345
Ellis, Robert V, 384
Ellis, Robert V, 385
Ellis, Robert V, 415
Ellis, Robert V, 560
Ellis, Robert V, 969
Ellis, Robt. John Robinson III, 109
Ellis, Roland VI, 385
Ellis, Ross I, 1151
Ellis, Rowland II, 514
Ellis, Rowland IV, 30
Ellis, Rowland IV, 84
Ellis, Rowland V, 51
Ellis, Rowland VI, 384
Ellis, Rowland VI, 385
Ellis, Rufus V, 236
Ellis, Ruth VI, 384
Ellis, Ruth VI, 426
Ellis, Ruth VI, 489
Ellis, Ruth VI, 490
Ellis, Ruth May V, 456
Ellis, S. H. V, 51
Ellis, S. Lydia V, 749
Ellis, Sam'l I, 1092
Ellis, Samuel I, 962
Ellis, Samuel I, 1077
Ellis, Samuel I, 1083
Ellis, Samuel I, 1092
Ellis, Samuel II, 172
Ellis, Samuel II, 217
Ellis, Samuel II, 286
Ellis, Samuel V, 51
Ellis, Samuel V, 236
Ellis, Samuel V, 384
Ellis, Samuel VI, 384
Ellis, Samuel VI, 385
Ellis, Samuel VI, 459
Ellis, Samuel VI, 594
Ellis, Samuel C. V, 167
Ellis, Samuel H. V, 167
Ellis, Samuel Henry V, 167
Ellis, Samuel P. II, 859
Ellis, Samuel P. II, 864
Ellis, Samuel W. I, 1083
Ellis, Samuel, Jr. I, 1092
Ellis, Sarah I, 301
Ellis, Sarah I, 306
Ellis, Sarah I, 497
Ellis, Sarah I, 1082
Ellis, Sarah I, 1083
Ellis, Sarah I, 1092
Ellis, Sarah I, 1101
Ellis, Sarah I, 1118
Ellis, Sarah II, 172
Ellis, Sarah II, 189
Ellis, Sarah II, 217
Ellis, Sarah II, 265
Ellis, Sarah II, 275
Ellis, Sarah II, 511
Ellis, Sarah II, 514
Ellis, Sarah IV, 144
Ellis, Sarah IV, 328
Ellis, Sarah IV, 355
Ellis, Sarah IV, 523
Ellis, Sarah IV, 552
Ellis, Sarah IV, 560
Ellis, Sarah IV, 561
Ellis, Sarah IV, 1278
Ellis, Sarah V, 51
Ellis, Sarah V, 167
Ellis, Sarah V, 219
Ellis, Sarah V, 235
Ellis, Sarah V, 236
Ellis, Sarah V, 330
Ellis, Sarah V, 335
Ellis, Sarah V, 384
Ellis, Sarah V, 385
Ellis, Sarah V, 389
Ellis, Sarah V, 488
Ellis, Sarah VI, 384
Ellis, Sarah VI, 385
Ellis, Sarah VI, 398
Ellis, Sarah VI, 440
Ellis, Sarah VI, 451
Ellis, Sarah VI, 457
Ellis, Sarah VI, 489
Ellis, Sarah VI, 586
Ellis, Sarah VI, 873
Ellis, Sarah A. V, 236
Ellis, Sarah Amanda V, 51
Ellis, Sarah Elizabeth IV, 522
Ellis, Sarah Elizabeth IV, 523
Ellis, Sarah L. V, 385
Ellis, Sarah L. VI, 912
Ellis, Sarah Lydia V, 737
Ellis, Sarah Lydia V, 750
Ellis, Selia I, 306
Ellis, Seth V, 384
Ellis, Seth V, 385
Ellis, Seth V, 560
Ellis, Seth V, 969
Ellis, Silas V, 384
Ellis, Solomon I, 1083
Ellis, Solomon I, 1151
Ellis, Solomon I, 1155
Ellis, Solomon IV, 523
Ellis, Solomon V, 235
Ellis, Solomon V, 236
Ellis, Solomon V, 302
Ellis, Solomon Jehu IV, 522
Ellis, Sophia V, 235
Ellis, Sophia V, 236
Ellis, Sophia V, 237
Ellis, Sophia V, 456
Ellis, Sophia V, 951
Ellis, Spencer VI, 911
Ellis, Stella V, 620
Ellis, Susan I, 1151
Ellis, Susan II, 779
Ellis, Susan V, 969
Ellis, Susan VI, 992
Ellis, Susanah I, 962
Ellis, Susanna I, 962
Ellis, Susanna I, 967
Ellis, Susanna I, 1084
Ellis, Susanna II, 217
Ellis, Susanna II, 859
Ellis, Susanna IV, 522
Ellis, Susanna V, 560
Ellis, Susanna V, 969
Ellis, Susanna A. IV, 523
Ellis, Susanna H. II, 859
Ellis, Susannah I, 1083
Ellis, Susannah II, 217
Ellis, Susannah IV, 522
Ellis, Susannah V, 51
Ellis, Susannah V, 219
Ellis, Susannah V, 236
Ellis, Susannah V, 330
Ellis, Susannah V, 345
Ellis, Susannah V, 363
Ellis, Susannah V, 384
Ellis, Susannah V, 488
Ellis, Susannah VI, 375
Ellis, Susannah VI, 384
Ellis, Susannah VI, 385
Ellis, Susannah VI, 911
Ellis, Susannah M. I, 1082
Ellis, Sylvester V, 237
Ellis, Syreaneas V, 237
Ellis, Tamar V, 51
Ellis, Tamar V, 167
Ellis, Tamar Ann V, 167
Ellis, Tamer I, 1083
Ellis, Tamer I, 1091
Ellis, Tamer I, 1092
Ellis, Tamer Ann V, 167
Ellis, Tamer Ann V, 210
Ellis, Tellitha VI, 911
Ellis, Theoder I, 497
Ellis, Theoder VI, 385
Ellis, Theodore I, 538
Ellis, Theodore IV, 144
Ellis, Theodore IV, 522
Ellis, Theodore IV, 523
Ellis, Theodore V, 237
Ellis, Theodore V, 302
Ellis, Theodore VI, 385
Ellis, Thomas I, 962
Ellis, Thomas I, 1083
Ellis, Thomas I, 1084
Ellis, Thomas I, 1090
Ellis, Thomas I, 1092
Ellis, Thomas I, 1099
Ellis, Thomas I, 1151
Ellis, Thomas II, 172
Ellis, Thomas II, 217
Ellis, Thomas II, 234
Ellis, Thomas II, 514
Ellis, Thomas IV, 144
Ellis, Thomas V, 51
Ellis, Thomas V, 167
Ellis, Thomas V, 235
Ellis, Thomas V, 236
Ellis, Thomas V, 237
Ellis, Thomas V, 292
Ellis, Thomas V, 456
Ellis, Thomas V, 945
Ellis, Thomas V, 951
Ellis, Thomas VI, 384
Ellis, Thomas VI, 385
Ellis, Thomas VI, 423
Ellis, Thomas VI, 435
Ellis, Thomas VI, 489
Ellis, Thomas VI, 912
Ellis, Thomas VI, 932
Ellis, Thomas B. II, 859
Ellis, Thomas Hannah Rebecca Jane Dinah Ellis VI, 384
Ellis, Thomas Jones VI, 384
Ellis, Thomas M. VI, 932
Ellis, Thomas R. V, 237
Ellis, Thomas Rees V, 236
Ellis, Thomas Rees V, 237
Ellis, Thomas, Jr. I, 962
Ellis, Thomas, Jr. V, 236
Ellis, Thomas, Jr. VI, 385
Ellis, Thomas, Sr. I, 962
Ellis, Thos. VI, 489
Ellis, Thos. B. II, 786
Ellis, Uriah V, 235
Ellis, Uriah V, 236
Ellis, Uriah V, 671
Ellis, Uriah VI, 911
Ellis, Ursula VI, 172
Ellis, Ursula VI, 203
Ellis, Ursula VI, 206
Ellis, Ury IV, 1130
Ellis, Ury IV, 1134
Ellis, Ury Ellen IV, 1130
Ellis, Walter V, 385
Ellis, Wesley M. V, 236
Ellis, Wesley Merrion V, 236
Ellis, Widow Mary I, 1091
Ellis, Widow Mary I, 1092
Ellis, Widow Mary I, 1095
Ellis, Widow Mary I, 1096
Ellis, William I, 1082
Ellis, William I, 1083
Ellis, William I, 1084
Ellis, William I, 1089
Ellis, William I, 1092
Ellis, William I, 1105
Ellis, William I, 1151
Ellis, William II, 172
Ellis, William II, 217
Ellis, William IV, 522
Ellis, William IV, 523
Ellis, William V, 167
Ellis, William V, 235
Ellis, William V, 236
Ellis, William V, 237
Ellis, William V, 330
Ellis, William V, 385
Ellis, William V, 945
Ellis, William VI, 13
Ellis, William VI, 384
Ellis, William VI, 876
Ellis, William VI, 892
Ellis, William VI, 894
Ellis, William VI, 911
Ellis, William VI, 912
Ellis, William VI, 1006
Ellis, William Brown I, 1083
Ellis, William H. II, 217
Ellis, Wm. I, 1084
Ellis, Wm. II, 738
Ellis, Wm. IV, 1110
Ellis, Wm. V, 167
Ellis, Wm. VI, 385
Ellis, Wm. VI, 489
Ellis, Wm. A. V, 456
Ellis, Wm. H. II, 792
Ellis, Wm. H. II, 859
Ellis, Wm. H. II, 925
Ellis, Zella V, 456
Ellis, Zimri S. I, 1083
Ellison, ??? III, 109
Ellison, ??? III, 110
Ellison, ??? III, 409
Ellison, A. L. I, 940
Ellison, Albert I, 924
Ellison, Alfonso L. I, 632
Ellison, Alfonso L. I, 940
Ellison, Alphonso L. I, 632
Ellison, Alphonso S. I, 924
Ellison, Amory III, 409
Ellison, Amy III, 110
Ellison, Anna V, 488
Ellison, Anna VI, 63
Ellison, Anthony III, 110
Ellison, Benjamin III, 482
Ellison, Beulah IV, 198
Ellison, Beulah C. IV, 198
Ellison, Caleb VI, 63
Ellison, Carl A. I, 924
Ellison, Carl A. I, 940
Ellison, Caroline III, 109
Ellison, Caroline III, 110
Ellison, Charles Edward I, 924
Ellison, Charles Edwin I, 940
Ellison, Charlotte III, 482
Ellison, Darcus VI, 106
Ellison, Dorcas VI, 104
Ellison, Dorcas VI, 106
Ellison, Edward I, 940
Ellison, Elijah VI, 106
Ellison, Eliza II, 196
Ellison, Eliza III, 482
Ellison, Elizabeth II, 172
Ellison, Elizabeth II, 196
Ellison, Elizabeth II, 217
Ellison, Elizabeth III, 109
Ellison, Elizabeth III, 110
Ellison, Elizabeth IV, 689
Ellison, Elizabeth Ann VI, 63
Ellison, Elizabeth Barker II, 217
Ellison, Elizabeth M. II, 859
Ellison, Elizabeth M. II, 904
Ellison, Emma S. IV, 198
Ellison, Eunice IV, 701
Ellison, Eunice IV, 704
Ellison, Ezra IV, 198
Ellison, Flora V, 237
Ellison, Frank V, 560
Ellison, Gerrard??? VI, 106
Ellison, Gerrot VI, 106
Ellison, Gideon VI, 200
Ellison, Gula VI, 63
Ellison, Gula VI, 69
Ellison, Hannah II, 172
Ellison, Hannah II, 217
Ellison, Hannah II, 230
Ellison, Hannah IV, 701
Ellison, Hannah M. II, 859
Ellison, Hannah M. II, 899
Ellison, Hannah N. II, 738
Ellison, Hannah N. II, 756
Ellison, Hannah N. II, 859
Ellison, Hannah N. II, 899
Ellison, Isaac IV, 30
Ellison, Isaac IV, 689
Ellison, Isaac IV, 701
Ellison, James II, 196
Ellison, James II, 217
Ellison, James II, 515
Ellison, James II, 792
Ellison, James VI, 63
Ellison, John I, 809
Ellison, John I, 962
Ellison, John II, 172
Ellison, John II, 196
Ellison, John II, 217
Ellison, John II, 230
Ellison, John II, 515
Ellison, John III, 109
Ellison, John IV, 950
Ellison, John VI, 63
Ellison, John VI, 242
Ellison, John B. II, 515
Ellison, John B. II, 859
Ellison, John B. II, 899
Ellison, John Barker II, 217
Ellison, John, Jr. II, 217
Ellison, Joseph II, 68
Ellison, Joseph II, 100
Ellison, Joseph II, 172
Ellison, Joseph II, 199
Ellison, Joseph II, 217
Ellison, Joseph II, 230
Ellison, Laura V, 488
Ellison, Lemuel VI, 63
Ellison, Lydia IV, 950
Ellison, Margaret II, 196
Ellison, Margaret II, 217
Ellison, Margaret II, 515
Ellison, Margaret II, 792
Ellison, Martha II, 217
Ellison, Martha VI, 739
Ellison, Mary I, 924
Ellison, Mary II, 217
Ellison, Mary III, 409
Ellison, Mary III, 420
Ellison, Mary IV, 1361
Ellison, Mary VI, 63
Ellison, Mary VI, 106
Ellison, Mary VI, 134
Ellison, Mary VI, 200
Ellison, Mason V, 237
Ellison, Matthew I, 962
Ellison, Milla I, 809
Ellison, Mille I, 962
Ellison, Milly I, 809
Ellison, Mozelle I, 940
Ellison, Mozelle K. I, 940
Ellison, Mozelle Kyle I, 924
Ellison, Nellie V, 560
Ellison, Octavia I, 632
Ellison, Octavia I, 940
Ellison, Octavia L. I, 940
Ellison, Octavia S. I, 924
Ellison, Octavo L. I, 632
Ellison, Oscar H. I, 924
Ellison, Oscar H. I, 940
Ellison, Phebe E. III, 109
Ellison, Phebe E. III, 110
Ellison, Rachel II, 68
Ellison, Rachel II, 100
Ellison, Rebecca IV, 814
Ellison, Robert II, 172
Ellison, Robert II, 217
Ellison, Robert II, 515
Ellison, Robert IV, 704
Ellison, Robert VI, 106
Ellison, Robert VI, 147
Ellison, Robert VI, 173
Ellison, Robert, Jr. IV, 701
Ellison, Rodman B. II, 859
Ellison, Rodman B. II, 899
Ellison, Samuel II, 68
Ellison, Samuel II, 100
Ellison, Samuel II, 172
Ellison, Samuel II, 217
Ellison, Samuel VI, 63
Ellison, Samuel VI, 134
Ellison, Samuel Wm. V, 620
Ellison, Sarah I, 962
Ellison, Sarah II, 172
Ellison, Sarah II, 199
Ellison, Sarah II, 217
Ellison, Sarah II, 859
Ellison, Sarah III, 109
Ellison, Sarah III, 110
Ellison, Sarah III, 480
Ellison, Sarah III, 482
Ellison, Sarah IV, 814
Ellison, Sarah IV, 850
Ellison, Sarah VI, 106
Ellison, Sarah VI, 173
Ellison, Sisilly VI, 147
Ellison, Susannah II, 217
Ellison, Susannah II, 230
Ellison, Susannah III, 420
Ellison, Thomas I, 962
Ellison, Thomas II, 172
Ellison, Thomas II, 217
Ellison, Thomas III, 110
Ellison, Thomas III, 480
Ellison, Thomas III, 482
Ellison, Thomas IV, 144
Ellison, Timothy III, 420
Ellison, William II, 217
Ellison, William II, 704
Ellison, William C. III, 110
Ellison, William C. VI, 739
Ellison, William Carlile II, 217
Ellison, Wm. C. II, 792
Elliss, Elizabeth VI, 594
Elliss, Enos VI, 594
Elliss, George VI, 912
Elliss, Jonathan VI, 594
Elliss, Jonathan VI, 607
Elliss, Josiah II, 358
Elliss, Lydia VI, 594
Elliss, Lydia VI, 607
Elliss, Permelia VI, 912
Ellisson, John I, 538
Elliston, Dorothy II, 358
Elliston, Naomy II, 358
Ellit, Ann I, 1118
Ellit, Deborah I, 445
Ellit, Hannah I, 98
Ellit, Lydde I, 98
Ellit, Rodah I, 98
Ellit, Sarah I, 98
Ellit, Thomas I, 98
Ellmore, Austin VI, 176
Ellmore, Cecilia VI, 176
Ellmore, Cicilia VI, 173
Ellmore, John VI, 161
Ellmore, John VI, 173
Ellmore, Thomas VI, 173
Ellmore, Thomas VI, 176
Ellmore, Thos. VI, 161
Ellot, Abraham I, 538
Ellot, Abraham I, 653
Ellot, Andrew II, 995
Ellot, Ann, Jr. II, 995
Ellot, Ann, Jr. II, 1025
Ellot, Benjamin I, 653
Ellot, Eliza I, 538
Ellot, Elizabeth I, 538
Ellot, Elizabeth II, 993
Ellot, Elizabeth II, 995
Ellot, Hannah I, 678
Ellot, Hannah I, 691
Ellot, Hannah II, 995
Ellot, Isaac I, 653
Ellot, Jacob I, 538
Ellot, Jacob I, 653
Ellot, John I, 653
Ellot, Joseph I, 653
Ellot, Mary II, 995
Ellot, Mary II, 1000
Ellot, Obediah I, 653
Ellot, Peter I, 653
Ellot, Rache I, 538
Ellot, Rachel I, 538
Ellot, Samuel I, 653
Ellot, Sarah II, 995

Ellot, Wd. Hannah II, 995
Ellot, William I, 538
Ellot, Wm. II, 993
Ellot, Wm. II, 995
Ellott, Andrew II, 959
Ellott, Elizabeth I, 538
Ellott, Hannah I, 538
Ellott, Hannah II, 959
Ellott, Hannah II, 993
Ellott, Hannah II, 995
Ellott, Israel I, 538
Ellott, Jacob I, 538
Ellott, John II, 68
Ellott, Mary II, 68
Ellott, Sarah II, 979
Ellott, Sarah II, 995
Ellott, William I, 538
Ellott, Wm. II, 995
Ellton, Mary II, 515
Elltson, Ellen B. IV, 973
Ellwell, David II, 515
Ellyson, ??? VI, 150
Ellyson, ??? VI, 174
Ellyson, Abigail IV, 627
Ellyson, Abigail IV, 943
Ellyson, Abigail IV, 950
Ellyson, Abigail IV, 964
Ellyson, Achiles VI, 173
Ellyson, Achilias VI, 174
Ellyson, Achsah IV, 617
Ellyson, Achsah IV, 942
Ellyson, Achsah IV, 950
Ellyson, Achsah IV, 951
Ellyson, Adella IV, 950
Ellyson, Agatha VI, 172
Ellyson, Agatha VI, 173
Ellyson, Agnes VI, 157
Ellyson, Agnes VI, 166
Ellyson, Agnes VI, 173
Ellyson, Agnes VI, 174
Ellyson, Agnes VI, 175
Ellyson, Agnes VI, 219
Ellyson, Agnes VI, 220
Ellyson, Agness VI, 157
Ellyson, Agness VI, 172
Ellyson, Agness VI, 173
Ellyson, Agness VI, 174
Ellyson, Albana VI, 175
Ellyson, Albanah VI, 173
Ellyson, Alfred IV, 950
Ellyson, Ann IV, 701
Ellyson, Ann IV, 949
Ellyson, Ann IV, 950
Ellyson, Ann IV, 998
Ellyson, Ann VI, 173
Ellyson, Ann VI, 174
Ellyson, Ann VI, 189
Ellyson, Anna IV, 30
Ellyson, Anna IV, 701
Ellyson, Anna IV, 949
Ellyson, Anna IV, 950
Ellyson, Anna IV, 989
Ellyson, Annaritta VI, 173
Ellyson, Annritta VI, 175
Ellyson, Benj. IV, 943
Ellyson, Benjamin IV, 389
Ellyson, Benjamin IV, 608
Ellyson, Benjamin IV, 622
Ellyson, Benjamin IV, 627
Ellyson, Benjamin IV, 701
Ellyson, Benjamin IV, 950
Ellyson, Benjamin IV, 964
Ellyson, Benjamin VI, 174
Ellyson, Benjamin VI, 189
Ellyson, Benjamin VI, 220
Ellyson, Benjamin, Jr. VI, 189
Ellyson, Betty IV, 701
Ellyson, Betty Jane IV, 950
Ellyson, Beulah IV, 79
Ellyson, Beulah IV, 84
Ellyson, Beulah C. IV, 84
Ellyson, Bobby IV, 701
Ellyson, Cecilia VI, 172
Ellyson, Cecilia VI, 176
Ellyson, Charles IV, 950
Ellyson, Charles IV, 951
Ellyson, Cicely VI, 175
Ellyson, Cicilia VI, 173
Ellyson, Cicilia VI, 175
Ellyson, Cicilia VI, 176
Ellyson, Cisilia VI, 174
Ellyson, Cisilia VI, 220
Ellyson, Clarence IV, 950
Ellyson, Clarence IV, 951
Ellyson, Daniel IV, 84
Ellyson, Daniel IV, 949
Ellyson, Daniel IV, 950
Ellyson, David IV, 622
Ellyson, David IV, 950
Ellyson, David IV, 951
Ellyson, David Edgerton IV, 1096
Ellyson, Deborah IV, 79
Ellyson, Deborah IV, 84
Ellyson, Deborah IV, 701
Ellyson, Deborah IV, 936
Ellyson, Deborah IV, 949
Ellyson, Deborah IV, 950
Ellyson, Drusilla IV, 950
Ellyson, Drusilla IV, 953
Ellyson, Edgar P. IV, 950
Ellyson, Edgar P. IV, 951
Ellyson, Eliz. VI, 173
Ellyson, Elizabeth IV, 84
Ellyson, Elizabeth IV, 701
Ellyson, Elizabeth IV, 936
Ellyson, Elizabeth IV, 949
Ellyson, Elizabeth IV, 950
Ellyson, Elizabeth IV, 998
Ellyson, Elizabeth VI, 164
Ellyson, Elizabeth VI, 165
Ellyson, Elizabeth VI, 167
Ellyson, Elizabeth VI, 172
Ellyson, Elizabeth VI, 173
Ellyson, Elizabeth VI, 174
Ellyson, Elizabeth VI, 175
Ellyson, Elizabeth VI, 189
Ellyson, Elizabeth VI, 192
Ellyson, Elizabeth VI, 213
Ellyson, Elizabeth VI, 268
Ellyson, Elizabeth VI, 321
Ellyson, Elizabeth, Jr. VI, 175
Ellyson, Ellen IV, 950
Ellyson, Ellen B. IV, 950
Ellyson, Ellen B. IV, 951
Ellyson, Elma C. IV, 389
Ellyson, Elma C. IV, 608
Ellyson, Elma C. IV, 622
Ellyson, Elma C. IV, 623
Ellyson, Emma IV, 950
Ellyson, Emma S. IV, 275
Ellyson, Emma S. IV, 951
Ellyson, Enoch IV, 701
Ellyson, Enoch IV, 949
Ellyson, Esther IV, 384
Ellyson, Esther IV, 388
Ellyson, Esther IV, 701
Ellyson, Esther IV, 949
Ellyson, Esther IV, 950
Ellyson, Esther IV, 1095
Ellyson, Esther IV, 1096
Ellyson, Ethel Bailey IV, 390
Ellyson, Ethel E. IV, 366
Ellyson, Ethel E. IV, 390
Ellyson, Eunice IV, 701
Ellyson, Eunice IV, 950
Ellyson, Eunice S. IV, 950
Ellyson, Eunice T. IV, 950
Ellyson, Ezra IV, 79
Ellyson, Ezra IV, 84
Ellyson, Ezra IV, 949
Ellyson, Ezra IV, 950
Ellyson, Fidelia IV, 950
Ellyson, Florence IV, 950
Ellyson, Florence IV, 951
Ellyson, G. R. VI, 173
Ellyson, G. Robert VI, 172
Ellyson, G. Robert VI, 173
Ellyson, G. Robert VI, 176
Ellyson, G. Robert VI, 192
Ellyson, G. Robt. VI, 161
Ellyson, Garerd R. VI, 189
Ellyson, Garerd Robert VI, 172
Ellyson, Garerd Robert VI, 173
Ellyson, Garret Robert VI, 172
Ellyson, Garrett VI, 242
Ellyson, Gerald Robert VI, 192
Ellyson, Gerard VI, 174
Ellyson, Gerard VI, 175
Ellyson, Gerard Robert VI, 167
Ellyson, Gerard Robert VI, 172
Ellyson, Gerard Robert VI, 173
Ellyson, Gerard Robert VI, 174
Ellyson, Gerard Robert VI, 175
Ellyson, Gerard Robert VI, 177
Ellyson, Gerard Robert VI, 185
Ellyson, Gerard Robert VI, 186
Ellyson, Gererd R. VI, 172
Ellyson, Gerrad Robert VI, 8
Ellyson, Gerrard VI, 173
Ellyson, Gerrard VI, 175
Ellyson, Gerrard Robert VI, 16
Ellyson, Gertrude IV, 951
Ellyson, Gertrude R. IV, 950
Ellyson, Gertrude Rachel IV, 950
Ellyson, Gideon IV, 30
Ellyson, Gideon IV, 701
Ellyson, Gideon IV, 949
Ellyson, Gideon VI, 16
Ellyson, Gideon VI, 173
Ellyson, Gideon VI, 174
Ellyson, Gideon VI, 175
Ellyson, Gideon VI, 242
Ellyson, Gideon VI, 268
Ellyson, Gideon VI, 269
Ellyson, Gideon VI, 636
Ellyson, Gideon, Jr. VI, 175
Ellyson, Gydeon VI, 173
Ellyson, Hannah IV, 622
Ellyson, Hannah IV, 701
Ellyson, Hannah IV, 949
Ellyson, Hannah IV, 950
Ellyson, Hannah IV, 953
Ellyson, Hannah IV, 990
Ellyson, Hannah VI, 172
Ellyson, Hannah VI, 173
Ellyson, Homer IV, 701
Ellyson, Homer IV, 950
Ellyson, Homer IV, 951
Ellyson, Homer M. IV, 950
Ellyson, Idella IV, 946
Ellyson, Idella D. IV, 947
Ellyson, Idella S. IV, 946
Ellyson, Idella S. IV, 951
Ellyson, Isaac IV, 30
Ellyson, Isaac IV, 84
Ellyson, Isaac IV, 701
Ellyson, Isaac IV, 936
Ellyson, Isaac IV, 949
Ellyson, Isaac IV, 950
Ellyson, Isaac IV, 998
Ellyson, Isaac VI, 636
Ellyson, Isaac Gideon VI, 717
Ellyson, Isaiah VI, 220
Ellyson, Isiah VI, 173
Ellyson, Isiah VI, 174
Ellyson, Isiah VI, 175
Ellyson, Isiah VI, 220
Ellyson, James IV, 950
Ellyson, James H. IV, 950
Ellyson, Jane VI, 172
Ellyson, Jane VI, 173
Ellyson, Jane VI, 174
Ellyson, Jane VI, 211
Ellyson, Jarrard VI, 242
Ellyson, Jeremiah IV, 701
Ellyson, Jesse VI, 173
Ellyson, John IV, 30
Ellyson, John IV, 701
Ellyson, John IV, 949
Ellyson, John IV, 950
Ellyson, John VI, 16
Ellyson, John VI, 150
Ellyson, John VI, 173
Ellyson, John VI, 174
Ellyson, John VI, 175
Ellyson, John VI, 214
Ellyson, John VI, 219
Ellyson, John VI, 220
Ellyson, John VI, 242
Ellyson, John, Jr. VI, 174
Ellyson, John, Jr. VI, 175
Ellyson, John, Sr. VI, 175
Ellyson, Jonathan VI, 173
Ellyson, Jonathan VI, 175
Ellyson, Jonathan VI, 636
Ellyson, Jonathan W. IV, 84
Ellyson, Joseph IV, 701
Ellyson, Joseph IV, 949
Ellyson, Joseph IV, 950
Ellyson, Joseph IV, 951
Ellyson, Joseph VI, 157
Ellyson, Joseph VI, 158
Ellyson, Joseph VI, 172
Ellyson, Joseph VI, 173
Ellyson, Joseph VI, 174
Ellyson, Joseph VI, 188
Ellyson, Joshua Storrs VI, 174
Ellyson, Josiah C. Ratcliff IV, 390
Ellyson, Josiah E. Ratcliff IV, 950
Ellyson, Judith VI, 172
Ellyson, Judith VI, 173
Ellyson, Laura IV, 950
Ellyson, Laura IV, 951
Ellyson, Lewis N. IV, 366
Ellyson, Lewis N. IV, 389
Ellyson, Lucy VI, 174
Ellyson, Lydia IV, 701
Ellyson, Lydia IV, 772
Ellyson, Lydia IV, 950
Ellyson, Majory VI, 268
Ellyson, Majory VI, 269
Ellyson, Margaret IV, 622
Ellyson, Margaret IV, 623
Ellyson, Margaret IV, 950
Ellyson, Margaret IV, 951
Ellyson, Margery IV, 30
Ellyson, Margery IV, 696
Ellyson, Margery IV, 701
Ellyson, Margery IV, 946
Ellyson, Margery IV, 949
Ellyson, Margery VI, 16
Ellyson, Margery VI, 173
Ellyson, Margery VI, 175
Ellyson, Margery VI, 268
Ellyson, Marjory VI, 242
Ellyson, Martha VI, 173
Ellyson, Mary IV, 30
Ellyson, Mary IV, 79
Ellyson, Mary IV, 84
Ellyson, Mary IV, 389
Ellyson, Mary IV, 390
Ellyson, Mary IV, 432
Ellyson, Mary IV, 607
Ellyson, Mary IV, 617
Ellyson, Mary IV, 622
Ellyson, Mary IV, 696
Ellyson, Mary IV, 701
Ellyson, Mary IV, 936
Ellyson, Mary IV, 942
Ellyson, Mary IV, 949
Ellyson, Mary IV, 950
Ellyson, Mary IV, 951
Ellyson, Mary IV, 984
Ellyson, Mary IV, 988
Ellyson, Mary IV, 989
Ellyson, Mary IV, 1037
Ellyson, Mary VI, 134
Ellyson, Mary VI, 157
Ellyson, Mary VI, 158
Ellyson, Mary VI, 166
Ellyson, Mary VI, 170
Ellyson, Mary VI, 172
Ellyson, Mary VI, 173
Ellyson, Mary VI, 174
Ellyson, Mary VI, 175
Ellyson, Mary VI, 176
Ellyson, Mary VI, 188
Ellyson, Mary VI, 189
Ellyson, Mary VI, 215
Ellyson, Mary VI, 636
Ellyson, Mary VI, 716
Ellyson, Mary Alice IV, 950
Ellyson, Mary, Jr. IV, 950
Ellyson, Matthew VI, 172
Ellyson, Matthew VI, 173
Ellyson, Matthew VI, 174
Ellyson, Matthew VI, 189
Ellyson, Matthew VI, 192
Ellyson, Micajah VI, 174
Ellyson, Milley V, 286
Ellyson, Milly V, 215
Ellyson, Miriam IV, 623
Ellyson, Miriam IV, 627
Ellyson, Miriam IV, 628
Ellyson, Miriam IV, 701
Ellyson, Miriam IV, 950
Ellyson, Miriam VI, 173
Ellyson, Molly VI, 173
Ellyson, Molly VI, 174
Ellyson, Molly VI, 185
Ellyson, Molly VI, 186
Ellyson, Orina VI, 175
Ellyson, Orinea VI, 175
Ellyson, Orinia VI, 173
Ellyson, Phebe IV, 622
Ellyson, Phebe IV, 623
Ellyson, Phebe IV, 665
Ellyson, Phebe IV, 701
Ellyson, Phebe IV, 950
Ellyson, Phebe IV, 951
Ellyson, Phebe IV, 1015
Ellyson, Pleasants VI, 189
Ellyson, Rachel IV, 951
Ellyson, Rachel VI, 175
Ellyson, Rebecca IV, 809
Ellyson, Rebecca IV, 814
Ellyson, Rebecca IV, 943
Ellyson, Rebecca IV, 950
Ellyson, Rebecca P. IV, 950
Ellyson, Robert IV, 30
Ellyson, Robert IV, 389
Ellyson, Robert IV, 432
Ellyson, Robert IV, 607
Ellyson, Robert IV, 617
Ellyson, Robert IV, 622
Ellyson, Robert IV, 623
Ellyson, Robert IV, 665
Ellyson, Robert IV, 701
Ellyson, Robert IV, 942
Ellyson, Robert IV, 949
Ellyson, Robert IV, 950
Ellyson, Robert IV, 951
Ellyson, Robert IV, 953
Ellyson, Robert IV, 988
Ellyson, Robert IV, 1015
Ellyson, Robert VI, 158
Ellyson, Robert VI, 167
Ellyson, Robert VI, 172
Ellyson, Robert VI, 173
Ellyson, Robert VI, 174
Ellyson, Robert VI, 175
Ellyson, Robert VI, 186
Ellyson, Robert VI, 189
Ellyson, Robert VI, 192
Ellyson, Robert VI, 242
Ellyson, Robert VI, 636
Ellyson, Robert Klar IV, 950
Ellyson, Robert M. IV, 950
Ellyson, Robert, Jr. IV, 701
Ellyson, Robert, Jr. IV, 950
Ellyson, Sadie IV, 701
Ellyson, Samuel VI, 173
Ellyson, Samuel VI, 175
Ellyson, Sarah IV, 84
Ellyson, Sarah IV, 950
Ellyson, Sarah VI, 148
Ellyson, Sarah VI, 172
Ellyson, Sarah VI, 173
Ellyson, Sarah VI, 174
Ellyson, Sarah VI, 175
Ellyson, Sarah VI, 185
Ellyson, Sarah VI, 186
Ellyson, Sarah VI, 717
Ellyson, Sarah A. IV, 951
Ellyson, Sarah A. IV, 1037
Ellyson, Sarah H. IV, 950
Ellyson, Susanna VI, 174
Ellyson, Susanna VI, 188
Ellyson, Susannah VI, 158
Ellyson, Susannah VI, 159
Ellyson, Susannah VI, 172
Ellyson, Susannah VI, 173
Ellyson, Susannah VI, 174
Ellyson, Tace IV, 950
Ellyson, Tacy IV, 950
Ellyson, Tacy M. IV, 607
Ellyson, Tacy M. IV, 623
Ellyson, Tacy M.. IV, 951
Ellyson, Thomas I, 962
Ellyson, Thomas VI, 164
Ellyson, Thomas VI, 166
Ellyson, Thomas VI, 167
Ellyson, Thomas VI, 172
Ellyson, Thomas VI, 173
Ellyson, Thomas VI, 174
Ellyson, Thomas VI, 175
Ellyson, Thomas VI, 189
Ellyson, Ursulah VI, 172
Ellyson, Ursulah VI, 173
Ellyson, Ursulah VI, 189
Ellyson, Ursulah VI, 191
Ellyson, Walter IV, 701
Ellyson, Walter J. IV, 950
Ellyson, Walter J. IV, 951
Ellyson, Wd. Elizabeth VI, 174
Ellyson, Wd. Elizabeth VI, 214
Ellyson, Wd. Sarah VI, 174
Ellyson, Webster IV, 950
Ellyson, William IV, 30
Ellyson, William IV, 701
Ellyson, William IV, 949
Ellyson, William IV, 950
Ellyson, William VI, 172
Ellyson, William VI, 173
Ellyson, William VI, 174
Ellyson, William VI, 175
Ellyson, William VI, 185
Ellyson, William VI, 186
Ellyson, William VI, 211
Ellyson, William VI, 213
Ellyson, William VI, 214
Ellyson, William, Jr. VI, 16
Ellyson, William, Jr. VI, 173
Ellyson, William, Jr. VI, 174
Ellyson, William, Jr. VI, 175
Ellyson, Wm. IV, 701
Ellyson, Wm. IV, 950
Ellyson, Wm. VI, 189
Ellyson, Wm. B. IV, 950
Ellyson, Wm., Jr. VI, 174
Ellyson, Wm., Jr. VI, 185
Ellyson, Zachariah IV, 30
Ellyson, Zachariah IV, 389
Ellyson, Zachariah IV, 622
Ellyson, Zachariah IV, 701
Ellyson, Zachariah IV, 919
Ellyson, Zachariah IV, 949
Ellyson, Zachariah IV, 950
Ellyson, Zachariah IV, 989
Ellyson, Zachariah VI, 173
Ellyson, Zachariah VI, 175
Ellyson, Zachariah VI, 636
Ellyson, Zachariah VI, 716
Ellyson, Zachariah, Jr. VI, 636
Ellyson, Zachariah, Jr. VI, 717
Ellyson, Zacheriah IV, 696
Ellyson, Zadoc IV, 950
Ellyson, Zechariah IV, 30
Ellyson, Zechariah IV, 950
Ellyson, Zechariah, Jr. IV, 30
Ellzey, Agatha I, 214
Ellzey, Agatha V, 51
Ellzey, Agatha VI, 114
Ellzey, Agatha VI, 134
Ellzey, Agathy I, 238

Ellzey, Agathy VI, 106
Ellzey, Easter VI, 106
Ellzey, Esther I, 238
Ellzey, Esther V, 51
Ellzey, Garard V, 51
Ellzey, Isaac I, 214
Ellzey, Kezia I, 238
Ellzey, Kezia I, 246
Ellzey, Keziah I, 238
Ellzey, Keziah V, 51
Ellzey, Kezier VI, 106
Ellzey, Lemuel V, 51
Ellzey, Mauld Alma V, 51
Ellzey, Priscilla V, 51
Ellzey, William I, 214
Ellzey, William I, 238
Ellzey, William V, 51
Ellzey, William VI, 106
Ellzey, William VI, 114
Ellzey, William VI, 134
Elma, Elina IV, 718
Elma, Levi IV, 718
Elma, Mary IV, 718
Elma, Rachel IV, 1361
Elman, Isaac V, 807
Elman, Mary V, 807
Elman, Owen V, 807
Elman, Rachel V, 807
Elmer, Clara II, 917
Elmlie, John II, 515
Elmon, Susanna I, 1092
Elmor, Abigail I, 1019
Elmor, Charity I, 1019
Elmor, David I, 1019
Elmor, John I, 1019
Elmor, Joseph I, 1019
Elmor, Mary I, 1019
Elmor, Rachel I, 1019
Elmor, Ridgeway I, 1019
Elmor, Sarah I, 1019
Elmor, Stephen I, 1019
Elmor, William I, 1019
Elmore, ??? V, 167
Elmore, Abigail I, 388
Elmore, Abigail V, 168
Elmore, Allen I, 1119
Elmore, Amelia VI, 252
Elmore, Andrew VI, 814
Elmore, Ann I, 538
Elmore, Ann I, 570
Elmore, Ann I, 780
Elmore, Ann I, 809
Elmore, Ann I, 820
Elmore, Ann I, 962
Elmore, Ann I, 1105
Elmore, Ann I, 1118
Elmore, Ann V, 445
Elmore, Ann V, 447
Elmore, Ann Elmore V, 445
Elmore, Archelaus I, 780
Elmore, Archelaus I, 809
Elmore, Archelaus I, 1119
Elmore, Archelus I, 1119
Elmore, Austin VI, 176
Elmore, Barbara Jane I, 616
Elmore, Barbara Jane I, 632
Elmore, Bertie I, 616
Elmore, Bertie I, 632
Elmore, Bertie Elmore I, 615
Elmore, Byron V, 168
Elmore, C. E. I, 616
Elmore, C. E. I, 632
Elmore, Cecilia VI, 172
Elmore, Cecilia VI, 176
Elmore, Cicila I, 809
Elmore, Cicilia I, 780
Elmore, Cicilia VI, 176
Elmore, Cicley VI, 253
Elmore, Cisily I, 1118
Elmore, Cisley VI, 242
Elmore, Cisley VI, 252
Elmore, Cisly I, 1118
Elmore, Cisly I, 1120
Elmore, Claud E. I, 615
Elmore, Claud E. I, 616
Elmore, Clementine A. G. VI, 912
Elmore, Cora V, 168
Elmore, Elisabeth I, 809
Elmore, Eliza A. VI, 823
Elmore, Elizabeth I, 780
Elmore, Elizabeth I, 1118
Elmore, Elizabeth I, 1135
Elmore, Elizabeth V, 488
Elmore, Elizabeth V, 498
Elmore, Elizabeth VI, 176
Elmore, Elizabeth VI, 245
Elmore, Elizabeth VI, 246
Elmore, Elizabeth VI, 262
Elmore, Ellen V, 168
Elmore, Evelyn Sue I, 616
Elmore, Evelyn Sue I, 632
Elmore, Hannah I, 1105
Elmore, Hannah I, 1119
Elmore, Isaac V, 167
Elmore, Isaac V, 168
Elmore, James A. VI, 806
Elmore, James A. VI, 912
Elmore, James Edward I, 1151
Elmore, Jane I, 780
Elmore, Jane I, 809
Elmore, Jane VI, 385
Elmore, Jemima Laura V, 168
Elmore, Jesse I, 1119
Elmore, Joel I, 780
Elmore, Joel I, 809
Elmore, Joel I, 962
Elmore, Joel I, 966
Elmore, Joel I, 1101
Elmore, Joel I, 1105
Elmore, John I, 780
Elmore, John I, 809
Elmore, John I, 1029
Elmore, John I, 1119
Elmore, John V, 237
Elmore, John V, 445
Elmore, John V, 447
Elmore, John VI, 149
Elmore, John VI, 176
Elmore, John VI, 242
Elmore, John VI, 245
Elmore, John VI, 246
Elmore, John Dixon I, 616
Elmore, John Dixon I, 632
Elmore, Joseph I, 1029
Elmore, Lavina I, 1119
Elmore, Lee Amy V, 168
Elmore, Lettie V, 167
Elmore, Louisa A. V, 167
Elmore, Luelma V, 168
Elmore, Luticia V, 168
Elmore, Mary I, 538
Elmore, Mary I, 570
Elmore, Mary I, 780
Elmore, Mary I, 1118
Elmore, Mary I, 1119
Elmore, Mary I, 1120
Elmore, Mary V, 167
Elmore, Mary VI, 176
Elmore, Mary VI, 814
Elmore, Mary Jane I, 1119
Elmore, Mordecai I, 1105
Elmore, Mordecai I, 1119
Elmore, Nancy I, 1119
Elmore, Nathan Thornborough V, 445
Elmore, Nora I, 615
Elmore, Orma V, 168
Elmore, Prudence I, 1029
Elmore, Prudence I, 1035
Elmore, Rachel I, 1029
Elmore, Rachel I, 1034
Elmore, Rachel V, 808
Elmore, Rachel V, 815
Elmore, Reason V, 167
Elmore, Rebecca I, 877
Elmore, Rebecca I, 962
Elmore, Rebecca I, 966
Elmore, Rebecca I, 1016
Elmore, Rebecca I, 1029
Elmore, Rebecca I, 1033
Elmore, Rebecca I, 1105
Elmore, Rebeckah VI, 176
Elmore, Rebekah I, 538
Elmore, Rebekah I, 1016
Elmore, Ridgeway I, 1029
Elmore, Rosanna V, 168
Elmore, Stephen I, 1029
Elmore, Stephen V, 168
Elmore, Thomas I, 538
Elmore, Thomas I, 570
Elmore, Thomas I, 773
Elmore, Thomas I, 780
Elmore, Thomas I, 809
Elmore, Thomas I, 962
Elmore, Thomas I, 1118
Elmore, Thomas I, 1119
Elmore, Thomas V, 168
Elmore, Thomas VI, 176
Elmore, Thomas VI, 216
Elmore, Thomas VI, 242
Elmore, Thomas VI, 252
Elmore, Thomas, Jr. VI, 172
Elmore, Thos., Sr. I, 1105
Elmore, Virginia Cicilia VI, 251
Elmore, Widow Cicilia I, 538
Elmore, William I, 388
Elmore, William VI, 823
Elmore, William A. I, 615
Elmsely, Elizabeth II, 515
Elmsely, George II, 515
Elmsely, Hannah II, 515
Elmsely, John II, 515
Elmsely, Mary II, 515
Elmsely, Sarah II, 515
Elmslie, Alexander II, 358
Elmslie, Alexander II, 471
Elmslie, Alexander II, 515
Elmslie, Barbara II, 515
Elmslie, Elizabeth II, 515
Elmslie, George II, 515
Elmslie, George II, 540
Elmslie, Hannah II, 515
Elmslie, James II, 515
Elmslie, John II, 515
Elmslie, John II, 540
Elmslie, John, Jr. II, 515
Elmslie, Margaret II, 358
Elmslie, Margaret II, 515
Elmslie, Mary II, 358
Elmslie, Mary II, 515
Elmslie, Mary II, 540
Elmslie, Sarah II, 515
Elmslie, Wd. Mary II, 471
Elmslie, Wd. Mary II, 515
Elmslie, Wm. II, 515
Elphrey, Elizabeth II, 357
Elphrey, Henry II, 357
Elphrey, Sarah II, 357
Elridge, Jonathan II, 513
Elridge, Jonathan II, 563
Elridge, Mary II, 513
Elridge, Mary II, 563
Elridge, Thomas II, 513
Elridge, Thomas II, 563
Elsay Oliver, Alma M. V, 30
Elsay, Agathy VI, 106
Elsay, Easter VI, 106
Elsay, Kezier VI, 106
Elsbery, Alcora Susan I, 18
Elsbery, James I, 18
Elsbery, Martha I, 18
Elsey, Agatha V, 215
Elston, Chas. V, 560
Elston, Horrace V, 560
Elston, Kemper V, 560
Elston, Lilbie V, 560
Elston, Mary Jane V, 560
Elston, Sallie E. V, 560
Elton, Ann M. II, 860
Elton, Ann Martha II, 793
Elton, Anna E. IV, 954
Elton, Annie M. II, 860
Elton, Annie M. II, 921
Elton, Anthony II, 217
Elton, Anthony III, 110
Elton, Bathsheba II, 207
Elton, Bathsheba II, 217
Elton, Chas. Shoemaker II, 793
Elton, Edith IV, 702
Elton, Elizabeth II, 217
Elton, Elizabeth II, 239
Elton, Elizabeth II, 358
Elton, Elizabeth II, 515
Elton, Emily IV, 701
Elton, Emily IV, 972
Elton, Flora B. II, 793
Elton, Francis II, 443
Elton, Frank V, 456
Elton, Grant IV, 702
Elton, Grant J. IV, 701
Elton, Hannah II, 172
Elton, Hannah II, 208
Elton, Hannah II, 217
Elton, Hannah II, 239
Elton, Hannah II, 267
Elton, Hannah II, 515
Elton, Hannah II, 543
Elton, Hannah, Jr. II, 217
Elton, James II, 543
Elton, Joseph IV, 972
Elton, Lela Leona IV, 972
Elton, Margaret II, 515
Elton, Margaret II, 543
Elton, Mary II, 217
Elton, Mary II, 267
Elton, Mary II, 515
Elton, Mary II, 543
Elton, Mary III, 110
Elton, Mary IV, 954
Elton, Mary Shoemaker II, 793
Elton, Rachel II, 515
Elton, Rachel II, 610
Elton, Richard IV, 701
Elton, Robert II, 358
Elton, Rose IV, 702
Elton, Rose M. IV, 701
Elton, Samuel R. II, 793
Elton, Samuel R. II, 860
Elton, Samuel R. II, 921
Elton, Sarah II, 217
Elton, Sarah II, 232
Elton, Susanna II, 443
Elton, Susannah II, 217
Elton, Susannah II, 244
Elton, Thos. R. IV, 954
Elton, William II, 172
Elton, William II, 217
Elton, William II, 267
Elton, William II, 443
Elton, William III, 110
Elventon, Sarah I, 306
Elventon, Sarah I, 309
Elvira, Mary IV, 1070
Elwell, ??? II, 358
Elwell, David II, 358
Elwell, David II, 440
Elwell, David II, 515
Elwell, David II, 586
Elwell, Mary II, 440
Elwell, Mary II, 460
Elwell, Rebecca II, 358
Elwell, Rebecca II, 515
Elwell, Rebecca II, 586
Elwell, Wd. Mary II, 515
Elwood, Alfred I, 210
Elwood, Cyrus V, 237
Elwood, Cyrus Arthur V, 237
Elwood, Emily L. I, 210
Elwood, Hannah E. IV, 835
Elwood, Herbert I, 530
Elwood, Joseph II, 291
Elwood, Kate V, 237
Elwood, Morgan II, 325
Elwood, Rebecca W. II, 325
Elwood, Ruth IV, 84
Elwood, Ruth IV, 98
Elwood, Thomas IV, 547
Elwood, Thomas IV, 835
Elwood, Will V, 237
Ely, ??? III, 269
Ely, Adele C. II, 807
Ely, Alonzo S. IV, 198
Ely, Amanda R. IV, 198
Ely, Ann II, 515
Ely, Ann II, 738
Ely, Ann II, 748
Ely, Anna II, 738
Ely, Anna W. II, 738
Ely, Anna W. II, 813
Ely, Anna W. II, 860
Ely, Caroline II, 286
Ely, Caroline A. II, 286
Ely, Caroline A. II, 297
Ely, Edward II, 860
Ely, Edward Waters IV, 328
Ely, Elias II, 286
Ely, Elias II, 297
Ely, Elizabeth III, 269
Ely, Elizabeth IV, 144
Ely, Elizabeth IV, 151
Ely, Elizabeth C. II, 831
Ely, Elizabeth C. II, 860
Ely, Emily IV, 390
Ely, Emily E. IV, 328
Ely, Emily E. IV, 336
Ely, Ernest S. VI, 385
Ely, Ernest S. VI, 458
Ely, Esther B. VI, 63
Ely, Fannie C. II, 831
Ely, Fannie C. II, 860
Ely, George II, 515
Ely, Gilbert W. II, 807
Ely, Grace C. III, 110
Ely, Hannah III, 110
Ely, Hannah M. III, 269
Ely, Henrietta VI, 814
Ely, Henry B. VI, 814
Ely, Henry S. III, 110
Ely, Jacob IV, 328
Ely, James S. IV, 328
Ely, James S. IV, 336
Ely, Jane VI, 104
Ely, Jane VI, 106
Ely, Jane VI, 134
Ely, Jeannie III, 101
Ely, Jeannie III, 110
Ely, John II, 841
Ely, John II, 860
Ely, Joseph II, 515
Ely, Joseph II, 704
Ely, Joseph O. II, 860
Ely, Josiah VI, 63
Ely, Lemuel VI, 104
Ely, Lemuel VI, 106
Ely, Lucretia VI, 458
Ely, Lucretia Nichols VI, 385
Ely, Lucretia Nichols VI, 458
Ely, Lucretia W. VI, 385
Ely, Margaret W. II, 738
Ely, Martha A. VI, 814
Ely, Mary W. II, 841
Ely, Mary W. II, 860
Ely, Oliver Wilson II, 738
Ely, Oliver Wilson II, 748
Ely, R. Amanda IV, 198
Ely, Rachel II, 828
Ely, Rebecca W. II, 841
Ely, Rebecca W. II, 860
Ely, Richard Elias II, 286
Ely, Richard Elias II, 297
Ely, Richard Elias II, 738
Ely, Ruth Anna II, 967
Ely, Ruthanna II, 738
Ely, S. G. III, 101
Ely, S. G. III, 110
Ely, Sarah II, 738
Ely, Sarah II, 748
Ely, Sarah IV, 328
Ely, Sarah Ann II, 860
Ely, Sarah B. IV, 328
Ely, Sarah D. II, 807
Ely, Sarah E. C. VI, 63
Ely, Sarah M. II, 286
Ely, Sarah M. II, 297
Ely, Sarah M. II, 738
Ely, Seth II, 831
Ely, Seth II, 860
Ely, William Brown Waters IV, 328
Elyson, ??? VI, 154
Elyson, Agatha VI, 164
Elyson, Agatha VI, 166
Elyson, Agatha VI, 172
Elyson, Agnes VI, 185
Elyson, Agness VI, 173
Elyson, Agness VI, 185
Elyson, Ann IV, 701
Elyson, Ann IV, 766
Elyson, Elizabeth VI, 172
Elyson, Elizabeth VI, 185
Elyson, G. R. VI, 154
Elyson, G. R. VI, 173
Elyson, Garerd Robert VI, 172
Elyson, Garerd Robert VI, 173
Elyson, Garerd Robert VI, 189
Elyson, Garrett VI, 242
Elyson, Gerard Robert VI, 173
Elyson, Hannah IV, 686
Elyson, Hannah VI, 164
Elyson, Hannah VI, 166
Elyson, Hannah VI, 172
Elyson, Judith VI, 172
Elyson, Judith VI, 173
Elyson, Judith VI, 189
Elyson, Judith VI, 191
Elyson, Robert IV, 686
Elyson, Robert VI, 164
Elyson, Robert VI, 166
Elyson, Robert VI, 172
Elyson, Robert VI, 242
Elyson, Sarah VI, 164
Elyson, Sarah VI, 166
Elyson, Sarah VI, 172
Elyson, Sarah VI, 173
Elyson, William VI, 173
Elyson, William VI, 185
Elzey, Agatha V, 237
Elzey, Esther V, 237
Elzey, Gerrard V, 237
Elzey, James M. V, 994
Elzey, Kezia V, 237
Elzey, Priscilla V, 237
Elzey, William V, 237
Elzy, Agatha VI, 134
Elzy, Agathy I, 238
Elzy, Mauld Alma V, 51
Emanuel, Calishta VI, 814
Emanuel, Charles VI, 814
Emanuel, Eliza VI, 814
Emanuel, Jeremiah VI, 814
Emanuel, Lucinda VI, 857
Emanuel, Martha A. VI, 814
Emanuel, Thos. VI, 857
Emanuel, William VI, 814
Emberson, Hannah II, 515
Emberson, Hannah II, 597
Emberson, Sarah I, 139
Embley, Hannah II, 358
Emblin, Mary II, 358
Embly, George II, 358
Embly, Hannah II, 358
Embly, Mariah IV, 814
Embly, Mary II, 358
Embly, Mary II, 515
Embly, Mary II, 546
Embly, Mary III, 110
Embly, Richard IV, 814
Embly, Ruth II, 515
Embly, Samuel II, 358
Embra, John V, 837
Embra, Mordecai IV, 198
Embray, Elihu I, 538
Embray, Elihu I, 962
Embray, Elijah I, 538
Embray, Elijah I, 962

Embray, Esther I, 538
Embray, Esther I, 962
Embray, Even I, 962
Embray, Jacob I, 962
Embray, Moses I, 962
Embray, Rachel I, 538
Embray, Rachel I, 962
Embray, Thomas I, 538
Embray, Thomas I, 962
Embre, Harriet IV, 171
Embre, Huldah IV, 171
Embre, John IV, 171
Embre, Jonathan I, 1048
Embre, Mercer V, 837
Embre, Rebekah I, 962
Embre, Rebekah I, 964
Embre, Sarah V, 837
Embree, ??? V, 795
Embree, ??? VI, 348
Embree, Abigail III, 39
Embree, Abigail III, 74
Embree, Abigail III, 110
Embree, Abigail III, 378
Embree, Abigail III, 379
Embree, Abigail IV, 198
Embree, Abigail IV, 390
Embree, Abigail IV, 616
Embree, Abigail IV, 623
Embree, Abigail VI, 351
Embree, Abigail VI, 354
Embree, Achsah IV, 390
Embree, Achsah IV, 1051
Embree, Achsah IV, 1055
Embree, Achsah IV, 1056
Embree, Achsah IV, 1089
Embree, Achsah IV, 1096
Embree, Amos I, 1019
Embree, Amos I, 1043
Embree, Amos I, 1048
Embree, Amos V, 51
Embree, Amos V, 837
Embree, Ann IV, 623
Embree, Ann IV, 643
Embree, Ann IV, 1064
Embree, Ann IV, 1130
Embree, Ann IV, 1133
Embree, Ann V, 749
Embree, Ann V, 808
Embree, Ann A. III, 110
Embree, Ann H. IV, 1130
Embree, Annes I, 1084
Embree, Annes I, 1092
Embree, Annes I, 1099
Embree, Ava IV, 577
Embree, Ava IV, 588
Embree, Ava IV, 1055
Embree, Ava IV, 1056
Embree, Ava IV, 1070
Embree, Avy IV, 1055
Embree, Barclay IV, 1055
Embree, Barclay IV, 1056
Embree, Caroline IV, 1055
Embree, Caroline IV, 1056
Embree, Caroline IV, 1076
Embree, Caroline IV, 1096
Embree, Carrie III, 379
Embree, Carrie III, 389
Embree, Charity III, 110
Embree, Charity IV, 623
Embree, Charles I, 1084
Embree, Charles I, 1093
Embree, Charles III, 110
Embree, Cynthia H. II, 704
Embree, Cynthia H. II, 738
Embree, Cyrenius Embree IV, 1096
Embree, Cyrenus IV, 1096
Embree, Daniel V, 903
Embree, Daniel V, 904
Embree, Daniel VI, 740
Embree, Daniel A. IV, 198
Embree, Daniel A. IV, 199
Embree, David IV, 1055
Embree, David IV, 1056
Embree, Davis V, 51
Embree, Davis V, 903
Embree, Deborah IV, 1055
Embree, Deborah IV, 1056
Embree, Deborah IV, 1065
Embree, Deborah L. III, 379
Embree, Deborah L. III, 389
Embree, Dianna T. IV, 198
Embree, Diannah F. IV, 199
Embree, Edith IV, 198
Embree, Edith IV, 390
Embree, Edith IV, 408
Embree, Edward III, 110
Embree, Effingham III, 379
Embree, Effingham III, 388
Embree, Egginingham III, 110
Embree, Elihu I, 962
Embree, Elihu I, 1084
Embree, Elihu I, 1089
Embree, Elihu I, 1090
Embree, Elihu I, 1092
Embree, Elihu I, 1093
Embree, Elihu I, 1097
Embree, Elihu I, 1098
Embree, Elihu I, 1099
Embree, Elihu VI, 594
Embree, Elijah I, 962
Embree, Elijah I, 1084
Embree, Elijah IV, 1096
Embree, Elijah V, 51
Embree, Elijah V, 168
Embree, Elijah VI, 594
Embree, Elisha V, 903
Embree, Eliza II, 793
Embree, Eliza IV, 390
Embree, Eliza IV, 1055
Embree, Eliza IV, 1096
Embree, Eliza IV, 1099
Embree, Eliza L. II, 860
Embree, Elizabeth I, 1084
Embree, Elizabeth I, 1090
Embree, Elizabeth IV, 198
Embree, Elizabeth IV, 328
Embree, Elizabeth IV, 365
Embree, Elizabeth IV, 1056
Embree, Elizabeth IV, 1084
Embree, Elizabeth L. II, 860
Embree, Elizabeth L. II, 916
Embree, Elizabeth P. II, 860
Embree, Ella IV, 1056
Embree, Esther I, 962
Embree, Esther I, 1084
Embree, Esther IV, 1278
Embree, Esther V, 51
Embree, Esther V, 168
Embree, Esther V, 951
Embree, Esther V, 960
Embree, Esther VI, 380
Embree, Esther VI, 385
Embree, Esther VI, 594
Embree, Evan I, 1019
Embree, Even I, 962
Embree, Eza IV, 1055
Embree, Ezra IV, 1056
Embree, F. Lawrence III, 110
Embree, Fanny III, 110
Embree, Franklin III, 110
Embree, George III, 74
Embree, George III, 110
Embree, George III, 378
Embree, George III, 379
Embree, Grace T. IV, 1055
Embree, Grace T. IV, 1056
Embree, Grace T. IV, 1064
Embree, Grace T. IV, 1083
Embree, Hannah I, 1026
Embree, Hannah I, 1029
Embree, Hannah III, 110
Embree, Hannah III, 379
Embree, Hannah III, 388
Embree, Hannah IV, 198
Embree, Hannah IV, 390
Embree, Hannah IV, 421
Embree, Hannah IV, 428
Embree, Hannah IV, 577
Embree, Hannah IV, 1055
Embree, Hannah IV, 1056
Embree, Hannah IV, 1059
Embree, Hannah IV, 1096
Embree, Hannah V, 51
Embree, Hannah V, 808
Embree, Hannah Mary V, 903
Embree, Hannah Mary VI, 740
Embree, Hannah, Jr. IV, 1056
Embree, Hannah, Jr. IV, 1096
Embree, Harriet IV, 198
Embree, Harriet IV, 328
Embree, Harriet IV, 367
Embree, Harriet IV, 390
Embree, Henry Corbit III, 125
Embree, Huldah IV, 198
Embree, Huldah IV, 328
Embree, Huldah IV, 390
Embree, Huldah IV, 623
Embree, Huldah IV, 701
Embree, Huldah VI, 351
Embree, Huldah VI, 354
Embree, Isaac I, 962
Embree, Isaac I, 1019
Embree, Isaac I, 1026
Embree, Isaac I, 1029
Embree, Isaac I, 1092
Embree, Isaac IV, 390
Embree, Isaac IV, 1055
Embree, Isaac IV, 1056
Embree, Isaac V, 51
Embree, Isaac V, 723
Embree, Isaac V, 808
Embree, Isaac V, 810
Embree, Isaac R. IV, 198
Embree, Isaac, Jr. V, 808
Embree, Israel IV, 198
Embree, Israel IV, 390
Embree, Israel IV, 450
Embree, Israel IV, 1055
Embree, Israel IV, 1056
Embree, Israel IV, 1096
Embree, Israel W. IV, 1056
Embree, Israel W. IV, 1096
Embree, Jacob I, 962
Embree, Jacob I, 1019
Embree, James I, 962
Embree, James II, 515
Embree, James II, 571
Embree, James IV, 198
Embree, James IV, 199
Embree, James IV, 328
Embree, James IV, 390
Embree, James IV, 1055
Embree, James IV, 1056
Embree, James IV, 1083
Embree, James V, 51
Embree, James V, 737
Embree, James V, 808
Embree, James V, 903
Embree, Jane L. III, 379
Embree, Jane L. III, 388
Embree, Jephtha IV, 1055
Embree, Jesse I, 1019
Embree, Jesse I, 1048
Embree, Jesse I Sup 1, 11
Embree, Jesse IV, 198
Embree, Jesse IV, 199
Embree, Jesse IV, 328
Embree, Jesse IV, 390
Embree, Jesse IV, 1055
Embree, Jesse IV, 1096
Embree, Jesse V, 51
Embree, Jesse V, 837
Embree, Jesse V, 902
Embree, Jesse V, 903
Embree, Jesse Gray IV, 1096
Embree, Joel Bundy IV, 1096
Embree, John I, 388
Embree, John I, 1019
Embree, John I, 1029
Embree, John I, 1043
Embree, John I, 1048
Embree, John III, 110
Embree, John IV, 198
Embree, John IV, 328
Embree, John IV, 390
Embree, John IV, 577
Embree, John IV, 588
Embree, John IV, 623
Embree, John IV, 701
Embree, John IV, 1055
Embree, John IV, 1056
Embree, John IV, 1059
Embree, John IV, 1070
Embree, John IV, 1096
Embree, John V, 51
Embree, John V, 828
Embree, John V, 837
Embree, John VI, 309
Embree, John VI, 336
Embree, John VI, 351
Embree, John VI, 354
Embree, John VI, 385
Embree, John VI, 386
Embree, John L. III, 379
Embree, John L. III, 389
Embree, John P. IV, 198
Embree, John P. IV, 199
Embree, John P. IV, 390
Embree, John, Jr. III, 407
Embree, John, Jr. III, 409
Embree, Jonah IV, 390
Embree, Jonathan I, 1019
Embree, Jonathan I, 1048
Embree, Joseph I, 1043
Embree, Joseph IV, 198
Embree, Joseph IV, 379
Embree, Joseph IV, 390
Embree, Joseph IV, 1053
Embree, Joseph IV, 1055
Embree, Joseph IV, 1056
Embree, Joseph IV, 1089
Embree, Joseph IV, 1096
Embree, Joseph V, 51
Embree, Joseph V, 837
Embree, Joseph L. II, 793
Embree, Joseph L. II, 860
Embree, Joshua II, 721
Embree, Kesiah IV, 390
Embree, Keziah IV, 170
Embree, Keziah IV, 198
Embree, Keziah IV, 199
Embree, Keziah IV, 390
Embree, Lawrence III, 110
Embree, Lawrence III, 251
Embree, Lawrence E. III, 110
Embree, Lawrence F. III, 125
Embree, Lawrence F. III, 243
Embree, Lemuel IV, 1096
Embree, Lindley IV, 1056
Embree, Lindley H. IV, 1055
Embree, Lindley H. IV, 1056
Embree, Lucinda IV, 198
Embree, Lucinda IV, 199
Embree, Lucinda IV, 390
Embree, Lydia I, 1019
Embree, Lydia I, 1047
Embree, Lydia I, 1048
Embree, Lydia IV, 198
Embree, Lydia IV, 390
Embree, Lydia IV, 421
Embree, Lydia IV, 1055
Embree, Margaret I, 388
Embree, Margaret I, 1019
Embree, Margaret V, 737
Embree, Margaret V, 903
Embree, Margaretta V, 903
Embree, Margaretta VI, 740
Embree, Maria II, 703
Embree, Maria IV, 390
Embree, Maria IV, 431
Embree, Maria IV, 1053
Embree, Maria IV, 1055
Embree, Maria IV, 1056
Embree, Maria IV, 1093
Embree, Maria IV, 1096
Embree, Marie III, 110
Embree, Marie III, 125
Embree, Martha III, 110
Embree, Martha IV, 1055
Embree, Martha IV, 1056
Embree, Martha IV, 1095
Embree, Martha IV, 1102
Embree, Martha IV, 1116
Embree, Martha W. III, 110
Embree, Mary I, 388
Embree, Mary I, 962
Embree, Mary I, 1019
Embree, Mary I, 1043
Embree, Mary I, 1048
Embree, Mary II, 860
Embree, Mary III, 110
Embree, Mary III, 200
Embree, Mary III, 379
Embree, Mary III, 388
Embree, Mary III, 456
Embree, Mary IV, 328
Embree, Mary IV, 523
Embree, Mary IV, 528
Embree, Mary IV, 623
Embree, Mary IV, 662
Embree, Mary IV, 1053
Embree, Mary IV, 1056
Embree, Mary IV, 1096
Embree, Mary V, 51
Embree, Mary V, 737
Embree, Mary V, 794
Embree, Mary V, 828
Embree, Mary V, 837
Embree, Mary V, 902
Embree, Mary V, 903
Embree, Mary V, 904
Embree, Mary VI, 309
Embree, Mary VI, 351
Embree, Mary VI, 385
Embree, Mary Ann II, 704
Embree, Mary Ann IV, 199
Embree, Mary Ann IV, 264
Embree, Mary Ann IV, 390
Embree, Mary Ann IV, 450
Embree, Mary Ann IV, 1055
Embree, Mary Ann IV, 1096
Embree, Mary Ellen IV, 1055
Embree, Mary L. IV, 199
Embree, Mary S. IV, 198
Embree, Maryann IV, 390
Embree, Matilda IV, 1055
Embree, Mercer I, 1043
Embree, Mercer V, 51
Embree, Mercer V, 837
Embree, Merrick IV, 1055
Embree, Merrick IV, 1096
Embree, Mordecai IV, 198
Embree, Mordecai IV, 390
Embree, Mordecai M. IV, 198
Embree, Moses I, 962
Embree, Moses I, 1015
Embree, Moses I, 1019
Embree, Moses I, 1029
Embree, Moses IV, 616
Embree, Moses IV, 623
Embree, Moses IV, 643
Embree, Moses V, 51
Embree, Moses V, 808
Embree, Moses VI, 309
Embree, Moses VI, 351
Embree, Moses VI, 354
Embree, Moses VI, 385
Embree, Moses VI, 386
Embree, Moses R. IV, 623
Embree, Moses, Jr. IV, 623
Embree, Mosses I, 388
Embree, Nathaniel III, 110
Embree, Norris J. II, 793
Embree, Norris J. II, 860
Embree, Norris Jones II, 358
Embree, Norris Jones II, 515
Embree, Pearson IV, 1055
Embree, Phebe III, 389
Embree, Phebe IV, 198
Embree, Phebe IV, 390
Embree, Phebe IV, 428
Embree, Phebe IV, 1055
Embree, Phebe S. III, 36
Embree, Phebe S. III, 110
Embree, Phebe S. III, 379
Embree, Philip D. V, 237
Embree, Rachel I, 962
Embree, Rachel I, 1019
Embree, Rachel I, 1048
Embree, Rachel I, 1084
Embree, Rachel IV, 616
Embree, Rachel IV, 623
Embree, Rachel IV, 942
Embree, Rachel IV, 1056
Embree, Rachel IV, 1070
Embree, Rachel V, 51
Embree, Rachel V, 236
Embree, Rachel V, 237
Embree, Rachel V, 469
Embree, Rachel V, 488
Embree, Rachel V, 534
Embree, Rachel V, 903
Embree, Rachel V, 960
Embree, Rachel VI, 309
Embree, Rachel VI, 385
Embree, Rachel VI, 594
Embree, Rachel VI, 740
Embree, Rebecca II, 358
Embree, Rebecca II, 515
Embree, Rebecca II, 571
Embree, Rebecca II, 721
Embree, Rebecca II, 738
Embree, Rebecca IV, 379
Embree, Rebecca IV, 390
Embree, Rebecca IV, 1053
Embree, Rebecca IV, 1055
Embree, Rebecca IV, 1056
Embree, Rebecca V, 51
Embree, Rebecca V, 903
Embree, Rebeccah V, 51
Embree, Rebeckah IV, 1055
Embree, Rebekah I, 962
Embree, Rebekah I, 1019
Embree, Rebekah I, 1043
Embree, Reuben IV, 1055
Embree, Robert III, 36
Embree, Robert III, 379
Embree, Robert IV, 1055
Embree, Robert C. III, 110
Embree, Robt. III, 389
Embree, Ruth III, 407
Embree, Ruth III, 409
Embree, Ruth IV, 124
Embree, Ruth IV, 125
Embree, Ruth IV, 1096
Embree, Ruth V, 808
Embree, Sabra I, 1084
Embree, Sally I, 1084
Embree, Samuel II, 704
Embree, Samuel III, 110
Embree, Samuel IV, 198
Embree, Samuel IV, 390
Embree, Samuel IV, 421
Embree, Samuel IV, 428
Embree, Samuel IV, 470
Embree, Samuel IV, 577
Embree, Samuel IV, 1055
Embree, Samuel IV, 1056
Embree, Samuel IV, 1075
Embree, Samuel IV, 1096
Embree, Samuel V, 236
Embree, Samuel V, 237
Embree, Samuel V, 837
Embree, Samuel, Jr. IV, 390
Embree, Sarah I, 1019
Embree, Sarah I, 1043
Embree, Sarah I, 1048
Embree, Sarah I, 1084
Embree, Sarah II, 358
Embree, Sarah II, 515
Embree, Sarah II, 571
Embree, Sarah III, 74
Embree, Sarah III, 110
Embree, Sarah III, 210

Embree, Sarah III, 251
Embree, Sarah III, 379
Embree, Sarah IV, 198
Embree, Sarah IV, 199
Embree, Sarah IV, 390
Embree, Sarah IV, 418
Embree, Sarah IV, 1096
Embree, Sarah V, 51
Embree, Sarah V, 168
Embree, Sarah V, 172
Embree, Sarah V, 808
Embree, Sarah V, 810
Embree, Sarah V, 828
Embree, Sarah V, 837
Embree, Sarah V, 903
Embree, Sarah VI, 740
Embree, Sarah Ann IV, 1056
Embree, Sarah Ann IV, 1075
Embree, Sarah Emma III, 378
Embree, Sarah J. II, 860
Embree, Sarah R. III, 110
Embree, Sarah R. III, 409
Embree, Sophia II, 721
Embree, Stephen IV, 623
Embree, Thomas I, 962
Embree, Thomas I, 1019
Embree, Thomas I, 1077
Embree, Thomas I, 1084
Embree, Thomas I, 1092
Embree, Thomas III, 409
Embree, Thomas V, 51
Embree, Thomas V, 168
Embree, Thomas V, 951
Embree, Thomas V, 960
Embree, Thomas VI, 380
Embree, Thomas VI, 385
Embree, Thomas VI, 594
Embree, Thomas VI, 604
Embree, Thomas C. III, 110
Embree, Thos. V, 207
Embree, Virginia V, 237
Embree, Wd. Eliz. B. III, 125
Embree, William II, 358
Embree, William IV, 390
Embree, William V, 837
Embree, William A. IV, 198
Embree, William A. IV, 199
Embree, William A. IV, 390
Embree, William F. III, 110
Embree, William L. III, 110
Embree, William L. VI, 740
Embree, Wm. II, 515
Embree, Wm. II, 571
Embree, Wm. IV, 623
Embree, Wm. IV, 1055
Embree, Wm. IV, 1056
Embree, Wm. IV, 1096
Embree, Wm. V, 903
Embree, Wm. A. IV, 199
Embree, Wm. Dewees IV, 1096
Embree, Wm. L. V, 903
Embree, Wm. L. VI, 740
Embree, Wm. N. II, 860
Embree, Worley I, 1084
Embree, Worley I, 1093
Embree, Zenas IV, 1064
Embrey, Frances VI, 912
Embrey, John IV, 814
Embrey, William VI, 912
Embry, ??? IV, 1047
Embry, Abigail IV, 523
Embry, Ann V, 808
Embry, Edith IV, 523
Embry, Elizabeth IV, 523
Embry, Harriett IV, 523
Embry, Huldah IV, 523
Embry, Isaac V, 808
Embry, James IV, 523
Embry, Jesse IV, 523
Embry, John IV, 523
Embry, Mary IV, 523
Embry, Mary Ann IV, 145
Embry, Mary Ann IV, 156
Embry, Mordecai IV, 523
Embry, Moses VI, 309
Embury, Herbert H. IV, 1037
Emeigh, Ann M. III, 510
Emeigh, Arden III, 510
Emeigh, Elizabeth III, 510
Emens, Edith V, 488
Emeree, Ann V, 809
Emeree, Isaac V, 809
Emerick, Ella E. II, 793
Emerick, Harry II, 793
Emerick, Howard II, 793
Emerick, Lucette V, 737
Emerick, Mrs. ??? IV, 1314
Emerick, Russell R. V, 837
Emerick, Sadie P. V, 994
Emerick, Wm. V, 994
Emerson, Amelia III, 110
Emerson, Amelia III, 122
Emerson, Ames III, 110
Emerson, Edw. Waldo III, 110
Emerson, Govey II, 515
Emerson, Hannah II, 515
Emerson, Joseph B. III, 110
Emerson, Love I, 99
Emerson, Mrs. Nicholas VI, 11
Emerson, Nicholas VI, 12
Emerson, Raymond III, 110
Emerson, Raymond III, 122
Emerson, Samaria J. III, 399
Emerson, Sarah H. III, 110
Emerson, Sarah Hooper III, 133
Emerson, Susan III, 110
Emerson, Tebitha I, 99
Emerson, William III, 133
Emerson, William, Jr. III, 110
Emerson, Wm. III, 110
Emerson, Wm. S. II, 860
Emery, Ella V, 560
Emery, Esther IV, 723
Emery, Esther IV, 766
Emery, Esther IV, 824
Emery, Esther IV, 844
Emery, Hannah II, 217
Emery, Ida IV, 1361
Emery, Jermain B. IV, 1361
Emery, Margaret I, 388
Emery, Mary I, 388
Emery, Minnie IV, 701
Emery, Sarah II, 217
Emery, Sarah VI, 489
Emery, Sarah VI, 505
Emery, Thomas V, 469
Emes, Eliza J. IV, 1037
Emes, Lillian M. IV, 1037
Emes, Luther IV, 1037
Emigh, Adam III, 482
Emigh, Adam III, 489
Emigh, Adam III, 497
Emigh, Ann III, 482
Emigh, Ann III, 489
Emigh, Ann M. III, 482
Emigh, Ann M. III, 497
Emigh, Elizabeth III, 482
Emigh, Elizabeth S. III, 482
Emigh, Elizabeth S. III, 489
Emigh, Margaret III, 482
Emigh, Margaret C. III, 489
Emigh, Margaret E. III, 482
Emigh, Philip III, 482
Emily, Martha IV, 854
Emily, Rebecca IV, 944
Emlem, Joshua II, 515
Emlem, Mary II, 515
Emlem, Wd. Hannah II, 515
Emlen, Ann II, 358
Emlen, Ann II, 516
Emlen, Ann II, 597
Emlen, Ann II, 623
Emlen, Ann, Jr. II, 516
Emlen, Anna II, 358
Emlen, Anna II, 516
Emlen, Anna II, 677
Emlen, Anne II, 516
Emlen, Beulah II, 359
Emlen, Beulah S. II, 516
Emlen, Beulah S. II, 673
Emlen, Beulah S. II, 738
Emlen, Caleb II, 358
Emlen, Caleb II, 359
Emlen, Caleb II, 497
Emlen, Caleb II, 516
Emlen, Caleb II, 623
Emlen, Caleb II, 677
Emlen, Caleb II, 738
Emlen, Deborah II, 516
Emlen, Deborah II, 626
Emlen, Deborah II, 704
Emlen, Dr. Samuel II, 704
Emlen, Elizabeth II, 215
Emlen, Elizabeth II, 217
Emlen, Elizabeth II, 516
Emlen, Elizabeth II, 599
Emlen, Elizabeth II, 704
Emlen, Elizabeth Ann II, 359
Emlen, Elizabeth Ann II, 738
Emlen, Ellinor II, 451
Emlen, Ellinor II, 515
Emlen, George II, 358
Emlen, George II, 451
Emlen, George II, 497
Emlen, George II, 515
Emlen, George II, 516
Emlen, George II, 556
Emlen, George II, 558
Emlen, George II, 584
Emlen, George II, 597
Emlen, George II, 677
Emlen, George, Jr. II, 358
Emlen, George, Jr. II, 516
Emlen, George, Sr. II, 358
Emlen, Hanah II, 515
Emlen, Hannah II, 358
Emlen, Hannah II, 516
Emlen, Hannah II, 584
Emlen, Hannah II, 668
Emlen, Hudson II, 358
Emlen, James II, 516
Emlen, James II, 606
Emlen, James II, 673
Emlen, James II, 704
Emlen, James II, 738
Emlen, James II, 770
Emlen, James III, 110
Emlen, James Valentine II, 359
Emlen, James Valentine II, 738
Emlen, Jeremiah II, 358
Emlen, John II, 358
Emlen, John J. II, 704
Emlen, John Thompson II, 704
Emlen, Joseph II, 358
Emlen, Joseph II, 516
Emlen, Joshua II, 358
Emlen, Joshua II, 516
Emlen, Joshua II, 558
Emlen, Joshua II, 599
Emlen, Joshua II, 604
Emlen, Joshua II, 626
Emlen, Luke VI, 357
Emlen, Lydia II, 704
Emlen, Margaret II, 516
Emlen, Margaret II, 556
Emlen, Mary II, 358
Emlen, Mary II, 464
Emlen, Mary II, 497
Emlen, Mary II, 516
Emlen, Mary II, 535
Emlen, Mary II, 558
Emlen, Mary II, 606
Emlen, Mary II, 623
Emlen, Mary C. II, 704
Emlen, Mary C. II, 738
Emlen, Mary P. II, 516
Emlen, Mary, Jr. II, 516
Emlen, Mary, Jr. II, 677
Emlen, Phebe II, 606
Emlen, Phebe II, 673
Emlen, Phebe P. II, 516
Emlen, Rachel II, 358
Emlen, Rachel II, 516
Emlen, Rachel II, 558
Emlen, Rachel II, 600
Emlen, Samuel II, 172
Emlen, Samuel II, 217
Emlen, Samuel II, 358
Emlen, Samuel II, 359
Emlen, Samuel II, 440
Emlen, Samuel II, 516
Emlen, Samuel II, 558
Emlen, Samuel II, 600
Emlen, Samuel II, 738
Emlen, Samuel II, 770
Emlen, Samuel VI, 270
Emlen, Samuel, Jr. II, 215
Emlen, Samuel, Jr. II, 217
Emlen, Samuel, Jr. II, 359
Emlen, Samuel, Jr. II, 516
Emlen, Samuel, Jr. II, 599
Emlen, Samuel, Jr. II, 604
Emlen, Samuel, Jr. II, 673
Emlen, Samuel, Sr. II, 358
Emlen, Sarah II, 497
Emlen, Sarah II, 516
Emlen, Sarah II, 600
Emlen, Sarah II, 604
Emlen, Sarah II, 738
Emlen, Sarah II, 767
Emlen, Sarah II, 770
Emlen, Susan II, 172
Emlen, Susan II, 704
Emlen, Susan T. II, 704
Emlen, Susan T. II, 738
Emlen, Susan T. II, 770
Emlen, Susanna II, 215
Emlen, Susanna II, 217
Emlen, Susannah II, 217
Emlen, Susannah II, 359
Emlen, Wd. Mary II, 358
Emlen, William II, 359
Emlen, Wm. II, 516
Emlen, Wm. F. II, 516
Emley, Adalaide Fenimore II, 856
Emley, Adalaide Fenimore II, 860
Emley, Adelaide Lancaster VI, 740
Emley, Ann II, 286
Emley, Ann II, 302
Emley, Ann L. II, 318
Emley, Ann Lancaster II, 796
Emley, Anna A. II, 856
Emley, Anna A. II, 860
Emley, Anna Amanda VI, 740
Emley, Anna Melvina II, 796
Emley, Annie Lucile VI, 740
Emley, Annie Lucile VI, 790
Emley, Henrietta D. II, 318
Emley, Henrietta D. II, 326
Emley, John C. V, 837
Emley, Joseph Cook II, 860
Emley, Margaret V, 837
Emley, Mary II, 172
Emley, Mary II, 516
Emley, Mary II, 546
Emley, Mary L. V, 51
Emley, Richard IV, 814
Emley, Ruth II, 172
Emley, Samuel II, 516
Emley, Sarah II, 217
Emley, Sarah S. II, 318
Emley, Susan W. II, 318
Emley, Susan W. II, 326
Emley, Thomas II, 172
Emley, Warren Edwards VI, 740
Emley, Warren Edwards VI, 790
Emley, Warren Edwards, Jr. VI, 740
Emley, William II, 172
Emley, William S. II, 318
Emley, Wm. II, 516
Emley, Wm. II, 546
Emley, Wm. II, 796
Emley, Wm. S. II, 856
Emley, Wm. S. II, 860
Emley, Wm. Stokes VI, 740
Emlin, Jeremiah II, 358
Emlin, Mary II, 454
Emlin, Mary II, 516
Emlin, Sarah V, 574
Emly, Ann L. II, 318
Emly, Ann L. II, 325
Emly, Deborah II, 359
Emly, Henrietta D. II, 318
Emly, Joseph Cook II, 860
Emly, Joshua II, 359
Emly, Mary II, 359
Emly, Samuel II, 359
Emly, Samuel II, 516
Emly, Susan W. II, 318
Emly, William S. II, 318
Emly, William S. II, 325
Emmanuel, John M. III, 110
Emmerson, Ann II, 359
Emmerson, Charles J. V, 737
Emmerson, Governeir II, 738
Emmerson, Govey II, 515
Emmerson, Lambert II, 359
Emmett, Elizabeth IV, 259
Emminger, Charles H. IV, 868
Emminger, Chas. H. IV, 814
Emminger, Herchel IV, 814
Emminger, Lena IV, 814
Emminger, Lena M. IV, 868
Emmins, Thomas IV, 858
Emmison, Widow Tabitha I, 139
Emmison, Widow Tabitha I, 165
Emmons, ??? IV, 1125
Emmons, Abner IV, 390
Emmons, Albert IV, 1056
Emmons, Albert IV, 1096
Emmons, Albert IV, 1129
Emmons, Albert IV, 1130
Emmons, Amy IV, 199
Emmons, Ann IV, 125
Emmons, Ann IV, 128
Emmons, Aurora E. IV, 375
Emmons, Aurora E. IV, 390
Emmons, Caroline S. IV, 903
Emmons, Caroline S. IV, 904
Emmons, Caroline S. IV, 914
Emmons, Caroline S. IV, 1096
Emmons, Caroline S. IV, 1130
Emmons, Caroline Susan IV, 1130
Emmons, Cassandra IV, 701
Emmons, Cassandra IV, 904
Emmons, Cassina C. V, 51
Emmons, Chester W. IV, 199
Emmons, Chester W. IV, 214
Emmons, Cyrenius IV, 904
Emmons, Cyrenius IV, 917
Emmons, David IV, 701
Emmons, Davis IV, 903
Emmons, Davis IV, 904
Emmons, Davis IV, 1096
Emmons, Delitha IV, 1056
Emmons, Delitha IV, 1092
Emmons, Delitha IV, 1096
Emmons, Delitha IV, 1130
Emmons, Edison C. IV, 1096
Emmons, Edwin IV, 1130
Emmons, Edwin C. IV, 1096
Emmons, Edwin C. IV, 1130
Emmons, Elias IV, 814
Emmons, Elizabeth IV, 903
Emmons, Elizabeth IV, 904
Emmons, Elizabeth IV, 1096
Emmons, Elizabeth D. IV, 987
Emmons, Elizabeth D. IV, 1056
Emmons, Elizabeth D. IV, 1096
Emmons, Elizabeth D. IV, 1130
Emmons, Ellwood Dean IV, 1096
Emmons, Elmina IV, 1096
Emmons, Elmira IV, 1056
Emmons, Elmira IV, 1130
Emmons, Elmira IV, 1136
Emmons, Elwood D. IV, 1096
Emmons, Elwood D. IV, 1130
Emmons, Emily IV, 972
Emmons, Enos IV, 814
Emmons, Florence IV, 199
Emmons, Florence IV, 214
Emmons, Frank IV, 1250
Emmons, Harry D. IV, 1056
Emmons, Harry Davis IV, 1096
Emmons, Harvey IV, 1130
Emmons, Harvey D. IV, 1056
Emmons, Harvey D. IV, 1130
Emmons, Harvey Davis IV, 1130
Emmons, Hervey D. IV, 1130
Emmons, Isaac IV, 904
Emmons, Jacob IV, 701
Emmons, Jacob IV, 904
Emmons, John IV, 1130
Emmons, John T. IV, 1130
Emmons, Jonathan IV, 814
Emmons, Joseph IV, 904
Emmons, Joseph V, 330
Emmons, Joseph V, 363
Emmons, Levi IV, 814
Emmons, Lindley IV, 1130
Emmons, Lindley F. IV, 1096
Emmons, Louis IV, 375
Emmons, Louis W. IV, 390
Emmons, Lydia IV, 814
Emmons, Lydia IV, 904
Emmons, Martin IV, 814
Emmons, Mary IV, 278
Emmons, Mary IV, 701
Emmons, Mary IV, 808
Emmons, Mary IV, 814
Emmons, Mary IV, 904
Emmons, Mary IV, 913
Emmons, Mary IV, 916
Emmons, Mary IV, 951
Emmons, Mary IV, 999
Emmons, Mary IV, 1056
Emmons, Mary IV, 1096
Emmons, Mary IV, 1130
Emmons, Mary IV, 1250
Emmons, Mary V, 330
Emmons, Mary C. IV, 1096
Emmons, Mary C. IV, 1130
Emmons, Mary Ellen IV, 1130
Emmons, Mary M. V, 330
Emmons, Mary W. IV, 904
Emmons, Mary W. V, 330
Emmons, Mary W. V, 363
Emmons, Meriam IV, 904
Emmons, Meriam IV, 917
Emmons, Micajah IV, 904
Emmons, Micajah IV, 1056
Emmons, Micajah IV, 1092
Emmons, Micajah IV, 1096
Emmons, Micajah IV, 1130
Emmons, Miriam IV, 904
Emmons, Orlando IV, 1130
Emmons, Orlin D. IV, 1130
Emmons, Phebe IV, 904
Emmons, Phebe IV, 913
Emmons, Phebe IV, 914
Emmons, Rachel IV, 390
Emmons, Rachel IV, 1129
Emmons, Rachel IV, 1130
Emmons, Randall IV, 390
Emmons, Rebecca IV, 701
Emmons, Rebecca IV, 814
Emmons, Rebecca IV, 904
Emmons, Rebecca IV, 913
Emmons, Rebecca IV, 914
Emmons, Sarah IV, 904
Emmons, Sarah IV, 917
Emmons, Serenius IV, 904
Emmons, Susanna IV, 814
Emmons, Susanna IV, 900
Emmons, Susanna IV, 904
Emmons, Thomas IV, 701
Emmons, Thomas IV, 814
Emmons, Thomas IV, 897
Emmons, Thomas IV, 904
Emmons, Thomas IV, 913
Emmons, Thomas IV, 999
Emmons, Thomas IV, 1096

Emmons, Thomas IV, 1130
Emmons, Thomas V, 330
Emmons, Thomas, Jr. IV, 808
Emmons, Thomas, Jr. IV, 814
Emmons, Thomas, Jr. IV, 904
Emmons, Thomas, Sr. IV, 1056
Emmons, Thos IV, 913
Emmons, Thos. IV, 904
Emmons, Thos. IV, 1130
Emmons, Will IV, 814
Emmons, Wilson B. IV, 1096
Emmons, Wilson R. IV, 1096
Emmons, Wilson T. IV, 199
Emmons, Wm. IV, 814
Emory, Anna III, 110
Emory, Clinton VI, 74
Emory, David Lloyd III, 409
Emory, Esther J. III, 418
Emory, Esther Jackson III, 409
Emory, George S. III, 409
Emory, Hannah W. III, 409
Emory, John III, 204
Emory, John Comegys III, 110
Emory, John Martin Groome III, 409
Emory, John Martin Groome III, 418
Emory, Lilly VI, 74
Emory, Rebecca V, 51
Emory, Rebecca V, 102
Emory, Sarah Hull III, 110
Emory, Sarah Hull III, 204
Emory, Stuart R. III, 110
Emperor, Mrs. ??? VI, 12
Emperor, Mrs. Mary VI, 11
Emperor, Mrs. Mary VI, 12
Empson, Cornelius II, 68
Empson, Cornelius II, 94
Empson, Cornelius II, 359
Empson, Cornelius II, 516
Empson, Cornelius II, 621
Empson, Cornelius, Jr. II, 359
Empson, Hannah II, 359
Empson, Mary II, 68
Empson, Mary II, 94
Empson, Mary II, 516
Empson, Mary II, 621
Empson, Sarah II, 359
Empson, William II, 359
Emrick, Bernice Lee V, 837
Emrick, Blanche V, 837
Emrick, Charles V, 837
Emrick, Elwood Richard V, 837
Emrick, Eva V, 837
Emrick, George P. V, 737
Emrick, Jessie V, 837
Emrick, Lilly V, 837
Emrick, Lucetta V, 737
Emrick, Lucette V, 737
Emrick, Russell R. V, 837
Emry, Isaac V, 808
Emry, Rachel II, 709
Emslie, Alexander II, 515
Emslie, Mary II, 515
Emson, Cornelius II, 443
Emson, James II, 443
Emson, Sarah II, 359
Emsweiler, Cora IV, 1206
Emsweiler, John D. IV, 1206
Enbody, Chas. V, 994
Enburg, Emily II, 715
Enburg, John Moore Clark II, 715
Enburg, Marion II, 715
Endell, Lois Evelyn IV, 1216
Endell, Ward IV, 1216
Endesley, Eugine I, 1151
Endesley, Herbert I, 1151
Endesley, Josie I, 1151
Endicott, Susannah IV, 390
Endicott, Susannah IV, 404
Endle, Catharine IV, 1314
Endley, Laura I. I, 1140
Endley, Mary Janes I, 1140
Endley, Sarah I. I, 1140
Endley, Wm. Henry Harrison I, 1140
Ends, Henry VI, 814
Ends, Missouri VI, 814
Endsley, Bettie G. I, 1151
Endsley, Ephraim L. I, 1151
Endsley, Eugine I, 1151
Endsley, Frank I, 1151
Endsley, Genevieve I, 1151
Endsley, Herbert I, 1151
Endsley, Hester I, 1151
Endsley, Hettie I, 1151
Endsley, J. A. I, 1151
Endsley, John I, 1151
Endsley, John C. I, 1151
Endsley, Joseph A. I, 1151
Endsley, Josie I, 1151
Endsley, Lula I, 1151
Endsley, Mollie I, 1151
Endsley, Nancy I, 1151
Endsley, W. H. H. I, 1151
Endsley, William I, 1151
Enearl, Almy Jane IV, 1359
Enearl, Almy Jane IV, 1361
Enfield, Henry IV, 199
Eng, Emeline III, 110
Engel, ??? IV, 1085
Englan, Elizabeth II, 473
Englan, Elizabeth II, 517
Englan, Mary VI, 775
Englan, Philip II, 516
England, Abraham II, 359
England, Abraham II, 517
England, Abraham II, 630
England, Ann II, 517
England, Ann IV, 30
England, Ann IV, 68
England, Ann IV, 702
England, Ann IV, 762
England, Betty IV, 702
England, Christian II, 450
England, Christian II, 516
England, Daniel II, 172
England, Daniel II, 359
England, Daniel II, 443
England, Daniel II, 491
England, Daniel II, 516
England, David IV, 17
England, David IV, 19
England, David IV, 30
England, David VI, 386
England, Don James IV, 702
England, Edith IV, 702
England, Elisabeth II, 517
England, Elizabeth II, 359
England, Elizabeth II, 491
England, Elizabeth II, 516
England, Elizabeth II, 517
England, Elizabeth II, 592
England, Elizabeth III, 379
England, Elizabeth III, 384
England, Elizabeth IV, 22
England, Elizabeth IV, 30
England, Elizabeth IV, 43
England, Elizabeth IV, 59
England, Elizabeth IV, 122
England, Elizabeth IV, 125
England, Elizabeth IV, 470
England, Elizabeth IV, 486
England, Elizabeth VI, 386
England, Elizabeth M. II, 286
England, Elizabeth M. II, 304
England, Emma IV, 31
England, Emma IV, 145
England, Emma IV, 147
England, Emma IV, 702
England, Esther IV, 30
England, Esther IV, 390
England, Fam IV, 31
England, George II, 517
England, George IV, 31
England, George IV, 702
England, George VI, 627
England, George VI, 636
England, Gideon IV, 702
England, Hannah II, 68
England, Hannah II, 112
England, Hannah II, 359
England, Hannah II, 517
England, Hannah IV, 30
England, Hannah IV, 59
England, Hannah IV, 64
England, Hannah IV, 69
England, Hannah IV, 702
England, Hannah IV, 792
England, Hannah IV, 814
England, Harold IV, 702
England, Howard II, 739
England, Isaac II, 517
England, Isaac IV, 30
England, Isaac VI, 386
England, Isaac VI, 814
England, Isaac VI, 823
England, Israel IV, 30
England, Israel VI, 386
England, James II, 739
England, James IV, 702
England, James R. IV, 702
England, Jane II, 359
England, Jane II, 517
England, Jane II, 630
England, Jane IV, 31
England, Jane IV, 702
England, Jane, Jr. IV, 30
England, Jemima II, 172
England, Jemima II, 516
England, Jemima II, 538
England, Joanna II, 819
England, John II, 517
England, John IV, 30
England, John IV, 199
England, John VI, 386
England, John VI, 489
England, Joseph II, 172
England, Joseph II, 359
England, Joseph II, 457
England, Joseph II, 517
England, Joseph IV, 30
England, Joseph IV, 40
England, Joseph IV, 59
England, Joseph IV, 69
England, Joseph IV, 702
England, Joseph IV, 792
England, Joseph VI, 814
England, Joseph, Jr. IV, 30
England, Joseph, Jr. IV, 702
England, Josiah IV, 30
England, Josiah IV, 675
England, Josiah IV, 702
England, Josiah IV, 792
England, Letitia C. VI, 627
England, Letitia C. VI, 636
England, Lindley M. II, 739
England, Margaret IV, 328
England, Mary I, 388
England, Mary I, 391
England, Mary II, 172
England, Mary II, 359
England, Mary II, 517
England, Mary IV, 17
England, Mary IV, 19
England, Mary IV, 22
England, Mary IV, 30
England, Mary IV, 40
England, Mary IV, 41
England, Mary IV, 702
England, Mary VI, 814
England, Mary Emma VI, 622
England, Mary Emma VI, 624
England, Mary Emma VI, 625
England, Mary Emma VI, 626
England, Mary Emma VI, 627
England, Mary Emma VI, 631
England, Mary Emma VI, 636
England, Mary Emma VI, 650
England, Mary Emma VI, 691
England, Matilda IV, 702
England, Matilda IV, 759
England, Matilda IV, 792
England, Milton IV, 199
England, Milton V. IV, 328
England, Milton V. IV, 814
England, Nancy VI, 814
England, Philip II, 359
England, Philip II, 443
England, Philip II, 516
England, Philip II, 545
England, Rachel III, 110
England, Richard III, 111
England, Robert IV, 30
England, Samuel II, 517
England, Samuel IV, 22
England, Samuel IV, 30
England, Samuel IV, 31
England, Samuel IV, 64
England, Samuel IV, 69
England, Samuel IV, 145
England, Samuel IV, 147
England, Samuel IV, 702
England, Samuel IV, 814
England, Samuel, Jr. IV, 31
England, Sarah II, 359
England, Sarah II, 451
England, Sarah II, 457
England, Sarah II, 510
England, Sarah II, 517
England, Sarah IV, 19
England, Sarah IV, 30
England, Sarah IV, 675
England, Sarah IV, 702
England, Sarah IV, 792
England, Sarah VI, 386
England, Sarah Ann IV, 814
England, Susanna IV, 30
England, Tacy IV, 22
England, Tacy IV, 30
England, Tacy IV, 31
England, Tacy IV, 64
England, Tacy IV, 69
England, Tacy IV, 145
England, Tacy IV, 702
England, Tacy, Jr. IV, 30
England, Tacy, Jr. IV, 702
England, Thomas II, 359
England, Thomas II, 443
England, Thomas II, 504
England, Thomas II, 516
England, Thomas Clement II, 704
England, Wd. Elizabeth II, 516
England, Wd. Elizabeth II, 545
England, Wd. Hannah II, 517
England, Wm. II, 510
England, Wm. II, 517
Englar, Alice III, 276
Englar, Mary III, 276
Englar, Mary III, 277
Engle, ??? IV, 951
Engle, ??? IV, 1125
Engle, Aaron II, 318
Engle, Aaron II, 319
Engle, Abraham II, 211
Engle, Abraham II, 217
Engle, Abraham IV, 145
Engle, Abraham IV, 147
Engle, Abraham IV, 328
Engle, Abraham IV, 346
Engle, Abraham IV, 390
Engle, Abraham V, 51
Engle, Albina II, 318
Engle, Albina II, 319
Engle, Allen A. II, 318
Engle, Allen A. II, 327
Engle, Amos W. III, 111
Engle, Ann IV, 145
Engle, Ann IV, 147
Engle, Ann IV, 610
Engle, Ann IV, 623
Engle, Ann IV, 951
Engle, Ann V, 52
Engle, Ann V, 77
Engle, Ann V, 140
Engle, Ann V, 168
Engle, Ann V, 838
Engle, Ann B. IV, 623
Engle, Ann B. IV, 951
Engle, Anna IV, 328
Engle, Anna IV, 390
Engle, Anna G. II, 318
Engle, Anna G. II, 325
Engle, Anna M. IV, 390
Engle, Anna Mercy IV, 419
Engle, Anne IV, 145
Engle, Annie II, 309
Engle, Annie II, 318
Engle, Annie S. II, 318
Engle, Arthur II, 172
Engle, Arthur II, 283
Engle, Arthur II, 287
Engle, Asa II, 136
Engle, Caleb II, 172
Engle, Caleb II, 211
Engle, Caleb II, 217
Engle, Caleb IV, 145
Engle, Caleb IV, 328
Engle, Caleb IV, 348
Engle, Caleb IV, 368
Engle, Caleb IV, 373
Engle, Caleb IV, 390
Engle, Caleb IV, 391
Engle, Caleb IV, 392
Engle, Caleb IV, 409
Engle, Caleb IV, 419
Engle, Caleb IV, 430
Engle, Caleb IV, 1056
Engle, Caleb IV, 1096
Engle, Caleb IV, 1123
Engle, Caleb IV, 1130
Engle, Caleb IV, 1131
Engle, Caleb T. IV, 1131
Engle, Caleb W. IV, 1130
Engle, Caleb, Jr. IV, 391
Engle, Caroline II, 309
Engle, Caroline S. II, 318
Engle, Caroline S. II, 326
Engle, Catharine IV, 623
Engle, Catharine IV, 702
Engle, Catharine IV, 868
Engle, Catharine IV, 873
Engle, Charles II, 117
Engle, Charles IV, 623
Engle, Charles IV, 643
Engle, Charles IV, 951
Engle, Charles IV, 978
Engle, Charles D. IV, 951
Engle, Charles H. IV, 702
Engle, Chas. IV, 623
Engle, Chas. D. IV, 1037
Engle, Cora V, 330
Engle, Cora V, 456
Engle, David III, 111
Engle, David D. II, 287
Engle, David D. III, 84
Engle, David D. III, 111
Engle, Deborah IV, 390
Engle, Deborah IV, 405
Engle, Deborah IV, 452
Engle, Deborah IV, 1098
Engle, Deborah IV, 1121
Engle, Deborah Jane IV, 1096
Engle, Deborah Jane IV, 1131
Engle, Dudley V, 330
Engle, Edith II, 172
Engle, Edith II, 283
Engle, Edith II, 287
Engle, Edith Ann II, 823
Engle, Edith E. III, 111
Engle, Edith E. III, 260
Engle, Edith R. II, 287
Engle, Edith R. II, 290
Engle, Edna Mae IV, 1314
Engle, Edward B. II, 131
Engle, Edward B. II, 148
Engle, Eliza IV, 951
Engle, Eliza V, 951
Engle, Eliza C. IV, 951
Engle, Eliza C. IV, 979
Engle, Elizabeth II, 217
Engle, Elizabeth IV, 145
Engle, Elizabeth IV, 328
Engle, Elizabeth IV, 368
Engle, Elizabeth IV, 390
Engle, Elizabeth IV, 391
Engle, Elizabeth IV, 454
Engle, Elizabeth IV, 523
Engle, Elizabeth IV, 540
Engle, Elizabeth IV, 951
Engle, Elizabeth IV, 1056
Engle, Elizabeth IV, 1079
Engle, Elizabeth IV, 1096
Engle, Elizabeth V, 52
Engle, Elizabeth V, 330
Engle, Elizabeth V, 343
Engle, Elizabeth V, 838
Engle, Elizabeth V, 951
Engle, Elizabeth S. II, 318
Engle, Elizabeth S. II, 327
Engle, Elma IV, 944
Engle, Elwood IV, 1130
Engle, Emily II, 309
Engle, Emily II, 318
Engle, Emily M. II, 318
Engle, Emily M. II, 319
Engle, Emily Maria II, 318
Engle, Emmer G. IV, 1037
Engle, Emmor IV, 1037
Engle, Emmor G. IV, 1037
Engle, Ephraim IV, 391
Engle, Ephraim W. IV, 391
Engle, Ephraim W. IV, 1096
Engle, Ephraim W. IV, 1131
Engle, Esther IV, 623
Engle, Esther IV, 702
Engle, Eva H. III, 111
Engle, Eva H. III, 260
Engle, Ezekiel IV, 1096
Engle, Ezra II, 283
Engle, Ezra II, 287
Engle, Ezra C. II, 283
Engle, Ezra C. II, 287
Engle, Grace IV, 145
Engle, Gulielma II, 132
Engle, Hannah IV, 328
Engle, Hannah IV, 390
Engle, Hannah IV, 1131
Engle, Hannah V, 52
Engle, Hannah V, 159
Engle, Hannah V, 168
Engle, Hannah V, 489
Engle, Hannah V, 951
Engle, Hannah Ann V, 52
Engle, Hannah Ann V, 488
Engle, Hannah Ann V, 489
Engle, Hannah Ann V, 537
Engle, Hannah Ann V, 951
Engle, Harmon V, 330
Engle, Harry IV, 199
Engle, Helena P. II, 318
Engle, Herbert II, 309
Engle, Herbert II, 318
Engle, Herbert S. II, 318
Engle, Herbert Stokes II, 860
Engle, Hope V, 838
Engle, Howard II, 309
Engle, Howard II, 318
Engle, Isaac IV, 951
Engle, Isaac V, 51
Engle, Isaac V, 52
Engle, Isaac V, 63
Engle, Isaac V, 838
Engle, Isaac V, 951
Engle, Isaac V, 956
Engle, J. H. V, 560
Engle, Jacob IV, 145
Engle, Jacob V, 838
Engle, James II, 217
Engle, James IV, 145
Engle, James IV, 951
Engle, Jane I, 1055
Engle, Jane IV, 145
Engle, Jane IV, 623

Engle, Jane IV, 643
Engle, Jane IV, 951
Engle, Jane IV, 978
Engle, Jane V, 51
Engle, Jane V, 52
Engle, Jane V, 159
Engle, Jane V, 168
Engle, Jane V, 951
Engle, Jane D. II, 287
Engle, Jane Elizabeth V, 168
Engle, Jesse V, 330
Engle, Jesse B. IV, 390
Engle, Joana IV, 623
Engle, Joana IV, 663
Engle, Joann IV, 623
Engle, Job II, 823
Engle, Job II, 860
Engle, Job IV, 145
Engle, Job IV, 328
Engle, John II, 172
Engle, John II, 217
Engle, John II, 287
Engle, John IV, 145
Engle, John IV, 328
Engle, John IV, 390
Engle, John IV, 391
Engle, John IV, 405
Engle, John IV, 452
Engle, John IV, 1056
Engle, John IV, 1079
Engle, John IV, 1096
Engle, John IV, 1098
Engle, John IV, 1121
Engle, John IV, 1130
Engle, John IV, 1131
Engle, John IV, 1132
Engle, John V, 330
Engle, John V, 838
Engle, John Calvin V, 737
Engle, Joseph II, 287
Engle, Joseph II, 309
Engle, Joseph II, 517
Engle, Joseph IV, 1096
Engle, Joseph W. III, 111
Engle, Joshua IV, 390
Engle, Joshua IV, 446
Engle, Joshua V, 52
Engle, Joshua V, 159
Engle, Joshua V, 168
Engle, Joshua V, 489
Engle, Joshua V, 838
Engle, Joshua V, 945
Engle, Joshua V, 951
Engle, Joshua W. V, 951
Engle, Joshua W. V, 960
Engle, Josiah II, 131
Engle, Josiah IV, 623
Engle, Josiah IV, 868
Engle, Josiah IV, 951
Engle, Josiah L. IV, 1037
Engle, Josiah, Jr. IV, 623
Engle, Leanore IV, 1037
Engle, Lemuel IV, 623
Engle, Lemuel IV, 702
Engle, Levi H. IV, 1130
Engle, Levi H. IV, 1131
Engle, Lewis IV, 951
Engle, Lindley V, 330
Engle, Louisa IV, 951
Engle, Louisa IV, 1130
Engle, Louisa IV, 1131
Engle, Louisa IV, 1132
Engle, Luanna II, 287
Engle, Luanna II, 290
Engle, Lucina IV, 951
Engle, Lucinda V, 838
Engle, Lydia II, 287
Engle, Marg. C. III, 84
Engle, Margaret III, 111
Engle, Margaret V, 560
Engle, Margaret C. III, 111
Engle, Maria IV, 328
Engle, Maria IV, 390
Engle, Maria IV, 391
Engle, Maria IV, 443
Engle, Maria IV, 1096
Engle, Maria IV, 1098
Engle, Mariah IV, 373
Engle, Mariah IV, 390
Engle, Mariah IV, 391
Engle, Mariah IV, 1096
Engle, Marie Madaline V, 560
Engle, Marie Madeline V, 560
Engle, Marion Fenimore III, 84
Engle, Marion Fenimore III, 111
Engle, Marion Fennimore III, 111
Engle, Marsey II, 172
Engle, Marsey II, 211
Engle, Marsey II, 217
Engle, Martha II, 117
Engle, Martha II, 136
Engle, Martha V, 37
Engle, Martha V, 52
Engle, Martha V, 330
Engle, Martha V, 951
Engle, Martha V, 961
Engle, Martha T. II, 283
Engle, Martha T. II, 287
Engle, Mary II, 172
Engle, Mary II, 217
Engle, Mary IV, 139
Engle, Mary IV, 145
Engle, Mary IV, 328
Engle, Mary IV, 390
Engle, Mary IV, 405
Engle, Mary IV, 409
Engle, Mary IV, 623
Engle, Mary IV, 722
Engle, Mary IV, 868
Engle, Mary IV, 951
Engle, Mary IV, 1096
Engle, Mary IV, 1123
Engle, Mary IV, 1131
Engle, Mary IV, 1138
Engle, Mary Ann II, 318
Engle, Mary E. V, 51
Engle, Mary E. V, 63
Engle, Mary E. V, 330
Engle, Mary Elma IV, 702
Engle, Mary Jane IV, 951
Engle, Mary Jane IV, 967
Engle, Mary M. II, 287
Engle, Mary S. IV, 1131
Engle, Mary T. IV, 1131
Engle, Mercy II, 217
Engle, Mercy IV, 145
Engle, Mercy IV, 328
Engle, Mercy IV, 368
Engle, Mercy IV, 373
Engle, Mercy IV, 390
Engle, Mercy IV, 391
Engle, Mercy IV, 409
Engle, Mercy IV, 419
Engle, Mercy IV, 951
Engle, Mercy IV, 1056
Engle, Mercy IV, 1096
Engle, Nathan IV, 623
Engle, Nathan IV, 702
Engle, Nathan IV, 868
Engle, Nathan IV, 873
Engle, Nathan V, 951
Engle, Nathaniel IV, 623
Engle, Obadiah II, 283
Engle, Obadiah II, 287
Engle, Patience II, 211
Engle, Patience II, 217
Engle, Patience II, 283
Engle, Patience II, 287
Engle, Patience IV, 145
Engle, Patience IV, 147
Engle, Patience IV, 390
Engle, Phebe IV, 346
Engle, Phebe IV, 523
Engle, Philena W. IV, 1131
Engle, Rachel IV, 145
Engle, Rachel IV, 147
Engle, Rachel IV, 328
Engle, Rachel IV, 348
Engle, Rachel IV, 390
Engle, Rachel IV, 430
Engle, Rachel IV, 1096
Engle, Rachel IV, 1131
Engle, Rachel V, 808
Engle, Rachel V, 809
Engle, Rachel A. IV, 1037
Engle, Rachel A. IV, 1043
Engle, Rachel Ann IV, 951
Engle, Rachel Ann IV, 1131
Engle, Rachel Ann IV, 1140
Engle, Rebecca IV, 328
Engle, Rebecca IV, 390
Engle, Rebecca IV, 391
Engle, Rebecca IV, 439
Engle, Rebecca IV, 951
Engle, Rebecca IV, 980
Engle, Rebecca IV, 1131
Engle, Rebecca IV, 1137
Engle, Rebecca V, 838
Engle, Rebecca H. III, 362
Engle, Rebecca M. IV, 951
Engle, Rebeccah IV, 145
Engle, Richard IV, 390
Engle, Richard IV, 391
Engle, Richard IV, 951
Engle, Richard IV, 1131
Engle, Richard B. IV, 951
Engle, Robert IV, 623
Engle, Robert IV, 702
Engle, Robert V, 51
Engle, Robert V, 838
Engle, Robert V, 951
Engle, Robert B. II, 287
Engle, Robert F. II, 287
Engle, Ruth V, 327
Engle, Ruth V, 330
Engle, Sabilla IV, 1130
Engle, Samuel II, 287
Engle, Samuel IV, 145
Engle, Samuel IV, 328
Engle, Samuel IV, 1096
Engle, Samuel IV, 1131
Engle, Samuel V, 330
Engle, Samuel V, 838
Engle, Samuel C. II, 217
Engle, Sarah II, 131
Engle, Sarah II, 823
Engle, Sarah II, 860
Engle, Sarah IV, 145
Engle, Sarah IV, 328
Engle, Sarah IV, 390
Engle, Sarah IV, 391
Engle, Sarah IV, 392
Engle, Sarah IV, 928
Engle, Sarah IV, 951
Engle, Sarah IV, 1096
Engle, Sarah IV, 1130
Engle, Sarah V, 52
Engle, Sarah V, 951
Engle, Sarah V, 956
Engle, Sarah A. II, 283
Engle, Sarah A. II, 287
Engle, Sarah A. IV, 390
Engle, Sarah A. IV, 391
Engle, Sarah A. IV, 446
Engle, Sarah Ann V, 951
Engle, Sarah Ann V, 960
Engle, Sarah B. IV, 390
Engle, Sarah B. IV, 1096
Engle, Sarah B. IV, 1121
Engle, Sarah E. IV, 1131
Engle, Sarah E. IV, 1138
Engle, Sarah Elizabeth IV, 1130
Engle, Sarah Jane IV, 927
Engle, Sarah Jane IV, 951
Engle, Sarah M. V, 52
Engle, Sarah M. V, 951
Engle, Stacy V, 330
Engle, Susanna V, 838
Engle, Susannah V, 838
Engle, Tily B. II, 318
Engle, Tylee B. II, 309
Engle, Tylee B. II, 318
Engle, Tylee B., Jr. II, 318
Engle, Tylee W. II, 318
Engle, Tylee W. II, 325
Engle, Walter V, 330
Engle, Warren V, 51
Engle, Wd Phebe IV, 328
Engle, William IV, 1130
Engle, William V, 838
Engle, William Clothier III, 111
Engle, Zimri IV, 610
Engle, Zimri IV, 623
Engle, Zimri IV, 951
Engle, Zimri, Jr. IV, 951
Engleby, Blaxton II, 443
Engleby, Elizabeth II, 443
Engledue, Blaxton II, 359
Engledue, Elizabeth II, 359
Engleright, Amelia V, 994
Engleright, Chas. V, 994
English, Abigail I, 853
English, Abigail I, 877
English, Abigail I, 885
English, Abigail II, 173
English, Abigail II, 218
English, Abigail C. I, 853
English, Abraham Hulings II, 217
English, Achsah II, 173
English, Achsah II, 218
English, Achsah II, 229
English, Adaliza I, 874
English, Adaliza I, 877
English, Addison I, 878
English, Adliza E. I, 853
English, Albert J. I, 852
English, Allen L. I, 852
English, Amy II, 173
English, Amy II, 218
English, Amy II, 271
English, Amy II, 474
English, Amy II, 517
English, Ann II, 173
English, Ann II, 217
English, Ann II, 218
English, Ann II, 990
English, Ann II, 995
English, Ann VI, 912
English, Armissa A. I, 809
English, Asenith A. I, 878
English, Betsey VI, 912
English, Caroline II, 860
English, Caroline II, 933
English, Charles VI, 912
English, Clara I, 924
English, Clara I, 940
English, Clara B. I, 940
English, Clen I, 877
English, Clen I, 883
English, Edith IV, 951
English, Edna I, 919
English, Edward I, 1029
English, Elen I, 877
English, Elen I, 883
English, Elisabeth II, 218
English, Elisabeth II, 219
English, Elisha II, 218
English, Elisha N. II, 218
English, Elisha N. II, 517
English, Eliza I, 852
English, Eliza I, 878
English, Eliza I, 893
English, Eliza II, 218
English, Elizabeth II, 173
English, Elizabeth II, 202
English, Elizabeth II, 217
English, Elizabeth II, 218
English, Elizabeth II, 229
English, Elizabeth VI, 912
English, Elizabeth B. II, 860
English, Elizabeth B. II, 933
English, Ellen I, 921
English, Emily I, 624
English, Emily I, 628
English, Emily E. I, 878
English, Emily E. I, 905
English, Emily Ellen I, 852
English, Enoch E. I, 852
English, Enos I, 903
English, Frances M. I, 853
English, George L. VI, 912
English, Hannah II, 132
English, Hannah II, 218
English, Hannah II, 252
English, Henry VI, 912
English, Hester II, 217
English, Isaac II, 173
English, Isaac II, 218
English, Isaac II, 990
English, Isaac II, 995
English, Israel II, 218
English, J. Roland I, 853
English, James II, 173
English, James II, 218
English, James VI, 912
English, James VI, 986
English, Jane VI, 912
English, Jane VI, 955
English, Jesse IV, 951
English, John I, 809
English, John I, 852
English, John I, 877
English, John I, 885
English, John I, 1029
English, John II, 173
English, John II, 218
English, John II, 739
English, John III, 111
English, John VI, 912
English, John B. I, 852
English, John B. I, 878
English, John Barton I, 853
English, John Barton I, 878
English, John E. II, 860
English, John E. II, 933
English, John W. VI, 885
English, John, Jr. I, 877
English, Joseph II, 173
English, Joseph II, 202
English, Joseph II, 217
English, Joseph II, 218
English, Joseph II, 224
English, Joseph IV, 951
English, Joseph H. IV, 951
English, Joseph, Jr. II, 218
English, Joshua I, 1029
English, Landonia C. VI, 885
English, Leah II, 739
English, Lindsey I, 852
English, Lou A. I, 853
English, Lucy VI, 882
English, Lucy VI, 912
English, Lurton I, 921
English, M. J. I, 853
English, Madison I, 852
English, Margaret I, 852
English, Margaret I, 877
English, Margaret I, 881
English, Margaret C. I, 853
English, Mariam I, 852
English, Martha I, 878
English, Martha I, 898
English, Martha I, 906
English, Martha I, 925
English, Martha I, 929
English, Martha I, 932
English, Martha VI, 912
English, Martha D. I, 621
English, Martha D. I, 852
English, Mary I, 809
English, Mary I, 834
English, Mary I, 869
English, Mary I, 878
English, Mary I, 1029
English, Mary II, 218
English, Mary II, 224
English, Mary A. I, 852
English, Mary A. I, 919
English, Mary Ann I, 852
English, Mary Ann I, 877
English, Mary Ann I, 903
English, Mary E. IV, 951
English, Mary H. IV, 951
English, Mary Kelly I, 1029
English, Melissa I, 852
English, Mercy II, 218
English, Mildred I, 617
English, Mildred R. I, 853
English, Mildred R. I, 877
English, Mildred R. I, 903
English, Mildred Ruth I, 853
English, Miriam I, 852
English, Miriam I, 877
English, Nereus C. I, 853
English, Parmenas VI, 912
English, Patsy VI, 912
English, Penninah I, 940
English, Penninah I, 941
English, Permenus VI, 912
English, Priscilla I, 852
English, Priscilla I, 877
English, Priscilla I, 878
English, Priscilla I, 898
English, Rachel I, 852
English, Rachel I, 865
English, Rachel I, 876
English, Rachel I, 877
English, Rachel I, 878
English, Rachel I, 903
English, Rebecca II, 173
English, Rebecca II, 218
English, Rebecca II, 221
English, Rebecca II, 359
English, Rebecca II, 990
English, Rebecca II, 995
English, Rebecca, Jr. II, 218
English, Rebeccah VI, 386
English, Rebeckah II, 173
English, Retta I, 617
English, Robert I, 852
English, Robert I, 877
English, Robert L. I, 878
English, Robert Lee V, 994
English, Robert Lorenzo I, 852
English, Robert S. I, 853
English, Rodema I, 878
English, Ruth I, 852
English, Ruth I, 877
English, Ruth I, 885
English, Sally VI, 912
English, Sally Ann VI, 967
English, Samira I, 809
English, Samira I, 844
English, Samira I, 921
English, Samira I, 928
English, Samuel I, 878
English, Samuel II, 173
English, Samuel II, 217
English, Samuel II, 218
English, Samuel II, 224
English, Samuel II, 517
English, Samuel II, 860
English, Samuel Ellis II, 218
English, Samuel Lee I, 853
English, Samuel R. I, 852
English, Samuel, Jr. II, 218
English, Samuel, Jr. II, 517
English, Sarah II, 217
English, Sarah II, 218
English, Sarah VI, 912
English, Sarah Ann I, 853
English, Sarah Ann I, 871
English, Sarah Ann I, 878
English, Semira I, 929
English, Stephen VI, 912
English, Stephen VI, 967
English, Susannah II, 217
English, Thomas I, 617
English, Thomas I, 852
English, Thomas I, 853
English, Thomas I, 877
English, Thomas I, 1029
English, Thomas II, 173
English, Thomas II, 217

English, Thomas II, 218
English, Thomas Madison I, 852
English, Thomasin II, 218
English, Thomasine II, 173
English, Triphene II, 173
English, Tryphena II, 218
English, Tryphenia II, 218
English, W. A. V, 620
English, Wd. Mercy II, 173
English, William I, 852
English, William I, 853
English, William I, 877
English, William II, 218
English, William III, 111
English, William VI, 885
English, William Allen I, 852
English, William L. I, 878
English, William Luter I, 852
English, William Wilson II, 173
English, Wm. S. II, 132
English, Zebulon I, 852
English, Zebulon I, 877
English, Zebulon A. I, 853
Engram, Mary II, 216
Engram, Mary II, 218
Engs, Philip III, 111
Enis, Mary Elizabeth V, 52
Enix, Abigail II, 218
Enix, Anna II, 218
Enix, Martha II, 218
Enix, Meriam II, 218
Enix, Thomas II, 218
Enke, Rachel IV, 929
Enke, Rachel IV, 951
Enke, Rachel IV, 1024
Enke, Rachel IV, 1025
Enloes, Huldah IV, 814
Enloes, Samuel IV, 814
Enloes, William S. IV, 814
Enloss, Isabel V, 52
Enlow, Emily IV, 84
Enlow, James IV, 84
Enlow, Luke IV, 84
Enlow, Oman IV, 84
Enlow, Ruth IV, 84
Enlow, Susanna IV, 84
Enlows, Emily IV, 125
Enlows, Huldah IV, 814
Enlows, Huldah IV, 853
Enlows, Huldah IV, 858
Enlows, James IV, 31
Enlows, James IV, 42
Enlows, James IV, 84
Enlows, James IV, 92
Enlows, James IV, 125
Enlows, John IV, 31
Enlows, John IV, 125
Enlows, Luke IV, 31
Enlows, Mary H. IV, 27
Enlows, Mary H. IV, 31
Enlows, Oliver Cope IV, 31
Enlows, Ruth IV, 92
Enlows, Ruth IV, 125
Enlows, Samuel IV, 814
Enlows, Samuel IV, 853
Enlows, Samuel IV, 858
Enlows, Sarah IV, 31
Enlows, Sarah IV, 42
Enlows, Susan IV, 814
Enlows, Susan IV, 853
Enlows, Susanna IV, 31
Enlows, Susannah IV, 125
Enlows, Thomas IV, 951
Enlows, William S. IV, 814
Enlows, Wm. IV, 858
Ennes, Clara V, 994
Ennes, John VI, 814
Ennes, Milly VI, 814
Ennis, Benjamin II, 359
Ennis, Cassandra II, 359
Ennis, Chas. V, 168
Ennis, Clara V, 168
Ennis, Clara V, 994
Ennis, Clifford V, 737
Ennis, Della May V, 168
Ennis, Dessie V, 671
Ennis, Driffy V, 168
Ennis, Duff V, 168
Ennis, Fam IV, 1314
Ennis, Forest V, 737
Ennis, Forrest Clifford IV, 1314
Ennis, Frances M. V, 737
Ennis, Frank IV, 1314
Ennis, Frank V, 737
Ennis, Geo V, 745
Ennis, Hannah V, 168
Ennis, Harriet V, 168
Ennis, Hattie N. V, 168
Ennis, James II, 359
Ennis, James II, 517
Ennis, James II, 682
Ennis, John VI, 814
Ennis, Josephine IV, 1314
Ennis, Josephine V, 737
Ennis, Lemuel V, 168
Ennis, Leota IV, 1314
Ennis, Leota V, 737
Ennis, Lydia II, 453
Ennis, Lydia II, 483
Ennis, Lydia II, 517
Ennis, Malord V, 994
Ennis, Mamie V, 994
Ennis, Margaret H. VI, 801
Ennis, Mary V, 168
Ennis, Mary V, 671
Ennis, Mary V, 994
Ennis, Mary E. V, 52
Ennis, Mary E. V, 95
Ennis, Mary Elizabeth V, 52
Ennis, Mary Elizabeth V, 745
Ennis, Mordecai V, 52
Ennis, Mordecai E. V, 52
Ennis, Myrtle V, 168
Ennis, Myrtle V, 671
Ennis, Nonna M. V, 994
Ennis, Paulina VI, 814
Ennis, Perry V, 168
Ennis, Queena V, 168
Ennis, Sarah II, 359
Ennis, Sarah II, 517
Ennis, Sarah II, 682
Ennis, Sarah E. V, 745
Ennis, T. J. V, 168
Ennis, Thomas V, 168
Ennis, Thomas J. V, 168
Ennis, Thompson V, 168
Ennis, W. M. V, 168
Ennis, William V, 168
Enns, Frances Jane VI, 983
Enns, John VI, 983
Enny, Diggery II, 443
Enny, Mary II, 443
Enny, Richard II, 443
Enoch, ??? II, 443
Enoch, Abigail II, 173
Enoch, Abigail II, 218
Enoch, Ann II, 218
Enoch, Anne II, 173
Enoch, David II, 359
Enoch, David II, 443
Enoch, Elizabeth II, 218
Enoch, Elizabeth II, 517
Enoch, Hannah II, 173
Enoch, Hannah II, 218
Enoch, Hope II, 173
Enoch, James L. II, 739
Enoch, Maggie V, 237
Enoch, Martha II, 173
Enoch, Martha II, 218
Enoch, Mary II, 173
Enoch, Mary II, 218
Enoch, Mary II, 359
Enoch, Melissa Jane V, 868
Enoch, Miriam II, 173
Enoch, Miriam II, 218
Enoch, Miriam II, 517
Enoch, Thomas II, 173
Enoch, Thomas II, 218
Enochs, Elizabeth II, 117
Enochs, Maggie V, 237
Enochs, Thomas II, 117
Enocks, Abigail II, 218
Enocks, Elizabeth II, 117
Enocks, Elizabeth II, 125
Enocks, Mary II, 218
Enocks, Miriam II, 218
Enocks, Miriam II, 220
Enocks, Thomas II, 218
Enos, Dorothy II, 218
Enos, Dorothy II, 230
Enos, Mary IV, 85
Enos, Robert IV, 84
Enos, Susannah II, 506
Enos, Susannah II, 517
Ensey, John V, 52
Ensign, Charles E. I, 1151
Ensly, Susannah V, 738
Ent, Clara V, 671
Ent, Emma V, 671
Ent, Emma J. V, 620
Ent, Margaret V, 671
Ent, Maria Estella V, 671
Ent, Mary V, 555
Ent, Milton L. V, 671
Entriken, Ellen B. II, 798
Entriken, Hannah M. II, 860
Entriken, Hannah M. II, 905
Entrikin, Emmor IV, 814
Entrikin, Franklin Wayne IV, 814
Entrikin, James Bennett IV, 814
Entrikin, Susanna IV, 814
Eperson, Edith V, 298
Eperson, Edith V, 302
Epison, Edith V, 302
Eppelsheimer, Frederick II, 852
Eppelsheimer, Mary L. II, 852
Eppendorff, Geo. A. W. III, 111
Eppendorff, Juliana III, 111
Eppendorff, Max III, 111
Eppendorff, Max III, 173
Eppendorff, Sarah III, 111
Eppendorff, Sarah R. III, 111
Eppendorff, Sarah R. III, 173
Epperson, Anney VI, 863
Epperson, Boley VI, 817
Epperson, Eliza Walker VI, 815
Epperson, Elizabeth VI, 815
Epperson, Elizabeth VI, 855
Epperson, Elizabeth E. VI, 815
Epperson, Jane B. VI, 815
Epperson, John VI, 815
Epperson, Joseph VI, 795
Epperson, Joseph VI, 815
Epperson, Joseph C. VI, 833
Epperson, Joseph C. P. VI, 815
Epperson, Lillie B. VI, 795
Epperson, Littleberry VI, 815
Epperson, Littleberry VI, 850
Epperson, Littleberry VI, 855
Epperson, Lucy VI, 827
Epperson, Martha A. VI, 817
Epperson, Martha V. VI, 815
Epperson, Mary VI, 815
Epperson, Nancy VI, 795
Epperson, Nancy VI, 879
Epperson, Nancy P. VI, 815
Epperson, Phebe VI, 850
Epperson, Polly VI, 815
Epperson, Polly VI, 848
Epperson, Rebeckah VI, 815
Epperson, Richard VI, 815
Epperson, Richard VI, 850
Epperson, Richard VI, 855
Epperson, Rosanna VI, 850
Epperson, Samuel VI, 815
Epperson, Susanna VI, 815
Epperson, William VI, 815
Epperson, William VI, 827
Epperson, William VI, 848
Epplesheimer, Frederick II, 860
Epplesheimer, Mary L. II, 860
Epps, Dolly V, 994
Epps, Hartwell VI, 815
Epps, Hartwell VI, 912
Epps, Mary C. VI, 815
Epps, Polly C. VI, 912
Epps, Rena I, 336
Epps, Robert VI, 834
Erbe, Dorothea Anna Nathalia VI, 631
Erbe, Dorothea Anna Nathalia VI, 636
Erbe, Henry VI, 636
Erbe, Vernon VI, 636
Erdman, Elizabeth C. II, 704
Erdman, Elizabeth C. II, 739
Erdman, Oscar M. II, 704
Erey, Richard II, 443
Erickson, Augusta III, 426
Erickson, Augusta III, 461
Erickson, Julia IV, 951
Eriom, James II, 359
Erlenwein, Howard IV, 1250
Erls, Sary I, 138
Ernest, Esq. Henry I, 1083
Ernest, Kate Elliott V, 671
Erns, Bartelemy IV, 199
Erns, Marie IV, 199
Erns, Mrs. ??? IV, 199
Ernshaw, Ann IV, 470
Ernshaw, George IV, 470
Ernshaw, Hannah IV, 470
Erott, Francis II, 517
Eroyd, Sarah M. IV, 199
Erp, George V, 168
Erskine, Addie V, 456
Erskine, Clarence V, 456
Erskine, Ethel V, 456
Erskine, Ethel Eulania V, 237
Erskine, Geo. W. IV, 1314
Erskine, Heressi V, 456
Erskine, Irene V, 456
Erskine, Jacob H. V, 237
Erskine, Joseph V, 456
Erskine, Lucile V, 456
Erskine, Maud V, 456
Erskine, Olive D. V, 226
Erskine, Olive D. V, 237
Erskine, Olive D. V, 456
Erskine, Phebe V, 456
Erskine, Rachel IV, 173
Erskine, Rachel IV, 199
Erskine, Robert V, 456
Erskine, Sarah V, 456
Erskine, Viola V, 456
Erskine, Wm. V, 456
Ertel, Jack V, 671
Erton, Mary V, 994
Erven, Willie S. V, 738
Ervin, Catherine V, 781
Ervin, Catherine V, 793
Ervin, Jane VI, 315
Ervin, John I, 539
Ervin, Magdalene VI, 315
Ervin, Mary VI, 315
Ervin, Susannah VI, 315
Ervine, Mary Virginia IV, 470
Erving, Mary E. V, 456
Erwin, ??? VI, 348
Erwin, Alfred Glen IV, 951
Erwin, Alfred Glen IV, 952
Erwin, Alice II, 517
Erwin, Alice II, 566
Erwin, Betsy VI, 1003
Erwin, Celicia IV, 623
Erwin, David II, 359
Erwin, Elisha IV, 623
Erwin, Elizabeth IV, 616
Erwin, Elizabeth IV, 623
Erwin, Elizabeth IV, 626
Erwin, Elma IV, 623
Erwin, Grace Irene V, 835
Erwin, Grace Irene V, 838
Erwin, Hannah IV, 623
Erwin, Hannah Ann IV, 623
Erwin, James II, 359
Erwin, James IV, 31
Erwin, James IV, 623
Erwin, James IV, 625
Erwin, James IV, 667
Erwin, James VI, 315
Erwin, James VI, 351
Erwin, James VI, 353
Erwin, James VI, 489
Erwin, Jane II, 517
Erwin, Jane II, 547
Erwin, Jane VI, 351
Erwin, Jane VI, 353
Erwin, Jane VI, 489
Erwin, Jane VI, 975
Erwin, Jesse IV, 623
Erwin, John II, 218
Erwin, John II, 359
Erwin, John II, 517
Erwin, John IV, 31
Erwin, John IV, 623
Erwin, John VI, 351
Erwin, Jonas VI, 907
Erwin, Jonas VI, 975
Erwin, Jonas VI, 1003
Erwin, Joseph VI, 982
Erwin, Joseph VI, 986
Erwin, Lawrence Francis IV, 951
Erwin, Lawrence Francis IV, 952
Erwin, Lester IV, 951
Erwin, Lydia Ann IV, 623
Erwin, Lydia Ann IV, 654
Erwin, Magdalen VI, 489
Erwin, Magdalen VI, 939
Erwin, Magdalene VI, 315
Erwin, Mahlon IV, 31
Erwin, Mahlon IV, 616
Erwin, Mahlon IV, 623
Erwin, Mahlon IV, 702
Erwin, Mahlon VI, 351
Erwin, Margaret IV, 623
Erwin, Marie IV, 951
Erwin, Marie IV, 952
Erwin, Mary II, 359
Erwin, Mary II, 517
Erwin, Mary IV, 31
Erwin, Mary IV, 623
Erwin, Mary IV, 646
Erwin, Mary VI, 315
Erwin, Mary VI, 351
Erwin, Mary VI, 489
Erwin, Mary Ann IV, 623
Erwin, Mary Elizabeth IV, 951
Erwin, Miriam VI, 982
Erwin, Rachel S. II, 793
Erwin, Rachel S. II, 860
Erwin, Reuben IV, 623
Erwin, Samuel IV, 31
Erwin, Samuel IV, 605
Erwin, Samuel IV, 623
Erwin, Samuel IV, 626
Erwin, Samuel IV, 646
Erwin, Samuel VI, 314
Erwin, Samuel VI, 315
Erwin, Samuel VI, 351
Erwin, Samuel VI, 489
Erwin, Samuel, Jr. IV, 623
Erwin, Sarah IV, 31
Erwin, Sarah IV, 605
Erwin, Sarah IV, 623
Erwin, Sarah IV, 626
Erwin, Sarah IV, 646
Erwin, Sarah VI, 314
Erwin, Sarah VI, 315
Erwin, Sarah VI, 351
Erwin, Sarah H. IV, 623
Erwin, Susanna VI, 351
Erwin, Susannah IV, 31
Erwin, Susannah IV, 623
Erwin, Susannah VI, 489
Erwin, Susannah, Jr. IV, 623
Erwin, Wd. Mary II, 359
Erwin, William IV, 31
Erwin, William IV, 623
Erwin, William VI, 351
Erwin, Wm. IV, 623
Erwine, Dorcas III, 111
Erwine, Dorcas III, 194
Erwine, Irwin VI, 515
Erwine, James VI, 515
Erwine, Jane VI, 489
Erwine, Magdalane VI, 515
Erwine, Mary VI, 515
Erwine, Susannah VI, 515
Erwyn, Jane II, 511
Erwyn, Jane II, 517
Esborn, John II, 359
Esburne, Robert II, 517
Eschwege, Bessie III, 111
Eschwege, Herman III, 111
Eschwege, Nina III, 111
Escolme, Edward IV, 1314
Eselick, Elnorah IV, 199
Eshner, Jerome IV, 1314
Eshner, Jerome Earle IV, 1314
Esly, Clarissa V, 994
Esly, Wm. V, 994
Esmond, Eseias III, 111
Esmond, Ethelwynne III, 111
Esmond, Frederick E. III, 111
Esmond, Frederick E. III, 239
Esmond, Jacob III, 111
Esmond, John III, 111
Esmond, Joseph III, 111
Esmond, Lulu III, 111
Esmond, Lulu III, 239
Esmond, Rhoda III, 111
Espy, Sarah I, 388
Essex, Elisabeth II, 638
Essex, Elizabeth II, 517
Essly, Clarissa V, 994
Estabrook, ??? III, 111
Estabrook, Alfred III, 111
Estabrook, Jane IV, 702
Estabrook, Jane IV, 792
Estabrook, John III, 111
Estabrook, Mary Elsie III, 111
Estabrook, Richard III, 111
Estabrook, Thomas III, 111
Estacke, Margrett II, 359
Estaugh, Hannah II, 517
Estaugh, Hannah II, 595
Estaugh, James II, 359
Estaugh, James II, 517
Estaugh, James II, 577
Estaugh, James II, 595
Estaugh, John II, 359
Estaugh, John II, 517
Estaugh, Mary II, 517
Estaugh, Mary II, 577
Estaw, Elizabeth II, 359
Estaw, Hannah II, 359
Estaw, James II, 359
Estaw, John II, 359
Estaw, Mary II, 359
Estell, Meribah V, 237
Estell, Rebecca IV, 699
Estell, Rebecca IV, 702
Estell, William V, 237
Estep, Charles S. V, 168
Estep, Dr. C. E. V, 168
Estep, Dr. Chas. S. V, 168
Estep, Fern V, 168
Estep, Jane IV, 903
Estep, Jane IV, 904
Estep, Jessie V, 168
Esterbrook, ??? III, 111
Esterbrook, Alfred III, 111
Esterbrook, John III, 111
Esterbrook, Mary Elsie III, 111
Esterbrook, Richard III, 111
Esterbrook, Thomas III, 111
Estes, Anna J. Hoag V, 671
Estes, Benj. VI, 937
Estes, Benjamin VI, 912
Estes, Benjamin VI, 913
Estes, Benjamin VI, 942
Estes, Benjamin VI, 967
Estes, Benjamin VI, 970
Estes, Benjamin VI, 987

Estes, Catharine VI, 912
Estes, Edward VI, 908
Estes, Edward VI, 912
Estes, Edward VI, 970
Estes, Edward VI, 1017
Estes, Elizabeth VI, 937
Estes, Elsie VI, 729
Estes, Huldah C. V, 671
Estes, Huldah H. V, 671
Estes, Jane VI, 1017
Estes, Jesse VI, 973
Estes, Joel VI, 918
Estes, Joel VI, 937
Estes, John T. VI, 987
Estes, Kisiah VI, 977
Estes, Lewis A. V, 671
Estes, Lewis A. V, 683
Estes, Lewis H. V, 671
Estes, Lucy VI, 987
Estes, Ludovic V, 671
Estes, Ludovica V, 671
Estes, Martha VI, 967
Estes, Nancy VI, 913
Estes, Peggy VI, 912
Estes, Sarah Ann VI, 970
Estes, Thomas Rowland V, 671
Estey, Abigail II, 517
Estey, Abigail II, 671
Estey, Eunice II, 517
Estey, Eunice II, 671
Estey, Moses II, 517
Estey, Moses II, 671
Esther, Esther Louise III, 293
Esther, Hester V, 840
Esther, Mary VI, 815
Esther, Matthew VI, 815
Esthill, Jonathan II, 517
Esthill, Thomas II, 517
Estis, Abigail II, 517
Estlack, Esther C. II, 758
Estlack, George II, 758
Estlack, Hezekiah II, 758
Estlack, Israel II, 793
Estlack, Israel II, 810
Estlack, Louise II, 810
Estlack, Margaret II, 216
Estlack, Margaret II, 758
Estlack, Thomas II, 287
Estlack, Wd. Louisa II, 793
Estlack, Wd. Mary White II, 810
Estle, James V, 456
Estle, Meriba V, 456
Estle, Rebecca V, 456
Estle, William V, 456
Etherton, Eliza IV, 523
Etherton, Eliza IV, 542
Ethridge, Blanch IV, 1314
Etris, Catharine II, 793
Etris, Catharine II, 795
Etzrodt, Anna IV, 935
Etzrodt, Anna IV, 952
Eubank, Achilles VI, 912
Eubank, Alley I, 269
Eubank, Ambros VI, 1021
Eubank, Ambrose VI, 912
Eubank, Ambrose VI, 931
Eubank, Ambrose VI, 935
Eubank, Anna VI, 1016
Eubank, Chas. T. V, 671
Eubank, Daniel I, 269
Eubank, Elias M. VI, 912
Eubank, Elijah I, 269
Eubank, Eliza VI, 914
Eubank, Elizabeth Jane VI, 912
Eubank, Hezekiah VI, 912
Eubank, John VI, 891
Eubank, John VI, 912
Eubank, John VI, 914
Eubank, John VI, 943
Eubank, John VI, 979
Eubank, John VI, 1003
Eubank, John M. VI, 883
Eubank, John M. VI, 887
Eubank, Joseph VI, 912
Eubank, Joseph VI, 914
Eubank, Joseph VI, 921
Eubank, Judith H. VI, 912
Eubank, Leonard S. VI, 912
Eubank, Lucy VI, 891
Eubank, Mary VI, 912
Eubank, Mary F. VI, 943
Eubank, Nancy VI, 912
Eubank, Patsy I. VI, 912
Eubank, Penelope E. VI, 871
Eubank, Polly VI, 912
Eubank, Polly VI, 979
Eubank, Polly VI, 1021
Eubank, Sally VI, 931
Eubank, Sarah VI, 912
Eubank, Sarah B. VI, 912
Eubank, Sarah M. VI, 1011
Eubank, Susan S. VI, 914
Eubank, Thomas VI, 912
Eubank, Thomas VI, 1016
Eubank, William VI, 871
Eubank, William VI, 891
Eubank, William VI, 912
Eubank, William VI, 979
Eubank, William VI, 1011
Eubanks, Alley I, 269
Eubanks, Ambrose VI, 899
Eubanks, Ambrose VI, 946
Eubanks, Jenny VI, 946
Eubanks, Nancy VI, 899
Euins, Saphire I, 36
Euins, Saphire I, 48
Euless, Sarah V, 781
Euphemia, Elizabeth V, 917
Eustace, Aaron II, 517
Eustis, Amelia V, 904
Eustis, Geo. Dexter V, 904
Eustis, Geo. Dexter V, 940
Eustis, Helen Lawson V, 904
Eustis, Helen Lawson V, 940
Eustis, Nancy V, 904
Evaleth, Mary III, 111
Evan, John II, 218
Evan, Owen II, 360
Evan, Sampson VI, 811
Evan, Smith IV, 679
Evan, Thomas II, 443
Evangeline, Garabell IV, 1253
Evans, ??? II, 360
Evans, ??? III, 36
Evans, ??? III, 112
Evans, ??? V, 385
Evans, ??? V, 443
Evans, ??? V, 823
Evans, Aaron II, 27
Evans, Aaron II, 68
Evans, Aaron II, 69
Evans, Aaron II, 102
Evans, Aaron V, 53
Evans, Aaron V, 738
Evans, Aaron V, 781
Evans, Abel V, 53
Evans, Abigail I, 193
Evans, Abigail I, 539
Evans, Abigail I, 1016
Evans, Abigail II, 454
Evans, Abigail II, 518
Evans, Abigail II, 519
Evans, Abigail II, 723
Evans, Abigail III, 111
Evans, Abigail III, 276
Evans, Abigail K. I, 878
Evans, Abigail K. I, 1016
Evans, Abigail R. V, 904
Evans, Abraham II, 287
Evans, Abraham II, 519
Evans, Abraham II, 542
Evans, Achsah I, 192
Evans, Achsah I, 539
Evans, Achsah I, 809
Evans, Albert I, 9
Evans, Albert I, 49
Evans, Alice I, 238
Evans, Alice II, 360
Evans, Alice II, 519
Evans, Alice II, 520
Evans, Alice II, 704
Evans, Alice II, 739
Evans, Alice II, 785
Evans, Alice II, 793
Evans, Alice II, 860
Evans, Alice III, 57
Evans, Alice III, 111
Evans, Alice III, 112
Evans, Alice C. II, 287
Evans, Alice C. II, 288
Evans, Alice Carter II, 739
Evans, Alva V, 456
Evans, Amanda IV, 471
Evans, Amanda IV, 486
Evans, Amelia II, 173
Evans, Amelia II, 218
Evans, Amelia II, 219
Evans, Amelia II, 519
Evans, Amirah Haines V, 969
Evans, Amos II, 287
Evans, Amos II, 359
Evans, Amos IV, 199
Evans, Amos IV, 471
Evans, Amos IV, 1056
Evans, Amos V, 238
Evans, Amos H. IV, 145
Evans, Amos H. IV, 1056
Evans, Amos Hutton IV, 145
Evans, Amos Hutton IV, 328
Evans, Amos Hutton IV, 470
Evans, Amos Hutton IV, 471
Evans, Amos Hutton IV, 523
Evans, Amy II, 68
Evans, Amy II, 69
Evans, Amy II, 518
Evans, Amy II, 739
Evans, Amy III, 95
Evans, Amy III, 111
Evans, Amy VI, 684
Evans, Amyrah V, 53
Evans, Amyrah V, 64
Evans, Angeline Elizabeth VI, 1021
Evans, Ann I, 1019
Evans, Ann I, 1029
Evans, Ann II, 27
Evans, Ann II, 68
Evans, Ann II, 69
Evans, Ann II, 219
Evans, Ann II, 359
Evans, Ann II, 443
Evans, Ann II, 518
Evans, Ann II, 519
Evans, Ann II, 520
Evans, Ann II, 793
Evans, Ann III, 107
Evans, Ann III, 111
Evans, Ann V, 52
Evans, Ann V, 55
Evans, Ann V, 90
Evans, Ann V, 790
Evans, Ann VI, 810
Evans, Ann C. V, 53
Evans, Ann C. V, 106
Evans, Ann C. V, 904
Evans, Ann P. IV, 200
Evans, Ann S. V, 53
Evans, Anna I, 9
Evans, Anna I, 193
Evans, Anna II, 117
Evans, Anna II, 518
Evans, Anna II, 519
Evans, Anna II, 520
Evans, Anna II, 606
Evans, Anna IV, 199
Evans, Anna IV, 1158
Evans, Anna IV, 1250
Evans, Anna V, 671
Evans, Anna V, 994
Evans, Anna Clare IV, 199
Evans, Anna D. IV, 296
Evans, Anna J. IV, 199
Evans, Anna L. V, 969
Evans, Anna R. II, 739
Evans, Anna R. II, 767
Evans, Anna Rhoads II, 738
Evans, Anna Rhoads II, 739
Evans, Anna S. IV, 199
Evans, Anna S. V, 26
Evans, Anna S. V, 53
Evans, Anne II, 219
Evans, Anne II, 359
Evans, Anne II, 518
Evans, Anne II, 519
Evans, Anne II, 739
Evans, Anne S. V, 967
Evans, Anne S. V, 969
Evans, Annie II, 793
Evans, Annie E. III, 111
Evans, Annie E. III, 134
Evans, Annie L. VI, 670
Evans, Anthony VI, 815
Evans, Anthony VI, 880
Evans, Anthony VI, 912
Evans, Anthony VI, 1021
Evans, Anthony, Jr. VI, 905
Evans, Anthony, Jr. VI, 912
Evans, Arthur IV, 199
Evans, Arthur IV, 296
Evans, Arthur V, 671
Evans, Asa V, 53
Evans, Asher IV, 31
Evans, Asher IV, 145
Evans, Asher IV, 199
Evans, Asher IV, 328
Evans, Asher IV, 470
Evans, Asher IV, 471
Evans, Asher IV, 523
Evans, Asher IV, 1056
Evans, Asher P. IV, 145
Evans, Asher P. IV, 1056
Evans, Asher Parker IV, 145
Evans, Asher Parker IV, 523
Evans, Austin IV, 199
Evans, Axcy I, 183
Evans, Barbra II, 499
Evans, Barbra II, 518
Evans, Barbra II, 519
Evans, Benj. V, 904
Evans, Benjamin I, 192
Evans, Benjamin I, 193
Evans, Benjamin I, 202
Evans, Benjamin I, 1029
Evans, Benjamin II, 69
Evans, Benjamin II, 359
Evans, Benjamin IV, 199
Evans, Benjamin IV, 470
Evans, Benjamin V, 41
Evans, Benjamin V, 52
Evans, Benjamin V, 53
Evans, Benjamin V, 109
Evans, Benjamin V, 904
Evans, Benjamin V, 969
Evans, Benjamin F. V, 904
Evans, Benjamin, Sr. V, 52
Evans, Benoni IV, 31
Evans, Benoni IV, 145
Evans, Benoni IV, 328
Evans, Benoni IV, 523
Evans, Bertha Phebe II, 793
Evans, Bertha Phebe II, 861
Evans, Bessie V, 560
Evans, Bettie H. I, 539
Evans, Beulah II, 1056
Evans, Beulah V, 53
Evans, Beulah V, 116
Evans, Beulah T. II, 965
Evans, Bridget VI, 801
Evans, Cadwalader II, 518
Evans, Cadwalader II, 519
Evans, Cadwalader IV, 145
Evans, Cadwalader IV, 328
Evans, Cadwalader IV, 471
Evans, Cadwalader IV, 523
Evans, Cadwalader, Jr. II, 518
Evans, Cadwallader II, 359
Evans, Cadwallader II, 360
Evans, Cadwallader II, 518
Evans, Cadwallader II, 519
Evans, Cadwallader II, 520
Evans, Cadwallader II, 551
Evans, Cadwallader II, 611
Evans, Cadwallader IV, 31
Evans, Cadwallader IV, 137
Evans, Caleb II, 359
Evans, Caleb II, 360
Evans, Caleb II, 518
Evans, Caleb G. II, 287
Evans, Caleb G. II, 739
Evans, Caleb G. III, 111
Evans, Caleb G. III, 112
Evans, Caleb J. V, 904
Evans, Carey V, 238
Evans, Carlton VI, 803
Evans, Caroline V, 54
Evans, Caroline E. V, 28
Evans, Caroline E. V, 52
Evans, Caron I, 539
Evans, Caron Happock I, 1016
Evans, Cary V, 238
Evans, Cassandra IV, 199
Evans, Catharine I, 673
Evans, Catharine I, 678
Evans, Catharine II, 117
Evans, Catharine II, 126
Evans, Catharine II, 359
Evans, Catharine II, 519
Evans, Catharine II, 551
Evans, Catharine II, 739
Evans, Catharine II, 769
Evans, Catharine VI, 386
Evans, Catharine VI, 636
Evans, Catharine VI, 716
Evans, Catharine VI, 801
Evans, Catharine VI, 885
Evans, Catherine II, 518
Evans, Catherine II, 739
Evans, Catherine V, 238
Evans, Catherine VI, 386
Evans, Catherine W. II, 739
Evans, Catherine W. II, 769
Evans, Celia I, 238
Evans, Celia E. I, 49
Evans, Celia E. I, 238
Evans, Chalkley I, 193
Evans, Charity V, 781
Evans, Charles I, 193
Evans, Charles II, 309
Evans, Charles II, 519
Evans, Charles II, 520
Evans, Charles II, 704
Evans, Charles II, 739
Evans, Charles II, 793
Evans, Charles II, 860
Evans, Charles V, 53
Evans, Charles V, 456
Evans, Charles M. II, 793
Evans, Charles M. II, 861
Evans, Chas. II, 793
Evans, Chas. II, 817
Evans, Chas. II, 860
Evans, Chas. II, 861
Evans, Chas. II, 864
Evans, Chas. II, 915
Evans, Chas. II, 940
Evans, Chas. Price II, 861
Evans, Christian I, 49
Evans, Christian I, 238
Evans, Christiana I, 238
Evans, Christiana V, 54
Evans, Christianna V, 54
Evans, Clara R. V, 456
Evans, Columbus C. IV, 199
Evans, Corda I, 632
Evans, Cornealy M. I, 878
Evans, Cornealy M. I, 1016
Evans, Crowell III, 111
Evans, Crowell III, 276
Evans, Cyrus V, 904
Evans, Daniel I, 183
Evans, Daniel I, 192
Evans, Daniel I, 539
Evans, Daniel I, 809
Evans, Daniel II, 173
Evans, Daniel II, 218
Evans, Daniel II, 484
Evans, Daniel II, 518
Evans, Daniel II, 519
Evans, Daniel IV, 1250
Evans, Daniel VI, 799
Evans, Daniel VI, 801
Evans, Daniel VI, 818
Evans, Daniel VI, 859
Evans, Darnie V, 238
Evans, David I, 388
Evans, David I, 497
Evans, David I, 539
Evans, David I, 809
Evans, David I, 1029
Evans, David II, 27
Evans, David II, 58
Evans, David II, 68
Evans, David II, 69
Evans, David II, 96
Evans, David II, 359
Evans, David II, 360
Evans, David II, 443
Evans, David II, 518
Evans, David II, 519
Evans, David II, 520
Evans, David II, 556
Evans, David II, 739
Evans, David II, 860
Evans, David II, 861
Evans, David V, 30
Evans, David V, 52
Evans, David V, 53
Evans, David V, 54
Evans, David VI, 310
Evans, David VI, 594
Evans, David, Jr. II, 519
Evans, Deborah I, 497
Evans, Deborah I, 539
Evans, Deborah II, 359
Evans, Deborah II, 518
Evans, Della IV, 1158
Evans, Delphina S. IV, 199
Evans, Delphine IV, 296
Evans, Dilla IV, 1158
Evans, Dorothy I, 48
Evans, Dorothy I, 139
Evans, Dorothy I, 152
Evans, Dorothy I, 169
Evans, Douty II, 359
Evans, Edmund II, 520
Evans, Edward II, 359
Evans, Edward II, 360
Evans, Edward II, 486
Evans, Edward II, 518
Evans, Eleanor II, 27
Evans, Eleanor II, 69
Evans, Eleanor II, 360
Evans, Eleanor II, 518
Evans, Eleanor II, 519
Evans, Eleanor II, 520
Evans, Eleanor II, 563
Evans, Eleanor II, 805
Evans, Eleanor III, 57
Evans, Eleanor III, 111
Evans, Eleanor IV, 31
Evans, Eleanor IV, 44
Evans, Eleanor V, 781
Evans, Eleanor Edwards II, 785
Evans, Eleanor H. V, 733
Evans, Eleanor H. V, 803
Evans, Elenor IV, 31
Evans, Elenor IV, 199
Evans, Elenor IV, 308
Evans, Elenor VI, 859
Evans, Elery Channing IV, 199
Evans, Elesabeth I, 48
Evans, Elesabeth I, 54
Evans, Eli IV, 624
Evans, Elias II, 518
Evans, Elioner II, 68

Evans, Elisabeth I, 9
Evans, Elisabeth I, 48
Evans, Elisabeth I, 49
Evans, Elisabeth I, 52
Evans, Elisabeth I, 139
Evans, Elisabeth I, 169
Evans, Elisabeth I, 171
Evans, Elisabeth I, 193
Evans, Elisabeth II, 518
Evans, Eliza III, 161
Evans, Eliza V, 53
Evans, Eliza A. II, 861
Evans, Eliza A. II, 892
Evans, Eliza G. III, 111
Evans, Eliza G. III, 112
Evans, Eliza H. VI, 815
Evans, Eliza M. VI, 815
Evans, Elizabeth I, 193
Evans, Elizabeth I, 1029
Evans, Elizabeth II, 27
Evans, Elizabeth II, 68
Evans, Elizabeth II, 173
Evans, Elizabeth II, 218
Evans, Elizabeth II, 219
Evans, Elizabeth II, 287
Evans, Elizabeth II, 359
Evans, Elizabeth II, 360
Evans, Elizabeth II, 484
Evans, Elizabeth II, 518
Evans, Elizabeth II, 528
Evans, Elizabeth II, 704
Evans, Elizabeth II, 791
Evans, Elizabeth II, 861
Evans, Elizabeth II, 875
Evans, Elizabeth II, 898
Evans, Elizabeth IV, 175
Evans, Elizabeth IV, 199
Evans, Elizabeth IV, 312
Evans, Elizabeth IV, 314
Evans, Elizabeth IV, 624
Evans, Elizabeth IV, 681
Evans, Elizabeth IV, 702
Evans, Elizabeth IV, 739
Evans, Elizabeth IV, 952
Evans, Elizabeth V, 28
Evans, Elizabeth V, 41
Evans, Elizabeth V, 52
Evans, Elizabeth V, 53
Evans, Elizabeth V, 64
Evans, Elizabeth V, 102
Evans, Elizabeth V, 115
Evans, Elizabeth V, 117
Evans, Elizabeth V, 738
Evans, Elizabeth V, 892
Evans, Elizabeth V, 904
Evans, Elizabeth VI, 106
Evans, Elizabeth VI, 636
Evans, Elizabeth VI, 638
Evans, Elizabeth VI, 815
Evans, Elizabeth VI, 834
Evans, Elizabeth VI, 880
Evans, Elizabeth G. II, 287
Evans, Elizabeth G. II, 704
Evans, Elizabeth G. II, 739
Evans, Elizabeth H. II, 861
Evans, Elizabeth H. II, 915
Evans, Elizabeth Hill II, 793
Evans, Elizabeth Hill II, 817
Evans, Elizabeth M. II, 861
Evans, Elizabeth M. V, 52
Evans, Elizabeth M. V, 53
Evans, Elizabeth M. V, 54
Evans, Elizabeth M. V, 969
Evans, Elizabeth M. V, 975
Evans, Elizabeth R. II, 739
Evans, Elizabeth S. III, 112
Evans, Elizabeth T. II, 861
Evans, Elizabeth Tatem II, 815
Evans, Elizabeth Tomlinson I, 139
Evans, Ella IV, 199
Evans, Ellen II, 520
Evans, Ellen III, 111
Evans, Ellen A. V, 904
Evans, Ellen C. II, 861
Evans, Ellen C. II, 898
Evans, Ellen H. II, 815
Evans, Ellen H. II, 861
Evans, Ellen H. II, 912
Evans, Ellinor II, 995
Evans, Elonar II, 68
Evans, Elonar II, 102
Evans, Elton V, 168
Evans, Elva I, 193
Evans, Elva V, 168
Evans, Elva A. V, 168
Evans, Elwood II, 793
Evans, Elwood II, 861
Evans, Emerson V, 238
Evans, Emerson V, 456
Evans, Emily T. II, 861
Evans, Emily T. II, 892
Evans, Emily Thomas II, 793
Evans, Emin II, 518
Evans, Emma I, 616
Evans, Emma V, 456
Evans, Emma L. II, 861
Evans, Emma L. II, 897
Evans, Emmor V, 53
Evans, Erma V, 168
Evans, Ester Elizabeth II, 148
Evans, Esther I, 539
Evans, Esther II, 406
Evans, Esther II, 861
Evans, Esther II, 875
Evans, Esther II, 909
Evans, Esther IV, 702
Evans, Esther IV, 744
Evans, Esther IV, 952
Evans, Esther IV, 981
Evans, Esther V, 52
Evans, Esther V, 53
Evans, Esther V, 70
Evans, Esther V, 445
Evans, Esther V, 446
Evans, Esther V, 733
Evans, Esther V, 738
Evans, Esther V, 739
Evans, Esther V, 781
Evans, Esther V, 786
Evans, Esther Elizabeth II, 148
Evans, Euphemia Cattell IV, 1037
Evans, Evan II, 359
Evans, Evan II, 360
Evans, Evan II, 518
Evans, Evan II, 519
Evans, Evan II, 542
Evans, Evan II, 551
Evans, Evan II, 676
Evans, Evan IV, 31
Evans, Evan IV, 145
Evans, Evan IV, 199
Evans, Evan IV, 328
Evans, Evan IV, 461
Evans, Evan IV, 465
Evans, Evan IV, 470
Evans, Evan IV, 471
Evans, Evan IV, 523
Evans, Evan IV, 1056
Evans, Evan V, 24
Evans, Evan V, 52
Evans, Evan V, 53
Evans, Evan V, 215
Evans, Evan V, 237
Evans, Evan VI, 386
Evans, Evan VI, 594
Evans, Evan VI, 597
Evans, Evan VI, 636
Evans, Evan VI, 740
Evans, Evan Griffith IV, 199
Evans, Exum I, 9
Evans, Exum I, 193
Evans, F. Algernon II, 739
Evans, Florence II, 861
Evans, Florence Johnson IV, 199
Evans, Florence W. II, 861
Evans, Florence W. II, 943
Evans, Frances II, 519
Evans, Frances II, 598
Evans, Frances III, 111
Evans, Frances III, 276
Evans, Frances V, 445
Evans, Frances W. II, 860
Evans, Francis II, 519
Evans, Francis Algernon II, 738
Evans, Francis J. III, 111
Evans, Francis W. II, 860
Evans, Francis W. II, 861
Evans, Francis W. V, 904
Evans, Frank IV, 1250
Evans, Franklin II, 861
Evans, Franklin S. II, 861
Evans, Franklin S. II, 897
Evans, Fronia V, 671
Evans, G. W. VI, 799
Evans, Geo. I. IV, 199
Evans, Geo. O. II, 898
Evans, George IV, 199
Evans, George V, 52
Evans, George V, 53
Evans, George V, 54
Evans, George V, 69
Evans, George VI, 815
Evans, George Fullerton V, 671
Evans, George H. V, 54
Evans, George I. IV, 311
Evans, George I. IV, 312
Evans, George J. IV, 199
Evans, George L. III, 111
Evans, George L. V, 52
Evans, George O. II, 861
Evans, George P. IV, 314
Evans, George W. II, 519
Evans, George W. V, 168
Evans, Glenn V, 238
Evans, Grace II, 704
Evans, Grace II, 739
Evans, Gulielma II, 408
Evans, Hannah I, 539
Evans, Hannah I, 1029
Evans, Hannah I, 1061
Evans, Hannah I, 1119
Evans, Hannah II, 49
Evans, Hannah II, 68
Evans, Hannah II, 117
Evans, Hannah II, 126
Evans, Hannah II, 359
Evans, Hannah II, 360
Evans, Hannah II, 457
Evans, Hannah II, 518
Evans, Hannah II, 519
Evans, Hannah II, 520
Evans, Hannah II, 559
Evans, Hannah II, 676
Evans, Hannah II, 739
Evans, Hannah II, 793
Evans, Hannah II, 860
Evans, Hannah II, 861
Evans, Hannah IV, 199
Evans, Hannah IV, 294
Evans, Hannah IV, 612
Evans, Hannah IV, 681
Evans, Hannah IV, 702
Evans, Hannah IV, 739
Evans, Hannah V, 24
Evans, Hannah V, 28
Evans, Hannah V, 29
Evans, Hannah V, 31
Evans, Hannah V, 35
Evans, Hannah V, 41
Evans, Hannah V, 43
Evans, Hannah V, 52
Evans, Hannah V, 53
Evans, Hannah V, 88
Evans, Hannah V, 90
Evans, Hannah V, 109
Evans, Hannah V, 969
Evans, Hannah VI, 594
Evans, Hannah Ann V, 53
Evans, Hannah Ann V, 137
Evans, Hannah B. II, 739
Evans, Hannah Bacon II, 739
Evans, Hannah I. IV, 311
Evans, Hannah I. IV, 314
Evans, Hannah J. IV, 199
Evans, Hannah J. IV, 200
Evans, Hannah J. IV, 273
Evans, Hannah Jane IV, 199
Evans, Hannah, Sr. V, 52
Evans, Harriet D. II, 861
Evans, Harriett Barret V, 168
Evans, Harry V, 238
Evans, Hattie IV, 1250
Evans, Henrietta IV, 145
Evans, Henrietta IV, 199
Evans, Henrietta IV, 471
Evans, Henrietta IV, 523
Evans, Henrietta IV, 1056
Evans, Henry I, 49
Evans, Henry I, 238
Evans, Henry V, 53
Evans, Henry F. I, 49
Evans, Henry F. I, 238
Evans, Henry H. VI, 912
Evans, Henry W. II, 861
Evans, Hepsabah V, 52
Evans, Hepsibah V, 53
Evans, Hepsibah V, 127
Evans, Hester V, 330
Evans, Hester V, 335
Evans, Highly I, 1119
Evans, Highly I, 1122
Evans, Hugh II, 359
Evans, Hugh II, 360
Evans, Hugh II, 384
Evans, Hugh II, 518
Evans, Huldah Chappel I, 48
Evans, Isaac I, 539
Evans, Isaac I, 878
Evans, Isaac I, 1016
Evans, Isaac II, 69
Evans, Isaac V, 26
Evans, Isaac V, 52
Evans, Isaac V, 53
Evans, Isaac V, 168
Evans, Isaac V, 967
Evans, Isaac V, 969
Evans, Isaac P. V, 53
Evans, Isam V, 385
Evans, Isom V, 385
Evans, J. Wistar II, 739
Evans, Jacob II, 68
Evans, Jacob II, 443
Evans, Jacob V, 53
Evans, Jacob V, 64
Evans, Jael II, 27
Evans, Jael II, 69
Evans, Jael II, 102
Evans, James I, 49
Evans, James I, 238
Evans, James I, 632
Evans, James II, 44
Evans, James II, 69
Evans, James II, 173
Evans, James IV, 31
Evans, James IV, 145
Evans, James IV, 328
Evans, James IV, 470
Evans, James IV, 471
Evans, James IV, 523
Evans, James IV, 702
Evans, James V, 55
Evans, James C. I, 616
Evans, James C. IV, 145
Evans, James Cadwallader IV, 470
Evans, James E. IV, 702
Evans, James P. II, 861
Evans, James P. II, 940
Evans, James Paul II, 793
Evans, Jane II, 27
Evans, Jane II, 58
Evans, Jane II, 68
Evans, Jane II, 76
Evans, Jane II, 218
Evans, Jane II, 219
Evans, Jane II, 359
Evans, Jane II, 518
Evans, Jane II, 519
Evans, Jane II, 611
Evans, Jane II, 791
Evans, Jane II, 814
Evans, Jane V, 781
Evans, Jane VI, 106
Evans, Jane VI, 114
Evans, Jane VI, 115
Evans, Jane VI, 815
Evans, Jasen V, 904
Evans, Jason V, 52
Evans, Jason V, 53
Evans, Jason V, 64
Evans, Jason V, 904
Evans, Jason V, 918
Evans, Jemima I, 9
Evans, Jemima I, 193
Evans, Jemimah I, 193
Evans, Jemimah I, 196
Evans, Jennie III, 112
Evans, Jennie V, 330
Evans, Jesse I, 497
Evans, Jesse I, 539
Evans, Jesse V, 52
Evans, Jesse V, 53
Evans, Jesse VI, 803
Evans, Jesse VI, 847
Evans, Jesse, Jr. I, 539
Evans, Jessie Viola III, 111
Evans, Jno, Sr. VI, 29
Evans, Joan II, 443
Evans, Joanna IV, 85
Evans, Joanna IV, 145
Evans, Joanna IV, 199
Evans, Joanna IV, 328
Evans, Job V, 53
Evans, Joel II, 359
Evans, Joel III, 111
Evans, Joel V, 52
Evans, Joel V, 53
Evans, John I, 183
Evans, John I, 192
Evans, John I, 539
Evans, John I, 809
Evans, John II, 27
Evans, John II, 68
Evans, John II, 69
Evans, John II, 76
Evans, John II, 89
Evans, John II, 218
Evans, John II, 359
Evans, John II, 360
Evans, John II, 443
Evans, John II, 451
Evans, John II, 499
Evans, John II, 517
Evans, John II, 518
Evans, John II, 519
Evans, John II, 611
Evans, John III, 111
Evans, John IV, 31
Evans, John IV, 145
Evans, John IV, 199
Evans, John IV, 471
Evans, John V, 28
Evans, John V, 52
Evans, John V, 53
Evans, John V, 168
Evans, John V, 237
Evans, John V, 904
Evans, John VI, 807
Evans, John VI, 815
Evans, John VI, 912
Evans, John B. II, 519
Evans, John Bonsall II, 519
Evans, John Bonsall II, 793
Evans, John C. II, 860
Evans, John C. II, 861
Evans, John C. II, 892
Evans, John Cadwallader II, 793
Evans, John Cadwallader II, 860
Evans, John Cadwallader II, 861
Evans, John Cox II, 793
Evans, John Emmerson V, 456
Evans, John S. V, 52
Evans, John S. V, 168
Evans, John Wilfred II, 793
Evans, John Wistar II, 739
Evans, John, Jr. II, 218
Evans, Jonathan I, 497
Evans, Jonathan I, 539
Evans, Jonathan II, 117
Evans, Jonathan II, 126
Evans, Jonathan II, 359
Evans, Jonathan II, 360
Evans, Jonathan II, 457
Evans, Jonathan II, 518
Evans, Jonathan II, 519
Evans, Jonathan II, 557
Evans, Jonathan II, 676
Evans, Jonathan II, 738
Evans, Jonathan II, 739
Evans, Jonathan IV, 145
Evans, Jonathan IV, 199
Evans, Jonathan IV, 681
Evans, Jonathan IV, 702
Evans, Jonathan IV, 739
Evans, Jonathan IV, 952
Evans, Jonathan IV, 1250
Evans, Jonathan M. IV, 702
Evans, Jonathan P. I, 539
Evans, Jonathan, Jr. II, 457
Evans, Jonathan, Jr. II, 519
Evans, Joseph I, 9
Evans, Joseph I, 48
Evans, Joseph I, 192
Evans, Joseph I, 193
Evans, Joseph I, 1019
Evans, Joseph I, 1029
Evans, Joseph I, 1034
Evans, Joseph II, 69
Evans, Joseph II, 287
Evans, Joseph II, 288
Evans, Joseph II, 360
Evans, Joseph II, 519
Evans, Joseph II, 520
Evans, Joseph II, 785
Evans, Joseph II, 793
Evans, Joseph II, 860
Evans, Joseph II, 861
Evans, Joseph III, 57
Evans, Joseph III, 111
Evans, Joseph III, 112
Evans, Joseph III, 161
Evans, Joseph V, 52
Evans, Joseph V, 53
Evans, Joseph V, 70
Evans, Joseph V, 117
Evans, Joseph V, 738
Evans, Joseph V, 739
Evans, Joseph V, 781
Evans, Joseph V, 828
Evans, Joseph V, 838
Evans, Joseph V, 889
Evans, Joseph V, 892
Evans, Joseph V, 904
Evans, Joseph Fulton V, 904
Evans, Joseph Morris II, 520
Evans, Joseph R. V, 28
Evans, Joseph R. V, 52
Evans, Joseph R. V, 54
Evans, Joseph S. II, 520
Evans, Joseph, Jr. V, 53
Evans, Joshua I, 9
Evans, Joshua II, 218
Evans, Joshua II, 287
Evans, Joshua II, 360
Evans, Joshua II, 518
Evans, Joshua II, 519
Evans, Joshua II, 520
Evans, Joshua II, 739
Evans, Joshua III, 111
Evans, Joshua IV, 702
Evans, Joshua D. II, 174
Evans, Joshua D. II, 287
Evans, Joshua D. II, 288

Evans, Joshua D. II, 704
Evans, Joshua D. II, 739
Evans, Joshua D. II, 861
Evans, Joshua D. II, 906
Evans, Joshua D. III, 60
Evans, Joshua D. III, 111
Evans, Joshua D. III, 112
Evans, Joshua D. III, 247
Evans, Joshua D., Jr. III, 112
Evans, Joshua David III, 111
Evans, Joshua R. II, 148
Evans, Joshua, Jr. II, 519
Evans, Josiah IV, 199
Evans, Josiah IV, 289
Evans, Julia I, 10
Evans, Julia III, 111
Evans, Julia A. I, 49
Evans, Julia Ann IV, 199
Evans, Julian M. V, 781
Evans, Julianna I, 9
Evans, Junitte V, 53
Evans, Juretee V, 52
Evans, Juretee V, 54
Evans, Karenhappuck I, 878
Evans, Katherine II, 443
Evans, Katie B. V, 168
Evans, Keranhappuck I, 1016
Evans, Kerenhappock I, 1030
Evans, Kerenhappock Gaunt I, 1029
Evans, Keziah V, 53
Evans, Keziah V, 131
Evans, Kiziah VI, 815
Evans, Lemuel II, 219
Evans, Lemuel II, 519
Evans, Lemuel III, 111
Evans, Leone Catherine V, 456
Evans, Leroy V, 238
Evans, Letitia II, 518
Evans, Letticia VI, 817
Evans, Letticia W. VI, 817
Evans, Levany VI, 912
Evans, Levi II, 68
Evans, Levi II, 69
Evans, Lewis III, 95
Evans, Lewis III, 111
Evans, Lewis B. III, 111
Evans, Lewis B. III, 112
Evans, Lidia I, 1029
Evans, Lidia I, 1030
Evans, Lillie IV, 702
Evans, Lincoln V, 994
Evans, Lottie Violette V, 994
Evans, Louis III, 111
Evans, Louisa IV, 184
Evans, Louisa IV, 199
Evans, Louisa A. II, 860
Evans, Louisa Ann II, 793
Evans, Louisa Emmeline I, 9
Evans, Louiza I, 49
Evans, Lowry II, 360
Evans, Lowry II, 384
Evans, Lowry II, 518
Evans, Luce II, 359
Evans, Lucia II, 360
Evans, Lucie II, 359
Evans, Lucie II, 360
Evans, Lucy II, 519
Evans, Lucy II, 520
Evans, Lucy II, 551
Evans, Lutitia A. I, 388
Evans, Lyda I, 139
Evans, Lyddia I, 48
Evans, Lyddia I, 86
Evans, Lyddia I, 715
Evans, Lydia I, 48
Evans, Lydia I, 139
Evans, Lydia I, 539
Evans, Lydia I, 571
Evans, Lydia I, 715
Evans, Lydia II, 287
Evans, Lydia II, 309
Evans, Lydia II, 518
Evans, Lydia II, 699
Evans, Lydia II, 861
Evans, Lydia II, 940
Evans, Lydia IV, 702
Evans, Lydia IV, 739
Evans, Lydia V, 43
Evans, Lydia V, 52
Evans, Lydia V, 53
Evans, Lydia V, 117
Evans, Lydia V, 237
Evans, Lydia V, 240
Evans, Lydia V, 780
Evans, Lydia V, 781
Evans, Lydia J. II, 287
Evans, Lydia J. III, 111
Evans, Lydia May II, 309
Evans, Lydia P. II, 965
Evans, Lydia Spears I, 539
Evans, Lydia W. II, 739
Evans, Lydia W. II, 775
Evans, M. V, 994
Evans, Margaret I, 9
Evans, Margaret I, 48
Evans, Margaret I, 49
Evans, Margaret I, 192
Evans, Margaret I, 193
Evans, Margaret II, 173
Evans, Margaret II, 218
Evans, Margaret II, 219
Evans, Margaret II, 360
Evans, Margaret II, 484
Evans, Margaret II, 518
Evans, Margaret II, 519
Evans, Margaret II, 560
Evans, Margaret II, 590
Evans, Margaret II, 710
Evans, Margaret II, 793
Evans, Margaret II, 861
Evans, Margaret V, 31
Evans, Margaret V, 52
Evans, Margaret V, 53
Evans, Margaret V, 238
Evans, Margaret V, 385
Evans, Margaret VI, 386
Evans, Margaret VI, 615
Evans, Margaret VI, 636
Evans, Margaret VI, 811
Evans, Margaret A. V, 560
Evans, Margaret A. V, 568
Evans, Margaret Ann V, 53
Evans, Margaret Ann V, 54
Evans, Margaret Ann V, 63
Evans, Margaret Ann V, 560
Evans, Margarett I, 1019
Evans, Margrett II, 360
Evans, Marianna V, 238
Evans, Marietta C. IV, 199
Evans, Maris V, 781
Evans, Mark VI, 912
Evans, Martha I, 9
Evans, Martha I, 193
Evans, Martha I, 238
Evans, Martha I, 920
Evans, Martha I, 1019
Evans, Martha I, 1029
Evans, Martha I, 1033
Evans, Martha II, 218
Evans, Martha II, 518
Evans, Martha II, 519
Evans, Martha II, 520
Evans, Martha IV, 196
Evans, Martha IV, 199
Evans, Martha IV, 328
Evans, Martha IV, 351
Evans, Martha V, 53
Evans, Martha V, 902
Evans, Martha V, 904
Evans, Martha VI, 386
Evans, Martha VI, 636
Evans, Martha VI, 703
Evans, Martha VI, 704
Evans, Martha A. I, 49
Evans, Martha A. I, 238
Evans, Martha Ann II, 520
Evans, Martha Ann II, 554
Evans, Martha Dilworth V, 904
Evans, Martha I. VI, 803
Evans, Martha J. VI, 815
Evans, Mary I, 9
Evans, Mary I, 48
Evans, Mary I, 49
Evans, Mary I, 139
Evans, Mary I, 157
Evans, Mary I, 193
Evans, Mary I, 202
Evans, Mary I, 238
Evans, Mary I, 359
Evans, Mary I, 497
Evans, Mary I, 539
Evans, Mary I, 878
Evans, Mary I, 1016
Evans, Mary I, 1019
Evans, Mary I, 1029
Evans, Mary I, 1039
Evans, Mary I, 1059
Evans, Mary I, 1060
Evans, Mary I, 1061
Evans, Mary II, 44
Evans, Mary II, 68
Evans, Mary II, 69
Evans, Mary II, 92
Evans, Mary II, 96
Evans, Mary II, 105
Evans, Mary II, 359
Evans, Mary II, 360
Evans, Mary II, 451
Evans, Mary II, 518
Evans, Mary II, 519
Evans, Mary II, 542
Evans, Mary II, 548
Evans, Mary II, 557
Evans, Mary II, 559
Evans, Mary II, 602
Evans, Mary II, 607
Evans, Mary II, 609
Evans, Mary II, 860
Evans, Mary III, 112
Evans, Mary III, 285
Evans, Mary IV, 31
Evans, Mary IV, 85
Evans, Mary IV, 103
Evans, Mary IV, 145
Evans, Mary IV, 199
Evans, Mary IV, 328
Evans, Mary IV, 465
Evans, Mary IV, 470
Evans, Mary IV, 471
Evans, Mary IV, 523
Evans, Mary IV, 892
Evans, Mary IV, 894
Evans, Mary IV, 949
Evans, Mary IV, 1056
Evans, Mary IV, 1158
Evans, Mary IV, 1250
Evans, Mary V, 19
Evans, Mary V, 52
Evans, Mary V, 53
Evans, Mary V, 64
Evans, Mary V, 69
Evans, Mary V, 70
Evans, Mary V, 109
Evans, Mary V, 127
Evans, Mary V, 137
Evans, Mary V, 385
Evans, Mary V, 424
Evans, Mary V, 427
Evans, Mary V, 814
Evans, Mary V, 828
Evans, Mary V, 904
Evans, Mary V, 918
Evans, Mary V, 969
Evans, Mary V, 970
Evans, Mary VI, 386
Evans, Mary VI, 594
Evans, Mary VI, 597
Evans, Mary VI, 636
Evans, Mary VI, 638
Evans, Mary VI, 682
Evans, Mary VI, 740
Evans, Mary VI, 815
Evans, Mary VI, 819
Evans, Mary VI, 912
Evans, Mary A. IV, 199
Evans, Mary Ann II, 519
Evans, Mary Ann II, 520
Evans, Mary Ann II, 603
Evans, Mary Ann II, 860
Evans, Mary Ann II, 861
Evans, Mary Ann V, 237
Evans, Mary Ann V, 456
Evans, Mary Ann V, 489
Evans, Mary Ann V, 491
Evans, Mary Ann Jones VI, 912
Evans, Mary E. V, 168
Evans, Mary Ellen IV, 1056
Evans, Mary Ellen IV, 1075
Evans, Mary Frances III, 111
Evans, Mary Frances III, 202
Evans, Mary G. II, 861
Evans, Mary G. II, 912
Evans, Mary Gertrude II, 815
Evans, Mary J. VI, 818
Evans, Mary Jane VI, 912
Evans, Mary K. II, 704
Evans, Mary K. II, 739
Evans, Mary K. II, 906
Evans, Mary K. III, 112
Evans, Mary K. III, 247
Evans, Mary L. II, 704
Evans, Mary L. II, 739
Evans, Mary P. IV, 199
Evans, Mary P. IV, 314
Evans, Mary P. V, 52
Evans, Mary P. V, 88
Evans, Mary W. II, 860
Evans, Mary, Jr. V, 53
Evans, Matilda V, 385
Evans, Matilda Ann V, 385
Evans, Matilda Ann V, 422
Evans, Mearum I, 183
Evans, Melissa V, 168
Evans, Mila I, 9
Evans, Milicent II, 68
Evans, Milisent I, 183
Evans, Milisent I, 539
Evans, Millah I, 809
Evans, Milliam V, 137
Evans, Millicent I, 192
Evans, Milliscent II, 69
Evans, Milliscent II, 105
Evans, Minerva I, 9
Evans, Minerva I, 38
Evans, Minerva I, 49
Evans, Minnie M. IV, 1158
Evans, Miriam I, 9
Evans, Miriam I, 48
Evans, Miriam I, 67
Evans, Miriam I, 192
Evans, Miriam I, 202
Evans, Morris II, 860
Evans, Morris A. III, 112
Evans, Morris James II, 815
Evans, Moses I, 539
Evans, Moses I, 878
Evans, Moses I, 1016
Evans, Moses I, 1019
Evans, Moses I, 1029
Evans, Moses I, 1030
Evans, Moses II, 360
Evans, Moses II, 518
Evans, Moses II, 520
Evans, Moses V, 385
Evans, Moses V, 781
Evans, Mourning I, 193
Evans, Mrs. Jennie IV, 702
Evans, Musgrave II, 359
Evans, Musgrave II, 518
Evans, Musgrove II, 360
Evans, Musgrove II, 518
Evans, Nancy I, 193
Evans, Nancy I, 497
Evans, Nancy I, 539
Evans, Nancy V, 53
Evans, Nancy V, 738
Evans, Nancy V, 894
Evans, Nancy V, 904
Evans, Nancy VI, 799
Evans, Nancy VI, 815
Evans, Nancy VI, 848
Evans, Nathan I, 497
Evans, Nathan II, 69
Evans, Nathan II, 519
Evans, Nathan IV, 199
Evans, Nathan R. II, 860
Evans, Nathan R. II, 995
Evans, Nathaniel II, 68
Evans, Nellie IV, 702
Evans, Nettie IV, 702
Evans, Oliver II, 360
Evans, Oliver II, 861
Evans, Oliver II, 898
Evans, Owen I, 359
Evans, Owen II, 218
Evans, Owen II, 360
Evans, Owen II, 518
Evans, Owen II, 607
Evans, Owen II, 965
Evans, Owen V, 52
Evans, Owen V, 53
Evans, P. II, 519
Evans, Pamela IV, 31
Evans, Pamela V, 445
Evans, Pamelia IV, 145
Evans, Pamelia IV, 467
Evans, Pamelia IV, 471
Evans, Park IV, 471
Evans, Parker IV, 199
Evans, Parker IV, 1056
Evans, Parmelia V, 53
Evans, Parmelia V, 445
Evans, Patience V, 53
Evans, Patsy VI, 912
Evans, Peter II, 359
Evans, Peter II, 360
Evans, Peter II, 519
Evans, Phebe II, 793
Evans, Phebe II, 807
Evans, Phebe II, 823
Evans, Phebe II, 861
Evans, Phebe V, 994
Evans, Phebe VI, 386
Evans, Phebe VI, 636
Evans, Phebe VI, 703
Evans, Phebe F. II, 861
Evans, Phebe F. II, 912
Evans, Phebe S. II, 861
Evans, Philip IV, 702
Evans, Philip IV, 744
Evans, Philip IV, 952
Evans, Philip IV, 981
Evans, Phineas I, 9
Evans, Phinehas I, 48
Evans, Phinehas I, 49
Evans, Phinehas I, 193
Evans, Polly VI, 815
Evans, Priscilla II, 218
Evans, Priscilla II, 855
Evans, Priscilla II, 860
Evans, Priscilla III, 112
Evans, Priscilla V, 330
Evans, Priscilla V, 385
Evans, Priscilla V, 828
Evans, Priscilla V, 838
Evans, Prudence II, 27
Evans, Quin II, 443
Evans, Rachel I, 9
Evans, Rachel I, 48
Evans, Rachel I, 54
Evans, Rachel I, 183
Evans, Rachel I, 192
Evans, Rachel I, 193
Evans, Rachel I, 195
Evans, Rachel I, 497
Evans, Rachel I, 539
Evans, Rachel I, 809
Evans, Rachel I, 1029
Evans, Rachel I, 1034
Evans, Rachel II, 406
Evans, Rachel II, 738
Evans, Rachel II, 739
Evans, Rachel II, 817
Evans, Rachel II, 861
Evans, Rachel II, 864
Evans, Rachel II, 909
Evans, Rachel IV, 702
Evans, Rachel V, 30
Evans, Rachel V, 52
Evans, Rachel V, 53
Evans, Rachel V, 55
Evans, Rachel V, 168
Evans, Rachel V, 170
Evans, Rachel V, 237
Evans, Rachel V, 248
Evans, Rachel V, 738
Evans, Rachel V, 892
Evans, Rachel V, 904
Evans, Rachel VI, 493
Evans, Rachel VI, 565
Evans, Rachel VI, 566
Evans, Rachel VI, 567
Evans, Rachel S. II, 860
Evans, Rachel S. II, 861
Evans, Rachel S. II, 915
Evans, Rachel S. II, 940
Evans, Rachel Steinmetz II, 793
Evans, Rachel, Jr. V, 53
Evans, Rankin V, 904
Evans, Rebecca I, 193
Evans, Rebecca I, 539
Evans, Rebecca I, 1029
Evans, Rebecca I, 1059
Evans, Rebecca II, 174
Evans, Rebecca II, 218
Evans, Rebecca II, 244
Evans, Rebecca II, 246
Evans, Rebecca II, 287
Evans, Rebecca II, 288
Evans, Rebecca II, 360
Evans, Rebecca II, 486
Evans, Rebecca II, 493
Evans, Rebecca II, 518
Evans, Rebecca II, 519
Evans, Rebecca II, 704
Evans, Rebecca II, 739
Evans, Rebecca II, 860
Evans, Rebecca II, 861
Evans, Rebecca IV, 145
Evans, Rebecca IV, 199
Evans, Rebecca IV, 328
Evans, Rebecca IV, 471
Evans, Rebecca IV, 523
Evans, Rebecca IV, 577
Evans, Rebecca IV, 597
Evans, Rebecca V, 28
Evans, Rebecca V, 52
Evans, Rebecca V, 53
Evans, Rebecca V, 738
Evans, Rebecca V, 741
Evans, Rebecca V, 790
Evans, Rebecca V, 904
Evans, Rebecca VI, 854
Evans, Rebecca B. III, 112
Evans, Rebecca C. I, 878
Evans, Rebecca C. I, 1016
Evans, Rebecca E. V, 53
Evans, Rebecca E. V, 129
Evans, Rebecca G. II, 287
Evans, Rebecca G. II, 704
Evans, Rebecca G. II, 739
Evans, Rebecca G. II, 861
Evans, Rebecca G. II, 906
Evans, Rebecca G. III, 60
Evans, Rebecca G. III, 111
Evans, Rebecca G. III, 112
Evans, Rebecca G. III, 244
Evans, Rebecca G. III, 247
Evans, Rebecca L. II, 318
Evans, Rebecca L. II, 325
Evans, Rebeccah II, 360
Evans, Rebeckah I, 1019
Evans, Rebeckah II, 68
Evans, Rebeckah II, 102

vans, Rebeckah IV, 470
vans, Rebekah I, 192
vans, Rebekah I, 193
vans, Rebekah I, 202
vans, Rebekah I, 539
vans, Rebekah I, 1029
vans, Rebekah I, 1030
vans, Rebekah II, 518
vans, Rebekah II, 597
vans, Rebekah V, 53
vans, Reece II, 360
vans, Reece VI, 817
vans, Rees II, 518
vans, Rees VI, 801
vans, Rees VI, 815
vans, Reese II, 360
vans, Reese II, 518
vans, Reese VI, 801
vans, Reese VI, 810
vans, Reese M. V, 904
vans, Rhoda I, 9
vans, Rian V, 52
vans, Rian V, 54
vans, Richard II, 360
vans, Richard II, 1033
vans, Richard VI, 386
vans, Richard VI, 636
vans, Richard VI, 703
vans, Risdon V, 52
vans, Risdon V, 53
vans, Risdon V, 54
vans, Robert I, 9
vans, Robert I, 48
vans, Robert I, 54
vans, Robert I, 86
vans, Robert I, 139
vans, Robert I, 183
vans, Robert I, 192
vans, Robert I, 539
vans, Robert I, 1015
vans, Robert I, 1016
vans, Robert I, 1019
vans, Robert I, 1029
vans, Robert I, 1030
vans, Robert I, 1059
vans, Robert II, 287
vans, Robert II, 359
vans, Robert II, 360
vans, Robert II, 518
vans, Robert II, 519
vans, Robert II, 861
vans, Robert II, 875
vans, Robert II, 995
vans, Robert V, 53
vans, Robert V, 733
vans, Robert V, 738
vans, Robert V, 741
vans, Robert V, 781
vans, Robert V, 786
vans, Robert V, 790
vans, Robert V, 803
vans, Robert V, 904
vans, Robert VI, 106
vans, Robert VI, 114
vans, Robert E. II, 860
vans, Robert E. III, 111
vans, Robert E. III, 112
vans, Robert Franklin V, 904
vans, Robert J. II, 520
vans, Robert, Jr. I, 48
vans, Robert, Jr. I, 139
vans, Robert, Jr. VI, 106
vans, Robertson I, 193
vans, Rowland II, 359
vans, Rowland II, 360
vans, Rowland II, 519
vans, Ruth II, 57
vans, Ruth II, 68
vans, Ruth II, 69
vans, Ruth II, 89
vans, Ruth II, 173
vans, Ruth II, 218
vans, Ruth II, 219
vans, Ruth II, 518
vans, Ruth II, 519
vans, Ruth II, 704
vans, Ruth II, 739
vans, Ruth V, 52
vans, Ruth V, 53
vans, Ruth V, 117
vans, Ryan V, 53
vans, S. Delphine IV, 199
vans, S. Delphine IV, 297
vans, S??? II, 359
vans, Sally IV, 328
vans, Sally IV, 345
vans, Sally V, 739
vans, Sally V, 781
vans, Salome II, 218
vans, Sampson VI, 815
vans, Sampson VI, 834
Evans, Sampson VI, 838
Evans, Sampson, Jr. VI, 833
Evans, Samuel II, 218
Evans, Samuel II, 244
Evans, Samuel II, 359
Evans, Samuel II, 360
Evans, Samuel II, 518
Evans, Samuel II, 520
Evans, Samuel II, 548
Evans, Samuel III, 111
Evans, Samuel III, 112
Evans, Samuel V, 53
Evans, Samuel V, 456
Evans, Sarah I, 48
Evans, Sarah I, 85
Evans, Sarah I, 183
Evans, Sarah I, 192
Evans, Sarah I, 359
Evans, Sarah I, 539
Evans, Sarah I, 809
Evans, Sarah I, 1019
Evans, Sarah I, 1029
Evans, Sarah I, 1035
Evans, Sarah II, 27
Evans, Sarah II, 44
Evans, Sarah II, 68
Evans, Sarah II, 69
Evans, Sarah II, 76
Evans, Sarah II, 105
Evans, Sarah II, 218
Evans, Sarah II, 360
Evans, Sarah II, 509
Evans, Sarah II, 512
Evans, Sarah II, 518
Evans, Sarah II, 519
Evans, Sarah II, 520
Evans, Sarah II, 546
Evans, Sarah II, 643
Evans, Sarah II, 793
Evans, Sarah II, 860
Evans, Sarah II, 861
Evans, Sarah II, 864
Evans, Sarah III, 95
Evans, Sarah III, 111
Evans, Sarah IV, 31
Evans, Sarah IV, 85
Evans, Sarah IV, 112
Evans, Sarah IV, 145
Evans, Sarah IV, 199
Evans, Sarah IV, 311
Evans, Sarah IV, 312
Evans, Sarah IV, 467
Evans, Sarah IV, 470
Evans, Sarah IV, 471
Evans, Sarah IV, 523
Evans, Sarah IV, 681
Evans, Sarah IV, 702
Evans, Sarah IV, 739
Evans, Sarah IV, 1056
Evans, Sarah V, 52
Evans, Sarah V, 53
Evans, Sarah V, 122
Evans, Sarah V, 238
Evans, Sarah V, 456
Evans, Sarah V, 489
Evans, Sarah V, 534
Evans, Sarah V, 738
Evans, Sarah V, 904
Evans, Sarah V, 918
Evans, Sarah VI, 156
Evans, Sarah VI, 176
Evans, Sarah VI, 386
Evans, Sarah VI, 594
Evans, Sarah VI, 597
Evans, Sarah VI, 636
Evans, Sarah VI, 638
Evans, Sarah VI, 815
Evans, Sarah Delphine IV, 199
Evans, Sarah Ella II, 148
Evans, Sarah Ella IV, 199
Evans, Sarah Ellen IV, 199
Evans, Sarah Henrietta IV, 145
Evans, Sarah I. I, 49
Evans, Sarah J. I, 232
Evans, Sarah J. I, 238
Evans, Sarah J. III, 111
Evans, Sarah Jane III, 112
Evans, Sarah Jane V, 457
Evans, Sarah M. III, 112
Evans, Sarah M. Dilworth V, 904
Evans, Sarah Margaret VI, 636
Evans, Sarah P. I, 238
Evans, Sarah R. V, 238
Evans, Sarrah II, 68
Evans, Seth II, 360
Evans, Seth V, 52
Evans, Seth V, 53
Evans, Sidney II, 519
Evans, Sidney II, 556
Evans, Sina VI, 847
Evans, Sophia M. I, 878
Evans, Sophia M. I, 1016
Evans, Stockton H. II, 739
Evans, Stockton H. II, 861
Evans, Stockton H. II, 864
Evans, Stockton Hill II, 793
Evans, Stockton Hill II, 860
Evans, Susan II, 793
Evans, Susan II, 861
Evans, Susan II, 897
Evans, Susan III, 112
Evans, Susan III, 290
Evans, Susan V, 52
Evans, Susan V, 53
Evans, Susan V, 108
Evans, Susan V, 237
Evans, Susan V, 738
Evans, Susan V, 904
Evans, Susan Ann III, 36
Evans, Susan M. IV, 199
Evans, Susan M. IV, 289
Evans, Susan T. II, 861
Evans, Susanna II, 59
Evans, Susanna II, 360
Evans, Susanna II, 384
Evans, Susanna V, 53
Evans, Susanna V, 69
Evans, Susanna VI, 691
Evans, Susanna VI, 815
Evans, Susannah II, 68
Evans, Susannah II, 69
Evans, Susannah II, 360
Evans, Susannah IV, 702
Evans, Susannah V, 53
Evans, Susannah V, 904
Evans, Susannah VI, 636
Evans, Susannah M. IV, 199
Evans, Susie E. V, 901
Evans, Susie E. V, 904
Evans, Sydna II, 518
Evans, Sydna II, 556
Evans, Tempy VI, 912
Evans, Thadeus I, 238
Evans, Thomas I, 9
Evans, Thomas I, 183
Evans, Thomas I, 192
Evans, Thomas I, 202
Evans, Thomas I, 1029
Evans, Thomas II, 218
Evans, Thomas II, 246
Evans, Thomas II, 359
Evans, Thomas II, 360
Evans, Thomas II, 518
Evans, Thomas II, 519
Evans, Thomas II, 520
Evans, Thomas II, 559
Evans, Thomas II, 704
Evans, Thomas II, 739
Evans, Thomas II, 769
Evans, Thomas III, 112
Evans, Thomas IV, 31
Evans, Thomas IV, 103
Evans, Thomas IV, 1056
Evans, Thomas V, 31
Evans, Thomas V, 43
Evans, Thomas V, 52
Evans, Thomas V, 53
Evans, Thomas V, 88
Evans, Thomas V, 90
Evans, Thomas V, 109
Evans, Thomas V, 115
Evans, Thomas V, 781
Evans, Thomas V, 969
Evans, Thomas VI, 386
Evans, Thomas VI, 636
Evans, Thomas VI, 815
Evans, Thomas VI, 847
Evans, Thomas VI, 848
Evans, Thomas J. V, 781
Evans, Thomas W. II, 704
Evans, Thomas Wistar II, 739
Evans, Thonas VI, 803
Evans, Thos. II, 117
Evans, Thos. II, 126
Evans, Thos. II, 520
Evans, Thos. II, 860
Evans, Thos. V, 780
Evans, Thos. V, 975
Evans, Thos. D. VI, 804
Evans, Thos. D. VI, 815
Evans, Thos. P. II, 912
Evans, Thos. Passmore II, 793
Evans, Thos. W. II, 860
Evans, Thos. W. II, 861
Evans, Thos. W. II, 912
Evans, Ulysses V, 904
Evans, Wd. Alice II, 793
Evans, Wd. Elizabeth II, 518
Evans, Wd. Mary II, 519
Evans, Wd. Mary II, 793
Evans, Wd. Mary Ann II, 793
Evans, Wd. Mary Ann II, 861
Evans, Wd. Rebecca II, 360
Evans, Whalen VI, 636
Evans, Wheelon VI, 386
Evans, Wight II, 360
Evans, Will V, 238
Evans, William I, 48
Evans, William I, 192
Evans, William I, 497
Evans, William I, 539
Evans, William II, 359
Evans, William II, 360
Evans, William II, 704
Evans, William II, 723
Evans, William IV, 199
Evans, William V, 53
Evans, William V, 127
Evans, William V, 238
Evans, William V, 781
Evans, William VI, 815
Evans, William VI, 818
Evans, William VI, 912
Evans, William A. VI, 815
Evans, William Bacon II, 704
Evans, William E. II, 793
Evans, William Gill II, 704
Evans, William Gill III, 112
Evans, William H. I, 616
Evans, William Jones IV, 1056
Evans, William P. III, 111
Evans, William P. III, 112
Evans, William Penn II, 360
Evans, William R. V, 52
Evans, William R. V, 53
Evans, William R. V, 54
Evans, William R. V, 63
Evans, William R. V, 560
Evans, Willis I, 193
Evans, Wilmot I, 799
Evans, Wilmot I, 809
Evans, Wilson II, 360
Evans, Wilson II, 519
Evans, Wilson II, 520
Evans, Wilson II, 793
Evans, Wilson II, 860
Evans, Wilson II, 861
Evans, Wilson II, 897
Evans, Wilson III, 111
Evans, Wilson III, 112
Evans, Wilson III, 290
Evans, Wilson, Jr. II, 861
Evans, Wm. II, 519
Evans, Wm. II, 739
Evans, Wm. IV, 1056
Evans, Wm. V, 781
Evans, Wm. Albert II, 793
Evans, Wm. Bacon II, 739
Evans, Wm. Gill III, 112
Evans, Wm. Henry V, 904
Evans, Wm. J. IV, 145
Evans, Wm. Jones IV, 145
Evans, Wm. Jones IV, 199
Evans, Wm. Jones IV, 471
Evans, Wm. P. II, 520
Evans, Wm. Penn II, 519
Evans, Wm. Penn II, 520
Evans, Wm. R. V, 568
Evans, Zillah IV, 199
Evarts, Alice III, 73
Evarts, Alice III, 112
Evarts, Annie V, 994
Evarts, David V, 994
Evarts, Effie V, 994
Evarts, Helen M. III, 112
Evarts, Jason V, 994
Evarts, Sherman III, 73
Evarts, Sherman III, 112
Evarts, Wm. Maxwell III, 112
Eve, Ann II, 520
Eve, Ann II, 600
Eve, George VI, 815
Eve, George VI, 838
Eve, George, Jr. VI, 817
Eve, Oswell II, 360
Eve, Patsy VI, 815
Eve, William II, 360
Evelyn, Clara V, 712
Evelyn, Morris V, 712
Evens, Achsah I, 539
Evens, Alice I, 214
Evens, Amy II, 68
Evens, Ann I, 545
Evens, Ann C. V, 904
Evens, Ann C. V, 915
Evens, Benjamin I, 193
Evens, Benjamin V, 904
Evens, Calvin I, 497
Evens, Charles V, 456
Evens, Daniel I, 539
Evens, David I, 497
Evens, David I, 545
Evens, David II, 68
Evens, Elisa I, 497
Evens, Elisabeth I, 194
Evens, Elizabeth I, 190
Evens, Elizabeth II, 68
Evens, Elizabeth II, 83
Evens, Esther I, 497
Evens, Esther I, 539
Evens, Esther I, 545
Evens, Francis W. V, 904
Evens, Hannah I, 539
Evens, Hannah I, 1061
Evens, Hannah I, 1063
Evens, Isam I, 545
Evens, Jacob II, 68
Evens, Jasen V, 904
Evens, Jemima I, 193
Evens, Jemima I, 201
Evens, Jesse I, 497
Evens, Jesse I, 539
Evens, Jesse I, 545
Evens, John I, 539
Evens, John IV, 199
Evens, John VI, 912
Evens, John B. II, 519
Evens, Jurete I, 497
Evens, Levi II, 68
Evens, Lydia I, 715
Evens, Margaret I, 192
Evens, Margaret I, 196
Evens, Mary I, 539
Evens, Mary I, 545
Evens, Mary I, 553
Evens, Mary II, 68
Evens, Mary V, 904
Evens, Milicent II, 68
Evens, Milisent I, 539
Evens, Nathaniel II, 68
Evens, Nathaniel II, 83
Evens, Patsy VI, 912
Evens, Polly I, 497
Evens, Rachel I, 539
Evens, Rebecca II, 218
Evens, Rebecca II, 861
Evens, Rian I, 497
Evens, Risdon I, 497
Evens, Robert I, 183
Evens, Robert II, 287
Evens, Robert VI, 106
Evens, Sarah II, 68
Evens, Sarah V, 456
Evens, Sarah V, 904
Evens, Sarrah II, 68
Evens, Susannah II, 68
Evens, Susannah V, 904
Evens, Thadyas I, 214
Evens, Thomas II, 218
Evens, William I, 190
Evens, William I, 192
Evenson, Jesse VI, 386
Everagin, Edward VI, 63
Everden, Thomas VI, 11
Everegin, Elizabeth I, 99
Everegin, Mary I, 99
Everegin, William I, 99
Everest, Cornelius Douglas V, 620
Everest, Cornelius J. V, 620
Everest, Elmer V, 620
Everest, Mary V, 619
Everest, Mary V, 620
Everest, Sherman V, 620
Everet, Agness I, 385
Everet, Agness I, 388
Everet, Emma V, 994
Everett, A. L. V, 994
Everett, Anderson VI, 815
Everett, Ann IV, 60
Everett, Ann V, 731
Everett, Ann VI, 529
Everett, Ann VI, 547
Everett, Ann VI, 565
Everett, Ann VI, 567
Everett, Ann VI, 576
Everett, Anne VI, 565
Everett, Annie Hunter I, 615
Everett, Benj. VI, 490
Everett, Charles VI, 544
Everett, Dorothy VI, 431
Everett, Elizabeth VI, 490
Everett, Elizabeth VI, 544
Everett, Elizabeth VI, 580
Everett, Elizabeth VI, 912
Everett, Elizabeth VI, 925
Everett, Hannah IV, 1158
Everett, Hannah VI, 544
Everett, Huldah VI, 988
Everett, Isaac VI, 544
Everett, James M. IV, 199
Everett, John IV, 199
Everett, John VI, 490
Everett, John VI, 544

Everett, John VI, 912
Everett, John VI, 961
Everett, John VI, 988
Everett, Joseph II, 360
Everett, Joseph VI, 490
Everett, Lucinda S. V, 731
Everett, Lucy Wheat VI, 912
Everett, Maria S. VI, 1001
Everett, Mary VI, 544
Everett, Mildred A. VI, 815
Everett, N. J. V, 994
Everett, Nancy VI, 961
Everett, Rachel VI, 490
Everett, Rachel VI, 544
Everett, Ruth VI, 544
Everett, S. V, 731
Everett, Sarah IV, 199
Everett, Sarah VI, 544
Everett, Simmonds VI, 988
Everett, Simmons VI, 915
Everett, Simmons VI, 981
Everett, Thomas VI, 912
Everett, Thomas VI, 1001
Everett, William IV, 1158
Everett, William VI, 544
Everett, Wm. IV, 1158
Everette, Simmons VI, 907
Everetts, A. L. V, 994
Everetts, Annie V, 994
Everetts, David V, 994
Everetts, Effie V, 994
Everetts, Emma V, 994
Everetts, Etta V, 994
Everetts, Eva V, 994
Everetts, Gladys M. V, 994
Everetts, Jason V, 994
Everetts, Kansas V, 994
Everetts, N. J. V, 994
Everham, Benjamin II, 219
Everham, Elizabeth II, 219
Everhart, ??? I, 616
Everhart, ??? I, 624
Everhart, Willis V, 168
Everigin, Elizabeth I, 139
Everigin, Elizabeth I, 142
Everigin, John I, 139
Everigin, Mary I, 139
Everigin, Mary I, 155
Everigin, Mary I, 172
Everigin, Sarah I, 139
Everigin, Sarah I, 141
Everigin, William I, 92
Everigin, William I, 139
Everigin, William I, 142
Everigin, William I, 172
Everingham, ??? III, 247
Everingham, Carrie IV, 1235
Everingham, Charles IV, 1278
Everingham, John IV, 1235
Everingham, Joseph II, 219
Everingham, Lydia II, 219
Everingham, Mary A. IV, 1278
Everingham, Sophrona IV, 1278
Everingham, Unity III, 247
Everit, Ann III, 112
Everit, Ann III, 147
Everit, Caroline L. III, 217
Everit, Eliz. III, 112
Everit, Elizabeth VI, 351
Everit, Mary III, 59
Everit, Richard III, 59
Everit, Susannah III, 147
Everit, Thos. III, 112
Everit, Thos. III, 147
Everitt, ??? VI, 580
Everitt, A. N. VI, 973
Everitt, Amelia III, 112
Everitt, Amelia III, 288
Everitt, Ann III, 112
Everitt, Ann IV, 31
Everitt, Ann IV, 59
Everitt, Ann VI, 471
Everitt, Ann VI, 565
Everitt, Ann VI, 618
Everitt, Ann VI, 708
Everitt, Anna R. III, 112
Everitt, Anna R. III, 179
Everitt, Anne VI, 489
Everitt, Anne VI, 490
Everitt, Barbary VI, 490
Everitt, Benj. VI, 490
Everitt, Beulah III, 112
Everitt, Beulah E. III, 112
Everitt, Beulah E. III, 194
Everitt, Caroline L. III, 112
Everitt, Caroline L. III, 216
Everitt, Carrie A. III, 112
Everitt, Carrie A. III, 198
Everitt, Catharine III, 112
Everitt, Catharine III, 164
Everitt, David B. III, 270
Everitt, Edward III, 112
Everitt, Edward VI, 490
Everitt, Edward VI, 505
Everitt, Edward Augustus III, 112
Everitt, Eliz. III, 112
Everitt, Elizabeth VI, 305
Everitt, Elizabeth VI, 309
Everitt, Elizabeth VI, 483
Everitt, Elizabeth VI, 490
Everitt, Elizabeth VI, 525
Everitt, Elizabeth VI, 538
Everitt, Elizabeth VI, 581
Everitt, Elizabeth VI, 582
Everitt, George III, 112
Everitt, George H. III, 112
Everitt, George W. III, 112
Everitt, George W. IV, 31
Everitt, George W. IV, 59
Everitt, Henry III, 76
Everitt, Henry III, 112
Everitt, Henry III, 194
Everitt, Henry III, 409
Everitt, Isaac IV, 31
Everitt, Isaac VI, 490
Everitt, Jane III, 112
Everitt, Jane VI, 490
Everitt, Jane VI, 505
Everitt, Jane E. III, 289
Everitt, Jane Elizabeth III, 112
Everitt, John II, 995
Everitt, John IV, 31
Everitt, John VI, 489
Everitt, John VI, 490
Everitt, John VI, 1011
Everitt, John F. VI, 1001
Everitt, Joseph VI, 309
Everitt, Joseph VI, 483
Everitt, Joseph VI, 490
Everitt, Martha VI, 490
Everitt, Mary III, 112
Everitt, Mary III, 287
Everitt, Mary III, 288
Everitt, Mary III, 289
Everitt, Mary III, 398
Everitt, Mary III, 409
Everitt, Mary VI, 489
Everitt, Mary VI, 653
Everitt, Mary VI, 670
Everitt, Mary C. III, 288
Everitt, Mary C. III, 409
Everitt, Mary E. III, 409
Everitt, Mary Jane Rebecca VI, 973
Everitt, Phebe III, 112
Everitt, Phebe III, 409
Everitt, Rachel VI, 483
Everitt, Rachel VI, 490
Everitt, Rachel VI, 544
Everitt, Rebecca IV, 31
Everitt, Rich. III, 398
Everitt, Richard III, 112
Everitt, Richard III, 288
Everitt, Richard III, 289
Everitt, Richard III, 409
Everitt, Sarah Ann III, 76
Everitt, Sarah Ann III, 112
Everitt, Sarah Ann III, 194
Everitt, Sarah Ann III, 409
Everitt, Susanna III, 112
Everitt, Susanna IV, 31
Everitt, Susannah III, 112
Everitt, Susannah V. III, 76
Everitt, Susannah V. III, 112
Everitt, Susannah Valentine III, 112
Everitt, Theodore Edgerton III, 112
Everitt, Thomas III, 112
Everitt, Thomas III, 198
Everitt, Thomas, Jr. III, 112
Everitt, Thos. III, 112
Everitt, Valentine III, 112
Everitt, Valentine III, 179
Everitt, Valentine III, 194
Everitt, Valentine III, 216
Everitt, Wd. Elizabeth VI, 526
Everitt, Wd. Elizabeth VI, 549
Everitt, Wd. Elizabeth VI, 580
Everly, ??? II, 360
Everly, Abigail II, 360
Everly, Adam IV, 200
Everly, Bertha A. IV, 200
Everly, Elizabeth II, 360
Everly, Elizabeth Ann IV, 200
Everly, Jacob II, 360
Everly, John II, 360
Everly, John, Jr. II, 360
Everly, Melissa M. IV, 200
Everly, Sarah II, 360
Everly, Thomas E. IV, 200
Everly, William IV, 200
Everngham, Abigail II, 823
Evernghim, ??? III, 343
Evernghim, Abigail III, 113
Evernghim, Abigail III, 315
Evernghim, Alice III, 362
Evernghim, Asa III, 113
Evernghim, Avis III, 113
Evernghim, Avis B. III, 113
Evernghim, Avis B. III, 235
Evernghim, Delaplaine III, 113
Evernghim, Elizabeth III, 113
Evernghim, Elizabeth M. III, 113
Evernghim, Elizabeth R. III, 113
Evernghim, Gilbert III, 99
Evernghim, Gilbert III, 113
Evernghim, Gilbert III, 315
Evernghim, Gilbert III, 343
Evernghim, Gilbert D. III, 113
Evernghim, Hannah III, 113
Evernghim, Helen Louisa III, 113
Evernghim, Henry III, 113
Evernghim, Jacob R. III, 113
Evernghim, James III, 113
Evernghim, Jos. D. III, 113
Evernghim, Jos. D. III, 361
Evernghim, Joseph III, 113
Evernghim, Joseph D. III, 113
Evernghim, Joseph D. III, 361
Evernghim, Julia Ross III, 113
Evernghim, Louisa III, 113
Evernghim, Louisa III, 361
Evernghim, Lydia W. III, 113
Evernghim, Margaret R. III, 113
Evernghim, Maria M. III, 113
Evernghim, Mary III, 113
Evernghim, Mary III, 362
Evernghim, Mary Josephine III, 113
Evernghim, Phebe III, 99
Evernghim, Phebe III, 113
Evernghim, Phebe III, 315
Evernghim, Phebe Anna III, 113
Evernghim, Samuel D. III, 362
Evernghim, Samuel M. III, 113
Evernghim, Sarah S. III, 113
Evernghim, Susan III, 113
Evernghim, Susan III, 361
Evernghim, Susan R. III, 29
Evernghim, Susan R. III, 113
Evernghim, Susan R. III, 361
Evernghim, Thomason III, 113
Evernghim, Unity III, 113
Evernghim, Victor III, 362
Evernghim, William Thurston III, 113
Evernham, Benjamin II, 219
Evernham, Elisabeth II, 218
Evernham, Elisabeth II, 219
Evernham, Elizabeth II, 219
Evernham, Elizabeth II, 254
Evernham, Joseph II, 219
Evernham, Lydia II, 219
Everritt, John VI, 925
Everritt, Polly Ann VI, 1011
Evers, ??? III, 350
Evers, Elizabeth III, 113
Evers, Elizabeth III, 350
Eversly, Abigail II, 360
Eversly, Sarah II, 360
Everstein, Lorna Pauline IV, 702
Everstine, Augusta IV, 702
Everstine, Augusta IV, 952
Everstine, Charles IV, 702
Everstine, Charles IV, 952
Everstine, Charles Hawkind IV, 952
Everstine, Chas. IV, 952
Everstine, Genevieve IV, 702
Everstine, Genevieve IV, 952
Everstine, George IV, 952
Everstine, George Henry IV, 702
Everstine, George Henry IV, 952
Everstine, Geraldine IV, 702
Everstine, Geraldine IV, 952
Everstine, Loma Pauline IV, 952
Everstine, Lorna Pauline IV, 702
Everstine, Maxine IV, 702
Everstine, Maxine IV, 952
Everstine, Pauline IV, 952
Evert, Etta V, 994
Everton, ??? II, 360
Everton, Nathaniel II, 360
Everts, A. L. V, 994
Everts, Annie V, 994
Everts, David V, 994
Everts, Effie V, 994
Everts, Jason V, 994
Everts, Kansas V, 994
Every, Elizabeth II, 360
Every, John II, 360
Every, Sarah II, 219
Eves, Agnes S. IV, 391
Eves, Amanda J. IV, 1096
Eves, Ann II, 520
Eves, Anna II, 173
Eves, Anna II, 219
Eves, Anna II, 238
Eves, Anne II, 520
Eves, Benjamin II, 173
Eves, Benjamin Cathrall II, 520
Eves, Catharine IV, 80
Eves, Catharine IV, 85
Eves, Daniel II, 173
Eves, Deborah III, 113
Eves, Dorothy II, 173
Eves, Dorothy II, 219
Eves, Dorothy II, 231
Eves, Edith III, 300
Eves, Edward III, 113
Eves, Ellen IV, 391
Eves, Hannah II, 219
Eves, Hannah II, 238
Eves, Hannah IV, 391
Eves, Hannah IV, 577
Eves, Hannah IV, 592
Eves, James IV, 391
Eves, James IV, 577
Eves, James IV, 1056
Eves, Jane II, 219
Eves, Jane II, 273
Eves, John II, 173
Eves, John II, 219
Eves, John II, 234
Eves, John II, 520
Eves, John IV, 391
Eves, John IV, 577
Eves, John IV, 1056
Eves, Lydia IV, 391
Eves, Lydia IV, 577
Eves, Lydia IV, 599
Eves, Mary II, 219
Eves, Mary II, 234
Eves, Mary II, 258
Eves, Mary II, 520
Eves, Mary II, 712
Eves, Mary II, 739
Eves, Mary IV, 391
Eves, Pamela II, 520
Eves, Ruthan IV, 391
Eves, Ruthann IV, 577
Eves, Ruthanna IV, 577
Eves, Ruthanna IV, 1056
Eves, Samuel II, 173
Eves, Samuel II, 219
Eves, Samuel II, 258
Eves, Samuel II, 273
Eves, Samuel II, 520
Eves, Susan IV, 391
Eves, Susan IV, 1056
Eves, Susanna IV, 144
Eves, Susanna IV, 391
Eves, Susanna IV, 577
Eves, Susanna IV, 1056
Eves, Susannah IV, 391
Eves, Thomas II, 163
Eves, Thomas II, 173
Eves, Thomas II, 219
Eves, Thomas II, 273
Eves, William III, 113
Evey, Abram II, 360
Evey, Adam II, 360
Evey, Adam II, 520
Evey, Hannah II, 360
Evey, Mary II, 520
Evey, Mary II, 687
Evey, Nichola II, 360
Evic, Adam F. V, 994
Evin, Hannah I, 1117
Evin, Hannah I, 1119
Evins, Ann I, 1029
Evins, Ann I, 1036
Evins, Asher IV, 328
Evins, B. D. IV, 1278
Evins, David VI, 309
Evins, David VI, 310
Evins, Elioner II, 68
Evins, Elioner II, 77
Evins, Elisabeth I, 48
Evins, Elisabeth I, 85
Evins, Elizabeth IV, 680
Evins, Elizabeth IV, 770
Evins, Elizabeth VI, 156
Evins, Hannah IV, 680
Evins, Jane II, 68
Evins, Jennie IV, 1278
Evins, John I, 192
Evins, John I, 202
Evins, John II, 218
Evins, Jonathan IV, 680
Evins, Jonathan IV, 770
Evins, Joseph I, 48
Evins, Joseph I, 85
Evins, Lyddia I, 715
Evins, Martha II, 218
Evins, Mary I, 48
Evins, Mary I, 57
Evins, Miriam I, 35
Evins, Miriam I, 48
Evins, Rebecca I, 1029
Evins, Robert I, 1029
Evins, Robert, Jr. I, 48
Evins, Sarah I, 192
Evins, Sarah I, 202
Evins, Sarah II, 218
Evins, Sarah VI, 156
Evins, Susannah IV, 702
Evins, Susannah IV, 770
Evins, William I, 35
Evins, William I, 48
Evirard, Edward II, 360
Evitt, Joseph II, 443
Evitt, Mary II, 443
Evitt, Rebekah II, 360
Evitt, Sarah II, 443
Evy, Adam II, 520
Evy, Nichola II, 360
Evys, Adam II, 360
Evys, Hannah II, 360
Ewan, Sarah II, 219
Ewbank, Charles V, 671
Ewbank, Chas. V, 677
Ewbank, Chas. T. V, 671
Ewbank, Olive V, 671
Ewbank, Olive V, 677
Ewen, Absolam II, 219
Ewen, Ambrose II, 861
Ewen, Ambrose II, 868
Ewen, David II, 219
Ewen, Elizabeth II, 69
Ewen, Elizabeth II, 861
Ewen, Elizabeth II, 868
Ewen, Ellen II, 793
Ewen, Ellen II, 861
Ewen, Ellen II, 868
Ewen, George II, 793
Ewen, Jedediah II, 793
Ewen, Jedediah II, 861
Ewen, Jedediah II, 868
Ewen, Rachel VI, 385
Ewen, Rachel VI, 386
Ewen, Susanna II, 69
Ewen, Susannah II, 204
Ewen, Susannah II, 219
Ewen, William G. II, 793
Ewer, Anna III, 113
Ewer, Edith R. III, 113
Ewer, Edith Rushmore III, 113
Ewer, Edmund R. III, 113
Ewer, Edward III, 113
Ewer, Elizabeth II, 360
Ewer, Mary II, 219
Ewer, Mary II, 520
Ewer, Mary II, 658
Ewer, Paul R. III, 113
Ewer, Robert II, 219
Ewer, Robert II, 246
Ewer, Robert II, 360
Ewers, ??? IV, 391
Ewers, Abigail IV, 391
Ewers, Abigail IV, 441
Ewers, Amy IV, 145
Ewers, Amy IV, 322
Ewers, Amy IV, 345
Ewers, Amy IV, 391
Ewers, Amy VI, 637
Ewers, Amy VI, 642
Ewers, Ann VI, 636
Ewers, Ann VI, 642
Ewers, Elizabeth IV, 328
Ewers, Elizabeth IV, 336
Ewers, Gladney IV, 328
Ewers, Gladney IV, 391
Ewers, Gulielma IV, 145
Ewers, Gulielma IV, 328
Ewers, Gulielma IV, 345
Ewers, Gulielma VI, 637
Ewers, Guly Elma IV, 590
Ewers, Jesse IV, 328
Ewers, Jesse IV, 391
Ewers, John IV, 391
Ewers, John VI, 637
Ewers, John VI, 642
Ewers, Lydia IV, 328
Ewers, Lydia IV, 336
Ewers, Lydia IV, 391
Ewers, Martha IV, 391
Ewers, Martha IV, 458
Ewers, Mary G. VI, 637
Ewers, Phebe VI, 636
Ewers, Phebe VI, 644
Ewers, Phebe Gregg VI, 637
Ewers, Rachel VI, 625

Ewers, Rachel VI, 637
Ewers, Rebecca IV, 145
Ewers, Rebeckah IV, 322
Ewers, Rebeckah IV, 328
Ewers, Rebeckah VI, 637
Ewers, Sarah IV, 391
Ewers, Sarah VI, 637
Ewers, Sarah VI, 642
Ewers, Thomas IV, 145
Ewers, Thomas IV, 328
Ewers, Thomas VI, 637
Ewers, William IV, 328
Ewers, William IV, 391
Ewers, William IV, 441
Ewers, William VI, 637
Ewers, William VI, 642
Ewers, Wm. IV, 145
Ewers, Wm. IV, 322
Ewers, Wm. IV, 345
Ewers, Zilpha W. IV, 391
Ewers, Zilpha W. IV, 404
Ewes, Abraham VI, 926
Ewes, Elizabeth VI, 926
Ewes, Sally VI, 926
Ewin, Betsy VI, 1003
Ewin, Mrs. Mary L. VI, 959
Ewin, Samuel IV, 814
Ewin, Sarah II, 219
Ewing, Anna VI, 913
Ewing, Beulah Stewart II, 704
Ewing, Beulah Stewart II, 712
Ewing, Beulah Stewart II, 719
Ewing, C. P. IV, 1314
Ewing, Caleb VI, 913
Ewing, Caleb VI, 929
Ewing, Charles H. VI, 913
Ewing, Chas. Cooper V, 456
Ewing, Chatham VI, 913
Ewing, Claire V, 168
Ewing, Claire V, 199
Ewing, Clara V, 168
Ewing, Clyde V, 168
Ewing, Cooper M. V, 456
Ewing, David II, 173
Ewing, Eliza F. VI, 913
Ewing, Elizabeth II, 69
Ewing, Elizabeth V, 397
Ewing, Elizabeth VI, 913
Ewing, Elizabeth Jane VI, 884
Ewing, Grace II, 739
Ewing, Grace S. II, 719
Ewing, Grace Stewart II, 704
Ewing, Grace Stewart II, 712
Ewing, Hannah II, 219
Ewing, Hannah II, 520
Ewing, Hannah II, 696
Ewing, Isabelle I, 616
Ewing, John VI, 911
Ewing, John VI, 913
Ewing, John VI, 987
Ewing, John J. VI, 913
Ewing, Julia V, 168
Ewing, Lydia VI, 913
Ewing, Martha I, 632
Ewing, Martha H. I, 616
Ewing, Martha H. I, 632
Ewing, Mary V, 238
Ewing, Mary V, 456
Ewing, Mary VI, 913
Ewing, Mary L. VI, 913
Ewing, Maskell II, 704
Ewing, Maskell II, 712
Ewing, Maskell II, 719
Ewing, Mitchell VI, 913
Ewing, Nancy VI, 884
Ewing, Nancy VI, 913
Ewing, Pamella VI, 911
Ewing, Patsey VI, 987
Ewing, Phebe VI, 913
Ewing, Rachel II, 219
Ewing, Rachel II, 229
Ewing, Rebecca II, 287
Ewing, Robert I, 616
Ewing, Roy V, 168
Ewing, Samuel IV, 814
Ewing, Samuel V, 238
Ewing, Samuel V, 456
Ewing, Sidney VI, 987
Ewing, Susanna II, 69
Ewing, Tabitha VI, 913
Ewing, William V, 456
Ewing, William VI, 889
Ewing, William VI, 913
Ewing, William VI, 987
Ewing, Wm. V, 168
Ewing, Wm. VI, 953
Ewing, Wm. VI, 958
Ewing, Wm. VI, 979
Ewing, Wm. VI, 990
Ewing, Wm. A. V, 168
Ewings, Absolam II, 219
Ewings, Absolum II, 219
Ewings, Ann II, 219
Ewings, Ann Burtis II, 219
Ewings, David II, 219
Ewings, Elizabeth II, 69
Ewings, Elizabeth II, 219
Ewings, Hannah II, 219
Ewings, Julius II, 219
Ewings, Rachel II, 219
Ewings, Robt. VI, 1021
Ewings, Sarah II, 219
Ewings, Susannah II, 204
Ewings, Susannah II, 219
Ewings, Tristrum II, 219
Ewins, Absolum II, 219
Ewins, Absolum II, 223
Ewins, Ann II, 219
Ewins, Hannah II, 219
Ewins, Hannah II, 223
Ewins, Julius II, 219
Ewins, Tristrum II, 219
Ewstes, Aaron II, 517
Ewstis, Aaron II, 231
Ewstis, Joseph II, 231
Exline, Jane IV, 85
Exline, Jane IV, 109
Exum, ??? VI, 39
Exum, Jeremiah VI, 29
Exum, Jeremiah VI, 35
Exum, Mary VI, 29
Exum, Mary VI, 35
Exum, Thomas VI, 207
Exum, Wd. Mary VI, 29
Eyer, Alexander II, 443
Eyer, John II, 443
Eyer, Susanna II, 443
Eyerdams, Anna Louisa IV, 1314
Eyeres, Jemima IV, 200
Eyeres, Sarah IV, 200
Eyers, Habakkuk II, 219
Eyers, Sarah II, 219
Eyler, Bessie V, 54
Eyre, Adam IV, 200
Eyre, Adam VI, 386
Eyre, Ann II, 219
Eyre, Ann IV, 200
Eyre, Ann VI, 386
Eyre, Ann P. IV, 85
Eyre, Ann P. IV, 88
Eyre, Ann P. IV, 205
Eyre, Anna IV, 200
Eyre, Anna R. II, 861
Eyre, Anna Rebecca II, 793
Eyre, Anna Wilson II, 793
Eyre, Anne VI, 386
Eyre, Asa II, 219
Eyre, Barclay VI, 637
Eyre, Barclay VI, 710
Eyre, Barclay VI, 711
Eyre, Barclay VI, 740
Eyre, Barclay VI, 768
Eyre, Clarence P. II, 861
Eyre, Clarence Preston II, 793
Eyre, Col. Benj. III, 409
Eyre, Col. Benj. III, 440
Eyre, Col. Benj. G. III, 461
Eyre, Edith VI, 740
Eyre, Edith VI, 768
Eyre, Edith C. II, 861
Eyre, Edith Clark II, 793
Eyre, Edward D. II, 861
Eyre, Edward D. III, 113
Eyre, Edward Davis II, 793
Eyre, Edward Davis II, 839
Eyre, Edward Davis II, 861
Eyre, Edward E. II, 861
Eyre, Eleanor II, 842
Eyre, Eleanor II, 855
Eyre, Eleanor II, 861
Eyre, Elizabeth II, 173
Eyre, Elizabeth II, 219
Eyre, Elizabeth II, 793
Eyre, Elizabeth Ann II, 793
Eyre, Elizabeth Ann II, 839
Eyre, Elizabeth Ann II, 855
Eyre, Elizabeth Ann II, 861
Eyre, Elizabeth Ann III, 113
Eyre, Elizabeth Ann III, 409
Eyre, Elizabeth Ann III, 461
Eyre, Elizabeth B. VI, 740
Eyre, Elizabeth D. II, 861
Eyre, Elleanor II, 793
Eyre, Emma D. VI, 637
Eyre, Emma D. VI, 740
Eyre, Emma Dutton VI, 710
Eyre, Emma Dutton VI, 711
Eyre, Emma E. VI, 768
Eyre, Florence II, 793
Eyre, Florence II, 861
Eyre, Habakkuk II, 219
Eyre, Habakuk II, 219
Eyre, Hannah II, 203
Eyre, Hannah II, 219
Eyre, Hannah II, 277
Eyre, Hannah IV, 200
Eyre, Hannah VI, 386
Eyre, Hannah H. VI, 740
Eyre, Hannah J. IV, 263
Eyre, Harriet III, 113
Eyre, Harriet III, 409
Eyre, Harriet III, 440
Eyre, Henry Russell II, 793
Eyre, Hope II, 219
Eyre, Hosea II, 219
Eyre, Isaac II, 793
Eyre, Isaac II, 842
Eyre, Isaac II, 855
Eyre, Isaac II, 861
Eyre, Isaac P. II, 861
Eyre, Isaac Preston II, 793
Eyre, Isaac W. VI, 740
Eyre, Isabella M. II, 793
Eyre, Jabez II, 793
Eyre, Jacob III, 113
Eyre, James III, 461
Eyre, James I. M. III, 461
Eyre, Jane R. III, 461
Eyre, Jemima IV, 200
Eyre, Jemima IV, 205
Eyre, Jemima IV, 210
Eyre, Jemima IV, 263
Eyre, John VI, 11
Eyre, John VI, 386
Eyre, Jonas P. II, 861
Eyre, Jonas Preston II, 793
Eyre, Joshua II, 793
Eyre, Joshua II, 861
Eyre, Keturah II, 219
Eyre, Kezia R. II, 842
Eyre, Kezia R. II, 861
Eyre, Levi II, 219
Eyre, Macre P. VI, 637
Eyre, Macre P. VI, 710
Eyre, Margaret II, 219
Eyre, Martha III, 461
Eyre, Martha IV, 200
Eyre, Martha IV, 287
Eyre, Mary II, 219
Eyre, Mary III, 409
Eyre, Mary III, 440
Eyre, Mary III, 461
Eyre, Mary VI, 386
Eyre, Mary E. II, 839
Eyre, Mary E. II, 861
Eyre, Mary Eachus II, 793
Eyre, Mary L. II, 793
Eyre, Miller Gibson IV, 85
Eyre, Miriam II, 793
Eyre, Miriam II, 861
Eyre, Preston VI, 637
Eyre, Preston VI, 710
Eyre, Rebecca II, 793
Eyre, Rebecca II, 816
Eyre, Rebecca II, 861
Eyre, Richard II, 203
Eyre, Richard II, 219
Eyre, Robert IV, 200
Eyre, Robert IV, 205
Eyre, Robert IV, 210
Eyre, Robert IV, 263
Eyre, Robert VI, 386
Eyre, Robert, Jr. IV, 200
Eyre, Robert, Jr. VI, 386
Eyre, Robert, Sr. IV, 200
Eyre, Robert, Sr. VI, 386
Eyre, Samuel II, 173
Eyre, Samuel VI, 386
Eyre, Sarah II, 219
Eyre, Sarah IV, 200
Eyre, Sarah VI, 386
Eyre, Sybil II, 793
Eyre, Sybil II, 861
Eyre, Thomas II, 173
Eyre, Thomas II, 219
Eyre, Thomas, Jr. II, 219
Eyre, Thomas, Sr. II, 219
Eyre, Wd. Kezia II, 793
Eyre, William II, 793
Eyre, William VI, 386
Eyre, Wm. II, 793
Eyre, Wm. II, 839
Eyre, Wm. II, 842
Eyre, Wm. II, 855
Eyre, Wm. II, 861
Eyre, Wm. Preston II, 793
Eyre, Wm. Preston II, 861
Eyres, Adam IV, 200
Eyres, Ann II, 219
Eyres, Hannah II, 219
Eyres, Hannah VI, 441
Eyres, Hope II, 219
Eyres, Keturah II, 219
Eyres, Keturah II, 272
Eyres, Mary II, 219
Eyres, Mary VI, 386
Eyres, Rebecca II, 219
Eyres, Sarah II, 232
Eyres, Sarah IV, 226
Eyres, Thomas, Jr. II, 219
Eyres, Thomas, Sr. II, 219

Fabrion, Ellen IV, 1250
Fabrion, Gustave R. IV, 1250
Fackler, John H. V, 994
Fackler, Sarah A. V, 994
Fackler, W. H. V, 994
Faeth, Amy V, 904
Faeth, Amy V, 908
Faeth, Erma V, 904
Faeth, Harold V, 904
Faeth, Harold V, 908
Fagan, Chas. V, 994
Fagan, Euphemy IV, 814
Fagan, Hannah IV, 868
Fagan, Hannah IV, 880
Fagan, Harman IV, 858
Fagan, Harmon IV, 814
Fagan, Lydia IV, 814
Fagan, Nora V, 994
Fagg, Alice N. I, 940
Fagg, Alice U. I, 924
Fagg, Onslow Parrish I, 940
Fagg, S. S. I, 878
Fahey, Anna V, 658
Fahey, Anna V, 671
Fahey, Anna Bayliss V, 671
Fahey, Richard V, 658
Fahey, Richard V, 671
Fahlstrom, Mrs. Viola IV, 1314
Fahnestock, Caroline III, 384
Faile, Mary I, 357
Failes, ??? III, 101
Failes, ??? III, 113
Failes, A. W. III, 166
Failes, Joshua III, 116
Fair, Adie V, 994
Fair, Alfred H. III, 114
Fair, Alice III, 98
Fair, Alice III, 114
Fair, Amie V, 994
Fair, Anie V, 994
Fair, Ann III, 114
Fair, Ann M. III, 98
Fair, Ann M. III, 114
Fair, Emeline III, 114
Fair, Martha Ellen V, 994
Fair, Mary B. V, 738
Fair, Mattie V, 994
Fair, Obadiah V, 994
Fair, Robert III, 98
Fair, Robert III, 114
Fair, Samuel V, 738
Fair, Samuel VI, 1007
Fair, Sarah V, 994
Fair, Thomas III, 114
Fair, Thomas V, 994
Fair, William John III, 114
Fair, Wm. H. V, 994
Fairbank, Ann II, 792
Fairbank, Mary D. II, 520
Fairbanke, Sarah II, 69
Fairbanke, Sarah II, 104
Fairbanks, Elizabeth II, 17
Fairbanks, Henry III, 114
Fairbanks, Robert II, 17
Fairbanoks, Elizabeth II, 27
Fairbanoks, Elizabeth II, 42
Fairbanoks, Robert II, 27
Fairbanoks, Robert II, 42
Fairbanoks, Sarah II, 27
Fairbanoks, Sarch II, 27
Fairby, Sophia V, 302
Fairby, Sophia V, 308
Fairchild, John VI, 913
Fairchild, Laura P. VI, 913
Fairchild, Rachel V, 46
Fairchild, Rachel V, 54
Fairchild, Rebecca IV, 1096
Fairchild, Rebecca IV, 1119
Faircloth, Cora E. VI, 63
Faircloth, Eva VI, 91
Faircloth, Franklin VI, 63
Faircloth, Julia VI, 91
Faircloth, Julia E. VI, 63
Faircloth, Julia E. VI, 74
Faircloth, Julia E. VI, 85
Faircloth, Julia F. VI, 63
Faircloth, Junius VI, 63
Faircloth, Junius F. VI, 63
Faircloth, Junius F. VI, 69
Faircloth, Martha VI, 91
Faircloth, Martha C. VI, 63
Faircloth, Martha C. VI, 74
Faircloth, Mary VI, 63
Faircloth, Nicholas VI, 63
Faircloth, Sarah C. VI, 63
Faircloth, Sarah C. VI, 69
Faircloth, William VI, 63
Faircloth, William VI, 74
Faircloth, William VI, 85
Faircloth, Wm. VI, 63
Fairclough, Caroline F. IV, 1314
Fairclough, Carrie IV, 1314
Fairclough, Florence Louise IV, 1314
Fairclough, Margaret Elizabeth IV, 1314
Fairclough, Wm. IV, 1314
Fairfax, Matilda Howard II, 789
Fairhurst, Ann VI, 481
Fairhurst, Ann VI, 490
Fairhurst, Ann VI, 587
Fairhurst, Eliza VI, 637
Fairhurst, Eliza VI, 724
Fairhurst, George VI, 490
Fairhurst, George VI, 637
Fairhurst, Hannah VI, 490
Fairhurst, Jane VI, 472
Fairhurst, Jane VI, 490
Fairhurst, Jeremiah VI, 490
Fairhurst, Jeremiah VI, 587
Fairhurst, John VI, 490
Fairhurst, Phebe VI, 490
Fairhurst, Rachel VI, 486
Fairhurst, Rachel VI, 490
Fairhurst, Rebecca VI, 490
Fairhurst, Rebecca VI, 540
Fairhurst, Ruth VI, 489
Fairhurst, Ruth VI, 490
Fairlamb, Anna Mary II, 792
Fairlamb, Bond II, 862
Fairlamb, Francis III, 114
Fairlamb, Hannah I. II, 862
Fairlamb, Hannah I. II, 901
Fairlamb, Jonathan T. II, 862
Fairlamb, Josiah II, 862
Fairlamb, Lucretia M. II, 839
Fairlamb, Lucretia M. II, 861
Fairlamb, Lucretia M. II, 862
Fairlamb, Martha II, 839
Fairlamb, Martha II, 862
Fairlamb, Martha A. II, 862
Fairlamb, Martha H. II, 862
Fairlamb, Mary II, 861
Fairlamb, Nicholas II, 520
Fairlamb, Nicholas II, 861
Fairlamb, Richard Crosby II, 839
Fairlamb, Richard Crosby II, 861
Fairlamb, Robert Crosby II, 792
Fairlamb, Ruth Ann II, 792
Fairlee, Eliza Ann III, 114
Fairley, C. Grant V, 671
Fairley, C. Grant V, 693
Fairley, Callie V, 456
Fairley, Callie V, 671
Fairley, Callie B. V, 671
Fairley, Charles E. V, 238
Fairley, Charley V, 456
Fairley, Christina V, 456
Fairley, Cyrus W. V, 456
Fairley, Grant V, 456
Fairley, Grant V, 671
Fairley, Hannah V, 456
Fairley, Herman V, 456
Fairley, James V, 456
Fairley, Jennie V, 238
Fairley, John V, 456
Fairley, Mary V, 238
Fairley, Mary V, 456
Fairley, Robert V, 456
Fairley, Rosa V, 456
Fairley, Ruth V, 456
Fairley, Sarah Ethel V, 671
Fairley, Sarah Ethel V, 693
Fairley, Walter V, 456
Fairley, Wilmer V, 456
Fairley, Winnie O. V, 238
Fairly, Charles E. V, 238
Fairly, Fanny VI, 913
Fairly, Jennie V, 238
Fairly, Mary V, 238
Fairly, Sophia V, 302
Fairly, Sophia V, 308
Fairly, William VI, 913
Fairly, Winnie O. V, 238
Fairman, Benjamin II, 360
Fairman, Benjamin II, 520
Fairman, Benjamin II, 588
Fairman, Benjamin II, 628
Fairman, Elizabeth II, 219
Fairman, Elizabeth II, 237
Fairman, Elizabeth II, 360
Fairman, Francis II, 360
Fairman, Mary II, 520

Fairman, Mary II, 628
Fairman, Robert II, 360
Fairman, Sarah II, 520
Fairman, Sarah II, 588
Fairman, Susannah II, 360
Fairman, Thomas II, 219
Fairman, Thomas II, 237
Fairman, Thomas II, 329
Fairman, Thomas II, 360
Fairman, Thomas II, 520
Fairman, Wd. Elizabeth II, 360
Fairman, William II, 360
Falcker, Wiliam V, 739
Falconar, David II, 541
Falconar, Gilbert II, 541
Falconar, Hanah II, 541
Falcone, Mary VI, 242
Falconer, David II, 520
Falconer, David IV, 31
Falconer, Elizabeth IV, 31
Falconer, Gilbert II, 520
Falconer, Hannah II, 360
Falconer, Hannah II, 520
Falconer, Hester III, 114
Falconer, Rachel III, 114
Falconer, Rachel M. III, 114
Falconer, Robert IV, 31
Falconer, Samuel III, 114
Falconer, Samuel III, 350
Falconer, Susanna IV, 31
Falconer, Thomas IV, 31
Faldwell, Nancy VI, 863
Faler, Martha V, 994
Faler, Mary V, 994
Faler, Samuel V, 994
Fales, ??? III, 166
Fales, Adelaide III, 114
Fales, Emily J. III, 114
Fales, Emily J. III, 270
Fales, Geo III, 114
Fales, Geo. III, 270
Fales, Hannah III, 114
Fales, Jonas III, 114
Fales, Mary III, 270
Fales, Mary Thomaston III, 114
Falkner, David V, 17
Falkner, Elizabeth VI, 594
Falkner, Ezra V, 994
Falkner, Ezra N. V, 994
Falkner, Hannah IV, 145
Falkner, Jane V, 54
Falkner, Jesse V, 54
Falkner, Jesse, Jr. VI, 387
Falkner, John B. V, 994
Falkner, Judith V, 54
Falkner, Robert IV, 31
Falkner, Robert V, 54
Falkner, Ruth V, 445
Falkner, Solomon V, 445
Falkner, Susanna V, 54
Falkner, Thomas V, 54
Falkner, Viola V, 490
Fallack, Rebecca IV, 952
Fallack, Rebecca IV, 976
Fallam, Robert VI, 289
Fallas, Isah V, 489
Fallice, George VI, 386
Fallice, Mary VI, 386
Fallis, Amos V, 401
Fallis, Amos V, 480
Fallis, Amos V, 489
Fallis, Amos V, 553
Fallis, Amos V, 560
Fallis, Amos V, 904
Fallis, Ann IV, 85
Fallis, Ann V, 560
Fallis, Clara Best V, 904
Fallis, Deborah V, 34
Fallis, Deborah V, 54
Fallis, Eli V, 489
Fallis, Eliza IV, 85
Fallis, Eliza V, 489
Fallis, Eliza V, 511
Fallis, Eliza V, 536
Fallis, Eliza V, 560
Fallis, Elizabeth IV, 85
Fallis, Elizabeth V, 54
Fallis, Elizabeth V, 489
Fallis, Elizabeth V, 560
Fallis, Elizabeth V, 951
Fallis, Elizabeth VI, 386
Fallis, Elizabeth VI, 594
Fallis, Elizabeth M. V, 489
Fallis, Ellan Wright V, 904
Fallis, Ellen V, 904
Fallis, Ellen V, 919
Fallis, Esther IV, 85
Fallis, Esther V, 54
Fallis, Esther V, 123
Fallis, Esther V, 489
Fallis, Esther V, 560
Fallis, Esther V, 951
Fallis, George VI, 386
Fallis, Harriet V, 54
Fallis, Harriet V, 489
Fallis, Harriett V, 54
Fallis, Harriett V, 136
Fallis, Harriett V, 560
Fallis, Isaac V, 489
Fallis, Isaac V, 904
Fallis, Isaac C. V, 489
Fallis, Isaac C. V, 560
Fallis, Isaac C. V, 895
Fallis, Isaac C. V, 904
Fallis, Isah V, 489
Fallis, Isaiah IV, 85
Fallis, Isaiah V, 54
Fallis, Isaiah V, 489
Fallis, Isaiah V, 560
Fallis, Isaiah V, 951
Fallis, Isaiah VI, 386
Fallis, Jacob VI, 386
Fallis, Jane V, 479
Fallis, Jane V, 489
Fallis, Jane V, 560
Fallis, Jane VI, 594
Fallis, Job VI, 386
Fallis, Job VI, 594
Fallis, John IV, 85
Fallis, John V, 54
Fallis, John V, 489
Fallis, John V, 560
Fallis, John V, 951
Fallis, John VI, 362
Fallis, John VI, 386
Fallis, John VI, 594
Fallis, John C. V, 54
Fallis, John, Jr. V, 54
Fallis, Jonathan IV, 85
Fallis, Jonathan V, 560
Fallis, Jonathan VI, 386
Fallis, Joseph B. V, 904
Fallis, Liddia VI, 386
Fallis, Lydia IV, 85
Fallis, Lydia V, 401
Fallis, Lydia V, 480
Fallis, Lydia V, 489
Fallis, Lydia V, 514
Fallis, Lydia V, 553
Fallis, Lydia V, 560
Fallis, Lydia V, 561
Fallis, Lydia V, 583
Fallis, Lydia V, 904
Fallis, Lydia McMillan V, 489
Fallis, Mary IV, 85
Fallis, Mary IV, 332
Fallis, Mary V, 111
Fallis, Mary V, 489
Fallis, Mary V, 548
Fallis, Mary V, 560
Fallis, Mary V, 592
Fallis, Mary V, 904
Fallis, Mary VI, 362
Fallis, Mary VI, 386
Fallis, Mary VI, 594
Fallis, Mary C. V, 895
Fallis, Mary C. V, 904
Fallis, Mary Esther V, 139
Fallis, Mary, Jr. IV, 85
Fallis, Miriam IV, 85
Fallis, Miriam V, 560
Fallis, Miriam V, 601
Fallis, Miriam VI, 386
Fallis, Miriam VI, 594
Fallis, Nancy V, 489
Fallis, Nancy V, 509
Fallis, Nancy V, 560
Fallis, Nancy Harriet Jane V, 489
Fallis, Phebe IV, 85
Fallis, Phebe V, 34
Fallis, Phebe V, 54
Fallis, Phebe V, 489
Fallis, Phebe V, 560
Fallis, Phebe VI, 386
Fallis, Rachel IV, 85
Fallis, Rachel V, 54
Fallis, Rachel V, 138
Fallis, Rachel V, 139
Fallis, Rachel V, 489
Fallis, Rachel V, 560
Fallis, Rachel V, 583
Fallis, Rachel V, 604
Fallis, Rachel VI, 386
Fallis, Rachel VI, 594
Fallis, Richard IV, 85
Fallis, Richard V, 34
Fallis, Richard V, 54
Fallis, Richard V, 489
Fallis, Richard V, 560
Fallis, Richard VI, 386
Fallis, Richard VI, 594
Fallis, Sarah IV, 85
Fallis, Sarah V, 489
Fallis, Sarah V, 560
Fallis, Sarah V, 572
Fallis, Sarah V, 573
Fallis, Susan V, 385
Fallis, Susan V, 401
Fallis, Susan A. V, 560
Fallis, Susan A. V, 583
Fallis, Susan M. V, 489
Fallis, Susan M. V, 514
Fallis, Susan M. V, 560
Fallis, Susan N. V, 385
Fallis, Thomas IV, 85
Fallis, Thomas V, 54
Fallis, Thomas V, 489
Fallis, Thomas V, 560
Fallis, Turner W. V, 489
Fallis, Turner W. V, 560
Fallman, Job II, 219
Fallman, Job II, 271
Fallman, Sarah II, 219
Fallman, Sarah II, 271
Falls, Benjamin VI, 911
Falls, Benjamin VI, 913
Falls, Benjamin VI, 930
Falls, Benjamin VI, 946
Falls, Daniel VI, 897
Falls, Daniel VI, 948
Falls, Eleanor VI, 990
Falls, Elizabeth VI, 897
Falls, Emily M. VI, 913
Falls, George VI, 913
Falls, George W. VI, 913
Falls, Israel VI, 913
Falls, John VI, 913
Falls, Joseph VI, 897
Falls, Joseph VI, 913
Falls, Joseph VI, 990
Falls, Kitty VI, 913
Falls, Malinda VI, 913
Falls, Margaret VI, 913
Falls, Mary M. VI, 930
Falls, Mildred F. VI, 946
Falls, Nancy VI, 913
Falls, Nancy VI, 933
Falls, Rachel VI, 924
Falls, Thomas M. VI, 946
Fallwell, Sarah VI, 837
Falor, Harold IV, 1314
Falquhar, Beulah IV, 492
Falquhar, Joseph IV, 492
Falquhar, Mary S. IV, 492
Faltner, Ezra V, 994
Faltner, Ezra N. V, 994
Falwell, John VI, 815
Falwell, Martha VI, 817
Falwell, Rebecca II, 520
Falwell, Sarah A. VI, 815
Fam, ??? VI, 84
Fanak, Ann IV, 1361
Fanak, Hannah IV, 1361
Fanak, Jane IV, 1361
Fanak, John IV, 1361
Fanak, Mary IV, 1361
Fanak, Robert IV, 1361
Fanak, Thomas IV, 1361
Fancair, Emily V, 995
Fance, Eliza Jane V, 994
Fancett, Mary IV, 1130
Fancett, Richard IV, 1130
Fancett, Sarah IV, 1130
Fancette, Anna I, 931
Fanchair, Emily V, 995
Fanchair, Isaac V, 995
Fanchair, Wm. A. V, 995
Fancher, Esther E. III, 114
Fancier, Wm. A. V, 995
Fancisco, John W. V, 995
Fandree, Catharine V, 994
Fandrel, Catharine V, 995
Fanghnder, Eva V, 489
Fanghnder, Paul I. V, 489
Fanghnder, Viola M. V, 489
Fanley, Martha IV, 702
Fanley, Thomas IV, 702
Fanley, Thomas VI, 389
Fanning, Carrie L. III, 410
Fanning, Carrie Lane III, 445
Fanning, David G. III, 410
Fanning, David G. III, 445
Fanning, Elizabeth III, 410
Fanning, Elizabeth III, 445
Fanning, Elizabeth VI, 63
Fanning, Elizabeth VI, 73
Fanning, John V, 330
Fanning, John V, 456
Fanning, Thomas VI, 63
Fanning, Thomas VI, 73
Faquhar, Benjamin V, 574
Faquhar, Ruth V, 574
Farber, Chas. K. V, 671
Farber, Etha V, 671
Farenton, Elizabeth I, 497
Fargo, John IV, 1158
Farguson, Anne VI, 295
Farguson, Anne VI, 310
Farguson, Nimrod VI, 295
Farguson, Nimrod VI, 310
Fari, John VI, 815
Fari, Mary VI, 815
Farington, Abraham IV, 703
Farington, Annie IV, 1278
Farington, Armelia IV, 1206
Farington, Caleb K. IV, 1158
Farington, Lida IV, 1278
Farington, Lizie IV, 1278
Farington, Mary IV, 1206
Farington, Moses IV, 1206
Farington, Sarah IV, 703
Farington, Sarah IV, 1206
Farington, T. P. IV, 1278
Farington, Theadore IV, 1278
Farington, Theodore IV, 1278
Faris, Alice VI, 827
Faris, Anderson C. VI, 963
Faris, Benjamin VI, 813
Faris, Benjamin VI, 856
Faris, Benjamin VI, 860
Faris, Easy VI, 815
Faris, Eliza R. VI, 992
Faris, Elizabeth V, 838
Faris, Elizabeth V, 860
Faris, Elizabeth VI, 815
Faris, Frasure VI, 310
Faris, Jacob VI, 866
Faris, James H. VI, 823
Faris, John II, 361
Faris, John IV, 145
Faris, John VI, 806
Faris, John VI, 822
Faris, John VI, 825
Faris, John VI, 827
Faris, John VI, 830
Faris, John VI, 866
Faris, John H. VI, 815
Faris, John R. VI, 865
Faris, Kezih VI, 810
Faris, Lucretia VI, 815
Faris, Margaret II, 361
Faris, Margaret VI, 310
Faris, Margaret VI, 312
Faris, Phebe VI, 833
Faris, Rachel II, 361
Faris, Sally VI, 866
Faris, Susanna IV, 145
Faris, Susanna IV, 152
Faris, Susanna VI, 847
Faris, Susannah IV, 145
Faris, Thomas V, 995
Faris, Valentine VI, 847
Faris, William VI, 866
Faris, Wm. A. VI, 815
Farish, Mary VI, 242
Farish, Mary VI, 269
Farish, Thomas VI, 242
Fariss, A. C. VI, 992
Fariss, Anderson VI, 913
Fariss, Anderson C. VI, 984
Fariss, Anderson C. VI, 1002
Fariss, Becky VI, 815
Fariss, Benj. VI, 815
Fariss, Benjamin VI, 815
Fariss, Benjamin VI, 831
Fariss, Benjamin VI, 854
Fariss, Claiborne VI, 815
Fariss, Deliley VI, 815
Fariss, Dorothy VI, 815
Fariss, Easy VI, 815
Fariss, Eliza VI, 815
Fariss, Elizabeth II, 522
Fariss, Elizabeth VI, 808
Fariss, Elizabeth VI, 815
Fariss, Elizabeth VI, 817
Fariss, Elizabeth VI, 854
Fariss, Elizabeth VI, 912
Fariss, Frances A. VI, 815
Fariss, Francis VI, 840
Fariss, George B. VI, 815
Fariss, George B. VI, 819
Fariss, James H. VI, 815
Fariss, Jane II, 522
Fariss, Jane II, 587
Fariss, Jane VI, 981
Fariss, Jesse VI, 815
Fariss, Jessie VI, 815
Fariss, John VI, 815
Fariss, John VI, 822
Fariss, John VI, 840
Fariss, John A. VI, 815
Fariss, John H. VI, 815
Fariss, John J. VI, 913
Fariss, John J. VI, 981
Fariss, John J. VI, 994
Fariss, Joseph VI, 815
Fariss, Joseph A. VI, 843
Fariss, Lucretia VI, 815
Fariss, Martha VI, 815
Fariss, Martha I. VI, 815
Fariss, Martha J. VI, 815
Fariss, Martin VI, 815
Fariss, Martin H. VI, 815
Fariss, Martin H. VI, 817
Fariss, Mary VI, 815
Fariss, Mary VI, 848
Fariss, Mary VI, 913
Fariss, Mary B. VI, 913
Fariss, Mary E. VI, 815
Fariss, Mary Jane VI, 913
Fariss, Nancy VI, 815
Fariss, Nancy VI, 822
Fariss, Nancy VI, 913
Fariss, Nancy VI, 1002
Fariss, Patara Ann VI, 815
Fariss, Polly VI, 815
Fariss, Rebecca VI, 947
Fariss, Sabra VI, 815
Fariss, Sallie VI, 815
Fariss, Sarah P. VI, 815
Fariss, Sophia VI, 856
Fariss, Susan Ann VI, 815
Fariss, Susanna VI, 831
Fariss, Thomas VI, 815
Fariss, Thomas A. VI, 913
Fariss, Thomas C. VI, 828
Fariss, William VI, 808
Fariss, William VI, 815
Fariss, Wm. A. VI, 815
Farland, Hannah IV, 702
Farland, Joseph IV, 702
Farler, Sarah I, 49
Farler, Sarah I, 66
Farley, ??? III, 334
Farley, Capt. James III, 402
Farley, David VI, 913
Farley, Edward VI, 343
Farley, Edward VI, 860
Farley, Edward VI, 913
Farley, Edward VI, 963
Farley, Eliz. III, 114
Farley, Eliza III, 334
Farley, Elizabeth III, 114
Farley, Elizabeth III, 334
Farley, Elvira VI, 913
Farley, Henry F. VI, 815
Farley, Henry T. VI, 343
Farley, Henry T. VI, 860
Farley, James III, 410
Farley, Judith VI, 815
Farley, Judy VI, 913
Farley, Keziah VI, 913
Farley, Lockey J. VI, 963
Farley, Lydia A. VI, 833
Farley, Margaret III, 402
Farley, Margaret III, 410
Farley, Mary VI, 343
Farley, Mary VI, 860
Farley, Mary J. VI, 992
Farley, Peter III, 114
Farley, Phebe VI, 908
Farley, Sally VI, 913
Farley, W. D. VI, 856
Farley, Zerriah III, 410
Farley, Zerviah III, 402
Farling, ??? V, 671
Farling, Abraham V, 671
Farling, Amos V, 671
Farling, Amos V, 995
Farling, Barbara V, 995
Farling, Barbara E. V, 671
Farling, Christopher V, 671
Farling, Fietta V, 671
Farling, Fietta Abraham V, 671
Farling, Frank V, 995
Farling, Grace V, 995
Farling, Lavina V, 671
Farling, Levina V, 671
Farling, Rhoda V, 671
Farling, Samuel V, 671
Farling, Samuel V, 995
Farling, Sarah V, 995
Farling, Sarah L. V, 671
Farlow, Abner I, 746
Farlow, Abner I, 924
Farlow, Absalom I, 746
Farlow, Absalom I, 760
Farlow, Absolom I, 761
Farlow, Ada I, 238
Farlow, Adela I, 761
Farlow, Adela P. I, 747
Farlow, Adela P. I, 760
Farlow, Adelia I, 745
Farlow, Alice I, 616
Farlow, Alice I, 746

Farlow, Allice I, 760
Farlow, Allice I, 770
Farlow, Alpheas I, 760
Farlow, Alpheus I, 747
Farlow, Alva Malinda I, 747
Farlow, Ann I, 352
Farlow, Ann I, 388
Farlow, Ann I, 653
Farlow, Ann I, 746
Farlow, Ann I, 747
Farlow, Ann I, 760
Farlow, Ann I, 762
Farlow, Archie C. I, 747
Farlow, Archie C. I, 760
Farlow, Armella I, 747
Farlow, Armony I, 746
Farlow, Belinda I, 760
Farlow, Bellinda I, 760
Farlow, Bellinda I, 770
Farlow, Beryn B. I, 632
Farlow, Bevan Breathwaite I, 616
Farlow, Candace I, 745
Farlow, Caroline I, 746
Farlow, Catharine Adella I, 746
Farlow, Cecil A. I, 746
Farlow, Cinderella I, 923
Farlow, Cindrella H. I, 746
Farlow, Clara Barton I, 924
Farlow, Clara Barton I, 941
Farlow, Clara Barton I, 948
Farlow, Clarissa I, 747
Farlow, Clarissa I, 760
Farlow, Cora I, 941
Farlow, Daniel I, 760
Farlow, Daniel B. I, 747
Farlow, David I, 474
Farlow, David I, 476
Farlow, David I, 479
Farlow, David I, 616
Farlow, David I, 632
Farlow, David I, 745
Farlow, David I, 746
Farlow, David I, 747
Farlow, David I, 760
Farlow, David I, 761
Farlow, David I, 924
Farlow, David Arthur I, 746
Farlow, David C. I, 632
Farlow, David Cary I, 616
Farlow, David S. I, 328
Farlow, David, Jr. I, 746
Farlow, Davis S. I, 328
Farlow, Deborah I, 352
Farlow, Deborah I, 388
Farlow, Deborah I, 747
Farlow, Deborah I, 760
Farlow, Deborah I, 764
Farlow, Deborah I, 765
Farlow, Deborah I, 769
Farlow, Deborah I, 928
Farlow, Deborah Ann I, 746
Farlow, Deborah Ann I, 749
Farlow, Deborah E. I, 747
Farlow, Della I, 238
Farlow, Delphinia A. I, 747
Farlow, Dorothy I, 924
Farlow, E. Edgar I, 941
Farlow, E. Wray I, 941
Farlow, Edgar Wilson I, 924
Farlow, Edith I, 747
Farlow, Edith I, 755
Farlow, Edith I, 760
Farlow, Effie I, 238
Farlow, Elbert Wray I, 924
Farlow, Eleanor I, 746
Farlow, Eleanor I, 760
Farlow, Eleanor I, 764
Farlow, Elihu I, 238
Farlow, Elihu B. I, 746
Farlow, Elisa I, 760
Farlow, Eliza I, 746
Farlow, Eliza I, 754
Farlow, Eliza I, 761
Farlow, Elizabeth I, 653
Farlow, Elizabeth I, 746
Farlow, Elizabeth I, 755
Farlow, Elizabeth I, 760
Farlow, Elizabeth Farlow I, 754
Farlow, Ellison I, 238
Farlow, Elma I, 238
Farlow, Elmira E. I, 747
Farlow, Emily I, 238
Farlow, Emily J. I, 760
Farlow, Emily J. I, 767
Farlow, Enoch I, 328
Farlow, Enoch I, 653
Farlow, Enoch I, 678
Farlow, Enoch I, 689
Farlow, Enoch I, 746
Farlow, Enoch I, 747
Farlow, Enoch I, 749
Farlow, Enoch I, 760
Farlow, Enoch Edgar I, 746
Farlow, Enoch Edgar I, 924
Farlow, Enoch Edgar I, 940
Farlow, Enoch Edgar I, 948
Farlow, Enoch Ernest I, 924
Farlow, Enoch T. I, 746
Farlow, Enoch, Jr. I, 746
Farlow, Enoch, Jr. I, 760
Farlow, Ernest I, 941
Farlow, Estella I, 746
Farlow, Eunice I, 746
Farlow, Eunice I, 747
Farlow, Eunice I, 760
Farlow, Eunice I, 764
Farlow, Eunice Samira I, 761
Farlow, Evangeline I, 746
Farlow, Fanny I, 924
Farlow, Fanny I, 940
Farlow, Fanny I, 948
Farlow, Frank V, 995
Farlow, George I, 653
Farlow, George I, 715
Farlow, George I, 727
Farlow, George I, 741
Farlow, George I, 746
Farlow, George I, 760
Farlow, George I, 924
Farlow, George D. I, 941
Farlow, George M. I, 747
Farlow, George M. I, 760
Farlow, Hannah I, 445
Farlow, Hannah I, 451
Farlow, Hannah I, 479
Farlow, Hannah I, 673
Farlow, Hannah I, 678
Farlow, Hannah I, 741
Farlow, Hannah I, 747
Farlow, Hannah I, 760
Farlow, Hannah I, 809
Farlow, Hannah E. I, 746
Farlow, Hannah Matilda I, 746
Farlow, Henry I. I, 760
Farlow, Henry J. I, 760
Farlow, Henry J. I, 770
Farlow, Herbert Leslie I, 746
Farlow, Honlolula I, 632
Farlow, Honolulu I, 616
Farlow, Isaac I, 445
Farlow, Isaac I, 447
Farlow, Isaac I, 653
Farlow, Isaac I, 741
Farlow, Isaac I, 746
Farlow, Isaac I, 760
Farlow, Isaac N. I, 747
Farlow, Isaac Newton I, 934
Farlow, Isaac, Jr. I, 760
Farlow, J. W. I, 613
Farlow, J. W. I, 616
Farlow, Jabez I, 746
Farlow, Jabez I, 747
Farlow, Jabez I, 760
Farlow, Jabez I, 764
Farlow, James I, 747
Farlow, James I, 760
Farlow, James I, 809
Farlow, James I, 840
Farlow, James Daniel I, 746
Farlow, James Garfield I, 746
Farlow, James Ralto I, 924
Farlow, James Ralto I, 941
Farlow, Jane I, 653
Farlow, Jane I, 741
Farlow, Jane I, 746
Farlow, Jane I, 760
Farlow, Jane I, 770
Farlow, Jeptha I, 747
Farlow, Jesse E. I, 746
Farlow, John I, 616
Farlow, John I, 746
Farlow, John I, 747
Farlow, John I, 757
Farlow, John I, 760
Farlow, John I, 761
Farlow, John I, 770
Farlow, John I, 921
Farlow, John I, 924
Farlow, John I, 940
Farlow, John C. I, 746
Farlow, John C. I, 761
Farlow, John F. I, 746
Farlow, John F. I, 760
Farlow, John Kemp I, 746
Farlow, John N. I, 761
Farlow, John Newton I, 746
Farlow, John, Jr. I, 924
Farlow, John, Jr. I, 941
Farlow, Jonathan I, 352
Farlow, Jonathan I, 746
Farlow, Jonathan C. I, 747
Farlow, Jonathan C. I, 760
Farlow, Joseph I, 352
Farlow, Joseph I, 388
Farlow, Joseph I, 445
Farlow, Joseph I, 449
Farlow, Joseph I, 616
Farlow, Joseph I, 653
Farlow, Joseph I, 746
Farlow, Joseph I, 754
Farlow, Joseph I, 755
Farlow, Joseph I, 760
Farlow, Joseph E. I, 746
Farlow, Laura I, 633
Farlow, Laura I, 638
Farlow, Laura A. I, 633
Farlow, Laura A. I, 638
Farlow, Laura M. I, 336
Farlow, Laura M. I, 338
Farlow, Laura Moore I, 616
Farlow, Lewallen I, 941
Farlow, Lewallen Worth I, 941
Farlow, Lewellen I, 920
Farlow, Lewellin I, 924
Farlow, Louisa I, 746
Farlow, Louisa I, 759
Farlow, Louisa I, 760
Farlow, Lovena I, 616
Farlow, Luellen I, 746
Farlow, Luzena M. I, 746
Farlow, Lydia I, 746
Farlow, Lydia I, 760
Farlow, Lydia I, 761
Farlow, Maffie Viola I, 924
Farlow, Maggie I, 920
Farlow, Maggie I, 941
Farlow, Mamie I, 941
Farlow, Margaret I, 853
Farlow, Margaret I, 878
Farlow, Margaret A. I, 747
Farlow, Margaret H. I, 941
Farlow, Margarette I, 940
Farlow, Martha I, 934
Farlow, Martha Jane I, 746
Farlow, Martha L. I, 761
Farlow, Martha Lutitia I, 746
Farlow, Mary I, 328
Farlow, Mary I, 445
Farlow, Mary I, 447
Farlow, Mary I, 474
Farlow, Mary I, 476
Farlow, Mary I, 479
Farlow, Mary I, 616
Farlow, Mary I, 632
Farlow, Mary I, 653
Farlow, Mary I, 678
Farlow, Mary I, 689
Farlow, Mary I, 741
Farlow, Mary I, 745
Farlow, Mary I, 746
Farlow, Mary I, 747
Farlow, Mary I, 749
Farlow, Mary I, 760
Farlow, Mary I, 761
Farlow, Mary I, 921
Farlow, Mary I, 924
Farlow, Mary A. I, 747
Farlow, Mary A. I, 759
Farlow, Mary A. I, 761
Farlow, Mary Ann I, 616
Farlow, Mary Ann I, 746
Farlow, Mary E. I, 613
Farlow, Mary E. I, 616
Farlow, Mary Ellen I, 746
Farlow, Mary Ellen I, 924
Farlow, Mary J. I, 747
Farlow, Michael I, 445
Farlow, Michael I, 451
Farlow, Michael I, 479
Farlow, Michael I, 653
Farlow, Michael I, 678
Farlow, Michael I, 741
Farlow, Michael I, 746
Farlow, Michael I, 747
Farlow, Michael I, 760
Farlow, Michael A. I, 616
Farlow, Michael A. I, 747
Farlow, Michael A. I, 760
Farlow, Michael Cox I, 745
Farlow, Michael Cox I, 747
Farlow, Michal I, 809
Farlow, Nancy I, 632
Farlow, Nancy I, 760
Farlow, Nancy I, 761
Farlow, Nancy I, 769
Farlow, Nancy E. I, 746
Farlow, Nancy E. I, 761
Farlow, Nancy Jane I, 746
Farlow, Nancy Jane I, 755
Farlow, Nancy Jane I, 760
Farlow, Nannie E. I, 616
Farlow, Nannie E. I, 632
Farlow, Naomi Ruth I, 924
Farlow, Naomi Ruth I, 941
Farlow, Nathan I, 445
Farlow, Nathan I, 653
Farlow, Nathan I, 678
Farlow, Nathan I, 715
Farlow, Nathan I, 746
Farlow, Nathan I, 747
Farlow, Nathan I, 760
Farlow, Nathan Hill I, 746
Farlow, Nathan, Jr. I, 760
Farlow, Nathan, Sr. I, 747
Farlow, Nelson I, 747
Farlow, Newby I, 746
Farlow, Newton I, 633
Farlow, Newton I, 638
Farlow, Newton F. I, 616
Farlow, Newton F. I, 633
Farlow, Pearl I, 931
Farlow, Rachel I, 760
Farlow, Rachel I, 809
Farlow, Rachel I, 840
Farlow, Rachel I, 934
Farlow, Rachel A. I, 747
Farlow, Rachel Cora I, 924
Farlow, Ralph Kelsey I, 924
Farlow, Ralph Mead I, 941
Farlow, Ralph Mead I, 948
Farlow, Rebecca I, 746
Farlow, Rhoda I, 615
Farlow, Rhoda I, 627
Farlow, Rodema I, 747
Farlow, Roy I, 940
Farlow, Rufus E. I, 747
Farlow, Ruth I, 352
Farlow, Ruth I, 388
Farlow, Ruth I, 445
Farlow, Ruth I, 449
Farlow, Ruth I, 539
Farlow, Ruth I, 653
Farlow, Ruth I, 678
Farlow, Ruth I, 746
Farlow, Ruth I, 747
Farlow, Ruth I, 760
Farlow, Ruth I, 767
Farlow, Sallie I, 625
Farlow, Samuel I, 653
Farlow, Samuel I, 747
Farlow, Samuel I, 760
Farlow, Samuel I, 761
Farlow, Samuel I, 762
Farlow, Sarah I, 653
Farlow, Sarah I, 715
Farlow, Sarah I, 727
Farlow, Sarah I, 746
Farlow, Sarah I, 747
Farlow, Sarah I, 757
Farlow, Sarah I, 760
Farlow, Sarah I, 763
Farlow, Sarah I, 767
Farlow, Sarah I, 770
Farlow, Sarah I, 933
Farlow, Sarah A. I, 761
Farlow, Sarah Annis I, 746
Farlow, Sarah E. I, 747
Farlow, Sarah Ellen I, 760
Farlow, Scovia I, 932
Farlow, Sewel I, 653
Farlow, Sewel I, 759
Farlow, Sewel I, 761
Farlow, Sewel I, 853
Farlow, Sewel I, 878
Farlow, Sewell I, 747
Farlow, Sewell I, 760
Farlow, Silas I, 746
Farlow, Silas I, 760
Farlow, Sophronia I, 746
Farlow, Sophronia I, 924
Farlow, Sophronia P. I, 328
Farlow, Sophronia P. I, 761
Farlow, Sue I, 941
Farlow, Sue VI, 81
Farlow, Sue F. I, 921
Farlow, Sue J. VI, 63
Farlow, Sue J. VI, 82
Farlow, Susan I, 924
Farlow, Susannah Jane I, 746
Farlow, Tamar I, 746
Farlow, Tamer I, 760
Farlow, Tamor Martitia I, 746
Farlow, Thomas E. I, 746
Farlow, Vera I, 920
Farlow, Vera I, 941
Farlow, Vera Gertrude I, 924
Farlow, Vera Gertrude I, 940
Farlow, William I, 653
Farlow, William I, 746
Farlow, William I, 760
Farlow, William I, 941
Farlow, William C. I, 760
Farlow, William Elbert I, 746
Farlow, William G. I, 747
Farlow, William H. I, 746
Farlow, William H. I, 747
Farlow, William S. I, 746
Farlow, William S. I, 760
Farlow, Worth L. I, 924
Farlow, Xantippe I, 747
Farlow, Zanteppe I, 760
Farlow, Zelma Leah I, 924
Farlow, Zelma Lee I, 941
Farlow, Zelma Lee I, 948
Farlow, Zimri I, 746
Farlow, Zimri I, 760
Farlowe, Beryn B. I, 632
Farmar, Luzena C. V, 904
Farmer, ??? IV, 391
Farmer, ??? IV, 952
Farmer, ??? VI, 293
Farmer, Abby Ann IV, 200
Farmer, Abby Ann IV, 904
Farmer, Abel Gilbert IV, 1057
Farmer, Abijah V, 738
Farmer, Ada IV, 1250
Farmer, Adaline IV, 391
Farmer, Adaline IV, 523
Farmer, Addie E. IV, 1250
Farmer, Adeline IV, 523
Farmer, Adeline IV, 545
Farmer, Agnes VI, 310
Farmer, Amelia IV, 391
Farmer, Amelia IV, 523
Farmer, Amelia IV, 577
Farmer, Amelia IV, 580
Farmer, Ann I, 389
Farmer, Ann I, 399
Farmer, Ann II, 520
Farmer, Ann IV, 381
Farmer, Ann IV, 385
Farmer, Ann IV, 391
Farmer, Ann IV, 425
Farmer, Ann IV, 523
Farmer, Ann IV, 538
Farmer, Ann IV, 624
Farmer, Ann IV, 702
Farmer, Ann IV, 733
Farmer, Ann IV, 814
Farmer, Ann IV, 904
Farmer, Ann IV, 905
Farmer, Ann IV, 912
Farmer, Ann IV, 952
Farmer, Ann IV, 974
Farmer, Ann IV, 1131
Farmer, Ann B. VI, 799
Farmer, Anna V, 738
Farmer, Anna V, 755
Farmer, Armelia IV, 1057
Farmer, Armelia IV, 1058
Farmer, Armila C. IV, 523
Farmer, Barnabas VI, 815
Farmer, Benj. V, 738
Farmer, Benjamin I, 389
Farmer, Benjamin I, 653
Farmer, Benjamin I, 1048
Farmer, Benjamin V, 738
Farmer, Benjamin VI, 816
Farmer, Benjamin VI, 861
Farmer, Betsy VI, 913
Farmer, Beulah IV, 904
Farmer, Beulah R. IV, 471
Farmer, Beulah R. IV, 493
Farmer, Brences VI, 843
Farmer, Cassander IV, 200
Farmer, Catharine I, 389
Farmer, Catharine I, 1048
Farmer, Catharine II, 360
Farmer, Catharine II, 520
Farmer, Catharine IV, 391
Farmer, Catharine VI, 386
Farmer, Catharine VI, 413
Farmer, Catherine I, 1048
Farmer, Ceziah VI, 876
Farmer, Charles VI, 816
Farmer, Charles E. VI, 997
Farmer, Clerelia A. V, 995
Farmer, Daniel V, 738
Farmer, Dearman Williams IV, 1057
Farmer, Delilah VI, 816
Farmer, Eda Ann VI, 913
Farmer, Edith IV, 814
Farmer, Elihu IV, 904
Farmer, Elijah IV, 391
Farmer, Elizabeth I, 653
Farmer, Elizabeth I, 1048
Farmer, Elizabeth IV, 702
Farmer, Elizabeth IV, 904
Farmer, Elizabeth V, 738
Farmer, Elizabeth V, 767
Farmer, Elizabeth VI, 815
Farmer, Elizabeth Ann VI, 1016
Farmer, Ellen IV, 904

Farmer, Ellen A. IV, 471
Farmer, Ellen A. IV, 493
Farmer, Emma II, 739
Farmer, Emmet S. IV, 523
Farmer, Fanny VI, 913
Farmer, Fanny VI, 975
Farmer, Hannah I, 389
Farmer, Hannah I, 539
Farmer, Hannah I, 653
Farmer, Hannah I, 878
Farmer, Hannah I, 1048
Farmer, Hannah V, 738
Farmer, Hannah V, 767
Farmer, Hannah VI, 361
Farmer, Hannah VI, 386
Farmer, Hannah VI, 389
Farmer, Harrison VI, 796
Farmer, Harrison VI, 816
Farmer, Harrison VI, 857
Farmer, Henry VI, 310
Farmer, Isaac P. IV, 200
Farmer, Isaac P. IV, 904
Farmer, Isaac Parker IV, 200
Farmer, Isaac Parker IV, 471
Farmer, Isaac Parker IV, 905
Farmer, Isaac T. V, 738
Farmer, Isabela IV, 1057
Farmer, Jacob IV, 471
Farmer, Jacob IV, 904
Farmer, Jacob IV, 905
Farmer, Jacob VI, 993
Farmer, James I, 715
Farmer, James IV, 702
Farmer, James IV, 904
Farmer, James IV, 912
Farmer, James IV, 932
Farmer, James IV, 952
Farmer, James IV, 1314
Farmer, James VI, 799
Farmer, James VI, 815
Farmer, James VI, 913
Farmer, Jesse I, 539
Farmer, Jesse IV, 391
Farmer, Jesse IV, 523
Farmer, Jesse IV, 952
Farmer, Jesse V, 738
Farmer, Jesse VI, 876
Farmer, Jessy V, 738
Farmer, John I, 49
Farmer, John I, 388
Farmer, John I, 389
Farmer, John I, 539
Farmer, John I, 653
Farmer, John I, 678
Farmer, John I, 715
Farmer, John I, 878
Farmer, John I, 1043
Farmer, John I, 1048
Farmer, John II, 443
Farmer, John II, 520
Farmer, John IV, 200
Farmer, John IV, 471
Farmer, John IV, 904
Farmer, John IV, 905
Farmer, John IV, 912
Farmer, John IV, 917
Farmer, John IV, 952
Farmer, John V, 54
Farmer, John V, 738
Farmer, John V, 767
Farmer, John Albert V, 738
Farmer, John T. IV, 523
Farmer, Joseph I, 49
Farmer, Joseph I, 139
Farmer, Joseph I, 142
Farmer, Joseph I, 389
Farmer, Joseph I, 1048
Farmer, Joseph IV, 391
Farmer, Joseph IV, 523
Farmer, Joseph IV, 952
Farmer, Joseph, Jr. I, 715
Farmer, Ketura IV, 523
Farmer, Keturah IV, 523
Farmer, Keturah IV, 904
Farmer, Keturah IV, 905
Farmer, Keturah IV, 911
Farmer, Kitura IV, 814
Farmer, Kiturah IV, 904
Farmer, Laban VI, 913
Farmer, Laura IV, 904
Farmer, Loray G. IV, 523
Farmer, Luzena C. V, 904
Farmer, Luzena C. V, 942
Farmer, Luzina C. V, 904
Farmer, Lydia I, 1008
Farmer, Lydia I, 1009
Farmer, Lydia IV, 904
Farmer, Lynden T. IV, 523
Farmer, Mahala VI, 815
Farmer, Maribah IV, 702
Farmer, Marshall B. VI, 997
Farmer, Marshall B. VI, 1016
Farmer, Martha I, 539
Farmer, Martha I, 878
Farmer, Martha IV, 200
Farmer, Martha IV, 904
Farmer, Martha VI, 815
Farmer, Martha A. VI, 816
Farmer, Martha M. VI, 997
Farmer, Mary I, 139
Farmer, Mary I, 142
Farmer, Mary I, 388
Farmer, Mary I, 389
Farmer, Mary I, 401
Farmer, Mary I, 539
Farmer, Mary I, 653
Farmer, Mary I, 678
Farmer, Mary I, 686
Farmer, Mary I, 715
Farmer, Mary I, 878
Farmer, Mary I, 1043
Farmer, Mary I, 1048
Farmer, Mary II, 520
Farmer, Mary IV, 200
Farmer, Mary IV, 259
Farmer, Mary IV, 385
Farmer, Mary IV, 391
Farmer, Mary IV, 471
Farmer, Mary IV, 624
Farmer, Mary IV, 904
Farmer, Mary IV, 905
Farmer, Mary IV, 912
Farmer, Mary IV, 917
Farmer, Mary IV, 952
Farmer, Mary IV, 1057
Farmer, Mary IV, 1082
Farmer, Mary V, 738
Farmer, Mary V, 767
Farmer, Mary V, 768
Farmer, Mary VI, 829
Farmer, Mary VI, 861
Farmer, Mary VI, 869
Farmer, Mary VI, 913
Farmer, Mary Ann I, 715
Farmer, Mary Ann I, 716
Farmer, Mary Ann IV, 391
Farmer, Mary Ann IV, 523
Farmer, Mary Ann IV, 524
Farmer, Mary Ann IV, 580
Farmer, Mary Ann V, 738
Farmer, Mary C. IV, 904
Farmer, Mary Casander IV, 905
Farmer, Mary Cassader IV, 471
Farmer, Mary Cassandra IV, 200
Farmer, Mary Hooks I, 336
Farmer, Mary Jackson I, 389
Farmer, Mary, Jr. IV, 814
Farmer, Maryann I, 653
Farmer, Maryann IV, 391
Farmer, Maryann IV, 523
Farmer, Maryanna I, 389
Farmer, Matilda V, 54
Farmer, Matilda V, 738
Farmer, Meribah IV, 905
Farmer, Meribah IV, 912
Farmer, Meribah IV, 932
Farmer, Meribah IV, 952
Farmer, Meriboh IV, 904
Farmer, Meriby IV, 905
Farmer, Merihab IV, 952
Farmer, Mildred VI, 816
Farmer, Minnie IV, 1250
Farmer, Moses I, 389
Farmer, Moses I, 539
Farmer, Moses I, 653
Farmer, Moses I, 678
Farmer, Moses I, 686
Farmer, Moses I, 715
Farmer, Moses I, 716
Farmer, Moses V, 738
Farmer, Moses V, 767
Farmer, Moses VI, 1001
Farmer, Mrs. Minnie IV, 1250
Farmer, Nancy VI, 815
Farmer, Nancy VI, 861
Farmer, Nancy VI, 876
Farmer, Nathan I, 388
Farmer, Nathan I, 389
Farmer, Nathan I, 539
Farmer, Nathan I, 809
Farmer, Nathan I, 878
Farmer, Nathan I, 971
Farmer, Nathan I, 986
Farmer, Naylor IV, 1057
Farmer, Oakley J. IV, 523
Farmer, Orry V, 738
Farmer, Parker IV, 200
Farmer, Phebe I, 389
Farmer, Phebe I, 413
Farmer, Phebe I, 653
Farmer, Phebe V, 728
Farmer, Phebe V, 738
Farmer, Pheby I, 986
Farmer, Philip I, 878
Farmer, Philip V, 738
Farmer, Philip V, 755
Farmer, Philip V, 767
Farmer, Phillip I, 539
Farmer, Polly VI, 913
Farmer, Prudence V, 54
Farmer, Prudence V, 738
Farmer, Rachel I, 374
Farmer, Rachel I, 388
Farmer, Rachel I, 389
Farmer, Rachel I, 653
Farmer, Rachel I, 678
Farmer, Rachel I, 715
Farmer, Rachel I, 1048
Farmer, Rachel IV, 381
Farmer, Rachel IV, 391
Farmer, Rachel IV, 523
Farmer, Rachel IV, 572
Farmer, Rachel IV, 577
Farmer, Rachel IV, 952
Farmer, Rachel V, 738
Farmer, Rachel Bradley I, 389
Farmer, Rachel Bradly I, 389
Farmer, Rebecca I, 539
Farmer, Rebecca IV, 624
Farmer, Rebecca IV, 904
Farmer, Rebecca IV, 905
Farmer, Rebecca IV, 912
Farmer, Rebecca IV, 1072
Farmer, Rebecca V, 738
Farmer, Rebekah I, 418
Farmer, Rebekah I, 1048
Farmer, Rebekah Saunders I, 389
Farmer, Reuben I, 539
Farmer, Reuben I, 878
Farmer, Reuben V, 728
Farmer, Reuben V, 738
Farmer, Rhoda IV, 523
Farmer, Rhoda IV, 904
Farmer, Rhoda IV, 912
Farmer, Ruth I, 49
Farmer, Ruth I, 66
Farmer, Ruth IV, 391
Farmer, Ruth IV, 455
Farmer, Ruth V, 738
Farmer, Sam C. VI, 816
Farmer, Sarah I, 388
Farmer, Sarah I, 389
Farmer, Sarah I, 418
Farmer, Sarah I, 539
Farmer, Sarah I, 653
Farmer, Sarah I, 715
Farmer, Sarah I, 716
Farmer, Sarah I, 878
Farmer, Sarah IV, 200
Farmer, Sarah IV, 224
Farmer, Sarah IV, 391
Farmer, Sarah IV, 471
Farmer, Sarah IV, 517
Farmer, Sarah IV, 523
Farmer, Sarah IV, 912
Farmer, Sarah V, 738
Farmer, Sarah V, 767
Farmer, Sarah P. IV, 200
Farmer, Sarah P. IV, 523
Farmer, Sarah P. IV, 904
Farmer, Sarah P. IV, 905
Farmer, Sarah P. V, 738
Farmer, Sarah Shepherd I, 389
Farmer, Saryann V, 738
Farmer, Serepta V, 738
Farmer, Smith H. VI, 816
Farmer, Solomon I, 715
Farmer, Stephen S. VI, 913
Farmer, Susanna IV, 523
Farmer, Susanna IV, 952
Farmer, Susannah IV, 367
Farmer, Susannah IV, 391
Farmer, Susannah IV, 523
Farmer, Susannah IV, 591
Farmer, Susannah IV, 624
Farmer, Susannah IV, 952
Farmer, Susannah V, 738
Farmer, Susannah V, 767
Farmer, Susannah VI, 797
Farmer, Susnna IV, 814
Farmer, Sydnor VI, 815
Farmer, Tabitha IV, 391
Farmer, Tabitha IV, 952
Farmer, Tabitha IV, 974
Farmer, Talitha IV, 523
Farmer, Taylor IV, 391
Farmer, Taylor IV, 523
Farmer, Taylor IV, 524
Farmer, Taylor IV, 580
Farmer, Taylor IV, 952
Farmer, Thomas I, 49
Farmer, Thomas I, 66
Farmer, Thomas I, 239
Farmer, Thomas I, 715
Farmer, Thomas I, 1048
Farmer, Thomas II, 360
Farmer, Thomas IV, 381
Farmer, Thomas IV, 385
Farmer, Thomas IV, 391
Farmer, Thomas IV, 523
Farmer, Thomas IV, 912
Farmer, Thomas IV, 952
Farmer, Thomas IV, 974
Farmer, Thomas IV, 1361
Farmer, Thomas VI, 815
Farmer, Thomas VI, 816
Farmer, Thomas VI, 861
Farmer, Thomas VI, 913
Farmer, Thomas E. IV, 523
Farmer, Thomas, Jr. I, 49
Farmer, Thos. B. VI, 829
Farmer, Thos. E. IV, 517
Farmer, Wd. Jane VI, 913
Farmer, Wd. Peggy VI, 975
Farmer, William I, 389
Farmer, William I, 1029
Farmer, William I, 1041
Farmer, William I, 1043
Farmer, William I, 1048
Farmer, William IV, 200
Farmer, William IV, 391
Farmer, William IV, 471
Farmer, William IV, 904
Farmer, William IV, 905
Farmer, William IV, 912
Farmer, William V, 54
Farmer, William V, 738
Farmer, William VI, 815
Farmer, William VI, 913
Farmer, William James IV, 624
Farmer, William, Jr. I, 389
Farmer, William, Jr. I, 1048
Farmer, William, Jr. V, 738
Farmer, William, Sr. I, 539
Farmer, Wilson VI, 815
Farmer, Wm. IV, 200
Farmer, Wm. IV, 259
Farmer, Wm. IV, 391
Farmer, Wm. IV, 455
Farmer, Wm. IV, 904
Farmer, Wm. V, 738
Farmingdale, Lucy G. III, 503
Farmingdale, Walter III, 503
Farnham, Baldwin VI, 913
Farnham, Caroline S. VI, 913
Farnham, Elizabeth H. II, 704
Farnham, John II, 704
Farnham, Mary II, 704
Farnham, Susan II, 704
Farnley, Hannah VI, 595
Farnley, Thomas VI, 389
Farnley, William VI, 595
Farnly, Martha VI, 600
Farnsworth, Daniel II, 219
Farnsworth, Daniel II, 249
Farnsworth, Mary IV, 1314
Farnsworth, Rachel II, 219
Farnsworth, Rachel II, 249
Farnum, Elizabeth H. II, 730
Farnum, Elizabeth H. II, 736
Farnum, Elizabeth H. II, 739
Farnum, John II, 730
Farnum, John II, 736
Farnum, John II, 739
Farnum, Mary II, 730
Farnum, Mary II, 739
Farnum, Peter II, 736
Farnum, Peter II, 739
Farnum, Susan F. II, 739
Farnum, Susan F. II, 774
Farnum, Susanna II, 736
Farnum, Susanna II, 739
Faro, Elizabeth III, 114
Faro, Elizabeth III, 360
Faro, Elizabeth III, 410
Faro, Elizabeth III, 468
Faro, Jarvis III, 114
Faro, Jarvis III, 360
Faro, Jarvis III, 410
Faro, Jarvis III, 468
Faro, Rachel IV, 391
Farquar, Adam II, 995
Farquar, Allen V, 489
Farquar, Benjamin V, 489
Farquar, Cyrus V, 489
Farquar, Edwin V, 489
Farquar, Elizabeth II, 995
Farquar, Francis V, 489
Farquar, Hannah Ann V, 489
Farquar, Harriet A. V, 489
Farquar, Henry B. V, 489
Farquar, Jonathan V, 489
Farquar, Josiah V, 489
Farquar, Lucinda IV, 1096
Farquar, Milton J. V, 489
Farquar, Rachel V, 489
Farquar, Rebecca II, 995
Farquar, Rebecca II, 1022
Farquar, Rebecca V, 489
Farquar, Susannah V, 489
Farquar, Uriah V, 489
Farquehar, William IV, 200
Farquer, Ann VI, 386
Farquer, Wm. VI, 386
Farquhar, ??? III, 329
Farquhar, Aaron Roberts IV, 524
Farquhar, Abi V, 489
Farquhar, Abi V, 510
Farquhar, Abi V, 530
Farquhar, Abi Sparks V, 489
Farquhar, Adam II, 995
Farquhar, Adam II, 1003
Farquhar, Alan II, 219
Farquhar, Alan IV, 31
Farquhar, Alan IV, 212
Farquhar, Alan IV, 328
Farquhar, Alan IV, 358
Farquhar, Alan IV, 471
Farquhar, Alice VI, 740
Farquhar, Allan II, 219
Farquhar, Allen IV, 31
Farquhar, Allen IV, 200
Farquhar, Allen IV, 471
Farquhar, Allen IV, 523
Farquhar, Allen IV, 524
Farquhar, Allen V, 54
Farquhar, Allen V, 168
Farquhar, Allen V, 330
Farquhar, Allen V, 489
Farquhar, Allen VI, 490
Farquhar, Allen VI, 491
Farquhar, Allen VI, 534
Farquhar, Allen, Jr. VI, 505
Farquhar, Allen, Sr. VI, 536
Farquhar, Amos II, 219
Farquhar, Amos IV, 200
Farquhar, Amos V, 54
Farquhar, Amos V, 169
Farquhar, Amos VI, 490
Farquhar, Amos VI, 733
Farquhar, Amos VI, 740
Farquhar, Amos VI, 760
Farquhar, Andrew V, 54
Farquhar, Andrew V, 168
Farquhar, Andrew V, 169
Farquhar, Ann IV, 29
Farquhar, Ann IV, 31
Farquhar, Ann IV, 56
Farquhar, Ann V, 168
Farquhar, Ann V, 181
Farquhar, Ann VI, 467
Farquhar, Ann VI, 490
Farquhar, Ann VI, 491
Farquhar, Ann VI, 505
Farquhar, Ann VI, 534
Farquhar, Ann VI, 585
Farquhar, Ann VI, 740
Farquhar, Anna M. VI, 740
Farquhar, Anna R. V, 511
Farquhar, B. Hallowell II, 862
Farquhar, B. Hallowell II, 890
Farquhar, Benajah II, 995
Farquhar, Benajah IV, 868
Farquhar, Benj. V, 671
Farquhar, Benj. V, 716
Farquhar, Benj. V, 904
Farquhar, Benjamin IV, 200
Farquhar, Benjamin IV, 471
Farquhar, Benjamin V, 54
Farquhar, Benjamin V, 168
Farquhar, Benjamin V, 181
Farquhar, Benjamin V, 469
Farquhar, Benjamin V, 489
Farquhar, Benjamin V, 545
Farquhar, Benjamin V, 560
Farquhar, Benjamin V, 561
Farquhar, Benjamin V, 568
Farquhar, Benjamin V, 671
Farquhar, Benjamin VI, 490
Farquhar, Benjamin Hallowell II, 793
Farquhar, Beulah IV, 463
Farquhar, Beulah IV, 467
Farquhar, Beulah IV, 471
Farquhar, Beulah IV, 498
Farquhar, Bula T. IV, 471
Farquhar, Caleb IV, 200
Farquhar, Caleb VI, 490
Farquhar, Camilla McMillan V, 672
Farquhar, Carmel IV, 703
Farquhar, Caroline IV, 31
Farquhar, Caroline IV, 66
Farquhar, Caroline V, 671

rquhar, Caroline S. VI, 740
rquhar, Caroline S. VI, 765
rquhar, Caroline S. VI, 766
rquhar, Caroline S. VI, 782
rquhar, Charles IV, 56
rquhar, Charles V, 561
rquhar, Charles V, 671
rquhar, Charles VI, 733
rquhar, Charles VI, 740
rquhar, Charles C. IV, 471
rquhar, Charles Henry VI, 740
rquhar, Chas. Benj. V, 671
rquhar, Cyrus V, 54
rquhar, Cyrus V, 489
rquhar, Cyrus V, 560
rquhar, Cyrus V, 561
rquhar, Cyrus V, 904
rquhar, D. J. V, 169
rquhar, David IV, 31
rquhar, David IV, 391
rquhar, David IV, 523
rquhar, David IV, 524
quhar, David Jay V, 169
quhar, Deborah VI, 491
quhar, Dinah IV, 200
quhar, Dr. Jonah VI, 490
quhar, Edith IV, 212
quhar, Edith IV, 328
quhar, Edith IV, 358
quhar, Edith IV, 410
quhar, Edith IV, 471
quhar, Edith IV, 523
quhar, Edith IV, 524
quhar, Edith V, 656
quhar, Edith V, 671
quhar, Edith Melrose V, 672
quhar, Edmund III, 114
quhar, Edward IV, 703
quhar, Edward IV, 869
quhar, Edward A. IV, 869
quhar, Edward Andrews IV, 869
quhar, Edwin IV, 1158
quhar, Edwin V, 489
quhar, Eli IV, 125
quhar, Elijah IV, 200
quhar, Eliza E. VI, 740
quhar, Elizabeth II, 520
quhar, Elizabeth II, 739
quhar, Elizabeth II, 995
quhar, Elizabeth II, 1003
quhar, Elizabeth IV, 31
quhar, Elizabeth IV, 85
quhar, Elizabeth IV, 145
quhar, Elizabeth IV, 463
quhar, Elizabeth IV, 467
quhar, Elizabeth IV, 471
quhar, Elizabeth IV, 703
quhar, Elizabeth IV, 792
quhar, Elizabeth IV, 868
quhar, Elizabeth IV, 869
quhar, Elizabeth IV, 1278
quhar, Elizabeth V, 54
quhar, Elizabeth V, 168
quhar, Elizabeth V, 169
quhar, Elizabeth V, 511
quhar, Elizabeth VI, 477
quhar, Elizabeth VI, 490
quhar, Elizabeth VI, 491
quhar, Elizabeth VI, 572
quhar, Elizabeth VI, 585
quhar, Elizabeth VI, 587
quhar, Elizabeth VI, 623
quhar, Elizabeth VI, 627
quhar, Elizabeth VI, 650
quhar, Elizabeth VI, 665
quhar, Elizabeth VI, 718
quhar, Elizabeth W. IV, 792
quhar, Elizabeth, Sr. IV, 471
quhar, Elizabeth, Sr. IV, 624
quhar, Esther II, 995
quhar, Esther II, 1003
quhar, Esther Lois V, 672
quhar, Eunice Ellen V, 168
quhar, Evelyn V, 671
quhar, Frances V, 489
quhar, Francis V, 489
quhar, Francis V, 514
quhar, Francis V, 671
quhar, Francis V, 672
quhar, Francis H. V, 671
quhar, Francis H. V, 688
quhar, Francis Hunt V, 672
quhar, Francis P. IV, 1158
quhar, George V, 904
quhar, George VI, 491
quhar, George B. VI, 740
quhar, Granville VI, 740
quhar, Granville S. VI, 740
quhar, Hannah IV, 31
quhar, Hannah IV, 34
Farquhar, Hannah IV, 200
Farquhar, Hannah IV, 270
Farquhar, Hannah IV, 328
Farquhar, Hannah IV, 463
Farquhar, Hannah IV, 467
Farquhar, Hannah IV, 471
Farquhar, Hannah IV, 499
Farquhar, Hannah IV, 523
Farquhar, Hannah IV, 524
Farquhar, Hannah V, 511
Farquhar, Hannah V, 671
Farquhar, Hannah V, 672
Farquhar, Hannah VI, 490
Farquhar, Hannah VI, 491
Farquhar, Hannah A. V, 672
Farquhar, Hannah Ann IV, 31
Farquhar, Hannah Ann IV, 200
Farquhar, Hannah Ann IV, 312
Farquhar, Hannah Ann IV, 315
Farquhar, Hannah Ann V, 489
Farquhar, Hannah Ann V, 514
Farquhar, Hannah Ann V, 671
Farquhar, Hannah Ann V, 672
Farquhar, Hannah Maria IV, 463
Farquhar, Hannah Maria IV, 471
Farquhar, Harold Francis V, 671
Farquhar, Harriet V, 659
Farquhar, Harriet A. V, 489
Farquhar, Harriet A. V, 672
Farquhar, Harriet A. V, 700
Farquhar, Harriet Alice V, 169
Farquhar, Harriett V, 671
Farquhar, Harriett A. V, 671
Farquhar, Helena Belle V, 169
Farquhar, Henry V, 489
Farquhar, Henry V, 672
Farquhar, Henry V, 904
Farquhar, Henry B. V, 489
Farquhar, Henry B. V, 671
Farquhar, Henry B. V, 672
Farquhar, Henry Hallowell VI, 740
Farquhar, Hildegarde V, 671
Farquhar, Hildegarde V, 686
Farquhar, Iradel V, 169
Farquhar, Isabella V, 54
Farquhar, Isaiah V, 511
Farquhar, Jacob V, 54
Farquhar, Jacob V, 168
Farquhar, Jacob V, 169
Farquhar, James IV, 1278
Farquhar, James VI, 491
Farquhar, James A. V, 169
Farquhar, James P. IV, 1278
Farquhar, James William V, 511
Farquhar, Joel VI, 491
Farquhar, John IV, 31
Farquhar, John IV, 471
Farquhar, John IV, 498
Farquhar, John V, 511
Farquhar, John VI, 491
Farquhar, Jonah V, 54
Farquhar, Jonah V, 168
Farquhar, Jonah V, 169
Farquhar, Jonah V, 489
Farquhar, Jonathan V, 54
Farquhar, Jonathan V, 489
Farquhar, Jonathan B. V, 511
Farquhar, Jos. IV, 463
Farquhar, Jos. IV, 471
Farquhar, Joseph IV, 31
Farquhar, Joseph IV, 467
Farquhar, Joseph IV, 471
Farquhar, Joseph IV, 498
Farquhar, Joseph IV, 1158
Farquhar, Joseph VI, 491
Farquhar, Joseph VI, 512
Farquhar, Josiah V, 54
Farquhar, Josiah V, 489
Farquhar, Josiah V, 510
Farquhar, Laurena Hunt V, 672
Farquhar, Laurenna V, 385
Farquhar, Laurenna V, 405
Farquhar, Laurenna V, 672
Farquhar, Lewis Cooper II, 793
Farquhar, Linden W. V, 169
Farquhar, Louisa V, 489
Farquhar, Louisa V, 501
Farquhar, Louisa V, 904
Farquhar, Lucinda IV, 1097
Farquhar, Lydia V, 489
Farquhar, Lydia V, 560
Farquhar, Lydia V, 561
Farquhar, Lydia V, 904
Farquhar, Lydia VI, 491
Farquhar, Lydia Maria V, 168
Farquhar, Mahlon V, 54
Farquhar, Mahlon V, 168
Farquhar, Mahlon V, 169
Farquhar, Mahlon V, 489
Farquhar, Mahlon VI, 491
Farquhar, Malcom VI, 740
Farquhar, Malon Andrew William V, 169
Farquhar, Margaret II, 862
Farquhar, Margaret II, 890
Farquhar, Margaret VI, 740
Farquhar, Margaret VI, 745
Farquhar, Maria VI, 491
Farquhar, Maria VI, 512
Farquhar, Martha IV, 56
Farquhar, Martha IV, 200
Farquhar, Martha IV, 212
Farquhar, Martha IV, 471
Farquhar, Martha IV, 524
Farquhar, Martha D. II, 793
Farquhar, Martha D. II, 862
Farquhar, Martha D. II, 890
Farquhar, Martha W. IV, 200
Farquhar, Martha W. IV, 523
Farquhar, Martha W. IV, 524
Farquhar, Mary IV, 31
Farquhar, Mary IV, 62
Farquhar, Mary V, 671
Farquhar, Mary V, 711
Farquhar, Mary V, 716
Farquhar, Mary VI, 467
Farquhar, Mary VI, 490
Farquhar, Mary VI, 491
Farquhar, Mary VI, 585
Farquhar, Mary VI, 733
Farquhar, Mary VI, 740
Farquhar, Mary VI, 760
Farquhar, Mary Ada V, 672
Farquhar, Mary Anna III, 114
Farquhar, Mary Anna III, 329
Farquhar, Mary B. IV, 1158
Farquhar, Mary B. V, 560
Farquhar, Mary B. V, 561
Farquhar, Mary B. V, 568
Farquhar, Mary B. V, 671
Farquhar, Mary C. IV, 471
Farquhar, Mary Edith VI, 740
Farquhar, Mary Elizabeth V, 671
Farquhar, Mary Evelyn V, 671
Farquhar, Mary Evelyn V, 688
Farquhar, Mary G. V, 671
Farquhar, Mary I. V, 169
Farquhar, Mary S. IV, 471
Farquhar, Mary T. IV, 471
Farquhar, Mary T. IV, 498
Farquhar, Mary Vandervoort V, 672
Farquhar, Mary Willis VI, 740
Farquhar, Mary Willis VI, 760
Farquhar, Massey IV, 1158
Farquhar, Massey VI, 491
Farquhar, Massie IV, 1158
Farquhar, Matilda IV, 200
Farquhar, Matilda IV, 270
Farquhar, Matilda IV, 524
Farquhar, Matilda IV, 547
Farquhar, Mercy IV, 1158
Farquhar, Milton J. V, 489
Farquhar, Milton J. V, 671
Farquhar, Milton J. V, 672
Farquhar, Milton Kelly V, 671
Farquhar, Milton P. V, 671
Farquhar, Minnie B. V, 561
Farquhar, Moses IV, 1158
Farquhar, Moses VI, 491
Farquhar, Moses B. IV, 1158
Farquhar, Moses B. VI, 491
Farquhar, Naomi J. V, 671
Farquhar, Naomi Jane V, 561
Farquhar, Nellie V, 667
Farquhar, Nellie V, 672
Farquhar, Oscar V, 672
Farquhar, Oscar J. V, 671
Farquhar, Phebe IV, 200
Farquhar, Phebe V, 54
Farquhar, Phebe V, 158
Farquhar, Phebe V, 169
Farquhar, Phebe VI, 490
Farquhar, Phebe VI, 491
Farquhar, Phebe VI, 505
Farquhar, Phebe S. III, 114
Farquhar, Pheobe VI, 491
Farquhar, Philip V, 54
Farquhar, Philip V, 169
Farquhar, Phillip V, 169
Farquhar, R. Henry V, 904
Farquhar, Rachael VI, 491
Farquhar, Rachel V, 34
Farquhar, Rachel V, 54
Farquhar, Rachel V, 479
Farquhar, Rachel V, 489
Farquhar, Rachel V, 511
Farquhar, Rachel VI, 490
Farquhar, Rachel VI, 491
Farquhar, Rachel VI, 585
Farquhar, Rachel F. V, 904
Farquhar, Rebecca II, 995
Farquhar, Rebecca IV, 471
Farquhar, Rebecca IV, 869
Farquhar, Rebecca V, 489
Farquhar, Rebecca V, 533
Farquhar, Rebecca V, 671
Farquhar, Rebecca V, 695
Farquhar, Rebecca Abi V, 672
Farquhar, Rebecca Avi V, 672
Farquhar, Rebecca P. IV, 869
Farquhar, Richard V, 489
Farquhar, Richard V, 904
Farquhar, Richard VI, 491
Farquhar, Richard Henry V, 904
Farquhar, Robert V, 671
Farquhar, Robert V, 686
Farquhar, Robert VI, 490
Farquhar, Robert Hamilton V, 672
Farquhar, Robert M. VI, 740
Farquhar, Robert Roy V, 672
Farquhar, Roger B. VI, 766
Farquhar, Roger Brook VI, 765
Farquhar, Roger Brooke VI, 740
Farquhar, Roger Brooke VI, 782
Farquhar, Ruth IV, 1158
Farquhar, Ruth V, 560
Farquhar, Ruth V, 561
Farquhar, Ruth V, 671
Farquhar, Ruth VI, 491
Farquhar, Ruth Elma V, 168
Farquhar, Ruth P. IV, 1158
Farquhar, Salathiel D. V, 169
Farquhar, Samuel IV, 31
Farquhar, Samuel IV, 85
Farquhar, Samuel IV, 200
Farquhar, Samuel VI, 490
Farquhar, Samuel VI, 491
Farquhar, Sarah IV, 31
Farquhar, Sarah IV, 85
Farquhar, Sarah IV, 145
Farquhar, Sarah IV, 200
Farquhar, Sarah IV, 202
Farquhar, Sarah IV, 471
Farquhar, Sarah IV, 703
Farquhar, Sarah IV, 868
Farquhar, Sarah IV, 869
Farquhar, Sarah V, 54
Farquhar, Sarah V, 511
Farquhar, Sarah VI, 490
Farquhar, Sarah VI, 491
Farquhar, Sarah VI, 536
Farquhar, Sarah VI, 733
Farquhar, Sarah VI, 740
Farquhar, Sarah A. IV, 1158
Farquhar, Sarah Ann V, 511
Farquhar, Sarah B. VI, 740
Farquhar, Sarah Brooke VI, 740
Farquhar, Sarah Brooke VI, 782
Farquhar, Sarah Brooks VI, 731
Farquhar, Sarah Brooks VI, 781
Farquhar, Sarah E. V, 169
Farquhar, Sarah W. IV, 703
Farquhar, Seth V, 511
Farquhar, Susan IV, 1158
Farquhar, Susan IV, 1197
Farquhar, Susanna VI, 491
Farquhar, Susannah V, 54
Farquhar, Susannah V, 489
Farquhar, Susannah V, 512
Farquhar, Susannah VI, 491
Farquhar, Susannah VI, 512
Farquhar, Susannah VI, 699
Farquhar, Susannah VI, 701
Farquhar, Susannah M. VI, 491
Farquhar, Susannah M. VI, 512
Farquhar, Thomas IV, 29
Farquhar, Thomas IV, 31
Farquhar, Thomas VI, 490
Farquhar, Thomas C. VI, 740
Farquhar, Thomas Carlton V, 671
Farquhar, Thos. IV, 328
Farquhar, Thos. IV, 471
Farquhar, Uriah V, 54
Farquhar, Uriah V, 489
Farquhar, Viola M. V, 169
Farquhar, Wilbert Morgan V, 169
Farquhar, William IV, 31
Farquhar, William IV, 85
Farquhar, William IV, 145
Farquhar, William IV, 200
Farquhar, William IV, 471
Farquhar, William V, 54
Farquhar, William V, 168
Farquhar, William VI, 490
Farquhar, William VI, 491
Farquhar, William VI, 505
Farquhar, William VI, 534
Farquhar, William VI, 585
Farquhar, William B. V, 54
Farquhar, William H. IV, 1158
Farquhar, William Henry V, 168
Farquhar, William, Jr. VI, 467
Farquhar, William, Jr. VI, 491
Farquhar, William, Jr. VI, 585
Farquhar, William, Sr. VI, 491
Farquhar, Wm. IV, 145
Farquhar, Wm. IV, 202
Farquhar, Wm. IV, 270
Farquhar, Wm. IV, 463
Farquhar, Wm. IV, 467
Farquhar, Wm. IV, 1158
Farquhar, Wm. VI, 467
Farquhar, Wm. VI, 490
Farquhar, Wm. H. IV, 1158
Farquhar, Wm. Henry II, 862
Farquhar, Wm. Henry II, 890
Farquhar, Wm., Jr. VI, 491
Farquhar, Wm., Jr. VI, 585
Farr, ??? IV, 1303
Farr, Abbie IV, 1314
Farr, Abbie E. IV, 703
Farr, Abigail VI, 376
Farr, Abigail VI, 386
Farr, Angelina V, 951
Farr, Angeline V, 951
Farr, Anna M. V, 322
Farr, Anna M. V, 330
Farr, Asenah Newlin VI, 386
Farr, Asenath IV, 200
Farr, Asenath IV, 203
Farr, Asenath N. V, 54
Farr, Asenath N. V, 139
Farr, Asenath N. VI, 386
Farr, Asenith V, 951
Farr, Catharine IV, 869
Farr, Catharine IV, 873
Farr, Cyrus V, 951
Farr, Cyrus Franklin V, 951
Farr, Edward V, 76
Farr, Edward V, 139
Farr, Edward V, 955
Farr, Edward VI, 386
Farr, Edwin IV, 1314
Farr, Edwin H. IV, 703
Farr, Edwin W. IV, 1314
Farr, Edwin Wilson IV, 703
Farr, Elizabeth V, 671
Farr, Elizabeth V, 951
Farr, Elizabeth V, 952
Farr, Elizabeth E. I, 1151
Farr, Fannie J. I, 1151
Farr, Faye F. V, 671
Farr, Florence Marion V, 671
Farr, Gibson V, 951
Farr, Hannah V, 951
Farr, Ira I, 1151
Farr, Isaac II, 520
Farr, Isaac V, 951
Farr, Isaac VI, 386
Farr, Isaac Musgrave V, 951
Farr, Isaiah Musgrove V, 951
Farr, J. Henderson I, 1151
Farr, James V, 951
Farr, James Gibson V, 951
Farr, Jane V, 951
Farr, John V, 952
Farr, John H. I, 1151
Farr, Joseph VI, 386
Farr, Leah V, 951
Farr, Leah V, 952
Farr, Leah VI, 386
Farr, Lizzie L. I, 1151
Farr, Mabel E. IV, 703
Farr, Mabel E. IV, 1314
Farr, Margaret V, 948
Farr, Margaret V, 951
Farr, Margaret VI, 386
Farr, Margaret VI, 740
Farr, Margaret VI, 741
Farr, Maria V, 951
Farr, Mariah V, 951
Farr, Mariah Theresa V, 951
Farr, Marion V, 671
Farr, Mary V, 54
Farr, Mary V, 76
Farr, Mary V, 139
Farr, Mary V, 951
Farr, Mary V, 955
Farr, Mary VI, 386
Farr, Mary VI, 426
Farr, Mary Jane V, 951
Farr, Mary M. I, 1151
Farr, Mary, Jr. V, 54
Farr, Mary, Jr. V, 90
Farr, Mary, Jr. V, 951
Farr, Rebecca I, 1151
Farr, Sallie I, 1151
Farr, Tamar V, 54
Farr, Tamar V, 76
Farr, Tamar VI, 386
Farr, Tamer V, 951

Farr, Thomas G. V, 951
Farr, Wendell G. V, 671
Farr, William I, 1151
Farr, Wm. B. I, 1151
Farr, Wm. E. IV, 703
Farr, Wm. E. IV, 1314
Farr, Wm. J. I, 1151
Farra, Levina IV, 391
Farra, Levina IV, 431
Farra, Rachel IV, 431
Farra, Rees IV, 431
Farrah, Ann IV, 1361
Farrah, Elizabeth IV, 1361
Farrah, Hannah IV, 1361
Farrah, Jane IV, 1361
Farrah, Jane IV, 1375
Farrah, John IV, 1361
Farrah, Mary IV, 1361
Farrah, Robert IV, 1361
Farrah, Thomas IV, 1361
Farrand, James III, 114
Farrand, Jane III, 114
Farrand, Jane III, 115
Farrand, Jane T. III, 114
Farrand, Mary Ann III, 71
Farrand, Mary Anne III, 114
Farrand, Matthew III, 114
Farrand, Matthew III, 115
Farrand, Sarah Harvey III, 114
Farrand, Sarah Harvey III, 335
Farrell, Alice III, 114
Farrell, Hannah III, 510
Farrell, Hannah VI, 296
Farrell, Hannah VI, 874
Farrell, John III, 114
Farrell, John D. III, 114
Farrell, Libbie III, 510
Farrell, Libbie A. III, 510
Farrell, Mary Ann III, 114
Farrell, Mary L. III, 114
Farrell, Tredwell III, 510
Farrell, William III, 510
Farrell, William VI, 310
Farren, Allen B. IV, 1314
Farren, Frances J. IV, 1314
Farren, Hattie M. IV, 1314
Farren, May IV, 1314
Farren, Mrs. M. J. IV, 1314
Farren, Robert Willard IV, 1314
Farren, Sadie E. IV, 1314
Farrer, Charity VI, 840
Farrer, Charity VI, 852
Farrer, Daniel VI, 840
Farrer, Henrietta VI, 852
Farrer, James VI, 852
Farrer, Jane VI, 840
Farrer, Polly VI, 934
Farrer, Sarah IV, 1158
Farrguson, Mary VI, 850
Farrington, ??? III, 114
Farrington, ??? III, 344
Farrington, Abigail II, 215
Farrington, Abigail II, 219
Farrington, Abigail III, 72
Farrington, Abigail III, 114
Farrington, Abigail III, 115
Farrington, Abigail III, 162
Farrington, Abigail III, 201
Farrington, Abigail V, 995
Farrington, Abraham II, 219
Farrington, Abraham IV, 31
Farrington, Abraham IV, 85
Farrington, Abraham IV, 96
Farrington, Abraham IV, 145
Farrington, Abraham IV, 200
Farrington, Abraham IV, 703
Farrington, Abraham IV, 728
Farrington, Abraham IV, 814
Farrington, Amelia III, 114
Farrington, Amelia III, 370
Farrington, Amelia III, 379
Farrington, Amelia III, 380
Farrington, Amelia IV, 814
Farrington, Amelia IV, 1158
Farrington, Amelia IV, 1175
Farrington, Amelia Jane IV, 1158
Farrington, Amelia Jane IV, 1206
Farrington, Amelia Jane IV, 1207
Farrington, Amos White III, 114
Farrington, Amos White III, 115
Farrington, Amy III, 115
Farrington, Amy III, 281
Farrington, Amy III, 443
Farrington, Ann III, 114
Farrington, Ann III, 115
Farrington, Ann III, 204
Farrington, Ann III, 248
Farrington, Ann III, 379
Farrington, Ann III, 382
Farrington, Anna III, 54
Farrington, Anna III, 114
Farrington, Anna M. III, 114
Farrington, Anna M. III, 132
Farrington, Anne III, 115
Farrington, Anne III, 380
Farrington, Annie IV, 1278
Farrington, Armelia IV, 1151
Farrington, Armelia IV, 1158
Farrington, Armelia IV, 1206
Farrington, Armelia Jane
IV, 1158
Farrington, Armella IV, 814
Farrington, Armella IV, 829
Farrington, Armella IV, 1158
Farrington, Bellion IV, 814
Farrington, Benjamin III, 115
Farrington, Billion IV, 85
Farrington, Billion IV, 703
Farrington, Bridget III, 114
Farrington, Bridget III, 268
Farrington, Caleb K. IV, 1158
Farrington, Caleb Kirk IV, 1158
Farrington, Caroline III, 379
Farrington, Caroline III, 387
Farrington, Catharine III, 320
Farrington, Catharine III, 380
Farrington, Catharine III, 385
Farrington, Catherine III, 114
Farrington, Charity III, 114
Farrington, Charity III, 115
Farrington, Charity III, 256
Farrington, Charles III, 115
Farrington, Charles III, 380
Farrington, Charles W. III, 115
Farrington, Clarance IV, 1158
Farrington, Clarence IV, 1207
Farrington, Clarence H. IV, 1158
Farrington, Deborah III, 115
Farrington, Deborah III, 240
Farrington, Deborah IV, 31
Farrington, Deborah IV, 85
Farrington, Deborah IV, 96
Farrington, Deborah IV, 145
Farrington, Deborah IV, 703
Farrington, Deborah IV, 814
Farrington, Deborah IV, 905
Farrington, Dorothy III, 115
Farrington, E. III, 114
Farrington, E. III, 115
Farrington, Eddy IV, 1158
Farrington, Edmund III, 380
Farrington, Edward III, 115
Farrington, Edward III, 293
Farrington, Edward III, 410
Farrington, Edward III, 447
Farrington, Eliz. III, 114
Farrington, Eliz. III, 370
Farrington, Eliz. III, 387
Farrington, Eliza III, 380
Farrington, Eliza F. III, 377
Farrington, Eliza Hartley
IV, 1207
Farrington, Elizabeth I, 539
Farrington, Elizabeth I, 566
Farrington, Elizabeth III, 115
Farrington, Elizabeth III, 355
Farrington, Elizabeth III, 377
Farrington, Elizabeth III, 379
Farrington, Elizabeth III, 380
Farrington, Elizabeth III, 385
Farrington, Elizabeth V, 238
Farrington, Elizabeth V, 268
Farrington, Elizabeth
Thornbrough I, 539
Farrington, Ethel May IV, 1206
Farrington, Ezra III, 114
Farrington, Ezra III, 115
Farrington, Ezra III, 256
Farrington, Ezra III, 312
Farrington, Ezra III, 410
Farrington, Frances III, 115
Farrington, Frances III, 293
Farrington, Frances III, 410
Farrington, Frances III, 447
Farrington, Geo. III, 114
Farrington, Geo. III, 355
Farrington, Geo. III, 370
Farrington, George II, 520
Farrington, George II, 592
Farrington, George III, 115
Farrington, George III, 377
Farrington, George III, 379
Farrington, George III, 380
Farrington, George III, 385
Farrington, George III, 387
Farrington, Hannah III, 114
Farrington, Hannah III, 115
Farrington, Hannah III, 162
Farrington, Hannah III, 237
Farrington, Hannah III, 256
Farrington, Hannah III, 312
Farrington, Hannah III, 314
Farrington, Hannah III, 406
Farrington, Hannah III, 410
Farrington, Hannah IV, 1158
Farrington, Hannah P. IV, 1158
Farrington, Hannah P. IV, 1165
Farrington, Helen H. III, 39
Farrington, Hiram III, 115
Farrington, J. J. IV, 1207
Farrington, Jane III, 114
Farrington, Jane III, 115
Farrington, Jane III, 380
Farrington, Jane VI, 741
Farrington, Jane F. III, 355
Farrington, Jesse III, 115
Farrington, Jesse III, 380
Farrington, Jesse IV, 471
Farrington, Jesse K. IV, 471
Farrington, Jesse Kirk IV, 85
Farrington, Jesse Kirk IV, 703
Farrington, Jesse Kirk IV, 814
Farrington, Jesse T. IV, 1158
Farrington, Jesse T. IV, 1206
Farrington, Jesse T. IV, 1207
Farrington, John II, 520
Farrington, John II, 592
Farrington, John III, 41
Farrington, John III, 86
Farrington, John III, 115
Farrington, John III, 153
Farrington, John III, 380
Farrington, John IV, 85
Farrington, John IV, 703
Farrington, John IV, 814
Farrington, John IV, 1158
Farrington, Joseph II, 220
Farrington, Joseph III, 115
Farrington, Joseph IV, 85
Farrington, Joseph IV, 703
Farrington, Joseph J. IV, 1206
Farrington, Joseph John IV, 1158
Farrington, Joseph John IV, 1207
Farrington, Joseph John V, 951
Farrington, Judith IV, 85
Farrington, Judith IV, 471
Farrington, Judith IV, 703
Farrington, Judith IV, 814
Farrington, Judith IV, 905
Farrington, Kexia III, 115
Farrington, Keziah III, 410
Farrington, Keziah III, 458
Farrington, Lydia III, 115
Farrington, Lydia III, 380
Farrington, Marcy III, 115
Farrington, Marey III, 115
Farrington, Margaret III, 114
Farrington, Margaret III, 115
Farrington, Margaret III, 132
Farrington, Maria III, 115
Farrington, Maria III, 380
Farrington, Maria III, 389
Farrington, Mary I, 539
Farrington, Mary II, 220
Farrington, Mary II, 520
Farrington, Mary II, 592
Farrington, Mary III, 41
Farrington, Mary III, 86
Farrington, Mary III, 115
Farrington, Mary III, 119
Farrington, Mary III, 153
Farrington, Mary III, 204
Farrington, Mary III, 254
Farrington, Mary III, 379
Farrington, Mary III, 380
Farrington, Mary III, 382
Farrington, Mary IV, 814
Farrington, Mary IV, 1158
Farrington, Mary IV, 1175
Farrington, Mary IV, 1206
Farrington, Mary IV, 1207
Farrington, Mary IV, 1218
Farrington, Mary Frances
IV, 1158
Farrington, Mary Frances
IV, 1206
Farrington, Mary Frances
IV, 1207
Farrington, Matt. III, 115
Farrington, Matthew III, 115
Farrington, Matthew III, 162
Farrington, Matthew III, 237
Farrington, Matthew III, 254
Farrington, Matthew III, 332
Farrington, Moses IV, 31
Farrington, Moses IV, 85
Farrington, Moses IV, 145
Farrington, Moses IV, 703
Farrington, Moses IV, 814
Farrington, Moses IV, 829
Farrington, Moses IV, 858
Farrington, Moses IV, 1158
Farrington, Moses IV, 1175
Farrington, Moses IV, 1206
Farrington, Nathan III, 115
Farrington, Permelia III, 86
Farrington, Permelia III, 115
Farrington, Phebe II, 173
Farrington, Phebe II, 220
Farrington, Phebe IV, 85
Farrington, Phebe IV, 703
Farrington, Phebe IV, 814
Farrington, Phebe IV, 905
Farrington, Phebe Ellen IV, 1158
Farrington, Phebe Ellen IV, 1206
Farrington, Phebe Ellen IV, 1207
Farrington, Phebe Ellin IV, 1158
Farrington, Priscilla IV, 1158
Farrington, Priscilla IV, 1207
Farrington, Priscillaann IV, 1207
Farrington, Sally D. III, 115
Farrington, Samuel II, 219
Farrington, Samuel II, 220
Farrington, Sarah II, 173
Farrington, Sarah II, 287
Farrington, Sarah III, 115
Farrington, Sarah III, 153
Farrington, Sarah III, 313
Farrington, Sarah III, 332
Farrington, Sarah III, 344
Farrington, Sarah III, 380
Farrington, Sarah IV, 703
Farrington, Sarah IV, 728
Farrington, Sarah IV, 814
Farrington, Sarah IV, 905
Farrington, Sarah IV, 1158
Farrington, Sarah IV, 1206
Farrington, Sarah IV, 1207
Farrington, Sarah IV, 1208
Farrington, Sarah D. III, 115
Farrington, Sarah D. III, 312
Farrington, Sarah Fowler III, 115
Farrington, Sarah J. IV, 1206
Farrington, Sarah Jane IV, 1158
Farrington, Sarah, Jr. III, 115
Farrington, Susannah III, 115
Farrington, Tacie Emma IV, 1158
Farrington, Tacy Emma IV, 1158
Farrington, Tacy Emma IV, 1206
Farrington, Tacy Emma IV, 1207
Farrington, Theodore IV, 1278
Farrington, Thomas III, 115
Farrington, Thomas III, 313
Farrington, Thomas III, 314
Farrington, Thomas III, 344
Farrington, Thos. III, 410
Farrington, Thos. III, 458
Farrington, Walter III, 115
Farrington, Walter III, 119
Farrington, Walter III, 201
Farrington, Walter III, 204
Farrington, Walter III, 281
Farrington, Walter III, 379
Farrington, Walter III, 380
Farrington, Walter III, 382
Farrington, Walter III, 443
Farrington, Wd. Abigail III, 114
Farrington, William Penn
IV, 1158
Farris, Elizabeth II, 794
Farris, Elizabeth P. II, 740
Farris, Francis II, 361
Farris, John VI, 805
Farris, John VI, 815
Farris, Joseph VI, 831
Farris, Martha VI, 815
Farris, Martin H. VI, 817
Farris, Mary II, 522
Farris, Mary II, 569
Farris, Mary E. VI, 815
Farris, Nancy C. VI, 797
Farris, Rebecca VI, 994
Farris, Valentine VI, 797
Farriss, Elizabeth P. II, 522
Farriss, Elizabeth T. VI, 831
Farriss, John VI, 808
Farriss, Mary Jane VI, 913
Farriss, Rebecca VI, 912
Farriss, Thomas A. VI, 913
Farriss, Wm. A. VI, 831
Farror, Belle IV, 1314
Farror, George IV, 1314
Farror, John D. IV, 1314
Farror, Nellie B. IV, 1314
Farrow, Ann II, 173
Farrow, Charity VI, 852
Farrow, Daniel VI, 796
Farrow, Daniel VI, 798
Farrow, Daniel VI, 816
Farrow, Daniel VI, 820
Farrow, Daniel VI, 842
Farrow, Elizabeth VI, 798
Farrow, Elizabeth VI, 842
Farrow, James II, 173
Farrow, James VI, 796
Farrow, James VI, 798
Farrow, John VI, 843
Farrow, Judith VI, 816
Farrow, Lucy VI, 796
Farrow, Mary II, 173
Farrow, Nelley VI, 843
Farrow, Rachel IV, 391
Farrow, Sarah VI, 852
Farson, Ann II, 521
Farson, Ann II, 739
Farthing, Agnes VI, 822
Farthing, Edney VI, 827
Farthing, Elizabeth VI, 813
Farthing, Fanny VI, 800
Farthing, John VI, 913
Farthing, Martha VI, 813
Farthing, Mary VI, 913
Farthing, Molly VI, 809
Farthing, Nancy VI, 809
Farthing, Sally VI, 817
Farthing, Thomas VI, 822
Farthing, William VI, 800
Farthing, William VI, 809
Farthing, William VI, 813
Farthing, William VI, 817
Farthing, William VI, 822
Farthing, William VI, 827
Farthing, Wm. VI, 809
Farungton, Armilla IV, 1217
Farungton, Moses IV, 1217
Farungton, Priscillaann IV, 120
Farungton, Priscillaann IV, 121
Farwell, Joseph III, 115
Fassell, Samuel II, 862
Fasset, Phebe V, 491
Fassett, Albert V, 995
Fassett, Annie M. V, 995
Fassett, Denard W. V, 995
Fassett, Eliza V, 995
Fassett, Emma III, 61
Fassett, Emma III, 115
Fassett, Emma V, 995
Fassett, Emory A. V, 995
Fassett, John B. V, 995
Fassett, Laura A. V, 995
Fassett, Mary V, 995
Fassett, Mary C. V, 995
Fassett, Nora V, 995
Fassett, Nora B. V, 995
Fassett, Wm. V, 995
Fassett, Wm. S. V, 995
Fatherly, Edna J. III, 410
Fatherly, Emeline III, 410
Fatherly, Emeline III, 463
Fatherly, Robert E. III, 115
Fatherly, Robert E. III, 410
Fatherly, Robert E. III, 463
Fatherly, Wm. E. III, 410
Faucet, Elijah V, 491
Faucet, Esther IV, 200
Faucet, John IV, 392
Faucet, Jonathan IV, 392
Faucett, ??? VI, 782
Faucett, Anna I, 935
Faucett, Benjamin IV, 578
Faucett, Charlotte Lucinda
V, 169
Faucett, Elijah R. V, 169
Faucett, Elizabeth II, 486
Faucett, Elizabeth II, 521
Faucett, Elizabeth IV, 577
Faucett, Elizabeth IV, 580
Faucett, Emma II, 360
Faucett, Emme II, 521
Faucett, Homer V, 169
Faucett, Huldah IV, 1159
Faucett, Huldah V, 169
Faucett, Jesse H. V, 169
Faucett, Jonathan IV, 524
Faucett, Jonathan V, 169
Faucett, Jonathan P. V, 169
Faucett, Joseph II, 486
Faucett, Joseph II, 521
Faucett, Martha VI, 595
Faucett, Mary VI, 595
Faucett, Mary Esther V, 169
Faucett, Milo IV, 1159
Faucett, Nathan II, 521
Faucett, Phebe VI, 595
Faucett, Philip II, 521
Faucett, Rachel IV, 159
Faucett, Rebecca Jane V, 169
Faucett, Samuel IV, 159
Faucett, Samuel VI, 595
Faucett, Susan VI, 741
Faucett, Susan VI, 782
Faucett, Sylvia M. V, 169
Faucett, Tamar Ann V, 169
Faucett, William IV, 919
Faucett, William Elihu V, 169

ucett, Wm. G. V, 951
ucette, Anna I, 865
ucette, Anna I, 935
ucette, Deborah I, 935
ucette, Simeon I, 935
ucit, Elizabeth II, 521
ucit, Jane II, 471
ucit, Jane II, 521
ucit, Jane II, 542
ucit, Jonathan II, 69
ucit, Lidya II, 69
ucit, Lidya II, 91
ucit, Nathan II, 471
ucit, Nathan II, 521
ucit, Walter II, 471
ucit, Walter II, 521
ucit, Wd. Jane II, 521
ucitt, John II, 360
ucitt, Nathan II, 360
ulk, Ann VI, 131
ulk, Aquilla VI, 131
ulk, Betsy VI, 63
ulk, Betsy VI, 67
ulk, Betsy VI, 242
ulk, Betsy VI, 248
ulk, David VI, 131
ulk, Elizabeth VI, 63
ulk, Elizabeth VI, 91
ulk, Elizabeth VI, 131
ulk, John VI, 63
ulk, John VI, 131
ulk, John VI, 134
ulk, Joseph VI, 131
ulk, Martha VI, 131
ulk, Martha VI, 134
ulk, Martha, Jr. VI, 131
ulk, Martha, Sr. VI, 131
ulk, Mary VI, 63
ulk, Mary VI, 64
ulk, Mary VI, 131
ulk, Mary VI, 134
ulk, Miriam VI, 131
ulk, Penninah VI, 131
ulk, Peter VI, 131
ulk, Richard VI, 131
ulk, Samuel VI, 131
ulk, Samuel B. VI, 131
ulk, Thomas V, 56
ulk, Thomas Elwood VI, 131
ulk, William VI, 63
ulk, William VI, 131
ulk, William H. VI, 64
ulk, William Henry VI, 63
ulk, William Hunnicutt VI, 131
ulke, Amelia V, 56
ulke, Cadwallader V, 56
ulke, Grace V, 56
ulke, Jesse Mary V, 56
ulke, John V, 56
ulke, Judah V, 56
ulke, Sarah V, 56
ulke, Silas V, 56
ulker, David VI, 387
ulker, Jesse, Senior VI, 387
ulker, Judith VI, 387
ulker, Martha VI, 387
ulker, Mary VI, 387
ulkman, Eva IV, 1158
ulkman, Mrs. ??? IV, 1158
ulknear, Elizabeth VI, 387
ulknear, Robert VI, 387
ulknear, Susannah VI, 387
ulkner, Abigail IV, 703
ulkner, Abigail IV, 748
ulkner, Abijah V, 490
ulkner, Adna A. V, 490
ulkner, Amos E. V, 490
ulkner, Angelina V, 490
ulkner, Angeline V, 490
ulkner, Ann VI, 387
ulkner, Anna V, 490
ulkner, Anna V, 543
ulkner, Bessie Cleora V, 490
ulkner, Cora Mary V, 490
ulkner, Cora May V, 490
ulkner, David IV, 31
ulkner, David IV, 32
ulkner, David V, 469
ulkner, David V, 473
ulkner, David V, 489
ulkner, David V, 490
ulkner, David V, 544
ulkner, David VI, 387
ulkner, David VI, 451
ulkner, David VI, 453
ulkner, David Walter V, 490
ulkner, David, Jr. V, 490
ulkner, Drusilla VI, 913
ulkner, Eleanor VI, 387
ulkner, Elias V, 490
Faulkner, Eliza V, 490
Faulkner, Eliza V, 951
Faulkner, Elizabeth IV, 31
Faulkner, Elizabeth V, 480
Faulkner, Elizabeth V, 490
Faulkner, Elizabeth V, 528
Faulkner, Elizabeth V, 544
Faulkner, Elizabeth V, 554
Faulkner, Elizabeth V, 561
Faulkner, Elizabeth VI, 387
Faulkner, Elizabeth VI, 427
Faulkner, Elizabeth VI, 594
Faulkner, Elizabeth VI, 602
Faulkner, Ellen V, 54
Faulkner, Ellen V, 469
Faulkner, Ellen V, 471
Faulkner, Ellen V, 490
Faulkner, Ellin VI, 387
Faulkner, Ethel V, 738
Faulkner, Etta Leona V, 490
Faulkner, Hannah II, 520
Faulkner, Hannah IV, 31
Faulkner, Hannah V, 54
Faulkner, Hannah V, 489
Faulkner, Hannah V, 490
Faulkner, Hannah V, 524
Faulkner, Hannah V, 532
Faulkner, Hannah VI, 387
Faulkner, Hannah VI, 393
Faulkner, Hannah VI, 431
Faulkner, Hannah VI, 443
Faulkner, Harry T. V, 490
Faulkner, Harvey C. V, 490
Faulkner, Howard P. V, 490
Faulkner, Isaac V, 995
Faulkner, Isaiah M. V, 490
Faulkner, James V, 490
Faulkner, James Dun VI, 387
Faulkner, James W. V, 490
Faulkner, Jane V, 54
Faulkner, Jane V, 490
Faulkner, Jane V, 533
Faulkner, Jane VI, 387
Faulkner, Jesse IV, 32
Faulkner, Jesse V, 54
Faulkner, Jesse V, 489
Faulkner, Jesse VI, 427
Faulkner, Jesse VI, 431
Faulkner, Jesse VI, 450
Faulkner, Jesse VI, 594
Faulkner, Jesse, Jr. V, 490
Faulkner, Jesse, Jr. VI, 387
Faulkner, Joel V, 489
Faulkner, Joel V, 490
Faulkner, Joel Wright V, 490
Faulkner, John V, 490
Faulkner, Judith IV, 32
Faulkner, Judith V, 17
Faulkner, Judith V, 54
Faulkner, Judith V, 469
Faulkner, Judith V, 489
Faulkner, Judith V, 490
Faulkner, Judith V, 492
Faulkner, Judith V, 505
Faulkner, Judith V, 544
Faulkner, Judith VI, 387
Faulkner, Judith VI, 451
Faulkner, Judith VI, 453
Faulkner, Juliann V, 490
Faulkner, Laura V, 738
Faulkner, Leah V, 473
Faulkner, Leah V, 490
Faulkner, Leah V, 544
Faulkner, Leroy H. V, 490
Faulkner, Lewis B. IV, 1250
Faulkner, Loren V, 738
Faulkner, Lucien V, 490
Faulkner, Lucina V, 490
Faulkner, Lucina V, 510
Faulkner, Lucinda V, 490
Faulkner, Lydia V, 489
Faulkner, Lydia V, 490
Faulkner, Lydia S. V, 490
Faulkner, Lydia S. V, 506
Faulkner, Mabel V, 738
Faulkner, Martha V, 54
Faulkner, Martha V, 469
Faulkner, Martha VI, 387
Faulkner, Martha VI, 427
Faulkner, Martha VI, 450
Faulkner, Martha VI, 453
Faulkner, Martha VI, 594
Faulkner, Mary IV, 32
Faulkner, Mary IV, 1250
Faulkner, Mary V, 472
Faulkner, Mary V, 489
Faulkner, Mary V, 490
Faulkner, Mary V, 498
Faulkner, Mary V, 505
Faulkner, Mary V, 544
Faulkner, Mary VI, 387
Faulkner, Merle V, 738
Faulkner, Minnie V, 490
Faulkner, Nathan V, 490
Faulkner, Phebe IV, 32
Faulkner, Phebe V, 474
Faulkner, Phebe V, 489
Faulkner, Phebe V, 490
Faulkner, Phebe V, 519
Faulkner, Phebe V, 543
Faulkner, Phebe V, 544
Faulkner, Phebe VI, 387
Faulkner, Rachel V, 472
Faulkner, Rachel V, 490
Faulkner, Rachel V, 513
Faulkner, Rachel V, 544
Faulkner, Robert IV, 31
Faulkner, Robert V, 54
Faulkner, Robert V, 490
Faulkner, Robert V, 544
Faulkner, Robert VI, 387
Faulkner, Robert VI, 427
Faulkner, Robert VI, 594
Faulkner, Robert VI, 602
Faulkner, Russell J. V, 490
Faulkner, Ruth V, 476
Faulkner, Ruth V, 490
Faulkner, Ruth V, 531
Faulkner, Ruth VI, 387
Faulkner, Ruth VI, 450
Faulkner, Samuel V, 490
Faulkner, Sarah V, 490
Faulkner, Sarah VI, 387
Faulkner, Sarah E. V, 490
Faulkner, Solomon IV, 32
Faulkner, Solomon V, 476
Faulkner, Solomon V, 490
Faulkner, Solomon VI, 387
Faulkner, Stephen VI, 387
Faulkner, Susanna IV, 31
Faulkner, Susanna V, 54
Faulkner, Susanna V, 469
Faulkner, Susannah V, 489
Faulkner, Susannah V, 490
Faulkner, Susannah V, 494
Faulkner, Susannah V, 502
Faulkner, Susannah VI, 387
Faulkner, Thomas IV, 31
Faulkner, Thomas V, 54
Faulkner, Thomas V, 490
Faulkner, Thomas VI, 387
Faulkner, Thomas H. V, 490
Faulkner, Viola V, 490
Faulkner, William I, 715
Faulkner, William VI, 387
Faulkner, William VI, 913
Faulknere, Jesse, Senior VI, 387
Faulknere, Mary VI, 387
Faullis, George VI, 386
Fauning, Mary I, 49
Fauning, Mary I, 77
Faurer, Frances I, 633
Faurer, Frances I, 639
Faus, Cora Harner V, 169
Fauset, Emma V, 995
Fauset, Ruth I, 431
Fauset, Ruth I, 445
Fausett, Albion VI, 388
Fausett, Anna VI, 388
Fausett, Atlantic VI, 388
Fausett, David VI, 388
Fausett, Dorcas VI, 388
Fausett, Druzilla VI, 388
Fausett, Eli VI, 388
Fausett, Elijah VI, 388
Fausett, Elisha VI, 388
Fausett, Elizabeth VI, 388
Fausett, Esther VI, 388
Fausett, Eunice VI, 388
Fausett, Franklin VI, 388
Fausett, Isaac VI, 388
Fausett, Jehu VI, 388
Fausett, Jesse VI, 388
Fausett, John VI, 388
Fausett, John, Jr. VI, 388
Fausett, Jonathan VI, 388
Fausett, Joseph VI, 388
Fausett, Joseph Janney VI, 388
Fausett, Joshua VI, 388
Fausett, Josiah VI, 388
Fausett, Levi VI, 388
Fausett, Louisa VI, 388
Fausett, Lydia VI, 388
Fausett, Lydia Ann VI, 388
Fausett, Mahlon VI, 388
Fausett, Mahlon Taylor VI, 388
Fausett, Martha VI, 388
Fausett, Mary VI, 388
Fausett, Mary Ellen VI, 388
Fausett, Mary Taylor VI, 388
Fausett, Nancy VI, 388
Fausett, Nathan VI, 388
Fausett, Oliver Goldsmith VI, 388
Fausett, Phebe VI, 388
Fausett, Philadelphia VI, 388
Fausett, Phineas Anderton VI, 388
Fausett, Rebecca II, 360
Fausett, Rebecca VI, 388
Fausett, Richard VI, 388
Fausett, Robert VI, 388
Fausett, Sarah VI, 388
Fausett, Sarah Eunice VI, 388
Fausett, Simeon VI, 388
Fausett, Susannah VI, 388
Fausett, Thomas VI, 388
Fausett, Thomas William VI, 388
Fausett, Unice VI, 388
Fausett, Washington VI, 388
Fausett, William VI, 388
Fausett, William Taylor VI, 388
Faushire, Emily V, 995
Faushire, Isaac V, 995
Faust, Dellie IV, 1158
Faust, Ella IV, 1158
Faust, Maud L. IV, 1158
Faust, Mirieth M. IV, 1158
Faust, Rena V, 995
Fauster, Elizabeth IV, 86
Fauster, Timothy Kirk IV, 76
Fauster, Wd. Elizabeth IV, 76
Faustman, Monica III, 116
Faustman, Monica III, 136
Fauver, Frances I, 624
Fawcet, Abigail IV, 704
Fawcet, Albert V, 995
Fawcet, Eli IV, 704
Fawcet, Elizabeth IV, 145
Fawcet, Elizabeth IV, 155
Fawcet, Elma IV, 704
Fawcet, Emory A. V, 995
Fawcet, Esther IV, 704
Fawcet, Hannah IV, 704
Fawcet, Jonathan IV, 703
Fawcet, Jonathan IV, 704
Fawcet, Laura A. V, 995
Fawcet, Levi IV, 704
Fawcet, Mary IV, 703
Fawcet, Mary IV, 704
Fawcet, Mary C. V, 995
Fawcet, Rebecca IV, 739
Fawcet, Richard B. IV, 739
Fawcet, Simeon IV, 704
Fawcet, Sina IV, 704
Fawcett, ??? IV, 391
Fawcett, Aaron IV, 740
Fawcett, Abbie T. IV, 926
Fawcett, Abbie T. IV, 953
Fawcett, Abigail IV, 85
Fawcett, Abigail IV, 328
Fawcett, Abigail IV, 329
Fawcett, Abigail IV, 392
Fawcett, Abigail IV, 524
Fawcett, Abigail IV, 534
Fawcett, Abigail IV, 703
Fawcett, Abigail IV, 704
Fawcett, Abigail IV, 718
Fawcett, Abigail IV, 723
Fawcett, Abigail IV, 926
Fawcett, Abigail IV, 952
Fawcett, Abigail IV, 953
Fawcett, Abigail IV, 1096
Fawcett, Abigail H. IV, 524
Fawcett, Abner IV, 85
Fawcett, Abner IV, 87
Fawcett, Abner IV, 392
Fawcett, Abner IV, 703
Fawcett, Abner IV, 952
Fawcett, Abner IV, 1094
Fawcett, Abner IV, 1096
Fawcett, Abner IV, 1097
Fawcett, Abner VI, 595
Fawcett, Alban V, 491
Fawcett, Albert IV, 704
Fawcett, Albion VI, 388
Fawcett, Alice S. IV, 704
Fawcett, Alice S. IV, 705
Fawcett, Alice S. IV, 1098
Fawcett, Allen B. IV, 524
Fawcett, Alpheus IV, 524
Fawcett, Alpheus Harrison IV, 1158
Fawcett, Alvira IV, 952
Fawcett, Alvira A. IV, 953
Fawcett, Alvira A. IV, 971
Fawcett, Amanda IV, 1097
Fawcett, Amanda J. IV, 1097
Fawcett, Amanda J. IV, 1115
Fawcett, Amelia IV, 524
Fawcett, Amelia IV, 536
Fawcett, Amelia IV, 1097
Fawcett, Amos IV, 329
Fawcett, Amos IV, 392
Fawcett, Amos IV, 704
Fawcett, Amos IV, 705
Fawcett, Amos IV, 748
Fawcett, Ann IV, 703
Fawcett, Ann VI, 451
Fawcett, Ann Eliza IV, 329
Fawcett, Ann M. IV, 1097
Fawcett, Anna IV, 697
Fawcett, Anna IV, 703
Fawcett, Anna IV, 704
Fawcett, Anna IV, 705
Fawcett, Anna IV, 729
Fawcett, Anna IV, 952
Fawcett, Anna IV, 953
Fawcett, Anna VI, 388
Fawcett, Anna Eliza IV, 577
Fawcett, Anna F. IV, 953
Fawcett, Anna F. IV, 1008
Fawcett, Anna Mariah IV, 1158
Fawcett, Anne IV, 1098
Fawcett, Anne IV, 1114
Fawcett, Armela IV, 392
Fawcett, Armela IV, 1057
Fawcett, Armelia IV, 524
Fawcett, Arthur IV, 1097
Fawcett, Atlantic IV, 323
Fawcett, Atlantic IV, 329
Fawcett, Atlantic VI, 388
Fawcett, Austin Simson IV, 1057
Fawcett, Benj. IV, 337
Fawcett, Benjamin IV, 200
Fawcett, Benjamin IV, 329
Fawcett, Benjamin IV, 391
Fawcett, Benjamin IV, 392
Fawcett, Benjamin IV, 524
Fawcett, Benjamin IV, 577
Fawcett, Benjamin IV, 578
Fawcett, Benjamin IV, 704
Fawcett, Benjamin T. IV, 524
Fawcett, Bertha V, 385
Fawcett, C. E. IV, 255
Fawcett, Carlos J. IV, 1097
Fawcett, Caroline V, 491
Fawcett, Caroline W. V, 491
Fawcett, Catharine IV, 704
Fawcett, Catharine IV, 765
Fawcett, Charles IV, 1278
Fawcett, Charles H. IV, 1097
Fawcett, Charlotte IV, 524
Fawcett, Charlotte V, 476
Fawcett, Charlotte V, 491
Fawcett, Charlotte T. V, 490
Fawcett, Clara IV, 705
Fawcett, Clara IV, 1314
Fawcett, Clarence IV, 950
Fawcett, Clarence IV, 951
Fawcett, Clarence Arthur IV, 1097
Fawcett, Clarence E. IV, 1098
Fawcett, Clarence Edward IV, 200
Fawcett, Clarence Edward IV, 1097
Fawcett, Clifford IV, 200
Fawcett, Clifford IV, 282
Fawcett, Clifford J. IV, 1097
Fawcett, Clifford J. IV, 1098
Fawcett, Clifford J. IV, 1116
Fawcett, Daniel IV, 1097
Fawcett, Darcus IV, 329
Fawcett, David IV, 329
Fawcett, David IV, 674
Fawcett, David IV, 703
Fawcett, David IV, 704
Fawcett, David IV, 757
Fawcett, David IV, 773
Fawcett, David IV, 1016
Fawcett, David VI, 388
Fawcett, David VI, 595
Fawcett, David Clifford IV, 1097
Fawcett, Debby IV, 1097
Fawcett, Deborah IV, 392
Fawcett, Deborah IV, 518
Fawcett, Deborah IV, 692
Fawcett, Deborah IV, 704
Fawcett, Deborah IV, 718
Fawcett, Deborah IV, 905
Fawcett, Deborah IV, 911
Fawcett, Deborah IV, 952
Fawcett, Deborah IV, 953
Fawcett, Deborah IV, 980
Fawcett, Deborah IV, 1097
Fawcett, Deborah IV, 1103
Fawcett, Deborah M. IV, 905
Fawcett, Deborah M. IV, 952
Fawcett, Deborah M. IV, 953
Fawcett, Deborah S. IV, 524
Fawcett, Deborah S. IV, 534
Fawcett, Deborah S. IV, 703
Fawcett, Deborah S. IV, 705

Fawcett, Deborah Simmons IV, 428
Fawcett, Dorcas IV, 524
Fawcett, Dorcas IV, 536
Fawcett, Dorcas VI, 388
Fawcett, Drucilla IV, 577
Fawcett, Drusilla IV, 329
Fawcett, Drusilla IV, 577
Fawcett, Drusilla IV, 686
Fawcett, Drusilla IV, 703
Fawcett, Drusilla IV, 704
Fawcett, Druzilla VI, 388
Fawcett, Edith IV, 673
Fawcett, Edith IV, 704
Fawcett, Edith IV, 775
Fawcett, Edith IV, 792
Fawcett, Edith L. IV, 1097
Fawcett, Edith M. IV, 792
Fawcett, Edward IV, 704
Fawcett, Edward IV, 705
Fawcett, Edward IV, 744
Fawcett, Edward IV, 1016
Fawcett, Edward C. IV, 704
Fawcett, Edward C., Jr. IV, 704
Fawcett, Edward Cloudsley IV, 704
Fawcett, Edward Gilbert IV, 1097
Fawcett, Edward P. IV, 718
Fawcett, Edward S. IV, 1158
Fawcett, Edward S. V, 951
Fawcett, Edward W. IV, 703
Fawcett, Edward W. IV, 705
Fawcett, Edwin IV, 703
Fawcett, Edwin IV, 952
Fawcett, Edwin IV, 953
Fawcett, Eli IV, 392
Fawcett, Eli IV, 524
Fawcett, Eli IV, 703
Fawcett, Eli IV, 704
Fawcett, Eli IV, 705
Fawcett, Eli IV, 1057
Fawcett, Eli IV, 1097
Fawcett, Eli IV, 1100
Fawcett, Eli VI, 388
Fawcett, Eli VI, 595
Fawcett, Eli S. IV, 1097
Fawcett, Elijah IV, 329
Fawcett, Elijah IV, 396
Fawcett, Elijah IV, 524
Fawcett, Elijah IV, 527
Fawcett, Elijah IV, 1096
Fawcett, Elijah IV, 1097
Fawcett, Elijah V, 491
Fawcett, Elijah VI, 388
Fawcett, Elijah VI, 595
Fawcett, Elina IV, 718
Fawcett, Elisha IV, 145
Fawcett, Elisha IV, 329
Fawcett, Elisha IV, 336
Fawcett, Elisha IV, 337
Fawcett, Elisha IV, 703
Fawcett, Elisha IV, 811
Fawcett, Elisha IV, 814
Fawcett, Elisha VI, 387
Fawcett, Elisha VI, 388
Fawcett, Elisha VI, 450
Fawcett, Elisha VI, 595
Fawcett, Elisha VI, 637
Fawcett, Elisha VI, 656
Fawcett, Elisha VI, 668
Fawcett, Elisha VI, 712
Fawcett, Eliza J. IV, 200
Fawcett, Eliza J. IV, 255
Fawcett, Eliza Jane IV, 524
Fawcett, Elizabeth II, 521
Fawcett, Elizabeth II, 576
Fawcett, Elizabeth IV, 85
Fawcett, Elizabeth IV, 87
Fawcett, Elizabeth IV, 145
Fawcett, Elizabeth IV, 200
Fawcett, Elizabeth IV, 329
Fawcett, Elizabeth IV, 391
Fawcett, Elizabeth IV, 392
Fawcett, Elizabeth IV, 394
Fawcett, Elizabeth IV, 524
Fawcett, Elizabeth IV, 577
Fawcett, Elizabeth IV, 588
Fawcett, Elizabeth IV, 703
Fawcett, Elizabeth IV, 704
Fawcett, Elizabeth IV, 705
Fawcett, Elizabeth IV, 723
Fawcett, Elizabeth IV, 745
Fawcett, Elizabeth IV, 952
Fawcett, Elizabeth IV, 1195
Fawcett, Elizabeth V, 490
Fawcett, Elizabeth V, 491
Fawcett, Elizabeth VI, 388
Fawcett, Elizabeth Ann V, 491
Fawcett, Elizabeth G. IV, 85
Fawcett, Elizabeth G. IV, 705
Fawcett, Elizabeth G. IV, 952
Fawcett, Elizabeth G. IV, 988
Fawcett, Elizabeth H. V, 491
Fawcett, Elizabeth H. V, 539
Fawcett, Elizabeth P. IV, 1158
Fawcett, Elizabeth R. IV, 703
Fawcett, Elizabeth R. IV, 775
Fawcett, Elizabeth W. IV, 1159
Fawcett, Elkana VI, 388
Fawcett, Elkanah VI, 388
Fawcett, Elma IV, 704
Fawcett, Elma IV, 705
Fawcett, Elma IV, 715
Fawcett, Elmina IV, 703
Fawcett, Elvira IV, 703
Fawcett, Elvira IV, 704
Fawcett, Elvira IV, 705
Fawcett, Elvira IV, 744
Fawcett, Elvira IV, 953
Fawcett, Elvira VI, 364
Fawcett, Elvira VI, 388
Fawcett, Elwood IV, 703
Fawcett, Elwood IV, 705
Fawcett, Elwood IV, 1097
Fawcett, Emeline IV, 761
Fawcett, Emeline IV, 814
Fawcett, Emeline IV, 818
Fawcett, Emma II, 360
Fawcett, Emma L. IV, 704
Fawcett, Emme II, 521
Fawcett, Emme II, 576
Fawcett, Emmer IV, 705
Fawcett, Emmir IV, 85
Fawcett, Emmir IV, 101
Fawcett, Emmor IV, 703
Fawcett, Emmor IV, 705
Fawcett, Emmor IV, 741
Fawcett, Eoizabeth G. IV, 753
Fawcett, Estella IV, 1097
Fawcett, Esther IV, 200
Fawcett, Esther IV, 524
Fawcett, Esther IV, 558
Fawcett, Esther IV, 683
Fawcett, Esther IV, 703
Fawcett, Esther IV, 704
Fawcett, Esther IV, 705
Fawcett, Esther IV, 739
Fawcett, Esther IV, 744
Fawcett, Esther IV, 788
Fawcett, Esther VI, 388
Fawcett, Esther N. IV, 705
Fawcett, Esther S. IV, 704
Fawcett, Esther Sidney II, 719
Fawcett, Esther Sidney IV, 704
Fawcett, Esther Sidney IV, 767
Fawcett, Eunice IV, 200
Fawcett, Eunice IV, 320
Fawcett, Eunice IV, 328
Fawcett, Eunice IV, 329
Fawcett, Eunice IV, 624
Fawcett, Eunice IV, 683
Fawcett, Eunice IV, 686
Fawcett, Eunice IV, 697
Fawcett, Eunice IV, 701
Fawcett, Eunice IV, 703
Fawcett, Eunice IV, 704
Fawcett, Eunice IV, 761
Fawcett, Eunice IV, 773
Fawcett, Eunice IV, 950
Fawcett, Eunice IV, 1158
Fawcett, Eunice VI, 388
Fawcett, Eunice VI, 595
Fawcett, Eunice T. IV, 950
Fawcett, Eunice T. IV, 952
Fawcett, Ezra IV, 704
Fawcett, Ezra IV, 705
Fawcett, Flora IV, 704
Fawcett, Flora IV, 1158
Fawcett, Flora B. IV, 705
Fawcett, Florence H. IV, 200
Fawcett, Florence H. IV, 282
Fawcett, Florence H. IV, 1097
Fawcett, Florence H. IV, 1098
Fawcett, Florence H. IV, 1116
Fawcett, Florence S. IV, 200
Fawcett, Florence S. IV, 1098
Fawcett, Franklin IV, 145
Fawcett, Franklin IV, 329
Fawcett, Franklin VI, 387
Fawcett, Franklin VI, 388
Fawcett, Franklin VI, 637
Fawcett, Frederick VI, 595
Fawcett, George IV, 524
Fawcett, George E. IV, 1097
Fawcett, George E. IV, 1098
Fawcett, George W. IV, 704
Fawcett, George W. IV, 952
Fawcett, Grace VI, 595
Fawcett, Gulielma VI, 364
Fawcett, Gulielma VI, 388
Fawcett, Gulielma Bean Elkanah VI, 368
Fawcett, Hannah IV, 145
Fawcett, Hannah IV, 323
Fawcett, Hannah IV, 674
Fawcett, Hannah IV, 703
Fawcett, Hannah IV, 704
Fawcett, Hannah IV, 705
Fawcett, Hannah IV, 740
Fawcett, Hannah IV, 748
Fawcett, Hannah IV, 757
Fawcett, Hannah IV, 773
Fawcett, Hannah IV, 1016
Fawcett, Hannah VI, 362
Fawcett, Hannah VI, 387
Fawcett, Hannah VI, 595
Fawcett, Hannah B. IV, 1016
Fawcett, Hannah C. IV, 703
Fawcett, Hannah C. IV, 704
Fawcett, Hannah C. IV, 723
Fawcett, Hannah F. IV, 713
Fawcett, Hannah R. IV, 704
Fawcett, Hannah R. IV, 739
Fawcett, Harry M. V, 385
Fawcett, Henry IV, 705
Fawcett, Henry B. IV, 703
Fawcett, Herophila IV, 811
Fawcett, Herophila IV, 814
Fawcett, Herphilia IV, 329
Fawcett, Hopewell VI, 387
Fawcett, Howard IV, 704
Fawcett, Howard IV, 705
Fawcett, Howard IV, 1097
Fawcett, Howard S. IV, 705
Fawcett, Howard S. IV, 1098
Fawcett, Huldah IV, 1159
Fawcett, Isaac IV, 703
Fawcett, Isaac IV, 705
Fawcett, Isaac VI, 388
Fawcett, Isaac VI, 595
Fawcett, Isaac P. V, 491
Fawcett, Jackson IV, 1278
Fawcett, Jacob IV, 145
Fawcett, Jacob IV, 329
Fawcett, Jacob IV, 703
Fawcett, Jacob IV, 705
Fawcett, Jacob VI, 595
Fawcett, James E. IV, 704
Fawcett, Jane II, 360
Fawcett, Jane II, 521
Fawcett, Jane IV, 329
Fawcett, Jane IV, 346
Fawcett, Jane IV, 392
Fawcett, Jane IV, 524
Fawcett, Jane IV, 952
Fawcett, Jane IV, 997
Fawcett, Jane IV, 1097
Fawcett, Jane IV, 1278
Fawcett, Jane IV, 1285
Fawcett, Jane V, 475
Fawcett, Jane V, 490
Fawcett, Jane V, 491
Fawcett, Janny IV, 329
Fawcett, Jason IV, 200
Fawcett, Jason IV, 375
Fawcett, Jason IV, 392
Fawcett, Jason IV, 703
Fawcett, Jason IV, 952
Fawcett, Jason IV, 1090
Fawcett, Jason IV, 1097
Fawcett, Jason IV, 1098
Fawcett, Jean S. IV, 1158
Fawcett, Jebtha IV, 1097
Fawcett, Jehu IV, 524
Fawcett, Jehu IV, 534
Fawcett, Jehu IV, 703
Fawcett, Jehu IV, 704
Fawcett, Jehu IV, 705
Fawcett, Jehu IV, 718
Fawcett, Jehu IV, 723
Fawcett, Jehu IV, 776
Fawcett, Jehu VI, 388
Fawcett, Jephtha IV, 797
Fawcett, Jephtha IV, 814
Fawcett, Jephtha Ann IV, 1097
Fawcett, Jephthah IV, 703
Fawcett, Jephthah IV, 952
Fawcett, Jephthah IV, 1087
Fawcett, Jephthah IV, 1097
Fawcett, Jeptha IV, 392
Fawcett, Jeptha IV, 455
Fawcett, Jeptha IV, 524
Fawcett, Jeptha IV, 952
Fawcett, Jeptha IV, 1015
Fawcett, Jeptha Ann IV, 524
Fawcett, Jeptha Anna IV, 524
Fawcett, Jeptha Anna IV, 557
Fawcett, Jepthaann IV, 1097
Fawcett, Jesse IV, 329
Fawcett, Jesse IV, 391
Fawcett, Jesse IV, 392
Fawcett, Jesse IV, 524
Fawcett, Jesse IV, 1057
Fawcett, Jesse IV, 1097
Fawcett, Jesse VI, 388
Fawcett, Joel IV, 329
Fawcett, Joel IV, 391
Fawcett, John II, 360
Fawcett, John IV, 328
Fawcett, John IV, 329
Fawcett, John IV, 392
Fawcett, John IV, 577
Fawcett, John IV, 704
Fawcett, John IV, 705
Fawcett, John V, 490
Fawcett, John V, 491
Fawcett, John V, 522
Fawcett, John VI, 371
Fawcett, John VI, 387
Fawcett, John VI, 388
Fawcett, John VI, 415
Fawcett, John VI, 434
Fawcett, John VI, 594
Fawcett, John VI, 595
Fawcett, John VI, 599
Fawcett, John VI, 602
Fawcett, John B. V, 995
Fawcett, John P. V, 491
Fawcett, John Painter VI, 387
Fawcett, John S. IV, 392
Fawcett, John Smith IV, 391
Fawcett, John W. IV, 761
Fawcett, John Wm. IV, 524
Fawcett, John, Jr. VI, 388
Fawcett, Jonah IV, 703
Fawcett, Jonas IV, 524
Fawcett, Jonathan IV, 145
Fawcett, Jonathan IV, 175
Fawcett, Jonathan IV, 200
Fawcett, Jonathan IV, 255
Fawcett, Jonathan IV, 329
Fawcett, Jonathan IV, 353
Fawcett, Jonathan IV, 391
Fawcett, Jonathan IV, 392
Fawcett, Jonathan IV, 444
Fawcett, Jonathan IV, 524
Fawcett, Jonathan IV, 692
Fawcett, Jonathan IV, 703
Fawcett, Jonathan IV, 704
Fawcett, Jonathan IV, 705
Fawcett, Jonathan IV, 744
Fawcett, Jonathan IV, 1057
Fawcett, Jonathan IV, 1097
Fawcett, Jonathan V, 491
Fawcett, Jonathan VI, 388
Fawcett, Jonathan VI, 595
Fawcett, Jonathan P. IV, 524
Fawcett, Jonathan P. V, 490
Fawcett, Jonathan P. V, 491
Fawcett, Jonathan W., Jr. IV, 705
Fawcett, Jos. VI, 388
Fawcett, Joseph II, 360
Fawcett, Joseph II, 521
Fawcett, Joseph II, 576
Fawcett, Joseph IV, 145
Fawcett, Joseph IV, 329
Fawcett, Joseph IV, 524
Fawcett, Joseph IV, 703
Fawcett, Joseph IV, 704
Fawcett, Joseph IV, 705
Fawcett, Joseph IV, 739
Fawcett, Joseph IV, 1096
Fawcett, Joseph VI, 367
Fawcett, Joseph VI, 369
Fawcett, Joseph VI, 387
Fawcett, Joseph VI, 388
Fawcett, Joseph VI, 595
Fawcett, Joseph Janney IV, 145
Fawcett, Joseph Janney VI, 387
Fawcett, Joseph Janney VI, 388
Fawcett, Joseph S. IV, 1090
Fawcett, Joseph S. IV, 1097
Fawcett, Joseph S. IV, 1098
Fawcett, Joseph, Jr. IV, 524
Fawcett, Joshua IV, 329
Fawcett, Joshua VI, 388
Fawcett, Joshua H. IV, 1096
Fawcett, Josiah IV, 624
Fawcett, Josiah IV, 650
Fawcett, Josiah IV, 701
Fawcett, Josiah IV, 704
Fawcett, Josiah IV, 705
Fawcett, Josiah IV, 746
Fawcett, Josiah IV, 765
Fawcett, Josiah IV, 1158
Fawcett, Josiah VI, 387
Fawcett, Josiah VI, 388
Fawcett, Josiah VI, 450
Fawcett, Josiah VI, 451
Fawcett, Josiah VI, 595
Fawcett, Lemuel IV, 704
Fawcett, Lemuel IV, 705
Fawcett, Levi IV, 329
Fawcett, Levi IV, 703
Fawcett, Levi IV, 704
Fawcett, Levi IV, 705
Fawcett, Levi IV, 788
Fawcett, Levi V, 491
Fawcett, Levi VI, 388
Fawcett, Levi E. V, 491
Fawcett, Lewis IV, 703
Fawcett, Lewis IV, 705
Fawcett, Lindley IV, 329
Fawcett, Lindley IV, 1097
Fawcett, Lindley IV, 1103
Fawcett, Lindley M. IV, 1097
Fawcett, Lindly IV, 524
Fawcett, Linley M. IV, 329
Fawcett, Lora V, 672
Fawcett, Lorenzo D. V, 491
Fawcett, Louisa IV, 1096
Fawcett, Louisa VI, 388
Fawcett, Louisa M. IV, 1097
Fawcett, Louisa M. IV, 1121
Fawcett, Louisa Penelope IV, 1158
Fawcett, Lucetta V, 951
Fawcett, Lucinda IV, 524
Fawcett, Lucinda IV, 703
Fawcett, Lucinda IV, 952
Fawcett, Lucinda IV, 959
Fawcett, Lucinda IV, 1096
Fawcett, Lucinda IV, 1097
Fawcett, Lucinda V, 491
Fawcett, Lucinda V, 520
Fawcett, Luther T. IV, 704
Fawcett, Luther T. IV, 705
Fawcett, Lydia IV, 336
Fawcett, Lydia IV, 391
Fawcett, Lydia IV, 392
Fawcett, Lydia IV, 421
Fawcett, Lydia IV, 692
Fawcett, Lydia IV, 703
Fawcett, Lydia IV, 757
Fawcett, Lydia IV, 792
Fawcett, Lydia IV, 814
Fawcett, Lydia IV, 1097
Fawcett, Lydia IV, 1113
Fawcett, Lydia VI, 373
Fawcett, Lydia VI, 387
Fawcett, Lydia VI, 388
Fawcett, Lydia VI, 450
Fawcett, Lydia VI, 594
Fawcett, Lydia VI, 595
Fawcett, Lydia VI, 599
Fawcett, Lydia VI, 637
Fawcett, Lydia VI, 712
Fawcett, Lydia VI, 741
Fawcett, Lydia VI, 750
Fawcett, Lydia Ann IV, 145
Fawcett, Lydia Ann IV, 329
Fawcett, Lydia Ann IV, 337
Fawcett, Lydia Ann IV, 524
Fawcett, Lydia Ann IV, 557
Fawcett, Lydia Ann IV, 577
Fawcett, Lydia Ann IV, 797
Fawcett, Lydia Ann IV, 814
Fawcett, Lydia Ann IV, 1087
Fawcett, Lydia Ann IV, 1097
Fawcett, Lydia Ann IV, 1120
Fawcett, Lydia Ann VI, 387
Fawcett, Lydia Ann VI, 388
Fawcett, Lydia Ann VI, 637
Fawcett, Lydia Anne IV, 524
Fawcett, Lydia Jane IV, 329
Fawcett, Lydia Jane IV, 577
Fawcett, Lydia Jane IV, 1098
Fawcett, Lydia Jane IV, 1114
Fawcett, Lydia M. IV, 85
Fawcett, Lydia M. IV, 703
Fawcett, Lydia M. IV, 705
Fawcett, Lydia W. IV, 85
Fawcett, Lydia W. IV, 101
Fawcett, Lydia W. IV, 705
Fawcett, Lydia W. IV, 741
Fawcett, Lydiann IV, 392
Fawcett, Mahlon IV, 329
Fawcett, Mahlon IV, 524
Fawcett, Mahlon IV, 705
Fawcett, Mahlon VI, 388
Fawcett, Mahlon T. IV, 329
Fawcett, Mahlon Taylor IV, 14
Fawcett, Mahlon Taylor IV, 32
Fawcett, Mahlon Taylor VI, 38
Fawcett, Mahlon Taylor VI, 38
Fawcett, Mahlon Taylor VI, 63
Fawcett, Margaret IV, 704
Fawcett, Margaret IV, 1096
Fawcett, Margaret VI, 371
Fawcett, Margaret VI, 387
Fawcett, Margaret VI, 595
Fawcett, Margaret F. IV, 1097
Fawcett, Margaret F. IV, 1099
Fawcett, Maria IV, 200
Fawcett, Maria IV, 392

wcett, Maria IV, 419
wcett, Maria IV, 524
wcett, Maria IV, 1057
wcett, Maria IV, 1097
wcett, Mariah IV, 329
wcett, Mariah IV, 391
wcett, Marie V, 668
wcett, Marie V, 672
wcett, Marietta IV, 1098
wcett, Marietta IV, 1114
wcett, Marietta B. IV, 1097
wcett, Marion V, 672
wcett, Martha IV, 320
wcett, Martha IV, 323
wcett, Martha IV, 328
wcett, Martha IV, 329
wcett, Martha IV, 354
wcett, Martha IV, 357
wcett, Martha IV, 392
wcett, Martha IV, 486
wcett, Martha IV, 524
wcett, Martha IV, 703
wcett, Martha IV, 705
wcett, Martha IV, 761
wcett, Martha IV, 952
wcett, Martha IV, 1097
wcett, Martha VI, 368
wcett, Martha VI, 387
wcett, Martha VI, 388
wcett, Martha VI, 593
wcett, Martha VI, 595
wcett, Martha B. IV, 1097
wcett, Martha D. IV, 1097
wcett, Martha Jr. IV, 1094
wcett, Martha M. IV, 704
wcett, Martha M. IV, 705
wcett, Martha M. IV, 774
wcett, Martha W. IV, 392
wcett, Martha W. IV, 524
wcett, Martha W. IV, 1057
wcett, Martha, Jr. IV, 1096
wcett, Mary IV, 145
wcett, Mary IV, 175
wcett, Mary IV, 200
wcett, Mary IV, 323
wcett, Mary IV, 328
wcett, Mary IV, 329
wcett, Mary IV, 346
wcett, Mary IV, 390
wcett, Mary IV, 391
wcett, Mary IV, 392
wcett, Mary IV, 437
wcett, Mary IV, 438
wcett, Mary IV, 454
wcett, Mary IV, 524
wcett, Mary IV, 554
wcett, Mary IV, 577
wcett, Mary IV, 579
wcett, Mary IV, 692
wcett, Mary IV, 703
wcett, Mary IV, 704
wcett, Mary IV, 705
wcett, Mary IV, 744
wcett, Mary IV, 776
wcett, Mary IV, 788
wcett, Mary IV, 1057
wcett, Mary IV, 1090
wcett, Mary IV, 1097
wcett, Mary IV, 1100
wcett, Mary IV, 1103
wcett, Mary IV, 1113
wcett, Mary V, 385
wcett, Mary V, 490
wcett, Mary V, 491
wcett, Mary V, 995
wcett, Mary VI, 367
wcett, Mary VI, 369
wcett, Mary VI, 371
wcett, Mary VI, 387
wcett, Mary VI, 388
wcett, Mary VI, 429
wcett, Mary VI, 595
wcett, Mary VI, 602
wcett, Mary VI, 603
wcett, Mary Ann IV, 392
wcett, Mary Ann IV, 523
wcett, Mary Ann IV, 524
wcett, Mary Ann IV, 952
wcett, Mary Ann IV, 1014
wcett, Mary Ann IV, 1057
wcett, Mary Ann IV, 1061
wcett, Mary Ann IV, 1097
wcett, Mary Ann V, 489
wcett, Mary Ann V, 490
wcett, Mary Ann V, 491
wcett, Mary B. IV, 1098
wcett, Mary E. IV, 200
wcett, Mary E. IV, 375
wcett, Mary E. IV, 392
wcett, Mary E. IV, 1090
wcett, Mary E. IV, 1097
Fawcett, Mary E. IV, 1098
Fawcett, Mary Ellen IV, 1158
Fawcett, Mary Ellen VI, 388
Fawcett, Mary Emma IV, 704
Fawcett, Mary Emma IV, 705
Fawcett, Mary G. IV, 704
Fawcett, Mary G. IV, 705
Fawcett, Mary G. IV, 761
Fawcett, Mary H. IV, 1098
Fawcett, Mary J. IV, 705
Fawcett, Mary J. IV, 731
Fawcett, Mary J. IV, 794
Fawcett, Mary N. IV, 200
Fawcett, Mary R. IV, 705
Fawcett, Mary R. IV, 739
Fawcett, Mary Rebecca IV, 200
Fawcett, Mary Rebecca IV, 255
Fawcett, Mary T. IV, 329
Fawcett, Mary T. IV, 336
Fawcett, Mary Taylor IV, 145
Fawcett, Mary Taylor IV, 329
Fawcett, Mary Taylor VI, 387
Fawcett, Mary Taylor VI, 388
Fawcett, Mary Taylor VI, 637
Fawcett, Maryann IV, 524
Fawcett, Maryann IV, 1097
Fawcett, Milo IV, 1158
Fawcett, Milo IV, 1159
Fawcett, Milton IV, 524
Fawcett, Milton V, 490
Fawcett, Milton V, 491
Fawcett, Milton V, 496
Fawcett, Mordecai H. V, 491
Fawcett, Myrl IV, 1250
Fawcett, Nancy IV, 329
Fawcett, Nancy IV, 511
Fawcett, Nancy IV, 513
Fawcett, Nancy IV, 524
Fawcett, Nancy VI, 388
Fawcett, Nathan II, 360
Fawcett, Nathan II, 521
Fawcett, Nathan IV, 329
Fawcett, Nathan IV, 705
Fawcett, Nathan VI, 388
Fawcett, Nathan B. IV, 703
Fawcett, O. H. IV, 1278
Fawcett, Oliver G. IV, 1158
Fawcett, Oliver Goldsmith IV, 1158
Fawcett, Oliver Goldsmith VI, 388
Fawcett, Patience IV, 1057
Fawcett, Patience IV, 1058
Fawcett, Patience IV, 1097
Fawcett, Phebe IV, 145
Fawcett, Phebe IV, 329
Fawcett, Phebe IV, 524
Fawcett, Phebe IV, 704
Fawcett, Phebe IV, 705
Fawcett, Phebe IV, 748
Fawcett, Phebe IV, 953
Fawcett, Phebe IV, 984
Fawcett, Phebe V, 491
Fawcett, Phebe V, 522
Fawcett, Phebe VI, 388
Fawcett, Phebe VI, 403
Fawcett, Phebe VI, 595
Fawcett, Phebe J. IV, 1016
Fawcett, Phebe W. V, 491
Fawcett, Phenias Anderton IV, 1158
Fawcett, Philadelphia VI, 388
Fawcett, Philip II, 521
Fawcett, Philip IV, 391
Fawcett, Phineas IV, 704
Fawcett, Phineas A. IV, 1158
Fawcett, Phineas Anderton VI, 388
Fawcett, Rachel IV, 145
Fawcett, Rachel IV, 200
Fawcett, Rachel IV, 328
Fawcett, Rachel IV, 329
Fawcett, Rachel IV, 343
Fawcett, Rachel IV, 354
Fawcett, Rachel IV, 391
Fawcett, Rachel IV, 392
Fawcett, Rachel IV, 455
Fawcett, Rachel IV, 486
Fawcett, Rachel IV, 577
Fawcett, Rachel IV, 952
Fawcett, Rachel IV, 1015
Fawcett, Rachel IV, 1097
Fawcett, Rachel IV, 1120
Fawcett, Rachel VI, 362
Fawcett, Rachel VI, 387
Fawcett, Rachel VI, 388
Fawcett, Rachel VI, 434
Fawcett, Rachel VI, 593
Fawcett, Rachel VI, 594
Fawcett, Rachel VI, 595
Fawcett, Rachel VI, 599
Fawcett, Rachel VI, 603
Fawcett, Rachel Ann IV, 329
Fawcett, Ralph F. IV, 704
Fawcett, Ralph F. IV, 705
Fawcett, Rease IV, 329
Fawcett, Rebecca II, 360
Fawcett, Rebecca IV, 145
Fawcett, Rebecca IV, 329
Fawcett, Rebecca IV, 337
Fawcett, Rebecca IV, 391
Fawcett, Rebecca IV, 392
Fawcett, Rebecca IV, 444
Fawcett, Rebecca IV, 524
Fawcett, Rebecca IV, 1057
Fawcett, Rebecca IV, 1097
Fawcett, Rebecca V, 491
Fawcett, Rebecca V, 542
Fawcett, Rebecca VI, 387
Fawcett, Rebecca VI, 388
Fawcett, Rebecca VI, 637
Fawcett, Rebecca VI, 668
Fawcett, Rebecca B. IV, 704
Fawcett, Rebecca B. IV, 705
Fawcett, Rebecca J. IV, 329
Fawcett, Rebecca J. IV, 337
Fawcett, Rebecca J. VI, 637
Fawcett, Rebecca J. VI, 656
Fawcett, Rebecca J. VI, 672
Fawcett, Rebecca Jane V, 167
Fawcett, Rebecca P. V, 491
Fawcett, Rebeckah VI, 387
Fawcett, Rebeckah VI, 388
Fawcett, Rebeckah VI, 434
Fawcett, Rebeckah VI, 594
Fawcett, Rebeckah VI, 595
Fawcett, Rebeckah VI, 599
Fawcett, Reece L. IV, 329
Fawcett, Reese IV, 524
Fawcett, Richard IV, 145
Fawcett, Richard IV, 147
Fawcett, Richard IV, 200
Fawcett, Richard IV, 329
Fawcett, Richard IV, 390
Fawcett, Richard IV, 391
Fawcett, Richard IV, 392
Fawcett, Richard IV, 394
Fawcett, Richard IV, 428
Fawcett, Richard IV, 437
Fawcett, Richard IV, 438
Fawcett, Richard IV, 454
Fawcett, Richard IV, 624
Fawcett, Richard IV, 683
Fawcett, Richard IV, 686
Fawcett, Richard IV, 697
Fawcett, Richard IV, 703
Fawcett, Richard IV, 704
Fawcett, Richard IV, 705
Fawcett, Richard IV, 761
Fawcett, Richard IV, 1057
Fawcett, Richard IV, 1097
Fawcett, Richard IV, 1113
Fawcett, Richard VI, 362
Fawcett, Richard VI, 387
Fawcett, Richard VI, 388
Fawcett, Richard VI, 429
Fawcett, Richard VI, 594
Fawcett, Richard VI, 595
Fawcett, Richard VI, 599
Fawcett, Richard VI, 603
Fawcett, Richard B. IV, 703
Fawcett, Richard B. IV, 704
Fawcett, Richard B. IV, 705
Fawcett, Richard B. IV, 775
Fawcett, Richard B. IV, 792
Fawcett, Richard Stanton IV, 1097
Fawcett, Robert IV, 328
Fawcett, Robert IV, 329
Fawcett, Robert IV, 346
Fawcett, Robert IV, 524
Fawcett, Robert V, 490
Fawcett, Robert V, 491
Fawcett, Robert VI, 388
Fawcett, Robert VI, 594
Fawcett, Robery Ellyson, Jr. IV, 952
Fawcett, Rosa V, 739
Fawcett, Ruth IV, 391
Fawcett, Ruth IV, 392
Fawcett, Ruth IV, 704
Fawcett, Ruth IV, 705
Fawcett, Ruth IV, 1097
Fawcett, Ruth V, 672
Fawcett, Samuel IV, 145
Fawcett, Samuel IV, 200
Fawcett, Samuel IV, 329
Fawcett, Samuel IV, 391
Fawcett, Samuel IV, 392
Fawcett, Samuel IV, 513
Fawcett, Samuel IV, 524
Fawcett, Samuel IV, 577
Fawcett, Samuel IV, 705
Fawcett, Samuel IV, 952
Fawcett, Samuel IV, 1057
Fawcett, Samuel IV, 1058
Fawcett, Samuel IV, 1061
Fawcett, Samuel IV, 1097
Fawcett, Samuel VI, 595
Fawcett, Samuel G. IV, 329
Fawcett, Samuel G. IV, 1097
Fawcett, Samuel G. IV, 1115
Fawcett, Samuel S. IV, 952
Fawcett, Samuel S. IV, 997
Fawcett, Samuel Sharp IV, 703
Fawcett, Samuel T. IV, 703
Fawcett, Sarah IV, 145
Fawcett, Sarah IV, 147
Fawcett, Sarah IV, 328
Fawcett, Sarah IV, 329
Fawcett, Sarah IV, 390
Fawcett, Sarah IV, 391
Fawcett, Sarah IV, 392
Fawcett, Sarah IV, 394
Fawcett, Sarah IV, 396
Fawcett, Sarah IV, 524
Fawcett, Sarah IV, 527
Fawcett, Sarah IV, 534
Fawcett, Sarah IV, 535
Fawcett, Sarah IV, 624
Fawcett, Sarah IV, 650
Fawcett, Sarah IV, 701
Fawcett, Sarah IV, 704
Fawcett, Sarah IV, 705
Fawcett, Sarah IV, 718
Fawcett, Sarah IV, 723
Fawcett, Sarah IV, 745
Fawcett, Sarah IV, 746
Fawcett, Sarah IV, 814
Fawcett, Sarah IV, 835
Fawcett, Sarah IV, 1057
Fawcett, Sarah IV, 1096
Fawcett, Sarah IV, 1097
Fawcett, Sarah IV, 1105
Fawcett, Sarah IV, 1158
Fawcett, Sarah V, 491
Fawcett, Sarah V, 496
Fawcett, Sarah VI, 387
Fawcett, Sarah VI, 388
Fawcett, Sarah VI, 415
Fawcett, Sarah VI, 448
Fawcett, Sarah VI, 450
Fawcett, Sarah VI, 592
Fawcett, Sarah VI, 594
Fawcett, Sarah VI, 595
Fawcett, Sarah VI, 637
Fawcett, Sarah VI, 668
Fawcett, Sarah VI, 712
Fawcett, Sarah VI, 741
Fawcett, Sarah VI, 750
Fawcett, Sarah A. IV, 329
Fawcett, Sarah Ann IV, 329
Fawcett, Sarah Ann IV, 1097
Fawcett, Sarah Ann IV, 1101
Fawcett, Sarah Anne IV, 329
Fawcett, Sarah B. IV, 524
Fawcett, Sarah B. IV, 1016
Fawcett, Sarah B. V, 491
Fawcett, Sarah C. IV, 692
Fawcett, Sarah C. IV, 705
Fawcett, Sarah Edna VI, 388
Fawcett, Sarah Eunice IV, 1158
Fawcett, Sarah Eunice VI, 388
Fawcett, Sarah J. IV, 1098
Fawcett, Sarah Josephine IV, 1097
Fawcett, Sarah L. IV, 704
Fawcett, Sarah L. IV, 773
Fawcett, Sarah P. V, 490
Fawcett, Sarah T. IV, 703
Fawcett, Sarah T. IV, 705
Fawcett, Sarah T. IV, 773
Fawcett, Sarah T. IV, 1158
Fawcett, Sarah W. IV, 1097
Fawcett, Semilda IV, 524
Fawcett, Sibilah IV, 1076
Fawcett, Sibilay IV, 1057
Fawcett, Sibilla IV, 391
Fawcett, Sibilla IV, 392
Fawcett, Sibilla IV, 437
Fawcett, Sidney IV, 704
Fawcett, Sidney A. II, 719
Fawcett, Sidney A. IV, 704
Fawcett, Sidney A. IV, 767
Fawcett, Sidney Ann IV, 681
Fawcett, Sidney Ann IV, 704
Fawcett, Simeon IV, 329
Fawcett, Simeon IV, 703
Fawcett, Simeon IV, 704
Fawcett, Simeon IV, 905
Fawcett, Simeon IV, 911
Fawcett, Simeon IV, 952
Fawcett, Simeon IV, 953
Fawcett, Simeon IV, 980
Fawcett, Simeon VI, 388
Fawcett, Sina IV, 329
Fawcett, Sina IV, 333
Fawcett, Sina IV, 704
Fawcett, Sina F. IV, 705
Fawcett, Sina F. IV, 750
Fawcett, Stephen IV, 1120
Fawcett, Susan VI, 741
Fawcett, Susanah IV, 1097
Fawcett, Susannah IV, 323
Fawcett, Susannah IV, 329
Fawcett, Susannah IV, 524
Fawcett, Susannah IV, 1057
Fawcett, Susannah VI, 388
Fawcett, Tacy IV, 1097
Fawcett, Tacy VI, 403
Fawcett, Tacy Jane IV, 1097
Fawcett, Thomas IV, 320
Fawcett, Thomas IV, 328
Fawcett, Thomas IV, 329
Fawcett, Thomas IV, 392
Fawcett, Thomas IV, 486
Fawcett, Thomas IV, 524
Fawcett, Thomas IV, 704
Fawcett, Thomas IV, 705
Fawcett, Thomas IV, 745
Fawcett, Thomas IV, 1097
Fawcett, Thomas VI, 368
Fawcett, Thomas VI, 387
Fawcett, Thomas VI, 388
Fawcett, Thomas VI, 592
Fawcett, Thomas VI, 593
Fawcett, Thomas VI, 594
Fawcett, Thomas VI, 595
Fawcett, Thomas VI, 597
Fawcett, Thomas VI, 598
Fawcett, Thomas VI, 599
Fawcett, Thomas VI, 637
Fawcett, Thomas VI, 668
Fawcett, Thomas VI, 712
Fawcett, Thomas VI, 741
Fawcett, Thomas VI, 750
Fawcett, Thomas F. II, 719
Fawcett, Thomas F. IV, 681
Fawcett, Thomas F. IV, 703
Fawcett, Thomas F. IV, 704
Fawcett, Thomas Hayes IV, 706
Fawcett, Thomas W. IV, 329
Fawcett, Thomas William VI, 388
Fawcett, Thomas Williams IV, 329
Fawcett, Thomas Wm. VI, 387
Fawcett, Thomas, Jr. IV, 329
Fawcett, Thos. IV, 323
Fawcett, Thos. IV, 328
Fawcett, Thos. IV, 354
Fawcett, Thos. IV, 524
Fawcett, Thos. VI, 637
Fawcett, Thos. F. IV, 767
Fawcett, Thos. Hayes IV, 704
Fawcett, Thos. Wm. IV, 145
Fawcett, Unice VI, 388
Fawcett, Virginia E. IV, 1158
Fawcett, Walter II, 521
Fawcett, Walter IV, 952
Fawcett, Walter IV, 953
Fawcett, Walter H. IV, 1097
Fawcett, Walter H. IV, 1098
Fawcett, Washington IV, 329
Fawcett, Washington VI, 388
Fawcett, Wd. Jane II, 521
Fawcett, William II, 360
Fawcett, William IV, 85
Fawcett, William IV, 328
Fawcett, William IV, 329
Fawcett, William IV, 392
Fawcett, William IV, 704
Fawcett, William IV, 952
Fawcett, William VI, 388
Fawcett, William VI, 595
Fawcett, William VI, 637
Fawcett, William E. IV, 705
Fawcett, William F. IV, 85
Fawcett, William T. IV, 705
Fawcett, William T. VI, 388
Fawcett, William Taylor IV, 1158
Fawcett, William Taylor VI, 388
Fawcett, Willis G. IV, 704
Fawcett, Willis G. IV, 705
Fawcett, Willis T. IV, 1097
Fawcett, Willis T. IV, 1098
Fawcett, Winchester VI, 387
Fawcett, Wm. II, 521
Fawcett, Wm. IV, 703
Fawcett, Wm. IV, 1096
Fawcett, Wm. Elmer IV, 704
Fawcett, Wm. F. IV, 703
Fawcett, Wm. F. IV, 723
Fawcett, Wm. F. IV, 775

Fawcett, Wm. F. IV, 1158
Fawcett, Wm. G. V, 951
Fawcett, Wm. H. IV, 952
Fawcett, Wm. H. IV, 1097
Fawcett, Wm. Henry IV, 1097
Fawcett, Wm. L. V, 385
Fawcett, Wm. McNichols IV, 577
Fawcett, Wm. T. IV, 704
Fawcett, Wm. T. IV, 1158
Fawcett, Wm. T. IV, 1159
Fawcett, Wm. T. IV, 1195
Fawcett, Zaccheus IV, 703
Fawcett, Zaccheus IV, 705
Fawcette, Anna I, 926
Fawcette, Anna I, 929
Fawcitt, Samuel IV, 145
Fawcitt, Sarah W. IV, 1123
Fawkes, Anna Trego II, 862
Fawkes, E. Lawrence II, 862
Fawkes, Emma T. II, 862
Fawkes, Emma T. II, 876
Fawkes, Esther Katharyn II, 862
Fawkes, Esther W. II, 862
Fawkes, Helen Jeanette II, 862
Fawkes, Lewis II, 717
Fawkes, Phebe Anna II, 717
Fawkes, Sarah D. II, 739
Fawkes, Sarah D. II, 764
Fawkes, Sarah Emma II, 862
Fawkes, Sarah F. II, 717
Fayle, Joshua III, 116
Fayle, Mary I, 357
Fayle, Thomas IV, 1314
Fayles, ??? III, 113
Fayre, Deborah III, 449
Fazer, Eliza III, 116
Fazier, Susanna I, 572
Feak, Eliz III, 410
Feak, Eliz. III, 410
Feak, Elizabeth III, 398
Feak, Elizabeth III, 410
Feak, John III, 398
Feak, John III, 410
Feak, Martha III, 398
Feak, Martha III, 410
Feake, Abigail III, 116
Feake, Deborah III, 116
Feake, Deborah III, 410
Feake, Deborah III, 466
Feake, Eliz. III, 116
Feake, Eliz. III, 410
Feake, Elizabeth III, 62
Feake, Elizabeth III, 74
Feake, Elizabeth III, 116
Feake, Elizabeth III, 260
Feake, Elizabeth III, 410
Feake, Elizabeth III, 438
Feake, Elizabeth III, 466
Feake, Hannah III, 41
Feake, Hannah III, 75
Feake, Hannah III, 116
Feake, John III, 62
Feake, John III, 74
Feake, John III, 75
Feake, John III, 116
Feake, John III, 260
Feake, John III, 410
Feake, John III, 438
Feake, John III, 466
Feake, Martha III, 62
Feake, Martha III, 116
Feake, Mary III, 74
Feake, Mary III, 116
Feake, Robert III, 116
Feake, Robert III, 410
Feake, Sarah III, 116
Feake, Wd. Elizabeth III, 410
Feaks, Abigail III, 116
Feaks, Benj. III, 118
Feaks, Benjamin III, 118
Feaks, Deborah III, 116
Feaks, Deborah III, 351
Feaks, Eliz. III, 116
Feaks, Elizabeth III, 116
Feaks, Elizabeth III, 118
Feaks, Hannah III, 116
Feaks, John III, 116
Feaks, John III, 118
Feaks, Martha III, 116
Feaks, Mary III, 116
Feaks, Robert III, 116
Feaks, Sarah III, 116
Feaks, Sarah III, 118
Feanley, Martha IV, 706
Feanley, Martin IV, 706
Feanley, Thos. IV, 706
Fear, Elizabeth IV, 85
Fear, Elizabeth IV, 109
Fear, Jane VI, 828
Fear, John VI, 913
Fear, Nancy VI, 828
Fear, Nancy VI, 913
Fear, W. L. VI, 811
Fearlam, Jane II, 995
Fearlamb, Jane II, 995
Fearlamb, Jane II, 1027
Fearman, Elizabeth II, 220
Fearman, Thomas II, 220
Fearnley, Hannah VI, 595
Fearnley, Martha VI, 591
Fearnley, Martha VI, 593
Fearnley, Martha VI, 595
Fearnley, Martha VI, 597
Fearnley, Martha VI, 598
Fearnley, Martha VI, 600
Fearnley, Thomas VI, 595
Fearnley, Unice VI, 595
Fearnley, William VI, 595
Fearon, Anne II, 220
Fearon, Anne II, 271
Fearon, Peter II, 220
Fearon, Peter II, 241
Fearon, Peter II, 521
Fearon, Susanah II, 220
Fearon, Susanah II, 241
Fears, Elizabeth VI, 816
Fears, Jesse VI, 913
Fears, John VI, 913
Fears, Nancy VI, 913
Fears, Thomas VI, 816
Fearter, Retta V, 995
Fearuley, Ann III, 120
Feast, Annie VI, 494
Feaster, Cora V, 995
Feaster, Drusella V, 995
Feaster, Louvina V, 995
Feaster, Rella V, 995
Feaster, Retta V, 995
Feather, Adam P. VI, 913
Feather, Ann E. VI, 913
Feather, Betsy VI, 935
Feather, Eve VI, 984
Feather, Henry P. VI, 984
Feather, Henry P. VI, 986
Feather, John VI, 913
Feather, John VI, 984
Feather, John VI, 986
Feather, Joseph VI, 913
Feather, Julian VI, 913
Feather, Mary Ann VI, 913
Feather, Mary C. VI, 913
Feather, Nancy VI, 984
Feather, Nancy VI, 986
Feather, Philip VI, 935
Feather, Polly VI, 913
Feather, Richard B. VI, 913
Feather, Rutha VI, 913
Feather, Sally VI, 935
Feather, Sarah VI, 928
Featherby, Benjamin II, 995
Featherby, Benjamin II, 1050
Featherby, George Washington II, 1050
Featherby, Jane II, 995
Featherby, Jane II, 1011
Featherby, Mary II, 995
Featherby, Mary II, 1011
Featherby, Mary II, 1050
Featherby, Mercy Ann II, 1050
Featherby, Nathaniel II, 995
Featherby, Nathaniel II, 1011
Featherly, Mary II, 1050
Featheroll, Marguerite IV, 1250
Feathers, Mary Ann VI, 913
Feathers, Richard B. VI, 913
Featherston, Howell VI, 913
Featherston, Martha S. VI, 913
Featherston, Richard VI, 913
Featherston, Silas VI, 913
Feazel, Aaron VI, 896
Feazel, Aaron VI, 914
Feazel, Amanda V. VI, 984
Feazel, Ann L. VI, 930
Feazel, Ann T. VI, 984
Feazel, Eliza VI, 914
Feazel, Elizabeth VI, 930
Feazel, J. VI, 1019
Feazel, Jacob VI, 310
Feazel, Jacob VI, 352
Feazel, Jacob VI, 896
Feazel, Jacob VI, 914
Feazel, John Cabell VI, 914
Feazel, Joseph VI, 914
Feazel, Juliet VI, 914
Feazel, Lockey VI, 914
Feazel, Martha VI, 914
Feazel, Mary M. VI, 1019
Feazel, Philip VI, 310
Feazel, Philip VI, 992
Feazel, Philip VI, 1019
Feazel, Rachel VI, 896
Feazel, Rachel VI, 914
Feazel, Susannah VI, 914
Feazel, William VI, 928
Feazel, Wm. VI, 905
Feazel, Wm. VI, 1021
Feazle, Aaron VI, 914
Feazle, Elizabeth VI, 875
Feazle, Jacob VI, 352
Feazle, Jacob VI, 875
Feazle, Jacob VI, 914
Feazle, Lockey VI, 914
Feazle, Mahala VI, 1019
Feazle, Martha VI, 914
Feazle, Martha VI, 1019
Feazle, Mary VI, 1019
Feazle, Philip VI, 310
Feazle, Philip VI, 352
Feazle, Polly VI, 998
Feazle, Sarah VI, 941
Febiger, Sarah S. V, 905
Febiger, Sarah T. V, 905
Federer, Mary IV, 1314
Federer, Mrs. Mary IV, 1314
Fedrick, ??? I, 715
Feek, Eliz. III, 116
Feek, Hannah III, 116
Feek, John III, 116
Feeks, Ann III, 400
Feeks, Catharine III, 400
Feeks, Deborah III, 465
Feeks, Hannah III, 401
Feeks, Hannah III, 410
Feeks, Mary III, 400
Feeks, Robt. III, 400
Feeks, William III, 410
Feeley, ??? VI, 741
Feeley, ??? VI, 742
Feeley, Irwin Chase VI, 742
Feeley, Lucretia M. VI, 742
Feeley, Sarah Chace Franklin VI, 741
Feeley, Sarah Chase VI, 742
Feen, Calla IV, 1250
Feen, Joanna Marie IV, 1250
Feese, Ezra V, 739
Feese, Sophia V, 739
Feezel, Bernard VI, 914
Feicht, Edgar IV, 706
Feicht, Ellsworth IV, 706
Feicht, Harry M. IV, 706
Feicht, Harry Morell IV, 706
Feicht, Minnie IV, 706
Feicht, Vera IV, 706
Feicht, Vera Smith IV, 706
Feicht, Verdie IV, 706
Feige, Maria A. E. III, 482
Feighner, Alice V, 995
Feighner, Max V, 995
Feight, Mariah IV, 1207
Feightner, Max V, 995
Feild, Ambrose II, 196
Feild, Ambrose II, 220
Feild, Benjamin II, 173
Feild, Benjamin II, 196
Feild, Benjamin II, 220
Feild, Mary II, 196
Feild, Mary II, 220
Feild, Susannah II, 173
Feister, Albert V, 995
Feke, Anne III, 403
Feke, Anne III, 410
Feke, Catharine III, 403
Feke, Catharine III, 410
Feke, Charles III, 410
Feke, Charley III, 403
Feke, Clemence III, 403
Feke, Daniel III, 401
Feke, Daniel III, 410
Feke, Deborah III, 410
Feke, Elder III, 402
Feke, Eliz. III, 410
Feke, Elizabeth III, 75
Feke, Elizabeth III, 401
Feke, Elizabeth III, 410
Feke, Hannah III, 75
Feke, Hannah III, 410
Feke, John III, 75
Feke, John III, 410
Feke, Martha III, 410
Feke, Mary III, 400
Feke, Mary III, 401
Feke, Mary III, 410
Feke, Robert III, 410
Feke, Wd. Elizabeth III, 410
Feke, William III, 410
Felger, Mrs. Eleanor V, 571
Felger, Mrs. F. IV, 1314
Felkins, John VI, 901
Felkins, Salley VI, 901
Fell, Aaron IV, 32
Fell, Aaron IV, 85
Fell, Aaron IV, 145
Fell, Aaron IV, 146
Fell, Aaron Townsend II, 793
Fell, Abigail II, 360
Fell, Abner G. VI, 741
Fell, Abner G. VI, 743
Fell, Ada II, 813
Fell, Alexander S. VI, 64
Fell, Alfred M. II, 862
Fell, Alpheus IV, 525
Fell, Ann II, 361
Fell, Ann II, 739
Fell, Ann II, 740
Fell, Ann II, 1050
Fell, Ann IV, 32
Fell, Ann IV, 85
Fell, Ann IV, 200
Fell, Ann IV, 524
Fell, Ann IV, 525
Fell, Ann IV, 1278
Fell, Ann Kitchen II, 793
Fell, Anna VI, 64
Fell, Anna G. VI, 64
Fell, Anna T. II, 862
Fell, Anna Trego II, 917
Fell, Benjamin II, 521
Fell, Benjamin II, 959
Fell, Bridget II, 959
Fell, Bridgett II, 959
Fell, Caroline VI, 64
Fell, Caroline G. VI, 64
Fell, Carrie G. VI, 64
Fell, Courtland J. II, 361
Fell, Courtland J. II, 739
Fell, D. Newlin II, 794
Fell, D. Newlin II, 862
Fell, David II, 1050
Fell, David II, 1072
Fell, David N. II, 862
Fell, David Newlin II, 862
Fell, David Newlin II, 917
Fell, Edgar Trainer II, 793
Fell, Edith N. II, 862
Fell, Edward H. II, 793
Fell, Edward H. II, 862
Fell, Edward W. II, 862
Fell, Eliza II, 361
Fell, Eliza II, 705
Fell, Eliza II, 740
Fell, Eliza VI, 741
Fell, Elizabeth II, 959
Fell, Elizabeth II, 993
Fell, Elizabeth II, 995
Fell, Elizabeth II, 1050
Fell, Elizabeth II, 1072
Fell, Elizabeth IV, 32
Fell, Elizabeth IV, 515
Fell, Elizabeth IV, 524
Fell, Emily II, 361
Fell, Emily II, 740
Fell, Emily IV, 524
Fell, Emily IV, 525
Fell, Emma II, 793
Fell, Emma II, 862
Fell, Emma T. II, 862
Fell, Esther II, 986
Fell, Esther II, 995
Fell, Esther II, 1009
Fell, Esther H. IV, 524
Fell, Esther H. IV, 525
Fell, Esther H. IV, 530
Fell, Ezra IV, 32
Fell, Ezra IV, 85
Fell, Franklin II, 361
Fell, Franklin II, 705
Fell, Franklin II, 739
Fell, Franklin II, 740
Fell, Grace IV, 182
Fell, Grace IV, 201
Fell, Hannah II, 946
Fell, Hannah II, 995
Fell, Hannah II, 1050
Fell, Hannah II, 1072
Fell, Howard II, 361
Fell, Howard IV, 524
Fell, Howard A. II, 862
Fell, Isaac II, 959
Fell, James B. II, 995
Fell, James B. II, 1050
Fell, James B. II, 1072
Fell, Jane II, 946
Fell, Jane II, 959
Fell, Jane II, 995
Fell, Jane II, 1050
Fell, Jane II, 1072
Fell, John II, 959
Fell, John II, 995
Fell, John II, 1019
Fell, John Duer II, 793
Fell, John W. IV, 524
Fell, Jonathan II, 361
Fell, Jonathan II, 521
Fell, Jonathan II, 705
Fell, Jonathan II, 739
Fell, Jonathan II, 740
Fell, Jonathan II, 959
Fell, Jonathan II, 995
Fell, Jonathan II, 1050
Fell, Jonathan II, 1072
Fell, Jonathan, Jr. II, 521
Fell, Jonathan, Sr. II, 361
Fell, Jos. IV, 524
Fell, Joseph II, 959
Fell, Joseph II, 986
Fell, Joseph II, 993
Fell, Joseph II, 995
Fell, Joseph II, 1009
Fell, Joseph IV, 85
Fell, Joseph IV, 145
Fell, Joseph IV, 200
Fell, Joseph IV, 201
Fell, Joseph IV, 524
Fell, Joseph IV, 525
Fell, Joseph E. VI, 64
Fell, Joseph J. IV, 524
Fell, Joseph Towsend IV, 524
Fell, Joseph W. II, 794
Fell, Joseph W. II, 862
Fell, Joseph, Jr. II, 740
Fell, Joshua II, 793
Fell, Joshua II, 813
Fell, Joshua II, 995
Fell, Joshua II, 1050
Fell, Joshua II, 1072
Fell, Latitia II, 1050
Fell, Laura VI, 64
Fell, Lewis IV, 524
Fell, Lewis L. IV, 524
Fell, Lizzie VI, 55
Fell, Lizzie VI, 64
Fell, Lydia Ann IV, 524
Fell, Lydia Ann IV, 525
Fell, Mahlon IV, 32
Fell, Mahlon IV, 85
Fell, Mahlon V, 781
Fell, Margaret II, 740
Fell, Margaret VI, 5
Fell, Margaret C. II, 740
Fell, Margery II, 825
Fell, Maria II, 739
Fell, Marshal IV, 524
Fell, Marshal, Jr. IV, 525
Fell, Marshall IV, 200
Fell, Marshall IV, 221
Fell, Marshall IV, 524
Fell, Marshall IV, 525
Fell, Marshall IV, 530
Fell, Martha II, 794
Fell, Martha II, 862
Fell, Martha II, 917
Fell, Martha IV, 525
Fell, Martha T. II, 862
Fell, Mary II, 220
Fell, Mary II, 361
Fell, Mary II, 739
Fell, Mary II, 740
Fell, Mary II, 794
Fell, Mary II, 813
Fell, Mary II, 959
Fell, Mary Ashman II, 793
Fell, Mary M. II, 833
Fell, Mary M. II, 862
Fell, Mary McKinstry VI, 741
Fell, Mary McKinstry VI, 743
Fell, Moses IV, 32
Fell, Moses IV, 85
Fell, Oliver Shaw II, 794
Fell, Penrose II, 739
Fell, Phebe L. IV, 524
Fell, Phebe L. IV, 559
Fell, Rachel II, 959
Fell, Rachel II, 995
Fell, Rachel IV, 32
Fell, Rachel IV, 85
Fell, Rachel IV, 145
Fell, Rachel IV, 201
Fell, Rachel IV, 260
Fell, Rebecca II, 361
Fell, Rebecca II, 521
Fell, Rebecca II, 705
Fell, Rebecca II, 739
Fell, Rebecca II, 740
Fell, Rebecca II, 995
Fell, Rebecca II, 1009
Fell, Rebecca IV, 200
Fell, Rebecca IV, 201
Fell, Rebecca IV, 221
Fell, Rebecca IV, 524
Fell, Rebecca IV, 530
Fell, Rebecca Ann II, 361
Fell, Rebecca Ann II, 740
Fell, Rebecca T. II, 862
Fell, Rebeckah II, 959

ell, Richard H. VI, 741
ell, Samuel VI, 64
ell, Samuel K. IV, 524
ell, Samuel S. VI, 55
ell, Samuel S. VI, 64
ell, Sarah II, 959
ell, Sarah II, 995
ell, Sarah II, 1019
ell, Sarah II, 1050
ell, Sarah II, 1072
ell, Sarah VI, 64
ell, Sarah Ann II, 948
ell, Susan L. II, 793
ell, Susan T. II, 862
ell, Susan W. II, 705
ell, Tamer II, 959
ell, Thomas II, 360
ell, Thomas IV, 524
ell, Thomas IV, 525
ell, Thomas Jenks II, 361
ell, Thomas Jenks II, 739
ell, William G. VI, 64
ell, William Jenks II, 705
ell, William W. IV, 524
ell, Wilson IV, 524
ell, Wm. II, 1050
ell, Wm. Jenks II, 740
eller, Elizabeth VI, 901
eller, Elizabeth VI, 914
eller, John VI, 914
eller, John VI, 922
eller, Milly VI, 914
eller, Peter VI, 901
eller, Peter VI, 914
ellers, Elizabeth VI, 914
ellers, John VI, 914
ellow, Abigail I, 287
ellow, Abigail I, 301
ellow, Abigail I, 306
ellow, Betty I, 287
ellow, Charity I, 287
ellow, Charity I, 306
ellow, Charity I, 307
ellow, Henry V, 672
ellow, Henry C. V, 672
ellow, John I, 287
ellow, John I, 288
ellow, John I, 301
ellow, John I, 306
ellow, Mary I, 287
ellow, Mary I, 288
ellow, Mary I, 306
ellow, Mary V, 808
ellow, Mary V, 817
ellow, Mary F. V, 815
ellow, Mary Rachel I, 306
ellow, Melissa V, 672
ellow, Phebe I, 302
ellow, Phebe I, 306
ellow, Price I, 287
ellow, Price I, 306
ellow, Rachel I, 287
ellow, Rachel I, 288
ellow, Rachel I, 306
ellow, Rachel I, 315
ellow, Robert I, 287
ellow, Robert I, 288
ellow, Robert I, 306
ellow, Robert I, 315
ellow, Sally I, 288
ellow, Sally I, 306
ellow, Sally V, 802
ellow, Sally V, 808
ellow, Samuel Miles V, 808
ellow, Sarah I, 287
ellow, William I, 288
ellows, A. M. IV, 1250
ellows, Alice III, 116
ellows, Augustus IV, 1250
ellows, F. E. IV, 1251
ellows, Frederick E. IV, 1250
ellows, J. L. IV, 1314
ellows, James III, 116
ellows, John III, 116
ellows, Thomas III, 116
ellows, William III, 116
elmont, Bertha Beal I, 1152
elps, Charlotte V, 227
elps, Eli V, 227
elps, Sarah V, 445
elps, Sarah V, 447
eltnerer, Albert V, 995
elts, Cherry IV, 706
elty, Mary VI, 388
elty, Mary VI, 401
ender, Fred V, 672
enemore, Ann II, 220
enemore, Ann II, 252
enemore, Isaac II, 361
enemore, Jason L. II, 521
enemore, Lucy II, 220
Fenemore, Rachel II, 220
Fenemore, Rachel II, 223
Fenemore, Richard II, 220
Fenemore, Samuel II, 220
Fenemore, Samuel II, 252
Fenemore, Sarah II, 210
Fenemore, Sarah II, 220
Fenemore, William II, 220
Fenher, Will V, 739
Fenher, William V, 739
Fenhrer, William V, 739
Fenimore, Allen III, 166
Fenimore, Amy II, 287
Fenimore, Amy II, 739
Fenimore, Amy II, 740
Fenimore, Amy II, 794
Fenimore, Amy II, 862
Fenimore, Ann II, 220
Fenimore, Elizabeth II, 173
Fenimore, Elizabeth II, 213
Fenimore, Elizabeth II, 287
Fenimore, Elizabeth II, 361
Fenimore, Emma W. II, 287
Fenimore, Enoch II, 220
Fenimore, Enock II, 220
Fenimore, Esther G. II, 287
Fenimore, Esther G. II, 862
Fenimore, Esther Gardner II, 794
Fenimore, Hannah II, 173
Fenimore, Hannah II, 220
Fenimore, Hannah II, 231
Fenimore, Hannah II, 267
Fenimore, Henry II, 213
Fenimore, Henry Isaac II, 287
Fenimore, Hester G. II, 862
Fenimore, Jason L. II, 287
Fenimore, Jason L. II, 521
Fenimore, Jason L. II, 739
Fenimore, Jason L. II, 740
Fenimore, Jason L. II, 862
Fenimore, John II, 739
Fenimore, John II, 740
Fenimore, John II, 794
Fenimore, Jonathan II, 220
Fenimore, Joseph II, 220
Fenimore, Joseph II, 234
Fenimore, Lucy II, 220
Fenimore, Marian H. II, 287
Fenimore, Marion H. II, 287
Fenimore, Mary II, 200
Fenimore, Mary II, 212
Fenimore, Mary II, 220
Fenimore, Mary II, 739
Fenimore, Mary II, 740
Fenimore, Miriam II, 173
Fenimore, Miriam II, 220
Fenimore, Miriam II, 287
Fenimore, Miriam H. II, 287
Fenimore, Nathaniel II, 220
Fenimore, Nathaniel II, 521
Fenimore, Priscilla II, 220
Fenimore, Priscilla II, 287
Fenimore, Rachel II, 220
Fenimore, Richard II, 173
Fenimore, Richard II, 212
Fenimore, Richard II, 220
Fenimore, Richard II, 267
Fenimore, Samuel II, 220
Fenimore, Sarah II, 220
Fenimore, Wd. Elizabeth II, 220
Fenimore, Wd. Elizabeth II, 234
Fenimore, William II, 200
Fenimore, William II, 220
Fenimore, William Nathaniel II, 220
Fenker, Hattie V, 620
Fenker, Henry V, 620
Fenley, Eunice IV, 329
Fenley, Hannah IV, 329
Fenly, Hannah IV, 354
Fenly, Martha IV, 354
Fenly, Thomas IV, 354
Fennamore, Hannah II, 220
Fennamore, Richard II, 220
Fennell, William Edward II, 705
Fennemore, Marian H. II, 740
Fenner, Charles V, 330
Fenner, Chas. V, 330
Fenner, Dwight V, 330
Fenner, Effie V, 330
Fenner, Frank V, 456
Fenner, Lucy V, 456
Fenner, Lydia E. V, 330
Fenner, Lydia E. V, 342
Fenner, Lydia Elizabeth V, 330
Fenner, Wright V, 330
Fennimore, Amy II, 740
Fennimore, Amy II, 862
Fennimore, Elizabeth II, 361
Fennimore, Emma W. II, 306
Fennimore, Enock II, 220
Fennimore, Hester G. II, 862
Fennimore, Isaac II, 361
Fennimore, Jason L. II, 287
Fennimore, Jason L. II, 521
Fennimore, Jason L. II, 740
Fennimore, John II, 740
Fennimore, Lucy II, 220
Fennimore, Lucy II, 245
Fennimore, Marian H. II, 287
Fennimore, Marian H. II, 740
Fennimore, Mary II, 220
Fennimore, Mary II, 251
Fennimore, Mary II, 440
Fennimore, Mary II, 740
Fennimore, Miriam II, 218
Fennimore, Miriam II, 220
Fennimore, Miriam H. II, 287
Fennimore, Nathaniel II, 220
Fennimore, Nathaniel II, 521
Fennimore, Priscilla II, 220
Fennimore, Priscilla II, 287
Fennimore, Rachel II, 231
Fennimore, Samuel II, 521
Fennimore, William II, 220
Fennimore, Wm. II, 521
Fennyere, ??? III, 116
Fennyere, John T. III, 116
Fennyere, Ruth III, 52
Fennyere, Ruth III, 116
Fennyere, Wilfred H. III, 116
Fenster, Solomon V, 995
Fenstermaker, Lottie IV, 201
Fentham, Ann II, 521
Fentham, Elizabeth Johns II, 521
Fentham, Henry Hale II, 521
Fentham, John Goldie II, 521
Fentham, John Goldie II, 529
Fentham, John Gouldie II, 361
Fentham, John Gouldie II, 521
Fentham, Mary II, 521
Fentham, Mary II, 627
Fentham, Philip II, 361
Fentham, Priscilla II, 361
Fentham, Priscilla II, 521
Fentham, Priscilla II, 529
Fentham, Priscilla II, 566
Fentham, Priscilla II, 627
Fentham, Sarah Florenza II, 462
Fentham, Sarah Florenza II, 521
Fentham, Sarah Garrigues II, 361
Fentham, Susanna II, 361
Fentham, Susanna II, 521
Fentham, Susanna II, 529
Fentham, Wm. II, 521
Fentham, Wm. Wyatt II, 521
Fentham, Wm. Wyatt II, 529
Fentham, Wm. Wyatt II, 627
Fenthem, Sarah Florenza II, 521
Fenton, Ann VI, 388
Fenton, Ann VI, 389
Fenton, Ann VI, 406
Fenton, Ann VI, 449
Fenton, Ann VI, 491
Fenton, Ann VI, 567
Fenton, Ann VI, 637
Fenton, Ann VI, 638
Fenton, Ann VI, 660
Fenton, Ann VI, 709
Fenton, Anna L. VI, 637
Fenton, Annie Virginia VI, 637
Fenton, Annie Virginia VI, 638
Fenton, Annie Virginia VI, 640
Fenton, Annie Virginia VI, 645
Fenton, Annie Virginia VI, 693
Fenton, Benj. Franklin VI, 686
Fenton, Benjamin VI, 388
Fenton, Benjamin VI, 389
Fenton, Benjamin VI, 449
Fenton, Benjamin VI, 491
Fenton, Benjamin VI, 567
Fenton, Benjamin VI, 637
Fenton, Benjamin VI, 638
Fenton, Benjamin VI, 660
Fenton, Benjamin VI, 709
Fenton, Benjamin Franklin VI, 637
Fenton, Benjamin Franklin VI, 638
Fenton, Benjamin Franklin VI, 640
Fenton, Benjamin Franklin VI, 645
Fenton, Benjamin Franklin VI, 693
Fenton, Cora A. V, 385
Fenton, Cora A. V, 905
Fenton, Cora Alice V, 385
Fenton, Edna A. VI, 637
Fenton, Edna A. VI, 640
Fenton, Eleazar II, 220
Fenton, Eleazar II, 259
Fenton, Eleazer II, 220
Fenton, Elizabeth II, 216
Fenton, Elizabeth II, 220
Fenton, Elizabeth II, 259
Fenton, Enoch VI, 637
Fenton, Enoch VI, 679
Fenton, Enoch VI, 683
Fenton, Enoch VI, 693
Fenton, Ephraim II, 979
Fenton, Ephraim II, 995
Fenton, Hannah II, 220
Fenton, Hannah II, 259
Fenton, J. Ellen VI, 637
Fenton, Jacob IV, 706
Fenton, James IV, 706
Fenton, Jane VI, 679
Fenton, John II, 220
Fenton, John VI, 367
Fenton, John VI, 388
Fenton, John VI, 389
Fenton, John VI, 491
Fenton, John VI, 492
Fenton, John VI, 566
Fenton, John VI, 567
Fenton, John, Jr. VI, 389
Fenton, Jos. S. VI, 492
Fenton, Joseph VI, 388
Fenton, Joseph S. VI, 389
Fenton, Joseph, Jr. VI, 389
Fenton, Joshua VI, 388
Fenton, Josiah J. VI, 389
Fenton, Josiah J. VI, 414
Fenton, Josiah J. VI, 637
Fenton, Josiah Jackson VI, 389
Fenton, Josiah, Jr. VI, 388
Fenton, Louisa J. VI, 637
Fenton, Louisa J. VI, 680
Fenton, Louisa Jane VI, 670
Fenton, Louisa Jane VI, 673
Fenton, Louisa Jane VI, 679
Fenton, Louisa Jane VI, 681
Fenton, Louisa Jane VI, 682
Fenton, Louisa Jane VI, 718
Fenton, Mary VI, 388
Fenton, Mary VI, 389
Fenton, Mary A. VI, 388
Fenton, Mary A. VI, 414
Fenton, Mary A. VI, 637
Fenton, Mary M. VI, 492
Fenton, Mary M. VI, 567
Fenton, Mary McPherson VI, 566
Fenton, Mary Virginia VI, 637
Fenton, Mary Virginia VI, 638
Fenton, Mary Virginia VI, 645
Fenton, Pricilla VI, 638
Fenton, Priscilla VI, 388
Fenton, Priscilla VI, 389
Fenton, Priscilla VI, 449
Fenton, Priscilla VI, 637
Fenton, Priscilla VI, 709
Fenton, Rachel VI, 406
Fenton, Rachel VI, 411
Fenton, Rachel Wilkinson VI, 388
Fenton, Ruth VI, 388
Fenton, Ruth Esther VI, 637
Fenton, Ruth Esther VI, 638
Fenton, Ruth Esther VI, 679
Fenton, Ruth Esther VI, 683
Fenton, Ruth Esther VI, 686
Fenton, Ruth Esther VI, 693
Fenton, Ruth Esther VI, 707
Fenton, Ruth Esther VI, 711
Fenton, Samuel II, 220
Fenton, Sarah VI, 382
Fenton, Sarah VI, 388
Fenton, Sarah Ann VI, 388
Fenton, Sarah Ann VI, 438
Fenton, Sidney VI, 389
Fenton, Sidney VI, 633
Fenton, Sidney VI, 638
Fenton, Sidny VI, 381
Fenton, Sudney VI, 388
Fenton, W. Annie Virginia VI, 686
Fentons, Edna A. VI, 637
Fentons, Mary Virginia VI, 637
Fentons, Ruth Esther VI, 637
Fentress, Betsey Ann I, 904
Fentress, Betsy Ann I, 878
Fentress, Caroline I, 711
Fentress, Caroline I, 715
Fentress, Caroline I, 757
Fentress, Caroline I, 761
Fentress, Eleazar I, 715
Fentress, Elizabeth I, 99
Fentress, Elizabeth I, 695
Fentress, Elizabeth I, 715
Fentress, Elizabeth I, 878
Fentress, Emsley I, 715
Fentress, Fred R. I, 616
Fentress, Frederick I, 99
Fentress, Frederick I, 715
Fentress, Frederick I, 737
Fentress, Luzanna I, 761
Fentress, Mary I, 678
Fentress, Mary I, 715
Fentress, Mary I, 737
Fentress, Mary E. I, 306
Fentress, Octavia I, 616
Fentress, Octavia I, 633
Fentress, Pharoah I, 99
Fentress, Pharoah I, 139
Fentress, Pharoah I, 695
Fentress, Pharoah I, 715
Fentress, Susannah I, 761
Fentress, Susannah I, 762
Fentris, ??? I, 867
Fentris, Elisabeth I, 139
Fentris, Elisabeth I, 152
Fentris, Elizabeth Ann I, 867
Fentris, Pharoah I, 139
Fentris, Pharoah I, 152
Fentriss, Elisabeth I, 139
Fentriss, Elizabeth I, 480
Fentriss, Elizabeth I, 712
Fentriss, Elizabeth I, 878
Fentriss, Elizabeth A. I, 853
Fentriss, Mary I, 715
Fentriss, Pharoah I, 139
Fentriss, Pharoh I, 139
Fenwick, John II, 17
Fenwick, John II, 18
Fenwick, John II, 163
Fenwick, Matthew II, 740
Fenwick, Susanna II, 521
Fenwick, Susanna II, 557
Ferbish, Lorena IV, 1314
Ferebee, Ruth I, 809
Ferebee, Ruth I, 821
Fereel, Rachel IV, 815
Fergason, Charles V, 169
Fergason, Elmer IV, 1251
Fergason, Sirus V, 169
Fergerson, Maggie V, 997
Fergerson, Mary V, 238
Ferguson, ??? IV, 146
Ferguson, Aaron V, 169
Ferguson, Aaron V, 492
Ferguson, Abbot S. II, 521
Ferguson, Abbott S. II, 521
Ferguson, Adam V, 620
Ferguson, Agnes I, 941
Ferguson, Albert III, 116
Ferguson, Alfred A. VI, 914
Ferguson, Alfred F. VI, 914
Ferguson, Allen VI, 816
Ferguson, Almira V, 620
Ferguson, Amelia A. III, 116
Ferguson, Amelia Anne III, 21
Ferguson, Andrew II, 521
Ferguson, Andrew VI, 816
Ferguson, Ann II, 361
Ferguson, Ann II, 521
Ferguson, Ann II, 605
Ferguson, Ann III, 116
Ferguson, Ann V, 55
Ferguson, Ann V, 169
Ferguson, Ann V, 238
Ferguson, Ann VI, 310
Ferguson, Anna V, 228
Ferguson, Anna V, 238
Ferguson, Anna VI, 310
Ferguson, Anne VI, 310
Ferguson, Anny VI, 914
Ferguson, Archibald VI, 914
Ferguson, Benjamin II, 131
Ferguson, Benjamin II, 361
Ferguson, Benjamin II, 521
Ferguson, Blanch IV, 1315
Ferguson, Caleb VI, 914
Ferguson, Caleb VI, 971
Ferguson, Catharine IV, 869
Ferguson, Catharine IV, 884
Ferguson, Catherine VI, 816
Ferguson, Celia Ann VI, 914
Ferguson, Charles II, 521
Ferguson, Charles III, 116
Ferguson, Charles V, 169
Ferguson, Charles V, 238
Ferguson, Chas. V, 169
Ferguson, Chas. V, 620
Ferguson, Cinthia VI, 914
Ferguson, Clark I, 1057
Ferguson, Clark V, 169
Ferguson, Clark V, 171
Ferguson, Clark V, 238
Ferguson, Clark V, 620
Ferguson, Claudia I, 941
Ferguson, Clement V, 561
Ferguson, Cynthia V, 561

Ferguson, Cynthia W. IV, 1362
Ferguson, Cyrus V, 169
Ferguson, Daniel VI, 914
Ferguson, David III, 116
Ferguson, David VI, 914
Ferguson, David R. III, 116
Ferguson, Deborah III, 116
Ferguson, Dwight IV, 1207
Ferguson, Dwight H. IV, 1207
Ferguson, Edith IV, 1315
Ferguson, Edward W. III, 116
Ferguson, Edward W. VI, 806
Ferguson, Eliza III, 116
Ferguson, Elizabeth III, 116
Ferguson, Elizabeth III, 335
Ferguson, Elizabeth V, 169
Ferguson, Elizabeth V, 238
Ferguson, Elizabeth VI, 816
Ferguson, Elizabeth VI, 914
Ferguson, Elizabeth J. III, 116
Ferguson, Elizabeth J. III, 335
Ferguson, Elizabeth Levi V, 169
Ferguson, Elizabeth V. III, 116
Ferguson, Elizabeth Van Everen III, 116
Ferguson, Ellen III, 116
Ferguson, Ellen Jane V, 620
Ferguson, Elsie L. III, 116
Ferguson, Esther Amanda V, 492
Ferguson, Esther Amanda V, 620
Ferguson, Evangeline V, 169
Ferguson, Fanny VI, 914
Ferguson, Florence V, 620
Ferguson, Geo. III, 116
Ferguson, George III, 116
Ferguson, George VI, 914
Ferguson, George A. III, 116
Ferguson, George F. III, 116
Ferguson, George W. II, 521
Ferguson, George, Jr. III, 116
Ferguson, H. V, 561
Ferguson, H. W. I, 941
Ferguson, Hannah III, 116
Ferguson, Hannah III, 211
Ferguson, Hannah L. III, 116
Ferguson, Hannah W. V, 169
Ferguson, Helen III, 116
Ferguson, Henrietta V, 169
Ferguson, Henry VI, 914
Ferguson, Isaac II, 521
Ferguson, Isaac V, 55
Ferguson, Isaac V, 169
Ferguson, Isaac V, 238
Ferguson, Isaac VI, 310
Ferguson, Israel III, 116
Ferguson, Jacob V, 169
Ferguson, James II, 131
Ferguson, James II, 521
Ferguson, James III, 116
Ferguson, James IV, 525
Ferguson, Jane VI, 816
Ferguson, Jane C. II, 740
Ferguson, Jane C. II, 752
Ferguson, Jemima VI, 914
Ferguson, Jeremiah VI, 914
Ferguson, Jeremiah VI, 929
Ferguson, Jesse VI, 914
Ferguson, Jessie VI, 953
Ferguson, John II, 361
Ferguson, John II, 521
Ferguson, John III, 89
Ferguson, John III, 116
Ferguson, John III, 117
Ferguson, John VI, 816
Ferguson, John VI, 914
Ferguson, John C. III, 116
Ferguson, John C. III, 335
Ferguson, John H. III, 116
Ferguson, John H. III, 335
Ferguson, John H. VI, 914
Ferguson, Joseph V, 169
Ferguson, Joseph VI, 798
Ferguson, Joseph VI, 816
Ferguson, Joseph VI, 914
Ferguson, Joseph Riley V, 169
Ferguson, Judy VI, 914
Ferguson, Julia III, 116
Ferguson, Julia VI, 914
Ferguson, Levi V, 169
Ferguson, Levi V, 238
Ferguson, Littleberry VI, 914
Ferguson, Lucinda Catherine V, 169
Ferguson, Lucy VI, 914
Ferguson, Malissa V, 620
Ferguson, Maria Eliza V, 620
Ferguson, Mary II, 361
Ferguson, Mary III, 116
Ferguson, Mary IV, 33
Ferguson, Mary IV, 517
Ferguson, Mary IV, 525
Ferguson, Mary V, 55
Ferguson, Mary V, 169
Ferguson, Mary V, 228
Ferguson, Mary V, 238
Ferguson, Mary V, 620
Ferguson, Mary VI, 310
Ferguson, Mary Ann V, 620
Ferguson, Mary E. III, 116
Ferguson, Mary E. V, 169
Ferguson, Mary Effie III, 116
Ferguson, Mary Effie III, 335
Ferguson, Mary Eliza V, 169
Ferguson, Mary Jane VI, 914
Ferguson, Mary V. III, 89
Ferguson, Mary V. III, 116
Ferguson, Melissa V, 620
Ferguson, Melissa V, 635
Ferguson, Mellissa V, 620
Ferguson, Minnie V, 561
Ferguson, Mrs. Edith IV, 1315
Ferguson, Nancy VI, 914
Ferguson, Nancy VI, 929
Ferguson, Nimrod V, 55
Ferguson, Nimrod V, 228
Ferguson, Nimrod V, 238
Ferguson, Nimrod VI, 310
Ferguson, Pamela VI, 914
Ferguson, Phoebe VI, 914
Ferguson, Pleasant VI, 914
Ferguson, Polly VI, 914
Ferguson, Prudence II, 361
Ferguson, Prudence II, 521
Ferguson, Rachel II, 131
Ferguson, Rachel II, 521
Ferguson, Rachel III, 116
Ferguson, Rachel V, 169
Ferguson, Rebecca V, 238
Ferguson, Richard V, 238
Ferguson, Richard VI, 914
Ferguson, Robert VI, 840
Ferguson, Rosanna V, 620
Ferguson, Ruth IV, 869
Ferguson, Ruth IV, 884
Ferguson, Samuel II, 521
Ferguson, Samuel V, 169
Ferguson, Samuel V, 238
Ferguson, Samuel V, 385
Ferguson, Samuel V, 445
Ferguson, Samuel V, 561
Ferguson, Samuel V, 635
Ferguson, Samuel VI, 914
Ferguson, Sarah I, 1057
Ferguson, Sarah II, 521
Ferguson, Sarah III, 29
Ferguson, Sarah III, 116
Ferguson, Sarah III, 139
Ferguson, Sarah III, 286
Ferguson, Sarah V, 169
Ferguson, Sarah V, 171
Ferguson, Sarah V, 238
Ferguson, Sarah V, 385
Ferguson, Sarah V, 561
Ferguson, Sarah VI, 816
Ferguson, Sarah VI, 818
Ferguson, Sarah VI, 953
Ferguson, Sarah E. V, 169
Ferguson, Sarah Emily V, 169
Ferguson, Sarah H. III, 116
Ferguson, Sarah L. III, 116
Ferguson, Sarah L. III, 117
Ferguson, Seneca VI, 310
Ferguson, Sidney L. V, 620
Ferguson, Sirus V, 169
Ferguson, Smmuel V, 620
Ferguson, Sophia VI, 914
Ferguson, Stella IV, 1207
Ferguson, Susan III, 89
Ferguson, Susan III, 116
Ferguson, Susan III, 117
Ferguson, Susan S. VI, 914
Ferguson, Susannah VI, 914
Ferguson, Thomas V, 561
Ferguson, Thomas VI, 914
Ferguson, Thos. IV, 1315
Ferguson, Virgil F. V, 620
Ferguson, Webster M. V, 561
Ferguson, Willey VI, 914
Ferguson, William III, 21
Ferguson, William III, 117
Ferguson, William VI, 816
Ferguson, William VI, 914
Ferguson, William Edney V, 238
Ferguson, Wm. IV, 814
Ferguson, Wm. V, 620
Ferguson, Wm. C. IV, 814
Ferguson, Wm. J. V, 620
Fergusson, Annie Elizabeth V, 597
Ferington, Lizie IV, 1278
Ferington, Lizie IV, 1299
Ferington, Theadore IV, 1278
Feris, Martha V, 995
Feris, Richd VI, 176
Feriss, Ann E. VI, 829
Feriss, John VI, 829
Ferman, Deborah II, 997
Ferman, Elizabeth II, 997
Ferman, Susannah S. II, 1051
Fern, Joshua II, 361
Fern, Mary II, 361
Fernald, Carrie Almenia II, 812
Fernean, Bertha V, 238
Fernean, Harry V, 238
Fernley, ??? II, 443
Fernley, Eunice IV, 352
Fernley, Hannah IV, 352
Fernley, Hannah VI, 389
Fernley, Martha VI, 389
Fernley, Stanley II, 443
Fernley, Thomas VI, 389
Fernley, Wm. IV, 352
Fernly, Eunice VI, 595
Fernly, Hannah VI, 595
Fernly, Martha VI, 389
Fernly, Martha VI, 422
Fernly, Martha VI, 595
Fernly, Thomas VI, 389
Fernly, Thomas VI, 422
Fernly, Thomas VI, 595
Fernly, Unice VI, 389
Fernly, Unice VI, 595
Fernly, William VI, 595
Fernow, Ida D. V, 238
Fernow, Jesse B. V, 238
Fernow, Thelma Lucile V, 238
Fernsly, Martha VI, 598
Fernsly, Rachel VI, 598
Ferqueran, Henry VI, 898
Ferqueran, Sejus VI, 898
Ferral, Benjamin IV, 624
Ferral, Nancy IV, 624
Ferrall, Benjamin IV, 624
Ferrall, Edmond IV, 624
Ferrall, Edmund IV, 624
Ferrall, James IV, 32
Ferrall, James IV, 624
Ferrall, James VI, 310
Ferrall, Judith IV, 624
Ferrall, Lucy Ann IV, 624
Ferrall, Martha IV, 624
Ferrall, Martha VI, 310
Ferrall, Martha VI, 904
Ferrall, Mary IV, 32
Ferrall, Mary IV, 624
Ferrall, Nancy IV, 624
Ferrall, Nancy VI, 311
Ferrall, William VI, 310
Ferrall, William VI, 904
Ferrand, Ruth III, 427
Ferree, Ray V, 672
Ferree, Susanna II, 521
Ferrel, Abner VI, 970
Ferrel, Ann VI, 979
Ferrel, Deborah I, 539
Ferrel, Jno. VI, 983
Ferrel, Lucy H. VI, 914
Ferrel, Mary M. VI, 879
Ferrel, Milton P. VI, 914
Ferrel, Rachel IV, 799
Ferrel, Rachel IV, 814
Ferrel, Rachel IV, 815
Ferrel, William VI, 310
Ferrell, ??? VI, 293
Ferrell, Abner VI, 879
Ferrell, Catherine VI, 310
Ferrell, Catherine VI, 340
Ferrell, Cornelia V, 55
Ferrell, Elizabeth VI, 310
Ferrell, Elizabeth VI, 335
Ferrell, Frasure VI, 310
Ferrell, Hannah VI, 310
Ferrell, Henry C. VI, 879
Ferrell, Henry C. VI, 914
Ferrell, James VI, 310
Ferrell, Jane VI, 310
Ferrell, Jane VI, 314
Ferrell, Jean VI, 1016
Ferrell, Judith VI, 310
Ferrell, Judith VI, 312
Ferrell, Lucy H. VI, 914
Ferrell, Margaret VI, 310
Ferrell, Margaret VI, 312
Ferrell, Martha VI, 310
Ferrell, Martha VI, 333
Ferrell, Mary VI, 296
Ferrell, Mary VI, 310
Ferrell, Mary VI, 816
Ferrell, Mary VI, 874
Ferrell, Milton P. VI, 914
Ferrell, Nancy IV, 639
Ferrell, Nancy VI, 311
Ferrell, Prudence VI, 310
Ferrell, Prudence VI, 914
Ferrell, Rebeckah VI, 310
Ferrell, Virginia J. VI, 914
Ferrell, William VI, 242
Ferrell, William VI, 296
Ferrell, William VI, 310
Ferrell, William VI, 816
Ferrell, William VI, 874
Ferrell, William VI, 914
Ferrell, William, Jr. VI, 310
Ferrell, William, Jr. VI, 312
Ferrier, Deborah III, 302
Ferril, Elma T. IV, 201
Ferril, George IV, 201
Ferrill, Abner VI, 930
Ferrill, Eliza VI, 970
Ferrill, Gabrel Farel VI, 930
Ferrill, Jane VI, 310
Ferrill, Jane VI, 314
Ferrill, Jane VI, 932
Ferrill, Jene VI, 1016
Ferrill, Mildred VI, 930
Ferrill, Rebeckah VI, 926
Ferrington, Jesse K. IV, 471
Ferris, ??? III, 117
Ferris, ??? III, 281
Ferris, ??? III, 428
Ferris, Abraham II, 361
Ferris, Alfred J. II, 309
Ferris, Alfred J. II, 862
Ferris, Alfred J. VI, 741
Ferris, Alfred Justice II, 862
Ferris, Alfred Justice VI, 741
Ferris, Alfred S. II, 318
Ferris, Amelia III, 117
Ferris, Amelia III, 283
Ferris, Ann III, 117
Ferris, Ann III, 281
Ferris, Anna II, 522
Ferris, Anna II, 872
Ferris, Anna III, 117
Ferris, Anna III, 281
Ferris, Anna III, 282
Ferris, Anna Amelia III, 283
Ferris, Anna H. III, 117
Ferris, Anna H. III, 307
Ferris, Anna Jenkins II, 794
Ferris, Anna Jenkins II, 862
Ferris, Anna Jenkins II, 872
Ferris, Anna L. IV, 1235
Ferris, Anne II, 361
Ferris, Anne III, 117
Ferris, Benjamin II, 361
Ferris, Benjamin II, 522
Ferris, Benjamin VI, 150
Ferris, Caroline III, 117
Ferris, Caroline M. III, 117
Ferris, Caroline Murray III, 117
Ferris, Catherine III, 428
Ferris, Clara E. IV, 1235
Ferris, Cornell III, 117
Ferris, David I, 389
Ferris, David II, 309
Ferris, David II, 318
Ferris, David II, 522
Ferris, David II, 592
Ferris, David II, 862
Ferris, David II, 912
Ferris, David VI, 741
Ferris, David Sands III, 117
Ferris, Deborah II, 361
Ferris, Deborah II, 522
Ferris, Deborah III, 117
Ferris, Direxa IV, 1235
Ferris, Dobbs Ferry III, 117
Ferris, Dr. Valentine III, 117
Ferris, Ebenezer III, 117
Ferris, Edward II, 361
Ferris, Edward II, 862
Ferris, Edward B. II, 740
Ferris, Edward B. II, 862
Ferris, Edward B. II, 882
Ferris, Edward Bringhurst II, 794
Ferris, Edward Bringhurst II, 862
Ferris, Edward Bringhurst II, 872
Ferris, Elijah III, 117
Ferris, Elijah III, 156
Ferris, Elijah III, 283
Ferris, Eliza II, 794
Ferris, Eliza M. II, 862
Ferris, Eliza M. II, 882
Ferris, Elizabeth II, 522
Ferris, Elizabeth II, 614
Ferris, Elizabeth II, 794
Ferris, Elizabeth II, 820
Ferris, Elizabeth II, 862
Ferris, Elizabeth II, 872
Ferris, Elizabeth II, 882
Ferris, Elizabeth III, 117
Ferris, Elizabeth IV, 1235
Ferris, Elizabeth P. II, 522
Ferris, Elizabeth P. II, 740
Ferris, Elsie E. IV, 1235
Ferris, Erastus III, 117
Ferris, Erastus III, 372
Ferris, Fanny II, 361
Ferris, Fanny II, 522
Ferris, Fanny II, 797
Ferris, Frances L. III, 342
Ferris, Francesca III, 117
Ferris, Francis II, 361
Ferris, Francis II, 521
Ferris, Francis C. II, 309
Ferris, Francis C. II, 318
Ferris, Francis Canby II, 318
Ferris, Gilbert V, 561
Ferris, Grace III, 117
Ferris, Gulielma A. II, 882
Ferris, Hannah III, 410
Ferris, Hannah III, 430
Ferris, Hannah Brinton II, 79
Ferris, Hannah Brinton II, 862
Ferris, Hannah Brinton II, 912
Ferris, Henry II, 309
Ferris, Henry II, 318
Ferris, Jane II, 522
Ferris, Jane III, 117
Ferris, Jane III, 328
Ferris, Jane U. III, 307
Ferris, Jane W. III, 117
Ferris, John II, 361
Ferris, John II, 522
Ferris, John III, 53
Ferris, John III, 54
Ferris, John III, 117
Ferris, John III, 151
Ferris, John III, 307
Ferris, John III, 410
Ferris, John III, 430
Ferris, John H. III, 117
Ferris, John H. III, 328
Ferris, John H., Jr. III, 117
Ferris, John Haviland III, 117
Ferris, John Price II, 794
Ferris, Jonathan III, 117
Ferris, L. Murray, Jr. III, 278
Ferris, L., Jr. III, 117
Ferris, Liba II, 862
Ferris, Liba II, 882
Ferris, Lidya II, 522
Ferris, Lindley M. III, 117
Ferris, Lindley Murray III, 11
Ferris, Lindley Murray III, 23
Ferris, Luther V, 561
Ferris, Lydia II, 361
Ferris, Lydia II, 522
Ferris, Mabel III, 117
Ferris, Mabel L. III, 117
Ferris, Mabel Livingston III, 2
Ferris, Margaret II, 361
Ferris, Marshie Hare V, 55
Ferris, Martha I. III, 117
Ferris, Martha I. III, 278
Ferris, Mary II, 522
Ferris, Mary II, 592
Ferris, Mary III, 54
Ferris, Mary III, 117
Ferris, Mary III, 151
Ferris, Mary III, 238
Ferris, Mary III, 330
Ferris, Mary III, 410
Ferris, Mary III, 430
Ferris, Mary IV, 1235
Ferris, Mary A. T. III, 117
Ferris, Mary A. T. III, 225
Ferris, Mary Abby III, 117
Ferris, Mary Abby III, 372
Ferris, Mary Anna III, 117
Ferris, Mary Anna T. III, 117
Ferris, Mary Louisa III, 117
Ferris, Matilda II, 309
Ferris, Matilda II, 318
Ferris, Matilda VI, 741
Ferris, O. W. IV, 1235
Ferris, Patience II, 882
Ferris, Phebe III, 54
Ferris, Phebe III, 117
Ferris, Phebe III, 156
Ferris, Phebe J. III, 117
Ferris, Phebe Jane III, 117
Ferris, Philip Livingston III, 1
Ferris, Rachel II, 361
Ferris, Rebecca Ann V, 51
Ferris, Rebecca Ann V, 55
Ferris, Reed III, 117
Ferris, Richd VI, 176
Ferris, Ridhd VI, 176
Ferris, Robert M. III, 117
Ferris, Robert M. III, 225

erris, Robert Murry, Jr. III, 117
erris, Robt. M. III, 117
erris, Sarah II, 862
erris, Sarah III, 117
erris, Sarah III, 151
erris, Sarah VI, 741
erris, Sarah A. II, 318
erris, Sarah A. II, 862
erris, Sarah A. II, 912
erris, Sarah A. VI, 741
erris, Sarah Alice IV, 1235
erris, Sarah Ann II, 309
erris, Sarah Ann II, 318
erris, Sarah Ann VI, 741
erris, Sherman IV, 1235
erris, Sophia III, 117
erris, Thomas IV, 1235
erris, Walter II, 309
erris, Walter II, 318
erris, Walter II, 794
erris, Walter II, 862
erris, Walter II, 912
erris, Walter VI, 741
erris, Walter H. IV, 1235
erris, Walton Canby II, 794
erris, William II, 361
erris, William III, 430
erris, William C. II, 309
erris, William Canby II, 318
erris, William Canby VI, 741
erris, William J. II, 318
erris, William L. III, 117
erris, William Taber III, 117
erris, William, Jr. III, 117
erris, Wm. C. VI, 741
erris, Zachariah II, 522
erris, Zachariah III, 117
erris, Zachary III, 117
erris, Ziba II, 522
erris, Ziba II, 794
erriss, Benjamin II, 522
erriss, David II, 522
erriss, Elizabeth II, 522
erriss, Elizabeth II, 697
erriss, John II, 522
erriss, John II, 697
erriss, Lydia II, 361
erriss, Lydia II, 522
erriss, Lydia II, 697
erriss, Mary II, 522
erriss, Zachariah II, 522
erriss, Zachariah II, 697
erry, Thomas II, 995
erst, Lizzie S. V, 838
erul, Franklin V, 995
esler, Asenath IV, 329
esler, Asenath IV, 333
esmire, Balaam M. I, 480
esmire, Balsam W. I, 467
esmire, Isaac B. I, 480
esmire, James G. I, 480
esmire, James S. I, 467
esmire, James S. I, 480
esmire, John M. I, 467
esmire, John M. I, 480
esmire, John W. I, 480
esmire, Molsey I, 469
essant, William V, 385
essent, William V, 385
eters, Grace II, 69
eters, Sarah II, 69
etheralt, Lillie IV, 1250
etheralt, Lulu IV, 1250
etherhoff, Cecile IV, 1250
etherolt, Beryl IV, 1250
etherolt, Cecil May IV, 1250
etherolt, Cecile IV, 1250
etherolt, Lillie IV, 1250
etherolt, Lulu IV, 1250
etherolt, Margaret IV, 1250
etherolt, Marguerite IV, 1250
etro, Amy V, 238
etro, Isabel V, 238
etro, Jacob V, 238
etro, Joseph V, 238
etro, Sarah V, 238
etter, Hannah Lawrence II, 995
etter, Manuel III, 75
etter, Manuel III, 117
etter, Manuel III, 378
etter, Manuel III, 380
etter, Sarah III, 75
etter, Sarah III, 117
etter, Sarah III, 378
etter, Sarah III, 380
ettering, Maude V, 330
ettering, Walter V, 330
etterling, Maud E. V, 330
etterling, Maude V, 330
etterling, Walter V, 330
etterling, Walter J. V, 330
Fetters, Christina C. V, 739
Fetters, Clyde IV, 1251
Fetters, Erasmus II, 69
Fetters, Erasmus II, 105
Fetters, Flora V, 739
Fetters, George V, 739
Fetters, Grace II, 69
Fetters, Marie V, 739
Fetters, Mary A. IV, 1251
Fetters, P. V, 739
Fetters, Rebeccah II, 69
Fetters, Rebeccah II, 105
Fetters, Sarah II, 69
Fettig, Margaret V, 734
Fettro, Amy V, 455
Fettro, Amy V, 456
Fettro, Amy V, 461
Fettro, Amy V, 465
Fettro, Ethel V, 457
Fettro, Grace V, 456
Fettro, Isabel V, 456
Fettro, Jacob V, 455
Fettro, Jacob V, 456
Fettro, Jacob V, 461
Fettro, Jacob V, 465
Fettro, Luella V, 456
Fettro, Rachel V, 461
Fettro, Sarah V, 455
Fettro, Tobitha V, 465
Fetz, Mary E. Carr V, 170
Feurgeson, John E. I, 715
Feuson, Elizabeth M. V, 952
Feuson, Elizabeth M. V, 959
Few, Ann II, 361
Few, Daniel II, 361
Few, Daniel II, 522
Few, Joseph II, 361
Few, Joseph V, 620
Few, Rachel I, 389
Few, Rachel I, 428
Few, Rachel II, 522
Few, Rachel II, 641
Few, Sarah II, 220
Few, Sarah II, 262
Fewman, Mary W. IV, 1362
Ffox, George VI, 7
Ffox, George VI, 21
Ffulsher, Mr. Thomas VI, 9
Fiales, ??? III, 166
Ficket, Phebe M. III, 380
Fickett, Cape Elizabeth III, 118
Fickett, Hannah III, 118
Fickett, Phebe III, 118
Fickett, Phebe M. III, 117
Fickett, Samuel III, 118
Fickett, Scott H. III, 118
Fiddler, Betty Rowland I, 924
Fiddles, Mary E. II, 740
Fidler, Arthur I, 941
Fidler, Edith I, 941
Fidler, Edith R. I, 941
Fidler, Eliza C. IV, 1235
Fidler, Elizabeth VI, 914
Fidler, Frances VI, 914
Fidler, Mary C. IV, 1235
Fidler, Norman I, 941
Fidler, Norman Brookshire I, 941
Fidler, Samuel VI, 914
Fie, July Ann V, 969
Fie, July Ann V, 972
Fiehn, Arthur III, 118
Fiehn, Arthur III, 280
Fiehn, Carl III, 118
Fiehn, Clara III, 118
Fiehn, Clara III, 280
Fiehn, Louisa III, 118
Field, ??? III, 119
Field, Aaron III, 118
Field, Aaron III, 119
Field, Aaron III, 120
Field, Aaron III, 139
Field, Aaron III, 155
Field, Abby Jane III, 118
Field, Abigail II, 996
Field, Abigail II, 1035
Field, Abigail III, 118
Field, Abraham II, 996
Field, Abraham II, 1035
Field, Abraham Warner II, 996
Field, Adelaide III, 119
Field, Adelaide III, 153
Field, Albany III, 118
Field, Ambrose II, 220
Field, Ambrose III, 118
Field, Ambrose III, 119
Field, Ambrose IV, 706
Field, Amelia II, 267
Field, Amos Bunting II, 996
Field, Andrew VI, 853
Field, Andrew VI, 914
Field, Andrew VI, 970
Field, Ann II, 361
Field, Ann II, 523
Field, Ann II, 554
Field, Ann II, 740
Field, Ann II, 981
Field, Ann II, 996
Field, Ann III, 41
Field, Ann III, 118
Field, Ann III, 248
Field, Ann III, 273
Field, Ann IV, 201
Field, Ann Matilda VI, 914
Field, Ann T. II, 862
Field, Anna III, 91
Field, Anna III, 118
Field, Anna III, 120
Field, Anna IV, 201
Field, Anna IV, 525
Field, Anna VI, 914
Field, Anna H. III, 121
Field, Anna P. III, 118
Field, Anna P. III, 212
Field, Annah H. III, 118
Field, Anne III, 118
Field, Anne III, 119
Field, Anthony III, 55
Field, Anthony III, 118
Field, Anthony III, 410
Field, Benj. III, 313
Field, Benj. III, 410
Field, Benjamin II, 220
Field, Benjamin II, 996
Field, Benjamin II, 1031
Field, Benjamin III, 17
Field, Benjamin III, 32
Field, Benjamin III, 40
Field, Benjamin III, 72
Field, Benjamin III, 116
Field, Benjamin III, 118
Field, Benjamin III, 119
Field, Benjamin III, 120
Field, Benjamin III, 310
Field, Benjamin III, 410
Field, Bessie III, 119
Field, Bessie G. I, 633
Field, Bessie Grey I, 616
Field, Caleb II, 221
Field, Caleb III, 41
Field, Caleb III, 115
Field, Caleb III, 118
Field, Caleb III, 120
Field, Caleb III, 273
Field, Caroline III, 118
Field, Catharine II, 221
Field, Catharine Ann II, 361
Field, Charity III, 120
Field, Charles II, 522
Field, Charles III, 118
Field, Charles III, 119
Field, Charles III, 237
Field, Charles M. III, 91
Field, Charles M. III, 118
Field, Charles M. III, 120
Field, Charles M., Jr. III, 212
Field, Charles Merritt III, 118
Field, Charlotte III, 119
Field, Charlotte III, 140
Field, Charlotte C. III, 118
Field, Charlotte C. III, 119
Field, Charlotte C. III, 139
Field, Christopher I, 653
Field, Cleopatra I, 761
Field, Cleopatra I, 762
Field, Cora L. I, 633
Field, Cora Lee I, 616
Field, Daniel VI, 914
Field, David Barton Taylor II, 996
Field, Deborah II, 687
Field, Deborah III, 32
Field, Deborah III, 118
Field, Deborah III, 119
Field, Deborah III, 225
Field, Deborah III, 255
Field, Deborah M. III, 118
Field, Deborah M. III, 298
Field, Donald M. III, 120
Field, Edw. S. III, 118
Field, Edw. S. III, 119
Field, Edw. S. III, 162
Field, Edward III, 118
Field, Edward III, 119
Field, Edward S. III, 108
Field, Edward S. III, 118
Field, Eleanor II, 220
Field, Eleanor II, 233
Field, Eleanor II, 522
Field, Eleanor III, 120
Field, Eleanor III, 137
Field, Eleanor III, 292
Field, Elenor I, 616
Field, Eliz. III, 119
Field, Eliza III, 128
Field, Eliza III, 262
Field, Elizabeth II, 361
Field, Elizabeth II, 522
Field, Elizabeth II, 523
Field, Elizabeth II, 531
Field, Elizabeth II, 689
Field, Elizabeth II, 695
Field, Elizabeth II, 802
Field, Elizabeth II, 829
Field, Elizabeth II, 959
Field, Elizabeth II, 996
Field, Elizabeth II, 1032
Field, Elizabeth III, 52
Field, Elizabeth III, 116
Field, Elizabeth III, 118
Field, Elizabeth III, 119
Field, Elizabeth III, 182
Field, Elizabeth III, 367
Field, Elizabeth III, 380
Field, Elizabeth III, 410
Field, Elizabeth IV, 706
Field, Elizabeth IV, 751
Field, Elizabeth VI, 914
Field, Elizabeth VI, 1018
Field, Elizabeth M. II, 959
Field, Ellen II, 361
Field, Elnathan III, 52
Field, Elnathan III, 119
Field, Emily L. I, 678
Field, Emily L. I, 692
Field, Experience III, 17
Field, Experience III, 118
Field, Fannie C. III, 139
Field, Fannie C. III, 140
Field, Fannie E. III, 118
Field, Fannie E. III, 119
Field, Frances Ann II, 361
Field, Frances Ann II, 522
Field, Frances Ann II, 554
Field, Franky VI, 914
Field, Frederick C. III, 118
Field, George II, 361
Field, George II, 522
Field, George B. I, 336
Field, George B. III, 248
Field, George W. II, 522
Field, Ginnins II, 522
Field, Grace E. I, 633
Field, Grace Eleanor I, 616
Field, Hamilton III, 119
Field, Hannah I, 878
Field, Hannah II, 220
Field, Hannah II, 221
Field, Hannah II, 486
Field, Hannah II, 996
Field, Hannah II, 1014
Field, Hannah II, 1031
Field, Hannah II, 1034
Field, Hannah II, 1035
Field, Hannah III, 40
Field, Hannah III, 55
Field, Hannah III, 72
Field, Hannah III, 118
Field, Hannah III, 119
Field, Hannah III, 120
Field, Hannah III, 255
Field, Hannah III, 263
Field, Hannah III, 336
Field, Hannah III, 380
Field, Hannah III, 410
Field, Hannah IV, 706
Field, Hannah B. III, 237
Field, Hannah Clark II, 996
Field, Hannah G. III, 44
Field, Hannah G. III, 119
Field, Hannah G. III, 120
Field, Harriet III, 119
Field, Harriet III, 296
Field, Helen III, 119
Field, Helen G. III, 120
Field, Helen G. III, 127
Field, Henrietta C. III, 118
Field, Henrietta R. II, 862
Field, Henry C. III, 118
Field, Henry C. III, 119
Field, Henry C. III, 153
Field, Henry C. III, 156
Field, Herbert H. III, 111
Field, Herbert H. III, 119
Field, Isaac C. II, 862
Field, Isaac Chapman II, 996
Field, James VI, 914
Field, James VI, 947
Field, James VI, 1001
Field, Jennings II, 522
Field, Jerusha III, 119
Field, Jesse III, 119
Field, John II, 220
Field, John II, 221
Field, John II, 361
Field, John II, 522
Field, John II, 687
Field, John II, 689
Field, John II, 996
Field, John II, 1035
Field, John III, 367
Field, John IV, 706
Field, John VI, 914
Field, John Brown II, 995
Field, John Haviland III, 120
Field, John, Jr. II, 522
Field, John, Jr. VI, 914
Field, Jonathan T. II, 996
Field, Joseph II, 221
Field, Joseph II, 522
Field, Joseph II, 531
Field, Joseph II, 554
Field, Joseph II, 740
Field, Joseph II, 794
Field, Joseph II, 862
Field, Joseph II, 883
Field, Joseph II, 959
Field, Joseph II, 1035
Field, Joseph III, 118
Field, Joseph III, 120
Field, Joseph III, 273
Field, Joseph Benjamin I, 616
Field, Joseph Coles III, 119
Field, Joseph F. I, 616
Field, Joseph, Jr. II, 996
Field, Josephine L. III, 118
Field, Josiah III, 44
Field, Josiah III, 120
Field, Josiah III, 146
Field, Katherine H. III, 119
Field, Katherine H. III, 162
Field, Katherine Hamilton III, 119
Field, L. Emily I, 653
Field, Latitia II, 996
Field, Latitia II, 1034
Field, Laura I, 619
Field, Laura I, 633
Field, Laura I, 878
Field, Laura I, 897
Field, Louisa M. III, 119
Field, Louisa M. III, 120
Field, Louisa M. III, 247
Field, Louisa M. III, 298
Field, Louisa W. VI, 915
Field, Louise Emily I, 653
Field, Lydia II, 1035
Field, Lydia III, 108
Field, Lydia R. III, 118
Field, Lydia R. E. III, 118
Field, Lydia R. E. III, 119
Field, Lydia R. E. III, 162
Field, Lydia S. III, 118
Field, Lydia S. III, 155
Field, Marcy II, 220
Field, Margaret II, 522
Field, Margaret II, 785
Field, Margaret II, 984
Field, Margaret II, 996
Field, Margarett II, 996
Field, Margit VI, 823
Field, Maria III, 119
Field, Maria M. III, 119
Field, Marielma III, 119
Field, Marielma III, 154
Field, Marielma III, 155
Field, Marielma III, 156
Field, Marielma III, 181
Field, Marielma III, 312
Field, Marielma F. III, 156
Field, Martha III, 118
Field, Martha III, 119
Field, Martha III, 237
Field, Martha III, 372
Field, Mary I, 898
Field, Mary II, 220
Field, Mary II, 221
Field, Mary II, 252
Field, Mary II, 267
Field, Mary II, 361
Field, Mary II, 487
Field, Mary II, 522
Field, Mary II, 523
Field, Mary II, 687
Field, Mary II, 740
Field, Mary II, 794
Field, Mary II, 862
Field, Mary II, 996
Field, Mary II, 1035
Field, Mary II, 1042
Field, Mary III, 115
Field, Mary III, 119
Field, Mary III, 120
Field, Mary III, 156
Field, Mary III, 246

Field, Mary III, 248
Field, Mary III, 273
Field, Mary III, 296
Field, Mary IV, 706
Field, Mary Ann II, 862
Field, Mary Ann II, 1035
Field, Mary C. III, 120
Field, Mary C. III, 218
Field, Mary Ella II, 855
Field, Mary Ella II, 862
Field, Mary, Jr. II, 522
Field, Mary, Jr. II, 523
Field, Mary, Jr. II, 996
Field, Mary, Jr. II, 1050
Field, Mary, Sr. II, 862
Field, Mercy II, 220
Field, Mercy II, 221
Field, Mercy II, 523
Field, Mercy II, 740
Field, Mercy II, 862
Field, Mercy II, 996
Field, Nathan II, 221
Field, Nathan II, 361
Field, Nathan II, 522
Field, Nathan II, 695
Field, Nathan II, 829
Field, Nathan II, 996
Field, Nathan III, 120
Field, Nathan III, 182
Field, Nathaniel III, 52
Field, Nathaniel III, 119
Field, Nellie V. I, 633
Field, Nellie Virginia I, 616
Field, Newberry II, 220
Field, Newberry II, 221
Field, Newberry II, 996
Field, Nina III, 111
Field, Nina III, 119
Field, Oliver III, 119
Field, Patience III, 52
Field, Patience III, 119
Field, Peggy VI, 823
Field, Phebe III, 119
Field, Phebe III, 281
Field, Phebe III, 318
Field, Phebe F. III, 326
Field, Phebe T. III, 137
Field, Phebe Titus III, 120
Field, R. Allen I, 653
Field, Rachel II, 794
Field, Rachel II, 862
Field, Rachel II, 883
Field, Rachel III, 119
Field, Rachel VI, 853
Field, Rachel J. II, 862
Field, Rebecca II, 221
Field, Rebecca II, 361
Field, Rebecca II, 522
Field, Rebecca II, 531
Field, Rebecca II, 554
Field, Rebecca II, 794
Field, Rebecca II, 862
Field, Rebecca II, 883
Field, Rebeckah II, 996
Field, Rebeckah III, 55
Field, Rebeckah III, 120
Field, Rhoda J. VI, 947
Field, Richard II, 794
Field, Richard III, 118
Field, Richard III, 120
Field, Richard III, 225
Field, Richard III, 298
Field, Richard B. III, 118
Field, Richard C. III, 120
Field, Richard C. III, 127
Field, Richard C. III, 218
Field, Richard M. III, 137
Field, Richard Manning III, 120
Field, Richard Manning III, 292
Field, Richard Mott III, 119
Field, Richard Mott III, 120
Field, Richard T. III, 120
Field, Richmond I, 616
Field, Robert II, 220
Field, Robert II, 241
Field, Robert III, 55
Field, Robert III, 118
Field, Robert III, 119
Field, Robert III, 120
Field, Robert III, 281
Field, Robert III, 318
Field, Robert III, 375
Field, Robert VI, 918
Field, Roberts III, 118
Field, Robt. III, 451
Field, Rodman III, 120
Field, S. Benjamin III, 120
Field, Sam'l I, 633
Field, Samuel II, 361
Field, Samuel II, 522
Field, Samuel II, 705
Field, Samuel II, 995
Field, Samuel III, 120
Field, Samuel III, 246
Field, Sarah II, 522
Field, Sarah II, 677
Field, Sarah II, 695
Field, Sarah II, 829
Field, Sarah II, 996
Field, Sarah II, 1035
Field, Sarah II, 1050
Field, Sarah III, 44
Field, Sarah III, 70
Field, Sarah III, 72
Field, Sarah III, 118
Field, Sarah III, 119
Field, Sarah III, 120
Field, Sarah III, 146
Field, Sarah III, 310
Field, Sarah IV, 525
Field, Sarah VI, 965
Field, Sarah Louise III, 119
Field, Sarah S. III, 44
Field, Sarah S. III, 120
Field, Sophia IV, 869
Field, Sophia IV, 875
Field, Stepen II, 996
Field, Stephen II, 996
Field, Stephen III, 120
Field, Susan I, 336
Field, Susanna II, 522
Field, Susanna II, 705
Field, Susanna III, 410
Field, Susannah II, 220
Field, Susannah II, 241
Field, Susannah III, 118
Field, Susannah III, 119
Field, Susannah III, 120
Field, Susannah III, 226
Field, Thomas II, 361
Field, Thomas II, 522
Field, Thomas III, 70
Field, Thomas S. III, 119
Field, Thos. S. II, 862
Field, Thos. S. II, 883
Field, Thos. Shreve II, 794
Field, Violet V. III, 120
Field, Violet V. III, 167
Field, Wd. Henrietta II, 794
Field, Wd. Phebe III, 120
Field, William II, 221
Field, William II, 361
Field, William III, 336
Field, William IV, 706
Field, William VI, 965
Field, William VI, 979
Field, William A. II, 361
Field, William C. III, 167
Field, William D. C. III, 118
Field, William D. C. III, 120
Field, William M. VI, 915
Field, William M. VI, 973
Field, William S. I, 633
Field, William Samuel I, 616
Field, William, Jr. VI, 914
Field, Winsfred Samuel I, 616
Field, Wm. II, 996
Field, Wm. II, 1031
Field, Wm. II, 1034
Field, Wm. III, 255
Field, Wm. VI, 872
Field, Wm. VI, 1007
Field, Wm. A. II, 554
Field, Wm. H. III, 119
Field, Wm. H. III, 296
Field, Zebulon III, 119
Fielder, Abram VI, 915
Fielder, Daniel VI, 915
Fielder, Elizabeth VI, 826
Fielder, George VI, 915
Fielder, George VI, 938
Fielder, Mary VI, 915
Fielder, Patsy VI, 938
Fielder, Permelia VI, 915
Fielder, Sally VI, 915
Fielder, Writtey VI, 938
Fielding, Ann III, 120
Fielding, Ann III, 121
Fielding, Esther II, 429
Fielding, Esther II, 523
Fielding, Esther II, 584
Fielding, Hester II, 672
Fielding, Thos. Peter III, 120
Fielding, William III, 120
Fielding, William III, 121
Fields, Andrew VI, 914
Fields, Ann VI, 949
Fields, Ann Matilda VI, 914
Fields, Anna IV, 525
Fields, Anna VI, 914
Fields, Betsy VI, 827
Fields, Caleb II, 221
Fields, Caleb II, 267
Fields, Catharine II, 221
Fields, Catharine II, 267
Fields, Daniel VI, 816
Fields, Daniel VI, 914
Fields, David VI, 816
Fields, Delphinia I, 678
Fields, Elizabeth IV, 953
Fields, Elizabeth VI, 914
Fields, Emily L. I, 678
Fields, Ezekiel VI, 816
Fields, Ezekiel VI, 852
Fields, Franky VI, 914
Fields, George B. I, 336
Fields, Henrietta R. II, 862
Fields, Henrietta R. II, 915
Fields, Isabella VI, 840
Fields, J. T. IV, 1278
Fields, James VI, 914
Fields, James W. VI, 1007
Fields, Jane V, 895
Fields, Jane V, 905
Fields, Jane VI, 798
Fields, Jane Bryant V, 905
Fields, Jemima H. VI, 827
Fields, John VI, 798
Fields, John VI, 914
Fields, John VI, 965
Fields, John VI, 969
Fields, John VI, 990
Fields, John B. VI, 914
Fields, Joseph II, 221
Fields, Joseph II, 267
Fields, Laura I, 633
Fields, Lefea IV, 1207
Fields, Lefy IV, 1207
Fields, Louisa W. VI, 915
Fields, Lucinda VI, 994
Fields, Margaret VI, 827
Fields, Margaret VI, 830
Fields, Margaret VI, 915
Fields, Margaret Ann VI, 990
Fields, Margret VI, 840
Fields, Margret VI, 915
Fields, Mary I, 934
Fields, Mary VI, 802
Fields, Mary VI, 816
Fields, Mary J. VI, 914
Fields, Mildred A. VI, 915
Fields, Mille VI, 914
Fields, Nancy VI, 830
Fields, Nancy VI, 965
Fields, Patsy VI, 802
Fields, Rachel IV, 32
Fields, Rachel VI, 816
Fields, Rebecca II, 221
Fields, Rebecca II, 267
Fields, Rebecca VI, 914
Fields, Richard II, 794
Fields, Rocksinancey VI, 816
Fields, Sally VI, 969
Fields, Samuel VI, 914
Fields, Samuel VI, 915
Fields, Sarah IV, 329
Fields, Sarah IV, 515
Fields, Sarah IV, 560
Fields, Wd. Henrietta II, 794
Fields, William VI, 990
Fields, William H. VI, 915
Fields, William M. VI, 915
Fields, William, Jr. VI, 914
Fields, Wm. VI, 994
Fields, Wm. S. V, 170
Fiers, Wm. V, 561
Fiester, Albert V, 995
Fiester, Cora V, 995
Fiester, John V, 995
Fiester, Rella V, 995
Fiets-Randolph, Margaret I, 31
Fife, Audna V, 672
Fife, Audna V, 673
Fife, Audra V, 672
Fife, Catharine VI, 741
Fife, Cleo V, 672
Fife, Cleo M. V, 666
Fife, Cleo M. V, 672
Fife, Clinton V, 672
Fife, Clinton V, 673
Fife, Elsie V, 670
Fife, Elsie V, 672
Fife, Elsie Jane V, 672
Fife, Ira Hundley V, 666
Fife, Ira Hundley V, 672
Fife, Jane V, 486
Fife, Jane V, 491
Fife, Wm. Clinton V, 672
Fifer, Isaac VI, 915
Fifer, Mary VI, 880
Fifer, Mary Margaret VI, 915
Fifer, Mathias VI, 915
Fifer, Melinda VI, 915
Fifer, Michael VI, 915
Fifer, Nancy V, 904
Figg, Benjamin VI, 242
Figg, Mary T. VI, 242
Figg, Mary T. VI, 246
Figg, Mary T. VI, 248
Figg, Sarah VI, 242
Figg, William L. VI, 176
Figg, William S. VI, 242
Figg, William S. VI, 246
Figg, William S. VI, 248
Figgans, Alice E. V, 457
Figgans, Elizabeth V, 457
Figgans, Nancy M. V, 457
Figgins, Alice V, 238
Figgins, Alice E. V, 457
Figgins, Cora V, 457
Figgins, Elijah V, 238
Figgins, Elijah, Jr. V, 238
Figgins, Elizabeth V, 238
Figgins, Elizabeth V, 457
Figgins, Minnie V, 457
Figgins, Nancy V, 238
Figgins, Nancy Ann V, 238
Figgins, Nancy M. V, 457
Figgins, Thomas E. V, 457
Figgins, Zadoc V, 238
Figgins, Zadock V, 238
Figgons, Elizabeth V, 457
Figgons, Minnie V, 457
Figgons, Thomas E. V, 457
File, Ada I, 941
File, Ada V. I, 941
File, Ada Virginia I, 925
File, Eliza I, 925
File, J. U. I, 925
File, James I, 941
File, James Addison I, 925
File, Mildred I, 925
File, Mildred I, 941
File, Sarah VI, 361
File, Sarah VI, 389
Files, C. A. V, 995
Files, John II, 443
Files, Mrs. C. A. V, 995
Files, William II, 443
Filson, Cornelia A. V, 146
Filson, Cornelia Ann V, 146
Filson, Cynthia E. V, 146
Filson, Cynthia Ellen V, 146
Filson, John V, 146
Filson, John C. V, 146
Finch, ??? III, 120
Finch, Ada M., Jr. III, 120
Finch, Ann II, 443
Finch, Ann B. VI, 816
Finch, Anna III, 120
Finch, Anna M. III, 120
Finch, Anna M. III, 245
Finch, B, Jr. VI, 846
Finch, Barnet VI, 797
Finch, Barnet VI, 802
Finch, Barnet VI, 810
Finch, Barnet VI, 816
Finch, Barnet VI, 818
Finch, Barnet VI, 833
Finch, Barnet VI, 835
Finch, Barnet VI, 845
Finch, Barnet VI, 857
Finch, Barnet VI, 860
Finch, Barnet VI, 863
Finch, Barnet VI, 865
Finch, Barnet VI, 866
Finch, Barnet W. VI, 821
Finch, Barnet William VI, 827
Finch, Barnet, Jr. VI, 824
Finch, Bernard VI, 866
Finch, Betsy VI, 810
Finch, Betsy VI, 818
Finch, Blagdon VI, 821
Finch, Blagdon VI, 851
Finch, Blagdon, Jr. VI, 816
Finch, Blegdon VI, 800
Finch, Blegdon VI, 805
Finch, Blegdon VI, 810
Finch, Caroline VI, 840
Finch, Catharine VI, 824
Finch, Charity III, 295
Finch, Charlotte III, 120
Finch, Chat III, 120
Finch, Daniel W. IV, 1362
Finch, David IV, 32
Finch, David IV, 85
Finch, David VI, 389
Finch, David L. III, 120
Finch, Easter VI, 816
Finch, Ede VI, 836
Finch, Eliza III, 120
Finch, Eliza Ann IV, 1362
Finch, Eliza K. VI, 846
Finch, Elizabeth IV, 28
Finch, Elizabeth IV, 32
Finch, Elizabeth IV, 85
Finch, Elizabeth VI, 389
Finch, Elizabeth VI, 795
Finch, Elizabeth VI, 802
Finch, Elizabeth VI, 816
Finch, Fanny VI, 810
Finch, Hannah III, 120
Finch, Hannah IV, 22
Finch, Hannah IV, 32
Finch, Hannah IV, 85
Finch, Hannah IV, 815
Finch, Hannah IV, 855
Finch, Hannah IV, 1362
Finch, Hannah VI, 389
Finch, Hannah VI, 863
Finch, Hannah B. W. III, 120
Finch, Henry VI, 816
Finch, Henry VI, 821
Finch, Henry VI, 840
Finch, Hudson III, 120
Finch, Jane VI, 816
Finch, Jane VI, 857
Finch, Jemima VI, 814
Finch, Jemima VI, 821
Finch, Jennie III, 120
Finch, Jennie III, 261
Finch, John VI, 802
Finch, John VI, 806
Finch, John VI, 810
Finch, John VI, 816
Finch, John VI, 831
Finch, John VI, 836
Finch, John VI, 841
Finch, John W. III, 120
Finch, John, Jr. VI, 816
Finch, Luviner VI, 835
Finch, Lydia IV, 32
Finch, Lydia IV, 85
Finch, Lydia VI, 389
Finch, Mahaley VI, 816
Finch, Margaret VI, 802
Finch, Martha VI, 805
Finch, Martha VI, 816
Finch, Martha A. VI, 865
Finch, Mary IV, 28
Finch, Mary IV, 32
Finch, Mary IV, 85
Finch, Mary VI, 389
Finch, Mary VI, 816
Finch, Mary VI, 833
Finch, Matilda VI, 892
Finch, Mildred VI, 800
Finch, Mina VI, 836
Finch, Mina VI, 845
Finch, Minor VI, 810
Finch, Nancy VI, 821
Finch, Nelly VI, 806
Finch, Ocelia III, 120
Finch, Orville III, 120
Finch, Otis D. IV, 1362
Finch, Patsey VI, 831
Finch, Peninah IV, 32
Finch, Peninah IV, 85
Finch, Peninah VI, 389
Finch, Polly VI, 802
Finch, Rachel IV, 32
Finch, Rachel IV, 85
Finch, Rachel VI, 389
Finch, Rachel VI, 797
Finch, Rebecca IV, 1362
Finch, Reuben IV, 1362
Finch, Richard S. H. III, 120
Finch, Ruth IV, 28
Finch, Ruth IV, 32
Finch, Ruth IV, 85
Finch, Ruth VI, 389
Finch, Sally VI, 816
Finch, Sally VI, 851
Finch, Sally VI, 866
Finch, Samuel IV, 32
Finch, Samuel IV, 85
Finch, Samuel IV, 125
Finch, Samuel IV, 1362
Finch, Samuel VI, 389
Finch, Samuel R. IV, 1362
Finch, Sarah IV, 32
Finch, Sarah IV, 40
Finch, Sarah IV, 85
Finch, Sarah IV, 578
Finch, Sarah IV, 594
Finch, Sarah VI, 389
Finch, Sarah VI, 841
Finch, Selah VI, 833
Finch, Susan VI, 799
Finch, Thomas III, 120
Finch, Thomas Ellwood III, 12(
Finch, Thomas Ellwood III, 24!
Finch, Trip IV, 1362
Finch, Tripp IV, 1362
Finch, William III, 120

inch, William VI, 816
inch, William B. VI, 816
inch, William Y. III, 120
inch, Willie M. III, 120
inch, Wm. Y. III, 261
incher, Armel I, 1019
incher, Armil I, 1015
incher, Armil I, 1029
incher, Arniel I, 1056
incher, Caleb II, 361
incher, Elizabeth I, 1019
incher, Elizabeth I, 1027
incher, Elizabeth I, 1029
incher, Elizabeth I, 1056
incher, Elizabeth II, 361
incher, Elizabeth II, 544
incher, Esther I, 1056
incher, Francis I, 1019
incher, Francis I, 1027
incher, Francis I, 1029
incher, Francis I, 1056
incher, Francis II, 361
incher, Francis II, 523
incher, Hester I, 1019
incher, Jesse I, 1029
incher, Jesse I Sup 1, 10
incher, John I, 1029
incher, Jonathan I, 389
incher, Joshua II, 361
incher, Joshua II, 523
incher, Joshua II, 544
incher, Mary I, 389
incher, Mary I, 404
incher, Mary II, 361
incher, Mary II, 523
incher, Mary II, 651
incher, Rachel I, 1060
incher, Rachel I, 1061
incher, Rebecca I, 1056
incher, Rebeccah I, 1056
incher, Rebekah I, 1019
incher, Rebekah I, 1053
incher, Rebekah I, 1061
incher, Rebekah I, 1062
incher, Sarah II, 523
incher, Sarah II, 525
incher, Thomas I, 1056
ncher, William II, 361
inck, Anna Lee Byerly II, 794
incks, Frances VI, 557
indley, Betsy VI, 816
indley, Hattie IV, 193
indley, Jackson IV, 193
indley, John VI, 816
indley, Loretta IV, 193
indley, Mary IV, 1150
inegan, Peter V, 672
ineout, Matilda V, 672
ineran, Jennie B. IV, 713
ineran, Martin IV, 713
ney, Catharine IV, 792
ney, Cordelia R. IV, 792
ney, Robert IV, 792
ney, Susanna VI, 64
ney, Susanna VI, 74
nger, Arthur Frank I, 1152
nger, Franklin I, 1152
nger, Marie Genieve I, 1152
ngulin, Anna IV, 1315
ngulin, Ferdinan J. IV, 1315
ngulin, Ferdinand IV, 1315
ngulin, Josephine IV, 1315
ngulin, Lilian IV, 1315
ngulin, Viola IV, 1315
nican, Mary VI, 542
nigan, Christopher II, 361
nigan, Ella V, 457
nikin, Mary VI, 492
nikin, Mary VI, 542
nison, Betsy I, 389
nison, Ellen I, 389
nison, Jeremieh I, 389
nister, Elizabeth II, 523
nister, Elizabeth II, 561
nister, Margaret II, 523
nister, Margaret II, 561
nister, Margaret II, 708
nister, Margaret II, 802
nister, Wm. II, 523
nister, Wm. II, 561
nk, ??? III, 120
nk, Ada III, 121
nk, Ada III, 246
nk, Ada B. II, 862
nk, Ada B. II, 905
nk, Ada P. III, 121
nk, Ada P. III, 343
nk, Anna II, 862
nk, Anna II, 905
nk, Anna III, 120
nk, Emil II, 862
Fink, Emil II, 905
Fink, Emil III, 58
Fink, Emil III, 120
Fink, Emil III, 246
Fink, Emil III, 343
Fink, Ernest III, 120
Fink, Ernst II, 862
Fink, Ernst II, 905
Fink, Eunice III, 30
Fink, Eunice III, 121
Fink, Helen III, 120
Fink, Helen III, 121
Fink, Helen III, 343
Fink, Herbert H. III, 30
Fink, Herbert H. III, 120
Fink, Herbert H. III, 121
Fink, Wd. Ada III, 58
Fink, Wd. Ada III, 120
Finkbine, Lydia V, 905
Finkbine, Lydia V, 934
Finkhouse, Mable V, 995
Finkhouse, Roy V, 995
Finks, Frances VI, 734
Finlaw, Cornelia II, 131
Finlaw, Cornelia Thompson II, 148
Finlaw, David II, 138
Finlaw, Elizabeth II, 132
Finlaw, Elizabeth II, 138
Finlaw, Ella II, 127
Finlaw, Harry Lummis II, 131
Finlaw, Harry S. II, 148
Finlaw, John M. II, 131
Finlaw, Lydia II, 138
Finlaw, Mary E. II, 131
Finley, Agness VI, 890
Finley, Elizabeth II, 523
Finley, Elizabeth VI, 890
Finley, Elizabeth VI, 915
Finley, Elsie IV, 392
Finley, Elsie IV, 402
Finley, Hattie IV, 173
Finley, Hattie IV, 196
Finley, James VI, 890
Finley, John Armour VI, 915
Finley, Mary II, 523
Finley, Melissa IV, 392
Finley, Mellisa IV, 406
Finley, Minnie IV, 392
Finley, Minnie IV, 407
Finley, Robert II, 523
Finley, Samuel VI, 890
Finley, Samuel VI, 915
Finley, Tamar II, 361
Finlow, Mary II, 523
Finlow, Robert II, 361
Finlow, Sarah II, 443
Finly, Thomas G. VI, 158
Finly, Thomas G. VI, 176
Finn, Bryn Mawr II, 873
Finn, Edith II, 862
Finn, Edith II, 873
Finn, Edwin R. II, 873
Finn, George Howell II, 862
Finn, George Howell II, 873
Finn, Martha H. II, 862
Finn, Martha H. II, 873
Finn, Mary L. II, 873
Finn, Wm. W. II, 862
Finn, Wm. W. II, 873
Finnemore, Nathaniel II, 521
Finnemore, Wm. II, 521
Finneran, William IV, 706
Finnester, William II, 361
Finney, Ann II, 221
Finney, Ann II, 233
Finney, Ann II, 361
Finney, Ann II, 523
Finney, Ann II, 551
Finney, Barbara IV, 953
Finney, Charles II, 221
Finney, Charles II, 233
Finney, Charles II, 361
Finney, Charles II, 523
Finney, Clara IV, 706
Finney, Clara A. IV, 706
Finney, Edward IV, 953
Finney, Elizabeth V, 739
Finney, Elizabeth VI, 915
Finney, Elizabeth VI, 939
Finney, Hannah II, 361
Finney, Hannah II, 523
Finney, Hannah V, 730
Finney, John VI, 952
Finney, John VI, 984
Finney, Nancy V, 731
Finney, Nancy V, 734
Finney, Nancy V, 799
Finney, Nancy V, 800
Finney, Peter VI, 952
Finney, Peter VI, 984
Finney, Polly VI, 984
Finney, Rachel II, 221
Finney, Rachel II, 233
Finney, Robert V, 734
Finney, Robert V, 739
Finney, Sally VI, 952
Finney, Samuel II, 221
Finney, Samuel II, 233
Finney, Seth C. C. III, 471
Finney, Sophia VI, 939
Finney, William VI, 915
Finnison, Betsy I, 389
Finnison, Elizabeth I, 389
Finnison, Ellen I, 389
Finnison, Ida I, 389
Finnison, Jeremiah I, 389
Finnison, Jeremieh I, 389
Finny, Ann II, 361
Finny, Charles II, 361
Finny, Hannah II, 361
Finout, Matilda V, 672
Fipps, Sarah II, 622
Firestone, Sally Ann IV, 606
Firestone, Sally Ann IV, 624
Firlong, Patsy VI, 962
Firman, Andrew V, 672
Firman, Benjamin II, 361
Firman, Hannah II, 997
Firman, Kinsey II, 361
Firman, Louisa V, 672
Firman, Richard Way II, 997
Firman, Sarah II, 997
Firman, Sarah II, 1023
Firman, Thomas II, 361
Firmin, Arthur E. III, 121
Firs, Ella IV, 1235
Firs, Wesley IV, 1235
Firsee, Elizabeth VI, 927
Firtchman, Mary F. IV, 823
Firth, Addie III, 410
Firth, Ann II, 832
Firth, Ann II, 862
Firth, Ann A. II, 148
Firth, Ann A. II, 862
Firth, Edward II, 27
Firth, Elizabeth II, 27
Firth, Elizabeth II, 60
Firth, Elizabeth II, 69
Firth, Elizabeth III, 410
Firth, Ezra II, 27
Firth, Ezra II, 60
Firth, Ezra II, 69
Firth, Hannah II, 69
Firth, Henrietta III, 410
Firth, Henry II, 27
Firth, Henry II, 69
Firth, J. E. III, 410
Firth, John II, 27
Firth, John II, 69
Firth, John II, 361
Firth, John III, 410
Firth, Judith II, 27
Firth, Louise III, 164
Firth, M. E. III, 410
Firth, Mary II, 862
Firth, Mary A. III, 121
Firth, Preston II, 69
Firth, Preston C. II, 862
Firth, Preston Carpenter II, 27
Firth, Preston Carpenter II, 794
Firth, Samuel II, 27
Firth, Samuel II, 69
Firth, Sarah II, 27
Firth, Sarah II, 69
Firth, Sarah II, 108
Firth, Sarah E. III, 410
Firth, Sidney III, 121
Firth, Thomas II, 69
Firth, Thomas III, 410
Firth, Thos. II, 27
Firth, William III, 164
Fiser, Jacob VI, 915
Fiser, Polly VI, 915
Fish, Albert IV, 624
Fish, Alma Blanche IV, 715
Fish, Amon IV, 624
Fish, Amy II, 862
Fish, Amy II, 930
Fish, Amy II, 996
Fish, Amy II, 1050
Fish, Amy II, 1072
Fish, Anna II, 1073
Fish, Anna IV, 624
Fish, Anna Erie II, 1084
Fish, Anne IV, 624
Fish, Benjamin II, 1050
Fish, Beulah II, 930
Fish, Celia IV, 624
Fish, Celia IV, 650
Fish, Chas. IV, 715
Fish, Clarence V, 995
Fish, Clarissa V, 995
Fish, Daniel II, 1073
Fish, Daniel II, 1084
Fish, Deborah IV, 624
Fish, Deborah IV, 650
Fish, Elias Wildman II, 996
Fish, Elijah II, 996
Fish, Elijah II, 1038
Fish, Elijah II, 1050
Fish, Elijah II, 1072
Fish, Elijah II, 1073
Fish, Elijah II, 1076
Fish, Elisha II, 996
Fish, Elisha II, 1038
Fish, Eliza F. IV, 1159
Fish, Elizabeth II, 996
Fish, Elizabeth II, 1038
Fish, Elizabeth II, 1050
Fish, Elizabeth II, 1072
Fish, Elizabeth II, 1073
Fish, Elizabeth II, 1076
Fish, Elizabeth IV, 1159
Fish, Emma Jane IV, 624
Fish, Emma Jean IV, 624
Fish, Esther B. II, 1073
Fish, Esther B. II, 1084
Fish, Gardner IV, 624
Fish, George C. II, 930
Fish, Hannah II, 996
Fish, Hannah II, 1038
Fish, Hannah II, 1050
Fish, Hannah II, 1056
Fish, Hannah II, 1072
Fish, Hannah II, 1076
Fish, Hannah IV, 624
Fish, Hannah K. IV, 624
Fish, Hannah K. IV, 629
Fish, Hannah K. IV, 706
Fish, Hannah K. IV, 716
Fish, Harry IV, 624
Fish, Heman B. II, 1073
Fish, Heman B. II, 1084
Fish, James V, 995
Fish, James Palmer II, 1073
Fish, John IV, 624
Fish, Joseph II, 1050
Fish, Joseph II, 1065
Fish, Joseph II, 1072
Fish, Joseph IV, 624
Fish, Joseph IV, 650
Fish, Lemuel IV, 624
Fish, Levi II, 798
Fish, Louise IV, 715
Fish, Lydia IV, 624
Fish, Manuel V, 995
Fish, Margaret IV, 715
Fish, Margaret VI, 242
Fish, Margaret L. VI, 242
Fish, Mariall H. V, 995
Fish, Mark II, 930
Fish, Mary II, 823
Fish, Mary II, 862
Fish, Mary II, 930
Fish, Mary II, 1050
Fish, Mary II, 1072
Fish, Mary II, 1080
Fish, Mary III, 121
Fish, Mary III, 380
Fish, Mary III, 410
Fish, Mary III, 420
Fish, Mary IV, 624
Fish, Phebe IV, 624
Fish, Preserved III, 380
Fish, Rachel V, 995
Fish, Rachel B. IV, 1159
Fish, Rebecca II, 798
Fish, Ruth II, 930
Fish, Salem IV, 624
Fish, Samuel II, 930
Fish, Samuel IV, 624
Fish, Sarah II, 959
Fish, Sarah II, 996
Fish, Sarah II, 1050
Fish, Sarah II, 1068
Fish, Sarah II, 1072
Fish, Sarah V, 995
Fish, Scott IV, 624
Fish, Selim IV, 624
Fish, Silas II, 862
Fish, Silas II, 930
Fish, Silas II, 996
Fish, Silas IV, 706
Fish, Solomon IV, 624
Fish, Stacy T. Gaunt II, 930
Fish, Stephen IV, 624
Fish, Stephen IV, 629
Fish, Stephen IV, 706
Fish, Stephen IV, 716
Fish, Susannah IV, 706
Fish, William II, 1065
Fish, Wm. II, 1073
Fishback, Ada V, 330
Fishback, Annie V, 238
Fishback, Harry V, 330
Fishback, Lydia Margaret V, 237
Fishback, Lydia Margaret V, 238
Fishback, Lydia Margaret V, 457
Fishback, Martha V, 456
Fishback, Mrs. Ada V, 330
Fishback, Thomas V, 456
Fishbaugh, Margaret E. V, 995
Fishbaugh, Wesley B. V, 995
Fishbourn, Hannah II, 523
Fishbourn, Hannah II, 583
Fishbourn, Jane II, 523
Fishbourn, Jane II, 528
Fishbourn, Mary II, 523
Fishbourn, Wm. II, 482
Fishbourn, Wm. II, 523
Fishbourn, Wm. II, 583
Fishbourne, Abraham II, 361
Fishbourne, Edward II, 361
Fishbourne, Hannah II, 361
Fishbourne, Hannah II, 523
Fishbourne, Jane II, 523
Fishbourne, Jane II, 636
Fishbourne, Mary II, 523
Fishbourne, Samuel II, 361
Fishbourne, Sarah II, 523
Fishbourne, Sarah II, 597
Fishbourne, William II, 361
Fishbourne, Wm. II, 523
Fishbourne, Wm. II, 636
Fishburn, Abraham II, 361
Fishburn, Edward II, 361
Fishburn, Hannah II, 361
Fishburn, Hannah Carpenter II, 361
Fishburn, Samuel II, 361
Fishburn, Sarah II, 361
Fishburn, William II, 361
Fisher, ??? III, 369
Fisher, ??? IV, 861
Fisher, ??? V, 905
Fisher, A. Packer IV, 525
Fisher, A. Ruth II, 767
Fisher, Abel IV, 32
Fisher, Abel IV, 85
Fisher, Abel John IV, 32
Fisher, Abigail II, 493
Fisher, Abigail II, 523
Fisher, Abraham I, 9
Fisher, Abraham I, 14
Fisher, Abraham I, 49
Fisher, Abraham I, 239
Fisher, Abram I, 49
Fisher, Abram I, 213
Fisher, Abram I, 214
Fisher, Abram II, 740
Fisher, Abram II, 764
Fisher, Abram II, 767
Fisher, Achsah V, 491
Fisher, Achsah V, 531
Fisher, Achsah V, 620
Fisher, Adia Ruth V, 385
Fisher, Albert V, 672
Fisher, Albert V, 685
Fisher, Alice IV, 32
Fisher, Alice IV, 69
Fisher, Alice IV, 81
Fisher, Alice IV, 85
Fisher, Alice V, 55
Fisher, Alice V, 238
Fisher, Alice V, 239
Fisher, Alice V, 621
Fisher, Alice VI, 389
Fisher, Amanda Ruth II, 740
Fisher, Amasa IV, 624
Fisher, Amasa IV, 706
Fisher, Amasa IV, 869
Fisher, Amasa VI, 311
Fisher, Amase IV, 869
Fisher, Amerous II, 443
Fisher, Amos I, 497
Fisher, Amos V, 238
Fisher, Amos V, 239
Fisher, Amos V, 302
Fisher, Amos V, 330
Fisher, Amos V, 331
Fisher, Amos V, 361
Fisher, Amos V, 620
Fisher, Amos VI, 492
Fisher, Andrew II, 819
Fisher, Ann II, 523
Fisher, Ann II, 524
Fisher, Ann II, 542
Fisher, Ann IV, 471
Fisher, Ann IV, 706
Fisher, Ann IV, 716
Fisher, Ann V, 995
Fisher, Ann VI, 311
Fisher, Ann VI, 389

Fisher, Ann VI, 492
Fisher, Ann VI, 915
Fisher, Ann Eliza IV, 1207
Fisher, Ann Eliza IV, 1213
Fisher, Ann K. V, 561
Fisher, Ann, Jr. VI, 492
Fisher, Anna II, 709
Fisher, Anna IV, 706
Fisher, Anna V, 107
Fisher, Anna V, 672
Fisher, Anna V, 739
Fisher, Anna V, 760
Fisher, Anna C. II, 740
Fisher, Anna C. II, 764
Fisher, Anna C. V, 55
Fisher, Anna Cloud V, 561
Fisher, Anna E. II, 137
Fisher, Anna Elizabeth IV, 768
Fisher, Anna H. V, 55
Fisher, Anna Jane I, 9
Fisher, Anna Jane I, 49
Fisher, Anna Jane I, 51
Fisher, Anna K. V, 561
Fisher, Anna K. V, 581
Fisher, Anna Knight IV, 624
Fisher, Anna Knight IV, 706
Fisher, Anna W. II, 524
Fisher, Anna W. II, 740
Fisher, Anna W. III, 121
Fisher, Anna, Jr. VI, 311
Fisher, Anne IV, 706
Fisher, Anne IV, 716
Fisher, Anne VI, 311
Fisher, Anne K. IV, 869
Fisher, Anne Knight IV, 869
Fisher, Aphas V, 239
Fisher, Asael V, 55
Fisher, Asahel IV, 706
Fisher, Asahel V, 561
Fisher, Asahel E. IV, 706
Fisher, Asahel E. V, 561
Fisher, Asahel Exchange IV, 706
Fisher, Asahel Exchange IV, 882
Fisher, Asahel Exchanze IV, 869
Fisher, Austin V, 331
Fisher, Avis V, 952
Fisher, Axhel E. V, 55
Fisher, Azariah V, 331
Fisher, Azariah V, 672
Fisher, Azariah V, 683
Fisher, Barack VI, 389
Fisher, Barak IV, 525
Fisher, Barak VI, 389
Fisher, Barak VI, 595
Fisher, Baruch IV, 146
Fisher, Baruch VI, 389
Fisher, Benjamin V, 995
Fisher, Bertha V, 672
Fisher, Bertha V, 685
Fisher, Betty VI, 311
Fisher, Betty VI, 389
Fisher, Betty VI, 492
Fisher, Bridgett II, 361
Fisher, Bridgett II, 362
Fisher, Caiphas VI, 389
Fisher, Caleb IV, 125
Fisher, Caleb V, 739
Fisher, Caphas VI, 389
Fisher, Casandra IV, 146
Fisher, Cassander IV, 85
Fisher, Cassander IV, 471
Fisher, Cassander IV, 488
Fisher, Catherine II, 473
Fisher, Catherine II, 523
Fisher, Cephas I, 1093
Fisher, Cephas V, 238
Fisher, Cephas V, 239
Fisher, Charles I, 539
Fisher, Charles II, 117
Fisher, Charles V, 55
Fisher, Charles V, 969
Fisher, Charles VI, 311
Fisher, Charles C. IV, 1159
Fisher, Charley VI, 311
Fisher, Charlie IV, 1159
Fisher, Charlotte V, 672
Fisher, Christopher VI, 311
Fisher, Clara IV, 1278
Fisher, Clesee Jean V, 331
Fisher, Clyde V, 672
Fisher, Coleman II, 361
Fisher, Coleman II, 524
Fisher, Cora IV, 1315
Fisher, Cyrus V, 55
Fisher, Cyrus V, 672
Fisher, Cyrus W. IV, 706
Fisher, Cyrus W. V, 55
Fisher, Dade M. VI, 816
Fisher, Damaris I, 539
Fisher, Damaris I, 574
Fisher, Daniel VI, 808
Fisher, Daniel VI, 834
Fisher, David I, 780
Fisher, David I, 809
Fisher, David IV, 86
Fisher, David IV, 125
Fisher, David IV, 1278
Fisher, David V, 739
Fisher, David V, 995
Fisher, David VI, 102
Fisher, David VI, 103
Fisher, David VI, 106
Fisher, Dawson Thomas VI, 741
Fisher, Deborah II, 361
Fisher, Deborah II, 826
Fisher, Dora IV, 1159
Fisher, E. Jane V, 385
Fisher, Earl V, 672
Fisher, Edatha L. VI, 1022
Fisher, Editha L. VI, 915
Fisher, Edney Elizabeth VI, 915
Fisher, Edward III, 121
Fisher, Eilizabeth VI, 389
Fisher, Eleanor Jane V, 385
Fisher, Eleanor Peel I, 49
Fisher, Eleanor Peet I, 9
Fisher, Elenor V, 385
Fisher, Elias IV, 624
Fisher, Elias IV, 869
Fisher, Elias V, 55
Fisher, Elias V, 107
Fisher, Elias V, 561
Fisher, Elias V, 889
Fisher, Elias V, 905
Fisher, Elias VI, 306
Fisher, Elias VI, 311
Fisher, Elias VI, 389
Fisher, Elias VI, 492
Fisher, Elias Fisher Cloud V, 561
Fisher, Elias M. V, 385
Fisher, Elisabeth D. I, 49
Fisher, Elisabeth Davis I, 9
Fisher, Elisabeth Davis I, 49
Fisher, Elise VI, 389
Fisher, Eliza I, 933
Fisher, Eliza II, 69
Fisher, Eliza II, 79
Fisher, Eliza H. II, 69
Fisher, Eliza J. V, 331
Fisher, Elizabeth II, 361
Fisher, Elizabeth II, 362
Fisher, Elizabeth II, 524
Fisher, Elizabeth II, 633
Fisher, Elizabeth II, 959
Fisher, Elizabeth II, 996
Fisher, Elizabeth II, 1025
Fisher, Elizabeth IV, 32
Fisher, Elizabeth IV, 69
Fisher, Elizabeth IV, 81
Fisher, Elizabeth IV, 85
Fisher, Elizabeth IV, 86
Fisher, Elizabeth IV, 92
Fisher, Elizabeth IV, 125
Fisher, Elizabeth IV, 129
Fisher, Elizabeth IV, 201
Fisher, Elizabeth V, 55
Fisher, Elizabeth V, 238
Fisher, Elizabeth V, 239
Fisher, Elizabeth V, 256
Fisher, Elizabeth V, 302
Fisher, Elizabeth V, 446
Fisher, Elizabeth V, 620
Fisher, Elizabeth V, 739
Fisher, Elizabeth V, 905
Fisher, Elizabeth VI, 311
Fisher, Elizabeth VI, 319
Fisher, Elizabeth VI, 325
Fisher, Elizabeth VI, 374
Fisher, Elizabeth VI, 389
Fisher, Elizabeth VI, 492
Fisher, Elizabeth VI, 883
Fisher, Elizabeth VI, 915
Fisher, Ella IV, 1251
Fisher, Ella VI, 741
Fisher, Ella VI, 742
Fisher, Ella VI, 743
Fisher, Ellwood V, 905
Fisher, Elver J. V, 331
Fisher, Elver J. V, 672
Fisher, Elwood VI, 311
Fisher, Emaline IV, 676
Fisher, Emaline IV, 706
Fisher, Emely I, 780
Fisher, Emily I, 809
Fisher, Emily W. V, 55
Fisher, Emily W. V, 138
Fisher, Emma IV, 1278
Fisher, Emma V, 55
Fisher, Emma V, 331
Fisher, Emma H. V, 672
Fisher, Emma L. V, 331
Fisher, Estel V, 331
Fisher, Esther I, 959
Fisher, Esther I, 962
Fisher, Esther II, 362
Fisher, Esther II, 524
Fisher, Esther II, 740
Fisher, Esther II, 767
Fisher, Esther II, 794
Fisher, Esther II, 863
Fisher, Etta Irena IV, 1251
Fisher, Eunice IV, 706
Fisher, Eunice V, 55
Fisher, Eva IV, 543
Fisher, Eve IV, 525
Fisher, Fenwick II, 523
Fisher, Frances IV, 32
Fisher, Frances IV, 85
Fisher, Frances IV, 146
Fisher, Frances A. V, 491
Fisher, Francis IV, 85
Fisher, Francis IV, 471
Fisher, Francis V, 55
Fisher, Francis Rotch II, 705
Fisher, Francis Rotch II, 740
Fisher, Francis Rotch III, 121
Fisher, Frank V, 491
Fisher, Frank V, 561
Fisher, Frank V, 995
Fisher, Gabriel S. VI, 915
Fisher, Garbutt II, 524
Fisher, Garbutt II, 740
Fisher, George II, 362
Fisher, George II, 443
Fisher, George IV, 1159
Fisher, George L. VI, 915
Fisher, Georgie IV, 1159
Fisher, Grace II, 221
Fisher, Grace II, 523
Fisher, Grace III, 121
Fisher, Hannah II, 362
Fisher, Hannah II, 523
Fisher, Hannah II, 524
Fisher, Hannah II, 597
Fisher, Hannah II, 767
Fisher, Hannah II, 790
Fisher, Hannah II, 794
Fisher, Hannah II, 853
Fisher, Hannah II, 863
Fisher, Hannah IV, 32
Fisher, Hannah IV, 44
Fisher, Hannah IV, 392
Fisher, Hannah IV, 405
Fisher, Hannah IV, 624
Fisher, Hannah IV, 706
Fisher, Hannah IV, 869
Fisher, Hannah V, 55
Fisher, Hannah V, 67
Fisher, Hannah V, 218
Fisher, Hannah V, 239
Fisher, Hannah V, 330
Fisher, Hannah V, 331
Fisher, Hannah V, 561
Fisher, Hannah V, 905
Fisher, Hannah V, 922
Fisher, Hannah VI, 306
Fisher, Hannah VI, 311
Fisher, Hannah VI, 352
Fisher, Hannah VI, 355
Fisher, Hannah VI, 386
Fisher, Hannah VI, 389
Fisher, Hannah VI, 492
Fisher, Hannah Logan II, 719
Fisher, Hannah Logan II, 723
Fisher, Harriet V, 331
Fisher, Harriet V, 995
Fisher, Harroett V, 995
Fisher, Helen V, 667
Fisher, Henry III, 121
Fisher, Henry IV, 471
Fisher, Henry V, 331
Fisher, Henry A. IV, 471
Fisher, Henry Hilary I, 49
Fisher, Henry Wright I, 9
Fisher, Henry Wright I, 49
Fisher, Hester V, 667
Fisher, Hester V, 672
Fisher, Hiram V, 55
Fisher, Hiram V, 238
Fisher, Hiram V, 239
Fisher, Hiram V, 302
Fisher, Hiram V, 331
Fisher, Hiram V, 446
Fisher, Hiram V, 620
Fisher, Hiram VI, 389
Fisher, Hiron I, 962
Fisher, Homer V, 672
Fisher, Horace V, 55
Fisher, Irene I, 780
Fisher, Irene I, 809
Fisher, Irene I, 815
Fisher, Irenia I, 809
Fisher, Isaac IV, 69
Fisher, Isaac IV, 81
Fisher, Isaac IV, 86
Fisher, Isaac IV, 92
Fisher, Isaac IV, 125
Fisher, Isaac IV, 624
Fisher, Isaac IV, 869
Fisher, Isaac V, 55
Fisher, Isaac V, 128
Fisher, Isaac V, 238
Fisher, Isaac V, 239
Fisher, Isaac V, 302
Fisher, Isaac V, 620
Fisher, Isaac V, 739
Fisher, Isaac, Sr. V, 739
Fisher, Jabez Maud II, 362
Fisher, Jabez Maud II, 524
Fisher, Jacob White VI, 1022
Fisher, James I, 962
Fisher, James I, 1077
Fisher, James I, 1093
Fisher, James II, 767
Fisher, James IV, 86
Fisher, James IV, 125
Fisher, James V, 55
Fisher, James V, 238
Fisher, James V, 239
Fisher, James V, 256
Fisher, James V, 331
Fisher, James V, 621
Fisher, James V, 672
Fisher, James V, 739
Fisher, James VI, 389
Fisher, James VI, 816
Fisher, James VI, 915
Fisher, James C. II, 524
Fisher, James H. IV, 1251
Fisher, James W. V, 491
Fisher, Jane I, 214
Fisher, Jane I, 962
Fisher, Jane I, 1093
Fisher, Jane V, 55
Fisher, Jane V, 238
Fisher, Jane V, 239
Fisher, Jane V, 256
Fisher, Jane V, 291
Fisher, Jane V, 331
Fisher, Jane V, 446
Fisher, Jane V, 620
Fisher, Jane V, 621
Fisher, Jane V, 633
Fisher, Jane VI, 389
Fisher, Jane Nancy V, 446
Fisher, Jemima V, 238
Fisher, Jemima V, 239
Fisher, Jemima V, 302
Fisher, Jemima V, 446
Fisher, Jemima V, 620
Fisher, Jemimah V, 620
Fisher, Jennie V, 331
Fisher, Jesse C. IV, 1278
Fisher, Joel IV, 85
Fisher, Joel IV, 146
Fisher, Joel IV, 471
Fisher, John I, 962
Fisher, John II, 362
Fisher, John II, 443
Fisher, John II, 473
Fisher, John II, 523
Fisher, John II, 550
Fisher, John II, 664
Fisher, John II, 959
Fisher, John II, 996
Fisher, John II, 1005
Fisher, John II, 1025
Fisher, John IV, 32
Fisher, John IV, 33
Fisher, John IV, 44
Fisher, John IV, 86
Fisher, John IV, 125
Fisher, John IV, 146
Fisher, John IV, 392
Fisher, John IV, 471
Fisher, John IV, 525
Fisher, John V, 55
Fisher, John V, 238
Fisher, John V, 239
Fisher, John V, 330
Fisher, John V, 446
Fisher, John V, 739
Fisher, John VI, 311
Fisher, John VI, 315
Fisher, John VI, 389
Fisher, John VI, 492
Fisher, John VI, 595
Fisher, John VI, 915
Fisher, John VI, 965
Fisher, John B. VI, 915
Fisher, John, Jr. II, 523
Fisher, John, Jr. V, 239
Fisher, John, Jr. V, 331
Fisher, John, Sr. V, 239
Fisher, John, Sr. V, 331
Fisher, Jonathan II, 362
Fisher, Jonathan IV, 624
Fisher, Jonathan V, 905
Fisher, Jos. VI, 311
Fisher, Joseph II, 362
Fisher, Joseph II, 443
Fisher, Joseph II, 532
Fisher, Joseph IV, 146
Fisher, Joseph IV, 329
Fisher, Joseph IV, 392
Fisher, Joseph IV, 405
Fisher, Joseph IV, 706
Fisher, Joseph IV, 716
Fisher, Joseph IV, 753
Fisher, Joseph IV, 869
Fisher, Joseph IV, 882
Fisher, Joseph V, 67
Fisher, Joseph V, 331
Fisher, Joseph VI, 311
Fisher, Joseph VI, 331
Fisher, Joseph VI, 352
Fisher, Joseph VI, 355
Fisher, Joseph VI, 389
Fisher, Joseph VI, 492
Fisher, Joseph Fawcett IV, 706
Fisher, Joseph Scarsborough IV, 624
Fisher, Joseph, Jr. IV, 624
Fisher, Joseph, Jr. VI, 304
Fisher, Joseph, Jr. VI, 311
Fisher, Joseph, Jr. VI, 352
Fisher, Joseph, Jr. VI, 492
Fisher, Joseph, Sr. VI, 311
Fisher, Josephine III, 121
Fisher, Josephine B. III, 369
Fisher, Joshua II, 362
Fisher, Joshua II, 523
Fisher, Joshua II, 584
Fisher, Joshua II, 631
Fisher, Joshua II, 794
Fisher, Joshua III, 121
Fisher, Joshua IV, 471
Fisher, Joshua V, 385
Fisher, Juleus I, 780
Fisher, Katherine II, 362
Fisher, Lamar W. II, 524
Fisher, Lamar W. II, 740
Fisher, Lamar W. III, 121
Fisher, Laura A. V, 385
Fisher, Letitia V, 55
Fisher, Letitia V, 64
Fisher, Letitia V, 107
Fisher, Lewis VI, 389
Fisher, Lina Ann V, 55
Fisher, Love II, 362
Fisher, Lucinda V, 905
Fisher, Lucinda VI, 311
Fisher, Lucinda VI, 816
Fisher, Lucy VI, 931
Fisher, Luranna V, 672
Fisher, Luranna V, 683
Fisher, Luranna A. V, 672
Fisher, Lydia I, 878
Fisher, Lydia I, 890
Fisher, Lydia II, 362
Fisher, Lydia II, 523
Fisher, Lydia II, 532
Fisher, Lydia IV, 32
Fisher, Lydia IV, 33
Fisher, Lydia IV, 39
Fisher, Lydia IV, 44
Fisher, Lydia V, 672
Fisher, Lydia Ann IV, 706
Fisher, Lydia Ann V, 55
Fisher, Lydia E. V, 331
Fisher, Lydia E. V, 672
Fisher, Maggie V, 995
Fisher, Malinda IV, 1159
Fisher, Margaret IV, 706
Fisher, Margaret IV, 753
Fisher, Margaret IV, 869
Fisher, Margaret IV, 882
Fisher, Margaret V, 238
Fisher, Margaret V, 239
Fisher, Margaret V, 247
Fisher, Margaret VI, 389
Fisher, Margery II, 443
Fisher, Margery II, 523
Fisher, Margery II, 589
Fisher, Margrett II, 362
Fisher, Maria I, 14
Fisher, Maria Wright I, 9
Fisher, Maria Wright I, 49
Fisher, Mariah I, 213
Fisher, Marietta IV, 624
Fisher, Martha I, 537
Fisher, Martha I, 539
Fisher, Martha I, 809
Fisher, Martha I, 814
Fisher, Martha V, 491

Fisher, Martha V, 620
Fisher, Martha VI, 102
Fisher, Martha VI, 103
Fisher, Martha VI, 107
Fisher, Martha VI, 389
Fisher, Martha VI, 401
Fisher, Martha VI, 816
Fisher, Martha VI, 915
Fisher, Mary I, 49
Fisher, Mary II, 362
Fisher, Mary II, 495
Fisher, Mary II, 523
Fisher, Mary II, 524
Fisher, Mary II, 527
Fisher, Mary II, 550
Fisher, Mary II, 588
Fisher, Mary II, 611
Fisher, Mary II, 794
Fisher, Mary II, 819
Fisher, Mary II, 959
Fisher, Mary II, 996
Fisher, Mary II, 1005
Fisher, Mary IV, 32
Fisher, Mary IV, 33
Fisher, Mary IV, 85
Fisher, Mary IV, 86
Fisher, Mary IV, 87
Fisher, Mary IV, 146
Fisher, Mary IV, 329
Fisher, Mary IV, 340
Fisher, Mary IV, 471
Fisher, Mary IV, 704
Fisher, Mary IV, 1278
Fisher, Mary IV, 1315
Fisher, Mary V, 55
Fisher, Mary V, 238
Fisher, Mary V, 239
Fisher, Mary V, 260
Fisher, Mary V, 331
Fisher, Mary V, 446
Fisher, Mary V, 620
Fisher, Mary V, 672
Fisher, Mary VI, 389
Fisher, Mary VI, 401
Fisher, Mary VI, 492
Fisher, Mary VI, 595
Fisher, Mary VI, 741
Fisher, Mary VI, 915
Fisher, Mary Amos V, 446
Fisher, Mary Ann III, 121
Fisher, Mary Ann V, 905
Fisher, Mary Ann VI, 311
Fisher, Mary Ann VI, 915
Fisher, Mary E. V, 331
Fisher, Mary Emma V, 385
Fisher, Mary Frances VI, 915
Fisher, Mary G. II, 362
Fisher, Mary G. II, 524
Fisher, Mary G. II, 740
Fisher, Mary G. II, 752
Fisher, Mary G. V, 55
Fisher, Mary Griffitts II, 524
Fisher, Mary J. V, 611
Fisher, Mary J. V, 620
Fisher, Mary Margaret VI, 915
Fisher, Mary R. IV, 705
Fisher, Mary R. IV, 706
Fisher, Mary Ruth V, 672
Fisher, Mary Ruth V, 720
Fisher, Mary T. V, 55
Fisher, Matilda V, 905
Fisher, Matilda VI, 311
Fisher, Matilda VI, 915
Fisher, Matthew VI, 915
Fisher, Maude J. IV, 471
Fisher, May IV, 1315
Fisher, Michael VI, 915
Fisher, Michael C. II, 69
Fisher, Michael C. II, 79
Fisher, Miers II, 362
Fisher, Miers II, 432
Fisher, Miers II, 524
Fisher, Miers II, 631
Fisher, Miers II, 740
Fisher, Miers III, 121
Fisher, Miers, Jr. II, 362
Fisher, Mildred VI, 834
Fisher, Mildred Ann VI, 949
Fisher, Millicent II, 362
Fisher, Milly VI, 808
Fisher, Milly VI, 915
Fisher, Nancy I, 797
Fisher, Nancy I, 809
Fisher, Nancy V, 238
Fisher, Nancy V, 239
Fisher, Nancy V, 705
Fisher, Nancy V, 995
Fisher, Nancy VI, 915
Fisher, Nancy T. V, 239
Fisher, Nancy T. V, 273
Fisher, Nathan V, 238
Fisher, Nicholas III, 121
Fisher, O. Clyde V, 672
Fisher, Oliver V, 672
Fisher, Ora IV, 1278
Fisher, Paul IV, 1251
Fisher, Penelope V, 239
Fisher, Penelope V, 255
Fisher, Permela I, 780
Fisher, Permelia I, 809
Fisher, Peter VI, 816
Fisher, Phebe III, 121
Fisher, Phebe IV, 201
Fisher, Phebe IV, 567
Fisher, Phebe IV, 578
Fisher, Phebe V, 385
Fisher, Phebe V, 419
Fisher, Phebe VI, 433
Fisher, Phebe J. V, 331
Fisher, Polly VI, 965
Fisher, Polly L. VI, 915
Fisher, Priscilla IV, 706
Fisher, Priscilla IV, 784
Fisher, Rachel II, 69
Fisher, Rachel II, 705
Fisher, Rachel II, 740
Fisher, Rachel IV, 32
Fisher, Rachel IV, 85
Fisher, Rachel IV, 146
Fisher, Rachel IV, 471
Fisher, Rachel IV, 492
Fisher, Rachel IV, 624
Fisher, Rachel IV, 706
Fisher, Rachel IV, 869
Fisher, Rachel V, 238
Fisher, Rachel V, 331
Fisher, Rachel VI, 311
Fisher, Rachel VI, 315
Fisher, Rachel VI, 389
Fisher, Rachel A. V, 331
Fisher, Rachel A. V, 905
Fisher, Rachel A. V, 912
Fisher, Raynette IV, 1315
Fisher, Rebecca II, 69
Fisher, Rebecca II, 79
Fisher, Rebecca II, 362
Fisher, Rebecca II, 524
Fisher, Rebecca II, 705
Fisher, Rebecca III, 121
Fisher, Rebecca IV, 32
Fisher, Rebecca IV, 37
Fisher, Rebecca IV, 392
Fisher, Rebecca IV, 429
Fisher, Rebecca IV, 525
Fisher, Rebecca V, 238
Fisher, Rebecca V, 239
Fisher, Rebecca V, 278
Fisher, Rebecca V, 302
Fisher, Rebecca V, 331
Fisher, Rebecca V, 385
Fisher, Rebecca V, 620
Fisher, Rebecca Cloud V, 561
Fisher, Rebecca W. II, 524
Fisher, Rebecca W. II, 740
Fisher, Rebeccah V, 446
Fisher, Rebeckah IV, 329
Fisher, Rebeckah IV, 392
Fisher, Rebeckah VI, 492
Fisher, Rebekah VI, 433
Fisher, Rebekah VI, 492
Fisher, Redwood II, 362
Fisher, Redwood II, 524
Fisher, Redwood II, 705
Fisher, Redwood II, 740
Fisher, Redwood III, 121
Fisher, Redwood VI, 638
Fisher, Rewood II, 362
Fisher, Rhoda I, 809
Fisher, Rhoda I, 878
Fisher, Rhoda I, 900
Fisher, Richard IV, 146
Fisher, Richard IV, 329
Fisher, Richard VI, 389
Fisher, Robert II, 959
Fisher, Robert IV, 624
Fisher, Robert VI, 311
Fisher, Robert VI, 389
Fisher, Robert VI, 492
Fisher, Rodah I, 912
Fisher, Russel Davis V, 491
Fisher, Ruth IV, 32
Fisher, Ruth IV, 85
Fisher, Ruth IV, 92
Fisher, Ruth IV, 146
Fisher, Ruth IV, 471
Fisher, Ruth IV, 624
Fisher, Ruth IV, 706
Fisher, Ruth IV, 762
Fisher, Ruth IV, 869
Fisher, Ruth IV, 953
Fisher, Ruth IV, 976
Fisher, Ruth V, 55
Fisher, Ruth V, 67
Fisher, Ruth V, 561
Fisher, Ruth V, 572
Fisher, Ruth V, 573
Fisher, Ruth A. V, 331
Fisher, Ruth A. V, 361
Fisher, Ruth Esther V, 672
Fisher, Ruth S. II, 740
Fisher, Samuel I, 539
Fisher, Samuel II, 221
Fisher, Samuel II, 237
Fisher, Samuel II, 362
Fisher, Samuel II, 523
Fisher, Samuel II, 863
Fisher, Samuel IV, 32
Fisher, Samuel IV, 85
Fisher, Samuel IV, 146
Fisher, Samuel IV, 525
Fisher, Samuel V, 239
Fisher, Samuel VI, 311
Fisher, Samuel VI, 319
Fisher, Samuel VI, 325
Fisher, Samuel VI, 389
Fisher, Samuel VI, 492
Fisher, Samuel B. II, 69
Fisher, Samuel B. II, 79
Fisher, Samuel B. VI, 915
Fisher, Samuel D. IV, 471
Fisher, Samuel Griffitts II, 524
Fisher, Samuel Rhoads II, 524
Fisher, Samuel Rowland II, 524
Fisher, Samuel Rowland II, 790
Fisher, Samuel Rowland II, 794
Fisher, Samuel Rowland II, 853
Fisher, Samuel Rowland II, 863
Fisher, Samuel W. II, 362
Fisher, Samuel W. II, 524
Fisher, Samuel W. II, 633
Fisher, Saphas I, 1093
Fisher, Sarah I, 9
Fisher, Sarah I, 14
Fisher, Sarah I, 49
Fisher, Sarah I, 128
Fisher, Sarah I, 213
Fisher, Sarah I, 247
Fisher, Sarah I, 539
Fisher, Sarah I, 570
Fisher, Sarah I, 962
Fisher, Sarah II, 221
Fisher, Sarah II, 237
Fisher, Sarah II, 362
Fisher, Sarah II, 443
Fisher, Sarah II, 523
Fisher, Sarah II, 524
Fisher, Sarah II, 584
Fisher, Sarah II, 631
Fisher, Sarah II, 633
Fisher, Sarah II, 664
Fisher, Sarah II, 740
Fisher, Sarah II, 764
Fisher, Sarah II, 767
Fisher, Sarah II, 790
Fisher, Sarah II, 794
Fisher, Sarah II, 853
Fisher, Sarah II, 863
Fisher, Sarah IV, 146
Fisher, Sarah IV, 392
Fisher, Sarah IV, 1057
Fisher, Sarah IV, 1098
Fisher, Sarah IV, 1251
Fisher, Sarah V, 126
Fisher, Sarah V, 805
Fisher, Sarah V, 808
Fisher, Sarah V, 905
Fisher, Sarah V, 912
Fisher, Sarah V, 995
Fisher, Sarah VI, 311
Fisher, Sarah VI, 331
Fisher, Sarah VI, 389
Fisher, Sarah VI, 430
Fisher, Sarah VI, 492
Fisher, Sarah VI, 595
Fisher, Sarah VI, 816
Fisher, Sarah Coleman II, 362
Fisher, Sarah E. IV, 1251
Fisher, Sarah F. V, 55
Fisher, Sarah Mitchell II, 819
Fisher, Sarah Moore I, 9
Fisher, Sarah Moore I, 49
Fisher, Sarah R. II, 524
Fisher, Sarah Redwood II, 806
Fisher, Sarah Redwood II, 812
Fisher, Sarah V. IV, 471
Fisher, Sarah W. II, 362
Fisher, Sidney V, 238
Fisher, Silvanus IV, 624
Fisher, Silvanus IV, 706
Fisher, Silvanus VI, 311
Fisher, Sina IV, 869
Fisher, Sina IV, 883
Fisher, Sinai V, 55
Fisher, Sucky VI, 915
Fisher, Susan III, 121
Fisher, Susan M. IV, 471
Fisher, Susanna I, 539
Fisher, Susanna I, 563
Fisher, Susanna IV, 471
Fisher, Susanna IV, 479
Fisher, Susanna V, 239
Fisher, Susanna Georganna I, 49
Fisher, Susannah V, 238
Fisher, Susannah V, 302
Fisher, Susannah V, 331
Fisher, Susannah V, 491
Fisher, Susannah V, 501
Fisher, Susannah V, 620
Fisher, Susannah V, 952
Fisher, Susannah V, 960
Fisher, Sussana Georganna I, 9
Fisher, Sylvannious VI, 311
Fisher, Sylvanus IV, 869
Fisher, Tabitha II, 361
Fisher, Tabitha II, 362
Fisher, Tabitha II, 523
Fisher, Tabitha II, 524
Fisher, Tabitha II, 564
Fisher, Telitha IV, 567
Fisher, Telitha IV, 578
Fisher, Thomas I, 962
Fisher, Thomas II, 361
Fisher, Thomas II, 362
Fisher, Thomas II, 493
Fisher, Thomas II, 523
Fisher, Thomas II, 584
Fisher, Thomas IV, 624
Fisher, Thomas IV, 882
Fisher, Thomas V, 55
Fisher, Thomas V, 238
Fisher, Thomas V, 239
Fisher, Thomas V, 331
Fisher, Thomas VI, 389
Fisher, Thomas VI, 492
Fisher, Thomas VI, 883
Fisher, Thomas VI, 889
Fisher, Thomas VI, 915
Fisher, Thomas VI, 949
Fisher, Thomas VI, 1018
Fisher, Thomas Dawson VI, 492
Fisher, Thomas J. VI, 915
Fisher, Thomas R. IV, 706
Fisher, Thomas Rawlings IV, 706
Fisher, Thomas Rawlings IV, 869
Fisher, Thomas Rollings IV, 869
Fisher, Thomas W. I, 49
Fisher, Thomas W. II, 740
Fisher, Thomas W. II, 764
Fisher, Thomas W. II, 767
Fisher, Thomas Wright I, 9
Fisher, Thomas Wright I, 49
Fisher, Thomas, Jr. VI, 389
Fisher, Thos. II, 794
Fisher, Thos. V, 331
Fisher, Thos. V, 905
Fisher, Thos. Elwood V, 905
Fisher, Thos. Jerome V, 995
Fisher, Unice V, 128
Fisher, Wager VI, 741
Fisher, Wager VI, 742
Fisher, Wager VI, 743
Fisher, Wd. Sarah II, 474
Fisher, Wd. Sarah II, 523
Fisher, William II, 221
Fisher, William II, 237
Fisher, William II, 361
Fisher, William II, 362
Fisher, William IV, 32
Fisher, William IV, 392
Fisher, William IV, 706
Fisher, William IV, 869
Fisher, William VI, 311
Fisher, William VI, 915
Fisher, William G. VI, 915
Fisher, William J. I, 49
Fisher, William Joseph I, 9
Fisher, William Joseph I, 49
Fisher, William Righter VI, 741
Fisher, William, Jr. II, 361
Fisher, William, Jr. VI, 311
Fisher, William, Sr. VI, 311
Fisher, Wm. II, 523
Fisher, Wm. II, 550
Fisher, Wm. II, 564
Fisher, Wm. II, 611
Fisher, Wm. II, 633
Fisher, Wm. IV, 624
Fisher, Wm. IV, 706
Fisher, Wm. IV, 762
Fisher, Wm. IV, 784
Fisher, Wm. IV, 1057
Fisher, Wm. IV, 1098
Fisher, Wm. H. V, 331
Fisher, Wm. Henry V, 672
Fisher, Wm. Redwood II, 524
Fisher, Wm. W. II, 524
Fishers, Mary II, 537
Fishers, Miers II, 537
Fishers, Redwood II, 537
Fishers, Sarah II, 537
Fishwater, George II, 362
Fishwater, Mary II, 362
Fisiold, William VI, 29
Fisk, Lida S. IV, 1159
Fisthler, Delia IV, 1315
Fistler, Anna IV, 1315
Fistler, Clara IV, 1315
Fistler, Delia IV, 1315
Fistler, Edward IV, 1315
Fistler, Edward A. IV, 1315
Fistler, Emma IV, 1315
Fistler, Frank IV, 815
Fistler, Franklin IV, 1315
Fistler, May IV, 815
Fitch, Agnes VI, 816
Fitch, Avis III, 382
Fitch, Avis L. III, 380
Fitch, Charles B. VI, 805
Fitch, Elma IV, 201
Fitch, Hezekiah III, 30
Fitch, Hezekiah III, 121
Fitch, Jane VI, 816
Fitch, John IV, 201
Fitch, John IV, 310
Fitch, Jos. III, 382
Fitch, Joseph III, 380
Fitch, Joseph III, 382
Fitch, Joseph III, 389
Fitch, Joseph, Jr. III, 380
Fitch, Mary III, 126
Fitch, Mary III, 380
Fitch, Mary IV, 201
Fitch, Polly VI, 854
Fitch, Sally VI, 836
Fitch, Samuel VI, 816
Fitch, Samuel VI, 836
Fitch, Sarah III, 30
Fitch, Sarah III, 121
Fitch, Thomas VI, 797
Fitch, Thomas VI, 816
Fitch, Thomas VI, 836
Fitchell, Virginia IV, 201
Fitchett, Anna IV, 201
Fitchett, George IV, 201
Fitchwater, Abraham II, 362
Fitchwater, Elizabeth II, 362
Fitchwater, George II, 362
Fitchwater, Mary II, 362
Fitchwater, Mary II, 996
Fitchwater, Thomas II, 362
Fitchwater, Thomas II, 996
Fitkins, Susie Noris IV, 1315
Fitler, Mary II, 838
Fitler, Mary II, 863
Fitler, Nathan Meyers II, 838
Fitler, Nathan Meyers II, 863
Fitpatrick, Elsie VI, 816
Fitpatrick, Hiram A. VI, 915
Fitpatrick, James VI, 816
Fitpatrick, Lucinda M. VI, 915
Fitspatrick, Eliza IV, 624
Fitspatrick, Eliza IV, 666
Fittro, Joseph V, 238
Fittro, Lawrence IV, 953
Fittro, Louis H. IV, 953
Fittro, Minerva V, 331
Fittro, Pearl Anna IV, 953
Fittro, Rosella IV, 953
Fitts Randolph, Edward IV, 624
Fitts Randolph, Richard IV, 625
Fitz Gerrald, Peter VI, 242
Fitz Randal, Mary II, 524
Fitz Randolf, Eliza III, 121
Fitz Randolph, ??? III, 121
Fitz Randolph, Abigail IV, 86
Fitz Randolph, Abraham IV, 32
Fitz Randolph, Anna IV, 32
Fitz Randolph, Anna IV, 68
Fitz Randolph, Caroline Eliza III, 121
Fitz Randolph, Caroline Eliza III, 152
Fitz Randolph, Dr. John Lindley III, 121
Fitz Randolph, Edmund III, 121
Fitz Randolph, Edward III, 121
Fitz Randolph, Edward IV, 32
Fitz Randolph, Edward IV, 624
Fitz Randolph, Edward IV, 625
Fitz Randolph, Edward IV, 869
Fitz Randolph, Eliza III, 121
Fitz Randolph, Eliza III, 152
Fitz Randolph, Elizabeth IV, 32
Fitz Randolph, Isaac IV, 32
Fitz Randolph, Israel IV, 32

Fitz Randolph, Israel IV, 86
Fitz Randolph, Jacob IV, 32
Fitz Randolph, James IV, 32
Fitz Randolph, James Cornwall III, 121
Fitz Randolph, James T. III, 410
Fitz Randolph, Joel IV, 32
Fitz Randolph, John L. III, 121
Fitz Randolph, John L. III, 152
Fitz Randolph, Jonah IV, 32
Fitz Randolph, Margaret IV, 32
Fitz Randolph, Margaret IV, 68
Fitz Randolph, Mary B. III, 410
Fitz Randolph, Phebe III, 121
Fitz Randolph, Phebe IV, 32
Fitz Randolph, Phebe IV, 39
Fitz Randolph, Richard IV, 32
Fitz Randolph, Richard IV, 624
Fitz Randolph, Richard IV, 625
Fitz Randolph, Robert III, 121
Fitz-Randolph, Jacob I, 49
Fitz-Randolph, James III, 397
Fitz-Randolph, Mary B. III, 397
Fitzgerald, Amelia III, 121
Fitzgerald, Amelia III, 286
Fitzgerald, Anna J. V, 739
Fitzgerald, Beatrice IV, 201
Fitzgerald, Caroline IV, 201
Fitzgerald, Charles H. IV, 201
Fitzgerald, Chas. IV, 201
Fitzgerald, Daniel III, 482
Fitzgerald, Donna V, 739
Fitzgerald, Donna M. V, 739
Fitzgerald, Dorcas IV, 283
Fitzgerald, Eliza IV, 283
Fitzgerald, Gerald III, 121
Fitzgerald, Gerald III, 286
Fitzgerald, Guy A. IV, 201
Fitzgerald, Herman H. IV, 201
Fitzgerald, Herman, Jr. IV, 201
Fitzgerald, James IV, 1315
Fitzgerald, Margaret III, 121
Fitzgerald, Margaret III, 286
Fitzgerald, Nathan IV, 283
Fitzgerald, Peter VI, 243
Fitzgerald, Sarah III, 482
Fitzgerald, William V, 739
Fitzgerrald, Peter VI, 243
Fitzhugh, Anne VI, 915
Fitzhugh, Hannah VI, 979
Fitzhugh, Nancy VI, 915
Fitzhugh, Peter VI, 915
Fitzhugh, Peter VI, 1000
Fitzhugh, Peter VI, 1019
Fitzhugh, Robert VI, 300
Fitzhugh, Robert VI, 882
Fitzhugh, Robert VI, 915
Fitzhugh, Robt. VI, 956
Fitzhugh, Robt. VI, 979
Fitzimmons, Lucy Gardner VI, 915
Fitzimmons, William VI, 915
Fitzpatrick, ??? III, 362
Fitzpatrick, Behethaline VI, 915
Fitzpatrick, Bessie III, 121
Fitzpatrick, Bessie III, 362
Fitzpatrick, Ellen V, 55
Fitzpatrick, Ellen V, 672
Fitzpatrick, Hiram A. VI, 915
Fitzpatrick, John VI, 915
Fitzpatrick, Lucinda M. VI, 915
Fitzpatrick, Nancy VI, 1008
Fitzpatrick, Thomas VI, 1008
Fitzrandolph, Caroline Eliza III, 262
Fitzrandolph, Edmund F. III, 262
Fitzrandolph, Edmund Kinsey II, 996
Fitzrandolph, Eliza III, 262
Fitzrandolph, Eliza F. III, 262
Fitzrandolph, Hannah S. F. III, 262
Fitzrandolph, Hannah Skinner III, 262
Fitzrandolph, Harriet Ann F. III, 262
Fitzrandolph, Harriet S. F. III, 262
Fitzrandolph, Hugh II, 362
Fitzrandolph, James III, 262
Fitzrandolph, James C. F. III, 262
Fitzrandolph, James F. III, 262
Fitzrandolph, Jane II, 996
Fitzrandolph, Jane II, 1007
Fitzrandolph, John III, 262
Fitzrandolph, John F. III, 262
Fitzrandolph, John L. III, 262
Fitzrandolph, John L. F. III, 262
Fitzrandolph, John R. F. III, 262
Fitzrandolph, John T. III, 262
Fitzrandolph, Joseph III, 262
Fitzrandolph, Joseph K. F. III, 262
Fitzrandolph, King III, 262
Fitzrandolph, Mary II, 362
Fitzrandolph, Mary III, 262
Fitzrandolph, Mary F. III, 262
Fitzrandolph, S. F. III, 262
Fitzrandolph, Samuel F. III, 262
Fitzrandolph, Sarah K. III, 262
Fitzrandolph, Sarah K. F. III, 262
Fitzrandolph, Sidney III, 262
Fitzrandolph, William W. F. III, 262
Fitzsimmons, Hannah IV, 324
Fitzsimmons, Lydia Ann IV, 324
Fitzsimmons, Lydia Ann IV, 329
Fitzsimmons, Mary VI, 915
Fitzsimmons, Stephen IV, 324
Fitzsimmons, Thomas VI, 915
Fitzwalter, Rebecca II, 524
Fitzwater, Deborah II, 489
Fitzwater, Deborah II, 524
Fitzwater, Elisabeth II, 524
Fitzwater, Elisabeth II, 555
Fitzwater, Elizabeth II, 612
Fitzwater, George II, 362
Fitzwater, George II, 491
Fitzwater, George II, 524
Fitzwater, George II, 537
Fitzwater, George II, 541
Fitzwater, George II, 602
Fitzwater, George II, 633
Fitzwater, Hannah II, 491
Fitzwater, Hannah II, 524
Fitzwater, Martha II, 524
Fitzwater, Martha II, 602
Fitzwater, Mary II, 524
Fitzwater, Mary II, 541
Fitzwater, Mary II, 633
Fitzwater, Rebecca II, 524
Fitzwater, Rebecca II, 550
Fitzwater, Rebecca II, 555
Fitzwater, Sarah II, 524
Fitzwater, Sarah II, 537
Fitzwater, Thomas II, 524
Fitzwater, Thomas II, 612
Fix, Martha V, 620
Fizer, Adam, Jr. VI, 876
Fizer, Ann VI, 908
Fizer, Charles B. VI, 915
Fizer, Daniel VI, 915
Fizer, Daniel VI, 991
Fizer, Elizabeth VI, 894
Fizer, Frances J. VI, 915
Fizer, George W. VI, 816
Fizer, Jacob VI, 915
Fizer, Jacob VI, 1018
Fizer, John VI, 894
Fizer, John VI, 908
Fizer, John VI, 915
Fizer, Lucy Ann G. VI, 816
Fizer, Lydia VI, 915
Fizer, Mary Jane VI, 1018
Fizer, Polly VI, 915
Fizer, William VI, 894
Fizer, William H. VI, 894
Fizer, Wilmoth VI, 915
Flack, James V, 561
Flack, Mary V, 561
Flack, Nancy V, 561
Flagg, Mary C. II, 863
Flagor, Albert IV, 201
Flagor, Margaret IV, 201
Flanagan, James VI, 918
Flanders, John V, 561
Flanders, John A. V, 672
Flandreau, Eleanor III, 121
Flandreau, Eleanor III, 242
Flandreau, Frances III, 121
Flandreau, Frances III, 242
Flandreau, Letitia III, 121
Flandreau, Nelson E. III, 242
Flandreau, Nelson Eugene III, 121
Flandreau, Nelson Eugene III, 321
Flannagan, Martha II, 863
Flanner, Abigail I, 214
Flanner, Abigail I, 539
Flanner, Abigail IV, 201
Flanner, Abigail IV, 202
Flanner, Abigail IV, 286
Flanner, Abigail IV, 392
Flanner, Abigail IV, 472
Flanner, Abigail IV, 499
Flanner, Ann IV, 295
Flanner, Ann U. IV, 201
Flanner, Ann U. IV, 202
Flanner, Anna IV, 201
Flanner, Anna IV, 815
Flanner, Anna E. IV, 815
Flanner, Annie E. IV, 202
Flanner, Casper Wister IV, 392
Flanner, Catharine IV, 201
Flanner, Catharine IV, 202
Flanner, Catharine IV, 392
Flanner, Catharine IV, 578
Flanner, Catherine Patterson IV, 450
Flanner, Charity IV, 175
Flanner, Charity IV, 201
Flanner, Charity IV, 243
Flanner, Charity B. IV, 201
Flanner, Charles IV, 201
Flanner, Charles IV, 202
Flanner, Dilwin IV, 201
Flanner, Eaton I, 544
Flanner, Eaton Hays IV, 201
Flanner, Eaton Haze I, 539
Flanner, Edmund IV, 201
Flanner, Edward IV, 201
Flanner, Henry IV, 201
Flanner, Henry IV, 202
Flanner, Jacob I, 214
Flanner, Jacob I, 239
Flanner, Jacob I, 539
Flanner, Jacob IV, 201
Flanner, Jacob IV, 243
Flanner, Jacob IV, 472
Flanner, Jacob B. IV, 201
Flanner, Jacob P. IV, 175
Flanner, Jacob P. IV, 201
Flanner, Jacob P. IV, 202
Flanner, Keziah IV, 385
Flanner, Keziah IV, 392
Flanner, Keziah IV, 407
Flanner, Luella IV, 201
Flanner, Luella IV, 202
Flanner, Mary IV, 201
Flanner, Mary IV, 243
Flanner, Mary Ann IV, 201
Flanner, Mary Ann IV, 202
Flanner, Mary Ann IV, 237
Flanner, Mary L. IV, 201
Flanner, Mary L. IV, 296
Flanner, Oliver IV, 201
Flanner, Oliver IV, 202
Flanner, Oliver IV, 237
Flanner, Penina IV, 201
Flanner, Peninah I, 214
Flanner, Peninah I, 539
Flanner, Peninah IV, 171
Flanner, Peninah IV, 201
Flanner, Peninah IV, 202
Flanner, Peninah IV, 251
Flanner, Peninah IV, 286
Flanner, Peninah IV, 297
Flanner, Peninah IV, 392
Flanner, Peninah IV, 472
Flanner, Peninah IV, 578
Flanner, Peninnah I, 230
Flanner, Peninnah I, 239
Flanner, Peninnah IV, 201
Flanner, Peninnah IV, 392
Flanner, Penninah IV, 202
Flanner, Phebe IV, 201
Flanner, Phenina I, 539
Flanner, Rebecca IV, 201
Flanner, Rebecca IV, 251
Flanner, Rebecca IV, 472
Flanner, Sarah IV, 171
Flanner, Sarah IV, 201
Flanner, Sarah IV, 472
Flanner, Sarah IV, 566
Flanner, Sarah IV, 572
Flanner, Sarah IV, 578
Flanner, Thomas I, 214
Flanner, Thomas I, 239
Flanner, Thomas I, 539
Flanner, Thomas IV, 201
Flanner, Thomas IV, 330
Flanner, Thomas IV, 392
Flanner, Thomas N. IV, 202
Flanner, Thomas W. IV, 392
Flanner, Trinity IV, 392
Flanner, William I, 214
Flanner, William I, 230
Flanner, William I, 239
Flanner, William I, 539
Flanner, William I, 544
Flanner, William IV, 201
Flanner, William IV, 202
Flanner, William IV, 392
Flanner, William IV, 472
Flanner, William IV, 578
Flanner, William, Jr. IV, 202
Flanner, Wm. IV, 171
Flanner, Wm. IV, 201
Flanner, Wm. IV, 220
Flanner, Wm. IV, 251
Flanner, Wm. IV, 286
Flanner, Wm. IV, 296
Flanner, Wm. IV, 392
Flanner, Wm. IV, 450
Flanner, Wm. IV, 578
Flanner, Wm. Bailey IV, 578
Flanner, Wm., Jr. IV, 201
Flansburgh, Catharine H. III, 121
Flansburgh, Catharine H. III, 363
Flansburgh, John H. III, 121
Flansburgh, John H. III, 363
Flansburgh, Maria III, 121
Flansburgh, Maria III, 363
Flascott, John II, 362
Flascott, Phebe II, 362
Flash, Alexander III, 121
Flash, Edward III, 121
Flash, Edward III, 284
Flash, Frances III, 121
Flash, Frances III, 284
Flash, Rachel III, 121
Flatter, Maggie V, 739
Flattery, Maggie V, 739
Flaud, Elizabeth I, 539
Flaud, Elizabeth I, 553
Flecher, Priscilla V, 55
Flecher, Sarah I, 306
Fleckles, Helen E. III, 410
Fleckles, Helen E. III, 420
Fleckles, Leopold Victor III, 410
Fleckles, Leopoldt Victor III, 420
Fleckles, Mary III, 410
Fleckles, Mary III, 420
Fleet, Abigail III, 482
Fleet, Elizabeth III, 401
Fleet, Elizabeth III, 410
Fleet, Jesse III, 482
Fleet, Jonathan G. III, 497
Fleet, Joseph III, 401
Fleet, Joseph III, 410
Fleet, Lydia III, 497
Fleet, Parret III, 482
Fleet, Susannah III, 401
Fleet, Susannah III, 410
Flemens, Rachel I, 986
Fleming, Abraham VI, 915
Fleming, Alse I, 986
Fleming, Ann II, 362
Fleming, Ann III, 120
Fleming, Ann III, 121
Fleming, Ann IV, 28
Fleming, Ann IV, 32
Fleming, Anne VI, 877
Fleming, Asenath I, 986
Fleming, Asenath I, 999
Fleming, Charles VI, 8
Fleming, Charles VI, 16
Fleming, Charles VI, 29
Fleming, Charles VI, 147
Fleming, Charles VI, 148
Fleming, Charles VI, 155
Fleming, Charles VI, 176
Fleming, Charles VI, 188
Fleming, Charles VI, 218
Fleming, Curles VI, 29
Fleming, Daniel I, 1075
Fleming, David I, 975
Fleming, David I, 986
Fleming, David VI, 816
Fleming, David VI, 977
Fleming, Elizabeth I, 1075
Fleming, Elizabeth VI, 176
Fleming, Elizabeth VI, 188
Fleming, Elizabeth VI, 816
Fleming, Elizabeth VI, 915
Fleming, Elizabeth VI, 977
Fleming, Esther II, 816
Fleming, Fanny VI, 915
Fleming, Frank IV, 1159
Fleming, George W. IV, 1278
Fleming, Grace VI, 155
Fleming, Grace VI, 176
Fleming, Gussie IV, 1192
Fleming, Hannah VI, 209
Fleming, Hannah VI, 210
Fleming, Harper IV, 1192
Fleming, Ida Underwood IV, 1159
Fleming, James III, 121
Fleming, James Howard VI, 176
Fleming, Jane Alice I, 986
Fleming, Janet VI, 816
Fleming, Jean I, 1075
Fleming, Jennie IV, 1251
Fleming, Jesse I, 986
Fleming, John I, 1075
Fleming, John V, 170
Fleming, John V, 491
Fleming, John VI, 816
Fleming, John D. V, 491
Fleming, John D. V, 672
Fleming, Joseph IV, 1251
Fleming, Joseph VI, 915
Fleming, Joseph H. IV, 1251
Fleming, Josephine IV, 1251
Fleming, Lena IV, 1251
Fleming, Lena M. IV, 1251
Fleming, Margaret I, 986
Fleming, Margaret II, 362
Fleming, Martha I, 1075
Fleming, Mary I, 986
Fleming, Mary IV, 1251
Fleming, Mary V, 491
Fleming, Mary VI, 816
Fleming, Mary B. V, 491
Fleming, Mary Dena V, 170
Fleming, Mary Dena V, 491
Fleming, May V, 170
Fleming, Mrs. James IV, 1251
Fleming, Mrs. Joseph IV, 1251
Fleming, Mrs. Myrtle IV, 1315
Fleming, Nancy VI, 803
Fleming, Nancy VI, 915
Fleming, Nellie V, 491
Fleming, Priscilla IV, 688
Fleming, Priscilla IV, 706
Fleming, Rachel I, 986
Fleming, Rebecca II, 483
Fleming, Rebecca II, 524
Fleming, Robert II, 362
Fleming, Ruth VI, 640
Fleming, Sampson I, 986
Fleming, Samuel IV, 1251
Fleming, Samuel VI, 803
Fleming, Samuel VI, 864
Fleming, Samuel VI, 915
Fleming, Sarah I, 1075
Fleming, Sarah III, 120
Fleming, Sarah III, 121
Fleming, Sarah III, 152
Fleming, Sarah VI, 148
Fleming, Sarah C. I, 986
Fleming, Stanley IV, 688
Fleming, Stanley IV, 706
Fleming, Susannah I, 986
Fleming, Susannah VI, 155
Fleming, Susannah VI, 176
Fleming, Susannah VI, 188
Fleming, Susannah, Jr. VI, 155
Fleming, Susannah, Jr. VI, 176
Fleming, Tarlton VI, 176
Fleming, Thomas I, 1075
Fleming, Thomas III, 120
Fleming, Thomas III, 121
Fleming, Thomas III, 152
Fleming, Urselah VI, 176
Fleming, Urselah VI, 218
Fleming, Urselah VI, 219
Fleming, Uselah VI, 176
Fleming, Viola IV, 1251
Fleming, William II, 362
Flemings, Jesse I, 986
Flemings, Margaret I, 986
Flemings, Mary B. V, 491
Flemings, Sampson I, 986
Flemings, Sampson I, 993
Flemings, Sarah C. I, 986
Flemings, Sarah C. I, 993
Flemings, Susannah I, 986
Flemings, Susannah I, 998
Flemmen, Alse I, 986
Flemmen, Rachel I, 986
Flemmen, Susannah I, 986
Flemmin, David I, 986
Flemming, Abigail V, 995
Flemming, Ann II, 362
Flemming, Chas. V, 996
Flemming, Dinah VI, 638
Flemming, Dinah VI, 639
Flemming, Donald V, 995
Flemming, Jennie IV, 1251
Flemming, John V, 170
Flemming, John D. V, 170
Flemming, Joseph H. IV, 1251
Flemming, Josephine IV, 1251
Flemming, Lester Dail V, 995
Flemming, Mary IV, 1251
Flemming, Mary Dena V, 170
Flemming, May V, 170
Flemming, Morris V, 995
Flemming, Mrs. James IV, 1251
Flemming, Mrs. Myrtle IV, 1315
Flemming, Nancy IV, 202
Flemming, Nancy IV, 206
Flemming, Nellie V, 491
Flemming, Robert II, 362
Flemming, Ruth VI, 638
Flemming, Thos. V, 995
Flemming, Thos. J. V, 995
Flemming, Viola IV, 1251
Flemming, William II, 362

Flemmings, Mary I, 986
Flemmings, Sarah II, 984
Flemmings, Sarah II, 996
Flemons, Rachel I, 982
Flenner, Nellie VI, 741
Flenner, Nellie VI, 762
Fleshley, Clara Kaiser IV, 706
Fleshman, Abraham VI, 816
Fleshman, Abraham VI, 842
Fleshman, Elnore VI, 816
Fleshman, H. S. VI, 842
Fleshman, Mary E. VI, 842
Fletcher, ??? III, 299
Fletcher, Achsah I, 288
Fletcher, Albert E. VI, 623
Fletcher, Albert E. VI, 638
Fletcher, Albert W. III, 121
Fletcher, Alfred P. III, 121
Fletcher, Alfred P. III, 257
Fletcher, Althea III, 121
Fletcher, Althea III, 257
Fletcher, Anna III, 122
Fletcher, Anna E. V, 905
Fletcher, Anna H. III, 121
Fletcher, Anna H. III, 122
Fletcher, Annah H. III, 118
Fletcher, Axey I, 301
Fletcher, Axey I, 306
Fletcher, Benj. V, 905
Fletcher, Bessie I, 941
Fletcher, Bessie F. I, 921
Fletcher, Bessie Luzana I, 925
Fletcher, Betsey I, 214
Fletcher, Betsey I, 306
Fletcher, Betsey I, 315
Fletcher, Betty I, 288
Fletcher, Charlotte III, 263
Fletcher, Chas. II, 798
Fletcher, Daniel II, 705
Fletcher, Daniel II, 740
Fletcher, E. B. V, 170
Fletcher, Edw. C. III, 121
Fletcher, Edward I, 921
Fletcher, Edward I, 925
Fletcher, Elizabeth II, 362
Fletcher, Elizabeth II, 798
Fletcher, Elizabeth IV, 1251
Fletcher, Elizabeth V, 996
Fletcher, Enoch Yardley II, 996
Fletcher, Exum I, 288
Fletcher, Francis IV, 1235
Fletcher, Geo. IV, 1315
Fletcher, George IV, 1315
Fletcher, George V, 170
Fletcher, Hannah II, 794
Fletcher, Hannah II, 863
Fletcher, Hannah Mary VI, 623
Fletcher, Hannah Mary VI, 638
Fletcher, Harriet VI, 638
Fletcher, Harriett VI, 623
Fletcher, Helen V, 170
Fletcher, Henry IV, 706
Fletcher, Henry V, 52
Fletcher, Henry V, 55
Fletcher, Henry V, 168
Fletcher, Henry V, 170
Fletcher, Howard S. III, 118
Fletcher, Howard S. III, 121
Fletcher, Howard S. III, 122
Fletcher, Howard Stetson, Jr. III, 122
Fletcher, Ida I, 921
Fletcher, Ida I, 925
Fletcher, Jane I, 49
Fletcher, Jane I, 56
Fletcher, Jane I Sup 1, 4
Fletcher, Jesse I, 49
Fletcher, John I, 214
Fletcher, John I, 288
Fletcher, John II, 362
Fletcher, John II, 740
Fletcher, John II, 764
Fletcher, John II, 969
Fletcher, John V, 55
Fletcher, John V, 170
Fletcher, John S. II, 740
Fletcher, John Wm. V, 170
Fletcher, Joseph IV, 1251
Fletcher, Joseph V, 996
Fletcher, Joseph Kirkbride, Jr. II, 996
Fletcher, Joseph W. IV, 1251
Fletcher, Joshua I, 49
Fletcher, Joshua I, 76
Fletcher, Joshua I, 180
Fletcher, Joshua I, 193
Fletcher, Joshua I, 214
Fletcher, Joshua I, 239
Fletcher, Joshua I, 288
Fletcher, Katharine III, 121
Fletcher, Katharine III, 257
Fletcher, Londa III, 122
Fletcher, Londa III, 299
Fletcher, Louise II, 810
Fletcher, Lydia R. C. III, 122
Fletcher, Margaret I, 49
Fletcher, Margaret I, 76
Fletcher, Margaret I, 80
Fletcher, Margaret I, 123
Fletcher, Margaret I, 189
Fletcher, Margaret I, 193
Fletcher, Margaretta B. II, 740
Fletcher, Margret I, 49
Fletcher, Mary I, 49
Fletcher, Mary I, 70
Fletcher, Mary I, 214
Fletcher, Mary I, 288
Fletcher, Mary I, 306
Fletcher, Mary I, 319
Fletcher, Mary II, 740
Fletcher, Mary II, 996
Fletcher, Mary II, 1041
Fletcher, Mary VI, 862
Fletcher, Mary Ann II, 118
Fletcher, Mary Ann II, 119
Fletcher, Mary Ann V, 239
Fletcher, Mary Ann V, 905
Fletcher, Mary Ann V, 908
Fletcher, Mary Chenoweth V, 170
Fletcher, Mary F. II, 740
Fletcher, Mary F. II, 775
Fletcher, Mary Sophia II, 804
Fletcher, May V, 170
Fletcher, Minnie IV, 706
Fletcher, Miriam I, 49
Fletcher, Miriam I, 68
Fletcher, Mordecai H. V, 905
Fletcher, Mordecai H. V, 926
Fletcher, Nancy V, 302
Fletcher, Nancy V, 307
Fletcher, Nancy V, 331
Fletcher, Phebe II, 740
Fletcher, Phebe II, 764
Fletcher, Phebe II, 960
Fletcher, Phebe B. II, 969
Fletcher, Phebe H. II, 740
Fletcher, Phebe H. II, 969
Fletcher, Priscilla I, 306
Fletcher, Priscilla I, 315
Fletcher, Priscilla V, 55
Fletcher, Priscilla V, 299
Fletcher, Priscilla V, 302
Fletcher, Prissilla I, 214
Fletcher, Rachel II, 705
Fletcher, Rachel II, 740
Fletcher, Rachel V, 52
Fletcher, Rachel V, 55
Fletcher, Rachel V, 168
Fletcher, Rachel V, 170
Fletcher, Ralph I, 9
Fletcher, Ralph I, 49
Fletcher, Ralph I, 62
Fletcher, Ralph I, 214
Fletcher, Ralph I, 288
Fletcher, Ralph I, 306
Fletcher, Ralph I, 308
Fletcher, Ralph I Sup 1, 4
Fletcher, Raymond V, 170
Fletcher, Raymond Kennedy V, 170
Fletcher, Rebecca V, 302
Fletcher, Rebecca V, 309
Fletcher, Robert II, 959
Fletcher, Robert II, 996
Fletcher, Robert II, 1007
Fletcher, Robert V, 905
Fletcher, Ruth I, 49
Fletcher, Ruth I, 87
Fletcher, Ruth I, 126
Fletcher, Ruth III, 121
Fletcher, Sally I, 288
Fletcher, Sarah I, 62
Fletcher, Sarah I, 193
Fletcher, Sarah I, 198
Fletcher, Sarah I, 206
Fletcher, Sarah I, 239
Fletcher, Sarah I, 288
Fletcher, Sarah I, 306
Fletcher, Sarah I, 308
Fletcher, Sarah V, 55
Fletcher, Sarah V, 317
Fletcher, Sarah V, 331
Fletcher, Sarah M. V, 239
Fletcher, Sarah, Jr. II, 996
Fletcher, Sarah, Jr. II, 1007
Fletcher, Tabitha VI, 856
Fletcher, Thomas III, 122
Fletcher, Thomas VI, 856
Fletcher, Widow Margaret I, 193
Fletcher, Widow Miriam I, 49
Fletcher, William I, 193
Fletcher, William II, 362
Fletcher, Wm. IV, 1235
Fletcher, Wm. VI, 623
Fletcher, Wm. VI, 638
Fletcher, Zachariah I, 193
Fletncher, Phebe H. II, 764
Flewellin, Albert III, 147
Flewellin, Albert III, 373
Flewellin, Geo. III, 373
Flewellin, Mary III, 373
Flewellin, Sarah Jane III, 147
Flewellin, Sarah Jane III, 373
Flexney, Daniel, Jr. II, 524
Flickinger, Louisa IV, 1018
Flin, Elizabeth VI, 916
Flin, Thomas VI, 916
Fling, Abigail II, 524
Fling, Abigail II, 562
Fling, Bennett II, 362
Fling, Bennett II, 524
Fling, David II, 524
Fling, David II, 562
Fling, Henry II, 362
Fling, Henry II, 740
Fling, John II, 362
Fling, John II, 524
Fling, John II, 536
Fling, John II, 546
Fling, John II, 562
Fling, Mary II, 362
Fling, Sally Ann II, 524
Fling, Sally Ann II, 536
Fling, Sarah Ann II, 362
Fling, Susanna II, 362
Fling, Susanna II, 524
Fling, Susanna II, 536
Fling, Susanna II, 546
Fling, Susanna II, 705
Fling, Susanna II, 740
Fling, Susanna H. II, 362
Fling, Susanna, Jr. II, 524
Fling, Susanna, Jr. II, 546
Fling, Susannah II, 524
Fling, Susannah II, 562
Fling, Susannah H. II, 794
Fling, Susannah H. II, 863
Fling, William II, 794
Fling, William B. II, 362
Fling, Wm. II, 863
Fling, Wm. B. II, 524
Fling, Wm. B. II, 546
Fling, Wm. B. II, 705
Fling, Wm. B. II, 740
Fling, Wm. B. II, 794
Fling, Wm. B. II, 863
Flink, Alice I, 625
Flink, Marion C. I, 625
Flink, Myrtle I, 625
Flinn, Sarah II, 524
Flinn, Sarah II, 672
Flinton, Sarah II, 221
Flippin, James M. I, 878
Flipping, Kitty Ann VI, 927
Flitcher, Jane I, 49
Flitcher, Jane I, 74
Flitcher, Jesse I, 49
Flitcher, Joshua I, 49
Flitcher, Joshua I, 239
Flitcher, Margaret I, 49
Flitcher, Margaret I, 79
Flitcher, Margaret I, 193
Flitcher, Margret I, 49
Flitcher, Miriam I, 49
Flitcher, Phebe H. II, 1050
Flitcher, Phebe H. II, 1059
Flitcher, Ralph I, 49
Flitcher, Ralph I, 68
Flitcher, Widow Miriam I, 49
Flitcher, Widow Miriam I, 68
Flitcher, Zachariah I, 193
Flitcraft, Allen II, 118
Flitcraft, Allen II, 863
Flitcraft, Alvanetha II, 863
Flitcraft, Alvanetha II, 920
Flitcraft, Ann II, 116
Flitcraft, Ann II, 118
Flitcraft, Clement B. III, 410
Flitcraft, Eliza Ann V, 882
Flitcraft, Ella II, 919
Flitcraft, Ella II, 920
Flitcraft, George II, 118
Flitcraft, Helen III, 409
Flitcraft, Helen III, 410
Flitcraft, Isaac II, 118
Flitcraft, Isaiah II, 863
Flitcraft, Isaiah V, 882
Flitcraft, Isaiah, Jr. II, 118
Flitcraft, Luella W. III, 410
Flitcraft, Mary II, 118
Flitcraft, Mary Ann II, 115
Flitcraft, Mary Ann II, 118
Flitcraft, Mary Ann V, 882
Flitcraft, Mary Ann V, 886
Flitcraft, Pembrook V, 882
Flitcraft, Prudence II, 118
Flitcraft, Ruth II, 115
Flitcraft, Ruth II, 118
Flitcraft, Stanley G. III, 409
Flitcraft, Stanley G. III, 410
Flood, Elisha VI, 816
Flood, Joel W. VI, 816
Flood, Joseph VI, 891
Flood, Joseph VI, 916
Flood, Joseph VI, 944
Flood, Joseph VI, 968
Flood, Joseph VI, 979
Flood, Joseph VI, 1003
Flood, Joseph VI, 1017
Flooi, Ina V, 170
Flora, Mary E. V, 672
Florence, ??? S. II, 875
Florence, Mary I, 56
Flota, Katy V, 620
Flota, Louisa Peebles V, 620
Flota, Wm. V, 620
Flouke, Martha S. VI, 848
Flounders, Edward II, 524
Flour, Essex II, 362
Flourney, Albert VI, 721
Flourney, Florence Inez VI, 721
Flourney, James, Sr. VI, 1002
Flournoy, Ann VI, 816
Flournoy, David VI, 816
Flournoy, Florence III, 122
Flournoy, Florence III, 361
Flournoy, James VI, 916
Flournoy, James VI, 1022
Flournoy, John Herbert III, 122
Flournoy, John Herbert III, 361
Flournoy, Laura III, 122
Flournoy, Lucinda VI, 1002
Flournoy, Nathaniel III, 122
Flournoy, Peggy VI, 916
Flournoy, Polly VI, 1022
Flower, Ann II, 525
Flower, Ann II, 567
Flower, Benjamin II, 362
Flower, Caleb II, 362
Flower, Charles II, 362
Flower, Daniel II, 362
Flower, Daniel II, 523
Flower, Daniel II, 525
Flower, Daniell II, 362
Flower, Elizabeth II, 362
Flower, Elizabeth II, 443
Flower, Elizabeth II, 525
Flower, Elizabeth II, 569
Flower, Elizabeth II, 591
Flower, Enoch II, 362
Flower, Enoch II, 525
Flower, Enoch II, 567
Flower, Enoch, Jr. II, 362
Flower, Essex II, 362
Flower, Essex II, 525
Flower, Esther II, 443
Flower, Fincher II, 362
Flower, Henry II, 362
Flower, Henry II, 443
Flower, Henry, Jr. II, 443
Flower, Hester II, 443
Flower, Joanna II, 362
Flower, John II, 362
Flower, John II, 443
Flower, Joseph II, 362
Flower, Mary II, 362
Flower, Mary II, 443
Flower, Mary II, 497
Flower, Mary II, 525
Flower, Mary II, 538
Flower, Mary VI, 389
Flower, Mary VI, 638
Flower, Mary Jones II, 525
Flower, Phebe IV, 32
Flower, Phebe IV, 37
Flower, Samuel II, 362
Flower, Samuel II, 525
Flower, Sarah II, 362
Flower, Sarah II, 523
Flower, Sarah II, 525
Flower, Seth II, 443
Flower, Thomas II, 362
Flower, Thomas II, 443
Flower, Wd. Ann II, 362
Flowers, Ann II, 443
Flowers, Canby II, 959
Flowers, Charles VI, 816
Flowers, Eleanor VI, 797
Flowers, Elizabeth II, 443
Flowers, Elizabeth II, 1073
Flowers, Elizabeth II, 1077
Flowers, Elizabeth VI, 856
Flowers, Franklin P. II, 863
Flowers, Henry II, 443
Flowers, Jane V, 620
Flowers, John VI, 816
Flowers, Joseph II, 1050
Flowers, Lenis VI, 816
Flowers, Lockey L. VI, 799
Flowers, Louisa VI, 816
Flowers, Mary VI, 367
Flowers, Mary VI, 389
Flowers, Mary VI, 816
Flowers, Milly VI, 816
Flowers, Nancy VI, 909
Flowers, Nasmis VI, 817
Flowers, Polly K. VI, 821
Flowers, Robin VI, 856
Flowers, Samuel VI, 816
Flowers, Samuel VI, 909
Flowers, Sarah M. II, 959
Flowers, Sarah M. II, 996
Flowers, Sarah M. II, 1038
Flowers, Sarah M. II, 1050
Flowers, Turza H. VI, 797
Flowers, Valentine VI, 817
Flowers, William VI, 797
Flowers, William VI, 799
Flowers, William VI, 816
Flowers, William VI, 821
Flowers, Wm. P. II, 148
Flowery, Ann II, 362
Floyd, Adelaide III, 360
Floyd, Adelaide O. III, 122
Floyd, Ann I, 497
Floyd, Ann I, 539
Floyd, Ann I, 553
Floyd, Ann Jessop I, 539
Floyd, Biddy VI, 916
Floyd, Biddy VI, 985
Floyd, Caleb VI, 492
Floyd, Daniel W. VI, 916
Floyd, Daniel W. VI, 985
Floyd, Elizabeth I, 497
Floyd, Elizabeth I, 509
Floyd, Elizabeth I, 539
Floyd, Elizabeth I, 550
Floyd, Elizabeth I, 553
Floyd, Elizabeth VI, 916
Floyd, Fanny VI, 982
Floyd, Francis II, 525
Floyd, Helen V, 672
Floyd, James VI, 916
Floyd, John I, 497
Floyd, John I, 509
Floyd, John I, 539
Floyd, Joseph V, 620
Floyd, Nancy VI, 915
Floyd, Nathaniel VI, 916
Floyd, Polly VI, 826
Floyd, Polly T. VI, 916
Floyd, Robert Wentworth III, 122
Floyd, Robert Wentworth III, 360
Floyd, Widow Ann I, 509
Floyd, William VI, 826
Floyd, William VI, 915
Floyd, Wm. VI, 982
Fluharty, Harry A. I, 617
Fluharty, Harry A. I, 633
Fluharty, Hazel I, 633
Fluharty, Robert Hazel I, 617
Fluke, Elizabeth I, 1029
Fluke, Elizabeth I, 1033
Flushing, Ann III, 41
Flynn, C. Washington VI, 816
Flynn, John M. P. VI, 817
Flynn, Martha E. VI, 816
Flynn, Maurice III, 122
Flynn, Maurice III, 254
Flynn, Sarah A. V, 331
Flynn, Selina A. III, 122
Flynn, Selina A. III, 254
Foalden, James VI, 916
Foalden, Jesse Y. VI, 916
Foalden, Polly VI, 916
Foalding, Nancy VI, 1002
Fockler, Susan V, 996
Foddrea, James I, 270
Foddrea, Melinda I, 270
Foddrea, William I, 270
Fodera, James I, 270
Fodra, William I, 270
Fodry, Melinda I, 270
Fodry, William I, 270
Fofer, Jas. M. VI, 1005
Fog, Elizabeth H. II, 525
Fog, Elizabeth H. II, 740
Fog, Samuel II, 740
Fog, Sarah IV, 707
Fogg, ??? IV, 953
Fogg, Aaron II, 28
Fogg, Aaron II, 35
Fogg, Aaron II, 50
Fogg, Aaron II, 70
Fogg, Aaron II, 90

Fogg, Aaron II, 131
Fogg, Aaron II, 135
Fogg, Aaron II, 136
Fogg, Aaron II, 794
Fogg, Aaron II, 810
Fogg, Aaron II, 863
Fogg, Aaron II, 900
Fogg, Aaron II, 910
Fogg, Aaron IV, 706
Fogg, Aaron IV, 707
Fogg, Aaron IV, 953
Fogg, Aaron A. II, 131
Fogg, Aaron A. II, 148
Fogg, Aaron L. II, 863
Fogg, Aaron L. II, 900
Fogg, Aaron, Jr. II, 28
Fogg, Adna IV, 707
Fogg, Adna IV, 922
Fogg, Adna IV, 953
Fogg, Adna S. IV, 202
Fogg, Adna S. IV, 275
Fogg, Adnah II, 118
Fogg, Adnah IV, 953
Fogg, Albert II, 863
Fogg, Albert II, 926
Fogg, Albert IV, 953
Fogg, Albert IV, 954
Fogg, Ann II, 28
Fogg, Ann II, 68
Fogg, Ann II, 69
Fogg, Ann II, 70
Fogg, Ann II, 131
Fogg, Ann II, 134
Fogg, Ann II, 794
Fogg, Ann III, 23
Fogg, Ann Elizabeth II, 131
Fogg, Anna II, 131
Fogg, Anna II, 133
Fogg, Anna II, 148
Fogg, Anna IV, 953
Fogg, Anna Amelia II, 794
Fogg, Anna Frances II, 131
Fogg, Anna M. IV, 948
Fogg, Anna M. IV, 953
Fogg, Anna S. II, 148
Fogg, Anna Ware II, 148
Fogg, Aron II, 70
Fogg, Aron II, 89
Fogg, Aron IV, 707
Fogg, Beulah IV, 757
Fogg, Beulah IV, 805
Fogg, Beulah IV, 813
Fogg, Beulah IV, 934
Fogg, Beulah IV, 949
Fogg, Beulah IV, 953
Fogg, Beulah IV, 960
Fogg, Blanche II, 863
Fogg, Blanche II, 926
Fogg, Bula IV, 805
Fogg, Bula IV, 815
Fogg, Carl Sayre II, 131
Fogg, Caroline M. II, 131
Fogg, Caroline Miller II, 131
Fogg, Carrie II, 148
Fogg, Catharine II, 131
Fogg, Catharine II, 525
Fogg, Catharine II, 544
Fogg, Charles II, 28
Fogg, Charles II, 42
Fogg, Charles II, 52
Fogg, Charles II, 70
Fogg, Charles II, 118
Fogg, Charles IV, 275
Fogg, Charles IV, 707
Fogg, Charles IV, 953
Fogg, Charles, Jr. II, 69
Fogg, Chas. II, 28
Fogg, Chas. II, 69
Fogg, Chas. II, 87
Fogg, Chas. II, 99
Fogg, Chas. IV, 202
Fogg, Clara IV, 954
Fogg, Clara D. IV, 953
Fogg, Clarkson II, 794
Fogg, Clarkson II, 863
Fogg, Comly IV, 953
Fogg, Daniel II, 28
Fogg, David II, 28
Fogg, David II, 57
Fogg, David II, 70
Fogg, David II, 131
Fogg, David II, 148
Fogg, David IV, 953
Fogg, David S. II, 131
Fogg, David S. II, 148
Fogg, David Tyler II, 131
Fogg, David Tyler II, 148
Fogg, Deborah Wood II, 794
Fogg, Drusilla IV, 950
Fogg, Drusilla IV, 953
Fogg, Druzilla IV, 953
Fogg, E. Wood II, 863
Fogg, Ebeneazer IV, 953
Fogg, Ebeneezer IV, 816
Fogg, Ebeneezer IV, 953
Fogg, Ebeneezer F. IV, 953
Fogg, Ebenezer II, 28
Fogg, Ebenezer IV, 707
Fogg, Ebenezer W. II, 863
Fogg, Ebenezer W. VI, 741
Fogg, Edgar IV, 953
Fogg, Edmin IV, 805
Fogg, Edmin IV, 946
Fogg, Edmin IV, 953
Fogg, Edmund IV, 707
Fogg, Edmund IV, 953
Fogg, Edward II, 131
Fogg, Edward B. IV, 953
Fogg, Edward T. II, 131
Fogg, Edward T., Jr. II, 131
Fogg, Edwin IV, 707
Fogg, Edwin IV, 813
Fogg, Edwin IV, 950
Fogg, Edwin IV, 953
Fogg, Edwin Edmund II, 118
Fogg, Eleazer IV, 953
Fogg, Elijah II, 28
Fogg, Elisha II, 28
Fogg, Elisha II, 70
Fogg, Elisha II, 794
Fogg, Elisha II, 863
Fogg, Elisha IV, 706
Fogg, Elisha IV, 707
Fogg, Elisha IV, 953
Fogg, Eliza A. IV, 805
Fogg, Eliza Ann IV, 813
Fogg, Eliza Ann IV, 946
Fogg, Eliza Ann IV, 953
Fogg, Eliza Mary IV, 1251
Fogg, Elizabeth II, 28
Fogg, Elizabeth II, 52
Fogg, Elizabeth II, 69
Fogg, Elizabeth II, 70
Fogg, Elizabeth II, 79
Fogg, Elizabeth II, 82
Fogg, Elizabeth II, 102
Fogg, Elizabeth II, 103
Fogg, Elizabeth II, 109
Fogg, Elizabeth II, 138
Fogg, Elizabeth IV, 922
Fogg, Elizabeth IV, 953
Fogg, Elizabeth V, 905
Fogg, Elizabeth H. II, 131
Fogg, Elizabeth H. II, 148
Fogg, Elizabeth H. II, 525
Fogg, Elizabeth Lippincott II, 148
Fogg, Elizabeth Lippincott II, 154
Fogg, Elizabeth Nelson II, 131
Fogg, Elizabeth Nelson II, 148
Fogg, Elizabeth P. II, 148
Fogg, Elizabeth T. II, 318
Fogg, Elizabeth W. II, 133
Fogg, Ellen II, 967
Fogg, Ellen IV, 949
Fogg, Ellen IV, 953
Fogg, Ellen Glover II, 794
Fogg, Elma IV, 953
Fogg, Elmor W. IV, 953
Fogg, Emeline L. II, 863
Fogg, Emily IV, 202
Fogg, Emily IV, 953
Fogg, Emmaline L. II, 900
Fogg, Emmaline Louisa II, 810
Fogg, Erma IV, 954
Fogg, Erma D. IV, 953
Fogg, Esther IV, 202
Fogg, Esther IV, 275
Fogg, Esther F. IV, 202
Fogg, H. Norman II, 131
Fogg, Hanna IV, 953
Fogg, Hannah II, 28
Fogg, Hannah II, 35
Fogg, Hannah II, 42
Fogg, Hannah II, 50
Fogg, Hannah II, 57
Fogg, Hannah II, 69
Fogg, Hannah II, 70
Fogg, Hannah II, 76
Fogg, Hannah II, 87
Fogg, Hannah II, 89
Fogg, Hannah II, 109
Fogg, Hannah II, 131
Fogg, Hannah II, 134
Fogg, Hannah II, 135
Fogg, Hannah II, 136
Fogg, Hannah II, 148
Fogg, Hannah II, 152
Fogg, Hannah II, 513
Fogg, Hannah II, 525
Fogg, Hannah II, 794
Fogg, Hannah II, 863
Fogg, Hannah II, 900
Fogg, Hannah II, 910
Fogg, Hannah IV, 706
Fogg, Hannah IV, 707
Fogg, Hannah IV, 953
Fogg, Hannah IV, 979
Fogg, Hannah IV, 1025
Fogg, Hannah IV, 1028
Fogg, Hannah Ann IV, 707
Fogg, Hannah H. II, 130
Fogg, Hannah Pancoast II, 794
Fogg, Hannah Pancoast II, 810
Fogg, Hannah W. II, 148
Fogg, Hannah Ware II, 131
Fogg, Helen Moore II, 794
Fogg, Hellen IV, 1251
Fogg, Henry II, 148
Fogg, Henry H. II, 131
Fogg, Henry H. II, 148
Fogg, Henry Heartly II, 131
Fogg, Henry W. II, 148
Fogg, Holme II, 28
Fogg, Holme II, 69
Fogg, Holme II, 94
Fogg, Holme, Jr. II, 28
Fogg, Ida II, 133
Fogg, Isaac II, 28
Fogg, Isaac II, 70
Fogg, Isabel IV, 843
Fogg, Isabel IV, 924
Fogg, Isabel IV, 953
Fogg, Isabel C. IV, 202
Fogg, Isabell C. IV, 275
Fogg, Isabella C. IV, 202
Fogg, J. Hildreth II, 148
Fogg, Jane IV, 816
Fogg, Jane IV, 953
Fogg, Job II, 28
Fogg, John Borton II, 131
Fogg, John Borton II, 148
Fogg, Jonathan H. II, 133
Fogg, Jonathan H. II, 138
Fogg, Jonathan R. II, 900
Fogg, Joseph II, 28
Fogg, Joseph II, 69
Fogg, Joseph II, 70
Fogg, Joseph II, 79
Fogg, Josiah IV, 706
Fogg, Josiah IV, 707
Fogg, Josiah IV, 953
Fogg, Josiah IV, 1025
Fogg, Kathryn II, 131
Fogg, Leatitia W. II, 133
Fogg, Letitia W. II, 131
Fogg, Letitia W. II, 148
Fogg, Letitia W. II, 154
Fogg, Lindley IV, 953
Fogg, Lucy II, 131
Fogg, Lucy Borton II, 148
Fogg, Lydia II, 28
Fogg, Lydia II, 69
Fogg, Lydia II, 94
Fogg, Lydia II, 118
Fogg, Lydia II, 131
Fogg, Mabel G. II, 148
Fogg, Maria K. II, 863
Fogg, Marianna IV, 953
Fogg, Maris K. II, 907
Fogg, Martha A. II, 794
Fogg, Martha M. II, 863
Fogg, Martha M. II, 901
Fogg, Mary II, 28
Fogg, Mary II, 70
Fogg, Mary II, 90
Fogg, Mary II, 131
Fogg, Mary II, 148
Fogg, Mary II, 150
Fogg, Mary II, 715
Fogg, Mary IV, 275
Fogg, Mary IV, 707
Fogg, Mary IV, 953
Fogg, Mary IV, 985
Fogg, Mary Betts II, 863
Fogg, Mary Betts II, 907
Fogg, Mary C. II, 863
Fogg, Mary Ella IV, 202
Fogg, Mary Ella IV, 275
Fogg, Mary G. II, 706
Fogg, Mary Jane IV, 710
Fogg, Mary Jane IV, 801
Fogg, Mary Jane IV, 812
Fogg, Mary Jane IV, 816
Fogg, Mary Jane IV, 839
Fogg, Mary Jane IV, 948
Fogg, Mary L. II, 148
Fogg, Mary Lee II, 131
Fogg, Mary S. II, 131
Fogg, Mary S. II, 148
Fogg, Mary Sayre II, 131
Fogg, Maryanna IV, 953
Fogg, Norman Allen II, 131
Fogg, Norman Allen II, 148
Fogg, Prudence II, 28
Fogg, Rachel II, 28
Fogg, Rachel II, 38
Fogg, Rachel II, 69
Fogg, Rachel II, 94
Fogg, Rebecca II, 28
Fogg, Rebecca II, 35
Fogg, Rebecca II, 57
Fogg, Rebecca II, 69
Fogg, Rebecca II, 70
Fogg, Rebecca II, 76
Fogg, Rebecca II, 89
Fogg, Rebecca II, 135
Fogg, Rebecca M. IV, 707
Fogg, Rebeckah II, 52
Fogg, Rebeckah II, 69
Fogg, Rebeckah II, 70
Fogg, Rebekah II, 28
Fogg, Richard II, 131
Fogg, Robert II, 148
Fogg, Robert II, 154
Fogg, Robert IV, 953
Fogg, Robert E. IV, 953
Fogg, Robert M. II, 131
Fogg, Robert M. II, 148
Fogg, Robert S. II, 131
Fogg, Robert S. II, 133
Fogg, Robert S. II, 148
Fogg, Robert S. II, 154
Fogg, Samuel II, 28
Fogg, Samuel II, 69
Fogg, Samuel II, 70
Fogg, Samuel II, 82
Fogg, Samuel II, 525
Fogg, Samuel V, 905
Fogg, Samuel, Jr. II, 69
Fogg, Sarah II, 28
Fogg, Sarah II, 69
Fogg, Sarah II, 99
Fogg, Sarah II, 102
Fogg, Sarah II, 136
Fogg, Sarah II, 900
Fogg, Sarah IV, 707
Fogg, Sarah IV, 928
Fogg, Sarah IV, 953
Fogg, Sarah V, 905
Fogg, Sarah Ann II, 717
Fogg, Sarah Ann V, 905
Fogg, Sarah F. IV, 683
Fogg, Sarah F. IV, 707
Fogg, Sarah W. II, 131
Fogg, Susan II, 131
Fogg, Susan II, 148
Fogg, Tacy IV, 706
Fogg, Tacy IV, 707
Fogg, Tacy IV, 953
Fogg, Tacy P. II, 863
Fogg, Tacy P. II, 910
Fogg, Tacy Pancoast II, 815
Fogg, Thomas II, 28
Fogg, Thomas II, 131
Fogg, Thomas II, 794
Fogg, Thos. II, 794
Fogg, Verna II, 131
Fogg, William II, 28
Fogg, William II, 794
Fogg, William IV, 1251
Fogg, William P. II, 794
Fogg, Wm. II, 148
Fogg, Wm. IV, 954
Fogg, Wm. E. II, 863
Fogg, Wm. E. D. IV, 953
Fogg, Wm. Edwin IV, 953
Fogg, Wm. P. II, 794
Fogg, Wm. P. II, 863
Fogg, Wm. R. II, 863
Fogg, Wm. Raymond II, 863
Fogg, Wm. Raymond II, 907
Fogg, Wm. W. II, 148
Fogg, Wm. W. II, 863
Fogg, Wm. W. II, 907
Fogg, Wm. Woolman II, 131
Fogle, Elizabeth Ann V, 610
Fogle, Elizabeth Ann V, 620
Fogle, Wm. B. V, 620
Fogleman, Hannah I, 345
Fogleman, Leticia I, 345
Fogleman, Peter I, 345
Foguson, Henry VI, 914
Foguson, Susannah VI, 914
Foland, Adolphus V, 170
Foland, Adolphus V. V, 170
Foland, Azariah V, 170
Foland, Ella M. V, 673
Foland, Ella McCon V, 673
Foland, Ella McCray V, 672
Foland, George V, 491
Foland, George V, 672
Foland, Jennie V, 491
Foland, Jennie V, 672
Foland, Julia V, 170
Foland, Martha J. V, 170
Foland, Ota V, 672
Folden, Elizabeth VI, 916
Folden, James VI, 916
Folden, John VI, 884
Folden, John VI, 919
Folden, John VI, 927
Folden, Molly VI, 919
Folder, Joseph II, 363
Foldin, Polly VI, 990
Folding, Adam VI, 916
Folding, Annis E. VI, 948
Folding, Elizabeth VI, 916
Folding, Nancy VI, 957
Folding, Sarah VI, 957
Folding, William VI, 916
Folding, William VI, 948
Foldsom, Polly I, 328
Foldsom, William F. I, 328
Foldsom, Zilpha I, 328
Foldson, David Franklin I, 324
Foldson, Jno. Nathaniel I, 324
Foldson, M. E. I, 324
Foldson, W. F. I, 324
Foles, Mrs. C. A. V, 995
Foley, Alveretta V, 996
Foley, Bertha V, 996
Foley, Clem V, 996
Foley, Earl V, 996
Foley, Ellen V, 996
Foley, Geo. V, 996
Foley, Geo. W. V, 996
Foley, Gretchen V, 996
Foley, James V, 996
Foley, James C. V, 996
Foley, Jasper W. V, 996
Foley, John H. V, 996
Foley, Lillian V, 996
Foley, Loretta V, 996
Foley, Margaret A. V, 996
Foley, Martha A. V, 996
Foley, Mrs. Henry V, 996
Foley, Nancy V, 996
Foley, Pearl V, 996
Foley, W. M. V, 996
Folgar, Elizabeth V, 55
Folgar, Margaret V, 55
Folgar, Mary V, 55
Folgar, Phebe V, 55
Folgar, Sarah V, 55
Folger, ??? III, 122
Folger, ??? III, 306
Folger, Abigail V, 920
Folger, Alexander C. III, 122
Folger, Anna II, 788
Folger, Anna II, 811
Folger, Anna V, 905
Folger, Asa I, 780
Folger, Asa I, 907
Folger, Asa I, 912
Folger, Avis V, 905
Folger, Avis C. III, 122
Folger, Beatrice V, 673
Folger, Benjamin III, 122
Folger, Benjamin VI, 311
Folger, Charles V, 905
Folger, Charles M. III, 70
Folger, Charles M. III, 122
Folger, Clarissa III, 78
Folger, Clarissa III, 122
Folger, Daniel V, 899
Folger, David V, 905
Folger, David V, 932
Folger, Dina I, 678
Folger, Dinah I, 780
Folger, Dinah I, 809
Folger, Dinah I, 810
Folger, Diodamia III, 122
Folger, Edward III, 122
Folger, Edward V, 905
Folger, Edward R. III, 122
Folger, Elihu V, 55
Folger, Elihu V, 905
Folger, Elihue V, 905
Folger, Elijah V, 55
Folger, Eliza V, 899
Folger, Eliza V, 905
Folger, Eliza Ann V, 905
Folger, Eliza Ann V, 932
Folger, Elizabeth I, 780
Folger, Elizabeth I, 809
Folger, Elizabeth I, 810
Folger, Elizabeth IV, 472
Folger, Elizabeth IV, 483
Folger, Elizabeth V, 55
Folger, Elizabeth V, 905
Folger, Elizabeth V, 932
Folger, Emily B. III, 122
Folger, Emily B. III, 306

Folger, Esther A. III, 70
Folger, Esther A. III, 122
Folger, Eunice I, 907
Folger, Eunice V, 55
Folger, Eunice V, 905
Folger, Francis R. III, 122
Folger, Franklin III, 122
Folger, Frederick Wm. III, 122
Folger, George I, 780
Folger, George I, 912
Folger, George V, 905
Folger, George M. V, 905
Folger, Hepsibah V, 37
Folger, Hepsibah V, 55
Folger, Hepzibeth V, 899
Folger, Hepzibeth V, 905
Folger, Hershel V, 673
Folger, Jared V, 55
Folger, Jared V, 905
Folger, Jethro I, 911
Folger, Jethro I, 912
Folger, Jethro V, 905
Folger, Joan Marie V, 673
Folger, Judith I, 780
Folger, Judith VI, 311
Folger, Latham I, 678
Folger, Latham I, 692
Folger, Latham I, 773
Folger, Latham I, 780
Folger, Latham I, 809
Folger, Latham I, 907
Folger, Latham I, 912
Folger, Latham I Sup 1, 10
Folger, Lydia I, 780
Folger, Lydia I, 809
Folger, Lydia I, 840
Folger, Lydia V, 899
Folger, Lydia V, 905
Folger, Mahew IV, 815
Folger, Margaret V, 55
Folger, Margaret V, 899
Folger, Margaret V, 905
Folger, Margaret V, 906
Folger, Margaret V, 920
Folger, Mary I, 780
Folger, Mary I, 911
Folger, Mary I, 912
Folger, Mary IV, 472
Folger, Mary V, 55
Folger, Mary V, 905
Folger, Mary V, 906
Folger, Mary Anne V, 905
Folger, Mary Way V, 905
Folger, Matilda I, 678
Folger, Matilda I, 692
Folger, Matilda I, 773
Folger, Matilda I, 780
Folger, Matilda I, 809
Folger, Matilda I, 825
Folger, Matilda I, 907
Folger, Matilda I, 912
Folger, Matilda IV, 821
Folger, Nathaniel V, 905
Folger, O. Hershel V, 673
Folger, Paul I, 912
Folger, Phebe II, 792
Folger, Phebe III, 122
Folger, Phebe V, 55
Folger, Phebe V, 905
Folger, Phebe Chadwick V, 37
Folger, Phebe Chadwick V, 55
Folger, Phebe R. V, 905
Folger, Rebecca I, 809
Folger, Rebecca I, 810
Folger, Rebecca V, 905
Folger, Reuben I, 678
Folger, Reuben I, 780
Folger, Reuben I, 809
Folger, Reuben I, 909
Folger, Reuben III, 122
Folger, Robert C. III, 122
Folger, Robert M. III, 78
Folger, Robert M. III, 122
Folger, Robt. C. III, 122
Folger, Samuel W. III, 122
Folger, Sarah IV, 892
Folger, Sarah V, 55
Folger, Sarah V, 901
Folger, Sarah V, 905
Folger, Sarah V, 906
Folger, Sarah J. III, 122
Folger, Sarah M. V, 905
Folger, Seth V, 905
Folger, Silvanus V, 905
Folger, Solomon V, 905
Folger, Susan III, 122
Folger, Susan III, 244
Folger, Susan M. III, 122
Folger, Susannah III, 122
Folger, Timothy V, 37
Folger, Timothy V, 55
Folger, Tristram V, 55
Folger, Tristram V, 889
Folger, Tristram V, 905
Folger, Tristram C. V, 905
Folger, Wd. William III, 122
Folger, William J. III, 122
Folgier, Matilda I, 809
Folie, Nancy V, 996
Folk, Anne II, 526
Folk, Anne II, 643
Folk, Cadwallader II, 363
Folk, Catharine IV, 1278
Folk, Etta J. IV, 1278
Folk, Frances V, 952
Folk, Isechar IV, 330
Folk, Judah II, 363
Folk, Mary II, 363
Folk, Owen II, 443
Folk, Samuel V, 331
Folker, Wiliam V, 739
Folker, William V, 739
Folkerth, Clarence V, 170
Folkerth, Clarence V. V, 170
Folkerth, Clarissa V, 170
Folkerth, Jesse V, 55
Folkerth, Jesse V, 170
Folkerth, Lucy V, 55
Folkes, Edward VI, 170
Folkes, Edward VI, 176
Folkes, Edward VI, 195
Folketh, Clarence V, 170
Folketh, Clarence V. V, 170
Folketh, Clarissa V, 170
Folketh, Jesse V, 170
Folketh, Lucy V, 170
Folles, George VI, 386
Follett, Thomas II, 363
Follett, Thomas II, 525
Folley, Samuel V, 620
Follin, James VI, 990
Follis, Erwin V, 996
Follis, Esther V, 54
Follis, George VI, 386
Follis, Gorden Rachel VI, 389
Follis, Jacob VI, 386
Follis, Jane VI, 594
Follis, John V, 54
Follis, John V, 489
Follis, Mary VI, 386
Follis, Peter VI, 961
Follis, Peter VI, 1001
Follis, Phebe VI, 383
Follis, Phebe VI, 386
Follis, Rachel IV, 85
Follis, Rachel IV, 89
Follis, Rachel VI, 392
Follis, Richard VI, 383
Follis, Richard VI, 386
Follis, Thomas V, 55
Follis, Turner W. V, 489
Followel, Isaac Ivins II, 525
Followell, Lydia II, 221
Follseth, Jesse V, 55
Follserth, Lucy V, 55
Follway, Elizabeth II, 70
Follway, John II, 70
Follway, Nathan II, 70
Follway, Samuel II, 70
Follway, Thomas II, 70
Follwell, Jacob II, 525
Follwell, John II, 221
Follwell, Joseph II, 221
Follwell, Mary II, 221
Follwell, Nathan, Jr. II, 221
Follwell, Patience II, 221
Follwell, Rebecca II, 525
Follwell, Wm. II, 525
Folsom, Ann III, 122
Folsom, Annie III, 122
Folsom, Chas. S. III, 122
Folsom, Mary I, 306
Folsom, Mary I, 313
Folsom, Morris III, 228
Folsom, Morris W. III, 122
Folsom, Rebecca III, 122
Folsom, Wm. III, 122
Folson, Annie III, 228
Folston, Albert Lee I, 324
Folston, Eliza I, 324
Folston, Franklin T. I, 329
Folston, Stephen I, 324
Foltz, Eugene C. IV, 1251
Foltz, Gladys IV, 1251
Folwell, Abigail II, 173
Folwell, Abigail II, 221
Folwell, Abigail II, 287
Folwell, Abigail II, 309
Folwell, Abigail II, 318
Folwell, Abigail II, 705
Folwell, Abigail S. II, 363
Folwell, Abigail S. II, 740
Folwell, Amos Ellis II, 173
Folwell, Amos Ellis II, 309
Folwell, Andrew II, 221
Folwell, Ann II, 221
Folwell, Ann II, 287
Folwell, Ann II, 525
Folwell, Ann II, 696
Folwell, Ann III, 199
Folwell, Ann L. II, 740
Folwell, Anna II, 525
Folwell, Benjamin II, 221
Folwell, Caleb II, 221
Folwell, Caleb S. II, 525
Folwell, Caleb Scattergood II, 221
Folwell, Charles E. II, 318
Folwell, Charles S. II, 363
Folwell, Charles S. II, 525
Folwell, Charles S. II, 740
Folwell, Charles S. III, 199
Folwell, Edward II, 221
Folwell, Edward II, 525
Folwell, Edward III, 122
Folwell, Edward VI, 492
Folwell, Elisabeth II, 221
Folwell, Eliza II, 705
Folwell, Elizabeth II, 70
Folwell, Elizabeth II, 173
Folwell, Elizabeth II, 194
Folwell, Elizabeth II, 221
Folwell, Elizabeth II, 252
Folwell, Elizabeth II, 363
Folwell, Elizabeth II, 525
Folwell, Elizabeth II, 623
Folwell, Elizabeth II, 696
Folwell, Elizabeth II, 955
Folwell, Elizabeth Ann II, 525
Folwell, Esther Earl II, 173
Folwell, Esther Earle II, 221
Folwell, Esther Earle II, 363
Folwell, Esther Earle II, 525
Folwell, George II, 221
Folwell, George Dillwyn II, 173
Folwell, George Dillwyn II, 221
Folwell, Hannah II, 363
Folwell, Hannah L. II, 740
Folwell, Hope II, 173
Folwell, Hope II, 194
Folwell, Hope II, 221
Folwell, Isaac Ivans II, 363
Folwell, Isaac Ivins II, 525
Folwell, Jacob II, 525
Folwell, Jacob S. II, 363
Folwell, James II, 221
Folwell, James II, 363
Folwell, James II, 525
Folwell, Jane II, 221
Folwell, Jane C. II, 221
Folwell, Jean II, 221
Folwell, John II, 70
Folwell, John II, 173
Folwell, John II, 220
Folwell, John II, 221
Folwell, John II, 363
Folwell, John II, 463
Folwell, John II, 491
Folwell, John II, 525
Folwell, John G. II, 221
Folwell, John G. II, 525
Folwell, John G. III, 122
Folwell, John Gardiner II, 221
Folwell, John Gardiner II, 363
Folwell, John Gardiner II, 525
Folwell, John M. II, 363
Folwell, John, Jr. II, 525
Folwell, Joseph II, 173
Folwell, Joseph II, 221
Folwell, Joseph II, 363
Folwell, Joseph D. II, 525
Folwell, Joseph D. II, 740
Folwell, Joseph David II, 525
Folwell, Josephine II, 818
Folwell, Joshua II, 173
Folwell, Joshua II, 221
Folwell, Joshua II, 287
Folwell, Joshua II, 309
Folwell, Joshua II, 318
Folwell, Lydia II, 221
Folwell, Martha C. II, 525
Folwell, Martha C. II, 740
Folwell, Mary II, 173
Folwell, Mary II, 220
Folwell, Mary II, 221
Folwell, Mary II, 363
Folwell, Mary II, 525
Folwell, Mary II, 577
Folwell, Mercy II, 173
Folwell, Mercy II, 220
Folwell, Mercy II, 221
Folwell, Mercy II, 996
Folwell, Nathan II, 70
Folwell, Nathan II, 173
Folwell, Nathan II, 221
Folwell, Nathan II, 231
Folwell, Nathan II, 309
Folwell, Nathan II, 318
Folwell, Nathan II, 525
Folwell, Nathan, Jr. II, 221
Folwell, Nathaniel II, 525
Folwell, Patience II, 173
Folwell, Patience II, 221
Folwell, Patience II, 252
Folwell, Rebecca II, 173
Folwell, Rebecca II, 218
Folwell, Rebecca II, 221
Folwell, Rebecca II, 363
Folwell, Rebecca II, 525
Folwell, Rebecca II, 623
Folwell, Rebecca II, 705
Folwell, Richard L. II, 740
Folwell, Robert II, 525
Folwell, Robert II, 740
Folwell, Samuel II, 70
Folwell, Samuel II, 173
Folwell, Samuel II, 221
Folwell, Sarah II, 173
Folwell, Sarah II, 221
Folwell, Sarah II, 231
Folwell, Sarah II, 309
Folwell, Sarah II, 363
Folwell, Sarah II, 482
Folwell, Sarah II, 525
Folwell, Sarah II, 705
Folwell, Spicer II, 363
Folwell, Susan II, 525
Folwell, Susanna II, 525
Folwell, Susannah II, 221
Folwell, Thomas II, 70
Folwell, Thomas II, 194
Folwell, Thomas II, 221
Folwell, Thomas II, 363
Folwell, Thomas II, 525
Folwell, Thomas II, 696
Folwell, Thomas Iredell II, 525
Folwell, Thomas Iredell II, 740
Folwell, Thos. II, 525
Folwell, William II, 173
Folwell, William II, 221
Folwell, William II, 287
Folwell, William II, 363
Folwell, William II, 705
Folwell, William J. II, 363
Folwell, Wm. II, 70
Folwell, Wm. II, 221
Folwell, Wm. II, 525
Folwell, Wm. II, 623
Folwell, Wm. II, 740
Folwell, Wm., Jr. II, 525
Folwell, Wm., Jr. II, 740
Fonderwhite, Benj. F. III, 122
Fonderwhite, Louisa Maria III, 122
Fonderwhite, Walter J. III, 122
Fondler, Eva V, 491
Fondler, Viola M. V, 491
Fones, Eliz III, 410
Fones, Eliz. III, 410
Fones, Wd. Elizabeth III, 410
Font, Ida IV, 1278
Fookes, Thomas VI, 11
Foolks, V. N. IV, 202
Foote, Minnie IV, 1315
Foote, Minnie A. IV, 1315
Foraker, Emma C. V, 457
Foraker, George J. V, 457
Foraker, John H. V, 457
Foraker, Mayme M. V, 457
Forbes, Amelia III, 110
Forbes, Amelia III, 122
Forbes, Calvin VI, 615
Forbes, Calvin VI, 638
Forbes, Catharine S. III, 410
Forbes, Edw. E. III, 420
Forbes, Edw. E. III, 431
Forbes, Edward E. III, 410
Forbes, Elizabeth III, 410
Forbes, Elizabeth III, 420
Forbes, Elizabeth III, 431
Forbes, Harlan L. VI, 638
Forbes, Hugh II, 363
Forbes, Hugh II, 525
Forbes, Hugh II, 602
Forbes, Hugh II, 667
Forbes, J. Malcolm III, 110
Forbes, J. Malcolm III, 122
Forbes, John III, 410
Forbes, John VI, 849
Forbes, John VI, 915
Forbes, John VI, 977
Forbes, Margaret VI, 615
Forbes, Margaret VI, 638
Forbes, Mary II, 464
Forbes, Mary II, 526
Forbes, Nancy VI, 849
Forbes, Rachel II, 363
Forbes, Rachel II, 525
Forbes, Rachel II, 667
Forbes, Samuel Dexter VI, 638
Forbes, Sarah VI, 748
Forbes, Sarah C. III, 110
Forbes, Sarah C. III, 122
Forbes, Tacy II, 525
Forbes, Tacy II, 602
Forbes, Wd. Tacy II, 363
Forby, Benjamin VI, 11
Forby, Benjamin VI, 12
Forby, Mrs. ??? VI, 11
Forby, Mrs. ??? VI, 12
Ford, Alice II, 526
Ford, Amelia Ann II, 324
Ford, Ann IV, 330
Ford, Ann IV, 525
Ford, Bertie H. IV, 1159
Ford, Calvin VI, 817
Ford, Calvin, Sr. VI, 846
Ford, Catherine W. VI, 817
Ford, Charles C. II, 131
Ford, Charles C. IV, 202
Ford, Charlie V, 620
Ford, Clara G. IV, 1315
Ford, Clara Guinness IV, 1315
Ford, Culvrain, Sr. VI, 815
Ford, David II, 318
Ford, David II, 324
Ford, David V, 996
Ford, Edward V, 996
Ford, Eliza V, 620
Ford, Elizabeth III, 122
Ford, Elizabeth III, 177
Ford, Elizabeth V, 620
Ford, Elizabeth VI, 817
Ford, Emmeline V, 996
Ford, Esther III, 122
Ford, Frances V, 996
Ford, Francis VI, 243
Ford, Francis VI, 272
Ford, Garland VI, 916
Ford, Geo. V, 996
Ford, George V, 996
Ford, Hannah II, 363
Ford, Hannah Ann II, 318
Ford, Hannah More II, 131
Ford, Hannah S. II, 309
Ford, Helen IV, 1315
Ford, Helen M. IV, 1315
Ford, Henry I, 539
Ford, Hezekiah VI, 815
Ford, Hezekiah VI, 817
Ford, Huldah V, 996
Ford, Jacob II, 526
Ford, Jacob IV, 472
Ford, James C. V, 996
Ford, James E. V, 331
Ford, James E. V, 358
Ford, Jane A. V, 673
Ford, Jefferson IV, 1315
Ford, Jefferson W. IV, 1315
Ford, John V, 620
Ford, John VI, 991
Ford, John J. V, 620
Ford, John Jessup II, 131
Ford, John R. VI, 823
Ford, John R. VI, 846
Ford, Joseph II, 794
Ford, Joseph IV, 472
Ford, Joshua IV, 472
Ford, Labourn VI, 817
Ford, Lena IV, 1159
Ford, Lewis IV, 1159
Ford, Lewis A. IV, 1159
Ford, Lovisa E. V, 996
Ford, Lucy VI, 856
Ford, Lydia V, 620
Ford, Margaret V, 331
Ford, Margaret V, 358
Ford, Martha II, 794
Ford, Martha V, 996
Ford, Martha VI, 817
Ford, Martha A. VI, 817
Ford, Mary II, 363
Ford, Mary Elizabeth V, 620
Ford, Mary Jane IV, 1278
Ford, Mary P. VI, 916
Ford, Mr. ??? IV, 1315
Ford, Mrs. T. G. IV, 1315
Ford, Olivia W. VI, 817
Ford, Phebe IV, 1362
Ford, Rebecca II, 309
Ford, Rebecca IV, 385
Ford, Rebecca IV, 393
Ford, Ruth V, 491
Ford, Ruth V, 506
Ford, Sally VI, 856

Ford, Sarah III, 43
Ford, Sarah III, 122
Ford, Sarah V, 620
Ford, Sarah B. II, 794
Ford, Sarah B. II, 863
Ford, Sarah B. II, 910
Ford, Sarah E. VI, 846
Ford, Sarah L. IV, 1278
Ford, Sarah M. VI, 817
Ford, Suckey VI, 991
Ford, Susan Ann V, 996
Ford, Susan Ann VI, 815
Ford, Susan Frances V, 558
Ford, Tailor V, 620
Ford, Thomas III, 122
Ford, Thomas III, 177
Ford, Thomas H. VI, 817
Ford, Thomas, Jr. III, 43
Ford, Thomas, Jr. III, 122
Ford, William II, 363
Ford, William IV, 202
Ford, William V, 620
Ford, William A. II, 309
Ford, William C. VI, 798
Ford, William C. VI, 817
Ford, William P. VI, 817
Ford, William T. IV, 202
Ford, Wm. II, 526
Ford, Wm. IV, 1315
Ford, Wm. Harrison IV, 1315
Fordham, Abel II, 526
Fordham, Abel II, 562
Fordham, Benjamin II, 443
Fordham, Benjamin II, 483
Fordham, Benjamin II, 526
Fordham, Hannah II, 464
Fordham, Hannah II, 526
Fordham, Jacob II, 526
Fordham, Jane II, 499
Fordham, Jane II, 526
Fordham, Jane II, 562
Fordham, Lydia II, 483
Fordham, Lydia II, 526
Fordham, Sarah II, 455
Fordham, Sarah II, 526
Fordham, Sarah II, 672
Fordice, Olive V, 331
Fordum, Abell II, 363
Fordyce, Ada V, 561
Fordyce, Albert C. V, 561
Fordyce, Alberta C. V, 561
Fordyce, Alice V, 561
Fordyce, Henrietta V, 561
Fordyce, Ida E. V, 561
Fordyce, Oscar V, 561
Fordyce, Permelia V, 561
Fordyce, Ray V, 561
Fordyce, William F. V, 561
Fordyce, Wm. V, 561
Fore, America A. VI, 825
Fore, Charles J. VI, 817
Fore, Eliza VI, 817
Fore, Elizabeth VI, 823
Fore, John VI, 817
Fore, John VI, 823
Fore, John W. VI, 825
Fore, John W. VI, 839
Fore, Margaret VI, 817
Fore, Milton VI, 817
Fore, Milton Lee VI, 825
Fore, Nancy VI, 817
Fore, Nancy E. VI, 823
Fore, Peter VI, 817
Fore, Peter VI, 823
Fore, Rebecca VI, 817
Fore, Tabitha VI, 817
Foredyce, Ada V, 561
Forehand, Alonzo I, 9
Forehand, Calvin I, 7
Forehand, Calvin I, 9
Forehand, Calvin I, 49
Forehand, Elisabeth I, 49
Forehand, Elisabeth Ellen I, 9
Forehand, Georgeanna I, 9
Forehand, Lydia I, 9
Forehand, Lydia I, 49
Forehand, Lydia L. I, 7
Forehand, Lydia L. I, 9
Forehand, Margaret J. I, 9
Forehand, Martha Jane I, 9
Forehand, Martha Jane I, 49
Forehand, Priscilla I, 9
Forehand, Priscilla I, 49
Forehand, Virginia I, 9
Forehand, Virginia E. I, 49
Foreman, Abner IV, 86
Foreman, Alexander II, 526
Foreman, Ann IV, 86
Foreman, Ann IV, 91
Foreman, Ann E. IV, 1278
Foreman, Anna I, 270
Foreman, Anna V, 673
Foreman, Deborah IV, 86
Foreman, Deborah IV, 91
Foreman, Elizabeth II, 526
Foreman, Elizabeth IV, 26
Foreman, Elizabeth IV, 32
Foreman, Elizabeth IV, 86
Foreman, Ellis IV, 86
Foreman, Elroy IV, 1278
Foreman, Hannah IV, 86
Foreman, Horace E. V, 673
Foreman, Isaac II, 526
Foreman, Isaac IV, 86
Foreman, J. W. IV, 1278
Foreman, James IV, 86
Foreman, Jane IV, 86
Foreman, Jane IV, 472
Foreman, Jesse IV, 86
Foreman, John IV, 86
Foreman, John IV, 472
Foreman, John IV, 1278
Foreman, Joseph IV, 32
Foreman, Mary IV, 86
Foreman, Mary IV, 1278
Foreman, Minnie IV, 1278
Foreman, Ollie Way IV, 202
Foreman, Philip II, 363
Foreman, Rachel IV, 86
Foreman, Rachel IV, 330
Foreman, Rachel IV, 340
Foreman, Rachel IV, 472
Foreman, Rachel IV, 489
Foreman, Rebecca IV, 86
Foreman, Rhoda IV, 86
Foreman, Richard IV, 86
Foreman, Robert IV, 86
Foreman, Samuel IV, 86
Foreman, Sarah IV, 86
Foreman, Sarah Jane V, 457
Foreman, Sidney II, 526
Foreman, Susanna II, 526
Foreman, Thomas II, 526
Foreman, Wm. B. IV, 1278
Forest, Rebecca V, 996
Forest, Rebecca J. V, 996
Forester, Anna IV, 1251
Forester, Freda S. IV, 1251
Forester, Gertrude IV, 1251
Forester, Lillian IV, 1251
Forfar, Grace Louise III, 123
Forfar, Louise III, 247
Forfar, Mary I. III, 123
Forfar, Mary I. III, 247
Forfar, Robt. III, 123
Forfar, Robt. III, 247
Forgason, Alfred I, 761
Forgason, Nathan H. I, 761
Forgason, Sarah I, 761
Forgason, Thomas J. I, 761
Forgee, Daniel VI, 817
Forgee, James II, 363
Forgee, Nasmis VI, 817
Forgerson, Jemima VI, 914
Forgerson, Jeremiah VI, 914
Forgerson, Mary IV, 26
Forgerson, Mary Coffin IV, 33
Forgie, D. K. VI, 927
Forgie, Daniel K. VI, 914
Forgie, Daniel K. VI, 916
Forgie, Nancy A. VI, 916
Forguson, Andrew II, 505
Forguson, Andrew II, 521
Forguson, Benjamin II, 505
Forguson, Benjamin II, 521
Forguson, Elizabeth VI, 914
Forguson, Jemimah VI, 991
Forguson, Jeremiah VI, 914
Forguson, Jeremiah VI, 991
Forguson, Jesse VI, 914
Forguson, Judy VI, 914
Forguson, Polly VI, 991
Forguson, Rachel II, 505
Forguson, Rachel II, 521
Forguson, Sarah II, 505
Forguson, Sarah II, 521
Forgusson, Martha VI, 869
Forice, Margaret I, 445
Fork, ??? VI, 283
Forker, Adam II, 192
Forker, Adam II, 221
Forker, Elizabeth II, 192
Forker, Elizabeth II, 221
Forkner, Judith V, 83
Forlens, John II, 443
Forman, Abner IV, 86
Forman, Ann II, 222
Forman, Ann IV, 86
Forman, Cath. III, 231
Forman, Catharine III, 123
Forman, Deborah II, 222
Forman, Deborah IV, 86
Forman, Elizabeth II, 222
Forman, Elizabeth II, 526
Forman, Elizabeth IV, 32
Forman, Elizabeth IV, 86
Forman, Elizabeth IV, 115
Forman, Ellis IV, 86
Forman, George II, 222
Forman, George III, 123
Forman, Hannah IV, 86
Forman, Hannah IV, 110
Forman, Isaac II, 526
Forman, Isaac IV, 32
Forman, James IV, 86
Forman, Jane IV, 32
Forman, Jane IV, 86
Forman, Jesse IV, 86
Forman, John IV, 32
Forman, John IV, 51
Forman, John IV, 86
Forman, Joseph IV, 32
Forman, Josiah II, 222
Forman, Keturah M. II, 830
Forman, Keturah M. II, 863
Forman, Margaret IV, 755
Forman, Mary IV, 32
Forman, Mary IV, 86
Forman, Mary IV, 115
Forman, Mary M. III, 123
Forman, Middleton II, 222
Forman, Rachel IV, 32
Forman, Rebecca IV, 32
Forman, Rebecca IV, 86
Forman, Rebeccah IV, 115
Forman, Rhoda IV, 86
Forman, Richard IV, 32
Forman, Richard IV, 86
Forman, Richard Way II, 222
Forman, Robert IV, 32
Forman, Robert IV, 86
Forman, Robert IV, 115
Forman, Ruth II, 222
Forman, Samuel IV, 86
Forman, Samuel IV, 115
Forman, Sarah IV, 32
Forman, Sarah IV, 51
Forman, Sarah IV, 86
Forman, Sidney II, 526
Forman, Thomas II, 526
Forman, Vera IV, 755
Forman, Wm. IV, 755
Forman, Wm. W. Allen II, 863
Forner, David H. IV, 472
Forner, H. D. IV, 472
Fornston, Elizabeth VI, 389
Forqueran, Harriet B. VI, 865
Forqueran, Henry VI, 865
Forqueran, Henry VI, 898
Forqueran, John VI, 869
Forqueran, John VI, 926
Forqueran, John VI, 927
Forqueran, John VI, 930
Forqueran, Nancy VI, 930
Forqueran, Polly VI, 869
Forqueran, Susan VI, 865
Forqueran, Susan L. VI, 898
Forquernan, Bar. VI, 988
Forqueron, Charles VI, 916
Forqueron, Henry VI, 916
Forqueron, John VI, 916
Forqueron, Littleberry VI, 916
Forqueron, Mary VI, 916
Forqueron, Mary Jane VI, 916
Forqueron, Milly VI, 916
Forqueron, Peter VI, 883
Forqueron, Susanna VI, 916
Forqueron, William VI, 916
Forquerson, Peter VI, 920
Forquhar, Alan II, 219
Forqurean, Peter VI, 929
Forqureau, Henry VI, 826
Forqureau, M. A. G. VI, 826
Forrer, Sarah IV, 1159
Forrer, Sarah IV, 1166
Forrer, Sarah V, 969
Forrest, Ann II, 363
Forrest, George II, 363
Forrest, Jane II, 363
Forrest, Joan II, 363
Forrest, Maria II, 363
Forrest, Mary II, 363
Forrest, Thomas II, 363
Forrest, Wd. Joan II, 363
Forrest, William II, 363
Forrester, Charlotte III, 123
Forrester, Elizabeth III, 123
Forrester, Hannah IV, 86
Forrester, Hannah IV, 97
Forrester, Margaret I, 1152
Forrester, Sarah II, 526
Forrester, Susannah II, 526
Forrist, Joan II, 363
Forrist, Mary II, 363
Forrist, William II, 363
Forrister, Elizabeth II, 222
Forrister, James II, 526
Forrister, Patrick II, 443
Forrow, Charity VI, 816
Forrow, Daniel VI, 816
Forrow, Elijah VI, 816
Forrow, Elizabeth VI, 816
Forrow, James VI, 816
Forrow, John VI, 816
Forsee, Mary VI, 907
Forsha, Amanda V, 239
Forsha, Elizabeth V, 239
Forsha, Wilson V, 239
Forster, Alice II, 363
Forster, Alice II, 462
Forster, Alice II, 526
Forster, Anna S. III, 123
Forster, Armeala I, 600
Forster, Barsheba I, 540
Forster, Deborah II, 363
Forster, Elizabeth II, 526
Forster, Elizabeth II, 545
Forster, Elizabeth III, 123
Forster, George II, 363
Forster, Hannah II, 363
Forster, Hugh I, 540
Forster, Hugh I, 606
Forster, James II, 363
Forster, John I, 600
Forster, John II, 363
Forster, John II, 526
Forster, Joseph I, 540
Forster, Joseph I, 573
Forster, Margaret I, 1152
Forster, Margaret III, 123
Forster, Margaret III, 290
Forster, Margaret III, 380
Forster, Mary I, 540
Forster, Mary I, 573
Forster, Mary II, 363
Forster, Mary II, 473
Forster, Miles III, 123
Forster, Moses II, 363
Forster, Moses II, 462
Forster, Moses II, 526
Forster, Nancy H. I, 606
Forster, Rachel II, 222
Forster, Rebecca III, 123
Forster, Reuben II, 363
Forster, Reuben II, 462
Forster, Reuben II, 526
Forster, Reuben II, 545
Forster, Ruben II, 363
Forster, Samuel I, 540
Forster, Sarah I, 606
Forster, Sarah II, 363
Forster, Thomas III, 123
Forster, Thomas III, 380
Forster, Thomas B. III, 123
Forster, Thomas B. III, 290
Forster, Wd. Hannah II, 363
Forster, William I, 540
Forster, William I, 1140
Forster, William I, 1152
Forster, William II, 363
Forsyth, Hannah II, 287
Forsyth, Joshua II, 287
Forsyth, Matthew II, 221
Forsyth, Matthew II, 261
Forsyth, Mercy II, 221
Forsyth, Mercy II, 261
Forsyth, Michael II, 287
Forsyth, Samuel II, 526
Forsythe, Anna IV, 841
Forsythe, Elma IV, 694
Forsythe, Elma IV, 707
Forsythe, Elma C. IV, 707
Forsythe, Frank W. IV, 707
Forsythe, Hannah II, 287
Forsythe, Helen IV, 841
Forsythe, Helen M. IV, 815
Forsythe, Helen M. IV, 842
Forsythe, Henry IV, 841
Forsythe, Jane II, 808
Forsythe, Joseph IV, 1315
Forsythe, Joseph W. IV, 1315
Forsythe, Joseph W. IV, 1333
Forsythe, Josephine IV, 1315
Forsythe, Martha IV, 707
Forsythe, Martha C. IV, 694
Forsythe, Martha C. IV, 707
Forsythe, Mary IV, 1315
Forsythe, Mary VI, 907
Forsythe, Mary Louisa IV, 1315
Forsythe, Wm. IV, 707
Fort, Mary P. II, 287
Fort, Mary P. II, 294
Forte, Fay V, 457
Forten, Harriet D. II, 816
Fortener, Daniel II, 526
Fortener, Simeon II, 526
Fortener, Susannah II, 526
Fortener, Uriah II, 526
Fortier, Elbert V, 457
Fortier, Henry V, 457
Fortier, Waunita N. V, 457
Fortiner, Daniel II, 526
Fortiner, Daniel II, 573
Fortiner, Hannah II, 221
Fortiner, Susannah II, 526
Fortiner, Susannah II, 573
Fortiner, Uriah II, 526
Fortiner, Uriah II, 573
Fortner, Elijah I, 1152
Fortner, Elizabeth I, 1152
Fortner, Ethel D. I, 1152
Fortner, Margaret I, 1152
Fortner, Rachel V, 20
Fortner, Simeon II, 526
Fortune, Lucy VI, 804
Forwalter, Christiana M. V, 996
Forward, Sarah E. IV, 1095
Forward, Sarah E. IV, 1098
Foscher, Daniel VI, 974
Foscher, Suana VI, 974
Fosdick, A. Leonard IV, 1315
Fosdick, Abigail III, 123
Fosdick, Abigail IV, 891
Fosdick, Abigail IV, 892
Fosdick, David III, 123
Fosdick, Deborah III, 123
Fosdick, Eliza III, 123
Fosdick, Eliza IV, 892
Fosdick, Elizabeth VI, 827
Fosdick, Epenetus III, 123
Fosdick, Frank IV, 1315
Fosdick, George VI, 817
Fosdick, Hamilton III, 123
Fosdick, Henry C. III, 123
Fosdick, Ida IV, 1315
Fosdick, Jerry IV, 1315
Fosdick, Lydia VI, 340
Fosdick, Lydia VI, 855
Fosdick, Mary VI, 817
Fosdick, Mary VI, 831
Fosdick, Mary A. VI, 817
Fosdick, Moses III, 123
Fosdick, Nora IV, 1315
Fosdick, Rebecca III, 123
Fosdick, Sally VI, 855
Fosdick, Samuel III, 123
Fosdick, Samuel T. III, 123
Fosdick, Tamar III, 123
Fosdick, Tamar IV, 892
Fosdick, Thamar III, 123
Fosdick, Timothy VI, 834
Fosdick, Underhill III, 123
Fosdick, William VI, 340
Fosdick, William VI, 827
Fosdick, William VI, 829
Fosdick, William VI, 855
Foset, Hannah II, 70
Fosher, Elizabeth VI, 817
Fosher, John VI, 817
Fosher, Matthias VI, 926
Fosher, Polly VI, 926
Fosot, Jonathan II, 70
Foss, Jennie V, 996
Fossell, Barbara II, 478
Fossell, Barbara II, 526
Fossell, Elizabeth II, 503
Fossell, Elizabeth II, 526
Fossell, Solomon II, 478
Fossell, Solomon II, 503
Fossell, Solomon II, 526
Fossett, Jesse IV, 1097
Fossett, Thomas VI, 592
Fossit, Hannah II, 70
Fossit, Jonathan II, 70
Fossit, Lydia II, 70
Fossmyer, Omelia IV, 1251
Foste, William VI, 811
Foster, ??? III, 73
Foster, ??? III, 348
Foster, ??? III, 410
Foster, Abigail I, 497
Foster, Abigail I, 498
Foster, Abigail I, 530
Foster, Abigail I, 540
Foster, Abigail I, 559
Foster, Abigail I, 572
Foster, Abigail I, 817
Foster, Abigail A. V, 385
Foster, Abner VI, 916
Foster, Agatha I, 526
Foster, Agatha I, 540
Foster, Agnes I, 498
Foster, Agnes I, 540
Foster, Agnes II, 705
Foster, Aletha I, 497

Foster, Alfred P. VI, 916
Foster, Alice II, 526
Foster, Alice Adella IV, 1315
Foster, Alice E. IV, 1315
Foster, Alis II, 473
Foster, Alis II, 526
Foster, Amy II, 221
Foster, Amy I. III, 410
Foster, Ann III, 123
Foster, Ann III, 139
Foster, Anna I, 498
Foster, Anna I, 540
Foster, Anna II, 222
Foster, Anna II, 287
Foster, Anna J. I, 540
Foster, Anna Jane I, 497
Foster, Anna L. II, 740
Foster, Anna L. II, 752
Foster, Anna M. III, 123
Foster, Anna M. III, 348
Foster, Anna Mills V, 673
Foster, Anny II, 19
Foster, Anthony VI, 817
Foster, Archibald VI, 817
Foster, Armely I, 538
Foster, Armely I, 540
Foster, Armilia I, 602
Foster, Armilla I, 540
Foster, Armillia I, 602
Foster, Asa V, 906
Foster, Asenath I, 540
Foster, Augusta S. III, 123
Foster, Barsheba I, 540
Foster, Baruba I, 602
Foster, Bathsheba I, 498
Foster, Bathsheba I, 540
Foster, Benjamin Franklin V, 906
Foster, Benjamin W. III, 123
Foster, Betsy III, 123
Foster, Betsy III, 302
Foster, Betsy VI, 833
Foster, Booker VI, 844
Foster, Bowker VI, 916
Foster, Brooks VI, 844
Foster, Bundy IV, 202
Foster, Caleb I, 497
Foster, Caleb I, 498
Foster, Caleb I, 540
Foster, Caleb I, 581
Foster, Carl IV, 1251
Foster, Catharine I, 602
Foster, Catherine H. VI, 817
Foster, Celia C. III, 123
Foster, Chalkly I, 498
Foster, Charity II, 173
Foster, Charity II, 269
Foster, Charity V, 239
Foster, Charity V, 252
Foster, Charles K. II, 1051
Foster, Charles Kenyon II, 959
Foster, Charles Kenyon II, 1050
Foster, Clementine VI, 916
Foster, Cornelia III, 217
Foster, Creed VI, 817
Foster, Creed VI, 826
Foster, Creed VI, 854
Foster, Daniel Quimba I, 498
Foster, David I, 541
Foster, David F. VI, 817
Foster, DeWitt IV, 1251
Foster, Dewitt L. IV, 1251
Foster, Drurester VI, 916
Foster, Ebanor IV, 86
Foster, Edith II, 1085
Foster, Edith Bailey V, 906
Foster, Edward II, 1085
Foster, Edward IV, 401
Foster, Edward H. II, 946
Foster, Edward H. II, 948
Foster, Edward H. II, 1085
Foster, Edward H. II, 1087
Foster, Edward H. II, 1089
Foster, Edward H. IV, 417
Foster, Eleanor IV, 815
Foster, Elihu I, 541
Foster, Eliza II, 946
Foster, Eliza II, 948
Foster, Eliza II, 1085
Foster, Eliza II, 1087
Foster, Eliza IV, 417
Foster, Eliza V, 896
Foster, Eliza V, 899
Foster, Eliza V, 906
Foster, Eliza A. VI, 804
Foster, Elizabeth I, 497
Foster, Elizabeth II, 118
Foster, Elizabeth II, 168
Foster, Elizabeth II, 222
Foster, Elizabeth II, 526
Foster, Elizabeth III, 34
Foster, Elizabeth IV, 86
Foster, Elizabeth IV, 815
Foster, Elizabeth VI, 811
Foster, Elizabeth VI, 817
Foster, Elizabeth VI, 916
Foster, Elizabeth VI, 971
Foster, Elizabeth J. VI, 916
Foster, Elizabeth T. III, 123
Foster, Ellen G. II, 794
Foster, Ellen G. II, 863
Foster, Elmina H. I, 533
Foster, Elmina H. I, 540
Foster, Elmira W. II, 705
Foster, Elmira W. II, 741
Foster, Elsie III, 123
Foster, Elsie A. III, 73
Foster, Elsie A. III, 123
Foster, Elvira M. III, 155
Foster, Elvira M. III, 281
Foster, Emily V, 882
Foster, Emily V, 883
Foster, Emma IV, 401
Foster, Emma IV, 750
Foster, Emma J. II, 948
Foster, Emma J. II, 1087
Foster, Emma J. II, 1089
Foster, Emma Jane IV, 417
Foster, Emma W. II, 946
Foster, Emma W. II, 948
Foster, Emma W. II, 1050
Foster, Emma W. II, 1063
Foster, Emma W. II, 1087
Foster, Emma??? II, 1085
Foster, Enos V, 996
Foster, Epp VI, 817
Foster, Erastes T. III, 410
Foster, Esther II, 526
Foster, Esther II, 740
Foster, Esther IV, 815
Foster, Esther IV, 844
Foster, Esther Brown IV, 86
Foster, Esther Brown IV, 815
Foster, Experience II, 221
Foster, Experience II, 271
Foster, Ezra I, 498
Foster, Fanny III, 410
Foster, Feris W. VI, 916
Foster, Flora IV, 1315
Foster, Frances G. VI, 937
Foster, Francis IV, 86
Foster, Francis IV, 815
Foster, Francis VI, 916
Foster, Francis Foster IV, 815
Foster, Frank III, 410
Foster, Frank Bryn III, 123
Foster, Frank Bryn III, 199
Foster, G. L. IV, 1315
Foster, George II, 173
Foster, George S. III, 410
Foster, George W. II, 287
Foster, George W. II, 740
Foster, George W. III, 123
Foster, George W. VI, 817
Foster, George W. VI, 821
Foster, Grace I, 497
Foster, Grace I, 498
Foster, Grace I, 536
Foster, Grace I, 540
Foster, Grace IV, 1251
Foster, Grace V, 996
Foster, Grace M. IV, 1251
Foster, Hallie III, 123
Foster, Hallie III, 302
Foster, Hannah I, 497
Foster, Hannah I, 540
Foster, Hannah I, 543
Foster, Hannah I, 581
Foster, Hannah II, 19
Foster, Hannah II, 70
Foster, Hannah II, 98
Foster, Hannah II, 168
Foster, Hannah II, 173
Foster, Hannah II, 205
Foster, Hannah II, 222
Foster, Hannah V, 170
Foster, Hannah V, 491
Foster, Hannel I, 602
Foster, Harriet C. VI, 817
Foster, Harry IV, 1315
Foster, Harry A. IV, 1315
Foster, Henry Cope IV, 393
Foster, Henry Cope IV, 420
Foster, Henry J. VI, 916
Foster, Hester II, 70
Foster, Homer V, 996
Foster, Horace II, 959
Foster, Horace B. II, 948
Foster, Horace B. II, 1087
Foster, Horace B. IV, 393
Foster, Hugh I, 498
Foster, Hugh I, 540
Foster, Hugh I, 602
Foster, Hugh I, 606
Foster, Isaac II, 526
Foster, Isaac V, 385
Foster, Isabella II, 863
Foster, Isiah C. V, 906
Foster, James II, 526
Foster, James IV, 1278
Foster, James VI, 916
Foster, James VI, 971
Foster, James, Jr. VI, 916
Foster, James, Sr. VI, 971
Foster, Jane II, 173
Foster, Jane II, 222
Foster, Jane V, 33
Foster, Jane V, 55
Foster, Jane W. V, 55
Foster, Jemima I, 540
Foster, Jemima I, 541
Foster, Jemima V, 331
Foster, Jesse I, 541
Foster, Jesse Edgerton IV, 954
Foster, Jno. II, 526
Foster, Joël E. VI, 916
Foster, John I, 497
Foster, John I, 498
Foster, John I, 536
Foster, John I, 538
Foster, John I, 540
Foster, John I, 602
Foster, John I, 606
Foster, John II, 222
Foster, John II, 526
Foster, John II, 1087
Foster, John III, 34
Foster, John III, 123
Foster, John III, 410
Foster, John V, 331
Foster, John VI, 817
Foster, John VI, 897
Foster, John VI, 904
Foster, John VI, 908
Foster, John A. I, 602
Foster, John B. III, 50
Foster, John B. III, 123
Foster, John Crumwell I, 498
Foster, John H. I, 540
Foster, John H. VI, 799
Foster, John P. VI, 817
Foster, John Randolph V, 239
Foster, John W. F. V, 55
Foster, John Wilbur II, 705
Foster, John, Jr. I, 540
Foster, Jonah II, 173
Foster, Jos. B. III, 123
Foster, Joseph I, 498
Foster, Joseph I, 540
Foster, Joseph II, 173
Foster, Joseph II, 705
Foster, Joseph V, 55
Foster, Joshua I, 497
Foster, Joshua I, 498
Foster, Joshua I, 540
Foster, Joshua II, 173
Foster, Joshua II, 222
Foster, Joshua IV, 86
Foster, Joshua IV, 815
Foster, Joshua V, 55
Foster, Josiah II, 19
Foster, Josiah II, 70
Foster, Josiah II, 173
Foster, Josiah II, 221
Foster, Josiah II, 222
Foster, Josiah II, 648
Foster, Josiah V, 55
Foster, Julia VI, 817
Foster, Larkin VI, 804
Foster, Larkin VI, 817
Foster, Lelia Young I, 633
Foster, Lester V, 673
Foster, Lillian III, 123
Foster, Lindley W. II, 1085
Foster, Lizzie M. III, 123
Foster, Lydia II, 70
Foster, Lydia V, 882
Foster, Lydia V, 885
Foster, Lydia VI, 389
Foster, Lydia VI, 451
Foster, Lydia VI, 813
Foster, Mabel III, 123
Foster, Mabel W. III, 123
Foster, Mabel W. III, 199
Foster, Margaret III, 123
Foster, Margaret IV, 86
Foster, Margaret IV, 815
Foster, Margaret VI, 846
Foster, Margaret J. II, 863
Foster, Maria III, 123
Foster, Maria E. III, 123
Foster, Mariana II, 1085
Foster, Mariana IV, 393
Foster, Mariana IV, 401
Foster, Mariana IV, 403
Foster, Marianna IV, 393
Foster, Mariannna IV, 961
Foster, Marietta IV, 1315
Foster, Martha I, 498
Foster, Martha III, 123
Foster, Martha VI, 817
Foster, Martha VI, 862
Foster, Martha VI, 916
Foster, Martha VI, 985
Foster, Martha Ann VI, 916
Foster, Martha D. VI, 985
Foster, Martha Jane VI, 999
Foster, Martha K. II, 1089
Foster, Mary I, 497
Foster, Mary I, 540
Foster, Mary I, 555
Foster, Mary I, 606
Foster, Mary II, 70
Foster, Mary II, 173
Foster, Mary II, 221
Foster, Mary II, 222
Foster, Mary II, 241
Foster, Mary II, 251
Foster, Mary II, 473
Foster, Mary II, 526
Foster, Mary II, 959
Foster, Mary III, 50
Foster, Mary III, 123
Foster, Mary III, 341
Foster, Mary VI, 821
Foster, Mary VI, 846
Foster, Mary VI, 908
Foster, Mary VI, 916
Foster, Mary A. IV, 949
Foster, Mary C. II, 948
Foster, Mary C. IV, 393
Foster, Mary E. III, 50
Foster, Mary E. F. Wattles V, 55
Foster, Mary J. IV, 949
Foster, Mary J. IV, 954
Foster, Mary L. VI, 916
Foster, Mary M. VI, 916
Foster, Mary S. II, 948
Foster, Mary S. II, 1087
Foster, Massy Ann VI, 949
Foster, Matilda III, 123
Foster, Matthew II, 863
Foster, Matthew S. II, 794
Foster, Matthew T. II, 863
Foster, Matthew Whillden II, 863
Foster, Matthew Whilldon II, 794
Foster, Millicent IV, 815
Foster, Millicent H. IV, 815
Foster, Millicent H. IV, 844
Foster, Millicent S. IV, 815
Foster, Milly VI, 909
Foster, Moses II, 473
Foster, Moses II, 526
Foster, Mrs. Flora IV, 1315
Foster, Nancy I, 602
Foster, Nancy VI, 832
Foster, Nancy VI, 916
Foster, Nancy H. I, 606
Foster, Nancy Isabelle V, 239
Foster, Nathan I, 497
Foster, Nathan I, 498
Foster, Nathan I, 540
Foster, Nathan I, 559
Foster, Nathan, Jr. I, 540
Foster, Nina Irvin V, 55
Foster, Nina Irwin V, 55
Foster, Ollie V, 808
Foster, Othniel III, 123
Foster, Patrick L. VI, 916
Foster, Patsey VI, 904
Foster, Patsy VI, 916
Foster, Paulina II, 1086
Foster, Paulina VI, 817
Foster, Pauline II, 1087
Foster, Payton VI, 891
Foster, Payton VI, 898
Foster, Payton VI, 949
Foster, Peyton VI, 916
Foster, Polly VI, 796
Foster, Polly VI, 971
Foster, Polly VI, 1015
Foster, Rachel II, 70
Foster, Rachel II, 222
Foster, Rachel IV, 86
Foster, Rebecca II, 70
Foster, Rebecca II, 173
Foster, Rebecca II, 221
Foster, Rebecca II, 227
Foster, Rebecca II, 803
Foster, Rebekah I, 541
Foster, Reuben II, 526
Foster, Reuben III, 123
Foster, Reuben III, 302
Foster, Reuben B. III, 123
Foster, Rhoda I, 541
Foster, Richard VI, 904
Foster, Richard VI, 916
Foster, Robert I, 497
Foster, Robert III, 123
Foster, Robert N. III, 123
Foster, Sally I, 540
Foster, Samuel I, 498
Foster, Samuel I, 540
Foster, Samuel IV, 86
Foster, Samuel IV, 815
Foster, Samuel V, 170
Foster, Samuel V, 491
Foster, Sarah I, 540
Foster, Sarah I, 606
Foster, Sarah II, 526
Foster, Sarah IV, 86
Foster, Sarah IV, 815
Foster, Sarah V, 906
Foster, Sarah VI, 897
Foster, Sarah A. VI, 826
Foster, Sarah K. III, 410
Foster, Susan VI, 916
Foster, Susan Ann
Temperance VI, 817
Foster, Susan M. III, 410
Foster, Susanah I, 540
Foster, Susanna VI, 817
Foster, Susannah I, 497
Foster, Susannah II, 526
Foster, Temperance VI, 817
Foster, Temple I, 497
Foster, Thomas I, 498
Foster, Thomas I, 541
Foster, Thomas II, 173
Foster, Thomas V, 906
Foster, Thomas Brown IV, 86
Foster, Thomas Brown IV, 815
Foster, Thyra Jane IV, 393
Foster, Thyra Jane IV, 420
Foster, Timothy IV, 86
Foster, Timothy IV, 815
Foster, Washington VI, 817
Foster, Wd. Elizabeth IV, 86
Foster, William I, 497
Foster, William I, 498
Foster, William I, 540
Foster, William II, 168
Foster, William II, 173
Foster, William II, 221
Foster, William II, 269
Foster, William II, 271
Foster, William III, 123
Foster, William VI, 796
Foster, William VI, 821
Foster, William VI, 832
Foster, William VI, 897
Foster, William VI, 916
Foster, William C. III, 410
Foster, William E. V, 906
Foster, William H. III, 123
Foster, William P. III, 123
Foster, William R. VI, 999
Foster, Willy VI, 916
Foster, Wm. II, 526
Foster, Wm. IV, 815
Foster, Wm. VI, 813
Foster, Wm. O. IV, 815
Foster, Wm. O. IV, 844
Fotch, John IV, 954
Fotch, John IV, 1037
Fotch, John E. IV, 1037
Fotch, Louisa IV, 954
Fotch, Louisa IV, 1037
Fothergill, Alice Haworth II, 118
Fothergill, Christopher
Wetherill II, 222
Fothergill, Margaret II, 118
Fothergill, Mary II, 222
Fothergill, Mary II, 271
Fothergill, Samuel II, 526
Fothergill, Susanna II, 118
Fothergill, Susanna II, 705
Fothergill, Susanna II, 741
Fothergill, Susannah II, 118
Fothergill, Wm. II, 526
Foughty, Anna IV, 707
Foughty, Anna IV, 766
Foughty, Charles E. IV, 707
Foughty, Deborah IV, 707
Foughty, Elihu IV, 707
Foughty, Elisha IV, 707
Foughty, Elisha B. IV, 707
Foughty, Elizabeth IV, 707
Foughty, Hannah C. IV, 707
Foughty, James IV, 707
Foughty, Joseph IV, 707
Foughty, Levi IV, 707
Foughty, Mary Ann IV, 707
Foughty, Maryann IV, 707
Foughty, Phebe IV, 707
Foughty, Samuel IV, 707

Foughty, Sarah IV, 707
Foulden, Adam VI, 916
Foulden, Appy VI, 919
Foulden, Elizabeth VI, 916
Foulden, George VI, 916
Foulden, George W. VI, 916
Foulden, George W. VI, 957
Foulden, Henry VI, 916
Foulden, James VI, 916
Foulden, James VI, 919
Foulden, Jesse Y. VI, 916
Foulden, John VI, 916
Foulden, Louisa VI, 916
Foulden, Mary VI, 916
Foulden, Nancy VI, 916
Foulden, Peachy Ann VI, 1003
Foulden, Polly VI, 916
Foulden, Robert VI, 916
Foulden, Salley VI, 916
Foulden, William VI, 916
Foulden, William VI, 1003
Fouldin, Adam VI, 1002
Fouldin, Susan VI, 1002
Foulding, Elizabeth M. VI, 987
Foulding, Henry VI, 916
Foulding, James VI, 916
Foulding, James VI, 987
Foulding, Polly VI, 916
Foulding, Robert VI, 916
Fouler, John VI, 177
Foulk, Amanda Jane IV, 202
Foulk, Amasa IV, 202
Foulk, Ann II, 222
Foulk, Ann IV, 202
Foulk, Anna IV, 202
Foulk, Cadwalader II, 363
Foulk, Cadwalader II, 996
Foulk, Cadwalader IV, 200
Foulk, Cadwaler II, 996
Foulk, Cadwallader II, 363
Foulk, Caleb II, 527
Foulk, Charles IV, 625
Foulk, Deborah II, 363
Foulk, Edward IV, 202
Foulk, Elizabeth IV, 202
Foulk, Francis E. IV, 202
Foulk, Francis Elwood IV, 202
Foulk, George IV, 202
Foulk, Hannah II, 527
Foulk, Hannah IV, 333
Foulk, Hannah Mary IV, 202
Foulk, Harris IV, 202
Foulk, Henry Bailey IV, 202
Foulk, Issachar IV, 333
Foulk, Jane II, 527
Foulk, Jane IV, 333
Foulk, Jesse IV, 202
Foulk, Jesse M. IV, 202
Foulk, John B. IV, 202
Foulk, Judah II, 363
Foulk, Margaret II, 363
Foulk, Mary II, 363
Foulk, Mary II, 996
Foulk, Mary II, 1013
Foulk, Mary IV, 202
Foulk, Mary IV, 312
Foulk, Phebe II, 996
Foulk, Phebe IV, 200
Foulk, Phebe Ann IV, 202
Foulk, Pheby II, 996
Foulk, Priscilla IV, 330
Foulk, Rebecca IV, 202
Foulk, Sarah II, 996
Foulk, Sarah IV, 200
Foulk, Sarah IV, 202
Foulk, Sarah IV, 330
Foulk, Sarah IV, 341
Foulk, Sarah Ann IV, 202
Foulk, Silas IV, 202
Foulk, Thomas II, 363
Foulk, William II, 363
Foulk, William IV, 202
Foulke, ??? II, 802
Foulke, ??? IV, 393
Foulke, Aaron IV, 330
Foulke, Aaron IV, 351
Foulke, Aaron IV, 393
Foulke, Aaron P. IV, 1057
Foulke, Alice Maria III, 380
Foulke, Amanda Jane IV, 146
Foulke, Amanda Jane IV, 312
Foulke, Amelia IV, 330
Foulke, Amelia IV, 558
Foulke, Amelia V, 56
Foulke, Amos II, 363
Foulke, Amos II, 526
Foulke, Amos II, 527
Foulke, Amos II, 569
Foulke, Ann II, 222
Foulke, Ann II, 805
Foulke, Ann IV, 146
Foulke, Ann IV, 326
Foulke, Ann IV, 330
Foulke, Ann IV, 525
Foulke, Ann IV, 1057
Foulke, Ann V, 56
Foulke, Ann V, 906
Foulke, Ann Eliza V, 906
Foulke, Ann Rachel V, 56
Foulke, Anna III, 79
Foulke, Anna III, 123
Foulke, Anna IV, 142
Foulke, Anna IV, 258
Foulke, Anna C. II, 863
Foulke, Anna C. II, 882
Foulke, Anna McIlvain II, 819
Foulke, Anne II, 526
Foulke, Anne IV, 146
Foulke, Anne IV, 520
Foulke, Anne Elsie IV, 1057
Foulke, Anthony IV, 330
Foulke, Anthony IV, 560
Foulke, Anthony VI, 741
Foulke, Barton IV, 330
Foulke, Barton IV, 343
Foulke, Barton IV, 393
Foulke, Bathsheba IV, 330
Foulke, Bathsheba IV, 359
Foulke, Cadwalader II, 363
Foulke, Cadwalader IV, 330
Foulke, Cadwallader II, 222
Foulke, Cadwallader II, 363
Foulke, Cadwallader II, 472
Foulke, Cadwallader II, 526
Foulke, Cadwallader IV, 142
Foulke, Cadwallader IV, 146
Foulke, Cadwallader IV, 578
Foulke, Cadwallader V, 56
Foulke, Cadwallader, Jr. IV, 578
Foulke, Caleb II, 363
Foulke, Caleb II, 526
Foulke, Caleb II, 527
Foulke, Caleb II, 568
Foulke, Cassandra V, 906
Foulke, Catharine II, 728
Foulke, Charles II, 526
Foulke, Charles II, 527
Foulke, Charles M. II, 863
Foulke, Chas. M. II, 863
Foulke, Daniel III, 79
Foulke, Daniel III, 123
Foulke, David Smith IV, 1098
Foulke, Deborah II, 363
Foulke, Deborah II, 527
Foulke, Deborah II, 618
Foulke, Edith W. IV, 1057
Foulke, Edward II, 527
Foulke, Edward II, 805
Foulke, Edward III, 123
Foulke, Edward IV, 146
Foulke, Edward IV, 162
Foulke, Edward V, 906
Foulke, Edwin III, 123
Foulke, Edwin M. III, 123
Foulke, Edwin M. III, 310
Foulke, Eleanor II, 363
Foulke, Eleanor II, 527
Foulke, Eleanor II, 613
Foulke, Eleanor II, 741
Foulke, Eleanor IV, 330
Foulke, Eleanor IV, 560
Foulke, Eleanor VI, 741
Foulke, Eleanor P. II, 741
Foulke, Eliz. C. III, 79
Foulke, Eliz. C. III, 123
Foulke, Eliza IV, 525
Foulke, Eliza IV, 555
Foulke, Eliza IV, 1057
Foulke, Eliza IV, 1076
Foulke, Elizabeth II, 363
Foulke, Elizabeth II, 804
Foulke, Elizabeth III, 123
Foulke, Elizabeth IV, 202
Foulke, Elizabeth IV, 275
Foulke, Elizabeth IV, 330
Foulke, Elizabeth IV, 525
Foulke, Elizabeth IV, 549
Foulke, Elizabeth IV, 1057
Foulke, Elizabeth V, 56
Foulke, Ellen II, 863
Foulke, Ellen III, 182
Foulke, Ellen III, 206
Foulke, Ellen IV, 330
Foulke, Ellen IV, 525
Foulke, Elva III, 123
Foulke, Elva III, 310
Foulke, Emma B. II, 863
Foulke, Evan IV, 146
Foulke, Everad V, 906
Foulke, Francis Elwood IV, 146
Foulke, Francis Elwood IV, 312
Foulke, George II, 527
Foulke, Grace IV, 330
Foulke, Grace IV, 578
Foulke, Grace IV, 584
Foulke, Grace V, 56
Foulke, Hannah II, 363
Foulke, Hannah II, 526
Foulke, Hannah II, 527
Foulke, Hannah II, 569
Foulke, Hannah II, 794
Foulke, Hannah II, 863
Foulke, Hannah III, 123
Foulke, Hannah III, 287
Foulke, Hannah IV, 330
Foulke, Hannah IV, 393
Foulke, Hannah IV, 453
Foulke, Hannah IV, 525
Foulke, Hannah IV, 539
Foulke, Hannah IV, 1057
Foulke, Hannah IV, 1077
Foulke, Hannah IV, 1159
Foulke, Hannah IV, 1171
Foulke, Hannah V, 56
Foulke, Hannah Mary IV, 146
Foulke, Hannah Mary IV, 312
Foulke, Hannah O. V, 69
Foulke, Isaac II, 363
Foulke, Isachar IV, 319
Foulke, Isachar IV, 327
Foulke, Isachar IV, 359
Foulke, Isechar IV, 330
Foulke, Issachar IV, 327
Foulke, Issachar IV, 330
Foulke, Issachar IV, 393
Foulke, J. Roberts II, 863
Foulke, James II, 363
Foulke, James II, 526
Foulke, James III, 123
Foulke, James Crozer IV, 525
Foulke, Jane II, 363
Foulke, Jane II, 526
Foulke, Jane II, 527
Foulke, Jane II, 568
Foulke, Jane II, 794
Foulke, Jane II, 863
Foulke, Jane IV, 319
Foulke, Jane IV, 325
Foulke, Jane IV, 327
Foulke, Jane IV, 330
Foulke, Jane IV, 359
Foulke, Jane IV, 393
Foulke, Jane Peirce II, 796
Foulke, Jesse IV, 330
Foulke, Jesse IV, 525
Foulke, Jesse IV, 578
Foulke, Jesse IV, 1057
Foulke, Jesse M. IV, 312
Foulke, Jesse M. IV, 315
Foulke, Jesse M. IV, 578
Foulke, Jesse M. V, 297
Foulke, Jesse M. V, 302
Foulke, Jesse Mary V, 56
Foulke, Jesse R. IV, 525
Foulke, Jesse R. IV, 1057
Foulke, Jesse, Jr. IV, 525
Foulke, John II, 363
Foulke, John II, 527
Foulke, John II, 613
Foulke, John IV, 330
Foulke, John IV, 393
Foulke, John IV, 578
Foulke, John V, 56
Foulke, John Lewis IV, 1159
Foulke, John M. V, 906
Foulke, Joseph III, 123
Foulke, Joshua IV, 393
Foulke, Joshua IV, 1057
Foulke, Joshua V, 56
Foulke, Joshua V, 69
Foulke, Juda IV, 393
Foulke, Judah II, 363
Foulke, Judah II, 472
Foulke, Judah II, 526
Foulke, Judah II, 527
Foulke, Judah II, 613
Foulke, Judah IV, 325
Foulke, Judah IV, 326
Foulke, Judah IV, 330
Foulke, Judah IV, 393
Foulke, Judah IV, 578
Foulke, Judah IV, 584
Foulke, Judah IV, 599
Foulke, Judah V, 56
Foulke, Judah V, 115
Foulke, Judah V, 302
Foulke, Judah V, 906
Foulke, Judith II, 527
Foulke, Judith II, 618
Foulke, Judith III, 123
Foulke, Judith III, 343
Foulke, Judith III, 380
Foulke, Levi V, 906
Foulke, Lewis W. IV, 1057
Foulke, Lowry II, 526
Foulke, Lowry II, 527
Foulke, Lowry II, 597
Foulke, Lucius W. IV, 1057
Foulke, Lydia III, 123
Foulke, Lydia III, 310
Foulke, Lydia V, 906
Foulke, Margaret II, 363
Foulke, Margaret II, 805
Foulke, Margaret IV, 146
Foulke, Margaret V, 56
Foulke, Margaret V, 69
Foulke, Margaret V, 906
Foulke, Margaret J. IV, 347
Foulke, Margaret Jane IV, 1053
Foulke, Margaret Jane IV, 1057
Foulke, Maria III, 380
Foulke, Martha IV, 1057
Foulke, Mary II, 363
Foulke, Mary II, 472
Foulke, Mary II, 526
Foulke, Mary II, 527
Foulke, Mary II, 590
Foulke, Mary II, 613
Foulke, Mary II, 618
Foulke, Mary II, 672
Foulke, Mary II, 741
Foulke, Mary IV, 202
Foulke, Mary IV, 312
Foulke, Mary IV, 315
Foulke, Mary IV, 319
Foulke, Mary IV, 330
Foulke, Mary IV, 343
Foulke, Mary IV, 393
Foulke, Mary IV, 1057
Foulke, Mary IV, 1076
Foulke, Mary IV, 1098
Foulke, Mary IV, 1115
Foulke, Mary V, 297
Foulke, Mary V, 302
Foulke, Mary V, 906
Foulke, Matilda III, 123
Foulke, Mercy IV, 330
Foulke, Mercy IV, 578
Foulke, Mercy IV, 599
Foulke, Mery IV, 578
Foulke, Miles IV, 393
Foulke, Milten IV, 393
Foulke, Milton IV, 393
Foulke, Milton IV, 1057
Foulke, Nathan IV, 393
Foulke, Owen II, 363
Foulke, Owen II, 527
Foulke, Phebe II, 222
Foulke, Phebe IV, 330
Foulke, Phebe IV, 351
Foulke, Phebe IV, 393
Foulke, Phebe IV, 560
Foulke, Phebe IV, 1057
Foulke, Phebe VI, 741
Foulke, Phebe Ann IV, 146
Foulke, Phebe Ann IV, 162
Foulke, Phebe Ann IV, 312
Foulke, Phebe W. II, 863
Foulke, Priscilla IV, 330
Foulke, Priscilla IV, 357
Foulke, Priscilla IV, 393
Foulke, Rachel IV, 258
Foulke, Rachel IV, 330
Foulke, Rachel IV, 525
Foulke, Rachel IV, 538
Foulke, Rebecca IV, 196
Foulke, Rebecca IV, 202
Foulke, Rebecca IV, 327
Foulke, Rebecca IV, 330
Foulke, Rebecca M. II, 863
Foulke, Richard II, 363
Foulke, Richard II, 527
Foulke, Richard P. II, 363
Foulke, Richard P. II, 527
Foulke, Richard P. II, 863
Foulke, Richard Parker II, 794
Foulke, Robert W. IV, 1057
Foulke, Roland R. II, 863
Foulke, Rosa Bell White IV, 330
Foulke, Rowland Roberts II, 863
Foulke, Samuel II, 802
Foulke, Samuel V, 906
Foulke, Samuel L. II, 863
Foulke, Sarah II, 222
Foulke, Sarah IV, 146
Foulke, Sarah IV, 325
Foulke, Sarah IV, 326
Foulke, Sarah IV, 327
Foulke, Sarah IV, 330
Foulke, Sarah IV, 333
Foulke, Sarah IV, 352
Foulke, Sarah IV, 389
Foulke, Sarah IV, 393
Foulke, Sarah IV, 525
Foulke, Sarah IV, 578
Foulke, Sarah IV, 584
Foulke, Sarah IV, 599
Foulke, Sarah IV, 1057
Foulke, Sarah IV, 1159
Foulke, Sarah V, 56
Foulke, Sarah V, 115
Foulke, Sarah V, 302
Foulke, Sarah V, 906
Foulke, Sarah Ann IV, 146
Foulke, Sarah Ann IV, 312
Foulke, Sarah Ann IV, 525
Foulke, Sarah P. IV, 330
Foulke, Sarah P. IV, 560
Foulke, Sarah P. VI, 741
Foulke, Sidney V, 906
Foulke, Silas IV, 330
Foulke, Silas IV, 393
Foulke, Silas IV, 578
Foulke, Silas V, 56
Foulke, Susanna II, 363
Foulke, Susanna II, 527
Foulke, Susanna II, 605
Foulke, Susanna Nancarrow II, 527
Foulke, Sylvas IV, 330
Foulke, Thomas II, 363
Foulke, Thomas III, 123
Foulke, Thomas III, 287
Foulke, Thomas IV, 258
Foulke, Thomas IV, 330
Foulke, Thomas IV, 352
Foulke, Thomas IV, 393
Foulke, Thomas IV, 1057
Foulke, Thomas V, 56
Foulke, Thomas V, 906
Foulke, Thomas D. V, 906
Foulke, Thos. D. V, 906
Foulke, William II, 363
Foulke, William II, 819
Foulke, William IV, 330
Foulke, William IV, 525
Foulke, William IV, 555
Foulke, William IV, 1057
Foulke, William VI, 741
Foulke, William A. V, 491
Foulke, William D. III, 123
Foulke, William Dudley III, 123
Foulke, William H. IV, 146
Foulke, William H. IV, 312
Foulke, William R. VI, 741
Foulke, William W. IV, 330
Foulke, William W. IV, 560
Foulke, Wm. II, 526
Foulke, Wm. II, 569
Foulke, Wm. IV, 525
Foulke, Wm. IV, 1053
Foulke, Wm. IV, 1057
Foulke, Wm. IV, 1076
Foulke, Wm. G. II, 863
Foulke, Wm. G. II, 882
Foulke, Wm. Henry II, 863
Foulke, Wm. Henry V, 969
Foulke, Wm. Jones II, 526
Foulkner, James W. V, 490
Foulks, Amelia IV, 358
Foulks, Judah IV, 358
Foulks, Sarah IV, 358
Fountain, Isaac I, 329
Fourd, Henry I, 539
Fourqueran, John VI, 916
Fourqueran, Mary VI, 916
Foust, Abigail V, 239
Foust, Albancia V, 996
Foust, Anna V, 996
Foust, Custer V, 996
Foust, Cynthia Ann V, 239
Foust, Ethel R. V, 996
Foust, Evaline V, 996
Foust, Frank V, 996
Foust, G. W. V, 996
Foust, Glenn R. V, 996
Foust, Hazel V, 996
Foust, Ida May V, 239
Foust, James I, 389
Foust, Kester V, 996
Foust, Laura V, 996
Foust, Loren V, 996
Foust, Lorrin V, 996
Foust, Louisa IV, 1251
Foust, Martha IV, 1251
Foust, Mary V, 996
Foust, Mrs. H. H. I, 941
Foust, Mrs. O. K. IV, 1159
Foust, P. C. V, 996
Foust, Perry IV, 1159
Foust, Perry V, 996
Foust, Samuel V, 239
Foust, Sarah V, 996
Foust, Sarah A. V, 996
Foust, Sarah Ann V, 996

Foust, Sibba I, 628
Foust, Turen V, 996
Fout, Cyrus IV, 1278
Fout, Susie IV, 1278
Fouts, ??? I, 715
Fouts, ??? I, 731
Fouts, Abraham VI, 916
Fouts, Beatrice V, 838
Fouts, Daniel VI, 916
Fouts, Elizabeth I, 715
Fouts, Elizabeth IV, 954
Fouts, Elizabeth V, 739
Fouts, Elizabeth V, 774
Fouts, Elizabeth V, 838
Fouts, Garrison Elsworth IV, 954
Fouts, George VI, 916
Fouts, Green B. VI, 917
Fouts, Greenville VI, 946
Fouts, Hannah IV, 954
Fouts, Hiram G. IV, 954
Fouts, Jacob I, 715
Fouts, John V, 838
Fouts, John Earl V, 838
Fouts, Leroy E. IV, 954
Fouts, Linnor I, 715
Fouts, Linor I, 715
Fouts, Martha A. VI, 917
Fouts, Mary I, 715
Fouts, Mary IV, 954
Fouts, Mary E. IV, 954
Fouts, Milly VI, 916
Fouts, Peter V, 739
Fouts, Polly VI, 916
Fouts, Rebeckah I, 714
Fouts, Rebeckah I, 715
Fouts, Roy IV, 954
Fouts, Roy Elton IV, 954
Fouts, William I, 715
Fouts, William V, 838
Foutz, ??? VI, 996
Foutz, Abraham VI, 916
Foutz, Abraham VI, 917
Foutz, Betsey VI, 981
Foutz, Daniel VI, 916
Foutz, Daniel VI, 991
Foutz, Elizabeth V, 773
Foutz, Frances VI, 917
Foutz, Frances E. VI, 904
Foutz, George VI, 916
Foutz, George VI, 981
Foutz, Glenn V, 996
Foutz, Grant V, 996
Foutz, Green B. VI, 917
Foutz, Henry V, 773
Foutz, Jacob VI, 981
Foutz, Jacob VI, 996
Foutz, John VI, 904
Foutz, John VI, 917
Foutz, John S. VI, 1013
Foutz, Martha A. VI, 917
Foutz, Mary V, 996
Foutz, Mary L. P. VI, 917
Foutz, Milly VI, 916
Foutz, Polly VI, 916
Foutz, Priscilla VI, 917
Foutz, William W. VI, 917
Fowke, Jesse IV, 167
Fowler, ??? III, 68
Fowler, Abigail III, 124
Fowler, Achsah IV, 1098
Fowler, Achsah IV, 1100
Fowler, Achsah O. IV, 1098
Fowler, Achsah Ogborn IV, 905
Fowler, Addison I. IV, 1131
Fowler, Addison J. IV, 1131
Fowler, Agnes VI, 817
Fowler, Alfred IV, 1131
Fowler, Alfred Irving IV, 815
Fowler, Alfred Irving IV, 1131
Fowler, Alice V, 996
Fowler, Alice A. III, 124
Fowler, Alice Maria III, 124
Fowler, Amanda III, 410
Fowler, Ammon III, 124
Fowler, Ann VI, 177
Fowler, Ann VI, 311
Fowler, Ann VI, 312
Fowler, Ann VI, 339
Fowler, Ann VI, 854
Fowler, Anna M. IV, 32
Fowler, Anna M. IV, 62
Fowler, Anna M. IV, 202
Fowler, Anna W. IV, 892
Fowler, Anne VI, 177
Fowler, Anne VI, 211
Fowler, Anne VI, 312
Fowler, Anne B. IV, 1131
Fowler, Belinda H. IV, 1131
Fowler, Belinda H. IV, 1133
Fowler, Benjamin III, 124
Fowler, Caleb III, 124
Fowler, Caleb IV, 625
Fowler, Caleb IV, 869
Fowler, Caleb IV, 882
Fowler, Caleb IV, 905
Fowler, Caleb IV, 1098
Fowler, Caleb IV, 1100
Fowler, Caleb IV, 1131
Fowler, Caleb IV, 1135
Fowler, Caroline III, 410
Fowler, Catharine III, 124
Fowler, Catharine V, 170
Fowler, Catharine Ann III, 124
Fowler, Chalkley T. IV, 1098
Fowler, Chalkley T. IV, 1131
Fowler, Chalkley T. IV, 1133
Fowler, Charity IV, 1278
Fowler, Charles III, 124
Fowler, Charles E. IV, 1131
Fowler, Chas. IV, 1315
Fowler, Christopher VI, 311
Fowler, Christopher VI, 312
Fowler, Christopher VI, 338
Fowler, Christopher VI, 817
Fowler, Christopher VI, 850
Fowler, Christopher VI, 941
Fowler, Conway VI, 817
Fowler, Cornelia III, 124
Fowler, Daniel S. IV, 892
Fowler, David VI, 312
Fowler, David H. IV, 1278
Fowler, Deborah III, 124
Fowler, Dorinda F. III, 45
Fowler, Dorinda F. III, 124
Fowler, Dorothy IV, 815
Fowler, Duncan III, 410
Fowler, Edgar L. IV, 815
Fowler, Edgar L. IV, 1131
Fowler, Edmond IV, 1131
Fowler, Edmund IV, 815
Fowler, Edmund IV, 851
Fowler, Edmund IV, 1138
Fowler, Edmund S. IV, 1098
Fowler, Edmund S. IV, 1131
Fowler, Edmund Smith IV, 815
Fowler, Edmund Smith IV, 905
Fowler, Edward III, 124
Fowler, Eli IV, 55
Fowler, Elisha B. IV, 815
Fowler, Elisha B. IV, 844
Fowler, Eliz. III, 28
Fowler, Eliz. III, 67
Fowler, Eliza VI, 107
Fowler, Eliza VI, 120
Fowler, Eliza B. III, 68
Fowler, Eliza B. III, 124
Fowler, Eliza J. IV, 1278
Fowler, Elizabeth IV, 1131
Fowler, Elizabeth IV, 1278
Fowler, Elizabeth VI, 107
Fowler, Elizabeth VI, 177
Fowler, Elizabeth VI, 961
Fowler, Elizabeth VI, 1015
Fowler, Elizabeth Blazebrook VI, 1014
Fowler, Elizabeth J. IV, 1133
Fowler, Elizabeth J. VI, 817
Fowler, Elizabeth Z. IV, 1098
Fowler, Ella M. IV, 1131
Fowler, Emerson IV, 1131
Fowler, Emerson J. IV, 815
Fowler, Emilada IV, 1131
Fowler, Emily IV, 892
Fowler, Emma E. IV, 815
Fowler, Emmerson J. IV, 815
Fowler, Emmerson J. IV, 1131
Fowler, Emmolada IV, 1131
Fowler, Emmolada IV, 1134
Fowler, Esther IV, 815
Fowler, Esther IV, 1098
Fowler, Esther IV, 1103
Fowler, Esther IV, 1131
Fowler, Ethelinda D. III, 124
Fowler, Eva Irene IV, 551
Fowler, Eva Irene IV, 1131
Fowler, Eva Irene IV, 1138
Fowler, Francis II, 527
Fowler, Francis II, 741
Fowler, Francis VI, 177
Fowler, Francis, Jr. II, 527
Fowler, Freelove III, 124
Fowler, Freelove III, 346
Fowler, George IV, 1278
Fowler, Gilbert III, 45
Fowler, Gilbert III, 124
Fowler, Gilbert, Jr. III, 124
Fowler, Godfrey VI, 160
Fowler, Godfrey VI, 162
Fowler, Godfrey VI, 177
Fowler, Godfrey VI, 211
Fowler, Gustavus Adolphus IV, 905
Fowler, Hannah II, 790
Fowler, Hannah II, 996
Fowler, Hannah III, 124
Fowler, Hannah IV, 815
Fowler, Hannah IV, 844
Fowler, Hannah IV, 892
Fowler, Hannah C. IV, 707
Fowler, Hannah C. IV, 768
Fowler, Hannah C. IV, 815
Fowler, Hannah C. IV, 844
Fowler, Hannah C. IV, 1130
Fowler, Hannah C. IV, 1131
Fowler, Henry III, 124
Fowler, Henry VI, 107
Fowler, Henry VI, 177
Fowler, Henry B. III, 124
Fowler, Henry H. III, 124
Fowler, Hester III, 124
Fowler, Horace III, 24
Fowler, Horace III, 124
Fowler, Isaac III, 124
Fowler, Isaac P. III, 124
Fowler, Jacob V, 739
Fowler, James III, 124
Fowler, James IV, 869
Fowler, James IV, 883
Fowler, James IV, 905
Fowler, James IV, 954
Fowler, James VI, 917
Fowler, Jane III, 124
Fowler, Jennie III, 423
Fowler, Jennie V, 996
Fowler, Jinny VI, 917
Fowler, John III, 124
Fowler, John IV, 1278
Fowler, John VI, 7
Fowler, John VI, 22
Fowler, John VI, 29
Fowler, John VI, 30
Fowler, John VI, 93
Fowler, John VI, 107
Fowler, John VI, 120
Fowler, John VI, 177
Fowler, John VI, 181
Fowler, John VI, 311
Fowler, John VI, 312
Fowler, John VI, 339
Fowler, John VI, 817
Fowler, John VI, 939
Fowler, John Christopher VI, 799
Fowler, John Lynch VI, 312
Fowler, John P. III, 124
Fowler, John S. IV, 1098
Fowler, John S. IV, 1103
Fowler, John S. IV, 1131
Fowler, John Smith IV, 905
Fowler, John, Jr. VI, 107
Fowler, John, Jr. VI, 312
Fowler, John, Jr. VI, 854
Fowler, John, Sr. VI, 107
Fowler, John, Sr. VI, 177
Fowler, John, Sr. VI, 312
Fowler, Jonathan III, 124
Fowler, Joseph IV, 707
Fowler, Joseph IV, 869
Fowler, Joseph IV, 954
Fowler, Judith VI, 312
Fowler, Judith VI, 338
Fowler, Judith VI, 852
Fowler, Judith G. VI, 939
Fowler, L. E. V, 996
Fowler, L. Frank III, 124
Fowler, Lena V, 996
Fowler, Libbie IV, 1315
Fowler, Lida IV, 1278
Fowler, Lindley M. IV, 1098
Fowler, Lindley M. IV, 1131
Fowler, Lindley M. IV, 1133
Fowler, Luther Frank III, 268
Fowler, Lydia III, 124
Fowler, Lydia IV, 625
Fowler, Lydia IV, 869
Fowler, Lydia IV, 883
Fowler, Lydia Ann III, 124
Fowler, Margaret IV, 815
Fowler, Maria III, 124
Fowler, Maria L. II, 741
Fowler, Maria L. II, 753
Fowler, Marion V, 996
Fowler, Martha III, 24
Fowler, Martha III, 124
Fowler, Martha III, 216
Fowler, Martha VI, 100
Fowler, Martha VI, 101
Fowler, Martha VI, 107
Fowler, Martha VI, 134
Fowler, Martha E. III, 124
Fowler, Mary I, 371
Fowler, Mary I, 389
Fowler, Mary II, 527
Fowler, Mary III, 24
Fowler, Mary III, 124
Fowler, Mary III, 313
Fowler, Mary IV, 625
Fowler, Mary IV, 815
Fowler, Mary IV, 851
Fowler, Mary IV, 869
Fowler, Mary IV, 882
Fowler, Mary IV, 883
Fowler, Mary IV, 905
Fowler, Mary IV, 954
Fowler, Mary IV, 1100
Fowler, Mary IV, 1136
Fowler, Mary IV, 1138
Fowler, Mary V, 996
Fowler, Mary VI, 107
Fowler, Mary VI, 134
Fowler, Mary VI, 141
Fowler, Mary VI, 311
Fowler, Mary VI, 312
Fowler, Mary VI, 339
Fowler, Mary VI, 852
Fowler, Mary Ann IV, 1131
Fowler, Mary Ann IV, 1140
Fowler, Mary Anna P. IV, 1131
Fowler, Mary E. IV, 815
Fowler, Mary M. IV, 815
Fowler, Mary M. IV, 1131
Fowler, Mary S. IV, 1131
Fowler, Mary S. IV, 1135
Fowler, Mary Sara IV, 815
Fowler, Mary Sara IV, 851
Fowler, Mary Sarah IV, 1131
Fowler, Meribah, Jr. II, 997
Fowler, Milton D. IV, 1098
Fowler, Milton D. IV, 1131
Fowler, Milton Dewberry IV, 905
Fowler, Miriam IV, 892
Fowler, Miriam IV, 895
Fowler, Mirian IV, 892
Fowler, Molly VI, 339
Fowler, Molly VI, 854
Fowler, Moses III, 124
Fowler, Nancy VI, 311
Fowler, Nancy VI, 312
Fowler, Nancy VI, 799
Fowler, Nancy VI, 864
Fowler, Nelson V, 996
Fowler, Orland R. IV, 815
Fowler, Orlando IV, 815
Fowler, Orlando R. IV, 1130
Fowler, Orlando R. IV, 1131
Fowler, Pebles VI, 177
Fowler, Phebe III, 124
Fowler, Phebe IV, 815
Fowler, Phebe IV, 905
Fowler, Phebe IV, 1131
Fowler, Phebe V, 239
Fowler, Phebe V, 247
Fowler, Phebe V, 446
Fowler, Phebe W. IV, 1133
Fowler, Rachel IV, 525
Fowler, Rachel IV, 544
Fowler, Raymond V, 996
Fowler, Rebecca III, 124
Fowler, Rebecca III, 234
Fowler, Rebecca IV, 625
Fowler, Rebecca IV, 867
Fowler, Rebecca IV, 869
Fowler, Robert VI, 24
Fowler, Ruth E. IV, 815
Fowler, Rye III, 124
Fowler, Sally IV, 32
Fowler, Sally IV, 55
Fowler, Sally IV, 202
Fowler, Sally IV, 266
Fowler, Samuel IV, 625
Fowler, Samuel IV, 815
Fowler, Samuel IV, 869
Fowler, Samuel IV, 905
Fowler, Sarah III, 124
Fowler, Sarah IV, 55
Fowler, Sarah IV, 815
Fowler, Sarah IV, 905
Fowler, Sarah IV, 916
Fowler, Sarah IV, 1098
Fowler, Sarah IV, 1131
Fowler, Sarah IV, 1135
Fowler, Sarah V, 996
Fowler, Sarah VI, 177
Fowler, Sarah VI, 917
Fowler, Sarah Ann III, 407
Fowler, Sarah H. III, 124
Fowler, Sarah H. III, 268
Fowler, Simmons VI, 107
Fowler, Simmons VI, 120
Fowler, Simmons VI, 134
Fowler, Simmons VI, 141
Fowler, Simmons VI, 177
Fowler, Solomon V, 996
Fowler, Susan III, 124
Fowler, Susan B. III, 124
Fowler, Susan J. IV, 1131
Fowler, Susanna III, 124
Fowler, Susanna J. IV, 1131
Fowler, Susannah VI, 160
Fowler, Susannah VI, 177
Fowler, Susannah VI, 203
Fowler, Tena V, 996
Fowler, Theodate IV, 1057
Fowler, Theodate IV, 1079
Fowler, Thomas VI, 312
Fowler, Thomas G. VI, 854
Fowler, Thos. VI, 817
Fowler, Viney VI, 974
Fowler, Viresta VI, 817
Fowler, Wd. ??? VI, 177
Fowler, Weeden III, 124
Fowler, William III, 124
Fowler, William III, 313
Fowler, William VI, 107
Fowler, William VI, 311
Fowler, William VI, 312
Fowler, William VI, 917
Fowler, William VI, 961
Fowler, William D. III, 124
Fowler, William D. VI, 817
Fowler, William D. VI, 823
Fowler, William D. VI, 826
Fowler, Wm. VI, 817
Fowler, Wm. C. VI, 932
Fowler, Wm. C. VI, 1018
Fowler, Wm. D. V, 170
Fowles, Nancy I, 389
Fowsler, Wm. D. III, 216
Fowzer, Mary II, 977
Fowzer, Mary II, 997
Fox, ??? VI, 22
Fox, ??? VI, 40
Fox, ??? VI, 41
Fox, ??? VI, 93
Fox, ??? VI, 94
Fox, A. A. VI, 1012
Fox, Abraham III, 124
Fox, Ada L. IV, 777
Fox, Alice M. V, 385
Fox, Almira V, 385
Fox, Ann II, 364
Fox, Ann II, 443
Fox, Ann II, 688
Fox, Ann IV, 156
Fox, Ann Mott III, 125
Fox, Ann W. II, 131
Fox, Anna IV, 143
Fox, Anna IV, 144
Fox, Anna IV, 146
Fox, Anna IV, 202
Fox, Anna IV, 203
Fox, Anna Applebee IV, 146
Fox, Anna M. III, 124
Fox, Anna M. III, 280
Fox, Anna W. II, 148
Fox, Anne II, 131
Fox, Bernard Johnson VI, 733
Fox, Bernard Johnson VI, 741
Fox, Caroline II, 363
Fox, Caroline V, 56
Fox, Caroline V, 68
Fox, Catharine III, 125
Fox, Catharine N. VI, 917
Fox, Catharine T. III, 125
Fox, Charles IV, 146
Fox, Charles IV, 202
Fox, Charles I. IV, 146
Fox, Charles James IV, 146
Fox, Charles James IV, 202
Fox, Charles Pemberton II, 364
Fox, Charlotte III, 125
Fox, Charlotte III, 203
Fox, Charlotte III, 316
Fox, Charlotte L. III, 125
Fox, Chas. J. VI, 1012
Fox, Clara V, 739
Fox, Clara D. V, 385
Fox, Clara P. V, 385
Fox, Clarissa L. L. VI, 817
Fox, David I, 131
Fox, Deborah III, 124
Fox, Deborah III, 125
Fox, Deborah III, 288
Fox, Delitha E. VI, 817
Fox, Dorthy II, 363
Fox, Edmund Kelley VI, 741
Fox, Edmund Kelly VI, 791
Fox, Edward B. III, 124
Fox, Eleanor B. II, 132
Fox, Eliza L. III, 124
Fox, Eliza L. III, 125
Fox, Eliza L. III, 225
Fox, Elizabeth II, 363
Fox, Elizabeth II, 364
Fox, Elizabeth II, 443
Fox, Elizabeth II, 527

Fox, Elizabeth II, 567
Fox, Elizabeth II, 596
Fox, Elizabeth II, 608
Fox, Elizabeth II, 620
Fox, Elizabeth II, 623
Fox, Elizabeth II, 637
Fox, Elizabeth III, 124
Fox, Elizabeth IV, 142
Fox, Elizabeth IV, 146
Fox, Elizabeth V, 385
Fox, Elizabeth V, 386
Fox, Elizabeth V, 781
Fox, Elizabeth V, 789
Fox, Elizabeth VI, 841
Fox, Elizabeth Hill II, 527
Fox, Elizabeth Hill II, 608
Fox, Elizabeth Mary II, 364
Fox, Elizabeth Miller IV, 146
Fox, Emeline II, 364
Fox, Emma V, 996
Fox, Emma Leonard V, 491
Fox, Erie Esther IV, 202
Fox, Ester II, 364
Fox, Esther III, 124
Fox, Esther III, 125
Fox, Esther III, 323
Fox, Esther IV, 202
Fox, Esther IV, 519
Fox, Esther IV, 525
Fox, Esther Cooper IV, 203
Fox, Esther J. IV, 202
Fox, Esther Moore IV, 203
Fox, Esther Shotwell) III, 288
Fox, Ethel V, 739
Fox, Florence Eyster VI, 741
Fox, Florence Eyster VI, 791
Fox, Francis II, 364
Fox, Francis IV, 146
Fox, Francis IV, 203
Fox, Francis Cooper IV, 202
Fox, Francis D. IV, 146
Fox, Francis D. IV, 161
Fox, Francis Drake IV, 146
Fox, Geo. V, 962
Fox, Geo. S. III, 225
Fox, George I, 131
Fox, George II, 17
Fox, George II, 222
Fox, George II, 227
Fox, George II, 364
Fox, George II, 527
Fox, George II, 538
Fox, George II, 620
Fox, George III, 71
Fox, George III, 125
Fox, George III, 280
Fox, George III, 288
Fox, George IV, 1315
Fox, George VI, 5
Fox, George VI, 7
Fox, George VI, 8
Fox, George VI, 21
Fox, George VI, 22
Fox, George VI, 24
Fox, George VI, 27
Fox, George VI, 28
Fox, George VI, 29
Fox, George VI, 30
Fox, George VI, 32
Fox, George VI, 34
Fox, George VI, 38
Fox, George VI, 39
Fox, George VI, 40
Fox, George VI, 41
Fox, George VI, 93
Fox, George VI, 225
Fox, George VI, 306
Fox, George VI, 809
Fox, George VI, 817
Fox, George D. III, 125
Fox, George Henry III, 125
Fox, George I. V, 385
Fox, George J. V, 386
Fox, George S. III, 124
Fox, George S. III, 125
Fox, George S. III, 323
Fox, George T. III, 288
Fox, George T. IV, 1315
Fox, Gus IV, 777
Fox, Hannah II, 364
Fox, Harriet II, 294
Fox, Herbert V, 739
Fox, Hester III, 124
Fox, Hiram V, 996
Fox, Huldah V, 996
Fox, Jacob V, 385
Fox, Jacob S. V, 385
Fox, James II, 363
Fox, James II, 364
Fox, James II, 527
Fox, James II, 567
Fox, James VI, 817
Fox, James, Jr. II, 363
Fox, James, Jr. II, 364
Fox, James, Jr. II, 527
Fox, James, Jr. II, 688
Fox, James, Sr. II, 363
Fox, Jane V, 838
Fox, Jane V, 873
Fox, Jane V, 996
Fox, John II, 443
Fox, John Francis IV, 202
Fox, Jonathan II, 222
Fox, Jonathan III, 124
Fox, Joseph II, 363
Fox, Joseph II, 364
Fox, Joseph II, 527
Fox, Joseph II, 596
Fox, Joseph II, 608
Fox, Joseph II, 620
Fox, Joseph II, 623
Fox, Joseph II, 637
Fox, Joseph Mickle II, 364
Fox, Joseph S. III, 288
Fox, Josiah IV, 146
Fox, Josiah IV, 156
Fox, Julia Fitzhugh VI, 733
Fox, Julia Fitzhugh VI, 741
Fox, Juliana D. IV, 161
Fox, Juliann IV, 203
Fox, Juliann IV, 296
Fox, Julianna D. IV, 146
Fox, Justenian II, 364
Fox, Justinian II, 443
Fox, Louisa II, 364
Fox, Lydia III, 124
Fox, Lydia III, 125
Fox, Lydia IV, 905
Fox, Lydia IV, 910
Fox, Margaret V, 239
Fox, Margaret V, 385
Fox, Margaret V, 952
Fox, Margaret V, 962
Fox, Margaret VI, 312
Fox, Margaret E. V, 385
Fox, Maria T. III, 71
Fox, Maria T. III, 125
Fox, Martha V, 860
Fox, Martha VI, 817
Fox, Mary II, 364
Fox, Mary II, 524
Fox, Mary II, 527
Fox, Mary II, 620
Fox, Mary III, 124
Fox, Mary III, 125
Fox, Mary V, 239
Fox, Mary V, 996
Fox, Mary A. V, 996
Fox, Mary E. II, 132
Fox, Mary L. III, 125
Fox, Mary Lydia III, 125
Fox, Mary Moore IV, 202
Fox, Mary Weaver VI, 741
Fox, Mary Weaver VI, 791
Fox, Mildred V, 996
Fox, Mildred Rosebud VI, 733
Fox, Mildred Rosebud VI, 741
Fox, Miller IV, 202
Fox, Minor H. II, 132
Fox, Nancy VI, 817
Fox, Nancy A. VI, 817
Fox, Patience VI, 817
Fox, Pemberton II, 364
Fox, Phebe I, 389
Fox, Phebe I, 402
Fox, Polly VI, 817
Fox, Pur. Rebecca L. III, 125
Fox, Rachel V, 170
Fox, Rachel M. V, 739
Fox, Rebecca III, 125
Fox, Rebecca L. III, 124
Fox, Rebecca L. III, 225
Fox, Rebecca L. III, 280
Fox, Rebecca L. III, 313
Fox, Rebecca L. III, 323
Fox, Rebecca Stephen IV, 146
Fox, Rebecca Stevens IV, 146
Fox, Rebecca Stevens IV, 156
Fox, Richard II, 364
Fox, Richard VI, 807
Fox, Richard VI, 817
Fox, Richard VI, 823
Fox, S. H. V, 996
Fox, Sally Ann VI, 1012
Fox, Samuel II, 364
Fox, Samuel M. II, 364
Fox, Samuel Mickle II, 527
Fox, Samuel Mickle II, 623
Fox, Samuel Pleasants II, 364
Fox, Sarah I, 878
Fox, Sarah II, 70
Fox, Sarah II, 93
Fox, Sarah II, 364
Fox, Sarah II, 527
Fox, Sarah II, 623
Fox, Sarah III, 125
Fox, Sarah IV, 203
Fox, Sarah V, 962
Fox, Sarah VI, 817
Fox, Sarah VI, 823
Fox, Sarah Clark III, 125
Fox, Sarah Cooper IV, 202
Fox, Sarah E. V, 860
Fox, Sarah Emily II, 311
Fox, Sarah S. IV, 144
Fox, Sarah S. IV, 146
Fox, Sarah Scantleberry IV, 146
Fox, Sarah Scantlebury IV, 146
Fox, Squire H. F. V, 996
Fox, Susanna II, 222
Fox, Susanna II, 364
Fox, Susanna II, 527
Fox, Susanna VI, 817
Fox, Susannah II, 222
Fox, Susannah II, 538
Fox, Susannah VI, 807
Fox, Susie V, 739
Fox, Thomas II, 443
Fox, Thomas VI, 817
Fox, Thomas VI, 866
Fox, Thomas G. VI, 817
Fox, Thomas G. VI, 917
Fox, Thomasine II, 527
Fox, Thomasine II, 637
Fox, Tillie IV, 777
Fox, Uriah V, 996
Fox, Wd. Ann II, 363
Fox, William III, 124
Fox, William III, 125
Fox, William V, 860
Fox, William VI, 813
Fox, William VI, 817
Fox, William H. VI, 817
Fox, William James III, 125
Fox, William Spicer IV, 202
Fox, William W. III, 125
Fox, William W. III, 203
Fox, William W., Jr. III, 125
Fox, Wm. Henry III, 125
Fox, Wm. N. II, 131
Fox, Wm. Spicer IV, 202
Fox, Wm. W. III, 125
Foy, Phebe III, 125
Fozdick, Elizabeth VI, 817
Fozdick, Jane VI, 817
Fozdick, Timothy VI, 817
Fozdick, William VI, 817
Frace, Clara III, 125
Fradley, Susan G. VI, 873
Frailey, Jane Chapman II, 735
Fraim, Asenath V, 952
Fraim, Elizabeth V, 952
Fraim, James V, 952
Fraim, John V, 952
Fraim, Mahlon V, 952
Fraim, Robert II, 364
Fraim, Wm. V, 952
Frair, Elizabeth VI, 965
Fraiser, Abner I, 540
Fraiser, Barbary I, 540
Fraiser, Beriah I, 540
Fraiser, Julia I, 540
Fraiser, Samuel I, 540
Fraiser, Sarah V, 621
Fraiser, Thomas I, 540
Fraisher, Ezekiel VI, 390
Fraishier, Sally VI, 827
Fraishier, Wm. VI, 827
Fraizer, Aaron I, 565
Fraizer, Aaron I, 653
Fraizer, Aaron I, 654
Fraizer, Aaron I, 678
Fraizer, Aaron I, 679
Fraizer, Abel I, 654
Fraizer, Abel I, 679
Fraizer, Abel I, 682
Fraizer, Abel I, 853
Fraizer, Abigail I, 654
Fraizer, Abigail I, 678
Fraizer, Abner I, 654
Fraizer, Abner I, 1119
Fraizer, Abraham I, 654
Fraizer, Abraham I, 1119
Fraizer, Alexander I, 653
Fraizer, Alexander V, 491
Fraizer, Alexander V, 621
Fraizer, Alice V, 621
Fraizer, Ann I, 679
Fraizer, Ann I, 682
Fraizer, Ann I, 1060
Fraizer, Catharine I, 677
Fraizer, Davis V, 239
Fraizer, Eli I, 654
Fraizer, Eli I, 1119
Fraizer, Elijah I, 654
Fraizer, Elisha V, 621
Fraizer, Eliza I, 1119
Fraizer, Elizabeth V, 621
Fraizer, Elza I, 1119
Fraizer, Enos I, 654
Fraizer, Frances V, 239
Fraizer, Francis V, 239
Fraizer, Gidian V, 239
Fraizer, Hannah I, 654
Fraizer, Hannah I, 1119
Fraizer, Hannah V, 621
Fraizer, Isaac I, 654
Fraizer, Isaac I, 679
Fraizer, Isabel I, 653
Fraizer, Isabel I, 659
Fraizer, Isabel I, 679
Fraizer, Isabel I, 681
Fraizer, James I, 654
Fraizer, Jane I, 654
Fraizer, Jane I, 1119
Fraizer, Jane V, 621
Fraizer, John I, 389
Fraizer, John I, 653
Fraizer, John I, 654
Fraizer, John I, 678
Fraizer, John I, 853
Fraizer, John I, 1119
Fraizer, John V, 621
Fraizer, Jonah V, 292
Fraizer, Jonah V, 621
Fraizer, Jonathan I, 654
Fraizer, Joshua V, 621
Fraizer, Lindley Murray V, 621
Fraizer, Lydia Ann V, 621
Fraizer, Martha I, 654
Fraizer, Martha I, 853
Fraizer, Martha W. V, 621
Fraizer, Mary I, 653
Fraizer, Mary I, 654
Fraizer, Mary I, 678
Fraizer, Mary I, 679
Fraizer, Mary I, 681
Fraizer, Mary I, 853
Fraizer, Mary V, 621
Fraizer, Mary Jane V, 621
Fraizer, Matthew I, 654
Fraizer, Matthew I, 679
Fraizer, Matthew I, 681
Fraizer, Nathan I, 853
Fraizer, Phebe I, 653
Fraizer, Phebe V, 619
Fraizer, Rachel I, 853
Fraizer, Rachel Wright V, 621
Fraizer, Rebecca I, 679
Fraizer, Rebecca I, 1089
Fraizer, Rebecca T. V, 621
Fraizer, Rebeccah I, 679
Fraizer, Rebeccah I, 682
Fraizer, Rebeckah I, 878
Fraizer, Rebeckah I, 891
Fraizer, Rebekah I, 853
Fraizer, Robert I, 654
Fraizer, Samuel I, 1119
Fraizer, Samuel, Sr. I, 1119
Fraizer, Sarah I, 565
Fraizer, Sarah I, 653
Fraizer, Sarah I, 654
Fraizer, Sarah I, 678
Fraizer, Sarah I, 679
Fraizer, Sarah I, 853
Fraizer, Sarah V, 292
Fraizer, Sarah V, 621
Fraizer, Solomon I, 654
Fraizer, Solomon I, 677
Fraizer, Susanna I, 654
Fraizer, Susanna I, 678
Fraizer, Susanna I, 692
Fraizer, Thomas V, 239
Fraizer, William I, 678
Fraizer, William I, 692
Fraizer, William I, 1119
Fraizer, William, Jr. I, 1119
Fraizer, Willis IV, 1207
Fraizure, Elizabeth V, 651
Fraizure, Hannah P. V, 651
Fraizure, John V, 651
Fraizure, Lydia V, 651
Fraizure, Mary V, 651
Fraklin, James VI, 1004
Fraklin, Mary Ann VI, 1004
Fraley, Frederick II, 863
Fraley, Frederick II, 871
Fraley, Jane II, 741
Fraley, Jane C. II, 863
Fraley, Jane C. II, 871
Fraley, Sallie C. II, 863
Fraley, Sallie C. II, 871
Fraley, Sarah II, 735
Fraley, Sarah II, 741
Fraley, Sarah Cresson II, 798
Fraling, Betsy VI, 917
Fraling, Daniel VI, 890
Fraling, Daniel VI, 917
Fraling, Edward VI, 890
Fraling, Henry VI, 917
Fraling, Mary J. VI, 890
Fraling, Nancy VI, 917
Frame, Aaron II, 705
Frame, Aaron IV, 203
Frame, Aaron IV, 281
Frame, Aaron IV, 292
Frame, Aaron IV, 330
Frame, Aaron IV, 375
Frame, Aaron IV, 394
Frame, Aaron IV, 410
Frame, Aaron IV, 443
Frame, Aaron IV, 459
Frame, Aaron IV, 525
Frame, Aaron IV, 534
Frame, Aaron IV, 550
Frame, Aaron IV, 559
Frame, Aaron IV, 686
Frame, Acenath V, 952
Frame, Achsah IV, 393
Frame, Achsah IV, 525
Frame, Achsah IV, 550
Frame, Alace V, 56
Frame, Amas IV, 393
Frame, Amasa IV, 203
Frame, Amasa IV, 393
Frame, Amasa IV, 414
Frame, Amasa IV, 431
Frame, Amasa IV, 445
Frame, Amasa IV, 707
Frame, Amasa IV, 771
Frame, Ann IV, 203
Frame, Ann IV, 410
Frame, Ann IV, 1207
Frame, Ann IV, 1220
Frame, Ann P. III, 380
Frame, Anna IV, 203
Frame, Anna IV, 272
Frame, Anna IV, 330
Frame, Anna IV, 496
Frame, Anna VI, 390
Frame, Anna H. VI, 621
Frame, Anna H. VI, 638
Frame, Asenath IV, 200
Frame, Asenath IV, 203
Frame, Asenath V, 952
Frame, Aseneth V, 952
Frame, Benj. IV, 203
Frame, Benjamin III, 125
Frame, Benjamin III, 380
Frame, Benjamin IV, 203
Frame, Benjamin IV, 320
Frame, Benjamin IV, 321
Frame, Benjamin IV, 330
Frame, Benjamin IV, 525
Frame, Benjamin VI, 390
Frame, Caroline III, 380
Frame, Caroline III, 387
Frame, Catharine III, 125
Frame, Catharine III, 380
Frame, Catharine C. III, 380
Frame, Catharine D. III, 125
Frame, Catharine D. III, 380
Frame, Catherine W. V, 56
Frame, Charles III, 380
Frame, Charles III, 387
Frame, Clara IV, 771
Frame, Clara E. IV, 393
Frame, Clara E. IV, 445
Frame, Clara E. IV, 707
Frame, Clara E. IV, 772
Frame, Corrine V, 170
Frame, Corrinne V, 183
Frame, David III, 125
Frame, David VI, 621
Frame, David VI, 638
Frame, David VI, 741
Frame, David James VI, 638
Frame, Eliza III, 125
Frame, Eliza III, 249
Frame, Eliza III, 250
Frame, Eliza III, 380
Frame, Eliza III, 383
Frame, Eliza VI, 621
Frame, Eliza VI, 622
Frame, Eliza VI, 623
Frame, Eliza VI, 638
Frame, Eliza VI, 651
Frame, Eliza VI, 702
Frame, Eliza VI, 706
Frame, Elizabeth II, 705
Frame, Elizabeth III, 380
Frame, Elizabeth IV, 203
Frame, Elizabeth IV, 320
Frame, Elizabeth IV, 321
Frame, Elizabeth IV, 330

Frame, Elizabeth IV, 375
Frame, Elizabeth IV, 393
Frame, Elizabeth IV, 410
Frame, Elizabeth IV, 420
Frame, Elizabeth IV, 434
Frame, Elizabeth IV, 447
Frame, Elizabeth IV, 578
Frame, Elizabeth IV, 596
Frame, Elizabeth V, 56
Frame, Elizabeth V, 952
Frame, Elizabeth VI, 390
Frame, Elizabeth Ann IV, 578
Frame, Elizabeth Ann IV, 581
Frame, Elizabeth B. II, 741
Frame, Elizabeth B. IV, 394
Frame, Elizabeth F. V, 56
Frame, Elizabeth K. IV, 393
Frame, Elizabeth R. IV, 393
Frame, Elizabeth R. IV, 394
Frame, Elizabeth R. IV, 414
Frame, Elizabeth S. V, 56
Frame, Emily IV, 374
Frame, Emily IV, 393
Frame, Emily D. II, 711
Frame, Emily D. IV, 393
Frame, Emily D. IV, 394
Frame, Emily Dennis IV, 393
Frame, Emily Dennis IV, 418
Frame, Esther VI, 621
Frame, Esther VI, 638
Frame, Esther E. V, 170
Frame, Esther G. V, 183
Frame, Eunice F. V, 56
Frame, Florence II, 711
Frame, Florence IV, 393
Frame, Florence IV, 418
Frame, Florence M. IV, 394
Frame, Geo. IV, 238
Frame, George IV, 203
Frame, George IV, 393
Frame, George IV, 434
Frame, George VI, 390
Frame, Georgia V, 98
Frame, Georgia Anna IV, 393
Frame, Georgia Anna V, 56
Frame, Georgianna V, 56
Frame, Hettie V, 170
Frame, Hettie C. V, 170
Frame, Ira E. IV, 203
Frame, Ira S. II, 705
Frame, Ira S. II, 741
Frame, Ira S. IV, 375
Frame, Ira S. IV, 393
Frame, Ira S. IV, 394
Frame, Itasca M. V, 170
Frame, James IV, 200
Frame, James IV, 203
Frame, James IV, 330
Frame, James IV, 525
Frame, James V, 952
Frame, James VI, 390
Frame, James M. VI, 621
Frame, James M. VI, 638
Frame, James T. IV, 203
Frame, James T. IV, 272
Frame, James T. IV, 330
Frame, James T. IV, 525
Frame, James Thomas V, 56
Frame, Jane IV, 203
Frame, Jane IV, 321
Frame, Jane IV, 330
Frame, Jane VI, 390
Frame, Jas. T. IV, 496
Frame, Jesse III, 125
Frame, Jesse III, 204
Frame, Jesse III, 380
Frame, Jesse III, 383
Frame, Jesse III, 386
Frame, Jesse III, 482
Frame, Jesse H. VI, 638
Frame, John V, 952
Frame, John T. IV, 203
Frame, Joseph III, 125
Frame, Joseph III, 380
Frame, Joseph VI, 638
Frame, Joseph A. IV, 393
Frame, Joseph A. IV, 394
Frame, Joseph E. IV, 394
Frame, Joseph L. III, 125
Frame, Joseph L. III, 380
Frame, Joseph W. IV, 203
Frame, Katharyne W. V, 56
Frame, Laura IV, 393
Frame, Laura L. IV, 394
Frame, Lavina H. IV, 394
Frame, Lavina H. IV, 459
Frame, Lavina H. IV, 525
Frame, Lavina H. IV, 559
Frame, Lavinia H. IV, 394
Frame, Leah V, 952
Frame, Leah V, 955
Frame, Lindley V, 98
Frame, Lura L. IV, 393
Frame, Lura L. IV, 394
Frame, Lyda G. IV, 393
Frame, Lyda G. IV, 440
Frame, Lydia IV, 203
Frame, Lydia IV, 209
Frame, Lydia IV, 238
Frame, Lydia IV, 393
Frame, Lydia IV, 434
Frame, Lydia IV, 578
Frame, Lydia IV, 581
Frame, Mahlon V, 952
Frame, Margaret H. IV, 393
Frame, Margaret H. IV, 420
Frame, Maria III, 125
Frame, Maria III, 380
Frame, Maria F. III, 386
Frame, Marie III, 380
Frame, Mary III, 125
Frame, Mary III, 204
Frame, Mary III, 380
Frame, Mary III, 383
Frame, Mary III, 386
Frame, Mary III, 482
Frame, Mary IV, 209
Frame, Mary IV, 393
Frame, Mary IV, 436
Frame, Mary V, 56
Frame, Mary V, 57
Frame, Mary Ann IV, 203
Frame, Mary Ann IV, 393
Frame, Mary Ann IV, 410
Frame, Mary Ann IV, 525
Frame, Mary Ann IV, 534
Frame, Mary E. IV, 394
Frame, Mary Elma IV, 393
Frame, Mary F. IV, 394
Frame, Mary F. IV, 448
Frame, Mary F. V, 56
Frame, Mary T. IV, 393
Frame, Melissa IV, 203
Frame, Nathan P. Grissell IV, 578
Frame, Nathan T. V, 170
Frame, Nathan T. V, 183
Frame, Oliver IV, 203
Frame, Oliver C. IV, 203
Frame, Oliver C. IV, 393
Frame, Oliver C. IV, 394
Frame, Peter IV, 203
Frame, Peter IV, 525
Frame, Phebe III, 380
Frame, Phebe III, 482
Frame, Phebe III, 506
Frame, Phebe Alice IV, 393
Frame, Phebe Alice V, 56
Frame, Rachel IV, 203
Frame, Rachel IV, 320
Frame, Rachel IV, 330
Frame, Rachel VI, 390
Frame, Rachel E. IV, 393
Frame, Rachel E. IV, 394
Frame, Rachel E. IV, 431
Frame, Rachel E. IV, 445
Frame, Rachel E. IV, 707
Frame, Rachel E. IV, 771
Frame, Rebecca IV, 203
Frame, Rebecca IV, 368
Frame, Rebecca IV, 393
Frame, Rebecca Ann IV, 203
Frame, Ruana IV, 393
Frame, Ruanna IV, 203
Frame, Ruanna IV, 281
Frame, Ruanna IV, 310
Frame, Ruanna IV, 330
Frame, Ruanna IV, 369
Frame, Ruanna IV, 375
Frame, Ruanna IV, 393
Frame, Ruanna IV, 411
Frame, Ruanna IV, 525
Frame, Ruanna IV, 686
Frame, Ruanna T. IV, 393
Frame, Ruannah IV, 203
Frame, Ruannah IV, 288
Frame, Ruannah T. IV, 203
Frame, Susan VI, 638
Frame, Tabitha IV, 375
Frame, Tabitha IV, 393
Frame, Tabitha IV, 443
Frame, Tabitha IV, 444
Frame, Tabitha IV, 525
Frame, Tabitha IV, 686
Frame, Tacy IV, 203
Frame, Tacy IV, 393
Frame, Tacy IV, 443
Frame, Tacy T. IV, 203
Frame, Tacy T. IV, 393
Frame, Talitha II, 705
Frame, Talitha IV, 281
Frame, Talitha IV, 410
Frame, Talitha IV, 534
Frame, Tassie V, 170
Frame, Telitha IV, 203
Frame, Telitha IV, 292
Frame, Thomas III, 125
Frame, Thomas III, 380
Frame, Thomas L. III, 125
Frame, Thomas L. IV, 203
Frame, Thomas L. IV, 393
Frame, Thomas L. IV, 447
Frame, Thomas L. V, 56
Frame, Thompson IV, 203
Frame, Thompson IV, 374
Frame, Thompson IV, 393
Frame, Thompson IV, 394
Frame, Thos. IV, 209
Frame, Thos. L. III, 380
Frame, Thos. L. IV, 420
Frame, William III, 125
Frame, William III, 380
Frame, William III, 482
Frame, William III, 506
Frame, William IV, 203
Frame, William IV, 330
Frame, William VI, 390
Frame, William A. IV, 203
Frame, William A. IV, 393
Frame, William A. IV, 394
Frame, William A. IV, 418
Frame, William F. IV, 203
Frame, William H. V, 56
Frame, William T. V, 56
Frame, William T. V, 57
Frame, Wm. II, 711
Frame, Wm. IV, 203
Frame, Wm. IV, 288
Frame, Wm. IV, 330
Frame, Wm. IV, 393
Frame, Wm. IV, 525
Frame, Wm. V, 56
Frame, Wm. V, 952
Frame, Wm. A. IV, 394
Frame, Wm. T. V, 56
Frames, Mary Ann IV, 393
Frampton, C. A. IV, 707
Frampton, Dessie IV, 707
Frampton, Elizabeth II, 273
Frampton, Elizabeth II, 460
Frampton, Elizabeth II, 527
Frampton, Elizabeth III, 125
Frampton, Elizabeth III, 261
Frampton, Mary III, 125
Frampton, Sarah II, 199
Frampton, Sarah II, 222
Frampton, William III, 125
Frampton, William III, 261
Frampton, Wm. II, 527
Frampton, Wm. II, 633
Framton, Elizabeth II, 222
Framton, Sarah II, 222
Framton, Thomas II, 222
Framton, Thomas II, 364
France, Eliza V, 996
France, Eliza Jane V, 996
France, Helen III, 125
France, Jane III, 125
France, Jane III, 229
France, Maria III, 125
France, Sanford Dewey III, 125
France, Sanford Dewey III, 229
France, Susan III, 125
France, Wm. Stewart III, 125
Frances, Lucy J. VI, 807
Frances, Martha IV, 944
Frances, Samuel Mifflin II, 364
Frances, Sarah III, 403
Franch, Charles C. II, 528
Franch, David II, 720
Franch, Eliza II, 720
Franch, Elma II, 948
Franch, Elma II, 949
Franch, James II, 528
Franch, Joseph II, 528
Franch, Mary II, 720
Franch, Mercy G. II, 528
Franch, Sarah Chapman II, 528
Franche, F. William III, 125
Franche, Marie III, 125
Franche, Marie III, 243
Franche, T. William III, 243
Francis, ??? III, 125
Francis, ??? III, 126
Francis, Agnes E. III, 126
Francis, Alfred Tench III, 125
Francis, Alfred Tench III, 323
Francis, Anna III, 125
Francis, Anna III, 208
Francis, Aug't T. III, 125
Francis, Augustus T. III, 125
Francis, Augustus T. III, 208
Francis, Dorothy T. III, 125
Francis, Dorothy T. III, 323
Francis, Edith Agnes III, 16
Francis, Edith Agnes III, 125
Francis, Edna III, 125
Francis, Edna D. III, 125
Francis, Elizabeth Austin IV, 1207
Francis, Ethel IV, 1315
Francis, Geo. Fitz R. III, 126
Francis, George W. IV, 1207
Francis, Grace III, 126
Francis, Grace Ann III, 125
Francis, Hannah II, 527
Francis, Hannah II, 637
Francis, Ida M. IV, 472
Francis, Joseph Parker IV, 1207
Francis, Lloyd W. III, 125
Francis, Lloyd West III, 125
Francis, Mary IV, 1207
Francis, Mary Ann IV, 1207
Francis, Mary J. VI, 817
Francis, Mary Taber IV, 1207
Francis, Philip Ward III, 16
Francis, Philip Ward III, 125
Francis, Samuel Mifflin II, 364
Francis, Sarah II, 364
Francis, William A. III, 126
Francis, Wilson VI, 817
Francis, Wm. Albert III, 125
Franck, Henrietta III, 183
Franck, Mariah I, 761
Franck, Mariah I, 762
Franer, Lida V, 870
Frank, Daniel D. IV, 972
Frank, John VI, 954
Frank, John VI, 981
Frank, John A. V, 561
Frank, Mariah I, 761
Frank, Maud S. IV, 972
Frank, Minnie Louise IV, 1315
Frank, Nancy VI, 981
Frank, Sarah C. IV, 972
Frank, Sukey VI, 954
Frankeberger, Betsey VI, 887
Frankeberger, William VI, 887
Frankfurt, Helen III, 32
Frankfurt, Myron III, 32
Frankfurt, Secunda III, 32
Frankhouser, Ruth IV, 86
Frankhouser, Ruth IV, 115
Frankland, Agnes V, 906
Frankland, Agnes V, 910
Frankland, Agnes Elizabeth V, 910
Frankland, Ann V, 906
Frankland, Anna V, 906
Frankland, Anne V, 910
Frankland, Benj. V, 906
Frankland, Benj. V, 910
Frankland, Benjamin V, 906
Frankland, Benjamin Frankland V, 910
Frankland, Frances V, 906
Frankland, Frances Maris V, 906
Frankland, Malcomb V, 910
Frankland, Maria V, 910
Frankland, Mary V, 906
Frankland, Mary V, 910
Frankland, Sarah V, 906
Frankland, Sarah V, 910
Frankland, Sarah M. V, 910
Frankland, Sarah Maria V, 910
Frankland, Thomas H. IV, 1235
Frankland, Thomas Henry IV, 1207
Frankland, Thomas Henry IV, 1235
Frankland, Thos. V, 906
Frankland, Thos. V, 910
Frankland, Thos. Milford V, 910
Frankland, Thos. Wilfred V, 910
Frankland, Wm. V, 910
Franklin, ??? III, 127
Franklin, ??? III, 296
Franklin, Abner VI, 917
Franklin, Abner H. VI, 917
Franklin, Abraham III, 126
Franklin, Almira III, 126
Franklin, Amelia III, 126
Franklin, Amelia III, 127
Franklin, Amelia III, 293
Franklin, Ann III, 127
Franklin, Ann Julicia L. VI, 917
Franklin, Ann M. III, 126
Franklin, Ann M. III, 127
Franklin, Ann M. III, 235
Franklin, Anna III, 127
Franklin, Anna T. III, 127
Franklin, Anne VI, 817
Franklin, Annie T. III, 410
Franklin, Annie T. III, 411
Franklin, Annie T. III, 458
Franklin, Anthony III, 126
Franklin, Anthony III, 380
Franklin, Anthony III, 384
Franklin, Anthony III, 389
Franklin, Archd. VI, 869
Franklin, Archd. VI, 987
Franklin, Archd. VI, 1012
Franklin, Archer VI, 917
Franklin, Archibald VI, 866
Franklin, Archibald VI, 917
Franklin, Archibald VI, 964
Franklin, Artridge VI, 546
Franklin, Artridge VI, 577
Franklin, Benj. S. V, 673
Franklin, Benjamin III, 127
Franklin, Benjamin VI, 818
Franklin, Benjamin VI, 827
Franklin, Benjamin VI, 829
Franklin, Benjamin VI, 856
Franklin, Benjamin VI, 857
Franklin, Benjamin VI, 917
Franklin, Benjamin H. III, 126
Franklin, Benjamin H. III, 127
Franklin, Betsey VI, 917
Franklin, Betsey VI, 976
Franklin, Bridget E. VI, 804
Franklin, Byron V, 673
Franklin, Calista H. VI, 818
Franklin, Camilla Susan VI, 1022
Franklin, Carleton Garretson VI, 742
Franklin, Catharine III, 385
Franklin, Catharine VI, 917
Franklin, Catharine VI, 969
Franklin, Catharine C. III, 126
Franklin, Catherine VI, 865
Franklin, Charles F. III, 410
Franklin, Charles F. III, 458
Franklin, Charlotte III, 75
Franklin, Daniel VI, 849
Franklin, Daniel E. VI, 818
Franklin, Deborah II, 527
Franklin, Deborah II, 602
Franklin, Deborah III, 87
Franklin, Deborah III, 126
Franklin, Deborah III, 127
Franklin, Deborah III, 294
Franklin, Deborah M. III, 70
Franklin, Deborah M. III, 126
Franklin, Deborah M. III, 127
Franklin, Dorothy III, 40
Franklin, Dorothy III, 126
Franklin, Edmond VI, 1015
Franklin, Edmund VI, 865
Franklin, Edmund VI, 917
Franklin, Edmund VI, 968
Franklin, Edward III, 126
Franklin, Edward III, 127
Franklin, Elias VI, 917
Franklin, Elina VI, 917
Franklin, Eliza Ann VI, 994
Franklin, Elizabeth III, 126
Franklin, Elizabeth III, 321
Franklin, Elizabeth III, 380
Franklin, Elizabeth III, 384
Franklin, Elizabeth III, 385
Franklin, Elizabeth III, 388
Franklin, Elizabeth VI, 816
Franklin, Elizabeth VI, 817
Franklin, Elizabeth VI, 818
Franklin, Elizabeth VI, 840
Franklin, Elizabeth VI, 844
Franklin, Elizabeth VI, 851
Franklin, Elizabeth VI, 855
Franklin, Elizabeth VI, 861
Franklin, Elizabeth VI, 866
Franklin, Elizabeth VI, 917
Franklin, Elizabeth VI, 1011
Franklin, Elizabeth R. VI, 917
Franklin, Emily III, 126
Franklin, Emily S. VI, 917
Franklin, Emma III, 77
Franklin, Emma III, 126
Franklin, Emma V, 673
Franklin, Esther II, 527
Franklin, Esther II, 599
Franklin, Esther III, 126
Franklin, Esther III, 232
Franklin, Esther III, 272
Franklin, Esther M. VI, 821
Franklin, Eugene IV, 1315
Franklin, Frances V. III, 380
Franklin, Francis III, 126
Franklin, Francis W. VI, 917
Franklin, Frederick P. III, 293
Franklin, Frederick Robert III, 385
Franklin, Geo. N. III, 126
Franklin, George N. III, 126

Franklin, George N. III, 127
Franklin, Hannah III, 127
Franklin, Hannah III, 264
Franklin, Hannah VI, 917
Franklin, Hannah C. III, 127
Franklin, Hariet VI, 1012
Franklin, Henry III, 40
Franklin, Henry III, 42
Franklin, Henry III, 75
Franklin, Henry III, 126
Franklin, Henry III, 236
Franklin, Henry III, 411
Franklin, Henry III, 444
Franklin, Henry VI, 817
Franklin, Henry VI, 851
Franklin, Henry J. III, 126
Franklin, Henry Mitchell III, 293
Franklin, Henry R. VI, 821
Franklin, Henry R. VI, 834
Franklin, Henry T. VI, 917
Franklin, Henry W. VI, 883
Franklin, Henry W. VI, 917
Franklin, Henry W. VI, 963
Franklin, Irwin VI, 742
Franklin, Irwin Chace VI, 741
Franklin, Irwin Chace VI, 779
Franklin, Irwin Chace VI, 793
Franklin, Irwin Chase VI, 741
Franklin, J. VI, 859
Franklin, Jackson W. VI, 917
Franklin, Jacob III, 294
Franklin, James I, 829
Franklin, James VI, 917
Franklin, James C. VI, 917
Franklin, James D. VI, 797
Franklin, James Emlen II, 364
Franklin, James Nelson VI, 741
Franklin, James T. VI, 917
Franklin, Jane VI, 866
Franklin, Janet VI, 816
Franklin, Jericho III, 126
Franklin, Jinsey VI, 917
Franklin, Joel VI, 917
Franklin, Joel VI, 921
Franklin, Joel VI, 992
Franklin, Joel VI, 1003
Franklin, Joel W. VI, 818
Franklin, John II, 527
Franklin, John II, 602
Franklin, John III, 126
Franklin, John III, 127
Franklin, John III, 329
Franklin, John III, 380
Franklin, John III, 388
Franklin, John III, 459
Franklin, John VI, 817
Franklin, John VI, 861
Franklin, John VI, 917
Franklin, John VI, 1021
Franklin, John Bryant VI, 917
Franklin, John C. III, 126
Franklin, John L. III, 380
Franklin, John L. III, 389
Franklin, John W. VI, 818
Franklin, John, Jr. III, 126
Franklin, John, Sr. VI, 963
Franklin, Jos. F. III, 382
Franklin, Jos. L. III, 126
Franklin, Jos. L. III, 380
Franklin, Joseph II, 664
Franklin, Joseph III, 293
Franklin, Joseph III, 294
Franklin, Joseph III, 380
Franklin, Joseph VI, 917
Franklin, Joseph VI, 976
Franklin, Joseph F. III, 126
Franklin, Joseph F. III, 204
Franklin, Joseph F. III, 380
Franklin, Joseph F. III, 382
Franklin, Joseph H. III, 294
Franklin, Joseph L. III, 380
Franklin, Judith VI, 963
Franklin, Judith E. VI, 818
Franklin, Judith W. VI, 818
Franklin, Judy B. VI, 841
Franklin, Kesiah VI, 859
Franklin, Kessiah VI, 866
Franklin, Laura I, 829
Franklin, Lawrence Haworth V, 673
Franklin, Lawson VI, 917
Franklin, Lawson VI, 979
Franklin, Lawson VI, 1003
Franklin, Lemuel IV, 707
Franklin, Leticia J. D. VI, 818
Franklin, Letitia III, 329
Franklin, Letticia VI, 817
Franklin, Letticia W. VI, 817
Franklin, Lewis VI, 834
Franklin, Lewis VI, 844
Franklin, Lewis VI, 859
Franklin, Lewis VI, 917
Franklin, Lewis, Jr. VI, 825
Franklin, Lidda VI, 797
Franklin, Linna VI, 976
Franklin, Locky VI, 893
Franklin, Locky VI, 917
Franklin, Louisa III, 126
Franklin, Louisa III, 127
Franklin, Lucretia M. VI, 741
Franklin, Lucretia M. VI, 742
Franklin, Lucretia M. VI, 779
Franklin, Lucretia M. VI, 793
Franklin, Lucy V, 673
Franklin, Lucy V, 680
Franklin, Lucy VI, 917
Franklin, Lucy Ann III, 385
Franklin, Lucy Maria Alice V, 673
Franklin, Lydia III, 380
Franklin, Lydia III, 384
Franklin, Lydia III, 389
Franklin, Lydia Franklin III, 385
Franklin, Margaret VI, 803
Franklin, Margaret VI, 831
Franklin, Margaret VI, 851
Franklin, Margaret VI, 917
Franklin, Margaret VI, 1021
Franklin, Marget VI, 917
Franklin, Maria III, 126
Franklin, Maria III, 127
Franklin, Marianna II, 863
Franklin, Martha VI, 917
Franklin, Martha VI, 964
Franklin, Martha Ann VI, 917
Franklin, Martha Ann VI, 1000
Franklin, Martha E. VI, 979
Franklin, Martha I. VI, 917
Franklin, Martha J. VI, 818
Franklin, Martha J. VI, 917
Franklin, Martha T. VI, 917
Franklin, Mary II, 527
Franklin, Mary II, 557
Franklin, Mary II, 632
Franklin, Mary III, 41
Franklin, Mary III, 82
Franklin, Mary III, 126
Franklin, Mary III, 127
Franklin, Mary III, 156
Franklin, Mary III, 164
Franklin, Mary III, 236
Franklin, Mary III, 244
Franklin, Mary III, 250
Franklin, Mary III, 293
Franklin, Mary III, 363
Franklin, Mary III, 380
Franklin, Mary III, 411
Franklin, Mary III, 417
Franklin, Mary III, 418
Franklin, Mary III, 444
Franklin, Mary V, 673
Franklin, Mary V, 689
Franklin, Mary VI, 817
Franklin, Mary VI, 827
Franklin, Mary VI, 844
Franklin, Mary VI, 915
Franklin, Mary VI, 917
Franklin, Mary VI, 1003
Franklin, Mary ??? III, 126
Franklin, Mary A. VI, 866
Franklin, Mary A. VI, 917
Franklin, Mary Ann VI, 910
Franklin, Mary C. VI, 828
Franklin, Mary E. III, 126
Franklin, Mary E. III, 296
Franklin, Mary J. VI, 818
Franklin, Mary J. VI, 914
Franklin, Mason VI, 917
Franklin, Mason VI, 995
Franklin, Matthew III, 87
Franklin, Matthew III, 126
Franklin, Milisant VI, 818
Franklin, Milly VI, 834
Franklin, Milton VI, 917
Franklin, Milton VI, 969
Franklin, Milton VI, 1000
Franklin, Minny VI, 869
Franklin, Miriam III, 126
Franklin, Miriam III, 380
Franklin, Miriam III, 382
Franklin, Miriam L. III, 126
Franklin, Miriam L. III, 204
Franklin, Morris III, 75
Franklin, Morris III, 126
Franklin, Morris III, 127
Franklin, Mrs. Polly VI, 999
Franklin, Nancey VI, 1004
Franklin, Nancy VI, 851
Franklin, Nancy VI, 856
Franklin, Nancy VI, 859
Franklin, Nancy VI, 917
Franklin, Nancy VI, 968
Franklin, Nancy VI, 987
Franklin, Nancy VI, 999
Franklin, Nancy Dowell VI, 992
Franklin, Nathan VI, 850
Franklin, Owen VI, 866
Franklin, Owen VI, 963
Franklin, Owen VI, 997
Franklin, Pamelia A. VI, 917
Franklin, Peter VI, 817
Franklin, Peter B. III, 126
Franklin, Peter B. III, 164
Franklin, Peter B. III, 411
Franklin, Peter B. III, 417
Franklin, Peter B. III, 418
Franklin, Phebe III, 126
Franklin, Phebe III, 158
Franklin, Pleasant VI, 992
Franklin, Polly VI, 829
Franklin, Polly M. VI, 917
Franklin, Rebecca III, 126
Franklin, Rebecca III, 321
Franklin, Rebecca VI, 917
Franklin, Rebecca T. III, 127
Franklin, Richard III, 126
Franklin, Richard V, 673
Franklin, Richard L. III, 380
Franklin, Robert VI, 817
Franklin, Robert VI, 818
Franklin, Robert VI, 828
Franklin, Robert VI, 833
Franklin, Robert VI, 844
Franklin, Robert VI, 856
Franklin, Robert VI, 861
Franklin, Robert VI, 866
Franklin, Robert, Jr. VI, 818
Franklin, Rosenah VI, 917
Franklin, Salley VI, 900
Franklin, Sally VI, 817
Franklin, Sally VI, 833
Franklin, Sally VI, 899
Franklin, Sally VI, 900
Franklin, Sally VI, 917
Franklin, Sally Ann III, 126
Franklin, Sam. VI, 917
Franklin, Saml VI, 1021
Franklin, Saml. VI, 917
Franklin, Saml. VI, 992
Franklin, Samuel II, 527
Franklin, Samuel II, 599
Franklin, Samuel II, 633
Franklin, Samuel III, 126
Franklin, Samuel III, 127
Franklin, Samuel III, 232
Franklin, Samuel III, 272
Franklin, Samuel VI, 917
Franklin, Samuel Glass V, 673
Franklin, Samuel, Jr. II, 633
Franklin, Sarah II, 364
Franklin, Sarah II, 527
Franklin, Sarah II, 557
Franklin, Sarah II, 633
Franklin, Sarah III, 75
Franklin, Sarah III, 126
Franklin, Sarah III, 127
Franklin, Sarah III, 236
Franklin, Sarah III, 270
Franklin, Sarah III, 272
Franklin, Sarah VI, 817
Franklin, Sarah VI, 818
Franklin, Sarah VI, 844
Franklin, Sarah VI, 917
Franklin, Sarah Ann III, 75
Franklin, Sarah Chace VI, 741
Franklin, Sarah Chace VI, 793
Franklin, Sarah Chase VI, 742
Franklin, Sarah H. III, 293
Franklin, Sarah J. VI, 818
Franklin, Sarah Jane VI, 917
Franklin, Sarah M. VI, 990
Franklin, Sarah P. III, 70
Franklin, Sarah P. III, 126
Franklin, Sarah P. III, 127
Franklin, Sarah P. VI, 741
Franklin, Sarah, Jr. III, 42
Franklin, Sarah, Jr. III, 126
Franklin, Stacy Byron V, 673
Franklin, Temperance Jane VI, 883
Franklin, Thomas II, 364
Franklin, Thomas II, 527
Franklin, Thomas II, 557
Franklin, Thomas II, 599
Franklin, Thomas II, 602
Franklin, Thomas II, 632
Franklin, Thomas III, 126
Franklin, Thomas III, 127
Franklin, Thomas III, 250
Franklin, Thomas VI, 797
Franklin, Thomas VI, 804
Franklin, Thomas VI, 816
Franklin, Thomas VI, 817
Franklin, Thomas VI, 818
Franklin, Thomas VI, 833
Franklin, Thomas VI, 834
Franklin, Thomas VI, 836
Franklin, Thomas VI, 837
Franklin, Thomas VI, 838
Franklin, Thomas VI, 841
Franklin, Thomas VI, 851
Franklin, Thomas VI, 859
Franklin, Thomas VI, 866
Franklin, Thomas VI, 917
Franklin, Thomas VI, 930
Franklin, Thomas VI, 996
Franklin, Thomas E. VI, 796
Franklin, Thomas E. VI, 831
Franklin, Thomas E. VI, 849
Franklin, Thomas Franklin III, 293
Franklin, Thomas H. VI, 818
Franklin, Thomas M. III, 127
Franklin, Thomas Morris III, 127
Franklin, Thomas, Jr. II, 527
Franklin, Thomas, Jr. II, 632
Franklin, Thomas, Jr. III, 127
Franklin, Thomas, Jr. III, 156
Franklin, Thos. III, 70
Franklin, Thos. III, 126
Franklin, Thos. III, 293
Franklin, Thos. VI, 817
Franklin, Thos. VI, 841
Franklin, Thos. D. VI, 818
Franklin, Thos. H. III, 380
Franklin, Thos. H. VI, 831
Franklin, W. L. VI, 844
Franklin, Walter II, 364
Franklin, Walter II, 527
Franklin, Walter II, 557
Franklin, Walter III, 41
Franklin, Walter III, 126
Franklin, Walter III, 127
Franklin, Walter III, 235
Franklin, Walter M. III, 126
Franklin, Walter, Jr. III, 127
Franklin, Wd. Letitia III, 126
Franklin, William III, 126
Franklin, William III, 385
Franklin, William VI, 917
Franklin, William Edward III, 385
Franklin, William H. III, 127
Franklin, William L. VI, 817
Franklin, Wm. VI, 870
Franklin, Wm. H. III, 127
Franklin, Wm. H. III, 264
Franklin, Wm. L VI, 816
Franklin, Wm. M. III, 77
Franklin, Wm. M. III, 126
Frankline, Lucretia M. VI, 741
Franks, Elisabeth II, 527
Franks, Elizabeth II, 527
Franks, George II, 527
Franks, George II, 559
Franks, John V, 561
Franks, John VI, 915
Franks, John A. V, 561
Franks, Katie V, 621
Franks, Lucy V, 621
Franks, Mary II, 527
Franks, Mary II, 559
Franks, Milly VI, 915
Franks, Sarah VI, 918
Franks, Washington VI, 918
Franser, ??? III, 297
Frantz, Martha IV, 954
Frantz, Matilda IV, 954
Frantz, Matilda IV, 1011
Fraser, ??? III, 127
Fraser, Alfred III, 411
Fraser, Alfred III, 429
Fraser, Alfred V. III, 411
Fraser, Alfred V. III, 431
Fraser, Alfred Valentine III, 411
Fraser, Dorothy Gladys III, 127
Fraser, Dorothy Gladys III, 297
Fraser, Edy IV, 1362
Fraser, Eleanor IV, 330
Fraser, Helen G. III, 120
Fraser, Helen G. III, 127
Fraser, James Whalen IV, 330
Fraser, John IV, 1362
Fraser, Lydia III, 429
Fraser, Margaret III, 411
Fraser, Margaret III, 475
Fraser, Maria Ann IV, 330
Fraser, Martha III, 411
Fraser, Martha III, 431
Fraser, Martha W. III, 411
Fraser, Martha W. M. III, 431
Fraser, Mary C. III, 411
Fraser, Mott III, 475
Fraser, Mrs. Henry W. I, 941
Fraser, Pandora I, 941
Fraser, Pandora H. I, 925
Fraser, Thomas Mott III, 411
Fraser, Thomas Smith IV, 330
Frasher, James VI, 918
Frasher, John VI, 918
Frasher, Margery I, 540
Frasher, Sally VI, 918
Frashier, Ann VI, 818
Frashier, Daniel VI, 818
Frashier, Elijah VI, 818
Frashier, Elizabeth VI, 818
Frashier, Henry VI, 818
Frashier, Joel VI, 818
Frashier, John VI, 818
Frashier, Lucy VI, 818
Frashier, Polly VI, 818
Frashier, Rhoda VI, 818
Frashier, Thomas VI, 818
Frashier, William VI, 818
Frashwel, Sarah VI, 918
Frashwell, James VI, 918
Frashwell, Sarah VI, 918
Frasier, Addie V, 996
Frasier, Elizabeth VI, 827
Frasier, James Whalen IV, 330
Frasier, John I, 389
Frasier, William VI, 827
Frasington, Elizabeth V, 302
Frasor, Isaac I, 1029
Frasor, Jamima I, 878
Frasor, Margery I, 878
Frasure, ??? V, 633
Frasure, Alice V, 239
Frasure, Lydia V, 239
Frasure, Lydia V, 633
Frasure, Margaret VI, 310
Frasure, Margaret VI, 312
Frasure, Moses V, 633
Frasure, Rebecca V, 621
Fraun, Jesse M. V, 331
Fravel, ??? V, 56
Fravel, Anna II, 864
Fravel, Anna II, 937
Fravel, Eleanor VI, 372
Fravel, Jacob IV, 342
Fravel, Jane IV, 342
Fravel, Maria J. V, 56
Fravel, Maria S. IV, 330
Fravel, Mary E. V, 56
Fravel, Myra J. II, 864
Fravel, Myra J. IV, 330
Fravel, Myra J. V, 56
Fravel, Owen U. II, 864
Fravel, Owen W. V, 56
Fravel, Rebecca V, 56
Fravel, Rebecca S. II, 864
Fravel, Rebecca S. IV, 330
Fravel, Rebecca S. IV, 342
Fravel, Rebecca S. V, 56
Fravel, Rebeckah V, 56
Fravel, William J. IV, 330
Fravel, William J. V, 56
Fravel, Wm. J. II, 864
Fravel, Wm. J. II, 937
Fravel, Wm. J. IV, 330
Frayser, Sarah I, 389
Frayzer, Elizabeth I, 389
Frazee, Augusta IV, 1315
Frazee, Geo. W. IV, 1315
Frazee, George IV, 1315
Frazee, Harry Albert IV, 1315
Frazee, Henry III, 127
Frazee, Martin V, 56
Frazee, Mary Eliza V, 33
Frazee, Mary Eliza V, 56
Frazee, Mrs. Augusta IV, 1315
Frazee, Rachel IV, 707
Frazee, Rufus III, 127
Frazee, Thos. L. IV, 1315
Frazee, Wm. D. IV, 1315
Frazell, Joshua IV, 1251
Frazell, Mary IV, 1251
Frazer, Aaron I, 540
Frazer, Abigail I, 540
Frazer, Abigail I, 562
Frazer, Abner I, 1119
Frazer, Abram V, 331
Frazer, Acsa M. II, 859
Frazer, Acsa M. II, 864
Frazer, Albert V, 56
Frazer, Albert E. I, 853
Frazer, Alexander V, 491
Frazer, Alice V, 491
Frazer, Alse V, 239
Frazer, Ann I, 1084
Frazer, Anna C. I, 853
Frazer, Anna E. I, 869
Frazer, Anna E. I, 879
Frazer, Ava VI, 243
Frazer, Ava F. VI, 243

zer, Benjamin VI, 918
zer, Boriah I, 1084
zer, Caleb I, 540
zer, Caleb II, 864
zer, Caleb S. II, 859
zer, Caleb T. II, 859
zer, Caleb T. II, 864
zer, Clarissa VI, 918
zer, Cyrus Piggott I, 853
zer, David I, 853
zer, Dell I, 853
zer, Dora I, 853
zer, Dorcas I, 679
zer, E. Winston I, 853
zer, Edward Winston I, 879
zer, Elijah II, 222
zer, Elizabeth I, 679
zer, Elizabeth V, 626
zer, Elza I, 1119
zer, Elza I, 1135
zer, Emily I, 853
zer, Emma A. I, 853
zer, Emmet VI, 243
zer, Emmet M. VI, 243
zer, Emmet Manly VI, 243
zer, Francis I, 679
zer, Franklin G. I, 853
zer, George V, 56
zer, Gertie V, 239
zer, Grace I, 853
zer, Hannah I, 809
zer, Hannah I, 853
zer, Hannah I, 879
zer, Harrison I, 853
zer, Isaac I, 853
zer, Isaac I, 1029
zer, Isaac I, 1035
zer, Isaac G. I, 853
zer, James I, 389
zer, James I, 540
zer, James I, 1029
zer, Jane V, 621
zer, Jane J. I, 853
zer, Jeams I, 540
zer, Jeffrey H. I, 853
zer, Jeremiah Ruffin I, 853
zer, Jessie VI, 243
zer, Jessie Ava VI, 243
zer, John I, 270
zer, John I, 540
zer, John I, 562
zer, John I, 679
zer, John I, 691
zer, John V, 491
zer, John Gurney I, 853
zer, Jonah V, 239
zer, Jonathan I, 853
zer, Joseph II, 222
zer, Julius C. I, 853
zer, Lottie I, 853
zer, Lottie H. I, 879
zer, Louisa I, 853
zer, Louisa J. I, 879
zer, Lucetta I, 853
zer, Lucetta I, 879
zer, Lydia I, 679
zer, Lydia I, 691
zer, Lydia IV, 1207
zer, Lydia P. V, 621
zer, Lydia P. V, 626
zer, Margery I, 540
zer, Mariam R. I, 853
zer, Martha I, 540
zer, Martha I, 853
zer, Mary I, 853
zer, Mary I, 878
zer, Mary I, 1029
zer, Mary I, 1035
zer, Mary II, 222
zer, Mary L. I, 853
zer, Mary M. V, 239
zer, Millikan I, 878
zer, Moses V, 626
zer, Nancy M. I, 853
zer, Oliver I, 853
zer, Phebe I, 878
zer, Rebecca V, 331
zer, Rebecca V, 353
azer, Ruby IV, 1315
azer, Rufus Winston I, 853
zer, Ruth II, 222
zer, Samuel I, 1119
azer, Sarah VI, 918
azer, Sarah J. II, 859
zer, Sarah J. II, 864
zer, Sollomon I, 853
azer, Solomon I, 853
azer, Solomon I, 879
azer, Susanna I, 878
azer, Susanna I, 906
azer, Thos. L. IV, 1315
Frazer, William I, 761
Frazer, William VI, 918
Frazier, Aaron I, 389
Frazier, Aaron I, 540
Frazier, Aaron I, 678
Frazier, Aaron I, 679
Frazier, Aaron I, 809
Frazier, Aaron V, 239
Frazier, Aaron V, 621
Frazier, Abel I, 679
Frazier, Abel I, 878
Frazier, Abel VI, 918
Frazier, Abigail I, 540
Frazier, Abigail I, 678
Frazier, Abigail I, 747
Frazier, Abigail I, 761
Frazier, Abigail I, 1105
Frazier, Abigail I, 1119
Frazier, Abigail I, 1124
Frazier, Abner I, 540
Frazier, Abner I, 962
Frazier, Abner I, 1093
Frazier, Abraham I, 962
Frazier, Abraham I, 1105
Frazier, Abraham V, 331
Frazier, Abram V, 331
Frazier, Addie V, 996
Frazier, Albert I, 879
Frazier, Alexander I, 540
Frazier, Alexander I, 962
Frazier, Alexander V, 491
Frazier, Alexander V, 621
Frazier, Alexander VI, 390
Frazier, Alexander VI, 813
Frazier, Alexandria I, 1093
Frazier, Alexandria VI, 390
Frazier, Alice V, 239
Frazier, Alice V, 491
Frazier, Alice V, 621
Frazier, Alice V, 637
Frazier, Alice V, 638
Frazier, Alice V, 647
Frazier, Alse V, 239
Frazier, Ammy VI, 854
Frazier, Andrew J. V, 673
Frazier, Andy V, 673
Frazier, Angelina VI, 809
Frazier, Angelina VI, 818
Frazier, Ann I, 679
Frazier, Ann I, 878
Frazier, Ann I, 1056
Frazier, Ann I, 1061
Frazier, Ann I, 1093
Frazier, Ann I, 1097
Frazier, Ann IV, 146
Frazier, Ann IV, 330
Frazier, Ann IV, 394
Frazier, Ann V, 239
Frazier, Ann V, 247
Frazier, Ann V, 331
Frazier, Ann C. I, 879
Frazier, Ann Freyser I, 389
Frazier, Anna IV, 330
Frazier, Anna IV, 349
Frazier, Anna IV, 394
Frazier, Anna IV, 578
Frazier, Anna E. I, 879
Frazier, Anne IV, 394
Frazier, Anne IV, 433
Frazier, Anne IV, 578
Frazier, Annie Grace I, 941
Frazier, Anselem VI, 809
Frazier, Ardelia E. VI, 832
Frazier, Arthur IV, 1278
Frazier, Ashley V, 621
Frazier, Auselem VI, 818
Frazier, Barbary I, 540
Frazier, Barclay I, 962
Frazier, Benjamin VI, 818
Frazier, Benjamin VI, 918
Frazier, Benjamin F. I, 679
Frazier, Beriah I, 540
Frazier, Beriah I, 962
Frazier, Beriah I, 1093
Frazier, Beriah I, 1097
Frazier, Berry I, 336
Frazier, Caleb I, 540
Frazier, Caroline Elizabeth V, 621
Frazier, Carsen V, 673
Frazier, Catharine I, 679
Frazier, Catharine J. VI, 918
Frazier, Charity IV, 578
Frazier, Charity IV, 600
Frazier, Charlotte V, 331
Frazier, Charlotte VI, 866
Frazier, Christopher VI, 818
Frazier, Clarissa VI, 918
Frazier, Clarkson V, 996
Frazier, Clifford I, 616
Frazier, Clifford V, 673
Frazier, Cora V, 673
Frazier, Corina I, 922
Frazier, Cyrus I, 625
Frazier, Cyrus P. I, 616
Frazier, Cyrus P. I, 633
Frazier, Cyrus P. I, 879
Frazier, Daniel I, 270
Frazier, Daniel IV, 32
Frazier, Daniel IV, 137
Frazier, Daniel IV, 146
Frazier, Daniel IV, 330
Frazier, Daniel IV, 388
Frazier, Daniel IV, 394
Frazier, Daniel IV, 578
Frazier, Daniel B. I, 679
Frazier, Daniel, Jr. I, 49
Frazier, Daniel, Jr. I, 270
Frazier, Daniel, Jr. I, 276
Frazier, David I, 389
Frazier, David I, 878
Frazier, David IV, 578
Frazier, David V, 162
Frazier, David V, 170
Frazier, David V, 331
Frazier, David L. I, 679
Frazier, David L. I, 878
Frazier, David L. I, 879
Frazier, David O. I, 941
Frazier, David P. VI, 818
Frazier, David R. VI, 860
Frazier, David W. I, 747
Frazier, David W. I, 761
Frazier, Davis V, 239
Frazier, Della E. I, 616
Frazier, Dora I, 879
Frazier, Dorcas I, 679
Frazier, Edgar V, 996
Frazier, Edith I, 614
Frazier, Edith V, 621
Frazier, Edward Winston I, 879
Frazier, Edwin G. VI, 818
Frazier, Effie I, 761
Frazier, Effie I, 767
Frazier, Effie Oma V, 331
Frazier, Eleanor IV, 330
Frazier, Elener IV, 330
Frazier, Eli I, 962
Frazier, Eli I, 1105
Frazier, Elihu V, 996
Frazier, Elinor IV, 330
Frazier, Elinor IV, 347
Frazier, Elisabeth H. I, 633
Frazier, Elisha I, 962
Frazier, Elisha V, 621
Frazier, Eliza I, 1105
Frazier, Eliza I, 1119
Frazier, Eliza I, 1128
Frazier, Elizabeth I, 389
Frazier, Elizabeth I, 540
Frazier, Elizabeth I, 616
Frazier, Elizabeth I, 633
Frazier, Elizabeth I, 634
Frazier, Elizabeth I, 679
Frazier, Elizabeth II, 364
Frazier, Elizabeth IV, 578
Frazier, Elizabeth V, 170
Frazier, Elizabeth V, 239
Frazier, Elizabeth V, 247
Frazier, Elizabeth V, 331
Frazier, Elizabeth V, 491
Frazier, Elizabeth V, 621
Frazier, Elizabeth V, 637
Frazier, Elizabeth V, 644
Frazier, Elizabeth V, 651
Frazier, Elizabeth V, 951
Frazier, Elizabeth V, 952
Frazier, Elizabeth VI, 818
Frazier, Elizabeth VI, 918
Frazier, Elizabeth A. VI, 818
Frazier, Elizabeth Ann V, 331
Frazier, Emily I, 878
Frazier, Emma I, 879
Frazier, Emma May I, 919
Frazier, Esther I, 623
Frazier, Eunice I, 931
Frazier, Eunice Worth I, 616
Frazier, Ezekiel I, 962
Frazier, Ezekiel I, 1077
Frazier, Ezekiel I, 1093
Frazier, Ezekiel V, 239
Frazier, Ezekiel V, 331
Frazier, Ezekiel V, 491
Frazier, Ezekiel V, 621
Frazier, Ezekiel V, 624
Frazier, Ezekiel V, 637
Frazier, Ezekiel V, 952
Frazier, Ezekiel VI, 390
Frazier, Ezekiel, Jr. V, 621
Frazier, Florella I, 747
Frazier, Florilla I, 761
Frazier, Frances I, 747
Frazier, Frances I, 761
Frazier, Frances V, 239
Frazier, Frances V, 331
Frazier, Francis I, 389
Frazier, Francis I, 679
Frazier, Francis V, 170
Frazier, Francis V, 239
Frazier, Francis V, 247
Frazier, Francis V, 331
Frazier, Francis VI, 818
Frazier, Francis Henry V, 331
Frazier, Frank I, 919
Frazier, Franklin VI, 64
Frazier, Franklin G. I, 879
Frazier, George VI, 52
Frazier, George VI, 64
Frazier, Gertie V, 239
Frazier, Gertrude I, 616
Frazier, Gertrude I, 625
Frazier, Gertrude I, 633
Frazier, Gertrude I, 640
Frazier, Gideon I, 389
Frazier, Gideon V, 239
Frazier, Gideon V, 247
Frazier, Gidian V, 239
Frazier, Glen V, 561
Frazier, Glenn V, 561
Frazier, Grace I, 616
Frazier, Gracset I, 878
Frazier, Gracset I, 898
Frazier, Guidean V, 331
Frazier, Hannah I, 679
Frazier, Hannah I, 809
Frazier, Hannah I, 879
Frazier, Hannah I, 919
Frazier, Hannah I, 1105
Frazier, Hannah V, 239
Frazier, Hannah V, 247
Frazier, Hannah V, 331
Frazier, Hannah V, 621
Frazier, Hannah V, 644
Frazier, Hannah V, 647
Frazier, Hannah V, 673
Frazier, Hannah VI, 390
Frazier, Hannah P. V, 651
Frazier, Harison I, 633
Frazier, Harison Lea I, 616
Frazier, Harrison I, 616
Frazier, Harrison I, 633
Frazier, Harrison I, 878
Frazier, Harrison I, 879
Frazier, Henry VI, 863
Frazier, Homer V, 673
Frazier, Hugh VI, 918
Frazier, Huldah V. V, 996
Frazier, Hyram IV, 1207
Frazier, Idella M. V, 996
Frazier, Isaac I, 679
Frazier, Isaac I, 747
Frazier, Isaac I, 761
Frazier, Isaac I, 1061
Frazier, Isaac G. I, 879
Frazier, Isaac N. I, 747
Frazier, Isaac N. I, 761
Frazier, Isabel I, 679
Frazier, Isaiah V, 331
Frazier, J. Farr V, 673
Frazier, J. G. I, 616
Frazier, J. G. I, 879
Frazier, Jacob I, 750
Frazier, James I, 389
Frazier, James I, 540
Frazier, James I, 878
Frazier, James I, 1119
Frazier, James V, 331
Frazier, James V, 621
Frazier, James V, 673
Frazier, James VI, 818
Frazier, James VI, 918
Frazier, James C. V, 673
Frazier, James D. I, 941
Frazier, James F. V, 621
Frazier, James Farr V, 673
Frazier, James H. I, 679
Frazier, James Whalen IV, 330
Frazier, Jamima I, 878
Frazier, Jane I, 747
Frazier, Jane I, 761
Frazier, Jane I, 919
Frazier, Jane I, 1105
Frazier, Jane I, 1119
Frazier, Jane I, 1130
Frazier, Jane V, 621
Frazier, Jane V, 638
Frazier, Jane J. I, 879
Frazier, Jeams I, 540
Frazier, Jeffrey H. I, 679
Frazier, Jemima VI, 813
Frazier, Jeremiah R. I, 879
Frazier, Jesse I, 747
Frazier, Jesse I, 761
Frazier, Jincy VI, 64
Frazier, John I, 49
Frazier, John I, 270
Frazier, John I, 389
Frazier, John I, 540
Frazier, John I, 678
Frazier, John I, 679
Frazier, John I, 878
Frazier, John I, 962
Frazier, John I, 1105
Frazier, John V, 239
Frazier, John V, 331
Frazier, John V, 491
Frazier, John V, 621
Frazier, John V, 637
Frazier, John V, 638
Frazier, John V, 647
Frazier, John V, 651
Frazier, John VI, 390
Frazier, John VI, 818
Frazier, John VI, 874
Frazier, John VI, 918
Frazier, John A. I, 747
Frazier, John A. I, 761
Frazier, John G. I, 879
Frazier, John Henry V, 673
Frazier, John T. I, 679
Frazier, John, Jr. I, 878
Frazier, Jonah V, 239
Frazier, Jonah V, 331
Frazier, Jonah V, 333
Frazier, Jonah V, 491
Frazier, Jonah V, 610
Frazier, Jonah V, 621
Frazier, Jonathan I, 878
Frazier, Jonathan A. I, 679
Frazier, Jonny I, 306
Frazier, Joseph V, 331
Frazier, Joseph VI, 818
Frazier, Joseph Burr V, 673
Frazier, Joshua V, 621
Frazier, Julia I, 540
Frazier, Julian I, 1093
Frazier, Julin I, 962
Frazier, Julius C. I, 879
Frazier, Kate J. V, 331
Frazier, Keziah I, 750
Frazier, Kora S. IV, 1207
Frazier, L. D. IV, 1207
Frazier, Levinah V, 239
Frazier, Lindley Murray V, 621
Frazier, Locky VI, 818
Frazier, Lona I, 622
Frazier, Lottie H. I, 879
Frazier, Louisa J. I, 879
Frazier, Louise I, 616
Frazier, Louise I, 633
Frazier, Louise Caroline I, 616
Frazier, Louise Caroline I, 633
Frazier, Lucetta I, 616
Frazier, Lucetta I, 625
Frazier, Lucetta I, 879
Frazier, Lucy VI, 818
Frazier, Lydia I, 679
Frazier, Lydia IV, 1207
Frazier, Lydia V, 239
Frazier, Lydia V, 331
Frazier, Lydia V, 356
Frazier, Lydia V, 491
Frazier, Lydia V, 520
Frazier, Lydia V, 621
Frazier, Lydia V, 637
Frazier, Lydia V, 638
Frazier, Lydia V, 651
Frazier, Lydia V, 838
Frazier, Lydia V, 855
Frazier, Lydia Ann V, 331
Frazier, Lydia Ann V, 621
Frazier, Lydia P. V, 331
Frazier, Lydia P. V, 339
Frazier, Lydia P. V, 621
Frazier, Lydia Pusey V, 621
Frazier, Margaret Jane Morris V, 673
Frazier, Margarette V, 331
Frazier, Margery I, 540
Frazier, Margery I, 878
Frazier, Maria V, 621
Frazier, Maria A. IV, 319
Frazier, Maria A. IV, 330
Frazier, Maria Ann IV, 330
Frazier, Martha I, 540
Frazier, Martha I, 878
Frazier, Martha I, 889
Frazier, Martha I, 902
Frazier, Martha I, 1119
Frazier, Martha I, 1127
Frazier, Martha A. V, 699
Frazier, Martha Ann V, 673
Frazier, Martha W. V, 492
Frazier, Martha W. V, 538

Frazier, Martha W. V, 621
Frazier, Mary I, 270
Frazier, Mary I, 678
Frazier, Mary I, 679
Frazier, Mary I, 747
Frazier, Mary I, 761
Frazier, Mary I, 878
Frazier, Mary II, 364
Frazier, Mary IV, 578
Frazier, Mary V, 331
Frazier, Mary V, 333
Frazier, Mary V, 491
Frazier, Mary V, 522
Frazier, Mary V, 621
Frazier, Mary V, 637
Frazier, Mary V, 638
Frazier, Mary V, 651
Frazier, Mary VI, 818
Frazier, Mary A. I, 761
Frazier, Mary A. VI, 818
Frazier, Mary D. V, 610
Frazier, Mary J. I, 747
Frazier, Mary Jane I, 761
Frazier, Mary Jane V, 621
Frazier, Mary Jane V, 673
Frazier, Mary L. I, 879
Frazier, Mary M. V, 239
Frazier, Mary N. I, 879
Frazier, Maryann V, 331
Frazier, Matthew I, 679
Frazier, Micajah VI, 818
Frazier, Mildred VI, 863
Frazier, Milikan I, 878
Frazier, Millikan I, 878
Frazier, Miriam R. I, 879
Frazier, Moses I, 962
Frazier, Moses V, 331
Frazier, Moses V, 356
Frazier, Moses V, 491
Frazier, Moses V, 621
Frazier, Moses V, 638
Frazier, Moses V, 644
Frazier, Moses V, 951
Frazier, Moses V, 952
Frazier, Moses VI, 390
Frazier, Mrs. Henry W. I, 941
Frazier, Nancy H. VI, 842
Frazier, Nancy M. I, 879
Frazier, Nannie I, 616
Frazier, Nannie I, 633
Frazier, Nathan I, 878
Frazier, Nathan V, 239
Frazier, Nathan V, 331
Frazier, Nathan V, 621
Frazier, Nelly I, 270
Frazier, Nelly IV, 32
Frazier, Nelly IV, 33
Frazier, Nelly IV, 146
Frazier, Nelly IV, 388
Frazier, Nelly IV, 394
Frazier, Nelly IV, 578
Frazier, Pandora I, 941
Frazier, Penina I, 750
Frazier, Phebe I, 878
Frazier, Phebe V, 621
Frazier, Phebe V, 624
Frazier, Phebe VI, 390
Frazier, Phebe VI, 638
Frazier, Polly VI, 809
Frazier, Polly VI, 864
Frazier, Polly VI, 918
Frazier, Rachel I, 878
Frazier, Rachel V, 673
Frazier, Rachel V, 996
Frazier, Rachel S. V, 673
Frazier, Rachel Wright V, 621
Frazier, Rebecca I, 679
Frazier, Rebecca I, 878
Frazier, Rebecca I, 1093
Frazier, Rebecca V, 162
Frazier, Rebecca V, 170
Frazier, Rebecca V, 239
Frazier, Rebecca V, 331
Frazier, Rebecca V, 491
Frazier, Rebecca V, 514
Frazier, Rebecca V, 561
Frazier, Rebecca V, 586
Frazier, Rebecca V, 621
Frazier, Rebecca V, 624
Frazier, Rebecca V, 637
Frazier, Rebecca V, 952
Frazier, Rebecca VI, 818
Frazier, Rebecca T. V, 610
Frazier, Rebecca T. V, 621
Frazier, Rebeccah I, 679
Frazier, Rebeccah I, 1093
Frazier, Rebeccah VI, 390
Frazier, Rebeckah I, 878
Frazier, Rebekah I, 878
Frazier, Rebekah VI, 390
Frazier, Reuben V, 838
Frazier, Rhoda VI, 809
Frazier, Richard VI, 64
Frazier, Richard VI, 638
Frazier, Robert II, 364
Frazier, Robert VI, 818
Frazier, Robert Haines I, 616
Frazier, Rufus I, 633
Frazier, Rufus W. I, 616
Frazier, Rufus W. I, 633
Frazier, Rufus W. I, 879
Frazier, Ruhama I, 679
Frazier, Sally VI, 795
Frazier, Sally VI, 818
Frazier, Sally VI, 918
Frazier, Samuel I, 540
Frazier, Samuel I, 878
Frazier, Samuel I, 953
Frazier, Samuel I, 962
Frazier, Samuel I, 1077
Frazier, Samuel I, 1093
Frazier, Samuel I, 1105
Frazier, Samuel V, 239
Frazier, Samuel V, 331
Frazier, Samuel Kinley I, 941
Frazier, Sarah I, 270
Frazier, Sarah I, 389
Frazier, Sarah I, 540
Frazier, Sarah I, 678
Frazier, Sarah I, 679
Frazier, Sarah I, 902
Frazier, Sarah I, 920
Frazier, Sarah IV, 330
Frazier, Sarah IV, 347
Frazier, Sarah V, 239
Frazier, Sarah V, 247
Frazier, Sarah V, 331
Frazier, Sarah V, 621
Frazier, Sarah VI, 52
Frazier, Sarah VI, 64
Frazier, Sarah VI, 636
Frazier, Sarah VI, 638
Frazier, Sarah VI, 818
Frazier, Sarah VI, 832
Frazier, Sarah VI, 918
Frazier, Sarah Rebecca I, 925
Frazier, Sarah Rebecca I, 941
Frazier, Seth V, 331
Frazier, Solomon I, 679
Frazier, Solomon I, 879
Frazier, Solomon I, 919
Frazier, Solomon I, 1105
Frazier, Solomon I, 1119
Frazier, Solomon K. I, 879
Frazier, Son V, 621
Frazier, Stanley I, 878
Frazier, Stanly I, 878
Frazier, Stephen V, 331
Frazier, Susanah I, 540
Frazier, Susanah V, 331
Frazier, Susanna I, 540
Frazier, Susanna I, 678
Frazier, Susanna I, 809
Frazier, Susanna I, 878
Frazier, Susanna V, 331
Frazier, Susanna VI, 918
Frazier, Susannah I, 1101
Frazier, Susannah I, 1105
Frazier, Susannah V, 239
Frazier, Susannah V, 331
Frazier, Susie Ridny I, 616
Frazier, Tamer Cox I, 389
Frazier, Thomas I, 270
Frazier, Thomas I, 389
Frazier, Thomas I, 540
Frazier, Thomas I, 878
Frazier, Thomas I, 962
Frazier, Thomas V, 239
Frazier, Thomas V, 247
Frazier, Thomas V, 331
Frazier, Thomas V, 996
Frazier, Thomas VI, 818
Frazier, Thomas Sharp VI, 390
Frazier, Thomas Smith IV, 330
Frazier, Thomas, Jr. I, 270
Frazier, Thos. VI, 842
Frazier, Virginia V, 673
Frazier, Widow Nelly I, 276
Frazier, William I, 270
Frazier, William I, 678
Frazier, William I, 761
Frazier, William I, 962
Frazier, William I, 1101
Frazier, William I, 1105
Frazier, William IV, 32
Frazier, William IV, 146
Frazier, William IV, 330
Frazier, William IV, 394
Frazier, William IV, 433
Frazier, William IV, 578
Frazier, William V, 491
Frazier, William V, 492
Frazier, William V, 621
Frazier, William VI, 795
Frazier, William VI, 818
Frazier, William VI, 832
Frazier, William VI, 854
Frazier, William VI, 863
Frazier, William VI, 864
Frazier, William VI, 918
Frazier, Willis IV, 1207
Frazier, Wm. IV, 349
Frazier, Wm. VI, 809
Frazier, Wm. VI, 813
Frazier, Wm. VI, 832
Frazier, Zephamah V, 673
Frazier, Zephaniah V, 673
Frazor, Aaron I, 540
Frazur, Hannah VI, 390
Frazur, Hannah VI, 442
Frazur, Thomas Sharp VI, 390
Frazure, Agnes IV, 125
Frazure, Agnes IV, 134
Frazure, Ann V, 331
Frazure, Elizabeth V, 491
Frazure, Ezekiel V, 491
Frazure, Guidean V, 331
Frazure, Hannah I, 809
Frazure, Hannah I, 818
Frazure, Jonah V, 491
Frazure, Lydia V, 491
Frazure, Margarette V, 331
Frazure, Moses V, 491
Frazure, Stephen V, 331
Frazure, Thomas V, 331
Freak, Marcy II, 997
Frear, Carrie L. III, 127
Frear, Carrie L. III, 337
Frear, Frank Burroughs III, 127
Frear, Frank Burroughs III, 337
Freas, Carolyn Bowen II, 138
Frech, Christina II, 705
Frech, Henry II, 705
Frech, Johann Adam II, 705
Frech, Pauline II, 705
Fred, Ann VI, 492
Fred, Ann VI, 530
Fred, Isaac VI, 483
Fred, Joseph VI, 492
Fred, Joseph VI, 638
Fred, Joshua VI, 492
Fred, Joshua VI, 638
Fred, Mary VI, 492
Fred, Mary W. V, 56
Fred, Rachel VI, 638
Fred, Rachel VI, 640
Fred, Rebecca VI, 620
Fred, Rebecca VI, 638
Fred, Ruth VI, 638
Fred, Ruth VI, 674
Fred, Sarah VI, 492
Fred, Sarah VI, 632
Fred, Sarah VI, 638
Fred, Thomas VI, 492
Fred, Viley W. IV, 331
Fred, Viley W. IV, 359
Fredd, Elizabeth B. II, 864
Frederic, Martha E. I, 809
Frederick, Alpheus I, 809
Frederick, Amos IV, 1037
Frederick, Betsey VI, 944
Frederick, Carroll VI, 649
Frederick, Cathrine VI, 918
Frederick, Delcena C. I, 809
Frederick, Elizabeth VI, 962
Frederick, Jacob VI, 918
Frederick, Jacob VI, 962
Frederick, James I, 809
Frederick, James Madison I, 809
Frederick, Jesse I, 809
Frederick, John VI, 918
Frederick, Machael VI, 944
Frederick, Martha E. I, 809
Frederick, Michl. VI, 903
Frederick, Nancy VI, 918
Frederick, Nellie IV, 1037
Frederick, Pauline III, 479
Frederick, Pearl IV, 1037
Frederick, Polly I, 809
Frederick, Polly VI, 903
Frederick, Romulus I, 809
Frederick, Russell IV, 1037
Fredric, Polly I, 809
Fredrick, Alpheus I, 809
Fredrick, James I, 809
Fredrick, James Madison I, 809
Fredrick, Jesse I, 809
Fredrick, Nellie IV, 1037
Fredrick, Romulus I, 809
Free, Austin Craig VI, 784
Free, Cornelia VI, 784
Free, Eunice B. I, 761
Free, Eunice B. I, 771
Free, Gertrude VI, 742
Free, Gertrude VI, 784
Free, Harry Stevenson VI, 742
Free, Harry Stevenson VI, 784
Free, Lydia I, 761
Free, Margaret VI, 742
Free, Margaret VI, 784
Free, Margaret Taylor VI, 784
Free, Reuben M. I, 761
Free, Robert Daouglas VI, 784
Freeborn, Alice III, 127
Freeborn, Alice III, 188
Freeborn, Ann Eliza V, 386
Freeborn, Ann Louisa III, 127
Freeborn, Anna Eliza V, 386
Freeborn, Benjamin III, 127
Freeborn, Caroline III, 127
Freeborn, David V, 386
Freeborn, David B. V, 386
Freeborn, Elizabeth III, 127
Freeborn, Elizabeth M. III, 127
Freeborn, Ella V, 386
Freeborn, Etta S. V, 386
Freeborn, Geo. III, 127
Freeborn, George III, 127
Freeborn, Gideon III, 127
Freeborn, Gideon L. III, 127
Freeborn, John W. III, 127
Freeborn, Joseph S. III, 127
Freeborn, Mary III, 127
Freeborn, Mary III, 188
Freeborn, Mary V, 386
Freeborn, Orcelia V, 386
Freeborn, Orcelia G. V, 386
Freeborn, Samuel IV, 146
Freeborn, Samuel IV, 472
Freeborn, Susan P. III, 127
Freeborn, Susanna III, 127
Freeborn, Thomas III, 127
Freeborn, Thomas III, 188
Freed, David II, 784
Freed, Matilda II, 784
Freed, Matilda II, 841
Freed, Matilda II, 864
Freedland, Charlotte II, 118
Freedland, Charlotte II, 126
Freedland, Charlotte N. II, 28
Freedland, Elizabeth II, 22
Freedland, Elizabeth II, 28
Freedland, Elizabeth II, 70
Freedland, Elizabeth II, 118
Freedland, Elizabeth II, 126
Freedland, Jonas II, 28
Freedland, Jonas II, 70
Freedland, Jonas II, 118
Freedland, Jonas II, 126
Freedland, Jonathan II, 28
Freedland, Jonathan II, 118
Freedland, Jonathan II, 126
Freedland, Jonos II, 22
Freedland, Lydia II, 22
Freedland, Lydia II, 28
Freedland, Lydia II, 70
Freedland, Sarah II, 28
Freedland, Sarah II, 70
Freedle, William H. I, 879
Freedley, Alice E. II, 793
Freedley, Angenetta V, 386
Freedley, Elizabeth Sinclair II, 793
Freedley, Harriet II, 793
Freedley, Howard C. II, 793
Freedley, Jacob II, 861
Freedley, Jacob II, 864
Freedley, Sarah II, 793
Freedley, Sarah II, 861
Freedley, Sarah II, 864
Freedley, Susan II, 861
Freedley, Susan II, 864
Freedley, Wilson, Jr. II, 793
Freeland, Amos V, 673
Freeland, Eliza V, 673
Freeland, Eliza Jane V, 673
Freeland, John Wesley V, 492
Freeland, Susanna II, 527
Freeland, Susannah II, 541
Freeland, Walter V, 492
Freeland, Wm. II, 527
Freeland, Wm. II, 541
Freelove, George III, 180
Freelove, Susanna III, 180
Freeman, Anna VI, 894
Freeman, Austin H. IV, 954
Freeman, Belle L. IV, 954
Freeman, Benjamin IV, 117
Freeman, Betsey Ann VI, 1005
Freeman, Betsy VI, 939
Freeman, Blanche F. III, 127
Freeman, Blanche F. III, 311
Freeman, Caroline Adelaide VI, 760
Freeman, Catey VI, 918
Freeman, Charity I, 389
Freeman, Charity I, 427
Freeman, Charles IV, 954
Freeman, Charlotte VI, 801
Freeman, Col. Edward VI, 818
Freeman, Daniel I, 352
Freeman, Daniel I, 389
Freeman, Daniel, Jr. I, 389
Freeman, Edwin H. VI, 983
Freeman, Eliza VI, 918
Freeman, Eliza Ellen V, 492
Freeman, Elizabeth I, 352
Freeman, Elizabeth I, 389
Freeman, Elizabeth I, 407
Freeman, Elizabeth VI, 914
Freeman, Emma J. IV, 954
Freeman, Evaline B. VI, 842
Freeman, Frances I, 352
Freeman, Frances I, 374
Freeman, Frances I, 389
Freeman, Frances VI, 986
Freeman, Francis VI, 818
Freeman, Frank VI, 799
Freeman, Frank VI, 822
Freeman, Frank VI, 837
Freeman, Frank VI, 850
Freeman, Garland H. VI, 914
Freeman, Garland H. VI, 918
Freeman, George IV, 954
Freeman, George W. IV, 954
Freeman, Granville V, 492
Freeman, Granville V, 673
Freeman, Hannah I, 352
Freeman, Hannah I, 389
Freeman, Harriet E. VI, 1018
Freeman, Helen III, 119
Freeman, Herbert Edgar I, 879
Freeman, Isaac I, 853
Freeman, James VI, 872
Freeman, James VI, 894
Freeman, James VI, 908
Freeman, James VI, 918
Freeman, James VI, 922
Freeman, James VI, 939
Freeman, James VI, 985
Freeman, James VI, 986
Freeman, James VI, 1013
Freeman, James O. VI, 1005
Freeman, James, Jr. VI, 918
Freeman, Jane I, 352
Freeman, Jane I, 389
Freeman, Jane VI, 243
Freeman, Jane VI, 259
Freeman, Jane VI, 908
Freeman, Jane M. VI, 983
Freeman, Jean I, 389
Freeman, Jesse VI, 918
Freeman, John I, 352
Freeman, John I, 389
Freeman, John I Sup 1, 9
Freeman, John II, 364
Freeman, John II, 527
Freeman, John VI, 914
Freeman, John L. I, 853
Freeman, John L. I, 879
Freeman, Joseph Wray I, 879
Freeman, Joshua I, 352
Freeman, Joshua I, 389
Freeman, Judith H. VI, 918
Freeman, Kesiah VI, 924
Freeman, Lena Caroline VI, 792
Freeman, Lewis IV, 1362
Freeman, Lucy VI, 799
Freeman, Lucy VI, 818
Freeman, Lydia IV, 33
Freeman, Lydia IV, 34
Freeman, Mable II, 717
Freeman, Mahala IV, 86
Freeman, Mahala IV, 117
Freeman, Malinda VI, 802
Freeman, Mariah I, 853
Freeman, Martha V, 779
Freeman, Martha V, 781
Freeman, Martin W. VI, 818
Freeman, Mary I, 376
Freeman, Mary I, 389
Freeman, Mary I, 853
Freeman, Mary VI, 818
Freeman, Mary VI, 918
Freeman, Mary VI, 985
Freeman, Mary F. IV, 954
Freeman, Mary Myrtle I, 879
Freeman, Milly VI, 872
Freeman, Minerva VI, 918
Freeman, Miza V, 492
Freeman, Morris VI, 814
Freeman, Morris VI, 818
Freeman, Moses VI, 818
Freeman, Nancy VI, 828
Freeman, Nancy VI, 918

eeman, Nathan I, 389
eeman, Nathan I Sup 1, 9
eeman, Nathaniel II, 997
eeman, Nicholas VI, 11
eeman, Nicie V, 492
eeman, Peggy VI, 939
eeman, Pleasant VI, 818
eeman, Polly VI, 870
eeman, Polly VI, 918
eeman, Rachel VI, 818
eeman, Rebecca I, 352
eeman, Rebekah I, 389
eeman, Richard VI, 914
eeman, Richard VI, 918
eeman, Richard VI, 923
eeman, Richard VI, 938
eeman, Richard VI, 962
eeman, Richard VI, 1005
eeman, Richard VI, 1006
eeman, Richard, Jr. VI, 972
eeman, Robert VI, 842
eeman, Robert VI, 983
eeman, Sally VI, 870
eeman, Sally VI, 918
eeman, Samantha V, 492
eeman, Samuel I, 389
eeman, Sarah I, 389
eeman, Sarah I, 420
eeman, Sarah II, 528
eeman, Sarah IV, 117
eeman, Sarah VI, 818
eeman, Sarah VI, 918
eeman, Sarah VI, 939
eeman, Sarah VI, 1013
eeman, Sarah Green VI, 828
eeman, Susannah VI, 1001
eeman, Sylvester V, 492
eeman, Thomas IV, 203
eeman, Thomas VI, 801
eeman, Viola V, 492
eeman, Walter VI, 918
eeman, Wd. Sarah II, 510
eeman, William VI, 918
eeman, William VI, 937
eeman, Wm. I, 352
eeman, Wm. VI, 1001
eer, Martha IV, 1316
eer, Vera Ruth IV, 1316
eer, Willard IV, 1315
eer, Willard IV, 1316
eer, Willard P. IV, 1315
eer, Wm. P. IV, 1315
eestone, Daniel V, 561
eestone, Martha V, 56
eestone, Martha V, 75
eestone, Martha VI, 492
eestone, Martha VI, 554
eestone, Mary Russell VI, 492
eet, Harry IV, 1037
eet, Rachel IV, 525
eet, Rachel IV, 542
eezan, Garland V, 673
eeze, Garland D. V, 673
eeze, Thomas V, 561
eidel, Audrey Mary III, 128
eidel, Conrad III, 128
eidel, Doris Edith III, 128
eidel, Edith M. III, 128
eidel, Edith M. III, 161
eidel, Elizabeth III, 128
eidel, Frank III, 128
eidel, Frank B., Jr. III, 128
eidel, Frank Burt III, 127
eidel, Frank Burt III, 128
eidel, Frank Burt III, 161
eidel, Grant III, 127
eidel, Grant III, 128
eidel, Grant III, 262
eidel, Mary E. III, 127
eidel, Mary Eliz. III, 128
eidel, Mary Elizabeth III, 262
eidel, Nelly III, 128
eidel, Phebe III, 128
eidel, Richard Grant III, 128
eidland, Elizabeth II, 55
eidland, Jonas II, 55
eidland, Lydia II, 55
eland, Amos V, 673
eland, Eliza V, 673
eland, Esther II, 443
eland, Robert II, 443
eland, William II, 443
eland, Wm. II, 443
eman, John II, 364
emont, C. F. V, 996
ench, ??? IV, 1303
ench, Abel IV, 955
ench, Albert II, 794
ench, Albert IV, 707
ench, Albert IV, 709
ench, Albert IV, 944
French, Albert IV, 954
French, Albert IV, 955
French, Albert E. IV, 709
French, Albert E. IV, 955
French, Albert Hewett IV, 955
French, Albert N. IV, 1038
French, Allen IV, 472
French, Allen T. IV, 472
French, Allen T. IV, 954
French, Allen T. IV, 1019
French, Alma IV, 955
French, Alma Hewett IV, 955
French, Amanda IV, 376
French, Amanda IV, 394
French, Amy IV, 708
French, Amy IV, 709
French, Ann IV, 707
French, Ann IV, 708
French, Ann IV, 728
French, Ann IV, 943
French, Ann IV, 954
French, Ann IV, 955
French, Ann IV, 1009
French, Ann V, 936
French, Ann W. IV, 955
French, Ann W. IV, 998
French, Anna II, 794
French, Anna II, 864
French, Anna II, 904
French, Anna IV, 525
French, Anna IV, 683
French, Anna IV, 707
French, Anna IV, 708
French, Anna IV, 709
French, Anna IV, 728
French, Anna IV, 772
French, Anna IV, 955
French, Anna IV, 1316
French, Anna B. II, 864
French, Anna D. II, 864
French, Anna Dora II, 812
French, Anna Dora II, 864
French, Anna Dora II, 904
French, Anna E. II, 173
French, Anna E. II, 287
French, Anna E. IV, 955
French, Anna S. IV, 179
French, Anna S. IV, 191
French, Anna S. IV, 203
French, Anna S. IV, 412
French, Anna S. IV, 708
French, Anna Street II, 700
French, Anne IV, 708
French, Anney VI, 918
French, Annie B. IV, 708
French, Annie B. IV, 791
French, Barberry VI, 918
French, Barzilla IV, 919
French, Barzillai IV, 611
French, Barzillai IV, 625
French, Barzillai IV, 679
French, Barzillai IV, 707
French, Barzillai IV, 708
French, Barzillai IV, 791
French, Barzillai IV, 815
French, Barzillai IV, 857
French, Barzillai IV, 905
French, Barzillai IV, 954
French, Barzillai IV, 955
French, Barzillai M. IV, 708
French, Barzillai Moris IV, 709
French, Barzillar IV, 955
French, Barzillar, Jr. IV, 955
French, Barzillia IV, 858
French, Barzillia, Jr. IV, 709
French, Bathsheba II, 827
French, Benjamin IV, 955
French, Benjamin J. IV, 955
French, Benjamin Wilson IV, 525
French, Caleb IV, 33
French, Caroline II, 785
French, Caroline Burr II, 794
French, Caroline M. IV, 1038
French, Charles II, 173
French, Charles II, 222
French, Charles II, 287
French, Charles II, 364
French, Charles II, 528
French, Charles IV, 707
French, Charles IV, 708
French, Charles IV, 954
French, Charles IV, 955
French, Charles V, 56
French, Charles C. II, 364
French, Charles C. II, 485
French, Charles C. II, 528
French, Charles C. II, 864
French, Charles C. V, 952
French, Charles Creighton II, 528
French, Charles Ogden IV, 708
French, Charles S. II, 864
French, Chas. S. II, 904
French, Chas. Strickland II, 794
French, Clarkson IV, 625
French, Clarkson IV, 708
French, Clarkson IV, 709
French, Clarkson IV, 791
French, Clarkson S. IV, 708
French, Cynthia E. II, 864
French, Daniel VI, 918
French, Daniel VI, 948
French, Daniel VI, 1012
French, David II, 948
French, David II, 949
French, David II, 1085
French, David II, 1087
French, David II, 1089
French, David IV, 552
French, David IV, 707
French, David IV, 708
French, David IV, 709
French, David IV, 770
French, David IV, 905
French, David IV, 918
French, David IV, 954
French, David IV, 955
French, David IV, 980
French, Deborah IV, 146
French, Deborah IV, 203
French, Deborah IV, 708
French, Deborah IV, 954
French, Deborah IV, 955
French, Deborah D. IV, 709
French, Deborah D. IV, 715
French, Deborah G. IV, 955
French, Deborah M. IV, 708
French, Deborah M. IV, 709
French, Deborah M. IV, 955
French, Edgar IV, 708
French, Edgar IV, 709
French, Edgar IV, 955
French, Edward IV, 708
French, Edward O. IV, 709
French, Elanor VI, 918
French, Eleanor Lukens II, 794
French, Eli IV, 708
French, Eli IV, 955
French, Eli IV, 1057
French, Eliel IV, 394
French, Elijah IV, 697
French, Elijah IV, 707
French, Elijah IV, 708
French, Elijah IV, 954
French, Elijah IV, 1362
French, Elisha L. IV, 708
French, Elisha S. IV, 708
French, Eliza IV, 552
French, Eliza IV, 708
French, Eliza IV, 905
French, Eliza IV, 918
French, Eliza IV, 955
French, Eliza IV, 980
French, Eliza Ann IV, 707
French, Eliza Ann IV, 708
French, Eliza Ann IV, 954
French, Eliza Ann IV, 1278
French, Eliza M. II, 948
French, Eliza M. II, 1087
French, Eliza M. II, 1089
French, Eliza M. IV, 709
French, Eliza M. IV, 770
French, Eliza W. II, 948
French, Elizabeth II, 364
French, Elizabeth II, 658
French, Elizabeth IV, 394
French, Elizabeth IV, 445
French, Elizabeth IV, 472
French, Elizabeth IV, 498
French, Elizabeth IV, 707
French, Elizabeth IV, 709
French, Elizabeth IV, 944
French, Elizabeth IV, 954
French, Elizabeth IV, 955
French, Elizabeth IV, 988
French, Elizabeth B. II, 864
French, Elizabeth Borton II, 785
French, Elizabeth Borton II, 794
French, Elizabeth C. II, 1051
French, Elizabeth C. II, 1060
French, Elizabeth F. V, 57
French, Elizabeth G. V, 57
French, Elizabeth M. IV, 954
French, Elizabeth M. IV, 955
French, Elizabeth T. IV, 955
French, Ella IV, 709
French, Ella IV, 1037
French, Ella B. IV, 709
French, Elma II, 948
French, Elma II, 1057
French, Elma II, 1087
French, Elma II, 1089
French, Elma IV, 708
French, Elma IV, 709
French, Elma F. IV, 709
French, Elma F. IV, 747
French, Elmira IV, 444
French, Elmira IV, 709
French, Elmira T. IV, 394
French, Elmira T. IV, 444
French, Elmira T. IV, 708
French, Elmira T. IV, 768
French, Emergene II, 287
French, Emergene L. II, 173
French, Emily II, 794
French, Emma IV, 146
French, Emma IV, 160
French, Emma IV, 394
French, Emma IV, 444
French, Emma IV, 709
French, Emma IV, 955
French, Emma Walton II, 864
French, Emmergene L. IV, 955
French, Emmor IV, 955
French, Emmorgene L. IV, 955
French, Enoch IV, 33
French, Enoch J. IV, 1038
French, Esther IV, 33
French, Esther IV, 78
French, Esther IV, 86
French, Esther IV, 707
French, Esther IV, 708
French, Esther IV, 946
French, Esther IV, 954
French, Esther IV, 955
French, Esther C. IV, 1037
French, Ezra IV, 707
French, Ezra IV, 954
French, Ezra IV, 955
French, Ezra IV, 970
French, Ezra IV, 998
French, George IV, 708
French, George IV, 709
French, George F. II, 287
French, George F. II, 741
French, Hannah II, 204
French, Hannah II, 222
French, Hannah II, 287
French, Hannah II, 741
French, Hannah IV, 472
French, Hannah IV, 708
French, Hannah IV, 709
French, Hannah IV, 955
French, Hannah IV, 1362
French, Hannah Ann II, 173
French, Hannah Ann II, 287
French, Hannah L. IV, 525
French, Hannah L. IV, 554
French, Hannah L. IV, 555
French, Hannah L. IV, 708
French, Hannah L. IV, 782
French, Haran IV, 954
French, Helen IV, 1362
French, Henrietta IV, 708
French, Henry IV, 955
French, Holland M. IV, 708
French, Hubert IV, 708
French, Hubert C. IV, 709
French, Huldah IV, 1278
French, Isabella IV, 1155
French, Israel IV, 146
French, Israel IV, 203
French, Israel IV, 394
French, Israel IV, 444
French, Israel, Jr. VI, 638
French, James II, 173
French, James II, 287
French, James II, 485
French, James II, 528
French, James IV, 86
French, James IV, 472
French, James IV, 707
French, James IV, 708
French, James IV, 954
French, James IV, 1009
French, James V, 56
French, James V, 936
French, James VI, 918
French, James Creighton IV, 955
French, James F. IV, 472
French, James F. IV, 954
French, James F. IV, 955
French, James G. IV, 955
French, James, Jr. II, 287
French, James, Jr. IV, 86
French, Jane II, 222
French, Jane II, 229
French, Jane Elizabeth V, 751
French, John IV, 558
French, John IV, 683
French, John IV, 707
French, John IV, 708
French, John IV, 709
French, John IV, 746
French, John IV, 768
French, John IV, 788
French, John IV, 954
French, John IV, 955
French, John VI, 918
French, John E. II, 864
French, John T. IV, 1362
French, Joseph II, 485
French, Joseph II, 528
French, Joseph IV, 707
French, Joseph IV, 708
French, Joseph IV, 709
French, Joseph C. IV, 707
French, Joseph C. IV, 708
French, Joseph C. IV, 954
French, Joseph T. IV, 472
French, Joseph T. IV, 954
French, Joseph, Jr. II, 528
French, Joshua II, 364
French, Joshua Hunt IV, 33
French, Judith IV, 696
French, Judith IV, 707
French, Judith IV, 946
French, Judith IV, 954
French, Judith IV, 955
French, Judith IV, 988
French, Judith IV, 1017
French, Judith, Jr. IV, 955
French, Julia A. II, 864
French, Julia Ann II, 794
French, Julia Ann IV, 191
French, Julia Anna II, 794
French, Julian IV, 146
French, Juliann IV, 203
French, Karon IV, 472
French, Kesiah II, 70
French, Keziah II, 70
French, Laura W. V, 906
French, Lewis IV, 708
French, Lewis IV, 709
French, Lewis B. IV, 709
French, Lewis G. IV, 709
French, Lewis G. IV, 1037
French, Lorinda IV, 708
French, Louis IV, 709
French, Lucetta IV, 1278
French, Lucetta IV, 1283
French, Lydia IV, 647
French, Lydia IV, 707
French, Lydia IV, 708
French, Lydia IV, 709
French, Lydia IV, 742
French, Lydia IV, 829
French, Lydia IV, 878
French, Lydia IV, 954
French, Lydia IV, 955
French, Lydia IV, 981
French, Lydia L. V, 952
French, Lydia L. V, 962
French, Lydia Lovegrove VI, 722
French, Lydiaann V, 64
French, Lydiaann French V, 56
French, Mahlon II, 528
French, Marcy IV, 86
French, Marcy G. V, 952
French, Margaret IV, 444
French, Maria IV, 707
French, Mariah IV, 954
French, Mariam IV, 708
French, Martha IV, 465
French, Martha IV, 472
French, Martha IV, 558
French, Martha IV, 611
French, Martha IV, 625
French, Martha IV, 679
French, Martha IV, 707
French, Martha IV, 708
French, Martha IV, 709
French, Martha IV, 931
French, Martha IV, 933
French, Martha IV, 954
French, Martha IV, 955
French, Martha IV, 957
French, Martha IV, 1007
French, Martha B. IV, 625
French, Martha B. IV, 708
French, Martha B. IV, 709
French, Martha H. IV, 683
French, Martha H. IV, 746
French, Martha H. IV, 768
French, Martha H. IV, 788
French, Mary I, 1152
French, Mary II, 204
French, Mary II, 222
French, Mary II, 864
French, Mary IV, 373
French, Mary IV, 394
French, Mary IV, 625
French, Mary IV, 707
French, Mary IV, 708

French, Mary IV, 709
French, Mary IV, 770
French, Mary IV, 791
French, Mary IV, 815
French, Mary IV, 857
French, Mary IV, 905
French, Mary IV, 954
French, Mary IV, 955
French, Mary IV, 969
French, Mary IV, 970
French, Mary IV, 1009
French, Mary IV, 1037
French, Mary IV, 1057
French, Mary V, 915
French, Mary A. II, 708
French, Mary A. IV, 525
French, Mary A. IV, 558
French, Mary A. IV, 708
French, Mary A. IV, 788
French, Mary Almyra IV, 955
French, Mary Ann IV, 558
French, Mary Ann IV, 708
French, Mary B. II, 173
French, Mary B. II, 287
French, Mary B. IV, 955
French, Mary C. IV, 954
French, Mary E. IV, 955
French, Mary F. IV, 552
French, Mary G. IV, 954
French, Mary Isabella IV, 948
French, Mary Isabella IV, 955
French, Mary J. IV, 525
French, Mary J. IV, 554
French, Mary J. IV, 708
French, Mary J. IV, 709
French, Mary J. IV, 748
French, Mary J. IV, 750
French, Mary J. IV, 782
French, Mary J. IV, 955
French, Mary Jane IV, 709
French, Mary Jane IV, 955
French, Mary Jane IV, 1007
French, Mary Lucile IV, 709
French, Mary Shaw II, 794
French, Mary W. II, 794
French, Mercy II, 364
French, Mercy II, 485
French, Mercy II, 528
French, Mercy IV, 707
French, Mercy G. II, 485
French, Mercy G. II, 528
French, Mercy G. V, 56
French, Mercy G. V, 63
French, Mercy G. V, 64
French, Meriam IV, 708
French, Meriam IV, 709
French, Miriam IV, 525
French, Miriam IV, 534
French, Moses Townsend IV, 708
French, Nancy P. VI, 918
French, Nathan IV, 33
French, Nelly IV, 394
French, Newton IV, 472
French, Newton IV, 954
French, Obadiah IV, 954
French, Obadiah C. IV, 955
French, Otho IV, 394
French, Otho IV, 445
French, Otho IV, 1057
French, Patience Thomas IV, 708
French, Paul C. IV, 708
French, Paul C. IV, 709
French, Pheraba IV, 1278
French, Pheraba A. IV, 1298
French, Rachel II, 801
French, Rachel II, 811
French, Rachel II, 823
French, Rachel II, 997
French, Rachel II, 1023
French, Rachel III, 128
French, Rachel IV, 21
French, Rachel IV, 33
French, Rachel Ann VI, 492
French, Rachel Ann VI, 511
French, Rachel Ann VI, 512
French, Rachel H. IV, 21
French, Rachel H. IV, 33
French, Rachel H. IV, 625
French, Rachel H. IV, 679
French, Rachel H. IV, 708
French, Rachel H. IV, 709
French, Rachel S. IV, 709
French, Rachel S. IV, 757
French, Rebecca II, 222
French, Rebecca II, 260
French, Rebecca II, 364
French, Rebecca II, 485
French, Rebecca II, 528
French, Rebecca IV, 707
French, Rebecca IV, 708
French, Rebecca IV, 954
French, Rebecca C. IV, 709
French, Rebecca C. IV, 955
French, Rhoda Ann IV, 394
French, Rhoda Ann IV, 445
French, Richard II, 222
French, Richard II, 257
French, Richard II, 260
French, Richard II, 287
French, Richard II, 741
French, Richard II, 794
French, Richard II, 864
French, Richard IV, 707
French, Richard IV, 708
French, Richard IV, 954
French, Richard A. II, 864
French, Richard Abbott II, 794
French, Robert IV, 86
French, Robert IV, 525
French, Robert IV, 707
French, Robert IV, 708
French, Robert IV, 709
French, Robert IV, 728
French, Robert IV, 772
French, Robert IV, 954
French, Robert P. IV, 955
French, Robert, Jr. IV, 707
French, Rosa Ermina IV, 709
French, Ruth IV, 708
French, Ruth Ann IV, 808
French, Ruth Ann IV, 815
French, Sally VI, 1012
French, Samuel IV, 525
French, Samuel IV, 554
French, Samuel IV, 707
French, Samuel IV, 708
French, Samuel IV, 709
French, Samuel IV, 748
French, Samuel IV, 750
French, Samuel IV, 782
French, Samuel H. IV, 708
French, Sarah II, 222
French, Sarah II, 257
French, Sarah II, 275
French, Sarah II, 287
French, Sarah II, 741
French, Sarah IV, 383
French, Sarah IV, 394
French, Sarah IV, 472
French, Sarah IV, 708
French, Sarah IV, 709
French, Sarah IV, 933
French, Sarah IV, 954
French, Sarah IV, 955
French, Sarah V, 63
French, Sarah B. II, 741
French, Sarah Baynes II, 794
French, Sarah Chapman II, 528
French, Sarah J. IV, 708
French, Sarah L. II, 287
French, Sarah L. II, 741
French, Shepherd III, 128
French, Sophia IV, 708
French, Stacy IV, 33
French, Susanna IV, 954
French, Susannah IV, 697
French, Susannah IV, 707
French, Susannah IV, 708
French, Terrill IV, 1362
French, Thomas II, 222
French, Thomas II, 528
French, Thomas II, 658
French, Thomas IV, 78
French, Thomas IV, 86
French, Thomas IV, 465
French, Thomas IV, 472
French, Thomas IV, 498
French, Thomas IV, 707
French, Thomas IV, 708
French, Thomas IV, 919
French, Thomas IV, 931
French, Thomas IV, 933
French, Thomas IV, 954
French, Thomas V, 63
French, Thomas E. IV, 955
French, Thomas E. IV, 1038
French, Thomas Emmor IV, 955
French, Thomas French IV, 33
French, Thomas Y. IV, 21
French, Thomas Y. IV, 33
French, Thomas Y. IV, 625
French, Thomas Y. IV, 679
French, Thomas Y. IV, 708
French, Thomas Y. IV, 709
French, Thos. IV, 707
French, Thos. Yates IV, 707
French, Unity IV, 954
French, Unity IV, 955
French, Uriah IV, 708
French, Uriah V, 57
French, Uriah V, 969
French, Wd. Eliza M. II, 1085
French, William IV, 394
French, William IV, 946
French, William IV, 1057
French, William V, 56
French, William VI, 918
French, William B. V, 57
French, William F. IV, 472
French, William F. IV, 954
French, William F. IV, 955
French, William G. II, 173
French, William G. II, 287
French, William Henry IV, 709
French, William R. IV, 708
French, William R. IV, 954
French, Wm. II, 528
French, Wm. II, 997
French, Wm. II, 1023
French, Wm. IV, 373
French, Wm. IV, 955
French, Wm. IV, 988
French, Wm. B. IV, 696
French, Wm. B. IV, 707
French, Wm. B. V, 906
French, Wm. B. V, 952
French, Wm. B. V, 962
French, Wm. B. VI, 722
French, Wm. F. IV, 954
French, Wm. G. IV, 955
French, Wm. H. II, 864
French, Wm. H. IV, 708
French, Wm. Hazleton II, 785
French, Wm. Henry IV, 955
French, Wm. J. IV, 955
French, Wm. James IV, 954
French, Wm. R. IV, 707
French, Wm. R. IV, 955
French, Wm. Rogers IV, 954
French, Wm. T. VI, 492
French, Wm. T. VI, 511
French, Wm. T. VI, 512
French, Zadok IV, 525
French, Zadok IV, 534
French, Zadok IV, 707
French, Zadok IV, 708
French, Zadok S. IV, 708
French, Zadok S. IV, 709
French, Zemah IV, 312
French, Zemah IV, 315
French, Zeruah IV, 203
Frescott, Ann IV, 686
Frescott, Ann IV, 687
Frescott, Ann IV, 709
Frescott, Benjamin IV, 687
Frescott, Clark IV, 686
Frescott, Clark IV, 709
Frescott, Ellener IV, 687
Frescott, Hannah IV, 687
Frescott, John IV, 687
Frescott, Lawrence IV, 687
Frescott, Lawrence W. IV, 687
Frescott, Meribah IV, 687
Frescott, Samuel IV, 709
Frescott, Sarah IV, 687
Frescott, Sophia IV, 709
Fresh, Caroline V, 386
Fresh, Caroline V, 422
Fresh, Priscilla I, 1119
Fresh, Priscilla I, 1134
Freth, John II, 70
Freth, Sarah II, 70
Freth, Sarah II, 95
Frettwell, Elizabeth II, 173
Frettwell, John II, 173
Frettwell, Peter II, 173
Fretwell, Anne VI, 835
Fretwell, Joshua II, 222
Fretwell, Lenard VI, 818
Fretwell, Lucy VI, 835
Fretwell, Margaret VI, 818
Fretwell, Margaret VI, 867
Fretwell, Nancy VI, 818
Fretwell, Ralph II, 528
Fretwell, Rebecca II, 222
Fretwell, Richard VI, 818
Fretwell, Samuel II, 222
Frey, Huldah V, 997
Frey, John V, 997
Frey, Mary IV, 1159
Frey, Mary IV, 1207
Frezer, Aaron V, 239
Frezer, Alice V, 238
Frezer, Alice V, 239
Frezer, John V, 238
Frezer, John V, 239
Friar, James M. V, 561
Frick, Ann II, 864
Frick, Jacob II, 794
Frick, Mary A. III, 310
Frick, Mary Amanda III, 263
Frick, Mary Amanda III, 372
Frick, Wd. Ann II, 794
Friedland, Elizabeth II, 94
Friedland, Jonas II, 94
Friedland, Lydia II, 70
Friedland, Sarah II, 70
Friedland, Sarah II, 94
Friedle, William H. I, 879
Friench, Elijah IV, 954
Friench, Eliza Ann IV, 954
Friench, Esther IV, 954
Friench, Joseph C. IV, 954
Friench, Mariah IV, 954
Friench, Rebecca IV, 954
Friench, Susanna IV, 954
Friench, Thomas IV, 954
Friend, Albert IV, 1251
Friend, Earl J. IV, 1251
Friend, Elizabeth IV, 203
Friend, Elizabeth V, 781
Friend, Maynard IV, 1251
Friend, Olive K. IV, 1251
Friend, Ollie IV, 1251
Friend, Orthodox II, 936
Friend, Wesley IV, 203
Fries, Ann II, 364
Fries, Ann II, 528
Fries, George S. VI, 390
Fries, John II, 364
Fries, John II, 528
Fries, Mary E. VI, 372
Fries, Mary Ella VI, 390
Fries, Rebecca VI, 390
Fries, Salome II, 364
Fries, Virginia III, 272
Fries, Virginia VI, 390
Fries, Virginia VI, 438
Fries, William Chandler II, 364
Friese, John II, 364
Friese, Salome II, 364
Friis-Holm, Astrid E. III, 128
Friis-Holm, Dr. Gudson III, 128
Friis-Holm, Edw. Holm III, 128
Frilher, Eliza E. IV, 1279
Frior, Anthony II, 222
Fris, Virginia VI, 390
Frisbee, Elizabeth W. III, 128
Frisbee, Ida V. III, 128
Frisbee, Lawrence III, 128
Frisbee, Willard C. III, 128
Frisbie, ??? III, 210
Frisbie, Arthur G. IV, 1316
Frisbie, Elizabeth III, 188
Frisbie, Elizabeth W. III, 128
Frisbie, Elizabeth W. III, 210
Frisbie, Esther Louise IV, 1316
Frisbie, Flonna IV, 1316
Frisbie, Ida V. III, 128
Frisbie, Ida V. III, 188
Frisbie, Lawrence III, 128
Frisbie, Lawrence III, 188
Frisbie, Mrs. Flonna IV, 1316
Frisbie, Willard C. III, 128
Frisby, Debora V, 997
Frisby, Louisa V, 997
Frisgoe, Elisabeth II, 528
Frisher, Arthur G. IV, 1316
Frishmuth, Elizabeth B. II, 838
Frishmuth, Elizabeth B. II, 864
Frishmuth, Hannah B. II, 864
Frisk, Thomas V, 386
Frismuth, Elizabeth II, 794
Frismuth, John C. W. II, 794
Fristo, Dollie IV, 1251
Fristo, Elma IV, 1251
Fristo, Elmer IV, 1251
Fristo, Nellie IV, 1251
Fristoe, Minnie IV, 1316
Fristoe, Walter W. IV, 1316
Fristre, Minnie IV, 1316
Fritchman, Addison H. IV, 815
Fritchman, Adison H. IV, 815
Fritchman, Ann IV, 815
Fritchman, Emerson B. IV, 709
Fritchman, Emerson B. IV, 815
Fritchman, Joel IV, 815
Fritchman, John IV, 815
Fritchman, John H. IV, 815
Fritchman, Joseph IV, 709
Fritchman, Joseph IV, 815
Fritchman, Joseph IV, 823
Fritchman, Lucy IV, 709
Fritchman, Lucy H. IV, 709
Fritchman, Mary IV, 135
Fritchman, Mary IV, 709
Fritchman, Mary IV, 815
Fritchman, Mary IV, 823
Fritchman, Mary F. IV, 815
Fritchman, Mary F. IV, 824
Fritchman, Mary H. IV, 815
Fritchman, Mary Louise IV, 709
Frith, Ann III, 462
Frith, Anna III, 411
Frith, Archibald VI, 911
Frith, Elizabeth VI, 967
Frith, Herbert VI, 918
Frith, Herbert VI, 1008
Frith, Jane VI, 1008
Frith, John II, 56
Frith, John II, 70
Frith, John II, 103
Frith, John VI, 918
Frith, John VI, 1008
Frith, John, Jr. II, 70
Frith, Joseph VI, 987
Frith, Margaretta A. III, 411
Frith, Margaretta A. III, 462
Frith, Mary VI, 918
Frith, Nancy VI, 987
Frith, Oscar III, 411
Frith, Oscar III, 462
Frith, Patsy VI, 1008
Frith, Patty VI, 918
Frith, Polly VI, 918
Frith, Rhoda VI, 798
Frith, Rhoda VI, 939
Frith, Rhoda VI, 967
Frith, Rhoda Mason VI, 918
Frith, Ruth A. VI, 918
Frith, Samuel II, 70
Frith, Sarah II, 56
Frith, Sarah II, 70
Frith, Sarah II, 103
Frith, Thomas II, 70
Frith, Thomas VI, 918
Frith, William VI, 918
Frith, William VI, 982
Fritts, Jasper V, 673
Fritts, Mary III, 223
Fritts, Mary Lee I, 1152
Fritts, Susannah V, 400
Fritz, Annabelle IV, 1207
Fritz, Annis B. IV, 1207
Fritz, Ella IV, 1207
Fritz, Hazel IV, 1207
Fritz, Henry IV, 1207
Fritz, Jane IV, 1207
Fritz, Kenneth M. IV, 1207
Fritz, Laur IV, 1207
Fritz, Lonzo IV, 1207
Fritz, Lonzo V. IV, 1207
Fritz, Matilda IV, 1207
Fritz, Pearl IV, 1207
Fritz, Wm. IV, 1207
Fritzgerald, Peter VI, 242
Froelicher, Deborah P. II, 705
Froelicher, Elizabeth II, 705
Froelicher, Elizabeth L. II, 705
Froelicher, Francis M. II, 705
Froelick, Cordelia IV, 1316
Froelicker, Deborah Lowry II, 741
Froelicker, Elizabeth II, 741
Froelicker, Elizabeth Lowry II, 741
Froelicker, Francis M. II, 741
Froelicker, Francis M., Jr. II, 7
Froggett, Thomas II, 443
Frohlicher, Francis Mitchell II, 864
Frohlicher, Hans II, 864
Frohlicker, Francis Mitchell II, 864
Frolicher, Hans II, 900
Fronefield, Alice G. V, 997
Fronefield, Alma V, 997
Fronefield, Anna V, 997
Fronefield, B. F. V, 997
Fronefield, Bertha V, 997
Fronefield, Christiana V, 997
Fronefield, Christina V, 997
Fronefield, Ella V, 997
Fronefield, Eva V, 997
Fronefield, Evaline V, 997
Fronefield, J. H. V, 997
Fronefield, Jacob V, 997
Fronefield, Maggie V, 997
Fronefield, Maggie A. V, 997
Fronefield, Margaret V, 997
Fronefield, Mary E. V, 997
Fronefield, Rosa V, 997
Fronefield, Rose V, 997
Fronefield, Solomon V, 997
Fronefield, Wm. V, 997
Fronefield, Wm., Sr. V, 997
Fronte, William Alfred V, 492
Frost, ??? III, 41
Frost, ??? III, 72
Frost, ??? III, 230
Frost, ??? III, 391
Frost, ??? III, 412
Frost, Aaron III, 128
Frost, Abigail III, 128
Frost, Abigail III, 129

rost, Abigail III, 227
rost, Abraham III, 128
rost, Adelbert IV, 869
rost, Alice III, 128
rost, Alice III, 411
rost, Alice III, 412
rost, Alice V. III, 93
rost, Alice V. III, 128
rost, Amelia III, 129
rost, Amy III, 411
rost, Amy III, 412
rost, Amy III, 482
rost, Amy IV, 1098
rost, Amy IV, 1116
rost, Ann H. III, 411
rost, Anna III, 129
rost, Anna III, 148
rost, Anna Elizabeth III, 411
rost, Anna H. III, 128
rost, Anna H. III, 148
rost, Anna Vail III, 227
rost, Anna W. III, 69
rost, Anne Elizabeth III, 475
rost, Annie A. II, 864
rost, Annie A. II, 879
rost, Caleb III, 128
rost, Caleb III, 403
rost, Caleb III, 411
rost, Caleb III, 412
rost, Caleb III, 414
rost, Caleb III, 438
rost, Caleb III, 466
rost, Caleb H. III, 128
rost, Caroline A. III, 128
rost, Catharine III, 128
rost, Catharine III, 249
rost, Catharine III, 430
rost, Catharine M. III, 411
rost, Catharine P. III, 129
rost, Charles III, 128
rost, Charles III, 129
rost, Charles III, 400
rost, Charles III, 411
rost, Charles III, 412
rost, Charles III, 430
rost, Charles III, 453
rost, Charles III, 455
rost, Charles III, 463
rost, Charles III, 482
rost, Charles L. III, 128
rost, Charles S. III, 93
rost, Charles Seely III, 128
rost, Charles Seely III, 129
rost, Chas. III, 441
rost, Cornelia III, 412
rost, Cornelia III, 461
rost, D. Anna II, 864
rost, D. Anna II, 905
rost, Daniel III, 427
rost, David M. III, 128
rost, David M. III, 255
rost, Deborah III, 74
rost, Dorothy III, 137
rost, Edw. L. III, 411
rost, Edw. L. III, 412
rost, Edward III, 129
rost, Edward III, 397
rost, Edward III, 411
rost, Edward L. III, 411
rost, Edward L. III, 420
rost, Edward L. III, 464
rost, Edward S. III, 128
rost, Edward T. III, 411
rost, Eleanor III, 90
rost, Eleanor III, 129
rost, Eliz. M. III, 147
rost, Eliza III, 129
rost, Eliza Hart III, 227
rost, Elizabeth III, 129
Frost, Elizabeth III, 241
Frost, Elizabeth III, 411
Frost, Elizabeth H. III, 438
Frost, Elizabeth M. III, 128
Frost, Elizabeth M. III, 129
Frost, Elizabeth M. III, 146
Frost, Elizabeth M. III, 147
Frost, Emily C. III, 129
Frost, Esther III, 400
Frost, Esther III, 411
Frost, Esther III, 412
Frost, Ettie W. III, 412
Frost, Freelove III, 129
Frost, Freelove III, 412
Frost, Gideon III, 128
Frost, Gideon III, 411
Frost, Gideon III, 412
Frost, Gideon III, 470
Frost, Goldie IV, 869
Frost, Grace III, 226
Frost, Grace III, 412
Frost, Grace III, 442
Frost, Grace Frost III, 227
Frost, Halstead H. III, 411
Frost, Hannah III, 129
Frost, Hannah III, 401
Frost, Hannah III, 405
Frost, Hannah III, 406
Frost, Hannah III, 411
Frost, Hannah III, 412
Frost, Hannah III, 420
Frost, Hannah III, 427
Frost, Hannah III, 464
Frost, Hannah III, 482
Frost, Hannah III, 503
Frost, Hannah H. III, 411
Frost, Hannah H. III, 412
Frost, Hannah L. III, 411
Frost, Hannah Matilda III, 128
Frost, Harriet III, 225
Frost, Harriet III, 227
Frost, Harriet III, 368
Frost, Harriet F. III, 128
Frost, Harriett III, 226
Frost, Henrietta III, 411
Frost, Henrietta III, 466
Frost, Henry III, 411
Frost, Henry T. III, 411
Frost, Henry T. III, 412
Frost, Henry T. III, 440
Frost, Herietta W. III, 464
Frost, Howard III, 411
Frost, Isaac III, 128
Frost, Isaac III, 411
Frost, Isaac III, 412
Frost, Isaac III, 482
Frost, Isaac III, 503
Frost, Isaac C. III, 47
Frost, Isaac C. III, 128
Frost, Isaac C. III, 129
Frost, Isaac D. III, 230
Frost, J. Sheldon III, 128
Frost, J. Sheldon III, 137
Frost, Jacob III, 128
Frost, Jacob III, 129
Frost, Jacob III, 208
Frost, Jacob III, 411
Frost, Jacob III, 412
Frost, Jacob III, 442
Frost, Jacob III, 455
Frost, Jacob III, 460
Frost, Jacob L. III, 412
Frost, James IV, 869
Frost, Jane Ann III, 128
Frost, Jane Ann III, 208
Frost, Jane W. III, 129
Frost, Jemima III, 406
Frost, Jemima III, 411
Frost, Jemima III, 412
Frost, John III, 380
Frost, John VI, 357
Frost, John VI, 390
Frost, John VI, 415
Frost, John D. III, 128
Frost, John Hicks III, 128
Frost, Jordan C. III, 74
Frost, Jos. III, 412
Frost, Joseph III, 411
Frost, Joseph III, 412
Frost, Josephine III, 129
Frost, Josephine B. III, 129
Frost, Josephine B. III, 230
Frost, Josephine L. III, 412
Frost, Josephine L. III, 433
Frost, Joshua IV, 1159
Frost, Lanah III, 400
Frost, Lanah III, 412
Frost, Leonard III, 411
Frost, Leonard III, 412
Frost, Leonard III, 426
Frost, Leonard J. III, 128
Frost, Leonard J. III, 129
Frost, Leonard T. III, 128
Frost, Lilla J. III, 128
Frost, Lilla J. III, 255
Frost, Lizzie J. III, 412
Frost, Lizzie J. III, 426
Frost, Louisa C. III, 412
Frost, Lydia V, 838
Frost, Lydia V, 874
Frost, M III, 438
Frost, Margaret III, 129
Frost, Margaret III, 411
Frost, Margaret III, 412
Frost, Margaret III, 463
Frost, Maria III, 411
Frost, Marquis C. III, 230
Frost, Marquis Chester III, 129
Frost, Marshall S. III, 411
Frost, Marshall S. III, 412
Frost, Marshall S. III, 433
Frost, Marshall S. III, 461
Frost, Martha III, 129
Frost, Martha III, 403
Frost, Martha III, 411
Frost, Martha III, 412
Frost, Martha III, 453
Frost, Martha III, 463
Frost, Mary III, 72
Frost, Mary III, 107
Frost, Mary III, 129
Frost, Mary III, 406
Frost, Mary III, 411
Frost, Mary III, 412
Frost, Mary III, 427
Frost, Mary III, 430
Frost, Mary III, 441
Frost, Mary III, 455
Frost, Mary III, 459
Frost, Mary III, 460
Frost, Mary III, 461
Frost, Mary III, 470
Frost, Mary III, 475
Frost, Mary III, 482
Frost, Mary III, 502
Frost, Mary IV, 1159
Frost, Mary VI, 390
Frost, Mary Ann III, 129
Frost, Mary D. III, 128
Frost, Mary S. III, 129
Frost, Mary U. III, 411
Frost, Mary W. III, 128
Frost, Mary W. III, 411
Frost, Mary W. III, 440
Frost, Matilda III, 41
Frost, Matilda III, 128
Frost, Matilda III, 129
Frost, Naomi III, 129
Frost, Newbury H. III, 412
Frost, Obadiah III, 128
Frost, Obadiah III, 129
Frost, Obadiah III, 148
Frost, Obediah III, 128
Frost, Obediah III, 147
Frost, Pamela III, 397
Frost, Pamela III, 411
Frost, Penn III, 107
Frost, Penn III, 129
Frost, Penn III, 400
Frost, Penn III, 412
Frost, Penn III, 460
Frost, Penn. III, 412
Frost, Phebe III, 128
Frost, Phebe III, 129
Frost, Phebe III, 146
Frost, Phebe III, 147
Frost, Phebe III, 148
Frost, Phebe III, 406
Frost, Phebe III, 411
Frost, Phebe III, 412
Frost, Phebe III, 455
Frost, Phebe V, 163
Frost, Phebe V, 170
Frost, Phebe A. III, 129
Frost, Phebe C. III, 225
Frost, Phebe E. III, 128
Frost, Phebe Elizabeth III, 128
Frost, Phebe Jane III, 47
Frost, Phebe Jane III, 128
Frost, Phebe Jane III, 129
Frost, Phebe Jane III, 230
Frost, Philemon H. III, 129
Frost, Rachel VI, 883
Frost, Rebecca III, 401
Frost, Rebecca III, 412
Frost, Richard III, 129
Frost, Richard K. III, 129
Frost, Richard, Jr. III, 227
Frost, Robert III, 129
Frost, Robert III, 412
Frost, Robert IV, 1159
Frost, Ruth IV, 869
Frost, Sally Ann C. III, 128
Frost, Samuel III, 129
Frost, Samuel III, 147
Frost, Samuel III, 223
Frost, Samuel III, 346
Frost, Sarah III, 129
Frost, Sarah III, 400
Frost, Sarah III, 403
Frost, Sarah III, 411
Frost, Sarah III, 412
Frost, Sarah III, 414
Frost, Sarah III, 427
Frost, Sarah III, 428
Frost, Sarah III, 429
Frost, Sarah III, 430
Frost, Sarah III, 438
Frost, Sarah III, 444
Frost, Sarah III, 455
Frost, Sarah III, 460
Frost, Sarah III, 465
Frost, Sarah III, 466
Frost, Sarah VI, 390
Frost, Sarah VI, 415
Frost, Sarah A. III, 249
Frost, Sarah Ann III, 128
Frost, Sarah Ann III, 129
Frost, Sarah Ann III, 412
Frost, Sarah E. II, 794
Frost, Sarah F. III, 48
Frost, Sarah L. II, 741
Frost, Sarah L. II, 761
Frost, Sarah M. III, 128
Frost, Sarah M. III, 411
Frost, Sarah M. III, 412
Frost, Sarah M. III, 463
Frost, Semantha III, 129
Frost, Semantha III, 346
Frost, Semantha Weeks III, 129
Frost, Sidney B. II, 864
Frost, Sidney B. II, 879
Frost, Smith P. III, 129
Frost, Solomon V. III, 128
Frost, Solomon V. III, 129
Frost, Solomon V. III, 227
Frost, Stephen III, 90
Frost, Stephen III, 128
Frost, Stephen III, 249
Frost, Stephen III, 406
Frost, Stephen III, 411
Frost, Stephen M. III, 128
Frost, Susan III, 129
Frost, Sydney B. II, 794
Frost, Thomas III, 129
Frost, Thomas III, 406
Frost, Thomas III, 411
Frost, Thomas IV, 869
Frost, Timothy T. III, 411
Frost, Walter L. III, 128
Frost, Wd. Eleanor III, 128
Frost, Wd. Eleanor III, 129
Frost, Wd. Mary III, 380
Frost, Wd. Susan III, 129
Frost, William III, 129
Frost, William III, 401
Frost, William III, 411
Frost, William III, 412
Frost, William III, 489
Frost, William H. III, 128
Frost, William S. III, 128
Frost, William S. III, 129
Frost, Wm. III, 502
Frost, Wright III, 129
Frost, Wright III, 412
Frost, Wright III, 459
Frost, Wright III, 475
Frothingham, ??? III, 129
Frothingham, ??? III, 256
Frothingham, Helen III, 129
Frothingham, Helen III, 256
Frowenfelter, Lucy II, 828
Frownfield, Maggie V, 997
Frudenberg, Amelia IV, 1316
Fruitt, Nancy W. VI, 832
Fry, Alice V, 240
Fry, Andrew Jackson V, 240
Fry, Ann II, 528
Fry, Ann IV, 77
Fry, Ann IV, 86
Fry, Ann W. II, 705
Fry, Anna II, 1048
Fry, Anna II, 1051
Fry, Bessie III, 129
Fry, Bessie M. III, 337
Fry, Bessie Marion III, 316
Fry, Blanch V, 561
Fry, Charles V, 332
Fry, Charles W. V, 57
Fry, Christena V, 240
Fry, Christina V, 240
Fry, Clifford S. III, 129
Fry, Clifford S. III, 316
Fry, Clifford S. III, 337
Fry, Cora Etta V, 239
Fry, Daniel V, 240
Fry, Eleanor Priscilla III, 129
Fry, Eleanor Priscilla III, 130
Fry, Eleanor Priscilla III, 262
Fry, Elizabeth IV, 1279
Fry, Elizabeth IV, 1289
Fry, Ellen V, 240
Fry, Frances III, 129
Fry, George IV, 472
Fry, George W. V, 240
Fry, Glendora V, 240
Fry, Glendora R. V, 239
Fry, Hannah J. V, 240
Fry, Harriet Jane V, 239
Fry, Hershel V, 561
Fry, Howard V, 332
Fry, Isaac V, 57
Fry, Isaac L. V, 57
Fry, J. W., Jr. V, 240
Fry, Jack V, 240
Fry, Jackson V, 331
Fry, Jacob W. II, 705
Fry, James V, 239
Fry, James V, 240
Fry, Jefferson V, 240
Fry, Jericho John III, 360
Fry, John II, 528
Fry, John III, 129
Fry, John III, 332
Fry, John III, 412
Fry, John III, 470
Fry, John III, 474
Fry, John V, 240
Fry, John V, 997
Fry, John W. V, 240
Fry, John William V, 240
Fry, John, Jr. III, 412
Fry, John, Jr. III, 460
Fry, Joseph III, 129
Fry, Joseph V, 240
Fry, Joseph William V, 240
Fry, Lillian III, 129
Fry, Lillian III, 262
Fry, Lue Ellen V, 561
Fry, Mahala V, 239
Fry, Malinda Catherine V, 239
Fry, Margaret V, 57
Fry, Margaret E. V, 57
Fry, Margaret Elizabeth V, 239
Fry, Maria V, 239
Fry, Martha III, 129
Fry, Martha Esther V, 240
Fry, Mary III, 129
Fry, Mary III, 135
Fry, Mary III, 332
Fry, Mary III, 360
Fry, Mary III, 412
Fry, Mary III, 413
Fry, Mary III, 460
Fry, Mary III, 470
Fry, Mary III, 474
Fry, Mary III, 507
Fry, Mary IV, 1207
Fry, Mary V, 240
Fry, Merlin IV, 709
Fry, Michael V, 239
Fry, Nettie V, 332
Fry, Nicholas V, 240
Fry, Nick V, 240
Fry, Olga V, 240
Fry, Olga V, 331
Fry, Olga J. V, 240
Fry, Oscar D. V, 240
Fry, Perlie V, 561
Fry, Phebe Ellen V, 240
Fry, Rebecca II, 705
Fry, Roy V, 492
Fry, Sallie A. V, 240
Fry, Samuel Willis III, 412
Fry, Sherman V, 240
Fry, Sophronia C. V, 240
Fry, Tamison III, 412
Fry, Thomas E. III, 129
Fry, Thomas Jefferson V, 239
Fry, Thomasin III, 129
Fry, Virginia V, 331
Fry, W. Raymond III, 129
Fry, W. Raymond III, 262
Fry, Walter Eleanor III, 130
Fry, Walter Raymond III, 130
Fry, Wd. Bessie M. III, 129
Fry, Wd. Elizabeth II, 364
Fry, Willard V, 561
Fry, William II, 364
Fry, William III, 129
Fry, William III, 130
Fry, William III, 412
Fry, William III, 413
Fry, William V, 332
Fry, Wm. Storrs II, 528
Frybarger, Abraham V, 57
Frybarger, Grace B. V, 57
Frye, Carl V, 492
Frye, Christina V, 240
Frye, Daniel V, 240
Frye, Edith V, 492
Frye, Everett V, 492
Frye, Glendora V, 240
Frye, J. W., Jr. V, 240
Frye, Jack V, 240
Frye, James V, 239
Frye, James J. V, 492
Frye, Jefferson V, 240
Frye, John V, 240
Frye, John W. V, 240
Frye, Joseph V, 240
Frye, Lavinna V, 492
Frye, Leona V, 492
Frye, Leroy V, 492
Frye, Levinna V, 673
Frye, Lovina V, 492

Frye, Mahala V, 217
Frye, Margaret Elizabeth V, 239
Frye, Maria V, 239
Frye, Mary A. V, 492
Frye, Merlin IV, 709
Frye, Merlin M. IV, 709
Frye, Nicholas V, 492
Frye, Nicholas V, 673
Frye, Nick V, 240
Frye, Nick V, 492
Frye, Olga V, 240
Frye, Oscar V, 492
Frye, Roy V, 492
Frye, Roy V, 673
Frye, Sallie A. V, 240
Frye, Sophronia C. V, 240
Fryer, Anna V, 561
Fryer, Annie V, 561
Fryer, James M. V, 561
Fryer, James Madison V, 561
Fryer, Leona V, 561
Fryer, Mathew V, 561
Fryer, Orville V, 561
Fryer, Thelma V, 561
Fryer, Wilbur V, 561
Frysinger, Alice C. II, 705
Frysinger, Alice Chappell II, 741
Frysinger, Howard L. II, 705
Fuchs, Caroline III, 135
Fuchs, Caroline III, 311
Fuchs, John III, 311
Fuchs, Marie III, 311
Fudge, Rachel V, 952
Fudge, Rachel V, 958
Fuester, John V, 997
Fuester, Louvina V, 997
Fugate, Annie E. V, 562
Fugate, Elizabeth IV, 815
Fugate, Elizabeth IV, 855
Fugate, Martha V, 561
Fugate, Merretta V, 561
Fuggitt, Frances VI, 691
Fuhr, John D. V, 739
Fuhrer, Ethel III, 130
Fuhrer, Harry III, 130
Fuhrer, Lillian III, 130
Fuhrer, Marie III, 130
Fulcher, Joseph VI, 243
Fulcher, William VI, 243
Fulerton, Ann IV, 146
Fulerton, Ann IV, 152
Fulgham, Michel VI, 64
Fulgham, Michel VI, 88
Fulghum, Amy V, 562
Fulghum, Ann I, 288
Fulghum, Anthony I, 288
Fulghum, Anthony I, 299
Fulghum, Anthony I, 306
Fulghum, Benjamin I, 306
Fulghum, Catherine V, 562
Fulghum, Catherine V, 591
Fulghum, Celia I, 288
Fulghum, Celia I, 299
Fulghum, Celia I, 306
Fulghum, Edeth I, 306
Fulghum, Elizabeth I, 306
Fulghum, Frederick I, 288
Fulghum, Frederick I, 306
Fulghum, Frederick I, 314
Fulghum, Hannah V, 562
Fulghum, Hannah V, 568
Fulghum, Jeremiah I, 306
Fulghum, Jeremiah H. I, 306
Fulghum, Jesse I, 288
Fulghum, Jesse I, 306
Fulghum, John I, 283
Fulghum, Joseph I, 288
Fulghum, Joseph I, 306
Fulghum, Josiah I, 306
Fulghum, Josiah J. I, 306
Fulghum, Martha I, 288
Fulghum, Mary I, 288
Fulghum, Mary I, 299
Fulghum, Mary I, 302
Fulghum, Mary I, 306
Fulghum, Michael I, 288
Fulghum, Michael I, 306
Fulghum, Michael I, 309
Fulghum, Michael I, 320
Fulghum, Mikel I, 306
Fulghum, Mildred I, 306
Fulghum, Molly I, 288
Fulghum, Molly I, 306
Fulghum, Nanna I, 306
Fulghum, Patience I, 283
Fulghum, Peninah I, 288
Fulghum, Peninah I, 302
Fulghum, Peninah I, 306
Fulghum, Phebe I, 306
Fulghum, Piety I, 306
Fulghum, Piety I, 309
Fulghum, Piety I, 314
Fulghum, Pinninah I, 306
Fulghum, Pinninah I, 309
Fulghum, Rebecca I, 288
Fulghum, Rebecka I, 306
Fulghum, Rebeckah I, 306
Fulghum, Sarah I, 283
Fulghum, Sarah I, 288
Fulghum, Sarah I, 299
Fulghum, Sarah I, 306
Fulghum, Sarah I, 320
Fulghum, Selia I, 306
Fulghum, Silia I, 306
Fulghum, William I, 306
Fulghum, Woodard I, 306
Fulghum, Woodard V, 562
Fulk, Adam IV, 1279
Fulk, Isa IV, 1279
Fulke, Sarah III, 93
Fulke, Sarah III, 130
Fulkersin, Ora Lucille III, 130
Fulkersin, Ora Lucille III, 244
Fulkersin, Wesley III, 130
Fulkersin, Wesley III, 244
Fulkerson, Sarah V, 457
Fulkerson, Sarah E. V, 457
Fulkerson, Susan V, 170
Fulks, Martha VI, 918
Fulks, Obediah VI, 918
Fullam, Esther IV, 709
Fullam, Mrs. Esther IV, 709
Fullen, John II, 364
Fullen, Mary II, 528
Fullen, Mary II, 667
Fuller, Abigail IV, 709
Fuller, Albert IV, 1316
Fuller, Anna C. IV, 987
Fuller, Cyrus IV, 1362
Fuller, Dean IV, 1316
Fuller, Dean D. IV, 1316
Fuller, Edward J. IV, 987
Fuller, Hannah III, 130
Fuller, Isabella IV, 1362
Fuller, Isabella IV, 1379
Fuller, James, Jr. III, 130
Fuller, John IV, 1312
Fuller, John Wilkinson V, 906
Fuller, Mary II, 528
Fuller, Mary IV, 709
Fuller, Mary IV, 751
Fuller, Mary IV, 955
Fuller, Mary IV, 987
Fuller, Maud IV, 1312
Fuller, Oliver II, 528
Fuller, Oliver II, 741
Fuller, Rebecca I, 715
Fuller, Rebecca I, 722
Fuller, Robert Charlton V, 906
Fuller, Samuel III, 130
Fuller, Sarah II, 506
Fuller, Sarah II, 528
Fuller, Sarah IV, 1312
Fuller, William VI, 29
Fuller, William VI, 158
Fuller, William VI, 177
Fuller, Wm. VI, 205
Fullerton, Eliza V, 906
Fullerton, Eliza V, 942
Fullerton, Elizabeth A. V, 997
Fullerton, Florence III, 130
Fullerton, John III, 412
Fulmer, Julia Ann V, 997
Fulmer, Lewis V, 997
Fulmer, Louis V, 997
Fulor, Nancy VI, 830
Fulsham, John VI, 107
Fulsher, William VI, 243
Fulstow, Charity IV, 1235
Fulstow, John IV, 1235
Fulstow, John D. IV, 1235
Fulstow, Robert IV, 1235
Fulstow, Sarah IV, 1235
Fulton, Amelia III, 130
Fulton, Bessie Luzana I, 925
Fulton, Dorcas III, 130
Fulton, E. K. I, 921
Fulton, E. K. I, 925
Fulton, Elisabeth I, 622
Fulton, Elizabeth VI, 636
Fulton, Elizabeth VI, 638
Fulton, Ella III, 130
Fulton, F. G. I, 921
Fulton, F. J. I, 925
Fulton, Flora Bessie I, 921
Fulton, Florrie Robbins I, 925
Fulton, Hannah IV, 472
Fulton, Hannah V, 57
Fulton, Hannah VI, 467
Fulton, Hannah VI, 492
Fulton, Hannah B. V, 906
Fulton, Hattie I, 925
Fulton, Hattie I, 941
Fulton, James I, 941
Fulton, James S. I, 925
Fulton, Jesse III, 232
Fulton, Jessie III, 130
Fulton, Jno. S. IV, 1316
Fulton, John III, 130
Fulton, John S. IV, 1316
Fulton, Joseph Sidney III, 130
Fulton, Maggie IV, 203
Fulton, Martha II, 699
Fulton, Martha II, 713
Fulton, Martha L. I, 925
Fulton, Mary V, 413
Fulton, Mary VI, 638
Fulton, Mary E. V, 413
Fulton, Mary Louise III, 130
Fulton, Nellie III, 130
Fulton, Nelly III, 130
Fulton, Paul J. III, 130
Fulton, Phebe VI, 638
Fulton, Rachel III, 130
Fulton, Rachel VI, 492
Fulton, Rachel VI, 562
Fulton, Richard VI, 638
Fulton, Robert III, 130
Fulton, Robert IV, 1316
Fulton, Robert V, 413
Fulton, Robert H. IV, 1316
Fulton, Sarah V, 673
Fulton, Sarah J. V, 673
Fulton, Sarah Jane III, 130
Fulton, Vera Geneva I, 925
Fulton, Vera Geneva I, 941
Fulton, William II, 713
Fults, Emma IV, 815
Fults, Nettie IV, 815
Fultz, Annie V, 673
Fultz, Jennie V, 673
Fultz, Mary R. V, 673
Funcanon, Mary Ann I, 736
Funcanon, Mary Ann I, 737
Funcanon, Sarah I, 736
Funcanon, Sarah I, 737
Funcke, Hallcarnia V, 739
Funcke, William V, 739
Funderburg, Jennie V, 57
Funkey, Clara M. V, 57
Funkey, Clara W. V, 57
Funkey, John A. V, 57
Funston, Alice IV, 1251
Funston, Atwood IV, 1251
Funston, Flora IV, 1316
Funston, Geo. F. IV, 1316
Funston, Joseph IV, 1251
Funston, Joseph E. IV, 1251
Fuqua, Aaron VI, 918
Fuqua, Abner VI, 918
Fuqua, Abraham VI, 918
Fuqua, Abram VI, 954
Fuqua, Abram VI, 985
Fuqua, Ann VI, 919
Fuqua, Anna VI, 884
Fuqua, Anney VI, 1016
Fuqua, Benj. B. VI, 919
Fuqua, Betsey VI, 1016
Fuqua, Caleb VI, 918
Fuqua, Caleb VI, 919
Fuqua, Caleb VI, 949
Fuqua, Caleb VI, 973
Fuqua, Caleb VI, 981
Fuqua, Capt. Moses VI, 902
Fuqua, Catharine VI, 892
Fuqua, Cele VI, 929
Fuqua, Celia VI, 918
Fuqua, Celia VI, 983
Fuqua, Delpha VI, 918
Fuqua, Delphia VI, 892
Fuqua, Delphia VI, 1012
Fuqua, Edy VI, 961
Fuqua, Eliza VI, 902
Fuqua, Eliza VI, 918
Fuqua, Eliza Ann VI, 1018
Fuqua, Elizabeth VI, 813
Fuqua, Elizabeth VI, 877
Fuqua, Elizabeth VI, 918
Fuqua, Elizabeth VI, 981
Fuqua, Elizabeth B. VI, 918
Fuqua, Emeline VI, 919
Fuqua, Ephraim VI, 918
Fuqua, Fanny VI, 918
Fuqua, Fanny VI, 962
Fuqua, Fanny VI, 985
Fuqua, Frances VI, 985
Fuqua, Granville L. VI, 919
Fuqua, Harriett VI, 1012
Fuqua, Henry VI, 955
Fuqua, Hezekiah VI, 918
Fuqua, Hezekiah VI, 949
Fuqua, Hezekiah VI, 979
Fuqua, Hezekiah VI, 1018
Fuqua, Isham VI, 877
Fuqua, Isham VI, 878
Fuqua, Isham VI, 889
Fuqua, Isham VI, 892
Fuqua, Isham VI, 900
Fuqua, Isham VI, 903
Fuqua, Isham VI, 906
Fuqua, Isham VI, 911
Fuqua, Isham VI, 912
Fuqua, Isham VI, 915
Fuqua, Isham VI, 917
Fuqua, Isham VI, 918
Fuqua, Isham VI, 920
Fuqua, Isham VI, 924
Fuqua, Isham VI, 926
Fuqua, Isham VI, 929
Fuqua, Isham VI, 932
Fuqua, Isham VI, 937
Fuqua, Isham VI, 940
Fuqua, Isham VI, 951
Fuqua, Isham VI, 962
Fuqua, Isham VI, 968
Fuqua, Isham VI, 969
Fuqua, Isham VI, 980
Fuqua, Isham VI, 981
Fuqua, Isham VI, 982
Fuqua, Isham VI, 983
Fuqua, Isham VI, 988
Fuqua, Isham VI, 1001
Fuqua, Isham VI, 1003
Fuqua, Isham VI, 1016
Fuqua, Isham VI, 1019
Fuqua, Isham VI, 1021
Fuqua, James I, 633
Fuqua, John VI, 884
Fuqua, John VI, 918
Fuqua, John VI, 961
Fuqua, Joseph VI, 918
Fuqua, Joseph VI, 961
Fuqua, Joseph VI, 979
Fuqua, Joseph VI, 983
Fuqua, Joseph VI, 985
Fuqua, Joseph VI, 999
Fuqua, Joseph VI, 1016
Fuqua, Judith VI, 949
Fuqua, Julia M. VI, 986
Fuqua, Julian VI, 1014
Fuqua, Lavina VI, 836
Fuqua, Laviner VI, 837
Fuqua, Levina VI, 951
Fuqua, Mariah VI, 985
Fuqua, Martha VI, 918
Fuqua, Martha J. VI, 919
Fuqua, Martha M. VI, 919
Fuqua, Martin L. VI, 919
Fuqua, Mary VI, 919
Fuqua, Mary VI, 949
Fuqua, Mary VI, 979
Fuqua, Mary F. VI, 954
Fuqua, Mille VI, 918
Fuqua, Milly VI, 949
Fuqua, Milly VI, 979
Fuqua, Moses VI, 807
Fuqua, Moses VI, 811
Fuqua, Moses VI, 813
Fuqua, Moses VI, 842
Fuqua, Moses VI, 893
Fuqua, Moses VI, 918
Fuqua, Moses VI, 919
Fuqua, Moses VI, 929
Fuqua, Moses VI, 985
Fuqua, Moses VI, 986
Fuqua, Nancy VI, 842
Fuqua, Nancy VI, 884
Fuqua, Nancy VI, 918
Fuqua, Nancy VI, 979
Fuqua, Nancy VI, 983
Fuqua, Nancy E. VI, 919
Fuqua, Narcissa VI, 893
Fuqua, P. J. VI, 919
Fuqua, Patsy VI, 918
Fuqua, Peter VI, 918
Fuqua, Polly VI, 918
Fuqua, Ralph VI, 918
Fuqua, Rhoda VI, 955
Fuqua, Sally VI, 807
Fuqua, Sally VI, 999
Fuqua, Sally M. VI, 918
Fuqua, Sarah VI, 918
Fuqua, Silas VI, 999
Fuqua, Thomas VI, 948
Fuqua, Thomas VI, 949
Fuqua, Thomas C. VI, 816
Fuqua, Thomas C. VI, 913
Fuqua, Thomas C. VI, 1010
Fuqua, Thos. VI, 929
Fuqua, Thos. VI, 1004
Fuqua, William VI, 918
Fuqua, William VI, 921
Fuqua, William VI, 924
Fuqua, William VI, 983
Fuqua, William M. VI, 919
Fuqua, Wm. VI, 842
Fuqua, Wm. VI, 934
Furbay, Caroline IV, 204
Furbay, Caroline IV, 1279
Furbay, Eliza IV, 204
Furbay, Elizabeth IV, 1207
Furbay, Emma IV, 204
Furbay, Ethel IV, 204
Furbay, Ethel IV, 1279
Furbay, Frances IV, 1207
Furbay, Francis IV, 1207
Furbay, Guy IV, 1207
Furbay, Guy W. IV, 1207
Furbay, Josie Irene IV, 204
Furbay, Leta Young IV, 1207
Furbay, Leta Young IV, 1251
Furbay, Lewis IV, 203
Furbay, Lewis IV, 204
Furbay, Lida IV, 204
Furbay, Oliver IV, 204
Furbay, Rebecca A. E. IV, 203
Furbay, Rebecca A. E. IV, 204
Furbay, Rev. James R. IV, 1279
Furbay, W. L. IV, 1207
Furbay, Walter R. IV, 1207
Furbay, Will IV, 1207
Furbay, Wm. IV, 1207
Furbish, Mrs. ??? IV, 1316
Furbush, Jane E. VI, 813
Furbush, Jefferson D. VI, 818
Furbush, John VI, 813
Furbush, Mary VI, 864
Furbush, Matilda J. VI, 818
Furbush, Polly VI, 977
Furbush, Sally VI, 919
Furbush, Sarah B. VI, 846
Furbush, William VI, 813
Furbush, William VI, 846
Furbush, William VI, 864
Furbush, William VI, 919
Furbush, Wm. VI, 849
Furgason, Aaron V, 169
Furgason, Aaron V, 492
Furgason, Arthur Hale V, 492
Furgason, Ellen Jane V, 492
Furgason, Esther Amanda V, 492
Furgason, Isaac V, 169
Furgason, Jacob V, 169
Furgason, James II, 118
Furgason, Maria Eliza V, 492
Furgason, Mary IV, 33
Furgason, Mary IV, 86
Furgason, Mary V, 169
Furgason, Mary Coffin IV, 33
Furgason, Melissa V, 492
Furgason, Samuel V, 492
Furgason, Thomas Clark V, 492
Furgason, Webster Monroe V, 492
Furgason, William IV, 204
Furgerson, Emma V, 997
Furgerson, Jeremiah VI, 914
Furgerson, Jesse VI, 914
Furgerson, Nancy VI, 914
Furgerson, Sarah V, 226
Furgerson, Sarah V, 238
Furgeson, Aaron V, 169
Furgeson, Ann V, 169
Furgeson, Charles V, 169
Furgeson, Clark V, 169
Furgeson, Cyrus V, 169
Furgeson, Elizabeth V, 169
Furgeson, Emma V, 997
Furgeson, Ida V, 997
Furgeson, Isaac V, 169
Furgeson, Jacob V, 169
Furgeson, Joseph V, 169
Furgeson, Levi V, 169
Furgeson, Mabel I. IV, 1316
Furgeson, Maggie V, 997
Furgeson, Margrit Jane V, 997
Furgeson, Martin N. IV, 1316
Furgeson, Mary V, 169
Furgeson, Mary V, 997
Furgeson, Mira F. IV, 1316
Furgeson, Rachel V, 169
Furgeson, Samuel V, 169
Furgeson, Sarah E. I, 925
Furgison, Alfred I, 747
Furgison, Edward Newton I, 747
Furgison, Nathan H. I, 747
Furgison, Sarah I, 747
Furgison, Thomas I, 747
Furguson, Adeline VI, 818
Furguson, Amelia VI, 870
Furguson, Edward VI, 818
Furguson, John H. VI, 818
Furguson, Mary IV, 86
Furguson, Mary E. VI, 818
Furguson, Rebecca VI, 818

urguson, Samuel V, 673
urguson, Sarah V, 673
urguson, William VI, 818
urgusson, Chas. V, 169
urlong, Christina V, 739
urlong, Dionitia VI, 978
urlong, Pearl E. V, 737
urlong, Pearl E. V, 739
urlong, Polly VI, 891
urlong, Samuel V, 739
urman, Abigail II, 808
urman, Abigail II, 864
urman, Abigail II, 896
urman, Abigail C. II, 864
urman, Abigail C. II, 883
urman, Abigail C. II, 896
urman, Abigail C. II, 907
urman, Abigail F. II, 896
urman, Ann II, 222
urman, Anna C. II, 803
urman, Anna C. II, 864
urman, Anna C. II, 883
urman, Barzillia II, 997
urman, Chancy IV, 1362
urman, Clement A. Woodnutt II, 864
urman, David II, 794
urman, David II, 864
urman, David II, 907
urman, David II, 924
urman, David II, 932
urman, David K. II, 794
urman, David Killy II, 864
urman, David Killy II, 880
urman, Deborah II, 222
urman, Deborah II, 287
urman, Deborah II, 318
urman, Deborah II, 997
urman, Deborah II, 1073
urman, Deborah II, 1078
urman, Deborah R. II, 837
urman, Deborah R. II, 856
urman, Deborah R. II, 864
urman, Deborah R. II, 865
urman, Elizabeth II, 222
urman, Elizabeth II, 997
urman, Elizabeth II, 1038
urman, Elizabeth II, 1051
urman, Elizabeth Ellis II, 779
urman, Elizabeth H. II, 864
urman, Elizabeth H. II, 942
urman, Elizabeth P. II, 794
urman, Elizabeth P. II, 864
urman, Elizabeth P. II, 924
urman, Elmer IV, 204
urman, Florence S. II, 794
urman, George II, 222
urman, George M. II, 794
urman, George M. II, 856
urman, George M. II, 864
urman, George M. II, 907
urman, Hannah II, 997
urman, Helen D. II, 837
urman, Helen D. II, 864
urman, Helen R. II, 896
urman, Horace S. II, 794
urman, Horace S. II, 864
urman, James B. II, 896
Furman, John II, 997
Furman, John II, 1038
Furman, Josiah II, 222
Furman, Lydia C. IV, 204
Furman, Margaret II, 794
Furman, Margaret II, 856
Furman, Margaret II, 864
Furman, Margaret II, 907
Furman, Margaret Divine II, 880
Furman, Margaret F. II, 864
Furman, Margaret L. II, 794
Furman, Margaret L. II, 864
Furman, Margaret L. II, 932
Furman, Margaret Longstreth II, 824
Furman, Margaret S. II, 864
Furman, Mary II, 794
Furman, Mary II, 864
Furman, Mary II, 907
Furman, Mary IV, 1188
Furman, Mary IV, 1362
Furman, Mary VI, 142
Furman, Mary C. II, 896
Furman, Mary P. II, 794
Furman, Mary P. II, 924
Furman, Mary P. II, 932
Furman, Middleton II, 222
Furman, Phebe W. II, 896
Furman, Phebe W. IV, 1362
Furman, Preston II, 896
Furman, Rebecca W. II, 813
Furman, Rebecca W. II, 864
Furman, Rebecca W. II, 907
Furman, Richard Way II, 222
Furman, Richard Way II, 997
Furman, Ruth II, 222
Furman, Samuel II, 837
Furman, Samuel II, 864
Furman, Samuel II, 865
Furman, Samuel T. II, 864
Furman, Samuel T. II, 883
Furman, Samuel T. II, 896
Furman, Samuel T. II, 907
Furman, Samuel Thurston II, 794
Furman, Sarah II, 997
Furman, Sarah II, 1051
Furman, Sarah II, 1073
Furman, Sidney II, 528
Furman, Sidney II, 630
Furman, Sidney Keen II, 794
Furman, Susan II, 779
Furman, Susanna S. II, 1059
Furman, Susannah II, 997
Furman, Susannah II, 1038
Furman, Susannah S. II, 997
Furman, Susannah S. II, 1051
Furman, Thos. II, 779
Furman, Wm. II, 997
Furman, Wm. II, 1038
Furman, Wm. II, 1051
Furnace, Anna V, 58
Furnace, Benjamin V, 739
Furnace, Bethia V, 58
Furnace, Calista IV, 1207
Furnace, Dinah V, 89
Furnace, Elizabeth V, 474
Furnace, Elizabeth V, 492
Furnace, Esley V, 492
Furnace, Esly V, 492
Furnace, Esther I, 1019
Furnace, Eunice V, 58
Furnace, Hannah I, 1029
Furnace, Isaac IV, 1207
Furnace, Isaac V, 57
Furnace, Isaac V, 492
Furnace, John I, 1019
Furnace, John V, 469
Furnace, John V, 739
Furnace, Joseph I, 1019
Furnace, Joseph V, 474
Furnace, Joseph V, 492
Furnace, Joseph V, 739
Furnace, Laura M. IV, 1207
Furnace, Lydia V, 789
Furnace, Martha V, 794
Furnace, Mary I, 1019
Furnace, Mary V, 739
Furnace, Mary V, 781
Furnace, Penelope II, 364
Furnace, Phebe V, 58
Furnace, Reba M. V, 58
Furnace, Rebecah I, 1019
Furnace, Robert I, 1019
Furnace, Robert I, 1029
Furnace, Robert I, 1030
Furnace, Robert F. V, 58
Furnace, Robert H. V, 58
Furnace, Salista IV, 1207
Furnace, Samuel V, 739
Furnace, Samuel V, 789
Furnace, Sarah V, 492
Furnace, Sarah V, 739
Furnace, Sarah V, 794
Furnace, Seth V, 89
Furnace, Sidney V, 58
Furnace, Thomas I, 1019
Furnace, Thomas II, 528
Furnace, William I, 1019
Furnace, William V, 739
Furnance, Ahira B. V, 492
Furnance, Ahiza B. V, 492
Furnance, Elizabeth V, 492
Furnance, Esley V, 492
Furnance, Esly V, 492
Furnance, Isaac V, 492
Furnance, Joseph V, 492
Furnance, Orlando V, 492
Furnance, Robert Barclay V, 492
Furnance, Samuel V, 492
Furnance, Samuel S. V, 492
Furnance, Sarah V, 492
Furnance, Sarah S. V, 492
Furnas, ??? V, 147
Furnas, Aaron V, 781
Furnas, Aaron V, 782
Furnas, Achsah V, 171
Furnas, Ada V, 58
Furnas, Adam V, 58
Furnas, Adam V, 739
Furnas, Alferd V, 57
Furnas, Allen V, 170
Furnas, Allen V, 171
Furnas, Ann V, 171
Furnas, Ann D. V, 25
Furnas, Anna V, 57
Furnas, Anna V, 58
Furnas, Anna V, 74
Furnas, Anna V, 171
Furnas, Anna V, 179
Furnas, Anna D. V, 57
Furnas, Anna Dinah V, 57
Furnas, Anne Maria V, 171
Furnas, Annie Maria V, 171
Furnas, Axey V, 194
Furnas, Benj. V, 789
Furnas, Benjamin V, 57
Furnas, Benjamin V, 739
Furnas, Benjamin V, 781
Furnas, Benjamin V, 782
Furnas, Benjamin V, 808
Furnas, Benjamin V, 809
Furnas, Benjamin V, 818
Furnas, Bethia V, 58
Furnas, Bethia M. V, 58
Furnas, Bethiah IV, 1159
Furnas, Bethiah IV, 1175
Furnas, Bethiah V, 57
Furnas, Bethiah M. IV, 1159
Furnas, Bethiah M. V, 56
Furnas, Bethiah M. V, 58
Furnas, Beulah V, 781
Furnas, Beulah V, 789
Furnas, Beulah V, 809
Furnas, Calista V, 57
Furnas, Calista V, 58
Furnas, Calista V, 103
Furnas, Charles V, 782
Furnas, Charles V, 808
Furnas, Charles C. V, 57
Furnas, Charles C. V, 58
Furnas, Charles M. V, 808
Furnas, Christiana V, 194
Furnas, Christopher V, 57
Furnas, Christopher V, 170
Furnas, Christopher V, 171
Furnas, Christopher V, 781
Furnas, Christopher V, 782
Furnas, Christopher, Jr. V, 781
Furnas, Christopher, Jr. V, 786
Furnas, David V, 25
Furnas, David V, 57
Furnas, David V, 58
Furnas, David V, 171
Furnas, David V, 739
Furnas, Davis II, 865
Furnas, Davis II, 932
Furnas, Davis III, 38
Furnas, Davis III, 130
Furnas, Davis V, 26
Furnas, Davis V, 57
Furnas, Davis V, 58
Furnas, Davis V, 134
Furnas, Davis V, 781
Furnas, Deborah White I, 616
Furnas, Dinah I, 1057
Furnas, Dinah I, 1058
Furnas, Dinah II, 865
Furnas, Dinah II, 932
Furnas, Dinah IV, 1159
Furnas, Dinah V, 57
Furnas, Dinah V, 58
Furnas, Dinah V, 103
Furnas, Dinah V, 170
Furnas, Dinah V, 171
Furnas, Dinah V, 184
Furnas, Dinah V, 190
Furnas, Edith V, 57
Furnas, Edith V, 58
Furnas, Edith V, 808
Furnas, Edith D. V, 57
Furnas, Edwin S. V, 57
Furnas, Edwin S. V, 135
Furnas, Elihu V, 57
Furnas, Elizabeth III, 130
Furnas, Elizabeth V, 26
Furnas, Elizabeth V, 57
Furnas, Elizabeth V, 58
Furnas, Elizabeth V, 171
Furnas, Elizabeth F. III, 38
Furnas, Elizabeth M. V, 739
Furnas, Ella III, 72
Furnas, Ella III, 130
Furnas, Ella III, 194
Furnas, Ella III, 336
Furnas, Ella V, 57
Furnas, Ella D. V, 58
Furnas, Emily V, 57
Furnas, Emily V, 58
Furnas, Emily M. V, 58
Furnas, Esley V, 171
Furnas, Esly V, 57
Furnas, Esly V, 170
Furnas, Esly V, 544
Furnas, Esther I, 1029
Furnas, Esther I, 1036
Furnas, Esther I, 1056
Furnas, Esther I, 1057
Furnas, Esther I, 1059
Furnas, Esther I, 1061
Furnas, Esther I, 1063
Furnas, Esther V, 57
Furnas, Esther V, 170
Furnas, Esther V, 191
Furnas, Esther V, 781
Furnas, Esther V, 797
Furnas, Esther V, 809
Furnas, Esther V, 815
Furnas, Esther V, 818
Furnas, Esther V, 819
Furnas, Eugene V, 57
Furnas, Eunice V, 57
Furnas, Eunice V, 58
Furnas, Eunice V, 120
Furnas, Eunice V, 163
Furnas, Eunice V, 171
Furnas, Eunice V, 809
Furnas, Fred V, 171
Furnas, Frederick W. V, 57
Furnas, Hannah I, 1029
Furnas, Hannah I, 1030
Furnas, Hannah I, 1056
Furnas, Hannah I, 1057
Furnas, Hannah I, 1059
Furnas, Hannah I, 1061
Furnas, Hannah I, 1063
Furnas, Hannah V, 57
Furnas, Hannah V, 162
Furnas, Hannah V, 170
Furnas, Hannah V, 171
Furnas, Hannah V, 190
Furnas, Hannah V, 191
Furnas, Hannah V, 206
Furnas, Hannah Anna V, 171
Furnas, Harriet V, 57
Furnas, Harriet V, 58
Furnas, Harriet E. V, 58
Furnas, Harriet E. V, 135
Furnas, Harvy V, 790
Furnas, Henry V, 808
Furnas, Henry S. V, 808
Furnas, Henry S. V, 809
Furnas, Horace V, 57
Furnas, Ina I, 633
Furnas, Ina I, 639
Furnas, Ina E. I, 616
Furnas, Isaac I, 1057
Furnas, Isaac V, 57
Furnas, Isaac V, 58
Furnas, Isaac V, 159
Furnas, Isaac V, 170
Furnas, Isaac V, 171
Furnas, Isaac V, 544
Furnas, J. D. III, 72
Furnas, James V, 739
Furnas, James V, 790
Furnas, Jane III, 38
Furnas, Jane III, 130
Furnas, Jane V, 25
Furnas, Jane V, 57
Furnas, Jane V, 117
Furnas, Jane V, 781
Furnas, Jane S. V, 26
Furnas, Jane S. V, 57
Furnas, Jason V, 808
Furnas, John I, 1015
Furnas, John I, 1028
Furnas, John I, 1029
Furnas, John I, 1030
Furnas, John I, 1056
Furnas, John I, 1057
Furnas, John I, 1059
Furnas, John I, 1061
Furnas, John I, 1063
Furnas, John V, 57
Furnas, John V, 159
Furnas, John V, 164
Furnas, John V, 170
Furnas, John V, 171
Furnas, John V, 739
Furnas, John V, 781
Furnas, John V, 782
Furnas, John V, 808
Furnas, John V, 809
Furnas, John V, 818
Furnas, John D. III, 130
Furnas, John D. III, 194
Furnas, John D. III, 336
Furnas, John D. V, 57
Furnas, John Davis V, 57
Furnas, John, Jr. V, 171
Furnas, Jolin V, 57
Furnas, Jos. V, 171
Furnas, Joseph I, 1029
Furnas, Joseph I, 1030
Furnas, Joseph I, 1036
Furnas, Joseph I, 1056
Furnas, Joseph I, 1057
Furnas, Joseph V, 57
Furnas, Joseph V, 100
Furnas, Joseph V, 161
Furnas, Joseph V, 163
Furnas, Joseph V, 166
Furnas, Joseph V, 170
Furnas, Joseph V, 171
Furnas, Joseph V, 176
Furnas, Joseph V, 194
Furnas, Joseph V, 739
Furnas, Joseph V, 740
Furnas, Joseph V, 745
Furnas, Joseph V, 781
Furnas, Joseph V, 808
Furnas, Joseph V, 810
Furnas, Joseph V, 811
Furnas, Joseph V, 816
Furnas, Joseph V, 817
Furnas, Joseph V, 819
Furnas, Joseph E. V, 782
Furnas, Joseph Evans V, 781
Furnas, Laura V, 57
Furnas, Laura V, 58
Furnas, Lawrence Webber V, 57
Furnas, Louisa V, 781
Furnas, Louisa V, 808
Furnas, Lucile V, 171
Furnas, Lydia V, 781
Furnas, Lydia V, 808
Furnas, Lydia V, 815
Furnas, Lydia Hasket V, 739
Furnas, Marcia Elisabeth Anne I, 616
Furnas, Marie III, 194
Furnas, Mark V, 790
Furnas, Martha V, 58
Furnas, Martha V, 781
Furnas, Mary I, 1029
Furnas, Mary I, 1056
Furnas, Mary I, 1057
Furnas, Mary I, 1061
Furnas, Mary V, 56
Furnas, Mary V, 57
Furnas, Mary V, 103
Furnas, Mary V, 162
Furnas, Mary V, 163
Furnas, Mary V, 164
Furnas, Mary V, 166
Furnas, Mary V, 170
Furnas, Mary V, 171
Furnas, Mary V, 739
Furnas, Mary V, 740
Furnas, Mary V, 781
Furnas, Mary V, 782
Furnas, Mary V, 786
Furnas, Mary V, 789
Furnas, Mary V, 799
Furnas, Mary V, 808
Furnas, Mary V, 812
Furnas, Mary V, 816
Furnas, Mary V, 818
Furnas, Mary Jane V, 171
Furnas, Mary Louisa V, 57
Furnas, Mary P. V, 808
Furnas, Mary P. V, 811
Furnas, Mary Pearson V, 745
Furnas, Maryan V, 781
Furnas, Matilda I, 1057
Furnas, Matilda V, 159
Furnas, Matilda V, 171
Furnas, Matilda V, 194
Furnas, Nancy E. I, 624
Furnas, Naomi V, 171
Furnas, Naomy V, 171
Furnas, Naomy V, 211
Furnas, Orlando V, 171
Furnas, Oscar M. V, 57
Furnas, Oscar M. V, 58
Furnas, Patience V, 57
Furnas, Patience V, 100
Furnas, Patience V, 740
Furnas, Patience V, 808
Furnas, Patience V, 816
Furnas, Patience V, 817
Furnas, Patience V, 819
Furnas, Patience N. V, 57
Furnas, Patty V, 171
Furnas, Patty V, 176
Furnas, Phebe V, 57
Furnas, Phebe V, 58
Furnas, Phebe V, 171
Furnas, Philip I, 624
Furnas, Philip Williams I, 616
Furnas, Phillip William I, 633
Furnas, Phillip William I, 639
Furnas, Priscilla V, 809
Furnas, Prudence V, 809
Furnas, Rachel I, 1056
Furnas, Rachel V, 781

Furnas, Rachel V, 782
Furnas, Rachel V, 792
Furnas, Rachel V, 808
Furnas, Rachel V, 819
Furnas, Rachel Dakin V, 57
Furnas, Reba M. V, 58
Furnas, Rebecca I, 1056
Furnas, Rebecca I, 1057
Furnas, Rebecca V, 58
Furnas, Rebecca V, 159
Furnas, Rebecca V, 161
Furnas, Rebecca V, 170
Furnas, Rebecca V, 171
Furnas, Rebecca V, 206
Furnas, Rebecca V, 799
Furnas, Rebecca V, 811
Furnas, Rebecca Millhouse I, 1056
Furnas, Rev. ??? V, 743
Furnas, Robert I, 1029
Furnas, Robert I, 1030
Furnas, Robert I, 1056
Furnas, Robert I, 1057
Furnas, Robert I, 1059
Furnas, Robert I, 1061
Furnas, Robert I, 1063
Furnas, Robert V, 17
Furnas, Robert V, 57
Furnas, Robert V, 74
Furnas, Robert V, 147
Furnas, Robert V, 162
Furnas, Robert V, 169
Furnas, Robert V, 170
Furnas, Robert V, 171
Furnas, Robert V, 190
Furnas, Robert V, 191
Furnas, Robert V, 206
Furnas, Robert V, 211
Furnas, Robert V, 781
Furnas, Robert V, 782
Furnas, Robert F. IV, 1159
Furnas, Robert F. IV, 1175
Furnas, Robert F. V, 56
Furnas, Robert F. V, 58
Furnas, Robert H. V, 57
Furnas, Robert H. V, 58
Furnas, Robert Julius I, 616
Furnas, Robert, Jr. V, 171
Furnas, Robert, Jr. V, 179
Furnas, Robert, Jr. V, 194
Furnas, Roscoe V, 58
Furnas, Ruth I, 1028
Furnas, Ruth I, 1030
Furnas, Ruth I, 1056
Furnas, Ruth V, 57
Furnas, Ruth V, 164
Furnas, Ruth V, 170
Furnas, Ruth V, 171
Furnas, Ruth Ellen V, 171
Furnas, Sally V, 74
Furnas, Sally V, 75
Furnas, Sally V, 739
Furnas, Sally V, 781
Furnas, Sally V, 808
Furnas, Sally V, 810
Furnas, Sally V, 811
Furnas, Samuel V, 57
Furnas, Samuel V, 171
Furnas, Samuel V, 739
Furnas, Samuel V, 781
Furnas, Samuel V, 782
Furnas, Samuel V, 786
Furnas, Samuel V, 808
Furnas, Samuel V, 812
Furnas, Samuel V, 815
Furnas, Sarah I, 1029
Furnas, Sarah I, 1036
Furnas, Sarah I, 1057
Furnas, Sarah V, 57
Furnas, Sarah V, 169
Furnas, Sarah V, 170
Furnas, Sarah V, 171
Furnas, Sarah V, 739
Furnas, Sarah V, 774
Furnas, Sarah V, 781
Furnas, Sarah V, 786
Furnas, Sarah Ellen V, 808
Furnas, Sarah Hill V, 58
Furnas, Sarah Jane III, 336
Furnas, Sarah Jane V, 57
Furnas, Sarah L. V, 58
Furnas, Sarah P. V, 781
Furnas, Sarah S. II, 865
Furnas, Sarah S. II, 932
Furnas, Sarah S. V, 58
Furnas, Sarah S. V, 134
Furnas, Savis V, 57
Furnas, Seth I, 1057
Furnas, Seth II, 865
Furnas, Seth II, 932
Furnas, Seth IV, 1159
Furnas, Seth V, 57
Furnas, Seth V, 58
Furnas, Seth V, 103
Furnas, Seth V, 170
Furnas, Seth V, 171
Furnas, Seth V, 184
Furnas, Seth Elisha V, 57
Furnas, Seth M. V, 58
Furnas, Seth W. V, 43
Furnas, Seth W. V, 57
Furnas, Seth W. V, 58
Furnas, Sidney V, 57
Furnas, Sidney V, 58
Furnas, Solomon V, 171
Furnas, Susannah V, 743
Furnas, Thomas W. V, 781
Furnas, Thomas Wilkinson I, 1029
Furnas, Thos. Wilkinson I, 1056
Furnas, Walter C. V, 171
Furnas, Walton C. V, 171
Furnas, Wilkinson V, 782
Furnas, William I, 1030
Furnas, William I, 1056
Furnas, William V, 57
Furnas, William V, 739
Furnas, William V, 781
Furnas, William V, 808
Furnas, William F. V, 58
Furnas, William Frame V, 57
Furnas, Wm. I, 616
Furnas, Wm. V, 781
Furnas, Wm. V, 782
Furnas, Wm. V, 789
Furnas, Wm. V, 809
Furnes, Esly V, 57
Furness, Benjamin II, 173
Furness, Elizabeth II, 222
Furness, Garner II, 997
Furness, Hannah II, 528
Furness, Henry II, 443
Furness, John I, 1029
Furness, John II, 364
Furness, Joseph II, 364
Furness, Martha II, 528
Furness, Mary II, 364
Furness, Rachel II, 528
Furness, Samuel II, 173
Furness, Susan II, 173
Furness, Thomas II, 528
Furness, Thomas Wilkinson I, 1029
Furnice, Sarah V, 794
Furnis, Anthony II, 222
Furnis, Anthony II, 528
Furnis, Benjamin II, 222
Furnis, Daniel II, 364
Furnis, Elizabeth II, 222
Furnis, Elizabeth II, 364
Furnis, Elizabeth V, 492
Furnis, Esther IV, 33
Furnis, Hannah II, 528
Furnis, Hannah IV, 33
Furnis, Henry II, 364
Furnis, John II, 364
Furnis, John IV, 33
Furnis, Joseph II, 222
Furnis, Joseph II, 364
Furnis, Martha II, 222
Furnis, Martha II, 528
Furnis, Mary II, 364
Furnis, Mary IV, 33
Furnis, Penelope II, 364
Furnis, Rachel II, 528
Furnis, Robert IV, 33
Furnis, Samuel II, 222
Furnis, Seth IV, 33
Furnis, Susannah II, 222
Furnis, Thomas II, 222
Furnis, Thomas II, 364
Furnis, Thomas II, 528
Furniss, Ann II, 443
Furniss, Elizabeth II, 364
Furniss, Henry II, 443
Furniss, John II, 443
Furniss, Joseph II, 222
Furniss, Penelope II, 443
Furniss, Susannah II, 222
Furniss, Susannah II, 275
Furniss, Thomas II, 222
Furniss, Thomas II, 364
Furniss, Thomas II, 443
Furqua, Isham VI, 927
Furqueran, Peter VI, 851
Furr, J. C. I, 941
Furr, John Alfred, Jr. I, 941
Furr, John Richard I, 941
Furr, Lula I, 941
Furrow, Clarissa IV, 1279
Furrow, John IV, 1279
Furry, Lydia II, 364
Furry, Mary IV, 125
Furry, Mary IV, 132
Furstenberger, Emma IV, 1207
Furstenberger, Henry IV, 1207
Fussel, Ann II, 528
Fussel, Elizabeth II, 528
Fussel, Esther II, 528
Fussel, Jacob II, 528
Fussel, Joseph II, 865
Fussel, Sarah Emily II, 865
Fussel, Susanna II, 528
Fussel, Wm. II, 528
Fussell, Ann II, 364
Fussell, Ann II, 410
Fussell, Ann II, 528
Fussell, Barbara II, 528
Fussell, Bart. III, 130
Fussell, Bartholomew II, 364
Fussell, Bartholomew II, 528
Fussell, Bartholomew II, 795
Fussell, Bartholomew II, 865
Fussell, Bartholomew III, 69
Fussell, Bartholomew III, 130
Fussell, Bartholomew III, 163
Fussell, Bartholomew, Sr. II, 824
Fussell, C. III, 130
Fussell, Elisabeth II, 528
Fussell, Eliz. D. III, 130
Fussell, Elizabeth II, 528
Fussell, Elizabeth III, 130
Fussell, Elizabeth D. III, 180
Fussell, Emily R. II, 795
Fussell, Emily R. II, 865
Fussell, Esther II, 528
Fussell, Esther II, 588
Fussell, Geo. D. III, 180
Fussell, George D. III, 130
Fussell, Hariet Jane II, 795
Fussell, Harriet Jane II, 865
Fussell, Henry B. II, 865
Fussell, Howard Lewis II, 865
Fussell, Howard Milton III, 130
Fussell, Jacob II, 364
Fussell, Jacob II, 528
Fussell, Jacob II, 588
Fussell, Jacob III, 130
Fussell, James II, 364
Fussell, Joseph II, 794
Fussell, Joseph II, 865
Fussell, Joshua Longstreth II, 865
Fussell, Laura Cecilia II, 795
Fussell, Laura L. II, 865
Fussell, Lydia II, 795
Fussell, Lydia Ada II, 795
Fussell, Lydia Ada II, 865
Fussell, M. Howard III, 130
Fussell, Margaret II, 364
Fussell, Marion II, 795
Fussell, Mary II, 364
Fussell, Mary II, 528
Fussell, Mary II, 689
Fussell, Mordecai III, 130
Fussell, Morris II, 865
Fussell, Rebecca II, 806
Fussell, Rebecca II, 824
Fussell, Rebecca II, 865
Fussell, Rebecca C. II, 865
Fussell, Rebecca C. III, 69
Fussell, Rebecca C. III, 130
Fussell, Rebecca C. III, 163
Fussell, Rebecca O. III, 130
Fussell, Sarah II, 364
Fussell, Sarah II, 528
Fussell, Sarah E. III, 130
Fussell, Sarah Emily II, 794
Fussell, Sarah Emily II, 865
Fussell, Solomon II, 364
Fussell, Solomon II, 498
Fussell, Solomon II, 528
Fussell, Solomon II, 588
Fussell, Solomon II, 689
Fussell, Susan II, 865
Fussell, Susanna II, 364
Fussell, Susanna II, 498
Fussell, Susanna II, 528
Fussell, Susannah II, 364
Fussell, Susannah II, 528
Fussell, Timothy II, 364
Fussell, Wd. Rebecca II, 824
Fussell, William II, 364
Fussell, William Lewis II, 795
Fussell, Willis II, 795
Fussell, Wm. II, 528
Fussell, Wm. H. II, 865
Fussell, Wm. Henry II, 795
Fussell, Wm. Lewis II, 865
Fuster, Cora V, 997
Futer, Cecil Raymond II, 705
Futer, Cecil Raymond II, 741
Futer, Hannah Mary II, 705
Futer, Jeremiah II, 705
Futrell, A. Rebecca I, 235
Futrell, A. Rebecca I, 239
Futrell, Aaron I, 239
Futrell, Amy Rebecca I, 212
Futrell, Amy Rebecca I, 214
Futrell, Anna E. I, 239
Futrell, Bessie M. I, 214
Futrell, Elijah N. I, 239
Futrell, Eliza Jane I, 211
Futrell, Eliza Jane I, 239
Futrell, Ella I, 214
Futrell, Ella Jane I, 214
Futrell, Frances Loraine I, 214
Futrell, George I, 239
Futrell, Harrison I, 214
Futrell, Horace I, 212
Futrell, Horace C. I, 214
Futrell, Horace C. I, 235
Futrell, Horace C. I, 239
Futrell, James I, 219
Futrell, James N. I, 211
Futrell, James N. I, 214
Futrell, James N. I, 222
Futrell, James N. I, 225
Futrell, James N. I, 239
Futrell, James T. I, 214
Futrell, James Thomas I, 214
Futrell, Jane E. I, 214
Futrell, Jane E. I, 235
Futrell, Jane E. I, 239
Futrell, Jane Stalker I, 239
Futrell, Jas. N. I, 214
Futrell, Jesse William I, 214
Futrell, Joseph Horace I, 214
Futrell, Joseph J. I, 214
Futrell, Joseph J. I, 239
Futrell, Josephine E. I, 239
Futrell, Josephine Elizabeth I, 214
Futrell, Judith I, 214
Futrell, Judith I, 225
Futrell, Judith A. I, 219
Futrell, Judith A. I, 222
Futrell, Judith A. I, 239
Futrell, Judith A. I, 255
Futrell, Judith Ann I, 211
Futrell, Judith Ann I, 214
Futrell, Lidia E. I, 239
Futrell, Lydia I, 214
Futrell, Lydia E. I, 235
Futrell, Lydia E. I, 239
Futrell, Lydia E. I, 761
Futrell, Lydia E. I, 770
Futrell, Margaret A. I, 225
Futrell, Margaret A. I, 239
Futrell, Margaret A. I, 255
Futrell, Margaret Ann I, 214
Futrell, Margaret F. I, 222
Futrell, Mary S. I, 213
Futrell, Mary S. I, 214
Futrell, Ollie P. I, 214
Futrell, Rachel I, 239
Futrell, Sallie F. I, 239
Futrell, Sallie F. I, 249
Futrell, Sarah Florence I, 214
Futrell, Sarah Florence I, 219
Futrell, William H. I, 214
Futrell, William H. I, 239
Futril, Rachel I, 237
Futril, Rachel I, 239

Gabel, Mary Ann V, 882
Gabell, Mary Ann V, 882
Gabell, Mary Ann V, 885
Gabitas, Abigail II, 364
Gabitas, Deborah II, 222
Gabitas, Deborah II, 226
Gabitas, Jeremiah II, 364
Gabitas, Rachel II, 222
Gabitas, Rachel II, 241
Gabitas, William II, 222
Gabitas, William II, 241
Gabitas, William II, 364
Gabrill, Thomas II, 443
Gachel, Hannah IV, 815
Gadd, James I, 99
Gadde, Elizabeth VI, 997
Gadde, Joseph VI, 919
Gadde, Joseph VI, 958
Gadde, Joseph VI, 997
Gadde, Joseph VI, 1001
Gadde, Joseph VI, 1014
Gadde, Peggy VI, 919
Gadde, Shearwood VI, 997
Gadde, Sherwood VI, 1014
Gaddes, William V, 739
Gaddey, Jemima VI, 958
Gaddey, Joseph VI, 958
Gaddie, Joseph VI, 850
Gaddis, Ann VI, 390
Gaddis, Carey B. V, 386
Gaddis, Carrie V, 386
Gaddis, Carrie B. V, 386
Gaddis, Ella V, 673
Gaddis, Ethel V, 386
Gaddis, Missouri V, 374
Gaddis, Sarah I, 928
Gaddis, Sarah VI, 390
Gaddis, Sarah VI, 408
Gaddis, Sarah Jane V, 171
Gaddis, Thomas B. V, 386
Gaddis, Thomas D. V, 386
Gaddis, Tilden H. V, 386
Gaddis, William V, 739
Gaddy, Ann VI, 890
Gaddy, Anne VI, 926
Gaddy, Bartholomew VI, 890
Gaddy, Bartholomew VI, 919
Gaddy, Bartholomew VI, 945
Gaddy, Batt. VI, 916
Gaddy, Elizabeth VI, 919
Gaddy, Francis VI, 919
Gaddy, George VI, 919
Gaddy, George VI, 926
Gaddy, George VI, 945
Gaddy, Jenny VI, 1014
Gaddy, Joseph VI, 919
Gaddy, Judith VI, 919
Gaddy, Kitturah VI, 974
Gaddy, Margaret VI, 919
Gaddy, Martha VI, 919
Gaddy, Martha VI, 974
Gaddy, Marthy VI, 894
Gaddy, Peggy VI, 919
Gaddy, Ruth VI, 945
Gaddy, Ruthy VI, 894
Gaddy, Sherwood VI, 1014
Gaddy, Susan VI, 988
Gaddy, Susanna VI, 916
Gaddy, Susannah VI, 914
Gaddy, Wiliam VI, 962
Gaddy, William VI, 826
Gaddy, William VI, 919
Gaddy, William VI, 962
Gaddy, William VI, 988
Gadis, Alaska V, 171
Gadis, Jane V, 171
Gadis, Sarah Jane V, 171
Gaewood, Susannah VI, 390
Gaffield, Mattie IV, 1159
Gaffney, Ann II, 997
Gaffney, Ann II, 1018
Gaffney, Bessie V, 332
Gaffney, Rachel V, 332
Gage, Mary IV, 1362
Gage, Mary Ann V, 492
Gage, Mary Ann V, 531
Gager, Mary III, 232
Gager, Mary III, 253
Gager, Mary III, 305
Gagger, Mary IV, 1213
Gagger, Nichodemus IV, 1213
Gahagan, Mary H. III, 267
Gail, Abel III, 130
Gail, Abigail III, 130
Gail, Abigail III, 291
Gail, Dinah III, 130
Gail, Elizabeth III, 130
Gail, Thomas III, 130
Gail, Thomas III, 291
Gailbreath, Leah IV, 956
Gaines, Barnard VI, 1006
Gaines, Elizabeth III, 130
Gaines, Elizabeth VI, 919
Gaines, Elizabeth C. III, 80
Gaines, Elizabeth C. III, 130
Gaines, Elizabeth W. III, 130
Gaines, Henry G. VI, 819
Gaines, James III, 130
Gaines, Jane IV, 1159
Gaines, John W. VI, 819
Gaines, Martha A. VI, 819
Gaines, Moses V, 171
Gaines, Mrs. Cora IV, 1316
Gaines, Mrs. Cora May IV, 131
Gaines, Robert F. VI, 919
Gaines, Stephen III, 80
Gaines, Stephen III, 130
Gaines, Wd. Frances III, 130
Gains, Jane IV, 1156
Galaday, Ruth V, 240
Galamore, Martha I, 809
Galamore, Martha I, 838
Galaway, J. C. IV, 1279
Galaway, J. M. IV, 1235
Galaway, Maggie IV, 1235
Galaway, Tace IV, 619
Galaway, Tace IV, 625
Galaway, Thomas H. IV, 1235
Galbraith, Charlotte II, 1069

Galbraith, Charlotte II, 1073
Galbraith, Elizabeth IV, 146
Galbraith, Elizabeth IV, 162
Galbraith, Francis C. IV, 816
Galbraith, Rachel P. VI, 830
Galbraith, Rhoda IV, 956
Galbraith, Samuel VI, 830
Galbrath, Hannah I, 809
Galbrath, James I, 796
Galbrath, James I, 809
Galbrath, Jane I, 796
Galbrath, Jane I, 809
Galbrath, William I, 809
Galbreath, ??? I, 1030
Galbreath, ??? I, 1037
Galbreath, ??? IV, 795
Galbreath, Albert S. IV, 956
Galbreath, Alizabeth I, 1048
Galbreath, Amanda IV, 816
Galbreath, Ann I, 541
Galbreath, Ann I, 809
Galbreath, Ann I, 1030
Galbreath, Ann IV, 625
Galbreath, Ann IV, 693
Galbreath, Ann IV, 797
Galbreath, Ann IV, 816
Galbreath, Ann IV, 820
Galbreath, Anne IV, 146
Galbreath, Asher IV, 146
Galbreath, Ashur IV, 625
Galbreath, Brinton IV, 956
Galbreath, Brinton R. IV, 956
Galbreath, Britain C. IV, 955
Galbreath, Briton G. IV, 956
Galbreath, Charity I, 780
Galbreath, Charity I, 809
Galbreath, Charity I, 1030
Galbreath, Charity I, 1037
Galbreath, Charity IV, 816
Galbreath, Cornelia IV, 709
Galbreath, David IV, 146
Galbreath, David IV, 625
Galbreath, David IV, 816
Galbreath, David IV, 837
Galbreath, David IV, 858
Galbreath, David L. IV, 816
Galbreath, Deborah G. IV, 709
Galbreath, Elizabeth I, 780
Galbreath, Elizabeth I, 809
Galbreath, Elizabeth I, 1049
Galbreath, Elizabeth IV, 146
Galbreath, Elizabeth IV, 816
Galbreath, Elizabeth IV, 849
Galbreath, Elizabeth B. IV, 800
Galbreath, Elizabeth B. IV, 816
Galbreath, Elizabeth P. IV, 816
Galbreath, Enoch Russell IV, 956
Galbreath, Esther Ann IV, 816
Galbreath, Esther Ann IV, 831
Galbreath, Francis C. IV, 709
Galbreath, Francis C. IV, 816
Galbreath, Hannah IV, 625
Galbreath, Hannah IV, 693
Galbreath, Hannah IV, 709
Galbreath, Hannah IV, 816
Galbreath, Hannah IV, 827
Galbreath, Ida May IV, 956
Galbreath, James I, 541
Galbreath, James I, 545
Galbreath, James I, 780
Galbreath, James I, 879
Galbreath, James I, 1016
Galbreath, James I, 1030
Galbreath, James IV, 146
Galbreath, James IV, 816
Galbreath, James H. IV, 816
Galbreath, James, Jr. I, 1030
Galbreath, Jane I, 780
Galbreath, Jane I, 809
Galbreath, Jane IV, 816
Galbreath, Jemima I, 780
Galbreath, John I, 1030
Galbreath, John I, 1048
Galbreath, Leah IV, 816
Galbreath, Leah IV, 955
Galbreath, Leah IV, 956
Galbreath, Leah IV, 962
Galbreath, Leah Y. IV, 956
Galbreath, Martha IV, 956
Galbreath, Martha IV, 1010
Galbreath, Martha J. IV, 956
Galbreath, Mary I, 1030
Galbreath, Mary IV, 816
Galbreath, Mary IV, 841
Galbreath, Mary V, 997
Galbreath, Mary VI, 819
Galbreath, Matilda IV, 816
Galbreath, Nathan I, 1030
Galbreath, Nathan IV, 815
Galbreath, Nathan IV, 816
Galbreath, Nathan IV, 831
Galbreath, Nathan IV, 858
Galbreath, Nathan, Jr. IV, 816
Galbreath, Oliver E. IV, 956
Galbreath, Rhoda IV, 625
Galbreath, Rhoda IV, 1001
Galbreath, Robert IV, 955
Galbreath, Roland IV, 816
Galbreath, Ruth IV, 815
Galbreath, Ruth IV, 816
Galbreath, Ruth IV, 858
Galbreath, Samuel IV, 816
Galbreath, Samuel IV, 955
Galbreath, Samuel VI, 819
Galbreath, Samuel VI, 865
Galbreath, Samuel B. V, 997
Galbreath, Sarah I, 780
Galbreath, Sarah I, 809
Galbreath, Sarah I, 1048
Galbreath, Sarah IV, 625
Galbreath, Sarah IV, 816
Galbreath, Sarah IV, 820
Galbreath, Sarah IV, 837
Galbreath, Sarah Ann IV, 816
Galbreath, Sarah Harris IV, 955
Galbreath, Susanna I, 541
Galbreath, Susanna I, 545
Galbreath, Susanna I, 1030
Galbreath, Susannah I, 1030
Galbreath, Susannah IV, 146
Galbreath, Susannah IV, 625
Galbreath, Susannah IV, 816
Galbreath, Thomas IV, 693
Galbreath, Thomas IV, 709
Galbreath, Thomas IV, 797
Galbreath, Thomas IV, 816
Galbreath, Thomas IV, 858
Galbreath, William I, 1030
Galbreath, William IV, 625
Galbreath, William F. IV, 709
Galbreath, Wm. IV, 816
Galbreath, Wm. IV, 841
Galbreath, Wm. IV, 858
Galbreathe, John I, 1048
Galbreathe, John I, 1050
Galbreathe, Sarah I, 1048
Galbreathe, Sarah I, 1050
Galbreth, Ann I, 809
Galbreth, Asher I, 809
Galbreth, Charity I, 809
Galbreth, David I, 809
Galbreth, Elizabeth I, 809
Galbreth, Hannah I, 809
Galbreth, James I, 809
Galbreth, James I, 879
Galbreth, Jane I, 809
Galbreth, Sarah I, 809
Galbreth, Susanna I, 809
Galbreth, William I, 809
Galbuth, Rhoda V, 734
Galdean, Jacob VI, 838
Galdean, Theziah VI, 836
Galding, Jacob VI, 818
Galding, Rachel VI, 818
Gale, Ailse VI, 64
Gale, Caroline III, 130
Gale, Elizabeth III, 55
Gale, George III, 130
Gale, Moses III, 130
Gale, Moses, Jr. III, 130
Gale, Sarah II, 791
Gale, Susan III, 130
Galeman, Alcinda V, 562
Galeman, Eunice W. V, 562
Galemore, Sally V, 622
Gales, Sarah I. V, 997
Gales, Warren V, 997
Galiger, Joseph J. V, 997
Galiger, Mary V, 997
Galimore, Amanda V, 58
Galimore, Amanda V, 123
Galiway, Elizabeth V, 997
Galiway, Woodford V, 997
Galladay, Ruth V, 22
Galladay, Ruth V, 58
Gallady, Ruth V, 492
Gallager, Anna Eliza IV, 727
Gallager, Hannah C. IV, 1316
Gallager, Matilda IV, 1316
Gallager, W. F. IV, 1316
Gallagher, Andrew C. V, 58
Gallagher, Andrew Cadwallader V, 58
Gallagher, Benjamin III, 131
Gallagher, Dora V, 58
Gallagher, Dora C. V, 58
Gallagher, Dora P. V, 34
Gallagher, Dora P. V, 58
Gallagher, Esther V, 58
Gallagher, Esther C. V, 58
Gallagher, Fred IV, 1316
Gallagher, Frederick W. IV, 1316
Gallagher, Hannah IV, 1316
Gallagher, Hannah C. IV, 1316
Gallagher, Harriet III, 131
Gallagher, Henry Newcomb III, 131
Gallagher, James V, 58
Gallagher, James G. V, 58
Gallagher, John D. V, 34
Gallagher, John D. V, 58
Gallagher, Matilda IV, 1316
Gallagher, Matilda C. IV, 1316
Gallagher, Phebe II, 70
Gallagher, Rachel V, 58
Gallagher, Rachel Shaw V, 58
Gallagher, Sally III, 131
Gallagher, Sterling IV, 1316
Gallagher, W. F. IV, 1316
Gallagher, Wm. F. IV, 1316
Gallaher, Ann V, 673
Gallaher, Dollie I, 1152
Gallaher, Harvey V, 673
Gallaher, James V, 673
Gallaher, Mary J. V, 673
Gallaher, Rebecca V, 661
Gallamore, Elijah V, 622
Gallamore, Elizabeth V, 622
Gallamore, James M. V, 622
Gallamore, John V, 622
Gallamore, Martha V, 622
Gallaspey, Hannah II, 502
Gallaway, Appy VI, 919
Gallaway, Daniel A. III, 131
Gallaway, Edmund VI, 919
Gallaway, Isham VI, 936
Gallaway, Sarah VI, 936
Gallbreath, Rhoda IV, 625
Gallemore, Adna R. V, 622
Gallemore, Amanda V, 58
Gallemore, Ann V, 618
Gallemore, Ann V, 621
Gallemore, Ann V, 622
Gallemore, Ann Eliza V, 622
Gallemore, Catharine V, 621
Gallemore, Catharine V, 622
Gallemore, Catharine V, 636
Gallemore, Catherine V, 621
Gallemore, Cyrus V, 622
Gallemore, Edgar R. V, 622
Gallemore, Elijah V, 622
Gallemore, Elisha V, 58
Gallemore, Elisha V, 621
Gallemore, Elisha V, 622
Gallemore, Elisha V, 644
Gallemore, Elisha, Jr. V, 622
Gallemore, Eliza V, 622
Gallemore, Elizabeth V, 612
Gallemore, Elizabeth V, 622
Gallemore, Elizabeth Elen V, 622
Gallemore, Elizabeth Ellen V, 622
Gallemore, Emily V, 622
Gallemore, Emily V, 627
Gallemore, Emily J. V, 622
Gallemore, Ettie V, 622
Gallemore, Flora V, 622
Gallemore, Florence V, 622
Gallemore, Isaiah V, 622
Gallemore, James V, 622
Gallemore, James M. V, 622
Gallemore, James William V, 622
Gallemore, James Wm. V, 622
Gallemore, Jennie G. V, 622
Gallemore, John V, 621
Gallemore, John V, 622
Gallemore, John W. V, 622
Gallemore, Joseph V, 622
Gallemore, Latham V, 622
Gallemore, Letha L. V, 622
Gallemore, Levicy V, 622
Gallemore, Levicy V, 634
Gallemore, Levisa V, 621
Gallemore, Lewis V, 621
Gallemore, Louisa L. V, 622
Gallemore, Marietta L. V, 622
Gallemore, Martha V, 622
Gallemore, Martha Jane V, 622
Gallemore, Mary V, 58
Gallemore, Mary V, 492
Gallemore, Mary V, 621
Gallemore, Mary V, 622
Gallemore, Mary V, 629
Gallemore, Mary J. V, 622
Gallemore, Mary Jane V, 613
Gallemore, Mary Jane V, 621
Gallemore, Mary Jane V, 622
Gallemore, Mary Jane V, 647
Gallemore, Meria V, 622
Gallemore, Moses V, 622
Gallemore, Nathan V, 621
Gallemore, Oscar V, 622
Gallemore, Phebe V, 621
Gallemore, Rebecca Jane V, 622
Gallemore, Rosanna V, 622
Gallemore, Sally V, 622
Gallemore, Sally V, 629
Gallemore, Sarah V, 621
Gallemore, Sarah Amanda V, 58
Gallemore, Sarah Amanda V, 622
Gallemore, Susannah V, 621
Gallemore, Syrus E. V, 622
Gallemore, William V, 58
Gallemore, William V, 621
Gallemore, William P. V, 622
Gallemore, William, Jr. V, 622
Gallemore, Wm. V, 622
Gallemore, Wm. B. V, 622
Gallemore, Wm. P. V, 613
Gallemore, Wm. P. V, 622
Gallentine, Hester IV, 1279
Gallentine, Mary IV, 1279
Gallentine, Sydner IV, 1279
Gallentine, William IV, 1279
Galley, Sampson II, 443
Galliday, Ruth V, 332
Galliett, Effa V, 673
Galliett, Henry B. V, 673
Galliher, Mary V, 386
Gallimore, Ann V, 621
Gallimore, Ann Eliza V, 622
Gallimore, Audna V, 672
Gallimore, Audna V, 673
Gallimore, Audna R. V, 673
Gallimore, Catharine V, 492
Gallimore, Catherine V, 621
Gallimore, Cyrus V, 622
Gallimore, Elisha V, 123
Gallimore, Elisha V, 492
Gallimore, Elisha V, 622
Gallimore, Eliza V, 622
Gallimore, Elizabeth Ellen V, 622
Gallimore, Emily J. V, 622
Gallimore, Ertie M. V, 492
Gallimore, Flora E. V, 673
Gallimore, Florence V, 673
Gallimore, Isaiah V, 622
Gallimore, Isaiah M. V, 492
Gallimore, James V, 622
Gallimore, James W. V, 673
Gallimore, James William V, 622
Gallimore, John V, 492
Gallimore, Joseph V, 622
Gallimore, Kathleen I, 933
Gallimore, Latham V, 622
Gallimore, Letha V, 673
Gallimore, Letha V, 707
Gallimore, Letha C. V, 673
Gallimore, Levicey V, 492
Gallimore, Lewis V, 621
Gallimore, Martha I, 809
Gallimore, Martha Jane V, 622
Gallimore, Mary I, 809
Gallimore, Mary I, 838
Gallimore, Mary V, 492
Gallimore, Mary V, 622
Gallimore, Mary V, 673
Gallimore, Mary J. V, 476
Gallimore, Mary J. V, 492
Gallimore, Mary J. V, 673
Gallimore, Mary Jane V, 492
Gallimore, Mary Jane V, 621
Gallimore, Moses V, 622
Gallimore, Nathan V, 621
Gallimore, Oscar V, 622
Gallimore, Oscar V, 673
Gallimore, Oscar M. V, 673
Gallimore, Phebe V, 621
Gallimore, Polly V, 492
Gallimore, Rebecca Jane V, 622
Gallimore, Rosanna V, 622
Gallimore, Sarah V, 621
Gallimore, Sarah Amanda V, 123
Gallimore, Susannah V, 621
Gallimore, Syrus E. V, 622
Gallimore, William V, 240
Gallimore, William V, 476
Gallimore, William V, 492
Gallimore, William V, 621
Gallimore, William P. V, 622
Gallimore, Wm. B. V, 673
Gallimore, Wm. Gallimore V, 673
Gallion, Levicy VI, 818
Gallion, Mitchell VI, 818
Gallion, Polly VI, 918
Gallion, Saml. VI, 918
Galliway, William VI, 29
Galloney, Phebe W. III, 33
Gallop, Cora V, 562
Gallop, Cora V, 674
Gallop, Emma V, 674
Gallop, Estella V, 674
Gallop, Etta V, 562
Gallop, Martha J. V, 562
Gallop, Martha Jane V, 562
Gallop, Martha Jane V, 674
Gallop, Susanna V, 562
Gallop, Susannah V, 545
Gallop, Susannah V, 562
Gallops, Susanna V, 562
Gallops, Susanna V, 570
Galloway, Aby L. IV, 575
Galloway, Ann II, 528
Galloway, Ann II, 619
Galloway, Anna IV, 575
Galloway, Annie M. IV, 401
Galloway, Appy VI, 919
Galloway, Archibald VI, 919
Galloway, Benjamin VI, 919
Galloway, Benjamin VI, 987
Galloway, Bertha L. IV, 575
Galloway, Bertha L. IV, 578
Galloway, Caleb IV, 394
Galloway, Caleb IV, 401
Galloway, Charles A. IV, 575
Galloway, Charlotte III, 482
Galloway, Charlotte B. III, 502
Galloway, Christiana VI, 888
Galloway, Daniel VI, 919
Galloway, Daniel A. III, 357
Galloway, David V, 838
Galloway, David J. V, 838
Galloway, Edmund VI, 919
Galloway, Eliza III, 482
Galloway, Eliza III, 502
Galloway, Elma IV, 204
Galloway, Emaline IV, 401
Galloway, Grace II, 364
Galloway, Hezekiah III, 357
Galloway, Isham VI, 889
Galloway, Isham VI, 1004
Galloway, Isum VI, 942
Galloway, James IV, 204
Galloway, James L. IV, 204
Galloway, Jane II, 523
Galloway, Jane II, 528
Galloway, John II, 523
Galloway, John II, 528
Galloway, John VI, 889
Galloway, Joseph II, 364
Galloway, Joseph II, 528
Galloway, Joseph II, 619
Galloway, L. Growden II, 364
Galloway, Laurence Growdon II, 364
Galloway, Mae IV, 204
Galloway, Maggie IV, 1235
Galloway, May IV, 204
Galloway, Molly VI, 919
Galloway, Nancy IV, 204
Galloway, Phebe VI, 809
Galloway, Rebeckah VI, 919
Galloway, Rhoda VI, 919
Galloway, Sarah Ellen IV, 378
Galloway, Sarah Ellen IV, 394
Galloway, Susannah II, 364
Galloway, Thomas H. IV, 1235
Galloway, William III, 502
Galloway, Wm. III, 482
Gallup, Cora V, 562
Gallup, Cora V, 674
Gallup, Emma V, 674
Gallup, Estella V, 674
Gallup, Etta V, 562
Gallup, George V, 673
Gallup, H. B. V, 674
Gallup, Martha V, 674
Gallup, Martha J. V, 562
Gallup, Martha Jane V, 674
Gallup, Susanna N. V, 673
Gallup, Susannah V, 673
Galongher, Joseph V, 997
Galoway, David J. V, 838
Gambell, Harrison P. IV, 710
Gambell, Mary II, 443
Gambell, Michaell II, 443
Gambell, Samuel IV, 710
Gambier, Frank IV, 1316
Gambier, Lillian IV, 1316
Gamble, Adelbert IV, 710
Gamble, Albert L. IV, 816
Gamble, Alice V, 997
Gamble, Alice Lena IV, 816
Gamble, Alice Lena IV, 956
Gamble, Alice M. IV, 817
Gamble, Alice M. IV, 956
Gamble, Altha E. IV, 816
Gamble, Alvin H. IV, 625
Gamble, Alvin H. IV, 710
Gamble, Alvin H. IV, 816
Gamble, Alvina H. IV, 816
Gamble, Amelia B. IV, 816
Gamble, Amelia B. IV, 824
Gamble, Arthur IV, 817
Gamble, Arthur S. IV, 816

Gamble, Bertha Amelia IV, 816
Gamble, Bertha Amelia IV, 824
Gamble, Bessie V. IV, 1288
Gamble, Bradway IV, 710
Gamble, Carl S. IV, 956
Gamble, Carl Samuel IV, 816
Gamble, Carol S. IV, 816
Gamble, Catharine Rebecca IV, 816
Gamble, Catherine Rebecca IV, 816
Gamble, Catherine Rebecca IV, 956
Gamble, Charles IV, 625
Gamble, Charles IV, 710
Gamble, Charles IV, 715
Gamble, Charles IV, 816
Gamble, Charles IV, 956
Gamble, Charles W. IV, 710
Gamble, Charles W. IV, 816
Gamble, Charles W. IV, 854
Gamble, Chas. IV, 710
Gamble, Chas. IV, 831
Gamble, Chas. W. IV, 710
Gamble, Chas. W. IV, 824
Gamble, Chas. W. IV, 834
Gamble, Clara I, 633
Gamble, Clara A. I, 627
Gamble, Clarence V, 997
Gamble, Daisy V, 997
Gamble, Edith M. IV, 816
Gamble, Edith M. IV, 834
Gamble, Edith May IV, 816
Gamble, Edith May IV, 834
Gamble, Edward Y. IV, 170
Gamble, Edward Y. IV, 204
Gamble, Edward Y. IV, 364
Gamble, Edward Y. IV, 394
Gamble, Edward Y. IV, 710
Gamble, Edward Y. IV, 816
Gamble, Edwin Y. IV, 394
Gamble, Elisha IV, 383
Gamble, Elisha IV, 394
Gamble, Elisha IV, 619
Gamble, Elisha IV, 625
Gamble, Elisha IV, 816
Gamble, Eliza IV, 625
Gamble, Elizabeth IV, 33
Gamble, Elizabeth IV, 86
Gamble, Elizabeth IV, 146
Gamble, Elizabeth IV, 394
Gamble, Elizabeth V, 240
Gamble, Emma V, 997
Gamble, Emma L. IV, 418
Gamble, Emma L. IV, 816
Gamble, Emma L. IV, 831
Gamble, Ernest J. IV, 816
Gamble, Francis II, 528
Gamble, G. Alfred IV, 817
Gamble, G. Alfred IV, 956
Gamble, Geo. Alfred IV, 956
Gamble, George V, 240
Gamble, George Alfred IV, 816
Gamble, Harrison IV, 394
Gamble, Harrison IV, 611
Gamble, Harrison IV, 625
Gamble, Harrison IV, 709
Gamble, Harrison IV, 710
Gamble, Harrison IV, 816
Gamble, Harrison IV, 869
Gamble, Harrison IV, 956
Gamble, Harrison P. IV, 625
Gamble, Harrison P. IV, 710
Gamble, Harrison P. IV, 956
Gamble, Harrison P. IV, 1057
Gamble, Homer IV, 710
Gamble, Homer IV, 956
Gamble, Homer J. IV, 816
Gamble, Homer S. IV, 816
Gamble, Homer S. IV, 817
Gamble, Homer S. IV, 956
Gamble, Homer, Jr. IV, 817
Gamble, Homer, Jr. IV, 956
Gamble, Irena H. IV, 710
Gamble, Irena H. IV, 816
Gamble, Irene H. IV, 710
Gamble, Irene H. IV, 839
Gamble, J. Howard IV, 625
Gamble, J. Howard IV, 710
Gamble, James I, 627
Gamble, James L. W. IV, 710
Gamble, Jane IV, 1057
Gamble, Jannette IV, 710
Gamble, John E. V, 997
Gamble, John H. VI, 821
Gamble, Joseph IV, 33
Gamble, Joseph IV, 86
Gamble, Joseph IV, 146
Gamble, Joseph H. IV, 869
Gamble, K. Rebecca IV, 956
Gamble, Karl S. IV, 817
Gamble, Karl S. IV, 956
Gamble, Karl Samuel IV, 956
Gamble, Kay Rebecca IV, 817
Gamble, Lena IV, 816
Gamble, Lena IV, 956
Gamble, Lena M. IV, 816
Gamble, Lena M. IV, 817
Gamble, Lena M. IV, 956
Gamble, Lenora I, 627
Gamble, Mabel IV, 710
Gamble, Mabel B. IV, 625
Gamble, Mabel B. IV, 710
Gamble, Mable B. IV, 625
Gamble, Martha IV, 710
Gamble, Martha IV, 715
Gamble, Martha IV, 816
Gamble, Martha E. V, 997
Gamble, Martha Ellen IV, 869
Gamble, Martha H. IV, 710
Gamble, Martha H. IV, 816
Gamble, Martha Jane IV, 816
Gamble, Martha Jane IV, 869
Gamble, Martitia I, 679
Gamble, Martitia I, 681
Gamble, Mary II, 222
Gamble, Mary IV, 699
Gamble, Mary IV, 710
Gamble, Mary IV, 816
Gamble, Mary IV, 1324
Gamble, Mary Gertrude IV, 625
Gamble, Mary Gertrude IV, 710
Gamble, Mary Jane IV, 204
Gamble, Mary Jane IV, 699
Gamble, Mary Jane IV, 710
Gamble, Mary Jane IV, 812
Gamble, Mary Jane IV, 816
Gamble, Mary Jane IV, 839
Gamble, Mary Jane IV, 948
Gamble, Mary Jane IV, 956
Gamble, Mary R. IV, 710
Gamble, Mary R. IV, 812
Gamble, Mary R. IV, 816
Gamble, Mary R. IV, 948
Gamble, Melvina IV, 383
Gamble, Melvina IV, 394
Gamble, Melvina IV, 619
Gamble, Melvina IV, 625
Gamble, Michell II, 443
Gamble, Morrison P. IV, 956
Gamble, Neil E. V, 997
Gamble, Nellie IV, 1324
Gamble, Ollin II, 364
Gamble, Orly V, 997
Gamble, Phebe IV, 394
Gamble, Phebe IV, 611
Gamble, Phebe IV, 625
Gamble, Phebe IV, 709
Gamble, Phebe IV, 710
Gamble, Phebe IV, 816
Gamble, Phebe IV, 869
Gamble, Phebe IV, 956
Gamble, Phebe IV, 1057
Gamble, Phebe Jane IV, 710
Gamble, Phebe Jane IV, 816
Gamble, R. W. V, 997
Gamble, Rachel IV, 824
Gamble, Rachel IV, 831
Gamble, Rachel IV, 834
Gamble, Rachel S. IV, 816
Gamble, Rachel S. IV, 854
Gamble, Rebecca A. IV, 710
Gamble, Rebecca W. IV, 170
Gamble, Rebecca W. IV, 204
Gamble, Rebecca W. IV, 364
Gamble, Rebecca W. IV, 394
Gamble, Rebecca W. IV, 710
Gamble, Richard III, 131
Gamble, Robert IV, 1324
Gamble, Robert S. IV, 625
Gamble, Robert S. IV, 710
Gamble, Rolland G. V, 997
Gamble, Ruth Ellen IV, 816
Gamble, Ruth Ellen IV, 869
Gamble, Samuel IV, 204
Gamble, Samuel IV, 625
Gamble, Samuel IV, 699
Gamble, Samuel IV, 710
Gamble, Samuel IV, 812
Gamble, Samuel IV, 816
Gamble, Samuel IV, 839
Gamble, Samuel IV, 948
Gamble, Samuel IV, 956
Gamble, Samuel IV, 1057
Gamble, Sarah IV, 625
Gamble, Sarah IV, 710
Gamble, Sarah IV, 816
Gamble, Sarah V, 997
Gamble, Sarah H. IV, 611
Gamble, Sarah H. IV, 667
Gamble, Thamer IV, 869
Gamble, Wesley V, 997
Gamble, Wilber V, 997
Gamble, Wilford E. IV, 816
Gamble, Wilford E. IV, 817
Gamble, Wilford Edward IV, 816
Gamble, Wilford Edward IV, 956
Gamble, Wilfred E. IV, 956
Gamble, William IV, 625
Gamble, William IV, 710
Gamble, William IV, 816
Gamble, Wm. IV, 710
Gamble, Wm. IV, 816
Gambler, Harrison P. IV, 1062
Gambler, Phebe IV, 1062
Gambler, Phebe Jane IV, 805
Gambol, Mary II, 222
Gambrale, Mary I, 193
Gambrale, Mary I, 198
Gambrel, Hannah I, 193
Gambrel, Mary I, 193
Gambril, Hannah I, 139
Gambril, Hannah I, 145
Games, Barbara IV, 1161
Gamlin, Jane II, 443
Gamlin, John II, 443
Gammel, Eliza IV, 625
Gammel, Eliza IV, 661
Gammon, Amelia III, 131
Gammon, Amelia J. III, 131
Gammon, Amelia J. III, 368
Gammon, Eliza D. IV, 367
Gammon, Eliza D. IV, 394
Gammon, Harold W. III, 131
Gammon, Harold W. III, 368
Gammon, Howard W., Jr. III, 131
Gamo, Flora IV, 1316
Gamo, Mrs. Flora A. IV, 1316
Ganaway, Elizabeth L. VI, 799
Ganaway, Jeffrey VI, 799
Gander, Robina VI, 818
Gander, Thomas VI, 818
Ganel, Altha V, 997
Gangos, Elizabeth I, 986
Gannaway, Elizabeth VI, 838
Gannaway, Jas VI, 291
Gannaway, Lydia VI, 818
Gannaway, Mary VI, 818
Gannaway, William G. VI, 818
Gannaway, Woodson VI, 818
Gannaway, Woodson VI, 838
Gannett, Anna Gannett II, 889
Gannett, Anna Hinsdale II, 865
Gannett, Charlotte Katharine III, 131
Gannett, Charlotte Katharine III, 213
Gannett, Ezra Stiles II, 865
Gannett, Ezra Stiles II, 889
Gannett, Mary T. II, 865
Gannett, Mary T. II, 889
Gannett, Mary T. L. III, 131
Gannett, Mary T. L. III, 213
Gannett, Wm. C. III, 131
Gannett, Wm. C. III, 213
Gannett, Wm. Channing II, 865
Gannett, Wm. Channing II, 889
Gano, Aaron V, 906
Gano, Aaron Goforth V, 906
Gano, Cornelia V, 906
Gano, Laura V, 906
Gano, Nixon V, 906
Gant, Cassie IV, 956
Gant, Hannah II, 224
Gant, John IV, 956
Gant, Killey I, 541
Gant, Mary V, 492
Gant, Mary V, 500
Gant, Samuel II, 224
Gant, Sarah Ann IV, 817
Gant, Sarah Ann IV, 821
Gant, Zeblon I, 541
Ganter, Helena IV, 1316
Ganter, Helena Franziska IV, 1316
Ganter, Michael I, 1030
Gantz, Celicia IV, 710
Gantz, Celicia IV, 779
Gantz, Celicia L. IV, 625
Gantz, Celicia L. IV, 661
Gantz, Ella IV, 1038
Gapen, Zachariah IV, 33
Garagus, Elizabeth M. II, 148
Garber, Ethel V, 739
Garbreath, Leah IV, 956
Garbreath, Rhoda IV, 956
Gard, Annie III, 131
Gard, Annie III, 272
Gard, David A. III, 131
Gard, David H. III, 272
Gard, Emma V, 171
Gard, Harry V, 171
Gard, J. H. V, 171
Gard, John V, 171
Gard, John V, 172
Gard, Margaret V, 171
Gard, Mary III, 131
Gard, Mary III, 272
Gard, Will V, 171
Gard, William V, 171
Garde, Patsy VI, 919
Garde, William VI, 919
Garden, Richard I, 540
Gardener, Ann B. II, 287
Gardener, Diana IV, 1362
Gardener, Elizabeth II, 222
Gardener, Flora M. I, 412
Gardener, Hannah II, 222
Gardener, Hannah II, 249
Gardener, James II, 287
Gardener, John I, 761
Gardener, Mary II, 222
Gardener, Mary II, 234
Gardener, Mary B. II, 287
Gardener, Matthew II, 222
Gardener, Matthew II, 234
Gardener, Patience II, 118
Gardener, William VI, 390
Gardham, Andrie III, 131
Gardham, Andrie Frances III, 131
Gardham, Chris. Walker III, 310
Gardham, Christopher Walker III, 131
Gardham, Frances III, 131
Gardham, Frances M. III, 131
Gardham, Frances M. III, 310
Gardham, Jos. III, 131
Gardham, Mary E. III, 131
Gardiner, Abigail II, 795
Gardiner, Abraham II, 174
Gardiner, Abraham II, 337
Gardiner, Amy II, 794
Gardiner, Ann II, 174
Gardiner, Ann II, 795
Gardiner, Ann II, 865
Gardiner, Ann II, 948
Gardiner, Ann B. II, 287
Gardiner, Ann B. II, 288
Gardiner, Ann B. II, 1046
Gardiner, Ann B. II, 1051
Gardiner, Ann B. II, 1087
Gardiner, Barclay II, 290
Gardiner, Benjamin II, 337
Gardiner, Benjamin VI, 919
Gardiner, Caroline II, 705
Gardiner, Caroline H. II, 701
Gardiner, Caroline H. II, 733
Gardiner, Caroline H. II, 741
Gardiner, Clara May II, 922
Gardiner, Cola IV, 1316
Gardiner, Damaris II, 705
Gardiner, Damarus II, 741
Gardiner, Donald IV, 1316
Gardiner, Edith II, 529
Gardiner, Elisa B. II, 174
Gardiner, Eliza II, 714
Gardiner, Eliza B. II, 288
Gardiner, Eliza B. II, 1051
Gardiner, Eliza L. II, 1046
Gardiner, Eliza L. II, 1051
Gardiner, Elizabeth II, 70
Gardiner, Elizabeth II, 196
Gardiner, Elizabeth II, 197
Gardiner, Elizabeth II, 222
Gardiner, Elizabeth II, 223
Gardiner, Elizabeth II, 290
Gardiner, Elizabeth II, 337
Gardiner, Elizabeth II, 529
Gardiner, Elizabeth W. VI, 919
Gardiner, Ellen III, 131
Gardiner, Emily B. II, 174
Gardiner, Emily B. II, 948
Gardiner, Ephraim II, 70
Gardiner, Erma IV, 1316
Gardiner, Erma Marie IV, 1316
Gardiner, Ernest H. II, 288
Gardiner, Esther W. II, 174
Gardiner, Franklin II, 290
Gardiner, Garrett VI, 64
Gardiner, Geo. IV, 1316
Gardiner, Hannah II, 222
Gardiner, Hannah II, 242
Gardiner, Hannah II, 337
Gardiner, Hannah II, 365
Gardiner, Hannah II, 528
Gardiner, Hannah II, 705
Gardiner, Hannah II, 922
Gardiner, Harriet I. II, 705
Gardiner, Harriett S. II, 701
Gardiner, Henry IV, 1159
Gardiner, Henry T. II, 701
Gardiner, Henry T. II, 705
Gardiner, Henry T. II, 741
Gardiner, Hettie W. II, 174
Gardiner, Isaac II, 337
Gardiner, James II, 174
Gardiner, James II, 287
Gardiner, James II, 288
Gardiner, James II, 290
Gardiner, James II, 946
Gardiner, James II, 1046
Gardiner, James II, 1051
Gardiner, James H. II, 529
Gardiner, James H. II, 741
Gardiner, Jane II, 222
Gardiner, Jane II, 230
Gardiner, Jane II, 288
Gardiner, Job II, 223
Gardiner, Job II, 529
Gardiner, John II, 222
Gardiner, John II, 223
Gardiner, John II, 254
Gardiner, John II, 705
Gardiner, Joseph II, 70
Gardiner, Joseph II, 714
Gardiner, Joseph II, 922
Gardiner, Joseph S. II, 290
Gardiner, Joseph W. II, 174
Gardiner, Joseph W. II, 288
Gardiner, Joseph W. II, 1046
Gardiner, Joseph W. II, 1051
Gardiner, Lenora IV, 1316
Gardiner, Louisa II, 288
Gardiner, Martha IV, 1159
Gardiner, Mary II, 174
Gardiner, Mary II, 222
Gardiner, Mary II, 237
Gardiner, Mary II, 337
Gardiner, Mary II, 471
Gardiner, Mary II, 528
Gardiner, Mary II, 714
Gardiner, Mary II, 718
Gardiner, Mary VI, 64
Gardiner, Mary Ann IV, 1159
Gardiner, Mary B. II, 287
Gardiner, Mary B. II, 288
Gardiner, Mary B. II, 290
Gardiner, Mary Elizabeth VI, 36
Gardiner, Mary Ella II, 288
Gardiner, Mary W. II, 290
Gardiner, Matthew II, 174
Gardiner, Matthew II, 222
Gardiner, Patience II, 223
Gardiner, Patience II, 288
Gardiner, Phebe II, 803
Gardiner, Prudence II, 70
Gardiner, Rebecca B. P. II, 290
Gardiner, Roswell IV, 1316
Gardiner, Roswell H. IV, 1316
Gardiner, Samuel II, 70
Gardiner, Samuel II, 290
Gardiner, Samuel II, 337
Gardiner, Sarah II, 174
Gardiner, Sarah II, 222
Gardiner, Sarah II, 254
Gardiner, Stacy II, 290
Gardiner, Susan J. II, 174
Gardiner, Susanna II, 337
Gardiner, Thomas II, 174
Gardiner, Thomas II, 196
Gardiner, Thomas II, 222
Gardiner, Thomas II, 223
Gardiner, Thomas II, 337
Gardiner, Thomas W. II, 705
Gardiner, Thomas W. II, 741
Gardiner, Thomas, Jr. II, 222
Gardiner, Thomas, Jr. II, 242
Gardiner, Wd. Ann B. II, 946
Gardiner, William II, 174
Gardiner, William II, 288
Gardiner, William IV, 1159
Gardiner, Wm. II, 529
Garding, Harriett E. IV, 204
Garding, Lemuel IV, 204
Garding, Samuel IV, 204
Gardner, Aaron I, 498
Gardner, Aaron III, 217
Gardner, Abagile I, 810
Gardner, Abel I, 498
Gardner, Abel I, 541
Gardner, Abel I, 780
Gardner, Abel I, 810
Gardner, Abigail I, 498
Gardner, Abigail I, 761
Gardner, Abigail I, 780
Gardner, Abigail I, 810
Gardner, Abigail I, 843
Gardner, Abigail I, 846
Gardner, Abraham II, 528
Gardner, Achelus II, 529
Gardner, Adelaide S. III, 412
Gardner, Agnes VI, 818
Gardner, Alfred I, 588
Gardner, Alfred I, 593

rdner, Alfred A. III, 412
rdner, Alfred H. III, 412
rdner, Alice III, 131
rdner, Alice H. III, 20
rdner, Alvin IV, 1159
rdner, Ammiel I, 498
rdner, Angelina I, 593
rdner, Ann I, 541
rdner, Ann I, 588
rdner, Ann I, 912
rdner, Ann I, 914
rdner, Ann V, 357
rdner, Ann V, 932
rdner, Ann B. II, 1085
rdner, Ann Eliza VI, 492
rdner, Ann Eliza VI, 494
rdner, Ann Eliza VI, 495
rdner, Anna I, 780
rdner, Anna I, 797
rdner, Anna I, 810
rdner, Anna III, 215
rdner, Anna D. W. III, 131
rdner, Anna Deacon III, 131
rdner, Anna Dean III, 131
rdner, Anna Gordon III, 131
rdner, Anna H. III, 131
rdner, Anna H. III, 217
rdner, Anna L. V, 332
rdner, Anna S. V, 332
rdner, Archelus III, 131
rdner, Archilaus II, 529
rdner, Asa III, 131
rdner, Asabel V, 782
rdner, Asael V, 838
rdner, Asahel A. V, 838
rdner, Bartlete I, 780
rdner, Bartlett I, 810
rdner, Barzilla I, 352
rdner, Barzilla I, 541
rdner, Barzilla I, 558
rdner, Barzilla I Sup 1, 9
rdner, Barzillai I, 352
rdner, Barzillai I, 498
rdner, Barzillai I, 540
rdner, Barzillai I, 541
rdner, Barzillia I, 541
rdner, Benjamin A. III, 132
rdner, Benjamin S. III, 131
rdner, Betsy VI, 818
rdner, Brazilla I, 787
rdner, C. L. IV, 1038
rdner, Calvin I, 588
rdner, Calvin I, 593
rdner, Catharine V, 332
rdner, Charles V, 58
rdner, Charles M. V, 332
rdner, Charles William
III, 131
rdner, Chas. M. V, 332
rdner, Cireny I, 588
rdner, Clarence Leon IV, 1038
rdner, Cleo IV, 1159
rdner, Cordelia A. III, 131
rdner, Cordelia A. III, 275
rdner, David I, 498
rdner, David I, 809
rdner, David I, 810
rdner, Deborah I, 536
rdner, Deborah I, 541
rdner, Deborah I, 577
rdner, Deborah I, 810
rdner, Deborah II, 479
rdner, Deborah II, 528
rdner, Delila I, 593
rdner, Delilah V, 753
rdner, Delilah V, 782
rdner, Delilah V, 789
rdner, Delphina I, 389
rdner, Delphina I, 405
rdner, Delphina I, 615
rdner, Delphina E. I, 389
rdner, Delphina E. I, 408
rdner, Delphina E. I, 787
rdner, Delphina Eliza I, 352
rdner, Demaris III, 131
rdner, Dinah I, 541
rdner, Dinah I, 809
rdner, Dinah I, 810
rdner, Dinah III, 131
rdner, E. F. VI, 808
rdner, Edith I, 588
rdner, Edith II, 365
rdner, Edith II, 529
rdner, Edith IV, 695
rdner, Edom V, 357
rdner, Edward I, 588
rdner, Edward I, 593
rdner, Edythe IV, 710
rdner, Eleanor V, 332
rdner, Eliab I, 780
rdner, Eliab I, 810
Gardner, Eliab I, 839
Gardner, Eliab V, 838
Gardner, Elihu I, 498
Gardner, Elisabeth II, 528
Gardner, Elisabeth II, 660
Gardner, Elisabeth V, 838
Gardner, Eliub I, 810
Gardner, Eliza III, 193
Gardner, Eliza V, 562
Gardner, Eliza J. IV, 1098
Gardner, Eliza J. IV, 1123
Gardner, Elizabeth I, 534
Gardner, Elizabeth I, 541
Gardner, Elizabeth I, 588
Gardner, Elizabeth I, 593
Gardner, Elizabeth I, 780
Gardner, Elizabeth I, 809
Gardner, Elizabeth I, 810
Gardner, Elizabeth I, 825
Gardner, Elizabeth I, 839
Gardner, Elizabeth II, 197
Gardner, Elizabeth II, 223
Gardner, Elizabeth II, 364
Gardner, Elizabeth II, 365
Gardner, Elizabeth II, 518
Gardner, Elizabeth II, 528
Gardner, Elizabeth II, 529
Gardner, Elizabeth IV, 710
Gardner, Elizabeth V, 332
Gardner, Elizabeth V, 356
Gardner, Elizabeth V, 782
Gardner, Elizabeth V, 932
Gardner, Elizabeth VI, 818
Gardner, Elnathan III, 131
Gardner, Elnathan III, 212
Gardner, Emily B. II, 1085
Gardner, Endoris V, 838
Gardner, Ephraim II, 70
Gardner, Ephraim VI, 638
Gardner, Ephraim VI, 713
Gardner, Ephrain VI, 818
Gardner, Ephriam VI, 801
Gardner, Ernest III, 131
Gardner, Ernest H. II, 288
Gardner, Ernest H. II, 306
Gardner, Ernest H. III, 131
Gardner, Ernest H. III, 215
Gardner, Esther V, 838
Gardner, Esther F. V, 838
Gardner, Ethel IV, 1159
Gardner, Eunice I, 498
Gardner, Eunice I, 541
Gardner, Eunice I, 715
Gardner, Eunice I, 780
Gardner, Eunice I, 806
Gardner, Eunice I, 810
Gardner, Eunice I, 839
Gardner, Eunice I, 846
Gardner, Eunice V, 788
Gardner, Eunis I, 781
Gardner, Fanny IV, 1159
Gardner, Flora I, 389
Gardner, Flora I, 405
Gardner, Flora Marzillia I, 352
Gardner, Florence L. III, 412
Gardner, Florence L. III, 449
Gardner, Forest IV, 1159
Gardner, Frank H. IV, 695
Gardner, Franklin I, 780
Gardner, Frederick III, 131
Gardner, Garret VI, 85
Gardner, Garret VI, 91
Gardner, Geo. L. III, 132
Gardner, George I, 498
Gardner, George I, 780
Gardner, George I, 810
Gardner, George F. III, 131
Gardner, George G. III, 131
Gardner, Gerald IV, 1038
Gardner, Grafton I, 780
Gardner, Grafton I, 810
Gardner, Hannah I, 541
Gardner, Hannah I, 586
Gardner, Hannah I, 810
Gardner, Hannah I, 840
Gardner, Hannah II, 365
Gardner, Hannah II, 528
Gardner, Hannah II, 529
Gardner, Hannah III, 131
Gardner, Hannah III, 212
Gardner, Harper Wills III, 131
Gardner, Harry M. V, 332
Gardner, Henry IV, 1159
Gardner, Henry V, 838
Gardner, Henry VI, 818
Gardner, Henry E. IV, 1159
Gardner, Hezekiah I, 810
Gardner, Hezekiah Barnard
III, 131
Gardner, Isaac I, 498
Gardner, Isaac I, 541
Gardner, Isaac I, 810
Gardner, Isaac I, 847
Gardner, Isaac I Sup 1, 9
Gardner, Isaac V, 788
Gardner, Isaac V, 969
Gardner, Isaac, Jr. I, 541
Gardner, Isaac, Jr. I, 809
Gardner, Isaac, Jr. I, 810
Gardner, Isaiah V, 357
Gardner, Jacob III, 131
Gardner, Jacob V, 357
Gardner, James I, 780
Gardner, James I, 810
Gardner, James I, 839
Gardner, James II, 70
Gardner, James III, 131
Gardner, James V, 332
Gardner, James VI, 638
Gardner, James VI, 713
Gardner, James VI, 714
Gardner, James H. II, 529
Gardner, James M. I, 593
Gardner, James R. V, 332
Gardner, Jane I, 761
Gardner, Jane II, 288
Gardner, Jane III, 131
Gardner, Jane Louisa II, 306
Gardner, Jelina I, 588
Gardner, Jemima I, 498
Gardner, Jemima I, 540
Gardner, Jemima I, 541
Gardner, Jemima I, 558
Gardner, Jemima I, 780
Gardner, Jemima I, 810
Gardner, Jemima V, 739
Gardner, Jesse I, 529
Gardner, Jesse I, 780
Gardner, Jesse I, 810
Gardner, Jesse V, 357
Gardner, Jesse B. V, 332
Gardner, Jessie B. V, 332
Gardner, Job II, 529
Gardner, Joel V, 357
Gardner, John I, 498
Gardner, John I, 761
Gardner, John II, 365
Gardner, John II, 528
Gardner, John II, 676
Gardner, John VI, 802
Gardner, John VI, 816
Gardner, John VI, 818
Gardner, John VI, 819
Gardner, John VI, 845
Gardner, John VI, 859
Gardner, John VI, 866
Gardner, John B. W. IV, 472
Gardner, John H. VI, 797
Gardner, John H. VI, 841
Gardner, John H. VI, 860
Gardner, John J. III, 412
Gardner, John J. III, 449
Gardner, Jonathan I, 593
Gardner, Jonathan I, 780
Gardner, Jonathan I, 810
Gardner, Joseph II, 70
Gardner, Joseph II, 365
Gardner, Joseph II, 528
Gardner, Joseph V, 562
Gardner, Joseph V, 838
Gardner, Joseph W. II, 288
Gardner, Judith I, 498
Gardner, Judith I, 525
Gardner, Judith I, 540
Gardner, Judith I, 541
Gardner, Judith I, 561
Gardner, Judith I, 780
Gardner, Judith I, 787
Gardner, Judith I, 810
Gardner, Judith I, 912
Gardner, Judith I, 913
Gardner, Kate V, 332
Gardner, Katherine T. W. III, 412
Gardner, Keturah IV, 1207
Gardner, Keturah IV, 1212
Gardner, Keturah V, 782
Gardner, Keturah V, 783
Gardner, Laban III, 131
Gardner, Lewis III, 131
Gardner, Libni I, 541
Gardner, Libni I, 586
Gardner, Libni I, 588
Gardner, Lizzie IV, 1038
Gardner, Lizzie Mae IV, 1038
Gardner, Louisa II, 288
Gardner, Lucy I, 623
Gardner, Lumina VI, 866
Gardner, Lydda I, 525
Gardner, Lydda I, 541
Gardner, Lydia I, 498
Gardner, Lydia I, 588
Gardner, Lydia I, 593
Gardner, Lydia I, 596
Gardner, Lydia I, 780
Gardner, Lydia I, 810
Gardner, Lydia I, 844
Gardner, Lydia III, 131
Gardner, Lydia III, 284
Gardner, Lydia III, 380
Gardner, Lydia III, 482
Gardner, Lydia V, 58
Gardner, Margaret V, 357
Gardner, Maria Clark IV, 710
Gardner, Martha II, 365
Gardner, Martha II, 528
Gardner, Martha IV, 1159
Gardner, Martha W. III, 412
Gardner, Mary I, 389
Gardner, Mary I, 405
Gardner, Mary I, 541
Gardner, Mary I, 593
Gardner, Mary I, 761
Gardner, Mary I, 780
Gardner, Mary I, 801
Gardner, Mary I, 810
Gardner, Mary I, 824
Gardner, Mary I, 825
Gardner, Mary I, 1119
Gardner, Mary I, 1135
Gardner, Mary II, 70
Gardner, Mary II, 222
Gardner, Mary II, 365
Gardner, Mary II, 528
Gardner, Mary III, 131
Gardner, Mary V, 562
Gardner, Mary V, 783
Gardner, Mary V, 788
Gardner, Mary V, 789
Gardner, Mary VI, 85
Gardner, Mary VI, 91
Gardner, Mary VI, 638
Gardner, Mary VI, 713
Gardner, Mary A. I, 593
Gardner, Mary A. I, 595
Gardner, Mary Ann II, 365
Gardner, Mary Ann III, 131
Gardner, Mary Ann III, 275
Gardner, Mary Ann IV, 1159
Gardner, Mary E. IV, 710
Gardner, Mary Elizabeth IV, 677
Gardner, Mary Ella II, 288
Gardner, Mary Ella II, 306
Gardner, Mary Ella III, 131
Gardner, Mary Ella III, 215
Gardner, Mary I. VI, 808
Gardner, Mary W. V, 838
Gardner, Maryann I, 588
Gardner, Matilda I, 498
Gardner, Matilda I, 525
Gardner, Merab VI, 742
Gardner, Meriam I, 810
Gardner, Merril Clair IV, 1038
Gardner, Merrill IV, 1038
Gardner, Metilda I, 541
Gardner, Micajah I, 498
Gardner, Minerva C. VI, 818
Gardner, Miriam I, 498
Gardner, Miriam I, 780
Gardner, Miriam I, 802
Gardner, Miriam I, 810
Gardner, Miriam I, 840
Gardner, Miriam I, 841
Gardner, Nancy VI, 638
Gardner, Nancy VI, 713
Gardner, Nancy VI, 714
Gardner, Nathan I, 498
Gardner, Nathan III, 132
Gardner, Nathaniel III, 131
Gardner, Nathaniel III, 217
Gardner, Nathaniel III, 306
Gardner, Nathaniel VI, 818
Gardner, Neomi I, 498
Gardner, Noah III, 131
Gardner, Noah III, 284
Gardner, Noah III, 412
Gardner, Noah III, 420
Gardner, Noah III, 476
Gardner, Obed I, 780
Gardner, Obed I, 810
Gardner, Ora IV, 1159
Gardner, Orlando E. I, 467
Gardner, Orlando E. I, 480
Gardner, Patience II, 223
Gardner, Paul I, 498
Gardner, Paul I, 541
Gardner, Paul I, 809
Gardner, Paul I, 810
Gardner, Penelope I, 715
Gardner, Penelope I, 810
Gardner, Penelope H. I, 781
Gardner, Penelope H. I, 810
Gardner, Pennelope I, 715
Gardner, Pennelope I, 720
Gardner, Phebe I, 780
Gardner, Phebe I, 810
Gardner, Phebe I, 819
Gardner, Phebe III, 131
Gardner, Phebe III, 412
Gardner, Phebe III, 420
Gardner, Phebe V, 912
Gardner, Philip A. IV, 710
Gardner, Priscilla I, 541
Gardner, Rachel I, 780
Gardner, Rachel I, 810
Gardner, Rachel I, 827
Gardner, Rachel V, 332
Gardner, Rachel V, 356
Gardner, Rachel V, 357
Gardner, Ralph V, 997
Gardner, Rebecca I, 809
Gardner, Rebecca I, 810
Gardner, Rebeckah I, 810
Gardner, Rebekah I, 541
Gardner, Reuben I, 541
Gardner, Reuben I, 588
Gardner, Reuben I, 593
Gardner, Rhoada I, 541
Gardner, Rhoada I, 558
Gardner, Rhoda I, 498
Gardner, Rhoda I, 529
Gardner, Rhoda I, 588
Gardner, Rhoda I, 593
Gardner, Rhoda I, 780
Gardner, Rhoda I, 804
Gardner, Rhoda I, 810
Gardner, Richard I, 540
Gardner, Richard I, 780
Gardner, Richard I, 809
Gardner, Richard I, 810
Gardner, Richard I Sup 1, 10
Gardner, Richard V, 838
Gardner, Richard L. III, 412
Gardner, Robert, Jr. V, 58
Gardner, Rodah I, 810
Gardner, Roselle V, 332
Gardner, Rosetta IV, 695
Gardner, Rosetta IV, 710
Gardner, Rowland H. III, 131
Gardner, Rowland H. III, 275
Gardner, Roza C. IV, 817
Gardner, Russel V, 332
Gardner, Ruth I, 810
Gardner, Ruth I, 839
Gardner, Ruth III, 131
Gardner, Ruth S. III, 131
Gardner, Sally I, 498
Gardner, Sally I, 588
Gardner, Sally B. VI, 819
Gardner, Sarah I, 780
Gardner, Sarah I, 796
Gardner, Sarah I, 810
Gardner, Sarah I, 839
Gardner, Sarah II, 365
Gardner, Sarah II, 529
Gardner, Sarah III, 131
Gardner, Sarah III, 244
Gardner, Sarah III, 284
Gardner, Sarah III, 412
Gardner, Sarah III, 420
Gardner, Sarah III, 476
Gardner, Sarah V, 357
Gardner, Sarah V, 838
Gardner, Sarah E. III, 131
Gardner, Sarah E. III, 132
Gardner, Sarah E. III, 266
Gardner, Sarah Eliz III, 306
Gardner, Sarah Eliz. III, 217
Gardner, Sarah Elizabeth
III, 131
Gardner, Seneca III, 131
Gardner, Seth I, 541
Gardner, Seth I, 588
Gardner, Seth III, 131
Gardner, Seth III, 132
Gardner, Seth III, 412
Gardner, Shubael I, 810
Gardner, Shubal I, 780
Gardner, Shubal I, 801
Gardner, Shubal I, 810
Gardner, Shubel I, 498
Gardner, Silvanus I, 541
Gardner, Silvanus I, 586
Gardner, Silvanus I, 588
Gardner, Silvanus I, 593
Gardner, Silvanus I, 809
Gardner, Silvanus I, 840
Gardner, Sith I, 593
Gardner, Smith III, 131
Gardner, Solomon I, 541
Gardner, Solomon I, 588
Gardner, Solomon I, 593
Gardner, Stephen I, 498
Gardner, Stephen I, 540
Gardner, Stephen I, 541

Gardner, Stephen I, 761
Gardner, Stephen I, 780
Gardner, Stephen I, 810
Gardner, Stephen I Sup 1, 9
Gardner, Stephen, Jr. I, 540
Gardner, Stephen, Jr. I, 810
Gardner, Susanna I, 780
Gardner, Susanna I, 810
Gardner, Susanna I, 827
Gardner, Susanna L. III, 132
Gardner, Susannah V, 899
Gardner, Sylvanus I, 541
Gardner, Sylvanus I, 810
Gardner, Sylvanus I Sup 1, 10
Gardner, Thaddeus I, 715
Gardner, Thaddeus I, 780
Gardner, Thaddeus I, 781
Gardner, Thadeus I, 810
Gardner, Thadeus I, 839
Gardner, Theodore V, 562
Gardner, Theodore V, 838
Gardner, Thomas I, 498
Gardner, Thomas I, 588
Gardner, Thomas II, 163
Gardner, Thomas II, 197
Gardner, Thomas II, 365
Gardner, Thomas II, 528
Gardner, Thomas V, 357
Gardner, Thomas W. III, 132
Gardner, Thos. V, 932
Gardner, Tiecia I, 593
Gardner, Tyrecy I, 588
Gardner, Unice, Jr. I, 541
Gardner, Unice, Sr. I, 541
Gardner, Viola A. IV, 710
Gardner, Walter Gerald IV, 1038
Gardner, Wanda IV, 1038
Gardner, Wanda Eileen IV, 1038
Gardner, Wd. Hannah II, 476
Gardner, Wd. Mary II, 62
Gardner, Widow Deborah I, 541
Gardner, Widow Jemima I, 498
Gardner, William I, 536
Gardner, William I, 540
Gardner, William I, 541
Gardner, William I, 715
Gardner, William I, 720
Gardner, William I, 780
Gardner, William I, 781
Gardner, William I, 810
Gardner, William I, 843
Gardner, William II, 288
Gardner, William II, 306
Gardner, William II, 364
Gardner, William IV, 1159
Gardner, William V, 783
Gardner, William V, 838
Gardner, William Elwood I, 588
Gardner, William G. V, 739
Gardner, William W. I, 593
Gardner, Wm. II, 528
Gardner, Wm. II, 529
Gardner, Wm. IV, 710
Gardner, Wm. IV, 1159
Gardner, Wm. V, 753
Gardner, Wm. V, 789
Gardner, Wm., Jr. II, 529
Gardnier, Alvin IV, 1159
Gardyne, Dorothy I, 941
Garee, Sarah IV, 86
Garee, Sarah IV, 109
Gareson, Anne IV, 817
Gareson, George IV, 817
Gareson, Hiram IV, 817
Gareson, Jesse IV, 817
Gareson, Joseph IV, 817
Gareson, Susana II, 71
Garet, Hanah II, 515
Garet, Hanah II, 529
Garetson, Mariah IV, 732
Garetson, Price IV, 710
Garey, Laura IV, 473
Garford, Samuel III, 132
Garges, Elizabeth I, 986
Garhite, Ephm VI, 148
Garhite, Ephm VI, 177
Garigues, Benjamin T. II, 865
Garigues, Betty II, 865
Garigues, Marshall II, 865
Garigus, Richard H. IV, 711
Gariot, Abigail I, 139
Gariot, Abigail I, 140
Garis, Zachariah I, 306
Garish, Comrade IV, 1251
Garish, Conrad IV, 1251
Garite, Samll VI, 148
Garite, Samuel VI, 177
Garland, Burr VI, 919
Garland, Burr VI, 963
Garland, Clara V, 386
Garland, Clarence V, 386
Garland, Daniel V, 386
Garland, David VI, 232
Garland, David VI, 243
Garland, David VI, 285
Garland, Edward VI, 243
Garland, Edward VI, 285
Garland, Joanna V, 386
Garland, John R. VI, 919
Garland, M. H. VI, 894
Garland, Mary VI, 232
Garland, Mary VI, 243
Garland, Mary VI, 285
Garland, Mary C. M. VI, 919
Garland, Mary L. VI, 919
Garland, Nicholas A. VI, 919
Garland, Paulina H. VI, 919
Garland, Robert I, 1152
Garland, Ruth II, 529
Garland, Ruth II, 665
Garland, Samuel VI, 919
Garland, Sarah VI, 919
Garlick, Dunckin II, 443
Garlick, Patrick II, 443
Garman, Anna M. V, 492
Garman, Ellie G. V, 457
Garman, Harry J. V, 492
Garman, Ida V, 172
Garman, Ida V, 623
Garman, Jacob V, 172
Garman, Jacob V, 623
Garman, Judith V, 492
Garman, Lydia P. IV, 688
Garman, Lydia P. IV, 710
Garman, Maude V, 623
Garman, Orval V, 492
Garman, Orvil Maude V, 172
Garman, Orville V, 492
Garman, Orville V, 623
Garman, Sophia Ann VI, 922
Garman, Viola Bell V, 172
Garman, Violet Belle V, 623
Garmen, Judith V, 490
Garmen, Judith V, 492
Garmier, Rachel II, 220
Garmier, Rachel II, 223
Garmon, Judith V, 492
Garmond, Orval V, 492
Garner, Albert V, 387
Garner, Alfred I, 616
Garner, Alice V, 674
Garner, Amaziah V, 386
Garner, Ameziah V, 387
Garner, Amos V, 386
Garner, Amos V, 387
Garner, Amos R. V, 387
Garner, Ann V, 240
Garner, Ann V, 371
Garner, Ann V, 381
Garner, Ann V, 386
Garner, Ann V, 387
Garner, Ann V, 389
Garner, Ann V, 400
Garner, Ann V, 422
Garner, Ann V, 427
Garner, Ann V, 441
Garner, Anna M. III, 114
Garner, Anna M. III, 132
Garner, Annie E. III, 482
Garner, Asa V, 386
Garner, Asenath Isabel V, 386
Garner, Birdie V, 674
Garner, Caroline III, 482
Garner, Caroline III, 483
Garner, Caroline E. III, 497
Garner, Caroline Elizabeth III, 482
Garner, Cecil V, 387
Garner, Charlie Augustus V, 386
Garner, Charlotte T. III, 482
Garner, Charlotte T. III, 483
Garner, Clara V, 562
Garner, Edmund B. V, 906
Garner, Eldon C. V, 387
Garner, Eleanor V, 332
Garner, Eleanor V, 387
Garner, Eleanor V, 391
Garner, Elenor V, 386
Garner, Elenor V, 430
Garner, Eliza III, 483
Garner, Eliza A. VI, 983
Garner, Elizabeth I, 383
Garner, Elizabeth I, 390
Garner, Elizabeth II, 70
Garner, Elizabeth III, 497
Garner, Elizabeth V, 371
Garner, Elizabeth V, 386
Garner, Elizabeth V, 387
Garner, Elizabeth A. V, 386
Garner, Elizabeth A. V, 387
Garner, Ephraim II, 70
Garner, Ethel V, 387
Garner, Felten I, 616
Garner, Felton I, 633
Garner, Felton, Jr. I, 616
Garner, Frank V, 387
Garner, George VI, 810
Garner, George VI, 843
Garner, George G. VI, 816
Garner, Grace V, 382
Garner, Grace V, 387
Garner, Grace V, 417
Garner, Hannah I, 1081
Garner, Hannah II, 443
Garner, Hattie V, 387
Garner, Henry M. V, 386
Garner, Hepsebah V, 899
Garner, Hepsebah V, 906
Garner, Hepzibah V, 906
Garner, Hyacinth V, 387
Garner, Ira V, 386
Garner, Ira V, 387
Garner, Irena V, 386
Garner, Irena V, 430
Garner, James V, 382
Garner, James V, 386
Garner, James V, 417
Garner, James V, 674
Garner, James Allen V, 386
Garner, James W. VI, 919
Garner, James W. VI, 975
Garner, Jephthah V, 240
Garner, Jephthat V, 386
Garner, Jeptha V, 412
Garner, Jesse V, 386
Garner, Jesse V, 387
Garner, Job S. V, 386
Garner, John III, 482
Garner, John V, 386
Garner, John V, 387
Garner, John V, 391
Garner, John V, 400
Garner, John V, 430
Garner, John Irwin V, 386
Garner, John, Jr. II, 443
Garner, Joseph II, 70
Garner, Joseph II, 71
Garner, Joseph V, 386
Garner, Joseph V, 387
Garner, Joseph Wm. V, 387
Garner, Julia A. V, 387
Garner, Levina V, 386
Garner, Lindley V, 386
Garner, Lindley V, 387
Garner, Linn Thomas I, 616
Garner, Louisa V, 387
Garner, Louiza V, 387
Garner, Lydia V, 906
Garner, Maranda V, 387
Garner, Margaret V, 386
Garner, Margaret V, 387
Garner, Margaret V, 391
Garner, Marion V, 674
Garner, Martha V, 381
Garner, Martha V, 386
Garner, Martha V, 441
Garner, Martha Ann V, 386
Garner, Martha Ann V, 387
Garner, Martha B. V, 240
Garner, Martha B. V, 261
Garner, Martha B. V, 387
Garner, Martha B. V, 412
Garner, Martha Ellen V, 386
Garner, Martha Ellen V, 387
Garner, Martha Emma V, 387
Garner, Martha L. V, 562
Garner, Martha L. V, 596
Garner, Martha S. V, 387
Garner, Martha S. V, 562
Garner, Mary I, 616
Garner, Mary V, 386
Garner, Mary V, 387
Garner, Mary V, 391
Garner, Mary V, 392
Garner, Mary VI, 843
Garner, Mary Ann V, 391
Garner, Mary B. V, 387
Garner, Mary Jane V, 384
Garner, Mary Jane V, 386
Garner, Mary Jane V, 387
Garner, Mary Matilda V, 386
Garner, Mary Matilda V, 387
Garner, Mattie V, 387
Garner, Milton V, 386
Garner, Milton V, 387
Garner, Mollie A. V, 387
Garner, Mont V, 387
Garner, Mont J. V, 387
Garner, Myrtle I, 616
Garner, Myrtle McGee I, 633
Garner, Nancy V, 386
Garner, Nancy V, 387
Garner, Nancy VI, 810
Garner, Ollive V, 386
Garner, Phebe V, 906
Garner, Pleasant V, 386
Garner, Pleasant B. V, 387
Garner, Prudence II, 70
Garner, Rachel V, 386
Garner, Rachel V, 422
Garner, Rachel V, 441
Garner, Rebecca IV, 86
Garner, Rebecca IV, 109
Garner, Rebecca V, 386
Garner, Rebecca V, 387
Garner, Rebecca V, 427
Garner, Rebecca V, 438
Garner, Rebecca V, 562
Garner, Rebecca V, 593
Garner, Rebecca V, 705
Garner, Rebecca Jane V, 386
Garner, Rebecca Jane V, 387
Garner, Richard V, 387
Garner, Richard G. V, 386
Garner, Rileigh V, 386
Garner, Rileigh V, 387
Garner, Robert V, 906
Garner, Ruth V, 371
Garner, Ruth V, 386
Garner, Samuel II, 70
Garner, Sarah III, 482
Garner, Sarah E. V, 387
Garner, Sarah E. VI, 919
Garner, Sarah M. V, 382
Garner, Sarah M. V, 386
Garner, Sarah M. V, 387
Garner, Sephthah V, 261
Garner, Susanna V, 389
Garner, Susanna V, 562
Garner, Susanna V, 563
Garner, Susannah V, 386
Garner, Thomas II, 365
Garner, Thomas E. V, 386
Garner, Thomas H. III, 114
Garner, Thomas H. III, 132
Garner, Velma V, 387
Garner, William III, 482
Garner, William III, 483
Garner, William III, 497
Garner, William V, 240
Garner, William V, 371
Garner, William V, 381
Garner, William V, 386
Garner, William V, 389
Garner, William V, 422
Garner, William H. III, 132
Garner, William H. V, 387
Garner, William O. V, 387
Garner, Wm. III, 482
Garner, Wm. III, 497
Garner, Wm. V, 371
Garner, Wm. V, 387
Garner, Wm. V, 427
Garnet, Absolem VI, 803
Garnet, Alexander VI, 819
Garnet, Frances VI, 819
Garnett, Augusta V, 332
Garnett, Augustus P. V, 332
Garnett, Joseph II, 529
Garns, John II, 365
Garone, August III, 132
Garone, August III, 279
Garone, Barbara Grace III, 132
Garone, Margaret III, 132
Garone, Margaret L. III, 279
Garrat, Josiah Gilbert I, 879
Garrat, William I, 879
Garratt, Ann II, 365
Garratt, James II, 365
Garratt, William VI, 29
Garraway, Charles II, 365
Garreson, Thos. V, 622
Garreston, Thos. V, 622
Garret, ??? VI, 39
Garret, Abigail I, 810
Garret, Abigail I, 827
Garret, Ann VI, 45
Garret, Ann VI, 46
Garret, Bulah I, 810
Garret, Caleb I, 810
Garret, Caleb I, 962
Garret, Cyrus I, 810
Garret, Elizabeth VI, 33
Garret, Henry A. III, 209
Garret, Jonathan I, 986
Garret, Katheren VI, 23
Garret, Mary IV, 526
Garret, Nathan I, 810
Garret, Rebecca V, 240
Garret, Rebecca V, 286
Garret, Samuel II, 513
Garret, Samuel II, 610
Garret, Sarah I, 49
Garret, Sarah K. III, 209
Garret, Virginia J. II, 925
Garret, Welcom I, 541
Garret, William I, 879
Garret, William IV, 394
Garret, William VI, 33
Garret, William VI, 40
Garret, Wm. VI, 31
Garret, Wm. VI, 33
Garretson, ??? IV, 1125
Garretson, ??? V, 965
Garretson, Aaron V, 492
Garretson, Almedia IV, 367
Garretson, Almedia IV, 395
Garretson, Amos IV, 331
Garretson, Amos IV, 472
Garretson, Amos IV, 525
Garretson, Amos IV, 526
Garretson, Amos IV, 560
Garretson, Angalina IV, 525
Garretson, Angelina IV, 526
Garretson, Angeline IV, 560
Garretson, Ann IV, 578
Garretson, Ann IV, 579
Garretson, Ann IV, 710
Garretson, Ann IV, 711
Garretson, Ann IV, 817
Garretson, Ann IV, 1030
Garretson, Ann P. IV, 711
Garretson, Ann P. IV, 1025
Garretson, Ann P. IV, 1028
Garretson, Anna IV, 33
Garretson, Anna IV, 65
Garretson, Anna IV, 146
Garretson, Anna IV, 204
Garretson, Anna IV, 394
Garretson, Anna IV, 472
Garretson, Anna IV, 710
Garretson, Anna IV, 1057
Garretson, Anna IV, 1058
Garretson, Anna M. IV, 711
Garretson, Anna M. IV, 714
Garretson, Anne IV, 817
Garretson, Anne P. IV, 1025
Garretson, Armel IV, 33
Garretson, Armela IV, 204
Garretson, Armele IV, 625
Garretson, Armella IV, 204
Garretson, Armella IV, 472
Garretson, Armella IV, 625
Garretson, Armelle IV, 146
Garretson, Asa IV, 146
Garretson, Asa IV, 204
Garretson, Asa IV, 383
Garretson, Asa IV, 394
Garretson, Asa IV, 576
Garretson, Asa IV, 578
Garretson, Asa IV, 579
Garretson, Asenath IV, 146
Garretson, Asenath IV, 386
Garretson, Asenath IV, 387
Garretson, Asenath IV, 394
Garretson, Asenath IV, 574
Garretson, Asenath IV, 578
Garretson, Asenith IV, 394
Garretson, Barclay IV, 710
Garretson, Barclay IV, 1025
Garretson, Beulah IV, 204
Garretson, Beulah IV, 235
Garretson, Beulah IV, 466
Garretson, Beulah IV, 472
Garretson, Beulah IV, 1057
Garretson, Beulah C. II, 865
Garretson, Bulah IV, 472
Garretson, Caspares IV, 33
Garretson, Casparis IV, 472
Garretson, Casparus IV, 146
Garretson, Casparus IV, 152
Garretson, Charles V, 59
Garretson, Charles F. V, 58
Garretson, Daniel IV, 1057
Garretson, David IV, 472
Garretson, David IV, 1057
Garretson, David IV, 1098
Garretson, David IV, 1132
Garretson, Eli IV, 472
Garretson, Eli IV, 673
Garretson, Eli IV, 692
Garretson, Eli IV, 710
Garretson, Eli IV, 711
Garretson, Eli IV, 817
Garretson, Eli IV, 1025
Garretson, Eli IV, 1057
Garretson, Eli IV, 1098
Garretson, Eli IV, 1132
Garretson, Eliakim II, 865
Garretson, Elijah II, 71
Garretson, Elisha IV, 331
Garretson, Eliza IV, 25
Garretson, Eliza IV, 33
Garretson, Eliza IV, 204
Garretson, Eliza IV, 466

Garretson, Eliza IV, 472
Garretson, Eliza IV, 509
Garretson, Eliza IV, 525
Garretson, Eliza IV, 526
Garretson, Eliza IV, 1057
Garretson, Eliza IV, 1088
Garretson, Eliza IV, 1098
Garretson, Eliza IV, 1128
Garretson, Eliza IV, 1132
Garretson, Eliza Ann II, 741
Garretson, Elizabeth IV, 146
Garretson, Elizabeth IV, 164
Garretson, Elizabeth IV, 392
Garretson, Elizabeth IV, 394
Garretson, Elizabeth IV, 395
Garretson, Elizabeth IV, 472
Garretson, Elizabeth IV, 574
Garretson, Elizabeth IV, 578
Garretson, ELizabeth IV, 600
Garretson, Elizabeth IV, 601
Garretson, Elizabeth IV, 1057
Garretson, Elizabeth IV, 1098
Garretson, Elizabeth IV, 1132
Garretson, Elizabeth V, 58
Garretson, Elizabeth R. II, 741
Garretson, Elizabeth R. II, 765
Garretson, Emily IV, 472
Garretson, Emily IV, 1057
Garretson, Emily IV, 1098
Garretson, Emily IV, 1114
Garretson, Emily S. IV, 1132
Garretson, Emily Sophia IV, 395
Garretson, Emily Sophia IV, 1132
Garretson, Franklin IV, 710
Garretson, Franklin IV, 1025
Garretson, George IV, 817
Garretson, George IV, 858
Garretson, Hannah IV, 146
Garretson, Hannah IV, 204
Garretson, Hannah IV, 331
Garretson, Hannah IV, 395
Garretson, Hannah IV, 472
Garretson, Hannah IV, 503
Garretson, Hannah IV, 578
Garretson, Hannah IV, 597
Garretson, Hannah IV, 673
Garretson, Hannah IV, 710
Garretson, Hannah IV, 817
Garretson, Hannah IV, 1132
Garretson, Hannah V, 492
Garretson, Hannah F. IV, 331
Garretson, Hannah J. II, 741
Garretson, Hannah J. II, 765
Garretson, Hannah L. IV, 560
Garretson, Hannah T. IV, 560
Garretson, Harriet I. II, 705
Garretson, Harriett S. II, 701
Garretson, Henrietta IV, 22
Garretson, Henrietta IV, 33
Garretson, Henrietta IV, 146
Garretson, Henrietta IV, 204
Garretson, Henrietta IV, 394
Garretson, Henrietta IV, 472
Garretson, Henrietta IV, 526
Garretson, Henrietta IV, 565
Garretson, Henrietta IV, 578
Garretson, Henrietta IV, 587
Garretson, Henrietta IV, 597
Garretson, Henrietta IV, 1058
Garretson, Hiram IV, 817
Garretson, Isaac IV, 466
Garretson, Isaac IV, 472
Garretson, Isaac IV, 578
Garretson, Isaac IV, 1057
Garretson, Isaac V, 59
Garretson, Isaac VI, 493
Garretson, Isaac H. V, 58
Garretson, Isaac P. IV, 578
Garretson, Isaac Parker IV, 204
Garretson, Isaac Parker IV, 578
Garretson, Jazar IV, 472
Garretson, Jazer IV, 204
Garretson, Jazer IV, 1025
Garretson, Jesse IV, 710
Garretson, Jesse IV, 711
Garretson, Jesse IV, 817
Garretson, Joanna IV, 33
Garretson, Joanna IV, 42
Garretson, Joel IV, 146
Garretson, Joel IV, 331
Garretson, Joel IV, 392
Garretson, Joel IV, 394
Garretson, Joel IV, 395
Garretson, Joel IV, 472
Garretson, Joel IV, 526
Garretson, Joel IV, 560
Garretson, Joel IV, 1057
Garretson, Joel IV, 1098
Garretson, Joel IV, 1132
Garretson, John IV, 22
Garretson, John IV, 33
Garretson, John IV, 146
Garretson, John IV, 204
Garretson, John IV, 394
Garretson, John IV, 472
Garretson, John IV, 526
Garretson, John IV, 565
Garretson, John IV, 587
Garretson, John IV, 597
Garretson, John IV, 710
Garretson, John IV, 711
Garretson, John IV, 750
Garretson, John IV, 817
Garretson, John IV, 1025
Garretson, John IV, 1030
Garretson, John IV, 1057
Garretson, John IV, 1058
Garretson, John IV, 1098
Garretson, John IV, 1132
Garretson, John V, 58
Garretson, John V, 59
Garretson, John V, 967
Garretson, John V, 969
Garretson, John V, 976
Garretson, John V, 977
Garretson, John V, 979
Garretson, Joseph II, 741
Garretson, Joseph II, 765
Garretson, Joseph IV, 33
Garretson, Joseph IV, 146
Garretson, Joseph IV, 164
Garretson, Joseph IV, 204
Garretson, Joseph IV, 365
Garretson, Joseph IV, 394
Garretson, Joseph IV, 395
Garretson, Joseph IV, 472
Garretson, Joseph IV, 519
Garretson, Joseph IV, 526
Garretson, Joseph IV, 574
Garretson, Joseph IV, 578
Garretson, Joseph IV, 710
Garretson, Joseph IV, 817
Garretson, Joseph F. IV, 571
Garretson, Joseph F. IV, 578
Garretson, Joseph F. IV, 1098
Garretson, Joseph L. V, 58
Garretson, Joseph L. V, 59
Garretson, Lavinia IV, 312
Garretson, Leora IV, 394
Garretson, Luceta IV, 526
Garretson, Luceta IV, 541
Garretson, Lucretia IV, 1025
Garretson, Lucretia M. IV, 673
Garretson, Lucretia M. IV, 710
Garretson, Lucretia M. IV, 711
Garretson, Lucretia M. IV, 1025
Garretson, Lydia II, 865
Garretson, Lydia V, 58
Garretson, Lydia V, 967
Garretson, Lydia V, 969
Garretson, Lydia M., Jr. II, 865
Garretson, Margaret V, 59
Garretson, Margaret V, 116
Garretson, Margaret A. IV, 711
Garretson, Maria IV, 710
Garretson, Maria IV, 750
Garretson, Maria M. IV, 710
Garretson, Mariah IV, 710
Garretson, Mariah IV, 711
Garretson, Mariah IV, 817
Garretson, Marsena IV, 1025
Garretson, Martha IV, 331
Garretson, Martha IV, 383
Garretson, Martha IV, 394
Garretson, Martha IV, 526
Garretson, Martha IV, 560
Garretson, Martha IV, 578
Garretson, Martha Luceta IV, 526
Garretson, Martha Lucetta IV, 331
Garretson, Martha Lucetta IV, 578
Garretson, Martha Lucette IV, 343
Garretson, Mary IV, 33
Garretson, Mary IV, 65
Garretson, Mary IV, 146
Garretson, Mary IV, 152
Garretson, Mary IV, 153
Garretson, Mary IV, 204
Garretson, Mary IV, 331
Garretson, Mary IV, 394
Garretson, Mary IV, 472
Garretson, Mary IV, 525
Garretson, Mary IV, 526
Garretson, Mary IV, 578
Garretson, Mary IV, 1025
Garretson, Mary IV, 1098
Garretson, Mary IV, 1132
Garretson, Mary V, 906
Garretson, Mary Ann IV, 319
Garretson, Mary Ann IV, 331
Garretson, Mary Ann IV, 472
Garretson, Mary Ann IV, 479
Garretson, Mary Ann IV, 526
Garretson, Mary Ann IV, 560
Garretson, Mary Ann IV, 686
Garretson, Mary Ann IV, 710
Garretson, Mary Ann IV, 711
Garretson, Mary Anne IV, 525
Garretson, Mary E. I, 1152
Garretson, Mary E. I, 1162
Garretson, Melvina IV, 365
Garretson, Melvina IV, 394
Garretson, Mot IV, 1025
Garretson, Nancy IV, 331
Garretson, Nathan IV, 472
Garretson, Newton IV, 1025
Garretson, Nicholas IV, 541
Garretson, Ora IV, 395
Garretson, Patience IV, 33
Garretson, Patience IV, 146
Garretson, Patience IV, 204
Garretson, Patience IV, 472
Garretson, Patience IV, 565
Garretson, Patience IV, 578
Garretson, Peggy IV, 525
Garretson, Peggy IV, 526
Garretson, Peggy IV, 560
Garretson, Peirce IV, 710
Garretson, Penina IV, 578
Garretson, Phebe V, 58
Garretson, Phebe V, 969
Garretson, Phebe V, 977
Garretson, Pierce IV, 710
Garretson, Pierce IV, 744
Garretson, Pierce IV, 817
Garretson, Pierce IV, 835
Garretson, Pierce IV, 1021
Garretson, Pierce IV, 1025
Garretson, Price IV, 710
Garretson, Rachel II, 71
Garretson, Rachel II, 79
Garretson, Rachel IV, 33
Garretson, Rachel IV, 472
Garretson, Rachel IV, 482
Garretson, Rachel IV, 1098
Garretson, Rachel IV, 1127
Garretson, Rachel IV, 1132
Garretson, Rebecca IV, 204
Garretson, Rebecca IV, 578
Garretson, Rebecca IV, 587
Garretson, Rebecca IV, 710
Garretson, Rebecca IV, 711
Garretson, Rebecca IV, 757
Garretson, Rebecca IV, 817
Garretson, Rebecca IV, 1025
Garretson, Rebecca IV, 1030
Garretson, Rebecca V, 58
Garretson, Rebecca V, 59
Garretson, Rebecca V, 967
Garretson, Rebecca V, 976
Garretson, Rebecca V, 977
Garretson, Rebecca V, 979
Garretson, Rebecca E. IV, 1025
Garretson, Rebecca Elma IV, 1025
Garretson, Rebecca J. V, 59
Garretson, Rebecca Jane V, 59
Garretson, Rebecca Maria IV, 710
Garretson, Rebecca W. IV, 710
Garretson, Rebecca W. IV, 711
Garretson, Rebecca W. IV, 750
Garretson, Reuben L. V, 59
Garretson, Reuben T. V, 58
Garretson, Reuben T. V, 70
Garretson, Rhoda V, 58
Garretson, Rhoda V, 969
Garretson, Rhoda V, 976
Garretson, Richard IV, 1057
Garretson, Richard IV, 1098
Garretson, Richard IV, 1132
Garretson, Rueben T. V, 969
Garretson, Rueben T. V, 971
Garretson, Ruth IV, 204
Garretson, Ruth IV, 383
Garretson, Ruth IV, 394
Garretson, Ruth IV, 576
Garretson, Ruth IV, 578
Garretson, Ruth IV, 579
Garretson, Ruth Ann IV, 710
Garretson, Ruth Ann IV, 711
Garretson, Ruth Ann IV, 734
Garretson, Ruth Anna V, 969
Garretson, Ruth Anna V, 970
Garretson, Ruthanna IV, 1057
Garretson, Ruthanna IV, 1098
Garretson, Ruthanna IV, 1132
Garretson, Ruthanna IV, 1140
Garretson, Ruthanna V, 58
Garretson, Samantha M. IV, 710
Garretson, Samantha M. IV, 1025
Garretson, Samuel, Jr. V, 58
Garretson, Sarah IV, 33
Garretson, Sarah IV, 146
Garretson, Sarah IV, 152
Garretson, Sarah IV, 204
Garretson, Sarah IV, 331
Garretson, Sarah IV, 342
Garretson, Sarah IV, 472
Garretson, Sarah IV, 526
Garretson, Sarah IV, 541
Garretson, Sarah IV, 571
Garretson, Sarah IV, 578
Garretson, Sarah IV, 589
Garretson, Sarah IV, 673
Garretson, Sarah IV, 711
Garretson, Sarah IV, 1025
Garretson, Sarah IV, 1057
Garretson, Sarah IV, 1098
Garretson, Sarah IV, 1111
Garretson, Sarah V, 58
Garretson, Sarah V, 59
Garretson, Sarah V, 70
Garretson, Sarah V, 969
Garretson, Sarah V, 971
Garretson, Sarah C. IV, 526
Garretson, Sarah C. IV, 578
Garretson, Sarah H. IV, 710
Garretson, Sarah H. IV, 744
Garretson, Sarah H. IV, 817
Garretson, Sarah H. IV, 835
Garretson, Sarah I. IV, 692
Garretson, Sarah I. IV, 710
Garretson, Sarah J. IV, 1025
Garretson, Sarah Jr. IV, 519
Garretson, Sarah Michener IV, 331
Garretson, Sarah W. IV, 1021
Garretson, Sidney IV, 710
Garretson, Sidney IV, 817
Garretson, Susanna IV, 1098
Garretson, Tabitha II, 71
Garretson, Talbert IV, 560
Garretson, Talbot IV, 331
Garretson, Talboth IV, 525
Garretson, Talbott IV, 472
Garretson, Talbott IV, 526
Garretson, Thomas V, 58
Garretson, Thomas V, 59
Garretson, Thomas V, 492
Garretson, Townsend II, 71
Garretson, William IV, 33
Garretson, William IV, 65
Garretson, William IV, 394
Garretson, William IV, 472
Garretson, William IV, 1057
Garretson, William IV, 1098
Garretson, William IV, 1132
Garretson, Wm. IV, 146
Garretson, Wm. IV, 152
Garretson, Wm. IV, 153
Garretson, Wm. IV, 1057
Garretson, Wm. IV, 1098
Garrett, Aaron II, 948
Garrett, Abel Noble II, 529
Garrett, Abigail I, 810
Garrett, Abner VI, 919
Garrett, Absolem VI, 819
Garrett, Alexander III, 132
Garrett, Alice III, 132
Garrett, Alice Biardot III, 132
Garrett, Alice Biardot III, 145
Garrett, Amelia III, 132
Garrett, Andrew Orvil V, 387
Garrett, Angelina Mary Jane VI, 919
Garrett, Ann II, 365
Garrett, Ann IV, 33
Garrett, Ann IV, 35
Garrett, Ann E. VI, 973
Garrett, Anna I, 879
Garrett, Anna II, 705
Garrett, Anna II, 721
Garrett, Anna Mary II, 865
Garrett, Anne II, 365
Garrett, Anne II, 741
Garrett, Annie II, 773
Garrett, Benjamin II, 795
Garrett, Benjamin II, 865
Garrett, Benjamin F. II, 851
Garrett, Benjamin G. VI, 980
Garrett, Bernard VI, 919
Garrett, Bernard VI, 937
Garrett, Betsy VI, 819
Garrett, Beulah I, 811
Garrett, Beulah I, 956
Garrett, Bulah I, 810
Garrett, Caleb I, 810
Garrett, Caleb I, 811
Garrett, Caleb I, 956
Garrett, Caleb I, 962
Garrett, Caroline I, 811
Garrett, Cath. Ann III, 132
Garrett, Catharine W. II, 865
Garrett, Catharine W. II, 925
Garrett, Catherine V, 240
Garrett, Charity IV, 902
Garrett, Charity IV, 913
Garrett, Charles L. II, 865
Garrett, Charles Leroy V, 387
Garrett, Charles Lewis II, 795
Garrett, Chas. L. II, 865
Garrett, Chas. L. II, 893
Garrett, Cyrus I, 810
Garrett, Cyrus I, 956
Garrett, David II, 705
Garrett, Dorothea F. III, 132
Garrett, Dorothy III, 70
Garrett, Dorothy III, 132
Garrett, Effie Viola V, 387
Garrett, Elijah VI, 819
Garrett, Eliz. III, 132
Garrett, Eliza I, 811
Garrett, Elizabeth II, 365
Garrett, Elizabeth II, 699
Garrett, Elizabeth II, 820
Garrett, Elizabeth VI, 38
Garrett, Elizabeth Biddle II, 705
Garrett, Elizabeth Biddle II, 741
Garrett, Elizabeth C. II, 741
Garrett, Elizabeth Williams VI, 819
Garrett, Emily I, 811
Garrett, Florence E. II, 789
Garrett, Florence E. II, 851
Garrett, Florence E. II, 865
Garrett, Frances II, 705
Garrett, Frances II, 728
Garrett, Frances II, 741
Garrett, Frances VI, 850
Garrett, Frances VI, 919
Garrett, Frances B. II, 705
Garrett, Frances B. II, 741
Garrett, George II, 795
Garrett, Hanah II, 529
Garrett, Hannah II, 365
Garrett, Hannah II, 795
Garrett, Hannah A. II, 865
Garrett, Hannah Ashbridge II, 795
Garrett, Helen III, 132
Garrett, Helen III, 294
Garrett, Henrietta II, 365
Garrett, Henrietta II, 529
Garrett, Henrietta II, 741
Garrett, Henrietta II, 772
Garrett, Henry III, 132
Garrett, Henry VI, 919
Garrett, Henry A. III, 132
Garrett, Hibbard II, 865
Garrett, Hibberd II, 795
Garrett, Hibberd II, 865
Garrett, Hiram I, 986
Garrett, Irene Marie III, 132
Garrett, Isham V, 240
Garrett, Isom I, 962
Garrett, Jacob VI, 919
Garrett, James II, 365
Garrett, James Creson II, 365
Garrett, Jane II, 795
Garrett, Jane II, 827
Garrett, Jesse II, 741
Garrett, John VI, 798
Garrett, John VI, 819
Garrett, John VI, 1020
Garrett, John Biddle II, 705
Garrett, John Biddle II, 741
Garrett, John G. VI, 919
Garrett, John K. II, 365
Garrett, John K. II, 529
Garrett, John Knowles II, 529
Garrett, Jonathan I, 986
Garrett, Joseph IV, 902
Garrett, Joseph IV, 913
Garrett, Joseph V, 387
Garrett, Joseph G. V, 387
Garrett, Joshua I, 962
Garrett, Josiah VI, 819
Garrett, Josiah VI, 985
Garrett, Josiah Gilbert I, 879
Garrett, July Ann I, 811
Garrett, Katheren VI, 37
Garrett, Katheren VI, 38
Garrett, Kathren VI, 38
Garrett, Laura B. III, 132
Garrett, Lena Nelson II, 795
Garrett, Lena Nelson II, 893
Garrett, Lewis I, 962
Garrett, Lewis Jones II, 365
Garrett, Lewis Jones II, 741
Garrett, Lewis P. II, 865
Garrett, Lucile E. III, 132
Garrett, Lucille E. III, 300

Garrett, Margaret I, 986
Garrett, Margaret II, 365
Garrett, Margaret II, 712
Garrett, Margaret II, 741
Garrett, Margaret II, 765
Garrett, Margarett VI, 38
Garrett, Marget VI, 919
Garrett, Margret I, 960
Garrett, Margrett VI, 38
Garrett, Maris III, 132
Garrett, Martha VI, 919
Garrett, Martha H. II, 365
Garrett, Martha H. II, 705
Garrett, Martha N. II, 741
Garrett, Martha Price II, 865
Garrett, Mary II, 608
Garrett, Mary II, 795
Garrett, Mary III, 132
Garrett, Mary III, 142
Garrett, Mary III, 145
Garrett, Mary III, 294
Garrett, Mary IV, 523
Garrett, Mary VI, 919
Garrett, Mary Ann VI, 985
Garrett, Mary Ann VI, 1020
Garrett, Mary B. IV, 204
Garrett, Mary E. V, 387
Garrett, Mary H. II, 865
Garrett, Mary J. VI, 973
Garrett, Mary Jane II, 865
Garrett, Maurice II, 865
Garrett, Maurice II, 925
Garrett, Minnie II, 795
Garrett, Molly VI, 919
Garrett, Nancy VI, 819
Garrett, Nathan I, 810
Garrett, Nathan II, 795
Garrett, Ophelia V, 246
Garrett, Patsy VI, 919
Garrett, Peggy VI, 919
Garrett, Percy H. II, 865
Garrett, Percy Hickman II, 795
Garrett, Philip II, 365
Garrett, Philip II, 497
Garrett, Philip II, 529
Garrett, Philip II, 728
Garrett, Philip II, 741
Garrett, Philip II, 765
Garrett, Philip C. II, 705
Garrett, Philip C. II, 741
Garrett, Philip, Jr. II, 741
Garrett, Polly VI, 919
Garrett, Rachel Davis II, 829
Garrett, Reason VI, 919
Garrett, Rebecca II, 365
Garrett, Rebecca II, 497
Garrett, Rebecca II, 529
Garrett, Rebecca II, 705
Garrett, Rebecca II, 728
Garrett, Rebecca II, 741
Garrett, Rebecca II, 765
Garrett, Rebecca V, 240
Garrett, Rebecca C. II, 741
Garrett, Robert T. II, 865
Garrett, Samuel L. II, 741
Garrett, Sarah I, 49
Garrett, Sarah I, 53
Garrett, Sarah II, 365
Garrett, Sarah II, 497
Garrett, Sarah II, 510
Garrett, Sarah II, 529
Garrett, Sarah II, 588
Garrett, Sarah II, 795
Garrett, Sarah III, 132
Garrett, Sarah IV, 902
Garrett, Sarah IV, 913
Garrett, Sarah VI, 819
Garrett, Sarah K. III, 132
Garrett, Sarah T. II, 851
Garrett, Sophia I, 49
Garrett, Sophia I, 53
Garrett, Stark VI, 819
Garrett, Stark B. VI, 919
Garrett, Stark B. VI, 972
Garrett, Stark B. VI, 973
Garrett, Stark B. VI, 1020
Garrett, Stephen VI, 819
Garrett, Stephenson P. II, 865
Garrett, Susan VI, 819
Garrett, Susan T. II, 865
Garrett, Susanna VI, 798
Garrett, Susanna N. II, 365
Garrett, Susannah H. II, 741
Garrett, T. Ellwood II, 741
Garrett, T. Elwood II, 705
Garrett, Thomas II, 365
Garrett, Thomas II, 497
Garrett, Thomas II, 529
Garrett, Thomas II, 705
Garrett, Thomas III, 132
Garrett, Thomas III, 145
Garrett, Thomas III, 294
Garrett, Thomas III, 300
Garrett, Thomas VI, 919
Garrett, Thomas C. II, 728
Garrett, Thomas C. II, 741
Garrett, Thomas S. III, 132
Garrett, Thomas S. III, 142
Garrett, Thos. II, 795
Garrett, Thos. II, 865
Garrett, Thos. II, 925
Garrett, Thos. III, 132
Garrett, Thos. III, 145
Garrett, Victor III, 70
Garrett, Victor III, 132
Garrett, Virginia J. II, 865
Garrett, Welcom I, 960
Garrett, Welcom I, 962
Garrett, Welcome I, 986
Garrett, William I, 879
Garrett, William II, 365
Garrett, William V, 387
Garrett, William VI, 38
Garrett, William VI, 919
Garrett, William S. IV, 204
Garrett, Wm. II, 529
Garrett, Wm. VI, 919
Garrett, Wm. H. II, 865
Garrett, Wm. Hickman II, 795
Garrett, Wm. L. II, 865
Garrett, Wm. Lewis II, 795
Garrettson, Eliakim II, 795
Garrettson, Lydia II, 795
Garrettson, Lydia M., Jr. II, 865
Garrettson, Lydia Maria II, 795
Garrigas, Charles IV, 817
Garrigas, Deborah IV, 817
Garrigas, Helen IV, 817
Garrigas, Helen M. IV, 817
Garrigas, Margaret E. IV, 817
Garrigas, Sally Ann IV, 817
Garriges, Samuel II, 365
Garrigue, Benjamin II, 365
Garrigue, Isaac II, 365
Garrigue, John II, 550
Garrigue, Joseph II, 365
Garrigue, Martha II, 365
Garrigue, Mary II, 550
Garrigue, Rebecca II, 550
Garrigue, Sarah VI, 474
Garrigue, Susannah II, 365
Garrigue, William II, 365
Garrigues, Abraham II, 365
Garrigues, Abraham II, 529
Garrigues, Abraham II, 530
Garrigues, Abraham II, 591
Garrigues, Abraham II, 865
Garrigues, Abraham M. II, 741
Garrigues, Abraham Mitchell II, 795
Garrigues, Alfred Haydock II, 795
Garrigues, Alfred Linde IV, 711
Garrigues, Ann II, 365
Garrigues, Ann II, 529
Garrigues, Ann II, 569
Garrigues, Ann H. IV, 711
Garrigues, Anna H. IV, 711
Garrigues, Anna Lee II, 311
Garrigues, Benjamin II, 365
Garrigues, Benjamin II, 529
Garrigues, Benjamin D. II, 530
Garrigues, Benjamin D. II, 742
Garrigues, Benjamin Franklin II, 529
Garrigues, Benjamin Tucker II, 795
Garrigues, Caspar II, 530
Garrigues, Caspar H. II, 741
Garrigues, Charles IV, 905
Garrigues, Charles H. II, 742
Garrigues, Charles Tanguy II, 530
Garrigues, Chas. P. II, 795
Garrigues, Christian II, 365
Garrigues, Christian II, 472
Garrigues, Deborah IV, 905
Garrigues, Deborah M. II, 530
Garrigues, Deborah M. II, 742
Garrigues, Edw. B. II, 530
Garrigues, Edward II, 365
Garrigues, Edward II, 529
Garrigues, Edward II, 530
Garrigues, Edward II, 627
Garrigues, Edward II, 865
Garrigues, Edward IV, 711
Garrigues, Edward B. II, 365
Garrigues, Edward B. II, 530
Garrigues, Edward B. II, 705
Garrigues, Edward B. II, 741
Garrigues, Edward B. II, 932
Garrigues, Edward H. II, 530
Garrigues, Edward H. II, 742
Garrigues, Edward H. IV, 711
Garrigues, Edward James II, 795
Garrigues, Eliza Ann II, 795
Garrigues, Elizabeth II, 529
Garrigues, Elizabeth II, 530
Garrigues, Elizabeth II, 654
Garrigues, Elizabeth II, 742
Garrigues, Elizabeth II, 771
Garrigues, Elizabeth II, 795
Garrigues, Elizabeth II, 865
Garrigues, Elizabeth IV, 905
Garrigues, Elizabeth H. II, 865
Garrigues, Elizabeth Haydock II, 365
Garrigues, Elizabeth Hill II, 795
Garrigues, Elizabeth M. II, 865
Garrigues, Elizabeth M. II, 917
Garrigues, Elizabeth M. II, 918
Garrigues, Elizabeth M. II, 924
Garrigues, Elizabeth Magdalen II, 795
Garrigues, Elmsley II, 529
Garrigues, Ester II, 530
Garrigues, Esther II, 365
Garrigues, Esther II, 530
Garrigues, Esther II, 591
Garrigues, Esther II, 741
Garrigues, Esther II, 795
Garrigues, Esther, Jr. II, 742
Garrigues, Francis Middleton II, 795
Garrigues, George B. II, 865
Garrigues, Guli Elma IV, 711
Garrigues, Gulielma IV, 711
Garrigues, Gulielma W. II, 742
Garrigues, Gulielma W. II, 747
Garrigues, Gulielma W. IV, 711
Garrigues, Hannah II, 529
Garrigues, Hannah II, 530
Garrigues, Hannah II, 544
Garrigues, Hannah II, 795
Garrigues, Hannah IV, 905
Garrigues, Hannah B. II, 865
Garrigues, Hannah B. II, 924
Garrigues, Hannah Humphreys II, 530
Garrigues, Hannah Marshall II, 530
Garrigues, Hannah Marshall II, 741
Garrigues, Hannah S. II, 530
Garrigues, Hannah S. II, 544
Garrigues, Haydock II, 365
Garrigues, Helen IV, 905
Garrigues, Helen IV, 906
Garrigues, Henry H. II, 865
Garrigues, Henry Hill II, 795
Garrigues, Henry M. II, 365
Garrigues, Henry M. II, 741
Garrigues, Hetty Marshall II, 795
Garrigues, Humphrey II, 705
Garrigues, Humphreys II, 742
Garrigues, Isaac II, 365
Garrigues, Isaac II, 472
Garrigues, Isaac II, 529
Garrigues, Isaac II, 553
Garrigues, Isaac II, 626
Garrigues, Isaac B. II, 530
Garrigues, Isaac B. II, 544
Garrigues, Isaac, Jr. II, 529
Garrigues, Jacob II, 365
Garrigues, Jacob II, 529
Garrigues, James II, 529
Garrigues, James II, 918
Garrigues, James R. II, 865
Garrigues, James R. II, 917
Garrigues, James R. II, 918
Garrigues, James R. II, 924
Garrigues, James Ralph II, 365
Garrigues, James Ralph II, 795
Garrigues, John II, 365
Garrigues, John II, 521
Garrigues, John II, 529
Garrigues, John II, 550
Garrigues, John II, 609
Garrigues, John II, 795
Garrigues, Joseph II, 365
Garrigues, Joseph Cruckshank II, 705
Garrigues, Joseph Crukshanks II, 742
Garrigues, Lizzie H. II, 865
Garrigues, Lizzie H. II, 917
Garrigues, Lydia S. II, 365
Garrigues, Lydia S. II, 865
Garrigues, Lydia S. II, 932
Garrigues, Lydia Smith II, 824
Garrigues, Lydis S. II, 741
Garrigues, Margaret II, 529
Garrigues, Margaret II, 530
Garrigues, Margaret II, 627
Garrigues, Margaret II, 705
Garrigues, Margaret II, 742
Garrigues, Margaret IV, 711
Garrigues, Margaret C. II, 705
Garrigues, Margaret H. II, 742
Garrigues, Margaret H. II, 747
Garrigues, Margaretta C. II, 742
Garrigues, Maria IV, 900
Garrigues, Maria IV, 905
Garrigues, Marshall II, 742
Garrigues, Marshall II, 795
Garrigues, Martha II, 365
Garrigues, Mary II, 365
Garrigues, Mary II, 470
Garrigues, Mary II, 529
Garrigues, Mary II, 530
Garrigues, Mary II, 546
Garrigues, Mary II, 569
Garrigues, Mary II, 591
Garrigues, Mary II, 599
Garrigues, Mary II, 741
Garrigues, Mary II, 795
Garrigues, Mary II, 865
Garrigues, Mary III, 132
Garrigues, Mary III, 165
Garrigues, Mary Ann II, 530
Garrigues, Mary Ann II, 741
Garrigues, Mary Ann IV, 905
Garrigues, Mary M. II, 850
Garrigues, Mary M. II, 865
Garrigues, Mary M. II, 918
Garrigues, Mary Miller II, 795
Garrigues, Mary Ralph II, 529
Garrigues, Mathew II, 472
Garrigues, Mathew II, 529
Garrigues, Rachel II, 365
Garrigues, Rachel II, 529
Garrigues, Rachel II, 566
Garrigues, Ralph II, 530
Garrigues, Rebecca II, 365
Garrigues, Rebecca II, 529
Garrigues, Rebecca II, 546
Garrigues, Rebecca II, 550
Garrigues, Rebecca II, 609
Garrigues, Rebecca II, 639
Garrigues, Rebecca C. II, 705
Garrigues, Rebecca C. II, 741
Garrigues, Rebeckah II, 529
Garrigues, Richard IV, 905
Garrigues, Richard H. II, 530
Garrigues, Richard H. II, 742
Garrigues, Richard H. IV, 711
Garrigues, Robert Steel II, 795
Garrigues, Sally Ann IV, 905
Garrigues, Samuel II, 365
Garrigues, Samuel II, 470
Garrigues, Samuel II, 529
Garrigues, Samuel II, 530
Garrigues, Samuel II, 546
Garrigues, Samuel II, 569
Garrigues, Samuel II, 599
Garrigues, Samuel J. II, 365
Garrigues, Samuel P. II, 365
Garrigues, Samuel P. II, 705
Garrigues, Samuel S. II, 741
Garrigues, Samuel Smith II, 705
Garrigues, Samuel, Jr. II, 365
Garrigues, Samuel, Jr. II, 529
Garrigues, Samuel, Jr. II, 546
Garrigues, Sarah II, 365
Garrigues, Sarah II, 521
Garrigues, Sarah II, 529
Garrigues, Sarah II, 553
Garrigues, Sarah II, 626
Garrigues, Sarah II, 705
Garrigues, Sarah II, 865
Garrigues, Sarah II, 932
Garrigues, Sarah Ann II, 705
Garrigues, Sarah Ann IV, 905
Garrigues, Sarah G. II, 530
Garrigues, Sarah G. II, 741
Garrigues, Sarah Marshall II, 530
Garrigues, Sarah Marshall II, 741
Garrigues, Sarah P. II, 530
Garrigues, Sarah P. II, 742
Garrigues, Susan II, 38
Garrigues, Susanna II, 365
Garrigues, Susanna II, 521
Garrigues, Susanna II, 529
Garrigues, Susanna II, 546
Garrigues, Susannah II, 365
Garrigues, Susannah II, 529
Garrigues, Susannah II, 799
Garrigues, Tacy II, 530
Garrigues, Tacy II, 742
Garrigues, Thomas II, 365
Garrigues, Thomas II, 529
Garrigues, William II, 365
Garrigues, William II, 705
Garrigues, William II, 795
Garrigues, William IV, 711
Garrigues, William IV, 905
Garrigues, William A. II, 795
Garrigues, William H. IV, 711
Garrigues, William Henry IV, 7
Garrigues, Wm. II, 529
Garrigues, Wm. II, 530
Garrigues, Wm. II, 544
Garrigues, Wm. II, 591
Garrigues, Wm. II, 599
Garrigues, Wm. II, 742
Garrigues, Wm. II, 747
Garrigues, Wm. II, 795
Garrigues, Wm. IV, 956
Garrigues, Wm. A. II, 741
Garrigues, Wm. A. II, 865
Garrigues, Wm. Henry II, 530
Garrigues, Wm. Henry II, 742
Garrigues, Wm. Henry II, 747
Garrigues, Wm. Henry IV, 711
Garrigues, Wm., Jr. II, 530
Garriguis, Richard H. IV, 711
Garrigus, A. L. IV, 1251
Garrigus, A. S. IV, 1251
Garrigus, Benjamin Franklin II, 529
Garrigus, Deborah IV, 905
Garrigus, Edward II, 529
Garrigus, Edward H. IV, 711
Garrigus, Elizabeth M. II, 148
Garrigus, Hannah II, 529
Garrigus, Hannah B. II, 148
Garrigus, Helen M. IV, 817
Garrigus, Isaac II, 529
Garrigus, James II, 148
Garrigus, Lydia IV, 1251
Garrigus, Margaret II, 529
Garrigus, Margaret IV, 891
Garrigus, Margaret IV, 892
Garrigus, Mary II, 529
Garrigus, Mary Ralph II, 529
Garrigus, Samuel IV, 1251
Garrihus, Helen M. IV, 819
Garris, Charity I, 288
Garris, Chase I, 306
Garris, Chasey I, 283
Garris, Exum I, 288
Garris, Gradda I, 288
Garris, Gradda I, 301
Garris, Gradda I, 306
Garris, Grady I, 306
Garris, Ida IV, 204
Garris, Joshua I, 283
Garris, Joshua I, 288
Garris, Joshua I, 306
Garris, Katie IV, 204
Garris, Martha IV, 204
Garris, Sarah I, 288
Garris, Sarah I, 301
Garris, Sarah I, 306
Garris, Temperance I, 283
Garris, Temperance I, 301
Garris, Temperance I, 306
Garris, Wiley I, 306
Garris, Wilie I, 306
Garris, William VI, 1017
Garris, Zachariah I, 288
Garris, Zachariah I, 306
Garrison, Alice I, 1009
Garrison, Alice I, 1011
Garrison, Anna IV, 87
Garrison, Anna IV, 113
Garrison, Catherine II, 365
Garrison, Eleanor II, 51
Garrison, Eleanor Ashton II, 71
Garrison, Elizabeth I, 879
Garrison, Elonar II, 71
Garrison, Elonar II, 99
Garrison, Esther II, 71
Garrison, George Walker IV, 86
Garrison, Hannah II, 71
Garrison, Hannah II, 108
Garrison, Hester III, 132
Garrison, Jacob II, 71
Garrison, Jacob II, 99
Garrison, Jeanne H. VI, 819
Garrison, John III, 132
Garrison, John R. VI, 819
Garrison, Levina IV, 312
Garrison, Lillie V, 674
Garrison, Rachel II, 69
Garrison, Rachel II, 71
Garrison, Rachel Fisher II, 71
Garrison, Rebecca IV, 986
Garrison, Richard II, 71
Garrison, Sarah I, 879
Garrison, Sarah I, 880
Garrison, Sarah I, 897

Garrison, Susana II, 71
Garrison, Thomas I, 811
Garrison, Thomas I, 853
Garrison, Thomas I, 879
Garrison, Thomas I, 897
Garrison, William IV, 1025
Garrod, Julia VI, 919
Garrod, Thomas B. VI, 919
Garrot, Elizabeth VI, 858
Garrot, Else I, 1060
Garrot, Else I, 1061
Garrot, Gregory, Elizabeth I, 1061
Garrot, John VI, 858
Garrott, Benjamin VI, 827
Garrott, Elijah VI, 798
Garrott, Eliza VI, 828
Garrott, John VI, 828
Garrott, John VI, 850
Garrott, Lucretia VI, 850
Garrott, William VI, 828
Garry, Elizabeth IV, 1251
Garthright, Judith VI, 177
Garthright, William VI, 161
Garthright, William VI, 177
Garthright, William VI, 220
Garthrite, Ephraim VI, 177
Gartley, Ann II, 742
Gartley, Ann H. II, 705
Gartley, Samuel II, 742
Gartright, Judith VI, 177
Gartright, Judith VI, 188
Gartrill, John VI, 359
Gartrite, Eph VI, 177
Gartrite, Epham VI, 177
Gartrite, Ephm VI, 177
Gartrite, Ephraim VI, 177
Gartrite, Ephrim VI, 177
Gartrite, Frans VI, 177
Gartrite, Jane VI, 177
Gartrite, John VI, 177
Gartrite, Judith VI, 177
Gartrite, Samuel VI, 177
Gartrite, William VI, 177
Garvin, Ann VI, 819
Garvin, Elizabeth VI, 819
Garvin, Elizabeth VI, 850
Garvin, Emily VI, 919
Garvin, Hugh VI, 819
Garvin, Jane V, 997
Garvin, John J. VI, 918
Garvin, John J. VI, 919
Garvin, Martha L. VI, 819
Garvin, Nancy VI, 860
Garvin, Robert T. VI, 819
Garvin, Susanna VI, 850
Garvin, Thomas VI, 819
Garvin, William VI, 860
Garvis, Eliza F. VI, 819
Garvis, Gilliam M. VI, 819
Garwood, Abijah V, 59
Garwood, Abner Fawcett IV, 956
Garwood, Abraham II, 365
Garwood, Abraham IV, 33
Garwood, Abraham IV, 87
Garwood, Abraham IV, 101
Garwood, Abram IV, 973
Garwood, Adam IV, 711
Garwood, Alice II, 223
Garwood, Alice IV, 625
Garwood, Alice IV, 626
Garwood, Allen II, 318
Garwood, Allen, Jr. II, 318
Garwood, Allice IV, 87
Garwood, Amy II, 223
Garwood, Ann IV, 663
Garwood, Ann IV, 711
Garwood, Ann IV, 817
Garwood, Ann Eliza IV, 626
Garwood, Ann Eliza IV, 711
Garwood, Ann Eliza IV, 817
Garwood, Anna IV, 626
Garwood, Anna P. IV, 817
Garwood, Anna P. IV, 956
Garwood, Anna Priscilla IV, 626
Garwood, Anna Priscilla IV, 711
Garwood, Anna Priscilla IV, 817
Garwood, Anna Priscilla IV, 932
Garwood, Anna Priscilla IV, 956
Garwood, Anne IV, 626
Garwood, Annie Priscilla IV, 956
Garwood, Asa IV, 626
Garwood, Ascenath H. IV, 956
Garwood, Ascenith IV, 817
Garwood, Asenath IV, 711
Garwood, Asenath IV, 817
Garwood, Asenath H. IV, 711
Garwood, Asenath H. IV, 956
Garwood, Asenith IV, 711
Garwood, Assenath IV, 626
Garwood, Barzilla VI, 742
Garwood, Barzillai II, 223
Garwood, Benjamin IV, 711
Garwood, Benjamin V. IV, 87
Garwood, Beulah II, 318
Garwood, Cattell IV, 87
Garwood, Charity II, 223
Garwood, Charity IV, 33
Garwood, Charity IV, 41
Garwood, Cloak IV, 1279
Garwood, Cynthia Ann IV, 1279
Garwood, Daniel II, 1087
Garwood, Daniel IV, 33
Garwood, Daniel IV, 625
Garwood, Daniel IV, 626
Garwood, Daniel IV, 635
Garwood, Daniel IV, 663
Garwood, Daniel IV, 711
Garwood, Daniel V, 59
Garwood, Daniel VI, 390
Garwood, Daniel VI, 591
Garwood, Daniel VI, 596
Garwood, Daniel, Jr. IV, 626
Garwood, Darby IV, 87
Garwood, David IV, 87
Garwood, David IV, 626
Garwood, David IV, 711
Garwood, David C. IV, 711
Garwood, Deborah V, 59
Garwood, Deborah V, 127
Garwood, Deborah VI, 596
Garwood, Dorothy II, 223
Garwood, Dorothy II, 231
Garwood, Edith G. IV, 87
Garwood, Edith G. IV, 973
Garwood, Edward VI, 591
Garwood, Elener II, 223
Garwood, Elener II, 246
Garwood, Eli H. IV, 87
Garwood, Elias IV, 625
Garwood, Elias IV, 626
Garwood, Eliza IV, 817
Garwood, Elizabeth II, 223
Garwood, Elizabeth IV, 85
Garwood, Elizabeth IV, 87
Garwood, Elizabeth IV, 99
Garwood, Elizabeth IV, 614
Garwood, Elizabeth IV, 623
Garwood, Elizabeth IV, 626
Garwood, Elizabeth IV, 952
Garwood, Elizabeth IV, 956
Garwood, Elizabeth IV, 1273
Garwood, Elizabeth IV, 1279
Garwood, Elizabeth V, 952
Garwood, Elizabeth VI, 390
Garwood, Elizabeth Jane IV, 626
Garwood, Elizabeth Jane IV, 711
Garwood, Elizabeth Jane IV, 817
Garwood, Emeline II, 318
Garwood, Emiline II, 318
Garwood, Empson H. II, 318
Garwood, Esther IV, 33
Garwood, Esther IV, 625
Garwood, Esther IV, 626
Garwood, Esther IV, 658
Garwood, Esther V, 59
Garwood, Esther VI, 390
Garwood, Esther VI, 595
Garwood, Esther VI, 596
Garwood, Esther VI, 597
Garwood, Esther VI, 598
Garwood, Esther VI, 600
Garwood, Esther VI, 604
Garwood, George IV, 626
Garwood, Griffith IV, 87
Garwood, Hannah II, 223
Garwood, Hannah IV, 33
Garwood, Hannah IV, 626
Garwood, Hannah IV, 638
Garwood, Hannah V, 59
Garwood, Hannah VI, 390
Garwood, Hannah VI, 596
Garwood, Hannah VI, 604
Garwood, Hester IV, 658
Garwood, Hezekiah II, 174
Garwood, Hezekiah II, 223
Garwood, Hope IV, 33
Garwood, Hope IV, 625
Garwood, Hope IV, 626
Garwood, Hope IV, 635
Garwood, Hope VI, 390
Garwood, Hope VI, 595
Garwood, Hope VI, 596
Garwood, Hope VI, 598
Garwood, Isaac IV, 625
Garwood, Isaac IV, 626
Garwood, Isaah VI, 390
Garwood, Isaiah IV, 33
Garwood, Isaiah IV, 623
Garwood, Isaiah IV, 625
Garwood, Isaiah IV, 626
Garwood, Isaiah IV, 635
Garwood, Isaiah IV, 638
Garwood, Isaiah IV, 658
Garwood, Isaiah VI, 596
Garwood, Isiah V, 59
Garwood, Israel Negus IV, 956
Garwood, Jacob II, 223
Garwood, Jacob II, 246
Garwood, Jacob, Jr. II, 223
Garwood, James IV, 1279
Garwood, Jane IV, 87
Garwood, Jane IV, 204
Garwood, Jason H. IV, 87
Garwood, Jesse IV, 33
Garwood, Jesse IV, 85
Garwood, Jesse IV, 87
Garwood, Jesse IV, 101
Garwood, Jesse IV, 103
Garwood, Jesse IV, 107
Garwood, Jesse IV, 114
Garwood, Jesse IV, 626
Garwood, Jesse R. IV, 33
Garwood, Jesse R. IV, 79
Garwood, Jesse R. IV, 87
Garwood, Jesse R. IV, 711
Garwood, Job II, 223
Garwood, Job II, 1045
Garwood, Job II, 1051
Garwood, Job II, 1087
Garwood, John II, 213
Garwood, John II, 223
Garwood, John II, 246
Garwood, John II, 1045
Garwood, John II, 1051
Garwood, John IV, 39
Garwood, John IV, 625
Garwood, John IV, 626
Garwood, John IV, 711
Garwood, John IV, 817
Garwood, John V, 59
Garwood, John VI, 390
Garwood, John VI, 478
Garwood, John VI, 591
Garwood, John VI, 593
Garwood, John VI, 595
Garwood, John VI, 596
Garwood, John VI, 598
Garwood, John VI, 600
Garwood, John VI, 604
Garwood, John R. Warrington IV, 956
Garwood, John S. II, 223
Garwood, John W. IV, 711
Garwood, John W. IV, 817
Garwood, John W. IV, 956
Garwood, John, Jr. V, 59
Garwood, Jonas IV, 626
Garwood, Jonathan V, 59
Garwood, Joseph II, 223
Garwood, Joseph IV, 33
Garwood, Joseph IV, 87
Garwood, Joseph IV, 626
Garwood, Joseph V, 59
Garwood, Joseph VI, 390
Garwood, Joseph B. II, 866
Garwood, Joseph D. IV, 711
Garwood, Joseph D. IV, 817
Garwood, Joseph D. IV, 956
Garwood, Joseph H. Miller IV, 33
Garwood, Levi IV, 625
Garwood, Levi IV, 626
Garwood, Levi V, 59
Garwood, Levi VI, 390
Garwood, Levi VI, 596
Garwood, Lewis IV, 626
Garwood, Lewis G. IV, 817
Garwood, Lewis J. IV, 711
Garwood, Lewis J. IV, 817
Garwood, Lot V, 59
Garwood, Lucy IV, 625
Garwood, Lucy Ann IV, 626
Garwood, Lucy Ann IV, 636
Garwood, Lydia IV, 33
Garwood, Lydia IV, 39
Garwood, Lydia IV, 85
Garwood, Lydia IV, 87
Garwood, Lydia IV, 89
Garwood, Lydia IV, 101
Garwood, Lydia IV, 103
Garwood, Lydia IV, 107
Garwood, Lydia IV, 114
Garwood, Lydia IV, 956
Garwood, Lydia IV, 983
Garwood, Lydia Ann IV, 87
Garwood, Lydia Margaret IV, 87
Garwood, Lydia Margaret IV, 711
Garwood, Macy V, 59
Garwood, Macy V, 71
Garwood, Margaret II, 71
Garwood, Margaret II, 76
Garwood, Margaret IV, 626
Garwood, Margaret IV, 711
Garwood, Margaret VI, 390
Garwood, Margaret VI, 596
Garwood, Mariam IV, 33
Garwood, Martha II, 365
Garwood, Martha II, 530
Garwood, Mary II, 223
Garwood, Mary II, 231
Garwood, Mary II, 365
Garwood, Mary II, 1045
Garwood, Mary II, 1051
Garwood, Mary II, 1087
Garwood, Mary IV, 32
Garwood, Mary IV, 33
Garwood, Mary IV, 39
Garwood, Mary IV, 76
Garwood, Mary IV, 86
Garwood, Mary IV, 87
Garwood, Mary IV, 113
Garwood, Mary IV, 610
Garwood, Mary IV, 625
Garwood, Mary IV, 626
Garwood, Mary IV, 635
Garwood, Mary IV, 638
Garwood, Mary IV, 649
Garwood, Mary IV, 658
Garwood, Mary IV, 873
Garwood, Mary IV, 973
Garwood, Mary VI, 390
Garwood, Mary VI, 591
Garwood, Mary VI, 596
Garwood, Mary Ann IV, 87
Garwood, Mary Ann IV, 101
Garwood, Mary B. II, 318
Garwood, Mary H. II, 318
Garwood, Mary H. II, 326
Garwood, Mary Heustis II, 223
Garwood, Mary, Sr. IV, 87
Garwood, Mary, Sr. IV, 626
Garwood, Mercy V, 59
Garwood, Mira C. IV, 711
Garwood, Miri C. IV, 33
Garwood, Myra IV, 79
Garwood, Myra IV, 87
Garwood, Obed IV, 17
Garwood, Obed IV, 32
Garwood, Obed IV, 33
Garwood, Obed IV, 71
Garwood, Obed IV, 86
Garwood, Obed IV, 87
Garwood, Obed VI, 390
Garwood, Obed, Jr. IV, 87
Garwood, Oliver J. IV, 87
Garwood, Orie IV, 1279
Garwood, Patience V, 59
Garwood, Phebe IV, 608
Garwood, Phebe IV, 626
Garwood, Priscilla IV, 711
Garwood, Rachel II, 202
Garwood, Rachel II, 223
Garwood, Rachel IV, 87
Garwood, Rachel IV, 114
Garwood, Rachel IV, 117
Garwood, Rachel IV, 956
Garwood, Rachel IV, 1013
Garwood, Rachel H. IV, 711
Garwood, Rachel H. IV, 817
Garwood, Rachel H. IV, 956
Garwood, Rachel K. IV, 817
Garwood, Rebecca II, 213
Garwood, Rebecca II, 223
Garwood, Rebecca II, 224
Garwood, Rebecca IV, 33
Garwood, Rebecca IV, 49
Garwood, Rebecca IV, 87
Garwood, Rebecca IV, 101
Garwood, Robert V, 59
Garwood, Roberts IV, 87
Garwood, Ruth IV, 607
Garwood, Ruth IV, 626
Garwood, Samuel II, 213
Garwood, Samuel II, 223
Garwood, Samuel IV, 33
Garwood, Samuel IV, 626
Garwood, Samuel VI, 390
Garwood, Sarah IV, 33
Garwood, Sarah IV, 626
Garwood, Sarah IV, 635
Garwood, Sarah IV, 711
Garwood, Sarah IV, 734
Garwood, Sarah V, 59
Garwood, Sarah VI, 390
Garwood, Sarah VI, 591
Garwood, Sarah VI, 595
Garwood, Sarah VI, 596
Garwood, Sarah Ann V, 59
Garwood, Sarah Ann V, 118
Garwood, Sarah Thorn V, 172
Garwood, Sidney IV, 87
Garwood, Sidney IV, 89
Garwood, Sidney IV, 625
Garwood, Sidney IV, 626
Garwood, Susannah VI, 596
Garwood, Susannah VI, 604
Garwood, Sylvanus IV, 711
Garwood, Sylvanus IV, 817
Garwood, Syvanus P. IV, 626
Garwood, Tacy VI, 390
Garwood, Thomas II, 71
Garwood, Thomas II, 76
Garwood, Thomas IV, 33
Garwood, Thomas IV, 626
Garwood, Thomas IV, 1279
Garwood, Thomas V, 59
Garwood, Thomas VI, 390
Garwood, Thomas VI, 596
Garwood, Thomas VI, 604
Garwood, Thos. IV, 625
Garwood, Thos. IV, 626
Garwood, Tilman IV, 626
Garwood, William II, 365
Garwood, William IV, 33
Garwood, William M. IV, 87
Garwood, Wm. IV, 125
Garwood, Wm. Miller IV, 87
Gary, James VI, 819
Gary, Wilmuth VI, 819
Gasaway, Carrie IV, 473
Gase, Bertha IV, 1316
Gash, Elizabeth VI, 819
Gash, Elizabeth VI, 919
Gash, Elizabeth VI, 955
Gash, Martha VI, 921
Gash, Michael VI, 819
Gash, Michael VI, 919
Gash, Michael VI, 920
Gash, Michael, Jr. VI, 920
Gash, Molly VI, 920
Gash, Thos. VI, 919
Gaskel, Amy II, 223
Gaskel, Amy II, 260
Gaskel, Huldah V, 981
Gaskel, Josias II, 223
Gaskel, Josias II, 260
Gaskel, Pamela IV, 1025
Gaskel, Pamela IV, 1029
Gaskell, Edward V, 59
Gaskell, Israel IV, 817
Gaskell, Louisa V, 59
Gaskell, Louisa V, 387
Gaskell, Louise V, 387
Gaskell, Margarett II, 118
Gaskell, Margarett II, 119
Gaskell, Mary V, 387
Gaskell, Milton S. V, 387
Gaskell, Nathan R. IV, 817
Gaskell, Nathan Robert IV, 817
Gaskell, Thomas V, 387
Gaskil, Ann II, 238
Gaskil, Ann II, 997
Gaskil, Benjamin II, 223
Gaskil, Caleb II, 224
Gaskil, Caleb II, 272
Gaskil, Cornelia II, 997
Gaskil, Cornelia C. II, 997
Gaskil, Daniel II, 223
Gaskil, Ebenezer II, 224
Gaskil, Ebenezer, Jr. II, 223
Gaskil, Edith II, 224
Gaskil, Edward II, 238
Gaskil, Edward, Jr. II, 223
Gaskil, Elizabeth II, 224
Gaskil, Elizabeth II, 272
Gaskil, Grace II, 167
Gaskil, Hannah II, 219
Gaskil, Hannah II, 223
Gaskil, Hannah II, 997
Gaskil, Hannah Ann II, 997
Gaskil, Job II, 174
Gaskil, Job II, 224
Gaskil, Joseph II, 167
Gaskil, Joseph II, 223
Gaskil, Levi II, 224
Gaskil, Lorobable II, 223
Gaskil, Lorobable II, 238
Gaskil, Mahlon R. V, 674
Gaskil, Martha II, 223
Gaskil, Samuel II, 224
Gaskil, Sarah II, 997
Gaskil, Sarah E. II, 997
Gaskil, Thomas II, 224
Gaskil, Virgin II, 167
Gaskile, Edward, Jr. II, 223
Gaskile, Grace II, 223
Gaskile, Jennings II, 224
Gaskile, Jonathan II, 223
Gaskile, Joseph II, 223
Gaskile, Josiah II, 223
Gaskile, Patience II, 223
Gaskile, Sarah II, 197
Gaskile, Sarah II, 223
Gaskile, Thomas II, 224
Gaskill, Aaron II, 223

Gaskill, Aaron II, 241
Gaskill, Aaron Wright II, 795
Gaskill, Abigail II, 795
Gaskill, Abigail II, 866
Gaskill, Abigail II, 940
Gaskill, Alfred R. II, 866
Gaskill, Alfred R. III, 132
Gaskill, Alonzo H. V, 997
Gaskill, Amy II, 223
Gaskill, Amy II, 866
Gaskill, Amy II, 917
Gaskill, Angeline IV, 929
Gaskill, Angeline IV, 956
Gaskill, Ann II, 223
Gaskill, Ann II, 530
Gaskill, Ann II, 997
Gaskill, Anna Elizabeth II, 866
Gaskill, Anna Elizabeth II, 940
Gaskill, Anna H. II, 288
Gaskill, Anna H. II, 705
Gaskill, Anna H. II, 742
Gaskill, Anna M. II, 288
Gaskill, Avaline IV, 712
Gaskill, Avaline IV, 753
Gaskill, Barzillia, Jr. II, 224
Gaskill, Benjamin II, 223
Gaskill, Benjamin II, 224
Gaskill, Beulah II, 131
Gaskill, Beulah II, 223
Gaskill, Beulah II, 224
Gaskill, Beulah A. II, 146
Gaskill, Beulah A. II, 148
Gaskill, Beulah A. II, 866
Gaskill, Beulah A. II, 941
Gaskill, Beulah Ann II, 131
Gaskill, Bulah II, 255
Gaskill, Caleb II, 174
Gaskill, Caleb II, 224
Gaskill, Caleb II, 287
Gaskill, Caleb II, 288
Gaskill, Caleb II, 293
Gaskill, Caleb II, 298
Gaskill, Caleb II, 866
Gaskill, Caleb II, 905
Gaskill, Caroline III, 132
Gaskill, Caroline E. II, 866
Gaskill, Caroline E. III, 132
Gaskill, Caroline E. C. II, 866
Gaskill, Caroline Elizabeth Cooper II, 795
Gaskill, Charles II, 131
Gaskill, Charles II, 146
Gaskill, Charles II, 148
Gaskill, Charles II, 530
Gaskill, Chas. II, 795
Gaskill, Chas. II, 866
Gaskill, Chas. II, 940
Gaskill, Chas. II, 941
Gaskill, Clara Hoffman II, 795
Gaskill, Clara Hoffman II, 866
Gaskill, Clayton II, 795
Gaskill, Clayton II, 866
Gaskill, Clayton II, 940
Gaskill, Cornelia II, 997
Gaskill, Daniel II, 223
Gaskill, Daniel II, 258
Gaskill, Daniel IV, 711
Gaskill, Ebenezer II, 223
Gaskill, Ebenezer II, 224
Gaskill, Ebenezer II, 530
Gaskill, Ebenezer, Jr. II, 223
Gaskill, Edith II, 71
Gaskill, Edith II, 223
Gaskill, Edith II, 224
Gaskill, Edith II, 288
Gaskill, Edward II, 174
Gaskill, Edward II, 223
Gaskill, Edward IV, 711
Gaskill, Edward, Jr. II, 223
Gaskill, Edwin A. II, 866
Gaskill, Edwin A. II, 914
Gaskill, Edwin Austin II, 795
Gaskill, Edwin Austin II, 866
Gaskill, Elizabeth II, 146
Gaskill, Elizabeth II, 148
Gaskill, Elizabeth II, 174
Gaskill, Elizabeth II, 223
Gaskill, Elizabeth II, 224
Gaskill, Elizabeth II, 263
Gaskill, Elizabeth II, 287
Gaskill, Elizabeth II, 288
Gaskill, Elizabeth II, 293
Gaskill, Elizabeth II, 298
Gaskill, Elizabeth II, 530
Gaskill, Elizabeth II, 866
Gaskill, Elizabeth II, 905
Gaskill, Elizabeth IV, 711
Gaskill, Elizabeth IV, 712
Gaskill, Elizabeth IV, 750
Gaskill, Elizabeth IV, 761
Gaskill, Elizabeth IV, 762
Gaskill, Elizabeth S. II, 866
Gaskill, Elizabeth S. II, 918
Gaskill, Elizabeth S. II, 922
Gaskill, Elizabeth W. II, 174
Gaskill, Elizabeth W. II, 288
Gaskill, Elizabeth W. II, 298
Gaskill, Elizabeth W. II, 866
Gaskill, Elizabeth W. II, 905
Gaskill, Elizabeth Williams II, 812
Gaskill, Emily M. II, 941
Gaskill, Emma A. W. II, 866
Gaskill, Emma S. II, 866
Gaskill, Emma S. II, 941
Gaskill, Emma S. W. II, 914
Gaskill, Emma Stratton II, 795
Gaskill, Esther II, 223
Gaskill, Esther II, 530
Gaskill, Esther II, 1051
Gaskill, Frank V, 997
Gaskill, George II, 174
Gaskill, George II, 288
Gaskill, George E. II, 941
Gaskill, Gertrude II, 795
Gaskill, Grace II, 223
Gaskill, Grace II, 250
Gaskill, Grace V, 828
Gaskill, Hannah II, 221
Gaskill, Hannah II, 223
Gaskill, Hannah II, 224
Gaskill, Hannah II, 288
Gaskill, Hannah II, 808
Gaskill, Hannah II, 816
Gaskill, Hannah II, 866
Gaskill, Hannah II, 997
Gaskill, Hannah IV, 33
Gaskill, Hannah IV, 60
Gaskill, Hannah IV, 711
Gaskill, Hannah V, 492
Gaskill, Hannah C. II, 288
Gaskill, Hannah E. II, 866
Gaskill, Hannah E. II, 889
Gaskill, Hannah Fortiner II, 223
Gaskill, Hannah Y. II, 866
Gaskill, Hannah Y. II, 914
Gaskill, Harrie T. IV, 1316
Gaskill, Helen May II, 866
Gaskill, Henry C. II, 866
Gaskill, Henry K. II, 866
Gaskill, Henry K. III, 132
Gaskill, Hope II, 223
Gaskill, Hulda II, 224
Gaskill, Hulda II, 244
Gaskill, Huldah II, 174
Gaskill, Huldah II, 288
Gaskill, Huldah IV, 711
Gaskill, Huldah IV, 712
Gaskill, Huldah V, 997
Gaskill, Isabella P. II, 131
Gaskill, Israel IV, 711
Gaskill, Israel IV, 712
Gaskill, Israel IV, 761
Gaskill, Israel IV, 817
Gaskill, J. Howard II, 866
Gaskill, J. Howard II, 917
Gaskill, Jacob II, 223
Gaskill, James II, 223
Gaskill, Jane II, 223
Gaskill, Jane II, 224
Gaskill, Jane II, 258
Gaskill, Jane V, 545
Gaskill, Jane V, 554
Gaskill, Jane V, 562
Gaskill, Jane C. II, 866
Gaskill, Jennie IV, 1316
Gaskill, Jennie M. IV, 1316
Gaskill, Jennings II, 224
Gaskill, Job II, 174
Gaskill, Job II, 224
Gaskill, Job II, 530
Gaskill, Job S. II, 288
Gaskill, Job S. II, 530
Gaskill, Job S. II, 808
Gaskill, Job S. II, 866
Gaskill, Job, Jr. II, 224
Gaskill, John II, 224
Gaskill, Jonathan II, 223
Gaskill, Jonathan II, 248
Gaskill, Jonathan II, 258
Gaskill, Joseph II, 218
Gaskill, Joseph II, 223
Gaskill, Joseph II, 224
Gaskill, Joseph II, 250
Gaskill, Joseph II, 318
Gaskill, Joseph Franklin II, 795
Gaskill, Joseph Franklin II, 866
Gaskill, Joshua II, 223
Gaskill, Joshua Howard III, 132
Gaskill, Joshua W. II, 866
Gaskill, Joshua W. III, 132
Gaskill, Joshua Wright II, 795
Gaskill, Josiah II, 130
Gaskill, Josiah II, 131
Gaskill, Josiah II, 146
Gaskill, Josiah II, 148
Gaskill, Josiah II, 223
Gaskill, Josiah II, 288
Gaskill, Josiah II, 866
Gaskill, Josiah, Jr. II, 866
Gaskill, Josias II, 223
Gaskill, Laura V, 674
Gaskill, Lavinia II, 223
Gaskill, Levi II, 224
Gaskill, Lorobable II, 223
Gaskill, Louisa V, 674
Gaskill, Louise V, 387
Gaskill, Lucretia Stevens II, 223
Gaskill, Lucy II, 130
Gaskill, Lucy II, 131
Gaskill, Lucy II, 288
Gaskill, Lucy W. II, 146
Gaskill, Lucy W. II, 148
Gaskill, Lydia II, 174
Gaskill, Lydia II, 288
Gaskill, Lydia II, 298
Gaskill, Lydia II, 318
Gaskill, Lydia II, 323
Gaskill, Lydia II, 530
Gaskill, Lydia II, 672
Gaskill, Mahlon V, 674
Gaskill, Mahlon R. V, 674
Gaskill, Margaret II, 174
Gaskill, Margarett II, 118
Gaskill, Maria Louisa V, 562
Gaskill, Marianna II, 941
Gaskill, Martha II, 116
Gaskill, Martha II, 118
Gaskill, Martha II, 130
Gaskill, Martha II, 146
Gaskill, Martha II, 148
Gaskill, Martha II, 223
Gaskill, Martha II, 258
Gaskill, Martha II, 795
Gaskill, Mary II, 174
Gaskill, Mary II, 218
Gaskill, Mary II, 223
Gaskill, Mary II, 224
Gaskill, Mary II, 254
Gaskill, Mary II, 288
Gaskill, Mary II, 293
Gaskill, Mary II, 700
Gaskill, Mary B. II, 118
Gaskill, Mary B. II, 131
Gaskill, Mary B. II, 159
Gaskill, Mary C. II, 866
Gaskill, Milton S. V, 387
Gaskill, Milton S. V, 674
Gaskill, Naomi II, 148
Gaskill, Naomi II, 866
Gaskill, Naomi II, 942
Gaskill, Nathan IV, 711
Gaskill, Nathan IV, 712
Gaskill, Nathan B. II, 131
Gaskill, Nathan B. II, 866
Gaskill, Nathan B. II, 914
Gaskill, Nathan B. II, 919
Gaskill, Nathan B. II, 941
Gaskill, Nathan B. II, 942
Gaskill, Nathan Buzby II, 795
Gaskill, Nathan R. IV, 712
Gaskill, Nathan R. IV, 817
Gaskill, Patience II, 223
Gaskill, Phebe IV, 204
Gaskill, Phebe IV, 283
Gaskill, Phebe S. IV, 204
Gaskill, Rebecca II, 174
Gaskill, Rebecca II, 224
Gaskill, Rebecca II, 229
Gaskill, Rebecca II, 287
Gaskill, Rebecca II, 288
Gaskill, Rebecca II, 301
Gaskill, Rebecca II, 318
Gaskill, Rebecca IV, 711
Gaskill, Rebecca IV, 753
Gaskill, Rebecca L. II, 174
Gaskill, Rebecca L. II, 288
Gaskill, Redman C. II, 866
Gaskill, Redman Cooper II, 795
Gaskill, Robert II, 530
Gaskill, Rodman C. III, 132
Gaskill, Rudderrow S. IV, 204
Gaskill, Ruthanna II, 131
Gaskill, Samuel II, 223
Gaskill, Samuel II, 224
Gaskill, Sarah II, 223
Gaskill, Sarah II, 224
Gaskill, Sarah II, 248
Gaskill, Sarah II, 250
Gaskill, Sarah II, 530
Gaskill, Sarah II, 821
Gaskill, Sarah II, 953
Gaskill, Sarah II, 997
Gaskill, Sarah Allennetta II, 795
Gaskill, Sarah E. II, 997
Gaskill, Solomon II, 223
Gaskill, Stephen II, 223
Gaskill, Susannah II, 223
Gaskill, Susannah II, 241
Gaskill, Thomas II, 223
Gaskill, Thomas II, 224
Gaskill, Thomas, Jr. II, 224
Gaskill, Thos. W. IV, 1316
Gaskill, Virgin II, 201
Gaskill, Virgin II, 224
Gaskill, Wd. Mary Carr II, 808
Gaskill, William II, 174
Gaskill, William V, 562
Gaskill, Wm. II, 530
Gaskill, Zarzillai II, 223
Gaskill, Zerobabel II, 221
Gaskill, Zerobabel II, 223
Gaskill, Zerubbabel II, 224
Gaskiln, Josiah II, 224
Gaskiln, Josiah II, 226
Gaskiln, Mary II, 224
Gaskiln, Mary II, 226
Gaskin, Josiah II, 224
Gaskin, Josiah II, 238
Gaskin, Mary II, 224
Gaskin, Rebecca II, 224
Gaskin, Rebecca II, 238
Gaskin, Samuel II, 224
Gaskins, Bartholomew Adams VI, 920
Gaskins, Celia Ann V, 674
Gaskins, Dr. Aaron J. V, 674
Gaskins, Essie Alton V, 674
Gaskins, James V, 674
Gaskins, Rachel Wood VI, 920
Gassett, Nancy V, 739
Gassner, Hattie VI, 784
Gassner, Hattie VI, 786
Gassoway, Ann VI, 547
Gassoway, Elizabeth VI, 547
Gassoway, Nicholas VI, 547
Gaston, Elizabeth VI, 865
Gaston, Enphraisah I, 935
Gatchal, Laura IV, 1207
Gatchel, Agnes II, 795
Gatchel, Agnes II, 831
Gatchel, Agnes II, 866
Gatchel, Catharine II, 530
Gatchel, Catharine II, 728
Gatchel, Catharine II, 742
Gatchel, Catharine II, 793
Gatchel, Catharine II, 795
Gatchel, Catharine Foulke II, 742
Gatchel, Collin II, 795
Gatchel, Collin M. II, 831
Gatchel, Collin M. II, 866
Gatchel, Collin Stevenson II, 866
Gatchel, Deborah IV, 331
Gatchel, Deborah IV, 459
Gatchel, Deborah Ann IV, 331
Gatchel, Elisha II, 795
Gatchel, Elizabeth IV, 331
Gatchel, Elizabeth IV, 526
Gatchel, Francis Read II, 795
Gatchel, Gainer IV, 395
Gatchel, Gainer IV, 459
Gatchel, Garner IV, 331
Gatchel, George II, 530
Gatchel, Hannah II, 795
Gatchel, Hannah IV, 331
Gatchel, Harry Amos II, 866
Gatchel, Helen Virginia II, 795
Gatchel, Israel II, 866
Gatchel, Jane II, 826
Gatchel, Jeremiah IV, 459
Gatchel, John IV, 331
Gatchel, Joseph II, 742
Gatchel, Joseph II, 793
Gatchel, Joseph II, 795
Gatchel, Laura IV, 1207
Gatchel, Laura L. IV, 1207
Gatchel, Lizzie II, 866
Gatchel, Louisa II, 858
Gatchel, Louise II, 810
Gatchel, Maria IV, 331
Gatchel, Rebecca II, 784
Gatchel, Robert IV, 331
Gatchel, Sarah Mason II, 795
Gatchel, Wayne IV, 1207
Gatchel, Wd. Louisa II, 793
Gatchell, Agnes II, 795
Gatchell, Agnes II, 866
Gatchell, Alfred V, 906
Gatchell, Alice III, 132
Gatchell, Ann IV, 331
Gatchell, C. Stevenson II, 866
Gatchell, Caroline H. II, 365
Gatchell, Caroline H. II, 730
Gatchell, Caroline H. II, 742
Gatchell, Caroline H. II, 841
Gatchell, Caroline H. II, 866
Gatchell, Catharine II, 530
Gatchell, Catharine II, 742
Gatchell, Catharine II, 837
Gatchell, Catharine II, 841
Gatchell, Catharine II, 866
Gatchell, Catharine Foulke II, 365
Gatchell, Catharine Foulke II, 866
Gatchell, Catherin II, 365
Gatchell, Colin McKenzie II, 365
Gatchell, Collin II, 795
Gatchell, Collin II, 903
Gatchell, Collin M. II, 841
Gatchell, Collin M. II, 866
Gatchell, Collin Makinzi II, 866
Gatchell, Collin McKensie II, 742
Gatchell, Collin Stevenson II, 866
Gatchell, Deborah IV, 331
Gatchell, Deborah Ann IV, 331
Gatchell, Edmund K. II, 365
Gatchell, Edmund K. II, 742
Gatchell, Edmund K. II, 866
Gatchell, Edmund kersey II, 866
Gatchell, Elisha II, 795
Gatchell, Elizabeth IV, 331
Gatchell, Elizabeth Crippen II, 854
Gatchell, Elizabeth Crippen II, 866
Gatchell, Elizabeth G. II, 866
Gatchell, Elizabeth G. II, 924
Gatchell, Frances Read II, 866
Gatchell, Frances Reed II, 365
Gatchell, Francis R. II, 866
Gatchell, Francis R. II, 916
Gatchell, Francis Reed II, 742
Gatchell, Gainer IV, 331
Gatchell, Garner IV, 331
Gatchell, George II, 530
Gatchell, George II, 742
Gatchell, Hannah II, 866
Gatchell, Hannah IV, 331
Gatchell, Hannah E. IV, 331
Gatchell, Harry Amos II, 866
Gatchell, Henry III, 132
Gatchell, Henry A. II, 854
Gatchell, Henry A. II, 866
Gatchell, Israel II, 866
Gatchell, James II, 365
Gatchell, Jeremiah IV, 331
Gatchell, John IV, 331
Gatchell, Joseph II, 365
Gatchell, Joseph II, 530
Gatchell, Joseph II, 742
Gatchell, Joseph II, 795
Gatchell, Joseph II, 841
Gatchell, Joseph II, 866
Gatchell, Joseph, Jr. II, 742
Gatchell, Lizzie II, 866
Gatchell, Louisa II, 530
Gatchell, Louisa G. II, 737
Gatchell, Louisa G. II, 742
Gatchell, Louise II, 866
Gatchell, Maria IV, 331
Gatchell, Nathan IV, 331
Gatchell, Rebecca II, 365
Gatchell, Rebecca II, 811
Gatchell, Rebecca Caroline II, 866
Gatchell, Rebecca G. II, 730
Gatchell, Rebecca G. II, 742
Gatchell, Rebecca G. II, 841
Gatchell, Rebecca G. II, 866
Gatchell, Robert IV, 331
Gatchell, Robert B. IV, 331
Gatchell, Sarah Ann II, 831
Gatchell, Sarah M. II, 866
Gatchell, Sarah M. II, 916
Gate, Richard W. I, 50
Gate, Richard W. VI, 64
Gates, Anna Bell IV, 1279
Gates, Belle IV, 1235
Gates, Belle IV, 1316
Gates, Cherrish II, 365
Gates, Daniel IV, 1279
Gates, Edwin Edgerton II, 850
Gates, Edwin Edgerton II, 866
Gates, Elijah VI, 920
Gates, Elizabeth VI, 920
Gates, Ethel Moore II, 788
Gates, Ethel Moore II, 850
Gates, Ethel Moore II, 866
Gates, Frances A. V, 906
Gates, Frances A. White V, 906
Gates, Georgiana H. M. II, 850
Gates, Georgiana H. M. II, 866
Gates, Horatio Hamilton III, 132

Gates, Jacob IV, 1279
Gates, Jennie IV, 1279
Gates, Joseph IV, 1279
Gates, Josiah II, 365
Gates, Josiah II, 530
Gates, Josiah II, 997
Gates, Mary III, 132
Gates, Mary U. III, 132
Gates, Mary U. III, 365
Gates, Merrill E., Jr. III, 132
Gates, Merrill Edward, Jr. III, 365
Gates, Mildred III, 132
Gates, Mildred III, 188
Gates, Philip III, 132
Gates, Samuel J. III, 132
Gates, Samuel J. III, 188
Gates, Sarah II, 366
Gates, Sarah II, 530
Gates, Susanna V, 59
Gates, Susanna V, 906
Gates, Susannah V, 59
Gates, Susannah V, 906
Gatewood, Emmy VI, 1020
Gatewood, James VI, 883
Gatewood, James VI, 892
Gatewood, James VI, 910
Gatewood, James VI, 1006
Gatewood, James VI, 1020
Gatewood, James VI, 1021
Gatewood, Lucy VI, 1021
Gatewood, Makey VI, 892
Gatewood, Martha VI, 1006
Gatewood, Sophia VI, 910
Gatewood, Thomas VI, 1020
Gathright, John VI, 177
Gatling, James I, 24
Gatling, Margaret C. I, 24
Gatrill, Thomas II, 443
Gatson, Elizabeth VI, 920
Gatson, William VI, 920
Gatterson, Ann IV, 750
Gatterson, John IV, 750
Gattin, Mary I, 50
Gattin, Sarah I, 43
Gattin, Sarah I, 50
Gatting, Mary I, 50
Gatting, Mary I, 74
Gatting, Sarah I, 50
Gattis, Ann VI, 408
Gatton, Mary II, 530
Gatyell, Wayne IV, 1207
Gaub, Anna IV, 1316
Gaub, Minnie IV, 1316
Gaucher, Margaret IV, 817
Gaucher, Margaret IV, 854
Gaudin, Patty VI, 857
Gaugh, Dresilla VI, 312
Gauker, Mary V, 968
Gauker, Mary V, 970
Gaulden, Anne VI, 857
Gaulden, Susannah VI, 987
Gauldin, Juriah VI, 819
Gauldin, Thomas VI, 819
Gaulding, Elizabeth VI, 863
Gaulding, Lucy VI, 863
Gaulding, Sarah L. VI, 944
Gaunt, ??? II, 224
Gaunt, Abigail I, 1030
Gaunt, Abigal I, 1033
Gaunt, Achsah II, 866
Gaunt, Achsah II, 930
Gaunt, Ann II, 118
Gaunt, Ann R. III, 132
Gaunt, Anna E. II, 134
Gaunt, Anna Maria II, 174
Gaunt, Annanias II, 224
Gaunt, Benjamin II, 174
Gaunt, Benjamin II, 224
Gaunt, Benjamin II, 288
Gaunt, Benjamin W. II, 866
Gaunt, Benjamin W. II, 895
Gaunt, Beulah V, 59
Gaunt, Beulah V, 114
Gaunt, Casse IV, 956
Gaunt, Charles I, 541
Gaunt, Charles II, 174
Gaunt, Charles S. II, 288
Gaunt, Clayton II, 118
Gaunt, Daniel II, 224
Gaunt, Daniel II, 366
Gaunt, Daniel II, 530
Gaunt, Delaplaine III, 132
Gaunt, Dr. Benj. U. II, 808
Gaunt, Elizabeth I, 1026
Gaunt, Elizabeth I, 1030
Gaunt, Elizabeth II, 118
Gaunt, Elizabeth II, 174
Gaunt, Elizabeth Louisa II, 174
Gaunt, Ester I, 1030
Gaunt, Esther II, 224
Gaunt, Eva H. II, 134
Gaunt, Filmore II, 134
Gaunt, Franklin II, 174
Gaunt, Franklin II, 288
Gaunt, Hannah II, 118
Gaunt, Hannah II, 213
Gaunt, Hannah II, 224
Gaunt, Hannah II, 253
Gaunt, Hannah II, 275
Gaunt, Hannah II, 366
Gaunt, Hannah II, 705
Gaunt, Hiram Cicero V, 172
Gaunt, Israel I, 390
Gaunt, Israel I, 541
Gaunt, Israel II, 224
Gaunt, Jane III, 132
Gaunt, Jane W. III, 132
Gaunt, Jefferson III, 132
Gaunt, Jemima I, 1039
Gaunt, John II, 118
Gaunt, John II, 270
Gaunt, Jonah I, 1039
Gaunt, Josephine II, 808
Gaunt, Josephine C. II, 866
Gaunt, Josephine C. II, 891
Gaunt, Josephine C. II, 895
Gaunt, Judith I, 1030
Gaunt, Judith I, 1039
Gaunt, Kerenhappock I, 1030
Gaunt, Killey I, 541
Gaunt, Le Clere II, 866
Gaunt, Louisa II, 174
Gaunt, M??? II, 270
Gaunt, Malachi I, 1093
Gaunt, Malichi I, 541
Gaunt, Maris I, 1030
Gaunt, Maris I, 1032
Gaunt, Martha A. V, 172
Gaunt, Mary I, 1019
Gaunt, Mary I, 1030
Gaunt, Mary II, 224
Gaunt, Mary II, 270
Gaunt, Mary V, 492
Gaunt, Maud Halcyon II, 808
Gaunt, Maud Halcyon II, 866
Gaunt, Maude Halcyon II, 866
Gaunt, Maude Halcyon II, 895
Gaunt, Nathan Cole II, 174
Gaunt, Nebo I, 1026
Gaunt, Nebo I, 1030
Gaunt, Nebo I, 1039
Gaunt, Pablias I, 1093
Gaunt, Phebe II, 224
Gaunt, Prudence V, 59
Gaunt, Prudence V, 78
Gaunt, Publias I, 541
Gaunt, Rachel II, 118
Gaunt, Ruth II, 866
Gaunt, Samuel I, 50
Gaunt, Samuel I, 541
Gaunt, Samuel I, 1030
Gaunt, Samuel I, 1033
Gaunt, Samuel I, 1093
Gaunt, Samuel II, 118
Gaunt, Samuel II, 224
Gaunt, Samuel II, 275
Gaunt, Samuel II, 866
Gaunt, Samuel II, 930
Gaunt, Samuel Kelly I, 541
Gaunt, Sarah I, 1028
Gaunt, Sarah I, 1030
Gaunt, Sarah I, 1031
Gaunt, Sarah II, 224
Gaunt, Sarah II, 259
Gaunt, Sarah V, 59
Gaunt, Sarah V, 144
Gaunt, Sarah C. V, 906
Gaunt, Sophia II, 224
Gaunt, Sophia II, 242
Gaunt, Sophiah II, 224
Gaunt, Stacy T. II, 866
Gaunt, Stacy T. III, 132
Gaunt, Susan II, 174
Gaunt, Susan W. II, 224
Gaunt, Susanna I, 541
Gaunt, Susanna I, 1030
Gaunt, Susanna I, 1033
Gaunt, Susanna I, 1093
Gaunt, Susanna V, 59
Gaunt, Susanna W. II, 288
Gaunt, Widow Mary I, 1033
Gaunt, William III, 132
Gaunt, Zeblon I, 541
Gaunt, Zebulon I, 344
Gaunt, Zebulon I, 390
Gaunt, Zebulon I, 1019
Gaunt, Zebulon I, 1030
Gaunt, Zebulon I, 1033
Gaunt, Zebulon II, 224
Gaunt, Zebulon II, 242
Gaunt, Zebulon II, 253
Gaunt, Zebulon II, 270
Gaunt, Zebulon, Jr. II, 224
Gaunt, Zimri I, 1028
Gaunt, Zimri I, 1030
Gauntt, Benjamin II, 265
Gauntt, Beula V, 59
Gauntt, Beulah V, 59
Gauntt, Charles V, 59
Gauntt, Charles S. II, 288
Gauntt, Elias V, 59
Gauntt, Ezekiel V, 59
Gauntt, Israel I, 541
Gauntt, Jane V, 59
Gauntt, Jefferson II, 742
Gauntt, Jefferson III, 132
Gauntt, Jemima V, 59
Gauntt, Jesse V, 59
Gauntt, Josephine C. II, 866
Gauntt, Judith V, 59
Gauntt, Le Clere II, 866
Gauntt, Matilda V, 59
Gauntt, Maud Halcyon II, 866
Gauntt, Nebo V, 59
Gauntt, Prudence V, 59
Gauntt, Publias I, 1084
Gauntt, Samuel I, 1084
Gauntt, Sarah II, 265
Gauntt, Sarah V, 59
Gauntt, Susan W. II, 265
Gauntt, Susanna I, 1084
Gauntt, Susanna V, 59
Gauntt, Susannah V, 59
Gauntt, Uriah V, 59
Gauntt, Zimri V, 59
Gaus, Drusilla IV, 675
Gaus, Drusilla IV, 712
Gaus, Enoch IV, 675
Gaus, Sarah IV, 675
Gaus, Sarah IV, 712
Gause, ??? IV, 87
Gause, ??? V, 877
Gause, Aaron V, 838
Gause, Aaron V, 839
Gause, Abraham IV, 87
Gause, Abraham V, 60
Gause, Abram V, 60
Gause, Alice V, 997
Gause, Amelia IV, 331
Gause, Amos IV, 87
Gause, Amy VI, 390
Gause, Amy VI, 411
Gause, Ann IV, 77
Gause, Ann IV, 87
Gause, Ann IV, 88
Gause, Ann V, 30
Gause, Ann V, 838
Gause, Ann V, 839
Gause, Ann C. V, 839
Gause, Ann C. V, 844
Gause, Ann E. V, 838
Gause, Ann R. IV, 817
Gause, Ann R. IV, 834
Gause, Anna V, 60
Gause, Anna V, 839
Gause, Anna R. V, 59
Gause, Anna R. V, 86
Gause, Anna Rebecca V, 59
Gause, Bathsheba V, 882
Gause, Bethsheba V, 839
Gause, Bethsheba V, 882
Gause, Charles IV, 87
Gause, Charles V, 838
Gause, Charles V, 839
Gause, Charles VI, 390
Gause, Clarkson V, 59
Gause, Clarkson V, 60
Gause, Clarkson V, 86
Gause, Clarkson V, 108
Gause, Clarkson V, 115
Gause, Clarkson V, 120
Gause, Clarkson V, 131
Gause, Drusilla IV, 712
Gause, Elcana B. V, 562
Gause, Eleana B. V, 60
Gause, Eli IV, 87
Gause, Eli IV, 88
Gause, Eli IV, 104
Gause, Eli V, 59
Gause, Eli V, 60
Gause, Eli V, 838
Gause, Eli V, 839
Gause, Eli V, 844
Gause, Eli C. I, 390
Gause, Eli D. V, 834
Gause, Eli D. V, 838
Gause, Eli D. V, 839
Gause, Eli D. V, 881
Gause, Eliza V, 59
Gause, Eliza V, 60
Gause, Eliza Cooper V, 838
Gause, Eliza V. V, 60
Gause, Elizabeth V, 34
Gause, Elizabeth V, 59
Gause, Elizabeth V, 60
Gause, Elizabeth V, 86
Gause, Elizabeth V, 120
Gause, Elizabeth V, 834
Gause, Elizabeth V, 839
Gause, Elizabeth V, 879
Gause, Elizabeth V, 882
Gause, Elkana B. V, 387
Gause, Elkana B. V, 562
Gause, Elkanah B. V, 60
Gause, Elkanah B. V, 562
Gause, Elkanah B. V, 674
Gause, Elkanah Beard V, 59
Gause, Elkanah Beard V, 674
Gause, Elva P. I, 306
Gause, Enoch IV, 87
Gause, Enoch IV, 712
Gause, Enos V, 562
Gause, Enos V, 674
Gause, Esther V, 492
Gause, Esther F. V, 387
Gause, Esther F. V, 562
Gause, Esther F. V, 674
Gause, Esther Frame V, 59
Gause, George R. V, 59
Gause, George R. V, 60
Gause, Hannah IV, 204
Gause, Hannah IV, 331
Gause, Hannah V, 59
Gause, Hannah V, 60
Gause, Hannah B. V, 838
Gause, Hannah B. V, 839
Gause, Hannah P. V, 952
Gause, Hannah R. V, 60
Gause, Harriet IV, 331
Gause, Harriet Amelia IV, 204
Gause, Henry M. V, 387
Gause, Hester F. V, 60
Gause, Isaac IV, 87
Gause, Isaac V, 60
Gause, Isaac V, 838
Gause, Isaac V, 839
Gause, Isaac V, 854
Gause, Isaac V, 882
Gause, Isaac VI, 390
Gause, Isaac V. V, 59
Gause, Isaac V. V, 60
Gause, Israel IV, 87
Gause, Israel V, 838
Gause, Israel V, 839
Gause, Israel V, 879
Gause, Israel V, 882
Gause, Jacob V, 838
Gause, James IV, 87
Gause, James V, 839
Gause, James P. V, 60
Gause, James P. V, 838
Gause, James P. V, 839
Gause, James Pearse IV, 87
Gause, Jane V, 60
Gause, Jane V, 136
Gause, Jesse IV, 87
Gause, Jesse IV, 204
Gause, Jesse IV, 331
Gause, Jesse V, 60
Gause, Jesse V, 838
Gause, Jesse V, 839
Gause, John IV, 87
Gause, John IV, 88
Gause, John V, 838
Gause, John V, 839
Gause, John V, 882
Gause, Joseph V, 838
Gause, Joseph V, 839
Gause, Lydia V, 834
Gause, Lydia V, 838
Gause, Lydia V, 839
Gause, Lydia V, 881
Gause, Mahlon V, 997
Gause, Mahlon S. V, 997
Gause, Martha IV, 87
Gause, Martha IV, 104
Gause, Martha IV, 204
Gause, Martha IV, 331
Gause, Martha IV, 1279
Gause, Martha IV, 1286
Gause, Martha V, 59
Gause, Martha V, 60
Gause, Martha V, 99
Gause, Martha V, 838
Gause, Martha V, 839
Gause, Martha V, 844
Gause, Martha P. V, 59
Gause, Mary IV, 19
Gause, Mary IV, 33
Gause, Mary IV, 87
Gause, Mary IV, 88
Gause, Mary IV, 104
Gause, Mary V, 59
Gause, Mary V, 60
Gause, Mary V, 88
Gause, Mary V, 99
Gause, Mary V, 838
Gause, Mary V, 839
Gause, Mary VI, 390
Gause, Mary E. V, 59
Gause, Mary E. V, 108
Gause, Mary Elizabeth V, 59
Gause, Mary J. V, 59
Gause, Mary J. V, 60
Gause, Mary J. V, 562
Gause, Mary J. V, 574
Gause, Mary Jane V, 387
Gause, Mary Jane V, 562
Gause, Mary Jane V, 674
Gause, Mary P. V, 59
Gause, Maryann V, 59
Gause, Maurice V, 562
Gause, Miriam IV, 87
Gause, Miriam V, 59
Gause, Miriam V, 60
Gause, Morris V, 387
Gause, Nathan IV, 19
Gause, Nathan IV, 33
Gause, Nathan IV, 87
Gause, Nathan IV, 88
Gause, Nathan V, 838
Gause, Nathan V, 839
Gause, Nathan V, 882
Gause, Noah Albert V, 59
Gause, Patience IV, 87
Gause, Patience V, 838
Gause, Patience V, 839
Gause, Pearce IV, 87
Gause, Rachel M. IV, 523
Gause, Rachel M. IV, 526
Gause, Rebecca Ann IV, 712
Gause, Richard V, 59
Gause, Richard V, 834
Gause, Richard V, 838
Gause, Richard V, 839
Gause, Richard P. V, 59
Gause, Richard P. V, 60
Gause, Ruth IV, 33
Gause, Ruth IV, 77
Gause, Ruth IV, 87
Gause, Ruth IV, 88
Gause, Ruth V, 28
Gause, Ruth V, 59
Gause, Ruth V, 60
Gause, Ruth V, 838
Gause, Ruth V, 839
Gause, Ruth V, 952
Gause, Ruth Ann V, 60
Gause, Ruth Anna V, 60
Gause, Ruth Anna V, 120
Gause, Ruthanna IV, 87
Gause, Ruthanna V, 59
Gause, Ruthanna V, 88
Gause, Ruthannah V, 59
Gause, Samuel IV, 87
Gause, Samuel IV, 104
Gause, Samuel V, 59
Gause, Samuel V, 60
Gause, Samuel V, 88
Gause, Samuel V, 99
Gause, Samuel V, 387
Gause, Samuel V, 562
Gause, Samuel V, 574
Gause, Samuel V, 674
Gause, Samuel V, 838
Gause, Samuel V, 882
Gause, Samuel C. V, 60
Gause, Samy V, 59
Gause, Sarah IV, 87
Gause, Sarah IV, 88
Gause, Sarah IV, 102
Gause, Sarah IV, 712
Gause, Sarah V, 839
Gause, Sarah V, 854
Gause, Sarah V, 882
Gause, Sarah M. V, 839
Gause, Sarah M. V, 882
Gause, Sidney V, 59
Gause, Sidney V, 108
Gause, Sidney V, 131
Gause, Solomon IV, 33
Gause, Solomon IV, 77
Gause, Solomon IV, 87
Gause, Solomon IV, 88
Gause, Solomon V, 28
Gause, Solomon V, 59
Gause, Solomon V, 60
Gause, Solomon V, 136
Gause, Solomon V, 838
Gause, Solomon V, 839
Gause, Sophia V, 60
Gause, Stephen A. V, 839
Gause, Steven V, 838
Gause, Thomas V, 882

Gause, Thomas E. V, 387
Gause, Wm. M. V, 882
Gauslin, Mary II, 55
Gauslin, Mary Bell II, 72
Gauthrop, James VI, 390
Gauthrop, Thomas VI, 390
Gauz, Vera IV, 1316
Gauze, Ann E. V, 883
Gauze, Sarah IV, 147
Gavin, David V, 174
Gavin, Lizzie V, 174
Gavin, Phoebe V, 174
Gawhrop, Hannah II, 866
Gawhrop, James II, 866
Gawhrop, James, Jr. II, 866
Gawhrop, Sarah C. II, 866
Gawthorp, Thomas III, 132
Gawthorp, Thomas VI, 243
Gawthrop, Edith VI, 390
Gawthrop, Edith VI, 450
Gawthrop, Hannah II, 915
Gawthrop, Hannah VI, 390
Gawthrop, Hannah VI, 408
Gawthrop, Henry II, 866
Gawthrop, Isabel VI, 390
Gawthrop, Isabel VI, 462
Gawthrop, James II, 915
Gawthrop, James VI, 390
Gawthrop, James VI, 408
Gawthrop, James, Jr. II, 915
Gawthrop, James, Jr. VI, 390
Gawthrop, John VI, 390
Gawthrop, Mary II, 801
Gawthrop, Mary T. II, 866
Gawthrop, Patience VI, 390
Gawthrop, Patience VI, 408
Gawthrop, Rachel VI, 382
Gawthrop, Rachel VI, 390
Gawthrop, Rachel Mott II, 801
Gawthrop, Sarah C. II, 915
Gawthrop, Thomas II, 530
Gawthrop, Thomas VI, 390
Gawthrop, Wm. II, 801
Gay, Asa IV, 331
Gay, Asa IV, 395
Gay, Charles IV, 331
Gay, Cyrus IV, 331
Gay, David IV, 331
Gay, Dorothy L. III, 133
Gay, Eliphilet IV, 331
Gay, Elvin IV, 331
Gay, Ephraim IV, 331
Gay, Grace III, 132
Gay, Grace V. III, 133
Gay, Hyram IV, 331
Gay, Jesse IV, 331
Gay, Joane Lawrence VI, 29
Gay, John I, 50
Gay, John I, 239
Gay, Jonathan VI, 107
Gay, Mary IV, 331
Gay, Nancy IV, 331
Gay, Nancy VI, 920
Gay, Rebecca VI, 29
Gay, Rebecca VI, 33
Gay, Robert IV, 331
Gay, Robert VI, 920
Gay, Roland III, 132
Gay, Roland E. III, 133
Gay, Sarah IV, 331
Gay, Sarah IV, 395
Gay, Sarah IV, 420
Gay, Sarah J. VI, 64
Gay, Sarah J. VI, 76
Gay, Thomas VI, 29
Gay, Thomas VI, 33
Gay, William IV, 331
Gaye, Mary IV, 959
Gaye, Phyllis IV, 959
Gaye, Wm. IV, 959
Gayham, Anes I, 390
Gayham, Anes I, 425
Gayle, John T. VI, 819
Gayle, Mary A. VI, 819
Gaylord, Anna IV, 1157
Gaylord, Anna IV, 1159
Gaylord, Catharine IV, 1159
Gaylord, Eleazer IV, 1159
Gaynor, Lucy IV, 204
Gaynor, Lucy A. IV, 204
Gearhaeart, Burwell VI, 920
Gearhaeart, Sarah Jane VI, 920
Gearhart, Leonard IV, 1279
Gearheart, Belle IV, 1279
Gearheart, Charlotte IV, 1279
Gearheart, John T. IV, 1279
Gearheart, Leonard IV, 1279
Gearheart, Mary IV, 1279
Geary, Elizabeth IV, 1251
Geary, Elizabeth M. IV, 1251
Geary, Laura IV, 473
Geary, Sarah VI, 493
Gebhart, George V, 970
Gebhart, Margaret V, 457
Geddes, Alexandria III, 133
Geddes, Susan III, 133
Geddes, Susan VI, 742
Gedds, Alexandria III, 133
Gedds, Susan III, 133
Geddy, Bartholomew VI, 974
Geddy, George VI, 974
Geddy, Martha VI, 974
Geddy, Mary VI, 974
Geddy, Wm. VI, 945
Gedney, Caleb III, 133
Gee, ??? III, 133
Gee, Benjamin VI, 865
Gee, Charles VI, 130
Gee, Charles VI, 134
Gee, Charles VI, 144
Gee, Elisabeth I, 239
Gee, Ellen Dodge IV, 1316
Gee, James VI, 64
Gee, James S. VI, 134
Gee, James S. VI, 136
Gee, James S. VI, 144
Gee, Jane VI, 865
Gee, Susie IV, 1316
Gee, Theron VI, 130
Gee, Theron VI, 134
Gee, Theron VI, 144
Geeting, Debrah Ann V, 839
Geho, Marshall IV, 1279
Geho, Paul IV, 1279
Gehron, Chris V, 387
Gehron, Edith V, 387
Gehron, Mondalee V, 387
Geiberson, Earl V, 172
Geiberson, Lillie G. V, 172
Geiberson, Roy V, 172
Geiger, Laura Todhunter V, 674
Geiger, Mabel Elizabeth III, 133
Geiger, Mabel Elizabeth III, 265
Geiger, Nancy M. III, 133
Geiger, Nancy M. III, 265
Geiger, Otto John III, 133
Geiger, Otto John III, 265
Geis, Henry F. III, 133
Geisey, William IV, 204
Geist, Ida II, 960
Gelaspy, Elijah B. VI, 921
Gelaspy, Mary F. VI, 921
Gelaspy, Rolling VI, 921
Gellar, Moses V, 240
Gellette, Mariam IV, 1316
Gelston, Anna III, 133
Gelston, Eliza C. III, 133
Genealogy, Janney VI, 482
Genhert, Ethel III, 133
Genhert, Ethel III, 136
Genhert, Rene III, 133
Genhert, Wolf III, 133
Gennet, Ellsbury J. IV, 395
Gennings, Levi II, 81
Gennings, Thomas II, 81
Gennit, Ellsberg L. IV, 395
Gennit, Ellsbury J. IV, 395
Gennit, Elsbury L. IV, 395
Genny, Samuel V, 954
Genny, Sarah V, 954
Gens, Vera Pearl IV, 1316
Gentry, Baxton VI, 990
Gentry, John II, 443
Gentry, Mary II, 443
George, Abel IV, 1159
George, Abel IV, 1160
George, Abel IV, 1279
George, Abigail IV, 1159
George, Able IV, 1159
George, Abner V, 302
George, Amos II, 530
George, Amos II, 560
George, Amos II, 655
George, Amy V, 302
George, Amy V, 332
George, Ann II, 530
George, Ann II, 655
George, Ann V, 311
George, Ann M. VI, 831
George, Anna V, 302
George, Bailey VI, 819
George, Betsey VI, 850
George, Caleb IV, 626
George, Caleb IV, 869
George, Caleb VI, 391
George, Charles L. VI, 819
George, Charley IV, 1207
George, Col. Mary A. VI, 821
George, Col. Reuben VI, 865
George, Cyrus V, 302
George, David V, 302
George, David V, 303
George, David VI, 391
George, David VI, 920
George, David VI, 922
George, Deltla VI, 819
George, Donald IV, 1208
George, Edith IV, 331
George, Edith R. IV, 331
George, Edith R. IV, 357
George, Edward I, 1119
George, Edward II, 530
George, Edward VI, 243
George, Edward VI, 267
George, Eleanor V, 220
George, Eleanor V, 240
George, Elias Hicks VI, 391
George, Elis VI, 390
George, Eliza VI, 851
George, Elizabeth II, 530
George, Elizabeth III, 31
George, Elizabeth V, 303
George, Elizabeth VI, 493
George, Elizabeth VI, 565
George, Elizabeth VI, 567
George, Elizabeth VI, 801
George, Elizabeth VI, 840
George, Elizabeth VI, 920
George, Ellen V, 457
George, Ellen VI, 493
George, Ellen VI, 566
George, Ellen VI, 567
George, Ellendar VI, 920
George, Ellis V, 303
George, Ellis VI, 362
George, Ellis VI, 390
George, Ellis VI, 391
George, Ellis VI, 416
George, Elva V, 240
George, Enon V, 60
George, Enos V, 300
George, Enos V, 302
George, Enos VI, 391
George, Esther IV, 817
George, Esther IV, 869
George, Esther VI, 639
George, Esther VI, 701
George, Evan V, 303
George, Evan VI, 366
George, Evan VI, 390
George, Evan VI, 391
George, Evan George VI, 391
George, Frances H. VI, 864
George, George VI, 391
George, Gideon Lea, Sr. VI, 352
George, Hannah II, 530
George, Hannah V, 303
George, Hannah VI, 366
George, Hannah VI, 390
George, Hannah VI, 391
George, Harriett IV, 331
George, Harry IV, 1207
George, Harry IV, 1208
George, Henry IV, 626
George, Henry IV, 817
George, Henry IV, 825
George, Henry IV, 869
George, Henry VI, 390
George, Henry VI, 391
George, Henry VI, 394
George, Henry VI, 819
George, Henry VI, 831
George, Henry C. V, 303
George, Hesther IV, 869
George, Isaac V, 60
George, Isaac V, 302
George, Isaac V, 311
George, Isaac VI, 390
George, Isaac VI, 391
George, Isaiah V, 303
George, James V, 60
George, James V, 303
George, James V, 309
George, James VI, 362
George, James VI, 390
George, James VI, 391
George, James H. VI, 819
George, James L. V, 303
George, James, Jr. VI, 391
George, Jesse II, 530
George, Jesse IV, 1159
George, Jesse IV, 1207
George, Jesse V, 60
George, Jesse V, 215
George, Jesse V, 240
George, Jesse V, 302
George, Jesse V, 303
George, Jesse VI, 390
George, Jesse VI, 391
George, Jesse VI, 416
George, Jesse B. V, 303
George, Joel VI, 363
George, Joel VI, 391
George, Joel VI, 392
George, John II, 530
George, John IV, 1159
George, John IV, 1160
George, John IV, 1279
George, John V, 302
George, John V, 303
George, John VI, 390
George, John VI, 840
George, John B., Jr. V, 303
George, John Band V, 303
George, John S. IV, 1159
George, John S. IV, 1160
George, John S. IV, 1279
George, Jonas VI, 363
George, Jonathan VI, 363
George, Jonathan VI, 391
George, Joseph Leech IV, 869
George, Joseph Leech Hoops IV, 817
George, Joseph Leech Hoops IV, 870
George, Krekor III, 232
George, Leah V, 302
George, Leah V, 303
George, Leah VI, 390
George, Leah VI, 391
George, Lewis IV, 1207
George, Lewis V, 303
George, Lewis VI, 391
George, Lewis B. VI, 392
George, Lydia IV, 817
George, Lydia IV, 825
George, Lydia IV, 869
George, Lydia V, 302
George, Lydia V, 303
George, Lydia V, 309
George, Lydia VI, 362
George, Lydia VI, 390
George, Lydia VI, 391
George, Lydia VI, 409
George, Lydia VI, 416
George, Margaret I, 116
George, Margaret I, 139
George, Margaret I, 164
George, Maria VI, 391
George, Maria VI, 418
George, Martha I, 941
George, Martha I, 1119
George, Martha L. I, 925
George, Mary II, 797
George, Mary IV, 204
George, Mary IV, 331
George, Mary IV, 332
George, Mary IV, 473
George, Mary IV, 494
George, Mary IV, 626
George, Mary IV, 869
George, Mary IV, 1159
George, Mary IV, 1160
George, Mary IV, 1208
George, Mary IV, 1279
George, Mary V, 60
George, Mary V, 303
George, Mary VI, 362
George, Mary VI, 363
George, Mary VI, 380
George, Mary VI, 390
George, Mary VI, 391
George, Mary VI, 409
George, Mary VI, 493
George, Mary VI, 566
George, Mary VI, 567
George, Mary VI, 819
George, Mary Ann IV, 1159
George, Mary B. VI, 391
George, Mary George VI, 391
George, Mary R. V, 302
George, Mary, Jr. V, 303
George, Mary, Jr. VI, 391
George, Mary, Sr. VI, 391
George, Mattie Wood V, 674
George, Melvina V, 240
George, Mercy V, 215
George, Mercy V, 303
George, Mercy VI, 390
George, Mercy VI, 391
George, Mercy VI, 416
George, Milley VI, 920
George, Milly VI, 865
George, Molly VI, 838
George, Nancy VI, 819
George, Patience IV, 1207
George, Penelope VI, 920
George, Phebe V, 60
George, Phebe V, 300
George, Phebe V, 302
George, Phebe VI, 391
George, Polly VI, 881
George, Rachel IV, 869
George, Rachel V, 303
George, Rachel VI, 363
George, Rachel VI, 390
George, Rachel VI, 391
George, Rebecca II, 530
George, Rebecca II, 560
George, Rebecca II, 655
George, Rebecca VI, 390
George, Rebecca VI, 391
George, Rebecca VI, 416
George, Rebekah VI, 391
George, Reuben VI, 920
George, Reubin VI, 352
George, Reubin VI, 353
George, Reubin VI, 821
George, Richard II, 366
George, Richard II, 530
George, Richard II, 560
George, Richard IV, 869
George, Richard V, 240
George, Richard V, 303
George, Richard VI, 380
George, Richard VI, 390
George, Richard VI, 391
George, Richard VI, 409
George, Richard George IV, 869
George, Richard George VI, 391
George, Richard H. II, 742
George, Richard Humphreys II, 366
George, Rithy VI, 920
George, Rose IV, 1207
George, Ruth V, 303
George, Ruth VI, 390
George, Ruth VI, 391
George, Sally V, 300
George, Sally V, 302
George, Sally VI, 838
George, Samuel I, 1119
George, Samuel IV, 1159
George, Samuel VI, 838
George, Samuel VI, 920
George, Sarah II, 530
George, Sarah IV, 473
George, Sarah IV, 494
George, Sarah IV, 526
George, Sarah IV, 1207
George, Sarah IV, 1208
George, Sarah V, 303
George, Sarah VI, 243
George, Sarah VI, 267
George, Sarah VI, 362
George, Sarah VI, 390
George, Sarah VI, 391
George, Sarah VI, 851
George, Sarah L. V, 302
George, Silas VI, 391
George, Susannah I Sup 1, 3
George, Susannah I Sup 1, 4
George, Tabitha V, 24
George, Tabitha V, 60
George, Tabitha V, 240
George, Tabitha V, 387
George, Tacy II, 366
George, Tacy II, 530
George, Tacy II, 560
George, Tamar VI, 390
George, Tamar VI, 391
George, Tamar VI, 394
George, Tamer IV, 626
George, Thomas II, 530
George, Tura IV, 1207
George, Valinda IV, 1159
George, Valinda IV, 1160
George, Valinda IV, 1279
George, Vilinda IV, 1159
George, Walter IV, 1207
George, Walter IV, 1208
George, Wd. Mary VI, 391
George, William VI, 352
George, William VI, 353
George, William VI, 849
George, William VI, 878
George, William VI, 920
George, William H. IV, 1159
George, William H. IV, 1279
George, William M. VI, 920
George, Wm. IV, 1159
George, Wm. VI, 363
George, Wm. VI, 833
George, Wm. A. IV, 1160
George, Wm. H. IV, 1159
Georgees, Edward I, 1093
Georke, Agnes G. III, 100
Georke, Benjamin III, 136
Georke, Frank III, 136
Georke, Isabella III, 277
Georke, Martha B. III, 136
Georke, Oscar III, 100
Gerald, Hannah III, 413
Gerald, Hannah III, 452
Gerald, Harriet III, 413

Gerald, Thomas J. III, 413
Gerald, Thomas J. III, 452
Gerald, Thos. J. III, 452
Gerard, Fanny Grand V, 674
Gerberding, C. O. VI, 920
Gerberding, Mary Jane VI, 920
Gerde, Patsy VI, 919
Gerde, William VI, 919
Gerhard, Christian V, 562
Gerhard, Louis V, 562
Gerhard, Mary V, 562
Gerhart, Mary II, 824
Geringer, Ira I, 935
Gerlager, ??? III, 133
Gerlager, Frederic III, 133
Gerlager, Henry III, 133
Germain, Isaac III, 452
Germain, Margaret III, 452
German, Mary VI, 680
Germon, John II, 366
Germon, Sarah II, 366
Germond, ??? III, 133
Germond, Earl III, 133
Germond, Earl III, 136
Germond, Earl Goerke III, 133
Germond, Helen III, 136
Germond, Henry III, 133
Germond, James III, 413
Germond, Norman Maurice III, 133
Germond, Oscar III, 133
Germond, Samuel III, 133
Germond, Sarah III, 413
Germond, Sarah III, 455
Germond, Seaman III, 413
Germond, Selma III, 133
Germond, Selma G. III, 133
Germond, Selma G. III, 136
Germond, Simon III, 413
Germond, Simon III, 455
Germond, William III, 133
Gernhardt, Anna III, 133
Gernhardt, Anna III, 317
Gernhardt, Henry III, 133
Gernhardt, Joseph H. III, 317
Gernhardt, Marie Josephine III, 133
Gernhardt, Marie Josephine III, 317
Gerow, Ellsworth IV, 993
Gerow, Lucy Ann III, 133
Gerow, Marilla L. IV, 993
Gerow, Mary IV, 993
Gerow, Sarah III, 133
Gerow, William P. III, 133
Gerrard, Dora C. IV, 1316
Gerrard, Dora C. IV, 1320
Gerrard, Robert II, 366
Gerren, C. Felba IV, 1251
Gerren, Feba O. IV, 1251
Gerrish, Conrad IV, 1251
Gerrison, Elizabeth I, 879
Gerrminhard, Ella IV, 1251
Gerrminhard, Gussie IV, 1251
Gerrminhard, Harry IV, 1251
Gerrminhard, Lizzie IV, 1251
Gerrminhard, Mathew IV, 1251
Gerrminhard, Samuel IV, 1251
Gerton, Milton I, 390
Gertright, Samuel VI, 177
Gertrite, Jane VI, 177
Gertrite, Jane Anna VI, 148
Gertrude, Anna M. III, 210
Gertrude, Benj. H. III, 210
Gertrude, Emily V, 121
Gertrude, Frances III, 210
Gertrude, Helen VI, 376
Gervas, Elizabeth II, 71
Gervas, Elizabeth II, 103
Gervis, Gerard VI, 317
Gesling, Ann II, 443
Gesling, Catherine II, 443
Gesling, Ceasar II, 443
Gest, Ann II, 797
Gest, Ann II, 870
Gest, Baker V, 60
Gest, Clarissa V, 907
Gest, Clifford H. V, 907
Gest, Clifford Haworth V, 907
Gest, Deborah II, 870
Gest, Deborah V, 906
Gest, Elizabeth II, 797
Gest, Elizabeth II, 870
Gest, Erasmus V, 907
Gest, Guion M. III, 133
Gest, Hannah II, 791
Gest, Hannah V, 60
Gest, Jacob T. II, 870
Gest, Jacob Thomas II, 797
Gest, James V, 60
Gest, James V, 907
Gest, Jennie III, 133
Gest, John II, 797
Gest, John II, 870
Gest, John V, 60
Gest, Joseph V, 906
Gest, Joseph V, 907
Gest, Joseph G. V, 907
Gest, Joseph Haywood III, 133
Gest, Joseph Haywood III, 298
Gest, Joseph Henry V, 907
Gest, Joseph J. V, 907
Gest, Joseph John V, 907
Gest, Lillian III, 133
Gest, Mary V, 60
Gest, Mary Ann II, 870
Gest, Pauline III, 133
Gest, Pauline III, 298
Gest, Rebecca V, 907
Gest, Roy E. III, 133
Gest, Sarah V, 60
Gest, Sarah V, 172
Gest, Sarah E. V, 172
Gest, Susan A. V, 892
Gest, Susan A. V, 907
Gester, Jemima I, 887
Gester, Jemima I, 902
Getchel, Hannah IV, 331
Getchel, Hannah IV, 349
Getchell, William III, 133
Gettis, Ann VI, 390
Geurekian, Arman III, 133
Geurekian, Bedras T. III, 133
Geurekian, Huart III, 133
Geurekian, Mary III, 133
Ghant, Michel IV, 367
Ghant, Michel IV, 395
Gheen, Elizabeth II, 826
Ghent, Jane V, 737
Ghent, Jane V, 740
Ghiseling, Elisabeth II, 530
Ghold, John C. IV, 712
Ghollar, Phebe II, 70
Ghollar, Phebe L. Gallagher II, 71
Ghourley, Adalaide I, 1152
Ghourley, Caroline I, 1152
Ghourley, Lydia I, 1152
Ghourley, Phebe I, 1152
Ghourley, Robert I, 1152
Ghrist, Deborah IV, 90
Ghrist, John IV, 35
Ghrist, John IV, 714
Ghrist, Joseph IV, 35
Ghrist, Joseph IV, 90
Ghrist, Margaret IV, 90
Ghrist, Margaret IV, 121
Ghrist, Margaret Bailey IV, 126
Ghrist, Thirza IV, 90
Ghrist, William IV, 35
Giar, Mary I, 542
Gibb, Florence May IV, 712
Gibb, Lucy IV, 712
Gibb, Oscar IV, 712
Gibbens, Helen IV, 1208
Gibbens, Lydia I, 270
Gibbens, Lydia I, 275
Gibbens, Samuel IV, 712
Gibbens, Susanna II, 530
Gibbens, Wm. II, 530
Gibbings, John II, 555
Gibbings, Sarah II, 555
Gibbins, Abigail III, 133
Gibbins, Bevington Henry III, 133
Gibbins, Edith Susan III, 133
Gibbins, John II, 530
Gibbins, John, Jr. II, 530
Gibbins, Mary Ann IV, 712
Gibbins, Sarah II, 530
Gibbins, Sarah Hooper III, 133
Gibbins, Sophia I, 541
Gibbins, Sophiah I, 541
Gibbins, Wm. IV, 712
Gibbon, Lydia IV, 593
Gibbons, Abby III, 234
Gibbons, Abel II, 224
Gibbons, Abigail II, 795
Gibbons, Abigail III, 110
Gibbons, Abigail III, 133
Gibbons, Abigail H. II, 867
Gibbons, Abigail H. III, 133
Gibbons, Adaline II, 820
Gibbons, Adaline II, 887
Gibbons, Adaline II, 924
Gibbons, Adrian IV, 1362
Gibbons, Albert Willard IV, 579
Gibbons, Almeda Ellen IV, 579
Gibbons, Amanda Ellen IV, 580
Gibbons, Amos E. IV, 205
Gibbons, Ann II, 118
Gibbons, Ann II, 821
Gibbons, Ann IV, 205
Gibbons, Ann IV, 578
Gibbons, Ann IV, 579
Gibbons, Ann IV, 580
Gibbons, Anna II, 28
Gibbons, Anna IV, 579
Gibbons, Anna IV, 594
Gibbons, Anne II, 117
Gibbons, Anne II, 118
Gibbons, Benjamin F. IV, 712
Gibbons, Beulah II, 224
Gibbons, Carlton IV, 526
Gibbons, Carlton IV, 1208
Gibbons, Caroline II, 843
Gibbons, Caroline II, 867
Gibbons, Caroline IV, 388
Gibbons, Charles II, 742
Gibbons, Charles III, 133
Gibbons, Charles III, 175
Gibbons, Charles E. IV, 580
Gibbons, Charles E. IV, 712
Gibbons, Clara IV, 579
Gibbons, Daniel II, 530
Gibbons, Daniel III, 133
Gibbons, David IV, 712
Gibbons, Deborah II, 821
Gibbons, Dillon IV, 135
Gibbons, Dillon IV, 136
Gibbons, Dillon IV, 205
Gibbons, Dillon IV, 580
Gibbons, Dillon IV, 712
Gibbons, Edith IV, 570
Gibbons, Edith Elmira IV, 579
Gibbons, Edith G. IV, 570
Gibbons, Edith G. IV, 580
Gibbons, Edith Glass IV, 712
Gibbons, Edmund IV, 579
Gibbons, Edmund IV, 580
Gibbons, Edward IV, 626
Gibbons, Edward IV, 712
Gibbons, Edward IV, 956
Gibbons, Edward J. IV, 712
Gibbons, Edward S. IV, 626
Gibbons, Edward V. IV, 579
Gibbons, Edward V. IV, 580
Gibbons, Edward V. IV, 591
Gibbons, Edwin Cope II, 821
Gibbons, Edwin D. IV, 579
Gibbons, Elam IV, 205
Gibbons, Elam IV, 580
Gibbons, Eleanor IV, 204
Gibbons, Eli IV, 205
Gibbons, Eli IV, 580
Gibbons, Eli W. IV, 204
Gibbons, Eli W. IV, 246
Gibbons, Eli W. IV, 570
Gibbons, Eli W. IV, 579
Gibbons, Eli W. IV, 580
Gibbons, Eli W. IV, 585
Gibbons, Eli W. IV, 587
Gibbons, Elisabeth IV, 1367
Gibbons, Eliz. III, 133
Gibbons, Eliza C. III, 133
Gibbons, Eliza E. III, 175
Gibbons, Eliza Jane IV, 204
Gibbons, Eliza Jane IV, 205
Gibbons, Eliza Jane IV, 246
Gibbons, Eliza Jane IV, 570
Gibbons, Eliza Jane IV, 579
Gibbons, Eliza Jane IV, 580
Gibbons, Eliza Jane IV, 585
Gibbons, Eliza Jane IV, 587
Gibbons, Eliza M. IV, 526
Gibbons, Eliza M. IV, 552
Gibbons, Eliza M. IV, 580
Gibbons, Eliza M. IV, 595
Gibbons, Elizabeth IV, 135
Gibbons, Elizabeth IV, 147
Gibbons, Elizabeth IV, 205
Gibbons, Elizabeth IV, 572
Gibbons, Elizabeth IV, 573
Gibbons, Elizabeth IV, 577
Gibbons, Elizabeth IV, 579
Gibbons, Elizabeth IV, 580
Gibbons, Elizabeth IV, 599
Gibbons, Elizabeth IV, 600
Gibbons, Elizabeth IV, 601
Gibbons, Elizabeth IV, 1362
Gibbons, Elizabeth P. IV, 1362
Gibbons, Elizabeth P. IV, 1368
Gibbons, Ellen IV, 712
Gibbons, Ellis Leeds II, 821
Gibbons, Ellis Leeds, Jr. II, 821
Gibbons, Elma IV, 205
Gibbons, Elma IV, 289
Gibbons, Elma IV, 579
Gibbons, Elma IV, 580
Gibbons, Elma IV, 596
Gibbons, Elma F. IV, 580
Gibbons, Elma T. IV, 205
Gibbons, Elvira IV, 580
Gibbons, Elvira W. IV, 579
Gibbons, Emma IV, 413
Gibbons, Emma Laura IV, 579
Gibbons, Emma Laura IV, 585
Gibbons, Enoch II, 224
Gibbons, Ernest M. IV, 579
Gibbons, Esther II, 366
Gibbons, Esther IV, 205
Gibbons, Esther IV, 580
Gibbons, Ethel M. IV, 1038
Gibbons, Francis III, 133
Gibbons, Francis IV, 626
Gibbons, Frederick R. IV, 579
Gibbons, George II, 530
Gibbons, George W. II, 531
Gibbons, George W. II, 866
Gibbons, George Washington II, 795
Gibbons, George Washington II, 820
Gibbons, Hannah II, 224
Gibbons, Hannah II, 530
Gibbons, Hannah IV, 147
Gibbons, Hannah IV, 205
Gibbons, Hannah IV, 262
Gibbons, Hartley IV, 1208
Gibbons, Helen IV, 1208
Gibbons, Henry II, 118
Gibbons, Homer IV, 205
Gibbons, Homer IV, 578
Gibbons, Homer IV, 580
Gibbons, Homer IV, 1058
Gibbons, Hugh IV, 712
Gibbons, Hugh Judge IV, 956
Gibbons, Ida IV, 370
Gibbons, Ida IV, 395
Gibbons, Iona Belle IV, 1208
Gibbons, Isaac IV, 712
Gibbons, Isaac IV, 956
Gibbons, Isaac H. III, 133
Gibbons, Isaac H. IV, 712
Gibbons, Isaac T. III, 133
Gibbons, Isaac Thomas IV, 205
Gibbons, Isabelle IV, 1208
Gibbons, Isaiah H. IV, 712
Gibbons, Isaiah K. IV, 712
Gibbons, J. IV, 1362
Gibbons, Jacob IV, 1362
Gibbons, James II, 117
Gibbons, James II, 118
Gibbons, James II, 530
Gibbons, James III, 133
Gibbons, James IV, 135
Gibbons, James IV, 204
Gibbons, James IV, 205
Gibbons, James IV, 526
Gibbons, James IV, 573
Gibbons, James IV, 580
Gibbons, James IV, 601
Gibbons, James IV, 1058
Gibbons, James IV, 1083
Gibbons, James E. IV, 526
Gibbons, James E. IV, 552
Gibbons, James E. IV, 579
Gibbons, James E. IV, 580
Gibbons, James E. IV, 595
Gibbons, James S. II, 742
Gibbons, James S. II, 795
Gibbons, James S. II, 866
Gibbons, James S. III, 110
Gibbons, James S. III, 133
Gibbons, James S. III, 234
Gibbons, James W. IV, 579
Gibbons, Jane II, 366
Gibbons, Jane II, 530
Gibbons, Jane IV, 147
Gibbons, Jane IV, 578
Gibbons, Jane IV, 579
Gibbons, Jane IV, 599
Gibbons, Janne I Sup 1, 4
Gibbons, John II, 366
Gibbons, John II, 530
Gibbons, John II, 546
Gibbons, John IV, 205
Gibbons, John IV, 395
Gibbons, John IV, 572
Gibbons, John IV, 599
Gibbons, John IV, 1208
Gibbons, John Edwin IV, 205
Gibbons, John F. IV, 579
Gibbons, John Franklin IV, 205
Gibbons, John Franklin IV, 580
Gibbons, John M. IV, 1208
Gibbons, John Taylor IV, 205
Gibbons, John Taylor IV, 580
Gibbons, John, Jr. II, 530
Gibbons, Jos. B. IV, 289
Gibbons, Joseph II, 288
Gibbons, Joseph II, 303
Gibbons, Joseph II, 705
Gibbons, Joseph III, 133
Gibbons, Joseph IV, 147
Gibbons, Joseph IV, 204
Gibbons, Joseph IV, 205
Gibbons, Joseph IV, 573
Gibbons, Joseph IV, 580
Gibbons, Joseph IV, 594
Gibbons, Joseph IV, 601
Gibbons, Joseph IV, 1362
Gibbons, Joseph IV, 1368
Gibbons, Joseph IV, 1381
Gibbons, Joseph IV, 1382
Gibbons, Joseph B. IV, 205
Gibbons, Joseph B. IV, 576
Gibbons, Joseph B. IV, 579
Gibbons, Joseph B. IV, 596
Gibbons, Joseph H. IV, 1362
Gibbons, Joseph, Jr. IV, 205
Gibbons, Joshua II, 224
Gibbons, Joshua II, 530
Gibbons, Joshua IV, 88
Gibbons, Judge Hugh IV, 712
Gibbons, Julia III, 133
Gibbons, Katharine Moore II, 821
Gibbons, Lavin IV, 205
Gibbons, Lavina H. IV, 579
Gibbons, Leanna Pearl IV, 1208
Gibbons, Leland S. IV, 579
Gibbons, Lida M. IV, 579
Gibbons, Lindley IV, 205
Gibbons, Lindley IV, 569
Gibbons, Lindley IV, 579
Gibbons, Lindley H. IV, 372
Gibbons, Lindley H. IV, 395
Gibbons, Lindley H. IV, 579
Gibbons, Lindley H. IV, 580
Gibbons, Louisa IV, 388
Gibbons, Lucas II, 224
Gibbons, Lucinda IV, 205
Gibbons, Lucinda IV, 579
Gibbons, Lucinda IV, 580
Gibbons, Lucy III, 133
Gibbons, Lucy III, 234
Gibbons, Lydia I, 270
Gibbons, Lydia II, 117
Gibbons, Lydia II, 118
Gibbons, Lydia II, 530
Gibbons, Lydia IV, 205
Gibbons, Lydia IV, 526
Gibbons, Lydia IV, 572
Gibbons, Lydia IV, 579
Gibbons, Lydia IV, 580
Gibbons, Lydia IV, 594
Gibbons, Lydia IV, 601
Gibbons, Lydia IV, 712
Gibbons, Lydia IV, 724
Gibbons, Lydia IV, 1058
Gibbons, Lydia IV, 1083
Gibbons, Lydia Ann IV, 205
Gibbons, Lydia Ann IV, 580
Gibbons, Lydia Ann V, 839
Gibbons, Lydia H. IV, 205
Gibbons, Lydia H. IV, 1362
Gibbons, Lydia H. IV, 1380
Gibbons, Lydia S. IV, 205
Gibbons, Maranda IV, 205
Gibbons, Maranda IV, 573
Gibbons, Maranda IV, 579
Gibbons, Maranda IV, 580
Gibbons, Margaret II, 288
Gibbons, Margaret II, 303
Gibbons, Margaret IV, 1362
Gibbons, Margaret W. IV, 579
Gibbons, Maria IV, 205
Gibbons, Maria IV, 579
Gibbons, Maria IV, 580
Gibbons, Maria IV, 712
Gibbons, Martha IV, 147
Gibbons, Martha IV, 176
Gibbons, Martha IV, 205
Gibbons, Martha IV, 567
Gibbons, Martha IV, 573
Gibbons, Martha IV, 579
Gibbons, Martha IV, 1058
Gibbons, Martha IV, 1362
Gibbons, Mary II, 224
Gibbons, Mary II, 530
Gibbons, Mary II, 780
Gibbons, Mary II, 787
Gibbons, Mary II, 821
Gibbons, Mary IV, 135
Gibbons, Mary IV, 136
Gibbons, Mary IV, 147
Gibbons, Mary IV, 395
Gibbons, Mary IV, 577
Gibbons, Mary IV, 579
Gibbons, Mary IV, 580
Gibbons, Mary IV, 594
Gibbons, Mary IV, 712
Gibbons, Mary Ann IV, 205
Gibbons, Mary Ann IV, 626
Gibbons, Mary Ann IV, 712

Gibbons, Mary Ann IV, 716
Gibbons, Mary G. IV, 712
Gibbons, Mary H. II, 531
Gibbons, Mary H. IV, 1093
Gibbons, Mary H. IV, 1098
Gibbons, Mary Hisham II, 531
Gibbons, Mary J. IV, 580
Gibbons, Mary J. IV, 1058
Gibbons, Mary P. II, 705
Gibbons, Mercy IV, 147
Gibbons, Miles II, 224
Gibbons, Mortimer Claude IV, 579
Gibbons, N. Allen IV, 580
Gibbons, Nathan Allen IV, 579
Gibbons, Nathan Allen IV, 580
Gibbons, Olive R. IV, 579
Gibbons, Olive R. IV, 591
Gibbons, Oliver H. IV, 205
Gibbons, Oliver H. IV, 579
Gibbons, Oliver H. IV, 580
Gibbons, Penina IV, 204
Gibbons, Penina IV, 205
Gibbons, Penina IV, 579
Gibbons, Penina IV, 580
Gibbons, Penina IV, 600
Gibbons, Penina IV, 601
Gibbons, Penina E. IV, 573
Gibbons, Penina E. IV, 579
Gibbons, Peninah IV, 573
Gibbons, Peninah IV, 579
Gibbons, Peninah IV, 580
Gibbons, Peninah IV, 594
Gibbons, Peninah IV, 600
Gibbons, Penninah IV, 205
Gibbons, Phebe II, 224
Gibbons, Phebe II, 530
Gibbons, Phebe II, 858
Gibbons, Phebe II, 867
Gibbons, Phebe III, 133
Gibbons, Phebe E. II, 867
Gibbons, Phebe G. IV, 290
Gibbons, Phebe G. IV, 1362
Gibbons, Phebe G. IV, 1382
Gibbons, Rachel II, 795
Gibbons, Rachel II, 807
Gibbons, Rachel II, 820
Gibbons, Rachel II, 866
Gibbons, Rachel IV, 205
Gibbons, Rachel IV, 372
Gibbons, Rachel IV, 395
Gibbons, Rachel IV, 569
Gibbons, Rachel IV, 579
Gibbons, Rachel IV, 580
Gibbons, Rachel IV, 600
Gibbons, Rachel Ann II, 866
Gibbons, Rachel Ann II, 867
Gibbons, Rachel Ann II, 943
Gibbons, Rachel B. IV, 395
Gibbons, Rachel B. IV, 580
Gibbons, Ray IV, 1208
Gibbons, Rebecca II, 224
Gibbons, Rebecca III, 133
Gibbons, Rebecca IV, 576
Gibbons, Rebecca IV, 579
Gibbons, Rebecca E. IV, 579
Gibbons, Rebecca W. IV, 205
Gibbons, Reulon II, 224
Gibbons, Rheuben IV, 1058
Gibbons, Richard IV, 205
Gibbons, Ronald D. IV, 526
Gibbons, Ronald D. IV, 579
Gibbons, Ruth II, 224
Gibbons, Ruth IV, 205
Gibbons, Ruth IV, 580
Gibbons, Ruth IV, 1382
Gibbons, Ruthanna IV, 205
Gibbons, Samuel IV, 579
Gibbons, Samuel IV, 712
Gibbons, Samuel IV, 956
Gibbons, Samuel Cope II, 821
Gibbons, Samuel W. IV, 712
Gibbons, Samuel, Jr. IV, 712
Gibbons, Sarah II, 224
Gibbons, Sarah II, 288
Gibbons, Sarah II, 303
Gibbons, Sarah II, 366
Gibbons, Sarah II, 530
Gibbons, Sarah II, 705
Gibbons, Sarah III, 110
Gibbons, Sarah III, 133
Gibbons, Sarah IV, 147
Gibbons, Sarah IV, 204
Gibbons, Sarah IV, 205
Gibbons, Sarah IV, 288
Gibbons, Sarah IV, 579
Gibbons, Sarah IV, 1362
Gibbons, Sarah Ann IV, 1058
Gibbons, Sarah E. IV, 205
Gibbons, Sarah E. IV, 579
Gibbons, Sarah Elizabeth IV, 580
Gibbons, Sarah H. III, 110
Gibbons, Steven I Sup 1, 4
Gibbons, Susan II, 118
Gibbons, Susan IV, 147
Gibbons, Susan IV, 526
Gibbons, Susan IV, 527
Gibbons, Susan IV, 579
Gibbons, Susanna II, 530
Gibbons, Susanna IV, 569
Gibbons, Susanna IV, 579
Gibbons, Susannah II, 821
Gibbons, Susannah IV, 147
Gibbons, Thomas IV, 204
Gibbons, Thomas IV, 205
Gibbons, Thomas IV, 288
Gibbons, Thomas IV, 712
Gibbons, Thomas IV, 1362
Gibbons, Thomas D. IV, 712
Gibbons, Thos. II, 821
Gibbons, Tilman IV, 205
Gibbons, Wager III, 133
Gibbons, Webster IV, 1382
Gibbons, Wilbert IV, 526
Gibbons, Wilbur Carlton IV, 579
Gibbons, William II, 366
Gibbons, William III, 133
Gibbons, William IV, 147
Gibbons, William IV, 205
Gibbons, William S. IV, 205
Gibbons, William, Jr. II, 795
Gibbons, Willis Hartley IV, 1208
Gibbons, Wm. II, 530
Gibbons, Wm. III, 133
Gibbons, Wm. IV, 147
Gibbons, Wm. IV, 388
Gibbons, Wm. IV, 580
Gibbons, Wm. IV, 712
Gibbons, Wm. A. II, 742
Gibbons, Wm. I. II, 117
Gibbons, Wm. I. II, 118
Gibbons, Wm. Melville IV, 1208
Gibbons, Wm. P. II, 742
Gibbons, Wm. P. II, 867
Gibbons, Zenas IV, 1058
Gibbons, Zinas Ruben Sarah Ann IV, 580
Gibbs, ??? II, 366
Gibbs, ??? III, 133
Gibbs, Abel III, 133
Gibbs, Abel III, 350
Gibbs, Alex VI, 942
Gibbs, Alex VI, 944
Gibbs, Alexander VI, 877
Gibbs, Alexander VI, 920
Gibbs, Alexander VI, 955
Gibbs, Alexander VI, 1009
Gibbs, Alexander, Jr. VI, 942
Gibbs, Alexr. VI, 932
Gibbs, Alexr. VI, 959
Gibbs, Alexr. VI, 967
Gibbs, Alexr. VI, 980
Gibbs, Alexr. VI, 986
Gibbs, Alfred M. VI, 920
Gibbs, Ann I, 982
Gibbs, Ann I, 986
Gibbs, Ann II, 194
Gibbs, Ann II, 225
Gibbs, Ann II, 366
Gibbs, Ann II, 531
Gibbs, Ann II, 551
Gibbs, Ann II, 780
Gibbs, Ann V, 60
Gibbs, Ann V, 64
Gibbs, Ann VI, 920
Gibbs, Ann P. VI, 920
Gibbs, Barclay II, 780
Gibbs, Benjamin II, 173
Gibbs, Benjamin II, 174
Gibbs, Benjamin II, 211
Gibbs, Benjamin II, 224
Gibbs, Benjamin II, 366
Gibbs, Benjamin II, 531
Gibbs, Borus II, 71
Gibbs, Burroughs II, 71
Gibbs, Burwell VI, 920
Gibbs, Carlton IV, 1208
Gibbs, Casann B. VI, 920
Gibbs, Catherine VI, 920
Gibbs, Chalkley Harris II, 71
Gibbs, Charlotte III, 133
Gibbs, Daniel IV, 1208
Gibbs, David VI, 877
Gibbs, David VI, 897
Gibbs, David VI, 920
Gibbs, David VI, 1002
Gibbs, Doshia VI, 911
Gibbs, Dr. Sam'l III, 133
Gibbs, Dr. Samuel E. III, 212
Gibbs, Drury C. VI, 964
Gibbs, Edmond Wetherby II, 71
Gibbs, Edward II, 28
Gibbs, Edward II, 71
Gibbs, Edward VI, 813
Gibbs, Eliz. III, 134
Gibbs, Eliz. III, 350
Gibbs, Eliza E. II, 288
Gibbs, Elizabeth II, 288
Gibbs, Elizabeth III, 133
Gibbs, Elizabeth VI, 877
Gibbs, Elizabeth VI, 920
Gibbs, Elizabeth VI, 973
Gibbs, Elizabeth VI, 1017
Gibbs, Elizabeth T. VI, 742
Gibbs, Emily VI, 819
Gibbs, Eneas II, 366
Gibbs, Enoch II, 28
Gibbs, Enoch II, 71
Gibbs, Enoch II, 131
Gibbs, Esther II, 28
Gibbs, Esther II, 71
Gibbs, Esther II, 531
Gibbs, Esther Garrison II, 71
Gibbs, Eva III, 76
Gibbs, Florence May IV, 712
Gibbs, Frances VI, 813
Gibbs, Frances VI, 994
Gibbs, George VI, 819
Gibbs, Gilbert VI, 920
Gibbs, Grace C. III, 133
Gibbs, Grace C. III, 232
Gibbs, Grace C. III, 292
Gibbs, Grace Carol III, 133
Gibbs, Grace Carol III, 292
Gibbs, Grace Caroline III, 134
Gibbs, Grace Caroline III, 212
Gibbs, Hannah II, 71
Gibbs, Hannah II, 224
Gibbs, Hannah II, 225
Gibbs, Hannah II, 240
Gibbs, Hannah II, 250
Gibbs, Hannah II, 522
Gibbs, Hannah II, 531
Gibbs, Hannah III, 100
Gibbs, Hannah III, 133
Gibbs, Hannah III, 134
Gibbs, Hannah III, 350
Gibbs, Hannah V, 60
Gibbs, Hannah V, 137
Gibbs, Hannah VI, 920
Gibbs, Hannah A. II, 705
Gibbs, Hannah Ann II, 280
Gibbs, Hannah Ann II, 288
Gibbs, Haydock III, 133
Gibbs, Henry C. VI, 920
Gibbs, Hephsibah II, 28
Gibbs, Hephzibah II, 28
Gibbs, Hepzabah II, 131
Gibbs, Hepzibah II, 71
Gibbs, Hepzibah II, 77
Gibbs, Herbert VI, 920
Gibbs, Isaac II, 213
Gibbs, Isaac II, 224
Gibbs, Isaac II, 240
Gibbs, Isaac II, 250
Gibbs, Isaac III, 100
Gibbs, Isaac III, 134
Gibbs, Isaac, Jr. II, 253
Gibbs, James VI, 920
Gibbs, James C. VI, 920
Gibbs, James C. VI, 955
Gibbs, Jemima VI, 920
Gibbs, Jemima Ann II, 288
Gibbs, Jesse R. VI, 973
Gibbs, Joel VI, 920
Gibbs, John II, 28
Gibbs, John II, 71
Gibbs, John II, 224
Gibbs, John II, 240
Gibbs, John II, 288
Gibbs, John II, 522
Gibbs, John II, 531
Gibbs, John III, 194
Gibbs, John III, 355
Gibbs, John VI, 906
Gibbs, John VI, 911
Gibbs, John VI, 920
Gibbs, John VI, 972
Gibbs, John W. IV, 205
Gibbs, John Wilber IV, 205
Gibbs, Jonathan II, 28
Gibbs, Jonathan II, 71
Gibbs, Jonathan II, 76
Gibbs, Jonathan II, 522
Gibbs, Jonathan II, 531
Gibbs, Jordan VI, 920
Gibbs, Joseph II, 224
Gibbs, Joseph II, 366
Gibbs, Joseph VI, 819
Gibbs, Joseph N. II, 288
Gibbs, Josephine II, 288
Gibbs, Joshua II, 225
Gibbs, Joshua III, 134
Gibbs, Judith II, 531
Gibbs, Kelly A. IV, 1208
Gibbs, Keziah VI, 920
Gibbs, Larkin VI, 920
Gibbs, Lewin VI, 920
Gibbs, Lidya II, 28
Gibbs, Lidya II, 71
Gibbs, Lidya II, 76
Gibbs, Lucas II, 71
Gibbs, Lucas II, 76
Gibbs, Lucas II, 110
Gibbs, Lucy IV, 712
Gibbs, Lucy J. VI, 920
Gibbs, Lucy Jane VI, 312
Gibbs, Lucy Jane VI, 334
Gibbs, Lydia II, 28
Gibbs, Lydia II, 71
Gibbs, Lydia IV, 1208
Gibbs, Lydia VI, 920
Gibbs, Maria L. VI, 729
Gibbs, Maria L. VI, 730
Gibbs, Maria L. VI, 742
Gibbs, Maria L. VI, 791
Gibbs, Maria Louisa VI, 920
Gibbs, Martha II, 71
Gibbs, Martha VI, 955
Gibbs, Martha Ann VI, 916
Gibbs, Martha Ann VI, 920
Gibbs, Martha D. II, 288
Gibbs, Martin II, 194
Gibbs, Martin II, 224
Gibbs, Martin II, 225
Gibbs, Martin II, 780
Gibbs, Mary II, 28
Gibbs, Mary II, 71
Gibbs, Mary II, 76
Gibbs, Mary II, 83
Gibbs, Mary II, 118
Gibbs, Mary II, 131
Gibbs, Mary II, 173
Gibbs, Mary II, 225
Gibbs, Mary II, 253
Gibbs, Mary II, 531
Gibbs, Mary II, 867
Gibbs, Mary III, 134
Gibbs, Mary III, 194
Gibbs, Mary III, 355
Gibbs, Mary V, 782
Gibbs, Mary V, 785
Gibbs, Mary VI, 819
Gibbs, Mary VI, 897
Gibbs, Mary VI, 942
Gibbs, Mary A. VI, 930
Gibbs, Mary Ann VI, 920
Gibbs, Mary Anna II, 288
Gibbs, Mary R. III, 134
Gibbs, Mary R. III, 483
Gibbs, Mary, Sr. II, 28
Gibbs, Mason VI, 986
Gibbs, Matilda VI, 880
Gibbs, Matthew VI, 920
Gibbs, Miles H. III, 134
Gibbs, Nancy VI, 920
Gibbs, Nancy VI, 932
Gibbs, Obadiah III, 134
Gibbs, Oscar IV, 712
Gibbs, Pamelia VI, 1002
Gibbs, Paschal A. VI, 869
Gibbs, Paschal A. VI, 898
Gibbs, Paschal A. VI, 920
Gibbs, Paschal A. VI, 998
Gibbs, Paschal N. VI, 920
Gibbs, Patsy VI, 920
Gibbs, Patty VI, 967
Gibbs, Perling VI, 819
Gibbs, Permelia VI, 920
Gibbs, Peter VI, 813
Gibbs, Peter VI, 819
Gibbs, Phebe II, 28
Gibbs, Phebe II, 70
Gibbs, Phebe II, 71
Gibbs, Phebe II, 83
Gibbs, Phebe II, 173
Gibbs, Phebe II, 194
Gibbs, Phebe II, 224
Gibbs, Phebe II, 225
Gibbs, Phebe III, 133
Gibbs, Phebe L. Gallagher II, 71
Gibbs, Philip VI, 819
Gibbs, Phillip VI, 803
Gibbs, Polly VI, 920
Gibbs, Polly VI, 930
Gibbs, Polly VI, 955
Gibbs, Rebecca II, 191
Gibbs, Rebecca II, 211
Gibbs, Rebecca II, 224
Gibbs, Rebecca II, 225
Gibbs, Rebecca II, 252
Gibbs, Rebecca II, 288
Gibbs, Rebecca II, 522
Gibbs, Rebecca II, 531
Gibbs, Rebecca II, 974
Gibbs, Rebecca II, 997
Gibbs, Rebecca H. II, 288
Gibbs, Rebecca N. VI, 730
Gibbs, Rebecca N. VI, 742
Gibbs, Rebeckah II, 225
Gibbs, Rebekah VI, 819
Gibbs, Reuben VI, 493
Gibbs, Richard II, 17
Gibbs, Richard II, 28
Gibbs, Richard II, 71
Gibbs, Richard II, 83
Gibbs, Richard III, 134
Gibbs, Richard, Jr. II, 71
Gibbs, Robert II, 224
Gibbs, Robert VI, 920
Gibbs, Robert VI, 930
Gibbs, Robert VI, 994
Gibbs, Robert VI, 1017
Gibbs, Sallie B. VI, 843
Gibbs, Sally VI, 920
Gibbs, Samuel E. III, 134
Gibbs, Samuel E. III, 232
Gibbs, Samuel E. III, 292
Gibbs, Samuel T. III, 134
Gibbs, Sarah II, 28
Gibbs, Sarah II, 71
Gibbs, Sarah II, 76
Gibbs, Sarah II, 118
Gibbs, Sarah II, 121
Gibbs, Sarah II, 202
Gibbs, Sarah II, 225
Gibbs, Sarah III, 134
Gibbs, Sarah III, 232
Gibbs, Sarah Hammett II, 71
Gibbs, Sarah Pancoast II, 911
Gibbs, Solomon II, 71
Gibbs, Sophia VI, 920
Gibbs, Susan II, 288
Gibbs, Susan II, 293
Gibbs, Susanna VI, 819
Gibbs, Susannah II, 28
Gibbs, Susannah II, 213
Gibbs, Susannah VI, 920
Gibbs, Thomas VI, 916
Gibbs, Thomas VI, 920
Gibbs, Thomas C. VI, 819
Gibbs, Violetta VI, 920
Gibbs, Wd. Ann II, 780
Gibbs, Wd. Mary II, 795
Gibbs, Wd. Rebecca II, 174
Gibbs, William II, 366
Gibbs, William VI, 911
Gibbs, William VI, 920
Gibbs, William S. II, 288
Gibbs, William W. VI, 920
Gibbs, Wilmuth VI, 920
Gibbs, Wm. A. VI, 930
Gibbs, Wyatt VI, 920
Gibbs, Wyatt VI, 999
Giberson, E. L. V, 172
Giberson, Earl V, 172
Giberson, Lillie V, 172
Giberson, Lillie G. V, 172
Giberson, Roy V, 172
Giberson, Roy Wilbur V, 172
Giblon, Anna V, 907
Giblon, Anne V, 941
Giblon, Earl Z. V, 907
Giblon, Earl Z. V, 941
Gibons, Thomas IV, 205
Gibs, Rebecca II, 288
Gibson, ??? V, 388
Gibson, A. G. V, 388
Gibson, Aaron IV, 712
Gibson, Aaron IV, 956
Gibson, Aaron IV, 957
Gibson, Aaron IV, 991
Gibson, Aaron VI, 639
Gibson, Abigail III, 171
Gibson, Abion M. V, 457
Gibson, Abner VI, 493
Gibson, Abner VI, 639
Gibson, Absalom V, 388
Gibson, Absalom V, 400
Gibson, Absolom V, 430
Gibson, Adie G. V, 388
Gibson, Albert IV, 205
Gibson, Albert V, 172
Gibson, Albian M. V, 332
Gibson, Albion IV, 957
Gibson, Albion V, 332
Gibson, Albion M. IV, 1038
Gibson, Albion M. V, 674
Gibson, Alice VI, 493
Gibson, Alice VI, 517
Gibson, Alice VI, 522
Gibson, Alice VI, 639
Gibson, Alice VI, 640
Gibson, Alice VI, 672
Gibson, Alta V, 388

bson, Amelia IV, 205
bson, Amos IV, 75
bson, Amos IV, 88
bson, Amos IV, 101
bson, Amos IV, 205
bson, Amos VI, 493
bson, Amos VI, 639
bson, Amos VI, 676
bson, Amos VI, 742
bson, Amos E. IV, 88
bson, Amos E. IV, 957
bson, Amos G. IV, 205
bson, Ann IV, 205
bson, Ann IV, 956
bson, Ann IV, 1010
bson, Ann V, 172
bson, Ann VI, 493
bson, Ann VI, 596
bson, Ann VI, 639
bson, Ann P. IV, 88
bson, Ann P. IV, 200
bson, Ann P. IV, 205
bson, Ann T. IV, 205
bson, Anna H. IV, 1235
bson, Anne IV, 957
bson, Annie M. IV, 205
bson, Arcada V, 303
bson, Asa II, 72
bson, Asa IV, 712
bson, Asa IV, 927
bson, Asa IV, 956
bson, Asa IV, 957
bson, Benjamin II, 225
bson, Betty IV, 33
bson, Betty IV, 88
bson, Caleb V, 388
ibson, Caleb L. V, 388
ibson, Caleb S. V, 388
ibson, Carrie IV, 1235
ibson, Carrie IV, 1240
ibson, Carrie W. IV, 1235
ibson, Catharine IV, 712
ibson, Charles A. V, 388
bson, Chas. V, 388
ibson, Christiana IV, 88
ibson, Christiana IV, 89
bson, Clementina VI, 639
ibson, Clementina VI, 640
bson, Clementina VI, 676
ibson, Daniel II, 71
bson, Daniel Stone VI, 493
ibson, David II, 531
bson, David VI, 493
ibson, David VI, 639
bson, Deborah V, 172
bson, Dinah VI, 638
ibson, Dinah VI, 639
ibson, Dorcas II, 28
ibson, Edna IV, 720
ibson, Edna VI, 637
ibson, Edna A. VI, 637
ibson, Edna A. VI, 640
ibson, Eli VI, 493
ibson, Elijah Alfred V, 172
ibson, Elisha VI, 640
ibson, Elisha VI, 742
ibson, Eliza IV, 88
bson, Eliza V, 901
ibson, Eliza V, 907
bson, Eliza VI, 820
ibson, Elizabeth II, 28
ibson, Elizabeth II, 71
ibson, Elizabeth II, 105
ibson, Elizabeth II, 366
ibson, Elizabeth II, 443
ibson, Elizabeth IV, 88
ibson, Elizabeth IV, 107
ibson, Elizabeth IV, 205
ibson, Elizabeth IV, 927
ibson, Elizabeth IV, 956
ibson, Elizabeth IV, 957
ibson, Elizabeth IV, 1157
ibson, Elizabeth IV, 1160
ibson, Elizabeth V, 951
ibson, Elizabeth VI, 620
ibson, Elizabeth VI, 639
ibson, Elizabeth VI, 879
ibson, Elizabeth H. IV, 957
ibson, Elizabeth H. IV, 991
ibson, Ella VI, 639
ibson, Ella VI, 640
ibson, Ella VI, 676
ibson, Ellen VI, 639
ibson, Emeline IV, 205
ibson, Emma II, 815
ibson, Emsey VI, 639
ibson, Emsey VI, 647
ibson, Esther IV, 786
ibson, Esther IV, 956
ibson, Esther IV, 957
ibson, Esther IV, 1279
Gibson, Esther V, 172
Gibson, Esther VI, 493
Gibson, Esther VI, 526
Gibson, Esther VI, 639
Gibson, Esther VI, 640
Gibson, Esther VI, 702
Gibson, Esther VI, 703
Gibson, Esther C. V, 196
Gibson, Esther Coulson V, 172
Gibson, Ethel IV, 712
Gibson, Ethel V, 386
Gibson, Ethel V, 388
Gibson, Eva M. V, 388
Gibson, Evan VI, 639
Gibson, Evi VI, 639
Gibson, Frances V, 172
Gibson, Francis M. V, 388
Gibson, Frank V, 388
Gibson, Garret I, 1119
Gibson, Garrett I, 962
Gibson, George I, 715
Gibson, George IV, 957
Gibson, George VI, 493
Gibson, George VI, 640
Gibson, Georgie Annie V, 674
Gibson, Gideon II, 54
Gibson, Gideon II, 71
Gibson, Gideon VI, 493
Gibson, Gideon VI, 574
Gibson, Gideon VI, 586
Gibson, Gidon II, 71
Gibson, Hannah II, 54
Gibson, Hannah II, 71
Gibson, Hannah IV, 75
Gibson, Hannah IV, 88
Gibson, Hannah IV, 97
Gibson, Hannah IV, 101
Gibson, Hannah IV, 205
Gibson, Hannah IV, 262
Gibson, Hannah IV, 956
Gibson, Hannah IV, 957
Gibson, Hannah IV, 972
Gibson, Hannah V, 172
Gibson, Hannah VI, 493
Gibson, Hannah VI, 574
Gibson, Hannah VI, 620
Gibson, Hannah VI, 639
Gibson, Hannah VI, 676
Gibson, Hannah VI, 882
Gibson, Hannah VI, 920
Gibson, Hannah Gibson IV, 88
Gibson, Hannah J. IV, 125
Gibson, Hannah J. IV, 205
Gibson, Hannah M. IV, 956
Gibson, Hannah S. II, 288
Gibson, Hannah S. II, 303
Gibson, Harrie IV, 205
Gibson, Harry IV, 205
Gibson, Harry C. IV, 205
Gibson, Harsha V, 388
Gibson, Helen V, 388
Gibson, Herber VI, 640
Gibson, Hezekiah II, 366
Gibson, Huldah IV, 1235
Gibson, Huldah IV, 1237
Gibson, Ida M. V, 388
Gibson, Isaac II, 225
Gibson, Isaac Thorn V, 172
Gibson, Isaac, Jr. VI, 639
Gibson, Isabella VI, 819
Gibson, Iscs VI, 493
Gibson, J. Donald II, 867
Gibson, J. W. IV, 1038
Gibson, Jack VI, 920
Gibson, James IV, 33
Gibson, James IV, 88
Gibson, James IV, 1279
Gibson, James VI, 493
Gibson, James VI, 503
Gibson, James S. III, 171
Gibson, Jane II, 28
Gibson, Jane II, 71
Gibson, Jane II, 92
Gibson, Jane VI, 798
Gibson, Jennie IV, 1235
Gibson, Jeremiah VI, 639
Gibson, Jerome IV, 1235
Gibson, Jerome G. IV, 1235
Gibson, Jess A. V, 674
Gibson, Jesse I, 480
Gibson, Jesse V, 388
Gibson, Jesse VI, 639
Gibson, Jesse A. V, 388
Gibson, Jesse A. V, 674
Gibson, Jessie E. V, 388
Gibson, John II, 225
Gibson, John II, 234
Gibson, John II, 807
Gibson, John II, 815
Gibson, John IV, 33
Gibson, John IV, 88
Gibson, John IV, 956
Gibson, John IV, 957
Gibson, John VI, 493
Gibson, John VI, 517
Gibson, John VI, 518
Gibson, John VI, 522
Gibson, John VI, 639
Gibson, John VI, 640
Gibson, John VI, 643
Gibson, John VI, 661
Gibson, John VI, 664
Gibson, John VI, 676
Gibson, John VI, 754
Gibson, John VI, 807
Gibson, John VI, 819
Gibson, John VI, 879
Gibson, John VI, 911
Gibson, John VI, 920
Gibson, John Edwin IV, 957
Gibson, John S. IV, 956
Gibson, John William VI, 493
Gibson, John, Jr. IV, 88
Gibson, John, Jr. VI, 493
Gibson, John, Jr. VI, 517
Gibson, John, Jr. VI, 522
Gibson, Jonathan VI, 640
Gibson, Joseph II, 28
Gibson, Joseph II, 71
Gibson, Joseph II, 92
Gibson, Joseph IV, 33
Gibson, Joseph IV, 88
Gibson, Joseph IV, 786
Gibson, Joseph IV, 956
Gibson, Joseph VI, 493
Gibson, Joseph VI, 637
Gibson, Joseph VI, 639
Gibson, Joseph VI, 640
Gibson, Joseph VI, 641
Gibson, Joseph VI, 676
Gibson, Joseph VI, 680
Gibson, Joseph VI, 700
Gibson, Joseph VI, 703
Gibson, Joseph VI, 920
Gibson, Joseph William IV, 957
Gibson, Joseph, Jr. II, 71
Gibson, Joseph, Jr. VI, 640
Gibson, Joshua II, 71
Gibson, Joshua IV, 33
Gibson, Joshua IV, 88
Gibson, Joshua IV, 97
Gibson, Joshua V, 907
Gibson, Juda VI, 920
Gibson, Keith IV, 712
Gibson, Kenneth IV, 712
Gibson, Kenneth IV, 1317
Gibson, Laura VI, 640
Gibson, Laura E. VI, 639
Gibson, Laura E. VI, 640
Gibson, Laura E. VI, 676
Gibson, Letitia IV, 712
Gibson, Letitia IV, 956
Gibson, Louisa M. V, 60
Gibson, Louiza V, 388
Gibson, Louiza V, 400
Gibson, Louiza Jane V, 388
Gibson, Lucetta IV, 956
Gibson, Lucina IV, 957
Gibson, Lucinda I, 480
Gibson, Lucinda L. IV, 956
Gibson, Lucretta IV, 957
Gibson, Lydia IV, 75
Gibson, Lydia IV, 88
Gibson, Lydia IV, 97
Gibson, Lydia IV, 125
Gibson, Lydia IV, 131
Gibson, Lydia IV, 957
Gibson, Lydia IV, 990
Gibson, Lydia V, 907
Gibson, Lydia V, 930
Gibson, Lydia VI, 493
Gibson, Lydia VI, 526
Gibson, Lydia VI, 640
Gibson, Lydia VI, 700
Gibson, Lydia Ann IV, 956
Gibson, Lydia Ann IV, 957
Gibson, Lydia S. IV, 88
Gibson, Lydia S. IV, 956
Gibson, Lydia S. IV, 957
Gibson, Mabel IV, 205
Gibson, Mabel IV, 1251
Gibson, Mable IV, 1251
Gibson, Mahlon VI, 639
Gibson, Margaret IV, 1279
Gibson, Maria L. V, 172
Gibson, Maria L. V, 211
Gibson, Maria L. V, 963
Gibson, Maria Louisa V, 172
Gibson, Martha II, 781
Gibson, Martha II, 807
Gibson, Martha II, 808
Gibson, Martha II, 852
Gibson, Martha IV, 712
Gibson, Martha IV, 817
Gibson, Martha IV, 955
Gibson, Martha IV, 957
Gibson, Martha V, 332
Gibson, Martha E. V, 388
Gibson, Martha E. V, 674
Gibson, Martha Emily V, 674
Gibson, Marthy IV, 1279
Gibson, Mary I, 715
Gibson, Mary I, 728
Gibson, Mary II, 531
Gibson, Mary IV, 33
Gibson, Mary IV, 205
Gibson, Mary IV, 712
Gibson, Mary IV, 817
Gibson, Mary IV, 840
Gibson, Mary IV, 956
Gibson, Mary IV, 1279
Gibson, Mary V, 388
Gibson, Mary V, 907
Gibson, Mary V, 951
Gibson, Mary V, 997
Gibson, Mary VI, 493
Gibson, Mary VI, 503
Gibson, Mary VI, 516
Gibson, Mary VI, 517
Gibson, Mary VI, 518
Gibson, Mary VI, 519
Gibson, Mary VI, 520
Gibson, Mary VI, 535
Gibson, Mary VI, 569
Gibson, Mary VI, 572
Gibson, Mary VI, 576
Gibson, Mary VI, 596
Gibson, Mary VI, 639
Gibson, Mary VI, 640
Gibson, Mary VI, 648
Gibson, Mary VI, 661
Gibson, Mary VI, 662
Gibson, Mary VI, 664
Gibson, Mary VI, 667
Gibson, Mary VI, 672
Gibson, Mary VI, 674
Gibson, Mary VI, 676
Gibson, Mary VI, 680
Gibson, Mary VI, 681
Gibson, Mary VI, 683
Gibson, Mary VI, 684
Gibson, Mary VI, 692
Gibson, Mary VI, 712
Gibson, Mary VI, 742
Gibson, Mary VI, 754
Gibson, Mary VI, 766
Gibson, Mary VI, 819
Gibson, Mary VI, 879
Gibson, Mary VI, 911
Gibson, Mary Ann IV, 88
Gibson, Mary Ann IV, 957
Gibson, Mary Emily V, 388
Gibson, Mathew B. IV, 957
Gibson, Miller IV, 88
Gibson, Miller IV, 200
Gibson, Miller IV, 205
Gibson, Miller V, 60
Gibson, Miller VI, 639
Gibson, Miriam VI, 493
Gibson, Miriam VI, 640
Gibson, Miriam VI, 709
Gibson, Montillion V, 196
Gibson, Montillion V, 211
Gibson, Moses VI, 493
Gibson, Moses VI, 526
Gibson, Moses VI, 640
Gibson, Moses VI, 700
Gibson, Moses, Jr. VI, 640
Gibson, Moses, Sr. VI, 640
Gibson, Myrtle IV, 712
Gibson, Myrtle IV, 1317
Gibson, Nancy V, 388
Gibson, Nathan II, 531
Gibson, Nathaniel IV, 88
Gibson, Nathaniel IV, 125
Gibson, Olive IV, 205
Gibson, Olive V, 457
Gibson, Oliver IV, 205
Gibson, Oliver E. IV, 205
Gibson, Oliver O. V, 388
Gibson, Orlando M. V, 388
Gibson, Oscar V, 388
Gibson, Patrick VI, 857
Gibson, Patsy VI, 911
Gibson, Pemelia IV, 1197
Gibson, Permelia IV, 1160
Gibson, Phebe II, 224
Gibson, Phebe II, 225
Gibson, Phebe IV, 88
Gibson, Phebe VI, 493
Gibson, Phebe VI, 640
Gibson, Phebe VI, 642
Gibson, Phebe VI, 643
Gibson, Phebe VI, 645
Gibson, Phebe VI, 680
Gibson, Phebe VI, 703
Gibson, Phebe VI, 721
Gibson, Phebe VI, 722
Gibson, Polly VI, 912
Gibson, Prudence IV, 712
Gibson, Prudence IV, 1279
Gibson, Prudence H. IV, 712
Gibson, Prudence H. IV, 786
Gibson, Rachel I, 715
Gibson, Rachel I, 721
Gibson, Rachel II, 225
Gibson, Rachel II, 249
Gibson, Rachel V, 388
Gibson, Rachel V, 400
Gibson, Rachel V, 404
Gibson, Rachel V, 430
Gibson, Rachel V, 562
Gibson, Rachel VI, 392
Gibson, Rachel VI, 638
Gibson, Rachel VI, 639
Gibson, Rachel VI, 640
Gibson, Rachel VI, 641
Gibson, Rachel VI, 650
Gibson, Rachel VI, 676
Gibson, Rachel VI, 700
Gibson, Rachel Jane V, 172
Gibson, Rebecca IV, 88
Gibson, Rebecca IV, 89
Gibson, Rebecca IV, 205
Gibson, Rebecca IV, 956
Gibson, Rebecca IV, 957
Gibson, Rebecca VI, 640
Gibson, Rebecca W. IV, 957
Gibson, Rebeckah II, 28
Gibson, Rebeckah VI, 539
Gibson, Rebekah VI, 493
Gibson, Rebekah VI, 640
Gibson, Rebekah VI, 716
Gibson, Robert IV, 205
Gibson, Robert V, 951
Gibson, Robert VI, 639
Gibson, Robert VI, 819
Gibson, Robert E. IV, 88
Gibson, Robert E. IV, 205
Gibson, Rose Valley V, 674
Gibson, Russell IV, 205
Gibson, Russell N. IV, 205
Gibson, Ruth II, 366
Gibson, Ruth IV, 75
Gibson, Ruth IV, 88
Gibson, Ruth V, 674
Gibson, Ruth V, 716
Gibson, Ruth V, 907
Gibson, Ruth VI, 493
Gibson, Ruth VI, 517
Gibson, Ruth VI, 518
Gibson, Ruth VI, 522
Gibson, Ruth VI, 638
Gibson, Ruth VI, 639
Gibson, Ruth VI, 640
Gibson, Ruth VI, 661
Gibson, Ruth VI, 664
Gibson, Ruth VI, 676
Gibson, Ruth VI, 754
Gibson, Ruth Anna IV, 957
Gibson, Ruth Eleanor V, 674
Gibson, Ruth N. I, 761
Gibson, Ruth N. I, 771
Gibson, Ruth R. IV, 712
Gibson, Sally VI, 928
Gibson, Sammy IV, 1235
Gibson, Samuel II, 531
Gibson, Samuel IV, 88
Gibson, Samuel IV, 957
Gibson, Samuel IV, 1010
Gibson, Samuel VI, 640
Gibson, Sarah I, 374
Gibson, Sarah I, 390
Gibson, Sarah II, 28
Gibson, Sarah II, 225
Gibson, Sarah II, 238
Gibson, Sarah II, 807
Gibson, Sarah II, 808
Gibson, Sarah II, 815
Gibson, Sarah IV, 205
Gibson, Sarah IV, 712
Gibson, Sarah IV, 956
Gibson, Sarah IV, 957
Gibson, Sarah V, 172
Gibson, Sarah V, 196
Gibson, Sarah V, 211
Gibson, Sarah V, 388
Gibson, Sarah VI, 493
Gibson, Sarah VI, 639
Gibson, Sarah VI, 640
Gibson, Sarah VI, 650
Gibson, Sarah A. V, 388
Gibson, Sarah A. V, 430
Gibson, Sarah E. V, 388

Gibson, Sarah Elizabeth V, 388
Gibson, Sarah Elizabeth V, 421
Gibson, Sarah H. IV, 712
Gibson, Sarah M. V, 674
Gibson, Solomon VI, 640
Gibson, Spicer II, 531
Gibson, Susanna IV, 88
Gibson, Susanna IV, 108
Gibson, Susanna IV, 1279
Gibson, Tabitha Jane IV, 956
Gibson, Tabitha Jane IV, 957
Gibson, Tacy IV, 957
Gibson, Tacy IV, 1001
Gibson, Tamar IV, 957
Gibson, Tamar S. IV, 956
Gibson, Thamar Ann V, 172
Gibson, Thomas IV, 88
Gibson, Thomas V, 172
Gibson, Thomas VI, 493
Gibson, Thomas VI, 640
Gibson, Thomas V. IV, 956
Gibson, Thomas V. IV, 957
Gibson, Thomas, Jr. IV, 88
Gibson, W. F. IV, 205
Gibson, W. T. V, 388
Gibson, Webster V, 882
Gibson, Webster VI, 639
Gibson, Webster VI, 640
Gibson, Webster VI, 641
Gibson, William IV, 89
Gibson, William IV, 205
Gibson, William IV, 956
Gibson, William IV, 957
Gibson, William IV, 1279
Gibson, William V, 997
Gibson, William VI, 392
Gibson, William VI, 493
Gibson, William VI, 641
Gibson, William VI, 974
Gibson, William S. IV, 957
Gibson, William Stanley IV, 88
Gibson, William T. V, 388
Gibson, William Thomas V, 388
Gibson, Wm. IV, 88
Gibson, Wm. IV, 957
Gibson, Wm. V, 997
Gibson, Wm. VI, 912
Gibson, Wm. S. IV, 957
Gibson, Wm. Stanley IV, 88
Giddens, Martha II, 366
Giddens, Rebecca II, 366
Gideon, Andrew J. II, 858
Gideon, Andrew J. II, 867
Gideon, Anna S. II, 858
Gideon, Anna S. II, 867
Gideon, Carrie II, 858
Gideon, Carrie II, 867
Gideon, Henry Ann VI, 600
Gideon, John IV, 126
Gideon, Martin VI, 600
Gidley, Amy IV, 1147
Gidley, Amy IV, 1160
Gidley, Anne B. II, 753
Gidley, Annie B. II, 742
Gidley, Arthur Emmett IV, 1160
Gidley, Bathsheba IV, 1208
Gidley, Cecelia A. Victoria IV, 1160
Gidley, Charles IV, 1208
Gidley, Chellis IV, 1160
Gidley, Clifton IV, 1160
Gidley, Daniel IV, 1160
Gidley, Daniel IV, 1165
Gidley, Daniel A. IV, 1160
Gidley, Daniel D. IV, 1160
Gidley, Daniel D. IV, 1362
Gidley, Darwin IV, 1160
Gidley, Darwin IV, 1279
Gidley, David IV, 1160
Gidley, Deborah IV, 1160
Gidley, Deborah IV, 1165
Gidley, Dorwin IV, 1160
Gidley, Dorwin IV, 1235
Gidley, Ella P. IV, 1160
Gidley, Ellen IV, 1160
Gidley, Ellen Ann IV, 1160
Gidley, Ellin IV, 1160
Gidley, Elwood Chellis IV, 1160
Gidley, Esther IV, 1160
Gidley, Esther IV, 1177
Gidley, Esther IV, 1222
Gidley, Griffith L. IV, 1160
Gidley, Hannah IV, 1147
Gidley, Hannah IV, 1157
Gidley, Hannah IV, 1160
Gidley, Hannah IV, 1197
Gidley, Hibertus IV, 1208
Gidley, Isaac IV, 1160
Gidley, Isaac M. IV, 1279
Gidley, Jesse Vernon IV, 1098
Gidley, Lorana L. IV, 1279
Gidley, Mary IV, 1279
Gidley, Minnie IV, 1160
Gidley, Moses IV, 1160
Gidley, Patience IV, 1098
Gidley, Patience IV, 1119
Gidley, Patience IV, 1160
Gidley, Patience IV, 1190
Gidley, Phebe IV, 1160
Gidley, Phebe IV, 1165
Gidley, Phebe IV, 1184
Gidley, Phebe IV, 1190
Gidley, Phebe D. IV, 1160
Gidley, Phebe Jr. IV, 1160
Gidley, Phebe, Jr. IV, 1147
Gidley, Robert Pharo Lowry II, 742
Gidley, Royal G. IV, 1160
Gidley, Royal G. IV, 1362
Gidley, Ruth IV, 1147
Gidley, Ruth IV, 1160
Gidley, Ruth IV, 1208
Gidley, Ruth O. IV, 1208
Gidley, Sarah IV, 1147
Gidley, Sarah IV, 1160
Gidley, Sarah IV, 1197
Gidley, Sarah IV, 1362
Gidley, Sarah Jane IV, 1208
Gidley, Semantha IV, 1279
Gidley, Seth IV, 1208
Gidley, Seth S. IV, 1208
Gidley, Seth S. IV, 1218
Gidley, Susan IV, 1160
Gidley, Terressa IV, 1160
Gidley, Terresse IV, 1160
Gidley, Walter Clifton IV, 1160
Gidley, William IV, 205
Gidley, William IV, 1160
Gidley, William IV, 1362
Gidley, Wm. IV, 1147
Gidley, Wm. IV, 1160
Gidley, Wm. IV, 1190
Gidley, Wm. IV, 1362
Gidley, Wm., Jr. IV, 1160
Gidney, Phebe IV, 1177
Giek, Geo. IV, 1317
Giek, Nina IV, 1317
Giek, Nina Angie IV, 1317
Gier, Mary I, 812
Giesy, Rose IV, 205
Giesy, William IV, 205
Giffen, George W. V, 674
Giffhorn, Bell V, 332
Giffhorn, Belle IV, 1317
Giffin, Anna V, 674
Giffin, David II, 444
Giffin, David V, 674
Giffin, George W. V, 674
Giffin, Katherine II, 444
Giffin, Mary II, 444
Giffin, Mary II, 531
Giffin, Mary II, 658
Giffin, Thomas II, 531
Giffin, Thomas II, 658
Giffin???, Elizabeth I, 716
Giffin???, Elizabeth I, 723
Giffing, David II, 444
Giffing, Deborah II, 118
Giffing, Deborah II, 119
Giffing, Katherine II, 444
Gifford, ??? IV, 1047
Gifford, Abel IV, 395
Gifford, Abel IV, 1058
Gifford, Abigail I, 352
Gifford, Abigail IV, 365
Gifford, Abigail IV, 395
Gifford, Abigail IV, 1058
Gifford, Abigail, Jr. IV, 1058
Gifford, Abraham IV, 395
Gifford, Abraham IV, 1058
Gifford, Abraham IV, 1160
Gifford, Abraham IV, 1235
Gifford, Abram IV, 1236
Gifford, Alexander IV, 395
Gifford, Alexander IV, 1058
Gifford, Alexander M. IV, 395
Gifford, Alexander M. IV, 1058
Gifford, Alva V, 840
Gifford, Alva Edwin V, 839
Gifford, Andrew I, 811
Gifford, Andrew V, 829
Gifford, Andrew V, 839
Gifford, Andrew G. V, 839
Gifford, Ann V, 839
Gifford, Ann V, 864
Gifford, Annie W. III, 134
Gifford, Annuel V, 839
Gifford, Annuel V, 840
Gifford, Asa Lindley V, 839
Gifford, Asa Lindly V, 839
Gifford, Benjamin I, 541
Gifford, Benjamin IV, 1160
Gifford, Benjamin IV, 1235
Gifford, Benjamin J. IV, 1236
Gifford, Benoni IV, 1363
Gifford, Bethena V, 839
Gifford, Bethuel II, 722
Gifford, Catharine IV, 1058
Gifford, Catharine IV, 1235
Gifford, Catherine D. IV, 1160
Gifford, Charles II, 288
Gifford, Charles IV, 1160
Gifford, Charles IV, 1235
Gifford, Charles IV, 1236
Gifford, Chas. III, 134
Gifford, Clara P. II, 742
Gifford, Clara Pennell II, 705
Gifford, Clara Pennell II, 742
Gifford, Clarissa IV, 1363
Gifford, Clarkson IV, 1058
Gifford, Cynthia IV, 1363
Gifford, Daniel V, 839
Gifford, David IV, 1160
Gifford, David V, 839
Gifford, Deborah P. II, 705
Gifford, Deborah P. II, 742
Gifford, Debrah Ann V, 839
Gifford, Edith V, 839
Gifford, Edith H. V, 840
Gifford, Edith H. V, 844
Gifford, Edith May V, 840
Gifford, Edward IV, 1160
Gifford, Edward S. I, 50
Gifford, Eliza IV, 1363
Gifford, Eliza Ann V, 839
Gifford, Eliza Ann V, 840
Gifford, Eliza Ann V, 857
Gifford, Eliza Ann V, 867
Gifford, Eliza J. IV, 1236
Gifford, Eliza Jane IV, 1160
Gifford, Eliza Jane IV, 1236
Gifford, Elizabeth II, 722
Gifford, Elizabeth IV, 1160
Gifford, Elizabeth IV, 1235
Gifford, Elizabeth V, 839
Gifford, Elizabeth A. V, 332
Gifford, Elizabeth A. V, 353
Gifford, Ellen V, 839
Gifford, Elma III, 134
Gifford, Elton B. II, 288
Gifford, Elton B. II, 705
Gifford, Elton B. II, 742
Gifford, Elton James II, 705
Gifford, Emlen IV, 1058
Gifford, Esther II, 288
Gifford, Esther II, 706
Gifford, Esther II, 742
Gifford, Esther V, 839
Gifford, Ethan B. II, 742
Gifford, Eunice I, 390
Gifford, Eunice I, 498
Gifford, Eunice I, 526
Gifford, Eunice I, 541
Gifford, Eunice I, 748
Gifford, Eunice I, 811
Gifford, Eunice I, 816
Gifford, Fred V, 839
Gifford, Freddie V, 840
Gifford, Giles J. IV, 1160
Gifford, Giles J. IV, 1161
Gifford, Giles J. IV, 1235
Gifford, Giles T. IV, 1160
Gifford, Hannah I, 498
Gifford, Hannah I, 799
Gifford, Hannah I, 811
Gifford, Hannah IV, 1058
Gifford, Hannah V, 837
Gifford, Hannah V, 839
Gifford, Hannah V, 863
Gifford, Hannah VI, 392
Gifford, Hannah VI, 455
Gifford, Hannah J. V, 826
Gifford, Hannah J. V, 839
Gifford, Hannah J. V, 840
Gifford, Hannah P. I, 879
Gifford, Hannah P. IV, 473
Gifford, Hannah P. IV, 483
Gifford, Henry I, 811
Gifford, Henry V, 839
Gifford, Henry R. V, 839
Gifford, Humphrey IV, 1160
Gifford, Humphrey IV, 1235
Gifford, Humphrey J. IV, 1160
Gifford, Humphrey, Jr. IV, 1236
Gifford, Isaac IV, 1363
Gifford, Isaac V, 839
Gifford, Isaac R. III, 413
Gifford, Isaac R. III, 441
Gifford, Isaac R. IV, 473
Gifford, Isaac Reynard IV, 473
Gifford, Isabell IV, 395
Gifford, Isabell IV, 415
Gifford, Isabella IV, 395
Gifford, Isabella IV, 1058
Gifford, Jane IV, 1160
Gifford, Jane IV, 1231
Gifford, Jane IV, 1235
Gifford, Jemima Ann II, 288
Gifford, Jemima Ann II, 706
Gifford, Jemima Ann II, 742
Gifford, Jennie V, 870
Gifford, Jesse I, 352
Gifford, Jesse I, 390
Gifford, Jesse IV, 1058
Gifford, Jesse V, 839
Gifford, Jesse John V, 839
Gifford, Job J. IV, 1160
Gifford, John J. IV, 1235
Gifford, John J. IV, 1236
Gifford, Jonas I, 748
Gifford, Jonathan I, 390
Gifford, Jonathan I, 498
Gifford, Jonathan I, 526
Gifford, Jonathan I, 541
Gifford, Jonathan I, 773
Gifford, Jonathan I, 811
Gifford, Joseph A. IV, 1160
Gifford, Joseph A. IV, 1235
Gifford, Joseph B. IV, 1160
Gifford, Joseph B. IV, 1235
Gifford, Joseph B. IV, 1236
Gifford, Judith V, 933
Gifford, Kate IV, 1236
Gifford, Kezia I, 390
Gifford, Kezia I, 402
Gifford, Kezia I, 811
Gifford, Kezia V, 839
Gifford, Keziah I, 811
Gifford, Keziah V, 839
Gifford, Kisiah V, 839
Gifford, Lavina I, 526
Gifford, Lavina I, 541
Gifford, Levi I, 352
Gifford, Levi I, 390
Gifford, Levi IV, 395
Gifford, Levi IV, 1058
Gifford, Lindley V, 839
Gifford, Lindley V, 840
Gifford, Lizzie B. V, 840
Gifford, Lucy IV, 1160
Gifford, Lucy IV, 1235
Gifford, Lucy V, 839
Gifford, Lucy Ann V, 839
Gifford, Lucy Marie V, 840
Gifford, Lurton Andrew V, 839
Gifford, Lydia I, 498
Gifford, Lydia IV, 205
Gifford, Lydia IV, 473
Gifford, Lydia IV, 482
Gifford, Margaret I, 352
Gifford, Margaret I, 390
Gifford, Margaret I, 427
Gifford, Margaret V, 839
Gifford, Margaret V, 840
Gifford, Maria IV, 1363
Gifford, Marven IV, 331
Gifford, Marven IV, 395
Gifford, Marvin IV, 365
Gifford, Marvin IV, 395
Gifford, Marvin IV, 1058
Gifford, Mary I, 498
Gifford, Mary I, 811
Gifford, Mary III, 335
Gifford, Mary Ann II, 722
Gifford, Mary B. V, 839
Gifford, Mary Elizabeth V, 839
Gifford, Mary Emma II, 705
Gifford, Mary I. IV, 1160
Gifford, Mary J. IV, 1235
Gifford, Mary P. II, 705
Gifford, Mary P. II, 742
Gifford, Masy IV, 1236
Gifford, Masy IV, 1240
Gifford, Micajah IV, 1160
Gifford, Michael IV, 1058
Gifford, Michael K. IV, 1058
Gifford, Michael King IV, 395
Gifford, Nathan I, 811
Gifford, Nathan V, 839
Gifford, Nathan V, 841
Gifford, Obadiah IV, 1160
Gifford, Obadiah IV, 1235
Gifford, Owen IV, 395
Gifford, Owen IV, 1058
Gifford, Patience IV, 395
Gifford, Patience IV, 1058
Gifford, Pearl Francis V, 839
Gifford, Pegeg I, 390
Gifford, Peleg I, 352
Gifford, Pelegg I, 390
Gifford, Phariba IV, 395
Gifford, Phariba IV, 1058
Gifford, Phariby IV, 1053
Gifford, Phariby IV, 1058
Gifford, Phebe I, 498
Gifford, Phebe R. IV, 473
Gifford, Phebe T. III, 413
Gifford, Phebe T. III, 441
Gifford, Priscilla VI, 392
Gifford, Priscilla VI, 455
Gifford, Rebecca III, 134
Gifford, Rebecca III, 229
Gifford, Rebecca IV, 1058
Gifford, Rebecca IV, 1083
Gifford, Rebecca V, 839
Gifford, Rebeccah V, 839
Gifford, Rebeccah V, 841
Gifford, Riley W. V, 840
Gifford, Robert Austin IV, 473
Gifford, Rufus IV, 1160
Gifford, Rufus IV, 1363
Gifford, Ruth IV, 1160
Gifford, Ruth B. III, 134
Gifford, Ruth B. III, 199
Gifford, Sarah I, 498
Gifford, Sarah I, 811
Gifford, Sarah I, 820
Gifford, Sarah IV, 395
Gifford, Sarah IV, 1058
Gifford, Sarah IV, 1160
Gifford, Sarah IV, 1208
Gifford, Sarah IV, 1235
Gifford, Sarah V, 839
Gifford, Sarah V, 840
Gifford, Sarah Ann IV, 1058
Gifford, Sarah Ann V, 839
Gifford, Sarah Ann V, 840
Gifford, Sarah Ann V, 860
Gifford, Sarah E. V, 829
Gifford, Sarah E. V, 839
Gifford, Sarah Jane IV, 1160
Gifford, Sarah Jane IV, 1235
Gifford, Sarah S. III, 134
Gifford, Sarah S. III, 229
Gifford, Susanna V, 839
Gifford, Susannah V, 839
Gifford, Susannah V, 840
Gifford, Susannah V, 865
Gifford, Susannah V, 867
Gifford, Sylvia IV, 1235
Gifford, Sylvia Ann IV, 1160
Gifford, Sylvia Ann IV, 1235
Gifford, Sylvia Ann IV, 1236
Gifford, Sylvia C. IV, 1160
Gifford, Sylvia C. IV, 1236
Gifford, Temperance IV, 1058
Gifford, Temperance IV, 1098
Gifford, Theophelus VI, 392
Gifford, Theophelus VI, 455
Gifford, Thomas IV, 473
Gifford, Unice I, 773
Gifford, Wd. Sarah E. V, 839
Gifford, William I, 390
Gifford, William I, 498
Gifford, William I, 811
Gifford, William IV, 473
Gifford, William IV, 1058
Gifford, William V, 839
Gifford, William V, 864
Gifford, William H. IV, 1236
Gifford, William Henry IV, 1160
Gifford, William Henry IV, 1236
Gifford, Wm. I, 402
Gifford, Wm. III, 134
Gifford, Wm. III, 229
Gifford, Wm. III, 413
Gifford, Wm. IV, 482
Gifford, Wm. IV, 1279
Gilaspie, Elijah B. VI, 921
Gilaspie, Mary F. VI, 921
Gilaspie, Rolling VI, 921
Gilbart, John II, 225
Gilber, Lydia I, 879
Gilberd, Miriam I, 716
Gilberd, Sarah I, 716
Gilberd, Sarah II, 997
Gilberd, Sarah II, 1007
Gilbert, ??? IV, 1047
Gilbert, ??? IV, 1125
Gilbert, Aaron I, 99
Gilbert, Aaron I, 193
Gilbert, Aaron I, 853
Gilbert, Aaron I, 879
Gilbert, Aaron I, 895
Gilbert, Aaron L. I, 879
Gilbert, Aaron Lancaster I, 99
Gilbert, Aaron Lancaster I, 140
Gilbert, Aaron Lancaster I, 879
Gilbert, Abegil I, 99
Gilbert, Abel I, 288
Gilbert, Abel IV, 147
Gilbert, Abel IV, 164
Gilbert, Abel IV, 331
Gilbert, Abel IV, 395
Gilbert, Abel IV, 580

Gilbert, Abel IV, 1050
Gilbert, Abel IV, 1057
Gilbert, Abel IV, 1058
Gilbert, Abel IV, 1061
Gilbert, Abel IV, 1072
Gilbert, Abel IV, 1098
Gilbert, Abel IV, 1099
Gilbert, Abel IV, 1131
Gilbert, Abel, Jr. IV, 1058
Gilbert, Abigail I, 139
Gilbert, Abigail I, 140
Gilbert, Abigail I, 193
Gilbert, Abigail I, 853
Gilbert, Abigail I, 879
Gilbert, Abigail II, 444
Gilbert, Abigail II, 531
Gilbert, Abigail II, 654
Gilbert, Abijah IV, 526
Gilbert, Able IV, 577
Gilbert, Able IV, 580
Gilbert, Abner IV, 88
Gilbert, Abner IV, 114
Gilbert, Abner IV, 124
Gilbert, Abner IV, 126
Gilbert, Abner IV, 129
Gilbert, Abner IV, 712
Gilbert, Abner IV, 713
Gilbert, Abner IV, 817
Gilbert, Abraham IV, 205
Gilbert, Abraham IV, 526
Gilbert, Abram IV, 205
Gilbert, Achsah I, 1020
Gilbert, Achsah I, 1030
Gilbert, Achsah I, 1037
Gilbert, Achsah IV, 331
Gilbert, Achsah IV, 395
Gilbert, Achsah IV, 1050
Gilbert, Achsah IV, 1058
Gilbert, Adda IV, 713
Gilbert, Addison IV, 88
Gilbert, Addison IV, 1132
Gilbert, Addison S. IV, 1131
Gilbert, Albert V, 739
Gilbert, Alfred IV, 839
Gilbert, Alice IV, 124
Gilbert, Alice IV, 126
Gilbert, Alice Cope IV, 88
Gilbert, Alice G. IV, 807
Gilbert, Amelia IV, 577
Gilbert, Amelia IV, 580
Gilbert, Amos VI, 641
Gilbert, Amos VI, 742
Gilbert, Amos Ball IV, 1058
Gilbert, Amy V, 332
Gilbert, Ann I, 99
Gilbert, Ann I Sup 1, 3
Gilbert, Ann I Sup 1, 4
Gilbert, Ann II, 788
Gilbert, Ann IV, 88
Gilbert, Ann IV, 124
Gilbert, Ann IV, 126
Gilbert, Ann IV, 129
Gilbert, Ann IV, 712
Gilbert, Ann IV, 713
Gilbert, Ann IV, 903
Gilbert, Ann IV, 1131
Gilbert, Ann V, 324
Gilbert, Ann VI, 493
Gilbert, Ann VI, 641
Gilbert, Ann VI, 819
Gilbert, Ann Eliza IV, 88
Gilbert, Ann Eliza IV, 126
Gilbert, Ann Eliza IV, 135
Gilbert, Ann Eliza IV, 817
Gilbert, Ann Hutton IV, 88
Gilbert, Anna I, 853
Gilbert, Anna I, 879
Gilbert, Anna IV, 580
Gilbert, Anna IV, 817
Gilbert, Anna IV, 1057
Gilbert, Anna IV, 1058
Gilbert, Anna IV, 1099
Gilbert, Anne IV, 473
Gilbert, Anne IV, 486
Gilbert, Annie IV, 88
Gilbert, Annie V, 332
Gilbert, Annie E. III, 111
Gilbert, Annie E. III, 134
Gilbert, Anzanetta IV, 88
Gilbert, Anzanette IV, 114
Gilbert, Anzonett IV, 713
Gilbert, Aquilla Crew IV, 577
Gilbert, Armela IV, 1131
Gilbert, Armela C. IV, 1131
Gilbert, Armelia IV, 577
Gilbert, Armelia IV, 1058
Gilbert, Armelia IV, 1131
Gilbert, Armelia C. IV, 580
Gilbert, Asenath I, 853
Gilbert, Asenath I, 879
Gilbert, Asher IV, 129
Gilbert, Averela VI, 819
Gilbert, Averilla V, 32
Gilbert, Barclay Penrose IV, 1058
Gilbert, Benj. II, 174
Gilbert, Benj. VI, 931
Gilbert, Benjamin I, 390
Gilbert, Benjamin I, 1020
Gilbert, Benjamin II, 366
Gilbert, Benjamin II, 997
Gilbert, Benjamin II, 1035
Gilbert, Benjamin IV, 19
Gilbert, Benjamin IV, 33
Gilbert, Benjamin IV, 88
Gilbert, Benjamin IV, 123
Gilbert, Benjamin IV, 126
Gilbert, Benjamin IV, 135
Gilbert, Benjamin IV, 621
Gilbert, Benjamin IV, 693
Gilbert, Benjamin IV, 700
Gilbert, Benjamin IV, 712
Gilbert, Benjamin VI, 819
Gilbert, Benjamin VI, 920
Gilbert, Benjamin, Jr. II, 531
Gilbert, Bertha V, 997
Gilbert, Beulah I, 1020
Gilbert, Beulah I, 1030
Gilbert, Cary I, 1019
Gilbert, Cary I, 1030
Gilbert, Cathrine II, 613
Gilbert, Charles IV, 1058
Gilbert, Charles VI, 302
Gilbert, Charles VI, 802
Gilbert, Charles VI, 819
Gilbert, Charles E. IV, 1058
Gilbert, Charles E. IV, 1131
Gilbert, Charles L. V, 332
Gilbert, Charles S. V, 332
Gilbert, Chas. E. IV, 1131
Gilbert, Clifton L. VI, 921
Gilbert, Cornelius I, 390
Gilbert, Cynthia Ann IV, 1058
Gilbert, Cynthia Ann IV, 1099
Gilbert, Cynthiann IV, 1127
Gilbert, Cynthiann IV, 1131
Gilbert, Daniel IV, 526
Gilbert, Daniel A. IV, 205
Gilbert, Daniel A. IV, 1058
Gilbert, Daniel A. IV, 1099
Gilbert, Daniel G. IV, 1099
Gilbert, Daniel W. IV, 395
Gilbert, Daniel W. IV, 1058
Gilbert, Daniel W. IV, 1064
Gilbert, Daniel W. IV, 1098
Gilbert, Daniel W. IV, 1131
Gilbert, Daniel Wm. IV, 1058
Gilbert, David II, 795
Gilbert, David IV, 735
Gilbert, David P. IV, 126
Gilbert, Debora IV, 126
Gilbert, Debora IV, 128
Gilbert, Deborah II, 997
Gilbert, Deborah II, 1021
Gilbert, Deborah IV, 88
Gilbert, Deborah IV, 94
Gilbert, Deborah IV, 135
Gilbert, Deborah IV, 722
Gilbert, Deborah IV, 817
Gilbert, Deborah IV, 823
Gilbert, Deborah S. IV, 135
Gilbert, Dillon IV, 580
Gilbert, Dillwin IV, 713
Gilbert, Dorathy I, 140
Gilbert, Dorathy I, 156
Gilbert, Dorathy I, 853
Gilbert, Dorathy I, 854
Gilbert, Doris Beryl V, 240
Gilbert, Dorithy I, 99
Gilbert, Dorothy I, 140
Gilbert, Dorothy I, 716
Gilbert, Dorothy I, 879
Gilbert, Dorothy L. IV, 957
Gilbert, Edgar K. IV, 1058
Gilbert, Edith IV, 126
Gilbert, Edith IV, 131
Gilbert, Edith IV, 205
Gilbert, Edith IV, 276
Gilbert, Edith IV, 713
Gilbert, Edith IV, 835
Gilbert, Edith IV, 841
Gilbert, Edith IV, 1058
Gilbert, Edith IV, 1098
Gilbert, Edith IV, 1099
Gilbert, Edith M. IV, 88
Gilbert, Edith M. IV, 757
Gilbert, Edith S. IV, 1131
Gilbert, Edward IV, 1279
Gilbert, Edwin D. IV, 126
Gilbert, Edwin D. IV, 135
Gilbert, Edwin D. IV, 817
Gilbert, Eli IV, 395
Gilbert, Eli IV, 1058
Gilbert, Eli IV, 1096
Gilbert, Eli IV, 1098
Gilbert, Eli IV, 1099
Gilbert, Eli IV, 1131
Gilbert, Elisabeth I, 139
Gilbert, Elisabeth I, 140
Gilbert, Elisabeth I, 148
Gilbert, Elisabeth I, 167
Gilbert, Elisabeth I, 169
Gilbert, Elisabeth I, 173
Gilbert, Elisabeth I, 239
Gilbert, Elisha K. VI, 819
Gilbert, Eliza IV, 124
Gilbert, Eliza IV, 126
Gilbert, Eliza IV, 135
Gilbert, Eliza IV, 136
Gilbert, Eliza IV, 693
Gilbert, Eliza C. IV, 88
Gilbert, Eliza C. IV, 126
Gilbert, Eliza Jane IV, 1099
Gilbert, Eliza T. L. IV, 957
Gilbert, Elizabeth I, 99
Gilbert, Elizabeth I, 139
Gilbert, Elizabeth I, 280
Gilbert, Elizabeth I, 288
Gilbert, Elizabeth I, 306
Gilbert, Elizabeth I, 853
Gilbert, Elizabeth I, 854
Gilbert, Elizabeth I, 879
Gilbert, Elizabeth I, 1043
Gilbert, Elizabeth II, 72
Gilbert, Elizabeth II, 531
Gilbert, Elizabeth II, 610
Gilbert, Elizabeth II, 613
Gilbert, Elizabeth II, 628
Gilbert, Elizabeth II, 783
Gilbert, Elizabeth II, 788
Gilbert, Elizabeth IV, 88
Gilbert, Elizabeth IV, 145
Gilbert, Elizabeth IV, 147
Gilbert, Elizabeth IV, 205
Gilbert, Elizabeth IV, 297
Gilbert, Elizabeth IV, 331
Gilbert, Elizabeth IV, 395
Gilbert, Elizabeth IV, 429
Gilbert, Elizabeth IV, 526
Gilbert, Elizabeth IV, 957
Gilbert, Elizabeth IV, 1058
Gilbert, Elizabeth IV, 1076
Gilbert, Elizabeth IV, 1098
Gilbert, Elizabeth IV, 1099
Gilbert, Elizabeth IV, 1127
Gilbert, Elizabeth IV, 1131
Gilbert, Elizabeth IV, 1137
Gilbert, Elizabeth VI, 919
Gilbert, Elizabeth H. IV, 1058
Gilbert, Elizabeth H. IV, 1099
Gilbert, Elizabeth Lloyd IV, 957
Gilbert, Elizabeth R. IV, 1058
Gilbert, Elizabeth R. IV, 1099
Gilbert, Elizabeth S. IV, 1058
Gilbert, Elizabeth S. IV, 1131
Gilbert, Elizabeth T. IV, 957
Gilbert, Ellen IV, 126
Gilbert, Ellen IV, 135
Gilbert, Ellen IV, 817
Gilbert, Ellen IV, 1097
Gilbert, Ellen B. IV, 817
Gilbert, Ellen C. II, 702
Gilbert, Ellen C. IV, 88
Gilbert, Ellen C. IV, 205
Gilbert, Ellen C. IV, 283
Gilbert, Ellen C. IV, 817
Gilbert, Ellen C. IV, 844
Gilbert, Ellen P. II, 867
Gilbert, Elma IV, 135
Gilbert, Elma IV, 722
Gilbert, Elma IV, 817
Gilbert, Elma G. IV, 817
Gilbert, Elma G. IV, 823
Gilbert, Elmira V, 739
Gilbert, Emily I, 925
Gilbert, Emma II, 823
Gilbert, Emma III, 315
Gilbert, Esther I, 390
Gilbert, Esther I, 419
Gilbert, Esther I, 879
Gilbert, Esther Swan I, 925
Gilbert, Fanny VI, 819
Gilbert, Finley IV, 88
Gilbert, Geo. IV, 802
Gilbert, Geo. D. IV, 123
Gilbert, Geo. D. IV, 807
Gilbert, Geo. D. IV, 817
Gilbert, Geo. D. IV, 839
Gilbert, George I, 390
Gilbert, George IV, 88
Gilbert, George IV, 124
Gilbert, George IV, 126
Gilbert, George IV, 129
Gilbert, George IV, 135
Gilbert, George IV, 817
Gilbert, George D. IV, 126
Gilbert, George D. IV, 817
Gilbert, Gertie IV, 713
Gilbert, Gertrude Francis III, 134
Gilbert, Gilbert II, 366
Gilbert, Gilbert IV, 88
Gilbert, Gurney IV, 957
Gilbert, Gurtie IV, 713
Gilbert, Hanameel I, 1019
Gilbert, Hannah I, 854
Gilbert, Hannah I, 879
Gilbert, Hannah II, 366
Gilbert, Hannah IV, 88
Gilbert, Hannah IV, 123
Gilbert, Hannah IV, 124
Gilbert, Hannah IV, 126
Gilbert, Hannah IV, 129
Gilbert, Hannah IV, 135
Gilbert, Hannah IV, 802
Gilbert, Hannah IV, 807
Gilbert, Hannah IV, 817
Gilbert, Hannah IV, 839
Gilbert, Hannah IV, 957
Gilbert, Hannah VI, 920
Gilbert, Helen Mae IV, 985
Gilbert, Henry C. VI, 921
Gilbert, Hepsbah I, 1020
Gilbert, Hepsibah I, 1035
Gilbert, Hepzibah I, 1030
Gilbert, Herman T. III, 111
Gilbert, Herman T. III, 134
Gilbert, Howard Kent IV, 713
Gilbert, Howard Leroy V, 240
Gilbert, Humphrey VI, 921
Gilbert, Ida A. Newlin IV, 817
Gilbert, Ida Armela IV, 1131
Gilbert, Isaac IV, 957
Gilbert, Isabell IV, 1317
Gilbert, J. Wendell IV, 957
Gilbert, James I, 390
Gilbert, James IV, 713
Gilbert, James VI, 12
Gilbert, James VI, 921
Gilbert, James A. IV, 735
Gilbert, Jane I, 410
Gilbert, Jane IV, 713
Gilbert, Jane Audrey IV, 713
Gilbert, Jane More I, 390
Gilbert, Jarvis VI, 920
Gilbert, Jemima I, 45
Gilbert, Jemima I, 50
Gilbert, Jemima I, 853
Gilbert, Jemima I, 879
Gilbert, Jemimah I, 879
Gilbert, Jemimah I, 895
Gilbert, Jemimah VI, 920
Gilbert, Jenny VI, 819
Gilbert, Jeremia I, 879
Gilbert, Jeremiah I, 50
Gilbert, Jeremiah I, 99
Gilbert, Jeremiah I, 139
Gilbert, Jeremiah I, 140
Gilbert, Jeremiah I, 149
Gilbert, Jeremiah I, 157
Gilbert, Jeremiah I, 716
Gilbert, Jeremiah I, 879
Gilbert, Jesse II, 997
Gilbert, Jesse IV, 88
Gilbert, Jesse IV, 126
Gilbert, Joel I, 99
Gilbert, Joel I, 139
Gilbert, Joel I, 147
Gilbert, Joel I, 173
Gilbert, Joel I, 193
Gilbert, Joel I, 288
Gilbert, Joel I, 853
Gilbert, Joel I, 879
Gilbert, Joel I, 1043
Gilbert, Joel IV, 145
Gilbert, Joel IV, 147
Gilbert, Joel IV, 331
Gilbert, Joel IV, 395
Gilbert, Joel IV, 429
Gilbert, Joel IV, 1058
Gilbert, Joel IV, 1076
Gilbert, Joel IV, 1098
Gilbert, Joel IV, 1099
Gilbert, Joel IV, 1127
Gilbert, Joel IV, 1131
Gilbert, Joel IV, 1136
Gilbert, Joel IV, 1137
Gilbert, John I, 99
Gilbert, John I, 140
Gilbert, John I, 390
Gilbert, John I Sup 1, 4
Gilbert, John I Sup 1, 6
Gilbert, John II, 72
Gilbert, John II, 225
Gilbert, John II, 366
Gilbert, John II, 444
Gilbert, John II, 531
Gilbert, John II, 610
Gilbert, John II, 628
Gilbert, John II, 658
Gilbert, John II, 788
Gilbert, John II, 800
Gilbert, John II, 997
Gilbert, John IV, 205
Gilbert, John IV, 258
Gilbert, John IV, 331
Gilbert, John IV, 395
Gilbert, John IV, 526
Gilbert, John IV, 543
Gilbert, John IV, 985
Gilbert, John V, 997
Gilbert, John VI, 819
Gilbert, John Gurney IV, 957
Gilbert, John J. IV, 957
Gilbert, John Lowell IV, 713
Gilbert, John W. VI, 836
Gilbert, John Wendell IV, 957
Gilbert, John, Jr. II, 531
Gilbert, John, Jr. II, 997
Gilbert, Jonathan I, 1019
Gilbert, Jonathan I, 1020
Gilbert, Jonathan I, 1030
Gilbert, Jonathan IV, 205
Gilbert, Jonathan IV, 1058
Gilbert, Jonathan IV, 1099
Gilbert, Joseph I, 35
Gilbert, Joseph I, 50
Gilbert, Joseph I, 98
Gilbert, Joseph I, 99
Gilbert, Joseph I, 390
Gilbert, Joseph I, 424
Gilbert, Joseph II, 366
Gilbert, Joseph II, 531
Gilbert, Joseph II, 976
Gilbert, Joseph II, 997
Gilbert, Joseph IV, 903
Gilbert, Joseph VI, 11
Gilbert, Joseph VI, 493
Gilbert, Joshua II, 366
Gilbert, Joshua II, 531
Gilbert, Joshua II, 610
Gilbert, Joshua II, 613
Gilbert, Joshua IV, 88
Gilbert, Joshua IV, 126
Gilbert, Joshua IV, 128
Gilbert, Joshua IV, 135
Gilbert, Joshua IV, 531
Gilbert, Joshua IV, 722
Gilbert, Joshua IV, 817
Gilbert, Joshua IV, 823
Gilbert, Joshua, Jr. II, 531
Gilbert, Joshua, Jr. II, 997
Gilbert, Josiah I, 99
Gilbert, Josiah I, 140
Gilbert, Josiah I, 156
Gilbert, Josiah I, 715
Gilbert, Josiah I, 716
Gilbert, Josiah I, 853
Gilbert, Josiah I, 854
Gilbert, Josiah I, 879
Gilbert, Josiah I Sup 1, 4
Gilbert, Josiah I Sup 1, 6
Gilbert, Katy IV, 1279
Gilbert, Kent IV, 713
Gilbert, Lavina VI, 825
Gilbert, Lewis B. III, 134
Gilbert, Lidda I, 193
Gilbert, Linneus IV, 88
Gilbert, Lowrana I, 413
Gilbert, Lowrana Phillips I, 390
Gilbert, Lula Mae IV, 957
Gilbert, Lulu Mae IV, 957
Gilbert, Lydia I, 140
Gilbert, Lydia I, 147
Gilbert, Lydia I, 193
Gilbert, Lydia I, 853
Gilbert, Lydia I, 854
Gilbert, Lydia I, 879
Gilbert, Lydia II, 531
Gilbert, Lydia II, 658
Gilbert, Lydia II, 997
Gilbert, Lydia II, 1037
Gilbert, Lydia IV, 88
Gilbert, Lydia IV, 123
Gilbert, Lydia IV, 126
Gilbert, Lydia IV, 135
Gilbert, Lydia IV, 621
Gilbert, Lydia IV, 693
Gilbert, Lydia IV, 700
Gilbert, Lydia IV, 712
Gilbert, Lydia IV, 903
Gilbert, Mabel E. V, 240
Gilbert, Maggie V, 997
Gilbert, Margaret I, 98
Gilbert, Margaret I, 137
Gilbert, Margaret I, 139

Gilbert, Margaret II, 366
Gilbert, Margaret IV, 19
Gilbert, Margaret IV, 33
Gilbert, Margaret IV, 126
Gilbert, Maria IV, 1096
Gilbert, Maria IV, 1098
Gilbert, Maria O. VI, 819
Gilbert, Martha I, 50
Gilbert, Martha I, 85
Gilbert, Martha II, 613
Gilbert, Martha VI, 292
Gilbert, Martha VI, 921
Gilbert, Martha VI, 931
Gilbert, Martha VI, 965
Gilbert, Mary I, 35
Gilbert, Mary I, 50
Gilbert, Mary I, 51
Gilbert, Mary I, 55
Gilbert, Mary I, 99
Gilbert, Mary I, 390
Gilbert, Mary I, 400
Gilbert, Mary I, 854
Gilbert, Mary I, 879
Gilbert, Mary II, 72
Gilbert, Mary II, 111
Gilbert, Mary II, 225
Gilbert, Mary II, 366
Gilbert, Mary II, 457
Gilbert, Mary II, 531
Gilbert, Mary II, 628
Gilbert, Mary II, 691
Gilbert, Mary II, 997
Gilbert, Mary IV, 88
Gilbert, Mary IV, 126
Gilbert, Mary IV, 135
Gilbert, Mary IV, 136
Gilbert, Mary IV, 205
Gilbert, Mary IV, 331
Gilbert, Mary IV, 395
Gilbert, Mary IV, 429
Gilbert, Mary IV, 526
Gilbert, Mary IV, 580
Gilbert, Mary IV, 712
Gilbert, Mary IV, 713
Gilbert, Mary IV, 957
Gilbert, Mary IV, 1058
Gilbert, Mary IV, 1072
Gilbert, Mary IV, 1098
Gilbert, Mary IV, 1131
Gilbert, Mary IV, 1136
Gilbert, Mary V, 997
Gilbert, Mary VI, 819
Gilbert, Mary A. II, 795
Gilbert, Mary A. II, 867
Gilbert, Mary Ann IV, 577
Gilbert, Mary Ann VI, 921
Gilbert, Mary C. IV, 713
Gilbert, Mary Hunter I, 390
Gilbert, Mary P. IV, 1058
Gilbert, Mary P. IV, 1072
Gilbert, Mary P. IV, 1131
Gilbert, Mary P. IV, 1137
Gilbert, Mary Pearson I, 1020
Gilbert, Mary S. IV, 205
Gilbert, Mary S. IV, 1058
Gilbert, Mary S. IV, 1064
Gilbert, Mary S. IV, 1099
Gilbert, Mary Wistar II, 72
Gilbert, Mary, Jr. II, 531
Gilbert, Mary, Jr. II, 997
Gilbert, Mary, Jr. II, 1033
Gilbert, Meriam I, 716
Gilbert, Michael VI, 819
Gilbert, Michael VI, 920
Gilbert, Milicent I, 853
Gilbert, Milly VI, 819
Gilbert, Miriam I, 99
Gilbert, Miriam I, 139
Gilbert, Miriam I, 140
Gilbert, Miriam I, 157
Gilbert, Miriam I, 716
Gilbert, Miriam I, 854
Gilbert, Miriam I, 879
Gilbert, Mordica VI, 819
Gilbert, Narcissa I, 921
Gilbert, Narcissa I, 925
Gilbert, Narcissa I, 929
Gilbert, Nathan I, 99
Gilbert, Nathan I, 853
Gilbert, Nathan V, 332
Gilbert, Nehemiah Thomas, Jr. V, 739
Gilbert, Nellie IV, 985
Gilbert, Oscar V, 674
Gilbert, Patty VI, 819
Gilbert, Pearson II, 795
Gilbert, Penninah I, 853
Gilbert, Peter I, 925
Gilbert, Phebe I, 377
Gilbert, Phebe I, 854
Gilbert, Phebe I, 879
Gilbert, Phebe II, 997
Gilbert, Phebe V, 740
Gilbert, Phebe V, 767
Gilbert, Phebe V, 769
Gilbert, Phebe Carrol I, 390
Gilbert, Preston VI, 920
Gilbert, Priscila I, 50
Gilbert, Priscilla II, 531
Gilbert, Rachel I, 390
Gilbert, Rachel I Sup 1, 4
Gilbert, Rachel I Sup 1, 6
Gilbert, Rachel II, 366
Gilbert, Rachel II, 531
Gilbert, Rachel II, 975
Gilbert, Rachel II, 997
Gilbert, Rachel IV, 395
Gilbert, Rachel IV, 577
Gilbert, Rachel IV, 1058
Gilbert, Rachel IV, 1061
Gilbert, Rachel IV, 1093
Gilbert, Rachel VI, 836
Gilbert, Rachel C. IV, 626
Gilbert, Rachel C. IV, 665
Gilbert, Rachel C. IV, 713
Gilbert, Rachel C. IV, 735
Gilbert, Rachel Eleanor IV, 1131
Gilbert, Rea IV, 1003
Gilbert, Rebecca I, 99
Gilbert, Rebecca I, 879
Gilbert, Rebecca II, 997
Gilbert, Rebecca IV, 88
Gilbert, Rebecca IV, 126
Gilbert, Rebecca IV, 129
Gilbert, Rebecca IV, 147
Gilbert, Rebecca IV, 164
Gilbert, Rebecca IV, 205
Gilbert, Rebecca IV, 250
Gilbert, Rebecca IV, 331
Gilbert, Rebecca IV, 395
Gilbert, Rebecca IV, 580
Gilbert, Rebecca IV, 817
Gilbert, Rebecca IV, 832
Gilbert, Rebecca IV, 839
Gilbert, Rebecca IV, 1050
Gilbert, Rebecca IV, 1058
Gilbert, Rebecca IV, 1061
Gilbert, Rebecca IV, 1072
Gilbert, Rebecca IV, 1096
Gilbert, Rebecca IV, 1098
Gilbert, Rebecca IV, 1099
Gilbert, Rebecca IV, 1131
Gilbert, Rebecca IV, 1135
Gilbert, Rebecca B. IV, 735
Gilbert, Rebecca McGrail IV, 88
Gilbert, Rebecca W. IV, 531
Gilbert, Rebeckah I, 140
Gilbert, Rebeckah II, 997
Gilbert, Rebeckah II, 1035
Gilbert, Rebeckah IV, 395
Gilbert, Rebekah I, 140
Gilbert, Rebekah I, 149
Gilbert, Rebekah I, 853
Gilbert, Rebekah I, 879
Gilbert, Rhea Stanley IV, 957
Gilbert, Rhoda IV, 577
Gilbert, Robert II, 366
Gilbert, Robert II, 531
Gilbert, Robert, Jr. II, 531
Gilbert, Rose V, 240
Gilbert, Ruth IV, 205
Gilbert, Ruth IV, 280
Gilbert, Ruth IV, 331
Gilbert, Ruth IV, 395
Gilbert, Ruth IV, 1058
Gilbert, Ruth IV, 1065
Gilbert, S. Peter I, 925
Gilbert, Sally VI, 920
Gilbert, Samuel VI, 819
Gilbert, Samuel VI, 920
Gilbert, Samuel C. IV, 88
Gilbert, Samuel C. IV, 126
Gilbert, Samuel C. IV, 713
Gilbert, Samuel Pryor II, 531
Gilbert, Sara IV, 817
Gilbert, Sara Ann IV, 1058
Gilbert, Sarah I, 50
Gilbert, Sarah I, 73
Gilbert, Sarah I, 99
Gilbert, Sarah I, 140
Gilbert, Sarah I, 156
Gilbert, Sarah I, 288
Gilbert, Sarah I, 388
Gilbert, Sarah I, 716
Gilbert, Sarah I, 719
Gilbert, Sarah I, 854
Gilbert, Sarah I, 879
Gilbert, Sarah I Sup 1, 4
Gilbert, Sarah I Sup 1, 6
Gilbert, Sarah II, 174
Gilbert, Sarah II, 225
Gilbert, Sarah II, 366
Gilbert, Sarah II, 513
Gilbert, Sarah II, 531
Gilbert, Sarah II, 976
Gilbert, Sarah II, 982
Gilbert, Sarah II, 997
Gilbert, Sarah IV, 33
Gilbert, Sarah IV, 88
Gilbert, Sarah IV, 126
Gilbert, Sarah IV, 135
Gilbert, Sarah IV, 145
Gilbert, Sarah IV, 147
Gilbert, Sarah IV, 205
Gilbert, Sarah IV, 312
Gilbert, Sarah IV, 331
Gilbert, Sarah IV, 395
Gilbert, Sarah IV, 526
Gilbert, Sarah IV, 802
Gilbert, Sarah IV, 803
Gilbert, Sarah IV, 817
Gilbert, Sarah IV, 1058
Gilbert, Sarah IV, 1098
Gilbert, Sarah IV, 1131
Gilbert, Sarah IV, 1134
Gilbert, Sarah V, 739
Gilbert, Sarah V, 740
Gilbert, Sarah Ann IV, 88
Gilbert, Sarah Ann IV, 126
Gilbert, Sarah Ann IV, 712
Gilbert, Sarah Ann IV, 1058
Gilbert, Sarah Ann IV, 1064
Gilbert, Sarah Ann IV, 1098
Gilbert, Sarah Ann IV, 1099
Gilbert, Sarah Ann V, 622
Gilbert, Sarah Ann V, 640
Gilbert, Sarah C. VI, 921
Gilbert, Sarah Ellett I, 390
Gilbert, Sarah J. III, 134
Gilbert, Seberah I, 390
Gilbert, Seberah I, 424
Gilbert, Susan IV, 88
Gilbert, Susan IV, 126
Gilbert, Susan IV, 205
Gilbert, Susan IV, 621
Gilbert, Susan IV, 700
Gilbert, Susan IV, 713
Gilbert, Susan IV, 813
Gilbert, Susan IV, 817
Gilbert, Susan M. IV, 88
Gilbert, Susan P. IV, 526
Gilbert, Susanna IV, 88
Gilbert, Susanna IV, 129
Gilbert, Susanna IV, 205
Gilbert, Susanna IV, 258
Gilbert, Susanna IV, 543
Gilbert, Susanna P. IV, 205
Gilbert, Susannah IV, 126
Gilbert, Susannah IV, 205
Gilbert, Susannah IV, 526
Gilbert, Tacy IV, 817
Gilbert, Tacy IV, 822
Gilbert, Taylor IV, 577
Gilbert, Taylor IV, 1131
Gilbert, Thomas I, 50
Gilbert, Thomas I, 99
Gilbert, Thomas I, 118
Gilbert, Thomas I, 139
Gilbert, Thomas I, 140
Gilbert, Thomas I, 148
Gilbert, Thomas I, 288
Gilbert, Thomas I, 715
Gilbert, Thomas I, 716
Gilbert, Thomas I, 719
Gilbert, Thomas I, 854
Gilbert, Thomas I, 879
Gilbert, Thomas I, 1020
Gilbert, Thomas I, 1043
Gilbert, Thomas II, 366
Gilbert, Thomas II, 457
Gilbert, Thomas II, 531
Gilbert, Thomas II, 997
Gilbert, Thomas II, 1037
Gilbert, Thomas IV, 205
Gilbert, Thomas IV, 331
Gilbert, Thomas IV, 395
Gilbert, Thomas IV, 577
Gilbert, Thomas IV, 1058
Gilbert, Thomas IV, 1098
Gilbert, Thomas IV, 1099
Gilbert, Thomas V, 740
Gilbert, Thomas Bee II, 531
Gilbert, Thomas Clarkson IV, 126
Gilbert, Thomas Smith IV, 1098
Gilbert, Thomas Smith IV, 1099
Gilbert, Thomas Wilson, Jr. II, 997
Gilbert, Thos. IV, 276
Gilbert, Thos. V, 739
Gilbert, Walter IV, 626
Gilbert, Walter V, 240
Gilbert, Walter C. III, 134
Gilbert, Wd Elizabeth II, 627
Gilbert, Wd. Joanna II, 795
Gilbert, Wd. Mary II, 111
Gilbert, Wendell IV, 957
Gilbert, William I, 50
Gilbert, William II, 706
Gilbert, William IV, 1098
Gilbert, William IV, 1131
Gilbert, William V, 240
Gilbert, William Garrat I, 879
Gilbert, William H. IV, 1058
Gilbert, William J. IV, 1058
Gilbert, Wilmer IV, 713
Gilbert, Wilmer H. IV, 126
Gilbert, Wilmer H. IV, 135
Gilbert, Wilmer H. IV, 817
Gilbord, Jemima I, 9
Gilbord, Joseph I, 9
Gilbord, Josiah I, 9
Gilbord, Sarah I, 9
Gilbord, Thos. I, 9
Gilbpin, John C. VI, 1017
Gilbraith, Susanna I, 541
Gilbreath, Amy J. H. I, 679
Gilbreath, Ann I, 541
Gilbreath, Anne VI, 835
Gilbreath, Charity I, 541
Gilbreath, Charity I, 1016
Gilbreath, Charity I, 1030
Gilbreath, Charity I, 1036
Gilbreath, Elizabeth VI, 921
Gilbreath, James I, 541
Gilbreath, James I, 879
Gilbreath, James I, 1016
Gilbreath, James I, 1030
Gilbreath, James IV, 206
Gilbreath, James, Jr. I, 541
Gilbreath, James, Jr. I, 1016
Gilbreath, Joel I, 541
Gilbreath, John I, 541
Gilbreath, John I, 1016
Gilbreath, John I, 1030
Gilbreath, Lydia I, 541
Gilbreath, Lydia I, 879
Gilbreath, Lydia I, 1016
Gilbreath, Martha V, 240
Gilbreath, Martha V, 254
Gilbreath, Mary I, 1030
Gilbreath, Mary I, 1038
Gilbreath, Susanna I, 541
Gilbreath, Susanna I, 809
Gilbreath, Thomas VI, 921
Gilbreth, Mary I, 617
Gilby, Martha H. II, 867
Gilby, Wm. F. II, 867
Gilchris, Charles F. VI, 853
Gilchrist, Andrew I, 1030
Gilchrist, Andrew II, 531
Gilchrist, Blanche L. IV, 1161
Gilchrist, Charles VI, 819
Gilchrist, Charles F. VI, 819
Gilchrist, David IV, 1161
Gilchrist, David D. IV, 1161
Gilchrist, Martha T. III, 134
Gilchrist, Mary III, 194
Gilchrist, Mary A. VI, 833
Gilchrist, Mary R. VI, 819
Gilchrist, Mina III, 134
Gilchrist, Mina III, 194
Gilchrist, Nancy VI, 819
Gilchrist, Nancy A. VI, 819
Gilchrist, Robert V. VI, 819
Gilchrist, Samuel III, 134
Gilchrist, William III, 194
Gildersleeve, ??? III, 293
Gildersleeve, Alfred Mosher III, 134
Gildersleeve, Florence L. III, 134
Gildersleeve, Florence L. III, 293
Gildersleeve, Henry B. III, 134
Gildersleeve, Jane III, 134
Gildersleeve, Mary J. III, 134
Gilen, Lydia IV, 1271
Gilen, Lydia IV, 1279
Gilenwater, Valentine VI, 867
Gilenwaters, Kessiah VI, 867
Gilerist, Andrew I, 541
Giles, Almeida I, 1152
Giles, Amanda Catharine VI, 976
Giles, Amelia III, 256
Giles, Anna II, 366
Giles, Anna II, 532
Giles, Anna III, 363
Giles, Anna, Jr. II, 488
Giles, Anna, Jr. II, 532
Giles, Anne III, 97
Giles, Anne III, 368
Giles, Annie III, 363
Giles, Aquilla II, 531
Giles, Aquilla II, 532
Giles, Columbus I, 920
Giles, Columbus I, 925
Giles, Cora I, 920
Giles, Cora May I, 925
Giles, Cora May I, 941
Giles, Dicey VI, 819
Giles, Dorothy II, 225
Giles, Dorothy II, 261
Giles, Edward II, 531
Giles, Edward II, 532
Giles, Elizabeth II, 366
Giles, Elizabeth II, 532
Giles, Elizabeth II, 603
Giles, Elizabeth VI, 819
Giles, Elizabeth VI, 822
Giles, Hannah II, 444
Giles, Henry II, 444
Giles, Jacob II, 366
Giles, Jacob II, 488
Giles, Jacob II, 531
Giles, Jacob II, 532
Giles, Jacob, Jr. II, 532
Giles, James II, 531
Giles, James II, 532
Giles, Jesse VI, 819
Giles, Joanna II, 488
Giles, Joanna II, 532
Giles, John VI, 930
Giles, Josiah VI, 819
Giles, Jubal VI, 921
Giles, Laura I, 879
Giles, Laura I, 882
Giles, Laura I, 920
Giles, Laura I, 925
Giles, Maria III, 483
Giles, Mary II, 225
Giles, Mary II, 240
Giles, Mary II, 997
Giles, Mary Ann VI, 921
Giles, Nancy VI, 930
Giles, Perrin VI, 819
Giles, Phebe P. III, 201
Giles, Rebeckah II, 444
Giles, Sally VI, 858
Giles, Sally VI, 941
Giles, Sarah VI, 819
Giles, Sarah VI, 866
Giles, Sarah Frances VI, 994
Giles, Sophia VI, 921
Giles, Thomas II, 531
Giles, Thomas II, 532
Giles, Thomas VI, 921
Giles, Thomas VI, 994
Gilford, Ann III, 134
Gilford, Ann III, 239
Gilgrist, Andrew II, 531
Gilham, John I, 445
Gilham, John Westly I, 445
Gilingham, Mary Wildman II, 856
Gilkesan, Mary VI, 576
Gilkesan, Mary S. VI, 493
Gilkesan, Mary S. VI, 576
Gilkeson, James VI, 392
Gilkeson, Mary Susan VI, 392
Gilkeson, Sarah Elizabeth VI, 392
Gilkeson, Sarah Elizabeth VI, 428
Gill, ??? VI, 42
Gill, Alexander VI, 921
Gill, Amie II, 65
Gill, Amie II, 72
Gill, Amy II, 72
Gill, Ann II, 532
Gill, Ann II, 795
Gill, Ann II, 867
Gill, Ann IV, 206
Gill, Ann VI, 392
Gill, Ann E. VI, 921
Gill, Anna L. IV, 206
Gill, C. W. VI, 929
Gill, C. W. VI, 992
Gill, Charles VI, 942
Gill, Charles VI, 949
Gill, Charles VI, 971
Gill, Charles VI, 985
Gill, Charles VI, 1009
Gill, Charles H. VI, 866
Gill, Charles W. VI, 921
Gill, Chas. W. VI, 967
Gill, David II, 72
Gill, Deborah IV, 206
Gill, Deborah IV, 300
Gill, Elizabeth II, 72
Gill, Elizabeth II, 105
Gill, Elizabeth IV, 147
Gill, Elizabeth IV, 206
Gill, Elizabeth IV, 224
Gill, Elizabeth IV, 464
Gill, Elizabeth VI, 796
Gill, Elizabeth Ann W. II, 867
Gill, Elizabeth Ann Wilson II, 79

Gill, Frances II, 532
Gill, Geo. IV, 957
Gill, George II, 72
Gill, George II, 105
Gill, George E. IV, 1252
Gill, Hanna II, 116
Gill, Hanna II, 118
Gill, Hannah II, 366
Gill, Hannah II, 451
Gill, Hannah II, 532
Gill, Hannah II, 706
Gill, Hannah E. IV, 206
Gill, Harry IV, 206
Gill, Harry C. IV, 206
Gill, Henry VI, 177
Gill, Henry S. VI, 921
Gill, Hewes II, 532
Gill, James II, 532
Gill, James IV, 206
Gill, James H. IV, 206
Gill, James I. II, 532
Gill, James W. IV, 206
Gill, Jenny VI, 949
Gill, John II, 65
Gill, John II, 72
Gill, John II, 105
Gill, John II, 532
Gill, John IV, 206
Gill, John IV, 224
Gill, John IV, 307
Gill, John IV, 464
Gill, John V, 240
Gill, John V, 952
Gill, John VI, 177
Gill, John VI, 392
Gill, John VI, 921
Gill, John S. VI, 921
Gill, John W. IV, 206
Gill, John, Jr. II, 72
Gill, Joseph II, 532
Gill, Joseph II, 795
Gill, Joseph II, 867
Gill, Joseph IV, 206
Gill, Joseph VI, 177
Gill, Joseph VI, 178
Gill, Joseph Hewes II, 366
Gill, Joseph John IV, 206
Gill, Joshua II, 72
Gill, Joshua II, 225
Gill, Joshua II, 366
Gill, Joshua II, 532
Gill, Joshua II, 997
Gill, Kitty VI, 942
Gill, Lottie W. IV, 957
Gill, Lottie Winona Cole IV, 1252
Gill, Louisa IV, 957
Gill, Louisa IV, 1252
Gill, Louisa W. II, 867
Gill, Louisa W. II, 919
Gill, Marcy II, 20
Gill, Margaret II, 532
Gill, Mary II, 366
Gill, Mary II, 532
Gill, Mary Ann IV, 206
Gill, Mary Ann IV, 259
Gill, Mary C. VI, 1009
Gill, Mary Elizabeth VI, 921
Gill, Mary Ellie IV, 206
Gill, Mary Eva IV, 206
Gill, Mary H. II, 795
Gill, Mary H. II, 867
Gill, Mary H. VI, 177
Gill, Mary H. VI, 178
Gill, Mary Virginia II, 795
Gill, Mercy II, 19
Gill, Mildred L. IV, 957
Gill, Nancy IV, 202
Gill, Nancy IV, 206
Gill, Nathaniel II, 366
Gill, Nathaniel II, 532
Gill, Peggy VI, 921
Gill, Polly VI, 921
Gill, Priscilla IV, 206
Gill, Priscilla IV, 307
Gill, Prudence II, 72
Gill, Prudence II, 105
Gill, Prudence VI, 177
Gill, Rebecca VI, 985
Gill, Rebecca F. VI, 820
Gill, Robert II, 366
Gill, Robert II, 532
Gill, Robert, Jr. II, 532
Gill, Roger II, 366
Gill, Roger VI, 13
Gill, Ruth W. IV, 957
Gill, Salkill V, 240
Gill, Sally VI, 971
Gill, Saltkil V, 952
Gill, Samuel IV, 206
Gill, Samuel VI, 392
Gill, Samuel C. IV, 206
Gill, Sarah II, 366
Gill, Sarah II, 532
Gill, Sarah VI, 796
Gill, Sarah Ann II, 118
Gill, Sarah C. IV, 464
Gill, Sarah H. VI, 807
Gill, Sarah H. VI, 921
Gill, Sunna IV, 307
Gill, Susanna IV, 206
Gill, Susanna IV, 224
Gill, Susanna V, 240
Gill, Susannah V, 303
Gill, Susannah V, 952
Gill, Tabitha VI, 921
Gill, Thomas VI, 392
Gill, Wallace IV, 1252
Gill, Wallace E. IV, 957
Gill, Washington VI, 921
Gill, William IV, 206
Gill, William S. IV, 206
Gillam, Dan V, 622
Gillam, Daniel V, 492
Gillam, Ernest Allen V, 492
Gillam, Hannah II, 795
Gillam, Hannah II, 816
Gillam, Hannah II, 867
Gillam, Hannah II, 914
Gillam, Hannah H. II, 867
Gillam, Harvey II, 795
Gillam, Harvey II, 844
Gillam, Harvey II, 867
Gillam, Harvey II, 886
Gillam, Harvey H. II, 867
Gillam, Jennie V, 622
Gillam, John Calvin V, 492
Gillam, Lear I, 446
Gillam, Lily May V, 492
Gillam, Mary IV, 713
Gillam, Mary L. II, 742
Gillam, Mary L. II, 766
Gillam, Mary W. II, 867
Gillam, Mary W. III, 16
Gillam, Mary W. III, 259
Gillam, Roger Miriam V, 622
Gillam, Sarah II, 844
Gillam, Sarah II, 867
Gillam, Sarah C. II, 886
Gillam, Sarah Grubb II, 795
Gillam, Sarah T. II, 867
Gillam, Susan II, 795
Gillam, Susanna VI, 1001
Gillam, Susannah II, 844
Gillam, Susannah II, 867
Gillam, Susannah W. II, 795
Gillam, Susannah Woolston II, 867
Gillam, Susannah Woolston II, 886
Gillam, Wm. II, 795
Gillam, Wm. II, 844
Gillam, Wm. Henry II, 867
Gilland, David J. V, 332
Gilland, Laura V, 332
Gillaspey, Hannah II, 532
Gillaspie, Elijah B. VI, 921
Gillaspie, Mahala VI, 921
Gillaspie, Mary F. VI, 921
Gillaspie, Penelope V, 60
Gillaspie, Penelope V, 84
Gillaspie, Rolling VI, 921
Gillaspie, Talton VI, 921
Gillaspy, Elizabeth M. VI, 943
Gillaspy, Hannah II, 502
Gillaspy, Roland VI, 943
Gillen, Dorothy IV, 1252
Gillen, Elba IV, 1252
Gillen, Eliza III, 61
Gillen, Eliza III, 297
Gillen, Floyd IV, 1252
Gillen, Grace IV, 1252
Gillenwaters, Elisha VI, 845
Gillenwaters, John VI, 845
Gillenwaters, Sophia VI, 845
Gillespey, Hannah II, 742
Gillespi, Edward J. IV, 1317
Gillespi, Geo. G. IV, 1317
Gillespi, Harlan Edward IV, 1317
Gillespi, Louise IV, 1317
Gillespie, Charles VI, 820
Gillespie, Edward J. IV, 1317
Gillespie, Elizabeth VI, 820
Gillespie, Margaret IV, 957
Gillespie, Margaret IV, 977
Gillespie, Penelope V, 60
Gillespie, Sarah III, 134
Gillespie, Sarah III, 173
Gillett, Elizabeth W. IV, 206
Gillham, Burwell VI, 107
Gilliam, Ann VI, 921
Gilliam, Anthony W. VI, 820
Gilliam, Archelaus VI, 921
Gilliam, Archerlous VI, 827
Gilliam, Archibald VI, 921
Gilliam, Blanch I, 930
Gilliam, Celia B. VI, 820
Gilliam, Charlotte VI, 954
Gilliam, Eliza B. VI, 820
Gilliam, Elizabeth VI, 811
Gilliam, Elizabeth VI, 820
Gilliam, Elizabeth VI, 827
Gilliam, Elizabeth VI, 903
Gilliam, Elizabeth J. D. VI, 921
Gilliam, Glover D. VI, 815
Gilliam, Glover D. VI, 820
Gilliam, James VI, 819
Gilliam, Jarrerd VI, 820
Gilliam, Jarrett VI, 827
Gilliam, Jarrett VI, 921
Gilliam, Martha V. VI, 815
Gilliam, Nancy VI, 811
Gilliam, Nancy VI, 921
Gilliam, Patterson VI, 820
Gilliam, Richard VI, 903
Gilliam, Richard VI, 921
Gilliam, Richard VI, 954
Gilliam, Richard VI, 997
Gilliam, Richard, Jr. VI, 921
Gilliam, Robert VI, 820
Gilliam, Sally VI, 997
Gilliam, Sally McKine VI, 819
Gilliam, Selina M. VI, 820
Gilliam, Susan VI, 820
Gilliam, Theodosia VI, 921
Gilliam, William Jarratt VI, 821
Gilliam, Zach. VI, 980
Gillilan, Susannah IV, 88
Gillilan, Susannah IV, 105
Gilliland, Charley V, 997
Gilliland, Harriet IV, 395
Gilliland, Harriet IV, 410
Gilliland, Maria V, 379
Gilliland, Maria V, 388
Gilliland, Mary E. V, 997
Gillim, Susannah I, 446
Gillingham, A. Scott VI, 742
Gillingham, A. Scott VI, 743
Gillingham, A. Scott VI, 751
Gillingham, A. Scott VI, 759
Gillingham, A. Scott VI, 763
Gillingham, Abigail A. VI, 743
Gillingham, Adrienne VI, 742
Gillingham, Albert J. II, 796
Gillingham, ALbert J. II, 867
Gillingham, Albert Victor II, 867
Gillingham, Ann II, 366
Gillingham, Ann II, 532
Gillingham, Ann II, 563
Gillingham, Ann II, 867
Gillingham, Ann II, 959
Gillingham, Ann II, 980
Gillingham, Ann II, 998
Gillingham, Ann II, 1049
Gillingham, Ann II, 1051
Gillingham, Ann B. II, 1046
Gillingham, Ann B. II, 1051
Gillingham, Ann Eliza II, 998
Gillingham, Ann Eliza II, 1009
Gillingham, Ann G. II, 1073
Gillingham, Ann W. II, 532
Gillingham, Anna II, 366
Gillingham, Anna II, 532
Gillingham, Anna II, 742
Gillingham, Anna L. VI, 742
Gillingham, Anna L. VI, 743
Gillingham, Anna L. VI, 774
Gillingham, Anna Maria II, 924
Gillingham, Anna W. II, 742
Gillingham, Anne II, 867
Gillingham, Annie B. II, 1085
Gillingham, Annie B. II, 1087
Gillingham, Benjamin II, 195
Gillingham, Benjamin II, 225
Gillingham, Benjamin II, 959
Gillingham, Benjamin R. VI, 743
Gillingham, Bertha VI, 742
Gillingham, Bertha VI, 743
Gillingham, Bertha VI, 751
Gillingham, Bertha VI, 759
Gillingham, Bertha VI, 763
Gillingham, Bridget II, 796
Gillingham, Bridget II, 997
Gillingham, Bridget II, 1017
Gillingham, Bridgit II, 997
Gillingham, Caroline II, 366
Gillingham, Caroline II, 742
Gillingham, Caroline S. II, 706
Gillingham, Caroline S. II, 742
Gillingham, Catharine II, 742
Gillingham, Catharine V, 907
Gillingham, Catharine VI, 743
Gillingham, Chalkey VI, 789
Gillingham, Chalkley VI, 737
Gillingham, Chalkley VI, 742
Gillingham, Charles II, 532
Gillingham, Charles II, 742
Gillingham, Charles Augustus II, 366
Gillingham, Charles Augustus II, 742
Gillingham, Charles Clarkson VI, 743
Gillingham, Chas. II, 796
Gillingham, Chas. II, 867
Gillingham, Clara Leedom II, 867
Gillingham, Clinton II, 796
Gillingham, Clinton II, 867
Gillingham, Edith Leslie III, 134
Gillingham, Edward C. II, 366
Gillingham, Edward C. II, 742
Gillingham, Eliza II, 133
Gillingham, Eliza V, 907
Gillingham, Eliza VI, 743
Gillingham, Elizabeth II, 366
Gillingham, Elizabeth II, 742
Gillingham, Elizabeth II, 867
Gillingham, Elizabeth II, 959
Gillingham, Elizabeth II, 997
Gillingham, Elizabeth II, 998
Gillingham, Elizabeth II, 1000
Gillingham, Elizabeth II, 1016
Gillingham, Elizabeth II, 1017
Gillingham, Elizabeth II, 1030
Gillingham, Elizabeth III, 134
Gillingham, Elizabeth III, 148
Gillingham, Elizabeth VI, 743
Gillingham, Elizabeth J. II, 867
Gillingham, Elizabeth J. VI, 743
Gillingham, Elizabeth Jane II, 796
Gillingham, Elizabeth Moon II, 532
Gillingham, Elizabeth T. III, 134
Gillingham, Ella VI, 741
Gillingham, Ella VI, 742
Gillingham, Ella VI, 743
Gillingham, Ellen R. II, 867
Gillingham, Ellen R. VI, 743
Gillingham, Ellwood W. II, 867
Gillingham, Ellwood William II, 796
Gillingham, Elvira II, 998
Gillingham, Elvira II, 1016
Gillingham, Elvira II, 1051
Gillingham, Elvira II, 1059
Gillingham, Elvira II, 1073
Gillingham, Elvira II, 1078
Gillingham, Elwood W. VI, 743
Gillingham, Emaline VI, 478
Gillingham, Emeline II, 366
Gillingham, Emeline VI, 734
Gillingham, Emeline VI, 742
Gillingham, Emiline II, 742
Gillingham, Emma II, 706
Gillingham, Emma II, 742
Gillingham, Emma II, 796
Gillingham, Emma II, 867
Gillingham, Emma II, 925
Gillingham, Emma Jane II, 796
Gillingham, Emma Jane II, 867
Gillingham, Emma Jane VI, 743
Gillingham, Emma K. VI, 742
Gillingham, Emma K. VI, 743
Gillingham, Emma K. VI, 762
Gillingham, Emma Kezia II, 889
Gillingham, Emma Keziah II, 868
Gillingham, Emmaline VI, 556
Gillingham, Esther II, 366
Gillingham, Esther II, 532
Gillingham, Esther V, 882
Gillingham, Esther VI, 743
Gillingham, Esther VI, 778
Gillingham, Esther A. VI, 742
Gillingham, Esther Ann V, 907
Gillingham, Esther H. V, 882
Gillingham, Esther H. V, 885
Gillingham, Esther H. VI, 742
Gillingham, Esther H. VI, 776
Gillingham, Esther Scott VI, 742
Gillingham, Esther Scott VI, 759
Gillingham, Francenia II, 366
Gillingham, Frances II, 742
Gillingham, Frances A. II, 924
Gillingham, Frances Ashbridge II, 796
Gillingham, Francinia II, 742
Gillingham, George II, 133
Gillingham, George C. VI, 734
Gillingham, George Chalkley VI, 742
Gillingham, George Chalkley VI, 743
Gillingham, George Chalkley VI, 786
Gillingham, George Lewis VI, 743
Gillingham, Grace II, 867
Gillingham, Hannah II, 366
Gillingham, Hannah II, 998
Gillingham, Hannah II, 1051
Gillingham, Hannah II, 1073
Gillingham, Hannah VI, 743
Gillingham, Hannah W. VI, 737
Gillingham, Hannah W. VI, 742
Gillingham, Harold Ellwood II, 867
Gillingham, Harper II, 867
Gillingham, Harper V, 907
Gillingham, Harriet II, 1051
Gillingham, Harriet II, 1056
Gillingham, Harriet II, 1073
Gillingham, Harriet II, 1076
Gillingham, Harvey II, 959
Gillingham, Harvey II, 1051
Gillingham, Harvey II, 1073
Gillingham, Harvy II, 998
Gillingham, Harvy II, 1016
Gillingham, Helen V, 907
Gillingham, Henrietta II, 796
Gillingham, Henrietta II, 867
Gillingham, Henry W. III, 64
Gillingham, Henry W. III, 134
Gillingham, Henry Warrington VI, 743
Gillingham, Hetty V, 907
Gillingham, Hetty V, 930
Gillingham, Isaac VI, 743
Gillingham, J. Reuben VI, 743
Gillingham, James II, 366
Gillingham, James II, 532
Gillingham, James II, 540
Gillingham, James II, 742
Gillingham, James II, 867
Gillingham, James W. II, 706
Gillingham, James Wood II, 532
Gillingham, Jane V, 907
Gillingham, Jane VI, 743
Gillingham, Jehu VI, 743
Gillingham, John II, 195
Gillingham, John II, 225
Gillingham, John II, 366
Gillingham, John II, 532
Gillingham, John II, 563
Gillingham, John II, 959
Gillingham, John II, 998
Gillingham, John II, 1031
Gillingham, John II, 1037
Gillingham, Jonathan II, 796
Gillingham, Jonathan II, 959
Gillingham, Joseph II, 366
Gillingham, Joseph II, 532
Gillingham, Joseph II, 742
Gillingham, Joseph II, 796
Gillingham, Joseph II, 959
Gillingham, Joseph II, 997
Gillingham, Joseph II, 998
Gillingham, Joseph II, 1000
Gillingham, Joseph II, 1016
Gillingham, Joseph II, 1017
Gillingham, Joseph IV, 818
Gillingham, Joseph VI, 734
Gillingham, Joseph VI, 742
Gillingham, Joseph Warrington VI, 742
Gillingham, Josephine II, 366
Gillingham, Keziah VI, 737
Gillingham, Keziah VI, 742
Gillingham, Keziah VI, 789
Gillingham, Lewis V, 882
Gillingham, Lewis V, 885
Gillingham, Lewis VI, 738
Gillingham, Lewis VI, 742
Gillingham, Lewis VI, 776
Gillingham, Lewis VI, 778
Gillingham, Lewis H. II, 867
Gillingham, Lewis Herndon VI, 742
Gillingham, Louisa H. II, 867
Gillingham, Lucas II, 796
Gillingham, Lucas II, 867
Gillingham, Lucas III, 134
Gillingham, Lucas VI, 743
Gillingham, Lydia II, 796
Gillingham, Lydia II, 867
Gillingham, Lydia E. II, 867
Gillingham, Lydia E. VI, 743
Gillingham, Mahlon II, 366
Gillingham, Mahlon II, 532
Gillingham, Mahlon II, 706
Gillingham, Mahlon II, 742

Gillingham, Mahlon Howard II, 366
Gillingham, Mahlon Howard II, 742
Gillingham, Martha II, 366
Gillingham, Martha II, 467
Gillingham, Martha II, 532
Gillingham, Martha II, 796
Gillingham, Martha II, 994
Gillingham, Martha II, 997
Gillingham, Martha R. VI, 742
Gillingham, Martha R. VI, 743
Gillingham, Martha R. VI, 786
Gillingham, Mary II, 366
Gillingham, Mary II, 796
Gillingham, Mary II, 959
Gillingham, Mary II, 998
Gillingham, Mary II, 1017
Gillingham, Mary II, 1051
Gillingham, Mary Ann II, 366
Gillingham, Mary Ann II, 867
Gillingham, Mary Ann II, 896
Gillingham, Mary Ann VI, 741
Gillingham, Mary Ann VI, 742
Gillingham, Mary Ann VI, 743
Gillingham, Mary Ann VI, 762
Gillingham, Mary Ann VI, 773
Gillingham, Mary Ann VI, 774
Gillingham, Mary Anna II, 366
Gillingham, Mary Anne II, 742
Gillingham, Mary E. III, 207
Gillingham, Mary H. II, 867
Gillingham, Mary Harper II, 796
Gillingham, Mary Hudson VI, 743
Gillingham, Mary Hudson VI, 763
Gillingham, Mary McKinstry VI, 741
Gillingham, Mary McKinstry VI, 743
Gillingham, Mary Warrington VI, 737
Gillingham, Mary Wildman II, 791
Gillingham, Mathias II, 867
Gillingham, Matthias II, 867
Gillingham, Matthias II, 998
Gillingham, Moses II, 796
Gillingham, Nathan H. III, 134
Gillingham, Phebe II, 366
Gillingham, Phebe II, 532
Gillingham, Phebe II, 540
Gillingham, Phebe II, 867
Gillingham, Phebe II, 1051
Gillingham, Phebe II, 1062
Gillingham, Phebe II, 1073
Gillingham, Phebe II, 1081
Gillingham, Phebe W. II, 532
Gillingham, Phebe W. II, 742
Gillingham, Phebe W. II, 867
Gillingham, Rachel II, 1049
Gillingham, Rachel II, 1051
Gillingham, Rachel II, 1073
Gillingham, Rachel Harrold II, 366
Gillingham, Rebecca II, 366
Gillingham, Rebecca II, 532
Gillingham, Rebecca II, 742
Gillingham, Rebecca II, 796
Gillingham, Rebecca II, 867
Gillingham, Rebecca VI, 734
Gillingham, Rebecca VI, 742
Gillingham, Reuben H. II, 867
Gillingham, Reuben Roberts VI, 743
Gillingham, Samuel II, 366
Gillingham, Samuel II, 532
Gillingham, Samuel II, 742
Gillingham, Samuel II, 867
Gillingham, Samuel II, 959
Gillingham, Samuel H. II, 532
Gillingham, Samuel H. II, 742
Gillingham, Samuel H. II, 867
Gillingham, Samuel Harrold II, 366
Gillingham, Sarah II, 195
Gillingham, Sarah II, 225
Gillingham, Sarah II, 366
Gillingham, Sarah II, 532
Gillingham, Sarah II, 680
Gillingham, Sarah II, 742
Gillingham, Sarah II, 796
Gillingham, Sarah II, 817
Gillingham, Sarah II, 867
Gillingham, Sarah II, 959
Gillingham, Sarah II, 997
Gillingham, Sarah II, 1031
Gillingham, Sarah II, 1037
Gillingham, Sarah III, 134
Gillingham, Sarah V, 907
Gillingham, Sarah Ann II, 796
Gillingham, Sarah H. II, 867
Gillingham, Sark Kirkner II, 796
Gillingham, Stacy II, 867
Gillingham, Susan II, 366
Gillingham, Susan II, 532
Gillingham, Susan II, 706
Gillingham, Susan II, 742
Gillingham, Susan C. II, 366
Gillingham, Susan E. VI, 743
Gillingham, Susan Elizabeth II, 1071
Gillingham, Susan Elizabeth II, 1073
Gillingham, Susan Esther VI, 743
Gillingham, Susan Esther VI, 778
Gillingham, Susanna II, 366
Gillingham, Tacie E. II, 1065
Gillingham, Tacie E. II, 1073
Gillingham, Tacy II, 867
Gillingham, Theodore III, 148
Gillingham, Theodore J. II, 867
Gillingham, Theodore T. II, 867
Gillingham, Theodore T. III, 134
Gillingham, Theodore T. VI, 743
Gillingham, Thomas II, 959
Gillingham, Thomas II, 998
Gillingham, Thos. II, 796
Gillingham, Walter II, 796
Gillingham, Warrington VI, 741
Gillingham, Warrington VI, 742
Gillingham, Warrington VI, 762
Gillingham, Warrington VI, 773
Gillingham, Warrington VI, 774
Gillingham, Wd. Pheebe II, 532
Gillingham, William II, 366
Gillingham, William II, 959
Gillingham, William II, 998
Gillingham, William VI, 743
Gillingham, William Jenks, Jr. II, 796
Gillingham, William Lawrie II, 366
Gillingham, Wm. II, 867
Gillingham, Wm. II, 998
Gillingham, Wm. II, 1051
Gillingham, Wm. V, 907
Gillingham, Wm. G. II, 924
Gillingham, Wm. Heyward II, 796
Gillingham, Yeamans II, 796
Gillingham, Yedmans II, 997
Gillingham, Yedmans II, 1017
Gillinghamy, Edward C. III, 134
Gillinghamy, Henry W. III, 134
Gillinghamy, Mary Ann III, 134
Gillinghamy, Sarah III, 134
Gillinghamy, Warrington III, 134
Gillinwaters, Elisha VI, 820
Gillinwaters, Eliza VI, 820
Gillinwaters, John VI, 820
Gills, Alexander VI, 921
Gills, Ambrose VI, 820
Gills, Ambrose VI, 921
Gills, Ann E. VI, 921
Gills, Archibald VI, 921
Gills, Asa VI, 921
Gills, Betsey VI, 921
Gills, Caroline E. VI, 921
Gills, Charles H. VI, 820
Gills, Charles W. VI, 921
Gills, Henry S. VI, 921
Gills, John VI, 326
Gills, John VI, 829
Gills, John VI, 888
Gills, John VI, 896
Gills, John VI, 921
Gills, John S. VI, 921
Gills, John W. VI, 921
Gills, Lucinda VI, 820
Gills, Lucy VI, 921
Gills, Mary VI, 921
Gills, Mary Elizabeth VI, 921
Gills, Peggy VI, 921
Gills, Polly VI, 820
Gills, Polly VI, 921
Gills, Richard R. VI, 834
Gills, Sarah VI, 921
Gills, Sarah H. VI, 921
Gills, Sarah W. VI, 921
Gills, Tabitha VI, 921
Gills, Washington VI, 921
Gills, William H. VI, 921
Gillum, Ara Anna I, 446
Gillum, Carmaliza I, 446
Gillum, Elizabeth I, 445
Gillum, Elizabeth I, 449
Gillum, Elizabeth II, 444
Gillum, James I, 445
Gillum, James II, 444
Gillum, John I, 445
Gillum, John I, 446
Gillum, John Westly I, 445
Gillum, Lear I, 446
Gillum, Mahala I, 446
Gillum, Ozburn I, 445
Gillum, Robert II, 444
Gillum, Susannah I, 446
Gillum, William Franklin I, 445
Gilmer, Emma W. VI, 883
Gilmer, George II, 366
Gilmer, Hannah II, 706
Gilmer, William W. VI, 883
Gilmore, ??? III, 71
Gilmore, Benjamin III, 134
Gilmore, Benjamin III, 345
Gilmore, Benjamin III, 346
Gilmore, Clarissa VI, 921
Gilmore, Eli VI, 921
Gilmore, Eli D. VI, 990
Gilmore, Eliza III, 413
Gilmore, George C. II, 848
Gilmore, George C. II, 868
Gilmore, Grace IV, 1317
Gilmore, Grace E. IV, 1317
Gilmore, Hannah II, 532
Gilmore, James III, 134
Gilmore, John III, 134
Gilmore, John III, 413
Gilmore, Lucy III, 134
Gilmore, Lydia III, 134
Gilmore, Malinda III, 71
Gilmore, Malinda III, 134
Gilmore, Maria III, 413
Gilmore, Mary III, 134
Gilmore, Mary III, 345
Gilmore, Mary E. II, 848
Gilmore, Mary E. II, 868
Gilmore, Mary E. C. II, 868
Gilmore, Mary H. III, 346
Gilmore, Sarah III, 413
Gilmore, Thomas III, 413
Gilmore, Thomas H. III, 413
Gilmore, Thomas H. III, 453
Gilmore, Thomas Henry III, 134
Gilmore, Warren V, 998
Gilmore, William W. III, 134
Gilpen, George III, 135
Gilpen, Henry V, 622
Gilpen, Joseph D. III, 135
Gilpen, Levisa V, 622
Gilpen, Lydia V, 519
Gilpen, Maria III, 135
Gilpen, Martha V, 622
Gilpen, Peggy VI, 932
Gilpen, Phebe V, 172
Gilpen, Phebe V, 195
Gilpen, Rachel V, 622
Gilpen, Rebecca Jane V, 622
Gilpen, Sydney Ann II, 805
Gilphin, Burrel G. VI, 889
Gilpin, Abigail II, 524
Gilpin, Alban VI, 243
Gilpin, Alban VI, 493
Gilpin, Albert Gallatin VI, 494
Gilpin, Alfred V, 60
Gilpin, Ann R. II, 877
Gilpin, Anna R. VI, 780
Gilpin, Anna R. VI, 783
Gilpin, Annie VI, 494
Gilpin, Barnard VI, 392
Gilpin, Benjamin III, 134
Gilpin, Bernard VI, 392
Gilpin, Bernard VI, 493
Gilpin, Bernard VI, 495
Gilpin, Bernard VI, 617
Gilpin, Bernard VI, 641
Gilpin, Bernard VI, 726
Gilpin, Betsey VI, 959
Gilpin, Burwell G. VI, 908
Gilpin, Burwell G. VI, 921
Gilpin, Burwell G. VI, 979
Gilpin, Charles II, 868
Gilpin, Charles III, 134
Gilpin, Chas. II, 868
Gilpin, Chas. II, 941
Gilpin, Edward Charles VI, 494
Gilpin, Elizabeth II, 366
Gilpin, Elizabeth II, 533
Gilpin, Elizabeth III, 134
Gilpin, Elizabeth V, 60
Gilpin, Elizabeth V, 332
Gilpin, Elizabeth V, 336
Gilpin, Elizabeth VI, 564
Gilpin, Elizabeth VI, 783
Gilpin, Elizabeth VI, 921
Gilpin, Emily VI, 494
Gilpin, Esther V, 172
Gilpin, Esther V, 492
Gilpin, Esther V, 493
Gilpin, Esther V, 622
Gilpin, Esther V, 637
Gilpin, Fannie E. VI, 494
Gilpin, Frances Ann VI, 494
Gilpin, Francis VI, 921
Gilpin, Francis G. VI, 993
Gilpin, Francis G. VI, 1019
Gilpin, Francis Green VI, 959
Gilpin, George II, 366
Gilpin, George II, 532
Gilpin, George II, 533
Gilpin, George III, 134
Gilpin, George III, 135
Gilpin, George III, 245
Gilpin, George III, 272
Gilpin, Gideon VI, 493
Gilpin, Hannah II, 532
Gilpin, Hannah II, 575
Gilpin, Hannah II, 868
Gilpin, Hannah VI, 617
Gilpin, Hannah VI, 641
Gilpin, Hannah James II, 794
Gilpin, Hannah James II, 803
Gilpin, Henry V, 172
Gilpin, Henry V, 492
Gilpin, Henry V, 493
Gilpin, Henry V, 622
Gilpin, Henry V, 637
Gilpin, Henry Dilworth II, 532
Gilpin, Henry Dilworth II, 533
Gilpin, Isaac II, 366
Gilpin, Isaac VI, 908
Gilpin, Isaac VI, 921
Gilpin, Isaac VI, 955
Gilpin, James II, 803
Gilpin, James V, 172
Gilpin, James VI, 921
Gilpin, Jane II, 532
Gilpin, Jane II, 613
Gilpin, Jane III, 134
Gilpin, Jane Lawson II, 366
Gilpin, John V, 60
Gilpin, John V, 172
Gilpin, John V, 493
Gilpin, John VI, 876
Gilpin, John Ferriss II, 533
Gilpin, John O. VI, 917
Gilpin, John O. VI, 921
Gilpin, John Thomas V, 172
Gilpin, John Thomas V, 493
Gilpin, John Thos. V, 493
Gilpin, Joseph II, 532
Gilpin, Joseph II, 533
Gilpin, Joseph II, 868
Gilpin, Joseph V, 172
Gilpin, Joseph Bernard VI, 494
Gilpin, Joseph D. III, 135
Gilpin, Joshua II, 366
Gilpin, Joshua II, 524
Gilpin, Joshua II, 532
Gilpin, Joshua II, 533
Gilpin, Lena V, 60
Gilpin, Levi V, 493
Gilpin, Levisa V, 622
Gilpin, Lizabeth VI, 980
Gilpin, Louisa V, 622
Gilpin, Louisa G. VI, 921
Gilpin, Lucy III, 134
Gilpin, Lucy III, 245
Gilpin, Lydia II, 523
Gilpin, Lydia II, 532
Gilpin, Lydia V, 172
Gilpin, Lydia V, 493
Gilpin, Lyman V, 240
Gilpin, Maria II, 532
Gilpin, Maria II, 533
Gilpin, Maria III, 135
Gilpin, Martha V, 622
Gilpin, Martha VI, 921
Gilpin, Martha VI, 980
Gilpin, Mary II, 366
Gilpin, Mary II, 367
Gilpin, Mary II, 532
Gilpin, Mary II, 533
Gilpin, Mary V, 172
Gilpin, Mary V, 492
Gilpin, Mary V, 493
Gilpin, Mary V, 500
Gilpin, Mary V, 622
Gilpin, Mary A. VI, 494
Gilpin, Mary Albina VI, 494
Gilpin, Mary C. VI, 913
Gilpin, Mary Jane VI, 921
Gilpin, Mary L. III, 47
Gilpin, Miles V, 240
Gilpin, Minerva VI, 921
Gilpin, Nancy VI, 995
Gilpin, Nancy Jane VI, 921
Gilpin, Phebe V, 172
Gilpin, Phebe V, 622
Gilpin, Polly VI, 984
Gilpin, Rachel II, 367
Gilpin, Rachel II, 533
Gilpin, Rachel III, 135
Gilpin, Rachel III, 272
Gilpin, Rachel V, 622
Gilpin, Rachel V, 650
Gilpin, Rachel VI, 493
Gilpin, Rachel VI, 494
Gilpin, Rachel VI, 495
Gilpin, Rachel VI, 1019
Gilpin, Rebecca III, 134
Gilpin, Rebecca V, 60
Gilpin, Rebecca V, 172
Gilpin, Rebecca V, 190
Gilpin, Rebecca V, 493
Gilpin, Rebecca Jane V, 622
Gilpin, Rebeccah V, 60
Gilpin, Rebeccah V, 135
Gilpin, Rebeckah V, 493
Gilpin, Rebeckah VI, 993
Gilpin, Richard Arthington II, 533
Gilpin, Richard B. II, 877
Gilpin, Ruth V, 493
Gilpin, Ruth VI, 921
Gilpin, Samuel II, 523
Gilpin, Samuel II, 524
Gilpin, Samuel II, 532
Gilpin, Samuel II, 613
Gilpin, Samuel VI, 178
Gilpin, Samuel VI, 493
Gilpin, Samuel VI, 495
Gilpin, Samuel VI, 921
Gilpin, Samuel S. VI, 243
Gilpin, Sarah II, 524
Gilpin, Sarah II, 803
Gilpin, Sarah III, 134
Gilpin, Sarah V, 63
Gilpin, Sarah V, 134
Gilpin, Sarah V, 172
Gilpin, Sarah V, 192
Gilpin, Sarah V, 493
Gilpin, Sarah VI, 493
Gilpin, Sarah VI, 494
Gilpin, Sarah VI, 495
Gilpin, Sarah VI, 617
Gilpin, Sarah VI, 641
Gilpin, Sarah Lydia II, 366
Gilpin, Sarah Lydia II, 533
Gilpin, Sarah P. VI, 474
Gilpin, Susanna VI, 999
Gilpin, Tacy V, 60
Gilpin, Tacy V, 111
Gilpin, Tacy V, 172
Gilpin, Thomas II, 367
Gilpin, Thomas II, 523
Gilpin, Thomas II, 524
Gilpin, Thomas II, 532
Gilpin, Thomas II, 575
Gilpin, Thomas V, 60
Gilpin, Thomas V, 111
Gilpin, Thomas V, 172
Gilpin, Thomas V, 493
Gilpin, Thomas V, 622
Gilpin, Thomas VI, 743
Gilpin, Thomas Harris VI, 494
Gilpin, Thomas Wm. II, 533
Gilpin, Thomas, Jr. V, 172
Gilpin, Tracy V, 172
Gilpin, Virginia Ann VI, 493
Gilpin, Wd. Laura II, 801
Gilpin, William VI, 921
Gilpin, William VI, 995
Gilpin, Wm. II, 524
Gilpin, Wm. II, 533
Gilpin, Wm. Gover VI, 494
Gilso, ??? III, 135
Gilso, Benjamin III, 135
Gilso, William III, 135
Gilson, Grace IV, 818
Gilson, Sarah V, 168
Gilson, Sarah V, 172
Gimberling, Adelaide III, 135
Gimberling, Horace E. III, 135
Gimberling, Juliet III, 135
Gimison, Mary II, 533
Gimnes, Margite II, 17
Ginder, Mary IV, 1252
Gingrich, Russel V, 740
Gingrich, Russell V, 740
Ginn, Anna V, 622
Ginn, Blanche B. V, 622
Ginn, Fannie V, 622
Ginn, John M. V, 622
Ginn, Sally V, 622
Ginn, Sarah V, 622
Ginnett, Abigail I, 300
Ginnett, Abigail I, 309
Ginnett, Ann I, 310
Ginnett, David I, 310
Ginnett, Joseph I, 311

Ginnett, Judith I, 309
Ginnett, Judith I, 313
Ginnett, Maryan I, 311
Ginnings, Alice I, 981
Ginnings, Alice I, 989
Ginter, Nora Stebbins IV, 1252
Ginter, Nora Stebbins IV, 1317
Gintner, Emma VI, 732
Gintner, Emma VI, 751
Giorgeschi, David VI, 743
Giorgeschi, Emilio VI, 733
Giorgeschi, Emilio VI, 743
Giorgeschi, Giuseppina VI, 743
Giorgeschi, Kathleen Maude VI, 733
Giorgeschi, Kathleen Maude VI, 743
Gipson, Ann VI, 596
Gipson, James VI, 921
Gipson, Ruth VI, 921
Girard, Nettie V, 622
Gire, Ida V, 458
Girrard, Doris IV, 1317
Girten, Edith V, 33
Girten, Edith V, 60
Girton, Augusta L. V, 941
Girton, Augusta Will V, 907
Girton, Geo. V, 907
Girton, Howard M. V, 907
Girton, Howard M. V, 941
Girton, Lydia V, 907
Gish, Barbary VI, 921
Gish, Betsy VI, 921
Gish, David VI, 921
Gish, John VI, 921
Gish, Polly VI, 921
Gissop, Enoch I, 54
Gissop, Enoch I, 67
Gissop, Mary I, 54
Gissop, Mary I, 67
Gist, Deborah Jane IV, 1074
Gitchell, Ann IV, 331
Gitchell, Deborah IV, 331
Gitchell, Elizabeth IV, 331
Gitchell, Emly II, 367
Gitchell, Gainer IV, 331
Gitchell, Hannah E. IV, 331
Gitchell, Jeremiah IV, 331
Gitchell, Joseph II, 367
Gitchell, Maria IV, 331
Gitchell, Nathan IV, 331
Gitchell, Robert B. IV, 331
Githens, Ida V, 172
Githens, Mary II, 533
Githens, Thomas II, 533
Gitson, Betsey VI, 907
Gitson, Petor VI, 907
Gitten, Magdalene II, 998
Gitten, Magdalene II, 1011
Gitthart, Charles II, 444
Giund, Delight Jane IV, 982
Given, Amon IV, 147
Given, Amon IV, 206
Given, Ann IV, 145
Given, Ann IV, 147
Given, Ann IV, 206
Given, Ann H. IV, 147
Given, Elizabeth IV, 147
Given, Elizabeth IV, 152
Given, Emma IV, 31
Given, Emma IV, 34
Given, Emma IV, 145
Given, Emma IV, 147
Given, Emma IV, 206
Given, Isaac IV, 147
Given, Isaac IV, 206
Given, Israel IV, 147
Given, Israel IV, 206
Given, James IV, 147
Given, James IV, 206
Given, Jane IV, 147
Given, Joel IV, 147
Given, Margaret A. IV, 206
Given, Moses IV, 145
Given, Moses IV, 147
Given, Rachel IV, 147
Given, Reuben IV, 147
Given, Samuel England IV, 34
Given, Sarah E. Boyle IV, 206
Givens, Mary Ann IV, 331
Giwdre, Maria III, 453
Gladall, Henry V, 457
Gladdell, Sarah V, 332
Gladden, Ann II, 533
Gladden, Mary II, 533
Gladden, Richard II, 533
Gladding, Nance P. VI, 878
Gladen, Mary II, 174
Gladen, Mary II, 533
Gladen, Thomas II, 174
Glading, Hope II, 225
Glading, Hope II, 238
Glading, Mary II, 206
Glading, Mary II, 225
Glading, Mary III, 129
Glading, Mary III, 135
Glading, Mary III, 413
Glading, Mary III, 442
Glading, Thomasin III, 135
Glading, William II, 225
Glading, William II, 238
Glading, William III, 129
Glading, William III, 135
Glading, William III, 413
Glading, William Fry III, 442
Glading, Wm. III, 412
Gladle, Euphemia V, 457
Gladle, Frant T. V, 457
Gladle, Harvey V, 457
Gladle, Henry V, 457
Gladle, Mary V, 457
Gladle, Myrta V, 457
Gladle, Thomas V, 457
Glaentzer, Helen III, 135
Glaentzer, Helen III, 138
Glaister, Joseph I, 99
Glaister, Joseph I, 140
Glaister, Joseph VI, 8
Glaister, Joseph VI, 13
Glaister, Joseph VI, 16
Glaister, Joseph VI, 25
Glaister, Joseph VI, 29
Glaister, Joseph VI, 32
Glaister, Joseph VI, 36
Glaister, Joseph VI, 41
Glaister, Joseph VI, 98
Glaister, Joseph VI, 154
Glaister, Mary I, 99
Glaister, Mary I, 140
Glaister, Ruth I, 140
Glaister, Ruth I, 165
Glaister, Sarah I, 140
Glaistor, Joseph I, 135
Glaistor, Mary I, 92
Glaistor, Mary I, 135
Glaistor, Sarah I, 143
Glaives, Hester II, 72
Glaives, Joseph Ware II, 72
Glancy, Mary V, 998
Glascho, Mary I, 140
Glasco, Mary I, 140
Glasco, Vilater I, 140
Glasco, Violate I, 140
Glascock, Margaret VI, 820
Glascock, Priscilla V, 240
Glascock, Priscilla V, 267
Glascock, William L. VI, 820
Glaser, Caroly C. III, 51
Glaser, Carolyn III, 135
Glaser, Carolyn C. III, 135
Glaser, Henrieta III, 51
Glaser, Henrietta III, 135
Glaser, Myron III, 51
Glaser, Myron III, 135
Glaser, Sam'l Jerome III, 51
Glaser, Sam'l Jerome III, 135
Glasgo, Josephine V, 388
Glasgo, Josephine V, 406
Glasgoe, Mary I, 140
Glasgoe, Solomon I, 140
Glasgoe, Vilateee I, 140
Glasgoe, Vilater I, 140
Glasgoe, Violate I, 140
Glasgow, Louis N. V, 675
Glasgow, Vilateee I, 140
Glass, Ada V, 998
Glass, Alice V, 674
Glass, Alice Emma V, 708
Glass, Alice Emma V, 721
Glass, Alice Nell V, 674
Glass, Ann II, 998
Glass, Anna IV, 1208
Glass, Anna L. IV, 1208
Glass, Anne E. IV, 206
Glass, Benj. H. V, 669
Glass, Benjamin H. V, 721
Glass, Betsy VI, 820
Glass, Brazella V, 674
Glass, Bruzilla V, 674
Glass, Caroline IV, 206
Glass, Caty VI, 866
Glass, Celia VI, 804
Glass, Charles VI, 820
Glass, Charles VI, 866
Glass, Chas. VI, 796
Glass, Chiswell VI, 820
Glass, Dolly VI, 820
Glass, Edith IV, 713
Glass, Edith V, 674
Glass, Edward M. VI, 921
Glass, Eliza VI, 820
Glass, Elizabeth VI, 820
Glass, Ella A. V, 674
Glass, Emma E. V, 674
Glass, Esther VI, 820
Glass, Frances VI, 796
Glass, Frances VI, 993
Glass, Geo. D. H. V, 674
Glass, George II, 998
Glass, George V, 674
Glass, Harry IV, 206
Glass, James VI, 819
Glass, James VI, 820
Glass, James VI, 864
Glass, Jane VI, 821
Glass, Jesse VI, 820
Glass, Jesse VI, 836
Glass, John VI, 820
Glass, Judy VI, 859
Glass, Julia V, 623
Glass, L. L. IV, 1208
Glass, Laban V, 623
Glass, Lavina VI, 820
Glass, Letty VI, 836
Glass, Logan IV, 1208
Glass, Logan L. IV, 1208
Glass, Louise V, 667
Glass, Louise V, 721
Glass, Martha Jane VI, 921
Glass, Mary V, 493
Glass, Mary V, 499
Glass, Mary V, 623
Glass, Mary V, 635
Glass, Mary VI, 824
Glass, Mary A. IV, 206
Glass, Mary B. V, 674
Glass, Mary E. IV, 206
Glass, Mary H. V, 674
Glass, Mary S. IV, 206
Glass, Mary S. IV, 286
Glass, Mattie H. V, 674
Glass, Nancy VI, 805
Glass, Nancy VI, 820
Glass, Nancy VI, 851
Glass, Paschal VI, 807
Glass, Paschal VI, 809
Glass, Paschal VI, 818
Glass, Paschal VI, 820
Glass, Paschal VI, 838
Glass, Paschal VI, 847
Glass, Paschal VI, 858
Glass, Paschal VI, 866
Glass, Pashal VI, 846
Glass, Rachel McDonald V, 669
Glass, Rachel McDonald V, 721
Glass, Robert V, 674
Glass, Robert G. V, 674
Glass, Ruby Irene V, 998
Glass, Ruth Ann IV, 206
Glass, Ruthanna IV, 206
Glass, Sabin V, 623
Glass, Samuel R. V, 674
Glass, Samuel W. V, 674
Glass, Sarah VI, 921
Glass, Sarah Ann VI, 921
Glass, Senator Carter H. VI, 289
Glass, Susan A. VI, 820
Glass, Susanna VI, 820
Glass, Susannah VI, 392
Glass, Thomas VI, 921
Glass, Thomas W. VI, 921
Glass, Vincent VI, 820
Glass, Vincent VI, 824
Glass, Vincent VI, 833
Glass, Vincent VI, 836
Glass, Vincent VI, 859
Glass, Vincent VI, 866
Glass, Vincent VI, 993
Glass, Vincent, Jr. VI, 820
Glass, Vincent, Jr. VI, 824
Glass, Vincent, Sr. VI, 820
Glass, Vinson VI, 804
Glass, Virginia V, 655
Glass, Virginia V, 674
Glass, Wd. Glass VI, 851
Glass, William II, 444
Glass, William IV, 206
Glass, William VI, 820
Glass, William VI, 921
Glass, William M. IV, 206
Glass, Willis VI, 824
Glass, Willis W. VI, 820
Glass, Wm. T. V, 998
Glasscock, Rhoda C. V, 623
Glasscoe, John I, 879
Glassford, ??? III, 175
Glassford, Catharine III, 135
Glassford, Esther K. III, 135
Glassford, Esther K. III, 175
Glassford, James III, 135
Glassford, Martha W. IV, 1279
Glassford, Robert IV, 1279
Glaster, Joseph VI, 29
Glaster, Sarah VI, 29
Glaster, Thomas VI, 29
Glaudis, David F. VI, 806
Glaudis, Elizabeth A. VI, 806
Glavin, J. Benjamin II, 706
Glavin, Michael II, 706
Glavin, Sophis II, 706
Glazebrook, Julius VI, 820
Glazebrook, Mary VI, 820
Glazier, ??? III, 135
Glazier, Adrian III, 135
Glazier, Anna III, 135
Glazier, Edward III, 135
Glazier, Elizabeth C. III, 135
Glazier, Elizabeth C. IV, 1363
Glazier, George III, 135
Glazier, George G. III, 135
Glazier, Goddard III, 135
Glazier, Lydia III, 135
Glazier, Lydia III, 309
Glazier, Lydia B. III, 135
Glazier, Lydia W. III, 135
Glazier, Mary III, 135
Glazier, Mary IV, 1363
Glazier, Nathaniel S. III, 135
Glazier, Richard IV, 1363
Glazier, Richard B. III, 135
Glazier, Richard, Jr. III, 135
Glazier, Robert B. IV, 1363
Glazier, Robert Barclay III, 135
Glazier, Russell W. III, 135
Glazier, Sarah K. III, 135
Gleadall, Ambrose V, 457
Gleadall, Euphemia V, 457
Gleadall, Hannah V, 457
Gleadall, Thomas V, 457
Gleadell, Ambrose V, 457
Gleadell, Elmer V, 457
Gleadell, Euphemia V, 457
Gleadell, Frank V, 457
Gleadell, Frant T. V, 457
Gleadell, Hannah V, 457
Gleadell, Harry V, 457
Gleadell, Harvey V, 457
Gleadell, Henry V, 457
Gleadell, Maggie V, 457
Gleadell, Mary V, 457
Gleadell, Minnie V, 457
Gleadell, Mirtie V, 457
Gleadell, Myrta V, 457
Gleadell, Myrtle V, 457
Gleadell, Pearl Leota V, 457
Gleadell, Thomas V, 457
Gleadell, Wm. V, 457
Gleason, Gad IV, 1236
Gleason, Jane IV, 1236
Gleason, Joseph IV, 1236
Gleave, Elizabeth II, 533
Gleave, Hannah II, 468
Gleave, Hannah II, 533
Gleave, Isaac II, 468
Gleave, Isaac II, 533
Gleave, James II, 533
Gleave, Mary II, 533
Gleave, Mary II, 560
Gleave, Rebecca II, 533
Gleave, Rebekah II, 533
Gleaves, Edith II, 72
Gleaves, Elizabeth II, 533
Gleaves, Hester II, 72
Gleaves, Hester II, 76
Gleaves, Rebecca II, 533
Glecknor, Mary IV, 1317
Gleeson, Alvah B. IV, 1317
Gleeson, Arthur C. IV, 1317
Gleeson, Chas. IV, 1317
Gleeson, Chas. D. IV, 1317
Gleeson, Frances IV, 1317
Gleeson, Franklin G. IV, 1317
Gleeson, Grace IV, 1317
Gleeson, Wm. IV, 1317
Gleeson, Wm. F. IV, 1317
Gleeves, Edith II, 72
Glen, Charles VI, 922
Glen, Jenny VI, 922
Glendenning, Stella IV, 1279
Glenn, Amanda J. V, 674
Glenn, Cora I, 621
Glenn, E. R. I, 625
Glenn, Edith IV, 206
Glenn, Edith IV, 292
Glenn, Effie V, 674
Glenn, Elizabeth V, 332
Glenn, Elizabeth V, 674
Glenn, Ella I, 616
Glenn, Ella B. I, 625
Glenn, Elmore Robert I, 616
Glenn, Emma V, 674
Glenn, Franklin Filmore I, 617
Glenn, Geo. V, 998
Glenn, Hassie I, 625
Glenn, Hassie Marion I, 633
Glenn, Hessie Marion I, 616
Glenn, John I, 616
Glenn, John I, 633
Glenn, John V, 674
Glenn, John A. V, 674
Glenn, John T. VI, 802
Glenn, Lacy Murrow I, 617
Glenn, Lacy Murrow VI, 243
Glenn, Leo S. V, 674
Glenn, Lizzie IV, 1161
Glenn, Mable I, 621
Glenn, Martha I, 617
Glenn, Martha Pearl I, 617
Glenn, Martha Pearl I, 633
Glenn, Martha Pearl VI, 243
Glenn, Mary II, 486
Glenn, Mary II, 533
Glenn, Mary V, 674
Glenn, Mary V, 907
Glenn, Mary Elizabeth V, 668
Glenn, Nancy VI, 820
Glenn, Peyton VI, 820
Glenn, Peyton VI, 867
Glenn, Robert I, 633
Glenn, Robert V, 998
Glenn, Robert G. VI, 820
Glenn, Robert Vernon I, 616
Glenn, Samuel V, 674
Glenn, Samuel E. V, 674
Glenn, Sarah II, 727
Glenn, Sarah II, 742
Glenn, Sarah V, 674
Glenn, Sarah M. VI, 820
Glenn, Susan E. V, 674
Glenn, Susie E. V, 674
Glenna, Sarah V, 674
Glenny, John II, 533
Glick, Bessie IV, 1252
Glick, Mrs. ??? IV, 1252
Glick, Sophia IV, 1252
Gloset, Geo. V, 998
Gloset, George V, 998
Gloset, Lavina V, 998
Glosir, August IV, 957
Glossen, Sarah I, 446
Glosser, August IV, 957
Glosser, H. III, 413
Glosser, Ida III, 413
Glosser, Mary E. III, 413
Glosson, Sarah I, 446
Gloster, Mary I, 140
Glover, Adeline II, 288
Glover, Amy IV, 905
Glover, Amy IV, 909
Glover, Ann IV, 905
Glover, Beatrice L. III, 135
Glover, Benj. C. III, 92
Glover, Benjamin C. III, 135
Glover, Benjamin G. III, 135
Glover, Caroline A. II, 868
Glover, Caroline Amelia II, 796
Glover, Clark V, 60
Glover, Daniel IV, 1317
Glover, Dinah II, 367
Glover, Edmund V, 623
Glover, Elizabeth II, 225
Glover, Elizabeth II, 253
Glover, Elizabeth II, 533
Glover, Elizabeth II, 581
Glover, Elizabeth Ann VI, 743
Glover, Elizabeth Ann VI, 744
Glover, Elizabeth M. II, 288
Glover, Elsie IV, 1317
Glover, Frances VI, 911
Glover, Frances G. VI, 922
Glover, Franky VI, 922
Glover, G. S. I, 617
Glover, George M. II, 288
Glover, Hannah IV, 88
Glover, Hannah E. VI, 743
Glover, Hannah Elizabeth VI, 785
Glover, Henrietta T. VI, 743
Glover, Henrietta T. VI, 744
Glover, Henry H. H. VI, 743
Glover, J. Wheeler III, 393
Glover, J. Wheeler III, 413
Glover, Jacob II, 796
Glover, James II, 533
Glover, James II, 581
Glover, Jemimah IV, 567
Glover, Jemimah IV, 580
Glover, John II, 225
Glover, John V, 623
Glover, John Thomas II, 533
Glover, John Thomas II, 581
Glover, John Thorn II, 225
Glover, Joshua L. VI, 743
Glover, Joshua L. VI, 744
Glover, Josiah V, 60

Glover, Katherine II, 225
Glover, Louisa C. III, 135
Glover, Louise III, 135
Glover, Louise C. III, 92
Glover, Margaret VI, 869
Glover, Martha II, 989
Glover, Martha II, 998
Glover, Martha C. I, 617
Glover, Martha C. I, 633
Glover, Martha Jane VI, 986
Glover, Mary II, 225
Glover, Mary II, 796
Glover, Mary IV, 580
Glover, Mary IV, 598
Glover, Mary IV, 713
Glover, Mary IV, 957
Glover, Milley VI, 922
Glover, Moses B. VI, 922
Glover, Mrs. Elsie IV, 1317
Glover, Nancy VI, 922
Glover, Nancy VI, 947
Glover, Noah G. VI, 743
Glover, Noah G. VI, 744
Glover, Phebe II, 288
Glover, Polly VI, 933
Glover, Rebecca IV, 88
Glover, Richard II, 989
Glover, Richard II, 998
Glover, Ruth Ann VI, 743
Glover, Ruth Ann VI, 744
Glover, Sally VI, 911
Glover, Samuel II, 367
Glover, Sarah III, 71
Glover, Sarah III, 237
Glover, Sarah III, 393
Glover, Sarah III, 413
Glover, Sarah V, 623
Glover, Sarah A. III, 413
Glover, Sarah A. III, 475
Glover, Sarah C. II, 288
Glover, Sophia II, 721
Glover, Sophia Ann VI, 922
Glover, Thomas VI, 922
Glover, Thomas B. VI, 743
Glover, Thomas B. VI, 744
Glover, Thomas B. VI, 785
Glover, William V, 60
Glover, William VI, 911
Glover, William VI, 922
Glover, William VI, 947
Glover, William VI, 986
Glover, William VI, 991
Glover, William S. VI, 743
Glover, Wm. IV, 88
Glun, Frank B. IV, 1363
Glunt, David E. V, 809
Gluyas, James M. I, 811
Gluyas, John I, 781
Gluyas, John B. I, 811
Gluyas, John B. I, 829
Gluyas, John Bennatts I, 781
Gluyas, Mary I, 781
Gluyas, Mildred B. I, 811
Gluyas, Mildred B. I, 829
Goad, Abraham VI, 922
Goad, Agathy VI, 967
Goad, Ann VI, 927
Goad, Cary VI, 820
Goad, Elizabeth VI, 922
Goad, Gincy VI, 874
Goad, James VI, 922
Goad, James M. VI, 901
Goad, James M. VI, 922
Goad, James M. VI, 936
Goad, Jonathan VI, 874
Goad, Joshua VI, 922
Goad, Juley VI, 820
Goad, Julian H. VI, 922
Goad, July VI, 922
Goad, Katey VI, 960
Goad, Lewis A. VI, 922
Goad, Lucinda Jane VI, 922
Goad, Marshall VI, 995
Goad, Martha F. VI, 922
Goad, Mary VI, 922
Goad, Mary F. VI, 922
Goad, Mary M. VI, 901
Goad, Milley VI, 922
Goad, Milly VI, 874
Goad, Milly VI, 922
Goad, Nancy VI, 922
Goad, Nancy VI, 995
Goad, Paulina VI, 874
Goad, Peggy VI, 922
Goad, Priscilla VI, 995
Goad, Richard VI, 874
Goad, Richard VI, 901
Goad, Richard VI, 922
Goad, Robert VI, 922
Goad, Robert VI, 960
Goad, Sally VI, 922
Goad, Tabythy VI, 967
Goad, Thomas VI, 820
Goad, Thomas VI, 922
Goad, Thomas VI, 960
Goad, Uriah VI, 922
Goad, Uriah VI, 1008
Goad, William VI, 820
Goad, William VI, 922
Goad, William VI, 967
Goad, William F. VI, 922
Goard, Mary F. VI, 922
Goard, William F. VI, 922
Gobbs, Ann I, 50
Gobson, Samuel II, 367
Godard, John II, 367
Godard, Joseph V, 907
Godard, Mary H. V, 907
Godard, Wm. Henry V, 907
Godbolt, Mary I, 879
Godbolt, Mary I, 887
Godby, Ann VI, 11
Goddard, Arthur H. III, 135
Goddard, Elizabeth IV, 957
Goddard, Gladys III, 483
Goddard, John A. V, 998
Goddard, Martha Belle V, 998
Goddard, Mary H. V, 907
Goddard, Reuben IV, 957
Goddard, Sarah W. VI, 64
Goddard, Sarah W. VI, 77
Goddard, Treva IV, 957
Godert, Frances IV, 627
Godert, Frances IV, 648
Godet, Margaret II, 868
Godet, Margaret W. III, 135
Godet, Margaret Washington II, 796
Godet, Thos. II, 796
Godet, Thos. Martin Du Brois II, 796
Godett, Thos. II, 796
Godfrey, Andrew II, 533
Godfrey, Deborah II, 533
Godfrey, Deborah II, 661
Godfrey, Eleanor II, 367
Godfrey, Ellener II, 533
Godfrey, Jane II, 533
Godfrey, Jane II, 540
Godfrey, John VI, 843
Godfrey, Lucea II, 533
Godfrey, Lucea II, 642
Godfrey, Lucy II, 533
Godfrey, Mary II, 444
Godfrey, Mary VI, 843
Godfrey, Thomas II, 533
Godfrey, Thomas II, 642
Godfrey, Thos. II, 547
Godfrey, William H. V, 60
Godfrey, Wm. II, 533
Godfrey, Wm. IV, 1279
Godfrey, Wm. H. IV, 1279
Godgin, Mary IV, 456
Godon, Solomon II, 367
Godsee, Henry VI, 820
Godsee, Margaret VI, 820
Godsey, Arianer VI, 820
Godsey, Bridget VI, 860
Godsey, Charles VI, 820
Godsey, Chas. VI, 860
Godsey, Daniel VI, 820
Godsey, Elizabeth J. VI, 839
Godsey, Henry VI, 820
Godsey, Henry VI, 839
Godsey, John VI, 839
Godsey, John H. VI, 832
Godsey, Joseph VI, 820
Godsey, Margaret VI, 820
Godsey, Mary A. E. VI, 820
Godsey, Molley VI, 867
Godsey, Perlina VI, 860
Godward, Martha IV, 1038
Godward, Martha Ann IV, 1038
Godwin, ??? VI, 39
Godwin, Ann I, 306
Godwin, Edward II, 61
Godwin, Frances II, 61
Godwin, Jeremiah VI, 63
Godwin, Jeremiah VI, 64
Godwin, Jeremiah VI, 70
Godwin, Joseph VI, 58
Godwin, Joseph VI, 64
Godwin, Kemuel II, 534
Godwin, Lloyd I, 306
Godwin, Lois I, 336
Godwin, Margaret VI, 64
Godwin, Rachel II, 534
Godwin, Remuel II, 534
Godwin, Tabitha II, 534
Godwin, Tho VI, 29
Godwin, Thomas VI, 25
Godwin, Thomas VI, 29
Godwin, Thomas VI, 32
Godwin, Virginia I, 306
Godwin, Winfred I, 336
Godwinn, Frances II, 485
Goede, Sophie II, 783
Goerke, Ada III, 135
Goerke, Ada III, 311
Goerke, Agnes III, 135
Goerke, Agnes III, 280
Goerke, Benjamin III, 135
Goerke, Benjamin III, 228
Goerke, Caroline III, 135
Goerke, Dr. Francis C. III, 135
Goerke, Edmund III, 135
Goerke, Edmund, Jr. III, 135
Goerke, Evelyn T. III, 135
Goerke, Francis III, 135
Goerke, Francis C. III, 311
Goerke, Francis C., Jr. III, 135
Goerke, Frank III, 136
Goerke, Frank William III, 228
Goerke, Frederick H. III, 135
Goerke, George III, 116
Goerke, George III, 135
Goerke, George III, 136
Goerke, Gerald George III, 135
Goerke, Helen III, 229
Goerke, Isabella III, 136
Goerke, Isabella III, 207
Goerke, Isabella III, 340
Goerke, Marguerite III, 135
Goerke, Marguerite Elizabeth III, 135
Goerke, Martha B. III, 136
Goerke, Martha B. III, 351
Goerke, Mary III, 136
Goerke, Mary III, 228
Goerke, Monica III, 116
Goerke, Monica III, 136
Goerke, Oscar III, 135
Goerke, Oscar III, 136
Goerke, Oscar III, 207
Goerke, Oscar III, 280
Goerke, Oscar III, 304
Goerke, Paulina III, 135
Goerke, Paulina III, 136
Goerke, Paulina III, 205
Goerke, Paulina III, 228
Goerke, Paulina III, 280
Goerke, Paulina III, 351
Goerke, Pauline III, 136
Goerke, Pauline III, 228
Goerke, Pauline L. III, 205
Goerke, Phebe III, 135
Goerke, Phebe III, 228
Goerke, Rudolph III, 135
Goerke, Rudolph III, 136
Goerke, Rudolph III, 205
Goerke, Rudolph III, 228
Goerke, Rudolph III, 280
Goerke, Rudolph III, 351
Goerke, Selma III, 135
Goerke, Selma III, 136
Goerke, Selma III, 280
Goerke, Selma G. III, 133
Goerke, Selma G. III, 136
Goerke, Sophia III, 304
Goerke, Walter III, 229
Goetz, Carl III, 136
Goetz, Frederick Carl III, 136
Goetz, Frederick Carl III, 143
Goetz, Katherine III, 136
Goetz, Ottillie III, 136
Goetz, Ottillie III, 143
Gofer, William II, 174
Goff, Aaron VI, 922
Goff, Abram VI, 922
Goff, Abram. VI, 880
Goff, Achbell VI, 957
Goff, Ambros VI, 976
Goff, Ambros VI, 982
Goff, Ambrose VI, 888
Goff, Ambrose VI, 976
Goff, Ann Eliza VI, 957
Goff, Anne VI, 828
Goff, Archd. VI, 955
Goff, Archd. VI, 974
Goff, Archebell VI, 922
Goff, Archibald VI, 889
Goff, Archibald VI, 922
Goff, Archibald VI, 970
Goff, Archibald VI, 996
Goff, Archibell VI, 922
Goff, Benjamin VI, 922
Goff, Catharine Scarlett II, 796
Goff, Clarey VI, 976
Goff, Clifton D. III, 413
Goff, Duett M. III, 413
Goff, Duett Mortimer III, 413
Goff, Edith IV, 206
Goff, Elcy VI, 990
Goff, Elizabeth VI, 885
Goff, Elizabeth VI, 886
Goff, Elizabeth VI, 982
Goff, Elizabeth VI, 990
Goff, Elizabeth VI, 1005
Goff, Ellen V, 240
Goff, Emily IV, 1279
Goff, Etta IV, 1279
Goff, Eva IV, 1279
Goff, Fannie M. III, 413
Goff, Fanny VI, 922
Goff, Frances VI, 970
Goff, Harriet VI, 922
Goff, Henry VI, 922
Goff, Horatio VI, 836
Goff, Horatio VI, 854
Goff, Horatio VI, 858
Goff, James IV, 1252
Goff, James VI, 922
Goff, James D. VI, 922
Goff, James J. IV, 1252
Goff, Jefferson VI, 943
Goff, Jefferson VI, 996
Goff, Jencey VI, 974
Goff, Jeremiah VI, 922
Goff, Joel VI, 922
Goff, John VI, 854
Goff, John VI, 886
Goff, John VI, 918
Goff, John VI, 922
Goff, John VI, 938
Goff, John VI, 971
Goff, John VI, 974
Goff, John VI, 997
Goff, John VI, 1005
Goff, John H. VI, 922
Goff, John H. VI, 1021
Goff, John, Jr. VI, 922
Goff, John, Jr. VI, 1021
Goff, John, Sr. VI, 955
Goff, Joseph VI, 886
Goff, Joseph VI, 890
Goff, Joseph VI, 918
Goff, Joseph VI, 922
Goff, Joseph VI, 938
Goff, Joseph VI, 975
Goff, Joseph VI, 1005
Goff, Joseph VI, 1021
Goff, Leonard VI, 922
Goff, Leonard VI, 1005
Goff, Lorenzo VI, 889
Goff, Lucey VI, 922
Goff, Lucy VI, 938
Goff, Lucy VI, 996
Goff, Mary VI, 922
Goff, Mary E. VI, 922
Goff, Mary H. VI, 971
Goff, Matilda VI, 880
Goff, McGhee VI, 922
Goff, Mege VI, 922
Goff, Melina VI, 889
Goff, Minerva Lewis VI, 922
Goff, Mortimer L. III, 413
Goff, Nancy VI, 918
Goff, Nancy VI, 922
Goff, Nancy VI, 1009
Goff, Nancy VI, 1021
Goff, Nora IV, 1279
Goff, Patience VI, 922
Goff, Patsy VI, 922
Goff, Pokehunters VI, 922
Goff, Polly VI, 922
Goff, Polly VI, 976
Goff, Priscilla VI, 312
Goff, Priscilla VI, 339
Goff, Priscilla VI, 922
Goff, Priscilla VI, 1005
Goff, Prissilla VI, 1005
Goff, Rhody VI, 922
Goff, Ruth A. VI, 918
Goff, Sally VI, 888
Goff, Sally VI, 922
Goff, Sam VI, 990
Goff, Sarah VI, 955
Goff, Sarah E. VI, 890
Goff, Sebia VI, 922
Goff, Susan S. III, 413
Goff, Vinea VI, 922
Goff, William VI, 880
Goff, William F. VI, 890
Goff, Wm. Dwight IV, 1279
Goff, Zachariah VI, 888
Goffen, Abraham Marks III, 133
Goffen, Abraham Marks III, 136
Goffen, Bernard S. III, 136
Goffen, Daniel III, 136
Goffen, Deborah S. III, 136
Goffen, Ethel III, 133
Goffen, Ethel III, 136
Goffen, Rene III, 136
Goffen, William III, 136
Goffen, Wolf III, 136
Goffney, Bessie V, 332
Gofney, Rachel V, 332
Goforth, Aaron II, 367
Goforth, Aaron II, 504
Goforth, Aaron II, 533
Goforth, Aaron II, 624
Goforth, Aaron II, 959
Goforth, Alice II, 465
Goforth, Alice II, 533
Goforth, Aron II, 367
Goforth, Aron, Jr. II, 367
Goforth, Elizabeth II, 367
Goforth, Elizabeth II, 533
Goforth, Frances II, 444
Goforth, George II, 444
Goforth, Hannah II, 367
Goforth, John II, 367
Goforth, Joseph II, 367
Goforth, Mary II, 367
Goforth, Mary II, 451
Goforth, Mary II, 504
Goforth, Mary II, 533
Goforth, Mary II, 624
Goforth, Mary II, 959
Goforth, Mary Dennis II, 533
Goforth, Miles II, 444
Goforth, Nathaniel II, 367
Goforth, Nathaniel II, 504
Goforth, Nathaniel II, 533
Goforth, Sarah II, 367
Goforth, Sarah II, 533
Goforth, Tabitha II, 367
Goforth, Wd. Mary II, 367
Goforth, Wm. II, 998
Goggens, Robart VI, 922
Goggens, Sally VI, 922
Goggin, Ann VI, 937
Goggin, Ann Elizabeth VI, 955
Goggin, Elizabeth VI, 860
Goggin, Elizabeth VI, 901
Goggin, Elizabeth VI, 914
Goggin, Elizabeth VI, 923
Goggin, Elizabeth Jane VI, 923
Goggin, Emily VI, 958
Goggin, Frances E. VI, 964
Goggin, Frances H. VI, 975
Goggin, James M. VI, 964
Goggin, Jeffrey R. VI, 923
Goggin, Jennett VI, 922
Goggin, Jno. O. L. VI, 923
Goggin, John VI, 922
Goggin, John A. VI, 923
Goggin, John M. VI, 955
Goggin, Letice VI, 812
Goggin, Lucy VI, 922
Goggin, Margaret VI, 923
Goggin, Mary C. VI, 922
Goggin, N. C. VI, 923
Goggin, Nancy VI, 820
Goggin, Nancy VI, 1001
Goggin, P. M. VI, 923
Goggin, Pamelia VI, 894
Goggin, Pamelia VI, 922
Goggin, Pleasant VI, 922
Goggin, Pleasant M. VI, 978
Goggin, Pleasant M. VI, 1022
Goggin, Polly VI, 921
Goggin, Polly VI, 922
Goggin, Rachel VI, 921
Goggin, Rachel VI, 922
Goggin, Rachel VI, 1001
Goggin, Richard VI, 812
Goggin, Richard VI, 820
Goggin, Rick VI, 860
Goggin, Robart VI, 922
Goggin, Robert VI, 820
Goggin, S. VI, 923
Goggin, Sally VI, 820
Goggin, Sally VI, 922
Goggin, Sarah VI, 902
Goggin, Stephen VI, 333
Goggin, Stephen VI, 812
Goggin, Stephen VI, 860
Goggin, Stephen VI, 922
Goggin, Stephen VI, 937
Goggin, Stephen VI, 955
Goggin, Stephen VI, 975
Goggin, Stephen VI, 987
Goggin, Stephen VI, 1001
Goggin, Stephen, Jr. VI, 919
Goggin, Stephen, Senr. VI, 902
Goggin, Stephen, Senr. VI, 922
Goggin, Stephen, Sr. VI, 333
Goggin, Susan S. S. VI, 923
Goggin, Susanna VI, 922
Goggin, T. C. VI, 899
Goggin, T. C. VI, 904
Goggin, T. C. VI, 907
Goggin, T. C. VI, 908
Goggin, T. C. VI, 913

oggin, T. C. VI, 919
oggin, T. C. VI, 921
oggin, T. C. VI, 923
oggin, T. C. VI, 940
oggin, T. C. VI, 951
oggin, T. C. VI, 1006
oggin, T. C. VI, 1022
oggin, T. M. VI, 958
oggin, Thomas VI, 914
oggin, Thomas VI, 922
oggin, Thomas VI, 926
oggin, Thomas VI, 976
oggin, Thomas VI, 993
oggin, Thomas VI, 1018
oggin, Thomas C. VI, 871
oggin, Thomas C. VI, 874
oggin, Thomas C. VI, 878
oggin, Thomas C. VI, 879
oggin, Thomas C. VI, 883
oggin, Thomas C. VI, 884
oggin, Thomas C. VI, 886
oggin, Thomas C. VI, 887
oggin, Thomas C. VI, 891
oggin, Thomas C. VI, 892
oggin, Thomas C. VI, 896
oggin, Thomas C. VI, 897
oggin, Thomas C. VI, 899
oggin, Thomas C. VI, 900
oggin, Thomas C. VI, 901
oggin, Thomas C. VI, 902
oggin, Thomas C. VI, 904
oggin, Thomas C. VI, 905
oggin, Thomas C. VI, 906
oggin, Thomas C. VI, 908
oggin, Thomas C. VI, 909
oggin, Thomas C. VI, 912
oggin, Thomas C. VI, 915
oggin, Thomas C. VI, 916
oggin, Thomas C. VI, 917
oggin, Thomas C. VI, 922
oggin, Thomas C. VI, 923
oggin, Thomas C. VI, 924
oggin, Thomas C. VI, 925
oggin, Thomas C. VI, 927
oggin, Thomas C. VI, 933
oggin, Thomas C. VI, 936
oggin, Thomas C. VI, 939
oggin, Thomas C. VI, 940
oggin, Thomas C. VI, 942
oggin, Thomas C. VI, 944
oggin, Thomas C. VI, 947
oggin, Thomas C. VI, 948
oggin, Thomas C. VI, 950
oggin, Thomas C. VI, 951
oggin, Thomas C. VI, 953
oggin, Thomas C. VI, 955
oggin, Thomas C. VI, 957
oggin, Thomas C. VI, 958
oggin, Thomas C. VI, 959
oggin, Thomas C. VI, 960
oggin, Thomas C. VI, 962
oggin, Thomas C. VI, 964
oggin, Thomas C. VI, 965
oggin, Thomas C. VI, 967
oggin, Thomas C. VI, 969
oggin, Thomas C. VI, 972
oggin, Thomas C. VI, 973
oggin, Thomas C. VI, 975
oggin, Thomas C. VI, 979
oggin, Thomas C. VI, 980
oggin, Thomas C. VI, 981
oggin, Thomas C. VI, 983
oggin, Thomas C. VI, 986
oggin, Thomas C. VI, 987
oggin, Thomas C. VI, 989
oggin, Thomas C. VI, 990
oggin, Thomas C. VI, 992
oggin, Thomas C. VI, 996
oggin, Thomas C. VI, 998
oggin, Thomas C. VI, 999
oggin, Thomas C. VI, 1002
oggin, Thomas C. VI, 1004
oggin, Thomas C. VI, 1010
oggin, Thomas C. VI, 1013
oggin, Thomas C. VI, 1014
oggin, Thomas C. VI, 1015
oggin, Thomas C. VI, 1017
oggin, Thomas C. VI, 1022
Goggin, Thomas G. VI, 923
Goggin, Thos. C. VI, 975
Goggin, Tomas C. VI, 881
Goggin, W. L. VI, 929
Goggin, W. L. VI, 949
Goggin, W. L. VI, 964
Goggin, William VI, 922
Goggin, William L. VI, 922
Goggin, William L. VI, 923
Goin, Isham VI, 923
Goin, Isham VI, 1008
Goin, Jeremiah VI, 1008
Goin, Ketura VI, 923
Goin, Manoah VI, 923
Goin, Nancy VI, 1008
Goin, Susanna VI, 923
Goin, William VI, 1008
Going, Anne VI, 923
Going, Emma II, 796
Going, Emma Ridgway II, 796
Going, Isham VI, 820
Going, Isham VI, 923
Going, James I, 962
Going, James II, 796
Going, John VI, 820
Going, John VI, 842
Going, Joseph VI, 923
Going, Judah VI, 811
Going, Judith VI, 923
Going, Ketura VI, 923
Going, Manerva VI, 820
Going, Manoah VI, 923
Going, Micajah VI, 923
Going, Noah VI, 897
Going, Polly VI, 923
Going, Sally VI, 820
Going, Samuel II, 796
Going, Susanna VI, 923
Goings, Berdyrine VI, 844
Goings, Elizabeth VI, 844
Goings, Samuel VI, 844
Goins, Chester V, 623
Goins, Inez V, 623
Golburt, Daniel II, 823
Golburt, Wd. Catharine II, 823
Gold, John C. IV, 713
Gold, Rosamond II, 1069
Gold, Rosamond II, 1073
Golden, Cornelia A. III, 413
Golden, Cornelia A. III, 420
Golden, Esther IV, 80
Golden, Esther IV, 89
Golden, Jane III, 136
Golden, Jane M. III, 136
Golden, Margaret V, 815
Golden, Mary IV, 1236
Golden, Mary IV, 1240
Golden, Mary A. III, 129
Golden, Nancy VI, 937
Golden, Sarah I, 1119
Golden, Sarah I, 1120
Golden, Sarah IV, 80
Golden, Sarah IV, 89
Golding, Abigail II, 533
Golding, Abigail II, 633
Goldry, Margaret II, 225
Goldsberry, Janette V, 388
Goldsberry, Jennie V, 388
Goldsberry, Leander V, 388
Goldsberry, Lula V, 388
Goldsberry, Robert V, 388
Goldsberry, William V, 388
Goldsborough, Catharine II, 533
Goldsborough, Catharine II, 637
Goldsmith, Eleanor II, 543
Goldsmith, Elijah II, 288
Goldsmith, Elijah III, 136
Goldsmith, Elizabeth II, 288
Goldsmith, Elizabeth II, 289
Goldsmith, Ellen II, 543
Goldsmith, George II, 367
Goldsmith, George II, 533
Goldsmith, George II, 543
Goldsmith, Isaac P. II, 289
Goldsmith, Isaac Procher II, 288
Goldsmith, Isaac Proctor II, 288
Goldsmith, Mary II, 288
Goldsmith, Mary VI, 11
Goldsmith, Mary VI, 12
Goldsmith, Mrs. ??? VI, 11
Goldsmith, William VI, 11
Goldsmith, William VI, 12
Goldsmith, William Henry II, 288
Goldsmith, William Henry II, 289
Goldy, D. C. IV, 713
Goldy, Edward S. IV, 713
Goldy, J. S. IV, 713
Goldy, Jennie B. IV, 713
Goll, Anna I, 1075
Goll, Christian I, 1075
Goll, Isabell I, 1076
Goll, Isabella I, 1075
Gollaher, Mary V, 562
Golliver, Martin V, 998
Golloway, John VI, 992
Gomere, Harland IV, 207
Gomere, William IV, 206
Gomery, Ann IV, 206
Gomery, Benjamin IV, 206
Gomery, Benjamin IV, 207
Gomery, Benjamin IV, 395
Gomery, Eli IV, 206
Gomery, Enoch IV, 206
Gomery, Enoch IV, 395
Gomery, Hannah IV, 206
Gomery, Hannah IV, 395
Gomery, Harlan IV, 206
Gomery, Harland IV, 207
Gomery, Harlem IV, 206
Gomery, Harlen IV, 206
Gomery, Isaac IV, 206
Gomery, John IV, 206
Gomery, John IV, 334
Gomery, John, Jr. IV, 206
Gomery, Joshua IV, 206
Gomery, Joshua IV, 395
Gomery, Lavina IV, 206
Gomery, Levina IV, 206
Gomery, Levina IV, 207
Gomery, Lewis IV, 206
Gomery, Lovina IV, 206
Gomery, Lovina IV, 395
Gomery, Lydia IV, 206
Gomery, Phebe IV, 89
Gomery, Phebe IV, 206
Gomery, Phebe IV, 207
Gomery, Phebe IV, 395
Gomery, Sarah IV, 334
Gomery, Swithen IV, 206
Gomery, Swithin IV, 206
Gomery, Thomas IV, 206
Gomery, Thomas Lewis IV, 206
Gomery, William IV, 206
Gomery, William IV, 395
Gomery, Wm. IV, 206
Gomery, Wm. IV, 207
Gomery, Wm. IV, 395
Gommere, John II, 227
Gongwer, Alice IV, 1038
Gongwer, Catharine IV, 713
Gongwer, Rosa IV, 713
Gooch, Louisa C. VI, 886
Gooch, Louisa C. VI, 923
Gooch, Tabbitha VI, 820
Gooch, Thomas VI, 820
Gooch, Thomas, Jr. VI, 820
Gooch, William B. VI, 923
Good, Albert V, 998
Good, Alzira V, 998
Good, Andrew Jackson V, 998
Good, Ann II, 533
Good, Ann II, 975
Good, Ann II, 998
Good, Anna II, 998
Good, Anna K. V, 61
Good, Annie V, 61
Good, Annie V, 76
Good, Betsy V, 60
Good, Betsy V, 61
Good, Betsy V, 493
Good, Caroline VI, 64
Good, Chalkly VI, 64
Good, Charles V, 60
Good, Charles V, 61
Good, Charles V, 493
Good, David IV, 957
Good, Eleanor II, 174
Good, Eleanor II, 289
Good, Eleanor II, 998
Good, Eleanor II, 1051
Good, Elenor II, 1051
Good, Elenor II, 1073
Good, Elizabeth F. V, 493
Good, Elizabeth T. V, 60
Good, Ellen V, 61
Good, Ellis V, 60
Good, Ellis V, 61
Good, Ellis V, 76
Good, Ellis V, 493
Good, Emma V, 998
Good, Evan V, 60
Good, Evan V, 61
Good, Evan V, 493
Good, Hannah IV, 957
Good, Jonathan II, 998
Good, Katie V, 998
Good, Latetia II, 959
Good, Latitia II, 1051
Good, Letitia II, 998
Good, Letitia II, 1073
Good, Lizzie V, 61
Good, Lydia V, 61
Good, Lydia C. V, 60
Good, Lydia C. V, 61
Good, Lydia C. V, 493
Good, Margaretta II, 868
Good, Margaretta II, 899
Good, Margaretta W. II, 868
Good, Martha V, 41
Good, Martha V, 61
Good, Martha E. V, 60
Good, Martha E. V, 493
Good, Mary II, 367
Good, Mary II, 533
Good, Mary II, 868
Good, Mary II, 899
Good, Mary V, 840
Good, Mary V, 998
Good, Mary A. VI, 64
Good, Mary Ann V, 25
Good, Mary Ann V, 60
Good, Mary Ann V, 61
Good, Mary Ann V, 493
Good, Nathan II, 868
Good, Nathan II, 899
Good, Pearson II, 868
Good, Pearson II, 899
Good, Peter II, 998
Good, Rachel V, 61
Good, Rachel L. V, 493
Good, Rachel M. V, 61
Good, Rachel M. V, 144
Good, Rebecca IV, 957
Good, Rebecca V, 41
Good, Susan V, 998
Good, Willie V, 998
Goodall, Charles P. VI, 243
Goodall, Charles P. VI, 256
Goodall, Elizabeth II, 868
Goodbar, Harvey V, 172
Goodbody, Agnes Eliz. III, 136
Goodbody, Agnes Elizabeth III, 136
Goodbody, Ann II, 533
Goodbody, Dora III, 136
Goodbody, Hannah Frances III, 136
Goodbody, Isabella Sophia III, 136
Goodbody, John Lister III, 136
Goodbody, Lydia III, 136
Goodbody, Lydia M. III, 65
Goodbody, Marcia B. III, 65
Goodbody, Marcia B. III, 136
Goodbody, Marcus III, 65
Goodbody, Marcus III, 136
Goodbody, Margaret Jane III, 136
Goodbody, Maurice F. III, 136
Goodbody, Maurice F. F. III, 136
Goodbody, Robert III, 136
Goodbody, Robt. III, 136
Goodbody, Susan III, 136
Goodbody, Thomas III, 136
Goodbody, Thomas Pim III, 136
Goodbody, Thos. Pim III, 136
Goode, Agnes VI, 178
Goode, Ann II, 477
Goode, Ann II, 533
Goode, Ann M. VI, 923
Goode, Ann Mary VI, 923
Goode, David VI, 923
Goode, Edmond VI, 932
Goode, Edmund VI, 883
Goode, Edmund VI, 923
Goode, Edwd, Jr. VI, 178
Goode, Francis II, 477
Goode, Francis II, 533
Goode, Jane VI, 923
Goode, Jno. VI, 1009
Goode, John III, 136
Goode, John VI, 923
Goode, John, Jr. VI, 934
Goode, Judith VI, 310
Goode, Judith VI, 312
Goode, Margaret V, 172
Goode, Margaret V, 187
Goode, Margaret VI, 178
Goode, Margaret VI, 826
Goode, Martha W. VI, 820
Goode, Mary II, 533
Goode, Mat VI, 803
Goode, Nancy VI, 803
Goode, Patty VI, 974
Goode, Phebe E. P. VI, 820
Goode, Robert VI, 820
Goode, Salley VI, 923
Goode, Sally VI, 932
Goode, Sarah II, 477
Goode, Sarah II, 533
Goode, Sarah VI, 312
Goode, Sarah VI, 322
Goode, Sarah VI, 342
Goode, Sarah B. VI, 796
Goode, Susan VI, 932
Goode, William A. VI, 820
Gooden, Mary II, 72
Gooden, Sarah II, 72
Gooden, Sarah II, 534
Gooden, Sarah II, 653
Gooden, Thomas II, 72
Gooden, Willem II, 72
Goodenough, Alice III, 136
Goodenough, Alice III, 137
Goodenough, Alice III, 349
Goodenough, Nancy A. III, 136
Goodenough, Nancy S. III, 349
Goodenough, Thos. III, 136
Goodenough, Thos. III, 349
Goodin, Lucy V, 907
Goodin, Nathan V, 882
Gooding, Anna IV, 1059
Gooding, Anna E. IV, 207
Gooding, Anna S. IV, 207
Gooding, Annie E. IV, 207
Gooding, Bertha IV, 1252
Gooding, Calvert IV, 207
Gooding, Danford Leigh IV, 207
Gooding, Danford S. IV, 207
Gooding, Deborah II, 534
Gooding, Edith IV, 1252
Gooding, Emma IV, 207
Gooding, Esther IV, 1252
Gooding, Eva Leona IV, 207
Gooding, G. A. IV, 207
Gooding, George II, 444
Gooding, George IV, 1059
Gooding, George A. IV, 207
Gooding, Harriet E. IV, 207
Gooding, Isaac IV, 1059
Gooding, Jacob I, 50
Gooding, James IV, 1058
Gooding, James IV, 1059
Gooding, James Calvert IV, 207
Gooding, John II, 534
Gooding, Joseph IV, 1059
Gooding, Lemuel IV, 207
Gooding, Lillie IV, 207
Gooding, Mahlon IV, 1059
Gooding, Margaret IV, 1058
Gooding, Martha P. IV, 207
Gooding, Mary IV, 207
Gooding, Mary L. IV, 207
Gooding, Monna IV, 207
Gooding, Neda IV, 1252
Gooding, Richard IV, 1059
Gooding, Richard IV, 1132
Gooding, Ruth IV, 1059
Gooding, Samuel IV, 207
Gooding, Sarah IV, 1059
Gooding, Stanley IV, 1252
Gooding, Susanna IV, 1059
Gooding, Susannah IV, 1058
Gooding, Susannah IV, 1070
Gooding, William IV, 207
Gooding, William IV, 1058
Gooding, William IV, 1059
Gooding, Wm. IV, 1059
Gooding, Wm. IV, 1070
Goodman, A. M. VI, 801
Goodman, A. M. VI, 834
Goodman, A. M. VI, 860
Goodman, A. M. VI, 1010
Goodman, Achilles VI, 805
Goodman, Achilles VI, 820
Goodman, Amanda VI, 866
Goodman, Ann VI, 923
Goodman, Anna Smith III, 137
Goodman, Anna Smith III, 371
Goodman, Bartlett) VI, 888
Goodman, Callum VI, 243
Goodman, Calum B. VI, 243
Goodman, Calvin VI, 243
Goodman, Carl M. IV, 1208
Goodman, Clifton IV, 1208
Goodman, Clifton D. IV, 1208
Goodman, Daniel III, 137
Goodman, Daniel III, 371
Goodman, David VI, 923
Goodman, Delia VI, 831
Goodman, Elizabeth III, 137
Goodman, Elizabeth VI, 820
Goodman, Elizabeth VI, 860
Goodman, Elizabeth VI, 890
Goodman, Ella IV, 713
Goodman, Ella IV, 1208
Goodman, Esther II, 868
Goodman, Esther II, 944
Goodman, Fanny VI, 923
Goodman, Frances VI, 974
Goodman, Gibson VI, 820
Goodman, Henrico VI, 243
Goodman, Henrietta VI, 860
Goodman, Henry S. VI, 1010
Goodman, James VI, 923
Goodman, James VI, 974
Goodman, James B. VI, 923
Goodman, James B. VI, 974
Goodman, James B. VI, 1018
Goodman, Jane III, 137
Goodman, Jane E. VI, 923
Goodman, Janet M. VI, 834
Goodman, Jesse VI, 820
Goodman, Jesse VI, 866
Goodman, Jesse B. VI, 923
Goodman, Jesse M. VI, 816
Goodman, Jesse M. VI, 831
Goodman, John III, 137

Goodman, John VI, 795
Goodman, John VI, 804
Goodman, John VI, 820
Goodman, John VI, 836
Goodman, John VI, 842
Goodman, John VI, 888
Goodman, John VI, 923
Goodman, Laura VI, 243
Goodman, Lucinda VI, 820
Goodman, Lucy VI, 923
Goodman, Lucy VI, 974
Goodman, Martha VI, 820
Goodman, Martha VI, 983
Goodman, Martha A. VI, 816
Goodman, Martha Susan VI, 923
Goodman, Mary Ann VI, 974
Goodman, Mary J. VI, 820
Goodman, Milly VI, 836
Goodman, Nancy VI, 923
Goodman, Nancy VI, 974
Goodman, Nancy VI, 1010
Goodman, Nicholas H. VI, 923
Goodman, Paulina VI, 1018
Goodman, Permelia VI, 860
Goodman, Rebecca F. VI, 820
Goodman, Reece IV, 1208
Goodman, Rhody VI, 888
Goodman, Robert VI, 923
Goodman, Robert VI, 967
Goodman, Sallie VI, 804
Goodman, Samuel III, 137
Goodman, Susan M. III, 97
Goodman, Thomas IV, 1208
Goodman, Viola IV, 1208
Goodman, William H. VI, 820
Goodman, William H. VI, 860
Goodrich, ??? III, 25
Goodrich, Alley VI, 983
Goodrich, Anna VI, 64
Goodrich, Anna G. VI, 64
Goodrich, Anna J. VI, 91
Goodrich, Daniel VI, 923
Goodrich, Elizabeth III, 25
Goodrich, Elizabeth III, 137
Goodrich, James VI, 983
Goodrich, Jane VI, 923
Goodrich, Stanley W. III, 137
Goodrich, Thomas VI, 983
Goodrich, William VI, 64
Goodrich, Wm. VI, 64
Goodring, Edith IV, 1252
Goodson, Alexander I, 879
Goodson, Alexander V, 240
Goodson, Bennet I, 811
Goodson, Bennet I, 879
Goodson, Bennett I, 536
Goodson, Bennett I, 542
Goodson, Bennett I, 811
Goodson, Bennett I, 879
Goodson, Harriet V, 240
Goodson, Harriett I, 879
Goodson, Hornett I, 879
Goodson, Jane II, 534
Goodson, Jane II, 590
Goodson, Jessie D. IV, 1317
Goodson, Job II, 367
Goodson, Job II, 534
Goodson, Job II, 590
Goodson, John II, 367
Goodson, John II, 534
Goodson, John II, 590
Goodson, Lydia I, 986
Goodson, Lydia II, 534
Goodson, Lydia II, 677
Goodson, Polly I, 879
Goodson, Polly V, 240
Goodson, Priscilla I, 536
Goodson, Priscilla I, 542
Goodson, Priscilla I, 879
Goodson, Priscilla V, 240
Goodson, Rhoda I, 879
Goodson, Rhoda V, 240
Goodson, Rhoda V, 291
Goodson, Rodah V, 240
Goodson, Sarah II, 367
Goodson, Sarah II, 534
Goodson, Solomon I, 879
Goodson, Solomon V, 240
Goodson, Uriah I, 879
Goodson, Uriah V, 240
Goodson, Wd. Cicely II, 534
Goodson, Wd. Jane II, 534
Goodson, Wd. Jane II, 673
Goodsonn, Cicely II, 668
Goodsonn, John II, 482
Goodsonn, John II, 534
Goodsonn, John II, 668
Goodsonn, Sarah II, 482
Goodsonn, Sarah II, 534
Goodsonn, Wd. Cicely II, 534
Goodwin, A. Helena II, 743
Goodwin, Abigail II, 29
Goodwin, Abigail II, 118
Goodwin, Abigail II, 132
Goodwin, Abigail IV, 207
Goodwin, Alice A. IV, 473
Goodwin, Alice Ann IV, 473
Goodwin, Ann I, 306
Goodwin, Ann I, 315
Goodwin, Ann IV, 207
Goodwin, Ann Lillie IV, 473
Goodwin, Anna VI, 616
Goodwin, Anna VI, 641
Goodwin, Anna T. II, 706
Goodwin, Anna T. II, 743
Goodwin, C. L. V, 840
Goodwin, C. L. V. V, 840
Goodwin, Caleb I, 50
Goodwin, Clement V, 840
Goodwin, Daniel II, 131
Goodwin, Deborah II, 367
Goodwin, Deborah II, 534
Goodwin, Deborah II, 682
Goodwin, Ebenezer V, 998
Goodwin, Edward II, 72
Goodwin, Eliza A. V, 562
Goodwin, Eliza A. V, 582
Goodwin, Elizabeth II, 28
Goodwin, Elizabeth II, 29
Goodwin, Elizabeth II, 47
Goodwin, Elizabeth II, 61
Goodwin, Elizabeth II, 72
Goodwin, Elizabeth II, 112
Goodwin, Elizabeth II, 118
Goodwin, Elizabeth II, 130
Goodwin, Elizabeth II, 132
Goodwin, Elizabeth II, 140
Goodwin, Elizabeth II, 682
Goodwin, Elizabeth VI, 494
Goodwin, Elizabeth Clement II, 72
Goodwin, Ella IV, 473
Goodwin, Ellen IV, 473
Goodwin, Ernest L. VI, 744
Goodwin, Ethel M. IV, 1317
Goodwin, Ethel M. IV, 1336
Goodwin, Ethel Russell IV, 1317
Goodwin, Ezra IV, 207
Goodwin, Ezra Israel VI, 494
Goodwin, Frances II, 72
Goodwin, George VI, 494
Goodwin, Gideon VI, 392
Goodwin, Gideon VI, 494
Goodwin, Hannah I, 46
Goodwin, Hannah I, 50
Goodwin, Hannah II, 72
Goodwin, Hannah T. G. II, 133
Goodwin, Helena A. II, 706
Goodwin, Henry V, 840
Goodwin, Hester II, 72
Goodwin, Howard S. IV, 1317
Goodwin, Howard S. IV, 1336
Goodwin, Huldah II, 131
Goodwin, Huldah II, 133
Goodwin, Huldah II, 148
Goodwin, Isaac I, 50
Goodwin, Isaac I, 193
Goodwin, James I, 39
Goodwin, James I, 50
Goodwin, James I, 193
Goodwin, Jane VI, 494
Goodwin, Jane H. V, 998
Goodwin, Jesse IV, 473
Goodwin, Jesse B. VI, 923
Goodwin, John I, 336
Goodwin, John II, 28
Goodwin, John II, 72
Goodwin, John II, 75
Goodwin, John II, 99
Goodwin, John II, 367
Goodwin, John II, 534
Goodwin, John V, 840
Goodwin, John VI, 494
Goodwin, John, Jr. II, 534
Goodwin, Joseph II, 28
Goodwin, Joseph II, 57
Goodwin, Joseph II, 72
Goodwin, Joseph II, 174
Goodwin, Joseph V, 840
Goodwin, Joseph V, 843
Goodwin, Joseph Brown II, 72
Goodwin, Julia I, 41
Goodwin, Julia I, 50
Goodwin, Katharine II, 28
Goodwin, Kemuel II, 534
Goodwin, Lena IV, 1252
Goodwin, Lewis I, 336
Goodwin, Lewis II, 28
Goodwin, Lewis II, 72
Goodwin, Lewis II, 113
Goodwin, Lois I, 336
Goodwin, Louis I, 336
Goodwin, Lucian VI, 923
Goodwin, Luciand VI, 919
Goodwin, Lydia I, 39
Goodwin, Lydia I, 50
Goodwin, Lydia I, 193
Goodwin, M. VI, 840
Goodwin, Margaret VI, 64
Goodwin, Martha II, 534
Goodwin, Martha IV, 207
Goodwin, Martha M. II, 534
Goodwin, Mary I, 50
Goodwin, Mary II, 28
Goodwin, Mary II, 47
Goodwin, Mary II, 72
Goodwin, Mary II, 76
Goodwin, Mary II, 82
Goodwin, Mary II, 112
Goodwin, Mary II, 131
Goodwin, Mary II, 174
Goodwin, Mary II, 828
Goodwin, Mary IV, 580
Goodwin, Mary IV, 587
Goodwin, Mary V, 840
Goodwin, Mary V, 843
Goodwin, Mary VI, 494
Goodwin, Mary VI, 501
Goodwin, Mary H. II, 534
Goodwin, Mary Hancock II, 72
Goodwin, Mary Ida IV, 473
Goodwin, Mary M. II, 140
Goodwin, Mary Morris II, 28
Goodwin, Mary S. V, 61
Goodwin, Micajah VI, 831
Goodwin, Micajah VI, 850
Goodwin, Miles V, 840
Goodwin, Morris II, 131
Goodwin, Morris, Jr. II, 706
Goodwin, Nathan I, 50
Goodwin, Nathan V, 61
Goodwin, Nathan V, 840
Goodwin, Nathan V, 882
Goodwin, Olive V, 840
Goodwin, Park V, 998
Goodwin, Penninah I, 48
Goodwin, Penninah I, 50
Goodwin, Pheby II, 28
Goodwin, Prudence II, 62
Goodwin, Prudence II, 72
Goodwin, Prudence II, 75
Goodwin, Prudence II, 130
Goodwin, Rachel I, 50
Goodwin, Rachel II, 29
Goodwin, Rachel II, 47
Goodwin, Rachel II, 72
Goodwin, Rachel II, 89
Goodwin, Rachel II, 112
Goodwin, Rachel II, 534
Goodwin, Rachel V, 840
Goodwin, Rachel N. II, 131
Goodwin, Rachel N. II, 148
Goodwin, Rebecca V, 840
Goodwin, Rebecca Ann II, 131
Goodwin, Rebecca Ann II, 148
Goodwin, Rebeckah II, 57
Goodwin, Rebeckah II, 72
Goodwin, Rebeckah, Jr. II, 72
Goodwin, Rebeckah, Jr. II, 113
Goodwin, Remuel II, 534
Goodwin, Richard I, 50
Goodwin, Richard II, 28
Goodwin, Richard V, 61
Goodwin, Richard V, 840
Goodwin, Russel V, 998
Goodwin, Ruth IV, 312
Goodwin, Ruthann IV, 1099
Goodwin, Ruthann IV, 1107
Goodwin, Sally VI, 923
Goodwin, Samuel V, 840
Goodwin, Sarah I, 50
Goodwin, Sarah II, 28
Goodwin, Sarah II, 29
Goodwin, Sarah II, 72
Goodwin, Sarah II, 81
Goodwin, Sarah II, 118
Goodwin, Sarah II, 132
Goodwin, Sarah II, 367
Goodwin, Sarah VI, 494
Goodwin, Sarah C. II, 140
Goodwin, Sarah L. II, 131
Goodwin, Sarah, Jr. II, 367
Goodwin, Sibba I, 50
Goodwin, Spicey VI, 840
Goodwin, Stephen V, 840
Goodwin, Susan II, 810
Goodwin, Susanna VI, 494
Goodwin, Susannah II, 28
Goodwin, Susannah II, 72
Goodwin, Susannah II, 86
Goodwin, Susannah II, 87
Goodwin, Susannah II, 99
Goodwin, Susannah Mason II, 72
Goodwin, Tabitha II, 534
Goodwin, Thomas II, 28
Goodwin, Thomas II, 72
Goodwin, Thomas II, 174
Goodwin, Thomas VI, 494
Goodwin, Thomas VI, 501
Goodwin, Thomas, Jr. VI, 494
Goodwin, Thomas, Jr. VI, 501
Goodwin, Thos. II, 28
Goodwin, Vannie Jonnie I, 336
Goodwin, Vannie L. I, 336
Goodwin, Wd. Elizabeth, Sr. II, 28
Goodwin, William I, 50
Goodwin, William II, 28
Goodwin, William II, 47
Goodwin, William II, 132
Goodwin, William II, 367
Goodwin, William IV, 207
Goodwin, William V, 840
Goodwin, Winfred I, 336
Goodwin, Wm. II, 28
Goodwin, Wm. II, 29
Goodwin, Wm. II, 72
Goodwin, Wm. II, 112
Goodwin, Wm. II, 130
Goodwin, Wm. II, 133
Goodwin, Wm. II, 140
Goodwin, Wm., Jr. II, 72
Goodwin, Wm., Jr. II, 112
Gookin, May III, 137
Gookin, May III, 313
Gooldey, Frederick VI, 982
Gooldy, Alfred VI, 923
Gooldy, Elizabeth VI, 883
Gooldy, Frederick VI, 883
Gooldy, Frederick VI, 959
Gooldy, Frederick VI, 997
Gooldy, Mary VI, 959
Gooldy, Mary T. VI, 923
Gooldy, Sophia VI, 923
Goolery, Frederick VI, 927
Goolman, Alcinda F. V, 562
Goolman, Eunice V, 61
Goolman, Eunice V, 68
Goolman, Eunice W. V, 562
Goolsberry, Janette V, 388
Goolsberry, Jennie V, 388
Goolsberry, Leander V, 388
Goolsberry, Lula V, 388
Goolsberry, Robert V, 388
Goolsberry, William V, 388
Goolsby, Arthur VI, 820
Goolsby, Polly C. VI, 820
Goose, Susanna I, 982
Goose, Susanna I, 986
Goosling, Letitia VI, 688
Goowin, Park V, 998
Goram, Daniel II, 367
Gord, July VI, 922
Gord, Mary VI, 922
Gord, Thomas VI, 922
Gord, William VI, 922
Gordan, Ann VI, 596
Gordan, Irene I, 811
Gordan, John I, 811
Gordan, Jonathan I, 811
Gordan, Laura I, 930
Gordan, Mary II, 462
Gordan, Mary II, 534
Gordan, Rachel VI, 385
Gorden, Alfred I, 498
Gorden, Ann VI, 596
Gorden, Ann C. VI, 107
Gorden, Anna I, 781
Gorden, Bertha V, 998
Gorden, Charity I, 811
Gorden, Charity I, 843
Gorden, Charles I, 541
Gorden, Charles I, 781
Gorden, Charles I, 811
Gorden, Deborah I, 811
Gorden, Deborah I, 823
Gorden, Eli I, 781
Gorden, Elizabeth I, 781
Gorden, Esther I, 781
Gorden, James I, 541
Gorden, James I, 781
Gorden, Jesse I, 781
Gorden, John I, 781
Gorden, John I, 811
Gorden, Jonathan I, 781
Gorden, Jonathan I, 811
Gorden, Lester V, 61
Gorden, Lydia I, 781
Gorden, Lydiann V, 31
Gorden, Lydiann V, 61
Gorden, Mary I, 541
Gorden, Mary I, 781
Gorden, Mary VI, 596
Gorden, Molley I, 781
Gorden, Mordecai Lewis II, 367
Gorden, Rachel I, 781
Gorden, Rachel VI, 392
Gorden, Rebecah I, 498
Gorden, Richard I, 498
Gorden, Richard I, 542
Gorden, Richard I, 781
Gorden, Ruth I, 541
Gorden, Ruth I, 781
Gorden, Ruth I, 811
Gorden, Sarah I, 781
Gorden, Sarah I, 811
Gorden, Sarah I, 822
Gorden, Seth I, 542
Gorden, Seth I, 781
Gorden, Sousanna I, 542
Gorden, Susanna I, 498
Gorden, Susanna I, 542
Gorden, W. P. V, 998
Gorden, William I, 781
Gorden, William M. V, 172
Gording, Samuel IV, 207
Gordon, ??? III, 137
Gordon, Abigail II, 367
Gordon, Abigail II, 534
Gordon, Abigail II, 580
Gordon, Abner I, 811
Gordon, Abraham II, 367
Gordon, Agnes W. VI, 820
Gordon, Alexandria VI, 178
Gordon, Alexandria VI, 198
Gordon, Ann II, 367
Gordon, Ann Eliza II, 796
Gordon, Ann Eliza II, 868
Gordon, Ann Eliza II, 923
Gordon, Anna V, 998
Gordon, Asa E. I, 811
Gordon, Bertha V, 998
Gordon, Bradford II, 868
Gordon, Carrie IV, 713
Gordon, Charity I, 811
Gordon, Charles I, 582
Gordon, Charles I, 811
Gordon, Charles IV, 1208
Gordon, Clementina III, 137
Gordon, Cynthia II, 706
Gordon, Cynthia II, 743
Gordon, Cyrus I, 811
Gordon, Deborah I, 811
Gordon, Deborah H. II, 868
Gordon, Druzilla IV, 754
Gordon, Edward VI, 817
Gordon, Edward VI, 821
Gordon, Edwin I, 811
Gordon, Eli I, 811
Gordon, Eliza VI, 178
Gordon, Eliza M. VI, 178
Gordon, Eliza M. VI, 198
Gordon, Elizabeth I, 811
Gordon, Elizabeth II, 367
Gordon, Elizabeth III, 166
Gordon, Elizabeth III, 322
Gordon, Elizabeth V, 840
Gordon, Elizabeth V, 841
Gordon, Ella II, 796
Gordon, Emily V, 493
Gordon, Emily V, 534
Gordon, Emily VI, 820
Gordon, Ferdinand II, 367
Gordon, George Washington IV, 1208
Gordon, Giles VI, 821
Gordon, Gove, Patience II, 534
Gordon, Hannah I, 811
Gordon, Harriet VI, 821
Gordon, Hartwell VI, 820
Gordon, Helen May III, 384
Gordon, Howard Baker II, 796
Gordon, Irena I, 811
Gordon, Irene I, 811
Gordon, J. W. I, 941
Gordon, James I, 811
Gordon, James N. VI, 834
Gordon, Jasper I, 811
Gordon, Jasper M. I, 811
Gordon, Jesse I, 811
Gordon, Jesse M. I, 811
Gordon, Joathar I, 811
Gordon, John I, 811
Gordon, John I, 843
Gordon, John V, 240
Gordon, John VI, 820
Gordon, John VI, 874
Gordon, John VI, 928
Gordon, John VI, 959
Gordon, John M. VI, 820
Gordon, John W. V, 240
Gordon, Jonathan I, 811
Gordon, Jonathan W. I, 811
Gordon, Joseph B. III, 137
Gordon, Judith A. VI, 821

ordon, Keziah I, 811
ordon, Keziah I, 842
ordon, Leroy V, 998
ordon, Lester V, 61
ordon, Lillie IV, 1208
ordon, Lolly IV, 1208
ordon, Louisa V, 998
ordon, Lydia I, 811
ordon, Lydia P. I, 328
ordon, Lydia P. I, 329
ordon, Marindy VI, 837
ordon, Mary I, 811
ordon, Mary I, 843
ordon, Mary II, 534
ordon, Mary V, 240
ordon, Mary VI, 198
ordon, Minerva IV, 1208
ordon, Molley I, 811
ordon, Mordecai II, 534
ordon, Mordecai L. II, 534
ordon, Mordecai Lewis II, 367
ordon, Myra V, 740
ordon, Nancy VI, 874
ordon, Oliver I, 811
ordon, Oliver C. I, 811
ordon, Otis D. IV, 1279
ordon, Polly VI, 928
ordon, Rachel I, 811
ordon, Richard I, 328
ordon, Richard I, 329
ordon, Richard I, 390
ordon, Richard I, 542
ordon, Richard I, 546
ordon, Richard II, 534
ordon, Ruth I, 582
ordon, Ruth I, 811
ordon, Samira I, 811
ordon, Samirah I, 811
ordon, Sarah I, 811
ordon, Sarah J. V, 240
ordon, Seth I, 811
ordon, Susanna I, 546
ordon, U. P. V, 998
ordon, Uwchlan II, 868
ordon, Virlinchege VI, 820
ordon, W. P. V, 998
ordon, Warner I, 811
ordon, William I, 811
ordon, William II, 706
ordon, Wm. II, 796
ore, Abbina IV, 356
ore, Abigail III, 49
ore, Albina IV, 356
ore, Amos VI, 856
ore, Amos. VI, 847
ore, Ann IV, 331
ore, Ann IV, 356
ore, Ann VI, 641
ore, Ann VI, 672
ore, Ann VI, 673
ore, Anna IV, 395
ore, Anna IV, 452
ore, Anna IV, 453
ore, Anne IV, 331
ore, Anne IV, 356
ore, Elizabeth VI, 482
ore, Elizabeth VI, 494
ore, Euphemia VI, 847
ore, Harriett VI, 744
ore, Henrietta VI, 641
ore, Henrietta VI, 711
ore, Herbert Charles VI, 744
ore, Jane VI, 392
ore, Jane VI, 487
ore, Jane VI, 494
ore, Jean VI, 494
ore, Jonathan VI, 641
ore, Jonathan VI, 673
ore, Jonathan VI, 711
ore, Jonathan VI, 713
ore, Joseph, Jr. VI, 641
ore, Joseph, Sr. VI, 641
ore, Joshua VI, 641
ore, Joshua VI, 672
ore, Joshua VI, 673
ore, Mahlon Smith VI, 673
ore, Margaret VI, 494
ore, Mary Ann VI, 673
ore, Mary S. VI, 668
ore, Mercy IV, 350
ore, Mercy IV, 356
ore, Mercy VI, 641
ore, Mercy VI, 704
ore, Pamela VI, 744
ore, Phebe VI, 494
ore, Phebe VI, 578
ore, Phebe VI, 641
ore, Phebe VI, 719
ore, Sarah IV, 331
ore, Sarah IV, 350
ore, Sarah VI, 482
Gore, Sarah VI, 494
Gore, Sarah VI, 500
Gore, Sarah VI, 506
Gore, Sarah VI, 578
Gore, Sarah VI, 641
Gore, Sarah VI, 644
Gore, Sarah VI, 673
Gore, Sarah VI, 719
Gore, Solomon VI, 641
Gore, Susan Carr VI, 641
Gore, Susan Carr VI, 711
Gore, Susan Carr VI, 713
Gore, Thomas IV, 350
Gore, Thomas IV, 356
Gore, Thomas VI, 494
Gore, Thomas VI, 641
Gore, Thomas VI, 668
Gore, William VI, 494
Gore, William VI, 641
Gore, William VI, 744
Gorforth, Mary II, 533
Gorham, ??? III, 137
Gorham, George III, 137
Gorham, Jennie IV, 1236
Gorham, Pamela III, 265
Gorham, Pamelia III, 137
Gorham, Susan C. II, 948
Gorham, Susan C. II, 949
Gorley, Mary V, 303
Gorm, Elizabeth III, 137
Gormack, Edward Mayo I, 140
Gorman, Anna V, 240
Gorman, Anna V, 332
Gorman, Annie V, 240
Gorman, Harriet F. IV, 1363
Gorman, Harry V, 240
Gorman, Harry V, 332
Gorman, Ida V, 623
Gorman, Jacob V, 623
Gorman, Jennie A. IV, 1317
Gorman, Joseph V, 240
Gorman, Maggie V, 240
Gorman, Mary V, 240
Gorman, Maude V, 623
Gorman, Mildred V, 240
Gorman, Mildred V, 332
Gorman, Modie V, 623
Gorman, Orville V, 240
Gorman, Orville V, 332
Gorman, Orville V, 623
Gorman, Thomas B. IV, 1317
Gorman, Violet Belle V, 623
Gorman, Willie V, 623
Gormin, Maggie V, 240
Gorral, Emma V, 998
Gorrel, Alta V, 998
Gorrel, Emma V, 998
Gorrel, Walter V, 998
Gorshate, Catherine II, 367
Gorsuch, Ann IV, 1279
Gortner, Dionetia VI, 923
Gortner, Jacob VI, 923
Gorton, Abigail IV, 1363
Gorton, Alice May III, 137
Gorton, Alice May III, 337
Gorton, Ann Eliza IV, 1363
Gorton, Charles III, 137
Gorton, Charles IV, 1363
Gorton, David IV, 1359
Gorton, David IV, 1363
Gorton, David IV, 1385
Gorton, Edward IV, 1363
Gorton, Eliza IV, 1363
Gorton, Eliza Ann IV, 1363
Gorton, Esther IV, 1363
Gorton, Esther M. IV, 1359
Gorton, Esther M. IV, 1363
Gorton, Hannah IV, 1359
Gorton, Hannah IV, 1363
Gorton, Hannah IV, 1385
Gorton, Hannah E. IV, 1363
Gorton, Hannah E. IV, 1385
Gorton, Horace Simmons III, 137
Gorton, Horace Simmons III, 337
Gorton, Job IV, 1363
Gorton, Job, Jr. IV, 1363
Gorton, Martha IV, 1363
Gorton, Martha IV, 1366
Gorton, Olive IV, 1363
Gorton, Polly IV, 1363
Gorton, Richard IV, 1363
Gorton, Richard IV, 1366
Gorton, Sarah IV, 1363
Gorton, Zilpha IV, 1363
Gosbey, Sarah I, 50
Gosbey, Sarah I, 76
Gosby, Hannah I Sup 1, 4
Gosby, Hannah I Sup 1, 5
Gosby, John I Sup 1, 4
Gosby, John I Sup 1, 5
Gosden, Gove, Patience II, 534
Gosden, Martha II, 534
Gosden, Patience II, 534
Goshart, Mary II, 534
Goshart, Mary II, 562
Goshen, Sarah III, 19
Goshen, Susan C. II, 948
Goslin, Ann II, 534
Goslin, Ann II, 686
Goslin, Elizabeth II, 72
Goslin, Hannah II, 998
Goslin, Hannah II, 1016
Goslin, Isabel II, 72
Goslin, Isabel II, 82
Goslin, John II, 72
Goslin, Mary Bell II, 72
Goslin, Priscilla IV, 713
Goslin, Priscilla C. IV, 694
Goslin, Priscilla C. IV, 713
Goslin, Rebecca II, 92
Goslin, Rebecca Pew II, 72
Goslin, Samuel II, 72
Goslin, Sarah Peterson II, 72
Goslin, Savery II, 72
Goslin, Savery II, 82
Goslin, Savety II, 72
Goslin, Wd. Eleanor III, 137
Goslin, Wm. IV, 713
Gosling, Anne II, 367
Gosling, Elizabeth II, 72
Gosling, Isabel II, 72
Gosling, John II, 72
Gosling, Mary II, 225
Gosling, Mary Bell II, 72
Gosling, Rebecca Pew II, 72
Gosling, Samuel II, 72
Gosling, Sarah II, 92
Gosling, Sarah Peterson II, 72
Gosling, Savery II, 72
Gosling, Savety II, 72
Gosnel, Dawson VI, 832
Gosnell, Benjamin VI, 821
Gosnell, Elizabeth VI, 821
Gosnell, Jane VI, 821
Gosnell, William VI, 821
Gosney, Benjamin VI, 821
Gosney, Elizabeth VI, 821
Gosney, Lotty VI, 855
Gosnold, Mary II, 367
Goss, Abigail I, 713
Goss, Abigail I, 716
Goss, Charles VI, 392
Goss, Clifford V, 998
Goss, Mary Ann IV, 1153
Goss, Mary Ann IV, 1161
Gosset, Charity I, 880
Gosset, Charity I, 893
Gosset, Cyrus Elwood I, 781
Gosset, Emely Permelia I, 781
Gosset, George Thomas I, 781
Gosset, James M. I, 811
Gosset, James Marshal I, 781
Gosset, Jonathan Wesley I, 781
Gosset, Judith I, 524
Gosset, Judith I, 542
Gosset, Nathan I, 781
Gosset, Nathan L. I, 781
Gosset, Nathan L. I, 811
Gosset, Phebe I, 811
Gosset, Phebe Roseline I, 781
Gosset, Prudence I, 542
Gosset, Prudence I, 569
Gosset, Rebecca I, 837
Gosset, Rebeccah Emily I, 781
Gosset, William Walter I, 781
Gossett, Amariah V, 240
Gossett, Anna E. I, 747
Gossett, Charety I, 747
Gossett, Charity I, 880
Gossett, George I, 761
Gossett, George I, 811
Gossett, George I, 826
Gossett, George Elwood I, 747
Gossett, George S. I, 747
Gossett, Hannah I, 811
Gossett, Hannah C. I, 747
Gossett, James M. I, 811
Gossett, John V, 240
Gossett, Keziah C. I, 747
Gossett, Lydia V, 237
Gossett, Lydia V, 240
Gossett, Martha I, 926
Gossett, Martha S. I, 747
Gossett, Nathan I, 747
Gossett, Nathan I, 761
Gossett, Nathan I, 811
Gossett, Nathan I, 812
Gossett, Nathan L. I, 811
Gossett, Phebe I, 761
Gossett, Phebe I, 811
Gossett, Phebe I, 826
Gossett, Rachel Z. I, 747
Gossett, Rebecca I, 811
Gossett, Rebecca E. I, 811
Gossett, Rebecca E. I, 812
Gossett, Williamson I, 811
Gossin, Emma V, 675
Gossitt, Hannah I, 811
Gossitt, Hannah I, 838
Gossling, John VI, 494
Gossling, John VI, 543
Gossling, John VI, 641
Gossling, John VI, 687
Gossling, Letitia VI, 494
Gossling, Letitia VI, 543
Gossling, Letitia VI, 544
Gossling, Letitia VI, 564
Gossling, Letitia VI, 641
Gossling, Letitia VI, 687
Gossling, Letitia VI, 708
Gossling, Letitia A. VI, 544
Gossling, Matilda VI, 494
Gossling, Matilda VI, 543
Gossling, Matilda VI, 641
Gossling, Matilda VI, 687
Gothard, Cordelia Belle I, 1152
Gothard, Cordelia Belle I, 1157
Gothard, Cordie L. I, 1152
Gothard, Joseph William I, 1152
Gothard, Joseph Wm. I, 1157
Gothard, Louis I, 1152
Gothard, Mattie I, 1152
Gothard, William I, 1152
Gotherman, James V, 623
Gottschick, Elizabeth II, 610
Gottschick, George II, 610
Gottshick, George II, 534
Goudy, Bernice A. III, 137
Gouge, Thomas VI, 878
Gough, Adna H. III, 137
Gough, Ann Eliza III, 137
Gough, Ann M. E. VI, 821
Gough, Horatio VI, 856
Gough, James J. IV, 1252
Gough, John III, 137
Gough, John M. III, 137
Gough, John M. III, 304
Gough, Mary V, 907
Gough, Mary A. VI, 821
Gough, Mary H. III, 137
Gough, Mary H. III, 304
Gough, Mary L. VI, 856
Gough, Mima VI, 890
Gough, Richard III, 137
Gough, Sarah III, 137
Gough, Sarah III, 304
Gough, Sarah VI, 821
Gough, William VI, 821
Gough, William VI, 859
Gould, ??? III, 369
Gould, Daniel III, 137
Gould, Dorothy III, 137
Gould, Florence III, 137
Gould, Gladys Kinghorn III, 137
Gould, Gladys Kinghorn III, 214
Gould, Hannah III, 369
Gould, James Ecroyd II, 1085
Gould, James Ecroyd II, 1087
Gould, John III, 137
Gould, John III, 260
Gould, Margaret II, 225
Gould, Margaret II, 273
Gould, Martha II, 1085
Gould, Martha S. II, 1087
Gould, Sarah II, 1087
Gould, Sarah III, 137
Gould, Sarah III, 260
Gould, Sarah M. II, 1085
Gould, Thomas B. II, 1085
Gould, Thomas B. II, 1087
Gould, Thos. III, 137
Gould, Wait III, 137
Gouldman, James E. VI, 1004
Goulman, Alcinda F. V, 562
Goulman, Eunice W. V, 562
Gourd, Jonathan VI, 923
Gourd, Mary VI, 923
Gourdon, Elizabeth II, 367
Gourley, Atkinson Hughs II, 868
Gourley, Atkinson Hughs II, 928
Gourley, Caroline I, 1152
Gourley, Emmer K. II, 928
Gourley, Emmor Kimber II, 796
Gourley, Grace II, 796
Gourley, Grace II, 928
Gourley, Howard II, 796
Gourley, Jessee M. K. II, 868
Gourley, Jessie M. II, 796
Gourley, John I, 586
Gourley, Robert I, 1152
Gourley, Ruth Anna II, 928
Gourly, Atkinson Hughs II, 868
Gourly, Emmer K. II, 868
Gourly, Grace II, 868
Gourly, Howard II, 868
Gourly, Jessee M. K. II, 868
Gourly, Joseph II, 998
Gourly, Ruth Anna II, 868
Gove, Anna Ellen IV, 207
Gove, Anna Ellen IV, 713
Gove, Bridget II, 485
Gove, Bridget II, 534
Gove, Bridgett II, 367
Gove, Elizabeth II, 367
Gove, Frederic Dennis IV, 713
Gove, Frederick D. IV, 207
Gove, Frederick D. IV, 713
Gove, Hannah IV, 207
Gove, Hannah V, 952
Gove, John Howard IV, 207
Gove, John Howard IV, 713
Gove, Jonathan V, 952
Gove, Lydia D. V, 952
Gove, Martha II, 367
Gove, Martha II, 635
Gove, Mary II, 367
Gove, Moses IV, 207
Gove, Moses B. IV, 285
Gove, Moses D. IV, 207
Gove, Moses D. IV, 713
Gove, Patience II, 367
Gove, Patience II, 534
Gove, Plymouth II, 534
Gove, Richard II, 367
Gove, Richard II, 485
Gove, Richard II, 534
Gove, Richard II, 635
Gove, Sallie B. IV, 713
Gove, Sally IV, 207
Gove, Sally B. IV, 207
Gove, Sally B. IV, 285
Gove, Sally B. IV, 713
Gove, Sarah II, 367
Gover, Albina Gregg VI, 664
Gover, Albinah VI, 495
Gover, Amos M. VI, 495
Gover, Ann VI, 494
Gover, Ann Eliza VI, 492
Gover, Ann Eliza VI, 493
Gover, Ann Eliza VI, 494
Gover, Ann Eliza VI, 495
Gover, Ann T. VI, 495
Gover, Anthony VI, 641
Gover, Anthony P. VI, 494
Gover, Anthony P. VI, 495
Gover, Anthony P. VI, 518
Gover, Anthony P. VI, 664
Gover, Anthony P. VI, 744
Gover, Anthony P. VI, 754
Gover, Anthony P. VI, 758
Gover, Anthony Poultney VI, 494
Gover, Anthony Poultney VI, 495
Gover, Anthony Poultney VI, 661
Gover, Anthony Poultney VI, 744
Gover, Caroline VI, 744
Gover, Cornelia VI, 744
Gover, Elizabeth VI, 494
Gover, Elizabeth VI, 495
Gover, Elizabeth VI, 641
Gover, Ellen M. VI, 495
Gover, Ephriam G. VI, 494
Gover, Hannah VI, 495
Gover, Hannah VI, 504
Gover, Henry T. VI, 493
Gover, Henry T. VI, 494
Gover, Henry T. VI, 495
Gover, Isaac VI, 494
Gover, Jacob Janney VI, 641
Gover, Jane VI, 744
Gover, Jesse VI, 392
Gover, Jesse VI, 494
Gover, Jesse VI, 495
Gover, Jesse VI, 531
Gover, Jesse VI, 532
Gover, Jesse VI, 542
Gover, Jesse VI, 572
Gover, Jonathan VI, 495
Gover, Margaret A. VI, 428
Gover, Margaret A. VI, 495
Gover, Margaret A. VI, 542
Gover, Margaret C. VI, 542
Gover, Martha G. VI, 494
Gover, Mary VI, 494
Gover, Mary VI, 495
Gover, Mary VI, 504
Gover, Mary VI, 641
Gover, Mary Albinah VI, 744
Gover, Mary Elizabeth VI, 641
Gover, Mary G. VI, 494
Gover, Miriam VI, 494
Gover, Miriam VI, 495
Gover, Miriam VI, 531
Gover, Miriam G. VI, 392
Gover, Miriam G. VI, 494

Gover, Miriam G. VI, 495
Gover, Miriam G. VI, 532
Gover, Miriam G. VI, 542
Gover, Miriam G. VI, 572
Gover, Moses VI, 641
Gover, Moses Janney VI, 641
Gover, Nathan Parkins VI, 392
Gover, Rachel VI, 493
Gover, Rachel VI, 495
Gover, Robert VI, 495
Gover, Robert VI, 502
Gover, Robert VI, 641
Gover, Robert H. VI, 495
Gover, Robert H. VI, 744
Gover, Samuel VI, 493
Gover, Samuel VI, 494
Gover, Samuel VI, 495
Gover, Samuel VI, 502
Gover, Samuel VI, 519
Gover, Samuel VI, 520
Gover, Samuel VI, 522
Gover, Samuel VI, 533
Gover, Samuel VI, 572
Gover, Samuel VI, 641
Gover, Samuel VI, 661
Gover, Samuel VI, 744
Gover, Samuel A. VI, 392
Gover, Samuel A. VI, 428
Gover, Samuel A. VI, 495
Gover, Samuel A. VI, 532
Gover, Samuel A. VI, 542
Gover, Samuel A. VI, 744
Gover, Samuel A., Sr. VI, 495
Gover, Samuel Arthur VI, 495
Gover, Samuel, Jr. VI, 495
Gover, Sarah VI, 493
Gover, Sarah VI, 494
Gover, Sarah VI, 495
Gover, Sarah VI, 518
Gover, Sarah VI, 572
Gover, Sarah VI, 641
Gover, Sarah VI, 661
Gover, Sarah VI, 744
Gover, Sarah VI, 754
Gover, Sarah VI, 758
Gover, Sarah A. VI, 541
Gover, Sarah A., Jr. VI, 495
Gover, Sarah A., Jr. VI, 541
Gover, Sarah G. VI, 495
Gover, Sarah H. VI, 495
Gover, Sarah H. VI, 531
Gover, Sarah H. VI, 532
Gover, Temperance VI, 495
Gover, Temperance VI, 532
Gover, Thamasin VI, 495
Gover, Wd. Sarah VI, 744
Gover, Widow Sarah VI, 495
Gover, Widow Sarah VI, 522
Gover, William VI, 495
Govet, Esther II, 225
Govet, Joseph II, 225
Govet, Lydia II, 534
Govet, Lydia II, 589
Govett, Annesley II, 796
Govett, Annesley II, 868
Govett, Eleanor II, 453
Govett, Eleanor II, 534
Govett, Eleanor II, 562
Govett, Eliza II, 796
Govett, Eliza II, 868
Govett, Elizabeth II, 367
Govett, Elizabeth II, 453
Govett, Elizabeth II, 534
Govett, Elizabeth II, 547
Govett, Elizabeth II, 861
Govett, Elizabeth II, 868
Govett, Ellen II, 793
Govett, Ellen II, 861
Govett, Ellen II, 868
Govett, Esther II, 225
Govett, Esther II, 270
Govett, Esther II, 367
Govett, Esther II, 534
Govett, Esther II, 796
Govett, Esther II, 868
Govett, George II, 861
Govett, James II, 534
Govett, Joseph II, 225
Govett, Joseph II, 270
Govett, Joseph II, 367
Govett, Joseph II, 453
Govett, Joseph II, 534
Govett, Joseph II, 562
Govett, Lydia II, 367
Govett, Lydia II, 534
Govett, Robert II, 534
Govett, Robert A. II, 868
Govett, Robert Annesley II, 796
Govett, Robert Annesley II, 868
Govett, Sarah II, 534
Govett, Sarah II, 706
Govett, William II, 225
Govett, William II, 270
Govett, William II, 367
Govett, Wm. II, 453
Govett, Wm. II, 861
Govett, Wm. II, 868
Govett, Wm., Jr. II, 534
Govette, Elizabeth II, 868
Govette, Ellen II, 868
Govette, Esther II, 868
Govot, Esther II, 225
Gow, John III, 137
Gowdy, Maud M. II, 777
Gower, Elizabeth VI, 923
Gower, John VI, 923
Gower, Polly VI, 935
Gowing, Aveline VI, 808
Gowing, Elizabeth VI, 923
Gowing, Isham VI, 923
Gowing, Micajah VI, 923
Gowing, Polly VI, 923
Gowing, Samuel VI, 808
Gowing, William VI, 923
Gowker, Esther II, 720
Grabel, Rachel IV, 85
Grabel, Rachel IV, 89
Grabel, Rachel IV, 126
Grabill, Anna S. J. IV, 1238
Grabill, Annie S. J. IV, 1236
Grace, Benajah IV, 207
Grace, Grace IV, 207
Grace, Isaac IV, 207
Grace, Rachel IV, 207
Gracery, Ella III, 137
Gracery, Jas. Travilla III, 137
Gracery, Raymond Rossiter III, 137
Gracery, Sarah F. III, 137
Gracery, Winola III, 137
Gracery, Winola D. III, 137
Gracery, Wm. N. III, 137
Gracey, Jane II, 817
Gracey, Raymond Rossiter III, 65
Gracey, Winola Dorothy III, 65
Gracy, George II, 367
Gracy, Mary II, 367
Graddy, ??? I, 336
Graddy, Luke I, 336
Graebe, Rosa L. IV, 186
Graebe, Rosa L. IV, 207
Graeff, Susan R. II, 826
Grafeustine, M. H. IV, 1252
Grafeustine, Mabel IV, 1252
Graff, Rebecca II, 534
Graff, Rebecca II, 657
Grafton, Emerson F. IV, 473
Grafton, Florence IV, 473
Grafton, Florence Carey IV, 1279
Grafton, G. W. IV, 473
Grafton, George W. IV, 473
Grafton, Hettie IV, 473
Grafton, Israel IV, 473
Grafton, James IV, 207
Grafton, James W. IV, 473
Grafton, Jane IV, 473
Grafton, Lucinda IV, 473
Grafton, Mary II, 534
Grafton, Mary IV, 207
Grafton, Mary IV, 473
Grafton, Sadie IV, 473
Grafton, Sarah IV, 473
Grafton, Victor IV, 473
Grag, Rebeckah II, 536
Gragg, Amy IV, 71
Graham, Addie VI, 770
Graham, Andrew J. III, 137
Graham, Andrew J. III, 274
Graham, Ann V, 341
Graham, Ann M. VI, 821
Graham, Anna M. II, 868
Graham, Betsey VI, 923
Graham, Carlis V, 998
Graham, Caroline III, 137
Graham, Caroline III, 274
Graham, Caroline Bell II, 868
Graham, Caroline T. II, 868
Graham, Carrie Bell II, 868
Graham, Charles VI, 923
Graham, Charles H. V, 61
Graham, Chas. V, 998
Graham, Clara J. II, 868
Graham, Clyde IV, 207
Graham, Davis V, 593
Graham, Deborah IV, 147
Graham, Deborah IV, 160
Graham, Edward VI, 892
Graham, Edward VI, 923
Graham, Effie M. V, 61
Graham, Eliza VI, 803
Graham, Eliza VI, 846
Graham, Elizabeth IV, 147
Graham, Elizabeth VI, 812
Graham, Elizabeth VI, 923
Graham, Elizabeth VI, 1010
Graham, Elizabeth VI, 1013
Graham, Elizabeth V. II, 743
Graham, Elizabeth V. II, 772
Graham, Ellen V, 998
Graham, Elma J. II, 868
Graham, Elma Jenkins II, 868
Graham, Enoch V, 388
Graham, Francis VI, 846
Graham, George II, 534
Graham, George V, 998
Graham, George H. II, 868
Graham, Hannah III, 137
Graham, Hannah IV, 581
Graham, Hannah I. V, 388
Graham, Hannah Isabel V, 388
Graham, Harry IV, 207
Graham, Harvey IV, 207
Graham, I. P. V, 998
Graham, Irene IV, 1333
Graham, Israel J. II, 868
Graham, Jacob V, 61
Graham, Jacob V, 341
Graham, Jacob R. V, 61
Graham, James IV, 147
Graham, James L. II, 868
Graham, Jane P. II, 868
Graham, Jennie II, 868
Graham, Jesse V, 388
Graham, Jesse V, 440
Graham, Jewse V, 388
Graham, Jno. D. V, 998
Graham, John W. V, 61
Graham, Jonathan V, 388
Graham, Joseph IV, 207
Graham, Josiah V, 388
Graham, Julia VI, 893
Graham, Lawson VI, 923
Graham, Lemuel III, 137
Graham, Leota V, 998
Graham, Lila V, 998
Graham, Lovina V, 388
Graham, Lydia V, 61
Graham, M. VI, 984
Graham, M. Thomas VI, 893
Graham, Maggie S. IV, 207
Graham, Margaret II, 534
Graham, Margaret II, 743
Graham, Maria IV, 627
Graham, Maria IV, 636
Graham, Martha VI, 923
Graham, Martha VI, 1013
Graham, Mary V, 61
Graham, Mary V, 332
Graham, Mary V, 388
Graham, Mary V, 562
Graham, Mary V, 593
Graham, Mary VI, 844
Graham, Mary E. IV, 1317
Graham, Michael IV, 147
Graham, Michael VI, 1010
Graham, Minnie M. V, 593
Graham, Nettie V, 61
Graham, Patience IV, 147
Graham, Phebe V, 388
Graham, Phebe V, 440
Graham, Philena W. IV, 126
Graham, Philena W. IV, 130
Graham, Rachel V, 332
Graham, Rachel V, 341
Graham, Rachel V, 388
Graham, Robert III, 137
Graham, Sarah VI, 821
Graham, Sarah J. V, 998
Graham, Susan VI, 984
Graham, Susana M. VI, 893
Graham, Susanna VI, 892
Graham, Susannah VI, 844
Graham, Thomas VI, 821
Graham, William V, 61
Graham, William VI, 812
Graham, William John III, 137
Graham, William L. VI, 821
Graham, Wm. V, 998
Graham, Wm. L. VI, 963
Grahame, Anna M. II, 868
Grahame, Caroline Bell II, 868
Grahame, Carrie Bell II, 868
Grahame, George II, 796
Grahame, George II, 819
Grahame, George H. II, 868
Grahame, Hicks Harris II, 796
Grahame, Israel J. II, 868
Grahame, Israel Janney II, 796
Grahame, Jane P. II, 868
Grahame, Jane Peirce II, 796
Grahame, Jennie II, 868
Grahame, Mary II, 796
Grahame, Mary II, 819
Grahame, Wd. Mary II, 819
Grainger, Chalkley II, 367
Grainger, Elizabeth II, 367
Grainger, Joshua II, 367
Grainger, Miriam II, 367
Graisberry, Abraham II, 444
Graisberry, Benjamin II, 444
Graisberry, Sarah II, 444
Graisbury, Ann II, 444
Graisbury, Elizabeth II, 444
Graisbury, James II, 444
Graisbury, Mary II, 444
Graisbury, Moses II, 444
Graisbury, Sarah II, 534
Grambo, Catherine IV, 1252
Gramm, Florence II, 960
Gramm, Florence II, 1051
Gramm, Herman II, 960
Gramm, Ida II, 960
Gramm, Johannes II, 960
Gramm, Johannes II, 1051
Grammer, Andrew VI, 484
Grammer, Ollie I, 1152
Gramwell, Mary M. II, 851
Gramwell, Mary M. II, 884
Grandell, Berta V, 457
Grandell, Hattie V, 457
Granderson, Nancy VI, 297
Grandine, Abigail II, 535
Grandle, Hattie V, 457
Grandle, Hettie V, 241
Grandom, Catherine II, 367
Grandom, Hart II, 535
Grandom, John II, 367
Grandom, John II, 535
Grandom, John II, 543
Grandom, Mary II, 367
Grandom, Mary II, 535
Grandom, Mary II, 543
Grandom, Sarah II, 367
Grandom, Sarah II, 535
Grandom, Thomas II, 367
Grandon, George IV, 207
Grandstaff, William V, 675
Grandstaff, Wm. V, 675
Grandum, Hart II, 535
Grandum, John II, 535
Grandum, Mary II, 535
Grandum, Sarah II, 535
Grandy, Anna IV, 1363
Grandy, Benjamin IV, 1363
Grandy, Daniel IV, 1363
Grandy, Dorcas IV, 1359
Grandy, Dorcas IV, 1363
Grandy, Edmund IV, 1359
Grandy, Edmund IV, 1363
Grandy, Elinor III, 137
Grandy, Enos IV, 1363
Grandy, Francis IV, 1363
Grandy, Francis M. IV, 1363
Grandy, George IV, 1363
Grandy, George IV, 1366
Grandy, James IV, 1363
Grandy, Jane IV, 1359
Grandy, Jane IV, 1363
Grandy, Joseph IV, 1363
Grandy, Parke IV, 1363
Grandy, Phebe IV, 1363
Grandy, Rheuhamah IV, 1363
Grandy, Sarah L. IV, 1363
Grandy, Sarah L. IV, 1366
Grandy, William IV, 1363
Granger, Annie W. III, 137
Granger, Arthur L. III, 137
Granger, Bert IV, 1317
Granger, Beryl IV, 1317
Granger, Elizabeth II, 535
Granger, Florence IV, 1317
Granger, Herbert C. IV, 1317
Granger, Mariana III, 67
Granger, Marina III, 137
Granger, Wm. L. III, 67
Granger, Wm. L. III, 137
Granstaff, Andrew N. V, 998
Granstaff, Beatrice V, 998
Granstaff, C. N. V, 998
Granstaff, Catharine V, 998
Granstaff, Clarence V, 998
Granstaff, Curtis V, 998
Granstaff, Curtis N. V, 998
Granstaff, Curtis W. V, 998
Granstaff, Elizabeth V, 998
Granstaff, Ella V, 998
Granstaff, Ethel V, 998
Granstaff, Flora V, 998
Granstaff, Florence V, 998
Granstaff, Fred V, 998
Granstaff, Frederic V, 998
Granstaff, Frederick V, 998
Granstaff, Harrold V, 998
Granstaff, Harry V, 998
Granstaff, James V, 998
Granstaff, Lemuel L. V, 998
Granstaff, Margaret V, 998
Granstaff, Martha V, 998
Granstaff, Martha M. V, 998
Granstaff, Mary V, 998
Granstaff, Maud V, 998
Granstaff, Mauda V, 998
Granstaff, Nellie J. V, 998
Granstaff, Owen V, 998
Granstaff, Ralf V, 998
Granstaff, Ralph V, 998
Granstaff, Ruby V, 998
Granstaff, Wabash V, 998
Grant, Alexander II, 444
Grant, Alice IV, 1161
Grant, Ann IV, 34
Grant, Ann IV, 39
Grant, Anna I, 336
Grant, Anna IV, 1161
Grant, Annzube IV, 34
Grant, Anthony IV, 34
Grant, Archilla IV, 870
Grant, Arthur IV, 1161
Grant, Asa IV, 1161
Grant, Asa T. IV, 1279
Grant, Catharine IV, 34
Grant, Charles R. III, 483
Grant, Delaplain III, 137
Grant, Duncan VI, 923
Grant, Edy VI, 923
Grant, Elizabeth II, 796
Grant, Emma I, 336
Grant, Esther II, 504
Grant, Esther II, 535
Grant, Eugene I, 336
Grant, Frances Ford IV, 870
Grant, Franklin Blair I, 1152
Grant, George N. IV, 207
Grant, James IV, 34
Grant, James Alexander I, 1152
Grant, Jennie IV, 1279
Grant, John I, 239
Grant, John IV, 34
Grant, John VI, 923
Grant, John VI, 978
Grant, John M. II, 796
Grant, John M. II, 818
Grant, John M. II, 868
Grant, John S. I, 1152
Grant, Jordan I, 208
Grant, Judith IV, 34
Grant, Judith IV, 61
Grant, Luella Mae IV, 1161
Grant, Luella May IV, 1161
Grant, Lula IV, 1196
Grant, Lulu Worth IV, 1161
Grant, Lydia IV, 33
Grant, Lydia IV, 34
Grant, Margaret IV, 1317
Grant, Margery IV, 34
Grant, Mariam I, 239
Grant, Mariam I, 240
Grant, Martha II, 367
Grant, Mary I, 239
Grant, Mary II, 796
Grant, Mary IV, 34
Grant, Mary IV, 1161
Grant, Mary V, 493
Grant, Mary V, 998
Grant, Mary Josephine I, 1152
Grant, Mary W. II, 868
Grant, May IV, 1161
Grant, Mildred I, 239
Grant, Mildred I, 251
Grant, Millicent I, 208
Grant, Miriam I, 239
Grant, Nancy I, 1152
Grant, Polly I, 231
Grant, Polly I, 239
Grant, Ruth VI, 978
Grant, Sarah IV, 34
Grant, Sarah V, 172
Grant, Sarah A. VI, 923
Grant, Sien A. I, 239
Grant, Sion A. I, 239
Grant, Stella Westbrook IV, 11
Grant, Susan I, 336
Grant, W. J. V, 998
Grant, Wd. Sally II, 818
Grant, Widow Sallie Ann I, 208
Grant, Wm. II, 796
Grantham, ??? I, 336
Grantham, Amelia I, 633
Grantham, Amelia L. P. I, 336
Grantham, Amy I, 336
Grantham, Amy I, 339
Grantham, Annie D. I, 336
Grantham, Annie D. I, 633
Grantham, Annie Daisy I, 336
Grantham, Barney I, 329

tham, Bertha I, 635
tham, Carson I, 635
tham, Carson H. I, 617
tham, Carson H. I, 633
tham, Claudius R. I, 617
tham, Daisy I, 612
tham, Daisy I, 617
tham, Daisy I, 630
tham, Daisy I, 633
tham, David J. I, 324
tham, David J. I, 329
tham, Edward Stanley
, 324
tham, Edward Stanley
, 329
tham, Elisabeth I, 617
tham, Elisabeth I, 633
tham, Elizabeth I, 307
tham, Elizabeth I, 633
tham, Elizabeth H. I, 633
tham, Emery P. I, 637
tham, Ezra I, 617
tham, Francis I, 637
tham, Ganzada Cox I, 324
tham, George H. I, 336
tham, George H. I, 612
tham, George H. I, 617
tham, George H. I, 633
tham, Hannah I, 637
tham, Herbert G. I, 617
tham, Lizzie I, 612
tham, Lizzie I, 617
tham, Lizzie H. I, 336
tham, Manard I, 329
tham, Manard Barny I, 324
tham, Mary Cumi I, 324
tham, Mittie I, 213
tham, Murray I, 617
tham, Murray F. I, 336
tham, Murray F. I, 633
tham, Omelia I, 633
tham, Omelia L. I, 336
tham, Polly I, 324
tham, Richard I, 617
tham, Richard I, 633
tham, Sarah E. I, 619
tham, Sarah Elizabeth
, 324
tham, Sarah M. I, 307
tham, Uriah I, 329
tham, Walter I, 633
tham, Walter J. I, 336
tham, Walter J. I, 617
tham, William I, 329
tham, William Uriah I, 324
tland, Jane II, 56
tland, Jane II, 72
tlin, Jane II, 469
tlin, Jane II, 535
tom, Elizabeth I, 303
tom, Elizabeth I, 307
tstaff, Curtis V, 998
ville, Richard F. V, 907
wood, Frances VI, 1001
wood, Samuel VI, 1001
e, George W. IV, 713
e, Lydia M. IV, 713
igny, Hannah IV, 426
igny, Hannah H. IV, 395
z, Caroline B. VI, 567
z, Robenia III, 17
z, Robenia III, 96
z, Simon VI, 567
att, Joseph V, 332
att, Joseph A. V, 332
ve, Albina IV, 34
ve, Albina IV, 42
ve, Alexander I, 390
ve, Allen IV, 89
ve, Ann IV, 34
ve, Ann IV, 42
ve, Betty IV, 34
ve, Betty IV, 89
ve, David IV, 24
ve, David IV, 34
ve, David IV, 89
ve, Edith IV, 24
ve, Elizabeth IV, 34
ve, Elwood IV, 89
ve, Enos IV, 34
ve, Enos IV, 89
ve, Hannah IV, 34
ve, Hannah IV, 89
ve, Hannah IV, 100
ve, Hannah L. V, 740
ve, Hannah L. V, 758
ve, Israel IV, 89
ve, Jacob IV, 34
ve, Jane I, 375
ve, Jane I, 390
ve, Jehu IV, 34
Grave, Jesse IV, 34
Grave, Jesse IV, 89
Grave, John L. IV, 89
Grave, Jonathan IV, 89
Grave, Jonathan L. IV, 89
Grave, Joshua IV, 42
Grave, Kersey IV, 89
Grave, Kersey IV, 1280
Grave, Kersey IV, 1286
Grave, Lella V, 241
Grave, Lydia IV, 89
Grave, Lydia IV, 1280
Grave, Lydia IV, 1286
Grave, Lydia Ann V, 740
Grave, Lydia Ann V, 749
Grave, Lydia Ann V, 750
Grave, Lydia Ann V, 840
Grave, Maris Taylor IV, 34
Grave, Mary I, 387
Grave, Mary I, 390
Grave, Mary I, 391
Grave, Mary V, 740
Grave, Mary Ann IV, 34
Grave, Mary Ann IV, 42
Grave, Nathan IV, 89
Grave, Pusey IV, 89
Grave, Rachel IV, 34
Grave, Rebecca IV, 89
Grave, Rebecca J. IV, 89
Grave, Rebeccah IV, 34
Grave, Rebekah I, 390
Grave, Rebekah I, 404
Grave, Ruth IV, 24
Grave, Ruth IV, 26
Grave, Ruth IV, 34
Grave, Ruth IV, 69
Grave, Ruthanna IV, 34
Grave, Samuel IV, 34
Grave, Sarah IV, 89
Grave, Sarahann IV, 89
Grave, Stephen IV, 89
Grave, Susanna IV, 89
Grave, Tacy IV, 34
Grave, Thomas I, 390
Grave, Warner IV, 89
Grave, William I, 390
Graven, John II, 535
Graven, Rebecca II, 535
Graven, Rebecca IV, 818
Gravenstine, Chas. II, 796
Gravenstine, John II, 535
Gravenstine, Rebecca II, 535
Gravenstine, Rebecca II, 630
Gravenstine, Rebecca Graven II, 535
Gravenstine, Wd. Hannah Wood II, 796
Graves, A. J. V, 332
Graves, Amy I, 390
Graves, Amy V, 303
Graves, Andrew V, 332
Graves, Ann II, 868
Graves, Ann II, 907
Graves, Ann IV, 892
Graves, Annie V, 241
Graves, Clara L. IV, 957
Graves, Curtis IV, 1252
Graves, Dorothy II, 72
Graves, Dorothy II, 225
Graves, Dorothy II, 256
Graves, E. Adelaide IV, 1317
Graves, Edith C. IV, 1317
Graves, Elizabeth II, 65
Graves, Elizabeth II, 73
Graves, Emeline IV, 1317
Graves, Evalyn T. V, 623
Graves, Fanny VI, 923
Graves, Gordon H. III, 137
Graves, Hannah V, 757
Graves, Jane II, 998
Graves, John V, 241
Graves, John VI, 15
Graves, John P. VI, 924
Graves, Jonathan II, 868
Graves, Jonathan II, 907
Graves, Jonathan IV, 892
Graves, Joseph II, 54
Graves, Joseph II, 72
Graves, Joseph II, 73
Graves, Joseph II, 535
Graves, Josephine III, 87
Graves, Josephine III, 303
Graves, Kennett II, 73
Graves, Lella V, 241
Graves, Lucy C. VI, 912
Graves, Lydia Ann V, 840
Graves, Margaret II, 72
Graves, Margaret II, 73
Graves, Margaret II, 90
Graves, Margreat II, 72
Graves, Maria II, 868
Graves, Maria II, 907
Graves, Mariah II, 868
Graves, Marina V, 241
Graves, Martha V, 332
Graves, Mary I, 390
Graves, Mary II, 516
Graves, Mary II, 535
Graves, Mary II, 998
Graves, Mary IV, 891
Graves, Mary IV, 892
Graves, Mary V, 241
Graves, Mary V, 303
Graves, Mary V, 305
Graves, Mary V, 740
Graves, Mary V, 769
Graves, Mary Ann IV, 34
Graves, Mary Ann IV, 42
Graves, Mary M. IV, 892
Graves, May H. IV, 1317
Graves, Miami V, 241
Graves, Myra E. IV, 1317
Graves, Nancy VI, 923
Graves, Naomi II, 535
Graves, Peyton VI, 923
Graves, Randolph I, 480
Graves, Rebecca II, 54
Graves, Rebecca II, 72
Graves, Rebecca II, 73
Graves, Rebecca II, 108
Graves, Rebecca II, 535
Graves, Rebeckah II, 29
Graves, Richard II, 72
Graves, Richard II, 73
Graves, Richard II, 225
Graves, Richard II, 256
Graves, Richard VI, 923
Graves, Robert II, 868
Graves, Robert II, 907
Graves, Robert IV, 891
Graves, Robert IV, 892
Graves, Salley VI, 923
Graves, Samuel II, 72
Graves, Samuel II, 73
Graves, Samuel II, 90
Graves, Samuel II, 998
Graves, Samuel IV, 34
Graves, Sarah IV, 957
Graves, Stella M. IV, 1317
Graves, Tabitha E. VI, 924
Graves, Thomas II, 29
Graves, Thomas II, 72
Graves, Thomas II, 73
Graves, Thomas II, 535
Graves, Wd. Mary II, 535
Graves, William I, 390
Graves, William V, 241
Graves, William VI, 923
Graves, Willis IV, 957
Graveyard, Randolph V, 787
Gravinstine, John II, 535
Gray, ??? IV, 239
Gray, ??? IV, 958
Gray, ??? VI, 768
Gray, Abigail I, 542
Gray, Abigail IV, 958
Gray, Abigail V, 61
Gray, Abigail L. IV, 959
Gray, Abigzil V, 61
Gray, Adam V, 675
Gray, Adelbert IV, 1161
Gray, Adelbert W. IV, 1161
Gray, Agness IV, 208
Gray, Alexander VI, 877
Gray, Alexander VI, 924
Gray, Alexander VI, 941
Gray, Alice I, 1152
Gray, Alice VI, 995
Gray, Amy IV, 1099
Gray, Amy IV, 1118
Gray, Amy VI, 924
Gray, Andrew II, 130
Gray, Andrew V, 551
Gray, Angeline V, 562
Gray, Angeline V, 675
Gray, Ann II, 367
Gray, Ann IV, 34
Gray, Ann IV, 60
Gray, Ann IV, 207
Gray, Ann IV, 208
Gray, Ann IV, 290
Gray, Ann IV, 526
Gray, Ann IV, 541
Gray, Ann IV, 580
Gray, Ann IV, 959
Gray, Ann V, 61
Gray, Ann V, 493
Gray, Ann V, 528
Gray, Ann E. R. VI, 924
Gray, Anna IV, 526
Gray, Anna V, 895
Gray, Anna V, 907
Gray, Anna Elizabeth V, 551
Gray, Annabella II, 368
Gray, Anne IV, 526
Gray, Apphia VI, 869
Gray, Asa IV, 395
Gray, Asenath V, 61
Gray, Atherton IV, 526
Gray, Atlantic IV, 395
Gray, Atlantic O. IV, 208
Gray, Atlantic O. IV, 312
Gray, Atlantic O. IV, 313
Gray, Atlantic Ocean IV, 208
Gray, Atlantic Ocean IV, 312
Gray, Atlantic Ocean IV, 395
Gray, Austin VI, 869
Gray, Austin VI, 916
Gray, B. VI, 900
Gray, Bennett IV, 1161
Gray, Betsy I, 542
Gray, Burkett VI, 883
Gray, Burkett VI, 900
Gray, Burkett VI, 1014
Gray, Callohill VI, 994
Gray, Caroline IV, 239
Gray, Catharine IV, 207
Gray, Catharine IV, 208
Gray, Catharine IV, 238
Gray, Catharine IV, 312
Gray, Catharine IV, 395
Gray, Catherine VI, 924
Gray, Chapman VI, 924
Gray, Charles II, 367
Gray, Charles Loren IV, 1161
Gray, Charlotte IV, 208
Gray, Charlotte IV, 891
Gray, Charlotte IV, 892
Gray, Christiana IV, 576
Gray, Christianna IV, 580
Gray, Christianna IV, 594
Gray, Cordelia Ellen IV, 1161
Gray, Cyrenius Embree IV, 1099
Gray, David IV, 89
Gray, David IV, 147
Gray, David IV, 207
Gray, David IV, 576
Gray, David IV, 580
Gray, David Howard III, 137
Gray, Deborah IV, 207
Gray, Deborah IV, 208
Gray, Deborah IV, 265
Gray, Deborah IV, 580
Gray, Dollie V, 666
Gray, Dollie V, 675
Gray, Dollie C. V, 675
Gray, Ebenezer IV, 526
Gray, Edgar E. IV, 1161
Gray, Edgar Emmet IV, 1161
Gray, Edwin N. IV, 1161
Gray, Elexander VI, 924
Gray, Eli I, 498
Gray, Eli I, 542
Gray, Eli Noble IV, 1161
Gray, Elijah IV, 34
Gray, Elijah IV, 89
Gray, Elijah IV, 147
Gray, Elijah IV, 207
Gray, Elijah IV, 208
Gray, Elijah IV, 249
Gray, Elijah IV, 370
Gray, Elijah IV, 395
Gray, Elijah IV, 580
Gray, Elijah IV, 1099
Gray, Elisha IV, 207
Gray, Elisha IV, 208
Gray, Elisha IV, 580
Gray, Eliza I, 239
Gray, Eliza II, 130
Gray, Eliza IV, 239
Gray, Eliza VI, 744
Gray, Elizabeth I, 498
Gray, Elizabeth I, 797
Gray, Elizabeth I, 811
Gray, Elizabeth II, 367
Gray, Elizabeth II, 368
Gray, Elizabeth II, 489
Gray, Elizabeth II, 535
Gray, Elizabeth II, 553
Gray, Elizabeth III, 137
Gray, Elizabeth III, 138
Gray, Elizabeth IV, 370
Gray, Elizabeth IV, 395
Gray, Elizabeth IV, 1161
Gray, Elizabeth VI, 392
Gray, Elizabeth VI, 834
Gray, Elizabeth F. IV, 208
Gray, Elizabeth N. VI, 1014
Gray, Elma IV, 239
Gray, Ema IV, 526
Gray, Emily IV, 208
Gray, Emma III, 137
Gray, Emma V, 623
Gray, Emmer I, 593
Gray, Esther IV, 34
Gray, Esther IV, 89
Gray, Esther IV, 147
Gray, Esther IV, 207
Gray, Esther IV, 208
Gray, Esther IV, 249
Gray, Florence V, 675
Gray, Frances J. VI, 924
Gray, Frances M. VI, 900
Gray, Gardner B. IV, 1161
Gray, Gardner Bennett IV, 1161
Gray, George II, 225
Gray, George II, 367
Gray, George II, 368
Gray, George II, 462
Gray, George II, 535
Gray, George II, 641
Gray, George II, 678
Gray, George V, 61
Gray, George V, 675
Gray, George VI, 924
Gray, George VI, 995
Gray, George K. VI, 392
Gray, George W. V, 675
Gray, Gibbens V, 623
Gray, Hannah I, 871
Gray, Hannah I, 880
Gray, Hannah IV, 169
Gray, Hannah IV, 207
Gray, Hannah IV, 208
Gray, Hannah IV, 306
Gray, Hannah IV, 526
Gray, Hannah IV, 959
Gray, Hannah IV, 1096
Gray, Hannah IV, 1099
Gray, Hannah Embree, Jr. IV, 1099
Gray, Hannah G. IV, 958
Gray, Harriet V, 597
Gray, Harry IV, 959
Gray, Harvey IV, 239
Gray, Henry IV, 239
Gray, Henry H. IV, 239
Gray, Horace IV, 959
Gray, Horrice B. IV, 958
Gray, Howard B. IV, 959
Gray, Howard Leonard V, 562
Gray, Isaac II, 368
Gray, Isaac II, 514
Gray, Isaac II, 535
Gray, Isaac IV, 208
Gray, Isaac IV, 239
Gray, Isaac IV, 526
Gray, Isaac, Jr. IV, 239
Gray, Jacob II, 535
Gray, James III, 137
Gray, James IV, 526
Gray, James VI, 392
Gray, James VI, 895
Gray, James VI, 979
Gray, James D. VI, 392
Gray, James W. V, 675
Gray, James, Sr. VI, 882
Gray, Jane I, 757
Gray, Jane I, 761
Gray, Jane II, 130
Gray, Jane V, 47
Gray, Jane V, 61
Gray, Jane VI, 816
Gray, Jeremiah II, 368
Gray, Jesse I, 593
Gray, Jesse I, 624
Gray, Jesse IV, 208
Gray, Jesse IV, 580
Gray, Jesse IV, 1099
Gray, Jessie IV, 1317
Gray, Jessie B. IV, 1317
Gray, John II, 368
Gray, John II, 535
Gray, John III, 137
Gray, John III, 138
Gray, John IV, 207
Gray, John IV, 208
Gray, John IV, 265
Gray, John IV, 526
Gray, John IV, 580
Gray, John V, 61
Gray, John VI, 744
Gray, John VI, 821
Gray, John VI, 924
Gray, John VI, 927
Gray, John C. VI, 900
Gray, John C. VI, 994
Gray, John Embree IV, 1099
Gray, John F. VI, 392
Gray, John G. IV, 239
Gray, John P. VI, 972
Gray, John P. VI, 1000
Gray, John S. I, 716
Gray, John T. V, 562

Gray, John T. VI, 905
Gray, John W. V, 562
Gray, John Warner II, 502
Gray, John White IV, 208
Gray, John White IV, 580
Gray, John Whittier IV, 580
Gray, Joseph II, 367
Gray, Joseph II, 368
Gray, Joseph II, 535
Gray, Joseph II, 545
Gray, Joseph II, 564
Gray, Joseph II, 678
Gray, Joseph IV, 580
Gray, Joseph IV, 1099
Gray, Joseph R. V, 675
Gray, Joseph, Jr. II, 368
Gray, Josie IV, 1280
Gray, L. Jane V, 61
Gray, Lemuel IV, 207
Gray, Lemuel IV, 208
Gray, Lemuel IV, 1099
Gray, Lewis IV, 239
Gray, Lewis C. IV, 580
Gray, Lilburn IV, 208
Gray, Lilly V, 457
Gray, Lina V, 551
Gray, Lina V, 562
Gray, Lizzie V, 457
Gray, Loren IV, 1146
Gray, Loren IV, 1161
Gray, Loren IV, 1163
Gray, Loren B. IV, 959
Gray, Louisa IV, 239
Gray, Louisa Olive IV, 1161
Gray, Lucinda IV, 1161
Gray, Lucinda IV, 1183
Gray, Lucinda VI, 924
Gray, Lucy VI, 392
Gray, Lucy Ann IV, 1357
Gray, Lucy Ann IV, 1363
Gray, Lydia I, 542
Gray, Lydia I, 1009
Gray, Lydia II, 368
Gray, Lydia IV, 239
Gray, Lydia IV, 526
Gray, Lydia IV, 543
Gray, Lydia IV, 1161
Gray, Lydia G. IV, 239
Gray, Lydia Jane IV, 1161
Gray, Lydia Jane IV, 1163
Gray, Lydia Jane IV, 1209
Gray, Mabel V, 623
Gray, Mabel Annette V, 562
Gray, Malakiah I, 542
Gray, Malekiah I, 498
Gray, Mallachi I, 542
Gray, Mallachi I, 578
Gray, Marcy II, 502
Gray, Margaret II, 368
Gray, Margrett II, 368
Gray, Marquis D. VI, 924
Gray, Marquis D. VI, 943
Gray, Martha II, 368
Gray, Martha II, 535
Gray, Martha V, 551
Gray, Martha Ann IV, 1065
Gray, Mary I, 542
Gray, Mary I, 624
Gray, Mary I, 797
Gray, Mary I, 811
Gray, Mary II, 367
Gray, Mary II, 368
Gray, Mary II, 481
Gray, Mary II, 494
Gray, Mary II, 514
Gray, Mary II, 535
Gray, Mary II, 542
Gray, Mary II, 545
Gray, Mary II, 564
Gray, Mary II, 641
Gray, Mary IV, 34
Gray, Mary IV, 49
Gray, Mary IV, 89
Gray, Mary IV, 147
Gray, Mary IV, 207
Gray, Mary IV, 208
Gray, Mary IV, 249
Gray, Mary IV, 312
Gray, Mary IV, 395
Gray, Mary IV, 580
Gray, Mary IV, 594
Gray, Mary IV, 1099
Gray, Mary IV, 1106
Gray, Mary V, 38
Gray, Mary V, 61
Gray, Mary V, 675
Gray, Mary VI, 900
Gray, Mary VI, 905
Gray, Mary VI, 924
Gray, Mary Ann I, 624
Gray, Mary Ann I, 626
Gray, Mary Ann IV, 208
Gray, Mary Ann IV, 395
Gray, Mary Ann IV, 451
Gray, Mary Ann VI, 744
Gray, Mary Ann VI, 768
Gray, Mary D. V, 675
Gray, Mary E. IV, 34
Gray, Mary Elizabeth IV, 239
Gray, Mary Jane I, 498
Gray, Mary Jane I, 542
Gray, Mary L. I, 716
Gray, Mary Letitia IV, 239
Gray, Mary W. VI, 924
Gray, Massy II, 587
Gray, Mathia II, 535
Gray, Mathias II, 587
Gray, Mercy II, 535
Gray, Mercy II, 587
Gray, Mercy II, 678
Gray, Milly V, 457
Gray, Milly VI, 821
Gray, Morgan IV, 239
Gray, Morgan IV, 395
Gray, Mrs. Ann E. VI, 882
Gray, Nancy IV, 395
Gray, Nancy V, 61
Gray, Nancy VI, 924
Gray, Naomi II, 368
Gray, Naomi II, 462
Gray, Nathan IV, 34
Gray, Nathan IV, 580
Gray, Nathan IV, 959
Gray, Noble IV, 1161
Gray, Orson VI, 924
Gray, Oscar V, 675
Gray, Park V, 675
Gray, Patience II, 368
Gray, Patience II, 514
Gray, Patience II, 535
Gray, Patience II, 556
Gray, Patience II, 636
Gray, Percy R. III, 137
Gray, Peter IV, 207
Gray, Peter IV, 208
Gray, Peter IV, 580
Gray, Phebe F. VI, 392
Gray, Phebe T. III, 137
Gray, Pinkney I, 593
Gray, Polly VI, 924
Gray, Rachel I, 593
Gray, Rachel IV, 207
Gray, Rachel IV, 208
Gray, Rachel IV, 580
Gray, Rachel VI, 924
Gray, Rebecca V, 61
Gray, Rebecca V, 493
Gray, Rebeckah VI, 924
Gray, Rees IV, 208
Gray, Rhoda VI, 900
Gray, Rhoda VI, 924
Gray, Richard I, 542
Gray, Richard IV, 594
Gray, Richard E. IV, 580
Gray, Robert II, 368
Gray, Robert IV, 207
Gray, Robert VI, 392
Gray, Robert VI, 924
Gray, Robert H. VI, 392
Gray, Robert Roberts II, 556
Gray, Robert U. III, 137
Gray, Rosetta IV, 239
Gray, Russell William V, 562
Gray, Russell Wm. V, 562
Gray, Ruth IV, 1099
Gray, Sally VI, 889
Gray, Samuel II, 368
Gray, Samuel II, 535
Gray, Samuel II, 553
Gray, Samuel II, 636
Gray, Samuel IV, 34
Gray, Samuel IV, 89
Gray, Samuel IV, 147
Gray, Samuel IV, 207
Gray, Samuel IV, 208
Gray, Samuel IV, 306
Gray, Samuel IV, 1099
Gray, Samuel VI, 945
Gray, Samuel VI, 994
Gray, Samuel N. II, 706
Gray, Samuel, Jr. II, 367
Gray, Samuel, Jr. II, 368
Gray, Samuell II, 514
Gray, Sanford P. V, 675
Gray, Sarah I, 593
Gray, Sarah I, 597
Gray, Sarah I, 1009
Gray, Sarah I, 1010
Gray, Sarah II, 368
Gray, Sarah IV, 27
Gray, Sarah IV, 34
Gray, Sarah IV, 395
Gray, Sarah IV, 580
Gray, Sarah IV, 1099
Gray, Sarah IV, 1161
Gray, Sarah IV, 1163
Gray, Sarah VI, 882
Gray, Sarah VI, 972
Gray, Sarah B. V, 562
Gray, Sarah Ellen IV, 1161
Gray, Sarah M. IV, 1146
Gray, Sarah M. IV, 1161
Gray, Suky VI, 881
Gray, Susan I, 761
Gray, Susan I, 811
Gray, Susan I, 815
Gray, Susan IV, 78
Gray, Susan IV, 89
Gray, Susan VI, 1003
Gray, Susanna IV, 207
Gray, Susanna IV, 301
Gray, Susannah IV, 239
Gray, Terrissa VI, 1000
Gray, Thomas IV, 207
Gray, Thomas IV, 208
Gray, Thomas IV, 238
Gray, Thomas IV, 312
Gray, Thomas IV, 395
Gray, Thomas IV, 526
Gray, Thomas IV, 580
Gray, Thomas V, 562
Gray, Thomas VI, 834
Gray, Thomas VI, 926
Gray, Thomas L. IV, 395
Gray, Thos. IV, 208
Gray, Walter V, 61
Gray, Walter V, 562
Gray, Walter V, 675
Gray, Wd. Mary II, 368
Gray, Wd. Patience II, 535
Gray, William II, 367
Gray, William II, 368
Gray, William IV, 208
Gray, William IV, 312
Gray, William IV, 395
Gray, William IV, 526
Gray, William IV, 1161
Gray, William V, 38
Gray, William V, 61
Gray, William VI, 392
Gray, William VI, 881
Gray, William VI, 889
Gray, William VI, 900
Gray, William B. IV, 1161
Gray, William S. IV, 207
Gray, William, Senr. VI, 889
Gray, Wm. II, 535
Gray, Wm. IV, 526
Gray, Wm. IV, 1317
Gray, Wm. B. IV, 1161
Gray, Wm. Pinkney I, 593
Gray, Wm. S. IV, 207
Graybill, Ed V, 388
Graybill, Nancy V, 388
Grayham, Enoch I, 962
Grayham, Mary V, 332
Graysbury, James II, 368
Graysbury, Sarah II, 368
Grayson, Bathsheba VI, 924
Grayson, James VI, 924
Grazier, Mary II, 368
Grear, Jimima VI, 925
Greater, Harold H. III, 138
Greater, Helen III, 135
Greater, Helen III, 138
Greater, Mildred III, 138
Greater, Mildred III, 206
Greater, Ralph George III, 135
Greater, Ralph George III, 138
Greater, Ralph George III, 206
Greater, Stephen Arlene III, 138
Greathouse, Charles V, 562
Greathouse, Charles Henry V, 562
Greathouse, Dora V, 562
Greathouse, Dora Amanda V, 562
Greathouse, Linton Smart V, 562
Greathouse, Mary Millie V, 562
Greathouse, Sarah V, 562
Greathouse, Sarah V, 581
Greathouse, Sarah Martin V, 562
Greave, Betty IV, 34
Greave, Betty IV, 43
Greave, Elizabeth IV, 34
Greave, Enos IV, 34
Greave, Enos IV, 43
Greave, Hannah IV, 34
Greave, Jacob IV, 34
Greave, Jesse IV, 34
Greave, Rebeccah IV, 34
Greave, Tacy IV, 34
Greave, Tacy IV, 80
Greave, Tacy IV, 89
Greaves, Alexander I, 390
Greaves, Alfred IV, 526
Greaves, Amy I, 390
Greaves, Charles IV, 526
Greaves, Emey I, 390
Greaves, Emma V, 61
Greaves, Emy I, 352
Greaves, George II, 796
Greaves, George IV, 526
Greaves, Hannah I, 390
Greaves, Isaac I, 390
Greaves, Jane I, 390
Greaves, Jane II, 1010
Greaves, John I, 352
Greaves, John I, 390
Greaves, John V, 61
Greaves, Lydia B. II, 743
Greaves, Lydia B. II, 759
Greaves, Mary I, 352
Greaves, Mary I, 390
Greaves, Mary II, 535
Greaves, Mary II, 998
Greaves, Mary V, 61
Greaves, Mary Ann I, 139
Greaves, Mary Ann I, 140
Greaves, Rebekah I, 390
Greaves, Sarah IV, 526
Greaves, Susanna II, 368
Greaves, Thomas I, 390
Greaves, Thomas II, 535
Greaves, Wd. Sarah Harrison II, 796
Greaves, William I, 390
Greaves, William V, 61
Grebbs, Frank IV, 1252
Grebhart, Edward V, 740
Greeg, James M. IV, 1252
Green, ??? III, 138
Green, ??? III, 201
Green, ??? III, 373
Green, ??? III, 503
Green, ??? V, 332
Green, ??? V, 443
Green, Aaron IV, 526
Green, Aaron IV, 527
Green, Aaron V, 389
Green, Aaron V, 493
Green, Aaron V, 527
Green, Abigail I, 1004
Green, Abigail IV, 331
Green, Abigail IV, 526
Green, Abigail IV, 1280
Green, Abigail V, 493
Green, Abigail V, 512
Green, Abigail V, 562
Green, Abigail V, 563
Green, Abigail V, 565
Green, Abigail V, 567
Green, Abigail V, 840
Green, Abigail VI, 392
Green, Abigail VI, 593
Green, Abigail VI, 596
Green, Abigail Jane I, 932
Green, Absillet V, 563
Green, Absillet V, 602
Green, Achsah IV, 1280
Green, Achsah V, 241
Green, Achsah V, 242
Green, Achsah P. V, 241
Green, Ada V, 655
Green, Ada V, 675
Green, Adaline V, 242
Green, Agnes E. III, 16
Green, Agnes E. III, 126
Green, Aimee III, 138
Green, Aimee III, 275
Green, Albert V, 61
Green, Albert V, 62
Green, Albert V, 563
Green, Albert L. V, 675
Green, Albert R. IV, 1280
Green, Alcinda V, 389
Green, Alexander IV, 208
Green, Alexander IV, 331
Green, Alexander IV, 395
Green, Alexander IV, 396
Green, Alexander IV, 529
Green, Alice I, 1001
Green, Alice I, 1009
Green, Alice II, 868
Green, Alice IV, 208
Green, Alice IV, 1280
Green, Alice V, 241
Green, Alice V, 242
Green, Alice V, 269
Green, Alice V, 493
Green, Alice V, 675
Green, Alice VI, 596
Green, Alice C. IV, 1363
Green, Alice D. V, 675
Green, Alice Doan V, 675
Green, Alice H. V, 242
Green, Alice H. V, 675
Green, Alice M. V, 233
Green, Alice M. V, 242
Green, Alie E. V, 389
Green, Alise H. V, 241
Green, Allen V, 493
Green, Allen V, 494
Green, Allice V, 494
Green, Alma V, 333
Green, Alma V, 334
Green, Almeda V. IV, 958
Green, Almeda V. IV, 992
Green, Almira III, 138
Green, Almira L. III, 259
Green, Alva E. III, 138
Green, Amanda II, 118
Green, Amanda V, 675
Green, Amanda V, 740
Green, Amanda Jane V, 389
Green, Amanda Jane V, 907
Green, Amos I, 542
Green, Amos I, 1016
Green, Amos I, 1043
Green, Amos I, 1048
Green, Amos V, 840
Green, Amos V, 845
Green, Amy A. VI, 846
Green, Amy Ellen V, 270
Green, Anabelle IV, 208
Green, Angaline P. IV, 1280
Green, Angeline G. V, 242
Green, Ann II, 226
Green, Ann II, 313
Green, Ann II, 318
Green, Ann II, 319
Green, Ann II, 536
Green, Ann III, 138
Green, Ann IV, 208
Green, Ann IV, 292
Green, Ann IV, 526
Green, Ann IV, 958
Green, Ann V, 62
Green, Ann VI, 924
Green, Ann B. VI, 816
Green, Ann Eliza III, 138
Green, Ann Louisa V, 61
Green, Ann R. III, 138
Green, Anna I, 1004
Green, Anna V, 241
Green, Anna V, 269
Green, Anna V, 411
Green, Anna V, 493
Green, Anna V, 494
Green, Anna V, 527
Green, Anna V, 562
Green, Anna V, 675
Green, Anna V, 687
Green, Anna Bell IV, 208
Green, Anna Elizabeth V, 27
Green, Anna J. V, 623
Green, Anna Jenkins V, 242
Green, Anna Louisa V, 61
Green, Anna Louisa V, 563
Green, Anna Louise V, 563
Green, Anna M. II, 869
Green, Anna M. V, 563
Green, Anna Maria IV, 1280
Green, Anna Mary IV, 208
Green, Anna Melvina II, 796
Green, Anna P. IV, 1280
Green, Anna P. V, 241
Green, Anne V, 389
Green, Anne V, 493
Green, Anne P. V, 242
Green, Annie V, 390
Green, Annie C. II, 868
Green, Anthony V, 227
Green, Arthur B. III, 138
Green, Arthur Edward V, 56
Green, Arthur Edward V, 56
Green, Arthur M. V, 389
Green, Asa I, 1004
Green, Asa V, 493
Green, Asa V, 554
Green, Asa V, 562
Green, Asa V, 563
Green, Asa V, 675
Green, Asa B. V, 61
Green, Asa B. V, 332
Green, Asa B. V, 386
Green, Asa B. V, 389
Green, Asa B. V, 562
Green, Asa B. V, 563
Green, Asa Oscar V, 61
Green, Asa Oscar V, 563
Green, Asaph V, 269
Green, Asaph V, 907
Green, Asaph Leander V, 49
Green, Ascenith V, 840
Green, Asenith V, 840

en, Aseph Leander V, 389
en, Aseph Leander V, 494
en, Aseph Leander V, 563
en, Aseph Leander V, 907
en, Barbara IV, 1161
en, Bell V, 333
en, Belle V, 333
en, Benjamin I, 654
en, Benjamin I, 679
en, Benjamin I, 690
en, Benjamin II, 796
en, Benjamin II, 907
en, Benjamin II, 921
en, Benjamin IV, 396
en, Benjamin IV, 1280
en, Bernice Ellen V, 563
en, Bernice Ellen V, 564
en, Bert Franklin V, 563
en, Bert Franklin V, 564
en, Bertha IV, 1148
en, Bertha IV, 1161
en, Bertha IV, 1173
en, Bertha V, 493
en, Bertha V, 494
en, Bessie V, 333
en, Blanche IV, 1208
en, Booker VI, 924
en, C. Herbert V, 242
en, C. Herbert V, 675
en, Caleb III, 138
en, Caleb III, 240
en, Caleb VI, 177
en, Caleb VI, 178
en, Caroline III, 138
en, Caroline V, 61
en, Carrie IV, 1280
en, Carrie IV, 1298
en, Carrie V, 389
en, Carrie E. V, 389
en, Carrie Estella V, 389
en, Catharine II, 226
en, Catherine E. V, 998
en, Catherine E. V, 999
en, Charity V, 833
en, Charity V, 840
en, Charles II, 118
en, Charles III, 138
en, Charles V, 390
en, Charles E. V, 389
en, Charles Edwin V, 389
en, Charles Herbert V, 242
en, Charles Herbert V, 675
en, Charlotte I, 1004
en, Charlotte V, 241
en, Charlotte V, 243
en, Charlotte V, 493
en, Charlotte V, 512
en, Charlotte D. V, 389
en, Charlotte D. V, 420
en, Charlotte D. V, 493
en, Charlotte D. V, 518
en, Charlotte E. V, 241
en, Charlotte H. V, 241
en, Chas. Herbert V, 655
en, Clara IV, 1280
en, Clarence V, 333
en, Clarkson T. V, 563
en, Claudia V, 563
en, Clementina II, 917
en, Cora V, 390
en, Cora A. V, 389
en, Cordelia Bays V, 227
en, Cordelia Bays V, 241
en, Cynthia II, 796
en, Cynthia V, 333
en, Cynthia Ann V, 333
en, Cynthia S. II, 868
en, Cyrus V, 563
en, Daniel II, 444
en, Daniel IV, 713
en, Daniel IV, 765
en, Daniel V, 278
en, Daniel V, 390
en, Daniel V, 907
en, Daniel M. V, 241
en, Daniel M. V, 242
en, Daniel M. V, 389
en, Daniel M. V, 390
en, David I, 956
en, David I, 1004
en, David II, 226
en, David IV, 1280
en, David V, 61
en, David V, 62
en, David V, 82
en, David V, 92
en, David V, 332
en, David V, 333
en, David V, 389
en, David V, 493
en, David V, 562
Green, David V, 563
Green, David V, 579
Green, David VI, 924
Green, David A. V, 333
Green, David Alonzo V, 333
Green, David Alonzo V, 907
Green, David C. V, 388
Green, David C. V, 389
Green, David C. V, 390
Green, David H. IV, 208
Green, David Warren V, 389
Green, Deborah II, 444
Green, Deborah IV, 1280
Green, Deborah A. IV, 1280
Green, Deborah A. IV, 1298
Green, Deborah A. V, 219
Green, Deborah A. V, 241
Green, Deborah Ann I, 613
Green, Deborah Ann V, 241
Green, Delfina IV, 1280
Green, Delilah IV, 1161
Green, Della IV, 1280
Green, Delphina IV, 1280
Green, Delphina M. IV, 1280
Green, Dr. Benjamin II, 796
Green, Dr. Israel III, 138
Green, Dr. Israel III, 257
Green, Dr. Lindley M. V, 242
Green, Earnest L. V, 242
Green, Edith Luella IV, 1280
Green, Edith M. V, 389
Green, Edna IV, 1363
Green, Edward III, 138
Green, Eleanor IV, 208
Green, Eli V, 61
Green, Eli V, 62
Green, Eli V, 332
Green, Eli V, 333
Green, Eli V, 388
Green, Eli V, 563
Green, Eli V, 840
Green, Eli H. V, 61
Green, Eli H. V, 333
Green, Eliah V, 389
Green, Elias I, 1004
Green, Elias IV, 1280
Green, Elias IV, 1298
Green, Elias V, 241
Green, Elias V, 242
Green, Elias G. V, 270
Green, Elie V, 62
Green, Eliel V, 388
Green, Elijah V, 61
Green, Elijah V, 563
Green, Elijah C. V, 61
Green, Elijah C. V, 67
Green, Elijah C. V, 563
Green, Elijah J. V, 62
Green, Eliza Ann V, 270
Green, Eliza Jane IV, 530
Green, Elizabeth II, 226
Green, Elizabeth II, 368
Green, Elizabeth II, 444
Green, Elizabeth II, 535
Green, Elizabeth II, 646
Green, Elizabeth III, 138
Green, Elizabeth III, 329
Green, Elizabeth III, 483
Green, Elizabeth III, 503
Green, Elizabeth IV, 1363
Green, Elizabeth IV, 1365
Green, Elizabeth V, 241
Green, Elizabeth V, 242
Green, Elizabeth V, 249
Green, Elizabeth V, 383
Green, Elizabeth V, 389
Green, Elizabeth V, 429
Green, Elizabeth V, 493
Green, Elizabeth V, 527
Green, Elizabeth V, 563
Green, Elizabeth V, 571
Green, Elizabeth V, 675
Green, Elizabeth V, 802
Green, Elizabeth V, 809
Green, Elizabeth V, 840
Green, Elizabeth VI, 924
Green, Ella V, 563
Green, Ella V, 675
Green, Ellen IV, 331
Green, Ellen IV, 395
Green, Ellen V, 563
Green, Ellen V, 675
Green, Ellen V, 802
Green, Ellen V, 809
Green, Ellen H. V, 563
Green, Ellen M. V, 564
Green, Ellis II, 536
Green, Ellis Lewis II, 536
Green, Elvira Ruth V, 241
Green, Emilie P. V, 67
Green, Emily V, 61
Green, Emily H. V, 62
Green, Emma V, 387
Green, Emma E. I, 932
Green, Enoch III, 138
Green, Enoch V, 840
Green, Enos V, 389
Green, Enos V, 494
Green, Ernest V, 675
Green, Ernest L. V, 242
Green, Ernest L. V, 494
Green, Ernest L. V, 675
Green, Esther I, 542
Green, Esther I, 1016
Green, Esther I, 1043
Green, Esther I, 1048
Green, Esther IV, 208
Green, Esther IV, 713
Green, Esther IV, 765
Green, Esther V, 61
Green, Esther V, 840
Green, Eunice IV, 1280
Green, Eva Ella III, 138
Green, Eva Ella III, 373
Green, Evelyn Strand IV, 1280
Green, Ezekiel VI, 392
Green, Ezekiel VI, 596
Green, F. K. IV, 1161
Green, Faith D. V, 623
Green, Flora Ellen IV, 1280
Green, Flora M. V, 563
Green, Florence J. II, 869
Green, Florence J. II, 924
Green, Florence Marice IV, 1161
Green, Florence Marise IV, 1161
Green, Florence N. V, 270
Green, Frances III, 138
Green, Frances III, 257
Green, Frances IV, 1161
Green, Frances IV, 1195
Green, Frances VI, 816
Green, Frances Marion V, 907
Green, Frances R. III, 138
Green, Frances R. III, 257
Green, Frances W. V, 242
Green, Frances Willard IV, 963
Green, Francetta IV, 1252
Green, Francis IV, 1252
Green, Francis M. V, 333
Green, Francis Marion V, 333
Green, Francis Marion V, 907
Green, Francis W. V, 494
Green, Francis W. V, 675
Green, Frank IV, 1195
Green, Frank E. III, 138
Green, Frank E. III, 197
Green, Frank K. IV, 1161
Green, Frank K. IV, 1173
Green, Frank L. IV, 1161
Green, Franklin E. II, 796
Green, Franklin E. II, 869
Green, Fred V, 998
Green, Fremont V, 999
Green, Fremont R. V, 998
Green, Gariah I, 390
Green, Geo. V, 411
Green, George V, 840
Green, George VI, 35
Green, George Dillwyn II, 869
Green, George Tatum, Jr. IV, 958
Green, Grace V, 241
Green, Grace V, 242
Green, Grace V, 253
Green, Grace V, 387
Green, Grace L. V, 242
Green, Grace L. V, 494
Green, Grace L. V, 675
Green, Gravner I, 679
Green, Gravner I, 686
Green, Griffen III, 138
Green, Gulielma V, 241
Green, Gulielma V, 242
Green, Gulielma V, 278
Green, Gulielma V, 389
Green, Gulielma V, 390
Green, Gulielma V, 563
Green, Gulielma V, 587
Green, Gulielma V, 698
Green, Gurnell Crafton III, 138
Green, Gurney V, 390
Green, Hannah I, 542
Green, Hannah I, 1004
Green, Hannah I, 1007
Green, Hannah I, 1009
Green, Hannah I, 1016
Green, Hannah I, 1043
Green, Hannah II, 73
Green, Hannah II, 104
Green, Hannah II, 194
Green, Hannah II, 225
Green, Hannah II, 226
Green, Hannah II, 235
Green, Hannah II, 792
Green, Hannah II, 800
Green, Hannah II, 998
Green, Hannah II, 1027
Green, Hannah II, 1042
Green, Hannah IV, 396
Green, Hannah IV, 446
Green, Hannah IV, 473
Green, Hannah IV, 958
Green, Hannah IV, 1006
Green, Hannah V, 241
Green, Hannah V, 269
Green, Hannah V, 284
Green, Hannah V, 377
Green, Hannah V, 389
Green, Hannah V, 493
Green, Hannah V, 675
Green, Hannah V, 840
Green, Hannah V, 845
Green, Hannah V, 871
Green, Hannah V, 952
Green, Hannah VI, 177
Green, Hannah VI, 178
Green, Hannah C. II, 868
Green, Hannah C. II, 869
Green, Hannah C. II, 887
Green, Hannah C. II, 933
Green, Hannah C. II, 938
Green, Hannah E. V, 242
Green, Hannah Elizabeth V, 242
Green, Hannah Ella II, 869
Green, Hannah Isabel V, 390
Green, Hannah Isabel V, 563
Green, Hannah Isabelle V, 563
Green, Hannah K. IV, 208
Green, Hannah K. IV, 288
Green, Hannah L. IV, 208
Green, Hannah M. II, 796
Green, Hannah M. II, 868
Green, Harlen P. V, 333
Green, Harley G. V, 998
Green, Harriett I, 925
Green, Harriett Florence IV, 1280
Green, Harry IV, 1208
Green, Harry F. IV, 1161
Green, Harry J. V, 389
Green, Harry T. IV, 1208
Green, Hazael D. V, 241
Green, Hazael D. V, 278
Green, Hazael D. V, 675
Green, Hazel D. V, 229
Green, Hazel D. V, 242
Green, Helen L. III, 138
Green, Helen L. III, 197
Green, Helen M. II, 289
Green, Herbert V, 494
Green, Herbert C. V, 494
Green, Hester V, 840
Green, Hilda R. V, 998
Green, Hilda R. V, 999
Green, Homer V, 172
Green, Homer V, 389
Green, Howard IV, 1161
Green, Howard IV, 1208
Green, Howard H. IV, 1161
Green, Hubert C. V, 675
Green, Hulda I, 679
Green, Huldah I, 654
Green, Huldah I, 679
Green, Huldah I, 690
Green, Ida II, 869
Green, Inez V, 675
Green, Inez A. V, 675
Green, Isaac I, 956
Green, Isaac I, 962
Green, Isaac I, 1004
Green, Isaac I, 1007
Green, Isaac I, 1009
Green, Isaac III, 138
Green, Isaac IV, 331
Green, Isaac V, 241
Green, Isaac V, 242
Green, Isaac V, 269
Green, Isaac V, 284
Green, Isaac V, 493
Green, Isaac V, 494
Green, Isaac V, 527
Green, Isaac V, 562
Green, Isaac V, 952
Green, Isaac VI, 596
Green, Isaac A. V, 242
Green, Isaac A. V, 244
Green, Isaac Anthony V, 241
Green, Isaac C. V, 389
Green, Isaac Linton V, 241
Green, Isaac William V, 241
Green, Isaac, Sr. I, 1004
Green, Isaiah II, 226
Green, Isaiah V, 563
Green, Isaiah V, 564
Green, Israel III, 138
Green, Israel III, 257
Green, Israel IV, 526
Green, Israel IV, 527
Green, Israel V, 388
Green, Israel VI, 243
Green, Israel C. V, 333
Green, Israel C. V, 389
Green, Israel C. V, 422
Green, Israel C. V, 623
Green, Israel C. V, 635
Green, Israel J. IV, 958
Green, Israel J. IV, 992
Green, J. Walter II, 869
Green, Jacob I, 715
Green, Jacob I, 716
Green, Jacob IV, 208
Green, Jacob IV, 526
Green, Jacob IV, 1280
Green, Jacob V, 563
Green, Jacob A. IV, 527
Green, Jacob A. IV, 957
Green, Jacob A. IV, 958
Green, Jacob A. IV, 970
Green, Jacob H. IV, 1280
Green, Jacob H. V, 563
Green, Jahiel V, 389
Green, James I, 542
Green, James I, 679
Green, James III, 138
Green, James IV, 331
Green, James IV, 396
Green, James IV, 526
Green, James IV, 527
Green, James V, 270
Green, James V, 387
Green, James VI, 924
Green, James B. II, 319
Green, James B. II, 796
Green, James B. II, 869
Green, James L. I, 932
Green, James Robert V, 389
Green, James Robert V, 493
Green, James Robert V, 494
Green, James Robert V, 563
Green, James Robert V, 907
Green, James Walter II, 869
Green, James, Jr. I, 542
Green, Jane II, 225
Green, Jane II, 796
Green, Jane V, 389
Green, Jane V, 420
Green, Jane V, 563
Green, Jane V, 586
Green, Jane M. IV, 1363
Green, Jehiel V, 388
Green, Jehiel V, 389
Green, Jehiel V, 493
Green, Jehiel V, 494
Green, Jehiel V, 512
Green, Jehiel V, 563
Green, Jehiel V, 907
Green, Jemima III, 138
Green, Jemima VI, 587
Green, Jemina VI, 495
Green, Jeptha V, 387
Green, Jesse I, 542
Green, Jesse I, 962
Green, Jesse I, 1016
Green, Jesse I, 1043
Green, Jesse IV, 1280
Green, Jesse V, 241
Green, Jesse V, 242
Green, Jesse V, 269
Green, Jesse V, 333
Green, Jesse V, 389
Green, Jesse V, 493
Green, Jesse V, 833
Green, Jesse V, 840
Green, Jesse VI, 596
Green, Jesse May IV, 713
Green, Jesse W. V, 242
Green, Jesse Wilson V, 241
Green, Jessie IV, 1161
Green, Jessie E. IV, 1208
Green, Joel V, 388
Green, Joel V, 389
Green, Joel V, 429
Green, Joel V, 494
Green, Joel V, 527
Green, Joel V, 563
Green, Joel William V, 493
Green, Joel Wm. V, 389
Green, Joel Wm. V, 907
Green, Johiel V, 389
Green, Johiel V, 411
Green, John I, 542
Green, John I, 654
Green, John I, 716
Green, John I, 811
Green, John I, 962
Green, John I, 1004

Green, John I, 1009
Green, John II, 194
Green, John II, 225
Green, John II, 226
Green, John II, 368
Green, John II, 444
Green, John II, 535
Green, John IV, 208
Green, John IV, 331
Green, John IV, 396
Green, John IV, 526
Green, John IV, 713
Green, John IV, 905
Green, John IV, 907
Green, John IV, 957
Green, John IV, 1007
Green, John IV, 1280
Green, John V, 61
Green, John V, 241
Green, John V, 242
Green, John V, 243
Green, John V, 253
Green, John V, 261
Green, John V, 270
Green, John V, 322
Green, John V, 332
Green, John V, 333
Green, John V, 388
Green, John V, 389
Green, John V, 493
Green, John V, 562
Green, John V, 563
Green, John V, 604
Green, John VI, 392
Green, John VI, 403
Green, John VI, 596
Green, John C. V, 389
Green, John C. V, 563
Green, John G. P. V, 241
Green, John G. P. V, 242
Green, John H. IV, 208
Green, John H. IV, 288
Green, John H. V, 242
Green, John Hamilton V, 241
Green, John P. IV, 1280
Green, John P. V, 907
Green, John Rileigh V, 389
Green, John Riley V, 61
Green, John Riley V, 389
Green, John S. IV, 396
Green, John S. V, 333
Green, John Sewel V, 333
Green, John Sewell V, 389
Green, John T. III, 138
Green, John Wm. V, 332
Green, John Wm. V, 333
Green, John, Jr. I, 1008
Green, John, Jr. I, 1009
Green, John, Jr. V, 241
Green, John, Jr. V, 242
Green, John, Jr. V, 269
Green, John, Jr. V, 389
Green, John, Jr. V, 493
Green, John, Sr. V, 493
Green, Jonathan IV, 1280
Green, Jonathan V, 61
Green, Jonathan V, 241
Green, Jonathan V, 242
Green, Jonathan V, 389
Green, Jonathan V, 563
Green, Jonathan E. V, 390
Green, Jonathan Evan V, 389
Green, Jonathan G. V, 270
Green, Jonathan H. IV, 1363
Green, Joseph I, 542
Green, Joseph I, 569
Green, Joseph I, 606
Green, Joseph I, 716
Green, Joseph II, 226
Green, Joseph II, 244
Green, Joseph II, 796
Green, Joseph II, 868
Green, Joseph IV, 34
Green, Joseph IV, 396
Green, Joseph IV, 473
Green, Joseph V, 61
Green, Joseph V, 241
Green, Joseph V, 332
Green, Joseph V, 333
Green, Joseph V, 388
Green, Joseph V, 390
Green, Joseph V, 437
Green, Joseph V, 840
Green, Joseph VI, 821
Green, Joseph Lindley V, 388
Green, Joseph Lindley V, 390
Green, Joseph P. V, 388
Green, Josiah IV, 396
Green, Josiah E. V, 389
Green, Judith A. VI, 821
Green, Julia V, 675
Green, Julia E. V, 242
Green, Julia E. V, 675
Green, Julia Ellen V, 241
Green, Juliann V, 387
Green, Kesiah VI, 924
Green, Keturah George IV, 1161
Green, Kezia V, 840
Green, Keziah V, 840
Green, L. M. V, 675
Green, La Vanchie May IV, 1208
Green, Laura E. V, 390
Green, Laura Elizabeth V, 563
Green, Laura Elma V, 389
Green, LaVanchie IV, 1161
Green, Leander V, 907
Green, Lena Smith IV, 1161
Green, Leslie IV, 1317
Green, Levi V, 61
Green, Levi V, 62
Green, Levi V, 219
Green, Levi V, 241
Green, Levi V, 242
Green, Levi V, 249
Green, Levi V, 253
Green, Levi V, 563
Green, Lewis IV, 1161
Green, Lewis C. II, 868
Green, Lewis G. II, 868
Green, Lieu Emma Catherine V, 389
Green, Lieuemma Catharine V, 907
Green, Lieuenna Catharine V, 563
Green, Lillian M. V, 332
Green, Lillian N. V, 333
Green, Lillie R. IV, 1161
Green, Lindley M. V, 675
Green, Lindley Murray V, 233
Green, Lindley Murray V, 242
Green, Linley Murray V, 241
Green, Lizzie IV, 1317
Green, Lizzie V, 564
Green, Lizzie V, 675
Green, Lizzie V, 710
Green, Lizzie E. V, 675
Green, Lois V, 675
Green, Louisa V, 387
Green, Lucy III, 138
Green, Lucy T. III, 138
Green, Lyda I, 962
Green, Lydda I, 962
Green, Lydda I, 964
Green, Lydia I, 1004
Green, Lydia II, 444
Green, Lydia II, 536
Green, Lydia II, 559
Green, Lydia II, 743
Green, Lydia II, 796
Green, Lydia II, 868
Green, Lydia III, 138
Green, Lydia III, 259
Green, Lydia IV, 34
Green, Lydia IV, 208
Green, Lydia IV, 396
Green, Lydia IV, 427
Green, Lydia IV, 627
Green, Lydia IV, 818
Green, Lydia V, 493
Green, Lydia V, 562
Green, Lydia V, 840
Green, Lydia VI, 178
Green, Lydia VI, 495
Green, Lydia VI, 513
Green, Lydia VI, 587
Green, Lydia Annetta V, 563
Green, Lydia C. III, 138
Green, Lydia C. III, 329
Green, Magalen VI, 924
Green, Mahala V, 563
Green, Mahlon V, 388
Green, Mahlon V, 389
Green, Malinda W. VI, 827
Green, Margaret I, 926
Green, Margaret I, 962
Green, Margaret I, 1008
Green, Margaret I, 1009
Green, Margaret II, 796
Green, Margaret II, 869
Green, Margaret Ann V, 270
Green, Margaret F. V, 241
Green, Margaret F. V, 269
Green, Margaret R. II, 869
Green, Margaret R. II, 933
Green, Margret VI, 596
Green, Maria IV, 331
Green, Maria IV, 340
Green, Maria IV, 395
Green, Maria Alma V, 333
Green, Maria Alma V, 907
Green, Maria Elma V, 333
Green, Maria M. V, 387
Green, Mariah Alma V, 332
Green, Mariah Alma V, 333
Green, Marius Edward IV, 208
Green, Martha I, 542
Green, Martha I, 880
Green, Martha III, 138
Green, Martha V, 387
Green, Martha Elizabeth V, 333
Green, Martha Elizabeth V, 389
Green, Martha Emily V, 389
Green, Martha G. IV, 970
Green, Martha G. Johnson IV, 958
Green, Martha Hannah V, 241
Green, Martha J. IV, 958
Green, Martishia I, 880
Green, Martitia I, 621
Green, Mary I, 527
Green, Mary I, 542
Green, Mary I, 569
Green, Mary I, 679
Green, Mary I, 716
Green, Mary I, 956
Green, Mary I, 962
Green, Mary I, 1001
Green, Mary I, 1004
Green, Mary II, 368
Green, Mary II, 536
Green, Mary II, 820
Green, Mary III, 323
Green, Mary IV, 89
Green, Mary IV, 102
Green, Mary IV, 208
Green, Mary IV, 282
Green, Mary IV, 290
Green, Mary IV, 331
Green, Mary IV, 359
Green, Mary IV, 395
Green, Mary IV, 396
Green, Mary IV, 444
Green, Mary IV, 473
Green, Mary IV, 518
Green, Mary IV, 526
Green, Mary IV, 529
Green, Mary IV, 560
Green, Mary IV, 561
Green, Mary IV, 713
Green, Mary IV, 905
Green, Mary IV, 907
Green, Mary IV, 957
Green, Mary IV, 1007
Green, Mary IV, 1161
Green, Mary IV, 1173
Green, Mary IV, 1195
Green, Mary IV, 1280
Green, Mary V, 61
Green, Mary V, 62
Green, Mary V, 82
Green, Mary V, 92
Green, Mary V, 227
Green, Mary V, 241
Green, Mary V, 242
Green, Mary V, 332
Green, Mary V, 388
Green, Mary V, 389
Green, Mary V, 390
Green, Mary V, 410
Green, Mary V, 411
Green, Mary V, 438
Green, Mary V, 493
Green, Mary V, 494
Green, Mary V, 538
Green, Mary V, 562
Green, Mary V, 563
Green, Mary V, 579
Green, Mary V, 603
Green, Mary V, 623
Green, Mary V, 809
Green, Mary V, 840
Green, Mary VI, 392
Green, Mary VI, 596
Green, Mary A. V, 576
Green, Mary Ada IV, 1280
Green, Mary Alice IV, 1161
Green, Mary Alice IV, 1208
Green, Mary Alice V, 242
Green, Mary Ann I, 715
Green, Mary Ann I, 716
Green, Mary Ann IV, 395
Green, Mary Ann IV, 396
Green, Mary Ann V, 242
Green, Mary Ann V, 389
Green, Mary Ann V, 397
Green, Mary Ann V, 563
Green, Mary Ann V, 576
Green, Mary Ann V, 604
Green, Mary Ann V, 675
Green, Mary Ann V, 683
Green, Mary Anna V, 241
Green, Mary E. IV, 208
Green, Mary E. V, 242
Green, Mary E. V, 389
Green, Mary E. V, 421
Green, Mary E. V, 494
Green, Mary E. V, 675
Green, Mary Elizabeth V, 493
Green, Mary Elmira II, 796
Green, Mary Elmira II, 868
Green, Mary Emely V, 563
Green, Mary Emily IV, 1280
Green, Mary Emily V, 61
Green, Mary Emily V, 388
Green, Mary Emily V, 563
Green, Mary Ethel V, 242
Green, Mary Ethel V, 675
Green, Mary H. V, 242
Green, Mary H. VI, 177
Green, Mary H. VI, 178
Green, Mary H. VI, 197
Green, Mary Hannah V, 241
Green, Mary Hannah V, 389
Green, Mary Jane V, 270
Green, Mary Jane V, 563
Green, Mary L. V, 389
Green, Mary L. V, 390
Green, Mary L. V, 494
Green, Mary Luela V, 333
Green, Mary Luella V, 242
Green, Mary M. V, 389
Green, Mary M. VI, 955
Green, Mary Pinkham IV, 208
Green, Mary S. IV, 713
Green, Mary T. IV, 1007
Green, Mary, Sr. I, 654
Green, Mary, Sr. I, 1004
Green, Matilda III, 123
Green, Matilda V, 242
Green, Matilda V, 494
Green, Matilda V, 675
Green, Matilda G. V, 242
Green, Matilda J. V, 242
Green, Matilda J. V, 333
Green, Matilda P. V, 242
Green, Maud G. V, 270
Green, Maud M. V, 998
Green, Meribah II, 796
Green, Milly V, 241
Green, Milly M. V, 241
Green, Minnie V, 172
Green, Miriam V, 389
Green, Miriam V, 429
Green, Moses II, 226
Green, Myrtle V, 172
Green, Myrtle Evelyn V, 563
Green, Myrtle Evelyn V, 564
Green, Nancy I, 593
Green, Nancy V, 689
Green, Nancy VI, 924
Green, Nancy E. V, 563
Green, Nancy E. V, 580
Green, Nancy Emily V, 563
Green, Nancy Jane V, 389
Green, Naomi V, 241
Green, Naomi V, 675
Green, Naomi C. V, 242
Green, Naomi C. V, 278
Green, Naomi C. V, 675
Green, Nelly VI, 956
Green, Noah IV, 1161
Green, Noah IV, 1236
Green, Obedience W. IV, 1280
Green, Olive V, 840
Green, Oliver III, 138
Green, Oralonzo V, 242
Green, Orie L. V, 242
Green, Orlando V, 563
Green, Orlando W. V, 563
Green, Owen W. V, 388
Green, Parker V, 389
Green, Parker V, 421
Green, Patience I, 654
Green, Patience I, 679
Green, Patience I, 691
Green, Paul IV, 1208
Green, Paul Franklin IV, 1161
Green, Paul Franklin IV, 1208
Green, Payton W. V, 389
Green, Pearl A. V, 998
Green, Pearl A. V, 999
Green, Percy V, 241
Green, Percy V, 242
Green, Percy V, 675
Green, Percy V, 687
Green, Percy E. V, 242
Green, Percy E. V, 494
Green, Percy E. V, 623
Green, Percy E. V, 675
Green, Peyton V, 390
Green, Peyton W. V, 389
Green, Phebe II, 536
Green, Phebe II, 743
Green, Phebe III, 85
Green, Phebe III, 86
Green, Phebe III, 138
Green, Phebe III, 257
Green, Phebe IV, 1252
Green, Phebe VI, 243
Green, Philip E. V, 623
Green, Phillis Pauline IV, 116
Green, Pliny F. V, 675
Green, Polly V, 61
Green, Polly V, 62
Green, Polly V, 494
Green, Polly V, 563
Green, Rachel I, 525
Green, Rachel I, 542
Green, Rachel I, 654
Green, Rachel I, 679
Green, Rachel I, 687
Green, Rachel I, 716
Green, Rachel I, 728
Green, Rachel I, 1004
Green, Rachel I, 1009
Green, Rachel II, 706
Green, Rachel III, 138
Green, Rachel IV, 208
Green, Rachel IV, 395
Green, Rachel IV, 396
Green, Rachel IV, 399
Green, Rachel IV, 427
Green, Rachel IV, 444
Green, Rachel IV, 446
Green, Rachel IV, 473
Green, Rachel IV, 478
Green, Rachel IV, 526
Green, Rachel IV, 527
Green, Rachel IV, 556
Green, Rachel IV, 1280
Green, Rachel V, 61
Green, Rachel V, 241
Green, Rachel V, 243
Green, Rachel V, 253
Green, Rachel V, 261
Green, Rachel V, 389
Green, Rachel V, 411
Green, Rachel V, 422
Green, Rachel V, 493
Green, Rachel V, 494
Green, Rachel V, 512
Green, Rachel V, 527
Green, Rachel V, 563
Green, Rachel V, 623
Green, Rachel V, 635
Green, Rachel V, 907
Green, Rachel Ann V, 241
Green, Rachel Ann V, 494
Green, Rachel Anna V, 242
Green, Rachel B. V, 61
Green, Rachel B. V, 563
Green, Rachel G. V, 270
Green, Rachel J. V, 227
Green, Rachel J. V, 241
Green, Rachel Jane IV, 1280
Green, Rachel M. V, 333
Green, Rachel M. V, 389
Green, Rachel M. V, 623
Green, Rachel, Jr. I, 1008
Green, Rachel, Jr. I, 1009
Green, Rebecca II, 226
Green, Rebecca III, 413
Green, Rebecca IV, 396
Green, Rebecca IV, 399
Green, Rebecca IV, 526
Green, Rebecca IV, 1059
Green, Rebecca IV, 1065
Green, Rebecca IV, 1149
Green, Rebecca IV, 1161
Green, Rebecca IV, 1280
Green, Rebecca V, 61
Green, Rebecca V, 62
Green, Rebecca V, 242
Green, Rebecca V, 244
Green, Rebecca V, 333
Green, Rebecca V, 563
Green, Rebecca V, 840
Green, Rebecca I. V, 388
Green, Rebecca S. II, 706
Green, Rebecca S. IV, 208
Green, Rebecca S. IV, 214
Green, Reuben I, 956
Green, Reuben I, 959
Green, Reuben I, 962
Green, Reuben I, 1004
Green, Reuben I, 1009
Green, Reuben IV, 1280
Green, Reuben V, 61
Green, Reuben V, 562
Green, Reuben V, 563
Green, Reuben V, 675
Green, Reuben VI, 924
Green, Rhoda I, 956
Green, Rhoda I, 959

een, Rhoda I, 962
een, Rhoda I, 1004
een, Rhoda I, 1009
een, Rhoda IV, 581
een, Rhoda V, 61
een, Rhoda V, 241
een, Rhoda V, 303
een, Rhoda V, 322
een, Rhoda V, 332
een, Rhoda V, 333
een, Rhoda V, 367
een, Rhoda V, 388
een, Rhoda V, 389
een, Rhoda V, 390
een, Rhoda V, 493
een, Rhoda V, 562
een, Rhoda V, 563
een, Rhoda V, 606
een, Rhoda Ann V, 61
een, Rhoda Ann V, 92
een, Rhoda Ann V, 563
een, Rhoda C. V, 333
een, Richard C. V, 232
een, Richard C. V, 241
een, Richard C. V, 242
een, Richard C. V, 494
een, Richard C. V, 563
een, Richard C. V, 675
een, Richard E. V, 675
een, Richard H. V, 242
een, Robert I, 654
een, Robert I, 962
een, Robert I, 1004
een, Robert II, 444
een, Robert II, 792
een, Robert IV, 1280
een, Robert V, 332
een, Robert V, 333
een, Robert V, 388
een, Robert V, 389
een, Robert V, 493
een, Robert V, 562
een, Robert V, 563
een, Robert V, 623
een, Robert A. V, 388
een, Robert Amos V, 390
een, Robert B. V, 388
een, Robert B. V, 389
een, Robert B. V, 390
een, Robert Barclay V, 389
een, Robert E. IV, 208
een, Robert Ellsworth V, 999
een, Robert Elsworth V, 998
een, Robert L. V, 333
een, Robert L. V, 388
een, Robert L. V, 389
een, Robert L. V, 493
een, Robert L. V, 494
een, Robert M. V, 623
een, Robert Meredith V, 241
een, Robert Oscar V, 333
een, Robert Oscar V, 389
een, Robert W. IV, 1280
een, Roda V, 388
een, Roda V, 437
een, Rodema Estel V, 241
een, Roland M. IV, 208
een, Ronald M. IV, 208
een, Rose II, 503
een, Rose II, 535
een, Rowland V, 493
een, Rowland V, 562
een, Rowland V, 563
een, Rowland V, 571
een, Rowland V, 602
een, Ruben V, 493
een, Ruby IV, 1320
een, Ruby J. IV, 1317
een, Rueben V, 493
een, Rufus III, 138
een, Ruth I, 679
een, Ruth I, 686
een, Ruth I, 962
een, Ruth I, 1001
een, Ruth I, 1004
een, Ruth I, 1009
een, Ruth IV, 395
een, Ruth IV, 1208
een, Ruth V, 241
een, Ruth V, 261
een, Ruth V, 284
een, Ruth V, 388
een, Ruth V, 389
een, Ruth V, 493
een, Ruth V, 494
een, Ruth V, 523
een, Ruth V, 952
een, Ruth VI, 392
een, Ruth VI, 403
een, Ruth VI, 596
een, Ruth Alice V, 270
Green, Ruth Emma V, 333
Green, Ruth L. IV, 527
Green, Ruth Lucile IV, 1161
Green, Ruth Lucile IV, 1208
Green, Ruth M. V, 241
Green, Ruth M. V, 623
Green, Ruth Matilda V, 241
Green, Ruth T. IV, 526
Green, S. V, 332
Green, Sadie V, 242
Green, Sadie V, 675
Green, Sadie D. V, 242
Green, Sadie D. V, 494
Green, Sadie D. V, 675
Green, Sadie M. V, 232
Green, Sadie M. V, 241
Green, Saline V, 333
Green, Sallie R. II, 868
Green, Sallie R. II, 869
Green, Sallie R. II, 887
Green, Sallie Rebecca II, 805
Green, Samantha V, 332
Green, Samantha N. V, 333
Green, Sampson IV, 395
Green, Sampson VI, 924
Green, Samson IV, 331
Green, Samuel II, 368
Green, Samuel IV, 208
Green, Samuel IV, 292
Green, Samuel IV, 331
Green, Samuel IV, 526
Green, Samuel IV, 958
Green, Samuel V, 388
Green, Samuel V, 563
Green, Samuel G. V, 563
Green, Samuel G. V, 675
Green, Samuel T. V, 563
Green, Sanford VI, 744
Green, Sarah I, 715
Green, Sarah I, 716
Green, Sarah II, 226
Green, Sarah II, 244
Green, Sarah II, 368
Green, Sarah II, 472
Green, Sarah II, 535
Green, Sarah II, 536
Green, Sarah III, 138
Green, Sarah III, 201
Green, Sarah III, 240
Green, Sarah III, 284
Green, Sarah III, 338
Green, Sarah IV, 395
Green, Sarah IV, 396
Green, Sarah IV, 425
Green, Sarah IV, 473
Green, Sarah IV, 526
Green, Sarah IV, 529
Green, Sarah V, 242
Green, Sarah V, 269
Green, Sarah V, 385
Green, Sarah V, 389
Green, Sarah V, 493
Green, Sarah V, 494
Green, Sarah V, 840
Green, Sarah V, 845
Green, Sarah VI, 744
Green, Sarah A. III, 138
Green, Sarah A. V, 389
Green, Sarah Alcinda V, 378
Green, Sarah Ann V, 389
Green, Sarah Ann V, 390
Green, Sarah Ann V, 907
Green, Sarah E. III, 222
Green, Sarah Ellen V, 388
Green, Sarah Ellen V, 390
Green, Sarah Huff V, 241
Green, Sarah Jane V, 389
Green, Sarah M. V, 493
Green, Serena B. II, 868
Green, Serena B. II, 869
Green, Serena B. II, 938
Green, Seth W. IV, 1320
Green, Sewel V, 332
Green, Sewel V, 493
Green, Sewel V, 907
Green, Sewell V, 333
Green, Sewell V, 907
Green, Sophia IV, 526
Green, Sophia IV, 527
Green, Sophia IV, 536
Green, Sophia V, 564
Green, Sophia Jane VI, 924
Green, Stanley IV, 1161
Green, Stella IV, 1161
Green, Stella Mae IV, 1208
Green, Stella May IV, 1161
Green, Stella May V, 242
Green, Stephen III, 138
Green, Stephen III, 259
Green, Stephen III, 329
Green, Susan Mary V, 333
Green, Susan Mary V, 389
Green, Susann V, 562
Green, Susanna I, 1001
Green, Susanna I, 1009
Green, Susanna I, 1010
Green, Susanna IV, 1280
Green, Susanna V, 389
Green, Susanna V, 562
Green, Susanna V, 563
Green, Susanna Catharine V, 907
Green, Susannah I, 962
Green, Susannah V, 61
Green, Susannah V, 386
Green, Susannah V, 389
Green, Susannah V, 493
Green, Susannah V, 494
Green, Susannah V, 554
Green, Susannah V, 563
Green, Susannah V, 587
Green, Susannah V, 675
Green, Sylvia VI, 821
Green, T. V, 332
Green, Tamar V, 333
Green, Tamer V, 333
Green, Tamer V, 907
Green, Temperance III, 138
Green, Theodocia Eva V, 333
Green, Theodocia Eva V, 389
Green, Thomas II, 194
Green, Thomas II, 225
Green, Thomas II, 226
Green, Thomas III, 138
Green, Thomas IV, 331
Green, Thomas IV, 526
Green, Thomas IV, 527
Green, Thomas IV, 713
Green, Thomas IV, 818
Green, Thomas V, 61
Green, Thomas V, 563
Green, Thomas V, 840
Green, Thomas A. III, 138
Green, Thomas E. V, 332
Green, Thomas E. V, 390
Green, Thomas Edgar V, 332
Green, Thomas Elwood V, 388
Green, Thomas F. V, 270
Green, Thomas Homer V, 333
Green, Thomas Homer V, 389
Green, Thomas T. V, 241
Green, Thomas T. V, 242
Green, Thomas, Jr. V, 61
Green, Thos. E. IV, 208
Green, Townsend III, 138
Green, Uriah IV, 1161
Green, Vanchie IV, 1208
Green, Viola IV, 208
Green, Walter II, 933
Green, Walter V, 390
Green, Walter Douglas V, 389
Green, Walter W. II, 868
Green, Walter W. II, 869
Green, Walter W. II, 887
Green, Walter W. II, 933
Green, Walter W. II, 938
Green, Warren J. V, 241
Green, Wd. Alice II, 796
Green, Wd. Ann V, 61
Green, Wd. Hannah M. II, 796
Green, Wd. Lydia M. II, 792
Green, William I, 542
Green, William I, 880
Green, William II, 706
Green, William III, 138
Green, William IV, 395
Green, William IV, 396
Green, William IV, 399
Green, William IV, 427
Green, William IV, 444
Green, William IV, 473
Green, William IV, 478
Green, William IV, 526
Green, William V, 61
Green, William V, 62
Green, William V, 269
Green, William V, 387
Green, William V, 390
Green, William V, 494
Green, William V, 563
Green, William VI, 744
Green, William VI, 821
Green, William VI, 924
Green, William D. V, 242
Green, William D. V, 494
Green, William D. V, 675
Green, William Dewsbury V, 241
Green, William E. V, 390
Green, William Edgerton V, 241
Green, William Edgerton V, 389
Green, William Edgerton V, 390
Green, William Edward I, 880
Green, William G. III, 138
Green, William G. V, 61
Green, William G. V, 389
Green, William G. V, 563
Green, William Henry III, 138
Green, William Jesse V, 840
Green, William Orlando V, 387
Green, William P. V, 241
Green, William P. V, 242
Green, William T. V, 563
Green, William W. V, 388
Green, William Walter V, 333
Green, Willie V, 172
Green, Willis IV, 1161
Green, Wilson V, 493
Green, Wilson V, 494
Green, Wm. II, 535
Green, Wm. III, 138
Green, Wm. IV, 395
Green, Wm. IV, 446
Green, Wm. IV, 473
Green, Wm. V, 563
Green, Wm. Chapman II, 869
Green, Wm. Chapman II, 924
Green, Wm. D. V, 675
Green, Wm. Edward I, 880
Green, Wm. G. V, 563
Green, Wm. Henry III, 275
Green, Wm. K. IV, 1363
Green, Wm. P. IV, 1280
Green, Zacharias I, 390
Greenamre, Iva M. IV, 958
Greenamyer, Charles IV, 958
Greenamyer, Charles E. IV, 958
Greenamyer, Clarence IV, 958
Greenamyer, Ella IV, 1317
Greenamyer, Elsie L. IV, 958
Greenamyer, Emma IV, 958
Greenamyer, Emma S. IV, 958
Greenamyer, Fannie IV, 1317
Greenamyer, Ira M. IV, 958
Greenamyer, Iva M. IV, 958
Greenamyer, John IV, 958
Greenamyer, John D. IV, 958
Greenamyer, Mary IV, 958
Greenamyer, Mary M. IV, 958
Greenamyer, Maud IV, 958
Greenamyer, Rosco L. IV, 958
Greenamyer, S. IV, 1317
Greenamyer, Wm. H. IV, 958
Greenawalt, Effie Marie IV, 958
Greenawalt, Effie Marie IV, 1018
Greenawalt, Fred C. IV, 1018
Greenawalt, Iva Ola IV, 925
Greenawalt, Iva Ola IV, 958
Greenawalt, John S. IV, 925
Greenawalt, John S. IV, 958
Greenawalt, John S. IV, 1018
Greenawalt, Lewis Leon IV, 958
Greenawalt, Louisa J. IV, 958
Greenawalt, Luella IV, 958
Greenawalt, Luella J. IV, 925
Greenawalt, Luella J. IV, 1018
Greenawalt, Mary IV, 958
Greenawalt, Theressa Mary IV, 958
Greenawalt, Theressa May IV, 958
Greenaway, Rebecca II, 368
Greenaway, Rebecca II, 463
Greenaway, Rebecca II, 536
Greenberg, Jacob III, 138
Greenberg, Julius III, 138
Greenberg, Julius R. III, 138
Greenberg, Louisa III, 138
Greenberg, Palma III, 138
Greene, Alice Doan V, 687
Greene, Anna V, 241
Greene, Anna Jenkins V, 242
Greene, Arthur B. III, 138
Greene, Arthur W. III, 342
Greene, Catharine III, 54
Greene, Charlotte E. V, 284
Greene, Dr. Lindley M. V, 242
Greene, Edward VI, 999
Greene, Emily VI, 744
Greene, Emily VI, 772
Greene, Emily Reynolds VI, 744
Greene, George VI, 744
Greene, Hannah M. VI, 744
Greene, Hazel V, 284
Greene, Isaac V, 242
Greene, John T. III, 138
Greene, Lucy III, 138
Greene, Lucy T. III, 138
Greene, Lydia VI, 744
Greene, Martha III, 138
Greene, Mary Elmira VI, 744
Greene, Mary Luella V, 242
Greene, Myra V, 922
Greene, N. III, 342
Greene, Naomi V, 284
Greene, Percy V, 241
Greene, Robert Meredith V, 241
Greene, Rufus III, 138
Greene, Ruth Matilda V, 241
Greene, Thomas III, 138
Greene, Thomas IV, 713
Greene, Thomas A. III, 138
Greene, Warren J. V, 241
Greene, Wd. Emily VI, 731
Greene, William VI, 772
Greene, Wm. VI, 731
Greenfield, Margaret II, 998
Greenfield, Margaret II, 1005
Greenfield, Mary IV, 527
Greenfield, Mary IV, 530
Greenfield, Mary IV, 713
Greenfield, Mary IV, 973
Greenfield, Verlin IV, 713
Greenhalgh, Sarah A. IV, 208
Greenleaf, Caspar II, 368
Greenleaf, Catharine II, 368
Greenleaf, Catharine, Jr. II, 368
Greenleaf, Dorothy II, 869
Greenleaf, Elizabeth II, 368
Greenleaf, Elizabeth II, 869
Greenleaf, Elizabeth II, 879
Greenleaf, Isaac II, 368
Greenleaf, Sarah II, 368
Greenleaf, Wm. II, 869
Greenleafe, Caspar II, 368
Greenleafe, Catharine, Jr. II, 368
Greenleafe, Catherine II, 536
Greenleafe, Catherine II, 651
Greenleafe, Cathrine II, 536
Greenleafe, Cathrine II, 690
Greenleafe, Elizabeth II, 480
Greenleafe, Elizabeth II, 536
Greenleafe, Elizabeth II, 651
Greenleafe, Isaac II, 368
Greenleafe, Isaac II, 480
Greenleafe, Isaac II, 536
Greenleafe, Isaac II, 651
Greenleafe, Isaac II, 690
Greenleafe, Sarah II, 368
Greenleafe, Sarah II, 501
Greenleafe, Sarah II, 536
Greenleafe, Wd. Dorothy II, 796
Greenleafe, William II, 796
Greenleafe, Wm. II, 796
Greenlease, Lydia VI, 624
Greenlease, Lydia VI, 641
Greenlee, Hannah IV, 31
Greenlee, Hannah IV, 34
Greenlief, Hannah IV, 323
Greenlief, Hannah IV, 331
Greenmayer, Eva IV, 708
Greenmayer, George IV, 708
Greenmayer, Lorinda IV, 708
Greenoak, Ann III, 138
Greenup, John Naylor II, 536
Greenup, Mary II, 536
Greenup, Mary II, 605
Greenwalt, Iva Ola IV, 958
Greenwalt, John S. IV, 958
Greenwalt, Louisa J. IV, 958
Greenwalt, Theressa Mary IV, 958
Greenwood, Abram VI, 976
Greenwood, Agnes V, 924
Greenwood, Bailey VI, 924
Greenwood, Bartlette VI, 821
Greenwood, Benj. V, 924
Greenwood, Benjamin IV, 1218
Greenwood, Benson VI, 924
Greenwood, Catharine VI, 966
Greenwood, Catherine VI, 924
Greenwood, Clemsey VI, 986
Greenwood, Demarcus VI, 950
Greenwood, Demarquis VI, 924
Greenwood, Elizabeth VI, 914
Greenwood, James VI, 924
Greenwood, Joannah VI, 976
Greenwood, John VI, 924
Greenwood, Lena VI, 984
Greenwood, Lucy VI, 924
Greenwood, Mariah VI, 976
Greenwood, Martha IV, 958
Greenwood, Martha IV, 1003
Greenwood, Mary III, 138
Greenwood, Minerva Ann VI, 924
Greenwood, Nancy VI, 821
Greenwood, Nancy VI, 924
Greenwood, Necy VI, 924
Greenwood, Richard VI, 914
Greenwood, Richard VI, 916
Greenwood, Richard VI, 924
Greenwood, Richard VI, 966
Greenwood, Richard VI, 986
Greenwood, Samuel VI, 994
Greenwood, Sinah VI, 976
Greenwood, Sinea VI, 946

Greenwood, Sophia VI, 984
Greenwood, Susanna V, 924
Greenwood, William VI, 960
Greenwood, Wm. VI, 976
Greer, Abraham I, 1140
Greer, Amanda I, 1152
Greer, Amanda M. I, 1140
Greer, Ann VI, 904
Greer, Ann Mallcum II, 998
Greer, Asa VI, 924
Greer, Bird VI, 924
Greer, Bowker W. VI, 924
Greer, Catharine VI, 924
Greer, Cora J. I, 1152
Greer, Dr. Will A. I, 1152
Greer, Drucilla VI, 924
Greer, Elizabeth C. I, 1140
Greer, Frank A. I, 1152
Greer, Henry VI, 924
Greer, James VI, 924
Greer, James W. VI, 924
Greer, Jane II, 998
Greer, Jane III, 138
Greer, John J. I, 1152
Greer, John Sherman I, 1140
Greer, Joseph VI, 924
Greer, Lewsey VI, 924
Greer, Lydia V, 62
Greer, Magdalene VI, 924
Greer, Martin VI, 924
Greer, Mary VI, 924
Greer, Nancy Demoss VI, 929
Greer, Nathan VI, 924
Greer, Parthenia V, 952
Greer, Rebeckah VI, 924
Greer, Robert B. VI, 627
Greer, Roscoe Leroy I, 1140
Greer, S. L. I, 1152
Greer, Samuel III, 138
Greer, Samuel III, 139
Greer, Samuel E. I, 1140
Greer, Samuel L. I, 1140
Greer, Sophia Jane VI, 924
Greer, Susanna VI, 924
Greer, Tempey VI, 929
Greer, Thomas B. VI, 890
Greer, Virginia Neill VI, 627
Greer, Wd. Anne VI, 924
Greer, William A. I, 1140
Greesey, Edmund VI, 1016
Greetham, Eva IV, 1317
Greeves, Dorothy II, 524
Greeves, Dorothy II, 536
Greeves, Elizabeth Coates II, 536
Greeves, Elizabeth Coates II, 616
Greeves, James R. II, 524
Greeves, James R. II, 536
Greeves, Mary II, 536
Greeves, Mary II, 616
Greeves, Robert II, 536
Greeves, Sally Ann II, 524
Greeves, Sally Ann II, 536
Greeves, Samuel II, 524
Greeves, Samuel II, 536
Greeves, Sarah II, 368
Greeves, Sarah II, 869
Greeves, Thomas II, 368
Greeves, Thomas II, 536
Greeves, Thomas II, 616
Greeves, Wm. II, 536
Greeves, Wm. II, 616
Greg, Armested VI, 723
Greg, Jacob I, 390
Greg, Lydia VI, 723
Greg, Mahlon II, 536
Greg, Rebekah I, 380
Greg, Rebekah I, 390
Greg, Susannah VI, 485
Gregg, ??? VI, 293
Gregg, ??? VI, 508
Gregg, ??? VI, 634
Gregg, Aaron VI, 498
Gregg, Aaron VI, 641
Gregg, Abel IV, 89
Gregg, Abel IV, 147
Gregg, Abel IV, 208
Gregg, Abel IV, 326
Gregg, Abel IV, 331
Gregg, Abel IV, 527
Gregg, Abel IV, 1162
Gregg, Abel VI, 644
Gregg, Abigail IV, 208
Gregg, Abigail IV, 332
Gregg, Abigail IV, 359
Gregg, Abigail IV, 396
Gregg, Abner IV, 34
Gregg, Abner IV, 147
Gregg, Abner IV, 156
Gregg, Abner IV, 331
Gregg, Abner IV, 332
Gregg, Abner IV, 333
Gregg, Abner IV, 356
Gregg, Abner IV, 357
Gregg, Abner IV, 358
Gregg, Abner IV, 396
Gregg, Abner V, 952
Gregg, Abner VI, 312
Gregg, Abner VI, 333
Gregg, Abner VI, 336
Gregg, Abner VI, 392
Gregg, Abner VI, 496
Gregg, Abner VI, 497
Gregg, Abner VI, 503
Gregg, Abner VI, 563
Gregg, Abner VI, 641
Gregg, Abner VI, 642
Gregg, Abner VI, 644
Gregg, Abner VI, 705
Gregg, Abner, Sr. IV, 332
Gregg, Abner, Sr. IV, 335
Gregg, Abner, Sr. VI, 642
Gregg, Abner, Sr. VI, 647
Gregg, Abner, Sr. VI, 648
Gregg, Abraham IV, 331
Gregg, Abraham IV, 349
Gregg, Agnes VI, 643
Gregg, Agnes VI, 645
Gregg, Agness VI, 643
Gregg, Agness VI, 723
Gregg, Albeniah VI, 312
Gregg, Albert IV, 333
Gregg, Albert VI, 642
Gregg, Albina II, 815
Gregg, Albina IV, 147
Gregg, Albina IV, 331
Gregg, Albina IV, 356
Gregg, Albina IV, 452
Gregg, Albina IV, 453
Gregg, Albina VI, 312
Gregg, Albina VI, 496
Gregg, Albina VI, 519
Gregg, Albinah IV, 396
Gregg, Albinah VI, 494
Gregg, Albinah VI, 518
Gregg, Albinah VI, 522
Gregg, Albinah VI, 642
Gregg, Albinah VI, 661
Gregg, Albinah VI, 664
Gregg, Albinah VI, 744
Gregg, Albinah VI, 754
Gregg, Albinah VI, 758
Gregg, Alfred IV, 332
Gregg, Alfred IV, 396
Gregg, Alice IV, 208
Gregg, Alma A. V, 62
Gregg, Alma J. IV, 1162
Gregg, Alma W. IV, 1162
Gregg, Almary V, 62
Gregg, Alphard IV, 147
Gregg, Amey VI, 498
Gregg, Amos II, 536
Gregg, Amos II, 590
Gregg, Amos II, 998
Gregg, Amos II, 1043
Gregg, Amos IV, 333
Gregg, Amos VI, 496
Gregg, Amos VI, 497
Gregg, Amy IV, 34
Gregg, Amy IV, 69
Gregg, Amy IV, 89
Gregg, Amy IV, 98
Gregg, Amy IV, 332
Gregg, Amy IV, 335
Gregg, Amy IV, 396
Gregg, Amy V, 840
Gregg, Amy VI, 393
Gregg, Amy VI, 496
Gregg, Amy VI, 498
Gregg, Amy VI, 637
Gregg, Amy VI, 642
Gregg, Ann II, 73
Gregg, Ann II, 112
Gregg, Ann II, 536
Gregg, Ann II, 590
Gregg, Ann IV, 33
Gregg, Ann IV, 34
Gregg, Ann IV, 35
Gregg, Ann IV, 89
Gregg, Ann IV, 147
Gregg, Ann IV, 208
Gregg, Ann IV, 331
Gregg, Ann IV, 332
Gregg, Ann IV, 333
Gregg, Ann IV, 336
Gregg, Ann IV, 337
Gregg, Ann IV, 527
Gregg, Ann IV, 534
Gregg, Ann IV, 1162
Gregg, Ann IV, 1197
Gregg, Ann IV, 1280
Gregg, Ann V, 62
Gregg, Ann VI, 312
Gregg, Ann VI, 336
Gregg, Ann VI, 392
Gregg, Ann VI, 467
Gregg, Ann VI, 495
Gregg, Ann VI, 496
Gregg, Ann VI, 497
Gregg, Ann VI, 561
Gregg, Ann VI, 636
Gregg, Ann VI, 642
Gregg, Ann VI, 644
Gregg, Ann VI, 701
Gregg, Anna IV, 147
Gregg, Anna IV, 149
Gregg, Anna IV, 332
Gregg, Anna IV, 335
Gregg, Anna VI, 643
Gregg, Anna Elizabeth V, 743
Gregg, Anna Maria VI, 642
Gregg, Anna Maria VI, 662
Gregg, Anna Maria VI, 663
Gregg, Anne IV, 527
Gregg, Anne VI, 312
Gregg, Annie E. V, 740
Gregg, Anthony Burton, Jr. II, 998
Gregg, Aquila IV, 147
Gregg, Aquilla IV, 396
Gregg, Armistead M. VI, 682
Gregg, Armisted M. VI, 642
Gregg, Armisted M. VI, 722
Gregg, Aron VI, 392
Gregg, Aron VI, 496
Gregg, Asa IV, 208
Gregg, Asa IV, 332
Gregg, Asa IV, 1162
Gregg, Asahel IV, 527
Gregg, Asenath IV, 147
Gregg, Asenath IV, 153
Gregg, Asenath IV, 329
Gregg, Asenath IV, 332
Gregg, Asenath IV, 333
Gregg, Asenath IV, 340
Gregg, Asenath IV, 342
Gregg, Asenath IV, 352
Gregg, Asenath IV, 396
Gregg, Asenath VI, 644
Gregg, Asenath VI, 675
Gregg, B. Mary VI, 656
Gregg, B. May VI, 642
Gregg, B. May VI, 643
Gregg, B. May VI, 674
Gregg, Balsena VI, 664
Gregg, Balsena VI, 714
Gregg, Bani IV, 89
Gregg, Barbara May VI, 642
Gregg, Benjamin V, 37
Gregg, Benjamin W. IV, 208
Gregg, Benjamin W. IV, 396
Gregg, Bennet IV, 396
Gregg, Bennett IV, 332
Gregg, Betsey VI, 642
Gregg, Betsey VI, 653
Gregg, Betsy Ann IV, 527
Gregg, Betty Ann IV, 208
Gregg, Betty Ann IV, 1162
Gregg, Beula Ann IV, 527
Gregg, Beulahann IV, 527
Gregg, Bula Ann IV, 581
Gregg, Burr IV, 332
Gregg, Burr IV, 396
Gregg, Caiphas IV, 34
Gregg, Caleb IV, 147
Gregg, Caleb IV, 332
Gregg, Caleb IV, 386
Gregg, Caleb IV, 396
Gregg, Caleb IV, 581
Gregg, Caleb IV, 713
Gregg, Caleb IV, 1059
Gregg, Caleb IV, 1082
Gregg, Caleb VI, 642
Gregg, Carleton IV, 527
Gregg, Carlton IV, 581
Gregg, Carrie D. V, 62
Gregg, Catharine IV, 69
Gregg, Catherine IV, 42
Gregg, Catherine IV, 89
Gregg, Cenith IV, 391
Gregg, Cephas IV, 34
Gregg, Cephas IV, 89
Gregg, Charles H. V, 740
Gregg, Charles H. V, 743
Gregg, Charles Lewis IV, 35
Gregg, Cinah IV, 396
Gregg, Cora Elma V. VI, 642
Gregg, Cora Elma V. VI, 692
Gregg, Daniel IV, 34
Gregg, Daniel IV, 1059
Gregg, Daniel VI, 642
Gregg, David IV, 208
Gregg, David IV, 527
Gregg, David IV, 1059
Gregg, David IV, 1162
Gregg, Deaf John VI, 485
Gregg, Deborah II, 536
Gregg, Deborah II, 590
Gregg, Deborah II, 998
Gregg, Deborah IV, 396
Gregg, Deborah IV, 397
Gregg, Deborah IV, 406
Gregg, Dinah IV, 34
Gregg, Dinah IV, 89
Gregg, Dinah VI, 496
Gregg, Dinah VI, 497
Gregg, Dinah VI, 498
Gregg, Dinah VI, 522
Gregg, Dinah VI, 549
Gregg, Dinah VI, 559
Gregg, Dinah VI, 562
Gregg, Dinah VI, 642
Gregg, Dinah VI, 660
Gregg, Dinah VI, 674
Gregg, Dinah VI, 714
Gregg, Dinah VI, 715
Gregg, Dinah VI, 716
Gregg, Doris Elaine VI, 643
Gregg, Dr. Mahlon II, 796
Gregg, Dumb John VI, 485
Gregg, Edgar IV, 1162
Gregg, Edgar V, 62
Gregg, Edgar A. V, 62
Gregg, Edgar B. VI, 642
Gregg, Edgar B. VI, 644
Gregg, Edgar B. VI, 682
Gregg, Edgar B. VI, 692
Gregg, Edgar Bentley VI, 642
Gregg, Edgar Bentley VI, 656
Gregg, Edgar Bently VI, 631
Gregg, Edgar Bently VI, 643
Gregg, Edgar Bently VI, 680
Gregg, Edith IV, 147
Gregg, Edith IV, 327
Gregg, Edith IV, 332
Gregg, Edith VI, 644
Gregg, Edith W. VI, 643
Gregg, Edward Bentley VI, 642
Gregg, Edward Bentley VI, 643
Gregg, Edward Bentley VI, 656
Gregg, Edward Bently VI, 674
Gregg, Eli IV, 89
Gregg, Eli IV, 208
Gregg, Eli IV, 308
Gregg, Eli IV, 332
Gregg, Eli IV, 1161
Gregg, Eli IV, 1162
Gregg, Eli V, 62
Gregg, Eli VI, 644
Gregg, Elias IV, 332
Gregg, Elias IV, 333
Gregg, Elias IV, 396
Gregg, Elihu IV, 89
Gregg, Elijah IV, 332
Gregg, Elijah IV, 333
Gregg, Elijah IV, 336
Gregg, Elijah IV, 352
Gregg, Elijah IV, 396
Gregg, Elijah IV, 397
Gregg, Elijah Burr IV, 147
Gregg, Elijah W. IV, 1059
Gregg, Elijah, W. IV, 396
Gregg, Elisha VI, 528
Gregg, Elisha VI, 744
Gregg, Eliza IV, 332
Gregg, Eliza IV, 356
Gregg, Eliza IV, 396
Gregg, Eliza IV, 527
Gregg, Elizabeth II, 368
Gregg, Elizabeth II, 536
Gregg, Elizabeth II, 869
Gregg, Elizabeth II, 998
Gregg, Elizabeth II, 1000
Gregg, Elizabeth II, 1043
Gregg, Elizabeth IV, 22
Gregg, Elizabeth IV, 34
Gregg, Elizabeth IV, 35
Gregg, Elizabeth IV, 40
Gregg, Elizabeth IV, 50
Gregg, Elizabeth IV, 69
Gregg, Elizabeth IV, 322
Gregg, Elizabeth IV, 332
Gregg, Elizabeth IV, 333
Gregg, Elizabeth IV, 343
Gregg, Elizabeth IV, 396
Gregg, Elizabeth IV, 417
Gregg, Elizabeth IV, 581
Gregg, Elizabeth IV, 1276
Gregg, Elizabeth IV, 1280
Gregg, Elizabeth VI, 392
Gregg, Elizabeth VI, 495
Gregg, Elizabeth VI, 496
Gregg, Elizabeth VI, 498
Gregg, Elizabeth VI, 528
Gregg, Elizabeth VI, 552
Gregg, Elizabeth VI, 553
Gregg, Elizabeth VI, 580
Gregg, Elizabeth VI, 642
Gregg, Elizabeth VI, 643
Gregg, Elizabeth VI, 664
Gregg, Elizabeth C. VI, 643
Gregg, Elizabeth C. VI, 645
Gregg, Elizabeth C. VI, 721
Gregg, Elizabeth C. VI, 723
Gregg, Elizabeth N. VI, 643
Gregg, Elizabeth W. IV, 396
Gregg, Elizabethson, Jr. VI, 49
Gregg, Ella IV, 208
Gregg, Ellis IV, 147
Gregg, Ellis V, 62
Gregg, Elmira IV, 208
Gregg, Elmira IV, 396
Gregg, Elwood IV, 1059
Gregg, Emer IV, 1059
Gregg, Emma Gibson VI, 643
Gregg, Emma W. VI, 645
Gregg, Emmer IV, 1059
Gregg, Emmett IV, 1236
Gregg, Ester IV, 321
Gregg, Ester IV, 332
Gregg, Esther IV, 147
Gregg, Esther V, 952
Gregg, Esther VI, 371
Gregg, Esther VI, 392
Gregg, Esther VI, 393
Gregg, Esther VI, 622
Gregg, Esther VI, 642
Gregg, Esther VI, 643
Gregg, Eula IV, 527
Gregg, Frank B. V, 62
Gregg, Geo. G. VI, 722
Gregg, George IV, 34
Gregg, George IV, 35
Gregg, George IV, 89
Gregg, George VI, 485
Gregg, George VI, 496
Gregg, George VI, 497
Gregg, George VI, 498
Gregg, George VI, 528
Gregg, George VI, 573
Gregg, George G. VI, 642
Gregg, George G. VI, 643
Gregg, George G. VI, 722
Gregg, George Holmes VI, 643
Gregg, George Holmes VI, 674
Gregg, George, Jr. VI, 392
Gregg, George, Jr. VI, 496
Gregg, Guli Elma IV, 147
Gregg, Guli Elma V, 62
Gregg, Gulielma IV, 89
Gregg, Gulielma IV, 147
Gregg, Gulielma IV, 208
Gregg, Gulielma IV, 218
Gregg, Gulielma IV, 332
Gregg, Gulielma IV, 339
Gregg, Gulielma VI, 644
Gregg, Hamelton IV, 333
Gregg, Hancock II, 536
Gregg, Hannah IV, 208
Gregg, Hannah IV, 319
Gregg, Hannah IV, 323
Gregg, Hannah IV, 326
Gregg, Hannah IV, 331
Gregg, Hannah IV, 332
Gregg, Hannah IV, 333
Gregg, Hannah IV, 341
Gregg, Hannah IV, 343
Gregg, Hannah IV, 346
Gregg, Hannah IV, 396
Gregg, Hannah IV, 421
Gregg, Hannah IV, 527
Gregg, Hannah IV, 581
Gregg, Hannah IV, 673
Gregg, Hannah IV, 713
Gregg, Hannah IV, 1059
Gregg, Hannah IV, 1162
Gregg, Hannah VI, 393
Gregg, Hannah VI, 496
Gregg, Hannah VI, 497
Gregg, Hannah VI, 499
Gregg, Hannah VI, 539
Gregg, Hannah VI, 565
Gregg, Hannah VI, 567
Gregg, Hannah VI, 622
Gregg, Hannah VI, 640
Gregg, Hannah VI, 643
Gregg, Hannah VI, 684
Gregg, Hannah B. IV, 333
Gregg, Hannah B. IV, 1025
Gregg, Hannah Maria VI, 642
Gregg, Hannah Priscilla IV, 32
Gregg, Hannah Priscilla IV, 33
Gregg, Hannah, Sr. IV, 396
Gregg, Hanson IV, 332
Gregg, Hanson IV, 333
Gregg, Hanson IV, 527

egg, Harman John VI, 642
egg, Harmon John VI, 663
egg, Harriet IV, 332
egg, Harriet IV, 352
egg, Harriet Ann VI, 643
egg, Harriet Ann VI, 721
egg, Harriett IV, 332
egg, Harriett IV, 396
egg, Harriett Ann VI, 723
egg, Hazel V, 675
egg, Helen Ely VI, 643
egg, Henly VI, 643
egg, Henry IV, 34
egg, Henry IV, 396
egg, Henry IV, 581
egg, Henry IV, 1059
egg, Henry H. VI, 642
egg, Hester VI, 642
egg, Hiram IV, 396
egg, Hiram V, 33
egg, Hiram V, 62
regg, Horace L. VI, 631
regg, Horace L. VI, 642
regg, Horace L. VI, 643
regg, Horace L., Jr. VI, 643
regg, Isaac IV, 34
regg, Isaac IV, 208
regg, Israel IV, 89
regg, Israel IV, 332
regg, Israel IV, 1162
regg, Israel VI, 497
regg, Israel VI, 596
regg, Israel VI, 643
regg, J. C. IV, 1252
regg, Jacob IV, 147
regg, Jacob IV, 321
regg, Jacob IV, 332
regg, Jacob IV, 335
regg, Jacob IV, 336
regg, Jacob IV, 345
regg, Jacob IV, 396
regg, Jacob VI, 643
regg, Jacob VI, 701
regg, James IV, 147
regg, James IV, 208
regg, James IV, 332
regg, James IV, 359
regg, James IV, 396
regg, James IV, 527
regg, James IV, 581
regg, James VI, 393
regg, James VI, 643
regg, James M. IV, 1252
regg, Jane II, 986
regg, Jane II, 998
regg, Jane IV, 332
regg, Jane VI, 559
regg, Jane Sheward VI, 497
regg, Jehu IV, 89
regg, Jesse IV, 89
regg, Jesse IV, 147
regg, Jesse IV, 208
regg, Jesse IV, 332
regg, Jesse IV, 527
regg, Jesse IV, 1162
regg, Jesse VI, 643
regg, Jesse VI, 644
regg, Jesse Medcelf IV, 147
regg, Jesse Thomas VI, 497
regg, Johb VI, 562
regg, John II, 536
regg, John II, 590
regg, John II, 998
regg, John II, 1000
regg, John IV, 34
regg, John IV, 89
regg, John IV, 147
regg, John IV, 332
regg, John IV, 334
regg, John IV, 335
regg, John IV, 340
regg, John IV, 396
regg, John VI, 312
regg, John VI, 371
regg, John VI, 392
regg, John VI, 393
regg, John VI, 485
regg, John VI, 495
regg, John VI, 496
regg, John VI, 497
regg, John VI, 498
regg, John VI, 500
regg, John VI, 506
regg, John VI, 559
regg, John VI, 563
regg, John VI, 565
regg, John VI, 567
regg, John VI, 622
regg, John VI, 640
regg, John VI, 641
regg, John VI, 643
Gregg, John VI, 644
Gregg, John VI, 645
Gregg, John VI, 648
Gregg, John VI, 652
Gregg, John VI, 653
Gregg, John VI, 654
Gregg, John VI, 705
Gregg, John VI, 707
Gregg, John VI, 721
Gregg, John VI, 722
Gregg, John VI, 723
Gregg, John Dumb VI, 496
Gregg, John William VI, 645
Gregg, John William VI, 723
Gregg, John Wm. VI, 643
Gregg, John Wm. VI, 723
Gregg, John, Jr. IV, 396
Gregg, John, Jr. VI, 497
Gregg, Jonas IV, 35
Gregg, Jonas IV, 332
Gregg, Jonas IV, 581
Gregg, Jonathan IV, 333
Gregg, Jonathan IV, 396
Gregg, Joseph IV, 34
Gregg, Joseph IV, 58
Gregg, Joseph IV, 89
Gregg, Joseph IV, 581
Gregg, Joseph IV, 1059
Gregg, Joseph V, 740
Gregg, Joseph VI, 643
Gregg, Joseph G. VI, 643
Gregg, Joseph W. IV, 208
Gregg, Joseph W. IV, 396
Gregg, Joseph Wright IV, 396
Gregg, Joshua IV, 396
Gregg, Joshua VI, 497
Gregg, Joshua VI, 596
Gregg, Joshua VI, 642
Gregg, Joshua VI, 643
Gregg, Joshua VI, 653
Gregg, Joshua C. II, 869
Gregg, Joshua C. IV, 333
Gregg, Joshua, Jr. IV, 332
Gregg, Josiah P. IV, 208
Gregg, Katharine VI, 643
Gregg, Kenworthy IV, 333
Gregg, Kenworthy IV, 1025
Gregg, L. F. I, 1152
Gregg, Laban IV, 147
Gregg, Laban IV, 332
Gregg, Laban IV, 333
Gregg, Laura J. VI, 645
Gregg, Leeson I, 1152
Gregg, Leonidus Houk I, 1152
Gregg, Levi IV, 34
Gregg, Levi VI, 496
Gregg, Levi VI, 644
Gregg, Lot IV, 319
Gregg, Lot IV, 332
Gregg, Lot IV, 333
Gregg, Lot IV, 396
Gregg, Lot IV, 447
Gregg, Lot IV, 673
Gregg, Lot IV, 713
Gregg, Lott IV, 356
Gregg, Louisa G. IV, 359
Gregg, Lucinda IV, 332
Gregg, Lucinda IV, 340
Gregg, Lucinda IV, 396
Gregg, Lucinda IV, 617
Gregg, Lucinda IV, 621
Gregg, Lucy IV, 527
Gregg, Lucy IV, 554
Gregg, Luola Lester VI, 642
Gregg, Lydia IV, 87
Gregg, Lydia IV, 89
Gregg, Lydia IV, 147
Gregg, Lydia IV, 332
Gregg, Lydia IV, 333
Gregg, Lydia IV, 356
Gregg, Lydia IV, 357
Gregg, Lydia IV, 396
Gregg, Lydia IV, 527
Gregg, Lydia IV, 581
Gregg, Lydia IV, 583
Gregg, Lydia VI, 312
Gregg, Lydia VI, 392
Gregg, Lydia VI, 496
Gregg, Lydia VI, 497
Gregg, Lydia VI, 513
Gregg, Lydia VI, 631
Gregg, Lydia VI, 643
Gregg, Lydia VI, 644
Gregg, Lydia VI, 653
Gregg, Lydia Ann IV, 35
Gregg, Lydia Ann IV, 45
Gregg, Lydia Ann IV, 332
Gregg, Lydia Ann IV, 340
Gregg, Lydia L. IV, 527
Gregg, Lydia N. VI, 642
Gregg, Lydia N. VI, 644
Gregg, Lydia N. VI, 682
Gregg, Lydia N. VI, 722
Gregg, Lydia S. IV, 324
Gregg, Lydia S. IV, 332
Gregg, Mahlon II, 536
Gregg, Mahlon II, 796
Gregg, Mahlon II, 869
Gregg, Mahlon II, 998
Gregg, Mahlon II, 1043
Gregg, Mahlon IV, 147
Gregg, Mahlon IV, 208
Gregg, Mahlon IV, 332
Gregg, Mahlon IV, 343
Gregg, Mahlon IV, 396
Gregg, Mahlon IV, 397
Gregg, Mahlon IV, 421
Gregg, Mahlon VI, 312
Gregg, Mahlon VI, 498
Gregg, Mahlon VI, 644
Gregg, Mahlon, Jr. IV, 396
Gregg, Malinda IV, 332
Gregg, Malinda IV, 345
Gregg, Margaret IV, 73
Gregg, Margaret IV, 89
Gregg, Margaret IV, 333
Gregg, Margaret IV, 334
Gregg, Margaret V, 743
Gregg, Margaret VI, 573
Gregg, Margaret S. IV, 332
Gregg, Margaret S. IV, 334
Gregg, Maria IV, 147
Gregg, Maria IV, 396
Gregg, Maria IV, 414
Gregg, Mariah IV, 332
Gregg, Mariah IV, 339
Gregg, Mariam IV, 333
Gregg, Mariam IV, 396
Gregg, Mark IV, 527
Gregg, Mark IV, 581
Gregg, Mark C. IV, 527
Gregg, Martha IV, 34
Gregg, Martha IV, 208
Gregg, Martha IV, 308
Gregg, Martha IV, 396
Gregg, Martha IV, 581
Gregg, Martha IV, 1059
Gregg, Martha IV, 1082
Gregg, Martha IV, 1161
Gregg, Martha IV, 1162
Gregg, Martha V, 62
Gregg, Martha VI, 392
Gregg, Martha VI, 483
Gregg, Martha VI, 496
Gregg, Martha VI, 498
Gregg, Martha VI, 528
Gregg, Martha VI, 644
Gregg, Martha Ann V, 740
Gregg, Martha Ann VI, 642
Gregg, Martha Ann VI, 643
Gregg, Martha Ann VI, 722
Gregg, Martha S. V, 740
Gregg, Martin IV, 35
Gregg, Martin IV, 332
Gregg, Martin IV, 581
Gregg, Mary II, 536
Gregg, Mary II, 706
Gregg, Mary IV, 34
Gregg, Mary IV, 35
Gregg, Mary IV, 51
Gregg, Mary IV, 58
Gregg, Mary IV, 89
Gregg, Mary IV, 147
Gregg, Mary IV, 321
Gregg, Mary IV, 327
Gregg, Mary IV, 331
Gregg, Mary IV, 332
Gregg, Mary IV, 333
Gregg, Mary IV, 334
Gregg, Mary IV, 335
Gregg, Mary IV, 336
Gregg, Mary IV, 340
Gregg, Mary IV, 345
Gregg, Mary IV, 346
Gregg, Mary IV, 349
Gregg, Mary IV, 396
Gregg, Mary IV, 527
Gregg, Mary IV, 1059
Gregg, Mary V, 740
Gregg, Mary VI, 496
Gregg, Mary VI, 497
Gregg, Mary VI, 503
Gregg, Mary VI, 513
Gregg, Mary VI, 631
Gregg, Mary VI, 642
Gregg, Mary VI, 643
Gregg, Mary VI, 644
Gregg, Mary VI, 647
Gregg, Mary VI, 648
Gregg, Mary VI, 680
Gregg, Mary VI, 754
Gregg, Mary Ann IV, 333
Gregg, Mary Ann IV, 348
Gregg, Mary Ann IV, 349
Gregg, Mary Ann IV, 396
Gregg, Mary Ann IV, 431
Gregg, Mary Ann V, 743
Gregg, Mary Ann V, 749
Gregg, Mary C. VI, 631
Gregg, Mary C. VI, 642
Gregg, Mary C. VI, 643
Gregg, Mary C. VI, 656
Gregg, Mary C. VI, 682
Gregg, Mary C. VI, 692
Gregg, Mary Cassandra VI, 680
Gregg, Mary Eliza IV, 333
Gregg, Mary Eliza IV, 359
Gregg, Mary Jane VI, 644
Gregg, Mary Jane VI, 685
Gregg, Mary L. IV, 208
Gregg, Mary N. VI, 723
Gregg, Mary Virginia VI, 643
Gregg, Mary W. IV, 1162
Gregg, Mary, Jr. IV, 396
Gregg, Mary, Jr. VI, 643
Gregg, Mary, Jr. VI, 701
Gregg, Massy VI, 312
Gregg, May VI, 719
Gregg, May H. VI, 656
Gregg, Maye I, 1152
Gregg, Mercy IV, 147
Gregg, Mercy VI, 312
Gregg, Michael VI, 496
Gregg, Michael VI, 642
Gregg, Michael VI, 661
Gregg, Michael VI, 664
Gregg, Michael VI, 744
Gregg, Michael VI, 754
Gregg, Milicent IV, 396
Gregg, Milicent IV, 1059
Gregg, Milisent IV, 386
Gregg, Milisent IV, 396
Gregg, Millicent IV, 1059
Gregg, Millicent IV, 1082
Gregg, Millisent IV, 581
Gregg, Milly V, 852
Gregg, Moses I, 971
Gregg, Nancy IV, 527
Gregg, Nancy IV, 1162
Gregg, Naomi VI, 644
Gregg, Naomi VI, 719
Gregg, Nathan IV, 35
Gregg, Nathan IV, 333
Gregg, Nathan IV, 348
Gregg, Nathan IV, 396
Gregg, Nathan IV, 431
Gregg, Nathan IV, 581
Gregg, Nathan VI, 497
Gregg, Nathan VI, 644
Gregg, Nathan Pusey IV, 35
Gregg, Nathan Pusey IV, 332
Gregg, Nathaniel IV, 34
Gregg, Nathaniel IV, 35
Gregg, Nathaniel IV, 50
Gregg, Nathaniel IV, 69
Gregg, Nathaniel IV, 147
Gregg, Nathaniel IV, 312
Gregg, Nathaniel IV, 332
Gregg, Nathaniel IV, 343
Gregg, Nathaniel IV, 581
Gregg, Nathaniel VI, 312
Gregg, Nathaniel VI, 642
Gregg, Newton IV, 396
Gregg, Nicholas IV, 333
Gregg, Nimrod IV, 34
Gregg, Nimrod IV, 35
Gregg, Nimrod IV, 42
Gregg, Nimrod IV, 69
Gregg, Nimrod IV, 89
Gregg, Nimrod IV, 332
Gregg, Nimrod VI, 498
Gregg, Oliver T. IV, 208
Gregg, Orpha IV, 34
Gregg, Orpha IV, 51
Gregg, Orpha IV, 89
Gregg, Patience V, 62
Gregg, Patience W. V, 33
Gregg, Patience W. V, 62
Gregg, Phebe IV, 89
Gregg, Phebe IV, 147
Gregg, Phebe IV, 331
Gregg, Phebe IV, 332
Gregg, Phebe IV, 333
Gregg, Phebe IV, 336
Gregg, Phebe IV, 337
Gregg, Phebe IV, 352
Gregg, Phebe IV, 396
Gregg, Phebe IV, 397
Gregg, Phebe IV, 527
Gregg, Phebe IV, 534
Gregg, Phebe IV, 581
Gregg, Phebe IV, 587
Gregg, Phebe IV, 1161
Gregg, Phebe IV, 1162
Gregg, Phebe V, 62
Gregg, Phebe V, 303
Gregg, Phebe VI, 393
Gregg, Phebe VI, 636
Gregg, Phebe VI, 640
Gregg, Phebe VI, 642
Gregg, Phebe VI, 643
Gregg, Phebe VI, 644
Gregg, Phebe VI, 645
Gregg, Phebe VI, 721
Gregg, Phebe VI, 722
Gregg, Phebe A. VI, 642
Gregg, Phebe H. IV, 527
Gregg, Phebe H. IV, 581
Gregg, Phebe H. V, 62
Gregg, Phebe P. IV, 332
Gregg, Phebe, Jr. VI, 637
Gregg, Phineas IV, 89
Gregg, Phineas IV, 208
Gregg, Phineas IV, 1162
Gregg, Phineas IV, 1280
Gregg, Phinehas IV, 147
Gregg, Phinehas IV, 332
Gregg, Pusey IV, 35
Gregg, Pusey IV, 332
Gregg, Rachel IV, 1161
Gregg, Rachel IV, 1162
Gregg, Rachel IV, 1181
Gregg, Rachel V, 62
Gregg, Rachel V, 114
Gregg, Rachel V, 740
Gregg, Rachel V, 782
Gregg, Rachel Persis V, 740
Gregg, Rachel Persis V, 743
Gregg, Rebecca IV, 147
Gregg, Rebecca IV, 396
Gregg, Rebecca VI, 392
Gregg, Rebecca VI, 497
Gregg, Rebecca VI, 498
Gregg, Rebecca VI, 561
Gregg, Rebecca VI, 580
Gregg, Rebecca VI, 642
Gregg, Rebecca VI, 643
Gregg, Rebecca VI, 644
Gregg, Rebecca VI, 701
Gregg, Rebecca VI, 715
Gregg, Rebeccah VI, 392
Gregg, Rebecka VI, 497
Gregg, Rebeckah II, 536
Gregg, Rebeckah VI, 522
Gregg, Rebeckah VI, 637
Gregg, Rebeka VI, 567
Gregg, Rebekah VI, 496
Gregg, Rebekah VI, 497
Gregg, Rebekah VI, 498
Gregg, Rebekah VI, 643
Gregg, Rebekah VI, 660
Gregg, Rebekah VI, 674
Gregg, Rebekah VI, 701
Gregg, Rhoda IV, 147
Gregg, Rhoda IV, 327
Gregg, Rhoda IV, 332
Gregg, Rhoda VI, 312
Gregg, Richard VI, 495
Gregg, Richard VI, 497
Gregg, Robert Danforth V, 62
Gregg, Robert W. IV, 1161
Gregg, Russell VI, 644
Gregg, Ruth IV, 34
Gregg, Ruth IV, 60
Gregg, Ruth IV, 89
Gregg, Ruth IV, 116
Gregg, Ruth IV, 147
Gregg, Ruth IV, 156
Gregg, Ruth IV, 332
Gregg, Ruth IV, 356
Gregg, Ruth IV, 396
Gregg, Ruth IV, 447
Gregg, Ruth VI, 312
Gregg, Ruth VI, 392
Gregg, Ruth VI, 458
Gregg, Ruth VI, 496
Gregg, Ruth VI, 497
Gregg, Ruth VI, 498
Gregg, Ruth VI, 500
Gregg, Ruth VI, 505
Gregg, Ruth VI, 506
Gregg, Ruth VI, 563
Gregg, Ruth VI, 574
Gregg, Ruth VI, 622
Gregg, Ruth VI, 641
Gregg, Ruth VI, 642
Gregg, Ruth VI, 643
Gregg, Ruth VI, 644
Gregg, Ruth VI, 648
Gregg, Ruth VI, 652
Gregg, Ruth VI, 653
Gregg, Ruth VI, 654
Gregg, Ruth VI, 705
Gregg, Ruth Ann IV, 332

Gregg, Ruth Anna IV, 332
Gregg, Ruth Smith VI, 559
Gregg, Ruthanna IV, 35
Gregg, Ruthanna IV, 332
Gregg, Ruthanna IV, 581
Gregg, S. V, 749
Gregg, Salathiel L. V, 62
Gregg, Sallie VI, 642
Gregg, Samuel IV, 34
Gregg, Samuel IV, 73
Gregg, Samuel IV, 89
Gregg, Samuel IV, 147
Gregg, Samuel IV, 208
Gregg, Samuel IV, 324
Gregg, Samuel IV, 331
Gregg, Samuel IV, 332
Gregg, Samuel IV, 337
Gregg, Samuel IV, 339
Gregg, Samuel IV, 396
Gregg, Samuel IV, 527
Gregg, Samuel IV, 534
Gregg, Samuel IV, 581
Gregg, Samuel IV, 1162
Gregg, Samuel IV, 1276
Gregg, Samuel IV, 1280
Gregg, Samuel V, 62
Gregg, Samuel VI, 393
Gregg, Samuel VI, 487
Gregg, Samuel VI, 496
Gregg, Samuel VI, 497
Gregg, Samuel VI, 498
Gregg, Samuel VI, 561
Gregg, Samuel VI, 644
Gregg, Samuel VI, 680
Gregg, Samuel VI, 701
Gregg, Samuel, Jr. VI, 497
Gregg, Samuel, Jr. VI, 644
Gregg, Sarah II, 796
Gregg, Sarah II, 869
Gregg, Sarah IV, 34
Gregg, Sarah IV, 147
Gregg, Sarah IV, 156
Gregg, Sarah IV, 331
Gregg, Sarah IV, 332
Gregg, Sarah IV, 356
Gregg, Sarah IV, 357
Gregg, Sarah IV, 358
Gregg, Sarah IV, 391
Gregg, Sarah IV, 396
Gregg, Sarah IV, 524
Gregg, Sarah IV, 527
Gregg, Sarah V, 740
Gregg, Sarah VI, 312
Gregg, Sarah VI, 380
Gregg, Sarah VI, 392
Gregg, Sarah VI, 393
Gregg, Sarah VI, 483
Gregg, Sarah VI, 485
Gregg, Sarah VI, 493
Gregg, Sarah VI, 496
Gregg, Sarah VI, 497
Gregg, Sarah VI, 498
Gregg, Sarah VI, 520
Gregg, Sarah VI, 521
Gregg, Sarah VI, 550
Gregg, Sarah VI, 563
Gregg, Sarah VI, 587
Gregg, Sarah VI, 641
Gregg, Sarah VI, 642
Gregg, Sarah VI, 644
Gregg, Sarah VI, 661
Gregg, Sarah VI, 664
Gregg, Sarah VI, 666
Gregg, Sarah VI, 668
Gregg, Sarah VI, 696
Gregg, Sarah VI, 699
Gregg, Sarah VI, 701
Gregg, Sarah VI, 703
Gregg, Sarah VI, 704
Gregg, Sarah VI, 705
Gregg, Sarah VI, 706
Gregg, Sarah VI, 707
Gregg, Sarah VI, 744
Gregg, Sarah VI, 754
Gregg, Sarah A. I, 1152
Gregg, Sarah A. III, 139
Gregg, Sarah Ann IV, 332
Gregg, Sarah Ann IV, 333
Gregg, Sarah Ann IV, 359
Gregg, Sarah Ann IV, 396
Gregg, Sarah Ann VI, 644
Gregg, Sarah Ann VI, 648
Gregg, Sarah Ann VI, 704
Gregg, Sarah Jane IV, 332
Gregg, Sarah Jane IV, 340
Gregg, Sarah Jane V, 37
Gregg, Sarah Jane V, 46
Gregg, Sarah Jane V, 62
Gregg, Sarah M. IV, 1059
Gregg, Sarahann IV, 527
Gregg, Sidney IV, 87
Gregg, Sidney IV, 89
Gregg, Sidney Daniel V, 37
Gregg, Sina IV, 329
Gregg, Sina IV, 333
Gregg, Smith V, 740
Gregg, Smith V, 743
Gregg, Smith V, 782
Gregg, Spencer IV, 333
Gregg, Stephan VI, 694
Gregg, Stephen IV, 147
Gregg, Stephen IV, 331
Gregg, Stephen IV, 332
Gregg, Stephen IV, 333
Gregg, Stephen IV, 340
Gregg, Stephen IV, 342
Gregg, Stephen IV, 346
Gregg, Stephen IV, 352
Gregg, Stephen IV, 391
Gregg, Stephen IV, 396
Gregg, Stephen IV, 527
Gregg, Stephen VI, 312
Gregg, Stephen VI, 487
Gregg, Stephen VI, 497
Gregg, Stephen VI, 549
Gregg, Stephen VI, 642
Gregg, Stephen C. IV, 333
Gregg, Stephen, Jr. IV, 332
Gregg, Stephen, Jr. VI, 644
Gregg, Stephen, Jr. VI, 675
Gregg, Sue VI, 643
Gregg, Sue VI, 674
Gregg, Susanna IV, 327
Gregg, Susanna IV, 332
Gregg, Susanna IV, 333
Gregg, Susanna IV, 527
Gregg, Susanna VI, 644
Gregg, Susanna VI, 709
Gregg, Susannah IV, 332
Gregg, Susannah IV, 396
Gregg, Susannah VI, 496
Gregg, Susannah VI, 497
Gregg, Susannah VI, 498
Gregg, Susannah VI, 549
Gregg, Sylvanes IV, 333
Gregg, Sylvanus IV, 396
Gregg, Sylvanus IV, 397
Gregg, Sylvanus L. IV, 208
Gregg, Tacy IV, 208
Gregg, Tacy IV, 332
Gregg, Tacy IV, 1162
Gregg, Tacy IV, 1172
Gregg, Thamasin VI, 634
Gregg, Thamasin VI, 642
Gregg, Thomas IV, 34
Gregg, Thomas IV, 69
Gregg, Thomas IV, 89
Gregg, Thomas IV, 396
Gregg, Thomas VI, 380
Gregg, Thomas VI, 392
Gregg, Thomas VI, 393
Gregg, Thomas VI, 483
Gregg, Thomas VI, 487
Gregg, Thomas VI, 496
Gregg, Thomas VI, 497
Gregg, Thomas VI, 498
Gregg, Thomas VI, 519
Gregg, Thomas VI, 522
Gregg, Thomas VI, 549
Gregg, Thomas VI, 559
Gregg, Thomas VI, 561
Gregg, Thomas VI, 562
Gregg, Thomas VI, 637
Gregg, Thomas VI, 642
Gregg, Thomas VI, 643
Gregg, Thomas VI, 644
Gregg, Thomas VI, 660
Gregg, Thomas VI, 668
Gregg, Thomas VI, 674
Gregg, Thomas VI, 701
Gregg, Thomas VI, 715
Gregg, Thomas VI, 820
Gregg, Thomas Hirst IV, 147
Gregg, Thomas, Jr. IV, 89
Gregg, Thomas, Jr. VI, 393
Gregg, Thomas, Jr. VI, 498
Gregg, Thomas, Jr. VI, 644
Gregg, Thomas, Jr. VI, 660
Gregg, Thos. VI, 806
Gregg, Uriah VI, 393
Gregg, Uriah VI, 644
Gregg, Vila IV, 208
Gregg, Vila IV, 225
Gregg, Walter III, 139
Gregg, Wd. Margaret S. V, 740
Gregg, Wd. Ruth Smith VI, 562
Gregg, Wd. Susannah VI, 487
Gregg, Widow Esther Allen VI, 622
Gregg, Widow Esther Allen VI, 643
Gregg, Widow Rebeckah VI, 674
Gregg, Widow Rebekah VI, 644
Gregg, Widow Ruth VI, 497
Gregg, Widow Sarah VI, 497
Gregg, Wilbur V, 740
Gregg, Wilbur S. V, 743
Gregg, William II, 796
Gregg, William IV, 34
Gregg, William IV, 208
Gregg, William IV, 332
Gregg, William IV, 333
Gregg, William IV, 527
Gregg, William IV, 581
Gregg, William IV, 1162
Gregg, William V, 62
Gregg, William VI, 312
Gregg, William VI, 495
Gregg, William VI, 496
Gregg, William VI, 498
Gregg, William VI, 580
Gregg, William VI, 642
Gregg, William VI, 643
Gregg, William VI, 644
Gregg, William VI, 721
Gregg, William E. V, 782
Gregg, William Henry III, 139
Gregg, William W. IV, 1162
Gregg, William W. V, 62
Gregg, William, Jr. VI, 498
Gregg, Willis V, 740
Gregg, Wm. II, 73
Gregg, Wm. II, 112
Gregg, Wm. II, 869
Gregg, Wm. IV, 147
Gregg, Wm. IV, 323
Gregg, Wm. IV, 581
Gregg, Wm. VI, 495
Gregg, Wm. VI, 723
Gregg, Wm. Elwood V, 740
Gregg, Wm. W. IV, 1162
Gregg, Zillah IV, 89
Gregory, Amelia Ann I, 9
Gregory, Benjamin IV, 1162
Gregory, Blanche V, 675
Gregory, Calvin I, 336
Gregory, Caroline V, 22
Gregory, Caroline V, 62
Gregory, Charles VI, 842
Gregory, Christian F. VI, 821
Gregory, Christine E. V, 675
Gregory, Dashy VI, 813
Gregory, Deborah W. VI, 906
Gregory, Edward VI, 910
Gregory, Elizabeth I, 1061
Gregory, Elizabeth M. VI, 863
Gregory, Elvira VI, 924
Gregory, George W. I, 9
Gregory, George W. I, 50
Gregory, Hannah II, 73
Gregory, Hannah II, 536
Gregory, Hannah II, 674
Gregory, Hazel Smith IV, 1162
Gregory, Henry T. VI, 821
Gregory, Isaac I, 1061
Gregory, James IV, 1162
Gregory, John VI, 178
Gregory, John VI, 193
Gregory, John VI, 813
Gregory, John VI, 825
Gregory, John VI, 832
Gregory, John VI, 841
Gregory, John VI, 863
Gregory, John, Jr. VI, 821
Gregory, Kennett H. V, 675
Gregory, Lucinda VI, 842
Gregory, Lydia D. IV, 1162
Gregory, Marcus A. VI, 924
Gregory, Margaret VI, 821
Gregory, Martha I, 1061
Gregory, Martha V, 675
Gregory, Martha A. V, 333
Gregory, Mary I, 193
Gregory, Mary I, 194
Gregory, Mary IV, 1162
Gregory, Mary IV, 1184
Gregory, Mary V, 333
Gregory, Mary A. VI, 823
Gregory, Mary Ann VI, 883
Gregory, Millisent Wade II, 536
Gregory, Nancy V, 675
Gregory, Nancy VI, 821
Gregory, Nathan V, 333
Gregory, Peter VI, 821
Gregory, Peter VI, 832
Gregory, Polly VI, 821
Gregory, Rachel II, 998
Gregory, Rachel II, 1017
Gregory, Raymond B. V, 675
Gregory, Rebecca I, 390
Gregory, Richard VI, 821
Gregory, Robert VI, 821
Gregory, Sally VI, 841
Gregory, Sally E. VI, 858
Gregory, Samuel II, 29
Gregory, Sarah I, 390
Gregory, Sarah II, 29
Gregory, Sarah II, 73
Gregory, Sarah Anna II, 472
Gregory, Sarah Anna II, 536
Gregory, Selah IV, 1162
Gregory, Selah IV, 1184
Gregory, Servetus V, 333
Gregory, Sherman V, 333
Gregory, Sirvetus V, 675
Gregory, Sophia I, 9
Gregory, Sophia I, 50
Gregory, Sophia VI, 832
Gregory, Survetus V, 333
Gregory, Sylvester V, 675
Gregory, Thomas VI, 178
Gregory, Walepole II, 73
Gregory, Walpole II, 29
Gregory, Walpole II, 73
Gregory, Walpole II, 226
Gregory, Walpole II, 536
Gregory, William I, 9
Gregory, William I, 50
Gregory, William VI, 821
Gregson, Albert Franklin I, 654
Gregson, Alfred Brails I, 654
Gregson, Barney James I, 654
Gregson, Charley Roscoe I, 654
Gregson, Elizabeth II, 706
Gregson, Hannah Elizabeth I, 654
Gregson, Henry Clay I, 654
Gregson, Hubert Clayton I, 654
Gregson, Martha Ann II, 706
Gregson, Martha Ann II, 743
Gregson, Walter Claudius I, 654
Gregson, Wm. II, 706
Greiner, Rebecca Ann IV, 713
Greiner, Rebecca Ann IV, 777
Greist, Ethel II, 869
Greist, Jane V, 62
Greist, Joseph V, 62
Greist, Joseph P. II, 869
Greist, Mabel H. II, 869
Greist, Peter V, 952
Greist, Rueben V, 952
Greist, Salathiel V, 952
Greist, Thos. H. II, 869
Greist, Wm. II, 869
Grelet, Stephen II, 226
Grellet, Rachel II, 226
Grellet, Rebecca II, 226
Grellet, Rebecca III, 81
Grellet, Stephen II, 174
Grellet, Stephen II, 226
Grellet, Stephen III, 81
Grellet, Wd. Rebecca II, 174
Grellett, Gabriel III, 139
Grellett, Joseph III, 139
Grellett, Rachel III, 139
Grellett, Rebecca III, 139
Grellett, Stephen III, 139
Grellett, Susannah III, 139
Grenawaugh, Rachel IV, 1059
Grenawaugh, Rachel IV, 1065
Grennell, Edwin Fordis IV, 1208
Grennell, Elisa Ellen IV, 1208
Grennell, Jeremiah IV, 1208
Grennell, Martha IV, 1208
Grennell, Priscilla IV, 681
Grennell, Priscilla IV, 713
Grennell, Sylvester IV, 1208
Grese, ??? VI, 744
Grese, ??? VI, 776
Grese, Sarah N. VI, 776
Greshaw, Elizabeth VI, 820
Greshaw, Isaac VI, 820
Greshaw, Isaac VI, 821
Greshaw, James VI, 821
Greshaw, James VI, 853
Greshaw, Jane VI, 821
Greshaw, Jemima VI, 821
Greshaw, Mary VI, 821
Greshaw, Samuel VI, 821
Greshaw, William VI, 821
Gress, Anna II, 1051
Gretsinger, Anna V, 172
Gretsinger, Annie V, 172
Gretsinger, Christopher V, 172
Gretsinger, Mamie V, 172
Gretsinger, Nellie Mariah V, 172
Grewel, Moses IV, 627
Grewell, Alice IV, 713
Grewell, Alice IV, 818
Grewell, Alice IV, 905
Grewell, Alice IV, 958
Grewell, Alice VI, 312
Grewell, Alice VI, 352
Grewell, Alice VI, 354
Grewell, Alice P. IV, 958
Grewell, Ann Eliza IV, 818
Grewell, Ann Eliza IV, 958
Grewell, Caroline IV, 958
Grewell, Caroline S. IV, 818
Grewell, Caroline S. IV, 905
Grewell, Caroline S. IV, 958
Grewell, Charles B. IV, 818
Grewell, Charles B. IV, 958
Grewell, Daniel IV, 527
Grewell, Deborah Ann IV, 905
Grewell, Deborah Ann IV, 958
Grewell, Elizabeth Clemens IV, 714
Grewell, Ezekiel IV, 527
Grewell, Hannah IV, 714
Grewell, Hannah IV, 766
Grewell, Isaac IV, 527
Grewell, James C. IV, 958
Grewell, John IV, 35
Grewell, John IV, 527
Grewell, John IV, 1099
Grewell, John P. IV, 713
Grewell, John P. IV, 714
Grewell, John P. IV, 748
Grewell, John P. IV, 818
Grewell, John P. IV, 905
Grewell, John P. IV, 958
Grewell, John R. IV, 905
Grewell, Mary IV, 333
Grewell, Mary IV, 527
Grewell, Mary IV, 714
Grewell, Mary VI, 312
Grewell, Mary Ann IV, 527
Grewell, Mary Ann IV, 555
Grewell, Mary Ann IV, 556
Grewell, Mary Jane IV, 958
Grewell, Moses IV, 627
Grewell, Peter VI, 352
Grewell, Phebe F. IV, 713
Grewell, Phebe F. IV, 714
Grewell, Phebe F. IV, 748
Grewell, Phebe F. IV, 792
Grewell, Phebe F. IV, 958
Grewell, Rachel IV, 333
Grewell, Rachel IV, 527
Grewell, Rhoda A. P. IV, 818
Grewell, Ruth IV, 527
Grewell, Sarah IV, 527
Grewell, Sarah IV, 542
Grewell, Sarah IV, 713
Grewell, Sarah IV, 818
Grewell, Sarah IV, 905
Grewell, Sarah IV, 958
Grewell, Sarah VI, 312
Grewell, Sarah VI, 352
Grewell, Sarah Ann IV, 333
Grewell, Sarah Ellen IV, 958
Grewell, Susan IV, 527
Grewell, Thomas IV, 527
Grewell, Thomas D. IV, 527
Grewell, Thomas P. Stanley IV, 714
Grewell, Thos. IV, 527
Grewell, Timothy IV, 713
Grewell, Timothy VI, 312
Grewell, Timothy VI, 352
Grewell, Timothy VI, 354
Grey, ??? IV, 958
Grey, Abigail I, 530
Grey, Abigail I, 542
Grey, Abigail IV, 958
Grey, Abigail L. IV, 959
Grey, Ann IV, 208
Grey, Ann IV, 224
Grey, Ann IV, 959
Grey, Ann V, 26
Grey, Ann V, 61
Grey, Asa IV, 395
Grey, Asenath V, 61
Grey, Asenath V, 102
Grey, Elijah IV, 208
Grey, Elijah IV, 1059
Grey, Elisha IV, 208
Grey, Elizabeth II, 822
Grey, Frances VI, 941
Grey, Francis VI, 834
Grey, George II, 368
Grey, Hannah IV, 959
Grey, Hannah IV, 1056
Grey, Hannah IV, 1059
Grey, Hannah G. IV, 958
Grey, Harry IV, 959
Grey, Horace IV, 959
Grey, Horrice B. IV, 958
Grey, Howard B. IV, 959
Grey, Isaac IV, 208
Grey, Jesse IV, 1059
Grey, Josie IV, 1280
Grey, Lemuel IV, 1059
Grey, Lilly V, 457

ey, Loren IV, 1161
ey, Loren B. IV, 959
ey, Louisa L. IV, 617
ey, Louisa L. IV, 627
ey, Lydia Jane I, 923
ey, Martha IV, 1280
ey, Martha Ann IV, 1059
ey, Mary I, 542
ey, Mary IV, 1056
ey, Mary IV, 1059
ey, Milly V, 457
ey, Nancy IV, 395
ey, Nancy VI, 800
ey, Naomi II, 368
ey, Nathan IV, 959
ey, Nathaniel VI, 134
ey, Nathaniel VI, 139
ey, Peter IV, 208
ey, Robert IV, 1056
ey, Samuel IV, 1059
ey, Thomas II, 869
ey, Thomas VI, 834
ey, Thos. IV, 208
ey, Walter V, 562
ey, William IV, 208
eyham, Joseph IV, 207
eyham, Mary V, 340
eysom, Eleanor V, 840
eysom, Eleanor V, 862
ian, John II, 444
ian, Katherine II, 444
ice, Alma J. V, 675
ice, Charles W. V, 675
ice, Elizabeth IV, 1025
ice, Flora M. V, 242
ice, Fred V, 242
ice, Fredson V, 242
ice, Fredson E. V, 242
ice, Harriet V, 333
ice, Harriet E. V, 333
ice, Hattie V, 242
ice, James V, 333
ice, James E. V, 333
ice, Jane V, 242
ice, Jane V, 333
ice, Jane V, 675
ice, Jane V, 713
ice, Jemima V, 390
ice, Jemima V, 394
ice, Jemima Jane V, 333
ice, Jesse V, 242
ice, Jesse H. V, 242
ice, John D. V, 333
ice, Lella E. V, 675
ice, Louisa IV, 959
ice, Louisa IV, 961
ice, Mary V, 242
ice, Mildred V, 675
ice, Mildred V, 711
ice, Nora Marie V, 675
ice, Pleasant A. V, 333
ice, Rachel A. V, 333
ice, Ruth V, 675
ice, Ruth V, 679
ice, Ruthanna V, 675
ice, Sarah E. V, 333
ice, Thomas E. V, 333
ice, William I, 336
ice, William V, 390
ice, William E. V, 333
ice, Wm. E. V, 333
idley, Anna II, 711
idley, Elizabeth II, 536
idley, Samuel II, 368
idley, Samuel II, 536
ieg, Sarah III, 175
ier, Amanda II, 132
ier, Amanda II, 148
ier, Amanda II, 149
ier, Anna B. II, 142
ier, Anna L. II, 129
ier, Anna V. II, 132
ier, Anna V. II, 149
ier, David F. II, 132
ier, David F. II, 136
ier, David Fogg II, 132
ier, David Fogg II, 149
ier, Elizabeth II, 132
ier, Elizabeth Mulford II, 132
ier, Elizabeth Mulford II, 149
ier, Frank Allen II, 132
ier, Gulielma II, 132
ier, Gulielma II, 136
ier, Gulielma Engle II, 132
ier, Gulielma Engle II, 149
ier, Hannah II, 132
ier, Hannah E. II, 149
ier, Joanna II, 136
ier, Joanna II, 151
ier, Joanna II, 156
ier, Joanna F. II, 149
Grier, Joanna F. II, 156
Grier, Jonathan II, 132
Grier, Jonathan B. II, 129
Grier, Jonathan B. II, 142
Grier, Jonathan B. II, 149
Grier, Jonathan B., Jr. II, 142
Grier, Jonathan B., Jr. II, 149
Grier, Katherine Elizabeth II, 132
Grier, Lydia V, 62
Grier, Lydia H. II, 129
Grier, Lydia S. II, 142
Grier, Lydia S. II, 149
Grier, Martha II, 156
Grier, Richard II, 132
Grier, Robert B. VI, 734
Grier, Sarah II, 118
Grier, Sarah II, 124
Grier, Sarah II, 148
Grier, Sarah II, 158
Grier, Virginia Neill VI, 734
Grier, Woodnutt P. II, 149
Grier, Woodnutt Pettit II, 132
Gries, Mary Ann IV, 714
Gries, Nathan IV, 714
Griese, ??? VI, 744
Griese, ??? VI, 776
Griese, Sarah N. VI, 776
Griest, Amy V, 62
Griest, Amy V, 494
Griest, Amy V, 970
Griest, Ann IV, 561
Griest, Ann V, 970
Griest, Anna V, 62
Griest, Anne V, 970
Griest, Asenath IV, 1099
Griest, Athelina Edwards V, 62
Griest, Catharine II, 869
Griest, Catharine P. II, 869
Griest, Deborah IV, 35
Griest, Edwin V, 564
Griest, Edwin V, 970
Griest, Ellen S. VI, 368
Griest, Ethel II, 869
Griest, Evalina Edwards V, 62
Griest, Frank VI, 368
Griest, Isaac V, 62
Griest, Isaac V, 494
Griest, Isaac V, 970
Griest, Jane V, 62
Griest, Jane V, 907
Griest, John IV, 35
Griest, John IV, 1099
Griest, John V, 62
Griest, John V, 494
Griest, John V, 970
Griest, Joseph IV, 35
Griest, Joseph IV, 90
Griest, Joseph V, 62
Griest, Joseph V, 494
Griest, Joseph V, 970
Griest, Joseph P. II, 869
Griest, Joseph Pownall II, 797
Griest, Joseph W. V, 62
Griest, Joseph W. V, 969
Griest, Joseph W. V, 970
Griest, Katharine II, 797
Griest, Lydia V, 970
Griest, Lydia V, 973
Griest, Mabel H. II, 869
Griest, Mabell II, 797
Griest, Margaret II, 797
Griest, Margaret IV, 90
Griest, Mary V, 62
Griest, Mary V, 87
Griest, Mary V, 494
Griest, Mary V, 970
Griest, Mary Eliza V, 970
Griest, Mary Kirk II, 797
Griest, Micajah V, 62
Griest, Micajah V, 494
Griest, Micajah V, 970
Griest, Milton IV, 1099
Griest, Peter V, 952
Griest, Rebecca Ann V, 970
Griest, Ruben V, 952
Griest, Rueben V, 952
Griest, Ruth Anna V, 969
Griest, Ruth Anna V, 970
Griest, Ruth M. IV, 35
Griest, Ruth M. IV, 90
Griest, Ruth M. V, 970
Griest, Ruth M. V, 979
Griest, Ruthanna V, 970
Griest, Salathiel V, 952
Griest, Sarah V, 952
Griest, Susan V, 970
Griest, Tabitha V, 952
Griest, Thomas II, 869
Griest, Thos. II, 869
Griest, Thos. H. II, 869
Griest, Virginia VI, 368
Griest, Virginia VI, 394
Griest, Virginia Preston VI, 368
Griest, William II, 797
Griest, William IV, 35
Griest, William V, 62
Griest, William V, 970
Griest, William Elmer IV, 561
Griest, Wm. II, 797
Griest, Wm. II, 869
Griest, Wm. V, 970
Griest, Wm. V, 973
Griest, Wm. P. V, 970
Grieves, Phebe C. II, 149
Grieze, ??? VI, 744
Grieze, ??? VI, 776
Grieze, Joseph L. VI, 744
Grieze, Mary VI, 744
Grieze, Sarah N. VI, 744
Grieze, Sarah N. VI, 776
Grifeth, Mary V, 242
Griffa, Rebecca VI, 938
Griffen, ??? III, 21
Griffen, ??? III, 141
Griffen, Aaron III, 139
Griffen, Abigail III, 141
Griffen, Abigail III, 236
Griffen, Abigail III, 423
Griffen, Abigail F. III, 139
Griffen, Abigail F. III, 140
Griffen, Abigail F. III, 355
Griffen, Abigail S. III, 365
Griffen, Abigail T. III, 139
Griffen, Alice III, 139
Griffen, Alice III, 141
Griffen, Alice L. III, 140
Griffen, Amy III, 139
Griffen, Amy T. III, 61
Griffen, Amy T. III, 63
Griffen, Amy T. III, 139
Griffen, Amy T. III, 141
Griffen, Amy T. III, 344
Griffen, Ann III, 123
Griffen, Ann III, 139
Griffen, Ann III, 141
Griffen, Ann D. III, 141
Griffen, Anna III, 139
Griffen, Anna III, 181
Griffen, Anna III, 338
Griffen, Anna III, 339
Griffen, Anna B. III, 139
Griffen, Anna L. III, 296
Griffen, Anna T. III, 139
Griffen, Beatrice J. III, 140
Griffen, Caroline III, 141
Griffen, Charles III, 139
Griffen, Charles III, 333
Griffen, Charles Field III, 140
Griffen, Charles H. III, 116
Griffen, Charles H. III, 139
Griffen, Charles, Jr. III, 140
Griffen, Charlotte III, 140
Griffen, Charlotte C. III, 139
Griffen, Clarissa III, 81
Griffen, Clarissa III, 139
Griffen, Clarissa III, 141
Griffen, Cornelia A. III, 140
Griffen, Cornelia A. III, 353
Griffen, Cornelia H. III, 50
Griffen, Cornelia H. III, 141
Griffen, Daniel M. III, 141
Griffen, Deborah III, 139
Griffen, Deborah III, 140
Griffen, Edith C. III, 139
Griffen, Edmond III, 139
Griffen, Edmond III, 140
Griffen, Edmond III, 355
Griffen, Edmund III, 139
Griffen, Edmund Field III, 139
Griffen, Edmund Field III, 141
Griffen, Edmund Field III, 202
Griffen, Edward Ellis III, 140
Griffen, Eliza III, 116
Griffen, Eliza III, 139
Griffen, Eliza III, 141
Griffen, Eliza B. III, 25
Griffen, Eliza B. III, 141
Griffen, Eliza D. III, 139
Griffen, Eliza D. III, 279
Griffen, Eliza H. III, 141
Griffen, Eliza M. III, 141
Griffen, Elizabeth III, 139
Griffen, Elizabeth III, 140
Griffen, Elizabeth III, 141
Griffen, Elizabeth III, 155
Griffen, Elizabeth III, 341
Griffen, Elizabeth V. III, 139
Griffen, Elizabeth V. III, 155
Griffen, Ella III, 140
Griffen, Ella III, 181
Griffen, Ella IV, 1317
Griffen, Ellwood B. III, 139
Griffen, Ellwood G. III, 279
Griffen, Elnathan III, 139
Griffen, Emily H. III, 139
Griffen, Emily H. III, 140
Griffen, Emily H. III, 332
Griffen, Esther III, 139
Griffen, Esther III, 140
Griffen, Esther III, 203
Griffen, Esther III, 230
Griffen, Esther III, 354
Griffen, Esther III, 355
Griffen, Esther H. III, 140
Griffen, Esther L. III, 139
Griffen, Esther S. III, 140
Griffen, Ezekiel III, 50
Griffen, Ezekiel III, 139
Griffen, Ezekiel III, 140
Griffen, Fannie III, 139
Griffen, Fannie C. III, 140
Griffen, Fannie E. III, 119
Griffen, Fannie T. III, 141
Griffen, Fannie T. III, 323
Griffen, George III, 139
Griffen, George J. III, 140
Griffen, George S. III, 139
Griffen, George Steinman II, 797
Griffen, Hannah I, 50
Griffen, Hannah I, 56
Griffen, Hannah III, 81
Griffen, Hannah III, 139
Griffen, Hannah III, 140
Griffen, Hannah III, 141
Griffen, Hannah III, 233
Griffen, Hannah III, 353
Griffen, Hannah III, 354
Griffen, Hannah III, 467
Griffen, Hannah T. III, 139
Griffen, Henry III, 139
Griffen, Henry III, 140
Griffen, Henry III, 141
Griffen, Henry III, 155
Griffen, Henry III, 181
Griffen, Henry III, 319
Griffen, Henry III, 333
Griffen, Henry III, 353
Griffen, Henry III, 467
Griffen, Henry E. III, 119
Griffen, Henry E. III, 139
Griffen, Henry E. III, 140
Griffen, Henry E. III, 141
Griffen, Henry E. III, 323
Griffen, Henry E., Jr. III, 140
Griffen, Henry Jesse III, 140
Griffen, Henry R. II, 869
Griffen, Henry R. III, 140
Griffen, Henry S. III, 140
Griffen, Hernry Clay III, 140
Griffen, Jacob III, 140
Griffen, Jacob V, 62
Griffen, Jacob V, 242
Griffen, James I, 50
Griffen, James I, 56
Griffen, James III, 139
Griffen, James III, 140
Griffen, James V, 62
Griffen, James V, 242
Griffen, James Henry III, 140
Griffen, Jane III, 140
Griffen, Jane III, 233
Griffen, Jane A. III, 139
Griffen, Jane A. III, 141
Griffen, Jane H. III, 140
Griffen, Jeannie III, 140
Griffen, Jeannie III, 271
Griffen, Jeannie H. III, 271
Griffen, Jerusha III, 141
Griffen, Jesse H. III, 141
Griffen, John II, 797
Griffen, John II, 869
Griffen, John III, 139
Griffen, John III, 140
Griffen, John III, 203
Griffen, John III, 204
Griffen, John III, 230
Griffen, John C. III, 140
Griffen, John D. III, 139
Griffen, John D. III, 140
Griffen, John D. III, 367
Griffen, John F. III, 140
Griffen, John F. III, 224
Griffen, John L. III, 139
Griffen, John L. III, 140
Griffen, John L. III, 141
Griffen, John L. III, 160
Griffen, John L. III, 271
Griffen, John L. III, 332
Griffen, John T. III, 139
Griffen, John T. III, 355
Griffen, Joseph III, 140
Griffen, Joseph T. III, 139
Griffen, Joseph T. III, 140
Griffen, Josephine III, 140
Griffen, Josephine III, 141
Griffen, Leila III, 140
Griffen, Leila III, 197
Griffen, Letitia III, 140
Griffen, Louisa III, 140
Griffen, Marcia III, 140
Griffen, Margaret C. III, 140
Griffen, Marguerite III, 140
Griffen, Marguerite III, 279
Griffen, Martha III, 139
Griffen, Martha III, 140
Griffen, Martha III, 145
Griffen, Martha III, 353
Griffen, Martha III, 367
Griffen, Martha A. III, 333
Griffen, Martha V. III, 139
Griffen, Martha V. III, 155
Griffen, Mary III, 21
Griffen, Mary III, 140
Griffen, Mary III, 141
Griffen, Mary III, 224
Griffen, Mary III, 230
Griffen, Mary E. II, 797
Griffen, Mary E. II, 869
Griffen, Mary E. III, 139
Griffen, Mary E. III, 140
Griffen, Mary E. III, 204
Griffen, Mary J. III, 20
Griffen, Mary J. III, 140
Griffen, Mary Jane III, 140
Griffen, Mary Jane III, 141
Griffen, Mary L. II, 135
Griffen, Mary L. III, 140
Griffen, Mary L. III, 230
Griffen, Mary M. III, 63
Griffen, Mary M. III, 139
Griffen, Mary M. III, 140
Griffen, Mary M. III, 141
Griffen, Minnie Victoria III, 139
Griffen, Minnie Victoria III, 202
Griffen, Obadiah III, 423
Griffen, Oliver III, 140
Griffen, Oliver III, 353
Griffen, Peter III, 319
Griffen, Phebe M. III, 50
Griffen, Phebe M. III, 139
Griffen, Phebe M. III, 140
Griffen, Richard III, 141
Griffen, Richard III, 279
Griffen, Richard F. III, 140
Griffen, Robert III, 140
Griffen, Robert III, 231
Griffen, Robert C. III, 140
Griffen, Robert C. III, 197
Griffen, Robert Cornell III, 141
Griffen, Robert E. III, 231
Griffen, Robert N. III, 140
Griffen, Samuel III, 140
Griffen, Samuel III, 141
Griffen, Samuel V, 62
Griffen, Sarah III, 21
Griffen, Sarah III, 50
Griffen, Sarah III, 139
Griffen, Sarah III, 140
Griffen, Sarah III, 141
Griffen, Sarah III, 144
Griffen, Sarah III, 160
Griffen, Sarah III, 166
Griffen, Sarah III, 271
Griffen, Sarah III, 319
Griffen, Sarah III, 454
Griffen, Sarah A. III, 139
Griffen, Sarah A. III, 140
Griffen, Sarah A. III, 141
Griffen, Sarah A. III, 323
Griffen, Sarah A. III, 333
Griffen, Sarah Ann III, 140
Griffen, Sarah Clark III, 50
Griffen, Sarah Clark III, 141
Griffen, Sarah Eliz. III, 21
Griffen, Sarah Elizabeth III, 21
Griffen, Sarah Elizabeth III, 141
Griffen, Sarah H. III, 139
Griffen, Sarah H. III, 141
Griffen, Sarah H. III, 332
Griffen, Sarah R. III, 139
Griffen, Solomon III, 81
Griffen, Solomon III, 139
Griffen, Solomon III, 141
Griffen, Stephen III, 139
Griffen, Stephen III, 140
Griffen, Stephen III, 141
Griffen, Stephen III, 233
Griffen, Susan Mott III, 139
Griffen, T. T. III, 141
Griffen, Thirzah H. III, 140
Griffen, Thomas III, 141
Griffen, Thomas P. III, 141
Griffen, Thomas T. III, 141

Griffen, Thomas T. III, 230
Griffen, Thomas W. III, 25
Griffen, Thomas W. III, 141
Griffen, Thos. III, 141
Griffen, Thos. T. III, 21
Griffen, Thos. T. III, 63
Griffen, Thos. T. III, 139
Griffen, Thos. T. III, 140
Griffen, Thos. T. III, 141
Griffen, Walter H. III, 140
Griffen, Walter H. III, 141
Griffen, Walter H. III, 296
Griffen, Wd. Abigail III, 139
Griffen, Wd. Anna III, 139
Griffen, William III, 141
Griffen, William J. III, 141
Griffen, Wm. Jay III, 141
Griffen, Wm. M. III, 140
Griffeth, David II, 368
Griffeth, David VI, 374
Griffeth, David VI, 393
Griffeth, Hannah VI, 387
Griffeth, Hannah VI, 393
Griffeth, John VI, 395
Griffeth, John, Jr. VI, 393
Griffeth, Levina IV, 312
Griffeth, Mary VI, 393
Griffeth, Rachel VI, 393
Griffeth, Rachel VI, 395
Griffeth, Rachel VI, 894
Griffeth, Robert VI, 871
Griffeth, Ruth VI, 374
Grifffith, A. H. VI, 394
Grifffith, Mary Anna VI, 394
Grifffith, Rachel VI, 394
Grifffith, Robert D. VI, 394
Grifffith, William P. VI, 394
Griffin, ??? VI, 64
Griffin, Abigail III, 413
Griffin, Abigail R. IV, 1363
Griffin, Abraham III, 413
Griffin, Absalom I, 880
Griffin, Ailee I, 36
Griffin, Ailee I, 50
Griffin, Alice III, 53
Griffin, Alice III, 188
Griffin, Amaziah I, 50
Griffin, Amaziah I, 140
Griffin, Amaziah I, 144
Griffin, Amos I, 9
Griffin, Amos I, 10
Griffin, Amos I, 50
Griffin, Amos I, 77
Griffin, Amy IV, 1236
Griffin, Amy J. IV, 1236
Griffin, Amy T. III, 63
Griffin, Ann I, 4
Griffin, Ann I, 51
Griffin, Ann I, 99
Griffin, Ann I, 140
Griffin, Ann I, 160
Griffin, Ann I, 239
Griffin, Ann II, 536
Griffin, Ann II, 680
Griffin, Ann III, 413
Griffin, Ann III, 447
Griffin, Ann E. I, 215
Griffin, Ann E. I, 239
Griffin, Anna I, 10
Griffin, Anna I, 51
Griffin, Anna I, 207
Griffin, Anna I, 239
Griffin, Anna E. I, 229
Griffin, Anna T. V. III, 338
Griffin, Anne I, 51
Griffin, Anne E. I, 239
Griffin, Annie E. I, 239
Griffin, Archibald IV, 382
Griffin, Bartholomew III, 413
Griffin, Beatrice J. III, 60
Griffin, Benjamin V, 333
Griffin, Blanch VI, 64
Griffin, Burruss VI, 895
Griffin, Caleb I, 9
Griffin, Ceborn I, 390
Griffin, Ceburn S. I, 390
Griffin, Charles III, 338
Griffin, Charles H. IV, 1363
Griffin, Charlotte VI, 993
Griffin, Charlotte VI, 1018
Griffin, Claud IV, 1236
Griffin, Claude IV, 1236
Griffin, Daniel VI, 243
Griffin, Daniel A. IV, 1363
Griffin, David I, 140
Griffin, David Starr I, 215
Griffin, Eliab I, 50
Griffin, Eliab I, 51
Griffin, Eliab I, 78
Griffin, Elisabeth I, 4
Griffin, Elisabeth I, 9
Griffin, Elisabeth I, 50
Griffin, Elisabeth I, 51
Griffin, Elisabeth I, 52
Griffin, Elisabeth I, 68
Griffin, Elisabeth I, 77
Griffin, Elisabeth I, 79
Griffin, Elisabeth I, 87
Griffin, Elisabeth I, 140
Griffin, Elisabeth I, 160
Griffin, Elisabeth, Jr. I, 51
Griffin, Eliza D. III, 413
Griffin, Elizabeth I, 10
Griffin, Elizabeth I, 99
Griffin, Elizabeth I, 716
Griffin, Elizabeth IV, 397
Griffin, Elizabeth IV, 426
Griffin, Elizabeth VI, 64
Griffin, Elizabeth VI, 65
Griffin, Elizabeth VI, 74
Griffin, Elizabeth VI, 91
Griffin, Elizabeth P. III, 61
Griffin, Elizabeth P. IV, 208
Griffin, Elizabeth P. IV, 252
Griffin, Ella VI, 64
Griffin, Ellen Jane VI, 64
Griffin, Ellen M. I, 239
Griffin, Ellen Manota I, 215
Griffin, Emigin I, 215
Griffin, Emmet VI, 64
Griffin, Ephraim I, 51
Griffin, Ephraim I, 215
Griffin, Ephraim I, 239
Griffin, Ephraim I, 248
Griffin, Ephraim I Sup 1, 7
Griffin, Ephriam I, 215
Griffin, Ephriam I, 219
Griffin, Ephriam I, 239
Griffin, Ephriam Jordon I, 215
Griffin, Esther I, 7
Griffin, Esther I, 43
Griffin, Esther I, 51
Griffin, Esther III, 76
Griffin, Esther VI, 243
Griffin, Esther A. VI, 243
Griffin, Esther S. II, 869
Griffin, Etta VI, 243
Griffin, Exum I, 215
Griffin, Exum I, 239
Griffin, Exum O. I, 207
Griffin, Exum O. I, 215
Griffin, Exum O. I, 229
Griffin, Exum O. I, 239
Griffin, Ezekiel III, 413
Griffin, Ezekiel III, 447
Griffin, Ezra G. I, 208
Griffin, Ezra G. I, 215
Griffin, Ezra G. I, 232
Griffin, Ezra G. I, 239
Griffin, Ezra G. I, 240
Griffin, Feraby V, 340
Griffin, Florence Virginia I, 1119
Griffin, Frank IV, 1236
Griffin, Franklin VI, 64
Griffin, Franklin VI, 65
Griffin, George S. II, 869
Griffin, Geulielma I, 307
Griffin, Geulielma I, 319
Griffin, Gillian I, 37
Griffin, Gillian I, 51
Griffin, Gulielma I, 8
Griffin, Gulielma I, 43
Griffin, Gulielma I, 51
Griffin, Hannah I, 7
Griffin, Hannah I, 50
Griffin, Hannah I, 51
Griffin, Hannah I, 61
Griffin, Hannah I, 69
Griffin, Hannah I, 87
Griffin, Hannah I, 99
Griffin, Hannah I, 102
Griffin, Hannah I, 140
Griffin, Hannah I, 144
Griffin, Hannah I, 147
Griffin, Hannah I, 716
Griffin, Hannah I, 880
Griffin, Hannah III, 413
Griffin, Hannah Jane I, 215
Griffin, Hattie Lavinia VI, 64
Griffin, Henry III, 413
Griffin, Henry R. II, 869
Griffin, Huldah I, 50
Griffin, Huldah I, 78
Griffin, Isaac I, 1030
Griffin, Isabella I, 230
Griffin, Isabella I, 239
Griffin, Isbel I, 239
Griffin, Jabez II, 536
Griffin, Jabez II, 680
Griffin, Jacob I, 99
Griffin, Jacob I, 140
Griffin, Jacob I, 712
Griffin, Jacob I, 716
Griffin, Jacob V, 62
Griffin, Jacob V, 242
Griffin, James I, 9
Griffin, James I, 10
Griffin, James I, 50
Griffin, James I, 51
Griffin, James I, 79
Griffin, James I, 99
Griffin, James I, 140
Griffin, James I, 144
Griffin, James I, 239
Griffin, James I, 390
Griffin, James I, 716
Griffin, James I, 812
Griffin, James I, 880
Griffin, James V, 62
Griffin, James V, 242
Griffin, James V, 315
Griffin, James V, 333
Griffin, James VI, 64
Griffin, James VI, 65
Griffin, James VI, 74
Griffin, James Henry I, 215
Griffin, James M. I, 390
Griffin, James W. VI, 53
Griffin, James W. VI, 65
Griffin, Jane A. III, 53
Griffin, Jeams I, 98
Griffin, Jeremiah I, 1119
Griffin, Jesse I, 51
Griffin, Joel I, 1030
Griffin, Joel T. IV, 1363
Griffin, John I, 50
Griffin, John I, 51
Griffin, John I, 52
Griffin, John I, 215
Griffin, John II, 869
Griffin, John III, 413
Griffin, John V, 852
Griffin, John VI, 58
Griffin, John VI, 65
Griffin, John B. I, 215
Griffin, John B. I, 239
Griffin, John B. I, 262
Griffin, John C. III, 60
Griffin, John C. F. I, 390
Griffin, Joseph I, 9
Griffin, Joseph I, 10
Griffin, Joseph I, 48
Griffin, Joseph I, 50
Griffin, Joseph I, 51
Griffin, Joseph I, 95
Griffin, Joseph I, 99
Griffin, Joseph I, 102
Griffin, Joseph I, 103
Griffin, Joseph I, 109
Griffin, Joseph I, 140
Griffin, Joseph I, 152
Griffin, Joseph I, 182
Griffin, Joseph II, 536
Griffin, Joshua I, 50
Griffin, Joshua I, 51
Griffin, Joshua I, 140
Griffin, Joshua I, 1030
Griffin, Josiah I, 4
Griffin, Josiah I, 9
Griffin, Josiah I, 51
Griffin, Josiah I, 77
Griffin, Josiah I, 140
Griffin, Josiah I, 160
Griffin, Julia VI, 64
Griffin, Keziah VI, 645
Griffin, Liddea I, 98
Griffin, Liddia I, 137
Griffin, Liddia I, 140
Griffin, Lizzie T. VI, 64
Griffin, Lucinda VI, 889
Griffin, Lyda I, 95
Griffin, Lydda I, 51
Griffin, Lydda I, 99
Griffin, Lyddia I, 78
Griffin, Lyddia I, 140
Griffin, Lydia I, 38
Griffin, Lydia I, 50
Griffin, Lydia I, 51
Griffin, Lydia I, 716
Griffin, Lydia I, 880
Griffin, Lydia I, 892
Griffin, Lydia I, 1030
Griffin, Lydia V, 564
Griffin, Lydia V, 595
Griffin, Margaret A. I, 219
Griffin, Margaret A. I, 239
Griffin, Margaret A. I, 249
Griffin, Margaret Ann I, 215
Griffin, Margaret E. I, 390
Griffin, Margaret E. VI, 924
Griffin, Martha I, 99
Griffin, Martha I, 140
Griffin, Martha I, 152
Griffin, Martha I, 164
Griffin, Martha Elen I, 215
Griffin, Martha J. VI, 58
Griffin, Martha J. VI, 64
Griffin, Mary I, 45
Griffin, Mary I, 50
Griffin, Mary I, 51
Griffin, Mary I, 64
Griffin, Mary I, 76
Griffin, Mary I, 99
Griffin, Mary I, 109
Griffin, Mary I, 127
Griffin, Mary I, 136
Griffin, Mary I, 140
Griffin, Mary I, 170
Griffin, Mary I, 182
Griffin, Mary I, 215
Griffin, Mary I, 231
Griffin, Mary I, 239
Griffin, Mary I, 300
Griffin, Mary I, 303
Griffin, Mary I, 307
Griffin, Mary I, 413
Griffin, Mary I, 712
Griffin, Mary I, 716
Griffin, Mary III, 59
Griffin, Mary V, 62
Griffin, Mary V, 242
Griffin, Mary V, 852
Griffin, Mary A. I, 239
Griffin, Mary B. I, 215
Griffin, Mary C. V, 36
Griffin, Mary C. V, 62
Griffin, Mary Catharine I, 390
Griffin, Mary E. I, 232
Griffin, Mary E. I, 239
Griffin, Mary E. II, 869
Griffin, Mary E. VI, 53
Griffin, Mary E. VI, 64
Griffin, Mary E. VI, 65
Griffin, Mary Elizabeth I, 215
Griffin, Mary Ellen I, 215
Griffin, Mary Jane V, 970
Griffin, Mary Jane VI, 91
Griffin, Mary Lizzie I, 208
Griffin, Mary Perry I, 390
Griffin, Melissa IV, 397
Griffin, Melissa IV, 453
Griffin, Meriam I, 50
Griffin, Meriam I, 68
Griffin, Milicent I, 51
Griffin, Milicent I, 77
Griffin, Miriam I, 9
Griffin, Miriam I, 10
Griffin, Miriam I, 50
Griffin, Miriam I, 51
Griffin, Miriam I, 57
Griffin, Miriam I, 61
Griffin, Miriam I, 99
Griffin, Miriam I, 103
Griffin, Miriam III, 413
Griffin, Mrs. John H. VI, 64
Griffin, Myriam I, 140
Griffin, Myriam I, 159
Griffin, Nancy I, 390
Griffin, Nancy I, 1119
Griffin, Nancy V, 852
Griffin, Nancy Mariah I, 390
Griffin, Nathan I, 51
Griffin, Noah I, 51
Griffin, Noah I, 88
Griffin, Obadiah III, 413
Griffin, Orpha I, 140
Griffin, Penina I, 68
Griffin, Pennina I, 51
Griffin, Penninah I, 9
Griffin, Pheriba I, 51
Griffin, Pheriba I, 88
Griffin, Philena IV, 1162
Griffin, Philena IV, 1191
Griffin, Polly I, 390
Griffin, Priscilla V, 333
Griffin, Rachel I, 10
Griffin, Rachel I, 43
Griffin, Rachel I, 51
Griffin, Rachel I, 390
Griffin, Rachel IV, 1363
Griffin, Rebecca I, 3
Griffin, Rebecca I, 39
Griffin, Rebecca I, 51
Griffin, Rebecca VI, 65
Griffin, Rebecca C. I, 390
Griffin, Reginald I, 215
Griffin, Reuben I, 50
Griffin, Robert I, 50
Griffin, Robert I, 239
Griffin, Robert I, 300
Griffin, Robert I, 307
Griffin, Robert II, 35
Griffin, Robert II, 37
Griffin, Robert II, 40
Griffin, Robert II, 45
Griffin, Robert VI, 65
Griffin, Robert B. I, 215
Griffin, Sabra I, 51
Griffin, Sabra I, 82
Griffin, Sallie I, 215
Griffin, Sallie I, 219
Griffin, Sallie I, 239
Griffin, Sallie I, 248
Griffin, Sally I, 215
Griffin, Samuel V, 62
Griffin, Samuel V, 564
Griffin, Samuel V, 595
Griffin, Samuel VI, 924
Griffin, Samuel Millikan I, 880
Griffin, Sarah I, 36
Griffin, Sarah I, 39
Griffin, Sarah I, 48
Griffin, Sarah I, 50
Griffin, Sarah I, 51
Griffin, Sarah I, 66
Griffin, Sarah I, 99
Griffin, Sarah I, 102
Griffin, Sarah I, 140
Griffin, Sarah I, 147
Griffin, Sarah I, 215
Griffin, Sarah I, 239
Griffin, Sarah I, 307
Griffin, Sarah I, 316
Griffin, Sarah I, 716
Griffin, Sarah I, 733
Griffin, Sarah II, 536
Griffin, Sarah II, 680
Griffin, Sarah II, 743
Griffin, Sarah II, 869
Griffin, Sarah III, 480
Griffin, Sarah A. III, 338
Griffin, Sarah Eleanor IV, 382
Griffin, Sarah M. III, 483
Griffin, Selah I, 307
Griffin, Seth I, 239
Griffin, Stephen III, 53
Griffin, Stephen IV, 1363
Griffin, Stephen W. IV, 1363
Griffin, Susanah I, 215
Griffin, Susanna I, 239
Griffin, Susanna I, 240
Griffin, Susanna IV, 382
Griffin, Susanna M. II, 536
Griffin, Susanna M. II, 743
Griffin, Susannah M. II, 869
Griffin, Thomas I, 140
Griffin, Thomas I, 1119
Griffin, W. A. III, 480
Griffin, W. A. III, 483
Griffin, Widow Jane I, 140
Griffin, Widow Jane I, 144
Griffin, William I, 7
Griffin, William I, 10
Griffin, William I, 43
Griffin, William I, 45
Griffin, William I, 50
Griffin, William I, 51
Griffin, William I, 87
Griffin, William I, 92
Griffin, William I, 127
Griffin, William I, 140
Griffin, William I, 239
Griffin, William I, 264
Griffin, William I, 307
Griffin, William I, 1030
Griffin, William H. III, 413
Griffin, William J. III, 188
Griffin, William S. II, 368
Griffin, Willis I, 3
Griffin, Wm. VI, 846
Griffin, Wm. Jay III, 61
Griffin, Wm. T. I, 215
Griffin, Wm. Thomas I, 215
Griffins, Richard III, 375
Griffit, Christopher VI, 807
Griffith, ??? IV, 795
Griffith, ??? IV, 1047
Griffith, ??? V, 172
Griffith, A. Rebecca IV, 35
Griffith, Aaron V, 892
Griffith, Aaron H. VI, 393
Griffith, Aaron H. VI, 402
Griffith, Aaron H. VI, 437
Griffith, Abel L. IV, 333
Griffith, Abraham II, 226
Griffith, Abraham II, 537
Griffith, Abraham II, 588
Griffith, Abraham IV, 90
Griffith, Abraham IV, 147
Griffith, Abraham IV, 208
Griffith, Abraham IV, 209
Griffith, Abraham IV, 312
Griffith, Abraham IV, 333
Griffith, Abraham IV, 397
Griffith, Abraham IV, 527

ffith, Abraham IV, 1059
ffith, Abraham VI, 498
ffith, Abraham VI, 552
ffith, Abraham VI, 572
ffith, Abraham VI, 587
ffith, Abraham VI, 596
ffith, Abram IV, 126
ffith, Abram IV, 333
ffith, Abram IV, 349
ffith, Addison IV, 1059
ffith, Albert IV, 818
ffith, Alice B. VI, 393
ffith, Allan IV, 35
ffith, Amos IV, 35
ffith, Amos IV, 70
ffith, Amos IV, 89
ffith, Amos IV, 90
ffith, Amos IV, 104
ffith, Amos IV, 105
ffith, Amos IV, 333
ffith, Amos IV, 473
ffith, Amos IV, 505
ffith, Amos IV, 714
ffith, Amos V, 242
ffith, Amos V, 952
ffith, Amos L. IV, 312
ffith, Amos L. IV, 314
ffith, Amos L. IV, 333
ffith, Amos L. IV, 354
ffith, Amos Lee IV, 208
ffith, Amos Lee IV, 209
ffith, Amos Lee IV, 333
ffith, Amos T. IV, 90
ffith, Amos T. IV, 116
ffith, Amos T. IV, 473
ffith, Amos T. IV, 714
ffith, Amos, Jr. IV, 35
ffith, Amy IV, 208
ffith, Amy IV, 209
ffith, Amy IV, 226
ffith, Amy IV, 312
ffith, Amy IV, 315
ffith, Ann IV, 147
ffith, Ann IV, 208
ffith, Ann IV, 209
ffith, Ann IV, 527
ffith, Ann IV, 818
ffith, Ann IV, 840
ffith, Ann VI, 498
ffith, Ann VI, 527
ffith, Ann VI, 572
ffith, Ann VI, 573
ffith, Ann VI, 587
ffith, Ann M. IV, 818
ffith, Ann Moor IV, 818
ffith, Ann Moore IV, 714
ffith, Ann More IV, 209
ffith, Anna V, 172
ffith, Anna Elizabeth II, 869
ffith, Anna Mary IV, 89
ffith, Anna Mary IV, 90
ffith, Anna Olive IV, 959
ffith, Anna R. IV, 209
ffith, Anna R. IV, 312
ffith, Anna R. IV, 333
ffith, Annie IV, 209
ffith, Annie V, 172
ffith, Anthony II, 537
ffith, Anzonetta IV, 209
ffith, Aquila VI, 532
ffith, Benajah IV, 1059
ffith, Benjamin IV, 35
ffith, Benjamin IV, 209
ffith, Benjamin V, 999
ffith, Carey V, 333
ffith, Charles IV, 209
ffith, Charles IV, 397
ffith, Charles IV, 1059
ffith, Charles Lee IV, 333
ffith, Charles P. IV, 209
ffith, Charles P. IV, 333
ffith, Charles R. IV, 208
ffith, Charles R. IV, 312
ffith, Charles W. IV, 208
ffith, Charles W. IV, 333
ffith, Charles William IV, 714
ffith, Charlotte Ellen IV, 959
ffith, Chas. W. IV, 208
ffith, Chas. W. IV, 238
ffith, Christiana IV, 88
ffith, Christiana IV, 89
ffith, Christiana IV, 90
ffith, Christianna IV, 90
ffith, Collins IV, 209
ffith, Collins IV, 397
iffith, Collins IV, 1059
ffith, Collins IV, 1099
ffith, Collins W. V, 907
ffith, Collins W. V, 908
ffith, Collins W. V, 970
ffith, Cynthea IV, 627
Griffith, Cynthia IV, 35
Griffith, Cynthia IV, 38
Griffith, Cynthia IV, 627
Griffith, Cynthia IV, 632
Griffith, Cynthia IV, 714
Griffith, Daniel P. IV, 35
Griffith, Daniel P. IV, 89
Griffith, Daniel P. IV, 90
Griffith, David II, 960
Griffith, David IV, 35
Griffith, David VI, 393
Griffith, David L. V, 62
Griffith, David L. VI, 393
Griffith, David P. IV, 89
Griffith, David P. IV, 93
Griffith, Deborah IV, 209
Griffith, Dona Martha V, 172
Griffith, Donald IV, 959
Griffith, Donald Eugene IV, 959
Griffith, Donald Otis IV, 959
Griffith, Donna V, 172
Griffith, Dora A. V, 457
Griffith, Dora G. V, 457
Griffith, Earl V, 333
Griffith, Edith IV, 35
Griffith, Edith IV, 70
Griffith, Edith IV, 89
Griffith, Edith IV, 90
Griffith, Edith IV, 105
Griffith, Edith IV, 473
Griffith, Edith IV, 714
Griffith, Edith A. IV, 35
Griffith, Edith A. IV, 90
Griffith, Edith Ann IV, 89
Griffith, Edith Ann IV, 90
Griffith, Edna IV, 1038
Griffith, Edna IV, 1317
Griffith, Edra Jean IV, 959
Griffith, Edward V, 457
Griffith, Edward M. V, 457
Griffith, Edward R. VI, 393
Griffith, Edwin IV, 1059
Griffith, Edwin IV, 1099
Griffith, Edwin IV, 1132
Griffith, Eleanor IV, 209
Griffith, Eleanor IV, 714
Griffith, Eleanor IV, 1059
Griffith, Eleanor IV, 1064
Griffith, Elenor IV, 208
Griffith, Eli IV, 35
Griffith, Eli IV, 89
Griffith, Eli IV, 90
Griffith, Eli IV, 126
Griffith, Eli IV, 147
Griffith, Eli IV, 209
Griffith, Eli IV, 333
Griffith, Eli IV, 397
Griffith, Eli IV, 428
Griffith, Eli IV, 1059
Griffith, Eli IV, 1099
Griffith, Eli V, 907
Griffith, Eli V, 908
Griffith, Eli V, 970
Griffith, Eli L. IV, 208
Griffith, Eli R. IV, 35
Griffith, Eli R. IV, 47
Griffith, Eli R. IV, 870
Griffith, Eli R. IV, 877
Griffith, Elina IV, 209
Griffith, Elisabeth II, 537
Griffith, Elisabeth IV, 1363
Griffith, Elisha IV, 90
Griffith, Elisha IV, 126
Griffith, Eliza IV, 35
Griffith, Eliza IV, 47
Griffith, Eliza IV, 48
Griffith, Eliza Ann IV, 209
Griffith, Eliza Jane IV, 35
Griffith, Eliza Jane IV, 714
Griffith, Elizabeth II, 226
Griffith, Elizabeth II, 368
Griffith, Elizabeth II, 537
Griffith, Elizabeth II, 588
Griffith, Elizabeth IV, 48
Griffith, Elizabeth IV, 104
Griffith, Elizabeth IV, 126
Griffith, Elizabeth IV, 134
Griffith, Elizabeth IV, 208
Griffith, Elizabeth IV, 209
Griffith, Elizabeth IV, 226
Griffith, Elizabeth IV, 333
Griffith, Elizabeth IV, 466
Griffith, Elizabeth IV, 473
Griffith, Elizabeth IV, 527
Griffith, Elizabeth IV, 714
Griffith, Elizabeth IV, 818
Griffith, Elizabeth IV, 858
Griffith, Elizabeth IV, 870
Griffith, Elizabeth IV, 877
Griffith, Elizabeth IV, 1356
Griffith, Elizabeth IV, 1363
Griffith, Elizabeth V, 62
Griffith, Elizabeth V, 140
Griffith, Elizabeth V, 476
Griffith, Elizabeth V, 494
Griffith, Elizabeth V, 505
Griffith, Elizabeth V, 675
Griffith, Elizabeth V, 676
Griffith, Elizabeth V, 892
Griffith, Elizabeth V, 908
Griffith, Elizabeth VI, 393
Griffith, Elizabeth VI, 498
Griffith, Elizabeth VI, 573
Griffith, Elizabeth VI, 596
Griffith, Elizabeth Ann IV, 209
Griffith, Elizabeth Ann IV, 312
Griffith, Elizabeth Ann IV, 314
Griffith, Elizabeth B. V, 893
Griffith, Elizabeth B. VI, 393
Griffith, Elizabeth Mary IV, 714
Griffith, Elizabeth P. IV, 35
Griffith, Elizabeth P. IV, 70
Griffith, Elizabeth P. IV, 209
Griffith, Elma IV, 90
Griffith, Elma IV, 126
Griffith, Elma IV, 208
Griffith, Elma IV, 209
Griffith, Elma IV, 311
Griffith, Elma IV, 312
Griffith, Elma IV, 527
Griffith, Elma IV, 1059
Griffith, Elma IV, 1099
Griffith, Elma IV, 1120
Griffith, Elma V, 301
Griffith, Elma V, 303
Griffith, Elma V, 333
Griffith, Emaline IV, 714
Griffith, Emeline IV, 714
Griffith, Emeline IV, 814
Griffith, Emeline IV, 818
Griffith, Emlen IV, 126
Griffith, Emlen IV, 397
Griffith, Emlen IV, 527
Griffith, Emlen IV, 1072
Griffith, Emlen IV, 1099
Griffith, Emlen IV, 1111
Griffith, Emlin IV, 90
Griffith, Emlin IV, 126
Griffith, Emma V, 333
Griffith, Emma V, 999
Griffith, Emmor IV, 714
Griffith, Emmor H. IV, 35
Griffith, Emmor H. IV, 38
Griffith, Emmor H. IV, 627
Griffith, Emmor H. IV, 632
Griffith, Emor IV, 35
Griffith, Esther IV, 35
Griffith, Esther IV, 53
Griffith, Esther IV, 54
Griffith, Esther IV, 209
Griffith, Esther VI, 393
Griffith, Esther P. IV, 35
Griffith, Esther P. IV, 89
Griffith, Esther P. IV, 90
Griffith, Esther P. IV, 104
Griffith, Esther P. IV, 261
Griffith, Eva I, 941
Griffith, Evan IV, 208
Griffith, Evan IV, 209
Griffith, Evan IV, 226
Griffith, Evan IV, 333
Griffith, Evan IV, 714
Griffith, Even IV, 209
Griffith, Even, Jr. IV, 208
Griffith, Even, Sr. IV, 208
Griffith, Frances II, 368
Griffith, Francis Marion V, 675
Griffith, Francis Marion V, 676
Griffith, Frank IV, 209
Griffith, Frank Lewis IV, 1317
Griffith, George IV, 90
Griffith, George IV, 208
Griffith, George IV, 209
Griffith, George A. IV, 209
Griffith, George P. IV, 90
Griffith, Gertrude II, 797
Griffith, Gilbert B. IV, 959
Griffith, Grace IV, 209
Griffith, Grace V, 172
Griffith, Gracie IV, 209
Griffith, Grant IV, 209
Griffith, Hannah II, 795
Griffith, Hannah IV, 27
Griffith, Hannah IV, 35
Griffith, Hannah IV, 208
Griffith, Hannah IV, 209
Griffith, Hannah IV, 238
Griffith, Hannah IV, 312
Griffith, Hannah IV, 330
Griffith, Hannah IV, 333
Griffith, Hannah IV, 397
Griffith, Hannah IV, 714
Griffith, Hannah V, 494
Griffith, Hannah VI, 393
Griffith, Hannah VI, 452
Griffith, Hannah VI, 498
Griffith, Hannah P. VI, 393
Griffith, Hannah Saunders VI, 393
Griffith, Harriet H. VI, 385
Griffith, Harriet H. VI, 393
Griffith, Harry IV, 714
Griffith, Hazel IV, 959
Griffith, Henry V, 494
Griffith, Ida V, 999
Griffith, Isaac II, 73
Griffith, Isaac II, 797
Griffith, Isaac II, 869
Griffith, Isaac II, 874
Griffith, Isaac II, 920
Griffith, Isaac III, 141
Griffith, Isaac IV, 35
Griffith, Isaac IV, 42
Griffith, Isaac IV, 208
Griffith, Isaac IV, 209
Griffith, Isaac V, 62
Griffith, Isaac V, 915
Griffith, Isaac VI, 478
Griffith, Isaac VI, 498
Griffith, Isaac VI, 532
Griffith, Isaac VI, 572
Griffith, Isaac VI, 587
Griffith, Isaac, Jr. II, 797
Griffith, Isaac, Jr. II, 869
Griffith, Israel IV, 35
Griffith, Israel IV, 47
Griffith, Israel IV, 57
Griffith, Israel IV, 627
Griffith, Israel IV, 714
Griffith, Israel IV, 870
Griffith, Israel L. IV, 35
Griffith, Israel, Jr. IV, 35
Griffith, Jacob IV, 27
Griffith, Jacob IV, 35
Griffith, Jacob IV, 48
Griffith, Jacob IV, 54
Griffith, Jacob Lewis IV, 333
Griffith, James I, 812
Griffith, James II, 226
Griffith, James II, 537
Griffith, James V, 999
Griffith, James VI, 498
Griffith, James A. IV, 209
Griffith, James H. VI, 393
Griffith, James William IV, 209
Griffith, Jane IV, 209
Griffith, Jane IV, 312
Griffith, Jane IV, 315
Griffith, Jane VI, 393
Griffith, Jane R. VI, 418
Griffith, Jason IV, 35
Griffith, Jene P. II, 706
Griffith, Joanna VI, 393
Griffith, Joel IV, 35
Griffith, Joel Emlen IV, 209
Griffith, Joel Emlin IV, 35
Griffith, John IV, 1038
Griffith, John V, 242
Griffith, John V, 952
Griffith, John VI, 393
Griffith, John VI, 401
Griffith, John VI, 424
Griffith, John VI, 445
Griffith, John VI, 460
Griffith, John VI, 498
Griffith, John VI, 594
Griffith, John VI, 596
Griffith, John McP. VI, 393
Griffith, John W. V, 333
Griffith, John W. VI, 393
Griffith, John W. VI, 445
Griffith, John, Jr. VI, 393
Griffith, John, Sr. V, 494
Griffith, Jonathan IV, 89
Griffith, Jonathan IV, 90
Griffith, Joseph II, 368
Griffith, Joseph II, 537
Griffith, Joseph IV, 47
Griffith, Joseph VI, 498
Griffith, Joseph A. IV, 209
Griffith, Joseph Clarkson VI, 393
Griffith, Joseph W. II, 226
Griffith, Joseph W. II, 289
Griffith, Joseph W. V, 172
Griffith, Josiah V, 333
Griffith, Judith II, 368
Griffith, Judith II, 504
Griffith, Julia IV, 803
Griffith, Julia IV, 818
Griffith, Juliann IV, 209
Griffith, Katurah IV, 714
Griffith, Keith Otis IV, 959
Griffith, Ketura IV, 818
Griffith, Keturah IV, 147
Griffith, Keturah IV, 209
Griffith, Keturah IV, 714
Griffith, Keturah P. IV, 714
Griffith, Kezia T. VI, 393
Griffith, Kezia T. VI, 445
Griffith, Keziah VI, 704
Griffith, Kitturah IV, 209
Griffith, Laetitia IV, 47
Griffith, Latitia IV, 35
Griffith, Latitia IV, 57
Griffith, Laura L. IV, 209
Griffith, Laurence V, 333
Griffith, Lavenia IV, 35
Griffith, Lavinia IV, 209
Griffith, Leslie V, 333
Griffith, Letitia IV, 35
Griffith, Letitia IV, 627
Griffith, Lettitia IV, 870
Griffith, Levina IV, 312
Griffith, Lucinda VI, 1002
Griffith, Lucy Amelia IV, 473
Griffith, Lucy Amelia IV, 714
Griffith, Lukens V, 62
Griffith, Lukens V, 140
Griffith, Lydia IV, 27
Griffith, Lydia IV, 35
Griffith, Lydia IV, 48
Griffith, Lydia IV, 54
Griffith, Lydia H. VI, 393
Griffith, Lydia H. VI, 460
Griffith, Lydia H. VI, 461
Griffith, M. Elma IV, 208
Griffith, M. Elma IV, 263
Griffith, M. W. I, 925
Griffith, Mabel IV, 959
Griffith, Mabel Sarah IV, 959
Griffith, Mable I, 941
Griffith, Mable Louisa I, 925
Griffith, Mahlon F. IV, 959
Griffith, Mahlon Franklin IV, 959
Griffith, Margaret IV, 126
Griffith, Margaretta V, 907
Griffith, Margaretta V, 908
Griffith, Margaretta V, 926
Griffith, Martha IV, 48
Griffith, Martha IV, 90
Griffith, Martha IV, 115
Griffith, Martha IV, 208
Griffith, Martha V, 359
Griffith, Martha VI, 393
Griffith, Martha VI, 424
Griffith, Martha VI, 498
Griffith, Martha VI, 536
Griffith, Martha Ann II, 699
Griffith, Martha Ann VI, 393
Griffith, Martha G. VI, 427
Griffith, Martha Gardner IV, 1317
Griffith, Martha Jane IV, 209
Griffith, Martha Jane IV, 312
Griffith, Mary II, 224
Griffith, Mary II, 226
Griffith, Mary II, 368
Griffith, Mary II, 524
Griffith, Mary II, 537
Griffith, Mary II, 706
Griffith, Mary II, 795
Griffith, Mary II, 797
Griffith, Mary II, 801
Griffith, Mary IV, 35
Griffith, Mary IV, 58
Griffith, Mary IV, 126
Griffith, Mary IV, 147
Griffith, Mary IV, 208
Griffith, Mary IV, 209
Griffith, Mary IV, 312
Griffith, Mary IV, 333
Griffith, Mary IV, 349
Griffith, Mary IV, 397
Griffith, Mary IV, 466
Griffith, Mary IV, 473
Griffith, Mary IV, 527
Griffith, Mary IV, 714
Griffith, Mary IV, 818
Griffith, Mary IV, 850
Griffith, Mary IV, 1038
Griffith, Mary IV, 1059
Griffith, Mary V, 242
Griffith, Mary V, 892
Griffith, Mary V, 952
Griffith, Mary V, 999
Griffith, Mary VI, 380
Griffith, Mary VI, 393
Griffith, Mary VI, 401
Griffith, Mary VI, 424
Griffith, Mary VI, 445
Griffith, Mary VI, 460
Griffith, Mary VI, 498
Griffith, Mary VI, 552
Griffith, Mary VI, 594

Griffith, Mary VI, 596
Griffith, Mary A. V, 333
Griffith, Mary Ann IV, 35
Griffith, Mary Ann IV, 208
Griffith, Mary Ann IV, 870
Griffith, Mary Ann IV, 877
Griffith, Mary Anna VI, 393
Griffith, Mary Anna J. VI, 393
Griffith, Mary E. IV, 90
Griffith, Mary E. IV, 116
Griffith, Mary E. IV, 473
Griffith, Mary E. IV, 505
Griffith, Mary E. IV, 714
Griffith, Mary E. IV, 959
Griffith, Mary E. IV, 981
Griffith, Mary Elizabeth VI, 393
Griffith, Mary Ellen IV, 182
Griffith, Mary Ellen IV, 209
Griffith, Mary Ellen IV, 333
Griffith, Mary Ellen IV, 959
Griffith, Mary Elma IV, 90
Griffith, Mary Elma IV, 105
Griffith, Mary Elma IV, 209
Griffith, Mary H. IV, 818
Griffith, Mary John IV, 47
Griffith, Mary P. V, 915
Griffith, Mary P. VI, 393
Griffith, Mary P. VI, 402
Griffith, Mary R. IV, 35
Griffith, Mary R. IV, 89
Griffith, Mary R. IV, 90
Griffith, Mary R. IV, 105
Griffith, Mary W. IV, 209
Griffith, Matha G. VI, 394
Griffith, Maud IV, 1038
Griffith, Maurice II, 797
Griffith, Mercy IV, 209
Griffith, Mercy Jane IV, 208
Griffith, Meriam VI, 498
Griffith, Meriam VI, 552
Griffith, Milton IV, 90
Griffith, Milton IV, 126
Griffith, Milton IV, 1059
Griffith, Milton IV, 1064
Griffith, Myrtle IV, 959
Griffith, Nancy V, 494
Griffith, Nancy V, 518
Griffith, Nancy Osborn V, 62
Griffith, Nancy Osborn V, 494
Griffith, Nannie I, 925
Griffith, Nannie V, 172
Griffith, Nannie Eva I, 925
Griffith, Nettie IV, 714
Griffith, Newlin IV, 126
Griffith, Newton IV, 90
Griffith, Newton IV, 126
Griffith, Newton IV, 209
Griffith, Newton IV, 1059
Griffith, Newton IV, 1099
Griffith, Oliver IV, 818
Griffith, Oliver Francis IV, 35
Griffith, Oliver Francis IV, 209
Griffith, Oliver R. IV, 35
Griffith, Oscar IV, 35
Griffith, Oscar IV, 90
Griffith, Oscar J. IV, 90
Griffith, Oscar J. IV, 105
Griffith, Oscar J. IV, 208
Griffith, Oscar J. IV, 209
Griffith, Oscar J. IV, 263
Griffith, Oscar J. IV, 714
Griffith, Owen II, 368
Griffith, Paulina P. V, 623
Griffith, Paulina P. V, 630
Griffith, Phebe II, 960
Griffith, Philena G. IV, 20
Griffith, Philena G. IV, 35
Griffith, Philis IV, 959
Griffith, Phyllis IV, 959
Griffith, Phyllis Gaye IV, 981
Griffith, Rachel I, 812
Griffith, Rachel II, 226
Griffith, Rachel II, 264
Griffith, Rachel II, 797
Griffith, Rachel II, 869
Griffith, Rachel II, 874
Griffith, Rachel IV, 147
Griffith, Rachel IV, 209
Griffith, Rachel IV, 333
Griffith, Rachel IV, 397
Griffith, Rachel IV, 428
Griffith, Rachel IV, 714
Griffith, Rachel IV, 1059
Griffith, Rachel IV, 1099
Griffith, Rachel V, 907
Griffith, Rachel V, 908
Griffith, Rachel V, 970
Griffith, Rachel VI, 393
Griffith, Rachel VI, 460
Griffith, Rachel VI, 572
Griffith, Rachel VI, 587
Griffith, Rachel Annah VI, 393
Griffith, Rachel H. IV, 714
Griffith, Rachel P. IV, 209
Griffith, Rachel P. IV, 397
Griffith, Rebecca I, 812
Griffith, Rebecca II, 960
Griffith, Rebecca IV, 35
Griffith, Rebecca IV, 42
Griffith, Rebecca IV, 47
Griffith, Rebecca IV, 48
Griffith, Rebecca IV, 209
Griffith, Rebecca IV, 714
Griffith, Rebecca IV, 748
Griffith, Rebecca IV, 818
Griffith, Rebecca E. I, 811
Griffith, Rebecca E. I, 812
Griffith, Rebecca J. II, 869
Griffith, Rebecca J. II, 933
Griffith, Rebecca Webster II, 797
Griffith, Rees IV, 209
Griffith, Rees L. IV, 209
Griffith, Rees L. IV, 312
Griffith, Rees L. IV, 333
Griffith, Reese IV, 527
Griffith, Reese S. IV, 208
Griffith, Reuben IV, 209
Griffith, Reuben IV, 466
Griffith, Reuben IV, 714
Griffith, Reuben IV, 818
Griffith, Reuben IV, 858
Griffith, Richard II, 797
Griffith, Richard II, 869
Griffith, Richard Kendall IV, 959
Griffith, Riley I, 1152
Griffith, Robert Daniel VI, 393
Griffith, Ruth II, 824
Griffith, Ruth II, 869
Griffith, Ruth II, 874
Griffith, Ruth IV, 90
Griffith, Ruth IV, 123
Griffith, Ruth IV, 126
Griffith, Ruth IV, 209
Griffith, Ruth IV, 312
Griffith, Ruth IV, 333
Griffith, Ruth V, 242
Griffith, Ruth V, 564
Griffith, Ruth V, 571
Griffith, Ruth V, 952
Griffith, Ruth VI, 393
Griffith, S. Brenneman IV, 959
Griffith, Samuel IV, 35
Griffith, Samuel IV, 89
Griffith, Samuel IV, 126
Griffith, Samuel IV, 208
Griffith, Samuel IV, 209
Griffith, Samuel IV, 330
Griffith, Samuel IV, 333
Griffith, Samuel V, 675
Griffith, Samuel B. V, 675
Griffith, Samuel B. V, 676
Griffith, Samuel C. IV, 1059
Griffith, Samuel Powell Griffiths II, 524
Griffith, Samuella IV, 714
Griffith, Sarah I, 812
Griffith, Sarah II, 226
Griffith, Sarah II, 368
Griffith, Sarah IV, 89
Griffith, Sarah IV, 90
Griffith, Sarah IV, 123
Griffith, Sarah IV, 126
Griffith, Sarah IV, 127
Griffith, Sarah IV, 208
Griffith, Sarah IV, 209
Griffith, Sarah IV, 311
Griffith, Sarah IV, 312
Griffith, Sarah IV, 333
Griffith, Sarah IV, 397
Griffith, Sarah IV, 527
Griffith, Sarah IV, 529
Griffith, Sarah IV, 714
Griffith, Sarah IV, 1059
Griffith, Sarah IV, 1062
Griffith, Sarah V, 915
Griffith, Sarah VI, 498
Griffith, Sarah Ann IV, 1059
Griffith, Sarah Ann IV, 1062
Griffith, Sarah Ann IV, 1072
Griffith, Sarah Ann IV, 1099
Griffith, Sarah Ann IV, 1111
Griffith, Sarah D. IV, 312
Griffith, Sarah D. IV, 314
Griffith, Sarah Eleanor VI, 498
Griffith, Sarah Eleanor VI, 578
Griffith, Sarah Emaline IV, 714
Griffith, Sarah Emily III, 141
Griffith, Sarah Louisa IV, 89
Griffith, Sarah Louisa IV, 93
Griffith, Sarah Louiza IV, 35
Griffith, Sarah R. V, 999
Griffith, Sarah Rebecca IV, 1059
Griffith, Sarah, Jr. IV, 90
Griffith, Sarah, Jr. IV, 126
Griffith, Sarahann IV, 1099
Griffith, Seth VI, 393
Griffith, Sibbill VI, 393
Griffith, Sophie IV, 1038
Griffith, Susan II, 819
Griffith, Susan II, 824
Griffith, Susanna II, 537
Griffith, Susanna VI, 821
Griffith, Susannah V, 242
Griffith, Susannah V, 490
Griffith, Susannah V, 494
Griffith, Susannah V, 952
Griffith, Sylvester V, 999
Griffith, Theodore IV, 1059
Griffith, Thomas II, 368
Griffith, Thomas II, 369
Griffith, Thomas II, 504
Griffith, Thomas II, 536
Griffith, Thomas II, 575
Griffith, Thomas IV, 48
Griffith, Thomas IV, 1059
Griffith, Thomas IV, 1062
Griffith, Verna IV, 1038
Griffith, Vialetta L. IV, 1059
Griffith, Violetta IV, 1059
Griffith, Violetta IV, 1064
Griffith, Violetta L. IV, 209
Griffith, Violetta L. IV, 397
Griffith, Virginia Ann VI, 393
Griffith, Virginia Rose IV, 959
Griffith, W. B. V, 676
Griffith, Walter III, 141
Griffith, Wayne B. IV, 959
Griffith, Wd. Ann VI, 478
Griffith, William IV, 89
Griffith, William IV, 90
Griffith, William IV, 209
Griffith, William IV, 333
Griffith, William IV, 627
Griffith, William IV, 858
Griffith, William IV, 959
Griffith, William IV, 1059
Griffith, William V, 242
Griffith, William VI, 393
Griffith, William VI, 596
Griffith, William VI, 821
Griffith, William Brooks V, 675
Griffith, William H. IV, 714
Griffith, William Mode IV, 90
Griffith, Wm. II, 824
Griffith, Wm. II, 869
Griffith, Wm. II, 874
Griffith, Wm. IV, 123
Griffith, Wm. IV, 126
Griffith, Wm. IV, 127
Griffith, Wm. IV, 333
Griffith, Wm. IV, 397
Griffith, Wm. IV, 818
Griffith, Wm. IV, 850
Griffith, Wm. IV, 858
Griffith, Wm. IV, 959
Griffith, Wm. IV, 981
Griffith, Wm. V, 952
Griffith, Wm. H. II, 797
Griffith, Wm. H. II, 869
Griffith, Wm. Mode IV, 126
Griffith, Wm. P. IV, 209
Griffith, Wm. P. IV, 397
Griffith, Wm. P. IV, 1099
Griffith, Wm. Patten IV, 1059
Griffith, Zachariah B. IV, 527
Griffiths, Abigail II, 537
Griffiths, Abigail II, 681
Griffiths, Abraham II, 588
Griffiths, Anna II, 537
Griffiths, Anna II, 596
Griffiths, Elisabeth II, 588
Griffiths, Elizabeth II, 457
Griffiths, Esther II, 581
Griffiths, Hannah II, 537
Griffiths, Hannah II, 601
Griffiths, Isaac III, 141
Griffiths, James I, 781
Griffiths, Mary II, 537
Griffiths, Mary II, 601
Griffiths, Mary II, 681
Griffiths, Nathaniel II, 457
Griffiths, Rebecca Emily I, 781
Griffiths, Samuel Powell II, 601
Griffiths, Samuel Powell II, 681
Griffiths, Sarah I, 781
Griffiths, Sarah Emily III, 141
Griffiths, Susannah II, 483
Griffiths, Susannah II, 536
Griffiths, Walter III, 141
Griffiths, William II, 369
Griffiths, Wm. II, 483
Griffiths, Wm. II, 536
Griffits, Elizabeth II, 368
Griffits, Lucy II, 368
Griffits, Mary II, 368
Griffits, Nathaniel II, 368
Griffits, Susanna II, 537
Griffitts, Abigail II, 368
Griffitts, Abigail II, 537
Griffitts, Abigail II, 626
Griffitts, Abraham II, 537
Griffitts, Ambrose Oliver I, 1152
Griffitts, Ann II, 368
Griffitts, Anthony II, 537
Griffitts, Charles I, 1152
Griffitts, David II, 368
Griffitts, Elisabeth II, 537
Griffitts, Elizabeth II, 368
Griffitts, Elizabeth II, 536
Griffitts, Elizabeth II, 537
Griffitts, Emma I, 1152
Griffitts, Esther II, 537
Griffitts, Frances II, 368
Griffitts, Francis Glen I, 1152
Griffitts, George II, 368
Griffitts, George II, 536
Griffitts, Hannah II, 368
Griffitts, Hannah II, 537
Griffitts, Henry II, 368
Griffitts, Hester II, 368
Griffitts, Isaac II, 368
Griffitts, Isaac II, 369
Griffitts, Isaac II, 524
Griffitts, Isaac II, 537
Griffitts, J. A. I, 1152
Griffitts, Jacob D. I, 1140
Griffitts, Jacob D. I, 1152
Griffitts, James II, 537
Griffitts, James II, 626
Griffitts, James A. I, 1152
Griffitts, John Lee I, 1152
Griffitts, John, Jr. I, 1152
Griffitts, Joseph II, 368
Griffitts, Joseph II, 537
Griffitts, Judith II, 368
Griffitts, Lucia II, 537
Griffitts, Lucia II, 564
Griffitts, Lucy II, 368
Griffitts, Martha II, 536
Griffitts, Mary II, 368
Griffitts, Mary II, 369
Griffitts, Mary II, 537
Griffitts, Mary II, 608
Griffitts, Mary, Jr. II, 368
Griffitts, Mary, Jr. II, 536
Griffitts, Nathan II, 368
Griffitts, Nathaniel II, 368
Griffitts, Nathaniel II, 536
Griffitts, Owen II, 368
Griffitts, Riley I, 1152
Griffitts, Samuel II, 537
Griffitts, Samuel P., Jr. II, 537
Griffitts, Samuel Powell II, 368
Griffitts, Sarah II, 368
Griffitts, Sarah II, 369
Griffitts, Sarah II, 524
Griffitts, Sarah II, 537
Griffitts, Sarah II, 767
Griffitts, Sarah Emlen II, 743
Griffitts, Sarah G. I, 1152
Griffitts, Susanna II, 537
Griffitts, Susannah II, 536
Griffitts, Thomas II, 368
Griffitts, Thomas II, 369
Griffitts, Thomas II, 524
Griffitts, Thomas II, 536
Griffitts, Thomas II, 537
Griffitts, Thomas II, 608
Griffitts, William II, 368
Griffitts, William II, 369
Griffitts, William Clarence I, 1152
Griffitts, William F. II, 368
Griffitts, Wm. II, 536
Griffitts, Wm. II, 537
Griffitts, Wm. II, 626
Griffitts, Wm. F. II, 537
Grifford, Abigail IV, 1057
Grifford, Marvin IV, 1057
Grifford, Patience IV, 1057
Griffy, Oliver V, 172
Griffy, William E. V, 172
Griffy, Wm. E. V, 172
Grigg, ??? II, 369
Grigg, Anderson I, 956
Grigg, Anderson I, 963
Grigg, Anna I, 963
Grigg, Anna I, 967
Grigg, Deborah II, 998
Grigg, Dr. Amos II, 369
Grigg, Elijah I, 956
Grigg, Elijah I, 963
Grigg, Elizabeth II, 998
Grigg, Jacob I, 498
Grigg, Jacob I, 963
Grigg, John I, 498
Grigg, John I, 963
Grigg, Joseph V. I, 963
Grigg, Joseph V. V, 242
Grigg, Joseph Vassor I, 963
Grigg, Leah I, 956
Grigg, Leah I, 963
Grigg, Martha I, 498
Grigg, Martha I, 956
Grigg, Martha I, 963
Grigg, Mary I, 498
Grigg, Mary I, 963
Grigg, Massor I, 498
Grigg, Moses I, 498
Grigg, Moses I, 542
Grigg, Moses I, 953
Grigg, Moses I, 956
Grigg, Moses I, 963
Grigg, Moses I, 969
Grigg, Moses H. I, 963
Grigg, Moses H. V, 242
Grigg, Oce I, 963
Grigg, Oce I, 969
Grigg, Phebe I, 963
Grigg, Phebe I, 969
Grigg, Phebe V, 242
Grigg, Sarah I, 498
Grigg, William I, 498
Grigg, William I, 956
Grigg, Wm. I, 963
Griggs, ??? III, 141
Griggs, Dorothy II, 537
Griggs, Eliza T. III, 141
Griggsby, Etchison VI, 924
Griggsby, Ethel Louise IV, 131
Griggsby, Henrietta H. VI, 924
Griggsby, James T. VI, 924
Griggsby, Sally VI, 924
Griggsby, Wm. B. IV, 1317
Grigory, Thomas VI, 178
Grigs, Dorothy II, 537
Grigsby, Benjamin VI, 939
Grigsby, Benjamin VI, 1019
Grigsby, Etchison VI, 895
Grigsby, Etchison VI, 939
Grigsby, Etchison VI, 1019
Grigsby, Henrietta H. VI, 924
Grigsby, James T. VI, 924
Grigsby, Rebecca VI, 1019
Grigsby, Sarah VI, 939
Grim, Barbary IV, 959
Grim, Elsa V, 457
Grim, Ethel V, 242
Grim, Ethel V, 274
Grim, John IV, 959
Grim, John V, 242
Grim, John V, 457
Grim, Martha V, 242
Grim, Martha V, 457
Grim, Mary A. IV, 959
Grim, Ostie Ridgway V, 333
Grim, Pearl V, 242
Grimacy, Lucinda IV, 714
Grimacy, Lucinda IV, 748
Grime, John VI, 744
Grimes, Alfred V, 494
Grimes, Amos D. V, 494
Grimes, Andrew J. I, 880
Grimes, Asa G. V, 494
Grimes, Asa G. V, 564
Grimes, Asa J. V, 494
Grimes, Caleb VI, 391
Grimes, Carl L. IV, 209
Grimes, Carl S. IV, 209
Grimes, Clara IV, 1280
Grimes, David V, 62
Grimes, Elizabeth V, 62
Grimes, Elizabeth V, 494
Grimes, Enoch I, 1093
Grimes, Evan VI, 391
Grimes, Frances III, 141
Grimes, George V, 62
Grimes, George V, 119
Grimes, George V, 494
Grimes, George V, 564
Grimes, George V, 597
Grimes, George M. V, 494
Grimes, Hannah IV, 144
Grimes, Hannah IV, 147
Grimes, Hannah IV, 209
Grimes, Hannah IV, 397
Grimes, Hannah IV, 1059
Grimes, Hannah VI, 391
Grimes, Harry J. IV, 209
Grimes, Harvey J. IV, 209
Grimes, Howard IV, 209
Grimes, Howard W. IV, 209
Grimes, Jacob I, 1093
Grimes, Jacob L. V, 494
Grimes, James III, 141

imes, Jesse V, 243
imes, John VI, 821
imes, Jonathan V, 242
imes, Joseph VI, 918
imes, Josiah V, 242
imes, Lenora IV, 1280
imes, Lucy VI, 818
imes, Lucy E. IV, 209
imes, Martha Jane V, 494
imes, Martha Jane V, 564
imes, Mary V, 243
imes, Mary VI, 821
imes, Mary VI, 918
imes, Memmry VI, 821
imes, Myra IV, 209
imes, Myre E. IV, 209
imes, Nathaniel IV, 147
imes, Rachel I, 1093
imes, Rachel IV, 147
imes, Rachel V, 242
imes, Rachel V, 243
imes, Rachel VI, 391
imes, Rachel VI, 394
imes, Richard VI, 821
imes, Sarah V, 494
imes, Susanna V, 62
imes, Susanna V, 119
imes, Susanna V, 564
imes, Susanna V, 597
imes, Susanna VI, 918
imes, Susannah V, 62
imes, Susannah V, 494
imes, Susannah V, 564
imes, Susannah S. V, 494
imes, Tamar VI, 390
imes, Tamar VI, 391
imes, Tamar VI, 394
imes, Thomas VI, 391
imes, Thomas VI, 394
imes, Uly S. IV, 1280
imes, Violet VI, 818
imes, Walker IV, 209
imes, Walker G. IV, 209
imes, Walker J. IV, 209
imes, Walter IV, 209
imes, William VI, 818
imiel, Belle IV, 1162
imke, Angelina E. II, 743
imke, Angelina E. G. II, 743
imke, Angelina E. G. II, 774
imke, Sarah II, 743
imke, Sarah Moore II, 537
imm, Edward Eugene III, 141
imm, Grace IV, 1317
imm, Harold IV, 1317
imm, Harold Hartford IV, 1317
imm, Helen Marie IV, 1317
imm, Mary Elizabeth VI, 377
imm, Mary Elizabeth VI, 394
imm, Mary Elizabeth VI, 406
immesy, Lucinda IV, 714
immesy, Lydia Ann IV, 714
immisy, Lydia Ann IV, 714
imshaw, Ann III, 141
imshaw, Ann Eliza III, 141
imshaw, Ann W. IV, 473
imshaw, Anna Jane I, 49
imshaw, Anna Jane I, 51
imshaw, Benjamin III, 141
imshaw, Catharine III, 141
imshaw, Charles I, 49
imshaw, Charles I, 51
imshaw, Elizabeth III, 141
rimshaw, Emma III, 141
rimshaw, Emma III, 153
rimshaw, Emma R. III, 141
imshaw, Emma R. III, 153
rimshaw, Frederick I, 51
rimshaw, George III, 141
rimshaw, Hannah III, 141
rimshaw, Hannah III, 309
rimshaw, Hannah IV, 397
rimshaw, Hannah IV, 473
rimshaw, Hannah IV, 1099
rimshaw, Hannah Holmes III, 141
rimshaw, Harriett I, 51
rimshaw, Henry Holmes III, 141
rimshaw, James IV, 818
imshaw, Jane IV, 473
rimshaw, Jane IV, 474
imshaw, Jane IV, 818
rimshaw, Jane IV, 870
imshaw, Jean IV, 473
rimshaw, John III, 141
rimshaw, John III, 153
imshaw, John IV, 473
rimshaw, John IV, 474
imshaw, John IV, 477
rimshaw, John IV, 496
Grimshaw, John IV, 498
Grimshaw, John IV, 506
Grimshaw, Joseph IV, 209
Grimshaw, Margaret IV, 399
Grimshaw, Margaret IV, 473
Grimshaw, Margaret IV, 474
Grimshaw, Margaret IV, 477
Grimshaw, Margaret IV, 496
Grimshaw, Margaret IV, 498
Grimshaw, Margaret IV, 506
Grimshaw, Phebe IV, 397
Grimshaw, Phebe IV, 435
Grimshaw, Phebe IV, 436
Grimshaw, Phebe IV, 473
Grimshaw, Phebe IV, 496
Grimshaw, Rachel IV, 473
Grimshaw, Rachel IV, 496
Grimshaw, Samuel III, 141
Grimshaw, Sarah III, 141
Grimshaw, Sarah III, 142
Grimshaw, Sarah III, 243
Grimshaw, Sarah IV, 473
Grimshaw, Sarah IV, 506
Grimshaw, Tabitha IV, 473
Grimshaw, Tabitha IV, 477
Grimsley, George L. V, 457
Grimsley, Isaiah V, 457
Grimsley, Lucinda V, 457
Grindell, Alice V, 740
Grindell, Amanda V, 740
Grindell, Amanda M. V, 740
Grindell, Daniel V, 740
Grindell, Daniel F. V, 740
Grindell, Ella Hall V, 740
Grindell, Francis A. V, 740
Grindell, Frank V, 740
Grindell, Lucinda V, 740
Grindell, Mary A. V, 740
Grindell, Sarah V, 740
Grindell, Sarah E. V, 740
Grindell, William H. V, 740
Grindle, Ella IV, 1317
Grindle, Gladys IV, 1317
Grindle, H. S. IV, 1317
Grindle, Mary A. V, 740
Grindle, Sarah E. V, 740
Grindle, Stewart IV, 1317
Grinke, Sarah II, 743
Grinnel, Belle IV, 1162
Grinnel, Jeremiah IV, 1162
Grinnell, Belle IV, 1162
Grinnell, Cornelius III, 309
Grinnell, Cornelius, Jr. III, 142
Grinnell, Edwin IV, 1208
Grinnell, Edwin Fordis IV, 1208
Grinnell, Elisa Ellen IV, 1208
Grinnell, Eliza III, 142
Grinnell, Eliza III, 309
Grinnell, Eliza Ellen IV, 1208
Grinnell, Eva I, 1152
Grinnell, Evalyn I, 1152
Grinnell, Evalyn IV, 937
Grinnell, Evalyn IV, 959
Grinnell, Fordyce IV, 1208
Grinnell, Henry III, 142
Grinnell, Jane M. IV, 959
Grinnell, Jane M. IV, 972
Grinnell, Jeremiah IV, 959
Grinnell, Jeremiah IV, 972
Grinnell, Jeremiah IV, 1208
Grinnell, Jeremiah IV, 1229
Grinnell, Jeremiah A. I, 1152
Grinnell, Jeremiah A. IV, 959
Grinnell, Joseph III, 142
Grinnell, M. Evalyn IV, 959
Grinnell, M. Evlyn I, 1152
Grinnell, Martha I, 1152
Grinnell, Martha IV, 1208
Grinnell, Martha IV, 1229
Grinnell, Mary I, 1152
Grinnell, Mary III, 296
Grinnell, Mary III, 352
Grinnell, Post III, 142
Grinnell, Rhoda IV, 959
Grinnell, Rhoda IV, 1208
Grinnell, Rhoda H. I, 1152
Grinnell, Russell III, 142
Grinnell, Sarah III, 142
Grinnell, Susan R. III, 142
Grinnell, Sylvester IV, 959
Grinnell, Sylvester IV, 1208
Grinnell, William III, 142
Grinnille, Jeremiah A. I, 1152
Grinslade, Elizabeth II, 29
Grinslade, Elizabeth II, 73
Grinslade, Elizabeth II, 86
Grinslade, Elizabeth II, 88
Grinslade, Hephzibah II, 73
Grinslade, John II, 29
Grinslade, John II, 73
Grinslade, John II, 86
Grinslade, John II, 88
Grinslade, Mary Matson II, 73
Grinslade, Mathias II, 73
Grinslade, Matson II, 73
Grinslade, Rebeccah II, 73
Grinslade, Rebeckah II, 73
Grinslade, Rebeckah II, 88
Grinslade, Sarah II, 73
Grinsley, Elizabeth II, 73
Grinsley, Elizabeth II, 86
Grinyer, Samuel III, 142
Griple, Elizabeth IV, 1280
Griple, Elizabeth IV, 1285
Gripman, Martha IV, 1363
Gripman, Phebe IV, 1363
Gripman, Phebe, Jr. IV, 1363
Gripman, Silas IV, 1363
Gripman, Uriah IV, 1363
Grisberry, Sarah II, 537
Grisberry, Sarah II, 543
Griscom, ??? II, 797
Griscom, ??? III, 142
Griscom, Abigail II, 174
Griscom, Abigail II, 226
Griscom, Abigail II, 233
Griscom, Abigail II, 369
Griscom, Abigail III, 142
Griscom, Acton II, 797
Griscom, Alice Butcher II, 149
Griscom, Allen II, 132
Griscom, Allen II, 149
Griscom, Andrew II, 29
Griscom, Andrew II, 49
Griscom, Andrew II, 73
Griscom, Andrew II, 74
Griscom, Andrew II, 106
Griscom, Andrew II, 107
Griscom, Andrew II, 118
Griscom, Andrew II, 128
Griscom, Andrew II, 132
Griscom, Andrew II, 144
Griscom, Andrew II, 149
Griscom, Andrew II, 444
Griscom, Andrew II, 507
Griscom, Andrew II, 537
Griscom, Andrew A. II, 149
Griscom, Ann II, 29
Griscom, Ann II, 73
Griscom, Ann II, 74
Griscom, Ann II, 101
Griscom, Ann II, 118
Griscom, Ann II, 132
Griscom, Ann II, 142
Griscom, Ann II, 144
Griscom, Ann II, 149
Griscom, Ann II, 369
Griscom, Ann II, 1045
Griscom, Ann II, 1051
Griscom, Ann Brown II, 706
Griscom, Anna II, 870
Griscom, Anna II, 925
Griscom, Anna B. II, 132
Griscom, Anna B. II, 149
Griscom, Anna Brown II, 743
Griscom, Anna Hilliard II, 138
Griscom, Barclay II, 29
Griscom, Barclay II, 118
Griscom, Barclay II, 132
Griscom, Barclay II, 144
Griscom, Barclay II, 149
Griscom, Barkley II, 132
Griscom, Barkley II, 149
Griscom, Barkly II, 149
Griscom, Benj. II, 132
Griscom, Benjamin II, 29
Griscom, Benjamin II, 49
Griscom, Benjamin II, 73
Griscom, Benjamin II, 74
Griscom, Benjamin II, 81
Griscom, Benjamin II, 91
Griscom, Benjamin II, 106
Griscom, Benjamin II, 118
Griscom, Benjamin II, 132
Griscom, Benjamin II, 138
Griscom, Benjamin II, 149
Griscom, Benjamin II, 159
Griscom, Beulah II, 743
Griscom, Beulah II, 747
Griscom, Beulah A. II, 139
Griscom, Beulah Ann II, 29
Griscom, Beulah Ann II, 132
Griscom, Beulah Ann II, 149
Griscom, Beulah Ann II, 159
Griscom, Beulah S. II, 132
Griscom, Beulah S. II, 149
Griscom, Caroline II, 132
Griscom, Charles II, 29
Griscom, Charles II, 74
Griscom, Charles II, 118
Griscom, Charles W. II, 132
Griscom, Charles W. II, 149
Griscom, Clement A. II, 838
Griscom, Clement A. II, 869
Griscom, Clement A. II, 902
Griscom, Clement Acton II, 797
Griscom, Clement Acton II, 837
Griscom, Clement Acton II, 869
Griscom, Clement Acton II, 893
Griscom, Clement Acton, Jr. II, 797
Griscom, Clement B. II, 132
Griscom, Daniel III, 142
Griscom, David II, 29
Griscom, David II, 73
Griscom, David II, 74
Griscom, David II, 101
Griscom, David II, 118
Griscom, David II, 814
Griscom, David III, 142
Griscom, David D. II, 132
Griscom, David D. II, 149
Griscom, David J. II, 797
Griscom, David J. II, 869
Griscom, David J. II, 908
Griscom, Deborah II, 29
Griscom, Dora Ingham II, 797
Griscom, Dr. ??? III, 142
Griscom, Edgar G. II, 132
Griscom, Edgar Y. II, 149
Griscom, Edward III, 142
Griscom, Edward IV, 1364
Griscom, Edward P. III, 142
Griscom, Edwin A. II, 743
Griscom, Edwin A. II, 747
Griscom, Eleanor B. II, 132
Griscom, Eleanor B. II, 149
Griscom, Elizabeth II, 132
Griscom, Elizabeth II, 174
Griscom, Elizabeth II, 226
Griscom, Elizabeth Allen II, 129
Griscom, Elizabeth Bradway II, 132
Griscom, Elizabeth Bradway II, 149
Griscom, Elizabeth D. II, 174
Griscom, Elizabeth D. II, 289
Griscom, Elizabeth D. III, 142
Griscom, Elizabeth M. III, 190
Griscom, Elizabeth W. II, 869
Griscom, Ella II, 149
Griscom, Ella II, 159
Griscom, Ella T. II, 149
Griscom, Ellen II, 814
Griscom, Ellen M. II, 869
Griscom, Ellen M. II, 908
Griscom, Elmer II, 132
Griscom, Elmer II, 146
Griscom, Elmer II, 149
Griscom, Emeline II, 149
Griscom, Emma II, 119
Griscom, Emma II, 132
Griscom, Emma II, 153
Griscom, Emmeline II, 808
Griscom, Ephraim B. II, 132
Griscom, Ephriam B. II, 149
Griscom, Everat II, 29
Griscom, Everatt II, 29
Griscom, Everatt II, 73
Griscom, Everett S. II, 851
Griscom, Everett S. II, 870
Griscom, Florence II, 851
Griscom, Florence L. II, 870
Griscom, Frances II, 869
Griscom, Frances C. II, 838
Griscom, Frances C. II, 869
Griscom, Frances Canby II, 797
Griscom, Frances Canby II, 837
Griscom, Frances H. III, 190
Griscom, Frances Margaret II, 132
Griscom, Frank II, 149
Griscom, Geneveive Sprigg II, 869
Griscom, Genevieve Sprigg II, 893
Griscom, Geo. H. III, 190
Griscom, George II, 29
Griscom, George II, 73
Griscom, George II, 74
Griscom, George II, 118
Griscom, George II, 132
Griscom, George II, 706
Griscom, George II, 743
Griscom, George II, 960
Griscom, George II, 1045
Griscom, George II, 1051
Griscom, Grace II, 369
Griscom, Grace II, 537
Griscom, Hannah Ann II, 149
Griscom, Hannah S. II, 149
Griscom, Hannah Stuart II, 808
Griscom, Hannah Woodnut II, 811
Griscom, Hannah Woodnut II, 869
Griscom, Hannah Woodnut II, 902
Griscom, Hannah Woodnutt II, 797
Griscom, Harriet L. II, 132
Griscom, Helen II, 797
Griscom, Helen Biddle II, 837
Griscom, Helen Biddle II, 869
Griscom, Helen Lydia II, 132
Griscom, Helen Lydia II, 149
Griscom, Henrietta III, 142
Griscom, Henry II, 149
Griscom, Henry R. II, 132
Griscom, J. Milton II, 149
Griscom, Jane II, 814
Griscom, Jane W. II, 869
Griscom, Jane W. II, 870
Griscom, Jane W. II, 908
Griscom, Jane W., Jr. II, 869
Griscom, Jane Whitelock, Jr. II, 908
Griscom, Jane Whitlock, Jr. II, 869
Griscom, John II, 29
Griscom, John II, 73
Griscom, John II, 74
Griscom, John II, 117
Griscom, John II, 118
Griscom, John II, 132
Griscom, John II, 149
Griscom, John II, 174
Griscom, John II, 226
Griscom, John II, 289
Griscom, John II, 902
Griscom, John III, 142
Griscom, John Acton II, 797
Griscom, John D. II, 132
Griscom, John D. II, 142
Griscom, John D. II, 149
Griscom, John D. II, 811
Griscom, John D. II, 838
Griscom, John D. II, 869
Griscom, John D., Jr. II, 797
Griscom, John Denn II, 797
Griscom, John Franklin II, 132
Griscom, John Hoskins III, 142
Griscom, John Milton II, 132
Griscom, Joseph II, 132
Griscom, Joseph II, 369
Griscom, Joseph D. II, 132
Griscom, L. Penns Neck II, 132
Griscom, Latitia II, 73
Griscom, Latitia II, 106
Griscom, Leatetia II, 29
Griscom, Leatitia II, 29
Griscom, Leatitia II, 73
Griscom, Leatitia II, 107
Griscom, Leslie II, 851
Griscom, Leslie II, 870
Griscom, Letitia II, 49
Griscom, Letitia II, 73
Griscom, Letitia II, 132
Griscom, Lloyd Carpenter II, 797
Griscom, Lydia II, 73
Griscom, Lydia II, 132
Griscom, Lydia B. II, 149
Griscom, Lydia P. II, 146
Griscom, Lydia P. II, 149
Griscom, Margaret II, 114
Griscom, Margaret II, 118
Griscom, Margaret II, 132
Griscom, Margaret II, 149
Griscom, Margaret II, 811
Griscom, Margaret II, 869
Griscom, Margaret II, 902
Griscom, Margaret A. II, 149
Griscom, Margaret A. II, 838
Griscom, Margaret A. II, 869
Griscom, Margaret E. II, 129
Griscom, Margaret E. II, 146
Griscom, Margaret E. II, 149
Griscom, Margaret M. II, 142
Griscom, Margaret M. II, 149
Griscom, Margaret Morris II, 132
Griscom, Margaret Morris II, 149
Griscom, Margaret R. II, 149
Griscom, Margaret Woodnutt II, 797
Griscom, Marianna II, 128
Griscom, Marianna II, 139
Griscom, Marianna II, 144
Griscom, Marianna II, 149
Griscom, Martha II, 29
Griscom, Martha II, 74
Griscom, Martha II, 118
Griscom, Martha II, 132
Griscom, Martha II, 144
Griscom, Martha II, 149
Griscom, Martha II, 369

Griscom, Martha D. II, 128
Griscom, Martha Jane II, 132
Griscom, Martha Jane II, 149
Griscom, Mary II, 29
Griscom, Mary II, 73
Griscom, Mary II, 74
Griscom, Mary II, 81
Griscom, Mary II, 118
Griscom, Mary II, 149
Griscom, Mary II, 174
Griscom, Mary II, 226
Griscom, Mary II, 537
Griscom, Mary Anna II, 128
Griscom, Mary Anna II, 132
Griscom, Mary Anna II, 149
Griscom, Mary Anna II, 870
Griscom, Mary Anne II, 851
Griscom, Mary E. II, 132
Griscom, Mary E. II, 149
Griscom, Mary H. II, 174
Griscom, Mary H. II, 226
Griscom, Mary H. II, 289
Griscom, Mary H. II, 706
Griscom, Mary H. II, 743
Griscom, Mary H. III, 142
Griscom, Mary M. II, 132
Griscom, Mary M. II, 144
Griscom, Mary M. II, 149
Griscom, Mary M. W. II, 149
Griscom, Mary W. II, 73
Griscom, Mary W. II, 74
Griscom, Mary W. II, 132
Griscom, Mary W. II, 743
Griscom, Mary W. II, 747
Griscom, Mary Wade II, 808
Griscom, Mary Wood II, 29
Griscom, Maurice H. II, 146
Griscom, Maurice H. II, 149
Griscom, Mercy II, 706
Griscom, Mercy II, 743
Griscom, Mercy II, 1045
Griscom, Mercy II, 1051
Griscom, Morris H. II, 129
Griscom, Morris H. II, 132
Griscom, Nancy II, 797
Griscom, Rachel II, 29
Griscom, Rachel II, 59
Griscom, Rachel II, 66
Griscom, Rachel II, 73
Griscom, Rachel II, 74
Griscom, Rachel II, 101
Griscom, Rachel II, 117
Griscom, Rachel II, 118
Griscom, Rachel II, 289
Griscom, Rachel II, 537
Griscom, Rachel J. II, 118
Griscom, Rachel J. II, 289
Griscom, Rebecca II, 29
Griscom, Rebecca II, 73
Griscom, Rebecca II, 106
Griscom, Rebecca II, 118
Griscom, Rebecca II, 132
Griscom, Rebecca II, 138
Griscom, Rebecca II, 149
Griscom, Rebecca II, 159
Griscom, Rebecca II, 369
Griscom, Rebecca B. II, 149
Griscom, Rebecca Burr II, 132
Griscom, Rebekah II, 537
Griscom, Richard B. II, 132
Griscom, Rodman Ellison II, 797
Griscom, Rodman Ellison II, 870
Griscom, Rodman Ellison II, 925
Griscom, Ruth Anna III, 142
Griscom, Ruth E. II, 132
Griscom, Saluel S. II, 74
Griscom, Samuel II, 29
Griscom, Samuel II, 73
Griscom, Samuel II, 369
Griscom, Samuel II, 537
Griscom, Samuel S. II, 73
Griscom, Samuel T. II, 74
Griscom, Sarah II, 29
Griscom, Sarah II, 65
Griscom, Sarah II, 73
Griscom, Sarah II, 74
Griscom, Sarah II, 91
Griscom, Sarah II, 102
Griscom, Sarah II, 369
Griscom, Sarah II, 507
Griscom, Sarah II, 537
Griscom, Sarah Ann II, 132
Griscom, Sarah Ann II, 144
Griscom, Sarah Ann II, 149
Griscom, Sarah L. III, 32
Griscom, Sarah L. III, 170
Griscom, Sarah Stretch II, 73
Griscom, Susan II, 132
Griscom, Susan II, 174
Griscom, Susan III, 142
Griscom, Susan D. II, 289
Griscom, Susanna II, 29
Griscom, Susanna III, 142
Griscom, Susannah II, 29
Griscom, Susannah II, 49
Griscom, Susannah II, 73
Griscom, Susannah II, 74
Griscom, Susannah II, 81
Griscom, Susannah II, 91
Griscom, Susannah II, 132
Griscom, Susannah II, 226
Griscom, Tobias II, 226
Griscom, Tobias II, 369
Griscom, Tobias II, 537
Griscom, Walter II, 132
Griscom, Walter II, 706
Griscom, Walter II, 743
Griscom, Walter II, 747
Griscom, Walter D. II, 132
Griscom, Walter D. II, 144
Griscom, Walter D. II, 149
Griscom, Wd. Hannah Ann II, 132
Griscom, Wd. Jane II, 797
Griscom, William II, 29
Griscom, William II, 132
Griscom, William H. III, 142
Griscom, William T. II, 132
Griscom, William Woodnutt II, 797
Griscom, Wm. II, 29
Griscom, Wm. II, 59
Griscom, Wm. II, 65
Griscom, Wm. II, 66
Griscom, Wm. II, 73
Griscom, Wm. II, 74
Griscom, Wm. II, 101
Griscom, Wm. II, 117
Griscom, Wm. II, 118
Griscom, Wm. II, 142
Griscom, Wm. II, 149
Griscom, Wm. II, 797
Griscom, Wm. II, 808
Griscom, Wm. II, 1045
Griscom, Wm. II, 1051
Griscom, Wm. Adams II, 29
Griscom, Wm. H. II, 149
Griscom, Wm. M. II, 869
Griscom, Wm. T. II, 132
Griscom, Wm. T. II, 149
Griscom, Wm. W. II, 869
Griscom, Wm., Jr. II, 29
Griscom, Wm., Jr. II, 73
Griscom, Wm., Jr. II, 74
Griscom, Wm., Jr. II, 101
Griscom, Wm., Jr. II, 118
Griscomb, Ann II, 369
Griscomb, Deborah II, 222
Griscomb, Deborah II, 467
Griscomb, Deborah II, 537
Griscomb, Martha II, 369
Griscomb, Mary II, 537
Griscomb, Rachel II, 537
Griscomb, Rebekah II, 537
Griscomb, Samuel II, 369
Griscomb, Samuel II, 537
Griscomb, Sarah II, 507
Griscomb, Sarah II, 537
Griscomb, Susanna II, 507
Griscomb, Susanna II, 537
Griscomb, Tobias II, 222
Griscomb, Tobias II, 226
Griscomb, Tobias II, 537
Griscomb, Wm. II, 73
Griscombe, Grace II, 537
Griscombe, Grace II, 629
Griscombe, Tobias II, 537
Griscombe, Tobias II, 629
Griscome, Andrew II, 73
Griscome, Wm., Jr. II, 73
Griscum, Andrew II, 51
Griscum, Andrew II, 73
Griscum, Ann II, 369
Griscum, Mary II, 51
Griscum, Mary II, 73
Griscum, Tobias II, 369
Grise, Augusta IV, 1162
Grisel, Ansel Rogers IV, 1364
Grisel, Cynthia IV, 1364
Grisel, Lydia Ann IV, 1364
Grisele, Martha IV, 1208
Grisele, Simeon IV, 1208
Grisele, Susana IV, 1202
Grisele, Susana IV, 1208
Grisele, Susannah IV, 1208
Grisele, Thomas IV, 1202
Grisele, Thomas IV, 1208
Grisell, Aden S. IV, 1182
Grisell, Agnes IV, 35
Grisell, Agnes IV, 36
Grisell, Agness IV, 35
Grisell, Agness IV, 64
Grisell, Almira IV, 1162
Grisell, Almira, Jr. IV, 1162
Grisell, Ann IV, 36
Grisell, Ann IV, 627
Grisell, Ann IV, 1162
Grisell, Benjamin IV, 1162
Grisell, Charles IV, 36
Grisell, Charles IV, 627
Grisell, Cynthia IV, 1162
Grisell, Cynthia IV, 1182
Grisell, Daniel IV, 1182
Grisell, Elizabeth IV, 984
Grisell, Elmira IV, 1162
Grisell, Hannah IV, 36
Grisell, Hannah IV, 627
Grisell, Harvey IV, 1162
Grisell, Joseph IV, 35
Grisell, Joseph IV, 36
Grisell, Joseph IV, 64
Grisell, Joseph IV, 627
Grisell, Joseph IV, 714
Grisell, Joseph IV, 1162
Grisell, Letitia IV, 714
Grisell, Lydia IV, 1182
Grisell, Lydia Ann IV, 1162
Grisell, Margaret IV, 36
Grisell, Margaret IV, 627
Grisell, Mariam IV, 1162
Grisell, Martha IV, 36
Grisell, Martha IV, 627
Grisell, Martha IV, 1162
Grisell, Martha Jane IV, 1162
Grisell, Mary IV, 1162
Grisell, Mary A. IV, 787
Grisell, Milo P. IV, 1162
Grisell, Miriam IV, 1162
Grisell, Nathan IV, 1162
Grisell, Nathan P. IV, 312
Grisell, Nathan P. IV, 314
Grisell, Priscilla IV, 35
Grisell, Priscilla IV, 64
Grisell, Priscilla IV, 1162
Grisell, Priscilla IV, 1182
Grisell, Rachel IV, 35
Grisell, Rachel IV, 36
Grisell, Rachel IV, 627
Grisell, Rachel IV, 1162
Grisell, Rebecca IV, 312
Grisell, Rebecca IV, 314
Grisell, Samuel IV, 36
Grisell, Samuel IV, 627
Grisell, Sarah IV, 1182
Grisell, Simeon IV, 1162
Grisell, Susannah IV, 1208
Grisell, Thomas IV, 35
Grisell, Thomas IV, 36
Grisell, Thomas IV, 627
Grisell, Thomas IV, 1162
Grisell, Thomas E. IV, 714
Grisell, Thomas E. IV, 787
Grisell, Thomas, Jr. IV, 1162
Grisell, William IV, 1162
Grisell, Wm. IV, 1162
Griselm, Agnes VI, 394
Grishaw, Elizabeth VI, 821
Grishaw, Isaac S. VI, 849
Grishaw, James VI, 821
Grishaw, Jeremiah VI, 800
Grishaw, Mary F. VI, 821
Grishaw, Samuel VI, 830
Grishaw, Sarah VI, 800
Grishaw, Sarah A. VI, 821
Grishaw, Sealy VI, 830
Grishaw, Susan VI, 849
Grishaw, William VI, 821
Grisley, Elizabeth II, 459
Grisley, Elizabeth II, 537
Grisley, Isaiah V, 457
Grisley, Thomas II, 459
Grisley, Thomas II, 537
Grisom, Eleanor C. V, 740
Grisom, Eleanor C. V, 764
Grissel, Agnes IV, 36
Grissel, Elizabeth IV, 581
Grissel, Hannah Ann IV, 597
Grissel, Margaret IV, 36
Grissel, Martha IV, 36
Grissel, Simeon IV, 581
Grissel, Simeon IV, 1208
Grissel, Thomas IV, 581
Grissel, Thomas IV, 1208
Grissell, Almira IV, 818
Grissell, Amos IV, 818
Grissell, Ann IV, 818
Grissell, Benjamin IV, 818
Grissell, Benjamin IV, 1162
Grissell, Caroline E. IV, 818
Grissell, Charles D. IV, 818
Grissell, Chas. D. IV, 843
Grissell, Cynthia IV, 1146
Grissell, David IV, 843
Grissell, David Smith IV, 843
Grissell, Edmund IV, 843
Grissell, Edward IV, 209
Grissell, Edward IV, 210
Grissell, Edward IV, 296
Grissell, Edward L. IV, 209
Grissell, Edward L. IV, 210
Grissell, Eliza IV, 210
Grissell, Eliza IV, 843
Grissell, Eliza N. IV, 210
Grissell, Elizabeth IV, 90
Grissell, Elizabeth IV, 209
Grissell, Elizabeth IV, 210
Grissell, Elizabeth IV, 296
Grissell, Elizabeth IV, 581
Grissell, Elizabeth Ann IV, 581
Grissell, Elizabeth H. IV, 209
Grissell, Elizabeth H. IV, 210
Grissell, Emily IV, 397
Grissell, Hannah IV, 209
Grissell, Hannah IV, 210
Grissell, Hannah IV, 296
Grissell, Hannah IV, 581
Grissell, Hannah IV, 818
Grissell, Hannah IV, 840
Grissell, Hannah Ann IV, 209
Grissell, Hannah Ann IV, 210
Grissell, Hannah Ann IV, 581
Grissell, Hannah T. IV, 397
Grissell, Hannah T. IV, 459
Grissell, Hiram IV, 818
Grissell, Jesse IV, 209
Grissell, Joanna IV, 843
Grissell, Joseph IV, 714
Grissell, Joseph IV, 818
Grissell, Joseph Dutton IV, 843
Grissell, Letitia IV, 714
Grissell, Lydia IV, 203
Grissell, Lydia IV, 209
Grissell, Lydia IV, 210
Grissell, Lydia IV, 459
Grissell, Lydia IV, 581
Grissell, Margaret IV, 818
Grissell, Maria IV, 843
Grissell, Mariah IV, 818
Grissell, Martha IV, 680
Grissell, Martha IV, 818
Grissell, Martha IV, 828
Grissell, Martha Jane IV, 1188
Grissell, Mary A. IV, 714
Grissell, Mary F. IV, 818
Grissell, Mary F. IV, 843
Grissell, Matilda IV, 843
Grissell, Miriam IV, 818
Grissell, Nathan IV, 581
Grissell, Nathan IV, 818
Grissell, Nathan IV, 1146
Grissell, Nathan P. IV, 203
Grissell, Nathan P. IV, 209
Grissell, Nathan P. IV, 333
Grissell, Nathan P. IV, 397
Grissell, Nathan P. IV, 434
Grissell, Nathan P. IV, 459
Grissell, Nathan P. IV, 581
Grissell, Oliver Griffith IV, 714
Grissell, Phebe IV, 843
Grissell, Priscilla IV, 1162
Grissell, Priscilla IV, 1177
Grissell, Rachel IV, 680
Grissell, Rachel IV, 714
Grissell, Rachel IV, 818
Grissell, Rebecca IV, 209
Grissell, Rebecca IV, 210
Grissell, Rebecca IV, 333
Grissell, Rebecca IV, 397
Grissell, Sabina IV, 818
Grissell, Samuel IV, 818
Grissell, Sarah IV, 818
Grissell, Sarah IV, 843
Grissell, Sarah Ann IV, 397
Grissell, Sarah Ann IV, 449
Grissell, Simeon IV, 209
Grissell, Simeon IV, 210
Grissell, Simeon IV, 581
Grissell, Simon IV, 210
Grissell, Subbina IV, 818
Grissell, Thomas IV, 209
Grissell, Thomas IV, 210
Grissell, Thomas IV, 581
Grissell, Thomas IV, 680
Grissell, Thomas IV, 858
Grissell, Thomas IV, 1208
Grissell, Thomas A. IV, 209
Grissell, Thomas E. IV, 714
Grissell, Thomas Henry IV, 843
Grissell, Thomas, Jr. IV, 818
Grissell, Thos. IV, 210
Grissell, William IV, 818
Grissell, Wm. IV, 818
Grissell, Wm. IV, 1162
Grissen, Elizabeth V, 676
Grissle, Ann IV, 856
Grissle, Lydia IV, 581
Grissle, Margaret IV, 818
Grissle, Margaret IV, 830
Grissle, Thomas, Jr. IV, 818
Grissom, Charlotte VI, 924
Grissom, Hattie I, 925
Grissom, Henry VI, 924
Grissom, Mary Jane VI, 892
Grissom, Mary Jane VI, 992
Grissom, Susanah VI, 985
Grissom, Susanna VI, 924
Grissom, Thomas VI, 892
Grissom, Thomas VI, 985
Grissom, Thomas VI, 992
Grissom, Willis VI, 924
Grissorn, Willis VI, 929
Grist, Amy V, 62
Grist, Amy V, 494
Grist, Ann IV, 210
Grist, Ann IV, 300
Grist, Ann V, 494
Grist, Ann W. IV, 473
Grist, Ann W. IV, 477
Grist, Deborah IV, 35
Grist, Deborah IV, 90
Grist, Deborah Jane IV, 1059
Grist, Edwin V, 564
Grist, Ellen VI, 394
Grist, Frank VI, 394
Grist, George IV, 90
Grist, George IV, 126
Grist, Isaac V, 62
Grist, Isaac V, 494
Grist, John II, 444
Grist, John IV, 714
Grist, John V, 62
Grist, John V, 494
Grist, Jos. IV, 477
Grist, Joseph II, 444
Grist, Joseph IV, 90
Grist, Joseph IV, 126
Grist, Joseph V, 62
Grist, Joseph V, 494
Grist, Joseph W. V, 62
Grist, Joseph, Jr. IV, 90
Grist, Lydia IV, 84
Grist, Lydia IV, 90
Grist, Margaret IV, 90
Grist, Margaret IV, 126
Grist, Margaret Bailey IV, 126
Grist, Mary IV, 477
Grist, Mary V, 62
Grist, Mary V, 494
Grist, Micajah V, 62
Grist, Micajah V, 494
Grist, Ohpha IV, 90
Grist, Orpha IV, 126
Grist, Phebe IV, 90
Grist, Phebe IV, 103
Grist, Rebecca IV, 90
Grist, Ruth VI, 380
Grist, Ruth M. IV, 90
Grist, Therza IV, 90
Grist, Virginia VI, 394
Grist, William IV, 90
Grist, William IV, 126
Grist, William Elmer IV, 210
Griste, Ann V, 494
Griswald, Agness IV, 90
Griswald, Agness IV, 113
Griswell, Priscilla IV, 1162
Griswold, Geo. III, 394
Griswold, Lydia III, 394
Gritman, Drusilla III, 413
Gritman, Drusilla III, 441
Grizell, Hannah V, 928
Grizell, Martha V, 928
Grizell, Thos. V, 928
Grizzell, Edward IV, 210
Grizzell, Edward L. IV, 210
Grizzell, Eliza IV, 210
Grizzell, Eliza N. IV, 210
Grizzell, Elizabeth IV, 210
Grizzell, Elizabeth H. IV, 210
Grizzell, Hannah IV, 210
Grizzell, Hannah IV, 581
Grizzell, Hannah Ann IV, 210
Grizzell, Lydia IV, 210
Grizzell, Rebecca IV, 209
Grizzell, Rebecca IV, 210
Grizzell, Simeon IV, 210
Grizzell, Simon IV, 210
Grizzell, Thomas IV, 210
Grizzell, Thos. IV, 210
Groaff, Abigail II, 74
Groaff, Elizabeth II, 52
Groaff, Elizabeth II, 74
Groaff, Elizabeth II, 104
Groaff, Leatitia II, 74
Groaff, Wm. II, 74

ce, Mary VI, 984
ofenstein, M. H. IV, 1252
ofenstein, Mabel IV, 1252
off, ??? III, 429
ff, Abigail II, 57
off, Abigail II, 74
off, De Graef III, 413
off, De Grove III, 413
off, Florence V, 908
off, Joseph II, 369
off, Leatitia II, 104
off, Mary III, 132
off, Mary III, 142
off, Mary III, 145
off, Mary III, 294
off, Rachel III, 413
off, Rachel III, 429
off, Sarah V, 908
off, Sarah Elizabeth V, 908
off, William V, 908
off, Willie Nesley V, 908
off, Wm. II, 74
off, Wm. II, 104
ogan, J. P. VI, 913
ogg, Andrew J. V, 286
ogg, Lida V, 286
ogg, Sarah V, 286
omett, Wm. II, 537
oner, Edgar IV, 714
oner, Lillian IV, 714
oner, Naomi IV, 714
oom, Jonathan VI, 886
oom, Jonathan VI, 964
oom, Katy VI, 964
oom, Polly M. VI, 886
oome, Jonathan VI, 1010
oome, Nancy M. VI, 1010
oome, Thomas S. I, 633
oome, William II, 17
oome, William II, 23
ooms, Jonathan VI, 869
ooms, Nancy VI, 869
oove, Anna M. IV, 711
oscosk, Alice V, 999
oscosk, J. L. V, 999
oscost, Alice V, 999
oscost, J. L. V, 999
oscost, Jesse Lewis V, 999
oscost, Louie S. V, 999
oscost, Lua V, 999
oscost, Ollie V, 999
oscost, Thelma V, 999
osdidier, Alma Muetzel IV, 1318
osdidier, Gertrude IV, 1318
osdidier, Gertrude Henderson IV, 1318
osdidier, Lloyd IV, 1318
ose, Phebe IV, 905
ose, Phebe IV, 909
oshon, Amelia III, 142
oshon, Amelia III, 337
oshon, Henry III, 142
oshon, Henry III, 337
oss, Abraham VI, 925
oss, Abraham VI, 954
oss, Abram VI, 925
oss, Caroline VI, 1014
oss, Catharine M. VI, 994
oss, George VI, 925
oss, George VI, 994
oss, George W. VI, 914
oss, George W. VI, 1014
oss, Henry VI, 885
oss, Henry VI, 888
oss, Henry VI, 924
oss, Henry VI, 925
oss, Isaac VI, 875
oss, Isaac VI, 896
oss, Isaac VI, 984
oss, Isaac, Jr. VI, 875
oss, Jane I, 542
oss, Joanna VI, 925
oss, John VI, 1017
oss, Juliet VI, 914
oss, Lucinda VI, 947
oss, Lucinda Oney VI, 925
oss, Lydia VI, 925
oss, Margaret VI, 914
oss, Margaret VI, 1014
oss, Marshall VI, 933
oss, Martha Jane Cundiff VI, 925
oss, Mary VI, 896
oss, Nancy VI, 821
oss, Nancy VI, 875
oss, Nancy VI, 925
oss, Nancy Jane VI, 933
oss, Pagy VI, 994
oss, Peggy VI, 924
oss, Polly VI, 933
Gross, Rebekah VI, 924
Gross, Richard VI, 821
Gross, Richard VI, 924
Gross, Sarah I, 498
Gross, Thomas VI, 947
Gross, William VI, 925
Grosscup, Amanda IV, 627
Grosscup, Amanda IV, 648
Grosscup, Louisa IV, 870
Grosscup, Louisa IV, 879
Grosse, Deborah IV, 818
Grosse, Eliz. III, 273
Grosse, Margaret III, 273
Grosse, Thomas III, 273
Grosvenor, Rev. P. S. III, 412
Grounds, Anny Lowry VI, 925
Grounds, George VI, 925
Grousser, E. J. IV, 1252
Grousser, Emily Jane IV, 1252
Grove, ??? VI, 39
Grove, Anna M. IV, 714
Grove, Annetta IV, 1252
Grove, Arthur V, 999
Grove, Chloe V, 564
Grove, Daniel V, 999
Grove, Dr. ??? VI, 23
Grove, Dr. John VI, 41
Grove, Elizabeth V, 457
Grove, Elizabeth V, 557
Grove, Elma IV, 126
Grove, Elma IV, 128
Grove, Elzie V, 809
Grove, George V, 457
Grove, Grace V, 557
Grove, Hamer V, 564
Grove, Heber V, 564
Grove, Homer V, 564
Grove, Howard V, 564
Grove, Ida V, 457
Grove, Lizzie V, 457
Grove, Lottie V, 999
Grove, Lucinda IV, 952
Grove, Lucinda IV, 959
Grove, Lydia V, 243
Grove, Lynn I, 1095
Grove, M. C. V, 457
Grove, Mark V, 457
Grove, Oscar V, 557
Grove, Oscar V, 564
Grove, Ross V, 809
Grove, Sarah IV, 319
Grove, Sarah IV, 333
Grove, Walter V, 457
Grove, Wm. V, 999
Grover, Etta Reed III, 311
Groves, Ada IV, 714
Groves, Alexander IV, 1252
Groves, Alvira IV, 1162
Groves, Anna M. IV, 714
Groves, Annetta IV, 1252
Groves, Chalmer IV, 714
Groves, Chalmer W. IV, 714
Groves, Clifford E. IV, 210
Groves, Curtis IV, 1252
Groves, Dr. John VI, 41
Groves, Edward IV, 714
Groves, Florence M. III, 142
Groves, Ida IV, 210
Groves, Jeffry VI, 637
Groves, Jennie III, 142
Groves, Jeoffry VI, 638
Groves, Jeoffry VI, 645
Groves, John IV, 210
Groves, John VI, 41
Groves, Joseph IV, 1162
Groves, Lizzie IV, 1252
Groves, Lizzie V, 457
Groves, Lola Ruth IV, 1318
Groves, Mary Virginia VI, 637
Groves, Mary Virginia VI, 638
Groves, Mary Virginia VI, 645
Grow, Joseph VI, 808
Growden, Elizabeth II, 537
Growden, Lawrence II, 537
Growden, Lawrence II, 998
Growden, Sarah II, 998
Growdon, Anne II, 477
Growdon, Anne II, 537
Growdon, Elizabeth II, 537
Growdon, Elizabeth II, 633
Growdon, Grace II, 537
Growdon, Grace II, 583
Growdon, Hannah II, 369
Growdon, Hannah II, 537
Growdon, Joseph II, 477
Growdon, Joseph II, 537
Growdon, Joseph II, 583
Growdon, Lawrance II, 979
Growdon, Lawrence II, 537
Growdon, Sarah II, 979
Grub, Jesse VI, 902
Grub, Leander V, 243
Grub, Robert II, 537
Grubb, ??? II, 165
Grubb, ??? R. II, 174
Grubb, Adam VI, 395
Grubb, Alfred VI, 925
Grubb, Andrew VI, 925
Grubb, Andrew VI, 1004
Grubb, Andrew W. VI, 925
Grubb, Andrew W. VI, 991
Grubb, Ann IV, 210
Grubb, Ann IV, 241
Grubb, Ann IV, 263
Grubb, Ann IV, 326
Grubb, Ann IV, 333
Grubb, Anna B. IV, 197
Grubb, Anna B. IV, 210
Grubb, Anna E. II, 870
Grubb, Annie II, 870
Grubb, Beulah VI, 395
Grubb, Beulah VI, 396
Grubb, Beulah VI, 744
Grubb, Beulah VI, 745
Grubb, Charity I, 649
Grubb, Charles W. V, 390
Grubb, Curtis IV, 210
Grubb, Curtis IV, 241
Grubb, Curtis IV, 263
Grubb, Curtis IV, 326
Grubb, Curtis IV, 333
Grubb, Curtis VI, 395
Grubb, Curtis VI, 498
Grubb, Dabney VI, 884
Grubb, Dabney VI, 925
Grubb, David II, 174
Grubb, Deborah II, 174
Grubb, Deborah II, 226
Grubb, Deborah II, 232
Grubb, Edith II, 174
Grubb, Edith A. IV, 210
Grubb, Edith Ann IV, 89
Grubb, Edith P. IV, 714
Grubb, Edward II, 870
Grubb, Edward Gilpin II, 797
Grubb, Elijah VI, 925
Grubb, Elizabeth II, 174
Grubb, Elizabeth II, 193
Grubb, Elizabeth II, 226
Grubb, Elizabeth II, 870
Grubb, Elizabeth IV, 210
Grubb, Elizabeth VI, 395
Grubb, Elizabeth VI, 421
Grubb, Elizabeth VI, 744
Grubb, Elizabeth VI, 763
Grubb, Elizabeth M. IV, 210
Grubb, Elizabeth M. IV, 241
Grubb, Elizabeth P. II, 870
Grubb, Etta IV, 1280
Grubb, George W. V, 243
Grubb, Gertrude IV, 210
Grubb, Hannah II, 165
Grubb, Hannah II, 174
Grubb, Hannah II, 194
Grubb, Hannah II, 226
Grubb, Hannah II, 797
Grubb, Hannah II, 870
Grubb, Hannah IV, 200
Grubb, Hannah IV, 210
Grubb, Hannah IV, 333
Grubb, Hannah VI, 395
Grubb, Hannah VI, 429
Grubb, Hannah G. IV, 210
Grubb, Hannah G. IV, 263
Grubb, Henry II, 74
Grubb, Henry II, 174
Grubb, Henry II, 226
Grubb, Henry II, 249
Grubb, Isaac II, 174
Grubb, J. M. IV, 1280
Grubb, Jacob VI, 925
Grubb, Jacob VI, 1007
Grubb, Jane V. V, 243
Grubb, Jemima IV, 200
Grubb, Jemima IV, 210
Grubb, Jeremith IV, 210
Grubb, Jesse VI, 925
Grubb, Jesse VI, 978
Grubb, Jesse VI, 991
Grubb, Jimima VI, 925
Grubb, John II, 226
Grubb, John IV, 200
Grubb, John IV, 210
Grubb, John IV, 333
Grubb, John VI, 395
Grubb, John VI, 396
Grubb, Joseph II, 174
Grubb, Joseph II, 226
Grubb, Joseph VI, 395
Grubb, Joseph B. II, 870
Grubb, Joseph C. II, 870
Grubb, Joseph Caldwell II, 797
Grubb, Katharine IV, 1280
Grubb, Katherine IV, 1289
Grubb, Leander V, 243
Grubb, Lidia II, 254
Grubb, Limerick III, 142
Grubb, Louisa VI, 1001
Grubb, Lydia II, 174
Grubb, Lydia II, 201
Grubb, Lydia II, 226
Grubb, Lydia II, 242
Grubb, Lydia IV, 210
Grubb, Lydia VI, 395
Grubb, Lydia VI, 457
Grubb, Martha II, 870
Grubb, Mary II, 174
Grubb, Mary II, 226
Grubb, Mary II, 249
Grubb, Mary II, 254
Grubb, Mary II, 277
Grubb, Mary II, 724
Grubb, Mary II, 795
Grubb, Mary IV, 193
Grubb, Mary IV, 210
Grubb, Mary VI, 395
Grubb, Mary VI, 744
Grubb, Mary E. IV, 1318
Grubb, Mary Elizabeth IV, 210
Grubb, Mary Elizabeth IV, 1318
Grubb, Mary V. V, 243
Grubb, Mary, Jr. II, 226
Grubb, Mary, Jr. II, 256
Grubb, Nancey VI, 925
Grubb, Nancy VI, 925
Grubb, Nathan IV, 1280
Grubb, Patsey VI, 925
Grubb, Polly VI, 925
Grubb, Rebeccah VI, 395
Grubb, Rebekah VI, 395
Grubb, Rebekah VI, 396
Grubb, Rob II, 174
Grubb, Robert II, 174
Grubb, Robert II, 193
Grubb, Robert II, 194
Grubb, Robert II, 226
Grubb, Robert II, 232
Grubb, Robert II, 242
Grubb, Robert II, 254
Grubb, Robert II, 277
Grubb, Robert II, 289
Grubb, Robert II, 537
Grubb, Ruth VI, 395
Grubb, Ruth VI, 396
Grubb, Sally VI, 925
Grubb, Samuel IV, 89
Grubb, Samuel IV, 210
Grubb, Samuel L. II, 870
Grubb, Samuel S. II, 870
Grubb, Samuel S. IV, 210
Grubb, Sarah II, 174
Grubb, Sarah II, 193
Grubb, Sarah II, 194
Grubb, Sarah II, 226
Grubb, Sarah II, 229
Grubb, Sarah II, 232
Grubb, Sarah II, 242
Grubb, Sarah II, 277
Grubb, Sarah IV, 210
Grubb, Sarah VI, 395
Grubb, Sarah VI, 744
Grubb, Sarah VI, 745
Grubb, Sarah Crozier IV, 333
Grubb, Solomon VI, 925
Grubb, Susanna III, 142
Grubb, Susanna IV, 90
Grubb, Susanna VI, 395
Grubb, Susannah VI, 395
Grubb, Susannah VI, 396
Grubb, Thomas III, 142
Grubb, Thomas J. V, 243
Grubb, Wd. Mary II, 174
Grubb, William II, 174
Grubb, William II, 226
Grubb, William II, 242
Grubb, William VI, 395
Grubb, William VI, 396
Grubb, William M. II, 226
Grubb, William Miller II, 174
Grubb, William R. II, 706
Grubb, William, Jr. VI, 395
Grubb, Wm. II, 254
Grubb, Wm. VI, 744
Grubb, Wm. VI, 745
Grubb, Wm. L. II, 870
Grubb, Wm. M. III, 142
Grubb, Wm. R. II, 743
Grubb, Wm. S. II, 870
Grubb, Wraty VI, 991
Grubbs, Andrew W. VI, 925
Grubbs, Ann IV, 90
Grubbs, Curtis IV, 90
Grubbs, Edith Ann IV, 90
Grubbs, Elizabeth IV, 1269
Grubbs, Elizabeth V, 840
Grubbs, Elizabeth V, 841
Grubbs, Jacob VI, 925
Grubbs, Jefferson IV, 90
Grubbs, Leander V, 243
Grubbs, Nancy VI, 925
Grubbs, Robert VI, 821
Grubbs, Samuel IV, 90
Grubbs, Sarah VI, 821
Grubbs, Susanna IV, 90
Grube, Henerie II, 17
Gruber, Charles W. VI, 821
Gruber, George VI, 821
Gruber, Harriet E. VI, 821
Gruber, Polly K. VI, 821
Grubham, Elizabeth II, 978
Grubham, Elizabeth II, 998
Grubham, Geo. II, 978
Grubham, George II, 960
Grubham, George II, 998
Grubham, Martha II, 978
Grubham, Martha II, 998
Grubham, Martha II, 1020
Grubham, Thomas II, 998
Grubs, Mary IV, 387
Grubs, Mary IV, 397
Grue, John II, 444
Gruel, Alice P. IV, 958
Gruell, Elizabeth IV, 549
Gruell, John P. IV, 958
Gruell, Phebe F. IV, 714
Gruell, Rachel IV, 527
Gruell, Susan IV, 526
Gruell, Susan IV, 527
Gruell, Thomas D. IV, 527
Grueniski, Mary L. III, 145
Gruesser, Emily J. IV, 1252
Gruffen, Jacob I, 698
Gruffen, Jeames I, 698
Gruffen, John I, 698
Gruffen, Mary I, 698
Grumley, Ebenezer II, 369
Grumman, Catherine V, 243
Grumman, Eddy V, 243
Grumman, Georgiana V, 243
Grumman, Georgianna V, 243
Grumman, Jesse V, 243
Grumman, Lovey V, 243
Grumman, Luty V, 243
Grumman, Monnie V, 243
Grummans, V. W. IV, 473
Grummen, V. W. IV, 473
Grummen, Victor W. IV, 473
Grundy, Alfred Allen III, 142
Grundy, Alfreda III, 142
Grundy, Alfreda Elizabeth III, 142
Grundy, Alice III, 142
Grundy, Edmund II, 799
Grundy, Rebecca II, 799
Grundy, Susan Hulme II, 799
Gruwell, Alice VI, 312
Gruwell, Alice VI, 352
Gruwell, Alice VI, 354
Gruwell, Alice P. IV, 958
Gruwell, John P. IV, 714
Gruwell, John P. IV, 911
Gruwell, John P. IV, 958
Gruwell, John R. IV, 905
Gruwell, Mary VI, 312
Gruwell, Phebe F. IV, 792
Gruwell, Phebe F. IV, 958
Gruwell, Sarah IV, 905
Gruwell, Sarah IV, 911
Gruwell, Sarah VI, 312
Gruwell, Timothy VI, 312
Gruwell, Timothy VI, 352
Gruwell, Timothy VI, 354
Grymes, Richard VI, 992
Grymes, Violet VI, 992
Gryms, Enoch I, 1084
Gryms, Jonathan I, 1084
Gryms, Josiah I, 1084
Guant, Charles I, 541
Guant, Charles I, 1016
Guant, Esther II, 224
Guant, Israel II, 224
Guant, Malichi I, 541
Guant, Malichi I, 1016
Guant, Publias I, 541
Guant, Publias I, 1016
Guant, Samuel I, 541
Guant, Samuel I, 1016
Guant, Samuel Kelly I, 541
Guant, Samuel Kelly I, 1016
Guant, Susanna I, 541
Guant, Susanna I, 1016
Guant, Zebulon, Jr. II, 224
Guardner, Elizabeth I, 593
Guardner, Rhoda I, 593

Guarrigues, Mary Ann IV, 905
Guathney, Elizabeth VI, 65
Guathney, Elizabeth VI, 91
Guchen, Lucinda I, 1119
Guder, George V, 999
Gudgeon, Mina V, 564
Gudgeon, Silas V, 564
Guerly, Joseph VI, 498
Guernsey, Benjamin Burling III, 172
Guernsey, Catharine III, 172
Guernsey, John III, 172
Guernsey, Margaret III, 172
Guernsey, Mary H. III, 142
Guernsey, Nathaniel III, 172
Guernsey, Sam'l B. III, 142
Guernsey, Samuel P. III, 172
Guernsey, Susan Amelia III, 172
Guesford, Mariam I, 880
Guess, Ann II, 369
Guess, Elizabeth II, 369
Guess, Hannah II, 989
Guess, Hannah II, 998
Guess, Jean II, 369
Guess, John II, 369
Guess, Jonathan II, 369
Guess, Rachel II, 369
Guess, Susanna II, 369
Guess, William II, 369
Guest, Alce II, 369
Guest, Alice II, 538
Guest, Alice II, 551
Guest, Alice II, 644
Guest, Amelia II, 227
Guest, Amelia II, 348
Guest, Amelia II, 490
Guest, Amelia II, 538
Guest, Amelia II, 596
Guest, Ann II, 208
Guest, Ann II, 226
Guest, Ann II, 227
Guest, Ann II, 369
Guest, Ann II, 797
Guest, Ann II, 870
Guest, Anna II, 226
Guest, Anna II, 490
Guest, Anna II, 538
Guest, Baker I, 1043
Guest, Baker V, 841
Guest, David V, 841
Guest, Deborah II, 870
Guest, Edith IV, 1318
Guest, Elizabeth II, 226
Guest, Elizabeth II, 241
Guest, Elizabeth II, 369
Guest, Elizabeth II, 538
Guest, Elizabeth II, 551
Guest, Elizabeth II, 652
Guest, Elizabeth II, 797
Guest, Elizabeth II, 870
Guest, Elizabeth V, 841
Guest, George II, 208
Guest, George II, 226
Guest, George II, 241
Guest, George II, 369
Guest, George II, 513
Guest, George II, 538
Guest, George II, 601
Guest, George II, 652
Guest, Hannah I, 1043
Guest, Hannah I, 1048
Guest, Hannah I, 1049
Guest, Hannah II, 208
Guest, Hannah II, 226
Guest, Hannah II, 369
Guest, Hannah II, 490
Guest, Hannah II, 512
Guest, Hannah II, 538
Guest, Hannah V, 841
Guest, Hezekiah II, 226
Guest, Jacob T. II, 870
Guest, Jacob Thomas II, 797
Guest, James I, 1043
Guest, James I, 1048
Guest, James I, 1049
Guest, James II, 226
Guest, James II, 369
Guest, James II, 490
Guest, James II, 512
Guest, James II, 538
Guest, James V, 841
Guest, Jean II, 369
Guest, John I, 1043
Guest, John II, 226
Guest, John II, 369
Guest, John II, 538
Guest, John II, 652
Guest, John II, 670
Guest, John II, 797
Guest, John II, 870
Guest, John V, 841
Guest, John, Jr. II, 538
Guest, Jonathan II, 226
Guest, Jonathan II, 227
Guest, Jonathan II, 272
Guest, Jonathan II, 369
Guest, Jonathan II, 512
Guest, Jonathan II, 538
Guest, Jonathan II, 596
Guest, Margaret II, 226
Guest, Margaret II, 227
Guest, Margaret II, 272
Guest, Margaret II, 369
Guest, Margaret II, 538
Guest, Margaret II, 596
Guest, Martha II, 369
Guest, Mary I, 1043
Guest, Mary II, 227
Guest, Mary II, 369
Guest, Mary II, 525
Guest, Mary II, 537
Guest, Mary II, 538
Guest, Mary II, 596
Guest, Mary II, 644
Guest, Mary II, 652
Guest, Mary Ann II, 870
Guest, Phebe II, 513
Guest, Phebe II, 601
Guest, Priscilla II, 369
Guest, Rachel II, 227
Guest, Rachel II, 369
Guest, Rachel II, 538
Guest, Richard II, 369
Guest, Sarah I, 1043
Guest, Sarah II, 226
Guest, Stephen V, 841
Guest, Susanna II, 369
Guest, Susannah II, 538
Guest, Susannah II, 670
Guest, Thomas II, 74
Guest, Thomas II, 538
Guest, Thomas V, 841
Guest, W. C. IV, 1318
Guest, William II, 369
Guest, Wm. II, 537
Guest, Wm. IV, 1318
Guffey, J. M. IV, 134
Guffin, Stephen IV, 1364
Guglass, David VI, 956
Guglass, Mary Ann VI, 956
Guian, Mary Ann IV, 334
Guier, Jesse I, 193
Guier, Mary I, 51
Guier, Rebekah I, 193
Guilbert, Katurah IV, 1280
Guilbert, Katurah IV, 1281
Guild, Catharine III, 299
Guilds, Edith Irene I, 619
Guill, Robert VI, 821
Guill, Susanna C. VI, 821
Guilpin, Louisa V, 625
Guina???, Lucy I, 627
Guindon, Albert W. IV, 397
Guindon, Albert W. IV, 401
Guindon, Bertha R. IV, 397
Guindon, Bertha R. IV, 401
Guindon, Carrol Taber IV, 397
Guindon, Carroll IV, 959
Guindon, Carroll T. IV, 959
Guindon, Carroll Taber IV, 397
Guindon, Carroll Taber IV, 959
Guindon, Clifford Joseph IV, 397
Guindon, Dorothy Inez IV, 397
Guindon, Frances IV, 959
Guindon, Frances Ruth IV, 397
Guindon, Frances Ruth IV, 959
Guindon, Francis T. IV, 397
Guindon, Francis T. IV, 714
Guindon, Francis T. IV, 959
Guindon, George IV, 959
Guindon, George A. IV, 959
Guindon, George Albert IV, 397
Guindon, George Albert IV, 959
Guindon, Joseph N. IV, 397
Guindon, Joseph N. IV, 959
Guindon, Joseph N. IV, 980
Guindon, Joseph W. IV, 397
Guindon, Lydia M. IV, 714
Guindon, Mary Eva IV, 397
Guindon, Susanna H. IV, 397
Guindon, Susanna H. IV, 959
Guindon, Susannah H. IV, 714
Guindon, Wilford Francis IV, 397
Guindon, William Raymond IV, 397
Guindon, Zoa IV, 959
Guindon, Zoa C. IV, 397
Guindon, Zoa C. IV, 980
Guindon, Zoa Caroline IV, 397
Guindon, Zoa Caroline IV, 959
Guindon, Zoa Miles IV, 959
Guinea, Col. Harry VI, 821
Guinea, Col. Mary A. VI, 821
Guinea, Morriss VI, 934
Guinn, Allen T. V, 676
Guinn, Asa V, 999
Guinn, Charles V, 999
Guinn, Hickman V, 999
Guinn, J. C. Fremont V, 999
Guinn, Laydock II, 369
Guinn, Mary V, 999
Guinn, Russel V, 999
Guinn, Sarah Amanda IV, 334
Guinn, Tina V, 999
Guinn, Vena V, 999
Guinn, William II, 369
Guion, Benjamin III, 142
Guion, Mary III, 142
Guion, Sarah III, 142
Guir, Exum I, 193
Guir, Jesse I, 193
Guir, Rebekah I, 193
Guir, Silous I, 193
Guire, John I, 812
Guire, Mary I, 51
Guire, Mary I, 542
Guire, Nathan W. I, 812
Guire, Rachel V, 303
Guire, Rachel V, 311
Guire, Sarah V, 303
Guiselman, Ezra V, 999
Guiselman, Sarah V, 999
Gulager, ??? III, 142
Gulager, Henry III, 142
Gulager, Louisa III, 142
Guldin, Faney VI, 1015
Gulliand, David V, 333
Gully, Ann II, 538
Gulson, Joshua II, 369
Gulson, Joshua II, 538
Gultery, Henry VI, 243
Gum, Anthony II, 369
Gumere, Ann IV, 206
Gumere, Ann IV, 527
Gumere, Eli IV, 206
Gumere, Eli IV, 334
Gumere, Eli IV, 527
Gumere, Enoch IV, 527
Gumere, Hannah IV, 527
Gumere, Harlan IV, 527
Gumere, Harlen IV, 206
Gumere, John IV, 206
Gumere, John IV, 527
Gumere, Joshua IV, 527
Gumere, Phebe IV, 206
Gumere, Phebe IV, 527
Gumere, Swithen IV, 206
Gumere, Swithen IV, 527
Gumere, Thomas IV, 527
Gumere, William IV, 527
Gumere, Wm. IV, 206
Gumeree, Eli IV, 333
Gumery, Ann IV, 206
Gumery, Ann IV, 210
Gumery, Ann IV, 259
Gumery, Ann IV, 293
Gumery, Ann IV, 312
Gumery, Ann IV, 333
Gumery, Benjamin IV, 206
Gumery, Benjamin IV, 312
Gumery, Benjamin IV, 333
Gumery, Eli IV, 312
Gumery, Eli IV, 333
Gumery, Eli IV, 334
Gumery, Elizabeth IV, 210
Gumery, Elizabeth IV, 293
Gumery, Elizabeth IV, 312
Gumery, Enoch IV, 206
Gumery, Enoch IV, 312
Gumery, Enoch IV, 333
Gumery, Ephraim J. Parker IV, 333
Gumery, Hannah IV, 206
Gumery, Hannah IV, 210
Gumery, Hannah IV, 312
Gumery, Hannah IV, 333
Gumery, Hannah IV, 334
Gumery, Hannah IV, 357
Gumery, Isaac IV, 206
Gumery, Isaac IV, 210
Gumery, Isaac IV, 334
Gumery, John IV, 206
Gumery, John IV, 210
Gumery, John IV, 293
Gumery, John IV, 334
Gumery, John, Jr. IV, 206
Gumery, John, Jr. IV, 333
Gumery, Joshua IV, 206
Gumery, Joshua IV, 312
Gumery, Joshua IV, 333
Gumery, Lavina IV, 206
Gumery, Lavina IV, 312
Gumery, Lavina IV, 333
Gumery, Levina IV, 206
Gumery, Levinah IV, 210
Gumery, Levinah IV, 293
Gumery, Lewis IV, 333
Gumery, Lydia IV, 210
Gumery, Lydia IV, 312
Gumery, Lydia IV, 313
Gumery, Nancy IV, 210
Gumery, Nancy IV, 312
Gumery, Nancy IV, 334
Gumery, Phebe IV, 259
Gumery, Phebe IV, 312
Gumery, Phebe IV, 333
Gumery, Sarah IV, 210
Gumery, Sarah IV, 312
Gumery, Sarah IV, 334
Gumery, Swithen IV, 312
Gumery, Swithen IV, 333
Gumery, Thomas IV, 333
Gumery, Thomas L. IV, 312
Gumery, William IV, 206
Gumery, William IV, 312
Gumery, William IV, 333
Gumley, Deborah II, 538
Gumley, Deborah II, 555
Gumley, Deborah II, 998
Gumley, Deborah II, 1003
Gumley, John II, 369
Gumley, John II, 538
Gumley, Mary II, 369
Gumley, Wd. Deborah II, 538
Gumley, William II, 369
Gummere, ??? III, 142
Gummere, Abel II, 289
Gummere, Abigail B. II, 175
Gummere, Abigail B. II, 289
Gummere, Amelia M. II, 175
Gummere, Amelia Mott II, 15
Gummere, Amelia Mott II, 163
Gummere, Amelia Smith II, 289
Gummere, Amelia Smith II, 297
Gummere, Anna II, 289
Gummere, Anna M. II, 175
Gummere, Anna M. II, 289
Gummere, Barker II, 175
Gummere, Benjamin V, 952
Gummere, Caroline E. II, 289
Gummere, Caroline Elizabeth II, 289
Gummere, Charles II, 175
Gummere, Charles II, 289
Gummere, Christiana II, 289
Gummere, Edward II, 175
Gummere, Edward II, 289
Gummere, Elisabeth II, 175
Gummere, Elizabeth II, 174
Gummere, Elizabeth II, 175
Gummere, Elizabeth II, 205
Gummere, Elizabeth II, 227
Gummere, Elizabeth II, 286
Gummere, Elizabeth II, 289
Gummere, Elizabeth II, 293
Gummere, Elizabeth B. II, 289
Gummere, Elizabeth B. II, 295
Gummere, Elizabeth D. II, 196
Gummere, Elizabeth D. II, 289
Gummere, Elizabeth H. II, 175
Gummere, Elizabeth H. II, 289
Gummere, Elizabeth J. II, 289
Gummere, Elizabeth J. II, 297
Gummere, Ellen II, 175
Gummere, Ellen II, 289
Gummere, Frances II, 175
Gummere, Frances II, 289
Gummere, Frances II, 295
Gummere, Frances M. II, 289
Gummere, Frances Marsh II, 289
Gummere, Francis II, 289
Gummere, Francis B. II, 174
Gummere, Francis B. II, 175
Gummere, Francis Barton II, 289
Gummere, Francis Barton II, 297
Gummere, Francis Barton, Jr. II, 289
Gummere, George II, 175
Gummere, Hannah II, 289
Gummere, Hannah V, 952
Gummere, Henry D. II, 289
Gummere, Henry Day II, 175
Gummere, Henry Day II, 289
Gummere, Isabella II, 175
Gummere, John II, 174
Gummere, John II, 175
Gummere, John II, 205
Gummere, John II, 227
Gummere, John II, 286
Gummere, John II, 289
Gummere, John II, 295
Gummere, John III, 142
Gummere, John J. II, 289
Gummere, John, Jr. II, 289
Gummere, Jonathan II, 289
Gummere, Joshua V, 952
Gummere, Levina V, 952
Gummere, Margaret II, 289
Gummere, Maria M. II, 289
Gummere, Maria Mott II, 175
Gummere, Martha II, 289
Gummere, Martha B. II, 175
Gummere, Martha B. II, 289
Gummere, Martha M. II, 289
Gummere, Martha M. II, 293
Gummere, Martha M. W. II, 1
Gummere, Mary II, 175
Gummere, Mary II, 289
Gummere, Mayberry II, 178
Gummere, Phebe IV, 80
Gummere, Phebe IV, 89
Gummere, Phebe IV, 339
Gummere, Phebe V, 952
Gummere, Phebe V, 957
Gummere, R. Morris II, 175
Gummere, R. Morris II, 289
Gummere, Rachel II, 175
Gummere, Rachel II, 178
Gummere, Rachel II, 196
Gummere, Rachel II, 205
Gummere, Rachel II, 227
Gummere, Rachel II, 236
Gummere, Rachel I. II, 227
Gummere, Rachel I. II, 236
Gummere, Rachel J. II, 227
Gummere, Rachel, Jr. II, 227
Gummere, Rebecca H. II, 289
Gummere, Rebecca Hunt II, 1
Gummere, Richard Morris II,
Gummere, Richard Morris II,
Gummere, Richard Mott II, 1
Gummere, Richard Mott II, 2
Gummere, Samuel II, 175
Gummere, Samuel II, 178
Gummere, Samuel II, 196
Gummere, Samuel II, 205
Gummere, Samuel II, 227
Gummere, Samuel II, 236
Gummere, Samuel J. II, 174
Gummere, Samuel J. II, 175
Gummere, Samuel J. II, 227
Gummere, Samuel J. II, 289
Gummere, Samuel J. II, 297
Gummere, Samuel James II,
Gummere, Samuel R. II, 174
Gummere, Samuel R. II, 175
Gummere, Samuel R. II, 196
Gummere, Samuel R. II, 289
Gummere, Samuel, Jr. II, 227
Gummere, Susan B. II, 286
Gummere, Susan B. II, 289
Gummere, Susanna B. II, 174
Gummere, Susannah B. II, 22
Gummere, Swithen V, 952
Gummere, Wd. Elizabeth II,
Gummere, Wd. Elizabeth B. II, 174
Gummere, Wd. Lydia II, 178
Gummere, William II, 289
Gummere, William II, 293
Gummere, William H. II, 289
Gummere, William Henry II,
Gummere, William, Jr. II, 175
Gummere, Wm. V, 952
Gummersal, Thomas III, 142
Gummerson, George S. III, 83
Gummerson, Mildred Laura III, 83
Gummery, Benjamin II, 369
Gummery, Benjamin IV, 312
Gummery, Deborah II, 369
Gummery, Eli IV, 312
Gummery, Enoch IV, 312
Gummery, Hannah II, 998
Gummery, Hannah II, 1017
Gummery, Hannah IV, 312
Gummery, Hepsebah V, 899
Gummery, John II, 369
Gummery, Joshua IV, 312
Gummery, Lavina IV, 312
Gummery, Phebe IV, 312
Gummery, Swithen IV, 312
Gummery, Thomas L. IV, 312
Gummery, William IV, 312
Gumminhart, Ella IV, 1252
Gumminhart, George IV, 1252
Gumminhart, Gussie IV, 1252
Gumminhart, Harry IV, 1252
Gumminhart, Lizzie IV, 1252
Gumminhart, Louisa IV, 1252
Gumminhart, Samuel IV, 125
Gumminhart, Wm. IV, 1252
Gumnerson, Alice T. III, 142
Gumnerson, Geo. J. III, 142
Gumnerson, George S. III, 14

mnerson, Mildred Laura
III, 142
mp, Florence E. IV, 1252
nderson, Gertrude L. II, 971
nderson, Katherine II, 971
nderson, Lewis II, 971
ndy, Cyrus V, 999
ndy, Joanna V, 999
nnall, Sally VI, 811
nnaway, Lucy VI, 805
nnaway, Woodson VI, 805
nter, Bruce I, 208
nter, Bruce L. I, 215
nter, Helen I, 215
nter, Helen Rachel I, 208
rley, Alfred I, 588
rley, Alpheus N. V, 623
rley, Alpheus Newton V, 623
rley, Arrelia G. I, 939
rley, Arrelia G. I, 941
rley, Aurelia E. I, 880
rley, Benjamin F. I, 588
rley, Benjamin Franklin I, 593
rley, C. Lee I, 941
rley, Calvin Lee I, 880
rley, Caroline VI, 744
rley, Charles I, 498
rley, Charles I, 542
rley, Charles I, 588
rley, Charles I, 593
rley, Charles I, 595
rley, Charles I, 679
rley, Charles I, 812
rley, Danyeal I, 290
rley, David S. I, 925
rley, David S. I, 941
rley, Derio I, 925
rley, Devro I, 941
rley, Edey I, 290
rley, Eliza I, 588
rley, Eliza I, 593
rley, Eliza I, 679
rley, Eliza I, 812
rley, Eliza H. I, 812
rley, Elizabeth I, 498
rley, Elizabeth I, 542
rley, Elmina I, 542
rley, Elmina I, 593
rley, Elmina J. I, 542
rley, Elmina J. I, 593
rley, Frances M. V, 623
rley, George I, 588
rley, George Anner I, 290
rley, Georgianna I, 621
rley, Hubert I, 941
rley, Isaac I, 498
rley, Isaac I, 588
rley, Isaac I, 593
rley, Isaac I, 596
rley, Jean I, 588
rley, Job I, 498
rley, John I, 498
rley, John I, 542
rley, John I, 574
rley, John I, 588
rley, John I, 593
rley, John I, 932
rley, John I, 963
rley, John W. V, 623
rley, John, Jr. I, 588
rley, John, Sr. I, 588
rley, Joseph Addison I, 593
rley, Lydda I, 963
rley, Lydia I, 542
rley, Lydia I, 572
rley, Mary I, 542
rley, Mary I, 572
rley, Nannie E. I, 880
rley, Nathan I, 588
rley, Nathan I, 593
rley, Patsey I, 925
rley, Penninah I, 940
rley, Penninah I, 941
rley, Rhoda I, 586
rley, Rhoda I, 588
rley, Rhoda I, 593
rley, Rhoda I, 679
rley, Rhoda I, 812
rley, Rhoda I, 822
rley, Rody I, 498
rley, Rohda I, 542
rley, Rohda I, 574
rley, Ruth I, 588
rley, Ruth I, 593
rley, Ruth I, 595
rley, Ruth I, 679
rley, Ruth I, 812
rley, Sally I, 588
rley, Sally I, 593
rley, Sally I, 595
rley, Sarah I, 542
Gurley, Sarah I, 932
Gurley, Sarah C. I, 932
Gurley, Susanna I, 588
Gurley, Susanna I, 593
Gurley, Susanna I, 596
Gurley, Thomas Chalkley I, 593
Gurley, Widow Lydia I, 542
Gurley, William I, 588
Gurley, William I, 593
Gurley, Zilpha I, 932
Gurly, Joseph VI, 645
Gurly, Ruth I, 812
Gurnee, Frances W. III, 295
Gurnee, Francis W. III, 143
Gurnee, Margaret E. III, 143
Gurnee, Margaret E. III, 295
Gurnee, Myra III, 295
Gurnee, Myra E. III, 143
Gurnee, Myra E. III, 295
Gurnee, Wd. Margaret E. III, 143
Gurney, Amy III, 167
Gurney, Amy H. III, 65
Gurney, Amy H. III, 167
Gurney, Amy H. III, 256
Gurney, Eliza P. II, 289
Gurney, Eliza Paul II, 289
Gurney, Emily Jane III, 59
Gurney, James I, 622
Gurney, Joseph John II, 175
Gurney, Joseph John VI, 243
Gurney, Roxie V. I, 622
Gurney, Wd. Eliza P. II, 175
Gurnsey, Ann IV, 334
Gurnsey, Elizabeth IV, 334
Gurnsey, Hannah IV, 334
Gurnsey, Isaac IV, 334
Gurnsey, John IV, 334
Gurnsey, Sarah IV, 334
Gurvis, Sylvester V, 999
Guryton, Isaac Oliver IV, 210
Gus, Mary I, 141
Gustin, Alice V, 676
Gustin, Jonathan V, 676
Gustin, Milburn V, 676
Gustin, Milburn V, 710
Gustin, Norah V, 676
Gustin, Phoebe V, 676
Gustin, Phoebe V, 710
Gustin, Wm. C. V, 676
Gustin, Wm. E. V, 676
Gusweiler, Amy V, 904
Gusweiler, Amy V, 908
Gusweiler, Amy A. V, 908
Gusweiler, Amy Annetta V, 908
Gusweiler, Anna Margaret V, 908
Gusweiler, Ellen Elverta V, 908
Gusweiler, Frank Morton V, 908
Gusweiler, Frank R. V, 908
Gusweiler, Frederick Walton
V, 908
Gusweiler, Joseph G. V, 908
Gusweiler, Joseph Geo. V, 908
Gusweiler, Joseph Geo., Jr.
V, 908
Gusweiler, Joseph George, Jr.
V, 908
Gusweiler, Joseph, Jr. V, 908
Gusweiler, Laura V, 908
Gusweiler, Laura U. B. V, 908
Gusweiler, Lura B. V, 908
Gusweiler, Mary Margaret V, 908
Gusweiler, Ripley Frank V, 908
Gutherie, Clayborn B. I, 618
Gutherie, Clayborn Braxton
I, 617
Gutherie, Edna Mae I, 617
Gutherie, John B. I, 617
Gutherie, Margaret A. I, 618
Gutherie, Mary A. V, 243
Gutherie, Mary Elsina I, 617
Gutherie, Nancy I, 617
Gutherie, Nancy Elisabeth I, 618
Gutherie, Nettie V, 243
Gutherie, Robert Hazel I, 617
Guthrey, Anney VI, 918
Guthrey, Reuben VI, 925
Guthrie, Alfred I, 446
Guthrie, Anna Lavonna V, 243
Guthrie, Austin T. V, 676
Guthrie, Bessie V, 676
Guthrie, Bessie N. V, 676
Guthrie, Candice I, 446
Guthrie, Candis I, 434
Guthrie, Carl V, 676
Guthrie, Carl L. V, 676
Guthrie, Caroline I, 446
Guthrie, Claborn I, 446
Guthrie, Clayborn B. I, 633
Guthrie, Claybourne I, 434
Guthrie, Elener I, 446
Guthrie, Elizabeth I, 446
Guthrie, Elizabeth VI, 821
Guthrie, Elsie I, 633
Guthrie, Elsie I, 634
Guthrie, Esther M. VI, 821
Guthrie, Forest G. V, 676
Guthrie, George I, 434
Guthrie, George I, 446
Guthrie, Hannibal Eugene V, 243
Guthrie, Hazel I, 633
Guthrie, Helena Elizabeth
III, 143
Guthrie, James V, 676
Guthrie, James VI, 925
Guthrie, James D. V, 676
Guthrie, John I, 434
Guthrie, John F. I, 446
Guthrie, John Henry V, 243
Guthrie, Kate IV, 1163
Guthrie, Katharine B. IV, 1163
Guthrie, Katherine IV, 1252
Guthrie, Katie IV, 1252
Guthrie, Katie, Jr. IV, 1163
Guthrie, Katie, Sr. IV, 1163
Guthrie, Margaret V, 243
Guthrie, Martha Elisabeth I, 622
Guthrie, Mary I, 434
Guthrie, Mary I, 446
Guthrie, Mary A. V, 243
Guthrie, Mary Caroline I, 434
Guthrie, Minnie V, 243
Guthrie, Nancy I, 434
Guthrie, Nancy I, 446
Guthrie, Nettie V, 243
Guthrie, Nicholas VI, 821
Guthrie, Oliver I, 434
Guthrie, Oliver I, 446
Guthrie, Oliver VI, 821
Guthrie, Rachel VI, 821
Guthrie, Richard Clarence I, 434
Guthrie, Robert V, 676
Guthrie, S. B. V, 243
Guthrie, Sallie V, 243
Guthrie, Samuel VI, 821
Guthrie, Sarah I, 434
Guthrie, Sarah I, 446
Guthrie, Sarah A. I, 446
Guthrie, Sarah Ann I, 434
Guthrie, Susan VI, 821
Guthrie, William VI, 821
Guthrie, Zachariah T. V, 243
Guthry, Agnes VI, 830
Guthry, Anna IV, 90
Guthry, Anna IV, 109
Guthry, Elizabeth VI, 925
Guthry, Henry VI, 830
Guthry, James VI, 312
Guthry, James VI, 925
Guthry, Jane VI, 821
Guthry, John VI, 821
Guthry, John VI, 904
Guthry, John VI, 925
Guthry, Mary VI, 916
Guthry, Milley VI, 904
Guthry, Nancy VI, 925
Guthry, Reuben VI, 925
Guthry, Richard VI, 925
Guthry, Ruth VI, 948
Guthry, S. Simmons VI, 925
Guthry, Sally VI, 925
Gutshall, Belle IV, 210
Gutshall, Clara B. IV, 210
Gutshall, Erma IV, 210
Gutshall, Irma IV, 210
Gutshall, Wm. IV, 210
Gutshaw, Clara B. IV, 210
Guttery, Elener I, 446
Guttery, Elener I, 451
Guttery, James VI, 867
Guttery, Martha VI, 867
Guttry, Penelope VI, 304
Guttry, Penelope VI, 803
Guy, Abigail I, 140
Guy, Abigail I, 307
Guy, Abigail Susan III, 143
Guy, Abigail Susan III, 238
Guy, Atlas I, 336
Guy, Bertha III, 143
Guy, Bridgett II, 227
Guy, Charlotte IV, 1099
Guy, Charlotte IV, 1112
Guy, Edward II, 444
Guy, Eliza IV, 1096
Guy, Eliza IV, 1099
Guy, Hannah I, 140
Guy, Hannah I, 307
Guy, Ichabod Ward I, 336
Guy, Isaac IV, 210
Guy, Iva IV, 1318
Guy, J. H. I, 336
Guy, Jemimah II, 369
Guy, Jeremiah II, 369
Guy, John I, 141
Guy, John II, 369
Guy, John II, 516
Guy, John II, 538
Guy, John Henry III, 143
Guy, Joseph IV, 210
Guy, Margaret I, 141
Guy, Margaret I, 147
Guy, Margrett II, 369
Guy, Mary I, 140
Guy, Mary I, 141
Guy, Mary III, 143
Guy, Mary III, 238
Guy, Mary L. II, 713
Guy, Miranda VI, 745
Guy, Mrs. Mamje I, 336
Guy, Myrtle V. IV, 1318
Guy, Percy C. II, 713
Guy, Percy C. III, 143
Guy, Percy C. III, 238
Guy, Richard II, 17
Guy, Richard II, 18
Guy, Richard II, 65
Guy, Richard II, 227
Guy, Sarah Morgan VI, 745
Guy, Susan A. II, 713
Guy, William I, 140
Guy, William I, 141
Guy, William VI, 745
Guy, Wm. H. IV, 1318
Guyar, Miriam, Jr. I, 193
Guyar, Miriam, Jr. I, 203
Guye, Bridgett II, 227
Guye, Richard II, 227
Guyer, Aaron I, 183
Guyer, Abigail I, 183
Guyer, Abigail I, 193
Guyer, Ausley IV, 1318
Guyer, Ausley E. IV, 1318
Guyer, Cornelia Adeline I, 781
Guyer, David Harper I, 781
Guyer, Esther I, 183
Guyer, Esther I, 193
Guyer, Esther I, 197
Guyer, Exum I, 183
Guyer, Exum I, 193
Guyer, Guley Elma I, 183
Guyer, Gulielma I, 193
Guyer, James Henry I, 781
Guyer, Jemima I, 781
Guyer, Jemima I, 812
Guyer, Jesse I, 183
Guyer, Jesse I, 193
Guyer, Jno. I, 51
Guyer, John I, 51
Guyer, John I, 68
Guyer, John I, 183
Guyer, John I, 193
Guyer, John I, 798
Guyer, John I, 812
Guyer, John B. I, 781
Guyer, John Marshal I, 781
Guyer, Joseph I, 36
Guyer, Joseph I, 51
Guyer, Joseph I, 193
Guyer, Joseph I, 716
Guyer, Joseph I, 812
Guyer, Joshua I, 51
Guyer, Lydia I, 798
Guyer, Lydia I, 812
Guyer, Lydia T. I, 781
Guyer, Mary I, 51
Guyer, Mary I, 193
Guyer, Mary I, 781
Guyer, Mary I, 812
Guyer, Miriam I, 36
Guyer, Miriam I, 51
Guyer, Miriam I, 68
Guyer, Miriam I, 193
Guyer, Miriam I, 808
Guyer, Miriam I, 812
Guyer, Miriam, Jr. I, 193
Guyer, Nathan I, 193
Guyer, Nathan I, 781
Guyer, Nathan I, 812
Guyer, Nathan W. I, 812
Guyer, Nathan, Sr. I, 781
Guyer, Nathan, Sr. I, 812
Guyer, Olive E. IV, 1163
Guyer, Ottillie III, 136
Guyer, Ottillie III, 143
Guyer, Rebekah I, 193
Guyer, Samuel I, 193
Guyer, Sarah I, 183
Guyer, Sarah I, 193
Guyer, Sarah I, 716
Guyer, Sarah I, 734
Guyer, Sarah I, 798
Guyer, Sarah I, 812
Guyer, Sarah V, 303
Guyer, Seth I, 183
Guyer, Silas I, 183
Guyer, Silous I, 193
Guyer, William I, 193
Guyin, Rachel IV, 315
Guyne, Allen VI, 934
Guyne, Peggy VI, 934
Guynn, Albert IV, 334
Guynn, Albert L. IV, 334
Guynn, Amanda IV, 334
Guynn, Elizabeth A. IV, 334
Guynn, Frank IV, 210
Guynn, Hannah IV, 210
Guynn, Hugh IV, 210
Guynn, Hugh Oliver IV, 334
Guynn, Jequette IV, 210
Guynn, John IV, 334
Guynn, Mary IV, 334
Guynn, Mary Ann IV, 334
Guynn, Mary Elizabeth IV, 334
Guynn, Mary L. IV, 334
Guynn, Minnie Wanita IV, 334
Guynn, Rachel IV, 334
Guynn, Sarah IV, 334
Guynn, Sarah Amanda IV, 334
Guynn, Thomas IV, 334
Guynn, Thomas F. IV, 334
Guynn, William S. IV, 334
Guyselman, E. L. V, 999
Gwaltney, Albert VI, 925
Gwaltney, Ann VI, 925
Gwaltney, Jemima VI, 925
Gwaltney, John R. VI, 1018
Gwaltney, Mary VI, 925
Gwaltney, Mary Ann VI, 960
Gwaltney, William VI, 925
Gwathny, Anne Maria VI, 925
Gwathny, George VI, 925
Gwatkin, Catharine VI, 885
Gwatkin, Charles VI, 925
Gwatkin, Charles VI, 1013
Gwatkin, Charles B. VI, 925
Gwatkin, Charlotte A. VI, 925
Gwatkin, Chas. VI, 951
Gwatkin, Chas. VI, 969
Gwatkin, Edward VI, 925
Gwatkin, Eliza Ann VI, 938
Gwatkin, Fanny VI, 969
Gwatkin, Frances O. VI, 972
Gwatkin, James VI, 925
Gwatkin, James VI, 1004
Gwatkin, Joshua VI, 925
Gwatkin, Lucy M. VI, 935
Gwatkin, Mary VI, 925
Gwatkin, Mary A. VI, 1013
Gwatkin, Mary J. VI, 938
Gwatkin, Molley VI, 963
Gwatkin, Nancy H. VI, 963
Gwatkin, Permelia C. VI, 925
Gwatkin, Polly VI, 925
Gwatkins, Charles VI, 925
Gwatkins, Charles B. VI, 1003
Gwatkins, Edward VI, 903
Gwatkins, Elizabeth VI, 894
Gwatkins, Kitty VI, 951
Gwatkins, Lucinda VI, 889
Gwatkins, Mary VI, 894
Gwatkins, Molly VI, 903
Gwatkins, Peggy VI, 894
Gwatkins, Polly VI, 1014
Gwatkins, Polly C. VI, 903
Gwattney, Ann Mariah VI, 821
Gwattney, Temple VI, 821
Gwin, Charity I, 1119
Gwin, Charity I, 1126
Gwin, Mary Ann IV, 334
Gwinn, Frank IV, 210
Gwinn, Hannah IV, 210
Gwinn, Hannah IV, 255
Gwinn, Hugh IV, 210
Gwinn, Isaac IV, 210
Gwinn, Jequette IV, 210
Gwinn, Mary Elizabeth IV, 210
Gwinn, Rachel IV, 210
Gwinn, Sarah Amanda IV, 341
Gwinn, Sarah Ann IV, 210
Gwinn, Susana IV, 210
Gwinn, Susanna IV, 210
Gwinn, Thomas IV, 210
Gwinn, William IV, 210
Gwoir, Anne M. IV, 555
Gwyer, Gwendolyn III, 143
Gwyer, Gwendolyn III, 339
Gwyn, Hannah IV, 210
Gwyn, Mary II, 369
Gwyn, Susanna IV, 210
Gwyn, Susanna IV, 248
Gwyn, Thomas IV, 210
Gwynedd, Sarah II, 538
Gwynn, Albert IV, 334
Gwynn, Hannah IV, 210
Gwynn, Hannah IV, 290

Gwynn, Mary Elizabeth IV, 334
Gwynn, Minnie Wanita IV, 334
Gwynn, Nancy VI, 925
Gwynn, Rachel IV, 334
Gwynn, Samuel VI, 925
Gwynn, Sarah Ann IV, 191
Gwynn, Sarah Ann IV, 311
Gwynn, Sarah Ann IV, 312
Gwynn, Thomas IV, 210
Gwynne, Julia III, 273
Gyer, Mary I, 812
Gyer, Mary I, 822
Gyger, Elma IV, 959
Gyger, Elma IV, 975
Gymer, Emma IV, 1318
Gymer, Mahala IV, 1318
Gypson, Garet I, 542
Gyre, Nathan I, 812

H???, Eliza III, 308
H???, Emily III, 361
Haack, Anna III, 176
Haack, Anna III, 268
Haas, Frederick VI, 821
Haas, John VI, 858
Haas, Lena V, 999
Haas, Lucy VI, 821
Haas, Mary VI, 858
Habbick, George Wm. III, 143
Habbick, Mary III, 143
Haberland, Fred IV, 1038
Hack, Fred IV, 1161
Hack, Lena IV, 1164
Hack, Lena IV, 1185
Hack, Lena Smith IV, 1161
Hack, Mary IV, 1161
Hackaday, Henry A. VI, 981
Hackenberg, Guy IV, 1318
Hackenberg, Hanna IV, 1318
Hackenberg, Hannah IV, 1318
Hackenberg, Henry W. IV, 1318
Hackenberg, Roy IV, 1318
Hacker, Anna II, 706
Hacker, Anna Hazen II, 538
Hacker, Anna Hazen II, 743
Hacker, Beulah II, 706
Hacker, Beulah II, 776
Hacker, Beulah M. II, 743
Hacker, Beulah M. II, 765
Hacker, Charles II, 706
Hacker, Charles II, 743
Hacker, Elizabeth II, 369
Hacker, Elizabeth Lloyd Mifflin II, 743
Hacker, Hannah II, 369
Hacker, Hannah J. II, 743
Hacker, Hannah J. II, 776
Hacker, Hannah Wistar II, 743
Hacker, Isaiah II, 369
Hacker, Isaiah II, 538
Hacker, Isaiah II, 706
Hacker, Isaiah II, 743
Hacker, J. Barclay II, 743
Hacker, Jeremiah II, 706
Hacker, Jeremiah II, 743
Hacker, Jeremiah II, 765
Hacker, Jeremiah II, 776
Hacker, John Barclay II, 706
Hacker, Lloyd Mifflin II, 706
Hacker, Mary II, 743
Hacker, Mary S. II, 743
Hacker, Paschall II, 743
Hacker, Paschall II, 765
Hacker, Rebecca II, 538
Hacker, Rebecca II, 743
Hacker, Wm. II, 743
Hacker, Wm. II, 776
Hacker, Wm. Brown II, 538
Hacket, Elizabeth II, 62
Hacket, Elizabeth II, 74
Hacket, Lucy VI, 814
Hacket, Sally VI, 820
Hacket, Sarah II, 74
Hackett, Amy VI, 840
Hackett, Col. Joseph VI, 822
Hackett, Col. Winney VI, 822
Hackett, Edna III, 64
Hackett, Edna Wallace III, 64
Hackett, Edna Wallace III, 143
Hackett, Elizabeth I, 818
Hackett, Elizabeth II, 74
Hackett, Elizabeth II, 89
Hackett, Ester VI, 865
Hackett, Isaac VI, 822
Hackett, Joseph I, 818
Hackett, Josephine Johns IV, 1318
Hackett, Lucy VI, 822
Hackett, Wm. N. III, 64
Hackley, Henry VI, 29
Hackney, A. F. I, 1153
Hackney, A. Thomas I, 1153
Hackney, Aaron I, 1119
Hackney, Aaron I, 1140
Hackney, Aaron I, 1152
Hackney, Aaron IV, 17
Hackney, Aaron IV, 90
Hackney, Aaron V, 62
Hackney, Aaron VI, 366
Hackney, Aaron VI, 395
Hackney, Aaron VI, 396
Hackney, Aaron VI, 399
Hackney, Aaron VI, 496
Hackney, Aaron VI, 499
Hackney, Aaron H. VI, 395
Hackney, Aaron H. VI, 396
Hackney, Aaron L. I, 1141
Hackney, Aaron T. I, 1153
Hackney, Aaron Thompson I, 1140
Hackney, Aaron Thos. I, 1141
Hackney, Aaron, Jr. IV, 90
Hackney, Aaron, Sr. VI, 396
Hackney, Agnes II, 227
Hackney, Agnes II, 232
Hackney, Alex H. VI, 395
Hackney, Amos V, 62
Hackney, Amos VI, 396
Hackney, Ann I, 1141
Hackney, Ann I, 1153
Hackney, Ann VI, 362
Hackney, Ann VI, 395
Hackney, Ann J. I, 1141
Hackney, Annie I, 1153
Hackney, Arabella Tennessee I, 1140
Hackney, Aron VI, 395
Hackney, Aron VI, 396
Hackney, Aron H. VI, 499
Hackney, Benj. F. I, 1141
Hackney, Benjamin I, 1153
Hackney, Benjamin F. I, 1141
Hackney, Benjamin F. I, 1153
Hackney, Betsey I, 1140
Hackney, Bond VI, 396
Hackney, Caladonia I, 1141
Hackney, Caledonia I, 1153
Hackney, Canby H. V, 62
Hackney, Canby H. V, 63
Hackney, Charity VI, 379
Hackney, Charity VI, 395
Hackney, Charity VI, 396
Hackney, Charity VI, 444
Hackney, Charity VI, 501
Hackney, Charity VI, 560
Hackney, Clay I, 1153
Hackney, David I, 1141
Hackney, David I, 1153
Hackney, David Jones I, 1153
Hackney, Deborah VI, 395
Hackney, Deborah L. V, 494
Hackney, Edith L. I, 1141
Hackney, Edith L. McClure I, 1153
Hackney, Edward V, 494
Hackney, Edward V, 676
Hackney, Edward VI, 396
Hackney, Edward Bond V, 62
Hackney, Eleanor VI, 396
Hackney, Eleanor W. V, 62
Hackney, Elijah I, 1141
Hackney, Elijah I, 1153
Hackney, Eliza I, 1153
Hackney, Eliza J. I, 1141
Hackney, Elizabeth I, 1141
Hackney, Elizabeth I, 1152
Hackney, Elizabeth I, 1153
Hackney, Elizabeth I, 1154
Hackney, Elizabeth I, 1155
Hackney, Elizabeth VI, 395
Hackney, Elizabeth VI, 499
Hackney, Elizabeth J. I, 1147
Hackney, Elizabeth J. I, 1153
Hackney, Elizabeth Jane I, 1141
Hackney, Elizabeth M. I, 1141
Hackney, Elmira B. V, 62
Hackney, Elmira B. V, 63
Hackney, Ephraim A. I, 1141
Hackney, Evan L. V, 63
Hackney, Evan Lewis V, 62
Hackney, F. R. I, 1153
Hackney, Francis I, 1140
Hackney, Francis I, 1141
Hackney, Francis J. I, 1153
Hackney, Francis N. I, 1141
Hackney, Francis N. I, 1153
Hackney, Francis R. I, 1141
Hackney, Francis R. I, 1153
Hackney, Frank J. I, 1150
Hackney, Frank J. I, 1153
Hackney, Frankis Ira I, 1141
Hackney, Franklin I, 1153
Hackney, George I, 1153
Hackney, George IV, 90
Hackney, George VI, 395
Hackney, George VI, 499
Hackney, George T. I, 1141
Hackney, George T. I, 1153
Hackney, George Thomson I, 1153
Hackney, Gulia Elma I, 1141
Hackney, Gustavus A. I, 1140
Hackney, Gustavus A. I, 1153
Hackney, Hannah IV, 90
Hackney, Hannah VI, 366
Hackney, Hannah VI, 395
Hackney, Hannah VI, 396
Hackney, Hannah VI, 440
Hackney, Hannah VI, 496
Hackney, Hannah VI, 499
Hackney, Hannah E. I, 1141
Hackney, Henry A. I, 1153
Hackney, Henry Adrian I, 1140
Hackney, Henry C. I, 628
Hackney, Henry Clay I, 1141
Hackney, Henry Clay I, 1153
Hackney, Henryanna I, 628
Hackney, Henryanna I, 1153
Hackney, Henryanna C. I, 633
Hackney, Henryanna C. I, 642
Hackney, Howard V, 494
Hackney, Hugh I, 1137
Hackney, Hugh I, 1141
Hackney, Hugh I, 1152
Hackney, Hugh V, 62
Hackney, Hugh VI, 396
Hackney, Hugh L. I, 1153
Hackney, Hugh L. W. I, 1141
Hackney, Hugh L. W. I, 1153
Hackney, Ira Lewis I, 1119
Hackney, J. Wesley I, 1153
Hackney, James L. I, 1140
Hackney, James L. I, 1153
Hackney, James L. V, 676
Hackney, James R. I, 1141
Hackney, James T. I, 1141
Hackney, Jane I, 1119
Hackney, Jane I, 1140
Hackney, Jane I, 1141
Hackney, Jane I, 1153
Hackney, Jehu VI, 395
Hackney, Jehu VI, 499
Hackney, Jno VI, 395
Hackney, Joe Dan I, 625
Hackney, John I, 1140
Hackney, John I, 1141
Hackney, John I, 1152
Hackney, John I, 1153
Hackney, John IV, 90
Hackney, John VI, 993
Hackney, John C. I, 1141
Hackney, John C. I, 1153
Hackney, John L. I, 1141
Hackney, John L. I, 1153
Hackney, John Lewis V, 62
Hackney, John Lewis V, 494
Hackney, John Lewis VI, 396
Hackney, John Westley I, 1141
Hackney, John, Jr. I, 1153
Hackney, Jos. VI, 395
Hackney, Joseph I, 1030
Hackney, Joseph II, 227
Hackney, Joseph II, 265
Hackney, Joseph II, 527
Hackney, Joseph II, 538
Hackney, Joseph IV, 90
Hackney, Joseph VI, 362
Hackney, Joseph VI, 363
Hackney, Joseph VI, 395
Hackney, Joseph VI, 396
Hackney, Joseph VI, 419
Hackney, Joseph VI, 444
Hackney, Joseph VI, 445
Hackney, Joseph VI, 447
Hackney, Joseph VI, 452
Hackney, Joseph VI, 499
Hackney, Joseph E. VI, 395
Hackney, Joseph W. VI, 395
Hackney, Joseph, Jr. II, 538
Hackney, Joseph, Jr. II, 706
Hackney, Joseph, Jr. VI, 395
Hackney, Josephine I, 262
Hackney, Josephine I, 1153
Hackney, Josephine I, 1162
Hackney, Junetta I, 1141
Hackney, Junette I, 1093
Hackney, Levi I, 1141
Hackney, Levi I, 1153
Hackney, Lucinda I, 1140
Hackney, Lucinda I, 1153
Hackney, Lucinda I, 1154
Hackney, Lutitia E. I, 1141
Hackney, Lydia IV, 73
Hackney, Lydia IV, 90
Hackney, Lydia IV, 108
Hackney, Lydia VI, 395
Hackney, Lydia VI, 444
Hackney, Lydia VI, 447
Hackney, Lydia VI, 449
Hackney, Lydia VI, 452
Hackney, Lydia VI, 499
Hackney, Margaret I, 262
Hackney, Margret I, 1153
Hackney, Mariam Ann I, 1141
Hackney, Martha V, 46
Hackney, Martha VI, 362
Hackney, Martha VI, 381
Hackney, Martha VI, 395
Hackney, Martha VI, 419
Hackney, Martha VI, 444
Hackney, Martha VI, 445
Hackney, Martha Ann I, 1141
Hackney, Martha S. I, 1141
Hackney, Martha S. I, 1153
Hackney, Mary I, 391
Hackney, Mary I, 404
Hackney, Mary I, 1030
Hackney, Mary I, 1141
Hackney, Mary I, 1152
Hackney, Mary IV, 90
Hackney, Mary IV, 95
Hackney, Mary V, 676
Hackney, Mary VI, 396
Hackney, Mary VI, 445
Hackney, Mary A. I, 1141
Hackney, Mary Adline I, 1149
Hackney, Mary Adline I, 1153
Hackney, Mary Ann I, 1140
Hackney, Mary Ann VI, 395
Hackney, Mary Ann VI, 452
Hackney, Mary J. I, 1141
Hackney, Mary Jane I, 1153
Hackney, Mary L. V, 62
Hackney, Mary S. VI, 395
Hackney, Mary S. VI, 396
Hackney, Mary S. VI, 499
Hackney, Mary T. VI, 396
Hackney, Maud Caroline I, 1141
Hackney, Maynard V, 676
Hackney, Miriam Ann I, 1153
Hackney, Mittie I, 625
Hackney, N. Catherine V, 172
Hackney, Nancy I, 1140
Hackney, Nancy E. I, 1141
Hackney, Phebe I, 1141
Hackney, Phebe I, 1153
Hackney, Phebe E. I, 1141
Hackney, Phebe Elizabeth I, 1141
Hackney, Phebe Elizabeth I, 1153
Hackney, Priscilla I, 617
Hackney, Priscilla I, 628
Hackney, Priscilla B. I, 593
Hackney, Priscilla B. I, 633
Hackney, Priscilla B. I, 1153
Hackney, Rachel II, 227
Hackney, Rachel II, 265
Hackney, Rachel II, 538
Hackney, Rachel II, 743
Hackney, Rachel V, 63
Hackney, Rachel V, 123
Hackney, Rachel VI, 393
Hackney, Rachel VI, 394
Hackney, Rachel VI, 395
Hackney, Rachel G. V, 123
Hackney, Rachel G. VI, 395
Hackney, Rachel G. VI, 447
Hackney, Raichel I, 1141
Hackney, Raymond V, 676
Hackney, Rebecah I, 1152
Hackney, Rebecca I, 1119
Hackney, Rebecca I, 1141
Hackney, Rebecca I, 1152
Hackney, Rebecca Jane VI, 395
Hackney, Rebeckah I, 1140
Hackney, Rebeckah I, 1141
Hackney, Richard Earl I, 1153
Hackney, Robert V, 494
Hackney, Robert H. VI, 395
Hackney, Robert H. VI, 396
Hackney, Rose V, 494
Hackney, Rose V, 676
Hackney, Rosetta Louisa I, 1141
Hackney, Sallie E. VI, 395
Hackney, Samuel II, 227
Hackney, Samuel B. V, 62
Hackney, Samuel B. VI, 396
Hackney, Samuel S. VI, 395
Hackney, Samuel S. VI, 396
Hackney, Samuel S. VI, 499
Hackney, Samuel T. VI, 396
Hackney, Sarah I, 1119
Hackney, Sarah I, 1120
Hackney, Sarah I, 1140
Hackney, Sarah I, 1141
Hackney, Sarah I, 1152
Hackney, Sarah VI, 395
Hackney, Sarah VI, 399
Hackney, Sarah VI, 499
Hackney, Sarah Ann I, 1119
Hackney, Sarah Ann I, 1141
Hackney, Sarah E. VI, 396
Hackney, Sarah E. VI, 499
Hackney, Sarah Elizabeth I, 1
Hackney, Sarah Elizabeth VI, 396
Hackney, Sarah Ellen VI, 395
Hackney, Sarah H. VI, 368
Hackney, Sarah H. VI, 396
Hackney, Sarah J. I, 625
Hackney, Sarah Jane I, 1141
Hackney, Sherman Raymond V, 494
Hackney, Sophronia P. I, 1141
Hackney, Susan I, 1141
Hackney, Susan I, 1153
Hackney, Susan V, 35
Hackney, Susan V, 62
Hackney, Susan V, 156
Hackney, Susan D. V, 62
Hackney, Susan D. V, 172
Hackney, Susanna II, 527
Hackney, Susannah II, 222
Hackney, Susannah II, 227
Hackney, Susannah II, 538
Hackney, Thomas I, 1141
Hackney, Thomas I, 1152
Hackney, Thomas I, 1155
Hackney, Thomas II, 227
Hackney, Thomas E. I, 1141
Hackney, Thomas E. I, 1153
Hackney, Thomas M. Jones I, 1153
Hackney, Thos. E. I, 1141
Hackney, Volcah V, 494
Hackney, Wilbur V, 494
Hackney, Wilford Haines V, 49
Hackney, Wilfred V, 676
Hackney, William V, 62
Hackney, William I. I, 1153
Hackney, William I. V, 62
Hackney, William J. I, 1141
Hackney, William J. I, 1153
Hackney, William J. V, 62
Hackney, William J. VI, 396
Hackney, William J., Jr. I, 114
Hackney, William R. I, 1141
Hackney, William Riley I, 115
Hackney, Willie B. I, 1141
Hackney, Wm. J. I, 1141
Hackworth, A. VI, 899
Hackworth, Anna VI, 906
Hackworth, Anne VI, 869
Hackworth, Anney VI, 949
Hackworth, Barbara VI, 947
Hackworth, Bethania W. VI, 9
Hackworth, Betsey VI, 872
Hackworth, Burwell VI, 925
Hackworth, Burwell VI, 998
Hackworth, Charity VI, 957
Hackworth, Charity VI, 990
Hackworth, Charlotte VI, 822
Hackworth, Daniel VI, 925
Hackworth, Dorothy VI, 925
Hackworth, Elijah H. VI, 925
Hackworth, Elijah Turner, Sr. VI, 925
Hackworth, Elizabeth VI, 925
Hackworth, Frances VI, 872
Hackworth, Frankey VI, 872
Hackworth, George VI, 925
Hackworth, George VI, 949
Hackworth, George VI, 1007
Hackworth, George D. VI, 898
Hackworth, Huldy VI, 949
Hackworth, James VI, 925
Hackworth, James VI, 948
Hackworth, Jane VI, 925
Hackworth, Jas. VI, 928
Hackworth, Jesse VI, 933
Hackworth, Jesse VI, 949
Hackworth, Jesse VI, 967
Hackworth, John VI, 925
Hackworth, Jos. VI, 928
Hackworth, Joseph VI, 966
Hackworth, Malinda VI, 934
Hackworth, Malinda H. VI, 92
Hackworth, Martha A. VI, 925
Hackworth, Mary VI, 925
Hackworth, Milly VI, 966
Hackworth, Nancy VI, 925
Hackworth, Nancy VI, 948
Hackworth, Nicholas VI, 822
Hackworth, Nicholas VI, 957
Hackworth, Peggy VI, 933

ackworth, Piety VI, 1007
ackworth, Polly VI, 925
ackworth, Polly VI, 949
ackworth, Reuben VI, 822
ackworth, Reuben VI, 925
ackworth, Reuben VI, 968
ackworth, Sally VI, 925
ackworth, Sally VI, 1006
ackworth, Suckey VI, 941
ackworth, Susan VI, 822
ackworth, Susanna VI, 925
ackworth, Susanna VI, 957
ackworth, Tabby VI, 928
ackworth, Thomas VI, 822
ackworth, Thomas VI, 925
ackworth, Thomas VI, 934
ackworth, Thomas VI, 1006
ackworth, Unity VI, 906
ackworth, Uriah VI, 958
ackworth, Washington VI, 925
ackworth, Washn. VI, 958
ackworth, Wesley VI, 925
ackworth, William VI, 869
ackworth, William VI, 925
ackworth, William VI, 926
ackworth, William VI, 928
ackworth, William VI, 941
ackworth, William VI, 947
ackworth, William VI, 957
ackworth, William VI, 990
ackworth, Wm. VI, 899
ackworth, Wm. VI, 925
acney, Aaron VI, 395
acney, Charity VI, 395
acney, Jno VI, 395
acney, Joseph VI, 395
acney, N. Catherine V, 172
adaway, Anna III, 143
adaway, Dorothy III, 143
adaway, Dorothy III, 193
adaway, Frank T. III, 143
adaway, Stratton III, 193
adaway, Wm. Stratton III, 143
addad, Gertrude IV, 1318
addock, ??? I, 544
addock, ??? III, 143
addock, Benjamin I, 394
addock, Benjamin I, 480
addock, Catharine III, 143
addock, Catharine III, 219
addock, Deborah III, 103
addock, Deborah III, 143
addock, Deborah Chapman III, 143
addock, Edwin Joseph III, 143
addock, Eleanor II, 745
addock, Frederick Wm. III, 143
addock, Hannah II, 546
addock, Hannah II, 874
addock, Hannah II, 875
addock, Hannah V, 50
addock, Hannah V, 71
addock, Henrietta L. III, 143
addock, Henrietta Louisa III, 143
addock, Henry II, 745
addock, Isaac III, 143
addock, James II, 546
addock, James II, 875
addock, James T. II, 745
addock, James Thompson II, 745
addock, John I, 384
addock, John I, 394
addock, John I, 716
addock, John II, 546
addock, June III, 335
addock, Lydia Ann III, 143
addock, Margaret I, 384
addock, Margaret I, 394
addock, Nathaniel III, 143
addock, Robert J. III, 143
addock, Robert James III, 143
addock, Ruth I, 480
addock, Sarah II, 546
addock, Sarah A. II, 874
addock, Sarah A. II, 875
addock, Sarah Ann II, 745
addock, Sarah Ann II, 874
addock, Sarah Ann III, 143
addock, Sarah J. III, 334
addock, Susanna II, 745
addock, Susanna II, 939
addock, Susanna H. II, 745
addock, Susanna Willard II, 874
addock, William J. III, 143
aden, Anthony VI, 815
aden, Anthony VI, 819
aden, Anthony VI, 821
aden, Benjamin VI, 796
Haden, Benjamin VI, 797
Haden, Benjamin VI, 803
Haden, Benjamin VI, 820
Haden, Benjamin VI, 826
Haden, Benjamin VI, 858
Haden, Benjamin VI, 931
Haden, Elizabeth VI, 821
Haden, ELizabeth E. VI, 805
Haden, James C. VI, 822
Haden, James M. VI, 929
Haden, Jane VI, 858
Haden, Jenny VI, 819
Haden, John VI, 822
Haden, John D. VI, 826
Haden, John M. Mason VI, 834
Haden, John, Sr. VI, 809
Haden, John, Sr. VI, 842
Haden, Margaret VI, 813
Haden, Maria B. IV, 892
Haden, Maria B. IV, 893
Haden, Milly VI, 809
Haden, Moses VI, 888
Haden, Nancy VI, 822
Haden, Polly VI, 826
Haden, Rachel VI, 822
Haden, Rachel VI, 842
Haden, Rebeckah VI, 815
Haden, Richard VI, 931
Haden, Richard D. VI, 962
Haden, Richard G. VI, 796
Haden, Richard P. VI, 815
Haden, Rutha VI, 888
Haden, Seley VI, 854
Haden, Susan A. D. VI, 834
Haden, Turner VI, 809
Haden, William V. VI, 858
Hadgecock, Catharine I, 942
Hadleigh, Joseph I, 446
Hadleigh, Joseph I, 455
Hadleigh, Susanna I, 446
Hadleigh, Susanna I, 455
Hadley, ??? V, 63
Hadley, ??? V, 600
Hadley, A. W. I, 1153
Hadley, Aaron I, 352
Hadley, Aaron I, 392
Hadley, Aaron I, 396
Hadley, Abel I, 467
Hadley, Abel I, 476
Hadley, Abel I, 480
Hadley, Abigail V, 563
Hadley, Abigail V, 565
Hadley, Abigail V, 566
Hadley, Abigail V, 567
Hadley, Abigail G. V, 555
Hadley, Abigail J. V, 391
Hadley, Abigail J. V, 567
Hadley, Abigail J. V, 569
Hadley, Abigail J. V, 676
Hadley, Abija I, 434
Hadley, Abraham V, 146
Hadley, Abraham V, 564
Hadley, Abraham V, 565
Hadley, Abraham H. V, 568
Hadley, Ada V, 568
Hadley, Ada E. V, 566
Hadley, Adalade IV, 1252
Hadley, Adalaide G. IV, 1252
Hadley, Adaline V, 568
Hadley, Addaline I, 1153
Hadley, Addison I, 435
Hadley, Adelaide IV, 1318
Hadley, Adelaide G. V, 569
Hadley, Adella V, 677
Hadley, Adilla V, 569
Hadley, Adilla M. V, 677
Hadley, Adison I, 447
Hadley, Alanta V, 569
Hadley, Albert V, 63
Hadley, Albert V, 565
Hadley, Albert V, 568
Hadley, Albert V, 677
Hadley, Albert H. V, 63
Hadley, Albert H. V, 677
Hadley, Albert J. V, 565
Hadley, Albert J. V, 568
Hadley, Alfred I, 392
Hadley, Alfred I, 426
Hadley, Alfred V, 63
Hadley, Alfred V, 243
Hadley, Alfred V, 268
Hadley, Alfred V, 390
Hadley, Alfred V, 677
Hadley, Alfred, Jr. V, 567
Hadley, Alice I, 679
Hadley, Alice II, 907
Hadley, Alice V, 566
Hadley, Alice V, 569
Hadley, Alice V, 676
Hadley, Alice V, 677
Hadley, Alice V, 714
Hadley, Alice C. II, 870
Hadley, Alice P. II, 870
Hadley, Allen V, 565
Hadley, Allen V, 568
Hadley, Almira V, 565
Hadley, Almira V, 567
Hadley, Almira V, 605
Hadley, Alonta V, 566
Hadley, Alonta V, 677
Hadley, Alontie V, 677
Hadley, Alonzo V, 565
Hadley, Alonzo V, 569
Hadley, Alonzo V, 676
Hadley, Alonzo V, 677
Hadley, Alonzo L. V, 676
Hadley, Aloutie V, 677
Hadley, Alva IV, 210
Hadley, Alvin V, 677
Hadley, Amanda V, 568
Hadley, Amanda M. V, 568
Hadley, Amanda Maria V, 566
Hadley, Amanda Maria V, 676
Hadley, Amanda Meriah V, 568
Hadley, Ambrose M. V, 457
Hadley, Amos L. V, 390
Hadley, Amos L. V, 908
Hadley, Amy I, 480
Hadley, Ann I, 391
Hadley, Ann I, 392
Hadley, Ann I, 435
Hadley, Ann V, 63
Hadley, Ann V, 243
Hadley, Ann V, 331
Hadley, Ann V, 333
Hadley, Ann V, 373
Hadley, Ann V, 390
Hadley, Ann V, 403
Hadley, Ann V, 436
Hadley, Ann V, 495
Hadley, Ann V, 507
Hadley, Ann V, 564
Hadley, Ann V, 565
Hadley, Ann V, 567
Hadley, Ann V, 570
Hadley, Ann V, 575
Hadley, Ann V, 576
Hadley, Ann V, 592
Hadley, Ann V, 605
Hadley, Ann V, 676
Hadley, Ann V, 952
Hadley, Ann V, 962
Hadley, Ann Elizabeth V, 566
Hadley, Ann Elizabeth V, 568
Hadley, Ann Jeanette V, 677
Hadley, Ann K. V, 564
Hadley, Ann K. V, 575
Hadley, Ann K. V, 681
Hadley, Ann M. V, 139
Hadley, Ann M. V, 495
Hadley, Ann M. V, 511
Hadley, Ann M. V, 567
Hadley, Ann M. V, 582
Hadley, Ann P. V, 568
Hadley, Anna V, 63
Hadley, Anna V, 373
Hadley, Anna V, 390
Hadley, Anna V, 565
Hadley, Anna V, 566
Hadley, Anna V, 567
Hadley, Anna V, 676
Hadley, Anna V, 677
Hadley, Anna Edith V, 566
Hadley, Anna Ethel V, 566
Hadley, Anna Ethel C. V, 569
Hadley, Anna M. V, 568
Hadley, Anna M. V, 604
Hadley, Anna P. V, 568
Hadley, Anna W. V, 568
Hadley, Anna W. V, 569
Hadley, Anna Wim V, 676
Hadley, Anna Winn V, 566
Hadley, Anne V, 243
Hadley, Anne V, 390
Hadley, Anne V, 495
Hadley, Anne V, 621
Hadley, Annie V, 63
Hadley, Annie V, 390
Hadley, Annie V, 568
Hadley, Annie J. V, 390
Hadley, Ansalem V, 565
Hadley, Ansalem V, 676
Hadley, Archabald V, 565
Hadley, Archibald V, 565
Hadley, Archibald V, 566
Hadley, Archibald V, 568
Hadley, Aron I, 447
Hadley, Artemus V, 567
Hadley, Artemus V, 568
Hadley, Artemus N. V, 63
Hadley, Artemus N. V, 86
Hadley, Artemus N. V, 565
Hadley, Artemus N. V, 568
Hadley, Artemus N. V, 579
Hadley, Arthalina V, 677
Hadley, Arthur V, 568
Hadley, Arthur V, 569
Hadley, Arthur E. V, 173
Hadley, Arthur E. V, 568
Hadley, Arthur E. V, 970
Hadley, Asenath I, 434
Hadley, Asenath I, 446
Hadley, Asenath I, 447
Hadley, Asenath I, 480
Hadley, Asenath I, 677
Hadley, Asenath I, 679
Hadley, Asenath I, 761
Hadley, Atwell V, 566
Hadley, Atwell V, 569
Hadley, Atwell M. V, 391
Hadley, Atwell M. V, 566
Hadley, Atwell M. V, 676
Hadley, Atwill V, 569
Hadley, Atwood V, 569
Hadley, Bell V, 390
Hadley, Belle V, 677
Hadley, Benjamin V, 677
Hadley, Benjamin B. V, 565
Hadley, Benjamin B. V, 568
Hadley, Benjamin B. V, 677
Hadley, Bertha IV, 1318
Hadley, Bertha A. V, 566
Hadley, Bertha M. V, 566
Hadley, Bertha M. V, 569
Hadley, Bertha M. V, 676
Hadley, Bessie V, 550
Hadley, Bessie V, 677
Hadley, Bessie V, 678
Hadley, Bessie V, 709
Hadley, Bessie L. V, 63
Hadley, Binjamin I, 391
Hadley, Bridget I, 781
Hadley, Bridget I, 812
Hadley, Bridget I, 971
Hadley, Bridget I, 975
Hadley, Bridget I, 977
Hadley, Byrom C. V, 566
Hadley, C. Jane V, 243
Hadley, C. Jane V, 283
Hadley, Caleb V, 567
Hadley, Calvin V, 63
Hadley, Calvin V, 565
Hadley, Calvin V, 566
Hadley, Calvin V, 568
Hadley, Calvin V, 677
Hadley, Calvin C. V, 565
Hadley, Calvin Charles V, 566
Hadley, Caroline II, 870
Hadley, Caroline V, 63
Hadley, Caroline V, 568
Hadley, Caroline V, 677
Hadley, Caroline Elizabeth V, 495
Hadley, Carrie V, 569
Hadley, Carrie V, 604
Hadley, Carrie V, 677
Hadley, Carrie B. V, 677
Hadley, Carrie Bell V, 566
Hadley, Carter V, 567
Hadley, Catharine I, 350
Hadley, Catharine I, 391
Hadley, Catharine I, 399
Hadley, Catharine I, 445
Hadley, Catharine I, 446
Hadley, Catharine I, 451
Hadley, Catherine I, 352
Hadley, Chambers V, 564
Hadley, Chambers V, 568
Hadley, Chambers V, 676
Hadley, Charles V, 63
Hadley, Charles V, 565
Hadley, Charles V, 568
Hadley, Charles V, 677
Hadley, Charles D. V, 63
Hadley, Chas. V, 677
Hadley, Chester V, 565
Hadley, Chester V, 567
Hadley, Chester G. V, 568
Hadley, Chester G. V, 569
Hadley, Clara M. V, 173
Hadley, Clara M. V, 569
Hadley, Clare M. V, 173
Hadley, Clarence V, 63
Hadley, Clarence V, 677
Hadley, Clarence Edwin V, 63
Hadley, Clark V, 565
Hadley, Clark Henman V, 495
Hadley, Clark Hinman V, 495
Hadley, Clark W. V, 568
Hadley, Clifford V. V, 569
Hadley, Clifford V. V, 676
Hadley, Clifton V, 390
Hadley, Clorinna V, 677
Hadley, Columbus V, 566
Hadley, Cora V, 677
Hadley, Cora C. V, 569
Hadley, Cora L. V, 569
Hadley, Cora L. V, 970
Hadley, Cora Louisa V, 676
Hadley, Corrilla M. V, 568
Hadley, Cynthia Jane V, 390
Hadley, Cyrus V, 623
Hadley, Cyrus V, 677
Hadley, Cyrus M. V, 565
Hadley, Cyrus M. V, 568
Hadley, Daniel H. V, 243
Hadley, Daniel H. V, 390
Hadley, David I, 392
Hadley, David I, 435
Hadley, David V, 564
Hadley, David V, 566
Hadley, David V, 567
Hadley, David L. V, 555
Hadley, David L. V, 567
Hadley, David L. V, 676
Hadley, Deborah I, 383
Hadley, Deborah I, 391
Hadley, Deborah I, 392
Hadley, Deborah I, 405
Hadley, Deborah V, 564
Hadley, Deborah V, 567
Hadley, Deborah V, 569
Hadley, Deborah V, 601
Hadley, Deborah J. V, 568
Hadley, Deborah L. V, 676
Hadley, Della V, 682
Hadley, Donald Leroy V, 566
Hadley, Doris V, 566
Hadley, Dorothy IV, 1318
Hadley, Dorothy Jean V, 569
Hadley, Dosha V, 676
Hadley, Earl IV, 1318
Hadley, Edgar V, 565
Hadley, Edgar V, 677
Hadley, Edgar L. V, 566
Hadley, Edgar L. V, 569
Hadley, Edgar L. V, 677
Hadley, Edith V, 333
Hadley, Edith V, 390
Hadley, Edith V, 393
Hadley, Edith V, 499
Hadley, Edith M. IV, 934
Hadley, Edith Mary Sarah V, 243
Hadley, Edith Vivian V, 391
Hadley, Edith W. V, 566
Hadley, Edith W. V, 569
Hadley, Edward J. IV, 1318
Hadley, Edwin V, 63
Hadley, Edwin V, 482
Hadley, Edwin V, 488
Hadley, Edwin V, 495
Hadley, Edwin V, 559
Hadley, Edwin V, 565
Hadley, Edwin V, 567
Hadley, Edwin V, 676
Hadley, Edwin C. V, 63
Hadley, Elaine IV, 211
Hadley, Eleanor I, 352
Hadley, Eleanor I, 446
Hadley, Eleanor I, 455
Hadley, Eleen V, 568
Hadley, Elener I, 391
Hadley, Elener I, 405
Hadley, Elenor I, 352
Hadley, Elenor I, 434
Hadley, Eli I, 391
Hadley, Eli I, 392
Hadley, Eli I, 446
Hadley, Eli I, 454
Hadley, Eli V, 494
Hadley, Eli V, 549
Hadley, Eli V, 563
Hadley, Eli V, 564
Hadley, Eli V, 565
Hadley, Eli V, 567
Hadley, Eli V, 589
Hadley, Eli V, 676
Hadley, Eli L. V, 567
Hadley, Eli S. V, 565
Hadley, Elias I, 352
Hadley, Elinor I, 391
Hadley, Elisa I, 447
Hadley, Elisabeth I, 446
Hadley, Elisabeth, Jr. I, 446
Hadley, Elisha I, 467
Hadley, Eliza I, 353
Hadley, Eliza V, 63
Hadley, Eliza V, 495
Hadley, Eliza V, 511
Hadley, Eliza V, 565
Hadley, Eliza V, 567
Hadley, Eliza V, 568
Hadley, Eliza V, 582
Hadley, Eliza A. V, 567
Hadley, Eliza A. V, 575

Hadley, Eliza Ann V, 564
Hadley, Eliza B. V, 495
Hadley, Eliza B. V, 515
Hadley, Eliza B. V, 567
Hadley, Eliza B. V, 584
Hadley, Elizabeth I, 352
Hadley, Elizabeth I, 373
Hadley, Elizabeth I, 391
Hadley, Elizabeth I, 392
Hadley, Elizabeth I, 423
Hadley, Elizabeth I, 435
Hadley, Elizabeth I, 446
Hadley, Elizabeth V, 494
Hadley, Elizabeth V, 495
Hadley, Elizabeth V, 503
Hadley, Elizabeth V, 547
Hadley, Elizabeth V, 553
Hadley, Elizabeth V, 564
Hadley, Elizabeth V, 565
Hadley, Elizabeth V, 567
Hadley, Elizabeth V, 568
Hadley, Elizabeth V, 569
Hadley, Elizabeth V, 579
Hadley, Elizabeth V, 602
Hadley, Elizabeth V, 677
Hadley, Elizabeth V, 684
Hadley, Elizabeth Elen V, 390
Hadley, Elizabeth Ellen V, 229
Hadley, Elizabeth Ellen V, 243
Hadley, Elizabeth Ellen V, 390
Hadley, Elizabeth M. V, 63
Hadley, Elizabeth M. V, 86
Hadley, Elizabeth M. V, 568
Hadley, Elizabeth N. V, 63
Hadley, Elizabeth T. V, 63
Hadley, Elizabeth T. V, 568
Hadley, Elizabeth T. V, 677
Hadley, Elizabeth W. V, 29
Hadley, Elizabeth W. V, 63
Hadley, Elizabeth W. V, 551
Hadley, Elizabeth W. V, 568
Hadley, Ella V, 550
Hadley, Ella V, 566
Hadley, Ella V, 664
Hadley, Ella V, 676
Hadley, Ella H. V, 550
Hadley, Ellen IV, 210
Hadley, Ellen V, 63
Hadley, Ellen V, 554
Hadley, Ellen V, 555
Hadley, Ellen V, 565
Hadley, Ellen V, 566
Hadley, Ellen V, 567
Hadley, Ellen V, 568
Hadley, Ellen V, 666
Hadley, Ellen V, 677
Hadley, Ellen C. V, 569
Hadley, Ellen C. V, 677
Hadley, Ellen J. V, 243
Hadley, Ellen W. V, 568
Hadley, Ellwood V, 565
Hadley, Elmer F. V, 390
Hadley, Elmer T. V, 390
Hadley, Elnora V, 566
Hadley, Elsa V, 678
Hadley, Elsie V, 568
Hadley, Elton P. V, 677
Hadley, Elwood V, 568
Hadley, Elwood V, 592
Hadley, Ematine I, 447
Hadley, Emeline I, 447
Hadley, Emeline V, 677
Hadley, Emiline V, 495
Hadley, Emily V, 63
Hadley, Emily V, 83
Hadley, Emily V, 566
Hadley, Emily V, 567
Hadley, Emily V, 579
Hadley, Emily C. V, 173
Hadley, Emily C. V, 568
Hadley, Emily C. V, 970
Hadley, Emily Caroline V, 568
Hadley, Emily G. V, 243
Hadley, Emily G. V, 275
Hadley, Emily G. V, 676
Hadley, Emily J. V, 63
Hadley, Emily J. V, 567
Hadley, Emma I, 353
Hadley, Emma V, 333
Hadley, Emma V, 390
Hadley, Emma V, 565
Hadley, Emma V, 566
Hadley, Emma V, 568
Hadley, Emma V, 676
Hadley, Emma V, 977
Hadley, Emma B. V, 568
Hadley, Emma C. V, 333
Hadley, Emma C. V, 677
Hadley, Emma S. V, 390
Hadley, Emma S. V, 566
Hadley, Enoch I, 391
Hadley, Enoch I, 392
Hadley, Esther I, 435
Hadley, Esther I, 447
Hadley, Esther V, 482
Hadley, Esther V, 494
Hadley, Esther V, 495
Hadley, Esther V, 529
Hadley, Esther V, 565
Hadley, Esther V, 908
Hadley, Esther C. V, 173
Hadley, Esther C. V, 495
Hadley, Esther C. V, 567
Hadley, Ethel I, 1153
Hadley, Ethel V, 391
Hadley, Ethel V, 677
Hadley, Ethel V, 710
Hadley, Ethel K. V, 566
Hadley, Ethel K. V, 569
Hadley, Eugene IV, 1318
Hadley, Eugene V, 545
Hadley, Eugnne V, 676
Hadley, Eunice I, 352
Hadley, Eunice I, 812
Hadley, Eunice M. V, 569
Hadley, Eunis I, 971
Hadley, Eva J. V, 569
Hadley, Eva J. V, 677
Hadley, Eva Jane V, 566
Hadley, Eva Jane V, 676
Hadley, Eva R. IV, 1252
Hadley, Evalina O. V, 63
Hadley, Evaline V, 63
Hadley, Evaline O. V, 677
Hadley, Evan V, 565
Hadley, Evan V, 566
Hadley, Evan V, 970
Hadley, Evan H. V, 63
Hadley, Evan H. V, 568
Hadley, Evan H. V, 676
Hadley, Evan H. V, 677
Hadley, Evan H. V, 970
Hadley, Eveline V, 568
Hadley, Everett Murray V, 566
Hadley, Everett Murry V, 566
Hadley, F. W. V, 390
Hadley, Farinda V, 566
Hadley, Farinda V, 569
Hadley, Flora V, 568
Hadley, Flora V, 569
Hadley, Flora M. V, 566
Hadley, Florence V, 63
Hadley, Florence V, 605
Hadley, Florence V, 678
Hadley, Florence E. V, 566
Hadley, Florence E. V, 569
Hadley, Florence E. V, 677
Hadley, Frances V, 63
Hadley, Frances V, 677
Hadley, Francis V, 565
Hadley, Francis V, 568
Hadley, Francis V, 677
Hadley, Frank V, 333
Hadley, Frank V, 677
Hadley, Frank W. V, 390
Hadley, Frank W. V, 391
Hadley, Frank W. V, 568
Hadley, Franklin Everett V, 566
Hadley, George I, 352
Hadley, George I, 383
Hadley, George I, 391
Hadley, George I, 392
Hadley, George C. V, 566
Hadley, George C. V, 569
Hadley, George C. V, 676
Hadley, Gertrude V, 566
Hadley, Gertrude W. V, 677
Hadley, Gilpin V, 566
Hadley, Gladys V, 333
Hadley, Gulielma V, 565
Hadley, Hannah I, 357
Hadley, Hannah I, 364
Hadley, Hannah I, 391
Hadley, Hannah I, 392
Hadley, Hannah I, 401
Hadley, Hannah I, 414
Hadley, Hannah I, 467
Hadley, Hannah I, 480
Hadley, Hannah II, 870
Hadley, Hannah II, 907
Hadley, Hannah V, 562
Hadley, Hannah V, 564
Hadley, Hannah V, 567
Hadley, Hannah V, 590
Hadley, Hannah V, 591
Hadley, Hariett E. I, 435
Hadley, Harlan H. V, 550
Hadley, Harlan H. V, 564
Hadley, Harlan H. V, 566
Hadley, Harlan H. V, 568
Hadley, Harlan H. V, 676
Hadley, Harriet V, 243
Hadley, Harriet V, 565
Hadley, Harriet V, 569
Hadley, Harriet E. V, 566
Hadley, Harriet E. V, 623
Hadley, Harriet E. V, 625
Hadley, Harriet M. V, 243
Hadley, Harriet M. V, 280
Hadley, Harriett E. V, 677
Hadley, Harriett Isabel V, 566
Hadley, Harriett Isabella V, 676
Hadley, Harriett J. V, 568
Hadley, Hattie E. V, 569
Hadley, Hattie E. V, 677
Hadley, Hattie E. V, 678
Hadley, Hattie I. V, 569
Hadley, Hattie J. V, 568
Hadley, Hazeldell V, 457
Hadley, Henrietta V, 979
Hadley, Henry V, 63
Hadley, Henry V, 565
Hadley, Henry V, 568
Hadley, Henry V, 970
Hadley, Henry V, 979
Hadley, Herbert V, 391
Hadley, Herbert V, 566
Hadley, Herbert H. V, 566
Hadley, Hershel V, 391
Hadley, Hershel T. V, 566
Hadley, Hershel T. V, 569
Hadley, Hiram II, 870
Hadley, Hiram II, 907
Hadley, Hiram V, 562
Hadley, Hiram V, 565
Hadley, Hiram V, 568
Hadley, Horace A. V, 566
Hadley, Horace A. V, 676
Hadley, Horace H. V, 569
Hadley, Howard J. V, 566
Hadley, Hubert H. V, 569
Hadley, Hugh Isaac V, 550
Hadley, Hulda I, 447
Hadley, Ida Belle V, 390
Hadley, Ida Belle V, 566
Hadley, Idabell V, 568
Hadley, Ira I, 352
Hadley, Isaac I, 352
Hadley, Isaac I, 391
Hadley, Isaac I, 392
Hadley, Isaac I, 716
Hadley, Isaac V, 494
Hadley, Isaac V, 564
Hadley, Isaac V, 567
Hadley, Isaac H. V, 63
Hadley, Isaac H. V, 566
Hadley, Isaac H. V, 568
Hadley, Isaac P. V, 566
Hadley, Isaac P. V, 569
Hadley, Isaac P. V, 676
Hadley, Isaac Parker V, 605
Hadley, Isabel V, 677
Hadley, Isabel A. V, 568
Hadley, Isabella V, 551
Hadley, Isabella A. V, 566
Hadley, Isabelle V, 583
Hadley, Isaiah V, 564
Hadley, Isaiah V, 567
Hadley, Izma V, 63
Hadley, J. V, 565
Hadley, J. C. IV, 1318
Hadley, J. C. V, 623
Hadley, J. Carlton V, 569
Hadley, Jabes H. V, 568
Hadley, Jabez H. V, 564
Hadley, Jack I, 446
Hadley, Jacob I, 352
Hadley, Jacob I, 391
Hadley, Jacob I, 392
Hadley, Jacob I, 434
Hadley, Jacob I, 435
Hadley, Jacob I, 446
Hadley, Jacob V, 63
Hadley, Jacob V, 231
Hadley, Jacob V, 243
Hadley, Jacob V, 494
Hadley, Jacob V, 545
Hadley, Jacob V, 552
Hadley, Jacob V, 564
Hadley, Jacob V, 566
Hadley, Jacob V, 676
Hadley, Jacob V, 952
Hadley, Jacob C. V, 557
Hadley, Jacob C. V, 568
Hadley, James I, 352
Hadley, James I, 392
Hadley, James I, 434
Hadley, James V, 229
Hadley, James V, 243
Hadley, James V, 275
Hadley, James V, 291
Hadley, James V, 315
Hadley, James V, 331
Hadley, James V, 333
Hadley, James V, 369
Hadley, James V, 373
Hadley, James V, 390
Hadley, James V, 402
Hadley, James V, 403
Hadley, James V, 436
Hadley, James V, 551
Hadley, James V, 565
Hadley, James V, 567
Hadley, James V, 568
Hadley, James V, 583
Hadley, James V, 621
Hadley, James V, 676
Hadley, James V, 677
Hadley, James V, 908
Hadley, James V, 970
Hadley, James Albert V, 243
Hadley, James B. I, 446
Hadley, James B. I, 447
Hadley, James Clark V, 676
Hadley, James D. V, 908
Hadley, James Dickey I, 352
Hadley, James E. V, 390
Hadley, James E. V, 970
Hadley, James F. V, 569
Hadley, James Murphy V, 566
Hadley, James Seth V, 677
Hadley, James Seth V, 709
Hadley, James W. V, 495
Hadley, James William V, 494
Hadley, James William V, 495
Hadley, James Wm. V, 908
Hadley, James, Jr. V, 243
Hadley, James, Jr. V, 249
Hadley, Jane I, 352
Hadley, Jane I, 391
Hadley, Jane I, 392
Hadley, Jane I, 396
Hadley, Jane I, 424
Hadley, Jane I, 434
Hadley, Jane I, 446
Hadley, Jane I, 447
Hadley, Jane I, 454
Hadley, Jane I, 467
Hadley, Jane I, 476
Hadley, Jane I, 480
Hadley, Jane V, 70
Hadley, Jane V, 146
Hadley, Jane V, 333
Hadley, Jane V, 390
Hadley, Jane V, 494
Hadley, Jane V, 495
Hadley, Jane V, 550
Hadley, Jane V, 559
Hadley, Jane V, 564
Hadley, Jane V, 565
Hadley, Jane V, 567
Hadley, Jane V, 568
Hadley, Jane V, 574
Hadley, Jane V, 605
Hadley, Jane V, 659
Hadley, Jane V, 698
Hadley, Jane Ann V, 495
Hadley, Jane Ann V, 908
Hadley, Jane Balard V, 567
Hadley, Jean I, 391
Hadley, Jeanette V, 677
Hadley, Jeanette V, 686
Hadley, Jemima I, 336
Hadley, Jemima V, 63
Hadley, Jemima V, 488
Hadley, Jemima V, 495
Hadley, Jemima V, 559
Hadley, Jemima V, 568
Hadley, Jemima D. V, 63
Hadley, Jemima D. V, 495
Hadley, Jemima D. V, 567
Hadley, Jennie IV, 211
Hadley, Jeremiah I, 352
Hadley, Jeremiah I, 353
Hadley, Jeremiah I, 391
Hadley, Jeremiah I, 392
Hadley, Jeremiah I, 406
Hadley, Jeremiah I, 462
Hadley, Jeremiah I, 467
Hadley, Jeremiah I, 476
Hadley, Jeremiah I, 480
Hadley, Jeremiah I, 761
Hadley, Jeremiah V, 243
Hadley, Jeremiah V, 333
Hadley, Jeremiah V, 390
Hadley, Jeremiah V, 494
Hadley, Jeremiah V, 495
Hadley, Jeremiah V, 529
Hadley, Jeremiah V, 568
Hadley, Jeremiah V, 841
Hadley, Jeremiah V, 908
Hadley, Jeremiah, Jr. I, 352
Hadley, Jeremieh I, 391
Hadley, Jesse V, 567
Hadley, Jesse William V, 566
Hadley, Joab I, 447
Hadley, Job I, 434
Hadley, Job I, 447
Hadley, Job V, 30
Hadley, Job V, 63
Hadley, Joel I, 446
Hadley, Joel I, 447
Hadley, John I, 352
Hadley, John I, 391
Hadley, John I, 392
Hadley, John I, 435
Hadley, John I, 446
Hadley, John I, 447
Hadley, John I, 467
Hadley, John I, 480
Hadley, John I, 679
Hadley, John I, 716
Hadley, John V, 243
Hadley, John V, 333
Hadley, John V, 390
Hadley, John V, 494
Hadley, John V, 495
Hadley, John V, 496
Hadley, John V, 564
Hadley, John V, 565
Hadley, John V, 567
Hadley, John V, 584
Hadley, John V, 589
Hadley, John V, 599
Hadley, John V, 676
Hadley, John V, 908
Hadley, John V, 952
Hadley, John V, 962
Hadley, John V, 970
Hadley, John V, 976
Hadley, John C. V, 495
Hadley, John C. V, 567
Hadley, John Henley I, 480
Hadley, John N. V, 565
Hadley, John S. V, 495
Hadley, John Smith V, 494
Hadley, John Smith V, 495
Hadley, John T. I, 446
Hadley, John T. I, 480
Hadley, John W. V, 566
Hadley, John William V, 565
Hadley, John Wm. V, 568
Hadley, John Wm. V, 606
Hadley, John Wm. V, 676
Hadley, John, Jr. V, 567
Hadley, John, Jr. V, 568
Hadley, John, Jr. V, 605
Hadley, Johnathan V, 63
Hadley, Jonathan I, 352
Hadley, Jonathan I, 391
Hadley, Jonathan I, 392
Hadley, Jonathan I, 435
Hadley, Jonathan I, 446
Hadley, Jonathan I, 447
Hadley, Jonathan V, 63
Hadley, Jonathan V, 494
Hadley, Jonathan V, 495
Hadley, Jonathan V, 498
Hadley, Jonathan V, 511
Hadley, Jonathan V, 515
Hadley, Jonathan V, 564
Hadley, Jonathan V, 567
Hadley, Jonathan V, 582
Hadley, Jonathan V, 584
Hadley, Jonathan V, 585
Hadley, Jonathan V, 602
Hadley, Jonathan V, 623
Hadley, Jonathan V, 677
Hadley, Jonathan B. Bowgill V, 568
Hadley, Jonathan D. V, 63
Hadley, Jonathan D. V, 555
Hadley, Jonathan D. V, 565
Hadley, Jonathan D. V, 567
Hadley, Jonathan D. V, 568
Hadley, Jonathan D. V, 970
Hadley, Jonathan Simon I, 447
Hadley, Jonathan T. V, 676
Hadley, Jonathan William I, 435
Hadley, Jos. I, 345
Hadley, Joseph I, 352
Hadley, Joseph I, 365
Hadley, Joseph I, 391
Hadley, Joseph I, 392
Hadley, Joseph I, 393
Hadley, Joseph I, 396
Hadley, Joseph I, 434
Hadley, Joseph I, 446
Hadley, Joseph I, 447
Hadley, Joseph V, 565
Hadley, Joseph V, 569
Hadley, Joseph V, 676
Hadley, Joseph V, 677
Hadley, Joseph C. IV, 1252
Hadley, Joseph C. IV, 1318

Hadley, Joseph C. V, 565
Hadley, Joseph C. V, 568
Hadley, Joseph C. V, 677
Hadley, Joseph W. V, 566
Hadley, Joseph W. V, 676
Hadley, Josephuns I, 447
Hadley, Joshua I, 350
Hadley, Joshua I, 352
Hadley, Joshua I, 353
Hadley, Joshua I, 357
Hadley, Joshua I, 360
Hadley, Joshua I, 362
Hadley, Joshua I, 368
Hadley, Joshua I, 373
Hadley, Joshua I, 391
Hadley, Joshua I, 398
Hadley, Joshua I, 434
Hadley, Joshua I, 435
Hadley, Joshua I, 446
Hadley, Joshua I, 447
Hadley, Joshua I, 542
Hadley, Joshua I Sup 1, 9
Hadley, Joshua V, 63
Hadley, Joshua V, 390
Hadley, Joshua V, 494
Hadley, Joshua V, 495
Hadley, Joshua V, 536
Hadley, Joshua V, 560
Hadley, Joshua V, 564
Hadley, Joshua V, 567
Hadley, Joshua V, 569
Hadley, Joshua VI, 178
Hadley, Joshua B. I, 392
Hadley, Joshua B. I, 446
Hadley, Joshua D. V, 390
Hadley, Joshua D. V, 411
Hadley, Joshua D. V, 908
Hadley, Joshua, Jr. I, 391
Hadley, Joshua, Jr. I, 446
Hadley, Joshua, Jr. I, 447
Hadley, Joshua, Sr. I, 392
Hadley, Joshua, Sr. I, 396
Hadley, Julia I, 447
Hadley, Julia V, 243
Hadley, Julia V, 272
Hadley, Julia V, 568
Hadley, Julia V, 583
Hadley, Julia Ann V, 564
Hadley, Juliet V, 243
Hadley, Juliet V, 390
Hadley, Kezia K. V, 243
Hadley, Kezia K. V, 268
Hadley, Keziah V, 243
Hadley, Keziah V, 390
Hadley, Keziah K. V, 243
Hadley, Keziah K. V, 390
Hadley, Keziah R. V, 390
Hadley, Larkin IV, 211
Hadley, Larkin J. IV, 210
Hadley, Laura V, 568
Hadley, Laura V, 569
Hadley, Leila V, 390
Hadley, Levi I, 447
Hadley, Lewis I. IV, 211
Hadley, Lindley V, 564
Hadley, Lindley V, 568
Hadley, Lizzie V, 550
Hadley, Lizzie V, 678
Hadley, Lizzie Ethel V, 63
Hadley, Lizzie V. V, 677
Hadley, Lois Irene IV, 1318
Hadley, Loren V, 677
Hadley, Loren V, 686
Hadley, Loren S. V, 678
Hadley, Lot Maris I, 352
Hadley, Louetta V, 569
Hadley, Louie M. V, 551
Hadley, Louie May V, 566
Hadley, Louie May V, 677
Hadley, Louisa V, 63
Hadley, Louisa V, 97
Hadley, Louisa V, 565
Hadley, Louisa V, 567
Hadley, Louisa V, 585
Hadley, Louisa Jane I, 392
Hadley, Louise V, 677
Hadley, Louise V, 714
Hadley, Lucetta W. V, 676
Hadley, Lucinda V, 231
Hadley, Lucinda V, 243
Hadley, Lucinda V, 557
Hadley, Lucinda V, 568
Hadley, Lucinda V, 569
Hadley, Lucinda V, 676
Hadley, Lucinda V, 677
Hadley, Lucy V, 566
Hadley, Lucy C. V, 568
Hadley, Lucy C. V, 574
Hadley, Lucy Caroline V, 565
Hadley, Lucy Caroline V, 680
Hadley, Lucy H. V, 573
Hadley, Lucy M. V, 63
Hadley, Lucy M. V, 567
Hadley, Luella V, 569
Hadley, Luetta V, 677
Hadley, Lyddia I, 542
Hadley, Lydia I, 352
Hadley, Lydia I, 381
Hadley, Lydia I, 391
Hadley, Lydia I, 392
Hadley, Lydia I, 398
Hadley, Lydia I, 434
Hadley, Lydia I, 446
Hadley, Lydia I, 542
Hadley, Lydia I, 545
Hadley, Lydia V, 243
Hadley, Lydia V, 494
Hadley, Lydia V, 495
Hadley, Lydia V, 564
Hadley, Lydia V, 566
Hadley, Lydia V, 567
Hadley, Lydia V, 598
Hadley, Lydia V, 952
Hadley, Lydia V, 970
Hadley, Lydia D. V, 676
Hadley, Lydia G. V, 970
Hadley, Lydia G. Stanton V, 568
Hadley, Lydia, Jr. V, 567
Hadley, M. Etta V, 566
Hadley, Mabel Alice V, 677
Hadley, Mabel Alice V, 686
Hadley, Mabel Elizabeth V, 677
Hadley, Mable V, 677
Hadley, Mable V, 710
Hadley, Mable E. V, 710
Hadley, Mahala V, 138
Hadley, Mahala H. V, 567
Hadley, Mahala H. V, 604
Hadley, Mahala J. V, 567
Hadley, Mahalah G. V, 565
Hadley, Mahama J. V, 602
Hadley, Mahlon V, 565
Hadley, Mahlon C. V, 173
Hadley, Mahlon C. V, 568
Hadley, Mahlon C. V, 970
Hadley, Mardeca I, 447
Hadley, Margaret I, 352
Hadley, Margaret I, 391
Hadley, Margaret I, 392
Hadley, Margaret I, 446
Hadley, Margaret I, 454
Hadley, Margaret I, 716
Hadley, Margaret II, 1051
Hadley, Margaret V, 52
Hadley, Margaret V, 333
Hadley, Margaret V, 390
Hadley, Margaret V, 403
Hadley, Margaret A. V, 560
Hadley, Margaret A. V, 568
Hadley, Margaret Ann V, 53
Hadley, Margaret Ann V, 63
Hadley, Margaret Ann V, 390
Hadley, Margaret Ann V, 565
Hadley, Margaret Louise V, 677
Hadley, Margret I, 391
Hadley, Margret I, 446
Hadley, Marie V, 569
Hadley, Marie V, 605
Hadley, Marietta V, 565
Hadley, Marietta V, 677
Hadley, Martha I, 353
Hadley, Martha I, 392
Hadley, Martha I, 446
Hadley, Martha I, 449
Hadley, Martha I, 454
Hadley, Martha V, 565
Hadley, Martha Ann V, 565
Hadley, Martha Annillie V, 495
Hadley, Martha E. V, 569
Hadley, Martha E. V, 677
Hadley, Martha Emeline V, 565
Hadley, Martha H. V, 567
Hadley, Martha H. V, 575
Hadley, Martha T. V, 569
Hadley, Mary I, 345
Hadley, Mary I, 352
Hadley, Mary I, 360
Hadley, Mary I, 362
Hadley, Mary I, 365
Hadley, Mary I, 391
Hadley, Mary I, 392
Hadley, Mary I, 396
Hadley, Mary I, 411
Hadley, Mary I, 434
Hadley, Mary I, 435
Hadley, Mary I, 446
Hadley, Mary I, 447
Hadley, Mary I, 453
Hadley, Mary I, 761
Hadley, Mary I, 986
Hadley, Mary V, 63
Hadley, Mary V, 243
Hadley, Mary V, 331
Hadley, Mary V, 333
Hadley, Mary V, 390
Hadley, Mary V, 495
Hadley, Mary V, 511
Hadley, Mary V, 549
Hadley, Mary V, 552
Hadley, Mary V, 564
Hadley, Mary V, 565
Hadley, Mary V, 566
Hadley, Mary V, 567
Hadley, Mary V, 568
Hadley, Mary V, 582
Hadley, Mary V, 583
Hadley, Mary V, 589
Hadley, Mary V, 593
Hadley, Mary V, 604
Hadley, Mary V, 621
Hadley, Mary V, 677
Hadley, Mary V, 952
Hadley, Mary V, 970
Hadley, Mary V, 974
Hadley, Mary A. V, 569
Hadley, Mary Ann I, 435
Hadley, Mary Ann V, 63
Hadley, Mary Ann V, 67
Hadley, Mary Ann V, 390
Hadley, Mary Ann V, 908
Hadley, Mary Anna V, 566
Hadley, Mary Anna V, 676
Hadley, Mary B. V, 560
Hadley, Mary B. V, 561
Hadley, Mary B. V, 565
Hadley, Mary B. V, 568
Hadley, Mary Catharine V, 566
Hadley, Mary D. V, 566
Hadley, Mary D. V, 676
Hadley, Mary E. V, 63
Hadley, Mary Edith V, 566
Hadley, Mary Emily I, 467
Hadley, Mary F. V, 390
Hadley, Mary F. V, 569
Hadley, Mary G. V, 676
Hadley, Mary Howard V, 569
Hadley, Mary J. I, 435
Hadley, Mary J. V, 567
Hadley, Mary J. V, 589
Hadley, Mary Jane I, 447
Hadley, Mary Jane V, 495
Hadley, Mary Jane V, 565
Hadley, Mary Jane V, 567
Hadley, Mary Jane V, 568
Hadley, Mary Jane V, 574
Hadley, Mary Katharine V, 677
Hadley, Mary Katharine V, 713
Hadley, Mary Katherine V, 677
Hadley, Mary L. V, 495
Hadley, Mary M. V, 564
Hadley, Mary N. V, 63
Hadley, Mary N. V, 565
Hadley, Mary N. V, 567
Hadley, Mary N. V, 676
Hadley, Mary Naomi V, 677
Hadley, Mary T. V, 565
Hadley, Mary T. V, 568
Hadley, Mary T. V, 569
Hadley, Mary T. V, 676
Hadley, Mary T. V, 970
Hadley, Mary V. V, 230
Hadley, Mary V. V, 243
Hadley, Mary V. V, 676
Hadley, Mary Velma I, 1153
Hadley, Mary Virginia V, 677
Hadley, Mary, Jr. V, 676
Hadley, Maryann I, 392
Hadley, Matilda I, 392
Hadley, Matilda I, 422
Hadley, Maurice V, 566
Hadley, Maurice V, 604
Hadley, Melvin IV, 1318
Hadley, Micajah C. V, 557
Hadley, Micajah C. V, 565
Hadley, Micajah C. V, 566
Hadley, Micajah C. V, 568
Hadley, Micajah C. V, 677
Hadley, Milden T. V, 677
Hadley, Miles V, 565
Hadley, Miles V, 568
Hadley, Miles V, 677
Hadley, Miles H. V, 568
Hadley, Milly V, 566
Hadley, Milton I, 434
Hadley, Milton I, 435
Hadley, Milton V, 63
Hadley, Milton V, 564
Hadley, Milton V, 566
Hadley, Milton V, 567
Hadley, Minnie Johns V, 566
Hadley, Minnie Johns V, 569
Hadley, Miriam V, 391
Hadley, Miriam G. V, 390
Hadley, Mordeca I, 435
Hadley, Morris W. V, 566
Hadley, Morris W. V, 569
Hadley, Morris W. V, 676
Hadley, Myrtle IV, 211
Hadley, Myrtle O. Allen IV, 1318
Hadley, Nancy I, 447
Hadley, Nancy I, 449
Hadley, Nancy I, 467
Hadley, Naomi V, 550
Hadley, Naomi V, 659
Hadley, Naomi V, 677
Hadley, Naomi C. V, 565
Hadley, Naomi C. V, 676
Hadley, Naomi M. V, 678
Hadley, Nathan I, 434
Hadley, Nathan I, 447
Hadley, Nathan I, 452
Hadley, Nathan V, 63
Hadley, Nathan V, 67
Hadley, Nathan V, 495
Hadley, Nathan V, 568
Hadley, Nathan V, 569
Hadley, Nathan V, 677
Hadley, Nathan L. V, 495
Hadley, Nettie I, 1153
Hadley, Nora V, 569
Hadley, Nora V, 592
Hadley, Norah C. V, 676
Hadley, Oda V, 390
Hadley, Olive I, 447
Hadley, Olive I, 452
Hadley, Olive V, 63
Hadley, Olive V, 565
Hadley, Olive V, 567
Hadley, Olive V, 568
Hadley, Olive V, 582
Hadley, Olive V, 585
Hadley, Olive V, 671
Hadley, Olive V, 677
Hadley, Olivia V, 678
Hadley, Oma C. V, 677
Hadley, Opal V, 677
Hadley, Opal V, 708
Hadley, Orlando V, 566
Hadley, Orlando V, 569
Hadley, Orlando V, 676
Hadley, Orlando V, 677
Hadley, Orlando V, 678
Hadley, Otis V, 63
Hadley, Otis V, 566
Hadley, Otis V, 568
Hadley, Otis M. V, 63
Hadley, Owen I, 447
Hadley, Park V, 569
Hadley, Parker V, 569
Hadley, Patience I, 352
Hadley, Patience I, 353
Hadley, Patience I, 357
Hadley, Patience I, 362
Hadley, Patience I, 391
Hadley, Patience I, 446
Hadley, Patience I, 453
Hadley, Patience I, 812
Hadley, Phebe I, 391
Hadley, Phebe I, 446
Hadley, Phebe I, 480
Hadley, Phebe V, 565
Hadley, Phebe D. V, 567
Hadley, Phebe D. V, 587
Hadley, Pheby I, 391
Hadley, R. V, 565
Hadley, R. J. V, 566
Hadley, Rachel I, 391
Hadley, Rachel I, 392
Hadley, Rachel I, 393
Hadley, Rachel I, 434
Hadley, Rachel I, 446
Hadley, Rachel I, 462
Hadley, Rachel I, 467
Hadley, Rachel I, 476
Hadley, Rachel I, 480
Hadley, Rachel I, 761
Hadley, Rachel V, 33
Hadley, Rachel V, 63
Hadley, Rachel V, 390
Hadley, Rachel V, 411
Hadley, Rachel V, 568
Hadley, Rachel V, 570
Hadley, Rachel V, 573
Hadley, Rachel V, 595
Hadley, Rachel V, 623
Hadley, Rachel V, 677
Hadley, Rachel V, 908
Hadley, Rachel A. I, 435
Hadley, Rachel A. V, 678
Hadley, Rachel Ann V, 495
Hadley, Rachel Ann V, 496
Hadley, Rachel Anna V, 568
Hadley, Rachel L. V, 567
Hadley, Rachel M. V, 549
Hadley, Rachel M. V, 567
Hadley, Rachel M. V, 611
Hadley, Rachel M. V, 623
Hadley, Rachel M. V, 677
Hadley, Ralph Newton I, 1153
Hadley, Raymond Morris V, 566
Hadley, Reba V, 391
Hadley, Reba M. V, 566
Hadley, Reba M. V, 569
Hadley, Rebecah I, 447
Hadley, Rebecca I, 345
Hadley, Rebecca I, 392
Hadley, Rebecca I, 434
Hadley, Rebecca I, 435
Hadley, Rebecca I, 446
Hadley, Rebecca I, 447
Hadley, Rebecca I, 467
Hadley, Rebecca V, 63
Hadley, Rebecca V, 495
Hadley, Rebecca V, 498
Hadley, Rebecca V, 536
Hadley, Rebecca V, 564
Hadley, Rebecca V, 567
Hadley, Rebecca V, 568
Hadley, Rebecca V, 623
Hadley, Rebecca V, 676
Hadley, Rebecca V, 678
Hadley, Rebecca C. V, 568
Hadley, Rebecca Helen V, 565
Hadley, Rebecca Helen V, 568
Hadley, Rebecca Helen V, 605
Hadley, Rebecca Jane V, 390
Hadley, Rebecca Jane V, 405
Hadley, Rebecca Jane V, 565
Hadley, Rebecca Jane V, 568
Hadley, Rebekah I, 391
Hadley, Rebekah I, 396
Hadley, Rebekah I, 434
Hadley, Rhoda I, 392
Hadley, Rhoda I, 426
Hadley, Rhoda V, 599
Hadley, Rhoda V, 970
Hadley, Rhoda V, 976
Hadley, Rhoda Ann V, 568
Hadley, Rhoda Ann V, 580
Hadley, Rhoda E. V, 565
Hadley, Rhoda E. V, 689
Hadley, Rhoda G. V, 568
Hadley, Rhoda G. V, 599
Hadley, Rhoda G. V, 970
Hadley, Rhoda G. V, 977
Hadley, Rhoda G. V, 979
Hadley, Rhodah I, 392
Hadley, Riley I, 447
Hadley, Robert V, 677
Hadley, Robert V, 710
Hadley, Robert Allen V, 677
Hadley, Robert E. V, 678
Hadley, Robert M. V, 63
Hadley, Rodney G. V, 566
Hadley, Ross A. III, 143
Hadley, Royal V, 390
Hadley, Ruth I, 350
Hadley, Ruth I, 352
Hadley, Ruth I, 353
Hadley, Ruth I, 358
Hadley, Ruth I, 360
Hadley, Ruth I, 362
Hadley, Ruth I, 364
Hadley, Ruth I, 365
Hadley, Ruth I, 368
Hadley, Ruth I, 391
Hadley, Ruth I, 392
Hadley, Ruth I, 404
Hadley, Ruth I, 406
Hadley, Ruth I, 407
Hadley, Ruth I, 434
Hadley, Ruth I, 435
Hadley, Ruth I, 446
Hadley, Ruth I, 447
Hadley, Ruth I, 453
Hadley, Ruth I, 455
Hadley, Ruth I, 716
Hadley, Ruth I, 781
Hadley, Ruth I, 812
Hadley, Ruth I, 826
Hadley, Ruth I, 977
Hadley, Ruth I, 978
Hadley, Ruth V, 494
Hadley, Ruth V, 495
Hadley, Ruth V, 496
Hadley, Ruth V, 498
Hadley, Ruth V, 547
Hadley, Ruth V, 560
Hadley, Ruth V, 564
Hadley, Ruth V, 566
Hadley, Ruth V, 567
Hadley, Ruth V, 572
Hadley, Ruth V, 589
Hadley, Ruth V, 598
Hadley, Ruth V, 952

Hadley, Ruth V, 959
Hadley, Ruth Ann I, 467
Hadley, Ruth Anna V, 677
Hadley, Ruth Annie V, 569
Hadley, Ruth E. V, 494
Hadley, Ruth E. V, 495
Hadley, Ruth E. V, 565
Hadley, Ruth E. V, 569
Hadley, Ruth Edna V, 566
Hadley, Ruth Edna V, 676
Hadley, Ruth L. V, 676
Hadley, Ruth S. V, 565
Hadley, Ruth S. V, 567
Hadley, Ruth S. V, 569
Hadley, Ruth S. V, 677
Hadley, Ruthanna V, 566
Hadley, Ruthanna V, 569
Hadley, Ruthanna V, 677
Hadley, Ruthanna V, 678
Hadley, S. H. V, 566
Hadley, Sallie L. V, 63
Hadley, Samuel I, 392
Hadley, Samuel I, 434
Hadley, Samuel I, 480
Hadley, Samuel I, 761
Hadley, Samuel V, 564
Hadley, Samuel V, 959
Hadley, Samuel Allen I, 761
Hadley, Samuel H. V, 63
Hadley, Samuel H. V, 83
Hadley, Samuel H. V, 567
Hadley, Samuel H. V, 598
Hadley, Samuel H. V, 676
Hadley, Samuel H. V, 952
Hadley, Samuel L. V, 566
Hadley, Samuel L. V, 567
Hadley, Samuel L. V, 574
Hadley, Samuel L. V, 676
Hadley, Samuel M. V, 567
Hadley, Samuel M. V, 579
Hadley, Samuel S. V, 495
Hadley, Samuel S. V, 908
Hadley, Samuel W. V, 568
Hadley, Sarah I, 352
Hadley, Sarah I, 362
Hadley, Sarah I, 391
Hadley, Sarah I, 392
Hadley, Sarah I, 411
Hadley, Sarah I, 434
Hadley, Sarah I, 435
Hadley, Sarah I, 446
Hadley, Sarah I, 447
Hadley, Sarah V, 229
Hadley, Sarah V, 243
Hadley, Sarah V, 249
Hadley, Sarah V, 291
Hadley, Sarah V, 333
Hadley, Sarah V, 390
Hadley, Sarah V, 402
Hadley, Sarah V, 436
Hadley, Sarah V, 454
Hadley, Sarah V, 495
Hadley, Sarah V, 564
Hadley, Sarah V, 567
Hadley, Sarah V, 569
Hadley, Sarah V, 590
Hadley, Sarah V, 591
Hadley, Sarah A. V, 390
Hadley, Sarah A. V, 391
Hadley, Sarah A. V, 566
Hadley, Sarah A. V, 569
Hadley, Sarah Ann V, 243
Hadley, Sarah Ann V, 291
Hadley, Sarah Ann V, 390
Hadley, Sarah C. V, 569
Hadley, Sarah Caroline V, 568
Hadley, Sarah Caroline V, 677
Hadley, Sarah E. V, 566
Hadley, Sarah E. V, 676
Hadley, Sarah E. V, 677
Hadley, Sarah Elizabeth V, 565
Hadley, Sarah Elizabeth V, 567
Hadley, Sarah Ellen V, 569
Hadley, Sarah Ellen V, 676
Hadley, Sarah Ellen V, 677
Hadley, Sarah Ellin V, 568
Hadley, Sarah Ellin V, 606
Hadley, Sarah Jane V, 565
Hadley, Sarah Jane V, 567
Hadley, Sarah Jane V, 587
Hadley, Sarah, Jr. I, 446
Hadley, Sarah, Sr. I, 446
Hadley, Seth V, 565
Hadley, Seth V, 569
Hadley, Seth V, 970
Hadley, Seth S. V, 63
Hadley, Seth S. V, 565
Hadley, Seth S. V, 568
Hadley, Seth Silver V, 495
Hadley, Seth Silvers V, 568
Hadley, Simon I, 352
Hadley, Simon I, 358
Hadley, Simon I, 364
Hadley, Simon I, 391
Hadley, Simon I, 392
Hadley, Simon I, 423
Hadley, Simon I, 435
Hadley, Simon I, 446
Hadley, Simon I, 716
Hadley, Simon I, 781
Hadley, Simon I, 812
Hadley, Simon I, 971
Hadley, Simon I, 977
Hadley, Simon I, 986
Hadley, Simon I Sup 1, 9
Hadley, Simon V, 63
Hadley, Simon V, 494
Hadley, Simon V, 495
Hadley, Simon V, 507
Hadley, Simon V, 549
Hadley, Simon V, 564
Hadley, Simon V, 567
Hadley, Simon V, 568
Hadley, Simon V, 573
Hadley, Simon V, 589
Hadley, Simon V, 611
Hadley, Simon V, 623
Hadley, Simon V, 677
Hadley, Simon V, 970
Hadley, Simon V, 974
Hadley, Simon B. I, 392
Hadley, Simon, Jr. I, 446
Hadley, Simon, Jr. I, 975
Hadley, Simon, Sr. I, 975
Hadley, Sinthy Jane V, 243
Hadley, Smith V, 908
Hadley, Sophia V, 390
Hadley, Sophia V, 565
Hadley, Sophia V, 567
Hadley, Sophia V, 602
Hadley, Sophia V, 604
Hadley, Stella V, 333
Hadley, Stephen M. I, 1153
Hadley, Susan V, 566
Hadley, Susan V, 569
Hadley, Susan N. V, 568
Hadley, Susan N. V, 677
Hadley, Susan W. V, 568
Hadley, Susan W. V, 677
Hadley, Susan W. V, 970
Hadley, Susana I, 352
Hadley, Susanah I, 446
Hadley, Susanna I, 446
Hadley, Susanna V, 390
Hadley, Susanna V, 566
Hadley, Susanna V, 567
Hadley, Susanna V, 569
Hadley, Susanna V, 580
Hadley, Susanna V, 601
Hadley, Susanna V, 676
Hadley, Susanna Jane V, 565
Hadley, Susanna Jane V, 676
Hadley, Susanna W. V, 63
Hadley, Susanna W. V, 555
Hadley, Susannah I, 375
Hadley, Susannah I, 392
Hadley, Susannah I, 434
Hadley, Susannah I, 446
Hadley, Susannah I, 447
Hadley, Susannah V, 390
Hadley, Susannah V, 550
Hadley, Susannah V, 565
Hadley, Susannah V, 567
Hadley, Susannah V, 568
Hadley, Susannah V, 676
Hadley, Susannah V, 970
Hadley, Susannah N. V, 566
Hadley, Susannah W. V, 567
Hadley, Susannah W. V, 568
Hadley, Susannah, Sr. V, 568
Hadley, Susie V, 676
Hadley, Tacy V, 30
Hadley, Tacy V, 63
Hadley, Tamar V, 436
Hadley, Tamer V, 333
Hadley, Tamer V, 390
Hadley, Tarinda V, 677
Hadley, Teston V, 979
Hadley, Thamar V, 243
Hadley, Thamer V, 390
Hadley, Theodocia V, 565
Hadley, Theodocia V, 589
Hadley, Theodocia V, 600
Hadley, Theodocia V, 676
Hadley, Theodore V, 566
Hadley, Theodosia V, 567
Hadley, Theodosia V, 599
Hadley, Thomas I, 352
Hadley, Thomas I, 391
Hadley, Thomas I, 392
Hadley, Thomas I, 411
Hadley, Thomas I, 446
Hadley, Thomas I Sup 1, 9
Hadley, Thomas V, 494
Hadley, Thomas V, 564
Hadley, Thomas V, 568
Hadley, Thomas V, 676
Hadley, Tobias Julian I, 761
Hadley, Veda V, 566
Hadley, Vivian M. V, 566
Hadley, Vivian M. V, 569
Hadley, W. A. VI, 243
Hadley, W. B. V, 566
Hadley, W. C. V, 569
Hadley, Walter V, 568
Hadley, Walter V, 970
Hadley, Walter C. II, 870
Hadley, Walter C. II, 907
Hadley, Warren V, 565
Hadley, Warren V, 676
Hadley, Wd. Anna V, 63
Hadley, Weldon S. V, 566
Hadley, Wendell V, 678
Hadley, Wilber S. V, 63
Hadley, Willard V, 677
Hadley, Willard V, 708
Hadley, Willard I. V, 678
Hadley, Willard Jesse V, 677
Hadley, William I, 352
Hadley, William I, 391
Hadley, William I, 392
Hadley, William I, 435
Hadley, William I, 446
Hadley, William I, 447
Hadley, William V, 390
Hadley, William V, 494
Hadley, William V, 495
Hadley, William V, 564
Hadley, William V, 566
Hadley, William V, 567
Hadley, William V, 676
Hadley, William V, 677
Hadley, William B. V, 390
Hadley, William B. V, 568
Hadley, William Beale V, 564
Hadley, William C. V, 676
Hadley, William Clark V, 565
Hadley, William Clark V, 676
Hadley, William Edgar V, 566
Hadley, William Edgar V, 676
Hadley, William L. V, 63
Hadley, William L. V, 676
Hadley, William Lawrence V, 495
Hadley, William P. V, 565
Hadley, William, Jr. V, 567
Hadley, Winnie V, 390
Hadley, Winnie V, 391
Hadley, Wm. V, 390
Hadley, Wm. V, 550
Hadley, Wm. V, 567
Hadley, Wm. V, 569
Hadley, Wm. V, 582
Hadley, Wm. V, 908
Hadley, Wm. B. V, 568
Hadley, Wm. Beal V, 568
Hadley, Wm. C. V, 567
Hadley, Wm. Edgar V, 677
Hadley, Wm. L. V, 565
Hadley, Wm. L. V, 567
Hadley, Wm. P. V, 569
Hadley, Wm. P. V, 677
Hadley, Wm. P. V, 678
Hadley, Wm., Jr. V, 567
Hadley, Woodro Warner V, 566
Hadley, Woodrow W. V, 569
Hadley, Woodrow Warner V, 676
Hadley, Zenas V, 566
Hadley, Zenas V, 677
Hadley, Zenas G. V, 569
Hadley, Zene G. V, 569
Hadley, Zenis Garland V, 676
Hadley, Zeno I, 434
Hadley, Zeno I, 446
Hadley, Zeno I, 447
Hadley, Zeno Tatum I, 435
Hadley, Zilpha I, 925
Hadly, Ann I, 391
Hadly, Ann I, 405
Hadly, Arthur IV, 212
Hadly, Asenath I, 761
Hadly, Bridget I, 812
Hadly, Catharine I, 446
Hadly, Catharine I, 447
Hadly, Edith M. IV, 962
Hadly, Elenor I, 434
Hadly, Elenor I, 435
Hadly, Elizabeth I, 431
Hadly, Elizabeth I, 435
Hadly, Elizabeth Mote IV, 212
Hadly, Hannah I, 370
Hadly, Hannah I, 391
Hadly, Helen A. IV, 962
Hadly, Herbert IV, 212
Hadly, Herbert H. IV, 962
Hadly, Herbert L. IV, 212
Hadly, Herbert L. IV, 962
Hadly, Jacob I, 391
Hadly, Jacob I, 414
Hadly, Jacob I, 444
Hadly, Jacob I, 446
Hadly, James I, 435
Hadly, Jeremiah I, 434
Hadly, Jeremiah I, 435
Hadly, Jeremieh I, 391
Hadly, John I, 370
Hadly, John I, 391
Hadly, John I, 435
Hadly, John I, 446
Hadly, John I, 447
Hadly, John I, 480
Hadly, Jonathan I, 391
Hadly, Jonathan I, 405
Hadly, Jonathan I, 435
Hadly, Joshua I, 356
Hadly, Joshua I, 391
Hadly, Joshua I, 394
Hadly, Joshua I, 434
Hadly, Joshua I, 435
Hadly, Joshua I, 446
Hadly, Joshua I, 447
Hadly, Josphine A. IV, 962
Hadly, Lydia I, 356
Hadly, Lydia I, 391
Hadly, Lydia I, 394
Hadly, Lydia I, 399
Hadly, Lydia I, 434
Hadly, Lydia I, 446
Hadly, Lydia I, 447
Hadly, Martha I, 435
Hadly, Mary I, 388
Hadly, Mary I, 390
Hadly, Mary I, 391
Hadly, Mary I, 392
Hadly, Mary I, 435
Hadly, Mary I, 445
Hadly, Mary I, 446
Hadly, Mary I, 453
Hadly, Mary I, 761
Hadly, Mary E. IV, 962
Hadly, Patience I, 356
Hadly, Patience I, 391
Hadly, Patience I, 402
Hadly, Patience I, 796
Hadly, Patience I, 812
Hadly, Phebe I, 391
Hadly, Phebe I, 414
Hadly, Pheby I, 391
Hadly, Rachel I, 431
Hadly, Rachel I, 446
Hadly, Ruth I, 391
Hadly, Ruth I, 431
Hadly, Ruth I, 434
Hadly, Ruth I, 435
Hadly, Ruth I, 446
Hadly, Ruth I, 451
Hadly, Ruth I, 455
Hadly, Sarah I, 379
Hadly, Sarah I, 391
Hadly, Sarah I, 418
Hadly, Sarah I, 435
Hadly, Sarah I, 444
Hadly, Sarah I, 446
Hadly, Simon I, 434
Hadly, Simon I, 435
Hadly, Simon I, 971
Hadly, Thomas I, 435
Hadly, William I, 391
Hadly, William I, 435
Hadly, Wm. I, 379
Hadock, Abigail I, 393
Hadock, Abigail I, 394
Hadock, Abigail I, 404
Hadock, James I, 394
Hadock, John I, 716
Hadock, Margret I, 986
Hadox, Evelyn IV, 1318
Hadwen, James II, 538
Hadwin, James III, 143
Hadwin, Mary IV, 438
Haering, Anna IV, 1252
Haering, Clarence L. IV, 1252
Haffe, James II, 369
Hafflick, Anna II, 870
Haffline, Sarah II, 870
Haffner, Charles IV, 1038
Hafford, Eloise Ada III, 143
Haflick, Anna II, 848
Haflick, Anna II, 870
Hafline, Sarah II, 870
Hagaman, Anna C. IV, 126
Hagaman, Anne IV, 127
Hagaman, Cornelia V, 906
Hagaman, Isaac IV, 127
Hagaman, Isaac C. IV, 126
Hagaman, John IV, 126
Hagaman, John IV, 127
Hagaman, John C. IV, 126
Hagaman, Joseph IV, 127
Hagaman, Maria IV, 126
Hagaman, Maria IV, 127
Hagaman, Martha IV, 127
Hagaman, Mary IV, 126
Hagaman, Michael IV, 36
Hagaman, Michael IV, 123
Hagaman, Michael IV, 126
Hagaman, Michael IV, 127
Hagaman, Rachel IV, 127
Hagaman, Ruth IV, 127
Hagaman, Ruth IV, 132
Hagaman, Ruth G. IV, 126
Hagaman, Sarah IV, 36
Hagaman, Sarah IV, 123
Hagaman, Sarah IV, 126
Hagaman, Sarah IV, 127
Hagaman, Sarah, Jr. IV, 127
Hagan, ??? III, 143
Hagan, Arthur Tyson III, 143
Hagan, Arthur Tyson III, 144
Hagan, Austin III, 144
Hagan, Austin Alexander III, 14:
Hagan, Austin Alexander III, 14
Hagan, Benjamin III, 144
Hagan, Benjamin Olive III, 144
Hagan, Eliz. L. III, 143
Hagan, Eliz. Leedom III, 143
Hagan, Eliz. Leedom III, 263
Hagan, Eliza Ann III, 144
Hagan, Elizabeth III, 144
Hagan, Elizabeth Leedom III, 143
Hagan, George III, 144
Hagan, James III, 143
Hagan, James Wallace III, 143
Hagan, Jane III, 144
Hagan, John III, 143
Hagan, John III, 144
Hagan, Jos. III, 143
Hagan, Joseph III, 63
Hagan, Joseph III, 86
Hagan, Joseph III, 143
Hagan, Joseph III, 144
Hagan, Joseph III, 197
Hagan, Joseph III, 263
Hagan, Margaret III, 143
Hagan, Margaret III, 144
Hagan, Margaret III, 312
Hagan, Margaret H. III, 86
Hagan, Margaret S. III, 143
Hagan, Margaret S. III, 144
Hagan, Mary III, 144
Hagan, Mary Henrietta III, 144
Hagan, Olive III, 143
Hagan, Olive III, 144
Hagan, Phebe C. III, 63
Hagan, Phebe C. III, 143
Hagan, Phebe C. III, 144
Hagan, Robert III, 144
Hagan, Sarah III, 143
Hagan, Sarah III, 144
Hagan, Sarah E. III, 86
Hagan, Sarah E. III, 143
Hagan, Sarah E. III, 144
Hagan, Sarah E. III, 197
Hagan, Sarah E. III, 263
Hagan, Sarah Eliz. III, 63
Hagan, Sarah Elizabeth III, 144
Hagan, Sarah J. III, 143
Hagan, Sarah Jane III, 143
Hagan, Sarah Jane III, 144
Hagan, Sarah Jane III, 197
Hagan, William III, 143
Hagan, William Levell III, 144
Hage, Francis II, 960
Hage, Hannah II, 960
Hage, Isaac II, 960
Hage, Mary I Sup 1, 4
Hage, Mary I Sup 1, 5
Hage, Pleasant II, 960
Hage, Pleasant II, 989
Hage, Pleasant II, 998
Hage, Rebecca II, 960
Hage, Rebeckah II, 999
Hage, William I Sup 1, 4
Hageman, James IV, 1318
Hageman, James C. IV, 1318
Hageman, Nettie C. II, 870
Hageman, Nettie C. II, 881
Hagen, ??? III, 219
Hagen, ??? III, 312
Hagen, Ann Eliza III, 219
Hagen, Margaret III, 312
Hagerman, Charlotte C. VI, 925
Hagerman, Chas. V, 999
Hagerman, Cliford V, 999
Hagerman, Elizabeth F. VI, 986

Hagerman, Everett V, 334
Hagerman, Florence V, 999
Hagerman, Geo. E. V, 908
Hagerman, George E. V, 334
Hagerman, George E. V, 908
Hagerman, Henrietta V, 841
Hagerman, Henrietta V, 854
Hagerman, Levin B. VI, 986
Hagerman, Levon Burr VI, 925
Hagerman, Lydia V, 391
Hagerman, Lydia V, 413
Hagerman, Margaret C. VI, 925
Hagerman, Mrs. Charlotte C. VI, 949
Hagerty, Basil V, 999
Hagerty, Bessie H. V, 999
Hagerty, Donald V, 999
Hagerty, Wm. H. V, 999
Hagey, Mary II, 816
Haggard, Jemimah V, 999
Haggardy, Homer V, 334
Haggerty, John IV, 714
Hagner, Emily II, 870
Hagner, Emily W. II, 870
Hagstog, Jacob II, 369
Hagstog, Sarah II, 369
Hague, Ann II, 960
Hague, Ann IV, 211
Hague, Ann IV, 272
Hague, Ann IV, 291
Hague, Ann VI, 499
Hague, Ann VI, 519
Hague, Ann VI, 523
Hague, Ann VI, 531
Hague, Ann VI, 554
Hague, Ann VI, 555
Hague, Ann VI, 579
Hague, Anna N. IV, 473
Hague, Clairee C. V, 678
Hague, Edith V, 678
Hague, Edith M. V, 678
Hague, Elizabeth IV, 211
Hague, Elizabeth A. IV, 211
Hague, Elizabeth A. IV, 271
Hague, Francis II, 960
Hague, Francis II, 998
Hague, Francis II, 999
Hague, Francis II, 1041
Hague, Francis IV, 211
Hague, Francis VI, 464
Hague, Francis VI, 499
Hague, Francis VI, 500
Hague, Francis VI, 519
Hague, Francis VI, 531
Hague, Francis VI, 550
Hague, Francis VI, 555
Hague, Francis VI, 573
Hague, Francis VI, 580
Hague, Francis VI, 586
Hague, Francis VI, 661
Hague, Hannah II, 960
Hague, Hannah VI, 471
Hague, Hannah VI, 500
Hague, Hannah VI, 539
Hague, Hannah VI, 587
Hague, Hannah VI, 591
Hague, Hannah VI, 596
Hague, Harry V, 678
Hague, Harry W. V, 678
Hague, Hazel E. V, 678
Hague, Helen IV, 1252
Hague, Henrietta IV, 211
Hague, Henrietta L. IV, 247
Hague, Henrietta T. IV, 211
Hague, Henrietta T. IV, 248
Hague, Henry B. IV, 211
Hague, Henry B. IV, 247
Hague, Henry B. IV, 291
Hague, Henry B. IV, 292
Hague, Henry Ball IV, 211
Hague, Henry W. IV, 1252
Hague, Hercules VI, 587
Hague, Hiram VI, 499
Hague, Hyram VI, 499
Hague, Isaac II, 960
Hague, Jacob VI, 587
Hague, James IV, 211
Hague, James R. IV, 211
Hague, James R. IV, 272
Hague, James R. IV, 473
Hague, James R., Jr. IV, 211
Hague, James Rattikane IV, 211
Hague, James Russell IV, 211
Hague, Jane II, 960
Hague, Jane II, 999
Hague, Jane II, 1041
Hague, Jane IV, 1099
Hague, Jane IV, 1109
Hague, Jane VI, 464
Hague, Jane VI, 499
Hague, Jane VI, 500
Hague, Jane VI, 519
Hague, Jane VI, 531
Hague, Jane VI, 555
Hague, Jane VI, 580
Hague, Jane VI, 586
Hague, Jane VI, 645
Hague, Jane VI, 658
Hague, Jane VI, 661
Hague, John II, 960
Hague, John IV, 211
Hague, John VI, 555
Hague, John VI, 587
Hague, John C. IV, 211
Hague, John Lupton IV, 211
Hague, John T. IV, 211
Hague, Jonah VI, 499
Hague, Jonah VI, 500
Hague, Jonah VI, 512
Hague, Jonah VI, 516
Hague, Jonas I, 548
Hague, Joseph IV, 211
Hague, Joseph IV, 1252
Hague, Joseph R. IV, 211
Hague, Joseph S. IV, 211
Hague, Joseph S. IV, 271
Hague, Joseph Sanders IV, 211
Hague, Lerura Ann VI, 645
Hague, Lerura Ann VI, 688
Hague, M. S. IV, 1252
Hague, Margaret V, 334
Hague, Margaret F. IV, 1097
Hague, Margaret F. IV, 1099
Hague, Margarett VI, 587
Hague, Martha Ann IV, 211
Hague, Martha Ann IV, 231
Hague, Martha T. V, 678
Hague, Mary II, 960
Hague, Mary IV, 219
Hague, Mary IV, 473
Hague, Mary V, 678
Hague, Mary VI, 467
Hague, Mary VI, 500
Hague, Mary H. IV, 211
Hague, Mary H. IV, 473
Hague, Mary T. V, 678
Hague, Nancy IV, 211
Hague, Pleasand VI, 519
Hague, Pleasant II, 981
Hague, Pleasant II, 998
Hague, Pleasant II, 999
Hague, Pleasant VI, 499
Hague, Pleasant VI, 500
Hague, Pleasant VI, 510
Hague, Pleasant VI, 511
Hague, Pleasant VI, 519
Hague, Pleasant VI, 522
Hague, Pleasant VI, 529
Hague, Pleasant VI, 586
Hague, Pleasant VI, 645
Hague, Pleasant VI, 658
Hague, Pleasant VI, 661
Hague, Pleasant VI, 668
Hague, Pleasant VI, 752
Hague, Pleasant VI, 757
Hague, R. E. IV, 1252
Hague, Rebecca II, 960
Hague, Rebecca IV, 211
Hague, Rebeckah II, 999
Hague, Rebeckah VI, 500
Hague, Rebekah VI, 513
Hague, Robert IV, 211
Hague, Robert IV, 231
Hague, Robert V, 678
Hague, Robert S. IV, 211
Hague, Robert S. V, 678
Hague, Rue Ann VI, 500
Hague, Rue Ann VI, 548
Hague, Rue Ann VI, 622
Hague, Rue Ann VI, 623
Hague, Rue Ann VI, 645
Hague, Rue Ann VI, 688
Hague, Ruth IV, 211
Hague, Ruth VI, 499
Hague, Ruth VI, 500
Hague, Ruth VI, 550
Hague, Samuel IV, 211
Hague, Samuel IV, 473
Hague, Samuel VI, 471
Hague, Samuel VI, 499
Hague, Samuel VI, 500
Hague, Samuel VI, 559
Hague, Samuel VI, 591
Hague, Samuel VI, 596
Hague, Samuel VI, 645
Hague, Samuel VI, 658
Hague, Samuel E. IV, 219
Hague, Samuel E. IV, 473
Hague, Samuel, Jr. VI, 500
Hague, Sarah IV, 211
Hague, Sarah IV, 275
Hague, Sarah VI, 494
Hague, Sarah VI, 500
Hague, Sarah VI, 509
Hague, Sarah VI, 573
Hague, Sarah VI, 580
Hague, Sarah VI, 587
Hague, Sarah Ann IV, 211
Hague, Sarah Ann IV, 247
Hague, Sarah Ann IV, 291
Hague, Sarah Ann IV, 292
Hague, Silas VI, 587
Hague, Susan IV, 1252
Hague, Tacy IV, 122
Hague, Thomas VI, 500
Hague, Thomas VI, 580
Hague, Thos. W. IV, 473
Hague, William II, 960
Hague, William IV, 211
Hague, William V, 334
Hague, William H. IV, 211
Hague, William H. IV, 473
Hague, William M. V, 678
Hague, Wm. V, 334
Hague, Wm. H. IV, 211
Hagy, Clayton L. II, 797
Hagy, Clayton L. II, 870
Hagy, Clayton L. II, 885
Hagy, Elizabeth II, 870
Hagy, Elizabeth II, 885
Hagy, Emma II, 797
Hagy, Emma W. II, 870
Hagy, Emma W. II, 885
Hagy, Joseph II, 870
Hagy, Joseph II, 885
Hagy, Lydia Ann II, 735
Hagy, Lydia Ann II, 743
Hahn, Mary IV, 1252
Haiden, William VI, 872
Haiden, William VI, 931
Haig, Mary I, 141
Haig, Mary III, 144
Haig, Mary III, 221
Haig, Sarah I, 139
Haig, Sarah I, 141
Haig, William I, 139
Haig, William I, 141
Haig, William III, 144
Haig, William III, 221
Haige, Francis II, 998
Haige, Francis II, 1015
Haige, Mary I, 99
Haige, Pleasant II, 998
Haige, Wd. Pleasant II, 1015
Haige, William I, 99
Haige, William, Jr. I, 99
Haight, ??? III, 144
Haight, Aaron III, 144
Haight, Alexander VI, 745
Haight, Amy III, 144
Haight, Amy VI, 745
Haight, Anna III, 131
Haight, Anna III, 144
Haight, Anna III, 212
Haight, Caroline A. III, 144
Haight, Caroline A. III, 212
Haight, Charity III, 144
Haight, Charles III, 144
Haight, David H. IV, 1364
Haight, Deborah III, 144
Haight, Deborah III, 326
Haight, Deborah III, 327
Haight, Edward III, 144
Haight, Eliza III, 184
Haight, Eliza L. III, 144
Haight, Elizabeth III, 144
Haight, Emeline III, 144
Haight, Francis IV, 1318
Haight, Frank IV, 1318
Haight, Franklin C. III, 144
Haight, Franklin C. III, 212
Haight, Hannah IV, 1364
Haight, Harriet III, 73
Haight, Harriet III, 74
Haight, Harriet III, 112
Haight, Huldah IV, 1364
Haight, Israel A. III, 144
Haight, Jacob III, 144
Haight, Jacob VI, 745
Haight, Jacob T. III, 144
Haight, Jacob T. III, 166
Haight, Jane III, 134
Haight, Jane III, 144
Haight, John III, 86
Haight, John III, 144
Haight, John III, 318
Haight, John III, 455
Haight, Keziah IV, 1364
Haight, Levi IV, 1364
Haight, Lydia IV, 1364
Haight, Mary III, 144
Haight, Mary III, 163
Haight, Mary A. III, 144
Haight, Mary Evelyn III, 144
Haight, Nicholas III, 144
Haight, Nicholas III, 318
Haight, Nicholas III, 413
Haight, Nicholas III, 451
Haight, Nicholas III, 454
Haight, Patience III, 144
Haight, Patience III, 318
Haight, Patience III, 413
Haight, Patience III, 451
Haight, Patience III, 454
Haight, Phebe III, 22
Haight, Phebe III, 144
Haight, Phebe III, 154
Haight, Phebe III, 318
Haight, Phebe III, 405
Haight, Phebe III, 413
Haight, Phebe III, 455
Haight, Phebe IV, 1364
Haight, Phebe A. III, 144
Haight, Reuben IV, 1364
Haight, Samuel III, 22
Haight, Samuel III, 144
Haight, Samuel III, 163
Haight, Samuel III, 319
Haight, Samuel III, 455
Haight, Samuel Carleton III, 144
Haight, Samuel L. III, 144
Haight, Samuel L. III, 327
Haight, Samuel, Jr. III, 144
Haight, Sarah III, 46
Haight, Sarah III, 144
Haight, Sarah III, 166
Haight, Sarah III, 319
Haight, Sarah III, 397
Haight, Sarah III, 451
Haight, Sarah III, 455
Haight, Selah III, 144
Haight, Selah III, 184
Haight, Stephen III, 144
Haight, Stephen S. III, 144
Haight, Susan A. III, 144
Haight, Wd. Phebe III, 86
Haight, Wd. Phebe III, 144
Haight, Wd. Susan A. III, 166
Hail, Benjamin VI, 926
Hail, Frances VI, 1004
Hail, John VI, 1004
Hail, Margaret E. III, 295
Hail, Margaret S. III, 37
Hail, Mary A. I, 880
Hail, Nancy VI, 982
Hail, Nathan VI, 396
Hail, Overstreet VI, 925
Hail, Polly VI, 979
Hail, Polly Moody VI, 926
Hail, Stephen, Junr. VI, 926
Hail, Susanna VI, 926
Hail, Thomas VI, 882
Haile, Anne VI, 875
Haile, Anne VI, 1020
Haile, Judith VI, 1007
Haile, Laban VI, 926
Haile, Mary VI, 29
Haile, Mary VI, 34
Haile, Molley VI, 926
Haile, Molly VI, 926
Haile, Nancey VI, 1020
Haile, Nancy VI, 965
Haile, Salley VI, 965
Haile, Stephen VI, 926
Haile, Stephen VI, 941
Haile, Stephen VI, 965
Haile, Stephen VI, 1020
Haile, Thomas VI, 925
Haile, William VI, 926
Hailey, Abigail I, 1066
Hailey, Elizabeth I, 716
Hailey, Elizabeth I, 812
Hailey, Elizabeth I, 1066
Hailey, Henry I, 1066
Hailey, Isau I, 716
Hailey, Isom I, 392
Hailey, Isom I, 812
Hailey, Isom I, 1066
Hailey, Mary Macy I, 1066
Hailey, Milla I, 812
Hailey, Phebe I, 812
Hailey, Phebe I, 876
Hailey, Phebe I, 880
Hailey, Pheebe I, 1066
Hailey, Silas I, 812
Hailey, William I, 392
Hailey, William I, 393
Hailey, William I, 1066
Haily, Elizabeth I, 392
Haily, Randle I, 393
Haily, Silas I, 393
Hain, Ann IV, 145
Hain, John IV, 145
Haine, Hannah V, 495
Haines, ??? II, 320
Haines, ??? III, 85
Haines, ??? V, 965
Haines, Aaron II, 175
Haines, Aaron II, 228
Haines, Aaron II, 229
Haines, Aaron V, 495
Haines, Aaron W. II, 290
Haines, Abel II, 175
Haines, Abel II, 204
Haines, Abel II, 228
Haines, Abel II, 241
Haines, Abel II, 309
Haines, Abel II, 319
Haines, Abel, Jr. II, 319
Haines, Abi V, 64
Haines, Abigail II, 216
Haines, Abigail II, 227
Haines, Abigail II, 228
Haines, Abigail II, 309
Haines, Abigail III, 39
Haines, Abigail III, 145
Haines, Abigail VI, 396
Haines, Abigail VI, 397
Haines, Abigail VI, 427
Haines, Abigail Ann II, 204
Haines, Abigail Ann II, 229
Haines, Abigail Ann II, 309
Haines, Abigail Ann II, 716
Haines, Abigail B. III, 85
Haines, Abigail B. III, 144
Haines, Abigail C. II, 319
Haines, Abigail C. II, 324
Haines, Abigail H. II, 870
Haines, Abigail H. II, 917
Haines, Abigail Mount II, 74
Haines, Abraham II, 74
Haines, Abraham II, 706
Haines, Abraham II, 743
Haines, Abraham V, 51
Haines, Abraham V, 826
Haines, Abraham VI, 500
Haines, Abraham VI, 645
Haines, Abraham VI, 692
Haines, Abram II, 706
Haines, Abram VI, 397
Haines, Abram VI, 550
Haines, Ada V, 678
Haines, Addie V, 496
Haines, Addison II, 797
Haines, Addison II, 870
Haines, Agnes II, 29
Haines, Agnes II, 706
Haines, Agnes II, 743
Haines, Agnes B. II, 706
Haines, Agnes B. II, 743
Haines, Agnes Huddy II, 74
Haines, Agness II, 74
Haines, Albert II, 319
Haines, Albert W. V, 570
Haines, Albina II, 289
Haines, Albina II, 309
Haines, Albina II, 318
Haines, Albina II, 319
Haines, Alfred V, 495
Haines, Alfred Cope II, 175
Haines, Alfred Cope II, 290
Haines, Alfred M. II, 310
Haines, Alfred M. II, 319
Haines, Alfred O. II, 290
Haines, Alfred S. IV, 715
Haines, Alice D. III, 145
Haines, Alice D. III, 284
Haines, Alice W. II, 310
Haines, Allen II, 290
Haines, Allen II, 870
Haines, Allen V, 173
Haines, Allen V, 570
Haines, Allen V, 623
Haines, Allen VI, 396
Haines, Allen R. II, 310
Haines, Allen R. II, 319
Haines, Allice W. II, 319
Haines, Alma Clarinda V, 457
Haines, Alveretta V, 457
Haines, Alvin II, 139
Haines, Alvin II, 870
Haines, Alvin Z. V, 495
Haines, Alvina VI, 396
Haines, Alvina VI, 500
Haines, Amelia C. III, 40
Haines, Amelia C. V, 64
Haines, Amelia E. V, 64
Haines, Amirah V, 64
Haines, Amos II, 227
Haines, Amos II, 228
Haines, Amos II, 309
Haines, Amos V, 63
Haines, Amos V, 64
Haines, Amos V, 173
Haines, Amos V, 495

Haines, Amos V, 496
Haines, Amos V, 569
Haines, Amos V, 578
Haines, Amos V, 908
Haines, Amos VI, 396
Haines, Amos W. II, 319
Haines, Amy II, 279
Haines, Amyrah V, 53
Haines, Amyrah V, 64
Haines, Andrew V, 391
Haines, Andrew J. V, 391
Haines, Angelina IV, 715
Haines, Ann II, 29
Haines, Ann II, 74
Haines, Ann II, 75
Haines, Ann II, 78
Haines, Ann II, 227
Haines, Ann II, 228
Haines, Ann II, 258
Haines, Ann II, 259
Haines, Ann II, 260
Haines, Ann II, 289
Haines, Ann II, 539
Haines, Ann II, 577
Haines, Ann II, 783
Haines, Ann II, 1087
Haines, Ann III, 428
Haines, Ann IV, 334
Haines, Ann IV, 397
Haines, Ann V, 49
Haines, Ann V, 64
Haines, Ann V, 229
Haines, Ann V, 243
Haines, Ann V, 970
Haines, Ann V, 974
Haines, Ann VI, 396
Haines, Ann VI, 397
Haines, Ann Hilderman II, 74
Haines, Ann Isabel V, 391
Haines, Ann Isabel V, 495
Haines, Ann Isabel V, 623
Haines, Ann Isabella V, 496
Haines, Ann Isabella V, 623
Haines, Ann L. II, 117
Haines, Ann L. II, 119
Haines, Ann L. II, 539
Haines, Ann L. II, 706
Haines, Ann L. II, 743
Haines, Ann L. II, 765
Haines, Ann L. II, 870
Haines, Anna II, 149
Haines, Anna II, 228
Haines, Anna II, 319
Haines, Anna II, 723
Haines, Anna II, 870
Haines, Anna II, 965
Haines, Anna II, 1087
Haines, Anna II, 1088
Haines, Anna IV, 334
Haines, Anna IV, 627
Haines, Anna V, 38
Haines, Anna V, 63
Haines, Anna V, 64
Haines, Anna E. V, 244
Haines, Anna H. II, 174
Haines, Anna J. V, 623
Haines, Anna L. II, 119
Haines, Anna M. V, 64
Haines, Anna P. IV, 211
Haines, Anna R. II, 870
Haines, Anna S. II, 117
Haines, Anna S. II, 119
Haines, Anna Satterthwait II, 797
Haines, Anna T. II, 319
Haines, Anne II, 214
Haines, Anne II, 228
Haines, Anne L. II, 706
Haines, Annie II, 175
Haines, Annie II, 290
Haines, Annie II, 871
Haines, Annie II, 948
Haines, Annie II, 1087
Haines, Annie M. V, 294
Haines, Anthony II, 29
Haines, Anthony II, 74
Haines, Apharacia V, 496
Haines, Apharacia V, 623
Haines, Apharacia V, 635
Haines, Apharacio V, 495
Haines, Apharacio V, 496
Haines, Aphracia V, 391
Haines, Arthur V, 391
Haines, Arthur Webster V, 678
Haines, Asaph V, 495
Haines, Asaph V, 496
Haines, Atlantic IV, 36
Haines, Atlantic IV, 90
Haines, Atlantic IV, 107
Haines, Atlantic IV, 473
Haines, Atlantic VI, 397
Haines, Atlantick IV, 90
Haines, Barclay II, 175
Haines, Bathsheba V, 64
Haines, Belle V, 391
Haines, Benajah II, 175
Haines, Benajah II, 290
Haines, Benjamin II, 117
Haines, Benjamin II, 119
Haines, Benjamin II, 309
Haines, Benjamin II, 369
Haines, Benjamin II, 538
Haines, Benjamin II, 577
Haines, Benjamin II, 870
Haines, Benjamin IV, 960
Haines, Benjamin B. II, 870
Haines, Benjamin D. II, 723
Haines, Benjamin L. IV, 960
Haines, Benjamin M. H. II, 706
Haines, Bernard V, 496
Haines, Bernard E. V, 678
Haines, Bernice V, 678
Haines, Bernice E. V, 496
Haines, Bethany VI, 396
Haines, Bethuel II, 539
Haines, Bethuel V, 63
Haines, Betty V, 64
Haines, Betty V, 173
Haines, Betty V, 243
Haines, Beulah II, 29
Haines, Beulah VI, 395
Haines, Beulah VI, 396
Haines, Beulah VI, 645
Haines, Beulah VI, 707
Haines, Beulah VI, 744
Haines, Beulah VI, 745
Haines, Biddle II, 144
Haines, Biddle II, 149
Haines, Bulah VI, 396
Haines, Bulah VI, 397
Haines, Burr II, 310
Haines, Burr II, 319
Haines, Burrwood M. II, 309
Haines, Caleb II, 132
Haines, Caleb II, 135
Haines, Caleb II, 199
Haines, Caleb II, 203
Haines, Caleb II, 216
Haines, Caleb II, 227
Haines, Caleb II, 228
Haines, Caleb II, 276
Haines, Caleb II, 289
Haines, Caleb II, 309
Haines, Caleb V, 569
Haines, Caleb V, 572
Haines, Caleb D. II, 132
Haines, Caleb D. II, 149
Haines, Caleb L. II, 290
Haines, Caleb Pierce II, 175
Haines, Calvin V, 569
Haines, Calvin V, 570
Haines, Carey Lee V, 173
Haines, Carey Leigh V, 173
Haines, Carl V, 678
Haines, Carl V, 716
Haines, Carlile VI, 397
Haines, Caroline II, 705
Haines, Caroline III, 145
Haines, Caroline M. II, 797
Haines, Caroline M. II, 870
Haines, Carrie E. V, 570
Haines, Caspar W. III, 145
Haines, Caspar Wistar II, 591
Haines, Casper II, 369
Haines, Casper W. II, 369
Haines, Catharine II, 544
Haines, Chalkley IV, 90
Haines, Chalkley IV, 91
Haines, Chalkley IV, 818
Haines, Chalkley IV, 922
Haines, Chalkley IV, 959
Haines, Chalkley IV, 960
Haines, Chalkley VI, 397
Haines, Charles II, 175
Haines, Charles II, 456
Haines, Charles IV, 334
Haines, Charles IV, 397
Haines, Charles IV, 398
Haines, Charles V, 64
Haines, Charles V, 173
Haines, Charles V, 908
Haines, Charles V, 970
Haines, Charles E. II, 139
Haines, Charles E. II, 744
Haines, Charles Edward II, 706
Haines, Charles M. V, 678
Haines, Charley C. V, 391
Haines, Charlotte III, 67
Haines, Charlotte V, 38
Haines, Charlotte V, 63
Haines, Charlotte V, 64
Haines, Charlotte V, 241
Haines, Charlotte V, 243
Haines, Charlotte C. IV, 1318
Haines, Charlotte E. II, 290
Haines, Charlotte Ellen II, 290
Haines, Charlotte Ellen II, 297
Haines, Chas. V, 908
Haines, Chas. E. II, 833
Haines, Chas. E. II, 871
Haines, Clara V, 244
Haines, Clara V, 678
Haines, Clara E. V, 244
Haines, Clara W. II, 310
Haines, Clara W. II, 319
Haines, Clara W. II, 323
Haines, Clark V, 64
Haines, Clark E. V, 970
Haines, Claudies E. V, 244
Haines, Clayton II, 319
Haines, Clayton II, 706
Haines, Clayton II, 743
Haines, Clayton II, 870
Haines, Clayton II, 953
Haines, Clayton IV, 211
Haines, Clayton IV, 246
Haines, Clayton V, 495
Haines, Clayton V, 496
Haines, Cora E. V, 391
Haines, Cora Ellen V, 391
Haines, Corwin V, 496
Haines, Corwin E. V, 496
Haines, D. W. V, 496
Haines, D. Webster V, 678
Haines, Daisy Lytle V, 173
Haines, Daniel II, 192
Haines, Daniel II, 200
Haines, Daniel II, 227
Haines, Daniel II, 228
Haines, Daniel VI, 395
Haines, Daniel VI, 396
Haines, Daniel VI, 397
Haines, Daniel VI, 500
Haines, Daniel VI, 501
Haines, Daniel VI, 549
Haines, Daniel VI, 645
Haines, Daniel VI, 659
Haines, Daniel VI, 744
Haines, Daniel VI, 745
Haines, Daniel Longstreath IV, 527
Haines, David II, 716
Haines, David IV, 212
Haines, David IV, 397
Haines, David V, 173
Haines, David V, 244
Haines, David V, 457
Haines, David V, 569
Haines, Davis IV, 212
Haines, Davis IV, 397
Haines, Davis IV, 1060
Haines, Deborah I, 1048
Haines, Deborah II, 29
Haines, Deborah II, 75
Haines, Deborah II, 119
Haines, Deborah II, 716
Haines, Deborah V, 63
Haines, Deborah V, 64
Haines, Deborah VI, 397
Haines, Deborah E. II, 743
Haines, Deborah E. II, 746
Haines, Deborah W. V, 64
Haines, Dempsy S. IV, 398
Haines, Dempsy T. IV, 334
Haines, Donald V, 244
Haines, Donald Eber V, 244
Haines, Donald L. V, 173
Haines, Dorothy Frances II, 797
Haines, Dr. ??? II, 309
Haines, Earl V, 496
Haines, Ebenezer VI, 396
Haines, Ebenezer VI, 397
Haines, Eber V, 495
Haines, Eber V, 496
Haines, Eber H. V, 244
Haines, Ebor K. V, 496
Haines, Edith II, 228
Haines, Edith II, 282
Haines, Edith II, 289
Haines, Edith II, 290
Haines, Edith II, 291
Haines, Edith III, 144
Haines, Edith III, 241
Haines, Edith IV, 715
Haines, Edith V, 173
Haines, Edith V, 496
Haines, Edith V, 678
Haines, Edith C. III, 144
Haines, Edith C. III, 145
Haines, Edith G. II, 319
Haines, Edith R. II, 287
Haines, Edith R. II, 290
Haines, Edith S. II, 319
Haines, Edith S. II, 323
Haines, Edith W. III, 85
Haines, Edith W. III, 144
Haines, Edith W. III, 145
Haines, Edmund Lipsy IV, 212
Haines, Edna V, 678
Haines, Edna Peelle V, 244
Haines, Edward VI, 396
Haines, Edward B. VI, 396
Haines, Edward K. V, 908
Haines, Edward Preston II, 175
Haines, Edward T. III, 145
Haines, Edwin II, 290
Haines, Edwin II, 319
Haines, Edwin IV, 212
Haines, Edwin IV, 334
Haines, Edwin IV, 527
Haines, Edwin IV, 561
Haines, Edwin V, 569
Haines, Edwin A. V, 570
Haines, Edwin M. II, 743
Haines, Edyth Laird V, 173
Haines, Elden V, 496
Haines, Eldon V, 496
Haines, Eldon V, 662
Haines, Eldon V, 678
Haines, Eldon V, 707
Haines, Eldon Ray V, 496
Haines, Eleanor II, 52
Haines, Eleanor II, 75
Haines, Eleanor V, 908
Haines, Eli IV, 36
Haines, Eli IV, 90
Haines, Eli IV, 91
Haines, Eli IV, 98
Haines, Eli IV, 107
Haines, Eli IV, 110
Haines, Eli IV, 113
Haines, Eli IV, 714
Haines, Eli IV, 850
Haines, Eli V, 173
Haines, Eli V, 212
Haines, Eli V, 243
Haines, Eli V, 261
Haines, Eli V, 495
Haines, Eli V, 496
Haines, Eli V, 515
Haines, Eli V, 569
Haines, Eli V, 678
Haines, Eli VI, 397
Haines, Eli C. V, 243
Haines, Eli J. IV, 960
Haines, Eli Jess IV, 960
Haines, Elias V, 243
Haines, Elisha IV, 334
Haines, Elisha IV, 397
Haines, Elisha V, 495
Haines, Elisha V, 496
Haines, Eliza II, 175
Haines, Eliza II, 714
Haines, Eliza IV, 334
Haines, Eliza IV, 336
Haines, Eliza V, 64
Haines, Eliza V, 73
Haines, Eliza Ann IV, 90
Haines, Eliza Ann IV, 91
Haines, Eliza Ann IV, 959
Haines, Eliza Ann IV, 960
Haines, Eliza C. II, 706
Haines, Eliza C. II, 743
Haines, Elizabet B. VI, 747
Haines, Elizabeth II, 29
Haines, Elizabeth II, 34
Haines, Elizabeth II, 53
Haines, Elizabeth II, 74
Haines, Elizabeth II, 119
Haines, Elizabeth II, 149
Haines, Elizabeth II, 175
Haines, Elizabeth II, 195
Haines, Elizabeth II, 200
Haines, Elizabeth II, 201
Haines, Elizabeth II, 204
Haines, Elizabeth II, 216
Haines, Elizabeth II, 227
Haines, Elizabeth II, 228
Haines, Elizabeth II, 229
Haines, Elizabeth II, 232
Haines, Elizabeth II, 240
Haines, Elizabeth II, 241
Haines, Elizabeth II, 252
Haines, Elizabeth II, 258
Haines, Elizabeth II, 276
Haines, Elizabeth II, 277
Haines, Elizabeth II, 289
Haines, Elizabeth II, 290
Haines, Elizabeth II, 291
Haines, Elizabeth II, 292
Haines, Elizabeth II, 309
Haines, Elizabeth II, 319
Haines, Elizabeth II, 369
Haines, Elizabeth II, 539
Haines, Elizabeth II, 577
Haines, Elizabeth II, 706
Haines, Elizabeth II, 743
Haines, Elizabeth II, 744
Haines, Elizabeth II, 759
Haines, Elizabeth II, 765
Haines, Elizabeth II, 791
Haines, Elizabeth II, 797
Haines, Elizabeth II, 799
Haines, Elizabeth II, 870
Haines, Elizabeth II, 916
Haines, Elizabeth III, 53
Haines, Elizabeth III, 145
Haines, Elizabeth IV, 211
Haines, Elizabeth IV, 212
Haines, Elizabeth IV, 398
Haines, Elizabeth IV, 421
Haines, Elizabeth IV, 473
Haines, Elizabeth IV, 627
Haines, Elizabeth IV, 714
Haines, Elizabeth V, 64
Haines, Elizabeth V, 160
Haines, Elizabeth V, 173
Haines, Elizabeth V, 243
Haines, Elizabeth V, 244
Haines, Elizabeth V, 334
Haines, Elizabeth V, 480
Haines, Elizabeth V, 487
Haines, Elizabeth V, 495
Haines, Elizabeth V, 496
Haines, Elizabeth V, 569
Haines, Elizabeth V, 623
Haines, Elizabeth V, 963
Haines, Elizabeth VI, 396
Haines, Elizabeth VI, 397
Haines, Elizabeth VI, 500
Haines, Elizabeth VI, 501
Haines, Elizabeth VI, 549
Haines, Elizabeth VI, 550
Haines, Elizabeth VI, 597
Haines, Elizabeth VI, 645
Haines, Elizabeth VI, 649
Haines, Elizabeth VI, 668
Haines, Elizabeth VI, 670
Haines, Elizabeth A. VI, 396
Haines, Elizabeth A. VI, 407
Haines, Elizabeth A. VI, 662
Haines, Elizabeth A. VI, 667
Haines, Elizabeth A. VI, 668
Haines, Elizabeth A. VI, 681
Haines, Elizabeth Ann V, 570
Haines, Elizabeth Ann V, 578
Haines, Elizabeth Avis VI, 642
Haines, Elizabeth Avis VI, 645
Haines, Elizabeth Avis VI, 663
Haines, Elizabeth Avis VI, 664
Haines, Elizabeth B. II, 149
Haines, Elizabeth B. II, 319
Haines, Elizabeth B. VI, 740
Haines, Elizabeth Ballenger II, 74
Haines, Elizabeth C. V, 495
Haines, Elizabeth C. V, 496
Haines, Elizabeth F. IV, 211
Haines, Elizabeth J. V, 334
Haines, Elizabeth L. II, 119
Haines, Elizabeth L. II, 149
Haines, Elizabeth L. II, 319
Haines, Elizabeth L. II, 870
Haines, Elizabeth L. VI, 397
Haines, Elizabeth Leeds II, 309
Haines, Elizabeth M. VI, 396
Haines, Elizabeth Mildred V, 173
Haines, Elizabeth Mitchner IV, 334
Haines, Elizabeth R. II, 309
Haines, Elizabeth R. II, 319
Haines, Elizabeth R. II, 870
Haines, Elizabeth S. II, 310
Haines, Elizabeth S. II, 319
Haines, Elizabeth T. IV, 397
Haines, Elizabeth T. IV, 417
Haines, Elizabeth W. II, 310
Haines, Elizabeth W. II, 960
Haines, Elizabeth W. II, 1051
Haines, Elizabeth W. II, 1060
Haines, Elizabeth Woolman II, 723
Haines, Elizabeth, II, 149
Haines, Ella V, 173
Haines, Ella V, 457
Haines, Ella Brown V, 244
Haines, Ellanora V, 213
Haines, Ellanora A. V, 173
Haines, Ellen II, 309
Haines, Ellen VI, 636
Haines, Ellen VI, 645
Haines, Ellen VI, 652
Haines, Ellen VI, 653
Haines, Ellen VI, 701
Haines, Ellen VI, 704

Haines, Ellen VI, 706
Haines, Ellen VI, 724
Haines, Ellen Glover II, 794
Haines, Ellis I, 1048
Haines, Ellis II, 175
Haines, Ellis II, 706
Haines, Ellis II, 744
Haines, Ellis V, 740
Haines, Ellis, Sr. I, 1048
Haines, Elma Ann II, 75
Haines, Elmer E. V, 570
Haines, Elnora V, 908
Haines, Elsie V, 670
Haines, Elsie V, 678
Haines, Elsie C. V, 678
Haines, Elvin V, 65
Haines, Elwood V, 391
Haines, Elwood V, 495
Haines, Elwood V, 496
Haines, Elwood V, 519
Haines, Elwood V, 623
Haines, Elwood V, 635
Haines, Emily II, 175
Haines, Emily V, 173
Haines, Emily V, 212
Haines, Emily V, 243
Haines, Emily V, 496
Haines, Emily V, 515
Haines, Emily Lucile V, 173
Haines, Emily M. II, 309
Haines, Emily M. II, 318
Haines, Emily M. II, 319
Haines, Emily Maria II, 290
Haines, Emily S. V, 173
Haines, Emily T. V, 243
Haines, Emily T. V, 261
Haines, Emlen II, 175
Haines, Emma V, 496
Haines, Emma V, 678
Haines, Emma VI, 649
Haines, Emma F. V, 391
Haines, Emma Hunt V, 496
Haines, Emmeline II, 119
Haines, Empson II, 310
Haines, Empson II, 319
Haines, Empson H. II, 319
Haines, Empson K. II, 309
Haines, Empson K. II, 319
Haines, Enos IV, 627
Haines, Enos IV, 818
Haines, Enos V, 229
Haines, Enos V, 243
Haines, Enos VI, 396
Haines, Enos VI, 397
Haines, Ephraim II, 29
Haines, Ephraim II, 74
Haines, Ephraim II, 110
Haines, Ephraim II, 149
Haines, Ephraim II, 187
Haines, Ephraim II, 228
Haines, Ephraim II, 319
Haines, Ephraim II, 870
Haines, Ephraim VI, 396
Haines, Ephraim VI, 416
Haines, Ephraim T. II, 149
Haines, Ephraim T. II, 319
Haines, Ephraim T. II, 870
Haines, Ephraim T. II, 928
Haines, Ephraim Tomlinson II, 797
Haines, Ephraim, Jr. II, 74
Haines, Ephriam T. II, 870
Haines, Erasmus W. II, 743
Haines, Errol Dean V, 173
Haines, Estella V, 496
Haines, Estella V, 678
Haines, Ester II, 227
Haines, Esther II, 227
Haines, Esther II, 870
Haines, Esther II, 916
Haines, Esther IV, 90
Haines, Esther IV, 91
Haines, Esther IV, 959
Haines, Esther IV, 960
Haines, Esther V, 64
Haines, Esther V, 173
Haines, Esther V, 446
Haines, Esther A. II, 290
Haines, Esther Ann IV, 334
Haines, Esther Ann IV, 715
Haines, Esther Jean V, 173
Haines, Esther W. IV, 922
Haines, Esther W. IV, 960
Haines, Ethel A. II, 309
Haines, Ethel A. II, 319
Haines, Eunice IV, 334
Haines, Eunice IV, 337
Haines, Eunice V, 496
Haines, Eunice Ann II, 119
Haines, Eunice Ann II, 149
Haines, Eunice Anna II, 797
Haines, Eva V, 391
Haines, Eva B. II, 286
Haines, Eva B. II, 290
Haines, Evan I, 1048
Haines, Even B. II, 290
Haines, Everett V, 173
Haines, Everett E. V, 173
Haines, Ezekiel II, 227
Haines, Ezekiel II, 228
Haines, Ezekiel VI, 396
Haines, Ezekiel VI, 397
Haines, Ezra II, 175
Haines, Ezra II, 228
Haines, Ezra II, 229
Haines, Ezra II, 290
Haines, Ezra II, 295
Haines, Ezra II, 303
Haines, Ezra II, 743
Haines, Ezra II, 759
Haines, Ezra II, 1085
Haines, Ezra II, 1087
Haines, Ezra II, 1088
Haines, Fannia A. VI, 645
Haines, Fannie A. VI, 500
Haines, Fannie S. II, 870
Haines, Fannie Saynor IV, 714
Haines, Fanny I. II, 871
Haines, Flora M. V, 570
Haines, Flora R. II, 870
Haines, Flora R. II, 871
Haines, Frances II, 228
Haines, Frances II, 232
Haines, Frances C. III, 145
Haines, Frances C. III, 343
Haines, Frances Marie V, 678
Haines, Frances Marie V, 716
Haines, Frances Strode Entriken II, 797
Haines, Francis E. V, 623
Haines, Frank III, 145
Haines, Frank V, 244
Haines, Frank V, 457
Haines, Frank E. V, 244
Haines, Franklin II, 175
Haines, Franklin II, 229
Haines, Franklin II, 870
Haines, Franklin II, 917
Haines, Franklin III, 39
Haines, Franklin III, 85
Haines, Franklin III, 144
Haines, Franklin III, 145
Haines, Franklin III, 343
Haines, Franklin B. II, 319
Haines, Franklin T. II, 319
Haines, Fred V, 678
Haines, Fred H. V, 678
Haines, Freddy Melville V, 391
Haines, G. Woolman II, 319
Haines, G. Woolman II, 324
Haines, Genevieve IV, 971
Haines, Genevieve W. IV, 960
Haines, Geo. III, 144
Haines, George II, 174
Haines, George II, 175
Haines, George II, 227
Haines, George II, 228
Haines, George II, 282
Haines, George II, 288
Haines, George II, 290
Haines, George II, 291
Haines, George II, 309
Haines, George II, 319
Haines, George A. II, 289
Haines, George E. II, 290
Haines, George E. II, 309
Haines, George E. II, 319
Haines, George W. II, 319
Haines, Gertrude H. II, 309
Haines, Gertrude J. II, 310
Haines, Godfrey III, 428
Haines, Grace II, 29
Haines, Grace II, 74
Haines, Grace II, 75
Haines, Grace II, 100
Haines, Grace II, 228
Haines, Grace VI, 396
Haines, Granvill II, 319
Haines, Granville B. II, 870
Haines, Granville B. II, 871
Haines, Granville Edward II, 309
Haines, Granville W. II, 310
Haines, Granville W. II, 319
Haines, Hanna Ann II, 319
Haines, Hanna M. IV, 190
Haines, Hanna M. IV, 211
Haines, Hannah II, 75
Haines, Hannah II, 175
Haines, Hannah II, 197
Haines, Hannah II, 198
Haines, Hannah II, 227
Haines, Hannah II, 228
Haines, Hannah II, 229
Haines, Hannah II, 260
Haines, Hannah II, 265
Haines, Hannah II, 283
Haines, Hannah II, 289
Haines, Hannah II, 290
Haines, Hannah II, 309
Haines, Hannah II, 310
Haines, Hannah II, 319
Haines, Hannah II, 369
Haines, Hannah II, 538
Haines, Hannah II, 591
Haines, Hannah II, 716
Haines, Hannah II, 791
Haines, Hannah II, 959
Haines, Hannah II, 960
Haines, Hannah III, 145
Haines, Hannah IV, 211
Haines, Hannah IV, 212
Haines, Hannah IV, 312
Haines, Hannah IV, 314
Haines, Hannah IV, 397
Haines, Hannah IV, 398
Haines, Hannah IV, 417
Haines, Hannah IV, 627
Haines, Hannah IV, 870
Haines, Hannah IV, 1060
Haines, Hannah IV, 1099
Haines, Hannah IV, 1100
Haines, Hannah V, 51
Haines, Hannah V, 64
Haines, Hannah V, 495
Haines, Hannah V, 569
Haines, Hannah V, 623
Haines, Hannah V, 826
Haines, Hannah V, 841
Haines, Hannah V, 882
Haines, Hannah A. II, 309
Haines, Hannah A. II, 319
Haines, Hannah Ann II, 309
Haines, Hannah Ann II, 310
Haines, Hannah Ann II, 319
Haines, Hannah Ann II, 327
Haines, Hannah B. II, 290
Haines, Hannah B. II, 306
Haines, Hannah B. III, 145
Haines, Hannah C. II, 319
Haines, Hannah C. II, 948
Haines, Hannah C. II, 1050
Haines, Hannah C. II, 1051
Haines, Hannah C. II, 1060
Haines, Hannah C. II, 1087
Haines, Hannah E. P. II, 290
Haines, Hannah F. II, 309
Haines, Hannah F. II, 319
Haines, Hannah H. II, 309
Haines, Hannah H. II, 310
Haines, Hannah H. II, 319
Haines, Hannah M. II, 175
Haines, Hannah M. II, 290
Haines, Hannah S. II, 706
Haines, Hannah W. II, 319
Haines, Hannah, Jr. II, 319
Haines, Harlin V, 495
Haines, Harriet II, 319
Haines, Harriet III, 145
Haines, Harriet III, 321
Haines, Harriet VI, 500
Haines, Harriet VI, 550
Haines, Harriet VI, 645
Haines, Harriet T. III, 145
Haines, Harriett II, 290
Haines, Harriett VI, 500
Haines, Harriett VI, 645
Haines, Harriett VI, 692
Haines, Harriot II, 309
Haines, Harry V, 334
Haines, Harry V, 678
Haines, Harvey V, 334
Haines, Harvey V, 570
Haines, Hattie V, 391
Haines, Helen IV, 211
Haines, Helen V, 65
Haines, Helen Josephine V, 244
Haines, Henry II, 290
Haines, Henry II, 706
Haines, Henry II, 743
Haines, Henry Ecroyd II, 279
Haines, Henry S. II, 309
Haines, Henry S. II, 319
Haines, Hesarkiah II, 52
Haines, Hesarkiah II, 75
Haines, Hester V, 243
Haines, Hew VI, 397
Haines, Hinchman IV, 870
Haines, Hiram IV, 90
Haines, Hiram VI, 397
Haines, Homer V, 173
Haines, Homer H. V, 173
Haines, Homer H. V, 207
Haines, Hope II, 132
Haines, Hope II, 135
Haines, Horace E. II, 309
Haines, Horace E. II, 310
Haines, Horace E. II, 319
Haines, Horrace E. II, 319
Haines, Howard V, 678
Haines, Hudson II, 175
Haines, Hudson B. II, 309
Haines, Hugh II, 74
Haines, Ica V, 334
Haines, Ida Bell V, 623
Haines, Idella II, 785
Haines, Ira V, 391
Haines, Isaac II, 227
Haines, Isaac II, 309
Haines, Isaac II, 791
Haines, Isaac II, 870
Haines, Isaac IV, 211
Haines, Isaac IV, 212
Haines, Isaac IV, 251
Haines, Isaac IV, 334
Haines, Isaac IV, 397
Haines, Isaac IV, 527
Haines, Isaac IV, 528
Haines, Isaac IV, 561
Haines, Isaac IV, 1059
Haines, Isaac IV, 1060
Haines, Isaac IV, 1099
Haines, Isaac IV, 1100
Haines, Isaac V, 63
Haines, Isaac V, 569
Haines, Isaac VI, 397
Haines, Isaac L. II, 870
Haines, Isaac S. II, 319
Haines, Isaac S. II, 870
Haines, Isaac W. II, 743
Haines, Isaac W. II, 765
Haines, Isaac W. V, 274
Haines, Israel IV, 870
Haines, Israel V, 173
Haines, Israel V, 495
Haines, Israel Thomas V, 391
Haines, Israel Thomas V, 496
Haines, Israel Thos. V, 623
Haines, J. Monroe V, 678
Haines, J. Rowland IV, 211
Haines, J. Rowland IV, 212
Haines, J. Rowland IV, 249
Haines, Jabe B. II, 776
Haines, Jacob II, 29
Haines, Jacob II, 74
Haines, Jacob II, 227
Haines, Jacob II, 265
Haines, Jacob II, 369
Haines, Jacob IV, 528
Haines, Jacob V, 495
Haines, Jacob VI, 396
Haines, Jacob VI, 397
Haines, Jacob M. IV, 527
Haines, James II, 75
Haines, James II, 228
Haines, James II, 369
Haines, James III, 85
Haines, James IV, 334
Haines, James IV, 398
Haines, James IV, 528
Haines, James IV, 870
Haines, James V, 63
Haines, James V, 64
Haines, James A. Brisben V, 391
Haines, James B. V, 391
Haines, James H. V, 64
Haines, James M. V, 64
Haines, James Oliver IV, 960
Haines, James W. V, 64
Haines, James, Jr. III, 85
Haines, Jane I, 1048
Haines, Jane II, 175
Haines, Jane II, 965
Haines, Jane III, 40
Haines, Jane III, 145
Haines, Jane V, 244
Haines, Jane V, 495
Haines, Jane V, 496
Haines, Jane B. II, 369
Haines, Jane B. II, 743
Haines, Jane B. III, 145
Haines, Jane Eves II, 953
Haines, Jane J. II, 319
Haines, Jane R. VI, 396
Haines, Janes II, 971
Haines, Janes R. VI, 364
Haines, Jarrett II, 309
Haines, Jedediah II, 29
Haines, Jedediah II, 75
Haines, Jemima II, 29
Haines, Jemima II, 53
Haines, Jemima V, 64
Haines, Jemima Ballinger II, 74
Haines, Jemima H. III, 40
Haines, Jennie Maria V, 173
Haines, Jennie Maria V, 212
Haines, Jeremiah II, 74
Haines, Jeremiah II, 175
Haines, Jeremiah II, 198
Haines, Jeremiah II, 227
Haines, Jeremiah II, 290
Haines, Jeremiah J. II, 289
Haines, Jeremiah, Jr. II, 228
Haines, Jervis II, 228
Haines, Jervis II, 229
Haines, Jervis II, 289
Haines, Jervis III, 145
Haines, Jervis W. II, 310
Haines, Jervis W. II, 319
Haines, Jesse II, 279
Haines, Jesse V, 569
Haines, Jesse VI, 397
Haines, Jesse Curtis V, 173
Haines, Jesse P. II, 369
Haines, Jessie V, 662
Haines, Jessie V, 678
Haines, Jno. II, 227
Haines, Jno. II, 228
Haines, Job II, 227
Haines, Job II, 229
Haines, Job II, 319
Haines, Job II, 706
Haines, Job II, 965
Haines, Joel II, 75
Haines, Joel II, 309
Haines, Joel II, 319
Haines, Joel V, 391
Haines, Joel E. V, 391
Haines, John II, 29
Haines, John II, 52
Haines, John II, 75
Haines, John II, 103
Haines, John II, 106
Haines, John II, 203
Haines, John II, 227
Haines, John II, 228
Haines, John II, 369
Haines, John II, 781
Haines, John II, 946
Haines, John II, 948
Haines, John II, 959
Haines, John II, 960
Haines, John II, 1051
Haines, John II, 1060
Haines, John IV, 90
Haines, John IV, 334
Haines, John IV, 397
Haines, John IV, 527
Haines, John IV, 528
Haines, John IV, 714
Haines, John V, 56
Haines, John V, 63
Haines, John V, 64
Haines, John V, 173
Haines, John V, 243
Haines, John V, 244
Haines, John V, 391
Haines, John V, 569
Haines, John V, 908
Haines, John V, 970
Haines, John VI, 395
Haines, John VI, 396
Haines, John VI, 397
Haines, John VI, 725
Haines, John VI, 822
Haines, John A. IV, 334
Haines, John A. IV, 397
Haines, John C. II, 960
Haines, John C. II, 1050
Haines, John C. II, 1051
Haines, John E. II, 1051
Haines, John E. II, 1060
Haines, John Edgar III, 85
Haines, John F. IV, 212
Haines, John G. II, 744
Haines, John G. II, 759
Haines, John G. V, 243
Haines, John L. V, 64
Haines, John M. IV, 527
Haines, John S. II, 228
Haines, John S. II, 229
Haines, John W. III, 85
Haines, John Willis IV, 334
Haines, John, Jr. IV, 398
Haines, Jonathan II, 228
Haines, Jonathan V, 63
Haines, Jonathan V, 64
Haines, Jos. B. II, 310
Haines, Jos. C. III, 145
Haines, Joseph II, 29
Haines, Joseph II, 74
Haines, Joseph II, 75
Haines, Joseph II, 175
Haines, Joseph II, 227
Haines, Joseph II, 228
Haines, Joseph II, 229

Haines, Joseph II, 252
Haines, Joseph II, 259
Haines, Joseph II, 283
Haines, Joseph II, 289
Haines, Joseph II, 290
Haines, Joseph II, 309
Haines, Joseph II, 310
Haines, Joseph II, 369
Haines, Joseph II, 746
Haines, Joseph II, 871
Haines, Joseph IV, 211
Haines, Joseph IV, 212
Haines, Joseph IV, 334
Haines, Joseph IV, 397
Haines, Joseph IV, 398
Haines, Joseph IV, 715
Haines, Joseph IV, 960
Haines, Joseph V, 244
Haines, Joseph VI, 396
Haines, Joseph VI, 397
Haines, Joseph VI, 500
Haines, Joseph VI, 501
Haines, Joseph VI, 549
Haines, Joseph VI, 645
Haines, Joseph A. II, 289
Haines, Joseph E. II, 319
Haines, Joseph E. II, 706
Haines, Joseph E. II, 743
Haines, Joseph E. II, 746
Haines, Joseph E. II, 871
Haines, Joseph Engle II, 833
Haines, Joseph Engle II, 871
Haines, Joseph H. II, 965
Haines, Joseph Henry II, 319
Haines, Joseph Howell II, 706
Haines, Joseph L. VI, 396
Haines, Joseph N. IV, 960
Haines, Joseph S. II, 706
Haines, Joseph Thompson II, 75
Haines, Joseph W. IV, 90
Haines, Joseph W. IV, 91
Haines, Joseph W. IV, 959
Haines, Joseph W. IV, 960
Haines, Joshua II, 228
Haines, Joshua II, 539
Haines, Joshua V, 243
Haines, Joshua V, 495
Haines, Joshua V, 496
Haines, Joshua V, 569
Haines, Joshua VI, 396
Haines, Joshua Bloomfield II, 290
Haines, Josiah II, 216
Haines, Josiah II, 227
Haines, Josiah II, 228
Haines, Josiah II, 229
Haines, Josiah II, 290
Haines, Josiah II, 309
Haines, Josiah II, 319
Haines, Josiah II, 369
Haines, Josiah II, 538
Haines, Josiah II, 690
Haines, Josiah V, 908
Haines, Judith V, 34
Haines, Judith V, 64
Haines, Judith V, 173
Haines, Judith V, 243
Haines, Judith V, 282
Haines, Judith V, 551
Haines, Judith V, 569
Haines, Judith V, 570
Haines, Judith V, 698
Haines, Judith VI, 822
Haines, Judith A. V, 569
Haines, Judith Ann V, 570
Haines, Judith J. V, 64
Haines, Judithann V, 173
Haines, Julia II, 1056
Haines, Julia French II, 1051
Haines, Julia French II, 1056
Haines, Julia H. II, 965
Haines, Juliann V, 495
Haines, Julie Ann V, 496
Haines, Latitia P. II, 319
Haines, Laura V, 496
Haines, Laura K. II, 319
Haines, Leatitia II, 29
Haines, Leatitia II, 74
Haines, Leticia II, 228
Haines, Letitia V, 55
Haines, Letitia V, 63
Haines, Letitia V, 64
Haines, Letitia P. II, 310
Haines, Levi IV, 627
Haines, Levi IV, 630
Haines, Levi IV, 870
Haines, Levi V, 241
Haines, Levi V, 243
Haines, Levi VI, 397
Haines, Levi A. IV, 870
Haines, Levy VI, 397
Haines, Lida V, 334
Haines, Lindley II, 706
Haines, Lindley II, 743
Haines, Lindley II, 744
Haines, Lindley II, 765
Haines, Lizzie IV, 474
Haines, Lizzie V, 496
Haines, Lizzie Bell V, 678
Haines, Lizzie M. V, 244
Haines, Lois V, 173
Haines, Lois A. V, 173
Haines, Lois A. V, 207
Haines, Lois T. V, 173
Haines, Louis Paul V, 457
Haines, Louisa V, 173
Haines, Louisa V, 678
Haines, Louisa E. V, 496
Haines, Louisa Martha II, 286
Haines, Louise II, 286
Haines, Louise II, 290
Haines, Louise E. V, 496
Haines, Louise M. II, 290
Haines, Louise Martha II, 290
Haines, Louise S. II, 290
Haines, Luanna II, 287
Haines, Luanna II, 290
Haines, Lucretia II, 228
Haines, Lucy II, 175
Haines, Lucy II, 290
Haines, Lucy II, 295
Haines, Lucy V, 623
Haines, Lucy A. II, 139
Haines, Lucy B. II, 175
Haines, Lucy B. II, 229
Haines, Lucy B. II, 290
Haines, Lucy B. II, 303
Haines, Lucy Maybel V, 457
Haines, Lulu May V, 391
Haines, Luther V, 173
Haines, Luther G. V, 173
Haines, Luther Grant V, 173
Haines, Lydia II, 29
Haines, Lydia II, 139
Haines, Lydia II, 175
Haines, Lydia II, 227
Haines, Lydia II, 228
Haines, Lydia II, 264
Haines, Lydia II, 265
Haines, Lydia II, 276
Haines, Lydia IV, 90
Haines, Lydia IV, 110
Haines, Lydia IV, 212
Haines, Lydia IV, 397
Haines, Lydia IV, 870
Haines, Lydia IV, 1050
Haines, Lydia IV, 1059
Haines, Lydia IV, 1060
Haines, Lydia IV, 1099
Haines, Lydia IV, 1100
Haines, Lydia V, 445
Haines, Lydia V, 446
Haines, Lydia V, 496
Haines, Lydia V, 678
Haines, Lydia Ann II, 289
Haines, Lydia Ann II, 307
Haines, Lydia Ann IV, 212
Haines, Lydia Ann IV, 397
Haines, Lydia Ann IV, 1060
Haines, Lydia Ann V, 243
Haines, Lydia Ann V, 570
Haines, Lydia B. IV, 211
Haines, Lydia B. IV, 212
Haines, Lydia B. IV, 246
Haines, Lydia Emily V, 391
Haines, Lydia Emily V, 495
Haines, Lydia Emily V, 496
Haines, Lydia Emily V, 623
Haines, Lydia H. II, 284
Haines, Lydia H. II, 290
Haines, Lydia Jane IV, 334
Haines, Lydia Jane IV, 357
Haines, Lydia M. IV, 90
Haines, Lydia M. IV, 91
Haines, Lydia M. IV, 960
Haines, Lydia N. VI, 396
Haines, Lydia N. VI, 407
Haines, Lydia N. VI, 518
Haines, Lydia N. VI, 627
Haines, Lydia N. VI, 645
Haines, Lydia N. VI, 661
Haines, Lydia N. VI, 662
Haines, Lydia N. VI, 664
Haines, Lydia N. VI, 667
Haines, Lydia Neill VI, 500
Haines, Lydia Neill VI, 518
Haines, Lydia Neill VI, 662
Haines, Lydia Neill VI, 745
Haines, Lydia Neill VI, 752
Haines, Lydia Neill VI, 753
Haines, Lydia R. II, 119
Haines, M. M. V, 391
Haines, Mabel L. II, 871
Haines, Mabell II, 797
Haines, Mahlon II, 539
Haines, Mahlon IV, 627
Haines, Mahlon IV, 630
Haines, Mahlon IV, 818
Haines, Mahlon IV, 870
Haines, Mahlon V, 243
Haines, Mahlon V, 244
Haines, Mahlon V, 446
Haines, Mahlon, Jr. V, 244
Haines, Malinda III, 145
Haines, Malinda III, 298
Haines, Malinda Elkinton III, 145
Haines, Malvern III, 145
Haines, Manite V, 334
Haines, Mantie V, 334
Haines, Mar V, 243
Haines, Marcy VI, 396
Haines, Margaret II, 204
Haines, Margaret II, 227
Haines, Margaret II, 235
Haines, Margaret II, 369
Haines, Margaret II, 538
Haines, Margaret II, 544
Haines, Margaret II, 591
Haines, Margaret II, 690
Haines, Margaret II, 841
Haines, Margaret II, 870
Haines, Margaret IV, 333
Haines, Margaret IV, 334
Haines, Margaret V, 63
Haines, Margaret V, 64
Haines, Margaret V, 391
Haines, Margaret V, 897
Haines, Margaret V, 908
Haines, Margaret VI, 396
Haines, Margaret VI, 397
Haines, Margaret VI, 444
Haines, Margaret C. VI, 645
Haines, Margaret Elizabeth V, 496
Haines, Margaret G. VI, 500
Haines, Margaret G. VI, 501
Haines, Margaret G. VI, 645
Haines, Margaret Hurley II, 870
Haines, Margaret J. VI, 745
Haines, Margaret M. V, 496
Haines, Margaret S. IV, 334
Haines, Margaret U. II, 743
Haines, Margaret U. II, 776
Haines, Margaret V. Wistar II, 743
Haines, Margaret, Jr. V, 64
Haines, Margaretta II, 968
Haines, Marget VI, 600
Haines, Maria V, 391
Haines, Maria VI, 397
Haines, Maria VI, 745
Haines, Maria Alice V, 496
Haines, Maria E. IV, 334
Haines, Maria E. IV, 398
Haines, Maria H. II, 322
Haines, Maria L. V, 391
Haines, Maria L. V, 419
Haines, Maria P. IV, 960
Haines, Maria R. II, 319
Haines, Mariah VI, 397
Haines, Marianna II, 959
Haines, Marianna II, 1050
Haines, Marianna II, 1051
Haines, Marjorie V, 244
Haines, Marjorie Jane V, 244
Haines, Mark II, 75
Haines, Mark II, 319
Haines, Martha II, 29
Haines, Martha II, 31
Haines, Martha II, 75
Haines, Martha II, 77
Haines, Martha II, 103
Haines, Martha II, 227
Haines, Martha II, 228
Haines, Martha II, 265
Haines, Martha II, 289
Haines, Martha II, 290
Haines, Martha II, 309
Haines, Martha II, 369
Haines, Martha IV, 211
Haines, Martha V, 64
Haines, Martha V, 569
Haines, Martha V, 570
Haines, Martha V, 587
Haines, Martha V, 698
Haines, Martha Alice V, 623
Haines, Martha Cheyney II, 809
Haines, Martha N. V, 173
Haines, Martha N. V, 570
Haines, Martha Virginia II, 149
Haines, Martha Virginia II, 319
Haines, Martha Virginia II, 870
Haines, Martha Virginia II, 928
Haines, Marvin Zimri V, 173
Haines, Mary I, 1048
Haines, Mary II, 29
Haines, Mary II, 74
Haines, Mary II, 75
Haines, Mary II, 83
Haines, Mary II, 135
Haines, Mary II, 175
Haines, Mary II, 198
Haines, Mary II, 199
Haines, Mary II, 216
Haines, Mary II, 227
Haines, Mary II, 228
Haines, Mary II, 230
Haines, Mary II, 232
Haines, Mary II, 252
Haines, Mary II, 264
Haines, Mary II, 276
Haines, Mary II, 289
Haines, Mary II, 290
Haines, Mary II, 299
Haines, Mary II, 309
Haines, Mary II, 317
Haines, Mary II, 319
Haines, Mary II, 320
Haines, Mary II, 706
Haines, Mary II, 743
Haines, Mary II, 759
Haines, Mary II, 795
Haines, Mary II, 870
Haines, Mary II, 871
Haines, Mary II, 999
Haines, Mary II, 1003
Haines, Mary IV, 90
Haines, Mary IV, 211
Haines, Mary IV, 212
Haines, Mary IV, 249
Haines, Mary IV, 334
Haines, Mary IV, 355
Haines, Mary IV, 397
Haines, Mary IV, 398
Haines, Mary IV, 473
Haines, Mary IV, 489
Haines, Mary IV, 627
Haines, Mary IV, 715
Haines, Mary IV, 870
Haines, Mary IV, 1060
Haines, Mary IV, 1099
Haines, Mary V, 52
Haines, Mary V, 53
Haines, Mary V, 64
Haines, Mary V, 65
Haines, Mary V, 70
Haines, Mary V, 100
Haines, Mary V, 173
Haines, Mary V, 207
Haines, Mary V, 229
Haines, Mary V, 233
Haines, Mary V, 243
Haines, Mary V, 244
Haines, Mary V, 457
Haines, Mary V, 495
Haines, Mary V, 496
Haines, Mary V, 569
Haines, Mary V, 678
Haines, Mary V, 908
Haines, Mary V, 969
Haines, Mary V, 970
Haines, Mary VI, 379
Haines, Mary VI, 395
Haines, Mary VI, 396
Haines, Mary VI, 397
Haines, Mary VI, 407
Haines, Mary VI, 424
Haines, Mary VI, 444
Haines, Mary VI, 453
Haines, Mary VI, 500
Haines, Mary VI, 501
Haines, Mary VI, 518
Haines, Mary VI, 549
Haines, Mary VI, 560
Haines, Mary VI, 576
Haines, Mary VI, 593
Haines, Mary VI, 598
Haines, Mary VI, 645
Haines, Mary VI, 659
Haines, Mary VI, 662
Haines, Mary VI, 663
Haines, Mary VI, 710
Haines, Mary VI, 717
Haines, Mary VI, 745
Haines, Mary VI, 753
Haines, Mary VI, 951
Haines, Mary A. IV, 1038
Haines, Mary Ann II, 119
Haines, Mary Ann II, 290
Haines, Mary Ann II, 296
Haines, Mary Ann II, 319
Haines, Mary Ann II, 369
Haines, Mary Ann II, 833
Haines, Mary Ann II, 871
Haines, Mary Ann IV, 1208
Haines, Mary Ann V, 391
Haines, Mary Ann V, 905
Haines, Mary Ann V, 908
Haines, Mary Anne II, 139
Haines, Mary B. II, 175
Haines, Mary B. II, 288
Haines, Mary B. II, 290
Haines, Mary B. II, 319
Haines, Mary B. III, 85
Haines, Mary C. II, 290
Haines, Mary C. II, 299
Haines, Mary E. III, 413
Haines, Mary E. III, 446
Haines, Mary E. V, 51
Haines, Mary E. V, 63
Haines, Mary E. V, 64
Haines, Mary E. V, 496
Haines, Mary E. V, 623
Haines, Mary Elizabeth V, 173
Haines, Mary Elizabeth V, 243
Haines, Mary Elizabeth V, 495
Haines, Mary Elizabeth V, 908
Haines, Mary Elmy II, 289
Haines, Mary Elmy II, 293
Haines, Mary Emily IV, 334
Haines, Mary Emily IV, 342
Haines, Mary Emma V, 495
Haines, Mary F. V, 678
Haines, Mary H. II, 290
Haines, Mary H. II, 319
Haines, Mary H. II, 321
Haines, Mary Homer II, 290
Haines, Mary Homer II, 299
Haines, Mary J. V, 678
Haines, Mary L. V, 64
Haines, Mary L. V, 94
Haines, Mary M. II, 311
Haines, Mary M. II, 870
Haines, Mary M. V, 391
Haines, Mary Maranda V, 391
Haines, Mary Maria V, 478
Haines, Mary Maria V, 496
Haines, Mary Mariah V, 495
Haines, Mary Miars V, 678
Haines, Mary R. II, 870
Haines, Mary R. IV, 334
Haines, Mary R. IV, 398
Haines, Mary Rosamond II, 833
Haines, Mary Rosamond II, 871
Haines, Mary Rowland III, 145
Haines, Mary S. II, 309
Haines, Mary S. II, 319
Haines, Mary S. II, 326
Haines, Mary T. IV, 960
Haines, Mary W. II, 175
Haines, Mary W. II, 229
Haines, Mary W. II, 279
Haines, Mary W. II, 286
Haines, Mary W. II, 290
Haines, Mary W. V, 64
Haines, Mary, Jr. II, 289
Haines, Matilda E. IV, 960
Haines, Matilda T. IV, 960
Haines, Mercy G. V, 56
Haines, Mercy G. V, 63
Haines, Mercy G. V, 64
Haines, Michael II, 310
Haines, Michael II, 319
Haines, Michael E. II, 319
Haines, Michael E. II, 327
Haines, Miller IV, 90
Haines, Miller VI, 397
Haines, Milton IV, 212
Haines, Milton IV, 397
Haines, Milton IV, 1060
Haines, Mina V, 841
Haines, Minnie B. V, 173
Haines, Mordeca II, 310
Haines, Mordecai II, 310
Haines, Mordecai V, 391
Haines, Mordecai V, 419
Haines, Mordecai M. V, 391
Haines, Mordecai S. II, 309
Haines, Mordecai S. II, 319
Haines, Mordicai S. II, 310
Haines, Morris IV, 1367
Haines, Moses II, 227
Haines, Mrs. Charlotte IV, 1318
Haines, Nancy II, 309
Haines, Nancy IV, 212
Haines, Nancy IV, 334
Haines, Nancy IV, 527
Haines, Naomi II, 74
Haines, Naomi V, 63
Haines, Naomi V, 64
Haines, Naomi V, 391
Haines, Naomi V, 419
Haines, Naomi Almira V, 64
Haines, Naomy II, 29

Haines, Narcissa V, 173
Haines, Nathan I, 1048
Haines, Nathan II, 29
Haines, Nathan II, 227
Haines, Nathan II, 310
Haines, Nathan II, 319
Haines, Nathan II, 539
Haines, Nathan II, 706
Haines, Nathan II, 870
Haines, Nathan II, 916
Haines, Nathan IV, 334
Haines, Nathan IV, 870
Haines, Nathan V, 64
Haines, Nathan VI, 364
Haines, Nathan VI, 395
Haines, Nathan VI, 396
Haines, Nathan VI, 397
Haines, Nathan VI, 407
Haines, Nathan VI, 444
Haines, Nathan VI, 453
Haines, Nathan VI, 500
Haines, Nathan VI, 501
Haines, Nathan VI, 518
Haines, Nathan VI, 549
Haines, Nathan VI, 560
Haines, Nathan VI, 645
Haines, Nathan VI, 662
Haines, Nathan VI, 663
Haines, Nathan VI, 704
Haines, Nathan VI, 707
Haines, Nathan VI, 745
Haines, Nathan VI, 753
Haines, Nathan B. II, 132
Haines, Nathan B. II, 149
Haines, Nathan B. V, 63
Haines, Nathan B. V, 64
Haines, Nathan B. V, 140
Haines, Nathan Haines VI, 705
Haines, Nathan Haines, Jr. VI, 705
Haines, Nathan J. Rogers IV, 36
Haines, Nathan O. V, 623
Haines, Nathan, Jr. VI, 397
Haines, Nathaniel II, 227
Haines, Nathaniel II, 230
Haines, Nathaniel IV, 145
Haines, Nathaniel IV, 328
Haines, Nathaniel IV, 397
Haines, Nehemiah II, 227
Haines, Nehemiah II, 260
Haines, Nelson William II, 175
Haines, Newbold II, 175
Haines, Newbold R. II, 743
Haines, Newbold R. II, 744
Haines, Newlin II, 175
Haines, Newlin II, 286
Haines, Newlin II, 290
Haines, Noah II, 228
Haines, Noah V, 38
Haines, Noah V, 63
Haines, Noah V, 64
Haines, Noah V, 146
Haines, Noah V, 569
Haines, Noah VI, 396
Haines, Noah S. V, 53
Haines, Noah S. V, 63
Haines, Noah S. V, 64
Haines, Norma L. V, 391
Haines, Norman VI, 705
Haines, Olive May V, 623
Haines, Ona Oberta V, 391
Haines, Opal E. V, 678
Haines, Oscar IV, 334
Haines, Patience II, 175
Haines, Patience II, 227
Haines, Patience VI, 396
Haines, Patience VI, 397
Haines, Pauline II, 781
Haines, Pauline IV, 627
Haines, Pearl V, 496
Haines, Phebe II, 175
Haines, Phebe II, 229
Haines, Phebe II, 289
Haines, Phebe II, 290
Haines, Phebe II, 295
Haines, Phebe II, 309
Haines, Phebe II, 369
Haines, Phebe II, 706
Haines, Phebe II, 743
Haines, Phebe II, 759
Haines, Phebe II, 946
Haines, Phebe II, 948
Haines, Phebe II, 1085
Haines, Phebe II, 1087
Haines, Phebe II, 1088
Haines, Phebe IV, 91
Haines, Phebe IV, 334
Haines, Phebe IV, 340
Haines, Phebe IV, 397
Haines, Phebe IV, 398
Haines, Phebe V, 485
Haines, Phebe V, 495
Haines, Phebe V, 496
Haines, Phebe Ann VI, 705
Haines, Phebe C. IV, 91
Haines, Phebe D. IV, 90
Haines, Phebe G. III, 85
Haines, Phebe P. II, 175
Haines, Phebe P. II, 290
Haines, Phebe P. II, 303
Haines, Phllis Ilene V, 173
Haines, Phyllis A. V, 173
Haines, Phyllis Irena V, 457
Haines, Portia V, 678
Haines, Portia V, 707
Haines, Portia VI, 396
Haines, Portia VI, 406
Haines, Portia VI, 622
Haines, Portia VI, 645
Haines, Portia VI, 660
Haines, Portia VI, 703
Haines, Portia VI, 706
Haines, Portia VI, 707
Haines, Portia R. VI, 397
Haines, Priscilla II, 192
Haines, Priscilla II, 227
Haines, Priscilla V, 495
Haines, Rachel II, 119
Haines, Rachel II, 175
Haines, Rachel II, 228
Haines, Rachel II, 290
Haines, Rachel II, 310
Haines, Rachel II, 319
Haines, Rachel II, 539
Haines, Rachel II, 743
Haines, Rachel IV, 145
Haines, Rachel IV, 211
Haines, Rachel IV, 251
Haines, Rachel IV, 328
Haines, Rachel IV, 334
Haines, Rachel IV, 345
Haines, Rachel IV, 397
Haines, Rachel IV, 527
Haines, Rachel IV, 528
Haines, Rachel IV, 561
Haines, Rachel IV, 627
Haines, Rachel IV, 630
Haines, Rachel IV, 715
Haines, Rachel IV, 818
Haines, Rachel V, 21
Haines, Rachel V, 63
Haines, Rachel V, 64
Haines, Rachel V, 69
Haines, Rachel V, 243
Haines, Rachel V, 952
Haines, Rachel V, 970
Haines, Rachel V, 971
Haines, Rachel VI, 397
Haines, Rachel VI, 420
Haines, Rachel VI, 705
Haines, Rachel A. IV, 211
Haines, Rachel A. IV, 271
Haines, Rachel E. II, 319
Haines, Rachel G. II, 319
Haines, Rachel M. II, 119
Haines, Rachel M. II, 149
Haines, Rachel M. II, 319
Haines, Rachel M. II, 323
Haines, Rachel Muckelray II, 74
Haines, Rachel N. II, 119
Haines, Rachel W. II, 175
Haines, Rachel W. II, 290
Haines, Rachel W. II, 291
Haines, Rachel W. II, 706
Haines, Ralph V, 496
Haines, Ralph A. IV, 1318
Haines, Rebecca II, 174
Haines, Rebecca II, 175
Haines, Rebecca II, 221
Haines, Rebecca II, 224
Haines, Rebecca II, 227
Haines, Rebecca II, 228
Haines, Rebecca II, 229
Haines, Rebecca II, 271
Haines, Rebecca II, 283
Haines, Rebecca II, 290
Haines, Rebecca II, 539
Haines, Rebecca II, 706
Haines, Rebecca II, 743
Haines, Rebecca II, 744
Haines, Rebecca II, 759
Haines, Rebecca II, 797
Haines, Rebecca II, 999
Haines, Rebecca II, 1051
Haines, Rebecca III, 144
Haines, Rebecca IV, 212
Haines, Rebecca IV, 397
Haines, Rebecca IV, 398
Haines, Rebecca IV, 527
Haines, Rebecca IV, 528
Haines, Rebecca IV, 552
Haines, Rebecca IV, 561
Haines, Rebecca IV, 562
Haines, Rebecca IV, 923
Haines, Rebecca IV, 960
Haines, Rebecca IV, 1038
Haines, Rebecca V, 47
Haines, Rebecca V, 63
Haines, Rebecca V, 64
Haines, Rebecca V, 140
Haines, Rebecca V, 146
Haines, Rebecca V, 496
Haines, Rebecca V, 569
Haines, Rebecca VI, 397
Haines, Rebecca VI, 399
Haines, Rebecca VI, 434
Haines, Rebecca VI, 745
Haines, Rebecca Ann II, 175
Haines, Rebecca Ann II, 229
Haines, Rebecca Ann II, 290
Haines, Rebecca Ann II, 306
Haines, Rebecca Ann II, 706
Haines, Rebecca Ann II, 743
Haines, Rebecca B. II, 1046
Haines, Rebecca B. II, 1051
Haines, Rebecca B. P. II, 175
Haines, Rebecca H. VI, 396
Haines, Rebecca H. VI, 397
Haines, Rebecca H. VI, 416
Haines, Rebecca Jane V, 391
Haines, Rebecca L. II, 706
Haines, Rebecca L. II, 743
Haines, Rebecca M. II, 870
Haines, Rebecca M. III, 145
Haines, Rebecca M. III, 241
Haines, Rebecca Mifflin II, 917
Haines, Rebecca P. II, 744
Haines, Rebecca R. II, 870
Haines, Rebecca Rowland II, 870
Haines, Rebecca S. II, 283
Haines, Rebecca S. II, 290
Haines, Rebecca Vickry II, 74
Haines, Rebecca W. II, 175
Haines, Rebecca W. II, 282
Haines, Rebecca W. II, 290
Haines, Rebecca Waters II, 74
Haines, Rebecca Worrel II, 781
Haines, Rebeckah II, 29
Haines, Rebeckah IV, 334
Haines, Rebeckah Barns II, 74
Haines, Rebekah II, 74
Haines, Rebekah II, 110
Haines, Rebekah VI, 379
Haines, Rebekah VI, 395
Haines, Rebekah VI, 396
Haines, Rebekah VI, 397
Haines, Remington II, 310
Haines, Remington II, 319
Haines, Reuben II, 29
Haines, Reuben II, 228
Haines, Reuben II, 369
Haines, Reuben II, 538
Haines, Reuben II, 544
Haines, Reuben II, 591
Haines, Reuben II, 690
Haines, Reuben II, 743
Haines, Reuben II, 776
Haines, Reuben III, 40
Haines, Reuben III, 145
Haines, Reuben V, 173
Haines, Reuben VI, 396
Haines, Reuben VI, 645
Haines, Reuben VI, 706
Haines, Reuben, Jr. II, 538
Haines, Richard II, 29
Haines, Richard II, 74
Haines, Richard II, 75
Haines, Richard II, 369
Haines, Richard VI, 396
Haines, Richard Allen V, 173
Haines, Richard R. III, 145
Haines, Richard R. III, 321
Haines, Richard R. VI, 397
Haines, Richard, Jr. II, 74
Haines, Robert II, 175
Haines, Robert V, 63
Haines, Robert V, 65
Haines, Robert V, 391
Haines, Robert VI, 396
Haines, Robert VI, 397
Haines, Robert VI, 444
Haines, Robert B. II, 743
Haines, Robert B. II, 776
Haines, Robert H. V, 64
Haines, Robert M. IV, 960
Haines, Robert W. II, 175
Haines, Robert W. II, 229
Haines, Robert, Jr. II, 290
Haines, Rowena M. V, 391
Haines, Rowland I. II, 871
Haines, Rowland J. II, 309
Haines, Rowland J. II, 319
Haines, Roy M. V, 496
Haines, Russell V, 65
Haines, Ruth IV, 90
Haines, Ruth IV, 91
Haines, Ruth IV, 98
Haines, Ruth IV, 107
Haines, Ruth IV, 110
Haines, Ruth IV, 113
Haines, Ruth IV, 527
Haines, Ruth IV, 850
Haines, Ruth V, 173
Haines, Ruth V, 243
Haines, Ruth V, 334
Haines, Ruth V, 469
Haines, Ruth V, 487
Haines, Ruth V, 496
Haines, Ruth VI, 395
Haines, Ruth VI, 396
Haines, Ruth VI, 397
Haines, Ruth Carey V, 173
Haines, S. Chester II, 797
Haines, Sadie V, 64
Haines, Sallie Mary V, 678
Haines, Sally Mary V, 678
Haines, Samantha V, 244
Haines, Samantha V, 457
Haines, Samuel II, 175
Haines, Samuel II, 197
Haines, Samuel II, 204
Haines, Samuel II, 227
Haines, Samuel II, 228
Haines, Samuel II, 232
Haines, Samuel II, 264
Haines, Samuel II, 265
Haines, Samuel II, 286
Haines, Samuel II, 369
Haines, Samuel II, 743
Haines, Samuel II, 759
Haines, Samuel IV, 212
Haines, Samuel IV, 397
Haines, Samuel IV, 1060
Haines, Samuel V, 173
Haines, Samuel V, 495
Haines, Samuel V, 496
Haines, Samuel V, 569
Haines, Samuel VI, 397
Haines, Samuel B. II, 228
Haines, Samuel B. II, 290
Haines, Samuel B. II, 870
Haines, Samuel B. II, 917
Haines, Samuel B. III, 144
Haines, Samuel B. III, 145
Haines, Samuel B. III, 241
Haines, Samuel D. II, 286
Haines, Samuel D. II, 290
Haines, Samuel D. II, 299
Haines, Samuel E. II, 797
Haines, Samuel E. II, 870
Haines, Samuel E. II, 871
Haines, Samuel Newbold II, 290
Haines, Samuel S. II, 175
Haines, Samuel S. II, 290
Haines, Samuel Stevenson II, 290
Haines, Samuel Stevenson II, 297
Haines, Samuel T. V, 569
Haines, Samuel, Jr. II, 228
Haines, Sarah II, 29
Haines, Sarah II, 74
Haines, Sarah II, 75
Haines, Sarah II, 113
Haines, Sarah II, 119
Haines, Sarah II, 149
Haines, Sarah II, 175
Haines, Sarah II, 199
Haines, Sarah II, 203
Haines, Sarah II, 227
Haines, Sarah II, 229
Haines, Sarah II, 232
Haines, Sarah II, 237
Haines, Sarah II, 244
Haines, Sarah II, 247
Haines, Sarah II, 289
Haines, Sarah II, 309
Haines, Sarah II, 310
Haines, Sarah II, 319
Haines, Sarah II, 369
Haines, Sarah II, 539
Haines, Sarah II, 706
Haines, Sarah II, 797
Haines, Sarah II, 965
Haines, Sarah IV, 90
Haines, Sarah IV, 91
Haines, Sarah IV, 98
Haines, Sarah IV, 212
Haines, Sarah IV, 240
Haines, Sarah IV, 334
Haines, Sarah IV, 397
Haines, Sarah IV, 398
Haines, Sarah IV, 627
Haines, Sarah IV, 630
Haines, Sarah IV, 715
Haines, Sarah IV, 748
Haines, Sarah IV, 818
Haines, Sarah IV, 870
Haines, Sarah IV, 960
Haines, Sarah V, 64
Haines, Sarah V, 88
Haines, Sarah V, 173
Haines, Sarah V, 243
Haines, Sarah V, 491
Haines, Sarah V, 496
Haines, Sarah V, 569
Haines, Sarah V, 970
Haines, Sarah VI, 396
Haines, Sarah VI, 397
Haines, Sarah VI, 410
Haines, Sarah VI, 416
Haines, Sarah VI, 645
Haines, Sarah VI, 706
Haines, Sarah A. II, 928
Haines, Sarah Ann IV, 870
Haines, Sarah B. II, 149
Haines, Sarah B. II, 319
Haines, Sarah B. II, 870
Haines, Sarah B. II, 928
Haines, Sarah B., Jr. II, 319
Haines, Sarah B., Jr. II, 870
Haines, Sarah Catharine V, 496
Haines, Sarah E. IV, 922
Haines, Sarah E. IV, 959
Haines, Sarah E. IV, 960
Haines, Sarah E. V, 569
Haines, Sarah Elizabeth V, 496
Haines, Sarah Elizabeth V, 557
Haines, Sarah Elizabeth V, 570
Haines, Sarah Emily V, 496
Haines, Sarah G. VI, 397
Haines, Sarah G. VI, 418
Haines, Sarah Lippincott VI, 397
Haines, Sarah Louisa V, 678
Haines, Sarah M. II, 290
Haines, Sarah M. II, 309
Haines, Sarah M. II, 319
Haines, Sarah R. II, 229
Haines, Sarah R. II, 265
Haines, Sarah R. II, 310
Haines, Sarah R. II, 319
Haines, Sarah S. II, 139
Haines, Sarah S. V, 678
Haines, Sarah T. II, 870
Haines, Sarah W. II, 288
Haines, Sarah Wray II, 74
Haines, Sarah, Jr. II, 149
Haines, Sary II, 74
Haines, Seldon T. IV, 334
Haines, Seldon T. IV, 398
Haines, Seth V, 64
Haines, Seth D. V, 64
Haines, Seth S. V, 63
Haines, Sidney R. III, 40
Haines, Silas M. V, 64
Haines, Silvenia V, 496
Haines, Simeon II, 228
Haines, Simeon III, 145
Haines, Simeon VI, 501
Haines, Simeon VI, 550
Haines, Simeon VI, 645
Haines, Simeon, Jr. II, 539
Haines, Simpson G. IV, 334
Haines, Simpson G. IV, 398
Haines, Smith IV, 212
Haines, Smith IV, 397
Haines, Smith IV, 1060
Haines, Sophia VI, 501
Haines, Sophia VI, 549
Haines, Sophronia V, 570
Haines, Sophronia Ann V, 393
Haines, Spencer II, 175
Haines, Spencer II, 948
Haines, Spencer II, 1085
Haines, Stacey II, 228
Haines, Stacey II, 259
Haines, Stacy II, 175
Haines, Stacy II, 229
Haines, Stacy V, 173
Haines, Stacy V, 243
Haines, Stacy V, 282
Haines, Stacy V, 569
Haines, Stacy V, 698
Haines, Stacy A. V, 569
Haines, Stacy Edwin V, 570
Haines, Stasia V, 173
Haines, Stella IV, 212
Haines, Stephen Allen V, 173
Haines, Stokes II, 175
Haines, Stokes II, 283
Haines, Stokes II, 290
Haines, Stokes II, 706
Haines, Susan II, 289
Haines, Susan V, 678
Haines, Susan VI, 397

Haines, Susan VI, 411
Haines, Susan VI, 649
Haines, Susan VI, 745
Haines, Susan B. II, 309
Haines, Susan Engle II, 817
Haines, Susan G. VI, 397
Haines, Susan N. II, 706
Haines, Susan N. II, 743
Haines, Susan N. II, 746
Haines, Susanna V, 979
Haines, Susanna C. II, 309
Haines, Susanna C. II, 310
Haines, Susanna C. II, 319
Haines, Susannah II, 29
Haines, Susannah II, 74
Haines, Susannah II, 75
Haines, Susannah II, 98
Haines, Susannah V, 64
Haines, Susannah V, 496
Haines, Susannah V, 512
Haines, Susannah V, 970
Haines, Sylvester T. V, 496
Haines, Sylvester T. V, 678
Haines, Tamasin VI, 560
Haines, Tamson IV, 90
Haines, Tamson IV, 113
Haines, Tamson IV, 114
Haines, Tamson IV, 555
Haines, Tamson IV, 850
Haines, Thaddeus A. V, 495
Haines, Thamasin VI, 396
Haines, Thamasin VI, 444
Haines, Thamasin VI, 544
Haines, Thamasin VI, 576
Haines, Thamsin VI, 560
Haines, Thomas II, 195
Haines, Thomas II, 221
Haines, Thomas II, 227
Haines, Thomas II, 228
Haines, Thomas II, 258
Haines, Thomas II, 743
Haines, Thomas VI, 396
Haines, Thomas C. IV, 960
Haines, Thomas H. V, 496
Haines, Thomas Lee II, 175
Haines, Thomas Lee II, 290
Haines, Thomas, Jr. II, 228
Haines, Thomasin VI, 501
Haines, Thos. B. II, 797
Haines, Thos. H. IV, 271
Haines, Thos. Harvey IV, 211
Haines, Timothy II, 539
Haines, Timothy IV, 211
Haines, Timothy IV, 212
Haines, Timothy IV, 334
Haines, Timothy IV, 398
Haines, Timothy IV, 417
Haines, Timothy IV, 527
Haines, Timothy IV, 528
Haines, Uriah W. II, 229
Haines, Uriah W. II, 310
Haines, Uriah W. II, 319
Haines, Valinda J. IV, 334
Haines, Venice V, 496
Haines, Vilinda J. IV, 398
Haines, W. Herbert IV, 190
Haines, W. Herbert IV, 211
Haines, Watts V, 495
Haines, Wd. Anna Rhoda II, 797
Haines, Wd. Edith II, 175
Haines, Wd. Elizabeth H. II, 187
Haines, Wd. Esther VI, 396
Haines, Wd. Hannah Ann II, 132
Haines, Wd. Hannah C. II, 946
Haines, Webster V, 495
Haines, Wilkins V, 64
Haines, Willard E. V, 173
Haines, William II, 29
Haines, William II, 175
Haines, William II, 227
Haines, William II, 230
Haines, William II, 247
Haines, William II, 290
Haines, William II, 309
Haines, William IV, 211
Haines, William IV, 212
Haines, William IV, 334
Haines, William IV, 527
Haines, William IV, 528
Haines, William IV, 561
Haines, William IV, 627
Haines, William IV, 818
Haines, William IV, 870
Haines, William V, 334
Haines, William V, 496
Haines, William VI, 397
Haines, William E. III, 145
Haines, William E. Staff III, 145
Haines, William Henry II, 706
Haines, William Mickle III, 145
Haines, William N. II, 175
Haines, William S. II, 369
Haines, William, Jr. II, 228
Haines, William, Jr. IV, 870
Haines, Willimene V, 495
Haines, Wilson V, 244
Haines, Wm. II, 74
Haines, Wm. II, 75
Haines, Wm. II, 98
Haines, Wm. II, 870
Haines, Wm. II, 916
Haines, Wm. IV, 211
Haines, Wm. IV, 334
Haines, Wm. IV, 337
Haines, Wm. V, 334
Haines, Wm. V, 678
Haines, Wm. D. V, 623
Haines, Wm. H. II, 744
Haines, Wm. Henry II, 706
Haines, Wm. Mickle III, 284
Haines, Woolman II, 319
Haines, Xenia V, 496
Haines, Zebedee II, 706
Haines, Zebedee II, 744
Haines, Zebedee II, 759
Haines, Zebedee IV, 211
Haines, Zimri V, 173
Haines, Zimri V, 243
Haines, Zimri V, 495
Haines, Zimri V, 496
Haines, Zimri V, 623
Haines, Zimri V, 678
Haines, Zimri D. V, 496
Haines, Zimri Dennison V, 495
Haines, Zimri Forster V, 173
Haines, Zimri Foster V, 173
Haines, Zimri L. V, 495
Haines, Zimri L. V, 623
Haines, Zimri S. V, 496
Haines, Zimri Samuel V, 391
Haines, Zimri, Jr. V, 496
Hains, Aaron II, 228
Hains, Aaron II, 229
Hains, Abigail II, 227
Hains, Abigail II, 228
Hains, Abigail II, 236
Hains, Abigail II, 259
Hains, Abigail VI, 397
Hains, Abram VI, 397
Hains, Agnes II, 80
Hains, Agnes Huddy II, 74
Hains, Allen VI, 596
Hains, Amos VI, 596
Hains, Angelina IV, 715
Hains, Angelina IV, 753
Hains, Ann II, 74
Hains, Ann II, 83
Hains, Ann II, 227
Hains, Ann II, 277
Hains, Ann IV, 147
Hains, Ann IV, 345
Hains, Ann IV, 351
Hains, Ann IV, 397
Hains, Ann V, 60
Hains, Ann V, 64
Hains, Ann VI, 596
Hains, Anna II, 228
Hains, Anna II, 264
Hains, Anna V, 121
Hains, Anthony II, 74
Hains, Atlantic VI, 597
Hains, Betty V, 64
Hains, Betty V, 152
Hains, Betty V, 173
Hains, Betty VI, 591
Hains, Betty VI, 597
Hains, Bulah VI, 397
Hains, Bulah VI, 597
Hains, Bulah VI, 602
Hains, Caleb II, 228
Hains, Carlile VI, 397
Hains, Chalkley IV, 818
Hains, Chalkley IV, 834
Hains, Charles IV, 397
Hains, Daniel II, 228
Hains, Daniel VI, 397
Hains, Deborah II, 75
Hains, Deborah II, 118
Hains, Deborah II, 119
Hains, Deborah VI, 397
Hains, Deborah VI, 597
Hains, Deborah VI, 601
Hains, Ebenezer VI, 397
Hains, Edith II, 228
Hains, Edith II, 275
Hains, Edwin IV, 334
Hains, Eli VI, 597
Hains, Eli VI, 601
Hains, Elisha IV, 397
Hains, Elizabeth I, 986
Hains, Elizabeth I, 997
Hains, Elizabeth II, 29
Hains, Elizabeth II, 54
Hains, Elizabeth II, 74
Hains, Elizabeth II, 104
Hains, Elizabeth II, 228
Hains, Elizabeth II, 275
Hains, Elizabeth IV, 653
Hains, Elizabeth V, 150
Hains, Elizabeth V, 173
Hains, Elizabeth V, 207
Hains, Elizabeth VI, 397
Hains, Elizabeth VI, 597
Hains, Elizabeth VI, 601
Hains, Elizabeth L. II, 119
Hains, Elma Ann II, 58
Hains, Elma Ann II, 75
Hains, Emmeline II, 119
Hains, Enos IV, 818
Hains, Enos V, 243
Hains, Enos VI, 397
Hains, Enos VI, 594
Hains, Enos VI, 596
Hains, Enos VI, 597
Hains, Ephraim II, 273
Hains, Ephraim, Jr. II, 74
Hains, Esther V, 64
Hains, Esther V, 173
Hains, Esther V, 207
Hains, Esther VI, 459
Hains, Esther VI, 596
Hains, Esther VI, 597
Hains, Evan I, 1048
Hains, Ezekiel II, 227
Hains, Ezekiel II, 236
Hains, Ezekiel VI, 397
Hains, George II, 228
Hains, George II, 275
Hains, Grace II, 209
Hains, Grace II, 228
Hains, Hannah I, 588
Hains, Hannah I, 812
Hains, Hannah II, 227
Hains, Hannah II, 228
Hains, Hannah II, 273
Hains, Hannah II, 369
Hains, Hannah IV, 653
Hains, Hannah V, 495
Hains, Hester V, 243
Hains, Hester VI, 597
Hains, Hugh II, 74
Hains, Isaac IV, 332
Hains, Isaac IV, 334
Hains, Isaac IV, 397
Hains, Isaac VI, 397
Hains, Isaac S. II, 870
Hains, Israel V, 173
Hains, Israel VI, 597
Hains, Jacob II, 227
Hains, Jacob VI, 397
Hains, Jacob VI, 597
Hains, James II, 75
Hains, James II, 369
Hains, James IV, 334
Hains, Jeremiah II, 74
Hains, Job II, 229
Hains, Joel II, 75
Hains, John II, 75
Hains, John II, 203
Hains, John II, 227
Hains, John II, 228
Hains, John II, 273
Hains, John II, 369
Hains, John IV, 147
Hains, John IV, 345
Hains, John IV, 351
Hains, John V, 64
Hains, John V, 150
Hains, John V, 173
Hains, John VI, 397
Hains, John VI, 591
Hains, John VI, 596
Hains, John VI, 597
Hains, John VI, 601
Hains, John A. IV, 397
Hains, John H. V, 207
Hains, John, Sr. VI, 597
Hains, Jonathan V, 63
Hains, Joseph II, 74
Hains, Joseph II, 228
Hains, Joseph II, 264
Hains, Joseph IV, 397
Hains, Joseph VI, 397
Hains, Joseph VI, 597
Hains, Joseph VI, 602
Hains, Joshua I, 812
Hains, Joshua II, 228
Hains, Joshua V, 243
Hains, Josiah II, 227
Hains, Josiah II, 538
Hains, Juliann V, 495
Hains, Leatitia II, 74
Hains, Leticia II, 228
Hains, Levi IV, 653
Hains, Levi V, 243
Hains, Levi VI, 397
Hains, Levi VI, 591
Hains, Levi VI, 597
Hains, Levi VI, 601
Hains, Levi VI, 603
Hains, Lydia I, 812
Hains, Lydia II, 227
Hains, Lydia II, 237
Hains, Lydia Ann V, 243
Hains, Lydia R. II, 119
Hains, Mahlon IV, 627
Hains, Mahlon IV, 818
Hains, Mahlon V, 243
Hains, Margaret V, 64
Hains, Margaret VI, 596
Hains, Margaret VI, 605
Hains, Margaret S. IV, 332
Hains, Margaret S. IV, 334
Hains, Marianna II, 1051
Hains, Martha II, 203
Hains, Martha II, 227
Hains, Martha II, 228
Hains, Mary I, 812
Hains, Mary II, 228
Hains, Mary II, 264
Hains, Mary II, 273
Hains, Mary IV, 334
Hains, Mary IV, 345
Hains, Mary V, 173
Hains, Mary V, 243
Hains, Mary VI, 379
Hains, Mary VI, 396
Hains, Mary VI, 397
Hains, Mary VI, 594
Hains, Mary VI, 596
Hains, Mary VI, 597
Hains, Mary VI, 600
Hains, Mary VI, 601
Hains, Mary VI, 602
Hains, Mary Ann II, 118
Hains, Mary Ann II, 119
Hains, Mary Ann IV, 1208
Hains, Moses II, 227
Hains, Nancy IV, 334
Hains, Naomi II, 74
Hains, Naomi V, 63
Hains, Narcissa V, 150
Hains, Narcissa V, 173
Hains, Narcissa VI, 597
Hains, Nathan II, 29
Hains, Nathan II, 227
Hains, Nathan IV, 334
Hains, Nathan V, 64
Hains, Nathan VI, 397
Hains, Nathaniel IV, 397
Hains, Noah V, 121
Hains, Noah VI, 596
Hains, Noah VI, 597
Hains, Patience II, 212
Hains, Patience II, 227
Hains, Patience VI, 397
Hains, Phebe II, 229
Hains, Phebe IV, 397
Hains, Rachel II, 119
Hains, Rachel II, 120
Hains, Rachel IV, 147
Hains, Rachel IV, 334
Hains, Rachel IV, 397
Hains, Rachel IV, 627
Hains, Rachel IV, 818
Hains, Rachel VI, 397
Hains, Rachel Muckelray II, 74
Hains, Rebecca II, 290
Hains, Rebecca IV, 397
Hains, Rebecca VI, 397
Hains, Rebecca S. II, 290
Hains, Rebeckah II, 54
Hains, Rebeckah IV, 334
Hains, Rebeckah Barns II, 74
Hains, Reuben V, 173
Hains, Richard II, 74
Hains, Richard II, 75
Hains, Richard II, 104
Hains, Richard II, 369
Hains, Robert IV, 459
Hains, Robert VI, 591
Hains, Robert VI, 595
Hains, Robert VI, 596
Hains, Robert VI, 597
Hains, Robert VI, 600
Hains, Robert VI, 605
Hains, Robert H. V, 64
Hains, Robert W. II, 229
Hains, Ruben VI, 597
Hains, Ruth IV, 91
Hains, Ruth V, 173
Hains, Ruth V, 280
Hains, Ruth VI, 397
Hains, Ruth VI, 597
Hains, Ruth VI, 601
Hains, Samuel II, 369
Hains, Samuel V, 495
Hains, Samuel VI, 397
Hains, Samuel Newbold II, 290
Hains, Sarah II, 29
Hains, Sarah II, 74
Hains, Sarah II, 84
Hains, Sarah II, 119
Hains, Sarah II, 227
Hains, Sarah IV, 334
Hains, Sarah IV, 351
Hains, Sarah IV, 818
Hains, Sarah IV, 834
Hains, Sarah V, 243
Hains, Sarah VI, 397
Hains, Sarah VI, 404
Hains, Sarah VI, 427
Hains, Sary II, 74
Hains, Simeon VI, 597
Hains, Stacia VI, 597
Hains, Stacy V, 173
Hains, Stasia V, 173
Hains, Stephen VI, 597
Hains, Stokes II, 290
Hains, Thomas II, 215
Hains, Thomas II, 228
Hains, Thomas II, 275
Hains, Timothy II, 539
Hains, Timothy IV, 334
Hains, William II, 29
Hains, William II, 227
Hains, William IV, 334
Hains, William IV, 818
Hains, Wm. II, 75
Hains, Zimri V, 173
Hainsworth, Eliza V, 457
Hair, Elizabeth II, 999
Hair, Harmon VI, 66
Hair, Henry VI, 65
Hair, Jesse VI, 107
Hair, Jesse VI, 109
Hair, John II, 999
Hair, Rosella VI, 66
Hair, Sarah VI, 107
Hair, Sarah VI, 109
Hair, William J. VI, 107
Hair, Zada Virlinda VI, 107
Haire, Martha VI, 66
Haire, Pheraba VI, 141
Hairengton, Elizabeth III, 413
Hairengton, John H. III, 413
Hairston, Hugh VI, 938
Hairston, Martha VI, 938
Hairston, Samuel VI, 915
Haisley, Abigail Emily V, 908
Haisley, Alexander I, 812
Haisley, Alexander I, 880
Haisley, Alfred V, 841
Haisley, Allen V, 830
Haisley, Allen V, 908
Haisley, Ann I, 909
Haisley, David I, 909
Haisley, Elexander I, 781
Haisley, Elexander I, 912
Haisley, Elizabeth I, 781
Haisley, Elizabeth I, 812
Haisley, Elizabeth I, 819
Haisley, Elizabeth I, 909
Haisley, Elizabeth I, 912
Haisley, Elizabeth I, 913
Haisley, Emily V, 405
Haisley, Emma V, 391
Haisley, Eunice I, 909
Haisley, Eunice V, 841
Haisley, Ezekiel I, 812
Haisley, Ezekiel I, 828
Haisley, Ezekiel I, 907
Haisley, Ezekiel I, 909
Haisley, Ezekiel I, 912
Haisley, Ezekiel, Jr. I, 907
Haisley, Grace I, 781
Haisley, Grace I, 812
Haisley, Grace I, 912
Haisley, Ira I, 909
Haisley, Jesse I, 812
Haisley, Jesse I, 880
Haisley, Jesse I, 889
Haisley, Jesse I, 909
Haisley, Jesse I, 912
Haisley, John I, 781
Haisley, John I, 812
Haisley, John I, 880
Haisley, John I, 909
Haisley, Joseph I, 812
Haisley, Joseph I, 827
Haisley, Joseph I, 907
Haisley, Joseph I, 909
Haisley, Joseph I, 912
Haisley, Josiah I, 909
Haisley, Lavina V, 841

aisley, Martha I, 812
aisley, Martha I, 909
aisley, Mary I, 781
aisley, Mary I, 812
aisley, Mary I, 828
aisley, Mary I, 907
aisley, Mary I, 909
aisley, Mary I, 912
aisley, Mary V, 841
aisley, Mary J. I, 912
aisley, Phebe I, 909
aisley, Ruth I, 880
aisley, Ruth I, 889
aisley, Ruth I, 909
aisley, Ruth I, 912
aisley, Sarah I, 812
aisley, Sarah I, 816
aisley, Sarah I, 827
aisley, Sarah I, 907
aisley, Sarah I, 909
aisley, Sarah I, 912
aisley, Wd. Mary V, 830
aisly, Alfred V, 841
aisly, Eunice V, 841
aisly, Eunice V, 873
aisly, Lavina V, 841
aisly, Mary V, 841
aisten, Joseph I, 717
aisten, William I, 717
aistings, Charlotte V, 391
aistings, Jacob VI, 398
aistins, John II, 372
aistins, Samuel II, 372
ait, Eliza L. III, 144
ait, Selah III, 144
aithcock, S. G. IV, 1280
aizley, Abigail Emily V, 937
ake, Frederick VI, 859
ake, Susannah VI, 859
aladay, Mary V, 678
aladay, Ruth I, 448
aladay, Ruth I, 449
alan, Jabez V, 497
albert, Leanora Latitia II, 871
albert, Leonora Latitia II, 797
aldeman, Abraham IV, 905
aldeman, Allen J. IV, 913
aldeman, Angelletta IV, 906
aldeman, Ann IV, 900
aldeman, Ann IV, 902
aldeman, Ann IV, 905
aldeman, Ann IV, 906
aldeman, Ann IV, 909
aldeman, Anna IV, 905
aldeman, Anna H. IV, 906
aldeman, Benjamin IV, 905
aldeman, Benjamin IV, 906
aldeman, David IV, 901
aldeman, David IV, 902
aldeman, David IV, 905
aldeman, David IV, 906
aldeman, David IV, 907
aldeman, David IV, 909
aldeman, David, Jr IV, 905
aldeman, David, Jr. IV, 906
aldeman, Elizabeth IV, 905
aldeman, Esther IV, 906
aldeman, Esther IV, 913
aldeman, Guly IV, 906
aldeman, Jacob IV, 715
aldeman, Jacob IV, 905
aldeman, Jacob IV, 906
aldeman, John Leondo IV, 906
aldeman, Joseph IV, 905
aldeman, Joseph IV, 906
aldeman, Joseph IV, 913
aldeman, Julia A. IV, 901
aldeman, Julia F. IV, 906
aldeman, Julia F. IV, 907
aldeman, Julia L. IV, 906
aldeman, Lauretta IV, 913
aldeman, Levina IV, 913
aldeman, Lovisa E. IV, 906
aldeman, Lovisa E. IV, 907
aldeman, Margery IV, 906
aldeman, Martha IV, 905
aldeman, Martha IV, 906
aldeman, Mary IV, 905
aldeman, Mary IV, 906
aldeman, Mary E. IV, 906
aldeman, Mary H. IV, 902
aldeman, Mary Isabel IV, 913
aldeman, Philena IV, 906
aldeman, Richard IV, 906
aldeman, Richard A. IV, 906
aldeman, Richard N. IV, 906
aldeman, Sandy Spring IV, 715
aldeman, Sina A. IV, 913
aldeman, Susanna IV, 905
aldeman, Susanna IV, 909
aldeman, Susannah IV, 906
Haldeman, Tamar IV, 905
Haldeman, Tamar IV, 906
Haldeman, Tamar S. IV, 901
Haldeman, Tamas S. IV, 906
Haldeman, Tamer IV, 906
Haldeman, Thomas IV, 906
Haldeman, Wm IV, 913
Halderman, Alonzo IV, 960
Halderman, Alonzo IV, 1038
Halderman, Alonzo O. IV, 960
Halderman, Ann IV, 715
Halderman, Ann IV, 819
Halderman, Ann IV, 906
Halderman, Ann IV, 960
Halderman, Anna IV, 212
Halderman, Anna IV, 960
Halderman, Anna H. IV, 819
Halderman, Anna H. IV, 856
Halderman, Anna J. IV, 960
Halderman, Anna J. IV, 1038
Halderman, Benj. IV, 960
Halderman, Benjamin IV, 715
Halderman, Benjamin IV, 819
Halderman, Christina IV, 960
Halderman, D. Ida IV, 923
Halderman, David IV, 715
Halderman, David IV, 819
Halderman, David IV, 897
Halderman, David IV, 905
Halderman, David IV, 906
Halderman, David IV, 960
Halderman, David Ellyson IV, 960
Halderman, David, Jr. IV, 715
Halderman, Delbert IV, 1038
Halderman, Edwin IV, 960
Halderman, Edwin G. IV, 960
Halderman, Elizabeth IV, 672
Halderman, Elizabeth IV, 715
Halderman, Elizabeth IV, 819
Halderman, Ervin G. IV, 960
Halderman, Esther IV, 946
Halderman, Esther IV, 960
Halderman, Esther IV, 987
Halderman, Esther IV, 1038
Halderman, Howard W. IV, 1038
Halderman, Ida D. IV, 960
Halderman, Jacob IV, 715
Halderman, Jacob IV, 819
Halderman, Jacob IV, 906
Halderman, Jacob IV, 910
Halderman, James IV, 715
Halderman, Joseph IV, 715
Halderman, Joseph IV, 906
Halderman, Joseph IV, 946
Halderman, Joseph IV, 960
Halderman, Joseph IV, 987
Halderman, Joseph IV, 1038
Halderman, Josephine IV, 960
Halderman, Lauretta IV, 960
Halderman, Lauretta IV, 987
Halderman, Loretta IV, 960
Halderman, Mabel IV, 960
Halderman, Margery IV, 715
Halderman, Margery IV, 906
Halderman, Margety IV, 910
Halderman, Maria IV, 960
Halderman, Martha IV, 715
Halderman, Martha IV, 819
Halderman, Martha IV, 906
Halderman, Mary IV, 715
Halderman, Mary IV, 906
Halderman, Mary IV, 1000
Halderman, Mary IV, 1005
Halderman, Mary Gladys IV, 960
Halderman, Oscar J. IV, 960
Halderman, Oscar J. IV, 1038
Halderman, Osker IV, 960
Halderman, Richard IV, 819
Halderman, Richard N. IV, 792
Halderman, Sandy Spring IV, 715
Halderman, Sarah B. IV, 960
Halderman, Susanna IV, 986
Halderman, Susannah IV, 715
Halderman, Susannah IV, 906
Halderman, Tamar IV, 715
Halderman, Tamar IV, 906
Halderman, Tamar Susannah IV, 819
Halderman, Tamer IV, 715
Halderman, Tamor IV, 715
Halderman, Thomas IV, 906
Haldi, Caroline IV, 1004
Haldi, Malissa IV, 1038
Haldi, Robert IV, 1038
Haldron, Bartholomew VI, 934
Haldron, Jane VI, 903
Haldy, Arthur IV, 1208
Haldy, Arthur IV, 1252
Haldy, Delia IV, 1318
Haldy, Eliza IV, 1208
Haldy, Herbert H. IV, 962
Haldy, Howard IV, 1252
Hale, ??? III, 145
Hale, ??? V, 570
Hale, Albert V. V, 570
Hale, Alfred V, 65
Hale, Alfred V, 570
Hale, Alfred V, 595
Hale, Alfred V, 678
Hale, Alfred C. V, 65
Hale, Alfred C. V, 570
Hale, Alice V, 570
Hale, Alice V, 678
Hale, Alice V, 706
Hale, Alice H. V, 595
Hale, Alice J. V, 678
Hale, Alice Pate V, 678
Hale, Ammonia V, 65
Hale, Ann V, 65
Hale, Ann V, 80
Hale, Ann V, 83
Hale, Ann V, 567
Hale, Ann V, 570
Hale, Ann V, 579
Hale, Ann Johnson V, 65
Hale, Anna V, 112
Hale, Anna V, 571
Hale, Annah VI, 999
Hale, Armoni V, 65
Hale, Armoni V, 496
Hale, Armonia V, 570
Hale, Armonia V, 571
Hale, Armonia V, 678
Hale, Asa I, 606
Hale, Benjamin VI, 926
Hale, Betsey VI, 902
Hale, Betsey VI, 925
Hale, Betsey VI, 926
Hale, Caleb III, 145
Hale, Caroline F. IV, 1318
Hale, Clara IV, 1318
Hale, Clark J. V, 570
Hale, Clark J. V, 678
Hale, Daniel VI, 926
Hale, Darinda I, 716
Hale, Darinda I, 733
Hale, Direndia I, 716
Hale, Dora Ingham II, 797
Hale, Edith V, 678
Hale, Edward I, 716
Hale, Edward H. I, 716
Hale, Edward Henley I, 698
Hale, Eli I, 392
Hale, Eli V, 80
Hale, Eli V, 112
Hale, Eli V, 496
Hale, Eli V, 567
Hale, Eli V, 570
Hale, Elie V, 65
Hale, Elizabeth I, 392
Hale, Elizabeth II, 539
Hale, Elizabeth II, 637
Hale, Elizabeth III, 145
Hale, Elizabeth V, 50
Hale, Elizabeth V, 65
Hale, Elizabeth V, 496
Hale, Elizabeth V, 516
Hale, Elizabeth V, 570
Hale, Elizabeth V, 571
Hale, Elizabeth V, 678
Hale, Elwood V, 570
Hale, Emma V, 570
Hale, Emma V, 678
Hale, Esther V, 570
Hale, Esther V, 678
Hale, Esther M. V, 678
Hale, Flora V, 555
Hale, Flora V, 556
Hale, Flora V, 570
Hale, Flora V, 665
Hale, Hannah V, 547
Hale, Hannah V, 570
Hale, Hannah V, 678
Hale, Hannah G. V, 678
Hale, Harlan B. I, 716
Hale, Harle B. I, 716
Hale, Harlen B. I, 698
Hale, Harlen Bolden I, 698
Hale, Harlin B. I, 880
Hale, Harrie V, 678
Hale, Hattie V, 678
Hale, Henry I, 606
Hale, Henry II, 29
Hale, Henry M. V, 678
Hale, Herman T. V, 678
Hale, Inez V, 570
Hale, Jacob I, 392
Hale, Jacob V, 65
Hale, Jacob V, 496
Hale, Jacob V, 547
Hale, Jacob V, 570
Hale, Jacob V, 678
Hale, Jane I, 698
Hale, Jane I, 716
Hale, Jane I, 725
Hale, Jenny VI, 925
Hale, Jessie V, 678
Hale, Jessie V, 692
Hale, John II, 29
Hale, John VI, 11
Hale, John VI, 902
Hale, John VI, 925
Hale, John VI, 926
Hale, Joseph V, 496
Hale, Joseph V, 570
Hale, Judith VI, 925
Hale, Julia Ann VI, 1012
Hale, Julian VI, 926
Hale, Kittie V, 457
Hale, Kittie V, 458
Hale, Laban VI, 926
Hale, Lawrence V, 65
Hale, Layton V, 678
Hale, Layton V, 692
Hale, Louisa V, 553
Hale, Louisa V, 570
Hale, Lucy VI, 926
Hale, Lydia V, 496
Hale, Lydia V, 497
Hale, Lydia V, 571
Hale, Malinda V, 120
Hale, Margaret I, 880
Hale, Margaret I, 886
Hale, Maria V, 65
Hale, Martha I, 392
Hale, Martha V, 65
Hale, Martha V, 496
Hale, Martha V, 570
Hale, Martha V, 585
Hale, Mary I, 606
Hale, Mary I, 698
Hale, Mary I, 716
Hale, Mary I, 738
Hale, Mary II, 29
Hale, Mary II, 498
Hale, Mary II, 539
Hale, Mary V, 65
Hale, Mary V, 80
Hale, Mary V, 496
Hale, Mary V, 526
Hale, Mary V, 555
Hale, Mary V, 570
Hale, Mary V, 678
Hale, Mary VI, 666
Hale, Mary A. I, 880
Hale, Mary A. I, 883
Hale, Mary Alice V, 570
Hale, Mary Alice V, 678
Hale, Mary Ann I, 716
Hale, Mary Ann V, 65
Hale, Matilda VI, 1017
Hale, Matthew I, 606
Hale, Mead VI, 925
Hale, Mershack VI, 926
Hale, Meshack VI, 926
Hale, Miles V, 65
Hale, Miles M. V, 65
Hale, Miles M. V, 570
Hale, Minnie Bell V, 570
Hale, Molley VI, 926
Hale, Nancy I, 698
Hale, Nancy I, 716
Hale, Nancy P. I, 716
Hale, Nancy P. I, 723
Hale, Naomi R. V, 570
Hale, Overstreet VI, 925
Hale, Overstreet VI, 1012
Hale, Phebe I, 542
Hale, Phebe I, 600
Hale, Phebe I, 606
Hale, Philip III, 145
Hale, Philip V, 65
Hale, Polly V, 570
Hale, Polly VI, 926
Hale, Polly Moody VI, 926
Hale, R. Edith V, 678
Hale, Rachel V, 570
Hale, Rachel V, 595
Hale, Rachel A. V, 678
Hale, Rachel Ann V, 495
Hale, Rachel Ann V, 496
Hale, Rachel Ann V, 570
Hale, Rachel Edith V, 678
Hale, Rebecca VI, 926
Hale, Rosa Belle V, 678
Hale, Ruth V, 495
Hale, Ruth V, 496
Hale, Samuel I, 392
Hale, Samuel I, 698
Hale, Samuel V, 496
Hale, Samuel H. I, 716
Hale, Samuel H. I, 880
Hale, Samuel H. I, 883
Hale, Samuel H. V, 496
Hale, Sarah I, 698
Hale, Sarah I, 716
Hale, Sarah I, 718
Hale, Sarah I, 879
Hale, Sarah I, 880
Hale, Sarah II, 539
Hale, Sarah II, 651
Hale, Sarah V, 678
Hale, Sarah VI, 822
Hale, Sarah A. V, 65
Hale, Sarah A. V, 112
Hale, Sarah Ann V, 65
Hale, Sarah Ann V, 570
Hale, Sarah C. V, 570
Hale, Sarah Collins V, 678
Hale, Sarah Tomlinson V, 570
Hale, Sophia VI, 926
Hale, Stephen, Junr. VI, 926
Hale, Street VI, 926
Hale, Suckey VI, 926
Hale, Susanna V, 562
Hale, Susanna V, 570
Hale, Susanna VI, 926
Hale, Susannah VI, 925
Hale, Tabitha VI, 926
Hale, Thomas II, 29
Hale, Thomas II, 539
Hale, Thomas VI, 925
Hale, Thomas VI, 926
Hale, William I, 392
Hale, William V, 65
Hale, William V, 496
Hale, William V, 570
Hale, William VI, 822
Hale, William VI, 926
Hale, William H. V, 65
Hale, William T. V, 570
Hale, Wm. V, 555
Hales, Edward I, 288
Hales, John VI, 178
Hales, John VI, 207
Hales, Mary VI, 963
Hales, Miles M. V, 65
Hales, Sallie I, 288
Hales, W. T. I, 307
Hales, William T. I, 288
Haley, ??? VI, 283
Haley, Agnes VI, 822
Haley, Archibald VI, 803
Haley, Archibald VI, 822
Haley, Bartlett VI, 244
Haley, Bartlitt VI, 244
Haley, Edmund VI, 822
Haley, Elizabeth I, 392
Haley, Elizabeth I, 393
Haley, Elizabeth I, 408
Haley, Elizabeth I, 812
Haley, Elizabeth V, 949
Haley, Elizabeth V, 952
Haley, Ella VI, 645
Haley, Ella VI, 653
Haley, Ella VI, 694
Haley, Esom VI, 244
Haley, George I, 393
Haley, Hannah VI, 852
Haley, Isom I, 392
Haley, Isom I, 408
Haley, John I, 393
Haley, John VI, 243
Haley, John VI, 244
Haley, John VI, 645
Haley, John VI, 711
Haley, John Clark VI, 244
Haley, Jonathan V, 495
Haley, Judith VI, 241
Haley, Judith VI, 243
Haley, Judith VI, 244
Haley, Lucy I, 392
Haley, Lucy I, 393
Haley, Lucy I, 410
Haley, Margaret E. VI, 645
Haley, Margaret E. VI, 677
Haley, Margaret E. VI, 687
Haley, Margaret E. VI, 695
Haley, Margaret E. VI, 711
Haley, Margaret E. VI, 712
Haley, Margaret E. VI, 713
Haley, Mary IV, 1247
Haley, Mary VI, 822
Haley, Milly I, 393
Haley, Phebe I, 880
Haley, Rachel VI, 822
Haley, Randle I, 393
Haley, Rebekah I, 393
Haley, Silas I, 393
Haley, Sophia I, 542
Haley, Thomas V, 496
Haley, Thomas S. V, 496

Haley, Ursula VI, 244
Haley, William I, 392
Haley, William I, 393
Haley, William VI, 243
Haley, William VI, 244
Haley, William VI, 285
Haley, Wm. I, 392
Halfdan-Nielson, Deborah III, 145
Halfdan-Nielson, Ellen III, 145
Halfdan-Nielson, Regnor III, 145
Haliday, James IV, 1318
Haliday, Maggie IV, 1318
Haliday, Marie IV, 1318
Haliman, Sarah Elizabeth IV, 1060
Haliman, Sarah Elizabeth IV, 1072
Hall, ??? I, 279
Hall, ??? III, 22
Hall, ??? III, 145
Hall, ??? III, 266
Hall, ??? IV, 212
Hall, ??? IV, 715
Hall, ??? VI, 726
Hall, A. M. I, 633
Hall, Abbie S. IV, 169
Hall, Abbie S. IV, 214
Hall, Abbie S. IV, 280
Hall, Abbie S. IV, 575
Hall, Abby IV, 213
Hall, Abel II, 29
Hall, Abel II, 30
Hall, Abel II, 75
Hall, Abel II, 77
Hall, Abel II, 78
Hall, Abi IV, 363
Hall, Abi IV, 400
Hall, Abi IV, 406
Hall, Abigail IV, 613
Hall, Abigail IV, 628
Hall, Abigail IV, 629
Hall, Abigail IV, 684
Hall, Abigail IV, 715
Hall, Abigail IV, 925
Hall, Abigail IV, 1035
Hall, Abigail IV, 1038
Hall, Abigail B. IV, 629
Hall, Abigail B. IV, 715
Hall, Abigail S. IV, 960
Hall, Abner I, 269
Hall, Abner I, 270
Hall, Abner IV, 36
Hall, Abner IV, 213
Hall, Abner IV, 215
Hall, Abner IV, 398
Hall, Abner IV, 399
Hall, Abner IV, 400
Hall, Abner IV, 401
Hall, Abner IV, 402
Hall, Abner IV, 407
Hall, Abner IV, 412
Hall, Abner G. IV, 628
Hall, Abner I. IV, 633
Hall, Abner I. IV, 664
Hall, Abner I. IV, 1012
Hall, Abner J. IV, 215
Hall, Abner J. IV, 627
Hall, Abner J. IV, 628
Hall, Abner P. IV, 627
Hall, Abner S. IV, 647
Hall, Abner T. IV, 715
Hall, Absalom VI, 926
Hall, Achsah IV, 212
Hall, Achsah IV, 215
Hall, Achsah IV, 398
Hall, Achsah IV, 960
Hall, Achsah IV, 961
Hall, Albert IV, 400
Hall, Albert IV, 402
Hall, Albert IV, 584
Hall, Albert E. IV, 213
Hall, Albert E. IV, 216
Hall, Albert Edwin IV, 961
Hall, Albert J. IV, 213
Hall, Albert J. IV, 819
Hall, Albert P. IV, 819
Hall, Alberta Sherron II, 154
Hall, Alexander I, 880
Hall, Alexander II, 444
Hall, Alexander II, 999
Hall, Alfred II, 871
Hall, Alfred IV, 819
Hall, Alfred IV, 906
Hall, Alfred V, 391
Hall, Alfred D. IV, 176
Hall, Alfred D. IV, 213
Hall, Alfred D. IV, 214
Hall, Alfred Henry IV, 1318
Hall, Alice II, 369
Hall, Alice II, 370
Hall, Alice II, 539
Hall, Alice II, 586
Hall, Alice II, 813
Hall, Alice V, 570
Hall, Alice Ann IV, 213
Hall, Alice Ann IV, 215
Hall, Alice Ann IV, 960
Hall, Alice Ann IV, 961
Hall, Alice Biardot III, 132
Hall, Alice Biardot III, 145
Hall, Alice L. III, 145
Hall, Alice M. IV, 213
Hall, Alice M. IV, 215
Hall, Alice M. IV, 250
Hall, Allan IV, 715
Hall, Allen IV, 410
Hall, Allen J. IV, 628
Hall, Allen J. IV, 629
Hall, Allen J. IV, 646
Hall, Allen J. IV, 741
Hall, Almeda V, 391
Hall, Almeda R. IV, 213
Hall, Almeda R. IV, 216
Hall, Alonzo IV, 400
Hall, Alpheus McK. I, 620
Hall, Alpheus McKendry I, 617
Hall, Altie IV, 368
Hall, Altie IV, 402
Hall, Altie Isabella IV, 399
Hall, Altie T. IV, 370
Hall, Alva IV, 215
Hall, Alva IV, 399
Hall, Alva B. IV, 402
Hall, Alvin E. IV, 399
Hall, Alvin E. IV, 402
Hall, Alvin Ernest IV, 400
Hall, Alvin J. II, 706
Hall, Alvin J. II, 744
Hall, Alvira IV, 856
Hall, Amanda I, 812
Hall, Amos IV, 398
Hall, Amos IV, 399
Hall, Amos IV, 453
Hall, Amos V, 391
Hall, Amy IV, 213
Hall, Amy IV, 215
Hall, Amy T. IV, 214
Hall, Amy T. IV, 215
Hall, Amy T. IV, 528
Hall, Amy T. IV, 553
Hall, Anderson I, 240
Hall, Andrew I, 880
Hall, Angelina I, 234
Hall, Angeline I, 211
Hall, Angeline I, 240
Hall, Ann I, 141
Hall, Ann I, 208
Hall, Ann I, 215
Hall, Ann I, 240
Hall, Ann I, 260
Hall, Ann I, 288
Hall, Ann I, 307
Hall, Ann II, 30
Hall, Ann II, 58
Hall, Ann II, 75
Hall, Ann II, 86
Hall, Ann II, 106
Hall, Ann II, 119
Hall, Ann II, 132
Hall, Ann II, 133
Hall, Ann II, 444
Hall, Ann II, 539
Hall, Ann III, 145
Hall, Ann IV, 147
Hall, Ann IV, 148
Hall, Ann IV, 213
Hall, Ann IV, 215
Hall, Ann IV, 370
Hall, Ann IV, 385
Hall, Ann IV, 398
Hall, Ann IV, 399
Hall, Ann IV, 400
Hall, Ann IV, 402
Hall, Ann IV, 412
Hall, Ann IV, 628
Hall, Ann IV, 848
Hall, Ann VI, 822
Hall, Ann Eliza IV, 513
Hall, Ann Eliza IV, 528
Hall, Ann H. IV, 402
Hall, Ann H. IV, 408
Hall, Ann Mary IV, 214
Hall, Ann W. IV, 169
Hall, Ann W. IV, 215
Hall, Ann W. IV, 401
Hall, Ann W. IV, 606
Hall, Ann W. IV, 627
Hall, Ann W. IV, 628
Hall, Ann W. IV, 644
Hall, Ann W. IV, 715
Hall, Ann W. IV, 738
Hall, Ann W. IV, 833
Hall, Ann W. IV, 960
Hall, Ann W. IV, 961
Hall, Anna I, 215
Hall, Anna I, 216
Hall, Anna I, 240
Hall, Anna I, 288
Hall, Anna I, 307
Hall, Anna I, 698
Hall, Anna I, 716
Hall, Anna II, 714
Hall, Anna II, 721
Hall, Anna IV, 189
Hall, Anna IV, 198
Hall, Anna IV, 199
Hall, Anna IV, 212
Hall, Anna IV, 214
Hall, Anna IV, 215
Hall, Anna IV, 216
Hall, Anna IV, 235
Hall, Anna IV, 254
Hall, Anna IV, 264
Hall, Anna IV, 289
Hall, Anna IV, 385
Hall, Anna IV, 388
Hall, Anna IV, 389
Hall, Anna IV, 398
Hall, Anna IV, 401
Hall, Anna IV, 407
Hall, Anna IV, 435
Hall, Anna IV, 518
Hall, Anna IV, 528
Hall, Anna IV, 573
Hall, Anna IV, 575
Hall, Anna IV, 576
Hall, Anna IV, 581
Hall, Anna IV, 583
Hall, Anna IV, 586
Hall, Anna IV, 628
Hall, Anna IV, 641
Hall, Anna IV, 647
Hall, Anna IV, 807
Hall, Anna IV, 819
Hall, Anna IV, 1012
Hall, Anna V, 782
Hall, Anna V, 789
Hall, Anna C. IV, 819
Hall, Anna Edgerton IV, 576
Hall, Anna F. IV, 694
Hall, Anna F. IV, 715
Hall, Anna Florence IV, 401
Hall, Anna Florence IV, 693
Hall, Anna Florence IV, 715
Hall, Anna M. IV, 212
Hall, Anna M. IV, 213
Hall, Anna M. IV, 214
Hall, Anna M. IV, 215
Hall, Anna M. IV, 237
Hall, Anna M. IV, 387
Hall, Anna M. IV, 402
Hall, Anna M. IV, 428
Hall, Anna M. IV, 444
Hall, Anna M. IV, 628
Hall, Anna M. IV, 633
Hall, Anna M. IV, 664
Hall, Anna M. IV, 715
Hall, Anna Mabel IV, 389
Hall, Anna Mabel IV, 402
Hall, Anna Mabel IV, 581
Hall, Anna Mabel IV, 813
Hall, Anna Mabel IV, 819
Hall, Anna Mable IV, 401
Hall, Anna Mary IV, 213
Hall, Anna Mary IV, 215
Hall, Anna T. II, 132
Hall, Anna T. IV, 402
Hall, Anna W. IV, 960
Hall, Anne IV, 148
Hall, Anne IV, 401
Hall, Annie I, 286
Hall, Annie II, 150
Hall, Annie II, 159
Hall, Annie IV, 518
Hall, Annie M. IV, 400
Hall, Annie M. IV, 401
Hall, Annie M. IV, 444
Hall, Annie T. II, 132
Hall, Annie T. II, 133
Hall, Annie T. II, 146
Hall, Annie T. II, 150
Hall, Aquila IV, 226
Hall, Ardith Eleanor IV, 961
Hall, Arthur IV, 213
Hall, Arthur IV, 215
Hall, Arthur IV, 528
Hall, Arthur D. II, 706
Hall, Arthur D. II, 744
Hall, Arthur H. IV, 402
Hall, Arthur Hartley IV, 400
Hall, Arthur T. IV, 215
Hall, Asa IV, 399
Hall, Asa IV, 402
Hall, Asaph VI, 736
Hall, Asaph VI, 745
Hall, Asenath I, 288
Hall, Asenath I, 307
Hall, Asenath IV, 182
Hall, Asenath IV, 212
Hall, Asenath IV, 213
Hall, Asenath IV, 398
Hall, Asenath IV, 399
Hall, Asenath IV, 401
Hall, Asenath IV, 426
Hall, Asenath IV, 453
Hall, Asenath IV, 590
Hall, Asenath W. IV, 899
Hall, Asenath W. IV, 906
Hall, Barcklay S. IV, 215
Hall, Barclay S. IV, 213
Hall, Barclay S. IV, 214
Hall, Barclay S. IV, 216
Hall, Barclay S. IV, 819
Hall, Barclay S. IV, 820
Hall, Barclay S. IV, 934
Hall, Barclay S. IV, 960
Hall, Barclay S. IV, 961
Hall, Bealah M. IV, 961
Hall, Beaulah Margaret IV, 961
Hall, Benjamin I, 99
Hall, Benjamin I, 100
Hall, Benjamin I, 138
Hall, Benjamin I, 141
Hall, Benjamin I, 654
Hall, Benjamin I, 679
Hall, Benjamin I, 685
Hall, Benjamin I, 698
Hall, Benjamin I, 716
Hall, Benjamin IV, 398
Hall, Benjamin IV, 399
Hall, Benjamin IV, 401
Hall, Benjamin IV, 402
Hall, Benjamin IV, 452
Hall, Benjamin IV, 581
Hall, Benjamin VI, 926
Hall, Bertha IV, 214
Hall, Bertha IV, 385
Hall, Bertha IV, 403
Hall, Bertha IV, 819
Hall, Bertha V, 999
Hall, Bertha A. IV, 628
Hall, Bertha D. IV, 627
Hall, Bertha D. IV, 628
Hall, Bertha Mary IV, 400
Hall, Bertha Mary IV, 401
Hall, Bertha Millicent IV, 819
Hall, Bertha R. IV, 397
Hall, Bertha R. IV, 400
Hall, Bertha R. IV, 401
Hall, Bertha R. IV, 402
Hall, Bertha Rosina IV, 1318
Hall, Bethany I, 270
Hall, Betsey Ann I, 215
Hall, Betsy IV, 401
Hall, Betsy VI, 822
Hall, Bettie Fleming I, 812
Hall, Betzy IV, 407
Hall, Beulah M. IV, 820
Hall, Beulah M. IV, 960
Hall, Beulah Margaret IV, 819
Hall, Beulah Marjorie IV, 819
Hall, Blance D. IV, 400
Hall, Blanche D. IV, 387
Hall, Blanche D. IV, 399
Hall, C. E. IV, 1236
Hall, Caleb I, 141
Hall, Caleb I, 240
Hall, Caleb I, 253
Hall, Caleb I, 288
Hall, Caleb I, 304
Hall, Caleb I, 307
Hall, Caleb I, 698
Hall, Caleb I, 716
Hall, Caleb IV, 363
Hall, Caleb IV, 398
Hall, Caleb IV, 399
Hall, Caleb IV, 401
Hall, Caleb IV, 408
Hall, Caleb IV, 426
Hall, Caleb VI, 926
Hall, Carl Whitcraft IV, 400
Hall, Caroline IV, 180
Hall, Caroline IV, 213
Hall, Caroline IV, 214
Hall, Caroline IV, 215
Hall, Caroline IV, 513
Hall, Caroline IV, 528
Hall, Caroline Ladd III, 145
Hall, Carolyn III, 145
Hall, Cassius IV, 400
Hall, Cassius C. IV, 399
Hall, Cassius C. IV, 401
Hall, Cassius C. IV, 406
Hall, Catharine I, 215
Hall, Catharine I, 240
Hall, Catharine M. II, 871
Hall, Catharine M. II, 888
Hall, Chalkley L. IV, 402
Hall, Chalkly V, 841
Hall, Charity I, 289
Hall, Charity I, 306
Hall, Charity I, 307
Hall, Charity IV, 398
Hall, Charity IV, 401
Hall, Charity IV, 528
Hall, Charity IV, 1236
Hall, Charity IV, 1240
Hall, Charity V, 809
Hall, Charity L. II, 132
Hall, Charles IV, 212
Hall, Charles IV, 213
Hall, Charles IV, 215
Hall, Charles IV, 960
Hall, Charles IV, 961
Hall, Charles VI, 822
Hall, Charles A. IV, 400
Hall, Charles Arthur IV, 400
Hall, Charles C. III, 145
Hall, Charles C. III, 295
Hall, Charles E. IV, 402
Hall, Charles H. IV, 960
Hall, Charles H. IV, 961
Hall, Charles Henry IV, 960
Hall, Charles Henry IV, 961
Hall, Charles Lyman III, 145
Hall, Charles P. IV, 215
Hall, Charles P. IV, 618
Hall, Charles P. IV, 628
Hall, Charles W. IV, 628
Hall, Charles W. IV, 629
Hall, Charles W. IV, 960
Hall, Charles W. IV, 961
Hall, Charley IV, 1208
Hall, Charlotte II, 30
Hall, Chas. Henry IV, 215
Hall, Chas. P. IV, 627
Hall, Chas. P. IV, 693
Hall, Chas. P. IV, 715
Hall, Chas. W. IV, 627
Hall, Chester B. IV, 400
Hall, Chester Blane IV, 400
Hall, Christena IV, 185
Hall, Christena IV, 212
Hall, Christian I, 240
Hall, Christian I, 253
Hall, Christian I, 288
Hall, Christian I, 307
Hall, Christian IV, 148
Hall, Christian IV, 198
Hall, Christian IV, 212
Hall, Christian IV, 323
Hall, Christian IV, 334
Hall, Christian IV, 1038
Hall, Christiana IV, 212
Hall, Christiana IV, 226
Hall, Christiana IV, 235
Hall, Christiana IV, 399
Hall, Christiana IV, 570
Hall, Christiana IV, 576
Hall, Christianna IV, 802
Hall, Christianna IV, 829
Hall, Christopher II, 75
Hall, Clara J. IV, 1163
Hall, Clara Lucile IV, 1318
Hall, Clara Luella IV, 401
Hall, Clara R. IV, 213
Hall, Clara R. IV, 214
Hall, Clara R. IV, 302
Hall, Clarabelle Osborn IV, 1163
Hall, Clarence IV, 399
Hall, Clarence James IV, 401
Hall, Clarence W. IV, 402
Hall, Clark J. V, 570
Hall, Clayton IV, 399
Hall, Clayton F. IV, 402
Hall, Clemenda III, 189
Hall, Clement II, 30
Hall, Clement II, 51
Hall, Clement II, 75
Hall, Clement II, 112
Hall, Clement II, 129
Hall, Clement II, 132
Hall, Clement II, 133
Hall, Clement II, 140
Hall, Clement II, 149
Hall, Clement II, 150
Hall, Clement II, 151
Hall, Clement II, 154
Hall, Clement II, 159
Hall, Clement H. II, 871
Hall, Clement Morris II, 30
Hall, Clifford D. IV, 819
Hall, Clifton IV, 214
Hall, Clifton D. IV, 264

Hall, Clifton P. IV, 213
Hall, Clifton P. IV, 216
Hall, Clifton P. IV, 289
Hall, Clifton P. IV, 819
Hall, Clifton P. IV, 848
Hall, Clinton P. IV, 213
Hall, Cora IV, 1236
Hall, Cora E. IV, 400
Hall, Cora E. IV, 402
Hall, Cornelius I, 215
Hall, Cornelius I, 240
Hall, Cristena IV, 185
Hall, Cynthia A. J. IV, 961
Hall, Cynthia A. J. IV, 971
Hall, Cyrus IV, 213
Hall, Cyrus IV, 215
Hall, Cyrus IV, 398
Hall, Cyrus IV, 401
Hall, Cyrus IV, 445
Hall, Cyrus IV, 627
Hall, Dan'l II, 222
Hall, Dan'l II, 229
Hall, Daniel II, 444
Hall, Daniel V, 391
Hall, Darby II, 539
Hall, David II, 30
Hall, David II, 75
Hall, David II, 539
Hall, David IV, 212
Hall, David IV, 215
Hall, David IV, 289
Hall, David IV, 402
Hall, David IV, 528
Hall, David IV, 553
Hall, David IV, 581
Hall, David IV, 819
Hall, David VI, 926
Hall, David Abner IV, 401
Hall, David F. II, 132
Hall, Dean R. IV, 402
Hall, Dean Robert IV, 401
Hall, Debby IV, 588
Hall, Debora IV, 214
Hall, Deborah IV, 213
Hall, Deborah IV, 214
Hall, Deborah IV, 215
Hall, Deborah IV, 276
Hall, Deborah IV, 280
Hall, Deborah IV, 305
Hall, Deborah IV, 364
Hall, Deborah IV, 384
Hall, Deborah IV, 398
Hall, Deborah IV, 399
Hall, Deborah IV, 402
Hall, Deborah IV, 407
Hall, Deborah IV, 429
Hall, Deborah IV, 453
Hall, Deborah IV, 520
Hall, Deborah IV, 528
Hall, Deborah IV, 557
Hall, Deborah IV, 558
Hall, Deborah B. IV, 214
Hall, Deborah C. IV, 401
Hall, Deborah C. IV, 406
Hall, Deborah Chambers IV, 452
Hall, Deborah D. IV, 581
Hall, Deborah D. IV, 582
Hall, Deborah D. IV, 588
Hall, Deborah D. IV, 709
Hall, Deborah D. IV, 715
Hall, Deborah D. IV, 792
Hall, Deborah D. IV, 819
Hall, Deborah D. IV, 906
Hall, Deborah D. IV, 911
Hall, Deborah E. IV, 400
Hall, Deborah K. II, 75
Hall, Deborah K. II, 81
Hall, Deborah Key II, 30
Hall, Deborah S. II, 706
Hall, Deborah S. IV, 193
Hall, Deborah S. IV, 214
Hall, Deborah S. IV, 423
Hall, Deborah S. IV, 528
Hall, Deborah S. IV, 673
Hall, Deborah W. IV, 215
Hall, Delbert Lester IV, 401
Hall, Delbert Lester IV, 403
Hall, Delbert Lester IV, 961
Hall, Della Lucile IV, 1318
Hall, Delora IV, 438
Hall, Dillwyn E. IV, 807
Hall, Dillwyn E. IV, 819
Hall, Dilwin E. IV, 213
Hall, Dilwyn E. IV, 819
Hall, Dinah IV, 148
Hall, Dinah IV, 157
Hall, Donald IV, 960
Hall, Donald Linton IV, 401
Hall, Donald Linton IV, 403
Hall, Donald Linton IV, 961
Hall, Dora IV, 581
Hall, Dora M. IV, 402
Hall, Dora M. IV, 581
Hall, Dora Myrtle IV, 402
Hall, Dora Myrtle IV, 570
Hall, Dorothy IV, 715
Hall, Dorothy L. IV, 402
Hall, Dorothy L. IV, 715
Hall, Dorothy Lucile IV, 401
Hall, Drucilla VI, 924
Hall, Drury VI, 813
Hall, Drury VI, 822
Hall, Drusala VI, 926
Hall, Drusilla V, 809
Hall, Ebenezer II, 30
Hall, Edgar A. I, 1154
Hall, Edgar Alvin IV, 400
Hall, Edith IV, 213
Hall, Edith IV, 215
Hall, Edith IV, 276
Hall, Edith IV, 289
Hall, Edith IV, 303
Hall, Edith IV, 410
Hall, Edith IV, 528
Hall, Edith IV, 925
Hall, Edith IV, 951
Hall, Edith IV, 960
Hall, Edith IV, 961
Hall, Edith IV, 998
Hall, Edith V, 570
Hall, Edith E. IV, 627
Hall, Edith E. IV, 628
Hall, Edith J. IV, 400
Hall, Edith Kirk IV, 1318
Hall, Edith Rachel IV, 819
Hall, Edna I, 215
Hall, Edna F. I, 208
Hall, Edna H. IV, 402
Hall, Edna H. IV, 414
Hall, Edna Virginia IV, 819
Hall, Edward I, 215
Hall, Edward I, 1154
Hall, Edward II, 30
Hall, Edward II, 75
Hall, Edward II, 111
Hall, Edward II, 133
Hall, Edward III, 145
Hall, Edward III, 171
Hall, Edward IV, 215
Hall, Edward IV, 627
Hall, Edward IV, 628
Hall, Edward IV, 819
Hall, Edward IV, 870
Hall, Edward Payson I, 812
Hall, Edward S. IV, 402
Hall, Edward S. IV, 961
Hall, Edward Stratton IV, 401
Hall, Edward Stratton IV, 960
Hall, Edwin IV, 213
Hall, Edwin IV, 214
Hall, Edwin IV, 215
Hall, Edwin IV, 528
Hall, Edwin IV, 819
Hall, Edwin C. II, 871
Hall, Edwin C. IV, 817
Hall, Edwin C. IV, 819
Hall, Edwin C. IV, 906
Hall, Edwin P. IV, 627
Hall, Edwin P. IV, 628
Hall, Edwin P. IV, 629
Hall, Edwin P. IV, 960
Hall, Edwin P. IV, 961
Hall, Edwind P. IV, 581
Hall, Eli I, 286
Hall, Eli IV, 398
Hall, Eli IV, 399
Hall, Eli IV, 401
Hall, Eli IV, 447
Hall, Elias IV, 36
Hall, Elihu IV, 581
Hall, Elijah Franklin I, 617
Hall, Elisabeth I, 240
Hall, Elisabeth I, 254
Hall, Elisabeth W. I, 240
Hall, Elisha I, 141
Hall, Elisha IV, 1060
Hall, Elisha VI, 884
Hall, Elisha VI, 886
Hall, Elisha VI, 924
Hall, Elisha VI, 926
Hall, Elisha VI, 932
Hall, Elisha VI, 965
Hall, Elisha VI, 967
Hall, Elisha VI, 991
Hall, Elisha, Jr. VI, 991
Hall, Eliz. A. III, 263
Hall, Eliza II, 444
Hall, Eliza IV, 213
Hall, Eliza IV, 215
Hall, Eliza IV, 246
Hall, Eliza IV, 398
Hall, Eliza IV, 419
Hall, Eliza IV, 444
Hall, Eliza VI, 814
Hall, Eliza D. IV, 214
Hall, Eliza D. IV, 215
Hall, Eliza D. IV, 276
Hall, Eliza D. IV, 402
Hall, Eliza D. IV, 438
Hall, Eliza D. IV, 528
Hall, Elizabeth I, 100
Hall, Elizabeth I, 130
Hall, Elizabeth I, 141
Hall, Elizabeth I, 215
Hall, Elizabeth I, 216
Hall, Elizabeth I, 288
Hall, Elizabeth I, 302
Hall, Elizabeth I, 307
Hall, Elizabeth I, 654
Hall, Elizabeth I, 679
Hall, Elizabeth I, 685
Hall, Elizabeth I, 698
Hall, Elizabeth I, 716
Hall, Elizabeth II, 30
Hall, Elizabeth II, 51
Hall, Elizabeth II, 75
Hall, Elizabeth II, 99
Hall, Elizabeth II, 100
Hall, Elizabeth II, 112
Hall, Elizabeth II, 119
Hall, Elizabeth II, 132
Hall, Elizabeth II, 137
Hall, Elizabeth II, 370
Hall, Elizabeth II, 444
Hall, Elizabeth II, 539
Hall, Elizabeth II, 617
Hall, Elizabeth II, 871
Hall, Elizabeth III, 145
Hall, Elizabeth III, 171
Hall, Elizabeth IV, 147
Hall, Elizabeth IV, 212
Hall, Elizabeth IV, 213
Hall, Elizabeth IV, 214
Hall, Elizabeth IV, 235
Hall, Elizabeth IV, 285
Hall, Elizabeth IV, 334
Hall, Elizabeth IV, 355
Hall, Elizabeth IV, 363
Hall, Elizabeth IV, 368
Hall, Elizabeth IV, 381
Hall, Elizabeth IV, 398
Hall, Elizabeth IV, 399
Hall, Elizabeth IV, 401
Hall, Elizabeth IV, 405
Hall, Elizabeth IV, 406
Hall, Elizabeth IV, 426
Hall, Elizabeth IV, 528
Hall, Elizabeth IV, 581
Hall, Elizabeth IV, 798
Hall, Elizabeth IV, 819
Hall, Elizabeth IV, 838
Hall, Elizabeth IV, 845
Hall, Elizabeth IV, 906
Hall, Elizabeth IV, 1060
Hall, Elizabeth IV, 1069
Hall, Elizabeth V, 65
Hall, Elizabeth V, 79
Hall, Elizabeth V, 806
Hall, Elizabeth V, 809
Hall, Elizabeth VI, 693
Hall, Elizabeth VI, 822
Hall, Elizabeth VI, 825
Hall, Elizabeth VI, 831
Hall, Elizabeth VI, 926
Hall, Elizabeth VI, 1016
Hall, Elizabeth A. VI, 666
Hall, Elizabeth A. VI, 693
Hall, Elizabeth A. VI, 704
Hall, Elizabeth Ann I, 307
Hall, Elizabeth B. IV, 213
Hall, Elizabeth B. IV, 214
Hall, Elizabeth B. IV, 276
Hall, Elizabeth Charity IV, 1236
Hall, Elizabeth D. IV, 215
Hall, Elizabeth D. IV, 288
Hall, Elizabeth H. IV, 215
Hall, Elizabeth H. IV, 845
Hall, Elizabeth J. IV, 402
Hall, Elizabeth J. IV, 407
Hall, Elizabeth J. IV, 581
Hall, Elizabeth J. IV, 583
Hall, Elizabeth T. IV, 364
Hall, Elizabeth T. IV, 400
Hall, Elizabeth T. IV, 402
Hall, Elizabeth T. IV, 673
Hall, Elizabeth, Jr. II, 119
Hall, Ella II, 711
Hall, Ella IV, 819
Hall, Ella H. II, 744
Hall, Ella H. II, 753
Hall, Ellen I, 1153
Hall, Ellen IV, 212
Hall, Ellen IV, 215
Hall, Ellen IV, 310
Hall, Ellen IV, 398
Hall, Ellen IV, 445
Hall, Ellsworth IV, 213
Hall, Ellwood V, 391
Hall, Elma IV, 213
Hall, Elma IV, 960
Hall, Elma C. IV, 400
Hall, Elma E. IV, 214
Hall, Elma E. IV, 528
Hall, Elma L. IV, 378
Hall, Elma L. IV, 400
Hall, Elma L. IV, 402
Hall, Elma M. IV, 402
Hall, Elma M. IV, 407
Hall, Elma Maria IV, 400
Hall, Elmer IV, 400
Hall, Elmer E. IV, 400
Hall, Elmer E. IV, 401
Hall, Elmer E. IV, 402
Hall, Elmer Elsworth IV, 399
Hall, Elmer I. IV, 387
Hall, Elmer I. IV, 401
Hall, Elmer I. IV, 402
Hall, Elsie IV, 392
Hall, Elsie IV, 402
Hall, Elsie H. IV, 400
Hall, Elsie May IV, 400
Hall, Elsie V. IV, 961
Hall, Elsie Virginia IV, 961
Hall, Elsworth IV, 213
Hall, Elton Harrold IV, 961
Hall, Elvira IV, 214
Hall, Elvira IV, 399
Hall, Elvira IV, 401
Hall, Elvira IV, 402
Hall, Elvira IV, 627
Hall, Elvira IV, 628
Hall, Elvira IV, 667
Hall, Elvira IV, 727
Hall, Elvira IV, 961
Hall, Elvira IV, 1017
Hall, Elvira IV, 1018
Hall, Elwood IV, 400
Hall, Elwood V, 391
Hall, Elza R. IV, 176
Hall, Elza R. IV, 214
Hall, Emily I, 240
Hall, Emily I, 812
Hall, Emily I, 829
Hall, Emily IV, 398
Hall, Emily IV, 843
Hall, Emily C. IV, 213
Hall, Emily C. IV, 819
Hall, Emily E. IV, 379
Hall, Emily E. IV, 399
Hall, Emily E. IV, 402
Hall, Emily S. IV, 213
Hall, Emily S. IV, 214
Hall, Emily S. IV, 272
Hall, Emily S. IV, 841
Hall, Emley I, 215
Hall, Emma II, 370
Hall, Emma III, 145
Hall, Emma C. V, 391
Hall, Emma L. III, 145
Hall, Emma L. III, 211
Hall, Emma L. III, 312
Hall, Emma Leona I, 617
Hall, Emmer Wm. IV, 213
Hall, Emmer Wm. IV, 215
Hall, Emmor W. IV, 960
Hall, Emmor W. IV, 1038
Hall, Emmor Wm. IV, 960
Hall, Emmor Wm. IV, 961
Hall, Ephraim IV, 528
Hall, Erma L. IV, 387
Hall, Erma L. IV, 401
Hall, Erma L. IV, 402
Hall, Estella V, 740
Hall, Estella May IV, 1038
Hall, Esther II, 75
Hall, Esther II, 111
Hall, Esther IV, 170
Hall, Esther Joyce I, 880
Hall, Ethel IV, 401
Hall, Ethel IV, 403
Hall, Ethel IV, 961
Hall, Ethel IV, 986
Hall, Ethel Margaret IV, 819
Hall, Ethelyn IV, 388
Hall, Ethelyn IV, 403
Hall, Etta V, 570
Hall, Etta B. IV, 1318
Hall, Etta Cleland V, 570
Hall, Euclid VI, 926
Hall, Evaline IV, 400
Hall, Eveline IV, 381
Hall, Eveline IV, 402
Hall, Everett IV, 402
Hall, Everett G. IV, 402
Hall, Everette G. IV, 399
Hall, Exum I, 288
Hall, Exum I, 307
Hall, Exum IV, 398
Hall, Exum IV, 401
Hall, Ezra IV, 213
Hall, Ezra IV, 960
Hall, Ezra B. IV, 961
Hall, Ezra Benjamin IV, 628
Hall, Ezra Benjamin IV, 629
Hall, Ezra Benjamin IV, 961
Hall, Ezra W. IV, 212
Hall, Fannie I, 617
Hall, Fannie I, 620
Hall, Fannie II, 133
Hall, Fanny II, 146
Hall, Fanny Pease II, 150
Hall, Felicia VI, 29
Hall, Felicia VI, 34
Hall, Florence IV, 199
Hall, Florence IV, 214
Hall, Florence G. VI, 730
Hall, Foster A. IV, 628
Hall, Foster A. IV, 629
Hall, Foster A. IV, 960
Hall, Foster A. IV, 961
Hall, Foster A. IV, 963
Hall, Foster Arthur IV, 961
Hall, Frances VI, 825
Hall, Frances Carpenter II, 133
Hall, Francis IV, 215
Hall, Francis D. IV, 399
Hall, Francis D. IV, 402
Hall, Francis Isabella I, 812
Hall, Francis Lindley IV, 960
Hall, Francis Lindley IV, 961
Hall, Francis W. II, 706
Hall, Francis W. II, 744
Hall, Francis W. IV, 213
Hall, Francis W. IV, 216
Hall, Frank G. IV, 1236
Hall, Frank T. II, 132
Hall, Franklin II, 30
Hall, Franklin IV, 528
Hall, Franklin IV, 582
Hall, Franklin B. IV, 213
Hall, Franklin B. IV, 215
Hall, Franklin B. IV, 528
Hall, Franklin G. IV, 1236
Hall, Franz K. IV, 402
Hall, Fred IV, 1236
Hall, Freda Blanche IV, 400
Hall, Geo. H. IV, 1318
Hall, Geo. T. VI, 730
Hall, George II, 138
Hall, George IV, 399
Hall, George IV, 401
Hall, George IV, 474
Hall, George B. IV, 960
Hall, George B. IV, 1038
Hall, George C. IV, 213
Hall, George C. IV, 216
Hall, George Dillwyn IV, 399
Hall, George E. IV, 819
Hall, George F. IV, 1236
Hall, George H. IV, 1318
Hall, George P. II, 154
Hall, George S. IV, 401
Hall, George S. IV, 528
Hall, George S. IV, 1208
Hall, George W. IV, 474
Hall, Georgia III, 22
Hall, Georgia III, 266
Hall, Gertrude M. IV, 402
Hall, Gertrude M. IV, 715
Hall, Gervas II, 30
Hall, Gervas Abner II, 132
Hall, Gervas Irving II, 132
Hall, Gervis II, 132
Hall, Golda IV, 459
Hall, Golda B. H. IV, 403
Hall, Golda B. H. IV, 459
Hall, Golda Bell IV, 400
Hall, Hall IV, 215
Hall, Hallie Olive IV, 402
Hall, Hallie Olive IV, 570
Hall, Hallie Olive IV, 581
Hall, Hallie Olive IV, 582
Hall, Hannah II, 30
Hall, Hannah II, 75
Hall, Hannah II, 89
Hall, Hannah II, 119
Hall, Hannah II, 121
Hall, Hannah II, 127
Hall, Hannah II, 138
Hall, Hannah II, 149
Hall, Hannah II, 154
Hall, Hannah II, 871
Hall, Hannah II, 975
Hall, Hannah II, 999
Hall, Hannah III, 145

Hall, Hannah IV, 195
Hall, Hannah IV, 212
Hall, Hannah IV, 213
Hall, Hannah IV, 214
Hall, Hannah IV, 215
Hall, Hannah IV, 226
Hall, Hannah IV, 305
Hall, Hannah IV, 399
Hall, Hannah IV, 400
Hall, Hannah IV, 401
Hall, Hannah IV, 528
Hall, Hannah IV, 558
Hall, Hannah IV, 581
Hall, Hannah IV, 627
Hall, Hannah IV, 1318
Hall, Hannah A. II, 119
Hall, Hannah A. II, 132
Hall, Hannah A. II, 149
Hall, Hannah A. II, 150
Hall, Hannah A. II, 871
Hall, Hannah A. IV, 398
Hall, Hannah A. IV, 400
Hall, Hannah Acton II, 30
Hall, Hannah Ann IV, 378
Hall, Hannah Ann IV, 387
Hall, Hannah Ann IV, 398
Hall, Hannah Ann IV, 399
Hall, Hannah Ann IV, 402
Hall, Hannah Ann IV, 453
Hall, Hannah Ann C. IV, 400
Hall, Hannah C. III, 209
Hall, Hannah Mary IV, 213
Hall, Hannah Mary IV, 215
Hall, Hannah Mary IV, 627
Hall, Hannah Mary IV, 628
Hall, Hannah Mary IV, 644
Hall, Hannah Mary IV, 738
Hall, Hannah Mary IV, 833
Hall, Hannah W. IV, 215
Hall, Harlon L. IV, 628
Hall, Harold IV, 403
Hall, Harold Laverne IV, 401
Hall, Harriet E. IV, 400
Hall, Harriett Ann IV, 1163
Hall, Harriett Ann IV, 1170
Hall, Harriett B. VI, 999
Hall, Harry IV, 1318
Hall, Harry E. IV, 961
Hall, Harry Edwin IV, 628
Hall, Harry Edwin IV, 629
Hall, Harry Edwin IV, 961
Hall, Harry Ervin IV, 628
Hall, Hartley IV, 528
Hall, Heil S. IV, 684
Hall, Heil S. IV, 715
Hall, Helen IV, 214
Hall, Helen IV, 905
Hall, Helen IV, 906
Hall, Helen E. IV, 400
Hall, Helen E. IV, 411
Hall, Helen Elizabeth II, 132
Hall, Helen G. III, 145
Hall, Helen Louisa IV, 213
Hall, Helen M. IV, 817
Hall, Helen M. IV, 819
Hall, Helen Phyllis IV, 290
Hall, Helen S. IV, 960
Hall, Henrietta III, 145
Hall, Henrietta M. II, 744
Hall, Henrietta M. II, 746
Hall, Henrietta M. II, 871
Hall, Henrietta M. II, 878
Hall, Henry I, 288
Hall, Henry IV, 148
Hall, Henry IV, 213
Hall, Henry IV, 215
Hall, Henry IV, 398
Hall, Henry IV, 399
Hall, Henry IV, 400
Hall, Henry IV, 452
Hall, Henry IV, 513
Hall, Henry IV, 528
Hall, Henry IV, 581
Hall, Henry IV, 813
Hall, Henry IV, 1318
Hall, Henry VI, 885
Hall, Henry VI, 926
Hall, Henry Alden IV, 389
Hall, Henry Alden IV, 400
Hall, Henry Alden IV, 401
Hall, Henry Alden IV, 402
Hall, Henry Alden IV, 819
Hall, Henry L. IV, 961
Hall, Henry Lee IV, 628
Hall, Henry Lee IV, 629
Hall, Henry Lee IV, 960
Hall, Henry Lee IV, 961
Hall, Henry Powell I, 679
Hall, Henry T. I, 216
Hall, Herbert D. IV, 628
Hall, Herbert D. IV, 629
Hall, Herbert D. IV, 657
Hall, Herbert D. IV, 768
Hall, Herbert David IV, 628
Hall, Herbert W. IV, 715
Hall, Herbert Walter IV, 401
Hall, Herman R. V, 570
Hall, Hervey IV, 334
Hall, Hervey IV, 581
Hall, Hervy IV, 528
Hall, Hester II, 75
Hall, Hester II, 111
Hall, Hezekiah VI, 995
Hall, Hial S. IV, 215
Hall, Hiel IV, 213
Hall, Hiel IV, 627
Hall, Hiel S. IV, 613
Hall, Hiel S. IV, 628
Hall, Hiel S. IV, 629
Hall, Homer IV, 400
Hall, Homer IV, 402
Hall, Homer C. IV, 400
Hall, Homer C. IV, 403
Hall, Homer Cecil IV, 400
Hall, Howard IV, 715
Hall, Howard E. IV, 715
Hall, Howard S. IV, 402
Hall, Howard Stanton IV, 401
Hall, Howard T. IV, 628
Hall, Howard T. IV, 629
Hall, Howard T. IV, 694
Hall, Howard T. IV, 715
Hall, Howard Theophilus IV, 401
Hall, Howard Theophilus IV, 693
Hall, Hyall IV, 215
Hall, Ida IV, 402
Hall, Ida IV, 715
Hall, Ida J. IV, 401
Hall, Ida J. IV, 442
Hall, Ida M. IV, 363
Hall, Ida M. IV, 402
Hall, Ida May IV, 363
Hall, Ida May IV, 400
Hall, Ida Stanton IV, 715
Hall, Ira K. IV, 215
Hall, Ira K. IV, 960
Hall, Ira K. IV, 961
Hall, Irene IV, 400
Hall, Irving Cassius IV, 401
Hall, Isaac I, 215
Hall, Isaac I, 216
Hall, Isaac I, 240
Hall, Isaac I, 251
Hall, Isaac I, 260
Hall, Isaac I, 288
Hall, Isaac I, 304
Hall, Isaac I, 307
Hall, Isaac II, 711
Hall, Isaac II, 744
Hall, Isaac II, 753
Hall, Isaac II, 797
Hall, Isaac III, 145
Hall, Isaac III, 211
Hall, Isaac IV, 147
Hall, Isaac IV, 148
Hall, Isaac IV, 157
Hall, Isaac IV, 355
Hall, Isaac IV, 365
Hall, Isaac IV, 381
Hall, Isaac IV, 385
Hall, Isaac IV, 398
Hall, Isaac IV, 399
Hall, Isaac IV, 402
Hall, Isaac IV, 405
Hall, Isaac IV, 447
Hall, Isaac IV, 627
Hall, Isaac V, 999
Hall, Isaac Key II, 30
Hall, Isaac W. IV, 334
Hall, Isaac W. IV, 399
Hall, Isaac, Jr. III, 145
Hall, Isaac, Jr. III, 312
Hall, Isaac, Jr. IV, 398
Hall, Isaac, Jr. IV, 401
Hall, Isaac, Jr. IV, 405
Hall, Isaac, Sr. IV, 401
Hall, Isabel I, 141
Hall, Isaiah I, 100
Hall, Isaiah I, 141
Hall, Isham VI, 818
Hall, Isham VI, 822
Hall, Isham. VI, 799
Hall, Israel IV, 212
Hall, Israel IV, 214
Hall, Israel IV, 627
Hall, Israel L. III, 312
Hall, J. H. Beals I, 1153
Hall, J. J. I, 1153
Hall, J. W. I, 240
Hall, J. Walter IV, 570
Hall, J. Wilmer IV, 581
Hall, Jacob V, 496
Hall, James I, 215
Hall, James I, 240
Hall, James I, 270
Hall, James II, 30
Hall, James II, 370
Hall, James II, 539
Hall, James IV, 212
Hall, James IV, 398
Hall, James IV, 401
Hall, James IV, 1163
Hall, James VI, 926
Hall, James C. I, 240
Hall, James E. IV, 215
Hall, James E. IV, 819
Hall, James Edgerton, Jr. IV, 401
Hall, James R. I, 215
Hall, James U. I, 240
Hall, James W. I, 215
Hall, James W. I, 231
Hall, James W. I, 240
Hall, James W. II, 119
Hall, James W. II, 132
Hall, James W. II, 149
Hall, James W. II, 150
Hall, James William I, 215
Hall, James Woodnutt II, 30
Hall, Jane I, 216
Hall, Jane I, 229
Hall, Jane I, 240
Hall, Jane II, 222
Hall, Jane II, 229
Hall, Jane II, 539
Hall, Jane II, 645
Hall, Jane II, 999
Hall, Jane III, 124
Hall, Jane III, 145
Hall, Jane III, 150
Hall, Jane III, 216
Hall, Jane III, 249
Hall, Jane IV, 400
Hall, Jane IV, 402
Hall, Jane IV, 819
Hall, Jane IV, 822
Hall, Jane C. I, 215
Hall, Jane C. I, 231
Hall, Jane H. III, 51
Hall, Jemima I, 692
Hall, Jenny VI, 822
Hall, Jeptha IV, 215
Hall, Jeptha IV, 399
Hall, Jeptha W. IV, 363
Hall, Jeptha W. IV, 400
Hall, Jeptha W. IV, 406
Hall, Jesse I, 208
Hall, Jesse I, 215
Hall, Jesse I, 216
Hall, Jesse I, 240
Hall, Jesse I, 288
Hall, Jesse I, 289
Hall, Jesse I, 307
Hall, Jesse I, 314
Hall, Jesse IV, 36
Hall, Jesse IV, 148
Hall, Jesse IV, 212
Hall, Jesse IV, 214
Hall, Jesse IV, 289
Hall, Jesse IV, 303
Hall, Jesse IV, 334
Hall, Jesse IV, 398
Hall, Jesse IV, 400
Hall, Jesse IV, 401
Hall, Jesse IV, 405
Hall, Jesse IV, 528
Hall, Jesse IV, 627
Hall, Jesse IV, 925
Hall, Jesse IV, 960
Hall, Jesse IV, 961
Hall, Jesse IV, 998
Hall, Jesse B. IV, 399
Hall, Jesse B. IV, 402
Hall, Jesse D. IV, 399
Hall, Jesse D. IV, 400
Hall, Jesse D. IV, 402
Hall, Jesse Franklin IV, 528
Hall, Jesse Ione V, 570
Hall, Jesse Stone V, 570
Hall, Jesse Thomas I, 215
Hall, Jesse W. IV, 819
Hall, Jesse Wilmer IV, 581
Hall, Jesse Wilmer IV, 582
Hall, Jesse Wilmer IV, 813
Hall, Jesse Wilmer IV, 819
Hall, Jessee VI, 926
Hall, Jessie M. IV, 628
Hall, Jessie M. IV, 629
Hall, Jessie M. IV, 960
Hall, Jessie M. IV, 961
Hall, Jno. IV, 400
Hall, Joan II, 539
Hall, Joanna VI, 927
Hall, Joel VI, 926
Hall, John I, 99
Hall, John I, 141
Hall, John I, 239
Hall, John I, 240
Hall, John I, 251
Hall, John I, 288
Hall, John I, 307
Hall, John II, 30
Hall, John II, 75
Hall, John II, 119
Hall, John II, 132
Hall, John II, 149
Hall, John II, 444
Hall, John II, 465
Hall, John II, 539
Hall, John II, 669
Hall, John II, 706
Hall, John II, 960
Hall, John II, 975
Hall, John II, 976
Hall, John II, 999
Hall, John II, 1022
Hall, John II, 1039
Hall, John III, 145
Hall, John III, 214
Hall, John IV, 147
Hall, John IV, 148
Hall, John IV, 163
Hall, John IV, 170
Hall, John IV, 193
Hall, John IV, 212
Hall, John IV, 213
Hall, John IV, 214
Hall, John IV, 215
Hall, John IV, 235
Hall, John IV, 260
Hall, John IV, 266
Hall, John IV, 276
Hall, John IV, 334
Hall, John IV, 364
Hall, John IV, 384
Hall, John IV, 398
Hall, John IV, 399
Hall, John IV, 400
Hall, John IV, 401
Hall, John IV, 402
Hall, John IV, 423
Hall, John IV, 435
Hall, John IV, 438
Hall, John IV, 520
Hall, John IV, 528
Hall, John IV, 576
Hall, John IV, 581
Hall, John IV, 586
Hall, John IV, 673
Hall, John IV, 819
Hall, John IV, 829
Hall, John IV, 960
Hall, John IV, 1099
Hall, John IV, 1318
Hall, John VI, 822
Hall, John VI, 924
Hall, John VI, 926
Hall, John A. IV, 402
Hall, John A. IV, 581
Hall, John A. IV, 601
Hall, John C. IV, 212
Hall, John C. IV, 215
Hall, John C. IV, 627
Hall, John C. IV, 628
Hall, John G. II, 1087
Hall, John G. IV, 528
Hall, John G. IV, 581
Hall, John G. IV, 582
Hall, John G. IV, 583
Hall, John G. IV, 628
Hall, John G. IV, 641
Hall, John G. IV, 794
Hall, John G. IV, 1318
Hall, John George II, 948
Hall, John George II, 1087
Hall, John Green IV, 528
Hall, John H. II, 132
Hall, John H. II, 150
Hall, John Robert IV, 581
Hall, John W. Smith IV, 401
Hall, John Wm. I, 216
Hall, John, Jr. I, 215
Hall, John, Jr. I, 240
Hall, John, Jr. IV, 401
Hall, John, Jr. VI, 886
Hall, John, Sr. VI, 926
Hall, Jonas M. IV, 1038
Hall, Joseph I, 141
Hall, Joseph I, 215
Hall, Joseph I, 216
Hall, Joseph I, 240
Hall, Joseph I, 253
Hall, Joseph I, 270
Hall, Joseph I, 288
Hall, Joseph I, 289
Hall, Joseph I, 302
Hall, Joseph I, 307
Hall, Joseph I, 698
Hall, Joseph I, 716
Hall, Joseph II, 30
Hall, Joseph II, 58
Hall, Joseph II, 75
Hall, Joseph II, 133
Hall, Joseph II, 539
Hall, Joseph II, 706
Hall, Joseph II, 744
Hall, Joseph II, 979
Hall, Joseph II, 999
Hall, Joseph IV, 29
Hall, Joseph IV, 36
Hall, Joseph IV, 137
Hall, Joseph IV, 148
Hall, Joseph IV, 185
Hall, Joseph IV, 198
Hall, Joseph IV, 200
Hall, Joseph IV, 208
Hall, Joseph IV, 212
Hall, Joseph IV, 213
Hall, Joseph IV, 214
Hall, Joseph IV, 215
Hall, Joseph IV, 226
Hall, Joseph IV, 256
Hall, Joseph IV, 368
Hall, Joseph IV, 396
Hall, Joseph IV, 399
Hall, Joseph IV, 401
Hall, Joseph IV, 402
Hall, Joseph IV, 528
Hall, Joseph IV, 574
Hall, Joseph IV, 581
Hall, Joseph IV, 627
Hall, Joseph IV, 628
Hall, Joseph IV, 667
Hall, Joseph IV, 819
Hall, Joseph IV, 836
Hall, Joseph IV, 843
Hall, Joseph IV, 1060
Hall, Joseph Anderson I, 215
Hall, Joseph D. IV, 36
Hall, Joseph D. IV, 39
Hall, Joseph D. IV, 214
Hall, Joseph Dew IV, 36
Hall, Joseph Edmon I, 215
Hall, Joseph G. I, 812
Hall, Joseph G. IV, 215
Hall, Joseph G. IV, 400
Hall, Joseph G. IV, 406
Hall, Joseph G. IV, 581
Hall, Joseph Gore IV, 399
Hall, Joseph H. I, 1154
Hall, Joseph H. IV, 401
Hall, Joseph Hall IV, 36
Hall, Joseph Hartley IV, 398
Hall, Joseph Heartly IV, 528
Hall, Joseph Hilles IV, 36
Hall, Joseph J. IV, 400
Hall, Joseph J. IV, 403
Hall, Joseph S. IV, 1163
Hall, Joseph W. IV, 370
Hall, Joseph W. IV, 387
Hall, Joseph W. IV, 398
Hall, Joseph W. IV, 399
Hall, Joseph W. IV, 400
Hall, Joseph W. IV, 452
Hall, Joseph, Jr. IV, 214
Hall, Josephine IV, 401
Hall, Joshua I, 216
Hall, Joshua I, 288
Hall, Joshua I, 289
Hall, Joshua I, 306
Hall, Joshua I, 307
Hall, Joshua IV, 213
Hall, Joshua V, 809
Hall, Josiah I, 251
Hall, Josiah II, 30
Hall, Josiah II, 75
Hall, Josiah IV, 212
Hall, Josiah IV, 213
Hall, Josiah IV, 214
Hall, Josiah IV, 215
Hall, Josiah IV, 280
Hall, Josiah IV, 305
Hall, Josiah IV, 528
Hall, Josiah IV, 557
Hall, Josiah IV, 558
Hall, Josiah IV, 1236
Hall, Josiah Parker I, 240
Hall, Judith I, 240
Hall, Judith I, 241
Hall, Judith Copeland I, 215
Hall, Judith Copeland I, 216
Hall, Judith D. V, 908
Hall, Judith Delphine V, 908
Hall, Judith Delphinia I, 812
Hall, Juicy VI, 822
Hall, Julia A. II, 146

ll, Julia A. VI, 822
ll, Julian I, 880
ll, Junius L. IV, 276
ll, Jurah VI, 795
ll, Katherine VI, 886
ll, Kenneth Franklin IV, 628
ll, Kezia VI, 967
ll, Keziah VI, 939
ll, Keziah VI, 950
ll, Lana IV, 572
ll, Lana IV, 581
ll, Lanah IV, 581
ll, Lany I, 270
ll, Lany IV, 36
ll, Lany IV, 214
ll, Lany IV, 228
ll, Laura IV, 1038
ll, Lavina I, 270
ll, Lavina IV, 36
ll, Lavina IV, 148
ll, Lavina IV, 198
ll, Lavina IV, 214
ll, Leiis Clifton IV, 819
ll, Leona I, 620
ll, Leona I, 633
ll, Leona I, 636
ll, Leonard VI, 926
ll, Leonard VI, 1014
ll, Leonard VI, 1016
ll, Lester IV, 808
ll, Lester G. IV, 401
ll, Letitia IV, 399
ll, Letitia IV, 401
ll, Levina IV, 148
ll, Levina IV, 214
ll, Levinah I, 269
ll, Levinah I, 270
ll, Levinah IV, 214
ll, Lewella L. IV, 819
ll, Lewis II, 30
ll, Lewis II, 133
ll, Lewis II, 146
ll, Lewis II, 150
ll, Lewis IV, 176
ll, Lewis IV, 183
ll, Lewis IV, 213
ll, Lewis IV, 215
ll, Lewis IV, 216
ll, Lewis IV, 276
ll, Lewis IV, 400
ll, Lewis IV, 575
ll, Lewis IV, 819
ll, Lewis IV, 960
ll, Lewis IV, 1163
ll, Lewis L. IV, 402
ll, Lewis M. II, 76
ll, Lewis M. II, 119
ll, Lewis M. II, 132
ll, Lewis M. II, 150
ll, Lewis M. II, 159
ll, Lewis W. IV, 402
ll, Liddia II, 999
ll, Lidy II, 132
ll, Lillian III, 145
ll, Lillian A. IV, 528
ll, Lillian B. IV, 627
ll, Lillian B. IV, 628
ll, Lillian M. III, 214
ll, Lillie M. IV, 584
ll, Lindley IV, 212
ll, Lindley IV, 213
ll, Lindley IV, 215
ll, Lindley IV, 261
ll, Lindley IV, 272
ll, Lindley IV, 282
ll, Lindley IV, 387
ll, Lindley IV, 399
ll, Lindley IV, 400
ll, Lindley IV, 401
ll, Lindley IV, 402
ll, Lindley IV, 528
ll, Lindley IV, 566
ll, Lindley IV, 581
ll, Lindley IV, 582
ll, Lindley IV, 715
ll, Lindley IV, 819
ll, Lindley IV, 841
ll, Lindley H. IV, 398
ll, Lindley H. IV, 402
ll, Lindley M. IV, 214
ll, Lindley W. IV, 819
ll, Lindley W. IV, 820
ll, Lindley W. IV, 838
ll, Linton IV, 169
ll, Linton IV, 212
ll, Linton IV, 213
ll, Linton IV, 215
ll, Linton IV, 401
ll, Linton IV, 606
ll, Linton IV, 627
ll, Linton IV, 628
Hall, Linton IV, 644
Hall, Linton IV, 715
Hall, Linton IV, 738
Hall, Linton IV, 833
Hall, Linton IV, 960
Hall, Linton IV, 961
Hall, Linton S. IV, 628
Hall, Lizzie IV, 276
Hall, Lizzie IV, 403
Hall, Lois J. IV, 402
Hall, Lois Josephine IV, 428
Hall, Lois L. IV, 428
Hall, Louis IV, 213
Hall, Louis L. IV, 387
Hall, Louis L. IV, 401
Hall, Louis Webster IV, 399
Hall, Louisa IV, 959
Hall, Louisa IV, 960
Hall, Louisa IV, 961
Hall, Louisa Bundy IV, 215
Hall, Louise E. II, 150
Hall, Louise Elizabeth II, 132
Hall, Lucella L. IV, 216
Hall, Lucile IV, 715
Hall, Lucinda I, 986
Hall, Lucinda I, 1153
Hall, Luella IV, 176
Hall, Luella IV, 183
Hall, Luella IV, 213
Hall, Luella IV, 214
Hall, Luella IV, 375
Hall, Luella IV, 376
Hall, Luella IV, 402
Hall, Luella L. IV, 216
Hall, Luella L. IV, 289
Hall, Luella L. IV, 291
Hall, Luella L. IV, 819
Hall, Luella L. IV, 847
Hall, Luella L. IV, 848
Hall, Luella Lucretia IV, 214
Hall, Lura IV, 214
Hall, Lura IV, 272
Hall, Lura D. IV, 213
Hall, Lydia I, 307
Hall, Lydia II, 30
Hall, Lydia II, 75
Hall, Lydia II, 93
Hall, Lydia II, 132
Hall, Lydia II, 140
Hall, Lydia II, 143
Hall, Lydia II, 149
Hall, Lydia II, 1039
Hall, Lydia IV, 213
Hall, Lydia IV, 398
Hall, Lydia IV, 528
Hall, Lydia IV, 544
Hall, Lydia IV, 819
Hall, Lydia IV, 847
Hall, Lydia V, 740
Hall, Lydia J. IV, 275
Hall, Lydia Jane II, 706
Hall, Lydia Jane IV, 214
Hall, Lydia Jane IV, 272
Hall, Lydia M. IV, 213
Hall, Lydia M. IV, 214
Hall, Lydia M. IV, 261
Hall, Lyman B. III, 145
Hall, M. J. IV, 400
Hall, Mabel Lucile IV, 628
Hall, Magalen VI, 924
Hall, Magdalean VI, 884
Hall, Magdalean VI, 967
Hall, Magdalena VI, 890
Hall, Magdalene VI, 924
Hall, Mahlon II, 539
Hall, Mahlon II, 999
Hall, Mahlon IV, 528
Hall, Malissa IV, 402
Hall, Malissa IV, 416
Hall, Mansel E. IV, 378
Hall, Mansel E. IV, 400
Hall, Mansel E. IV, 401
Hall, Mansel E. IV, 406
Hall, Mansel E. IV, 444
Hall, Mansel Eugene IV, 399
Hall, Mansell E. IV, 215
Hall, Manuel E. IV, 401
Hall, Mareb IV, 627
Hall, Mareh IV, 628
Hall, Margaret I, 215
Hall, Margaret I, 229
Hall, Margaret I, 240
Hall, Margaret II, 30
Hall, Margaret II, 66
Hall, Margaret II, 75
Hall, Margaret II, 79
Hall, Margaret II, 129
Hall, Margaret II, 539
Hall, Margaret II, 687
Hall, Margaret IV, 213
Hall, Margaret IV, 399
Hall, Margaret IV, 447
Hall, Margaret V, 391
Hall, Margaret A. IV, 276
Hall, Margaret Ann IV, 176
Hall, Margaret Ann IV, 183
Hall, Margaret Ann IV, 213
Hall, Margaret Ann IV, 819
Hall, Margaret Ann IV, 960
Hall, Margaret Ann Leonora I, 812
Hall, Margaret Evalyn IV, 819
Hall, Margaret Louise II, 706
Hall, Margaret Louise IV, 628
Hall, Margaret Morris II, 30
Hall, Margaret W. II, 119
Hall, Margaret W. II, 132
Hall, Margaret Woodnutt II, 30
Hall, Margaretta W. II, 137
Hall, Margaretta W. II, 150
Hall, Margaretta W. II, 156
Hall, Margary II, 871
Hall, Margret II, 75
Hall, Margret VI, 28
Hall, Margrett VI, 30
Hall, Maria IV, 212
Hall, Maria IV, 214
Hall, Maria IV, 369
Hall, Maria IV, 398
Hall, Maria IV, 399
Hall, Maria IV, 401
Hall, Maria IV, 439
Hall, Maria IV, 511
Hall, Maria IV, 528
Hall, Mariam I, 216
Hall, Mariam I, 231
Hall, Mariam I, 239
Hall, Mariam I, 240
Hall, Mariam I, 301
Hall, Mariam I, 307
Hall, Mariam P. IV, 384
Hall, Mariam P. IV, 400
Hall, Mariam P. IV, 402
Hall, Marian E. IV, 402
Hall, Marian Ethelyn IV, 575
Hall, Marian Ethelyn IV, 582
Hall, Marian Ethlyn IV, 575
Hall, Marian Helen IV, 401
Hall, Marian Helen IV, 960
Hall, Marian Helen IV, 961
Hall, Marian Hellen IV, 961
Hall, Mariana IV, 401
Hall, Mariana IV, 403
Hall, Marianna IV, 393
Hall, Mariannna IV, 961
Hall, Marie V, 153
Hall, Marion V, 391
Hall, Marion Ellen IV, 402
Hall, Marion Ethlyn IV, 387
Hall, Marion Ethlyn IV, 401
Hall, Mark II, 30
Hall, Martha I, 215
Hall, Martha I, 240
Hall, Martha II, 30
Hall, Martha II, 159
Hall, Martha III, 140
Hall, Martha III, 145
Hall, Martha IV, 200
Hall, Martha IV, 212
Hall, Martha IV, 215
Hall, Martha IV, 334
Hall, Martha IV, 368
Hall, Martha IV, 378
Hall, Martha IV, 399
Hall, Martha IV, 400
Hall, Martha IV, 401
Hall, Martha IV, 406
Hall, Martha IV, 410
Hall, Martha IV, 444
Hall, Martha IV, 528
Hall, Martha IV, 558
Hall, Martha IV, 581
Hall, Martha IV, 582
Hall, Martha IV, 594
Hall, Martha IV, 628
Hall, Martha IV, 629
Hall, Martha IV, 635
Hall, Martha IV, 657
Hall, Martha IV, 667
Hall, Martha IV, 699
Hall, Martha IV, 710
Hall, Martha IV, 715
Hall, Martha IV, 740
Hall, Martha IV, 768
Hall, Martha IV, 816
Hall, Martha IV, 1318
Hall, Martha VI, 799
Hall, Martha VI, 823
Hall, Martha VI, 926
Hall, Martha A. I, 215
Hall, Martha Ann I, 234
Hall, Martha Ann I, 240
Hall, Martha B. IV, 215
Hall, Martha E. IV, 387
Hall, Martha E. IV, 400
Hall, Martha F. IV, 629
Hall, Martha F. IV, 646
Hall, Martha F. IV, 715
Hall, Martha Farquhar IV, 399
Hall, Martha Frances IV, 628
Hall, Martha Frances IV, 629
Hall, Martha Frances IV, 715
Hall, Martha Frances IV, 741
Hall, Martha H. IV, 195
Hall, Martha H. IV, 401
Hall, Martha Hollingsworth IV, 402
Hall, Martha Hollingsworth IV, 628
Hall, Martha Hollingsworth IV, 819
Hall, Martha J. I, 240
Hall, Martha Jane I, 215
Hall, Martha P. IV, 627
Hall, Martha P. IV, 629
Hall, Martha P. IV, 657
Hall, Martha S. II, 150
Hall, Martha S. IV, 628
Hall, Martha S. IV, 629
Hall, Martha S. IV, 715
Hall, Martha W. IV, 1054
Hall, Martha W. IV, 1060
Hall, Mary I, 215
Hall, Mary I, 240
Hall, Mary I, 288
Hall, Mary I, 302
Hall, Mary I, 304
Hall, Mary I, 307
Hall, Mary I, 542
Hall, Mary I, 812
Hall, Mary I, 815
Hall, Mary I, 932
Hall, Mary I, 1027
Hall, Mary I, 1030
Hall, Mary II, 30
Hall, Mary II, 58
Hall, Mary II, 68
Hall, Mary II, 75
Hall, Mary II, 100
Hall, Mary II, 444
Hall, Mary II, 539
Hall, Mary III, 145
Hall, Mary III, 171
Hall, Mary IV, 36
Hall, Mary IV, 39
Hall, Mary IV, 148
Hall, Mary IV, 170
Hall, Mary IV, 176
Hall, Mary IV, 182
Hall, Mary IV, 189
Hall, Mary IV, 198
Hall, Mary IV, 212
Hall, Mary IV, 214
Hall, Mary IV, 215
Hall, Mary IV, 216
Hall, Mary IV, 260
Hall, Mary IV, 266
Hall, Mary IV, 276
Hall, Mary IV, 289
Hall, Mary IV, 334
Hall, Mary IV, 365
Hall, Mary IV, 366
Hall, Mary IV, 369
Hall, Mary IV, 381
Hall, Mary IV, 388
Hall, Mary IV, 398
Hall, Mary IV, 399
Hall, Mary IV, 401
Hall, Mary IV, 402
Hall, Mary IV, 405
Hall, Mary IV, 444
Hall, Mary IV, 474
Hall, Mary IV, 511
Hall, Mary IV, 518
Hall, Mary IV, 521
Hall, Mary IV, 528
Hall, Mary IV, 569
Hall, Mary IV, 576
Hall, Mary IV, 578
Hall, Mary IV, 581
Hall, Mary IV, 584
Hall, Mary IV, 588
Hall, Mary IV, 627
Hall, Mary IV, 628
Hall, Mary IV, 710
Hall, Mary IV, 715
Hall, Mary IV, 740
Hall, Mary IV, 816
Hall, Mary IV, 819
Hall, Mary IV, 845
Hall, Mary IV, 906
Hall, Mary IV, 911
Hall, Mary IV, 934
Hall, Mary IV, 942
Hall, Mary IV, 960
Hall, Mary IV, 961
Hall, Mary IV, 1093
Hall, Mary IV, 1099
Hall, Mary IV, 1208
Hall, Mary IV, 1214
Hall, Mary V, 65
Hall, Mary VI, 29
Hall, Mary VI, 36
Hall, Mary VI, 397
Hall, Mary VI, 408
Hall, Mary VI, 494
Hall, Mary VI, 501
Hall, Mary VI, 926
Hall, Mary VI, 991
Hall, Mary A. II, 779
Hall, Mary Alice IV, 378
Hall, Mary Alice IV, 400
Hall, Mary Alice IV, 402
Hall, Mary Alice VI, 645
Hall, Mary Alice VI, 672
Hall, Mary Ann IV, 401
Hall, Mary Anna IV, 401
Hall, Mary Anna IV, 621
Hall, Mary Anna IV, 628
Hall, Mary Anna IV, 960
Hall, Mary Anna IV, 961
Hall, Mary Anna E. IV, 402
Hall, Mary B. II, 706
Hall, Mary B. II, 744
Hall, Mary B. IV, 400
Hall, Mary B. IV, 401
Hall, Mary B. IV, 402
Hall, Mary B. IV, 1208
Hall, Mary B. IV, 1236
Hall, Mary Bailey IV, 408
Hall, Mary Bell IV, 400
Hall, Mary Belle IV, 400
Hall, Mary C. IV, 171
Hall, Mary C. IV, 213
Hall, Mary C. IV, 214
Hall, Mary C. IV, 215
Hall, Mary C. IV, 282
Hall, Mary C. IV, 528
Hall, Mary C. IV, 797
Hall, Mary C. IV, 815
Hall, Mary C. IV, 819
Hall, Mary C. IV, 820
Hall, Mary C. IV, 826
Hall, Mary C. IV, 839
Hall, Mary C. IV, 844
Hall, Mary C. IV, 961
Hall, Mary Cameron IV, 216
Hall, Mary D. IV, 369
Hall, Mary D. IV, 402
Hall, Mary E. IV, 961
Hall, Mary E. IV, 1038
Hall, Mary E. V, 999
Hall, Mary E. VI, 957
Hall, Mary Edith IV, 276
Hall, Mary Eliza IV, 213
Hall, Mary Eliza IV, 215
Hall, Mary Eliza IV, 234
Hall, Mary Eliza IV, 960
Hall, Mary Eliza IV, 961
Hall, Mary Elizabeth II, 669
Hall, Mary Ellen II, 706
Hall, Mary Ellen IV, 960
Hall, Mary Emiline V, 391
Hall, Mary Estella VI, 736
Hall, Mary Estella VI, 745
Hall, Mary Esther IV, 961
Hall, Mary Eva IV, 400
Hall, Mary Eva IV, 401
Hall, Mary Eva IV, 402
Hall, Mary Eva IV, 459
Hall, Mary F. III, 145
Hall, Mary F. III, 214
Hall, Mary H. IV, 582
Hall, Mary H. IV, 792
Hall, Mary Jones I, 812
Hall, Mary L. I, 1154
Hall, Mary L. III, 145
Hall, Mary L. IV, 401
Hall, Mary L. IV, 528
Hall, Mary O. I, 240
Hall, Mary P. IV, 213
Hall, Mary P. IV, 276
Hall, Mary P. IV, 399
Hall, Mary P. IV, 550
Hall, Mary Rebecca IV, 581
Hall, Mary Rebecca IV, 601
Hall, Mary S. IV, 366
Hall, Mary T. IV, 176
Hall, Mary T. IV, 180
Hall, Mary T. IV, 213
Hall, Mary T. IV, 214
Hall, Mary T. IV, 246
Hall, Mary T. IV, 282
Hall, Mary T. IV, 285

Hall, Mary T. IV, 528
Hall, Mary W. IV, 400
Hall, Mary Webster IV, 400
Hall, Maryanna IV, 629
Hall, Maryanna E. IV, 961
Hall, Matthew II, 999
Hall, Matthew VI, 926
Hall, Matthew VI, 957
Hall, Matthew, Jr. VI, 891
Hall, Matthew, Jr. VI, 926
Hall, Matthew, Jr. VI, 957
Hall, Matthew, Sr. VI, 890
Hall, Matthew, Sr. VI, 939
Hall, May IV, 215
Hall, May Vestal I, 941
Hall, Melinda VI, 926
Hall, Melissa IV, 618
Hall, Melissa IV, 627
Hall, Melissa IV, 628
Hall, Melissa IV, 693
Hall, Melissa IV, 715
Hall, Melissa C. IV, 715
Hall, Melissa H. IV, 400
Hall, Mellisa C. IV, 628
Hall, Merab IV, 212
Hall, Merab IV, 214
Hall, Merab IV, 215
Hall, Merab IV, 324
Hall, Merab IV, 334
Hall, Merel IV, 715
Hall, Meriam I, 307
Hall, Meriba IV, 215
Hall, Meribah II, 974
Hall, Meribah II, 999
Hall, Mic IV, 215
Hall, Mic??? IV, 215
Hall, Midlred R. IV, 582
Hall, Mifflin IV, 401
Hall, Mildred IV, 581
Hall, Mildred IV, 628
Hall, Mildred IV, 629
Hall, Mildred IV, 960
Hall, Mildred IV, 961
Hall, Mildred Olive IV, 819
Hall, Mildred R. IV, 820
Hall, Mildred Rachel IV, 582
Hall, Mildred Rachel IV, 813
Hall, Mildred Rachel IV, 819
Hall, Milford T. IV, 399
Hall, Milicent IV, 261
Hall, Milicent IV, 398
Hall, Milicent IV, 405
Hall, Milicent IV, 528
Hall, Milicent IV, 581
Hall, Millicent IV, 213
Hall, Millicent IV, 215
Hall, Millicent IV, 272
Hall, Millicent IV, 282
Hall, Millicent IV, 398
Hall, Millicent IV, 401
Hall, Millicent IV, 581
Hall, Millicent IV, 715
Hall, Millicent IV, 819
Hall, Millicent IV, 841
Hall, Milton IV, 399
Hall, Milton IV, 402
Hall, Milton J. VI, 926
Hall, Minerva A. VI, 926
Hall, Minnie IV, 628
Hall, Minnie C. IV, 629
Hall, Minnie C. IV, 961
Hall, Minnie Catharine IV, 581
Hall, Minnie Catharine IV, 629
Hall, Minnie Catharine IV, 960
Hall, Minnie Catharine IV, 961
Hall, Minnie Catherine IV, 961
Hall, Miriam I, 240
Hall, Miriam I, 288
Hall, Miriam I, 304
Hall, Miriam I, 307
Hall, Miriam IV, 213
Hall, Miriam IV, 214
Hall, Miriam IV, 385
Hall, Miriam IV, 398
Hall, Miriam IV, 574
Hall, Miriam IV, 585
Hall, Miriam IV, 623
Hall, Miriam IV, 627
Hall, Miriam IV, 628
Hall, Miriam C. IV, 213
Hall, Miriam P. IV, 1054
Hall, Miriam P. IV, 1060
Hall, Mollie I, 286
Hall, Molly VI, 926
Hall, Morris II, 30
Hall, Morris II, 75
Hall, Morris II, 93
Hall, Morris II, 112
Hall, Morris II, 132
Hall, Morris II, 137
Hall, Morris II, 143
Hall, Morris II, 149
Hall, Morris II, 797
Hall, Morris Franklin II, 30
Hall, Morris, Jr. II, 119
Hall, Morris, Jr. II, 133
Hall, Moses I, 51
Hall, Moses I, 216
Hall, Moses I, 233
Hall, Moses I, 240
Hall, Moses I, 288
Hall, Moses IV, 147
Hall, Moses IV, 148
Hall, Moses IV, 398
Hall, Moses IV, 426
Hall, Moses IV, 581
Hall, Moses V, 391
Hall, Moses VI, 23
Hall, Moses VI, 28
Hall, Moses VI, 29
Hall, Moses VI, 30
Hall, Moses VI, 34
Hall, Mr. ??? VI, 9
Hall, Myrtle D. IV, 402
Hall, Myrtle D. IV, 429
Hall, Myrtle E. I, 1154
Hall, Nancy IV, 401
Hall, Nancy IV, 449
Hall, Nancy IV, 819
Hall, Nancy VI, 844
Hall, Nancy VI, 926
Hall, Naomi II, 75
Hall, Naomia II, 75
Hall, Narville Lloyd IV, 401
Hall, Nathan I, 288
Hall, Nathan I, 307
Hall, Nathan IV, 148
Hall, Nathan IV, 212
Hall, Nathan IV, 213
Hall, Nathan IV, 214
Hall, Nathan IV, 215
Hall, Nathan IV, 304
Hall, Nathan IV, 305
Hall, Nathan IV, 398
Hall, Nathan IV, 399
Hall, Nathan IV, 401
Hall, Nathan IV, 429
Hall, Nathan IV, 435
Hall, Nathan IV, 453
Hall, Nathan IV, 455
Hall, Nathan IV, 528
Hall, Nathan IV, 558
Hall, Nathan L. IV, 214
Hall, Nathan L. IV, 215
Hall, Nathan P. II, 706
Hall, Nathan P. II, 871
Hall, Nathan P. II, 878
Hall, Nathan P. IV, 212
Hall, Nathan P. IV, 213
Hall, Nathan P. IV, 214
Hall, Nathan P. IV, 215
Hall, Nathan P. IV, 288
Hall, Nathan P. IV, 305
Hall, Nathan P. IV, 324
Hall, Nathan P. IV, 334
Hall, Nathan P. IV, 399
Hall, Nathan P. IV, 528
Hall, Nathan P. IV, 558
Hall, Nathan P. IV, 627
Hall, Nathan P. IV, 628
Hall, Nathan P. IV, 715
Hall, Nathan R. IV, 715
Hall, Nathaniel II, 30
Hall, Nathaniel II, 75
Hall, Nathaniel II, 100
Hall, Nathel IV, 215
Hall, Nellie IV, 1318
Hall, Nellie R. IV, 582
Hall, Nellie R. IV, 961
Hall, Nellie Ruth IV, 581
Hall, Nellie Ruth IV, 628
Hall, Nellie Ruth IV, 629
Hall, Nellie Ruth IV, 960
Hall, Nellie Ruth IV, 961
Hall, Nethaniel II, 58
Hall, Nethaniel II, 75
Hall, Nettie M. IV, 628
Hall, Nettie M. IV, 629
Hall, Nettie M. IV, 960
Hall, Nettie M. IV, 961
Hall, Noah IV, 398
Hall, Noah IV, 401
Hall, Noah IV, 528
Hall, Norris Folger III, 132
Hall, Norris Folger III, 145
Hall, Ogden R. IV, 213
Hall, Olive IV, 213
Hall, Olive IV, 819
Hall, Olive IV, 843
Hall, Olive H. IV, 215
Hall, Olive H. IV, 256
Hall, Olive H. IV, 819
Hall, Olive H. IV, 836
Hall, Olive W. IV, 402
Hall, Olive W. IV, 403
Hall, Olive W. IV, 424
Hall, Olive Winifred IV, 401
Hall, Oliver Horace IV, 961
Hall, Oliver Margaret IV, 581
Hall, Oliver W. IV, 213
Hall, Orpha IV, 838
Hall, Orpha J. IV, 819
Hall, Orpha J. IV, 820
Hall, Oscar C. IV, 961
Hall, Oscar Charles IV, 628
Hall, Oscar Charles IV, 629
Hall, Oscar Charles IV, 961
Hall, P. Sharpless II, 871
Hall, Parker IV, 184
Hall, Parker IV, 212
Hall, Parker IV, 213
Hall, Parker IV, 214
Hall, Parker IV, 215
Hall, Parker IV, 222
Hall, Parker IV, 302
Hall, Parker IV, 375
Hall, Parker IV, 400
Hall, Parker IV, 528
Hall, Parker IV, 531
Hall, Parthena II, 370
Hall, Patsy VI, 926
Hall, Paxton IV, 213
Hall, Payson I, 812
Hall, Pearson IV, 213
Hall, Pearson IV, 215
Hall, Pearson IV, 623
Hall, Pearson IV, 627
Hall, Pearson IV, 628
Hall, Penina IV, 400
Hall, Peninah I, 289
Hall, Peninah I, 307
Hall, Peninah I, 314
Hall, Peninah IV, 212
Hall, Peninah IV, 334
Hall, Peninah IV, 381
Hall, Peninah IV, 398
Hall, Peninah IV, 399
Hall, Penninah IV, 148
Hall, Penninah IV, 215
Hall, Perley IV, 403
Hall, Perley J. IV, 400
Hall, Peter IV, 276
Hall, Pharaba I, 233
Hall, Pharaba I, 240
Hall, Pharaby I, 216
Hall, Phebe I, 1048
Hall, Phebe II, 871
Hall, Phebe IV, 147
Hall, Phebe IV, 163
Hall, Phebe IV, 215
Hall, Phebe IV, 334
Hall, Phebe IV, 398
Hall, Phebe IV, 399
Hall, Phebe IV, 400
Hall, Phebe IV, 401
Hall, Phebe IV, 402
Hall, Phebe IV, 412
Hall, Phebe IV, 414
Hall, Phebe IV, 435
Hall, Phebe IV, 452
Hall, Phebe IV, 528
Hall, Phebe IV, 819
Hall, Phebe IV, 1236
Hall, Phebe V, 391
Hall, Phebe E. IV, 629
Hall, Phebe E. IV, 633
Hall, Phebe Elma IV, 213
Hall, Phebe Elma IV, 215
Hall, Phebe Elma IV, 627
Hall, Phebe Elma IV, 628
Hall, Phebe H. IV, 402
Hall, Phebe Jane IV, 401
Hall, Phebe T. II, 711
Hall, Phebe T. II, 744
Hall, Phebe T. II, 753
Hall, Philip Sharpless II, 871
Hall, Phineas I, 215
Hall, Phinehas I, 240
Hall, Piety I, 288
Hall, Piety I, 307
Hall, Piety IV, 398
Hall, Piety IV, 401
Hall, Piety IV, 407
Hall, Polly VI, 799
Hall, Polly VI, 926
Hall, Preston II, 30
Hall, Price I, 289
Hall, Price I, 307
Hall, Price F. V, 806
Hall, Price F. V, 809
Hall, Pricilla VI, 926
Hall, Priscilla II, 960
Hall, Priscilla IV, 398
Hall, Priscilla IV, 399
Hall, Priscilla IV, 401
Hall, Priscilla IV, 407
Hall, Priscilla IV, 447
Hall, Prudence II, 30
Hall, Prudence II, 72
Hall, Prudence II, 75
Hall, Prudence II, 119
Hall, Prudence II, 132
Hall, Prudence II, 149
Hall, Prudence II, 154
Hall, R. Edith V, 570
Hall, Rachel I, 270
Hall, Rachel I, 289
Hall, Rachel I, 307
Hall, Rachel II, 30
Hall, Rachel II, 75
Hall, Rachel II, 97
Hall, Rachel II, 444
Hall, Rachel II, 706
Hall, Rachel IV, 36
Hall, Rachel IV, 169
Hall, Rachel IV, 212
Hall, Rachel IV, 214
Hall, Rachel IV, 215
Hall, Rachel IV, 289
Hall, Rachel IV, 305
Hall, Rachel IV, 399
Hall, Rachel IV, 402
Hall, Rachel IV, 404
Hall, Rachel IV, 528
Hall, Rachel IV, 558
Hall, Rachel IV, 579
Hall, Rachel IV, 581
Hall, Rachel IV, 627
Hall, Rachel IV, 628
Hall, Rachel IV, 715
Hall, Rachel Amy IV, 215
Hall, Rachel G. II, 706
Hall, Rachel G. II, 744
Hall, Rachel G. IV, 399
Hall, Rachel G. IV, 402
Hall, Rachel M. IV, 213
Hall, Rachel M. IV, 214
Hall, Rachel W. II, 706
Hall, Rachel W. II, 744
Hall, Rachel W. III, 145
Hall, Rachel W. III, 295
Hall, Rachel W. IV, 528
Hall, Rachel W. IV, 627
Hall, Rachel W. IV, 628
Hall, Ralph IV, 819
Hall, Ralph Harlan IV, 628
Hall, Raymond Lindley IV, 819
Hall, Rebecca II, 30
Hall, Rebecca II, 75
Hall, Rebecca II, 76
Hall, Rebecca II, 98
Hall, Rebecca II, 110
Hall, Rebecca II, 112
Hall, Rebecca II, 119
Hall, Rebecca II, 132
Hall, Rebecca II, 133
Hall, Rebecca II, 149
Hall, Rebecca II, 154
Hall, Rebecca II, 960
Hall, Rebecca II, 999
Hall, Rebecca II, 1022
Hall, Rebecca IV, 176
Hall, Rebecca IV, 212
Hall, Rebecca IV, 213
Hall, Rebecca IV, 214
Hall, Rebecca IV, 215
Hall, Rebecca IV, 222
Hall, Rebecca IV, 396
Hall, Rebecca IV, 399
Hall, Rebecca IV, 528
Hall, Rebecca IV, 531
Hall, Rebecca IV, 960
Hall, Rebecca IV, 1060
Hall, Rebecca IV, 1075
Hall, Rebecca B. II, 133
Hall, Rebecca B. II, 150
Hall, Rebecca B. III, 145
Hall, Rebecca B. III, 150
Hall, Rebecca K. II, 133
Hall, Rebecca K. II, 150
Hall, Rebecca S. II, 706
Hall, Rebecca S. II, 744
Hall, Rebecca S. IV, 208
Hall, Rebecca S. IV, 214
Hall, Rebecca S. IV, 627
Hall, Rebecca S. IV, 628
Hall, Rebecca S. IV, 961
Hall, Rebecca W. IV, 387
Hall, Rebecca W. IV, 399
Hall, Rebecca W. IV, 1060
Hall, Rebecca W. IV, 1075
Hall, Rebecka II, 75
Hall, Rebeckah II, 29
Hall, Rebeckah II, 30
Hall, Rebeckah II, 52
Hall, Rebeckah II, 75
Hall, Rebeckah II, 77
Hall, Rebeckah II, 78
Hall, Rhoda I, 716
Hall, Richard I, 289
Hall, Richard I, 307
Hall, Richard VI, 795
Hall, Richard VI, 926
Hall, Richard Albert IV, 401
Hall, Rinda I, 1154
Hall, Robert I, 215
Hall, Robert I, 240
Hall, Robert I, 288
Hall, Robert II, 960
Hall, Robert IV, 212
Hall, Robert IV, 214
Hall, Robert IV, 334
Hall, Robert IV, 521
Hall, Robert IV, 528
Hall, Robert IV, 558
Hall, Robert IV, 581
Hall, Robert IV, 594
Hall, Robert IV, 710
Hall, Robert IV, 816
Hall, Robert IV, 1093
Hall, Robert IV, 1099
Hall, Robert VI, 825
Hall, Robert M. I, 812
Hall, Rodah I, 698
Hall, Rodra II, 30
Hall, Ronald J. IV, 402
Hall, Ronald J. IV, 581
Hall, Ronald Joseph IV, 402
Hall, Rosetta IV, 387
Hall, Rosetta IV, 399
Hall, Rosetta IV, 400
Hall, Rosetta IV, 566
Hall, Rosetta IV, 574
Hall, Rosetta IV, 575
Hall, Rosetta IV, 583
Hall, Rosetta IV, 586
Hall, Rosetta H. IV, 574
Hall, Rowland VI, 926
Hall, Rufus II, 871
Hall, Rufus IV, 819
Hall, Rufus M. IV, 906
Hall, Ruth I, 215
Hall, Ruth II, 465
Hall, Ruth II, 539
Hall, Ruth II, 999
Hall, Ruth IV, 398
Hall, Ruth IV, 401
Hall, Ruth V, 391
Hall, Ruth A. IV, 963
Hall, Ruthann IV, 399
Hall, Ruthanna IV, 961
Hall, Salley VI, 926
Hall, Sally VI, 818
Hall, Sally VI, 926
Hall, Sally B. VI, 926
Hall, Samuel I, 654
Hall, Samuel I, 698
Hall, Samuel I, 716
Hall, Samuel II, 30
Hall, Samuel II, 75
Hall, Samuel II, 110
Hall, Samuel IV, 199
Hall, Samuel IV, 213
Hall, Samuel IV, 214
Hall, Samuel IV, 215
Hall, Samuel IV, 235
Hall, Samuel IV, 254
Hall, Samuel IV, 400
Hall, Samuel VI, 926
Hall, Samuel D. II, 871
Hall, Sana A. IV, 693
Hall, Sara IV, 581
Hall, Sara Mabel IV, 1013
Hall, Sara T. IV, 819
Hall, Sarah I, 51
Hall, Sarah I, 99
Hall, Sarah I, 100
Hall, Sarah I, 130
Hall, Sarah I, 138
Hall, Sarah I, 141
Hall, Sarah I, 158
Hall, Sarah I, 206
Hall, Sarah I, 215
Hall, Sarah I, 216
Hall, Sarah I, 231
Hall, Sarah I, 234
Hall, Sarah I, 240
Hall, Sarah I, 242
Hall, Sarah I, 251
Hall, Sarah I, 270
Hall, Sarah I, 288
Hall, Sarah I, 289
Hall, Sarah I, 304
Hall, Sarah I, 307
Hall, Sarah I, 312

ll, Sarah I, 679
ll, Sarah I, 698
ll, Sarah I, 716
ll, Sarah I, 812
ll, Sarah I, 1027
ll, Sarah I, 1030
ll, Sarah II, 30
ll, Sarah II, 49
ll, Sarah II, 56
ll, Sarah II, 58
ll, Sarah II, 75
ll, Sarah II, 82
ll, Sarah II, 95
ll, Sarah II, 110
ll, Sarah II, 119
ll, Sarah II, 127
ll, Sarah II, 129
ll, Sarah II, 132
ll, Sarah II, 133
ll, Sarah II, 140
ll, Sarah II, 143
ll, Sarah II, 144
ll, Sarah II, 149
ll, Sarah II, 150
ll, Sarah II, 151
ll, Sarah II, 229
ll, Sarah II, 539
ll, Sarah II, 871
ll, Sarah II, 960
ll, Sarah II, 999
ll, Sarah IV, 36
ll, Sarah IV, 91
ll, Sarah IV, 92
ll, Sarah IV, 148
ll, Sarah IV, 186
ll, Sarah IV, 212
ll, Sarah IV, 214
ll, Sarah IV, 215
ll, Sarah IV, 226
ll, Sarah IV, 289
ll, Sarah IV, 304
ll, Sarah IV, 369
ll, Sarah IV, 370
ll, Sarah IV, 387
ll, Sarah IV, 398
ll, Sarah IV, 399
ll, Sarah IV, 400
ll, Sarah IV, 401
ll, Sarah IV, 402
ll, Sarah IV, 405
ll, Sarah IV, 406
ll, Sarah IV, 416
ll, Sarah IV, 438
ll, Sarah IV, 442
ll, Sarah IV, 446
ll, Sarah IV, 452
ll, Sarah IV, 455
ll, Sarah IV, 528
ll, Sarah IV, 574
ll, Sarah IV, 581
ll, Sarah IV, 582
ll, Sarah IV, 586
ll, Sarah IV, 1207
ll, Sarah IV, 1208
ll, Sarah IV, 1236
ll, Sarah V, 391
ll, Sarah VI, 745
ll, Sarah VI, 926
ll, Sarah VI, 965
ll, Sarah VI, 995
ll, Sarah VI, 1014
ll, Sarah A. I, 1153
ll, Sarah Anise IV, 400
ll, Sarah Ann II, 871
ll, Sarah B. IV, 397
ll, Sarah B. IV, 399
ll, Sarah B. IV, 400
ll, Sarah B. IV, 402
ll, Sarah B. IV, 411
ll, Sarah B. IV, 459
ll, Sarah D. V, 809
ll, Sarah Doudna IV, 400
ll, Sarah E. IV, 960
ll, Sarah E. IV, 961
ll, Sarah Elizabeth I, 215
ll, Sarah Elma IV, 1038
ll, Sarah H. I, 812
ll, Sarah H. IV, 1038
ll, Sarah Honor I, 812
ll, Sarah J. II, 151
ll, Sarah L. II, 154
ll, Sarah L. IV, 627
ll, Sarah L. IV, 629
ll, Sarah L. IV, 637
ll, Sarah Louisa IV, 376
ll, Sarah Louisa Bundy IV, 402
ll, Sarah M. IV, 214
ll, Sarah M. IV, 402
ll, Sarah Mabel IV, 628
ll, Sarah Mabel IV, 961
Hall, Sarah Mable IV, 628
Hall, Sarah Mable IV, 664
Hall, Sarah Mable IV, 1012
Hall, Sarah Myrtie IV, 400
Hall, Sarah O. VI, 745
Hall, Sarah P. IV, 819
Hall, Sarah R. IV, 582
Hall, Sarah R. IV, 715
Hall, Sarah R. IV, 740
Hall, Sarah R. IV, 758
Hall, Sarah R. IV, 819
Hall, Sarah R. IV, 906
Hall, Sarah S. IV, 581
Hall, Sarah T. IV, 212
Hall, Sarah T. IV, 215
Hall, Sarah T. IV, 304
Hall, Sarah W. IV, 400
Hall, Silas I, 288
Hall, Silas I, 307
Hall, Silas IV, 214
Hall, Silas IV, 215
Hall, Silas IV, 401
Hall, Silas Hartley IV, 402
Hall, Silva I, 240
Hall, Silva I, 253
Hall, Silva I, 288
Hall, Silva IV, 363
Hall, Silvia IV, 398
Hall, Silvia IV, 426
Hall, Silvia Jane I, 307
Hall, Silvy I, 240
Hall, Silvy IV, 399
Hall, Sina IV, 215
Hall, Sina IV, 285
Hall, Sina IV, 617
Hall, Sina IV, 627
Hall, Sina IV, 628
Hall, Sina IV, 715
Hall, Sina IV, 770
Hall, Sina IV, 870
Hall, Sina A. IV, 400
Hall, Sina A. IV, 423
Hall, Sina Ann IV, 402
Hall, Sina Ann IV, 528
Hall, Sina W. IV, 213
Hall, Sina W. IV, 214
Hall, Sina W. IV, 303
Hall, Sinah IV, 628
Hall, Sinclair Smith IV, 402
Hall, Stanton IV, 715
Hall, Stephen I, 100
Hall, Stephen I, 141
Hall, Stephen II, 75
Hall, Stephen II, 100
Hall, Stephen III, 145
Hall, Stephen III, 150
Hall, Stephen IV, 369
Hall, Stephen IV, 398
Hall, Stephen IV, 401
Hall, Stephen IV, 528
Hall, Steven I, 99
Hall, Susan D. II, 871
Hall, Susan J. III, 312
Hall, Susanah I, 215
Hall, Susanah II, 539
Hall, Susanna I, 239
Hall, Susanna I, 240
Hall, Susanna I, 270
Hall, Susanna II, 628
Hall, Susanna II, 871
Hall, Susanna IV, 36
Hall, Susanna IV, 566
Hall, Susannah I, 215
Hall, Sylvia IV, 398
Hall, Sylvia IV, 399
Hall, Sylvia Jane IV, 401
Hall, Sylvia Jane IV, 439
Hall, Tabitah VI, 932
Hall, Tabitha IV, 214
Hall, Tabitha VI, 884
Hall, Tabitha VI, 902
Hall, Tabitha D. IV, 184
Hall, Tabitha D. IV, 215
Hall, Tabitha D. IV, 302
Hall, Tabitha D. IV, 375
Hall, Tabitha D. IV, 376
Hall, Tabitha D. IV, 400
Hall, Tabitha D. IV, 402
Hall, Tace IV, 213
Hall, Tacey IV, 212
Hall, Tacey IV, 260
Hall, Tacy IV, 212
Hall, Tacy IV, 215
Hall, Tacy IV, 235
Hall, Tacy IV, 266
Hall, Tacy IV, 334
Hall, Tacy IV, 381
Hall, Tacy IV, 389
Hall, Tacy IV, 399
Hall, Tacy IV, 400
Hall, Tacy IV, 438
Hall, Tacy IV, 528
Hall, Tacy IV, 581
Hall, Tacy IV, 819
Hall, Tacy IV, 829
Hall, Tacy IV, 960
Hall, Tacy IV, 1099
Hall, Tacy Ellen IV, 402
Hall, Tacy Ellen IV, 528
Hall, Tacy M. IV, 214
Hall, Tacy M. IV, 235
Hall, Tacy M. IV, 402
Hall, Tacy M. IV, 439
Hall, Tacy M. IV, 581
Hall, Tacy M. IV, 594
Hall, Tacy M. IV, 629
Hall, Tacy M. IV, 640
Hall, Tamson II, 138
Hall, Teresa I, 617
Hall, Theodore III, 145
Hall, Theodore G. III, 145
Hall, Theodore H. III, 145
Hall, Thomas I, 215
Hall, Thomas I, 240
Hall, Thomas I, 288
Hall, Thomas II, 30
Hall, Thomas II, 444
Hall, Thomas II, 999
Hall, Thomas II, 1043
Hall, Thomas IV, 212
Hall, Thomas IV, 213
Hall, Thomas IV, 215
Hall, Thomas IV, 260
Hall, Thomas IV, 398
Hall, Thomas IV, 528
Hall, Thomas IV, 906
Hall, Thomas V, 570
Hall, Thomas VI, 494
Hall, Thomas VI, 501
Hall, Thomas VI, 822
Hall, Thomas VI, 926
Hall, Thomas Austin IV, 213
Hall, Thomas Austin IV, 215
Hall, Thomas C. IV, 400
Hall, Thomas H. IV, 819
Hall, Thomas Henry IV, 399
Hall, Thomas Henry IV, 402
Hall, Thomas M. II, 132
Hall, Thomas P. IV, 387
Hall, Thomas P. IV, 399
Hall, Thomas Samuel VI, 745
Hall, Thomas V. II, 871
Hall, Thomas V. IV, 819
Hall, Thomas, Jr. IV, 214
Hall, Thomas, Jr. IV, 215
Hall, Thomas, Sr. IV, 213
Hall, Thos. IV, 176
Hall, Thos. IV, 182
Hall, Thos. IV, 189
Hall, Thos. IV, 212
Hall, Thos. IV, 276
Hall, Thos. IV, 289
Hall, Thos. V. II, 871
Hall, Tillman IV, 215
Hall, Tillman IV, 961
Hall, Tillman L. IV, 400
Hall, Tillman L. IV, 402
Hall, Tilman IV, 212
Hall, Tilman IV, 213
Hall, Tilman IV, 215
Hall, Tilman IV, 234
Hall, Tilman IV, 960
Hall, Tilman L. IV, 399
Hall, Tilman L. IV, 400
Hall, Tilman L. IV, 402
Hall, Usly VI, 926
Hall, Velina M. IV, 629
Hall, Velma M. IV, 628
Hall, Verna C. IV, 581
Hall, Verna C. IV, 584
Hall, Verna Cecelia IV, 582
Hall, Verna Idella IV, 400
Hall, Vesta M. IV, 402
Hall, Vesta M. IV, 407
Hall, Vesta M. IV, 628
Hall, Vesta M. IV, 633
Hall, Vestal M. IV, 407
Hall, Vestal M. IV, 628
Hall, W. Mifflin IV, 393
Hall, W. Mifflin IV, 401
Hall, W. Mifflin IV, 961
Hall, Walter II, 133
Hall, Walter II, 146
Hall, Walter II, 150
Hall, Walter IV, 400
Hall, Walter IV, 402
Hall, Walter IV, 581
Hall, Walter L. IV, 961
Hall, Walter Linton IV, 628
Hall, Walter Linton IV, 629
Hall, Walter Linton IV, 961
Hall, Walter N. IV, 213
Hall, Walter W. IV, 960
Hall, Walter W. IV, 961
Hall, Wd. Emma L. III, 145
Hall, Wd. Georgia III, 145
Hall, Wd. Hannah II, 979
Hall, Wd. Hannah II, 1043
Hall, Wd. Mary II, 539
Hall, Wd. Susannah II, 797
Hall, Wesley V, 740
Hall, Widow Jemima I, 679
Hall, Wilford IV, 400
Hall, Wilford IV, 402
Hall, Wilford IV, 411
Hall, Wilford IV, 459
Hall, Wilford F. IV, 628
Hall, Wilford L. IV, 403
Hall, Wilford L. IV, 961
Hall, Wilford L. IV, 986
Hall, Wilford Leland IV, 401
Hall, Wilford Leland IV, 403
Hall, Wilford Leland IV, 961
Hall, Wilford Linton IV, 401
Hall, Wilford Linton IV, 629
Hall, Wilford Linton IV, 960
Hall, Wilford Linton IV, 961
Hall, Wilford T. IV, 397
Hall, Wilford T. IV, 399
Hall, Wilfred Linton IV, 961
Hall, Willard IV, 214
Hall, Willard B. IV, 819
Hall, Willard B. IV, 820
Hall, Willard B. IV, 960
Hall, Willard B. IV, 961
Hall, Willard Barclay IV, 961
Hall, William I, 215
Hall, William I, 288
Hall, William I, 307
Hall, William I, 698
Hall, William I, 716
Hall, William II, 17
Hall, William II, 30
Hall, William IV, 212
Hall, William IV, 213
Hall, William IV, 214
Hall, William IV, 215
Hall, William IV, 398
Hall, William IV, 399
Hall, William IV, 400
Hall, William IV, 401
Hall, William IV, 410
Hall, William IV, 528
Hall, William IV, 627
Hall, William IV, 628
Hall, William IV, 819
Hall, William IV, 906
Hall, William V, 740
Hall, William VI, 822
Hall, William VI, 926
Hall, William A. I, 240
Hall, William Albert I, 215
Hall, William B. II, 706
Hall, William G. IV, 399
Hall, William G. IV, 628
Hall, William R. IV, 214
Hall, William R. IV, 216
Hall, William T. IV, 400
Hall, William, Jr. VI, 822
Hall, William, Sr. IV, 213
Hall, Williard B. IV, 216
Hall, Willis D. IV, 627
Hall, Willis D. IV, 628
Hall, Willis Herbert IV, 400
Hall, Wilmer IV, 399
Hall, Wilmer IV, 402
Hall, Wilmer Esther IV, 400
Hall, Wilmer J. IV, 961
Hall, Wilmer Jeremiah IV, 961
Hall, Wilmer L. IV, 213
Hall, Wilmer L. IV, 216
Hall, Wilmer L. IV, 401
Hall, Wilmer L. IV, 442
Hall, Wilmer L. IV, 715
Hall, Wilson IV, 212
Hall, Wilson IV, 215
Hall, Wilson IV, 285
Hall, Wilson IV, 627
Hall, Wilson IV, 628
Hall, Wilson IV, 715
Hall, Wilson IV, 770
Hall, Wilson IV, 870
Hall, Wilson Luther IV, 961
Hall, Wilson M. IV, 215
Hall, Wilson M. IV, 621
Hall, Wilson M. IV, 627
Hall, Wilson M. IV, 628
Hall, Wilson M. IV, 629
Hall, Wilson M. IV, 960
Hall, Wilson M. IV, 961
Hall, Wilson Mifflin IV, 401
Hall, Wilson Mifflin IV, 402
Hall, Wilson Mifflin IV, 961
Hall, Wm. II, 56
Hall, Wm. II, 75
Hall, Wm. II, 99
Hall, Wm. II, 127
Hall, Wm. II, 444
Hall, Wm. II, 539
Hall, Wm. II, 871
Hall, Wm. IV, 176
Hall, Wm. IV, 180
Hall, Wm. IV, 195
Hall, Wm. IV, 212
Hall, Wm. IV, 213
Hall, Wm. IV, 246
Hall, Wm. IV, 285
Hall, Wm. IV, 528
Hall, Wm. IV, 588
Hall, Wm. IV, 819
Hall, Wm. IV, 845
Hall, Wm. B. IV, 213
Hall, Wm. B. IV, 214
Hall, Wm. B. IV, 272
Hall, Wm. B. IV, 275
Hall, Wm. G. II, 706
Hall, Wm. G. II, 744
Hall, Wm. G. IV, 627
Hall, Wm. P. IV, 528
Hall, Wm. R. IV, 214
Hall, Wm. W. IV, 819
Hall, Wm., Jr. IV, 214
Hall, Wm., Jr. IV, 444
Hall, Zilpah IV, 148
Hall, Zilpah IV, 398
Hall, Zilpha I, 307
Hall, Zilpha IV, 401
Hall, Zilpha IV, 402
Hall, Zilpha IV, 405
Hall, Zilpha IV, 415
Hall, Zilpha IV, 416
Hall, Zilphia I, 288
Halladay, Abigail II, 744
Hallam, Elisabeth I, 141
Hallam, Elisabeth I, 169
Hallam, Elizabeth I, 141
Hallam, Thomas I, 141
Hallam, Thomas I, 172
Hallam, Widow Elizabeth I, 172
Hallam, William VI, 244
Halleck, Sarah E. IV, 794
Hallenbach, Fred W. III, 145
Hallet, Child III, 146
Hallet, Lydia III, 287
Hallet, Mary C. III, 146
Hallet, Phebe Ann III, 146
Hallet, Phebe Cornell III, 146
Hallet, Sarah III, 146
Hallet, William III, 146
Hallett, ??? III, 146
Hallett, Abraham S. III, 145
Hallett, Abraham S. III, 146
Hallett, Amy III, 40
Hallett, Amy III, 145
Hallett, Amy III, 146
Hallett, Amy III, 287
Hallett, Ann III, 145
Hallett, Ann III, 146
Hallett, Ann III, 344
Hallett, Eliza W. III, 145
Hallett, Elizabeth C. III, 146
Hallett, Esther II, 791
Hallett, Esther III, 145
Hallett, Esther III, 321
Hallett, Gideon III, 146
Hallett, Gideon III, 380
Hallett, Gideon III, 413
Hallett, Hannah III, 146
Hallett, Hannah Ann III, 146
Hallett, Hester III, 145
Hallett, Israel III, 146
Hallett, Israel C. III, 146
Hallett, James III, 87
Hallett, James III, 119
Hallett, James III, 146
Hallett, Jerimiah III, 146
Hallett, Joseph D. III, 146
Hallett, Lydia III, 146
Hallett, Mary III, 56
Hallett, Mary III, 146
Hallett, Mary III, 343
Hallett, Mary III, 413
Hallett, Mary Jane III, 243
Hallett, Naomi III, 107
Hallett, Naomi III, 146
Hallett, Oswego III, 119
Hallett, Phebe III, 87
Hallett, Phebe III, 119
Hallett, Phebe III, 145
Hallett, Phebe III, 146
Hallett, Phebe III, 233
Hallett, Phebe III, 321
Hallett, Phebe E. III, 413
Hallett, Phebe E. III, 439

Hallett, Priscilla A. III, 380
Hallett, Priscilla A. III, 381
Hallett, Rachel C. III, 146
Hallett, Richard III, 40
Hallett, Richard III, 145
Hallett, Richard III, 146
Hallett, Richard III, 343
Hallett, Richard S. III, 146
Hallett, Richard T. III, 413
Hallett, Sarah III, 119
Hallett, Sarah III, 146
Hallett, Sarah III, 344
Hallett, Thomas III, 145
Hallett, Thomas III, 146
Hallett, Thomas III, 321
Hallett, Thomas III, 413
Hallett, Wd. Naomi III, 146
Hallett, William P. III, 413
Hallett, Wm. Paxson III, 146
Halley, Alice A. VI, 930
Halley, Ann VI, 926
Halley, Anna VI, 926
Halley, Anne VI, 926
Halley, Augustine VI, 926
Halley, Bailey VI, 926
Halley, Bailey VI, 951
Halley, Bartholomew VI, 926
Halley, Bartholomew VI, 928
Halley, Benjamin VI, 926
Halley, Betsey VI, 926
Halley, Betsy VI, 926
Halley, Charles P. VI, 926
Halley, Cornelius VI, 920
Halley, Elijah VI, 887
Halley, Elijah VI, 926
Halley, Elijah VI, 958
Halley, Elijah VI, 983
Halley, Elizabeth VI, 920
Halley, Elizabeth VI, 926
Halley, Elizabeth VI, 930
Halley, Elizabeth H. VI, 1000
Halley, Fanny VI, 1018
Halley, Frances Ann VI, 958
Halley, Francis VI, 310
Halley, Francis VI, 885
Halley, Francis VI, 914
Halley, Francis VI, 922
Halley, Francis VI, 926
Halley, Francis VI, 1000
Halley, Francis VI, 1018
Halley, Francis, Jr. VI, 1019
Halley, Frankey VI, 949
Halley, Giles VI, 926
Halley, Giles VI, 1016
Halley, Grace I, 134
Halley, Grace I, 141
Halley, Henry VI, 926
Halley, Henry VI, 988
Halley, Henry VI, 989
Halley, John VI, 926
Halley, John VI, 983
Halley, John VI, 1004
Halley, Joshua VI, 877
Halley, Joshua VI, 926
Halley, Josiah C. VI, 930
Halley, Maildred VI, 926
Halley, Margaret VI, 926
Halley, Mary VI, 1016
Halley, Mary F. VI, 926
Halley, Mary P. VI, 989
Halley, Nancey VI, 1019
Halley, Nancy VI, 926
Halley, Nancy S. VI, 926
Halley, Prudence VI, 310
Halley, Prudence VI, 914
Halley, Rebeckah VI, 926
Halley, Richard VI, 926
Halley, Ruth VI, 928
Halley, Ruth VI, 983
Halley, Sally VI, 926
Halley, Samuel VI, 926
Halley, Sanford VI, 874
Halley, Sanford VI, 922
Halley, Sanford VI, 926
Halley, Sanford VI, 1007
Halley, Sarah VI, 926
Halley, Sarah Elizabeth VI, 926
Halley, Sebia VI, 922
Halley, Sophia P. VI, 926
Halley, Thomas VI, 926
Halley, Thomas VI, 930
Halley, Thomas T. VI, 926
Halley, Thos. M. VI, 926
Halley, William VI, 244
Halley, William VI, 310
Halley, William VI, 874
Halley, William VI, 914
Halley, William VI, 926
Halley, William VI, 981
Halley, William VI, 1021
Halley, Wm. VI, 924
Halliday, Abigail II, 744
Halliday, Alvah V, 683
Halliday, Amanda V, 683
Halliday, Elizabeth II, 539
Halliday, Hiram E. V, 683
Halliday, James IV, 1318
Halliday, James W. V, 683
Halliday, Jesse F. V, 683
Halliday, Jesse H. V, 683
Halliday, John III, 146
Halliday, Lorenzo D. V, 683
Halliday, Maggie IV, 1318
Halliday, Ruth V, 683
Hallingam, Catherine II, 539
Hallingam, Katherine II, 539
Hallman, Alma IV, 929
Hallman, Alma IV, 961
Hallock, ??? III, 148
Hallock, ??? III, 242
Hallock, ??? III, 422
Hallock, A. A. III, 483
Hallock, Aaron B. III, 146
Hallock, Aaron L. IV, 1364
Hallock, Abel IV, 1364
Hallock, Abigail III, 146
Hallock, Abigail III, 147
Hallock, Abigail III, 258
Hallock, Abigail III, 360
Hallock, Abigail III, 413
Hallock, Abigail III, 414
Hallock, Abigail III, 436
Hallock, Abigail III, 437
Hallock, Abigail III, 466
Hallock, Abigail III, 468
Hallock, Abigail III, 470
Hallock, Abigail III, 471
Hallock, Alfred H. III, 483
Hallock, Alice J. III, 146
Hallock, Allan C. III, 146
Hallock, Allen C. III, 146
Hallock, Amey III, 414
Hallock, Amy III, 413
Hallock, Amy III, 459
Hallock, Ann III, 112
Hallock, Ann III, 146
Hallock, Ann III, 147
Hallock, Ann L. III, 60
Hallock, Ann L. III, 146
Hallock, Ann L. III, 151
Hallock, Anna III, 26
Hallock, Anna III, 147
Hallock, Anna III, 148
Hallock, Anna III, 320
Hallock, Anna III, 347
Hallock, Anna III, 414
Hallock, Anna III, 499
Hallock, Anna B. III, 146
Hallock, Anna B. III, 147
Hallock, Anna B. III, 242
Hallock, Anna B. III, 370
Hallock, Anna L. III, 146
Hallock, Anna U. III, 483
Hallock, Anna W. III, 146
Hallock, Anna W. III, 169
Hallock, Benajah IV, 1364
Hallock, Burling I, 216
Hallock, Burling III, 147
Hallock, Burling III, 242
Hallock, C. D. III, 483
Hallock, Cath. III, 437
Hallock, Catharine III, 413
Hallock, Catharine III, 414
Hallock, Catherine III, 146
Hallock, Catherine III, 360
Hallock, Catherine IV, 1364
Hallock, Charles III, 318
Hallock, Charles B. III, 148
Hallock, Clemence III, 468
Hallock, Clement III, 413
Hallock, Clement III, 414
Hallock, Daniel III, 146
Hallock, Daniel P. IV, 1364
Hallock, David III, 146
Hallock, David III, 413
Hallock, David III, 488
Hallock, David S. III, 483
Hallock, David S. III, 488
Hallock, Dinah III, 407
Hallock, Dinah III, 414
Hallock, Dorcas III, 413
Hallock, Dorothy Vail III, 147
Hallock, Dr. James C. III, 147
Hallock, Drake III, 318
Hallock, Edward III, 148
Hallock, Edward III, 399
Hallock, Edward III, 413
Hallock, Edward III, 414
Hallock, Edward III, 483
Hallock, Edward III, 499
Hallock, Edward B. III, 146
Hallock, Edward V. III, 413
Hallock, Eleanor III, 218
Hallock, Elinor III, 146
Hallock, Eliz P. III, 146
Hallock, Eliz. III, 147
Hallock, Eliz. III, 148
Hallock, Eliz. M. III, 147
Hallock, Eliz. M. III, 217
Hallock, Eliza. III, 483
Hallock, Elizabeh III, 148
Hallock, Elizabeth III, 91
Hallock, Elizabeth III, 146
Hallock, Elizabeth III, 147
Hallock, Elizabeth III, 241
Hallock, Elizabeth III, 381
Hallock, Elizabeth III, 385
Hallock, Elizabeth III, 413
Hallock, Elizabeth III, 414
Hallock, Elizabeth III, 447
Hallock, Elizabeth III, 483
Hallock, Elizabeth A. III, 147
Hallock, Elizabeth A. III, 370
Hallock, Elizabeth C. III, 146
Hallock, Elizabeth F. III, 218
Hallock, Elizabeth M. III, 128
Hallock, Elizabeth M. III, 146
Hallock, Elizabeth M. III, 147
Hallock, Emma Amelia III, 147
Hallock, Ernest A. III, 320
Hallock, Frederick E. III, 218
Hallock, George III, 147
Hallock, George D. III, 147
Hallock, Grace III, 147
Hallock, Grace III, 242
Hallock, Guildford III, 147
Hallock, Hallock R. III, 218
Hallock, Hannah III, 62
Hallock, Hannah III, 63
Hallock, Hannah III, 64
Hallock, Hannah III, 213
Hallock, Hannah III, 413
Hallock, Hannah III, 414
Hallock, Hannah III, 436
Hallock, Hannah III, 437
Hallock, Hannah III, 442
Hallock, Hannah III, 459
Hallock, Hannah IV, 1163
Hallock, Hannah IV, 1364
Hallock, Hannah J. IV, 1364
Hallock, Hannah L. III, 147
Hallock, Henrietta III, 397
Hallock, Henrietta III, 413
Hallock, Henrietta III, 414
Hallock, Henrietta B. III, 148
Hallock, Henry III, 26
Hallock, Henry III, 147
Hallock, Henry B. III, 146
Hallock, Henry B. III, 147
Hallock, Henry B. III, 242
Hallock, Henry B. III, 370
Hallock, Henry G. III, 147
Hallock, Henry H. III, 60
Hallock, Henry J. III, 146
Hallock, Henry J. III, 151
Hallock, Henry James III, 147
Hallock, Henry L. III, 147
Hallock, Henry L. III, 332
Hallock, Henry Lindsley III, 147
Hallock, Isaac C. III, 147
Hallock, Isaac P. III, 147
Hallock, Israel III, 147
Hallock, James III, 147
Hallock, James III, 148
Hallock, James III, 381
Hallock, James III, 483
Hallock, James VI, 177
Hallock, James VI, 178
Hallock, James VI, 397
Hallock, James C. III, 128
Hallock, James C. III, 146
Hallock, James C. III, 147
Hallock, James C. III, 217
Hallock, James C. III, 241
Hallock, James S. III, 488
Hallock, James, Jr. III, 147
Hallock, Jane III, 146
Hallock, Jane S. III, 488
Hallock, Jared C. IV, 1364
Hallock, Jas. C. III, 217
Hallock, Jesse III, 147
Hallock, Jesse III, 414
Hallock, John III, 146
Hallock, John III, 147
Hallock, John III, 258
Hallock, John III, 360
Hallock, John III, 413
Hallock, John III, 414
Hallock, John III, 436
Hallock, John III, 437
Hallock, John III, 458
Hallock, John III, 459
Hallock, John III, 466
Hallock, John III, 468
Hallock, John III, 471
Hallock, John D. III, 218
Hallock, John Townsend III, 112
Hallock, John Townsend III, 147
Hallock, John W. III, 147
Hallock, John, Jr. III, 147
Hallock, John, Jr. III, 177
Hallock, John, Jr. III, 414
Hallock, Josephine III, 147
Hallock, Josephine III, 332
Hallock, Joshua III, 488
Hallock, Juliette III, 261
Hallock, Katharine III, 414
Hallock, Katharine III, 436
Hallock, Katharine III, 471
Hallock, Katharine III, 473
Hallock, Keziah III, 488
Hallock, Latitia III, 488
Hallock, Lucy IV, 1364
Hallock, Lydia I, 216
Hallock, Lydia III, 147
Hallock, Lydia C. III, 147
Hallock, Lydia C. III, 241
Hallock, Malcolm T., Jr. III, 218
Hallock, Margaret III, 147
Hallock, Margaret III, 258
Hallock, Margaret III, 414
Hallock, Margaret III, 436
Hallock, Margaret E. III, 488
Hallock, Margt III, 437
Hallock, Marianna III, 147
Hallock, Marianna III, 242
Hallock, Martha III, 75
Hallock, Martha III, 147
Hallock, Martha III, 447
Hallock, Martha III, 488
Hallock, Martha M. IV, 1364
Hallock, Martha S. III, 483
Hallock, Martha S. III, 488
Hallock, Martha T. III, 483
Hallock, Martha T. III, 488
Hallock, Mary III, 147
Hallock, Mary III, 318
Hallock, Mary III, 373
Hallock, Mary III, 413
Hallock, Mary III, 414
Hallock, Mary III, 466
Hallock, Mary B. III, 147
Hallock, Mary E. III, 408
Hallock, Mary E. III, 414
Hallock, Mary Emma III, 147
Hallock, Mary Emma III, 242
Hallock, Mary M. III, 147
Hallock, Mary M. IV, 1364
Hallock, Mary M. ??? III, 147
Hallock, Mary W. III, 147
Hallock, Mercy W. III, 105
Hallock, Mercy W. III, 318
Hallock, Monzo IV, 1364
Hallock, Nathaniel III, 147
Hallock, Nicholas III, 381
Hallock, Nicholas III, 385
Hallock, Nicholas III, 408
Hallock, Nicholas III, 414
Hallock, Nicholas III, 483
Hallock, P. Francena III, 147
Hallock, P. Francena III, 217
Hallock, Patience III, 148
Hallock, Peter III, 414
Hallock, Peter III, 437
Hallock, Peter, Jr. III, 414
Hallock, Phebe III, 147
Hallock, Phebe III, 399
Hallock, Phebe III, 413
Hallock, Phebe III, 414
Hallock, Phebe III, 458
Hallock, Phebe III, 488
Hallock, Phebe Ann III, 148
Hallock, Phebe Ann III, 176
Hallock, Phebe B. III, 318
Hallock, Phebe F. III, 217
Hallock, Phebe F. III, 275
Hallock, Phebe Francena III, 147
Hallock, Phebe Francena III, 217
Hallock, Phebe H. Underhill III, 147
Hallock, Philadelphia III, 147
Hallock, Powel C. IV, 1364
Hallock, Powell IV, 1364
Hallock, Powell C. IV, 1364
Hallock, Rebekah III, 148
Hallock, Rebekah III, 279
Hallock, Reuben III, 147
Hallock, Reuben L. III, 147
Hallock, Richard III, 75
Hallock, Richard III, 414
Hallock, Richard B. III, 147
Hallock, Richard F. III, 147
Hallock, Richard Frost III, 147
Hallock, Samuel III, 146
Hallock, Samuel III, 414
Hallock, Sarah III, 147
Hallock, Sarah III, 148
Hallock, Sarah III, 177
Hallock, Sarah III, 340
Hallock, Sarah III, 407
Hallock, Sarah III, 414
Hallock, Sarah III, 421
Hallock, Sarah E. I, 216
Hallock, Sarah E. I, 240
Hallock, Sarah E. IV, 794
Hallock, Sarah Elizabeth III, 14
Hallock, Sarah Emily III, 147
Hallock, Sarah J. III, 147
Hallock, Sarah Jane III, 147
Hallock, Sarah W. III, 146
Hallock, Sarah W. III, 169
Hallock, Sherman N. III, 414
Hallock, Stephen III, 147
Hallock, Sybil J. III, 147
Hallock, Sybil J. III, 242
Hallock, Therese Marie III, 320
Hallock, Thomas III, 414
Hallock, Thomas B. III, 91
Hallock, Thomas B. III, 146
Hallock, Thomas B. III, 147
Hallock, Thomas B. III, 169
Hallock, Thomas B. III, 340
Hallock, Thomas Burling III, 27
Hallock, Thos. IV, 127
Hallock, Thos. B. III, 148
Hallock, Townsend S. III, 488
Hallock, Valentine H. III, 148
Hallock, Valentine H. III, 397
Hallock, Valentine H. III, 413
Hallock, Valentine H. III, 414
Hallock, William III, 146
Hallock, William III, 148
Hallock, William III, 176
Hallock, William III, 407
Hallock, William III, 413
Hallock, William III, 414
Hallock, William III, 447
Hallock, William Penn III, 147
Halloway, Abel VI, 403
Halloway, Abigail II, 466
Halloway, Abigail VI, 403
Halloway, Abner VI, 403
Halloway, Amos VI, 403
Halloway, Amos VI, 598
Halloway, Anna M. B. II, 744
Halloway, Anna Mary II, 744
Halloway, Asa VI, 403
Halloway, Charlotte VI, 403
Halloway, Clement P. II, 744
Halloway, Clementine II, 744
Halloway, David VI, 403
Halloway, Deborah IV, 549
Halloway, Deborah S. IV, 524
Halloway, Elizabeth V, 248
Halloway, Elizabeth VI, 403
Halloway, Ephraim VI, 403
Halloway, Ephraim W. II, 744
Halloway, George VI, 403
Halloway, Isaac IV, 524
Halloway, Isaac VI, 403
Halloway, Jacob, Jr. IV, 524
Halloway, James VI, 403
Halloway, James Arthur II, 744
Halloway, Jane II, 370
Halloway, John II, 540
Halloway, Levi VI, 403
Halloway, Margaret II, 370
Halloway, Maria IV, 73
Halloway, Mary II, 548
Halloway, Mary VI, 403
Halloway, Paton VI, 403
Halloway, Phebe VI, 403
Halloway, Philadelphia VI, 403
Halloway, Rachel VI, 403
Halloway, Rachel A. II, 744
Halloway, Rachel A. II, 753
Halloway, Rebecca IV, 524
Halloway, Rebecca IV, 539
Halloway, Rebecca Ann II, 744
Halloway, Rebekah VI, 592
Halloway, Rhoda IV, 75
Halloway, Robert VI, 403
Halloway, Robert S. IV, 549
Halloway, Ruth VI, 403
Halloway, Samuel VI, 403
Halloway, Sarah II, 540
Halloway, Sarah IV, 524
Halloway, Sarah VI, 403
Halloway, Tacy VI, 403
Halloway, Thomas VI, 403
Halloway, Thos. II, 370
Halloway, Tobias II, 466
Halloway, Tobias II, 540
Halloway, Tobias II, 548
Halloway, William VI, 403

Hallowel, Elizabeth II, 540
Hallowell, ??? II, 370
Hallowell, Abbie III, 148
Hallowell, Agnes II, 820
Hallowell, Alice VI, 746
Hallowell, Alice Sarah II, 799
Hallowell, Amelia II, 797
Hallowell, Amelia VI, 782
Hallowell, Amelia B. VI, 745
Hallowell, Amy II, 871
Hallowell, Amy II, 910
Hallowell, Ann II, 370
Hallowell, Ann II, 540
Hallowell, Ann II, 667
Hallowell, Ann II, 744
Hallowell, Ann II, 797
Hallowell, Ann II, 798
Hallowell, Ann II, 863
Hallowell, Ann II, 871
Hallowell, Ann II, 909
Hallowell, Ann II, 935
Hallowell, Ann VI, 745
Hallowell, Ann N. III, 148
Hallowell, Ann R. II, 871
Hallowell, Ann R. VI, 745
Hallowell, Anna II, 797
Hallowell, Anna II, 798
Hallowell, Anna II, 862
Hallowell, Anna II, 872
Hallowell, Anna III, 97
Hallowell, Anna C. II, 855
Hallowell, Anna C. II, 871
Hallowell, Anna E. II, 129
Hallowell, Anna Elgar II, 781
Hallowell, Anna Jenkins II, 862
Hallowell, Anna Jenkins II, 872
Hallowell, Anna N. III, 96
Hallowell, Anna Norwood III, 148
Hallowell, Anna R. VI, 745
Hallowell, Anna T. II, 871
Hallowell, Anna T. II, 923
Hallowell, Anna T. III, 107
Hallowell, Anna T. III, 148
Hallowell, Anna W. II, 129
Hallowell, Anne R. II, 871
Hallowell, Annie II, 825
Hallowell, Annie VI, 746
Hallowell, Anthony II, 370
Hallowell, Anthony II, 540
Hallowell, Anthony VI, 740
Hallowell, Anthony VI, 745
Hallowell, Barton II, 799
Hallowell, Belle II, 797
Hallowell, Benj. VI, 745
Hallowell, Benj. Shoemaker II, 797
Hallowell, Benjamin II, 370
Hallowell, Benjamin II, 911
Hallowell, Benjamin VI, 740
Hallowell, Benjamin VI, 745
Hallowell, Benjamin VI, 746
Hallowell, Benjamin VI, 760
Hallowell, Benjamin VI, 765
Hallowell, Benjamin VI, 766
Hallowell, Benjamin, Jr. II, 871
Hallowell, Benjamin, Jr. II, 872
Hallowell, Benjamin, Jr. II, 911
Hallowell, Benjamin, Jr. VI, 745
Hallowell, Caleb II, 540
Hallowell, Caleb II, 744
Hallowell, Caleb II, 797
Hallowell, Caleb II, 871
Hallowell, Caleb S. II, 797
Hallowell, Caleb S. II, 871
Hallowell, Caleb Shreve VI, 745
Hallowell, Caleb, Jr. II, 540
Hallowell, Caroline VI, 666
Hallowell, Caroline VI, 745
Hallowell, Caroline VI, 765
Hallowell, Caroline VI, 766
Hallowell, Catharine II, 370
Hallowell, Catherine II, 488
Hallowell, Charles II, 744
Hallowell, Charles II, 797
Hallowell, Charles II, 798
Hallowell, Charles II, 871
Hallowell, Charles VI, 745
Hallowell, Charles F. II, 871
Hallowell, Charles Fessenden III, 234
Hallowell, Charles I. II, 872
Hallowell, Charles T. II, 370
Hallowell, Charles T. II, 540
Hallowell, Charles T. II, 744
Hallowell, Charlotte B. W. II, 871
Hallowell, Charlotte B. W. II, 927
Hallowell, Charlotte Bartlett Wilhelmina II, 798
Hallowell, Chas T. II, 863
Hallowell, Chas. II, 797
Hallowell, Chas. II, 798
Hallowell, Chas. II, 871
Hallowell, Chas. Shreve II, 797
Hallowell, Chas. T. II, 798
Hallowell, Chas. T. II, 871
Hallowell, Chas. T. II, 909
Hallowell, Chas. T. II, 935
Hallowell, Chas. Tyson II, 797
Hallowell, Cornelia VI, 745
Hallowell, Daniel II, 825
Hallowell, Dorothy II, 540
Hallowell, Dr. Wm. II, 798
Hallowell, Edith VI, 745
Hallowell, Edith Macy II, 799
Hallowell, Edward II, 370
Hallowell, Edward II, 706
Hallowell, Edward II, 744
Hallowell, Edward II, 871
Hallowell, Edward Davis II, 798
Hallowell, Edward Hicks II, 798
Hallowell, Edward N. II, 871
Hallowell, Edward N. II, 927
Hallowell, Edward Needles II, 798
Hallowell, Edward S. VI, 746
Hallowell, Eleanor II, 370
Hallowell, Eleanor II, 540
Hallowell, Eleanor II, 744
Hallowell, Eleanor III, 107
Hallowell, Eleanor III, 148
Hallowell, Eleanor H. II, 769
Hallowell, Eliza Ann II, 799
Hallowell, Eliza M. VI, 746
Hallowell, Elizabeth II, 370
Hallowell, Elizabeth II, 540
Hallowell, Elizabeth II, 550
Hallowell, Elizabeth II, 613
Hallowell, Elizabeth II, 622
Hallowell, Elizabeth II, 796
Hallowell, Elizabeth II, 798
Hallowell, Elizabeth II, 826
Hallowell, Elizabeth II, 871
Hallowell, Elizabeth II, 999
Hallowell, Elizabeth III, 134
Hallowell, Elizabeth III, 148
Hallowell, Elizabeth V, 76
Hallowell, Elizabeth C. II, 855
Hallowell, Elizabeth C. II, 871
Hallowell, Elizabeth D. II, 871
Hallowell, Elizabeth K. II, 871
Hallowell, Elizabeth Kirk II, 820
Hallowell, Elizabeth Kirk II, 871
Hallowell, Elizabeth Kirk II, 923
Hallowell, Elizabeth M. II, 871
Hallowell, Elizabeth M. II, 872
Hallowell, Elizabeth M. VI, 745
Hallowell, Ellwood II, 798
Hallowell, Elmira II, 797
Hallowell, Emily II, 798
Hallowell, Emma II, 871
Hallowell, Emma VI, 745
Hallowell, Esther II, 799
Hallowell, Esther VI, 747
Hallowell, Esther F. III, 148
Hallowell, Esther F. III, 234
Hallowell, Esther Fisher III, 97
Hallowell, Esther Fisher III, 148
Hallowell, Fanny II, 797
Hallowell, Fanny F. II, 871
Hallowell, Florence VI, 746
Hallowell, Francis Jackson III, 148
Hallowell, Francis Miller VI, 746
Hallowell, Franklin II, 798
Hallowell, Franklin II, 871
Hallowell, Fred A. III, 234
Hallowell, Frederick T. III, 148
Hallowell, Garald W. II, 872
Hallowell, George II, 370
Hallowell, Gerald Wetherald II, 797
Hallowell, Hallowell III, 97
Hallowell, Hannah II, 370
Hallowell, Hannah II, 540
Hallowell, Hannah II, 577
Hallowell, Hannah Fletcher II, 787
Hallowell, Hannah Fletcher II, 788
Hallowell, Hannah P. II, 855
Hallowell, Hannah P. II, 856
Hallowell, Hannah P. II, 871
Hallowell, Hannah P. II, 927
Hallowell, Hannah P. III, 148
Hallowell, Hannah S. II, 871
Hallowell, Hannah S. II, 909
Hallowell, Harry II, 798
Hallowell, Henry C. VI, 745
Hallowell, Henry C. VI, 746
Hallowell, Henry C. VI, 766
Hallowell, Horace A. III, 97
Hallowell, Horace Bancroft III, 97
Hallowell, Irene III, 234
Hallowell, Isaac II, 798
Hallowell, Isaac R. Davis II, 871
Hallowell, Israel II, 370
Hallowell, Israel II, 540
Hallowell, Israel II, 613
Hallowell, Israel II, 681
Hallowell, Israel II, 813
Hallowell, J. Edgar II, 871
Hallowell, J. Elgar II, 923
Hallowell, J. Elgar VI, 746
Hallowell, J. W. III, 148
Hallowell, Jacob II, 370
Hallowell, James II, 540
Hallowell, James II, 797
Hallowell, James VI, 745
Hallowell, James B. VI, 746
Hallowell, James R. III, 148
Hallowell, James S. II, 292
Hallowell, James S. VI, 746
Hallowell, James S. VI, 782
Hallowell, Jane II, 540
Hallowell, Jane II, 871
Hallowell, Jane VI, 740
Hallowell, Jane VI, 745
Hallowell, Jeffries III, 483
Hallowell, Jeffries III, 489
Hallowell, John II, 370
Hallowell, John II, 488
Hallowell, John II, 515
Hallowell, John II, 532
Hallowell, John II, 540
Hallowell, John II, 550
Hallowell, John II, 577
Hallowell, John II, 613
Hallowell, John II, 667
Hallowell, John II, 706
Hallowell, John II, 744
Hallowell, John II, 769
Hallowell, John II, 798
Hallowell, John II, 871
Hallowell, John Edgar II, 129
Hallowell, John Elgar VI, 745
Hallowell, John W. III, 148
Hallowell, John White III, 148
Hallowell, John White, Jr. III, 148
Hallowell, John, Jr. II, 540
Hallowell, Joseph II, 370
Hallowell, Joseph II, 540
Hallowell, Joseph II, 550
Hallowell, Joseph II, 799
Hallowell, Joseph II, 806
Hallowell, Joseph G. III, 148
Hallowell, Joseph T. II, 540
Hallowell, Joshua L. II, 370
Hallowell, Joshua L. II, 540
Hallowell, Joshua L. II, 744
Hallowell, Joshua L. II, 797
Hallowell, Joshua L. II, 863
Hallowell, Joshua L. II, 871
Hallowell, Joshua Longstreth II, 797
Hallowell, Joshua Longstreth II, 798
Hallowell, Julia A. VI, 746
Hallowell, Julia Ann II, 799
Hallowell, Katherine II, 540
Hallowell, Lewis Bush II, 797
Hallowell, Lucretia Macy II, 799
Hallowell, Lydia III, 483
Hallowell, Lydia T. II, 871
Hallowell, Lydia T. II, 911
Hallowell, Margaret VI, 740
Hallowell, Margaret VI, 745
Hallowell, Margaret VI, 746
Hallowell, Margaret VI, 782
Hallowell, Margaret E. II, 871
Hallowell, Margaret E. II, 911
Hallowell, Margaret F. VI, 745
Hallowell, Margaret F. VI, 765
Hallowell, Maria II, 370
Hallowell, Marian III, 97
Hallowell, Marian H. III, 148
Hallowell, Martha II, 370
Hallowell, Martha II, 813
Hallowell, Mary II, 370
Hallowell, Mary II, 512
Hallowell, Mary II, 515
Hallowell, Mary II, 540
Hallowell, Mary II, 613
Hallowell, Mary II, 622
Hallowell, Mary II, 681
Hallowell, Mary II, 744
Hallowell, Mary II, 798
Hallowell, Mary II, 806
Hallowell, Mary II, 813
Hallowell, Mary II, 825
Hallowell, Mary II, 871
Hallowell, Mary II, 933
Hallowell, Mary III, 234
Hallowell, Mary VI, 745
Hallowell, Mary Ashbridge II, 798
Hallowell, Mary Ashbridge II, 820
Hallowell, Mary J. II, 797
Hallowell, Mary J. II, 798
Hallowell, Mary J. II, 871
Hallowell, Mary J. II, 909
Hallowell, Mary S. VI, 745
Hallowell, Mary S. VI, 746
Hallowell, Morris II, 909
Hallowell, Morris J., Jr. II, 871
Hallowell, Morris L. II, 540
Hallowell, Morris L. II, 744
Hallowell, Morris L. II, 855
Hallowell, Morris L. II, 856
Hallowell, Morris L. II, 871
Hallowell, Morris L. II, 927
Hallowell, Morris L. III, 148
Hallowell, Morris Longstreth II, 797
Hallowell, N. P. III, 96
Hallowell, Nathan III, 483
Hallowell, Nathan H. III, 148
Hallowell, Norwood III, 148
Hallowell, Norwood III, 160
Hallowell, Norwood P. II, 871
Hallowell, Norwood P. III, 47
Hallowell, Norwood P. III, 96
Hallowell, Norwood P. III, 148
Hallowell, Norwood Penrose II, 798
Hallowell, Norwood Penrose, Jr. III, 148
Hallowell, Phebe II, 370
Hallowell, Phebe II, 532
Hallowell, Phebe II, 540
Hallowell, Phebe III, 483
Hallowell, Phebe III, 488
Hallowell, Philip III, 148
Hallowell, Priscilla II, 797
Hallowell, Rachel II, 799
Hallowell, Rebecca II, 370
Hallowell, Rebecca II, 540
Hallowell, Rebecca II, 613
Hallowell, Rebecca II, 706
Hallowell, Rebecca II, 744
Hallowell, Rebecca II, 769
Hallowell, Rebecca B. III, 148
Hallowell, Rebecca B. III, 182
Hallowell, Rebecca P. II, 744
Hallowell, Rich. L. III, 148
Hallowell, Richard L. III, 148
Hallowell, Richard P. II, 856
Hallowell, Richard P. II, 871
Hallowell, Richard Price II, 798
Hallowell, Robert H. III, 148
Hallowell, Robert H. III, 182
Hallowell, Robert Haydock III, 148
Hallowell, Robert Haydock, Jr. III, 148
Hallowell, Robert S. VI, 745
Hallowell, Robt. Miller VI, 746
Hallowell, Roger Haydock III, 148
Hallowell, Ruth II, 232
Hallowell, Sallie C. II, 863
Hallowell, Sallie C. II, 871
Hallowell, Samuel Haydock III, 148
Hallowell, Samuel L. II, 370
Hallowell, Samuel L. II, 540
Hallowell, Samuel L. II, 871
Hallowell, Samuel Longstreth II, 797
Hallowell, Sara Ann II, 1073
Hallowell, Sarah II, 665
Hallowell, Sarah II, 667
Hallowell, Sarah II, 744
Hallowell, Sarah III, 148
Hallowell, Sarah VI, 745
Hallowell, Sarah VI, 746
Hallowell, Sarah VI, 766
Hallowell, Sarah Ann II, 798
Hallowell, Sarah Ann II, 1051
Hallowell, Sarah Ann II, 1059
Hallowell, Sarah Ann II, 1073
Hallowell, Sarah B. III, 160
Hallowell, Sarah Haydock III, 97
Hallowell, Sarah L. III, 483
Hallowell, Sarah L. III, 489
Hallowell, Sarah R. II, 730
Hallowell, Sarah R. II, 744
Hallowell, Sarah W. III, 47
Hallowell, Sarah W. III, 96
Hallowell, Sarah W. III, 148
Hallowell, Susan II, 772
Hallowell, Susan II, 798
Hallowell, Susan M. II, 871
Hallowell, Susan M. II, 935
Hallowell, Susan M. III, 47
Hallowell, Susan M. III, 148
Hallowell, Susan Morris II, 744
Hallowell, Susan Morris III, 148
Hallowell, Susan Verree II, 796
Hallowell, Susan Verree II, 820
Hallowell, Susan W. III, 234
Hallowell, Susanna II, 370
Hallowell, Susanna II, 986
Hallowell, Susanna II, 999
Hallowell, Susanna M. II, 540
Hallowell, Susanna Morris II, 540
Hallowell, Susannah II, 785
Hallowell, Susannah II, 871
Hallowell, Susannah Morris II, 825
Hallowell, Taressa K. II, 871
Hallowell, Theresa II, 797
Hallowell, Theresa II, 798
Hallowell, Thomas II, 370
Hallowell, Thomas II, 540
Hallowell, Thomas II, 665
Hallowell, Thomas II, 667
Hallowell, Thomas III, 488
Hallowell, Thomas C. III, 483
Hallowell, Thomas R. VI, 745
Hallowell, Wd. Caroline II, 825
Hallowell, William III, 107
Hallowell, William III, 148
Hallowell, William Ladd III, 148
Hallowell, William Penrose II, 798
Hallowell, William R. III, 414
Hallowell, Wm. II, 622
Hallowell, Wm. II, 999
Hallowell, Wm. Antrim II, 799
Hallowell, Wm. Antrim, Jr. II, 799
Hallowell, Wm. Ferris II, 797
Hallowell, Wm. Ferris II, 872
Hallowell, Wm. P. II, 855
Hallowell, Wm. P. II, 871
Hallowell, Wm. P., Jr. II, 871
Hallowell, Wm. R. II, 862
Hallowell, Wm. R. II, 872
Hallowell, Wm. S. II, 540
Hallowell, Wm. S. II, 622
Hallowell, Wm. S. II, 744
Hallowell, Wm. Satterthwaite II, 862
Hallowell, Wm. Satterthwaite II, 872
Hallowell, Wm., Jr. II, 999
Hallowell, Yarnall II, 798
Hallowell, Yarnall II, 820
Hallsey, William VI, 501
Hallwood, Henry IV, 1252
Hally, Elizabeth VI, 930
Hally, Permelia VI, 930
Hally, Terreal C. VI, 930
Halns, Lydia I, 824
Halsey, Amy V, 841
Halsey, Amy V, 868
Halsey, Edith III, 148
Halsey, Edith Judson III, 334
Halsey, George A. III, 148
Halsey, George A. III, 334
Halsey, Julia D. B. VI, 926
Halsey, Seth VI, 926
Halstead, ??? III, 369
Halstead, Adelaide III, 414
Halstead, Adelaide III, 442
Halstead, Catharine III, 311
Halstead, David, Jr. III, 483
Halstead, DeElla Harvey V, 570
Halstead, Hannah C. III, 369
Halstead, Henry P. III, 414
Halstead, Henry P. III, 442
Halstead, Jane III, 411
Halstead, Jane III, 414
Halstead, John III, 148
Halstead, John III, 179
Halstead, John F. III, 311
Halstead, Jonathan III, 148
Halstead, Mary III, 148
Halstead, Mary III, 179
Halstead, Phebe III, 129
Halstead, Phebe III, 148
Halstead, Philemon III, 411
Halstead, Philemon III, 414
Halstead, Samuel III, 148
Halstead, Sarah III, 411
Halstead, Sarah III, 414
Halstead, Sarah III, 462
Halstead, Sidney I, 935
Halstead, Sophia III, 148
Halstead, Sophia III, 253
Halstead, Stephen III, 129
Halstead, T. III, 369

Halstead, Thomas V, 173
Halstead, Timothy III, 462
Halsted, ??? III, 148
Halsted, Amanda III, 148
Halsted, Ann B. III, 148
Halsted, Anna III, 148
Halsted, Anna H. III, 148
Halsted, Catharine III, 148
Halsted, Catharine Ann III, 66
Halsted, Catharine Ann III, 148
Halsted, Catharine T. III, 148
Halsted, Catherine III, 148
Halsted, David III, 65
Halsted, David III, 148
Halsted, David F. III, 66
Halsted, David F. III, 148
Halsted, Esther III, 65
Halsted, Ezekiel III, 148
Halsted, Hannah C. T. III, 148
Halsted, John III, 148
Halsted, John F. III, 148
Halsted, Jonathan III, 148
Halsted, Mary III, 148
Halsted, Moses III, 148
Halsted, Naomi III, 65
Halsted, Patience III, 60
Halsted, Phebe III, 148
Halsted, Samuel III, 148
Halsted, Sophia III, 148
Halsted, Stephen III, 148
Halster, Anna H. III, 128
Halster, Moses III, 128
Halton, Abraham V, 496
Halton, Amos V, 496
Halton, Ann V, 496
Halton, Robert V, 496
Haly, Isom I, 1066
Haly, Lucy I, 393
Haly, Lucy I, 421
Ham, Alfred I, 542
Ham, Ann I, 781
Ham, Ann I, 812
Ham, Ann I, 822
Ham, Charles V, 65
Ham, Elisabeth I, 812
Ham, Elisabeth I, 822
Ham, Elizabeth I, 542
Ham, Elizabeth I, 781
Ham, Elizabeth I, 812
Ham, Elizabeth I, 813
Ham, Elizabeth I, 819
Ham, Emsley I, 812
Ham, Emsly I, 781
Ham, F. F. V, 570
Ham, Finley F. V, 570
Ham, Frankie IV, 1252
Ham, Fred V, 570
Ham, Hannah II, 540
Ham, Hannah II, 569
Ham, Hezekiah I, 542
Ham, Hezekiah I, 781
Ham, Hezekiah I, 812
Ham, Hezekiah I, 813
Ham, Hezekiah I, 839
Ham, Hezekiah I, 880
Ham, James IV, 1252
Ham, Jane I, 542
Ham, Jane I, 781
Ham, Jason I, 781
Ham, Jehu I, 781
Ham, Jehu I, 812
Ham, Joel I, 781
Ham, John I, 542
Ham, John I, 781
Ham, John I, 812
Ham, John I, 813
Ham, John I, 819
Ham, Lucy Elizabeth V, 570
Ham, Lucy Elizabeth V, 678
Ham, Marion F. V, 65
Ham, Martha I, 542
Ham, Martha I, 781
Ham, Martha V, 30
Ham, Martha V, 65
Ham, Martha V, 570
Ham, Martha V, 678
Ham, Martha Elizabeth V, 908
Ham, Martha J. V, 678
Ham, Martha Jane V, 570
Ham, Mary I, 781
Ham, Mary I, 812
Ham, Mary I, 880
Ham, Mary V, 65
Ham, Philip I, 542
Ham, Philip I, 773
Ham, Philip I, 781
Ham, Philip I, 812
Ham, Phillip I, 781
Ham, Priscilla I, 542
Ham, Priscilla I, 570
Ham, Priscilla I, 773
Ham, Priscilla I, 781
Ham, Priscilla I, 812
Ham, Priscilla I, 813
Ham, Priscilla I, 814
Ham, Priscilla I, 880
Ham, Rachel III, 414
Ham, Rachel III, 435
Ham, Robert II, 540
Ham, Sarah I, 781
Ham, Sarah I, 812
Ham, Sarah I, 813
Ham, Sarah I, 839
Ham, Sarah I, 880
Ham, Sarah, Jr. V, 334
Ham, Sarah, Jr. V, 358
Ham, Tacy V, 65
Ham, Tacy V, 94
Ham, Tacy Ellen V, 65
Ham, Thomas V, 65
Ham, William V, 65
Hambar, Martha II, 540
Hamblem, Mary I, 999
Hamblem, Rachel I, 999
Hamblen, Mary I, 986
Hambleton, Alexander VI, 927
Hambleton, Angelina II, 872
Hambleton, Ann IV, 629
Hambleton, Ann IV, 816
Hambleton, Ann IV, 820
Hambleton, Ann IV, 870
Hambleton, Ann IV, 944
Hambleton, Ann IV, 961
Hambleton, Ann IV, 1025
Hambleton, Ann VI, 953
Hambleton, Benj. IV, 629
Hambleton, Benjamin IV, 216
Hambleton, Benjamin IV, 629
Hambleton, Benjamin IV, 820
Hambleton, Benjamin IV, 870
Hambleton, Benjamin VI, 822
Hambleton, Benjamin K. IV, 875
Hambleton, Bennitt VI, 1017
Hambleton, Catharine H. IV, 870
Hambleton, Catherine H. IV, 820
Hambleton, Charles IV, 474
Hambleton, Charles IV, 629
Hambleton, Charles IV, 820
Hambleton, Charles IV, 870
Hambleton, Chas. IV, 473
Hambleton, Chas. IV, 870
Hambleton, David M. II, 872
Hambleton, David Moore II, 798
Hambleton, Edward IV, 629
Hambleton, Edward IV, 870
Hambleton, Edward Carroll, Jr. IV, 820
Hambleton, Elijah VI, 927
Hambleton, Eliza IV, 820
Hambleton, Eliza IV, 870
Hambleton, Elizabeth VI, 822
Hambleton, Elizabeth Edwards VI, 927
Hambleton, Elwood IV, 820
Hambleton, Emaline IV, 870
Hambleton, Emeline IV, 870
Hambleton, Emeline IV, 879
Hambleton, Emily IV, 865
Hambleton, Emily IV, 870
Hambleton, Emily H. IV, 865
Hambleton, Emlie IV, 870
Hambleton, Fanny VI, 994
Hambleton, Frank IV, 870
Hambleton, Franklin IV, 870
Hambleton, George IV, 870
Hambleton, George W. IV, 870
Hambleton, Hannah IV, 820
Hambleton, Hannah IV, 870
Hambleton, Hannah IV, 886
Hambleton, Hannah IV, 1025
Hambleton, Isaac Herbert IV, 820
Hambleton, Isaac Herbert IV, 870
Hambleton, Isaac Howard IV, 870
Hambleton, Isaac P. IV, 870
Hambleton, James IV, 629
Hambleton, James IV, 715
Hambleton, James IV, 870
Hambleton, James VI, 927
Hambleton, James VI, 964
Hambleton, James VI, 1021
Hambleton, Jane IV, 473
Hambleton, Jane IV, 474
Hambleton, Jane IV, 870
Hambleton, Joel G. IV, 820
Hambleton, Joel G. IV, 870
Hambleton, John IV, 629
Hambleton, John IV, 1060
Hambleton, Joseph IV, 216
Hambleton, Joseph W. III, 149
Hambleton, Joseph W. III, 280
Hambleton, Kitty Ann VI, 927
Hambleton, Levi IV, 820
Hambleton, Levi IV, 870
Hambleton, Lewis IV, 870
Hambleton, Louis IV, 870
Hambleton, Lydia Ann IV, 870
Hambleton, Martha IV, 629
Hambleton, Martha IV, 870
Hambleton, Mary II, 999
Hambleton, Mary IV, 474
Hambleton, Mary IV, 506
Hambleton, Mary IV, 614
Hambleton, Mary IV, 629
Hambleton, Mary IV, 661
Hambleton, Mary IV, 820
Hambleton, Mary IV, 870
Hambleton, Mary IV, 871
Hambleton, Moses IV, 816
Hambleton, Moses IV, 820
Hambleton, Moses IV, 870
Hambleton, Nancy VI, 980
Hambleton, Osborn IV, 820
Hambleton, Osborn IV, 870
Hambleton, Peter A. VI, 994
Hambleton, Polly VI, 994
Hambleton, Polly VI, 1017
Hambleton, Rachel IV, 403
Hambleton, Rachel IV, 614
Hambleton, Rachel IV, 629
Hambleton, Rachel IV, 820
Hambleton, Rachel IV, 870
Hambleton, Rachel IV, 875
Hambleton, Rachel IV, 1060
Hambleton, Richard VI, 927
Hambleton, Ruth Ann IV, 870
Hambleton, Sarah III, 149
Hambleton, Sarah III, 280
Hambleton, Sarah IV, 816
Hambleton, Sarah IV, 820
Hambleton, Sarah IV, 870
Hambleton, Sarah VI, 927
Hambleton, Sarah A. VI, 822
Hambleton, Sarah L. IV, 870
Hambleton, Sarah L. IV, 875
Hambleton, Stephen IV, 816
Hambleton, Stephen IV, 820
Hambleton, Stephen IV, 870
Hambleton, Susanna IV, 820
Hambleton, Susannah IV, 820
Hambleton, Susannah IV, 870
Hambleton, Thomas IV, 820
Hambleton, Thomas Elwood IV, 870
Hambleton, William IV, 216
Hambleton, William IV, 334
Hambleton, William IV, 614
Hambleton, William IV, 1025
Hambleton, William VI, 822
Hambleton, William, Jr. IV, 528
Hambleton, Wm. II, 999
Hambleton, Wm. IV, 474
Hambling, Charles I, 51
Hambling, Charles I, 60
Hambling, Martha I, 51
Hambling, Martha I, 60
Hambly, Hannah II, 540
Hambly, Hannah II, 682
Hambrick, James VI, 927
Hambrick, Mary C. VI, 927
Hamburger, Margaret III, 149
Hamel, A. F. V, 740
Hamel, John V, 740
Hamel, Mary V, 740
Hamel, Mercy II, 229
Hamel, W. H. V, 740
Hamell, Mary II, 229
Hamell, Mercy II, 229
Hamelton, Bessie V, 65
Hamelton, Martha W. VI, 822
Hamelton, Mary II, 999
Hamelton, Thomas VI, 822
Hamelton, Wm. II, 999
Hamer, Carol IV, 1252
Hamer, Catharine I, 716
Hamer, David I, 1030
Hamer, Don P. IV, 1252
Hamer, Eli II, 370
Hamer, Eli II, 540
Hamer, Eli II, 744
Hamer, Eli II, 798
Hamer, Eli II, 872
Hamer, Elisha I, 1120
Hamer, Elizabeth II, 540
Hamer, Elizabeth IV, 123
Hamer, Elizabeth IV, 127
Hamer, Ellis II, 370
Hamer, Ellis II, 744
Hamer, Ellis II, 872
Hamer, Hannah I, 1120
Hamer, Hannah I, 1127
Hamer, Hannah II, 370
Hamer, Hannah II, 744
Hamer, Hannah II, 798
Hamer, Hannah II, 872
Hamer, Henry I, 1120
Hamer, Henry I, 1127
Hamer, Ida IV, 1252
Hamer, Jacob II, 370
Hamer, Jacob II, 744
Hamer, Jacob II, 798
Hamer, Jacob II, 848
Hamer, Jacob II, 872
Hamer, Jacob, Jr. II, 744
Hamer, Jacob, Jr. II, 848
Hamer, Jacob, Jr. II, 872
Hamer, John II, 804
Hamer, Kathleen Patricia IV, 1318
Hamer, Mary II, 370
Hamer, Mary II, 744
Hamer, Mary II, 798
Hamer, Mary II, 848
Hamer, Mary II, 872
Hamer, Mary Elizabeth VI, 736
Hamer, Mary Elizabeth VI, 745
Hamer, Nicholas II, 798
Hamer, Rachel I, 1120
Hamer, Rosanna II, 804
Hamer, Sarah Ann II, 848
Hamer, Sarah Ann II, 872
Hamer, Susan II, 804
Hamer, Victor IV, 1253
Hamer, Wd. Susan II, 804
Hamer, William II, 370
Hamer, William W. II, 370
Hamers, Rachel VI, 839
Hamersley, Ann E. VI, 822
Hamersley, David VI, 822
Hamersley, Elizabeth VI, 822
Hamersley, Frances VI, 826
Hamersley, James B. VI, 815
Hamersley, James B. VI, 822
Hamersley, Jas. VI, 806
Hamersley, Jas. B. VI, 826
Hamersley, Jas. B. VI, 857
Hamersley, Lucy VI, 822
Hamersley, Mary VI, 841
Hamersley, Mary K. VI, 822
Hamersley, Maurice VI, 822
Hamersley, Nancy VI, 822
Hamersley, Nancy J. VI, 823
Hamersley, Richard VI, 822
Hamersley, Sarah VI, 806
Hamersley, Sarah VI, 822
Hamersley, Sarah VI, 857
Hamersley, Susan VI, 822
Hamersley, Susanna VI, 795
Hamersley, Susanna VI, 822
Hamersley, Thomas VI, 822
Hamersley, William VI, 822
Hamersley, William VI, 826
Hamersley, Wm. VI, 841
Hamersly, Elizabeth VI, 837
Hamersly, Richard VI, 837
Hamersly, William G. VI, 837
Hames, James VI, 850
Hamiel, Mrs. A. J. V, 740
Hamiger, Israel J. IV, 1253
Hamilton, ??? V, 678
Hamilton, Ada I, 633
Hamilton, Ada I, 941
Hamilton, Ada P. I, 880
Hamilton, Alexander VI, 927
Hamilton, Amanda V, 999
Hamilton, Amandah V, 999
Hamilton, Ann IV, 820
Hamilton, Ann IV, 1025
Hamilton, Ann VI, 510
Hamilton, Ann VI, 735
Hamilton, Ann VI, 746
Hamilton, Ann VI, 750
Hamilton, Anna I, 925
Hamilton, Anna I, 930
Hamilton, Anna V, 334
Hamilton, Annie I, 941
Hamilton, Annie V, 999
Hamilton, Asa G. I, 880
Hamilton, Benjamin IV, 216
Hamilton, Benjamin IV, 629
Hamilton, Bertie IV, 1280
Hamilton, Bessie V, 65
Hamilton, Caroline V, 969
Hamilton, Caroline V, 970
Hamilton, Celestia T. M. I, 880
Hamilton, Charles IV, 629
Hamilton, Chas. L. V, 623
Hamilton, Cornelia VI, 663
Hamilton, Cornelia VI, 664
Hamilton, Corwin V, 65
Hamilton, Corwin B. V, 65
Hamilton, D. Emery I, 941
Hamilton, D. Emory I, 941
Hamilton, D. Emory I, 942
Hamilton, David VI, 735
Hamilton, David VI, 746
Hamilton, David VI, 927
Hamilton, David Emory I, 925
Hamilton, David Emory, Jr. I, 925
Hamilton, Deborah II, 540
Hamilton, Deborah II, 649
Hamilton, Deborah III, 253
Hamilton, Dr. Adelbert VI, 746
Hamilton, Dr. Adelbert VI, 782
Hamilton, Edward Burr VI, 646
Hamilton, Eleanor IV, 216
Hamilton, Eli Elizabeth J. V, 623
Hamilton, Elijah VI, 927
Hamilton, Elizabeth II, 540
Hamilton, Elizabeth II, 614
Hamilton, Elizabeth II, 706
Hamilton, Elizabeth II, 872
Hamilton, Elizabeth II, 935
Hamilton, Elizabeth VI, 573
Hamilton, Elizabeth VI, 927
Hamilton, Elizabeth Edwards VI, 927
Hamilton, Ella I, 628
Hamilton, Elma I, 880
Hamilton, Elmer U. V, 679
Hamilton, Elwood Burr VI, 646
Hamilton, Emma V, 65
Hamilton, Emma V, 841
Hamilton, Esther IV, 1364
Hamilton, Evan VI, 927
Hamilton, Fanny VI, 836
Hamilton, Frances E. V, 679
Hamilton, Frank V, 65
Hamilton, Frank William V, 65
Hamilton, Gale W. IV, 1253
Hamilton, George V, 65
Hamilton, George R. V, 65
Hamilton, Grace V, 679
Hamilton, Grace V, 706
Hamilton, Grace J. V, 679
Hamilton, H. H. V, 496
Hamilton, Hallie V, 661
Hamilton, Hallie V, 678
Hamilton, Hallie V, 679
Hamilton, Harry B. V, 65
Hamilton, Harry Blaine V, 65
Hamilton, Helen Euphemia V, 458
Hamilton, Henry S. II, 706
Hamilton, Houston V, 458
Hamilton, Hubert Floyd V, 458
Hamilton, Huston V, 458
Hamilton, Ida E. V, 244
Hamilton, Isaac Herbert IV, 870
Hamilton, James II, 706
Hamilton, James II, 978
Hamilton, James II, 999
Hamilton, James IV, 216
Hamilton, James IV, 715
Hamilton, James V, 999
Hamilton, James VI, 822
Hamilton, James VI, 927
Hamilton, James VI, 1019
Hamilton, Jane II, 533
Hamilton, Jane II, 540
Hamilton, Jenny VI, 836
Hamilton, Jenny VI, 927
Hamilton, John V, 65
Hamilton, John V, 623
Hamilton, John VI, 573
Hamilton, John VI, 646
Hamilton, John H. VI, 646
Hamilton, John H. VI, 682
Hamilton, John H. VI, 684
Hamilton, John H. VI, 708
Hamilton, John H. VI, 712
Hamilton, John W. V, 623
Hamilton, John W. VI, 927
Hamilton, Jonah VI, 441
Hamilton, Joseph IV, 216
Hamilton, Joseph V, 65
Hamilton, Katharine I, 925
Hamilton, Katie V, 999
Hamilton, Keziah McCoun VI, 822
Hamilton, Kitty Ann VI, 927
Hamilton, Lewis V, 999
Hamilton, Lewis M. V, 999
Hamilton, Lloyd Wesley V, 458
Hamilton, Lorina V, 65
Hamilton, Lou I, 942
Hamilton, Louis V. II, 706
Hamilton, Louisa H. I, 925
Hamilton, Lula I, 880
Hamilton, Lula I, 891
Hamilton, M. E. II, 706
Hamilton, M. O. V, 458
Hamilton, Mabel IV, 1253
Hamilton, Maggie V, 458

Hamilton, Margaret V, 999
Hamilton, Maria I, 633
Hamilton, Maria E. I, 880
Hamilton, Maria Louisa V, 65
Hamilton, Marie I, 633
Hamilton, Marion V, 679
Hamilton, Martha I, 880
Hamilton, Martha I, 895
Hamilton, Martha I, 925
Hamilton, Martha A. V, 623
Hamilton, Martha Almeda I, 925
Hamilton, Martha J. I, 854
Hamilton, Martha W. VI, 822
Hamilton, Mary I, 941
Hamilton, Mary II, 471
Hamilton, Mary II, 540
Hamilton, Mary II, 978
Hamilton, Mary II, 999
Hamilton, Mary III, 180
Hamilton, Mary IV, 629
Hamilton, Mary IV, 631
Hamilton, Mary V, 678
Hamilton, Mary V, 712
Hamilton, Mary VI, 646
Hamilton, Mary VI, 682
Hamilton, Mary VI, 684
Hamilton, Mary VI, 708
Hamilton, Mary VI, 712
Hamilton, Mary VI, 718
Hamilton, Mary VI, 927
Hamilton, Mary A. I, 633
Hamilton, Mary A. I, 937
Hamilton, Mary A. I, 941
Hamilton, Mary A. V, 999
Hamilton, Mary Alice VI, 746
Hamilton, Mary Alice VI, 782
Hamilton, Mary Almina I, 925
Hamilton, Mary An I, 937
Hamilton, Mary Ann III, 149
Hamilton, Mary Ann III, 214
Hamilton, Mary Ann V, 65
Hamilton, Mary Anne V, 65
Hamilton, Mary B. II, 370
Hamilton, Mary E. II, 706
Hamilton, Mary E. V, 65
Hamilton, Mary E. V, 334
Hamilton, Mary E. V, 679
Hamilton, Mary L. I, 880
Hamilton, Midred V, 623
Hamilton, Milton L. II, 706
Hamilton, Milton L. II, 744
Hamilton, Minnie V, 458
Hamilton, Minnie V, 678
Hamilton, Minnie V, 679
Hamilton, Minnie V, 699
Hamilton, Moses IV, 820
Hamilton, Myrtle V, 334
Hamilton, Nancy VI, 1019
Hamilton, Nannie VI, 664
Hamilton, Oliver IV, 715
Hamilton, Pamelia VI, 822
Hamilton, Pamelia VI, 927
Hamilton, Paul I, 925
Hamilton, Paulina VI, 927
Hamilton, Paulina A. VI, 927
Hamilton, Phebe Susanna VI, 646
Hamilton, Pleasie V, 999
Hamilton, Pleza J. V, 999
Hamilton, R. F. V, 458
Hamilton, R. Hildegarde V, 686
Hamilton, Rachel IV, 216
Hamilton, Rachel IV, 239
Hamilton, Rachel IV, 805
Hamilton, Rachel IV, 820
Hamilton, Rachel Ann IV, 216
Hamilton, Rachel Ann IV, 257
Hamilton, Rachel Ann IV, 474
Hamilton, Rachel Ann IV, 491
Hamilton, Ray V, 496
Hamilton, Rebecca IV, 403
Hamilton, Rebecca IV, 447
Hamilton, Rebecca VI, 646
Hamilton, Rebecca E. VI, 646
Hamilton, Rebecca E. VI, 712
Hamilton, Rebecca E. VI, 714
Hamilton, Rexie Ione V, 458
Hamilton, Richard VI, 927
Hamilton, Robert V, 686
Hamilton, Rosco V, 458
Hamilton, Rowland VI, 927
Hamilton, Roy IV, 1318
Hamilton, Roy V, 679
Hamilton, S. H. V, 334
Hamilton, Sally IV, 1280
Hamilton, Samuel I, 925
Hamilton, Samuel V, 334
Hamilton, Sarah IV, 870
Hamilton, Sarah VI, 927
Hamilton, Sarah Catharine VI, 646
Hamilton, Sarah Catherine VI, 646
Hamilton, Sarah E. VI, 746
Hamilton, Sarah E. VI, 780
Hamilton, Sarah E. VI, 782
Hamilton, Sarah Grace V, 65
Hamilton, Sarah Jane V, 65
Hamilton, Stephen IV, 870
Hamilton, Steward V, 999
Hamilton, Susan B. VI, 746
Hamilton, Susannah I, 880
Hamilton, Swithin VI, 646
Hamilton, Swithin N. VI, 646
Hamilton, Tacy Ann VI, 646
Hamilton, Tacy Ann VI, 708
Hamilton, Thomas II, 540
Hamilton, Thomas VI, 822
Hamilton, Thomas VI, 927
Hamilton, Thomas Elwood IV, 870
Hamilton, Thomas Y. I, 633
Hamilton, Thomas Y. I, 937
Hamilton, Thomas Y. I, 941
Hamilton, Thomas Yardley I, 925
Hamilton, Thos. Y. I, 941
Hamilton, Troy I, 941
Hamilton, Troy A. I, 633
Hamilton, Troy Anderson I, 941
Hamilton, Truman Leslie V, 458
Hamilton, W. G. IV, 1280
Hamilton, William II, 370
Hamilton, William IV, 216
Hamilton, William IV, 561
Hamilton, William VI, 822
Hamilton, William K. II, 370
Hamilton, William, Jr. IV, 216
Hamilton, Wm. II, 999
Hamilton, Wm. V, 679
Hamilton, Wm. V, 700
Hamilton, Wm. VI, 810
Hamilton, Wm. V. V, 679
Hamilton, Wm. Vance V, 679
Hamilton, Zella V, 679
Hamilton, Zella V, 700
Hamit, Abigail II, 370
Hamlen, Asa IV, 891
Hamlen, Asa IV, 892
Hamlen, Hannah IV, 892
Hamlen, Sarah IV, 891
Hamlen, Sarah IV, 892
Hamlen, Wm. IV, 892
Hamlet, James VI, 822
Hamlet, Lucy VI, 822
Hamlet, Mary A. VI, 847
Hamlet, Thomas VI, 847
Hamlett, Dorothy VI, 815
Hamlett, Elizabeth VI, 865
Hamlett, James, Jr. VI, 865
Hamlett, James, Sr. VI, 865
Hamlett, Jas. VI, 815
Hamlett, Sarah E. VI, 804
Hamlett, Thos. VI, 804
Hamlett, William VI, 815
Hamlin, ??? VI, 95
Hamlin, Abigail IV, 961
Hamlin, Ann VI, 107
Hamlin, Charles IV, 629
Hamlin, Charles IV, 716
Hamlin, Charles VI, 107
Hamlin, Charles VI, 134
Hamlin, Elizabeth IV, 715
Hamlin, Elizabeth IV, 716
Hamlin, Elizabeth VI, 107
Hamlin, Elizabeth J. IV, 1280
Hamlin, Hannah IV, 629
Hamlin, Hannah IV, 635
Hamlin, John IV, 715
Hamlin, John IV, 716
Hamlin, John VI, 107
Hamlin, Joshua IV, 716
Hamlin, Joshua VI, 134
Hamlin, Lydia IV, 715
Hamlin, Lydia VI, 107
Hamlin, Martha IV, 629
Hamlin, Martha IV, 715
Hamlin, Martha VI, 107
Hamlin, Mary IV, 716
Hamlin, Mary VI, 134
Hamlin, Nancy VI, 107
Hamlin, Pharaby IV, 716
Hamlin, Phariba IV, 715
Hamlin, Phariba VI, 107
Hamlin, Sally IV, 715
Hamlin, Sally IV, 716
Hamlin, Sally VI, 107
Hamlin, Sarah VI, 42
Hamlin, Sarah VI, 107
Hamlin, Steaphen VI, 107
Hamlin, Stephen IV, 716
Hamlin, Stephen IV, 961
Hamlin, Stephen VI, 16
Hamlin, Stephen VI, 107
Hamlin, Susanna VI, 108
Hamlin, Susannah IV, 716
Hamlin, Susannah VI, 107
Hamlin, Susannah VI, 108
Hamlin, William IV, 629
Hamlin, William IV, 635
Hamlin, William IV, 716
Hamlin, William VI, 107
Hamlin, William VI, 134
Hamlinton, Lewis V, 999
Hamm, Minnie Price IV, 1318
Hamm, Rebecca Ann II, 792
Hammack, Betsy VI, 822
Hammack, Daniel VI, 940
Hammack, John H. V, 623
Hammack, John Henry V, 623
Hammack, Lewis VI, 822
Hammack, Lydia V, 623
Hammack, Lydia V, 640
Hammar, Charlotte V, 173
Hammar, David V, 173
Hammar, David V, 496
Hammar, Margaret V, 173
Hammar, Mary J. I, 617
Hammar, Williard I, 617
Hammarstrom, Carl Johan III, 149
Hammarstrom, Erik III, 94
Hammarstrom, Erik III, 149
Hammarstrom, Inez III, 149
Hammarstrom, Inez H. III, 94
Hammarstrom, Inez H. III, 149
Hammarstrom, Maria C. III, 149
Hammel, A. F. V, 740
Hammel, A. J. V, 740
Hammel, Alice V, 740
Hammel, Dora V, 740
Hammel, Elizabeth V, 740
Hammel, J. W. V, 740
Hammel, John V, 740
Hammel, Laura V, 740
Hammel, Mary V, 740
Hammel, Minnie V, 740
Hammel, Mrs. A. J. V, 740
Hammel, W. H. V, 740
Hammer, ??? I, 1140
Hammer, ??? V, 391
Hammer, Aaron I, 1082
Hammer, Aaron I, 1084
Hammer, Aaron I, 1085
Hammer, Aaron I, 1092
Hammer, Aaron I, 1093
Hammer, Aaron I, 1096
Hammer, Aaron I, 1105
Hammer, Aaron I, 1120
Hammer, Aaron I, 1154
Hammer, Aaron II, 540
Hammer, Aaron Francis I, 1105
Hammer, Abijah I, 467
Hammer, Abijah I, 480
Hammer, Abijah I, 716
Hammer, Abraham I, 393
Hammer, Abraham I, 457
Hammer, Abraham I, 467
Hammer, Abraham I, 480
Hammer, Abraham I, 698
Hammer, Abraham I, 716
Hammer, Abraham I, 813
Hammer, Abraham I, 1105
Hammer, Abraham I, 1119
Hammer, Abraham, Jr. I, 393
Hammer, Abraham, Jr. I, 716
Hammer, Abram I, 467
Hammer, Abram I, 716
Hammer, Alma V, 333
Hammer, Alma V, 334
Hammer, Amanda V, 392
Hammer, Amos V, 392
Hammer, Amos G. V, 391
Hammer, Amos G. V, 392
Hammer, Andy T. I, 1154
Hammer, Ann II, 540
Hammer, Anna V, 65
Hammer, Audsley D. V, 392
Hammer, Calvin I, 1084
Hammer, Catharine I, 467
Hammer, Catharine I, 480
Hammer, Catharine I, 698
Hammer, Catharine I, 716
Hammer, Catherine I, 1084
Hammer, Catherine I, 1093
Hammer, Charity I, 1105
Hammer, Charles V, 392
Hammer, Charlotte I, 925
Hammer, Charlotte I, 1030
Hammer, Charlotte V, 65
Hammer, Charlotte V, 153
Hammer, Clara V, 570
Hammer, Curtis V, 392
Hammer, Daisy V, 392
Hammer, David I, 393
Hammer, David I, 1030
Hammer, David V, 65
Hammer, David V, 153
Hammer, Delos E. I, 941
Hammer, Delos Edgar I, 925
Hammer, Diann I, 1120
Hammer, Dorotha V, 406
Hammer, Dorothy V, 391
Hammer, Drusilla V, 387
Hammer, Eleanor V, 392
Hammer, Eleanor Jane V, 385
Hammer, Eli II, 540
Hammer, Elisha I, 467
Hammer, Elisha I, 480
Hammer, Elisha I, 482
Hammer, Elisha I, 716
Hammer, Elisha I, 1093
Hammer, Elisha I, 1105
Hammer, Elisha I, 1120
Hammer, Elisha I, 1123
Hammer, Elisha I, 1154
Hammer, Elisha V, 385
Hammer, Elisha V, 391
Hammer, Elisha V, 392
Hammer, Elisha V, 433
Hammer, Elizabeth I, 1120
Hammer, Elizabeth I, 1153
Hammer, Elizabeth I, 1154
Hammer, Elizabeth II, 540
Hammer, Elizabeth V, 385
Hammer, Elizabeth V, 391
Hammer, Elizabeth V, 392
Hammer, Elizabeth V, 433
Hammer, Elizabeth VI, 312
Hammer, Elizabeth VI, 336
Hammer, Elizabeth VI, 397
Hammer, Elizabeth VI, 431
Hammer, Elleanor Jane V, 392
Hammer, Emeline V, 384
Hammer, Emerson V, 391
Hammer, Emily I, 1120
Hammer, Emma V, 391
Hammer, Emma V, 392
Hammer, Emma Hastings V, 679
Hammer, Emory I, 925
Hammer, Esther V, 384
Hammer, Esther V, 391
Hammer, Esther V, 418
Hammer, Esther Ann V, 391
Hammer, Esther Ann V, 392
Hammer, Esther Ann V, 436
Hammer, Eugene V, 570
Hammer, Florella V, 391
Hammer, Florella V, 392
Hammer, Frances I, 1120
Hammer, Francis V, 392
Hammer, Francis M. V, 391
Hammer, Hannah I, 1084
Hammer, Hannah I, 1093
Hammer, Hannah I, 1095
Hammer, Hannah I, 1105
Hammer, Hannah I, 1119
Hammer, Hannah I, 1120
Hammer, Hannah I, 1126
Hammer, Hannah I, 1141
Hammer, Hannah II, 540
Hammer, Harriet E. Jay I, 1154
Hammer, Hattie S. V, 841
Hammer, Henrietta Wilkerson I, 617
Hammer, Henry I, 1105
Hammer, Henry I, 1120
Hammer, Henry Lewis I, 1084
Hammer, Infant II, 540
Hammer, Ira I, 1120
Hammer, Ira Lewis I, 1105
Hammer, Ira Lewis I, 1119
Hammer, Ira Lewis I, 1120
Hammer, Ira Louis I, 1105
Hammer, Irena V, 391
Hammer, Isaac I, 467
Hammer, Isaac I, 480
Hammer, Isaac I, 716
Hammer, Isaac I, 1084
Hammer, Isaac I, 1089
Hammer, Isaac I, 1093
Hammer, Isaac I, 1094
Hammer, Isaac I, 1097
Hammer, Isaac I, 1102
Hammer, Isaac I, 1105
Hammer, Isaac I, 1119
Hammer, Isaac I, 1120
Hammer, Isaac I, 1126
Hammer, Isaac V, 384
Hammer, Isaac V, 391
Hammer, Isaac V, 418
Hammer, Isaac Rauley V, 391
Hammer, Jacob II, 540
Hammer, James V, 391
Hammer, James G. V, 391
Hammer, James G. V, 392
Hammer, James Riley V, 391
Hammer, Jane I, 1084
Hammer, Jane I, 1085
Hammer, Jane I, 1093
Hammer, Jane I, 1095
Hammer, Jane I, 1144
Hammer, Jane V, 383
Hammer, Jane V, 391
Hammer, Jane V, 392
Hammer, Jane V, 406
Hammer, Jesse I, 1093
Hammer, Jesse I, 1105
Hammer, Jesse I, 1120
Hammer, Jesse I, 1141
Hammer, Jesse I, 1153
Hammer, Jesse I, 1154
Hammer, Jesse V, 392
Hammer, Jessee I, 1154
Hammer, John I, 467
Hammer, John I, 480
Hammer, John I, 698
Hammer, John I, 1030
Hammer, John I, 1084
Hammer, John I, 1120
Hammer, John I, 1154
Hammer, John I, 1158
Hammer, John II, 370
Hammer, John V, 387
Hammer, John VI, 312
Hammer, John VI, 336
Hammer, John G. V, 391
Hammer, John H. IV, 1236
Hammer, Johnathan I, 1120
Hammer, Jonathan I, 1093
Hammer, Jonathan I, 1105
Hammer, Joseph I, 1120
Hammer, Joseph I, 1154
Hammer, Katharine I, 480
Hammer, Laban I, 1105
Hammer, Laban I, 1120
Hammer, Lacy V, 458
Hammer, Leroy V, 392
Hammer, Leuisa I, 716
Hammer, Levi V, 391
Hammer, Levisee I, 480
Hammer, Levisia I, 467
Hammer, Louisa V, 387
Hammer, Lucinda I, 1120
Hammer, Lucinda I, 1153
Hammer, Lucinda I, 1154
Hammer, Lydia I, 1084
Hammer, Lydia I, 1093
Hammer, Lydia I, 1105
Hammer, Lydia I, 1120
Hammer, Lydia I, 1128
Hammer, Lydia Jane V, 418
Hammer, Mahlon I, 1105
Hammer, Manford V, 392
Hammer, Maretta V, 392
Hammer, Margaret I, 393
Hammer, Margaret I, 1030
Hammer, Margaret I, 1031
Hammer, Margaret V, 65
Hammer, Margaret V, 153
Hammer, Margaret E. V, 391
Hammer, Margaret E. V, 433
Hammer, Margaret Emily V, 392
Hammer, Margaret Jane V, 392
Hammer, Martha I, 1154
Hammer, Martha V, 391
Hammer, Martha V, 392
Hammer, Martha V, 421
Hammer, Martha R. IV, 216
Hammer, Mary I, 370
Hammer, Mary I, 393
Hammer, Mary I, 467
Hammer, Mary I, 480
Hammer, Mary I, 716
Hammer, Mary I, 813
Hammer, Mary I, 1082
Hammer, Mary I, 1084
Hammer, Mary I, 1085
Hammer, Mary I, 1093
Hammer, Mary I, 1096
Hammer, Mary I, 1154
Hammer, Mary II, 540
Hammer, Mary IV, 523
Hammer, Mary IV, 528
Hammer, Mary V, 383
Hammer, Mary V, 387
Hammer, Mary V, 391
Hammer, Mary V, 392
Hammer, Mary Ann I, 1105
Hammer, Mary Ann I, 1154
Hammer, Mary E. V, 418
Hammer, Mary Ellen V, 391
Hammer, Mary Emily V, 392
Hammer, Mary Emily V, 433
Hammer, Mary G. I, 1093
Hammer, Mary Jane I, 1105

Hammer, Matilda I, 467
Hammer, Matilda I, 480
Hammer, Matilda I, 716
Hammer, Mattie V, 392
Hammer, Melvina V, 391
Hammer, Moses II, 540
Hammer, Nancy I, 480
Hammer, Nancy I, 482
Hammer, Nancy I, 1120
Hammer, Narcissa I, 1084
Hammer, Narcissus I, 1154
Hammer, Narcissus I, 1158
Hammer, Nathan I, 1105
Hammer, Nathan I, 1120
Hammer, Noah V, 391
Hammer, Peter V, 392
Hammer, Rachel I, 393
Hammer, Rachel I, 467
Hammer, Rachel I, 480
Hammer, Rachel I, 716
Hammer, Rachel I, 813
Hammer, Rachel I, 1030
Hammer, Rachel I, 1082
Hammer, Rachel I, 1084
Hammer, Rachel I, 1089
Hammer, Rachel I, 1091
Hammer, Rachel I, 1092
Hammer, Rachel I, 1093
Hammer, Rachel I, 1094
Hammer, Rachel I, 1105
Hammer, Rachel I, 1119
Hammer, Rachel I, 1120
Hammer, Rachel I, 1123
Hammer, Rachel I, 1154
Hammer, Rachel V, 65
Hammer, Rachel VI, 312
Hammer, Rachel VI, 336
Hammer, Rebecca I, 1093
Hammer, Rebecca II, 540
Hammer, Rebeckah I, 1084
Hammer, Rebeckah I, 1120
Hammer, Rebekah I, 393
Hammer, Rebekah I, 1120
Hammer, Riley V, 392
Hammer, Robert Thomas V, 570
Hammer, Sarah I, 1115
Hammer, Sarah I, 1120
Hammer, Sarah I, 1140
Hammer, Sarah I, 1154
Hammer, Sarah V, 391
Hammer, Sarah E. V, 392
Hammer, Sarah E. V, 421
Hammer, Sarah Jane I, 1084
Hammer, Sarry I, 1105
Hammer, Seth I, 1105
Hammer, Seth I, 1120
Hammer, Seth I, 1153
Hammer, Seth I, 1154
Hammer, Solomon II, 540
Hammer, Susanna I, 1120
Hammer, Susanna I, 1122
Hammer, Susannah I, 1105
Hammer, Thomas V, 392
Hammer, Victor V, 570
Hammer, Wilford V, 392
Hammer, Wilfred V, 391
Hammer, William II, 370
Hammer, William V, 391
Hammer, William R. V, 391
Hammer, Wm. V, 383
Hammer, Wm. V, 391
Hammer, Wm. V, 406
Hammers, George VI, 822
Hammers, Nelly VI, 822
Hammersley, David F. V, 392
Hammersley, Elizabeth E. V, 392
Hammersley, Fannie A. V, 392
Hammersley, James P. VI, 826
Hammersley, Lucy VI, 822
Hammersley, Richard VI, 822
Hammersley, William VI, 843
Hammet, Sarah II, 76
Hammet, Sarah II, 119
Hammet, Sarah IV, 36
Hammet, Sarah IV, 716
Hammet, Sarah IV, 1079
Hammet, Sarah V, 65
Hammett, Sarah II, 76
Hammett, Sarah II, 119
Hammett, Sarah II, 150
Hammett, Sarah R. II, 119
Hammill, Mary II, 229
Hammit, Ann II, 555
Hammit, Ellen IV, 961
Hammit, Ellen IV, 989
Hammit, Sarah II, 150
Hammit, Sarah IV, 91
Hammit, Sarah IV, 148
Hammitt, Ann II, 540
Hammitt, Edward IV, 1116
Hammitt, Elizabeth IV, 1116
Hammitt, Ellen IV, 1060
Hammitt, Ellen IV, 1099
Hammitt, Sarah A. IV, 1116
Hammitt, Sarah R. II, 119
Hammitt, Sarah R. IV, 1099
Hammock, Andrew VI, 927
Hammock, Ann VI, 927
Hammock, Catherine Emeline VI, 889
Hammock, John VI, 1009
Hammock, John Henry V, 623
Hammock, Lydia V, 623
Hammock, Martha S. VI, 927
Hammock, Mrs. Margaret VI, 976
Hammock, Nancy VI, 889
Hammock, Nancy VI, 927
Hammock, Oliver VI, 927
Hammock, Polly VI, 1009
Hammock, Susan VI, 976
Hammock, Thomas VI, 1009
Hammock, William L. VI, 927
Hammon, A. J. V, 999
Hammon, Aaron I, 717
Hammon, Branson I, 717
Hammon, Grace I, 717
Hammon, Hannah II, 370
Hammon, Jack V, 999
Hammon, Martha J. IV, 1163
Hammon, Minnie V, 999
Hammon, Moses I, 480
Hammon, Moses I, 482
Hammon, Polly I, 717
Hammon, Ruth I, 480
Hammon, Sarah I, 393
Hammon, Sarah I, 717
Hammon, Selemma IV, 1163
Hammond, ??? II, 370
Hammond, Aaron I, 698
Hammond, Aaron I, 717
Hammond, Abigail I, 393
Hammond, Abigail I, 716
Hammond, Abigail I, 1105
Hammond, Abigail I, 1120
Hammond, Abigail I, 1122
Hammond, Abigail III, 149
Hammond, Abigail, Jun'r I, 1120
Hammond, Addie I, 633
Hammond, Alexander I, 698
Hammond, Alexander I, 717
Hammond, Alice I, 713
Hammond, Alice I, 717
Hammond, Allen I, 717
Hammond, Amanda IV, 474
Hammond, Amanda IV, 475
Hammond, Amanda IV, 716
Hammond, Amor P. IV, 474
Hammond, Amos P. IV, 216
Hammond, Amos P. IV, 474
Hammond, Amy IV, 474
Hammond, Amy IV, 487
Hammond, Amy L. IV, 700
Hammond, Anderson I, 941
Hammond, Anderson IV, 216
Hammond, Anderson IV, 474
Hammond, Anderson IV, 475
Hammond, Ann I, 717
Hammond, Ann I, 1120
Hammond, Ann IV, 474
Hammond, Ann IV, 487
Hammond, Anna IV, 474
Hammond, Anna IV, 475
Hammond, Anna IV, 716
Hammond, Anna B. IV, 716
Hammond, Annie C. IV, 474
Hammond, Arthur III, 149
Hammond, Arthur W. IV, 906
Hammond, Asenath Duritta I, 480
Hammond, Asenath J. I, 467
Hammond, Asenath J. I, 699
Hammond, Asenath Jurita I, 467
Hammond, Augusta I, 634
Hammond, Augusta Clara I, 617
Hammond, Belinda I, 717
Hammond, Benj. IV, 488
Hammond, Benj. IV, 504
Hammond, Benjamin IV, 91
Hammond, Benjamin IV, 148
Hammond, Benjamin IV, 216
Hammond, Benjamin IV, 474
Hammond, Benjamin IV, 475
Hammond, Bezaleel IV, 474
Hammond, Bezaleel IV, 475
Hammond, Branson I, 699
Hammond, Branson I, 717
Hammond, Caroline B. IV, 529
Hammond, Caroline B. IV, 530
Hammond, Catharine IV, 475
Hammond, Catharine IV, 716
Hammond, Clarence IV, 474
Hammond, Cora IV, 470
Hammond, Cordelia IV, 216
Hammond, Cordelia IV, 474
Hammond, Cornelia Mary I, 854
Hammond, D. Anderson I, 941
Hammond, D. Anderson VI, 244
Hammond, Daniel IV, 36
Hammond, David IV, 1038
Hammond, Deborah I, 717
Hammond, Deborah IV, 91
Hammond, Deborah IV, 148
Hammond, Deborah IV, 216
Hammond, Deborah IV, 245
Hammond, Deborah IV, 474
Hammond, Deborah IV, 475
Hammond, Deborah IV, 485
Hammond, Deborah IV, 486
Hammond, Deborah IV, 488
Hammond, Deborah IV, 1197
Hammond, Elbert L. I, 941
Hammond, Eliza Ann IV, 474
Hammond, Eliza Ann IV, 475
Hammond, Elizabeth I, 698
Hammond, Elizabeth I, 699
Hammond, Elizabeth I, 717
Hammond, Elizabeth I, 724
Hammond, Elizabeth II, 541
Hammond, Elizabeth III, 149
Hammond, Elizabeth IV, 36
Hammond, Elizabeth IV, 463
Hammond, Elizabeth IV, 470
Hammond, Elizabeth IV, 474
Hammond, Elizabeth IV, 475
Hammond, Elizabeth C. IV, 474
Hammond, Elizabeth M. III, 149
Hammond, Ellen Martitia I, 854
Hammond, Ellick I, 699
Hammond, Emma I, 717
Hammond, Emma Eliza I, 854
Hammond, Enoch I, 699
Hammond, Ezra I, 698
Hammond, Ezra I, 699
Hammond, Ezra I, 708
Hammond, Ezra I, 717
Hammond, Frank IV, 475
Hammond, Frank N. IV, 474
Hammond, Frederick M. IV, 474
Hammond, Geo. IV, 245
Hammond, Geo. IV, 474
Hammond, Geo. IV, 488
Hammond, George I, 854
Hammond, George IV, 91
Hammond, George IV, 148
Hammond, George IV, 216
Hammond, George IV, 474
Hammond, George IV, 475
Hammond, George N. IV, 474
Hammond, George N. IV, 475
Hammond, Grace I, 717
Hammond, Grace I, 725
Hammond, Grace V, 303
Hammond, Grace L. V, 458
Hammond, Graces I, 699
Hammond, Hannah I, 1120
Hammond, Hannah IV, 475
Hammond, Hannah IV, 716
Hammond, Hannah M. IV, 474
Hammond, Hannah M. IV, 475
Hammond, Harriet IV, 216
Hammond, Harriet IV, 474
Hammond, Harriet IV, 475
Hammond, Harriet IV, 492
Hammond, Harriet IV, 1060
Hammond, Harriet IV, 1073
Hammond, Henry I, 467
Hammond, Henry I, 480
Hammond, Henry I, 699
Hammond, Henry I, 717
Hammond, Henry IV, 475
Hammond, Henry N. IV, 474
Hammond, Hiram IV, 216
Hammond, Hiram IV, 474
Hammond, Hiram IV, 475
Hammond, Hugh IV, 474
Hammond, Hugh IV, 475
Hammond, Ida IV, 475
Hammond, Ida E. IV, 474
Hammond, Ida Varana I, 617
Hammond, Iola I, 633
Hammond, Isaac I, 699
Hammond, Isaac I, 717
Hammond, Isaac IV, 216
Hammond, Isaac IV, 474
Hammond, Isaac N. IV, 475
Hammond, J. Edgar IV, 474
Hammond, James IV, 91
Hammond, James IV, 148
Hammond, James IV, 216
Hammond, James IV, 474
Hammond, James IV, 475
Hammond, James IV, 1060
Hammond, James C. IV, 216
Hammond, James C. IV, 475
Hammond, James C. IV, 1060
Hammond, James Clarkson I, 717
Hammond, Jane I, 699
Hammond, Jane IV, 474
Hammond, Jane L. IV, 716
Hammond, Jane L. IV, 733
Hammond, Jane N. IV, 216
Hammond, Jean I, 716
Hammond, Jemima III, 149
Hammond, Jesse I, 699
Hammond, Jesse I, 717
Hammond, Jesse IV, 475
Hammond, Jesse M. I, 467
Hammond, Jesse M. I, 699
Hammond, Jesse Monroe I, 480
Hammond, Jessee Monroe I, 467
Hammond, Jessie IV, 475
Hammond, Jessie F. IV, 474
Hammond, John I, 393
Hammond, John I, 395
Hammond, John I, 480
Hammond, John I, 698
Hammond, John I, 699
Hammond, John I, 717
Hammond, John IV, 216
Hammond, John IV, 474
Hammond, John IV, 487
Hammond, John IV, 492
Hammond, John IV, 1060
Hammond, John A. I, 617
Hammond, John Milton I, 699
Hammond, John N. IV, 474
Hammond, John T. IV, 474
Hammond, John, Jr. IV, 475
Hammond, John, Sr. I, 699
Hammond, Joseph I, 699
Hammond, Joseph IV, 216
Hammond, Joseph IV, 474
Hammond, Joseph IV, 475
Hammond, Joseph IV, 492
Hammond, Joseph IV, 1060
Hammond, Joseph IV, 1073
Hammond, Joseph I. IV, 474
Hammond, Joseph J. IV, 216
Hammond, Kittie IV, 475
Hammond, Kittie S. IV, 475
Hammond, Laura E. IV, 475
Hammond, Laura E. IV, 480
Hammond, Leroy V, 303
Hammond, Levy I, 699
Hammond, Lida IV, 1253
Hammond, Lillian IV, 906
Hammond, Lois Maria IV, 906
Hammond, Louisa IV, 474
Hammond, Louise V, 303
Hammond, Madison I, 717
Hammond, Mahala IV, 474
Hammond, Malina I, 698
Hammond, Margaret IV, 91
Hammond, Margaret IV, 99
Hammond, Margaret IV, 148
Hammond, Margaret IV, 216
Hammond, Margaret IV, 245
Hammond, Margaret IV, 303
Hammond, Margaret IV, 474
Hammond, Margaret IV, 475
Hammond, Margaret IV, 485
Hammond, Margaret IV, 488
Hammond, Margaret IV, 504
Hammond, Maria IV, 91
Hammond, Maria IV, 115
Hammond, Maria IV, 216
Hammond, Maria IV, 474
Hammond, Maria IV, 504
Hammond, Martha E. I, 880
Hammond, Martha J. IV, 1163
Hammond, Martha Jay I, 854
Hammond, Mary I, 699
Hammond, Mary I, 717
Hammond, Mary I, 736
Hammond, Mary IV, 91
Hammond, Mary IV, 148
Hammond, Mary IV, 216
Hammond, Mary IV, 474
Hammond, Mary IV, 492
Hammond, Mary IV, 504
Hammond, Mary Ann IV, 216
Hammond, Mary Ann IV, 474
Hammond, Mary C. I, 880
Hammond, Mary C. IV, 474
Hammond, Mary E. IV, 307
Hammond, Mary E. IV, 474
Hammond, Mary E. IV, 475
Hammond, Mary Ellen I, 925
Hammond, Mary J. I, 699
Hammond, Mary Jane I, 467
Hammond, Mary Jane I, 480
Hammond, Mary Jane I, 717
Hammond, Mary Marshill I, 395
Hammond, Mary Olive VI, 281
Hammond, Matilda IV, 1038
Hammond, Michael II, 541
Hammond, Milo A. I, 699
Hammond, Milo Arlendo I, 467
Hammond, Milo Orlando I, 480
Hammond, Moses I, 393
Hammond, Moses I, 467
Hammond, Moses I, 480
Hammond, Moses I, 482
Hammond, Moses I, 699
Hammond, Moses I, 717
Hammond, Moses I, 854
Hammond, Moses I, 880
Hammond, Moses, Sr. I, 1105
Hammond, Nancy I, 699
Hammond, Nancy I, 717
Hammond, Nancy I, 736
Hammond, Nancy I, 854
Hammond, Nancy J. I, 880
Hammond, Nathan I, 699
Hammond, Nathan I, 717
Hammond, Nathan IV, 474
Hammond, Nathan IV, 475
Hammond, Olive I, 941
Hammond, Olive VI, 244
Hammond, Olive Lena IV, 475
Hammond, Oliver B. IV, 216
Hammond, Oliver B. IV, 474
Hammond, Oliver B. IV, 475
Hammond, Ora IV, 474
Hammond, Orah W. IV, 475
Hammond, Phariba I, 699
Hammond, Phariba I, 717
Hammond, Pharibe I, 698
Hammond, Pharibe I, 699
Hammond, Pheriby I, 708
Hammond, Pheriby I, 717
Hammond, Pluma I, 634
Hammond, Pluma Evalia Sue I, 617
Hammond, Polly I, 699
Hammond, Polly I, 717
Hammond, Rachel IV, 216
Hammond, Rachel IV, 474
Hammond, Rachel IV, 475
Hammond, Rachel IV, 487
Hammond, Rachel IV, 1060
Hammond, Rachel E. IV, 216
Hammond, Rachel E. IV, 474
Hammond, Rebecca I, 717
Hammond, Robert I, 716
Hammond, Robert IV, 216
Hammond, Robert IV, 474
Hammond, Ruth I, 467
Hammond, Ruth I, 480
Hammond, Ruth I, 699
Hammond, Ruth I, 717
Hammond, Ruth IV, 91
Hammond, Ruth IV, 148
Hammond, Ruth IV, 474
Hammond, Ruth IV, 488
Hammond, Ruth IV, 716
Hammond, Ruth Ione I, 925
Hammond, Ruth J. I, 941
Hammond, Sabarah I, 761
Hammond, Sabarah I, 763
Hammond, Sabina I, 467
Hammond, Sabina I, 480
Hammond, Sabina I, 717
Hammond, Samuel I, 698
Hammond, Samuel I, 717
Hammond, Samuel IV, 474
Hammond, Sarah I, 393
Hammond, Sarah I, 480
Hammond, Sarah I, 698
Hammond, Sarah I, 699
Hammond, Sarah I, 713
Hammond, Sarah I, 717
Hammond, Sarah I, 719
Hammond, Sarah IV, 91
Hammond, Sarah IV, 112
Hammond, Sarah IV, 148
Hammond, Sarah IV, 216
Hammond, Sarah Addie Eliza I, 617
Hammond, Sarah L. I, 699
Hammond, Sarah Luzena I, 467
Hammond, Sarah Luzena I, 480
Hammond, Sophia VI, 677
Hammond, Sylvia V, 303
Hammond, Thomas I, 699
Hammond, Thomas I, 717
Hammond, Thomas IV, 216
Hammond, Thomas IV, 474
Hammond, Thomas IV, 475
Hammond, Thos. IV, 487
Hammond, Vernon V, 458
Hammond, Walter Monroe I, 854
Hammond, William I, 699

Hammond, William I, 717
Hammond, William I, 925
Hammond, William IV, 91
Hammond, William IV, 148
Hammond, William IV, 216
Hammond, William IV, 474
Hammond, William IV, 475
Hammond, William Baily I, 717
Hammond, William, Sr. I, 717
Hammond, Wm. I, 1105
Hammond, Wm. IV, 463
Hammond, Wm. IV, 474
Hammond, Wm. IV, 1038
Hammons, Abigail I, 716
Hammons, Ann I, 1120
Hammons, Hannah I, 1120
Hammons, Jean I, 716
Hammons, Jean I, 723
Hammons, Martha E. I, 880
Hammons, Mary C. I, 880
Hammons, Nancy J. I, 880
Hammons, Sabina I, 480
Hamms, Francis II, 370
Hamms, Henry II, 370
Hamms, Rebecka II, 370
Hamner, Elvira Coots VI, 822
Hamner, Emeline VI, 822
Hamner, James A. VI, 822
Hamner, John C. VI, 822
Hamners, Elizabeth VI, 817
Hamners, John VI, 817
Hamond, Lida IV, 1253
Hamond, Lyda IV, 1253
Hamond, Mary Olive VI, 244
Hamond, Richard II, 1033
Hamparsoomian, James II, 872
Hampson, John IV, 92
Hampson, Sarah IV, 92
Hampton, ??? IV, 403
Hampton, ??? IV, 1047
Hampton, ??? IV, 1125
Hampton, Adam III, 149
Hampton, Adam III, 182
Hampton, Adam H. III, 149
Hampton, Albert E. II, 872
Hampton, Alice V, 679
Hampton, Alva J. IV, 820
Hampton, Alva J. IV, 838
Hampton, Alva Jesse IV, 820
Hampton, Amos IV, 335
Hampton, Amos IV, 403
Hampton, Amos IV, 582
Hampton, Amos IV, 1060
Hampton, Amos IV, 1099
Hampton, Amos W. IV, 216
Hampton, Amos W. IV, 335
Hampton, Amos W. IV, 403
Hampton, Amos W. IV, 569
Hampton, Amos W. IV, 582
Hampton, Amy R. II, 946
Hampton, Amy R. IV, 794
Hampton, Andrew V, 44
Hampton, Andrew V, 65
Hampton, Andrew V, 100
Hampton, Andrew V, 623
Hampton, Ann II, 541
Hampton, Ann II, 563
Hampton, Ann II, 744
Hampton, Ann III, 149
Hampton, Ann III, 182
Hampton, Ann IV, 182
Hampton, Ann IV, 216
Hampton, Ann IV, 1060
Hampton, Ann IV, 1099
Hampton, Ann IV, 1100
Hampton, Ann B. IV, 216
Hampton, Ann P. IV, 1060
Hampton, Anna IV, 582
Hampton, Anna V, 65
Hampton, Anna V, 174
Hampton, Anna W. IV, 216
Hampton, Annie P. II, 872
Hampton, Asa IV, 582
Hampton, Asa IV, 1060
Hampton, Asa IV, 1100
Hampton, Asa C. IV, 403
Hampton, Asa C. IV, 427
Hampton, Asa C. IV, 582
Hampton, Asa C. IV, 1060
Hampton, Asa C. IV, 1071
Hampton, Asa C. IV, 1100
Hampton, Asenath IV, 403
Hampton, Asenath IV, 1055
Hampton, Asenath IV, 1060
Hampton, Augusta Artemesa V, 623
Hampton, Benjamin IV, 582
Hampton, Benjamin IV, 1060
Hampton, Benjamin IV, 1100
Hampton, Benjamin W. IV, 1099
Hampton, Bersheba VI, 930
Hampton, Bessie Sanders V, 334
Hampton, Bethula IV, 403
Hampton, Bethula IV, 565
Hampton, Bethula IV, 582
Hampton, Bethula IV, 601
Hampton, Bethula IV, 1049
Hampton, Bethula IV, 1060
Hampton, Bethula Ann IV, 1100
Hampton, Carey IV, 582
Hampton, Cary IV, 403
Hampton, Cary IV, 582
Hampton, Cary IV, 1060
Hampton, Cary IV, 1099
Hampton, Cary IV, 1120
Hampton, Cary P. IV, 1132
Hampton, Charity II, 946
Hampton, Charity II, 947
Hampton, Charity IV, 529
Hampton, Charity IV, 794
Hampton, Charles IV, 403
Hampton, Charles D. IV, 216
Hampton, Chas. IV, 216
Hampton, Chas. V, 570
Hampton, Chas. V, 970
Hampton, Christiana II, 825
Hampton, Christiana Lamb II, 798
Hampton, Clara V, 497
Hampton, Clara W. II, 872
Hampton, Clinton E. IV, 716
Hampton, Clinton E. IV, 820
Hampton, Clinton E. IV, 985
Hampton, Daniel C. IV, 794
Hampton, David II, 946
Hampton, David II, 999
Hampton, David IV, 1100
Hampton, David V, 65
Hampton, David V, 101
Hampton, David N. IV, 1132
Hampton, Edward IV, 582
Hampton, Edward B. II, 872
Hampton, Eleanor V, 65
Hampton, Eli IV, 1060
Hampton, Eli IV, 1100
Hampton, Elisha V, 65
Hampton, Eliz. III, 186
Hampton, Eliz. III, 347
Hampton, Eliza V, 970
Hampton, Eliza C. V, 570
Hampton, Eliza C. V, 970
Hampton, Elizabeth II, 541
Hampton, Elizabeth II, 549
Hampton, Elizabeth III, 149
Hampton, Elizabeth IV, 403
Hampton, Elizabeth IV, 582
Hampton, Elizabeth IV, 1060
Hampton, Elizabeth IV, 1074
Hampton, Elizabeth IV, 1099
Hampton, Elizabeth IV, 1100
Hampton, Elizabeth V, 65
Hampton, Elizabeth V, 136
Hampton, Elmer N. IV, 820
Hampton, Elvira IV, 1100
Hampton, Elvira IV, 1132
Hampton, Elvira E. II, 872
Hampton, Elvira E. II, 922
Hampton, Elwood III, 149
Hampton, Emeline III, 149
Hampton, Emily IV, 216
Hampton, Emily IV, 335
Hampton, Emily IV, 403
Hampton, Emily IV, 582
Hampton, Emily V, 570
Hampton, Emily V, 908
Hampton, Emlen IV, 794
Hampton, Emlen Griffith IV, 529
Hampton, Esther IV, 403
Hampton, Esther IV, 427
Hampton, Esther IV, 582
Hampton, Esther IV, 1060
Hampton, Esther IV, 1071
Hampton, Esther IV, 1100
Hampton, Ethel May V, 496
Hampton, Eunice IV, 403
Hampton, Eunice IV, 422
Hampton, Eunice IV, 1060
Hampton, Eunice IV, 1100
Hampton, Eunice IV, 1117
Hampton, Eunice V, 65
Hampton, Eunice V, 136
Hampton, Ezekiel V, 623
Hampton, Flora V, 623
Hampton, Flora B. V, 623
Hampton, George Smedley II, 541
Hampton, George Smedley II, 600
Hampton, Hannah II, 806
Hampton, Hannah II, 1011
Hampton, Hannah IV, 403
Hampton, Hannah IV, 962
Hampton, Hannah IV, 1060
Hampton, Hannah IV, 1099
Hampton, Hannah IV, 1100
Hampton, Hannah IV, 1117
Hampton, Hannah Ann IV, 1100
Hampton, Hannah Ann IV, 1132
Hampton, Hannah J. II, 844
Hampton, Hannah J. II, 872
Hampton, Henry Dennis IV, 216
Hampton, Henry Dennis V, 570
Hampton, Henry Dennis V, 908
Hampton, Henry T. II, 872
Hampton, Hiram IV, 335
Hampton, Hiram IV, 403
Hampton, Isaac IV, 1099
Hampton, Isaac IV, 1100
Hampton, Isaac V, 496
Hampton, Jacob V, 65
Hampton, Jacob V, 136
Hampton, Jacob, Jr. V, 65
Hampton, James II, 541
Hampton, James IV, 216
Hampton, James IV, 335
Hampton, James IV, 403
Hampton, James IV, 582
Hampton, James IV, 1100
Hampton, James H. IV, 582
Hampton, James H. IV, 1060
Hampton, James Hiram IV, 582
Hampton, James Hiram IV, 1061
Hampton, Jane V, 65
Hampton, Jane V, 101
Hampton, Jason IV, 403
Hampton, Jason IV, 962
Hampton, Jason IV, 1011
Hampton, Jason IV, 1060
Hampton, Jason IV, 1100
Hampton, Jason IV, 1120
Hampton, Jehiel V, 65
Hampton, Jesse IV, 1100
Hampton, Jessie Sanders V, 334
Hampton, Jno VI, 291
Hampton, Jno. VI, 930
Hampton, John II, 541
Hampton, John III, 149
Hampton, John IV, 127
Hampton, John IV, 216
Hampton, John IV, 403
Hampton, John IV, 582
Hampton, John IV, 589
Hampton, John IV, 593
Hampton, John IV, 600
Hampton, John IV, 1049
Hampton, John IV, 1055
Hampton, John IV, 1060
Hampton, John IV, 1100
Hampton, John VI, 312
Hampton, John VI, 975
Hampton, John C. II, 946
Hampton, John C. IV, 794
Hampton, John W. II, 872
Hampton, John W. II, 922
Hampton, John W. II, 923
Hampton, John W. IV, 582
Hampton, John W. V, 570
Hampton, John Watts II, 798
Hampton, John Watts II, 825
Hampton, John, Jr. IV, 582
Hampton, John, Jr. IV, 1060
Hampton, Jonathan IV, 1100
Hampton, Jonathan P. IV, 1060
Hampton, Jonathan P. IV, 1099
Hampton, Joseph III, 149
Hampton, Joseph IV, 582
Hampton, Joseph IV, 1060
Hampton, Joseph Arnold IV, 582
Hampton, Julia IV, 216
Hampton, Julia V, 570
Hampton, Julia V, 908
Hampton, Katherine T. III, 149
Hampton, Lavina IV, 582
Hampton, Levi IV, 216
Hampton, Levi IV, 335
Hampton, Levi IV, 403
Hampton, Levi IV, 582
Hampton, Levi IV, 591
Hampton, Levi Hampton IV, 582
Hampton, Levi Hampton IV, 1060
Hampton, Lewis II, 948
Hampton, Lewis Pusey II, 1085
Hampton, Lewis Pusey IV, 794
Hampton, Lizzie V, 623
Hampton, Louisa IV, 794
Hampton, Louisa M. IV, 985
Hampton, Lovicia E. III, 149
Hampton, Lucinda IV, 582
Hampton, Lucinda IV, 617
Hampton, Lucinda IV, 621
Hampton, Lucinda IV, 1100
Hampton, Lucy II, 798
Hampton, Lura Louise IV, 820
Hampton, Lydia IV, 1060
Hampton, Lydia A. IV, 794
Hampton, Lydia Ann IV, 582
Hampton, Lydia Ann IV, 591
Hampton, Lydia Ann IV, 794
Hampton, Margaret V, 496
Hampton, Margaret V, 529
Hampton, Maria IV, 820
Hampton, Martha II, 872
Hampton, Martha IV, 582
Hampton, Martha IV, 1060
Hampton, Martha IV, 1100
Hampton, Martha E. V, 623
Hampton, Mary II, 370
Hampton, Mary II, 541
Hampton, Mary III, 149
Hampton, Mary IV, 127
Hampton, Mary IV, 216
Hampton, Mary IV, 335
Hampton, Mary IV, 403
Hampton, Mary IV, 565
Hampton, Mary IV, 569
Hampton, Mary IV, 577
Hampton, Mary IV, 582
Hampton, Mary IV, 589
Hampton, Mary IV, 593
Hampton, Mary IV, 600
Hampton, Mary IV, 1049
Hampton, Mary IV, 1055
Hampton, Mary IV, 1060
Hampton, Mary IV, 1096
Hampton, Mary IV, 1099
Hampton, Mary IV, 1100
Hampton, Mary V, 65
Hampton, Mary Ann IV, 403
Hampton, Mary Ann IV, 582
Hampton, Mary Ann IV, 593
Hampton, Mary Ann IV, 962
Hampton, Mary Ann IV, 1011
Hampton, Mary Ann IV, 1060
Hampton, Mary Anna IV, 582
Hampton, Mary E. IV, 716
Hampton, Mary E. IV, 757
Hampton, Mary E. IV, 820
Hampton, Mary E. IV, 842
Hampton, Mary Eliza IV, 794
Hampton, Mary Ellen IV, 716
Hampton, Mary Elma IV, 1060
Hampton, Mary Lamb II, 825
Hampton, Maryann IV, 1100
Hampton, Maryann IV, 1120
Hampton, Milton V, 570
Hampton, Naomi V, 623
Hampton, Olive IV, 1060
Hampton, Oliver IV, 216
Hampton, Oliver IV, 582
Hampton, Oliver IV, 1060
Hampton, Oliver IV, 1100
Hampton, Oliver V, 570
Hampton, Oliver V, 908
Hampton, Oliver V, 970
Hampton, Orange V, 496
Hampton, Orange V, 497
Hampton, Phebe IV, 1100
Hampton, Rachel V, 44
Hampton, Rachel V, 65
Hampton, Rachel M. V, 496
Hampton, Rachel M. V, 541
Hampton, Rebecca II, 370
Hampton, Rebecca II, 798
Hampton, Rebecca V, 496
Hampton, Rebecca V, 570
Hampton, Rebecca F. II, 872
Hampton, Rebecca F. II, 922
Hampton, Richard IV, 820
Hampton, Richard IV, 1060
Hampton, Richard IV, 1100
Hampton, Richard B. IV, 1060
Hampton, Richard B. IV, 1099
Hampton, Robert IV, 582
Hampton, Robert IV, 1060
Hampton, Robert IV, 1100
Hampton, Robert W. IV, 182
Hampton, Robert W. IV, 216
Hampton, Robert W. V, 570
Hampton, Russell B. IV, 716
Hampton, Russell B. IV, 757
Hampton, Russell B. IV, 820
Hampton, Russell B. IV, 842
Hampton, Ruth IV, 1061
Hampton, Ruth IV, 1100
Hampton, Ruth Amy IV, 820
Hampton, Ruth Amy IV, 838
Hampton, Ruth Ann IV, 456
Hampton, Ruth Anna IV, 403
Hampton, Ruth C. IV, 1060
Hampton, Samuel II, 370
Hampton, Samuel II, 541
Hampton, Samuel IV, 403
Hampton, Samuel IV, 582
Hampton, Samuel B. IV, 1060
Hampton, Samuel B. IV, 1074
Hampton, Samuel B. IV, 1099
Hampton, Samuel B. IV, 1100
Hampton, Sara IV, 214
Hampton, Sarah II, 541
Hampton, Sarah II, 600
Hampton, Sarah III, 149
Hampton, Sarah IV, 126
Hampton, Sarah IV, 127
Hampton, Sarah IV, 403
Hampton, Sarah IV, 527
Hampton, Sarah IV, 529
Hampton, Sarah IV, 582
Hampton, Sarah IV, 716
Hampton, Sarah IV, 794
Hampton, Sarah IV, 820
Hampton, Sarah IV, 985
Hampton, Sarah IV, 1060
Hampton, Sarah IV, 1099
Hampton, Sarah IV, 1100
Hampton, Sarah IV, 1120
Hampton, Sarah IV, 1132
Hampton, Sarah V, 65
Hampton, Sarah V, 100
Hampton, Sarah G. IV, 794
Hampton, Sarah G. IV, 1060
Hampton, Sarah G. IV, 1061
Hampton, Sarah W. IV, 423
Hampton, Sarah W. IV, 582
Hampton, Sarah W. IV, 589
Hampton, Susan IV, 1056
Hampton, Susan IV, 1060
Hampton, Thomas IV, 403
Hampton, Thomas IV, 962
Hampton, Thomas IV, 1060
Hampton, Thomas IV, 1099
Hampton, Thomas IV, 1117
Hampton, Thomas IV, 1132
Hampton, Thomas VI, 30
Hampton, Thomas P. IV, 1100
Hampton, Thos. VI, 48
Hampton, Wd. Sarah II, 600
Hampton, William II, 946
Hampton, William II, 948
Hampton, William II, 1085
Hampton, William IV, 529
Hampton, William IV, 1060
Hampton, William R. IV, 820
Hampton, William S. IV, 1060
Hampton, Wm. IV, 794
Hampton, Wm. IV, 1061
Hampton, Wm. R. IV, 820
Hampton, Wm. S. IV, 1061
Hampton, Zachariah II, 1085
Hampton, Zachariah IV, 529
Hampton, Zachariah IV, 794
Hampton, Zachariah IV, 1060
Hampton, Zachariah B. IV, 126
Hampton, Zachariah B. IV, 127
Hampton, Zachariah B. IV, 529
Hampton, Zachariah B. VI, 646
Hamson, John II, 541
Hamton, David II, 999
Hamton, Eunice V, 44
Hamton, Hannah IV, 403
Hamton, Jacob V, 44
Hamton, Mary V, 44
Hamton, Sarah II, 541
Hana, Robert IV, 870
Hanan, Addison G. III, 83
Hanan, Addison G. III, 149
Hanan, Anna L. III, 83
Hanan, Anna L. III, 149
Hanan, Anna Livingston III, 149
Hanan, Charles Burton III, 149
Hanan, Henrietta F. III, 149
Hanan, John H. III, 149
Hanan, Jos. T. III, 273
Hanan, Leonard McDowell III, 149
Hanan, Lillian III, 83
Hanan, Lillian III, 149
Hanan, Lillian J. III, 149
Hanan, Richard Addison III, 149
Hanan, Wd. Lillian J. III, 273
Hanbee, Clarky I, 66
Hanby, Ann II, 76
Hanby, Ann II, 83
Hanby, Jno. VI, 501
Hanby, Mary II, 76
Hanby, Mary II, 91
Hanby, Mary VI, 501
Hanby, Wm. II, 76
Hanby, Wm. II, 91
Hanbys, Mary II, 76
Hance, ??? III, 149
Hance, Abram IV, 1163
Hance, Albert E. II, 798
Hance, Albert E. II, 1065
Hance, Albert E. II, 1073

Hance, Amy L. III, 149
Hance, Amy L. III, 233
Hance, Angelina III, 149
Hance, Ann II, 76
Hance, Ann II, 229
Hance, Ann II, 238
Hance, Ann II, 999
Hance, Ann A. II, 1044
Hance, Ann A. II, 1051
Hance, Ann A. II, 1068
Hance, Ann A. II, 1073
Hance, Anne II, 798
Hance, Anne II, 872
Hance, Anne II, 1073
Hance, Anne II, 1078
Hance, Annie II, 784
Hance, Annie P. II, 1073
Hance, Anselm III, 149
Hance, Anselm B. III, 39
Hance, Anselm B. III, 149
Hance, Anselm B. III, 241
Hance, Anselm B. III, 369
Hance, Anseln B. III, 228
Hance, Benj. B. III, 149
Hance, Benj. B. III, 155
Hance, Benjamin IV, 1163
Hance, Beulah C. II, 1071
Hance, Beulah C. II, 1073
Hance, David II, 229
Hance, David II, 320
Hance, David II, 999
Hance, Deborah II, 133
Hance, Ebenezer II, 798
Hance, Ebenezer II, 999
Hance, Ebenezer II, 1051
Hance, Ebenezer II, 1068
Hance, Ebenezer II, 1073
Hance, Ebenezer II, 1077
Hance, Ebenezer II, 1078
Hance, Edward II, 119
Hance, Edward II, 229
Hance, Edward II, 872
Hance, Edward II, 1073
Hance, Edward B. II, 76
Hance, Elisabeth II, 193
Hance, Elisabeth II, 229
Hance, Eliza II, 229
Hance, Eliza II, 1065
Hance, Eliza IV, 1163
Hance, Elizabeth II, 229
Hance, Elizabeth II, 1073
Hance, Elizabeth II, 1075
Hance, Elizabeth A. III, 149
Hance, Elizabeth L. II, 1073
Hance, Ellen III, 39
Hance, Ellen III, 149
Hance, Ellen III, 241
Hance, Ellen III, 369
Hance, Ellen Coddington III, 149
Hance, Esther II, 999
Hance, Esther II, 1051
Hance, Esther II, 1065
Hance, Esther II, 1073
Hance, Esther II, 1077
Hance, Esther IV, 1163
Hance, Evaline IV, 892
Hance, George A. II, 1073
Hance, Hannah II, 76
Hance, Hannah II, 102
Hance, Hannah II, 119
Hance, Hannah II, 133
Hance, Hannah II, 229
Hance, Hannah II, 541
Hance, Hannah II, 744
Hance, Hannah II, 872
Hance, Hannah B. III, 149
Hance, Hannah L. III, 149
Hance, Hannah L. III, 228
Hance, Henry T. II, 798
Hance, Henry T. II, 1065
Hance, Henry T. II, 1073
Hance, Horace II, 872
Hance, Horace II, 1073
Hance, Isaac II, 30
Hance, Isaac II, 76
Hance, Isaac II, 105
Hance, Isaac II, 119
Hance, Isaac II, 133
Hance, Isaiah P. II, 872
Hance, Isaiah P. II, 1073
Hance, Isaiah Price II, 798
Hance, James II, 76
Hance, James II, 102
Hance, James II, 119
Hance, James II, 133
Hance, James II, 229
Hance, Jane E. III, 39
Hance, Jane Eliza III, 149
Hance, Jedediah II, 229
Hance, Jediah II, 193
Hance, Jediah II, 229
Hance, Jediah II, 238
Hance, Jemima III, 149
Hance, John II, 76
Hance, John II, 119
Hance, John II, 133
Hance, John II, 150
Hance, John, Jr. II, 119
Hance, John, Jr. II, 150
Hance, Joseph II, 30
Hance, Joseph II, 76
Hance, Joseph II, 744
Hance, Juliet VI, 927
Hance, Lydia II, 999
Hance, Lydia II, 1017
Hance, Lydia II, 1051
Hance, Martha II, 30
Hance, Martha II, 1073
Hance, Martha II, 1077
Hance, Mary II, 30
Hance, Mary II, 76
Hance, Mary II, 105
Hance, Mary II, 192
Hance, Mary II, 229
Hance, Mary II, 707
Hance, Mary Ann II, 76
Hance, Mary Ann II, 119
Hance, Mary Ann II, 150
Hance, Mary J. II, 798
Hance, Meliscent II, 76
Hance, Milesant II, 150
Hance, Milicent II, 76
Hance, Milisent II, 119
Hance, Millicent II, 133
Hance, Obadiah III, 149
Hance, Peter VI, 927
Hance, Phebe II, 798
Hance, Phebe II, 840
Hance, Phebe II, 872
Hance, Phebe II, 999
Hance, Phebe II, 1051
Hance, Phebe II, 1068
Hance, Phebe II, 1073
Hance, Phebe II, 1078
Hance, Rachel III, 149
Hance, Rachel III, 369
Hance, Rachel Rebecca III, 149
Hance, Rebecca Ann II, 119
Hance, Rebecca Ann II, 150
Hance, Rebecca P. II, 744
Hance, Reco C. III, 149
Hance, Robert William III, 149
Hance, Sarah II, 30
Hance, Sarah II, 541
Hance, Sarah II, 872
Hance, Sarah III, 233
Hance, Sarah III, 241
Hance, Sarah IV, 1163
Hance, Sarah Ann III, 149
Hance, Sarah Ann III, 241
Hance, Sarah D. IV, 892
Hance, Sarah D. IV, 1031
Hance, Sarah Lavinia III, 149
Hance, Sarah Lavinia III, 155
Hance, Sarepta II, 229
Hance, Sarepta II, 238
Hance, Susan III, 155
Hance, Susan B. III, 149
Hance, Susan B. III, 155
Hance, Susan Woolley III, 149
Hance, Sylvanus III, 233
Hance, Thomas III, 149
Hance, Thomas IV, 892
Hance, Thomas IV, 1163
Hance, Thomas C. IV, 1163
Hance, Timothy II, 784
Hance, Timothy II, 798
Hance, Timothy II, 872
Hance, Timothy II, 999
Hance, Timothy II, 1051
Hance, Timothy II, 1073
Hance, Timothy II, 1078
Hance, William II, 30
Hance, William IV, 1163
Hance, Wm. II, 76
Hancher, Hannah VI, 365
Hancher, Hannah VI, 397
Hancher, Leonard V, 458
Hanckey, Aaron I, 1153
Hanckey, Aaron, Jr. I, 1153
Hanckey, Francis I, 1153
Hanckey, William I, 1153
Hancks, Abraham VI, 822
Hancks, James VI, 826
Hancks, Lucy VI, 822
Hancock, ??? II, 781
Hancock, ??? III, 150
Hancock, Achsah II, 218
Hancock, Achsah II, 229
Hancock, Ambrose VI, 927
Hancock, Ammon VI, 927
Hancock, Ammon G. VI, 927
Hancock, Ammon G. VI, 992
Hancock, Amos T. II, 291
Hancock, Amy II, 176
Hancock, Amy II, 212
Hancock, Amy II, 229
Hancock, Amy II, 310
Hancock, Anay VI, 927
Hancock, Ann II, 30
Hancock, Ann II, 310
Hancock, Ann II, 798
Hancock, Ann II, 960
Hancock, Ann III, 149
Hancock, Ann III, 150
Hancock, Ann M. II, 872
Hancock, Anna II, 176
Hancock, Anna II, 291
Hancock, Anna II, 300
Hancock, Anna II, 320
Hancock, Anna II, 324
Hancock, Anna C. II, 927
Hancock, Anna Simmons II, 872
Hancock, Anna Simmons II, 886
Hancock, Anna T. II, 150
Hancock, Anna T. II, 291
Hancock, Anna T. II, 303
Hancock, Anne I Sup 1, 4
Hancock, Anne II, 320
Hancock, Anne S. II, 310
Hancock, Anne S. II, 320
Hancock, Asa II, 176
Hancock, Asa II, 229
Hancock, Asa II, 291
Hancock, Asa II, 310
Hancock, Benj. VI, 90
Hancock, Benj. Franklin VI, 65
Hancock, Benjamin F. VI, 65
Hancock, Bethiah V, 841
Hancock, Bethiah V, 882
Hancock, Betsy Ann VI, 927
Hancock, Beulah II, 282
Hancock, Beulah II, 291
Hancock, Beulah II, 310
Hancock, Beulah II, 320
Hancock, Beulah II, 852
Hancock, Beulah II, 872
Hancock, Biddle II, 144
Hancock, Biddle II, 150
Hancock, Biddle II, 291
Hancock, Biddle II, 310
Hancock, Biddle II, 320
Hancock, Biddle II, 781
Hancock, Biddle II, 834
Hancock, Biddle II, 872
Hancock, Burtis II, 781
Hancock, Caleb II, 229
Hancock, Caleb II, 310
Hancock, Caleb II, 320
Hancock, Caleb II, 852
Hancock, Caleb II, 872
Hancock, Caroline VI, 958
Hancock, Caroline D. II, 798
Hancock, Caroline D. II, 852
Hancock, Caroline D. II, 872
Hancock, Carrie B. II, 798
Hancock, Charles II, 310
Hancock, Charles II, 320
Hancock, Charlotte II, 310
Hancock, Charlotte II, 320
Hancock, Charlotte E. VI, 927
Hancock, Chas. W. II, 872
Hancock, Christopher VI, 927
Hancock, Clayton II, 229
Hancock, Clayton II, 267
Hancock, Clayton II, 291
Hancock, Clement James II, 798
Hancock, D. B. VI, 859
Hancock, Daniel II, 229
Hancock, Daniel II, 802
Hancock, Dillwyn II, 150
Hancock, Dilwyn II, 150
Hancock, Edw. VI, 927
Hancock, Edward II, 30
Hancock, Edward II, 31
Hancock, Edward II, 77
Hancock, Edward VI, 927
Hancock, Edward VI, 942
Hancock, Edward VI, 958
Hancock, Edward VI, 993
Hancock, Edward Clinton II, 798
Hancock, Edward P. II, 150
Hancock, Edward P. II, 158
Hancock, Eliza Ann VI, 927
Hancock, Eliza W. II, 119
Hancock, Eliza W. II, 121
Hancock, Elizabeth II, 30
Hancock, Elizabeth II, 31
Hancock, Elizabeth II, 34
Hancock, Elizabeth II, 64
Hancock, Elizabeth II, 76
Hancock, Elizabeth II, 77
Hancock, Elizabeth II, 86
Hancock, Elizabeth II, 109
Hancock, Elizabeth II, 111
Hancock, Elizabeth II, 291
Hancock, Elizabeth II, 310
Hancock, Elizabeth II, 798
Hancock, Elizabeth II, 872
Hancock, Elizabeth II, 886
Hancock, Elizabeth IV, 36
Hancock, Elizabeth V, 841
Hancock, Elizabeth V, 882
Hancock, Elizabeth Ann II, 176
Hancock, Elizabeth Ann II, 279
Hancock, Elizabeth Ann II, 291
Hancock, Elizabeth Ann II, 310
Hancock, Elizabeth H. V, 886
Hancock, Elizabeth J. II, 872
Hancock, Elizabeth S. II, 316
Hancock, Elizabeth S. II, 320
Hancock, Elizaqbeth VI, 941
Hancock, Ellis II, 176
Hancock, Ellis II, 310
Hancock, Ellis H. II, 291
Hancock, Elsie II, 137
Hancock, Elvira VI, 826
Hancock, Emily II, 872
Hancock, Emma Alice VI, 65
Hancock, Emma J. VI, 65
Hancock, Ephraim II, 291
Hancock, Ephriam II, 310
Hancock, Ester II, 90
Hancock, Esther II, 31
Hancock, Esther II, 76
Hancock, Esther II, 144
Hancock, Esther II, 150
Hancock, Esther II, 781
Hancock, Esther II, 834
Hancock, Esther II, 836
Hancock, Esther II, 872
Hancock, Esther M. II, 872
Hancock, Flora II, 133
Hancock, Flora L. II, 133
Hancock, Frances VI, 927
Hancock, George IV, 36
Hancock, George IV, 716
Hancock, George B. II, 310
Hancock, George B. II, 320
Hancock, George B. II, 872
Hancock, George C. II, 176
Hancock, George C. II, 291
Hancock, George W. II, 798
Hancock, George W. II, 872
Hancock, George Washington II, 798
Hancock, Grace II, 31
Hancock, Hannah I, 542
Hancock, Hannah II, 30
Hancock, Hannah II, 31
Hancock, Hannah II, 34
Hancock, Hannah II, 51
Hancock, Hannah II, 69
Hancock, Hannah II, 76
Hancock, Hannah II, 77
Hancock, Hannah II, 86
Hancock, Hannah II, 105
Hancock, Hannah II, 150
Hancock, Hannah II, 158
Hancock, Hannah II, 228
Hancock, Hannah II, 229
Hancock, Hannah II, 798
Hancock, Hannah II, 872
Hancock, Hannah III, 149
Hancock, Hannah IV, 36
Hancock, Hannah IV, 716
Hancock, Hannah, Jr. II, 77
Hancock, Hariet II, 320
Hancock, Harriet II, 229
Hancock, Harriet II, 291
Hancock, Harriet II, 310
Hancock, Harriett VI, 927
Hancock, Helen II, 798
Hancock, Henry II, 30
Hancock, Henry J. II, 872
Hancock, Henry James II, 872
Hancock, Henry W. II, 144
Hancock, Henry W. II, 150
Hancock, Herbert Phillips VI, 65
Hancock, Hester II, 72
Hancock, Hester II, 76
Hancock, Howard Buzby II, 133
Hancock, Ida II, 133
Hancock, Irvin Thomas VI, 65
Hancock, Isabella V, 908
Hancock, Isabella V, 909
Hancock, Jacob V, 908
Hancock, Jane II, 30
Hancock, Jane II, 31
Hancock, Jane II, 68
Hancock, Jane II, 76
Hancock, Jane II, 229
Hancock, Jane II, 267
Hancock, Jane II, 291
Hancock, Jane II, 320
Hancock, Jane II, 541
Hancock, Jane VI, 910
Hancock, Jeanette Dyer II, 133
Hancock, Jenny VI, 891
Hancock, Jesse IV, 36
Hancock, Jesse IV, 716
Hancock, Jesse VI, 927
Hancock, Jno. VI, 927
Hancock, Joel IV, 36
Hancock, John II, 30
Hancock, John II, 31
Hancock, John II, 76
Hancock, John II, 119
Hancock, John II, 229
Hancock, John II, 370
Hancock, John III, 149
Hancock, John III, 231
Hancock, John IV, 36
Hancock, John VI, 834
Hancock, John VI, 871
Hancock, John VI, 916
Hancock, John VI, 919
Hancock, John VI, 927
Hancock, John VI, 938
Hancock, John VI, 960
Hancock, John VI, 968
Hancock, John C. II, 175
Hancock, John C. II, 176
Hancock, John C. II, 212
Hancock, John C. II, 229
Hancock, John C. II, 310
Hancock, John C. II, 320
Hancock, John C. II, 798
Hancock, John C. II, 852
Hancock, John C. II, 872
Hancock, John H. VI, 1013
Hancock, Jonathan II, 31
Hancock, Joseph II, 31
Hancock, Joseph II, 34
Hancock, Joseph II, 77
Hancock, Joseph II, 86
Hancock, Joseph II, 176
Hancock, Joseph II, 212
Hancock, Joseph II, 229
Hancock, Joseph II, 267
Hancock, Joseph II, 291
Hancock, Joseph II, 310
Hancock, Joseph II, 320
Hancock, Joseph V, 909
Hancock, Joseph B. II, 310
Hancock, Joseph B. II, 320
Hancock, Joseph B. II, 872
Hancock, Joseph B. II, 886
Hancock, Joseph C. II, 310
Hancock, Joseph G. II, 133
Hancock, Joseph L. II, 798
Hancock, Joseph Lee II, 791
Hancock, Joseph M. II, 872
Hancock, Joseph, Jr. II, 310
Hancock, Joseph, Jr. II, 320
Hancock, Joshua S. II, 310
Hancock, Joshua S. II, 320
Hancock, Julia Ann VI, 927
Hancock, Justus VI, 922
Hancock, Justus VI, 927
Hancock, Justus VI, 992
Hancock, Leannah VI, 835
Hancock, Lidya II, 31
Hancock, Lidya II, 71
Hancock, Lidya II, 76
Hancock, Lucy VI, 931
Hancock, Lula VI, 65
Hancock, Lulu VI, 65
Hancock, Lulu VI, 90
Hancock, Lydia II, 64
Hancock, Lydia II, 76
Hancock, Lydia II, 310
Hancock, Lydia L. II, 320
Hancock, Lydia L. II, 321
Hancock, Mabil II, 76
Hancock, Margaret II, 31
Hancock, Margaret II, 51
Hancock, Margaret II, 71
Hancock, Margaret II, 76
Hancock, Maria III, 150
Hancock, Martha II, 133
Hancock, Martha II, 150
Hancock, Martha II, 291
Hancock, Martha VI, 927
Hancock, Martha A. VI, 1013
Hancock, Martha J. II, 781
Hancock, Martha J. II, 834
Hancock, Martha J. II, 872
Hancock, Martha M. VI, 919
Hancock, Mary II, 30
Hancock, Mary II, 31
Hancock, Mary II, 61
Hancock, Mary II, 76
Hancock, Mary II, 133
Hancock, Mary II, 150

Hancock, Mary II, 291
Hancock, Mary II, 310
Hancock, Mary II, 319
Hancock, Mary II, 320
Hancock, Mary II, 872
Hancock, Mary II, 917
Hancock, Mary IV, 36
Hancock, Mary IV, 716
Hancock, Mary IV, 741
Hancock, Mary V, 841
Hancock, Mary V, 882
Hancock, Mary V, 885
Hancock, Mary Ann II, 320
Hancock, Mary Ann II, 326
Hancock, Mary Ann P. II, 310
Hancock, Mary Anna II, 791
Hancock, Mary C. II, 320
Hancock, Mary E. II, 144
Hancock, Mary E. II, 150
Hancock, Mary E. B. II, 150
Hancock, Mary Fogg II, 133
Hancock, Mary Jane VI, 992
Hancock, Mary L. II, 320
Hancock, Mary M. II, 872
Hancock, Milley VI, 927
Hancock, Miriam II, 214
Hancock, Miriam II, 229
Hancock, Miriam VI, 107
Hancock, Miriam VI, 108
Hancock, Moses II, 960
Hancock, N. H. VI, 859
Hancock, Nancy VI, 927
Hancock, Nancy VI, 993
Hancock, Nathan VI, 822
Hancock, Nathaniel II, 31
Hancock, Nathaniel II, 310
Hancock, Nethaniel II, 76
Hancock, Patience II, 176
Hancock, Patience II, 209
Hancock, Patience II, 212
Hancock, Patience II, 229
Hancock, Patience II, 267
Hancock, Patience II, 291
Hancock, Patience II, 310
Hancock, Patience II, 320
Hancock, Patience Ann II, 310
Hancock, Patience Ann II, 320
Hancock, Peggy VI, 825
Hancock, Perlina K. VI, 822
Hancock, Phebe II, 229
Hancock, Phebe II, 706
Hancock, Phebe H. II, 960
Hancock, Polly VI, 884
Hancock, Prudence II, 31
Hancock, Rachel II, 31
Hancock, Rachel II, 59
Hancock, Rachel II, 76
Hancock, Rachel II, 150
Hancock, Rachel II, 798
Hancock, Rachel II, 872
Hancock, Reading R. II, 176
Hancock, Reading R. II, 291
Hancock, Rebecca II, 31
Hancock, Rebecca II, 69
Hancock, Rebecca II, 76
Hancock, Rebecca II, 99
Hancock, Rebecca II, 133
Hancock, Rebeckah II, 31
Hancock, Rebeckah II, 76
Hancock, Rebeckah II, 109
Hancock, Rena Jane II, 310
Hancock, Richard II, 31
Hancock, Richard II, 72
Hancock, Richard II, 76
Hancock, Richard II, 133
Hancock, Richard VI, 109
Hancock, Ridgway II, 291
Hancock, Ridgway II, 310
Hancock, Ridgway II, 320
Hancock, Robert III, 150
Hancock, Romie Whitehead VI, 65
Hancock, Sabina IV, 36
Hancock, Sabina IV, 63
Hancock, Sabina IV, 716
Hancock, Sally B. VI, 834
Hancock, Saml. VI, 884
Hancock, Saml. VI, 930
Hancock, Samuel II, 30
Hancock, Samuel II, 31
Hancock, Samuel II, 59
Hancock, Samuel II, 69
Hancock, Samuel II, 76
Hancock, Samuel II, 150
Hancock, Samuel II, 158
Hancock, Samuel II, 798
Hancock, Samuel II, 872
Hancock, Samuel VI, 804
Hancock, Samuel VI, 894
Hancock, Samuel VI, 927
Hancock, Samuel VI, 941
Hancock, Samuel VI, 988
Hancock, Sarah I, 542
Hancock, Sarah I, 1120
Hancock, Sarah II, 31
Hancock, Sarah II, 57
Hancock, Sarah II, 61
Hancock, Sarah II, 68
Hancock, Sarah II, 76
Hancock, Sarah II, 104
Hancock, Sarah II, 105
Hancock, Sarah II, 133
Hancock, Sarah II, 370
Hancock, Sarah II, 541
Hancock, Sarah II, 802
Hancock, Sarah II, 812
Hancock, Sarah III, 149
Hancock, Sarah III, 150
Hancock, Sarah III, 231
Hancock, Sarah VI, 884
Hancock, Sarah VI, 927
Hancock, Sarah J. VI, 859
Hancock, Sarah M. II, 960
Hancock, Sarah Mulford II, 133
Hancock, Silas VI, 109
Hancock, Simon III, 149
Hancock, Simon VI, 927
Hancock, Sophia VI, 942
Hancock, Sophia Ann VI, 968
Hancock, Steven I Sup 1, 4
Hancock, Susan II, 133
Hancock, Susan C. II, 176
Hancock, Susan C. II, 291
Hancock, Susan C. II, 295
Hancock, Susan G. II, 119
Hancock, Susan G. II, 150
Hancock, Susan G. II, 158
Hancock, Susan Prior II, 791
Hancock, Susan R. II, 320
Hancock, Susana II, 76
Hancock, Susanna R. II, 310
Hancock, Susannah II, 76
Hancock, Susannah II, 99
Hancock, Thomas II, 31
Hancock, Thomas II, 76
Hancock, Thomas II, 133
Hancock, Thomas V, 908
Hancock, Thomas V, 909
Hancock, Thornton Conrow II, 872
Hancock, Thornton Conrow II, 886
Hancock, Walter II, 872
Hancock, Walter C. II, 798
Hancock, Walter C. II, 872
Hancock, Wd. Amy II, 175
Hancock, Wd. Mary VI, 109
Hancock, William II, 30
Hancock, William II, 31
Hancock, William II, 291
Hancock, William IV, 36
Hancock, William IV, 63
Hancock, William VI, 988
Hancock, William VI, 997
Hancock, William B. II, 320
Hancock, William C. II, 310
Hancock, William C. II, 320
Hancock, William C. II, 324
Hancock, William C. II, 798
Hancock, William P. II, 798
Hancock, William R. II, 291
Hancock, William, Jr. II, 31
Hancock, Winfred VI, 988
Hancock, Wm. II, 30
Hancock, Wm. II, 76
Hancock, Wm. II, 104
Hancock, Wm. II, 541
Hancock, Wm. II, 872
Hancock, Wm. IV, 716
Hancock, Wm. VI, 927
Hancock, Wm. C. II, 133
Hancock, Wm. C. II, 872
Hancock, Wm. Chambless, Jr. II, 133
Hancock, Wm. Thompson II, 150
Hancock, Wm., Jr. II, 30
Hancock, Wm., Jr. II, 68
Hancock, Wm., Jr. II, 69
Hancock, Wm., Jr. II, 76
Hand, James II, 444
Hand, Margaret B. III, 150
Hand, Margaret B. III, 197
Hand, Sarah III, 101
Hand, Sarah III, 150
Hand, Sarah III, 197
Hand, Silvanus III, 150
Hand, Silvanus III, 197
Handal, Blanche B. IV, 216
Handal, Clarence B. IV, 216
Handal, Daisy M. IV, 216
Handal, Mary R. IV, 216
Handcher, Ann VI, 397
Handcher, John VI, 397
Handcher, Mary VI, 397
Handcher, Mary VI, 448
Handcher, William VI, 397
Handcock, Hannah II, 58
Handcock, Hannah II, 76
Handcock, Miriam I, 393
Handcock, Miriam I, 418
Handcock, Sarah I, 382
Handcock, Sarah I, 393
Handcock, Thomas II, 58
Handcock, Thomas II, 76
Handley, ??? III, 150
Handley, Anne VI, 178
Handley, Brian Coaker VI, 178
Handley, Brian Croaker VI, 178
Handley, Charity I, 307
Handley, Charity I, 318
Handley, Charles III, 150
Handley, Daniel, Jr. V, 909
Handley, Dr. Daniel E. V, 909
Handley, Elizabeth IV, 1163
Handley, Jacob III, 150
Handley, Lucy J. I, 336
Handley, Margaret Matilda V, 909
Handley, Rachel VI, 171
Handley, Rachel VI, 178
Handley, Ruth I, 762
Handley, Theodore W. III, 150
Handley, Thomas VI, 161
Handley, Thomas VI, 171
Handley, Thomas VI, 178
Handman, Ally Compton V, 679
Handsher, Ann VI, 384
Handwert, Harry V, 999
Handwert, Mary A. V, 999
Handwork, Harry V, 999
Handwork, Mary A. V, 999
Handy, Eliza Frances Gordon II, 800
Handy, Herbert A. IV, 1253
Hane, Rachel III, 414
Hane, Rachel III, 435
Hanen, Rebecca H. V, 909
Hanen, Rebecca H. V, 925
Hanes, Catharine VI, 908
Hanes, David VI, 908
Hanes, Edward VI, 933
Hanes, Elizabeth III, 150
Hanes, Elizabeth III, 289
Hanes, Elizabeth III, 310
Hanes, Elizabeth V, 243
Hanes, Elizabeth V, 266
Hanes, Enos V, 266
Hanes, Esther Ann IV, 715
Hanes, Hannah I, 907
Hanes, Hannah I, 912
Hanes, Harriet A. III, 289
Hanes, John VI, 822
Hanes, Jonathan I, 963
Hanes, Joseph IV, 715
Hanes, Margaret S. III, 289
Hanes, Martha II, 75
Hanes, Martha V, 64
Hanes, Mary I, 812
Hanes, Mary I, 1048
Hanes, Mary II, 74
Hanes, Mary II, 105
Hanes, Mary II, 1002
Hanes, Mary III, 150
Hanes, Mary III, 310
Hanes, Mary IV, 715
Hanes, Mary V, 266
Hanes, Mary T. VI, 822
Hanes, Nathan VI, 397
Hanes, Nathan B. II, 149
Hanes, Rachel IV, 715
Hanes, Rebecca II, 108
Hanes, Rebecca Vickry II, 74
Hanes, Samuel V, 495
Hanes, Stephen III, 289
Hanes, Thomas III, 150
Hanes, Thomas III, 310
Hanes, Wm. III, 150
Hanes, Wm. III, 289
Hanes, Wm. Alex III, 289
Haney, A. M. V, 679
Haney, Abraham M. V, 570
Haney, Abraham M. V, 679
Haney, Abram V, 570
Haney, Abram V, 679
Haney, Abram M. V, 570
Haney, Alice I, 942
Haney, Archibald I, 880
Haney, Cassandra IV, 91
Haney, Cassandra IV, 101
Haney, Charles V, 570
Haney, Charles V, 571
Haney, Charles V, 679
Haney, Chas. V, 679
Haney, Delila C. V, 679
Haney, Delilah C. V, 679
Haney, Eliza II, 444
Haney, Elizabeth II, 370
Haney, Elizabeth V, 556
Haney, Elizabeth V, 570
Haney, Elizabeth V, 571
Haney, Elizabeth V, 679
Haney, Elizabeth B. V, 570
Haney, Elizabeth B. V, 679
Haney, Ella V, 570
Haney, Ella Mary V, 570
Haney, Ella Mary V, 679
Haney, Emma V, 679
Haney, Eva V, 571
Haney, Eva D. V, 570
Haney, Eva D. V, 679
Haney, James IV, 1319
Haney, Jerviss II, 370
Haney, John II, 370
Haney, John II, 444
Haney, John C. V, 570
Haney, John Charles V, 679
Haney, Joseph J. V, 570
Haney, Joseph W. V, 570
Haney, Joseph W. V, 679
Haney, Lila V, 570
Haney, Lila V, 679
Haney, Lila V, 716
Haney, Lila C. V, 679
Haney, Martin Jerviss II, 370
Haney, Mary I, 880
Haney, Mary E. IV, 1319
Haney, Rebecca I, 942
Haney, Sarah IV, 716
Haney, Thomas I, 942
Haney, Wm. IV, 1319
Hanglin, John H. IV, 1280
Hangrave, Samuel I, 61
Hanifer, Michael V, 334
Hanifur, Michael V, 334
Hank, Elenor VI, 397
Hank, Elleanor VI, 397
Hank, Hannah II, 176
Hank, Hannah II, 229
Hank, Hannah VI, 397
Hank, Hannah VI, 398
Hank, Hannah VI, 416
Hank, Hannah VI, 597
Hank, John II, 176
Hank, John II, 200
Hank, John II, 219
Hank, John II, 229
Hank, John II, 291
Hank, John II, 541
Hank, John IV, 23
Hank, John IV, 51
Hank, John VI, 397
Hank, John VI, 416
Hank, John VI, 597
Hank, Judith IV, 23
Hank, Judith IV, 36
Hank, Judith IV, 127
Hank, Judith IV, 962
Hank, Luke II, 229
Hank, Margaret VI, 376
Hank, Margaret VI, 397
Hank, Margaret VI, 398
Hank, Margaret VI, 416
Hank, Margrat VI, 397
Hank, Margret VI, 397
Hank, Rachel II, 219
Hank, Rachel II, 229
Hank, Rebecca II, 176
Hank, Rebecca II, 200
Hank, Rebecca II, 229
Hank, Sarah II, 229
Hank, Susannah VI, 374
Hank, Susannah VI, 397
Hank, Wd. Judith IV, 36
Hank, Widower John IV, 36
Hankel, Elizabeth VI, 732
Hankel, John Emmett VI, 732
Hankins, Jean VI, 398
Hankinson, Ambrose III, 150
Hankinson, Ann III, 150
Hankinson, Ann III, 373
Hankinson, Edward Y. IV, 529
Hankison, Holmes V, 623
Hankison, James V, 623
Hankison, Joseph H. V, 623
Hankison, Sarah J. V, 623
Hankle, Elizabeth VI, 927
Hankle, Jacob VI, 927
Hanks, Abraham VI, 839
Hanks, Ann VI, 501
Hanks, Austin J. V, 679
Hanks, Benson VI, 924
Hanks, Clara V, 679
Hanks, Eliza VI, 899
Hanks, Elizabeth VI, 994
Hanks, Fleetwood VI, 934
Hanks, Frances VI, 822
Hanks, Francis VI, 840
Hanks, Harmony VI, 927
Hanks, James V, 740
Hanks, James V, 809
Hanks, James, Sr. VI, 798
Hanks, John III, 150
Hanks, John V, 740
Hanks, John VI, 822
Hanks, Keziah V, 740
Hanks, Keziah V, 809
Hanks, Keziah V, 812
Hanks, Laura V, 679
Hanks, Martha V, 740
Hanks, Martha V, 752
Hanks, Martha V, 809
Hanks, Mary V, 725
Hanks, Mary V, 740
Hanks, Mary V, 752
Hanks, Mary V, 809
Hanks, Nancy VI, 822
Hanks, Nancy VI, 934
Hanks, Noah V, 740
Hanks, Noah V, 809
Hanks, Phebe V, 809
Hanks, Rachel V, 740
Hanks, Rachel V, 808
Hanks, Rachel V, 809
Hanks, Rachel VI, 501
Hanks, Rachel VI, 580
Hanks, Ruth I, 542
Hanks, Sally VI, 805
Hanks, Sarah C. V, 679
Hanks, Sarah Jane V, 392
Hanks, Sarah Jane V, 427
Hanks, Susan Jane VI, 873
Hanks, Tabitha VI, 798
Hanks, Thomas V, 740
Hanks, Thomas V, 809
Hanks, Thomas VI, 822
Hanks, Thomas VI, 841
Hanks, Thos. VI, 805
Hanks, William I, 1030
Hanks, William VI, 501
Hanks, William VI, 873
Hanks, William VI, 899
Hanks, William VI, 908
Hanks, William VI, 924
Hanks, William VI, 927
Hanks, William VI, 934
Hanks, William VI, 994
Hanks, Wm. VI, 993
Hanley, Benjamin IV, 870
Hanley, Caleb IV, 870
Hanley, Caleb P. IV, 870
Hanley, Catharine IV, 870
Hanley, James IV, 870
Hanley, Joseph IV, 870
Hanley, Latham IV, 870
Hanley, Phebe Ann IV, 870
Hanlin, Anna V, 47
Hanlin, Anna V, 65
Hanlin, Annie V, 392
Hanlon, Susanna IV, 382
Hanly, Benjamin IV, 716
Hann, Della V, 999
Hann, Enos V, 999
Hann, Hannah V, 999
Hann, Lydia IV, 1061
Hann, Lydia IV, 1082
Hann, Mrs. L. B. V, 999
Hanna, ??? IV, 603
Hanna, ??? VI, 293
Hanna, Ann IV, 36
Hanna, Ann IV, 629
Hanna, Ann VI, 313
Hanna, Anna IV, 629
Hanna, Anna IV, 820
Hanna, Anne IV, 629
Hanna, Anne IV, 645
Hanna, Anne IV, 706
Hanna, Anne IV, 716
Hanna, Benj. IV, 629
Hanna, Benjamin IV, 36
Hanna, Benjamin IV, 620
Hanna, Benjamin IV, 629
Hanna, Benjamin IV, 693
Hanna, Benjamin IV, 716
Hanna, Benjamin IV, 820
Hanna, Benjamin VI, 312
Hanna, Benjamin VI, 313
Hanna, Benjamin VI, 597
Hanna, Benjamin VI, 646
Hanna, Caleb IV, 629
Hanna, Caleb VI, 313
Hanna, Caleb VI, 597
Hanna, Catharine IV, 629
Hanna, Catharine IV, 634
Hanna, Catharine IV, 716
Hanna, Catharine IV, 820

Hanna, Catharine VI, 313
Hanna, Catharine VI, 597
Hanna, Catherine IV, 36
Hanna, Catherine IV, 629
Hanna, Catherine VI, 312
Hanna, Catherine VI, 313
Hanna, David IV, 629
Hanna, David VI, 313
Hanna, David VI, 597
Hanna, Eleanor III, 300
Hanna, Eleanor III, 357
Hanna, Eleanor G. III, 175
Hanna, Elizabeth Kersey IV, 706
Hanna, Esther IV, 36
Hanna, Esther IV, 629
Hanna, Esther IV, 634
Hanna, Esther VI, 313
Hanna, Esther VI, 597
Hanna, Hannah K. IV, 624
Hanna, Hannah K. IV, 629
Hanna, Hannah K. IV, 706
Hanna, Hannah K. IV, 716
Hanna, Hannah R. IV, 693
Hanna, Hannah R. IV, 716
Hanna, Hole Catharine IV, 629
Hanna, Jesse IV, 706
Hanna, Joshua IV, 629
Hanna, Joshua IV, 716
Hanna, Joshua IV, 820
Hanna, Leonard IV, 629
Hanna, Leonard IV, 716
Hanna, Leonard IV, 820
Hanna, Levi IV, 629
Hanna, Levi IV, 716
Hanna, Levi IV, 820
Hanna, Lewis IV, 716
Hanna, Lucy IV, 1253
Hanna, Malcolm B. III, 150
Hanna, Mary VI, 313
Hanna, Rachel IV, 620
Hanna, Rachel IV, 629
Hanna, Rachel IV, 716
Hanna, Rachel IV, 820
Hanna, Rachel VI, 646
Hanna, Rebecca III, 175
Hanna, Rebecca IV, 820
Hanna, Rebecca B. III, 145
Hanna, Rebecca B. III, 150
Hanna, Robert IV, 36
Hanna, Robert IV, 629
Hanna, Robert IV, 716
Hanna, Robert IV, 820
Hanna, Robert VI, 312
Hanna, Robert VI, 313
Hanna, Robert VI, 340
Hanna, Robert VI, 597
Hanna, Robert, Jr. IV, 629
Hanna, Robt. IV, 634
Hanna, Samuel Nichols IV, 629
Hanna, Sarah Glover II, 787
Hanna, Thomas IV, 36
Hanna, Thomas IV, 629
Hanna, Thomas IV, 706
Hanna, Thomas IV, 716
Hanna, Thomas IV, 820
Hanna, Thomas VI, 312
Hanna, Thomas VI, 313
Hanna, Thomas VI, 597
Hanna, Thos. IV, 629
Hanna, Triphena IV, 629
Hanna, Triphena IV, 649
Hanna, Triphena IV, 820
Hanna, Triphena IV, 835
Hanna, Triphenia IV, 716
Hanna, Tryphena IV, 629
Hanna, Tryphena IV, 716
Hanna, Tryphena VI, 646
Hanna, Tryphena VI, 683
Hanna, Tryphena VI, 685
Hanna, Tryphosa IV, 629
Hanna, Tryphosea IV, 716
Hanna, William III, 145
Hanna, William III, 150
Hanna, William III, 175
Hanna, William Betts VI, 313
Hanna, Zalinda IV, 629
Hanna, Zalinda IV, 716
Hanna, Zalinda IV, 820
Hanna, Zalinda IV, 825
Hanna, Zelinda IV, 820
Hannabass, David VI, 932
Hannabass, Elizabeth Ann VI, 1006
Hannabass, James VI, 912
Hannah, ??? IV, 861
Hannah, Addison G. III, 214
Hannah, Alice M. III, 234
Hannah, Anna IV, 629
Hannah, Anna IV, 806
Hannah, Anna IV, 820
Hannah, Anne IV, 820
Hannah, Anne IV, 870
Hannah, Arena V, 392
Hannah, Benjamin IV, 820
Hannah, Benjamin IV, 858
Hannah, Benjamin VI, 398
Hannah, Betsey VI, 927
Hannah, Catharine IV, 820
Hannah, Catharine IV, 870
Hannah, Catharine IV, 873
Hannah, Catharine IV, 907
Hannah, Catharine VI, 313
Hannah, Catharine VI, 822
Hannah, Catherine VI, 343
Hannah, Catherine VI, 398
Hannah, Deborah I, 393
Hannah, Eleanor III, 363
Hannah, Esther VI, 398
Hannah, Eva V, 679
Hannah, Florence V, 679
Hannah, Florence V, 682
Hannah, George VI, 927
Hannah, George B. VI, 822
Hannah, Hannah IV, 820
Hannah, Inman VI, 124
Hannah, James V, 679
Hannah, James VI, 822
Hannah, John VI, 927
Hannah, Joshua IV, 820
Hannah, Leonard IV, 820
Hannah, Levi IV, 820
Hannah, Martha VI, 822
Hannah, Mary I, 679
Hannah, Mary I, 717
Hannah, Mary II, 148
Hannah, Mary II, 150
Hannah, Mary VI, 646
Hannah, Mary VI, 675
Hannah, Netta VI, 718
Hannah, Pleasant T. VI, 928
Hannah, Rachel IV, 820
Hannah, Rebecca IV, 127
Hannah, Rebecca IV, 128
Hannah, Rebecca IV, 820
Hannah, Rebecca IV, 824
Hannah, Robert IV, 820
Hannah, Robert IV, 870
Hannah, Robert IV, 873
Hannah, Robert IV, 906
Hannah, Robert IV, 907
Hannah, Robert VI, 398
Hannah, Sarah VI, 822
Hannah, Sarah E. VI, 822
Hannah, Thomas IV, 629
Hannah, Thomas IV, 716
Hannah, Thomas IV, 820
Hannah, Thomas IV, 870
Hannah, Thomas VI, 398
Hannah, Triphena IV, 820
Hannah, Tryphena IV, 820
Hannah, William IV, 1280
Hannah, William VI, 822
Hannah, William L. VI, 822
Hannah, Wm. VI, 866
Hannah, Zalinda IV, 820
Hannah, Zelinda IV, 820
Hannan, Lydia VI, 398
Hannan, Lydia VI, 456
Hannas, Geo. VI, 859
Hannay, Charles H. IV, 962
Hannay, Mary IV, 962
Hanneman, Eleanor Rebecca III, 150
Hanneman, Frdk. Wm. John III, 150
Hanneman, William J. III, 150
Hanner, Marietta Shaw I, 634
Hanner, Paul Shaw I, 634
Hanner, Thelma B. Shaw I, 634
Hanney, Elizabeth II, 370
Hanney, Jerviss II, 370
Hanney, John II, 370
Hannicutt, Elizabeth VI, 118
Hannicutt, Thomas VI, 118
Hannon, William IV, 216
Hannon, William IV, 217
Hannum, Alce II, 541
Hannum, Alice II, 541
Hansburg, Sarah VI, 501
Hansburg, Sarah VI, 538
Hansbury, Sarah VI, 501
Hansbury, Sarah VI, 538
Hanse, David II, 291
Hanse, Edmund Edward II, 176
Hanse, Eliza II, 218
Hanse, Elizabeth II, 229
Hanse, Hannah II, 229
Hanse, Isaac II, 76
Hanse, James II, 76
Hanse, Jediah II, 176
Hanse, John II, 76
Hanse, Joseph II, 76
Hanse, Martha II, 71
Hanse, Martha II, 76
Hanse, Mary II, 71
Hanse, Mary II, 76
Hanse, Sarah II, 872
Hansel, Bessie V, 174
Hansel, Frances V, 497
Hansel, Oliver W. V, 497
Hansell, Albert II, 310
Hansell, Amos II, 310
Hansell, Ann II, 872
Hansell, Ann II, 907
Hansell, Anna II, 311
Hansell, Anna S. II, 310
Hansell, Anna S. II, 320
Hansell, Dudley Rex II, 310
Hansell, Dudley Rex II, 320
Hansell, Elizabeth II, 310
Hansell, Ella III, 207
Hansell, Ella III, 357
Hansell, Frances V, 497
Hansell, Hannah II, 310
Hansell, Hannah II, 320
Hansell, Hannah II, 872
Hansell, Hannah II, 874
Hansell, Hannah VI, 361
Hansell, Hannah VI, 398
Hansell, James II, 874
Hansell, James S. II, 872
Hansell, Lydia II, 310
Hansell, Mary II, 707
Hansell, Maurice II, 310
Hansell, Maurice II, 320
Hansell, Perry V, 66
Hansell, Virginia II, 310
Hansell, Virginia II, 320
Hansell, Wilmot II, 310
Hansen, Anna C. III, 150
Hansen, Anna C. III, 274
Hansen, C. F. A. III, 150
Hansen, C. F. A. III, 274
Hansen, C. William III, 414
Hansen, C. Wm. III, 447
Hansen, Caroline III, 150
Hansen, Christian Wm. III, 414
Hansen, Dorothy C. III, 150
Hansen, Harold R. III, 150
Hansen, Hazel III, 150
Hansen, Hazel III, 225
Hansen, Helen D. III, 414
Hansen, Keziah III, 150
Hansen, Lillian III, 414
Hansen, Lillian III, 447
Hansen, Nathaniel III, 150
Hansen, Olivia III, 150
Hansen, Olivia III, 274
Hansen, Robert B. III, 150
Hansen, Rudy III, 150
Hansen, Rudy C. III, 150
Hansen, Rudy C. III, 225
Hansen, Wd. Hazel III, 225
Hansen, William IV, 1364
Hansford, John VI, 975
Hansford, Sally VI, 975
Hanshaw, Ann VI, 397
Hanson, ??? IV, 403
Hanson, Almeda IV, 1095
Hanson, Almeda IV, 1100
Hanson, Ann IV, 404
Hanson, Ann IV, 582
Hanson, Ann E. IV, 1132
Hanson, Ann Eliza IV, 387
Hanson, Ann Eliza IV, 404
Hanson, Ann Eliza IV, 1132
Hanson, Asa IV, 217
Hanson, Asa IV, 404
Hanson, Asa IV, 582
Hanson, Benjamin IV, 403
Hanson, Benjamin IV, 433
Hanson, Benjamin H. IV, 375
Hanson, Benjamin H. IV, 404
Hanson, Benjamin Herman IV, 404
Hanson, Borden IV, 381
Hanson, Borden IV, 403
Hanson, Borden IV, 582
Hanson, Caleb L. IV, 404
Hanson, Caroline III, 150
Hanson, Cidney IV, 404
Hanson, Cidney IV, 1061
Hanson, Clarkey IV, 403
Hanson, Clarkey IV, 404
Hanson, Clarkey IV, 458
Hanson, Clarkson IV, 404
Hanson, Cora IV, 404
Hanson, Cora IV, 450
Hanson, Cora Sarah IV, 404
Hanson, Daniel VI, 134
Hanson, David IV, 403
Hanson, Deborah IV, 374
Hanson, Deborah IV, 403
Hanson, Deborah IV, 404
Hanson, Deborah IV, 438
Hanson, Deborah IV, 442
Hanson, Deborah IV, 450
Hanson, Deborah Bundy IV, 375
Hanson, Deborah H. IV, 374
Hanson, Deborah H. IV, 404
Hanson, Dempsey B. IV, 1132
Hanson, Demsey IV, 403
Hanson, Demsey B. IV, 404
Hanson, Demsey B. IV, 1132
Hanson, Edo IV, 404
Hanson, Edwin IV, 582
Hanson, Edwin Morris IV, 1100
Hanson, Elijah IV, 148
Hanson, Elijah IV, 217
Hanson, Elijah IV, 374
Hanson, Elijah IV, 380
Hanson, Elijah IV, 388
Hanson, Elijah IV, 403
Hanson, Elijah IV, 404
Hanson, Elijah IV, 446
Hanson, Elijah IV, 458
Hanson, Elijah IV, 582
Hanson, Elijah IV, 1061
Hanson, Elijah IV, 1100
Hanson, Elijah, Jr. IV, 404
Hanson, Elisha IV, 582
Hanson, Eliza IV, 217
Hanson, Eliza IV, 374
Hanson, Eliza IV, 403
Hanson, Eliza IV, 404
Hanson, Eliza IV, 441
Hanson, Eliza IV, 446
Hanson, Eliza IV, 450
Hanson, Eliza IV, 582
Hanson, Eliza IV, 1100
Hanson, Elizabeth II, 541
Hanson, Elizabeth IV, 403
Hanson, Elizabeth IV, 404
Hanson, Elizabeth IV, 454
Hanson, Emily Allen V, 909
Hanson, Emma J. IV, 1100
Hanson, Florence V, 497
Hanson, Florence V, 679
Hanson, Florence N. V, 679
Hanson, George F. IV, 404
Hanson, George T. IV, 1132
Hanson, Greenbury D. II, 370
Hanson, Gulielma II, 872
Hanson, Gulielma II, 924
Hanson, Gulielma M. II, 872
Hanson, Gulielma Maria II, 798
Hanson, Harold R. III, 150
Hanson, Henry IV, 404
Hanson, Henry IV, 1132
Hanson, Ida IV, 403
Hanson, Iddo IV, 404
Hanson, Isaac IV, 403
Hanson, Isaac IV, 404
Hanson, Isaac IV, 1061
Hanson, Isaac, Jr. IV, 404
Hanson, James IV, 1061
Hanson, Jesse IV, 403
Hanson, Joan II, 541
Hanson, Joan II, 669
Hanson, Joanna IV, 403
Hanson, Joanna IV, 404
Hanson, Joanna IV, 408
Hanson, Joanna IV, 1061
Hanson, Joannah IV, 404
Hanson, John IV, 404
Hanson, John IV, 582
Hanson, John C. IV, 1132
Hanson, John Clarkson IV, 1132
Hanson, John M. IV, 404
Hanson, John M. IV, 1132
Hanson, John Milton IV, 403
Hanson, Joseph IV, 403
Hanson, Joseph IV, 404
Hanson, Joseph IV, 408
Hanson, Joseph IV, 582
Hanson, Joseph IV, 1132
Hanson, Joseph B. II, 541
Hanson, Joseph B. II, 872
Hanson, Joseph B. II, 924
Hanson, Joseph Berry II, 798
Hanson, Joseph S. IV, 582
Hanson, Joseph S. IV, 1091
Hanson, Joseph S. IV, 1100
Hanson, Keziah III, 150
Hanson, Lavisa IV, 404
Hanson, Lavisa IV, 456
Hanson, Levi IV, 582
Hanson, Levica IV, 1100
Hanson, Levisa IV, 404
Hanson, Levisa IV, 1132
Hanson, Levisa IV, 1138
Hanson, Levisa W. IV, 1132
Hanson, Lovice IV, 380
Hanson, Lovice IV, 403
Hanson, Lovisa IV, 1100
Hanson, Lovisa W. IV, 404
Hanson, Lovise IV, 403
Hanson, Lucinda IV, 375
Hanson, Lucinda IV, 404
Hanson, Lucinda IV, 433
Hanson, Lydia IV, 217
Hanson, Lydia IV, 403
Hanson, Lydia IV, 408
Hanson, Lydia IV, 1100
Hanson, Lydia IV, 1132
Hanson, Lydia M. II, 707
Hanson, Malinda IV, 404
Hanson, Malinda IV, 1061
Hanson, Manoah IV, 403
Hanson, Manoah IV, 422
Hanson, Manoah IV, 450
Hanson, Manoah IV, 1100
Hanson, Manoah IV, 1120
Hanson, Manoah IV, 1132
Hanson, Manoah, Jr. IV, 404
Hanson, Margaret II, 541
Hanson, Margaret II, 597
Hanson, Martha IV, 404
Hanson, Martha IV, 422
Hanson, Martha IV, 582
Hanson, Martha IV, 1132
Hanson, Mary II, 541
Hanson, Mary II, 625
Hanson, Mary IV, 404
Hanson, Mary IV, 406
Hanson, Mary IV, 417
Hanson, Mary IV, 1132
Hanson, Mary E. II, 872
Hanson, Mary E. II, 924
Hanson, Mary E. IV, 404
Hanson, Mary E. IV, 433
Hanson, Mary E. IV, 1132
Hanson, Mary Z. IV, 1095
Hanson, Mary Z. IV, 1100
Hanson, Maud IV, 404
Hanson, Maud Ella IV, 404
Hanson, Menoah IV, 148
Hanson, Menoah IV, 160
Hanson, Milicent IV, 404
Hanson, Milicent IV, 1130
Hanson, Milicent IV, 1132
Hanson, Milisant IV, 1100
Hanson, Millicent IV, 403
Hanson, Millicent IV, 1120
Hanson, Millicent IV, 1132
Hanson, Nathaniel III, 150
Hanson, Patience IV, 388
Hanson, Patience IV, 403
Hanson, Phebe IV, 148
Hanson, Phebe IV, 404
Hanson, Phebe IV, 1100
Hanson, Phebe J. IV, 404
Hanson, Phebe J. IV, 1132
Hanson, Phebe Jane IV, 1132
Hanson, Phebe Jane IV, 1137
Hanson, Phoebe IV, 403
Hanson, Prudence IV, 404
Hanson, Prudence IV, 419
Hanson, Prudence IV, 582
Hanson, Prudence IV, 1100
Hanson, Prudence IV, 1132
Hanson, Rachel IV, 148
Hanson, Rachel IV, 160
Hanson, Rachel IV, 381
Hanson, Rachel IV, 402
Hanson, Rachel IV, 403
Hanson, Rachel IV, 404
Hanson, Rachel IV, 422
Hanson, Rachel IV, 450
Hanson, Rachel IV, 582
Hanson, Rachel IV, 1100
Hanson, Rachel IV, 1107
Hanson, Rachel IV, 1132
Hanson, Rachel B. IV, 1091
Hanson, Rachel B. IV, 1100
Hanson, Rebecca II, 798
Hanson, Rebecca IV, 381
Hanson, Rebecca IV, 404
Hanson, Robert IV, 403
Hanson, Robert IV, 404
Hanson, Robert IV, 419
Hanson, Robert IV, 582
Hanson, Robert IV, 1100
Hanson, Robert IV, 1132
Hanson, Rudy C. III, 150
Hanson, Samuel II, 496
Hanson, Samuel II, 541
Hanson, Samuel II, 669
Hanson, Samuel Howell II, 541
Hanson, Susan II, 496
Hanson, Susanna II, 527
Hanson, Susanna II, 541
Hanson, Susanna II, 556
Hanson, Susanna IV, 380
Hanson, Susanna IV, 403

nson, Susanna IV, 458
nson, Susanna IV, 582
nson, Susannah II, 541
nson, Susannah IV, 388
nson, Susannah IV, 390
nson, Susannah IV, 403
nson, Susannah IV, 404
nson, Thomas II, 541
nson, Thomas II, 625
nson, Thomas IV, 582
nson, Thomas IV, 1100
nson, Thomas Osborn IV, 1100
nson, Thomas Osborn IV, 1132
nson, Thomas Osburn IV, 582
nson, Timothy II, 541
nson, Timothy II, 625
nson, Timothy II, 798
nson, Timothy, Jr. II, 527
nson, Timothy, Jr. II, 541
nson, Wesley H. IV, 403
nson, William IV, 403
nson, William IV, 404
nson, William IV, 408
nson, William IV, 582
nson, William IV, 1061
nson, William Lindley IV, 404
nson, Wm. IV, 1061
nson, Wm. Lindley IV, 1132
nson, Zilpha IV, 404
nson, Zilpha IV, 582
nson, Zilpha W. IV, 391
nson, Zilpha W. IV, 404
nthon, Mary IV, 217
pgood, Adeline IV, 629
pgood, George IV, 629
pgood, George N. IV, 620
pgood, George N. IV, 629
pgood, Rebecca A. IV, 620
pgood, Rebecca A. IV, 629
pgood, Rebecca A. IV, 716
ppock, Caron I, 539
raway, Clement VI, 823
raway, Epa VI, 823
raway, Jane VI, 823
raway, Mary VI, 823
rbart, Mary III, 150
rbert, ??? III, 163
rbert, Alizabeth I, 1020
rbert, Ann I, 1020
rbert, Ann I, 1030
rbert, Charity I, 1020
rbert, Elizabeth II, 872
rbert, Felix III, 150
rbert, Isaac I, 883
rbert, Isaac I, 1016
rbert, John I, 1020
rbert, John I, 1030
rbert, Mary I, 1020
rbert, Mary III, 150
rbert, Peter I, 1020
rbert, Rachel I, 1020
rbert, Rachel I, 1030
rbert, Rebecah I, 1020
rbert, Rebecah I, 1030
rbert, Ruth III, 169
rbert, Shrews III, 150
rbert, Thomas I, 1020
rbert, Walter I, 1020
rbert, Walter I, 1030
rbeson, Lizzie W. II, 839
rbeson, Lizzie Webb II, 783
rbin, Margaret IV, 1274
rbin, Margaret IV, 1280
rbison, Elanor VI, 979
rbough, Rachel IV, 799
rbough, Rachel IV, 820
rbour, Rachel I, 1030
rbour, Walter I, 1030
rcher, Rebekah VI, 680
rcourt, Mary III, 25
rcourt, Mary III, 141
rcurt, Dorothy III, 75
rcurt, Elizabeth III, 75
rcurt, Richard III, 75
rcut, Dorothy III, 401
rcut, Elizabeth III, 401
rcut, Richard III, 401
rd, Eliza II, 370
rd, William II, 444
rdaway, Ann VI, 927
rdaway, Drewry VI, 927
rdaway, Drury VI, 823
rdaway, Drury VI, 856
rdaway, Lucy A. VI, 856
rdaway, Martha VI, 823
rden, Abraham II, 999
rden, Abraham II, 1073
rden, Agnes III, 150
rden, Agnes III, 151
rden, Bettie R. I, 880
rden, Caty VI, 927
Harden, Cynthia I, 621
Harden, David II, 229
Harden, Elizabeth II, 229
Harden, Elizabeth II, 444
Harden, Francis II, 370
Harden, John III, 150
Harden, Maria IV, 892
Harden, Mary II, 229
Harden, Mary VI, 501
Harden, Rettie R. I, 893
Harden, Sarah I, 983
Harden, Sarah I, 986
Harden, Sarah Ann V, 392
Harden, Thomas II, 444
Harden, Thomas VI, 927
Harden, William VI, 927
Hardenburg, Mary A. II, 873
Hardenburg, Mary A. II, 884
Harder, Winifred VI, 731
Harderster, Hannah I, 721
Hardester, Hannah I, 717
Hardester, Jemimah I, 717
Hardester, Jemimah I, 727
Hardesty, Charles V, 999
Hardesty, Chas. V, 999
Hardesty, Della V, 334
Hardesty, Ella M. V, 999
Hardesty, Flora V, 334
Hardesty, Frank V, 999
Hardesty, Hannah IV, 820
Hardesty, Hannah IV, 822
Hardesty, James V, 334
Hardesty, James J. V, 334
Hardesty, James T. V, 334
Hardesty, Mary V, 952
Hardesty, Mary V, 954
Hardesty, Mary VI, 398
Hardesty, Mary VI, 439
Hardesty, Nancy V, 999
Hardesty, Nancy A. V, 999
Hardesty, Nora V, 999
Hardesty, Ona V, 999
Hardey, Mary II, 370
Hardey, Sarah II, 370
Hardgrove, Mary VI, 381
Hardgrove, Mary VI, 398
Hardie, Andrew VI, 927
Hardie, Martha VI, 927
Hardiman, Abraham II, 230
Hardiman, Abraham II, 370
Hardiman, Abraham II, 487
Hardiman, Abraham II, 520
Hardiman, Abraham II, 524
Hardiman, Abraham II, 541
Hardiman, Deborah II, 487
Hardiman, Deborah II, 541
Hardiman, Dyana II, 370
Hardiman, Hanah II, 541
Hardiman, Hannah II, 344
Hardiman, Hannah II, 482
Hardiman, Hannah II, 520
Hardiman, Hannah II, 541
Hardiman, Mary II, 524
Hardiman, Mary II, 541
Hardiman, Rebecca II, 274
Hardin, Abigail III, 150
Hardin, Ann II, 999
Hardin, Ann II, 1024
Hardin, Bettie I, 670
Hardin, Charles I, 617
Hardin, Christopher V. I, 628
Hardin, Cladora I, 628
Hardin, Cynthia I, 622
Hardin, Elizabeth II, 370
Hardin, Elizabeth II, 541
Hardin, Elizabeth II, 562
Hardin, Estes II, 370
Hardin, Flushing III, 150
Hardin, Francis II, 370
Hardin, Francis II, 444
Hardin, Francis II, 541
Hardin, Francis II, 562
Hardin, J. R. I, 634
Hardin, James III, 150
Hardin, Mary I, 617
Hardin, Nathaniel II, 370
Hardin, Nathaniel II, 541
Hardin, Nathaniel II, 562
Hardin, Obedience VI, 244
Hardin, Retta I, 617
Hardin, Retta E. I, 634
Hardin, Robert I, 617
Hardin, Sarah II, 370
Hardin, Sarah Ann V, 422
Hardin, Sibba I, 628
Hardin, Thomas II, 370
Harding, Abraham II, 960
Harding, Abraham II, 999
Harding, Abraham II, 1011
Harding, Abraham, Jr. II, 999
Harding, Abraham, Jr. II, 1011
Harding, Ann II, 999
Harding, Cassie E. IV, 987
Harding, Charles II, 229
Harding, David II, 229
Harding, Deborah II, 176
Harding, Dr. John VI, 927
Harding, Eliza IV, 968
Harding, Elizabeth II, 176
Harding, Elizabeth II, 229
Harding, Elizabeth II, 541
Harding, Elizabeth III, 150
Harding, Ester II, 444
Harding, Esther II, 370
Harding, Esther II, 444
Harding, Francis II, 370
Harding, Francis II, 541
Harding, Francis, Jr. II, 541
Harding, Harriet H. VI, 927
Harding, Henry II, 458
Harding, Hope II, 176
Harding, John B. VI, 927
Harding, Kate IV, 1253
Harding, Mary II, 195
Harding, Mary II, 229
Harding, Mary II, 230
Harding, Mary II, 541
Harding, Mary II, 999
Harding, Mary II, 1011
Harding, Mary IV, 1209
Harding, Mary VI, 468
Harding, Mary VI, 585
Harding, Nathaniel II, 541
Harding, Obediance VI, 244
Harding, Obedience I, 986
Harding, Obedience VI, 244
Harding, Peter IV, 1253
Harding, Rachel II, 999
Harding, Rachel II, 1011
Harding, Rebecca II, 176
Harding, Rebekah II, 458
Harding, Rebekah II, 541
Harding, Samuel II, 370
Harding, Sarah II, 507
Harding, Sarah II, 541
Harding, Susan V, 999
Harding, Thomas II, 163
Harding, Thomas II, 176
Harding, Thomas II, 229
Harding, Thomas II, 245
Harding, Thomas II, 370
Harding, Thomas II, 444
Harding, Thomas II, 477
Harding, Thomas II, 541
Hardley, Ann V, 393
Hardley, James V, 393
Hardman, Abraham II, 230
Hardman, Ally Compton V, 679
Hardman, Ally Compton V, 706
Hardman, Charles V, 679
Hardman, Chas. V, 706
Hardman, Edward II, 230
Hardman, Mary Ann IV, 712
Hardman, Mary Ann IV, 716
Hardon, Sarah IV, 404
Hardon, Zachariah B. IV, 404
Hardway, Charles VI, 795
Hardway, John VI, 795
Hardway, Polly VI, 795
Hardwick, ??? V, 942
Hardwick, Betsey VI, 887
Hardwick, Charles, Sr. VI, 927
Hardwick, Elizabeth VI, 888
Hardwick, Elizabeth VI, 941
Hardwick, Elizabeth VI, 963
Hardwick, Frances VI, 941
Hardwick, George VI, 927
Hardwick, Joanna VI, 927
Hardwick, John VI, 887
Hardwick, John VI, 988
Hardwick, John, Jr. VI, 927
Hardwick, Leonard VI, 927
Hardwick, Leoney VI, 835
Hardwick, Lindsay C. VI, 844
Hardwick, Lucy VI, 899
Hardwick, Patsy VI, 823
Hardwick, Pleasant VI, 941
Hardwick, Robert VI, 899
Hardwick, Robert VI, 963
Hardwick, Robert VI, 979
Hardwick, Sally VI, 988
Hardwick, Susanna VI, 927
Hardwick, Usley VI, 979
Hardwick, William VI, 823
Hardwicke, Sally VI, 1021
Hardwood, Francis G. VI, 929
Hardwood, Tirzah Bond VI, 929
Hardy, Aaron V, 244
Hardy, Aaron B. V, 244
Hardy, Aholibama VI, 927
Hardy, Aldo V, 334
Hardy, Andrew VI, 927
Hardy, Ann VI, 823
Hardy, Ann E. VI, 970
Hardy, Baptis VI, 950
Hardy, Benjamin IV, 630
Hardy, Benjamin F. II, 744
Hardy, Benjamin F. IV, 630
Hardy, Capt. William A. VI, 992
Hardy, Catherine VI, 927
Hardy, Celia V, 334
Hardy, Cena VI, 928
Hardy, Charity I, 1104
Hardy, Charity I, 1105
Hardy, Chesley VI, 823
Hardy, Dabney VI, 928
Hardy, Darius E. V, 244
Hardy, Davis V, 244
Hardy, Dennis VI, 928
Hardy, Dennis VI, 1018
Hardy, E. D. V, 244
Hardy, Ed V, 244
Hardy, Edith VI, 313
Hardy, Edward V, 244
Hardy, Eleanor VI, 930
Hardy, Elener VI, 927
Hardy, Eliza J. VI, 960
Hardy, Eliza M. VI, 992
Hardy, Elizabeth II, 395
Hardy, Elizabeth II, 541
Hardy, Elizabeth II, 596
Hardy, Elizabeth VI, 927
Hardy, Ellen C. V, 244
Hardy, Elnor VI, 885
Hardy, Essa VI, 928
Hardy, Essa VI, 1018
Hardy, Ezra W. V, 244
Hardy, Frances S. J. VI, 948
Hardy, Fred V, 244
Hardy, Fred E. V, 244
Hardy, George VI, 928
Hardy, George W. VI, 930
Hardy, Henry B. VI, 928
Hardy, James VI, 928
Hardy, James VI, 992
Hardy, James A. VI, 921
Hardy, Jane VI, 928
Hardy, John VI, 927
Hardy, John VI, 928
Hardy, John VI, 960
Hardy, John VI, 973
Hardy, John S. VI, 823
Hardy, John W. V, 244
Hardy, Jonathan VI, 976
Hardy, Joseph VI, 914
Hardy, Joseph VI, 939
Hardy, Joseph VI, 940
Hardy, Joseph VI, 953
Hardy, Joseph VI, 960
Hardy, Joseph VI, 977
Hardy, Joseph VI, 987
Hardy, Joseph S. VI, 928
Hardy, Joseph S. VI, 948
Hardy, Joseph Y. VI, 1022
Hardy, Joseph, Jr. VI, 967
Hardy, Keziah VI, 927
Hardy, Mahala S. VI, 823
Hardy, Maria V, 222
Hardy, Maria V, 244
Hardy, Mariah V, 244
Hardy, Martha VI, 927
Hardy, Mary VI, 928
Hardy, Mary F. I, 336
Hardy, Mary Francis I, 336
Hardy, Mourning VI, 888
Hardy, Nancy V, 229
Hardy, Nancy V, 244
Hardy, Nancy A. V, 244
Hardy, Nancy R. VI, 989
Hardy, Nancy S. VI, 926
Hardy, Nettie V, 244
Hardy, Olive V, 244
Hardy, Olive V, 334
Hardy, Ollie V, 244
Hardy, Pauline A. VI, 928
Hardy, Peggy VI, 928
Hardy, Peggy VI, 987
Hardy, Polly VI, 940
Hardy, Polly VI, 976
Hardy, Rachel VI, 950
Hardy, Robert VI, 927
Hardy, Robert VI, 984
Hardy, Robert VI, 989
Hardy, Robert, Jr. VI, 1021
Hardy, Robt, Sr. VI, 1021
Hardy, Robt. VI, 993
Hardy, Ruth VI, 928
Hardy, Ruth VI, 970
Hardy, Sally VI, 953
Hardy, Sally VI, 1021
Hardy, Samuel VI, 888
Hardy, Samuel VI, 927
Hardy, Sarah V, 230
Hardy, Sarah V, 244
Hardy, Sarah VI, 823
Hardy, Sarah VI, 921
Hardy, Solomon VI, 823
Hardy, Solomon VI, 888
Hardy, Solomon VI, 927
Hardy, Solomon VI, 928
Hardy, Solomon VI, 930
Hardy, Sophia VI, 928
Hardy, Susan VI, 1018
Hardy, Susannah VI, 914
Hardy, Thomas VI, 885
Hardy, Thomas VI, 926
Hardy, Thomas VI, 927
Hardy, Thomas VI, 928
Hardy, William V, 244
Hardy, William V, 334
Hardy, William VI, 927
Hardy, William A. VI, 921
Hardy, William A. VI, 928
Hardy, William A. VI, 948
Hardy, William H. VI, 928
Hardy, William W. V, 334
Hardy, William, Jr. V, 244
Hardy, Wm. A. VI, 978
Hardy, Wm. A. VI, 987
Hardyman, Abraham II, 370
Hardyman, Dyana II, 370
Hardyman, Hannah II, 541
Hare, Abigail II, 960
Hare, Alice V, 66
Hare, Ann VI, 65
Hare, Ann M. I, 329
Hare, Ann M. VI, 66
Hare, Ann Mc. I, 329
Hare, Anne VI, 66
Hare, Anne VI, 69
Hare, Annie B. VI, 65
Hare, Aquila VI, 66
Hare, Benjamin F. VI, 65
Hare, Brian VI, 59
Hare, Brian VI, 66
Hare, Brian VI, 78
Hare, Bryant I, 51
Hare, Bryant I, 73
Hare, Christian V, 970
Hare, Christiana VI, 92
Hare, Christianna VI, 66
Hare, Cordelia IV, 1280
Hare, David V, 970
Hare, David V, 973
Hare, David VI, 66
Hare, Demsey VI, 66
Hare, Donald E. V, 675
Hare, Donald E. V, 679
Hare, Edith M. V, 623
Hare, Edith M. V, 679
Hare, Edna VI, 65
Hare, Edna VI, 66
Hare, Edna VI, 78
Hare, Edna VI, 91
Hare, Edny I, 329
Hare, Elijah I, 240
Hare, Elijah VI, 65
Hare, Elijah VI, 66
Hare, Elijah VI, 69
Hare, Elijah VI, 78
Hare, Elijah H. VI, 65
Hare, Elisabeth I, 613
Hare, Eliza V, 623
Hare, Eliza VI, 66
Hare, Eliza Ophelia VI, 65
Hare, Eliza W. V, 679
Hare, Elizabeth I, 923
Hare, Elizabeth III, 150
Hare, Elizabeth VI, 59
Hare, Elizabeth VI, 66
Hare, Elizabeth VI, 67
Hare, Elizabeth A. VI, 65
Hare, Elizabeth A. VI, 69
Hare, Elizabeth Ann VI, 65
Hare, Elizabeth V. VI, 65
Hare, Elizabeth V. VI, 66
Hare, Elizabeth V. VI, 81
Hare, Elizabeth Virginia VI, 92
Hare, Elma E. V, 970
Hare, Emma T. V, 334
Hare, Frances A. V, 970
Hare, George V, 66
Hare, Girl VI, 65
Hare, Gulielma VI, 65
Hare, Harmon VI, 66
Hare, Harriet M. VI, 65
Hare, Harriet M. VI, 66
Hare, Harriet M. VI, 69
Hare, Harrison VI, 69
Hare, Henry V, 623
Hare, Henry V, 679
Hare, Henry V, 704
Hare, Henry VI, 65
Hare, Henry VI, 66

Hare, Henry VI, 92
Hare, Henry D. V, 623
Hare, Henry I. V, 679
Hare, Hermon VI, 59
Hare, Hermon VI, 66
Hare, James I, 212
Hare, James VI, 59
Hare, James VI, 65
Hare, James R. VI, 66
Hare, James Walter VI, 65
Hare, Jane VI, 66
Hare, Jemima V, 66
Hare, Jemima V, 909
Hare, Jemima VI, 66
Hare, Jephta V. VI, 65
Hare, Jesse V, 970
Hare, Jesse VI, 65
Hare, Jesse VI, 66
Hare, Jesse, Sr. VI, 66
Hare, John I, 329
Hare, John II, 999
Hare, John V, 909
Hare, John VI, 59
Hare, John VI, 65
Hare, John VI, 66
Hare, John Hare VI, 78
Hare, John K. VI, 65
Hare, John L. VI, 65
Hare, John, Jr. V, 909
Hare, John, Jr. VI, 66
Hare, John, Sr. VI, 66
Hare, Jonathan C. VI, 66
Hare, Jonathan Cox VI, 65
Hare, Joseph V, 66
Hare, Joseph V, 970
Hare, Joseph VI, 65
Hare, Joseph VI, 66
Hare, Joseph VI, 81
Hare, Joseph E. V, 334
Hare, Joseph J. VI, 65
Hare, Joseph J. VI, 66
Hare, Joseph J. VI, 67
Hare, Joseph J. VI, 92
Hare, Joseph L. VI, 65
Hare, Joseph L. VI, 69
Hare, Joseph L. VI, 89
Hare, Julier VI, 65
Hare, Katherine V, 679
Hare, Katherine V, 704
Hare, Marcia J. V, 970
Hare, Margaret I, 226
Hare, Margaret VI, 65
Hare, Margaret VI, 66
Hare, Margaret VI, 89
Hare, Margaret A. I, 216
Hare, Margaret A. I, 240
Hare, Margaret A. I, 255
Hare, Margaret A. VI, 65
Hare, Margaret A. VI, 66
Hare, Margaret A. VI, 78
Hare, Margra VI, 59
Hare, Margra VI, 65
Hare, Margra VI, 66
Hare, Maria V, 970
Hare, Marsha V, 970
Hare, Marsha VI, 66
Hare, Martha VI, 66
Hare, Mary I, 51
Hare, Mary I, 73
Hare, Mary I, 212
Hare, Mary I, 240
Hare, Mary II, 960
Hare, Mary V, 66
Hare, Mary V, 909
Hare, Mary VI, 59
Hare, Mary VI, 65
Hare, Mary VI, 66
Hare, Mary VI, 78
Hare, Mary VI, 80
Hare, Mary VI, 88
Hare, Mary VI, 92
Hare, Mary E. V, 970
Hare, Mary H. I, 212
Hare, Mary J. VI, 65
Hare, Mary J. VI, 92
Hare, Mary V. VI, 65
Hare, Mary V. VI, 81
Hare, Metta IV, 1209
Hare, Nathaniel II, 960
Hare, Nettie V, 66
Hare, Penelope VI, 53
Hare, Penelope VI, 66
Hare, Pharaby VI, 66
Hare, Pharaby VI, 86
Hare, Pheraba VI, 141
Hare, Pheriba VI, 66
Hare, Rebecca I. VI, 65
Hare, Rhoda V, 970
Hare, Rhoda V, 973
Hare, Richard Henry VI, 65
Hare, Robert V, 970
Hare, Robert V, 979
Hare, Robert VI, 66
Hare, Rosella VI, 66
Hare, Roy IV, 1209
Hare, Ruth V, 675
Hare, Ruth V, 679
Hare, Ruth VI, 66
Hare, Ruth VI, 78
Hare, Ruth Esther IV, 1163
Hare, Ruthanna V, 623
Hare, Sarah VI, 65
Hare, Sarah VI, 66
Hare, Sarah E. VI, 65
Hare, Walter T. V, 623
Hare, Walter T. V, 679
Hare, William VI, 65
Hare, William H. I, 329
Hare, William H. VI, 65
Hare, William H. VI, 66
Hare, William H. VI, 69
Hare, William Henry I, 329
Hare, William J. VI, 107
Hare, William P. I, 240
Hare, William P. I, 255
Hare, William P. VI, 59
Hare, William P. VI, 65
Hare, William P. VI, 66
Hare, William P. VI, 78
Hare, William T. VI, 66
Hare, William Thomas VI, 65
Hare, Wm. H. V, 970
Hare, Wm. H. VI, 65
Hare, Wm. H. VI, 66
Hare, Wm. P. VI, 89
Hare, Zada VI, 65
Hare, Zada Verlinda VI, 65
Hare, Zada Verlinda VI, 89
Hare, Zada Virlinda VI, 107
Harfield, Matthew VI, 866
Harford, Isaac VI, 244
Harford, Lorretta III, 150
Harford, Samuel III, 150
Harford, Virgil III, 150
Hargis, Amanda III, 150
Hargis, Merton L. III, 150
Hargis, Morton L. III, 150
Hargrave, ??? VI, 95
Hargrave, Albert I, 921
Hargrave, Albert I, 925
Hargrave, Albert I, 929
Hargrave, Albert I, 942
Hargrave, Ann IV, 217
Hargrave, Ann VI, 107
Hargrave, Ann VI, 108
Hargrave, Ann VI, 113
Hargrave, Ann VI, 178
Hargrave, Ann VI, 179
Hargrave, Ann VI, 240
Hargrave, Anna IV, 217
Hargrave, Anna VI, 166
Hargrave, Anna VI, 170
Hargrave, Anna VI, 178
Hargrave, Anna VI, 179
Hargrave, Anne IV, 218
Hargrave, Anselm VI, 66
Hargrave, Anselm VI, 108
Hargrave, Anselm VI, 109
Hargrave, Benjamin IV, 217
Hargrave, Benjamin VI, 108
Hargrave, Benjamin VI, 109
Hargrave, Bessie I, 613
Hargrave, Ceiley VI, 108
Hargrave, Cely VI, 103
Hargrave, Charles II, 370
Hargrave, Charles II, 444
Hargrave, Charles IV, 217
Hargrave, Charles VI, 178
Hargrave, Charles VI, 179
Hargrave, Charles VI, 191
Hargrave, Charles VI, 195
Hargrave, Charles E. IV, 217
Hargrave, Charles L. IV, 217
Hargrave, Chas. IV, 217
Hargrave, Chas. E. IV, 217
Hargrave, David VI, 134
Hargrave, Deborah IV, 217
Hargrave, Deborah IV, 464
Hargrave, Deborah IV, 475
Hargrave, Deborah VI, 229
Hargrave, Deborah VI, 244
Hargrave, Deborah VI, 245
Hargrave, Deborah Ann IV, 193
Hargrave, Deborah Ann IV, 217
Hargrave, Deborah Ann VI, 179
Hargrave, Edith Emily I, 925
Hargrave, Elisha IV, 217
Hargrave, Elisha IV, 218
Hargrave, Elizabeth II, 370
Hargrave, Elizabeth IV, 217
Hargrave, Elizabeth IV, 218
Hargrave, Elizabeth VI, 45
Hargrave, Elizabeth VI, 98
Hargrave, Elizabeth VI, 108
Hargrave, Elizabeth VI, 135
Hargrave, Elizabeth VI, 155
Hargrave, Elizabeth VI, 163
Hargrave, Elizabeth VI, 166
Hargrave, Elizabeth VI, 178
Hargrave, Elizabeth VI, 179
Hargrave, Elizabeth VI, 182
Hargrave, Elizabeth VI, 244
Hargrave, Elizabeth VI, 245
Hargrave, Elizabeth VI, 313
Hargrave, Elizabeth A. IV, 217
Hargrave, Elizabeth Abb IV, 220
Hargrave, Elizabeth Ann IV, 217
Hargrave, Elizabeth Ann VI, 178
Hargrave, Elizabeth Ann VI, 179
Hargrave, Elizabeth Ann VI, 245
Hargrave, Elizabeth D. IV, 230
Hargrave, Elizabeth D. VI, 313
Hargrave, Elizabeth D. J. IV, 217
Hargrave, Elizabeth O. IV, 217
Hargrave, Elsie Bertha I, 925
Hargrave, Emily C. IV, 217
Hargrave, Emily C. IV, 307
Hargrave, Fanny VI, 245
Hargrave, Fanny Garland VI, 245
Hargrave, Fredarack I, 543
Hargrave, Frederick I, 543
Hargrave, Garland VI, 244
Hargrave, George VI, 108
Hargrave, George VI, 134
Hargrave, George VI, 182
Hargrave, Georgia H. I, 929
Hargrave, Georgie I, 942
Hargrave, Hamlin VI, 108
Hargrave, Hamlin VI, 109
Hargrave, Hannah VI, 108
Hargrave, Hannah VI, 116
Hargrave, Hartwell VI, 108
Hargrave, Hartwill VI, 98
Hargrave, Hartwill VI, 108
Hargrave, Herman VI, 108
Hargrave, James VI, 108
Hargrave, James Harris VI, 244
Hargrave, Jane II, 370
Hargrave, Jane IV, 217
Hargrave, Jane VI, 178
Hargrave, Jane VI, 179
Hargrave, Jesse I, 543
Hargrave, Jesse VI, 45
Hargrave, Jesse VI, 46
Hargrave, Jesse VI, 107
Hargrave, Jesse VI, 108
Hargrave, Jesse VI, 134
Hargrave, Jesse VI, 135
Hargrave, Jesse VI, 139
Hargrave, Jesse VI, 178
Hargrave, Jesse VI, 179
Hargrave, Jesse VI, 203
Hargrave, Jesse VI, 207
Hargrave, Jesse VI, 244
Hargrave, Jesse VI, 245
Hargrave, John II, 444
Hargrave, John IV, 217
Hargrave, John VI, 108
Hargrave, John VI, 113
Hargrave, John VI, 134
Hargrave, John VI, 244
Hargrave, John Garland VI, 245
Hargrave, John Gregory VI, 163
Hargrave, John H. IV, 217
Hargrave, John W. IV, 217
Hargrave, John Wilson IV, 217
Hargrave, Jordan VI, 66
Hargrave, Jordan VI, 109
Hargrave, Joseph I, 543
Hargrave, Joseph IV, 217
Hargrave, Joseph IV, 239
Hargrave, Joseph IV, 464
Hargrave, Joseph IV, 475
Hargrave, Joseph VI, 98
Hargrave, Joseph VI, 108
Hargrave, Joseph VI, 134
Hargrave, Joseph VI, 179
Hargrave, Joseph VI, 229
Hargrave, Joseph VI, 244
Hargrave, Joseph VI, 274
Hargrave, Joseph VI, 276
Hargrave, Joseph Lewis IV, 217
Hargrave, Joseph, Jr. VI, 108
Hargrave, Josiah VI, 108
Hargrave, Lemuel IV, 217
Hargrave, Lemuel IV, 230
Hargrave, Lemuel VI, 66
Hargrave, Lemuel VI, 178
Hargrave, Lemuel VI, 179
Hargrave, Lemuel VI, 182
Hargrave, Lena I, 921
Hargrave, Lena Gilbert I, 925
Hargrave, Lewis IV, 218
Hargrave, Lucy IV, 217
Hargrave, Lucy VI, 178
Hargrave, Lucy VI, 179
Hargrave, Lucy VI, 191
Hargrave, Lucy VI, 195
Hargrave, Lucy VI, 244
Hargrave, Lucy VI, 245
Hargrave, Lucy VI, 274
Hargrave, Lucy VI, 276
Hargrave, Lucy C. VI, 245
Hargrave, Lucy Cheadle VI, 245
Hargrave, Lucy F. VI, 245
Hargrave, Lydia IV, 217
Hargrave, Lydia IV, 227
Hargrave, Margaret IV, 239
Hargrave, Margaret J. IV, 217
Hargrave, Margart IV, 217
Hargrave, Mariah IV, 217
Hargrave, Martha IV, 217
Hargrave, Martha VI, 42
Hargrave, Martha VI, 96
Hargrave, Martha VI, 105
Hargrave, Martha VI, 108
Hargrave, Martha VI, 135
Hargrave, Martha VI, 139
Hargrave, Martha VI, 178
Hargrave, Martha VI, 179
Hargrave, Martha VI, 232
Hargrave, Martha VI, 244
Hargrave, Martha VI, 245
Hargrave, Martha VI, 252
Hargrave, Martha VI, 255
Hargrave, Martha VI, 318
Hargrave, Martha VI, 322
Hargrave, Martha Jane IV, 217
Hargrave, Mary I, 543
Hargrave, Mary I, 554
Hargrave, Mary IV, 217
Hargrave, Mary VI, 45
Hargrave, Mary VI, 108
Hargrave, Mary VI, 113
Hargrave, Mary VI, 155
Hargrave, Mary VI, 157
Hargrave, Mary VI, 178
Hargrave, Mary VI, 179
Hargrave, Mary VI, 203
Hargrave, Mary VI, 207
Hargrave, Mary VI, 244
Hargrave, Mary VI, 245
Hargrave, Mary VI, 255
Hargrave, Mary VI, 316
Hargrave, Mary VI, 317
Hargrave, Mary A. VI, 178
Hargrave, Mary Ann IV, 217
Hargrave, Mary Ann VI, 178
Hargrave, Mary Ann VI, 179
Hargrave, Mary Ann VI, 182
Hargrave, Mary Catharine IV, 217
Hargrave, Mary Catharine IV, 293
Hargrave, Mary Louisa IV, 217
Hargrave, Mary Louiza IV, 217
Hargrave, Matthew VI, 245
Hargrave, Matthew J. VI, 179
Hargrave, Matthew J. VI, 191
Hargrave, Matthew J. VI, 196
Hargrave, Matthew Jones VI, 108
Hargrave, Matthew Jones VI, 135
Hargrave, Matthew Jones VI, 179
Hargrave, Micajah Bates VI, 179
Hargrave, Michal Bailey VI, 108
Hargrave, Millicent VI, 245
Hargrave, Millicent VI, 251
Hargrave, Millicent VI, 255
Hargrave, Millicent VI, 323
Hargrave, Millicent VI, 345
Hargrave, Miriam VI, 107
Hargrave, Miriam VI, 108
Hargrave, Mourning VI, 117
Hargrave, Mourning III VI, 108
Hargrave, Nancy VI, 179
Hargrave, Nancy H. VI, 179
Hargrave, Nancy H. VI, 191
Hargrave, Nancy H. VI, 196
Hargrave, Naomey VI, 45
Hargrave, Naomey VI, 46
Hargrave, Naomh VI, 108
Hargrave, Naomy VI, 108
Hargrave, Narcissa I, 921
Hargrave, Narcissa I, 925
Hargrave, Narcissa I, 929
Hargrave, Nathan II, 370
Hargrave, Nehemiah Matson IV, 217
Hargrave, Oliver C. IV, 217
Hargrave, Oliver C. IV, 307
Hargrave, Pleasant VI, 244
Hargrave, Pleasant Terrell VI, 245
Hargrave, Polly VI, 134
Hargrave, Polly VI, 138
Hargrave, Priscilla VI, 182
Hargrave, Rachel IV, 217
Hargrave, Rachel VI, 244
Hargrave, Rachel VI, 245
Hargrave, Rachel VI, 274
Hargrave, Rachel VI, 276
Hargrave, Rachel M. IV, 217
Hargrave, Richard VI, 107
Hargrave, Richard VI, 108
Hargrave, Richard VI, 112
Hargrave, Richard VI, 179
Hargrave, Robert VI, 108
Hargrave, Robert VI, 134
Hargrave, Robert F. IV, 217
Hargrave, Robert Fleming IV, 217
Hargrave, Robert Fleming VI, 179
Hargrave, Robt. T. IV, 236
Hargrave, Ruanna IV, 217
Hargrave, Ruannah T. IV, 217
Hargrave, Ruannah T. IV, 236
Hargrave, Ruthanna T. IV, 217
Hargrave, Sally VI, 108
Hargrave, Sally Ann IV, 217
Hargrave, Sally Ann IV, 219
Hargrave, Samuel I, 51
Hargrave, Samuel I, 543
Hargrave, Samuel IV, 217
Hargrave, Samuel VI, 16
Hargrave, Samuel VI, 18
Hargrave, Samuel VI, 45
Hargrave, Samuel VI, 46
Hargrave, Samuel VI, 47
Hargrave, Samuel VI, 108
Hargrave, Samuel VI, 155
Hargrave, Samuel VI, 163
Hargrave, Samuel VI, 166
Hargrave, Samuel VI, 178
Hargrave, Samuel VI, 179
Hargrave, Samuel VI, 182
Hargrave, Samuel VI, 232
Hargrave, Samuel VI, 239
Hargrave, Samuel VI, 244
Hargrave, Samuel VI, 252
Hargrave, Samuel VI, 255
Hargrave, Samuel VI, 262
Hargrave, Samuel VI, 276
Hargrave, Samuel, Jr. VI, 274
Hargrave, Sarah IV, 217
Hargrave, Sarah IV, 220
Hargrave, Sarah VI, 45
Hargrave, Sarah VI, 46
Hargrave, Sarah VI, 108
Hargrave, Sarah VI, 117
Hargrave, Sarah VI, 178
Hargrave, Sarah VI, 244
Hargrave, Sarah VI, 252
Hargrave, Sarah VI, 255
Hargrave, Sarah VI, 301
Hargrave, Sarah VI, 322
Hargrave, Sarah E. IV, 217
Hargrave, Sarah Elizabeth IV, 217
Hargrave, Sarah Elizabeth IV, 218
Hargrave, Sarah Elizabeth VI, 179
Hargrave, Sarah H. VI, 30
Hargrave, Sarah H. VI, 178
Hargrave, Sarah H. VI, 179
Hargrave, Sarah H. VI, 182
Hargrave, Silas VI, 108
Hargrave, Silvah VI, 66
Hargrave, Silviah VI, 108
Hargrave, Susanna VI, 108
Hargrave, Susannah VI, 107
Hargrave, Susannah VI, 108
Hargrave, Sylvia VI, 66
Hargrave, Sylvia VI, 70
Hargrave, Tacy B. IV, 217
Hargrave, Thomas IV, 217
Hargrave, Thomas IV, 464
Hargrave, Thomas VI, 30
Hargrave, Thomas VI, 178
Hargrave, Thomas VI, 179
Hargrave, Thomas VI, 182
Hargrave, Thomas VI, 244
Hargrave, Thomas VI, 251
Hargrave, Thomas E. IV, 217
Hargrave, Thomas Exum IV, 21
Hargrave, Thomas Exum VI, 1
Hargrave, Thos. IV, 220
Hargrave, Widow Sarah I, 51
Hargrave, Widow Sarah I, 61
Hargrave, William IV, 217

Hargrave, William VI, 108
Hargrave, William VI, 117
Hargrave, William H. IV, 217
Hargrave, William R. IV, 217
Hargrave, William S. IV, 464
Hargrave, Wm. Henry IV, 217
Hargraves, Margaret II, 808
Hargrove, Hamlin VI, 109
Hargrove, Jane II, 370
Hargrove, Martha VI, 322
Hargrove, Nathan II, 370
Hargrove, Patty VI, 823
Hargrove, William VI, 823
Harimon, Mary IV, 1280
Haris, Beulah IV, 1100
Haris, Beuly IV, 1100
Haris, Daniel VI, 184
Haris, Hariet A. I, 435
Haris, Mary VI, 184
Haris, Richard IV, 1100
Harison, Ann V, 497
Harison, Anna V, 497
Harison, Elizabeth IV, 630
Harison, John A. V, 497
Harison, Rachel IV, 630
Harison, William H. V, 497
Hariston, Robt. VI, 938
Hariston, Ruth VI, 938
Harker, Adam II, 230
Harker, Adam II, 370
Harker, Adam II, 541
Harker, Adam II, 999
Harker, Adam II, 1026
Harker, Ann II, 230
Harker, Annie VI, 245
Harker, Annie A. VI, 245
Harker, Dr. F. S. VI, 245
Harker, Elizabeth II, 230
Harker, Elizabeth II, 371
Harker, Emma VI, 245
Harker, Emma Mellor VI, 245
Harker, Frances James VI, 245
Harker, Francis J. VI, 245
Harker, Francis James VI, 245
Harker, Frank VI, 245
Harker, Frank Butler VI, 245
Harker, Frank S. VI, 245
Harker, Frank Scott VI, 245
Harker, Frederick VI, 245
Harker, Grace II, 230
Harker, Grace II, 371
Harker, Grace II, 960
Harker, Herbert VI, 245
Harker, James II, 960
Harker, Jane II, 230
Harker, John II, 371
Harker, John II, 960
Harker, Joseph II, 371
Harker, Joshua II, 371
Harker, Martha II, 960
Harker, Martha II, 999
Harker, Martha II, 1026
Harker, Mary II, 77
Harker, Mary II, 81
Harker, Samuel II, 960
Harker, Samuel II, 999
Harker, Samuel II, 1026
Harker, William VI, 245
Harkins, Caroline M. III, 150
Harkins, John III, 150
Harkins, John B. III, 254
Harkins, Josephine III, 150
Harkins, Mary J. III, 150
Harkins, Mercy II, 31
Harkins, Samuel II, 31
Harkins, Susan G. III, 150
Harkins, Thomas II, 31
Harkloo, Stella May V, 841
Harkness, Abbey Jane IV, 1364
Harkness, Abigail IV, 1364
Harkness, Adam III, 150
Harkness, Adam IV, 1364
Harkness, Amy IV, 1349
Harkness, Amy IV, 1364
Harkness, Charles IV, 1364
Harkness, Cynthia S. IV, 1163
Harkness, Cynthia T. IV, 1163
Harkness, Cynthia T. V, 334
Harkness, D. A., Jr. IV, 1364
Harkness, Daniel W. IV, 1364
Harkness, David III, 66
Harkness, David III, 150
Harkness, David III, 359
Harkness, David IV, 1355
Harkness, David IV, 1364
Harkness, David IV, 1374
Harkness, David Smith IV, 1364
Harkness, David, Jr. IV, 1364
Harkness, David, Jr. IV, 1371
Harkness, Deborah IV, 1364
Harkness, Deborah R. IV, 1359
Harkness, Deborah R. IV, 1364
Harkness, Deborah R. IV, 1365
Harkness, Deborah R. IV, 1386
Harkness, Elizabeth IV, 1364
Harkness, Elizabeth IV, 1382
Harkness, Eva IV, 1365
Harkness, Flora E. IV, 1364
Harkness, Flora E. IV, 1374
Harkness, G. IV, 1364
Harkness, Gideon IV, 1364
Harkness, Gideon IV, 1382
Harkness, Jesse V, 334
Harkness, Jesse S. IV, 1163
Harkness, Jesse S. V, 334
Harkness, Jesse T. IV, 1163
Harkness, John IV, 1364
Harkness, Mary III, 66
Harkness, Mary III, 150
Harkness, Mary IV, 1355
Harkness, Mary IV, 1364
Harkness, Mary C. IV, 1355
Harkness, Mary C. IV, 1364
Harkness, Mary C. IV, 1386
Harkness, Phebe IV, 1364
Harkness, Richard IV, 1359
Harkness, Richard IV, 1364
Harkness, Richard IV, 1365
Harkness, Richard IV, 1386
Harkness, Robert P. V, 909
Harkness, Ruth IV, 1364
Harkness, Ruth Amy IV, 1364
Harkness, Sarah IV, 1364
Harkness, Sarah Maria IV, 1364
Harkness, Sarah Maria IV, 1365
Harkness, Sarah Maria IV, 1371
Harkness, Sarah R. IV, 1364
Harkness, Stephen IV, 1365
Harkness, Thankful III, 150
Harkness, Thankful IV, 1364
Harkness, William IV, 1364
Harkness, Wm. IV, 1364
Harlan, ??? IV, 404
Harlan, A. H. V, 174
Harlan, Aaron IV, 91
Harlan, Aaron V, 66
Harlan, Aaron V, 571
Harlan, Aaron VI, 628
Harlan, Aaron VI, 646
Harlan, Abigail I, 761
Harlan, Abigail I, 880
Harlan, Abigail II, 541
Harlan, Ahi I, 880
Harlan, Alice I, 679
Harlan, Alice I, 880
Harlan, Alice II, 542
Harlan, Alice A. V, 605
Harlan, Alice A. V, 720
Harlan, Almira P. II, 873
Harlan, Alpheus H. V, 174
Harlan, Amy IV, 1209
Harlan, Amy D. IV, 1163
Harlan, Amy D. IV, 1186
Harlan, Amy Drusilla IV, 1209
Harlan, Amy Drusilla IV, 1223
Harlan, Ann I, 654
Harlan, Ann I, 813
Harlan, Ann I, 880
Harlan, Ann I, 892
Harlan, Ann V, 571
Harlan, Ann V, 603
Harlan, Anna II, 542
Harlan, Anna II, 744
Harlan, Anna III, 368
Harlan, Anna V, 571
Harlan, Anna B. III, 150
Harlan, Anna Maud V, 174
Harlan, Anne II, 542
Harlan, Annie D. V, 665
Harlan, Barclay V, 497
Harlan, Barclay W. V, 571
Harlan, Caleb IV, 404
Harlan, Caleb IV, 1163
Harlan, Caroline V, 497
Harlan, Caroline E. V, 679
Harlan, Caroline Elizabeth V, 497
Harlan, Caroline Elizabeth V, 499
Harlan, Carter V, 66
Harlan, Carter V, 571
Harlan, Carter B. V, 66
Harlan, Carter B. V, 571
Harlan, Charity I, 880
Harlan, Charity V, 497
Harlan, Charity V, 571
Harlan, Charles II, 542
Harlan, Charles M. II, 744
Harlan, Chas. IV, 1026
Harlan, Credilla II, 541
Harlan, David I, 654
Harlan, David I, 813
Harlan, David I, 880
Harlan, David V, 497
Harlan, David V, 571
Harlan, David F. V, 571
Harlan, David Ferris V, 571
Harlan, David Ferris V, 624
Harlan, David K. V, 571
Harlan, David R. V, 66
Harlan, David R. V, 497
Harlan, Diadem V, 174
Harlan, Diadema V, 174
Harlan, Dinah VI, 496
Harlan, Dinah VI, 497
Harlan, Dinah VI, 522
Harlan, Dinah VI, 549
Harlan, Dinah VI, 559
Harlan, Dinah VI, 562
Harlan, Dinah VI, 660
Harlan, Edith I, 654
Harlan, Edith I, 813
Harlan, Edith I, 847
Harlan, Edith I, 854
Harlan, Edith I, 880
Harlan, Edith I, 1053
Harlan, Edith IV, 1026
Harlan, Edith V, 66
Harlan, Edith V, 497
Harlan, Edith V, 571
Harlan, Edith G. VI, 646
Harlan, Edward II, 542
Harlan, Edward II, 744
Harlan, Edward IV, 404
Harlan, Edward IV, 1163
Harlan, Edward IV, 1186
Harlan, Edward T. II, 798
Harlan, Edward T. II, 873
Harlan, Eleazar I, 881
Harlan, Eleazer I, 880
Harlan, Eli I, 880
Harlan, Eli VI, 628
Harlan, Eli VI, 646
Harlan, Eliza II, 798
Harlan, Elizabeth I, 747
Harlan, Elizabeth I, 757
Harlan, Elizabeth I, 761
Harlan, Elizabeth I, 881
Harlan, Elizabeth II, 541
Harlan, Elizabeth IV, 36
Harlan, Elizabeth V, 66
Harlan, Elizabeth V, 497
Harlan, Elizabeth V, 498
Harlan, Elizabeth V, 571
Harlan, Elizabeth V, 593
Harlan, Elizabeth V, 679
Harlan, Elizabeth A. IV, 1209
Harlan, Ellen B. II, 798
Harlan, Ellen B. E. II, 873
Harlan, Elwood V, 66
Harlan, Emery B. V, 497
Harlan, Emily IV, 1026
Harlan, Emma V, 571
Harlan, Emma V, 679
Harlan, Emory B. V, 66
Harlan, Enoch I, 654
Harlan, Enoch I, 679
Harlan, Enoch I, 686
Harlan, Enoch I, 761
Harlan, Enoch I, 813
Harlan, Enoch I, 847
Harlan, Enoch I, 854
Harlan, Enoch I, 880
Harlan, Enoch I, 881
Harlan, Enoch IV, 404
Harlan, Enoch IV, 444
Harlan, Enoch V, 66
Harlan, Enoch V, 497
Harlan, Enoch V, 498
Harlan, Enoch V, 571
Harlan, Enoch V, 679
Harlan, Enoch V, 909
Harlan, Enoch L. I, 748
Harlan, Enoch Lindsey I, 761
Harlan, Enoch, Jr. V, 571
Harlan, Enochy, Jr. V, 552
Harlan, Evan P. Bailey II, 873
Harlan, Everett V, 66
Harlan, F. Margaret V, 679
Harlan, Flora E. V, 174
Harlan, G. Passmore II, 873
Harlan, Geo. W. V, 909
Harlan, George II, 798
Harlan, George IV, 91
Harlan, George IV, 404
Harlan, George V, 66
Harlan, George V, 497
Harlan, George VI, 646
Harlan, George Passmore II, 798
Harlan, George W. IV, 1061
Harlan, George W. V, 909
Harlan, George, Jr. IV, 36
Harlan, Gibbons IV, 404
Harlan, Gibbons IV, 1061
Harlan, Hannah I, 654
Harlan, Hannah I, 813
Harlan, Hannah I, 880
Harlan, Hannah II, 371
Harlan, Hannah II, 541
Harlan, Hannah II, 542
Harlan, Hannah IV, 404
Harlan, Hannah IV, 444
Harlan, Hannah IV, 716
Harlan, Hannah IV, 779
Harlan, Hannah IV, 962
Harlan, Hannah IV, 1026
Harlan, Hannah IV, 1031
Harlan, Hannah IV, 1061
Harlan, Hannah V, 66
Harlan, Hannah V, 497
Harlan, Hannah V, 519
Harlan, Hannah V, 571
Harlan, Hannah V, 679
Harlan, Hannah V, 909
Harlan, Hannah V, 933
Harlan, Hannah Mary II, 798
Harlan, Hannah Mary II, 873
Harlan, Hannahmariah Elizabeth V, 571
Harlan, Harriet IV, 282
Harlan, Harriet IV, 404
Harlan, Harriet A. IV, 404
Harlan, Harriet A. IV, 444
Harlan, Harvey V, 66
Harlan, Henry IV, 404
Harlan, Henry IV, 1163
Harlan, Hinchman II, 542
Harlan, Hiram I, 679
Harlan, Hiram I, 680
Harlan, Hiram I, 880
Harlan, Hiram I, 881
Harlan, Humphrey IV, 404
Harlan, Humphrey M. IV, 1061
Harlan, I. A. V, 679
Harlan, Inez IV, 1026
Harlan, Isaac V, 571
Harlan, Isaac A. VI, 646
Harlan, Isaac F. V, 497
Harlan, Isaac H. V, 679
Harlan, Isaac J. I, 748
Harlan, Isaac Jones I, 761
Harlan, Isaac S. V, 66
Harlan, J. Comly IV, 1031
Harlan, J. Way IV, 1026
Harlan, Jabez V, 497
Harlan, Jabez V, 571
Harlan, Jacob V, 571
Harlan, Jacob V, 579
Harlan, James V, 571
Harlan, James V, 605
Harlan, Jane IV, 1026
Harlan, Jane V, 571
Harlan, John I, 854
Harlan, John I, 880
Harlan, John I, 881
Harlan, John IV, 404
Harlan, John V, 66
Harlan, John V, 496
Harlan, John V, 497
Harlan, John V, 571
Harlan, John V, 593
Harlan, John V, 679
Harlan, John C. V, 66
Harlan, John C. V, 571
Harlan, John M. V, 571
Harlan, John Man II, 371
Harlan, John Man II, 542
Harlan, John Milton V, 571
Harlan, John W. IV, 404
Harlan, John W. IV, 1163
Harlan, John, Jr. V, 571
Harlan, Jonathan I, 654
Harlan, Jonathan I, 747
Harlan, Jonathan I, 757
Harlan, Jonathan I, 880
Harlan, Jonathan V, 571
Harlan, Jonathan V, 624
Harlan, Jonothan I, 761
Harlan, Joseph II, 371
Harlan, Joseph II, 542
Harlan, Joseph IV, 716
Harlan, Joseph IV, 779
Harlan, Joseph IV, 962
Harlan, Joseph IV, 1026
Harlan, Joseph IV, 1031
Harlan, Joseph A. VI, 646
Harlan, Joseph G. III, 150
Harlan, Joseph G. III, 368
Harlan, Joseph, Jr. IV, 962
Harlan, Josephine V, 66
Harlan, Josephine G. III, 150
Harlan, Josephine G. III, 368
Harlan, Joshua II, 371
Harlan, Joshua II, 541
Harlan, Joshua II, 542
Harlan, Joshua II, 744
Harlan, Joshua III, 414
Harlan, Joshua IV, 36
Harlan, Joshua, Jr. II, 371
Harlan, Joshua, Jr. II, 542
Harlan, Josiah II, 542
Harlan, Josiah II, 744
Harlan, Laura IV, 1209
Harlan, Lewis IV, 404
Harlan, Lewis IV, 1163
Harlan, Lewis Oliver IV, 1163
Harlan, Louisa B. II, 707
Harlan, Lucy V, 497
Harlan, Lucy V, 552
Harlan, Lucy V, 571
Harlan, Lucy B. V, 571
Harlan, Lucy M. V, 679
Harlan, Lucy W. V, 679
Harlan, Lydia II, 371
Harlan, Lydia II, 542
Harlan, Lydia V, 66
Harlan, Lydia V, 496
Harlan, Lydia V, 497
Harlan, Lydia V, 571
Harlan, Lydia V, 596
Harlan, Lydia V, 679
Harlan, Mahlon V, 571
Harlan, Manelva IV, 1163
Harlan, Margaret I, 679
Harlan, Margaret V, 497
Harlan, Margaret V, 526
Harlan, Margaret A. V, 66
Harlan, Margaret Ann V, 571
Harlan, Margaret Ann V, 589
Harlan, Margaretann V, 497
Harlan, Margery IV, 91
Harlan, Margery V, 66
Harlan, Margret I, 880
Harlan, Maria V, 66
Harlan, Maria V, 571
Harlan, Mariah V, 571
Harlan, Marion E. II, 798
Harlan, Marion E. II, 873
Harlan, Martha IV, 1031
Harlan, Martha V, 66
Harlan, Martha V, 303
Harlan, Martha V, 310
Harlan, Martha V, 497
Harlan, Martha V, 569
Harlan, Martha V, 571
Harlan, Martha E. VI, 646
Harlan, Martin R. V, 571
Harlan, Mary I, 679
Harlan, Mary I, 761
Harlan, Mary II, 542
Harlan, Mary II, 744
Harlan, Mary III, 414
Harlan, Mary IV, 1026
Harlan, Mary V, 66
Harlan, Mary V, 79
Harlan, Mary V, 497
Harlan, Mary V, 516
Harlan, Mary V, 571
Harlan, Mary Ann IV, 716
Harlan, Mary Ann IV, 924
Harlan, Mary Ann IV, 962
Harlan, Mary Ann IV, 1026
Harlan, Mary Ann V, 571
Harlan, Mary E. V, 66
Harlan, Mary Elizabeth V, 66
Harlan, Mary Elizabeth V, 571
Harlan, Mary Ellen V, 579
Harlan, Mary Jane IV, 404
Harlan, Mary Jane IV, 1163
Harlan, Mary Jane IV, 1192
Harlan, Mary L. IV, 1209
Harlan, Mary R. VI, 646
Harlan, Mary T. II, 873
Harlan, Mary T. Spray V, 174
Harlan, Maxine V, 679
Harlan, May V, 571
Harlan, May V, 679
Harlan, May T. II, 873
Harlan, Michael VI, 496
Harlan, Milton V, 66
Harlan, Minerva V, 66
Harlan, Mornelvia IV, 1209
Harlan, Mornilva IV, 1209
Harlan, Moses IV, 91
Harlan, Moses V, 66
Harlan, Nancy I, 761
Harlan, Nancy V, 66
Harlan, Nathan I, 654
Harlan, Nathan I, 813
Harlan, Nathan I, 880
Harlan, Nathan I, 881
Harlan, Nathan I, 886
Harlan, Nathan V, 497
Harlan, Nathan V, 571
Harlan, Nathan, Jr. V, 571

Harlan, Nathaniel I, 654
Harlan, Nathaniel I, 813
Harlan, Nathaniel I, 880
Harlan, Nathaniel V, 66
Harlan, Nathaniel V, 334
Harlan, Nathaniel V, 571
Harlan, Nathaniel V, 679
Harlan, Nathaniel E. V, 66
Harlan, Nathaniel E. V, 497
Harlan, Nathaniel F. V, 334
Harlan, Nathaniel F. V, 571
Harlan, Newton V, 679
Harlan, Olive V, 593
Harlan, Oliver IV, 404
Harlan, Oliver IV, 1209
Harlan, Oliver V, 571
Harlan, Oliver T. V, 679
Harlan, Pamelia IV, 404
Harlan, Pamelia IV, 1163
Harlan, Parmelia IV, 1163
Harlan, Parmelia IV, 1209
Harlan, Parnelia IV, 1209
Harlan, Pemela IV, 1163
Harlan, Phebe IV, 1023
Harlan, Phebe IV, 1026
Harlan, Phebe A. IV, 1026
Harlan, Phebe Ann IV, 404
Harlan, Phebe Ann IV, 1163
Harlan, Phineas II, 541
Harlan, Prudence V, 571
Harlan, Rachel I, 679
Harlan, Rachel I, 686
Harlan, Rachel I, 881
Harlan, Rachel A. I, 748
Harlan, Rachel Abigail I, 755
Harlan, Rachel Abigail I, 761
Harlan, Rachel Abigail Adams I, 761
Harlan, Rachel Ann II, 833
Harlan, Rachel Ann II, 873
Harlan, Rachel Fallis V, 571
Harlan, Rachel Fallis V, 624
Harlan, Rebeca I, 881
Harlan, Rebecca I, 881
Harlan, Rebecca IV, 404
Harlan, Rebecca IV, 1061
Harlan, Rebecca V, 497
Harlan, Rebecca Ann V, 571
Harlan, Rebecca L. V, 711
Harlan, Rebeckah I, 880
Harlan, Rebekah I, 854
Harlan, Richard II, 542
Harlan, Richard II, 744
Harlan, Ruth I, 761
Harlan, Ruth I, 880
Harlan, Ruth V, 66
Harlan, Ruth V, 497
Harlan, Ruth V, 564
Harlan, Ruth V, 571
Harlan, Sally Coltrane I, 747
Harlan, Sally Margaret I, 761
Harlan, Samuel III, 414
Harlan, Samuel IV, 91
Harlan, Samuel IV, 404
Harlan, Samuel IV, 962
Harlan, Samuel IV, 1061
Harlan, Samuel V, 66
Harlan, Samuel V, 571
Harlan, Samuel V, 679
Harlan, Samuel C. IV, 1023
Harlan, Samuel C. IV, 1026
Harlan, Sara IV, 1026
Harlan, Sarah I, 679
Harlan, Sarah I, 680
Harlan, Sarah I, 761
Harlan, Sarah I, 880
Harlan, Sarah I, 881
Harlan, Sarah I, 886
Harlan, Sarah II, 371
Harlan, Sarah II, 541
Harlan, Sarah II, 542
Harlan, Sarah II, 744
Harlan, Sarah III, 414
Harlan, Sarah IV, 91
Harlan, Sarah V, 66
Harlan, Sarah V, 334
Harlan, Sarah V, 497
Harlan, Sarah V, 571
Harlan, Sarah V, 579
Harlan, Sarah V, 605
Harlan, Sarah A. V, 66
Harlan, Sarah A. V, 79
Harlan, Sarah A. V, 571
Harlan, Sarah Ann IV, 716
Harlan, Sarah Ann IV, 779
Harlan, Sarah Ann IV, 962
Harlan, Sarah Ann IV, 1031
Harlan, Sarah Caroline V, 571
Harlan, Solomon I, 654
Harlan, Solomon I, 813
Harlan, Solomon I, 880
Harlan, Solomon V, 497
Harlan, Solomon V, 571
Harlan, Solomon V, 624
Harlan, Stephen I, 679
Harlan, Stephen I, 880
Harlan, Stephen I, 881
Harlan, Stephen II, 371
Harlan, Susannah V, 497
Harlan, Susannah M. V, 571
Harlan, Thomas M. V, 174
Harlan, Thomas P. V, 174
Harlan, Viola V, 66
Harlan, Warren V, 66
Harlan, Warren V, 571
Harlan, Warren E. V, 66
Harlan, Warren E. V, 334
Harlan, Warren E. V, 909
Harlan, William I, 654
Harlan, William I, 748
Harlan, William I, 813
Harlan, William I, 880
Harlan, William IV, 404
Harlan, William IV, 1163
Harlan, William V, 66
Harlan, William V, 497
Harlan, William V, 571
Harlan, William Forster V, 624
Harlan, William Lynden I, 761
Harlan, Wilson IV, 1026
Harlan, Wilson V, 571
Harlan, Wilson V, 679
Harlan, Wilson B. IV, 1026
Harlan, Wm. II, 542
Harlan, Wm. V, 571
Harlan, Wm. Foster V, 571
Harlan, Wm. H. V, 571
Harlan, Wm. H. V, 679
Harlan, Wm. Haydock V, 174
Harland, Aaron VI, 398
Harland, Alice II, 542
Harland, Anna B. III, 150
Harland, Anna Maud V, 174
Harland, Diadem V, 174
Harland, Elizabeth VI, 398
Harland, Ezekiel VI, 398
Harland, Flora E. V, 174
Harland, Frank IV, 1319
Harland, George VI, 398
Harland, Joseph G. III, 150
Harland, Josephine G. III, 150
Harland, Joshua VI, 398
Harland, Moses VI, 398
Harland, Samuel III, 402
Harland, Samuel VI, 398
Harland, Sarah III, 402
Harland, Sarah VI, 398
Harland, Stephen VI, 398
Harland, Thomas P. V, 174
Harlen, Ann I, 813
Harlen, Anna II, 47
Harlen, Anna A. II, 119
Harlen, Anna A. II, 126
Harlen, Anna B. II, 119
Harlen, Anna B. II, 126
Harlen, Edith I, 813
Harlen, Edith I, 880
Harlen, George VI, 398
Harlen, Hannah I, 813
Harlen, Hannah II, 541
Harlen, Hannah IV, 716
Harlen, Hannah V, 66
Harlen, Hannah V, 103
Harlen, Harriet IV, 218
Harlen, John V, 66
Harlen, Joseph II, 47
Harlen, Joseph IV, 716
Harlen, Joseph IV, 820
Harlen, Joseph IV, 962
Harlen, Joseph G. II, 119
Harlen, Joseph G. II, 126
Harlen, Mary Ann IV, 716
Harlen, Moses V, 66
Harlen, Nathan I, 881
Harlen, Samuel IV, 716
Harlen, Samuel Steer IV, 218
Harlen, Sarah I, 761
Harlen, Sarah IV, 820
Harlen, Sarah IV, 825
Harlen, Sarah Ann IV, 716
Harlen, Solomon V, 497
Harley, Elizabeth V, 504
Harley, Mary II, 371
Harley, Rebecca V, 782
Harlin, Abigail I, 747
Harlin, Barclay V, 497
Harlin, Caroline V, 497
Harlin, Charity V, 497
Harlin, David V, 497
Harlin, Edith V, 66
Harlin, Edith V, 114
Harlin, Edith V, 497
Harlin, Eleazar I, 881
Harlin, Elizabeth I, 757
Harlin, Elizabeth I, 761
Harlin, Enoch I, 747
Harlin, Enoch V, 497
Harlin, George I, 393
Harlin, George V, 497
Harlin, Hannah IV, 962
Harlin, Hannah V, 497
Harlin, Hannah V, 519
Harlin, Jonathan I, 747
Harlin, Joseph IV, 820
Harlin, Lydia V, 497
Harlin, Margaret I, 673
Harlin, Margaret I, 679
Harlin, Margaret V, 497
Harlin, Martha V, 497
Harlin, Martin R. V, 571
Harlin, Mary I, 747
Harlin, Moses I, 747
Harlin, Moses VI, 398
Harlin, Nancy I, 747
Harlin, Nathan V, 497
Harlin, Rachel Abigail I, 757
Harlin, Rachel Abigail I, 761
Harlin, Ruth I, 747
Harlin, Ruth V, 497
Harlin, Sarah I, 747
Harlin, Sarah II, 371
Harlin, Sarah IV, 97
Harlin, Sarah V, 497
Harlin, Stephen I, 881
Harlin, Stephen II, 371
Harlin, Susannah V, 497
Harlin, William V, 497
Harlon, Alice II, 542
Harlon, Edith V, 497
Harlon, Eleazar I, 881
Harlon, Elizabeth I, 393
Harlon, Enoch I, 761
Harlon, Enoch V, 497
Harlon, George I, 393
Harlon, Hannah II, 542
Harlon, Hannah IV, 716
Harlon, Hannah V, 497
Harlon, John V, 497
Harlon, Joseph IV, 716
Harlon, Margery I, 393
Harlon, Mary I, 393
Harlon, Mary Ann IV, 675
Harlon, Rebeca I, 881
Harlon, Rebeca I, 885
Harlon, Rebecca V, 497
Harlon, Solomon V, 497
Harlon, Stephen I, 880
Harlond, Stephen VI, 398
Harlow, Enoch V, 497
Harlow, Harriet V. IV, 1319
Harlow, Mary IV, 1319
Harlow, Thomas VI, 245
Harman, ??? V, 174
Harman, Andrew II, 744
Harman, Andrew II, 770
Harman, Anne II, 542
Harman, Annie III, 95
Harman, Barbara VI, 952
Harman, Charity II, 371
Harman, Charles VI, 924
Harman, Charles VI, 928
Harman, Clara I, 936
Harman, David G. V, 174
Harman, David I. V, 174
Harman, Eleanor II, 542
Harman, Elisabeth II, 542
Harman, Elizabeth II, 371
Harman, Elizabeth IV, 218
Harman, Elizabeth IV, 283
Harman, Elizabeth V, 174
Harman, Elizabeth VI, 928
Harman, Exum I, 936
Harman, Fanny VI, 928
Harman, George II, 542
Harman, George W. I, 881
Harman, Henry VI, 928
Harman, Ida V, 174
Harman, Ida A. V, 174
Harman, Isaac II, 371
Harman, Jacob II, 371
Harman, Jacob II, 542
Harman, Jacob VI, 367
Harman, Jacob VI, 398
Harman, Jamima Woolman V, 909
Harman, Jane II, 542
Harman, Jane II, 544
Harman, Joel II, 371
Harman, John II, 707
Harman, Joseph II, 77
Harman, Josiah II, 371
Harman, Lizzie V, 174
Harman, Lizzie D. V, 174
Harman, Mary II, 371
Harman, Mary II, 519
Harman, Mary II, 542
Harman, Mary VI, 974
Harman, Naomi II, 371
Harman, Naomi II, 542
Harman, Peter VI, 952
Harman, Rach. A. VI, 368
Harman, Rachel II, 371
Harman, Rachel A. VI, 367
Harman, Rachel A. VI, 398
Harman, Rebeckah II, 77
Harman, Sarah II, 542
Harman, Sarah II, 565
Harman, Sarah II, 665
Harman, Sarah II, 713
Harman, Sarah II, 744
Harman, Sarah II, 770
Harman, Susan I, 936
Harman, Tubal II, 519
Harman, Tubal II, 542
Harman, Tubal II, 544
Harman, Tuball II, 371
Harman, William IV, 218
Harman, William VI, 928
Harmanes, Ester Riune II, 444
Harmar, Amos II, 542
Harmar, Hannah II, 542
Harmar, John II, 542
Harmar, Katharine II, 542
Harmar, Mary II, 535
Harmar, Mary II, 542
Harmar, Ruth II, 542
Harmar, Samuel II, 542
Harmar, Sarah II, 542
Harmell, Joseph V, 66
Harmer, Abraham II, 542
Harmer, Amos II, 542
Harmer, Amos IV, 148
Harmer, Amos IV, 1057
Harmer, Amos IV, 1061
Harmer, Amos R. IV, 148
Harmer, Amos R. IV, 1061
Harmer, Amos Roberts IV, 218
Harmer, Ann II, 150
Harmer, Ann II, 157
Harmer, Ann II, 523
Harmer, Ann II, 542
Harmer, Ann II, 706
Harmer, Ann II, 707
Harmer, Ann II, 718
Harmer, Anna IV, 276
Harmer, Anna IV, 1053
Harmer, Anna IV, 1061
Harmer, Anna IV, 1093
Harmer, Anna T. II, 706
Harmer, Benjamin II, 371
Harmer, Benjamin Tyler II, 150
Harmer, Benjamin Tyler II, 157
Harmer, Beulah Stewart II, 704
Harmer, Beulah Stewart II, 712
Harmer, Beulah Stewart II, 719
Harmer, Chalkley IV, 1061
Harmer, Charles II, 133
Harmer, Charles II, 150
Harmer, Charles II, 157
Harmer, Charles B. II, 133
Harmer, Charles B. II, 150
Harmer, Charles B., Jr. II, 150
Harmer, Charles B., Jr. II, 873
Harmer, Chas. II, 157
Harmer, Daniel IV, 1061
Harmer, David II, 320
Harmer, Ebeneezer II, 77
Harmer, Ebenezer II, 77
Harmer, Edward T. IV, 1061
Harmer, Elizabeth II, 371
Harmer, Elizabeth IV, 148
Harmer, Elizabeth IV, 218
Harmer, Elizabeth IV, 290
Harmer, Elizabeth IV, 1057
Harmer, Elizabeth IV, 1061
Harmer, Elwood IV, 148
Harmer, Elwood IV, 218
Harmer, Elwood IV, 1061
Harmer, Emaline B. II, 150
Harmer, Emaline B. II, 157
Harmer, Emeline B. II, 133
Harmer, Francis II, 282
Harmer, Francis II, 291
Harmer, George II, 371
Harmer, George II, 542
Harmer, George II, 611
Harmer, George IV, 148
Harmer, George IV, 218
Harmer, George IV, 1061
Harmer, George W. IV, 1061
Harmer, Hannah II, 542
Harmer, Hannah IV, 561
Harmer, Hannah Ann II, 134
Harmer, Hannah Ann II, 135
Harmer, Hannah Ann II, 150
Harmer, Hannah Ann II, 157
Harmer, Hannah Ann II, 818
Harmer, Honnor II, 371
Harmer, Honour II, 371
Harmer, Honour II, 611
Harmer, Isaac II, 371
Harmer, Isabella IV, 148
Harmer, Isabella IV, 150
Harmer, Isabella IV, 218
Harmer, Isabella IV, 1061
Harmer, Isaiah C. IV, 561
Harmer, J. Barton II, 133
Harmer, Jacob II, 371
Harmer, John II, 542
Harmer, John IV, 561
Harmer, John VI, 179
Harmer, Joseph II, 77
Harmer, Joseph II, 371
Harmer, Joseph II, 542
Harmer, Joshua II, 291
Harmer, Joshua L. II, 282
Harmer, Joshua L. II, 291
Harmer, Josiah II, 818
Harmer, Justice II, 873
Harmer, Justus II, 873
Harmer, Katharine II, 542
Harmer, Leah II, 542
Harmer, Leatitia II, 119
Harmer, Lemuel IV, 1061
Harmer, Lemuel J. IV, 1061
Harmer, Letitia II, 119
Harmer, Lettitia II, 119
Harmer, Lettitia II, 125
Harmer, Lillie T. II, 133
Harmer, Lydia IV, 1061
Harmer, Lydia Ann IV, 1061
Harmer, Lydia T. II, 134
Harmer, Lydia T. II, 150
Harmer, Margaret Emma IV, 820
Harmer, Margaret Emma IV, 830
Harmer, Mark II, 706
Harmer, Mark II, 707
Harmer, Mark II, 718
Harmer, Martha IV, 1061
Harmer, Martha IV, 1072
Harmer, Martha M. IV, 1061
Harmer, Mary II, 133
Harmer, Mary II, 150
Harmer, Mary II, 157
Harmer, Mary II, 160
Harmer, Mary II, 371
Harmer, Mary II, 542
Harmer, Mary IV, 1052
Harmer, Mary IV, 1061
Harmer, Mary Ann IV, 148
Harmer, Mary Ann IV, 218
Harmer, Mary Ann IV, 1057
Harmer, Mary Ann IV, 1061
Harmer, Mary H. II, 706
Harmer, Mary T. II, 133
Harmer, Mary W. II, 707
Harmer, Mary W. II, 745
Harmer, Mary White II, 119
Harmer, Naylor IV, 148
Harmer, Naylor IV, 150
Harmer, Naylor IV, 218
Harmer, Naylor IV, 1061
Harmer, Parthenia IV, 561
Harmer, Phebe II, 282
Harmer, Phebe II, 291
Harmer, Priscilla W. II, 282
Harmer, Priscilla W. II, 291
Harmer, Rachel II, 371
Harmer, Rachel IV, 1053
Harmer, Rachel IV, 1058
Harmer, Rachel IV, 1061
Harmer, Rachel IV, 1072
Harmer, Rachel IV, 1093
Harmer, Rebecca II, 135
Harmer, Rebecca II, 150
Harmer, Rebecca II, 154
Harmer, Rebecca IV, 1061
Harmer, Rebecca B. II, 150
Harmer, Rebeckah II, 77
Harmer, Ruth II, 119
Harmer, Ruth II, 371
Harmer, Ruth II, 542
Harmer, Ruth II, 718
Harmer, Samuel II, 542
Harmer, Sarah II, 542
Harmer, Susan F. II, 919
Harmer, Susan S. II, 150
Harmer, Susan S. II, 873
Harmer, Susie S. II, 133
Harmer, Thomas IV, 1061
Harmer, William II, 371
Harmer, William IV, 218
Harmer, William IV, 1061
Harmer, Wm. II, 542
Harmer, Wm. IV, 1053

Harmer, Wm. IV, 1058
Harmer, Wm. IV, 1061
Harmer, Wm. IV, 1072
Harmer, Wm. IV, 1093
Harmes, Maude IV, 1280
Harmon, Anne I, 51
Harmon, Anne I, 55
Harmon, Annie III, 255
Harmon, Billie V, 740
Harmon, Blanch I, 925
Harmon, Blanch I, 942
Harmon, Carrie V, 999
Harmon, Cary V, 999
Harmon, Charity II, 371
Harmon, Clara I, 925
Harmon, Clara I, 942
Harmon, E. T. I, 881
Harmon, Edward IV, 1253
Harmon, Eunice V, 497
Harmon, Exum I, 921
Harmon, Exum I, 922
Harmon, Exum I, 925
Harmon, Finley V, 999
Harmon, George W. I, 881
Harmon, George Wiseman I, 881
Harmon, Hattie IV, 1253
Harmon, Hattie E. IV, 1253
Harmon, Hazel I, 921
Harmon, Hazel I, 942
Harmon, Hazel I. I, 938
Harmon, Hazel I. I, 942
Harmon, Hazel Irene I, 925
Harmon, Katharine I, 942
Harmon, Katharine Whittier I, 925
Harmon, Lucy IV, 1253
Harmon, Mary I, 942
Harmon, Mary IV, 1253
Harmon, Mary Gladys I, 925
Harmon, Maude V, 999
Harmon, Mildred I, 922
Harmon, Mildred I, 925
Harmon, Mildred I, 942
Harmon, Peter VI, 883
Harmon, Rebecca VI, 746
Harmon, Rebecca VI, 773
Harmon, Rebecca VI, 774
Harmon, Robert I Sup 1, 4
Harmon, Sarah VI, 883
Harmon, Susan I, 881
Harmon, Susan I, 898
Harmon, Susan I, 921
Harmon, Susan I, 922
Harmon, Susan B. I, 942
Harmon, Susan B. I, 948
Harmon, Susan Belle I, 925
Harmon, Tuball II, 371
Harmon, Wanda V, 740
Harmor, Amos IV, 148
Harmor, Amos R. IV, 148
Harmor, Amos Roberts IV, 148
Harmor, Elizabeth IV, 148
Harmor, Elwood IV, 148
Harmor, George II, 371
Harmor, George IV, 148
Harmor, Isabella IV, 148
Harmor, Mary Ann IV, 148
Harmor, Nailor IV, 148
Harmor, Naylor IV, 148
Harmor, William IV, 148
Harned, Ada K. III, 150
Harned, Alfred III, 180
Harned, Alida C. V, 841
Harned, Andrew J. III, 150
Harned, Andrew J. III, 151
Harned, Anna III, 150
Harned, Anne III, 150
Harned, Catherine V, 832
Harned, Charles T. II, 873
Harned, Edith C. III, 151
Harned, Edith C. III, 180
Harned, Edward IV, 1365
Harned, Edward E. II, 873
Harned, Elizabeth II, 873
Harned, Eunice III, 15
Harned, Eunice III, 150
Harned, Helen III, 151
Harned, Helen III, 253
Harned, Hugh W. III, 151
Harned, Irving Alfred III, 151
Harned, Irving Alfred, Jr. III, 151
Harned, Jacob III, 483
Harned, Jacob III, 491
Harned, Jacob L. II, 873
Harned, Jacob Laing II, 798
Harned, James A. III, 100
Harned, James A. III, 151
Harned, James A. III, 162
Harned, Jas. A. III, 151
Harned, John II, 798
Harned, John IV, 1365
Harned, Jonathan IV, 1365
Harned, Katharine A. III, 151
Harned, Katie III, 151
Harned, Katie A. III, 100
Harned, Katie A. III, 151
Harned, Laura II, 873
Harned, Lucy III, 483
Harned, Lucy G. III, 258
Harned, Lucy G. III, 349
Harned, Lucy G. III, 494
Harned, Lucy G. III, 503
Harned, Margaret K. III, 151
Harned, Marion U. III, 150
Harned, Marion U. III, 151
Harned, Marion Virginia III, 151
Harned, Mary III, 151
Harned, Mary III, 483
Harned, Mary III, 491
Harned, Nathan IV, 1365
Harned, Phebe II, 798
Harned, Phineas III, 151
Harned, Rachel II, 873
Harned, Robert V, 832
Harned, Sarah S. II, 873
Harned, Sarah Shotwell II, 798
Harned, Wd. Alida C. V, 832
Harned, Wd. Alida C. V, 841
Harned, William VI, 646
Harned, Wm. VI, 501
Harned, Wm. Hutchinson III, 151
Harner, ??? V, 174
Harner, Ada V, 174
Harner, Ada L. V, 174
Harner, Arena B. V, 174
Harner, Arena C. V, 174
Harner, Charles T. V, 174
Harner, Clement V, 174
Harner, Clement M. V, 174
Harner, Clement S. V, 174
Harner, Cleora V, 174
Harner, Clyde V, 174
Harner, Clyde M. V, 174
Harner, Cracie Belle V, 174
Harner, Ebenezer II, 77
Harner, Edna V, 174
Harner, Elizabeth V, 174
Harner, Emily Alice V, 174
Harner, Eva Moon V, 174
Harner, Frank V, 174
Harner, Frank Wilson V, 174
Harner, Grace V, 174
Harner, Grace B. V, 174
Harner, Guy V, 174
Harner, Harriet P. V, 174
Harner, Harry V, 174
Harner, Hattie Lukens V, 679
Harner, Horace H. V, 174
Harner, James R. V, 174
Harner, Jennie Marie V, 174
Harner, Jennie Mills V, 174
Harner, Jesse V, 174
Harner, Lella V, 174
Harner, Lester A. V, 174
Harner, Lillie M. V, 174
Harner, Martha V, 174
Harner, Martha J. V, 174
Harner, Martin V, 174
Harner, Mary Eva V, 174
Harner, Marybelle V, 174
Harner, Ross V, 174
Harner, Ruth V, 174
Harner, Samuel V, 174
Harner, Stella Jane V, 174
Harner, Wm. H. V, 174
Harness, Cynthia V, 624
Harness, Cynthia L. V, 624
Harness, Samuel V, 624
Harness, Samuel Augustus V, 624
Harnett, Anna III, 151
Harney, Thomas II, 371
Harnley, John V, 1000
Harnods, Fanny VI, 828
Harold, Albert H. IV, 1280
Harold, Alice V, 679
Harold, Alice V, 700
Harold, Amasa IV, 583
Harold, Andrew I, 881
Harold, Andrew V, 497
Harold, Ann V, 497
Harold, Anna V, 410
Harold, Anna V, 497
Harold, Anna Elizabeth V, 497
Harold, Anna Kester V, 392
Harold, Anna W. IV, 1280
Harold, Annie Cox I, 634
Harold, Benjamin I, 912
Harold, Betta I, 813
Harold, Caroline V, 624
Harold, Caty IV, 583
Harold, Charity IV, 583
Harold, Clara I, 634
Harold, Clara V, 679
Harold, Clara O. V, 679
Harold, Clifford B. I, 942
Harold, David IV, 1280
Harold, David B. I, 942
Harold, David H. I, 942
Harold, Earl J. I, 634
Harold, Earl J. V, 679
Harold, Eli V, 497
Harold, Elizabeth V, 497
Harold, Elizabeth V, 563
Harold, Elizabeth V, 571
Harold, Harvey V, 624
Harold, Henrietta V, 624
Harold, Jacob IV, 583
Harold, James V, 497
Harold, James J. V, 497
Harold, James Johnson V, 497
Harold, James T. V, 497
Harold, John I, 594
Harold, John I, 597
Harold, John I, 912
Harold, Jonathan I, 594
Harold, Jonathan I, 813
Harold, Jonathan I, 836
Harold, Jonathan V, 497
Harold, Jonathan, Jr. V, 497
Harold, Jones E. V, 679
Harold, Jones E. V, 700
Harold, Joseph IV, 583
Harold, Leah S. V, 497
Harold, Leah Schooley V, 497
Harold, Leah T. V, 497
Harold, Lettitia I, 543
Harold, Margaret I, 634
Harold, Margaret I, 813
Harold, Margaret I, 836
Harold, Margaret V, 497
Harold, Margaret C. V, 679
Harold, Margareth I, 594
Harold, Margarett V, 497
Harold, Martha I, 594
Harold, Mary I, 594
Harold, Mary I, 597
Harold, Mary I, 813
Harold, Mary IV, 583
Harold, Mary V, 497
Harold, Mary V, 624
Harold, Mary Alice V, 497
Harold, Mary Allice V, 497
Harold, Mary Elizabeth I, 634
Harold, Mary Elizabeth V, 679
Harold, Mary L. V, 497
Harold, Mary R. V, 624
Harold, Matilda V, 624
Harold, Nathan V, 497
Harold, Ora J. IV, 1280
Harold, Pastor Earl I, 634
Harold, Rebecca V, 242
Harold, Rebecca V, 244
Harold, Rebecca VI, 478
Harold, Rosco C. IV, 1280
Harold, Russel E. V, 930
Harold, Sally V, 497
Harold, Samuel V, 497
Harold, Tacy I, 942
Harold, Tacy B. I, 942
Harp, Bertie IV, 1163
Harp, Lewis L. IV, 1163
Harp, Mary I, 50
Harp, Mary I, 51
Harper, ??? VI, 634
Harper, Alice II, 371
Harper, Alice II, 542
Harper, Alice V, 66
Harper, Alice V, 118
Harper, Ann II, 542
Harper, Ann II, 674
Harper, Ann IV, 217
Harper, Ann VI, 746
Harper, Ann R. II, 745
Harper, Anna M. III, 151
Harper, Anne IV, 218
Harper, Benjamin V, 440
Harper, Charles VI, 501
Harper, Charles VI, 521
Harper, Charles VI, 522
Harper, Chas. V, 1000
Harper, Daniel V, 66
Harper, Daniel V, 970
Harper, David II, 371
Harper, Dicey VI, 823
Harper, Edward II, 542
Harper, Edward R. II, 745
Harper, Eliphal II, 542
Harper, Elizabeth II, 320
Harper, Elizabeth II, 999
Harper, Elizabeth III, 151
Harper, Elizabeth VI, 858
Harper, Elizabeth F. VI, 823
Harper, Elizabeth W. III, 151
Harper, Elsie Morgan VI, 634
Harper, Emma II, 873
Harper, Emma II, 933
Harper, Emma V, 66
Harper, Emma V, 118
Harper, Frances V, 440
Harper, Franklin III, 151
Harper, Grace II, 796
Harper, Gustavus II, 371
Harper, Hannah II, 444
Harper, Hannah II, 542
Harper, Hannah II, 545
Harper, Hannah Ann II, 798
Harper, Henry II, 745
Harper, Hester II, 542
Harper, Hester II, 609
Harper, Ida V, 1000
Harper, James II, 542
Harper, Jane II, 230
Harper, Jane II, 371
Harper, Jane II, 542
Harper, Jane Massey II, 542
Harper, Jane Massey II, 745
Harper, Jenny VI, 928
Harper, Jesse II, 798
Harper, Jesse K. II, 1071
Harper, Jesse K. II, 1072
Harper, Jesse K. II, 1073
Harper, John II, 371
Harper, John II, 521
Harper, John II, 542
Harper, John II, 669
Harper, John II, 796
Harper, John VI, 823
Harper, John VI, 928
Harper, Jonathan II, 999
Harper, Joseph II, 371
Harper, Joseph II, 999
Harper, Joseph M. II, 873
Harper, Joseph M. III, 151
Harper, Joseph Monroe II, 798
Harper, Joseph W. VI, 135
Harper, Louisa V, 440
Harper, Lydia II, 999
Harper, Lydia IV, 583
Harper, Lydia IV, 599
Harper, Margaret II, 371
Harper, Margaret II, 542
Harper, Margaret II, 707
Harper, Margory VI, 928
Harper, Martha II, 999
Harper, Martha Ann V, 66
Harper, Mary II, 371
Harper, Mary II, 431
Harper, Mary II, 542
Harper, Mary II, 669
Harper, Mary II, 780
Harper, Mary Ann V, 970
Harper, Mary Martha II, 1071
Harper, Mary Martha II, 1073
Harper, Mattie Miller V, 1000
Harper, Nanch VI, 634
Harper, Nathan II, 861
Harper, Nathan II, 897
Harper, Nathan III, 151
Harper, Phebe II, 796
Harper, Rachel II, 371
Harper, Rachel H. II, 1072
Harper, Rachel H. II, 1073
Harper, Reuben II, 444
Harper, Rhoda IV, 583
Harper, Rhoda IV, 599
Harper, Robert VI, 823
Harper, Robert VI, 854
Harper, Robert VI, 928
Harper, Roberts II, 542
Harper, Rody VI, 854
Harper, Ruth V, 244
Harper, Ruth C. II, 1073
Harper, Samuel II, 371
Harper, Samuel II, 542
Harper, Samuel II, 672
Harper, Samuel II, 707
Harper, Sarah II, 542
Harper, Sarah II, 681
Harper, Sarah II, 999
Harper, Sarah V, 66
Harper, Sarah VI, 501
Harper, Sarah VI, 521
Harper, Sarah VI, 522
Harper, Sarah VI, 561
Harper, Sarah VI, 870
Harper, Sarah H. II, 1072
Harper, Sarah H. II, 1073
Harper, Sarah K. II, 1071
Harper, Sarah K. II, 1073
Harper, Sarah P. III, 151
Harper, Sarah S. V, 66
Harper, Sarah S. V, 970
Harper, Susanna II, 371
Harper, Susannah II, 999
Harper, Thomas II, 999
Harper, Thomas R. II, 873
Harper, Wd. Jane II, 521
Harper, William VI, 179
Harper, William VI, 218
Harplit, Susan B. V, 66
Harr, Elizabeth II, 542
Harr, Elizabeth II, 589
Harr, Elizabeth II, 593
Harra, C. S. VI, 134
Harra, C. S. VI, 135
Harra, D. VI, 135
Harral, Jonathan, Jr. I, 543
Harrar, Ida M. II, 857
Harras, Lydia IV, 581
Harras, Lydia IV, 583
Harrel, Arcada V, 244
Harrel, Dempsey I, 73
Harrel, Demsey I, 52
Harrel, Eleanor I, 52
Harrel, Hannah I, 52
Harrel, Hannah I, 73
Harrel, Jacob I, 52
Harrel, Jason I, 52
Harrel, Lauvenia Sarah I, 52
Harrel, Martin I, 52
Harrel, Mary V, 244
Harrel, Miriam I, 52
Harrel, Miriam I, 63
Harrel, Obed I, 52
Harrel, Rachel I, 48
Harrel, Rachel I, 52
Harrel, Rachel I, 594
Harrel, Rebecca I, 813
Harrel, Rebecca V, 244
Harrel, Silas I, 48
Harrel, Silas, Jr. I, 52
Harreld, Sarah I, 52
Harrell, Abigail I, 52
Harrell, Abigail I, 75
Harrell, Adom VI, 66
Harrell, Albertson I, 52
Harrell, Amey VI, 67
Harrell, Amos IV, 405
Harrell, Ann VI, 67
Harrell, Annie I, 617
Harrell, Annie C. I, 617
Harrell, Annie Cox I, 634
Harrell, Benj. V, 571
Harrell, Benjamin V, 571
Harrell, Bettie Ann I, 617
Harrell, Caroline IV, 906
Harrell, Charles I, 52
Harrell, Charles I, 57
Harrell, David I, 617
Harrell, David L. IV, 906
Harrell, David Wallace I, 617
Harrell, Demcey I, 52
Harrell, Demsey I, 52
Harrell, Dolly M. V, 571
Harrell, Ed. I, 52
Harrell, Edward J. IV, 906
Harrell, Eleanor I, 52
Harrell, Elijah I, 52
Harrell, Elizabeth I, 881
Harrell, Ella E. V, 571
Harrell, Euler I, 216
Harrell, Gabriel VI, 67
Harrell, Hannah I, 52
Harrell, Harvey I, 52
Harrell, Housen IV, 143
Harrell, Housen IV, 148
Harrell, Housen IV, 405
Harrell, Huldah I, 52
Harrell, Jacob I, 52
Harrell, James VI, 66
Harrell, James VI, 67
Harrell, Jason I, 52
Harrell, Jason IV, 906
Harrell, Jemima I, 52
Harrell, John VI, 67
Harrell, Lauvenia Sarah I, 52
Harrell, Louisa V, 571
Harrell, Lura M. V, 571
Harrell, Margaret I, 209
Harrell, Margaret I, 216
Harrell, Martha I, 209
Harrell, Martha IV, 148
Harrell, Martha Iola I, 216
Harrell, Martha J. I, 216
Harrell, Martha Jane I, 216
Harrell, Martin I, 52
Harrell, Mary I, 47
Harrell, Mary I, 52
Harrell, Mary IV, 405
Harrell, Minnie I, 52
Harrell, Minnie I, 77
Harrell, Miriam I, 52
Harrell, Ninna I, 307

Harrell, Obed I, 52
Harrell, Oliver I, 216
Harrell, Rachel I, 52
Harrell, Rachel I, 57
Harrell, Rachel IV, 143
Harrell, Rachel IV, 148
Harrell, Rachel IV, 405
Harrell, Robert IV, 906
Harrell, Samuel IV, 148
Harrell, Sarah I, 52
Harrell, Silas I, 52
Harrell, Silas, Jr. I, 52
Harrell, Tamer IV, 405
Harrell, Thomas I, 52
Harrell, Thomas I, 57
Harrell, Thomas I, 75
Harrell, Thomas IV, 906
Harrell, Thomas VI, 67
Harrell, Widow Sarah I, 52
Harrell, Widow Sarah I, 57
Harrell, William T. I, 216
Harrell, Winnie I, 303
Harrell, Winnie I, 307
Harrell, Wm. F. I, 209
Harres, Thomas V, 841
Harrier, Albert V, 571
Harrier, Florence V, 571
Harrier, Florence Elizabeth V, 571
Harrier, Helen Jane V, 571
Harrier, Laura V, 571
Harrimah, Amos IV, 1280
Harrimah, James IV, 1280
Harrimah, Mary IV, 1280
Harrington, Abraham II, 230
Harrington, Anna C. III, 151
Harrington, Anna Leora IV, 404
Harrington, Celia IV, 1253
Harrington, Cyrus J. IV, 404
Harrington, Elizabeth V, 244
Harrington, Geo. IV, 1319
Harrington, Harry G. III, 151
Harrington, Helen A. III, 314
Harrington, Joseph III, 151
Harrington, Lineus IV, 404
Harrington, Louise Belle IV, 1319
Harrington, Mary II, 745
Harrington, Mary II, 773
Harrington, Mary IV, 1319
Harrington, Mary E. IV, 1319
Harrington, Mary Ellen IV, 404
Harrington, Naomi V, 740
Harrington, Naomi V, 771
Harrington, Phebe II, 230
Harrington, Phebe Elma IV, 404
Harrington, Sara Etta IV, 404
Harrington, Sina B. IV, 404
Harrington, Taylor IV, 1253
Harriot, Samuel II, 542
Harriot, Samuel II, 631
Harriot, Sarah II, 542
Harriot, Sarah II, 544
Harriot, Sarah II, 631
Harriott, Jane II, 222
Harriott, Jane II, 230
Harriott, Jane II, 542
Harriott, Jane II, 544
Harriott, Jane II, 611
Harriott, John II, 371
Harriott, Miriam II, 371
Harriott, Samuel II, 222
Harriott, Samuel II, 230
Harriott, Samuel II, 371
Harriott, Samuel II, 542
Harriott, Samuel II, 611
Harriott, Sarah II, 542
Harriott, William II, 371
Harris, ??? III, 146
Harris, ??? IV, 717
Harris, ??? IV, 795
Harris, ??? VI, 223
Harris, ??? VI, 247
Harris, ??? VI, 293
Harris, ??? VI, 348
Harris, Aaron II, 31
Harris, Aaron II, 77
Harris, Abigale Roberson I, 271
Harris, Abner II, 31
Harris, Abram III, 151
Harris, Abram C. III, 151
Harris, Abram C. III, 373
Harris, Abram. C. III, 305
Harris, Absalom VI, 928
Harris, Adaline V, 1000
Harris, Adolphus V, 679
Harris, Agnes III, 57
Harris, Agnes III, 151
Harris, Albert Peele I, 435
Harris, Alce II, 371
Harris, Alfred I, 435
Harris, Alfred V, 572
Harris, Alfred H. I, 447
Harris, Alfred H. I, 626
Harris, Alice I, 271
Harris, Alice II, 371
Harris, Alis VI, 30
Harris, Alma E. V, 572
Harris, Alma J. IV, 717
Harris, Alvis I, 435
Harris, Amarilla IV, 1280
Harris, Amelia I, 270
Harris, Amelia I, 271
Harris, Amelia I, 274
Harris, Amos I, 270
Harris, Amos I, 271
Harris, Amos II, 133
Harris, Amos VI, 501
Harris, Amy IV, 36
Harris, Angelina IV, 300
Harris, Angelina G. V, 841
Harris, Ann I, 270
Harris, Ann I, 274
Harris, Ann II, 960
Harris, Ann II, 990
Harris, Ann II, 992
Harris, Ann II, 999
Harris, Ann II, 1026
Harris, Ann IV, 91
Harris, Ann IV, 218
Harris, Ann IV, 717
Harris, Ann IV, 721
Harris, Ann IV, 821
Harris, Ann IV, 840
Harris, Ann IV, 1021
Harris, Ann IV, 1026
Harris, Ann VI, 233
Harris, Ann VI, 246
Harris, Ann VI, 247
Harris, Ann VI, 483
Harris, Ann VI, 501
Harris, Ann Eliza IV, 821
Harris, Ann Eliza IV, 832
Harris, Ann Elizabeth II, 873
Harris, Ann Elizabeth IV, 630
Harris, Ann L. III, 151
Harris, Ann M. VI, 746
Harris, Ann M. VI, 792
Harris, Anna I, 265
Harris, Anna I, 270
Harris, Anna I, 271
Harris, Anna I, 307
Harris, Anna II, 943
Harris, Anna III, 387
Harris, Anna IV, 174
Harris, Anna IV, 218
Harris, Anna IV, 335
Harris, Anna IV, 717
Harris, Anna V, 741
Harris, Anna E. II, 873
Harris, Anna E. IV, 832
Harris, Anna E. IV, 1253
Harris, Anna E. V, 971
Harris, Anna E. V, 979
Harris, Anna H. II, 873
Harris, Anna H. II, 943
Harris, Anna J. IV, 847
Harris, Anna L. III, 146
Harris, Anna M. V, 361
Harris, Anna Maria IV, 717
Harris, Anna Mary V, 66
Harris, Anna Stanton I, 271
Harris, Anne VI, 30
Harris, Arthur III, 151
Harris, Arthur III, 252
Harris, Arthur III, 305
Harris, Arthur E. VI, 67
Harris, Arthur E. VI, 68
Harris, Asa VI, 501
Harris, Avarilla VI, 835
Harris, Averela VI, 819
Harris, Azubah II, 320
Harris, Barshaba I, 813
Harris, Barsheba I, 782
Harris, Benj. VI, 245
Harris, Benjamin I, 271
Harris, Benjamin I, 307
Harris, Benjamin I, 782
Harris, Benjamin I, 813
Harris, Benjamin II, 960
Harris, Benjamin II, 990
Harris, Benjamin II, 999
Harris, Benjamin II, 1026
Harris, Benjamin IV, 821
Harris, Benjamin V, 66
Harris, Benjamin VI, 61
Harris, Benjamin VI, 67
Harris, Benjamin VI, 179
Harris, Benjamin VI, 180
Harris, Benjamin VI, 238
Harris, Benjamin VI, 245
Harris, Benjamin VI, 246
Harris, Benjamin VI, 247
Harris, Benjamin VI, 248
Harris, Benjamin VI, 257
Harris, Benjamin VI, 267
Harris, Benjamin VI, 302
Harris, Benjamin VI, 802
Harris, Benjamin VI, 803
Harris, Benjamin VI, 823
Harris, Benjamin VI, 835
Harris, Benjamin T. VI, 63
Harris, Benjamin T. VI, 67
Harris, Benjamin T. VI, 248
Harris, Bersheba V, 66
Harris, Betsy I, 782
Harris, Betsy I, 1067
Harris, Betsy V, 174
Harris, Betsy VI, 63
Harris, Betsy VI, 67
Harris, Betsy VI, 242
Harris, Betsy VI, 248
Harris, Betty IV, 169
Harris, Betty IV, 218
Harris, Betty VI, 840
Harris, Beulah II, 799
Harris, Beulah II, 873
Harris, Beulah IV, 218
Harris, Beulah IV, 1061
Harris, Beulah Emily IV, 1054
Harris, Beulah Emily IV, 1061
Harris, Binjamin I, 813
Harris, Brin I, 270
Harris, Burgrub D. VI, 823
Harris, Burtha May I, 435
Harris, C. E. IV, 717
Harris, C. Esther III, 151
Harris, Callie V, 741
Harris, Callie Elsie I, 617
Harris, Carney IV, 717
Harris, Carney IV, 821
Harris, Carney IV, 857
Harris, Carolina III, 47
Harris, Caroline I, 271
Harris, Caroline III, 151
Harris, Caroline III, 252
Harris, Caroline IV, 218
Harris, Caroline IV, 335
Harris, Caroline PM VI, 247
Harris, Caroline S. III, 151
Harris, Caroline S. III, 157
Harris, Catharine VI, 805
Harris, Catharine VI, 823
Harris, Catharine S. II, 150
Harris, Chalkley II, 77
Harris, Chalkley IV, 717
Harris, Chalkley IV, 821
Harris, Chalkley IV, 828
Harris, Chalkly II, 31
Harris, Channing Page III, 18
Harris, Channing Page III, 151
Harris, Charity IV, 630
Harris, Charles III, 151
Harris, Charles VI, 823
Harris, Charles H. V, 334
Harris, Charles Wm. II, 707
Harris, Chas. VI, 1006
Harris, Chas. H. V, 334
Harris, Cheadle VI, 246
Harris, Cheadle VI, 247
Harris, Chester F. V, 740
Harris, Chlotilda VI, 179
Harris, Chlotilda VI, 190
Harris, Chlotilda VI, 194
Harris, Chlotilda VI, 235
Harris, Chlotilda VI, 246
Harris, Chlotilda VI, 247
Harris, Chlotilda VI, 257
Harris, Christiana IV, 218
Harris, Christiana IV, 226
Harris, Christiana VI, 92
Harris, Clara V, 741
Harris, Clara Cluxton V, 392
Harris, Clara Jane IV, 821
Harris, Clotilda VI, 248
Harris, Clotilda VI, 257
Harris, Cornelia M. III, 151
Harris, Cornelia W. III, 215
Harris, Cornelious VI, 246
Harris, Cornelius VI, 16
Harris, Cornelius VI, 245
Harris, Cuthbert I, 813
Harris, Daniel I, 265
Harris, Daniel I, 270
Harris, Daniel I, 271
Harris, Daniel II, 371
Harris, Daniel IV, 36
Harris, Daniel IV, 91
Harris, Daniel V, 66
Harris, Daniel VI, 179
Harris, Daniel VI, 245
Harris, Daniel VI, 246
Harris, Daniel VI, 247
Harris, Daniel VI, 398
Harris, Daniel VI, 501
Harris, Daniel VI, 502
Harris, Daniel VI, 597
Harris, Daniel VI, 928
Harris, Daniel, Jr. VI, 247
Harris, David I, 271
Harris, David I, 273
Harris, David I, 307
Harris, David I, 782
Harris, David I, 813
Harris, David I, 1030
Harris, David I, 1067
Harris, David I, 1070
Harris, David II, 31
Harris, David II, 77
Harris, David IV, 148
Harris, David IV, 218
Harris, David IV, 404
Harris, David IV, 529
Harris, David IV, 821
Harris, David V, 66
Harris, David V, 174
Harris, David V, 741
Harris, David VI, 501
Harris, David VI, 927
Harris, David E. IV, 821
Harris, David F. IV, 717
Harris, David F. IV, 784
Harris, David S. IV, 821
Harris, David, Jr. IV, 858
Harris, Deborah IV, 300
Harris, Deborah V, 66
Harris, Deborah VI, 67
Harris, Deborah VI, 235
Harris, Deborah VI, 246
Harris, Deborah VI, 248
Harris, Deborah VI, 501
Harris, Deborah VI, 552
Harris, Deborah VI, 597
Harris, Dinah VI, 928
Harris, Dorothy V, 741
Harris, Doshia VI, 893
Harris, Doshia VI, 928
Harris, Doshia VI, 977
Harris, E. Ann V, 22
Harris, E. Ann V, 66
Harris, Easter I, 270
Harris, Edgar V, 741
Harris, Edith II, 31
Harris, Edith II, 77
Harris, Edith II, 106
Harris, Edith VI, 16
Harris, Edith VI, 245
Harris, Edith VI, 246
Harris, Edith R. IV, 1253
Harris, Edith R. V, 971
Harris, Edith R. V, 979
Harris, Edward VI, 928
Harris, Elana IV, 529
Harris, Elana Eliza IV, 404
Harris, Elana Eliza IV, 418
Harris, Eleanor IV, 404
Harris, Electa V, 741
Harris, Eli IV, 218
Harris, Eli IV, 1061
Harris, Elijah I, 270
Harris, Elijah I, 271
Harris, Elijah I, 275
Harris, Elijah I, 276
Harris, Elijah I, 307
Harris, Elijah III, 350
Harris, Elijah, Sr. VI, 928
Harris, Elisha IV, 335
Harris, Eliza VI, 66
Harris, Eliza VI, 67
Harris, Eliza VI, 92
Harris, Eliza VI, 928
Harris, Eliza A. VI, 823
Harris, Eliza J. VI, 52
Harris, Eliza J. VI, 67
Harris, Elizabeth I, 265
Harris, Elizabeth I, 270
Harris, Elizabeth I, 271
Harris, Elizabeth I, 782
Harris, Elizabeth I, 813
Harris, Elizabeth I, 1030
Harris, Elizabeth I, 1037
Harris, Elizabeth IV, 300
Harris, Elizabeth IV, 630
Harris, Elizabeth V, 66
Harris, Elizabeth V, 174
Harris, Elizabeth V, 741
Harris, Elizabeth V, 970
Harris, Elizabeth VI, 5
Harris, Elizabeth VI, 6
Harris, Elizabeth VI, 30
Harris, Elizabeth VI, 39
Harris, Elizabeth VI, 67
Harris, Elizabeth VI, 179
Harris, Elizabeth VI, 180
Harris, Elizabeth VI, 215
Harris, Elizabeth VI, 242
Harris, Elizabeth VI, 245
Harris, Elizabeth VI, 246
Harris, Elizabeth VI, 247
Harris, Elizabeth VI, 248
Harris, Elizabeth VI, 301
Harris, Elizabeth VI, 313
Harris, Elizabeth VI, 335
Harris, Elizabeth VI, 352
Harris, Elizabeth VI, 398
Harris, Elizabeth VI, 494
Harris, Elizabeth VI, 495
Harris, Elizabeth VI, 502
Harris, Elizabeth VI, 508
Harris, Elizabeth VI, 519
Harris, Elizabeth VI, 520
Harris, Elizabeth VI, 641
Harris, Elizabeth VI, 646
Harris, Elizabeth VI, 647
Harris, Elizabeth VI, 661
Harris, Elizabeth VI, 744
Harris, Elizabeth VI, 802
Harris, Elizabeth VI, 813
Harris, Elizabeth VI, 823
Harris, Elizabeth VI, 928
Harris, Elizabeth VI, 1020
Harris, Elizabeth A. V, 66
Harris, Elizabeth A. VI, 54
Harris, Elizabeth A. VI, 67
Harris, Elizabeth A. VI, 823
Harris, Elizabeth Ann II, 828
Harris, Elizabeth Ann V, 66
Harris, Elizabeth D. VI, 215
Harris, Elizabeth S. VI, 951
Harris, Elizabeth T. VI, 879
Harris, Elizabeth V. VI, 65
Harris, Elizabeth V. VI, 66
Harris, Elizabeth Virginia VI, 92
Harris, Ella IV, 782
Harris, Ellen IV, 717
Harris, Ellen IV, 1021
Harris, Ellen IV, 1026
Harris, Ellen B. II, 138
Harris, Ellin IV, 1026
Harris, Ellin IV, 1031
Harris, Elsa VI, 893
Harris, Elsie II, 707
Harris, Elvah V, 66
Harris, Elwood B. I, 435
Harris, Emily IV, 127
Harris, Emily IV, 129
Harris, Emily IV, 218
Harris, Emily IV, 717
Harris, Emily H. IV, 717
Harris, Emily M. IV, 127
Harris, Emily M. IV, 717
Harris, Emmor IV, 821
Harris, Enoch I, 269
Harris, Enoch I, 270
Harris, Enoch II, 31
Harris, Enoch II, 77
Harris, Enoch IV, 137
Harris, Enoch IV, 148
Harris, Enoch IV, 218
Harris, Enoch IV, 335
Harris, Enoch IV, 717
Harris, Enoch IV, 962
Harris, Enoch Gibbs II, 77
Harris, Enoch R. IV, 962
Harris, Enoch, Jr. IV, 218
Harris, Ernest V, 66
Harris, Ernest V, 497
Harris, Essie M. I, 435
Harris, Estelle Kite III, 151
Harris, Esther I, 265
Harris, Esther I, 270
Harris, Esther II, 28
Harris, Esther II, 31
Harris, Esther II, 77
Harris, Esther II, 106
Harris, Esther III, 18
Harris, Esther III, 151
Harris, Esther IV, 36
Harris, Esther IV, 91
Harris, Esther IV, 821
Harris, Esther IV, 848
Harris, Esther IV, 1026
Harris, Esther V, 66
Harris, Esther VI, 398
Harris, Esther VI, 464
Harris, Esther VI, 468
Harris, Esther VI, 476
Harris, Esther VI, 501
Harris, Esther VI, 502
Harris, Esther C. IV, 717
Harris, Esther C. IV, 821
Harris, Esther C. IV, 1021
Harris, Esther, Jr. VI, 475
Harris, Estus V, 679
Harris, Eunis E. I, 435
Harris, Evan H. IV, 218

Harris, Ezekiel I, 270
Harris, Ezekiel IV, 148
Harris, Ezekiel IV, 174
Harris, Ezekiel IV, 194
Harris, Ezekiel IV, 218
Harris, Ezekiel IV, 233
Harris, Ezekiel IV, 335
Harris, Fannah IV, 194
Harris, Fannah IV, 218
Harris, Fannie I, 924
Harris, Fanny IV, 218
Harris, Feriba I, 270
Harris, Feribah I, 270
Harris, Feribah I, 273
Harris, Fleming Bates VI, 248
Harris, Floyd V, 741
Harris, Fran. VI, 928
Harris, Frances I, 930
Harris, Frances VI, 996
Harris, Frances R. VI, 977
Harris, Francis II, 371
Harris, Francis VI, 928
Harris, Francis VI, 1020
Harris, Francis M. V, 392
Harris, Fred V, 741
Harris, Frederick III, 47
Harris, Frederick III, 151
Harris, Frederick V, 741
Harris, Frederick A. VI, 928
Harris, Fredk. A. VI, 977
Harris, Geo. VI, 595
Harris, George I, 265
Harris, George I, 270
Harris, George I, 271
Harris, George II, 230
Harris, George II, 269
Harris, George II, 542
Harris, George II, 543
Harris, George II, 799
Harris, George II, 804
Harris, George II, 873
Harris, George IV, 36
Harris, George IV, 91
Harris, George V, 66
Harris, George V, 741
Harris, George VI, 179
Harris, George VI, 501
Harris, George VI, 527
Harris, George VI, 596
Harris, George VI, 597
Harris, George VI, 598
Harris, George Brin I, 270
Harris, George Brin I, 274
Harris, George W. V, 624
Harris, Gertrude E. IV, 717
Harris, Giles VI, 823
Harris, Grace II, 371
Harris, Gulielma IV, 208
Harris, Gulielma IV, 218
Harris, Gulielma VI, 501
Harris, Gulielma VI, 537
Harris, Hanna VI, 313
Harris, Hannah I, 271
Harris, Hannah I, 273
Harris, Hannah I, 275
Harris, Hannah I, 289
Harris, Hannah I, 307
Harris, Hannah I, 537
Harris, Hannah I, 543
Harris, Hannah I, 1061
Harris, Hannah I, 1063
Harris, Hannah II, 31
Harris, Hannah II, 65
Harris, Hannah II, 77
Harris, Hannah II, 542
Harris, Hannah II, 543
Harris, Hannah II, 707
Harris, Hannah IV, 20
Harris, Hannah IV, 36
Harris, Hannah IV, 529
Harris, Hannah IV, 541
Harris, Hannah IV, 630
Harris, Hannah IV, 717
Harris, Hannah IV, 784
Harris, Hannah V, 22
Harris, Hannah V, 740
Harris, Hannah V, 809
Harris, Hannah VI, 352
Harris, Hannah VI, 354
Harris, Hannah VI, 398
Harris, Hannah VI, 501
Harris, Hannah VI, 502
Harris, Hannah VI, 508
Harris, Hannah VI, 513
Harris, Hannah VI, 575
Harris, Hannah VI, 586
Harris, Hannah VI, 646
Harris, Hannah VI, 954
Harris, Hannah E. V, 244
Harris, Hannah W. IV, 717
Harris, Harriet VI, 67
Harris, Harriet VI, 68
Harris, Harriet VI, 92
Harris, Harriet C. VI, 823
Harris, Harris VI, 313
Harris, Hattie I, 869
Harris, Hattie I, 881
Harris, Hattie J. I, 942
Harris, Hector VI, 823
Harris, Helen III, 305
Harris, Helen L. V, 22
Harris, Helen S. III, 151
Harris, Helen S. III, 305
Harris, Henrietta IV, 1253
Harris, Henry I, 271
Harris, Henry I, 307
Harris, Henry IV, 630
Harris, Henry V, 572
Harris, Henry VI, 67
Harris, Henry VI, 823
Harris, Henry VI, 928
Harris, Henry Knight III, 151
Harris, Henry R. V, 572
Harris, Henry T. VI, 805
Harris, Hephzibah II, 28
Harris, Hephzibah II, 31
Harris, Hepsibah IV, 717
Harris, Hepzibah II, 71
Harris, Hepzibah II, 77
Harris, Hester I, 1030
Harris, Hester I, 1032
Harris, Hester II, 53
Harris, Hester II, 77
Harris, Hope V, 66
Harris, Hope VI, 595
Harris, Hope VI, 596
Harris, Hope VI, 597
Harris, Hope VI, 598
Harris, Howard V, 741
Harris, Ichabod I, 270
Harris, Isaac II, 31
Harris, Isaac V, 572
Harris, Isaac S. II, 320
Harris, Isabella VI, 30
Harris, Isabella VI, 246
Harris, Isabella VI, 248
Harris, Isabella VI, 257
Harris, Isaiah I, 270
Harris, Isaiah IV, 148
Harris, Isaiah IV, 717
Harris, Isaiah V, 66
Harris, Isaiah VI, 597
Harris, Isaiah Enoch I, 270
Harris, J. M. I, 942
Harris, J. Warren IV, 1253
Harris, J. Wistar III, 151
Harris, Jacob II, 31
Harris, Jacob IV, 36
Harris, Jacob IV, 630
Harris, Jacob IV, 716
Harris, Jacob IV, 717
Harris, Jacob IV, 721
Harris, Jacob IV, 782
Harris, Jacob IV, 1021
Harris, Jacob VI, 928
Harris, Jacob B. IV, 717
Harris, Jacob Benjamin IV, 717
Harris, Jacob T. V, 244
Harris, James I, 543
Harris, James I, 782
Harris, James I, 813
Harris, James II, 543
Harris, James V, 66
Harris, James V, 334
Harris, James VI, 54
Harris, James VI, 67
Harris, James VI, 68
Harris, James VI, 179
Harris, James VI, 180
Harris, James VI, 215
Harris, James VI, 217
Harris, James VI, 232
Harris, James VI, 233
Harris, James VI, 246
Harris, James VI, 247
Harris, James VI, 879
Harris, James VI, 910
Harris, James VI, 922
Harris, James VI, 928
Harris, James VI, 931
Harris, James VI, 940
Harris, James VI, 962
Harris, James VI, 990
Harris, James A. IV, 218
Harris, James A. IV, 717
Harris, James Alvis I, 435
Harris, James Crew VI, 247
Harris, James H. II, 873
Harris, James L. V, 334
Harris, James M. VI, 928
Harris, James N. III, 151
Harris, James N. III, 157
Harris, James O. III, 151
Harris, James W. II, 745
Harris, James W. II, 873
Harris, James W. III, 151
Harris, Jane I, 543
Harris, Jane I, 593
Harris, Jane I, 594
Harris, Jane I, 782
Harris, Jane III, 350
Harris, Jane IV, 821
Harris, Jane IV, 847
Harris, Jane V, 446
Harris, Jane VI, 823
Harris, Jane VI, 857
Harris, Jane VI, 993
Harris, Jane W. IV, 717
Harris, Jemima I, 782
Harris, Jemima IV, 91
Harris, Jemimah IV, 36
Harris, Jeremiah VI, 233
Harris, Jeremiah VI, 245
Harris, Jeremiah VI, 246
Harris, Jeremiah VI, 247
Harris, Jeremiah E. VI, 67
Harris, Jeremiah E. VI, 68
Harris, Jesse I, 270
Harris, Jesse I, 271
Harris, Jesse I, 305
Harris, Jesse I, 307
Harris, Jesse IV, 630
Harris, Jesse VI, 398
Harris, Jesse VI, 502
Harris, Jessey I, 271
Harris, Jessie IV, 755
Harris, Jessie IV, 1253
Harris, Jim V, 741
Harris, Joel IV, 717
Harris, Joel IV, 1021
Harris, Joel G. IV, 717
Harris, John I, 270
Harris, John I, 782
Harris, John I, 1067
Harris, John II, 28
Harris, John II, 31
Harris, John II, 53
Harris, John II, 75
Harris, John II, 77
Harris, John II, 104
Harris, John II, 106
Harris, John II, 371
Harris, John IV, 300
Harris, John IV, 716
Harris, John IV, 821
Harris, John V, 66
Harris, John V, 174
Harris, John VI, 16
Harris, John VI, 30
Harris, John VI, 65
Harris, John VI, 67
Harris, John VI, 68
Harris, John VI, 81
Harris, John VI, 109
Harris, John VI, 179
Harris, John VI, 180
Harris, John VI, 213
Harris, John VI, 223
Harris, John VI, 224
Harris, John VI, 245
Harris, John VI, 246
Harris, John VI, 247
Harris, John VI, 259
Harris, John VI, 267
Harris, John VI, 269
Harris, John VI, 313
Harris, John VI, 398
Harris, John VI, 810
Harris, John VI, 823
Harris, John VI, 865
Harris, John VI, 928
Harris, John VI, 939
Harris, John C. VI, 922
Harris, John G. VI, 823
Harris, John J. VI, 835
Harris, John L. I, 813
Harris, John M. VI, 819
Harris, John M. VI, 823
Harris, John Milton V, 841
Harris, John Stuart I, 782
Harris, John W. IV, 218
Harris, John W. IV, 300
Harris, John Wilson V, 841
Harris, John, Jr. VI, 16
Harris, Johnson I, 271
Harris, Johnson I, 289
Harris, Johnson I, 307
Harris, Jonas IV, 20
Harris, Jonas IV, 36
Harris, Jonas IV, 630
Harris, Jonas VI, 313
Harris, Jonas VI, 352
Harris, Jonas VI, 502
Harris, Jonas VI, 646
Harris, Jonathan I, 270
Harris, Jonathan I, 782
Harris, Jonathan I, 813
Harris, Jonathan I, 840
Harris, Jonathan I, 1067
Harris, Jonathan I, 1070
Harris, Jonathan II, 31
Harris, Jonathan IV, 218
Harris, Jonathan IV, 821
Harris, Jonathan IV, 1061
Harris, Jonathan V, 174
Harris, Jordan P. IV, 218
Harris, Jordan P. IV, 1061
Harris, Joseph I, 271
Harris, Joseph I, 307
Harris, Joseph II, 371
Harris, Joseph IV, 218
Harris, Joseph IV, 226
Harris, Joseph IV, 300
Harris, Joseph IV, 717
Harris, Joseph VI, 56
Harris, Joseph VI, 61
Harris, Joseph VI, 67
Harris, Joseph VI, 246
Harris, Joseph VI, 247
Harris, Joseph VI, 286
Harris, Joseph VI, 502
Harris, Joseph VI, 514
Harris, Joseph VI, 823
Harris, Joseph VI, 928
Harris, Josephine IV, 821
Harris, Josiah I, 265
Harris, Josiah I, 270
Harris, Josiah IV, 36
Harris, Josiah IV, 91
Harris, Judith I, 782
Harris, Judith I, 806
Harris, Judith I, 813
Harris, Judith II, 542
Harris, Judith VI, 179
Harris, Judith VI, 180
Harris, Judith VI, 210
Harris, Judith VI, 217
Harris, Judith VI, 238
Harris, Judith VI, 239
Harris, Judith VI, 245
Harris, Judith VI, 246
Harris, Judith VI, 247
Harris, Judith VI, 823
Harris, Julia III, 151
Harris, Julia VI, 58
Harris, Julia VI, 68
Harris, Julia Ann VI, 928
Harris, Jurdan IV, 1061
Harris, Kate V, 679
Harris, Katharene VI, 398
Harris, L. L. I, 942
Harris, Laney I, 270
Harris, Laney Ann IV, 805
Harris, Laney Ann IV, 821
Harris, Lany I, 269
Harris, Lany I, 270
Harris, Lany IV, 148
Harris, Lany IV, 218
Harris, Lany IV, 529
Harris, Lavina VI, 67
Harris, Lavinia VI, 76
Harris, Laymond VI, 973
Harris, Leah IV, 821
Harris, Leah IV, 956
Harris, Leah IV, 962
Harris, Leatitia II, 31
Harris, Lelia I, 634
Harris, Lelia I, 641
Harris, Lelia B. VI, 823
Harris, Lelia M. I, 435
Harris, Lelia Mable I, 626
Harris, Lemoyne Albert IV, 534
Harris, Lemuel IV, 962
Harris, Lena V, 392
Harris, Lenna V, 409
Harris, Leticia II, 77
Harris, Letitia II, 86
Harris, Lettice IV, 218
Harris, Lettice IV, 529
Harris, Lettis IV, 218
Harris, Lettis IV, 268
Harris, Lettuce IV, 404
Harris, Lettuce IV, 529
Harris, Levi IV, 630
Harris, Levi VI, 313
Harris, Levi VI, 352
Harris, Levi VI, 502
Harris, Levi VI, 646
Harris, Levi VI, 925
Harris, Levi VI, 928
Harris, Levi VI, 996
Harris, Levina VI, 54
Harris, Levina VI, 67
Harris, Lewis V, 392
Harris, Linley IV, 717
Harris, Lloyd V, 741
Harris, Loren V, 741
Harris, Louis V, 392
Harris, Louisa I, 782
Harris, Louisa I, 813
Harris, Louisa I, 840
Harris, Louisa M. VI, 928
Harris, Louisa T. VI, 928
Harris, Lovina VI, 67
Harris, Lowell Edwin V, 741
Harris, Lucilla I, 717
Harris, Lucilla I, 718
Harris, Lucina IV, 821
Harris, Lucinda IV, 300
Harris, Lucy V, 334
Harris, Lucy VI, 180
Harris, Lucy VI, 246
Harris, Lucy VI, 247
Harris, Lucy A. VI, 248
Harris, Lucy Anne VI, 248
Harris, Lusina IV, 821
Harris, Lusinda IV, 218
Harris, Lusinda IV, 300
Harris, Lusine IV, 821
Harris, Lusine IV, 847
Harris, Lydia I, 393
Harris, Lydia I, 424
Harris, Lydia I, 543
Harris, Lydia I, 813
Harris, Lydia IV, 300
Harris, Lydia IV, 630
Harris, Lydia V, 741
Harris, Lydia VI, 109
Harris, Lythea VI, 865
Harris, Mail VI, 928
Harris, Major William VI, 289
Harris, Malinda V, 392
Harris, Malinda V, 497
Harris, Malinda J. V, 392
Harris, Mamie V, 741
Harris, Margaret I, 543
Harris, Margaret I, 782
Harris, Margaret I, 813
Harris, Margaret IV, 1026
Harris, Margaret V, 66
Harris, Margaret V, 741
Harris, Margaret VI, 67
Harris, Margaret VI, 68
Harris, Margaret VI, 76
Harris, Margaret VI, 502
Harris, Margaret VI, 503
Harris, Margaret VI, 508
Harris, Margaret VI, 1013
Harris, Margaret Alsop III, 151
Harris, Margaret M. VI, 68
Harris, Margret VI, 30
Harris, Margrett VI, 30
Harris, Marion IV, 717
Harris, Marion IV, 755
Harris, Marion V, 392
Harris, Marion V, 497
Harris, Maris I, 782
Harris, Maris I, 881
Harris, Mark II, 31
Harris, Marlin V, 741
Harris, Marris I, 813
Harris, Martha I, 782
Harris, Martha II, 31
Harris, Martha II, 75
Harris, Martha II, 77
Harris, Martha IV, 821
Harris, Martha V, 66
Harris, Martha V, 740
Harris, Martha V, 741
Harris, Martha VI, 52
Harris, Martha VI, 67
Harris, Martha VI, 68
Harris, Martha VI, 92
Harris, Martha VI, 398
Harris, Martha VI, 502
Harris, Martha VI, 597
Harris, Martha VI, 817
Harris, Martha VI, 931
Harris, Martha VI, 1018
Harris, Martha F. VI, 67
Harris, Martha F. VI, 68
Harris, Martha F. VI, 92
Harris, Martha H. IV, 529
Harris, Martha H. IV, 536
Harris, Martha I. VI, 823
Harris, Martha M. J. VI, 67
Harris, Martha M. J. VI, 68
Harris, Martha M. J. VI, 81
Harris, Martha Mary IV, 534
Harris, Mary I, 265
Harris, Mary I, 270
Harris, Mary I, 271
Harris, Mary I, 273
Harris, Mary I, 289
Harris, Mary I, 782

Harris, Mary I, 803
Harris, Mary I, 813
Harris, Mary I, 881
Harris, Mary I, 1067
Harris, Mary I, 1070
Harris, Mary I, 1071
Harris, Mary II, 31
Harris, Mary II, 77
Harris, Mary II, 119
Harris, Mary II, 133
Harris, Mary II, 230
Harris, Mary II, 269
Harris, Mary II, 371
Harris, Mary II, 542
Harris, Mary II, 543
Harris, Mary II, 796
Harris, Mary II, 819
Harris, Mary II, 960
Harris, Mary II, 999
Harris, Mary IV, 36
Harris, Mary IV, 91
Harris, Mary IV, 218
Harris, Mary IV, 335
Harris, Mary IV, 630
Harris, Mary IV, 716
Harris, Mary IV, 717
Harris, Mary IV, 721
Harris, Mary IV, 780
Harris, Mary IV, 821
Harris, Mary IV, 1021
Harris, Mary IV, 1026
Harris, Mary V, 174
Harris, Mary V, 334
Harris, Mary V, 831
Harris, Mary V, 979
Harris, Mary VI, 30
Harris, Mary VI, 61
Harris, Mary VI, 65
Harris, Mary VI, 67
Harris, Mary VI, 81
Harris, Mary VI, 109
Harris, Mary VI, 179
Harris, Mary VI, 180
Harris, Mary VI, 232
Harris, Mary VI, 233
Harris, Mary VI, 245
Harris, Mary VI, 246
Harris, Mary VI, 247
Harris, Mary VI, 259
Harris, Mary VI, 313
Harris, Mary VI, 352
Harris, Mary VI, 356
Harris, Mary VI, 398
Harris, Mary VI, 502
Harris, Mary VI, 646
Harris, Mary VI, 803
Harris, Mary VI, 823
Harris, Mary VI, 922
Harris, Mary VI, 928
Harris, Mary VI, 1014
Harris, Mary VI, 1017
Harris, Mary Ann IV, 148
Harris, Mary Ann IV, 158
Harris, Mary Ann IV, 716
Harris, Mary Ann IV, 717
Harris, Mary Ann IV, 721
Harris, Mary Ann IV, 1026
Harris, Mary Ann VI, 997
Harris, Mary B. II, 133
Harris, Mary B. II, 138
Harris, Mary B. II, 150
Harris, Mary E. V, 334
Harris, Mary Elizabeth I, 782
Harris, Mary Elizabeth VI, 67
Harris, Mary H. IV, 1253
Harris, Mary H. V, 970
Harris, Mary H. V, 971
Harris, Mary I. I, 435
Harris, Mary J. I, 626
Harris, Mary Jane I, 435
Harris, Mary Jane I, 619
Harris, Mary L. IV, 1054
Harris, Mary L. IV, 1061
Harris, Mary M. VI, 928
Harris, Mary M. VI, 977
Harris, Mary P. III, 151
Harris, Mary T. VI, 242
Harris, Mary T. VI, 246
Harris, Mary T. VI, 248
Harris, Mary T. VI, 928
Harris, Mary, Jr. II, 230
Harris, Mary, Jr. VI, 246
Harris, Mathew VI, 67
Harris, Matthew VI, 51
Harris, Matthew VI, 67
Harris, Matthew VI, 68
Harris, Matthew VI, 109
Harris, Matthew VI, 928
Harris, Mattie IV, 218
Harris, Mattie VI, 83
Harris, May I, 270
Harris, Mellie M. IV, 1319
Harris, Mendenhall I, 813
Harris, Meriam I, 543
Harris, Meriam I, 561
Harris, Micajah VI, 247
Harris, Michael VI, 141
Harris, Michal VI, 109
Harris, Michal VI, 135
Harris, Milicent IV, 962
Harris, Millicent II, 31
Harris, Millie I, 270
Harris, Millison S. IV, 962
Harris, Miriam I, 543
Harris, Miriam I, 813
Harris, Miriam I, 828
Harris, Mittie I, 268
Harris, Mittie I, 270
Harris, Molly I, 782
Harris, Molly VI, 928
Harris, Moses VI, 63
Harris, Moses VI, 67
Harris, Moses VI, 244
Harris, Moses VI, 245
Harris, Moses VI, 246
Harris, Moses VI, 247
Harris, Moses VI, 313
Harris, Moses VI, 494
Harris, Moses VI, 495
Harris, Moses VI, 502
Harris, Moses VI, 519
Harris, Moses VI, 520
Harris, Moses VI, 641
Harris, Moses VI, 661
Harris, Moses VI, 744
Harris, Moses VI, 928
Harris, Moses Harris VI, 247
Harris, Mrs. Sarah III, 483
Harris, Myrtle V, 741
Harris, Nancy VI, 51
Harris, Nancy VI, 67
Harris, Nancy VI, 68
Harris, Nancy VI, 302
Harris, Nancy VI, 802
Harris, Nancy VI, 823
Harris, Nancy VI, 928
Harris, Nancy VI, 994
Harris, Nancy A. VI, 928
Harris, Nancy L. VI, 67
Harris, Nancy L. VI, 68
Harris, Nannie M. I, 927
Harris, Nathan I, 289
Harris, Nathan II, 31
Harris, Nathan IV, 717
Harris, Nathan IV, 821
Harris, Nathan VI, 823
Harris, Nathaniel VI, 911
Harris, Nathaniel VI, 928
Harris, Nathaniel VI, 1017
Harris, Nehemiah I, 265
Harris, Nehemiah I, 270
Harris, Nehemiah IV, 91
Harris, Nicholas VI, 245
Harris, Norma Jean V, 741
Harris, Obadiah I, 543
Harris, Obadiah I, 561
Harris, Obadiah I, 773
Harris, Obadiah I, 782
Harris, Obadiah I, 847
Harris, Obadiah I, 1067
Harris, Obadiah I, 1070
Harris, Obadiah I, 1071
Harris, Obadiah V, 174
Harris, Obediah I, 782
Harris, Obediah I, 813
Harris, Obediah I, 881
Harris, Obediah I, 892
Harris, Obediah I, 953
Harris, Obediah I, 1070
Harris, Obediah V, 787
Harris, Obediah VI, 179
Harris, Obediah VI, 185
Harris, Obediah VI, 186
Harris, Obediah VI, 246
Harris, Obediah, Jr. I, 813
Harris, Obidiah V, 66
Harris, Olive V, 741
Harris, Oliver IV, 962
Harris, Olover IV, 962
Harris, Oren IV, 1280
Harris, Orin IV, 1280
Harris, Orvilla IV, 821
Harris, Overton VI, 248
Harris, Owen VI, 928
Harris, Patara Ann VI, 815
Harris, Peal II, 371
Harris, Pearl V, 741
Harris, Pearle V, 741
Harris, Peggy VI, 61
Harris, Peggy VI, 67
Harris, Penelope IV, 821
Harris, Penelope IV, 828
Harris, Penelopy IV, 821
Harris, Penine I, 271
Harris, Peter VI, 928
Harris, Pheba I, 307
Harris, Phebe I, 271
Harris, Phebe I, 305
Harris, Phebe I, 307
Harris, Phebe II, 77
Harris, Phebe VI, 544
Harris, Phebe VI, 682
Harris, Phebe VI, 690
Harris, Phebe Jane IV, 1026
Harris, Pleasant I, 782
Harris, Pleasant I, 813
Harris, Pleasant V, 66
Harris, Plummer VI, 180
Harris, Plummer VI, 247
Harris, Polley VI, 928
Harris, Polly VI, 810
Harris, Polly VI, 928
Harris, Polly VI, 940
Harris, Polly VI, 962
Harris, Polly VI, 1013
Harris, Priscilla Lowes VI, 245
Harris, Prudence I, 270
Harris, Quinton P. II, 133
Harris, Quinton P. II, 138
Harris, Rachel I, 782
Harris, Rachel I, 813
Harris, Rachel I, 822
Harris, Rachel I, 1067
Harris, Rachel IV, 404
Harris, Rachel IV, 411
Harris, Rachel IV, 529
Harris, Rachel IV, 717
Harris, Rachel IV, 821
Harris, Rachel IV, 857
Harris, Rachel IV, 1021
Harris, Rachel V, 174
Harris, Rachel V, 787
Harris, Rachel VI, 246
Harris, Rachel VI, 247
Harris, Rachel VI, 248
Harris, Rachel VI, 261
Harris, Rachel VI, 269
Harris, Rachel VI, 271
Harris, Rachel VI, 501
Harris, Rachel Ann IV, 218
Harris, Rachel Ann IV, 404
Harris, Rachel Ann IV, 529
Harris, Rachel Griscom III, 151
Harris, Rachel M. VI, 67
Harris, Rachel M. VI, 68
Harris, Rebeca VI, 246
Harris, Rebecah I, 782
Harris, Rebecca I, 271
Harris, Rebecca I, 813
Harris, Rebecca II, 203
Harris, Rebecca II, 230
Harris, Rebecca IV, 218
Harris, Rebecca IV, 233
Harris, Rebecca IV, 717
Harris, Rebecca IV, 1026
Harris, Rebecca IV, 1061
Harris, Rebecca V, 66
Harris, Rebecca V, 787
Harris, Rebecca VI, 179
Harris, Rebecca VI, 185
Harris, Rebecca VI, 186
Harris, Rebecca VI, 246
Harris, Rebecca VI, 248
Harris, Rebecca VI, 257
Harris, Rebecca VI, 473
Harris, Rebecca VI, 479
Harris, Rebecca VI, 502
Harris, Rebecca VI, 928
Harris, Rebecca, Jr. I, 813
Harris, Rebeccah I, 271
Harris, Rebeckah I, 813
Harris, Rebeckah II, 542
Harris, Rebeckah II, 684
Harris, Rebeckah VI, 179
Harris, Rebeckah VI, 246
Harris, Rebekah I, 773
Harris, Rebekah I, 782
Harris, Rebekah I, 881
Harris, Rees IV, 218
Harris, Rees IV, 717
Harris, Rhoda Ann VI, 971
Harris, Richard III, 151
Harris, Richard IV, 218
Harris, Richard IV, 1061
Harris, Richard VI, 180
Harris, Richard VI, 247
Harris, Richard B. III, 215
Harris, Robert IV, 218
Harris, Robert IV, 300
Harris, Robert IV, 821
Harris, Robert IV, 847
Harris, Robert IV, 857
Harris, Robert IV, 962
Harris, Robert V, 334
Harris, Robert VI, 11
Harris, Robert VI, 813
Harris, Robert C. VI, 928
Harris, Robert J. IV, 300
Harris, Robert Lee I, 617
Harris, Robert P. VI, 935
Harris, Robert T. VI, 67
Harris, Robert T. VI, 68
Harris, Robert T. VI, 76
Harris, Robert, Jr. IV, 821
Harris, Robery IV, 962
Harris, Rosa V, 741
Harris, Rose V, 741
Harris, Roy V, 679
Harris, Ruby Lavern V, 741
Harris, Ruth I, 271
Harris, Ruth I, 276
Harris, Ruth II, 31
Harris, Ruth II, 77
Harris, Ruth II, 86
Harris, Ruth II, 88
Harris, Ruth II, 104
Harris, Ruth V, 409
Harris, Ruth V, 741
Harris, Ruth VI, 30
Harris, Ruth Ann V, 392
Harris, Ruth Anna IV, 717
Harris, Ruth Anna IV, 780
Harris, Ruth Ellen V, 66
Harris, Ruth Ellen V, 572
Harris, Ruthanna IV, 717
Harris, Salley VI, 911
Harris, Salley Lowes VI, 245
Harris, Sallie C. VI, 68
Harris, Sally IV, 717
Harris, Sally VI, 246
Harris, Sally VI, 823
Harris, Sally VI, 922
Harris, Sally VI, 928
Harris, Sally VI, 965
Harris, Sally D. VI, 982
Harris, Samuel I, 271
Harris, Samuel II, 31
Harris, Samuel II, 77
Harris, Samuel II, 106
Harris, Samuel III, 151
Harris, Samuel IV, 716
Harris, Samuel IV, 1021
Harris, Samuel IV, 1026
Harris, Samuel V, 392
Harris, Samuel V, 409
Harris, Samuel V, 741
Harris, Samuel VI, 67
Harris, Samuel VI, 109
Harris, Samuel VI, 398
Harris, Samuel VI, 464
Harris, Samuel VI, 486
Harris, Samuel VI, 501
Harris, Samuel VI, 502
Harris, Samuel VI, 503
Harris, Samuel VI, 508
Harris, Samuel VI, 513
Harris, Samuel VI, 597
Harris, Samuel VI, 646
Harris, Samuel VI, 647
Harris, Samuel VI, 813
Harris, Samuel VI, 928
Harris, Samuel VI, 954
Harris, Samuel VI, 1013
Harris, Samuel C. I, 271
Harris, Samuel Hargrave VI, 247
Harris, Samuel Terrell VI, 180
Harris, Samuel Westly IV, 717
Harris, Samuel, Jr. III, 151
Harris, Samuel, Jr. VI, 928
Harris, Samuel, Sr. VI, 928
Harris, Sarah I, 265
Harris, Sarah I, 270
Harris, Sarah I, 271
Harris, Sarah I, 543
Harris, Sarah I, 782
Harris, Sarah I, 813
Harris, Sarah I, 827
Harris, Sarah I, 837
Harris, Sarah II, 31
Harris, Sarah II, 77
Harris, Sarah II, 82
Harris, Sarah II, 371
Harris, Sarah III, 151
Harris, Sarah III, 169
Harris, Sarah IV, 36
Harris, Sarah IV, 52
Harris, Sarah IV, 91
Harris, Sarah IV, 194
Harris, Sarah IV, 218
Harris, Sarah IV, 233
Harris, Sarah IV, 257
Harris, Sarah IV, 265
Harris, Sarah IV, 335
Harris, Sarah IV, 404
Harris, Sarah IV, 717
Harris, Sarah IV, 821
Harris, Sarah IV, 857
Harris, Sarah IV, 962
Harris, Sarah IV, 1061
Harris, Sarah V, 831
Harris, Sarah V, 841
Harris, Sarah V, 847
Harris, Sarah VI, 68
Harris, Sarah VI, 107
Harris, Sarah VI, 109
Harris, Sarah VI, 245
Harris, Sarah VI, 246
Harris, Sarah VI, 247
Harris, Sarah VI, 502
Harris, Sarah VI, 519
Harris, Sarah VI, 520
Harris, Sarah VI, 521
Harris, Sarah VI, 526
Harris, Sarah VI, 533
Harris, Sarah VI, 547
Harris, Sarah VI, 563
Harris, Sarah VI, 641
Harris, Sarah VI, 661
Harris, Sarah VI, 755
Harris, Sarah VI, 757
Harris, Sarah VI, 928
Harris, Sarah A. VI, 92
Harris, Sarah Ann II, 873
Harris, Sarah Ann IV, 817
Harris, Sarah Ann IV, 821
Harris, Sarah Ann VI, 246
Harris, Sarah Ann VI, 248
Harris, Sarah Ann VI, 501
Harris, Sarah Ann VI, 527
Harris, Sarah B. II, 133
Harris, Sarah B. II, 150
Harris, Sarah B. VI, 928
Harris, Sarah C. VI, 67
Harris, Sarah C. VI, 68
Harris, Sarah D. VI, 1004
Harris, Sarah E. I, 617
Harris, Sarah Eliza IV, 529
Harris, Sarah Evaline I, 617
Harris, Sarah Jane VI, 398
Harris, Sarah M. III, 151
Harris, Sarah M. III, 305
Harris, Sarah M. III, 373
Harris, Sarah Maria IV, 1364
Harris, Sarah Maria IV, 1365
Harris, Sarah W. VI, 248
Harris, Sarah Y. IV, 962
Harris, Selia I, 271
Harris, Shadrack VI, 247
Harris, Shadrack Stanley VI, 247
Harris, Sidney IV, 218
Harris, Sidney IV, 1049
Harris, Sidney IV, 1061
Harris, Silas IV, 716
Harris, Silas IV, 717
Harris, Silas IV, 721
Harris, Silas IV, 1021
Harris, Silas IV, 1026
Harris, Simeon I, 271
Harris, Simmeon I, 271
Harris, Sophia VI, 245
Harris, Sophia VI, 247
Harris, Sophia M. VI, 928
Harris, Sophine VI, 63
Harris, Sophine VI, 67
Harris, Sparel VI, 977
Harris, Stanley VI, 246
Harris, Stanley VI, 247
Harris, Stanley VI, 270
Harris, Stanley VI, 271
Harris, Stephen I, 271
Harris, Stephen I, 273
Harris, Stephen I, 289
Harris, Stephen I, 307
Harris, Stephen VI, 1003
Harris, Stephen G. I, 289
Harris, Stokeley I, 270
Harris, Susan IV, 404
Harris, Susan IV, 529
Harris, Susan IV, 782
Harris, Susanah I, 270
Harris, Susanah I, 435
Harris, Susanna I, 271
Harris, Susanna I, 307
Harris, Susanna IV, 91
Harris, Susanna IV, 218
Harris, Susanna IV, 233
Harris, Susanna IV, 300
Harris, Susanna IV, 1061
Harris, Susanna IV, 1063
Harris, Susanna VI, 30
Harris, Susanna VI, 398
Harris, Susanna VI, 823
Harris, Susannah I, 307
Harris, Susannah I, 1067
Harris, Susannah II, 799

arris, Susannah II, 804
arris, Susannah V, 174
arris, Susannah VI, 398
arris, Susannah VI, 409
arris, Susannah VI, 501
arris, Susannah VI, 527
arris, Susannah VI, 823
arris, Susannah VI, 928
arris, Tabby VI, 928
arris, Talitha I, 271
arris, Tallitha I, 269
arris, Tallitha I, 271
arris, Thomas I, 270
arris, Thomas I, 782
arris, Thomas I, 1067
arris, Thomas I, 1070
arris, Thomas II, 31
arris, Thomas IV, 148
arris, Thomas IV, 218
arris, Thomas IV, 1061
arris, Thomas V, 174
arris, Thomas V, 841
arris, Thomas VI, 147
arris, Thomas VI, 179
arris, Thomas VI, 180
arris, Thomas VI, 190
arris, Thomas VI, 194
arris, Thomas VI, 235
arris, Thomas VI, 245
arris, Thomas VI, 246
arris, Thomas VI, 247
arris, Thomas VI, 248
arris, Thomas VI, 257
arris, Thomas VI, 502
arris, Thomas VI, 540
arris, Thomas VI, 823
arris, Thomas VI, 928
arris, Thomas VI, 988
arris, Thomas H. III, 60
arris, Thomas H. III, 146
arris, Thomas H. III, 151
arris, Thomas T. VI, 980
arris, Thomas, Jr. VI, 247
arris, Thomas, Jr. VI, 248
arris, Thomas, Sr. VI, 179
arris, Thomas, Sr. VI, 191
arris, Thomas, Sr. VI, 247
arris, Thompson V, 841
arris, Thompson V, 847
arris, Tilman VI, 67
arris, Tilman VI, 68
arris, Tilman VI, 76
arris, Tyre VI, 247
arris, Unity VI, 179
arris, Unity VI, 180
arris, Unity VI, 191
arris, Unity VI, 194
arris, Unity VI, 245
arris, Unity VI, 246
arris, Unity VI, 247
arris, Unity VI, 248
arris, Unity VI, 257
arris, Uriah I, 270
arris, Uriah IV, 148
arris, Uriah IV, 218
arris, Valearia V, 841
arris, Valearia V, 847
arris, Valeria V, 841
arris, Valerie V, 831
arris, Valerie V, 841
arris, Valerie V, 846
arris, Waddy Thomson VI, 928
arris, Watson IV, 218
arris, Watson IV, 1061
arris, Wd. Ann II, 804
arris, Wd. Elizabeth VI, 501
arris, Wd. Mary VI, 246
arris, Wd. Sarah III, 151
arris, Wd. Sarah M. III, 151
arris, Widow Dianna I, 270
arris, Widow Dianna I, 274
arris, Wiley VI, 928
arris, William I, 271
arris, William I, 307
arris, William II, 31
arris, William II, 371
arris, William IV, 300
arris, William IV, 335
arris, William IV, 630
arris, William V, 66
arris, William V, 392
arris, William V, 741
arris, William V, 970
arris, William VI, 52
arris, William VI, 66
arris, William VI, 67
arris, William VI, 68
arris, William VI, 246
arris, William VI, 275
arris, William VI, 301
arris, William VI, 302
Harris, William VI, 352
Harris, William VI, 354
Harris, William VI, 398
Harris, William VI, 502
Harris, William VI, 508
Harris, William VI, 802
Harris, William VI, 803
Harris, William VI, 804
Harris, William VI, 817
Harris, William VI, 819
Harris, William VI, 823
Harris, William VI, 835
Harris, William VI, 840
Harris, William VI, 857
Harris, William VI, 870
Harris, William VI, 871
Harris, William VI, 872
Harris, William VI, 874
Harris, William VI, 875
Harris, William VI, 876
Harris, William VI, 877
Harris, William VI, 878
Harris, William VI, 879
Harris, William VI, 882
Harris, William VI, 883
Harris, William VI, 885
Harris, William VI, 886
Harris, William VI, 887
Harris, William VI, 889
Harris, William VI, 891
Harris, William VI, 892
Harris, William VI, 893
Harris, William VI, 894
Harris, William VI, 895
Harris, William VI, 896
Harris, William VI, 897
Harris, William VI, 898
Harris, William VI, 899
Harris, William VI, 900
Harris, William VI, 902
Harris, William VI, 904
Harris, William VI, 905
Harris, William VI, 907
Harris, William VI, 908
Harris, William VI, 909
Harris, William VI, 910
Harris, William VI, 911
Harris, William VI, 912
Harris, William VI, 913
Harris, William VI, 914
Harris, William VI, 915
Harris, William VI, 916
Harris, William VI, 917
Harris, William VI, 918
Harris, William VI, 919
Harris, William VI, 920
Harris, William VI, 921
Harris, William VI, 922
Harris, William VI, 923
Harris, William VI, 924
Harris, William VI, 925
Harris, William VI, 927
Harris, William VI, 928
Harris, William VI, 929
Harris, William VI, 930
Harris, William VI, 931
Harris, William VI, 933
Harris, William VI, 934
Harris, William VI, 935
Harris, William VI, 936
Harris, William VI, 937
Harris, William VI, 938
Harris, William VI, 939
Harris, William VI, 940
Harris, William VI, 941
Harris, William VI, 942
Harris, William VI, 943
Harris, William VI, 944
Harris, William VI, 945
Harris, William VI, 946
Harris, William VI, 947
Harris, William VI, 949
Harris, William VI, 950
Harris, William VI, 951
Harris, William VI, 952
Harris, William VI, 953
Harris, William VI, 954
Harris, William VI, 955
Harris, William VI, 956
Harris, William VI, 957
Harris, William VI, 958
Harris, William VI, 959
Harris, William VI, 960
Harris, William VI, 961
Harris, William VI, 962
Harris, William VI, 963
Harris, William VI, 964
Harris, William VI, 965
Harris, William VI, 966
Harris, William VI, 967
Harris, William VI, 968
Harris, William VI, 970
Harris, William VI, 971
Harris, William VI, 972
Harris, William VI, 973
Harris, William VI, 974
Harris, William VI, 975
Harris, William VI, 977
Harris, William VI, 978
Harris, William VI, 979
Harris, William VI, 981
Harris, William VI, 982
Harris, William VI, 983
Harris, William VI, 984
Harris, William VI, 986
Harris, William VI, 988
Harris, William VI, 989
Harris, William VI, 990
Harris, William VI, 991
Harris, William VI, 992
Harris, William VI, 993
Harris, William VI, 994
Harris, William VI, 995
Harris, William VI, 996
Harris, William VI, 997
Harris, William VI, 998
Harris, William VI, 999
Harris, William VI, 1000
Harris, William VI, 1001
Harris, William VI, 1002
Harris, William VI, 1003
Harris, William VI, 1004
Harris, William VI, 1005
Harris, William VI, 1006
Harris, William VI, 1007
Harris, William VI, 1008
Harris, William VI, 1009
Harris, William VI, 1010
Harris, William VI, 1011
Harris, William VI, 1012
Harris, William VI, 1013
Harris, William VI, 1014
Harris, William VI, 1015
Harris, William VI, 1016
Harris, William VI, 1017
Harris, William VI, 1018
Harris, William VI, 1019
Harris, William VI, 1020
Harris, William VI, 1021
Harris, William VI, 1022
Harris, William B. VI, 935
Harris, William E. IV, 218
Harris, William E. VI, 247
Harris, William Eley VI, 245
Harris, William H. V, 979
Harris, William H. VI, 68
Harris, William H. VI, 823
Harris, William N. I, 435
Harris, William N. I, 447
Harris, William Paul I, 435
Harris, William, Jr. VI, 313
Harris, William, Jr. VI, 398
Harris, William, Jr. VI, 502
Harris, William, Jr. VI, 503
Harris, William, Jr. VI, 508
Harris, Willis I, 271
Harris, Wm. II, 77
Harris, Wm. II, 133
Harris, Wm. IV, 218
Harris, Wm. IV, 630
Harris, Wm. IV, 717
Harris, Wm. IV, 1061
Harris, Wm. VI, 67
Harris, Wm. VI, 68
Harris, Wm. VI, 501
Harris, Wm. VI, 502
Harris, Wm. VI, 503
Harris, Wm. VI, 508
Harris, Wm. VI, 937
Harris, Wm. D. IV, 1061
Harris, Wm. H. IV, 1253
Harris, Wm. H. V, 971
Harris, Wm. H., Sr. V, 970
Harris, Wm. Henry V, 970
Harris, Wm., Jr. VI, 501
Harris, Wm., Jr. VI, 502
Harris, Wm., Jr. VI, 503
Harris, Wm., Jr. VI, 540
Harris, Wm., Jr. VI, 646
Harris, Yancey B. VI, 928
Harris, Zemeriah I, 270
Harris, Zemeriah I, 271
Harris, Zemeriah I, 274
Harris, Zemeriah IV, 91
Harris-Janney, Sarah VI, 493
Harris-Janney, Sarah VI, 494
Harris-Janney, Sarah VI, 495
Harris-Janney, Sarah VI, 504
Harris-Janney, Sarah VI, 510
Harris-Janney, Sarah VI, 572
Harris-Janney, Sarah VI, 744
Harrison, Abbie P. V, 953
Harrison, Abbie P. V, 957
Harrison, Abby A. V, 953
Harrison, Abby Ann V, 953
Harrison, Abigail V, 953
Harrison, Agnes III, 150
Harrison, Agnes III, 151
Harrison, Agnes P. V, 953
Harrison, Alice VI, 647
Harrison, Alice VI, 698
Harrison, Amy IV, 612
Harrison, Amy IV, 630
Harrison, Ann IV, 630
Harrison, Ann IV, 638
Harrison, Ann V, 66
Harrison, Ann V, 497
Harrison, Ann V, 624
Harrison, Ann V, 953
Harrison, Ann Eliza V, 953
Harrison, Ann S. VI, 823
Harrison, Anna V, 66
Harrison, Anna V, 497
Harrison, Anna V, 624
Harrison, Anna H. V, 947
Harrison, Anna H. V, 953
Harrison, Anna J. IV, 219
Harrison, Anne V, 497
Harrison, Anne V, 532
Harrison, Arthur Dudley III, 414
Harrison, Arthur Dudley III, 435
Harrison, Arthur J. III, 414
Harrison, Bateal VI, 922
Harrison, Batiel VI, 924
Harrison, Battaile VI, 922
Harrison, Benj. IV, 607
Harrison, Benj. IV, 717
Harrison, Benjamin I, 240
Harrison, Benjamin IV, 630
Harrison, Benjamin IV, 638
Harrison, Benjamin IV, 717
Harrison, Benjamin IV, 871
Harrison, Benjamin IV, 1209
Harrison, Benjamin IV, 1281
Harrison, Benjamin VI, 130
Harrison, Benjamin VI, 135
Harrison, Benjamin, Jr. IV, 868
Harrison, Benjamin, Jr. IV, 871
Harrison, Bernard III, 151
Harrison, Betheny VI, 933
Harrison, Betsy VI, 928
Harrison, Blakey IV, 219
Harrison, Catharine V, 953
Harrison, Charlotte II, 543
Harrison, Charlotte VI, 928
Harrison, Clara V, 334
Harrison, Clara E. V, 334
Harrison, Clarabel V, 151
Harrison, Clarabel V, 174
Harrison, Claribel V, 174
Harrison, Clement II, 444
Harrison, Cornelia J. V, 953
Harrison, Daniel III, 151
Harrison, Daniel W. VI, 928
Harrison, David IV, 871
Harrison, Deborah II, 77
Harrison, Deborah II, 444
Harrison, Deborah IV, 219
Harrison, Deborah IV, 235
Harrison, Deborah IV, 1281
Harrison, Deborah VI, 180
Harrison, Deborah D. IV, 1281
Harrison, Deborah D. IV, 1298
Harrison, Deborah R. IV, 219
Harrison, Deborah R. IV, 237
Harrison, Easter II, 77
Harrison, Easter II, 110
Harrison, Edward V, 953
Harrison, Edward E. V, 953
Harrison, Edward H. IV, 630
Harrison, Edward H. IV, 871
Harrison, Eleanor II, 533
Harrison, Eleanor II, 543
Harrison, Elenore E. IV, 1281
Harrison, Elisha VI, 180
Harrison, Eliza IV, 380
Harrison, Eliza IV, 615
Harrison, Eliza IV, 630
Harrison, Eliza IV, 717
Harrison, Eliza V, 953
Harrison, Eliza V, 962
Harrison, Elizabeth II, 371
Harrison, Elizabeth II, 543
Harrison, Elizabeth III, 151
Harrison, Elizabeth IV, 37
Harrison, Elizabeth IV, 91
Harrison, Elizabeth IV, 211
Harrison, Elizabeth IV, 630
Harrison, Elizabeth IV, 821
Harrison, Elizabeth IV, 855
Harrison, Elizabeth IV, 867
Harrison, Elizabeth IV, 868
Harrison, Elizabeth IV, 871
Harrison, Elizabeth IV, 886
Harrison, Elizabeth IV, 1281
Harrison, Elizabeth V, 953
Harrison, Elizabeth V, 957
Harrison, Elizabeth V, 961
Harrison, Elizabeth V, 962
Harrison, Elizabeth VI, 155
Harrison, Elizabeth VI, 156
Harrison, Elizabeth VI, 180
Harrison, Elizabeth Ann IV, 1281
Harrison, Elizabeth C. IV, 871
Harrison, Elizabeth D. II, 543
Harrison, Elizabeth Fleming IV, 219
Harrison, Elizabeth P. V, 953
Harrison, Elizabeth U. III, 414
Harrison, Elizabeth U. III, 435
Harrison, Elkrun IV, 630
Harrison, Ellen II, 533
Harrison, Ellen II, 543
Harrison, Ellen Gordan IV, 219
Harrison, Ellwood G. V, 953
Harrison, Emma IV, 37
Harrison, Esther V, 953
Harrison, Ethel III, 414
Harrison, F. VI, 929
Harrison, Frances VI, 847
Harrison, Francis III, 152
Harrison, George II, 371
Harrison, George III, 345
Harrison, Hannah II, 77
Harrison, Hannah II, 230
Harrison, Hannah II, 371
Harrison, Hannah II, 543
Harrison, Hannah II, 608
Harrison, Hannah II, 745
Harrison, Hannah II, 768
Harrison, Hannah III, 151
Harrison, Hannah IV, 194
Harrison, Hannah IV, 219
Harrison, Hannah Bates VI, 180
Harrison, Henry II, 444
Harrison, Henry IV, 871
Harrison, Hester II, 31
Harrison, Hester II, 51
Harrison, Hester II, 77
Harrison, Hosea IV, 1281
Harrison, Isaac II, 799
Harrison, Isaac II, 873
Harrison, Isaac IV, 871
Harrison, Israel II, 31
Harrison, Israell II, 77
Harrison, Israell II, 110
Harrison, James II, 952
Harrison, James II, 999
Harrison, James V, 953
Harrison, James VI, 929
Harrison, James Hiatt IV, 1100
Harrison, James J. VI, 842
Harrison, James P. V, 953
Harrison, Jane II, 543
Harrison, Jane II, 629
Harrison, Jenny H. Leftwich VI, 928
Harrison, Jesse IV, 219
Harrison, John I, 271
Harrison, John II, 371
Harrison, John II, 543
Harrison, John III, 151
Harrison, John IV, 867
Harrison, John IV, 871
Harrison, John V, 334
Harrison, John V, 497
Harrison, John V, 624
Harrison, John V, 953
Harrison, John A. V, 66
Harrison, John A. V, 497
Harrison, John F. IV, 37
Harrison, John F. V, 953
Harrison, John F. V, 957
Harrison, John F. V, 961
Harrison, John F. V, 962
Harrison, John Franklin IV, 630
Harrison, John Franklin IV, 717
Harrison, John Franklin IV, 871
Harrison, John R. VI, 929
Harrison, John Stephen V, 624
Harrison, Jordain VI, 16
Harrison, Jordan IV, 218
Harrison, Jordan IV, 219
Harrison, Jordan IV, 241
Harrison, Jordan VI, 180
Harrison, Jordon IV, 219
Harrison, Joseph II, 77
Harrison, Joseph II, 371
Harrison, Joseph II, 444
Harrison, Joseph VI, 823
Harrison, Joshua V, 953
Harrison, Josias VI, 928
Harrison, Latham IV, 630
Harrison, Latham IV, 638

Harrison, Latham IV, 717
Harrison, Latham IV, 867
Harrison, Latham IV, 868
Harrison, Latham IV, 870
Harrison, Latham IV, 871
Harrison, Lucina Ann IV, 717
Harrison, Lucinda Ann IV, 607
Harrison, Lucinda Ann IV, 630
Harrison, Lucinda Ann IV, 871
Harrison, Lucinda Ann IV, 1209
Harrison, Lucinda Ann IV, 1281
Harrison, Lucy Newman VI, 929
Harrison, Lydia IV, 219
Harrison, Lydia IV, 228
Harrison, Lydia IV, 529
Harrison, Lydia A. IV, 717
Harrison, Lydia Ann IV, 37
Harrison, Macon IV, 1253
Harrison, Malinda VI, 953
Harrison, Margaret IV, 218
Harrison, Margaret IV, 219
Harrison, Margaret IV, 229
Harrison, Margaret IV, 235
Harrison, Margaret IV, 241
Harrison, Margaret IV, 1281
Harrison, Margaret VI, 180
Harrison, Margaret VI, 188
Harrison, Margaret I. IV, 219
Harrison, Margaret I. IV, 237
Harrison, Margaret J. IV, 219
Harrison, Margery III, 151
Harrison, Mariam IV, 630
Harrison, Martha Ann V, 66
Harrison, Martha Ann V, 497
Harrison, Martha Ann V, 624
Harrison, Martha Ann V, 953
Harrison, Marthaann V, 66
Harrison, Mary II, 371
Harrison, Mary II, 444
Harrison, Mary II, 543
Harrison, Mary II, 627
Harrison, Mary III, 151
Harrison, Mary IV, 37
Harrison, Mary IV, 211
Harrison, Mary IV, 219
Harrison, Mary IV, 607
Harrison, Mary IV, 620
Harrison, Mary IV, 630
Harrison, Mary IV, 638
Harrison, Mary IV, 717
Harrison, Mary IV, 867
Harrison, Mary IV, 870
Harrison, Mary IV, 871
Harrison, Mary IV, 882
Harrison, Mary IV, 883
Harrison, Mary IV, 1209
Harrison, Mary IV, 1281
Harrison, Mary V, 953
Harrison, Mary VI, 180
Harrison, Mary A. VI, 823
Harrison, Mary Ann II, 839
Harrison, Mary Ann II, 873
Harrison, Mary Ann IV, 871
Harrison, Mary Ann IV, 876
Harrison, Mary E. I, 543
Harrison, Mary E. IV, 1100
Harrison, Mary E. IV, 1101
Harrison, Mary Elizabeth IV, 630
Harrison, Mary Elizabeth IV, 717
Harrison, Mary Elizabeth IV, 871
Harrison, Mary Elizabeth IV, 1209
Harrison, Mary Hannah V, 953
Harrison, Mary William VI, 180
Harrison, Mary, Sr. VI, 100
Harrison, Matilda E. IV, 630
Harrison, Matilda Ellen IV, 630
Harrison, Matilda Ellen IV, 717
Harrison, Matilda Ellen IV, 871
Harrison, Matilda Ellen IV, 1209
Harrison, Melinda Stone VI, 929
Harrison, Mercy Ann IV, 219
Harrison, Meriam IV, 638
Harrison, Mildred IV, 871
Harrison, Mildred IV, 878
Harrison, Mildred P. IV, 871
Harrison, Milly VI, 928
Harrison, Miriam I, 622
Harrison, Miriam IV, 630
Harrison, Miriam IV, 867
Harrison, Miriam IV, 871
Harrison, Mirium IV, 871
Harrison, Nancy IV, 1281
Harrison, Nancy VI, 922
Harrison, Nancy VI, 929
Harrison, Naomi I, 622
Harrison, Naomi V, 174
Harrison, Paules E. VI, 823
Harrison, Peter IV, 91
Harrison, Peter IV, 194
Harrison, Peter IV, 262
Harrison, Phebe IV, 219
Harrison, Phebe IV, 870
Harrison, Phebe IV, 871
Harrison, Phebe IV, 882
Harrison, Polly VI, 180
Harrison, Polly VI, 922
Harrison, Priscilla J. IV, 219
Harrison, Rachel III, 151
Harrison, Rachel IV, 91
Harrison, Rachel IV, 219
Harrison, Rachel IV, 583
Harrison, Rachel IV, 630
Harrison, Rachel IV, 821
Harrison, Rachel IV, 1163
Harrison, Rachel IV, 1166
Harrison, Ray E. IV, 1319
Harrison, Rebecca III, 152
Harrison, Rebecca IV, 32
Harrison, Rebecca IV, 37
Harrison, Rebecca IV, 717
Harrison, Rebecca V, 953
Harrison, Rebecca P. V, 953
Harrison, Rebecca P. V, 961
Harrison, Richard II, 371
Harrison, Richard II, 543
Harrison, Richard II, 608
Harrison, Richard III, 151
Harrison, Richard IV, 211
Harrison, Richard P. VI, 902
Harrison, Robert II, 371
Harrison, Robert II, 543
Harrison, Robert V, 909
Harrison, Robert VI, 928
Harrison, Roger III, 151
Harrison, Roger III, 345
Harrison, Rowland II, 633
Harrison, Ruth II, 371
Harrison, Ruth II, 543
Harrison, Ruth IV, 219
Harrison, Ruth IV, 241
Harrison, Ruth VI, 180
Harrison, Ruth Anna V, 624
Harrison, Ruthanna V, 66
Harrison, Sabina Jane IV, 630
Harrison, Sabina Jane IV, 717
Harrison, Sabina Jane IV, 871
Harrison, Sally I, 543
Harrison, Sally VI, 823
Harrison, Sally VI, 834
Harrison, Sally VI, 928
Harrison, Sally Ann IV, 217
Harrison, Sally Ann IV, 219
Harrison, Sally S. VI, 100
Harrison, Samuel II, 371
Harrison, Samuel III, 117
Harrison, Samuel III, 151
Harrison, Samuel IV, 237
Harrison, Samuel VI, 810
Harrison, Samuel VI, 823
Harrison, Samuel I. VI, 802
Harrison, Samuel Irving IV, 219
Harrison, Samuel J. IV, 219
Harrison, Samuel J. VI, 823
Harrison, Samuel Jordan VI, 180
Harrison, Samuel Jordan VI, 313
Harrison, Samuel Pancoast II, 543
Harrison, Samuel T. IV, 219
Harrison, Sarah I, 543
Harrison, Sarah II, 31
Harrison, Sarah II, 371
Harrison, Sarah II, 543
Harrison, Sarah II, 633
Harrison, Sarah II, 799
Harrison, Sarah III, 117
Harrison, Sarah III, 151
Harrison, Sarah III, 246
Harrison, Sarah IV, 91
Harrison, Sarah IV, 194
Harrison, Sarah IV, 219
Harrison, Sarah IV, 262
Harrison, Sarah IV, 867
Harrison, Sarah IV, 871
Harrison, Sarah IV, 883
Harrison, Sarah Jordan VI, 155
Harrison, Sarah Jordan VI, 156
Harrison, Sarah Jordan VI, 180
Harrison, Sarah S. II, 799
Harrison, Sarah, Jr. II, 371
Harrison, Stella Clark IV, 717
Harrison, Stephen V, 497
Harrison, Stephen V, 624
Harrison, Stephen V, 953
Harrison, Stephen VI, 100
Harrison, Stephen L. V, 66
Harrison, Stephen S. V, 66
Harrison, Susan IV, 219
Harrison, Susan IV, 241
Harrison, Susan Hulme II, 799
Harrison, Susan L. IV, 219
Harrison, Susan Lloyd IV, 219
Harrison, Susanna VI, 924
Harrison, Susannah VI, 503
Harrison, Susannah VI, 540
Harrison, Tacy IV, 871
Harrison, Thomas II, 371
Harrison, Thomas II, 543
Harrison, Thomas II, 633
Harrison, Thomas IV, 335
Harrison, Thomas IV, 630
Harrison, Thomas IV, 870
Harrison, Thomas VI, 180
Harrison, Thomas H. V, 174
Harrison, Thomas Pancoast II, 543
Harrison, Thomason IV, 405
Harrison, Thompson II, 745
Harrison, Thos. II, 799
Harrison, Thos. H. V, 151
Harrison, Timothy I, 622
Harrison, Timothy V, 174
Harrison, Tirzah VI, 982
Harrison, Unity IV, 219
Harrison, Unity IV, 262
Harrison, Unity IV, 871
Harrison, Virginia VI, 823
Harrison, Walter L. IV, 219
Harrison, Wd. Mary III, 151
Harrison, Wd. Mary III, 345
Harrison, William III, 151
Harrison, William IV, 37
Harrison, William IV, 91
Harrison, William IV, 218
Harrison, William IV, 219
Harrison, William IV, 620
Harrison, William IV, 630
Harrison, William IV, 717
Harrison, William V, 66
Harrison, William V, 497
Harrison, William VI, 109
Harrison, William VI, 121
Harrison, William VI, 155
Harrison, William VI, 180
Harrison, William VI, 313
Harrison, William VI, 928
Harrison, William H. V, 66
Harrison, William H. V, 497
Harrison, William H. V, 532
Harrison, William H. V, 953
Harrison, William Henry IV, 37
Harrison, William Henry IV, 717
Harrison, William J. IV, 219
Harrison, William R. VI, 929
Harrison, William, Jr. IV, 630
Harrison, William, Jr. VI, 180
Harrison, William, Jr. VI, 313
Harrison, Wm. II, 543
Harrison, Wm. IV, 229
Harrison, Wm. IV, 235
Harrison, Wm. IV, 241
Harrison, Wm. IV, 1281
Harrison, Wm. V, 458
Harrison, Wm. V, 953
Harrison, Wm. VI, 99
Harrison, Wm. H. IV, 1281
Harrison, Wm. H. V, 624
Harrison, Wm. H. V, 953
Harrison, Wm. Henry IV, 1281
Harrison, Wm. J. IV, 219
Harrison, Wm. J. IV, 237
Harrison, Wm. Jordan IV, 219
Harrison, Wm. L. V, 953
Harrison, Z. E. VI, 897
Harrison, Z. E. VI, 900
Harrison, Z. E. VI, 972
Harrison, Z. E. VI, 1021
Harrison, Zachariah VI, 928
Harrison, Zachariah VI, 1015
Harriss, Alce II, 371
Harriss, Amos I, 265
Harriss, Anna I, 265
Harriss, David I, 265
Harriss, Elijah I, 265
Harriss, Elizabeth VI, 245
Harriss, Elizabeth VI, 801
Harriss, Francis II, 371
Harriss, Henry VI, 67
Harriss, James II, 444
Harriss, James VI, 67
Harriss, James VI, 71
Harriss, Jesse I, 265
Harriss, John II, 371
Harriss, John VI, 67
Harriss, John VI, 135
Harriss, Joseph I, 265
Harriss, Joseph VI, 67
Harriss, Kezziah I, 265
Harriss, Lovina VI, 67
Harriss, Lovina VI, 71
Harriss, Martha VI, 801
Harriss, Mary I, 265
Harriss, Mary VI, 67
Harriss, Mary VI, 109
Harriss, Mary VI, 110
Harriss, Matthew VI, 51
Harriss, Matthew VI, 67
Harriss, Matthew VI, 109
Harriss, Matthew VI, 110
Harriss, Michal VI, 135
Harriss, Moses VI, 67
Harriss, Nancy VI, 51
Harriss, Samuel VI, 67
Harriss, Samuel VI, 135
Harriss, Sarah I, 265
Harriss, Sarah VI, 107
Harriss, Simeon I, 265
Harriss, Sophine VI, 67
Harriss, Stephen I, 265
Harriss, Susanna I, 265
Harriss, Wd. Sarah VI, 744
Harriss, William II, 371
Harriss, William VI, 67
Harriss, Zemeriah I, 265
Harrod, Calvennetta V, 1000
Harrod, Elizabeth VI, 856
Harrod, Mahala V, 1000
Harrod, Mary V, 1000
Harrod, Millie V, 1000
Harrold, Abner II, 956
Harrold, Aletha I, 543
Harrold, Alfred I, 543
Harrold, Alfred I, 813
Harrold, Alice V, 392
Harrold, Alpherd I, 543
Harrold, Alpherd I, 584
Harrold, Amasa IV, 405
Harrold, Amos IV, 405
Harrold, Andrew I, 537
Harrold, Andrew I, 543
Harrold, Andrew I, 782
Harrold, Andrew I, 881
Harrold, Andrew I, 909
Harrold, Andrew I, 912
Harrold, Andrew V, 392
Harrold, Andrew V, 497
Harrold, Ann I, 813
Harrold, Ann I, 824
Harrold, Anna V, 392
Harrold, Anna V, 409
Harrold, Anna V, 497
Harrold, Anna Elizabeth V, 392
Harrold, Anna Kester V, 392
Harrold, Anne V, 392
Harrold, Arcada I, 956
Harrold, Arcada V, 244
Harrold, Arcada V, 303
Harrold, Benjamin I, 594
Harrold, Benjamin I, 597
Harrold, Benjamin I, 782
Harrold, Benjamin I, 909
Harrold, Benjamin I, 912
Harrold, Betta I, 813
Harrold, Catharan I, 956
Harrold, Catharine I, 813
Harrold, Catharine I, 963
Harrold, Catherine I, 956
Harrold, Caty IV, 583
Harrold, Charity IV, 405
Harrold, Clara I, 617
Harrold, Cordelia I, 617
Harrold, D. L. I, 881
Harrold, Daniel I, 543
Harrold, Daniel Baker I, 1004
Harrold, Darius Wilson I, 1004
Harrold, David Lee I, 881
Harrold, Dotty IV, 405
Harrold, Earl John I, 617
Harrold, Eli V, 497
Harrold, Elijah I, 543
Harrold, Elijah I, 813
Harrold, Elisabeth I, 617
Harrold, Elizabeth I, 813
Harrold, Elizabeth I, 835
Harrold, Elizabeth I, 881
Harrold, Elizabeth I, 909
Harrold, Elizabeth I, 1004
Harrold, Hannah I, 813
Harrold, Hannah I, 824
Harrold, Hannah I, 956
Harrold, Housen IV, 405
Harrold, Howsen IV, 405
Harrold, Hulda I, 1004
Harrold, Isaac S. I, 617
Harrold, Jacob I, 543
Harrold, Jacob I, 813
Harrold, Jacob I, 845
Harrold, Jacob I, 912
Harrold, Jacob I, 956
Harrold, Jacob I, 959
Harrold, Jacob I, 963
Harrold, Jacob I Sup 1, 10
Harrold, Jacob IV, 405
Harrold, Jacob V, 303
Harrold, James J. V, 392
Harrold, James Johnson V, 497
Harrold, Jane VI, 799
Harrold, Jesse I, 963
Harrold, John I, 543
Harrold, John I, 588
Harrold, John I, 594
Harrold, John I, 782
Harrold, John I, 813
Harrold, John I, 909
Harrold, John I, 912
Harrold, John I, 955
Harrold, John I, 963
Harrold, John V, 66
Harrold, Johnathan I, 543
Harrold, Jonathan I, 343
Harrold, Jonathan I, 393
Harrold, Jonathan I, 543
Harrold, Jonathan I, 594
Harrold, Jonathan I, 600
Harrold, Jonathan I, 773
Harrold, Jonathan I, 782
Harrold, Jonathan I, 813
Harrold, Jonathan I, 907
Harrold, Jonathan I, 909
Harrold, Jonathan I, 912
Harrold, Jonathan I, 956
Harrold, Jonathan I, 963
Harrold, Jonathan VI, 398
Harrold, Jonathan, Jr. I, 543
Harrold, Jonathan, Jr. I, 912
Harrold, Jonathan, Jr. V, 497
Harrold, Jonithan I, 956
Harrold, Jonithan I, 963
Harrold, Joseph IV, 405
Harrold, Latina I, 543
Harrold, Leah S. V, 392
Harrold, Leah Schooley V, 497
Harrold, Letha I, 813
Harrold, Letitia I, 813
Harrold, Lettitia I, 543
Harrold, Levi I, 813
Harrold, Levi I, 963
Harrold, Liddea I, 956
Harrold, Margaret I, 543
Harrold, Margaret I, 594
Harrold, Margaret I, 782
Harrold, Margaret I, 813
Harrold, Margaret I, 907
Harrold, Margaret I, 909
Harrold, Margaret V, 497
Harrold, Margaret Cordelia I, 617
Harrold, Margareth I, 594
Harrold, Martha I, 594
Harrold, Martha I, 1004
Harrold, Mary I, 543
Harrold, Mary I, 567
Harrold, Mary I, 594
Harrold, Mary I, 782
Harrold, Mary I, 798
Harrold, Mary I, 813
Harrold, Mary I, 825
Harrold, Mary I, 845
Harrold, Mary I, 909
Harrold, Mary I, 912
Harrold, Mary I, 956
Harrold, Mary I, 959
Harrold, Mary I, 963
Harrold, Mary I, 1004
Harrold, Mary IV, 405
Harrold, Mary V, 244
Harrold, Mary V, 392
Harrold, Mary V, 497
Harrold, Mary Alice V, 392
Harrold, Mary E. I, 543
Harrold, Mary Elizabeth V, 392
Harrold, Mary L. I, 537
Harrold, Mary L. I, 543
Harrold, Mary L. I, 912
Harrold, Moses Pitts I, 1004
Harrold, Nancy I, 1004
Harrold, Nathan I, 813
Harrold, Nathan I, 909
Harrold, Nathan I, 912
Harrold, Nathan I, 963
Harrold, Nathan V, 392
Harrold, Nathan V, 409
Harrold, Peninah I, 193
Harrold, Peninah I, 194
Harrold, Phebe I, 955
Harrold, Phebe I, 963
Harrold, Rachel I, 594
Harrold, Rachel I, 597
Harrold, Rachel I, 912
Harrold, Rachel I, 955
Harrold, Rachel I, 960
Harrold, Rachel I, 963
Harrold, Rachel IV, 220
Harrold, Rachel IV, 405
Harrold, Rachel Smith II, 796

rrold, Ranuel I, 543
rrold, Rebeca I, 813
rrold, Rebecah I, 584
rrold, Rebecca I, 543
rrold, Rebecca I, 813
rrold, Rebecca II, 796
rrold, Rebecca V, 244
rrold, Rebecca VI, 734
rrold, Rebecca VI, 742
rrold, Rebeccah I, 543
rrold, Rebekah I, 956
rrold, Rhoda I, 543
rrold, Rhoda I, 1004
rrold, Richard I, 543
rrold, Richard I, 567
rrold, Richard I, 813
rrold, Richard I, 825
rrold, Richard I, 909
rrold, Richard I, 912
rrold, Richard I, 963
rrold, Richard I, 1004
rrold, Richard V, 244
rrold, Ruth I, 961
rrold, Ruth I, 963
rrold, Samuel I, 909
rrold, Samuel I, 912
rrold, Samuel II, 796
rrold, Samuel V, 497
rrold, Syrus Lundy I, 1004
rrold, Tamer IV, 405
rrold, Thomas I, 956
rrold, Thomas V, 244
rrold, Widow Mary I, 588
rrold, William I, 543
rrold, William I, 813
rrold, William I, 956
rrold, William V, 244
rrold, Wm. V, 303
arroll, James V, 1000
arroll, Phebe V, 1000
arron, Edith IV, 1253
arrop, Eliza II, 873
arrop, Eliza II, 900
arrop, John II, 799
arrop, John II, 873
arrop, John II, 900
arrop, Sarah II, 799
arrop, Sarah II, 873
arrop, Sarah II, 900
arrop, Thomas II, 799
arrop, Wd. Elizabeth II, 799
arrott, Samuel II, 371
arrow, John VI, 398
arry, ??? IV, 405
arry, Aberry II, 371
arry, Absalom IV, 405
arry, Absalom IV, 392
arry, Absolom IV, 1061
arry, Auberry II, 371
arry, Comley IV, 37
arry, Cyrus IV, 37
arry, Cyrus IV, 91
arry, David II, 371
arry, David II, 543
arry, Eliza Jane IV, 37
arry, Eliza Jane IV, 55
arry, Elizabeth II, 543
arry, Elizabeth II, 672
arry, Frances VI, 503
arry, George IV, 37
arry, George IV, 91
arry, Hannah II, 460
arry, Hannah II, 461
arry, Hannah II, 543
arry, Hannah II, 707
arry, Hannah IV, 37
arry, Hannah IV, 91
arry, Hannah IV, 392
arry, Hannah IV, 405
arry, Hannah IV, 1061
arry, Herbert II, 371
arry, Jacob IV, 37
arry, Jesse IV, 37
arry, John II, 459
arry, John II, 461
arry, John II, 543
arry, John IV, 37
arry, John IV, 91
arry, John IV, 405
arry, John IV, 1061
arry, John IV, 1062
arry, Joseph II, 460
arry, Lewis IV, 37
arry, Lewis C. IV, 37
arry, Lydia II, 459
arry, Lydia II, 543
arry, Mary II, 371
arry, Mary II, 460
arry, Mary II, 543
arry, Mary II, 634
arry, Mary IV, 37
Harry, Mary IV, 91
Harry, Mary IV, 405
Harry, Mary IV, 1052
Harry, Mary IV, 1061
Harry, Mary IV, 1062
Harry, Mary VI, 507
Harry, Mary VI, 647
Harry, Mary VI, 655
Harry, Mary E. IV, 741
Harry, Mrs. ??? V, 472
Harry, Naomi IV, 37
Harry, Naomi IV, 46
Harry, Natella V, 208
Harry, Phebe IV, 37
Harry, Phebe IV, 91
Harry, Rachel VI, 647
Harry, Rachel VI, 655
Harry, Rebecca IV, 392
Harry, Rebecca IV, 405
Harry, Rebecca IV, 1061
Harry, Rebecca IV, 1062
Harry, Sarah II, 371
Harry, Sarah II, 453
Harry, Sarah II, 543
Harry, Sarah II, 634
Harry, Sarah II, 999
Harry, Sarah IV, 37
Harry, Sarah IV, 717
Harry, Susanna IV, 37
Harry, Thomas IV, 37
Harry, Thomas IV, 91
Harry, Thomas VI, 647
Harry, Thomas VI, 655
Harry, William IV, 405
Harry, William G. IV, 37
Harry, Wm. IV, 1061
Harsha, Rose Althea V, 679
Harshbarger, ??? V, 809
Harshbarger, Bertha V, 809
Harshbarger, Catharine V, 809
Harshbarger, Catherine V, 809
Harshbarger, Edgar V, 174
Harshbarger, Ethel V, 809
Harshbarger, Glen D. V, 174
Harshbarger, Gracia V, 809
Harshbarger, Guy F. V, 174
Harshbarger, Iva V, 174
Harshbarger, Julia V, 174
Harshbarger, Lena May V, 809
Harshbarger, Mary Opal V, 174
Harshbarger, May V, 809
Harshbarger, Wd. Abigail V, 765
Harshberger, Noara D. IV, 1163
Harshberger, Nora D. IV, 1163
Harshburger, E. V, 748
Harshburger, Elizabeth H. V, 748
Harshburger, H. V, 748
Harshman, Angeline V, 1000
Harshman, Angeline S. V, 1000
Harshman, James V, 1000
Harshman, Janet Auld IV, 717
Harshman, Mary M. IV, 717
Harshman, Robert IV, 717
Harstshorne, Hannah II, 176
Harstshorne, John II, 176
Hart, ??? VI, 283
Hart, Alfred IV, 717
Hart, Alice V, 741
Hart, Ann II, 31
Hart, Ann II, 59
Hart, Ann II, 77
Hart, Ann II, 372
Hart, Ann VI, 1010
Hart, Anne II, 371
Hart, Arrie L. V, 741
Hart, Caroline V, 624
Hart, Caroline E. II, 873
Hart, Catharine L. II, 856
Hart, Catharine L. II, 873
Hart, Charles H. V, 679
Hart, David Morris II, 371
Hart, Eleanor V, 379
Hart, Eleanor V, 392
Hart, Eliz. III, 227
Hart, Eliza II, 862
Hart, Eliza II, 917
Hart, Eliza III, 226
Hart, Elizabeth II, 371
Hart, Elizabeth II, 508
Hart, Elizabeth II, 543
Hart, Elizabeth II, 589
Hart, Elizabeth V, 66
Hart, Elizabeth V, 303
Hart, Elizabeth V, 841
Hart, Elizabeth VI, 248
Hart, Elizabeth VI, 286
Hart, Elizabeth VI, 503
Hart, Elizabeth VI, 575
Hart, Emily II, 371
Hart, Emma V, 741
Hart, Esther I, 1048
Hart, Esther V, 66
Hart, Esther V, 841
Hart, Esther V, 869
Hart, Frances III, 152
Hart, Fred I. III, 152
Hart, Fred I. III, 334
Hart, George II, 371
Hart, George V, 741
Hart, Grace A. IV, 821
Hart, Gracie IV, 821
Hart, Hannah II, 61
Hart, Hannah II, 77
Hart, Hannah II, 371
Hart, Hannah II, 372
Hart, Hannah II, 508
Hart, Hannah II, 543
Hart, Hannah II, 588
Hart, Hannah V, 841
Hart, Hannah VI, 487
Hart, Hannah VI, 535
Hart, Hannah VI, 738
Hart, Hannah VI, 766
Hart, Hannah S. II, 372
Hart, Hannah S. II, 530
Hart, Hannah S. II, 544
Hart, Harriet IV, 1319
Hart, Harriet C. V, 1000
Hart, Hastings H. III, 152
Hart, Henry Philips VI, 248
Hart, Henry Phillips VI, 248
Hart, Henry Phillips VI, 286
Hart, Isaac V, 66
Hart, Isaac V, 839
Hart, Isaac V, 841
Hart, James E. V, 741
Hart, James Philips VI, 248
Hart, James Phillips VI, 286
Hart, Jane II, 31
Hart, Jane II, 372
Hart, Jennie B. IV, 1319
Hart, Jimmy V, 841
Hart, Joab V, 624
Hart, John II, 31
Hart, John II, 59
Hart, John II, 61
Hart, John II, 77
Hart, John II, 371
Hart, John II, 372
Hart, John II, 508
Hart, John II, 530
Hart, John II, 535
Hart, John II, 543
Hart, John II, 588
Hart, John II, 589
Hart, John II, 645
Hart, John II, 657
Hart, John II, 707
Hart, John II, 745
Hart, John II, 762
Hart, John II, 777
Hart, John V, 303
Hart, John V, 624
Hart, John V, 741
Hart, John VI, 248
Hart, John VI, 286
Hart, John S. II, 372
Hart, John, Jr. II, 371
Hart, Joseph I, 543
Hart, Joseph I, 953
Hart, Joseph II, 372
Hart, Joseph II, 444
Hart, Joseph VI, 248
Hart, Joseph VI, 286
Hart, Laura III, 152
Hart, Louie V, 458
Hart, Lucy VI, 104
Hart, Lucy VI, 109
Hart, Lydia II, 372
Hart, Lydia II, 530
Hart, Lydia II, 543
Hart, Lydia II, 544
Hart, Lydia II, 657
Hart, Lydia II, 745
Hart, Lydia II, 762
Hart, Lydia II, 777
Hart, Lyman V, 1000
Hart, Mabel Mancher V, 392
Hart, Margaret II, 372
Hart, Margaret II, 515
Hart, Margaret II, 543
Hart, Margaret II, 657
Hart, Margaret II, 745
Hart, Margaret V, 66
Hart, Margaret V, 841
Hart, Martha II, 473
Hart, Martha II, 543
Hart, Martha IV, 1211
Hart, Martha Hobson IV, 1209
Hart, Mary II, 372
Hart, Mary II, 492
Hart, Mary II, 515
Hart, Mary II, 535
Hart, Mary II, 543
Hart, Mary II, 645
Hart, Mary II, 658
Hart, Mary II, 745
Hart, Mary V, 679
Hart, Mary V, 741
Hart, Mary V, 909
Hart, Mary V, 927
Hart, Mary VI, 104
Hart, Mary VI, 109
Hart, Mary VI, 119
Hart, Mary VI, 248
Hart, Mary VI, 286
Hart, Mary VI, 823
Hart, Mary A. V, 909
Hart, N. Hoover V, 741
Hart, Nellie E. III, 152
Hart, Nellie E. III, 334
Hart, Nettie III, 152
Hart, Nettie III, 334
Hart, Phineas V, 67
Hart, Phineas V, 841
Hart, Phinehas I, 543
Hart, Phinehas I, 1016
Hart, Rebecca II, 372
Hart, Rebecca II, 745
Hart, Rebecca V, 66
Hart, Rebecca V, 303
Hart, Rebecca V, 841
Hart, Rebecca S. II, 372
Hart, Rebeccah II, 372
Hart, Rebeccah V, 839
Hart, Rebeccah V, 841
Hart, Samuel II, 372
Hart, Samuel V, 841
Hart, Samuel VI, 823
Hart, Samuel C. II, 372
Hart, Samuel C. II, 707
Hart, Sarah II, 372
Hart, Sarah II, 537
Hart, Sarah II, 543
Hart, Sarah II, 552
Hart, Sarah V, 66
Hart, Sarah V, 741
Hart, Sarah V, 839
Hart, Sarah V, 841
Hart, Sarah VI, 104
Hart, Sarah VI, 109
Hart, Sarah S. II, 372
Hart, Sarah S. II, 745
Hart, Sarah S. II, 777
Hart, Sarah S. II, 829
Hart, Semour II, 372
Hart, Seymor II, 543
Hart, Seymor II, 657
Hart, Seymour II, 543
Hart, Silas V, 303
Hart, Susan V, 624
Hart, Susanna III, 353
Hart, Susannah II, 543
Hart, Susannah II, 618
Hart, Susannah II, 814
Hart, Thomas I, 543
Hart, Thomas I, 1016
Hart, Thomas II, 371
Hart, Thomas II, 372
Hart, Thomas II, 492
Hart, Thomas II, 508
Hart, Thomas II, 543
Hart, Thomas II, 618
Hart, Thomas V, 66
Hart, Thomas V, 841
Hart, Thomas L. II, 745
Hart, Thomas Lloyd II, 372
Hart, Thos. Corwin V, 741
Hart, Wd. Catherine L. II, 791
Hart, Wd. Hannah II, 77
Hart, William II, 372
Hart, William VI, 248
Hart, William VI, 286
Hart, William VI, 1010
Hart, Willie V, 741
Hart, Wm. S. II, 745
Hartbe, Mary II, 372
Hartberger, Noara D. IV, 1163
Hartegrove, Martha I, 543
Harter, Chas. V, 1000
Harter, Elizabeth V, 1000
Harter, Julia A. V, 1000
Harter, Mariah V, 1000
Harter, Sarah IV, 1253
Harter, Sarah V, 174
Harter, Thomas V, 1000
Harter, William IV, 1253
Harter, William V, 174
Harter, Wilson H. V, 1000
Harter, Wilson M. V, 1000
Hartgrave, Oliver C. IV, 217
Hartgrave, Ruanna IV, 217
Hartgrave, Thomas E. IV, 217
Hartgrave, William H. IV, 217
Hartgrove, Benjamin I, 543
Hartgrove, Martha I, 543
Hartgrove, Sophia Haley I, 543
Hartie, Mary Ann IV, 968
Hartland, Frank IV, 1319
Hartle, Anna III, 337
Hartley, A. L. IV, 1209
Hartley, Aaron IV, 335
Hartley, Aaron IV, 406
Hartley, Aaron IV, 1281
Hartley, Aaron Dewees IV, 601
Hartley, Abbie IV, 219
Hartley, Abi IV, 363
Hartley, Abi IV, 400
Hartley, Abi IV, 405
Hartley, Abi IV, 406
Hartley, Abia IV, 406
Hartley, Abijah Tipton IV, 601
Hartley, Abner W. IV, 405
Hartley, Aby IV, 406
Hartley, Agness IV, 37
Hartley, Albert L. IV, 1209
Hartley, Albert T. IV, 583
Hartley, Alfred IV, 821
Hartley, Alfred J. IV, 406
Hartley, Alfred J. IV, 407
Hartley, Alfred J. IV, 440
Hartley, Alfred J. IV, 821
Hartley, Alice II, 799
Hartley, Alice IV, 821
Hartley, Alice T. IV, 1209
Hartley, Alma V, 624
Hartley, Almeda IV, 601
Hartley, Alva IV, 405
Hartley, Alva B. IV, 388
Hartley, Alva B. IV, 406
Hartley, Alva B. IV, 407
Hartley, Alva B. IV, 575
Hartley, Alva B. IV, 583
Hartley, Amos IV, 1026
Hartley, Ann IV, 37
Hartley, Ann Lundy IV, 335
Hartley, Anna IV, 219
Hartley, Anna IV, 405
Hartley, Anna IV, 455
Hartley, Anna IV, 1209
Hartley, Anna Lundy IV, 335
Hartley, Anna M. IV, 407
Hartley, Anna M. IV, 583
Hartley, Anna Mabel IV, 406
Hartley, Anna Mabel IV, 581
Hartley, Anna Maria IV, 1209
Hartley, Anthony II, 984
Hartley, Anthony II, 1000
Hartley, Arthur J. IV, 219
Hartley, Arthur J. IV, 302
Hartley, Arthur J. IV, 406
Hartley, Arthur J. IV, 407
Hartley, Arthur J. IV, 583
Hartley, Avi IV, 451
Hartley, Barbara IV, 91
Hartley, Barbara IV, 127
Hartley, Barbara V, 842
Hartley, Barbara V, 909
Hartley, Barbary V, 841
Hartley, Barbera V, 909
Hartley, Benjamin II, 372
Hartley, Benjamin IV, 405
Hartley, Caleb IV, 219
Hartley, Caleb IV, 405
Hartley, Caleb IV, 406
Hartley, Caroline V, 842
Hartley, Catharine II, 31
Hartley, Catharine II, 77
Hartley, Catharine II, 107
Hartley, Catharine II, 525
Hartley, Catharine II, 544
Hartley, Cecil IV, 583
Hartley, Charity IV, 91
Hartley, Charity IV, 108
Hartley, Charity IV, 398
Hartley, Charity IV, 405
Hartley, Charity IV, 406
Hartley, Charity IV, 415
Hartley, Charity IV, 475
Hartley, Charles Andrew IV, 406
Hartley, Chester Earl IV, 406
Hartley, Cidney IV, 601
Hartley, Clarkson IV, 219
Hartley, Clarkson IV, 406
Hartley, Clarkson IV, 583
Hartley, Clifford B. IV, 406
Hartley, Clifford B. IV, 407
Hartley, Clifford B. IV, 583
Hartley, Cyrus IV, 405
Hartley, David IV, 405
Hartley, David IV, 406
Hartley, Debora IV, 406
Hartley, Deborah IV, 396
Hartley, Deborah IV, 406

Hartley, Deborah Ann V, 841
Hartley, Deborah Ann V, 842
Hartley, Deborah Ann V, 845
Hartley, Deborah C. IV, 401
Hartley, Deborah C. IV, 406
Hartley, Deborah E. IV, 400
Hartley, Deborah V. IV, 1026
Hartley, Dinah IV, 1021
Hartley, Dinah IV, 1026
Hartley, Dorothy Lucile IV, 406
Hartley, Dorothy Lucile IV, 407
Hartley, Dorothy Lucile IV, 821
Hartley, Ebi IV, 475
Hartley, Edith Alice IV, 821
Hartley, Edward II, 1000
Hartley, Edward IV, 37
Hartley, Edward E. V, 842
Hartley, Edwin IV, 1163
Hartley, Edwin A. IV, 1209
Hartley, Edwin M. IV, 1209
Hartley, Eli IV, 405
Hartley, Elias IV, 37
Hartley, Elias IV, 148
Hartley, Elias IV, 219
Hartley, Elias IV, 1163
Hartley, Elias V, 842
Hartley, Elias VI, 746
Hartley, Elias VI, 777
Hartley, Elisa C. IV, 1209
Hartley, Eliza II, 372
Hartley, Eliza IV, 127
Hartley, Eliza IV, 1209
Hartley, Eliza V, 909
Hartley, Eliza H. IV, 1209
Hartley, Eliza M. IV, 1209
Hartley, Elizabeth II, 31
Hartley, Elizabeth II, 57
Hartley, Elizabeth II, 77
Hartley, Elizabeth II, 493
Hartley, Elizabeth II, 544
Hartley, Elizabeth II, 799
Hartley, Elizabeth II, 868
Hartley, Elizabeth II, 873
Hartley, Elizabeth II, 984
Hartley, Elizabeth II, 1000
Hartley, Elizabeth IV, 37
Hartley, Elizabeth IV, 51
Hartley, Elizabeth IV, 91
Hartley, Elizabeth IV, 148
Hartley, Elizabeth IV, 219
Hartley, Elizabeth IV, 335
Hartley, Elizabeth IV, 398
Hartley, Elizabeth IV, 405
Hartley, Elizabeth IV, 406
Hartley, Elizabeth IV, 475
Hartley, Elizabeth IV, 581
Hartley, Elizabeth V, 67
Hartley, Elizabeth V, 842
Hartley, Elizabeth V, 848
Hartley, Elizabeth C. IV, 388
Hartley, Elizabeth C. IV, 407
Hartley, Elizabeth C. IV, 575
Hartley, Elizabeth C. IV, 583
Hartley, Elizabeth C. IV, 584
Hartley, Elizabeth Goodall II, 873
Hartley, Elizabeth H. IV, 37
Hartley, Elizabeth H. IV, 60
Hartley, Elizabeth J. IV, 407
Hartley, Elizabeth J. IV, 581
Hartley, Elizabeth J. IV, 583
Hartley, Elizabeth L. V, 842
Hartley, Ella V. IV, 1026
Hartley, Ella V. IV, 1031
Hartley, Ellen Graham IV, 583
Hartley, Ellis P. IV, 37
Hartley, Ellis P. IV, 59
Hartley, Ellis Pugh IV, 37
Hartley, Elma D. IV, 601
Hartley, Elma M. IV, 402
Hartley, Elma M. IV, 407
Hartley, Elmer C. IV, 406
Hartley, Elmira B. IV, 1209
Hartley, Elmira Mianda IV, 1209
Hartley, Elwood IV, 370
Hartley, Elwood IV, 406
Hartley, Elwood IV, 821
Hartley, Emma L. IV, 1209
Hartley, Esther II, 31
Hartley, Esther II, 77
Hartley, Esther II, 106
Hartley, Esther IV, 127
Hartley, Esther IV, 601
Hartley, Esther V, 909
Hartley, Ethel IV, 406
Hartley, Ethel IV, 821
Hartley, Ethel A. IV, 407
Hartley, Ethel A. IV, 440
Hartley, Ethel Alice IV, 821
Hartley, Eva Rebecca IV, 406
Hartley, Flora S. IV, 583
Hartley, Flora Sina IV, 583
Hartley, Frances VI, 746
Hartley, Frances VI, 763
Hartley, Frances VI, 777
Hartley, Frances E. V, 882
Hartley, Frances E. V, 886
Hartley, Fred M. IV, 406
Hartley, G. N. I, 543
Hartley, George II, 372
Hartley, George V, 842
Hartley, George N. I, 543
Hartley, Hannah II, 792
Hartley, Hannah II, 1000
Hartley, Hannah II, 1017
Hartley, Hannah IV, 28
Hartley, Hannah IV, 37
Hartley, Hannah IV, 1209
Hartley, Hannah V, 842
Hartley, Hannah F. V, 842
Hartley, Hannah J. IV, 1209
Hartley, Hannah Jane IV, 335
Hartley, Harold V, 334
Hartley, Harriet IV, 37
Hartley, Harriet IV, 57
Hartley, Harriet B. IV, 406
Hartley, Harriet West IV, 37
Hartley, Harry J. IV, 407
Hartley, Harry J. IV, 583
Hartley, Harry John IV, 406
Hartley, Harry John IV, 583
Hartley, Haworth II, 799
Hartley, Haworth W. II, 873
Hartley, Henry IV, 219
Hartley, Henry IV, 400
Hartley, Henry IV, 405
Hartley, Henry IV, 406
Hartley, Henry IV, 407
Hartley, Henry IV, 453
Hartley, Henry IV, 456
Hartley, Henry IV, 717
Hartley, Homer J. IV, 406
Hartley, Homer J. IV, 418
Hartley, Homer T. IV, 406
Hartley, Huldah IV, 1209
Hartley, Huldah H. IV, 1209
Hartley, Isaac IV, 219
Hartley, Isaac IV, 390
Hartley, Isaac IV, 400
Hartley, Isaac IV, 405
Hartley, Isaac W. IV, 406
Hartley, James II, 544
Hartley, James IV, 405
Hartley, James IV, 1021
Hartley, James IV, 1026
Hartley, James V, 842
Hartley, James Vernon IV, 601
Hartley, Jane Jones IV, 601
Hartley, Jennet IV, 1026
Hartley, Jeremiah II, 544
Hartley, Jeremiah II, 745
Hartley, Jeremiah II, 799
Hartley, Jeremiah II, 873
Hartley, Jesse IV, 405
Hartley, Jesse IV, 1209
Hartley, Jesse IV, 1214
Hartley, Jesse G. IV, 1209
Hartley, Jesse M. I, 543
Hartley, Jesse N. I, 543
Hartley, Jesse N. I, 1154
Hartley, Jesse N. IV, 1209
Hartley, Jesse T. IV, 1209
Hartley, Joel IV, 219
Hartley, Joel IV, 405
Hartley, John II, 372
Hartley, John IV, 219
Hartley, John IV, 398
Hartley, John IV, 405
Hartley, John IV, 406
Hartley, John IV, 435
Hartley, John IV, 455
Hartley, John IV, 475
Hartley, John IV, 601
Hartley, John V, 842
Hartley, John, Jr. IV, 406
Hartley, Jonathan II, 984
Hartley, Jonathan II, 1000
Hartley, Joseph I, 1154
Hartley, Joseph II, 799
Hartley, Joseph IV, 219
Hartley, Joseph IV, 335
Hartley, Joseph IV, 398
Hartley, Joseph IV, 400
Hartley, Joseph IV, 405
Hartley, Joseph IV, 475
Hartley, Joseph IV, 717
Hartley, Joseph IV, 1026
Hartley, Joseph IV, 1209
Hartley, Joseph A. IV, 365
Hartley, Joseph A. IV, 405
Hartley, Joseph B. IV, 405
Hartley, Joseph M. I, 543
Hartley, Joseph S. IV, 1021
Hartley, Joseph S. IV, 1026
Hartley, Joseph, Jr. IV, 406
Hartley, Josiah IV, 438
Hartley, Laura E. IV, 406
Hartley, Laura E. IV, 407
Hartley, Laura E. IV, 583
Hartley, Leah IV, 91
Hartley, Leah IV, 127
Hartley, Leah V, 909
Hartley, Letitia IV, 717
Hartley, Letitia IV, 1025
Hartley, Letitia IV, 1026
Hartley, Letitia, Jr. IV, 717
Hartley, Levi Mead IV, 1209
Hartley, Lewis IV, 405
Hartley, Lizzie C. IV, 584
Hartley, Lucila IV, 583
Hartley, Lucile IV, 219
Hartley, Lucile IV, 406
Hartley, Lucile IV, 407
Hartley, Lucile IV, 583
Hartley, Lucile IV, 585
Hartley, Lucinda V, 842
Hartley, Luella IV, 583
Hartley, Lydia IV, 37
Hartley, Lydia IV, 50
Hartley, Lydia V, 842
Hartley, Lydia Caroline V, 842
Hartley, Lydia Jane IV, 1161
Hartley, Lydia Jane IV, 1163
Hartley, Lydia Jane IV, 1209
Hartley, M. Elizabeth IV, 418
Hartley, M. Libbie V, 680
Hartley, Mahlon II, 999
Hartley, Mahlon II, 1000
Hartley, Mahlon II, 1017
Hartley, Mahlon IV, 37
Hartley, Mahlon IV, 219
Hartley, Mahlon IV, 398
Hartley, Mahlon IV, 405
Hartley, Mahlon IV, 406
Hartley, Mahlon IV, 415
Hartley, Mahlon IV, 475
Hartley, Mahlon IV, 583
Hartley, Mahlon IV, 591
Hartley, Mahlon IV, 1026
Hartley, Malinda IV, 378
Hartley, Malinda IV, 405
Hartley, Malinda IV, 406
Hartley, Malinda IV, 415
Hartley, Malinda IV, 475
Hartley, Margaret C. IV, 407
Hartley, Margaret C. IV, 456
Hartley, Maria IV, 219
Hartley, Maria IV, 365
Hartley, Maria IV, 405
Hartley, Maria Elma IV, 406
Hartley, Marietta IV, 1026
Hartley, Marilla IV, 1209
Hartley, Marilla R. IV, 1209
Hartley, Marion IV, 400
Hartley, Mark II, 31
Hartley, Mark II, 77
Hartley, Mark II, 372
Hartley, Mark II, 544
Hartley, Mark II, 647
Hartley, Martha II, 372
Hartley, Martha IV, 219
Hartley, Martha IV, 378
Hartley, Martha IV, 400
Hartley, Martha IV, 401
Hartley, Martha IV, 405
Hartley, Martha IV, 406
Hartley, Martha IV, 438
Hartley, Martha IV, 444
Hartley, Martha IV, 601
Hartley, Martha IV, 717
Hartley, Martha VI, 746
Hartley, Martha VI, 777
Hartley, Martha Eliza IV, 406
Hartley, Mary II, 31
Hartley, Mary II, 77
Hartley, Mary II, 106
Hartley, Mary II, 502
Hartley, Mary II, 544
Hartley, Mary II, 799
Hartley, Mary IV, 37
Hartley, Mary IV, 66
Hartley, Mary IV, 91
Hartley, Mary IV, 108
Hartley, Mary IV, 219
Hartley, Mary IV, 390
Hartley, Mary IV, 400
Hartley, Mary IV, 404
Hartley, Mary IV, 405
Hartley, Mary IV, 406
Hartley, Mary IV, 410
Hartley, Mary IV, 443
Hartley, Mary IV, 453
Hartley, Mary IV, 475
Hartley, Mary IV, 583
Hartley, Mary IV, 591
Hartley, Mary IV, 601
Hartley, Mary IV, 962
Hartley, Mary IV, 1209
Hartley, Mary IV, 1214
Hartley, Mary Ann IV, 335
Hartley, Mary Ann IV, 367
Hartley, Mary Ann IV, 406
Hartley, Mary Ann IV, 415
Hartley, Mary Ann IV, 428
Hartley, Mary B. IV, 400
Hartley, Mary B. IV, 401
Hartley, Mary Bell IV, 400
Hartley, Mary D. IV, 405
Hartley, Mary E. IV, 1209
Hartley, Mary Edith IV, 219
Hartley, Mary Edith IV, 302
Hartley, Mary Edith IV, 406
Hartley, Mary Edith IV, 407
Hartley, Mary Edith IV, 583
Hartley, Mary Edith IV, 584
Hartley, Mary Ellen IV, 1209
Hartley, Mary Emily IV, 1026
Hartley, Mary Etta IV, 406
Hartley, Mary R. IV, 406
Hartley, Mary R. IV, 407
Hartley, Mary R. IV, 583
Hartley, Mary R. IV, 601
Hartley, Mary Rebecca IV, 581
Hartley, Mary Rebecca IV, 601
Hartley, Mary Webster IV, 400
Hartley, Maryann IV, 335
Hartley, Maryann IV, 405
Hartley, Matthias II, 544
Hartley, Melinda IV, 406
Hartley, Melinda IV, 475
Hartley, Melissa IV, 392
Hartley, Melissa IV, 406
Hartley, Mellisa IV, 406
Hartley, Melva J. IV, 1209
Hartley, Meribah IV, 37
Hartley, Meribah IV, 59
Hartley, Merilla IV, 1209
Hartley, Milicent IV, 363
Hartley, Milicent IV, 398
Hartley, Milicent IV, 405
Hartley, Milicent IV, 583
Hartley, Millie IV, 219
Hartley, Minnie IV, 392
Hartley, Minnie IV, 406
Hartley, Minnie IV, 407
Hartley, Myron B. IV, 1209
Hartley, Myron T. IV, 1161
Hartley, Myron T. IV, 1163
Hartley, Myron T. IV, 1209
Hartley, Nancy IV, 400
Hartley, Naomi Louise IV, 406
Hartley, Noah IV, 219
Hartley, Noah IV, 363
Hartley, Noah IV, 398
Hartley, Noah IV, 405
Hartley, Noah IV, 406
Hartley, Noah IV, 475
Hartley, Noah IV, 583
Hartley, Noah E. IV, 406
Hartley, Noah P. IV, 405
Hartley, Noah, Jr. IV, 406
Hartley, Nora IV, 575
Hartley, Nora IV, 583
Hartley, Nora E. IV, 406
Hartley, Nora Elma IV, 574
Hartley, Nora Elma IV, 575
Hartley, Nora Elmer IV, 406
Hartley, Norah E. IV, 387
Hartley, Norton IV, 127
Hartley, Norton V, 909
Hartley, Norton D. V, 841
Hartley, Norton D. V, 842
Hartley, Norton D. V, 845
Hartley, Peninah IV, 405
Hartley, Peter IV, 37
Hartley, Peter V. IV, 37
Hartley, Peter Vickers IV, 37
Hartley, Phebe IV, 32
Hartley, Phebe IV, 37
Hartley, Phebe IV, 335
Hartley, Phebe IV, 363
Hartley, Phebe IV, 405
Hartley, Phebe IV, 406
Hartley, Phebe IV, 413
Hartley, Phebe E. IV, 378
Hartley, Phebe E. IV, 407
Hartley, Philena IV, 1025
Hartley, Philena IV, 1026
Hartley, Philip IV, 1209
Hartley, Prudence IV, 601
Hartley, Rachel II, 372
Hartley, Rachel II, 544
Hartley, Rachel IV, 127
Hartley, Rachel IV, 601
Hartley, Rachel V, 909
Hartley, Rachel J. I, 1154
Hartley, Rachel J. IV, 1209
Hartley, Rachel L. V, 842
Hartley, Ray IV, 1209
Hartley, Rebecca II, 455
Hartley, Rebecca II, 544
Hartley, Rebecca IV, 405
Hartley, Rebecca IV, 1026
Hartley, Rebecca V, 909
Hartley, Rebecca Aspden II, 54
Hartley, Reuben H. IV, 1209
Hartley, Reuben H. V, 680
Hartley, Richard G. IV, 1026
Hartley, Richard G. IV, 1031
Hartley, Richard Griffith IV, 10
Hartley, Roanice IV, 406
Hartley, Roanice IV, 428
Hartley, Robert E. IV, 583
Hartley, Robert Elmer IV, 583
Hartley, Roger II, 999
Hartley, Roger II, 1000
Hartley, Roger IV, 37
Hartley, Roger M. IV, 37
Hartley, Rosa R. IV, 406
Hartley, Rosela J. IV, 406
Hartley, Rosella IV, 219
Hartley, Rosella IV, 387
Hartley, Rosella IV, 406
Hartley, Rosella IV, 583
Hartley, Rosella J. IV, 574
Hartley, Rosella J. IV, 583
Hartley, Ruth IV, 1209
Hartley, Ruth M. IV, 1163
Hartley, Ruth W. IV, 1209
Hartley, Samuel I, 1154
Hartley, Samuel II, 31
Hartley, Samuel IV, 219
Hartley, Samuel IV, 406
Hartley, Samuel IV, 1021
Hartley, Samuel IV, 1209
Hartley, Samuel S. IV, 405
Hartley, Sara IV, 581
Hartley, Sara A. IV, 583
Hartley, Sara Alice IV, 583
Hartley, Sarah I, 543
Hartley, Sarah II, 31
Hartley, Sarah III, 120
Hartley, Sarah III, 121
Hartley, Sarah III, 152
Hartley, Sarah IV, 127
Hartley, Sarah IV, 219
Hartley, Sarah IV, 398
Hartley, Sarah IV, 400
Hartley, Sarah IV, 405
Hartley, Sarah IV, 406
Hartley, Sarah IV, 429
Hartley, Sarah IV, 435
Hartley, Sarah IV, 438
Hartley, Sarah IV, 475
Hartley, Sarah A. IV, 370
Hartley, Sarah A. IV, 406
Hartley, Sarah Alice IV, 406
Hartley, Sarah Alice IV, 407
Hartley, Sarah Alice IV, 583
Hartley, Sarah Ann IV, 1026
Hartley, Sarah Ann IV, 1028
Hartley, Sarah Anne IV, 1026
Hartley, Sarah Eleanor IV, 405
Hartley, Sarah Eliza IV, 1209
Hartley, Sarah Ellen IV, 219
Hartley, Sarah M. IV, 1026
Hartley, Sarah Norton V, 909
Hartley, Shirley IV, 406
Hartley, Sidney IV, 601
Hartley, Silas IV, 407
Hartley, Silas IV, 581
Hartley, Silas IV, 583
Hartley, Silas H. IV, 406
Hartley, Silas H. IV, 407
Hartley, Silas H. IV, 581
Hartley, Susannah II, 31
Hartley, Susannah II, 77
Hartley, Susannah II, 78
Hartley, Susannah II, 95
Hartley, Susie E. V, 842
Hartley, Tabitha IV, 1209
Hartley, Tabitha IV, 1217
Hartley, Tamar II, 799
Hartley, Tamar II, 873
Hartley, Thomas II, 31
Hartley, Thomas II, 77
Hartley, Thomas II, 999
Hartley, Thomas II, 1000
Hartley, Thomas II, 1017
Hartley, Thomas III, 152
Hartley, Thomas IV, 37
Hartley, Thomas IV, 91
Hartley, Thomas IV, 127
Hartley, Thomas IV, 219
Hartley, Thomas IV, 387

artley, Thomas IV, 405
artley, Thomas IV, 406
artley, Thomas IV, 574
artley, Thomas IV, 583
artley, Thomas IV, 1209
artley, Thomas V, 841
artley, Thomas V, 842
artley, Thomas C. V, 842
artley, Thomas E. I, 1154
artley, Thomas E. IV, 1209
artley, Thos. II, 77
artley, Thos. II, 78
artley, Thos. II, 106
artley, Thos. II, 107
artley, Thos. IV, 406
artley, Thos. V, 909
artley, Thos. E. IV, 1217
artley, Uriah IV, 219
artley, Uriah IV, 405
artley, Uriah IV, 406
artley, Uriah IV, 428
artley, Viola R. IV, 406
artley, W. Everet IV, 583
artley, W. Everett IV, 407
artley, W. H. I, 1154
artley, Walter Earl V, 680
artley, Walter G. IV, 583
artley, Walter T. IV, 1209
artley, Walter Thomas IV, 1209
artley, Willard Everet IV, 583
artley, Willard Everett IV, 406
artley, Willard Everett IV, 407
artley, Willard Everett IV, 583
artley, William IV, 405
artley, William IV, 406
artley, William V, 842
artley, William H. IV, 1209
artley, William Jones V, 841
artley, William L. IV, 717
artley, William Watson IV, 335
artley, Wilson IV, 335
artley, Wm. IV, 335
artley, Wm. Elwood IV, 407
artley, Wm. Elwood IV, 821
artley, Wm. Henry IV, 1209
artley, Zilpah IV, 398
artley, Zilpha IV, 405
artley, Zimri IV, 219
artley, Zimri IV, 405
artley, Zimri IV, 406
artly, Caroline V, 842
artly, Catharine II, 77
artly, Catharine II, 544
artly, Deborah Ann V, 842
artly, Elizabeth II, 1000
artly, Elizabeth V, 842
artly, Elizabeth L. V, 842
artly, George V, 842
artly, Hannah V, 842
artly, Hannah F. V, 842
artly, James V, 842
artly, John V, 842
artly, Jonathan II, 1000
artly, Joseph IV, 717
artly, Lydia V, 842
artly, Mahlon II, 1000
artly, Mary IV, 414
artly, Norton D. V, 842
artly, Sarah Ellen IV, 406
artly, Sarah Ellen IV, 439
artly, Thomas IV, 37
artly, Thomas V, 842
artly, William V, 842
artman, ??? II, 799
artman, Anna V, 392
artman, Anna V, 572
artman, Anna M. V, 710
artman, Arthur V, 175
artman, Arthur V, 680
artman, Artie IV, 1253
artman, Attie IV, 1209
artman, Bernice II, 291
artman, Bernice II, 302
artman, Bernice V, 680
artman, Bernice E. Hawkins V, 175
artman, Bernice H. V, 175
artman, Blanch V, 680
artman, Carrie II, 714
artman, Cecil Arthur V, 175
artman, Cecil Arthur V, 680
artman, Cyril F. IV, 1253
artman, Cyrus IV, 1253
artman, Cyrus M. IV, 1253
artman, Earl IV, 1319
artman, Earle IV, 1319
artman, Edna IV, 1253
artman, Edna M. IV, 1253
artman, Elda V, 1000
artman, Eliza V, 244
artman, Elizabeth V, 680
Hartman, Ella V, 1000
Hartman, Emma A. IV, 1319
Hartman, Estella V, 1000
Hartman, Geo. IV, 1319
Hartman, Geo. Elmore IV, 1319
Hartman, Geoge W. VI, 943
Hartman, George V, 392
Hartman, George Cyrus II, 714
Hartman, Hiram Ellsworth V, 680
Hartman, Isaac V, 244
Hartman, J. Arthur V, 680
Hartman, Jacob II, 372
Hartman, James V, 572
Hartman, James V, 680
Hartman, James William V, 572
Hartman, James William V, 680
Hartman, Jane W. V, 572
Hartman, John V, 174
Hartman, John C. V, 175
Hartman, John C. V, 458
Hartman, John L. V, 175
Hartman, Lewis Cole V, 458
Hartman, Lida V, 497
Hartman, Margaret V, 842
Hartman, Margaret Ruth V, 175
Hartman, Margaret Ruth V, 680
Hartman, Maris V, 572
Hartman, Maris V, 624
Hartman, Mary IV, 1319
Hartman, Mary V, 175
Hartman, Mary V, 458
Hartman, Mary Ann II, 799
Hartman, Mary Ann II, 804
Hartman, Mary C. V, 174
Hartman, Mary Melvine V, 1000
Hartman, Mrs. ??? IV, 1319
Hartman, Mrs. Emma A. IV, 1319
Hartman, Mrs. Geo IV, 1319
Hartman, Nellie V, 392
Hartman, Nora May V, 572
Hartman, Nora May V, 680
Hartman, Ora V, 303
Hartman, Ora L. V, 174
Hartman, Phebe V, 680
Hartman, Prudence V, 624
Hartman, Rachel V, 680
Hartman, Rachel Nancy V, 175
Hartman, Rachel Nancy V, 680
Hartman, Reason V, 1000
Hartman, Rebecca Jane II, 714
Hartman, Susan V, 572
Hartman, Susan V, 680
Hartman, Susan V, 1000
Hartman, Thos. Rowland II, 799
Hartman, Wm. Henry V, 1000
Harts, John II, 604
Hartshore, Rebecca VI, 543
Hartshorene, Susanna Saunders VI, 758
Hartshorene, William VI, 758
Hartshorn, Anna VI, 398
Hartshorn, Anna VI, 442
Hartshorn, Catharine II, 544
Hartshorn, Dr. Joseph VI, 398
Hartshorn, Dr. Joseph VI, 442
Hartshorn, Elizabeth II, 998
Hartshorn, Elizabeth V, 909
Hartshorn, Elizabeth V, 929
Hartshorn, Elizabeth H. V, 909
Hartshorn, Hannah II, 77
Hartshorn, Hannah II, 78
Hartshorn, Hugh II, 372
Hartshorn, Hugh II, 544
Hartshorn, James V, 909
Hartshorn, Jane VI, 398
Hartshorn, Jane VI, 442
Hartshorn, John D. V, 909
Hartshorn, Joseph II, 544
Hartshorn, Mary V, 909
Hartshorn, Patterson V, 909
Hartshorn, Richard II, 544
Hartshorn, Robert II, 77
Hartshorn, Robert II, 78
Hartshorn, Sarah II, 544
Hartshorn, Sarah V, 909
Hartshorn, William II, 372
Hartshorn, Wm. II, 544
Hartshorne, Alexandria III, 152
Hartshorne, Amy Ann VI, 766
Hartshorne, Ann II, 539
Hartshorne, Anna II, 468
Hartshorne, Anna II, 544
Hartshorne, Anna II, 730
Hartshorne, Anna II, 745
Hartshorne, Anna VI, 766
Hartshorne, Anna E. VI, 746
Hartshorne, Catharine II, 230
Hartshorne, Catharine II, 539
Hartshorne, Catharine II, 544
Hartshorne, Charles II, 539
Hartshorne, Elisabeth II, 176
Hartshorne, Elisha VI, 766
Hartshorne, Elizabeth II, 1000
Hartshorne, Hannah II, 176
Hartshorne, Hannah II, 178
Hartshorne, Hannah II, 217
Hartshorne, Hannah II, 230
Hartshorne, Hannah II, 248
Hartshorne, Hannah II, 291
Hartshorne, Hannah II, 294
Hartshorne, Hannah II, 372
Hartshorne, Hannah II, 539
Hartshorne, Hannah II, 544
Hartshorne, Hannah II, 1000
Hartshorne, Hannah II, 1001
Hartshorne, Hannah III, 108
Hartshorne, Hannah III, 152
Hartshorne, Hannah VI, 503
Hartshorne, Hannah VI, 555
Hartshorne, Hannah VI, 746
Hartshorne, Henry II, 730
Hartshorne, Henry II, 745
Hartshorne, Hugh II, 230
Hartshorne, Hugh II, 248
Hartshorne, Hugh II, 372
Hartshorne, Hugh II, 539
Hartshorne, Hugh II, 544
Hartshorne, Hugh II, 643
Hartshorne, Hugh II, 1000
Hartshorne, Hugh II, 1009
Hartshorne, Hugh III, 152
Hartshorne, Hugh VI, 503
Hartshorne, Hugh VI, 555
Hartshorne, Hugh VI, 746
Hartshorne, Jacob II, 539
Hartshorne, Jane II, 1000
Hartshorne, Jane II, 1009
Hartshorne, Jane III, 42
Hartshorne, Jane B. II, 539
Hartshorne, Jesse II, 539
Hartshorne, Jesse P. II, 539
Hartshorne, John II, 176
Hartshorne, John II, 178
Hartshorne, John II, 291
Hartshorne, John II, 294
Hartshorne, John III, 108
Hartshorne, John III, 152
Hartshorne, John, Jr. III, 152
Hartshorne, Joseph II, 372
Hartshorne, Joseph II, 468
Hartshorne, Joseph II, 544
Hartshorne, Joseph II, 730
Hartshorne, Joseph II, 745
Hartshorne, Joseph VI, 503
Hartshorne, Katherine II, 176
Hartshorne, Lucy II, 291
Hartshorne, Lucy II, 294
Hartshorne, Lucy III, 108
Hartshorne, Lucy III, 152
Hartshorne, Margaret II, 176
Hartshorne, Mary II, 539
Hartshorne, Mary VI, 564
Hartshorne, Mary VI, 741
Hartshorne, Mary VI, 746
Hartshorne, Mary VI, 766
Hartshorne, Mary VI, 780
Hartshorne, Mary VI, 781
Hartshorne, Mary VI, 782
Hartshorne, Mary Annie VI, 746
Hartshorne, Mary E. II, 730
Hartshorne, Mary E. II, 745
Hartshorne, Mary L. III, 152
Hartshorne, Mary Pine II, 539
Hartshorne, Patterson II, 1000
Hartshorne, Patterson III, 152
Hartshorne, Patterson, Sr. VI, 746
Hartshorne, Patteson VI, 746
Hartshorne, Pattison III, 152
Hartshorne, Pattison VI, 746
Hartshorne, Peter S. VI, 746
Hartshorne, Phebe II, 539
Hartshorne, Rachel II, 1043
Hartshorne, Rachel VI, 503
Hartshorne, Rachel Robert VI, 535
Hartshorne, Rebecca VI, 503
Hartshorne, Rebecca VI, 517
Hartshorne, Rebecca VI, 535
Hartshorne, Rebecca VI, 663
Hartshorne, Rebecca VI, 746
Hartshorne, Rebecca VI, 766
Hartshorne, Rebeckah VI, 503
Hartshorne, Rebeckah VI, 746
Hartshorne, Richard II, 539
Hartshorne, Richard II, 544
Hartshorne, Richard II, 1000
Hartshorne, Richard II, 1001
Hartshorne, Richard II, 1009
Hartshorne, Richard III, 42
Hartshorne, Richard III, 152
Hartshorne, Robert II, 176
Hartshorne, Robert II, 217
Hartshorne, Robert II, 230
Hartshorne, Robert III, 152
Hartshorne, Robert VI, 503
Hartshorne, Robert VI, 746
Hartshorne, Robert H. III, 152
Hartshorne, Robinson Stabler VI, 746
Hartshorne, Samuel II, 539
Hartshorne, Sarah II, 176
Hartshorne, Sarah II, 544
Hartshorne, Sarah II, 1000
Hartshorne, Sarah II, 1043
Hartshorne, Sarah III, 152
Hartshorne, Sarah VI, 503
Hartshorne, Sarah S. VI, 757
Hartshorne, Sarah Saunders VI, 519
Hartshorne, Sarah Saunders VI, 668
Hartshorne, Sarah Saunders VI, 746
Hartshorne, Sarah, Jr. III, 42
Hartshorne, Susanna II, 468
Hartshorne, Susanna II, 544
Hartshorne, Susanna II, 643
Hartshorne, Susanna VI, 503
Hartshorne, Susanna VI, 555
Hartshorne, Susanna VI, 746
Hartshorne, Susannah II, 1000
Hartshorne, Susannah VI, 503
Hartshorne, Susannah VI, 535
Hartshorne, Susannah VI, 746
Hartshorne, Susannah VI, 766
Hartshorne, Susannah VI, 775
Hartshorne, Thomas II, 176
Hartshorne, Thomazin II, 539
Hartshorne, Wd. Lucy II, 178
Hartshorne, Wd. Susanna Wood VI, 747
Hartshorne, Wd. Susannah VI, 778
Hartshorne, Wd. Susannah Wood VI, 503
Hartshorne, William II, 230
Hartshorne, William II, 248
Hartshorne, William II, 372
Hartshorne, William III, 152
Hartshorne, William VI, 535
Hartshorne, William VI, 555
Hartshorne, William VI, 746
Hartshorne, William VI, 766
Hartshorne, William VI, 775
Hartshorne, William VI, 778
Hartshorne, William, Jr. VI, 503
Hartshorne, William, Jr. VI, 725
Hartshorne, Wm. II, 468
Hartshorne, Wm. II, 544
Hartshorne, Wm. II, 643
Hartshorne, Wm. VI, 503
Hartshorne, Wm. VI, 746
Hartshorne, Wm. VI, 747
Hartsman, Sarah II, 544
Hartsock, Allen Z. V, 572
Hartsock, Anna Louise V, 572
Hartsock, Edna V, 67
Hartsock, Florence L. V, 67
Hartsock, Helen V, 67
Hartsock, Jane V, 67
Hartsock, Jean V, 67
Hartsock, Joseph Walter V, 572
Hartsock, Kenneth J. V, 572
Hartsock, Lena B. V, 67
Hartsock, M. V, 67
Hartsock, Owen Francis V, 67
Hartsock, Ross V, 67
Hartsock, Sarah Katharine V, 572
Hartsock, Viola V, 572
Hartsock, Wilton Heber V, 67
Hartsough, Maggie IV, 821
Hartsuck, J. Edward IV, 1305
Hartsuck, J. Edward IV, 1319
Hartsuck, Laura IV, 1305
Hartsuck, Laura IV, 1319
Hartsuck, Laura A. IV, 1319
Hartt, Caroline III, 450
Hartt, Henry III, 450
Hartt, Joseph I, 963
Hartwell, Ann M. VI, 751
Hartwell, Anna IV, 1253
Hartwell, Cornelia VI, 751
Hartwell, Cosmelia VI, 751
Hartwell, Eveline IV, 1253
Hartwell, Evelyn IV, 1253
Hartwell, Garabell IV, 1253
Hartwell, Hannah VI, 751
Hartwell, Herman IV, 1253
Hartwell, J. Wm. Hartwell VI, 751
Hartwell, John VI, 751
Hartwell, Mary VI, 751
Hartwell, Olive IV, 1253
Hartwell, Olive Matilda IV, 1253
Hartwell, Richardson VI, 751
Hartwell, Samuel VI, 751
Hartwell, Virginia VI, 751
Hartwell, Washington IV, 1253
Hartwell, Wm. VI, 751
Hartwig, Helen III, 280
Hartwig, Helen III, 344
Hartz, ??? IV, 717
Hartz, Alfred IV, 717
Hartz, Anna J. II, 707
Hartz, Anna Leitz II, 745
Hartz, Edith Sara II, 707
Hartz, Elias II, 710
Hartz, Elias II, 717
Hartz, F. Carroll II, 707
Hartz, John S. II, 707
Hartz, John S. II, 745
Hartz, Joseph II, 745
Hartz, Joseph J. II, 707
Hartz, Joseph James II, 745
Hartz, Lee II, 745
Hartz, Lee D. II, 707
Hartz, Lee D. II, 745
Hartz, Lydia II, 701
Hartz, Lydia II, 710
Hartz, Lydia II, 717
Hartz, Lydia Ann II, 701
Hartz, Lydia Ann II, 707
Hartz, Lydia Ann II, 732
Hartz, Lydia Ann II, 745
Hartz, Mary II, 707
Hartz, Mary II, 710
Hartz, Phyllis Klander II, 745
Hartz, Phyllis Klauder II, 707
Hartz, Rachel D. II, 717
Hartz, Ruth Anna II, 707
Hartz, Ruth Anna II, 745
Hartz, Sarah E. II, 701
Hartz, Sarah E. II, 707
Hartz, Sarah E. II, 745
Hartz, Sarah Elizabeth II, 732
Hartz, Sarah Elizabeth II, 745
Hartz, William II, 701
Hartz, William II, 707
Hartz, William A. IV, 717
Hartz, William Albert IV, 717
Hartz, Wm. II, 707
Hartz, Wm. D. II, 732
Hartz, Wm. D. II, 745
Hartz, Zenaida II, 707
Hartzel, Myra IV, 1253
Hartzell, Lucinda V, 731
Hartzell, Lucy IV, 709
Hartzell, Mary Ellen IV, 962
Hartzell, Mary Ellen IV, 1003
Harvard, Ann II, 544
Harvard, Ann II, 626
Harvard, David II, 544
Harvard, David II, 626
Harvey, ??? II, 150
Harvey, Aaron V, 67
Harvey, Aaron V, 68
Harvey, Aaron V, 69
Harvey, Aaron V, 574
Harvey, Aaron V, 680
Harvey, Abi V, 67
Harvey, Abigail V, 574
Harvey, Abigail C. V, 572
Harvey, Abner II, 372
Harvey, Abraham II, 544
Harvey, Abraham II, 1000
Harvey, Abraham II, 1019
Harvey, Abraham V, 573
Harvey, Abraham V, 680
Harvey, Ada B. II, 850
Harvey, Ada B. II, 873
Harvey, Agatha V, 67
Harvey, Agatha V, 68
Harvey, Agatha V, 498
Harvey, Agatha V, 573
Harvey, Agatha V, 902
Harvey, Agatha V, 909
Harvey, Agnes I, 353
Harvey, Agnes I, 435
Harvey, Agnes I, 543
Harvey, Agnes I, 813
Harvey, Agnes I, 814
Harvey, Agnes I, 817
Harvey, Agnes III, 152
Harvey, Agnes VI, 816
Harvey, Agness I, 393
Harvey, Agness I, 447
Harvey, Albert P. V, 69
Harvey, Alfred V, 67
Harvey, Alice II, 1000
Harvey, Alice II, 1019
Harvey, Alice II, 1051

Harvey, Alice V, 554
Harvey, Alice V, 573
Harvey, Alice V, 574
Harvey, Alice V, 680
Harvey, Alice V, 741
Harvey, Alice C. V, 680
Harvey, Alice S. V, 574
Harvey, Alice W. V, 574
Harvey, Allise II, 48
Harvey, Almeda I, 543
Harvey, Almeda I, 577
Harvey, Almeda Baker I, 1120
Harvey, Almedy I, 499
Harvey, Amos II, 799
Harvey, Amos IV, 37
Harvey, Amos IV, 91
Harvey, Amos IV, 475
Harvey, Amos V, 572
Harvey, Amos V, 842
Harvey, Amos VI, 398
Harvey, Amos B. V, 68
Harvey, Amos P. V, 573
Harvey, Andromeda IV, 630
Harvey, Ann I, 353
Harvey, Ann I, 435
Harvey, Ann I, 445
Harvey, Ann I, 447
Harvey, Ann I, 543
Harvey, Ann I, 556
Harvey, Ann II, 230
Harvey, Ann II, 268
Harvey, Ann II, 372
Harvey, Ann II, 977
Harvey, Ann II, 1000
Harvey, Ann IV, 86
Harvey, Ann IV, 91
Harvey, Ann V, 50
Harvey, Ann V, 67
Harvey, Ann V, 68
Harvey, Ann V, 192
Harvey, Ann V, 334
Harvey, Ann V, 345
Harvey, Ann V, 498
Harvey, Ann V, 516
Harvey, Ann V, 555
Harvey, Ann V, 559
Harvey, Ann V, 567
Harvey, Ann V, 572
Harvey, Ann V, 573
Harvey, Ann V, 574
Harvey, Ann V, 581
Harvey, Ann V, 586
Harvey, Ann V, 680
Harvey, Ann V, 1000
Harvey, Ann VI, 823
Harvey, Ann B. V, 572
Harvey, Ann C. V, 574
Harvey, Ann M. V, 574
Harvey, Ann M. VI, 844
Harvey, Anna I, 699
Harvey, Anna II, 1000
Harvey, Anna II, 1027
Harvey, Anna IV, 1236
Harvey, Anna V, 557
Harvey, Anna V, 572
Harvey, Anna V, 573
Harvey, Anna V, 574
Harvey, Anna V, 680
Harvey, Anna B. V, 69
Harvey, Anna B. V, 680
Harvey, Anna Mary IV, 630
Harvey, Annie V, 1000
Harvey, Anson B. II, 707
Harvey, Anson B. II, 745
Harvey, Anthony I, 353
Harvey, Anthony I, 435
Harvey, Anthony I, 447
Harvey, Anthony I, 543
Harvey, Anthony I, 556
Harvey, Anthony I, 580
Harvey, Archilles D. V, 573
Harvey, Asael I, 435
Harvey, Asenath I, 435
Harvey, Asenath V, 68
Harvey, Asenath V, 572
Harvey, Asenith V, 573
Harvey, Barbara I, 926
Harvey, Barzilla IV, 1365
Harvey, Bathsheba V, 68
Harvey, Bathsheba V, 175
Harvey, Bathsheba V, 195
Harvey, Bathsheba V, 573
Harvey, Bathshebe V, 572
Harvey, Benjamin II, 503
Harvey, Benjamin II, 544
Harvey, Bernard V, 574
Harvey, Betsy VI, 822
Harvey, Betsy VI, 823
Harvey, Beverly VI, 823
Harvey, Blancha V, 680
Harvey, C. W. I, 241
Harvey, Caleb I, 353
Harvey, Caleb I, 393
Harvey, Caleb I, 410
Harvey, Caleb I, 447
Harvey, Caleb I, 454
Harvey, Caleb V, 67
Harvey, Caleb V, 68
Harvey, Caleb V, 112
Harvey, Caleb V, 175
Harvey, Caleb V, 195
Harvey, Caleb V, 244
Harvey, Caleb V, 334
Harvey, Caleb V, 345
Harvey, Caleb V, 498
Harvey, Caleb V, 504
Harvey, Caleb V, 572
Harvey, Caleb V, 581
Harvey, Caleb E. V, 392
Harvey, Caleb E. V, 574
Harvey, Caleb Elwood V, 572
Harvey, Caleb J. V, 498
Harvey, Caleb J. V, 574
Harvey, Caleb J. V, 579
Harvey, Caleb, Jr. V, 573
Harvey, Caroline V, 56
Harvey, Caroline V, 67
Harvey, Caroline V, 68
Harvey, Caroline V, 573
Harvey, Caroline C. VI, 845
Harvey, Caroline Eliza III, 121
Harvey, Caroline Eliza III, 152
Harvey, Caroline Eliza III, 262
Harvey, Carrie H. V, 593
Harvey, Carter V, 67
Harvey, Carter V, 68
Harvey, Catharine IV, 91
Harvey, Catharine IV, 109
Harvey, Catharine IV, 630
Harvey, Catharine IV, 657
Harvey, Catharine VI, 823
Harvey, Catherine Harvey IV, 91
Harvey, Catherine Harvy IV, 37
Harvey, Chalkley I, 543
Harvey, Charles II, 544
Harvey, Charles V, 67
Harvey, Charles V, 498
Harvey, Charles V, 574
Harvey, Charles VI, 823
Harvey, Charles E. V, 680
Harvey, Charles T. II, 873
Harvey, Charley V, 1000
Harvey, Charlie E. V, 574
Harvey, Chas. T. V, 909
Harvey, Chas. Townsend V, 909
Harvey, Chloe Theodosia IV, 971
Harvey, Clara Frances V, 741
Harvey, Clarissa VI, 823
Harvey, Clement VI, 823
Harvey, Cynthia V, 572
Harvey, Cynthia V, 573
Harvey, Cyrus I, 435
Harvey, Cyrus W. I, 240
Harvey, Cyrus W. II, 707
Harvey, Cyrus Wilson I, 240
Harvey, Cyrus Wilson I, 255
Harvey, David I, 436
Harvey, David IV, 91
Harvey, David IV, 1236
Harvey, David V, 68
Harvey, David V, 497
Harvey, David V, 572
Harvey, David V, 573
Harvey, Davis V, 68
Harvey, Davis V, 573
Harvey, Davis Harvey V, 68
Harvey, De Ella V, 573
Harvey, Deborah IV, 86
Harvey, Deborah IV, 91
Harvey, Deborah V, 67
Harvey, Deborah V, 68
Harvey, Deborah V, 73
Harvey, Deborah V, 498
Harvey, Deborah V, 572
Harvey, Deborah L. V, 498
Harvey, Deborah L. V, 527
Harvey, Deborah L. V, 596
Harvey, DeElla V, 574
Harvey, Della V, 392
Harvey, Dorothea II, 560
Harvey, Dorothea Hunt II, 544
Harvey, Earnest V, 680
Harvey, Edith S. II, 792
Harvey, Edith Sharpless II, 826
Harvey, Edward II, 544
Harvey, Edward Stratton V, 68
Harvey, Edwin V, 741
Harvey, Eleanor II, 1000
Harvey, Eleanor IV, 469
Harvey, Eleanor VI, 384
Harvey, Eleanor VI, 398
Harvey, Eleanor VI, 757
Harvey, Elenor VI, 824
Harvey, Eleonor IV, 37
Harvey, Eli I, 353
Harvey, Eli I, 393
Harvey, Eli I, 436
Harvey, Eli I, 814
Harvey, Eli I, 838
Harvey, Eli V, 55
Harvey, Eli V, 67
Harvey, Eli V, 68
Harvey, Eli V, 497
Harvey, Eli V, 498
Harvey, Eli V, 560
Harvey, Eli V, 561
Harvey, Eli V, 572
Harvey, Eli V, 573
Harvey, Eli V, 574
Harvey, Eli V, 680
Harvey, Eli V, 909
Harvey, Eli P. V, 67
Harvey, Elias V, 67
Harvey, Elias V, 68
Harvey, Elias V, 244
Harvey, Elias V, 572
Harvey, Elias V, 573
Harvey, Elinor II, 1000
Harvey, Elisha V, 67
Harvey, Elisha B. V, 67
Harvey, Elizabeth I, 353
Harvey, Elizabeth I, 393
Harvey, Elizabeth I, 435
Harvey, Elizabeth I, 447
Harvey, Elizabeth I, 453
Harvey, Elizabeth I, 654
Harvey, Elizabeth I, 679
Harvey, Elizabeth I, 699
Harvey, Elizabeth I, 717
Harvey, Elizabeth I, 814
Harvey, Elizabeth II, 176
Harvey, Elizabeth II, 204
Harvey, Elizabeth II, 230
Harvey, Elizabeth II, 372
Harvey, Elizabeth II, 997
Harvey, Elizabeth II, 1000
Harvey, Elizabeth II, 1004
Harvey, Elizabeth II, 1041
Harvey, Elizabeth IV, 971
Harvey, Elizabeth V, 30
Harvey, Elizabeth V, 67
Harvey, Elizabeth V, 68
Harvey, Elizabeth V, 225
Harvey, Elizabeth V, 244
Harvey, Elizabeth V, 334
Harvey, Elizabeth V, 488
Harvey, Elizabeth V, 497
Harvey, Elizabeth V, 498
Harvey, Elizabeth V, 552
Harvey, Elizabeth V, 554
Harvey, Elizabeth V, 572
Harvey, Elizabeth V, 573
Harvey, Elizabeth V, 574
Harvey, Elizabeth V, 602
Harvey, Elizabeth V, 680
Harvey, Elizabeth V, 909
Harvey, Elizabeth VI, 814
Harvey, Elizabeth VI, 823
Harvey, Elizabeth VI, 845
Harvey, Elizabeth G. VI, 823
Harvey, Elizabeth Meda IV, 630
Harvey, Elizabeth R. V, 69
Harvey, Elizabeth W. VI, 822
Harvey, Elizabeth, Sr. I, 447
Harvey, Ella V, 1000
Harvey, Ella M. V, 549
Harvey, Ella M. V, 574
Harvey, Ellinor II, 1000
Harvey, Ellwood V, 68
Harvey, Ellwood V, 573
Harvey, Elsie R. V, 573
Harvey, Elsie R. V, 680
Harvey, Elzina V, 1000
Harvey, Emilie P. V, 67
Harvey, Emily V, 61
Harvey, Emily V, 67
Harvey, Enos I, 925
Harvey, Enos I, 942
Harvey, Enos F. V, 572
Harvey, Ernest V, 573
Harvey, Ernest V, 574
Harvey, Esther II, 1051
Harvey, Esther V, 572
Harvey, Esther V, 574
Harvey, Esther V, 580
Harvey, Etta V, 1000
Harvey, Eugene II, 873
Harvey, Eunice V, 61
Harvey, Eunice V, 67
Harvey, Eunice V, 68
Harvey, Eunice V, 572
Harvey, Eunice V, 573
Harvey, Evan VI, 964
Harvey, Ezekiel Horneday V, 498
Harvey, Fred H. V, 574
Harvey, Freddy H. V, 680
Harvey, Frederic V, 680
Harvey, Genetta V, 392
Harvey, Geo. M. V, 573
Harvey, Geo. W. V, 680
Harvey, George V, 68
Harvey, George V, 573
Harvey, George M. V, 574
Harvey, George Maden V, 572
Harvey, George Maden V, 573
Harvey, George S. V, 574
Harvey, George W. V, 574
Harvey, Gertrude V, 589
Harvey, Glenn V, 673
Harvey, Glenn V, 680
Harvey, Glover VI, 823
Harvey, Glover VI, 833
Harvey, Grace I, 543
Harvey, Grace I, 881
Harvey, Grace D. I, 881
Harvey, Grace D. I, 894
Harvey, Grace Dix I, 435
Harvey, Guli E. V, 51
Harvey, Guli E. V, 69
Harvey, Gulielma V, 67
Harvey, Gulielma Maria IV, 37
Harvey, Hannah I, 435
Harvey, Hannah I, 447
Harvey, Hannah I, 453
Harvey, Hannah I, 540
Harvey, Hannah I, 543
Harvey, Hannah I, 881
Harvey, Hannah II, 1000
Harvey, Hannah II, 1015
Harvey, Hannah II, 1030
Harvey, Hannah IV, 37
Harvey, Hannah IV, 43
Harvey, Hannah V, 47
Harvey, Hannah V, 67
Harvey, Hannah V, 68
Harvey, Hannah V, 92
Harvey, Hannah V, 96
Harvey, Hannah V, 498
Harvey, Hannah V, 572
Harvey, Hannah V, 573
Harvey, Hannah V, 574
Harvey, Hannah V, 581
Harvey, Hannah C. V, 574
Harvey, Hannah C. V, 584
Harvey, Hannah F. V, 572
Harvey, Hannah F. V, 574
Harvey, Harker VI, 823
Harvey, Harlan V, 67
Harvey, Harlan V, 68
Harvey, Harlan V, 498
Harvey, Harlan V, 554
Harvey, Harlan V, 573
Harvey, Harlin V, 68
Harvey, Henry II, 1000
Harvey, Henry II, 1027
Harvey, Henry II, 1038
Harvey, Henry II, 1041
Harvey, Henry V, 498
Harvey, Henry V, 516
Harvey, Henry V, 549
Harvey, Henry V, 572
Harvey, Henry V, 573
Harvey, Henry V, 574
Harvey, Henry V, 909
Harvey, Henry C. II, 873
Harvey, Henry C. V, 572
Harvey, Henry M. I, 543
Harvey, Henry McKinzie I, 435
Harvey, Henry S. IV, 630
Harvey, Henry Salonis IV, 620
Harvey, Henry Salonis IV, 630
Harvey, Henry, Jr. II, 1000
Harvey, Hezekiah VI, 823
Harvey, Homer V, 680
Harvey, Homer A. V, 680
Harvey, Inda V, 573
Harvey, Inda V, 574
Harvey, Inda V, 680
Harvey, Irena V, 392
Harvey, Irena V, 421
Harvey, Irena V, 573
Harvey, Irena V, 574
Harvey, Irena V, 589
Harvey, Isaac I, 346
Harvey, Isaac I, 353
Harvey, Isaac I, 385
Harvey, Isaac I, 393
Harvey, Isaac I, 435
Harvey, Isaac I, 447
Harvey, Isaac I, 814
Harvey, Isaac II, 544
Harvey, Isaac V, 20
Harvey, Isaac V, 50
Harvey, Isaac V, 67
Harvey, Isaac V, 68
Harvey, Isaac V, 73
Harvey, Isaac V, 244
Harvey, Isaac V, 392
Harvey, Isaac V, 498
Harvey, Isaac V, 503
Harvey, Isaac V, 572
Harvey, Isaac V, 573
Harvey, Isaac V, 574
Harvey, Isaac V, 680
Harvey, Isaac V, 902
Harvey, Isaac V, 909
Harvey, Isaac, Jr. I, 393
Harvey, Isaac, Jr. II, 544
Harvey, Isaac, Jr. III, 152
Harvey, Isaac, Sr. I, 435
Harvey, Isac I, 447
Harvey, Isac I, 453
Harvey, Isham VI, 817
Harvey, Isham VI, 823
Harvey, J. M. I, 942
Harvey, Jabez IV, 91
Harvey, Jack VI, 823
Harvey, Jacob III, 152
Harvey, Jacob IV, 657
Harvey, Jacob Marvin IV, 630
Harvey, Jacob W. II, 873
Harvey, James I, 543
Harvey, James II, 372
Harvey, James II, 544
Harvey, James II, 799
Harvey, James V, 67
Harvey, James V, 68
Harvey, James V, 303
Harvey, James V, 306
Harvey, James V, 572
Harvey, James V, 573
Harvey, James V, 574
Harvey, James V, 680
Harvey, James VI, 823
Harvey, James A. VI, 823
Harvey, James Boyle II, 544
Harvey, James Johnston I, 435
Harvey, James W. V, 572
Harvey, James W. V, 574
Harvey, Jane I, 654
Harvey, Jane II, 542
Harvey, Jane II, 544
Harvey, Jane II, 981
Harvey, Jane II, 1000
Harvey, Jane II, 1034
Harvey, Jane IV, 27
Harvey, Jane IV, 37
Harvey, Jane IV, 91
Harvey, Jane IV, 657
Harvey, Jane V, 67
Harvey, Jane V, 68
Harvey, Jane L. II, 707
Harvey, Jean I, 382
Harvey, Jean I, 393
Harvey, Jean I, 717
Harvey, Jehu IV, 91
Harvey, Jehu V, 498
Harvey, Jehu V, 572
Harvey, Jehu V, 574
Harvey, Jehu V, 757
Harvey, Jehu Coulson IV, 91
Harvey, Jenetta V, 573
Harvey, Jennette V, 574
Harvey, Jennie V, 573
Harvey, Jennie V, 574
Harvey, Jennie V, 680
Harvey, Jeremiah V, 498
Harvey, Jervis V, 68
Harvey, Jess I, 393
Harvey, Jesse I, 240
Harvey, Jesse I, 654
Harvey, Jesse I, 679
Harvey, Jesse I, 691
Harvey, Jesse I, 699
Harvey, Jesse I, 717
Harvey, Jesse V, 67
Harvey, Jesse V, 68
Harvey, Jesse V, 225
Harvey, Jesse V, 244
Harvey, Jesse V, 498
Harvey, Jesse V, 552
Harvey, Jesse V, 573
Harvey, Jesse V, 593
Harvey, Jesse VI, 807
Harvey, Jesse VI, 823
Harvey, Jesse Coulson IV, 91
Harvey, Jesse H. V, 568
Harvey, Jesse H. V, 572
Harvey, Jesse H. V, 573
Harvey, Jesse H. V, 574
Harvey, Jesse H. V, 680
Harvey, Jesse Henry IV, 630
Harvey, Jessie H. V, 574
Harvey, Joanna V, 1000
Harvey, Job II, 230
Harvey, Job II, 372

arvey, Job II, 542
arvey, Job II, 544
arvey, Job II, 650
arvey, Job IV, 37
arvey, Job IV, 43
arvey, Job IV, 469
arvey, Job VI, 384
arvey, Job VI, 398
arvey, Joel V, 97
arvey, John I, 435
arvey, John I, 436
arvey, John I, 543
arvey, John I, 654
arvey, John I, 922
arvey, John I, 929
arvey, John II, 176
arvey, John II, 230
arvey, John II, 268
arvey, John II, 1000
arvey, John II, 1030
arvey, John V, 61
arvey, John V, 63
arvey, John V, 67
arvey, John V, 68
arvey, John V, 69
arvey, John V, 111
arvey, John V, 497
arvey, John V, 545
arvey, John V, 549
arvey, John V, 572
arvey, John V, 573
arvey, John V, 574
arvey, John V, 592
arvey, John V, 680
arvey, John VI, 13
arvey, John VI, 398
arvey, John VI, 823
arvey, John C. VI, 823
arvey, John Elis David V, 498
arvey, John Foster I, 435
arvey, John H. V, 572
arvey, John Haley I, 926
arvey, John M. V, 67
arvey, John M. VI, 929
arvey, John Meader V, 573
arvey, John Medder V, 68
arvey, John W. VI, 795
arvey, John W. VI, 823
arvey, John W. VI, 838
arvey, Jonathan II, 1051
arvey, Jonathan V, 572
arvey, Jonathan V, 573
arvey, Joseph II, 372
arvey, Joseph II, 542
arvey, Joseph II, 544
arvey, Joseph III, 152
arvey, Joseph V, 67
arvey, Joseph V, 68
arvey, Joseph V, 498
arvey, Joseph D. V, 67
arvey, Joseph D. V, 68
arvey, Joseph F. V, 572
arvey, Joshua I, 353
arvey, Joshua I, 447
arvey, Joshua I, 451
arvey, Joshua II, 799
arvey, Joshua II, 873
arvey, Joshua V, 68
arvey, Joshua V, 175
arvey, Joshua V, 497
arvey, Joshua V, 498
arvey, Joshua V, 518
arvey, Joshua V, 554
arvey, Joshua V, 572
arvey, Joshua V, 573
arvey, Joshua V, 574
arvey, Joshua V, 680
arvey, Joshua V, 909
arvey, Josiah I, 543
arvey, Josiah L. III, 121
arvey, Josiah L. III, 152
arvey, Josiah L. III, 262
arvey, Judith II, 544
arvey, Judith II, 610
arvey, Julian VI, 807
arvey, Julianna I, 216
arvey, Julianna I, 225
arvey, Julianna I, 240
arvey, Julianna I, 255
arvey, Junetta V, 392
arvey, Kate V, 573
arvey, Kezia I, 679
arvey, Kezia I, 691
arvey, Keziah I, 699
arvey, Keziah I, 717
arvey, Keziah IV, 37
arvey, Kinsey II, 1051
arvey, Kissiah VI, 398
arvey, Latitia II, 995
arvey, Latitia II, 1000
arvey, Lavinia II, 799
Harvey, Lavinia II, 873
Harvey, Lavinia V, 909
Harvey, Lela M. IV, 1319
Harvey, Leonard II, 48
Harvey, Lettie I, 942
Harvey, Lettie I, 945
Harvey, Levi V, 498
Harvey, Levi V, 557
Harvey, Levi V, 572
Harvey, Levi V, 574
Harvey, Levina V, 909
Harvey, Lidia I, 353
Harvey, Lillie Green I, 926
Harvey, Lillie Green I, 942
Harvey, Lillie H. I, 929
Harvey, Lina V, 574
Harvey, Lina C. V, 574
Harvey, Lindley M. V, 67
Harvey, Lindley M. V, 68
Harvey, Lindly M. V, 67
Harvey, Lizzie V, 550
Harvey, Lizzie V, 573
Harvey, Lizzie V. V, 677
Harvey, Lizzie Viola V, 680
Harvey, Lucile V, 69
Harvey, Lucile V, 157
Harvey, Lucile V, 680
Harvey, Lucinda VI, 823
Harvey, Lucy V, 673
Harvey, Lucy V, 680
Harvey, Lucy C. V, 568
Harvey, Lucy C. V, 574
Harvey, Lucy Caroline V, 680
Harvey, Lucy Franklin V, 680
Harvey, Lucy H. V, 573
Harvey, Luetta I, 922
Harvey, Luretta I, 929
Harvey, Luretta Lea I, 926
Harvey, Luther T. V, 574
Harvey, Lydia I, 385
Harvey, Lydia I, 393
Harvey, Lydia I, 446
Harvey, Lydia I, 447
Harvey, Lydia I, 654
Harvey, Lydia I, 679
Harvey, Lydia I, 680
Harvey, Lydia I, 699
Harvey, Lydia I, 717
Harvey, Lydia II, 133
Harvey, Lydia II, 230
Harvey, Lydia V, 20
Harvey, Lydia V, 63
Harvey, Lydia V, 67
Harvey, Lydia V, 68
Harvey, Lydia V, 69
Harvey, Lydia V, 73
Harvey, Lydia V, 244
Harvey, Lydia V, 498
Harvey, Lydia V, 518
Harvey, Lydia V, 549
Harvey, Lydia V, 564
Harvey, Lydia V, 572
Harvey, Lydia V, 573
Harvey, Lydia V, 574
Harvey, Lydia V, 582
Harvey, Lydia Ann V, 67
Harvey, Lydia Ann V, 69
Harvey, Lydia Beulah IV, 630
Harvey, Lydia H. V, 69
Harvey, Lydia Overman I, 240
Harvey, Mahala V, 61
Harvey, Mahala V, 67
Harvey, Mahala V, 69
Harvey, Mahala V, 111
Harvey, Mahala V, 573
Harvey, Mahala V, 592
Harvey, Mahlon I, 925
Harvey, Mahlon V, 573
Harvey, Major VI, 818
Harvey, Malinda V, 67
Harvey, Malinda V, 68
Harvey, Manerva V, 68
Harvey, Margaret I, 654
Harvey, Margaret II, 544
Harvey, Margaret II, 986
Harvey, Margaret II, 1000
Harvey, Margaret IV, 37
Harvey, Margaret IV, 50
Harvey, Margaret IV, 335
Harvey, Margaret IV, 343
Harvey, Margary I, 717
Harvey, Margery Ann I, 543
Harvey, Maria V, 67
Harvey, Maria A. V, 680
Harvey, Maria E. V, 574
Harvey, Maria E. V, 680
Harvey, Mariah V, 68
Harvey, Martha I, 346
Harvey, Martha I, 353
Harvey, Martha I, 393
Harvey, Martha I, 435
Harvey, Martha I, 453
Harvey, Martha I, 814
Harvey, Martha II, 1000
Harvey, Martha II, 1019
Harvey, Martha V, 20
Harvey, Martha V, 65
Harvey, Martha V, 67
Harvey, Martha V, 68
Harvey, Martha V, 124
Harvey, Martha V, 498
Harvey, Martha V, 572
Harvey, Martha V, 573
Harvey, Martha V, 680
Harvey, Martha VI, 823
Harvey, Martha VI, 838
Harvey, Martha A. VI, 823
Harvey, Martha Eunice V, 68
Harvey, Martha Louise V, 67
Harvey, Martha W. V, 67
HArvey, Martha, Jr. II, 1000
Harvey, Martha, Sr. I, 435
Harvey, Mary I, 353
Harvey, Mary I, 393
Harvey, Mary I, 410
Harvey, Mary I, 426
Harvey, Mary I, 435
Harvey, Mary I, 436
Harvey, Mary I, 447
Harvey, Mary I, 451
Harvey, Mary I, 455
Harvey, Mary I, 543
Harvey, Mary I, 654
Harvey, Mary I, 717
Harvey, Mary I, 814
Harvey, Mary I, 838
Harvey, Mary I, 925
Harvey, Mary I, 942
Harvey, Mary II, 204
Harvey, Mary II, 230
Harvey, Mary II, 372
Harvey, Mary II, 544
Harvey, Mary II, 799
Harvey, Mary II, 895
Harvey, Mary II, 1000
Harvey, Mary II, 1002
Harvey, Mary II, 1041
Harvey, Mary II, 1051
Harvey, Mary IV, 37
Harvey, Mary IV, 469
Harvey, Mary IV, 475
Harvey, Mary V, 67
Harvey, Mary V, 68
Harvey, Mary V, 69
Harvey, Mary V, 175
Harvey, Mary V, 232
Harvey, Mary V, 244
Harvey, Mary V, 497
Harvey, Mary V, 498
Harvey, Mary V, 518
Harvey, Mary V, 552
Harvey, Mary V, 557
Harvey, Mary V, 566
Harvey, Mary V, 572
Harvey, Mary V, 573
Harvey, Mary V, 584
Harvey, Mary A. VI, 833
Harvey, Mary Alice V, 67
Harvey, Mary Ann I, 499
Harvey, Mary Ann V, 63
Harvey, Mary Ann V, 67
Harvey, Mary Ann V, 68
Harvey, Mary Ann V, 572
Harvey, Mary Ann V, 573
Harvey, Mary C. V, 68
Harvey, Mary C. VI, 929
Harvey, Mary G. V, 676
Harvey, Mary H. V, 65
Harvey, Mary H. V, 68
Harvey, Mary H. V, 225
Harvey, Mary H. V, 244
Harvey, Mary J. V, 244
Harvey, Mary J. V, 562
Harvey, Mary J. V, 574
Harvey, Mary Jane V, 565
Harvey, Mary Jane V, 567
Harvey, Mary Jane V, 572
Harvey, Mary Jane V, 574
Harvey, Mary Jane V, 674
Harvey, Mary L. VI, 829
Harvey, Mary M. I, 942
Harvey, Mary M. V, 574
Harvey, Mathias II, 1051
Harvey, Matthew VI, 929
Harvey, Matthias II, 1051
Harvey, Mercy II, 1000
Harvey, Micajah V, 68
Harvey, Micajah V, 680
Harvey, Micajah M. V, 67
Harvey, Micajah M. V, 69
Harvey, Michael I, 654
Harvey, Michael I, 679
Harvey, Michael I, 695
Harvey, Michael V, 244
Harvey, Michael, Sr. I, 699
Harvey, Michel V, 244
Harvey, Miles V, 67
Harvey, Miles V, 68
Harvey, Miles V, 69
Harvey, Miles V, 680
Harvey, Miles W. V, 680
Harvey, Milton V, 68
Harvey, Milton V, 573
Harvey, Miner II, 320
Harvey, Minerva V, 303
Harvey, Minerva V, 306
Harvey, Minnie V, 1000
Harvey, Minor II, 133
Harvey, Minor II, 230
Harvey, Moses I, 435
Harvey, Moses I, 447
Harvey, Moses I, 540
Harvey, Moses I, 543
Harvey, Moses I, 881
Harvey, Moses II, 1000
Harvey, Moses II, 1019
Harvey, Moses V, 573
Harvey, Moses B. V, 67
Harvey, Moses B. V, 68
Harvey, Mynor II, 291
Harvey, Myra V, 593
Harvey, Nancy IV, 1365
Harvey, Nancy V, 68
Harvey, Nancy V, 560
Harvey, Nancy V, 572
Harvey, Nancy V, 573
Harvey, Nancy V, 587
Harvey, Nancy V, 680
Harvey, Nancy VI, 797
Harvey, Nancy VI, 823
Harvey, Nancy VI, 845
Harvey, Nancy E. VI, 823
Harvey, Nancy J. VI, 823
Harvey, Nary V, 558
Harvey, Nathan I, 353
Harvey, Nathan I, 393
Harvey, Nathan I, 435
Harvey, Nathan I, 447
Harvey, Nathan I, 543
Harvey, Nathan I, 814
Harvey, Nathan I, 817
Harvey, Nathan V, 69
Harvey, Nathan V, 572
Harvey, Nathan VI, 823
Harvey, Nathaniel V, 392
Harvey, Nathaniel V, 572
Harvey, Nathaniel V, 573
Harvey, Nathaniel V, 574
Harvey, Nathaniel V, 589
Harvey, Nathaniel V, 680
Harvey, Nathaniel F. V, 573
Harvey, Nellie E. V, 574
Harvey, Nelliford E. V, 680
Harvey, Nora V, 175
Harvey, Olive Etta V, 680
Harvey, Oliver V, 67
Harvey, Oliver V, 69
Harvey, Ora V, 175
Harvey, Ora V, 201
Harvey, Peggy VI, 823
Harvey, Peter II, 176
Harvey, Peter II, 230
Harvey, Peter II, 291
Harvey, Peter II, 320
Harvey, Peter II, 817
Harvey, Peter V, 1000
Harvey, Peter VI, 747
Harvey, Peter VI, 772
Harvey, Phebe I, 435
Harvey, Phebe I, 436
Harvey, Polly IV, 1365
Harvey, Polly VI, 829
Harvey, Rachel I, 391
Harvey, Rachel I, 393
Harvey, Rachel I, 699
Harvey, Rachel II, 781
Harvey, Rachel IV, 91
Harvey, Rachel IV, 105
Harvey, Rachel V, 67
Harvey, Rachel V, 68
Harvey, Rachel V, 133
Harvey, Rachel Myra V, 573
Harvey, Rachel Myra V, 680
Harvey, Randall I, 926
Harvey, Rebecca I, 435
Harvey, Rebecca I, 922
Harvey, Rebecca I, 942
Harvey, Rebecca II, 230
Harvey, Rebecca II, 291
Harvey, Rebecca II, 299
Harvey, Rebecca II, 817
Harvey, Rebecca III, 152
Harvey, Rebecca IV, 620
Harvey, Rebecca IV, 630
Harvey, Rebecca V, 67
Harvey, Rebecca V, 68
Harvey, Rebecca V, 112
Harvey, Rebecca V, 495
Harvey, Rebecca V, 498
Harvey, Rebecca V, 504
Harvey, Rebecca V, 564
Harvey, Rebecca V, 572
Harvey, Rebecca V, 573
Harvey, Rebecca V, 574
Harvey, Rebecca V, 579
Harvey, Rebecca V, 600
Harvey, Rebecca V, 676
Harvey, Rebecca V, 680
Harvey, Rebecca VI, 747
Harvey, Rebecca VI, 772
Harvey, Rebecca VI, 773
Harvey, Rebecca Ann V, 67
Harvey, Rebecca Ann V, 68
Harvey, Rebecca D. IV, 630
Harvey, Rebecca H. V, 741
Harvey, Rebecca J. V, 498
Harvey, Rebecca J. V, 574
Harvey, Rebecca Stratton V, 573
Harvey, Rebeckah V, 498
Harvey, Rebekah V, 67
Harvey, Rebekah V, 89
Harvey, Rhoda I, 435
Harvey, Richard II, 544
Harvey, Richard VI, 16
Harvey, Richard VI, 797
Harvey, Richard VI, 798
Harvey, Richard VI, 823
Harvey, Richard VI, 829
Harvey, Richard VI, 853
Harvey, Richard VI, 854
Harvey, Richard VI, 859
Harvey, Richard Jones II, 544
Harvey, Robert II, 1000
Harvey, Robert V, 498
Harvey, Robert V, 573
Harvey, Rosella V, 1000
Harvey, Rowland IV, 971
Harvey, Rumford Dawes II, 544
Harvey, Ruth I, 346
Harvey, Ruth I, 372
Harvey, Ruth I, 393
Harvey, Ruth V, 55
Harvey, Ruth V, 67
Harvey, Ruth V, 68
Harvey, Ruth V, 495
Harvey, Ruth V, 498
Harvey, Ruth V, 536
Harvey, Ruth V, 554
Harvey, Ruth V, 561
Harvey, Ruth V, 572
Harvey, Ruth V, 573
Harvey, Ruth V, 741
Harvey, S. Bernard V, 574
Harvey, S. Bernard V, 680
Harvey, Sally VI, 823
Harvey, Sally A. VI, 845
Harvey, Sally P. VI, 929
Harvey, Samuel V, 67
Harvey, Samuel V, 68
Harvey, Samuel V, 89
Harvey, Samuel V, 574
Harvey, Samuel B. V, 572
Harvey, Samuel C. V, 680
Harvey, Samuel Clayton V, 680
Harvey, Samuel H. V, 600
Harvey, Sarah I, 447
Harvey, Sarah I, 454
Harvey, Sarah I, 543
Harvey, Sarah I, 580
Harvey, Sarah I, 654
Harvey, Sarah I, 814
Harvey, Sarah I, 837
Harvey, Sarah II, 176
Harvey, Sarah II, 202
Harvey, Sarah II, 230
Harvey, Sarah II, 544
Harvey, Sarah II, 650
Harvey, Sarah II, 786
Harvey, Sarah II, 817
Harvey, Sarah II, 1000
Harvey, Sarah II, 1020
Harvey, Sarah II, 1038
Harvey, Sarah II, 1051
Harvey, Sarah III, 152
Harvey, Sarah V, 38
Harvey, Sarah V, 50
Harvey, Sarah V, 67
Harvey, Sarah V, 68
Harvey, Sarah V, 112
Harvey, Sarah V, 244
Harvey, Sarah V, 392
Harvey, Sarah V, 497
Harvey, Sarah V, 498
Harvey, Sarah V, 549

Harvey, Sarah V, 559
Harvey, Sarah V, 560
Harvey, Sarah V, 572
Harvey, Sarah V, 573
Harvey, Sarah V, 574
Harvey, Sarah V, 680
Harvey, Sarah VI, 747
Harvey, Sarah VI, 772
Harvey, Sarah VI, 802
Harvey, Sarah VI, 814
Harvey, Sarah VI, 845
Harvey, Sarah A. VI, 859
Harvey, Sarah Ann V, 680
Harvey, Sarah B. V, 97
Harvey, Sarah E. V, 574
Harvey, Sarah E. VI, 822
Harvey, Sarah Ellen V, 574
Harvey, Sarah Elma V, 574
Harvey, Sarah Elma V, 576
Harvey, Sarah F. V, 67
Harvey, Sarah Jay V, 741
Harvey, Sarah L. V, 69
Harvey, Sarah L. V, 94
Harvey, Sarah T. V, 68
Harvey, Sarah T. V, 573
Harvey, Seth V, 573
Harvey, Seth V, 574
Harvey, Seth V, 680
Harvey, Silas V, 68
Harvey, Silas V, 572
Harvey, Silas V, 573
Harvey, Simon V, 68
Harvey, Simon V, 498
Harvey, Simon V, 680
Harvey, Simon D. V, 65
Harvey, Simon D. V, 67
Harvey, Simon D. V, 68
Harvey, Simon D. V, 69
Harvey, Simon D. V, 175
Harvey, Simon D. V, 225
Harvey, Simon D. V, 244
Harvey, Simon D. V, 552
Harvey, Simon, Jr. V, 573
Harvey, Sina Ann V, 572
Harvey, Son V, 572
Harvey, Stella Rebecca I, 926
Harvey, Susan A. VI, 823
Harvey, Susanna I, 699
Harvey, Susanna V, 574
Harvey, Susannah II, 799
Harvey, Susannah II, 981
Harvey, Susannah II, 1000
Harvey, Susannah V, 572
Harvey, Susannah V, 574
Harvey, Susannah Matthews I, 543
Harvey, T. C. V, 69
Harvey, Tabitha VI, 817
Harvey, Tacy Ellen Ham V, 68
Harvey, Tamar II, 1000
Harvey, Thomas I, 543
Harvey, Thomas I, 699
Harvey, Thomas I, 717
Harvey, Thomas II, 997
Harvey, Thomas II, 1000
Harvey, Thomas II, 1015
Harvey, Thomas VI, 823
Harvey, Thomas VI, 845
Harvey, Thomas B. V, 67
Harvey, Thomas B. V, 68
Harvey, Thomas B. V, 573
Harvey, Thomas B. VI, 816
Harvey, Thomas Chalkley I, 499
Harvey, Thomas Clarkson V, 67
Harvey, Thomas Pritlow VI, 16
Harvey, Thos. V, 741
Harvey, Thos. VI, 848
Harvey, Thos. B. VI, 823
Harvey, Thos. W. VI, 823
Harvey, Uriah IV, 91
Harvey, Viola V, 573
Harvey, Walter Miles, Jr. VI, 757
Harvey, Wd. Mary A. II, 799
Harvey, Wd. Rebecca V, 757
Harvey, Widow Almeda I, 543
Harvey, William I, 353
Harvey, William I, 393
Harvey, William I, 426
Harvey, William I, 435
Harvey, William I, 436
Harvey, William I, 447
Harvey, William I, 543
Harvey, William I, 577
Harvey, William I, 654
Harvey, William I, 717
Harvey, William I, 814
Harvey, William II, 372
Harvey, William V, 67
Harvey, William V, 68
Harvey, William V, 133
Harvey, William V, 334
Harvey, William V, 469
Harvey, William V, 495
Harvey, William V, 497
Harvey, William V, 498
Harvey, William V, 557
Harvey, William V, 572
Harvey, William V, 573
Harvey, William V, 574
Harvey, William V, 909
Harvey, William VI, 797
Harvey, William VI, 817
Harvey, William VI, 822
Harvey, William VI, 829
Harvey, William A. V, 67
Harvey, William Chalkley I, 499
Harvey, William F. V, 67
Harvey, William F. V, 68
Harvey, William Foster V, 68
Harvey, William Harlan V, 68
Harvey, William J. VI, 800
Harvey, William J. VI, 802
Harvey, William J. VI, 807
Harvey, William J. VI, 823
Harvey, William J. VI, 826
Harvey, William J. VI, 829
Harvey, William J. VI, 845
Harvey, William J. VI, 851
Harvey, William L. I, 499
Harvey, William Lambert I, 435
Harvey, William P. I, 1113
Harvey, William P. I, 1120
Harvey, William P. V, 574
Harvey, William P. VI, 829
Harvey, William Penn V, 572
Harvey, William R. V, 741
Harvey, William T. V, 574
Harvey, William, Jr. V, 498
Harvey, William, Jr. V, 573
Harvey, Willis V, 573
Harvey, Willis M. V, 572
Harvey, Willis M. V, 680
Harvey, Wilson V, 67
Harvey, Wilson V, 69
Harvey, Winifred V, 69
Harvey, Wm. I, 353
Harvey, Wm. I, 393
Harvey, Wm. II, 544
Harvey, Wm. II, 610
Harvey, Wm. II, 799
Harvey, Wm. V, 576
Harvey, Wm. VI, 845
Harvey, Wm. Foster V, 573
Harvey, Wm. H. IV, 1319
Harvey, Wm. P. V, 573
Harvey, Wm. P. V, 574
Harvey, Wm. P. V, 587
Harvey, Wm. P. V, 680
Harvey, Wm. T. V, 555
Harvey, Wm., Jr. V, 573
Harvey, Zilpha I, 925
Harvy, Agness I, 393
Harvy, Ann I, 543
Harvy, Ann I, 576
Harvy, Ann V, 334
Harvy, Archilles D. V, 573
Harvy, Dorathy I, 91
Harvy, Grace I, 543
Harvy, Hannah V, 558
Harvy, Hannah V, 573
Harvy, Henry II, 1034
Harvy, Jane II, 960
Harvy, Jesse I, 717
Harvy, John V, 68
Harvy, Keziah VI, 964
Harvy, Lydia I, 717
Harvy, Martha I, 392
Harvy, Martha I, 393
Harvy, Martha I, 418
Harvy, Mary I, 393
Harvy, Mary I, 447
Harvy, Mary I, 457
Harvy, Mary II, 960
Harvy, Mary II, 1000
Harvy, Mary II, 1034
Harvy, Mathias II, 960
Harvy, Rachel I, 393
Harvy, Ruth I, 393
Harvy, Sarah I, 447
Harvy, Thomas I, 717
Harvye, Abraham II, 982
Harvye, Abraham II, 1000
Harvye, Eleanor II, 1000
Harvye, Elinor II, 1000
Harvye, Elizabeth II, 1010
Harvye, Hannah II, 1000
Harvye, Henry, Jr. II, 1000
Harvye, Martha II, 982
Harvye, Martha, Jr. II, 982
Harvye, Martha, Jr. II, 1000
Harvye, Mercy II, 1031
Harvye, Sarah II, 981
Harwaggon, Ann II, 1000
Harwaggon, Peter II, 1000
Harwagon, Ann II, 977
Harwagon, Ann II, 1000
Harwagon, Peter II, 1000
Harwood, Abigail II, 372
Harwood, Andrew II, 444
Harwood, Elizabeth II, 523
Harwood, Elizabeth II, 544
Harwood, Elizabeth P. VI, 248
Harwood, Elizabeth P. VI, 266
Harwood, Francis G. VI, 959
Harwood, George II, 372
Harwood, James II, 444
Harwood, Jane II, 542
Harwood, Jane II, 544
Harwood, Jane II, 611
Harwood, Jessie S. V, 680
Harwood, John II, 372
Harwood, Mary II, 372
Harwood, Philip II, 444
Harwood, Ruth II, 372
Harwood, Samuel II, 372
Harwood, Sarah II, 372
Harwood, Sarah II, 542
Harwood, Sarah II, 544
Harwood, Sarah II, 631
Harwood, Susanna II, 372
Harwood, William II, 372
Harwood, Wm. II, 523
Harwood, Wm. II, 525
Hase, John I, 544
Haselton, Anna II, 372
Haselton, John II, 372
Haselton, Margarett II, 372
Haselton, Margrett II, 372
Haselton, Miriam II, 372
Haselton, Richard II, 372
Haselton, William II, 372
Hasenpflug, Arthur W. IV, 1319
Hasenpflug, Elizabeth IV, 1319
Hasenpflug, Ezra IV, 1319
Hasenpflug, Geo. IV, 1319
Hasenpflug, George IV, 1319
Hasenpflug, John A. IV, 1319
Hasenpflug, Leroy J. IV, 1319
Hasenpflug, Mildred IV, 1319
Hasenpflug, Sarah E. IV, 1319
Hasenpflug, Sarah S. IV, 1319
Hasenpflug, Sophia IV, 1319
Hashagen, Caroline III, 152
Hashagen, Caroline III, 339
Hashagen, Henry O. III, 152
Hashagen, Henry O. III, 339
Hashagen, Lillian B. III, 152
Hashagen, Lillian B. III, 339
Hashman, Charles IV, 475
Haskell, Almira III, 163
Haskell, Almira III, 226
Haskers, William II, 230
Haskers, Wm. II, 244
Hasket, ??? V, 795
Hasket, Abraham I, 52
Hasket, Abraham I, 56
Hasket, Abraham I, 100
Hasket, Abraham I, 141
Hasket, Alfred I, 141
Hasket, Alice I, 52
Hasket, Alice I, 56
Hasket, Allen I, 141
Hasket, Allien I, 141
Hasket, Alvin V, 741
Hasket, Alvine V, 742
Hasket, Ann I, 141
Hasket, Ann I, 1030
Hasket, Ann V, 69
Hasket, Ann V, 175
Hasket, Ann V, 971
Hasket, Ann V, 979
Hasket, Anna I, 100
Hasket, Anna V, 69
Hasket, Anne I, 184
Hasket, Anthony I, 194
Hasket, Bagley I, 184
Hasket, Betsy V, 498
Hasket, Byron V, 741
Hasket, Charity I, 1020
Hasket, Charity V, 69
Hasket, Charity V, 175
Hasket, Chas. A. V, 741
Hasket, Chas. L. V, 741
Hasket, Chas. Lewis V, 741
Hasket, Daniel Y. I, 194
Hasket, Dinah I Sup 1, 7
Hasket, Edith I, 38
Hasket, Edith I, 52
Hasket, Edna May V, 741
Hasket, Elisabeth I, 52
Hasket, Elisabeth I, 141
Hasket, Elisabeth I, 194
Hasket, Elizabeth I, 100
Hasket, Elizabeth I, 141
Hasket, Elizabeth I, 184
Hasket, Elizabeth I, 814
Hasket, Elizabeth I, 818
Hasket, Elizabeth V, 742
Hasket, Gemima I, 141
Hasket, Gemima I, 168
Hasket, Geo. Lester V, 741
Hasket, Hannah I, 141
Hasket, Hannah I, 184
Hasket, Hannah I, 1020
Hasket, Isaac I, 100
Hasket, Isaac I, 141
Hasket, Isaac I, 1020
Hasket, Isaac I, 1029
Hasket, Isaac I, 1030
Hasket, Isaac V, 69
Hasket, Isaac V, 175
Hasket, Isaac V, 741
Hasket, Isaac V, 742
Hasket, Isaac V, 757
Hasket, Isaac V, 765
Hasket, Isaac V, 809
Hasket, Isaac V, 842
Hasket, Isaac V, 970
Hasket, Isaac V, 971
Hasket, Isaac H. V, 979
Hasket, Isaac Reece V, 741
Hasket, Jemima I, 52
Hasket, Jemima I, 56
Hasket, Jemima I, 100
Hasket, Jemima I, 141
Hasket, Jemima I, 194
Hasket, Jemima I, 1020
Hasket, Jesse I, 100
Hasket, Jesse I, 141
Hasket, Jesse V, 498
Hasket, Joel V, 69
Hasket, Joel V, 971
Hasket, Joel V, 979
Hasket, John I, 52
Hasket, John I, 100
Hasket, John I, 141
Hasket, John I, 184
Hasket, John V, 741
Hasket, John V, 742
Hasket, John V, 752
Hasket, John V, 753
Hasket, John V, 842
Hasket, John V, 851
Hasket, John Cook V, 69
Hasket, John Woodly I, 184
Hasket, Joseph I, 38
Hasket, Joseph I, 52
Hasket, Joseph I, 100
Hasket, Joseph I, 141
Hasket, Joseph I, 168
Hasket, Joseph I, 194
Hasket, Joseph I, 1030
Hasket, Joseph V, 741
Hasket, Joseph V, 742
Hasket, Joseph Forster V, 741
Hasket, Joseph Henry V, 741
Hasket, Joshua I, 52
Hasket, Joshua I, 56
Hasket, Ledru C. V, 741
Hasket, Levi Cook V, 69
Hasket, Lidia I, 1029
Hasket, Lidia I, 1030
Hasket, Lucy V, 742
Hasket, Lucy A. V, 741
Hasket, Lucy A. V, 742
Hasket, Luvenia V, 741
Hasket, Luvenia V, 742
Hasket, Luvinia V, 741
Hasket, Lyda I, 1030
Hasket, Lyddia I, 37
Hasket, Lyddia I, 52
Hasket, Lyddia I, 141
Hasket, Lyddia I, 1020
Hasket, Lydia V, 69
Hasket, Lydia V, 100
Hasket, Lydia V, 175
Hasket, Lydia V, 741
Hasket, Lydia V, 742
Hasket, Lydia V, 757
Hasket, Lydia Alice V, 741
Hasket, Maime V, 742
Hasket, Martha I, 141
Hasket, Mary I, 100
Hasket, Mary I, 141
Hasket, Mary I, 184
Hasket, Mary I, 194
Hasket, Mary I, 566
Hasket, Mary I, 1020
Hasket, Mary I, 1027
Hasket, Mary I, 1030
Hasket, Mary V, 69
Hasket, Mary V, 175
Hasket, Mary V, 741
Hasket, Mary V, 742
Hasket, Mary V, 752
Hasket, Mary V, 753
Hasket, Mary V, 799
Hasket, Mary V, 811
Hasket, Mary V, 842
Hasket, Mary V, 851
Hasket, Mary V, 971
Hasket, Mary V, 979
Hasket, Mary Ann I, 193
Hasket, Mary Persons I, 543
Hasket, Melinda V, 741
Hasket, Miles I, 194
Hasket, Miriam I, 52
Hasket, Miriam I, 141
Hasket, Moses V, 741
Hasket, Moses V, 742
Hasket, Nancy Ann V, 100
Hasket, Nathan I, 52
Hasket, Nathan I, 194
Hasket, Ner V, 971
Hasket, Ner V, 979
Hasket, Orpha I, 717
Hasket, Orpha I, 733
Hasket, Penninah I, 194
Hasket, Phebe Ellen V, 741
Hasket, Rachel I, 56
Hasket, Rachel I, 1020
Hasket, Rachel V, 69
Hasket, Rachel V, 970
Hasket, Rachel V, 971
Hasket, Rachel V, 979
Hasket, Ralph I, 194
Hasket, Rebecca V, 69
Hasket, Rebecca V, 741
Hasket, Rebecca V, 742
Hasket, Rebecca V, 752
Hasket, Rebecca V, 757
Hasket, Rebecca V, 765
Hasket, Rebecca V, 842
Hasket, Rebecca, Jr. V, 741
Hasket, Rebekah I, 1029
Hasket, Rebekah I, 1030
Hasket, Rhoda V, 741
Hasket, Rhoda V, 765
Hasket, Robert V, 741
Hasket, Robert V, 742
Hasket, Robert E. V, 742
Hasket, Robert Evans V, 741
Hasket, Ruth I, 141
Hasket, Sarah I, 34
Hasket, Sarah I, 52
Hasket, Sarah I, 100
Hasket, Sarah I, 141
Hasket, Sarah I, 184
Hasket, Sarah I, 1020
Hasket, Sarah I, 1027
Hasket, Sarah I, 1030
Hasket, Silas I, 100
Hasket, Silas I, 141
Hasket, Silas I, 193
Hasket, Susan V, 69
Hasket, Susanna I, 241
Hasket, Susannah I, 141
Hasket, Susannah V, 69
Hasket, Susannah V, 971
Hasket, Susannah V, 979
Hasket, Thomas I, 34
Hasket, Thomas I, 52
Hasket, Thomas I, 100
Hasket, Thomas I, 141
Hasket, Thomas I, 271
Hasket, Thomas I, 1020
Hasket, Thomas I, 1030
Hasket, Thomas V, 69
Hasket, Thomas V, 100
Hasket, Thomas V, 741
Hasket, Thomas V, 742
Hasket, Thomas V, 979
Hasket, Thomas Wheaten I, 184
Hasket, Thos. V, 741
Hasket, Thos. V, 742
Hasket, Thos. Ellwood V, 741
Hasket, William I, 100
Hasket, William I, 141
Hasket, William I, 184
Hasket, William I, 194
Hasket, William I, 271
Hasket, William V, 69
Hasket, William H. I, 194
Hasket, William Low I, 184
Hasket, Wm. Lindley V, 741
Haskett, Abigail I, 184
Haskett, Alfred I, 141
Haskett, Allen I, 141
Haskett, Allien I, 141
Haskett, Ann V, 971
Haskett, Asa I, 184
Haskett, Elisabeth I, 141
Haskett, Elizabeth I, 141
Haskett, Elizabeth I, 184
Haskett, Henby I, 184

askett, I. V, 757
askett, Isaac I, 141
askett, Isaac V, 64
askett, Isaac V, 69
askett, Isaac V, 971
askett, Jesse I, 184
askett, Joel V, 971
askett, John I, 184
askett, Joseph I, 1030
askett, Joshua I, 52
askett, Joshua I, 184
askett, Josiah I, 193
askett, Lydia V, 69
askett, Lydia V, 757
askett, Mary I, 184
askett, Mary I, 194
askett, Mary I, 195
askett, Mary V, 798
askett, Mary V, 971
askett, Nathan I, 184
askett, Rachel I, 184
askett, Rachel V, 64
askett, Rachel V, 971
askett, Rebecca V, 69
askett, Silas I, 141
askett, Susannah V, 971
askett, Sylvanus A. I, 184
askett, Thomas I, 141
askett, Thomas I, 184
askett, Thomas I, 271
askett, Thomas I, 1030
askett, Thomas, II I, 184
askett, William I, 271
askings, Mary I, 393
askings, Mary I, 420
askins, ??? III, 152
askins, ??? III, 264
askins, Anna V, 607
askins, Barbara VI, 248
askins, Eli V, 503
askins, Frank VI, 242
askins, Frank VI, 248
askins, Frank W. VI, 248
askins, Hannah V, 503
askins, Henry III, 152
askins, Isaac V, 607
askins, Isabelle VI, 248
askins, John B. III, 152
askins, Joseph V, 503
askins, Josiah V, 607
askins, Margaret L. VI, 242
askins, Margaret L. VI, 248
askins, Mary III, 152
askins, Mary Peterson III, 152
askins, Moses V, 503
askins, Moses VI, 900
askins, Rachel Alma V, 249
askins, Ruth V, 503
askins, Sarah III, 152
askins, Sarah Eliz. III, 264
askins, Sarah Elizabeth III, 152
askins, Thomas C. VI, 248
askit, Abraham I, 141
askit, Ann I, 141
askit, Ann I, 143
askit, Ann I, 194
askit, Ann V, 52
askit, Ann V, 69
askit, Anna I, 194
askit, Anna I, 198
askit, Anthony I, 184
askit, Anthony I, 193
askit, Anthony I, 194
askit, Asa I, 194
askit, Charity V, 69
askit, Daniel Y. I, 194
askit, David I, 194
askit, Davis I, 184
askit, Elisabeth I, 52
askit, Elisabeth I, 53
askit, Elisabeth I, 189
askit, Elisabeth I, 193
askit, Elisabeth I, 194
askit, Elizabeth I, 193
askit, Elizabeth I, 195
askit, Elizabeth E. I, 184
askit, Elvy I, 194
askit, Elwood I, 194
askit, Gulielma I, 184
askit, Gulielma I, 193
Haskit, Hanah Levinae I, 184
Haskit, Hannah I, 128
Haskit, Hannah I, 141
Haskit, Hannah I, 193
Haskit, Hannah I, 194
Haskit, Henby I, 194
Haskit, Henry I, 193
Haskit, Henry I, 194
Haskit, Henry I, 196
Haskit, Isaac V, 69
Haskit, Isabel I, 194
Haskit, Jemima I, 141
Haskit, Jemima I, 193
Haskit, Jemima I, 194
Haskit, Jesse I, 141
Haskit, Jesse I, 193
Haskit, Jesse I, 194
Haskit, John I, 180
Haskit, John I, 184
Haskit, John I, 193
Haskit, John I, 194
Haskit, John F. I, 194
Haskit, John Sinkler I, 184
Haskit, John W. I, 194
Haskit, John, Jr. I, 193
Haskit, Joseph I, 193
Haskit, Joseph I, 194
Haskit, Joseph, Jr. I, 194
Haskit, Joshua I, 52
Haskit, Joshua I, 53
Haskit, Joshua I, 193
Haskit, Joshua I, 194
Haskit, Josiah I, 193
Haskit, Josiah I, 200
Haskit, Lear I, 194
Haskit, Lyda I, 190
Haskit, Lyda I, 194
Haskit, Lyddia I, 141
Haskit, Lydia I, 184
Haskit, Lydia V, 69
Haskit, Margaret I, 184
Haskit, Margaret I, 194
Haskit, Martha Ann I, 184
Haskit, Martha Ann I, 194
Haskit, Martha Carolin I, 184
Haskit, Mary I, 193
Haskit, Mary I, 194
Haskit, Mary V, 52
Haskit, Mary V, 69
Haskit, Mary A. I, 184
Haskit, Mary Ann I, 193
Haskit, Mary Ann I, 194
Haskit, Mary, Jr. I, 194
Haskit, Maza I, 194
Haskit, Miles I, 193
Haskit, Miles I, 194
Haskit, Morgan I, 194
Haskit, Nancy I, 194
Haskit, Nathan I, 194
Haskit, Palan I, 194
Haskit, Penninah I, 194
Haskit, Pininah I, 200
Haskit, Pinnah I, 193
Haskit, Pleasant I, 193
Haskit, Pleasant I, 195
Haskit, Rachel I, 193
Haskit, Rachel I, 196
Haskit, Ralph I, 194
Haskit, Ruth I, 152
Haskit, Ruth I, 194
Haskit, Ruth I, 196
Haskit, Samuel Y. I, 184
Haskit, Sarah I, 193
Haskit, Sarah I, 194
Haskit, Sarah I, 197
Haskit, Silas I, 141
Haskit, Silas I, 152
Haskit, Silas I, 193
Haskit, Susanna I, 241
Haskit, Thomas I, 141
Haskit, Thomas I, 193
Haskit, Thomas I, 194
Haskit, Thomas V, 52
Haskit, Thomas V, 69
Haskit, William I, 128
Haskit, William I, 141
Haskit, William I, 180
Haskit, William I, 184
Haskit, William I, 193
Haskit, William I, 194
Haskit, William V, 69
Haskit, William H. I, 194
Haskit, William, Jr. I, 194
Haskitt, Alice I, 183
Haskitt, Ann I, 191
Haskitt, Ann I, 194
Haskitt, Anna I, 194
Haskitt, Edith I, 184
Haskitt, Elisabeth I, 49
Haskitt, Elisabeth I, 52
Haskitt, Elisabeth I, 141
Haskitt, Henry I, 184
Haskitt, Isbel I, 184
Haskitt, Jemima I, 193
Haskitt, Jemima I, 695
Haskitt, Jesse I, 141
Haskitt, Jesse I, 159
Haskitt, Jesse I, 184
Haskitt, Joseph I, 184
Haskitt, Joshua I, 184
Haskitt, Leah I, 184
Haskitt, Lear I, 194
Haskitt, Mary I, 184
Haskitt, Mary I, 194
Haskitt, Mary I, 199
Haskitt, Miles I, 184
Haskitt, Miriam I, 52
Haskitt, Miriam I, 141
Haskitt, Miriam I, 159
Haskitt, Miriam I, 184
Haskitt, Nancy I, 194
Haskitt, Nancy I, 196
Haskitt, Sarah I, 141
Haskitt, Sarah I, 149
Haskitt, Thomas I, 194
Haskitt, William I, 194
Hasley, Ezekiel I, 912
Hasley, John I, 880
Hasley, Laura IV, 1319
Hasley, Mary I, 812
Hassam, Elizabeth VI, 663
Hassard, Aaron II, 372
Hassel, E. W. I, 814
Hassel, Elisha W. I, 814
Hassel, Emaline I, 814
Hassel, John W. I, 814
Hassel, Laura D. I, 814
Hassel, Laura D. I, 823
Hassel, Webster I, 814
Hasserd, Hannah II, 372
Hassert, Aaron II, 372
Hassert, Arent II, 372
Hassert, Hannah II, 372
Hassert, Jane II, 372
Hassert, Martha II, 372
Hassinger, ??? III, 152
Hassinger, ??? III, 298
Hassinger, Hazel III, 152
Hassinger, Hazel D. III, 152
Hassinger, Hezel D. III, 298
Hassong, Emma IV, 1319
Hastens, Joshua I, 717
Haster, Joseph V, 71
Hasting, Martha VI, 897
Hasting, Mary VI, 929
Hasting, Mary J. V, 244
Hasting, Melissa V, 244
Hasting, Reese VI, 398
Hasting, William V, 742
Hasting, Zachariah VI, 929
Hastings, Abraham VI, 398
Hastings, Alice III, 82
Hastings, Alice III, 152
Hastings, Alice D. VI, 747
Hastings, Ann I, 289
Hastings, Ann I, 307
Hastings, Ann I, 314
Hastings, Ann I, 699
Hastings, Ann I, 717
Hastings, Ann II, 545
Hastings, Ann V, 69
Hastings, Ann V, 742
Hastings, Ann Sarah I, 307
Hastings, Ann, Jr. I, 717
Hastings, Atta V, 1000
Hastings, Cassius V, 334
Hastings, Catharine I, 699
Hastings, Catharine I, 717
Hastings, Catharine V, 742
Hastings, Catherine V, 69
Hastings, Charity VI, 398
Hastings, Charles H. VI, 747
Hastings, Charles R. IV, 1365
Hastings, Easter I, 302
Hastings, Easter I, 307
Hastings, Easter I, 318
Hastings, Edith V, 1000
Hastings, Edith VI, 732
Hastings, Edith VI, 747
Hastings, Elba V, 1000
Hastings, Eliza II, 545
Hastings, Elizabeth II, 372
Hastings, Elizabeth II, 450
Hastings, Elizabeth II, 545
Hastings, Elizabeth II, 546
Hastings, Elizabeth IV, 519
Hastings, Elizabeth IV, 529
Hastings, Emma V, 680
Hastings, Ernest C. III, 152
Hastings, Ernest E. I, 1154
Hastings, Ernest E. III, 152
Hastings, Esther I, 307
Hastings, Esther II, 545
Hastings, Eunice I, 699
Hastings, Eunice I, 717
Hastings, Eunice V, 742
Hastings, George II, 545
Hastings, George Sands VI, 732
Hastings, George Sands VI, 747
Hastings, Gertrude R. IV, 1319
Hastings, Grace II, 372
Hastings, Grace II, 545
Hastings, Grace Molmes IV, 219
Hastings, Hannah II, 372
Hastings, Hannah II, 545
Hastings, Hannah II, 669
Hastings, Hannah IV, 148
Hastings, Hannah IV, 150
Hastings, Hannah VI, 398
Hastings, Hannah VI, 420
Hastings, Horton Howard IV, 148
Hastings, Isaac F. V, 1000
Hastings, Jacob VI, 398
Hastings, Job VI, 398
Hastings, Job VI, 444
Hastings, John II, 372
Hastings, John II, 450
Hastings, John II, 669
Hastings, John S. III, 82
Hastings, John S. III, 152
Hastings, Joseph I, 717
Hastings, Joseph II, 545
Hastings, Joseph V, 69
Hastings, Joseph Gray II, 545
Hastings, Joshua I, 289
Hastings, Joshua I, 717
Hastings, Joshua II, 372
Hastings, Joshua II, 545
Hastings, Joshua II, 614
Hastings, Joshua Sr. I, 314
Hastings, Joshua, Sr. I, 307
Hastings, Luzena S. B. I, 1154
Hastings, Martha II, 545
Hastings, Martha II, 614
Hastings, Martha II, 657
Hastings, Martha J. V, 334
Hastings, Mary I, 307
Hastings, Mary I, 717
Hastings, Mary II, 372
Hastings, Mary II, 535
Hastings, Mary II, 545
Hastings, Mary VI, 387
Hastings, Mary VI, 398
Hastings, Mary VI, 444
Hastings, Matilda L. III, 82
Hastings, Matilda L. III, 152
Hastings, Melissa V, 244
Hastings, Milicent I, 717
Hastings, Nancey I, 699
Hastings, Nancy I, 717
Hastings, Reese VI, 398
Hastings, Samuel II, 372
Hastings, Samuel II, 545
Hastings, Samuel II, 546
Hastings, Samuel II, 657
Hastings, Sarah I, 307
Hastings, Sarah I, 313
Hastings, Sarah I, 699
Hastings, Sarah I, 717
Hastings, Sarah II, 545
Hastings, Sarah V, 69
Hastings, Sarah V, 742
Hastings, Sarah VI, 385
Hastings, Sarah VI, 398
Hastings, Seth G. V, 1000
Hastings, Susan V, 334
Hastings, Susannah II, 545
Hastings, Thomas II, 372
Hastings, Unice V, 69
Hastings, Wellmet V, 69
Hastings, Wellmet V, 742
Hastings, Welmet I, 699
Hastings, Wilber V, 334
Hastings, Wilbur V, 334
Hastings, William I, 699
Hastings, William I, 717
Hastings, William I, 1154
Hastings, William II, 372
Hastings, William V, 69
Hastings, William V, 742
Hastings, William P. III, 152
Hastings, William W. III, 152
Hastings, Willie W. I, 1154
Hastings, Wm. II, 545
Hastings, Wm. P. III, 152
Hastins, Ann V, 69
Hastins, Catherine V, 69
Hastins, Elizabeth II, 372
Hastins, Hannah II, 372
Hastins, John II, 372
Hastins, Joshua II, 372
Hastins, Mary II, 372
Hastins, Samuel II, 372
Hastins, Sarah V, 69
Hastins, Unice V, 69
Hastins, Wellmet V, 69
Haston, Frances VI, 929
Haston, John VI, 929
Hatch, Andrew MacConnell VI, 747
Hatch, Isaac III, 152
Hatch, Isaac III, 365
Hatch, Isaac S. III, 152
Hatch, Jane VI, 109
Hatch, Jane VI, 113
Hatch, John E. IV, 219
Hatch, Julia V, 1000
Hatch, Katherine VI, 747
Hatch, Latitia III, 152
Hatch, Lida IV, 219
Hatch, Margaret Jane V, 742
Hatch, Mary Crete VI, 747
Hatch, Mary W. III, 152
Hatch, Ora B. V, 624
Hatch, Phebe III, 152
Hatch, Phebe III, 365
Hatch, Samuel W. III, 152
Hatch, Thomas I, 336
Hatch, Timothy V, 1000
Hatcheer, James VI, 679
Hatcher, A. Virginia VI, 647
Hatcher, Abigail IV, 1281
Hatcher, Albert H. VI, 648
Hatcher, Albert M. VI, 930
Hatcher, Albert M. VI, 1004
Hatcher, Alexander M. VI, 930
Hatcher, Allen D. VI, 930
Hatcher, Amanda VI, 631
Hatcher, Amanda VI, 647
Hatcher, Angeline VI, 943
Hatcher, Angeline W. VI, 929
Hatcher, Ann IV, 630
Hatcher, Ann VI, 486
Hatcher, Ann VI, 503
Hatcher, Ann VI, 634
Hatcher, Ann VI, 647
Hatcher, Ann VI, 709
Hatcher, Ann VI, 931
Hatcher, Ann VI, 969
Hatcher, Ann VI, 1002
Hatcher, Anna IV, 615
Hatcher, Anna IV, 631
Hatcher, Anna VI, 647
Hatcher, Anna VI, 693
Hatcher, Anna VI, 929
Hatcher, Anne VI, 970
Hatcher, Archd. VI, 970
Hatcher, Archd. VI, 973
Hatcher, Archd. VI, 1004
Hatcher, Archibald VI, 905
Hatcher, Archibald VI, 930
Hatcher, Archibald P. VI, 929
Hatcher, Ben VI, 924
Hatcher, Bengeman VI, 873
Hatcher, Benjamin VI, 146
Hatcher, Benjamin VI, 876
Hatcher, Benjamin VI, 915
Hatcher, Benjamin VI, 930
Hatcher, Benjamin VI, 995
Hatcher, Betsy VI, 929
Hatcher, Betsy Rucker VI, 929
Hatcher, Caleb H. VI, 929
Hatcher, Calistia VI, 930
Hatcher, Caroline VI, 929
Hatcher, Caroline M. VI, 941
Hatcher, Cassandra VI, 971
Hatcher, Catharine VI, 647
Hatcher, Catharine VI, 648
Hatcher, Catharine VI, 684
Hatcher, Catharine VI, 693
Hatcher, Catharine VI, 698
Hatcher, Catharine VI, 929
Hatcher, Catharine VI, 970
Hatcher, Catherine VI, 503
Hatcher, Catherine VI, 538
Hatcher, Catherine VI, 642
Hatcher, Catherine VI, 678
Hatcher, Catherine, Jr. VI, 503
Hatcher, Cealy VI, 908
Hatcher, Cele VI, 929
Hatcher, Cincinnatus VI, 970
Hatcher, Clara L. VI, 648
Hatcher, Clara Louisa VI, 621
Hatcher, Clara Louisa VI, 628
Hatcher, Clara Louisa VI, 648
Hatcher, Daniel IV, 219
Hatcher, Daniel Hains IV, 219
Hatcher, Daniel Hains VI, 647
Hatcher, David B. VI, 929
Hatcher, Demaris A. VI, 977
Hatcher, Deme VI, 908
Hatcher, E. H. VI, 1004
Hatcher, Ed. H. VI, 893
Hatcher, Edith VI, 503
Hatcher, Edith VI, 647
Hatcher, Edward VI, 893
Hatcher, Edward VI, 929
Hatcher, Edward H. VI, 977
Hatcher, Edwin M. VI, 929
Hatcher, Eli VI, 929
Hatcher, Elijah IV, 335
Hatcher, Elijah VI, 621
Hatcher, Elijah VI, 647
Hatcher, Elijah VI, 648

Hatcher, Elijah VI, 929
Hatcher, Eliza VI, 930
Hatcher, Eliza Ann IV, 631
Hatcher, Elizabeth IV, 197
Hatcher, Elizabeth IV, 219
Hatcher, Elizabeth VI, 313
Hatcher, Elizabeth VI, 503
Hatcher, Elizabeth VI, 647
Hatcher, Elizabeth VI, 724
Hatcher, Elizabeth VI, 914
Hatcher, Elizabeth VI, 929
Hatcher, Elizabeth VI, 930
Hatcher, Elizabeth A. VI, 930
Hatcher, Elizabeth N. VI, 929
Hatcher, Emily A. VI, 930
Hatcher, Emsey VI, 639
Hatcher, Emsey VI, 647
Hatcher, Esther IV, 1281
Hatcher, Farley VI, 952
Hatcher, Florentine M. VI, 929
Hatcher, Frances B. VI, 929
Hatcher, George VI, 503
Hatcher, George VI, 584
Hatcher, Gourley R. VI, 647
Hatcher, Granville L. VI, 930
Hatcher, Halley Francis VI, 926
Hatcher, Hannah IV, 84
Hatcher, Hannah IV, 91
Hatcher, Hannah IV, 630
Hatcher, Hannah IV, 631
Hatcher, Hannah IV, 821
Hatcher, Hannah VI, 647
Hatcher, Hannah VI, 648
Hatcher, Hannah VI, 679
Hatcher, Hannah VI, 694
Hatcher, Hardway VI, 892
Hatcher, Hardway VI, 929
Hatcher, Henry VI, 823
Hatcher, Henry VI, 893
Hatcher, Henry VI, 894
Hatcher, Henry VI, 929
Hatcher, Henry VI, 930
Hatcher, Henry VI, 931
Hatcher, Henry VI, 941
Hatcher, Henry VI, 970
Hatcher, Henry VI, 977
Hatcher, Henry VI, 987
Hatcher, Henry VI, 991
Hatcher, Henry VI, 1002
Hatcher, Henry VI, 1004
Hatcher, Henry VI, 1018
Hatcher, Henry M. VI, 929
Hatcher, Hillary VI, 929
Hatcher, Hnery VI, 1013
Hatcher, Hope IV, 1281
Hatcher, Isaac IV, 219
Hatcher, Isaac VI, 313
Hatcher, Isaac VI, 338
Hatcher, Isaac VI, 503
Hatcher, Isaac VI, 647
Hatcher, Isaac VI, 649
Hatcher, Isaac VI, 693
Hatcher, Isaac VI, 854
Hatcher, J. VI, 888
Hatcher, J. R. VI, 951
Hatcher, Jacob W. VI, 930
Hatcher, James IV, 630
Hatcher, James IV, 631
Hatcher, James IV, 821
Hatcher, James VI, 313
Hatcher, James VI, 399
Hatcher, James VI, 503
Hatcher, James VI, 538
Hatcher, James VI, 642
Hatcher, James VI, 647
Hatcher, James VI, 678
Hatcher, James VI, 684
Hatcher, James VI, 693
Hatcher, James VI, 698
Hatcher, James, Jr. VI, 503
Hatcher, James, Jr. VI, 647
Hatcher, Jane IV, 37
Hatcher, Jane IV, 332
Hatcher, Jane IV, 336
Hatcher, Jane IV, 407
Hatcher, Jane VI, 621
Hatcher, Jane VI, 648
Hatcher, Jenny VI, 940
Hatcher, Jeremiah VI, 870
Hatcher, Jeremiah VI, 871
Hatcher, Jeremiah VI, 873
Hatcher, Jeremiah VI, 874
Hatcher, Jeremiah VI, 875
Hatcher, Jeremiah VI, 877
Hatcher, Jeremiah VI, 879
Hatcher, Jeremiah VI, 881
Hatcher, Jeremiah VI, 883
Hatcher, Jeremiah VI, 884
Hatcher, Jeremiah VI, 885
Hatcher, Jeremiah VI, 888
Hatcher, Jeremiah VI, 889
Hatcher, Jeremiah VI, 890
Hatcher, Jeremiah VI, 891
Hatcher, Jeremiah VI, 892
Hatcher, Jeremiah VI, 893
Hatcher, Jeremiah VI, 896
Hatcher, Jeremiah VI, 899
Hatcher, Jeremiah VI, 900
Hatcher, Jeremiah VI, 902
Hatcher, Jeremiah VI, 903
Hatcher, Jeremiah VI, 907
Hatcher, Jeremiah VI, 908
Hatcher, Jeremiah VI, 911
Hatcher, Jeremiah VI, 912
Hatcher, Jeremiah VI, 913
Hatcher, Jeremiah VI, 915
Hatcher, Jeremiah VI, 918
Hatcher, Jeremiah VI, 919
Hatcher, Jeremiah VI, 920
Hatcher, Jeremiah VI, 922
Hatcher, Jeremiah VI, 923
Hatcher, Jeremiah VI, 924
Hatcher, Jeremiah VI, 925
Hatcher, Jeremiah VI, 926
Hatcher, Jeremiah VI, 927
Hatcher, Jeremiah VI, 928
Hatcher, Jeremiah VI, 929
Hatcher, Jeremiah VI, 930
Hatcher, Jeremiah VI, 931
Hatcher, Jeremiah VI, 936
Hatcher, Jeremiah VI, 937
Hatcher, Jeremiah VI, 938
Hatcher, Jeremiah VI, 939
Hatcher, Jeremiah VI, 940
Hatcher, Jeremiah VI, 942
Hatcher, Jeremiah VI, 945
Hatcher, Jeremiah VI, 947
Hatcher, Jeremiah VI, 950
Hatcher, Jeremiah VI, 951
Hatcher, Jeremiah VI, 952
Hatcher, Jeremiah VI, 955
Hatcher, Jeremiah VI, 959
Hatcher, Jeremiah VI, 961
Hatcher, Jeremiah VI, 965
Hatcher, Jeremiah VI, 966
Hatcher, Jeremiah VI, 967
Hatcher, Jeremiah VI, 970
Hatcher, Jeremiah VI, 971
Hatcher, Jeremiah VI, 972
Hatcher, Jeremiah VI, 973
Hatcher, Jeremiah VI, 977
Hatcher, Jeremiah VI, 978
Hatcher, Jeremiah VI, 979
Hatcher, Jeremiah VI, 981
Hatcher, Jeremiah VI, 983
Hatcher, Jeremiah VI, 987
Hatcher, Jeremiah VI, 988
Hatcher, Jeremiah VI, 990
Hatcher, Jeremiah VI, 992
Hatcher, Jeremiah VI, 993
Hatcher, Jeremiah VI, 995
Hatcher, Jeremiah VI, 996
Hatcher, Jeremiah VI, 997
Hatcher, Jeremiah VI, 998
Hatcher, Jeremiah VI, 1000
Hatcher, Jeremiah VI, 1002
Hatcher, Jeremiah VI, 1003
Hatcher, Jeremiah VI, 1004
Hatcher, Jeremiah VI, 1005
Hatcher, Jeremiah VI, 1006
Hatcher, Jeremiah VI, 1009
Hatcher, Jeremiah VI, 1010
Hatcher, Jeremiah VI, 1011
Hatcher, Jeremiah VI, 1012
Hatcher, Jeremiah VI, 1015
Hatcher, Jeremiah VI, 1016
Hatcher, Jeremiah VI, 1018
Hatcher, Jeremiah VI, 1019
Hatcher, Jeremiah VI, 1020
Hatcher, Jeremiah VI, 1021
Hatcher, Jeremiah G. VI, 923
Hatcher, Jeremiah G. VI, 929
Hatcher, Jesse IV, 630
Hatcher, Jesse VI, 647
Hatcher, Jno. A. VI, 929
Hatcher, Joanna Elizabet VI, 929
Hatcher, John IV, 37
Hatcher, John IV, 148
Hatcher, John IV, 605
Hatcher, John IV, 630
Hatcher, John IV, 631
Hatcher, John IV, 645
Hatcher, John VI, 503
Hatcher, John VI, 514
Hatcher, John VI, 616
Hatcher, John VI, 648
Hatcher, John VI, 649
Hatcher, John VI, 704
Hatcher, John VI, 929
Hatcher, John C. VI, 929
Hatcher, John F. VI, 621
Hatcher, John F. VI, 628
Hatcher, John F. VI, 648
Hatcher, John, Jr. VI, 647
Hatcher, Jonah VI, 648
Hatcher, Jonah VI, 649
Hatcher, Jonathan VI, 503
Hatcher, Jonathan VI, 823
Hatcher, Joseph IV, 631
Hatcher, Joseph VI, 503
Hatcher, Joseph VI, 648
Hatcher, Joseph VI, 649
Hatcher, Joseph VI, 694
Hatcher, Joshua IV, 37
Hatcher, Joshua IV, 137
Hatcher, Joshua IV, 219
Hatcher, Joshua IV, 332
Hatcher, Joshua IV, 336
Hatcher, Joshua IV, 407
Hatcher, Joshua IV, 630
Hatcher, Joshua IV, 631
Hatcher, Joshua IV, 1281
Hatcher, Joshua VI, 503
Hatcher, Joshua VI, 644
Hatcher, Joshua VI, 647
Hatcher, Joshua VI, 648
Hatcher, Joshua VI, 704
Hatcher, Judith VI, 823
Hatcher, Judith VI, 969
Hatcher, Judith M. VI, 970
Hatcher, Julia Kennedy VI, 929
Hatcher, Julianna VI, 897
Hatcher, Julius VI, 897
Hatcher, Julius VI, 929
Hatcher, Julius VI, 943
Hatcher, Julius VI, 970
Hatcher, Julius VI, 1002
Hatcher, Julius H. VI, 929
Hatcher, Julius H. VI, 970
Hatcher, Julius W. VI, 929
Hatcher, Julius, Jr. VI, 929
Hatcher, Julius, Sr. VI, 892
Hatcher, Julius, Sr. VI, 1002
Hatcher, Kitty F. VI, 929
Hatcher, Laura VI, 648
Hatcher, Laura S. VI, 647
Hatcher, Louisa J. VI, 929
Hatcher, Lucy VI, 892
Hatcher, Lucy VI, 929
Hatcher, Lucy VI, 1007
Hatcher, Lydia IV, 631
Hatcher, Lydia VI, 313
Hatcher, Lydia VI, 648
Hatcher, Lydia VI, 681
Hatcher, Lydia Ann IV, 631
Hatcher, Lydia Ann IV, 666
Hatcher, Mahlon IV, 37
Hatcher, Mahlon IV, 148
Hatcher, Mahlon VI, 648
Hatcher, Margaret VI, 929
Hatcher, Margaret VI, 1004
Hatcher, Margarett VI, 987
Hatcher, Margery VI, 503
Hatcher, Margery VI, 647
Hatcher, Margery VI, 648
Hatcher, Margery VI, 649
Hatcher, Margery VI, 682
Hatcher, Margery VI, 698
Hatcher, Martha VI, 929
Hatcher, Martha VI, 995
Hatcher, Mary IV, 37
Hatcher, Mary IV, 84
Hatcher, Mary IV, 91
Hatcher, Mary IV, 197
Hatcher, Mary IV, 219
Hatcher, Mary IV, 332
Hatcher, Mary IV, 335
Hatcher, Mary IV, 339
Hatcher, Mary IV, 627
Hatcher, Mary IV, 629
Hatcher, Mary IV, 630
Hatcher, Mary IV, 631
Hatcher, Mary VI, 313
Hatcher, Mary VI, 493
Hatcher, Mary VI, 503
Hatcher, Mary VI, 530
Hatcher, Mary VI, 642
Hatcher, Mary VI, 644
Hatcher, Mary VI, 647
Hatcher, Mary VI, 648
Hatcher, Mary VI, 649
Hatcher, Mary VI, 679
Hatcher, Mary VI, 689
Hatcher, Mary VI, 694
Hatcher, Mary VI, 873
Hatcher, Mary VI, 930
Hatcher, Mary A. VI, 929
Hatcher, Mary Ann IV, 630
Hatcher, Mary M. VI, 929
Hatcher, Mary M. VI, 930
Hatcher, Mary, Jr. VI, 563
Hatcher, Mary, Jr. VI, 704
Hatcher, Milly VI, 930
Hatcher, Nancy VI, 648
Hatcher, Nancy VI, 823
Hatcher, Nancy VI, 891
Hatcher, Nancy VI, 929
Hatcher, Nancy VI, 1002
Hatcher, Nancy E. VI, 930
Hatcher, Nathan IV, 630
Hatcher, Nelly I, 543
Hatcher, Nelson VI, 819
Hatcher, Noah VI, 616
Hatcher, Noah VI, 648
Hatcher, Pamelia VI, 908
Hatcher, Peggy VI, 1002
Hatcher, Peyton VI, 970
Hatcher, Peyton VI, 1003
Hatcher, Peyton VI, 1019
Hatcher, Phebe VI, 930
Hatcher, Polly VI, 929
Hatcher, Polly VI, 1002
Hatcher, Polly VI, 1018
Hatcher, Prudence VI, 648
Hatcher, Rachel IV, 37
Hatcher, Rachel IV, 219
Hatcher, Rachel IV, 335
Hatcher, Rachel IV, 627
Hatcher, Rachel IV, 630
Hatcher, Rachel IV, 631
Hatcher, Rachel IV, 645
Hatcher, Rachel VI, 313
Hatcher, Rachel VI, 503
Hatcher, Rachel VI, 616
Hatcher, Rachel VI, 647
Hatcher, Rachel VI, 648
Hatcher, Rachel VI, 649
Hatcher, Rachel VI, 693
Hatcher, Rebecca IV, 219
Hatcher, Rebecca IV, 605
Hatcher, Rebecca IV, 630
Hatcher, Rebecca IV, 631
Hatcher, Rebecca IV, 645
Hatcher, Rebecca VI, 503
Hatcher, Rebecca VI, 646
Hatcher, Rebecca VI, 647
Hatcher, Rebecca VI, 660
Hatcher, Rebecca VI, 679
Hatcher, Rebecca VI, 680
Hatcher, Rebecca VI, 682
Hatcher, Rebecca VI, 693
Hatcher, Rebecca VI, 705
Hatcher, Rebecca VI, 929
Hatcher, Rebecca VI, 988
Hatcher, Rebecca M. VI, 690
Hatcher, Rebecca Mary VI, 648
Hatcher, Rebecca Mary VI, 681
Hatcher, Rebecca Mary VI, 689
Hatcher, Rebeccah VI, 649
Hatcher, Rebeccah VI, 683
Hatcher, Rebeckah VI, 647
Hatcher, Rebeckah VI, 648
Hatcher, Rebekah VI, 503
Hatcher, Rebekah VI, 539
Hatcher, Rebekah VI, 625
Hatcher, Rebekah VI, 679
Hatcher, Rebekah VI, 684
Hatcher, Rhoda VI, 952
Hatcher, Richard VI, 969
Hatcher, Robert VI, 908
Hatcher, Ruth IV, 605
Hatcher, Ruth IV, 630
Hatcher, Ruth IV, 821
Hatcher, Ruth IV, 1281
Hatcher, Ruth IV, 1296
Hatcher, Ruth VI, 649
Hatcher, Ruth Hannah VI, 648
Hatcher, Ruth Hannah VI, 716
Hatcher, Salinia VI, 897
Hatcher, Salley VI, 931
Hatcher, Sally VI, 931
Hatcher, Samuel IV, 219
Hatcher, Samuel IV, 630
Hatcher, Samuel IV, 631
Hatcher, Samuel IV, 1281
Hatcher, Samuel VI, 644
Hatcher, Samuel VI, 647
Hatcher, Samuel VI, 648
Hatcher, Samuel VI, 649
Hatcher, Samuel VI, 689
Hatcher, Samuel VI, 693
Hatcher, Samuel VI, 873
Hatcher, Samuel VI, 924
Hatcher, Samuel VI, 929
Hatcher, Samuel VI, 967
Hatcher, Samuel VI, 988
Hatcher, Samuel VI, 995
Hatcher, Samuel VI, 1012
Hatcher, Sarah IV, 37
Hatcher, Sarah IV, 335
Hatcher, Sarah IV, 336
Hatcher, Sarah IV, 627
Hatcher, Sarah IV, 630
Hatcher, Sarah VI, 503
Hatcher, Sarah VI, 514
Hatcher, Sarah VI, 616
Hatcher, Sarah VI, 644
Hatcher, Sarah VI, 647
Hatcher, Sarah VI, 648
Hatcher, Sarah VI, 649
Hatcher, Sarah VI, 689
Hatcher, Sarah VI, 693
Hatcher, Sarah VI, 704
Hatcher, Sarah VI, 708
Hatcher, Sarah VI, 872
Hatcher, Sarah Ann VI, 644
Hatcher, Sarah Ann VI, 648
Hatcher, Sarah Ann VI, 704
Hatcher, Sarah Borling VI, 929
Hatcher, Sarah E. VI, 648
Hatcher, Sarah Ellen VI, 648
Hatcher, Sarah Ellen VI, 652
Hatcher, Sarah Ellen VI, 704
Hatcher, Sophia VI, 910
Hatcher, Sophia VI, 929
Hatcher, Spencer VI, 929
Hatcher, Susan VI, 1003
Hatcher, Susanna VI, 924
Hatcher, Tabitha VI, 995
Hatcher, Tempey VI, 929
Hatcher, Theodacia C. N. VI, 9
Hatcher, Thomas IV, 37
Hatcher, Thomas IV, 605
Hatcher, Thomas IV, 630
Hatcher, Thomas IV, 631
Hatcher, Thomas IV, 821
Hatcher, Thomas VI, 503
Hatcher, Thomas VI, 539
Hatcher, Thomas VI, 648
Hatcher, Thomas VI, 649
Hatcher, Thomas VI, 650
Hatcher, Thomas VI, 683
Hatcher, Thomas VI, 687
Hatcher, Thomas VI, 693
Hatcher, Thomas VI, 929
Hatcher, Thomas Elwood VI, 6
Hatcher, Thomas Hardaway VI, 1012
Hatcher, Thomas, Jr. VI, 649
Hatcher, Thos. IV, 630
Hatcher, Ulysses VI, 929
Hatcher, Uriah VI, 891
Hatcher, Uriah VI, 929
Hatcher, Uriah VI, 943
Hatcher, Uriah VI, 970
Hatcher, Uriah VI, 971
Hatcher, Uriah VI, 1003
Hatcher, Ward VI, 929
Hatcher, Ward VI, 969
Hatcher, William IV, 37
Hatcher, William IV, 335
Hatcher, William IV, 627
Hatcher, William IV, 630
Hatcher, William VI, 313
Hatcher, William VI, 503
Hatcher, William VI, 570
Hatcher, William VI, 647
Hatcher, William VI, 648
Hatcher, William VI, 649
Hatcher, William VI, 929
Hatcher, William VI, 931
Hatcher, William D. VI, 1014
Hatcher, William L. VI, 929
Hatcher, William L. VI, 991
Hatcher, William, Jr. IV, 631
Hatcher, William, Jr. VI, 503
Hatcher, William, Jr. VI, 530
Hatcher, William, Jr. VI, 563
Hatcher, William, Jr. VI, 649
Hatcher, William, Jr. VI, 704
Hatcher, Wm. IV, 630
Hatcher, Wm. VI, 649
Hatcher, Zedekiah VI, 952
Hatcherm, Jeremiah VI, 1004
Hatchers, Betsey VI, 1002
Hatfield, ??? V, 823
Hatfield, Abel IV, 37
Hatfield, Abel Janney IV, 37
Hatfield, Ann IV, 37
Hatfield, Charity VI, 399
Hatfield, Deborah IV, 37
Hatfield, George II, 545
Hatfield, James IV, 631
Hatfield, John IV, 37
Hatfield, John VI, 68
Hatfield, Jonas IV, 37
Hatfield, Jonas V, 842
Hatfield, Lydia II, 372
Hatfield, Lydia IV, 37
Hatfield, Lydia IV, 46
Hatfield, Martha IV, 37
Hatfield, Mary II, 545
Hatfield, Mary IV, 37
Hatfield, Nathan IV, 37
Hatfield, Rachel IV, 37

tfield, Sarah III, 152
tfield, Sarah V, 842
tfield, Stephen IV, 1365
tfield, Thomas IV, 37
tfield, Thomas V, 842
tfield, Thomas VI, 399
tfield, W. R. V, 742
tfield, William VI, 68
thaway, ??? IV, 219
thaway, Abraham V, 69
thaway, Albert T. IV, 1365
thaway, Alfred IV, 962
thaway, Alfred C. IV, 962
thaway, Alfred C. V, 680
thaway, Alfred Caleb IV, 1236
thaway, Alfred R. IV, 1236
thaway, Alfred R. IV, 1365
thaway, Alfrod C. IV, 962
thaway, Alonzo H. IV, 1365
thaway, Ann V, 175
thaway, Anna IV, 717
thaway, Anna IV, 781
thaway, Benj. III, 341
thaway, Benjamin H. III, 152
thaway, Benoni III, 152
thaway, Benoni III, 156
thaway, Betsy IV, 1236
thaway, Betsy IV, 1241
thaway, Caleb IV, 962
thaway, Caleb IV, 1147
thaway, Caleb IV, 1163
thaway, Caleb IV, 1164
haway, Caleb IV, 1195
thaway, Caleb IV, 1236
thaway, Caleb Alfred IV, 1236
thaway, Caleb, Jr. II, 230
haway, Caleb, Jr. IV, 1163
haway, Caleb, Jr. IV, 1236
thaway, Caroline III, 152
thaway, Caspar Henry IV, 962
thaway, Casper Henry IV, 1236
thaway, Charity IV, 1365
thaway, Charity IV, 1378
thaway, Charity G. IV, 1365
haway, Charles H. IV, 1236
haway, Chas. Henry IV, 1236
thaway, Direxa IV, 1231
thaway, Dorothy IV, 1365
haway, Earnest IV, 962
haway, Edith Alice IV, 962
thaway, Edith Alice IV, 1236
thaway, Edith R. IV, 962
thaway, Edward IV, 1236
haway, Elisabeth Ann IV, 1365
thaway, Elizabeth III, 152
thaway, Elizabeth IV, 1164
haway, Elizabeth IV, 1236
haway, Elizabeth IV, 1363
thaway, Elizabeth IV, 1365
thaway, Esther III, 152
haway, Esther IV, 1189
haway, Esther IV, 1236
thaway, Esther W. IV, 1163
thaway, Esther W. IV, 1164
thaway, Esther W. IV, 1236
haway, Francis Herman IV, 962
thaway, Francis Herman IV, 1236
thaway, Francis W. V, 680
thaway, Garrett V, 175
thaway, Geo. Smith III, 152
thaway, Goldie V, 69
thaway, Grace V, 909
thaway, Hannah III, 173
thaway, Harriet E. III, 152
thaway, Henry IV, 1163
thaway, Henry IV, 1189
thaway, Henry IV, 1236
thaway, Henry B. III, 152
thaway, Ida Eliza IV, 962
thaway, Ida Eliza IV, 1236
thaway, Isaac N. IV, 1164
thaway, Isaac N. IV, 1236
thaway, Isaac N. IV, 1365
thaway, Israel IV, 1163
thaway, Israel IV, 1236
thaway, Ivanetta V, 175
thaway, James IV, 1365
thaway, Jane IV, 1365
thaway, Jane IV, 1386
thaway, John V, 175
thaway, Joshua IV, 1163
thaway, Joshua IV, 1236
thaway, Julia S. IV, 1365
thaway, Lillie V, 909
thaway, Lillie F. V, 909
thaway, Lillie T. V, 909
thaway, Lily T. V, 909
Hathaway, Lydia II, 707
Hathaway, Lydia III, 153
Hathaway, Lydia Ann III, 152
Hathaway, Lydia S. III, 152
Hathaway, Maisey L. VI, 399
Hathaway, Maisy L. VI, 417
Hathaway, Martha V, 909
Hathaway, Martha J. V, 909
Hathaway, Martha T. V, 909
Hathaway, Mary II, 811
Hathaway, Mary III, 152
Hathaway, Mary IV, 1163
Hathaway, Mary IV, 1231
Hathaway, Mary IV, 1236
Hathaway, Mary Elma IV, 1236
Hathaway, Mary Eva IV, 962
Hathaway, Mildred VI, 399
Hathaway, Mildred VI, 417
Hathaway, Minnie V, 680
Hathaway, Minnie R. V, 680
Hathaway, Mrs. ??? IV, 219
Hathaway, Nancy Ann IV, 1236
Hathaway, Nancy Ann IV, 1239
Hathaway, Obed II, 372
Hathaway, Orvel Payne IV, 1365
Hathaway, Pearl V, 69
Hathaway, Peter IV, 1163
Hathaway, Peter IV, 1164
Hathaway, Peter IV, 1236
Hathaway, Peter IV, 1239
Hathaway, Peter IV, 1241
Hathaway, Peter, Sr. IV, 1236
Hathaway, Phebe III, 152
Hathaway, Phebe III, 341
Hathaway, Phebe IV, 1163
Hathaway, Phebe V, 69
Hathaway, Phebe B. IV, 1164
Hathaway, Phebe B. IV, 1236
Hathaway, Phebe B. IV, 1365
Hathaway, Phebe E. IV, 1365
Hathaway, Phebe R. IV, 1163
Hathaway, Phebe R. IV, 1164
Hathaway, Phebe R. IV, 1170
Hathaway, Phebe R. IV, 1236
Hathaway, Phebe R. IV, 1238
Hathaway, Phoebe R. I, 620
Hathaway, Prudence D. IV, 1164
Hathaway, Prudence D. IV, 1236
Hathaway, Prudence D. IV, 1239
Hathaway, Prudence Direxa IV, 1164
Hathaway, Rachel IV, 1147
Hathaway, Rachel IV, 1163
Hathaway, Rachel IV, 1231
Hathaway, Rachel IV, 1236
Hathaway, Rachel IV, 1242
Hathaway, Rachel Jr. IV, 1163
Hathaway, Rachel, Jr. IV, 1195
Hathaway, Richmond IV, 1163
Hathaway, Richmond IV, 1164
Hathaway, Richmond IV, 1236
Hathaway, Richmond IV, 1365
Hathaway, Samuel IV, 1236
Hathaway, Samuel B. IV, 1164
Hathaway, Samuel B. IV, 1236
Hathaway, Samuel B. IV, 1365
Hathaway, Sarah III, 152
Hathaway, Sarah IV, 962
Hathaway, Sarah IV, 1236
Hathaway, Sarah D. IV, 962
Hathaway, Sarah D. IV, 1236
Hathaway, Sarah D. IV, 1281
Hathaway, Seneca James IV, 1164
Hathaway, Smith III, 152
Hathaway, Stephen III, 152
Hathaway, Stephen, Jr. III, 152
Hathaway, Susan IV, 1147
Hathaway, Susan IV, 1163
Hathaway, Susan IV, 1164
Hathaway, Susan IV, 1236
Hathaway, Susan B. III, 152
Hathaway, Sylvester R. IV, 1365
Hathaway, Thomas IV, 1164
Hathaway, Thomas Edson VI, 399
Hathaway, Thomas Edson VI, 417
Hathaway, Thomas F. IV, 1236
Hathaway, Thomas T. IV, 1236
Hathaway, Thomas W. IV, 1163
Hathaway, William IV, 1163
Hathaway, William IV, 1236
Hathaway, William IV, 1365
Hathaway, William A. IV, 962
Hathaway, William P. IV, 1236
Hathaway, William P. IV, 1365
Hathaway, William S. III, 153
Hathaway, Wm. V, 909
Hathaway, Wm. A. IV, 962
Hathaway, Wm. Baxter V, 909
Hathaway, Wm. E. IV, 1236
Hathaway, Wm. E. V, 909
Hathaway, Wm. P. IV, 1236
Hathaway, Wm. Penn IV, 1163
Hathaway, Wm. Penn IV, 1164
Hathborn, Hannah I, 1048
Hathborn, Hannah I, 1050
Hatkinson, Ann II, 176
Hatkinson, Elisabeth II, 545
Hatkinson, Elizabeth II, 176
Hatkinson, Elizabeth II, 230
Hatkinson, Elizabeth II, 545
Hatkinson, Hinchman II, 176
Hatkinson, John II, 176
Hatkinson, John II, 230
Hatkinson, John II, 372
Hatkinson, John II, 545
Hatkinson, Joseph II, 176
Hatkinson, Joseph II, 545
Hatkinson, Martha II, 545
Hatkinson, Mary II, 176
Hatkinson, Rachel II, 176
Hatkinson, Rachel II, 372
Hatkinson, Rachel II, 451
Hatkinson, Rachel II, 545
Hatkinson, Wd. Elizabeth II, 176
Hatten, Ann V, 69
Hatten, Anna IV, 1164
Hatten, Annie Marie IV, 1164
Hatten, Bertha IV, 1164
Hatten, Chloe IV, 1164
Hatten, Clifton IV, 1164
Hatten, Delilah IV, 1164
Hatten, Edmond E. V, 953
Hatten, Edmund E. V, 953
Hatten, Eliza V, 953
Hatten, Elizabeth E. V, 953
Hatten, Ella G. IV, 1164
Hatten, Ellen IV, 1164
Hatten, Elma Elnora IV, 1164
Hatten, Frances IV, 1164
Hatten, Geo. W. IV, 1164
Hatten, George IV, 1164
Hatten, George W. IV, 1164
Hatten, Harry Lloyd IV, 1164
Hatten, Harvey IV, 1164
Hatten, Hugh W. IV, 1164
Hatten, Imo IV, 1164
Hatten, Imo Martin IV, 1164
Hatten, Josephine IV, 1164
Hatten, Leora IV, 1164
Hatten, Lewis IV, 1164
Hatten, Lorenzo V, 953
Hatten, Lorenzo M. V, 953
Hatten, Margaret V, 953
Hatten, Marian IV, 1164
Hatten, Marion IV, 1164
Hatten, Mary IV, 1161
Hatten, Mary IV, 1164
Hatten, Mary IV, 1173
Hatten, Mary IV, 1195
Hatten, Mary E. IV, 1164
Hatten, Newell, Nora IV, 1164
Hatten, Norma Jean IV, 1164
Hatten, Paul IV, 1164
Hatten, Rilla B. IV, 1164
Hatten, Robert IV, 1164
Hatten, Robert V, 953
Hatten, Robert M. IV, 1164
Hatten, Robert Willets V, 953
Hatten, Robert, Jr. IV, 1164
Hatten, Rosa IV, 1164
Hatten, Rosalene Mary IV, 1164
Hatten, Sarah V, 953
Hatten, Sidney IV, 1164
Hatten, Susannah V, 953
Hatten, Susannah E. V, 953
Hatten, Walter IV, 1164
Hatten, Willard IV, 1164
Hatten, Willard E. IV, 1164
Hatten, Willets V, 953
Hattersley, John II, 119
Hattfield, Charity VI, 399
Hattfield, Charity VI, 414
Hattfield, Elizabeth VI, 503
Hattfield, Elizabeth VI, 504
Hattfield, George II, 545
Hattfield, Jno. VI, 504
Hattfield, John Keziah VI, 504
Hattfield, Keziah VI, 504
Hattfield, Martha VI, 504
Hattfield, Rachel VI, 504
Hattfield, Tabitha VI, 504
Hattfield, Thomas VI, 504
Hattie Belle, Mehetable I, 339
Hatton, Ann V, 69
Hatton, Ann V, 70
Hatton, Ann V, 88
Hatton, Anna IV, 1164
Hatton, Anna V, 88
Hatton, Bertha IV, 1164
Hatton, Chalkley II, 873
Hatton, Chloe IV, 1164
Hatton, Clifton IV, 1164
Hatton, Constance III, 153
Hatton, Daisy Georgia III, 414
Hatton, Daisy Georgia III, 442
Hatton, Daisy Georgia III, 483
Hatton, Daisy Georgia III, 496
Hatton, Deborah V, 45
Hatton, Deborah V, 69
Hatton, Deborah V, 70
Hatton, Dr. Jos. III, 414
Hatton, Dr. Joseph III, 443
Hatton, Dr. Joseph III, 496
Hatton, Edmond E. V, 69
Hatton, Edmond E. V, 70
Hatton, Edmund E. V, 953
Hatton, Edward III, 153
Hatton, Edward IV, 407
Hatton, Edward V, 69
Hatton, Edward V, 70
Hatton, Edward V, 88
Hatton, Edward V, 94
Hatton, Edward V, 498
Hatton, Edward V, 910
Hatton, Edward VI, 180
Hatton, Edward VI, 248
Hatton, Edward B. V, 69
Hatton, Edward B. V, 70
Hatton, Elisa V, 70
Hatton, Eliza V, 69
Hatton, Eliza V, 70
Hatton, Eliza V, 110
Hatton, Elizabeth II, 372
Hatton, Elizabeth II, 516
Hatton, Elizabeth II, 545
Hatton, Elizabeth V, 69
Hatton, Elizabeth E. V, 70
Hatton, Frances IV, 1164
Hatton, Geo. V, 910
Hatton, George IV, 1164
Hatton, George V, 56
Hatton, George V, 69
Hatton, George V, 70
Hatton, George V, 498
Hatton, George VI, 504
Hatton, Georgianna III, 414
Hatton, Georgianna III, 443
Hatton, Georgianna III, 483
Hatton, Georgianna III, 496
Hatton, Hannah II, 873
Hatton, Hannah V, 69
Hatton, Hannah V, 70
Hatton, Harvey IV, 1164
Hatton, Imo Martin IV, 1164
Hatton, Jane II, 372
Hatton, Jervis V, 70
Hatton, Jervis J. V, 69
Hatton, Jesse VI, 180
Hatton, Joseph III, 483
Hatton, Joseph V, 69
Hatton, Joseph V, 70
Hatton, Leora IV, 1164
Hatton, Lettice II, 545
Hatton, Levi V, 69
Hatton, Levi L. V, 70
Hatton, Lewis IV, 1164
Hatton, Lewis V, 69
Hatton, Lorenzo M. V, 69
Hatton, Lorenzo M. V, 70
Hatton, Lorenzo M. V, 953
Hatton, Margaret V, 56
Hatton, Margaret V, 69
Hatton, Margaret V, 70
Hatton, Margaret V, 910
Hatton, Margaret V, 953
Hatton, Marian IV, 1164
Hatton, Mary IV, 1164
Hatton, Mary VI, 180
Hatton, Mary VI, 248
Hatton, Mary E. V, 69
Hatton, Newell, Nora IV, 1164
Hatton, Paul IV, 1164
Hatton, Peter II, 373
Hatton, Peter VI, 549
Hatton, Phebe T. II, 711
Hatton, Pleasant VI, 180
Hatton, Pleasant VI, 248
Hatton, Rachel V, 69
Hatton, Rachel V, 70
Hatton, Rachel V, 88
Hatton, Rachel V, 94
Hatton, Rachel V, 910
Hatton, Rachel V, 971
Hatton, Robert II, 545
Hatton, Robert III, 153
Hatton, Robert V, 69
Hatton, Robert V, 70
Hatton, Robert V, 910
Hatton, Robert V, 953
Hatton, Robert, Jr. IV, 1164
Hatton, Sarah II, 373
Hatton, Sarah IV, 1253
Hatton, Sarah V, 69
Hatton, Sarah V, 70
Hatton, Sarah VI, 180
Hatton, Sarah VI, 248
Hatton, Sarah VI, 549
Hatton, Susanna V, 69
Hatton, Susanna VI, 180
Hatton, Susanna VI, 304
Hatton, Susannah V, 69
Hatton, Susannah V, 70
Hatton, Susannah V, 953
Hatton, Susannah VI, 248
Hatton, Susannah E. V, 70
Hatton, Thomas II, 372
Hatton, Thomas II, 373
Hatton, Thomas VI, 180
Hatton, Thomas VI, 248
Hatton, Thomas VI, 549
Hatton, Thomas, Jr. VI, 248
Hatton, Thomas, Sr. VI, 248
Hatton, Wd. Elizabeth II, 516
Hatton, Wd. Elizabeth II, 545
Hatton, Willard IV, 1164
Hatton, Willets V, 70
Hatton, William VI, 992
Hatton, Willits V, 69
Hatton, Willits V, 70
Haucher, Leonard V, 244
Haughe, Allen B. V, 624
Haughe, Barnet V, 624
Haughe, Elizabeth V, 624
Haughe, Elizabeth Turner V, 624
Haughe, John A. V, 624
Haughe, Margaret V, 624
Haughe, Nancy V, 624
Haughe, Polly Ann V, 624
Haughe, Stephen S. V, 624
Haughey, Polly Ann V, 624
Haughey, Polly Ann V, 645
Haughn, Willie IV, 1281
Haught, Hazel IV, 1038
Haughton, ??? III, 210
Haughton, ??? III, 381
Haughton, ??? III, 382
Haughton, Agnes V, 906
Haughton, Agnes V, 910
Haughton, Anna V, 910
Haughton, Benjamin V, 910
Haughton, Eliza III, 381
Haughton, Eliza III, 382
Haughton, Eliza L. III, 153
Haughton, Eliza L. III, 210
Haughton, Elizabeth III, 382
Haughton, Elizabeth Agnes V, 894
Haughton, Elwood V, 334
Haughton, Henry I, 141
Haughton, Lucy V, 334
Haughton, Maria V, 334
Haughton, Richard V, 334
Haughton, Richard Elwood V, 334
Haughton, Salley V, 334
Haughton, Sally V, 334
Haughton, Samuel V, 906
Haughton, Samuel V, 910
Haughton, Wm. V, 334
Hauheil, Lillie Jane IV, 1253
Hauheil, Nellie Margaret IV, 1253
Hauldren, Bartholmew VI, 977
Hauldren, Mildred Ann VI, 977
Hauldron, Jackson VI, 977
Hauner, Thomas K. I, 679
Haus, Adelia V, 910
Hausefelt, Harmon V, 498
Hausefelt, Harmon A. V, 498
Hauser, Annie I, 942
Hauser, Annie I, 950
Hauser, Annie T. I, 926
Hauser, Charles I, 942
Hauser, Charles I, 950
Hauser, Charles M. I, 942
Hauser, Charles Merimon I, 926
Hauser, Margaret Louise I, 926
Hauser, Martha I, 926
Hauser, Theophilus I, 926
Hausman, John II, 444
Hausman, Margaret II, 444
Hauxhurst, ??? III, 56
Hauxhurst, Ann III, 397
Hauxhurst, Anna III, 189
Hauxhurst, Anna Maria VI, 747
Hauxhurst, Betts VI, 747
Hauxhurst, Catharine III, 284
Hauxhurst, Charles III, 381
Hauxhurst, Daisy Elizabeth III, 244
Hauxhurst, Daniel K. II, 874

Hauxhurst, Daniel K. VI, 747
Hauxhurst, Daniel K. VI, 786
Hauxhurst, Edward W. VI, 747
Hauxhurst, Eliz. III, 399
Hauxhurst, Esther P. VI, 747
Hauxhurst, Florence Amelia III, 398
Hauxhurst, George III, 397
Hauxhurst, George W. VI, 747
Hauxhurst, Hannah III, 396
Hauxhurst, Jacob L. VI, 747
Hauxhurst, James III, 284
Hauxhurst, James III, 381
Hauxhurst, James C. III, 172
Hauxhurst, Jane III, 194
Hauxhurst, Jane VI, 747
Hauxhurst, Jane VI, 760
Hauxhurst, Jane I. VI, 747
Hauxhurst, Jennie K. VI, 747
Hauxhurst, Joanah III, 396
Hauxhurst, Job VI, 747
Hauxhurst, Job VI, 761
Hauxhurst, John III, 194
Hauxhurst, John VI, 747
Hauxhurst, John VI, 760
Hauxhurst, John Thomas VI, 747
Hauxhurst, Julia E. III, 172
Hauxhurst, Lizzie E. VI, 747
Hauxhurst, Maria III, 395
Hauxhurst, Maria VI, 747
Hauxhurst, Maria S. VI, 747
Hauxhurst, Maria S. VI, 786
Hauxhurst, Maria W. VI, 747
Hauxhurst, Maria W. VI, 761
Hauxhurst, Maria W. VI, 789
Hauxhurst, Marianna III, 398
Hauxhurst, Nath. O. III, 399
Hauxhurst, Penelope III, 381
Hauxhurst, Phebe III, 126
Hauxhurst, Phebe A. III, 399
Hauxhurst, Phila VI, 747
Hauxhurst, Rachel III, 283
Hauxhurst, Rebecca III, 395
Hauxhurst, Rebecca VI, 747
Hauxhurst, Robert III, 381
Hauxhurst, Samson III, 396
Hauxhurst, Sarah III, 220
Hauxhurst, Sarah III, 381
Hauxhurst, Sarah E. III, 409
Hauxhurst, Stephen III, 381
Hauxhurst, Timothy S. K. III, 244
Hauxhurst, Townsend III, 395
Hauxhurst, Townsend VI, 747
Hauxhurst, Wm. E. III, 398
Havard, James II, 444
Havard, Jane II, 373
Havard, John II, 373
Havard, Mary II, 373
Havard, Sarah II, 373
Haveard, James II, 444
Havell, Capt. ??? VI, 36
Haven, Ella Paddock V, 910
Haven, Fannie Belle V, 910
Haven, George Irwin V, 910
Haven, Georgetta Paddock V, 910
Haven, James L. V, 910
Haven, Marion IV, 717
Haven, Phebe Paddock V, 910
Haven, Rebecca V, 910
Haven, Sarah Paddock V, 910
Haven, Susan III, 110
Haven, Willie Augustus V, 910
Havenridge, James VI, 109
Havenridge, John VI, 109
Havenridge, Margaret VI, 109
Havens, Anna III, 153
Havens, Cora V, 70
Havens, Eliza III, 153
Havens, Elizabeth III, 153
Havens, Joseph III, 153
Havens, Lucy IV, 1365
Havens, Lucy IV, 1373
Havens, Pelham III, 153
Havens, Samuel V, 70
Havens, Samuel V, 742
Havens, Thomas III, 153
Haverd, James II, 444
Haverd, Mary II, 444
Haverdc, Jane II, 373
Haverlo, Ella IV, 1165
Haviland, ??? III, 119
Haviland, ??? III, 157
Haviland, ??? III, 297
Haviland, A. Morris III, 155
Haviland, A. Walter III, 153
Haviland, Aaron III, 153
Haviland, Aaron III, 156
Haviland, Aaron III, 306
Haviland, Aaron G. III, 153
Haviland, Aaron G. III, 154
Haviland, Aaron G. III, 256
Haviland, Aaron G. III, 353
Haviland, Abbie J. IV, 1237
Haviland, Abbie Jane IV, 1237
Haviland, Abigail III, 153
Haviland, Abigail III, 292
Haviland, Abigail IV, 1349
Haviland, Abigail IV, 1365
Haviland, Abigail IV, 1366
Haviland, Adelaide III, 119
Haviland, Adelaide III, 153
Haviland, Agnes Maude III, 157
Haviland, Albert III, 154
Haviland, Albert E. III, 153
Haviland, Albert E. III, 154
Haviland, Alfred III, 153
Haviland, Alfred III, 157
Haviland, Alfred IV, 1237
Haviland, Alfred S. IV, 1164
Haviland, Alfred S. IV, 1237
Haviland, Alice III, 153
Haviland, Alice III, 156
Haviland, Alice III, 311
Haviland, Alice III, 418
Haviland, Alice IV, 718
Haviland, Alice IV, 1349
Haviland, Alice IV, 1365
Haviland, Alice IV, 1366
Haviland, Alice H. III, 312
Haviland, Alma V. IV, 718
Haviland, Ann III, 55
Haviland, Ann III, 153
Haviland, Ann IV, 1366
Haviland, Ann C. III, 153
Haviland, Anna III, 108
Haviland, Anna III, 118
Haviland, Anna III, 153
Haviland, Anna III, 154
Haviland, Anna III, 155
Haviland, Anna III, 340
Haviland, Anna III, 414
Haviland, Anna III, 483
Haviland, Anna IV, 718
Haviland, Anna IV, 1365
Haviland, Anna IV, 1366
Haviland, Anna C. III, 154
Haviland, Anna Chase IV, 1366
Haviland, Anna F. III, 155
Haviland, Anna G. III, 154
Haviland, Anna G. III, 156
Haviland, Anna Griffen III, 153
Haviland, Anna M. III, 153
Haviland, Anna M. III, 155
Haviland, Anne III, 108
Haviland, Anne III, 119
Haviland, Anne III, 154
Haviland, Anne III, 155
Haviland, Anne III, 157
Haviland, Anne C. IV, 1367
Haviland, Annie III, 154
Haviland, Annie S. III, 156
Haviland, Anthony III, 154
Haviland, Anthony B. III, 153
Haviland, Anthony B. III, 157
Haviland, Anthony Bartow III, 157
Haviland, Anthony M. III, 155
Haviland, Armenia III, 154
Haviland, Artemas C. IV, 1366
Haviland, Arthur III, 56
Haviland, Arthur III, 153
Haviland, Arthur III, 154
Haviland, Asenath IV, 1366
Haviland, Asineth IV, 1366
Haviland, Benj. III, 153
Haviland, Benj. III, 156
Haviland, Benj. H. III, 155
Haviland, Benj. S. III, 141
Haviland, Benj. S. III, 154
Haviland, Benj. S. III, 155
Haviland, Benj. S. III, 157
Haviland, Benjamin III, 115
Haviland, Benjamin III, 127
Haviland, Benjamin III, 152
Haviland, Benjamin III, 153
Haviland, Benjamin III, 156
Haviland, Benjamin III, 292
Haviland, Benjamin III, 396
Haviland, Benjamin H. III, 153
Haviland, Benjamin S. III, 153
Haviland, Bruena III, 155
Haviland, Caroline III, 153
Haviland, Caroline III, 154
Haviland, Caroline III, 156
Haviland, Caroline III, 164
Haviland, Caroline E. III, 107
Haviland, Caroline E. III, 176
Haviland, Caroline H. III, 418
Haviland, Carrie III, 155
Haviland, Catharine III, 153
Haviland, Catharine III, 155
Haviland, Catharine III, 156
Haviland, Catharine IV, 718
Haviland, Chancy IV, 1366
Haviland, Charity III, 153
Haviland, Charity III, 157
Haviland, Charles IV, 821
Haviland, Charles IV, 1347
Haviland, Charles IV, 1363
Haviland, Charles IV, 1365
Haviland, Charles IV, 1366
Haviland, Charles IV, 1376
Haviland, Charles A. IV, 718
Haviland, Charles C. III, 157
Haviland, Charles E. III, 154
Haviland, Charles F. III, 153
Haviland, Charles F. III, 156
Haviland, Charles M. III, 154
Haviland, Charles T. III, 156
Haviland, Charles, Jr. IV, 1366
Haviland, Charlotte III, 154
Haviland, Chas. IV, 821
Haviland, Chas. A. IV, 821
Haviland, Clarence M. III, 83
Haviland, Clarence M. III, 153
Haviland, Clarence M. III, 154
Haviland, Clement III, 153
Haviland, Clement III, 291
Haviland, Cora II, 846
Haviland, Cora II, 873
Haviland, Cora III, 65
Haviland, Cora III, 153
Haviland, Cora III, 154
Haviland, Cornelia III, 153
Haviland, Cornelia III, 154
Haviland, Cornelia III, 156
Haviland, Daniel III, 154
Haviland, Daniel III, 155
Haviland, Daniel III, 156
Haviland, Daniel III, 157
Haviland, Daniel III, 418
Haviland, Daniel IV, 821
Haviland, Daniel IV, 1365
Haviland, Daniel IV, 1366
Haviland, Daniel IV, 1367
Haviland, Daniel IV, 1378
Haviland, Daniel C. III, 154
Haviland, Daniel E. III, 76
Haviland, Daniel E. III, 153
Haviland, Daniel E. III, 154
Haviland, Daniel G. III, 140
Haviland, Daniel G. III, 153
Haviland, Daniel G. III, 154
Haviland, Daniel G. III, 155
Haviland, Daniel G. III, 164
Haviland, Daniel G. III, 261
Haviland, Daniel M. IV, 1352
Haviland, Daniel M. IV, 1366
Haviland, Daniel M. IV, 1367
Haviland, Daniel S. IV, 1365
Haviland, Daniel S. IV, 1367
Haviland, David III, 39
Haviland, David III, 154
Haviland, David III, 156
Haviland, David A. III, 97
Haviland, David A. III, 154
Haviland, David A. III, 156
Haviland, David C. III, 156
Haviland, David S. III, 64
Haviland, David S. III, 65
Haviland, David S. III, 87
Haviland, David S. III, 153
Haviland, David S. III, 154
Haviland, David S. III, 157
Haviland, Deborah III, 154
Haviland, Deborah IV, 1365
Haviland, Ebenezer III, 55
Haviland, Ebenezer III, 87
Haviland, Ebenezer III, 153
Haviland, Ebenezer III, 154
Haviland, Ebenezer III, 156
Haviland, Edgar IV, 821
Haviland, Edgar IV, 1367
Haviland, Edith A. IV, 1237
Haviland, Edith Ann IV, 1237
Haviland, Edith Maria IV, 1366
Haviland, Edmund III, 154
Haviland, Edmund III, 157
Haviland, Edna IV, 821
Haviland, Edna IV, 1367
Haviland, Edw. III, 154
Haviland, Edward III, 21
Haviland, Edward III, 154
Haviland, Edward III, 157
Haviland, Edward III, 343
Haviland, Edward E. III, 156
Haviland, Edwin III, 153
Haviland, Edwin III, 154
Haviland, Edwin III, 155
Haviland, Edwin III, 226
Haviland, Edwin III, 483
Haviland, Edwin, Jr. III, 154
Haviland, Eleanor Hortense III, 157
Haviland, Eli IV, 1366
Haviland, Eli C. IV, 1366
Haviland, Eli C. IV, 1367
Haviland, Eli C. IV, 1376
Haviland, Elijah III, 117
Haviland, Eliz. III, 155
Haviland, Eliza Jane IV, 1366
Haviland, Elizabeth III, 82
Haviland, Elizabeth III, 144
Haviland, Elizabeth III, 153
Haviland, Elizabeth III, 154
Haviland, Elizabeth III, 155
Haviland, Elizabeth III, 157
Haviland, Elizabeth III, 256
Haviland, Elizabeth III, 281
Haviland, Elizabeth III, 341
Haviland, Elizabeth III, 353
Haviland, Elizabeth C. III, 153
Haviland, Elizabeth C. III, 154
Haviland, Elizabeth H. III, 157
Haviland, Elizabeth H. III, 187
Haviland, Elizabeth V. III, 139
Haviland, Elizabeth V. III, 155
Haviland, Elizabeth W. III, 154
Haviland, Ella III, 154
Haviland, Ellen III, 157
Haviland, Elsie III, 21
Haviland, Elsie III, 154
Haviland, Emily III, 154
Haviland, Emily W. II, 745
Haviland, Emily W. III, 154
Haviland, Emma III, 39
Haviland, Emma III, 154
Haviland, Emma III, 244
Haviland, Emma R. III, 141
Haviland, Emma R. III, 153
Haviland, Emma R. III, 154
Haviland, Emma R. III, 155
Haviland, Emma R. III, 157
Haviland, Emma S. III, 153
Haviland, Emma S. III, 154
Haviland, Emma S. III, 256
Haviland, Esther III, 87
Haviland, Esther III, 153
Haviland, Esther III, 154
Haviland, Esther III, 155
Haviland, Esther III, 156
Haviland, Esther III, 157
Haviland, Esther III, 360
Haviland, Esther III, 483
Haviland, Esther III, 497
Haviland, Esther IV, 1355
Haviland, Esther IV, 1363
Haviland, Esther IV, 1365
Haviland, Esther IV, 1366
Haviland, Esther IV, 1367
Haviland, Esther G. III, 154
Haviland, Esther M. IV, 1366
Haviland, Esther P. III, 155
Haviland, Eugene III, 156
Haviland, Eunice S. IV, 1366
Haviland, Florence III, 483
Haviland, Florence III, 497
Haviland, Francis III, 157
Haviland, Frank III, 155
Haviland, Frank III, 181
Haviland, Frank III, 281
Haviland, Frank III, 391
Haviland, Frank III, 477
Haviland, Frank Bernard III, 155
Haviland, Franklin III, 153
Haviland, Franklin III, 155
Haviland, Frederick III, 155
Haviland, Frederick III, 156
Haviland, Frederick A. III, 154
Haviland, Geo. Samuel IV, 1237
Haviland, George III, 153
Haviland, George III, 154
Haviland, George III, 155
Haviland, George W. IV, 1237
Haviland, Gertrude III, 83
Haviland, Gertrude III, 153
Haviland, Gertrude III, 155
Haviland, Grace III, 153
Haviland, Grace III, 157
Haviland, Grace III, 297
Haviland, Grace A. III, 59
Haviland, Grace A. III, 157
Haviland, Grace R. III, 157
Haviland, Grace R. III, 364
Haviland, Hamilton Easter III, 118
Haviland, Hannah III, 119
Haviland, Hannah III, 153
Haviland, Hannah III, 154
Haviland, Hannah III, 155
Haviland, Hannah III, 156
Haviland, Hannah III, 164
Haviland, Hannah III, 261
Haviland, Hannah III, 418
Haviland, Harriet IV, 407
Haviland, Harriet M. IV, 1352
Haviland, Harriet M. IV, 1366
Haviland, Harry C. IV, 718
Haviland, Harvey IV, 1367
Haviland, Harvey S. IV, 1365
Haviland, Helena III, 156
Haviland, Helena III, 157
Haviland, Helena III, 246
Haviland, Henrietta III, 155
Haviland, Henrietta III, 156
Haviland, Henrietta B. III, 156
Haviland, Henry III, 155
Haviland, Henry III, 156
Haviland, Henry III, 483
Haviland, Henry F. III, 78
Haviland, Henry F. III, 155
Haviland, Henry F. III, 156
Haviland, Henry Louis III, 154
Haviland, Henry M. III, 149
Haviland, Henry M. III, 155
Haviland, Henry Morris III, 15
Haviland, Herbert H. III, 118
Haviland, Herbert Hance III, 1
Haviland, Howard III, 156
Haviland, Huldah IV, 1367
Haviland, Huldah IV, 1382
Haviland, Ingersoll IV, 1365
Haviland, Ingersoll IV, 1366
Haviland, Ingerson IV, 1349
Haviland, Ingerson IV, 1365
Haviland, Ira IV, 1365
Haviland, Ira IV, 1366
Haviland, Isaac III, 414
Haviland, Isaac IV, 91
Haviland, Isaac IV, 1365
Haviland, Isaac IV, 1366
Haviland, Isaac E. III, 414
Haviland, J. C. III, 108
Haviland, James IV, 1365
Haviland, James IV, 1366
Haviland, James C. III, 108
Haviland, James C. III, 118
Haviland, James C. III, 153
Haviland, James C. III, 154
Haviland, James C. III, 155
Haviland, James C. III, 156
Haviland, James C. III, 225
Haviland, James C. III, 483
Haviland, James C. III, 498
Haviland, James C. VI, 747
Haviland, James Jun. IV, 1365
Haviland, James S. III, 139
Haviland, James S. III, 155
Haviland, James S. III, 341
Haviland, James V. III, 155
Haviland, James V. III, 156
Haviland, Jane III, 55
Haviland, Jane III, 154
Haviland, Jane III, 155
Haviland, Jane III, 156
Haviland, Jane IV, 1366
Haviland, Jared C. IV, 1366
Haviland, Jas. C. III, 497
Haviland, Jemima III, 21
Haviland, Jemima III, 154
Haviland, Jemima III, 343
Haviland, Jericho III, 118
Haviland, John III, 55
Haviland, John III, 153
Haviland, John III, 155
Haviland, John III, 156
Haviland, John IV, 1366
Haviland, John IV, 1367
Haviland, John A. III, 153
Haviland, John A. III, 154
Haviland, John Case IV, 1237
Haviland, John E. III, 154
Haviland, John G. III, 153
Haviland, John G. III, 155
Haviland, John G. III, 156
Haviland, John G. III, 157
Haviland, John G. III, 176
Haviland, John Howard III, 15
Haviland, John Linton Carver II, 873
Haviland, John W. IV, 1353
Haviland, John W. IV, 1365
Haviland, John W. IV, 1366
Haviland, Joseph IV, 91
Haviland, Joseph IV, 110
Haviland, Joseph IV, 718
Haviland, Joseph B. IV, 1366
Haviland, Joseph B. IV, 1367
Haviland, Julia III, 95
Haviland, Julia III, 156
Haviland, Julia IV, 1366
Haviland, Julina IV, 1366
Haviland, Kate L. III, 155
Haviland, Kate L. III, 181

'iland, Laura IV, 1365
'iland, Laura IV, 1366
'iland, Laura IV, 1378
'iland, Laura Jane IV, 1366
'iland, Lavina IV, 1164
'iland, Lavina IV, 1231
'iland, Lavina IV, 1237
'iland, Leonard IV, 1365
'iland, Leonard IV, 1366
'iland, Lindley IV, 718
'iland, Lindley IV, 1367
iland, Louisa III, 153
iland, Louisa III, 154
iland, Louisa III, 226
'iland, Louise III, 155
iland, Louise III, 341
iland, Lucinda IV, 750
iland, Lucinda IV, 821
iland, Lucinda B. IV, 821
iland, Lucinda B. IV, 1366
iland, Lucinda B. IV, 1367
iland, Lucinda M. IV, 718
iland, Lucy III, 82
iland, Lucy III, 153
iland, Lucy III, 154
'iland, Lucy III, 156
iland, Lucy Jane IV, 1367
iland, Lydia III, 483
iland, Lydia IV, 91
'iland, Lydia IV, 110
iland, Lydia Aaron III, 118
iland, Lydia H. IV, 91
iland, Lydia H. IV, 718
'iland, Lydia K. IV, 37
iland, Lydia K. IV, 60
iland, Lydia S. III, 118
iland, Lydia S. III, 155
iland, Lyman III, 155
iland, Lyman III, 156
iland, M. Laura III, 78
iland, M. Laura III, 155
iland, Mae IV, 718
iland, Margaret III, 155
iland, Margaret IV, 1353
iland, Margaret IV, 1366
iland, Margaret A. III, 56
iland, Margaret A. III, 153
iland, Margaret M. III, 155
iland, Margery III, 155
iland, Margery III, 157
iland, Maria III, 155
iland, Maria III, 483
iland, Maria Louisa III, 25
iland, Maria Louisa III, 156
iland, Marielma III, 119
iland, Marielma III, 154
iland, Marielma III, 155
iland, Marielma III, 156
iland, Marielma III, 181
iland, Marielma III, 312
iland, Marielma F. III, 156
iland, Marseilma III, 156
iland, Martha IV, 1363
iland, Martha IV, 1365
iland, Martha IV, 1366
iland, Martha C. III, 156
iland, Mary III, 61
iland, Mary III, 127
iland, Mary III, 153
iland, Mary III, 154
iland, Mary III, 155
iland, Mary III, 156
iland, Mary III, 157
iland, Mary III, 176
iland, Mary III, 246
iland, Mary III, 340
iland, Mary III, 358
iland, Mary IV, 1366
iland, Mary Abbie III, 153
iland, Mary Abbie III, 291
iland, Mary Amelia III, 155
iland, Mary Ann IV, 1365
iland, Mary Ann VI, 406
iland, Mary Ann VI, 514
iland, Mary Ann VI, 660
iland, Mary Ann VI, 673
iland, Mary Ann VI, 752
iland, Mary Anna III, 154
iland, Mary Anna III, 156
iland, Mary B. III, 155
iland, Mary B. III, 156
iland, Mary C. III, 39
iland, Mary C. III, 154
iland, Mary C. III, 156
iland, Mary C. III, 157
iland, Mary E. III, 156
iland, Mary E. III, 157
iland, Mary Eliz. III, 156
iland, Mary Elizabeth III, 156
iland, Mary Elizabeth III, 312
iland, Mary H. III, 153
Haviland, Mary H. III, 155
Haviland, Mary Jane III, 154
Haviland, Mary S. III, 154
Haviland, Mary S. IV, 1366
Haviland, Mary S. IV, 1367
Haviland, Mary S. IV, 1368
Haviland, Matilda III, 156
Haviland, Matilda III, 414
Haviland, Matilda H. III, 25
Haviland, Maude III, 320
Haviland, Maurice B. III, 156
Haviland, Maurice R. III, 153
Haviland, Minerva IV, 1365
Haviland, Minerva IV, 1366
Haviland, N. M. IV, 1237
Haviland, Naomi III, 26
Haviland, Naomi IV, 1366
Haviland, Naomi IV, 1367
Haviland, Naomi C. III, 147
Haviland, Naomy IV, 1366
Haviland, Nellie Elma III, 156
Haviland, Nellie Elma III, 181
Haviland, Nelson IV, 1366
Haviland, Nelson Merritt IV, 1237
Haviland, Nelson Morris IV, 1164
Haviland, Ola G. IV, 718
Haviland, Paulina III, 156
Haviland, Peleg C. IV, 1365
Haviland, Peleg C. IV, 1366
Haviland, Phebe III, 82
Haviland, Phebe III, 108
Haviland, Phebe III, 117
Haviland, Phebe III, 118
Haviland, Phebe III, 152
Haviland, Phebe III, 153
Haviland, Phebe III, 154
Haviland, Phebe III, 155
Haviland, Phebe III, 156
Haviland, Phebe III, 225
Haviland, Phebe III, 271
Haviland, Phebe III, 341
Haviland, Phebe III, 483
Haviland, Phebe III, 497
Haviland, Phebe III, 498
Haviland, Phebe IV, 1365
Haviland, Phebe IV, 1366
Haviland, Phebe IV, 1378
Haviland, Phebe Ann III, 155
Haviland, Phebe Ann III, 156
Haviland, Phebe C. III, 76
Haviland, Phebe C. III, 153
Haviland, Phebe C. III, 154
Haviland, Phebe H. III, 55
Haviland, Phebe L. IV, 1367
Haviland, Phebe S. III, 156
Haviland, Philo IV, 1365
Haviland, Philo D. IV, 1365
Haviland, Philo D. IV, 1366
Haviland, Rebecca III, 153
Haviland, Rebecca III, 155
Haviland, Rebecca III, 156
Haviland, Rebecca III, 176
Haviland, Rebecca III, 306
Haviland, Rebecca III, 311
Haviland, Rebecca III, 312
Haviland, Rebecca IV, 407
Haviland, Rich F. III, 25
Haviland, Rich'd F. III, 156
Haviland, Richard III, 154
Haviland, Richard III, 155
Haviland, Richard F. III, 156
Haviland, Richard F. III, 414
Haviland, Robert III, 153
Haviland, Robert III, 155
Haviland, Robert III, 156
Haviland, Robert III, 312
Haviland, Robert B. III, 82
Haviland, Robert B. III, 153
Haviland, Robert B. III, 154
Haviland, Robert B. III, 156
Haviland, Robert B. III, 176
Haviland, Robert H. III, 156
Haviland, Robt. B. III, 153
Haviland, Robt. B. III, 155
Haviland, Robt. B. III, 311
Haviland, Robt. R. III, 155
Haviland, Ruth III, 97
Haviland, Ruth III, 154
Haviland, Ruth III, 414
Haviland, S. Willets III, 153
Haviland, S. Willets III, 154
Haviland, Samuel IV, 1164
Haviland, Samuel IV, 1236
Haviland, Samuel IV, 1237
Haviland, Samuel IV, 1242
Haviland, Samuel IV, 1365
Haviland, Samuel IV, 1366
Haviland, Samuel D. III, 156
Haviland, Samuel P. IV, 1164
Haviland, Samuel P. IV, 1237
Haviland, Samuel, Jr. IV, 1237
Haviland, Sarah III, 87
Haviland, Sarah III, 115
Haviland, Sarah III, 127
Haviland, Sarah III, 153
Haviland, Sarah III, 155
Haviland, Sarah III, 156
Haviland, Sarah III, 225
Haviland, Sarah III, 292
Haviland, Sarah III, 344
Haviland, Sarah III, 483
Haviland, Sarah A. III, 64
Haviland, Sarah A. III, 65
Haviland, Sarah A. III, 153
Haviland, Sarah A. III, 154
Haviland, Sarah Ann III, 155
Haviland, Sarah C. III, 154
Haviland, Sarah C. III, 155
Haviland, Sarah D. IV, 1365
Haviland, Sarah Eliz. III, 156
Haviland, Sarah Elizabeth III, 156
Haviland, Sarah L. IV, 1363
Haviland, Sarah L. IV, 1366
Haviland, Sarah L. IV, 1367
Haviland, Sarah L. IV, 1376
Haviland, Sarah Louise III, 153
Haviland, Sarah M. III, 155
Haviland, Sarah S. III, 156
Haviland, Sarah W. II, 745
Haviland, Sarah W. III, 154
Haviland, Seneca IV, 1365
Haviland, Seneca IV, 1366
Haviland, Seneca IV, 1367
Haviland, Seneca IV, 1368
Haviland, Smith Samuel IV, 1237
Haviland, Solomon III, 119
Haviland, Solomon III, 154
Haviland, Solomon III, 155
Haviland, Solomon III, 156
Haviland, Solomon III, 181
Haviland, Solomon III, 312
Haviland, Solomon J. III, 156
Haviland, Stephen III, 153
Haviland, Stephen III, 156
Haviland, Stewart Benjamin III, 153
Haviland, Susan III, 155
Haviland, Susan B. III, 149
Haviland, Susan B. III, 155
Haviland, Susan C. IV, 1367
Haviland, Susan C. IV, 1369
Haviland, Susan E. IV, 1236
Haviland, Susan E. IV, 1237
Haviland, Susan E. IV, 1242
Haviland, Susanna C. IV, 1366
Haviland, Susannah IV, 1365
Haviland, Susannah IV, 1366
Haviland, Susannah C. IV, 1366
Haviland, Theodore III, 95
Haviland, Theodore III, 154
Haviland, Theodore III, 156
Haviland, Thomas III, 156
Haviland, Thomas III, 157
Haviland, Thomas III, 246
Haviland, Thos. III, 156
Haviland, Vicena IV, 1366
Haviland, Vicena IV, 1367
Haviland, Vicena IV, 1376
Haviland, Viola G. IV, 821
Haviland, Wallace J. III, 153
Haviland, Walter III, 154
Haviland, Walter III, 155
Haviland, Walter III, 157
Haviland, Walter III, 187
Haviland, Walter Alfred IV, 1237
Haviland, Wd. Charity Farrington III, 396
Haviland, Wd. Hannah B. III, 155
Haviland, Willard III, 154
Haviland, William III, 153
Haviland, William III, 154
Haviland, William III, 156
Haviland, William III, 157
Haviland, William B. IV, 1164
Haviland, William B. IV, 1237
Haviland, William C. III, 59
Haviland, William R. III, 153
Haviland, William R. III, 157
Haviland, William Robert III, 155
Haviland, William S. III, 155
Haviland, William S. III, 483
Haviland, William, Jr. III, 483
Haviland, William, Jr. III, 497
Haviland, Wing IV, 1365
Haviland, Wing IV, 1366
Haviland, Wm. III, 155
Haviland, Wm. III, 156
Haviland, Wm. III, 157
Haviland, Wm. III, 414
Haviland, Wm. III, 483
Haviland, Wm. III, 497
Haviland, Wm. B. IV, 1164
Haviland, Wm. B. IV, 1237
Haviland, Wm. C. III, 157
Haviland, Wm. Edward IV, 1237
Haviland, Wm. Robert III, 157
Haviland, Wm. Robert III, 364
Haviland, Wm. T. III, 155
Haviland, Wm., Jr. III, 154
Haviland, Zilpha Ann IV, 1366
Haviland, Zilphana IV, 1366
Hawes, Katie V, 175
Hawes, Mary V, 64
Hawes, Mary V, 70
Hawes, Nathan V, 175
Hawes, Reuben VI, 930
Hawes, Tabitha VI, 930
Hawes, Vesta VI, 248
Hawes, Vesta A. VI, 248
Hawes, Vesta H. VI, 248
Haweson, Ebenezer III, 157
Hawhay, Elizabeth V, 648
Hawhay, Elizabeth Turner V, 624
Hawhay, Margaret V, 624
Hawhurst, Daniel III, 445
Hawhurst, Mary III, 26
Hawhurst, Phila. III, 445
Hawhurst, Sarah III, 445
Hawith, Solomon I, 814
Hawk, Albert V, 392
Hawk, Araminta V, 392
Hawk, Eli V, 392
Hawke, Sarah A. V, 70
Hawke, Sarah A. V, 121
Hawkens, Samuel VI, 597
Hawkes, Alice VI, 248
Hawkes, Alice W. VI, 248
Hawkes, Charles D. III, 415
Hawkes, Dr. I. J. VI, 248
Hawkes, Dr. Isiah J. VI, 248
Hawkes, Elizabeth VI, 248
Hawkes, Elvira VI, 248
Hawkes, Ezra VI, 248
Hawkes, Ezra J. VI, 248
Hawkes, Frederick C. VI, 248
Hawkes, Henrietta III, 63
Hawkes, Herbert S. VI, 248
Hawkes, Isaac VI, 248
Hawkes, Lydia IV, 962
Hawkes, Lydia Maria IV, 962
Hawkes, Lydia Maria IV, 999
Hawkes, Lydia Mariah IV, 962
Hawkes, Martha IV, 999
Hawkes, Martha S. IV, 962
Hawkes, Vira VI, 248
Hawkes, Wm. IV, 718
Hawkes, Wm. IV, 999
Hawkings, Dorothy II, 218
Hawkings, Dorothy II, 230
Hawkings, Sarah V, 969
Hawkings, Sarah V, 971
Hawkings, William II, 218
Hawkings, William II, 230
Hawkins, ??? II, 799
Hawkins, ??? V, 823
Hawkins, Abraham V, 70
Hawkins, Abraham V, 567
Hawkins, Abraham V, 574
Hawkins, Abraham V, 575
Hawkins, Adeline VI, 930
Hawkins, Alfred VI, 930
Hawkins, Alice A. VI, 930
Hawkins, Amos I, 1020
Hawkins, Amos I, 1031
Hawkins, Amos I, 1057
Hawkins, Amos I, 1058
Hawkins, Amos I, 1059
Hawkins, Amos I, 1060
Hawkins, Amos I, 1061
Hawkins, Amos I, 1062
Hawkins, Amos I, 1063
Hawkins, Amos V, 70
Hawkins, Amos V, 86
Hawkins, Amos V, 175
Hawkins, Amos V, 176
Hawkins, Amos V, 181
Hawkins, Amos V, 191
Hawkins, Amos V, 195
Hawkins, Amos V, 196
Hawkins, Amos V, 204
Hawkins, Amos V, 498
Hawkins, Amos V, 842
Hawkins, Amos VI, 504
Hawkins, Amos James V, 177
Hawkins, Ann I, 1020
Hawkins, Ann I, 1027
Hawkins, Ann I, 1031
Hawkins, Ann I, 1053
Hawkins, Ann I, 1055
Hawkins, Ann I, 1057
Hawkins, Ann I, 1058
Hawkins, Ann I, 1061
Hawkins, Ann II, 545
Hawkins, Ann V, 25
Hawkins, Ann V, 70
Hawkins, Ann V, 141
Hawkins, Ann V, 175
Hawkins, Ann V, 176
Hawkins, Ann V, 177
Hawkins, Ann V, 181
Hawkins, Ann V, 191
Hawkins, Ann V, 498
Hawkins, Ann V, 858
Hawkins, Anna I, 1057
Hawkins, Anna V, 153
Hawkins, Anna V, 175
Hawkins, Anna V, 177
Hawkins, Anna V, 196
Hawkins, Anna VI, 399
Hawkins, Anne I, 1060
Hawkins, Anne I, 1061
Hawkins, Annetta V, 575
Hawkins, Annette V, 574
Hawkins, Benjamin I, 1020
Hawkins, Benjamin I, 1031
Hawkins, Benjamin I, 1057
Hawkins, Benjamin I, 1060
Hawkins, Benjamin I, 1061
Hawkins, Benjamin V, 70
Hawkins, Benjamin V, 175
Hawkins, Benjamin V, 177
Hawkins, Benjamin V, 181
Hawkins, Benjamin V, 191
Hawkins, Benjamin V, 194
Hawkins, Benjamin V, 680
Hawkins, Benjamin V, 842
Hawkins, Benjamin V, 843
Hawkins, Benjamin VI, 504
Hawkins, Benjamin VI, 808
Hawkins, Benjamin VI, 930
Hawkins, Bernice V, 680
Hawkins, Bernice E. V, 176
Hawkins, Bernice E. H. V, 680
Hawkins, Betcy IV, 407
Hawkins, Betsy IV, 366
Hawkins, Betsy VI, 930
Hawkins, Caroline Margaret V, 574
Hawkins, Carrie C. V, 176
Hawkins, Catharine VI, 912
Hawkins, Catherine VI, 909
Hawkins, Celine VI, 930
Hawkins, Charity V, 175
Hawkins, Charity V, 176
Hawkins, Charity V, 198
Hawkins, Charity Cook V, 70
Hawkins, Charles II, 799
Hawkins, Charles V, 175
Hawkins, Chas. II, 873
Hawkins, Chas. IV, 1319
Hawkins, Chas. V, 177
Hawkins, Chas. B. III, 157
Hawkins, Chas. B. III, 362
Hawkins, Christiana V, 171
Hawkins, Christopher I, 1057
Hawkins, Christopher V, 70
Hawkins, Christopher V, 166
Hawkins, Christopher V, 175
Hawkins, Christopher V, 498
Hawkins, Cornelia C. III, 157
Hawkins, David I, 1057
Hawkins, David V, 175
Hawkins, Deborah T. V, 176
Hawkins, Deborah T. V, 177
Hawkins, Deborah T. V, 498
Hawkins, Deborah T. V, 499
Hawkins, Deborah T. V, 515
Hawkins, Dinah I, 1057
Hawkins, Dinah V, 70
Hawkins, Dinah V, 175
Hawkins, Dinah V, 176
Hawkins, Dinah V, 190
Hawkins, Dinah V, 206
Hawkins, Dorothy II, 230
Hawkins, Edith II, 862
Hawkins, Edith II, 873
Hawkins, Edith V, 166
Hawkins, Edith V, 175
Hawkins, Edith V, 176
Hawkins, Edith V, 574
Hawkins, Edward Lamb II, 799
Hawkins, Edwin R. II, 862
Hawkins, Edwin R. II, 873
Hawkins, Edwin Rover II, 799
Hawkins, Eleanor VI, 930
Hawkins, Eli I, 1020
Hawkins, Eli V, 175
Hawkins, Eli V, 177
Hawkins, Eli V, 574
Hawkins, Eli N. V, 575

Hawkins, Elijah V, 175
Hawkins, Elijah V, 177
Hawkins, Elin II, 960
Hawkins, Elisabeth II, 545
Hawkins, Eliza VI, 883
Hawkins, Eliza VI, 930
Hawkins, Elizabeth I, 1061
Hawkins, Elizabeth II, 230
Hawkins, Elizabeth II, 545
Hawkins, Elizabeth II, 599
Hawkins, Elizabeth II, 799
Hawkins, Elizabeth II, 806
Hawkins, Elizabeth II, 1000
Hawkins, Elizabeth IV, 1319
Hawkins, Elizabeth V, 30
Hawkins, Elizabeth V, 70
Hawkins, Elizabeth V, 176
Hawkins, Elizabeth V, 574
Hawkins, Elizabeth VI, 399
Hawkins, Elizabeth VI, 597
Hawkins, Elizabeth VI, 930
Hawkins, Elizabeth M. V, 498
Hawkins, Emelen W. III, 19
Hawkins, Emelene W. III, 157
Hawkins, Emeline V, 807
Hawkins, Emeline W. III, 19
Hawkins, Emeline W. III, 185
Hawkins, Emeline W. III, 290
Hawkins, Esther V, 842
Hawkins, Esther L. V, 585
Hawkins, Ethel E. V, 585
Hawkins, Ethel Mary V, 498
Hawkins, Ethel May V, 498
Hawkins, F. Luisey V, 177
Hawkins, Fleming VI, 930
Hawkins, Florence III, 97
Hawkins, Florence III, 275
Hawkins, Fountain M. VI, 930
Hawkins, Fountain M. VI, 1003
Hawkins, George W. VI, 923
Hawkins, George W. VI, 929
Hawkins, George W. VI, 930
Hawkins, Gregory, Elizabeth I, 1061
Hawkins, Hannah I, 1057
Hawkins, Hannah II, 373
Hawkins, Hannah II, 542
Hawkins, Hannah II, 545
Hawkins, Hannah IV, 1367
Hawkins, Hannah V, 70
Hawkins, Hannah V, 175
Hawkins, Hannah V, 176
Hawkins, Hannah V, 196
Hawkins, Hannah V, 345
Hawkins, Hannah V, 842
Hawkins, Hannah V, 843
Hawkins, Hannah T. IV, 1367
Hawkins, Harriet VI, 951
Hawkins, Harry A. III, 157
Hawkins, Harvey V, 176
Hawkins, Harvey V, 177
Hawkins, Helen V, 680
Hawkins, Helen E. V, 70
Hawkins, Helen E. V, 680
Hawkins, Helen Esther V, 70
Hawkins, Helen Esther V, 176
Hawkins, Helen Esther V, 177
Hawkins, Henry I, 1057
Hawkins, Henry V, 70
Hawkins, Henry V, 175
Hawkins, Henry V, 177
Hawkins, Henry V, 196
Hawkins, Henry V, 498
Hawkins, Henry V, 842
Hawkins, Henry C. II, 799
Hawkins, Henry C. II, 873
Hawkins, Howard II, 799
Hawkins, Isaac I, 543
Hawkins, Isaac I, 1015
Hawkins, Isaac I, 1020
Hawkins, Isaac I, 1031
Hawkins, Isaac I, 1056
Hawkins, Isaac I, 1057
Hawkins, Isaac I, 1059
Hawkins, Isaac I, 1060
Hawkins, Isaac I, 1061
Hawkins, Isaac I, 1062
Hawkins, Isaac V, 30
Hawkins, Isaac V, 58
Hawkins, Isaac V, 70
Hawkins, Isaac V, 86
Hawkins, Isaac V, 113
Hawkins, Isaac V, 125
Hawkins, Isaac V, 147
Hawkins, Isaac V, 175
Hawkins, Isaac V, 176
Hawkins, Isaac V, 177
Hawkins, Isaac V, 191
Hawkins, Isaac V, 574
Hawkins, Isaac VI, 504
Hawkins, Isaac C. V, 575
Hawkins, Isaac C. V, 585
Hawkins, Isaac E. V, 70
Hawkins, Isaac E. V, 97
Hawkins, Isaac, Sr. I, 1057
Hawkins, Isaac, Sr. V, 175
Hawkins, Isabel M. V, 177
Hawkins, Isabella M. V, 176
Hawkins, Israel V, 574
Hawkins, Israel V, 593
Hawkins, James I, 1020
Hawkins, James I, 1031
Hawkins, James I, 1056
Hawkins, James I, 1057
Hawkins, James I, 1059
Hawkins, James I, 1061
Hawkins, James II, 373
Hawkins, James II, 995
Hawkins, James II, 1000
Hawkins, James V, 70
Hawkins, James V, 159
Hawkins, James V, 162
Hawkins, James V, 175
Hawkins, James V, 177
Hawkins, James V, 190
Hawkins, James V, 192
Hawkins, James V, 842
Hawkins, James VI, 504
Hawkins, James VI, 930
Hawkins, James VI, 931
Hawkins, James B. VI, 930
Hawkins, James F. VI, 890
Hawkins, James William IV, 1367
Hawkins, James, Jr. I, 1057
Hawkins, Jane II, 373
Hawkins, Jane III, 157
Hawkins, Jane V, 70
Hawkins, Jane V, 177
Hawkins, Jane V, 192
Hawkins, Jane V, 567
Hawkins, Jane V, 574
Hawkins, Jane V, 575
Hawkins, Jane VI, 824
Hawkins, Jane E. VI, 923
Hawkins, Jeffery II, 1000
Hawkins, Jehu I, 1057
Hawkins, Jehu V, 70
Hawkins, Jehu V, 175
Hawkins, Jehu V, 176
Hawkins, Jehu V, 177
Hawkins, Jehu V, 192
Hawkins, Jehu V, 198
Hawkins, Jehu V, 206
Hawkins, Jehu V, 208
Hawkins, Jemima V, 166
Hawkins, Jesse I, 1057
Hawkins, Jesse V, 70
Hawkins, Jesse V, 175
Hawkins, Jesse V, 176
Hawkins, Jesse F. V, 176
Hawkins, Jesse F. V, 498
Hawkins, John I, 100
Hawkins, John I, 141
Hawkins, John I, 1020
Hawkins, John I, 1031
Hawkins, John I, 1055
Hawkins, John I, 1057
Hawkins, John I, 1060
Hawkins, John I, 1061
Hawkins, John I, 1062
Hawkins, John III, 157
Hawkins, John III, 189
Hawkins, John V, 70
Hawkins, John V, 77
Hawkins, John V, 166
Hawkins, John V, 175
Hawkins, John V, 176
Hawkins, John V, 177
Hawkins, John V, 179
Hawkins, John V, 196
Hawkins, John V, 345
Hawkins, John V, 498
Hawkins, John V, 499
Hawkins, John V, 574
Hawkins, John V, 575
Hawkins, John V, 842
Hawkins, John VI, 504
Hawkins, John VI, 909
Hawkins, John F. VI, 906
Hawkins, John F. VI, 930
Hawkins, John F. VI, 1014
Hawkins, John H. IV, 1367
Hawkins, John H. V, 574
Hawkins, John H. VI, 885
Hawkins, John H. VI, 930
Hawkins, John H. VI, 967
Hawkins, John R. IV, 1367
Hawkins, Jonathan I, 543
Hawkins, Jonathan I, 1015
Hawkins, Jonathan I, 1057
Hawkins, Jonathan V, 70
Hawkins, Jonathan V, 175
Hawkins, Jonathan V, 176
Hawkins, Jonathan V, 498
Hawkins, Jonathan VI, 504
Hawkins, Jonathan VI, 547
Hawkins, Jos. C. V, 193
Hawkins, Joseph I, 1020
Hawkins, Joseph V, 160
Hawkins, Joseph V, 171
Hawkins, Joseph V, 176
Hawkins, Joseph V, 177
Hawkins, Joseph VI, 909
Hawkins, Joseph VI, 930
Hawkins, Joseph VI, 967
Hawkins, Joseph Benjamin V, 842
Hawkins, Joseph C. V, 176
Hawkins, Joseph C. V, 177
Hawkins, Juliet VI, 951
Hawkins, Katherine VI, 930
Hawkins, Lee V, 680
Hawkins, Lena V, 680
Hawkins, Levi V, 52
Hawkins, Levi V, 70
Hawkins, Levi V, 177
Hawkins, Levi V, 680
Hawkins, Levi V, 842
Hawkins, Levi M. V, 176
Hawkins, Levi M. V, 680
Hawkins, Lewis M. III, 157
Hawkins, Lewis W. III, 19
Hawkins, Lewis W. III, 157
Hawkins, Linza E. V, 175
Hawkins, Little B. VI, 974
Hawkins, Littleberry VI, 824
Hawkins, Littleberry VI, 894
Hawkins, Louiza Jane V, 574
Hawkins, Lucas M. VI, 930
Hawkins, Lucinda Ann VI, 930
Hawkins, Lucinda L. VI, 906
Hawkins, Lydia I, 1060
Hawkins, Lydia I, 1061
Hawkins, Lydia V, 163
Hawkins, Lydia V, 175
Hawkins, Lydia V, 177
Hawkins, Margaret I, 1057
Hawkins, Margaret I, 1059
Hawkins, Margaret I, 1061
Hawkins, Margaret V, 70
Hawkins, Margaret V, 86
Hawkins, Margaret V, 87
Hawkins, Margaret V, 175
Hawkins, Margaret V, 196
Hawkins, Margery V, 70
Hawkins, Margery V, 77
Hawkins, Margery V, 176
Hawkins, Margery V, 179
Hawkins, Margret I, 1057
Hawkins, Mark V, 175
Hawkins, Mark V, 177
Hawkins, Martha I, 1020
Hawkins, Martha I, 1027
Hawkins, Martha I, 1031
Hawkins, Martha I, 1055
Hawkins, Martha I, 1056
Hawkins, Martha I, 1057
Hawkins, Martha I, 1060
Hawkins, Martha I, 1061
Hawkins, Martha I, 1062
Hawkins, Martha III, 157
Hawkins, Martha III, 362
Hawkins, Martha V, 70
Hawkins, Martha V, 175
Hawkins, Martha V, 176
Hawkins, Martha V, 181
Hawkins, Martha V, 192
Hawkins, Martha V, 498
Hawkins, Martha V, 843
Hawkins, Martha VI, 504
Hawkins, Martha VI, 824
Hawkins, Martha Ann V, 176
Hawkins, Martha L. III, 157
Hawkins, Martha L. III, 362
Hawkins, Marther I, 1031
Hawkins, Mary I, 1020
Hawkins, Mary I, 1055
Hawkins, Mary I, 1056
Hawkins, Mary I, 1057
Hawkins, Mary I, 1060
Hawkins, Mary I, 1061
Hawkins, Mary II, 1000
Hawkins, Mary V, 30
Hawkins, Mary V, 52
Hawkins, Mary V, 58
Hawkins, Mary V, 70
Hawkins, Mary V, 86
Hawkins, Mary V, 125
Hawkins, Mary V, 166
Hawkins, Mary V, 175
Hawkins, Mary V, 176
Hawkins, Mary V, 177
Hawkins, Mary V, 191
Hawkins, Mary V, 197
Hawkins, Mary V, 490
Hawkins, Mary V, 498
Hawkins, Mary V, 574
Hawkins, Mary V, 842
Hawkins, Mary V, 858
Hawkins, Mary A. V, 585
Hawkins, Mary A. VI, 930
Hawkins, Mary Ann IV, 1367
Hawkins, Mary Ann V, 176
Hawkins, Mary Ann V, 177
Hawkins, Mary Ann V, 195
Hawkins, Mary Ann V, 574
Hawkins, Mary Ann VI, 930
Hawkins, Mary E. V, 680
Hawkins, Mary Elizabeth V, 177
Hawkins, Mary Elizabeth V, 574
Hawkins, Mary Elizabeth V, 680
Hawkins, Mary Ellen V, 574
Hawkins, Mary Ellen V, 575
Hawkins, Mary F. VI, 824
Hawkins, Mary I. V, 680
Hawkins, Mary J. III, 157
Hawkins, Mary J. III, 189
Hawkins, Mary Jane V, 345
Hawkins, Mary L. II, 862
Hawkins, Mary L. II, 873
Hawkins, Mary Lamb II, 799
Hawkins, Mary Margaret V, 498
Hawkins, Mary Mills V, 177
Hawkins, Mary S. V, 176
Hawkins, Mary S. V, 207
Hawkins, Mary Susannah V, 177
Hawkins, Mary W. II, 799
Hawkins, Mary Walker V, 680
Hawkins, Mary, Jr. V, 176
Hawkins, Mary, Jr. V, 192
Hawkins, Massey I, 1057
Hawkins, Massey V, 176
Hawkins, Massey V, 204
Hawkins, Mildred VI, 825
Hawkins, Milly VI, 885
Hawkins, Milton V, 681
Hawkins, Milton J. V, 499
Hawkins, Milton J. V, 680
Hawkins, Milton T. V, 176
Hawkins, Milton T. V, 177
Hawkins, Milton T. V, 499
Hawkins, Miriam II, 799
Hawkins, Miriam II, 873
Hawkins, Morris J. V, 176
Hawkins, Moses VI, 930
Hawkins, Nancey VI, 919
Hawkins, Nancy VI, 823
Hawkins, Nancy VI, 909
Hawkins, Nancy VI, 930
Hawkins, Nancy VI, 965
Hawkins, Nancy VI, 967
Hawkins, Nancy C. V, 176
Hawkins, Nancy C. V, 177
Hawkins, Nancy Clarinda V, 680
Hawkins, Nancy E. VI, 930
Hawkins, Naomi V, 176
Hawkins, Naomi V, 177
Hawkins, Nathan I, 1015
Hawkins, Nathan I, 1020
Hawkins, Nathan I, 1027
Hawkins, Nathan I, 1031
Hawkins, Nathan I, 1055
Hawkins, Nathan I, 1057
Hawkins, Nathan I, 1061
Hawkins, Nathan V, 70
Hawkins, Nathan V, 115
Hawkins, Nathan V, 176
Hawkins, Nathan V, 498
Hawkins, Nathan V, 842
Hawkins, Nathan V, 858
Hawkins, Nathan VI, 504
Hawkins, Noah V, 175
Hawkins, Noah V, 177
Hawkins, Olive I, 1060
Hawkins, Olive I, 1061
Hawkins, Olive V, 70
Hawkins, Olive V, 842
Hawkins, Omar B. V, 585
Hawkins, Parkey VI, 812
Hawkins, Patty I, 1057
Hawkins, Patty V, 70
Hawkins, Patty V, 159
Hawkins, Patty V, 171
Hawkins, Patty V, 176
Hawkins, Paul V, 176
Hawkins, Peggy VI, 919
Hawkins, Permelia VI, 930
Hawkins, Peterson VI, 930
Hawkins, Phamay I, 1057
Hawkins, Phamy V, 176
Hawkins, Phamy V, 181
Hawkins, Phamy V, 191
Hawkins, Phamy V, 194
Hawkins, Phebe I, 543
Hawkins, Phebe I, 1015
Hawkins, Phebe I, 1057
Hawkins, Phebe I, 1059
Hawkins, Phebe I, 1061
Hawkins, Phebe I, 1063
Hawkins, Phebe V, 70
Hawkins, Phebe V, 175
Hawkins, Phebe V, 177
Hawkins, Phebe V, 191
Hawkins, Phebe V, 193
Hawkins, Phebe V, 196
Hawkins, Phebe V, 498
Hawkins, Phebe E. V, 585
Hawkins, Polly VI, 930
Hawkins, Polly VI, 940
Hawkins, R. C. VI, 824
Hawkins, Rachel II, 545
Hawkins, Rachel II, 624
Hawkins, Rachel II, 672
Hawkins, Rachel V, 70
Hawkins, Rachel V, 86
Hawkins, Rebecca I, 1057
Hawkins, Rebecca II, 799
Hawkins, Rebecca II, 873
Hawkins, Rebecca V, 70
Hawkins, Rebecca V, 115
Hawkins, Rebecca V, 175
Hawkins, Rebecca V, 176
Hawkins, Rebecca V, 498
Hawkins, Rebecca VI, 931
Hawkins, Rebeckah I, 1020
Hawkins, Rebeckah V, 175
Hawkins, Rebeckah V, 181
Hawkins, Rebekah I, 543
Hawkins, Rebekah I, 881
Hawkins, Rebekah I, 1016
Hawkins, Rebekah I, 1055
Hawkins, Rebekah I, 1060
Hawkins, Rebekah I, 1061
Hawkins, Robert V, 842
Hawkins, Robert VI, 825
Hawkins, Robert VI, 881
Hawkins, Robert VI, 930
Hawkins, Robert C. VI, 906
Hawkins, Robert, Jr. II, 230
Hawkins, Roger II, 1000
Hawkins, Rose Ann IV, 1367
Hawkins, Ruth I, 1055
Hawkins, Ruth I, 1056
Hawkins, Ruth I, 1057
Hawkins, Ruth V, 42
Hawkins, Ruth V, 70
Hawkins, Ruth V, 113
Hawkins, Ruth V, 125
Hawkins, Ruth V, 160
Hawkins, Ruth V, 161
Hawkins, Ruth V, 162
Hawkins, Ruth V, 175
Hawkins, Ruth V, 176
Hawkins, Ruth V, 195
Hawkins, Ruth V, 208
Hawkins, Ruth V, 561
Hawkins, Ruth V, 574
Hawkins, Ruth V, 593
Hawkins, Sally V, 70
Hawkins, Sally VI, 930
Hawkins, Samuel VI, 399
Hawkins, Samuel VI, 597
Hawkins, Sarah I, 100
Hawkins, Sarah I, 1057
Hawkins, Sarah I, 1059
Hawkins, Sarah I, 1060
Hawkins, Sarah I, 1061
Hawkins, Sarah I, 1062
Hawkins, Sarah I, 1063
Hawkins, Sarah III, 19
Hawkins, Sarah III, 157
Hawkins, Sarah V, 58
Hawkins, Sarah V, 70
Hawkins, Sarah V, 160
Hawkins, Sarah V, 162
Hawkins, Sarah V, 163
Hawkins, Sarah V, 175
Hawkins, Sarah V, 177
Hawkins, Sarah V, 190
Hawkins, Sarah V, 196
Hawkins, Sarah V, 469
Hawkins, Sarah V, 574
Hawkins, Sarah V, 842
Hawkins, Sarah VI, 399
Hawkins, Sarah A. VI, 832
Hawkins, Sarah H. V, 70
Hawkins, Sarah H. V, 85
Hawkins, Sarah H. V, 574
Hawkins, Sarah N. V, 574
Hawkins, Sarah N. V, 579
Hawkins, Sarah W. V, 176
Hawkins, Sarah W. V, 191
Hawkins, Seth V, 70
Hawkins, Seth V, 574

wkins, Son V, 574
wkins, Stephen I, 1057
wkins, Stephen I, 1061
wkins, Stephen V, 175
wkins, Susan V, 70
wkins, Susan V, 97
wkins, Susan V, 575
wkins, Susan V, 585
wkins, Susan B. VI, 930
wkins, Susanna I, 1057
wkins, Susanna V, 155
wkins, Susanna V, 175
wkins, Susanna V, 176
wkins, Susanna V, 198
wkins, Susanna V, 206
wkins, Susannah V, 176
wkins, Susannah V, 208
wkins, Tamer I, 1061
wkins, Thomas I, 1020
wkins, Thomas II, 373
wkins, Thomas V, 176
wkins, Thomas V, 181
wkins, Thomas V, 490
wkins, Thomas V, 498
wkins, Veny VI, 930
wkins, Viola V, 680
wkins, Viola J. V, 177
wkins, Viola K. V, 70
wkins, Viola K. V, 176
wkins, Viola K. V, 177
wkins, Viola K. V, 680
wkins, Violet Rose V, 499
wkins, Walter C. V, 574
wkins, Walter C. V, 575
wkins, William I, 1020
wkins, William I, 1057
wkins, William I, 1061
wkins, William II, 230
wkins, William V, 166
wkins, William V, 175
wkins, William V, 176
wkins, William V, 574
wkins, William V, 842
wkins, William VI, 823
wkins, William VI, 824
wkins, William VI, 825
wkins, William VI, 885
wkins, William VI, 919
wkins, William VI, 930
wkins, William VI, 940
wkins, William VI, 951
wkins, William A. V, 176
wkins, William E. VI, 930
wkins, William H. V, 574
wkins, William P. V, 574
wkins, William, Jr. VI, 940
wkins, William, Sr. VI, 930
wkins, William, Sr. VI, 965
wkins, Wm. II, 873
wkins, Wm. VI, 504
wkins, Wm. VI, 912
wkins, Wm. H. V, 574
wkins, Wm. H. V, 575
wkins, Wm. Pearson II, 873
wks, Edward IV, 765
wks, Elvira W. IV, 718
wks, George W. III, 157
wks, Isaiah J. IV, 718
wks, Isaiah Jones IV, 718
wks, Lydia Maria IV, 718
wks, Lydia Mariah IV, 962
wks, Martha IV, 765
wks, Martha S. IV, 718
wks, Martha S. IV, 962
wks, Martha S. IV, 1002
wks, Mary IV, 1253
wks, Phebe IV, 765
wks, William IV, 718
wks, Wm. IV, 718
wks, Wm. VI, 908
wksworth, Elizabeth II, 545
wksworth, John II, 545
wksworth, Wm. II, 545
wle, Elizabeth VI, 805
wle, Jno. T. VI, 805
wley, Amanda IV, 631
wley, Amos IV, 37
wley, Amos IV, 631
wley, Ann IV, 335
wley, Benj. IV, 697
wley, Benjamin IV, 37
wley, Benjamin IV, 631
wley, Benjamin IV, 718
wley, Benjamin IV, 821
wley, Benjamin IV, 871
wley, Benjamin IV, 963
wley, Caleb IV, 37
wley, Caleb IV, 335
wley, Caleb IV, 611
wley, Caleb IV, 631
wley, Caleb IV, 638
Hawley, Caleb IV, 718
Hawley, Caleb IV, 821
Hawley, Caleb IV, 871
Hawley, Caleb IV, 873
Hawley, Caleb IV, 897
Hawley, Caleb IV, 906
Hawley, Caleb P. IV, 871
Hawley, Catharine IV, 631
Hawley, Catharine IV, 638
Hawley, Catharine IV, 821
Hawley, Catharine IV, 871
Hawley, Catharine IV, 906
Hawley, David IV, 37
Hawley, David IV, 613
Hawley, David IV, 631
Hawley, Elisha IV, 37
Hawley, Elisha IV, 631
Hawley, Elisha IV, 718
Hawley, Eliza IV, 718
Hawley, Eliza IV, 777
Hawley, Eliza IV, 821
Hawley, Elizabeth IV, 613
Hawley, Elizabeth IV, 631
Hawley, Esther II, 137
Hawley, Hannah IV, 37
Hawley, Hannah IV, 335
Hawley, Hannah IV, 611
Hawley, Hannah IV, 631
Hawley, Hannah IV, 718
Hawley, Hannah IV, 821
Hawley, Hannah IV, 871
Hawley, Hannah IV, 892
Hawley, Hannah, Jr. IV, 631
Hawley, Hannah, Jr. IV, 718
Hawley, Hannah, Sr. IV, 631
Hawley, Hannah, Sr. IV, 718
Hawley, James IV, 871
Hawley, Jesse II, 137
Hawley, Jesse IV, 37
Hawley, Jesse IV, 631
Hawley, Jesse IV, 718
Hawley, Joseph IV, 821
Hawley, Joseph IV, 871
Hawley, Latham IV, 871
Hawley, Martha J. V, 910
Hawley, Martha J. V, 914
Hawley, Mary II, 796
Hawley, Mary IV, 37
Hawley, Mary IV, 611
Hawley, Mary IV, 631
Hawley, Mary IV, 697
Hawley, Mary IV, 718
Hawley, Mary IV, 821
Hawley, Mary IV, 891
Hawley, Mary IV, 892
Hawley, Mary IV, 963
Hawley, Mary Ann IV, 906
Hawley, Mary Ann IV, 909
Hawley, Nathan IV, 37
Hawley, Nathan IV, 38
Hawley, Phebe II, 721
Hawley, Phebe Ann IV, 871
Hawley, Rachel IV, 335
Hawley, Rachel IV, 345
Hawley, Rachel IV, 613
Hawley, Rachel IV, 631
Hawley, Rachel IV, 651
Hawley, Rebecca II, 137
Hawley, Richard IV, 37
Hawley, Richard IV, 335
Hawley, Richard IV, 345
Hawley, Richard IV, 631
Hawley, Richard IV, 651
Hawley, Robert IV, 718
Hawley, Samuel D. IV, 718
Hawley, Sarah IV, 718
Hawley, Sarah IV, 821
Hawley, Sarah B. IV, 1024
Hawley, Sarah B. IV, 1026
Hawley, Tacy IV, 871
Hawley, Tacy IV, 873
Hawley, Wm. IV, 718
Hawly, David IV, 610
Hawly, Elizabeth IV, 1367
Hawly, Rachel IV, 610
Hawly, Thomas IV, 1367
Hawly, Vicena IV, 1367
Hawmire, Liewella IV, 219
Hawn, Helen IV, 924
Hawn, Helen Ball IV, 963
Hawood, Ann II, 444
Hawood, John II, 373
Hawood, John II, 444
Hawood, Mary II, 373
Hawood, Samuel II, 373
Hawood, Sarah II, 444
Haworth, Abigail I, 782
Haworth, Abigail I, 794
Haworth, Abigail I, 854
Haworth, Abigail I, 881
Haworth, Abigail R. I, 882
Haworth, Absalom I, 1031
Haworth, Absalom VI, 399
Haworth, Absolem VI, 399
Haworth, Adaliza I, 882
Haworth, Adam B. I, 854
Haworth, Albert W. I, 1154
Haworth, Alla Jane V, 624
Haworth, Allen V, 499
Haworth, Alma Gladys IV, 1319
Haworth, Alvida V, 625
Haworth, Alvida V, 681
Haworth, Alvida Elizabeth V, 624
Haworth, Alvin I, 882
Haworth, Alvin H. I, 882
Haworth, Alvira T. I, 624
Haworth, Amanda I, 1106
Haworth, Amanda Emeline I, 882
Haworth, Amelia F. I, 854
Haworth, Ann I, 544
Haworth, Ann I, 854
Haworth, Ann I, 881
Haworth, Ann I, 963
Haworth, Ann I, 1028
Haworth, Ann I, 1031
Haworth, Ann I, 1101
Haworth, Ann I, 1106
Haworth, Ann I, 1116
Haworth, Ann I, 1120
Haworth, Ann V, 749
Haworth, Ann V, 806
Haworth, Ann V, 809
Haworth, Ann V, 813
Haworth, Ann B. IV, 822
Haworth, Ann B. IV, 842
Haworth, Anna I, 1116
Haworth, Anna I, 1121
Haworth, Anna V, 617
Haworth, Anna Elizabeth V, 624
Haworth, Anne V, 499
Haworth, Annie B. I, 1154
Haworth, Arthur J. IV, 475
Haworth, Asenath I, 854
Haworth, Asenath IV, 718
Haworth, Benjamin V, 617
Haworth, Benjamin C. I, 1106
Haworth, Benjamin Franklin I, 854
Haworth, Bertha Anna I, 926
Haworth, Bertha H. I, 930
Haworth, Bethany I, 814
Haworth, Betsy I, 854
Haworth, Betsy V, 807
Haworth, Betsy Davis V, 742
Haworth, Betsy Jane I, 1106
Haworth, Betty V, 809
Haworth, Bonnie Lou IV, 718
Haworth, Caroline V, 499
Haworth, Caroline V, 624
Haworth, Caroline E. V, 499
Haworth, Caroline Elizabeth V, 497
Haworth, Caroline Elizabeth V, 499
Haworth, Carrie Antram V, 681
Haworth, Catharine An I, 854
Haworth, Catharine L. I, 854
Haworth, Catherine I, 882
Haworth, Catherine I, 895
Haworth, Catherine L. I, 882
Haworth, Chamness I, 544
Haworth, Charity I, 531
Haworth, Charity I, 544
Haworth, Charity I, 963
Haworth, Charity I, 1106
Haworth, Charity I, 1116
Haworth, Charity I, 1121
Haworth, Charity V, 70
Haworth, Charity V, 244
Haworth, Charity V, 272
Haworth, Charity Chamney I, 544
Haworth, Charles IV, 963
Haworth, Charles V, 625
Haworth, Charles V, 681
Haworth, Charles E. IV, 718
Haworth, Charles Edgar IV, 963
Haworth, Chas. V, 617
Haworth, Chas. C. V, 625
Haworth, Chester C. I, 926
Haworth, Chester C. I, 942
Haworth, Chester C. I, 948
Haworth, Cinthy V, 809
Haworth, Cisilia I, 1106
Haworth, Cisily I, 1121
Haworth, Cisly I, 1118
Haworth, Cisly I, 1120
Haworth, Clarkson I, 854
Haworth, Clarkson I, 882
Haworth, Clayton M. V, 393
Haworth, Clemmons I, 882
Haworth, Clemons G. I, 854
Haworth, Clifford L. VI, 747
Haworth, Clifford L. VI, 759
Haworth, Clinton V, 624
Haworth, Clinton V, 625
Haworth, Clinton V, 681
Haworth, Cornelia I, 882
Haworth, Cynthia I, 854
Haworth, Cynthia I, 870
Haworth, Cynthia I, 882
Haworth, Cynthia V, 809
Haworth, Cynthy V, 805
Haworth, Cynthy V, 809
Haworth, Cyrus I, 882
Haworth, Cyrus B. I, 854
Haworth, Cyrus B. I, 882
Haworth, D. Henry I, 854
Haworth, D. Riley I, 1154
Haworth, Daisy S. IV, 475
Haworth, Daniel V, 335
Haworth, Daniel B. I, 1106
Haworth, David I, 544
Haworth, David I, 963
Haworth, David I, 1105
Haworth, David I, 1106
Haworth, David V, 70
Haworth, David V, 335
Haworth, David M. V, 809
Haworth, Dayton D. IV, 1319
Haworth, Deborah I, 877
Haworth, Deborah I, 881
Haworth, Delphina I, 875
Haworth, Delphina I, 882
Haworth, Dillon V, 70
Haworth, Dillon V, 499
Haworth, Doctor H. I, 882
Haworth, E. C. V, 625
Haworth, Edgar IV, 718
Haworth, Edgar IV, 963
Haworth, Edgar G. IV, 718
Haworth, Edgar G. IV, 963
Haworth, Edith I, 931
Haworth, Edith V, 393
Haworth, Edith V, 499
Haworth, Edith V, 624
Haworth, Edith V, 681
Haworth, Edith V, 695
Haworth, Edith V, 718
Haworth, Edith Emeline V, 499
Haworth, Edith Emily V, 499
Haworth, Edith Emily V, 517
Haworth, Edith Floy I, 926
Haworth, Edward V, 625
Haworth, Edward V, 681
Haworth, Eli I, 854
Haworth, Eli I, 881
Haworth, Eli I, 882
Haworth, Eli V, 192
Haworth, Eli V, 499
Haworth, Eli C. I, 882
Haworth, Eli J. I, 882
Haworth, Eli S. I, 854
Haworth, Elie, Jr. I, 882
Haworth, Elijah I, 499
Haworth, Elijah I, 881
Haworth, Elijah V, 393
Haworth, Elijah V, 624
Haworth, Elijah V, 649
Haworth, Elijah M. V, 625
Haworth, Elim, Jr. I, 882
Haworth, Elisa V, 809
Haworth, Elisabeth V, 244
Haworth, Eliza I, 854
Haworth, Elizabeth I, 537
Haworth, Elizabeth I, 544
Haworth, Elizabeth I, 570
Haworth, Elizabeth I, 782
Haworth, Elizabeth I, 854
Haworth, Elizabeth I, 881
Haworth, Elizabeth I, 1089
Haworth, Elizabeth I, 1093
Haworth, Elizabeth I, 1094
Haworth, Elizabeth I, 1120
Haworth, Elizabeth I, 1121
Haworth, Elizabeth I, 1125
Haworth, Elizabeth V, 71
Haworth, Elizabeth V, 393
Haworth, Elizabeth V, 403
Haworth, Elizabeth V, 436
Haworth, Elizabeth V, 499
Haworth, Elizabeth V, 566
Haworth, Elizabeth V, 624
Haworth, Elizabeth V, 625
Haworth, Elizabeth V, 649
Haworth, Elizabeth V, 681
Haworth, Elizabeth V, 735
Haworth, Elizabeth V, 809
Haworth, Elizabeth C. I, 854
Haworth, Elizabeth C. I, 882
Haworth, Elizabeth P. V, 681
Haworth, Elizabeth Shepard I, 782
Haworth, Elkanah V, 499
Haworth, Ella I, 926
Haworth, Ella I, 930
Haworth, Elvira I, 882
Haworth, Elwood IV, 821
Haworth, Elwood IV, 1132
Haworth, Elwood V, 617
Haworth, Emilia V, 393
Haworth, Emiline I, 926
Haworth, Emily I, 882
Haworth, Emily F. I, 882
Haworth, Emma IV, 1319
Haworth, Emma V, 681
Haworth, Emma C. V, 681
Haworth, Emma G. IV, 1319
Haworth, English I, 854
Haworth, English I, 882
Haworth, Enos E. V, 809
Haworth, Ester I, 881
Haworth, Esther IV, 1319
Haworth, Esther V, 335
Haworth, Esther V, 742
Haworth, Ethel Louisa V, 681
Haworth, Eunice V, 192
Haworth, Eunice Emma V, 624
Haworth, Evalin M. I, 1154
Haworth, Evelyn I, 942
Haworth, Ezekiel V, 71
Haworth, Ezekiel V, 335
Haworth, Ezekiel V, 393
Haworth, Ezekiel V, 403
Haworth, Ezekiel V, 436
Haworth, Ezekiel V, 499
Haworth, Ezekiel V, 624
Haworth, Ezekiel V, 625
Haworth, Ezekiel, Jr. V, 335
Haworth, Ezekiel, Jr. V, 393
Haworth, Flemmon V, 393
Haworth, Flora I, 854
Haworth, Flora I, 882
Haworth, Flora V, 335
Haworth, Flora A. V, 335
Haworth, Flora A. V, 393
Haworth, Frances IV, 718
Haworth, Frances IV, 963
Haworth, Frances V, 244
Haworth, Frances Emily B. V, 624
Haworth, Frances Willard IV, 963
Haworth, Francis Murray IV, 475
Haworth, Francis Murry IV, 475
Haworth, Frank I, 1154
Haworth, Frank V, 681
Haworth, Frank White V, 499
Haworth, Geo. V, 624
Haworth, Geo. D. V, 624
Haworth, Geo. D. V, 681
Haworth, Geo. D. V, 695
Haworth, George I, 394
Haworth, George I, 499
Haworth, George I, 544
Haworth, George I, 624
Haworth, George I, 854
Haworth, George I, 877
Haworth, George I, 881
Haworth, George I, 1031
Haworth, George I, 1077
Haworth, George I, 1093
Haworth, George I, 1094
Haworth, George II, 545
Haworth, George II, 609
Haworth, George II, 1000
Haworth, George II, 1025
Haworth, George V, 70
Haworth, George V, 71
Haworth, George V, 244
Haworth, George V, 335
Haworth, George V, 499
Haworth, George V, 537
Haworth, George V, 624
Haworth, George B. I, 854
Haworth, George B. I, 882
Haworth, George D. V, 393
Haworth, George D. V, 481
Haworth, George D. V, 499
Haworth, George D. V, 681
Haworth, George D., Jr. V, 499
Haworth, George H. V, 499
Haworth, George, Jr. I, 881
Haworth, George, Jr. V, 499
Haworth, Glenna V, 335
Haworth, Hanna V, 681
Haworth, Hannah I, 814
Haworth, Hannah I, 854
Haworth, Hannah I, 882
Haworth, Hannah I, 893
Haworth, Hannah I, 901
Haworth, Hannah I, 1106
Haworth, Hannah I, 1121
Haworth, Hannah I, 1126

Haworth, Hannah V, 161
Haworth, Hannah V, 177
Haworth, Hannah V, 624
Haworth, Hannah V, 681
Haworth, Hannah VI, 399
Haworth, Hannah C. V, 625
Haworth, Hannah C. B. I, 882
Haworth, Hannah E. I, 1106
Haworth, Harper I, 926
Haworth, Harriet E. V, 566
Haworth, Harriet E. V, 623
Haworth, Harriet E. V, 625
Haworth, Harriet Ellen V, 624
Haworth, Harriet M. I, 1106
Haworth, Harriett V, 681
Haworth, Harriett E. V, 677
Haworth, Helen Curl V, 681
Haworth, Henriann V, 624
Haworth, Henrietta IV, 718
Haworth, Henrietta IV, 963
Haworth, Henry I, 854
Haworth, Henry I, 881
Haworth, Henry I, 882
Haworth, Henry T. I, 854
Haworth, Henry T. I, 882
Haworth, Herman V, 499
Haworth, Hester V, 330
Haworth, Hester V, 335
Haworth, Hicajah H. V, 616
Haworth, Homer Franklin I, 926
Haworth, Horace Starbuck I, 926
Haworth, Hubert O. I, 882
Haworth, Ida V, 625
Haworth, Ida M. V, 625
Haworth, Ila V, 513
Haworth, Isaac I, 1106
Haworth, Isaac Joseph I, 1106
Haworth, Isaiah V, 393
Haworth, Isaiah V, 499
Haworth, Isaiah V, 506
Haworth, Isaiah M. V, 624
Haworth, Isaiah M. V, 625
Haworth, J. G. I, 930
Haworth, James I, 544
Haworth, James I, 854
Haworth, James I, 881
Haworth, James I, 882
Haworth, James I, 963
Haworth, James I, 1015
Haworth, James I, 1031
Haworth, James I, 1077
Haworth, James I, 1093
Haworth, James I, 1094
Haworth, James I, 1106
Haworth, James V, 70
Haworth, James V, 71
Haworth, James V, 244
Haworth, James V, 248
Haworth, James V, 272
Haworth, James V, 499
Haworth, James V, 624
Haworth, James V, 681
Haworth, James V, 799
Haworth, James V, 807
Haworth, James V, 813
Haworth, James VI, 399
Haworth, James E. V, 681
Haworth, James L. I, 854
Haworth, James L. I, 882
Haworth, James M. V, 624
Haworth, James M. V, 681
Haworth, James Malon V, 499
Haworth, James R. V, 499
Haworth, James Ridgley V, 681
Haworth, James S. V, 681
Haworth, James W. V, 393
Haworth, James Wright V, 499
Haworth, Jane I, 1106
Haworth, Jane II, 545
Haworth, Jane IV, 617
Haworth, Jane IV, 819
Haworth, Jane V, 244
Haworth, Jane V, 284
Haworth, Jane V, 393
Haworth, Jane V, 407
Haworth, Jane V, 625
Haworth, Jehu I, 1093
Haworth, Jehu V, 617
Haworth, Jemima I, 1031
Haworth, Jemima I, 1039
Haworth, Jennie V, 625
Haworth, Jennie V, 681
Haworth, Jeremiah I, 881
Haworth, Joanna V, 499
Haworth, Joanna V, 537
Haworth, Joanna Buskler V, 499
Haworth, Joel I, 544
Haworth, Joel I, 963
Haworth, Joel I, 1106
Haworth, Joel I, 1120
Haworth, Joel I, 1125
Haworth, Joel V, 335
Haworth, John I, 499
Haworth, John I, 544
Haworth, John I, 814
Haworth, John I, 854
Haworth, John I, 881
Haworth, John I, 882
Haworth, John I, 963
Haworth, John I, 1084
Haworth, John I, 1089
Haworth, John I, 1093
Haworth, John I, 1106
Haworth, John I, 1118
Haworth, John I, 1120
Haworth, John I, 1121
Haworth, John II, 545
Haworth, John II, 609
Haworth, John II, 707
Haworth, John V, 71
Haworth, John V, 499
Haworth, John VI, 399
Haworth, John A. I, 882
Haworth, John Allen I, 854
Haworth, John F. I, 926
Haworth, John F. V, 624
Haworth, John H. I, 1154
Haworth, Jonah V, 499
Haworth, Jonah V, 624
Haworth, Jonah F. V, 499
Haworth, Jonathan I, 544
Haworth, Jonathan I, 963
Haworth, Jonathan I, 1105
Haworth, Jonathan I, 1106
Haworth, Jonathan V, 70
Haworth, Jonathan V, 244
Haworth, Jonathan V, 261
Haworth, Jonathan V, 330
Haworth, Jonathan V, 335
Haworth, Jonathan V, 499
Haworth, Josiah I, 881
Haworth, Julia A. IV, 1128
Haworth, Julia A. IV, 1132
Haworth, Julian V, 809
Haworth, Julius Jasper I, 926
Haworth, Katy V, 617
Haworth, Keziah V, 809
Haworth, Laura I, 854
Haworth, Laura I, 882
Haworth, Laura Bell V, 499
Haworth, Lawrence V, 624
Haworth, Lenora P. V, 625
Haworth, Lida E. I, 1154
Haworth, Lilissa V, 393
Haworth, Lindsay I, 854
Haworth, Linsay I, 882
Haworth, Louisa IV, 812
Haworth, Louisa IV, 822
Haworth, Louisa V, 622
Haworth, Louisa V, 625
Haworth, Louisa D. IV, 822
Haworth, Lucinda I, 882
Haworth, Lucinda V, 809
Haworth, Lydia I, 1106
Haworth, Lydia I, 1121
Haworth, M. M. I, 925
Haworth, M. Victoria I, 626
Haworth, Mabel V, 742
Haworth, Mabel Doan V, 393
Haworth, Mabel Doan V, 625
Haworth, Madison I, 882
Haworth, Maggie I, 920
Haworth, Mahlon I, 1093
Haworth, Mahlon I, 1094
Haworth, Mahlon I, 1106
Haworth, Mahlon I, 1154
Haworth, Mahlon V, 71
Haworth, Mahlon V, 335
Haworth, Mahlon V, 393
Haworth, Mahlon V, 499
Haworth, Mahlon V, 610
Haworth, Mahlon V, 624
Haworth, Malissa V, 393
Haworth, Malon V, 393
Haworth, Margaret I, 544
Haworth, Margaret I, 854
Haworth, Margaret I, 881
Haworth, Margaret I, 882
Haworth, Margaret I, 902
Haworth, Margaret I, 926
Haworth, Margaret VI, 747
Haworth, Margaret VI, 759
Haworth, Margaret L. I, 882
Haworth, Margret I, 881
Haworth, Marmaduke I, 854
Haworth, Marmaduke I, 882
Haworth, Marmaduke M. I, 854
Haworth, Martha I, 782
Haworth, Martha II, 545
Haworth, Martha II, 609
Haworth, Martha V, 335
Haworth, Martha V, 624
Haworth, Martha V, 625
Haworth, Martha V, 627
Haworth, Martha E. I, 882
Haworth, Mary I, 499
Haworth, Mary I, 544
Haworth, Mary I, 773
Haworth, Mary I, 854
Haworth, Mary I, 881
Haworth, Mary I, 882
Haworth, Mary I, 901
Haworth, Mary I, 925
Haworth, Mary I, 963
Haworth, Mary I, 1093
Haworth, Mary I, 1106
Haworth, Mary I, 1116
Haworth, Mary I, 1121
Haworth, Mary I, 1154
Haworth, Mary II, 545
Haworth, Mary II, 609
Haworth, Mary V, 70
Haworth, Mary V, 248
Haworth, Mary V, 272
Haworth, Mary V, 335
Haworth, Mary V, 393
Haworth, Mary V, 493
Haworth, Mary V, 499
Haworth, Mary V, 506
Haworth, Mary V, 624
Haworth, Mary V, 625
Haworth, Mary V, 681
Haworth, Mary V, 809
Haworth, Mary V, 813
Haworth, Mary A. V, 335
Haworth, Mary C. I, 854
Haworth, Mary C. I, 882
Haworth, Mary E. IV, 718
Haworth, Mary J. V, 393
Haworth, Mary Jane V, 625
Haworth, Mary R. V, 681
Haworth, Mary Victoria I, 619
Haworth, Mary Victoria I, 624
Haworth, Matilda IV, 821
Haworth, Matilda IV, 1132
Haworth, Melissa V, 499
Haworth, Micajah I, 499
Haworth, Micajah I, 544
Haworth, Micajah I, 773
Haworth, Micajah I, 847
Haworth, Micajah I, 881
Haworth, Micajah H. V, 624
Haworth, Micajah H. V, 625
Haworth, Micajah, Jr. I, 881
Haworth, Micjah Henry V, 624
Haworth, Mildred Maria I, 882
Haworth, Minerva I, 882
Haworth, Minerva V, 499
Haworth, Moorman I, 1084
Haworth, Moorman V, 71
Haworth, Moorman V, 499
Haworth, Nancy V, 335
Haworth, Nancy V, 393
Haworth, Nancy V, 394
Haworth, Nancy V, 681
Haworth, Nathan I, 881
Haworth, Nathan I, 882
Haworth, Nathan J. I, 854
Haworth, Nathaniel V, 809
Haworth, Noah I, 1106
Haworth, Nora I, 882
Haworth, Nora I, 900
Haworth, Ora V, 625
Haworth, Orian V, 681
Haworth, Orion V, 625
Haworth, Orpha IV, 1319
Haworth, Otis V, 681
Haworth, Otis L. V, 681
Haworth, Owen V, 393
Haworth, Pandora H. I, 925
Haworth, Pearl V, 177
Haworth, Pearl V, 625
Haworth, Peggy I, 881
Haworth, Peggy I, 887
Haworth, Pharibe I, 881
Haworth, Phebe I, 544
Haworth, Phebe I, 773
Haworth, Phebe I, 814
Haworth, Phebe I, 827
Haworth, Phebe V, 71
Haworth, Phebe V, 244
Haworth, Phebe V, 284
Haworth, Phebe V, 393
Haworth, Phebe V, 403
Haworth, Phebe V, 499
Haworth, Phebe V, 505
Haworth, Phebe V, 610
Haworth, Phebe V, 624
Haworth, Phebe V, 696
Haworth, Phebe V, 799
Haworth, Phebe A. V, 616
Haworth, Phebe A. V, 625
Haworth, Phebe Ann V, 177
Haworth, Phebe Ann V, 192
Haworth, Phebe Ann V, 624
Haworth, Phebe Ann V, 625
Haworth, Phebe E. V, 624
Haworth, Pleasent I, 1105
Haworth, Ploly I, 854
Haworth, Polly I, 854
Haworth, Preston I, 1106
Haworth, Prudence V, 809
Haworth, Rachel I, 394
Haworth, Rachel I, 531
Haworth, Rachel I, 544
Haworth, Rachel I, 814
Haworth, Rachel I, 820
Haworth, Rachel I, 823
Haworth, Rachel I, 854
Haworth, Rachel I, 882
Haworth, Rachel V, 71
Haworth, Rachel V, 499
Haworth, Racher V, 499
Haworth, Ralph V, 681
Haworth, Rebecca II, 373
Haworth, Rebecca II, 545
Haworth, Rebecca V, 71
Haworth, Rebecca V, 393
Haworth, Rebecca V, 429
Haworth, Rebecca V, 499
Haworth, Rebecca V, 624
Haworth, Rebecca V, 681
Haworth, Rebecca J. V, 335
Haworth, Rebecca Jane V, 335
Haworth, Rebecca Jane V, 681
Haworth, Regina I, 882
Haworth, Rejoina I, 854
Haworth, Richard I, 544
Haworth, Richard I, 782
Haworth, Richard I, 794
Haworth, Richard I, 881
Haworth, Richard I, 889
Haworth, Richard I, 963
Haworth, Richard I, 1101
Haworth, Richard I, 1105
Haworth, Richard I, 1106
Haworth, Richard I, 1120
Haworth, Richard IV, 812
Haworth, Richard IV, 821
Haworth, Richard IV, 842
Haworth, Richard IV, 1128
Haworth, Richard IV, 1132
Haworth, Richard V, 70
Haworth, Richard V, 499
Haworth, Richard V, 566
Haworth, Richard V, 624
Haworth, Richard V, 625
Haworth, Richard Harden I, 1106
Haworth, Robert T. I, 1154
Haworth, Ruth I, 782
Haworth, Ruth I, 794
Haworth, Ruth I, 881
Haworth, Ruth I, 889
Haworth, Ruth V, 499
Haworth, Ruth V, 681
Haworth, Ruth V, 696
Haworth, Ruth Esther IV, 475
Haworth, Ruth Olive V, 681
Haworth, Sally I, 882
Haworth, Sampson V, 742
Haworth, Samuel I, 499
Haworth, Samuel I, 881
Haworth, Samuel V, 70
Haworth, Samuel V, 499
Haworth, Samuel C. V, 335
Haworth, Samuel C. V, 393
Haworth, Samuel L. I, 1154
Haworth, Sara I, 948
Haworth, Sarah I, 544
Haworth, Sarah I, 877
Haworth, Sarah I, 881
Haworth, Sarah I, 882
Haworth, Sarah I, 963
Haworth, Sarah I, 1031
Haworth, Sarah I, 1106
Haworth, Sarah I, 1121
Haworth, Sarah II, 1000
Haworth, Sarah II, 1025
Haworth, Sarah V, 70
Haworth, Sarah V, 244
Haworth, Sarah V, 248
Haworth, Sarah V, 261
Haworth, Sarah V, 335
Haworth, Sarah V, 481
Haworth, Sarah V, 499
Haworth, Sarah V, 681
Haworth, Sarah VI, 399
Haworth, Sarah Ann I, 1106
Haworth, Sarah Deborah I, 854
Haworth, Sarah E. V, 335
Haworth, Sarah E. V, 393
Haworth, Sarah E. T. I, 1154
Haworth, Sarah Jane I, 1106
Haworth, Sarah Jane V, 809
Haworth, Sarah T. I, 1121
Haworth, Solomon I, 854
Haworth, Solomon I, 881
Haworth, Solomon I, 882
Haworth, Stephanas I, 881
Haworth, Stephanas I, 1093
Haworth, Stephans I, 881
Haworth, Stephanus I, 782
Haworth, Stephanus I, 881
Haworth, Stephenas I, 499
Haworth, Stephenas I, 544
Haworth, Stephenas I, 570
Haworth, Stephenas I, 854
Haworth, Stephenes I, 881
Haworth, Stephenus VI, 399
Haworth, Susanah I, 1084
Haworth, Susanah I, 1106
Haworth, Susann V, 499
Haworth, Susanna I, 1115
Haworth, Susanna I, 1121
Haworth, Susanna II, 707
Haworth, Susanna V, 71
Haworth, Susanna V, 809
Haworth, Susannah I, 1093
Haworth, Susannah I, 1105
Haworth, Susannah V, 70
Haworth, Susannah V, 71
Haworth, Susannah V, 393
Haworth, Susannah V, 499
Haworth, Susannah V, 613
Haworth, Susannah V, 624
Haworth, Susannah V, 809
Haworth, Sylvester V, 335
Haworth, Sylvester V, 624
Haworth, Sylvester V, 625
Haworth, Thelma IV, 718
Haworth, Thomas I, 1106
Haworth, Thomas C. V, 335
Haworth, Thomas C. V, 681
Haworth, Thomas Mahlon V,
Haworth, Thos. M. V, 625
Haworth, Uriah V, 393
Haworth, Verginia Adaline I, 1106
Haworth, Victory I, 882
Haworth, W. Oliver I, 1154
Haworth, Walter T. V, 742
Haworth, Welmet I, 854
Haworth, Welmett I, 394
Haworth, Welmett I, 402
Haworth, Wesley I, 1106
Haworth, William I, 544
Haworth, William I, 882
Haworth, William I, 963
Haworth, William I, 1093
Haworth, William I, 1106
Haworth, William V, 70
Haworth, William V, 335
Haworth, William V, 499
Haworth, William V, 624
Haworth, William M. I, 882
Haworth, Wm. V, 625
Haworth, Wm. Lewes I, 1106
Hawot, Evelyn G. I, 942
Hawot, Evelyn L. I, 942
Hawot, Frances I, 942
Hawot, George B. I, 942
Hawot, Helen I, 942
Hawot, Horace S. I, 942
Hawot, Ila I, 942
Hawot, Ila Bennett I, 942
Hawot, James I, 942
Hawot, Jerome I, 942
Hawot, Jerome W. I, 942
Hawot, Jesse B. I, 942
Hawot, Katharine I, 942
Hawot, Laura Lamb I, 942
Hawot, Louise I, 942
Haws, Elizabeth VI, 826
Haws, George W. V, 625
Haws, Harriet A. V, 625
Haws, Hattie V, 625
Haws, James L. V, 625
Haws, Martha V, 625
Haws, Reuben VI, 930
Haws, Sarah V, 625
Haws, Sarah L. V, 625
Haws, Tabitha VI, 930
Haws, Thos. V, 625
Haws, William VI, 930
Hawson, Dorothy VI, 824
Hawson, William VI, 824
Hawthorn, Catherine E. V, 57
Hawthorn, Ellis Lemoin IV, 2
Hawthorn, Ethel V, 575
Hawthorn, Geo. V, 575
Hawthorn, George W. V, 575
Hawthorn, Gertrude IV, 219
Hawthorn, Helen IV, 175
Hawthorn, Helen IV, 219
Hawthorn, Mabel IV, 219

Hawthorn, Mable IV, 219
Hawthorn, Ruby IV, 1319
Hawthorn, Samantha V, 575
Hawxhurst, ??? III, 159
Hawxhurst, Almy III, 159
Hawxhurst, Amy III, 65
Hawxhurst, Amy III, 157
Hawxhurst, Ann III, 157
Hawxhurst, Ann III, 158
Hawxhurst, Ann III, 414
Hawxhurst, Ann III, 484
Hawxhurst, Anna III, 414
Hawxhurst, Anna III, 415
Hawxhurst, Augustus III, 415
Hawxhurst, Benj. III, 158
Hawxhurst, Benjamin III, 157
Hawxhurst, Benjamin III, 414
Hawxhurst, Benjamin III, 432
Hawxhurst, Bertha III, 414
Hawxhurst, Bertha III, 415
Hawxhurst, Bertha III, 458
Hawxhurst, Caroline III, 158
Hawxhurst, Caroline III, 414
Hawxhurst, Caroline III, 415
Hawxhurst, Caroline III, 446
Hawxhurst, Caroline III, 484
Hawxhurst, Caroline S. III, 157
Hawxhurst, Caroline S. III, 158
Hawxhurst, Cath. III, 158
Hawxhurst, Catharine III, 89
Hawxhurst, Catharine III, 157
Hawxhurst, Catharine III, 158
Hawxhurst, Catharine III, 483
Hawxhurst, Charity III, 414
Hawxhurst, Charity III, 415
Hawxhurst, Charity III, 450
Hawxhurst, Charles P. III, 484
Hawxhurst, Clarissa III, 415
Hawxhurst, Daisy III, 158
Hawxhurst, Daisy Eliz III, 158
Hawxhurst, Daniel III, 65
Hawxhurst, Daniel III, 157
Hawxhurst, Daniel III, 322
Hawxhurst, Daniel III, 414
Hawxhurst, Daniel K. II, 799
Hawxhurst, Daniel K. II, 874
Hawxhurst, Daniel K. III, 157
Hawxhurst, Daniel K. III, 158
Hawxhurst, Daniel K. III, 299
Hawxhurst, Daniel K. III, 311
Hawxhurst, Daniel S. III, 157
Hawxhurst, Deborah III, 158
Hawxhurst, Deborah III, 414
Hawxhurst, Edmund III, 157
Hawxhurst, Edmund III, 159
Hawxhurst, Eleanor III, 415
Hawxhurst, Eleanor III, 416
Hawxhurst, Elisha III, 158
Hawxhurst, Elisha III, 414
Hawxhurst, Elisha III, 483
Hawxhurst, Eliz. III, 415
Hawxhurst, Eliz. III, 483
Hawxhurst, Eliza III, 483
Hawxhurst, Elizabeth III, 414
Hawxhurst, Elizabeth III, 415
Hawxhurst, Elizabeth III, 462
Hawxhurst, Elizabeth III, 463
Hawxhurst, Elizabeth III, 464
Hawxhurst, Elizabeth III, 483
Hawxhurst, Elizabeth III, 484
Hawxhurst, Elizabeth III, 491
Hawxhurst, Elizabeth Anna III, 415
Hawxhurst, Emma III, 81
Hawxhurst, Emma III, 158
Hawxhurst, Ephraim III, 415
Hawxhurst, Ephraim III, 424
Hawxhurst, Ephraim III, 426
Hawxhurst, Ephraim III, 450
Hawxhurst, Ephraim C. III, 414
Hawxhurst, Ephraim C. III, 415
Hawxhurst, Esther III, 415
Hawxhurst, Florence Amelia III, 415
Hawxhurst, Franklin III, 158
Hawxhurst, G. III, 415
Hawxhurst, G. III, 484
Hawxhurst, Geo. Washington III, 484
Hawxhurst, George III, 415
Hawxhurst, George Henry III, 415
Hawxhurst, George W. III, 415
Hawxhurst, Hannah III, 65
Hawxhurst, Hannah III, 157
Hawxhurst, Hannah III, 158
Hawxhurst, Hannah III, 322
Hawxhurst, Hannah III, 414
Hawxhurst, Hannah III, 415
Hawxhurst, Hannah III, 432
Hawxhurst, Hannah B. III, 158
Hawxhurst, Hannah S. III, 158
Hawxhurst, Hariet III, 158
Hawxhurst, Harold III, 415
Hawxhurst, Harold III, 448
Hawxhurst, Harriet III, 159
Hawxhurst, Hazel Blossom III, 415
Hawxhurst, Hazel Blossom III, 448
Hawxhurst, Henry, Sr. III, 415
Hawxhurst, Ida III, 415
Hawxhurst, Ida III, 421
Hawxhurst, Isaac III, 483
Hawxhurst, Isabella R. III, 415
Hawxhurst, Israel III, 415
Hawxhurst, Israel III, 483
Hawxhurst, Israel III, 484
Hawxhurst, Israel III, 499
Hawxhurst, Jacob III, 415
Hawxhurst, Jacob III, 483
Hawxhurst, James III, 89
Hawxhurst, James III, 157
Hawxhurst, James III, 158
Hawxhurst, James III, 436
Hawxhurst, James III, 483
Hawxhurst, James III, 484
Hawxhurst, James III, 491
Hawxhurst, James C. III, 38
Hawxhurst, James C. III, 158
Hawxhurst, James C. III, 299
Hawxhurst, James G. III, 158
Hawxhurst, James J. III, 158
Hawxhurst, James O. III, 157
Hawxhurst, James O. III, 415
Hawxhurst, James O. III, 483
Hawxhurst, James O. III, 484
Hawxhurst, Jane III, 158
Hawxhurst, Jane III, 415
Hawxhurst, Jane S. III, 158
Hawxhurst, Jas. III, 415
Hawxhurst, Jennie II, 874
Hawxhurst, Jennie K. III, 157
Hawxhurst, Jennie K. III, 158
Hawxhurst, Jennie K. III, 299
Hawxhurst, Jericho III, 158
Hawxhurst, Joana III, 415
Hawxhurst, Job III, 415
Hawxhurst, John III, 158
Hawxhurst, John III, 415
Hawxhurst, John III, 436
Hawxhurst, John Thomas II, 874
Hawxhurst, John Thomas III, 157
Hawxhurst, Joseph III, 415
Hawxhurst, Julia III, 151
Hawxhurst, Julia III, 157
Hawxhurst, Julia III, 415
Hawxhurst, Julia III, 424
Hawxhurst, Julia III, 484
Hawxhurst, Julia E. III, 38
Hawxhurst, Julia E. III, 158
Hawxhurst, Julia E. III, 299
Hawxhurst, Julia E. III, 415
Hawxhurst, Julia E. III, 484
Hawxhurst, Leonard III, 415
Hawxhurst, Letitia III, 483
Hawxhurst, Letitia O. III, 415
Hawxhurst, Lydia III, 479
Hawxhurst, Margaret T. III, 415
Hawxhurst, Maria III, 158
Hawxhurst, Maria III, 311
Hawxhurst, Maria III, 415
Hawxhurst, Maria III, 483
Hawxhurst, Maria VI, 730
Hawxhurst, Maria VI, 747
Hawxhurst, Maria S. II, 874
Hawxhurst, Maria S. III, 157
Hawxhurst, Maria S. III, 158
Hawxhurst, Maria S. III, 299
Hawxhurst, Maria Shoemaker II, 799
Hawxhurst, Mariah E. III, 458
Hawxhurst, Marianna III, 414
Hawxhurst, Marianna III, 415
Hawxhurst, Marianna III, 418
Hawxhurst, Marianna III, 446
Hawxhurst, Marianna III, 458
Hawxhurst, Martha III, 158
Hawxhurst, Martha III, 414
Hawxhurst, Martha Jane III, 484
Hawxhurst, Martha P. III, 158
Hawxhurst, Mary III, 81
Hawxhurst, Mary III, 157
Hawxhurst, Mary III, 158
Hawxhurst, Mary III, 159
Hawxhurst, Mary III, 394
Hawxhurst, Mary III, 414
Hawxhurst, Mary III, 415
Hawxhurst, Mary III, 483
Hawxhurst, Mary III, 484
Hawxhurst, Mary Ann III, 415
Hawxhurst, Mary Ann III, 426
Hawxhurst, Mary B. III, 157
Hawxhurst, Mary B. III, 158
Hawxhurst, Mary B. III, 322
Hawxhurst, Mary Etta III, 415
Hawxhurst, Mary F. III, 158
Hawxhurst, Mary K. II, 874
Hawxhurst, Mary K. III, 157
Hawxhurst, Mary S. III, 158
Hawxhurst, Mary W. III, 415
Hawxhurst, Mary W. III, 458
Hawxhurst, Nath. O. III, 484
Hawxhurst, Nath., Jr. III, 158
Hawxhurst, Nathaniel III, 81
Hawxhurst, Nathaniel III, 158
Hawxhurst, Nathaniel III, 463
Hawxhurst, Nathaniel III, 484
Hawxhurst, Nathaniel O. III, 415
Hawxhurst, Nathaniel P. III, 484
Hawxhurst, Nathaniel, Jr. III, 158
Hawxhurst, Penelope III, 158
Hawxhurst, Penelope III, 436
Hawxhurst, Peter III, 159
Hawxhurst, Phebe III, 158
Hawxhurst, Phebe III, 484
Hawxhurst, Phebe A. III, 415
Hawxhurst, Phebe Ann III, 483
Hawxhurst, Phebe C. III, 38
Hawxhurst, Phebe C. III, 158
Hawxhurst, Phebe C. III, 484
Hawxhurst, Phebe F. III, 158
Hawxhurst, Phebe M. III, 158
Hawxhurst, Rachel III, 158
Hawxhurst, Rachel III, 483
Hawxhurst, Rachel III, 484
Hawxhurst, Rebecca III, 415
Hawxhurst, Rebecca III, 446
Hawxhurst, Rebecca VI, 730
Hawxhurst, Rebecca VI, 747
Hawxhurst, Richard III, 415
Hawxhurst, Richard III, 483
Hawxhurst, Richard F. III, 158
Hawxhurst, Richard S. III, 415
Hawxhurst, Richard, Sr. III, 415
Hawxhurst, Richard, Sr. III, 416
Hawxhurst, Robert III, 158
Hawxhurst, Samson III, 414
Hawxhurst, Samson III, 415
Hawxhurst, Sarah III, 81
Hawxhurst, Sarah III, 157
Hawxhurst, Sarah III, 158
Hawxhurst, Sarah III, 414
Hawxhurst, Sarah III, 415
Hawxhurst, Sarah III, 436
Hawxhurst, Sarah III, 483
Hawxhurst, Sarah III, 484
Hawxhurst, Sarah III, 499
Hawxhurst, Sarah Ann III, 484
Hawxhurst, Sarah C. III, 158
Hawxhurst, Sarah E. III, 415
Hawxhurst, Sarah H. III, 89
Hawxhurst, Sarah M. III, 158
Hawxhurst, Sarah P. III, 89
Hawxhurst, Sarah P. III, 158
Hawxhurst, Seaman III, 158
Hawxhurst, Simon III, 415
Hawxhurst, Susan III, 479
Hawxhurst, Susan III, 483
Hawxhurst, Susan III, 484
Hawxhurst, Sylvester III, 484
Hawxhurst, Thomas III, 158
Hawxhurst, Thos. III, 415
Hawxhurst, Timothy III, 158
Hawxhurst, Timothy S. K. III, 158
Hawxhurst, Townsend III, 415
Hawxhurst, Townsend III, 446
Hawxhurst, Townsend VI, 730
Hawxhurst, Townsend VI, 747
Hawxhurst, Vileta III, 415
Hawxhurst, Violetta III, 394
Hawxhurst, Violetta III, 415
Hawxhurst, Wallace III, 415
Hawxhurst, Wallace III, 421
Hawxhurst, Walter III, 158
Hawxhurst, Wd. Hannah B. III, 158
Hawxhurst, William III, 159
Hawxhurst, William III, 394
Hawxhurst, William III, 415
Hawxhurst, William E. III, 418
Hawxhurst, William H. III, 484
Hawxhurst, Wm. III, 81
Hawxhurst, Wm. III, 157
Hawxhurst, Wm. III, 158
Hawxhurst, Wm. III, 394
Hawxhurst, Wm. C. III, 484
Hawxhurst, Wm. E. III, 414
Hawxhurst, Wm. E. III, 415
Hawxhurst, Wm. E. III, 446
Hawxhurst, Wm. E. III, 458
Hawxhurst, Wm. Ephraim III, 415
Hawxhurst, Wright III, 158
Hawxhurst, Wright III, 159
Hay, Allice V, 1000
Hay, Catharine III, 159
Hay, Catharine VI, 811
Hay, Florence V, 71
Hay, Florence V, 110
Hay, Frank III, 159
Hay, Frank III, 282
Hay, Hannah V, 1000
Hay, James B. VI, 834
Hay, James R. VI, 811
Hay, James R. VI, 815
Hay, James R. VI, 830
Hay, James R. VI, 851
Hay, Jane VI, 863
Hay, John VI, 834
Hay, John VI, 863
Hay, Lizzie V, 245
Hay, Lucinda VI, 834
Hay, Margaret IV, 1319
Hay, Margaret O. IV, 1319
Hay, Martha VI, 851
Hay, Mary I, 714
Hay, Mary I, 717
Hay, Mary V, 1000
Hay, Maud Jarvis III, 159
Hay, Nancy V, 1000
Hay, Nancy VI, 811
Hay, Paulina VI, 824
Hay, Sarah R. III, 159
Hay, Sarah R. III, 282
Hay, Thomas VI, 824
Hay, Wd. George W. III, 159
Haycock, Abigail II, 545
Haycock, Alice IV, 1027
Haycock, Ann Sarah IV, 631
Haycock, Anna Maria IV, 220
Haycock, Barton IV, 675
Haycock, Barton IV, 1027
Haycock, Benj. IV, 217
Haycock, Benj. IV, 271
Haycock, Benjamin IV, 219
Haycock, Benjamin IV, 220
Haycock, Burton IV, 719
Haycock, Clarkson Oliver IV, 1027
Haycock, Dinah IV, 719
Haycock, Elizabeth IV, 631
Haycock, Elizabeth A. IV, 217
Haycock, Elizabeth Abb IV, 220
Haycock, Elizabeth Ann IV, 220
Haycock, Elvira IV, 1027
Haycock, Esther IV, 38
Haycock, Esther IV, 61
Haycock, Esther IV, 219
Haycock, George Albert IV, 220
Haycock, Hannah IV, 38
Haycock, Hannah IV, 42
Haycock, Hannah IV, 292
Haycock, Hannah IV, 675
Haycock, Hannah IV, 719
Haycock, Hannah A. IV, 220
Haycock, Hannah Ann IV, 220
Haycock, Hannah Ann IV, 271
Haycock, Irving IV, 1164
Haycock, Isaac William IV, 1027
Haycock, Jacob IV, 631
Haycock, Jane IV, 219
Haycock, Jane IV, 220
Haycock, Jane IV, 271
Haycock, Jane IV, 272
Haycock, Jane IV, 292
Haycock, Jane V, 499
Haycock, Jesse II, 545
Haycock, John IV, 38
Haycock, Jonah II, 545
Haycock, Jonathan II, 545
Haycock, Jonathan IV, 631
Haycock, Joseph II, 545
Haycock, Joseph IV, 292
Haycock, Larkin IV, 220
Haycock, Larkin A. IV, 220
Haycock, Lemuel IV, 220
Haycock, Lemuel P. IV, 220
Haycock, Malissa IV, 1164
Haycock, Mariam IV, 38
Haycock, Martha IV, 822
Haycock, Melissa IV, 1027
Haycock, Meriam IV, 220
Haycock, Nathan IV, 38
Haycock, Nathan IV, 42
Haycock, Nathan IV, 719
Haycock, Parker IV, 220
Haycock, Rachel IV, 675
Haycock, Rachel IV, 719
Haycock, Rachel IV, 1027
Haycock, Rebecca L. IV, 1027
Haycock, Samuel IV, 219
Haycock, Sarah IV, 631
Haycock, Sarah IV, 662
Haycock, Sarah A. IV, 1027
Haycock, Sarah B. IV, 1024
Haycock, Sarah B. IV, 1027
Haycock, Sarah T. IV, 220
Haycock, Sarah Thomas IV, 220
Haycock, Susanna IV, 631
Haycock, Susannah IV, 631
Haycock, Tacy II, 545
Haycock, Tacy IV, 1025
Haycock, Tacy IV, 1027
Hayden, Dora IV, 1209
Hayden, Esther I, 938
Hayden, Esther I, 942
Hayden, George IV, 1209
Hayden, Hubert IV, 1209
Hayden, Mary VI, 910
Haydock, ??? I, 544
Haydock, ??? III, 159
Haydock, ??? III, 160
Haydock, Abigail I, 393
Haydock, Abigail I, 394
Haydock, Agnes C. III, 201
Haydock, Alice III, 201
Haydock, Amelia III, 160
Haydock, Angeline III, 160
Haydock, Ann III, 200
Haydock, Ann Jones II, 373
Haydock, Ann Maria III, 160
Haydock, Anna Maria III, 159
Haydock, Annie III, 159
Haydock, Annie III, 160
Haydock, Arthur Kerr III, 168
Haydock, Barnard M. III, 159
Haydock, Benjamin I, 386
Haydock, Benjamin I, 394
Haydock, Benjamin I, 457
Haydock, Benjamin I, 480
Haydock, Benjamin II, 373
Haydock, Benjamin II, 745
Haydock, Catharine III, 159
Haydock, Catharine III, 273
Haydock, Charlotte Louisa III, 159
Haydock, Charlotte Louisa III, 160
Haydock, Child III, 201
Haydock, Clara N. III, 159
Haydock, Daniel V, 71
Haydock, Eden II, 176
Haydock, Eden II, 373
Haydock, Eden II, 524
Haydock, Eden II, 526
Haydock, Eden II, 529
Haydock, Eden II, 545
Haydock, Eden II, 546
Haydock, Eden II, 556
Haydock, Eden II, 670
Haydock, Eden II, 745
Haydock, Eden III, 159
Haydock, Edin II, 373
Haydock, Edith III, 159
Haydock, Edith III, 160
Haydock, Edith III, 168
Haydock, Edith Dorothy III, 168
Haydock, Edmund III, 159
Haydock, Edmund III, 160
Haydock, Edward II, 745
Haydock, Edward II, 874
Haydock, Edward J. II, 373
Haydock, Edward M. III, 159
Haydock, Edward M. III, 242
Haydock, Eleanor II, 745
Haydock, Eleanor III, 159
Haydock, Eleanor III, 288
Haydock, Eleanor Lowe III, 160
Haydock, Elinor S. II, 874
Haydock, Eliz. III, 159
Haydock, Eliz. A. III, 168
Haydock, Elizabeth II, 373
Haydock, Elizabeth II, 526
Haydock, Elizabeth II, 529
Haydock, Elizabeth II, 545
Haydock, Elizabeth II, 546
Haydock, Elizabeth II, 556
Haydock, Elizabeth III, 159
Haydock, Elizabeth III, 160
Haydock, Elizabeth III, 168
Haydock, Elizabeth III, 349
Haydock, Elizabeth III, 416
Haydock, Elizabeth III, 451
Haydock, Elizabeth B. III, 159
Haydock, Elizabeth Moode III, 159
Haydock, Elizabeth W. II, 546
Haydock, Elizabeth W. II, 670
Haydock, Ellen III, 201
Haydock, Ellen S. II, 874
Haydock, Elzabeth Ann Ethel III, 168

Haydock, Emily III, 415
Haydock, Emily V, 897
Haydock, Emily V, 910
Haydock, Emily L. V, 335
Haydock, Emily W. III, 77
Haydock, Emily W. III, 160
Haydock, Emily W. III, 415
Haydock, Ephraim III, 159
Haydock, Ephraim III, 160
Haydock, Francis III, 254
Haydock, George G. II, 373
Haydock, George G. II, 874
Haydock, George G. III, 86
Haydock, George G., Jr. III, 160
Haydock, George Guest II, 745
Haydock, George Guest II, 874
Haydock, George Guest III, 159
Haydock, George W. II, 373
Haydock, Hannah II, 373
Haydock, Hannah II, 546
Haydock, Hannah II, 556
Haydock, Hannah II, 599
Haydock, Hannah II, 874
Haydock, Hannah III, 148
Haydock, Hannah III, 159
Haydock, Hannah III, 160
Haydock, Hannah III, 200
Haydock, Hannah III, 201
Haydock, Hannah III, 259
Haydock, Hannah III, 358
Haydock, Hannah III, 415
Haydock, Hannah III, 416
Haydock, Hannah III, 438
Haydock, Hannah V, 71
Haydock, Hannah Edwards V, 71
Haydock, Hannah S. III, 349
Haydock, Hannah T. III, 159
Haydock, Hannah T. III, 160
Haydock, Hannah W. III, 160
Haydock, Henry II, 373
Haydock, Henry II, 545
Haydock, Henry II, 599
Haydock, Henry II, 745
Haydock, Henry III, 41
Haydock, Henry III, 159
Haydock, Henry III, 160
Haydock, Henry III, 200
Haydock, Henry III, 236
Haydock, Henry III, 259
Haydock, Henry III, 273
Haydock, Henry III, 415
Haydock, Henry III, 416
Haydock, Henry III, 419
Haydock, Henry III, 438
Haydock, Henry III, 484
Haydock, Henry R. III, 159
Haydock, Henry, Jr. III, 159
Haydock, Henry, Jr. III, 250
Haydock, Herbert III, 160
Haydock, Howard Wooding III, 168
Haydock, Isaac Henry III, 160
Haydock, Isabel M. V, 177
Haydock, James I, 394
Haydock, James II, 546
Haydock, James II, 874
Haydock, James III, 159
Haydock, James T. II, 745
Haydock, James Thompson II, 745
Haydock, James, Jr. III, 159
Haydock, Jane III, 17
Haydock, Jane III, 46
Haydock, Jane III, 50
Haydock, Jane III, 159
Haydock, Jane III, 160
Haydock, Jane III, 287
Haydock, Jane III, 416
Haydock, Jane H. III, 201
Haydock, Jesse Eleanor V, 177
Haydock, John I, 393
Haydock, John I, 394
Haydock, John I, 544
Haydock, John I, 986
Haydock, John II, 373
Haydock, John II, 545
Haydock, John II, 546
Haydock, John III, 17
Haydock, John III, 46
Haydock, John III, 50
Haydock, John III, 159
Haydock, John III, 160
Haydock, John III, 416
Haydock, John III, 451
Haydock, John V, 910
Haydock, John Mlburn III, 168
Haydock, John W. III, 159
Haydock, John W. III, 160
Haydock, John W. III, 165
Haydock, John W. III, 349
Haydock, John, Jr. III, 160
Haydock, Joseph II, 373
Haydock, Joseph III, 160
Haydock, Joseph W. III, 160
Haydock, June III, 335
Haydock, Kate J. III, 159
Haydock, Kate J. III, 242
Haydock, Katharine III, 159
Haydock, Lois III, 159
Haydock, Louisa Low III, 160
Haydock, Margaret I, 394
Haydock, Margaret I, 544
Haydock, Margaret I, 986
Haydock, Margaret III, 109
Haydock, Margaret III, 160
Haydock, Margaret B. III, 159
Haydock, Margaret B. III, 250
Haydock, Margret I, 986
Haydock, Maria W. III, 160
Haydock, Maria W. III, 254
Haydock, Martha II, 373
Haydock, Martha III, 159
Haydock, Martha B. III, 159
Haydock, Martha B. III, 236
Haydock, Martha W. II, 291
Haydock, Martha W. II, 745
Haydock, Mary II, 291
Haydock, Mary II, 373
Haydock, Mary II, 546
Haydock, Mary III, 41
Haydock, Mary III, 159
Haydock, Mary III, 160
Haydock, Mary III, 259
Haydock, Mary III, 416
Haydock, Mary III, 433
Haydock, Mary III, 438
Haydock, Mary A. II, 524
Haydock, Mary A. II, 546
Haydock, Mary A. II, 670
Haydock, Mary Ann II, 373
Haydock, Mary Ann II, 745
Haydock, Mary Ann II, 799
Haydock, Mary Ann II, 874
Haydock, Mary Ann III, 160
Haydock, Mary Ash II, 176
Haydock, Mary Ash II, 373
Haydock, Mary Ash II, 546
Haydock, Mary Ash II, 745
Haydock, Mary B. III, 160
Haydock, Mary B. III, 358
Haydock, Mary B. III, 359
Haydock, Mary Barker III, 160
Haydock, Mary Bowne II, 373
Haydock, Mary R. III, 416
Haydock, Mary W. III, 160
Haydock, Mary W. III, 254
Haydock, Mery III, 159
Haydock, Millie V, 335
Haydock, Millie V, 910
Haydock, Patience II, 373
Haydock, Patience II, 745
Haydock, Patience II, 874
Haydock, Patience II, 888
Haydock, Patience C. III, 86
Haydock, Patience Caroline III, 159
Haydock, Priscilla P. II, 874
Haydock, R. III, 358
Haydock, Rebecca II, 373
Haydock, Rebecca II, 529
Haydock, Rebecca II, 546
Haydock, Rebecca III, 27
Haydock, Rebecca III, 159
Haydock, Rebecca III, 160
Haydock, Rebecca III, 177
Haydock, Rebecca III, 288
Haydock, Rich III, 159
Haydock, Rich. III, 168
Haydock, Rich. III, 201
Haydock, Richard III, 159
Haydock, Richard III, 201
Haydock, Richard L. III, 159
Haydock, Richard L. III, 160
Haydock, Richard L. III, 416
Haydock, Richard R. III, 160
Haydock, Richard R. III, 201
Haydock, Richhill III, 160
Haydock, Robert II, 373
Haydock, Robert II, 526
Haydock, Robert II, 529
Haydock, Robert II, 545
Haydock, Robert II, 546
Haydock, Robert II, 599
Haydock, Robert II, 799
Haydock, Robert III, 148
Haydock, Robert III, 159
Haydock, Robert III, 177
Haydock, Robert III, 288
Haydock, Robert III, 358
Haydock, Robert H. III, 160
Haydock, Robert H. III, 254
Haydock, Robert H. III, 415
Haydock, Robert H. III, 416
Haydock, Robert Roger III, 160
Haydock, Robert W. III, 201
Haydock, Robert, Jr. II, 546
Haydock, Robert, Jr. III, 160
Haydock, Robt. III, 160
Haydock, Robt. J. III, 160
Haydock, Russell B. III, 168
Haydock, Russell B., Jr. III, 168
Haydock, Russell Benjamin III, 168
Haydock, Ruth I, 386
Haydock, Ruth I, 394
Haydock, Ruth I, 457
Haydock, Samuel II, 373
Haydock, Samuel II, 546
Haydock, Samuel II, 745
Haydock, Samuel II, 799
Haydock, Samuel II, 857
Haydock, Samuel II, 874
Haydock, Samuel II, 888
Haydock, Samuel III, 159
Haydock, Samuel C. II, 874
Haydock, Sarah II, 373
Haydock, Sarah II, 546
Haydock, Sarah II, 799
Haydock, Sarah II, 857
Haydock, Sarah II, 874
Haydock, Sarah II, 888
Haydock, Sarah III, 140
Haydock, Sarah III, 148
Haydock, Sarah III, 159
Haydock, Sarah III, 160
Haydock, Sarah III, 165
Haydock, Sarah III, 271
Haydock, Sarah III, 415
Haydock, Sarah III, 416
Haydock, Sarah III, 419
Haydock, Sarah A. II, 874
Haydock, Sarah Ann II, 745
Haydock, Sarah Ann II, 874
Haydock, Sarah Ann III, 159
Haydock, Sarah Anne III, 159
Haydock, Sarah Anne III, 160
Haydock, Sarah Anne III, 168
Haydock, Sarah B. III, 160
Haydock, Sarah Emily III, 77
Haydock, Sarah Emily III, 160
Haydock, Sarah J. III, 159
Haydock, Sarah Jane III, 46
Haydock, Sarah Jane III, 50
Haydock, Sarah Jane III, 109
Haydock, Sarah Jane III, 160
Haydock, Sarah W. III, 148
Haydock, Sarah Wharton III, 160
Haydock, Sophia III, 168
Haydock, Susanna I, 394
Haydock, Susanna II, 373
Haydock, Susanna II, 546
Haydock, Susanna II, 745
Haydock, Susanna H. II, 745
Haydock, Susanna Willard II, 874
Haydock, Susanna, Jr. II, 524
Haydock, Susanna, Jr. II, 546
Haydock, Susanna, Jr. II, 745
Haydock, Susannah II, 529
Haydock, Susannah II, 792
Haydock, Susannah II, 799
Haydock, Susannah II, 857
Haydock, Susannah II, 874
Haydock, Susannah H. II, 874
Haydock, Thomas V, 910
Haydock, Thomas T. V, 71
Haydock, Thomas T. V, 910
Haydock, Trevor C. V, 177
Haydock, Walter W. III, 416
Haydock, Wd. Eden II, 373
Haydock, Wd. Susannah II, 799
Haydock, William II, 373
Haydock, William III, 159
Haydock, William III, 160
Haydock, William V, 71
Haydock, William Moode III, 415
Haydock, William Russell III, 168
Haydock, William Titus III, 160
Haydock, Wm. II, 546
Haydock, Wm. V, 335
Haydock, Wm. M. III, 77
Haydock, Wm. M. III, 160
Haydock, Wm. Russell III, 168
Haydock, Wm. T. V, 335
Haydocks, Elizabeth II, 373
Haydon, Samuel II, 444
Haydon, William II, 444
Hayes, Abner V, 1000
Hayes, Albert IV, 513
Hayes, Albert IV, 529
Hayes, Albert IV, 718
Hayes, Alpha V, 625
Hayes, Ann IV, 718
Hayes, Ann VI, 399
Hayes, Anna V, 71
Hayes, Annie I, 924
Hayes, Betzy IV, 407
Hayes, Caddy J. IV, 1281
Hayes, Calvin C. IV, 906
Hayes, Charles I. IV, 718
Hayes, Charles T. II, 119
Hayes, Charles T. IV, 704
Hayes, Chas. IV, 529
Hayes, Chas. I. IV, 691
Hayes, Chas. I. IV, 692
Hayes, Chas. I. IV, 704
Hayes, Chas. I. IV, 715
Hayes, Chas. I. IV, 718
Hayes, Chas. I. IV, 760
Hayes, Chas. T. IV, 518
Hayes, David VI, 399
Hayes, Deborah IV, 402
Hayes, Deborah IV, 407
Hayes, Deborah IV, 518
Hayes, Deborah IV, 692
Hayes, Deborah IV, 704
Hayes, Deborah IV, 718
Hayes, Deborah F. IV, 518
Hayes, Deborah F. IV, 529
Hayes, Deborah F. IV, 691
Hayes, Deborah F. IV, 718
Hayes, E. Marie V, 393
Hayes, Earl B. V, 499
Hayes, Eaton IV, 407
Hayes, Edith IV, 715
Hayes, Edith IV, 718
Hayes, Edith IV, 760
Hayes, Edward II, 989
Hayes, Edward IV, 1237
Hayes, Eliza Jane IV, 906
Hayes, Elizabeth II, 546
Hayes, Elizabeth II, 685
Hayes, Elizabeth IV, 906
Hayes, Ellen IV, 718
Hayes, Elma IV, 704
Hayes, Elma IV, 715
Hayes, Elma IV, 718
Hayes, Elma IV, 760
Hayes, Esther IV, 718
Hayes, Esther IV, 735
Hayes, Florence A. IV, 1281
Hayes, Gertrude III, 23
Hayes, Gertrude III, 161
Hayes, Gertude III, 27
Hayes, Hannah II, 546
Hayes, Henry H. III, 161
Hayes, Henry, Jr. II, 546
Hayes, Hugh V, 1000
Hayes, Hugh Ellis V, 1000
Hayes, Israel IV, 718
Hayes, James II, 373
Hayes, James H. IV, 906
Hayes, Joel V, 393
Hayes, John II, 546
Hayes, John V, 71
Hayes, John VI, 931
Hayes, John H. IV, 1281
Hayes, John L. IV, 1319
Hayes, John W. IV, 1281
Hayes, Joseph H. IV, 1281
Hayes, Leah IV, 22
Hayes, Leah IV, 38
Hayes, Lillian Rebecca IV, 718
Hayes, Lizetta IV, 718
Hayes, Lydia IV, 718
Hayes, Lydia VI, 518
Hayes, Lydia VI, 539
Hayes, Lydia VI, 661
Hayes, Lydia Ellen IV, 718
Hayes, Maria V, 393
Hayes, Mariah V, 393
Hayes, Marie Pearl V, 71
Hayes, Marietta III, 27
Hayes, Marietta E. III, 161
Hayes, Mary II, 373
Hayes, Mary II, 546
Hayes, Mary IV, 407
Hayes, Mary IV, 718
Hayes, Mary Ann IV, 906
Hayes, Mary Ann V, 393
Hayes, Mary E. V, 499
Hayes, Mary H. IV, 692
Hayes, Mildred V, 681
Hayes, Mira D. IV, 513
Hayes, Mordecai IV, 718
Hayes, Mordecai IV, 735
Hayes, Myra D. IV, 513
Hayes, Myra D. IV, 529
Hayes, Myra D. IV, 718
Hayes, Nathan VI, 399
Hayes, Orange IV, 1281
Hayes, Orange M. IV, 1281
Hayes, Pearl V, 499
Hayes, Phebe II, 801
Hayes, Phebe IV, 902
Hayes, Phebe IV, 906
Hayes, Piety IV, 407
Hayes, Priscilla IV, 401
Hayes, Priscilla IV, 407
Hayes, Rachel II, 373
Hayes, Rachel II, 546
Hayes, Rebecca II, 710
Hayes, Rebecca A. IV, 1281
Hayes, Richard II, 373
Hayes, Richard II, 546
Hayes, Ruth IV, 871
Hayes, Ruth IV, 872
Hayes, Ruth V, 1000
Hayes, Ruth Esther V, 1000
Hayes, Samuel E. IV, 1281
Hayes, Sarah I, 717
Hayes, Sarah I, 730
Hayes, Sarah II, 373
Hayes, Sarah II, 546
Hayes, Sarah IV, 704
Hayes, Sarah IV, 718
Hayes, Sharpless III, 23
Hayes, Susan IV, 906
Hayes, Susannah II, 373
Hayes, Tazetta IV, 718
Hayes, Venice V, 499
Hayes, Virginia IV, 718
Hayes, Walter W. III, 161
Hayes, William II, 373
Hayes, William H. V, 499
Hayes, Wm. IV, 906
Hayes, Wm. V, 1000
Hayes, Wm. Donald IV, 718
Hayes, Wm. O. IV, 1281
Hayhurst, Bazaleel IV, 963
Hayhurst, Bazebel IV, 719
Hayhurst, Bezabel IV, 719
Hayhurst, Bezaleel IV, 1026
Hayhurst, Caroline E. II, 800
Hayhurst, Cuthbert VI, 399
Hayhurst, Deliverance VI, 399
Hayhurst, Eli IV, 38
Hayhurst, Eli IV, 92
Hayhurst, Elizabeth II, 1000
Hayhurst, Elizabeth II, 1008
Hayhurst, Elizabeth IV, 719
Hayhurst, Elizabeth IV, 963
Hayhurst, Elizabeth M. IV, 1026
Hayhurst, Elizabeth M. IV, 1031
Hayhurst, Elizabeth T. II, 874
Hayhurst, Elizabeth Tatem II, 815
Hayhurst, Ellis IV, 1026
Hayhurst, Ezra IV, 719
Hayhurst, Hannah IV, 38
Hayhurst, Hannah IV, 892
Hayhurst, Hannah IV, 893
Hayhurst, Hannah IV, 1026
Hayhurst, Isaac II, 800
Hayhurst, Israel Cortney IV, 719
Hayhurst, James IV, 38
Hayhurst, James T. II, 800
Hayhurst, Jane IV, 695
Hayhurst, Jane IV, 718
Hayhurst, Jane IV, 719
Hayhurst, Jane IV, 963
Hayhurst, Jane IV, 1024
Hayhurst, Jane IV, 1031
Hayhurst, Jeremiah II, 874
Hayhurst, Job IV, 38
Hayhurst, Job IV, 92
Hayhurst, John IV, 92
Hayhurst, Joseph II, 1000
Hayhurst, Joseph IV, 719
Hayhurst, Lydia IV, 718
Hayhurst, Lydia IV, 719
Hayhurst, Lydia IV, 963
Hayhurst, Lydia IV, 1021
Hayhurst, Martha II, 874
Hayhurst, Mary IV, 38
Hayhurst, Mary IV, 719
Hayhurst, Mary IV, 963
Hayhurst, Mary Ann IV, 963
Hayhurst, Mary Ann IV, 1007
Hayhurst, Mary F. IV, 1024
Hayhurst, Mary F. IV, 1026
Hayhurst, Rachel II, 960
Hayhurst, Rachel IV, 38
Hayhurst, Rachel IV, 92
Hayhurst, Rachel IV, 117
Hayhurst, Samuel T. II, 800
Hayhurst, Sarah IV, 38
Hayhurst, Sarah IV, 91
Hayhurst, Sarah IV, 92
Hayhurst, Sarah IV, 719
Hayhurst, Susan II, 874
Hayhurst, Susan IV, 695
Hayhurst, Susan IV, 719

yhurst, Susan IV, 963
yhurst, Susanna II, 874
yhurst, Susannah IV, 719
yhurst, Thomas II, 1000
yhurst, Thomas IV, 719
yhurst, Thomas IV, 963
yhurst, Thos. Mather IV, 719
yhurst, Warner M. II, 874
yhurst, Warner Mifflin II, 799
yhurst, William IV, 719
yhurst, William IV, 963
yhurst, Wm. IV, 695
yhurst, Wm. IV, 718
yhurst, Wm. IV, 719
yhurst, Wm. IV, 963
yhurst, Wm. IV, 1024
yhurst, Wm. IV, 1031
yhurst, Wm., Jr. IV, 963
yle, Elizabeth I, 392
yle, Martha I, 392
yle, Martha I, 393
yle, William VI, 244
ymaker, ??? VI, 747
ymaker, ??? VI, 760
ymaker, ??? VI, 761
ymaker, Anna VI, 747
ymaker, Anna VI, 760
ymaker, Anna VI, 761
ymore, Annetta Boyd I, 882
ymore, Bluman Willas I, 882
ymore, Keziah I, 882
ymore, Keziah Ann I, 882
ymore, William D. I, 882
ymore, Wm. Welcher I, 882
ynam, Louisa G. IV, 963
ynam, Louisa G. IV, 1008
ynes, ??? VI, 903
ynes, Abigail IV, 1385
ynes, Ada V, 678
ynes, Adaline VI, 930
ynes, Agnes VI, 930
ynes, Allen V, 173
ynes, Allen VI, 824
ynes, Amos V, 173
ynes, Austin VI, 824
ynes, Barsheba VI, 1014
ynes, Bersheba VI, 930
ynes, Betsey VI, 912
ynes, Betsey VI, 923
ynes, Betsey VI, 995
ynes, Betsy VI, 930
ynes, Betty VI, 975
ynes, Caleb VI, 930
ynes, Caleb, Jr. VI, 930
ynes, Caleb, Sr. VI, 930
ynes, Daniel VI, 904
ynes, Daniel VI, 930
ynes, David V, 173
ynes, David VI, 930
ynes, Dorcas IV, 1367
ynes, Dorcas IV, 1385
ynes, Earl V, 496
ynes, Edith V, 694
ynes, Edmond VI, 942
ynes, Edmund VI, 885
ynes, Edmund VI, 921
ynes, Edmund VI, 930
ynes, Edmund VI, 1013
ynes, Edward IV, 1237
ynes, Edward VI, 923
ynes, Eliza V, 938
ynes, Elizabeth II, 74
ynes, Elizabeth IV, 473
ynes, Elizabeth IV, 489
ynes, Elizabeth IV, 1237
ynes, Elizabeth V, 173
ynes, Elizabeth VI, 848
ynes, Elizabeth VI, 904
ynes, Elizabeth VI, 930
ynes, Elizabeth VI, 946
ynes, Elvin V, 65
ynes, Emma V, 496
ynes, Emma V, 678
ynes, Ester II, 227
ynes, Esther II, 199
ynes, Flanders VI, 966
ynes, Frances VI, 959
ynes, Francis VI, 930
ynes, Francis E. V, 623
ynes, George VI, 930
ynes, George A. VI, 824
ynes, George C. VI, 824
ynes, Hampton VI, 930
ynes, Hampton VI, 978
ynes, Hampton VI, 1021
ynes, Hannah VI, 937
ynes, Hannah VI, 942
ynes, Harry V, 334
ynes, Harry V, 694
ynes, Harvey V, 334
aynes, Hattie IV, 1237
Haynes, Helen V, 65
Haynes, Henry VI, 848
Haynes, Henry VI, 894
Haynes, Henry VI, 930
Haynes, Henry VI, 975
Haynes, Henry VI, 995
Haynes, Henry VI, 1014
Haynes, Henry, Jr. VI, 930
Haynes, Ibbey VI, 930
Haynes, Ica V, 334
Haynes, Ira V, 938
Haynes, Isbel VI, 942
Haynes, Jacob VI, 930
Haynes, James VI, 903
Haynes, James VI, 930
Haynes, Jane F. VI, 966
Haynes, John II, 199
Haynes, John II, 227
Haynes, John VI, 930
Haynes, John VI, 949
Haynes, John VI, 980
Haynes, John VI, 990
Haynes, John VI, 1000
Haynes, John F. IV, 212
Haynes, John P. VI, 894
Haynes, John P. VI, 930
Haynes, Joshua IV, 1385
Haynes, Judith V, 173
Haynes, Judith J. V, 64
Haynes, Judithann V, 173
Haynes, Laura V, 496
Haynes, Lida V, 334
Haynes, Lizzie IV, 474
Haynes, Lizzie IV, 491
Haynes, Louisa VI, 824
Haynes, Lucinda VI, 930
Haynes, Lucinda VI, 978
Haynes, Lucy VI, 930
Haynes, Lucy VI, 933
Haynes, Martha II, 369
Haynes, Martha V, 569
Haynes, Martha V, 571
Haynes, Martha VI, 921
Haynes, Martha A. B. VI, 930
Haynes, Martha N. V, 173
Haynes, Mary V, 64
Haynes, Mary V, 65
Haynes, Mary V, 94
Haynes, Mary V, 938
Haynes, Mary VI, 1000
Haynes, Mary VI, 1021
Haynes, Mary Ann VI, 885
Haynes, Mary H. VI, 930
Haynes, Mary L. VI, 824
Haynes, Matilda VI, 973
Haynes, Mildred VI, 930
Haynes, Millener VI, 930
Haynes, Milley VI, 1014
Haynes, Milly VI, 988
Haynes, Morrica VI, 824
Haynes, Morris IV, 1367
Haynes, Nancy VI, 853
Haynes, Nancy VI, 894
Haynes, Nancy VI, 930
Haynes, Nancy VI, 1013
Haynes, Naomi Almira V, 64
Haynes, Parmenas VI, 924
Haynes, Permeneas VI, 853
Haynes, Phebe VI, 930
Haynes, Queen Matilda VI, 930
Haynes, Rebekah II, 74
Haynes, Reuben II, 369
Haynes, Reuben V, 173
Haynes, Robert V, 65
Haynes, Robert VI, 847
Haynes, Robert VI, 930
Haynes, Russell V, 65
Haynes, Ruth V, 161
Haynes, Ruth V, 173
Haynes, Ruth V, 334
Haynes, Sally VI, 894
Haynes, Sally VI, 930
Haynes, Samuel V, 173
Haynes, Sarah II, 74
Haynes, Sarah II, 84
Haynes, Sarah V, 173
Haynes, Sarah VI, 912
Haynes, Sarah Catharine V, 496
Haynes, Sophronia Ann V, 393
Haynes, Sophronia Ann V, 432
Haynes, Stacy V, 173
Haynes, Tabitha VI, 894
Haynes, Tabitha VI, 930
Haynes, Thomas VI, 930
Haynes, William V, 496
Haynes, William VI, 885
Haynes, William VI, 930
Haynes, William VI, 988
Haynes, William VI, 1014
Haynes, Wm. II, 74
Haynes, Wm. II, 84
Haynes, Wm. V, 678
Haynie, Nettie L. V, 71
Hayns, Margaret II, 202
Hayns, Margaret II, 227
Hayns, Richard II, 74
Hayns, William, Jr. II, 228
Hayres, Joshua II, 77
Hays, Albert IV, 683
Hays, Albert IV, 718
Hays, Alice V, 575
Hays, Alice VI, 720
Hays, Andrew II, 68
Hays, Andrew II, 77
Hays, Ann II, 291
Hays, Anna V, 575
Hays, Anne V, 325
Hays, Anne V, 335
Hays, Annie V, 575
Hays, Bell V, 575
Hays, Benjamin VI, 720
Hays, Betsy IV, 401
Hays, Betzy IV, 407
Hays, Caddy J. IV, 1281
Hays, Calvin IV, 1209
Hays, Calvin C. IV, 1209
Hays, Carrie VI, 85
Hays, Charles G. IV, 704
Hays, Charles I. IV, 718
Hays, Charles J. II, 119
Hays, Charles T. II, 119
Hays, David VI, 399
Hays, Deborah IV, 704
Hays, Eaton IV, 220
Hays, Elioner II, 68
Hays, Elioner II, 77
Hays, Elizabeth IV, 1209
Hays, Elizabeth IV, 1228
Hays, Elizabeth VI, 824
Hays, Elizabeth VI, 921
Hays, Elizajane IV, 1209
Hays, Erskine R. V, 681
Hays, Esther II, 77
Hays, Esther IV, 718
Hays, Ethel V, 681
Hays, Florence A. IV, 1281
Hays, Hannah II, 546
Hays, Hannah VI, 720
Hays, Henry L. VI, 931
Hays, Jacob I, 394
Hays, James IV, 1209
Hays, James VI, 824
Hays, James H. IV, 1209
Hays, Jenny VI, 931
Hays, Jeremiah VI, 824
Hays, Joel V, 393
Hays, Joel V, 575
Hays, John V, 575
Hays, John VI, 720
Hays, John VI, 824
Hays, John VI, 921
Hays, John VI, 931
Hays, John W. IV, 1281
Hays, Joseph H. IV, 1281
Hays, Laura V, 575
Hays, Lucy VI, 931
Hays, Maggie IV, 1209
Hays, Maggie IV, 1210
Hays, Maria Walker V, 681
Hays, Marie V, 575
Hays, Mary II, 230
Hays, Mary II, 373
Hays, Mary IV, 407
Hays, Mary IV, 718
Hays, Mary Ann IV, 1228
Hays, Mary Ann V, 393
Hays, Mary Ann V, 575
Hays, Mary B. Ryan VI, 931
Hays, Maryann IV, 1209
Hays, Mildred V, 681
Hays, Myra D. IV, 683
Hays, Myra D. IV, 718
Hays, Nancy VI, 824
Hays, Naomi VI, 720
Hays, Nathan VI, 399
Hays, Orange IV, 1281
Hays, Orange M. IV, 1281
Hays, Pearl V, 575
Hays, Phebe IV, 1209
Hays, Piety IV, 401
Hays, Piety IV, 407
Hays, Rebecca A. IV, 1281
Hays, Rosa IV, 1209
Hays, Rosa IV, 1210
Hays, Samuel E. IV, 1281
Hays, Sarah II, 373
Hays, Sarah II, 519
Hays, Sarah II, 546
Hays, Sarah VI, 649
Hays, Sarah VI, 720
Hays, Sarah VI, 824
Hays, Scott VI, 85
Hays, Susan IV, 906
Hays, Susan IV, 1209
Hays, Tamer VI, 720
Hays, Thomas VI, 720
Hays, Walter W. III, 161
Hays, Warren V, 575
Hays, Wm. O. IV, 1281
Hayse, Andrew II, 61
Hayse, Andrew II, 77
Hayse, Eaton IV, 220
Hayse, Esther II, 61
Hayse, Esther II, 66
Hayse, Esther II, 77
Hayse, Susan IV, 1209
Hayslit, James R. V, 71
Hayslit, Susan B. V, 71
Hayslitt, James R. V, 71
Hayth, Achilles M. VI, 824
Hayth, Ann E. VI, 824
Hayth, Benjamin VI, 824
Hayth, Catharine VI, 824
Hayth, Frances H. VI, 860
Hayth, Joseph N. VI, 824
Hayth, Martha VI, 866
Hayth, Martha VI, 931
Hayth, Mary VI, 856
Hayth, Mary E. VI, 856
Hayth, Nancy B. VI, 824
Hayth, Polly VI, 824
Hayth, Polly VI, 857
Hayth, Sally VI, 854
Hayth, Thomas VI, 854
Hayth, Thomas VI, 857
Hayth, Thomas VI, 931
Hayth, Thomas C. VI, 860
Hayth, Thos. VI, 861
Hayth, William VI, 824
Hayth, William VI, 860
Hayth, William VI, 866
Hayth, William P. VI, 856
Hayth, Wm. VI, 856
Haythe, Buford VI, 837
Haythe, Catherine VI, 816
Haythe, Elizabeth VI, 827
Haythe, Emeline VI, 846
Haythe, Gilbert VI, 819
Haythe, Joseph N. VI, 824
Haythe, Juicy VI, 822
Haythe, Levica VI, 843
Haythe, Levina VI, 840
Haythe, Martha A. VI, 850
Haythe, Missouri VI, 853
Haythe, Nancy B. VI, 824
Haythe, Patsy VI, 832
Haythe, Sally B. VI, 819
Haythe, Thomas VI, 819
Haythe, Thomas VI, 822
Haythe, Thomas VI, 832
Haythe, Thomas VI, 843
Haythe, Thomas VI, 850
Haythe, Thomas, Jr. VI, 827
Haythe, William VI, 816
Haythe, William VI, 832
Haythe, William VI, 846
Haythe, William VI, 853
Haythe, William P. VI, 846
Haythe, Wm. VI, 857
Hayton, ??? III, 161
Hayton, John II, 230
Hayward, Ann II, 546
Hayward, Ann VI, 504
Hayward, Ann VI, 558
Hayward, Ann VI, 698
Hayward, Elizabeth IV, 1367
Hayward, Elizabeth VI, 583
Hayward, Elizabeth VI, 698
Hayward, Elizabeth VI, 722
Hayward, Elizabeth, VI, 558
Hayward, Geo. V, 953
Hayward, Hannah VI, 537
Hayward, Jacob V, 882
Hayward, John II, 515
Hayward, John II, 546
Hayward, Judith W. IV, 1367
Hayward, Keziah V, 953
Hayward, Leonard II, 513
Hayward, Leonard II, 546
Hayward, Lydia R. III, 161
Hayward, Mary II, 546
Hayward, Mary Ann V, 953
Hayward, Micajah IV, 1367
Hayward, Mildred K. V, 953
Hayward, Mildred Keane V, 873
Hayward, Roseann IV, 1367
Hayward, Roswell IV, 1367
Hayward, Sarah II, 373
Hayward, Sarah III, 66
Hayward, Sarah W. III, 161
Hayward, Stephen W. IV, 1367
Hayward, Thomas II, 513
Hayward, Thomas II, 546
Hayward, Thomas V, 882
Hayward, Wd. Martha II, 513
Hayward, Wd. Martha II, 546
Hayward, William V, 842
Hayward, William, Jr. V, 842
Hayward, William, Jr. V, 873
Hayward, Wm. V, 953
Haywood, Ann VI, 504
Haywood, Bessie V, 458
Haywood, Elizabeth II, 546
Haywood, Elizabeth V, 303
Haywood, Hannah VI, 504
Haywood, John II, 373
Haywood, John II, 516
Haywood, John II, 546
Haywood, Joseph V, 303
Haywood, Joseph V, 458
Haywood, Joseph VI, 504
Haywood, Lillian III, 133
Haywood, Mary II, 373
Haywood, Mary II, 516
Haywood, Mary II, 546
Haywood, Mary II, 658
Haywood, Rebecca II, 510
Haywood, Rebecca II, 546
Haywood, Rebecca II, 641
Haywood, Rebeckah II, 546
Haywood, Samuel II, 373
Haywood, Sarah II, 530
Haywood, Sarah II, 546
Haywood, Thomas II, 230
Hayworth, ??? V, 443
Hayworth, Abigail I, 814
Hayworth, Abigail I, 844
Hayworth, Absalom VI, 399
Hayworth, Absolem VI, 399
Hayworth, Adaliza I, 882
Hayworth, Adliza E. I, 855
Hayworth, Alina I, 926
Hayworth, Allen V, 499
Hayworth, Alvin H. I, 882
Hayworth, Alvira I, 854
Hayworth, Alvira I, 863
Hayworth, Amanda E. I, 854
Hayworth, Amanda Emeline I, 882
Hayworth, Ann I, 499
Hayworth, Ann I, 872
Hayworth, Ann I, 881
Hayworth, Ann I, 899
Hayworth, Ann I, 963
Hayworth, Ann I, 1120
Hayworth, Ann VI, 399
Hayworth, Anna Elizabeth V, 624
Hayworth, Asenath I, 882
Hayworth, Asenath I, 891
Hayworth, Barthena I, 814
Hayworth, Bell I, 855
Hayworth, Bertha I, 942
Hayworth, Bertha I, 946
Hayworth, Berthe I, 942
Hayworth, Bethany I, 814
Hayworth, Caroline V, 624
Hayworth, Catharine A. I, 926
Hayworth, Catharine A. I, 942
Hayworth, Catherine L. I, 882
Hayworth, Charity I, 963
Hayworth, Charity I, 1114
Hayworth, Charity I, 1120
Hayworth, Charity I, 1121
Hayworth, Chester C. I, 942
Hayworth, Chrissie I, 923
Hayworth, Cisily I, 1121
Hayworth, Cisly I, 1120
Hayworth, Clarkson I, 882
Hayworth, Clemmons I, 882
Hayworth, Clinton V, 624
Hayworth, Cornelia I, 882
Hayworth, Cornelia I, 902
Hayworth, Cornelia I, 922
Hayworth, Cornelia I, 934
Hayworth, Cyrus I, 882
Hayworth, Cyrus B. I, 882
Hayworth, David I, 499
Hayworth, David I, 963
Hayworth, David I, 1121
Hayworth, David V, 446
Hayworth, Deborah I, 942
Hayworth, Dillon I, 1120
Hayworth, Doctor F. I, 855
Hayworth, Edith I, 942
Hayworth, Edith V, 499
Hayworth, Eduth I, 622
Hayworth, Edward V, 446
Hayworth, Edward Vernon I, 926
Hayworth, Eli I, 782
Hayworth, Eli I, 881
Hayworth, Eli I, 882
Hayworth, Eli V, 499
Hayworth, Eli C. I, 882
Hayworth, Eli J. I, 882

Hayworth, Elie, Jr. I, 882
Hayworth, Elijah I, 782
Hayworth, Elijah I, 881
Hayworth, Elijah V, 177
Hayworth, Elisabeth V, 244
Hayworth, Elisabeth V, 283
Hayworth, Eliza I, 882
Hayworth, Eliza I, 898
Hayworth, Elizabeth I, 814
Hayworth, Elizabeth I, 855
Hayworth, Elizabeth I, 881
Hayworth, Elizabeth I, 1094
Hayworth, Elizabeth I, 1120
Hayworth, Elizabeth I, 1121
Hayworth, Elizabeth V, 177
Hayworth, Elizabeth V, 393
Hayworth, Elizabeth V, 434
Hayworth, Elizabeth V, 499
Hayworth, Elizabeth V, 624
Hayworth, Elizabeth C. I, 882
Hayworth, Ella I, 942
Hayworth, Elvira I, 882
Hayworth, Elvira Hayworth I, 903
Hayworth, Emeline I, 882
Hayworth, Emeline I, 898
Hayworth, Emilia V, 438
Hayworth, Emily I, 882
Hayworth, Emily I, 890
Hayworth, Emily F. I, 882
Hayworth, Emla A. I, 942
Hayworth, Ester I, 881
Hayworth, Esther V, 445
Hayworth, Esther V, 446
Hayworth, Evelyn I, 942
Hayworth, Evelyn G. I, 942
Hayworth, Evelyn L. I, 942
Hayworth, Everett I, 942
Hayworth, Everett E. I, 926
Hayworth, Everett E., Jr. I, 926
Hayworth, Fannie B. I, 942
Hayworth, Fannie Brown I, 926
Hayworth, Fannie Brown I, 942
Hayworth, Fannie H. I, 927
Hayworth, Flora I, 882
Hayworth, Frances I, 942
Hayworth, Frances V, 244
Hayworth, Frances E. I, 926
Hayworth, Frances E. I, 942
Hayworth, Frances Emily B. V, 624
Hayworth, Frances Morris I, 942
Hayworth, Frank I, 1154
Hayworth, George I, 394
Hayworth, George I, 782
Hayworth, George I, 854
Hayworth, George I, 863
Hayworth, George I, 881
Hayworth, George I, 926
Hayworth, George I, 956
Hayworth, George I, 963
Hayworth, George I, 1084
Hayworth, George II, 1000
Hayworth, George V, 469
Hayworth, George V, 499
Hayworth, George B. I, 854
Hayworth, George B. I, 882
Hayworth, George B. I, 942
Hayworth, George D., Jr. V, 499
Hayworth, George, Jr. I, 881
Hayworth, Hannah I, 814
Hayworth, Hannah I, 1121
Hayworth, Hannah V, 177
Hayworth, Hannah VI, 399
Hayworth, Hannah C. B. I, 882
Hayworth, Harriet Ellen V, 624
Hayworth, Harriett M. I, 942
Hayworth, Hattie I, 942
Hayworth, Hattie Corella I, 942
Hayworth, Hattie Corilla I, 926
Hayworth, Helen I, 942
Hayworth, Henry I, 782
Hayworth, Henry I, 855
Hayworth, Henry I, 882
Hayworth, Henry I, 924
Hayworth, Henry A. I, 854
Hayworth, Henry Alvin I, 926
Hayworth, Henry T. I, 882
Hayworth, Herman V, 499
Hayworth, Homer I, 942
Hayworth, Horace I, 942
Hayworth, Horace S. I, 942
Hayworth, Hubert I, 942
Hayworth, Hubert O. I, 942
Hayworth, Hubert Oscar I, 926
Hayworth, Ila I, 938
Hayworth, Ila I, 942
Hayworth, Ila Bennett I, 942
Hayworth, Isaac J. M. I, 855
Hayworth, Isabel II, 1000
Hayworth, Isabel II, 1012
Hayworth, Isabell II, 960
Hayworth, Isaiah M. V, 624
Hayworth, Isaiah M. V, 625
Hayworth, Isaiah M. V, 631
Hayworth, J. M. I, 926
Hayworth, J. M. I, 927
Hayworth, J. Madison I, 942
Hayworth, James I, 499
Hayworth, James I, 855
Hayworth, James I, 881
Hayworth, James I, 882
Hayworth, James I, 926
Hayworth, James I, 942
Hayworth, James I, 963
Hayworth, James I, 1084
Hayworth, James I, 1120
Hayworth, James II, 960
Hayworth, James V, 244
Hayworth, James V, 446
Hayworth, James V, 499
Hayworth, James VI, 399
Hayworth, James L. I, 882
Hayworth, James M. I, 942
Hayworth, James M. V, 624
Hayworth, James Madison I, 926
Hayworth, James Milton I, 926
Hayworth, James Milton I, 942
Hayworth, James Walton I, 926
Hayworth, James, Jr. V, 446
Hayworth, Jane I, 963
Hayworth, Jane I, 1120
Hayworth, Jane II, 545
Hayworth, Jas. M. I, 942
Hayworth, Jasper I, 942
Hayworth, Jeams I, 956
Hayworth, Jennie I, 942
Hayworth, Jennie Reitzel I, 926
Hayworth, Jeremiah I, 782
Hayworth, Jeremiah I, 881
Hayworth, Jerome I, 938
Hayworth, Jerome I, 942
Hayworth, Jerome W. I, 942
Hayworth, Jerome Winston I, 926
Hayworth, Jerome Winston I, 942
Hayworth, Jesse B. I, 942
Hayworth, Joanna V, 469
Hayworth, Joanna V, 479
Hayworth, Joanna V, 499
Hayworth, Job I, 855
Hayworth, Joel I, 499
Hayworth, Joel I, 963
Hayworth, Joel I, 1120
Hayworth, Joel I, 1121
Hayworth, Joel V, 446
Hayworth, John I, 782
Hayworth, John I, 814
Hayworth, John I, 855
Hayworth, John I, 881
Hayworth, John I, 882
Hayworth, John I, 956
Hayworth, John I, 963
Hayworth, John I, 1084
Hayworth, John I, 1120
Hayworth, John I, 1121
Hayworth, John V, 499
Hayworth, John VI, 399
Hayworth, John A. I, 882
Hayworth, John Maxwell I, 1120
Hayworth, Johnathan I, 1120
Hayworth, Jonathan I, 499
Hayworth, Jonathan I, 963
Hayworth, Jonathan I, 1120
Hayworth, Jonathan I, 1121
Hayworth, Jonathan V, 445
Hayworth, Jonathan V, 446
Hayworth, Jonathan V, 499
Hayworth, Josiah I, 782
Hayworth, Josiah I, 855
Hayworth, Josiah I, 881
Hayworth, Kate I, 926
Hayworth, Kate Lucile I, 926
Hayworth, Kate Lucile I, 942
Hayworth, Katharine I, 942
Hayworth, Laura I, 879
Hayworth, Laura I, 882
Hayworth, Laura I, 920
Hayworth, Laura I, 925
Hayworth, Laura Lamb I, 942
Hayworth, Lavania I, 924
Hayworth, Lewis I, 942
Hayworth, Linsay I, 882
Hayworth, Louise I, 942
Hayworth, Lucinda I, 814
Hayworth, Lucinda I, 855
Hayworth, Lucinda I, 882
Hayworth, Lucinda I, 903
Hayworth, Lydia I, 1121
Hayworth, Madison I, 882
Hayworth, Maffie Viola I, 924
Hayworth, Mahlon V, 499
Hayworth, Mahlon V, 624
Hayworth, Margaret I, 782
Hayworth, Margaret I, 847
Hayworth, Margaret I, 855
Hayworth, Margaret I, 877
Hayworth, Margaret I, 881
Hayworth, Margaret I, 882
Hayworth, Margaret I, 926
Hayworth, Margaret I, 1120
Hayworth, Margaret L. I, 854
Hayworth, Margaret L. I, 882
Hayworth, Margret I, 881
Hayworth, Maria I, 882
Hayworth, Maria I, 903
Hayworth, Mariah I, 853
Hayworth, Marmaduke I, 882
Hayworth, Marriam V. I, 942
Hayworth, Martha I, 809
Hayworth, Martha I, 814
Hayworth, Martha E. I, 854
Hayworth, Martha E. I, 882
Hayworth, Mary I, 499
Hayworth, Mary I, 782
Hayworth, Mary I, 847
Hayworth, Mary I, 855
Hayworth, Mary I, 881
Hayworth, Mary I, 882
Hayworth, Mary I, 899
Hayworth, Mary I, 905
Hayworth, Mary I, 956
Hayworth, Mary I, 963
Hayworth, Mary I, 1084
Hayworth, Mary I, 1119
Hayworth, Mary I, 1120
Hayworth, Mary I, 1121
Hayworth, Mary II, 960
Hayworth, Mary II, 989
Hayworth, Mary II, 1000
Hayworth, Mary V, 469
Hayworth, Mary V, 473
Hayworth, Mary V, 499
Hayworth, Mary V, 625
Hayworth, Mary V, 631
Hayworth, Mary VI, 399
Hayworth, Mary Ann V, 446
Hayworth, Mary Bernice I, 926
Hayworth, Mary Bernice I, 942
Hayworth, Mary C. I, 882
Hayworth, Mary E. IV, 733
Hayworth, Mary Ellen I, 926
Hayworth, Mary Ellen I, 942
Hayworth, Mary Regina I, 934
Hayworth, Mary Victoria I, 863
Hayworth, Micajah I, 782
Hayworth, Micajah I, 855
Hayworth, Micajah I, 881
Hayworth, Micajah V, 160
Hayworth, Micajah H. V, 177
Hayworth, Mildred A. I, 926
Hayworth, Mildred A. I, 942
Hayworth, Mildred M. I, 854
Hayworth, Mildred Maria I, 882
Hayworth, Minerva V, 499
Hayworth, Minnie I, 942
Hayworth, Minnie S. I, 926
Hayworth, Minnie Shepard I, 942
Hayworth, Miriam V. I, 926
Hayworth, Moorman V, 499
Hayworth, Moses I, 855
Hayworth, Nathan I, 882
Hayworth, Nereus I, 926
Hayworth, Newton Sylvester I, 926
Hayworth, Pearl V, 177
Hayworth, Pharibe I, 881
Hayworth, Phebe I, 544
Hayworth, Phebe I, 547
Hayworth, Phebe I, 814
Hayworth, Phebe V, 244
Hayworth, Phebe V, 469
Hayworth, Phebe V, 624
Hayworth, Phebe Ann V, 160
Hayworth, Phebe Ann V, 177
Hayworth, Pherebe I, 855
Hayworth, Rachel I, 367
Hayworth, Rachel I, 394
Hayworth, Rachel I, 782
Hayworth, Rachel I, 814
Hayworth, Racher V, 499
Hayworth, Randolph I, 926
Hayworth, Rebecca V, 499
Hayworth, Rebecca V, 502
Hayworth, Rebecca J. V, 335
Hayworth, Regina I, 882
Hayworth, Richard I, 499
Hayworth, Richard I, 544
Hayworth, Richard I, 814
Hayworth, Richard I, 956
Hayworth, Richard I, 963
Hayworth, Richard I, 1084
Hayworth, Richard I, 1101
Hayworth, Richard I, 1120
Hayworth, Richard I, 1121
Hayworth, Richard V, 499
Hayworth, Richard V, 624
Hayworth, Richard VI, 399
Hayworth, Richard, Jr. I, 1120
Hayworth, Roxana I, 942
Hayworth, Roxanna I, 926
Hayworth, Roxanna I, 927
Hayworth, Roxie I, 942
Hayworth, Rufus I, 942
Hayworth, Rufus K. I, 942
Hayworth, Rufus King I, 926
Hayworth, Rufus King I, 942
Hayworth, Ruth I, 814
Hayworth, Ruth I, 855
Hayworth, Ruth I, 881
Hayworth, Ruth I, 942
Hayworth, Ruth V, 499
Hayworth, Ruth V, 543
Hayworth, Sally I, 882
Hayworth, Samuel I, 782
Hayworth, Samuel I, 855
Hayworth, Samuel I, 881
Hayworth, Samuel I, 942
Hayworth, Samuel L. I, 942
Hayworth, Sarah I, 394
Hayworth, Sarah I, 428
Hayworth, Sarah I, 499
Hayworth, Sarah I, 882
Hayworth, Sarah I, 956
Hayworth, Sarah I, 963
Hayworth, Sarah I, 1084
Hayworth, Sarah I, 1119
Hayworth, Sarah I, 1120
Hayworth, Sarah I, 1121
Hayworth, Sarah II, 1000
Hayworth, Sarah V, 469
Hayworth, Sarah V, 499
Hayworth, Sarah V, 524
Hayworth, Sarah VI, 399
Hayworth, Sarah T. I, 1121
Hayworth, Shubal I, 934
Hayworth, Solomon I, 814
Hayworth, Solomon I, 881
Hayworth, Solomon I, 882
Hayworth, Stephanes I, 1120
Hayworth, Stephanus I, 367
Hayworth, Stephanus I, 881
Hayworth, Stephenas I, 394
Hayworth, Stephenas I, 782
Hayworth, Stephenes I, 881
Hayworth, Stephens I, 814
Hayworth, Stephenus VI, 399
Hayworth, Susann V, 499
Hayworth, Susanna I, 499
Hayworth, Susanna I, 1121
Hayworth, Susannah I, 956
Hayworth, Susannah I, 1084
Hayworth, Susannah V, 393
Hayworth, Susannah V, 425
Hayworth, Susannah V, 499
Hayworth, Susannah VI, 399
Hayworth, Theodore S. I, 926
Hayworth, Theodore Shepard I, 942
Hayworth, Thomas Mahlon V, 624
Hayworth, Thos. M. V, 625
Hayworth, Thursey Ruth I, 926
Hayworth, Thursey Ruth I, 942
Hayworth, Valeria M. I, 942
Hayworth, Velma Virginia I, 942
Hayworth, Velna Virginia I, 926
Hayworth, Velura Mildred I, 942
Hayworth, Victory I, 882
Hayworth, Victory I, 891
Hayworth, W. Madison I, 926
Hayworth, Welmett I, 394
Hayworth, Welmett I, 782
Hayworth, William I, 499
Hayworth, William I, 882
Hayworth, William I, 903
Hayworth, William I, 956
Hayworth, William I, 963
Hayworth, William I, 1084
Hayworth, William I, 1120
Hayworth, William V, 446
Hayworth, William V, 499
Hayworth, William V, 842
Hayworth, William A. I, 942
Hayworth, William W. I, 855
Hayworth, William, Jr. I, 1121
Hayworth, Wm. V, 446
Hayworth, Wm. Winborn I, 855
Hayze, Mary II, 546
Hazard, ??? III, 268
Hazard, Allen V, 575
Hazard, Allen V, 681
Hazard, Allen E. V, 681
Hazard, Amanda III, 285
Hazard, Amanda III, 345
Hazard, Amy Ellen V, 681
Hazard, Ann V, 567
Hazard, Ann V, 575
Hazard, Ann Catharine III, 161
Hazard, Ann K. V, 575
Hazard, Ann K. V, 681
Hazard, Anna III, 25
Hazard, Anna III, 153
Hazard, Anna III, 161
Hazard, Anna R. III, 161
Hazard, Anna R. V, 499
Hazard, Barbara Lee V, 681
Hazard, C. Howard II, 1085
Hazard, Charles De Charante II, 1085
Hazard, Charles H. III, 161
Hazard, Clara V, 499
Hazard, Clara V, 681
Hazard, Clara S. V, 499
Hazard, Clifton V, 500
Hazard, Clifton V, 681
Hazard, Dorothy F. VI, 747
Hazard, Earnest V, 681
Hazard, Edward III, 161
Hazard, Eli B. III, 161
Hazard, Eliza III, 161
Hazard, Elizabeth III, 324
Hazard, Elizabeth V, 681
Hazard, Elizabeth Irwin V, 681
Hazard, Ellen V, 393
Hazard, Emma V, 681
Hazard, Ernest V, 393
Hazard, Ernest V, 681
Hazard, Ernest R. V, 681
Hazard, Ethelbert V, 499
Hazard, Ethelbert V, 681
Hazard, Flora V, 500
Hazard, Flora V, 681
Hazard, Francis D. V, 499
Hazard, Frank V, 499
Hazard, Frank V, 681
Hazard, Frank O. V, 681
Hazard, Frank T. V, 681
Hazard, George II, 1088
Hazard, George F. II, 1085
Hazard, Gulia R. V, 681
Hazard, Hannah V, 499
Hazard, Harriet H. V, 575
Hazard, Harriet H. V, 681
Hazard, Henrietta V, 575
Hazard, Herbert V, 499
Hazard, Herbert V, 500
Hazard, Herbert V, 681
Hazard, James III, 161
Hazard, James III, 268
Hazard, John III, 161
Hazard, John V, 499
Hazard, John VI, 747
Hazard, John F. II, 874
Hazard, John F. VI, 747
Hazard, Julia R. V, 575
Hazard, Julia Rebecca V, 575
Hazard, Lorain V, 499
Hazard, Loren V, 681
Hazard, Loren W. V, 681
Hazard, Louella V, 499
Hazard, Louella V, 681
Hazard, Louella J. V, 681
Hazard, Lydia J. V, 575
Hazard, Lydia Jane V, 575
Hazard, Lydia Jane V, 681
Hazard, Lydia R. III, 161
Hazard, M. Rebecca I, 211
Hazard, Margaret C. III, 161
Hazard, Margaretta III, 161
Hazard, Margaretta E. III, 161
Hazard, Marie Louise II, 1085
Hazard, Marion J. II, 1085
Hazard, Martha C. III, 161
Hazard, Martha E. VI, 747
Hazard, Mary V, 500
Hazard, Mary V, 681
Hazard, Mary V, 715
Hazard, Mary Alice III, 161
Hazard, Mary Ellen V, 681
Hazard, Mary W. III, 94
Hazard, Mary W. III, 161
Hazard, Mary W. III, 195
Hazard, Mary W. III, 267
Hazard, Mary W. III, 268
Hazard, Nellie V, 681
Hazard, Pearl V, 393
Hazard, Pearl V, 681
Hazard, Pearle V, 681
Hazard, Pearle Certain V, 681
Hazard, Phebe Ann II, 1085
Hazard, Phebe Ann II, 1088
Hazard, Phebe Ann II, 1089
Hazard, Rebecca III, 161

ızard, Roberta V, 681
ızard, Rowland H. II, 1085
ızard, Rowland H. II, 1088
ızard, Rowland H. II, 1089
ızard, Rtth A. V, 681
ızard, Ruth V, 681
ızard, S. Carolina III, 161
ızard, Samuel III, 161
ızard, Samuel VI, 358
ızard, Samuel VI, 463
ızard, Samuel VI, 515
ızard, Sarah III, 161
ızard, Sarah III, 268
ızard, Sarah B. III, 161
ızard, Sarah L. V, 575
ızard, Sarah W. III, 161
ızard, Seth V, 681
ızard, T. III, 153
ızard, Thomas VI, 747
ızard, Thomas R. III, 161
ızard, Thomas W. III, 161
ızard, Thomas, Jr. III, 161
ızard, Troy III, 161
ızard, William II, 1085
ızard, William II, 1088
ızard, William III, 161
ıze, Andrew II, 77
ıze, Eaton I, 544
ıze, John I, 544
ızel, Ezikiel I, 814
ızel, John I, 814
ızel, Joseph I, 814
ızel, Martha Shealds I, 814
ızelett, Keziah IV, 392
ızelett, Keziah IV, 407
ızelle, Martha I, 837
ızelle, Martha Shealds I, 814
ızellwood, George II, 204
ızellwood, George II, 230
ızellwood, Margarett II, 230
ızellwood, Wd. Margarett II, 204
ızelton, Margrett II, 372
ızelwood, Benjamin VI, 824
ızelwood, Elizabeth VI, 810
ızelwood, Elizabeth VI, 824
ızelwood, H. VI, 841
ızelwood, John VI, 824
ızelwood, Littleberry VI, 831
ızelwood, Martha VI, 824
ızelwood, Mary VI, 810
ızelwood, Molly VI, 824
ızelwood, Richard VI, 824
ızelwood, Sally VI, 824
ızelwood, Sarah VI, 824
ızelwood, Sarah VI, 831
ızelwood, Thomas VI, 824
ızelwood, Thomas VI, 855
ızelwood, William VI, 824
ızen, Elizabeth E. IV, 892
ızen, Elizabeth E. IV, 895
ızer, William I, 722
ızle, Elizabeth I, 882
ızle, Mary I, 882
ızleton, Mary B. V, 71
ızlett, William VI, 828
ızlewood, Lilly VI, 931
ızlewood, Pleasant VI, 931
ızley, Alfred V, 842
ızley, Allen V, 842
ızley, Eunice V, 842
ızley, Lavina V, 842
ızley, Mary H. V, 842
ızzard, Clara V, 499
ızzard, Sarah L. V, 575
eacock, Abigail II, 545
eacock, Abigail II, 678
eacock, Addie IV, 1027
eacock, Addie J. IV, 1031
eacock, Addis J. IV, 1031
eacock, Alice IV, 1027
eacock, Alice IV, 1164
eacock, Alice B. IV, 1027
eacock, Alverda J. IV, 1027
eacock, Alvira IV, 1164
eacock, Amos IV, 719
eacock, Amos IV, 963
eacock, Amos D. IV, 719
eacock, Amos D. IV, 963
eacock, Amos D. IV, 1026
eacock, Ann II, 827
eacock, Ann IV, 871
eacock, Ann IV, 884
eacock, Ann IV, 963
eacock, Ann IV, 1027
eacock, Ann IV, 1031
eacock, Ann Eliza IV, 719
eacock, Ann Eliza IV, 1027
eacock, Anna M. II, 709
eacock, Anna M. II, 715
eacock, Ariah A. IV, 963
Heacock, Arthur G. IV, 1027
Heacock, Asenath IV, 719
Heacock, Asenath IV, 776
Heacock, Asenath IV, 963
Heacock, Asenath IV, 1026
Heacock, Barclay IV, 1027
Heacock, Barclay B. II, 874
Heacock, Barclay Barber II, 799
Heacock, Barclay Barber IV, 1027
Heacock, Barclay Barber IV, 1030
Heacock, Barton IV, 719
Heacock, Barton IV, 963
Heacock, Barton IV, 1023
Heacock, Barton IV, 1024
Heacock, Barton IV, 1026
Heacock, Barton IV, 1027
Heacock, Barton IV, 1164
Heacock, Benjamin IV, 38
Heacock, Benjamin IV, 220
Heacock, Bertha Olive IV, 1027
Heacock, Borton IV, 963
Heacock, Burton IV, 719
Heacock, Caleb IV, 38
Heacock, Chalkley IV, 1027
Heacock, Charles IV, 1027
Heacock, Charles D. IV, 1027
Heacock, Chas. II, 874
Heacock, Chas. Wayne II, 874
Heacock, Clara III, 161
Heacock, Clara IV, 1027
Heacock, Clara Hazel IV, 1027
Heacock, Clarkson IV, 963
Heacock, Clarkson IV, 1023
Heacock, Clarkson IV, 1027
Heacock, Clarkson IV, 1164
Heacock, Clarkson Oliver IV, 1027
Heacock, Clyde L. IV, 1027
Heacock, Corin IV, 1027
Heacock, Deborah E. IV, 1027
Heacock, Deborah E. IV, 1030
Heacock, Deborah Ellen II, 799
Heacock, Dennis IV, 719
Heacock, Dinah IV, 682
Heacock, Dinah IV, 719
Heacock, Dinah IV, 776
Heacock, Dinah IV, 963
Heacock, Dinah IV, 1021
Heacock, Dinah IV, 1026
Heacock, Dinah IV, 1027
Heacock, Edgar IV, 1027
Heacock, Edith M. III, 128
Heacock, Edith M. III, 161
Heacock, Edith Mary II, 874
Heacock, Edith R. IV, 1027
Heacock, Edward II, 874
Heacock, Edwin IV, 719
Heacock, Edwin IV, 963
Heacock, Edwin IV, 1026
Heacock, Edwin IV, 1027
Heacock, Elias IV, 777
Heacock, Elias H. IV, 719
Heacock, Elias H. IV, 963
Heacock, Elias H. IV, 1026
Heacock, Elias N. IV, 719
Heacock, Eliza II, 874
Heacock, Eliza IV, 38
Heacock, Eliza IV, 719
Heacock, Eliza IV, 777
Heacock, Eliza IV, 1164
Heacock, Eliza VI, 747
Heacock, Eliza Ann IV, 1210
Heacock, Elizabeth II, 874
Heacock, Elizabeth IV, 871
Heacock, Elizabeth IV, 880
Heacock, Elizabeth IV, 963
Heacock, Elizabeth A. IV, 1023
Heacock, Elizabeth A. IV, 1027
Heacock, Elizabeth Ann IV, 1027
Heacock, Elizabeth C. II, 704
Heacock, Ellwood II, 874
Heacock, Elvira IV, 1027
Heacock, Emeline II, 874
Heacock, Emma II, 732
Heacock, Emma II, 757
Heacock, Emma IV, 1027
Heacock, Emma A. IV, 1027
Heacock, Emma G. III, 161
Heacock, Emma G. III, 244
Heacock, Emma R. II, 874
Heacock, Emma R. IV, 1027
Heacock, Enos IV, 719
Heacock, Enos IV, 963
Heacock, Enos IV, 1026
Heacock, Enos IV, 1027
Heacock, Enos IV, 1031
Heacock, Enos George IV, 1027
Heacock, Ephraim IV, 1027
Heacock, Esther IV, 19
Heacock, Esther IV, 38
Heacock, Esther VI, 747
Heacock, Eunice IV, 719
Heacock, Ezra Borton IV, 719
Heacock, Frances VI, 649
Heacock, Frances VI, 703
Heacock, George W. IV, 1027
Heacock, Hannah IV, 38
Heacock, Hannah IV, 719
Heacock, Hannah IV, 871
Heacock, Hannah IV, 894
Heacock, Hannah IV, 895
Heacock, Hannah IV, 924
Heacock, Hannah IV, 963
Heacock, Hannah IV, 1027
Heacock, Hannah Ann IV, 1029
Heacock, Hannah H. IV, 871
Heacock, Hannah H. IV, 877
Heacock, Hannah P. IV, 864
Heacock, Hannah P. IV, 871
Heacock, Homer Barclay II, 799
Heacock, Ida E. II, 874
Heacock, Ida Elizabeth II, 799
Heacock, Ida Elizabeth II, 874
Heacock, Irving IV, 1164
Heacock, Isaac IV, 871
Heacock, Isaac IV, 1027
Heacock, Isaac B. IV, 1164
Heacock, Isaac William IV, 1027
Heacock, Israel II, 799
Heacock, Israel II, 874
Heacock, Jacob IV, 631
Heacock, Jacob IV, 871
Heacock, Jacob, Jr. IV, 871
Heacock, James IV, 871
Heacock, James IV, 872
Heacock, James D. IV, 872
Heacock, James D. IV, 1026
Heacock, Jane IV, 698
Heacock, Jane IV, 719
Heacock, Jane IV, 928
Heacock, Jane IV, 963
Heacock, Jane VI, 747
Heacock, Jane D. IV, 682
Heacock, Jane D. IV, 719
Heacock, Jane D. IV, 963
Heacock, Jane Dennis IV, 719
Heacock, Jemima II, 874
Heacock, Jemima Parsons II, 799
Heacock, Jesse II, 545
Heacock, Jesse II, 678
Heacock, Jesse II, 715
Heacock, Jesse IV, 92
Heacock, John IV, 38
Heacock, John IV, 871
Heacock, John IV, 963
Heacock, John G. IV, 38
Heacock, John P. II, 799
Heacock, John P. II, 874
Heacock, Jonah II, 545
Heacock, Jonah II, 678
Heacock, Jonathan IV, 631
Heacock, Jonathan IV, 864
Heacock, Jonathan IV, 871
Heacock, Jonathan N. IV, 871
Heacock, Jonathan N. IV, 877
Heacock, Jonathan, Jr. IV, 871
Heacock, Joseph IV, 38
Heacock, Joseph IV, 719
Heacock, Joseph IV, 1210
Heacock, Joseph VI, 747
Heacock, Joseph Lindley IV, 1027
Heacock, Josiah W. IV, 719
Heacock, Josiah W. IV, 963
Heacock, Josiah W. IV, 1026
Heacock, Josiah Wilson IV, 719
Heacock, Josiah Wilson IV, 1027
Heacock, Julia A. II, 874
Heacock, Julia A. II, 904
Heacock, Larkin IV, 38
Heacock, Larkin A. IV, 38
Heacock, Laura IV, 963
Heacock, Laura J. II, 714
Heacock, Lillian M. II, 874
Heacock, Lucretia M. II, 874
Heacock, Lucretia M. III, 128
Heacock, Lucretia M. III, 161
Heacock, Lucretia M. IV, 1027
Heacock, Lucretia M. IV, 1030
Heacock, Lula M. IV, 1027
Heacock, Lulu M. II, 874
Heacock, Lydia II, 715
Heacock, Madge II, 874
Heacock, Malissa IV, 1164
Heacock, Mariam IV, 38
Heacock, Marian IV, 730
Heacock, Martha IV, 38
Heacock, Martha IV, 719
Heacock, Martha IV, 730
Heacock, Mary IV, 870
Heacock, Mary IV, 871
Heacock, Mary IV, 872
Heacock, Mary IV, 878
Heacock, Mary Ann IV, 1164
Heacock, Mary P. II, 874
Heacock, Melissa IV, 1024
Heacock, Melissa IV, 1027
Heacock, Melissa IV, 1031
Heacock, Melissa IV, 1164
Heacock, Meriam IV, 38
Heacock, Milton IV, 719
Heacock, Milton IV, 776
Heacock, Milton IV, 963
Heacock, Milton IV, 1021
Heacock, Milton IV, 1026
Heacock, Milton IV, 1027
Heacock, Milton IV, 1029
Heacock, Miriam IV, 719
Heacock, Miriam IV, 727
Heacock, N. E. IV, 1027
Heacock, Nancy L. IV, 1027
Heacock, Nathan IV, 38
Heacock, Nathan IV, 682
Heacock, Nathan IV, 719
Heacock, Nathan IV, 776
Heacock, Nathan IV, 894
Heacock, Nathan IV, 895
Heacock, Nathan IV, 963
Heacock, Nathan IV, 1021
Heacock, Nathan IV, 1026
Heacock, Nathan IV, 1027
Heacock, Oliver IV, 1027
Heacock, Oliver IV, 1164
Heacock, Oscar Edison IV, 1027
Heacock, Phebe II, 874
Heacock, Phebe IV, 38
Heacock, Phebe IV, 719
Heacock, Phebe IV, 892
Heacock, Phebe IV, 894
Heacock, Preston IV, 1210
Heacock, Preston Emerson IV, 1027
Heacock, Rachel IV, 719
Heacock, Rachel IV, 924
Heacock, Rachel IV, 963
Heacock, Rachel IV, 1023
Heacock, Rachel IV, 1024
Heacock, Rachel IV, 1027
Heacock, Rachel IV, 1164
Heacock, Rachel Ann IV, 1027
Heacock, Rachel M. IV, 1027
Heacock, Ralph Henderson II, 799
Heacock, Rebecca IV, 719
Heacock, Rebecca IV, 1023
Heacock, Rebecca IV, 1027
Heacock, Rebecca Jane IV, 1027
Heacock, Rebecca Jane IV, 1164
Heacock, Rebecca Jr. IV, 776
Heacock, Rebecca L. IV, 1027
Heacock, Rebecca Leona IV, 1027
Heacock, Rosaltha V. IV, 710
Heacock, Rosamond IV, 719
Heacock, Roy A. II, 874
Heacock, Roy Antrim II, 799
Heacock, Samuel II, 704
Heacock, Samuel II, 714
Heacock, Samuel III, 244
Heacock, Samuel IV, 38
Heacock, Sarah IV, 675
Heacock, Sarah IV, 719
Heacock, Sarah IV, 864
Heacock, Sarah IV, 871
Heacock, Sarah IV, 880
Heacock, Sarah IV, 895
Heacock, Sarah IV, 924
Heacock, Sarah IV, 963
Heacock, Sarah IV, 1027
Heacock, Sarah A. IV, 1027
Heacock, Sarah Ann IV, 1027
Heacock, Sarah Ann IV, 1164
Heacock, Sarah Anne IV, 1164
Heacock, Sarah B. IV, 1027
Heacock, Sarah Jane IV, 719
Heacock, Sarah Jane IV, 1027
Heacock, Sarah M. IV, 892
Heacock, Sarah M. IV, 894
Heacock, Susan II, 704
Heacock, Susan II, 714
Heacock, Susan IV, 871
Heacock, Susan IV, 873
Heacock, Susanna III, 244
Heacock, Susanna IV, 871
Heacock, Susanna, Jr. IV, 871
Heacock, Susannah IV, 871
Heacock, T. Chalkley IV, 1027
Heacock, Tacy II, 545
Heacock, Tacy II, 678
Heacock, Tacy IV, 719
Heacock, Tacy IV, 963
Heacock, Tacy IV, 1027
Heacock, Tacy L. IV, 719
Heacock, Tacy L. IV, 729
Heacock, Taylor IV, 1027
Heacock, Uriah IV, 675
Heacock, Uriah IV, 719
Heacock, Uriah A. IV, 719
Heacock, Uriah A. IV, 1021
Heacock, Uriah A. IV, 1026
Heacock, Uriah A. IV, 1027
Heacock, Uriah Antrim IV, 719
Heacock, Uriah Antrim IV, 1027
Heacock, W. S. IV, 1210
Heacock, Wd. Lucretia M. II, 874
Heacock, Wd. Sarah IV, 871
Heacock, William II, 799
Heacock, William IV, 871
Heacock, William IV, 872
Heacock, William IV, 892
Heacock, William A. IV, 1027
Heacock, William A. IV, 1030
Heacock, William Antrim IV, 1027
Heacock, William W. III, 161
Heacock, Wm. II, 874
Heacock, Wm. II, 904
Heacock, Wm. IV, 730
Heacock, Wm. IV, 1210
Heacock, Wm. A. II, 874
Heacock, Wm. A. III, 128
Heacock, Wm. A. III, 161
Heacock, Wm. A. IV, 1027
Heacock, Wm. Antrim IV, 1027
Heacock, Wm. Antrim IV, 1164
Heacock, Wm. Channing IV, 1027
Heacock, Wm. S. IV, 1210
Head, Anna II, 547
Head, Anna II, 660
Head, Charlotte II, 373
Head, Daniel II, 373
Head, Eliza II, 430
Head, Eliza II, 673
Head, Elizabeth II, 373
Head, Elizabeth II, 545
Head, Elizabeth II, 546
Head, Elizabeth II, 547
Head, Elizabeth II, 643
Head, Elizabeth II, 644
Head, Elizabeth II, 660
Head, Elizabeth II, 721
Head, Elizabeth IV, 335
Head, Elizabeth IV, 357
Head, Ella I, 307
Head, Esther II, 457
Head, Esther II, 546
Head, George I, 1075
Head, Hannah II, 373
Head, Hannah II, 546
Head, Hannah II, 552
Head, Hannah VI, 504
Head, Israel II, 373
Head, John II, 373
Head, John II, 456
Head, John II, 457
Head, John II, 475
Head, John II, 545
Head, John II, 546
Head, John II, 547
Head, John II, 552
Head, John II, 558
Head, John II, 567
Head, John II, 575
Head, John II, 643
Head, John II, 644
Head, John II, 660
Head, John II, 677
Head, John, Jr. II, 373
Head, Joseph II, 373
Head, Joseph II, 547
Head, Joseph II, 707
Head, Judith II, 373
Head, Margaret II, 373
Head, Margaret II, 546
Head, Margaret II, 978
Head, Martha II, 546
Head, Martha II, 577
Head, Mary II, 373
Head, Mary II, 432
Head, Mary II, 546
Head, Mary II, 558
Head, Mary II, 677
Head, Mary III, 161
Head, Mary VI, 494
Head, Mary VI, 495
Head, Mary VI, 504
Head, Rachel II, 373
Head, Rebecca II, 373
Head, Rebecca II, 546
Head, Rebecca II, 567
Head, Rebecca VI, 521
Head, Rebecca VI, 523
Head, Samuel II, 373
Head, Samuel VI, 504
Head, Sarah II, 373
Head, Sarah II, 475

Head, Sarah II, 546
Head, Sarah VI, 504
Head, Susanna II, 546
Head, Susanna II, 547
Head, Susanna II, 575
Head, Susannah II, 643
Head, W. S. I, 336
Head, Wd. Margaret II, 456
Head, Wm. II, 643
Headen, Emilia VI, 992
Headen, Franklin VI, 982
Headen, Franklin VI, 992
Headen, Franklin VI, 1005
Headen, Franklin VI, 1018
Headen, John VI, 992
Headen, Lidia VI, 1005
Headen, Lidia P. VI, 1005
Headen, Mary VI, 352
Headen, Mary VI, 1017
Headen, Polly M. VI, 992
Headen, William VI, 1017
Headen, Winny VI, 992
Headland, Della IV, 719
Headland, Elmer IV, 719
Headland, Kenneth IV, 719
Headland, Mamie IV, 719
Headland, Mrs. ??? IV, 719
Headley, ??? II, 1000
Headley, Abigail II, 1001
Headley, Abigail II, 1036
Headley, Amos II, 1001
Headley, Ann II, 1052
Headley, Anna II, 960
Headley, Anna IV, 719
Headley, Benjamin II, 1001
Headley, Benjamin II, 1052
Headley, Catharine II, 1001
Headley, Christian II, 960
Headley, Christian II, 984
Headley, Christian II, 1001
Headley, Christiana II, 977
Headley, Christiana II, 980
Headley, Christiana II, 1001
Headley, Daniel II, 960
Headley, Daniel II, 1001
Headley, David II, 960
Headley, David II, 984
Headley, David II, 1001
Headley, David B. II, 960
Headley, David B. IV, 719
Headley, De Bonsall II, 960
Headley, Ebenezer II, 781
Headley, Ebenezer II, 1001
Headley, Ebenezer II, 1030
Headley, Ebenezer II, 1051
Headley, Edith II, 960
Headley, Edith II, 1001
Headley, Edith M. IV, 719
Headley, Edward II, 1052
Headley, Edward IV, 719
Headley, Edward H. II, 960
Headley, Edward Herbert IV, 719
Headley, Elizabeth II, 231
Headley, Elizabeth II, 781
Headley, Elizabeth II, 986
Headley, Elizabeth II, 1001
Headley, Elizabeth II, 1030
Headley, Gladys Lucile II, 960
Headley, Hannah II, 960
Headley, Hannah II, 979
Headley, Hannah II, 1001
Headley, Hannah II, 1018
Headley, Hannah II, 1073
Headley, Hannah IV, 719
Headley, Hannah W. IV, 719
Headley, Hannah, Jr. II, 981
Headley, Hannah, Jr. II, 1001
Headley, Hartis IV, 719
Headley, Henry II, 1073
Headley, James II, 1073
Headley, James Roger IV, 719
Headley, Jane IV, 407
Headley, John II, 960
Headley, John II, 979
Headley, John II, 1001
Headley, John II, 1036
Headley, John II, 1052
Headley, Jonathan II, 1073
Headley, Joseph II, 946
Headley, Joseph II, 960
Headley, Joseph II, 979
Headley, Joseph II, 984
Headley, Joseph II, 1001
Headley, Joseph II, 1018
Headley, Joseph II, 1085
Headley, Joshua II, 844
Headley, Joshua II, 874
Headley, Joshua II, 960
Headley, Joshua II, 986
Headley, Joshua II, 1001
Headley, Joshua VI, 178
Headley, Joshua, Jr. II, 1001
Headley, Laura IV, 719
Headley, Liddia II, 1001
Headley, Lidia II, 960
Headley, Louisa M. II, 844
Headley, Louisa M. II, 874
Headley, Lucy II, 1001
Headley, Lucy II, 1016
Headley, Luella II, 960
Headley, Lydia II, 960
Headley, Lydia II, 1001
Headley, Lydia II, 1040
Headley, Margaret II, 960
Headley, Margaret II, 1052
Headley, Mary II, 231
Headley, Mary II, 236
Headley, Mary II, 813
Headley, Mary II, 986
Headley, Mary II, 1001
Headley, Mary E. IV, 719
Headley, Mary, Jr. II, 1001
Headley, Mary, Jr. II, 1007
Headley, Meriah II, 1001
Headley, Nathan II, 781
Headley, Phebe II, 1001
Headley, Phebe II, 1032
Headley, Philip Dennis II, 1073
Headley, Rachel II, 1001
Headley, Rebecca II, 984
Headley, Rebecca II, 1001
Headley, Rebecca IV, 719
Headley, Rebecca K. II, 844
Headley, Rebecca K. II, 874
Headley, Robert B. IV, 407
Headley, Robert Barclay IV, 407
Headley, Rosanna II, 960
Headley, Ruth II, 1001
Headley, Samuel II, 1001
Headley, Samuel H. IV, 407
Headley, Sarah II, 987
Headley, Sarah II, 1001
Headley, Sarah II, 1037
Headley, Sarah M. II, 960
Headley, Solomon II, 960
Headley, Solomon II, 1001
Headley, Thomas II, 960
Headley, Thomas II, 1001
Headley, Thomas II, 1052
Headley, Ursula II, 1001
Headley, Violet Garrigues II, 960
Headley, Wd. Hannah II, 960
Headley, Wd. Margaret A. II, 1085
Headley, William II, 230
Headley, Wm. II, 1001
Headly, Amos II, 1001
Headly, Amy II, 977
Headly, Amy II, 1001
Headly, Ann II, 1052
Headly, Ann Elizabeth II, 1073
Headly, Anna Maria II, 1073
Headly, Benjamin II, 1052
Headly, Benjamin II, 1069
Headly, Benjamin II, 1074
Headly, Catharine II, 1001
Headly, Catharine II, 1036
Headly, Charles C. II, 547
Headly, Daniel II, 1001
Headly, De Bonsall II, 1052
Headly, Ebenezer II, 547
Headly, Ebenezer II, 682
Headly, Ebenezer II, 1001
Headly, Ebenezer II, 1051
Headly, Ebenezer II, 1068
Headly, Ebenezer II, 1069
Headly, Ebenezer II, 1073
Headly, Edith II, 985
Headly, Edith II, 988
Headly, Edith II, 1001
Headly, Edith II, 1044
Headly, Edith II, 1052
Headly, Edith II, 1073
Headly, Edward II, 1052
Headly, Edward II, 1073
Headly, Edward IV, 681
Headly, Edward IV, 719
Headly, Edward B. II, 1073
Headly, Edward H. II, 1052
Headly, Eliza II, 1068
Headly, Eliza II, 1073
Headly, Elizabeth II, 236
Headly, Elizabeth II, 1001
Headly, Elizabeth II, 1051
Headly, Elizabeth II, 1068
Headly, Elizabeth II, 1069
Headly, Elizabeth II, 1073
Headly, Elizabeth, Jr. II, 1051
Headly, Gladys Lucile II, 1052
Headly, Hannah II, 1051
Headly, Hannah II, 1052
Headly, Hannah II, 1072
Headly, Hannah II, 1073
Headly, Hannah IV, 681
Headly, Hannah IV, 719
Headly, Hannah, Jr. II, 1051
Headly, Hartis IV, 719
Headly, Henry II, 1073
Headly, Henry S. II, 1073
Headly, James II, 1073
Headly, James D. II, 1073
Headly, Jane II, 1069
Headly, Jane II, 1073
Headly, Jane II, 1074
Headly, Jane IV, 407
Headly, John II, 291
Headly, John II, 1001
Headly, John II, 1052
Headly, John II, 1073
Headly, John P. II, 1073
Headly, Jonathan II, 1052
Headly, Jonathan II, 1073
Headly, Joseph II, 985
Headly, Joseph II, 1001
Headly, Joseph II, 1044
Headly, Joseph II, 1052
Headly, Joseph II, 1073
Headly, Joshua II, 985
Headly, Joshua II, 1001
Headly, Joshua II, 1073
Headly, Liddia II, 984
Headly, Liddia II, 1001
Headly, Louisa II, 1073
Headly, Luella II, 1052
Headly, Lydia II, 1001
Headly, Margaret II, 1044
Headly, Margaret II, 1052
Headly, Martha II, 1073
Headly, Martha B. II, 1073
Headly, Mary II, 77
Headly, Mary II, 231
Headly, Mary II, 1073
Headly, Mary B. II, 1073
Headly, Mary T. II, 547
Headly, Moriah II, 1051
Headly, Morris II, 1073
Headly, Morris L. II, 1073
Headly, Philip Dennis II, 1073
Headly, Rachel II, 1001
Headly, Rachel II, 1073
Headly, Rebecca II, 1073
Headly, Rebecca IV, 719
Headly, Rebecca P. II, 1073
Headly, Rebecca T. II, 547
Headly, Robert B. IV, 407
Headly, Robert Barclay IV, 407
Headly, Rosanna Rosaque II, 1052
Headly, Ruth II, 1001
Headly, Samuel II, 1001
Headly, Samuel H. IV, 407
Headly, Sarah II, 985
Headly, Sarah II, 1001
Headly, Sarah II, 1037
Headly, Sarah Jane II, 1073
Headly, Thomas II, 1001
Headly, Thomas II, 1052
Headly, Thomas, Jr. II, 1073
Headly, Ursula II, 1001
Headly, Violet Garrigues II, 1052
Headly, Wm. II, 1001
Headly, Wm. II, 1073
Headon, Annie M. I, 394
Headon, Benjamin VI, 931
Headon, Emelia L. VI, 931
Headon, Franklin VI, 931
Headon, Joseph VI, 931
Headon, Martha VI, 931
Headon, Mary VI, 649
Headon, Mary VI, 671
Headon, Mary VI, 931
Headon, Minerva Ann VI, 931
Headon, Nancy VI, 931
Headon, Richard VI, 931
Headon, Sarah Farley VI, 931
Headon, Stephen D. I, 394
Headon, William VI, 931
Headon, William V. VI, 931
Heag, Mary I, 141
Heahurst, William IV, 1021
Heakes, Helen Isabel III, 396
Heakes, Helen Isabel III, 416
Heakes, Isabel N. III, 396
Heakes, Isabel N. III, 416
Heakes, Jas. B. III, 396
Heakes, Jas. R. III, 416
Heald, ??? IV, 603
Heald, ??? IV, 861
Heald, ??? IV, 1125
Heald, Abi IV, 631
Heald, Abi IV, 632
Heald, Abi IV, 633
Heald, Abi IV, 822
Heald, Abi IV, 846
Heald, Abi ??? IV, 872
Heald, Abner IV, 83
Heald, Abner IV, 92
Heald, Abner IV, 220
Heald, Abner IV, 274
Heald, Abner IV, 621
Heald, Abner IV, 622
Heald, Abner IV, 631
Heald, Abner IV, 632
Heald, Abner IV, 633
Heald, Abner IV, 657
Heald, Abner IV, 872
Heald, Abner J. IV, 1132
Heald, Abner T. IV, 1210
Heald, Abner Titus IV, 1210
Heald, Achsah IV, 1098
Heald, Achsah IV, 1100
Heald, Achsah IV, 1132
Heald, Achsah IV, 1136
Heald, Adaline IV, 632
Heald, Adaline IV, 657
Heald, Adeline S. IV, 633
Heald, Alfred IV, 1132
Heald, Alfred W. IV, 1132
Heald, Alice IV, 633
Heald, Alice Taylor II, 799
Heald, Allen IV, 632
Heald, Allen IV, 633
Heald, Allen IV, 648
Heald, Allen IV, 720
Heald, Allen IV, 872
Heald, Allen IV, 879
Heald, Amy IV, 332
Heald, Amy IV, 335
Heald, Amy IV, 631
Heald, Amy IV, 632
Heald, Amy IV, 1210
Heald, Ann IV, 612
Heald, Ann IV, 632
Heald, Ann IV, 872
Heald, Ann M. IV, 872
Heald, Anna M. IV, 1132
Heald, Anna M. IV, 1133
Heald, Anne IV, 631
Heald, Anne IV, 872
Heald, Bancroft II, 373
Heald, Betsey IV, 1062
Heald, Betsy IV, 611
Heald, Betsy H. IV, 872
Heald, Betsy H. IV, 873
Heald, Betsy Hole IV, 872
Heald, Caleb IV, 1136
Heald, Caleb Marshall IV, 1100
Heald, Caroline L. IV, 1132
Heald, Caroline S. IV, 1132
Heald, Caroline S. IV, 1140
Heald, Carrie IV, 1164
Heald, Celina IV, 632
Heald, Celina IV, 1210
Heald, Celina IV, 1217
Heald, Charles IV, 220
Heald, Charles IV, 632
Heald, Charles IV, 633
Heald, Charles IV, 822
Heald, Charles IV, 872
Heald, Chas. IV, 631
Heald, Cinah IV, 632
Heald, Cineh IV, 220
Heald, Cineh IV, 274
Heald, Clara Louise II, 799
Heald, Clarence IV, 633
Heald, Cynthea IV, 627
Heald, Cynthia IV, 35
Heald, Cynthia IV, 38
Heald, Cynthia IV, 632
Heald, Cynthia IV, 633
Heald, Cynthia IV, 720
Heald, Cyrus IV, 633
Heald, David IV, 632
Heald, David M. IV, 632
Heald, David M. IV, 633
Heald, Delbert IV, 961
Heald, Dosie IV, 1210
Heald, Edgar Wayne II, 799
Heald, Edith IV, 632
Heald, Edith IV, 642
Heald, Edna Marion II, 799
Heald, Edwin IV, 633
Heald, Edwin IV, 822
Heald, Edwin C. IV, 632
Heald, Edwin C. IV, 633
Heald, Edwin T. IV, 633
Heald, Edwin T. IV, 822
Heald, Edwin T. IV, 872
Heald, Eli II, 874
Heald, Eliza IV, 475
Heald, Eliza IV, 502
Heald, Eliza IV, 532
Heald, Eliza IV, 822
Heald, Eliza IV, 906
Heald, Eliza Ann IV, 407
Heald, Elizabeth IV, 631
Heald, Elizabeth IV, 632
Heald, Elizabeth IV, 650
Heald, Elizabeth IV, 906
Heald, Elizabeth IV, 907
Heald, Elizabeth IV, 1210
Heald, Elizabeth D. IV, 987
Heald, Elma Alice IV, 1210
Heald, Elmira IV, 872
Heald, Elmira IV, 877
Heald, Elmira IV, 1100
Heald, Elmira IV, 1106
Heald, Elnora S. IV, 633
Heald, Elnora S. IV, 657
Heald, Emma Leota IV, 987
Heald, Esther IV, 632
Heald, Esther IV, 961
Heald, Eva A. IV, 632
Heald, Eva A. IV, 633
Heald, Eva A. IV, 637
Heald, Evaline IV, 1132
Heald, Evva Wilson II, 799
Heald, Ezra IV, 632
Heald, Ezra IV, 633
Heald, Frances IV, 822
Heald, Francis IV, 633
Heald, Francis IV, 822
Heald, Francis IV, 872
Heald, Francis C. IV, 1164
Heald, Frank IV, 1164
Heald, H. C. IV, 1253
Heald, Hannah IV, 19
Heald, Hannah IV, 38
Heald, Hannah IV, 631
Heald, Hannah IV, 633
Heald, Hannah IV, 656
Heald, Hannah IV, 842
Heald, Hannah IV, 872
Heald, Hannah IV, 884
Heald, Hannah IV, 1210
Heald, Hannah IV, 1222
Heald, Harriet IV, 1164
Heald, Harriet IV, 1172
Heald, Harriet IV, 1210
Heald, Harriett IV, 1210
Heald, Helen H. II, 799
Heald, Henry IV, 632
Heald, Henry IV, 633
Heald, Henry IV, 720
Heald, Henry IV, 822
Heald, Henry IV, 1062
Heald, Hiel IV, 632
Heald, Hiel IV, 872
Heald, Howard T. II, 799
Heald, Ida Mabel II, 799
Heald, Isaac IV, 633
Heald, Israel IV, 605
Heald, Israel IV, 631
Heald, Israel IV, 632
Heald, Israel IV, 633
Heald, Israel IV, 634
Heald, Israel IV, 720
Heald, Israel IV, 872
Heald, Israel IV, 873
Heald, J. Wilson II, 874
Heald, James IV, 632
Heald, James IV, 633
Heald, James IV, 665
Heald, James IV, 822
Heald, James IV, 846
Heald, James IV, 858
Heald, James IV, 872
Heald, James IV, 906
Heald, Jane IV, 631
Heald, Jane IV, 632
Heald, Jane IV, 633
Heald, Jane IV, 663
Heald, Jane IV, 719
Heald, Jane IV, 720
Heald, Jane IV, 1100
Heald, Jane IV, 1101
Heald, Jane IV, 1132
Heald, Jesse IV, 631
Heald, Jesse IV, 872
Heald, Joel IV, 632
Heald, Joel IV, 1210
Heald, John IV, 17
Heald, John IV, 38
Heald, John IV, 40
Heald, John IV, 607
Heald, John IV, 622
Heald, John IV, 631
Heald, John IV, 632
Heald, John IV, 633
Heald, John IV, 647
Heald, John IV, 720
Heald, John IV, 872
Heald, John IV, 899
Heald, John K. IV, 1210
Heald, John Oliphant IV, 720

ald, John Wilson II, 799
ald, John, Jr. IV, 632
ald, Jonah IV, 872
ald, Jonathan IV, 632
ald, Joseph IV, 631
ald, Joseph IV, 632
ald, Joseph IV, 634
ald, Joseph IV, 656
ald, Joseph IV, 657
ald, Joseph IV, 863
ald, Joseph IV, 872
ald, Joseph IV, 873
ald, Joseph IV, 877
ald, Joseph IV, 883
ald, Joseph IV, 1210
ald, Joseph IV, 1217
ald, Joseph E. IV, 1210
ald, Joseph S. IV, 633
ald, Joseph S. IV, 822
ald, Joseph S. IV, 872
ald, Joseph S. IV, 987
ald, Leota IV, 822
ald, Levi IV, 631
ald, Levi IV, 632
ald, Levi IV, 808
ald, Levi IV, 822
ald, Levi IV, 963
ald, Levi IV, 1100
ald, Levi IV, 1130
ald, Levi IV, 1133
ald, Lewis J. IV, 633
ald, Lindley IV, 632
ald, Lindley IV, 633
ald, Lindley IV, 720
ald, Lizzie Stokes IV, 872
ald, Lizzy Stokes IV, 631
ald, Louis IV, 632
ald, Louis J. IV, 872
ald, Louisa IV, 963
ald, Louisa IV, 1130
ald, Louisa IV, 1132
ald, Louisa T. II, 874
ald, Louisa Wright II, 799
ald, Lucena H. IV, 633
ald, Lucena H. IV, 645
ald, Lucina IV, 720
ald, Lucina IV, 963
ald, Lucina IV, 1132
ald, Luiza IV, 1062
ald, Lydia IV, 605
ald, Lydia IV, 631
ald, Lydia IV, 632
ald, Lydia IV, 633
ald, Lydia IV, 655
ald, Lydia IV, 808
ald, Lydia IV, 822
ald, Lydia IV, 872
ald, Lydia IV, 906
ald, Lydia IV, 963
ald, Lydia IV, 1062
ald, Lydia IV, 1100
ald, Lydia IV, 1130
ald, Lydia IV, 1132
ald, Lydia IV, 1133
ald, Lydia A. IV, 632
ald, Lydia Ann IV, 1210
ald, Lydia Price II, 799
ald, Lydiann IV, 1210
ald, M. IV, 642
ald, Mahlon IV, 632
ald, Maria IV, 632
ald, Maria IV, 650
ald, Maria IV, 720
ald, Maria IV, 746
ald, Mariam IV, 627
ald, Mariam IV, 642
ald, Marietta IV, 1132
ald, Martha IV, 631
ald, Martha IV, 632
ald, Martha IV, 1132
ald, Martha Elma IV, 1210
ald, Martha Jane IV, 633
ald, Martha Jane IV, 872
ald, Martha Jane IV, 1128
ald, Martha Jane IV, 1132
ald, Mary II, 547
ald, Mary IV, 69
ald, Mary IV, 70
ald, Mary IV, 607
eald, Mary IV, 631
eald, Mary IV, 632
ald, Mary IV, 633
ald, Mary IV, 665
eald, Mary IV, 676
eald, Mary IV, 720
ald, Mary IV, 822
ald, Mary IV, 846
ald, Mary IV, 899
eald, Mary IV, 906
ald, Mary IV, 963
eald, Mary IV, 1100
Heald, Mary IV, 1136
Heald, Mary Ann II, 704
Heald, Mary Ann IV, 632
Heald, Mary Ann IV, 633
Heald, Mary Ann IV, 720
Heald, Mary Ann IV, 1132
Heald, Mary Ann IV, 1133
Heald, Mary B. IV, 1132
Heald, Mary Ruanna IV, 872
Heald, Mary S. IV, 1210
Heald, Mary S. IV, 1213
Heald, Mathew IV, 633
Heald, Mathew IV, 822
Heald, Mathew IV, 872
Heald, Matthew IV, 632
Heald, Matthew F. IV, 633
Heald, Matthew W. IV, 633
Heald, Matthew Watson IV, 475
Heald, Meriam IV, 720
Heald, Milton IV, 1132
Heald, Miriam IV, 632
Heald, Miriam IV, 633
Heald, Miriam IV, 643
Heald, Miriam IV, 650
Heald, Miriam IV, 656
Heald, Miriam IV, 872
Heald, Miriam IV, 877
Heald, Nathan IV, 38
Heald, Nathan IV, 69
Heald, Nathan IV, 532
Heald, Nathan IV, 612
Heald, Nathan IV, 631
Heald, Nathan IV, 632
Heald, Nathan IV, 655
Heald, Nathan IV, 864
Heald, Nathan IV, 872
Heald, Nathan IV, 884
Heald, Nathan IV, 906
Heald, Nathan IV, 1100
Heald, Nathan IV, 1210
Heald, Nathan IV, 1213
Heald, Nathan H. IV, 872
Heald, Nathan H. IV, 1210
Heald, Nathan Hole IV, 872
Heald, Nathan, Jr IV, 906
Heald, Nathan, Jr. IV, 38
Heald, Nathan, Jr. IV, 59
Heald, Nathan, Jr. IV, 631
Heald, Nathan, Jr. IV, 632
Heald, Nathan, Jr. IV, 633
Heald, Nathan, Jr. IV, 872
Heald, Nathan, Jr. IV, 907
Heald, Norman M. II, 799
Heald, Penina IV, 656
Heald, Penina IV, 872
Heald, Penina IV, 883
Heald, Peninah IV, 632
Heald, Phebe IV, 38
Heald, Phebe IV, 40
Heald, Phebe IV, 607
Heald, Phebe IV, 622
Heald, Phebe IV, 631
Heald, Phebe IV, 632
Heald, Phebe IV, 647
Heald, Phebe IV, 656
Heald, Phebe IV, 899
Heald, Phebe E. IV, 633
Heald, Phebe Elma IV, 607
Heald, Phebe Elma IV, 632
Heald, Phebe Elma IV, 863
Heald, Phebe Elma IV, 872
Heald, Rachel IV, 38
Heald, Rachel IV, 59
Heald, Rachel IV, 612
Heald, Rachel IV, 631
Heald, Rachel IV, 632
Heald, Rachel IV, 650
Heald, Rachel IV, 655
Heald, Rachel IV, 822
Heald, Rachel IV, 842
Heald, Rachel IV, 864
Heald, Rachel IV, 872
Heald, Rachel IV, 884
Heald, Rachel IV, 1100
Heald, Rachel IV, 1210
Heald, Rachel IV, 1217
Heald, Rachel Smith IV, 631
Heald, Rachel Smith IV, 872
Heald, Rebecca IV, 38
Heald, Rebecca IV, 69
Heald, Rebecca IV, 610
Heald, Rebecca IV, 631
Heald, Rebecca IV, 632
Heald, Rebecca IV, 633
Heald, Rebecca IV, 634
Heald, Rebecca IV, 647
Heald, Rebecca IV, 648
Heald, Rebecca IV, 655
Heald, Rebecca IV, 720
Heald, Rebecca IV, 822
Heald, Rebecca IV, 864
Heald, Rebecca IV, 872
Heald, Rebecca IV, 873
Heald, Rebecca IV, 878
Heald, Rebecca IV, 879
Heald, Rebecca IV, 906
Heald, Rebecca IV, 963
Heald, Ruth IV, 83
Heald, Ruth IV, 621
Heald, Ruth IV, 622
Heald, Ruth IV, 631
Heald, Ruth IV, 632
Heald, Ruth IV, 868
Heald, Ruth IV, 871
Heald, Ruth IV, 872
Heald, Ruth A. IV, 963
Heald, Ruthann IV, 1132
Heald, Ruthanna IV, 961
Heald, Ruthanna IV, 963
Heald, Samuel II, 373
Heald, Samuel II, 547
Heald, Samuel IV, 822
Heald, Samuel IV, 963
Heald, Samuel IV, 1100
Heald, Samuel IV, 1101
Heald, Samuel IV, 1132
Heald, Samuel Lusina IV, 1062
Heald, Sarah IV, 38
Heald, Sarah IV, 67
Heald, Sarah IV, 92
Heald, Sarah IV, 220
Heald, Sarah IV, 631
Heald, Sarah IV, 632
Heald, Sarah IV, 633
Heald, Sarah IV, 635
Heald, Sarah IV, 650
Heald, Sarah IV, 655
Heald, Sarah IV, 720
Heald, Sarah IV, 872
Heald, Sarah IV, 1210
Heald, Sarah V, 910
Heald, Sarah Ellen IV, 632
Heald, Sarah Ellen IV, 633
Heald, Sarah Ellen IV, 720
Heald, Sarah Elnora IV, 633
Heald, Sarah L. IV, 822
Heald, Sarah L. IV, 872
Heald, Sarah Roanna IV, 1210
Heald, Sarah Ruanna IV, 1210
Heald, Sidwell IV, 632
Heald, Sidwell IV, 633
Heald, Sidwell IV, 1164
Heald, Sidwell IV, 1210
Heald, Sina IV, 622
Heald, Sina IV, 632
Heald, Sina IV, 1062
Heald, Sina Ellen IV, 633
Heald, Sina Ellen IV, 1052
Heald, Sina Ellen IV, 1062
Heald, Sina L. IV, 633
Heald, Sina S. IV, 1062
Heald, Sinah IV, 220
Heald, Sinah IV, 632
Heald, Sinia S. IV, 720
Heald, Sllen IV, 632
Heald, Smith IV, 872
Heald, Smith IV, 1098
Heald, Smith IV, 1100
Heald, Smith IV, 1132
Heald, Smith Nathan IV, 631
Heald, Susanna IV, 631
Heald, Susanna IV, 842
Heald, Susanna IV, 1210
Heald, Susanna IV, 1218
Heald, Susanna IV, 1222
Heald, Susanna Neville V, 910
Heald, Susannah IV, 637
Heald, Susannah IV, 663
Heald, Susannah IV, 1210
Heald, Susannah V, 910
Heald, Susannah V, 924
Heald, T. IV, 642
Heald, Tacy IV, 632
Heald, Tacy IV, 817
Heald, Tacy IV, 822
Heald, Thomas IV, 627
Heald, Thomas IV, 632
Heald, Thomas IV, 633
Heald, Thomas IV, 643
Heald, Thomas IV, 650
Heald, Thomas IV, 656
Heald, Thomas IV, 720
Heald, Thomas IV, 877
Heald, Thomas S. IV, 872
Heald, Thos. IV, 631
Heald, Ury IV, 632
Heald, Ury IV, 656
Heald, Ury IV, 1210
Heald, Ury B. IV, 633
Heald, Ury B. IV, 863
Heald, Ury B. IV, 872
Heald, Ury B. IV, 873
Heald, Ury B. IV, 877
Heald, Ury B. IV, 883
Heald, Ury B. IV, 1132
Heald, Ury Betsy IV, 631
Heald, Ury Betsy IV, 634
Heald, Ury Betsy IV, 872
Heald, Wilford Lewis IV, 1132
Heald, William IV, 38
Heald, William IV, 67
Heald, William IV, 92
Heald, William IV, 632
Heald, William IV, 633
Heald, William IV, 720
Heald, William IV, 872
Heald, William A. IV, 1210
Heald, William F. IV, 633
Heald, William S. IV, 872
Heald, William W. IV, 631
Heald, William W. IV, 632
Heald, William W. IV, 637
Heald, William W. IV, 663
Heald, William, Jr. IV, 632
Heald, Wm. IV, 220
Heald, Wm. IV, 631
Heald, Wm. IV, 632
Heald, Wm. IV, 635
Heald, Wm. IV, 650
Heald, Wm. IV, 655
Heald, Wm. IV, 872
Heald, Wm. IV, 1062
Heald, Wm. IV, 1210
Heald, Wm. V, 910
Heald, Wm. H. IV, 1210
Heald, Wm. H. V, 910
Heald, Wm. W. IV, 631
Heald, Wm. W. IV, 822
Heald, Wm. W. IV, 842
Heald, Wm. W. IV, 1100
Heald, Wm. W. IV, 1210
Heald, Wm. W. IV, 1218
Heald, Wm. W. IV, 1222
Heald, Wm. W. V, 924
Heald, Wm., Jr. IV, 872
Healea, Nora Beheler IV, 1210
Healea, Wm. IV, 1210
Healey, ??? III, 35
Healey, Alice III, 416
Healey, Alice III, 435
Healey, Christopher III, 416
Healey, Christopher III, 435
Healey, Jonathan III, 71
Healey, Mary III, 409
Healey, Mary P. III, 35
Healey, Mary P. III, 71
Healey, Mary P. III, 161
Healey, Rachel III, 416
Healey, Rachel III, 435
Healey, Sarah III, 71
Healey, Wm. P. IV, 1062
Healton, Eunice I, 986
Healton, John I, 980
Healton, John I, 986
Healton, Rebeckah I, 986
Healton, Sarah I, 980
Healton, Sarah I, 986
Healy, ??? IV, 1047
Healy, Abigail III, 161
Healy, Abraham IV, 1164
Healy, Abraham IV, 1237
Healy, Abram IV, 1165
Healy, Abram IV, 1191
Healy, Alfred IV, 1237
Healy, Alse IV, 1055
Healy, Alse IV, 1062
Healy, Ann II, 960
Healy, Ann II, 1001
Healy, Ann II, 1052
Healy, Ann IV, 1164
Healy, Ann IV, 1231
Healy, Ann IV, 1237
Healy, Anna IV, 1165
Healy, Anna IV, 1237
Healy, Caleb IV, 1165
Healy, Caleb IV, 1237
Healy, Carrie IV, 1237
Healy, Charles IV, 220
Healy, Christopher II, 953
Healy, Christopher II, 960
Healy, Christopher II, 961
Healy, Christopher II, 966
Healy, Christopher II, 1001
Healy, Christopher II, 1015
Healy, Christopher II, 1044
Healy, Christopher II, 1052
Healy, Christopher II, 1053
Healy, Christopher II, 1057
Healy, Christopher II, 1074
Healy, David C. III, 161
Healy, Delila IV, 220
Healy, Edith A. IV, 1237
Healy, Edith Ann IV, 1164
Healy, Edith Ann IV, 1165
Healy, Edith Ann IV, 1237
Healy, Edward H. III, 161
Healy, Edward Hicks III, 162
Healy, Edwin III, 161
Healy, Edwin IV, 1237
Healy, Elizabeth IV, 1164
Healy, Elizabeth IV, 1165
Healy, Elizabeth IV, 1237
Healy, Elizabeth P. IV, 1164
Healy, Elizabeth P. IV, 1237
Healy, Emma W. II, 745
Healy, Emma W. II, 753
Healy, Emma Wales II, 707
Healy, Fannie IV, 1237
Healy, Fanny IV, 1237
Healy, Hannah III, 161
Healy, Hannah IV, 1062
Healy, Hannah IV, 1073
Healy, Hannah IV, 1240
Healy, Hannah M. IV, 1237
Healy, Hannah Maria IV, 1165
Healy, Hannah Maria IV, 1237
Healy, Hannah W. II, 961
Healy, Henry A. IV, 1165
Healy, Henry A. IV, 1237
Healy, Huldah IV, 1164
Healy, Huldah IV, 1235
Healy, Huldah IV, 1237
Healy, Isaac III, 71
Healy, Isaac III, 161
Healy, Isaac IV, 1164
Healy, Jacob IV, 1164
Healy, Jacob IV, 1165
Healy, Jacob IV, 1195
Healy, Jacob IV, 1237
Healy, Jemima IV, 1165
Healy, Jemima IV, 1195
Healy, Jemima IV, 1231
Healy, Jemima IV, 1237
Healy, Jeremiah II, 961
Healy, Jeremiah II, 1052
Healy, John II, 745
Healy, John II, 960
Healy, John II, 1052
Healy, John III, 161
Healy, John B. IV, 1165
Healy, John B. IV, 1237
Healy, Joseph II, 707
Healy, Joseph II, 745
Healy, Joseph II, 960
Healy, Joseph II, 1001
Healy, Joseph II, 1015
Healy, Joseph IV, 1164
Healy, Joseph IV, 1165
Healy, Joseph, Jr. II, 707
Healy, Joshua III, 161
Healy, Lucy II, 745
Healy, Lucy II, 762
Healy, Lucy E. II, 745
Healy, Lydia II, 961
Healy, Lydia II, 1001
Healy, Lydia II, 1052
Healy, Lydia II, 1053
Healy, Lydia IV, 220
Healy, Lydia IV, 1062
Healy, Lydia H. II, 709
Healy, Mark II, 961
Healy, Mary II, 1001
Healy, Mary III, 71
Healy, Mary III, 161
Healy, Mary IV, 1237
Healy, Mary E. IV, 1234
Healy, Mary E. IV, 1237
Healy, Mary Elizabeth IV, 1164
Healy, Mary Elizabeth IV, 1237
Healy, Mary P. III, 161
Healy, Mary P. IV, 1062
Healy, Mary S. III, 161
Healy, Mary W. III, 162
Healy, Mercy II, 961
Healy, Mercy II, 1052
Healy, Mercy II, 1053
Healy, Oliver IV, 220
Healy, Phebe I, 773
Healy, Phebe IV, 1164
Healy, Phebe IV, 1165
Healy, Phebe IV, 1237
Healy, Phebe C. IV, 1165
Healy, Phebe C. IV, 1191
Healy, Phebe S. IV, 1164
Healy, Rachel II, 960
Healy, Rachel II, 1001
Healy, Rachel II, 1015
Healy, Rachel III, 484
Healy, Rachel IV, 1165
Healy, Rachel IV, 1237
Healy, Rachel W. II, 707
Healy, Rachel W. II, 745
Healy, Rebecca II, 961
Healy, Rebecca II, 966

Healy, Rebecca II, 1052
Healy, Rebecca II, 1057
Healy, Renhama III, 161
Healy, Reuhama III, 162
Healy, Ruth II, 961
Healy, Samuel III, 162
Healy, Samuel V. III, 161
Healy, Sarah II, 953
Healy, Sarah II, 960
Healy, Sarah II, 961
Healy, Sarah II, 962
Healy, Sarah II, 966
Healy, Sarah II, 1001
Healy, Sarah II, 1052
Healy, Sarah II, 1053
Healy, Sarah II, 1057
Healy, Sarah II, 1074
Healy, Sarah IV, 220
Healy, Sarah IV, 407
Healy, Sarah IV, 426
Healy, Sarah IV, 583
Healy, Sarah IV, 591
Healy, Sarah IV, 1062
Healy, Sarah IV, 1237
Healy, Sarah Ann III, 162
Healy, Sarah E. II, 745
Healy, Sarah E. II, 751
Healy, Sarah H. II, 1044
Healy, Sarah Jane IV, 1164
Healy, Sarah Jane IV, 1237
Healy, Sarah M. II, 953
Healy, Sarah M. II, 960
Healy, Sarah M. II, 1044
Healy, Sarah M. II, 1052
Healy, Sarah, Jr. II, 1001
Healy, Sarah, Jr. II, 1015
Healy, Smith IV, 1164
Healy, Smith IV, 1165
Healy, Smith IV, 1237
Healy, Smith Alvin IV, 1165
Healy, Smith Alvin IV, 1237
Healy, Thomas II, 961
Healy, Thomas IV, 220
Healy, Thomas IV, 426
Healy, Thomas IV, 1062
Healy, Warren IV, 1237
Healy, Warren A. IV, 1237
Healy, William III, 161
Healy, William III, 162
Healy, William IV, 220
Healy, Wm. P. IV, 1062
Heanaker, Thomas II, 547
Heans, Hannah II, 547
Heard, Ann VI, 931
Heard, Anne VI, 937
Heard, George VI, 931
Heardley, Jane VI, 580
Heareld, Sally V, 497
Hearing, Grace Gertrude IV, 1253
Hearing, Raymond J. IV, 1253
Hearl, Daniel I, 543
Hearl, Rebeccah I, 543
Hearld, Tamer IV, 220
Hearly, Henry II, 31
Hearly, John II, 31
Hearly, Mary II, 31
Hearn, Sarah II, 374
Hearn, Sarah II, 547
Hearn, Susanna II, 475
Hearn, Susanna II, 547
Hearn, Susannah II, 475
Hearn, Susannah II, 547
Hearn, Thomas Brian, Jr. II, 547
Hearn, William II, 374
Hearne, Sarah II, 374
Hearne, William II, 374
Hearon, Rachel II, 547
Heartgrove, Sophia I, 542
Heartgrove, Sophia Haley I, 543
Heartley, Dinah IV, 822
Heartley, Dinah IV, 830
Heartley, Elisa C. IV, 1206
Heartley, Elisa C. IV, 1209
Heartley, Isaac W. IV, 406
Heartley, James IV, 822
Heartley, James IV, 830
Heartley, James IV, 1026
Heartley, Jesse IV, 1206
Heartley, Mary IV, 1206
Heartley, Penninah IV, 380
Heartley, Thomas IV, 1253
Heartly, Joseph S. IV, 1026
Heartshorne, Hannah II, 1001
Heartshorne, Hugh II, 1000
Heartshorne, Jane II, 1000
Heartshorne, Richard II, 1000
Heartshorne, Richard II, 1001
Heartsock, Arabelle J. V, 393
Heartsock, Byron V, 393
Heartt, Emily II, 371
Hearvey, Nathan I, 435
Heary, Carrie IV, 1281
Heary, James C. IV, 1281
Heater, Guy Carlton III, 162
Heater, Katharine III, 162
Heater, Katherine H. III, 162
Heater, Minnie H. III, 162
Heater, Nelson E. V. III, 162
Heath, Alec VI, 68
Heath, Ann II, 547
Heath, Ann II, 675
Heath, Charles III, 162
Heath, Charles D. V. III, 151
Heath, Charles DeVol III, 162
Heath, Christopher V, 315
Heath, Diodama VI, 504
Heath, Dorothy W. I, 208
Heath, E. H. VI, 68
Heath, Eleanor IV, 407
Heath, Elijah VI, 850
Heath, Elizabeth IV, 407
Heath, Hannah III, 162
Heath, Ida IV, 1281
Heath, Isaac IV, 407
Heath, James V, 625
Heath, Jane VI, 861
Heath, Joanna IV, 407
Heath, John II, 444
Heath, John IV, 407
Heath, John H. III, 162
Heath, John Hardy III, 162
Heath, Joseph VI, 130
Heath, Joseph VI, 135
Heath, Joshua IV, 407
Heath, Katharien D. III, 162
Heath, Katie III, 151
Heath, Lydia III, 162
Heath, Malissa IV, 1281
Heath, Malissa IV, 1291
Heath, Martha VI, 831
Heath, Martha VI, 861
Heath, Mary II, 444
Heath, Mary VI, 831
Heath, Mary F. I, 611
Heath, Mary Ray IV, 1253
Heath, Noble III, 162
Heath, Ralph IV, 407
Heath, Richard II, 373
Heath, Richard Walln II, 547
Heath, Robert II, 373
Heath, Robert II, 613
Heath, Robert IV, 407
Heath, Sarah III, 162
Heath, Susannah II, 373
Heath, William IV, 1281
Heath, William Philpot IV, 407
Heath, Wm. VI, 811
Heathcoate, Mary II, 373
Heathcoe, Susanna V, 809
Heathcott, John II, 373
Heathcott, Mary II, 373
Heathman, C. T. I, 617
Heathman, C. T. I, 634
Heathman, Elisabeth I, 617
Heathman, Ella B. I, 617
Heathman, Richard I, 617
Heaton, ??? III, 161
Heaton, Abel Thomas I, 544
Heaton, Adnah III, 162
Heaton, Adnah III, 213
Heaton, Amos II, 176
Heaton, Amos IV, 475
Heaton, Ann II, 373
Heaton, Ann Margaret II, 291
Heaton, Anna M. II, 874
Heaton, Anna M. II, 920
Heaton, Anna Margaret II, 176
Heaton, Anna Margaret II, 320
Heaton, Anna Margaret II, 819
Heaton, Anna Margaretta II, 874
Heaton, Benjamin I, 36
Heaton, Benjamin I, 52
Heaton, Benjamin I, 544
Heaton, Benjamin I, 1031
Heaton, Benjamin I, 1039
Heaton, Cassie IV, 475
Heaton, Comley T. IV, 475
Heaton, Comly T. IV, 475
Heaton, Cornelius IV, 220
Heaton, Death I, 1154
Heaton, Deborah I, 36
Heaton, Deborah I, 52
Heaton, Eliza III, 162
Heaton, Eliza III, 210
Heaton, Eliza III, 308
Heaton, Elizabeth I, 1026
Heaton, Elizabeth I, 1031
Heaton, Elizabeth I, 1154
Heaton, Elizabeth III, 162
Heaton, Elizabeth III, 358
Heaton, Elizabeth C. II, 698
Heaton, Esther IV, 220
Heaton, Evan P. IV, 475
Heaton, Gladys IV, 220
Heaton, Grace VI, 484
Heaton, Hannah II, 176
Heaton, Hannah II, 205
Heaton, Hannah II, 231
Heaton, Hannah II, 291
Heaton, Hannah II, 310
Heaton, Hannah II, 320
Heaton, Hannah II, 819
Heaton, Hannah II, 869
Heaton, Hannah II, 872
Heaton, Hannah II, 874
Heaton, Hannah II, 891
Heaton, Hannah II, 920
Heaton, Hannah L. II, 799
Heaton, Hannah Livezey II, 799
Heaton, Hannah, Jr. II, 291
Heaton, Hannah, Jr. II, 320
Heaton, Hannah, Jr. II, 874
Heaton, James P. IV, 475
Heaton, Jeremiah II, 373
Heaton, John II, 205
Heaton, John II, 220
Heaton, John II, 231
Heaton, John II, 373
Heaton, John III, 162
Heaton, John IV, 38
Heaton, John C. IV, 475
Heaton, John C. V, 842
Heaton, John P. IV, 475
Heaton, John Weeks I, 1031
Heaton, Joseph I, 1031
Heaton, Joseph II, 799
Heaton, Leada I, 1031
Heaton, Maggie J. III, 162
Heaton, Maggie J. III, 213
Heaton, Margaret IV, 220
Heaton, Margaretta IV, 220
Heaton, Martha IV, 220
Heaton, Mary I, 544
Heaton, Mary I, 577
Heaton, Mary II, 231
Heaton, Mary II, 374
Heaton, Mary II, 745
Heaton, Mary II, 785
Heaton, Mary II, 874
Heaton, Mary V, 177
Heaton, Mary Edna IV, 475
Heaton, Mary G. V, 30
Heaton, Mary G. V, 71
Heaton, Mary H. II, 843
Heaton, Mary H. II, 874
Heaton, Mayne IV, 220
Heaton, Nellie S. V, 177
Heaton, Rachel II, 205
Heaton, Rachel II, 220
Heaton, Rachel II, 231
Heaton, Rachel II, 745
Heaton, Rachel II, 797
Heaton, Rachel II, 869
Heaton, Rachel II, 874
Heaton, Rachel II, 1052
Heaton, Rachel II, 1061
Heaton, Rachel IV, 220
Heaton, Ralph V, 177
Heaton, Rebecca II, 231
Heaton, Rebecca II, 745
Heaton, Rebecca II, 764
Heaton, Rebecca II, 818
Heaton, Rebecca II, 874
Heaton, Rebecca II, 918
Heaton, Rebecca IV, 20
Heaton, Rebecca IV, 38
Heaton, Rebecca IV, 319
Heaton, Rebecca IV, 335
Heaton, Richard II, 176
Heaton, Richard II, 205
Heaton, Richard II, 231
Heaton, Richard II, 819
Heaton, Richard II, 869
Heaton, Richard II, 874
Heaton, Richard II, 920
Heaton, Robert II, 547
Heaton, Rutherford B. IV, 475
Heaton, Sarah IV, 38
Heaton, Sarah IV, 42
Heaton, Sarah IV, 475
Heaton, Squire II, 374
Heaton, Wd. Rachel II, 231
Heaton, Wd. Rachel II, 267
Heavenridge, Hannah I, 1091
Heavenridge, Hannah I, 1094
Heavenridge, Hannah VI, 109
Heavenridge, Isabel VI, 109
Heavenridge, James VI, 109
Heavenridge, John I, 1094
Heavenridge, John VI, 109
Heavenridge, John, Jr. I, 1094
Heavenridge, Margaret I, 1094
Heavenridge, Margaret VI, 109
Heavenridge, Samuel I, 1094
Heavenridge, William I, 1094
Heavenridge, William VI, 109
Heaworth, Mary E. IV, 718
Heband, Mary III, 234
Heberling, G. H. IV, 220
Heberling, George IV, 220
Heberling, George R. IV, 220
Heberling, Hannah IV, 220
Heberling, Hannah IV, 239
Heberling, Hannah IV, 312
Heberling, Hannah IV, 313
Heberling, Henry G. IV, 220
Heberling, Mary J. IV, 220
Heberling, Matilda IV, 220
Heberton, Ann II, 547
Heberton, Ann II, 561
Hebron, Margaret VI, 504
Heck, Amos Robert III, 484
Heck, Anna Caroline III, 484
Heck, Carl August III, 484
Heckel, Sarah V. IV, 963
Heckel, Sarah V. IV, 1002
Heckley, Fred, Jr. V, 681
Heckley, Fred, Jr. V, 691
Heckley, Helen Leroy V, 681
Heckley, Helen Leroy V, 691
Heckley, John IV, 1281
Heckman, Abbie L. V, 742
Heckman, Anson H. V, 742
Heckman, George E. V, 742
Heckman, Jesse V, 742
Heckman, John V, 809
Heckman, Mary V, 742
Heckman, Mary V, 809
Heckman, Ora M. V, 742
Heckman, Sarah Elizabeth V, 742
Heckman, William H. V, 742
Heddington, Clara IV, 1165
Heddington, Mamie IV, 1165
Hedg, Hanah II, 77
Hedgcock, Abigail I, 805
Hedgcock, Abigail I, 814
Hedgcock, Amanda I, 1154
Hedgcock, Charles I, 1154
Hedgcock, Clen I, 877
Hedgcock, Cordie I, 1154
Hedgcock, Elen I, 877
Hedgcock, Henry I, 1154
Hedgcock, Jacob I, 855
Hedgcock, John I, 1154
Hedgcock, Naomi I, 883
Hedgcock, Naomi I, 903
Hedgcock, Sarah I, 814
Hedgcock, Sarah I, 834
Hedgcock, William I, 1154
Hedgcock, Willis I, 1154
Hedge, Adeline E. III, 325
Hedge, Wm. N. III, 325
Hedgecock, Achsah C. I, 874
Hedgecock, Achsah C. I, 883
Hedgecock, Achsah Catharine I, 926
Hedgecock, Addison J. I, 883
Hedgecock, Amanda I, 1154
Hedgecock, Barnabas I, 882
Hedgecock, Basil I, 943
Hedgecock, Catharine I, 855
Hedgecock, Catharine I, 926
Hedgecock, Catharine I, 942
Hedgecock, Charles I, 1154
Hedgecock, Clen I, 883
Hedgecock, D. M. I, 941
Hedgecock, David I, 855
Hedgecock, David I, 883
Hedgecock, David I, 926
Hedgecock, David M. I, 925
Hedgecock, David M. I, 942
Hedgecock, David Madison I, 926
Hedgecock, Deborah I, 882
Hedgecock, Delphina I, 877
Hedgecock, Delphina I, 883
Hedgecock, Edgar A. I, 943
Hedgecock, Edith Moore I, 926
Hedgecock, Elen I, 883
Hedgecock, Elizabeth I, 883
Hedgecock, Elizabeth I, 943
Hedgecock, Ellen I, 921
Hedgecock, Emily I, 883
Hedgecock, Emily I, 888
Hedgecock, Emily A. I, 855
Hedgecock, Emily Almeda I, 926
Hedgecock, Emma I, 942
Hedgecock, Erie I, 943
Hedgecock, Esther I, 926
Hedgecock, Florence May I, 919
Hedgecock, Grace I, 882
Hedgecock, Hannah I, 882
Hedgecock, Henry I, 1154
Hedgecock, Huldah I, 883
Hedgecock, Ila I, 926
Hedgecock, Ila I, 943
Hedgecock, Ila H. I, 933
Hedgecock, Jacob I, 882
Hedgecock, Jacob I, 919
Hedgecock, James M. I, 926
Hedgecock, James M. I, 933
Hedgecock, John I, 1154
Hedgecock, Joseph I, 882
Hedgecock, Joseph, Jr. I, 883
Hedgecock, Joshua I, 882
Hedgecock, Joshua I, 926
Hedgecock, Joshua Edgar I, 92
Hedgecock, Julius I, 883
Hedgecock, L. F. I, 943
Hedgecock, Lois Ray I, 943
Hedgecock, Lou I, 942
Hedgecock, Louisa H. I, 925
Hedgecock, Louizer I, 855
Hedgecock, Luezer I, 883
Hedgecock, Lydia I, 882
Hedgecock, Margaret F. I, 943
Hedgecock, Marmaduke C. I, 8
Hedgecock, Martha I, 926
Hedgecock, Mary I, 919
Hedgecock, Mary A. I, 926
Hedgecock, Mary A. I, 933
Hedgecock, Mathew I, 882
Hedgecock, Miriam I, 873
Hedgecock, Miriam I, 883
Hedgecock, Nannie I, 943
Hedgecock, Nannie Virginia I, 926
Hedgecock, Priscilla I, 882
Hedgecock, Ruth I, 883
Hedgecock, Ruth I, 904
Hedgecock, Sarah I, 882
Hedgecock, Sarah I, 883
Hedgecock, Shubal G. I, 883
Hedgecock, Sophronia I, 883
Hedgecock, William I, 882
Hedgecock, William I, 883
Hedgecock, William P. I, 855
Hedgecock, William P. I, 943
Hedgecock, William Pugh I, 92
Hedgepeth, Ada VI, 68
Hedgepeth, Ada J. VI, 68
Hedgepeth, Ada J. VI, 82
Hedgepeth, Ann E. VI, 68
Hedgepeth, Ann E. VI, 86
Hedgepeth, Annie S. VI, 68
Hedgepeth, Annie S. VI, 82
Hedgepeth, Eliza A. VI, 68
Hedgepeth, Ella VI, 68
Hedgepeth, Ella D. VI, 68
Hedgepeth, Ella D. VI, 82
Hedgepeth, James VI, 68
Hedgepeth, James VI, 82
Hedgepeth, James VI, 87
Hedgepeth, James B. VI, 68
Hedgepeth, James B. VI, 69
Hedgepeth, Jane VI, 68
Hedgepeth, Jane VI, 69
Hedgepeth, John W. VI, 68
Hedgepeth, John W. VI, 69
Hedgepeth, Lavina VI, 68
Hedgepeth, Levina VI, 68
Hedgepeth, Levina VI, 69
Hedgepeth, Levina VI, 82
Hedgepeth, Levina VI, 87
Hedgepeth, Madison VI, 68
Hedgepeth, Margaret A. VI, 68
Hedgepeth, Margaret A. VI, 87
Hedgepeth, Murphey VI, 68
Hedgepeth, Murphey VI, 86
Hedgepeth, Murphrey VI, 86
Hedgepeth, Murphry VI, 68
Hedgepeth, Nancy VI, 68
Hedgepeth, Robert VI, 68
Hedgepeth, Vicotria VI, 68
Hedgepeth, Victoria VI, 68
Hedgepeth, Victoria VI, 86
Hedgepeth, Vinney VI, 92
Hedgepeth, Wilbon VI, 68
Hedger, Abigail III, 114
Hedger, Abigail III, 162
Hedger, Adeline E. III, 162
Hedger, Adeline E. III, 325
Hedger, Amy III, 162
Hedger, Ann III, 162
Hedger, Ann III, 198
Hedger, Benjamin III, 162
Hedger, Claude V, 71
Hedger, Deborah III, 162
Hedger, Eliakam II, 231
Hedger, Eliakam II, 264
Hedger, Eliakim III, 162
Hedger, Elizabeth III, 162
Hedger, George III, 162
Hedger, Hannah III, 21

dger, Hannah III, 115
dger, Hannah III, 162
dger, Joseph II, 231
dger, Joseph II, 264
dger, Joseph III, 162
dger, Joseph III, 366
dger, Keziah III, 162
dger, Keziah III, 366
dger, Mary III, 162
dger, Samuel II, 231
dger, Samuel III, 162
dger, Sarah II, 231
dger, Sarah II, 264
dger, Sarah III, 162
dger, Stephen III, 162
dger, Susannah III, 162
dger, Susannah III, 326
dger, Thomas III, 114
dger, Thomas III, 162
dger, Wm. N. III, 162
dger, Wm. N. III, 325
dges, Abigail III, 114
dges, Thomas III, 114
dgpath, Mary VI, 92
dgpeth, Ada J. VI, 92
dgpeth, Annie VI, 92
dgpeth, Elizabeth VI, 92
dgpeth, Ella VI, 92
dgpeth, Maggie VI, 92
dgpeth, Mary VI, 92
dgpeth, Victoria VI, 92
dgpeth, Vinney VI, 92
dgson, Hur I, 547
dley, Anna II, 960
dley, David B. II, 960
dley, De Bonsall II, 960
dley, De Bonsall II, 1052
dley, Edward H. II, 960
dley, Edward H. II, 1052
dley, Elizabeth II, 231
dley, Gladys Lucile II, 960
dley, Gladys Lucile II, 1052
dley, Hannah W. IV, 719
dley, Luella II, 960
dley, Luella II, 1052
dley, Mary II, 231
dley, Rosanna II, 960
dley, Rosanna Rosaque II, 1052
dley, Violet Garrigues II, 960
dley, Violet Garrigues II, 1052
dley, William II, 230
drick, Angie May V, 335
drick, Flora V, 335
drick, Lillian H. I, 927
drick, Lillian M. I, 943
drick, Lydia V, 335
drick, Martha V, 335
drick, Martha J. V, 335
drick, Mary V, 335
drick, Mary Ann VI, 931
drick, Mary E. V, 335
drick, Oliver V, 335
drick, Oliver Elmer V, 335
drick, Oliver R. V, 335
drick, Phillip VI, 931
drick, Theodore I, 927
drick, Theodore I, 943
ed, Mary II, 1001
ed, Thomas II, 1001
ed, Thomas II, 1024
eley, Ann IV, 1164
eley, Edith Ann IV, 1164
eley, Elizabeth P. IV, 1164
eley, Huldah IV, 1164
eley, Mary P. IV, 1062
eley, Sarah Jane IV, 1164
eley, Smith IV, 1164
ely, Abraham IV, 1164
ely, Elizabeth IV, 1164
ely, Isaac IV, 1164
ely, Jacob IV, 1164
ely, Joseph IV, 1164
ely, Phebe IV, 1164
ely, Phebe S. IV, 1164
es, Albert F. III, 33
es, Albert F. III, 162
es, Amelia III, 33
es, Amelia III, 162
es, Gertrude III, 33
es, Gertrude III, 162
ess, Amelia II, 948
estand, Martha J. IV, 720
estand, Milan IV, 720
estand, Samuel IV, 720
estand, Sarah IV, 720
eston, Ada Odessa IV, 963
eston, Homer IV, 963
effernan, Anne C. III, 162
effernan, James B. J. III, 162
effernan, Wm. III, 162
Heffner, Harry IV, 720
Hefner, Mary V, 625
Hefner, Phebe V, 177
Hefner, Phebe V, 192
Hefner, Samuel V, 625
Hegeman, Anna III, 416
Hegeman, Jacob III, 416
Hegeman, Jane III, 162
Hegeman, John C. III, 162
Hegeman, Jonah III, 162
Hegeman, Louia III, 162
Hegeman, Peter III, 162
Hegeman, Sarah III, 162
Hegerling, C. IV, 1319
Hegerling, Christopher IV, 1319
Hegerling, Lottie IV, 1319
Hegerman, John C. III, 162
Heiden, Sophia VI, 762
Heiden, Sophia VI, 770
Heiferd, Sarah IV, 494
Heighes, Alice III, 162
Heighes, John Intaglio III, 162
Heighway, Mary V, 71
Heighway, Mary V, 116
Heild, Elizabeth VI, 399
Heild, Hannah VI, 399
Heild, John VI, 399
Heild, Mary VI, 399
Heild, Nathan VI, 399
Heild, Rachel VI, 399
Heild, Rebecca VI, 399
Heild, Richard VI, 399
Heild, Sarah VI, 399
Heild, William VI, 399
Heileker, George IV, 1237
Heilson, Margaret I, 194
Heim, Grace IV, 720
Heine, Amelia C. II, 710
Heine, Grace IV, 1319
Heinley, Addie V, 71
Heinn, Grace IV, 1319
Heinn, Lydia A. IV, 1319
Heinsay, Hannah II, 547
Heinton, Arthur IV, 1319
Heinton, Kate IV, 1319
Heinton, Louisa K. IV, 1319
Heinton, Louise K. IV, 1320
Heinton, Robert IV, 1319
Heise, Chris IV, 1253
Heise, Dorothy IV, 1253
Heise, Esther Ellen IV, 1253
Heise, Frances Louise IV, 1253
Heise, Mary E. IV, 1253
Heise, Mary Elizabeth IV, 1253
Heise, Maud IV, 1253
Heise, Oneida IV, 1253
Heisey, Bertha V, 742
Heisey, Clara V, 742
Heisey, Dorothy V, 742
Heisey, Herman V, 742
Heisey, Naomi V, 742
Heisey, Ralph V, 742
Heisey, Ruth Esther V, 742
Heisey, Wilbur David V, 742
Heisey, Willard Julius V, 742
Heiskel, Mary V, 953
Heiskel, Mary V, 957
Heison, John II, 374
Heison, Sarah II, 374
Heister, John Fries II, 374
Heister, Margaret II, 374
Heister, Mary Morgan II, 875
Heisy, Aubry V, 809
Heisy, Isabelle V, 809
Heisy, Samuel V, 809
Heith, John V, 1000
Heitman, Lillie Estella I, 617
Heitman, Numa Ray I, 617
Heitman, Numa Ray I, 634
Heitman, Sara I, 617
Heitman, William C. I, 617
Helar, Martha V, 71
Held, Isabelle B. IV, 1038
Held, S. W. IV, 1038
Held, Stanton IV, 1038
Helena, Elsa II, 1060
Helenthal, Paul Raymond IV, 1253
Helenthal, Raymond IV, 1253
Helenthal, Stella M. IV, 1253
Hellen, Abigail I, 271
Hellen, Alice I, 271
Hellen, Brian I, 271
Hellen, Caroline I, 271
Hellen, Caroline P. I, 271
Hellen, Elizabeth I, 271
Hellen, Elizabeth I, 272
Hellen, John West I, 271
Hellen, Mary I, 271
Hellencamp, Elizabeth III, 162
Hellens, Mary II, 547
Hellens, Mary II, 586
Heller, Dudley V, 177
Heller, Dudley V, 245
Heller, Elizabeth III, 416
Heller, Elizabeth B. V, 335
Heller, Hannah III, 416
Heller, Ida V, 245
Heller, Ina Frye V, 177
Heller, Jediah P. III, 416
Heller, Martha V, 335
Heller, Martha V, 363
Heller, Martha R. V, 303
Heller, Martha R. V, 312
Heller, Rebecca IV, 1319
Heller, Rebecca VI, 397
Heller, Rebecca VI, 399
Heller, Richard III, 416
Hellerman, Wm. V, 910
Hellings, William II, 374
Hellins, Mary II, 547
Hellins, Wm. II, 547
Hellton, Robert II, 444
Helm, Betsey VI, 889
Helm, Elizabeth VI, 835
Helm, Elizabeth VI, 863
Helm, Elizabeth VI, 942
Helm, Frances VI, 931
Helm, James VI, 824
Helm, James VI, 835
Helm, James VI, 863
Helm, Jane VI, 812
Helm, John VI, 812
Helm, John VI, 835
Helm, John, Sr. VI, 812
Helm, Mary VI, 812
Helm, Moses VI, 906
Helm, Moses VI, 931
Helm, Nancy VI, 931
Helm, Nancy VI, 987
Helm, Sarah VI, 824
Helm, Susanna VI, 906
Helm, Thomas VI, 931
Helm, Thomas, Sr. VI, 931
Helman, Martha II, 119
Helmbold, Molly Paul II, 547
Helmbold, Molly Paul II, 679
Helmcamp, ??? III, 162
Helmcamp, Augustus III, 162
Helmer, Mary VI, 597
Helmet, J. T. V, 335
Helminger, Newton V, 1000
Helmit, J. T. V, 335
Helmkemp, Elizabeth III, 416
Helms, Frances VI, 931
Helms, Geo. W. V, 681
Helms, Rachel III, 55
Helms, Rachel III, 162
Helms, Sally VI, 975
Helms, Thomas VI, 931
Helms, Thomas, Sr. VI, 931
Helmstether, Catherine V, 71
Helsel, Jesse IV, 1038
Helsel, Mary IV, 1038
Helsel, Peter IV, 1038
Helton, Abigail I, 1010
Helton, Allen I, 975
Helton, Elizabeth I, 814
Helton, Eunce I, 999
Helton, Eunice I, 986
Helton, Joel I, 975
Helton, John I, 975
Helton, Jonathan I, 975
Helton, Rebeckah I, 975
Helton, Sarah I, 975
Heltz, John IV, 220
Helzer, William IV, 1253
Hembey, Eleanor II, 547
Hembey, Eleanor II, 562
Hembey, Joseph II, 547
Hembey, Joseph II, 562
Hemby, Clarky I, 308
Hemby, Clarky I, 309
Hemby, Marium I, 194
Hemby, Mary I, 194
Hemby, Peninah I, 193
Hemby, Peninah I, 194
Hemby, Pharaba I, 308
Hemby, Pharabe I, 310
Hemelright, Elizabeth V, 500
Hemelwright, Elizabeth V, 500
Hemilright, Elizabeth V, 575
Heminger, Dora IV, 1281
Heminger, Elmer IV, 1281
Heminger, Elwood IV, 1281
Heminger, Emery G. IV, 1281
Heminger, Emory IV, 1281
Heminger, Jane IV, 1281
Heminger, Joseph IV, 1281
Heminger, Mary IV, 1281
Hemingson, Andrew C. IV, 1320
Hemingson, Chas. K. IV, 1320
Hemingson, Emma C. IV, 1320
Hemingson, Esther Olina IV, 1320
Hemingson, Lizzie IV, 1320
Hemingson, Wm. F. IV, 1320
Hemingway, Abigail II, 1074
Hemingway, Abigail IV, 720
Hemingway, Abigail IV, 943
Hemingway, Abigail IV, 950
Hemingway, Abigail IV, 963
Hemingway, Abigail IV, 964
Hemingway, Alfred IV, 950
Hemingway, Benjamin IV, 964
Hemingway, David IV, 964
Hemingway, Eleazer IV, 963
Hemingway, Eleazer IV, 964
Hemingway, Elijah IV, 720
Hemingway, Elizabeth IV, 963
Hemingway, Elizabeth C. IV, 964
Hemingway, Fidelia IV, 950
Hemingway, Hope IV, 720
Hemingway, Hope IV, 932
Hemingway, Hope IV, 950
Hemingway, Hope IV, 963
Hemingway, Hope IV, 964
Hemingway, Isaac IV, 963
Hemingway, Isaac IV, 964
Hemingway, James IV, 720
Hemingway, James IV, 932
Hemingway, James IV, 950
Hemingway, James IV, 963
Hemingway, James IV, 964
Hemingway, James H. IV, 950
Hemingway, James, Jr. IV, 720
Hemingway, Jane M. IV, 932
Hemingway, Jane M. IV, 963
Hemingway, Jane M. IV, 964
Hemingway, John IV, 963
Hemingway, John W. IV, 964
Hemingway, Joseph IV, 963
Hemingway, Joseph IV, 964
Hemingway, Miriam IV, 950
Hemingway, Rebecca P. IV, 950
Hemingway, Robert M. IV, 950
Hemingway, Sarah IV, 964
Hemingway, William B. IV, 950
Hemmelright, Elizabeth VI, 399
Hemmeter, John G. IV, 1319
Hemming, Jane IV, 1281
Hemming, Joseph IV, 1281
Hemminger, Dora IV, 1281
Hemminger, Emory IV, 1281
Hemmings, Amanda VI, 888
Hemmings, Elmer IV, 1281
Hemmings, John A. G. VI, 931
Hemmings, Martha VI, 931
Hemmings, Mrs. Elizabeth VI, 888
Hemmingway, Abigail II, 875
Hemmingway, Abigail IV, 720
Hemmingway, Abigail IV, 964
Hemmingway, Emma Ratcliff IV, 220
Hemmingway, James IV, 720
Hemmingway, James IV, 964
Hemmingway, Joseph IV, 964
Hemphill, Catherine I, 883
Hemphill, Dorcas I, 883
Hemphill, Mary Catherine T. I, 855
Hemphill, Tabitha G. I, 855
Hempson, John IV, 92
Hempson, Mary Jane VI, 920
Hempson, Sarah IV, 92
Hempson, Sarah IV, 108
Hempstead, David Kinkead V, 681
Hempy, Elizabeth IV, 1100
Hempy, Elizabeth IV, 1119
Hemsley, Howard IV, 475
Hemsley, Mary E. IV, 475
Hemsley, William R. IV, 475
Hemsley, Wm. IV, 475
Hen, Elinor II, 444
Hen, John II, 444
Henbee, Clarkey I, 52
Henberry, Ellinor II, 1001
Henberry, Ellinor II, 1005
Henberry, Joseph II, 1001
Henberry, Joseph II, 1005
Henbey, Elisabeth I, 52
Henbey, Elisabeth I, 53
Henbey, Elizabeth I, 34
Henbey, John I, 53
Henbey, Silvanus I, 53
Henbey, Thomas I, 34
Henbey, Thomas I, 52
Henbey, Thomas I, 53
Henbey, Widow Hannah I, 53
Henbey, Widow Hannah I, 72
Henby, Abigail I, 100
Henby, Abigail I, 194
Henby, Abigail I, 307
Henby, Anna I, 194
Henby, Anna I, 198
Henby, Clarkey I, 52
Henby, Clarkey I, 53
Henby, Clarkey I, 66
Henby, Clarkey I, 69
Henby, Clarkey I, 142
Henby, Clarkey I, 194
Henby, Clarky I, 194
Henby, Clarky I, 307
Henby, Clerkey I, 100
Henby, Dorothy I, 142
Henby, Eli I, 194
Henby, Elias I, 194
Henby, Elijah I, 194
Henby, Elisabeth I, 34
Henby, Elisabeth I, 38
Henby, Elisabeth I, 50
Henby, Elisabeth I, 52
Henby, Elisabeth I, 53
Henby, Elisabeth I, 54
Henby, Elisabeth I, 194
Henby, Elisha I, 100
Henby, Elisha I, 194
Henby, Ephraim B. I, 194
Henby, Hanah I, 36
Henby, Hannah I, 52
Henby, Hannah I, 142
Henby, Hannah I, 147
Henby, Hannah I, 189
Henby, Hannah I, 193
Henby, Hannah I, 194
Henby, Hannah I, 307
Henby, Hannah I Sup 1, 4
Henby, Henry I, 195
Henby, James I, 34
Henby, James I, 52
Henby, James I Sup 1, 7
Henby, Jesse I, 194
Henby, John I, 53
Henby, John I, 100
Henby, John I, 142
Henby, John I, 147
Henby, John I, 194
Henby, John I Sup 1, 4
Henby, John I Sup 1, 7
Henby, John, Jr. I, 194
Henby, Joseph I, 35
Henby, Joseph I, 52
Henby, Joseph I, 142
Henby, Lucinda Lane I, 12
Henby, Margaret I, 52
Henby, Margaret I, 77
Henby, Mariam I, 307
Henby, Marium I, 194
Henby, Martha I, 194
Henby, Mary I, 40
Henby, Mary I, 52
Henby, Mary I, 194
Henby, Miriam I, 34
Henby, Miriam I, 53
Henby, Miriam I, 194
Henby, Miriam I, 307
Henby, Nathan I, 194
Henby, Peninah I, 184
Henby, Peninah I, 194
Henby, Penninah I, 189
Henby, Penninah I, 194
Henby, Pharaba I, 307
Henby, Pharaby I, 194
Henby, Sarah I, 35
Henby, Sarah I, 52
Henby, Sarah I, 194
Henby, Sarah I, 302
Henby, Sarah I, 307
Henby, Silvanus I, 34
Henby, Silvanus I, 52
Henby, Silvanus I, 53
Henby, Silvanus I, 77
Henby, Sylvaneous I, 194
Henby, Sylvanus I, 194
Henby, Thomas I, 52
Henby, Thomas I, 53
Henby, Thomas I, 66
Henby, Thomas I, 100
Henby, Thomas I, 184
Henby, Thomas I, 189
Henby, Thomas I, 193
Henby, Thomas I, 194
Henby, Widow Hannah I, 53
Henby, William I, 12
Henby, William I, 194
Henby, William, Jr. I, 12
Henby, Willis I, 194
Henchman, Barclay V, 971
Hencock, Sarah I, 542
Hencock, Sarah II, 374
Hendee, A. L. V, 409
Hendee, Ann V, 386

Hendee, Anna Eliza V, 386
Hendee, Mary V, 409
Hendee, Minnie L. V, 409
Hendee, Wm. V, 386
Henden, Carrollton IV, 220
Henden, Carrolton IV, 220
Henderlighter, Isaac VI, 931
Henderlighter, Spicy VI, 931
Hendershot, ??? IV, 220
Hendershot, Angeline IV, 220
Hendershot, C. O. IV, 220
Hendershot, Catherine Floretta IV, 220
Hendershot, Clyde IV, 220
Hendershot, Elizabeth IV, 220
Hendershot, Elizabeth IV, 246
Hendershot, Emma V, 500
Hendershot, Icie IV, 220
Hendershot, J. A. IV, 220
Hendershot, John IV, 220
Hendershot, John W. IV, 220
Hendershot, Jonathan IV, 220
Hendershot, Katharine IV, 220
Hendershot, Lawrence IV, 220
Hendershot, Lawrence E. IV, 220
Hendershot, Lola V, 500
Hendershot, Mildred IV, 220
Hendershot, Raymond IV, 220
Hendershot, Sarah IV, 220
Hendershot, Will Francis IV, 220
Hendershott, Lena V, 177
Henderson, ??? V, 177
Henderson, A??? IV, 1319
Henderson, Abner I. IV, 633
Henderson, Alisabeth I, 1020
Henderson, Almira III, 163
Henderson, Almira III, 226
Henderson, Andrew IV, 1319
Henderson, Ann I, 394
Henderson, Ann I, 403
Henderson, Anna C. IV, 720
Henderson, Anna M. IV, 633
Henderson, Anna Marie IV, 720
Henderson, Beatrice Eva IV, 407
Henderson, Betsy VI, 833
Henderson, Catharine IV, 1319
Henderson, Catharine VI, 960
Henderson, Catherine IV, 1319
Henderson, Charles V, 245
Henderson, Chas V, 269
Henderson, Chloe V, 245
Henderson, Christianna VI, 824
Henderson, Damon Vernon V, 245
Henderson, Daniel I, 1020
Henderson, Daniel VI, 824
Henderson, Earl Brown V, 245
Henderson, Edith J. IV, 407
Henderson, Edith J. IV, 408
Henderson, Edith J. IV, 437
Henderson, Edith Jeanette IV, 407
Henderson, Edith M. IV, 720
Henderson, Edith M. IV, 757
Henderson, Eli I, 1020
Henderson, Eli V, 71
Henderson, Elija W. II, 746
Henderson, Elija W. II, 750
Henderson, Eliza II, 707
Henderson, Eliza W. II, 746
Henderson, Eliza W. II, 775
Henderson, Elizabeth I, 394
Henderson, Elizabeth I, 883
Henderson, Elizabeth I, 1121
Henderson, Elizabeth I, 1128
Henderson, Elizabeth II, 374
Henderson, Elizabeth II, 534
Henderson, Elizabeth II, 547
Henderson, Elizabeth II, 707
Henderson, Elizabeth II, 722
Henderson, Elizabeth II, 745
Henderson, Elizabeth II, 746
Henderson, Elizabeth II, 750
Henderson, Elizabeth VI, 931
Henderson, Ella V, 269
Henderson, Ellen IV, 720
Henderson, Ellen IV, 758
Henderson, Ellen R. IV, 720
Henderson, Emily VI, 1014
Henderson, Esta V, 269
Henderson, Estie V, 245
Henderson, Ethel III, 163
Henderson, Eunice II, 707
Henderson, Eunice II, 746
Henderson, Eunice IV, 633
Henderson, Eunice H. IV, 407
Henderson, Eunice H. IV, 438
Henderson, Frances VI, 878
Henderson, Frances VI, 980
Henderson, Franklin David IV, 720
Henderson, George V, 245
Henderson, Gertrude IV, 1319
Henderson, Hannah W. II, 722
Henderson, Ida Jean IV, 720
Henderson, Ida M. IV, 475
Henderson, Isaac V, 71
Henderson, Isaac V, 500
Henderson, Isabel II, 444
Henderson, Isabella II, 707
Henderson, Isabella IV, 407
Henderson, J. Edward IV, 720
Henderson, J. H. VI, 796
Henderson, J. R. VI, 804
Henderson, James I, 1031
Henderson, James I Sup 1, 10
Henderson, James II, 707
Henderson, James II, 722
Henderson, James II, 746
Henderson, James II, 750
Henderson, James II, 775
Henderson, James IV, 407
Henderson, James IV, 438
Henderson, James IV, 633
Henderson, James Chalmers IV, 407
Henderson, James D. IV, 407
Henderson, James Wesley V, 177
Henderson, James Westley V, 500
Henderson, Janet IV, 838
Henderson, Jas. III, 163
Henderson, Jas. III, 226
Henderson, John I, 394
Henderson, John VI, 931
Henderson, John VI, 1014
Henderson, John Charles I, 1154
Henderson, Joseph II, 707
Henderson, Joseph IV, 407
Henderson, Joseph IV, 720
Henderson, Joseph D. II, 707
Henderson, Joseph D. II, 746
Henderson, Joseph D. IV, 402
Henderson, Joseph D. IV, 407
Henderson, Joseph D. IV, 628
Henderson, Joseph D. IV, 633
Henderson, Joseph W. II, 707
Henderson, Joseph W. II, 746
Henderson, Joseph W. II, 775
Henderson, Joshua IV, 720
Henderson, Joshua E. IV, 720
Henderson, Joshua E. IV, 757
Henderson, Kesiah I, 1020
Henderson, Kezia I, 1028
Henderson, Kezia I, 1031
Henderson, Keziah V, 71
Henderson, Keziah V, 500
Henderson, L. VI, 833
Henderson, Lloyd Israel IV, 407
Henderson, Locky VI, 931
Henderson, Lucinda IV, 407
Henderson, Lucinda IV, 448
Henderson, Margaret III, 163
Henderson, Margaret C. III, 163
Henderson, Martha I, 1020
Henderson, Martha I, 1031
Henderson, Martha II, 135
Henderson, Mary I, 912
Henderson, Mary I, 914
Henderson, Mary I, 1020
Henderson, Mary VI, 802
Henderson, Mary VI, 824
Henderson, Mary Ann VI, 824
Henderson, Mary Eliza II, 707
Henderson, Mary Ester V, 245
Henderson, Mourning V, 177
Henderson, Mourning V, 475
Henderson, Mourning V, 500
Henderson, Nancy VI, 995
Henderson, Nathan I, 1031
Henderson, Nathaniel I, 394
Henderson, Nathaniel I, 424
Henderson, Nathaniel I, 1020
Henderson, Nathaniel I, 1031
Henderson, Nathaniel V, 71
Henderson, Rachel I, 394
Henderson, Rachel I, 424
Henderson, Rachel I, 1031
Henderson, Rachel V, 71
Henderson, Rachel V, 469
Henderson, Rachel V, 500
Henderson, Rebecah I, 1020
Henderson, Rebecah I, 1031
Henderson, Rebecca I, 1031
Henderson, Rebecca I, 1154
Henderson, Rebecca VI, 931
Henderson, Rebeccah I, 394
Henderson, Rebeccah I, 424
Henderson, Rebekah I, 394
Henderson, Rebekah I, 1031
Henderson, Rebekah V, 71
Henderson, Reuben VI, 931
Henderson, Richard I, 343
Henderson, Richard I, 394
Henderson, Richard I, 1015
Henderson, Richard I, 1020
Henderson, Richard I, 1031
Henderson, Richard V, 71
Henderson, Richard V, 469
Henderson, Richard V, 500
Henderson, Richard VI, 180
Henderson, Richard VI, 186
Henderson, Richard VI, 197
Henderson, Richard VI, 286
Henderson, Robert III, 163
Henderson, Robert C. VI, 824
Henderson, Ruth II, 707
Henderson, Ruth C. IV, 688
Henderson, Ruth C. IV, 720
Henderson, Ruth K. II, 746
Henderson, Sally V, 303
Henderson, Sally V, 306
Henderson, Samuel VI, 824
Henderson, Sarah II, 707
Henderson, Sarah II, 746
Henderson, Sarah II, 775
Henderson, Sarah V, 71
Henderson, Sarah V, 500
Henderson, Sarah VI, 878
Henderson, Sarah VI, 960
Henderson, Sarah Frances V, 177
Henderson, Sarah Frances V, 500
Henderson, Selemma V, 245
Henderson, Shadrick I, 1031
Henderson, Sucky VI, 233
Henderson, Susan V, 910
Henderson, Susan V, 914
Henderson, Susannah I, 544
Henderson, Susannah I, 1016
Henderson, Susannah V, 71
Henderson, Talbert II, 746
Henderson, Thaniel I, 1020
Henderson, Thomas I, 394
Henderson, Thomas I, 1020
Henderson, Thomas I, 1031
Henderson, Thomas II, 707
Henderson, Thomas II, 746
Henderson, Thomas V, 71
Henderson, Thomas A. II, 707
Henderson, Thomas Albert II, 707
Henderson, Thomas, Jr. I, 1031
Henderson, Thos. C. IV, 1320
Henderson, Vesta M. IV, 402
Henderson, Vesta M. IV, 407
Henderson, Vesta M. IV, 633
Henderson, Vestal M. IV, 407
Henderson, Vestal M. IV, 628
Henderson, Virginia Eunice IV, 407
Henderson, William I, 394
Henderson, William I, 1020
Henderson, William I, 1031
Henderson, William V, 500
Henderson, William A. VI, 824
Henderson, William James II, 707
Henderson, William Judkins V, 910
Henderson, William, Jr. I, 1031
Henderson, Williamm VI, 931
Henderson, Winifred Ann IV, 407
Henderson, Wm. I, 403
Henderson, Wm. VI, 980
Hendix, Velna I, 943
Hendley, Ann III, 163
Hendley, Mary Emily I, 480
Hendley, Miriam Aletha I, 480
Hendley, Priscilla I, 814
Hendrake, ??? VI, 293
Hendrake, Amos VI, 313
Hendrake, Betsy VI, 313
Hendrake, Betty VI, 300
Hendrake, Betty VI, 313
Hendrake, Betty VI, 314
Hendrake, Chloe VI, 313
Hendrake, Ezekiah VI, 313
Hendrake, Jeremiah VI, 313
Hendrake, Jeremiah VI, 314
Hendrake, Judith VI, 313
Hendrake, Mary VI, 313
Hendrake, Moses VI, 313
Hendrake, Moses, Jr. VI, 313
Hendrake, Obed VI, 314
Hendrake, Obediah VI, 313
Hendrake, Orphah VI, 313
Hendrake, Richard VI, 313
Hendrake, Robert Bufkin VI, 314
Hendrake, Ruth VI, 313
Hendrake, Ruth VI, 314
Hendrake, Sarah VI, 313
Hendrake, Sarah VI, 314
Hendrake, William Payne VI, 313
Hendreckson, Mary II, 78
Hendrick, Absalom VI, 829
Hendrick, Bernard VI, 818
Hendrick, Bernard VI, 987
Hendrick, Bernard G. VI, 931
Hendrick, Betsy VI, 300
Hendrick, Betsy VI, 313
Hendrick, Betty VI, 314
Hendrick, Chloe VI, 313
Hendrick, Chloe VI, 344
Hendrick, Content I, 394
Hendrick, Content I, 425
Hendrick, Ezekiel VI, 848
Hendrick, James VI, 823
Hendrick, James VI, 838
Hendrick, James S. VI, 847
Hendrick, John VI, 344
Hendrick, John S. VI, 839
Hendrick, Julia E. VI, 874
Hendrick, Lucy VI, 931
Hendrick, Mary I, 394
Hendrick, Mary VI, 845
Hendrick, Mary VI, 848
Hendrick, Moses VI, 300
Hendrick, Moses VI, 344
Hendrick, Moses, Jr. VI, 313
Hendrick, Pemberton VI, 818
Hendrick, Pendleton VI, 818
Hendrick, Polly VI, 856
Hendrick, Ruth V, 245
Hendrick, Ruth VI, 313
Hendrick, Ruth VI, 314
Hendrick, Ruth VI, 328
Hendrick, Ruth VI, 344
Hendrick, Sarah VI, 313
Hendrick, Sarah VI, 314
Hendrick, Sarah VI, 343
Hendrick, Sarah B. VI, 832
Hendrick, Thomas VI, 344
Hendrick, Turner VI, 344
Hendrick, William VI, 846
Hendrick, Wm. VI, 832
Hendricks, Abeagal I, 195
Hendricks, Abel I, 195
Hendricks, Abraham I, 142
Hendricks, Abraham Hendrix I, 142
Hendricks, Absolem VI, 824
Hendricks, Ada S. I, 883
Hendricks, Albert II, 547
Hendricks, Albert II, 681
Hendricks, Ann I, 142
Hendricks, Ann IV, 127
Hendricks, Ann IV, 720
Hendricks, Ann E. VI, 824
Hendricks, Austin I, 883
Hendricks, Bernard VI, 824
Hendricks, Bernard VI, 829
Hendricks, Catherine VI, 843
Hendricks, Elisabeth I, 142
Hendricks, Elisabeth I, 174
Hendricks, Eliza IV, 720
Hendricks, Elizabeth VI, 824
Hendricks, Elizabeth VI, 836
Hendricks, Elizabeth VI, 841
Hendricks, Epsie I, 611
Hendricks, Ezekial VI, 841
Hendricks, Ezekiel VI, 830
Hendricks, Frances II, 374
Hendricks, Hadley I, 883
Hendricks, Harriett J. I, 53
Hendricks, Hattie I, 53
Hendricks, Ibbie I, 53
Hendricks, J. VI, 840
Hendricks, James II, 374
Hendricks, James VI, 824
Hendricks, James L. VI, 830
Hendricks, James S. VI, 830
Hendricks, Job I, 49
Hendricks, Job I, 53
Hendricks, Job I, 195
Hendricks, Job, Jr. I, 53
Hendricks, John II, 53
Hendricks, John II, 77
Hendricks, John II, 374
Hendricks, John II, 547
Hendricks, John II, 681
Hendricks, John F. VI, 824
Hendricks, Joseph VI, 824
Hendricks, Levi I, 195
Hendricks, Lucy VI, 811
Hendricks, Lucy VI, 824
Hendricks, Lucy May IV, 720
Hendricks, Lydia I, 883
Hendricks, Lydia E. I, 883
Hendricks, Lydia Elmira I, 883
Hendricks, Lydia Elmira I, 886
Hendricks, Marcy II, 53
Hendricks, Marcy II, 77
Hendricks, Martha I, 142
Hendricks, Martha I, 195
Hendricks, Martha VI, 824
Hendricks, Martha VI, 830
Hendricks, Mary I, 194
Hendricks, Mary I, 195
Hendricks, Mary I, 394
Hendricks, Mary II, 374
Hendricks, Mary IV, 720
Hendricks, Mary IV, 747
Hendricks, Mary B. I, 53
Hendricks, Milo IV, 720
Hendricks, Moses VI, 824
Hendricks, Moses VI, 836
Hendricks, Moses VI, 843
Hendricks, Nancy VI, 824
Hendricks, Nancy T. VI, 824
Hendricks, Nathan IV, 747
Hendricks, Pendelon VI, 811
Hendricks, Pennina I, 195
Hendricks, Phebe IV, 92
Hendricks, Pininah I, 195
Hendricks, Pininah I, 203
Hendricks, Rachel VI, 824
Hendricks, Rebeckah II, 681
Hendricks, Robert VI, 824
Hendricks, Ruth V, 245
Hendricks, Samuel I, 142
Hendricks, Samuel IV, 92
Hendricks, Sarah I, 142
Hendricks, Sarah VI, 824
Hendricks, Sarah Davis I, 634
Hendricks, Sarah J. I, 53
Hendricks, Solomon I, 53
Hendricks, Solomon I, 194
Hendricks, Solomon I, 195
Hendricks, Solomon I, 203
Hendricks, Solomon I Sup 1, 7
Hendricks, Sophia I, 49
Hendricks, Sophia I, 53
Hendricks, Susan VI, 840
Hendricks, Susannah I, 142
Hendricks, Susannah I, 156
Hendricks, Thomas I, 53
Hendricks, Wd. Rebeckah Wells II, 547
Hendricks, William J. VI, 824
Hendrickson, Amos II, 221
Hendrickson, Amos II, 231
Hendrickson, Anna III, 484
Hendrickson, Anna III, 500
Hendrickson, Benjamin E. VI, 740
Hendrickson, Benjamin E. VI, 747
Hendrickson, Benjamin E. VI, 748
Hendrickson, Benjamin E. VI, 786
Hendrickson, Blanche Elizabeth VI, 748
Hendrickson, Blanche Elizabeth VI, 786
Hendrickson, Caleb F. II, 310
Hendrickson, Caleb F. II, 320
Hendrickson, Caleb Folwell II, 799
Hendrickson, Charles III, 484
Hendrickson, Charlotte S. VI, 748
Hendrickson, Charlotte Stole VI, 731
Hendrickson, Charlotte Stole VI, 748
Hendrickson, Eleanor III, 415
Hendrickson, Eleanor III, 416
Hendrickson, Elizabeth II, 221
Hendrickson, Elizabeth II, 231
Hendrickson, Elizabeth II, 290
Hendrickson, Elizabeth II, 291
Hendrickson, Elizabeth II, 310
Hendrickson, Elizabeth II, 706
Hendrickson, Elizabeth II, 799
Hendrickson, Elizabeth H. II, 320
Hendrickson, Elizabeth H. II, 875
Hendrickson, Elizabeth, Jr. II, 291
Hendrickson, Emma II, 320
Hendrickson, Emma II, 840
Hendrickson, Emma II, 875
Hendrickson, Emma T. II, 310
Hendrickson, Emma T. II, 875
Hendrickson, Hanaah H. VI, 748
Hendrickson, Hannah VI, 748
Hendrickson, Hannah Eayre VI, 748
Hendrickson, Hannah Eayre VI, 786
Hendrickson, Hannah H. VI, 740
Hendrickson, Hannah H. VI, 747
Hendrickson, Hannah H. VI, 748

ndrickson, Hannah H. Eayre VI, 786
ndrickson, Henry B. II, 310
ndrickson, Henry B. II, 320
ndrickson, Henry B. II, 875
ndrickson, Henry Burr II, 799
ndrickson, Henry Smith II, 875
ndrickson, J. Eayre VI, 748
ndrickson, Jesse III, 484
ndrickson, Jesse III, 500
ndrickson, John II, 78
ndrickson, Joseph II, 221
ndrickson, Joseph II, 231
ndrickson, Joseph VI, 747
ndrickson, Joseph Eayre VI, 748
ndrickson, Joseph Eayre VI, 786
ndrickson, Julia A. III, 484
ndrickson, Julia Ann III, 163
ndrickson, Louisa III, 107
ndrickson, Mabel VI, 748
ndrickson, Mary II, 78
ndrickson, Rebecca C. VI, 747
ndrickson, Richard H. VI, 731
ndrickson, Richard H. VI, 748
ndrickson, Samuel III, 163
ndrickson, Samuel J. III, 484
ndrickson, Sarah I, 49
ndrickson, Sarah I, 53
ndrickson, Sarah II, 221
ndrickson, Sarah II, 231
ndrickson, Sarah A. III, 416
ndrickson, Sarah S. II, 231
ndrickson, Solomon I, 49
ndrickson, Solomon I, 53
ndrickson, Tylee B. II, 320
ndrickson, Tylee B. II, 875
ndrickson, Tyler B. II, 310
ndrickson, Tyler B. II, 320
ndrickson, William K. II, 291
ndrickson, William L. II, 310
ndrickson, William L. II, 320
endrix, Abel I, 195
endrix, Abraham I, 131
endrix, Ada S. I, 623
endrix, Ann I, 131
endrix, Ann IV, 92
endrix, Ann IV, 720
endrix, Ann IV, 755
endrix, Austin I, 883
endrix, Catharine I, 814
endrix, Catharine I, 815
endrix, D. K. I, 617
endrix, H. I, 623
endrix, Hannah I, 761
endrix, Hannah I, 771
endrix, Harriett J. I, 10
endrix, Harriett J. I, 53
endrix, Hattie I, 53
endrix, Isaac IV, 92
endrix, Jacob IV, 92
endrix, Joel IV, 1027
endrix, Josiah I, 10
endrix, Lydia I, 623
endrix, Lydia I, 883
endrix, Martha I, 142
endrix, Martha I, 160
endrix, Martha IV, 92
endrix, Martha IV, 112
endrix, Mary IV, 92
endrix, Mary IV, 100
endrix, Mary IV, 220
endrix, Mary IV, 287
endrix, Mary IV, 720
endrix, Mary B. I, 53
endrix, Mary R. I, 10
endrix, Nannie I, 625
endrix, Phebe IV, 76
endrix, Phebe IV, 92
endrix, Samuel IV, 92
endrix, Sarah I, 10
endrix, Sarah I, 142
endrix, Sarah I, 617
endrix, Sarah IV, 1253
endrix, Sarah J. I, 10
endrix, Sarah J. I, 53
endrix, Stephen IV, 92
endrix, Thomas I, 10
endrix, Thomas I, 53
endrix, Velna I, 949
endry, Annie Rulon II, 789
endry, George I, 394
endry, John II, 547
endry, Mary II, 547
endry, Samuel II, 231
enegar, Israel I. IV, 1253
eneks, E. B. IV, 1320
eniton, Louisa IV, 1320
eniton, Louise K. IV, 1320
Heniton, Robert IV, 1320
Heniton, Robert H. IV, 1320
Henley, ??? I, 685
Henley, Aaron Morris, Jr. I, 142
Henley, Aaron Morris, Sr. I, 142
Henley, Abel Trueblood I, 142
Henley, Abigail I, 142
Henley, Abigail I, 171
Henley, Abigail I, 594
Henley, Abigail I, 597
Henley, Abigail V, 404
Henley, Abraham I, 700
Henley, Abram I, 718
Henley, Agatha I, 654
Henley, Agatha I, 717
Henley, Agatha I, 722
Henley, Alpheus White I, 718
Henley, Amanda M. I, 719
Henley, Ann I, 100
Henley, Ann I, 142
Henley, Ann I, 150
Henley, Ann I, 654
Henley, Ann I, 679
Henley, Ann I, 699
Henley, Ann I, 713
Henley, Ann I, 717
Henley, Ann I, 718
Henley, Ann I, 719
Henley, Ann I, 762
Henley, Ann I, 814
Henley, Ann I, 819
Henley, Ann V, 393
Henley, Ann V, 405
Henley, Anna I, 700
Henley, Anna I, 718
Henley, Anna I, 719
Henley, Anna I, 730
Henley, Anna I, 748
Henley, Anna I, 757
Henley, Anna I, 762
Henley, Anna B. V, 742
Henley, Anna M. I, 699
Henley, Anna P. I, 814
Henley, Anne I, 142
Henley, Anne I, 152
Henley, Annie M. I, 814
Henley, Annie Mariah I, 719
Henley, Asenath I, 480
Henley, Asenath I, 700
Henley, Asenath I, 719
Henley, Asenath M. I, 699
Henley, Asenath M. I, 814
Henley, Benjamin Morris I, 142
Henley, Bernice I, 617
Henley, Bernice I, 634
Henley, Bernice III, 49
Henley, Caleb Trueblood I, 142
Henley, Camie I, 931
Henley, Carolyn I, 943
Henley, Carrie I, 634
Henley, Carrie Louisa I, 613
Henley, Carrie Louise I, 618
Henley, Carrie Louise I, 634
Henley, Carrie Louise I, 815
Henley, Carrie S. I, 634
Henley, Catharine I, 718
Henley, Charles I, 700
Henley, Charles I, 718
Henley, Charles A. I, 634
Henley, Charles A. V. I, 634
Henley, Charles A. V. I, 815
Henley, Charles H. I, 617
Henley, Charles V. I, 618
Henley, Charlie A. V. I, 634
Henley, Clarence Jay H. V, 742
Henley, Cleopatra I, 748
Henley, Cleopatra I, 761
Henley, Cleopatra I, 762
Henley, Crisse I, 700
Henley, Daniel W. I, 480
Henley, David I, 927
Henley, David Martin I, 814
Henley, David V. I, 618
Henley, David V. I, 699
Henley, David V. I, 700
Henley, David V. I, 719
Henley, David V. I, 814
Henley, Davis I, 628
Henley, Dougan C. I, 699
Henley, Dougan C. I, 719
Henley, Dougan C. I, 814
Henley, Eleanor I, 618
Henley, Eleanor I, 628
Henley, Eleanor I, 927
Henley, Elenor I, 719
Henley, Eleonor I, 699
Henley, Elias I, 473
Henley, Elias I, 480
Henley, Elias I, 654
Henley, Elias I, 699
Henley, Elias I, 700
Henley, Elias I, 718
Henley, Elias I, 814
Henley, Elias I, 819
Henley, Elias Albertson I, 142
Henley, Elisabeth I, 142
Henley, Elisabeth I, 147
Henley, Elisabeth I, 195
Henley, Elisabeth I, 814
Henley, Eliza A. V, 567
Henley, Eliza A. V, 575
Henley, Eliza Ann V, 575
Henley, Elizabeth I, 100
Henley, Elizabeth I, 132
Henley, Elizabeth I, 139
Henley, Elizabeth I, 142
Henley, Elizabeth I, 700
Henley, Elizabeth I, 718
Henley, Elizabeth I, 719
Henley, Elizabeth I, 737
Henley, Elizabeth I, 738
Henley, Elizabeth I, 814
Henley, Elizabeth I, 883
Henley, Elizabeth I, 912
Henley, Elizabeth W. I, 533
Henley, Elizabeth W. I, 544
Henley, Elizabeth W. I, 718
Henley, Elleanor I, 814
Henley, Elwood I, 586
Henley, Elwood I, 594
Henley, Elwood I, 719
Henley, Emma I, 938
Henley, Emma V, 742
Henley, Erasmus B. I, 719
Henley, Eunice I, 262
Henley, Eunice I, 748
Henley, Eunice I, 762
Henley, Eunice I, 814
Henley, Eunice I, 927
Henley, Eunice C. I, 814
Henley, Eunice C. I, 846
Henley, Eunice N. I, 762
Henley, Eunice N. I, 772
Henley, Florence V, 910
Henley, Frank Arthur I, 927
Henley, Frank Arthur I, 943
Henley, Franklin I, 719
Henley, Franklin A. I, 719
Henley, Frederi I, 699
Henley, Frederic I, 719
Henley, Frederick I, 544
Henley, Frederick I, 560
Henley, Frederick I, 719
Henley, G. H. I, 909
Henley, Gabral I, 700
Henley, Gabriel I, 654
Henley, Gabriel I, 718
Henley, George H. I, 594
Henley, George Ricks I, 100
Henley, George Rix I, 142
Henley, George Rix I, 171
Henley, Gertrude I, 815
Henley, Grace V, 910
Henley, Gulielma I, 711
Henley, Gulielma I, 718
Henley, Gulielma V, 403
Henley, Hannah Victoria I, 814
Henley, Harvey G. V, 742
Henley, Henry I, 100
Henley, Henry I, 654
Henley, Henry I, 699
Henley, Henry I, 700
Henley, Henry I, 717
Henley, Henry I, 718
Henley, Henry I, 719
Henley, Henry I, 762
Henley, Henry I, 814
Henley, Henry I, 836
Henley, Henry V, 71
Henley, Hezekiah I, 394
Henley, Hezekiah I, 699
Henley, Hezekiah I, 718
Henley, Hezekiah I, 813
Henley, Hezekiah I, 814
Henley, Hezekiah I, 883
Henley, Hezekiah V, 71
Henley, Hickson I, 588
Henley, Isabel I, 142
Henley, Isabel I, 162
Henley, Isabel I, 699
Henley, Isabell I, 654
Henley, Isabella I, 700
Henley, J. B. I, 719
Henley, Jabes I, 699
Henley, Jabez I, 718
Henley, Jabez I, 814
Henley, Jacob I, 700
Henley, Jacob I, 718
Henley, Jacob I, 719
Henley, Jacob V, 71
Henley, James I, 748
Henley, James I, 762
Henley, James D. I, 762
Henley, Jane I, 699
Henley, Jane I, 762
Henley, Jane I, 814
Henley, Jane I, 819
Henley, Jason V, 742
Henley, Jesse I, 53
Henley, Jesse I, 100
Henley, Jesse I, 142
Henley, Jesse I, 163
Henley, Jesse I, 544
Henley, Jesse I, 645
Henley, Jesse I, 654
Henley, Jesse I, 679
Henley, Jesse I, 695
Henley, Jesse I, 700
Henley, Jesse I, 710
Henley, Jesse I, 717
Henley, Jesse I, 718
Henley, Jesse I, 719
Henley, Jesse V, 71
Henley, Jesse A. I, 699
Henley, Jesse A. I, 814
Henley, Jesse Ambrose I, 719
Henley, Jesse B. I, 480
Henley, Jesse G. I, 638
Henley, Jesse M. I, 719
Henley, Jesse Milton I, 700
Henley, Jesse Ralph I, 699
Henley, Jesse, Jr. I, 717
Henley, Jesse, Jr. I, 718
Henley, Jessie I, 634
Henley, Jessie I, 815
Henley, Jessie Gertrude I, 618
Henley, Jessie Gertrude I, 623
Henley, Jessie Gertrude I, 634
Henley, Jessie Gertrude I, 931
Henley, John I, 53
Henley, John I, 65
Henley, John I, 100
Henley, John I, 108
Henley, John I, 127
Henley, John I, 142
Henley, John I, 143
Henley, John I, 155
Henley, John I, 195
Henley, John I, 203
Henley, John I, 480
Henley, John I, 533
Henley, John I, 544
Henley, John I, 654
Henley, John I, 679
Henley, John I, 695
Henley, John I, 699
Henley, John I, 700
Henley, John I, 717
Henley, John I, 718
Henley, John I, 719
Henley, John I, 737
Henley, John I, 762
Henley, John I, 814
Henley, John I, 819
Henley, John I, 909
Henley, John V, 71
Henley, John V, 245
Henley, John V, 303
Henley, John V, 335
Henley, John V, 469
Henley, John B. I, 700
Henley, John C. I, 480
Henley, John G. I, 719
Henley, John Goss I, 700
Henley, John H. I, 912
Henley, John Milton I, 814
Henley, John P. I, 719
Henley, John Price I, 142
Henley, John R. I, 718
Henley, John Symons, Sr. I, 142
Henley, John, Jr. I, 100
Henley, John, Jr. I, 142
Henley, John, Jr. I, 700
Henley, John, Jr. I, 719
Henley, John, Sr. I, 700
Henley, Jonathan Price I, 142
Henley, Jordan I, 142
Henley, Jordan I, 147
Henley, Jordon I, 100
Henley, Joseph I, 53
Henley, Joseph I, 100
Henley, Joseph I, 127
Henley, Joseph I, 142
Henley, Joseph I, 163
Henley, Joseph I, 169
Henley, Joseph I, 171
Henley, Joseph I, 594
Henley, Joseph I, 654
Henley, Joseph I, 699
Henley, Joseph I, 700
Henley, Joseph I, 718
Henley, Joseph I, 726
Henley, Joseph V, 71
Henley, Joseph Henley I, 142
Henley, Joseph John I, 700
Henley, Josiah Bundy I, 142
Henley, Judith I, 620
Henley, Judith I, 699
Henley, Judith I, 718
Henley, Kezia I, 695
Henley, Kezia I, 718
Henley, Keziah I, 142
Henley, Keziah I, 155
Henley, Keziah I, 480
Henley, Keziah I, 700
Henley, Keziah I, 762
Henley, Keziah Ann I, 718
Henley, Levi I, 719
Henley, Lindley H. I, 719
Henley, Louise F. I, 719
Henley, Lucilla I, 717
Henley, Lucilla I, 718
Henley, Lucilla Stanley I, 700
Henley, Lucretia I, 100
Henley, Lucretia I, 142
Henley, Lucretia I, 149
Henley, Lucretia I, 718
Henley, Lucretia I, 720
Henley, Luella I, 814
Henley, Lydea I, 700
Henley, Lydia I, 718
Henley, Lydia I, 723
Henley, Lydia L. I, 710
Henley, Lydia L. I, 719
Henley, M. C. I, 634
Henley, Mamie C. I, 719
Henley, Margaret I, 100
Henley, Margaret I, 142
Henley, Margaret I, 149
Henley, Margaret I, 544
Henley, Margaret I, 700
Henley, Margaret I, 711
Henley, Margaret I, 718
Henley, Margaret I, 719
Henley, Margaret Keziah I, 700
Henley, Maria I, 719
Henley, Maria Elma I, 699
Henley, Mariam I, 710
Henley, Mariam I, 718
Henley, Marie I, 394
Henley, Martha I, 699
Henley, Martha I, 717
Henley, Martha I, 718
Henley, Martha I, 814
Henley, Martha I, 836
Henley, Martha I, 911
Henley, Martha I, 912
Henley, Martha V, 71
Henley, Martha V, 215
Henley, Martha V, 245
Henley, Martha V, 259
Henley, Martha A. I, 719
Henley, Martha J. I, 699
Henley, Martha J. I, 814
Henley, Martha Jane I, 699
Henley, Martha Jane I, 719
Henley, Marvin V, 681
Henley, Marvin J. V, 681
Henley, Mary I, 53
Henley, Mary I, 100
Henley, Mary I, 108
Henley, Mary I, 127
Henley, Mary I, 139
Henley, Mary I, 142
Henley, Mary I, 143
Henley, Mary I, 154
Henley, Mary I, 163
Henley, Mary I, 170
Henley, Mary I, 480
Henley, Mary I, 654
Henley, Mary I, 695
Henley, Mary I, 699
Henley, Mary I, 700
Henley, Mary I, 709
Henley, Mary I, 710
Henley, Mary I, 718
Henley, Mary I, 719
Henley, Mary I, 738
Henley, Mary I, 814
Henley, Mary I, 912
Henley, Mary V, 71
Henley, Mary A. I, 480
Henley, Mary E. I, 714
Henley, Mary E. I, 719
Henley, Mary Elizabeth I, 700
Henley, Mary Ellen I, 814
Henley, Mary Emily I, 480
Henley, Mary H. I, 628
Henley, Mathew I, 719
Henley, Matthew I, 480
Henley, Matthew I, 719
Henley, Melicent I, 100
Henley, Micajah I, 623
Henley, Micajah I, 634

Henley, Micajah I, 699
Henley, Micajah I, 700
Henley, Micajah I, 718
Henley, Micajah I, 719
Henley, Micajah I, 814
Henley, Micajah I, 815
Henley, Micajah I, 931
Henley, Micajah I, 943
Henley, Micajah V, 403
Henley, Micajah C. I, 613
Henley, Micajah C. I, 618
Henley, Micajah C. I, 634
Henley, Micajah C. I, 927
Henley, Micajah C. I, 943
Henley, Milicen I, 679
Henley, Milicent I, 53
Henley, Milicent I, 78
Henley, Milicent I, 142
Henley, Milicent I, 173
Henley, Milicent I, 654
Henley, Miliscent I, 142
Henley, Milisent I, 53
Henley, Milisent I, 87
Henley, Minerva I, 719
Henley, Miriam I, 100
Henley, Miriam I, 544
Henley, Miriam I, 718
Henley, Miriam I, 724
Henley, Miriam Aletha I, 480
Henley, Mourning I, 35
Henley, Mourning I, 53
Henley, Mourning I, 100
Henley, Mourning I, 142
Henley, Nancey I, 700
Henley, Nancy I, 700
Henley, Nancy I, 718
Henley, Nancy E. I, 699
Henley, Nancy E. I, 814
Henley, Nancy J. I, 719
Henley, Nancy J. I, 729
Henley, Nanna I, 718
Henley, Nathan I, 142
Henley, Nathan I, 184
Henley, Nathan I, 195
Henley, Nathan I, 544
Henley, Nathan I, 628
Henley, Nathan I, 700
Henley, Nathan I, 717
Henley, Nathan I, 718
Henley, Nathan I, 748
Henley, Nathan I, 759
Henley, Nathan I, 762
Henley, Nathan P. I, 699
Henley, Nathan P. I, 814
Henley, Nathan P. I, 846
Henley, Nathan Pearson I, 719
Henley, Nereus Nixon I, 700
Henley, Nixon I, 473
Henley, Nixon I, 480
Henley, Nixon I, 700
Henley, Nixon I, 709
Henley, Nixon I, 718
Henley, Nixon I, 762
Henley, Nixon I, 770
Henley, Noah V, 71
Henley, Owner Eleanor I, 814
Henley, Parthenia I, 241
Henley, Parthenia I, 258
Henley, Parthenia I, 814
Henley, Parthenis I, 719
Henley, Parthina I, 699
Henley, Penelope I, 100
Henley, Penelope I, 654
Henley, Penelope I, 679
Henley, Penelope I, 685
Henley, Penelope I, 699
Henley, Penelope I, 700
Henley, Penelope I, 718
Henley, Pennina I, 718
Henley, Penninah I, 594
Henley, Penninah I, 700
Henley, Penninah I, 718
Henley, Penninah I, 726
Henley, Penninah I, 738
Henley, Phinehas I, 700
Henley, Phinehas I, 718
Henley, Pinina I, 718
Henley, Prim L. I, 617
Henley, Priscilla I, 813
Henley, Priscilla I, 814
Henley, Rachel I, 544
Henley, Rachel I, 583
Henley, Rachel I, 700
Henley, Rachel I, 718
Henley, Rachel I, 770
Henley, Rachel E. I, 544
Henley, Rachel E. I, 762
Henley, Rachel Esther I, 748
Henley, Rachel Esther I, 762
Henley, Rachel Stalker I, 762
Henley, Ralph I, 719
Henley, Rebecah I, 718
Henley, Rebecca I, 480
Henley, Rebecca I, 714
Henley, Rebecca I, 718
Henley, Rebecca V, 71
Henley, Rebecca V, 393
Henley, Rebecca V, 404
Henley, Rebecca E. V, 742
Henley, Rebeckah I, 699
Henley, Rebekah I, 480
Henley, Rebekah I, 700
Henley, Robert I, 700
Henley, Robert I, 718
Henley, Robert B. V, 910
Henley, Robert Barclay V, 910
Henley, Ruth I, 544
Henley, Ruth I, 628
Henley, Ruth I, 718
Henley, Ruth I, 748
Henley, Ruth I, 759
Henley, Ruth I, 762
Henley, Ruth V, 910
Henley, Ruth Dicks I, 762
Henley, S. A. I, 719
Henley, S. Carrie I, 634
Henley, S. Carrie I, 815
Henley, S. Ellen I, 625
Henley, Sallie I, 814
Henley, Sallie M. I, 583
Henley, Sallie M. I, 624
Henley, Sallie M. I, 625
Henley, Sallie M. I, 762
Henley, Sallie M. I, 772
Henley, Sallie M. Worth I, 544
Henley, Sallie Mallette I, 628
Henley, Samuel V, 567
Henley, Samuel V, 575
Henley, Samuel A. I, 927
Henley, Samuel Allen I, 700
Henley, Samuel E. I, 719
Henley, Samuel Hadley I, 700
Henley, Sarah I, 613
Henley, Sarah I, 700
Henley, Sarah I, 709
Henley, Sarah I, 716
Henley, Sarah I, 717
Henley, Sarah I, 718
Henley, Sarah I, 719
Henley, Sarah I, 726
Henley, Sarah I, 735
Henley, Sarah I, 748
Henley, Sarah I, 762
Henley, Sarah II, 547
Henley, Sarah II, 628
Henley, Sarah VI, 824
Henley, Sarah A. I, 986
Henley, Sarah Caroline I, 618
Henley, Sarah Caroline I, 927
Henley, Sarah E. I, 699
Henley, Sarah E. I, 814
Henley, Sarah Elen I, 719
Henley, Sarah J. I, 544
Henley, Sarah J. I, 719
Henley, Sarah J. VI, 953
Henley, Sarah Jane I, 544
Henley, Sarah Jane I, 560
Henley, Sarah Jane I, 719
Henley, Sarah Keziah I, 700
Henley, Sona Caroline I, 623
Henley, Stephen I, 457
Henley, Stephen I, 700
Henley, Stephen I, 718
Henley, Stephen I, 719
Henley, Stephen I, 730
Henley, Stephen I, 741
Henley, Stephen I, 748
Henley, Stephen I, 762
Henley, Stephen V, 71
Henley, Stephen Franklin I, 699
Henley, Susan I, 699
Henley, Susanna I, 588
Henley, Susanna I, 700
Henley, Susanna I, 718
Henley, Susanna I, 814
Henley, Susanna I, 819
Henley, Susanna I, 907
Henley, Susanna I, 909
Henley, Susannah I, 718
Henley, Susannah I, 733
Henley, Tamer I, 142
Henley, Thamer I, 142
Henley, Thomas I, 142
Henley, Thomas I, 588
Henley, Thomas I, 594
Henley, Thomas I, 597
Henley, Thomas I, 700
Henley, Thomas I, 718
Henley, Thomas E. I, 142
Henley, Thomas Elwood I, 100
Henley, Thomas Jordan I, 142
Henley, Thomas Wilson I, 699
Henley, Thos. V, 404
Henley, Vivean I, 618
Henley, Vivian J. I, 634
Henley, Vivian J. I, 638
Henley, Widow Elisabeth I, 203
Henley, Widow Mary I, 142
Henley, Widow Mary I, 163
Henley, William I, 719
Henley, William I, 748
Henley, William I, 762
Henley, William VI, 824
Henley, William C. I, 814
Henley, William D. I, 394
Henley, William D. I, 762
Henley, William F. I, 480
Henley, William Fluke I, 480
Henley, William Hubbard I, 699
Henley, William P. I, 588
Henley, William P. I, 594
Henley, William Penn I, 719
Henly, Ann VI, 109
Henly, Anna I, 718
Henly, Anna I, 722
Henly, Elias I, 480
Henly, Elizabeth I, 100
Henly, Elizabeth I, 912
Henly, Elizabeth I, 913
Henly, Franklin A. I, 719
Henly, Henry IV, 1367
Henly, Hezekiah I, 883
Henly, Ida IV, 1367
Henly, Ida IV, 1380
Henly, Ida S. IV, 1367
Henly, James I Sup 1, 7
Henly, Jane I, 814
Henly, Jesse I, 53
Henly, Jesse I, 55
Henly, Jesse VI, 109
Henly, Jesse VI, 118
Henly, John I, 53
Henly, John I, 100
Henly, John V, 245
Henly, Joseph I, 142
Henly, Marie I, 386
Henly, Mary I, 53
Henly, Mary I, 55
Henly, Mary I, 100
Henly, Mary I, 142
Henly, Mary I, 480
Henly, Matthew I, 480
Henly, Miaram I, 100
Henly, Milisent I, 53
Henly, Nixon I, 480
Henly, Otto IV, 1320
Henly, Patrick II, 444
Henly, Rebecca I, 480
Henly, Rebecca I, 718
Henly, Rebecca I, 721
Henly, Ruth IV, 1367
Henly, Warren IV, 1237
Henly, William P. IV, 1367
Henly, William P. IV, 1380
Henness, Nancy VI, 824
Henness, William VI, 824
Henney, Chas. V, 1000
Henney, Harriet V, 1000
Henney, Solomon V, 1000
Hennin, Ella IV, 1281
Hennin, Opa IV, 1281
Henninger, Sarah Elma V, 879
Henninger, Sarah Elma V, 882
Henningsen, Andrew IV, 1320
Henningsen, Andrew C. IV, 1320
Henningsen, Chas. IV, 1320
Henningsen, Chas. K. IV, 1320
Henningsen, Emma C. IV, 1320
Henningsen, Esther Olina IV, 1320
Henningsen, Lizzie IV, 1320
Henningsen, Wm. F. IV, 1320
Henninss, Patience VI, 848
Hennion, Andrew J. III, 416
Hennion, Jane III, 416
Hennis, Clara Bell IV, 220
Hennis, Nancy IV, 220
Hennis, Thomas IV, 220
Henny, Benjamin VI, 931
Henny, Easter VI, 931
Henny, Mikel VI, 931
Henny, Milly VI, 931
Henny, Sarah VI, 931
Henny, William VI, 931
Henri, Elizabeth II, 547
Henri, Elizabeth II, 707
Henri, Henrietta II, 707
Henris, Martha I, 195
Henry, ??? V, 71
Henry, A. T. VI, 844
Henry, Alexander IV, 1281
Henry, Alexander V, 1000
Henry, Alexander VI, 824
Henry, Alexander L. VI, 804
Henry, Amelia II, 547
Henry, Amelia II, 746
Henry, Ames IV, 1210
Henry, Amos IV, 1165
Henry, Amos IV, 1210
Henry, Amos Neal IV, 1165
Henry, Ann Elizabeth V, 700
Henry, Carrie V, 1000
Henry, Carrie Corrinne Baylies V, 71
Henry, Charles V, 575
Henry, Charles V, 681
Henry, Charles Edward IV, 1165
Henry, Chas. A. V, 681
Henry, Cynthia V, 575
Henry, Dinah VI, 837
Henry, Eleanor II, 547
Henry, Elizabeth II, 231
Henry, Elizabeth II, 547
Henry, Elizabeth II, 610
Henry, Elizabeth II, 709
Henry, Elwood V, 377
Henry, Frances Maria III, 163
Henry, Francis I, 1154
Henry, Frankie IV, 1165
Henry, Frankie IV, 1210
Henry, Geo. F. VI, 812
Henry, George I, 394
Henry, George IV, 873
Henry, George F. VI, 824
Henry, Hannah V, 575
Henry, Hannah V, 971
Henry, Hannah V, 979
Henry, Harley V, 377
Henry, Hattie Lavinia III, 190
Henry, Hattie Lavinia III, 342
Henry, Hazel IV, 1210
Henry, Helen C. IV, 1165
Henry, Herbert Wilson V, 1000
Henry, Homer V, 377
Henry, Hugh V, 971
Henry, Ida V, 575
Henry, Ina V, 575
Henry, J. B. IV, 1165
Henry, Jamed V, 1000
Henry, James V, 575
Henry, James E. V, 1000
Henry, James M. V, 575
Henry, Jefferson IV, 1165
Henry, Jennie IV, 1253
Henry, John C. III, 163
Henry, John C. III, 361
Henry, John K. V, 1000
Henry, Josiah IV, 906
Henry, Julia V, 335
Henry, Julia V, 625
Henry, Julia V, 681
Henry, Julia A. V, 681
Henry, Junius V, 681
Henry, Lavina V, 1000
Henry, Lorrin V, 1000
Henry, Louise II, 707
Henry, Lula V, 575
Henry, Lulu V, 575
Henry, Lydia IV, 873
Henry, Lydia V, 39
Henry, Lydia V, 71
Henry, Lydia V, 625
Henry, Lydia V, 627
Henry, Margaret A. VI, 824
Henry, Mariah Evaline IV, 906
Henry, Marietta Bellows III, 163
Henry, Marietta Bellows III, 361
Henry, Marion Sylvester IV, 906
Henry, Mary II, 547
Henry, Mary VI, 879
Henry, Mary VI, 983
Henry, Melissa V, 377
Henry, Milley VI, 920
Henry, Minnie Wynn IV, 1281
Henry, Mrs. Katheryn IV, 476
Henry, Nancy V, 377
Henry, Noah II, 707
Henry, Patrick VI, 284
Henry, Paul IV, 1165
Henry, Paul IV, 1210
Henry, Pauline J. VI, 824
Henry, Rachel Ann IV, 906
Henry, Rachel B. V, 24
Henry, Rachel B. V, 33
Henry, Rachel B. V, 71
Henry, Rachel M. B. V, 71
Henry, Ralph IV, 1165
Henry, Ralph IV, 1210
Henry, Ralph Forest IV, 1165
Henry, Retta V, 575
Henry, Rettie V, 575
Henry, Robert L. I, 1154
Henry, Rosco D. IV, 220
Henry, Ruby Wilson IV, 1320
Henry, Ruth Ellen IV, 1165
Henry, Samuel II, 231
Henry, Samuel V, 842
Henry, Sarah IV, 872
Henry, Sarah IV, 880
Henry, Sarah IV, 1100
Henry, Sarah IV, 1109
Henry, Sarah E. I, 1154
Henry, Sarah J. IV, 906
Henry, Sewell IV, 1281
Henry, Stella IV, 1165
Henry, Stella IV, 1210
Henry, Stella V, 575
Henry, Stella Belle IV, 1165
Henry, Susanna II, 231
Henry, Susannah II, 231
Henry, Susannah IV, 633
Henry, Susannah IV, 640
Henry, Thomas VI, 871
Henry, Thomas VI, 879
Henry, Thomas B. V, 71
Henry, Thomas J. I, 394
Henry, Tom VI, 920
Henry, Verda IV, 1210
Henry, Virgil IV, 220
Henry, Walter D. V, 377
Henry, Wesley IV, 1210
Henry, Wilbur Ellis IV, 1165
Henry, William IV, 1165
Henry, William V, 335
Henry, William V, 681
Henry, William E. V, 71
Henry, William H. V, 377
Henry, Winny VI, 879
Henry, Wm. II, 1001
Henry, Wm. IV, 1165
Henry, Wm. IV, 1210
Henry, Wm. V, 335
Henry, Wm. V, 377
Henry, Wm. V, 681
Henry, Wm. A. V, 681
Henry, Wm., Jr. V, 681
Henry, Wm., Sr. V, 681
Henry, Zenas V, 575
Hensell, Rachel VI, 399
Hensey, Rebecca P. II, 875
Hensey, Sarah A. II, 875
Henshaw, Abel V, 395
Henshaw, Absolem V, 395
Henshaw, Benjamin I, 783
Henshaw, Eadeth V, 395
Henshaw, Jesse I, 783
Henshaw, John I, 783
Henshaw, John V, 395
Henshaw, Jonathan I, 783
Henshaw, Margaret V, 395
Henshaw, Mary I, 783
Henshaw, Michael I, 397
Henshaw, Nancy V, 395
Henshaw, Rachel II, 78
Henshaw, Ruth I, 783
Henshaw, Seth I, 783
Henshaw, Susanna I, 783
Hensle, Florence IV, 1254
Henslee, H. C. IV, 1254
Hensley, Benjamin VI, 931
Hensley, Benjamin VI, 1021
Hensley, Benjn. VI, 912
Hensley, Benjn. VI, 929
Hensley, Benjn. VI, 946
Hensley, Benjn. VI, 983
Hensley, Benjn. VI, 1009
Hensley, Carriline VI, 931
Hensley, Cora IV, 1254
Hensley, Eliza VI, 931
Hensley, Elizabeth VI, 326
Hensley, Elizabeth VI, 829
Hensley, Elizabeth VI, 931
Hensley, Florence IV, 1254
Hensley, H. C. IV, 1254
Hensley, H. Millam VI, 932
Hensley, Harry C. IV, 1254
Hensley, Henry F. VI, 931
Hensley, Henry F. VI, 937
Hensley, James VI, 931
Hensley, James VI, 994
Hensley, James VI, 1005
Hensley, James VI, 1006
Hensley, James M. VI, 931
Hensley, James O. VI, 931
Hensley, James O. VI, 995
Hensley, Joel F. VI, 899
Hensley, Joel F. VI, 931
Hensley, Joel F. VI, 989
Hensley, John VI, 931
Hensley, John L. VI, 923
Hensley, John L. VI, 931
Hensley, John L. VI, 937
Hensley, Kitty F. VI, 929
Hensley, Lillay VI, 994
Hensley, Lilley Ann VI, 946

Hensley, Lucinda VI, 931
Hensley, Luveney E. VI, 931
Hensley, Margaret VI, 929
Hensley, Mary II, 547
Hensley, Mary II, 669
Hensley, Mary VI, 931
Hensley, Milley VI, 994
Hensley, Nancy VI, 931
Hensley, Nancy VI, 946
Hensley, Nancy B. VI, 1006
Hensley, Narcissa VI, 995
Hensley, Polly VI, 1005
Hensley, Ruth IV, 1254
Hensley, Salley VI, 931
Hensley, Sally VI, 876
Hensley, Samuel VI, 931
Hensley, Samuel W. VI, 931
Hensley, Sillay VI, 994
Hensley, Sophrony W. VI, 931
Hensley, Susan VI, 931
Hensley, William VI, 905
Hensley, William VI, 912
Hensley, William VI, 929
Hensley, William VI, 931
Hensley, William VI, 1006
Hensley, Willis VI, 931
Hensley, Willis VI, 946
Hensly, Mary II, 78
Henson, Abbey VI, 989
Henson, Alice IV, 1320
Henson, Eleanor I, 467
Henson, Elizabeth I, 397
Henson, Elizabeth I, 719
Henson, Elizabeth I, 733
Henson, Elizabeth I, 1009
Henson, Elizabeth I, 1012
Henson, Isham I, 467
Henson, Isham I, 481
Henston, Abraham IV, 41
Henston, Deborah IV, 41
Henszey, Amy Sides II, 799
Henszey, Ann II, 799
Henszey, Ann II, 861
Henszey, Ann II, 875
Henszey, Annie D. II, 875
Henszey, Annie Deborah II, 800
Henszey, Caroline II, 799
Henszey, Caroline II, 800
Henszey, Deborah II, 547
Henszey, Deborah II, 591
Henszey, Deborah II, 799
Henszey, Deborah Ann II, 799
Henszey, Deborah Ann II, 875
Henszey, Edwin II, 800
Henszey, Eliza Frances Gordon II, 800
Henszey, Elizabeth II, 800
Henszey, Elizabeth B. II, 875
Henszey, Elizabeth B. II, 922
Henszey, Elizabeth Sides II, 799
Henszey, Elizabeth Sides II, 800
Henszey, Ella Frances Ann II, 800
Henszey, Esther II, 861
Henszey, Esther II, 875
Henszey, Esther II, 922
Henszey, Esther E. II, 875
Henszey, Esther Evans II, 799
Henszey, Frances II, 875
Henszey, George II, 875
Henszey, George P. II, 874
Henszey, George P. II, 875
Henszey, Hannah II, 547
Henszey, Helen May II, 799
Henszey, Jacob Sides II, 800
Henszey, Joseph II, 547
Henszey, Joseph II, 591
Henszey, Joseph II, 799
Henszey, Joseph G. II, 875
Henszey, Joseph G. II, 887
Henszey, Joseph Wilmer II, 800
Henszey, Joshua II, 547
Henszey, Joshua II, 591
Henszey, Joshua II, 799
Henszey, Joshua II, 861
Henszey, Joshua II, 875
Henszey, Margaret P. II, 800
Henszey, Margaret P. II, 875
Henszey, Marshall II, 799
Henszey, Marshall II, 875
Henszey, Mary II, 547
Henszey, Mary Elizabeth II, 800
Henszey, Nary II, 591
Henszey, Priscilla H. II, 875
Henszey, Priscilla H. II, 887
Henszey, Priscilla P. II, 875
Henszey, Rebecca P. II, 875
Henszey, Rebeckah P. II, 875
Henszey, Rebeckah P. II, 887
Henszey, Robert E. II, 875
Henszey, Robert E. II, 922
Henszey, Robert Evans II, 799
Henszey, Robert Evans, Jr. II, 799
Henszey, Samuel C. II, 861
Henszey, Samuel C. II, 875
Henszey, Samuel C. II, 887
Henszey, Samuel C., Jr. II, 800
Henszey, Samuel C., Jr. II, 875
Henszey, Samuel Couch II, 799
Henszey, Samuel E. II, 875
Henszey, Samuel E. II, 922
Henszey, Sarah A. II, 874
Henszey, Sarah A. II, 875
Henszey, Theodosia II, 875
Henszey, Theodosia Githens II, 800
Henszey, Wm. C. II, 875
Henwood, Anna IV, 1320
Henwood, Jennie IV, 1320
Henwood, Marshall IV, 1320
Henwood, Merritt IV, 1320
Henwood, Willie IV, 1320
Henzey, Alexander W. II, 291
Henzey, Alexander Wilson II, 291
Henzey, George P. II, 291
Henzey, Margaret P. II, 291
Henzey, Mary II, 547
Henzey, Samuel C. II, 291
Henzey, Samuel C. II, 1001
Henzie, Hannah II, 547
Henzie, Hannah II, 684
Henzie, Joshua II, 684
Hepbourn, Ann W. IV, 633
Hepbourn, Cyrus IV, 633
Hepbourn, Linton IV, 633
Hepbourn, Lydia IV, 633
Hepbourn, Phebe Elma IV, 633
Hepburn, Emeline IV, 879
Hepburn, Nancy Ann IV, 872
Hepburn, Nancy Ann IV, 879
Hepburn, Thomas IV, 872
Hepfer, Rebecca V, 1000
Heplar, Ellan Anderson I, 927
Heplar, Jack I, 927
Hepler, Ella I, 943
Hepler, Odell H. I, 943
Heppenstall, Tabitah VI, 932
Heppenstall, Thomas VI, 932
Heptinstall, Wm. G. VI, 931
Herald, Amos IV, 220
Herald, Amos IV, 529
Herald, Andrew V, 393
Herald, Andrew V, 497
Herald, Daniel I, 543
Herald, David Lee I, 881
Herald, Eli V, 497
Herald, Elizabeth V, 497
Herald, Houseen IV, 220
Herald, Housen IV, 220
Herald, Housen IV, 529
Herald, Housin IV, 148
Herald, Housin IV, 220
Herald, James J. V, 393
Herald, James J. V, 417
Herald, James J. V, 497
Herald, Leah V, 393
Herald, Leah V, 420
Herald, Leah T. V, 497
Herald, Margarett V, 497
Herald, Mary IV, 220
Herald, Mary IV, 529
Herald, Mary IV, 1100
Herald, Mary V, 497
Herald, Mary L. I, 543
Herald, Mary L. V, 393
Herald, Mary, Jr. IV, 583
Herald, Nathan V, 497
Herald, Rachel IV, 220
Herald, Rachel IV, 529
Herald, Rebecca I, 543
Herald, Rebecca IV, 220
Herald, Rebecca IV, 529
Herald, Rosa VI, 369
Herald, Rosa VI, 732
Herald, Sally V, 497
Herald, Samuel V, 497
Herald, Sarah V, 393
Herald, Sarah V, 417
Herald, Susannah I, 1121
Herald, Tamar IV, 529
Herald, Tamer IV, 220
Herbart, Rebecah I, 1030
Herbart, Rebecah I, 1032
Herberdick, Levine II, 374
Herberdinck, Levine II, 374
Herberdinck, Mary II, 374
Herberdink, Katherine II, 374
Herberdink, Leven II, 547
Herberdink, Levin II, 374
Herberdink, Levin II, 586
Herberdink, Levine II, 374
Herberdink, Mary II, 374
Herberdink, Mary II, 586
Herbert, ??? III, 163
Herbert, Ann I, 544
Herbert, Ann I, 883
Herbert, Ann I, 1016
Herbert, Ann IV, 38
Herbert, Ann IV, 148
Herbert, Ann, Sr. I, 544
Herbert, Ann, Sr. I, 1016
Herbert, Anna Mary IV, 720
Herbert, Donna Jean IV, 720
Herbert, Eleanor I, 544
Herbert, Eleanor I, 1016
Herbert, Esther I, 544
Herbert, Esther I, 1016
Herbert, Hannah I, 544
Herbert, Hannah I, 1016
Herbert, Hester I, 544
Herbert, Isaac I, 544
Herbert, Isaac I, 883
Herbert, Isaac I, 1016
Herbert, James IV, 720
Herbert, Jobe I, 544
Herbert, Jobe I, 1016
Herbert, Joseph IV, 720
Herbert, Joseph Scott IV, 720
Herbert, Kenneth James IV, 720
Herbert, Loren IV, 720
Herbert, Loren P. IV, 720
Herbert, Louise IV, 720
Herbert, Lydia I, 544
Herbert, Lydia I, 1016
Herbert, Martha I, 544
Herbert, Martha I, 1016
Herbert, Mary IV, 720
Herbert, Mary A. IV, 720
Herbert, Maude IV, 720
Herbert, Minnie IV, 720
Herbert, Monroe Mercer IV, 720
Herbert, Norma Jane IV, 720
Herbert, Peter I, 544
Herbert, Peter I, 883
Herbert, Peter I, 1016
Herbert, Rebecca II, 547
Herbert, Rebecca II, 649
Herbert, Ruth IV, 720
Herbert, Scott IV, 720
Herbert, Wesley IV, 720
Herbert, William I, 544
Herbert, William I, 666
Herbert, William I, 883
Herbert, William I, 1016
Herbert, William IV, 148
Herborn, ??? VI, 581
Herborn, Margaret VI, 581
Herd, Hannah II, 560
Herd, Hannah II, 593
Herd, Robert V, 79
Herd, Rosamond V, 79
Herd, Susanna II, 628
Herd, Susannah II, 547
Herd, Susannah II, 560
Here, Pheriba VI, 86
Herel, Rebecca I, 543
Herendeen, Anna IV, 1165
Herendeen, Anna W. IV, 1210
Herendeen, Elizabeth IV, 1165
Herendeen, Elizabeth IV, 1210
Herendeen, Elizabeth IV, 1214
Herendeen, Huldah IV, 1165
Herendeen, Huldah H. IV, 1210
Herendeen, Joseph IV, 1165
Herendeen, Joseph IV, 1210
Herendeen, Joshua IV, 1165
Herendeen, Judith IV, 1165
Herendeen, Mary IV, 1165
Herendeen, Mary S. P. IV, 1210
Herendeen, Nathan IV, 1165
Herendeen, Nathan IV, 1210
Herendeen, Nathan, Jr. IV, 1165
Herendeen, Pennsylvania IV, 1165
Herendeen, Pennsylvania B. IV, 1210
Herendeen, Sarah IV, 1165
Herendeen, Sarah IV, 1210
Herendeen, Sarah IV, 1214
Herendeen, Welcome IV, 1165
Herendeen, Welcome IV, 1210
Herenden, Nathan IV, 1210
Hergrave, Fredarack I, 543
Herin, Ruth I, 394
Herior, John III, 367
Heritage, Benjamin II, 150
Heritage, Benjamin II, 160
Heritage, Benjamin W. II, 150
Heritage, Hannah II, 150
Heritage, Hannah II, 160
Heritage, John II, 231
Heritage, John II, 548
Heritage, Joseph II, 78
Heritage, Mary II, 231
Heritage, Mary B. II, 160
Heritage, Mary R. II, 150
Heritage, Naomi II, 119
Heritage, Naomi II, 122
Heritage, William Clark II, 231
Herlow, Martha IV, 1173
Herman, Anna IV, 1320
Herman, Florence IV, 1320
Herman, George II, 374
Herman, Jacob IV, 1320
Herman, Joseph II, 78
Herman, La Vern B. IV, 1320
Herman, Lenna V, 177
Herman, Margaret IV, 1320
Herman, Mary V, 1000
Herman, Rosanna I, 53
Herman, Rosanna I, 74
Herman, Wm. V, 1000
Hermer, Ellenor II, 548
Hermer, Joseph II, 31
Hermer, Joseph II, 78
Hermer, Joseph II, 87
Hermer, Rebeckah II, 31
Hermer, Rebeckah II, 75
Hermer, Rebeckah II, 78
Hermer, Rebekah II, 78
Hermer, Rebekah II, 87
Hermon, Leah II, 548
Hern, Hennery II, 374
Hern, Sarah II, 374
Hern, William II, 374
Herndon, Achiles VI, 824
Herndon, Achilles VI, 866
Herndon, Anie VI, 633
Herndon, Annette VI, 633
Herndon, Annie VI, 633
Herndon, Annie VI, 649
Herndon, Arthur VI, 824
Herndon, Betsey A. VI, 824
Herndon, Clarence VI, 633
Herndon, Daniel VI, 824
Herndon, Dave D. VI, 806
Herndon, David VI, 797
Herndon, David VI, 830
Herndon, Edmund VI, 815
Herndon, Edmund VI, 823
Herndon, Edmund VI, 824
Herndon, Edmund VI, 829
Herndon, Edmund VI, 858
Herndon, Edward VI, 797
Herndon, Edward VI, 807
Herndon, Elenor VI, 824
Herndon, Elizabeth VI, 633
Herndon, Elizabeth VI, 634
Herndon, Elizabeth VI, 824
Herndon, Elizabeth VI, 866
Herndon, Frances VI, 803
Herndon, Frederick Arnold VI, 633
Herndon, Gideon VI, 633
Herndon, Gideon VI, 634
Herndon, Herophilia VI, 633
Herndon, Jacob W. VI, 824
Herndon, Jane VI, 807
Herndon, John Morgan VI, 634
Herndon, Lettie VI, 807
Herndon, Louisa VI, 864
Herndon, Louise VI, 633
Herndon, Lucy VI, 829
Herndon, Lucy J. VI, 825
Herndon, Martha VI, 815
Herndon, Mary VI, 823
Herndon, Mary VI, 824
Herndon, Nancy VI, 633
Herndon, Rodney VI, 633
Herndon, Rodney VI, 634
Herndon, Sarah E. B. VI, 824
Herndon, William VI, 807
Herndon, William VI, 824
Herndon, Zerilda VI, 806
Herne, Sarah II, 547
Herne, Sarah II, 667
Herne, Wm. II, 667
Herold, Alfred I, 813
Herold, Mary E. I, 543
Herold, Rhoda I, 1009
Herold, Rhoda I, 1011
Heron, ??? III, 84
Heron, Fannie III, 84
Heron, Fannie III, 163
Herr, Fanny A. III, 163
Herr, Frances II, 820
Herr, Frances III, 293
Herr, Frances B. III, 163
Herr, Frank S. III, 163
Herr, Frank S. III, 293
Herr, George V, 742
Herr, Grace V, 742
Herr, Harry V, 742
Herr, Henry C. II, 310
Herr, Henry C. III, 163
Herr, Ruth E. III, 163
Herr, Walter V, 742
Herral, Alfred I, 543
Herral, Mary I, 594
Herrald, Mary I, 813
Herrel, Aletha I, 543
Herrel, Amos IV, 220
Herrel, Houseen IV, 220
Herrel, Mary IV, 194
Herrel, Mary IV, 220
Herrel, Rachel IV, 220
Herrel, Rebecca I, 543
Herrel, Tamer IV, 220
Herreld, Arcada V, 303
Herreld, Jacob V, 303
Herreld, Rebeckah V, 303
Herreld, Rebeckah V, 311
Herreld, Wm. V, 303
Herrell, Alfred I, 543
Herrell, Obediah V, 842
Herrick, Charlotte III, 163
Herrick, Charlotte III, 276
Herrick, Emily III, 163
Herrick, Emily III, 276
Herrick, George III, 163
Herrick, George III, 276
Herricks, Mary III, 411
Herriel, Jonathan I, 813
Herrier, Elinore Felger IV, 1320
Herrier, Florence V, 571
Herrier, Mrs. Eleanor V, 571
Herril, Howsen IV, 405
Herril, Mary IV, 405
Herril, Rachel IV, 405
Herril, Tamer IV, 405
Herrin, Clara V, 393
Herrin, Clyde V, 393
Herrin, Henderson I, 394
Herrin, John W. V, 393
Herrin, Rhoda V, 393
Herrin, Ruth I, 394
Herring, Bayard M. I, 336
Herring, Celia I, 338
Herring, Celie I, 336
Herring, Edith IV, 1254
Herring, Floyd V, 1000
Herring, Julia I, 336
Herring, Lloyd V, 1000
Herring, Lorenzo M. V, 1000
Herring, Lottie I, 336
Herring, Louisa I, 336
Herring, Louise I, 336
Herring, Matthew I, 336
Herring, Minnie V, 1000
Herring, Nellie I, 336
Herring, Rachel II, 483
Herring, Rachel II, 548
Herring, Robert I, 336
Herring, Susan I, 336
Herring, Willie I, 336
Herrington, Matilda IV, 1320
Herrington, Mrs. Matilda IV, 1320
Herrington, Ruth I, 1154
Herritage, Benjamin II, 140
Herritage, Hannah II, 140
Herritage, Mary II, 207
Herritage, Mary II, 231
Herritage, Richard II, 207
Herritage, Richard II, 231
Herrod, Callie V, 1000
Herrod, Mary V, 1000
Herrod, Viola V, 1000
Herrol, Amos IV, 405
Herrold, Anna V, 410
Herrold, Daniel V, 410
Herrold, Elizabeth V, 410
Herron, Bula May Frances I, 1154
Herron, Chas. O. V, 393
Herron, Clara V, 393
Herron, Clyde V, 393
Herron, John V, 393
Herron, John W. V, 393
Herron, Martha I, 1154
Herron, May V, 742
Herron, Nellie V, 742
Herron, Rachel D. V, 393
Herron, Rhoda V, 393
Herron, Thomas I, 1154
Herron, William Carl I, 1154
Herschel, Katharine III, 323
Herschel, Melvin III, 323
Hersey, Alice II, 548
Hersey, Alice II, 579
Hershey, John II, 707
Hershey, Mary D. II, 707
Hershey, Mary D. II, 736
Hershey, Mary D. II, 746

Hersley, Anna IV, 1004
Herson, Ann V, 245
Herson, Benjamin Levi I, 394
Herson, Henderson I, 394
Herson, John Gurney I, 394
Herst, Charlotte VI, 399
Herst, Edna IV, 720
Herst, Eli VI, 399
Herst, Hannah VI, 399
Herst, Jonathan VI, 399
Herton, Gilbert III, 163
Herve, Katherine II, 444
Herve, William II, 444
Hervey, Ann V, 498
Hervey, Elizabeth V, 498
Hervey, Hannah II, 227
Hervey, Isaac II, 78
Hervey, Job II, 230
Hervey, John II, 227
Hervey, John II, 230
Hervey, John II, 234
Hervey, Mary II, 227
Hervey, Mary II, 230
Hervey, Robert II, 78
Hervy, Agness I, 431
Hervy, Elizabeth I, 431
Herzog, Henrieta III, 51
Herzog, Henrietta III, 135
Hesket, Alice IV, 1210
Hesket, N. W. IV, 1210
Hesket, Norville W. IV, 1210
Heskett, Ann II, 511
Heskett, Ann II, 548
Heslet, Bertha VI, 748
Heslet, James VI, 748
Heson, Eliza V, 742
Hess, Amelia II, 948
Hess, Amelia M. II, 948
Hess, Amelia M. II, 1087
Hess, Amelia M. II, 1088
Hess, Catherine VI, 936
Hess, Charles V, 742
Hess, Christian II, 1087
Hess, Christian II, 1088
Hess, Dorothy W. II, 1087
Hess, Dorothy W. II, 1088
Hess, Emma V, 177
Hess, Emma Moon V, 177
Hess, Flora V, 742
Hess, Ida I, 903
Hess, Jacob VI, 936
Hess, Jean Jacques III, 273
Hess, John VI, 32
Hess, Marie III, 273
Hess, Mary M. III, 273
Hess, Nettie V, 742
Hess, Nina V, 458
Hess, Treva V, 742
Hessey, Christopher I, 400
Hessinger, Dudley J. IV, 1254
Hessinger, J. Dudley IV, 1254
Hessinger, Minnie IV, 1254
Hessinger, Paul J. IV, 1254
Hesson, Eliza V, 742
Hesson, Samuel V, 742
Hessy, Elizabeth V, 1001
Hessy, Louisa V, 1001
Hessy, Peter V, 1001
Hester, Amos V, 393
Hester, Amos V, 396
Hester, Amos V, 625
Hester, Ann IV, 408
Hester, Ann Maria V, 1001
Hester, David IV, 408
Hester, Elizabeth I, 499
Hester, Elizabeth I, 544
Hester, Elizabeth V, 71
Hester, Elizabeth V, 500
Hester, Elizabeth V, 530
Hester, Emerson V, 1001
Hester, Esther V, 393
Hester, Esther V, 396
Hester, Francis I, 499
Hester, Francis I, 544
Hester, Francis I, 547
Hester, Francis V, 71
Hester, Francis V, 469
Hester, Francis V, 500
Hester, Francis V, 625
Hester, Gaynor V, 631
Hester, Guy Carlton III, 119
Hester, Henry V, 500
Hester, Isaac V, 500
Hester, Joel V, 625
Hester, John I, 499
Hester, John V, 71
Hester, Joseph V, 71
Hester, Katherine H. III, 119
Hester, Mary I, 499
Hester, Mary I, 544
Hester, Mary I, 547
Hester, Mary V, 71
Hester, Mary V, 393
Hester, Mary V, 469
Hester, Mary V, 493
Hester, Mary V, 500
Hester, Mary V, 509
Hester, Mary V, 625
Hester, Mary V, 631
Hester, Mary V, 645
Hester, Minerva V, 1001
Hester, Phebe IV, 408
Hester, Rachel V, 500
Hester, Rebecca I, 1121
Hester, Rebecca I, 1131
Hester, Robert I, 499
Hester, Robert I, 544
Hester, Robert V, 71
Hester, Robert V, 393
Hester, Robert V, 625
Hester, Robert V, 645
Hester, Ruth I, 499
Hester, Ruth IV, 335
Hester, Ruth V, 71
Hester, Ruth V, 500
Hester, Ruth V, 530
Hester, Susan III, 177
Hester, Susannah V, 631
Hester, Thomas I, 499
Hester, Thomas II, 1001
Hester, Thomas V, 71
Hester, Thomas V, 500
Hester, Thomas V, 509
Hester, William V, 500
Hester, Zimri V, 625
Heston, Abraham IV, 38
Heston, Abraham IV, 819
Heston, Abraham IV, 822
Heston, Agnes IV, 964
Heston, Albert V, 71
Heston, Albert V, 72
Heston, Amos IV, 92
Heston, Amos IV, 97
Heston, Amos IV, 221
Heston, Amos IV, 822
Heston, Amos V, 177
Heston, Amos VI, 649
Heston, Ann II, 1002
Heston, Ann IV, 38
Heston, Ann IV, 43
Heston, Ann IV, 54
Heston, Ann IV, 92
Heston, Ann IV, 97
Heston, Ann IV, 822
Heston, Ann IV, 907
Heston, Ann V, 71
Heston, Ann V, 177
Heston, Anna II, 946
Heston, Anna II, 961
Heston, Anna II, 1044
Heston, Anna II, 1052
Heston, Anna II, 1054
Heston, Anna II, 1074
Heston, Anna II, 1085
Heston, Anna IV, 38
Heston, Anna IV, 221
Heston, Anna IV, 822
Heston, Anne II, 961
Heston, Anne II, 963
Heston, Anne IV, 148
Heston, Arthur L. V, 500
Heston, Benjamin II, 374
Heston, Charles VI, 748
Heston, Charles Albert V, 71
Heston, Charles B. II, 961
Heston, Charles B. II, 1052
Heston, Charles B. II, 1088
Heston, Chester IV, 721
Heston, Clifford IV, 721
Heston, David II, 961
Heston, David II, 963
Heston, David II, 1002
Heston, David II, 1028
Heston, David II, 1044
Heston, David II, 1052
Heston, David II, 1054
Heston, David II, 1074
Heston, David II, 1085
Heston, David II, 1088
Heston, David IV, 38
Heston, David IV, 221
Heston, David IV, 720
Heston, David IV, 822
Heston, David IV, 899
Heston, David IV, 906
Heston, David V, 177
Heston, David VI, 248
Heston, David, Jr. II, 1002
Heston, David, Jr. II, 1052
Heston, Deborah IV, 38
Heston, Deborah IV, 822
Heston, Dorithy II, 1001
Heston, Eber IV, 38
Heston, Eber IV, 43
Heston, Eber IV, 54
Heston, Eber, Jr. IV, 38
Heston, Edward T. V, 500
Heston, Edward W. V, 72
Heston, Elizabeth II, 961
Heston, Elizabeth IV, 38
Heston, Elizabeth IV, 92
Heston, Elizabeth IV, 148
Heston, Elizabeth IV, 221
Heston, Elizabeth IV, 273
Heston, Elizabeth IV, 632
Heston, Elizabeth IV, 822
Heston, Elizabeth IV, 843
Heston, Elizabeth IV, 906
Heston, Elizabeth IV, 907
Heston, Elizabeth V, 35
Heston, Elizabeth V, 71
Heston, Elizabeth V, 156
Heston, Elizabeth V, 177
Heston, Elizabeth V, 178
Heston, Elizabeth C. V, 178
Heston, Emma Jane V, 71
Heston, Euphemia IV, 38
Heston, Euphemy IV, 822
Heston, Euphemy IV, 828
Heston, Euphrimia IV, 822
Heston, George G. V, 500
Heston, Gilbert III, 163
Heston, Hannah IV, 221
Heston, Hannah IV, 822
Heston, Homer IV, 964
Heston, Howell L. VI, 814
Heston, Isaac II, 374
Heston, Isaiah II, 548
Heston, Jacob II, 548
Heston, Jacob II, 666
Heston, Jacob, Jr. II, 548
Heston, James IV, 720
Heston, Jane IV, 819
Heston, Jane IV, 822
Heston, Jane V, 500
Heston, Jane VI, 748
Heston, Jefferson IV, 720
Heston, Jesse II, 548
Heston, Jesse H. II, 548
Heston, Jesse H. II, 666
Heston, John IV, 38
Heston, John IV, 92
Heston, John IV, 148
Heston, John IV, 221
Heston, John IV, 273
Heston, John IV, 822
Heston, John IV, 906
Heston, John VI, 649
Heston, John B. II, 961
Heston, John B. II, 1044
Heston, John B. II, 1052
Heston, John B. II, 1088
Heston, John B. VI, 237
Heston, John Balderston VI, 248
Heston, Jonathan II, 800
Heston, Joseph IV, 720
Heston, Joseph VI, 748
Heston, Joseph L. V, 500
Heston, Josiah II, 548
Heston, Judith II, 548
Heston, Judith A. VI, 248
Heston, Lavay IV, 721
Heston, Letitia II, 1044
Heston, Letitia IV, 38
Heston, Letitia IV, 54
Heston, Letitia V, 500
Heston, Letitia VI, 748
Heston, Lydia IV, 607
Heston, Macy V, 59
Heston, Macy V, 71
Heston, Mahlon IV, 335
Heston, Mahlon IV, 408
Heston, Mahlon IV, 529
Heston, Mahlon V, 177
Heston, Margaret IV, 38
Heston, Margaret IV, 92
Heston, Margaret IV, 148
Heston, Margaret IV, 220
Heston, Margaret IV, 273
Heston, Margery V, 177
Heston, Maria IV, 813
Heston, Maria IV, 822
Heston, Maria Ann IV, 38
Heston, Mariah IV, 822
Heston, Martha II, 548
Heston, Martha II, 666
Heston, Martha Jane IV, 720
Heston, Mary II, 548
Heston, Mary II, 961
Heston, Mary II, 964
Heston, Mary II, 1001
Heston, Mary II, 1012
Heston, Mary II, 1044
Heston, Mary II, 1052
Heston, Mary II, 1088
Heston, Mary IV, 38
Heston, Mary V, 177
Heston, Mary V, 193
Heston, Mary VI, 623
Heston, Mary VI, 650
Heston, Mary B. II, 666
Heston, Mary B. VI, 248
Heston, Mary Elizabeth IV, 720
Heston, Massa V, 157
Heston, Massa V, 177
Heston, Massey V, 177
Heston, Mercy IV, 92
Heston, Mercy V, 71
Heston, Mercy VI, 649
Heston, Mercy VI, 716
Heston, Mrs. ??? IV, 721
Heston, Odessa IV, 964
Heston, Phebe II, 1002
Heston, Phebe II, 1028
Heston, Phebe IV, 899
Heston, Phebe IV, 907
Heston, Phebe V, 177
Heston, Phebe V, 188
Heston, Phebe Ann II, 961
Heston, Phebe Ann II, 963
Heston, Phebe Ann II, 1002
Heston, Phebe Ann II, 1052
Heston, Phebe Ann II, 1054
Heston, Phebe E. IV, 629
Heston, Phineas V, 177
Heston, Phinehas IV, 92
Heston, Phinehas VI, 649
Heston, Rachel II, 548
Heston, Rachel II, 666
Heston, Rebecca II, 1001
Heston, Rebecca II, 1038
Heston, Rebecca IV, 38
Heston, Rebecca IV, 148
Heston, Rebecca IV, 221
Heston, Rebecca IV, 822
Heston, Rebecca IV, 907
Heston, Rebecca IV, 914
Heston, Rebecca V, 177
Heston, Rebecca Ann V, 500
Heston, Rebekah II, 1001
Heston, Ruby May IV, 721
Heston, Ruth IV, 720
Heston, Ruth IV, 899
Heston, Ruth IV, 906
Heston, Ruth IV, 907
Heston, Samuel V, 500
Heston, Samuel VI, 748
Heston, Sara W. VI, 237
Heston, Sara Willets VI, 237
Heston, Sara Willets VI, 248
Heston, Sarah IV, 38
Heston, Sarah IV, 54
Heston, Sarah IV, 92
Heston, Sarah IV, 822
Heston, Sarah V, 177
Heston, Sarah Willits VI, 237
Heston, Sue IV, 721
Heston, Susan R. V, 500
Heston, Susannah V, 500
Heston, Tacy IV, 38
Heston, Tacy IV, 148
Heston, Tacy IV, 221
Heston, Tacy IV, 822
Heston, Thomas II, 548
Heston, Titus IV, 38
Heston, Titus IV, 92
Heston, Titus IV, 822
Heston, Uphemia IV, 92
Heston, Uphimea IV, 38
Heston, Vallaise IV, 721
Heston, William II, 961
Heston, William II, 1088
Heston, William IV, 92
Heston, William V, 71
Heston, William V, 177
Heston, William VI, 649
Heston, William VI, 748
Heston, Wm. II, 548
Heston, Wm. II, 1052
Heston, Zebulon IV, 38
Heston, Zebulon IV, 148
Heston, Zebulon IV, 221
Heston, Zebulon IV, 822
Heterick, Mary VI, 399
Heterick, Mary Cary VI, 395
Heterick, Robert VI, 395
Heterick, Robert VI, 399
Heterick, Sarah VI, 395
Heterick, Sarah VI, 399
Hetherington, Abigail II, 548
Hetherington, Pharaby IV, 221
Hetherington, Pheraba IV, 225
Hetzler, Mary V, 1001
Heulings, Abraham II, 231
Heulings, Ann II, 231
Heulings, Easter II, 231
Heulings, Easter II, 277
Heulings, Hester II, 231
Heulings, Hester II, 277
Heulings, Jacob II, 231
Heulings, Jacob II, 277
Heulings, Jonathan II, 231
Heulings, Mary Woodward II, 806
Heulings, William II, 231
Heulings, William II, 277
Heuser, Augustus III, 484
Heuser, Katharina III, 484
Heuser, Martha III, 484
Heuser, Mary III, 484
Heustes, Mary II, 231
Heustis, Aaron II, 231
Heustis, Aaron IV, 873
Heustis, Aholiab II, 231
Heustis, Ann II, 231
Heustis, Ann II, 255
Heustis, Bezaleel II, 231
Heustis, David III, 144
Heustis, Elizabeth IV, 637
Heustis, Hannah II, 231
Heustis, Joseph II, 231
Heustis, Mary II, 231
Heustis, Mary III, 144
Heustis, Mary Ann IV, 873
Heustis, Moses II, 231
Heustis, Moses Brendwith II, 23
Heustis, Robert III, 163
Heustis, Sarah II, 176
Heustis, Sarah II, 231
Hevens, Mary II, 78
Heverlo, Ella IV, 1165
Heverlo, Ella N. IV, 1165
Heverlo, Hattie IV, 1165
Heverlo, Hattie A. IV, 1165
Hew, Ann II, 444
Hew, John II, 444
Hewes, ??? III, 69
Hewes, Aaron II, 78
Hewes, Aaron II, 558
Hewes, Aaron II, 559
Hewes, Aaron VI, 513
Hewes, Aaron VI, 725
Hewes, Aaron VI, 748
Hewes, Aaron, Jr. VI, 183
Hewes, Aaron, Jr. VI, 748
Hewes, Abigail II, 379
Hewes, Abraham VI, 587
Hewes, Abram VI, 513
Hewes, Abram VI, 535
Hewes, Abram VI, 748
Hewes, Adrienne Gillingham VI, 748
Hewes, Alan Marple III, 175
Hewes, Albert M. II, 150
Hewes, Alena VI, 679
Hewes, Alice II, 379
Hewes, Amey II, 559
Hewes, Ann II, 78
Hewes, Anna Margaret II, 150
Hewes, Anna Margaret II, 151
Hewes, Archabel II, 32
Hewes, Bartholomew III, 130
Hewes, Benjamin II, 78
Hewes, Benjamin VI, 748
Hewes, C. III, 130
Hewes, Caleb II, 379
Hewes, Caleb II, 558
Hewes, Caroline S. II, 148
Hewes, Caroline S. II, 150
Hewes, Caroline S. II, 151
Hewes, Celia III, 175
Hewes, Chas. C. III, 175
Hewes, Christiana VI, 748
Hewes, Constantine VI, 513
Hewes, Daniel II, 379
Hewes, David VI, 513
Hewes, Deborah II, 78
Hewes, Deborah VI, 748
Hewes, Deborah VI, 781
Hewes, Deborah VI, 783
Hewes, Dorothea Murray VI, 74
Hewes, Edith IV, 637
Hewes, Edw. III, 130
Hewes, Edw. III, 163
Hewes, Edward II, 78
Hewes, Edward II, 558
Hewes, Eliz. R. III, 175
Hewes, Eliza VI, 748
Hewes, Elizabeth II, 31
Hewes, Elizabeth II, 78
Hewes, Elizabeth II, 80
Hewes, Elizabeth II, 113
Hewes, Elizabeth II, 127
Hewes, Elizabeth II, 133
Hewes, Elizabeth II, 150

Hewes, Elizabeth II, 151
Hewes, Elizabeth IV, 17
Hewes, Elizabeth IV, 92
Hewes, Elizabeth VI, 663
Hewes, Elizabeth VI, 748
Hewes, Elizabeth A. II, 150
Hewes, Elizabeth A. M. II, 148
Hewes, Elizabeth Hughes VI, 513
Hewes, Elizabeth M. II, 133
Hewes, Ellis IV, 637
Hewes, Emma III, 175
Hewes, Ezekiah II, 31
Hewes, Ezekiah II, 78
Hewes, Ezekiah II, 113
Hewes, Ezekiah II, 127
Hewes, George Chalkley Gillingham VI, 748
Hewes, Gideon IV, 637
Hewes, Hannah II, 32
Hewes, Hannah II, 78
Hewes, Hannah II, 119
Hewes, Hannah II, 123
Hewes, Hezekiah II, 78
Hewes, Hezekiah II, 119
Hewes, Howard II, 133
Hewes, Howard II, 151
Hewes, Isaiah III, 175
Hewes, Isaiah B. VI, 748
Hewes, Jacob II, 558
Hewes, James II, 78
Hewes, James II, 80
Hewes, James II, 85
Hewes, James VI, 513
Hewes, James VI, 535
Hewes, James VI, 587
Hewes, James A. VI, 748
Hewes, James, Jr. II, 78
Hewes, Jane II, 31
Hewes, Jane II, 32
Hewes, Jane II, 51
Hewes, Jane II, 78
Hewes, Jane II, 85
Hewes, Jane II, 127
Hewes, Jane II, 379
Hewes, Jemima II, 379
Hewes, Jemimah II, 78
Hewes, Jemimah II, 558
Hewes, Jemimah II, 609
Hewes, John II, 32
Hewes, John II, 78
Hewes, John II, 119
Hewes, John II, 123
Hewes, John II, 558
Hewes, John VI, 748
Hewes, John G. II, 747
Hewes, John Peter III, 175
Hewes, Jonathan II, 78
Hewes, Joseph II, 78
Hewes, Josiah II, 379
Hewes, Kennett VI, 649
Hewes, Lidya II, 78
Hewes, Lydia VI, 495
Hewes, Lydia VI, 513
Hewes, Lydia VI, 587
Hewes, Lydia E. VI, 649
Hewes, Lydia E. VI, 679
Hewes, Lydia E. VI, 681
Hewes, Margaret VI, 748
Hewes, Marion III, 175
Hewes, Martha II, 78
Hewes, Martha R. VI, 748
Hewes, Mary II, 32
Hewes, Mary II, 78
Hewes, Mary II, 83
Hewes, Mary II, 119
Hewes, Mary II, 123
Hewes, Mary II, 158
Hewes, Mary II, 559
Hewes, Mary II, 708
Hewes, Mary VI, 513
Hewes, Mary VI, 535
Hewes, Mary VI, 748
Hewes, Mary Ann II, 747
Hewes, Mary Ann Copeland VI, 748
Hewes, Mary H. II, 133
Hewes, Mary Hewes II, 150
Hewes, Mary M. II, 150
Hewes, Mary M. VI, 748
Hewes, Mary Rowley II, 150
Hewes, Mathias VI, 649
Hewes, Mathias VI, 676
Hewes, Mathias VI, 679
Hewes, Matthew VI, 513
Hewes, Mildred M. III, 175
Hewes, Moses II, 379
Hewes, Moses II, 558
Hewes, Moses II, 609
Hewes, Nancy VI, 748
Hewes, Rachel II, 78
Hewes, Rachel VI, 513
Hewes, Rachel VI, 535
Hewes, Rachel VI, 587
Hewes, Rachel VI, 748
Hewes, Rachel VI, 779
Hewes, Reb. III, 130
Hewes, Reb. III, 163
Hewes, Rebecca II, 32
Hewes, Rebecca II, 78
Hewes, Rebecca II, 559
Hewes, Rebecca II, 666
Hewes, Rebecca II, 667
Hewes, Rebecca II, 809
Hewes, Rebecca II, 822
Hewes, Rebecca IV, 637
Hewes, Rebecca C. III, 130
Hewes, Rebecca C. III, 163
Hewes, Rebecca O. III, 130
Hewes, Rogers II, 444
Hewes, Ruth II, 78
Hewes, Ruth VI, 513
Hewes, Ruth VI, 587
Hewes, Ruth VI, 649
Hewes, Ruth VI, 676
Hewes, Ruth VI, 679
Hewes, Ruth A. VI, 649
Hewes, Samuel II, 32
Hewes, Samuel II, 78
Hewes, Samuel II, 119
Hewes, Samuel II, 123
Hewes, Samuel II, 379
Hewes, Samuel II, 558
Hewes, Sarah II, 78
Hewes, Sarah II, 90
Hewes, Sarah II, 559
Hewes, Sarah III, 175
Hewes, Sarah VI, 513
Hewes, Sarah VI, 748
Hewes, Sarah Ann VI, 748
Hewes, Sarah Powers II, 747
Hewes, Sarah Powers VI, 748
Hewes, Susan V, 681
Hewes, Susannah II, 77
Hewes, Susannah II, 78
Hewes, Tabitha II, 78
Hewes, Thomas II, 31
Hewes, Thomas II, 32
Hewes, Thomas II, 78
Hewes, Thomas II, 133
Hewes, Thomas II, 148
Hewes, Thomas II, 150
Hewes, Thomas II, 151
Hewes, Thomas II, 558
Hewes, Thomas VI, 513
Hewes, Thomas Howard II, 150
Hewes, Ursula VI, 513
Hewes, Ursula VI, 535
Hewes, Ursula VI, 587
Hewes, Wd. Elizabeth VI, 513
Hewes, Wilmer VI, 679
Hewes, Wm. Hastings VI, 748
Hewes, Wm. J. VI, 748
Hewet, Lydia I, 241
Hewet, Lydia I, 248
Hewett, George III, 163
Hewett, H. Agnes II, 782
Hewett, Isabella III, 163
Hewett, Joseph H. I, 241
Hewett, Lydia I, 241
Hewett, Susanna IV, 721
Hewhall, Eliz. H. III, 25
Hewhall, Joseph P. III, 25
Hewit, Abel IV, 29
Hewit, Abel IV, 38
Hewit, Ann IV, 38
Hewit, Ann IV, 84
Hewit, Daniel IV, 721
Hewit, Jane IV, 721
Hewit, John II, 445
Hewit, John IV, 721
Hewit, Jonathan IV, 38
Hewit, Jonathan IV, 84
Hewit, Martha IV, 721
Hewit, Mary IV, 721
Hewit, Mary Jane IV, 677
Hewit, Mary Jane IV, 721
Hewit, Rachel IV, 29
Hewit, Rachel IV, 38
Hewit, Rachel IV, 39
Hewit, Rebecca IV, 38
Hewit, Ruth IV, 84
Hewit, Ruth IV, 92
Hewit, Sarah IV, 39
Hewit, Sarah IV, 92
Hewit, Sarah IV, 721
Hewit, William T. IV, 721
Hewitt, Abel IV, 38
Hewitt, Abel IV, 92
Hewitt, Abel IV, 121
Hewitt, Abel IV, 127
Hewitt, Abel IV, 611
Hewitt, Abel IV, 1367
Hewitt, Able IV, 92
Hewitt, Adaline VI, 930
Hewitt, Albert Hewitt IV, 955
Hewitt, Allen IV, 955
Hewitt, Allen T. IV, 955
Hewitt, Alma IV, 955
Hewitt, Almira IV, 955
Hewitt, Amos IV, 92
Hewitt, Amos IV, 127
Hewitt, Ann IV, 21
Hewitt, Ann IV, 38
Hewitt, Ann IV, 39
Hewitt, Ann IV, 76
Hewitt, Ann IV, 92
Hewitt, Ann IV, 121
Hewitt, Ann IV, 127
Hewitt, Ann IV, 611
Hewitt, Ann IV, 754
Hewitt, Ann IV, 927
Hewitt, Ann P. VI, 920
Hewitt, Anna II, 733
Hewitt, Anna II, 746
Hewitt, Anna IV, 121
Hewitt, Anna IV, 127
Hewitt, Anna IV, 679
Hewitt, Anne IV, 679
Hewitt, Benjamin VI, 932
Hewitt, Bessie N. IV, 1320
Hewitt, Charles IV, 38
Hewitt, Charles IV, 92
Hewitt, Charles IV, 127
Hewitt, Charlotte E. VI, 927
Hewitt, Cynthiann IV, 127
Hewitt, Cyrus IV, 92
Hewitt, Cyrus IV, 127
Hewitt, Daniel IV, 721
Hewitt, David IV, 127
Hewitt, David IV, 721
Hewitt, David Porter IV, 127
Hewitt, Edmond VI, 932
Hewitt, Edward J. VI, 924
Hewitt, Eliza VI, 932
Hewitt, Elizabeth IV, 38
Hewitt, Elizabeth IV, 121
Hewitt, Elizabeth IV, 127
Hewitt, Elizabeth IV, 955
Hewitt, Elizabeth VI, 932
Hewitt, Elizal VI, 900
Hewitt, Elmira IV, 124
Hewitt, Elmira IV, 127
Hewitt, Elmira VI, 994
Hewitt, Fanny VI, 1009
Hewitt, Frances VI, 911
Hewitt, Frances VI, 918
Hewitt, Frances D. VI, 824
Hewitt, George III, 163
Hewitt, George VI, 932
Hewitt, Hannah VI, 932
Hewitt, Haram IV, 955
Hewitt, Henrietta H. VI, 924
Hewitt, Henry H. VI, 824
Hewitt, Henry H. VI, 919
Hewitt, Isaac VI, 932
Hewitt, Isabella III, 91
Hewitt, Isabella III, 163
Hewitt, Israel IV, 127
Hewitt, James IV, 721
Hewitt, James IV, 955
Hewitt, James Creigton IV, 955
Hewitt, James, Jr. IV, 955
Hewitt, Jane IV, 721
Hewitt, Jane VI, 924
Hewitt, Jane VI, 935
Hewitt, Jemima VI, 824
Hewitt, Jesse IV, 127
Hewitt, John IV, 127
Hewitt, John IV, 721
Hewitt, John VI, 802
Hewitt, John VI, 824
Hewitt, John VI, 847
Hewitt, John VI, 892
Hewitt, John VI, 924
Hewitt, John VI, 930
Hewitt, John VI, 935
Hewitt, John VI, 1022
Hewitt, Jonathan IV, 38
Hewitt, Jonathan IV, 71
Hewitt, Jonathan IV, 76
Hewitt, Jonathan IV, 92
Hewitt, Jonathan IV, 121
Hewitt, Jonathan IV, 127
Hewitt, Jonathan IV, 754
Hewitt, Jonathan, Jr. IV, 127
Hewitt, Joseph IV, 38
Hewitt, Joseph IV, 85
Hewitt, Joseph IV, 92
Hewitt, Joseph IV, 124
Hewitt, Joseph IV, 127
Hewitt, Joseph IV, 1367
Hewitt, Joseph IV, 1373
Hewitt, Joseph D. IV, 1367
Hewitt, Joseph T. IV, 955
Hewitt, Joseph, Jr. IV, 127
Hewitt, Julian VI, 937
Hewitt, Juliet VI, 927
Hewitt, Juliet VI, 932
Hewitt, Laura IV, 822
Hewitt, Laura M. IV, 721
Hewitt, Lenna VI, 1022
Hewitt, Margaret IV, 1367
Hewitt, Margaret IV, 1373
Hewitt, Margaret K. IV, 1367
Hewitt, Martha IV, 92
Hewitt, Martha IV, 127
Hewitt, Martha IV, 721
Hewitt, Martha IV, 955
Hewitt, Martha IV, 1367
Hewitt, Mary IV, 127
Hewitt, Mary IV, 133
Hewitt, Mary IV, 721
Hewitt, Mary VI, 869
Hewitt, Mary VI, 933
Hewitt, Mary Almyra IV, 955
Hewitt, Mary Jane IV, 721
Hewitt, Matilda VI, 1009
Hewitt, Milly VI, 935
Hewitt, Milton IV, 127
Hewitt, Nancy VI, 911
Hewitt, Nancy VI, 932
Hewitt, Nancy VI, 1002
Hewitt, Newton IV, 955
Hewitt, Ollie M. IV, 1254
Hewitt, Patsy VI, 918
Hewitt, Polly VI, 892
Hewitt, Polly VI, 930
Hewitt, Rachel IV, 38
Hewitt, Rachel IV, 39
Hewitt, Rachel IV, 92
Hewitt, Rachel IV, 121
Hewitt, Rachel IV, 127
Hewitt, Rachel IV, 611
Hewitt, Rachel IV, 1367
Hewitt, Rebecca IV, 38
Hewitt, Rebecca IV, 92
Hewitt, Rebecca IV, 127
Hewitt, Rebecca C. VI, 932
Hewitt, Richard IV, 955
Hewitt, Richard VI, 921
Hewitt, Richard N. VI, 824
Hewitt, Robert IV, 955
Hewitt, Robert VI, 935
Hewitt, Ruth IV, 85
Hewitt, Ruth IV, 92
Hewitt, Ruth IV, 124
Hewitt, Ruth IV, 127
Hewitt, Sally VI, 892
Hewitt, Sally VI, 930
Hewitt, Samuel IV, 721
Hewitt, Sarah IV, 38
Hewitt, Sarah IV, 39
Hewitt, Sarah IV, 76
Hewitt, Sarah IV, 92
Hewitt, Sarah IV, 127
Hewitt, Sarah IV, 721
Hewitt, Sarah VI, 824
Hewitt, Sarah A. IV, 121
Hewitt, Sarah A. IV, 127
Hewitt, Spotswood VI, 932
Hewitt, Stephen VI, 920
Hewitt, Stephen VI, 932
Hewitt, Stephen VI, 933
Hewitt, Susanna IV, 92
Hewitt, Susanna IV, 721
Hewitt, Susannah IV, 721
Hewitt, Susannah IV, 754
Hewitt, Susannah L. IV, 1367
Hewitt, Thirza IV, 721
Hewitt, Thomas IV, 955
Hewitt, Thomas VI, 911
Hewitt, Thomas VI, 918
Hewitt, Thomas VI, 1009
Hewitt, Thomas Y. IV, 955
Hewitt, W. C. VI, 947
Hewitt, W. C. VI, 972
Hewitt, Warner VI, 1002
Hewitt, Warren VI, 900
Hewitt, William IV, 721
Hewitt, William VI, 1002
Hewitt, William H. VI, 824
Hewitt, William T. IV, 721
Hewitt, Wilson C. N. VI, 888
Hewitt, Wm. F. IV, 721
Hewitt, Wm. F. IV, 955
Hewitt, Worner VI, 892
Hewlett, Amelia III, 403
Hewlett, Amelia III, 404
Hewlett, Amelia III, 416
Hewlett, Ann III, 403
Hewlett, Ann III, 404
Hewlett, Ann III, 416
Hewlett, Anne III, 416
Hewlett, Daniel III, 416
Hewlett, Divine III, 404
Hewlett, Divine III, 416
Hewlett, Eliz. III, 487
Hewlett, Elizabeth III, 416
Hewlett, Elizabeth III, 422
Hewlett, Elizabeth III, 472
Hewlett, Emery III, 394
Hewlett, Emery III, 416
Hewlett, Frances III, 505
Hewlett, Frances III, 507
Hewlett, Fred IV, 822
Hewlett, George III, 416
Hewlett, George III, 472
Hewlett, Grace III, 416
Hewlett, Hannah III, 416
Hewlett, Hannah III, 484
Hewlett, Hannah III, 487
Hewlett, James III, 416
Hewlett, James III, 440
Hewlett, Jane III, 416
Hewlett, John III, 416
Hewlett, John III, 484
Hewlett, Lewis III, 416
Hewlett, Linneus IV, 822
Hewlett, Malva L. IV, 822
Hewlett, Margaret III, 416
Hewlett, Martha III, 404
Hewlett, Martha III, 416
Hewlett, Mary III, 394
Hewlett, Mary III, 416
Hewlett, Mary E. III, 416
Hewlett, Mary E. III, 440
Hewlett, Melva W. IV, 822
Hewlett, Melva W. IV, 852
Hewlett, Molly III, 416
Hewlett, Phebe III, 422
Hewlett, Phebe III, 487
Hewlett, Ruth III, 416
Hewlett, Ruth III, 474
Hewlett, Samuel III, 416
Hewlett, Samuel III, 474
Hewlett, Sarah III, 416
Hewlett, Sarah III, 484
Hewlett, Sina IV, 822
Hewlett, Townsend III, 416
Hewlett, Wm. M. III, 403
Hewlett, Wm. M. III, 404
Hewlett, Wm. Moyles III, 416
Hewling, Lydia S. IV, 633
Hewlings, Abraham II, 176
Hewlings, Abraham II, 231
Hewlings, Abraham II, 548
Hewlings, Abram II, 176
Hewlings, Ann II, 231
Hewlings, Ann II, 291
Hewlings, Caleb II, 548
Hewlings, Dorothy II, 219
Hewlings, Easter II, 231
Hewlings, Elizabeth II, 231
Hewlings, Elizabeth II, 272
Hewlings, Elizabeth V, 26
Hewlings, Elizabeth V, 30
Hewlings, Elizabeth V, 72
Hewlings, Esther II, 176
Hewlings, Esther II, 482
Hewlings, Esther II, 548
Hewlings, Franklin L. IV, 221
Hewlings, Hannah II, 548
Hewlings, Hester II, 176
Hewlings, Hester II, 231
Hewlings, Isaac Carmalt II, 548
Hewlings, Israel II, 231
Hewlings, Jacob II, 231
Hewlings, John II, 231
Hewlings, Jonathan II, 231
Hewlings, Jonathan II, 786
Hewlings, Joseph II, 231
Hewlings, Keturah II, 746
Hewlings, Lydia S. IV, 221
Hewlings, Lydia S. IV, 633
Hewlings, Mary II, 176
Hewlings, Mary II, 283
Hewlings, Mary II, 291
Hewlings, Ruth Anna IV, 221
Hewlings, Susanna II, 548
Hewlings, William II, 176
Hewlings, William II, 219
Hewlings, William II, 231
Hewlings, William, Jr. II, 231
Hews, Aaron II, 78
Hews, Aaron II, 234
Hews, Abram VI, 513
Hews, Albert M. II, 133
Hews, Ann I, 308
Hews, Anna Margaret II, 133
Hews, Anna Margaret II, 151
Hews, Benjamin II, 31
Hews, Caroline Senat II, 133
Hews, Charles Pennel II, 747
Hews, Charles Pennell II, 747
Hews, Clemmency I, 308

Hews, David II, 468
Hews, David II, 558
Hews, Dorothy II, 468
Hews, Dorothy II, 558
Hews, Edith II, 31
Hews, Edward II, 31
Hews, Edward II, 49
Hews, Edward II, 78
Hews, Elihu II, 31
Hews, Elizabeth II, 31
Hews, Elizabeth II, 32
Hews, Elizabeth II, 131
Hews, Elizabeth II, 133
Hews, Elizabeth M. II, 133
Hews, Ellis IV, 725
Hews, Ezekiah II, 31
Hews, Ezekiah II, 78
Hews, Ezekiah II, 133
Hews, Ezhiah II, 133
Hews, Frances C. V, 1001
Hews, Hannah II, 31
Hews, Hannah II, 49
Hews, Hannah II, 78
Hews, Hannah II, 91
Hews, Hannah II, 105
Hews, Hezekiah II, 78
Hews, Hezekiah II, 1003
Hews, Hiram II, 31
Hews, Howard II, 133
Hews, Howard II, 151
Hews, Isaac II, 31
Hews, Jacob II, 559
Hews, James II, 32
Hews, James, Jr. II, 78
Hews, Jane II, 31
Hews, Jane II, 78
Hews, Jane II, 97
Hews, Jane II, 133
Hews, Jane II, 234
Hews, Jemimah II, 78
Hews, John II, 78
Hews, John II, 91
Hews, John G. II, 747
Hews, Lidya II, 78
Hews, Mary II, 78
Hews, Mary II, 559
Hews, Mary II, 747
Hews, Mary H. II, 133
Hews, Mary Miller II, 133
Hews, Rachel II, 54
Hews, Rachel II, 78
Hews, Samuel II, 78
Hews, Samuel II, 747
Hews, Sarah I, 308
Hews, Sarah I, 320
Hews, Sarah II, 78
Hews, Sarah A. V, 1001
Hews, Sarah Ann II, 747
Hews, Tabitha II, 31
Hews, Tabitha II, 78
Hews, Tabitha II, 91
Hews, Thomas II, 31
Hews, Thomas II, 78
Hews, Thomas II, 97
Hews, Thomas II, 133
Hews, Thos. Howard II, 133
Hews, Wm. II, 558
Hewson, Abigail III, 100
Hewson, Abigail III, 163
Hewson, Hannah III, 163
Hewson, Margaret III, 163
Hewstis, ??? III, 175
Hewstis, Carpenter III, 163
Hewstis, David III, 163
Hewstis, Elizabeth III, 163
Hewstis, Elizabeth III, 237
Hewstis, James III, 163
Hewstis, Jonathan III, 45
Hewstis, Jonathan III, 163
Hewstis, Mary III, 45
Hewstis, Mary III, 163
Hewstis, Robert III, 163
Hewstis, Robert III, 237
Hewston, Margaret II, 234
Hewston, Mary VI, 824
Hewston, Peter VI, 824
Hewzey, Alexander W. II, 291
Hewzey, Samuel C. II, 291
Hexton, Maria IV, 476
Hexton, Maria IV, 493
Hey, Margaret O. IV, 1319
Heyburn, Gheretein Y. VI, 749
Heyd, Martha S. T. II, 1074
Heyderpool, Henry VI, 932
Heyderpool, Polly VI, 932
Heydorn, Ida Mabel IV, 1320
Heyl, Jane C. II, 849
Heyl, Jane C. II, 875
Heyl, John B. II, 849
Heyl, John B. II, 875
Heyl, Mary Jackson II, 849
Heyl, Mary Jackson II, 875
Heyl, Wm. Esher II, 849
Heyl, Wm. Esher II, 875
Heyman, Louisa IV, 1132
Heyman, Louise IV, 1138
Heyton, Elizabeth I, 1141
Heytower, Rachel I, 1121
Heyward, Mary II, 796
Heyward, Wd. Hannah II, 796
Heyward, Wm. II, 796
Heywood, Annie III, 160
Heywood, Elizabeth II, 513
Heywood, Elizabeth II, 546
Heywood, John II, 513
Hiat, Edith IV, 408
Hiat, George I, 399
Hiat, Isaac V, 72
Hiat, Jehu IV, 408
Hiat, Jehu IV, 450
Hiat, Joel I, 545
Hiat, Joel I, 579
Hiat, John I, 398
Hiat, John I, 399
Hiat, Joseph I, 815
Hiat, Lydia I, 394
Hiat, Margaret V, 501
Hiat, Martha I, 394
Hiat, Martha IV, 1165
Hiat, Mary I, 394
Hiat, Mary I, 579
Hiat, Mary Ann V, 72
Hiat, Mattie IV, 1165
Hiat, Rebecca I, 579
Hiat, Ruthanna IV, 221
Hiat, Sarah I, 394
Hiat, Susanna I, 399
Hiat, Susannah W. IV, 1281
Hiat, Tamer IV, 408
Hiat, Tamer IV, 450
Hiat, William I, 815
Hiat, William VI, 399
Hiatt, ??? IV, 1085
Hiatt, Aaron I, 956
Hiatt, Aaron I, 1004
Hiatt, Aaron V, 245
Hiatt, Aaron V, 304
Hiatt, Aaron Lindley I, 1005
Hiatt, Aaron Lindley V, 394
Hiatt, Abbigail I, 815
Hiatt, Abigail I, 499
Hiatt, Abigail I, 855
Hiatt, Abigail I, 883
Hiatt, Abigail I, 899
Hiatt, Abigail I, 1009
Hiatt, Ablenaugh I, 815
Hiatt, Abner I, 545
Hiatt, Abner I, 582
Hiatt, Abner V, 304
Hiatt, Abner V, 394
Hiatt, Absalom I, 986
Hiatt, Absalom V, 245
Hiatt, Absalom V, 304
Hiatt, Absolem I, 956
Hiatt, Absolom I, 986
Hiatt, Absolom I, 1004
Hiatt, Absolom I, 1009
Hiatt, Achsah I, 499
Hiatt, Achsah I, 545
Hiatt, Achsah I, 546
Hiatt, Achsah I, 582
Hiatt, Achsah I, 679
Hiatt, Albanah I, 782
Hiatt, Albert V, 72
Hiatt, Albert P. V, 72
Hiatt, Albert P. V, 394
Hiatt, Alce I, 815
Hiatt, Alice I, 815
Hiatt, Alice V, 394
Hiatt, Alice V, 682
Hiatt, Alice V, 692
Hiatt, Alice V, 900
Hiatt, Alice VI, 399
Hiatt, Alice VI, 415
Hiatt, Alice H. V, 394
Hiatt, Alice L. V, 682
Hiatt, Allen I, 500
Hiatt, Allen I, 545
Hiatt, Allen I, 883
Hiatt, Allen V, 72
Hiatt, Allen V, 500
Hiatt, Allen V, 575
Hiatt, Allis V, 394
Hiatt, Almeda IV, 1281
Hiatt, Alonzo V, 575
Hiatt, Alonzo A. V, 575
Hiatt, Amaziah I, 1005
Hiatt, Amaziah V, 245
Hiatt, Amaziah V, 298
Hiatt, Amaziah V, 304
Hiatt, Amer I, 499
Hiatt, Amer I, 546
Hiatt, Ameriah I, 815
Hiatt, Amos I, 499
Hiatt, Amos I, 545
Hiatt, Amos I, 963
Hiatt, Amos I, 1005
Hiatt, Amos IV, 408
Hiatt, Amos IV, 583
Hiatt, Amos IV, 1100
Hiatt, Amos IV, 1101
Hiatt, Amos V, 72
Hiatt, Amos V, 303
Hiatt, Amos V, 304
Hiatt, Amos V, 335
Hiatt, Amos V, 336
Hiatt, Amos V, 394
Hiatt, Amos V, 396
Hiatt, Amos V, 500
Hiatt, Amos C. V, 72
Hiatt, Amos C. V, 501
Hiatt, Amos G. V, 394
Hiatt, Amos J. V, 336
Hiatt, Amos J. V, 394
Hiatt, Amos J. V, 682
Hiatt, Angeline V, 682
Hiatt, Angie V, 501
Hiatt, Ann I, 499
Hiatt, Ann I, 500
Hiatt, Ann I, 804
Hiatt, Ann I, 815
Hiatt, Ann I, 956
Hiatt, Ann I, 1004
Hiatt, Ann I, 1009
Hiatt, Ann IV, 408
Hiatt, Ann IV, 583
Hiatt, Ann V, 72
Hiatt, Ann V, 178
Hiatt, Ann V, 245
Hiatt, Ann V, 304
Hiatt, Ann V, 327
Hiatt, Ann V, 335
Hiatt, Ann V, 336
Hiatt, Ann V, 394
Hiatt, Ann V, 477
Hiatt, Ann V, 500
Hiatt, Ann V, 523
Hiatt, Ann V, 540
Hiatt, Anna I, 499
Hiatt, Anna I, 532
Hiatt, Anna I, 545
Hiatt, Anna I, 546
Hiatt, Anna I, 579
Hiatt, Anna I, 582
Hiatt, Anna I, 815
Hiatt, Anna I, 1005
Hiatt, Anna IV, 408
Hiatt, Anna IV, 583
Hiatt, Anna IV, 1062
Hiatt, Anna IV, 1281
Hiatt, Anna V, 72
Hiatt, Anna V, 304
Hiatt, Anna V, 394
Hiatt, Anna V, 441
Hiatt, Anna V, 500
Hiatt, Anna B. I, 782
Hiatt, Anna Jane V, 336
Hiatt, Anna Jane V, 682
Hiatt, Anna Jean V, 682
Hiatt, Anna M. II, 721
Hiatt, Anna Rachel V, 245
Hiatt, Anna Rachel V, 500
Hiatt, Anne I, 546
Hiatt, Anne IV, 408
Hiatt, Anne IV, 583
Hiatt, Anne V, 178
Hiatt, Anne V, 245
Hiatt, Anne V, 368
Hiatt, Anne Jean V, 682
Hiatt, Annie J. V, 682
Hiatt, Ansalem I, 587
Hiatt, Ansalem I, 588
Hiatt, Ansalom I, 529
Hiatt, Ansalom I, 545
Hiatt, Anslem I, 594
Hiatt, Anslom I, 815
Hiatt, Armelia V, 178
Hiatt, Asaph I, 499
Hiatt, Asaph V, 245
Hiatt, Asaph V, 250
Hiatt, Asaph V, 368
Hiatt, Asaph V, 393
Hiatt, Asaph V, 394
Hiatt, Asaph V, 432
Hiatt, Asaph Hiatt V, 72
Hiatt, Ascenith V, 72
Hiatt, Asenath I, 815
Hiatt, Asenath I, 832
Hiatt, Asenath IV, 1101
Hiatt, Asenath IV, 1108
Hiatt, Asenath V, 178
Hiatt, Asenath C. I, 782
Hiatt, Asenath Ellen V, 245
Hiatt, Asenath P. IV, 1100
Hiatt, Aseneth I, 808
Hiatt, Aseneth I, 815
Hiatt, Asher I, 499
Hiatt, Asher I, 500
Hiatt, Asher I, 545
Hiatt, Asher I, 555
Hiatt, Asher I, 1005
Hiatt, Asher V, 245
Hiatt, Asher V, 393
Hiatt, Asher V, 394
Hiatt, Azariah I, 1005
Hiatt, Azariah V, 304
Hiatt, Beajah I, 546
Hiatt, Benajah I, 499
Hiatt, Benajah I, 546
Hiatt, Benajah V, 178
Hiatt, Benjamin I, 963
Hiatt, Benjamin I, 970
Hiatt, Benjamin I, 1005
Hiatt, Benjamin I, 1009
Hiatt, Benjamin V, 245
Hiatt, Benjamin V, 304
Hiatt, Benjamin V, 305
Hiatt, Benjamin V, 335
Hiatt, Benjamin K. I, 762
Hiatt, Benjamin K. I, 883
Hiatt, Benjamin Keys I, 975
Hiatt, Benjamin, Jr. V, 304
Hiatt, Bennajah I, 500
Hiatt, Bennajah I, 545
Hiatt, Bennajah I, 581
Hiatt, Bertha M. V, 682
Hiatt, Bertha May V, 336
Hiatt, Bertha May V, 682
Hiatt, Bessie V, 682
Hiatt, Bessie S. V, 682
Hiatt, Betsy IV, 1281
Hiatt, Betsy Ann V, 625
Hiatt, Bladen I, 544
Hiatt, Burrett V, 682
Hiatt, Burritt V, 682
Hiatt, Burritt M. V, 703
Hiatt, Caleb I, 986
Hiatt, Caleb V, 393
Hiatt, Caleb V, 394
Hiatt, Caroline V, 336
Hiatt, Caroline H. V, 336
Hiatt, Catharine I, 814
Hiatt, Catharine I, 815
Hiatt, Catharine I, 986
Hiatt, Catharine I, 1009
Hiatt, Catharine V, 304
Hiatt, Catherine I, 986
Hiatt, Catherine V, 394
Hiatt, Catherine VI, 384
Hiatt, Catherine VI, 399
Hiatt, Charity I, 500
Hiatt, Charity I, 544
Hiatt, Charity I, 545
Hiatt, Charity I, 546
Hiatt, Charity I, 581
Hiatt, Charity I, 815
Hiatt, Charity V, 575
Hiatt, Charity V, 580
Hiatt, Charles I, 855
Hiatt, Charles I, 975
Hiatt, Charles I, 986
Hiatt, Charles V, 245
Hiatt, Charles V, 501
Hiatt, Charles C. V, 682
Hiatt, Charles Everett V, 682
Hiatt, Chas. V, 682
Hiatt, Christie V, 304
Hiatt, Christine V, 245
Hiatt, Christine V, 299
Hiatt, Christopher I, 394
Hiatt, Christopher I, 499
Hiatt, Christopher I, 500
Hiatt, Christopher I, 525
Hiatt, Christopher I, 544
Hiatt, Christopher I, 545
Hiatt, Christopher I, 562
Hiatt, Christopher I, 847
Hiatt, Christopher I, 963
Hiatt, Christopher I, 1005
Hiatt, Christopher I, 1009
Hiatt, Christopher I, 1010
Hiatt, Christopher V, 72
Hiatt, Christopher V, 245
Hiatt, Christopher V, 246
Hiatt, Christopher V, 303
Hiatt, Christopher V, 368
Hiatt, Christopher V, 369
Hiatt, Christopher V, 394
Hiatt, Christopher V, 433
Hiatt, Christopher V, 440
Hiatt, Christopher V, 446
Hiatt, Christopher C. V, 394
Hiatt, Christopher, Sr. I, 499
Hiatt, Clarissa V, 270
Hiatt, Clarkson V, 72
Hiatt, Clarkson V, 74
Hiatt, Clarkson V, 304
Hiatt, Clarkson V, 380
Hiatt, Clarkson V, 394
Hiatt, Collumbus V, 394
Hiatt, Columbus V, 394
Hiatt, Cornelia I, 924
Hiatt, Cornelius V, 245
Hiatt, Curtis V, 394
Hiatt, Curtis V, 625
Hiatt, Cuthbert I, 594
Hiatt, Cuthbert I, 782
Hiatt, Cuthbert I, 815
Hiatt, Cuthbert I, 816
Hiatt, Daniel V, 72
Hiatt, Daniel V, 335
Hiatt, Daniel V, 500
Hiatt, Daniel Matthews VI, 504
Hiatt, Daniel W. V, 842
Hiatt, David I, 499
Hiatt, David I, 855
Hiatt, David I, 874
Hiatt, David I, 883
Hiatt, David I, 956
Hiatt, David I, 1004
Hiatt, David V, 245
Hiatt, David V, 304
Hiatt, David Ballard I, 545
Hiatt, Deborah IV, 1100
Hiatt, Deborah IV, 1101
Hiatt, Deborah V, 246
Hiatt, Deborah V, 336
Hiatt, Delilah V, 246
Hiatt, Della V, 682
Hiatt, Dempsey IV, 583
Hiatt, Dempsey IV, 1062
Hiatt, Dempsey IV, 1100
Hiatt, Demsey IV, 408
Hiatt, Demsey IV, 1062
Hiatt, Donald L. V, 682
Hiatt, Dorothy V, 682
Hiatt, Duella V, 394
Hiatt, Duella V, 682
Hiatt, Eber V, 500
Hiatt, Eddie V, 394
Hiatt, Edeth I, 782
Hiatt, Edith I, 815
Hiatt, Edith I, 830
Hiatt, Edith IV, 390
Hiatt, Edith IV, 408
Hiatt, Edmon I, 956
Hiatt, Edwin V, 72
Hiatt, Edwin J. V, 394
Hiatt, Edwin J. V, 682
Hiatt, Effie I, 357
Hiatt, Ele I, 883
Hiatt, Eleazar I, 499
Hiatt, Eleazar I, 500
Hiatt, Eleazar I, 545
Hiatt, Eleazar I, 546
Hiatt, Eleazar V, 335
Hiatt, Eleazar V, 358
Hiatt, Eleazar V, 500
Hiatt, Eleazer V, 72
Hiatt, Eli I, 986
Hiatt, Eli IV, 1281
Hiatt, Eli V, 394
Hiatt, Eliazar I, 545
Hiatt, Eliazer V, 72
Hiatt, Elieb I, 1005
Hiatt, Eliet I, 963
Hiatt, Elihu V, 231
Hiatt, Elihu V, 245
Hiatt, Elihu V, 246
Hiatt, Elihu V, 466
Hiatt, Elihu V, 501
Hiatt, Elihue John Reuben V, 245
Hiatt, Elijah IV, 408
Hiatt, Elijah IV, 583
Hiatt, Elijah IV, 1062
Hiatt, Elijah IV, 1099
Hiatt, Elijah IV, 1100
Hiatt, Elijah IV, 1101
Hiatt, Elijah V, 335
Hiatt, Elijah V, 336
Hiatt, Elijah J. IV, 1100
Hiatt, Elijah J. IV, 1110
Hiatt, Elisha I, 499
Hiatt, Elisha IV, 408
Hiatt, Elisha IV, 583
Hiatt, Elisha IV, 1062
Hiatt, Elisha IV, 1101
Hiatt, Elisha V, 246
Hiatt, Elisha V, 335
Hiatt, Elisha V, 336
Hiatt, Eliza I, 499
Hiatt, Eliza V, 72
Hiatt, Eliza V, 500
Hiatt, Eliza Emily V, 1003
Hiatt, Elizabeth I, 499

att, Elizabeth I, 500
att, Elizabeth I, 544
att, Elizabeth I, 545
att, Elizabeth I, 546
att, Elizabeth I, 562
att, Elizabeth I, 581
att, Elizabeth I, 782
att, Elizabeth I, 815
att, Elizabeth I, 816
att, Elizabeth I, 818
att, Elizabeth I, 843
att, Elizabeth I, 855
att, Elizabeth I, 883
att, Elizabeth I, 890
att, Elizabeth I, 975
att, Elizabeth I, 1005
att, Elizabeth I, 1008
att, Elizabeth I, 1009
att, Elizabeth V, 219
att, Elizabeth V, 222
att, Elizabeth V, 245
att, Elizabeth V, 246
att, Elizabeth V, 336
att, Elizabeth V, 368
att, Elizabeth V, 394
att, Elizabeth V, 440
att, Elizabeth V, 500
att, Elizabeth V, 575
att, Elizabeth V, 580
att, Elizabeth V, 689
att, Elizabeth VI, 399
att, Elizabeth VI, 400
att, Elizabeth Ann V, 625
att, Ella V, 394
att, Ellen V, 394
att, Elliott IV, 1281
iatt, Elvinah V, 245
iatt, Elvira Ann V, 246
att, Elvira Ann V, 260
iatt, Elwood IV, 1101
iatt, Elwood V, 72
iatt, Elwood V, 304
att, Elwood V, 394
iatt, Elwood D. IV, 1101
iatt, Elwood D. IV, 1132
iatt, Emily I, 883
att, Emily A. I, 855
att, Emily A. V, 682
att, Emily Alace V, 682
att, Emily Alice V, 336
iatt, Emily Ann I, 874
iatt, Emily Ann I, 883
iatt, Emily Jean V, 682
iatt, Emlen V, 394
iatt, Emma V, 394
iatt, Enoch I, 986
iatt, Enoch IV, 1281
iatt, Enoch V, 245
iatt, Enoch V, 246
iatt, Enoch V, 304
iatt, Enos I, 500
iatt, Enos I, 544
iatt, Enos I, 545
att, Enos I, 782
iatt, Enos I, 815
iatt, Enos I, 986
iatt, Enos V, 246
iatt, Esther I, 499
iatt, Esther I, 500
iatt, Esther I, 539
iatt, Esther I, 545
iatt, Esther I, 555
iatt, Esther V, 246
iatt, Esther V, 446
iatt, Esther VI, 399
iatt, Esther VI, 459
iatt, Esther G. I, 499
iatt, Eunice IV, 1281
iatt, Eunice V, 246
iatt, Evan I, 500
iatt, Evan I, 544
iatt, Evan VI, 399
iatt, Evelyn V, 39
iatt, Evelyn V, 72
iatt, Evelyn V, 380
iatt, Evelyn V, 394
iatt, Eviline V, 379
iatt, Eviline V, 394
iatt, Ezekiel I, 815
iatt, Ezra IV, 1281
iatt, Flora V, 178
iatt, Florence E. V, 336
iatt, Florence E. V, 362
iatt, Francis V, 72
iatt, Francis M. V, 394
iatt, Francis T. V, 72
iatt, Francisco V, 394
iatt, Frank V, 178
iatt, Frank V, 394
iatt, Frederick I, 544
iatt, Geo. A. V, 682
Hiatt, Geo. J. IV, 851
Hiatt, George I, 343
Hiatt, George I, 499
Hiatt, George I, 500
Hiatt, George I, 544
Hiatt, George I, 545
Hiatt, George I, 546
Hiatt, George I, 572
Hiatt, George I, 815
Hiatt, George V, 368
Hiatt, George V, 682
Hiatt, George VI, 400
Hiatt, George VI, 504
Hiatt, George VI, 505
Hiatt, George A. V, 682
Hiatt, George C. I, 855
Hiatt, George J. IV, 822
Hiatt, George J. IV, 1101
Hiatt, George Richard V, 245
Hiatt, Georgiana V, 682
Hiatt, Georgiana V, 685
Hiatt, Georgiana B. V, 246
Hiatt, Georgianna V, 658
Hiatt, Georgianna V, 682
Hiatt, Georgianna B. V, 682
Hiatt, Gertrude V, 231
Hiatt, Gertrude V, 245
Hiatt, Gideon V, 178
Hiatt, Gideon V, 368
Hiatt, Gideon V, 500
Hiatt, Grace IV, 1100
Hiatt, Grace IV, 1101
Hiatt, Grace IV, 1115
Hiatt, Greenberry V, 245
Hiatt, Guilford I, 545
Hiatt, Guilford I, 546
Hiatt, Guli Elma V, 500
Hiatt, Gulielma I, 500
Hiatt, Gulielma I, 883
Hiatt, Gulielma V, 335
Hiatt, Gulielma V, 358
Hiatt, Gulielma V, 559
Hiatt, Gulielma V, 575
Hiatt, Gulielman I, 545
Hiatt, Hannah I, 545
Hiatt, Hannah I, 575
Hiatt, Hannah I, 594
Hiatt, Hannah I, 815
Hiatt, Hannah I, 817
Hiatt, Hannah I, 956
Hiatt, Hannah I, 963
Hiatt, Hannah I, 968
Hiatt, Hannah I, 986
Hiatt, Hannah I, 1009
Hiatt, Hannah I, 1010
Hiatt, Hannah IV, 1099
Hiatt, Hannah IV, 1100
Hiatt, Hannah IV, 1101
Hiatt, Hannah V, 245
Hiatt, Hannah V, 246
Hiatt, Hannah V, 304
Hiatt, Hannah V, 305
Hiatt, Hannah V, 335
Hiatt, Hannah V, 547
Hiatt, Hannah V, 575
Hiatt, Hannah F. I, 499
Hiatt, Hannah, Sr. I, 1009
Hiatt, Harmon I, 1005
Hiatt, Harmon V, 245
Hiatt, Harmon V, 304
Hiatt, Harmon V, 335
Hiatt, Harold V, 682
Hiatt, Harold C. V, 658
Hiatt, Harold C. V, 682
Hiatt, Harriet V, 245
Hiatt, Harriet V, 394
Hiatt, Harriet Ellen V, 394
Hiatt, Harriett V, 336
Hiatt, Harriett V, 377
Hiatt, Harriett V, 394
Hiatt, Henry V, 178
Hiatt, Henry V, 245
Hiatt, Henry V, 304
Hiatt, Herman I, 499
Hiatt, Hermin V, 246
Hiatt, Hermon V, 245
Hiatt, Hervey V, 245
Hiatt, Hester V, 500
Hiatt, Hezekiah I, 500
Hiatt, Hezekiah I, 545
Hiatt, Hezekiah V, 72
Hiatt, Hezekiah V, 477
Hiatt, Hezekiah V, 500
Hiatt, Hezekiah V, 523
Hiatt, Hezekiah V, 540
Hiatt, Hiram I, 956
Hiatt, Hiram I, 1004
Hiatt, Hiram V, 245
Hiatt, Howard V, 304
Hiatt, Howard V, 394
Hiatt, Howard Allen V, 682
Hiatt, Huldah I, 883
Hiatt, Ida Bell V, 575
Hiatt, Ira V, 500
Hiatt, Ira S. IV, 1281
Hiatt, Irene I, 809
Hiatt, Irene I, 815
Hiatt, Irene V, 72
Hiatt, Irrena V, 178
Hiatt, Isaac I, 499
Hiatt, Isaac I, 546
Hiatt, Isaac I, 815
Hiatt, Isaac IV, 1101
Hiatt, Isaac V, 72
Hiatt, Isaac V, 129
Hiatt, Isaac V, 335
Hiatt, Isaac V, 500
Hiatt, Isaac V, 501
Hiatt, Isaac V, 842
Hiatt, Isaac VI, 399
Hiatt, Isaac P. V, 72
Hiatt, Isam I, 500
Hiatt, Isam I, 545
Hiatt, Isham V, 625
Hiatt, Isom I, 545
Hiatt, Isom IV, 1281
Hiatt, Isom V, 500
Hiatt, Isom V, 575
Hiatt, Isom V, 625
Hiatt, Ithamar V, 245
Hiatt, J. Wade I, 943
Hiatt, Jacob I, 500
Hiatt, Jacob I, 956
Hiatt, Jacob I, 1009
Hiatt, Jacob V, 245
Hiatt, Jacob V, 246
Hiatt, James I, 679
Hiatt, James I, 815
Hiatt, James I, 1004
Hiatt, James IV, 1100
Hiatt, James IV, 1101
Hiatt, James IV, 1132
Hiatt, James V, 245
Hiatt, James V, 304
Hiatt, James VI, 399
Hiatt, James Russell IV, 1101
Hiatt, Jamima I, 1005
Hiatt, Jamima V, 394
Hiatt, Jamima V, 440
Hiatt, Jane I, 499
Hiatt, Jane I, 782
Hiatt, Jane I, 815
Hiatt, Jane I, 855
Hiatt, Jane I, 883
Hiatt, Jane I, 890
Hiatt, Jane V, 72
Hiatt, Jane V, 74
Hiatt, Jane V, 304
Hiatt, Jane V, 380
Hiatt, Jane V, 394
Hiatt, Jane VI, 400
Hiatt, Jehu I, 499
Hiatt, Jehu I, 545
Hiatt, Jehu I, 571
Hiatt, Jehu I, 883
Hiatt, Jehu IV, 221
Hiatt, Jehu IV, 408
Hiatt, Jehu IV, 583
Hiatt, Jehu IV, 584
Hiatt, Jehu IV, 1062
Hiatt, Jehu IV, 1100
Hiatt, Jehu IV, 1107
Hiatt, Jehu V, 327
Hiatt, Jehu V, 335
Hiatt, Jehu V, 336
Hiatt, Jehu V, 500
Hiatt, Jemima I, 1005
Hiatt, Jemima I, 1009
Hiatt, Jemima I, 1010
Hiatt, Jemima IV, 583
Hiatt, Jemima V, 72
Hiatt, Jemima V, 245
Hiatt, Jemima V, 303
Hiatt, Jemima V, 335
Hiatt, Jemima V, 390
Hiatt, Jemima V, 394
Hiatt, Jemimah I, 956
Hiatt, Jemimah I, 1005
Hiatt, Jemimah I, 1009
Hiatt, Jemimah V, 335
Hiatt, Jemimah V, 394
Hiatt, Jesse I, 499
Hiatt, Jesse I, 500
Hiatt, Jesse I, 956
Hiatt, Jesse I, 1005
Hiatt, Jesse IV, 221
Hiatt, Jesse IV, 297
Hiatt, Jesse IV, 408
Hiatt, Jesse IV, 583
Hiatt, Jesse IV, 598
Hiatt, Jesse IV, 1062
Hiatt, Jesse IV, 1097
Hiatt, Jesse IV, 1100
Hiatt, Jesse IV, 1101
Hiatt, Jesse IV, 1132
Hiatt, Jesse V, 72
Hiatt, Jesse V, 178
Hiatt, Jesse V, 245
Hiatt, Jesse V, 270
Hiatt, Jesse V, 335
Hiatt, Jesse V, 336
Hiatt, Jesse V, 368
Hiatt, Jesse V, 394
Hiatt, Jesse V, 500
Hiatt, Jesse V, 516
Hiatt, Jesse V, 575
Hiatt, Jesse V, 625
Hiatt, Jesse L. IV, 1101
Hiatt, Jesse Thomas V, 575
Hiatt, Jesse, Jr. IV, 1101
Hiatt, Jether I, 499
Hiatt, Job I, 782
Hiatt, Job I, 815
Hiatt, Joel I, 499
Hiatt, Joel I, 500
Hiatt, Joel I, 545
Hiatt, Joel I, 815
Hiatt, Joel I, 883
Hiatt, Joel V, 500
Hiatt, Joel V, 575
Hiatt, John I, 215
Hiatt, John I, 343
Hiatt, John I, 394
Hiatt, John I, 499
Hiatt, John I, 500
Hiatt, John I, 529
Hiatt, John I, 544
Hiatt, John I, 545
Hiatt, John I, 546
Hiatt, John I, 577
Hiatt, John I, 580
Hiatt, John I, 679
Hiatt, John I, 782
Hiatt, John I, 815
Hiatt, John I, 883
Hiatt, John I, 943
Hiatt, John I, 953
Hiatt, John I, 963
Hiatt, John I, 986
Hiatt, John I, 1005
Hiatt, John I, 1009
Hiatt, John I, 1012
Hiatt, John V, 178
Hiatt, John V, 245
Hiatt, John V, 304
Hiatt, John V, 335
Hiatt, John V, 343
Hiatt, John V, 368
Hiatt, John V, 394
Hiatt, John V, 500
Hiatt, John VI, 357
Hiatt, John VI, 399
Hiatt, John VI, 400
Hiatt, John C. I, 855
Hiatt, John G. V, 394
Hiatt, John K. W. V, 575
Hiatt, John Owen I, 943
Hiatt, John, Jr. I, 544
Hiatt, John, Jr. V, 368
Hiatt, John, Sr. I, 773
Hiatt, Jonathan I, 499
Hiatt, Jonathan I, 500
Hiatt, Jonathan I, 545
Hiatt, Jonathan I, 582
Hiatt, Jonathan I, 1009
Hiatt, Jonathan IV, 408
Hiatt, Jonathan IV, 583
Hiatt, Jonathan IV, 1062
Hiatt, Jonathan IV, 1100
Hiatt, Jonathan IV, 1101
Hiatt, Jonathan V, 245
Hiatt, Jonathan V, 246
Hiatt, Jonathan V, 327
Hiatt, Jonathan V, 335
Hiatt, Jonathan V, 336
Hiatt, Jonathan V, 368
Hiatt, Jonathan V, 394
Hiatt, Jonathan V, 446
Hiatt, Jonathan V, 500
Hiatt, Jonathan V, 625
Hiatt, Jonathan Williams VI, 504
Hiatt, Jorden V, 72
Hiatt, Jordon V, 178
Hiatt, Josep I, 883
Hiatt, Joseph I, 499
Hiatt, Joseph I, 500
Hiatt, Joseph I, 544
Hiatt, Joseph I, 545
Hiatt, Joseph I, 815
Hiatt, Joseph I, 829
Hiatt, Joseph I, 855
Hiatt, Joseph I, 883
Hiatt, Joseph I, 898
Hiatt, Joseph I, 953
Hiatt, Joseph I, 956
Hiatt, Joseph I, 986
Hiatt, Joseph I, 1004
Hiatt, Joseph I, 1005
Hiatt, Joseph I, 1009
Hiatt, Joseph I, 1053
Hiatt, Joseph IV, 1062
Hiatt, Joseph IV, 1101
Hiatt, Joseph V, 219
Hiatt, Joseph V, 245
Hiatt, Joseph V, 246
Hiatt, Joseph V, 304
Hiatt, Joseph V, 335
Hiatt, Joseph V, 500
Hiatt, Joseph V, 575
Hiatt, Joseph V, 842
Hiatt, Joseph VI, 399
Hiatt, Joseph P. V, 72
Hiatt, Joseph, Jr. I, 815
Hiatt, Joseph, Jr. I, 953
Hiatt, Joseph, Jr. I, 963
Hiatt, Joseph, Jr. I, 968
Hiatt, Joseph, Jr. V, 245
Hiatt, Joshua I, 545
Hiatt, Joshua V, 575
Hiatt, Josiah I, 956
Hiatt, Josiah V, 245
Hiatt, Josiah V, 368
Hiatt, Josiah V, 900
Hiatt, Judith I, 240
Hiatt, Judith I, 241
Hiatt, Judith Copeland I, 215
Hiatt, Judith Copeland I, 216
Hiatt, Julia I, 986
Hiatt, July I, 956
Hiatt, Katharine I, 815
Hiatt, Katharine I, 840
Hiatt, Katharine V, 304
Hiatt, Katharine V, 312
Hiatt, Katurah IV, 1280
Hiatt, Katurah IV, 1281
Hiatt, Kezia I, 500
Hiatt, Kezia I, 815
Hiatt, Kezia I, 829
Hiatt, Keziah I, 815
Hiatt, Keziah I, 883
Hiatt, Keziah I, 986
Hiatt, Keziah I, 994
Hiatt, Lavina V, 304
Hiatt, Lavisa V, 625
Hiatt, Levi J. I, 855
Hiatt, Levina I, 545
Hiatt, Levina I, 580
Hiatt, Levina V, 245
Hiatt, Levina V, 246
Hiatt, Levina V, 298
Hiatt, Levina V, 368
Hiatt, Levinah I, 500
Hiatt, Levinah I, 1005
Hiatt, Levinah V, 368
Hiatt, Levisa V, 625
Hiatt, Levisha V, 625
Hiatt, Lewis IV, 583
Hiatt, Lewis IV, 1062
Hiatt, Lewis IV, 1101
Hiatt, Lewis V, 335
Hiatt, Lewis V, 336
Hiatt, Lewis V, 500
Hiatt, Lewis V, 501
Hiatt, Lewis V, 575
Hiatt, Lewis V, 580
Hiatt, Linden I, 855
Hiatt, Lora V, 72
Hiatt, Lora V, 394
Hiatt, Lora M. V, 72
Hiatt, Lora M. V, 115
Hiatt, Lorenza V, 72
Hiatt, Lorenzo V, 72
Hiatt, Louisa V, 245
Hiatt, Louisa V, 246
Hiatt, Louisa V, 262
Hiatt, Louisa V, 270
Hiatt, Louisa V, 625
Hiatt, Louisa V, 640
Hiatt, Lucy V, 394
Hiatt, Lydia I, 391
Hiatt, Lydia I, 394
Hiatt, Lydia I, 499
Hiatt, Lydia I, 525
Hiatt, Lydia I, 542
Hiatt, Lydia I, 544
Hiatt, Lydia I, 545
Hiatt, Lydia I, 550
Hiatt, Lydia I, 571
Hiatt, Lydia I, 883
Hiatt, Lydia I, 1005
Hiatt, Lydia I, 1009
Hiatt, Lydia I, 1053
Hiatt, Lydia IV, 408
Hiatt, Lydia IV, 409

Hiatt, Lydia V, 72
Hiatt, Lydia V, 245
Hiatt, Lydia V, 335
Hiatt, Lydia V, 336
Hiatt, Lydia V, 368
Hiatt, Lydia V, 394
Hiatt, Lydia V, 396
Hiatt, Lydia V, 426
Hiatt, Lydia V, 500
Hiatt, Lydia V, 501
Hiatt, Lydia V, 505
Hiatt, Lydia V, 533
Hiatt, Lydia V, 842
Hiatt, Lydia VI, 504
Hiatt, Lydia Ann IV, 1100
Hiatt, Lydia Ann IV, 1101
Hiatt, Lydia Ann V, 246
Hiatt, Lydia Ann V, 336
Hiatt, Lydia D. V, 335
Hiatt, Lydia, Jr. I, 544
Hiatt, Macie M. V, 394
Hiatt, Mahala V, 245
Hiatt, Mahala V, 393
Hiatt, Mahala V, 625
Hiatt, Mamie M. V, 500
Hiatt, Margaret I, 548
Hiatt, Margaret V, 500
Hiatt, Margaret V, 501
Hiatt, Margaret V, 575
Hiatt, Margaret Chapman V, 72
Hiatt, Mariam I, 215
Hiatt, Marshal T. I, 816
Hiatt, Martha I, 308
Hiatt, Martha I, 319
Hiatt, Martha I, 343
Hiatt, Martha I, 394
Hiatt, Martha I, 499
Hiatt, Martha I, 500
Hiatt, Martha I, 501
Hiatt, Martha I, 545
Hiatt, Martha I, 550
Hiatt, Martha I, 560
Hiatt, Martha I, 618
Hiatt, Martha I, 632
Hiatt, Martha I, 634
Hiatt, Martha I, 782
Hiatt, Martha I, 815
Hiatt, Martha I, 834
Hiatt, Martha I, 836
Hiatt, Martha I, 855
Hiatt, Martha I, 883
Hiatt, Martha I, 1009
Hiatt, Martha IV, 1062
Hiatt, Martha IV, 1101
Hiatt, Martha V, 72
Hiatt, Martha V, 75
Hiatt, Martha V, 246
Hiatt, Martha V, 335
Hiatt, Martha V, 336
Hiatt, Martha V, 394
Hiatt, Martha V, 433
Hiatt, Martha V, 501
Hiatt, Martha V, 682
Hiatt, Martha VI, 399
Hiatt, Martha VI, 504
Hiatt, Martha VI, 505
Hiatt, Martha Ann V, 575
Hiatt, Martha D. V, 501
Hiatt, Martha D. V, 504
Hiatt, Martha Delilah I, 615
Hiatt, Martha H. V, 394
Hiatt, Martha H. V, 567
Hiatt, Martha H. V, 575
Hiatt, Martha Jane V, 72
Hiatt, Martha Jane V, 842
Hiatt, Martha, Jr. I, 815
Hiatt, Mary I, 394
Hiatt, Mary I, 499
Hiatt, Mary I, 500
Hiatt, Mary I, 529
Hiatt, Mary I, 544
Hiatt, Mary I, 545
Hiatt, Mary I, 546
Hiatt, Mary I, 547
Hiatt, Mary I, 553
Hiatt, Mary I, 555
Hiatt, Mary I, 562
Hiatt, Mary I, 577
Hiatt, Mary I, 578
Hiatt, Mary I, 679
Hiatt, Mary I, 773
Hiatt, Mary I, 782
Hiatt, Mary I, 812
Hiatt, Mary I, 815
Hiatt, Mary I, 883
Hiatt, Mary I, 963
Hiatt, Mary I, 970
Hiatt, Mary I, 975
Hiatt, Mary I, 986
Hiatt, Mary I, 1005
Hiatt, Mary I, 1007
Hiatt, Mary I, 1009
Hiatt, Mary IV, 571
Hiatt, Mary IV, 584
Hiatt, Mary IV, 1062
Hiatt, Mary IV, 1091
Hiatt, Mary IV, 1097
Hiatt, Mary IV, 1100
Hiatt, Mary IV, 1101
Hiatt, Mary IV, 1281
Hiatt, Mary V, 178
Hiatt, Mary V, 245
Hiatt, Mary V, 246
Hiatt, Mary V, 270
Hiatt, Mary V, 282
Hiatt, Mary V, 304
Hiatt, Mary V, 305
Hiatt, Mary V, 306
Hiatt, Mary V, 327
Hiatt, Mary V, 335
Hiatt, Mary V, 336
Hiatt, Mary V, 344
Hiatt, Mary V, 368
Hiatt, Mary V, 383
Hiatt, Mary V, 394
Hiatt, Mary V, 410
Hiatt, Mary V, 476
Hiatt, Mary V, 492
Hiatt, Mary V, 500
Hiatt, Mary V, 501
Hiatt, Mary V, 575
Hiatt, Mary V, 625
Hiatt, Mary V, 635
Hiatt, Mary VI, 399
Hiatt, Mary VI, 400
Hiatt, Mary Ann V, 72
Hiatt, Mary Ann V, 304
Hiatt, Mary Ann V, 394
Hiatt, Mary Ann V, 411
Hiatt, Mary Ann V, 477
Hiatt, Mary Ann V, 500
Hiatt, Mary Ann V, 501
Hiatt, Mary B. V, 394
Hiatt, Mary B. V, 625
Hiatt, Mary Beals V, 72
Hiatt, Mary E. IV, 1101
Hiatt, Mary E. IV, 1132
Hiatt, Mary Elizabeth I, 634
Hiatt, Mary Elma IV, 822
Hiatt, Mary Elma IV, 851
Hiatt, Mary Elma IV, 1101
Hiatt, Mary Elma W. IV, 822
Hiatt, Mary Eva I, 943
Hiatt, Mary F. IV, 1100
Hiatt, Mary Haines V, 500
Hiatt, Mary Hannah Mason V, 500
Hiatt, Mary Jane I, 783
Hiatt, Mary Jane I, 815
Hiatt, Mary Jane I, 818
Hiatt, Mary M. V, 72
Hiatt, Mary M. V, 91
Hiatt, Mary T. V, 394
Hiatt, Mary Thornburgh I, 500
Hiatt, Mary Warrington IV, 1101
Hiatt, Maryann V, 500
Hiatt, Matilda I, 956
Hiatt, Matilda I, 980
Hiatt, Matilda I, 986
Hiatt, Mattie Davis I, 634
Hiatt, Mehala V, 394
Hiatt, Milford V, 246
Hiatt, Milla V, 72
Hiatt, Milton V, 575
Hiatt, Minnie B. V, 682
Hiatt, Minnie Isabel V, 336
Hiatt, Minnie Isabel V, 682
Hiatt, Mordecai I, 499
Hiatt, Mordecai I, 546
Hiatt, Mordicai I, 499
Hiatt, Mordicai I, 537
Hiatt, Mordicai I, 546
Hiatt, Moses I, 215
Hiatt, Mourning V, 304
Hiatt, Nancy IV, 1281
Hiatt, Nancy V, 393
Hiatt, Nancy V, 394
Hiatt, Naomi I, 499
Hiatt, Naomy I, 533
Hiatt, Naomy I, 546
Hiatt, Narcissa V, 72
Hiatt, Narcissa V, 500
Hiatt, Nathan I, 499
Hiatt, Nathan I, 500
Hiatt, Nathan I, 545
Hiatt, Nathan I, 578
Hiatt, Nathan I, 956
Hiatt, Nathan I, 1005
Hiatt, Nathan V, 245
Hiatt, Nathan V, 368
Hiatt, Nathan V, 394
Hiatt, Nathan V, 625
Hiatt, Nathan Litler VI, 400
Hiatt, Newton V, 394
Hiatt, Nina Lowenia I, 943
Hiatt, Noah V, 1003
Hiatt, Odsar Thompson V, 336
Hiatt, Olive V, 245
Hiatt, Olive V, 246
Hiatt, Olive V, 297
Hiatt, Olive V, 304
Hiatt, Olive Catharine V, 304
Hiatt, Oliver V, 245
Hiatt, Oliver V, 246
Hiatt, Oliver V, 682
Hiatt, Oliver V, 692
Hiatt, Opeckon I, 544
Hiatt, Othnial I, 815
Hiatt, Pearl V, 682
Hiatt, Pearl V, 703
Hiatt, Pearl Peelle V, 682
Hiatt, Phaniah V, 501
Hiatt, Phaniah V, 520
Hiatt, Phebe I, 499
Hiatt, Phebe I, 546
Hiatt, Phebe I, 559
Hiatt, Phebe I, 815
Hiatt, Phebe I, 855
Hiatt, Phebe I, 970
Hiatt, Phebe I, 1004
Hiatt, Phebe V, 72
Hiatt, Phebe V, 129
Hiatt, Phebe V, 245
Hiatt, Phebe V, 304
Hiatt, Phebe V, 309
Hiatt, Phebe V, 842
Hiatt, Phebe A. V, 270
Hiatt, Phebe T. V, 72
Hiatt, Pheby I, 782
Hiatt, Pheniah V, 72
Hiatt, Pheniah V, 500
Hiatt, Pheniah V, 501
Hiatt, Pheniah V, 520
Hiatt, Priscilla I, 1005
Hiatt, Priscilla V, 394
Hiatt, Priscilla V, 396
Hiatt, Priscillah I, 1009
Hiatt, Prudence I, 500
Hiatt, Prudence I, 545
Hiatt, Prudence I, 572
Hiatt, R. Ida V, 575
Hiatt, Rachel I, 499
Hiatt, Rachel I, 500
Hiatt, Rachel I, 545
Hiatt, Rachel I, 555
Hiatt, Rachel I, 582
Hiatt, Rachel I, 815
Hiatt, Rachel I, 826
Hiatt, Rachel I, 956
Hiatt, Rachel I, 1005
Hiatt, Rachel I, 1009
Hiatt, Rachel I, 1012
Hiatt, Rachel IV, 1062
Hiatt, Rachel IV, 1100
Hiatt, Rachel IV, 1281
Hiatt, Rachel V, 178
Hiatt, Rachel V, 245
Hiatt, Rachel V, 246
Hiatt, Rachel V, 286
Hiatt, Rachel V, 304
Hiatt, Rachel V, 308
Hiatt, Rachel V, 312
Hiatt, Rachel V, 335
Hiatt, Rachel V, 336
Hiatt, Rachel V, 368
Hiatt, Rachel V, 466
Hiatt, Rebecca I, 500
Hiatt, Rebecca I, 546
Hiatt, Rebecca I, 580
Hiatt, Rebecca I, 815
Hiatt, Rebecca I, 956
Hiatt, Rebecca IV, 1281
Hiatt, Rebecca V, 72
Hiatt, Rebecca V, 245
Hiatt, Rebecca V, 246
Hiatt, Rebecca V, 250
Hiatt, Rebecca V, 322
Hiatt, Rebecca V, 336
Hiatt, Rebecca V, 368
Hiatt, Rebecca V, 377
Hiatt, Rebecca V, 393
Hiatt, Rebecca V, 394
Hiatt, Rebecca V, 842
Hiatt, Rebecca VI, 384
Hiatt, Rebecca VI, 399
Hiatt, Rebeckah I, 546
Hiatt, Rebeckah I, 580
Hiatt, Rebeckah V, 309
Hiatt, Rebekah I, 499
Hiatt, Rebekah I, 594
Hiatt, Rebekah I, 677
Hiatt, Rebekah I, 679
Hiatt, Rebekah I, 815
Hiatt, Rebekah I, 1005
Hiatt, Rebekah V, 245
Hiatt, Rebekah V, 246
Hiatt, Rebekah V, 304
Hiatt, Rettie Sophia V, 394
Hiatt, Reuben V, 178
Hiatt, Reuben V, 501
Hiatt, Reubin V, 500
Hiatt, Rhoda I, 537
Hiatt, Rhoda I, 546
Hiatt, Rhoda IV, 1095
Hiatt, Rhoda IV, 1101
Hiatt, Rhoda V, 575
Hiatt, Rhoda V, 900
Hiatt, Richard I, 500
Hiatt, Richard I, 1009
Hiatt, Richard V, 304
Hiatt, Richard V, 368
Hiatt, Richard Mills V, 682
Hiatt, Robert I, 815
Hiatt, Robert IV, 409
Hiatt, Robert Barrett V, 682
Hiatt, Robert Burritt V, 682
Hiatt, Robert Stuart I, 815
Hiatt, Rolin D. IV, 1100
Hiatt, Rollin R. IV, 1101
Hiatt, Rosabell V, 394
Hiatt, Rosanah V, 245
Hiatt, Rosanna V, 600
Hiatt, Rosannah V, 178
Hiatt, Rosemeal V, 178
Hiatt, Rozannah V, 368
Hiatt, Ruben V, 178
Hiatt, Rueben V, 368
Hiatt, Rueben V, 501
Hiatt, Russell V, 682
Hiatt, Ruth I, 499
Hiatt, Ruth I, 500
Hiatt, Ruth I, 536
Hiatt, Ruth I, 544
Hiatt, Ruth I, 545
Hiatt, Ruth I, 571
Hiatt, Ruth I, 572
Hiatt, Ruth V, 245
Hiatt, Ruth V, 304
Hiatt, Ruth V, 305
Hiatt, Ruth V, 394
Hiatt, Ruth V, 406
Hiatt, Ruth V, 500
Hiatt, Ruth Anna IV, 1100
Hiatt, Ruth Anna V, 336
Hiatt, Ruth Hannah Mourning V, 245
Hiatt, Ruthanna IV, 221
Hiatt, Ruthanna IV, 297
Hiatt, Ruthanna IV, 583
Hiatt, Ruthanna IV, 598
Hiatt, Ruthanna IV, 1062
Hiatt, Ruthanna IV, 1097
Hiatt, Ruthanna IV, 1100
Hiatt, Ruthanna IV, 1101
Hiatt, Ruthanna IV, 1132
Hiatt, Ruthanna V, 335
Hiatt, Ruthanna B. IV, 1106
Hiatt, Samuel IV, 1281
Hiatt, Samuel V, 245
Hiatt, Samuel V, 500
Hiatt, Samuel V, 575
Hiatt, Samuel M. V, 501
Hiatt, Sarah I, 343
Hiatt, Sarah I, 394
Hiatt, Sarah I, 499
Hiatt, Sarah I, 500
Hiatt, Sarah I, 523
Hiatt, Sarah I, 544
Hiatt, Sarah I, 545
Hiatt, Sarah I, 546
Hiatt, Sarah I, 572
Hiatt, Sarah I, 594
Hiatt, Sarah I, 595
Hiatt, Sarah I, 783
Hiatt, Sarah I, 815
Hiatt, Sarah I, 855
Hiatt, Sarah I, 883
Hiatt, Sarah I, 898
Hiatt, Sarah I, 1005
Hiatt, Sarah I, 1009
Hiatt, Sarah V, 72
Hiatt, Sarah V, 140
Hiatt, Sarah V, 245
Hiatt, Sarah V, 297
Hiatt, Sarah V, 304
Hiatt, Sarah V, 335
Hiatt, Sarah V, 343
Hiatt, Sarah V, 368
Hiatt, Sarah V, 394
Hiatt, Sarah V, 432
Hiatt, Sarah V, 500
Hiatt, Sarah V, 501
Hiatt, Sarah V, 516
Hiatt, Sarah V, 540
Hiatt, Sarah V, 625
Hiatt, Sarah VI, 400
Hiatt, Sarah VI, 419
Hiatt, Sarah Ann IV, 571
Hiatt, Sarah Ann IV, 1097
Hiatt, Sarah Ann IV, 1100
Hiatt, Sarah Ann IV, 1101
Hiatt, Sarah Ann IV, 1281
Hiatt, Sarah E. IV, 221
Hiatt, Sarah J. I, 855
Hiatt, Sarah J. V, 575
Hiatt, Sarah Jane I, 500
Hiatt, Sarah Jane V, 575
Hiatt, Sarah M. V, 394
Hiatt, Shanna D. I, 546
Hiatt, Shanna D. I, 548
Hiatt, Shanna D. V, 842
Hiatt, Shannah I, 546
Hiatt, Shannah V, 129
Hiatt, Shannah D. V, 842
Hiatt, Shanny V, 72
Hiatt, Shanny D. V, 72
Hiatt, Sibbilla IV, 1100
Hiatt, Sibbilla IV, 1110
Hiatt, Sidneyann IV, 1281
Hiatt, Silas I, 500
Hiatt, Silas I, 532
Hiatt, Silas I, 545
Hiatt, Silas V, 72
Hiatt, Silas V, 178
Hiatt, Silas V, 245
Hiatt, Silas V, 335
Hiatt, Silas V, 368
Hiatt, Sinthann IV, 1281
Hiatt, Solomon I, 499
Hiatt, Solomon I, 500
Hiatt, Solomon I, 545
Hiatt, Solomon I, 594
Hiatt, Solomon I, 595
Hiatt, Solomon I, 783
Hiatt, Solomon I, 815
Hiatt, Solomon I, 956
Hiatt, Solomon V, 245
Hiatt, Solomon V, 246
Hiatt, Solomon V, 335
Hiatt, Solomon V, 368
Hiatt, Solomon V, 446
Hiatt, Sophronia I, 816
Hiatt, Stephen I, 782
Hiatt, Stephen I, 956
Hiatt, Stephen I, 963
Hiatt, Stephen I, 1005
Hiatt, Stephen I, 1009
Hiatt, Stephen V, 270
Hiatt, Stephen V, 500
Hiatt, Stephen V, 501
Hiatt, Susan I, 811
Hiatt, Susan I, 815
Hiatt, Susanah I, 500
Hiatt, Susanna I, 499
Hiatt, Susanna I, 500
Hiatt, Susanna I, 541
Hiatt, Susanna I, 542
Hiatt, Susanna I, 544
Hiatt, Susanna I, 545
Hiatt, Susanna I, 546
Hiatt, Susanna I, 1009
Hiatt, Susanna IV, 408
Hiatt, Susanna IV, 583
Hiatt, Susanna IV, 1062
Hiatt, Susanna IV, 1092
Hiatt, Susanna IV, 1100
Hiatt, Susanna IV, 1101
Hiatt, Susanna IV, 1107
Hiatt, Susanna IV, 1281
Hiatt, Susanna V, 245
Hiatt, Susannah I, 545
Hiatt, Susannah I, 782
Hiatt, Susannah V, 72
Hiatt, Susannah V, 246
Hiatt, Susannah V, 304
Hiatt, Susannah V, 335
Hiatt, Susannah V, 336
Hiatt, Susannah V, 500
Hiatt, Susannah V, 575
Hiatt, Susannah V, 625
Hiatt, Susannah V, 639
Hiatt, Susannah W. IV, 1281
Hiatt, Sybilla IV, 1101
Hiatt, Tamar IV, 583
Hiatt, Tamar IV, 1100
Hiatt, Tamar IV, 1107
Hiatt, Tamer IV, 221
Hiatt, Tamer IV, 408
Hiatt, Tamer IV, 1062
Hiatt, Tamer IV, 1101
Hiatt, Tamer IV, 1110
Hiatt, Tamer V, 327
Hiatt, Tamer V, 335
Hiatt, Tamer V, 336
Hiatt, Tamor IV, 1101

Hiatt, Thamar I, 1005
Hiatt, Thamer IV, 583
Hiatt, Thamer V, 318
Hiatt, Thamer V, 336
Hiatt, Thomas I, 1005
Hiatt, Thomas V, 336
Hiatt, Thomas V, 377
Hiatt, Thomas V, 394
Hiatt, Thomas Beals I, 545
Hiatt, Thomas L. V, 682
Hiatt, Thomas Lincoln V, 336
Hiatt, Thomas Lincoln V, 682
Hiatt, Ursula I, 499
Hiatt, Ursula I, 544
Hiatt, Ursula I, 575
Hiatt, Viry V, 394
Hiatt, Walter I, 632
Hiatt, Walter I, 634
Hiatt, Walter A. I, 615
Hiatt, Walter A. I, 618
Hiatt, Warren V, 72
Hiatt, Widow Mary I, 545
Hiatt, Widow Mary I, 782
Hiatt, Widow Sarah I, 500
Hiatt, William I, 343
Hiatt, William I, 394
Hiatt, William I, 499
Hiatt, William I, 500
Hiatt, William I, 525
Hiatt, William I, 544
Hiatt, William I, 545
Hiatt, William I, 546
Hiatt, William I, 581
Hiatt, William I, 606
Hiatt, William I, 677
Hiatt, William I, 679
Hiatt, William I, 782
Hiatt, William I, 815
Hiatt, William I, 953
Hiatt, William I, 956
Hiatt, William I, 963
Hiatt, William I, 986
Hiatt, William I, 1005
Hiatt, William IV, 1281
Hiatt, William V, 245
Hiatt, William V, 304
Hiatt, William VI, 399
Hiatt, William VI, 400
Hiatt, William VI, 415
Hiatt, William D. I, 855
Hiatt, William H. V, 394
Hiatt, Willie Grant V, 682
Hiatt, Wilson I, 816
Hiatt, Wilson IV, 583
Hiatt, Wilson IV, 1101
Hiatt, Wilson V, 246
Hiatt, Wilson V, 335
Hiatt, Wilson V, 336
Hiatt, Wm. IV, 1062
Hiatt, Wm. V, 304
Hiatt, Wm. V, 394
Hiatt, Wm. G. V, 682
Hiatt, Wm. Grant V, 336
Hiatt, Wm. Henry IV, 1281
Hiatt, Zachariah I, 500
Hiatt, Zachariah I, 815
Hiatt, Zacharias I, 883
Hiatt, Zadock I, 499
Hiatt, Zebulon I, 816
Hiatt, Zimri IV, 1281
Hiatt, Zimri V, 393
Hiatt, Zimry I, 1005
Hiatte, John Owen I, 943
Hibard, James V, 971
Hibard, Joseph V, 971
Hibbard, Aaron VI, 400
Hibbard, Benjamin VI, 400
Hibbard, Benjamin VI, 490
Hibbard, Benjamin VI, 505
Hibbard, Caleb IV, 529
Hibbard, Caleb IV, 561
Hibbard, Elizabeth II, 548
Hibbard, Hannah IV, 148
Hibbard, Hezekiah II, 548
Hibbard, Israel V, 971
Hibbard, James II, 548
Hibbard, James M. V, 72
Hibbard, James M. V, 106
Hibbard, Jehu L. IV, 964
Hibbard, Jehu R. IV, 964
Hibbard, John II, 548
Hibbard, Joseph II, 548
Hibbard, Joseph V, 971
Hibbard, Lydia V, 971
Hibbard, Margaret IV, 148
Hibbard, Mary II, 548
Hibbard, Mary V, 843
Hibbard, Phebe VI, 490
Hibbard, Phebe VI, 505
Hibbard, Rachel V, 971
Hibbard, Thomas IV, 148
Hibbard, Wm. P. II, 912
Hibben, Patience M. V, 682
Hibber, Martha VI, 400
Hibberd, ??? S. II, 875
Hibberd, Aaron V, 842
Hibberd, Aaron VI, 382
Hibberd, Aaron VI, 400
Hibberd, Aaron VI, 422
Hibberd, Aaron W. VI, 400
Hibberd, Allen II, 800
Hibberd, Allen II, 875
Hibberd, Allen V, 882
Hibberd, Allen VI, 400
Hibberd, Allice Ann V, 971
Hibberd, Amos II, 548
Hibberd, Benjamin V, 971
Hibberd, Benjamin VI, 364
Hibberd, Benjamin VI, 400
Hibberd, Benjamin VI, 490
Hibberd, Benjamin VI, 505
Hibberd, Caleb IV, 529
Hibberd, Carroll VI, 649
Hibberd, Charity V, 971
Hibberd, Charity VI, 364
Hibberd, Charity VI, 400
Hibberd, Charles J. VI, 649
Hibberd, Dalton V, 336
Hibberd, Earl M. II, 800
Hibberd, Elisha VI, 649
Hibberd, Elizabeth II, 548
Hibberd, Elizabeth V, 971
Hibberd, Elizabeth VI, 649
Hibberd, Elizabeth VI, 668
Hibberd, Emma VI, 649
Hibberd, Florence Barnes II, 800
Hibberd, Hannah II, 548
Hibberd, Hannah II, 552
Hibberd, Hannah V, 304
Hibberd, Hannah V, 336
Hibberd, Harriett H. VI, 649
Hibberd, Henry H. V, 882
Hibberd, Henry H. VI, 400
Hibberd, Henry Homer V, 882
Hibberd, Hezekiah II, 540
Hibberd, Hezekiah II, 548
Hibberd, Isaac V, 336
Hibberd, Israel V, 971
Hibberd, Jacob V, 336
Hibberd, Jacob V, 971
Hibberd, James II, 548
Hibberd, James V, 971
Hibberd, James VI, 400
Hibberd, James Edward V, 882
Hibberd, James Edward VI, 400
Hibberd, James F. VI, 400
Hibberd, James M. V, 842
Hibberd, James M. V, 854
Hibberd, James M. V, 882
Hibberd, James M. VI, 382
Hibberd, James M. VI, 400
Hibberd, Jane VI, 400
Hibberd, Jane VI, 505
Hibberd, Jane VI, 524
Hibberd, Jane Sarah V, 971
Hibberd, Jesse V, 336
Hibberd, Jesse V, 971
Hibberd, Job VI, 649
Hibberd, Job VI, 664
Hibberd, Job VI, 668
Hibberd, John II, 548
Hibberd, Joseph II, 540
Hibberd, Joseph II, 548
Hibberd, Joseph V, 971
Hibberd, Joseph VI, 400
Hibberd, Joseph VI, 505
Hibberd, Josiah II, 548
Hibberd, Josiah II, 552
Hibberd, Louisa A. II, 800
Hibberd, Lydia II, 875
Hibberd, Lydia V, 336
Hibberd, Lydia V, 971
Hibberd, Lydia VI, 400
Hibberd, Lydia D. V, 882
Hibberd, Lydia D. VI, 400
Hibberd, Lydia M. VI, 382
Hibberd, Lydia M. VI, 400
Hibberd, Margaret VI, 765
Hibberd, Martha V, 842
Hibberd, Martha VI, 382
Hibberd, Martha VI, 400
Hibberd, Martha VI, 422
Hibberd, Mary II, 540
Hibberd, Mary II, 548
Hibberd, Mary V, 842
Hibberd, Mary V, 843
Hibberd, Mary V, 854
Hibberd, Mary V, 882
Hibberd, Mary VI, 367
Hibberd, Mary VI, 400
Hibberd, Mary Ann V, 336
Hibberd, Mary Ann V, 971
Hibberd, Mary Ann VI, 400
Hibberd, Mary R. V, 882
Hibberd, Mary R. VI, 382
Hibberd, Naomi II, 716
Hibberd, Owen II, 548
Hibberd, Owen II, 552
Hibberd, Phebe V, 336
Hibberd, Phebe VI, 490
Hibberd, Phebe VI, 491
Hibberd, Phebe VI, 505
Hibberd, Rachel V, 971
Hibberd, Rebekah V, 304
Hibberd, Ruth Anna VI, 649
Hibberd, Ruth Anna VI, 664
Hibberd, Ruth Hannah VI, 649
Hibberd, Ruth Hannah VI, 668
Hibberd, Ruthanna VI, 668
Hibberd, Samuel V, 971
Hibberd, Samuel P. V, 910
Hibberd, Sarah V, 304
Hibberd, Sarah D. V, 336
Hibberd, Sarah Jane VI, 382
Hibberd, Sarah Jane VI, 400
Hibberd, Silas VI, 649
Hibberd, Silas VI, 668
Hibberd, Susan VI, 649
Hibberd, Susanna II, 548
Hibberd, Susanna II, 552
Hibberd, Tacy S. VI, 383
Hibberd, Tacy S. VI, 400
Hibberd, William VI, 400
Hibberd, Wm. V, 971
Hibberd, Wm. P. II, 841
Hibbern, Thomas IV, 872
Hibbert, Aaron VI, 400
Hibbert, Allen II, 875
Hibbert, Amos II, 548
Hibbert, Caleb IV, 408
Hibbert, Hannah II, 548
Hibbert, James VI, 400
Hibbert, James F. VI, 400
Hibbert, Jane VI, 400
Hibbert, Lydia VI, 400
Hibbert, Martha VI, 400
Hibberts, ??? II, 374
Hibberts, Hezekiah II, 374
Hibbourn, Elizabeth II, 1002
Hibbourn, Elizabeth II, 1031
Hibbs, Abraham II, 1002
Hibbs, Abraham IV, 529
Hibbs, Abraham IV, 530
Hibbs, Abraham IV, 551
Hibbs, Albert S. II, 1074
Hibbs, Alfred II, 1052
Hibbs, Amasa IV, 529
Hibbs, Amasa IV, 530
Hibbs, Amos IV, 221
Hibbs, Amos IV, 266
Hibbs, Amos IV, 529
Hibbs, Amos IV, 551
Hibbs, Amos VI, 505
Hibbs, Amos VI, 649
Hibbs, Amos VI, 690
Hibbs, Amos E. IV, 529
Hibbs, Amos, Jr. IV, 530
Hibbs, Ann IV, 510
Hibbs, Ann IV, 527
Hibbs, Ann IV, 529
Hibbs, Anne IV, 529
Hibbs, Anne IV, 530
Hibbs, Barclay IV, 529
Hibbs, Barclay IV, 530
Hibbs, Benjamin II, 1052
Hibbs, Benjamin IV, 529
Hibbs, Benjamin IV, 551
Hibbs, Benjamin VI, 649
Hibbs, Candace IV, 551
Hibbs, Catharine IV, 551
Hibbs, Catharine B. IV, 551
Hibbs, Catharine L. IV, 551
Hibbs, Daniel II, 1052
Hibbs, Deborah T. IV, 551
Hibbs, Edith VI, 699
Hibbs, Edith M. VI, 649
Hibbs, Edith M. VI, 700
Hibbs, Elijah IV, 529
Hibbs, Elisha IV, 551
Hibbs, Eliza II, 1065
Hibbs, Eliza II, 1072
Hibbs, Eliza II, 1074
Hibbs, Eliza Jane IV, 527
Hibbs, Elizabeth II, 1002
Hibbs, Elizabeth II, 1052
Hibbs, Elizabeth IV, 221
Hibbs, Elizabeth IV, 266
Hibbs, Elizabeth IV, 514
Hibbs, Elizabeth IV, 529
Hibbs, Elizabeth IV, 530
Hibbs, Elizabeth VI, 504
Hibbs, Elizabeth VI, 505
Hibbs, Elizabeth VI, 569
Hibbs, Elizabeth VI, 994
Hibbs, Elizabeth P. IV, 551
Hibbs, Elizabeth R. IV, 529
Hibbs, Elizabeth, Jr. VI, 505
Hibbs, Elwood Thomas IV, 551
Hibbs, Eva James VI, 932
Hibbs, Francis D. IV, 551
Hibbs, Frankey VI, 932
Hibbs, Franklin IV, 529
Hibbs, Franklin VI, 649
Hibbs, Franklin VI, 700
Hibbs, Geo. S. IV, 530
Hibbs, George IV, 529
Hibbs, George IV, 551
Hibbs, George S. IV, 529
Hibbs, George, Jr. IV, 551
Hibbs, Hannah V, 911
Hibbs, Hannah VI, 885
Hibbs, Henry V, 911
Hibbs, Isaac IV, 551
Hibbs, Isaac VI, 885
Hibbs, Isaac VI, 886
Hibbs, Isaac VI, 971
Hibbs, Israel IV, 551
Hibbs, James II, 1002
Hibbs, James II, 1052
Hibbs, Jane II, 1002
Hibbs, Jason IV, 529
Hibbs, Jason A. IV, 510
Hibbs, Jason A. IV, 529
Hibbs, Jason A. IV, 530
Hibbs, John IV, 527
Hibbs, John G. IV, 529
Hibbs, John G. IV, 530
Hibbs, John M. IV, 551
Hibbs, John R. IV, 529
Hibbs, John R. IV, 530
Hibbs, John W. IV, 551
Hibbs, Jonathan II, 444
Hibbs, Joseph VI, 505
Hibbs, Joseph VI, 886
Hibbs, Joseph VI, 932
Hibbs, Joseph VI, 936
Hibbs, Josephine IV, 221
Hibbs, Josephine IV, 263
Hibbs, Joshua IV, 551
Hibbs, Josiah R. IV, 530
Hibbs, Lambert II, 1002
Hibbs, Lambert II, 1052
Hibbs, Lemual K. IV, 551
Hibbs, Lewis IV, 551
Hibbs, Lydia IV, 530
Hibbs, Lydia IV, 550
Hibbs, Lydia IV, 551
Hibbs, Mahlon II, 1002
Hibbs, Margaret IV, 529
Hibbs, Maria IV, 529
Hibbs, Maria IV, 530
Hibbs, Maria H. IV, 551
Hibbs, Martha IV, 529
Hibbs, Martha IV, 530
Hibbs, Martha IV, 545
Hibbs, Martha IV, 551
Hibbs, Mary II, 986
Hibbs, Mary II, 1002
Hibbs, Mary IV, 221
Hibbs, Mary IV, 527
Hibbs, Mary IV, 529
Hibbs, Mary IV, 530
Hibbs, Mary VI, 505
Hibbs, Mary VI, 649
Hibbs, Mary VI, 650
Hibbs, Mary VI, 690
Hibbs, Mary VI, 704
Hibbs, Mary Ann IV, 78
Hibbs, Mary Ann IV, 92
Hibbs, Mary Ann IV, 527
Hibbs, Mary C. IV, 529
Hibbs, Mary C. IV, 530
Hibbs, Mary Jane IV, 551
Hibbs, Matthew II, 1002
Hibbs, Mercy VI, 505
Hibbs, Nancy IV, 529
Hibbs, Nathan IV, 551
Hibbs, Oliver II, 1052
Hibbs, Phebe II, 1002
Hibbs, Phebe II, 1052
Hibbs, Phebe Ann IV, 529
Hibbs, Phebe Ann IV, 530
Hibbs, Phebe R. IV, 551
Hibbs, Pheby II, 1002
Hibbs, Rachel VI, 971
Hibbs, Rachel Ann IV, 530
Hibbs, Rachel R. IV, 529
Hibbs, Rachel R. IV, 530
Hibbs, Robert F. R. IV, 529
Hibbs, Ruth IV, 550
Hibbs, Ruth VI, 505
Hibbs, Ruth VI, 649
Hibbs, Ruth VI, 690
Hibbs, Ruth VI, 886
Hibbs, Ruth S. IV, 387
Hibbs, Ruth S. IV, 408
Hibbs, Samuel IV, 527
Hibbs, Samuel VI, 932
Hibbs, Sarah IV, 526
Hibbs, Sarah IV, 527
Hibbs, Sarah IV, 529
Hibbs, Sarah IV, 530
Hibbs, Sarah IV, 551
Hibbs, Sarah VI, 489
Hibbs, Sarah VI, 505
Hibbs, Sarah VI, 650
Hibbs, Sarah VI, 674
Hibbs, Sarah VI, 675
Hibbs, Sarah VI, 715
Hibbs, Sarah G. IV, 529
Hibbs, Sarah G. IV, 530
Hibbs, Stephen VI, 650
Hibbs, Susanna W. II, 1074
Hibbs, Susannah II, 1002
Hibbs, Tacy IV, 551
Hibbs, Valentine IV, 526
Hibbs, Valentine IV, 529
Hibbs, Valentine IV, 530
Hibbs, William IV, 527
Hibbs, William IV, 529
Hibbs, William IV, 530
Hibbs, William VI, 505
Hibbs, William VI, 650
Hibbs, William VI, 690
Hibbs, William B. IV, 529
Hibbs, William G. IV, 529
Hibbs, Wm. IV, 221
Hibbs, Wm. IV, 529
Hibbs, Wm. IV, 545
Hibbs, Wm. VI, 649
Hibbs, Wm. B. IV, 530
Hibbs, Wm. G. IV, 530
Hibbs, Wm. K. IV, 551
Hibbs, Wm. P. IV, 551
Hibert, Thomas IV, 335
Hichcock, Elietas V, 178
Hichcock, Jacob I, 882
Hichcock, Mathew I, 882
Hick, Amelia III, 399
Hick, Hannah U. III, 399
Hick, Levena IV, 982
Hick, Levena Naylor IV, 964
Hick, Stephen R. III, 399
Hick, Wm. Mott III, 441
Hickerson, Lydia Jane IV, 1064
Hickerson, Lydia Lane IV, 1062
Hickfield, Susan V, 1001
Hickings, Rebeckah II, 78
Hickings, Rebeckah II, 85
Hicklan, Jane IV, 84
Hicklan, Jane IV, 92
Hickland, John IV, 1223
Hickland, Mary Ann IV, 1223
Hickland, Ruth IV, 721
Hickland, Samuel IV, 721
Hickland, Sarah A. IV, 1223
Hickland, Sarah Ann IV, 1210
Hicklen, Alice IV, 895
Hicklen, Ann IV, 892
Hicklen, Ann IV, 895
Hicklen, Dinah IV, 892
Hicklen, Hannah IV, 721
Hicklen, Hannah IV, 891
Hicklen, Hannah IV, 892
Hicklen, Hannah IV, 893
Hicklen, Hannah H. IV, 892
Hicklen, Jane IV, 620
Hicklen, Jane IV, 633
Hicklen, Jane IV, 721
Hicklen, Jane IV, 892
Hicklen, John IV, 633
Hicklen, John IV, 650
Hicklen, Joseph IV, 895
Hicklen, Joshua IV, 893
Hicklen, Lydia IV, 620
Hicklen, Lydia IV, 633
Hicklen, Lydia IV, 721
Hicklen, Martha IV, 633
Hicklen, Mary IV, 632
Hicklen, Mary IV, 633
Hicklen, Mary IV, 891
Hicklen, Mary IV, 892
Hicklen, Mary Ann IV, 633
Hicklen, Mary Ann IV, 638
Hicklen, Mary Ann IV, 650
Hicklen, Mary Ann IV, 721
Hicklen, Mary Ann IV, 1213
Hicklen, Mary Ann Jackson IV, 1210
Hicklen, Maryann IV, 1210
Hicklen, Rebecca IV, 892
Hicklen, Rebecca IV, 894
Hicklen, Ruth IV, 721
Hicklen, Ruth D. IV, 633
Hicklen, Samuel IV, 620

Hicklen, Samuel IV, 632
Hicklen, Samuel IV, 633
Hicklen, Samuel IV, 721
Hicklen, Sarah Ann IV, 721
Hicklen, Sarah Ann IV, 1210
Hicklen, Sarah Ann IV, 1213
Hicklen, Susannah IV, 632
Hicklen, Susannah IV, 633
Hicklen, Susannah, Jr. IV, 633
Hicklen, Tamer IV, 893
Hicklen, Thomason IV, 892
Hicklin, Elizabeth IV, 727
Hicklin, Ephraim IV, 727
Hicklin, Jane IV, 92
Hicklin, Mary Ann IV, 721
Hicklin, Mary Ann IV, 727
Hicklin, Samuel IV, 83
Hicklin, Samuel IV, 92
Hicklin, Samuel IV, 919
Hicklin, Susanna IV, 83
Hicklin, Susanna IV, 92
Hicklin, Susannah IV, 92
Hicklin, William IV, 92
Hickman, ??? V, 178
Hickman, ??? V, 756
Hickman, Abbey H. V, 742
Hickman, Abbey L. V, 742
Hickman, Abbie L. V, 742
Hickman, Ann II, 548
Hickman, Anson H. V, 742
Hickman, Benjamin II, 374
Hickman, Benjamin II, 548
Hickman, Benjamin, Jr. II, 548
Hickman, Bertha E. V, 963
Hickman, Catherine II, 548
Hickman, Cora V, 178
Hickman, Cora M. V, 178
Hickman, David II, 548
Hickman, David V, 178
Hickman, Dr. Joseph II, 795
Hickman, Elizabeth II, 548
Hickman, Elizabeth VI, 976
Hickman, Ella V, 178
Hickman, Geo. IV, 1211
Hickman, George IV, 1210
Hickman, George IV, 1211
Hickman, George IV, 1254
Hickman, George Alfred Townsend IV, 1210
Hickman, Gilpin II, 800
Hickman, Gwin V, 1001
Hickman, Halwin H. IV, 1210
Hickman, Hannah Ashbridge II, 795
Hickman, Hannah B. II, 875
Hickman, Harry V, 178
Hickman, Harry C. V, 178
Hickman, J. Freemont V, 963
Hickman, J. W. IV, 1210
Hickman, Jane IV, 1210
Hickman, Jennie IV, 1210
Hickman, Jer. V, 765
Hickman, Jeremiah V, 742
Hickman, Jesse V, 742
Hickman, John II, 548
Hickman, John M. IV, 1210
Hickman, Joseph V, 742
Hickman, Joseph VI, 976
Hickman, L. Parson VI, 624
Hickman, L. Parson VI, 627
Hickman, L. Parson VI, 650
Hickman, Leafy B. IV, 1210
Hickman, Louella Frances VI, 624
Hickman, Louella Frances VI, 627
Hickman, Louella Frances VI, 650
Hickman, Lydia IV, 892
Hickman, Martha IV, 645
Hickman, Mary I, 986
Hickman, Mary I, 989
Hickman, Mary II, 548
Hickman, Mary II, 795
Hickman, Mary II, 809
Hickman, Mary II, 821
Hickman, Mary II, 824
Hickman, Mary V, 742
Hickman, Mary V, 756
Hickman, Mary Ellen V, 178
Hickman, Mina V, 178
Hickman, Mrs. Eleanor IV, 1320
Hickman, Nina L. V, 178
Hickman, Ora M. V, 742
Hickman, Orey May V, 742
Hickman, Pearl IV, 1211
Hickman, Pearl IV, 1254
Hickman, Rhoda IV, 1211
Hickman, Robert F. IV, 1210
Hickman, Robert T. IV, 1210
Hickman, Ruthanna II, 822
Hickman, Sarah II, 548
Hickman, Sarah Elizabeth V, 742
Hickman, Susan R. V, 178
Hickman, T. N. IV, 1210
Hickman, T. S. IV, 1210
Hickman, Thomas I, 883
Hickman, Thomas IV, 1210
Hickman, Thomas N. IV, 1165
Hickman, Thomas N. IV, 1210
Hickman, Wd. Abigail V, 765
Hickman, Wd. Hannah B. II, 800
Hickman, William H. V, 742
Hickman, Wm. V, 742
Hickmore, Dinah I, 984
Hickmore, Dinah I, 986
Hickok, Cornelius C. III, 163
Hickok, Deborah IV, 1160
Hickok, Deborah IV, 1165
Hickok, Gerardine III, 163
Hickok, Hannah IV, 1160
Hickok, Harry IV, 1160
Hickox, William B. III, 163
Hickox, Wm. B. III, 189
Hickox, Zaydee B. III, 163
Hickox, Zaydee Bancroft III, 189
Hicks, ??? III, 112
Hicks, Abigail III, 164
Hicks, Abigail III, 165
Hicks, Abigail III, 417
Hicks, Abigail III, 419
Hicks, Abigail III, 484
Hicks, Abigail III, 485
Hicks, Abigail III, 498
Hicks, Abigail III, 501
Hicks, Abm. III, 443
Hicks, Abraham III, 416
Hicks, Abraham III, 444
Hicks, Adoniah, Jr. III, 501
Hicks, Agnes III, 47
Hicks, Albert III, 164
Hicks, Albert III, 418
Hicks, Alberta Flossie I, 927
Hicks, Albertson W. III, 416
Hicks, Albertson W. III, 418
Hicks, Albertson W. III, 443
Hicks, Albertson, Jr. III, 416
Hicks, Alexander III, 47
Hicks, Alfred III, 416
Hicks, Alice III, 418
Hicks, Alice A. III, 418
Hicks, Alice H. III, 417
Hicks, Alice Pennell III, 47
Hicks, Allan H. III, 47
Hicks, Alvin III, 47
Hicks, Amelia III, 403
Hicks, Amelia III, 416
Hicks, Amelia III, 417
Hicks, Amelia III, 418
Hicks, Amelia III, 419
Hicks, Amelia III, 466
Hicks, Amelia III, 471
Hicks, Amy III, 419
Hicks, Ann I, 241
Hicks, Ann Eliza II, 875
Hicks, Ann Louise III, 416
Hicks, Ann Louise III, 443
Hicks, Ann Mott III, 164
Hicks, Anna III, 47
Hicks, Anna III, 76
Hicks, Anna III, 165
Hicks, Anna III, 381
Hicks, Anna III, 419
Hicks, Anna IV, 381
Hicks, Anna IV, 408
Hicks, Anna C. III, 47
Hicks, Anna D. III, 381
Hicks, Anna D. III, 389
Hicks, Anna Mott III, 419
Hicks, Anna W. III, 417
Hicks, Anna W. III, 420
Hicks, Anne V, 246
Hicks, Anny VI, 825
Hicks, Arabella II, 715
Hicks, Asa IV, 149
Hicks, Asa IV, 381
Hicks, Asa IV, 408
Hicks, Asa VI, 109
Hicks, Asenath IV, 408
Hicks, Asenath IV, 435
Hicks, Asenith IV, 408
Hicks, Augus II, 374
Hicks, Augustine II, 374
Hicks, Augustine II, 548
Hicks, Augustine II, 568
Hicks, Augustine II, 660
Hicks, Augustine III, 416
Hicks, Augustine III, 424
Hicks, Augustis II, 548
Hicks, Austin III, 163
Hicks, Barbara III, 416
Hicks, Benj. III, 417
Hicks, Benj. III, 418
Hicks, Benj. III, 419
Hicks, Benj. III, 420
Hicks, Benj. III, 428
Hicks, Benj. III, 440
Hicks, Benj. D. III, 82
Hicks, Benj. D. III, 164
Hicks, Benj. D. III, 366
Hicks, Benj. D. III, 417
Hicks, Benjamin III, 163
Hicks, Benjamin III, 164
Hicks, Benjamin III, 165
Hicks, Benjamin III, 273
Hicks, Benjamin III, 381
Hicks, Benjamin III, 397
Hicks, Benjamin III, 398
Hicks, Benjamin III, 400
Hicks, Benjamin III, 403
Hicks, Benjamin III, 415
Hicks, Benjamin III, 416
Hicks, Benjamin III, 417
Hicks, Benjamin III, 418
Hicks, Benjamin III, 419
Hicks, Benjamin III, 427
Hicks, Benjamin III, 429
Hicks, Benjamin III, 432
Hicks, Benjamin III, 454
Hicks, Benjamin III, 470
Hicks, Benjamin III, 471
Hicks, Benjamin III, 473
Hicks, Benjamin III, 484
Hicks, Benjamin D. III, 163
Hicks, Benjamin D. III, 417
Hicks, Benjamin D. III, 418
Hicks, Benjamin E. III, 417
Hicks, Benjamin Embree III, 163
Hicks, Benjamin Embree III, 164
Hicks, Benjamin I. III, 165
Hicks, Benjamin L. III, 164
Hicks, Benjamin M. III, 417
Hicks, Benjamin T. III, 165
Hicks, Bertha III, 47
Hicks, Bethany IV, 365
Hicks, Bethany IV, 403
Hicks, Bethany IV, 408
Hicks, Bethany IV, 450
Hicks, Bethany IV, 584
Hicks, Bethena IV, 408
Hicks, Bethena IV, 457
Hicks, Caroline III, 153
Hicks, Caroline III, 164
Hicks, Caroline III, 165
Hicks, Caroline III, 416
Hicks, Caroline III, 417
Hicks, Caroline III, 418
Hicks, Caroline III, 419
Hicks, Caroline III, 440
Hicks, Caroline III, 484
Hicks, Caroline III, 485
Hicks, Caroline III, 497
Hicks, Caroline III, 498
Hicks, Caroline A. III, 418
Hicks, Caroline A. III, 443
Hicks, Caroline H. III, 397
Hicks, Caroline H. III, 409
Hicks, Caroline H. III, 417
Hicks, Caroline H. III, 418
Hicks, Caroline J. III, 409
Hicks, Caroline J. III, 417
Hicks, Caroline J. III, 418
Hicks, Caroline R. III, 403
Hicks, Caroline R. III, 417
Hicks, Caroline R. III, 419
Hicks, Caroline U. III, 485
Hicks, Caroline U. III, 486
Hicks, Caroline V. III, 418
Hicks, Caroline V. III, 421
Hicks, Carrie III, 419
Hicks, Carrie III, 464
Hicks, Carrie A. III, 418
Hicks, Catharine III, 112
Hicks, Catharine III, 164
Hicks, Catharine III, 165
Hicks, Catharine III, 417
Hicks, Catharine III, 418
Hicks, Catharine III, 429
Hicks, Charles III, 381
Hicks, Charles III, 419
Hicks, Charles IV, 476
Hicks, Charles V, 246
Hicks, Charles H. V, 246
Hicks, Charlie IV, 476
Hicks, Chas. II, 800
Hicks, Chas. II, 875
Hicks, Chas. III, 457
Hicks, Chas. M. II, 875
Hicks, Clark D. V, 246
Hicks, Clemens IV, 408
Hicks, Clement I, 927
Hicks, Clement IV, 148
Hicks, Clements VI, 99
Hicks, Clements VI, 109
Hicks, Clemmon IV, 408
Hicks, Clemons IV, 408
Hicks, Columbus I, 920
Hicks, Columbus I, 927
Hicks, Columbus C. I, 943
Hicks, Columbus Calvin I, 927
Hicks, Cordelia III, 417
Hicks, Daniel IV, 476
Hicks, Deborah III, 164
Hicks, Deborah W. III, 418
Hicks, Delilah J. VI, 847
Hicks, Dorothy Ellen IV, 1320
Hicks, Dorothy Ione I, 927
Hicks, Dr. John III, 164
Hicks, Dwight T. III, 417
Hicks, E. Jane I, 920
Hicks, E. Jane I, 927
Hicks, Edda Willets III, 443
Hicks, Edmund III, 484
Hicks, Edw. H. III, 47
Hicks, Edw. Jackson III, 420
Hicks, Edward II, 805
Hicks, Edward II, 1052
Hicks, Edward III, 417
Hicks, Edward III, 418
Hicks, Edward III, 422
Hicks, Edward III, 431
Hicks, Edward Fisher Sanderson III, 164
Hicks, Edward H. II, 875
Hicks, Edward J. III, 417
Hicks, Edward M. III, 165
Hicks, Edwin Willie III, 418
Hicks, Edwin Willis III, 417
Hicks, Edwin Willis III, 424
Hicks, Eleanor IV, 377
Hicks, Eleanor IV, 408
Hicks, Eli IV, 408
Hicks, Elias III, 126
Hicks, Elias III, 164
Hicks, Elias III, 165
Hicks, Elias III, 411
Hicks, Elias III, 417
Hicks, Elias III, 419
Hicks, Elias III, 444
Hicks, Elias III, 469
Hicks, Elias III, 479
Hicks, Elias III, 484
Hicks, Elias III, 485
Hicks, Elias III, 498
Hicks, Elias III, 506
Hicks, Elias IV, 584
Hicks, Elias V, 17
Hicks, Elias VI, 466
Hicks, Elias VI, 611
Hicks, Elias W. III, 417
Hicks, Elias, Jr. III, 417
Hicks, Eliz. III, 457
Hicks, Eliz. III, 482
Hicks, Eliz. W. III, 440
Hicks, Eliza III, 164
Hicks, Eliza III, 165
Hicks, Eliza III, 268
Hicks, Eliza Jane I, 927
Hicks, Eliza Sanderson III, 164
Hicks, Elizabeth II, 1052
Hicks, Elizabeth III, 47
Hicks, Elizabeth III, 82
Hicks, Elizabeth III, 163
Hicks, Elizabeth III, 164
Hicks, Elizabeth III, 165
Hicks, Elizabeth III, 273
Hicks, Elizabeth III, 320
Hicks, Elizabeth III, 400
Hicks, Elizabeth III, 416
Hicks, Elizabeth III, 417
Hicks, Elizabeth III, 418
Hicks, Elizabeth III, 419
Hicks, Elizabeth III, 427
Hicks, Elizabeth III, 429
Hicks, Elizabeth III, 440
Hicks, Elizabeth III, 445
Hicks, Elizabeth III, 468
Hicks, Elizabeth III, 473
Hicks, Elizabeth III, 484
Hicks, Elizabeth III, 485
Hicks, Elizabeth IV, 382
Hicks, Elizabeth IV, 408
Hicks, Elizabeth VI, 109
Hicks, Elizabeth VI, 813
Hicks, Elizabeth VI, 825
Hicks, Elizabeth A. VI, 806
Hicks, Elizabeth B. III, 485
Hicks, Elizabeth S. III, 164
Hicks, Elizabeth S. III, 416
Hicks, Elizabeth S. III, 484
Hicks, Elizabeth S. III, 490
Hicks, Elizabeth T. III, 163
Hicks, Elizabeth T. III, 165
Hicks, Elizabeth T. III, 417
Hicks, Elizabeth W. III, 417
Hicks, Elizabeth W. III, 419
Hicks, Ellen IV, 408
Hicks, Eloise W. III, 424
Hicks, Eloise Wentworth III, 41
Hicks, Elwood IV, 408
Hicks, Emaline IV, 408
Hicks, Emily I, 919
Hicks, Emily I, 927
Hicks, Emily III, 417
Hicks, Emily III, 419
Hicks, Emily III, 431
Hicks, Emma III, 417
Hicks, Emma III, 418
Hicks, Emma IV, 476
Hicks, Emma E. III, 417
Hicks, Emma E. III, 422
Hicks, Emma E. III, 431
Hicks, Emma E. III, 484
Hicks, Esther III, 164
Hicks, Esther III, 417
Hicks, Esther III, 486
Hicks, Esther J. III, 418
Hicks, Esther Jackson III, 409
Hicks, Eva V, 835
Hicks, Eva V, 843
Hicks, Fanny VI, 109
Hicks, Fletcher I, 919
Hicks, Fletcher I, 927
Hicks, Frances III, 164
Hicks, Francis W. II, 875
Hicks, Francis W. II, 877
Hicks, Frank IV, 476
Hicks, Frederick III, 417
Hicks, Frederick C. III, 418
Hicks, Frederick C. III, 448
Hicks, Geo. E. III, 163
Hicks, Geo. Lawrence IV, 476
Hicks, Geo. M. IV, 476
Hicks, Geo. M. IV, 1320
Hicks, George III, 164
Hicks, George III, 418
Hicks, George IV, 476
Hicks, George E. III, 164
Hicks, George E. III, 417
Hicks, George Embree III, 164
Hicks, George H. III, 47
Hicks, George Lawrence IV, 476
Hicks, George Lawrence IV, 132
Hicks, George M. IV, 476
Hicks, George N. IV, 1320
Hicks, Georgina III, 418
Hicks, Georgina III, 448
Hicks, Gertrude R. III, 419
Hicks, Gideon S. III, 416
Hicks, Gilbert III, 164
Hicks, Gilbert III, 165
Hicks, Gilbert III, 251
Hicks, Gilbert III, 418
Hicks, Gilbert III, 419
Hicks, Gilbert III, 466
Hicks, Grace III, 417
Hicks, Grace A. III, 32
Hicks, Grace A. III, 164
Hicks, Grace A. III, 418
Hicks, H. III, 68
Hicks, H. Sherwood II, 875
Hicks, Hannah II, 548
Hicks, Hannah II, 568
Hicks, Hannah II, 814
Hicks, Hannah III, 165
Hicks, Hannah III, 328
Hicks, Hannah III, 381
Hicks, Hannah III, 416
Hicks, Hannah III, 417
Hicks, Hannah III, 418
Hicks, Hannah III, 419
Hicks, Hannah III, 451
Hicks, Hannah III, 459
Hicks, Hannah III, 484
Hicks, Hannah C. III, 429
Hicks, Hannah M. III, 429
Hicks, Hannah U. III, 419
Hicks, Hannah U. III, 434
Hicks, Hannah W. III, 460
Hicks, Harriet III, 420
Hicks, Harriet III, 448
Hicks, Harriet III, 484
Hicks, Harriet III, 490
Hicks, Harriet L. III, 484
Hicks, Harrison IV, 408
Hicks, Hartwell I, 241
Hicks, Helen III, 409
Hicks, Helen III, 418
Hicks, Henrietta III, 165
Hicks, Henrietta III, 418
Hicks, Henry III, 164
Hicks, Henry III, 409
Hicks, Henry III, 417
Hicks, Henry III, 418
Hicks, Henry III, 421

icks, Henry III, 484
icks, Henry III, 485
icks, Henry III, 486
icks, Henry H. V, 246
icks, Henry W. III, 164
icks, Henry W. III, 165
icks, Henry William III, 164
icks, Horace I, 927
icks, Howard E. III, 418
icks, Howard Ellis III, 418
icks, I. I. VI, 889
icks, I. I. VI, 979
icks, I. I. VI, 1021
icks, Ida III, 418
icks, Ida III, 425
icks, Ida Willets III, 418
icks, Isaac I, 719
icks, Isaac II, 1052
icks, Isaac III, 25
icks, Isaac III, 105
icks, Isaac III, 163
icks, Isaac III, 164
icks, Isaac III, 185
icks, Isaac III, 281
icks, Isaac III, 286
icks, Isaac III, 415
icks, Isaac III, 417
icks, Isaac III, 418
icks, Isaac III, 419
icks, Isaac III, 445
icks, Isaac III, 473
icks, Isaac III, 484
icks, Isaac III, 507
icks, Isaac Cox III, 401
icks, Isaac H. III, 418
icks, Isaac H. III, 425
icks, Israel IV, 408
icks, J. Cromwell III, 429
icks, Jacob III, 416
icks, Jacob III, 417
icks, Jacob III, 418
icks, Jacob III, 419
icks, Jacob III, 429
icks, Jacob III, 451
icks, James I, 241
icks, James III, 417
icks, James III, 429
icks, James III, 484
icks, James IV, 149
icks, James IV, 365
icks, James IV, 403
icks, James IV, 408
icks, James IV, 450
icks, James IV, 584
icks, James VI, 109
icks, James VI, 817
icks, James VI, 825
icks, James VI, 847
icks, James M. III, 164
icks, James M. III, 417
icks, James M. III, 418
icks, James M. III, 419
icks, James, Jr. IV, 408
icks, Jane II, 374
icks, Jane II, 548
icks, Jane III, 164
icks, Jane III, 165
icks, Jane III, 416
icks, Jane III, 418
icks, Jane III, 424
icks, Jane VI, 310
icks, Jane VI, 314
icks, Jemima III, 417
icks, Jemima III, 444
icks, Jemima III, 469
icks, Jemima III, 479
icks, Jemima III, 484
icks, Jemima III, 498
icks, Jemima III, 506
icks, Jennie IV, 476
icks, Jennie IV, 1320
icks, Jennie M. IV, 476
icks, Jesse III, 484
icks, Jesse III, 498
icks, Jesse Hix VI, 314
icks, Joanna IV, 403
icks, Joanna IV, 408
icks, Joanna IV, 584
icks, Job I, 53
icks, John II, 548
icks, John III, 163
icks, John III, 165
icks, John III, 417
icks, John III, 418
icks, John III, 429
icks, John III, 436
icks, John III, 484
icks, John IV, 408
icks, John IV, 476
icks, John D. III, 153
icks, John D. III, 164
Hicks, John D. III, 165
Hicks, John D. III, 409
Hicks, John D. III, 418
Hicks, John D. III, 419
Hicks, John D. III, 441
Hicks, John D. III, 484
Hicks, John Haydock III, 165
Hicks, John Haydock, Jr. III, 164
Hicks, John S. III, 405
Hicks, John S. III, 416
Hicks, John S. III, 418
Hicks, John S. III, 419
Hicks, John S. III, 443
Hicks, John S. III, 464
Hicks, John Samuel III, 418
Hicks, Jos. III, 417
Hicks, Joseph II, 548
Hicks, Joseph III, 164
Hicks, Joseph III, 381
Hicks, Joseph III, 418
Hicks, Joseph III, 419
Hicks, Joseph III, 429
Hicks, Joseph IV, 148
Hicks, Joseph IV, 149
Hicks, Joseph IV, 161
Hicks, Joseph IV, 398
Hicks, Joseph IV, 408
Hicks, Joseph VI, 109
Hicks, Joseph Robert IV, 408
Hicks, Joseph W. III, 417
Hicks, Joshua T. III, 32
Hicks, Joshua T. III, 163
Hicks, Joshua T. III, 164
Hicks, Joshua T. III, 418
Hicks, Julia III, 165
Hicks, Julia III, 419
Hicks, Kezia III, 429
Hicks, Laban IV, 149
Hicks, Laban IV, 408
Hicks, Laban IV, 584
Hicks, Laban VI, 109
Hicks, Laben IV, 382
Hicks, Laben IV, 408
Hicks, Latitia III, 498
Hicks, Laura III, 418
Hicks, Lawrence IV, 1320
Hicks, Leona Rita I, 927
Hicks, Leonard III, 429
Hicks, Letitia III, 484
Hicks, Letitia III, 485
Hicks, Letitia III, 490
Hicks, Lillian I, 920
Hicks, Lillian B. N. III, 419
Hicks, Lillian H. I, 927
Hicks, Lillian M. I, 943
Hicks, Lillian Madison I, 927
Hicks, Lillian Madison I, 943
Hicks, Lillie III, 419
Hicks, Loiza IV, 584
Hicks, Louise III, 164
Hicks, Lucina IV, 408
Hicks, Lucinda IV, 149
Hicks, Lucinda IV, 161
Hicks, Lucinda IV, 408
Hicks, Lucy VI, 109
Hicks, Lurana I, 241
Hicks, Lydia I, 927
Hicks, Lydia III, 417
Hicks, Lydia III, 418
Hicks, Lydia III, 419
Hicks, Lydia IV, 403
Hicks, Lydia IV, 408
Hicks, Lydia IV, 584
Hicks, Lydia Ann IV, 408
Hicks, Malinda IV, 408
Hicks, Margaret I, 679
Hicks, Margaret II, 548
Hicks, Margaret II, 666
Hicks, Margaret II, 875
Hicks, Margaret II, 1002
Hicks, Margaret III, 163
Hicks, Margaret III, 164
Hicks, Margaret III, 165
Hicks, Margaret III, 251
Hicks, Margaret III, 417
Hicks, Margaret III, 418
Hicks, Margaret A. II, 875
Hicks, Margaret A. II, 877
Hicks, Margaret L. III, 445
Hicks, Margie I, 943
Hicks, Maria III, 416
Hicks, Maria L. III, 164
Hicks, Marianna III, 163
Hicks, Marianna III, 415
Hicks, Marianna III, 418
Hicks, Marie III, 418
Hicks, Marie III, 448
Hicks, Marietta III, 417
Hicks, Marjorie III, 405
Hicks, Marjorie III, 418
Hicks, Martha III, 163
Hicks, Martha III, 164
Hicks, Martha III, 165
Hicks, Martha III, 321
Hicks, Martha III, 408
Hicks, Martha III, 417
Hicks, Martha III, 418
Hicks, Martha III, 454
Hicks, Martha III, 457
Hicks, Martha III, 479
Hicks, Martha III, 484
Hicks, Martha IV, 408
Hicks, Martha IV, 450
Hicks, Martha IV, 476
Hicks, Martha IV, 584
Hicks, Martha M. III, 68
Hicks, Martha M. III, 164
Hicks, Martha T. III, 417
Hicks, Martha T. III, 418
Hicks, Martha W. III, 484
Hicks, Mary I, 241
Hicks, Mary I, 250
Hicks, Mary II, 374
Hicks, Mary II, 519
Hicks, Mary II, 548
Hicks, Mary II, 875
Hicks, Mary II, 877
Hicks, Mary II, 1052
Hicks, Mary III, 68
Hicks, Mary III, 126
Hicks, Mary III, 163
Hicks, Mary III, 164
Hicks, Mary III, 165
Hicks, Mary III, 251
Hicks, Mary III, 273
Hicks, Mary III, 381
Hicks, Mary III, 397
Hicks, Mary III, 411
Hicks, Mary III, 415
Hicks, Mary III, 416
Hicks, Mary III, 417
Hicks, Mary III, 418
Hicks, Mary III, 419
Hicks, Mary III, 422
Hicks, Mary III, 428
Hicks, Mary III, 429
Hicks, Mary III, 473
Hicks, Mary III, 484
Hicks, Mary III, 485
Hicks, Mary III, 498
Hicks, Mary IV, 148
Hicks, Mary IV, 149
Hicks, Mary IV, 398
Hicks, Mary IV, 408
Hicks, Mary IV, 584
Hicks, Mary VI, 99
Hicks, Mary VI, 109
Hicks, Mary A. III, 419
Hicks, Mary A. III, 426
Hicks, Mary Ann III, 484
Hicks, Mary Ann III, 485
Hicks, Mary Ann III, 498
Hicks, Mary Ann III, 510
Hicks, Mary Ann IV, 1275
Hicks, Mary Ann IV, 1281
Hicks, Mary Bailey IV, 408
Hicks, Mary C. III, 164
Hicks, Mary E. III, 82
Hicks, Mary E. III, 378
Hicks, Mary E. III, 381
Hicks, Mary E. III, 487
Hicks, Mary Elizabeth I, 927
Hicks, Mary Elizabeth III, 165
Hicks, Mary Elizabeth III, 381
Hicks, Mary F. III, 417
Hicks, Mary F. III, 418
Hicks, Mary F. III, 473
Hicks, Mary F. III, 484
Hicks, Mary F. III, 507
Hicks, Mary Jane IV, 408
Hicks, Mary M. III, 164
Hicks, Mary M. III, 400
Hicks, Mary M. III, 417
Hicks, Mary M. III, 419
Hicks, Mary M. III, 510
Hicks, Mary N. III, 164
Hicks, Mary P. III, 165
Hicks, Mary P. III, 419
Hicks, Mary R. III, 47
Hicks, Mary S. III, 165
Hicks, Mary S. III, 484
Hicks, Mary Titus III, 419
Hicks, Mary U. III, 419
Hicks, Mary W. III, 418
Hicks, Matilda III, 156
Hicks, Matilda III, 164
Hicks, Matilda III, 414
Hicks, Matilda III, 419
Hicks, Matt. III, 164
Hicks, Media I, 943
Hicks, Merritt III, 485
Hicks, Merritt III, 510
Hicks, Mesheck VI, 956
Hicks, Mildred VI, 825
Hicks, Milten IV, 408
Hicks, Milton IV, 408
Hicks, Miriam I, 241
Hicks, Miriam I, 251
Hicks, Mott III, 417
Hicks, Nathan P. II, 875
Hicks, Oliver III, 164
Hicks, Peggay I, 241
Hicks, Peggay I, 246
Hicks, Peggy I, 241
Hicks, Peggy III, 318
Hicks, Peggy III, 419
Hicks, Peggy III, 454
Hicks, Peter I, 241
Hicks, Phebe III, 47
Hicks, Phebe III, 163
Hicks, Phebe III, 164
Hicks, Phebe III, 165
Hicks, Phebe III, 397
Hicks, Phebe III, 398
Hicks, Phebe III, 399
Hicks, Phebe III, 416
Hicks, Phebe III, 417
Hicks, Phebe III, 418
Hicks, Phebe III, 419
Hicks, Phebe III, 434
Hicks, Phebe III, 436
Hicks, Phebe III, 444
Hicks, Phebe III, 451
Hicks, Phebe III, 454
Hicks, Phebe III, 469
Hicks, Phebe III, 484
Hicks, Phebe III, 487
Hicks, Phebe III, 490
Hicks, Phebe III, 501
Hicks, Phebe III, 503
Hicks, Phebe III, 506
Hicks, Phebe Amelia III, 484
Hicks, Phebe Amelia III, 503
Hicks, Phebe Amelia W. III, 484
Hicks, Phebe B. III, 417
Hicks, Phebe M. III, 419
Hicks, Phebe M. III, 484
Hicks, Priscilla Alden III, 381
Hicks, Rachel III, 165
Hicks, Rachel III, 417
Hicks, Rachel III, 418
Hicks, Rachel III, 419
Hicks, Rachel III, 420
Hicks, Rachel III, 443
Hicks, Rachel III, 444
Hicks, Rachel III, 469
Hicks, Rachel III, 470
Hicks, Rachel III, 474
Hicks, Rachel III, 484
Hicks, Rachel III, 507
Hicks, Rachel IV, 149
Hicks, Rachel IV, 408
Hicks, Rachel IV, 426
Hicks, Rachel VI, 109
Hicks, Rachel VI, 640
Hicks, Rachel VI, 650
Hicks, Rachel Ann III, 164
Hicks, Rachel Ann III, 199
Hicks, Rachel C. III, 416
Hicks, Rachel V. III, 418
Hicks, Rachel V. III, 419
Hicks, Rachel V. III, 464
Hicks, Rachel W. III, 419
Hicks, Rachel, Jr. VI, 400
Hicks, Ralph III, 419
Hicks, Rebecca I, 241
Hicks, Rebecca III, 429
Hicks, Rebecca IV, 476
Hicks, Rev. ??? V, 835
Hicks, Richard W. VI, 824
Hicks, Richard W. VI, 825
Hicks, Richard Y. III, 419
Hicks, Robert I, 241
Hicks, Robert III, 164
Hicks, Robert III, 165
Hicks, Robert III, 417
Hicks, Robert III, 419
Hicks, Robert IV, 149
Hicks, Robert IV, 408
Hicks, Robert IV, 584
Hicks, Robert VI, 109
Hicks, Robert A. III, 419
Hicks, Robert H. III, 418
Hicks, Robert M. III, 164
Hicks, Robert M. III, 204
Hicks, Robert M. III, 414
Hicks, Robert M. III, 417
Hicks, Robert M. III, 419
Hicks, Robert T. III, 164
Hicks, Robert T. III, 165
Hicks, Robt. III, 48
Hicks, Robt. M. III, 47
Hicks, Rosana III, 419
Hicks, Rosana III, 420
Hicks, Rosana III, 441
Hicks, Rosanna III, 48
Hicks, Rosanna F. III, 164
Hicks, Rosanna F. III, 204
Hicks, Rosannah III, 414
Hicks, Rosannah III, 419
Hicks, Rose Anna III, 47
Hicks, Rose Anna III, 164
Hicks, Rosita III, 420
Hicks, Rosita S. III, 419
Hicks, Rosita S. III, 420
Hicks, Rosita S. III, 441
Hicks, Ruth III, 164
Hicks, Ruth III, 419
Hicks, Ruth T. III, 420
Hicks, Ruth T. III, 422
Hicks, Sadie Agnes I, 927
Hicks, Sallie I, 919
Hicks, Sallie I, 943
Hicks, Sallie A. I, 927
Hicks, Sampson IV, 476
Hicks, Samuel III, 112
Hicks, Samuel III, 160
Hicks, Samuel III, 164
Hicks, Samuel III, 165
Hicks, Samuel III, 268
Hicks, Samuel III, 399
Hicks, Samuel III, 408
Hicks, Samuel III, 416
Hicks, Samuel III, 418
Hicks, Samuel III, 419
Hicks, Samuel III, 429
Hicks, Samuel III, 444
Hicks, Samuel III, 446
Hicks, Samuel III, 474
Hicks, Samuel III, 484
Hicks, Samuel III, 507
Hicks, Samuel M. III, 419
Hicks, Sarah II, 800
Hicks, Sarah II, 1052
Hicks, Sarah III, 105
Hicks, Sarah III, 160
Hicks, Sarah III, 163
Hicks, Sarah III, 164
Hicks, Sarah III, 165
Hicks, Sarah III, 268
Hicks, Sarah III, 355
Hicks, Sarah III, 378
Hicks, Sarah III, 381
Hicks, Sarah III, 385
Hicks, Sarah III, 403
Hicks, Sarah III, 411
Hicks, Sarah III, 415
Hicks, Sarah III, 417
Hicks, Sarah III, 418
Hicks, Sarah III, 419
Hicks, Sarah III, 429
Hicks, Sarah III, 441
Hicks, Sarah III, 445
Hicks, Sarah III, 471
Hicks, Sarah III, 484
Hicks, Sarah III, 498
Hicks, Sarah IV, 476
Hicks, Sarah A. III, 403
Hicks, Sarah A. III, 419
Hicks, Sarah A. III, 420
Hicks, Sarah A. III, 429
Hicks, Sarah Cornelia III, 484
Hicks, Sarah Cornelia III, 487
Hicks, Sarah Cornelia S. III, 484
Hicks, Sarah H. III, 126
Hicks, Sarah H. III, 164
Hicks, Sarah H. III, 165
Hicks, Sarah H. III, 417
Hicks, Sarah H. III, 418
Hicks, Sarah H. III, 419
Hicks, Sarah M. II, 875
Hicks, Sarah R. III, 164
Hicks, Sarah R. III, 165
Hicks, Sarah R. III, 418
Hicks, Sarah R. III, 419
Hicks, Sarah R. III, 484
Hicks, Sarah R. III, 497
Hicks, Sarah T. III, 165
Hicks, Sarah T. III, 381
Hicks, Sarah T. III, 389
Hicks, Sarah T. III, 417
Hicks, Sarah T. III, 419
Hicks, Sarah T. III, 440
Hicks, Sarah W. III, 419
Hicks, Sheffield III, 164
Hicks, Silas III, 76
Hicks, Silas III, 163
Hicks, Silas III, 165
Hicks, Silas III, 378
Hicks, Silas III, 381
Hicks, Silas III, 385
Hicks, Silas III, 389
Hicks, Silas III, 416
Hicks, Silas III, 417

Hicks, Silas III, 418
Hicks, Silas III, 419
Hicks, Silas III, 444
Hicks, Silas, Jr. III, 165
Hicks, Silas, Jr. III, 381
Hicks, Smith III, 165
Hicks, Smith III, 419
Hicks, Smith III, 484
Hicks, Smith III, 487
Hicks, Smith III, 490
Hicks, Smith III, 503
Hicks, Stephen III, 416
Hicks, Stephen III, 419
Hicks, Stephen III, 485
Hicks, Stephen R. III, 165
Hicks, Stephen R. III, 328
Hicks, Stephen R. III, 416
Hicks, Stephen R. III, 418
Hicks, Stephen R. III, 419
Hicks, Stephen R. III, 434
Hicks, Stephen R. III, 459
Hicks, Stephen R. III, 460
Hicks, Surany I, 241
Hicks, Susan II, 1052
Hicks, Susan III, 165
Hicks, Susan III, 396
Hicks, Susan III, 398
Hicks, Susan III, 417
Hicks, Susan III, 419
Hicks, Susan H. III, 59
Hicks, Susannah II, 799
Hicks, Tabitha I, 241
Hicks, Tabitha I, 246
Hicks, Temperance III, 163
Hicks, Temperance III, 417
Hicks, Temperance III, 419
Hicks, Temperance III, 428
Hicks, These III, 416
Hicks, Thomas I, 241
Hicks, Thomas I, 246
Hicks, Thomas III, 163
Hicks, Thomas III, 164
Hicks, Thomas III, 165
Hicks, Thomas III, 419
Hicks, Thomas VI, 932
Hicks, Thomas Askew II, 800
Hicks, Thomas M. III, 419
Hicks, Thos. A. II, 875
Hicks, Valentine III, 164
Hicks, Valentine III, 165
Hicks, Valentine III, 417
Hicks, Valentine III, 418
Hicks, Valentine III, 419
Hicks, Valentine III, 484
Hicks, Valentine III, 498
Hicks, Valentine III, 501
Hicks, Viola Lee I, 927
Hicks, Virginia III, 418
Hicks, Walter I, 943
Hicks, Walter III, 165
Hicks, Walter III, 418
Hicks, Walter III, 419
Hicks, Walter III, 422
Hicks, Walter L. I, 943
Hicks, Walter Lee I, 927
Hicks, Wd. Amy III, 419
Hicks, Wd. Elizabeth H. III, 281
Hicks, Wd. Phebe III, 484
Hicks, Whitehead III, 163
Hicks, Whitehead III, 164
Hicks, Whitehead III, 165
Hicks, Whitehead III, 318
Hicks, Whitehead III, 417
Hicks, Whitehead III, 418
Hicks, Whitehead III, 419
Hicks, Whitehead III, 426
Hicks, Whitehead III, 454
Hicks, Whitehead III, 485
Hicks, Whitehead III, 490
Hicks, Whitehead III, 510
Hicks, Willet II, 1074
Hicks, Willet III, 68
Hicks, Willet III, 164
Hicks, Willet III, 403
Hicks, Willet III, 417
Hicks, Willet III, 419
Hicks, Willet III, 420
Hicks, Willet III, 429
Hicks, Willet H. III, 164
Hicks, Willet J. III, 419
Hicks, Willett III, 165
Hicks, William I, 241
Hicks, William III, 165
Hicks, William III, 273
Hicks, William III, 381
Hicks, William III, 416
Hicks, William III, 419
Hicks, William III, 420
Hicks, William III, 422
Hicks, William III, 485
Hicks, William III, 498
Hicks, William IV, 408
Hicks, William IV, 584
Hicks, William VI, 109
Hicks, William VI, 932
Hicks, William C. III, 418
Hicks, William C. III, 419
Hicks, William H. VI, 932
Hicks, William L. III, 420
Hicks, William S. III, 485
Hicks, William T. III, 165
Hicks, Willit III, 419
Hicks, Wm. II, 875
Hicks, Wm. II, 877
Hicks, Wm. IV, 584
Hicks, Wm. VI, 813
Hicks, Wm. L. III, 419
Hicks, Wm. L. III, 441
Hicks, Wm. Leonard III, 420
Hicks, Wm. Mott III, 420
Hicks, Wm. Mott III, 448
Hicks, Wm. Preston III, 418
Hicks, Wm. S. III, 484
Hicks, Wm. S. III, 490
Hicks, Wm. S. III, 498
Hicks, Y. III, 417
Hicks, Zilpah IV, 408
Hicks, Zilpha IV, 408
Hicks, Zilpha IV, 450
Hicksites, ??? V, 17
Hickson, Anna IV, 1237
Hickson, David IV, 1211
Hickson, Grace IV, 1211
Hickson, Hattie IV, 1211
Hickson, Lucy IV, 1211
Hickson, Mary I, 1047
Hickson, Mary I, 1048
Hickson, Sarah IV, 1165
Hickson, Sarah VI, 640
Hickson, Sarah VI, 650
Hickson, Will IV, 1211
Hickson, Willie IV, 1165
Hickson, Wm. IV, 1165
Hiday, Elizabeth V, 72
Hiday, Elizabeth V, 111
Hide, Anne IV, 1197
Hide, Edmund II, 548
Hide, Sarah II, 548
Hide, Sarah II, 549
Hidy, G. H. V, 1001
Hidy, Israel V, 1001
Hidy, Josephine V, 1001
Hiefield, Susan V, 1001
Hiel, Sally V, 612
Hiel, Sally V, 625
Hiet, Absolom I, 986
Hiet, Caleb I, 986
Hiet, Catherine I, 986
Hiet, Eli I, 986
Hiet, Enos I, 986
Hiet, Frank V, 178
Hiet, Hannah I, 986
Hiet, John I, 986
Hiet, Joseph I, 986
Hiet, Mary I, 986
Hiett, Abigail I, 1009
Hiett, Abigail I, 1010
Hiett, Absolem I, 1094
Hiett, Absolom I, 963
Hiett, Absolom I, 968
Hiett, Amaziah V, 245
Hiett, Amos I, 963
Hiett, Amos I, 964
Hiett, Ann I, 956
Hiett, Ann I, 963
Hiett, Ann I, 968
Hiett, Ann I, 1001
Hiett, Anna I, 963
Hiett, Anna V, 304
Hiett, Anne IV, 568
Hiett, Anne IV, 583
Hiett, Anne V, 178
Hiett, Asher I, 963
Hiett, Azariah I, 955
Hiett, Azariah I, 963
Hiett, Benjamin I, 963
Hiett, Benjamin V, 245
Hiett, Benjamin V, 330
Hiett, Catharine I, 963
Hiett, Charity I, 815
Hiett, Charity I, 817
Hiett, Charles I, 963
Hiett, Charles I, 986
Hiett, Charles I, 991
Hiett, Christopher I, 545
Hiett, Christopher I, 963
Hiett, Daniel Matthews VI, 504
Hiett, David V, 304
Hiett, Eli I, 963
Hiett, Eli I, 986
Hiett, Eli I, 1094
Hiett, Eliet I, 963
Hiett, Elihu V, 245
Hiett, Elihue John Reuben V, 245
Hiett, Elijah IV, 568
Hiett, Elijah IV, 583
Hiett, Elisha I, 963
Hiett, Elisha IV, 583
Hiett, Elizabeth I, 1001
Hiett, Elizabeth Reece I, 963
Hiett, Enoch I, 986
Hiett, Enos I, 544
Hiett, Evan I, 544
Hiett, Evan VI, 399
Hiett, Flora V, 178
Hiett, George I, 956
Hiett, George VI, 400
Hiett, George VI, 504
Hiett, Gertrude V, 245
Hiett, Gideon V, 178
Hiett, Hannah I, 963
Hiett, Hannah I, 968
Hiett, Hannah I, 1001
Hiett, Hannah I, 1094
Hiett, Hannah V, 246
Hiett, Harmon V, 245
Hiett, Henry V, 245
Hiett, Hermin V, 246
Hiett, Howard I, 963
Hiett, Ithamar V, 245
Hiett, Jacob I, 956
Hiett, Jacob I, 961
Hiett, Jacob I, 963
Hiett, Jacob V, 245
Hiett, Jacob V, 246
Hiett, James VI, 399
Hiett, Jather I, 963
Hiett, Jehu I, 963
Hiett, Jehu IV, 583
Hiett, Jemima I, 955
Hiett, Jemima I, 959
Hiett, Jemima I, 963
Hiett, Jemima I, 1009
Hiett, Jemima I, 1011
Hiett, Jemima IV, 573
Hiett, Jemima IV, 583
Hiett, Jesse I, 956
Hiett, Jesse I, 963
Hiett, Jesse V, 178
Hiett, Jesse V, 245
Hiett, Joel I, 545
Hiett, John I, 394
Hiett, John I, 544
Hiett, John I, 956
Hiett, John I, 963
Hiett, John V, 178
Hiett, John V, 207
Hiett, John V, 245
Hiett, John VI, 399
Hiett, John, Jr. I, 544
Hiett, Jonah I, 963
Hiett, Jonathan I, 963
Hiett, Jonathan I, 1009
Hiett, Jonathan IV, 573
Hiett, Jonathan IV, 583
Hiett, Jonathan Williams VI, 504
Hiett, Joseph I, 544
Hiett, Joseph I, 545
Hiett, Joseph I, 783
Hiett, Joseph I, 956
Hiett, Joseph I, 963
Hiett, Joseph I, 986
Hiett, Joseph V, 245
Hiett, Joseph V, 246
Hiett, Joseph, Jr. I, 963
Hiett, Joseph, Jr. V, 245
Hiett, Kezia I, 783
Hiett, Levina V, 245
Hiett, Lewis IV, 583
Hiett, Lydda I, 963
Hiett, Lydia VI, 504
Hiett, Lydia, Jr. I, 544
Hiett, Martha I, 783
Hiett, Martha I, 1009
Hiett, Martha I, 1011
Hiett, Martha VI, 504
Hiett, Martha VI, 505
Hiett, Mary I, 955
Hiett, Mary I, 963
Hiett, Mary I, 991
Hiett, Mary V, 178
Hiett, Mary V, 207
Hiett, Mary V, 245
Hiett, Mary V, 330
Hiett, Mary VI, 399
Hiett, Mary VI, 432
Hiett, Moses I, 963
Hiett, Nathan V, 245
Hiett, Olive I, 963
Hiett, Olive V, 246
Hiett, Phebe I, 963
Hiett, Phebe I, 1001
Hiett, Priscilla I, 963
Hiett, Priscilla I, 964
Hiett, Rachel I, 956
Hiett, Rachel I, 959
Hiett, Rachel I, 963
Hiett, Rachel I, 1001
Hiett, Rachel I, 1009
Hiett, Rachel V, 178
Hiett, Rebecca V, 245
Hiett, Rebecca V, 246
Hiett, Richard I, 956
Hiett, Richard V, 304
Hiett, Rosannah V, 178
Hiett, Rosannah V, 207
Hiett, Rosemeal V, 178
Hiett, Ruben V, 178
Hiett, Ruth I, 956
Hiett, Ruth Hannah Mourning V, 245
Hiett, Sarah I, 545
Hiett, Sarah I, 579
Hiett, Sarah I, 783
Hiett, Sarah I, 956
Hiett, Sarah I, 1009
Hiett, Sarah I, 1011
Hiett, Sarah V, 245
Hiett, Sarah V, 304
Hiett, Silas I, 963
Hiett, Solomon I, 545
Hiett, Solomon I, 963
Hiett, Stephen I, 963
Hiett, Surry I, 963
Hiett, Susanah I, 961
Hiett, Susanna I, 963
Hiett, Susanna V, 245
Hiett, Susannah I, 545
Hiett, Susannah I, 956
Hiett, Susannah I, 963
Hiett, Susannah V, 246
Hiett, Susannah V, 304
Hiett, Tamar IV, 583
Hiett, Thomas I, 963
Hiett, Triot I, 963
Hiett, William I, 544
Hiett, William I, 545
Hiett, William I, 956
Hiett, William I, 963
Hiett, William V, 304
Hiett, William VI, 399
Hiett, William, Jr. I, 963
Hiett, Zachariah I, 783
Hiett, Zacharias I, 963
Hiette, Priscillah I, 1009
Hifford, Davis V, 1001
Hifford, Margaret E. V, 1001
Higbee, Ann Eliza V, 882
Higbee, Ann Eliza V, 887
Higbie, Elias B. III, 420
Higbie, Henry III, 420
Higbie, Joseph III, 397
Higbie, Joseph III, 420
Higbie, Rhoda III, 420
Higbie, Sarah III, 397
Higbie, Sarah III, 420
Higbie, Sarah III, 439
Higby, ??? III, 114
Higby, Ann III, 114
Higby, Mary II, 374
Higby, Phebe III, 165
Higby, Rachel II, 78
Higby, Rachel II, 93
Higgenbotham, Eliza VI, 976
Higgenbotham, Eliza A. VI, 932
Higgenbotham, James W. VI, 932
Higgenbotham, James, Jr. VI, 932
Higgenbotham, Jos. C. VI, 976
Higgenbotham, Nancy Ann VI, 932
Higgens, Ann W. VI, 932
Higgens, Joshua VI, 932
Higginbotham, Joanna VI, 932
Higginbotham, Jos. C. VI, 903
Higginbotham, Jos. C. VI, 1011
Higginbotham, Joseph C. VI, 932
Higginbotham, Lucinda Catharine VI, 1011
Higginbotham, Lucy VI, 800
Higginbotham, Mary III, 132
Higginbotham, Mary III, 165
Higginbotham, Mary VI, 903
Higginbotham, Thomas VI, 864
Higgins, Ann V, 676
Higgins, Ann Elizabeth V, 566
Higgins, Bethany III, 165
Higgins, Bethany III, 316
Higgins, Dr. ??? III, 165
Higgins, Dr. ??? III, 316
Higgins, Emma II, 875
Higgins, Emma Dyer II, 800
Higgins, Franklin Rickert II, 800
Higgins, Geo. E. IV, 1320
Higgins, George II, 875
Higgins, George Frank II, 875
Higgins, George Franklin II, 80
Higgins, Jane III, 165
Higgins, Jane III, 323
Higgins, John III, 165
Higgins, John V, 395
Higgins, John VI, 877
Higgins, John Hale III, 165
Higgins, John Hale III, 323
Higgins, Joseph V, 430
Higgins, Katharine V, 430
Higgins, Margaret VI, 895
Higgins, Mary III, 165
Higgins, Mary VI, 400
Higgins, Mary VI, 410
Higgins, Nancy VI, 877
Higgins, Polly Ann VI, 972
Higgins, Sara E. II, 800
Higgins, Sarah E. V, 430
Higginson, Agnes III, 165
Higginson, Ethel III, 165
Higginson, Ethel III, 166
Higginson, Frederick III, 165
Higginson, Wm. John III, 165
Higginson, Wm. John III, 166
Higgs, Ann II, 961
Higgs, Elizabeth II, 961
Higgs, Elizabeth II, 974
Higgs, Elizabeth II, 1002
Higgs, Elizabeth II, 1004
Higgs, James II, 961
Higgs, James II, 974
Higgs, James II, 999
Higgs, James II, 1002
Higgs, Jane II, 961
Higgs, Jane II, 999
Higgs, Jane II, 1002
Higgs, John II, 961
Higgs, Mary II, 961
Higgs, Sarah II, 961
High, Flora A. V, 1001
High, Henry V, 1001
High, James V, 1001
High, Josie V, 1001
High, Marion V, 1001
High, Mary E. V, 1001
High, Sadie M. V, 1001
High, Sarah V, 1001
High, Sarah E. V, 1001
High, Susan E. V, 1001
Highat, Isaac VI, 399
Highat, John VI, 399
Highatt, Lydia I, 1053
Highet, Anna IV, 408
Highet, Elisha IV, 408
Highet, Jehu IV, 408
Highet, Julia I, 986
Highet, Lydia IV, 408
Highett, Joseph V, 245
Highland, Cora Spencer I, 1154
Highly, James VI, 825
Highly, Nancy VI, 825
Highmiller, Ellie V, 458
Highmiller, John V, 458
Highot, Jehu I, 883
Highot, Joseph I, 883
Highot, Keziah I, 883
Highot, Lydia I, 883
Highot, Mary I, 883
Hight, Albert VI, 825
Hight, America A. VI, 825
Hight, Anna Rachel V, 245
Hight, Hartwell VI, 847
Hight, Hartwell VI, 854
Hight, John VI, 799
Hight, John VI, 825
Hight, Martha VI, 825
Hight, Martha VI, 857
Hight, Martha E. V, 625
Hight, Mary V, 245
Hight, Mary VI, 825
Hight, Mary VI, 854
Hight, Phebe IV, 1356
Hight, Phebe IV, 1367
Hight, Phebe VI, 825
Hight, Richard VI, 825
Hight, Rosanah V, 245
Hight, Samuel VI, 825
Hight, Susan VI, 825
Hightower, Catherine Ann I, 1121
Hightower, Eliza VI, 807
Hightower, Frances VI, 825
Hightower, George VI, 807
Hightower, George VI, 825
Hightower, George VI, 830
Hightower, Jency VI, 830
Hightower, Joseph Albert I, 112
Hightower, Polly VI, 825
Hightower, Rachel I, 1121

ightower, Rachel I, 1127
ightower, Richard VI, 825
ightower, Sarah C. I, 1121
ightower, Susanna VI, 856
ightower, Thomas VI, 856
igley, Frank V, 1001
igth, Mary A. VI, 825
igth, Robert VI, 825
ilborn, Howard P. IV, 1320
ilborn, John II, 375
ilborn, Mary II, 231
ilborn, Mary II, 260
ilborn, Mary S. II, 876
ilborn, Miles II, 375
ilborn, Paul A. IV, 1320
ilborn, Robert II, 231
ilborn, Thomas II, 231
ilborn, Thos. II, 260
ilborne, Elizabeth II, 374
ilbourn, Ann II, 1002
ilbourn, Frances II, 549
ilbourn, John II, 375
ilbourn, Katharine II, 1002
ilbourn, Kathrine II, 1002
ilbourn, Mary II, 231
ilbourn, Thomas II, 231
ilbourn, Thomas II, 1002
ilburne, Joseph II, 375
ilburne, Miles II, 375
ildabourn, Elizabeth II, 541
ildabourn, Elizabeth II, 549
ildbran, Rachel V, 809
ildebold, Lenora IV, 1211
ildebran, Anson V, 809
ildebran, John V, 809
ildebran, Rachel V, 809
ildebrand, Effie IV, 1211
ildebrand, Elizabeth II, 541
ildebrand, Elizabeth II, 549
ildebrand, Martin II, 549
ildebrand, Mary Ann II, 78
ildebrandt, T. Q. V, 682
ildebrandt, Thomas Q. V, 682
ildebrant, Elizabeth W. V, 682
ildebrant, Elizabeth W. V, 697
ildebrant, Henry V, 682
ildebrant, Henry V, 697
ildebrant, T. Q. V, 682
ildebrant, Thomas Q. V, 682
ildebrant, Thos. Q. V, 910
ildeburn, Elizabeth II, 512
ildeburn, Elizabeth II, 549
ildeburn, John II, 549
ildeburn, John Martin II, 375
ildeburn, Martin II, 512
ildeburn, Martin II, 549
ildeburn, Phebe II, 549
ildeburn, Phebe II, 589
ildeburn, Sarah II, 512
ildeburn, Sarah II, 549
ildeburn, Sarah II, 792
ildegarde, Jacob R. V, 672
ilderbrand, Mary Ann II, 78
ilderbrand, Mary Ann II, 81
ilderman, Ann II, 78
ildreth, Malinda IV, 1281
ildreth, Sarah V, 682
ildreth, Sarah E. V, 395
ildreth, Sarah E. V, 682
ildreth, Warren IV, 1281
ileman, Celina V, 1001
iler, Catharine IV, 476
ilerman, Rachel IV, 296
ilers, Nettie III, 152
iles, Mary II, 151
iles, Mary II, 154
iles, Mary Ann II, 119
iles, Mary Ann II, 121
iles, Nettie III, 334
iles, Rachel IV, 722
iles, Rachel IV, 964
iley, Ann VI, 400
ilgeneck, Lucy IV, 1320
ill, Aaron I, 53
ill, Aaron I, 100
ill, Aaron I, 101
ill, Aaron I, 113
ill, Aaron I, 142
ill, Aaron I, 143
ill, Aaron I, 157
ill, Aaron I, 395
ill, Aaron I, 481
ill, Aaron I, 654
ill, Aaron I, 655
ill, Aaron I, 679
ill, Aaron I, 688
ill, Aaron I, 700
ill, Aaron I, 701
ill, Aaron I, 710
ill, Aaron I, 719
ill, Aaron I, 720
Hill, Aaron I, 721
Hill, Aaron I, 735
Hill, Aaron I, 738
Hill, Aaron I, 816
Hill, Aaron VI, 162
Hill, Aaron VI, 180
Hill, Aaron Linus I, 701
Hill, Aaron Linus I, 783
Hill, Aaron O. I, 721
Hill, Aaron, Sr. I, 701
Hill, Aaron, Sr. I, 720
Hill, Abigail I, 748
Hill, Abigail I, 762
Hill, Abigail N. I, 700
Hill, Abigail N. I, 720
Hill, Abigail N. I, 726
Hill, Abram I, 701
Hill, Achas I, 395
Hill, Achas I, 426
Hill, Achsah I, 395
Hill, Achsah I, 700
Hill, Achsah I, 720
Hill, Achsah I, 730
Hill, Achsah V, 336
Hill, Achsah V, 953
Hill, Acksah II, 549
Hill, Adaline V, 336
Hill, Adliza J. I, 721
Hill, Adliza J. I, 738
Hill, Agnes II, 961
Hill, Alice V, 682
Hill, Alice VI, 561
Hill, Alice VI, 562
Hill, Alice VI, 563
Hill, Alice VI, 571
Hill, Alice VI, 644
Hill, Alice VI, 702
Hill, Alice VI, 705
Hill, Alice VI, 706
Hill, Alice VI, 707
Hill, Alice VI, 710
Hill, Alice, Jr. VI, 562
Hill, Allin I, 701
Hill, Almira IV, 39
Hill, Almira IV, 42
Hill, Alvin I, 927
Hill, Amelia C. V, 625
Hill, Amos IV, 475
Hill, Amos Line IV, 633
Hill, Ana I, 719
Hill, Andrew J. I, 308
Hill, Ann I, 100
Hill, Ann I, 141
Hill, Ann I, 143
Hill, Ann I, 353
Hill, Ann I, 379
Hill, Ann I, 394
Hill, Ann I, 395
Hill, Ann I, 426
Hill, Ann I, 701
Hill, Ann I, 719
Hill, Ann I, 720
Hill, Ann I, 726
Hill, Ann I, 741
Hill, Ann I, 748
Hill, Ann I, 760
Hill, Ann I, 855
Hill, Ann I, 883
Hill, Ann I, 894
Hill, Ann I, 919
Hill, Ann I, 927
Hill, Ann II, 374
Hill, Ann II, 549
Hill, Ann VI, 30
Hill, Ann E. I, 701
Hill, Anna I, 395
Hill, Anna I, 425
Hill, Anna I, 695
Hill, Anna I, 701
Hill, Anna I, 719
Hill, Anna V, 747
Hill, Anna V, 1001
Hill, Anne M. VI, 256
Hill, Annie VI, 249
Hill, Annie M. VI, 249
Hill, Annie M. VI, 256
Hill, Annis V, 1001
Hill, Arbulissa B. I, 618
Hill, Aron I, 720
Hill, Aron Orlando I, 700
Hill, Artalissa B. I, 634
Hill, Artilissa I, 927
Hill, Artilissa B. I, 943
Hill, Artlissa I, 943
Hill, Asenath I, 700
Hill, Asenath E. I, 481
Hill, Asenath E. I, 720
Hill, Asenath H. I, 700
Hill, Asenath H. I, 720
Hill, Asenath H. I, 732
Hill, Asher II, 549
Hill, Axum I, 720
Hill, Benjamin I, 546
Hill, Benjamin I, 553
Hill, Benjamin I, 655
Hill, Benjamin I, 700
Hill, Benjamin I, 719
Hill, Benjamin I, 730
Hill, Benjamin I, 1005
Hill, Benjamin I, 1010
Hill, Benjamin V, 72
Hill, Benjamin V, 742
Hill, Benoni I, 701
Hill, Benoni I, 709
Hill, Benoni I, 720
Hill, Benony I, 720
Hill, Bertha V, 458
Hill, Bertha V, 682
Hill, Caroline V, 575
Hill, Carson I, 943
Hill, Catharine II, 809
Hill, Catharine II, 898
Hill, Celia VI, 966
Hill, Charles II, 1052
Hill, Charles VI, 825
Hill, Charles Alpheus I, 701
Hill, Charles Alpheus I, 783
Hill, Charles E. III, 166
Hill, Charles Moore II, 549
Hill, Charles S. I, 816
Hill, Charlotte III, 369
Hill, Chas. II, 800
Hill, Chas. R. V, 336
Hill, Chas. R. V, 911
Hill, Christopher I, 701
Hill, Christopher I, 719
Hill, Clark I, 353
Hill, Clark I, 395
Hill, Clark I, 719
Hill, Clifton G. VI, 951
Hill, Cophire VI, 983
Hill, Cornelia I, 876
Hill, Daniel I, 353
Hill, Daniel I, 395
Hill, Daniel I, 748
Hill, Daniel I, 762
Hill, Daniel V, 336
Hill, Daniel V, 341
Hill, Daniel V, 782
Hill, Daniel V, 910
Hill, Daniel V, 911
Hill, Daniel V, 912
Hill, Daniel V, 953
Hill, Daniel V, 960
Hill, Daniel M. I, 701
Hill, Daniel M. I, 783
Hill, Daniel M. I, 816
Hill, Deborah II, 549
Hill, Deborah II, 1002
Hill, Deborah III, 165
Hill, Deborah IV, 221
Hill, Deborah IV, 260
Hill, Delphina I, 876
Hill, Delphina I, 884
Hill, Dora V, 73
Hill, Dora V, 178
Hill, Dorcas V, 782
Hill, Dove II, 374
Hill, Dr. Nathan Branson I, 701
Hill, Edith I, 748
Hill, Edith I, 762
Hill, Edith I, 943
Hill, Edna I, 943
Hill, Edna M. I, 927
Hill, Edward II, 374
Hill, Edward III, 165
Hill, Edwin IV, 475
Hill, Elihu IV, 633
Hill, Elijah V, 178
Hill, Eliner II, 374
Hill, Elisabeth II, 549
Hill, Eliza I, 701
Hill, Eliza I, 720
Hill, Eliza I, 724
Hill, Eliza V, 336
Hill, Eliza L. I, 701
Hill, Eliza L. I, 720
Hill, Eliza L. I, 816
Hill, Eliza L. I, 829
Hill, Eliza T. I, 816
Hill, Elizabeth I, 701
Hill, Elizabeth I, 719
Hill, Elizabeth I, 720
Hill, Elizabeth I, 728
Hill, Elizabeth II, 32
Hill, Elizabeth II, 49
Hill, Elizabeth II, 78
Hill, Elizabeth II, 86
Hill, Elizabeth II, 176
Hill, Elizabeth II, 205
Hill, Elizabeth II, 231
Hill, Elizabeth II, 374
Hill, Elizabeth II, 400
Hill, Elizabeth II, 549
Hill, Elizabeth II, 608
Hill, Elizabeth II, 645
Hill, Elizabeth II, 793
Hill, Elizabeth II, 795
Hill, Elizabeth II, 803
Hill, Elizabeth II, 818
Hill, Elizabeth II, 875
Hill, Elizabeth II, 1052
Hill, Elizabeth III, 165
Hill, Elizabeth III, 166
Hill, Elizabeth III, 213
Hill, Elizabeth IV, 39
Hill, Elizabeth IV, 57
Hill, Elizabeth IV, 335
Hill, Elizabeth IV, 354
Hill, Elizabeth V, 332
Hill, Elizabeth V, 336
Hill, Elizabeth V, 742
Hill, Elizabeth V, 747
Hill, Elizabeth V, 782
Hill, Elizabeth V, 911
Hill, Elizabeth VI, 30
Hill, Elizabeth VI, 816
Hill, Elizabeth VI, 828
Hill, Elizabeth VI, 912
Hill, Elizabeth VI, 952
Hill, Elizabeth VI, 966
Hill, Elizabeth Josephine V, 911
Hill, Elizabeth L. IV, 221
Hill, Elizabeth L. IV, 235
Hill, Elizabeth L. IV, 476
Hill, Elizabeth L. IV, 481
Hill, Elizabeth Magdalen II, 795
Hill, Elizabeth R. III, 165
Hill, Elizabeth W. II, 875
Hill, Elizabeth Z. V, 782
Hill, Elizabeth Z. V, 783
Hill, Ella V, 575
Hill, Ellen III, 165
Hill, Ellen M. III, 439
Hill, Emily Lathrop V, 72
Hill, Emma V, 336
Hill, Emma V, 458
Hill, Emma V, 682
Hill, Emma D. III, 165
Hill, Emma Mary III, 100
Hill, Emma Mary III, 165
Hill, Enos V, 178
Hill, Enos W. V, 73
Hill, Enos W. V, 178
Hill, Esther IV, 221
Hill, Esther IV, 229
Hill, Eugene III, 485
Hill, Eugene V, 911
Hill, Eugene M. V, 911
Hill, Eugene Manning, Jr. V, 911
Hill, Eunice I, 701
Hill, Eunice A. I, 711
Hill, Eunice A. I, 720
Hill, Exum I, 701
Hill, Exum I, 720
Hill, Ezekiel VI, 1016
Hill, Florence V, 1001
Hill, Fowel B. I, 720
Hill, Fowel Buxton I, 701
Hill, George II, 374
Hill, George II, 549
Hill, George R. V, 682
Hill, Gordon W. VI, 257
Hill, Grace II, 374
Hill, Gulielma VI, 257
Hill, H. Cornelia I, 883
Hill, H. M. Doss VI, 820
Hill, Hannah I, 1
Hill, Hannah I, 700
Hill, Hannah I, 701
Hill, Hannah I, 719
Hill, Hannah I, 720
Hill, Hannah I, 730
Hill, Hannah I, 1007
Hill, Hannah I, 1010
Hill, Hannah I Sup 1, 4
Hill, Hannah I Sup 1, 6
Hill, Hannah II, 32
Hill, Hannah II, 77
Hill, Hannah II, 78
Hill, Hannah II, 99
Hill, Hannah II, 374
Hill, Hannah II, 504
Hill, Hannah II, 549
Hill, Hannah II, 797
Hill, Hannah II, 800
Hill, Hannah II, 870
Hill, Hannah III, 104
Hill, Hannah III, 165
Hill, Hannah IV, 221
Hill, Hannah IV, 236
Hill, Hannah V, 336
Hill, Hannah V, 953
Hill, Hannah C. I, 855
Hill, Hannah C. I, 883
Hill, Hannah Elizabeth V, 336
Hill, Hannah S. IV, 221
Hill, Hannah S. IV, 476
Hill, Hannah S. IV, 482
Hill, Hanner VI, 990
Hill, Hattie V, 246
Hill, Helen Irene V, 575
Hill, Henrietta B. II, 819
Hill, Henrietta B. II, 875
Hill, Henrietta R. II, 875
Hill, Henrietta S. II, 921
Hill, Henry I, 700
Hill, Henry I, 701
Hill, Henry I, 720
Hill, Henry I, 730
Hill, Henry II, 374
Hill, Henry V, 336
Hill, Henry V, 953
Hill, Henry B. I, 718
Hill, Henry B. I, 720
Hill, Horace P. IV, 221
Hill, Howard II, 374
Hill, Howard II, 549
Hill, Hugh II, 374
Hill, Hulda I, 719
Hill, Huldah I, 100
Hill, Huldah I, 132
Hill, Huldah I, 142
Hill, Huldah I, 143
Hill, Huldah I, 164
Hill, Huldah I, 675
Hill, Huldah I, 679
Hill, Huldah I, 701
Hill, Humphrey II, 374
Hill, Humphrey II, 549
Hill, Irma B. IV, 746
Hill, Isaac II, 374
Hill, Isaac V, 743
Hill, Isaac V, 809
Hill, J. C. IV, 221
Hill, J. C. IV, 746
Hill, J. Carl I, 940
Hill, J. Carl I, 943
Hill, J. Carson I, 927
Hill, J. Carson I, 943
Hill, J. E. IV, 474
Hill, J. Harvey III, 100
Hill, J. Harvey III, 165
Hill, Jackson J. V, 1001
Hill, Jacob I, 100
Hill, Jacob I, 143
Hill, Jacob I, 654
Hill, Jacob I, 700
Hill, Jacob I, 720
Hill, Jacob V, 72
Hill, Jacob V, 742
Hill, James I, 1
Hill, James I Sup 1, 5
Hill, James II, 176
Hill, James II, 374
Hill, James II, 549
Hill, James II, 1002
Hill, James VI, 825
Hill, James A. V, 575
Hill, James Christian III, 485
Hill, James Christian III, 489
Hill, James M. I, 701
Hill, James M. I, 783
Hill, James M. I, 816
Hill, Jane I, 701
Hill, Jane II, 698
Hill, Jane E. I, 925
Hill, Jeams VI, 30
Hill, Jeffry VI, 990
Hill, Jesse I, 100
Hill, Jesse I, 143
Hill, Jesse I, 163
Hill, Jesse I, 695
Hill, Jesse I, 701
Hill, Jesse I, 719
Hill, Jesse I, 720
Hill, Jesse I, 730
Hill, Jesse I, 748
Hill, Jesse I, 762
Hill, Jesse V, 458
Hill, Jesse V, 742
Hill, Jesse E. V, 178
Hill, Joanna II, 374
Hill, Joanna II, 549
Hill, Joanna VI, 932
Hill, John I, 101
Hill, John I, 353
Hill, John I, 395
Hill, John I, 654
Hill, John I, 655
Hill, John I, 700
Hill, John I, 701
Hill, John I, 719
Hill, John I, 720

Hill, John I, 783
Hill, John I, 816
Hill, John I, 839
Hill, John I, 1005
Hill, John II, 374
Hill, John II, 549
Hill, John II, 987
Hill, John II, 1002
Hill, John III, 104
Hill, John III, 165
Hill, John III, 166
Hill, John III, 213
Hill, John IV, 221
Hill, John IV, 476
Hill, John V, 178
Hill, John V, 682
Hill, John V, 742
Hill, John VI, 932
Hill, John VI, 966
Hill, John VI, 1003
Hill, John A. I, 855
Hill, John A. I, 883
Hill, John C. I, 720
Hill, John C. IV, 221
Hill, John C. IV, 236
Hill, John C. IV, 286
Hill, John C. IV, 304
Hill, John C. IV, 476
Hill, John C. IV, 482
Hill, John Denny I, 927
Hill, John Denny I, 943
Hill, John G. IV, 221
Hill, John H. III, 144
Hill, John H. III, 166
Hill, John M. V, 178
Hill, John Thomas V, 743
Hill, John, Jr. III, 165
Hill, Jonathan I, 701
Hill, Jonathan V, 742
Hill, Jos. IV, 481
Hill, Joseph I, 101
Hill, Joseph I, 353
Hill, Joseph I, 379
Hill, Joseph I, 394
Hill, Joseph I, 395
Hill, Joseph I, 426
Hill, Joseph I, 655
Hill, Joseph I, 695
Hill, Joseph I, 701
Hill, Joseph I, 719
Hill, Joseph I, 741
Hill, Joseph I, 1005
Hill, Joseph II, 374
Hill, Joseph II, 549
Hill, Joseph II, 800
Hill, Joseph IV, 221
Hill, Joseph IV, 235
Hill, Joseph IV, 260
Hill, Joseph IV, 476
Hill, Joseph V, 72
Hill, Joseph V, 742
Hill, Joseph B. I, 700
Hill, Joseph B. I, 720
Hill, Joseph H. V, 178
Hill, Joshua A. I, 762
Hill, Josiah II, 374
Hill, Josije VI, 30
Hill, Julia III, 485
Hill, Katharyn V, 682
Hill, Kathryn V, 716
Hill, Kelly W. I, 855
Hill, Kelly W. I, 883
Hill, Laura Shearman V, 911
Hill, Laura Shermen Hill V, 911
Hill, Lauretta C. B. III, 166
Hill, Leah I, 53
Hill, Leah I, 60
Hill, Lela I, 943
Hill, Lelia I, 927
Hill, Lelia I, 940
Hill, Lelia I, 943
Hill, Leola K. V, 178
Hill, Leona King V, 178
Hill, Lewis P. IV, 221
Hill, Lewis T. IV, 221
Hill, Lillian Coffman IV, 221
Hill, Louisa IV, 1237
Hill, Louisa V, 489
Hill, Louisa V, 501
Hill, Louisa V, 682
Hill, Louisa V, 1001
Hill, Lucretia I, 718
Hill, Lucretia I, 720
Hill, Lucy Hazel IV, 221
Hill, Lula A. I, 943
Hill, Lula Agnes I, 927
Hill, Lydia I, 701
Hill, Lydia I, 719
Hill, Lydia I, 816
Hill, Lydia IV, 149
Hill, Lydia IV, 156
Hill, Lydia B. I, 701
Hill, Lydia B. I, 720
Hill, Lydia B. I, 734
Hill, Lydia B. I, 783
Hill, Lydia B. I, 796
Hill, Lydia B. I, 816
Hill, Lydia B. I, 839
Hill, Lydia B., Jr. I, 816
Hill, Lydia J. V, 178
Hill, Lydia Jane I, 783
Hill, Lynn F. V, 682
Hill, M. Edith I, 943
Hill, Madora V, 178
Hill, Mahlon P. IV, 221
Hill, Mahol P. IV, 221
Hill, Margaret I, 100
Hill, Margaret I, 101
Hill, Margaret I, 655
Hill, Margaret I, 675
Hill, Margaret I, 679
Hill, Margaret I, 713
Hill, Margaret I, 720
Hill, Margaret II, 549
Hill, Margaret VI, 162
Hill, Margaret VI, 180
Hill, Margaret D. I, 855
Hill, Margaret D. I, 883
Hill, Margaret Edith I, 927
Hill, Margaret F. I, 783
Hill, Margaret F. I, 816
Hill, Margaret Fell I, 701
Hill, Margarett VI, 966
Hill, Margret II, 602
Hill, Margrett II, 78
Hill, Margrett II, 96
Hill, Margrett II, 374
Hill, Maria I, 329
Hill, Maria I, 330
Hill, Maria I, 720
Hill, Maria I, 762
Hill, Mariah I, 761
Hill, Mariah I, 762
Hill, Mariah V, 682
Hill, Mariam I, 481
Hill, Mariam Ella I, 720
Hill, Mariam M. I, 783
Hill, Marjorie Jane V, 178
Hill, Martha I, 481
Hill, Martha I, 719
Hill, Martha I, 798
Hill, Martha I, 805
Hill, Martha I, 816
Hill, Martha II, 176
Hill, Martha IV, 39
Hill, Martha V, 72
Hill, Martha VI, 956
Hill, Martha VI, 1003
Hill, Martha A. I, 473
Hill, Martha A. I, 481
Hill, Martha A. I, 720
Hill, Martha A. V, 910
Hill, Martha A. VI, 825
Hill, Martha Ann V, 336
Hill, Martha Ann V, 341
Hill, Martha Ann V, 911
Hill, Martha Ann V, 912
Hill, Martha E. V, 178
Hill, Marthann V, 28
Hill, Mary I, 53
Hill, Mary I, 74
Hill, Mary I, 100
Hill, Mary I, 109
Hill, Mary I, 113
Hill, Mary I, 143
Hill, Mary I, 159
Hill, Mary I, 163
Hill, Mary I, 353
Hill, Mary I, 395
Hill, Mary I, 447
Hill, Mary I, 546
Hill, Mary I, 553
Hill, Mary I, 655
Hill, Mary I, 679
Hill, Mary I, 689
Hill, Mary I, 695
Hill, Mary I, 700
Hill, Mary I, 701
Hill, Mary I, 709
Hill, Mary I, 718
Hill, Mary I, 719
Hill, Mary I, 720
Hill, Mary I, 721
Hill, Mary I, 762
Hill, Mary I, 770
Hill, Mary I, 816
Hill, Mary I, 1005
Hill, Mary I, 1009
Hill, Mary I, 1010
Hill, Mary II, 176
Hill, Mary II, 374
Hill, Mary II, 549
Hill, Mary II, 552
Hill, Mary II, 658
Hill, Mary II, 668
Hill, Mary II, 809
Hill, Mary II, 1052
Hill, Mary IV, 27
Hill, Mary IV, 39
Hill, Mary IV, 221
Hill, Mary IV, 475
Hill, Mary IV, 476
Hill, Mary IV, 622
Hill, Mary IV, 633
Hill, Mary V, 72
Hill, Mary V, 246
Hill, Mary V, 742
Hill, Mary VI, 1003
Hill, Mary A. I, 855
Hill, Mary A. I, 880
Hill, Mary A. I, 883
Hill, Mary A. I, 884
Hill, Mary A. V, 178
Hill, Mary Ann I, 701
Hill, Mary Ann I, 783
Hill, Mary Ann I, 808
Hill, Mary Ann I, 816
Hill, Mary Ann II, 875
Hill, Mary Ann IV, 221
Hill, Mary Ann IV, 286
Hill, Mary Ann IV, 409
Hill, Mary Ann IV, 980
Hill, Mary Ann V, 29
Hill, Mary Ann V, 72
Hill, Mary Ann V, 178
Hill, Mary B. VI, 249
Hill, Mary E. I, 816
Hill, Mary E. III, 165
Hill, Mary E. III, 166
Hill, Mary E. III, 213
Hill, Mary Emeline I, 701
Hill, Mary Emeline I, 783
Hill, Mary Gibson II, 785
Hill, Mary J. I, 762
Hill, Mary Jane I, 821
Hill, Mary Janes I, 816
Hill, Maryann Ellen I, 481
Hill, Mathew I, 701
Hill, Matthew V, 742
Hill, Maud V, 458
Hill, May V, 458
Hill, Melissa V, 336
Hill, Melissa V, 337
Hill, Meriam I, 701
Hill, Meriam I, 720
Hill, Meriam I, 735
Hill, Meriom E. I, 700
Hill, Micajah I, 395
Hill, Micajah I, 416
Hill, Micajah I, 701
Hill, Micajah I, 720
Hill, Micajah I, 783
Hill, Micajah I, 816
Hill, Micajah I, 828
Hill, Micajah A. I, 783
Hill, Micajah Aaron I, 701
Hill, Micajah C. I, 783
Hill, Milcah II, 549
Hill, Milcah II, 600
Hill, Milicent Rosalie IV, 364
Hill, Milicent Rosaline IV, 408
Hill, Milissa V, 336
Hill, Milly VI, 842
Hill, Minerva IV, 1367
Hill, Miriam I, 100
Hill, Miriam I, 142
Hill, Miriam I, 157
Hill, Miriam I, 654
Hill, Miriam I, 700
Hill, Miriam I, 701
Hill, Miriam I, 719
Hill, Miriam I, 720
Hill, Miriam V, 743
Hill, Miriam V, 768
Hill, Miriam M. I, 701
Hill, Miriam M. I, 816
Hill, Miriam M. I, 837
Hill, Mordica I, 701
Hill, Moses I, 100
Hill, Moses II, 793
Hill, Moses II, 795
Hill, Moses II, 800
Hill, Mr. ??? VI, 12
Hill, Mr. John VI, 11
Hill, Murray V, 336
Hill, Nancy I, 713
Hill, Nancy I, 720
Hill, Nancy I, 738
Hill, Nancy V, 458
Hill, Nancy V, 575
Hill, Nancy VI, 912
Hill, Nancy VI, 1012
Hill, Nancy VI, 1016
Hill, Nancy H. I, 447
Hill, Nancy H. I, 452
Hill, Nancy H. I, 720
Hill, Nancy Harris I, 927
Hill, Nannie I, 920
Hill, Nannie I, 928
Hill, Nannie I, 934
Hill, Nannie A. I, 919
Hill, Nannie M. I, 927
Hill, Naomi I, 395
Hill, Naomi I, 416
Hill, Naomi I, 701
Hill, Naomi P. I, 701
Hill, Naomi P. I, 783
Hill, Nathan I, 655
Hill, Nathan I, 701
Hill, Nathan I, 719
Hill, Nathan I, 720
Hill, Nathan I, 816
Hill, Nathan V, 336
Hill, Nathan B. I, 720
Hill, Nathan B. I, 816
Hill, Nathan B. I, 829
Hill, Nathan Branson I, 701
Hill, Nathan H. I, 700
Hill, Nathan H. I, 721
Hill, Nathan H. I, 927
Hill, Nicey VI, 939
Hill, Nina V, 246
Hill, Oliver II, 549
Hill, Ora IV, 474
Hill, Peggy VI, 932
Hill, Penelope F. I, 816
Hill, Penelope Florina I, 701
Hill, Penelope Florine I, 783
Hill, Penina I, 720
Hill, Peninah I, 719
Hill, Peninah V, 953
Hill, Peninah V, 959
Hill, Peninnah V, 119
Hill, Pennelope I, 715
Hill, Pennelope I, 720
Hill, Penninah I, 701
Hill, Phebe IV, 633
Hill, Phebe IV, 634
Hill, Phebe IV, 646
Hill, Polly I, 821
Hill, Polly VI, 825
Hill, Polly VI, 990
Hill, Polly Jeanes I, 816
Hill, Priscilla V, 809
Hill, Priscilla VI, 1005
Hill, Rachel I, 142
Hill, Rachel I, 655
Hill, Rachel I, 719
Hill, Rachel I, 724
Hill, Rachel II, 444
Hill, Rachel II, 549
Hill, Rachel II, 681
Hill, Rachel II, 791
Hill, Rachel II, 817
Hill, Rachel IV, 221
Hill, Rachel IV, 286
Hill, Rachel IV, 304
Hill, Rachel IV, 476
Hill, Rachel VI, 30
Hill, Rachel VI, 966
Hill, Rachel Steinmetz II, 793
Hill, Ralph V, 73
Hill, Ralph J. V, 73
Hill, Ralph J. V, 178
Hill, Rebeah I, 353
Hill, Rebeca I, 720
Hill, Rebeca I, 721
Hill, Rebecca I, 395
Hill, Rebecca I, 399
Hill, Rebecca I, 762
Hill, Rebecca IV, 23
Hill, Rebecca IV, 39
Hill, Rebecca V, 72
Hill, Rebecca V, 91
Hill, Rebecca V, 178
Hill, Rebecca H. I, 720
Hill, Rebeckah I, 719
Hill, Rebeckah II, 32
Hill, Rebekah I, 395
Hill, Rebekah I, 701
Hill, Reuben VI, 825
Hill, Rhoda M. I, 783
Hill, Rhoda Maria I, 816
Hill, Richard II, 176
Hill, Richard II, 374
Hill, Richard II, 504
Hill, Richard II, 506
Hill, Richard II, 549
Hill, Richard II, 602
Hill, Richard II, 658
Hill, Richard II, 681
Hill, Richard II, 961
Hill, Richard II, 991
Hill, Richard II, 1002
Hill, Richard, Jr. II, 549
Hill, Roanna I, 927
Hill, Robert I, 655
Hill, Robert I, 719
Hill, Robert I, 726
Hill, Robert IV, 39
Hill, Robert V, 72
Hill, Robert V, 91
Hill, Robert VI, 825
Hill, Robert VI, 966
Hill, Robert Barclay I, 783
Hill, Robert Barkley I, 701
Hill, Roda E. Mariah I, 701
Hill, Rosimond II, 549
Hill, Rowland V, 910
Hill, Rowland VI, 249
Hill, Rowland VI, 256
Hill, Ruth I, 38
Hill, Ruth I, 53
Hill, Ruth I, 701
Hill, Ruth I, 719
Hill, Ruth IV, 92
Hill, Ruth IV, 105
Hill, Ruth IV, 633
Hill, Ruth IV, 634
Hill, Ruth IV, 644
Hill, Ruth Mary III, 485
Hill, Ruth Mary III, 489
Hill, Samuel I, 91
Hill, Samuel I, 329
Hill, Samuel I, 330
Hill, Samuel I, 353
Hill, Samuel I, 395
Hill, Samuel I, 447
Hill, Samuel I, 457
Hill, Samuel I, 655
Hill, Samuel I, 701
Hill, Samuel I, 709
Hill, Samuel I, 720
Hill, Samuel I, 816
Hill, Samuel II, 549
Hill, Samuel V, 72
Hill, Samuel V, 1001
Hill, Samuel VI, 257
Hill, Samuel B. I, 447
Hill, Samuel B. I, 452
Hill, Samuel B. I, 720
Hill, Samuel Bette I, 701
Hill, Samuel C. V, 782
Hill, Samuel C. V, 783
Hill, Samuel, Jr. I, 720
Hill, Sarah I, 206
Hill, Sarah I, 353
Hill, Sarah I, 654
Hill, Sarah I, 655
Hill, Sarah I, 679
Hill, Sarah I, 688
Hill, Sarah I, 700
Hill, Sarah I, 701
Hill, Sarah I, 716
Hill, Sarah I, 719
Hill, Sarah I, 720
Hill, Sarah I, 730
Hill, Sarah I, 732
Hill, Sarah I, 1005
Hill, Sarah I, 1009
Hill, Sarah I, 1010
Hill, Sarah II, 32
Hill, Sarah II, 78
Hill, Sarah II, 99
Hill, Sarah II, 176
Hill, Sarah II, 374
Hill, Sarah II, 506
Hill, Sarah II, 549
Hill, Sarah II, 987
Hill, Sarah II, 1002
Hill, Sarah V, 72
Hill, Sarah V, 742
Hill, Sarah VI, 825
Hill, Sarah Ann V, 336
Hill, Sarah E. II, 875
Hill, Sarah J. I, 701
Hill, Sarah J. I, 783
Hill, Sarah Jane I, 701
Hill, Sarah Jane I, 720
Hill, Sarah Jane I, 783
Hill, Sarah Jane I, 816
Hill, Sarah Jane I, 828
Hill, Sarah, Jr. II, 485
Hill, Seth II, 176
Hill, Shem II, 549
Hill, Sidney T. I, 855
Hill, Sidney T. I, 883
Hill, Sophronia I, 883
Hill, Susan V, 72
Hill, Susan VI, 825
Hill, Susan A. III, 144
Hill, Susan A. VI, 820
Hill, Susan F. III, 166
Hill, Susan M. V, 22
Hill, Susan M. V, 72

Hill, Susanah V, 72
Hill, Susanna I, 142
Hill, Susanna I, 172
Hill, Susanna I, 701
Hill, Susanna I, 719
Hill, Susanna I, 726
Hill, Susanna IV, 39
Hill, Susanna V, 72
Hill, Susanna VI, 825
Hill, Susannah II, 176
Hill, Susannah IV, 92
Hill, Susannah IV, 117
Hill, Susannah V, 42
Hill, Susannah V, 72
Hill, Susannah VI, 816
Hill, Sylvannus VI, 257
Hill, Sylvanus VI, 257
Hill, Tabitha I, 720
Hill, Tabitha I, 734
Hill, Tamar V, 336
Hill, Tamar T. V, 336
Hill, Tamer V, 960
Hill, Terelius A. I, 855
Hill, Terelius A. I, 884
Hill, Terileous A. I, 883
Hill, Thamar V, 953
Hill, Thomas I, 100
Hill, Thomas I, 141
Hill, Thomas I, 143
Hill, Thomas I, 655
Hill, Thomas I, 701
Hill, Thomas I, 719
Hill, Thomas I, 720
Hill, Thomas I, 732
Hill, Thomas II, 32
Hill, Thomas II, 78
Hill, Thomas II, 96
Hill, Thomas II, 374
Hill, Thomas II, 444
Hill, Thomas II, 549
Hill, Thomas V, 336
Hill, Thomas V, 742
Hill, Thomas V, 747
Hill, Thomas C. I, 720
Hill, Thomas Clarkson I, 701
Hill, Thomas J. VI, 932
Hill, Thomas T. I, 700
Hill, Thomas T. I, 720
Hill, Thomas, Jr. I, 701
Hill, Thomas, Jr. V, 336
Hill, Thos. V, 337
Hill, Thos. J. VI, 932
Hill, Walter V, 682
Hill, Wayne V, 72
Hill, Wd. Elizabeth II, 800
Hill, Wd. Mary II, 374
Hill, Wd. Mary II, 549
Hill, Wd. Mary II, 571
Hill, Wd. Mary Ann II, 800
Hill, Wd. Susan A. III, 166
Hill, Widow Elizabeth I, 730
Hill, Widow Lydia I, 710
Hill, Widow Miriam I, 143
Hill, Widow Miriam I, 148
Hill, William I, 53
Hill, William I, 74
Hill, William I, 100
Hill, William I, 101
Hill, William I, 143
Hill, William I, 264
Hill, William I, 271
Hill, William I, 353
Hill, William I, 395
Hill, William I, 481
Hill, William I, 546
Hill, William I, 654
Hill, William I, 655
Hill, William I, 679
Hill, William I, 689
Hill, William I, 695
Hill, William I, 700
Hill, William I, 701
Hill, William I, 719
Hill, William I, 720
Hill, William I, 721
Hill, William I, 748
Hill, William I, 762
Hill, William I, 855
Hill, William I, 883
Hill, William I, 919
Hill, William I, 927
Hill, William I, 953
Hill, William I, 1005
Hill, William II, 374
Hill, William II, 961
Hill, William IV, 633
Hill, William V, 72
Hill, William V, 246
Hill, William V, 742
Hill, William VI, 249
Hill, William Alfred VI, 257
Hill, William Allen I, 701
Hill, William C. I, 618
Hill, William C. I, 883
Hill, William C. I, 927
Hill, William G. I, 783
Hill, William T. I, 473
Hill, William T. I, 481
Hill, William T. I, 700
Hill, William T. I, 720
Hill, William W. VI, 825
Hill, William Wilson V, 336
Hill, William, Jr. I, 53
Hill, William, Jr. IV, 633
Hill, William, Sr. I, 762
Hill, Wm. I, 394
Hill, Wm. I, 395
Hill, Wm. I, 426
Hill, Wm. II, 549
Hill, Wm. II, 875
Hill, Wm. II, 1002
Hill, Wm. V, 458
Hill, Wm. A. V, 682
Hill, Wm. C. I, 855
Hill, Wm. C. I, 943
Hill, Wm. H. V, 458
Hill, Wm. Wilson V, 336
Hill, Zachariah VI, 966
Hill, Zack VI, 842
Hillard, Ann II, 132
Hillard, Harriet L. III, 209
Hillard, Mary II, 231
Hillard, Mary II, 256
Hillard, Mary III, 166
Hillard, Reuben II, 232
Hillard, Samuel VI, 314
Hillarl, Harriet III, 209
Hillarl, John III, 209
Hillarl, Mary III, 209
Hillary, Henry II, 374
Hillary, Henry II, 549
Hillary, Jane II, 374
Hillary, Jane II, 549
Hillary, Jane II, 679
Hillary, Samuel II, 374
Hillary, Samuel II, 549
Hillary, Samuel II, 679
Hillas, Nathan IV, 721
Hillas, Robert IV, 721
Hillas, Robert IV, 1028
Hillas, Samuel IV, 721
Hillas, Sarah IV, 721
Hillas, Skipwith C. IV, 721
Hillas, William IV, 721
Hillas, William IV, 1028
Hillborn, Albert Smith II, 800
Hillborn, Amos II, 374
Hillborn, Amos II, 549
Hillborn, Amos II, 800
Hillborn, Amos II, 831
Hillborn, Amos II, 875
Hillborn, Amos II, 876
Hillborn, Anna H. II, 876
Hillborn, Anna H. II, 923
Hillborn, Annie II, 800
Hillborn, Annie II, 876
Hillborn, Caroline B. II, 876
Hillborn, Elizabeth II, 374
Hillborn, Elizabeth II, 549
Hillborn, Elizabeth P. II, 800
Hillborn, Frances II, 374
Hillborn, Frances II, 549
Hillborn, Helen R. II, 800
Hillborn, Helen R. II, 876
Hillborn, Isaac H. II, 876
Hillborn, Isaac H. II, 923
Hillborn, James P. II, 800
Hillborn, James T. II, 876
Hillborn, Jane II, 800
Hillborn, Jane II, 856
Hillborn, Jane II, 876
Hillborn, John II, 374
Hillborn, John II, 375
Hillborn, John II, 549
Hillborn, John II, 662
Hillborn, John II, 800
Hillborn, John II, 831
Hillborn, John II, 875
Hillborn, John Martin II, 375
Hillborn, Joseph II, 374
Hillborn, Joseph II, 375
Hillborn, Joseph II, 549
Hillborn, Joseph Watson II, 549
Hillborn, Martha II, 876
Hillborn, Martin II, 549
Hillborn, Mary II, 800
Hillborn, Mary II, 831
Hillborn, Mary II, 875
Hillborn, Mary II, 876
Hillborn, Mary Letitia II, 800
Hillborn, Mary S. II, 876
Hillborn, Mary Simpson II, 800
Hillborn, Mary Smith II, 800
Hillborn, Miles II, 375
Hillborn, Miles II, 549
Hillborn, Miriam II, 800
Hillborn, Myles II, 374
Hillborn, Phebe II, 549
Hillborn, Rachel II, 374
Hillborn, Rachel II, 375
Hillborn, Rachel II, 549
Hillborn, Rachel II, 662
Hillborn, Rachel II, 923
Hillborn, Rachel W. II, 831
Hillborn, Rachel W. II, 876
Hillborn, Rachel Ward II, 800
Hillborn, Rebecca W. II, 800
Hillborn, Rebecca W. II, 876
Hillborn, Ruth Ann II, 876
Hillborn, Ruth Anna II, 800
Hillborn, Ruth Anna II, 876
Hillborn, Samuel T. II, 876
Hillborn, Samuel T. II, 923
Hillborn, Sarah II, 549
Hillborn, Thomas II, 374
Hillborn, Thomas II, 375
Hillborn, Wm. II, 800
Hillbourn, Ann II, 975
Hillbourn, Ann II, 1002
Hillbourn, Frances II, 549
Hillbourn, Frances II, 679
Hillbourn, John II, 549
Hillbourn, Joseph II, 549
Hillbourn, Katharine II, 1002
Hillbourn, Kathrine II, 1002
Hillbourn, Miles II, 375
Hillbourn, Miles II, 549
Hillbourn, Rachel II, 375
Hillbourn, Rachel II, 549
Hillbourn, Thomas II, 375
Hillbourn, Thomas II, 975
Hillbourn, Thomas II, 1002
Hillburn, Mary II, 876
Hiller, Charles E. III, 381
Hiller, Charles E. III, 382
Hiller, Chas. Eldrige III, 384
Hiller, Elizabeth III, 434
Hiller, Hannah II, 194
Hiller, Helen May III, 379
Hiller, Helen May III, 381
Hiller, Helen May III, 382
Hiller, Helen May III, 384
Hiller, Ira R. III, 380
Hiller, Ira R. III, 381
Hiller, Jedediah III, 421
Hiller, Jedediah III, 434
Hiller, Jediah P. III, 420
Hiller, Louise III, 384
Hiller, Louise Hemstreet III, 381
Hiller, Martha B. III, 381
Hiller, Martha B. III, 382
Hiller, Mary III, 434
Hiller, Mary Elizabeth III, 381
Hiller, Mary Elizabeth III, 382
Hiller, Priscilla A. III, 380
Hiller, Priscilla A. III, 381
Hiller, Samuel II, 194
Hiller, Wd. Elizabeth P. III, 421
Hillerman, Ann IV, 822
Hillerman, Ann IV, 823
Hillerman, Ann IV, 830
Hillerman, Ann S. H. IV, 822
Hillerman, Hannah IV, 820
Hillerman, Hannah IV, 822
Hillerman, Hannah I. IV, 822
Hillerman, Hannah J. IV, 822
Hillerman, John I. IV, 822
Hillerman, Joseph IV, 822
Hillerman, Joseph L. IV, 822
Hillerman, Loranzo D. IV, 822
Hillerman, Lorenzo IV, 822
Hillerman, Rachel IV, 221
Hillerman, Sarah IV, 822
Hillerman, William IV, 822
Hillerman, William R. IV, 721
Hillerman, Wm. IV, 822
Hillerman, Wm. I. IV, 822
Hilles, Amy G. V, 911
Hilles, Amy T. V, 911
Hilles, Ann IV, 39
Hilles, Ann IV, 45
Hilles, Ann IV, 823
Hilles, Ann Eliza IV, 39
Hilles, Charles IV, 39
Hilles, David IV, 29
Hilles, David IV, 39
Hilles, David Pugh IV, 39
Hilles, Edmund IV, 39
Hilles, Eleanor V, 911
Hilles, Eli II, 196
Hilles, Eli II, 231
Hilles, Eli IV, 39
Hilles, Elizabeth IV, 39
Hilles, Elizabeth IV, 67
Hilles, Enos IV, 717
Hilles, Enos IV, 721
Hilles, Enos IV, 1021
Hilles, Hannah IV, 29
Hilles, Hannah IV, 39
Hilles, Hannah IV, 812
Hilles, Hannah IV, 823
Hilles, Hugh IV, 39
Hilles, Hugh IV, 67
Hilles, Hugh IV, 858
Hilles, Jane IV, 721
Hilles, Margaret Mary II, 718
Hilles, Martha II, 196
Hilles, Martha II, 231
Hilles, Martha IV, 39
Hilles, Mary IV, 36
Hilles, Mary IV, 39
Hilles, Mary Ann IV, 717
Hilles, Mary Ann IV, 721
Hilles, Mary Ann IV, 1021
Hilles, Rachel IV, 1023
Hilles, Rachel IV, 1028
Hilles, Rebecca II, 196
Hilles, Rebecca II, 231
Hilles, Rebecca IV, 36
Hilles, Rebecca IV, 39
Hilles, Richard II, 675
Hilles, Robert IV, 721
Hilles, Robert IV, 1021
Hilles, Samuel IV, 39
Hilles, Samuel E. V, 911
Hilles, Samuel Eli V, 911
Hilles, Samuel F. V, 911
Hilles, Sarah IV, 39
Hilles, Scipwith C. IV, 335
Hilles, T. Clarkson IV, 1023
Hilles, Wd. Hannah II, 675
Hilles, William II, 196
Hilles, William II, 231
Hilles, William IV, 36
Hilles, William IV, 39
Hilles, William V, 911
Hilles, William D. IV, 39
Hilles, Wm. IV, 812
Hilles, Wm. IV, 823
Hilles, Wm. V, 911
Hilles, Wm. T. V, 911
Hilles, Wm. Tatum V, 911
Hilley, Elizabeth VI, 1020
Hilley, Susanna VI, 961
Hilliar, Abraham II, 232
Hilliar, Abraham II, 549
Hilliar, Edward II, 232
Hilliar, Grace II, 232
Hilliar, Joseph II, 232
Hilliar, Rebecca II, 232
Hilliar, Rebecca II, 255
Hilliar, Sarah II, 217
Hilliar, Sarah II, 232
Hilliard, Abraham II, 176
Hilliard, Adelaide III, 114
Hilliard, Adelaide D. II, 151
Hilliard, Adelaide W. III, 101
Hilliard, Adelaide W. III, 166
Hilliard, Amy III, 82
Hilliard, Amy Mary III, 166
Hilliard, Ann II, 133
Hilliard, Ann II, 151
Hilliard, Ann II, 176
Hilliard, Ann III, 114
Hilliard, Ann III, 166
Hilliard, Anna II, 79
Hilliard, Anna II, 145
Hilliard, Anna II, 151
Hilliard, Anna II, 158
Hilliard, Anna C. II, 783
Hilliard, Anna Maria II, 820
Hilliard, Benjamin Rowland II, 176
Hilliard, Bernard Aubry II, 133
Hilliard, Bessie III, 32
Hilliard, Charles II, 176
Hilliard, Charlotte II, 32
Hilliard, Charlotte II, 119
Hilliard, Charlotte II, 133
Hilliard, Charlotte W. II, 145
Hilliard, Charlotte W. II, 151
Hilliard, Deborah II, 176
Hilliard, Deborah G. II, 176
Hilliard, Eber II, 176
Hilliard, Edward II, 176
Hilliard, Eliza II, 133
Hilliard, Eliza G. II, 143
Hilliard, Eliza G. II, 151
Hilliard, Elizabeth II, 32
Hilliard, Elizabeth II, 79
Hilliard, Elizabeth II, 232
Hilliard, Elizabeth II, 268
Hilliard, Elizabeth T. II, 831
Hilliard, Elizabeth T. II, 876
Hilliard, Emeline II, 177
Hilliard, Frances II, 176
Hilliard, Franklin W. II, 177
Hilliard, George II, 176
Hilliard, George L. II, 133
Hilliard, Hannah II, 32
Hilliard, Hannah II, 78
Hilliard, Hannah II, 79
Hilliard, Hannah II, 119
Hilliard, Hannah II, 133
Hilliard, Hannah II, 151
Hilliard, Hannah II, 154
Hilliard, Hannah II, 232
Hilliard, Hannah II, 831
Hilliard, Hannah II, 832
Hilliard, Hannah II, 876
Hilliard, Hannah B. II, 151
Hilliard, Hannah K. II, 151
Hilliard, Hannah K. II, 154
Hilliard, Hannah K. II, 820
Hilliard, Hannah R. II, 177
Hilliard, Hannah R. II, 232
Hilliard, Hannah T. G. II, 133
Hilliard, Hannah T. G. II, 142
Hilliard, Hannah T. G. II, 145
Hilliard, Hannah T. G. II, 151
Hilliard, Helen M. II, 133
Hilliard, Helen Mary II, 151
Hilliard, Henrietta II, 151
Hilliard, Henry III, 82
Hilliard, Henry III, 166
Hilliard, Isaac II, 176
Hilliard, J. Bernard II, 142
Hilliard, J. Bernard II, 151
Hilliard, Jacob II, 176
Hilliard, Jacob II, 177
Hilliard, James I, 884
Hilliard, James II, 176
Hilliard, James S. II, 176
Hilliard, Joel II, 550
Hilliard, John II, 176
Hilliard, Jonathan II, 176
Hilliard, Jonathan II, 177
Hilliard, Jonathan II, 232
Hilliard, Jonathan Barclay II, 177
Hilliard, Jos. III, 114
Hilliard, Joseph II, 79
Hilliard, Joseph II, 119
Hilliard, Joseph II, 133
Hilliard, Joseph II, 176
Hilliard, Joseph II, 232
Hilliard, Joseph III, 166
Hilliard, Joseph Bernard II, 133
Hilliard, Joseph W. II, 177
Hilliard, Josiah Hilliard II, 783
Hilliard, Keziah II, 176
Hilliard, Keziah II, 177
Hilliard, Leonora II, 783
Hilliard, Lizzie Webb II, 783
Hilliard, Lucretta Mott II, 783
Hilliard, Margaret II, 32
Hilliard, Margaret II, 79
Hilliard, Margaret II, 101
Hilliard, Margaret II, 133
Hilliard, Margaret II, 145
Hilliard, Margaret II, 151
Hilliard, Margaret II, 176
Hilliard, Margaret II, 232
Hilliard, Margaret II, 783
Hilliard, Margarett II, 118
Hilliard, Margarett II, 119
Hilliard, Martha II, 32
Hilliard, Martha II, 119
Hilliard, Martha II, 133
Hilliard, Martha II, 145
Hilliard, Martha II, 151
Hilliard, Martha II, 176
Hilliard, Martha II, 177
Hilliard, Martha II, 783
Hilliard, Martha A. II, 783
Hilliard, Martha H. II, 320
Hilliard, Martha H. II, 325
Hilliard, Mary II, 32
Hilliard, Mary II, 79
Hilliard, Mary II, 136
Hilliard, Mary II, 143
Hilliard, Mary II, 176
Hilliard, Mary II, 177
Hilliard, Mary II, 232
Hilliard, Mary II, 549
Hilliard, Mary II, 550
Hilliard, Mary II, 746
Hilliard, Mary II, 780
Hilliard, Mary II, 783
Hilliard, Mary II, 832
Hilliard, Mary II, 876
Hilliard, Mary Amanda III, 82
Hilliard, Mary Amando III, 166
Hilliard, Mary Ann II, 783
Hilliard, Mary Atkinson II, 820

Hilliard, Mary Cayton II, 151
Hilliard, Mary Clayton II, 151
Hilliard, Mary E. II, 177
Hilliard, Mary Elizabeth II, 128
Hilliard, Mary Elizabeth II, 133
Hilliard, Mary Elizabeth II, 143
Hilliard, Mary Elizabeth II, 151
Hilliard, Mary L. II, 133
Hilliard, Mary, Jr. II, 177
Hilliard, Rachel II, 79
Hilliard, Rachel II, 101
Hilliard, Rachel II, 176
Hilliard, Rachel II, 232
Hilliard, Reuben II, 32
Hilliard, Reuben II, 78
Hilliard, Reuben II, 79
Hilliard, Reuben II, 151
Hilliard, Reuben II, 154
Hilliard, Reuben II, 232
Hilliard, Reuben II, 831
Hilliard, Reuben II, 876
Hilliard, Rheuben II, 119
Hilliard, Rheuben II, 832
Hilliard, Ruben II, 79
Hilliard, Ruben II, 133
Hilliard, Samuel II, 32
Hilliard, Samuel II, 79
Hilliard, Samuel II, 101
Hilliard, Samuel II, 119
Hilliard, Samuel II, 133
Hilliard, Samuel II, 145
Hilliard, Samuel II, 151
Hilliard, Samuel II, 176
Hilliard, Samuel II, 177
Hilliard, Samuel II, 232
Hilliard, Samuel II, 783
Hilliard, Sarah II, 133
Hilliard, Sarah II, 151
Hilliard, Sarah II, 176
Hilliard, Sarah II, 177
Hilliard, Sarah II, 232
Hilliard, Sarah Hall II, 133
Hilliard, Sarah Hall II, 142
Hilliard, Susan D. II, 130
Hilliard, Thomas II, 151
Hilliard, Thomas G. II, 133
Hilliard, Thomas T. II, 133
Hilliard, Thomas T. II, 142
Hilliard, Thomas T. II, 145
Hilliard, Thomas T. II, 151
Hilliard, Thomas T. III, 114
Hilliard, Thomas T. III, 166
Hilliard, Thos. T. III, 101
Hilliard, Townsend II, 32
Hilliard, Townsend II, 79
Hilliard, Townsend II, 151
Hilliard, Townsend II, 154
Hilliard, Townsend II, 232
Hilliard, Townsend II, 820
Hilliard, Viola V, 178
Hilliard, Wd. Mary II, 177
Hilliard, William I, 447
Hilliard, William II, 176
Hilliard, William II, 177
Hilliard, William II, 232
Hilliard, William II, 291
Hilliard, Wm. II, 79
Hilliard, Wm. G. II, 133
Hilliard, Wm. T. II, 133
Hilliard, Wm. T. II, 143
Hilliard, Wm. T. II, 145
Hilliard, Wm. T. II, 151
Hilliard, Wm. T., III II, 151
Hilliard, Wm. T., Jr. II, 133
Hilliard, Wm. T., Jr. II, 151
Hilliard, Wm. T.,, III II, 133
Hillier, Abraham II, 176
Hillier, Eber II, 176
Hillier, Edward II, 176
Hillier, Edward II, 232
Hillier, Frances II, 228
Hillier, Grace II, 232
Hillier, Jacob II, 177
Hillier, Jacob II, 232
Hillier, John II, 176
Hillier, John II, 231
Hillier, John II, 232
Hillier, Jonathan II, 176
Hillier, Jonathan II, 232
Hillier, Keziah II, 176
Hillier, Keziah II, 177
Hillier, Margaret II, 176
Hillier, Martha II, 176
Hillier, Martha II, 177
Hillier, Martha II, 232
Hillier, Mary II, 176
Hillier, Mary II, 177
Hillier, Mary II, 231
Hillier, Mary II, 232
Hillier, Samuel II, 176
Hillier, Sarah II, 176
Hillier, Sarah II, 177
Hillingshead, Rachel V, 887
Hillior, Martha II, 177
Hillior, William II, 177
Hillis, Ann IV, 717
Hillis, Ann IV, 721
Hillis, Ann IV, 823
Hillis, Anna U. IV, 296
Hillis, Anne U. IV, 221
Hillis, Arthur T. IV, 721
Hillis, Arthur T. IV, 1027
Hillis, David L. IV, 721
Hillis, Eli II, 231
Hillis, Elihu IV, 823
Hillis, Elizabeth IV, 721
Hillis, Elizabeth IV, 823
Hillis, Enos IV, 721
Hillis, Enos IV, 1027
Hillis, Enos IV, 1028
Hillis, Hannah II, 550
Hillis, Hannah IV, 823
Hillis, Howard IV, 1028
Hillis, Hugh IV, 823
Hillis, Hugh IV, 858
Hillis, Isaac IV, 721
Hillis, Jacob Davies IV, 721
Hillis, Jacob Davis IV, 721
Hillis, Jane IV, 717
Hillis, Jane IV, 721
Hillis, Jane IV, 1028
Hillis, Jane Mary IV, 1028
Hillis, Jeremiah IV, 721
Hillis, John P. IV, 335
Hillis, John P. IV, 634
Hillis, Martha II, 231
Hillis, Martha IV, 823
Hillis, Mary IV, 823
Hillis, Mary Ann IV, 721
Hillis, Mary Ann IV, 1027
Hillis, Mary Ann IV, 1028
Hillis, Nathan IV, 335
Hillis, Nathan IV, 634
Hillis, Nathan IV, 721
Hillis, Phebe IV, 721
Hillis, Rachel IV, 1028
Hillis, Rachel Ann IV, 335
Hillis, Rachel Ann IV, 634
Hillis, Rachel Ann IV, 721
Hillis, Rebecca II, 231
Hillis, Rebecca IV, 823
Hillis, Rebecca IV, 826
Hillis, Richard II, 550
Hillis, Robert IV, 335
Hillis, Robert IV, 634
Hillis, Robert IV, 717
Hillis, Robert IV, 721
Hillis, Robert IV, 1028
Hillis, Ruth L. IV, 721
Hillis, Samuel IV, 335
Hillis, Samuel IV, 634
Hillis, Samuel IV, 721
Hillis, Sarah IV, 335
Hillis, Sarah IV, 634
Hillis, Sarah IV, 721
Hillis, Sarah IV, 823
Hillis, Sarah IV, 850
Hillis, Scipwith C. IV, 335
Hillis, Seth II, 231
Hillis, Skipwith C. IV, 335
Hillis, Skipwith C. IV, 634
Hillis, Skipwith C. IV, 721
Hillis, William II, 231
Hillis, William IV, 634
Hillis, William IV, 721
Hillis, William IV, 1028
Hillis, Wm. IV, 335
Hillis, Wm. IV, 721
Hillis, Wm. IV, 823
Hillman, Abigail Mulhollon V, 843
Hillman, Aland M. V, 73
Hillman, Edmond V, 843
Hillman, Edmond V, 882
Hillman, Elizabeth V, 843
Hillman, Hannah II, 550
Hillman, Jacob II, 375
Hillman, Jonathan II, 550
Hillman, Martha II, 120
Hillman, Martha II, 123
Hillman, Martha IV, 721
Hillman, Martha F. IV, 721
Hillman, N. H. IV, 1320
Hillman, Rachel II, 79
Hillman, Rachel V, 843
Hillman, Samuel V, 843
Hillman, Sarah II, 32
Hillman, Sarah II, 79
Hillman, Sarah V, 843
Hillman, Sarah Brown V, 843
Hillman, W. H. IV, 1320
Hillman, Waldren V, 73
Hillman, Walter V, 73
Hillman, Wm. V, 911
Hillmen, Martha II, 120
Hills, Artlissa I, 943
Hills, Seth II, 231
Hillsman, Sterling VI, 826
Hillts, Hannah Matilda IV, 1038
Hillts, James W. IV, 1038
Hillts, John IV, 1038
Hillyard, Ann II, 232
Hillyard, Ann W. II, 291
Hillyard, George D. II, 291
Hillyard, James II, 292
Hillyard, Jonathan, Jr. II, 292
Hillyard, Joseph II, 444
Hillyard, Mary II, 444
Hillyard, Mary II, 876
Hillyard, Richard II, 444
Hillyard, Samuel II, 232
Hillyard, William II, 232
Hilman, Abigail V, 882
Hilman, Abigail M. V, 881
Hilman, Abigail M. V, 882
Hilman, Edmond V, 882
Hilman, Edmund V, 882
Hilman, Elizabeth V, 882
Hilman, Martha II, 120
Hilman, Martha J. VI, 932
Hilman, N. H. IV, 1320
Hilman, Samuel V, 882
Hilman, Sarah V, 882
Hilman, Uriah VI, 932
Hilmen, Rachel II, 79
Hilmkamp, ??? III, 166
Hilmkamp, John III, 166
Hilton, Abigail I, 1009
Hilton, Abigail I, 1010
Hilton, Abigail W. II, 320
Hilton, Ann IV, 335
Hilton, Ann IV, 348
Hilton, Ann H. IV, 402
Hilton, Ann H. IV, 408
Hilton, Charity Balinder VI, 1021
Hilton, Daniel II, 79
Hilton, Edway VI, 249
Hilton, Elisabeth II, 231
Hilton, Emma III, 168
Hilton, Fred IV, 1320
Hilton, Frederick IV, 1320
Hilton, James VI, 932
Hilton, Jeremiah VI, 890
Hilton, Jeremiah VI, 897
Hilton, Jeremiah VI, 932
Hilton, Jeremiah VI, 937
Hilton, Jeremiah VI, 993
Hilton, Jesse VI, 988
Hilton, John II, 231
Hilton, Kitturah VI, 897
Hilton, Lucy VI, 897
Hilton, Lucy VI, 1021
Hilton, Mary VI, 932
Hilton, Phebe II, 231
Hilton, Phebe II, 240
Hilton, Samuel V, 246
Hilton, Susan VI, 967
Hilton, Susanna VI, 932
Hilton, Susannah VI, 901
Hilton, William II, 231
Hilton, William II, 240
Hilton, Wm. II, 231
Hilts, Hannah Matilda IV, 1038
Hiltzeimer, Hannah II, 375
Hiltzheimer, Elizabeth II, 375
Hiltzheimer, Hannah II, 375
Hiltzheimer, Jacob II, 375
Hiltzheimer, William II, 375
Hilyard, Abraham II, 232
Hilyard, Abraham II, 707
Hilyard, Adelaide III, 166
Hilyard, Adelaide W. III, 166
Hilyard, Alice Emily III, 166
Hilyard, Amelia III, 166
Hilyard, Amy Mary III, 166
Hilyard, Ann II, 232
Hilyard, Ann II, 285
Hilyard, Ann II, 292
Hilyard, Ann III, 166
Hilyard, Ann III, 351
Hilyard, Ann W. II, 284
Hilyard, Ann W. II, 291
Hilyard, Ann W. II, 292
Hilyard, Ann W. II, 306
Hilyard, Ann W. III, 166
Hilyard, Anna II, 61
Hilyard, Anna II, 79
Hilyard, Anna II, 292
Hilyard, Anna D. III, 166
Hilyard, Anna D. III, 361
Hilyard, Anna M. II, 285
Hilyard, Anna M. II, 292
Hilyard, Anna Maria III, 166
Hilyard, Benjamin II, 310
Hilyard, Benjamin II, 320
Hilyard, Benjamin II, 324
Hilyard, Charles II, 176
Hilyard, Clary VI, 180
Hilyard, Cornelia II, 292
Hilyard, Cornelia III, 166
Hilyard, Deborah II, 226
Hilyard, Deborah II, 232
Hilyard, Eber II, 232
Hilyard, Edward II, 232
Hilyard, Eliz. R. III, 166
Hilyard, Eliz. R. III, 315
Hilyard, Elizabeth II, 232
Hilyard, Elizabeth II, 290
Hilyard, Elizabeth II, 292
Hilyard, Elizabeth III, 361
Hilyard, Elizabeth R. II, 292
Hilyard, Elizabeth R. II, 306
Hilyard, Elizabeth R. III, 166
Hilyard, Elizabeth T. II, 876
Hilyard, Elizabeth W. II, 292
Hilyard, Elizabeth W. III, 166
Hilyard, Elizabeth Woolman II, 723
Hilyard, Ellen II, 320
Hilyard, Ellen II, 324
Hilyard, Ellen S. II, 310
Hilyard, Emeline II, 177
Hilyard, Emeline E. II, 292
Hilyard, Emely II, 292
Hilyard, Emily II, 292
Hilyard, Emily II, 304
Hilyard, Emily III, 166
Hilyard, Emily H. II, 292
Hilyard, Emily H. II, 304
Hilyard, Emily H. III, 166
Hilyard, Frances II, 203
Hilyard, Frances II, 232
Hilyard, Frances II, 268
Hilyard, Franklin W. II, 177
Hilyard, Franklin W. II, 292
Hilyard, Geo. D. III, 166
Hilyard, George D. II, 291
Hilyard, George D. II, 292
Hilyard, George D. II, 306
Hilyard, George D. III, 166
Hilyard, George D. III, 361
Hilyard, George D., Jr. III, 166
Hilyard, George E. II, 310
Hilyard, Grace II, 232
Hilyard, Hannah II, 78
Hilyard, Hannah II, 205
Hilyard, Hannah II, 232
Hilyard, Hannah II, 268
Hilyard, Hannah II, 284
Hilyard, Hannah II, 291
Hilyard, Hannah II, 292
Hilyard, Hannah II, 310
Hilyard, Hannah II, 876
Hilyard, Hannah III, 166
Hilyard, Hannah III, 294
Hilyard, Hannah Emily II, 292
Hilyard, Hannah R. II, 232
Hilyard, Hannah T. II, 292
Hilyard, Hannah T. III, 166
Hilyard, Hannah T. III, 338
Hilyard, Henry III, 166
Hilyard, Isaac II, 232
Hilyard, Jacob II, 216
Hilyard, Jacob II, 232
Hilyard, Jacob II, 310
Hilyard, James I, 884
Hilyard, James II, 176
Hilyard, James II, 187
Hilyard, James II, 232
Hilyard, James II, 290
Hilyard, James II, 291
Hilyard, James II, 292
Hilyard, James III, 166
Hilyard, James Franklin II, 292
Hilyard, James Franklin III, 166
Hilyard, James S. II, 176
Hilyard, James, Jr. II, 292
Hilyard, James, Jr. III, 166
Hilyard, Jarrett II, 310
Hilyard, Joel II, 550
Hilyard, John II, 176
Hilyard, John II, 203
Hilyard, John II, 226
Hilyard, John II, 232
Hilyard, John II, 268
Hilyard, John II, 275
Hilyard, John II, 285
Hilyard, John II, 292
Hilyard, John II, 306
Hilyard, John III, 166
Hilyard, John III, 351
Hilyard, John W. II, 292
Hilyard, John W. III, 166
Hilyard, Jonathan II, 176
Hilyard, Jonathan II, 177
Hilyard, Jonathan II, 232
Hilyard, Jonathan II, 275
Hilyard, Jonathan II, 290
Hilyard, Jonathan II, 291
Hilyard, Jonathan III, 166
Hilyard, Jonathan Barclay II, 177
Hilyard, Jonathan Henry II, 29
Hilyard, Jonathan Henry III, 16
Hilyard, Jonathan, Jr. II, 232
Hilyard, Jonathan, Jr. II, 291
Hilyard, Jonathan, Jr. II, 292
Hilyard, Jos. W. III, 166
Hilyard, Joseph II, 176
Hilyard, Joseph II, 232
Hilyard, Joseph II, 284
Hilyard, Joseph II, 292
Hilyard, Joseph III, 166
Hilyard, Joseph Seth III, 166
Hilyard, Joseph W. II, 291
Hilyard, Joseph W. II, 292
Hilyard, Joseph W. III, 166
Hilyard, Joseph W. III, 338
Hilyard, Joseph W., Jr. III, 166
Hilyard, Joseph W., Jr. III, 242
Hilyard, Keziah II, 291
Hilyard, Keziah II, 304
Hilyard, Maggie I, 395
Hilyard, Margaret II, 79
Hilyard, Margaret II, 205
Hilyard, Margaret II, 216
Hilyard, Margaret II, 232
Hilyard, Maria II, 292
Hilyard, Martha II, 216
Hilyard, Martha II, 232
Hilyard, Martha II, 253
Hilyard, Martha II, 310
Hilyard, Martha H. II, 320
Hilyard, Martha W. III, 166
Hilyard, Mary II, 79
Hilyard, Mary II, 176
Hilyard, Mary II, 177
Hilyard, Mary II, 203
Hilyard, Mary II, 226
Hilyard, Mary II, 231
Hilyard, Mary II, 232
Hilyard, Mary II, 275
Hilyard, Mary II, 290
Hilyard, Mary II, 291
Hilyard, Mary II, 292
Hilyard, Mary II, 310
Hilyard, Mary II, 876
Hilyard, Mary III, 166
Hilyard, Mary Amando III, 166
Hilyard, Mary E. II, 177
Hilyard, Mary H. II, 305
Hilyard, Mary H. Walker II, 292
Hilyard, Mary R. II, 310
Hilyard, Mary R. II, 876
Hilyard, Mary T. II, 320
Hilyard, Mary T. III, 166
Hilyard, Mary T. III, 338
Hilyard, Rachel II, 79
Hilyard, Rachel II, 176
Hilyard, Rachel II, 232
Hilyard, Rachel III, 166
Hilyard, Rachel H. II, 187
Hilyard, Rachel L. II, 292
Hilyard, Rachel Louisa III, 166
Hilyard, Rachel W. II, 290
Hilyard, Rachel W. II, 291
Hilyard, Rachel W. III, 166
Hilyard, Rebecca II, 232
Hilyard, Reuben II, 78
Hilyard, Reuben II, 232
Hilyard, Reuben II, 876
Hilyard, Ruben II, 61
Hilyard, Ruben II, 71
Hilyard, Ruben II, 79
Hilyard, Samuel II, 79
Hilyard, Samuel II, 205
Hilyard, Samuel II, 226
Hilyard, Samuel II, 232
Hilyard, Sarah II, 227
Hilyard, Sarah II, 232
Hilyard, Sarah H. II, 292
Hilyard, Sarah H. II, 304
Hilyard, Sarah T. II, 292
Hilyard, Sarah T. III, 166
Hilyard, Thomas T. III, 166
Hilyard, Thos. T. III, 166
Hilyard, Townsend II, 79
Hilyard, Townsend II, 232
Hilyard, Townsend II, 876
Hilyard, Wd. Adelaide W. III, 16
Hilyard, William II, 232
Hilyard, William II, 291
Hilyard, William II, 310
Hilyard, William S. II, 310

lyard, Wm. II, 79
lyer, Sarah II, 219
lyer, Sarah II, 232
melwright, Margaret C. V, 697
miller, William V, 336
miller, Wm. V, 336
mles, Arnold B. V, 953
mmelright, Elizabeth VI, 400
mmelwright, Hannah II, 798
mmelwright, Mary II, 798
mmelwright, Philip II, 798
nant, Thomas I, 336
nchliffe, Emma II, 812
nchman, Allen V, 911
nchman, Anna II, 292
nchman, Anna B. II, 292
nchman, Barclay II, 292
nchman, Barclay V, 971
nchman, Benjamin II, 79
nchman, Benjamin II, 550
nchman, Benjamin M. II, 550
nchman, Charles II, 177
nchman, Charles Russell II, 292
nchman, Charles S. II, 292
nchman, Clemence A. II, 144
nchman, Clemence A. II, 151
nchman, Clement A. II, 144
nchman, Clement A. II, 151
nchman, Eliza II, 69
nchman, Eliza II, 79
nchman, Eliza V, 64
nchman, Eliza V, 73
nchman, Eliza W. II, 292
nchman, Elizabeth III, 166
nchman, Elizabeth IV, 679
nchman, Elizabeth IV, 721
nchman, Elizabeth B. II, 144
nchman, Elizabeth B. II, 151
nchman, Griffith II, 79
nchman, Griffith V, 73
nchman, Henry IV, 679
nchman, James II, 69
nchman, James II, 79
nchman, James II, 550
nchman, James Wilson II, 550
nchman, John II, 177
nchman, John II, 550
nchman, John III, 166
nchman, Joseph II, 550
nchman, Lydia II, 177
nchman, Lydia S. II, 292
nchman, Margaretta L. V, 911
nchman, Margaretta S. II, 292
nchman, Margaretta S. V, 911
nchman, Mary II, 550
nchman, Mary II, 689
nchman, Mary II, 690
nchman, Mary II, 779
nchman, Mary V, 73
nchman, Mary B. II, 725
nchman, Mary B. II, 746
nchman, Mary B. V, 73
nchman, Mary M. II, 292
nchman, Mary Mitchell II, 292
nchman, Rebecca T. IV, 683
nchman, Rebecca T. IV, 721
nchman, Rebecca T. IV, 928
nchman, Rebecca T. IV, 964
nchman, Russell II, 292
inchman, Ruth IV, 679
inchman, Sarah II, 69
inchman, Sarah II, 79
nchman, Sarah IV, 799
nchman, Sarah IV, 823
nchman, Sarah IV, 827
nchman, Sinah IV, 805
inchman, Sinah IV, 823
inchman, Walter II, 177
inchman, Walter S. II, 292
inchman, Wd. Eliza W. II, 177
inckle, Addie I, 616
inckle, Addie I, 619
inckle, Addie M. I, 618
inckle, Addie M. I, 634
inckle, Elsie I, 633
inckle, Elsie I, 634
inckle, Ethelda I, 619
inckle, Ethelda Elmore I, 616
inckle, Ethelda S. I, 634
inckle, Hoyle I, 633
inckle, Hoyle I, 634
inckle, John H. I, 618
inckle, Julia E. I, 618
inckle, Milo S. I, 616
inckle, Milo S. I, 618
inckle, Milo S. I, 619
inckle, Milo S. I, 634
incksman, Benjamin II, 550
ind, Ann II, 375
ind, Hannah II, 375
Hind, Mary II, 375
Hind, Mary II, 550
Hind, Rachel II, 550
Hind, Rachel II, 665
Hind, Robert II, 375
Hind, Robert II, 550
Hinderlong, Chares Ross IV, 1165
Hinderlong, Charles IV, 1165
Hinderlong, Charley IV, 1165
Hinderlong, Charlie IV, 1165
Hinderlong, Clara IV, 1165
Hinderlong, Edna Pearl IV, 1165
Hinderson, Charlotte I, 618
Hindricks, Sarah I, 629
Hinds, Ethel III, 165
Hinds, Ethel III, 166
Hinds, Hannah I, 280
Hinds, Hannah I, 308
Hinds, Hannah I, 312
Hinds, Jesse V, 501
Hinds, Jesse V, 531
Hinds, Julia III, 165
Hinds, Julia III, 166
Hinds, Peter I, 53
Hinds, Peter I, 308
Hinds, Peter I, 312
Hinds, Sarah V, 501
Hinds, Sarah V, 508
Hinds, Sarah V, 531
Hinds, William III, 165
Hinds, William III, 166
Hindshaw, W. W. VI, 524
Hine, Edwin I, 308
Hine, Lydia IV, 1320
Hine, Willis E. IV, 1320
Hiner, David VI, 932
Hiner, Dolly VI, 932
Hiner, Lillie IV, 823
Hiner, Robert IV, 823
Hines, Aaron I, 289
Hines, Ann II, 375
Hines, Anna E. I, 324
Hines, Caroline B. VI, 825
Hines, Charity V. I, 324
Hines, Charles McKenny V, 682
Hines, Clara IV, 721
Hines, Clara E. IV, 721
Hines, Clarkey I, 289
Hines, David VI, 883
Hines, Dock I, 308
Hines, Edgar V, 682
Hines, Edwin I, 308
Hines, Elizabeth I, 289
Hines, Elizabeth I, 302
Hines, Elizabeth I, 308
Hines, Elizabeth III, 166
Hines, Elizabeth III, 322
Hines, Emma G. I, 324
Hines, Essie IV, 749
Hines, George VI, 69
Hines, Hannah I, 289
Hines, Hannah I, 308
Hines, Hannah V, 501
Hines, Hannah V, 541
Hines, Hannah, Jr. I, 308
Hines, Harvey IV, 721
Hines, Harvey Ellsworth IV, 721
Hines, Isaac IV, 149
Hines, Isaac V, 501
Hines, J. Z. I, 308
Hines, James III, 166
Hines, James III, 322
Hines, James VI, 825
Hines, James, Jr. VI, 832
Hines, Jesse V, 501
Hines, Jesse V, 682
Hines, Jessie IV, 1254
Hines, Joel IV, 149
Hines, John I, 289
Hines, John I, 302
Hines, John I, 308
Hines, John V, 336
Hines, Joseph F. I, 324
Hines, Joshua I, 329
Hines, Joshuay F. I, 324
Hines, Kelly VI, 825
Hines, Lucy VI, 825
Hines, Lydia IV, 149
Hines, Martha I, 289
Hines, Martha I, 308
Hines, Mary I, 289
Hines, Mary I, 300
Hines, Mary I, 308
Hines, Mary I, 546
Hines, Mary E. I, 324
Hines, Maxwell IV, 1254
Hines, Mrs. Edna V, 743
Hines, Nathan I, 546
Hines, Nathan I, 547
Hines, Nathan IV, 149
Hines, Nathan V, 501
Hines, Nathaniel I, 546
Hines, Patience I, 546
Hines, Patience IV, 149
Hines, Patience V, 469
Hines, Patience V, 501
Hines, Peter I, 289
Hines, Peter I, 308
Hines, Rachel IV, 149
Hines, Rachel V, 487
Hines, Rachel V, 501
Hines, Rachel V, 682
Hines, Rebecca V, 336
Hines, Sarah I, 289
Hines, Sarah I, 308
Hines, Sarah I, 319
Hines, Sarah IV, 149
Hines, Sarah V, 501
Hines, Susanna IV, 149
Hines, Widow Patience I, 547
Hines, William I, 289
Hines, William VI, 796
Hines, William T. I, 324
Hines, Willis E. IV, 1320
Hines, Zelma Irene IV, 721
Hines, Zodock I, 308
Hing, Nancy VI, 825
Hing, Nathe VI, 825
Hinge, Ambrose VI, 825
Hinge, Jane VI, 825
Hings, Peyton VI, 825
Hings, Sally VI, 825
Hinkle, Achsah VI, 505
Hinkle, Achsah VI, 545
Hinkle, Alcesta K. II, 876
Hinkle, Alcesta K. II, 926
Hinkle, Benjamin VI, 825
Hinkle, Francis II, 79
Hinkle, George VI, 505
Hinkle, George VI, 545
Hinkle, Hayle I, 617
Hinkle, Job VI, 861
Hinkle, Jobe VI, 825
Hinkle, John I, 924
Hinkle, Joseph IV, 221
Hinkle, Lou I, 926
Hinkle, Lula S. I, 924
Hinkle, Mable I, 943
Hinkle, Mary Elsina I, 617
Hinkle, Nancy VI, 825
Hinkle, Olive IV, 1320
Hinkle, Sallie I, 924
Hinkle, Sarah E. VI, 521
Hinkley, Francis II, 79
Hinksman, Sinah IV, 805
Hinksman, Sinah IV, 823
Hinkson, Anna V, 682
Hinkson, Frank V, 682
Hinkson, Grace V, 682
Hinkson, Katharine IV, 149
Hinkson, Maud V, 682
Hinman, Annie IV, 1320
Hinman, Charles IV, 1320
Hinman, Chas. A. IV, 1316
Hinman, Chas. A. IV, 1320
Hinman, Chas. A., Jr. IV, 1320
Hinman, Dora IV, 1320
Hinman, Dora C. IV, 1316
Hinman, Dora C. IV, 1320
Hinman, Dorothy G. IV, 1320
Hinman, Frank IV, 1320
Hinman, Frank T. IV, 1320
Hinman, Fred IV, 1320
Hinman, Fred C. IV, 1320
Hinman, Harold B. IV, 1320
Hinman, Harriett V, 532
Hinman, M. S. IV, 1320
Hinman, Mrs. Cecil IV, 1320
Hinman, Percy IV, 1320
Hinman, Percy A. IV, 1320
Hinman, Phila F. IV, 1320
Hinman, Ruby IV, 1320
Hinman, Sarah III, 166
Hinman, Sarah III, 420
Hinman, Sarah IV, 1219
Hinman, Sarah Ann IV, 1211
Hinman, Seth W. IV, 1320
Hinman, Thekla IV, 1320
Hinnant, ??? I, 628
Hinnant, Alice I, 336
Hinnant, Bettie I, 337
Hinnant, Bettie L. I, 336
Hinnant, C. M. I, 336
Hinnant, Ed. I, 337
Hinnant, Elbert T. I, 336
Hinnant, Eleanor Ruby I, 628
Hinnant, J. H. I, 336
Hinnant, Jack I, 336
Hinnant, Margaret I, 336
Hinnant, Penniah I, 336
Hinnant, Penninah I, 336
Hinnant, Robert I, 337
Hinnant, Sarah A. I, 336
Hinnant, Thomas I, 336
Hinnant, Thomas, Jr. I, 337
Hinnant, Victoria I, 336
Hinnant, Zachariah I, 336
Hinnard, John I, 1094
Hinne, Ed. V, 834
Hinne, John II, 375
Hinne, Mina V, 834
Hinne, William II, 375
Hinrichs, C. F. A. III, 120
Hinrichs, Louisa III, 120
Hinrichs, Violet V. III, 120
Hinricks, C. F. A. III, 167
Hinricks, Louisa III, 167
Hinricks, Violet V. III, 167
Hinsdale, Anna B. III, 167
Hinsdale, Anna B. III, 364
Hinsdale, Daniel D. III, 167
Hinsdale, Deborah III, 167
Hinsdale, Deborah C. III, 167
Hinsdale, Deborah C. III, 311
Hinsdale, Henry II, 232
Hinsdale, Henry II, 256
Hinsdale, Henry III, 167
Hinsdale, Henry III, 311
Hinsdale, Henry III, 364
Hinsdale, Mary II, 232
Hinsdale, Mary II, 256
Hinsdale, Mary III, 167
Hinsdale, Mary III, 311
Hinsdale, Mary III, 364
Hinsdale, Rebecca III, 167
Hinsdale, Samuel III, 167
Hinsdale, Sarah II, 232
Hinsdale, Sarah II, 256
Hinsdale, Stephen G. III, 167
Hinsdale, William II, 232
Hinsdale, William II, 256
Hinselwood, Alexander II, 375
Hinselwood, Amy II, 375
Hinselwood, Ann II, 375
Hinselwood, Anne II, 375
Hinselwood, Barbara II, 375
Hinselwood, Robert II, 375
Hinsen, Elsie IV, 1330
Hinshaw, Aaron I, 353
Hinshaw, Aaron I, 354
Hinshaw, Aaron I, 396
Hinshaw, Aaron I, 481
Hinshaw, Abel I, 481
Hinshaw, Abel V, 395
Hinshaw, Abigail I, 353
Hinshaw, Abigail I, 354
Hinshaw, Abigail I, 355
Hinshaw, Abigail I, 361
Hinshaw, Abigail I, 378
Hinshaw, Abigail I, 395
Hinshaw, Abigail I, 396
Hinshaw, Abigail I, 397
Hinshaw, Abigail I, 404
Hinshaw, Abigail I, 409
Hinshaw, Abigail I, 427
Hinshaw, Abigail I, 464
Hinshaw, Abigail I, 467
Hinshaw, Abigail I, 468
Hinshaw, Abigail I, 477
Hinshaw, Abigail I, 481
Hinshaw, Abigail I, 749
Hinshaw, Abigail I, 762
Hinshaw, Abigail I, 763
Hinshaw, Abigail I, 768
Hinshaw, Abijah I, 354
Hinshaw, Abijah I, 396
Hinshaw, Abijah G. I, 481
Hinshaw, Abijah Goldsmith I, 467
Hinshaw, Absalom I, 353
Hinshaw, Absalom I, 468
Hinshaw, Absalom I, 481
Hinshaw, Absalom V, 395
Hinshaw, Absalom, Jr. I, 395
Hinshaw, Absolam I, 395
Hinshaw, Absolem I, 353
Hinshaw, Absolem I, 395
Hinshaw, Absolem V, 395
Hinshaw, Absolom I, 395
Hinshaw, Absolom I, 396
Hinshaw, Absolom I, 467
Hinshaw, Absolom, Jr. I, 467
Hinshaw, Adam I, 655
Hinshaw, Adam I, 679
Hinshaw, Adam I, 691
Hinshaw, Adam I, 987
Hinshaw, Adam I, 1121
Hinshaw, Adam Brown I, 748
Hinshaw, Alan I, 467
Hinshaw, Aletha S. I, 468
Hinshaw, Alice I, 353
Hinshaw, Alice I, 395
Hinshaw, Alice I, 546
Hinshaw, Alice I, 1106
Hinshaw, Allen I, 748
Hinshaw, Amanda E. I, 655
Hinshaw, Amos I, 468
Hinshaw, Amos G. I, 468
Hinshaw, Amos S. I, 467
Hinshaw, Amos S. I, 481
Hinshaw, Amy I, 397
Hinshaw, Amy I, 412
Hinshaw, Amy I, 422
Hinshaw, Amy I, 481
Hinshaw, Amy Nixon I, 396
Hinshaw, Andrew IV, 408
Hinshaw, Angelina I, 1106
Hinshaw, Angeline I, 1141
Hinshaw, Ann I, 353
Hinshaw, Ann I, 354
Hinshaw, Ann I, 396
Hinshaw, Ann I, 410
Hinshaw, Ann I, 425
Hinshaw, Ann I, 816
Hinshaw, Ann I, 975
Hinshaw, Ann I, 987
Hinshaw, Ann I, 1121
Hinshaw, Anna I, 748
Hinshaw, Anna I, 758
Hinshaw, Anna I, 763
Hinshaw, Anna I, 816
Hinshaw, Anna I, 828
Hinshaw, Anna I, 1121
Hinshaw, Anna I, 1130
Hinshaw, Anna V, 395
Hinshaw, Anna Cox I, 763
Hinshaw, Anna M. I, 749
Hinshaw, Anna Martitia I, 763
Hinshaw, Annas I, 748
Hinshaw, Anne I, 353
Hinshaw, Annes I, 762
Hinshaw, Anney I, 816
Hinshaw, Annie V, 682
Hinshaw, Annis I, 527
Hinshaw, Annis I, 546
Hinshaw, Annis I, 741
Hinshaw, Annis I, 762
Hinshaw, Annis I, 816
Hinshaw, Armelia I, 749
Hinshaw, Armelia I, 760
Hinshaw, Armella I, 762
Hinshaw, Ascenath I, 749
Hinshaw, Asenath I, 462
Hinshaw, Asenath I, 468
Hinshaw, Asenath I, 477
Hinshaw, Asenath I, 481
Hinshaw, Asenath I, 762
Hinshaw, Asenath I, 763
Hinshaw, Asenath I, 1106
Hinshaw, Asenath G. I, 701
Hinshaw, Augusta III, 167
Hinshaw, Augusta W. III, 167
Hinshaw, Barclay V, 625
Hinshaw, Barzilla I, 354
Hinshaw, Barzillia I, 354
Hinshaw, Benj. I, 353
Hinshaw, Benj. I, 354
Hinshaw, Benj. I, 355
Hinshaw, Benjamin I, 354
Hinshaw, Benjamin I, 355
Hinshaw, Benjamin I, 395
Hinshaw, Benjamin I, 396
Hinshaw, Benjamin I, 397
Hinshaw, Benjamin I, 407
Hinshaw, Benjamin I, 467
Hinshaw, Benjamin I, 481
Hinshaw, Benjamin I, 482
Hinshaw, Benjamin I, 527
Hinshaw, Benjamin I, 546
Hinshaw, Benjamin I, 741
Hinshaw, Benjamin I, 748
Hinshaw, Benjamin I, 762
Hinshaw, Benjamin I, 816
Hinshaw, Benjamin, Jr. I, 762
Hinshaw, Bertha A. I, 701
Hinshaw, Betsy I, 763
Hinshaw, Betsy Luzina I, 748
Hinshaw, Binjamin I, 655
Hinshaw, Calvin I, 461
Hinshaw, Carl I, 468
Hinshaw, Caroline I, 481
Hinshaw, Caroline I, 655
Hinshaw, Caroline I, 680
Hinshaw, Caroline E. V, 395
Hinshaw, Charles I, 354
Hinshaw, Charles I, 481
Hinshaw, Charles I, 1106
Hinshaw, Charles I, 1154
Hinshaw, Clara I, 467
Hinshaw, Clyde I, 467
Hinshaw, Cordelia E. I, 467
Hinshaw, Cyrus I, 353
Hinshaw, Cyrus C. I, 748
Hinshaw, Cyrus Clarkson I, 748

Hinshaw, Cyrus Franklin I, 397
Hinshaw, Cyrus N. I, 468
Hinshaw, Daniel I, 353
Hinshaw, Daniel I, 397
Hinshaw, Darius I, 748
Hinshaw, Darius I, 762
Hinshaw, Darius I, 763
Hinshaw, Darius B. I, 748
Hinshaw, David I, 1106
Hinshaw, David I, 1141
Hinshaw, David I, 1154
Hinshaw, David I, 1158
Hinshaw, David S. III, 167
Hinshaw, Deborah I, 353
Hinshaw, Deborah I, 395
Hinshaw, Deborah I, 397
Hinshaw, Deborah I, 407
Hinshaw, Deborah I, 749
Hinshaw, Deborah I, 768
Hinshaw, Delphina E. I, 468
Hinshaw, Delphina E. I, 481
Hinshaw, Delphine I, 355
Hinshaw, Delphine I, 397
Hinshaw, Dennis I, 353
Hinshaw, Dianna I, 749
Hinshaw, Dinah I, 355
Hinshaw, Dinah I, 396
Hinshaw, Dinah I, 405
Hinshaw, E. M. Mariah I, 687
Hinshaw, Eadeth V, 395
Hinshaw, Edith V, 395
Hinshaw, Edith V, 438
Hinshaw, Edmond I, 748
Hinshaw, Eli N. I, 481
Hinshaw, Eli Newlin I, 467
Hinshaw, Eli Newlin I, 481
Hinshaw, Elias I, 467
Hinshaw, Elias I, 468
Hinshaw, Elias I, 481
Hinshaw, Elihu B. I, 481
Hinshaw, Elihu Bennett I, 468
Hinshaw, Elijah I, 467
Hinshaw, Elisabeth I, 481
Hinshaw, Eliza I. I, 749
Hinshaw, Eliza Jane I, 756
Hinshaw, Eliza Jane I, 763
Hinshaw, Elizabeth I, 353
Hinshaw, Elizabeth I, 354
Hinshaw, Elizabeth I, 355
Hinshaw, Elizabeth I, 364
Hinshaw, Elizabeth I, 383
Hinshaw, Elizabeth I, 395
Hinshaw, Elizabeth I, 396
Hinshaw, Elizabeth I, 397
Hinshaw, Elizabeth I, 466
Hinshaw, Elizabeth I, 467
Hinshaw, Elizabeth I, 468
Hinshaw, Elizabeth I, 475
Hinshaw, Elizabeth I, 476
Hinshaw, Elizabeth I, 481
Hinshaw, Elizabeth I, 755
Hinshaw, Elizabeth I, 763
Hinshaw, Elizabeth I, 987
Hinshaw, Elizabeth I, 1121
Hinshaw, Elizabeth I, 1141
Hinshaw, Elizabeth IV, 408
Hinshaw, Elizabeth A. I, 1154
Hinshaw, Elizabeth A. I, 1158
Hinshaw, Elizabeth B. IV, 408
Hinshaw, Elizabeth B. IV, 438
Hinshaw, Elmina V, 73
Hinshaw, Elmina V, 83
Hinshaw, Elmina V, 85
Hinshaw, Elva V, 395
Hinshaw, Elva V, 682
Hinshaw, Elvan O. I, 655
Hinshaw, Elvira I, 353
Hinshaw, Elvisa B. I, 748
Hinshaw, Elwin I, 1121
Hinshaw, Emey I, 354
Hinshaw, Emily I, 619
Hinshaw, Emily I, 748
Hinshaw, Emily Lavina I, 748
Hinshaw, Emily M. I, 619
Hinshaw, Enoch I, 354
Hinshaw, Enoch I, 396
Hinshaw, Enoch I, 655
Hinshaw, Enos I, 468
Hinshaw, Ethel I, 467
Hinshaw, Ethel V, 682
Hinshaw, Eunice I, 461
Hinshaw, Eunice I, 468
Hinshaw, Eunice I, 741
Hinshaw, Eunice I, 748
Hinshaw, Eunice I, 762
Hinshaw, Eunice I, 811
Hinshaw, Eunice I, 816
Hinshaw, Eunice M. I, 749
Hinshaw, Eunice M. M. I, 679
Hinshaw, Eunice Mildred Maria I, 763
Hinshaw, Evan I, 1106
Hinshaw, Evan I, 1154
Hinshaw, Evelyn I, 467
Hinshaw, Ezra I, 353
Hinshaw, Ezra I, 354
Hinshaw, Ezra I, 395
Hinshaw, Ezra I, 396
Hinshaw, Ezra I, 407
Hinshaw, Ezra I, 679
Hinshaw, Ezra I, 1106
Hinshaw, Ezra I, 1121
Hinshaw, Ezra I, 1135
Hinshaw, Ezra I, 1142
Hinshaw, Ezra I, 1154
Hinshaw, Fernando A. I, 655
Hinshaw, Florence M. V, 395
Hinshaw, Florence N. V, 395
Hinshaw, Frances T. I, 481
Hinshaw, Francis T. I, 468
Hinshaw, Francis T. I, 481
Hinshaw, Frank W. V, 395
Hinshaw, Franklin A. I, 701
Hinshaw, Garner V, 395
Hinshaw, Garner V, 682
Hinshaw, George I, 355
Hinshaw, George I, 396
Hinshaw, George I, 748
Hinshaw, George I, 816
Hinshaw, George I, 975
Hinshaw, George I, 986
Hinshaw, George I, 1094
Hinshaw, George I, 1121
Hinshaw, George F. I, 481
Hinshaw, George Franklin I, 467
Hinshaw, George Franklin I, 481
Hinshaw, George M. I, 763
Hinshaw, Gulielma Maria I, 721
Hinshaw, Hannah I, 353
Hinshaw, Hannah I, 354
Hinshaw, Hannah I, 355
Hinshaw, Hannah I, 377
Hinshaw, Hannah I, 387
Hinshaw, Hannah I, 395
Hinshaw, Hannah I, 396
Hinshaw, Hannah I, 405
Hinshaw, Hannah I, 415
Hinshaw, Hannah I, 425
Hinshaw, Hannah I, 468
Hinshaw, Hannah I, 469
Hinshaw, Hannah I, 479
Hinshaw, Hannah I, 481
Hinshaw, Hannah I, 546
Hinshaw, Hannah I, 655
Hinshaw, Hannah I, 674
Hinshaw, Hannah I, 679
Hinshaw, Hannah I, 680
Hinshaw, Hannah I, 741
Hinshaw, Hannah I, 749
Hinshaw, Hannah I, 762
Hinshaw, Hannah I, 763
Hinshaw, Hannah I, 765
Hinshaw, Hannah I, 768
Hinshaw, Hannah I, 805
Hinshaw, Hannah I, 816
Hinshaw, Hannah I, 817
Hinshaw, Hannah I, 828
Hinshaw, Hannah I, 964
Hinshaw, Hannah I, 987
Hinshaw, Hannah I, 988
Hinshaw, Hannah I, 1106
Hinshaw, Hannah I, 1121
Hinshaw, Hannah I, 1124
Hinshaw, Hannah E. I, 481
Hinshaw, Hannah M. I, 481
Hinshaw, Hannah S. I, 655
Hinshaw, Hannah S. I, 680
Hinshaw, Henrietta V, 395
Hinshaw, Henrietta J. V, 395
Hinshaw, Henry I, 397
Hinshaw, Henry I, 481
Hinshaw, Henry I, 1106
Hinshaw, Henry Alexander I, 397
Hinshaw, Henry Lewis I, 1141
Hinshaw, Howard B. IV, 408
Hinshaw, Huldah I, 468
Hinshaw, Ira I, 354
Hinshaw, Ira I, 396
Hinshaw, Ira I, 397
Hinshaw, Ira I, 1106
Hinshaw, Isaac I, 353
Hinshaw, Isaac I, 354
Hinshaw, Isaac I, 396
Hinshaw, Isaac I, 397
Hinshaw, Isaac G. I, 763
Hinshaw, Isaac Gaston I, 748
Hinshaw, Isaac N. I, 763
Hinshaw, Isaac Newton I, 749
Hinshaw, Isabelle I, 748
Hinshaw, Isabelle I, 763
Hinshaw, Isaiah M. I, 481
Hinshaw, Isaiah Manley I, 467
Hinshaw, Isaiah Manly I, 481
Hinshaw, Isam I, 397
Hinshaw, Isham J. I, 397
Hinshaw, Isom I, 353
Hinshaw, Jabez I, 679
Hinshaw, Jabez I, 683
Hinshaw, Jabez I, 749
Hinshaw, Jabez I, 763
Hinshaw, Jabin I, 353
Hinshaw, Jacob I, 354
Hinshaw, Jacob I, 355
Hinshaw, Jacob I, 370
Hinshaw, Jacob I, 384
Hinshaw, Jacob I, 395
Hinshaw, Jacob I, 396
Hinshaw, Jacob I, 397
Hinshaw, Jacob I, 457
Hinshaw, Jacob I, 461
Hinshaw, Jacob I, 467
Hinshaw, Jacob I, 468
Hinshaw, Jacob I, 469
Hinshaw, Jacob I, 481
Hinshaw, Jacob I, 741
Hinshaw, Jacob I, 755
Hinshaw, Jacob I, 763
Hinshaw, Jacob I, 816
Hinshaw, Jacob L. I, 481
Hinshaw, Jacob Lindley I, 467
Hinshaw, Jacob Lindley I, 481
Hinshaw, Jacob, II I, 355
Hinshaw, Jacob, Jr. I, 395
Hinshaw, Jacob, Jr. I, 457
Hinshaw, James I, 748
Hinshaw, James I, 762
Hinshaw, James I, 763
Hinshaw, James I, 1121
Hinshaw, James H. I, 655
Hinshaw, James M. I, 763
Hinshaw, James W. I, 763
Hinshaw, James Washington I, 397
Hinshaw, James Williard I, 748
Hinshaw, Jane I, 354
Hinshaw, Jane I, 391
Hinshaw, Jane I, 395
Hinshaw, Jane I, 396
Hinshaw, Jane I, 464
Hinshaw, Jane I, 468
Hinshaw, Jane I, 477
Hinshaw, Jane I, 481
Hinshaw, Jane I, 721
Hinshaw, Jane I, 1106
Hinshaw, Jane I, 1121
Hinshaw, Jane I, 1135
Hinshaw, Jediahah I, 353
Hinshaw, Jedida I, 396
Hinshaw, Jedida I, 397
Hinshaw, Jedidah I, 353
Hinshaw, Jedidah I, 355
Hinshaw, Jemima I, 355
Hinshaw, Jesse I, 353
Hinshaw, Jesse I, 354
Hinshaw, Jesse I, 355
Hinshaw, Jesse I, 361
Hinshaw, Jesse I, 364
Hinshaw, Jesse I, 395
Hinshaw, Jesse I, 396
Hinshaw, Jesse I, 407
Hinshaw, Jesse I, 457
Hinshaw, Jesse I, 546
Hinshaw, Jesse I, 741
Hinshaw, Jesse I, 748
Hinshaw, Jesse I, 749
Hinshaw, Jesse I, 762
Hinshaw, Jesse I, 763
Hinshaw, Jesse I, 768
Hinshaw, Jesse I, 811
Hinshaw, Jesse I, 816
Hinshaw, Jesse I, 987
Hinshaw, Jesse I, 1106
Hinshaw, Jesse I, 1121
Hinshaw, Jesse, Jr. I, 354
Hinshaw, Jesse, Jr. I, 396
Hinshaw, Jesse, Jr. I, 763
Hinshaw, Job I, 355
Hinshaw, Job I, 721
Hinshaw, Job I, 763
Hinshaw, Job H. I, 701
Hinshaw, Job Harlan I, 748
Hinshaw, Jobe I, 721
Hinshaw, John I, 354
Hinshaw, John I, 355
Hinshaw, John I, 395
Hinshaw, John I, 396
Hinshaw, John I, 408
Hinshaw, John I, 468
Hinshaw, John I, 546
Hinshaw, John I, 580
Hinshaw, John I, 679
Hinshaw, John I, 721
Hinshaw, John I, 748
Hinshaw, John I, 749
Hinshaw, John I, 760
Hinshaw, John I, 762
Hinshaw, John I, 763
Hinshaw, John I, 783
Hinshaw, John I, 816
Hinshaw, John I, 825
Hinshaw, John I, 833
Hinshaw, John I, 912
Hinshaw, John I, 975
Hinshaw, John I, 986
Hinshaw, John I, 1094
Hinshaw, John I Sup 1, 9
Hinshaw, John V, 395
Hinshaw, John E. IV, 408
Hinshaw, John E. IV, 438
Hinshaw, John Garner V, 395
Hinshaw, John M. I, 748
Hinshaw, John R. I, 481
Hinshaw, John Randolph I, 467
Hinshaw, John Randolph I, 481
Hinshaw, John W. I, 397
Hinshaw, John, Jr. I, 1121
Hinshaw, Jonathan B. I, 468
Hinshaw, Jonathan P. I, 748
Hinshaw, Jonathan P. I, 763
Hinshaw, Joseph I, 354
Hinshaw, Joseph I, 395
Hinshaw, Joseph I, 396
Hinshaw, Joseph I, 402
Hinshaw, Joseph I, 407
Hinshaw, Joseph I, 481
Hinshaw, Joseph I, 816
Hinshaw, Joseph Lewis I, 468
Hinshaw, Joseph M. I, 763
Hinshaw, Joseph Moore I, 748
Hinshaw, Joseph Philips I, 987
Hinshaw, Joseph Phillips I, 816
Hinshaw, Joshua I, 1121
Hinshaw, Juneous R. I, 701
Hinshaw, Juretta I, 758
Hinshaw, Juretta I, 763
Hinshaw, Jurilla I, 762
Hinshaw, Larehoma I, 749
Hinshaw, Larken Irvin I, 1121
Hinshaw, Laura Catherine I, 1121
Hinshaw, Leanna E. I, 397
Hinshaw, Lewis I, 468
Hinshaw, Lorohame I, 674
Hinshaw, Lorohame I, 679
Hinshaw, Louisa I, 763
Hinshaw, Louisa Jane I, 748
Hinshaw, Lucinda I, 1106
Hinshaw, Lucinda I, 1121
Hinshaw, Lucinda I, 1124
Hinshaw, Lucinda I Sup 1, 12
Hinshaw, Lucy J. I, 468
Hinshaw, Luzena I, 763
Hinshaw, Lydia I, 354
Hinshaw, Lydia I, 748
Hinshaw, Lydia I, 749
Hinshaw, Lydia I, 762
Hinshaw, Lydia I, 763
Hinshaw, Lydia I, 766
Hinshaw, Lydia I, 816
Hinshaw, Lydia I, 825
Hinshaw, Lydia I, 912
Hinshaw, Maban I, 748
Hinshaw, Maben Luther I, 748
Hinshaw, Mahala I, 749
Hinshaw, Mahla I, 763
Hinshaw, Mahla I, 765
Hinshaw, Malinda I, 355
Hinshaw, Malinda I, 749
Hinshaw, Malinda I, 755
Hinshaw, Malinda I, 762
Hinshaw, Margaret I, 354
Hinshaw, Margaret I, 355
Hinshaw, Margaret I, 397
Hinshaw, Margaret I, 419
Hinshaw, Margaret I, 500
Hinshaw, Margaret I, 546
Hinshaw, Margaret I, 816
Hinshaw, Margaret I, 820
Hinshaw, Margaret I, 964
Hinshaw, Margaret I, 1101
Hinshaw, Margaret I, 1106
Hinshaw, Margaret I, 1121
Hinshaw, Margaret I, 1132
Hinshaw, Margaret V, 336
Hinshaw, Margaret V, 337
Hinshaw, Margaret V, 395
Hinshaw, Margaret V, 424
Hinshaw, Margaret G. V, 395
Hinshaw, Margery I, 354
Hinshaw, Margery I, 395
Hinshaw, Margery I, 402
Hinshaw, Margery I, 816
Hinshaw, Margret I, 1121
Hinshaw, Margret I, 1154
Hinshaw, Maria V, 395
Hinshaw, Maria H. V, 682
Hinshaw, Mariah I, 680
Hinshaw, Martha I, 748
Hinshaw, Martha I, 749
Hinshaw, Martha I, 762
Hinshaw, Martha I, 763
Hinshaw, Martha A. I, 701
Hinshaw, Martha Jane I, 749
Hinshaw, Martin I, 355
Hinshaw, Martin I, 397
Hinshaw, Martitia I, 467
Hinshaw, Martitia I, 481
Hinshaw, Mary I, 353
Hinshaw, Mary I, 354
Hinshaw, Mary I, 355
Hinshaw, Mary I, 364
Hinshaw, Mary I, 384
Hinshaw, Mary I, 391
Hinshaw, Mary I, 392
Hinshaw, Mary I, 395
Hinshaw, Mary I, 396
Hinshaw, Mary I, 397
Hinshaw, Mary I, 407
Hinshaw, Mary I, 408
Hinshaw, Mary I, 415
Hinshaw, Mary I, 467
Hinshaw, Mary I, 468
Hinshaw, Mary I, 474
Hinshaw, Mary I, 481
Hinshaw, Mary I, 482
Hinshaw, Mary I, 655
Hinshaw, Mary I, 679
Hinshaw, Mary I, 680
Hinshaw, Mary I, 683
Hinshaw, Mary I, 721
Hinshaw, Mary I, 748
Hinshaw, Mary I, 749
Hinshaw, Mary I, 762
Hinshaw, Mary I, 763
Hinshaw, Mary I, 771
Hinshaw, Mary I, 975
Hinshaw, Mary I, 986
Hinshaw, Mary I, 987
Hinshaw, Mary I, 1106
Hinshaw, Mary I, 1117
Hinshaw, Mary I, 1121
Hinshaw, Mary I, 1123
Hinshaw, Mary I, 1130
Hinshaw, Mary I, 1141
Hinshaw, Mary I, 1142
Hinshaw, Mary I, 1154
Hinshaw, Mary V, 246
Hinshaw, Mary E. I, 655
Hinshaw, Mary L. I, 748
Hinshaw, Mary Lunda I, 748
Hinshaw, Mary Marshill I, 395
Hinshaw, Mary Philips I, 987
Hinshaw, Mary Sarah Ann I, 98
Hinshaw, Matilda I, 1121
Hinshaw, Mebane I, 763
Hinshaw, Mebane L. I, 763
Hinshaw, Melinda I, 397
Hinshaw, Michael I, 355
Hinshaw, Michael I, 397
Hinshaw, Milecent I, 468
Hinshaw, Milicent I, 474
Hinshaw, Milicent I, 481
Hinshaw, Mille I, 762
Hinshaw, Mille I, 768
Hinshaw, Milli I, 748
Hinshaw, Millon, Jr. I, 763
Hinshaw, Milly I, 763
Hinshaw, Milton I, 763
Hinshaw, Milton W. I, 397
Hinshaw, Mines I, 748
Hinshaw, Minnie D. V, 395
Hinshaw, Minnie Delilah I, 748
Hinshaw, Minnie Dora V, 395
Hinshaw, Minus I, 763
Hinshaw, Miriam I, 748
Hinshaw, Miriam I, 755
Hinshaw, Miriam I, 762
Hinshaw, Miriam E. I, 749
Hinshaw, Miriam E. I, 817
Hinshaw, Miriam E. I, 835
Hinshaw, Miriam Emaline I, 76
Hinshaw, Miriam Emeline I, 81
Hinshaw, Nancy V, 395
Hinshaw, Nancy Ann I, 748
Hinshaw, Nancy Ann I, 763
Hinshaw, Nancy Jane I, 1121
Hinshaw, Nathan I, 353
Hinshaw, Nathan I, 397
Hinshaw, Nathan I, 467
Hinshaw, Nathan I, 481
Hinshaw, Nathan I, 655
Hinshaw, Nathan I, 762
Hinshaw, Nathan I, 763
Hinshaw, Nathan T. I, 749
Hinshaw, Newton I, 353

nshaw, Newton I, 397
nshaw, Noah I, 748
nshaw, Noah I, 763
nshaw, Olah I, 468
nshaw, Oliver E. I, 748
nshaw, Ollie I, 468
nshaw, Orie V, 395
nshaw, Orlando I, 763
nshaw, Orlando B. I, 749
nshaw, Orlindo I, 353
nshaw, Orrie V, 395
nshaw, Orris V, 682
nshaw, Phebe I, 354
nshaw, Phebe I, 370
nshaw, Phebe I, 396
nshaw, Phebe I, 457
nshaw, Phebe I, 467
nshaw, Phebe I, 481
nshaw, Phebe J. I, 701
nshaw, Phebe J. I, 721
nshaw, Rabacha I, 987
nshaw, Rachel I, 395
nshaw, Rachel I, 396
nshaw, Rachel I, 397
nshaw, Rachel I, 402
nshaw, Rachel I, 408
nshaw, Rachel I, 468
nshaw, Rachel I, 655
nshaw, Rachel I, 679
nshaw, Rachel I, 987
nshaw, Rachel I, 1121
nshaw, Rebeca I, 749
nshaw, Rebecca I, 354
nshaw, Rebecca I, 355
nshaw, Rebecca I, 396
nshaw, Rebecca I, 397
nshaw, Rebecca I, 467
nshaw, Rebecca I, 468
nshaw, Rebecca I, 655
nshaw, Rebecca I, 679
nshaw, Rebecca I, 680
nshaw, Rebecca I, 741
nshaw, Rebecca I, 749
nshaw, Rebecca I, 762
nshaw, Rebecca I, 763
nshaw, Rebecca I, 1147
nshaw, Rebecca I, 1154
nshaw, Rebeccah I, 395
nshaw, Rebeckah I, 395
nshaw, Rebeckah I, 407
nshaw, Rebeckah I, 816
nshaw, Rebekah I, 354
nshaw, Rebekah I, 381
nshaw, Rebekah I, 391
nshaw, Rebekah I, 395
nshaw, Rebekah I, 396
nshaw, Rebekah I, 406
nshaw, Rebekah I, 1121
nshaw, Reuben I, 354
nshaw, Reuben I, 396
nshaw, Rheuhamia I, 748
nshaw, Rhoda I, 464
nshaw, Rhoda I, 468
nshaw, Richard I, 1106
nshaw, Richard I, 1154
nshaw, Richard V, 809
nshaw, Richard T. I, 1142
nshaw, Robert III, 167
nshaw, Roswell Erastus I, 748
nshaw, Ruhanna I, 928
nshaw, Ruth I, 353
nshaw, Ruth I, 354
nshaw, Ruth I, 355
nshaw, Ruth I, 361
nshaw, Ruth I, 395
nshaw, Ruth I, 396
nshaw, Ruth I, 407
nshaw, Ruth I, 409
nshaw, Ruth I, 468
nshaw, Ruth I, 474
nshaw, Ruth I, 481
nshaw, Ruth I, 546
nshaw, Ruth I, 679
nshaw, Ruth I, 748
nshaw, Ruth I, 749
nshaw, Ruth I, 762
nshaw, Ruth I, 763
nshaw, Ruth I, 767
nshaw, Ruth I, 773
nshaw, Ruth I, 816
nshaw, Ruth I, 912
nshaw, Ruth I, 971
nshaw, Ruth I, 987
nshaw, Ruth I, 993
nshaw, Ruth I, 1106
nshaw, Ruth I, 1121
nshaw, Ruth I, 1123
nshaw, Ruth M. I, 397
nshaw, Ruth U. I, 748
nshaw, Sabarah I, 761
nshaw, Sabarah I, 762
Hinshaw, Sabarah I, 763
Hinshaw, Sabra R. I, 655
Hinshaw, Sabra R. I, 677
Hinshaw, Sabra R. I, 680
Hinshaw, Samuel I, 355
Hinshaw, Samuel I, 396
Hinshaw, Sarah I, 354
Hinshaw, Sarah I, 393
Hinshaw, Sarah I, 395
Hinshaw, Sarah I, 396
Hinshaw, Sarah I, 426
Hinshaw, Sarah I, 469
Hinshaw, Sarah I, 546
Hinshaw, Sarah I, 655
Hinshaw, Sarah I, 679
Hinshaw, Sarah I, 691
Hinshaw, Sarah I, 741
Hinshaw, Sarah I, 748
Hinshaw, Sarah I, 749
Hinshaw, Sarah I, 760
Hinshaw, Sarah I, 762
Hinshaw, Sarah I, 763
Hinshaw, Sarah I, 765
Hinshaw, Sarah I, 768
Hinshaw, Sarah I, 816
Hinshaw, Sarah I, 964
Hinshaw, Sarah I, 987
Hinshaw, Sarah I, 1106
Hinshaw, Sarah I, 1123
Hinshaw, Sarah I, 1144
Hinshaw, Sarah III, 167
Hinshaw, Sarah A. IV, 408
Hinshaw, Sarah A. V, 395
Hinshaw, Sarah Addie V, 395
Hinshaw, Sarah Elizabeth I, 1121
Hinshaw, Scytha I, 397
Hinshaw, Sebarah I, 749
Hinshaw, Serena I, 1106
Hinshaw, Seth I, 467
Hinshaw, Seth I, 674
Hinshaw, Seth I, 679
Hinshaw, Seth I, 741
Hinshaw, Seth I, 748
Hinshaw, Seth I, 749
Hinshaw, Seth I, 762
Hinshaw, Seth I, 763
Hinshaw, Seth I, 768
Hinshaw, Seth I, 816
Hinshaw, Seth I, 964
Hinshaw, Seth J. I, 481
Hinshaw, Seth Jacob I, 468
Hinshaw, Sibyl A. I, 353
Hinshaw, Silas I, 467
Hinshaw, Silas I, 468
Hinshaw, Silas I, 476
Hinshaw, Silas I, 481
Hinshaw, Simeon I, 655
Hinshaw, Simon I, 354
Hinshaw, Simon I, 396
Hinshaw, Solomon I, 468
Hinshaw, Stephen I, 468
Hinshaw, Stephen I, 479
Hinshaw, Stephen I, 481
Hinshaw, Stephen I, 749
Hinshaw, Stephen I, 763
Hinshaw, Stephen F. I, 481
Hinshaw, Stephen F. I, 655
Hinshaw, Stephen Frances I, 467
Hinshaw, Stephen Frances I, 481
Hinshaw, Susanna I, 428
Hinshaw, Susanna I, 655
Hinshaw, Susanna I, 679
Hinshaw, Susanna I, 748
Hinshaw, Susanna V, 843
Hinshaw, Susanna V, 855
Hinshaw, Susanna White I, 396
Hinshaw, Susannah I, 748
Hinshaw, Susannah I, 761
Hinshaw, Susannah I, 762
Hinshaw, Susannah I, 816
Hinshaw, Susannah R. I, 748
Hinshaw, Sybil A. I, 397
Hinshaw, Sybil A. I, 423
Hinshaw, Tace I, 468
Hinshaw, Tamar A. I, 397
Hinshaw, Tamer I, 397
Hinshaw, Thomas I, 354
Hinshaw, Thomas I, 395
Hinshaw, Thomas I, 396
Hinshaw, Thomas I, 415
Hinshaw, Thomas I, 467
Hinshaw, Thomas I, 468
Hinshaw, Thomas I, 474
Hinshaw, Thomas I, 481
Hinshaw, Thomas I, 741
Hinshaw, Thomas I, 749
Hinshaw, Thomas I, 762
Hinshaw, Thomas I, 763
Hinshaw, Thomas I, 975
Hinshaw, Thomas I, 986
Hinshaw, Thomas B. I, 467
Hinshaw, Thomas Benoni I, 467
Hinshaw, Thomas Benoni I, 481
Hinshaw, Thos. I, 354
Hinshaw, Thos. I, 355
Hinshaw, Thos. I, 407
Hinshaw, Tristram I, 748
Hinshaw, Tristrim I, 762
Hinshaw, Tristum I, 749
Hinshaw, Trustum I, 762
Hinshaw, Unice I, 816
Hinshaw, Uriah I, 500
Hinshaw, Uriah I, 546
Hinshaw, Uriah I, 964
Hinshaw, Uriah I, 1106
Hinshaw, Uriah I, 1121
Hinshaw, Uriah I, 1123
Hinshaw, Uriah I, 1141
Hinshaw, Uriah I, 1142
Hinshaw, Uriah I, 1147
Hinshaw, Uriah I, 1154
Hinshaw, Viola V, 395
Hinshaw, Viola A. V, 395
Hinshaw, Virena I, 748
Hinshaw, Virena Elma I, 763
Hinshaw, Virena Elma I, 772
Hinshaw, Walter C. I, 701
Hinshaw, Wellimet T. I, 436
Hinshaw, Welmet I, 396
Hinshaw, Welmet I, 429
Hinshaw, Widow Ann I, 816
Hinshaw, Widow Ann I, 833
Hinshaw, Widow Ruth I, 580
Hinshaw, Wilimet T. I, 436
Hinshaw, William I, 143
Hinshaw, William I, 353
Hinshaw, William I, 354
Hinshaw, William I, 355
Hinshaw, William I, 395
Hinshaw, William I, 396
Hinshaw, William I, 397
Hinshaw, William I, 546
Hinshaw, William I, 655
Hinshaw, William I, 674
Hinshaw, William I, 679
Hinshaw, William I, 680
Hinshaw, William I, 748
Hinshaw, William I, 749
Hinshaw, William I, 762
Hinshaw, William I, 763
Hinshaw, William I, 816
Hinshaw, William I, 817
Hinshaw, William I, 820
Hinshaw, William I, 828
Hinshaw, William I, 964
Hinshaw, William I, 975
Hinshaw, William I, 987
Hinshaw, William I, 1101
Hinshaw, William I, 1106
Hinshaw, William I, 1121
Hinshaw, William I, 1154
Hinshaw, William B. I, 762
Hinshaw, William B. I, 763
Hinshaw, William B. I, 805
Hinshaw, William Barton I, 748
Hinshaw, William O. I, 701
Hinshaw, William T. V, 395
Hinshaw, William Wade VI, 321
Hinshaw, William Wade VI, 360
Hinshaw, William Wade VI, 466
Hinshaw, William Wade VI, 614
Hinshaw, William Wade VI, 728
Hinshaw, William Zahan I, 748
Hinshaw, William, Jr. I, 395
Hinshaw, William, Jr. I, 396
Hinshaw, William, Jr. I, 397
Hinshaw, William, Jr. I, 546
Hinshaw, William, Jr. I, 679
Hinshaw, William, Jr. I, 762
Hinshaw, William, Sr. I, 749
Hinshaw, Wm. I, 353
Hinshaw, Wm. I, 354
Hinshaw, Wm. I, 355
Hinshaw, Wm. I, 396
Hinshaw, Wm. I, 408
Hinshaw, Wm. I, 500
Hinshaw, Wm. I, 1094
Hinshaw, Wm. I, 1106
Hinshaw, Wm. Wade VI, 476
Hinshaw, Wm. Wade VI, 496
Hinshaw, Wm. Wade VI, 515
Hinshaw, Wm. Wade VI, 660
Hinshaw, Wm., Sr. I, 1106
Hinshaw, Zebedee I, 762
Hinshaw, Zebedee M. I, 655
Hinshaw, Zebedee M. I, 680
Hinshaw, Zeno I, 354
Hinshaw, Zeno I, 396
Hinshaw, Zeno I, 748
Hinshaw, Zeno I, 763
Hinshaw, Zimri I, 355
Hinshaw, Zimri I, 397
Hinshaw, Zimri I, 1106
Hinshaw, Zimri I, 1154
Hinshelwood, Robert II, 375
Hinson, Aaron H. I, 386
Hinson, Aaron H. I, 397
Hinson, Abigal VI, 825
Hinson, Agness I, 379
Hinson, Agness I, 397
Hinson, Borden I, 289
Hinson, Borden IV, 149
Hinson, Charles VI, 825
Hinson, Charles VI, 855
Hinson, Clarkey I, 308
Hinson, Clarky I, 289
Hinson, Clerky IV, 149
Hinson, Eddie I, 337
Hinson, Effie I, 337
Hinson, Elijah I, 289
Hinson, Elijah I, 308
Hinson, Elijah IV, 149
Hinson, Elizabeth I, 308
Hinson, Elizabeth I, 397
Hinson, Emily V, 911
Hinson, Emily N. V, 911
Hinson, Flora I, 397
Hinson, Isaac I, 289
Hinson, Joseph V, 911
Hinson, Joshua I, 308
Hinson, Louisa I, 308
Hinson, Louise I, 308
Hinson, Lydia I, 397
Hinson, Manoah IV, 149
Hinson, Moses B. I, 329
Hinson, Nancy I, 337
Hinson, Nancy J. I, 337
Hinson, Nancy Jane I, 337
Hinson, Patience I, 308
Hinson, Susan I, 337
Hinson, Susanna I, 289
Hinson, Susanna I, 308
Hinson, Susanna IV, 149
Hinson, Susannah I, 308
Hinton, A. A. I, 634
Hinton, Adelaide I, 620
Hinton, Alonzo I, 618
Hinton, Alonzo A. I, 634
Hinton, Alonzo Alfred I, 618
Hinton, Ann VI, 860
Hinton, Bessie Gutherie I, 634
Hinton, Delilah I, 932
Hinton, F. M. V, 1001
Hinton, Francis V, 1001
Hinton, George I, 31
Hinton, Jane II, 375
Hinton, Jane II, 550
Hinton, Jemima VI, 825
Hinton, Jerusha III, 428
Hinton, John II, 375
Hinton, John II, 550
Hinton, Louvina V, 1001
Hinton, Mary I, 618
Hinton, Mary A. I, 31
Hinton, Mary Isabella I, 5
Hinton, Mary Isabella I, 53
Hinton, Mary Luella V, 1001
Hinton, Millard V, 1001
Hinton, Milliard M. V, 1001
Hinton, Minnie I, 618
Hinton, Mrs. M. D. I, 634
Hinton, Nancy Elisabeth I, 618
Hinton, Phebe V, 232
Hinton, Phebe V, 246
Hinton, Rebecca V, 1001
Hinton, Sarah V, 246
Hinton, Sarah V, 276
Hinton, Sarah V, 310
Hinton, Susanna II, 458
Hinton, Susanna II, 550
Hinton, Susannah II, 457
Hinton, Wiley N. I, 618
Hinton, William I, 634
Hinton, William II, 375
Hinton, William II, 457
Hinton, William VI, 809
Hinton, William VI, 825
Hinton, William VI, 850
Hinton, William VI, 860
Hinton, William Dick I, 618
Hinton, William T. I, 618
Hinton, Wm. I, 5
Hinton, Wm. II, 458
Hinton, Wm. II, 550
Hinton, Wm. II, 575
Hintz, Anne Kathryne III, 420
Hintz, Helen E. III, 410
Hintz, Helen E. III, 420
Hintz, Howard W. III, 410
Hintz, Howard W. III, 420
Hintz, Katharine III, 420
Hintz, Mary Helen III, 420
Hintz, Wm. E. III, 420
Hipinstall, Anny VI, 914
Hippenstall, Elizabeth VI, 878
Hippenstall, Minerva Ann VI, 931
Hippinstall, Sophia VI, 914
Hippley, Ann Eliza IV, 722
Hipsher, Daniel V, 1001
Hipsher, Esther V, 1001
Hipshier, Daniel V, 1001
Hipshire, Esther V, 1001
Hire, Alice V, 1001
Hire, Bertha V, 1001
Hire, Eliza M. V, 1001
Hire, Ernest Wilbur V, 1001
Hire, Fern V, 1001
Hire, Flora A. V, 178
Hire, Flora A. V, 1001
Hire, Hattie E. V, 178
Hire, James V, 1001
Hire, James W. V, 1001
Hire, John V, 1001
Hire, Josephine V, 1001
Hire, Lola V, 1001
Hire, Lola Marjorie V, 1001
Hire, Lucy V, 1001
Hire, Lula V, 1001
Hire, Maggie V, 1001
Hire, Mary V, 1001
Hire, Russell V, 1001
Hire, Sadie V, 1001
Hire, Sarah V, 1001
Hire, Sullivan J. V, 1001
Hire, Thos. V, 1001
Hire, Viola V, 1001
Hire, Wilson F. V, 1001
Hire, Wm. V, 1001
Hire, Wm. G. V, 1001
Hires, Ann II, 134
Hires, Anna II, 133
Hires, Anna F. II, 151
Hires, Anne II, 133
Hires, Charles II, 133
Hires, Charles II, 134
Hires, Charles II, 151
Hires, Charles II, 153
Hires, Charles R. II, 133
Hires, Charles R. II, 134
Hires, Charles R. II, 151
Hires, Charles R., Jr. II, 134
Hires, Elizabeth W. II, 854
Hires, Elizabeth W. II, 876
Hires, Elizabeth W. C. II, 876
Hires, Elizabeth Walton II, 800
Hires, Frank Shepherd II, 800
Hires, Letitia Fogg II, 134
Hires, Letitia Fogg II, 151
Hires, Louis Ayres II, 800
Hires, Mary II, 134
Hires, Mary II, 151
Hires, Mary Hildreth II, 151
Hires, Mary Hildreth II, 153
Hires, Mary Stretch II, 134
Hires, Mary Stretch II, 151
Hires, Nathaniel II, 151
Hires, Nathaniel S. II, 151
Hires, Nathaniel Stretch II, 134
Hires, Nathaniel Stretch II, 151
Hires, Nathaniel Stretch II, 153
Hires, Nathaniel Stretch, Jr. II, 134
Hires, Nathaniel Stretch, Jr. II, 151
Hires, Ruth Natalie II, 134
Hires, Ruth Natalie II, 151
Hires, Sullivan J. V, 1001
Hires, Susanna II, 134
Hires, Susanna II, 153
Hires, Susanna B. II, 133
Hires, Susanna DuBois II, 151
Hires, Wm. Morris II, 133
Hires, Wm. Morris II, 134
Hires, Wm. Morris II, 151
Hirsch, Annie IV, 1321
Hirschman, August IV, 1321
Hirschman, Florence Slade IV, 1321
Hirschman, Milburn IV, 1321
Hirschman, Ruth IV, 1321
Hirshey, Mary D. II, 746
Hirst, ??? IV, 409
Hirst, Abbie VI, 651
Hirst, Alpheus IV, 149
Hirst, Alpheus IV, 525
Hirst, Alpheus IV, 530
Hirst, Amanda IV, 335
Hirst, Amanda IV, 530
Hirst, Amanda IV, 538
Hirst, Amanda IV, 1101
Hirst, Amanda IV, 1104
Hirst, Ann IV, 149
Hirst, Ann IV, 200

Hirst, Ann IV, 221
Hirst, Ann IV, 222
Hirst, Ann IV, 266
Hirst, Ann IV, 335
Hirst, Ann IV, 530
Hirst, Ann IV, 531
Hirst, Ann IV, 539
Hirst, Ann IV, 1101
Hirst, Ann IV, 1130
Hirst, Ann IV, 1133
Hirst, Ann VI, 476
Hirst, Ann VI, 505
Hirst, Ann VI, 556
Hirst, Ann VI, 561
Hirst, Ann VI, 572
Hirst, Ann VI, 623
Hirst, Ann VI, 624
Hirst, Ann VI, 650
Hirst, Ann VI, 697
Hirst, Ann VI, 701
Hirst, Ann Maria IV, 530
Hirst, Ann R. IV, 221
Hirst, Ann Raley IV, 530
Hirst, Ann, Jr. IV, 222
Hirst, Anna IV, 149
Hirst, Anna IV, 298
Hirst, Anna IV, 332
Hirst, Anna IV, 335
Hirst, Anna IV, 530
Hirst, Anna VI, 505
Hirst, Anna VI, 650
Hirst, Anne IV, 538
Hirst, Anne VI, 505
Hirst, Annie A. VI, 631
Hirst, Annie A. VI, 650
Hirst, Annie A. VI, 651
Hirst, Asa Raley IV, 149
Hirst, Asenath IV, 149
Hirst, Asenath IV, 158
Hirst, Asenath IV, 221
Hirst, Asenath IV, 432
Hirst, Asenath IV, 530
Hirst, Asenath IV, 545
Hirst, Asenath IV, 770
Hirst, Calvin C. IV, 1133
Hirst, Caroline IV, 530
Hirst, Caroline VI, 650
Hirst, Caroline VI, 651
Hirst, Caroline B. IV, 529
Hirst, Caroline B. IV, 530
Hirst, Catharine IV, 149
Hirst, Catharine IV, 165
Hirst, Catharine IV, 512
Hirst, Catharine IV, 513
Hirst, Catharine IV, 530
Hirst, Charles Mason VI, 651
Hirst, Charlotte VI, 623
Hirst, Charlotte VI, 650
Hirst, Charlotte VI, 651
Hirst, Charlotte VI, 710
Hirst, Cornelia V, 953
Hirst, Cornelia VI, 650
Hirst, Cornelia VI, 651
Hirst, Cosmelia V, 953
Hirst, Cosmelia VI, 650
Hirst, Cosmelia VI, 651
Hirst, Daisy VI, 621
Hirst, Daisy VI, 650
Hirst, Daisy VI, 651
Hirst, David IV, 149
Hirst, David IV, 221
Hirst, David IV, 335
Hirst, David IV, 530
Hirst, David IV, 531
Hirst, David IV, 539
Hirst, David VI, 505
Hirst, David VI, 561
Hirst, David VI, 650
Hirst, David VI, 701
Hirst, Dillwyn G. IV, 1133
Hirst, Edgar H. VI, 621
Hirst, Edgar H. VI, 631
Hirst, Edgar H. VI, 650
Hirst, Edgar H. VI, 651
Hirst, Eli VI, 651
Hirst, Eli P. V, 953
Hirst, Eli P. VI, 650
Hirst, Eli P. VI, 651
Hirst, Eli P. VI, 665
Hirst, Elisha F. VI, 651
Hirst, Eliza Jane IV, 149
Hirst, Eliza Jane IV, 527
Hirst, Eliza Jane IV, 530
Hirst, Elizabeth IV, 149
Hirst, Elizabeth IV, 513
Hirst, Elizabeth IV, 519
Hirst, Elizabeth IV, 530
Hirst, Elizabeth IV, 1101
Hirst, Elizabeth VI, 475
Hirst, Elizabeth VI, 505
Hirst, Elizajane IV, 530
Hirst, Emma VI, 628
Hirst, Emma VI, 651
Hirst, Emma Virginia VI, 628
Hirst, Emma Virginia VI, 651
Hirst, Esther IV, 530
Hirst, Esther VI, 548
Hirst, Esther H. IV, 530
Hirst, Folio VI, 651
Hirst, Francinia VI, 621
Hirst, Francinia VI, 623
Hirst, Francinia VI, 650
Hirst, Francinia VI, 651
Hirst, Hannah IV, 149
Hirst, Hannah IV, 335
Hirst, Hannah IV, 530
Hirst, Hannah IV, 539
Hirst, Hannah V, 953
Hirst, Hannah VI, 650
Hirst, Hannah VI, 651
Hirst, Hannah VI, 665
Hirst, Hannah VI, 754
Hirst, Heston VI, 400
Hirst, Heston VI, 619
Hirst, Heston VI, 621
Hirst, Heston VI, 628
Hirst, Heston VI, 631
Hirst, Heston VI, 650
Hirst, Heston VI, 651
Hirst, Heston VI, 704
Hirst, Israel IV, 149
Hirst, Israel IV, 165
Hirst, Israel IV, 221
Hirst, Israel IV, 512
Hirst, Israel IV, 513
Hirst, Israel IV, 530
Hirst, Israel T. IV, 530
Hirst, Israel Wilson IV, 530
Hirst, James IV, 221
Hirst, James IV, 222
Hirst, James IV, 530
Hirst, James IV, 1101
Hirst, James IV, 1112
Hirst, James IV, 1133
Hirst, James P. IV, 1101
Hirst, James R. IV, 1133
Hirst, Jesse VI, 505
Hirst, Jesse VI, 548
Hirst, Jesse VI, 650
Hirst, Jesse VI, 651
Hirst, Jesse VI, 665
Hirst, Jesse VI, 688
Hirst, Jesse VI, 704
Hirst, Jesse VI, 710
Hirst, John IV, 149
Hirst, John IV, 221
Hirst, John IV, 305
Hirst, John IV, 409
Hirst, John IV, 513
Hirst, John IV, 530
Hirst, John VI, 464
Hirst, John VI, 476
Hirst, John VI, 505
Hirst, John VI, 536
Hirst, John VI, 548
Hirst, John VI, 561
Hirst, John VI, 569
Hirst, John VI, 570
Hirst, John VI, 597
Hirst, John VI, 623
Hirst, John VI, 650
Hirst, John VI, 651
Hirst, John VI, 688
Hirst, John VI, 701
Hirst, John VI, 709
Hirst, John VI, 725
Hirst, John J. VI, 651
Hirst, John Janney VI, 651
Hirst, John P. VI, 651
Hirst, John S. IV, 221
Hirst, John Townsend VI, 651
Hirst, John Townshend VI, 619
Hirst, John, Jr. VI, 505
Hirst, Jonathan VI, 623
Hirst, Jonathan VI, 650
Hirst, Jonathan VI, 651
Hirst, Jonathan VI, 710
Hirst, Joseph Addison IV, 530
Hirst, Leah VI, 400
Hirst, Leah VI, 619
Hirst, Leah VI, 621
Hirst, Leah VI, 628
Hirst, Leah VI, 631
Hirst, Leah VI, 650
Hirst, Leah VI, 651
Hirst, Leah VI, 704
Hirst, Lindley Murray IV, 530
Hirst, Lydia IV, 530
Hirst, Lydia IV, 532
Hirst, Lydia VI, 651
Hirst, Maria IV, 221
Hirst, Maria IV, 222
Hirst, Maria IV, 305
Hirst, Maria IV, 409
Hirst, Maria IV, 530
Hirst, Mary II, 699
Hirst, Mary IV, 149
Hirst, Mary IV, 221
Hirst, Mary IV, 285
Hirst, Mary IV, 410
Hirst, Mary IV, 512
Hirst, Mary IV, 530
Hirst, Mary IV, 531
Hirst, Mary IV, 553
Hirst, Mary IV, 634
Hirst, Mary VI, 400
Hirst, Mary VI, 476
Hirst, Mary VI, 505
Hirst, Mary VI, 536
Hirst, Mary VI, 548
Hirst, Mary VI, 561
Hirst, Mary VI, 569
Hirst, Mary VI, 570
Hirst, Mary VI, 623
Hirst, Mary VI, 650
Hirst, Mary VI, 651
Hirst, Mary VI, 665
Hirst, Mary VI, 688
Hirst, Mary VI, 701
Hirst, Mary VI, 704
Hirst, Mary VI, 709
Hirst, Mary VI, 710
Hirst, Mary Ann IV, 221
Hirst, Mary Ann IV, 519
Hirst, Mary Ann IV, 530
Hirst, Mary Ann IV, 634
Hirst, Mary Ann IV, 1129
Hirst, Mary Ann IV, 1133
Hirst, Mary Ellen VI, 651
Hirst, Mary Louisa VI, 651
Hirst, Minda V, 1001
Hirst, Miriah IV, 530
Hirst, Oliver VI, 651
Hirst, Oliver W. IV, 530
Hirst, Phebe IV, 335
Hirst, Rachel IV, 149
Hirst, Rachel IV, 221
Hirst, Rachel IV, 244
Hirst, Rachel IV, 409
Hirst, Rachel IV, 530
Hirst, Rachel IV, 1101
Hirst, Rachel IV, 1112
Hirst, Rachel VI, 650
Hirst, Rachel H. IV, 221
Hirst, Rachel H. IV, 286
Hirst, Rachel M. IV, 170
Hirst, Rachel M. IV, 221
Hirst, Rachel M. IV, 222
Hirst, Rachel Taber IV, 222
Hirst, Rebecca IV, 149
Hirst, Rebecca IV, 200
Hirst, Rebecca IV, 221
Hirst, Rebecca IV, 335
Hirst, Rebecca IV, 524
Hirst, Rebecca IV, 530
Hirst, Rebecca IV, 546
Hirst, Rebecca VI, 400
Hirst, Rebecca VI, 576
Hirst, Rebecca VI, 651
Hirst, Rebeckah VI, 505
Hirst, Rebekah VI, 505
Hirst, Rebekah VI, 569
Hirst, Rebekah VI, 570
Hirst, Rebekah VI, 651
Hirst, Rebekah VI, 709
Hirst, Ruthanna IV, 149
Hirst, Ruthanna IV, 221
Hirst, Ruthanna IV, 222
Hirst, Ruthanna IV, 298
Hirst, Ruthanna IV, 530
Hirst, Samuel Smith VI, 651
Hirst, Sarah VI, 505
Hirst, Sarah VI, 562
Hirst, Sarah Ellen VI, 651
Hirst, Smith IV, 149
Hirst, Smith IV, 221
Hirst, Smith IV, 530
Hirst, Smith V, 1001
Hirst, Theodore VI, 651
Hirst, Thomas IV, 149
Hirst, Thomas IV, 200
Hirst, Thomas IV, 221
Hirst, Thomas IV, 222
Hirst, Thomas IV, 332
Hirst, Thomas IV, 335
Hirst, Thomas IV, 530
Hirst, Thomas IV, 538
Hirst, Thomas IV, 553
Hirst, Thomas IV, 1101
Hirst, Thomas IV, 1129
Hirst, Thomas IV, 1133
Hirst, Thomas VI, 400
Hirst, Thomas VI, 505
Hirst, Thomas VI, 650
Hirst, Thomas VI, 651
Hirst, Thomas C. VI, 650
Hirst, Thomas C. VI, 651
Hirst, Thos. IV, 266
Hirst, Thos. IV, 285
Hirst, Thos. IV, 298
Hirst, Thos. IV, 530
Hirst, Virginia VI, 619
Hirst, Virginia VI, 651
Hirst, Wd. Rebeckah Talbott VI, 505
Hirst, Widow Rebecca VI, 536
Hirst, Wilson C. IV, 170
Hirst, Wilson C. IV, 221
Hirst, Wilson C. IV, 286
Hirst, Wilson C. IV, 409
Hirt, Alida V, 682
Hirt, Ernest V, 679
Hirt, Ernest V, 682
Hirt, Florence V, 679
Hirt, Florence V, 682
Hirt, Grace V, 682
Hirt, Grace V, 683
Hirt, James Edwin V, 682
Hirt, Lida V, 625
Hirt, Valentine V, 625
Hirt, Valentine V, 682
Hiselwood, Amy II, 375
Hiselwood, Anne II, 375
Hisler, Lydia Maria IV, 844
Hisler, Martha S. IV, 844
Hisler, Martha W. IV, 844
Hisler, Rhoda IV, 823
Hisler, Rhoda IV, 844
Hisler, Robert C. IV, 844
Hisler, Rosco R. IV, 844
Hisler, Sina E. IV, 844
Hisler, Wilmer W. IV, 844
Hissmeyer, Minnie IV, 1254
Hissong, ??? V, 743
Hissong, Clyde V, 743
Hissong, Delbert V, 743
Hissong, Elbert V, 743
Hissong, Frank V, 743
Hissong, Glenna V, 743
Hissong, La Von Arlene V, 743
Hissong, Merle V, 743
Hissong, Merlie V, 743
Hissong, Patricia Marie V, 743
Hissong, Raymond Lee V, 743
Histe, Maria V, 1001
Histon, Robert II, 444
Hitch, Australia J. V, 419
Hitch, John V, 682
Hitch, John C. V, 682
Hitch, Laura V, 682
Hitch, Nancy V, 419
Hitch, Thomas B. V, 682
Hitch, Vernon V, 682
Hitch, W. Vernon V, 682
Hitch, Wm. V, 419
Hitchcock, Anna II, 375
Hitchcock, Elietas V, 178
Hitchcock, Elistus V, 178
Hitchcock, Elizabeth I, 855
Hitchcock, Elizabeth II, 375
Hitchcock, Elizabeth II, 550
Hitchcock, Elizabeth II, 592
Hitchcock, Emma IV, 1321
Hitchcock, Eunice IV, 1321
Hitchcock, Grace I, 855
Hitchcock, Grace I, 875
Hitchcock, Grace I, 882
Hitchcock, Hannah I, 855
Hitchcock, Hannah I, 882
Hitchcock, Hannah I, 898
Hitchcock, Huldah I, 855
Hitchcock, Jacob I, 855
Hitchcock, James I, 855
Hitchcock, Jane IV, 1367
Hitchcock, Jane IV, 1385
Hitchcock, John II, 550
Hitchcock, Joseph I, 855
Hitchcock, Joseph I, 875
Hitchcock, Joseph I, 882
Hitchcock, Joseph II, 375
Hitchcock, Joseph II, 550
Hitchcock, Mariam I, 855
Hitchcock, Mary II, 375
Hitchcock, Matthew I, 855
Hitchcock, Naoma I, 855
Hitchcock, Nicholas II, 375
Hitchcock, Nicholas II, 550
Hitchcock, Nicholas II, 592
Hitchcock, Ruth I, 855
Hitchcock, Sarah I, 881
Hitchcock, Sarah I, 882
Hitchcock, William I, 882
Hitchcocks, Jacob I, 855
Hitchcocks, Jacob S. I, 855
Hitchcocks, Jane E. I, 855
Hitchcocks, John T. I, 855
Hitchcocks, Joseph A. I, 855
Hitchcocks, Julius M. I, 855
Hitchcocks, Marmaduke I, 855
Hitchcocks, Naomi I, 855
Hitchcocks, Ruth I, 855
Hitchcocks, Ruth D. I, 855
Hitchcocks, Sally L. I, 855
Hitchcocks, Saphronia A. I, 855
Hitchcocks, Shuble C. I, 855
Hitchcocks, William I, 855
Hitchcoke, Lydia I, 882
Hitchcoke, Priscilla I, 882
Hitchins, Elizabeth VI, 33
Hitchinson, Becca IV, 456
Hitchinson, John F. II, 876
Hitchner, Hannah R. II, 151
Hitchner, Hannah R. II, 156
Hitchner, Howard C. II, 134
Hitchner, Howard Cleveland II, 151
Hitchner, Howard Cleveland II, 156
Hitchner, Martha Grier II, 134
Hitchner, Martha Grier II, 151
Hitchner, Martha Grier II, 156
Hitchner, Wilbert B. II, 151
Hitchner, Wilbert B. II, 156
Hitchpeth, Agathy I, 817
Hitchpeth, Agathy I, 820
Hitchwater, Mary II, 1002
Hitchwater, Thomas II, 1002
Hite, Eleanor VI, 472
Hite, Eleanor VI, 475
Hite, Eleanor VI, 481
Hite, Eleanor VI, 505
Hite, Eleanor VI, 509
Hite, Eleanor VI, 510
Hite, Eleanor VI, 512
Hite, Eleanor VI, 543
Hite, Eleanor VI, 556
Hite, Eleanor VI, 565
Hite, Eleanor VI, 568
Hite, Eleanor VI, 573
Hite, Martha VI, 825
Hite, Sarah IV, 1152
Hite, Sarah IV, 1167
Hite, Thomas VI, 825
Hitson, Albert IV, 1321
Hitt, Clar III, 19
Hitt, Clara III, 29
Hitt, Clara III, 334
Hitt, Clara III, 353
Hitt, Clara III, 354
Hitt, Clara III, 356
Hitt, Clarissa III, 356
Hitt, Hiram III, 356
Hiveley, Martin V, 1001
Hiveley, Sarah C. V, 1001
Hively, Ann Eliza IV, 722
Hively, Elmer IV, 964
Hively, Elmor IV, 964
Hively, Emor IV, 964
Hively, George IV, 964
Hively, Louisa IV, 964
Hiverly, Katie IV, 1040
Hiverly, Katie Miles IV, 1038
Hix, Adeline R. VI, 932
Hix, Ann H. VI, 932
Hix, Avey VI, 932
Hix, Betsey VI, 957
Hix, Betsey VI, 1007
Hix, Betsy VI, 932
Hix, Caleb VI, 1019
Hix, Caroline VI, 932
Hix, Celia VI, 932
Hix, Christopher VI, 932
Hix, Dosha VI, 932
Hix, Drury VI, 911
Hix, Drury VI, 932
Hix, Edney VI, 807
Hix, Eliza I, 1154
Hix, Eliza Jane I, 884
Hix, Eliza Jane I, 893
Hix, Elizabeth VI, 909
Hix, Fanny I, 893
Hix, Fanny VI, 914
Hix, Farthing VI, 914
Hix, Farthing VI, 932
Hix, Florentine VI, 932
Hix, Hannah S. VI, 957
Hix, James VI, 932
Hix, James VI, 957
Hix, James H. VI, 932
Hix, James W. VI, 953
Hix, Jane VI, 310
Hix, Jane VI, 912
Hix, Jane VI, 932
Hix, Jemimah VI, 909
Hix, Jeremiah VI, 932

, Jesse VI, 310
, Jesse VI, 900
, Jesse VI, 925
, Jesse VI, 932
, Jesse VI, 957
, Jesse VI, 959
, Jesse VI, 974
, Jesse VI, 999
, John VI, 808
, John VI, 815
, John VI, 825
, John VI, 850
, John VI, 855
, John VI, 932
, John VI, 937
, John VI, 979
, John VI, 1006
, John VI, 1007
, Laban IV, 408
, Laban IV, 584
, Libby VI, 855
, Louisa IV, 584
, Louisa IV, 600
, Lucinda VI, 932
, Lucy VI, 109
, Marshall I, 1154
, Martha VI, 824
, Mary I, 241
, Mary VI, 104
, Mary VI, 109
, Mary VI, 851
, Mary VI, 932
, Mildred VI, 825
, Nancy VI, 932
, Nancy VI, 1003
, Patrick VI, 884
, Peggy I, 241
, Peggy VI, 932
, Philip VI, 910
, Philip VI, 932
, Philips VI, 1003
, Phillip VI, 909
, Polly VI, 910
, Polly Ann VI, 932
, Rebecca VI, 850
, Rebecca VI, 914
, Rebecker VI, 909
, Rhoda VI, 932
, Sabra VI, 815
, Sally VI, 881
, Sarah VI, 937
, Seany VI, 851
, Susanna VI, 884
, Tabitha I, 241
, William VI, 808
, William VI, 824
, William VI, 850
, William VI, 912
, William VI, 932
, William VI, 934
, William VI, 1007
, William H. VI, 932
, Wm. VI, 956
on, Anna V, 337
on, Annie V, 337
on, Arthur V, 337
on, C. L. V, 395
on, Carl V, 395
on, Christian V, 395
on, Christian E. V, 395
on, Elizabeth V, 843
on, Emily V, 395
on, Esther V, 843
on, Isaac V, 843
on, John V, 843
on, John V, 857
on, Joseph V, 395
on, Lelia V, 395
on, Marianna V, 395
on, Martha B. IV, 222
on, Mary V, 843
on, Mary E. V, 395
on, May V, 337
on, Melcena V, 395
on, Minnie M. V, 337
on, Mirtie M. V, 337
on, Nancy V, 843
on, Orlie C. V, 337
on, Phebe V, 843
on, Phebe V, 857
on, Rachel V, 843
on, Rachel, Jr. V, 843
on, Rebecca V, 843
on, Samuel V, 843
on, Sarah IV, 1165
on, Sarah V, 843
on, Sarah E. V, 337
on, Thomas V, 395
on, William V, 843
on, William V, 883
on, William, Jr. V, 843
Hixon, Wm. V, 843
Hixson, Addie V, 246
Hixson, Ann V, 246
Hixson, Annie Rose V, 246
Hixson, C. L. V, 395
Hixson, Emily V, 395
Hixson, Joseph V, 395
Hixson, Lelia V, 395
Hixson, Marianna V, 395
Hixson, Martha Ann VI, 684
Hixson, Mary V, 840
Hixson, Mary V, 843
Hixson, Maud V, 246
Hixson, Melcena V, 395
Hixson, Newton L. VI, 684
Hixson, Rachel V, 840
Hixson, Rebecca V, 843
Hixson, Rebecca VI, 505
Hixson, Rebecca VI, 580
Hixson, Ruth VI, 497
Hixson, Ruth VI, 505
Hixson, Sarah E. V, 246
Hixson, Walter V, 246
Hixson, William V, 843
Hixson, Wm. V, 840
Hixzon, Mirtie M. V, 337
Hoadley, Clarence II, 876
Hoadley, Clarence II, 923
Hoadley, Elizabeth II, 876
Hoadley, Elizabeth II, 923
Hoag, Abbie A. III, 167
Hoag, Abel T. IV, 1367
Hoag, Ada Hepzibah III, 167
Hoag, Ada Hepzibah III, 311
Hoag, Addison IV, 1369
Hoag, Addison C. IV, 1368
Hoag, Alice A. III, 167
Hoag, Alice Ada III, 311
Hoag, Amos IV, 1367
Hoag, Amos IV, 1368
Hoag, Amos IV, 1376
Hoag, Amos Edgar IV, 1368
Hoag, Amy III, 167
Hoag, Amy Ann IV, 1368
Hoag, Amy H. III, 65
Hoag, Amy H. III, 167
Hoag, Amy H. III, 256
Hoag, Ann IV, 1368
Hoag, Ann Eliza III, 167
Hoag, Ann Eliza IV, 1359
Hoag, Ann Eliza IV, 1367
Hoag, Ann Eliza IV, 1368
Hoag, Ann Maria III, 167
Hoag, Anna IV, 1367
Hoag, Anna V, 683
Hoag, Anna Eliza III, 167
Hoag, Anna J. V, 683
Hoag, Anna Maria III, 44
Hoag, Anna Maria III, 167
Hoag, Betsey IV, 1368
Hoag, Caleb L. I, 1121
Hoag, Caroline IV, 1368
Hoag, Caroline IV, 1369
Hoag, Caroline A. IV, 1356
Hoag, Caroline A. IV, 1368
Hoag, Catharine IV, 1368
Hoag, Chalkley IV, 1367
Hoag, Chalkley IV, 1368
Hoag, Charles II, 1052
Hoag, Charles III, 167
Hoag, Charles B. III, 167
Hoag, Charles B. III, 352
Hoag, Charlotte V. IV, 1368
Hoag, Chester IV, 1369
Hoag, Chester J. IV, 1369
Hoag, Chilian W. IV, 1368
Hoag, Cornelia Jane IV, 1368
Hoag, Cornelis IV, 1369
Hoag, Darius IV, 1368
Hoag, David III, 167
Hoag, David III, 356
Hoag, Dorcas IV, 634
Hoag, Dorcas IV, 1368
Hoag, Dorcas T. IV, 634
Hoag, Edward IV, 1368
Hoag, Edward IV, 1369
Hoag, Edward H. IV, 1369
Hoag, Edwin A. IV, 1369
Hoag, Edwin Amos IV, 1368
Hoag, Edwin W. III, 167
Hoag, Edwin W. III, 311
Hoag, Elihu IV, 1368
Hoag, Elihu IV, 1369
Hoag, Elihu V, 73
Hoag, Elisabeth IV, 1367
Hoag, Elisabeth IV, 1368
Hoag, Elisha IV, 823
Hoag, Elisha IV, 895
Hoag, Elisha IV, 1368
Hoag, Elisha W. IV, 891
Hoag, Elisha Wm. IV, 823
Hoag, Elisha Wm. IV, 858
Hoag, Elizabeth III, 167
Hoag, Elizabeth III, 352
Hoag, Elizabeth IV, 1368
Hoag, Elizabeth IV, 1374
Hoag, Elizabeth A. III, 167
Hoag, Elizabeth P. IV, 1362
Hoag, Elizabeth P. IV, 1368
Hoag, Ellen Maria IV, 1368
Hoag, Elma III, 167
Hoag, Elma A. III, 356
Hoag, Elma H. III, 167
Hoag, Emaline Amelia IV, 1368
Hoag, Emeline IV, 1368
Hoag, Emeline IV, 1376
Hoag, Emeline IV, 1384
Hoag, Emeline A. IV, 1368
Hoag, Emily III, 167
Hoag, Emily III, 256
Hoag, Emily IV, 1368
Hoag, Emily IV, 1380
Hoag, Esther III, 49
Hoag, Esther III, 167
Hoag, Fannie III, 65
Hoag, Fannie III, 167
Hoag, George IV, 1367
Hoag, Hannah IV, 893
Hoag, Hannah IV, 1367
Hoag, Hannah IV, 1368
Hoag, Hannah IV, 1369
Hoag, Hannah IV, 1371
Hoag, Hannah IV, 1374
Hoag, Hannah G. IV, 677
Hoag, Hannah G. IV, 722
Hoag, Hannah G. IV, 891
Hoag, Hannah G. IV, 893
Hoag, Hannah H. III, 167
Hoag, Hannah H. III, 205
Hoag, Hannah Mosher IV, 1368
Hoag, Harriet Temple IV, 1165
Hoag, Harriett IV, 1237
Hoag, Harriett IV, 1241
Hoag, Harriett Temple IV, 1237
Hoag, Hazael IV, 1367
Hoag, Hazael IV, 1368
Hoag, Hazael IV, 1374
Hoag, Hazael IV, 1380
Hoag, Hervey IV, 823
Hoag, Huldah III, 205
Hoag, Huldah C. V, 683
Hoag, Huldah S. II, 1052
Hoag, Huldale III, 167
Hoag, Ira W. III, 167
Hoag, Isabel IV, 1359
Hoag, Isabel IV, 1368
Hoag, Isabella IV, 1367
Hoag, Isabella IV, 1368
Hoag, Israel IV, 1357
Hoag, Israel IV, 1367
Hoag, Israel IV, 1368
Hoag, Israel G. III, 167
Hoag, Issabella IV, 1380
Hoag, Jackson IV, 1367
Hoag, Jacob IV, 1362
Hoag, Jacob IV, 1366
Hoag, Jacob IV, 1367
Hoag, Jacob IV, 1368
Hoag, Jacob IV, 1380
Hoag, Jacob S. IV, 1368
Hoag, Jacob Smith IV, 1368
Hoag, Jane III, 167
Hoag, Jay IV, 1369
Hoag, Jesse IV, 1165
Hoag, Jesse IV, 1192
Hoag, Jesse IV, 1237
Hoag, Jesse IV, 1367
Hoag, Jesse IV, 1369
Hoag, Jesse IV, 1386
Hoag, Joanna IV, 823
Hoag, Joanna IV, 893
Hoag, Joanna B. IV, 893
Hoag, Joel IV, 823
Hoag, Joel IV, 1028
Hoag, John III, 44
Hoag, John III, 167
Hoag, John IV, 1356
Hoag, John IV, 1367
Hoag, John Gurney IV, 1368
Hoag, John M., Jr. III, 65
Hoag, John Milton IV, 1368
Hoag, John S. III, 167
Hoag, Jonathan IV, 1165
Hoag, Jonathan IV, 1367
Hoag, Jonathan IV, 1369
Hoag, Joseph D. IV, 634
Hoag, Joseph Jonathan IV, 634
Hoag, Kempton III, 167
Hoag, Lewis A. V, 683
Hoag, Lindley I, 856
Hoag, Lindley M. I, 771
Hoag, Lindley M. III, 167
Hoag, Lindley M. III, 205
Hoag, Lodema IV, 1354
Hoag, Lodema IV, 1367
Hoag, Lodema IV, 1368
Hoag, Lodema IV, 1386
Hoag, Lorenzo IV, 1367
Hoag, Louisa L. III, 167
Hoag, Lydia III, 134
Hoag, Lydia III, 167
Hoag, Lydia III, 345
Hoag, Lydia IV, 823
Hoag, Lydia IV, 891
Hoag, Lydia IV, 893
Hoag, Lydia IV, 895
Hoag, Lydia IV, 896
Hoag, Lydia IV, 1351
Hoag, Lydia IV, 1369
Hoag, Mahlon IV, 1368
Hoag, Martha IV, 1386
Hoag, Martha Ann IV, 1367
Hoag, Martin W. IV, 1368
Hoag, Mary III, 167
Hoag, Mary III, 345
Hoag, Mary III, 369
Hoag, Mary IV, 893
Hoag, Mary IV, 1165
Hoag, Mary IV, 1192
Hoag, Mary IV, 1237
Hoag, Mary IV, 1367
Hoag, Mary IV, 1378
Hoag, Mary B. IV, 1369
Hoag, Mary C. IV, 1282
Hoag, Mary E. III, 167
Hoag, Mary Ellen II, 1074
Hoag, Mary Ellen II, 1084
Hoag, Mary K. III, 167
Hoag, Mary M. IV, 1368
Hoag, Mary P. IV, 1368
Hoag, Mary S. IV, 722
Hoag, Mary S. IV, 892
Hoag, Mary S. IV, 895
Hoag, Mary S. IV, 1366
Hoag, Mary S. IV, 1367
Hoag, Mary S. IV, 1368
Hoag, Mary W. IV, 1369
Hoag, Merritt III, 167
Hoag, Millard IV, 1369
Hoag, Nathan Chase IV, 1378
Hoag, Nathan Lindley IV, 634
Hoag, Nathaniel P. IV, 1359
Hoag, Nathaniel P. IV, 1367
Hoag, Nathaniel P. IV, 1368
Hoag, Nathaniel P. IV, 1380
Hoag, Olive I. III, 167
Hoag, Parley IV, 1368
Hoag, Parley Ann IV, 1368
Hoag, Paulina IV, 1368
Hoag, Percilla IV, 1368
Hoag, Persis IV, 1367
Hoag, Persis IV, 1368
Hoag, Persis IV, 1369
Hoag, Phebe III, 49
Hoag, Phebe III, 167
Hoag, Phebe IV, 1165
Hoag, Phebe IV, 1361
Hoag, Phebe IV, 1367
Hoag, Phebe IV, 1368
Hoag, Phebe E. III, 167
Hoag, Phebe F. III, 167
Hoag, Phebe T. III, 167
Hoag, Rachel IV, 1357
Hoag, Rachel IV, 1368
Hoag, Rachel IV, 1369
Hoag, Rachel, Jr. III, 65
Hoag, Richard Shotwell IV, 1378
Hoag, Ruth IV, 1165
Hoag, Ruth Temple IV, 1165
Hoag, Ruth Temple IV, 1237
Hoag, Sanford III, 49
Hoag, Sanford III, 167
Hoag, Sarah IV, 1356
Hoag, Sarah IV, 1362
Hoag, Sarah IV, 1366
Hoag, Sarah IV, 1367
Hoag, Sarah IV, 1368
Hoag, Sarah IV, 1374
Hoag, Sarah IV, 1380
Hoag, Sarah Ann III, 229
Hoag, Sarah B. IV, 1380
Hoag, Sarah H. III, 167
Hoag, Sarah H. III, 356
Hoag, Sarah I. III, 167
Hoag, Sarah I. III, 321
Hoag, Sarah Jane IV, 1368
Hoag, Sarah Jane IV, 1380
Hoag, Sarah Sanford III, 167
Hoag, Stephen IV, 1368
Hoag, Stephen Z. IV, 1368
Hoag, Stephen Z. IV, 1371
Hoag, Susan IV, 1356
Hoag, Susan IV, 1367
Hoag, Susan IV, 1368
Hoag, Susan IV, 1369
Hoag, Susan C. IV, 1369
Hoag, Susan E. IV, 1369
Hoag, Susanna IV, 1367
Hoag, Susanna IV, 1368
Hoag, Thomas IV, 1368
Hoag, Thos. Rowland V, 683
Hoag, William III, 65
Hoag, William III, 167
Hoag, William III, 256
Hoag, William IV, 1367
Hoag, William IV, 1368
Hoag, William E. III, 167
Hoage, Isaac IV, 223
Hoage, Rebecca II, 122
Hoage, Rebecca V, 499
Hoage, Rebecca V, 502
Hoagland, Caroline III, 167
Hoagland, Caroline IV, 21
Hoagland, Caroline IV, 39
Hoagland, Caroline IV, 611
Hoagland, Caroline IV, 679
Hoagland, Elbert III, 420
Hoagland, Isaac III, 167
Hoagland, James IV, 611
Hoagland, Margaret III, 167
Hoagland, Maria III, 315
Hoagland, Maria III, 420
Hoagland, Mary E. II, 707
Hoagland, Mary E. II, 722
Hoagland, Sarah IV, 611
Hoagland, Susan III, 167
Hoagland, Willemptje III, 420
Hoaglon, Mac V, 1001
Hoague, John C. IV, 178
Hoague, Rebecca IV, 178
Hoak, Anna Louise V, 73
Hoak, Benton Kellar V, 73
Hoak, Ena IV, 1254
Hoak, Monimia V, 73
Hoak, Seth V, 73
Hoal, Ann II, 444
Hoal, Elick II, 444
Hoan, Joseph II, 79
Hoar, Alfred IV, 1321
Hoar, George IV, 222
Hoar, George B. IV, 222
Hoar, Harry IV, 222
Hoar, Mabel IV, 222
Hoar, Mamie IV, 1321
Hoar, Margaret IV, 222
Hoar, Mary IV, 222
Hoar, Mr. ??? IV, 1321
Hoar, Mrs. A. K. IV, 1321
Hoar, Mrs. James IV, 1321
Hoar, Ruth IV, 1321
Hoar, Virginia Ruth IV, 1321
Hoarn, Jacob, Jr. II, 554
Hoarn, Phebe II, 554
Hoath, Lydia May IV, 1321
Hobaby, Johanna III, 168
Hobbs, Abigail I, 712
Hobbs, Abigail I, 721
Hobbs, Ann I, 77
Hobbs, Ann II, 444
Hobbs, Ann Louisa V, 911
Hobbs, Anna Louisa V, 902
Hobbs, Anna Louisa V, 911
Hobbs, Anslem V, 73
Hobbs, Barnabas IV, 222
Hobbs, Barnabas C. IV, 222
Hobbs, Barnabas C. IV, 287
Hobbs, Barnabas C. IV, 964
Hobbs, Barnabas C. IV, 1006
Hobbs, Barnaby I, 721
Hobbs, Deborah I, 702
Hobbs, Deborah V, 67
Hobbs, Deborah V, 73
Hobbs, Delilah I, 702
Hobbs, Elisha I, 695
Hobbs, Elisha I, 702
Hobbs, Elisha I, 721
Hobbs, Elisha I, 875
Hobbs, Elisha I, 884
Hobbs, Elisha V, 67
Hobbs, Elisha V, 73
Hobbs, Elisha, Jr. I, 721
Hobbs, Elisha, Jr. I, 884
Hobbs, Ester II, 375
Hobbs, Fanny I, 695
Hobbs, Fanny I, 721
Hobbs, Fanny I, 884
Hobbs, Frances I, 721
Hobbs, Gretchen A. I, 634
Hobbs, Gretchen Arnold I, 618
Hobbs, Grimsley Taylor I, 618
Hobbs, Hannah I, 702
Hobbs, Hannah V, 788
Hobbs, Hannah V, 911
Hobbs, Harvey V, 73

Hobbs, Henry V, 73
Hobbs, Henry V, 911
Hobbs, James VI, 932
Hobbs, Jason V, 73
Hobbs, John I, 308
Hobbs, Joseph John V, 911
Hobbs, Juliann IV, 530
Hobbs, L. Lyndeon I, 618
Hobbs, Lewis I, 817
Hobbs, Lewis Lindon I, 546
Hobbs, Lewis Lyndon I, 817
Hobbs, Lidda I, 721
Hobbs, Louisa V, 73
Hobbs, Lydia I, 39
Hobbs, Lydia I, 53
Hobbs, Lydia I, 702
Hobbs, Lydia I, 875
Hobbs, Lydia I, 884
Hobbs, Lyndon I, 817
Hobbs, Lyndon I, 829
Hobbs, Martha V, 73
Hobbs, Mary I, 546
Hobbs, Mary I, 618
Hobbs, Mary I, 702
Hobbs, Mary I, 721
Hobbs, Mary I, 724
Hobbs, Mary I, 817
Hobbs, Mary I, 829
Hobbs, Mary VI, 932
Hobbs, Mary M. I, 546
Hobbs, Mary M. I, 817
Hobbs, Mary Zelinda V, 575
Hobbs, Nancy I, 53
Hobbs, Orville A. W. V, 575
Hobbs, Penina I, 721
Hobbs, Penina I, 727
Hobbs, Penina V, 73
Hobbs, Peninah I, 702
Hobbs, Phebe I, 546
Hobbs, Phebe I, 817
Hobbs, Prisalah I, 721
Hobbs, Priscilla I, 702
Hobbs, Priscilla IV, 964
Hobbs, Priscilla V, 73
Hobbs, R. J. M. I, 634
Hobbs, Rachel Ann IV, 584
Hobbs, Rachel Ann IV, 594
Hobbs, Rebecca IV, 222
Hobbs, Rebecca IV, 287
Hobbs, Rebecca IV, 964
Hobbs, Rebecca IV, 1006
Hobbs, Rebecca T. IV, 964
Hobbs, Reuben I, 53
Hobbs, Richard J. M. I, 618
Hobbs, Richard M. I, 634
Hobbs, Richard Mendenhall I, 618
Hobbs, Richard Mendenhall I, 634
Hobbs, Samuel I, 702
Hobbs, Sarah I, 721
Hobbs, Sarah I, 724
Hobbs, Susan IV, 1177
Hobbs, Susannah I, 308
Hobbs, Thomas II, 375
Hobbs, Thomas II, 444
Hobbs, Walter I, 546
Hobbs, Walter M. I, 817
Hobbs, Walter Mendenhall I, 546
Hobbs, Walton V, 575
Hobbs, William I, 702
Hobbs, William I, 721
Hobbs, William IV, 964
Hobbs, William V, 73
Hobbs, Wilson IV, 530
Hobbs, Wilson V, 575
Hobbs, Wilson V, 605
Hobbs, Zalinda V, 575
Hobbs, Zalinda V, 605
Hobbs, Zelinda V, 575
Hobday, Jerusha IV, 947
Hobert, Nancy IV, 92
Hobert, Nancy IV, 93
Hobert, Nancy IV, 112
Hoblet, Lydia V, 971
Hoblet, Lydia V, 976
Hoblet, Lydia V, 979
Hobs, Abigail I, 680
Hobs, Abigail I, 686
Hobs, Abigil I, 702
Hobs, Barnabas I, 702
Hobs, Delila I, 702
Hobs, Delilah I, 677
Hobs, Delilah I, 680
Hobs, Elisha I, 680
Hobs, Elisha I, 702
Hobs, Fanna I, 702
Hobs, Fanney I, 680
Hobs, George V, 501
Hobs, Lydia I, 884
Hobs, Mary I, 702
Hobs, Penina I, 721
Hobs, Peninah I, 702
Hobs, Prisalah I, 712
Hobs, Prisalah I, 721
Hobs, Sarah I, 702
Hobs, Susannah I, 318
Hobs, Thomas I, 680
Hobs, William I, 702
Hobs, William I, 712
Hobs, William I, 721
Hobson, ??? IV, 222
Hobson, ??? IV, 964
Hobson, ??? IV, 1125
Hobson, Aaron I, 355
Hobson, Aaron V, 575
Hobson, Abigail R. I, 398
Hobson, Abigail Ruth I, 355
Hobson, Abraham I, 987
Hobson, Abraham IV, 222
Hobson, Abraham IV, 476
Hobson, Abraham J. IV, 473
Hobson, Abraham J. IV, 477
Hobson, Abraham Johns IV, 477
Hobson, Abram IV, 476
Hobson, Abram IV, 845
Hobson, Achsa V, 547
Hobson, Achsah V, 576
Hobson, Adaliza IV, 1133
Hobson, Adaliza IV, 1134
Hobson, Agness IV, 92
Hobson, Alden IV, 1090
Hobson, Alfred IV, 531
Hobson, Alice IV, 531
Hobson, Alicia III, 251
Hobson, Allen V, 576
Hobson, Amelia I, 987
Hobson, Amy I, 397
Hobson, Amy I, 398
Hobson, Amy I, 447
Hobson, Amy IV, 1205
Hobson, Amy IV, 1211
Hobson, Amy IV, 1223
Hobson, Amy P. IV, 1206
Hobson, Amy P. IV, 1211
Hobson, Andrew IV, 1133
Hobson, Angelina I, 398
Hobson, Ann I, 355
Hobson, Ann I, 356
Hobson, Ann I, 364
Hobson, Ann I, 397
Hobson, Ann I, 398
Hobson, Ann I, 420
Hobson, Ann I, 546
Hobson, Ann I, 975
Hobson, Ann I, 987
Hobson, Ann I, 993
Hobson, Ann I, 994
Hobson, Ann I, 1106
Hobson, Ann II, 876
Hobson, Ann II, 937
Hobson, Ann IV, 92
Hobson, Ann IV, 179
Hobson, Ann IV, 222
Hobson, Ann IV, 335
Hobson, Ann IV, 467
Hobson, Ann IV, 476
Hobson, Ann IV, 477
Hobson, Ann IV, 488
Hobson, Ann IV, 501
Hobson, Ann IV, 531
Hobson, Ann IV, 1133
Hobson, Ann IV, 1211
Hobson, Ann IV, 1212
Hobson, Ann M. IV, 477
Hobson, Ann M. IV, 502
Hobson, Ann M. IV, 634
Hobson, Ann M. IV, 872
Hobson, Ann M. VI, 896
Hobson, Ann Stout I, 397
Hobson, Ann W. IV, 473
Hobson, Ann W. IV, 477
Hobson, Anna I, 975
Hobson, Anna IV, 531
Hobson, Anna IV, 1101
Hobson, Anna IV, 1211
Hobson, Anna M. IV, 1132
Hobson, Anna M. IV, 1133
Hobson, Anna S. IV, 531
Hobson, Anna W. IV, 476
Hobson, Anne I, 356
Hobson, Anne I, 364
Hobson, Anne I, 975
Hobson, Anne IV, 149
Hobson, Anne IV, 530
Hobson, Anne IV, 1101
Hobson, Anne IV, 1118
Hobson, Anne H. IV, 476
Hobson, Arabella VI, 994
Hobson, Ariadna I, 546
Hobson, Ariadna I, 563
Hobson, Ariadna I, 976
Hobson, Ariadna I, 987
Hobson, Ariadny I, 976
Hobson, Arthur IV, 1211
Hobson, Arthur Brunson IV, 1133
Hobson, Asenath I, 355
Hobson, Asenath I, 465
Hobson, Asenath J. I, 383
Hobson, Asenath J. I, 398
Hobson, Bailey V, 501
Hobson, Baley I, 987
Hobson, Baly I, 397
Hobson, Barkly Stratton IV, 722
Hobson, Bayley I, 397
Hobson, Bedy I, 987
Hobson, Belina IV, 1101
Hobson, Belinda IV, 222
Hobson, Belinda IV, 369
Hobson, Belinda IV, 387
Hobson, Belinda IV, 409
Hobson, Belinda IV, 476
Hobson, Belinda IV, 477
Hobson, Belinda IV, 531
Hobson, Belinda IV, 678
Hobson, Belinda IV, 699
Hobson, Belinda IV, 722
Hobson, Belinda IV, 789
Hobson, Belinda IV, 800
Hobson, Belinda IV, 856
Hobson, Belinda IV, 1109
Hobson, Belinda IV, 1113
Hobson, Belinda IV, 1118
Hobson, Belinda IV, 1127
Hobson, Belinda IV, 1133
Hobson, Belinda A. IV, 521
Hobson, Belinda A. IV, 531
Hobson, Belinda F. IV, 1101
Hobson, Belinda H. IV, 477
Hobson, Belinda H. IV, 1131
Hobson, Belinda H. IV, 1133
Hobson, Belinda S. IV, 1101
Hobson, Belinda S. IV, 1114
Hobson, Belinda S. IV, 1133
Hobson, Belinda S. IV, 1137
Hobson, Bellinda IV, 411
Hobson, Benj. I, 356
Hobson, Benj. VI, 932
Hobson, Benj. D. IV, 845
Hobson, Benj. J. IV, 1130
Hobson, Benj. J. IV, 1135
Hobson, Benjamin I, 398
Hobson, Benjamin II, 707
Hobson, Benjamin IV, 222
Hobson, Benjamin IV, 477
Hobson, Benjamin IV, 480
Hobson, Benjamin IV, 823
Hobson, Benjamin IV, 828
Hobson, Benjamin IV, 1211
Hobson, Benjamin VI, 933
Hobson, Benjamin G. IV, 477
Hobson, Benjamin J. IV, 222
Hobson, Benjamin J. IV, 477
Hobson, Benjamin J. IV, 1101
Hobson, Benjamin J. IV, 1133
Hobson, Benjn. VI, 954
Hobson, Beverly Jean IV, 1211
Hobson, Bridget I, 985
Hobson, Bridget I, 987
Hobson, Caleb I, 976
Hobson, Caleb P. IV, 477
Hobson, Carl Edwin IV, 964
Hobson, Catharine I, 481
Hobson, Charles I, 354
Hobson, Charles I, 355
Hobson, Charles I, 397
Hobson, Charles I, 398
Hobson, Charles I, 884
Hobson, Charles I, 895
Hobson, Charles I, 976
Hobson, Charles I, 1106
Hobson, Charles IV, 222
Hobson, Charles IV, 476
Hobson, Charles IV, 1211
Hobson, Charles M. III, 168
Hobson, Charles M. III, 251
Hobson, Chas. I, 354
Hobson, Clarence C. IV, 531
Hobson, Daniel Brown I, 355
Hobson, David I, 356
Hobson, David I, 397
Hobson, David I, 975
Hobson, David I, 987
Hobson, David V, 576
Hobson, David, Jr. I, 987
Hobson, Deborah I, 356
Hobson, Deborah I, 397
Hobson, Deborah I, 398
Hobson, Deborah I, 763
Hobson, Deborah I, 987
Hobson, Deborah I, 992
Hobson, Deborah I Sup 1, 10
Hobson, Deborah Hinshaw I, 407
Hobson, Dinah I, 355
Hobson, Dinah I, 356
Hobson, Dinah I, 366
Hobson, Dinah I, 397
Hobson, Dinah I, 398
Hobson, Dinah I, 407
Hobson, Dinah I, 423
Hobson, Dinah I, 975
Hobson, Dinah I, 987
Hobson, Dinah I, 988
Hobson, Dinah K. I, 398
Hobson, Dinah K. I, 481
Hobson, Dorath I, 980
Hobson, Dorath I, 987
Hobson, Dorothy I, 987
Hobson, Dorothy IV, 222
Hobson, Dorothy IV, 477
Hobson, Dorothy IV, 509
Hobson, Dorothy IV, 552
Hobson, Dorothy IV, 845
Hobson, Dorothy IV, 846
Hobson, Dorothy IV, 1133
Hobson, Dorothy IV, 1138
Hobson, E. Gertrude IV, 1101
Hobson, Eber IV, 1211
Hobson, Eber S. IV, 823
Hobson, Eber S. IV, 1211
Hobson, Edith III, 159
Hobson, Edith III, 168
Hobson, Edith IV, 1090
Hobson, Edith IV, 1101
Hobson, Editha VI, 933
Hobson, Edward L. IV, 531
Hobson, Edwin F. IV, 477
Hobson, Edwin L. IV, 477
Hobson, Edwin S. IV, 964
Hobson, Edwin T. IV, 222
Hobson, Edwin T. IV, 964
Hobson, Eleany I, 975
Hobson, Eliz. C. III, 168
Hobson, Eliza I, 680
Hobson, Eliza II, 792
Hobson, Eliza A. IV, 1101
Hobson, Eliza A. IV, 1133
Hobson, Eliza A. IV, 1140
Hobson, Elizabeth I, 355
Hobson, Elizabeth I, 356
Hobson, Elizabeth I, 360
Hobson, Elizabeth I, 366
Hobson, Elizabeth I, 397
Hobson, Elizabeth I, 398
Hobson, Elizabeth I, 407
Hobson, Elizabeth I, 423
Hobson, Elizabeth I, 721
Hobson, Elizabeth I, 975
Hobson, Elizabeth I, 976
Hobson, Elizabeth I, 987
Hobson, Elizabeth I, 1000
Hobson, Elizabeth II, 375
Hobson, Elizabeth II, 550
Hobson, Elizabeth II, 800
Hobson, Elizabeth II, 876
Hobson, Elizabeth II, 937
Hobson, Elizabeth IV, 222
Hobson, Elizabeth IV, 964
Hobson, Elizabeth IV, 1101
Hobson, Elizabeth IV, 1131
Hobson, Elizabeth IV, 1133
Hobson, Elizabeth IV, 1211
Hobson, Elizabeth V, 575
Hobson, Elizabeth VI, 939
Hobson, Elizabeth VI, 954
Hobson, Elizabeth F. IV, 476
Hobson, Elizabeth Farquhar IV, 477
Hobson, Elizabeth J. IV, 1101
Hobson, Elizabeth J. IV, 1133
Hobson, Elizabeth K. VI, 848
Hobson, Elizabeth T. IV, 1206
Hobson, Elizabeth T. IV, 1211
Hobson, Elizabeth T. IV, 1277
Hobson, Elizabeth T. IV, 1281
Hobson, Elizabeth W. II, 876
Hobson, Ellen I, 976
Hobson, Ellen I, 980
Hobson, Ellen I, 987
Hobson, Emay I, 355
Hobson, Emey I, 355
Hobson, Emilia I, 975
Hobson, Emily VI, 933
Hobson, Emma IV, 1133
Hobson, Emma Gertrude IV, 531
Hobson, Emmerson IV, 1133
Hobson, Emy I, 355
Hobson, Emy I, 360
Hobson, Emy I, 397
Hobson, Emy I, 407
Hobson, Esther IV, 92
Hobson, Esther IV, 222
Hobson, Esther IV, 335
Hobson, Esther IV, 476
Hobson, Esther IV, 477
Hobson, Esther IV, 530
Hobson, Esther IV, 531
Hobson, Esther IV, 964
Hobson, Esther M. IV, 222
Hobson, Esther Phebe IV, 149
Hobson, Eunice I, 680
Hobson, Eunice I, 987
Hobson, Eunice I, 992
Hobson, Evan V, 575
Hobson, Evan B. I, 976
Hobson, Flora IV, 964
Hobson, Flora IV, 985
Hobson, Frances Adeline III, 1
Hobson, Francis II, 746
Hobson, Francis II, 876
Hobson, Francis II, 937
Hobson, Francis IV, 92
Hobson, Francis IV, 149
Hobson, Francis IV, 222
Hobson, Francis IV, 251
Hobson, Francis IV, 335
Hobson, Francis IV, 476
Hobson, Francis IV, 477
Hobson, Francis IV, 530
Hobson, Francis IV, 531
Hobson, George I, 355
Hobson, George I, 356
Hobson, George I, 366
Hobson, George I, 397
Hobson, George I, 398
Hobson, George I, 407
Hobson, George I, 975
Hobson, George I, 976
Hobson, George I, 987
Hobson, George I, 992
Hobson, George I, 1106
Hobson, George I, 1122
Hobson, George I Sup 1, 10
Hobson, George V, 501
Hobson, George Henry III, 16
Hobson, George K. I, 398
Hobson, George W. IV, 845
Hobson, George W. IV, 1133
Hobson, George, Jr. VI, 357
Hobson, George, Sr. VI, 357
Hobson, Gertrude IV, 1133
Hobson, Grace IV, 222
Hobson, Grace IV, 251
Hobson, Grace IV, 335
Hobson, Grace IV, 476
Hobson, Grace IV, 477
Hobson, Grace IV, 530
Hobson, Grace IV, 531
Hobson, Hannah I, 356
Hobson, Hannah I, 397
Hobson, Hannah I, 975
Hobson, Hannah I, 987
Hobson, Hannah IV, 476
Hobson, Hannah IV, 531
Hobson, Hannah IV, 552
Hobson, Hannah IV, 722
Hobson, Hannah IV, 771
Hobson, Hannah IV, 845
Hobson, Hannah V, 501
Hobson, Hannah V, 524
Hobson, Hannah D. IV, 845
Hobson, Hannah H. IV, 845
Hobson, Hazel IV, 1211
Hobson, Helen Hargrave III, 1
Hobson, Henrietta VI, 859
Hobson, Hinson I, 763
Hobson, Hollowill V, 73
Hobson, Homer H. III, 168
Hobson, Howard IV, 1133
Hobson, Howard E. IV, 1101
Hobson, Isaac I, 355
Hobson, Isaac I, 356
Hobson, Isaac I, 360
Hobson, Isaac I, 397
Hobson, Isaac I, 398
Hobson, Isaac I, 407
Hobson, Isaac I, 447
Hobson, Isaac I, 762
Hobson, Isaac I, 763
Hobson, Isaac I, 975
Hobson, Isaac Nuten I, 976
Hobson, Isaac, Jr. I, 398
Hobson, Isabella IV, 477
Hobson, Isabella IV, 485
Hobson, Isadore Pearl IV, 964
Hobson, J. IV, 476
Hobson, J. J. IV, 1211
Hobson, Jacob I, 356
Hobson, Jacob I, 397
Hobson, Jacob I, 976
Hobson, James IV, 92
Hobson, James IV, 149
Hobson, James IV, 477
Hobson, James IV, 1101
Hobson, James IV, 1133

obson, James David IV, 531
obson, James E. IV, 1211
obson, Jane I, 356
obson, Jane I, 397
obson, Jane I, 398
obson, Jane I, 424
obson, Jane IV, 92
obson, Jane IV, 149
obson, Jane IV, 222
obson, Jane IV, 252
obson, Jane IV, 476
obson, Jane IV, 477
obson, Jane IV, 488
obson, Jane IV, 1100
obson, Jane IV, 1101
obson, Jane IV, 1133
obson, Jane V, 575
obson, Jean I, 397
obson, Jesse I, 355
obson, Jesse I, 397
obson, Jesse I, 398
obson, Jesse I, 447
obson, Jesse I, 452
obson, Jesse I, 975
obson, Jesse I, 987
obson, Jesse I, 1106
obson, Jesse I, 1121
obson, John I, 308
obson, John I, 355
obson, John I, 356
obson, John I, 397
obson, John I, 679
obson, John I, 680
obson, John I, 721
obson, John I, 975
obson, John I, 976
obson, John I, 987
obson, John I, 1121
obson, John III, 168
obson, John IV, 92
obson, John IV, 222
obson, John IV, 335
obson, John IV, 467
obson, John IV, 476
obson, John IV, 477
obson, John IV, 485
obson, John IV, 531
obson, John IV, 722
obson, John IV, 872
obson, John IV, 1101
obson, John IV, 1118
obson, John IV, 1131
obson, John IV, 1133
obson, John IV, 1211
obson, John V, 73
obson, John V, 576
obson, John VI, 825
obson, John VI, 933
obson, John A. IV, 222
obson, John A. IV, 477
obson, John A. IV, 513
obson, John A. IV, 531
obson, John A. IV, 964
obson, John A. IV, 1101
obson, John A. IV, 1116
obson, John A. IV, 1128
obson, John A. IV, 1133
obson, John M. IV, 477
obson, John M. IV, 530
obson, John T. IV, 477
obson, John T. IV, 1211
obson, John W. IV, 1132
obson, John W. IV, 1133
obson, John, Jr. II, 375
obson, John, Jr. IV, 476
obson, John, Jr. IV, 488
obson, Jonathan I, 356
obson, Jos. I, 356
obson, Jos. IV, 476
obson, Jos. IV, 477
obson, Jos. IV, 531
obson, Jose I, 355
obson, Jose I, 398
obson, Jose I, 402
obson, Joseph I, 355
obson, Joseph I, 356
obson, Joseph I, 370
obson, Joseph I, 397
obson, Joseph I, 398
obson, Joseph I, 424
obson, Joseph I, 546
obson, Joseph IV, 92
obson, Joseph IV, 149
obson, Joseph IV, 179
obson, Joseph IV, 222
obson, Joseph IV, 463
obson, Joseph IV, 467
obson, Joseph IV, 476
obson, Joseph IV, 477
obson, Joseph IV, 488
obson, Joseph IV, 501
Hobson, Joseph IV, 502
Hobson, Joseph IV, 521
Hobson, Joseph IV, 528
Hobson, Joseph IV, 531
Hobson, Joseph IV, 552
Hobson, Joseph IV, 584
Hobson, Joseph IV, 722
Hobson, Joseph IV, 845
Hobson, Joseph IV, 1205
Hobson, Joseph IV, 1206
Hobson, Joseph IV, 1211
Hobson, Joseph IV, 1223
Hobson, Joseph V, 73
Hobson, Joseph V, 501
Hobson, Joseph C. I, 398
Hobson, Joseph C. IV, 1211
Hobson, Joseph Crew I, 355
Hobson, Joseph Doudna IV, 409
Hobson, Joseph F. IV, 531
Hobson, Joseph G. IV, 1133
Hobson, Joseph J. I, 398
Hobson, Joseph John I, 355
Hobson, Joseph P. IV, 222
Hobson, Joseph P. IV, 476
Hobson, Joseph T. IV, 531
Hobson, Joseph, Jr. IV, 477
Hobson, Joseph, Jr. IV, 499
Hobson, Joseph, Sr. IV, 476
Hobson, Joshua I, 987
Hobson, Joshua I, 1106
Hobson, Juliann D. IV, 1211
Hobson, Larkin I, 763
Hobson, Laura IV, 943
Hobson, Laura IV, 944
Hobson, Laura IV, 964
Hobson, Laura Levering IV, 1211
Hobson, Lavina I, 355
Hobson, Lavina I, 356
Hobson, Lavina A. I, 398
Hobson, Lee Stanley IV, 964
Hobson, Lena M. IV, 1133
Hobson, Lena May IV, 1095
Hobson, Lena May IV, 1101
Hobson, Lewis Dale IV, 1211
Hobson, Lidia I, 447
Hobson, Lilburn IV, 1211
Hobson, Lilbwm IV, 1211
Hobson, Lillian Shaffer IV, 1254
Hobson, Linneaus D. IV, 1133
Hobson, Louisa IV, 1205
Hobson, Louisa IV, 1211
Hobson, Louisa VI, 825
Hobson, Louisa W. VI, 825
Hobson, Lovenie I, 398
Hobson, Lucy VI, 939
Hobson, Luzena I, 987
Hobson, Lyda I, 721
Hobson, Lydia I, 355
Hobson, Lydia I, 392
Hobson, Lydia I, 397
Hobson, Lydia I, 398
Hobson, Lydia I, 447
Hobson, Lydia I, 452
Hobson, Lydia I, 679
Hobson, Lydia I, 680
Hobson, Lydia I, 987
Hobson, Lydia I, 1121
Hobson, Lydia IV, 476
Hobson, Lydia IV, 477
Hobson, Lydia IV, 1100
Hobson, Lydia IV, 1101
Hobson, Lydia IV, 1129
Hobson, Lydia IV, 1133
Hobson, Lydia IV, 1137
Hobson, M. IV, 476
Hobson, M. Watson IV, 476
Hobson, Mahala IV, 477
Hobson, Mahala IV, 497
Hobson, Mahale IV, 476
Hobson, Mahale IV, 492
Hobson, Mahlon I, 356
Hobson, Malinda I, 356
Hobson, Marcia Morris III, 168
Hobson, Margaret I, 987
Hobson, Margaret IV, 509
Hobson, Margaret IV, 531
Hobson, Margaret IV, 566
Hobson, Margaret IV, 584
Hobson, Margaret IV, 964
Hobson, Margaret E. VI, 971
Hobson, Mariam I, 308
Hobson, Marianna IV, 1133
Hobson, Marianna IV, 1134
Hobson, Martha I, 355
Hobson, Martha I, 356
Hobson, Martha I, 387
Hobson, Martha I, 397
Hobson, Martha I, 975
Hobson, Martha I, 987
Hobson, Martha I, 997
Hobson, Martha IV, 335
Hobson, Martha IV, 476
Hobson, Martha IV, 477
Hobson, Martha IV, 530
Hobson, Martha IV, 531
Hobson, Martha IV, 1133
Hobson, Martha IV, 1211
Hobson, Martha VI, 947
Hobson, Martha VI, 999
Hobson, Martha Ann IV, 222
Hobson, Martha Ann IV, 477
Hobson, Martha E. IV, 1133
Hobson, Martha E. IV, 1135
Hobson, Martha H. IV, 513
Hobson, Martha H. IV, 531
Hobson, Martha H. IV, 1128
Hobson, Martha H. IV, 1133
Hobson, Martha J. I, 988
Hobson, Martha J. I, 996
Hobson, Mary I, 355
Hobson, Mary I, 356
Hobson, Mary I, 370
Hobson, Mary I, 383
Hobson, Mary I, 397
Hobson, Mary I, 398
Hobson, Mary I, 405
Hobson, Mary I, 680
Hobson, Mary I, 976
Hobson, Mary I, 981
Hobson, Mary I, 987
Hobson, Mary I, 996
Hobson, Mary I, 999
Hobson, Mary I, 1121
Hobson, Mary IV, 92
Hobson, Mary IV, 149
Hobson, Mary IV, 222
Hobson, Mary IV, 467
Hobson, Mary IV, 476
Hobson, Mary IV, 477
Hobson, Mary IV, 722
Hobson, Mary IV, 765
Hobson, Mary IV, 1133
Hobson, Mary IV, 1138
Hobson, Mary IV, 1211
Hobson, Mary V, 575
Hobson, Mary A. VI, 859
Hobson, Mary Ann I, 356
Hobson, Mary Ann I, 984
Hobson, Mary Ann I, 987
Hobson, Mary Ann IV, 222
Hobson, Mary Ann IV, 476
Hobson, Mary Ann IV, 477
Hobson, Mary Ann IV, 502
Hobson, Mary Ann IV, 811
Hobson, Mary Ann IV, 903
Hobson, Mary Ann IV, 907
Hobson, Mary Ann IV, 1101
Hobson, Mary Ann IV, 1129
Hobson, Mary Ann IV, 1132
Hobson, Mary Ann IV, 1133
Hobson, Mary Ann IV, 1134
Hobson, Mary Anne I, 355
Hobson, Mary Bertha IV, 531
Hobson, Mary E. IV, 477
Hobson, Mary E. IV, 1211
Hobson, Mary Elizabeth III, 168
Hobson, Mary Elizabeth IV, 1211
Hobson, Mary J. IV, 222
Hobson, Mary J. IV, 518
Hobson, Mary J. IV, 1091
Hobson, Mary J. IV, 1101
Hobson, Mary J. IV, 1133
Hobson, Mary Lucile IV, 1101
Hobson, Mary R. IV, 1116
Hobson, Mary S. IV, 531
Hobson, Mary S. IV, 722
Hobson, Mary S. IV, 1133
Hobson, Mary T. IV, 222
Hobson, Mary T. IV, 476
Hobson, Mary Williams I, 356
Hobson, Maryan I, 975
Hobson, Maryann IV, 476
Hobson, Maryanne IV, 1133
Hobson, Matthew VI, 894
Hobson, Melinda I, 398
Hobson, Melinda I, 423
Hobson, Meriam V, 73
Hobson, Michael I, 397
Hobson, Michael I, 987
Hobson, Michael I, 1121
Hobson, Michal I, 987
Hobson, Michel I, 987
Hobson, Miles I, 355
Hobson, Miles I, 356
Hobson, Miles I, 398
Hobson, Miles I, 423
Hobson, Milley I, 355
Hobson, Miriam I, 308
Hobson, Miriam I, 987
Hobson, Nathan I, 356
Hobson, Nathan I, 397
Hobson, Nathan I, 987
Hobson, Nathan I, 1121
Hobson, Nathan Ellis I, 976
Hobson, Nicholas I, 975
Hobson, Nicholas I, 987
Hobson, Parmelia VI, 825
Hobson, Pegg I, 397
Hobson, Peggy I, 397
Hobson, Peggy I, 987
Hobson, Peggy V, 501
Hobson, Penelope I, 721
Hobson, Peniah I, 355
Hobson, Peninah I, 398
Hobson, Phebe I, 354
Hobson, Phebe IV, 92
Hobson, Phebe IV, 476
Hobson, Phebe IV, 477
Hobson, Phebe IV, 501
Hobson, Phebe IV, 1101
Hobson, Phebe IV, 1131
Hobson, Phebe N. IV, 477
Hobson, Phebe V. IV, 1211
Hobson, Phebe W. IV, 1133
Hobson, R. IV, 476
Hobson, R. L. VI, 825
Hobson, Rachel I, 356
Hobson, Rachel I, 397
Hobson, Rachel I, 425
Hobson, Rachel I, 546
Hobson, Rachel I, 817
Hobson, Rachel I, 975
Hobson, Rachel I, 976
Hobson, Rachel I, 981
Hobson, Rachel I, 987
Hobson, Rachel I, 999
Hobson, Rachel Ann IV, 488
Hobson, Rebecca I, 354
Hobson, Rebecca I, 356
Hobson, Rebecca I, 370
Hobson, Rebecca I, 398
Hobson, Rebecca I, 971
Hobson, Rebecca I, 975
Hobson, Rebecca I, 982
Hobson, Rebecca I, 987
Hobson, Rebecca I, 1106
Hobson, Rebecca IV, 222
Hobson, Rebecca IV, 467
Hobson, Rebecca IV, 476
Hobson, Rebecca IV, 477
Hobson, Rebecca IV, 496
Hobson, Rebecca IV, 502
Hobson, Rebecca IV, 528
Hobson, Rebecca IV, 531
Hobson, Rebecca IV, 1131
Hobson, Rebecca IV, 1133
Hobson, Rebecca IV, 1202
Hobson, Rebecca IV, 1211
Hobson, Rebecca Jane IV, 1130
Hobson, Rebecca Jane IV, 1133
Hobson, Rebecca P. IV, 476
Hobson, Rebecca P. IV, 488
Hobson, Rebecca P. IV, 872
Hobson, Rebecca P. IV, 1131
Hobson, Rebecca T. IV, 1211
Hobson, Rebeccah I, 1122
Hobson, Rebeccah I, 1125
Hobson, Rebekah I, 397
Hobson, Rebekah I, 1122
Hobson, Rebekah IV, 477
Hobson, Rebekah IV, 499
Hobson, Reuben IV, 1211
Hobson, Rhoda I, 355
Hobson, Rhoda I, 380
Hobson, Rhoda I, 398
Hobson, Rhoda Ann IV, 1211
Hobson, Rich., Jr. VI, 899
Hobson, Richard VI, 825
Hobson, Richard VI, 933
Hobson, Richard VI, 1011
Hobson, Richard, Jr. VI, 884
Hobson, Richard, Jr. VI, 899
Hobson, Richd. VI, 891
Hobson, Robert Leland IV, 964
Hobson, Rufus I, 355
Hobson, Rufus I, 398
Hobson, Russell Benj. III, 159
Hobson, Russell Benj. III, 168
Hobson, Ruth I, 355
Hobson, Ruth I, 398
Hobson, Ruth I, 402
Hobson, Ruth I, 412
Hobson, Ruth I, 680
Hobson, Ruth I, 762
Hobson, Ruth I, 763
Hobson, Ruth IV, 387
Hobson, Ruth IV, 463
Hobson, Ruth IV, 476
Hobson, Ruth IV, 477
Hobson, Ruth IV, 521
Hobson, Ruth IV, 528
Hobson, Ruth IV, 531
Hobson, Ruth IV, 552
Hobson, Ruth IV, 584
Hobson, Ruth IV, 845
Hobson, Ruth IV, 964
Hobson, Ruth IV, 1133
Hobson, Ruth Aldine IV, 1211
Hobson, Sally P. VI, 891
Hobson, Saml. VI, 994
Hobson, Samuel I, 356
Hobson, Samuel I, 397
Hobson, Samuel I, 987
Hobson, Samuel IV, 476
Hobson, Samuel IV, 1133
Hobson, Samuel VI, 896
Hobson, Samuel VI, 932
Hobson, Samuel VI, 971
Hobson, Samuel N. IV, 477
Hobson, Samuel N. IV, 872
Hobson, Samuel N. IV, 1132
Hobson, Samuel N. IV, 1133
Hobson, Sara Ann IV, 823
Hobson, Sara Ann IV, 833
Hobson, Sarah I, 354
Hobson, Sarah I, 355
Hobson, Sarah I, 356
Hobson, Sarah I, 397
Hobson, Sarah I, 398
Hobson, Sarah I, 408
Hobson, Sarah I, 409
Hobson, Sarah I, 546
Hobson, Sarah I, 565
Hobson, Sarah I, 975
Hobson, Sarah I, 987
Hobson, Sarah I, 989
Hobson, Sarah I, 998
Hobson, Sarah I, 1106
Hobson, Sarah I, 1121
Hobson, Sarah III, 168
Hobson, Sarah III, 170
Hobson, Sarah V, 501
Hobson, Sarah VI, 933
Hobson, Sarah A. IV, 222
Hobson, Sarah A. IV, 1130
Hobson, Sarah A. IV, 1133
Hobson, Sarah Ann II, 800
Hobson, Sarah Ann II, 876
Hobson, Sarah Ann IV, 222
Hobson, Sarah Ann IV, 477
Hobson, Sarah Ann IV, 480
Hobson, Sarah Ann IV, 823
Hobson, Sarah Ann IV, 828
Hobson, Sarah Ann IV, 964
Hobson, Sarah B. IV, 1211
Hobson, Sarah B. IV, 1219
Hobson, Silas I, 355
Hobson, Silas I, 356
Hobson, Silas I, 397
Hobson, Silas I, 398
Hobson, Silas I, 975
Hobson, Silas I, 987
Hobson, Silas I, 989
Hobson, Simon I, 355
Hobson, Stephen I, 355
Hobson, Stephen I, 356
Hobson, Stephen I, 364
Hobson, Stephen I, 383
Hobson, Stephen I, 397
Hobson, Stephen I, 398
Hobson, Stephen I, 407
Hobson, Stephen I, 423
Hobson, Stephen I, 425
Hobson, Stephen I, 546
Hobson, Stephen I, 563
Hobson, Stephen I, 763
Hobson, Stephen I, 817
Hobson, Stephen I, 971
Hobson, Stephen I, 975
Hobson, Stephen I, 976
Hobson, Stephen I, 980
Hobson, Stephen I, 981
Hobson, Stephen I, 987
Hobson, Stephen I, 999
Hobson, Stephen IV, 476
Hobson, Stephen IV, 477
Hobson, Stephen IV, 509
Hobson, Stephen IV, 531
Hobson, Stephen IV, 566
Hobson, Stephen IV, 584
Hobson, Stephen IV, 1100
Hobson, Stephen IV, 1101
Hobson, Stephen IV, 1129
Hobson, Stephen IV, 1133
Hobson, Stephen IV, 1137
Hobson, Stephen H. I, 987
Hobson, Stephen J. IV, 1133
Hobson, Stephen, Jr. I, 975
Hobson, Susa I, 987
Hobson, Susan VI, 932
Hobson, Susanna I, 356
Hobson, Susanna I, 377
Hobson, Susanna I, 398
Hobson, Sylvester IV, 1211

Hobson, Tacy IV, 1090
Hobson, Tacy A. IV, 1101
Hobson, Tacy Ann IV, 1129
Hobson, Tacy Ann IV, 1133
Hobson, Thomas I, 975
Hobson, Thomas I, 976
Hobson, Thomas I, 987
Hobson, Thomas I, 1106
Hobson, Thomas I, 1122
Hobson, Thomas IV, 222
Hobson, Thomas IV, 476
Hobson, Thomas IV, 480
Hobson, Thomas IV, 722
Hobson, Thomas IV, 765
Hobson, Thomas IV, 823
Hobson, Thomas IV, 828
Hobson, Thomas IV, 845
Hobson, Thomas IV, 1101
Hobson, Thomas IV, 1127
Hobson, Thomas IV, 1138
Hobson, Thomas IV, 1140
Hobson, Thomas IV, 1211
Hobson, Thomas IV, 1212
Hobson, Thomas Alden IV, 1101
Hobson, Thomas Alden IV, 1129
Hobson, Thomas Alden IV, 1133
Hobson, Thomas C. IV, 222
Hobson, Thomas C. IV, 477
Hobson, Thomas C. IV, 823
Hobson, Thomas C. IV, 1133
Hobson, Thomas C. IV, 1211
Hobson, Thomas Chalkley IV, 477
Hobson, Thomas Chalkley IV, 964
Hobson, Thomas, Jr. II, 800
Hobson, Thomas, Jr. II, 876
Hobson, Thos. II, 876
Hobson, Thos. II, 937
Hobson, Thos. IV, 509
Hobson, Thos. IV, 531
Hobson, Thos. IV, 1133
Hobson, Thos. VI, 933
Hobson, Thos., Jr. II, 876
Hobson, Truman Ellsworth IV, 1211
Hobson, Unity IV, 222
Hobson, Unity IV, 476
Hobson, Unity IV, 477
Hobson, Unity IV, 480
Hobson, Unity IV, 509
Hobson, Unity IV, 531
Hobson, Unity IV, 823
Hobson, Unity IV, 828
Hobson, Unity IV, 845
Hobson, Unity IV, 1127
Hobson, Unity IV, 1133
Hobson, Unity IV, 1138
Hobson, Unity Jane IV, 1211
Hobson, Virena I, 680
Hobson, Virginia IV, 964
Hobson, Virginia IV, 1211
Hobson, Waddy VI, 933
Hobson, William I, 308
Hobson, William I, 355
Hobson, William I, 356
Hobson, William I, 397
Hobson, William I, 398
Hobson, William I, 680
Hobson, William I, 817
Hobson, William I, 975
Hobson, William I, 998
Hobson, William I, 1121
Hobson, William IV, 92
Hobson, William IV, 149
Hobson, William IV, 476
Hobson, William IV, 477
Hobson, William IV, 1101
Hobson, William IV, 1133
Hobson, William V, 73
Hobson, William V, 501
Hobson, William VI, 939
Hobson, William VI, 958
Hobson, William VI, 999
Hobson, William C. IV, 1133
Hobson, William Penn II, 800
Hobson, William, Jr. I, 397
Hobson, William, Sr. I, 397
Hobson, William, Sr. I, 976
Hobson, Wm. I, 356
Hobson, Wm. I, 397
Hobson, Wm. I, 412
Hobson, Wm. III, 168
Hobson, Wm. IV, 222
Hobson, Wm. IV, 476
Hobson, Wm. IV, 492
Hobson, Wm. IV, 823
Hobson, Wm. IV, 1101
Hobson, Wm. IV, 1133
Hobson, Wm. IV, 1211
Hobson, Wm. VI, 894
Hobson, Wm. E. IV, 1101
Hobson, Wm. Penn II, 876
Hobson, Zelinga II, 699
Hobson, Zeruah I, 355
Hobson, Zeruah I, 398
Hobson, Zeruah I, 884
Hobson, Zeruah I, 895
Hockaday, ??? IV, 222
Hockaday, Benjamin IV, 222
Hockaday, Benjamin VI, 181
Hockaday, Benjamin VI, 195
Hockaday, Benjamin B. IV, 222
Hockaday, Benjamin B. VI, 180
Hockaday, Benjamin B. VI, 181
Hockaday, Benjamin B. VI, 191
Hockaday, Benjamin B. VI, 195
Hockaday, Benjamin, Jr. IV, 222
Hockaday, Henry A. VI, 995
Hockaday, James IV, 222
Hockaday, James VI, 181
Hockaday, John VI, 180
Hockaday, John VI, 181
Hockaday, John F. VI, 181
Hockaday, Joseph VI, 180
Hockaday, Joseph VI, 181
Hockaday, Mary VI, 181
Hockaday, Mary Ann IV, 222
Hockaday, Robert IV, 222
Hockaday, Robert VI, 181
Hockaday, Robert L. IV, 222
Hockaday, Robert Ladd IV, 222
Hockaday, Robert Ladd VI, 181
Hockaday, Sarah IV, 222
Hockaday, Sarah VI, 180
Hockaday, Sarah VI, 181
Hockaday, Sarah VI, 191
Hockaday, Sarah VI, 195
Hockaday, Sarah John Ladd VI, 181
Hockaday, Susanna VI, 180
Hockaday, Susanna VI, 181
Hockaday, Susannah VI, 181
Hockaday, Susannah F. VI, 181
Hockeday, Amelia VI, 825
Hockeday, Isaac VI, 825
Hockeday, John VI, 825
Hockeday, Kessiah VI, 825
Hocket, Allen V, 626
Hocket, Anna I, 1010
Hocket, Charlie V, 626
Hocket, David IV, 1281
Hocket, David IV, 1282
Hocket, David V, 626
Hocket, Della V, 626
Hocket, Elizabeth I, 885
Hocket, Elizabeth A. I, 677
Hocket, Elizabeth A. I, 680
Hocket, Emma IV, 1281
Hocket, Frank V, 626
Hocket, Hattie V, 626
Hocket, Himelius I, 680
Hocket, Homer V, 626
Hocket, Ida May V, 626
Hocket, Jacob V, 73
Hocket, Jacob V, 304
Hocket, Jacob V, 626
Hocket, Jane I, 680
Hocket, Jeremiah IV, 1281
Hocket, Jesse I, 885
Hocket, Jesse V, 625
Hocket, Jesse V, 626
Hocket, Jesse M. I, 680
Hocket, John I, 680
Hocket, John I, 953
Hocket, John V, 626
Hocket, John C. I, 680
Hocket, John Henry V, 626
Hocket, Jonathan I, 1010
Hocket, Joseph I, 886
Hocket, Julia Elma V, 625
Hocket, Julia Elma V, 626
Hocket, Lucinda V, 304
Hocket, Lucinda V, 305
Hocket, Luzena I, 885
Hocket, Malinda Ann V, 626
Hocket, Malinda Jane V, 626
Hocket, Margaret V, 502
Hocket, Mary V, 161
Hocket, Mary V, 178
Hocket, Mary V, 248
Hocket, Mary V, 502
Hocket, Mary V, 626
Hocket, Mary Roxanna I, 680
Hocket, Matilda Jane V, 625
Hocket, Moses IV, 39
Hocket, Moses V, 502
Hocket, Moses, Jr. IV, 39
Hocket, Naomi T. V, 73
Hocket, Newton IV, 1281
Hocket, Olive IV, 39
Hocket, Olive V, 502
Hocket, Philip I, 271
Hocket, Phillips I, 271
Hocket, Pleasant V, 625
Hocket, Pleasant V, 626
Hocket, Prudence V, 502
Hocket, Rachel I, 680
Hocket, Rachel V, 626
Hocket, Rebecca S. V, 626
Hocket, Rhoda V, 73
Hocket, Rhoda V, 304
Hocket, Ruth IV, 39
Hocket, Ruth V, 178
Hocket, Sarah V, 502
Hocket, Sarah V, 626
Hocket, Sarah E. I, 680
Hocket, Ulysses IV, 1281
Hocket, Uriah V, 626
Hocket, William V, 626
Hocket, William B. I, 680
Hocket, Wm. IV, 1281
Hocket, Wm. V, 626
Hockett, ??? V, 443
Hockett, ??? V, 576
Hockett, Achsah R. I, 680
Hockett, Adaline V, 396
Hockett, Agnes V, 396
Hockett, Agnes V, 413
Hockett, Agnes V, 502
Hockett, Agness V, 247
Hockett, Agness V, 446
Hockett, Albert V, 396
Hockett, Albert V, 398
Hockett, Albert Elwood V, 398
Hockett, Alce V, 73
Hockett, Alice V, 247
Hockett, Alice V, 337
Hockett, Allen V, 396
Hockett, Allen V, 397
Hockett, Allen V, 398
Hockett, Alma V, 399
Hockett, Almedia V, 398
Hockett, Alonzo V, 396
Hockett, Alonzo V, 397
Hockett, Alonzo V, 398
Hockett, Alonzo V, 399
Hockett, Alpheus V, 396
Hockett, Alpheus V, 576
Hockett, Alva V, 398
Hockett, Alvah V, 395
Hockett, Alvah V, 396
Hockett, Alvah V, 403
Hockett, Alvin V, 399
Hockett, Alwilda V, 396
Hockett, Alwilda V, 398
Hockett, Amos V, 396
Hockett, Amos V, 398
Hockett, Amos V, 399
Hockett, Amos V, 683
Hockett, Ann I, 680
Hockett, Ann I, 874
Hockett, Ann V, 73
Hockett, Ann V, 326
Hockett, Ann V, 337
Hockett, Ann V, 340
Hockett, Ann V, 342
Hockett, Ann V, 386
Hockett, Ann V, 396
Hockett, Ann V, 401
Hockett, Ann V, 502
Hockett, Ann V, 843
Hockett, Anna V, 220
Hockett, Anna V, 247
Hockett, Anna V, 372
Hockett, Anna V, 373
Hockett, Anna V, 395
Hockett, Anna V, 397
Hockett, Anna V, 398
Hockett, Anna V, 400
Hockett, Anna V, 403
Hockett, Anna V, 404
Hockett, Anna V, 417
Hockett, Anna V, 431
Hockett, Anna V, 436
Hockett, Anna V, 547
Hockett, Anna V, 576
Hockett, Anna B. V, 248
Hockett, Anna B. V, 398
Hockett, Anna J. I, 656
Hockett, Anna Jane V, 396
Hockett, Anna Jane V, 398
Hockett, Anna Moon V, 415
Hockett, Anne V, 397
Hockett, Anne V, 399
Hockett, Anne V, 419
Hockett, Anne V, 425
Hockett, Annie E. V, 397
Hockett, Annie Elizabeth V, 398
Hockett, Anthony V, 178
Hockett, Asa I, 931
Hockett, Asa V, 220
Hockett, Asa V, 395
Hockett, Asa V, 396
Hockett, Asa V, 397
Hockett, Asa V, 398
Hockett, Asa V, 436
Hockett, Asa C. V, 399
Hockett, Asa S. V, 247
Hockett, Asa S. V, 373
Hockett, Asa S. V, 398
Hockett, Barclay V, 337
Hockett, Barclay V, 396
Hockett, Barclay V, 397
Hockett, Benajah I, 656
Hockett, Benj. V, 415
Hockett, Benjamin I, 886
Hockett, Benjamin V, 373
Hockett, Benjamin V, 395
Hockett, Benjamin V, 396
Hockett, Benjamin V, 397
Hockett, Benjamin V, 413
Hockett, Benjamin V, 415
Hockett, Benjamin V, 416
Hockett, Benjamin V, 446
Hockett, Bessie M. I, 656
Hockett, Betsey V, 400
Hockett, Betsy V, 396
Hockett, Callie I, 611
Hockett, Callie I, 612
Hockett, Caroline V, 398
Hockett, Caroline D. I, 656
Hockett, Charity V, 373
Hockett, Charity V, 395
Hockett, Charity V, 396
Hockett, Charity V, 397
Hockett, Charity V, 413
Hockett, Charity V, 415
Hockett, Charity V, 416
Hockett, Charles V, 395
Hockett, Charles S. V, 397
Hockett, Charles S. V, 399
Hockett, Charley V, 398
Hockett, Charlotte V, 396
Hockett, Cina V, 247
Hockett, Clara V, 397
Hockett, Clara V, 398
Hockett, Clara V, 399
Hockett, Clara V, 669
Hockett, Clara V, 683
Hockett, Clarinda V, 396
Hockett, Clarinda V, 398
Hockett, Clarinda V, 559
Hockett, Clarinda V, 576
Hockett, Clarkson M. V, 399
Hockett, Clorinda V, 576
Hockett, Cora V, 576
Hockett, Cora E. I, 656
Hockett, Cyrus I, 655
Hockett, Cyrus I, 680
Hockett, Cyrus V, 337
Hockett, Cyrus Elwood I, 655
Hockett, Daniel V, 395
Hockett, Daniel V, 396
Hockett, Daniel V, 398
Hockett, Daniel V, 400
Hockett, Daniel H. V, 73
Hockett, David I, 656
Hockett, David V, 73
Hockett, David V, 247
Hockett, David V, 394
Hockett, David V, 396
Hockett, David V, 397
Hockett, David V, 399
Hockett, David V, 413
Hockett, David V, 441
Hockett, David V, 446
Hockett, David V, 683
Hockett, David A. V, 576
Hockett, David F. I, 655
Hockett, David W. V, 398
Hockett, David W. V, 399
Hockett, Della V, 397
Hockett, Della V, 398
Hockett, Dorcas V, 395
Hockett, Dorcas V, 396
Hockett, Dorcas V, 413
Hockett, Earl J. V, 337
Hockett, Edith I, 398
Hockett, Edith I, 426
Hockett, Edith V, 395
Hockett, Edith V, 397
Hockett, Edith V, 409
Hockett, Edith V, 683
Hockett, Edna V, 397
Hockett, Edward V, 576
Hockett, Edwin V, 398
Hockett, Elbridge V, 397
Hockett, Elden E. V, 576
Hockett, Eleanor C. V, 398
Hockett, Eleazer V, 337
Hockett, Eleazor V, 337
Hockett, Eli V, 395
Hockett, Eli V, 397
Hockett, Eliza I, 655
Hockett, Eliza V, 395
Hockett, Eliza V, 397
Hockett, Eliza Evaline I, 655
Hockett, Eliza J. I, 656
Hockett, Elizabeth I, 655
Hockett, Elizabeth I, 656
Hockett, Elizabeth I, 673
Hockett, Elizabeth I, 680
Hockett, Elizabeth I, 818
Hockett, Elizabeth I, 886
Hockett, Elizabeth I, 931
Hockett, Elizabeth V, 73
Hockett, Elizabeth V, 248
Hockett, Elizabeth V, 250
Hockett, Elizabeth V, 337
Hockett, Elizabeth V, 382
Hockett, Elizabeth V, 395
Hockett, Elizabeth V, 396
Hockett, Elizabeth V, 397
Hockett, Elizabeth V, 398
Hockett, Elizabeth V, 419
Hockett, Elizabeth V, 424
Hockett, Elizabeth V, 436
Hockett, Elizabeth V, 683
Hockett, Elizabeth A. I, 680
Hockett, Elizabeth W. V, 398
Hockett, Elizann V, 337
Hockett, Elldridge V, 398
Hockett, Ellen V, 337
Hockett, Ellen V, 397
Hockett, Ellen B. V, 396
Hockett, Ellwood V, 396
Hockett, Elma V, 398
Hockett, Elma V, 431
Hockett, Emely V, 337
Hockett, Emma V, 396
Hockett, Emma V, 398
Hockett, Emma V, 399
Hockett, Esther V, 337
Hockett, Esther V, 393
Hockett, Esther V, 396
Hockett, Esther V, 397
Hockett, Eugene V, 397
Hockett, Eugene V, 398
Hockett, Eunice Ellen I, 657
Hockett, Eva V, 576
Hockett, Fannie V, 399
Hockett, Fanny V, 398
Hockett, Francis V, 396
Hockett, Francis V, 398
Hockett, Francis A. V, 398
Hockett, Francis Alvin V, 396
Hockett, Francis Alvin V, 398
Hockett, Francis L. V, 397
Hockett, Francis L. V, 398
Hockett, Francis L. V, 399
Hockett, Francis L. V, 683
Hockett, Frank V, 683
Hockett, Frank E. V, 397
Hockett, Franklin C. V, 398
Hockett, Gertrude V, 576
Hockett, Guli Elma V, 396
Hockett, Gulielma Semans V, 39
Hockett, Hannah I, 329
Hockett, Hannah I, 348
Hockett, Hannah I, 474
Hockett, Hannah I, 481
Hockett, Hannah I, 655
Hockett, Hannah I, 656
Hockett, Hannah I, 661
Hockett, Hannah I, 680
Hockett, Hannah I, 692
Hockett, Hannah I, 721
Hockett, Hannah I, 758
Hockett, Hannah I, 764
Hockett, Hannah V, 329
Hockett, Hannah V, 337
Hockett, Hannah V, 395
Hockett, Hannah V, 398
Hockett, Hannah V, 404
Hockett, Hannah V, 446
Hockett, Hannah Ann V, 337
Hockett, Hannah Caroline I, 65
Hockett, Hannah D. I, 655
Hockett, Hannah Elizabeth I, 655
Hockett, Hannah Jane I, 655
Hockett, Hattie V, 399
Hockett, Hattie A. V, 397
Hockett, Hattie A. V, 399
Hockett, Hattie E. V, 683
Hockett, Hattie M. V, 397
Hockett, Hattie M. V, 398
Hockett, Henry V, 337
Hockett, Henry V, 396
Hockett, Henry V, 397
Hockett, Henry V, 399
Hockett, Henry A. V, 395
Hockett, Henry A. V, 398
Hockett, Henry N. V, 397

ckett, Hensie V, 576
ckett, Hezekiah I, 680
ckett, Hezekiah V, 446
ckett, Himelias M. I, 655
ckett, Himelius I, 680
ckett, Himelius M. I, 618
ckett, Himelius M. I, 656
ckett, Homer V, 399
ckett, Homer C. V, 397
ckett, Homer C. V, 683
ckett, Irene V, 397
ckett, Irene V, 398
ckett, Isaac I, 655
ckett, Isaac I, 680
ckett, Isaac V, 397
ckett, Isaac V, 502
ckett, Isaac V, 576
ckett, J. A. V, 576
ckett, J. D. I, 655
ckett, J. M. I, 655
ckett, Jabez V, 337
ckett, Jabez V, 396
ckett, Jacob V, 73
ckett, Jacob V, 337
ckett, Jacob V, 396
ckett, Jacob V, 397
ckett, Jacob V, 417
ckett, Jacob Semans V, 395
ckett, James V, 395
ckett, James V, 396
ckett, James V, 397
ckett, James V, 398
ckett, James A. V, 398
ckett, James G. V, 398
ckett, Jane I, 398
ckett, Jane I, 655
ckett, Jane I, 677
ckett, Jane I, 680
ckett, Jane V, 337
ckett, Jane V, 340
ckett, Jane V, 395
ckett, Jane V, 434
ckett, Jared V, 73
ckett, Jemima V, 398
ckett, Jesse I, 680
ckett, Jesse I, 874
ckett, Jesse V, 73
ckett, Jesse V, 337
ckett, Jesse V, 395
ckett, Jesse V, 396
ckett, Jesse V, 397
ckett, Jesse V, 399
ckett, Jesse V, 400
ckett, Jesse D. I, 655
ckett, Jesse D. I, 656
ckett, Jesse D. I, 677
ckett, Jesse D. I, 680
ckett, Jesse J. V, 399
ckett, Jesse J. V, 576
ckett, Jesse M. I, 680
ckett, Jesse P. V, 396
ckett, John I, 398
ckett, John I, 655
ckett, John I, 680
ckett, John I, 683
ckett, John I, 692
ckett, John V, 326
ckett, John V, 337
ckett, John V, 389
ckett, John V, 395
ckett, John V, 396
ckett, John V, 397
ckett, John V, 398
ckett, John V, 399
ckett, John V, 415
ckett, John V, 563
ckett, John V, 576
ckett, John V, 683
ockett, John Alpheus V, 398
ockett, John Alpheus V, 576
ockett, John Alpheus V, 683
ockett, John B. I, 656
ockett, John Beals I, 655
ockett, John C. I, 656
ockett, John C. I, 680
ockett, John Clarkson I, 656
ockett, John E. I, 655
ockett, John Edwin V, 396
ockett, John Edwin V, 398
ockett, John Semans V, 395
ockett, John, Jr. I, 680
ockett, Jonas V, 396
ockett, Jonas V, 398
ockett, Jonas V, 399
ockett, Jonathan V, 247
ockett, Jonathan V, 337
ockett, Jonathan V, 352
ockett, Jonathan V, 393
ockett, Jonathan V, 395
ockett, Jonathan V, 396
ockett, Jonathan V, 397
Hockett, Jonathan V, 398
Hockett, Jonathan V, 423
Hockett, Jonathan M. V, 399
Hockett, Joseph I, 818
Hockett, Joseph I, 886
Hockett, Joseph V, 73
Hockett, Joseph V, 315
Hockett, Joseph V, 326
Hockett, Joseph V, 337
Hockett, Joseph V, 340
Hockett, Joseph V, 342
Hockett, Joseph V, 386
Hockett, Joseph V, 397
Hockett, Joseph V, 416
Hockett, Joseph V, 446
Hockett, Josiah V, 337
Hockett, Josiah V, 356
Hockett, Josiah V, 397
Hockett, Josiah V, 398
Hockett, Julian V, 398
Hockett, Julian Edgar V, 396
Hockett, Julian Edgar V, 398
Hockett, Julielma V, 398
Hockett, Leah V, 395
Hockett, Leah V, 397
Hockett, Leah V, 407
Hockett, Lester Emlon I, 656
Hockett, Levi V, 337
Hockett, Levi V, 355
Hockett, Levi V, 395
Hockett, Levi V, 396
Hockett, Levi V, 398
Hockett, Levi V, 399
Hockett, Levi V, 425
Hockett, Lewis V, 337
Hockett, Lewis V, 396
Hockett, Lewis V, 397
Hockett, Lewis V, 398
Hockett, Lewis V, 399
Hockett, Lewis V, 683
Hockett, Lewis Edgar V, 396
Hockett, Lillie Perkins VI, 249
Hockett, Lindley V, 396
Hockett, Loes V, 395
Hockett, Loes V, 397
Hockett, Lois V, 337
Hockett, Lois V, 396
Hockett, Lois V, 397
Hockett, Lois V, 413
Hockett, Lorenzo V, 396
Hockett, Lou V, 683
Hockett, Loucinda V, 683
Hockett, Louisa V, 398
Hockett, Louise V, 683
Hockett, Louiza V, 396
Hockett, Louiza V, 398
Hockett, Louzena I, 985
Hockett, Louzena I, 988
Hockett, Lucinda V, 73
Hockett, Lucinda V, 396
Hockett, Lucinda V, 397
Hockett, Lucinda V, 398
Hockett, Lucinda V, 399
Hockett, Lucinda V, 406
Hockett, Lucinda V, 683
Hockett, Lucinda B. V, 418
Hockett, Lucinda J. V, 399
Hockett, Luzena S. I, 988
Hockett, Lydia I, 348
Hockett, Lydia I, 655
Hockett, Lydia I, 656
Hockett, Lydia I, 675
Hockett, Lydia I, 680
Hockett, Lydia I, 683
Hockett, Lydia V, 337
Hockett, Lydia V, 355
Hockett, Lydia V, 394
Hockett, Lydia V, 396
Hockett, Lydia V, 397
Hockett, Lydia V, 398
Hockett, Lydia V, 403
Hockett, Lydia V, 417
Hockett, Lydia V, 425
Hockett, Lydia V, 435
Hockett, Lydia Jane V, 396
Hockett, Mahlon I, 398
Hockett, Mahlon I, 474
Hockett, Mahlon I, 481
Hockett, Mahlon I, 680
Hockett, Mahlon I, 886
Hockett, Mahlon I, 985
Hockett, Mahlon I, 988
Hockett, Mahlon V, 372
Hockett, Mahlon V, 395
Hockett, Mahlon V, 396
Hockett, Mahlon V, 397
Hockett, Mahlon V, 398
Hockett, Mahlon V, 400
Hockett, Mahlon V, 401
Hockett, Mahlon V, 403
Hockett, Mahlon V, 404
Hockett, Mahlon V, 431
Hockett, Mahlon V, 547
Hockett, Mahlon V, 576
Hockett, Mahlon, Jr. V, 398
Hockett, Malon I, 655
Hockett, Malon I, 666
Hockett, Malon I, 680
Hockett, Margaret I, 626
Hockett, Margaret I, 680
Hockett, Margaret D. I, 657
Hockett, Margaret Ellen V, 398
Hockett, Marietta V, 576
Hockett, Martha I, 680
Hockett, Martha V, 326
Hockett, Martha V, 337
Hockett, Martha V, 396
Hockett, Martha E. V, 397
Hockett, Martha E. V, 398
Hockett, Martha Ellen I, 931
Hockett, Martha J. V, 398
Hockett, Martha J. V, 399
Hockett, Martha Jane V, 337
Hockett, Martha Jane V, 396
Hockett, Martha Jane V, 398
Hockett, Martha Jane V, 399
Hockett, Marvin Clinton I, 656
Hockett, Mary I, 721
Hockett, Mary V, 178
Hockett, Mary V, 247
Hockett, Mary V, 337
Hockett, Mary V, 345
Hockett, Mary V, 352
Hockett, Mary V, 384
Hockett, Mary V, 393
Hockett, Mary V, 395
Hockett, Mary V, 396
Hockett, Mary V, 397
Hockett, Mary V, 398
Hockett, Mary V, 400
Hockett, Mary V, 415
Hockett, Mary V, 423
Hockett, Mary A. I, 680
Hockett, Mary A. I, 692
Hockett, Mary A. V, 576
Hockett, Mary Alice I, 656
Hockett, Mary Ann V, 389
Hockett, Mary Ann V, 397
Hockett, Mary Ann V, 398
Hockett, Mary Ann V, 399
Hockett, Mary Ann V, 563
Hockett, Mary Ann V, 576
Hockett, Mary Ann V, 683
Hockett, Mary E. I, 662
Hockett, Mary E. V, 396
Hockett, Mary E. V, 576
Hockett, Mary Eliza I, 656
Hockett, Mary Elizabeth V, 397
Hockett, Mary Etta V, 576
Hockett, Mary Jane I, 655
Hockett, Mary Jane V, 395
Hockett, Mary Jane V, 396
Hockett, Mary Jane V, 398
Hockett, Mary Jane V, 403
Hockett, Mary Roxanna I, 655
Hockett, Mary Roxanna I, 680
Hockett, Mary, Jr. V, 398
Hockett, Matilda V, 248
Hockett, Matilda V, 277
Hockett, Matilda V, 396
Hockett, Matilda V, 398
Hockett, Mattie V, 397
Hockett, Milton I, 656
Hockett, Milton V, 396
Hockett, Milton V, 398
Hockett, Moses V, 162
Hockett, Moses V, 178
Hockett, Moses V, 502
Hockett, Moses, Jr. IV, 60
Hockett, Murray V, 398
Hockett, Myrtle B. V, 576
Hockett, Nancy V, 337
Hockett, Nancy V, 382
Hockett, Nancy V, 395
Hockett, Nancy V, 396
Hockett, Nancy V, 397
Hockett, Nancy V, 398
Hockett, Nancy Elen V, 396
Hockett, Nancy Ellen V, 398
Hockett, Nancy Ellen V, 399
Hockett, Nancy Jane V, 398
Hockett, Nancy Jane V, 576
Hockett, Nancy Jane V, 683
Hockett, Nancy M. I, 677
Hockett, Nancy M. I, 680
Hockett, Nancy Maria I, 655
Hockett, Naomi V, 337
Hockett, Naomi T. V, 73
Hockett, Nathan V, 337
Hockett, Nathan V, 397
Hockett, Nathan V, 398
Hockett, Nathan V, 418
Hockett, Neri V, 395
Hockett, Neri V, 396
Hockett, Neri V, 397
Hockett, Neri V, 431
Hockett, Newton V, 398
Hockett, Newton V, 399
Hockett, Nora I, 656
Hockett, Nuton V, 396
Hockett, Olive V, 162
Hockett, Olive V, 178
Hockett, Olive V, 502
Hockett, Oliver J. V, 337
Hockett, Orpha V, 73
Hockett, Orthey V, 399
Hockett, Oscar B. V, 337
Hockett, Oscar C. I, 656
Hockett, Phebe I, 666
Hockett, Phebe I, 680
Hockett, Phebe I, 687
Hockett, Phebe V, 247
Hockett, Phebe V, 395
Hockett, Phebe V, 397
Hockett, Phebe V, 416
Hockett, Phebe Alice Mary V, 446
Hockett, Phebe Ann V, 337
Hockett, Philip V, 337
Hockett, Phillip I, 398
Hockett, Phillip I, 721
Hockett, Phillip V, 337
Hockett, Pleasant V, 395
Hockett, Pleasant V, 396
Hockett, Pleasant V, 397
Hockett, Pleasant V, 398
Hockett, Polly V, 418
Hockett, Powell V, 337
Hockett, Rachel I, 618
Hockett, Rachel I, 655
Hockett, Rachel I, 656
Hockett, Rachel I, 674
Hockett, Rachel I, 680
Hockett, Rachel V, 326
Hockett, Rachel V, 337
Hockett, Rachel V, 395
Hockett, Rachel V, 396
Hockett, Rachel V, 397
Hockett, Rachel V, 399
Hockett, Rachel V, 415
Hockett, Rachel V, 416
Hockett, Rachel V, 419
Hockett, Rachel V, 431
Hockett, Rachel V, 683
Hockett, Rachel B. I, 661
Hockett, Rachel Rhodema I, 655
Hockett, Rebecca I, 655
Hockett, Rebecca I, 677
Hockett, Rebecca I, 680
Hockett, Rebecca V, 247
Hockett, Rebecca V, 277
Hockett, Rebecca V, 395
Hockett, Rebecca V, 396
Hockett, Rebecca V, 397
Hockett, Rebecca V, 398
Hockett, Rebecca V, 399
Hockett, Rebecca V, 431
Hockett, Rebecca V, 441
Hockett, Rebecca V, 502
Hockett, Rebecca V, 626
Hockett, Rebecca V, 643
Hockett, Rebecca R. V, 248
Hockett, Rebecca S. V, 398
Hockett, Retta V, 576
Hockett, Rhoda V, 73
Hockett, Rhoda A. V, 576
Hockett, Rodema I, 618
Hockett, Ruth I, 680
Hockett, Ruth IV, 60
Hockett, Ruth V, 73
Hockett, Ruth V, 178
Hockett, Ruth V, 386
Hockett, Ruth V, 395
Hockett, Ruth V, 396
Hockett, Ruth V, 397
Hockett, Ruth V, 400
Hockett, Ruth V, 414
Hockett, Ruth V, 416
Hockett, Ruth A. V, 398
Hockett, Sallie I, 329
Hockett, Sally I, 328
Hockett, Sally I, 329
Hockett, Sally I, 655
Hockett, Sally I, 680
Hockett, Samantha V, 337
Hockett, Samantha V, 399
Hockett, Saml. V, 397
Hockett, Samuel I, 398
Hockett, Samuel I, 426
Hockett, Sarah I, 398
Hockett, Sarah I, 481
Hockett, Sarah I, 666
Hockett, Sarah I, 680
Hockett, Sarah I, 681
Hockett, Sarah I, 885
Hockett, Sarah I, 988
Hockett, Sarah V, 247
Hockett, Sarah V, 337
Hockett, Sarah V, 351
Hockett, Sarah V, 395
Hockett, Sarah V, 396
Hockett, Sarah V, 397
Hockett, Sarah V, 398
Hockett, Sarah V, 399
Hockett, Sarah V, 415
Hockett, Sarah V, 446
Hockett, Sarah V, 576
Hockett, Sarah V, 683
Hockett, Sarah A. V, 396
Hockett, Sarah Ann V, 337
Hockett, Sarah Ann V, 399
Hockett, Sarah Ann V, 576
Hockett, Sarah E. I, 680
Hockett, Sarah E. V, 399
Hockett, Sarah E. V, 574
Hockett, Sarah E. V, 911
Hockett, Sarah Elizabeth V, 395
Hockett, Sarah Elizabeth V, 397
Hockett, Sarah Elizabeth V, 431
Hockett, Sarah Elma I, 656
Hockett, Sarah Elma I, 680
Hockett, Sarah Elma V, 574
Hockett, Sarah Elma V, 576
Hockett, Sarah J. I, 308
Hockett, Sarah J. I, 316
Hockett, Sena V, 396
Hockett, Seth V, 247
Hockett, Seth V, 277
Hockett, Seth V, 382
Hockett, Seth V, 395
Hockett, Seth V, 396
Hockett, Seth V, 397
Hockett, Seth V, 398
Hockett, Seth V, 431
Hockett, Seth B. I, 656
Hockett, Seth B. I, 680
Hockett, Seth W. V, 398
Hockett, Sibyl I, 618
Hockett, Sibyl I, 626
Hockett, Sibyl I, 656
Hockett, Sibyl I, 657
Hockett, Sibyl I, 721
Hockett, Sibyl B. I, 662
Hockett, Sibyl B. I, 680
Hockett, Sibyle I, 709
Hockett, Sibyle I, 721
Hockett, Silas V, 396
Hockett, Silas V, 398
Hockett, Silas V, 399
Hockett, Sina V, 399
Hockett, Sinia V, 397
Hockett, Sinia V, 432
Hockett, Sophronia P. I, 680
Hockett, Susan Alice V, 396
Hockett, Susan Alice V, 398
Hockett, Susanna I, 656
Hockett, Susanna V, 396
Hockett, Susanna V, 397
Hockett, Susanna Elma I, 655
Hockett, Susanna Maria I, 656
Hockett, Susannah V, 395
Hockett, Susannah V, 397
Hockett, Susannah V, 401
Hockett, Susannah V, 414
Hockett, Sylvia V, 396
Hockett, Thomas V, 337
Hockett, Thomas V, 396
Hockett, Thomas V, 398
Hockett, Thomas V, 399
Hockett, Thomas A. V, 397
Hockett, Thomas J. I, 656
Hockett, Thomas Lisbon V, 396
Hockett, Thomas Lisbon V, 398
Hockett, Thomas S. V, 398
Hockett, Thos. V, 396
Hockett, Thos. V, 397
Hockett, Uriah V, 395
Hockett, Uriah V, 398
Hockett, Uriah V, 399
Hockett, Uriah V, 911
Hockett, Uriah J. V, 399
Hockett, Warner M. I, 656
Hockett, Warner M. I, 680
Hockett, William I, 328
Hockett, William I, 329
Hockett, William I, 398
Hockett, William I, 655
Hockett, William I, 657
Hockett, William I, 680
Hockett, William I, 709
Hockett, William I, 721
Hockett, William I, 758
Hockett, William I, 764
Hockett, William I, 886
Hockett, William V, 247

Hockett, William V, 396
Hockett, William V, 397
Hockett, William V, 398
Hockett, William V, 399
Hockett, William A. V, 397
Hockett, William B. I, 618
Hockett, William B. I, 656
Hockett, William B. I, 680
Hockett, William C. I, 618
Hockett, William E. I, 634
Hockett, William Edwin V, 395
Hockett, William H. I, 655
Hockett, William P. V, 396
Hockett, William P. V, 398
Hockett, William P. V, 399
Hockett, William W. I, 655
Hockett, William, Sr. I, 656
Hockett, William, Sr. I, 680
Hockett, Wm. I, 348
Hockett, Wm. I, 661
Hockett, Wm. V, 337
Hockett, Wm. V, 397
Hockett, Wm. V, 446
Hockett, Wm. B. I, 626
Hockett, Wm. B. I, 662
Hockett, Wm. E. I, 634
Hockett, Wm. Moon V, 397
Hockett, Wm. P. V, 399
Hockett, Wm. R. V, 396
Hockett, Wm. R. V, 397
Hockett, Woodrow W. V, 576
Hockett, Zimri I, 655
Hockett, Zimri I, 680
Hockett, Zimri V, 395
Hockett, Zimri V, 396
Hockett, Zimri V, 397
Hockett, Zimri V, 398
Hockett, Zimri V, 399
Hockley, Hannah VI, 634
Hockley, Hannah VI, 651
Hockley, Hawkins VI, 651
Hockley, Lydia Ann VI, 634
Hockman, Ada B. V, 399
Hockman, Ada D. V, 399
Hockman, Anna T. V, 399
Hockman, Granville V, 399
Hockman, Granville P. V, 399
Hockman, Michael V, 399
Hockman, Minerva V, 399
Hockman, Rosa Bell V, 399
Hockman, Rosa Belle V, 399
Hockman, Tilford E. V, 399
Hoddock, Thomas T. V, 71
Hodgdon, Belle VI, 739
Hodgdon, Belle VI, 749
Hodgdon, Charles E. VI, 749
Hodgdon, Ella Abby VI, 749
Hodgdon, Ernest Franklin VI, 739
Hodgdon, Ernest Franklin VI, 749
Hodge, Asill II, 444
Hodge, Elizabeth II, 375
Hodge, Ella V, 626
Hodge, Frances II, 375
Hodge, Frances II, 550
Hodge, Frances II, 615
Hodge, Hanah II, 644
Hodge, Henry II, 375
Hodge, Henry II, 464
Hodge, Henry II, 523
Hodge, Henry II, 550
Hodge, Henry II, 615
Hodge, Henry II, 630
Hodge, Henry II, 644
Hodge, Howard V, 683
Hodge, Howard M. VI, 706
Hodge, Jane VI, 490
Hodge, Jane VI, 505
Hodge, John II, 444
Hodge, John Paschall II, 550
Hodge, Knight II, 464
Hodge, Knight II, 550
Hodge, Margaret II, 550
Hodge, Margrett II, 444
Hodge, Mary II, 523
Hodge, Mary II, 550
Hodge, Mary IV, 634
Hodge, Mary IV, 659
Hodge, Mary VI, 389
Hodge, Sarah Ann VI, 706
Hodge, Sarah H. VI, 706
Hodge, Solomon VI, 389
Hodge, Susanna II, 464
Hodge, Susanna II, 550
Hodge, Susanna II, 686
Hodge, Thomas I, 763
Hodge, Wd. Hanah II, 550
Hodge, Wd. Hannah II, 375
Hodgen, ??? IV, 1047
Hodgen, Agnes I, 1048
Hodgen, Ann V, 743
Hodgen, Benjamin I, 764
Hodgen, Daniel G. IV, 1254
Hodgen, David G. IV, 222
Hodgen, Eli IV, 722
Hodgen, Elsie F. IV, 222
Hodgen, Frances Kyne IV, 222
Hodgen, John I, 1048
Hodgen, John I, 1101
Hodgen, John I, 1122
Hodgen, John IV, 1062
Hodgen, Jonathan Theodore IV, 222
Hodgen, Joseph I, 763
Hodgen, Mary I, 1048
Hodgen, Mary IV, 722
Hodgen, Rebecca IV, 722
Hodgen, Robert V, 743
Hodgen, Sarah Jane I, 721
Hodgen, Stephen IV, 722
Hodgens, John I, 398
Hodgens, John E. IV, 1139
Hodgens, Joseph I, 398
Hodgens, Mary V, 501
Hodgens, Mary V, 530
Hodgens, Tamar E. IV, 1139
Hodgens, Theodate I, 398
Hodges, Andrew VI, 933
Hodges, Arnold IV, 1254
Hodges, Benjamin VI, 933
Hodges, Betsey VI, 963
Hodges, Betsy VI, 933
Hodges, Caleb III, 168
Hodges, Caleb H. III, 168
Hodges, Caleb Horatio III, 168
Hodges, Catharine Emma III, 168
Hodges, Charles VI, 825
Hodges, Edgar T. III, 168
Hodges, Eliza I, 634
Hodges, Elizabeth I, 616
Hodges, Elizabeth I, 633
Hodges, Elizabeth I, 634
Hodges, Emma III, 168
Hodges, Emma Hilton III, 168
Hodges, Fanny III, 168
Hodges, Florence III, 168
Hodges, Frances VI, 904
Hodges, Frances VI, 933
Hodges, Frances VI, 950
Hodges, Francis VI, 963
Hodges, Hannah II, 79
Hodges, Harriet S. VI, 933
Hodges, Ida M. I, 922
Hodges, Jane II, 375
Hodges, Jesse VI, 933
Hodges, Jesse VI, 950
Hodges, Jesse VI, 1020
Hodges, John IV, 1237
Hodges, John C. III, 168
Hodges, John Crossley III, 168
Hodges, Joseph Taber III, 168
Hodges, Lavina VI, 825
Hodges, Lillie IV, 222
Hodges, Margaret II, 375
Hodges, Margaret II, 1002
Hodges, Margaret II, 1020
Hodges, Martha D. III, 168
Hodges, Martha Dodrell III, 168
Hodges, Mary II, 375
Hodges, Mary E. VI, 1020
Hodges, Mary Eliza I, 634
Hodges, Mary Hilton III, 168
Hodges, Milton VI, 933
Hodges, Nancy VI, 904
Hodges, Phebe III, 168
Hodges, Phoebe III, 168
Hodges, Polly VI, 933
Hodges, Polly E. VI, 1008
Hodges, Raine A. I, 612
Hodges, Robert, Sr. VI, 933
Hodges, Ruth Emma III, 168
Hodges, Ruth R. III, 168
Hodges, Sally VI, 925
Hodges, Sally VI, 933
Hodges, Samson III, 168
Hodges, Samuel H. III, 168
Hodges, Samuel Horatio Second III, 168
Hodges, Sarah Ann VI, 933
Hodges, Thomas II, 375
Hodges, Thomas II, 550
Hodges, Thomas II, 675
Hodges, Thomas C. VI, 933
Hodges, W. G. IV, 222
Hodggens, Joseph I, 546
Hodggins, Joseph I, 546
Hodggins, Robert I, 645
Hodgin, A. Addison I, 635
Hodgin, Abba IV, 409
Hodgin, Abba IV, 455
Hodgin, Abbie I, 618
Hodgin, Abijah I, 657
Hodgin, Abijah I, 680
Hodgin, Abijah I, 681
Hodgin, Abijah I, 815
Hodgin, Abijah I, 817
Hodgin, Absalom I, 618
Hodgin, Agnes I, 1048
Hodgin, Agnes IV, 149
Hodgin, Agnes IV, 382
Hodgin, Agnes IV, 409
Hodgin, Agness IV, 139
Hodgin, Agness IV, 584
Hodgin, Aileen R. I, 634
Hodgin, Aileen Ross I, 618
Hodgin, Aileen Ross I, 634
Hodgin, Alice IV, 964
Hodgin, Alone P. I, 681
Hodgin, Amos IV, 409
Hodgin, Amos IV, 410
Hodgin, Amos M. I, 658
Hodgin, Amos M. I, 681
Hodgin, Amy I, 398
Hodgin, Amy IV, 149
Hodgin, Amy IV, 379
Hodgin, Amy IV, 409
Hodgin, Amy R. IV, 823
Hodgin, Ann I, 398
Hodgin, Ann I, 680
Hodgin, Ann I, 1047
Hodgin, Ann I, 1048
Hodgin, Ann IV, 149
Hodgin, Ann IV, 409
Hodgin, Ann IV, 584
Hodgin, Ann IV, 600
Hodgin, Ann IV, 1102
Hodgin, Ann IV, 1118
Hodgin, Anna I, 721
Hodgin, Anna I, 724
Hodgin, Anna E. I, 681
Hodgin, Anna J. I, 635
Hodgin, Anna Louise I, 635
Hodgin, Anna Mendenhall I, 634
Hodgin, Annie I, 618
Hodgin, Annie Jay I, 619
Hodgin, Annie Jay I, 622
Hodgin, Annie Louise I, 618
Hodgin, Asa I, 680
Hodgin, Asa M. I, 658
Hodgin, Asenath I, 762
Hodgin, Asenath I, 763
Hodgin, Asenath IV, 149
Hodgin, Asenath IV, 388
Hodgin, Asenath IV, 409
Hodgin, Asenath IV, 443
Hodgin, Asenath IV, 577
Hodgin, Asenath IV, 584
Hodgin, Barclay IV, 409
Hodgin, Barclay IV, 434
Hodgin, Benjamin I, 657
Hodgin, Benjamin I, 764
Hodgin, Benjamin IV, 584
Hodgin, Berneice IV, 823
Hodgin, Bernice I, 10
Hodgin, Bernice I, 939
Hodgin, Bertha Emily I, 289
Hodgin, Broughton I, 613
Hodgin, Bulah I, 614
Hodgin, Bynum I, 618
Hodgin, Bynum I, 634
Hodgin, Caroline M. I, 606
Hodgin, Caroline M. I, 763
Hodgin, Catharine I, 763
Hodgin, Catharine W. I, 634
Hodgin, Charles IV, 1062
Hodgin, Charles IV, 1133
Hodgin, Charles Broughton I, 619
Hodgin, Chas. Broughton I, 618
Hodgin, Clara Francis I, 10
Hodgin, Clarkson IV, 409
Hodgin, Clarkson IV, 442
Hodgin, Clarkson IV, 1062
Hodgin, Clarkson IV, 1133
Hodgin, Content I, 376
Hodgin, Content I, 398
Hodgin, Cora Eva I, 289
Hodgin, Cordelia I, 617
Hodgin, Cordelia B. I, 657
Hodgin, D. L. I, 658
Hodgin, Daniel IV, 383
Hodgin, Daniel IV, 409
Hodgin, Daniel IV, 410
Hodgin, Daniel IV, 1101
Hodgin, Daniel IV, 1102
Hodgin, Daniel W. IV, 409
Hodgin, Daniel W. IV, 1102
Hodgin, David I, 618
Hodgin, David I, 619
Hodgin, David I, 657
Hodgin, David I, 681
Hodgin, David Franklin I, 657
Hodgin, David G. IV, 222
Hodgin, David L. I, 681
Hodgin, David Lindley I, 657
Hodgin, David Lindley I, 658
Hodgin, David R. I, 634
Hodgin, David Reid I, 618
Hodgin, David S. I, 658
Hodgin, David S. I, 681
Hodgin, Davis S. I, 658
Hodgin, Deborah I, 657
Hodgin, Deborah I, 680
Hodgin, Deborah I, 884
Hodgin, Deborah A. I, 681
Hodgin, Deborah A. I, 689
Hodgin, Deborah Ann I, 657
Hodgin, Deborah Ann I, 658
Hodgin, Delilah I, 677
Hodgin, Delilah I, 681
Hodgin, Dicks I, 658
Hodgin, Dicks I, 680
Hodgin, Dora I, 618
Hodgin, Dorcas I, 398
Hodgin, Dorcas I, 416
Hodgin, Dorcas I, 680
Hodgin, Dwight H. I, 634
Hodgin, E. B. I, 634
Hodgin, Ed J. I, 614
Hodgin, Ed. A. I, 618
Hodgin, Edgar A. I, 681
Hodgin, Edmund C. Stanton IV, 410
Hodgin, Edward I, 634
Hodgin, Edwin IV, 409
Hodgin, Edwin IV, 1102
Hodgin, Edwin B. I, 618
Hodgin, Edwin B. I, 657
Hodgin, Edwin C. IV, 1062
Hodgin, Edwin E. IV, 409
Hodgin, Eleanor I, 680
Hodgin, Eli IV, 149
Hodgin, Eli IV, 376
Hodgin, Eli IV, 388
Hodgin, Eli IV, 409
Hodgin, Eli IV, 410
Hodgin, Eli IV, 1062
Hodgin, Eli IV, 1089
Hodgin, Eli IV, 1101
Hodgin, Eli, Jr. IV, 410
Hodgin, Elias I, 602
Hodgin, Elias I, 606
Hodgin, Elias I, 763
Hodgin, Elias IV, 409
Hodgin, Elias IV, 584
Hodgin, Elias IV, 1062
Hodgin, Elias IV, 1102
Hodgin, Elisabeth I, 618
Hodgin, Elisabeth White I, 613
Hodgin, Eliza I, 681
Hodgin, Elizabeth I, 658
Hodgin, Elizabeth I, 680
Hodgin, Elizabeth I, 684
Hodgin, Elizabeth I, 817
Hodgin, Elizabeth IV, 149
Hodgin, Elizabeth IV, 379
Hodgin, Elizabeth IV, 409
Hodgin, Elizabeth IV, 441
Hodgin, Elizabeth IV, 442
Hodgin, Elizabeth IV, 1101
Hodgin, Elma E. I, 658
Hodgin, Elsie F. IV, 222
Hodgin, Elza IV, 964
Hodgin, Emerson I, 657
Hodgin, Emily I, 619
Hodgin, Emily M. I, 619
Hodgin, Erastus W. I, 602
Hodgin, Esther I, 658
Hodgin, Esther I, 680
Hodgin, Esther I, 690
Hodgin, Esther I, 763
Hodgin, Esther I, 930
Hodgin, Esther IV, 1102
Hodgin, Esther Bernice I, 922
Hodgin, Esther Bundy IV, 409
Hodgin, Esther J. I, 676
Hodgin, Esther J. I, 681
Hodgin, Eunice I, 623
Hodgin, Eunice I, 658
Hodgin, Eunice I, 681
Hodgin, Eunice I, 691
Hodgin, Eunice IV, 409
Hodgin, Eunice IV, 445
Hodgin, Eunice Eleanor I, 658
Hodgin, Eva I, 613
Hodgin, Eva E. I, 618
Hodgin, Eva E. I, 634
Hodgin, Ezekiel IV, 409
Hodgin, Fatima J. I, 681
Hodgin, Fatima J. I, 689
Hodgin, Fatima Jane I, 658
Hodgin, Fatima Jane I, 681
Hodgin, Flarrs A. I, 681
Hodgin, Frances IV, 409
Hodgin, Frances IV, 1062
Hodgin, Frances IV, 1102
Hodgin, Frances IV, 1108
Hodgin, Frances Chase I, 618
Hodgin, Francis IV, 409
Hodgin, Francis IV, 1102
Hodgin, Francis T. I, 657
Hodgin, George I, 613
Hodgin, George Fox I, 658
Hodgin, George M. I, 634
Hodgin, George M. I, 681
Hodgin, George Marion I, 618
Hodgin, George W. I, 657
Hodgin, George W. I, 681
Hodgin, Gerney Edgar I, 289
Hodgin, Gurney I, 681
Hodgin, H. A. I, 618
Hodgin, Hannah I, 657
Hodgin, Hannah I, 658
Hodgin, Hannah I, 680
Hodgin, Hannah I, 681
Hodgin, Hannah I, 815
Hodgin, Hannah I, 817
Hodgin, Hannah I, 1041
Hodgin, Hannah C. I, 681
Hodgin, Hannah C. I, 689
Hodgin, Hannah Caroline I, 65
Hodgin, Hannah Caroline I, 68
Hodgin, Hannah P. IV, 1158
Hodgin, Hannah P. IV, 1165
Hodgin, Hariet IV, 1102
Hodgin, Harriet IV, 395
Hodgin, Harriet IV, 410
Hodgin, Harriet IV, 1102
Hodgin, Hattie E. I, 681
Hodgin, Hattie N. I, 657
Hodgin, Hattie N. I, 681
Hodgin, Henry I, 681
Hodgin, Henry I, 721
Hodgin, Henry A. I, 681
Hodgin, Hulda Jane I, 657
Hodgin, Huldah I, 626
Hodgin, Huldah I. I, 681
Hodgin, Huldah I. I, 689
Hodgin, Huldah L. J. I, 615
Hodgin, Ida M. I, 10
Hodgin, Ida M. I, 922
Hodgin, Ida M. IV, 477
Hodgin, Ida M. IV, 823
Hodgin, Irena Jane I, 681
Hodgin, Irene Jane I, 657
Hodgin, Irving C. I, 634
Hodgin, Irving Chase I, 657
Hodgin, Isaac C. I, 657
Hodgin, J. Addison I, 634
Hodgin, J. Ed. I, 618
Hodgin, Jabez I, 286
Hodgin, Jabez I, 289
Hodgin, Jabez I, 618
Hodgin, Jabez I, 657
Hodgin, Jabez C. I, 657
Hodgin, James I, 718
Hodgin, James I, 721
Hodgin, James I, 741
Hodgin, James I, 763
Hodgin, James A. I, 634
Hodgin, James A. I, 681
Hodgin, James Addison I, 618
Hodgin, James Addison I, 657
Hodgin, James M. I, 681
Hodgin, James W. I, 657
Hodgin, Jane I, 657
Hodgin, Jane I, 680
Hodgin, Jane I, 681
Hodgin, Jane I, 763
Hodgin, Jane I, 884
Hodgin, Jane I, 894
Hodgin, Jane IV, 409
Hodgin, Jas. A. I, 634
Hodgin, Jemima I, 398
Hodgin, Jemima I, 419
Hodgin, Jesse IV, 409
Hodgin, Jesse A. I, 634
Hodgin, Jesse Augustine I, 618
Hodgin, Jesse D. IV, 1101
Hodgin, Joab I, 398
Hodgin, John I, 398
Hodgin, John I, 657
Hodgin, John I, 658
Hodgin, John I, 681
Hodgin, John I, 817
Hodgin, John I, 1041
Hodgin, John I, 1048
Hodgin, John IV, 149
Hodgin, John IV, 365
Hodgin, John IV, 409
Hodgin, John IV, 410
Hodgin, John IV, 584
Hodgin, John IV, 1062

gin, John D. I, 602
gin, John E. I, 618
gin, John E. I, 634
gin, John E. I, 635
gin, John E. IV, 409
gin, John E. IV, 964
gin, John E. IV, 1102
gin, John E., Jr. I, 618
gin, John Edgerton IV, 584
gin, John Franklin I, 658
gin, John Garney I, 619
gin, John Gurney I, 619
gin, John Osker I, 657
gin, John T. I, 657
gin, John T. I, 681
gin, John, Jr. I, 546
gin, Jonathan I, 657
gin, Jonathan I, 658
gin, Jonathan I, 680
gin, Jonathan I, 681
gin, Jonathan I, 856
gin, Jonathan I, 884
gin, Jonathan B. I, 681
gin, Jonathan Backhouse I, 657
gin, Jonathan Theodore IV, 222
gin, Jonathan, Jr. I, 657
gin, Jonathan, Jr. I, 681
gin, Jonathan, Jr. I, 884
gin, Jonathan, Jr. I, 894
gin, Jonathan, Sr. I, 657
gin, Joseph I, 398
gin, Joseph I, 546
gin, Joseph I, 618
gin, Joseph I, 635
gin, Joseph I, 657
gin, Joseph I, 658
gin, Joseph I, 680
gin, Joseph I, 681
gin, Joseph I, 763
gin, Joseph IV, 584
gin, Joseph A. I, 657
gin, Joseph A. I, 681
gin, Joseph Brantingham IV, 823
gin, Joseph J. I, 681
gin, Joseph John Gurney I, 657
gin, Joseph W. I, 602
gin, Joseph, Jr. I, 681
gin, Joshua I, 680
gin, Josiah I, 763
gin, Joushua I, 398
gin, Julia I, 398
gin, Julia I, 618
gin, Julia I, 619
gin, Julia I, 625
gin, Julia I, 627
gin, Julia Blair I, 618
gin, Julia Blair I, 634
gin, Julia E. I, 681
gin, Junius R. I, 657
gin, Junius R. I, 681
gin, Kate I, 618
gin, Kate Cheston I, 619
gin, Katharine I, 763
gin, Kyle C. I, 635
gin, Kyle Colwell I, 618
gin, Laban IV, 149
gin, Laban IV, 409
gin, Laura I, 614
gin, Laura I, 619
gin, Laura I, 624
gin, Laura P. I, 634
gin, Lavina E. I, 602
gin, Leah IV, 409
gin, Leah IV, 1062
gin, Leake IV, 584
gin, Lenna IV, 477
gin, Lennah I, 10
gin, Leroy I, 618
gin, Linney I, 657
gin, Louisa I, 634
gin, Louisa I, 658
gin, Luzena I, 680
gin, Luzena M. I, 602
gin, Lydia I, 1048
gin, Lydia IV, 408
gin, Lydia IV, 409
gin, Lydia IV, 600
gin, Lydia Jane IV, 1102
gin, Lydia Jane IV, 1118
gin, Lydia Martitia I, 658
gin, Lydie IV, 409
gin, M. Cora I, 635
gin, Mammie Dowd I, 618
gin, Margaret I, 10
gin, Margaret I, 657
gin, Margaret I, 658
gin, Margaret I, 680
Hodgin, Margaret I, 681
Hodgin, Margaret I, 690
Hodgin, Margaret IV, 409
Hodgin, Margaret IV, 1101
Hodgin, Margaret IV, 1102
Hodgin, Margaret IV, 1122
Hodgin, Margaret Edna I, 657
Hodgin, Margery IV, 964
Hodgin, Margery Alice IV, 964
Hodgin, Maria IV, 514
Hodgin, Maria IV, 531
Hodgin, Marian I, 635
Hodgin, Martha I, 618
Hodgin, Martha I, 619
Hodgin, Martha I, 657
Hodgin, Martha I, 681
Hodgin, Martha I, 884
Hodgin, Martha IV, 149
Hodgin, Martha IV, 382
Hodgin, Martha IV, 409
Hodgin, Martha IV, 410
Hodgin, Martha IV, 444
Hodgin, Martha IV, 1101
Hodgin, Martha IV, 1102
Hodgin, Martha IV, 1113
Hodgin, Martha A. I, 904
Hodgin, Martha Ann I, 658
Hodgin, Martha Blanch I, 618
Hodgin, Martha D. I, 615
Hodgin, Martha Doraline I, 618
Hodgin, Martha Doraline I, 635
Hodgin, Martha Eleanor I, 657
Hodgin, Martha M. I, 618
Hodgin, Martitia I, 657
Hodgin, Martitia I, 679
Hodgin, Martitia I, 681
Hodgin, Martitia Jane I, 681
Hodgin, Mary I, 398
Hodgin, Mary I, 546
Hodgin, Mary I, 614
Hodgin, Mary I, 618
Hodgin, Mary I, 1048
Hodgin, Mary IV, 139
Hodgin, Mary IV, 149
Hodgin, Mary IV, 365
Hodgin, Mary IV, 388
Hodgin, Mary IV, 409
Hodgin, Mary IV, 441
Hodgin, Mary IV, 455
Hodgin, Mary IV, 584
Hodgin, Mary IV, 1062
Hodgin, Mary IV, 1102
Hodgin, Mary A. I, 884
Hodgin, Mary Ann I, 398
Hodgin, Mary Ann I, 416
Hodgin, Mary Ann IV, 409
Hodgin, Mary E. IV, 409
Hodgin, Mary E. IV, 434
Hodgin, Mary E. IV, 584
Hodgin, Mary E. IV, 596
Hodgin, Mary Eliza IV, 1101
Hodgin, Mary Eliza IV, 1102
Hodgin, Mary Elizabeth I, 658
Hodgin, Mary Esther IV, 803
Hodgin, Mary Esther IV, 823
Hodgin, Mary Esther IV, 1133
Hodgin, Mary J. I, 481
Hodgin, Mary J. I, 677
Hodgin, Mary J. I, 681
Hodgin, Mary Jane I, 615
Hodgin, Mary Jane I, 617
Hodgin, Mary Jane I, 618
Hodgin, Mary Jane I, 657
Hodgin, Mary Jane I, 681
Hodgin, Mary L. IV, 1092
Hodgin, Mary L. IV, 1102
Hodgin, Mary V. I, 657
Hodgin, Matilda I, 602
Hodgin, Matilda IV, 575
Hodgin, Matilda IV, 584
Hodgin, Maud E. I, 618
Hodgin, Maude Kirkman I, 635
Hodgin, Melinda I, 763
Hodgin, Melinda I, 767
Hodgin, Micaijah I, 658
Hodgin, Micaijah C. I, 657
Hodgin, Micajah C. I, 658
Hodgin, Micajah C. I, 680
Hodgin, Micajah C. I, 689
Hodgin, Minnie I, 635
Hodgin, Miriam I, 658
Hodgin, Miriam Pauline I, 618
Hodgin, Miriam Pauline I, 634
Hodgin, Mornen I, 757
Hodgin, Mornen I, 763
Hodgin, Mournen I, 763
Hodgin, Mozelle I, 10
Hodgin, Nancy I, 657
Hodgin, Nancy I, 681
Hodgin, Nancy I, 856
Hodgin, Nancy IV, 365
Hodgin, Nancy IV, 409
Hodgin, Nancy IV, 1062
Hodgin, Nancy Eliza I, 657
Hodgin, Nannie L. I, 481
Hodgin, Nathan I, 680
Hodgin, Nathan I, 681
Hodgin, Nathan I, 757
Hodgin, Nathan I, 763
Hodgin, Nellie I, 613
Hodgin, Nellie A. I, 634
Hodgin, Nellie Armfield I, 618
Hodgin, Nereus I, 657
Hodgin, Nereus I, 884
Hodgin, Nereus M. I, 884
Hodgin, Olive I, 635
Hodgin, Olive J. I, 619
Hodgin, Olive J. I, 635
Hodgin, Olive J. V, 683
Hodgin, Olive M. V, 683
Hodgin, Olive Mariam I, 619
Hodgin, Olive Marion I, 635
Hodgin, Olive Marion V, 683
Hodgin, Pauline I, 618
Hodgin, Peter I, 657
Hodgin, Phebe Jane I, 657
Hodgin, Phebe Jane I, 681
Hodgin, Prudence IV, 365
Hodgin, Prudence IV, 409
Hodgin, Prudence IV, 410
Hodgin, Prudence IV, 584
Hodgin, Prudence IV, 1062
Hodgin, Prudence IV, 1101
Hodgin, Prudence IV, 1102
Hodgin, R. Rodema I, 657
Hodgin, Rachel I, 10
Hodgin, Rachel I, 657
Hodgin, Rachel I, 680
Hodgin, Rachel I, 681
Hodgin, Rachel E. I, 10
Hodgin, Rebeca I, 720
Hodgin, Rebeca I, 721
Hodgin, Rebecca I, 658
Hodgin, Rebecca I, 681
Hodgin, Rebecca I, 718
Hodgin, Rebecca I, 721
Hodgin, Rebecca IV, 374
Hodgin, Rebecca IV, 386
Hodgin, Rebecca IV, 400
Hodgin, Rebecca IV, 409
Hodgin, Rebecca IV, 762
Hodgin, Rebecca M. I, 721
Hodgin, Rebecca M. I, 722
Hodgin, Robert I, 398
Hodgin, Robert I, 680
Hodgin, Robert I, 1041
Hodgin, Robert IV, 409
Hodgin, Robert IV, 584
Hodgin, Robert A. I, 681
Hodgin, Robert L. I, 657
Hodgin, Rodema I, 618
Hodgin, Rodema I, 634
Hodgin, Roy I, 635
Hodgin, Ruth I, 657
Hodgin, Ruth I, 680
Hodgin, Ruth I, 711
Hodgin, Ruth I, 721
Hodgin, Ruth I, 763
Hodgin, Ruth I, 817
Hodgin, Ruth Ann I, 657
Hodgin, Ruth Ann I, 658
Hodgin, Ruth H. I, 634
Hodgin, Ruth Harriet I, 618
Hodgin, Ruthanna IV, 409
Hodgin, Ruthanna IV, 1102
Hodgin, S. A. I, 635
Hodgin, Sallie I, 658
Hodgin, Sally I, 657
Hodgin, Sally I, 680
Hodgin, Sally I, 681
Hodgin, Sam'l H. I, 635
Hodgin, Sam'l H., Jr. I, 635
Hodgin, Samuel I, 635
Hodgin, Samuel H. I, 619
Hodgin, Samuel H. I, 635
Hodgin, Samuel H. V, 683
Hodgin, Samuel H., Jr. I, 619
Hodgin, Samuel H., Jr. I, 635
Hodgin, Samuel H., Jr. V, 683
Hodgin, Samuel Horace, Jr. V, 683
Hodgin, Sarah I, 289
Hodgin, Sarah I, 305
Hodgin, Sarah I, 308
Hodgin, Sarah I, 343
Hodgin, Sarah I, 398
Hodgin, Sarah I, 402
Hodgin, Sarah I, 615
Hodgin, Sarah I, 618
Hodgin, Sarah I, 623
Hodgin, Sarah I, 657
Hodgin, Sarah I, 658
Hodgin, Sarah I, 669
Hodgin, Sarah I, 679
Hodgin, Sarah I, 680
Hodgin, Sarah I, 681
Hodgin, Sarah I, 689
Hodgin, Sarah IV, 149
Hodgin, Sarah IV, 376
Hodgin, Sarah IV, 382
Hodgin, Sarah IV, 409
Hodgin, Sarah IV, 410
Hodgin, Sarah IV, 422
Hodgin, Sarah IV, 531
Hodgin, Sarah IV, 964
Hodgin, Sarah IV, 1062
Hodgin, Sarah IV, 1068
Hodgin, Sarah IV, 1088
Hodgin, Sarah IV, 1089
Hodgin, Sarah IV, 1101
Hodgin, Sarah IV, 1102
Hodgin, Sarah IV, 1133
Hodgin, Sarah V, 246
Hodgin, Sarah A. I, 602
Hodgin, Sarah A. I, 678
Hodgin, Sarah A. I, 681
Hodgin, Sarah E. I, 286
Hodgin, Sarah E. I, 657
Hodgin, Sarah E. I, 678
Hodgin, Sarah E. I, 681
Hodgin, Sarah Elizabeth I, 657
Hodgin, Sarah Hiatt I, 657
Hodgin, Sarah Hiatt I, 681
Hodgin, Sarah J. I, 721
Hodgin, Sarah Jane I, 721
Hodgin, Sarah M. IV, 409
Hodgin, Sarah M. IV, 410
Hodgin, Sarah M. IV, 1062
Hodgin, Sarah P. IV, 964
Hodgin, Sarah S. I, 286
Hodgin, Sarah V. I, 681
Hodgin, Sarah Verlinda I, 657
Hodgin, Scott I, 635
Hodgin, Shobar I, 10
Hodgin, Shubal I, 618
Hodgin, Shubal I, 622
Hodgin, Shubal G. I, 634
Hodgin, Shubal G. I, 681
Hodgin, Shubal Gurney I, 619
Hodgin, Simeon A. I, 634
Hodgin, Simeon Addison I, 619
Hodgin, Simeon Addison I, 624
Hodgin, Sina M. IV, 410
Hodgin, Sina M. IV, 442
Hodgin, Solomon I, 398
Hodgin, Solomon I, 658
Hodgin, Solomon I, 680
Hodgin, Sophronia I, 681
Hodgin, Sophronia E. I, 681
Hodgin, Sophronia Emiline I, 658
Hodgin, Sophronia Page I, 657
Hodgin, Stephen I, 623
Hodgin, Stephen I, 721
Hodgin, Stephen IV, 149
Hodgin, Stephen IV, 379
Hodgin, Stephen IV, 409
Hodgin, Stephen IV, 410
Hodgin, Stephen IV, 441
Hodgin, Stephen IV, 455
Hodgin, Stephen IV, 531
Hodgin, Stephen IV, 584
Hodgin, Stephen IV, 722
Hodgin, Stephen IV, 762
Hodgin, Stephen IV, 823
Hodgin, Stephen IV, 1062
Hodgin, Stephen IV, 1068
Hodgin, Stephen IV, 1101
Hodgin, Stephen IV, 1133
Hodgin, Stephen H. I, 721
Hodgin, Stephen P. I, 615
Hodgin, Stephen, Jr. IV, 409
Hodgin, Stephen, Jr. IV, 422
Hodgin, Sydnor Gladstone I, 619
Hodgin, T. C. IV, 477
Hodgin, T. C. IV, 823
Hodgin, Tabitha O. I, 289
Hodgin, Tamar IV, 409
Hodgin, Tamer I, 658
Hodgin, Tamer I, 680
Hodgin, Tamer IV, 1101
Hodgin, Tamer IV, 1102
Hodgin, Tamer D. IV, 1102
Hodgin, Tamer Jane IV, 1101
Hodgin, Tamer Jane IV, 1102
Hodgin, Tamir D. IV, 964
Hodgin, Tamor IV, 383
Hodgin, Tamor IV, 410
Hodgin, Theodate I, 398
Hodgin, Thomas I, 658
Hodgin, Thomas C. I, 10
Hodgin, Thomas C. I, 634
Hodgin, Thomas C. I, 657
Hodgin, Thomas C. I, 681
Hodgin, Thomas C. I, 922
Hodgin, Thomas C. IV, 477
Hodgin, Thomas E. I, 308
Hodgin, Thomas E. I, 681
Hodgin, Thomas Elbridge I, 289
Hodgin, Thomas Elbridge I, 657
Hodgin, Thomas George Fox I, 10
Hodgin, Thomas Thomasson IV, 584
Hodgin, Thos. IV, 823
Hodgin, Velna I, 623
Hodgin, Velna I, 634
Hodgin, Velna R. I, 681
Hodgin, Velna R. I, 683
Hodgin, Vivian I, 657
Hodgin, Vivian R. I, 618
Hodgin, Vivian R. I, 634
Hodgin, W. Milton I, 681
Hodgin, Waldeen Mendenhall I, 619
Hodgin, Walter I, 634
Hodgin, Walter T. I, 634
Hodgin, Widow Esther I, 657
Hodgin, Widow Sarah I, 658
Hodgin, Willard Scott I, 658
Hodgin, William I, 658
Hodgin, William I, 681
Hodgin, William I, 1048
Hodgin, William IV, 409
Hodgin, William IV, 410
Hodgin, William IV, 584
Hodgin, William IV, 1062
Hodgin, William A. I, 681
Hodgin, William H. H. I, 602
Hodgin, William L. I, 658
Hodgin, William M. I, 681
Hodgin, William S. I, 681
Hodgin, William V. I, 398
Hodgin, William Wyatt I, 658
Hodgin, Wilson IV, 514
Hodgin, Wilson IV, 531
Hodgin, Wilson IV, 1062
Hodgin, Wilson IV, 1133
Hodgin, Wm. IV, 139
Hodgin, Wm. IV, 149
Hodgin, Wm. IV, 382
Hodgin, Wm. IV, 409
Hodgin, Wm. IV, 455
Hodgin, Wm. IV, 584
Hodgin, Wm. IV, 1101
Hodgin, Wm. IV, 1102
Hodgin, Wm. IV, 1122
Hodgin, Wm. Abijah I, 657
Hodgin, Wm. Schooley IV, 409
Hodgin, Worth I, 657
Hodgin, Wyatt Yancey I, 681
Hodgin, Zebulon I, 657
Hodgin, Zimri I, 657
Hodgin, Zimri I, 658
Hodgin, Zimri I, 669
Hodgin, Zimri I, 681
Hodgins, Agnes IV, 386
Hodgins, Arnold IV, 1254
Hodgins, Caroline M. I, 763
Hodgins, Charles IV, 1133
Hodgins, Clarkson IV, 1133
Hodgins, Daniel IV, 1254
Hodgins, Daniel G. IV, 1254
Hodgins, David G. IV, 1254
Hodgins, Eli IV, 390
Hodgins, Eli IV, 1133
Hodgins, Elizabeth II, 1002
Hodgins, Elsie IV, 1254
Hodgins, Elsie F. IV, 1254
Hodgins, Frances IV, 1254
Hodgins, G. Arnold IV, 1254
Hodgins, Hannah I, 817
Hodgins, Henry S. IV, 531
Hodgins, Jennie IV, 1254
Hodgins, Joab I, 398
Hodgins, Joab I, 426
Hodgins, John I, 398
Hodgins, John I, 425
Hodgins, John I, 1122
Hodgins, John E. IV, 1133
Hodgins, Jonathan IV, 1254
Hodgins, Joseph I, 741
Hodgins, Maria IV, 531
Hodgins, Maria B. IV, 531
Hodgins, Mary I, 398
Hodgins, Mary I, 425
Hodgins, Mary I, 426
Hodgins, Mary I, 546
Hodgins, Mary IV, 149
Hodgins, Mary IV, 390
Hodgins, Mary IV, 587
Hodgins, Mary IV, 1133
Hodgins, Mary Esther IV, 1133
Hodgins, Mendel IV, 1254
Hodgins, Rebecca IV, 386
Hodgins, Robert I, 398

Hodgins, Robert V, 794
Hodgins, Sarah IV, 531
Hodgins, Sarah IV, 1133
Hodgins, Sarah B. IV, 531
Hodgins, Sarah M. IV, 1062
Hodgins, Sarah P. IV, 531
Hodgins, Stephen IV, 531
Hodgins, Stephen IV, 1133
Hodgins, Tamer D. IV, 1133
Hodgins, Wilson IV, 531
Hodgins, Wilson IV, 1133
Hodgins, Wm. IV, 386
Hodgkins, Bridget II, 523
Hodgkins, Bridget II, 550
Hodgkins, Mary II, 79
Hodgkins, Mary II, 97
Hodgkins, Mary II, 550
Hodgkins, Thomas II, 79
Hodgkins, Thomas II, 97
Hodgkins, Thomas II, 550
Hodgskin, Mary II, 550
Hodgskin, Thomas II, 550
Hodgson, ??? II, 375
Hodgson, Abigail I, 546
Hodgson, Abigail I, 572
Hodgson, Abigail I, 659
Hodgson, Abigail V, 247
Hodgson, Abigail V, 338
Hodgson, Abigail F. I, 547
Hodgson, Abner VI, 597
Hodgson, Achsah I, 537
Hodgson, Achsah I, 547
Hodgson, Achsah V, 469
Hodgson, Achsah V, 501
Hodgson, Achsah V, 626
Hodgson, Acsah V, 73
Hodgson, Alice II, 1002
Hodgson, Alice II, 1021
Hodgson, Allen V, 337
Hodgson, Allen V, 338
Hodgson, Allen V, 626
Hodgson, Alonzo V, 247
Hodgson, Amos I, 547
Hodgson, Amos I, 783
Hodgson, Amos V, 73
Hodgson, Amos V, 469
Hodgson, Amos V, 501
Hodgson, Amos V, 626
Hodgson, Ann I, 546
Hodgson, Ann I, 547
Hodgson, Ann I, 658
Hodgson, Ann I, 817
Hodgson, Ann V, 230
Hodgson, Ann V, 246
Hodgson, Ann V, 247
Hodgson, Anna II, 707
Hodgson, Anna II, 746
Hodgson, Anna V, 247
Hodgson, Anna V, 338
Hodgson, Anna V, 446
Hodgson, Anna V, 501
Hodgson, Ariedna I, 547
Hodgson, Armilly Adelia I, 547
Hodgson, Bathsheba C. I, 547
Hodgson, Benjamin I, 658
Hodgson, Benjamin V, 246
Hodgson, Benjamin V, 337
Hodgson, Carey V, 683
Hodgson, Carey V. V, 683
Hodgson, Caroline II, 746
Hodgson, Carrie V. V, 683
Hodgson, Charity I, 658
Hodgson, Charity V, 246
Hodgson, Charity V, 247
Hodgson, Chloe V, 246
Hodgson, Chloe V, 247
Hodgson, Christopher Hiatt I, 547
Hodgson, Cloe I, 547
Hodgson, Cloey I, 501
Hodgson, Cyrus V, 247
Hodgson, Cyrus V, 338
Hodgson, Cyrus L. V, 626
Hodgson, Daniel I, 547
Hodgson, Daniel II, 375
Hodgson, Daniel II, 1002
Hodgson, Daniel V, 626
Hodgson, Daniell II, 375
Hodgson, David I, 547
Hodgson, David I, 658
Hodgson, David I, 783
Hodgson, Deborah VI, 400
Hodgson, Deborah VI, 592
Hodgson, Deborah VI, 597
Hodgson, Delilah V, 247
Hodgson, Delilah V, 337
Hodgson, Dr. ??? II, 375
Hodgson, Drucilla V, 626
Hodgson, Edith V, 626
Hodgson, Edith V, 683
Hodgson, Eli I, 501
Hodgson, Eli I, 547
Hodgson, Elisabeth I, 817
Hodgson, Eliza H. V, 246
Hodgson, Eliza P. I, 547
Hodgson, Elizabeth I, 501
Hodgson, Elizabeth I, 546
Hodgson, Elizabeth I, 547
Hodgson, Elizabeth I, 562
Hodgson, Elizabeth I, 578
Hodgson, Elizabeth I, 817
Hodgson, Elizabeth I, 884
Hodgson, Elizabeth II, 746
Hodgson, Elizabeth V, 73
Hodgson, Elizabeth V, 247
Hodgson, Elizabeth V, 337
Hodgson, Elizabeth V, 501
Hodgson, Elizabeth VI, 400
Hodgson, Elizabeth H. II, 746
Hodgson, Elizabeth R. II, 707
Hodgson, Elizabeth R. II, 946
Hodgson, Elizabeth R. II, 1087
Hodgson, Elizabeth R. II, 1088
Hodgson, Ellsworth V, 626
Hodgson, Emily V, 246
Hodgson, Emily V, 247
Hodgson, Emma IV, 410
Hodgson, Enos V, 247
Hodgson, Enos V, 337
Hodgson, Enos V, 338
Hodgson, Esther VI, 400
Hodgson, Esther VI, 597
Hodgson, Flavious V, 247
Hodgson, Flavious J. V, 246
Hodgson, Flavius V, 246
Hodgson, Flavius V, 247
Hodgson, Geo. V, 338
Hodgson, George I, 487
Hodgson, George I, 546
Hodgson, George I, 547
Hodgson, George I, 817
Hodgson, George V, 215
Hodgson, George V, 246
Hodgson, George V, 268
Hodgson, George V, 337
Hodgson, George, Jr. I, 546
Hodgson, George, Jr. I, 564
Hodgson, George, Jr. V, 338
Hodgson, H. Clay VI, 400
Hodgson, Hannah I, 887
Hodgson, Hannah I, 1009
Hodgson, Hannah I, 1010
Hodgson, Hannah V, 246
Hodgson, Hannah V, 337
Hodgson, Hannah V, 338
Hodgson, Hannah V, 340
Hodgson, Hannah V, 446
Hodgson, Hannah V, 501
Hodgson, Hannah V, 509
Hodgson, Hannah VI, 597
Hodgson, Hannah A. VI, 400
Hodgson, Hannah A. VI, 461
Hodgson, Hannah W. VI, 400
Hodgson, Henry I, 658
Hodgson, Henry V, 246
Hodgson, Henry V, 337
Hodgson, Her V, 73
Hodgson, Hezekiah I, 501
Hodgson, Hezekiah V, 247
Hodgson, Hezekiah V, 446
Hodgson, Hur I, 537
Hodgson, Hur I, 546
Hodgson, Hur I, 547
Hodgson, Hur I, 578
Hodgson, Hur I, 817
Hodgson, Hur V, 501
Hodgson, Hur V, 626
Hodgson, Ira V, 501
Hodgson, Isaac I, 547
Hodgson, Isaac I, 817
Hodgson, Isaac II, 1002
Hodgson, Isaac V, 73
Hodgson, Isaac V, 501
Hodgson, Isaac V, 509
Hodgson, Isabel L. I, 547
Hodgson, Isaiah V, 626
Hodgson, James V, 337
Hodgson, James VI, 400
Hodgson, Jane V, 221
Hodgson, Jane V, 246
Hodgson, Jane V, 337
Hodgson, Jane V, 348
Hodgson, Jane V, 446
Hodgson, Jane V, 626
Hodgson, Jane Ann V, 246
Hodgson, Jehu I, 547
Hodgson, Jehu V, 73
Hodgson, Jehu V, 501
Hodgson, Jehu V, 626
Hodgson, Jemima V, 247
Hodgson, Jemima V, 501
Hodgson, Jess I, 884
Hodgson, Jesse V, 73
Hodgson, Jesse V, 501
Hodgson, Jesse V, 626
Hodgson, Joel I, 501
Hodgson, Joel I, 547
Hodgson, Joel V, 501
Hodgson, John I, 546
Hodgson, John I, 547
Hodgson, John I, 658
Hodgson, John I, 659
Hodgson, John I, 884
Hodgson, John V, 73
Hodgson, John V, 178
Hodgson, John V, 221
Hodgson, John V, 230
Hodgson, John V, 246
Hodgson, John V, 247
Hodgson, John V, 264
Hodgson, John V, 337
Hodgson, John V, 338
Hodgson, John V, 446
Hodgson, John V, 501
Hodgson, John Hezekiah V, 247
Hodgson, John Milton V, 338
Hodgson, John William V, 246
Hodgson, John, Jr. V, 337
Hodgson, Jonathan I, 546
Hodgson, Jonathan I, 547
Hodgson, Jonathan I, 572
Hodgson, Jonathan V, 73
Hodgson, Jonathan V, 247
Hodgson, Jonathan V, 304
Hodgson, Jonathan V, 311
Hodgson, Jonathan V, 337
Hodgson, Jonathan V, 443
Hodgson, Jonathan V, 501
Hodgson, Jonathan V, 626
Hodgson, Joseph I, 547
Hodgson, Joseph I, 884
Hodgson, Joseph I, 887
Hodgson, Joseph V, 247
Hodgson, Katherine V, 246
Hodgson, Levi V, 626
Hodgson, Levina V, 337
Hodgson, Lewis V, 247
Hodgson, Lewis V, 626
Hodgson, Lidia V, 501
Hodgson, Lydia I, 501
Hodgson, Lydia I, 537
Hodgson, Lydia I, 547
Hodgson, Lydia V, 246
Hodgson, Lydia V, 247
Hodgson, Lydia V, 338
Hodgson, Lydia V, 501
Hodgson, Lydia V, 503
Hodgson, Malinda V, 246
Hodgson, Margaret I, 547
Hodgson, Maria II, 746
Hodgson, Martha I, 547
Hodgson, Martha I, 659
Hodgson, Martha V, 247
Hodgson, Mary I, 501
Hodgson, Mary I, 544
Hodgson, Mary I, 545
Hodgson, Mary I, 546
Hodgson, Mary I, 547
Hodgson, Mary I, 659
Hodgson, Mary I, 817
Hodgson, Mary II, 746
Hodgson, Mary IV, 149
Hodgson, Mary V, 73
Hodgson, Mary V, 246
Hodgson, Mary V, 247
Hodgson, Mary V, 268
Hodgson, Mary V, 337
Hodgson, Mary V, 338
Hodgson, Mary V, 350
Hodgson, Mary V, 501
Hodgson, Mary V, 535
Hodgson, Mary V, 626
Hodgson, Mary VI, 597
Hodgson, Mary A. V, 247
Hodgson, Mary Ann V, 246
Hodgson, Mary R. II, 707
Hodgson, Mary R. II, 746
Hodgson, Mary R. II, 948
Hodgson, Mary R. II, 1087
Hodgson, Mary R. II, 1088
Hodgson, Mary, Jr. II, 746
Hodgson, Mathew V, 247
Hodgson, Mathew V, 446
Hodgson, Matilda II, 746
Hodgson, Matthew V, 337
Hodgson, Matthew V, 338
Hodgson, Matthew V, 340
Hodgson, Melissa V, 338
Hodgson, Mertie V, 247
Hodgson, Moses V, 446
Hodgson, Moses V, 501
Hodgson, Nancy V, 626
Hodgson, Naomi I, 501
Hodgson, Naomi I, 547
Hodgson, Naomi I, 658
Hodgson, Naomi I, 659
Hodgson, Naomi V, 246
Hodgson, Naomi V, 247
Hodgson, Naomi V, 338
Hodgson, Naomi V, 359
Hodgson, Naomi V, 501
Hodgson, Naomy V, 230
Hodgson, Naomy V, 246
Hodgson, Nathan I, 659
Hodgson, Nathan V, 247
Hodgson, Nathan V, 337
Hodgson, Nathan V, 501
Hodgson, Nathan V, 626
Hodgson, Nathan Hines V, 501
Hodgson, Neomi I, 547
Hodgson, Patience I, 501
Hodgson, Patience I, 537
Hodgson, Patience I, 546
Hodgson, Patience I, 547
Hodgson, Patience I, 783
Hodgson, Patience I, 817
Hodgson, Phebe V, 304
Hodgson, Phebe V, 311
Hodgson, Rachel I, 501
Hodgson, Rachel I, 546
Hodgson, Rachel I, 547
Hodgson, Rachel I, 562
Hodgson, Rachel I, 659
Hodgson, Rachel V, 247
Hodgson, Rachel V, 337
Hodgson, Rachel V, 501
Hodgson, Rachel V, 502
Hodgson, Rebecca I, 547
Hodgson, Rebecca I, 557
Hodgson, Rebecca I, 659
Hodgson, Rebecca I, 783
Hodgson, Rebecca V, 246
Hodgson, Rebecca V, 247
Hodgson, Rebecca V, 338
Hodgson, Rebecca V, 446
Hodgson, Rebecca V, 626
Hodgson, Rebeccah I, 681
Hodgson, Rebeccah I, 690
Hodgson, Rebekah I, 1007
Hodgson, Rhoda V, 247
Hodgson, Rhoda V, 337
Hodgson, Richard I, 884
Hodgson, Robert I, 487
Hodgson, Robert I, 546
Hodgson, Robert I, 547
Hodgson, Robert I, 562
Hodgson, Robert I, 659
Hodgson, Robert I, 884
Hodgson, Robert IV, 410
Hodgson, Robert VI, 6
Hodgson, Robert VI, 597
Hodgson, Ruth I, 546
Hodgson, Ruth V, 247
Hodgson, Ruth VI, 597
Hodgson, Sarah I, 501
Hodgson, Sarah I, 546
Hodgson, Sarah I, 658
Hodgson, Sarah I, 659
Hodgson, Sarah I, 884
Hodgson, Sarah I, 887
Hodgson, Sarah II, 375
Hodgson, Sarah II, 550
Hodgson, Sarah II, 746
Hodgson, Sarah II, 1002
Hodgson, Sarah V, 246
Hodgson, Sarah V, 247
Hodgson, Sarah V, 264
Hodgson, Sarah V, 315
Hodgson, Sarah V, 337
Hodgson, Sarah V, 338
Hodgson, Sarah V, 626
Hodgson, Sarah VI, 597
Hodgson, Sarah Ann V, 338
Hodgson, Sarah Ann V, 339
Hodgson, Sarah M. V, 247
Hodgson, Solomon I, 501
Hodgson, Solomon I, 547
Hodgson, Solomon I, 562
Hodgson, Solomon I, 658
Hodgson, Solomon I, 817
Hodgson, Solomon V, 73
Hodgson, Solomon V, 178
Hodgson, Solomon V, 246
Hodgson, Solomon V, 247
Hodgson, Solomon V, 443
Hodgson, Solomon V, 501
Hodgson, Susanna I, 546
Hodgson, Susanna I, 547
Hodgson, Susanna I, 783
Hodgson, Susannah V, 491
Hodgson, Susannah V, 501
Hodgson, Thomas I, 501
Hodgson, Thomas I, 537
Hodgson, Thomas I, 546
Hodgson, Thomas I, 547
Hodgson, Thomas I, 658
Hodgson, Thomas I, 783
Hodgson, Thomas I, 817
Hodgson, Thomas II, 1002
Hodgson, Thomas V, 247
Hodgson, Thomas V, 337
Hodgson, Thomas V, 501
Hodgson, Thomas V, 626
Hodgson, Thos. V, 626
Hodgson, Uri V, 501
Hodgson, Uriah I, 659
Hodgson, Uriah V, 246
Hodgson, Uriah V, 338
Hodgson, Virginia V, 247
Hodgson, Wd. Elizabeth VI, 59
Hodgson, Widow Mary I, 545
Hodgson, Widow Patience I, 5
Hodgson, William I, 545
Hodgson, William I, 547
Hodgson, William I, 659
Hodgson, William II, 946
Hodgson, William II, 952
Hodgson, William II, 1085
Hodgson, William II, 1087
Hodgson, William II, 1088
Hodgson, William V, 626
Hodgson, William VI, 597
Hodgson, William, Jr. II, 707
Hodgson, Willie V, 626
Hodgson, Wm. II, 746
Hodgson, Wm., Jr. II, 746
Hodgson, Zachariah I, 658
Hodgson, Zachariah V, 246
Hodgson, Zachariah V, 247
Hodgson, Zacheriah V, 247
Hodgson, Zimri V, 626
Hodgsons, ??? II, 375
Hodgsons, Dr. ??? II, 375
Hodson, A. I, 856
Hodson, Aaron I, 798
Hodson, Aaron I, 817
Hodson, Aaron I, 884
Hodson, Abigail I, 817
Hodson, Abigail V, 338
Hodson, Abigail F. I, 500
Hodson, Achsa I, 817
Hodson, Achsah I, 658
Hodson, Achsah I, 817
Hodson, Achsah I, 856
Hodson, Adella I, 500
Hodson, Adella I, 817
Hodson, Alice II, 232
Hodson, Alice II, 249
Hodson, Aliza I, 500
Hodson, Allen V, 337
Hodson, Allen V, 338
Hodson, Alonzo V, 247
Hodson, Amelia I, 885
Hodson, Amos V, 475
Hodson, Amos V, 501
Hodson, Ann I, 500
Hodson, Ann I, 546
Hodson, Ann I, 560
Hodson, Ann I, 678
Hodson, Ann I, 679
Hodson, Ann I, 681
Hodson, Ann I, 682
Hodson, Ann I, 817
Hodson, Ann V, 246
Hodson, Ann V, 317
Hodson, Ann V, 338
Hodson, Anna I, 884
Hodson, Anna IV, 1321
Hodson, Anna V, 337
Hodson, Anna V, 338
Hodson, Anna V, 339
Hodson, Anna V, 399
Hodson, Anna Jane V, 337
Hodson, Anne I, 870
Hodson, Anne I, 884
Hodson, Anne V, 338
Hodson, Annie V, 399
Hodson, Annuel I, 884
Hodson, Ariedna I, 547
Hodson, Armela I, 500
Hodson, Armelia I, 876
Hodson, Armelia I, 885
Hodson, Armella I, 817
Hodson, Aron I, 659
Hodson, Asa V, 338
Hodson, Baley I, 987
Hodson, Bathsheba Caroline I, 500
Hodson, Bathsheba Caroline I, 817
Hodson, Bathshebe Caroline I, 885
Hodson, Benjamin V, 337
Hodson, Bertha I, 934
Hodson, Caroline V, 338
Hodson, Caroline B. I, 885
Hodson, Carry V, 338

son, Catharine I, 884
son, Catharine I, 896
son, Charity I, 673
son, Charity I, 682
son, Charles V, 399
son, Charles H. V, 399
son, Chloe V, 338
son, Clarissa V, 338
son, Cloe I, 677
son, Cloe I, 681
son, Cyrus V, 338
son, Cyrus L. V, 626
son, Daniel II, 1002
son, David I, 500
son, David I, 547
son, David I, 658
son, David I, 681
son, David I, 682
son, David I, 817
son, David I, 884
son, David I, 987
son, Deborah I, 682
son, Deborah VI, 592
son, Deborah VI, 597
son, Delila V, 178
son, Delilah V, 337
son, Drucilla V, 626
son, Edith V, 626
son, Edwin V, 399
son, Edwin W. V, 399
son, Eli I, 547
son, Eli I, 856
son, Eli I, 885
son, Elias I, 659
son, Elias I, 927
son, Elina V, 337
son, Elisabeth I, 685
son, Elisabeth I, 817
son, Eliza I, 885
son, Eliza I, 899
son, Eliza V, 338
son, Eliza E. V, 399
son, Eliza Emma V, 399
son, Eliza H. V, 246
son, Eliza P. I, 817
son, Elizabeth I, 658
son, Elizabeth I, 659
son, Elizabeth I, 681
son, Elizabeth I, 682
son, Elizabeth I, 686
son, Elizabeth I, 817
son, Elizabeth I, 856
son, Elizabeth I, 884
son, Elizabeth I, 885
son, Elizabeth I, 890
son, Elizabeth I, 1010
son, Elizabeth V, 73
son, Elizabeth V, 178
son, Elizabeth V, 337
son, Elizabeth VI, 592
son, Ella N. V, 338
son, Ellsworth V, 626
son, Emily V, 246
son, Emily V, 247
son, Emily V, 264
son, Emily V, 338
son, Emily V, 399
son, Emily V, 413
son, Emily J. V, 338
son, Emma I, 885
son, Enos I, 659
son, Enos V, 337
son, Enos V, 338
son, Erwin I, 884
son, Esther I, 658
son, Esther I, 681
son, Esther I, 682
son, Etta V, 399
son, Ettie V, 338
son, Eva V, 338
son, Evelena V, 338
son, Flavious V, 247
son, Flavius V, 246
son, Flavius V, 247
son, Flavius V, 338
son, Florence V, 399
son, Geo. V, 338
son, George I, 343
son, George I, 500
son, George I, 501
son, George I, 546
son, George I, 560
son, George I, 681
son, George I, 682
son, George I, 817
son, George I, 884
son, George V, 178
son, George V, 337
son, George V, 399
son, George G. V, 399
son, George, Jr. V, 338
Hodson, Hannah I, 884
Hodson, Hannah I, 1010
Hodson, Hannah V, 246
Hodson, Hannah V, 336
Hodson, Hannah V, 337
Hodson, Hannah V, 338
Hodson, Hannah V, 501
Hodson, Harry V, 683
Hodson, Helen V, 683
Hodson, Henry I, 885
Hodson, Henry V, 337
Hodson, Hezekiah V, 338
Hodson, Hur I, 501
Hodson, Hur I, 659
Hodson, Hur I, 682
Hodson, Hur I, 686
Hodson, Hur I, 817
Hodson, Ida V, 338
Hodson, Ira V, 338
Hodson, Ira V, 399
Hodson, Ira V, 501
Hodson, Irene I, 927
Hodson, Isaac I, 659
Hodson, Isaac I, 679
Hodson, Isaac I, 682
Hodson, Isaac I, 817
Hodson, Isaac I, 884
Hodson, Isabel I, 659
Hodson, Isabel I, 679
Hodson, Isabel I, 681
Hodson, Isabel I, 817
Hodson, Isabel I, 884
Hodson, Isaiah V, 626
Hodson, Iva V, 338
Hodson, Izabel Lutesha I, 500
Hodson, Izabel Lutitia I, 817
Hodson, J. V, 683
Hodson, Jabez I, 682
Hodson, Jabez I, 689
Hodson, James I, 659
Hodson, James V, 337
Hodson, Jane I, 500
Hodson, Jane I, 817
Hodson, Jane I, 818
Hodson, Jane I, 884
Hodson, Jane I, 885
Hodson, Jeffrey I, 885
Hodson, Jemima I, 884
Hodson, Jemima V, 178
Hodson, Jennie V, 683
Hodson, Jeremiah I, 856
Hodson, Jeremiah I, 884
Hodson, Jeremiah W. I, 799
Hodson, Jeremiah W. I, 817
Hodson, Jess I, 884
Hodson, Jesse I, 501
Hodson, Jesse I, 658
Hodson, Jesse I, 659
Hodson, Jesse I, 681
Hodson, Jesse I, 692
Hodson, Jesse I, 817
Hodson, Jesse I, 856
Hodson, Jesse I, 884
Hodson, Jesse I, 885
Hodson, Jesse I, 987
Hodson, Jesse W. I, 856
Hodson, Joab I, 398
Hodson, Joab I, 884
Hodson, Joel I, 856
Hodson, Joel I, 884
Hodson, Joel I, 885
Hodson, Joel V, 501
Hodson, John I, 343
Hodson, John I, 457
Hodson, John I, 500
Hodson, John I, 501
Hodson, John I, 546
Hodson, John I, 547
Hodson, John I, 562
Hodson, John I, 659
Hodson, John I, 681
Hodson, John I, 682
Hodson, John I, 884
Hodson, John I, 885
Hodson, John I, 987
Hodson, John V, 178
Hodson, John V, 215
Hodson, John V, 246
Hodson, John V, 247
Hodson, John V, 264
Hodson, John V, 337
Hodson, John V, 338
Hodson, John V, 446
Hodson, John D. V, 399
Hodson, John Dalton V, 399
Hodson, John F. I, 500
Hodson, John G. IV, 1321
Hodson, John Milton I, 856
Hodson, John Milton V, 338
Hodson, John, Jr. V, 337
Hodson, Jonathan I, 501
Hodson, Jonathan I, 659
Hodson, Jonathan I, 679
Hodson, Jonathan I, 681
Hodson, Jonathan I, 682
Hodson, Jonathan I, 817
Hodson, Jonathan I, 818
Hodson, Jonathan I, 884
Hodson, Jonathan V, 247
Hodson, Jonathan V, 337
Hodson, Jonathan V, 338
Hodson, Joseph I, 501
Hodson, Joseph I, 547
Hodson, Joseph I, 659
Hodson, Joseph I, 678
Hodson, Joseph I, 681
Hodson, Joseph I, 884
Hodson, Joseph V, 247
Hodson, Joseph, Jr. V, 338
Hodson, Joshua V, 1001
Hodson, Katharine I, 856
Hodson, Katherine V, 246
Hodson, Katherine V, 250
Hodson, Lavina I, 1010
Hodson, Levica I, 884
Hodson, Levina V, 337
Hodson, Lewis V, 338
Hodson, Lewis A. V, 338
Hodson, Lidia V, 501
Hodson, Lillie V, 338
Hodson, Lindley I, 856
Hodson, Louisa Ann I, 856
Hodson, Luranna V, 672
Hodson, Luranna V, 683
Hodson, Luzena I, 884
Hodson, Lydia V, 246
Hodson, Lydia V, 247
Hodson, Lydia V, 258
Hodson, Lydia V, 338
Hodson, Malinda V, 246
Hodson, Margaret I, 658
Hodson, Margaret I, 673
Hodson, Margaret I, 681
Hodson, Margaret I, 682
Hodson, Margaret I, 884
Hodson, Margret I, 681
Hodson, Marietta V, 399
Hodson, Martha I, 500
Hodson, Martha I, 547
Hodson, Martha I, 682
Hodson, Martha I, 685
Hodson, Martha I, 799
Hodson, Martha I, 817
Hodson, Martha I, 856
Hodson, Martha I, 871
Hodson, Martha I, 884
Hodson, Martha I, 885
Hodson, Martha V, 337
Hodson, Martha V, 338
Hodson, Martha Adelia I, 885
Hodson, Martha J. V, 398
Hodson, Martha J. V, 399
Hodson, Martha Jane V, 399
Hodson, Mary I, 343
Hodson, Mary I, 398
Hodson, Mary I, 500
Hodson, Mary I, 501
Hodson, Mary I, 546
Hodson, Mary I, 562
Hodson, Mary I, 658
Hodson, Mary I, 659
Hodson, Mary I, 678
Hodson, Mary I, 679
Hodson, Mary I, 681
Hodson, Mary I, 682
Hodson, Mary I, 691
Hodson, Mary I, 692
Hodson, Mary I, 798
Hodson, Mary I, 817
Hodson, Mary I, 856
Hodson, Mary I, 884
Hodson, Mary I, 1010
Hodson, Mary V, 247
Hodson, Mary V, 337
Hodson, Mary V, 338
Hodson, Mary V, 399
Hodson, Mary V, 475
Hodson, Mary V, 501
Hodson, Mary V, 626
Hodson, Mary A. V, 247
Hodson, Mary Ann I, 884
Hodson, Mary Ann V, 399
Hodson, Mary L. V, 399
Hodson, Mary Mariah I, 856
Hodson, Mary, Jr. I, 884
Hodson, Mary, Jr. V, 399
Hodson, Mary, Sr. I, 884
Hodson, Matthew I, 659
Hodson, Matthew V, 336
Hodson, Matthew V, 337
Hodson, Matthew V, 338
Hodson, Melissa V, 336
Hodson, Melissa V, 337
Hodson, Melissa V, 338
Hodson, Mertie V, 247
Hodson, Michel I, 987
Hodson, Milly I, 677
Hodson, Milly I, 682
Hodson, Milton V, 338
Hodson, Miriam I, 987
Hodson, Nancy I, 817
Hodson, Nancy I, 818
Hodson, Nancy I, 884
Hodson, Nancy I, 885
Hodson, Nancy Ellen V, 398
Hodson, Nancy Ellen V, 399
Hodson, Naomi I, 547
Hodson, Naomi I, 658
Hodson, Naomi V, 178
Hodson, Naomi V, 246
Hodson, Nathan I, 501
Hodson, Nathan I, 659
Hodson, Nathan I, 884
Hodson, Nathan V, 178
Hodson, Nathan V, 337
Hodson, Nellie M. V, 338
Hodson, Nereus I, 885
Hodson, Nereus M. I, 885
Hodson, Nereus Milton I, 927
Hodson, Patience I, 546
Hodson, Patience I, 817
Hodson, Peggy I, 987
Hodson, Pheba A. I, 885
Hodson, Phebe I, 681
Hodson, Phebe I, 685
Hodson, Phebe V, 338
Hodson, Phila A. I, 870
Hodson, Phila A. I, 885
Hodson, Rachel I, 501
Hodson, Rachel I, 658
Hodson, Rachel I, 659
Hodson, Rachel I, 681
Hodson, Rachel I, 682
Hodson, Rachel I, 692
Hodson, Rachel I, 856
Hodson, Rachel I, 884
Hodson, Rachel I, 1010
Hodson, Rachel V, 337
Hodson, Rachel V, 399
Hodson, Rebeca I, 881
Hodson, Rebeca I, 885
Hodson, Rebecca I, 885
Hodson, Rebecca I, 893
Hodson, Rebecca V, 246
Hodson, Rebecca V, 247
Hodson, Rebecca V, 264
Hodson, Rebecca V, 338
Hodson, Rebecca V, 446
Hodson, Rebecca V, 645
Hodson, Rebeccah I, 679
Hodson, Rebeccah I, 681
Hodson, Rebeccah I, 682
Hodson, Rebeckah I, 885
Hodson, Rebeckah I, 1010
Hodson, Rebekah I, 1010
Hodson, Reuben I, 884
Hodson, Rhoda V, 178
Hodson, Rhoda V, 337
Hodson, Richard I, 501
Hodson, Richard I, 884
Hodson, Richard II, 550
Hodson, Robert I, 501
Hodson, Robert I, 658
Hodson, Robert I, 659
Hodson, Robert I, 679
Hodson, Robert I, 681
Hodson, Robert I, 682
Hodson, Robert I, 695
Hodson, Robert I, 817
Hodson, Robert I, 856
Hodson, Robert I, 884
Hodson, Robert I, 896
Hodson, Robert I, 897
Hodson, Robert VI, 592
Hodson, Robert F. I, 884
Hodson, Robert W. I, 884
Hodson, Robert, Jr. I, 659
Hodson, Robert, Jr. I, 884
Hodson, Rosanna I, 856
Hodson, Rosannah I, 885
Hodson, Rosetta V, 338
Hodson, Russell V, 338
Hodson, Ruth I, 501
Hodson, Ruth I, 546
Hodson, Ruth I, 548
Hodson, Ruth I, 659
Hodson, Ruth I, 678
Hodson, Ruth I, 681
Hodson, Ruth I, 682
Hodson, Ruth I, 741
Hodson, Ruth I, 856
Hodson, Sarah I, 343
Hodson, Sarah I, 394
Hodson, Sarah I, 398
Hodson, Sarah I, 399
Hodson, Sarah I, 500
Hodson, Sarah I, 544
Hodson, Sarah I, 546
Hodson, Sarah I, 659
Hodson, Sarah I, 682
Hodson, Sarah I, 689
Hodson, Sarah I, 884
Hodson, Sarah I, 897
Hodson, Sarah I, 902
Hodson, Sarah II, 550
Hodson, Sarah V, 178
Hodson, Sarah V, 337
Hodson, Sarah V, 338
Hodson, Sarah V, 399
Hodson, Sarah Ann V, 337
Hodson, Sarah Ann V, 338
Hodson, Simeon I, 658
Hodson, Simeon V, 399
Hodson, Solomon I, 501
Hodson, Solomon I, 677
Hodson, Solomon I, 678
Hodson, Solomon I, 681
Hodson, Solomon I, 817
Hodson, Solomon V, 73
Hodson, Solomon V, 178
Hodson, Solomon V, 247
Hodson, Stella V, 338
Hodson, Stephen I, 885
Hodson, Stephen G. I, 856
Hodson, Susanna I, 544
Hodson, Susanna I, 546
Hodson, Susanna I, 682
Hodson, Susanna I, 684
Hodson, Tamar I, 678
Hodson, Thomas I, 500
Hodson, Thomas I, 501
Hodson, Thomas I, 817
Hodson, Thomas I, 884
Hodson, Thomas V, 178
Hodson, Thomas V, 338
Hodson, Thos. V, 338
Hodson, Uriah V, 338
Hodson, Virgil V, 338
Hodson, Virginia V, 247
Hodson, Virginia V, 338
Hodson, Widow Patience I, 547
Hodson, William I, 884
Hodson, William V, 337
Hodson, William V, 338
Hodson, Willie V, 626
Hodson, Zachariah V, 246
Hodson, Zachariah V, 250
Hodson, Zaruiah I, 856
Hoe, Mary E. III, 168
Hoeg, Elisha IV, 823
Hoeg, Elisha Wm. IV, 823
Hoeg, Hervey IV, 823
Hoeg, Joanna IV, 823
Hoeg, Joel IV, 823
Hoeg, Joseph VI, 401
Hoeg, Lydia IV, 823
Hoeg, Mary II, 232
Hoeg, Mary VI, 506
Hoeg, William II, 232
Hoeg, Wm. VI, 506
Hoekstra, Alice III, 64
Hoekstra, Eliza A. III, 64
Hoekstra, Jacob A. III, 64
Hoelcher, Lucile IV, 1254
Hoelestra, Alice III, 168
Hoelestra, Eliza A. III, 168
Hoelestra, Jacob A. III, 168
Hoell, David VI, 972
Hoelle, Bertha V, 1001
Hoelly, Bertha V, 1001
Hoelly, Emma V, 1001
Hoelly, John V, 1001
Hoet, Caspar III, 168
Hoet, Elizabeth III, 168
Hoet, Jacob III, 168
Hoff, Daniel IV, 1321
Hoff, David III, 510
Hoff, Edgar III, 510
Hoff, Fanny III, 510
Hoff, Frankie III, 510
Hoff, Henry III, 510
Hoff, Mary A. III, 510
Hoff, Mary E. IV, 335
Hoff, Nelson III, 510
Hoff, William Watson III, 510
Hofferd, David V, 1001
Hofferd, Margaret V, 1002
Hofferd, Marshall V, 1001
Hoffhine, Cora IV, 1254
Hoffman, ??? II, 32
Hoffman, ??? III, 103
Hoffman, ??? III, 238
Hoffman, Abigail II, 32
Hoffman, Abigail II, 375

Hoffman, Almina W. II, 134
Hoffman, Almina W. II, 151
Hoffman, Angeline E. VI, 933
Hoffman, Anna M. III, 168
Hoffman, Anna M. III, 368
Hoffman, Annie E. II, 876
Hoffman, Beulah II, 375
Hoffman, Beulah III, 168
Hoffman, Beulah III, 238
Hoffman, Bruce IV, 1321
Hoffman, Bruce D. IV, 1321
Hoffman, Catharine III, 168
Hoffman, Charlotte III, 168
Hoffman, Charlotte III, 267
Hoffman, David VI, 825
Hoffman, Edwin VI, 933
Hoffman, Elizabeth II, 32
Hoffman, Elizabeth II, 79
Hoffman, Elizabeth N. II, 876
Hoffman, Elmira III, 168
Hoffman, Emma S. II, 876
Hoffman, Emma S. II, 894
Hoffman, Eugene I, 927
Hoffman, Fannie I, 943
Hoffman, Fannie H. I, 927
Hoffman, Frances VI, 933
Hoffman, Geo. III, 168
Hoffman, Harry N. III, 168
Hoffman, Harry N. III, 368
Hoffman, Isaac II, 32
Hoffman, Isaac II, 79
Hoffman, Isaac II, 94
Hoffman, Jacob II, 32
Hoffman, Jacob II, 79
Hoffman, Job II, 79
Hoffman, John II, 32
Hoffman, John II, 66
Hoffman, John II, 79
Hoffman, John III, 168
Hoffman, John VI, 912
Hoffman, John VI, 983
Hoffman, John, Jr. VI, 933
Hoffman, Jonathan II, 32
Hoffman, Jonathan III, 168
Hoffman, Joseph R. III, 168
Hoffman, Lidia V, 146
Hoffman, Lydia III, 168
Hoffman, Lydia V, 73
Hoffman, Lydia A. III, 168
Hoffman, Lydia A. III, 267
Hoffman, Lydia Thomas V, 73
Hoffman, Marmaduke II, 375
Hoffman, Martha Ann VI, 983
Hoffman, Martin II, 375
Hoffman, Mary II, 32
Hoffman, Mary II, 66
Hoffman, Mary II, 79
Hoffman, Mary II, 84
Hoffman, Mary II, 100
Hoffman, Mary VI, 933
Hoffman, Mary Ann II, 79
Hoffman, Mary Ann II, 90
Hoffman, Mary Anne II, 32
Hoffman, Mary E. VI, 825
Hoffman, Mary Jane VI, 912
Hoffman, Mary M. V, 73
Hoffman, Mary S. II, 876
Hoffman, Mrs. Anna IV, 1321
Hoffman, Mrs. Annie C. IV, 1321
Hoffman, Naomi II, 79
Hoffman, Naomi II, 91
Hoffman, Neomy II, 32
Hoffman, Phebe III, 128
Hoffman, Rebecca II, 79
Hoffman, Samuel II, 32
Hoffman, Samuel VI, 933
Hoffman, Sara III, 168
Hoffman, Sarah II, 79
Hoffman, Sarah II, 94
Hoffman, Sarah II, 375
Hoffman, Sarah II, 876
Hoffman, Sarah II, 896
Hoffman, Sarah V, 73
Hoffman, Sarah M. III, 168
Hoffman, Susanna IV, 1321
Hoffman, Wm. A. III, 168
Hoffman, Wm. A. III, 267
Hoffmire, Ann IV, 1211
Hoffmire, Ann IV, 1214
Hoffmire, Luella M. IV, 222
Hoffmire, Mabel Smith IV, 1211
Hoffmire, Mary IV, 1202
Hoffmire, Mary Brollier IV, 1211
Hoffmire, Sarah M. IV, 1211
Hoffner, Harry IV, 720
Hofford, David V, 1001
Hofman, Abigail II, 375
Hofman, Marmaduke II, 375
Hofman, Mary Louisa II, 804
Hog, Rebecca II, 375
Hogan, Amy VI, 876
Hogan, Ann VI, 898
Hogan, Ann VI, 933
Hogan, Anna VI, 873
Hogan, Annis VI, 869
Hogan, Avey VI, 933
Hogan, Betsy VI, 863
Hogan, Catharine VI, 873
Hogan, Catharine VI, 960
Hogan, Charles VI, 869
Hogan, Charles VI, 898
Hogan, Charles VI, 904
Hogan, Charles VI, 917
Hogan, Charles VI, 933
Hogan, Charles VI, 934
Hogan, Charles VI, 946
Hogan, Charles VI, 947
Hogan, Charles VI, 951
Hogan, Charles VI, 1019
Hogan, Cona VI, 863
Hogan, Daniel VI, 900
Hogan, Daniel VI, 933
Hogan, Daukes Johnson VI, 937
Hogan, David VI, 933
Hogan, Denny VI, 933
Hogan, Dorcas VI, 941
Hogan, Eliza Ann VI, 946
Hogan, Elizabeth VI, 825
Hogan, Elizabeth VI, 910
Hogan, Elizabeth VI, 912
Hogan, Elizabeth VI, 933
Hogan, Elizabeth VI, 934
Hogan, Elizabeth VI, 937
Hogan, Elizabeth VI, 941
Hogan, Emeline VI, 1019
Hogan, Enoch VI, 863
Hogan, Enoch VI, 864
Hogan, Enoch VI, 933
Hogan, Enoch VI, 934
Hogan, Enoch VI, 941
Hogan, Enoch VI, 956
Hogan, Enos VI, 933
Hogan, Enuch VI, 869
Hogan, Frances Elizabeth VI, 933
Hogan, Giles Q. VI, 946
Hogan, Giles Q. VI, 1019
Hogan, Heatha VI, 960
Hogan, Israel VI, 933
Hogan, James VI, 876
Hogan, James VI, 910
Hogan, James VI, 933
Hogan, James VI, 939
Hogan, James VI, 942
Hogan, Jane VI, 898
Hogan, John VI, 825
Hogan, John VI, 933
Hogan, Joseph VI, 892
Hogan, Joseph VI, 933
Hogan, Lizy VI, 933
Hogan, Lucinda VI, 933
Hogan, Lucy VI, 933
Hogan, Lydia S. VI, 892
Hogan, Malinda VI, 898
Hogan, Malinda VI, 933
Hogan, Margaret VI, 869
Hogan, Margaret VI, 933
Hogan, Marget VI, 900
Hogan, Martha Ann VI, 917
Hogan, Mary VI, 899
Hogan, Mary VI, 933
Hogan, Mary F. VI, 922
Hogan, Matilda VI, 899
Hogan, Milbern VI, 933
Hogan, Mille VI, 863
Hogan, Milley VI, 863
Hogan, Milley VI, 934
Hogan, Milly VI, 933
Hogan, Milly VI, 942
Hogan, Mourning VI, 933
Hogan, Nancy VI, 933
Hogan, Nancy F. VI, 933
Hogan, Nancy Jane VI, 933
Hogan, Obediah VI, 933
Hogan, Obediah VI, 1007
Hogan, Patsy VI, 1007
Hogan, Peggy VI, 933
Hogan, Peter VI, 933
Hogan, Peter VI, 1012
Hogan, Polly VI, 900
Hogan, Polly VI, 933
Hogan, Polly VI, 939
Hogan, Polly VI, 942
Hogan, Ruthanna IV, 964
Hogan, Sally VI, 869
Hogan, Sally VI, 933
Hogan, Samuel VI, 869
Hogan, Samuel VI, 933
Hogan, Sarah Frances VI, 951
Hogan, Thomas VI, 933
Hogan, Thomas VI, 941
Hogan, Thomas VI, 977
Hogan, Washington VI, 933
Hogan, Washington VI, 994
Hogan, William VI, 933
Hogan, Zachariah VI, 933
Hogatt, Ann V, 73
Hogatt, Elizabeth V, 73
Hogatt, Jacob V, 73
Hogatt, Jesse V, 73
Hogatt, Joseph V, 73
Hogatt, Josiah V, 304
Hogatt, Ruth V, 73
Hogbin, Leatitia II, 79
Hogbin, Leatitia II, 90
Hogbin, Mary II, 79
Hogbin, Mary II, 92
Hogden, Ann IV, 708
Hogden, Eli IV, 222
Hogden, Eli, Jr. IV, 222
Hogden, Elizabeth I, 547
Hogden, Harriet IV, 222
Hogden, John IV, 708
Hogden, Martha IV, 708
Hogden, William IV, 222
Hoge, Abigail M. IV, 312
Hoge, Abigail M. IV, 313
Hoge, Abigail M. IV, 314
Hoge, Abner IV, 336
Hoge, Abner E. IV, 336
Hoge, Absalom IV, 222
Hoge, Absalom IV, 223
Hoge, Absalom IV, 324
Hoge, Absalom IV, 336
Hoge, Absalom IV, 531
Hoge, Absalom IV, 532
Hoge, Absalom IV, 539
Hoge, Absalom IV, 722
Hoge, Absolam IV, 223
Hoge, Absolam IV, 531
Hoge, Absolam IV, 533
Hoge, Absolem IV, 223
Hoge, Absolum VI, 653
Hoge, Agnes Ann IV, 322
Hoge, Agnes Ann IV, 336
Hoge, Amos IV, 559
Hoge, Amy IV, 336
Hoge, Amy VI, 506
Hoge, Amy VI, 654
Hoge, Ann IV, 39
Hoge, Ann IV, 59
Hoge, Ann IV, 93
Hoge, Ann IV, 332
Hoge, Ann IV, 336
Hoge, Ann IV, 354
Hoge, Ann VI, 401
Hoge, Ann VI, 505
Hoge, Ann VI, 506
Hoge, Ann VI, 524
Hoge, Ann VI, 539
Hoge, Ann VI, 652
Hoge, Ann VI, 654
Hoge, Ann VI, 749
Hoge, Ann VI, 759
Hoge, Ann B. IV, 531
Hoge, Ann B. IV, 558
Hoge, Ann B. IV, 559
Hoge, Anna IV, 93
Hoge, Anna IV, 532
Hoge, Anna VI, 403
Hoge, Anna M. IV, 223
Hoge, Anna M. IV, 283
Hoge, Anna M. IV, 444
Hoge, Anne IV, 100
Hoge, Asa IV, 223
Hoge, Asa IV, 336
Hoge, Asa IV, 531
Hoge, Asa V, 502
Hoge, Asa VI, 393
Hoge, Asa VI, 401
Hoge, Asa VI, 653
Hoge, Asa B. VI, 402
Hoge, Asa Benjamin VI, 402
Hoge, Asa H. V, 502
Hoge, Asa H. V, 911
Hoge, Asa H. VI, 401
Hoge, Asa M. V, 911
Hoge, Asahel IV, 335
Hoge, Asahel IV, 336
Hoge, Asahel VI, 652
Hoge, Barak IV, 39
Hoge, Benjamin VI, 654
Hoge, Benjamin Battin IV, 722
Hoge, Betsey VI, 642
Hoge, Betsey VI, 653
Hoge, Betsy VI, 652
Hoge, Bushrod IV, 336
Hoge, Charles L. IV, 223
Hoge, Charles Malcolm VI, 652
Hoge, Charles William VI, 651
Hoge, Charles William VI, 652
Hoge, Charles William VI, 654
Hoge, Charles Wm. VI, 658
Hoge, Charlotta IV, 93
Hoge, Charlotte IV, 93
Hoge, Chas. Wm. VI, 659
Hoge, Clara V. IV, 223
Hoge, Clara V. VI, 651
Hoge, Clara V. VI, 654
Hoge, Clara V. VI, 658
Hoge, Clara V. VI, 659
Hoge, Clayton IV, 223
Hoge, Comley K. IV, 223
Hoge, Cosmelia J. VI, 652
Hoge, Cosmelia Janney VI, 652
Hoge, Cosmelia Janney VI, 664
Hoge, Craven IV, 223
Hoge, Craven IV, 336
Hoge, Craven IV, 532
Hoge, Craven VI, 653
Hoge, Craver IV, 223
Hoge, Daniel VI, 652
Hoge, Daniel VI, 706
Hoge, Daniel J. VI, 652
Hoge, Daniel J. VI, 704
Hoge, Daniel J. VI, 711
Hoge, Daniel J. VI, 713
Hoge, David IV, 93
Hoge, David IV, 222
Hoge, David IV, 336
Hoge, David IV, 531
Hoge, David IV, 532
Hoge, David VI, 506
Hoge, David VI, 644
Hoge, David VI, 652
Hoge, David VI, 654
Hoge, David E. IV, 336
Hoge, David J. IV, 532
Hoge, David Newcomer VI, 653
Hoge, David Newcomer VI, 694
Hoge, Edward IV, 336
Hoge, Edward Abijah VI, 654
Hoge, Edward B. IV, 531
Hoge, Edward B. IV, 532
Hoge, Eli J. VI, 652
Hoge, Eli J. VI, 653
Hoge, Eli J. VI, 654
Hoge, Eli J. VI, 660
Hoge, Eli J. VI, 664
Hoge, Eli J. VI, 665
Hoge, Eli J. VI, 718
Hoge, Eli J. VI, 749
Hoge, Eli J. VI, 789
Hoge, Elibeth VI, 402
Hoge, Elihu V, 73
Hoge, Elijah IV, 336
Hoge, Elijah VI, 654
Hoge, Elisha IV, 509
Hoge, Elisha IV, 531
Hoge, Elisha IV, 532
Hoge, Elisha IV, 554
Hoge, Elisha V, 304
Hoge, Elisha V, 312
Hoge, Eliz. III, 37
Hoge, Eliza IV, 334
Hoge, Eliza IV, 336
Hoge, Eliza IV, 532
Hoge, Eliza Jane IV, 189
Hoge, Eliza Jane IV, 222
Hoge, Eliza Jane IV, 223
Hoge, Eliza Pleasant VI, 652
Hoge, Eliza Pleasant VI, 653
Hoge, Eliza Pleasant VI, 654
Hoge, Eliza Pleasant VI, 660
Hoge, Eliza Pleasant VI, 664
Hoge, Eliza Pleasant VI, 749
Hoge, Eliza Pleasant VI, 789
Hoge, Eliza Pleasants VI, 665
Hoge, Elizabeth IV, 39
Hoge, Elizabeth IV, 222
Hoge, Elizabeth IV, 336
Hoge, Elizabeth IV, 389
Hoge, Elizabeth IV, 531
Hoge, Elizabeth VI, 400
Hoge, Elizabeth VI, 401
Hoge, Elizabeth VI, 408
Hoge, Elizabeth VI, 412
Hoge, Elizabeth VI, 441
Hoge, Elizabeth VI, 506
Hoge, Elizabeth VI, 520
Hoge, Elizabeth VI, 653
Hoge, Elizabeth VI, 654
Hoge, Elizabeth VI, 664
Hoge, Elizabeth VI, 665
Hoge, Elizabeth VI, 666
Hoge, Elizabeth VI, 721
Hoge, Elizabeth J. VI, 652
Hoge, Elizabeth J. VI, 653
Hoge, Elizabeth J. VI, 670
Hoge, Elizabeth Jane VI, 401
Hoge, Elizabeth S. I, 548
Hoge, Elizabeth S. VI, 401
Hoge, Elizabeth S. VI, 402
Hoge, Ella VI, 652
Hoge, Ella VI, 653
Hoge, Ella VI, 660
Hoge, Ellazan IV, 531
Hoge, Elmer IV, 389
Hoge, Elmina R. VI, 653
Hoge, Elmina R. VI, 656
Hoge, Emily E. IV, 336
Hoge, Emma IV, 223
Hoge, Ernest K. IV, 223
Hoge, Estella IV, 532
Hoge, Esther IV, 39
Hoge, Esther IV, 93
Hoge, Esther VI, 401
Hoge, Eulyssus IV, 532
Hoge, Eunice IV, 531
Hoge, Eunice W. IV, 531
Hoge, Eunice W. IV, 534
Hoge, Florence IV, 532
Hoge, Folio VI, 652
Hoge, Francis VI, 401
Hoge, Frederica VI, 400
Hoge, Frederica VI, 401
Hoge, Fredericia P. VI, 402
Hoge, Fredericia P. VI, 443
Hoge, George VI, 401
Hoge, George VI, 506
Hoge, George VI, 622
Hoge, George VI, 628
Hoge, George VI, 652
Hoge, George VI, 654
Hoge, Grace IV, 532
Hoge, Grace VI, 682
Hoge, Gracetta VI, 652
Hoge, Gracetta VI, 653
Hoge, Gregg VI, 652
Hoge, Gulielma P. VI, 616
Hoge, Gulielma Penn VI, 622
Hoge, Gulielma Penn VI, 652
Hoge, Gulielma Penn VI, 654
Hoge, Gulilema Pann VI, 628
Hoge, Hannah II, 232
Hoge, Hannah IV, 336
Hoge, Hannah IV, 358
Hoge, Hannah IV, 559
Hoge, Hannah V, 73
Hoge, Hannah VI, 375
Hoge, Hannah VI, 401
Hoge, Hannah VI, 402
Hoge, Hannah VI, 407
Hoge, Hannah VI, 506
Hoge, Hannah VI, 520
Hoge, Hannah VI, 622
Hoge, Hannah VI, 652
Hoge, Hannah VI, 653
Hoge, Hannah VI, 654
Hoge, Hannah VI, 665
Hoge, Hannah VI, 666
Hoge, Hannah Ann VI, 401
Hoge, Hannah B. IV, 336
Hoge, Hannah E. IV, 336
Hoge, Hannah Elma IV, 336
Hoge, Hannah Elma IV, 531
Hoge, Hannah Elma IV, 532
Hoge, Hannah Elma IV, 534
Hoge, Hannah G. IV, 722
Hoge, Hannah Pancoast II, 2
Hoge, Haseal IV, 410
Hoge, Henrietta VI, 653
Hoge, Henry J. VI, 652
Hoge, Henry J. VI, 704
Hoge, Howard M. VI, 636
Hoge, Howard M. VI, 652
Hoge, Howard M. VI, 706
Hoge, Isaac IV, 222
Hoge, Isaac IV, 223
Hoge, Isaac IV, 336
Hoge, Isaac IV, 531
Hoge, Isaac VI, 400
Hoge, Isaac VI, 401
Hoge, Isaac VI, 402
Hoge, Isaac VI, 441
Hoge, Isaac VI, 506
Hoge, Isaac VI, 520
Hoge, Isaac VI, 653
Hoge, Isaac VI, 654
Hoge, Isaac VI, 656
Hoge, Isaac VI, 665
Hoge, Isaac VI, 666
Hoge, Isaac C. VI, 402
Hoge, Isaac C. VI, 653
Hoge, Isaac C. VI, 656
Hoge, Isaac, Jr. VI, 401
Hoge, Isaiah IV, 39
Hoge, Israel VI, 401
Hoge, Israel VI, 402
Hoge, Jacob I, 1031
Hoge, Jacob I, 1048
Hoge, Jacob IV, 39
Hoge, Jacob IV, 93
Hoge, Jacob IV, 127
Hoge, Jacob VI, 401

e, Jacob Jenkins IV, 93
e, Jacob Ward VI, 653
e, Jacob Ward-Rees VI, 694
e, James IV, 223
e, James IV, 336
e, James IV, 531
e, James IV, 559
e, James IV, 964
e, James VI, 400
e, James VI, 401
e, James VI, 520
e, James VI, 653
e, James VI, 664
e, James VI, 665
e, James VI, 666
e, James D. VI, 400
e, James Edwin IV, 532
e, James L. VI, 402
e, James Laurence VI, 401
e, James M. VI, 402
e, James S. IV, 532
e, Jane IV, 336
e, Jane IV, 510
e, Jane IV, 532
e, Jesse IV, 39
e, Jesse IV, 222
e, Jesse IV, 234
e, Jesse IV, 336
e, Jesse IV, 339
e, Jesse VI, 401
e, Jesse VI, 506
e, Jesse VI, 551
e, Jesse VI, 577
e, Jesse VI, 632
e, Jesse VI, 642
e, Jesse VI, 652
e, Jesse VI, 653
e, Jesse VI, 654
e, Jesse VI, 670
e, Jesse VI, 685
e, Jesse VI, 694
e, Jesse VI, 711
e, Jesse VI, 713
ge, John IV, 39
ge, John IV, 71
ge, John IV, 93
ge, John IV, 127
ge, John IV, 223
ge, John IV, 336
ge, John IV, 512
ge, John IV, 531
ge, John IV, 532
ge, John IV, 559
ge, John IV, 1282
ge, John VI, 400
ge, John VI, 401
ge, John VI, 408
ge, John VI, 506
ge, John B. IV, 559
ge, John B. VI, 402
ge, John Barclay IV, 531
ge, John Barclay IV, 532
ge, John Barclay IV, 559
ge, John C. IV, 223
ge, John C. IV, 336
ge, John C. IV, 531
ge, John C. IV, 532
ge, John C. IV, 534
ge, John C. IV, 558
ge, John C. IV, 681
ge, John C. IV, 722
ge, John Clayton IV, 223
ge, John J. VI, 654
ge, John M. V, 502
ge, John M. VI, 401
ge, John McPherson V, 502
ge, John Mcpherson VI, 401
ge, John Mead VI, 654
ge, John Thomas, Jr. IV, 722
ge, John, Jr. IV, 93
ge, John, Jr. IV, 559
oge, Jonathan IV, 39
oge, Jonathan IV, 93
oge, Jonathan IV, 100
oge, Jonathan IV, 336
oge, Jonathan VI, 400
oge, Jonathan VI, 401
oge, Joseph IV, 223
oge, Joseph IV, 531
oge, Joseph IV, 559
oge, Joseph VI, 401
oge, Joseph VI, 506
oge, Joseph VI, 654
oge, Joseph L. IV, 532
oge, Joseph Phil VI, 654
oge, Joseph Philo VI, 654
oge, Joseph S. IV, 223
oge, Joseph S. IV, 283
oge, Joseph S. IV, 444
oge, Josephine VI, 401
oge, Joshua IV, 336
Hoge, Joshua VI, 506
Hoge, Joshua VI, 644
Hoge, Joshua VI, 652
Hoge, Joshua VI, 653
Hoge, Joshua VI, 654
Hoge, Joshua H. IV, 336
Hoge, Joshua, Jr. VI, 644
Hoge, Kenworthy IV, 223
Hoge, L. N., Jr. VI, 402
Hoge, Laura IV, 223
Hoge, Laura VI, 652
Hoge, Laura VI, 704
Hoge, Laura S. VI, 647
Hoge, Lavina IV, 39
Hoge, Lavina H. IV, 559
Hoge, Leah IV, 39
Hoge, Leah IV, 44
Hoge, Lelia IV, 223
Hoge, Levi IV, 530
Hoge, Levi IV, 531
Hoge, Lewis VI, 69
Hoge, Lewis VI, 400
Hoge, Lewis VI, 441
Hoge, Lewis N. I, 548
Hoge, Lewis N. VI, 400
Hoge, Lewis N. VI, 401
Hoge, Lewis N. VI, 402
Hoge, Lewis N., Jr. I, 548
Hoge, Lindley IV, 336
Hoge, Lindley IV, 532
Hoge, Lindley M. IV, 222
Hoge, Lindley M. IV, 336
Hoge, Lindley M. IV, 531
Hoge, Lindley M. IV, 532
Hoge, Lindley M. IV, 551
Hoge, Louis VI, 410
Hoge, Louis N., Jr. VI, 402
Hoge, Louis Neil VI, 401
Hoge, Lundy B. IV, 336
Hoge, Lydia IV, 322
Hoge, Lydia IV, 328
Hoge, Lydia IV, 336
Hoge, Lydia IV, 509
Hoge, Lydia IV, 512
Hoge, Lydia IV, 530
Hoge, Lydia IV, 531
Hoge, Lydia IV, 532
Hoge, Lydia V, 304
Hoge, Lydia V, 312
Hoge, Lydia VI, 506
Hoge, Lydia VI, 643
Hoge, Lydia VI, 644
Hoge, Lydia VI, 652
Hoge, Lydia VI, 653
Hoge, Lydia VI, 654
Hoge, Lydia Ann VI, 652
Hoge, Lydia Ann VI, 653
Hoge, Lydia Ann VI, 694
Hoge, Lydia Ann VI, 789
Hoge, Lydia Anna VI, 653
Hoge, Lydia Anna VI, 718
Hoge, Lydia Anna VI, 749
Hoge, Lydia Anna VI, 789
Hoge, Lydia M. IV, 366
Hoge, Margaret VI, 632
Hoge, Margaret VI, 652
Hoge, Margaret VI, 685
Hoge, Margaret VI, 694
Hoge, Margaret B. IV, 223
Hoge, Margaretta R. VI, 401
Hoge, Margery VI, 506
Hoge, Margery VI, 654
Hoge, Marie VI, 69
Hoge, Martha IV, 532
Hoge, Martha VI, 389
Hoge, Martha VI, 401
Hoge, Martha C. IV, 532
Hoge, Martha C. IV, 551
Hoge, Martha S. IV, 532
Hoge, Mary II, 232
Hoge, Mary II, 247
Hoge, Mary IV, 23
Hoge, Mary IV, 39
Hoge, Mary IV, 93
Hoge, Mary IV, 336
Hoge, Mary IV, 345
Hoge, Mary IV, 410
Hoge, Mary IV, 530
Hoge, Mary IV, 531
Hoge, Mary IV, 532
Hoge, Mary IV, 533
Hoge, Mary IV, 534
Hoge, Mary IV, 559
Hoge, Mary VI, 374
Hoge, Mary VI, 388
Hoge, Mary VI, 393
Hoge, Mary VI, 400
Hoge, Mary VI, 401
Hoge, Mary VI, 408
Hoge, Mary VI, 506
Hoge, Mary VI, 539
Hoge, Mary VI, 551
Hoge, Mary VI, 577
Hoge, Mary VI, 587
Hoge, Mary VI, 643
Hoge, Mary VI, 652
Hoge, Mary VI, 653
Hoge, Mary VI, 654
Hoge, Mary VI, 657
Hoge, Mary VI, 664
Hoge, Mary VI, 668
Hoge, Mary VI, 674
Hoge, Mary VI, 682
Hoge, Mary VI, 694
Hoge, Mary VI, 713
Hoge, Mary VI, 749
Hoge, Mary Alma IV, 223
Hoge, Mary Ann IV, 222
Hoge, Mary Ann IV, 223
Hoge, Mary Ann IV, 531
Hoge, Mary Ann IV, 532
Hoge, Mary Ann IV, 533
Hoge, Mary Ann IV, 534
Hoge, Mary B. IV, 223
Hoge, Mary C. IV, 1282
Hoge, Mary E. II, 746
Hoge, Mary Elizabeth IV, 223
Hoge, Mary Elizabeth IV, 336
Hoge, Mary Ellen VI, 652
Hoge, Mary Ellen VI, 653
Hoge, Mary Ellen VI, 654
Hoge, Mary Ellen VI, 660
Hoge, Mary Ellen VI, 670
Hoge, Mary Ellen VI, 711
Hoge, Mary Ellen VI, 713
Hoge, Mary Elma IV, 223
Hoge, Mary Emily IV, 336
Hoge, Mary Estella IV, 532
Hoge, Mary H. IV, 223
Hoge, Mary Jane IV, 532
Hoge, Mary S. IV, 722
Hoge, Mary T. IV, 329
Hoge, Mary T. IV, 336
Hoge, Mary T. VI, 401
Hoge, Mary Thomasin V, 502
Hoge, Maryann IV, 336
Hoge, Miller IV, 93
Hoge, Nathan VI, 653
Hoge, Nimrod IV, 336
Hoge, Nimrod VI, 652
Hoge, Owen VI, 400
Hoge, Peter IV, 93
Hoge, Peter Miller IV, 93
Hoge, Peter Miller IV, 532
Hoge, Phebe I, 1031
Hoge, Phebe I, 1048
Hoge, Phebe IV, 32
Hoge, Phebe IV, 39
Hoge, Phebe IV, 332
Hoge, Phebe IV, 336
Hoge, Phebe IV, 559
Hoge, Phebe V, 73
Hoge, Phebe VI, 249
Hoge, Phebe VI, 400
Hoge, Phebe VI, 401
Hoge, Phebe VI, 402
Hoge, Phebe W. IV, 509
Hoge, Phebe W. IV, 510
Hoge, Phebe W. IV, 531
Hoge, Phebe W. IV, 532
Hoge, Phila VI, 653
Hoge, Phila VI, 657
Hoge, Pleasant IV, 336
Hoge, Pleasant IV, 344
Hoge, Pleasant VI, 653
Hoge, Rachel IV, 25
Hoge, Rachel IV, 39
Hoge, Rachel IV, 93
Hoge, Rachel IV, 107
Hoge, Rachel IV, 222
Hoge, Rachel IV, 223
Hoge, Rachel IV, 324
Hoge, Rachel IV, 336
Hoge, Rachel IV, 366
Hoge, Rachel IV, 531
Hoge, Rachel IV, 532
Hoge, Rachel IV, 533
Hoge, Rachel IV, 539
Hoge, Rachel IV, 559
Hoge, Rachel IV, 722
Hoge, Rachel VI, 236
Hoge, Rachel VI, 237
Hoge, Rachel VI, 381
Hoge, Rachel VI, 401
Hoge, Rachel VI, 402
Hoge, Rachel VI, 622
Hoge, Rachel VI, 651
Hoge, Rachel VI, 652
Hoge, Rachel VI, 654
Hoge, Rachel VI, 658
Hoge, Rachel VI, 668
Hoge, Rachel B. IV, 532
Hoge, Rachel Ellicott VI, 749
Hoge, Rachel Louise VI, 652
Hoge, Rachel N. VI, 401
Hoge, Rachel N. VI, 402
Hoge, Rachel N. VI, 441
Hoge, Rachel P. IV, 222
Hoge, Rachel P. IV, 477
Hoge, Rachel P. IV, 486
Hoge, Rachel P. IV, 531
Hoge, Rachel P. IV, 532
Hoge, Rachel P. IV, 539
Hoge, Rachel T. IV, 223
Hoge, Rachell Ellicott VI, 753
Hoge, Rebecca II, 36
Hoge, Rebecca IV, 327
Hoge, Rebecca IV, 336
Hoge, Rebecca IV, 531
Hoge, Rebecca IV, 532
Hoge, Rebecca IV, 534
Hoge, Rebecca IV, 559
Hoge, Rebecca IV, 681
Hoge, Rebecca IV, 722
Hoge, Rebecca V, 502
Hoge, Rebecca VI, 401
Hoge, Rebecca VI, 524
Hoge, Rebecca VI, 653
Hoge, Rebecca VI, 670
Hoge, Rebecca B. IV, 336
Hoge, Rebecca Lupton V, 502
Hoge, Rebecca M. VI, 401
Hoge, Rebecca McPherson V, 502
Hoge, Rebecca P. IV, 722
Hoge, Rebecca W. IV, 531
Hoge, Rebecca W. IV, 532
Hoge, Rebeckah II, 1039
Hoge, Rebeckah IV, 559
Hoge, Rebekah VI, 506
Hoge, Rebekah VI, 652
Hoge, Rebekah VI, 654
Hoge, Rebekah VI, 749
Hoge, Rebekah VI, 759
Hoge, Rmbk VI, 652
Hoge, Ross C. VI, 652
Hoge, Ruth IV, 336
Hoge, Ruth VI, 401
Hoge, Ruth VI, 506
Hoge, Ruth VI, 644
Hoge, Ruth VI, 652
Hoge, Ruth VI, 654
Hoge, Ruthanna IV, 193
Hoge, Ruthanna IV, 223
Hoge, Ruthanna IV, 336
Hoge, Ruthanna IV, 348
Hoge, Sabina C. IV, 223
Hoge, Sallie J. VI, 402
Hoge, Sallie J. VI, 446
Hoge, Sallie Janney VI, 401
Hoge, Samuel IV, 336
Hoge, Samuel IV, 532
Hoge, Samuel VI, 506
Hoge, Samuel VI, 653
Hoge, Samuel VI, 654
Hoge, Samuel VI, 657
Hoge, Samuel E. IV, 223
Hoge, Samuel G. IV, 532
Hoge, Samuel T. IV, 532
Hoge, Samuel, Jr. IV, 336
Hoge, Sarah IV, 24
Hoge, Sarah IV, 39
Hoge, Sarah IV, 93
Hoge, Sarah IV, 125
Hoge, Sarah IV, 127
Hoge, Sarah IV, 222
Hoge, Sarah IV, 335
Hoge, Sarah IV, 336
Hoge, Sarah IV, 338
Hoge, Sarah IV, 359
Hoge, Sarah IV, 410
Hoge, Sarah IV, 531
Hoge, Sarah IV, 533
Hoge, Sarah IV, 534
Hoge, Sarah IV, 559
Hoge, Sarah VI, 494
Hoge, Sarah VI, 496
Hoge, Sarah VI, 506
Hoge, Sarah VI, 652
Hoge, Sarah VI, 654
Hoge, Sarah A. IV, 964
Hoge, Sarah A. IV, 971
Hoge, Sarah Ann IV, 223
Hoge, Sarah Ann IV, 1282
Hoge, Sarah Ann VI, 654
Hoge, Sarah Ann VI, 664
Hoge, Sarah B. IV, 964
Hoge, Sarah E. VI, 401
Hoge, Sarah E. VI, 632
Hoge, Sarah E. VI, 652
Hoge, Sarah E. VI, 685
Hoge, Sarah E. VI, 699
Hoge, Sarah E. VI, 706
Hoge, Sarah Eleanor VI, 654
Hoge, Sarah Eleanor VI, 682
Hoge, Sarah Elizabeth VI, 652
Hoge, Sarah Elizabeth VI, 704
Hoge, Sarah Elizabeth VI, 711
Hoge, Sarah Elizabeth VI, 713
Hoge, Sarah H. VI, 615
Hoge, Sarah H. VI, 652
Hoge, Sarah H. VI, 706
Hoge, Sarah J. VI, 400
Hoge, Sarah Jane IV, 336
Hoge, Sarah, Jr. IV, 322
Hoge, Schooley IV, 559
Hoge, Smith B. IV, 532
Hoge, Solomon IV, 39
Hoge, Solomon IV, 336
Hoge, Solomon VI, 401
Hoge, Solomon VI, 505
Hoge, Solomon VI, 506
Hoge, Solomon VI, 524
Hoge, Solomon VI, 539
Hoge, Solomon VI, 643
Hoge, Solomon VI, 644
Hoge, Solomon VI, 652
Hoge, Solomon VI, 653
Hoge, Solomon VI, 654
Hoge, Solomon VI, 657
Hoge, Solomon VI, 670
Hoge, Solomon VI, 682
Hoge, Solomon VI, 749
Hoge, Solomon VI, 759
Hoge, Solomon Elijah VI, 654
Hoge, Solomon, Jr. VI, 506
Hoge, Solomon, Jr. VI, 654
Hoge, Solomon, Sr. VI, 654
Hoge, Susan IV, 223
Hoge, Susan IV, 336
Hoge, Susan VI, 625
Hoge, Susan VI, 654
Hoge, Susan VI, 679
Hoge, Susan B. I, 548
Hoge, Susan B. VI, 69
Hoge, Susan B. VI, 400
Hoge, Susan B. VI, 402
Hoge, Susan B. VI, 441
Hoge, Susan Catharine VI, 664
Hoge, Susana B. VI, 410
Hoge, Susanna IV, 336
Hoge, Susanna VI, 624
Hoge, Susanna VI, 654
Hoge, Susanna B. VI, 401
Hoge, Susanna B. VI, 402
Hoge, Susannah IV, 234
Hoge, Susannah IV, 336
Hoge, Susannah IV, 339
Hoge, Susannah VI, 401
Hoge, Sussanah IV, 222
Hoge, Tacy IV, 93
Hoge, Tacy IV, 127
Hoge, Tamar VI, 506
Hoge, Tamar VI, 654
Hoge, Theodoric IV, 336
Hoge, Thomas IV, 39
Hoge, Thomas IV, 531
Hoge, Thomas C. IV, 532
Hoge, Thomas E. IV, 332
Hoge, Thomas E. IV, 336
Hoge, Thomas Elwood IV, 336
Hoge, Thomas Elwood VI, 654
Hoge, Thomas R. IV, 336
Hoge, Thomas Wilson IV, 223
Hoge, Thos. R. IV, 329
Hoge, Thos. W. IV, 223
Hoge, Ulyssus IV, 532
Hoge, W. T. VI, 402
Hoge, Washington IV, 332
Hoge, Washington IV, 336
Hoge, Washington VI, 654
Hoge, Wd. Margaret VI, 551
Hoge, Wd. Margaret Ward VI, 506
Hoge, Wd. Mary Holmes VI, 506
Hoge, Widow Grace VI, 632
Hoge, Widow Grace VI, 652
Hoge, Widow Grace VI, 685
Hoge, Widow Margaret VI, 653
Hoge, Widow Margaret VI, 654
Hoge, Widow Margaret VI, 694
Hoge, Widow Margaret Reese VI, 577
Hoge, Widow Mary VI, 654
Hoge, Widow Mary VI, 657
Hoge, William I, 1031
Hoge, William I, 1048
Hoge, William II, 232
Hoge, William II, 247
Hoge, William IV, 39
Hoge, William IV, 93
Hoge, William IV, 167
Hoge, William IV, 223
Hoge, William IV, 336
Hoge, William IV, 531

Hoge, William IV, 532
Hoge, William IV, 533
Hoge, William IV, 534
Hoge, William IV, 559
Hoge, William VI, 400
Hoge, William VI, 401
Hoge, William VI, 506
Hoge, William VI, 577
Hoge, William VI, 653
Hoge, William VI, 654
Hoge, William VI, 658
Hoge, William VI, 668
Hoge, William VI, 674
Hoge, William VI, 713
Hoge, William VI, 753
Hoge, William H. IV, 223
Hoge, William H. IV, 336
Hoge, William S. VI, 401
Hoge, William, Jr. VI, 401
Hoge, Willie S. VI, 402
Hoge, Wm. IV, 93
Hoge, Wm. IV, 359
Hoge, Wm. IV, 366
Hoge, Wm. IV, 531
Hoge, Wm. VI, 401
Hoge, Wm. VI, 506
Hoge, Wm. VI, 551
Hoge, Wm. VI, 622
Hoge, Wm. VI, 651
Hoge, Wm. VI, 652
Hoge, Wm. VI, 654
Hoge, Wm. VI, 664
Hoge, Wm. VI, 668
Hoge, Wm. VI, 694
Hoge, Wm. VI, 749
Hoge, Wm. K. VI, 664
Hoge, Zebulon II, 232
Hoge-Craven, Grace VI, 669
Hoge-Craven, Grace VI, 678
Hoge???, Mary VI, 676
Hoge???, Samuel VI, 676
Hoge???, Solomon VI, 676
Hoge???, Widow Mary VI, 676
Hogeland, Enoch V, 981
Hoges, William II, 444
Hoget, Mary I, 988
Hogg, Charles Edward III, 168
Hogg, Edward Charles III, 223
Hogg, Emily III, 168
Hogg, Emily A. III, 168
Hogg, Emily A. III, 223
Hogg, Emma F. II, 876
Hogg, Emma T. II, 862
Hogg, Emma T. II, 876
Hogg, Hannah II, 232
Hogg, Hannah II, 270
Hogg, Hannah II, 273
Hogg, James I, 1
Hogg, James II, 550
Hogg, James II, 594
Hogg, John VI, 181
Hogg, Martha VI, 181
Hogg, Martha VI, 197
Hogg, Rebecca II, 375
Hogg, Rebecca II, 524
Hogg, Rebecca II, 550
Hogg, Rebeccah II, 375
Hogg, Samuel VI, 181
Hogg, Sarah VI, 485
Hogg, Sarah VI, 496
Hogg, Susannah II, 550
Hogg, Susannah II, 594
Hogg, Thomas II, 375
Hogg, Thomas VI, 181
Hogg, Thomas VI, 197
Hogg, William VI, 357
Hoggard, Anna IV, 223
Hoggard, John T. IV, 223
Hoggart, Elizabeth I, 551
Hoggart, Nathan I, 551
Hoggat, Anthony I, 956
Hoggat, Anthony VI, 268
Hoggat, Benjamin I, 956
Hoggat, Benjamin I, 957
Hoggat, Charity I, 956
Hoggat, Charity I, 957
Hoggat, David I, 547
Hoggat, Deborah I, 885
Hoggat, Ede VI, 268
Hoggat, Eli I, 957
Hoggat, Elizabeth V, 73
Hoggat, Esther I, 957
Hoggat, Hannah I, 886
Hoggat, Hannah I, 957
Hoggat, Jared V, 73
Hoggat, Joseph V, 73
Hoggat, Leah I, 957
Hoggat, Margaret I, 1084
Hoggat, Mary I, 956
Hoggat, Mary I, 957
Hoggat, Mary I, 1085
Hoggat, Mary VI, 268
Hoggat, Moses I, 1084
Hoggat, Moses I, 1085
Hoggat, Neri I, 957
Hoggat, Orpha V, 73
Hoggat, Phillips I, 271
Hoggat, Prudence I, 1085
Hoggat, Rachel I, 957
Hoggat, Rebecah I, 1084
Hoggat, Rebecah I, 1085
Hoggat, Rebeccah I, 1085
Hoggat, Samuel I, 547
Hoggat, Sarah I, 957
Hoggat, Sarah I, 1085
Hoggath, William I, 764
Hoggatt, ??? V, 315
Hoggatt, Aaron I, 501
Hoggatt, Aaron I, 856
Hoggatt, Aaron I, 885
Hoggatt, Aaron V, 73
Hoggatt, Abigail I, 856
Hoggatt, Abigail I, 877
Hoggatt, Abigail I, 885
Hoggatt, Abner I, 856
Hoggatt, Agnes I, 814
Hoggatt, Agnes I, 817
Hoggatt, Agnes V, 338
Hoggatt, Agnes V, 502
Hoggatt, Agness I, 501
Hoggatt, Agness I, 1005
Hoggatt, Agness V, 247
Hoggatt, Alca I, 501
Hoggatt, Alce V, 73
Hoggatt, Alice I, 501
Hoggatt, Alice I, 547
Hoggatt, Alice I, 548
Hoggatt, Alice I, 581
Hoggatt, Alice V, 247
Hoggatt, Alice V, 338
Hoggatt, Alphonzo I, 856
Hoggatt, Ann I, 547
Hoggatt, Ann I, 548
Hoggatt, Ann I, 578
Hoggatt, Ann I, 656
Hoggatt, Ann I, 783
Hoggatt, Ann I, 856
Hoggatt, Ann I, 885
Hoggatt, Ann V, 239
Hoggatt, Ann V, 247
Hoggatt, Ann V, 338
Hoggatt, Ann V, 502
Hoggatt, Anna I, 818
Hoggatt, Anna I, 856
Hoggatt, Anna I, 885
Hoggatt, Anna I, 886
Hoggatt, Anna I, 1005
Hoggatt, Anna I, 1010
Hoggatt, Anna I, 1107
Hoggatt, Anna V, 247
Hoggatt, Anna V, 338
Hoggatt, Anna B. V, 248
Hoggatt, Anthony I, 487
Hoggatt, Anthony I, 501
Hoggatt, Anthony I, 547
Hoggatt, Anthony I, 783
Hoggatt, Anthony I, 817
Hoggatt, Anthony I, 818
Hoggatt, Anthony I, 957
Hoggatt, Anthony I, 964
Hoggatt, Anthony I, 1094
Hoggatt, Anthony V, 247
Hoggatt, Asa S. V, 247
Hoggatt, Benj. I, 959
Hoggatt, Benjamin I, 501
Hoggatt, Benjamin I, 856
Hoggatt, Benjamin I, 885
Hoggatt, Benjamin I, 886
Hoggatt, Benjamin I, 964
Hoggatt, Benjamin I, 1094
Hoggatt, Benjamin V, 247
Hoggatt, Betsy I, 856
Hoggatt, Betsy V, 248
Hoggatt, Catharine I, 501
Hoggatt, Charity I, 547
Hoggatt, Charity I, 783
Hoggatt, Charity I, 815
Hoggatt, Charity I, 817
Hoggatt, Charity I, 829
Hoggatt, Charity I, 856
Hoggatt, Charity I, 885
Hoggatt, Charity I, 959
Hoggatt, Charity I, 964
Hoggatt, Charity V, 247
Hoggatt, Cina V, 247
Hoggatt, Daniel H. V, 73
Hoggatt, David I, 501
Hoggatt, David I, 547
Hoggatt, David I, 548
Hoggatt, David I, 578
Hoggatt, David I, 582
Hoggatt, David I, 783
Hoggatt, David I, 817
Hoggatt, David I, 818
Hoggatt, David I, 1005
Hoggatt, David I, 1010
Hoggatt, David V, 73
Hoggatt, David V, 247
Hoggatt, David V, 338
Hoggatt, Deborah I, 885
Hoggatt, Deborah V, 73
Hoggatt, Dorcas I, 547
Hoggatt, Dorcas I, 582
Hoggatt, Dorcas I, 783
Hoggatt, Dorcas I, 818
Hoggatt, Dorcas I, 1005
Hoggatt, Dorcas I, 1010
Hoggatt, Dorcas V, 338
Hoggatt, Dorcious I, 817
Hoggatt, Earl V, 73
Hoggatt, Eda I, 1107
Hoggatt, Edith I, 655
Hoggatt, Edith I, 885
Hoggatt, Edith V, 247
Hoggatt, Edward I, 656
Hoggatt, Edward V, 248
Hoggatt, Eleazor V, 338
Hoggatt, Eli I, 885
Hoggatt, Eli V, 247
Hoggatt, Elisha I, 856
Hoggatt, Eliza V, 338
Hoggatt, Elizabeth I, 547
Hoggatt, Elizabeth I, 548
Hoggatt, Elizabeth I, 656
Hoggatt, Elizabeth I, 818
Hoggatt, Elizabeth I, 856
Hoggatt, Elizabeth I, 875
Hoggatt, Elizabeth I, 884
Hoggatt, Elizabeth I, 885
Hoggatt, Elizabeth I, 886
Hoggatt, Elizabeth I, 898
Hoggatt, Elizabeth I, 899
Hoggatt, Elizabeth V, 73
Hoggatt, Elizabeth V, 247
Hoggatt, Elizabeth V, 248
Hoggatt, Elizabeth V, 338
Hoggatt, Elizabeth V, 364
Hoggatt, Elsie V, 73
Hoggatt, Elve I, 856
Hoggatt, George I, 501
Hoggatt, Hannah I, 501
Hoggatt, Hannah I, 525
Hoggatt, Hannah I, 547
Hoggatt, Hannah I, 656
Hoggatt, Hannah I, 674
Hoggatt, Hannah I, 676
Hoggatt, Hannah I, 680
Hoggatt, Hannah I, 687
Hoggatt, Hannah I, 764
Hoggatt, Hannah I, 886
Hoggatt, Hannah V, 239
Hoggatt, Hannah V, 247
Hoggatt, Hezekiah I, 655
Hoggatt, Hezekiah I, 680
Hoggatt, Hezekiah I, 687
Hoggatt, Hezekiah V, 247
Hoggatt, Higby I, 1122
Hoggatt, Highla I, 957
Hoggatt, Highla I, 976
Hoggatt, Highla I, 1010
Hoggatt, Highly I, 1119
Hoggatt, Highly I, 1122
Hoggatt, Idith I, 885
Hoggatt, Isaac I, 547
Hoggatt, Isaac I, 656
Hoggatt, Isaac I, 1085
Hoggatt, Isaac I, 1122
Hoggatt, Isaac V, 239
Hoggatt, Isaac V, 247
Hoggatt, Isaac V, 502
Hoggatt, Isaac Mendenhall I, 547
Hoggatt, Isaiah I, 885
Hoggatt, Jacob I, 856
Hoggatt, Jacob V, 73
Hoggatt, Jane I, 398
Hoggatt, Jane I, 408
Hoggatt, Jane I, 548
Hoggatt, Jane I, 656
Hoggatt, Jane I, 680
Hoggatt, Jane I, 817
Hoggatt, Jane I, 856
Hoggatt, Jane I, 885
Hoggatt, Jane V, 247
Hoggatt, Jared V, 73
Hoggatt, Jean I, 547
Hoggatt, Jean V, 73
Hoggatt, Jesse I, 501
Hoggatt, Jesse I, 680
Hoggatt, Jesse I, 685
Hoggatt, Jesse I, 817
Hoggatt, Jesse I, 847
Hoggatt, Jesse I, 856
Hoggatt, Jesse I, 885
Hoggatt, Jesse I, 964
Hoggatt, Jesse I, 1005
Hoggatt, Jesse V, 338
Hoggatt, Joel I, 885
Hoggatt, Joel I, 957
Hoggatt, Joel I, 988
Hoggatt, Joel I, 1094
Hoggatt, Joel I, 1122
Hoggatt, John I, 343
Hoggatt, John I, 398
Hoggatt, John I, 501
Hoggatt, John I, 525
Hoggatt, John I, 547
Hoggatt, John I, 656
Hoggatt, John I, 680
Hoggatt, John I, 773
Hoggatt, John I, 847
Hoggatt, John I, 856
Hoggatt, John I, 885
Hoggatt, John I, 1085
Hoggatt, John I, 1122
Hoggatt, John V, 247
Hoggatt, John V, 248
Hoggatt, John V, 338
Hoggatt, Jonathan I, 501
Hoggatt, Jonathan I, 547
Hoggatt, Jonathan I, 582
Hoggatt, Jonathan I, 783
Hoggatt, Jonathan I, 817
Hoggatt, Jonathan I, 964
Hoggatt, Jonathan I, 1005
Hoggatt, Jonathan I, 1010
Hoggatt, Jonathan V, 247
Hoggatt, Jonathan V, 338
Hoggatt, Joseph I, 487
Hoggatt, Joseph I, 501
Hoggatt, Joseph I, 544
Hoggatt, Joseph I, 547
Hoggatt, Joseph I, 548
Hoggatt, Joseph I, 578
Hoggatt, Joseph I, 656
Hoggatt, Joseph I, 773
Hoggatt, Joseph I, 783
Hoggatt, Joseph I, 817
Hoggatt, Joseph I, 818
Hoggatt, Joseph I, 847
Hoggatt, Joseph I, 856
Hoggatt, Joseph I, 885
Hoggatt, Joseph I, 886
Hoggatt, Joseph I, 898
Hoggatt, Joseph I, 964
Hoggatt, Joseph I, 971
Hoggatt, Joseph I, 1094
Hoggatt, Joseph V, 73
Hoggatt, Joseph V, 247
Hoggatt, Joseph V, 248
Hoggatt, Joseph D. I, 857
Hoggatt, Joseph, Jr. I, 885
Hoggatt, Josiah I, 957
Hoggatt, Josiah I, 1094
Hoggatt, Josiah I, 1122
Hoggatt, Julia I, 885
Hoggatt, Julia V, 73
Hoggatt, Lebitha I, 655
Hoggatt, Louzena I, 856
Hoggatt, Louzena I, 988
Hoggatt, Lucinda V, 73
Hoggatt, Luzena I, 885
Hoggatt, Luzena S. I, 988
Hoggatt, Lydia I, 501
Hoggatt, Lydia I, 547
Hoggatt, Lydia I, 550
Hoggatt, Lydia I, 1085
Hoggatt, Lydia I, 1122
Hoggatt, Lydia V, 338
Hoggatt, Mahlon I, 501
Hoggatt, Mahlon I, 656
Hoggatt, Mahlon I, 783
Hoggatt, Mahlon I, 856
Hoggatt, Mahlon I, 885
Hoggatt, Mahlon I, 886
Hoggatt, Mahlon I, 894
Hoggatt, Mahlon I, 988
Hoggatt, Mahlon V, 338
Hoggatt, Mahlon, Jr. I, 885
Hoggatt, Malon I, 1005
Hoggatt, Margaret I, 501
Hoggatt, Margaret I, 547
Hoggatt, Margaret I, 548
Hoggatt, Margaret I, 578
Hoggatt, Margaret I, 656
Hoggatt, Margaret I, 674
Hoggatt, Margaret I, 680
Hoggatt, Margaret V, 73
Hoggatt, Margaret V, 238
Hoggatt, Margaret V, 239
Hoggatt, Margaret V, 247
Hoggatt, Margaret V, 248
Hoggatt, Margaret V, 502
Hoggatt, Margarett V, 247
Hoggatt, Margret I, 656
Hoggatt, Martha I, 501
Hoggatt, Martha I, 655
Hoggatt, Martha I, 680
Hoggatt, Martha I, 687
Hoggatt, Martha I, 856
Hoggatt, Martha I, 885
Hoggatt, Martha I, 886
Hoggatt, Martha V, 247
Hoggatt, Martha L. I, 857
Hoggatt, Mary I, 408
Hoggatt, Mary I, 501
Hoggatt, Mary I, 547
Hoggatt, Mary I, 548
Hoggatt, Mary I, 582
Hoggatt, Mary I, 655
Hoggatt, Mary I, 719
Hoggatt, Mary I, 721
Hoggatt, Mary I, 783
Hoggatt, Mary I, 797
Hoggatt, Mary I, 817
Hoggatt, Mary I, 818
Hoggatt, Mary I, 841
Hoggatt, Mary I, 856
Hoggatt, Mary I, 957
Hoggatt, Mary I, 964
Hoggatt, Mary I, 967
Hoggatt, Mary I, 976
Hoggatt, Mary I, 988
Hoggatt, Mary I, 1005
Hoggatt, Mary I, 1010
Hoggatt, Mary I, 1085
Hoggatt, Mary I, 1094
Hoggatt, Mary I, 1106
Hoggatt, Mary I, 1122
Hoggatt, Mary V, 73
Hoggatt, Mary V, 247
Hoggatt, Mary V, 248
Hoggatt, Mary V, 483
Hoggatt, Mary V, 502
Hoggatt, Maryan I, 856
Hoggatt, Matilda V, 248
Hoggatt, Meriam I, 885
Hoggatt, Meriam V, 73
Hoggatt, Milly V, 247
Hoggatt, Milton I, 656
Hoggatt, Miriam I, 501
Hoggatt, Miriam I, 885
Hoggatt, Miriam I, 891
Hoggatt, Moses I, 501
Hoggatt, Moses I, 817
Hoggatt, Moses I, 856
Hoggatt, Moses I, 885
Hoggatt, Moses I, 962
Hoggatt, Moses I, 964
Hoggatt, Moses I, 1077
Hoggatt, Moses I, 1094
Hoggatt, Moses V, 73
Hoggatt, Moses V, 247
Hoggatt, Moses V, 502
Hoggatt, Nancy Edna I, 856
Hoggatt, Naomi T. V, 73
Hoggatt, Nathan I, 501
Hoggatt, Nathan I, 548
Hoggatt, Nathan I, 655
Hoggatt, Nathan I, 656
Hoggatt, Nathan I, 783
Hoggatt, Nathan I, 856
Hoggatt, Nathan I, 885
Hoggatt, Nathan I, 901
Hoggatt, Nathan I, 957
Hoggatt, Nathan I, 1094
Hoggatt, Nathan I, 1122
Hoggatt, Nathan V, 247
Hoggatt, Nathan V, 338
Hoggatt, Nathan, Jr. I, 856
Hoggatt, Neri V, 247
Hoggatt, Noah I, 1107
Hoggatt, Olive V, 502
Hoggatt, Orpha V, 73
Hoggatt, Phebe I, 501
Hoggatt, Phebe I, 544
Hoggatt, Phebe I, 547
Hoggatt, Phebe I, 656
Hoggatt, Phebe I, 773
Hoggatt, Phebe I, 783
Hoggatt, Phebe I, 817
Hoggatt, Phebe I, 847
Hoggatt, Phebe I, 856
Hoggatt, Phebe I, 885
Hoggatt, Phebe I, 896
Hoggatt, Phebe V, 73
Hoggatt, Phebe V, 239
Hoggatt, Phebe V, 247
Hoggatt, Phebe Elizabeth I, 85
Hoggatt, Phebe, Jr. I, 847
Hoggatt, Pheby I, 783
Hoggatt, Philip I, 501
Hoggatt, Philip I, 547
Hoggatt, Philip I, 548
Hoggatt, Philip I, 581
Hoggatt, Philip I, 783

ggatt, Philip I, 817
ggatt, Philip I, 841
ggatt, Philip I, 885
ggatt, Philip V, 247
ggatt, Phillip I, 501
ggatt, Phillip I, 721
ggatt, Phillip I, 856
ggatt, Phillip V, 338
ggatt, Prudence V, 73
ggatt, Prudence V, 502
ggatt, Rachel I, 501
ggatt, Rachel I, 547
ggatt, Rachel I, 561
ggatt, Rachel I, 856
ggatt, Rachel I, 885
ggatt, Rachel V, 73
ggatt, Rachel V, 247
ggatt, Rachel V, 501
ggatt, Rachel V, 502
ggatt, Rebecca V, 247
ggatt, Rebecca V, 502
ggatt, Rebecca R. V, 248
ggatt, Rebekah I, 962
ggatt, Rebekah I, 964
ggatt, Rhoda V, 73
ggatt, Robert V, 73
ggatt, Ruth I, 501
ggatt, Ruth I, 525
ggatt, Ruth I, 547
ggatt, Ruth I, 680
ggatt, Ruth I, 773
ggatt, Ruth I, 783
ggatt, Ruth I, 847
ggatt, Ruth I, 856
ggatt, Ruth I, 877
ggatt, Ruth I, 885
ggatt, Ruth I, 891
ggatt, Ruth I, 964
ggatt, Ruth V, 74
ggatt, Ruth V, 224
ggatt, Ruth V, 247
ggatt, Ruth V, 338
ggatt, Sallie I, 656
ggatt, Sally I, 656
ggatt, Samuel I, 501
ggatt, Samuel I, 547
ggatt, Samuel I, 550
ggatt, Samuel I, 783
ggatt, Samuel I, 817
ggatt, Samuel I, 829
ggatt, Samuel I, 856
ggatt, Samuel I, 957
ggatt, Samuel I, 964
ggatt, Samuel I, 967
ggatt, Samuel I, 976
ggatt, Samuel I, 988
ggatt, Samuel I, 1085
ggatt, Samuel I, 1094
ggatt, Samuel I, 1106
ggatt, Samuel I, 1122
ggatt, Sarah I, 548
ggatt, Sarah I, 578
ggatt, Sarah I, 656
ggatt, Sarah I, 856
ggatt, Sarah I, 871
ggatt, Sarah I, 885
ggatt, Sarah I, 894
ggatt, Sarah I, 901
ggatt, Sarah I, 957
ggatt, Sarah I, 988
ggatt, Sarah I, 1010
ggatt, Sarah I, 1122
ggatt, Sarah I, 1133
ggatt, Sarah V, 73
ggatt, Sarah V, 239
ggatt, Sarah V, 247
ggatt, Sarah V, 502
ggatt, Sarah, Jr. I, 885
ggatt, Sarrah V, 247
ggatt, Seth I, 783
ggatt, Seth I, 964
ggatt, Seth I, 1005
ggatt, Seth V, 247
ggatt, Seth V, 338
ggatt, Solomon I, 501
ggatt, Solomon I, 964
ggatt, Stephanas I, 885
ggatt, Stephanus I, 501
ggatt, Stephanus I, 783
ggatt, Stephanus I, 817
ggatt, Stephen I, 547
ggatt, Stephen I, 548
ggatt, Stephen I, 578
ggatt, Stephen I, 656
ggatt, Stephen V, 239
ggatt, Stephen V, 247
ggatt, Stephen V, 248
ggatt, Stephenus I, 817
ggatt, Susanna I, 856
ggatt, Susannah J. I, 886
ggatt, Susannah J. I, 889
Hoggatt, Tabitha I, 885
Hoggatt, Tabitha V, 247
Hoggatt, Warner I, 856
Hoggatt, Warner I, 885
Hoggatt, Wellmet I, 885
Hoggatt, William I, 343
Hoggatt, William I, 398
Hoggatt, William I, 501
Hoggatt, William I, 525
Hoggatt, William I, 547
Hoggatt, William I, 656
Hoggatt, William I, 687
Hoggatt, William I, 764
Hoggatt, William I, 783
Hoggatt, William I, 856
Hoggatt, William I, 871
Hoggatt, William I, 875
Hoggatt, William I, 885
Hoggatt, William I, 886
Hoggatt, William V, 247
Hoggatt, William V, 501
Hoggatt, William V, 502
Hoggatt, Zadock V, 247
Hoggatt, Zimri I, 783
Hoggatt, Zimri I, 856
Hoggatt, Zimri I, 885
Hoggatt, Zimri I, 886
Hoggatt, Zimri I, 889
Hoggatt, Zimri Rowland I, 857
Hoggatt, Zodok I, 655
Hogge, Susannah VI, 413
Hoggen, Nathan I, 763
Hoggeon, Josiah I, 763
Hoggerty, Anna F. V, 399
Hoggerty, Leslie T. V, 399
Hoggerty, William F. V, 399
Hogget, Dorcious I, 817
Hoggett, Mahlon I, 457
Hoggett, Sarah I, 457
Hoggins, Hannah II, 550
Hoggitt, ??? VI, 283
Hoggitt, Anthony VI, 249
Hoggitt, Anthony VI, 269
Hoggitt, Anthony VI, 286
Hoggitt, Anthony, Jr. VI, 249
Hoggitt, Jane VI, 249
Hoggitt, Jane VI, 269
Hoggitt, Jane VI, 286
Hoggitt, Joseph VI, 249
Hoggitt, Lillie Perkins VI, 249
Hoggitt, Mary VI, 249
Hoggitt, Mary VI, 269
Hoggitt, Philip VI, 249
Hoggitt, Philip VI, 286
Hoggitt, Phillip VI, 249
Hoggitt, William VI, 286
Hoggitt, William E. VI, 249
Hogitt, Phillip VI, 249
Hogue, Absalom IV, 149
Hogue, Absalom IV, 222
Hogue, Absalom IV, 223
Hogue, Absolem IV, 223
Hogue, Agnes Ann IV, 372
Hogue, Agnes Ann IV, 410
Hogue, Amy IV, 410
Hogue, Amy VI, 654
Hogue, Ann IV, 149
Hogue, Ann IV, 410
Hogue, Ann VI, 401
Hogue, Ann VI, 654
Hogue, Anna M. IV, 410
Hogue, Annie IV, 211
Hogue, Asa IV, 149
Hogue, Asa IV, 336
Hogue, Asa Benjamin IV, 410
Hogue, Asael IV, 149
Hogue, Benjamin VI, 654
Hogue, Betsy IV, 149
Hogue, Bushrod IV, 336
Hogue, Bushrod IV, 410
Hogue, Charles L. IV, 410
Hogue, Charles William VI, 654
Hogue, Charles Wm. VI, 749
Hogue, Clara V. VI, 654
Hogue, Clara V. VI, 749
Hogue, Comley K. IV, 223
Hogue, Craven IV, 149
Hogue, Craven IV, 223
Hogue, David IV, 93
Hogue, David IV, 149
Hogue, David IV, 410
Hogue, David VI, 654
Hogue, David, Jr. IV, 410
Hogue, Edward IV, 336
Hogue, Edward Abijah VI, 654
Hogue, Edward Abijah VI, 749
Hogue, Eli J. VI, 654
Hogue, Elijah VI, 654
Hogue, Eliza IV, 336
Hogue, Eliza Pleasant VI, 654
Hogue, Elizabeth IV, 149
Hogue, Elizabeth IV, 328
Hogue, Elizabeth IV, 336
Hogue, Elizabeth IV, 344
Hogue, Elizabeth IV, 410
Hogue, Elizabeth VI, 654
Hogue, Elizabeth A. IV, 211
Hogue, Elizabeth R. IV, 394
Hogue, Elizabeth S. I, 548
Hogue, Elnor IV, 363
Hogue, Elnora IV, 410
Hogue, Emily E. IV, 328
Hogue, Emily E. IV, 336
Hogue, Esther IV, 93
Hogue, Francis VI, 401
Hogue, George VI, 654
Hogue, George VI, 749
Hogue, Gulielma Penn VI, 654
Hogue, Gulielma Penn VI, 749
Hogue, Hannah IV, 836
Hogue, Hannah VI, 654
Hogue, Hannah Elma IV, 336
Hogue, Haseal IV, 410
Hogue, Isaac IV, 149
Hogue, Isaac IV, 223
Hogue, Isaac IV, 410
Hogue, Isaac VI, 654
Hogue, Isaac N. IV, 410
Hogue, James IV, 149
Hogue, James IV, 223
Hogue, James VI, 401
Hogue, James Russel IV, 211
Hogue, Jesse VI, 654
Hogue, John C. IV, 223
Hogue, John C. IV, 336
Hogue, John J. VI, 654
Hogue, John J. VI, 749
Hogue, John Mead VI, 654
Hogue, John, Jr. IV, 93
Hogue, Jonas I, 548
Hogue, Jonathan IV, 39
Hogue, Jonathan IV, 93
Hogue, Jonathan IV, 336
Hogue, Jonathan IV, 410
Hogue, Jonathan L. IV, 410
Hogue, Joseph VI, 654
Hogue, Joseph G. IV, 410
Hogue, Joseph Phil VI, 654
Hogue, Joseph Philo VI, 654
Hogue, Joseph S. IV, 410
Hogue, Joshua IV, 149
Hogue, Joshua IV, 410
Hogue, Joshua VI, 654
Hogue, Laura IV, 223
Hogue, Levi IV, 410
Hogue, Lewis N. I, 548
Hogue, Lewis N., Jr. I, 548
Hogue, Lindley IV, 336
Hogue, Lindley M. IV, 222
Hogue, Lundy B. IV, 336
Hogue, Lydia IV, 149
Hogue, Lydia IV, 410
Hogue, Lydia VI, 654
Hogue, Margarett I, 548
Hogue, Margery VI, 654
Hogue, Mary IV, 71
Hogue, Mary IV, 211
Hogue, Mary IV, 328
Hogue, Mary IV, 410
Hogue, Mary VI, 653
Hogue, Mary VI, 654
Hogue, Mary VI, 676
Hogue, Mary VI, 749
Hogue, Mary Ann IV, 223
Hogue, Mary Elizabeth IV, 223
Hogue, Mary Ellen VI, 654
Hogue, Mary Emily IV, 410
Hogue, Orilla C. IV, 410
Hogue, Orison IV, 410
Hogue, Penninah IV, 569
Hogue, Penninah IV, 584
Hogue, Pilo Mead IV, 410
Hogue, Pleasant IV, 149
Hogue, Pleasant VI, 673
Hogue, Rachel IV, 222
Hogue, Rachel IV, 223
Hogue, Rachel VI, 654
Hogue, Rachel Ellicott VI, 749
Hogue, Rachel P. IV, 222
Hogue, Rachel T. IV, 223
Hogue, Rebecca IV, 149
Hogue, Rebecca IV, 336
Hogue, Rebekah VI, 654
Hogue, Romona IV, 410
Hogue, Ruth IV, 149
Hogue, Ruth IV, 336
Hogue, Ruth IV, 345
Hogue, Ruth IV, 410
Hogue, Ruth VI, 654
Hogue, Samuel IV, 328
Hogue, Samuel IV, 372
Hogue, Samuel IV, 410
Hogue, Samuel VI, 653
Hogue, Samuel VI, 654
Hogue, Samuel VI, 657
Hogue, Samuel VI, 676
Hogue, Samuel E. IV, 211
Hogue, Sarah IV, 149
Hogue, Sarah IV, 410
Hogue, Sarah VI, 654
Hogue, Sarah Ann IV, 223
Hogue, Sarah Ann IV, 1282
Hogue, Sarah Ann VI, 654
Hogue, Sarah Ann VI, 669
Hogue, Sarah B. IV, 964
Hogue, Sarah Eleanor VI, 654
Hogue, Sarah Jane IV, 324
Hogue, Sarah Jane IV, 336
Hogue, Shanna D. I, 546
Hogue, Shanna D. I, 548
Hogue, Shanna Doughteage I, 548
Hogue, Solomon IV, 149
Hogue, Solomon VI, 401
Hogue, Solomon VI, 653
Hogue, Solomon VI, 654
Hogue, Solomon VI, 676
Hogue, Solomon Elijah VI, 654
Hogue, Solomon, Jr. VI, 654
Hogue, Solomon, Sr. VI, 654
Hogue, Sophia I, 548
Hogue, Susan IV, 223
Hogue, Susan VI, 654
Hogue, Susan B. I, 548
Hogue, Susanna VI, 654
Hogue, Susannah IV, 410
Hogue, Sylvanus G. IV, 410
Hogue, Tacy IV, 127
Hogue, Tamar VI, 654
Hogue, Tamar Jane IV, 373
Hogue, Tamar Jane IV, 410
Hogue, Theodoric IV, 410
Hogue, Thomas E. IV, 410
Hogue, Thomas Elwood VI, 654
Hogue, Washington VI, 654
Hogue, Widow Margaret VI, 654
Hogue, Widow Mary VI, 654
Hogue, Widow Mary VI, 657
Hogue, Widow Mary VI, 676
Hogue, Wilbern M. VI, 988
Hogue, William IV, 223
Hogue, William VI, 654
Hogue, William VI, 749
Hogue, William Homes IV, 410
Hogue, William, Jr. VI, 401
Hogue, Wm. VI, 654
Hogue, Wm. VI, 749
Hohoff, Anna III, 320
Hohoff, Anna W. III, 146
Hohoff, Anna W. III, 169
Hohoff, Carrie III, 169
Hohoff, Ernest A. III, 146
Hohoff, Ernest A. III, 169
Hohoff, Ernest A. III, 320
Hohoff, Therese Marie III, 320
Hohoff-Hallock, Anna III, 347
Hohoff-Hallock, Ernest A. III, 347
Hohoff-Hallock, Therese Marie III, 347
Hoile, Margaret II, 292
Hoiles, James II, 550
Hoiles, Martha IV, 722
Hoiles, Martha IV, 751
Hoiles, Rachel IV, 722
Hoiles, Rachel IV, 964
Hoit, Eliza Jane V, 576
Holaday, Abigail I, 436
Holaday, Abraham I, 436
Holaday, Alva V, 400
Holaday, Alva V, 683
Holaday, Alvah V, 400
Holaday, Alvah V, 401
Holaday, Alvah V, 683
Holaday, Amanda V, 400
Holaday, Amanda V, 401
Holaday, Amanda V, 683
Holaday, Ana I, 448
Holaday, Angeline V, 338
Holaday, Angeline V, 400
Holaday, Angeline V, 401
Holaday, Angeline V, 440
Holaday, Angie V, 338
Holaday, Ann I, 436
Holaday, Ann V, 386
Holaday, Ann V, 400
Holaday, Ann V, 576
Holaday, Anna Delilah V, 400
Holaday, Anna Osborn V, 683
Holaday, Asa V, 400
Holaday, Asa V, 401
Holaday, Asa V, 576
Holaday, Asa V, 683
Holaday, Benjamin I, 448
Holaday, Bertie V, 339
Holaday, Bessie V, 683
Holaday, Betsey V, 400
Holaday, Betsy V, 396
Holaday, Betsy V, 399
Holaday, Betsy V, 400
Holaday, Betsy V, 576
Holaday, Betsy Jane V, 400
Holaday, Betsy Jane V, 576
Holaday, Betty V, 400
Holaday, Betty H. V, 421
Holaday, Betty J. V, 400
Holaday, Betty J. V, 429
Holaday, Binjam I, 448
Holaday, Camella V, 683
Holaday, Carey V, 682
Holaday, Carey V, 683
Holaday, Catharine I, 391
Holaday, Catharine I, 399
Holaday, Catharine I, 431
Holaday, Catharine I, 436
Holaday, Catharine I, 446
Holaday, Catharine I, 447
Holaday, Charles V, 338
Holaday, Charles V, 339
Holaday, Charles V, 400
Holaday, Charles V, 401
Holaday, Charles V, 683
Holaday, Charles E. V, 339
Holaday, Charles Emmett V, 401
Holaday, Charles, Sr. V, 338
Holaday, Chester V, 401
Holaday, Daniel V, 400
Holaday, David V, 400
Holaday, Deborah I, 436
Holaday, DeWitt V, 683
Holaday, Earnest V, 339
Holaday, Edith I, 677
Holaday, Edith I, 682
Holaday, Edna V, 401
Holaday, Elbridge V, 400
Holaday, Eliza I, 448
Holaday, Elizabeth V, 683
Holaday, Ellworth V, 400
Holaday, Elsworth V, 401
Holaday, Elva V, 401
Holaday, Elwood V, 400
Holaday, Emily Jane V, 400
Holaday, Enoch V, 400
Holaday, Enoch V, 576
Holaday, Enoch V, 604
Holaday, Ethel V, 401
Holaday, Ethel B. V, 401
Holaday, Eva V, 604
Holaday, Evaline A. V, 400
Holaday, Francis M. V, 400
Holaday, Frederick V, 683
Holaday, Frederick Samuel V, 683
Holaday, Gold Arrosmith V, 683
Holaday, Golda V, 683
Holaday, Goldam V, 656
Holaday, Grace V, 682
Holaday, Grace V, 683
Holaday, Hannah I, 431
Holaday, Hannah I, 436
Holaday, Hannah I, 443
Holaday, Hannah I, 447
Holaday, Hannah I, 448
Holaday, Hannah I, 857
Holaday, Hannah V, 399
Holaday, Hannah V, 400
Holaday, Hannah V, 547
Holaday, Hannah V, 576
Holaday, Harley C. V, 400
Holaday, Hattie V, 683
Holaday, Henry I, 399
Holaday, Henry I, 436
Holaday, Hiram E. V, 400
Holaday, Hiram E. V, 401
Holaday, Hiram E. V, 683
Holaday, Jacob I, 436
Holaday, Jain I, 447
Holaday, Jain I, 450
Holaday, James W. V, 400
Holaday, James W. V, 401
Holaday, James W. V, 683
Holaday, Jane I, 436
Holaday, Jane I, 447
Holaday, Jane I, 448
Holaday, Jane I, 682
Holaday, Jesse V, 400
Holaday, Jesse V, 656
Holaday, Jesse V, 683
Holaday, Jesse F. V, 399
Holaday, Jesse F. V, 400
Holaday, Jesse F. V, 401
Holaday, Jesse F. V, 576
Holaday, Jesse F. V, 683
Holaday, Jesse H. V, 400

Holaday, Jesse H. V, 401
Holaday, Jesse H. V, 683
Holaday, Jesse, Jr. V, 683
Holaday, Job V, 400
Holaday, John I, 436
Holaday, John I, 448
Holaday, John V, 386
Holaday, John V, 399
Holaday, John V, 400
Holaday, John V, 576
Holaday, John C. V, 400
Holaday, John H. V, 399
Holaday, John Henry V, 400
Holaday, Jonathan V, 399
Holaday, Jonathan V, 400
Holaday, Jonathan V, 576
Holaday, Joseph I, 399
Holaday, Joseph I, 436
Holaday, Joseph J. I, 448
Holaday, Joseph James I, 436
Holaday, Joseph M. V, 400
Holaday, Joseph P. I, 448
Holaday, Joshua I, 448
Holaday, Joshua I, 857
Holaday, Joshua I, 870
Holaday, Joshua I, 886
Holaday, Joushaua I, 448
Holaday, Lafayette V, 400
Holaday, Laura V, 401
Holaday, Lavina Caroline I, 436
Holaday, Leona V, 683
Holaday, Lida Evaline V, 400
Holaday, Lidia I, 448
Holaday, Lillian V, 683
Holaday, Lillie Maud V, 248
Holaday, Lillie Maud V, 683
Holaday, Lilly V, 683
Holaday, Lilly Adaline V, 400
Holaday, Lilly Maud V, 683
Holaday, Lindley V, 400
Holaday, Liza J. I, 436
Holaday, Lizzie A. V, 400
Holaday, Lora V, 401
Holaday, Loren V, 338
Holaday, Lorenzo D. V, 338
Holaday, Lorenzo D. V, 400
Holaday, Lorenzo D. V, 401
Holaday, Lorenzo D. V, 683
Holaday, Lorie O. V, 338
Holaday, Louisa V, 400
Holaday, Louisa V, 576
Holaday, Louisa J. V, 400
Holaday, Louiza V, 388
Holaday, Louiza V, 399
Holaday, Louiza V, 400
Holaday, Lydia I, 391
Holaday, Lydia I, 399
Holaday, Lydia I, 431
Holaday, Lydia I, 436
Holaday, Lydia I, 447
Holaday, Lydia I, 448
Holaday, Lydia I, 857
Holaday, Lydia I, 886
Holaday, Maggie E. V, 400
Holaday, Mahalah V, 683
Holaday, Malon V, 400
Holaday, Martha I, 436
Holaday, Martha I, 448
Holaday, Martha I, 857
Holaday, Mary I, 399
Holaday, Mary I, 436
Holaday, Mary I, 445
Holaday, Mary I, 447
Holaday, Mary I, 448
Holaday, Mary I, 455
Holaday, Mary V, 400
Holaday, Mary V, 401
Holaday, Mary Alice V, 400
Holaday, Mary Ann V, 399
Holaday, Mary Ann V, 400
Holaday, Mary Ann V, 576
Holaday, Mary Catharine I, 448
Holaday, Mary E. V, 400
Holaday, Milton V, 400
Holaday, Milton M. V, 399
Holaday, Nancy V, 339
Holaday, Nancy V, 401
Holaday, Nancy V, 683
Holaday, Nancy B. V, 400
Holaday, Nancy B. V, 439
Holaday, Nancy J. V, 338
Holaday, Nancy J. V, 401
Holaday, Nancy J. V, 683
Holaday, Naomi Belle V, 683
Holaday, Nellie V, 339
Holaday, Nellie V, 683
Holaday, Nellie V, 702
Holaday, Nora V, 338
Holaday, Nora V, 339
Holaday, Nora V, 683
Holaday, Owen I, 436
Holaday, Owen I, 448
Holaday, Owen V, 400
Holaday, Patience I, 399
Holaday, Patience I, 436
Holaday, Patience I, 448
Holaday, Patience I, 450
Holaday, Patience V, 400
Holaday, Patience V, 683
Holaday, Pheba Adelade I, 436
Holaday, Pleasant V, 400
Holaday, Raleigh V, 338
Holaday, Raleigh V, 401
Holaday, Rebeckah I, 436
Holaday, Rebekah I, 436
Holaday, Rhody I, 436
Holaday, Rhody I, 448
Holaday, Robert I, 399
Holaday, Robert I, 436
Holaday, Robert I, 677
Holaday, Robert I, 682
Holaday, Robert V, 399
Holaday, Robert V, 400
Holaday, Robert V, 547
Holaday, Robert V, 576
Holaday, Robert V, 683
Holaday, Robert Clayton V, 400
Holaday, Robert E. V, 683
Holaday, Robert Owen I, 436
Holaday, Robert Owen I, 448
Holaday, Rolla V, 400
Holaday, Ross V, 683
Holaday, Rosse E. V, 400
Holaday, Ruth I, 448
Holaday, Ruth V, 339
Holaday, Ruth V, 400
Holaday, Ruth V, 401
Holaday, Ruth V, 683
Holaday, Ruth M. V, 400
Holaday, Samuel I, 436
Holaday, Samuel I, 447
Holaday, Samuel I, 448
Holaday, Samuel I, 886
Holaday, Samuel V, 399
Holaday, Samuel V, 400
Holaday, Samuel V, 683
Holaday, Samuel A. V, 400
Holaday, Samuel, Sr. I, 448
Holaday, Sarah I, 399
Holaday, Sarah I, 436
Holaday, Sarah I, 447
Holaday, Sarah I, 448
Holaday, Sarah I, 450
Holaday, Sarah I, 451
Holaday, Sarah I, 453
Holaday, Sarah I, 857
Holaday, Sarah I, 870
Holaday, Sarah I, 886
Holaday, Sarah V, 604
Holaday, Sarah A. V, 400
Holaday, Sarah A. V, 401
Holaday, Sarah Ann V, 401
Holaday, Sarah Catherine I, 436
Holaday, Sarah J. I, 436
Holaday, Sarah J. I, 448
Holaday, Sarah J. V, 400
Holaday, Sarah Jane V, 338
Holaday, Simon I, 448
Holaday, Susanna V, 399
Holaday, Susanna V, 400
Holaday, Susanna V, 576
Holaday, Susannah V, 386
Holaday, Susannah V, 396
Holaday, Susannah V, 399
Holaday, Susannah V, 400
Holaday, Susannah V, 431
Holaday, Susie V, 683
Holaday, Thomas I, 399
Holaday, Thomas I, 436
Holaday, Thomas I, 447
Holaday, Thomas I, 448
Holaday, Thomas V, 400
Holaday, Thomas V, 576
Holaday, Thomas F. V, 399
Holaday, Thomas F. V, 400
Holaday, Thomas F. V, 401
Holaday, Thomas Ladd I, 436
Holaday, Viola V, 339
Holaday, Walter V, 400
Holaday, William I, 399
Holaday, William I, 436
Holaday, William I, 447
Holaday, William I, 448
Holaday, William I, 682
Holaday, William V, 399
Holaday, William V, 400
Holaday, William V, 576
Holaday, William V, 683
Holaday, William W. V, 400
Holaday, Wm. V, 339
Holaday, Wm. V, 400
Holaday, Wm. V, 683
Holagan, Patrick VI, 925
Holahan, Agnes A. IV, 433
Holand, Sarah Ida V, 1002
Holaway, Abner V, 401
Holaway, Abner V, 426
Holaway, Amos IV, 894
Holaway, Amos V, 401
Holaway, Asenath V, 401
Holaway, Betsy V, 401
Holaway, Betsy V, 446
Holaway, Cynthia V, 401
Holaway, Elizabeth V, 426
Holaway, Elizabeth V, 446
Holaway, Ellenor V, 401
Holaway, George V, 446
Holaway, Hepzabath IV, 894
Holaway, Isaac V, 401
Holaway, Isaac V, 446
Holaway, Jesse V, 401
Holaway, Joab V, 446
Holaway, John V, 401
Holaway, John V, 446
Holaway, Lavina I, 1010
Holaway, Louvicy V, 446
Holaway, Margaret V, 401
Holaway, Margaret V, 402
Holaway, Margaret V, 414
Holaway, Mary V, 426
Holaway, Matilda V, 401
Holaway, Pleasant V, 446
Holaway, Rachel V, 402
Holaway, Samuel V, 446
Holaway, Sarah IV, 893
Holaway, Sarah IV, 894
Holaway, Sarah V, 446
Holaway, William V, 446
Holaway, Wm. V, 446
Holbein, Edward II, 746
Holbein, Edwin II, 746
Holbert, Mary H. II, 800
Holbert, Mary H. II, 876
Holbrook, Addie Burrus I, 927
Holbrook, Anna Lily III, 60
Holbrook, H. Alma I, 927
Holbrook, Ila I, 943
Holbrook, Ila M. I, 927
Holbrook, James I, 927
Holbrook, Julian I, 943
Holbrook, Julian Harvey I, 927
Holbrook, Louise I, 927
Holbrook, Mildred I, 927
Holbrook, Myra V, 48
Holbrook, R. C. I, 943
Holbrook, Robert O. I, 927
Holbrook, Robert Russell III, 60
Holbrook, Robert Russell, Jr. III, 169
Holbrook, Robt. III, 169
Holbrook, Robt. Russell III, 169
Holbrook, Ruth III, 169
Holbrook, Sarah F. III, 169
Holbrook, Susanna I, 444
Holcomb, Amanda III, 169
Holcomb, Ann Amelia II, 1002
Holcomb, Ann Amelia II, 1052
Holcomb, Cynthia S. III, 169
Holcomb, Daisy IV, 1254
Holcomb, Donald IV, 1254
Holcomb, Dr Chas. III, 169
Holcomb, Eleanor M. III, 271
Holcomb, Eleanor Maxwell II, 800
Holcomb, Eleanor Maxwell II, 876
Holcomb, Eleonor Maxwell III, 169
Holcomb, Elisabeth II, 550
Holcomb, Eliz. Clark III, 229
Holcomb, Elizabeth II, 232
Holcomb, Elizabeth II, 550
Holcomb, Elizabeth III, 169
Holcomb, Elizabeth Clark II, 800
Holcomb, Elizabeth Clark III, 169
Holcomb, Ellwood IV, 1254
Holcomb, Elmira IV, 1254
Holcomb, Hannah II, 550
Holcomb, Hannah II, 858
Holcomb, Hannah II, 876
Holcomb, Henry IV, 1254
Holcomb, Jacob II, 550
Holcomb, Jacob II, 1002
Holcomb, Jacob III, 169
Holcomb, Jennetta IV, 1254
Holcomb, Jennie IV, 1254
Holcomb, Jennie R. IV, 1321
Holcomb, Jennie R. J. IV, 1321
Holcomb, John Miller II, 876
Holcomb, John Miller III, 169
Holcomb, July Ann II, 550
Holcomb, July Ann II, 560
Holcomb, Katie III, 217
Holcomb, Lewis IV, 1254
Holcomb, Louis IV, 1254
Holcomb, Margaret III, 169
Holcomb, Margaret III, 341
Holcomb, Mary II, 375
Holcomb, Mary II, 550
Holcomb, Mary II, 609
Holcomb, Mary II, 803
Holcomb, Mary II, 1000
Holcomb, Mary II, 1002
Holcomb, Mary II, 1052
Holcomb, Oliver H. III, 169
Holcomb, Rachel IV, 1062
Holcomb, Rachel IV, 1073
Holcomb, Rebekah II, 550
Holcomb, Richard II, 1000
Holcomb, Richard II, 1002
Holcomb, Ruth III, 169
Holcomb, Sarah II, 1002
Holcomb, Sarah M. II, 858
Holcomb, Sarah M. II, 876
Holcomb, Sophia II, 550
Holcomb, Swartmore III, 169
Holcomb, Wm. III, 169
Holcomb, Wm. Martindale II, 858
Holcomb, Wm. Martindale II, 876
Holcomb, Wm. P. II, 876
Holcomb, Wm. Penn II, 800
Holcomb, Wm. Penn II, 876
Holcomb, Wm. Penn III, 229
Holcombe, Betsy M. VI, 804
Holcombe, Charles VI, 821
Holcombe, Charles A. VI, 825
Holcombe, Elizabeth II, 540
Holcombe, Elizabeth II, 550
Holcombe, Elizabeth H. VI, 825
Holcombe, Helen III, 189
Holcombe, J. VI, 862
Holcombe, Jacob II, 540
Holcombe, Jacob II, 550
Holcombe, Jacob II, 1040
Holcombe, John VI, 867
Holcombe, Lucy J. VI, 825
Holcombe, Martha VI, 867
Holcombe, Sarah VI, 821
Holcombe, Sarah VI, 862
Hold, John W. VI, 876
Holdaman, David, Jr. IV, 715
Holdeman, Ann IV, 900
Holdeman, Edwin G. IV, 1038
Holden, Charles II, 375
Holden, Charles Thomas II, 550
Holden, Delaney VI, 822
Holden, Elijah II, 962
Holden, George V, 809
Holden, Jane II, 962
Holden, Nancy II, 962
Holden, Rosa IV, 1282
Holden, Rose IV, 1282
Holden, Susan VI, 822
Holder, Charles III, 169
Holder, Charles Frederick III, 169
Holder, Charles W. III, 169
Holder, Christopher VI, 6
Holder, Christopher VI, 24
Holder, Daniel III, 151
Holder, Daniel III, 169
Holder, Elijah VI, 825
Holder, Elizabeth I, 548
Holder, Emily A. I, 548
Holder, Emily A. III, 169
Holder, John I, 548
Holder, Joseph B. III, 169
Holder, Orlando I, 548
Holder, Richard Houghton III, 169
Holder, Sophia VI, 825
Holder, Warren III, 169
Holder, Wd. Sarah III, 151
Holderman, Ann IV, 715
Holderman, Ann IV, 804
Holderman, Ann IV, 823
Holderman, Ann IV, 900
Holderman, Benjamin IV, 715
Holderman, David IV, 715
Holderman, David IV, 900
Holderman, Esther IV, 1038
Holderman, James IV, 715
Holderman, John IV, 823
Holderman, Joseph IV, 715
Holderman, Joseph IV, 1038
Holderman, Joshua Brown IV, 823
Holderman, Mary IV, 715
Holderman, Susanna IV, 937
Holderman, Susannah IV, 715
Holdman, Sarah IV, 722
Holdman, Sarah IV, 728
Holdrege, Ellen III, 234
Holdren, Abraham VI, 934
Holdren, Adam. VI, 934
Holdren, Bartholomew VI, 97
Holdren, Becky VI, 904
Holdren, Frances S. VI, 934
Holdren, Harmony VI, 908
Holdren, Henry VI, 934
Holdren, Jacob VI, 934
Holdren, Joel VI, 934
Holdren, Kessiah VI, 934
Holdren, Malinda VI, 934
Holdren, Patsy VI, 934
Holdren, Polly VI, 904
Holdren, Rebecca VI, 908
Holdren, Sarah VI, 934
Holdren, Thomas VI, 934
Holdron, Abraham VI, 934
Holdron, Adam. VI, 934
Holdron, Archibald VI, 934
Holdron, Bartholomew VI, 92
Holdron, Bartholomew VI, 93
Holdron, Cornelius VI, 932
Holdron, Cornelius VI, 934
Holdron, Cornelous VI, 993
Holdron, Elizabeth VI, 934
Holdron, Elizabeth S. VI, 934
Holdron, Enoch VI, 934
Holdron, Frances S. VI, 934
Holdron, George VI, 934
Holdron, Harmony VI, 927
Holdron, Heatty VI, 934
Holdron, Henry VI, 934
Holdron, Jacob VI, 934
Holdron, Jane VI, 934
Holdron, Jane VI, 993
Holdron, Joel VI, 934
Holdron, John VI, 934
Holdron, Kessiah VI, 934
Holdron, Levi VI, 934
Holdron, Malinda VI, 934
Holdron, Martha VI, 934
Holdron, Matilda R. VI, 934
Holdron, Milley VI, 934
Holdron, Nancy VI, 934
Holdron, Patsy VI, 934
Holdron, Sarah VI, 934
Holdron, Thomas VI, 934
Holdron, Weatty VI, 934
Holdsworth, Florence II, 711
Hole, ??? IV, 861
Hole, ??? VI, 348
Hole, Abi VI, 980
Hole, Adam VI, 933
Hole, Adelaide IV, 1321
Hole, Adelaide M. IV, 1321
Hole, Adelaide M. IV, 1342
Hole, Adelaide W. III, 169
Hole, Adelaide W. III, 228
Hole, Alfred Clark V, 576
Hole, Alliance IV, 907
Hole, Amoret VI, 1017
Hole, Ann IV, 39
Hole, Ann IV, 634
Hole, Ann IV, 722
Hole, Ann IV, 823
Hole, Ann IV, 834
Hole, Ann IV, 873
Hole, Ann IV, 878
Hole, Ann IV, 901
Hole, Ann IV, 907
Hole, Ann IV, 908
Hole, Ann IV, 911
Hole, Ann V, 576
Hole, Ann Elizabeth V, 401
Hole, Anna IV, 871
Hole, Anna IV, 872
Hole, Anna IV, 873
Hole, Anna IV, 907
Hole, Anna E. IV, 193
Hole, Anna E. IV, 223
Hole, Anna E. IV, 946
Hole, Anna E. IV, 965
Hole, Anna E. V, 338
Hole, Anna Elizabeth V, 401
Hole, Anna L. IV, 907
Hole, Anna L. IV, 965
Hole, Anna S. IV, 965
Hole, Anne IV, 39
Hole, Anne IV, 634
Hole, Anne IV, 872
Hole, Anne IV, 878
Hole, Benjamin IV, 634
Hole, Benjamin IV, 722
Hole, Benjamin IV, 872
Hole, Benjamin IV, 907
Hole, Benjamin IV, 908
Hole, Benjamin IV, 988
Hole, Betsy IV, 631
Hole, Beulah Ann IV, 39
Hole, Beulah Ann IV, 873
Hole, Beulah Ann IV, 881

ole, Burla Ann IV, 722
ole, Caleb IV, 907
ole, Caleb IV, 965
ole, Carl C. IV, 965
ole, Carle C. IV, 965
ole, Caroline V, 576
ole, Cashann IV, 907
ole, Catharine IV, 623
ole, Catharine IV, 634
ole, Catharine IV, 823
ole, Catharine IV, 868
ole, Catharine IV, 869
ole, Catharine IV, 870
ole, Catharine IV, 872
ole, Catharine IV, 873
ole, Catharine IV, 878
ole, Catharine IV, 907
ole, Catharine IV, 908
ole, Catharine IV, 924
ole, Catharine IV, 964
ole, Catharine IV, 965
ole, Catharine Elizabeth IV, 907
ole, Catherine IV, 39
ole, Catherine IV, 634
ole, Catherine IV, 964
ole, Catherine E. IV, 965
ole, Charles IV, 629
ole, Charles IV, 634
ole, Charles IV, 645
ole, Charles IV, 722
ole, Charles IV, 866
ole, Charles IV, 868
ole, Charles IV, 872
ole, Charles IV, 873
ole, Charles IV, 874
ole, Charles IV, 887
ole, Charles IV, 907
ole, Charles IV, 1211
ole, Charles VI, 352
ole, Charles VI, 977
ole, Charles VI, 980
ole, Charles Emerson V, 401
ole, Charles S. IV, 965
ole, Charles Stanley IV, 907
ole, Charlotte IV, 722
ole, Charlotte IV, 907
ole, Charlotte IV, 908
ole, Charlotte IV, 912
ole, Charlotte IV, 913
ole, Chas IV, 911
ole, Chas. IV, 623
ole, Chas. IV, 632
ole, Chas. IV, 634
ole, Chas. IV, 873
ole, Chas. M. IV, 823
ole, Chas. Stanley IV, 965
ole, David IV, 39
ole, David IV, 634
ole, David IV, 722
ole, David IV, 871
ole, David IV, 872
ole, David IV, 873
ole, David IV, 878
ole, E. A. IV, 634
ole, Edgar T. III, 169
ole, Edgar T. III, 228
ole, Edgar T. IV, 1321
ole, Edgar T. IV, 1342
ole, Edward L. IV, 965
ole, Edward S. IV, 965
ole, Eli V, 576
ole, Elias IV, 907
ole, Elisha IV, 722
ole, Elisha IV, 907
ole, Elisha IV, 908
ole, Eliza IV, 552
ole, Eliza Ann IV, 964
ole, Eliza Ann IV, 965
ole, Eliza Anna IV, 907
ole, Elizabeth IV, 523
ole, Elizabeth IV, 532
ole, Elizabeth IV, 634
ole, Elizabeth IV, 866
ole, Elizabeth IV, 873
ole, Elizabeth IV, 964
ole, Elizabeth IV, 965
ole, Elizabeth IV, 988
ole, Elizabeth IV, 1282
ole, Elizabeth V, 401
ole, Elizabeth VI, 933
ole, Elizabeth Esther IV, 965
ole, Ella IV, 823
ole, Ellen IV, 634
ole, Elma IV, 722
ole, Elma G. IV, 723
ole, Elma G. IV, 817
ole, Elma G. IV, 823
ole, Elma G. IV, 824
ole, Elon IV, 33
ole, Elon IV, 39
Hole, Elon IV, 722
Hole, Elon IV, 872
Hole, Elon IV, 873
Hole, Elon IV, 881
Hole, Emerson IV, 634
Hole, Emerson B. IV, 722
Hole, Emerson B. IV, 1166
Hole, Emerson B. IV, 1211
Hole, Emerson Bennett IV, 634
Hole, Emmerson B. IV, 1166
Hole, Emmerson B. IV, 1211
Hole, Erwin Jay IV, 1038
Hole, Erwing Jay IV, 907
Hole, Esther IV, 623
Hole, Esther IV, 629
Hole, Esther IV, 632
Hole, Esther IV, 634
Hole, Esther IV, 868
Hole, Esther IV, 872
Hole, Esther IV, 873
Hole, Esther IV, 874
Hole, Esther IV, 881
Hole, Esther IV, 907
Hole, Esther IV, 965
Hole, Esther E. IV, 977
Hole, Esther Elma IV, 907
Hole, Esther Elma IV, 965
Hole, Esther M. IV, 881
Hole, Ethan IV, 873
Hole, Ethan IV, 907
Hole, Ethan Allen IV, 616
Hole, Ethan Allen IV, 634
Hole, Ethan Allen IV, 666
Hole, Ethan Allen IV, 866
Hole, Ethan Allen IV, 873
Hole, Eva V, 401
Hole, Florena-Eva V, 401
Hole, Florence Eva V, 401
Hole, Florence Eva V, 418
Hole, Francis Orlando V, 401
Hole, Francis Rolland V, 401
Hole, Frank V, 401
Hole, Frank V, 683
Hole, Franklin IV, 634
Hole, Gertrude IV, 823
Hole, Gertrude F. IV, 823
Hole, Gertrude F. IV, 907
Hole, Gulaelma IV, 907
Hole, Hannah IV, 609
Hole, Hannah IV, 634
Hole, Hannah IV, 666
Hole, Hannah IV, 722
Hole, Hannah IV, 873
Hole, Hannah IV, 965
Hole, Hannah VI, 977
Hole, Hannah B. IV, 634
Hole, Hannah B. IV, 722
Hole, Hannah B. IV, 965
Hole, Hannah W. IV, 965
Hole, Harrison V, 626
Hole, Harrison H. V, 248
Hole, Harry R. V, 248
Hole, Harry R. V, 626
Hole, Hogn IV, 870
Hole, Ida M. IV, 907
Hole, Ida M. IV, 908
Hole, Ida M. IV, 1038
Hole, Isabel IV, 722
Hole, Isabel W. IV, 722
Hole, Israel IV, 722
Hole, Israel IV, 907
Hole, Israel IV, 908
Hole, Israel P. IV, 965
Hole, J. M. IV, 823
Hole, J. Melville IV, 907
Hole, J. Melville IV, 908
Hole, J. W. IV, 1237
Hole, Jacob IV, 634
Hole, Jacob IV, 722
Hole, Jacob IV, 823
Hole, Jacob IV, 873
Hole, Jacob IV, 897
Hole, Jacob IV, 907
Hole, Jacob IV, 908
Hole, Jacob IV, 1165
Hole, Jacob VI, 977
Hole, Jacob VI, 980
Hole, Jacob T. IV, 964
Hole, Jacob Thomas IV, 965
Hole, Jacob Thos. IV, 907
Hole, Jacob, Jr. IV, 901
Hole, Jacob, Jr. IV, 907
Hole, Jacob, Jr. IV, 908
Hole, James IV, 873
Hole, James IV, 907
Hole, James M. IV, 609
Hole, James M. IV, 722
Hole, James M. IV, 864
Hole, James M. IV, 873
Hole, James M. IV, 965
Hole, Jane IV, 616
Hole, Jane IV, 866
Hole, Jane IV, 873
Hole, Jane IV, 907
Hole, Jane VI, 966
Hole, Jared IV, 722
Hole, Jared IV, 907
Hole, Jared IV, 908
Hole, Jesse IV, 872
Hole, Jesse IV, 873
Hole, John IV, 823
Hole, John IV, 873
Hole, John IV, 897
Hole, John IV, 907
Hole, John IV, 908
Hole, John IV, 964
Hole, John IV, 965
Hole, John VI, 933
Hole, John Franklin IV, 634
Hole, John Franklin IV, 907
Hole, John Green IV, 336
Hole, Jonah IV, 523
Hole, Jonah IV, 532
Hole, Jonah IV, 631
Hole, Jonah IV, 823
Hole, Jonah IV, 907
Hole, Jonah IV, 1146
Hole, Jonah IV, 1165
Hole, Jonah IV, 1166
Hole, Jonah V, 401
Hole, Jonah VI, 933
Hole, Jonah, Jr. V, 401
Hole, Jonathan IV, 532
Hole, Jonathan IV, 1165
Hole, Jonathan V, 396
Hole, Jonathan V, 401
Hole, Jonathan V, 418
Hole, Joseph IV, 873
Hole, Joseph IV, 881
Hole, Joseph IV, 907
Hole, Joshua IV, 907
Hole, Laura Elliott V, 401
Hole, Leander IV, 1038
Hole, Leander H. IV, 907
Hole, Leander H. IV, 908
Hole, Lemuel IV, 823
Hole, Lemuel IV, 873
Hole, Lemuel IV, 907
Hole, Lemuel IV, 908
Hole, Lemuel IV, 946
Hole, Lemuel IV, 964
Hole, Lemuel IV, 965
Hole, Lemuel IV, 998
Hole, Lemuel Homer III, 169
Hole, Lemuel Penrose IV, 907
Hole, Lemuel Penrose IV, 965
Hole, Lena May III, 169
Hole, Leona May III, 228
Hole, Leonard H. IV, 907
Hole, Leonard Hanna III, 169
Hole, Leora V, 626
Hole, Leora E. V, 248
Hole, Leora E. V, 626
Hole, Levi Miller IV, 823
Hole, Linnaeus E. IV, 965
Hole, Linneas E. IV, 722
Hole, Linneaus C. IV, 965
Hole, Linneus C. IV, 722
Hole, Linnois C. IV, 722
Hole, Louisa IV, 722
Hole, Louisa IV, 1211
Hole, Louisa V, 576
Hole, Lovely VI, 933
Hole, Lovisa E. IV, 907
Hole, Lovisa E. IV, 908
Hole, Lucinda IV, 616
Hole, Lydia IV, 39
Hole, Lydia IV, 722
Hole, Lydia IV, 873
Hole, Lydia IV, 907
Hole, Lydia IV, 908
Hole, Lydia Ann IV, 532
Hole, Lydia H. IV, 965
Hole, Lydia H. IV, 975
Hole, Mahala VI, 937
Hole, Mahaley VI, 966
Hole, Mahlon IV, 722
Hole, Mahlon IV, 759
Hole, Mahlon IV, 823
Hole, Mahlon IV, 842
Hole, Mahlon IV, 897
Hole, Mahlon IV, 907
Hole, Mahlon IV, 908
Hole, Mahlon IV, 912
Hole, Mahlon IV, 965
Hole, Mahlon W. IV, 965
Hole, Malinda V, 576
Hole, Maria V, 401
Hole, Marlan N. III, 169
Hole, Martha Jane V, 576
Hole, Mary IV, 33
Hole, Mary IV, 39
Hole, Mary IV, 331
Hole, Mary IV, 336
Hole, Mary IV, 532
Hole, Mary IV, 634
Hole, Mary IV, 645
Hole, Mary IV, 659
Hole, Mary IV, 722
Hole, Mary IV, 753
Hole, Mary IV, 823
Hole, Mary IV, 866
Hole, Mary IV, 872
Hole, Mary IV, 873
Hole, Mary IV, 905
Hole, Mary IV, 907
Hole, Mary IV, 908
Hole, Mary IV, 911
Hole, Mary IV, 917
Hole, Mary IV, 965
Hole, Mary IV, 1165
Hole, Mary V, 576
Hole, Mary VI, 352
Hole, Mary VI, 354
Hole, Mary Ann IV, 872
Hole, Mary Ann IV, 873
Hole, Mary Ann IV, 874
Hole, Mary Ellen IV, 907
Hole, Mary F. IV, 815
Hole, Mary F. IV, 823
Hole, Mary F. IV, 824
Hole, Mary Louisa IV, 634
Hole, Mary Louisa IV, 667
Hole, Mary M. IV, 965
Hole, Mary N. IV, 616
Hole, Mary N. IV, 634
Hole, Mary Nichols IV, 634
Hole, Mary V. IV, 873
Hole, Matilda IV, 759
Hole, Maurice IV, 722
Hole, Maurice IV, 723
Hole, Mellvin IV, 824
Hole, Mildred VI, 933
Hole, Miles Miller V, 576
Hole, Miriam L. V, 248
Hole, Morlan N. III, 169
Hole, Morris J. IV, 965
Hole, Myra H. IV, 722
Hole, Nancy VI, 933
Hole, Narcissa IV, 872
Hole, Narcissa IV, 873
Hole, Narcissa IV, 874
Hole, Nathan IV, 607
Hole, Nathan IV, 616
Hole, Nathan IV, 634
Hole, Nathan IV, 722
Hole, Nathan IV, 797
Hole, Nathan IV, 823
Hole, Nathan IV, 859
Hole, Nathan IV, 866
Hole, Nathan IV, 873
Hole, Nathan IV, 907
Hole, Nathan IV, 908
Hole, Nathan IV, 964
Hole, Nathan IV, 965
Hole, Nathan VI, 314
Hole, Nathan VI, 352
Hole, Norman W. IV, 907
Hole, Norman W. IV, 965
Hole, Patsy Ann VI, 909
Hole, Penrose IV, 965
Hole, Phebe IV, 616
Hole, Phebe IV, 866
Hole, Phebe IV, 873
Hole, Phebe IV, 907
Hole, Phebe IV, 908
Hole, Philip V, 65
Hole, Rachel IV, 722
Hole, Rachel IV, 759
Hole, Rachel IV, 823
Hole, Rachel IV, 842
Hole, Rachel IV, 907
Hole, Rachel IV, 908
Hole, Rachel IV, 912
Hole, Rachel IV, 965
Hole, Rachel Ann IV, 965
Hole, Rachel Ann IV, 984
Hole, Ralph J. III, 169
Hole, Ransom VI, 933
Hole, Rebecca IV, 632
Hole, Rebecca IV, 634
Hole, Rebecca IV, 666
Hole, Rebecca IV, 722
Hole, Rebecca IV, 823
Hole, Rebecca IV, 872
Hole, Rebecca IV, 873
Hole, Rebecca IV, 1211
Hole, Rebecca Jane IV, 907
Hole, Robert IV, 722
Hole, Robert IV, 873
Hole, Robert IV, 907
Hole, Robert IV, 908
Hole, Robert H. IV, 907
Hole, Robert H. IV, 965
Hole, Robert H. IV, 975
Hole, Ruth IV, 872
Hole, Ruth IV, 873
Hole, Ruth Ann IV, 1211
Hole, Ruth Anna IV, 634
Hole, Ruth Anna IV, 722
Hole, Ruth Anna IV, 965
Hole, Ruthanna IV, 965
Hole, Ruthanna IV, 984
Hole, Samuel IV, 666
Hole, Samuel IV, 873
Hole, Samuel IV, 907
Hole, Samuel IV, 1211
Hole, Samuel J. IV, 634
Hole, Samuel J. IV, 722
Hole, Samuel J. IV, 1211
Hole, Samuel T. IV, 634
Hole, Sarah III, 169
Hole, Sarah IV, 607
Hole, Sarah IV, 616
Hole, Sarah IV, 634
Hole, Sarah IV, 654
Hole, Sarah IV, 722
Hole, Sarah IV, 797
Hole, Sarah IV, 823
Hole, Sarah IV, 866
Hole, Sarah IV, 873
Hole, Sarah IV, 907
Hole, Sarah IV, 908
Hole, Sarah IV, 964
Hole, Sarah IV, 965
Hole, Sarah IV, 1146
Hole, Sarah IV, 1165
Hole, Sarah IV, 1166
Hole, Sarah IV, 1197
Hole, Sarah Ann V, 576
Hole, Sarah, Jr. IV, 634
Hole, Sarah, Jr. IV, 873
Hole, Sophia IV, 823
Hole, Sophia IV, 907
Hole, Sophia IV, 908
Hole, Sophia IV, 911
Hole, Sophia IV, 965
Hole, Sophia IV, 1165
Hole, Sophia IV, 1166
Hole, Sophia IV, 1237
Hole, Sophia A. IV, 965
Hole, Sophia M. IV, 965
Hole, Susan IV, 722
Hole, Susan IV, 871
Hole, Susan IV, 873
Hole, Susan V, 418
Hole, Susan VI, 933
Hole, Susanna V, 396
Hole, Susannah V, 401
Hole, Susie E. IV, 722
Hole, Tace IV, 872
Hole, Tacy IV, 634
Hole, Tacy IV, 645
Hole, Tacy IV, 871
Hole, Tacy IV, 873
Hole, Thomas IV, 872
Hole, Thomas IV, 873
Hole, Thomas IV, 907
Hole, Thomas VI, 933
Hole, Thomas B. IV, 722
Hole, Thos. IV, 634
Hole, Tirzah IV, 634
Hole, Tirzah IV, 872
Hole, Tirzah IV, 873
Hole, Tirzah IV, 876
Hole, Unity IV, 908
Hole, Unity IV, 965
Hole, Unity IV, 988
Hole, Unity C. IV, 907
Hole, Unity C. IV, 908
Hole, Unity C. IV, 946
Hole, Unity C. IV, 964
Hole, Unity C. IV, 965
Hole, Unity C. IV, 988
Hole, Unity C. IV, 998
Hole, Ury Betsy IV, 631
Hole, Ury Betsy IV, 634
Hole, William IV, 907
Hole, William VI, 909
Hole, William VI, 933
Hole, William Hadley V, 576
Hole, William Russell IV, 965
Hole, Willis IV, 722
Hole, Willis IV, 823
Hole, Willis R. IV, 723
Hole, Wilmer IV, 1321
Hole, Wilmer D. IV, 1321
Hole, Wilmouth Ann VI, 933
Hole, Winston L. V, 248
Hole, Wm. F. IV, 1211
Hole, Wm. Russell IV, 965
Holebrook, Florence V, 48
Holebrook, Myra V, 48
Holeman, Mary I, 988

Holeman, Rachel V, 237
Holeman, Rachel V, 248
Holesapple, Nancy VI, 804
Holesapple, Philip VI, 804
Holeson, Elizabeth VI, 869
Holgate, Mary H. II, 707
Holgate, Naomi II, 707
Holgate, Samuel II, 707
Holiday, Alvah V, 683
Holiday, Ann V, 400
Holiday, Asa V, 400
Holiday, Asa V, 683
Holiday, Betsy V, 400
Holiday, Carrie E. V, 458
Holiday, Eliza I, 448
Holiday, Enoch V, 400
Holiday, James V, 248
Holiday, Jesse F. V, 683
Holiday, Jesse, Jr. V, 683
Holiday, John V, 400
Holiday, Lillian V, 683
Holiday, Lillie Maud V, 248
Holiday, Lilly V, 683
Holiday, Lilly M. V, 248
Holiday, Mary Ann V, 400
Holiday, Mary Catharine I, 399
Holiday, Mary Catharine I, 444
Holiday, Mary Catharine I, 448
Holiday, Mary Catherine I, 376
Holiday, Mrs. James V, 248
Holiday, Naomi V, 248
Holiday, Patience V, 683
Holiday, Phebe IV, 1152
Holiday, Phebe IV, 1166
Holiday, Robert V, 400
Holiday, Ross V, 683
Holiday, Ruth V, 683
Holiday, Samuel V, 683
Holiday, Sarah Jane V, 338
Holiday, William V, 400
Holiday, Wm. V, 683
Holigan, Mary Jane VI, 934
Holigan, Thomas VI, 934
Holingshead, Agnes II, 177
Holingshead, John II, 177
Holingshead, Thomas II, 177
Holingshead, William II, 177
Holingsworth, Ann II, 79
Holingsworth, Ann II, 104
Holingsworth, Catrin II, 79
Holingsworth, Catrin II, 107
Holingsworth, Hariet V, 953
Holingsworth, Hariet V, 960
Holingsworth, James Thompson II, 79
Holingsworth, John II, 79
Holingsworth, John II, 107
Holingsworth, Jonah VI, 598
Holinsworth, Sarah G. I, 548
Holiway, Isaac V, 402
Holladay, A. W. I, 635
Holladay, Abigail I, 356
Holladay, Alfred W. I, 611
Holladay, Alfred W. I, 635
Holladay, Angeline V, 338
Holladay, Ann I, 357
Holladay, Ann V, 372
Holladay, Ann V, 400
Holladay, Ann V, 431
Holladay, Ann VI, 825
Holladay, Anna Delilah V, 372
Holladay, Anna Delilah V, 400
Holladay, Anne I, 356
Holladay, Asa V, 400
Holladay, Betheny VI, 933
Holladay, Betsy V, 399
Holladay, Camella V, 683
Holladay, Catharine I, 357
Holladay, Catharine I, 399
Holladay, Charles V, 338
Holladay, Charles V, 400
Holladay, Charles V, 683
Holladay, David V, 400
Holladay, David VI, 825
Holladay, David VI, 933
Holladay, Deborah I, 346
Holladay, Deborah I, 356
Holladay, Deborah I, 372
Holladay, Deborah I, 399
Holladay, Eli I, 635
Holladay, Emily Jane V, 400
Holladay, Enoch V, 400
Holladay, Frances VI, 933
Holladay, Hannah I, 356
Holladay, Hannah I, 399
Holladay, Hannah I, 411
Holladay, Hannah I, 448
Holladay, Hannah I, 886
Holladay, Hannah V, 399
Holladay, Hannah V, 400
Holladay, Hannah V, 430
Holladay, Hattie V, 683
Holladay, Henry I, 346
Holladay, Henry I, 356
Holladay, Henry I, 357
Holladay, Henry I, 362
Holladay, Henry I, 399
Holladay, Jacob I, 356
Holladay, Jane I, 357
Holladay, Jane I, 372
Holladay, Jane I, 399
Holladay, Jane I, 431
Holladay, Jane I, 886
Holladay, Jesse F. V, 399
Holladay, John I, 356
Holladay, John I, 357
Holladay, John V, 399
Holladay, John V, 430
Holladay, John V, 490
Holladay, John V, 502
Holladay, John VI, 933
Holladay, John C. V, 400
Holladay, Joseph I, 399
Holladay, Joshua I, 356
Holladay, Joshua I, 448
Holladay, Joshua I, 886
Holladay, Lewis VI, 933
Holladay, Loren V, 338
Holladay, Lydia I, 356
Holladay, Lydia I, 357
Holladay, Lydia I, 399
Holladay, Lydia I, 886
Holladay, Lyiah I, 357
Holladay, Maggie E. I, 635
Holladay, Manley L. I, 399
Holladay, Margaret I, 611
Holladay, Martha I, 444
Holladay, Martha I, 448
Holladay, Martha I, 886
Holladay, Martha VI, 933
Holladay, Mary I, 346
Holladay, Mary I, 356
Holladay, Mary I, 357
Holladay, Mary I, 362
Holladay, Mary I, 399
Holladay, Mary Ann V, 399
Holladay, Mary Catharine I, 399
Holladay, Nora V, 338
Holladay, Nora V, 683
Holladay, Ora I, 611
Holladay, Ora I, 629
Holladay, Ora I, 635
Holladay, Patience I, 356
Holladay, Patience I, 357
Holladay, Patience I, 399
Holladay, Polly VI, 933
Holladay, Raleigh V, 338
Holladay, Rebecca I, 357
Holladay, Rebeccah I, 357
Holladay, Robert I, 356
Holladay, Robert I, 399
Holladay, Robert I, 411
Holladay, Robert V, 399
Holladay, Ruth I, 356
Holladay, Ruth VI, 933
Holladay, Saml I, 356
Holladay, Saml I, 357
Holladay, Samuel I, 356
Holladay, Samuel I, 357
Holladay, Samuel I, 399
Holladay, Samuel I, 886
Holladay, Sarah I, 356
Holladay, Sarah I, 357
Holladay, Sarah I, 362
Holladay, Sarah I, 399
Holladay, Sarah I, 411
Holladay, Sarah I, 448
Holladay, Sarah I, 886
Holladay, Sarah VI, 933
Holladay, Simon I, 356
Holladay, Simon I, 448
Holladay, Susanna V, 399
Holladay, Susanna V, 400
Holladay, Susanna G. V, 431
Holladay, Susannah V, 399
Holladay, Susannah V, 430
Holladay, Susannah V, 490
Holladay, Susannah V, 502
Holladay, Thomas I, 399
Holladay, Thomas VI, 933
Holladay, William I, 357
Holladay, William I, 399
Holladay, William V, 399
Holladay, William V, 400
Holladay, William V, 502
Holladay, William VI, 933
Holladay, Wm. I, 356
Holladay, Wm. I, 357
Holladay, Wm. V, 372
Holladay, Wm. V, 431
Hollady, Alfred W. I, 635
Hollady, Maggie E. I, 635
Hollady, Ora I, 635
Hollagan, Jno. VI, 908
Hollagan, John VI, 934
Hollagan, Nancy VI, 934
Hollan, Elizabeth I, 305
Holland, Algermon Sydney III, 173
Holland, Allen III, 173
Holland, Allice IV, 1282
Holland, America VI, 934
Holland, Ann II, 375
Holland, Ann Eliza III, 173
Holland, Anna V, 179
Holland, Bathsheba VI, 996
Holland, Bershaba VI, 996
Holland, Bowker VI, 934
Holland, Catharine IV, 824
Holland, Catharine IV, 918
Holland, Catherine IV, 634
Holland, Charity V, 179
Holland, Charles V, 179
Holland, Charles VI, 960
Holland, Charles H. III, 173
Holland, Clarence Leon V, 179
Holland, Dicy VI, 892
Holland, Donald V, 1002
Holland, Doralee V, 1002
Holland, Doshia VI, 934
Holland, Drury VI, 825
Holland, Drury VI, 892
Holland, Drury VI, 933
Holland, Drury VI, 941
Holland, Drury VI, 970
Holland, Drury VI, 1005
Holland, Drury VI, 1007
Holland, Drury VI, 1016
Holland, Earl L. V, 179
Holland, Elgin V, 179
Holland, Elijah VI, 876
Holland, Elijah VI, 933
Holland, Eliza III, 173
Holland, Eliza H. III, 173
Holland, Elizabeth I, 304
Holland, Elizabeth I, 308
Holland, Elizabeth A. VI, 65
Holland, Elizabeth A. VI, 69
Holland, Elizabeth Ann VI, 65
Holland, Emma III, 173
Holland, Ermel E. V, 178
Holland, Ethel V, 179
Holland, Ethel R. V, 178
Holland, Frances Ann VI, 1014
Holland, Franky VI, 914
Holland, Free W. IV, 1211
Holland, Gertrude E. VI, 69
Holland, Gertrude E. VI, 79
Holland, Gideon III, 173
Holland, Gilbert Jr III, 173
Holland, Hallie May V, 179
Holland, Hannah III, 173
Holland, Hannah IV, 634
Holland, Hannah IV, 824
Holland, Hannah IV, 918
Holland, Hannah H. III, 173
Holland, Harry C. V, 179
Holland, Heleand VI, 69
Holland, Heleand B. VI, 71
Holland, Henry J. III, 173
Holland, I. III, 173
Holland, Isaac III, 173
Holland, Isabel VI, 506
Holland, James VI, 69
Holland, James VI, 72
Holland, James B. I, 308
Holland, John II, 551
Holland, John IV, 634
Holland, John IV, 824
Holland, John V, 178
Holland, John V, 179
Holland, John VI, 917
Holland, John VI, 933
Holland, John B. IV, 634
Holland, John B. VI, 876
Holland, John B. VI, 909
Holland, John B. VI, 969
Holland, John B. VI, 1022
Holland, John H. III, 173
Holland, John Jr III, 173
Holland, John W. VI, 968
Holland, John W. VI, 973
Holland, John W. VI, 1017
Holland, Jos. Brown III, 173
Holland, Joseph IV, 1211
Holland, Joseph VI, 826
Holland, Joseph J. VI, 249
Holland, Joseph T. III, 173
Holland, Joshua V, 179
Holland, Joshua Hudilson III, 169
Holland, Judith H. VI, 918
Holland, Julia Ann VI, 897
Holland, Kenneth V, 1002
Holland, Kent C. V, 179
Holland, Lavinia VI, 69
Holland, Lavinia VI, 72
Holland, Lenora V, 178
Holland, Lewis Smith V, 179
Holland, Lillie IV, 223
Holland, Lizzie A. VI, 92
Holland, Lucinda C. VI, 249
Holland, Lucy L. VI, 1022
Holland, Maggie IV, 223
Holland, Maggie V, 207
Holland, Mahala VI, 876
Holland, Margaret II, 551
Holland, Margaret VI, 69
Holland, Margaret VI, 90
Holland, Margaret VI, 506
Holland, Martha VI, 969
Holland, Martha A. III, 173
Holland, Martha Hazard III, 173
Holland, Mary C. V, 179
Holland, Mary Catherine V, 179
Holland, Mary E. V, 178
Holland, Mary H. Delano III, 173
Holland, Mary R. III, 173
Holland, Mary Rodman III, 173
Holland, Mary Turner VI, 909
Holland, Matilda VI, 69
Holland, Matilda VI, 135
Holland, Matilda VI, 825
Holland, Mattie V, 179
Holland, Mildred A. VI, 826
Holland, Milton V, 178
Holland, Milton V, 179
Holland, Morgan VI, 934
Holland, Myrtle V, 179
Holland, Nancy VI, 954
Holland, Nancy VI, 1022
Holland, Nathaniel II, 551
Holland, Nellie V, 178
Holland, Nina IV, 223
Holland, Nora V, 179
Holland, Oma V, 1002
Holland, Peggy VI, 825
Holland, Peggy VI, 933
Holland, Peter VI, 291
Holland, Peter VI, 314
Holland, Peter VI, 871
Holland, Peter D. VI, 934
Holland, Phares C. V, 179
Holland, Polly VI, 933
Holland, Polly VI, 996
Holland, Pontius III, 173
Holland, Raymond C. V, 178
Holland, Raymond C. V, 179
Holland, Rd. VI, 181
Holland, Rebecca VI, 69
Holland, Rebecca VI, 72
Holland, Rece VI, 934
Holland, Rhoda VI, 970
Holland, Richard IV, 1282
Holland, Richard VI, 506
Holland, Richard VI, 825
Holland, Richard VI, 860
Holland, Richard G. III, 173
Holland, Robert Bowne III, 173
Holland, Rolena Compton V, 179
Holland, Rollena V, 179
Holland, Ruby V, 1002
Holland, Ruth III, 169
Holland, Ruth VI, 506
Holland, Salina V, 502
Holland, Sally VI, 933
Holland, Sally VI, 934
Holland, Samuel II, 551
Holland, Samuel IV, 824
Holland, Samuel IV, 911
Holland, Samuel V, 178
Holland, Samuel V, 179
Holland, Samuel H. IV, 634
Holland, Sarah II, 375
Holland, Sarah III, 169
Holland, Sarah III, 173
Holland, Sarah IV, 410
Holland, Sarah IV, 415
Holland, Sarah IV, 634
Holland, Sarah IV, 824
Holland, Sarah IV, 911
Holland, Sarah IV, 918
Holland, Sarah VI, 860
Holland, Sarah VI, 1005
Holland, Sarah F. IV, 1211
Holland, Sarah Ida V, 1002
Holland, Sarah J. VI, 960
Holland, Sarah Jane V, 179
Holland, Sarah R. III, 173
Holland, Sarah, Jr. IV, 918
Holland, Savoury VI, 933
Holland, Stephen VI, 918
Holland, Stephen VI, 934
Holland, Stephen VI, 954
Holland, Stephen VI, 959
Holland, Stephen VI, 996
Holland, Stephen VI, 1014
Holland, Stephen, Jr. VI, 933
Holland, Stephen, Sr. VI, 985
Holland, Susan VI, 826
Holland, Susan VI, 941
Holland, Susanna K. IV, 911
Holland, Susannah IV, 634
Holland, Susannah IV, 824
Holland, Susannah K. IV, 918
Holland, Tenta III, 173
Holland, Theodore V, 179
Holland, Thomas VI, 506
Holland, Thomas VI, 934
Holland, Thomas C. III, 173
Holland, Thomas L. III, 169
Holland, Virginia VI, 506
Holland, Virginia H. VI, 567
Holland, Widower Susannah VI, 871
Holland, William II, 375
Holland, William IV, 634
Holland, William IV, 824
Holland, William VI, 69
Holland, William VI, 79
Holland, William H. III, 173
Holland, William Hazard III, 1
Holland, William T. VI, 826
Holland, William W. III, 173
Holland, William W. IV, 634
Holland, Willie V, 178
Holland, Wilma W. V, 1002
Holland, Wm. V, 179
Holland, Wm. VI, 79
Holland, Wm. P. III, 173
Holland, Wm. W. Jr III, 173
Holland, Zachariah VI, 69
Holland, Zachariah E. VI, 65
Hollaway, Abigail VI, 598
Hollaway, Asa, Jr. VI, 598
Hollaway, Elizabeth I, 988
Hollaway, Elizabeth V, 339
Hollaway, Elizabeth V, 446
Hollaway, Elizabeth V, 447
Hollaway, Elizabeth VI, 598
Hollaway, Elvira I, 548
Hollaway, George V, 339
Hollaway, George VI, 598
Hollaway, Isaac V, 339
Hollaway, John V, 339
Hollaway, Mary VI, 598
Hollaway, Mary Ann IV, 393
Hollaway, Mary, Jr. VI, 598
Hollaway, Phebe VI, 388
Hollaway, Pleasant V, 339
Hollaway, Samuel V, 339
Hollaway, Sarah V, 339
Hollaway, Sarah VI, 598
Hollaway, Thomas VI, 598
Hollaway, William V, 339
Hollaway, William VI, 598
Hollaway, Wm. H. IV, 393
Holleman, Josiah VI, 58
Holleman, Josiah VI, 69
Holleman, Sarah VI, 109
Holleman, Sarah VI, 110
Holleman, Wm. VI, 79
Hollen, Susanna IV, 93
Hollen, Susanna IV, 109
Hollenshead, ??? II, 177
Hollenshead, John II, 177
Hollenshead, John II, 232
Hollenshead, Rebecca II, 177
Hollenshead, William II, 177
Hollensworth, Hannah I, 818
Holler, Lovina IV, 1211
Holler, Lovina IV, 1221
Holler, Sarah E. V, 1002
Hollet, Hannah Elizabeth IV, 5
Hollet, Joseph IV, 561
Hollet, Mary P. IV, 561
Hollett, Harriet III, 76
Hollett, Mary Jane III, 169
Holley, Ann VI, 826
Holley, Ann Eliza III, 32
Holley, Ann Eliza III, 169
Holley, Ann Eliza III, 219
Holley, Ann Eliza III, 377
Holley, Ann Eliza III, 381
Holley, Ann Eliza III, 420
Holley, Ann Eliza III, 466
Holley, Cassandra VI, 940
Holley, Dosha VI, 955
Holley, Edmund VI, 834
Holley, Elizabeth VI, 940
Holley, Ella E. III, 32
Holley, Ella E. III, 377
Holley, Ella E. III, 381
Holley, Ellen VI, 989
Holley, Florence Amelia III, 21

olley, George V, 179
olley, Henry VI, 989
olley, James VI, 826
olley, James VI, 844
olley, Jenny VI, 951
olley, John V, 1002
olley, John VI, 826
olley, Josiah VI, 940
olley, Lemuel P. III, 169
olley, Lemuel P. III, 219
olley, Lemuel P. III, 420
olley, Lemuel P. III, 466
olley, Mary V, 1002
olley, Mary VI, 834
olley, Mary A. VI, 827
olley, Mary E. V, 1002
olley, Maud III, 466
olley, Maud E. III, 420
olley, Maud E. III, 466
olley, Nancy Randal VI, 827
olley, Polly VI, 826
olley, Samuel P. III, 32
olley, Samuel P. III, 169
olley, Samuel P. III, 377
olley, Samuel P. III, 381
olley, Sarah VI, 826
olley, Sarah E. V, 1002
olley, Thomas VI, 826
olley, Thomas VI, 940
olliday, Abigail II, 744
olliday, Adda May IV, 223
olliday, Aggie VI, 936
olliday, Alfred W. I, 619
olliday, Alvah V, 683
olliday, Amanda V, 683
olliday, Angie V, 338
olliday, Ann V, 554
olliday, Ann V, 576
olliday, Bertie R. I, 619
olliday, Betsey VI, 941
olliday, Charles V, 338
olliday, Charles, Sr. V, 338
olliday, Clyde C. IV, 1321
olliday, Clyde Cecil III, 169
olliday, Clyde Cecil III, 368
olliday, Clyde Wray IV, 1321
olliday, David IV, 223
olliday, David K. IV, 223
olliday, Edith IV, 223
olliday, Edith Sophia III, 169
olliday, Edith Sophia III, 368
olliday, Edith W. IV, 1321
olliday, Edward I, 1075
olliday, Eva V, 583
olliday, Fanny IV, 336
olliday, Fanny IV, 343
olliday, Frances VI, 933
olliday, Hannah II, 79
olliday, Hannah V, 576
olliday, Hannah V, 597
olliday, Hannah B. III, 169
olliday, Hiram E. V, 683
olliday, James II, 79
olliday, James W. V, 683
olliday, Jesse F. V, 683
olliday, Jesse H. V, 683
olliday, John IV, 223
olliday, Joseph B. III, 169
olliday, Joshua I, 886
olliday, Lewis VI, 933
olliday, Lillian IV, 223
olliday, Lorenzo D. V, 338
olliday, Lorenzo D. V, 683
olliday, Lorie O. V, 338
olliday, Manley L. I, 399
Holliday, Margaret E. I, 619
Holliday, Marth I, 450
Holliday, Nancy J. V, 338
Holliday, Ora I, 635
Holliday, Orah I, 619
Holliday, Patience V, 400
Holliday, Rhoda May I, 619
Holliday, Robert V, 683
Holliday, Robert E. V, 683
Holliday, Ross V, 683
Holliday, Ruth V, 683
Holliday, Ruth VI, 933
Holliday, Samuel I, 448
Holliday, Samuel I, 450
Holliday, Samuel, Sr. I, 448
Holliday, Thomas VI, 933
Holliday, William IV, 223
Holliday, William V, 576
Holliday, William VI, 941
Holliday, William VI, 982
Holliday, Wm. V, 554
Holliday, Wm. R. III, 169
Holligan, Elizabeth VI, 934
Holligan, Frankey VI, 934
Holligan, Hannah VI, 966
Holligan, James VI, 896
Holligan, Jane VI, 925
Holligan, Jno. VI, 966
Holligan, John VI, 925
Holligan, John VI, 934
Holligan, John VI, 966
Holligan, Katy VI, 896
Holligan, Mary Jane VI, 934
Holligan, Nancy VI, 934
Holligan, Patrick VI, 934
Holligan, Patrick VI, 1008
Holligan, Polly VI, 925
Holligan, Thomas VI, 934
Holliman, Elizabeth I, 1048
Holliman, Sarah VI, 110
Hollinger, Adda V, 1002
Hollinger, Agnes II, 707
Hollinger, Burley V, 1002
Hollinger, C. E. V, 1002
Hollinger, Chas. V, 1002
Hollinger, Chas. E. V, 1002
Hollinger, John II, 707
Hollinger, John II, 746
Hollingham, Catherine II, 539
Hollinghead, Goly I, 1154
Hollinghead, Lucy II, 551
Hollinghead, W. H. I, 1154
Hollingshead, Alice II, 551
Hollingshead, Amanda E. V, 883
Hollingshead, Andrew V, 883
Hollingshead, Anna II, 746
Hollingshead, Anna H. II, 375
Hollingshead, Benjamin M. II, 551
Hollingshead, Caroline H. II, 551
Hollingshead, Caroline M. II, 707
Hollingshead, Charles II, 375
Hollingshead, Deborah V, 883
Hollingshead, Edmond, Jr. II, 551
Hollingshead, Edmund II, 551
Hollingshead, Edmund II, 746
Hollingshead, Edmund J. II, 551
Hollingshead, Eliza W. II, 707
Hollingshead, Eliza W. II, 746
Hollingshead, Elizabeth II, 551
Hollingshead, Ellen II, 375
Hollingshead, Ellen II, 746
Hollingshead, Franklin R. V, 883
Hollingshead, George F. II, 876
Hollingshead, George F. V, 883
Hollingshead, Goly I, 1154
Hollingshead, Hannah II, 551
Hollingshead, Hannah II, 707
Hollingshead, Henry II, 375
Hollingshead, Henry II, 707
Hollingshead, Hudson II, 551
Hollingshead, Hugh II, 375
Hollingshead, Hugh II, 707
Hollingshead, Hugh F. II, 551
Hollingshead, Hugh F. II, 746
Hollingshead, Jacob II, 551
Hollingshead, Jacob, Jr. II, 551
Hollingshead, James II, 551
Hollingshead, John II, 551
Hollingshead, John II, 814
Hollingshead, Joseph II, 232
Hollingshead, Joseph M. II, 375
Hollingshead, Joseph M. II, 746
Hollingshead, Lucy II, 519
Hollingshead, Lucy II, 551
Hollingshead, Martha II, 375
Hollingshead, Martha II, 551
Hollingshead, Martha II, 707
Hollingshead, Martha II, 746
Hollingshead, Martha II, 814
Hollingshead, Mary II, 551
Hollingshead, Mary IV, 410
Hollingshead, Mary V, 883
Hollingshead, Morgan II, 519
Hollingshead, Morgan II, 551
Hollingshead, Morgan E. V, 883
Hollingshead, Nicholas II, 375
Hollingshead, Ona I, 1154
Hollingshead, Onea I, 1154
Hollingshead, Rachel V, 883
Hollingshead, Rachel F. V, 883
Hollingshead, Rebecca W. V, 883
Hollingshead, Rebeckah II, 519
Hollingshead, Rebeckah II, 551
Hollingshead, Samuel II, 551
Hollingshead, Sarah II, 551
Hollingshead, Susana V, 883
Hollingshead, Thomas II, 375
Hollingshead, Thomas II, 551
Hollingshead, W. H. I, 1154
Hollingshead, Wd. Sarah H. II, 814
Hollingsworht, Isaac V, 803
Hollingsworht, Jane V, 803
Hollingsworth, ??? V, 795
Hollingsworth, ??? VI, 495
Hollingsworth, A. D. V, 76
Hollingsworth, Abigail VI, 402
Hollingsworth, Abigail VI, 428
Hollingsworth, Abigail VI, 507
Hollingsworth, Abigail VI, 508
Hollingsworth, Abigail VI, 542
Hollingsworth, Abigail VI, 568
Hollingsworth, Abigail VI, 578
Hollingsworth, Abigail VI, 654
Hollingsworth, Abigail VI, 719
Hollingsworth, Abner V, 74
Hollingsworth, Abner V, 75
Hollingsworth, Abner V, 401
Hollingsworth, Abraham I, 1020
Hollingsworth, Abraham I, 1031
Hollingsworth, Abraham I, 1032
Hollingsworth, Abraham I, 1038
Hollingsworth, Abraham V, 57
Hollingsworth, Abraham V, 74
Hollingsworth, Abraham V, 75
Hollingsworth, Abraham V, 111
Hollingsworth, Abraham V, 810
Hollingsworth, Abraham VI, 357
Hollingsworth, Abraham VI, 402
Hollingsworth, Abraham VI, 507
Hollingsworth, Absalom V, 810
Hollingsworth, Absolom V, 810
Hollingsworth, Addie Mary V, 74
Hollingsworth, Adella V, 684
Hollingsworth, Albert V, 743
Hollingsworth, Albert R. V, 76
Hollingsworth, Albert Rudolph V, 74
Hollingsworth, Albert W. V, 743
Hollingsworth, Alice II, 551
Hollingsworth, Alice V, 74
Hollingsworth, Alice V, 81
Hollingsworth, Alice E. IV, 1139
Hollingsworth, Alice Unice IV, 1139
Hollingsworth, Allen IV, 875
Hollingsworth, Allen V, 74
Hollingsworth, Allen V, 75
Hollingsworth, Alpheus D. V, 74
Hollingsworth, Amanda Melvina II, 800
Hollingsworth, Amey I, 1020
Hollingsworth, Amey I, 1057
Hollingsworth, Amos I, 1031
Hollingsworth, Angeline V, 74
Hollingsworth, Angeline E. V, 75
Hollingsworth, Ann I, 548
Hollingsworth, Ann I, 1016
Hollingsworth, Ann I, 1020
Hollingsworth, Ann I, 1028
Hollingsworth, Ann I, 1031
Hollingsworth, Ann I, 1032
Hollingsworth, Ann I, 1035
Hollingsworth, Ann I, 1061
Hollingsworth, Ann IV, 635
Hollingsworth, Ann IV, 873
Hollingsworth, Ann IV, 875
Hollingsworth, Ann V, 74
Hollingsworth, Ann V, 76
Hollingsworth, Ann V, 127
Hollingsworth, Ann V, 171
Hollingsworth, Ann V, 502
Hollingsworth, Ann V, 743
Hollingsworth, Ann V, 769
Hollingsworth, Ann V, 810
Hollingsworth, Ann VI, 506
Hollingsworth, Ann VI, 507
Hollingsworth, Ann VI, 538
Hollingsworth, Anna IV, 1062
Hollingsworth, Anna IV, 1080
Hollingsworth, Anna V, 57
Hollingsworth, Anna V, 74
Hollingsworth, Anna V, 75
Hollingsworth, Anna V, 171
Hollingsworth, Anna V, 179
Hollingsworth, Anna V, 433
Hollingsworth, Anna V, 502
Hollingsworth, Anna V, 529
Hollingsworth, Anna V, 542
Hollingsworth, Anna V, 743
Hollingsworth, Anna V, 761
Hollingsworth, Anna V, 809
Hollingsworth, Anna V, 810
Hollingsworth, Anne IV, 1062
Hollingsworth, Anne V, 544
Hollingsworth, Anne V, 728
Hollingsworth, Anne V, 743
Hollingsworth, Anne V, 810
Hollingsworth, Anne V, 953
Hollingsworth, Annie V, 74
Hollingsworth, Anny V, 803
Hollingsworth, Aquilla VI, 506
Hollingsworth, Aquilla VI, 507
Hollingsworth, Aquilla W. V, 503
Hollingsworth, Arthur Everett IV, 1139
Hollingsworth, Asaph V, 502
Hollingsworth, Asaph V, 542
Hollingsworth, Asaph V, 544
Hollingsworth, Asaph V, 953
Hollingsworth, Asaph E. V, 502
Hollingsworth, Ascenith V, 843
Hollingsworth, Asenath VI, 586
Hollingsworth, Benj. V, 806
Hollingsworth, Benjamin I, 548
Hollingsworth, Benjamin I, 1031
Hollingsworth, Benjamin I, 1061
Hollingsworth, Benjamin I Sup 1, 11
Hollingsworth, Benjamin V, 810
Hollingsworth, Benjamin VI, 506
Hollingsworth, Benjamin VI, 507
Hollingsworth, Benjamin P. II, 876
Hollingsworth, Benjamin Powell II, 800
Hollingsworth, Betsey IV, 1062
Hollingsworth, Betsey IV, 1133
Hollingsworth, Betsey IV, 1134
Hollingsworth, Betsey IV, 1138
Hollingsworth, Betsy IV, 611
Hollingsworth, Betsy IV, 1062
Hollingsworth, Betsy IV, 1102
Hollingsworth, Betsy IV, 1127
Hollingsworth, Betsy IV, 1129
Hollingsworth, Betsy H. IV, 635
Hollingsworth, Betsy H. IV, 872
Hollingsworth, Betsy H. IV, 873
Hollingsworth, Betsy H. IV, 1134
Hollingsworth, Betty VI, 402
Hollingsworth, Calvin R. V, 502
Hollingsworth, Caroline VI, 472
Hollingsworth, Carrie VI, 472
Hollingsworth, Carrie VI, 507
Hollingsworth, Carrie VI, 655
Hollingsworth, Carter V, 743
Hollingsworth, Catharine I, 1031
Hollingsworth, Catherine V, 75
Hollingsworth, Celeste S. V, 75
Hollingsworth, Celeste Susan V, 74
Hollingsworth, Charity I, 1031
Hollingsworth, Charity V, 44
Hollingsworth, Charity V, 74
Hollingsworth, Charity V, 75
Hollingsworth, Charity V, 803
Hollingsworth, Charity V, 804
Hollingsworth, Charity V, 810
Hollingsworth, Charles IV, 149
Hollingsworth, Charles IV, 336
Hollingsworth, Charles IV, 723
Hollingsworth, Charles V, 76
Hollingsworth, Charles B. IV, 1062
Hollingsworth, Charles D. IV, 1134
Hollingsworth, Charles Daniel IV, 1063
Hollingsworth, Charles E. V, 74
Hollingsworth, Charles L. VI, 402
Hollingsworth, Charles L. VI, 507
Hollingsworth, Charles L. VI, 508
Hollingsworth, Charles L. VI, 543
Hollingsworth, Charles L. VI, 578
Hollingsworth, Charles L. VI, 654
Hollingsworth, Charles L. VI, 719
Hollingsworth, Charles M. V, 74
Hollingsworth, Charles M. V, 75
Hollingsworth, Charles M. V, 304
Hollingsworth, Charles M. V, 503
Hollingsworth, Christopher IV, 149
Hollingsworth, Christopher IV, 336
Hollingsworth, Christopher IV, 723
Hollingsworth, Christopher IV, 1369
Hollingsworth, Cissiah I, 1020
Hollingsworth, Clarence Wildie V, 74
Hollingsworth, Clifford V, 75
Hollingsworth, Clifford V, 684
Hollingsworth, Cynthia May IV, 1063
Hollingsworth, Cynthia May IV, 1134
Hollingsworth, Cyrus I, 588
Hollingsworth, Cyrus I, 594
Hollingsworth, Cyrus V, 810
Hollingsworth, Daniel V, 503
Hollingsworth, Daniel V, 743
Hollingsworth, David I, 1031
Hollingsworth, David I, 1032
Hollingsworth, David IV, 149
Hollingsworth, David IV, 336
Hollingsworth, David IV, 338
Hollingsworth, David IV, 520
Hollingsworth, David IV, 532
Hollingsworth, David IV, 640
Hollingsworth, David V, 74
Hollingsworth, David V, 75
Hollingsworth, David V, 502
Hollingsworth, David V, 503
Hollingsworth, David VI, 402
Hollingsworth, David VI, 647
Hollingsworth, David VI, 655
Hollingsworth, Dinah I, 548
Hollingsworth, Dinah I, 1015
Hollingsworth, Dinah I, 1031
Hollingsworth, Dinah I, 1061
Hollingsworth, Douglas V, 74
Hollingsworth, Douglas V, 76
Hollingsworth, Eamy I, 1061
Hollingsworth, Earl V, 75
Hollingsworth, Eber V, 75
Hollingsworth, Eber V, 76
Hollingsworth, Eber V, 684
Hollingsworth, Eber V, 743
Hollingsworth, Eda R. IV, 1211
Hollingsworth, Edith IV, 1139
Hollingsworth, Edmond IV, 1102
Hollingsworth, Edna P. IV, 1139
Hollingsworth, Edna V. IV, 1139
Hollingsworth, Edward IV, 336
Hollingsworth, Edward IV, 723
Hollingsworth, Edward V, 74
Hollingsworth, Edward VI, 506
Hollingsworth, Edward VI, 655
Hollingsworth, Edward H. V, 304
Hollingsworth, Edward W. V, 75
Hollingsworth, Edward W. V, 503
Hollingsworth, Edwin IV, 611
Hollingsworth, Edwin IV, 635
Hollingsworth, Edwin IV, 872
Hollingsworth, Edwin IV, 873
Hollingsworth, Edwin IV, 1062
Hollingsworth, Edwin IV, 1102
Hollingsworth, Edwin IV, 1127
Hollingsworth, Edwin IV, 1129
Hollingsworth, Edwin IV, 1133
Hollingsworth, Edwin IV, 1134
Hollingsworth, Edwin IV, 1138
Hollingsworth, Eleanor E. VI, 477
Hollingsworth, Eleanor E. VI, 506
Hollingsworth, Eleanor E. VI, 628
Hollingsworth, Eleanor E. VI, 655
Hollingsworth, Eli IV, 523
Hollingsworth, Eli IV, 532
Hollingsworth, Eli IV, 875
Hollingsworth, Eli V, 75
Hollingsworth, Eli V, 503
Hollingsworth, Eli V, 810
Hollingsworth, Eli VI, 655
Hollingsworth, Elias I, 1015
Hollingsworth, Elias I, 1031
Hollingsworth, Elias I Sup 1, 11
Hollingsworth, Elias V, 74
Hollingsworth, Elias V, 75
Hollingsworth, Elias V, 76
Hollingsworth, Elias V, 120
Hollingsworth, Elias V, 433
Hollingsworth, Elias VI, 506
Hollingsworth, Elihu IV, 532
Hollingsworth, Elihu V, 843
Hollingsworth, Elihu VI, 655
Hollingsworth, Elijah II, 375
Hollingsworth, Elinor E. VI, 627
Hollingsworth, Elisabeth S. VI, 655
Hollingsworth, Elisha IV, 523
Hollingsworth, Elisha IV, 632
Hollingsworth, Elisha IV, 634
Hollingsworth, Elisha IV, 635
Hollingsworth, Elisha IV, 873
Hollingsworth, Elisha IV, 1057
Hollingsworth, Elisha IV, 1059
Hollingsworth, Elisha IV, 1062
Hollingsworth, Elisha IV, 1066
Hollingsworth, Elisha IV, 1071
Hollingsworth, Elisha V, 743
Hollingsworth, Eliza IV, 532
Hollingsworth, Eliza IV, 535
Hollingsworth, Eliza V, 179
Hollingsworth, Eliza V, 401
Hollingsworth, Eliza V, 576
Hollingsworth, Eliza V, 740

Hollingsworth, Eliza A. IV, 875
Hollingsworth, Eliza Ann IV, 875
Hollingsworth, Elizabeth I, 399
Hollingsworth, Elizabeth IV, 149
Hollingsworth, Elizabeth IV, 336
Hollingsworth, Elizabeth IV, 520
Hollingsworth, Elizabeth IV, 523
Hollingsworth, Elizabeth IV, 532
Hollingsworth, Elizabeth IV, 723
Hollingsworth, Elizabeth IV, 875
Hollingsworth, Elizabeth IV, 926
Hollingsworth, Elizabeth IV, 965
Hollingsworth, Elizabeth V, 74
Hollingsworth, Elizabeth V, 75
Hollingsworth, Elizabeth V, 502
Hollingsworth, Elizabeth V, 794
Hollingsworth, Elizabeth B. IV, 965
Hollingsworth, ELizabeth H. VI, 369
Hollingsworth, Elizabeth P. VI, 402
Hollingsworth, Elizabeth P. VI, 507
Hollingsworth, Elizabeth S. VI, 506
Hollingsworth, Ella V, 502
Hollingsworth, Ella V, 503
Hollingsworth, Ella V, 684
Hollingsworth, Ellen E. VI, 508
Hollingsworth, Ellwood V, 76
Hollingsworth, Elva T. V, 401
Hollingsworth, Elwood IV, 532
Hollingsworth, Elwood IV, 533
Hollingsworth, Elwood V, 74
Hollingsworth, Emily V, 74
Hollingsworth, Emily V, 502
Hollingsworth, Emily V, 508
Hollingsworth, Emma V, 179
Hollingsworth, Emma V, 502
Hollingsworth, Emma J. V, 74
Hollingsworth, Emmer Asaph V, 503
Hollingsworth, Emmor IV, 1062
Hollingsworth, Emmor IV, 1063
Hollingsworth, Emmor IV, 1134
Hollingsworth, Enoch I, 548
Hollingsworth, Enoch I, 1016
Hollingsworth, Enoch I, 1031
Hollingsworth, Enoch V, 502
Hollingsworth, Enoch V, 684
Hollingsworth, Enos V, 743
Hollingsworth, Equille I, 1031
Hollingsworth, Equille I Sup 1, 11
Hollingsworth, Er IV, 410
Hollingsworth, Er IV, 634
Hollingsworth, Er IV, 635
Hollingsworth, Er IV, 873
Hollingsworth, Er IV, 1062
Hollingsworth, Erv VI, 507
Hollingsworth, Esther V, 33
Hollingsworth, Esther V, 72
Hollingsworth, Esther V, 74
Hollingsworth, Esther V, 75
Hollingsworth, Esther V, 248
Hollingsworth, Esther V, 401
Hollingsworth, Esther V, 435
Hollingsworth, Esther Jane V, 503
Hollingsworth, Eunice I, 1031
Hollingsworth, Eunice I, 1038
Hollingsworth, Eunice V, 57
Hollingsworth, Eunice V, 74
Hollingsworth, Eunice F. V, 74
Hollingsworth, Ezekiel I, 1032
Hollingsworth, Ezra IV, 635
Hollingsworth, Ezra IV, 1062
Hollingsworth, Faris IV, 336
Hollingsworth, Florence N. V, 74
Hollingsworth, Frank V, 401
Hollingsworth, Franklin V, 74
Hollingsworth, Franklin V, 76
Hollingsworth, Franklin V, 401
Hollingsworth, George I, 1031
Hollingsworth, George V, 75
Hollingsworth, George V, 103
Hollingsworth, George V, 743
Hollingsworth, George VI, 402
Hollingsworth, George, Jr. I, 1032
Hollingsworth, George, Jr. V, 743
Hollingsworth, George, Sr. V, 743
Hollingsworth, Glen V, 76
Hollingsworth, Grace IV, 532
Hollingsworth, Grace IV, 557
Hollingsworth, Grace IV, 1102
Hollingsworth, Grace IV, 1105
Hollingsworth, Grace E. IV, 1062
Hollingsworth, Grace E. IV, 1134
Hollingsworth, Grace Elizabeth IV, 1063
Hollingsworth, Grace Elizabeth V, 248
Hollingsworth, Gulielma I, 588
Hollingsworth, Gulielma I, 594
Hollingsworth, Gulielma V, 75
Hollingsworth, Guly E. I, 764
Hollingsworth, Guly Elma I, 756
Hollingsworth, Guly Elma I, 764
Hollingsworth, Hanah I, 1020
Hollingsworth, Hannah I, 594
Hollingsworth, Hannah I, 818
Hollingsworth, Hannah I, 1020
Hollingsworth, Hannah I, 1031
Hollingsworth, Hannah I, 1060
Hollingsworth, Hannah I, 1061
Hollingsworth, Hannah II, 551
Hollingsworth, Hannah II, 615
Hollingsworth, Hannah IV, 125
Hollingsworth, Hannah IV, 149
Hollingsworth, Hannah IV, 336
Hollingsworth, Hannah IV, 338
Hollingsworth, Hannah IV, 523
Hollingsworth, Hannah IV, 532
Hollingsworth, Hannah IV, 635
Hollingsworth, Hannah V, 35
Hollingsworth, Hannah V, 74
Hollingsworth, Hannah V, 75
Hollingsworth, Hannah V, 502
Hollingsworth, Hannah V, 503
Hollingsworth, Hannah V, 529
Hollingsworth, Hannah V, 794
Hollingsworth, Hannah V, 810
Hollingsworth, Hannah V, 842
Hollingsworth, Hannah V, 843
Hollingsworth, Hannah VI, 402
Hollingsworth, Hannah VI, 458
Hollingsworth, Hannah VI, 507
Hollingsworth, Hannah VI, 591
Hollingsworth, Hannah VI, 592
Hollingsworth, Hannah VI, 595
Hollingsworth, Hannah VI, 596
Hollingsworth, Hannah VI, 598
Hollingsworth, Hannah VI, 655
Hollingsworth, Hannah C. IV, 704
Hollingsworth, Hannah C. IV, 723
Hollingsworth, Hannah C. IV, 1062
Hollingsworth, Hannah Y. IV, 635
Hollingsworth, Hannah Y. IV, 667
Hollingsworth, Hannah Y. IV, 692
Hollingsworth, Hannah Y. IV, 693
Hollingsworth, Hannah Y. IV, 707
Hollingsworth, Hannah Y. IV, 713
Hollingsworth, Hannah Y. IV, 731
Hollingsworth, Hariet V, 953
Hollingsworth, Harriet V, 503
Hollingsworth, Harrison P. Gamble IV, 723
Hollingsworth, Henry I, 1030
Hollingsworth, Henry I, 1031
Hollingsworth, Henry I, 1032
Hollingsworth, Henry V, 74
Hollingsworth, Henry V, 75
Hollingsworth, Henry V, 743
Hollingsworth, Henry V, 803
Hollingsworth, Henry V, 810
Hollingsworth, Henry VI, 472
Hollingsworth, Henry D. VI, 472
Hollingsworth, Henry D. VI, 506
Hollingsworth, Henry D. VI, 507
Hollingsworth, Henry D. VI, 655
Hollingsworth, Hestar A. V, 684
Hollingsworth, Hester V, 684
Hollingsworth, Hester Ann V, 502
Hollingsworth, Hester Ann V, 503
Hollingsworth, Hester Ann V, 529
Hollingsworth, Hester Ann V, 684
Hollingsworth, I. V, 749
Hollingsworth, Ida IV, 1211
Hollingsworth, Ida V, 248
Hollingsworth, Idella V, 75
Hollingsworth, Idella V, 684
Hollingsworth, Inez V, 503
Hollingsworth, Inez V, 684
Hollingsworth, Ira V, 75
Hollingsworth, Ira V, 743
Hollingsworth, Irie V, 743
Hollingsworth, Irvin T. V, 401
Hollingsworth, Isaac I, 501
Hollingsworth, Isaac I, 548
Hollingsworth, Isaac I, 588
Hollingsworth, Isaac I, 594
Hollingsworth, Isaac I, 598
Hollingsworth, Isaac I, 818
Hollingsworth, Isaac I, 1015
Hollingsworth, Isaac I, 1020
Hollingsworth, Isaac I, 1028
Hollingsworth, Isaac I, 1031
Hollingsworth, Isaac I, 1032
Hollingsworth, Isaac I, 1039
Hollingsworth, Isaac I, 1061
Hollingsworth, Isaac IV, 93
Hollingsworth, Isaac IV, 149
Hollingsworth, Isaac IV, 532
Hollingsworth, Isaac IV, 561
Hollingsworth, Isaac V, 74
Hollingsworth, Isaac V, 75
Hollingsworth, Isaac V, 86
Hollingsworth, Isaac V, 503
Hollingsworth, Isaac V, 723
Hollingsworth, Isaac V, 740
Hollingsworth, Isaac V, 743
Hollingsworth, Isaac V, 747
Hollingsworth, Isaac V, 809
Hollingsworth, Isaac V, 810
Hollingsworth, Isaac VI, 415
Hollingsworth, Isaac VI, 506
Hollingsworth, Isaac VI, 507
Hollingsworth, Isaac VI, 511
Hollingsworth, Isaac VI, 538
Hollingsworth, Isaac VI, 565
Hollingsworth, Isaac VI, 655
Hollingsworth, Isaac H. IV, 875
Hollingsworth, Isaac, Jr. I, 1031
Hollingsworth, Isadore V, 502
Hollingsworth, Isaiah V, 743
Hollingsworth, Isaiah V, 843
Hollingsworth, Isaiah V, 861
Hollingsworth, Isaiah V, 862
Hollingsworth, Isiah V, 843
Hollingsworth, Israel V, 502
Hollingsworth, Israel H. V, 502
Hollingsworth, Israel H. V, 953
Hollingsworth, Israel H. V, 962
Hollingsworth, Iwrael V, 502
Hollingsworth, J. Furnace V, 75
Hollingsworth, J. Furnas V, 75
Hollingsworth, J. Furnas V, 684
Hollingsworth, Jabez V, 74
Hollingsworth, Jabez V, 75
Hollingsworth, Jacob I, 1031
Hollingsworth, Jacob I, 1032
Hollingsworth, Jacob V, 75
Hollingsworth, James I, 1031
Hollingsworth, James I, 1032
Hollingsworth, James I, 1039
Hollingsworth, James V, 33
Hollingsworth, James V, 72
Hollingsworth, James V, 74
Hollingsworth, James V, 75
Hollingsworth, James V, 339
Hollingsworth, James V, 401
Hollingsworth, James V, 435
Hollingsworth, James V, 723
Hollingsworth, James V, 743
Hollingsworth, James V, 782
Hollingsworth, James Er IV, 635
Hollingsworth, James H. V, 401
Hollingsworth, James M. V, 75
Hollingsworth, James M. V, 304
Hollingsworth, James M. V, 503
Hollingsworth, James N. V, 503
Hollingsworth, James W. V, 502
Hollingsworth, Jamima VI, 507
Hollingsworth, Jane I, 1020
Hollingsworth, Jane I, 1031
Hollingsworth, Jane IV, 635
Hollingsworth, Jane IV, 639
Hollingsworth, Jane V, 35
Hollingsworth, Jane V, 72
Hollingsworth, Jane V, 74
Hollingsworth, Jane V, 75
Hollingsworth, Jane V, 103
Hollingsworth, Jane V, 304
Hollingsworth, Jane V, 806
Hollingsworth, Jane V, 810
Hollingsworth, Jane VI, 507
Hollingsworth, Jane VI, 538
Hollingsworth, Jane VI, 587
Hollingsworth, Jane VI, 647
Hollingsworth, Jane VI, 655
Hollingsworth, Jane A. V, 502
Hollingsworth, Jane Ann V, 502
Hollingsworth, Jane Ann V, 514
Hollingsworth, Jane M. V, 810
Hollingsworth, Jarrus V, 502
Hollingsworth, Jas. V, 784
Hollingsworth, Jehu VI, 507
Hollingsworth, Jemima VI, 507
Hollingsworth, Jemima, Jr. VI, 507
Hollingsworth, Jesse I, 1057
Hollingsworth, Jesse I, 1061
Hollingsworth, Jesse II, 551
Hollingsworth, Jesse II, 800
Hollingsworth, Jesse IV, 875
Hollingsworth, Joel I, 1020
Hollingsworth, Joel I, 1032
Hollingsworth, Joel V, 75
Hollingsworth, Joel V, 761
Hollingsworth, Joel V, 803
Hollingsworth, Joel V, 809
Hollingsworth, Joel V, 810
Hollingsworth, Joel VI, 416
Hollingsworth, Joel G. IV, 1134
Hollingsworth, John I, 548
Hollingsworth, John I, 588
Hollingsworth, John I, 594
Hollingsworth, John I, 1020
Hollingsworth, John I, 1031
Hollingsworth, John I, 1032
Hollingsworth, John I, 1039
Hollingsworth, John I, 1061
Hollingsworth, John IV, 336
Hollingsworth, John IV, 532
Hollingsworth, John IV, 723
Hollingsworth, John V, 35
Hollingsworth, John V, 44
Hollingsworth, John V, 74
Hollingsworth, John V, 75
Hollingsworth, John V, 502
Hollingsworth, John V, 743
Hollingsworth, John V, 843
Hollingsworth, John VI, 507
Hollingsworth, John VI, 655
Hollingsworth, John Fares IV, 723
Hollingsworth, John Ferris IV, 149
Hollingsworth, John Ferris IV, 336
Hollingsworth, John Gurney V, 74
Hollingsworth, John Hough VI, 507
Hollingsworth, John Neill VI, 507
Hollingsworth, Jonah V, 74
Hollingsworth, Jonah VI, 402
Hollingsworth, Jonah VI, 423
Hollingsworth, Jonah VI, 507
Hollingsworth, Jonah VI, 598
Hollingsworth, Jonah VI, 602
Hollingsworth, Jonah H. VI, 416
Hollingsworth, Jonah Robert V, 74
Hollingsworth, Jonathan I, 1031
Hollingsworth, Jonathan I, 1032
Hollingsworth, Jonathan V, 75
Hollingsworth, Jonathan V, 502
Hollingsworth, Jonathan V, 843
Hollingsworth, Jonathan M. IV, 532
Hollingsworth, Jonathan M. E. IV, 532
Hollingsworth, Jonothan V, 75
Hollingsworth, Joseph I, 548
Hollingsworth, Joseph I, 1016
Hollingsworth, Joseph I, 1020
Hollingsworth, Joseph I, 1030
Hollingsworth, Joseph I, 1031
Hollingsworth, Joseph I, 1041
Hollingsworth, Joseph I, 1048
Hollingsworth, Joseph I, 1061
Hollingsworth, Joseph IV, 875
Hollingsworth, Joseph IV, 1062
Hollingsworth, Joseph V, 74
Hollingsworth, Joseph V, 75
Hollingsworth, Joseph V, 81
Hollingsworth, Joseph V, 140
Hollingsworth, Joseph V, 743
Hollingsworth, Joseph V, 799
Hollingsworth, Joseph V, 808
Hollingsworth, Joseph V, 810
Hollingsworth, Joseph V, 842
Hollingsworth, Joseph V, 843
Hollingsworth, Joseph VI, 359
Hollingsworth, Joseph VI, 402
Hollingsworth, Joseph VI, 507
Hollingsworth, Joseph Earl IV, 1139
Hollingsworth, Joseph Earl V, 76
Hollingsworth, Joseph Earl V, 743
Hollingsworth, Joseph F. V, 75
Hollingsworth, Joseph Furnace V, 76
Hollingsworth, Joseph Furnas V, 74
Hollingsworth, Joseph Furnas V, 75
Hollingsworth, Joseph Furnas V, 76
Hollingsworth, Joseph Furnas V, 743
Hollingsworth, Joseph Hall IV, 635
Hollingsworth, Joseph Hall IV, 824
Hollingsworth, Joseph P. IV, 875
Hollingsworth, Joseph Smith V, 74
Hollingsworth, Josiah V, 503
Hollingsworth, Josiah V, 743
Hollingsworth, Judith VI, 507
Hollingsworth, Kennet IV, 149
Hollingsworth, Kennett VI, 506
Hollingsworth, Keturah V, 75
Hollingsworth, Keturah V, 784
Hollingsworth, Keziah V, 819
Hollingsworth, Levi I, 1020
Hollingsworth, Levi I, 1031
Hollingsworth, Levi I, 1057
Hollingsworth, Levi II, 375
Hollingsworth, Levi II, 551
Hollingsworth, Levi IV, 149
Hollingsworth, Levi IV, 336
Hollingsworth, Levi IV, 532
Hollingsworth, Levi IV, 533
Hollingsworth, Levi IV, 875
Hollingsworth, Levi VI, 507
Hollingsworth, Levi VI, 647
Hollingsworth, Levi VI, 655
Hollingsworth, Lewis IV, 635
Hollingsworth, Lewis IV, 723
Hollingsworth, Lewis VI, 402
Hollingsworth, Lewis VI, 416
Hollingsworth, Lewis VI, 428
Hollingsworth, Lewis VI, 507
Hollingsworth, Lewis VI, 542
Hollingsworth, Lewis VI, 568
Hollingsworth, Lewis VI, 578
Hollingsworth, Lewis VI, 654
Hollingsworth, Lewis VI, 719
Hollingsworth, Lewis D. VI, 507
Hollingsworth, Lidia V, 74
Hollingsworth, Lodica V, 810
Hollingsworth, Louis IV, 635
Hollingsworth, Louis IV, 704
Hollingsworth, Louis IV, 723
Hollingsworth, Louis IV, 875
Hollingsworth, Louis IV, 1062
Hollingsworth, Louisa IV, 635
Hollingsworth, Lucy II, 551
Hollingsworth, Luella IV, 1062
Hollingsworth, Lula V, 179
Hollingsworth, Lulu V, 179
Hollingsworth, Lydia I, 380
Hollingsworth, Lydia I, 399
Hollingsworth, Lydia I, 1058
Hollingsworth, Lydia IV, 561
Hollingsworth, Lydia IV, 579
Hollingsworth, Lydia IV, 635
Hollingsworth, Lydia IV, 1084
Hollingsworth, Lydia V, 75
Hollingsworth, Lydia V, 120
Hollingsworth, Lydia V, 377
Hollingsworth, Lydia V, 401
Hollingsworth, Lydia V, 433
Hollingsworth, Lydia V, 502
Hollingsworth, Lydia V, 782
Hollingsworth, Lydia VI, 359
Hollingsworth, Lydia VI, 402
Hollingsworth, Lydia VI, 506
Hollingsworth, Lydia VI, 507
Hollingsworth, Lydia VI, 510
Hollingsworth, Lydia VI, 511
Hollingsworth, Lydia VI, 522
Hollingsworth, Lydia VI, 538
Hollingsworth, Lydia Ann IV, 1062
Hollingsworth, Lydia H. V, 502
Hollingsworth, Lydia H. V, 525
Hollingsworth, Lydia Jane VI, 402
Hollingsworth, Lydia Jane VI, 507
Hollingsworth, Mahlon IV, 635
Hollingsworth, Mahlon IV, 640
Hollingsworth, Mahlon IV, 873
Hollingsworth, Mahlon V, 74
Hollingsworth, Mahlon V, 141
Hollingsworth, Mahlon V, 304
Hollingsworth, Mahlon V, 503
Hollingsworth, Mahlon C. V, 75
Hollingsworth, Malon V, 75
Hollingsworth, Margaret I, 1030
Hollingsworth, Margaret I, 1031
Hollingsworth, Margaret IV, 622
Hollingsworth, Margaret IV, 635
Hollingsworth, Margaret IV, 640
Hollingsworth, Margaret IV, 663
Hollingsworth, Margaret IV, 667
Hollingsworth, Margaret IV, 693
Hollingsworth, Margaret IV, 723
Hollingsworth, Margaret IV, 873
Hollingsworth, Margaret IV, 875
Hollingsworth, Margaret IV, 110
Hollingsworth, Margaret IV, 111
Hollingsworth, Margaret V, 74
Hollingsworth, Margaret V, 743
Hollingsworth, Margaret V, 799
Hollingsworth, Margaret V, 810

llingsworth, Margaret V, 843
llingsworth, Margaret VI, 507
llingsworth, Margaret A. V, 75
llingsworth, Margaret A. V, 120
llingsworth, Margaret Ann V, 74
llingsworth, Margaret S. V, 743
llingsworth, Margy VI, 506
llingsworth, Marion V, 248
llingsworth, Marion V, 503
llingsworth, Mark V, 75
ollingsworth, Martha I, 548
ollingsworth, Martha I, 1016
ollingsworth, Martha I, 1020
ollingsworth, Martha I, 1031
ollingsworth, Martha I, 1057
ollingsworth, Martha I, 1058
ollingsworth, Martha I, 1061
ollingsworth, Martha IV, 410
ollingsworth, Martha IV, 628
ollingsworth, Martha IV, 635
ollingsworth, Martha IV, 641
ollingsworth, Martha IV, 768
ollingsworth, Martha IV, 824
ollingsworth, Martha IV, 965
ollingsworth, Martha IV, 1062
ollingsworth, Martha IV, 1066
ollingsworth, Martha IV, 1105
ollingsworth, Martha V, 56
ollingsworth, Martha V, 72
ollingsworth, Martha V, 74
ollingsworth, Martha V, 75
ollingsworth, Martha V, 76
ollingsworth, Martha VI, 416
ollingsworth, Martha Farquhar IV, 399
ollingsworth, Marther I, 1031
ollingsworth, Mary I, 504
ollingsworth, Mary I, 548
ollingsworth, Mary I, 594
ollingsworth, Mary I, 598
ollingsworth, Mary I, 1020
ollingsworth, Mary I, 1057
ollingsworth, Mary I, 1061
ollingsworth, Mary I, 1063
ollingsworth, Mary II, 551
ollingsworth, Mary II, 626
ollingsworth, Mary II, 800
ollingsworth, Mary IV, 149
ollingsworth, Mary IV, 336
ollingsworth, Mary IV, 532
ollingsworth, Mary IV, 965
ollingsworth, Mary V, 74
ollingsworth, Mary V, 75
ollingsworth, Mary V, 141
ollingsworth, Mary V, 304
ollingsworth, Mary V, 502
ollingsworth, Mary V, 728
ollingsworth, Mary V, 743
ollingsworth, Mary V, 833
ollingsworth, Mary V, 843
ollingsworth, Mary VI, 402
ollingsworth, Mary VI, 415
ollingsworth, Mary VI, 431
ollingsworth, Mary VI, 506
ollingsworth, Mary VI, 507
ollingsworth, Mary VI, 522
ollingsworth, Mary VI, 529
ollingsworth, Mary VI, 647
ollingsworth, Mary VI, 655
ollingsworth, Mary VI, 668
Hollingsworth, Mary VI, 673
Hollingsworth, Mary VI, 757
Hollingsworth, Mary VI, 763
Hollingsworth, Mary A. IV, 1134
Hollingsworth, Mary A. IV, 1138
Hollingsworth, Mary A. IV, 1139
Hollingsworth, Mary Ann IV, 532
Hollingsworth, Mary Ann IV, 1133
Hollingsworth, Mary Ann IV, 1139
Hollingsworth, Mary Anne IV, 532
Hollingsworth, Mary B. V, 74
Hollingsworth, Mary B. V, 75
Hollingsworth, Mary C. V, 74
Hollingsworth, Mary Catharine IV, 875
Hollingsworth, Mary Ellen VI, 506
Hollingsworth, Mary Ellen VI, 655
Hollingsworth, Mary Hall IV, 635
Hollingsworth, Mary I. V, 74
Hollingsworth, Mary J. IV, 532
Hollingsworth, Mary L. IV, 635
Hollingsworth, Mary L. W. V, 75
Hollingsworth, Mary L. W. V, 684
Hollingsworth, Mary P. V, 141
Hollingsworth, Mary P. V, 503
Hollingsworth, Mary P. VI, 393
Hollingsworth, Mary P. VI, 402
Hollingsworth, Mary W. IV, 687
Hollingsworth, Mary W. IV, 723
Hollingsworth, Mary W. V, 75
Hollingsworth, Mary W. V, 502
Hollingsworth, Maurice A. V, 76
Hollingsworth, Maurice Baxter V, 74
Hollingsworth, May VI, 655
Hollingsworth, May E. VI, 508
Hollingsworth, Michael V, 743
Hollingsworth, Midian V, 843
Hollingsworth, Milton IV, 926
Hollingsworth, Milton IV, 965
Hollingsworth, Milton V, 385
Hollingsworth, Milton V, 401
Hollingsworth, Miriam V, 782
Hollingsworth, Mirza V, 502
Hollingsworth, Moses V, 75
Hollingsworth, Moses V, 743
Hollingsworth, Moses W. V, 74
Hollingsworth, Nancy VI, 719
Hollingsworth, Nancy Catharine VI, 578
Hollingsworth, Nancy Catharine VI, 654
Hollingsworth, Nancy Catharine Whetherall VI, 507
Hollingsworth, Nancy Catherine VI, 507
Hollingsworth, Nancy Catherine VI, 508
Hollingsworth, Nancy Catherine VI, 543
Hollingsworth, Naomi VI, 506
Hollingsworth, Naomi VI, 507
Hollingsworth, Nathan I, 1031
Hollingsworth, Nathan I, 1032
Hollingsworth, Nathan IV, 1139
Hollingsworth, Nathan V, 74
Hollingsworth, Nathan V, 75
Hollingsworth, Nathan V, 179
Hollingsworth, Nathan V, 401
Hollingsworth, Nathan V, 576
Hollingsworth, Nathan V, 723
Hollingsworth, Nathan V, 810
Hollingsworth, Nathan Omor V, 74
Hollingsworth, Olive V, 782
Hollingsworth, Olive V, 843
Hollingsworth, Parker V, 743
Hollingsworth, Patience V, 843
Hollingsworth, Patience V, 861
Hollingsworth, Patience V, 862
Hollingsworth, Penina IV, 811
Hollingsworth, Penina IV, 824
Hollingsworth, Penina IV, 1129
Hollingsworth, Penina IV, 1134
Hollingsworth, Peninah IV, 1062
Hollingsworth, Pennina IV, 1134
Hollingsworth, Petter I, 1020
Hollingsworth, Phebe I, 588
Hollingsworth, Phebe I, 594
Hollingsworth, Phebe I, 626
Hollingsworth, Phebe IV, 410
Hollingsworth, Phebe IV, 561
Hollingsworth, Phebe IV, 634
Hollingsworth, Phebe IV, 635
Hollingsworth, Phebe IV, 640
Hollingsworth, Phebe IV, 710
Hollingsworth, Phebe IV, 723
Hollingsworth, Phebe IV, 816
Hollingsworth, Phebe IV, 873
Hollingsworth, Phebe IV, 876
Hollingsworth, Phebe IV, 1057
Hollingsworth, Phebe IV, 1062
Hollingsworth, Phebe V, 75
Hollingsworth, Phebe V, 502
Hollingsworth, Phebe V, 504
Hollingsworth, Phebe VI, 402
Hollingsworth, Phebe VI, 447
Hollingsworth, Phebe VI, 476
Hollingsworth, Phebe VI, 482
Hollingsworth, Phebe VI, 507
Hollingsworth, Phebe VI, 512
Hollingsworth, Phebe VI, 536
Hollingsworth, Phebe VI, 554
Hollingsworth, Phebe VI, 565
Hollingsworth, Phebe VI, 567
Hollingsworth, Phebe VI, 568
Hollingsworth, Phebe VI, 583
Hollingsworth, Phebe VI, 584
Hollingsworth, Phebe VI, 767
Hollingsworth, Phebe Ann IV, 622
Hollingsworth, Phebe Ann IV, 635
Hollingsworth, Phebe Ann V, 810
Hollingsworth, Phebe Leech IV, 635
Hollingsworth, Pierce V, 502
Hollingsworth, Pierce V, 503
Hollingsworth, Pierce V, 541
Hollingsworth, Rachel I, 1020
Hollingsworth, Rachel I, 1031
Hollingsworth, Rachel I, 1039
Hollingsworth, Rachel IV, 532
Hollingsworth, Rachel IV, 873
Hollingsworth, Rachel IV, 874
Hollingsworth, Rachel V, 35
Hollingsworth, Rachel V, 44
Hollingsworth, Rachel V, 74
Hollingsworth, Rachel V, 75
Hollingsworth, Rachel V, 133
Hollingsworth, Rachel V, 502
Hollingsworth, Rachel V, 509
Hollingsworth, Rachel V, 801
Hollingsworth, Rachel V, 803
Hollingsworth, Rachel V, 810
Hollingsworth, Rachel VI, 402
Hollingsworth, Rachel VI, 415
Hollingsworth, Rachel VI, 447
Hollingsworth, Rachel VI, 506
Hollingsworth, Rachel VI, 507
Hollingsworth, Rachel VI, 538
Hollingsworth, Rachel VI, 565
Hollingsworth, Rachel VI, 592
Hollingsworth, Rachel VI, 593
Hollingsworth, Rachel VI, 597
Hollingsworth, Rachel VI, 602
Hollingsworth, Rachel VI, 603
Hollingsworth, Rachel VI, 628
Hollingsworth, Rachel VI, 655
Hollingsworth, Rachel Ann V, 74
Hollingsworth, Rachel Ann V, 75
Hollingsworth, Rachel Ann V, 304
Hollingsworth, Rachel Ann V, 503
Hollingsworth, Rachel E. V, 953
Hollingsworth, Rachel E. V, 962
Hollingsworth, Rachel J. VI, 477
Hollingsworth, Rachel J. VI, 507
Hollingsworth, Rachel Jane VI, 402
Hollingsworth, Rachel Jane VI, 568
Hollingsworth, Rachel Suffiah Susannah V, 743
Hollingsworth, Rebecca II, 615
Hollingsworth, Rebecca V, 75
Hollingsworth, Rebecca C. V, 74
Hollingsworth, Rebecca C. V, 75
Hollingsworth, Rebecca C. V, 304
Hollingsworth, Rebeckah I, 1020
Hollingsworth, Reece J. II, 876
Hollingsworth, Reese Jones II, 800
Hollingsworth, Rhoda V, 74
Hollingsworth, Rhoda V, 75
Hollingsworth, Rhoda V, 140
Hollingsworth, Rhoda V, 576
Hollingsworth, Rhoda V, 810
Hollingsworth, Rhoda Ann V, 179
Hollingsworth, Rhoda Ann V, 401
Hollingsworth, Richard V, 743
Hollingsworth, Robert VI, 402
Hollingsworth, Robert VI, 542
Hollingsworth, Robert I. VI, 477
Hollingsworth, Robert I. VI, 507
Hollingsworth, Robert I. VI, 628
Hollingsworth, Robert I. VI, 655
Hollingsworth, Robert Isaac VI, 402
Hollingsworth, Robert Isaac VI, 507
Hollingsworth, Robert Isaac VI, 568
Hollingsworth, Robert P. VI, 506
Hollingsworth, Robert P. VI, 655
Hollingsworth, Robt. I. VI, 568
Hollingsworth, Roda V, 179
Hollingsworth, Ruth I, 1020
Hollingsworth, Ruth I, 1061
Hollingsworth, Ruth I, 1063
Hollingsworth, Ruth IV, 635
Hollingsworth, Ruth IV, 1062
Hollingsworth, Ruth IV, 1071
Hollingsworth, Ruth V, 749
Hollingsworth, Ruth V, 759
Hollingsworth, Ruth V, 810
Hollingsworth, Ruthanna V, 74
Hollingsworth, Sally V, 74
Hollingsworth, Sally V, 75
Hollingsworth, Sally V, 81
Hollingsworth, Sally V, 743
Hollingsworth, Sally V, 808
Hollingsworth, Sally V, 810
Hollingsworth, Sally VI, 899
Hollingsworth, Saml. IV, 399
Hollingsworth, Samuel IV, 149
Hollingsworth, Samuel IV, 336
Hollingsworth, Samuel IV, 410
Hollingsworth, Samuel IV, 622
Hollingsworth, Samuel IV, 628
Hollingsworth, Samuel IV, 635
Hollingsworth, Samuel IV, 640
Hollingsworth, Samuel IV, 663
Hollingsworth, Samuel IV, 667
Hollingsworth, Samuel IV, 693
Hollingsworth, Samuel IV, 723
Hollingsworth, Samuel IV, 873
Hollingsworth, Samuel IV, 875
Hollingsworth, Samuel V, 74
Hollingsworth, Samuel V, 75
Hollingsworth, Samuel V, 502
Hollingsworth, Samuel V, 503
Hollingsworth, Samuel V, 508
Hollingsworth, Samuel V, 514
Hollingsworth, Samuel VI, 402
Hollingsworth, Samuel A. IV, 635
Hollingsworth, Samuel Aseph Lydia James V, 502
Hollingsworth, Sara C. IV, 927
Hollingsworth, Sarah I, 548
Hollingsworth, Sarah I, 588
Hollingsworth, Sarah I, 594
Hollingsworth, Sarah I, 1020
Hollingsworth, Sarah I, 1028
Hollingsworth, Sarah I, 1030
Hollingsworth, Sarah I, 1031
Hollingsworth, Sarah I, 1032
Hollingsworth, Sarah I, 1037
Hollingsworth, Sarah I, 1039
Hollingsworth, Sarah I, 1058
Hollingsworth, Sarah IV, 149
Hollingsworth, Sarah IV, 336
Hollingsworth, Sarah IV, 345
Hollingsworth, Sarah IV, 517
Hollingsworth, Sarah IV, 532
Hollingsworth, Sarah IV, 533
Hollingsworth, Sarah IV, 556
Hollingsworth, Sarah IV, 611
Hollingsworth, Sarah IV, 614
Hollingsworth, Sarah IV, 632
Hollingsworth, Sarah IV, 634
Hollingsworth, Sarah IV, 635
Hollingsworth, Sarah IV, 640
Hollingsworth, Sarah IV, 873
Hollingsworth, Sarah IV, 1057
Hollingsworth, Sarah IV, 1058
Hollingsworth, Sarah IV, 1062
Hollingsworth, Sarah IV, 1063
Hollingsworth, Sarah IV, 1066
Hollingsworth, Sarah IV, 1071
Hollingsworth, Sarah IV, 1127
Hollingsworth, Sarah IV, 1131
Hollingsworth, Sarah IV, 1133
Hollingsworth, Sarah IV, 1134
Hollingsworth, Sarah V, 26
Hollingsworth, Sarah V, 74
Hollingsworth, Sarah V, 75
Hollingsworth, Sarah V, 111
Hollingsworth, Sarah V, 502
Hollingsworth, Sarah V, 723
Hollingsworth, Sarah V, 743
Hollingsworth, Sarah V, 769
Hollingsworth, Sarah V, 782
Hollingsworth, Sarah V, 784
Hollingsworth, Sarah V, 803
Hollingsworth, Sarah V, 808
Hollingsworth, Sarah V, 810
Hollingsworth, Sarah V, 843
Hollingsworth, Sarah VI, 402
Hollingsworth, Sarah VI, 416
Hollingsworth, Sarah VI, 431
Hollingsworth, Sarah VI, 507
Hollingsworth, Sarah VI, 655
Hollingsworth, Sarah VI, 683
Hollingsworth, Sarah Ann IV, 149
Hollingsworth, Sarah Ann IV, 336
Hollingsworth, Sarah Ann IV, 723
Hollingsworth, Sarah Ann IV, 875
Hollingsworth, Sarah Ann IV, 1059
Hollingsworth, Sarah Ann IV, 1062
Hollingsworth, Sarah Ann V, 502
Hollingsworth, Sarah C. IV, 611
Hollingsworth, Sarah C. IV, 615
Hollingsworth, Sarah G. I, 548
Hollingsworth, Sarah Jane IV, 635
Hollingsworth, Sarah Jane V, 502
Hollingsworth, Sarah Jane V, 503
Hollingsworth, Sarah Jane V, 541
Hollingsworth, Seth V, 74
Hollingsworth, Seth V, 75
Hollingsworth, Simon V, 179
Hollingsworth, Sintha M. IV, 1134
Hollingsworth, Smith IV, 875
Hollingsworth, Solomon V, 75
Hollingsworth, Solomon VI, 402
Hollingsworth, Sophia V, 502
Hollingsworth, Sophia V, 512
Hollingsworth, Sophia V, 810
Hollingsworth, Stephen II, 375
Hollingsworth, Stephen V, 782
Hollingsworth, Stephen VI, 359
Hollingsworth, Stephen VI, 402
Hollingsworth, Stephen VI, 410
Hollingsworth, Susan V, 385
Hollingsworth, Susan V, 401
Hollingsworth, Susan M. V, 401
Hollingsworth, Susan P. V, 76
Hollingsworth, Susanna I, 548
Hollingsworth, Susanna I, 588
Hollingsworth, Susanna I, 594
Hollingsworth, Susanna I, 818
Hollingsworth, Susanna I, 1031
Hollingsworth, Susanna IV, 149
Hollingsworth, Susanna IV, 532
Hollingsworth, Susanna IV, 548
Hollingsworth, Susanna IV, 875
Hollingsworth, Susanna V, 74
Hollingsworth, Susanna V, 75
Hollingsworth, Susanna V, 76
Hollingsworth, Susanna V, 86
Hollingsworth, Susanna V, 103
Hollingsworth, Susanna V, 179
Hollingsworth, Susanna V, 748
Hollingsworth, Susanna V, 757
Hollingsworth, Susanna V, 784
Hollingsworth, Susanna V, 810
Hollingsworth, Susanna P. V, 75
Hollingsworth, Susanna P. V, 810
Hollingsworth, Susannah I, 1020
Hollingsworth, Susannah I, 1031
Hollingsworth, Susannah I, 1032
Hollingsworth, Susannah I, 1039
Hollingsworth, Susannah IV, 532
Hollingsworth, Susannah V, 75
Hollingsworth, Susannah V, 401
Hollingsworth, Susannah V, 502
Hollingsworth, Susannah V, 684
Hollingsworth, Susannah V, 723
Hollingsworth, Susannah V, 743
Hollingsworth, Susannah V, 747
Hollingsworth, Susannah V, 761
Hollingsworth, Susannah V, 803
Hollingsworth, Susannah V, 809
Hollingsworth, Susannah V, 810
Hollingsworth, Susannah V, 843
Hollingsworth, Susannah VI, 402
Hollingsworth, Susannah VI, 506
Hollingsworth, Susannah VI, 542
Hollingsworth, Susannah VI, 655
Hollingsworth, Susannah P. V, 75
Hollingsworth, Susannah P. V, 684
Hollingsworth, Syrus I, 548
Hollingsworth, Thomas I, 1020
Hollingsworth, Thomas I, 1031
Hollingsworth, Thomas II, 232
Hollingsworth, Thomas IV, 149
Hollingsworth, Thomas IV, 532
Hollingsworth, Thomas IV, 635
Hollingsworth, Thomas IV, 723
Hollingsworth, Thomas V, 74
Hollingsworth, Thomas V, 75
Hollingsworth, Thomas V, 401
Hollingsworth, Thomas VI, 402
Hollingsworth, Thomas VI, 431
Hollingsworth, Thomas VI, 507
Hollingsworth, Thomas VI, 647
Hollingsworth, Thomas VI, 655
Hollingsworth, Thompson L. VI, 506
Hollingsworth, Thompson L. VI, 508
Hollingsworth, Thompson L. VI, 543
Hollingsworth, Thompson L. VI, 655
Hollingsworth, Thos. C. II, 876
Hollingsworth, Unice V, 810
Hollingsworth, Ury IV, 1062
Hollingsworth, Ury IV, 1102
Hollingsworth, Ury IV, 1130
Hollingsworth, Ury IV, 1134
Hollingsworth, Valentine V, 502
Hollingsworth, Valentine V, 782
Hollingsworth, Valentine VI, 507
Hollingsworth, Wd. Margaret S. V, 740
Hollingsworth, Widow Margaret VI, 655

Hollingsworth, Wildie B. V, 76
Hollingsworth, William I, 548
Hollingsworth, William I, 1015
Hollingsworth, William I, 1016
Hollingsworth, William I, 1020
Hollingsworth, William I, 1032
Hollingsworth, William I, 1061
Hollingsworth, William IV, 635
Hollingsworth, William IV, 875
Hollingsworth, William V, 74
Hollingsworth, William V, 75
Hollingsworth, William V, 833
Hollingsworth, William V, 843
Hollingsworth, William S. VI, 508
Hollingsworth, Wm. IV, 635
Hollingsworth, Wm. IV, 965
Hollingsworth, Wm. IV, 1062
Hollingsworth, Wm. P. II, 746
Hollingsworth, Wright V, 740
Hollingsworth, Wright V, 743
Hollingsworth, Yates V, 810
Hollingsworth, Zebulon V, 74
Hollingsworth, Zebulon V, 75
Hollingsworth, Zimri V, 26
Hollingsworth, Zimri V, 74
Hollingsworth, Zimri V, 75
Hollingworth, Abigail VI, 506
Hollingworth, Asenath VI, 506
Hollingworth, Charles L. VI, 506
Hollingworth, Lewis VI, 506
Hollingworth, Lydia Ann IV, 1074
Hollingworth, Nancy Catharine VI, 506
Hollins, Angeline G. VI, 832
Hollins, Casandra VI, 845
Hollins, George VI, 826
Hollins, Hardinea VI, 826
Hollins, Mary VI, 832
Hollins, William VI, 826
Hollinshead, ??? II, 177
Hollinshead, Agnes II, 177
Hollinshead, Alice II, 551
Hollinshead, Anna II, 746
Hollinshead, Benjamin M. II, 551
Hollinshead, Benjamin S. II, 746
Hollinshead, Caroline H. II, 551
Hollinshead, Edmund II, 418
Hollinshead, Edmund II, 551
Hollinshead, Edmund II, 746
Hollinshead, Eliza W. II, 746
Hollinshead, Elizabeth II, 551
Hollinshead, Elizabeth II, 743
Hollinshead, Elizabeth II, 746
Hollinshead, Ellen II, 746
Hollinshead, George F. II, 876
Hollinshead, Hannah II, 418
Hollinshead, Hudson II, 551
Hollinshead, Hugh F. II, 746
Hollinshead, Jacob II, 79
Hollinshead, Jacob II, 228
Hollinshead, Jacob II, 232
Hollinshead, Jacob, Jr. II, 551
Hollinshead, John II, 177
Hollinshead, John II, 227
Hollinshead, John II, 232
Hollinshead, John II, 249
Hollinshead, Joseph II, 232
Hollinshead, Joseph II, 249
Hollinshead, Joseph M. II, 746
Hollinshead, Josiah F. II, 743
Hollinshead, Josiah F. II, 746
Hollinshead, Lucy II, 551
Hollinshead, Lydia II, 177
Hollinshead, Lydia II, 232
Hollinshead, Martha II, 746
Hollinshead, Mary II, 204
Hollinshead, Mary II, 228
Hollinshead, Mary II, 232
Hollinshead, Mary II, 551
Hollinshead, Mary II, 667
Hollinshead, Mary II, 746
Hollinshead, Mary IV, 406
Hollinshead, Morgan Elwood II, 320
Hollinshead, Rebecca II, 177
Hollinshead, Rebecca W. II, 320
Hollinshead, Sarah II, 79
Hollinshead, Sarah II, 94
Hollinshead, Sarah II, 232
Hollinshead, Sarah II, 249
Hollinshead, Sarah II, 746
Hollinshead, Susan N. II, 743
Hollinshead, Susan N. II, 746
Hollinshead, Thomas II, 177
Hollinshead, Thomas II, 375
Hollinshead, Thomas II, 551
Hollinshead, William II, 177
Hollinshead, William II, 232
Hollinsworth, Phebe I, 596
Hollis, Mary II, 551
Hollister, Laura IV, 1254
Holliway, Aaron VI, 403
Holliway, Aaron VI, 598
Holliway, Aaron S. VI, 403
Holliway, Asa VI, 403
Holliway, Daten VI, 598
Holliway, David VI, 598
Holliway, Elizabeth VI, 453
Holliway, Eunice VI, 598
Holliway, George VI, 403
Holliway, Hannah VI, 598
Holliway, Jesse VI, 403
Holliway, Jesse VI, 598
Holliway, Joel VI, 598
Holliway, Lydia VI, 598
Holliway, Margaret VI, 598
Holliway, Mary S. VI, 403
Holliway, Nancy VI, 892
Holliway, Nathan VI, 403
Holliway, Olive IV, 723
Holliway, Phebe VI, 403
Holliway, Rachel VI, 403
Holliway, Robert VI, 403
Holliway, Samuel VI, 598
Holliway, Samuel VI, 892
Holliway, Sarah VI, 598
Holliway, Susannah VI, 598
Holliwell, Jennie V, 1002
Holloday, Simon I, 448
Holloman, John I, 329
Holloman, Josiah VI, 69
Holloman, Sarah VI, 109
Holloman, Sarah VI, 110
Holloman, William VI, 69
Holloman, Wm. VI, 79
Holloway, ??? IV, 531
Holloway, ??? IV, 603
Holloway, ??? V, 439
Holloway, ??? VI, 293
Holloway, A. IV, 533
Holloway, A. Howard IV, 636
Holloway, A. Howard IV, 724
Holloway, A. Howard IV, 824
Holloway, Aaron IV, 223
Holloway, Aaron IV, 533
Holloway, Aaron IV, 534
Holloway, Aaron IV, 626
Holloway, Aaron IV, 635
Holloway, Aaron IV, 645
Holloway, Aaron IV, 723
Holloway, Aaron IV, 724
Holloway, Aaron IV, 740
Holloway, Aaron IV, 893
Holloway, Aaron VI, 314
Holloway, Aaron VI, 403
Holloway, Aaron VI, 598
Holloway, Aaron VI, 655
Holloway, Aaron VI, 705
Holloway, Aaron S. VI, 403
Holloway, Aaron Smith VI, 655
Holloway, Aaron, Jr. IV, 535
Holloway, Aaron, Sr. IV, 534
Holloway, Abbie IV, 223
Holloway, Abbie IV, 534
Holloway, Abbie IV, 549
Holloway, Abby IV, 223
Holloway, Abby IV, 275
Holloway, Abby IV, 535
Holloway, Abby IV, 553
Holloway, Abby P. IV, 337
Holloway, Abby T. IV, 223
Holloway, Abby T. IV, 533
Holloway, Abby T. IV, 535
Holloway, Abel VI, 592
Holloway, Abel VI, 597
Holloway, Abel VI, 598
Holloway, Abigail IV, 223
Holloway, Abigail IV, 259
Holloway, Abigail IV, 337
Holloway, Abigail IV, 410
Holloway, Abigail IV, 436
Holloway, Abigail IV, 512
Holloway, Abigail IV, 533
Holloway, Abigail IV, 534
Holloway, Abigail IV, 535
Holloway, Abigail IV, 543
Holloway, Abigail IV, 548
Holloway, Abigail IV, 557
Holloway, Abigail V, 76
Holloway, Abigail V, 911
Holloway, Abigail VI, 592
Holloway, Abigail VI, 598
Holloway, Abigail VI, 655
Holloway, Abigail VI, 705
Holloway, Abner I, 988
Holloway, Abner V, 248
Holloway, Abner V, 401
Holloway, Abner V, 402
Holloway, Abner VI, 314
Holloway, Abner VI, 339
Holloway, Abner VI, 598
Holloway, Abraham B. IV, 533
Holloway, Albert Leland IV, 824
Holloway, Alfred H. IV, 723
Holloway, Alfred Howard IV, 635
Holloway, Alfred Howard IV, 724
Holloway, Alfred Howard IV, 731
Holloway, Alfred Howard IV, 824
Holloway, Alice IV, 411
Holloway, Alice IV, 450
Holloway, Alice A. IV, 965
Holloway, Alice A. IV, 966
Holloway, Alice A. IV, 1018
Holloway, Alice Ann IV, 723
Holloway, Alice Ann IV, 724
Holloway, Alice Ann IV, 965
Holloway, Alice Marie IV, 836
Holloway, Amelia B. IV, 824
Holloway, Amos IV, 93
Holloway, Amos IV, 635
Holloway, Amos IV, 686
Holloway, Amos IV, 723
Holloway, Amos IV, 919
Holloway, Amos V, 401
Holloway, Amos V, 402
Holloway, Amos VI, 314
Holloway, Amos VI, 339
Holloway, Amos VI, 598
Holloway, Amos, Jr. IV, 636
Holloway, Amy IV, 337
Holloway, Amy IV, 533
Holloway, Amy VI, 714
Holloway, Angeline IV, 1102
Holloway, Angeline IV, 1112
Holloway, Ann IV, 93
Holloway, Ann IV, 116
Holloway, Ann IV, 337
Holloway, Ann IV, 355
Holloway, Ann IV, 534
Holloway, Ann IV, 535
Holloway, Ann B. IV, 535
Holloway, Ann B. IV, 1102
Holloway, Ann Sharp IV, 411
Holloway, Anna IV, 411
Holloway, Anna IV, 534
Holloway, Anna IV, 723
Holloway, Anna IV, 742
Holloway, Anna VI, 314
Holloway, Anna B. IV, 836
Holloway, Anna M. II, 708
Holloway, Anna M. IV, 536
Holloway, Anna M. B. II, 744
Holloway, Anna M. B. IV, 536
Holloway, Anna M. B. IV, 824
Holloway, Anna M. B. IV, 836
Holloway, Anna Mary II, 729
Holloway, Anna Mary II, 744
Holloway, Anna Mary IV, 534
Holloway, Anne B. IV, 533
Holloway, Armstead I, 548
Holloway, Asa IV, 39
Holloway, Asa IV, 149
Holloway, Asa IV, 173
Holloway, Asa IV, 223
Holloway, Asa IV, 337
Holloway, Asa IV, 410
Holloway, Asa IV, 531
Holloway, Asa IV, 533
Holloway, Asa IV, 534
Holloway, Asa IV, 535
Holloway, Asa IV, 555
Holloway, Asa IV, 625
Holloway, Asa IV, 629
Holloway, Asa IV, 635
Holloway, Asa IV, 655
Holloway, Asa IV, 1102
Holloway, Asa VI, 314
Holloway, Asa VI, 403
Holloway, Asa VI, 592
Holloway, Asa VI, 598
Holloway, Asa VI, 655
Holloway, Asa VI, 656
Holloway, Asa VI, 682
Holloway, Asa VI, 690
Holloway, Asa VI, 705
Holloway, Asa C. IV, 533
Holloway, Asa G. IV, 532
Holloway, Asa G. IV, 534
Holloway, Asa G. IV, 542
Holloway, Asa G. IV, 836
Holloway, Asa, Jr. IV, 223
Holloway, Asa, Jr. IV, 337
Holloway, Asa, Jr. IV, 635
Holloway, Asa, Jr. VI, 314
Holloway, Asa, Jr. VI, 598
Holloway, Asenath V, 401
Holloway, Asenith V, 402
Holloway, Avis II, 780
Holloway, Barnes VI, 934
Holloway, Bertha Amelia IV, 816
Holloway, Bertha Amelia IV, 824
Holloway, Betsey I, 988
Holloway, Betsy IV, 514
Holloway, Betsy IV, 533
Holloway, Betsy IV, 534
Holloway, Betsy IV, 722
Holloway, Betsy V, 248
Holloway, Betsy V, 401
Holloway, Betsy V, 446
Holloway, Betsy VI, 314
Holloway, Betsy VI, 339
Holloway, Betsy Ann IV, 533
Holloway, Branson IV, 534
Holloway, Carol T. IV, 636
Holloway, Carol T. IV, 824
Holloway, Carol Thelma IV, 636
Holloway, Carol Thelma IV, 723
Holloway, Carol Thelma IV, 724
Holloway, Carol Thelma IV, 824
Holloway, Catharine IV, 533
Holloway, Catharine IV, 534
Holloway, Catharine IV, 535
Holloway, Catharine IV, 542
Holloway, Catherine VI, 598
Holloway, Catherine VI, 606
Holloway, Chalkley C. IV, 535
Holloway, Chalkley Clinton IV, 534
Holloway, Chalkley T. IV, 533
Holloway, Chalkley T. IV, 535
Holloway, Charles IV, 375
Holloway, Charles IV, 410
Holloway, Charles IV, 535
Holloway, Charles IV, 536
Holloway, Charles IV, 636
Holloway, Charles E. IV, 411
Holloway, Charles Francis IV, 411
Holloway, Charles P. IV, 742
Holloway, Charlotte VI, 402
Holloway, Charlotte VI, 594
Holloway, Charlotte VI, 598
Holloway, Chas. IV, 635
Holloway, Clement IV, 534
Holloway, Clement P. IV, 536
Holloway, Clement Purviance II, 708
Holloway, Clementine II, 729
Holloway, Clementine II, 744
Holloway, Cornelius IV, 1102
Holloway, Cornelius B. IV, 533
Holloway, Cornelius B. IV, 535
Holloway, Cornelius B. IV, 1102
Holloway, Cynthia V, 401
Holloway, Cynthia Ann V, 402
Holloway, Cyrus IV, 824
Holloway, Cyrus IV, 844
Holloway, Cyrus D. IV, 635
Holloway, Cyrus D. IV, 636
Holloway, Cyrus D. IV, 723
Holloway, Cyrus D. IV, 766
Holloway, D. IV, 647
Holloway, Daniel IV, 222
Holloway, Daniel IV, 223
Holloway, Daniel IV, 532
Holloway, Daniel IV, 533
Holloway, Daniel IV, 534
Holloway, Daniel IV, 535
Holloway, Daniel IV, 723
Holloway, Daniel IV, 724
Holloway, Daniel B. IV, 533
Holloway, Daniel B. IV, 534
Holloway, Daniel W. IV, 535
Holloway, Daten IV, 39
Holloway, Daten VI, 402
Holloway, Daten VI, 595
Holloway, Daten VI, 596
Holloway, Daten VI, 598
Holloway, Daton V, 76
Holloway, David IV, 39
Holloway, David IV, 410
Holloway, David IV, 411
Holloway, David IV, 533
Holloway, David IV, 535
Holloway, David IV, 557
Holloway, David IV, 611
Holloway, David IV, 723
Holloway, David IV, 724
Holloway, David IV, 742
Holloway, David IV, 751
Holloway, David IV, 927
Holloway, David IV, 965
Holloway, David IV, 966
Holloway, David V, 17
Holloway, David V, 76
Holloway, David V, 889
Holloway, David V, 911
Holloway, David V, 925
Holloway, David VI, 402
Holloway, David VI, 598
Holloway, David VI, 604
Holloway, David M. IV, 742
Holloway, David P. V, 911
Holloway, David, Jr. V, 911
Holloway, Dayton V, 911
Holloway, Deaton VI, 598
Holloway, Deborah IV, 411
Holloway, Deborah IV, 449
Holloway, Deborah IV, 533
Holloway, Deborah IV, 534
Holloway, Deborah IV, 554
Holloway, Deborah S. IV, 534
Holloway, Deborah S. IV, 705
Holloway, Deborah S. IV, 724
Holloway, Dorothy IV, 173
Holloway, Dorothy IV, 223
Holloway, Dorothy IV, 533
Holloway, Dorothy IV, 534
Holloway, Dorothy IV, 535
Holloway, Dorothy IV, 1102
Holloway, Dorothy Louella IV, 411
Holloway, Edgar B. IV, 636
Holloway, Edgar B. IV, 824
Holloway, Edgar Bertram IV, 82
Holloway, Edith IV, 636
Holloway, Edith L. IV, 636
Holloway, Edith L. IV, 724
Holloway, Edith L. IV, 731
Holloway, Edith L. IV, 824
Holloway, Edith Lydia IV, 635
Holloway, Edith Lydia IV, 640
Holloway, Edith Lydia IV, 723
Holloway, Edith Lydia K. IV, 63
Holloway, Edith Lydia K. IV, 72
Holloway, Edwin IV, 723
Holloway, Edwin IV, 724
Holloway, Edwin IV, 770
Holloway, Edwin IV, 965
Holloway, Edwin IV, 966
Holloway, Edwin F. IV, 513
Holloway, Edwin F. IV, 534
Holloway, Edwin F. IV, 535
Holloway, Edwin F. IV, 536
Holloway, Edwin F. IV, 540
Holloway, Edwin F. IV, 635
Holloway, Eleanor IV, 149
Holloway, Eleanor IV, 533
Holloway, Eleanor IV, 535
Holloway, Eli IV, 39
Holloway, Eli IV, 635
Holloway, Eli VI, 314
Holloway, Elias IV, 635
Holloway, Elisha IV, 533
Holloway, Elisha IV, 535
Holloway, Elisha IV, 1102
Holloway, Elisha J. II, 1085
Holloway, Elisha J. IV, 337
Holloway, Elisha J. IV, 355
Holloway, Elisha J. IV, 535
Holloway, Elisha J. IV, 554
Holloway, Elisha J. IV, 794
Holloway, Elisha J. IV, 1102
Holloway, Elisha J. IV, 1134
Holloway, Eliza IV, 532
Holloway, Eliza IV, 533
Holloway, Eliza IV, 534
Holloway, Eliza IV, 535
Holloway, Eliza B. IV, 533
Holloway, Eliza F. IV, 509
Holloway, Eliza F. IV, 534
Holloway, Eliza F. IV, 609
Holloway, Eliza F. IV, 636
Holloway, Eliza M. IV, 410
Holloway, Eliza M. IV, 411
Holloway, Eliza T. IV, 534
Holloway, Elizabeth I, 988
Holloway, Elizabeth IV, 223
Holloway, Elizabeth IV, 533
Holloway, Elizabeth IV, 535
Holloway, Elizabeth IV, 723
Holloway, Elizabeth IV, 1102
Holloway, Elizabeth V, 248
Holloway, Elizabeth V, 401
Holloway, Elizabeth V, 402
Holloway, Elizabeth VI, 314
Holloway, Elizabeth VI, 403
Holloway, Elizabeth VI, 598
Holloway, Elizabeth VI, 606
Holloway, Elizabeth VI, 655
Holloway, Elizabeth VI, 656
Holloway, Elizabeth VI, 690
Holloway, Elizabeth VI, 826
Holloway, Ella H. IV, 535
Holloway, Ella H. IV, 543
Holloway, Ellazan IV, 836
Holloway, Ellazan R. IV, 534
Holloway, Ellazan R. IV, 542
Holloway, Ellen Leeds IV, 534
Holloway, Ellenor V, 401
Holloway, Elma IV, 513
Holloway, Elma B. IV, 536
Holloway, Elma B. IV, 540
Holloway, Elma B. M. IV, 536

Holloway, Elvira I, 548
Holloway, Elvira I, 581
Holloway, Elvira IV, 337
Holloway, Elvira IV, 535
Holloway, Elvira VI, 655
Holloway, Emeline IV, 965
Holloway, Emeline IV, 1004
Holloway, Emerson IV, 535
Holloway, Emerson W. IV, 411
Holloway, Emerson W. IV, 534
Holloway, Emery C. IV, 816
Holloway, Emery C. IV, 824
Holloway, Emery P. IV, 824
Holloway, Emily IV, 611
Holloway, Emily IV, 635
Holloway, Emily IV, 636
Holloway, Emily IV, 723
Holloway, Emily IV, 724
Holloway, Emily IV, 923
Holloway, Emily IV, 927
Holloway, Emily IV, 965
Holloway, Emma IV, 534
Holloway, Emma F. IV, 534
Holloway, Ephraim IV, 533
Holloway, Ephraim IV, 534
Holloway, Ephraim IV, 535
Holloway, Ephraim IV, 545
Holloway, Ephraim IV, 1102
Holloway, Ephraim VI, 402
Holloway, Ephraim Asab IV, 534
Holloway, Ephraim W. II, 729
Holloway, Ephraim W. II, 744
Holloway, Ephraim W. IV, 534
Holloway, Ephraim W. IV, 552
Holloway, Ernest IV, 411
Holloway, Esther IV, 723
Holloway, Esther IV, 766
Holloway, Esther IV, 824
Holloway, Esther IV, 844
Holloway, Esther IV, 893
Holloway, Esther VI, 597
Holloway, Esther E. IV, 635
Holloway, Esther E. IV, 636
Holloway, Esther Rachel IV, 824
Holloway, Eunice IV, 723
Holloway, Eunice IV, 724
Holloway, Eunice VI, 598
Holloway, Eunice W. IV, 531
Holloway, Eunice W. IV, 534
Holloway, Eunice W. IV, 535
Holloway, Francis Taber IV, 533
Holloway, Geo. VI, 655
Holloway, George II, 232
Holloway, George II, 233
Holloway, George IV, 635
Holloway, George V, 248
Holloway, George VI, 314
Holloway, George VI, 402
Holloway, George VI, 403
Holloway, George VI, 597
Holloway, George VI, 598
Holloway, George VI, 606
Holloway, George VI, 655
Holloway, George VI, 682
Holloway, George VI, 690
Holloway, George VI, 707
Holloway, Gula VI, 63
Holloway, Gula VI, 69
Holloway, Hannah I, 548
Holloway, Hannah IV, 39
Holloway, Hannah IV, 533
Holloway, Hannah IV, 535
Holloway, Hannah IV, 629
Holloway, Hannah IV, 635
Holloway, Hannah IV, 636
Holloway, Hannah IV, 659
Holloway, Hannah IV, 723
Holloway, Hannah IV, 724
Holloway, Hannah IV, 739
Holloway, Hannah IV, 756
Holloway, Hannah IV, 836
Holloway, Hannah IV, 893
Holloway, Hannah V, 76
Holloway, Hannah V, 911
Holloway, Hannah V, 925
Holloway, Hannah VI, 314
Holloway, Hannah VI, 598
Holloway, Hannah VI, 604
Holloway, Hannah Elma IV, 532
Holloway, Hannah Elma IV, 534
Holloway, Hannah Elma IV, 542
Holloway, Harold L. IV, 411
Holloway, Harold Lindley IV, 411
Holloway, Harold Lindley IV, 535
Holloway, Harold Lindley IV, 536
Holloway, Harold, Jr. IV, 411
Holloway, Henry Earle IV, 534
Holloway, Hephzabah VI, 339
Holloway, Hephzibah IV, 635
Holloway, Hephzibah IV, 686
Holloway, Hephzibah IV, 723
Holloway, Hepsiba IV, 723
Holloway, Hepsibah IV, 93
Holloway, Hepzabah VI, 314
Holloway, Hepzebah VI, 339
Holloway, Hope IV, 626
Holloway, Hope IV, 635
Holloway, Hope IV, 636
Holloway, Hope VI, 596
Holloway, Hope VI, 597
Holloway, Hope VI, 598
Holloway, Howard IV, 636
Holloway, Howard IV, 640
Holloway, Howard John IV, 534
Holloway, Howard S. IV, 635
Holloway, Huldah IV, 723
Holloway, Huldah VI, 314
Holloway, Imlah IV, 723
Holloway, Imlah IV, 724
Holloway, Iral IV, 411
Holloway, Isaa, Sr. VI, 314
Holloway, Isaac II, 232
Holloway, Isaac IV, 39
Holloway, Isaac IV, 626
Holloway, Isaac IV, 635
Holloway, Isaac IV, 723
Holloway, Isaac IV, 724
Holloway, Isaac V, 248
Holloway, Isaac V, 401
Holloway, Isaac V, 402
Holloway, Isaac V, 446
Holloway, Isaac VI, 314
Holloway, Isaac VI, 340
Holloway, Isaac VI, 597
Holloway, Isaac VI, 826
Holloway, Isaac VI, 997
Holloway, Isaac P. IV, 337
Holloway, Isaac Parker IV, 223
Holloway, Isaac Parker IV, 337
Holloway, Isaac Parker IV, 535
Holloway, Isaiah IV, 635
Holloway, Isiah IV, 636
Holloway, J. Edwin IV, 534
Holloway, J. Howard IV, 636
Holloway, Jacob IV, 149
Holloway, Jacob IV, 167
Holloway, Jacob IV, 223
Holloway, Jacob IV, 299
Holloway, Jacob IV, 337
Holloway, Jacob IV, 509
Holloway, Jacob IV, 513
Holloway, Jacob IV, 533
Holloway, Jacob IV, 534
Holloway, Jacob IV, 535
Holloway, Jacob IV, 549
Holloway, Jacob IV, 554
Holloway, Jacob IV, 635
Holloway, Jacob IV, 704
Holloway, Jacob IV, 723
Holloway, Jacob IV, 1102
Holloway, Jacob VI, 598
Holloway, Jacob A. IV, 535
Holloway, Jacob M. IV, 533
Holloway, Jacob, Jr. IV, 511
Holloway, Jacob, Jr. IV, 535
Holloway, Jacob, Sr. IV, 534
Holloway, James IV, 39
Holloway, James IV, 149
Holloway, James IV, 331
Holloway, James IV, 337
Holloway, James IV, 533
Holloway, James IV, 534
Holloway, James IV, 535
Holloway, James IV, 635
Holloway, James IV, 1102
Holloway, James VI, 314
Holloway, James VI, 655
Holloway, James Arthur II, 708
Holloway, James Arthur II, 729
Holloway, James Arthur II, 744
Holloway, James Arthur IV, 513
Holloway, James Arthur IV, 534
Holloway, James Arthur IV, 536
Holloway, James B. IV, 534
Holloway, James D. IV, 533
Holloway, James, Jr. IV, 534
Holloway, James, Sr. IV, 533
Holloway, Jane IV, 533
Holloway, Jason IV, 723
Holloway, Jason IV, 893
Holloway, Jason VI, 314
Holloway, Jehu Fawcett IV, 724
Holloway, Jephtha IV, 636
Holloway, Jeptha IV, 535
Holloway, Jeptha IV, 635
Holloway, Jeptha V. IV, 534
Holloway, Jesse I, 988
Holloway, Jesse IV, 635
Holloway, Jesse IV, 683
Holloway, Jesse IV, 723
Holloway, Jesse IV, 724
Holloway, Jesse IV, 764
Holloway, Jesse IV, 965
Holloway, Jesse IV, 966
Holloway, Jesse V, 401
Holloway, Jesse V, 911
Holloway, Jesse VI, 314
Holloway, Jesse VI, 403
Holloway, Jesse VI, 427
Holloway, Jesse VI, 597
Holloway, Jesse VI, 598
Holloway, Jesse O. IV, 635
Holloway, Jesse O. IV, 636
Holloway, Jesse Painter VI, 402
Holloway, Joab V, 248
Holloway, Joab V, 401
Holloway, Joab V, 446
Holloway, Job IV, 93
Holloway, Job IV, 116
Holloway, Job IV, 723
Holloway, Job VI, 314
Holloway, Joel IV, 723
Holloway, Joel IV, 724
Holloway, Joel IV, 824
Holloway, Joel VI, 598
Holloway, Joel Bailey IV, 411
Holloway, John IV, 410
Holloway, John IV, 532
Holloway, John IV, 533
Holloway, John IV, 534
Holloway, John IV, 535
Holloway, John V, 76
Holloway, John V, 248
Holloway, John V, 401
Holloway, John V, 402
Holloway, John V, 446
Holloway, John VI, 23
Holloway, John VI, 30
Holloway, John VI, 314
Holloway, John VI, 402
Holloway, John VI, 403
Holloway, John VI, 594
Holloway, John VI, 597
Holloway, John VI, 598
Holloway, John VI, 605
Holloway, John VI, 934
Holloway, John B. IV, 411
Holloway, John W. V, 248
Holloway, John Warfield IV, 337
Holloway, Jonas IV, 533
Holloway, Jonas IV, 534
Holloway, Jonas IV, 535
Holloway, Jos. IV, 535
Holloway, Jos. IV, 836
Holloway, Joseph IV, 149
Holloway, Joseph IV, 533
Holloway, Joseph IV, 534
Holloway, Joseph IV, 535
Holloway, Joseph IV, 723
Holloway, Joseph IV, 724
Holloway, Joseph IV, 965
Holloway, Joseph IV, 966
Holloway, Joseph VI, 598
Holloway, Joseph Branson II, 708
Holloway, Joseph H. VI, 934
Holloway, Joseph S. IV, 723
Holloway, Joseph S. IV, 724
Holloway, Joseph S. IV, 965
Holloway, Joshua IV, 723
Holloway, Joshua IV, 724
Holloway, Jpseph B. IV, 536
Holloway, Katharine VI, 606
Holloway, Katherine VI, 598
Holloway, Lavania I, 924
Holloway, Lavina V, 435
Holloway, Lavinah VI, 598
Holloway, Lavini VI, 608
Holloway, Leland W. IV, 824
Holloway, Leroy IV, 411
Holloway, Leslie IV, 411
Holloway, Leslie Mervin IV, 824
Holloway, Levi VI, 403
Holloway, Levina VI, 598
Holloway, Levina VI, 608
Holloway, Levincy VI, 461
Holloway, Lewis T. IV, 742
Holloway, Lindley IV, 535
Holloway, Lindley IV, 723
Holloway, Lindley IV, 965
Holloway, Lindley Hoge IV, 533
Holloway, Lindley Hoge IV, 534
Holloway, Lindley M. IV, 516
Holloway, Lindley M. IV, 534
Holloway, Lindley M. IV, 554
Holloway, Lindley M. IV, 966
Holloway, Lindley Murray IV, 533
Holloway, Lindley T. IV, 724
Holloway, Loda IV, 724
Holloway, Lois M. IV, 636
Holloway, Lois M. IV, 824
Holloway, Lois Marjorie IV, 636
Holloway, Lois Marjorie IV, 723
Holloway, Lois Marjorie IV, 724
Holloway, Lois Marjorie IV, 824
Holloway, Louisa IV, 411
Holloway, Louisa IV, 533
Holloway, Louisa IV, 534
Holloway, Louisa S. IV, 411
Holloway, Louisa T. IV, 535
Holloway, Lovicy V, 248
Holloway, Luanna C. IV, 635
Holloway, Luanna C. IV, 636
Holloway, Lucinda IV, 534
Holloway, Lucinda IV, 535
Holloway, Lucinda IV, 1102
Holloway, Lucinda IV, 1116
Holloway, Lucinda IV, 1134
Holloway, Lucy Ann IV, 626
Holloway, Lucy Ann IV, 636
Holloway, Lydia IV, 39
Holloway, Lydia IV, 355
Holloway, Lydia IV, 367
Holloway, Lydia IV, 411
Holloway, Lydia IV, 509
Holloway, Lydia IV, 532
Holloway, Lydia IV, 533
Holloway, Lydia IV, 534
Holloway, Lydia IV, 535
Holloway, Lydia IV, 635
Holloway, Lydia IV, 641
Holloway, Lydia IV, 698
Holloway, Lydia IV, 724
Holloway, Lydia IV, 758
Holloway, Lydia IV, 891
Holloway, Lydia IV, 893
Holloway, Lydia IV, 1102
Holloway, Lydia IV, 1134
Holloway, Lydia V, 76
Holloway, Lydia V, 911
Holloway, Lydia V, 925
Holloway, Lydia VI, 598
Holloway, Lydia Ann IV, 621
Holloway, Lydia Ann IV, 636
Holloway, Lydia D. IV, 724
Holloway, Lydia D. IV, 965
Holloway, Lydia J. IV, 1134
Holloway, Lydia S. IV, 337
Holloway, Lydia S. IV, 533
Holloway, Lydia S. IV, 535
Holloway, Lydia S. IV, 794
Holloway, Lydia S. IV, 1102
Holloway, Lydia T. IV, 533
Holloway, Lynn Alvin IV, 824
Holloway, Mabel Ann IV, 535
Holloway, Mabel Ann IV, 536
Holloway, Mabel Anna IV, 411
Holloway, Mabel L. IV, 636
Holloway, Mabel L. IV, 824
Holloway, Mabel Lyda IV, 724
Holloway, Mabel Lydia IV, 636
Holloway, Mabel Lydia IV, 723
Holloway, Mable IV, 411
Holloway, Mable Lyda IV, 824
Holloway, Magaret VI, 655
Holloway, Mahala IV, 533
Holloway, Mahala IV, 534
Holloway, Margaet IV, 39
Holloway, Margaret IV, 149
Holloway, Margaret IV, 337
Holloway, Margaret IV, 533
Holloway, Margaret IV, 534
Holloway, Margaret IV, 535
Holloway, Margaret IV, 683
Holloway, Margaret IV, 723
Holloway, Margaret V, 76
Holloway, Margaret V, 401
Holloway, Margaret V, 911
Holloway, Margaret VI, 402
Holloway, Margaret VI, 403
Holloway, Margaret VI, 594
Holloway, Margaret VI, 597
Holloway, Margaret VI, 598
Holloway, Margaret VI, 656
Holloway, Margaret VI, 682
Holloway, Margaret W. IV, 534
Holloway, Margaret W. IV, 536
Holloway, Margret VI, 598
Holloway, Maria IV, 93
Holloway, Maria IV, 514
Holloway, Maria IV, 533
Holloway, Maria IV, 534
Holloway, Maria IV, 535
Holloway, Maria IV, 554
Holloway, Maria IV, 555
Holloway, Mariah IV, 337
Holloway, Martha IV, 223
Holloway, Martha IV, 299
Holloway, Martha IV, 337
Holloway, Martha IV, 513
Holloway, Martha IV, 516
Holloway, Martha IV, 533
Holloway, Martha IV, 534
Holloway, Martha IV, 554
Holloway, Martha IV, 723
Holloway, Martha IV, 966
Holloway, Martha B. IV, 724
Holloway, Martha H. IV, 529
Holloway, Martha H. IV, 534
Holloway, Martha H. IV, 536
Holloway, Martha H. IV, 554
Holloway, Martha M. IV, 511
Holloway, Martha M. IV, 534
Holloway, Martha Mary IV, 534
Holloway, Martin B. IV, 724
Holloway, Mary I, 919
Holloway, Mary IV, 39
Holloway, Mary IV, 337
Holloway, Mary IV, 410
Holloway, Mary IV, 531
Holloway, Mary IV, 533
Holloway, Mary IV, 534
Holloway, Mary IV, 535
Holloway, Mary IV, 545
Holloway, Mary IV, 555
Holloway, Mary IV, 625
Holloway, Mary IV, 629
Holloway, Mary IV, 635
Holloway, Mary IV, 655
Holloway, Mary IV, 723
Holloway, Mary IV, 724
Holloway, Mary IV, 824
Holloway, Mary IV, 1102
Holloway, Mary V, 401
Holloway, Mary VI, 314
Holloway, Mary VI, 340
Holloway, Mary VI, 597
Holloway, Mary VI, 598
Holloway, Mary VI, 605
Holloway, Mary VI, 997
Holloway, Mary Ann IV, 222
Holloway, Mary Ann IV, 223
Holloway, Mary Ann IV, 410
Holloway, Mary Ann IV, 525
Holloway, Mary Ann IV, 531
Holloway, Mary Ann IV, 532
Holloway, Mary Ann IV, 533
Holloway, Mary Ann IV, 534
Holloway, Mary Ann IV, 535
Holloway, Mary Ann F. IV, 411
Holloway, Mary Ann F. IV, 535
Holloway, Mary B. VI, 934
Holloway, Mary C. IV, 534
Holloway, Mary C. IV, 536
Holloway, Mary C. IV, 636
Holloway, Mary E. IV, 223
Holloway, Mary E. IV, 337
Holloway, Mary E. IV, 535
Holloway, Mary Edith IV, 583
Holloway, Mary Edith IV, 584
Holloway, Mary H. IV, 536
Holloway, Mary H. IV, 537
Holloway, Mary Jane V, 402
Holloway, Mary Lucy IV, 533
Holloway, Mary R. IV, 411
Holloway, Mary R. IV, 516
Holloway, Mary R. IV, 535
Holloway, Mary R. H. IV, 516
Holloway, Mary Rebecca IV, 534
Holloway, Mary Ruanna IV, 411
Holloway, Mary Ruanna IV, 536
Holloway, Mary S. IV, 535
Holloway, Mary S. IV, 1102
Holloway, Mary S. VI, 403
Holloway, Mary Scattergood IV, 534
Holloway, Mary, Jr. IV, 636
Holloway, Mary, Jr. VI, 598
Holloway, Matilda V, 401
Holloway, Melva Willets IV, 534
Holloway, Meriam IV, 708
Holloway, Meriam IV, 724
Holloway, Mildred Lydia IV, 723
Holloway, Minerva W. IV, 534
Holloway, Minerva W. IV, 552
Holloway, Miriam IV, 525
Holloway, Miriam IV, 533
Holloway, Miriam IV, 534
Holloway, Mrs. ??? VI, 11
Holloway, Mrs. W. S. IV, 1321
Holloway, Murray S. IV, 534
Holloway, Murray S. IV, 536
Holloway, Myra May IV, 724
Holloway, Nancy IV, 533
Holloway, Nancy IV, 535
Holloway, Nancy VI, 934
Holloway, Nancy B. V, 439
Holloway, Nathan I, 988
Holloway, Nathan IV, 93
Holloway, Nathan VI, 314
Holloway, Nathan VI, 403
Holloway, Nathan VI, 597
Holloway, Oliva IV, 723
Holloway, Olive IV, 635
Holloway, Olive IV, 645

Holloway, Olive IV, 723
Holloway, Olive IV, 724
Holloway, Olive IV, 740
Holloway, Paul Sears IV, 411
Holloway, Paul W. IV, 411
Holloway, Phebe IV, 331
Holloway, Phebe IV, 337
Holloway, Phebe IV, 533
Holloway, Phebe IV, 534
Holloway, Phebe IV, 535
Holloway, Phebe IV, 723
Holloway, Phebe IV, 1134
Holloway, Phebe VI, 314
Holloway, Phebe VI, 403
Holloway, Phebe VI, 597
Holloway, Phebe Louisa IV, 535
Holloway, Phebe Louisa IV, 1102
Holloway, Phebe Louisa IV, 1134
Holloway, Philadelphia VI, 388
Holloway, Philadelphia VI, 403
Holloway, Pleasant V, 248
Holloway, Pleasant VI, 314
Holloway, Purviance IV, 534
Holloway, R. IV, 647
Holloway, Rachel IV, 223
Holloway, Rachel IV, 410
Holloway, Rachel IV, 533
Holloway, Rachel IV, 534
Holloway, Rachel IV, 535
Holloway, Rachel IV, 611
Holloway, Rachel IV, 636
Holloway, Rachel IV, 641
Holloway, Rachel IV, 723
Holloway, Rachel IV, 724
Holloway, Rachel IV, 742
Holloway, Rachel IV, 751
Holloway, Rachel IV, 927
Holloway, Rachel IV, 965
Holloway, Rachel IV, 980
Holloway, Rachel V, 402
Holloway, Rachel VI, 403
Holloway, Rachel VI, 592
Holloway, Rachel VI, 597
Holloway, Rachel VI, 598
Holloway, Rachel VI, 655
Holloway, Rachel VI, 656
Holloway, Rachel VI, 705
Holloway, Rachel A. IV, 535
Holloway, Rachel A. IV, 641
Holloway, Rachel Anna IV, 636
Holloway, Rachel M. IV, 533
Holloway, Rebecca II, 779
Holloway, Rebecca IV, 337
Holloway, Rebecca IV, 346
Holloway, Rebecca IV, 509
Holloway, Rebecca IV, 512
Holloway, Rebecca IV, 514
Holloway, Rebecca IV, 525
Holloway, Rebecca IV, 533
Holloway, Rebecca IV, 535
Holloway, Rebecca IV, 548
Holloway, Rebecca IV, 556
Holloway, Rebecca IV, 641
Holloway, Rebecca Ann II, 744
Holloway, Rebecca Ann IV, 534
Holloway, Rebecca Ann IV, 535
Holloway, Rebecca B. IV, 533
Holloway, Rebecca B. IV, 534
Holloway, Rebecca B. IV, 556
Holloway, Rebecca B. IV, 713
Holloway, Rebecca B. IV, 735
Holloway, Rebecca D. IV, 723
Holloway, Rebecca D. IV, 724
Holloway, Rebecca D. IV, 770
Holloway, Rebecca D. IV, 965
Holloway, Rebecca D. IV, 966
Holloway, Rebecca R. IV, 636
Holloway, Rebecca R. IV, 665
Holloway, Rebecca S. IV, 534
Holloway, Rebecca S. IV, 535
Holloway, Rebecka VI, 592
Holloway, Rebeckah VI, 598
Holloway, Rhoda IV, 93
Holloway, Rhoda IV, 686
Holloway, Rhoda IV, 723
Holloway, Rhoda IV, 966
Holloway, Rhoda IV, 987
Holloway, Rhoda VI, 314
Holloway, Rhoda Ann IV, 724
Holloway, Rhoda E. IV, 723
Holloway, Rhoda E. IV, 724
Holloway, Rhoda E. IV, 965
Holloway, Rhoda Elizabeth IV, 965
Holloway, Rhoda Johnson VI, 314
Holloway, Robert IV, 337
Holloway, Robert IV, 346
Holloway, Robert IV, 509
Holloway, Robert IV, 514
Holloway, Robert IV, 525
Holloway, Robert IV, 533
Holloway, Robert IV, 534
Holloway, Robert IV, 548
Holloway, Robert IV, 556
Holloway, Robert VI, 403
Holloway, Robert A. IV, 535
Holloway, Robert S. IV, 223
Holloway, Robert S. IV, 533
Holloway, Robert S. IV, 535
Holloway, Robert S. IV, 553
Holloway, Robert Smith VI, 655
Holloway, Rody VI, 934
Holloway, Ruth II, 232
Holloway, Ruth II, 233
Holloway, Ruth V, 911
Holloway, Ruth VI, 392
Holloway, Ruth VI, 402
Holloway, Ruth VI, 403
Holloway, Ruth VI, 655
Holloway, Ruth VI, 682
Holloway, Ruth VI, 690
Holloway, Ruth VI, 707
Holloway, Ruthanna Stratton IV, 836
Holloway, Sally V, 248
Holloway, Sally VI, 314
Holloway, Sally VI, 934
Holloway, Samuel IV, 149
Holloway, Samuel IV, 167
Holloway, Samuel IV, 337
Holloway, Samuel IV, 410
Holloway, Samuel IV, 533
Holloway, Samuel IV, 534
Holloway, Samuel IV, 535
Holloway, Samuel IV, 635
Holloway, Samuel IV, 723
Holloway, Samuel IV, 724
Holloway, Samuel V, 248
Holloway, Samuel VI, 314
Holloway, Samuel VI, 598
Holloway, Samuel VI, 655
Holloway, Samuel VI, 714
Holloway, Samuel VI, 847
Holloway, Samuel VI, 934
Holloway, Samuel B. IV, 535
Holloway, Samuel B. IV, 1102
Holloway, Samuel Barber IV, 533
Holloway, Samuel E. IV, 1102
Holloway, Samuel G. IV, 531
Holloway, Samuel G. IV, 533
Holloway, Samuel G. IV, 534
Holloway, Samuel G. IV, 535
Holloway, Samuel G. IV, 1102
Holloway, Samuel L. IV, 223
Holloway, Samuel S. IV, 223
Holloway, Samuel S. IV, 535
Holloway, Samuel T. IV, 223
Holloway, Sarah I, 271
Holloway, Sarah IV, 39
Holloway, Sarah IV, 410
Holloway, Sarah IV, 411
Holloway, Sarah IV, 436
Holloway, Sarah IV, 511
Holloway, Sarah IV, 533
Holloway, Sarah IV, 534
Holloway, Sarah IV, 535
Holloway, Sarah IV, 549
Holloway, Sarah IV, 626
Holloway, Sarah IV, 635
Holloway, Sarah IV, 655
Holloway, Sarah IV, 681
Holloway, Sarah IV, 683
Holloway, Sarah IV, 704
Holloway, Sarah IV, 718
Holloway, Sarah IV, 723
Holloway, Sarah IV, 724
Holloway, Sarah IV, 764
Holloway, Sarah IV, 880
Holloway, Sarah IV, 893
Holloway, Sarah IV, 935
Holloway, Sarah IV, 965
Holloway, Sarah IV, 966
Holloway, Sarah IV, 1102
Holloway, Sarah V, 401
Holloway, Sarah V, 911
Holloway, Sarah VI, 314
Holloway, Sarah VI, 331
Holloway, Sarah VI, 339
Holloway, Sarah VI, 403
Holloway, Sarah VI, 427
Holloway, Sarah VI, 598
Holloway, Sarah VI, 934
Holloway, Sarah B. II, 703
Holloway, Sarah B. IV, 276
Holloway, Sarah B. IV, 513
Holloway, Sarah B. IV, 534
Holloway, Sarah C. IV, 375
Holloway, Sarah C. IV, 411
Holloway, Sarah C. IV, 535
Holloway, Sarah C. IV, 536
Holloway, Sarah F. IV, 509
Holloway, Sarah F. IV, 535
Holloway, Sarah F. IV, 549
Holloway, Sarah F. IV, 554
Holloway, Sarah F. IV, 635
Holloway, Sarah F. IV, 724
Holloway, Sarah I. IV, 534
Holloway, Sarah J. IV, 535
Holloway, Sarah Jane IV, 533
Holloway, Sarah Jane IV, 535
Holloway, Sarah Jane IV, 1102
Holloway, Sarah Louise IV, 724
Holloway, Sarah M. V, 248
Holloway, Sarah O. V, 382
Holloway, Sarah P. IV, 647
Holloway, Sarah P. IV, 723
Holloway, Sarah P. IV, 742
Holloway, Sarah P. IV, 878
Holloway, Sarah P. IV, 965
Holloway, Sarah P. IV, 981
Holloway, Sarah S. IV, 557
Holloway, Sarah T. IV, 965
Holloway, Sarah T. Lindley IV, 965
Holloway, Semira Clementine IV, 534
Holloway, Semira Clementine IV, 545
Holloway, Semira Clementine IV, 552
Holloway, Sina Emily IV, 766
Holloway, Sina Emily IV, 844
Holloway, Smith IV, 223
Holloway, Smith IV, 259
Holloway, Smith IV, 337
Holloway, Smith IV, 535
Holloway, Smith IV, 543
Holloway, Stanton IV, 39
Holloway, Stanton VI, 314
Holloway, Stephen IV, 723
Holloway, Stephen VI, 314
Holloway, Susan IV, 724
Holloway, Susan IV, 748
Holloway, Susannah IV, 635
Holloway, Susannah IV, 723
Holloway, Susannah IV, 764
Holloway, Susannah VI, 598
Holloway, Tabitha IV, 534
Holloway, Tacy VI, 403
Holloway, Tacy VI, 462
Holloway, Thama I, 548
Holloway, Thelma Leah IV, 824
Holloway, Thomas V, 248
Holloway, Thomas VI, 11
Holloway, Thomas VI, 12
Holloway, Thomas VI, 402
Holloway, Thomas VI, 403
Holloway, Thomas VI, 598
Holloway, Timothy V, 402
Holloway, Walter IV, 536
Holloway, Walter E. Vail IV, 411
Holloway, Walter S. IV, 534
Holloway, Warren O. IV, 636
Holloway, Warren Oliver IV, 824
Holloway, Widow Margaret VI, 707
Holloway, Widower Asa VI, 707
Holloway, Wilid F. IV, 635
Holloway, William IV, 533
Holloway, William IV, 535
Holloway, William V, 248
Holloway, William VI, 314
Holloway, William VI, 339
Holloway, William VI, 403
Holloway, William VI, 598
Holloway, William C. IV, 534
Holloway, William C. IV, 535
Holloway, William H. IV, 410
Holloway, William H. IV, 411
Holloway, William L. Ashton IV, 636
Holloway, William Mather IV, 724
Holloway, Willid IV, 636
Holloway, Willis L. IV, 411
Holloway, Wm. IV, 535
Holloway, Wm. IV, 554
Holloway, Wm. IV, 1102
Holloway, Wm. Coffee IV, 533
Holloway, Wm. D. Oliphant IV, 824
Holloway, Wm. E. IV, 635
Holloway, Wm. E. IV, 641
Holloway, Wm. E. IV, 965
Holloway, Wm. H. IV, 525
Holloway, Wm. H. IV, 534
Holloway, Wm. H. IV, 535
Holloway, Wm. W. IV, 535
Holloway, Zadok French IV, 724
Hollowday, Daniel V, 400
Hollowell, ??? I, 279
Hollowell, ??? VI, 95
Hollowell, Aaron I, 53
Hollowell, Aaron I, 54
Hollowell, Aaron I, 64
Hollowell, Aaron I, 184
Hollowell, Aaron I, 289
Hollowell, Abba I, 308
Hollowell, Abbie I, 242
Hollowell, Abbie III, 148
Hollowell, Abbie A. I, 241
Hollowell, Abbie A. I, 242
Hollowell, Abbie Ann I, 329
Hollowell, Abby I, 324
Hollowell, Abby V, 76
Hollowell, Abigail I, 216
Hollowell, Abigail I, 308
Hollowell, Abigail I, 318
Hollowell, Absalom I, 53
Hollowell, Absalom I, 206
Hollowell, Absalom I, 216
Hollowell, Absalom I, 241
Hollowell, Absolum I, 241
Hollowell, Absolum VI, 45
Hollowell, Agatha I, 308
Hollowell, Agatha I, 313
Hollowell, Albert P. I, 241
Hollowell, Albert P. I, 324
Hollowell, Alce VI, 30
Hollowell, Alce VI, 36
Hollowell, Alfred I, 943
Hollowell, Alfred J. I, 943
Hollowell, Alfred Jones I, 927
Hollowell, Alic VI, 30
Hollowell, Alice VI, 21
Hollowell, Alice VI, 30
Hollowell, Alice VI, 33
Hollowell, Alice A. I, 241
Hollowell, Alice A. I, 242
Hollowell, Alise VI, 30
Hollowell, Ann N. III, 148
Hollowell, Anna V, 76
Hollowell, Anna M. I, 309
Hollowell, Anna Maria I, 309
Hollowell, Anna Norwood III, 148
Hollowell, Anna T. III, 148
Hollowell, Anna W. I, 309
Hollowell, Anne E. I, 309
Hollowell, Annie I, 620
Hollowell, Annie V, 61
Hollowell, Annie V, 76
Hollowell, Annie E. I, 329
Hollowell, Benjamin VI, 30
Hollowell, Bertha V, 25
Hollowell, Bertha V, 76
Hollowell, Betcy I, 324
Hollowell, Betsy I, 184
Hollowell, Caleb I, 308
Hollowell, Caleb I, 548
Hollowell, Caleb I, 563
Hollowell, Carrie B. I, 943
Hollowell, Catharine I, 308
Hollowell, Catharine I, 309
Hollowell, Catharine I, 310
Hollowell, Catharine I, 324
Hollowell, Catharine D. I, 329
Hollowell, Catharine D. I, 330
Hollowell, Catharine Demareoe I, 324
Hollowell, Celia I, 289
Hollowell, Cephas I, 216
Hollowell, Charity I, 308
Hollowell, Charity I, 311
Hollowell, Charles Jesse I, 927
Hollowell, Charlotte I, 289
Hollowell, Charlotty I, 308
Hollowell, Charlotty I, 312
Hollowell, Chella I, 324
Hollowell, Chelly I, 303
Hollowell, Chelly I, 308
Hollowell, Christian I, 216
Hollowell, Christian I, 241
Hollowell, Christian I, 246
Hollowell, Cilas I, 241
Hollowell, Cora E. I, 54
Hollowell, Cora E. I, 241
Hollowell, Cora E. I, 324
Hollowell, David III, 411
Hollowell, David III, 420
Hollowell, David F. I, 635
Hollowell, David J. I, 241
Hollowell, David J. I, 242
Hollowell, David P. I, 241
Hollowell, David P. I, 242
Hollowell, David T. III, 169
Hollowell, Delphina I, 54
Hollowell, Delphina M. I, 44
Hollowell, Delphina M. I, 54
Hollowell, Dinah I Sup 1, 7
Hollowell, Earnest I, 337
Hollowell, Edgar V, 76
Hollowell, Edith I, 943
Hollowell, Edith Elizabeth I, 927
Hollowell, Edith Irene I, 619
Hollowell, Edmond VI, 30
Hollowell, Eleanor III, 148
Hollowell, Eli I, 289
Hollowell, Elijah J. I, 329
Hollowell, Elisabeth I, 195
Hollowell, Elisabeth I, 203
Hollowell, Elisabeth I, 235
Hollowell, Eliza I, 216
Hollowell, Eliza I, 241
Hollowell, Eliza I, 324
Hollowell, Eliza I, 329
Hollowell, Eliza I, 927
Hollowell, Elizabeth I, 184
Hollowell, Elizabeth I, 216
Hollowell, Elizabeth I, 235
Hollowell, Elizabeth I, 241
Hollowell, Elizabeth I, 289
Hollowell, Elizabeth I, 302
Hollowell, Elizabeth I, 308
Hollowell, Elizabeth I, 318
Hollowell, Elizabeth I, 325
Hollowell, Elizabeth I, 329
Hollowell, Elizabeth I, 927
Hollowell, Elizabeth II, 999
Hollowell, Elizabeth III, 148
Hollowell, Elizabeth V, 76
Hollowell, Elizabeth VI, 28
Hollowell, Elizabeth VI, 30
Hollowell, Elizabeth VI, 34
Hollowell, Elizabeth VI, 36
Hollowell, Elizabeth C. I, 928
Hollowell, Elwood V, 25
Hollowell, Elwood V, 60
Hollowell, Elwood V, 61
Hollowell, Elwood V, 76
Hollowell, Emma L. I, 619
Hollowell, Emma L. I, 635
Hollowell, Ernest I, 309
Hollowell, Esther I, 54
Hollowell, Esther I, 64
Hollowell, Esther I, 216
Hollowell, Esther I, 241
Hollowell, Esther I, 252
Hollowell, Esther F. III, 148
Hollowell, Esther Fisher III, 14
Hollowell, F. I, 329
Hollowell, Frances I, 308
Hollowell, Frances I, 511
Hollowell, Frances I, 548
Hollowell, Frances I, 563
Hollowell, Francis I, 241
Hollowell, Francis I, 246
Hollowell, Francis Jackson III, 148
Hollowell, Fred T. I, 241
Hollowell, Frederick T. I, 242
Hollowell, Frederick T. III, 148
Hollowell, Geo. I, 337
Hollowell, George A. I, 241
Hollowell, George A. I, 337
Hollowell, George Alson I, 324
Hollowell, Girusah I, 216
Hollowell, Gulia Anna Maria I, 289
Hollowell, Hannah III, 411
Hollowell, Hannah III, 420
Hollowell, Hannah L. III, 411
Hollowell, Hannah P. III, 148
Hollowell, Hattie I, 337
Hollowell, Henry I, 289
Hollowell, Henry VI, 22
Hollowell, Henry VI, 28
Hollowell, Henry VI, 29
Hollowell, Henry VI, 30
Hollowell, Henry VI, 34
Hollowell, Henry VI, 36
Hollowell, Henry O. I, 241
Hollowell, Henry O. III, 170
Hollowell, Herbert F. I, 241
Hollowell, Herbert T. I, 242
Hollowell, Herman F. I, 241
Hollowell, Hettie I, 337
Hollowell, Hettie I, 339
Hollowell, Hettie I, 635
Hollowell, Hettie O. I, 619
Hollowell, Hettie O. I, 635
Hollowell, Hettie O. III, 169
Hollowell, J. E. I, 324
Hollowell, J. W. III, 148
Hollowell, J. William I, 241
Hollowell, J. William I, 242
Hollowell, Jabez R. I, 309
Hollowell, Jahue Jessop I, 324
Hollowell, James V, 911
Hollowell, James R. I, 619
Hollowell, James R. I, 635
Hollowell, James R. III, 148
Hollowell, James R. III, 169
Hollowell, James S. II, 292
Hollowell, James S. V, 911
Hollowell, Jane IV, 223
Hollowell, Jehu I, 241

Hollowell, Jehu J. I, 242
Hollowell, Jess T. I, 943
Hollowell, Jesse I, 216
Hollowell, Jesse I, 241
Hollowell, Jesse I, 289
Hollowell, Jesse I, 309
Hollowell, Jesse I, 321
Hollowell, Jesse I, 324
Hollowell, Jesse I, 328
Hollowell, Jesse I, 329
Hollowell, Jesse I, 927
Hollowell, Jesse V, 76
Hollowell, Jesse E. I, 329
Hollowell, Jesse Elij. I, 324
Hollowell, Jesse F. I, 329
Hollowell, Jesse F. I, 927
Hollowell, Jesse T. I, 235
Hollowell, Jesse T. I, 241
Hollowell, Jesse T. I, 337
Hollowell, Jesse Thomas I, 324
Hollowell, Jesse Thomas I, 329
Hollowell, Jesse Thomas I, 927
Hollowell, Jesse Thomas I, 928
Hollowell, Jno. William I, 324
Hollowell, Joab I, 216
Hollowell, John I, 184
Hollowell, John I, 195
Hollowell, John I, 216
Hollowell, John I, 241
Hollowell, John I, 289
Hollowell, John I, 308
Hollowell, John I, 309
Hollowell, John I, 313
Hollowell, John I, 321
Hollowell, John I, 324
Hollowell, John I, 329
Hollowell, John V, 76
Hollowell, John VI, 30
Hollowell, John F. I, 44
Hollowell, John F. I, 54
Hollowell, John F. I, 216
Hollowell, John F. I, 241
Hollowell, John F. I, 309
Hollowell, John Francis I, 289
Hollowell, John H. I, 337
Hollowell, John Henry I, 325
Hollowell, John M. I, 241
Hollowell, John M. I, 242
Hollowell, John O. I, 635
Hollowell, John T. I, 241
Hollowell, John W. I, 309
Hollowell, John W. I, 329
Hollowell, John W. I, 619
Hollowell, John W. III, 148
Hollowell, John W. III, 169
Hollowell, John White III, 148
Hollowell, John White III, 196
Hollowell, John White, Jr. III, 148
Hollowell, John William I, 241
Hollowell, John William I, 324
Hollowell, John William I, 329
Hollowell, Jonathan I, 289
Hollowell, Jonothan V, 76
Hollowell, Jordon I, 241
Hollowell, Joseph I, 53
Hollowell, Joseph I, 60
Hollowell, Joseph I, 216
Hollowell, Joseph I, 241
Hollowell, Joseph I, 289
Hollowell, Joseph I, 308
Hollowell, Joseph I, 324
Hollowell, Joseph I, 548
Hollowell, Joseph VI, 30
Hollowell, Joseph VI, 45
Hollowell, Joseph VI, 46
Hollowell, Joseph G. I, 337
Hollowell, Joseph G. I, 619
Hollowell, Joseph G. I, 635
Hollowell, Joseph G. III, 148
Hollowell, Joseph G. III, 169
Hollowell, Joseph Gurney I, 325
Hollowell, Joseph J. I, 324
Hollowell, Joseph J. Cox I, 548
Hollowell, Julia Ann I, 216
Hollowell, Julia Ann I, 241
Hollowell, Julia Ann I, 258
Hollowell, Katie B. I, 241
Hollowell, Lara F. I, 309
Hollowell, Laura F. I, 309
Hollowell, Laura Frances I, 329
Hollowell, Leah I, 53
Hollowell, Leah I, 60
Hollowell, Leah I, 241
Hollowell, Leanry F. I, 289
Hollowell, Lena I, 242
Hollowell, Leslie T. I, 635
Hollowell, Leslie Theron I, 619
Hollowell, Leslie Theron I, 635
Hollowell, Levi I, 303
Hollowell, Levi I, 308
Hollowell, Levi I, 309
Hollowell, Levi I, 313
Hollowell, Levi I, 321
Hollowell, Levi I, 324
Hollowell, Levi I, 329
Hollowell, Lina I, 241
Hollowell, Lindley I, 241
Hollowell, Lindley M. I, 309
Hollowell, Lindley Murray I, 289
Hollowell, Lindley Murrey I, 325
Hollowell, Lindly Murray I, 216
Hollowell, Live I, 309
Hollowell, Lizzie I, 612
Hollowell, Lizzie I, 617
Hollowell, Lizzie I, 943
Hollowell, Lou I, 337
Hollowell, Louisa I, 241
Hollowell, Louisa V, 92
Hollowell, Lowry I, 329
Hollowell, Lula E. I, 241
Hollowell, Lydia IV, 411
Hollowell, Mamie Edward I, 337
Hollowell, Mamie Edwards I, 635
Hollowell, Mammie Cox I, 619
Hollowell, Margaret I, 195
Hollowell, Margaret I, 203
Hollowell, Margaret A. I, 309
Hollowell, Margaret B. I, 216
Hollowell, Margaret B. I, 241
Hollowell, Margaret B. I, 256
Hollowell, Margaret P. I, 229
Hollowell, Margaret P. I, 241
Hollowell, Maria Annie I, 305
Hollowell, Maria Annie I, 309
Hollowell, Mariah I, 308
Hollowell, Mariam I, 308
Hollowell, Marian H. III, 148
Hollowell, Marian H. III, 196
Hollowell, Marianna I, 927
Hollowell, Martha I, 216
Hollowell, Martha I, 241
Hollowell, Martha I, 289
Hollowell, Martha I, 308
Hollowell, Martha I, 313
Hollowell, Martha I, 548
Hollowell, Martha VI, 45
Hollowell, Martha VI, 46
Hollowell, Mary I, 53
Hollowell, Mary I, 57
Hollowell, Mary I, 180
Hollowell, Mary I, 184
Hollowell, Mary I, 188
Hollowell, Mary I, 195
Hollowell, Mary I, 216
Hollowell, Mary I, 241
Hollowell, Mary I, 253
Hollowell, Mary I, 289
Hollowell, Mary I, 308
Hollowell, Mary I, 309
Hollowell, Mary I, 316
Hollowell, Mary I, 324
Hollowell, Mary I, 329
Hollowell, Mary I, 511
Hollowell, Mary I, 943
Hollowell, Mary II, 730
Hollowell, Mary V, 76
Hollowell, Mary VI, 45
Hollowell, Mary A. I, 329
Hollowell, Mary A. I, 330
Hollowell, Mary A. I, 622
Hollowell, Mary Abigail I, 325
Hollowell, Mary Anna I, 943
Hollowell, Mary Anna V, 339
Hollowell, Mary C. I, 309
Hollowell, Mary D. I, 184
Hollowell, Mary D. V, 25
Hollowell, Mary D. V, 61
Hollowell, Mary D. V, 76
Hollowell, Mary E. I, 54
Hollowell, Mary E. I, 324
Hollowell, Mary E. I, 328
Hollowell, Mary E. I, 329
Hollowell, Mary E. I, 337
Hollowell, Mary E. I, 535
Hollowell, Mary E. I, 548
Hollowell, Mary E. I, 619
Hollowell, Mary Elisabeth I, 4
Hollowell, Mary Eliza I, 324
Hollowell, Mary Elizabeth I, 324
Hollowell, Mary J. I, 54
Hollowell, Mary J. I, 216
Hollowell, Mary J. I, 289
Hollowell, Mary J. I, 305
Hollowell, Mary J. I, 309
Hollowell, Mary J. I, 329
Hollowell, Mary J. V, 31
Hollowell, Mary J. V, 76
Hollowell, Mary Jane I, 54
Hollowell, Mary Jane I, 216
Hollowell, Mary Jane I, 241
Hollowell, Mary Jane I, 243
Hollowell, Maurice Lyndon I, 619
Hollowell, Maurice Lyndon I, 635
Hollowell, Merrey Robert I, 324
Hollowell, Michal I, 289
Hollowell, Michel I, 308
Hollowell, Michel V, 76
Hollowell, Milicent I, 189
Hollowell, Milicent I, 195
Hollowell, Miriam I, 216
Hollowell, Miriam I, 289
Hollowell, Miriam I, 308
Hollowell, Miriam I, 313
Hollowell, Miriam V, 76
Hollowell, Morening I, 206
Hollowell, Morris L. III, 148
Hollowell, Mournen I, 216
Hollowell, Murray R. I, 241
Hollowell, Murray R. I, 242
Hollowell, N. C. I, 309
Hollowell, Nathan I, 184
Hollowell, Nathan I, 195
Hollowell, Nathan I, 289
Hollowell, Nathan V, 76
Hollowell, Nathan H. III, 148
Hollowell, Nathan J. I, 329
Hollowell, Nathan Thomas I, 325
Hollowell, Nathan W. I, 54
Hollowell, Nettie C. I, 309
Hollowell, Nettie Catharine I, 337
Hollowell, Norman J. I, 337
Hollowell, Norwood III, 148
Hollowell, Norwood P. III, 148
Hollowell, Norwood Penrose, Jr. III, 148
Hollowell, Oliff I, 216
Hollowell, Oliff I, 233
Hollowell, Oliff I, 241
Hollowell, Olive I, 241
Hollowell, Pearl V. I, 241
Hollowell, Pearl V. I, 242
Hollowell, Pegga I, 308
Hollowell, Peggy I, 289
Hollowell, Peggy V, 76
Hollowell, Penina I, 324
Hollowell, Phebe I, 289
Hollowell, Phebe I, 303
Hollowell, Phebe I, 308
Hollowell, Philip III, 148
Hollowell, Piety I, 324
Hollowell, Polley I, 308
Hollowell, Polley I, 324
Hollowell, Polley I, 329
Hollowell, Polly I, 184
Hollowell, Polly I, 308
Hollowell, Polly I, 311
Hollowell, Polly Ann I, 329
Hollowell, Rachel I, 54
Hollowell, Rachel I, 184
Hollowell, Rebecca B. III, 148
Hollowell, Rebekah I, 184
Hollowell, Rena I, 337
Hollowell, Rena I, 620
Hollowell, Rena I, 635
Hollowell, Rich. L. III, 148
Hollowell, Rich. L. III, 169
Hollowell, Richard I, 635
Hollowell, Richard J., Jr. I, 635
Hollowell, Richard L. I, 619
Hollowell, Richard L. I, 635
Hollowell, Richard L. III, 148
Hollowell, Richard L. III, 169
Hollowell, Richard L. III, 170
Hollowell, Richard L., Jr. III, 169
Hollowell, Richard Lloyd I, 325
Hollowell, Richard T. L. I, 337
Hollowell, Robert I, 216
Hollowell, Robert I, 289
Hollowell, Robert I, 302
Hollowell, Robert I, 308
Hollowell, Robert V, 76
Hollowell, Robert Edward I, 619
Hollowell, Robert Edward I, 635
Hollowell, Robert H. III, 148
Hollowell, Robert Haydock III, 148
Hollowell, Robert Haydock, Jr. III, 148
Hollowell, Roger Haydock III, 148
Hollowell, Sallie I, 337
Hollowell, Sally A. I, 324
Hollowell, Samuel I, 216
Hollowell, Samuel I, 241
Hollowell, Samuel I, 250
Hollowell, Samuel Haydock III, 148
Hollowell, Sara Ann II, 1078
Hollowell, Sarah I, 53
Hollowell, Sarah I, 60
Hollowell, Sarah I, 184
Hollowell, Sarah I, 195
Hollowell, Sarah I, 206
Hollowell, Sarah I, 216
Hollowell, Sarah I, 241
Hollowell, Sarah I, 248
Hollowell, Sarah I, 289
Hollowell, Sarah I, 300
Hollowell, Sarah I, 306
Hollowell, Sarah I, 308
Hollowell, Sarah III, 148
Hollowell, Sarah V, 76
Hollowell, Sarah VI, 30
Hollowell, Sarah VI, 45
Hollowell, Sarah VI, 110
Hollowell, Sarah VI, 117
Hollowell, Sarah VI, 118
Hollowell, Sarah A. I, 44
Hollowell, Sarah A. I, 54
Hollowell, Sarah E. I, 329
Hollowell, Sarah M. I, 241
Hollowell, Sarah M. I, 289
Hollowell, Sarah M. I, 309
Hollowell, Sarah M. I, 329
Hollowell, Sarah Menville I, 329
Hollowell, Sarah W. III, 148
Hollowell, Sarah W. III, 170
Hollowell, Selia I, 306
Hollowell, Selia I, 308
Hollowell, Sidney I, 635
Hollowell, Silas I, 206
Hollowell, Silas I, 216
Hollowell, Silas I, 241
Hollowell, Silas I, 289
Hollowell, Silas I, 300
Hollowell, Silas I, 308
Hollowell, Silas I, 324
Hollowell, Silas I, 329
Hollowell, Smithson I, 289
Hollowell, Smithson V, 76
Hollowell, Stephen R. I, 309
Hollowell, Stephen R. I, 324
Hollowell, Stephen R. I, 329
Hollowell, Sue V. I, 337
Hollowell, Sue V. I, 635
Hollowell, Sue V. I, 642
Hollowell, Susan M. III, 148
Hollowell, Susan Morris III, 148
Hollowell, Susanna II, 999
Hollowell, Susanna VI, 110
Hollowell, Susanna VI, 118
Hollowell, T. S. I, 279
Hollowell, T. S. I, 309
Hollowell, Tabitha E. I, 329
Hollowell, Tabitha E. I, 330
Hollowell, Tabitha Edith I, 324
Hollowell, Tho. VI, 30
Hollowell, Thomas I, 53
Hollowell, Thomas I, 54
Hollowell, Thomas I, 57
Hollowell, Thomas I, 180
Hollowell, Thomas I, 195
Hollowell, Thomas I, 206
Hollowell, Thomas I, 216
Hollowell, Thomas I, 233
Hollowell, Thomas I, 241
Hollowell, Thomas I, 253
Hollowell, Thomas I, 264
Hollowell, Thomas I, 299
Hollowell, Thomas I, 308
Hollowell, Thomas I, 309
Hollowell, Thomas I, 310
Hollowell, Thomas I, 314
Hollowell, Thomas I, 321
Hollowell, Thomas I, 324
Hollowell, Thomas I, 337
Hollowell, Thomas I Sup 1, 7
Hollowell, Thomas VI, 7
Hollowell, Thomas VI, 21
Hollowell, Thomas VI, 22
Hollowell, Thomas VI, 29
Hollowell, Thomas VI, 30
Hollowell, Thomas C. IV, 411
Hollowell, Thomas L. I, 305
Hollowell, Thomas L. I, 309
Hollowell, Thomas L. I, 321
Hollowell, Thomas L. I, 324
Hollowell, Thomas L. I, 329
Hollowell, Thomas L. I, 617
Hollowell, Thomas L. I, 619
Hollowell, Thomas L. I, 622
Hollowell, Thomas S. I, 54
Hollowell, Thomas S. I, 216
Hollowell, Thomas S. I, 229
Hollowell, Thomas S. I, 241
Hollowell, Thomas S. I, 289
Hollowell, Thomas S. I, 305
Hollowell, Thomas S. I, 309
Hollowell, Thomas S. I, 324
Hollowell, Thomas S. I, 329
Hollowell, Thomas, Jr. I, 53
Hollowell, Thos. I, 184
Hollowell, Thos. VI, 30
Hollowell, Tom I, 4
Hollowell, Viola F. I, 309
Hollowell, Viola F. I, 337
Hollowell, W. R. I, 337
Hollowell, Walter A. I, 242
Hollowell, Walter L. I, 241
Hollowell, Walter P. I, 635
Hollowell, Walter P. III, 169
Hollowell, Wd. Alice VI, 30
Hollowell, Widow Mary I, 313
Hollowell, Wilie I, 329
Hollowell, Willey I, 324
Hollowell, William I, 216
Hollowell, William I, 242
Hollowell, William I, 289
Hollowell, William I, 303
Hollowell, William I, 308
Hollowell, William I, 309
Hollowell, William III, 148
Hollowell, William V, 76
Hollowell, William VI, 45
Hollowell, William VI, 110
Hollowell, William VI, 118
Hollowell, William B. I, 324
Hollowell, William E. I, 241
Hollowell, William E. I, 324
Hollowell, William E. I, 635
Hollowell, William E. III, 169
Hollowell, William Edgar I, 241
Hollowell, William F. I, 241
Hollowell, William H. I, 241
Hollowell, William Ladd III, 148
Hollowell, William Overman I, 329
Hollowell, William R. I, 325
Hollowell, William R. I, 620
Hollowell, William T. I, 44
Hollowell, William T. I, 54
Hollowell, William T. I, 309
Hollowell, William Thomas I, 289
Hollowell, William Thomas I, 324
Hollowell, Wm. C. III, 170
Hollowell, Wm. E. I, 619
Hollowell, Wm. S. II, 730
Hollowell, Zerusah I, 241
Hollowell, Zerusah I, 250
Hollowell, Zilpah I, 330
Hollowell, Zilpha I, 305
Hollowell, Zilpha I, 309
Hollowell, Zilpha I, 324
Hollowell, Zilpha I, 329
Hollowell, Zilpha I, 337
Hollowell, Zilpha I, 617
Hollowell, Zilpha I, 619
Hollowell, Zilpha Catherine I, 325
Hollowell, Zilphia I, 622
Hollowelll, Elizabeth VI, 33
Hollowy, Hannah I, 548
Holly, Anna IV, 1010
Holly, Anna V. IV, 966
Holly, Chole VI, 1003
Holly, Edith May V, 179
Holly, Elizabeth A. V, 179
Holly, Fannie O. IV, 966
Holly, Fanny O. IV, 966
Holly, Fanny O. IV, 1166
Holly, George V, 179
Holly, George W. V, 179
Holly, J. B. IV, 1166
Holly, James VI, 802
Holly, James VI, 838
Holly, John IV, 966
Holly, John V, 1002
Holly, John B. IV, 966
Holly, John B. IV, 1166
Holly, Mary V, 154
Holly, Mary V, 1002
Holly, Mary Ellen V, 179
Holly, Sanford VI, 955
Holly, Warren Lester V, 179
Hollyman, Mary II, 551
Hollyman, Mary II, 639
Hollyman, Sarah II, 504
Hollyman, Sarah II, 551
Hollyman, Thomas II, 375
Holm, Benjamin VI, 183
Holm, Eva May IV, 1321
Holman, ??? III, 196
Holman, Emma S. II, 833
Holman, Emma S. II, 876
Holman, Henry O. III, 170
Holman, James III, 170
Holman, Lafetra III, 170
Holman, Nathan III, 170
Holman, Nathan III, 196
Holman, Sarah III, 170
Holman, Sarah III, 196
Holme, ??? III, 128
Holme, Alida Alice III, 72

Holme, Alida Alice III, 170
Holme, Amy J. III, 187
Holme, Anna W. II, 151
Holme, Arthur Joseph III, 170
Holme, Benjamin II, 134
Holme, Benjamin II, 159
Holme, Benjamin VI, 94
Holme, Benjamin VI, 149
Holme, Benjamin S. II, 151
Holme, Charles III, 230
Holme, Charles E. III, 170
Holme, Charles E., Jr. III, 170
Holme, Charles O. III, 170
Holme, Chas. E. III, 72
Holme, Chas. E. III, 170
Holme, Edith M. III, 170
Holme, Effie III, 272
Holme, Eleanor III, 129
Holme, Eleanor III, 187
Holme, Eleanor III, 272
Holme, Elenor Gibbon II, 151
Holme, Eleonor III, 170
Holme, Elizabeth II, 134
Holme, Elizabeth S. II, 151
Holme, Elizabeth S. II, 159
Holme, Ethel Mary III, 170
Holme, Eunice A. III, 170
Holme, George II, 233
Holme, Helenn W. II, 134
Holme, Henry D. II, 151
Holme, Henry R. II, 134
Holme, Isabella T. III, 170
Holme, John II, 444
Holme, John G. II, 134
Holme, Joseph G. III, 170
Holme, Margaret Morris II, 151
Holme, Marion Florence III, 170
Holme, Martha II, 212
Holme, Martha II, 233
Holme, Mary II, 444
Holme, Mary VI, 181
Holme, Mary VI, 213
Holme, Mary T III, 170
Holme, Mary T. III, 72
Holme, Mary T. III, 170
Holme, Mary T. III, 230
Holme, Mrs. Louise IV, 1321
Holme, Pauline II, 151
Holme, Pauline II, 159
Holme, Pauline Hilda II, 151
Holme, Pauline W. II, 134
Holme, R. Henry II, 151
Holme, Richard Henry II, 151
Holme, Richard Henry II, 159
Holme, Tho. VI, 146
Holme, Thomas II, 551
Holme, Thomas W. III, 170
Holme, Thomas Wynne III, 90
Holme, Thos. Wynne III, 129
Holme, Wd. Eleanor III, 128
Holme, William V, 339
Holmes Mead, Mary VI, 654
Holmes, ??? III, 239
Holmes, Abigail VI, 656
Holmes, Agnes Haines II, 800
Holmes, Amasa W. VI, 934
Holmes, Andrew VI, 657
Holmes, Ann II, 221
Holmes, Ann II, 233
Holmes, Ann II, 523
Holmes, Ann II, 551
Holmes, Ann VI, 624
Holmes, Ann VI, 625
Holmes, Ann VI, 626
Holmes, Ann VI, 627
Holmes, Ann VI, 656
Holmes, Ann VI, 680
Holmes, Ann VI, 684
Holmes, Ann VI, 686
Holmes, Ann Eliza II, 120
Holmes, Ann Eliza VI, 656
Holmes, Ann Eliza VI, 657
Holmes, Ann Eliza VI, 672
Holmes, Anna VI, 403
Holmes, Anna Eliza VI, 656
Holmes, Anna Eliza VI, 672
Holmes, Anna R. II, 877
Holmes, Anna W. II, 151
Holmes, Anne III, 267
Holmes, Anne W. II, 134
Holmes, Annie V, 402
Holmes, Annie V, 414
Holmes, Archibald I, 143
Holmes, Archibald I, 195
Holmes, Arnold Boon VI, 508
Holmes, Arnold Boone VI, 508
Holmes, Arnold Boone VI, 656
Holmes, B. Mary VI, 656
Holmes, B. May VI, 642
Holmes, B. May VI, 643
Holmes, B. May VI, 674
Holmes, Bell V, 1002
Holmes, Benjamin II, 134
Holmes, Benjamin S. II, 151
Holmes, Bertha V, 576
Holmes, Bruce IV, 1321
Holmes, Caroline M. II, 134
Holmes, Caroline M. II, 151
Holmes, Charles V, 248
Holmes, Cora V, 458
Holmes, Daniel V, 76
Holmes, David IV, 224
Holmes, David V, 76
Holmes, David Ira V, 684
Holmes, Deborah VI, 508
Holmes, Edward R. II, 877
Holmes, Edward Wilson II, 800
Holmes, Edwin R. II, 877
Holmes, Eldon V, 684
Holmes, Eleanor Gibbon II, 134
Holmes, Elenor Gibbon II, 151
Holmes, Elhena II, 1002
Holmes, Elijah VI, 369
Holmes, Elijah VI, 403
Holmes, Elijah VI, 620
Holmes, Elijah VI, 653
Holmes, Elijah VI, 656
Holmes, Elijah VI, 657
Holmes, Elijah VI, 690
Holmes, Elijah VI, 695
Holmes, Elijah VI, 732
Holmes, Elijah VI, 749
Holmes, Elijah D. VI, 656
Holmes, Elijah D. VI, 657
Holmes, Elijah D. VI, 692
Holmes, Elisha VI, 656
Holmes, Elisha VI, 657
Holmes, Elisha VI, 714
Holmes, Elisha H. VI, 656
Holmes, Eliza II, 876
Holmes, Eliza II, 941
Holmes, Eliza III, 32
Holmes, Eliza IV, 620
Holmes, Eliza IV, 636
Holmes, Eliza VI, 657
Holmes, Eliza D. III, 170
Holmes, Eliza T. IV, 337
Holmes, Eliza T. VI, 508
Holmes, Eliza T. VI, 509
Holmes, Eliza T. VI, 629
Holmes, Eliza T. VI, 656
Holmes, Eliza T. VI, 657
Holmes, Elizabeth II, 69
Holmes, Elizabeth II, 79
Holmes, Elizabeth II, 134
Holmes, Elizabeth II, 151
Holmes, Elizabeth III, 104
Holmes, Elizabeth IV, 337
Holmes, Elizabeth IV, 636
Holmes, Elizabeth V, 684
Holmes, Elizabeth VI, 403
Holmes, Elizabeth VI, 502
Holmes, Elizabeth VI, 506
Holmes, Elizabeth VI, 508
Holmes, Elizabeth VI, 509
Holmes, Elizabeth VI, 620
Holmes, Elizabeth VI, 646
Holmes, Elizabeth VI, 653
Holmes, Elizabeth VI, 656
Holmes, Elizabeth VI, 657
Holmes, Elizabeth VI, 675
Holmes, Elizabeth VI, 684
Holmes, Elizabeth VI, 685
Holmes, Elizabeth VI, 690
Holmes, Elizabeth VI, 692
Holmes, Elizabeth VI, 695
Holmes, Elizabeth VI, 732
Holmes, Elizabeth VI, 749
Holmes, Elizabeth D. VI, 688
Holmes, Elizabeth Dinah VI, 656
Holmes, Elizabeth Dinah VI, 690
Holmes, Elizabeth H. IV, 724
Holmes, Elizabeth Holmes VI, 629
Holmes, Elizabeth Rogers VI, 369
Holmes, Elizabeth Rogers VI, 690
Holmes, Elizabeth S. II, 151
Holmes, Elizaeth VI, 676
Holmes, Ella Genette IV, 224
Holmes, Ellen VI, 508
Holmes, Elmina R. VI, 653
Holmes, Elmina R. VI, 656
Holmes, Elmina R. VI, 695
Holmes, Emily IV, 966
Holmes, Emily IV, 1005
Holmes, Emily VI, 656
Holmes, Emily VI, 662
Holmes, Emily VI, 679
Holmes, Emily VI, 680
Holmes, Emily VI, 681
Holmes, Emily VI, 685
Holmes, Emily VI, 707
Holmes, Emily VI, 934
Holmes, Emma J. V, 248
Holmes, Esther VI, 656
Holmes, Ethel Pearl V, 248
Holmes, Eva May IV, 1321
Holmes, Faye V, 684
Holmes, Frank V, 458
Holmes, Frank V, 684
Holmes, George II, 233
Holmes, George II, 1002
Holmes, George VI, 642
Holmes, George VI, 656
Holmes, George W. VI, 656
Holmes, Giles V, 1002
Holmes, Grace IV, 224
Holmes, Grace Holmes Hastings IV, 224
Holmes, Hannah IV, 337
Holmes, Hannah V, 76
Holmes, Hannah VI, 314
Holmes, Hannah VI, 508
Holmes, Hannah S. VI, 508
Holmes, Hannah S. VI, 656
Holmes, Hannah Shoemaker VI, 508
Holmes, Hannah Shoemaker VI, 619
Holmes, Hannah Shoemaker VI, 732
Holmes, Hannah Shoemaker VI, 749
Holmes, Harley S. V, 458
Holmes, Hattie VI, 657
Holmes, Helen IV, 224
Holmes, Helena S. II, 134
Holmes, Helena W. II, 151
Holmes, Helenn W. II, 134
Holmes, Henry D. II, 151
Holmes, Henry Dennis II, 134
Holmes, Henry R. II, 134
Holmes, Hester VI, 656
Holmes, Hester VI, 714
Holmes, Hugh Rogers VI, 656
Holmes, Isaac VI, 508
Holmes, Isaac VI, 619
Holmes, Isaac VI, 656
Holmes, Isaac VI, 732
Holmes, Isaac VI, 749
Holmes, Isaac Lot VI, 508
Holmes, J. C. I, 635
Holmes, J. Nathan IV, 224
Holmes, James III, 170
Holmes, James B. II, 800
Holmes, James Cicero I, 399
Holmes, James Woolman II, 134
Holmes, Jas. VI, 934
Holmes, Jennie B. V, 248
Holmes, Jennie B. V, 458
Holmes, Jesse II, 877
Holmes, Jesse II, 937
Holmes, Jesse IV, 337
Holmes, Jesse IV, 341
Holmes, Jesse IV, 636
Holmes, Jesse VI, 656
Holmes, Jesse H. II, 877
Holmes, Jesse H. II, 937
Holmes, Jesse H. VI, 749
Holmes, Jesse H. VI, 790
Holmes, Job II, 800
Holmes, John II, 134
Holmes, John VI, 826
Holmes, John VI, 832
Holmes, John Alexander IV, 224
Holmes, John G. II, 134
Holmes, John W. IV, 224
Holmes, John, Jr. II, 1002
Holmes, John, Jr. II, 1015
Holmes, Jonathan III, 144
Holmes, Jonathan III, 170
Holmes, Jonothan V, 76
Holmes, Joseph IV, 337
Holmes, Joseph IV, 636
Holmes, Joseph V, 76
Holmes, Joseph VI, 506
Holmes, Joseph VI, 508
Holmes, Joseph VI, 629
Holmes, Joseph VI, 653
Holmes, Joseph VI, 656
Holmes, Joseph VI, 657
Holmes, Joseph VI, 675
Holmes, Joseph VI, 676
Holmes, Joseph VI, 684
Holmes, Joseph VI, 685
Holmes, Joseph VI, 732
Holmes, Joseph VI, 749
Holmes, Joseph Hamilton VI, 656
Holmes, Joseph W. IV, 329
Holmes, Joseph W. IV, 337
Holmes, Joseph W. VI, 656
Holmes, Joseph W. VI, 657
Holmes, Joseph William VI, 509
Holmes, Joseph William VI, 656
Holmes, Joseph William VI, 657
Holmes, Joseph Wm. VI, 672
Holmes, Joshua VI, 657
Holmes, Julia E. VI, 679
Holmes, Juliet Catharine VI, 509
Holmes, Juliet Catharine VI, 657
Holmes, Juliette III, 239
Holmes, Kate C. III, 239
Holmes, Kerry Orlando IV, 337
Holmes, Kersey C. IV, 724
Holmes, Kezia VI, 631
Holmes, Kezia VI, 657
Holmes, Keziah VI, 657
Holmes, Laura G. II, 877
Holmes, Laura G. II, 905
Holmes, Laura Mary IV, 224
Holmes, Lorena M. VI, 657
Holmes, Lot IV, 620
Holmes, Lot IV, 636
Holmes, Lot IV, 664
Holmes, Lot VI, 403
Holmes, Lot VI, 657
Holmes, Lot VI, 685
Holmes, Lott VI, 508
Holmes, Lott VI, 657
Holmes, Lott VI, 684
Holmes, Lucinda I, 399
Holmes, Lucinda I, 635
Holmes, Lucinda C. I, 399
Holmes, Lydia A. VI, 657
Holmes, Lydia Ann VI, 656
Holmes, Lydia Elmira I, 883
Holmes, Lydia Elmira I, 886
Holmes, Marcy IV, 337
Holmes, Margaret II, 75
Holmes, Margaret II, 79
Holmes, Margaret II, 134
Holmes, Margaret II, 151
Holmes, Margaret II, 221
Holmes, Margaret II, 233
Holmes, Margaret II, 1002
Holmes, Margaret V, 684
Holmes, Margaret VI, 503
Holmes, Margaret VI, 508
Holmes, Margaret VI, 676
Holmes, Margaret Morris II, 134
Holmes, Margaret Morris II, 151
Holmes, Maria Oca V, 248
Holmes, Martha II, 120
Holmes, Martha II, 233
Holmes, Martha VI, 826
Holmes, Martha Jane VI, 656
Holmes, Mary II, 79
Holmes, Mary II, 80
Holmes, Mary II, 1002
Holmes, Mary IV, 224
Holmes, Mary IV, 636
Holmes, Mary IV, 664
Holmes, Mary V, 76
Holmes, Mary VI, 181
Holmes, Mary VI, 314
Holmes, Mary VI, 315
Holmes, Mary VI, 508
Holmes, Mary VI, 519
Holmes, Mary VI, 521
Holmes, Mary VI, 637
Holmes, Mary VI, 657
Holmes, Mary VI, 661
Holmes, Mary VI, 665
Holmes, Mary VI, 667
Holmes, Mary VI, 669
Holmes, Mary VI, 673
Holmes, Mary VI, 675
Holmes, Mary VI, 691
Holmes, Mary VI, 712
Holmes, Mary Ann II, 120
Holmes, Mary Ann II, 125
Holmes, Mary Ann VI, 508
Holmes, Mary C. III, 379
Holmes, Mary Elizabeth VI, 509
Holmes, Mary Elizabeth VI, 657
Holmes, Mary Ellen VI, 656
Holmes, Mary Ellen VI, 657
Holmes, Mary Ellen VI, 692
Holmes, Mary J. IV, 224
Holmes, Mary R. VI, 657
Holmes, Maud H. V, 248
Holmes, Maud H. V, 458
Holmes, Maude V, 248
Holmes, May VI, 719
Holmes, May H. VI, 656
Holmes, Melvin V, 458
Holmes, Mercy IV, 341
Holmes, Mercy L. IV, 337
Holmes, Mrs. L. IV, 1321
Holmes, Mrs. Louise IV, 1321
Holmes, Nancy VI, 369
Holmes, Nancy VI, 403
Holmes, Nancy VI, 620
Holmes, Nancy VI, 656
Holmes, Nancy VI, 657
Holmes, Nancy VI, 732
Holmes, Nancy VI, 749
Holmes, Nancy H. VI, 370
Holmes, Nancy H. VI, 403
Holmes, Nancy H. VI, 620
Holmes, Orlando Wm. IV, 337
Holmes, Orville VI, 656
Holmes, Orville VI, 657
Holmes, Otho Eugene V, 684
Holmes, Pauline II, 151
Holmes, Pauline Hilda II, 134
Holmes, Pauline Hilda II, 151
Holmes, Pauline W. II, 134
Holmes, Phebe III, 144
Holmes, Phebe III, 420
Holmes, Phila VI, 653
Holmes, Phila VI, 657
Holmes, R. Henry II, 151
Holmes, Rachel II, 800
Holmes, Rachel VI, 508
Holmes, Rachel VI, 555
Holmes, Rachel R. II, 877
Holmes, Raleigh V, 248
Holmes, Raleigh V, 458
Holmes, Ralph E. V, 248
Holmes, Raymond Waldo V, 684
Holmes, Rebecca II, 877
Holmes, Rebecca II, 1002
Holmes, Rebecca II, 1015
Holmes, Rebecca IV, 337
Holmes, Rebecca IV, 820
Holmes, Rebecca VI, 642
Holmes, Rebecca VI, 656
Holmes, Rebecca J. IV, 329
Holmes, Rebecca J. IV, 337
Holmes, Rebecca J. VI, 656
Holmes, Rebecca J. VI, 657
Holmes, Rebecca J. VI, 672
Holmes, Rebecca S. II, 877
Holmes, Rebecca S. II, 937
Holmes, Rebecca Sinclair VI, 749
Holmes, Rebecca Sinclair VI, 790
Holmes, Richard Henry II, 151
Holmes, Rollie H. V, 458
Holmes, S. E. I, 922
Holmes, Sallie V, 243
Holmes, Sallie V, 248
Holmes, Sallie B. II, 800
Holmes, Sallie B. II, 876
Holmes, Sallie B. II, 941
Holmes, Sallie B. VI, 657
Holmes, Samuel II, 877
Holmes, Samuel III, 170
Holmes, Samuel C. II, 876
Holmes, Samuel C. II, 877
Holmes, Samuel C. II, 941
Holmes, Samuel C. VI, 657
Holmes, Samuel Canby II, 800
Holmes, Samuel G. II, 877
Holmes, Samuel P. II, 877
Holmes, Samuel Thomas VI, 509
Holmes, Sarah II, 120
Holmes, Sarah II, 233
Holmes, Sarah II, 876
Holmes, Sarah II, 877
Holmes, Sarah II, 937
Holmes, Sarah IV, 636
Holmes, Sarah IV, 664
Holmes, Sarah VI, 314
Holmes, Sarah VI, 315
Holmes, Sarah VI, 508
Holmes, Sarah VI, 619
Holmes, Sarah VI, 657
Holmes, Sarah VI, 684
Holmes, Sarah VI, 685
Holmes, Sarah C. VI, 509
Holmes, Sarah C. VI, 657
Holmes, Sarah Canby VI, 509
Holmes, Sarah L. III, 32
Holmes, Sarah L. III, 170
Holmes, Scott VI, 508
Holmes, Sue VI, 642
Holmes, Tabitha VI, 845
Holmes, Tacy IV, 224
Holmes, Tacy IV, 292
Holmes, Thomas II, 221
Holmes, Thomas II, 233
Holmes, Thomas II, 375
Holmes, Thomas II, 551
Holmes, Thomas VI, 146
Holmes, Thomas D. III, 32
Holmes, Thos. D. III, 170
Holmes, Walter II, 877
Holmes, Walter II, 905
Holmes, Warner VI, 657
Holmes, Wd. Sarah II, 800
Holmes, Widow Emily VI, 685
Holmes, Widow Mary VI, 653
Holmes, Widow Mary VI, 654
Holmes, Widow Mary VI, 657

Holmes, William IV, 337
Holmes, William V, 339
Holmes, William VI, 314
Holmes, William VI, 315
Holmes, William VI, 403
Holmes, William VI, 508
Holmes, William VI, 509
Holmes, William VI, 629
Holmes, William VI, 656
Holmes, William VI, 657
Holmes, William F. VI, 656
Holmes, William F. VI, 657
Holmes, William, Sr. VI, 657
Holmes, Wm. II, 79
Holmes, Wm. II, 120
Holmes, Wm. II, 876
Holmes, Wm. II, 941
Holmes, Wm. VI, 508
Holmes, Wm. VI, 519
Holmes, Wm. VI, 521
Holmes, Wm. VI, 656
Holmes, Wm. VI, 657
Holmes, Wm. VI, 661
Holmes, Wm. VI, 673
Holmes, Zebulon II, 233
Holmes, Zebulon II, 800
Holmes, Zebulon II, 876
Holms, Ann II, 551
Holms, Archibald I, 195
Holms, Branson V, 339
Holms, Ellen VI, 508
Holms, Hannah VI, 508
Holms, Isaac VI, 508
Holms, Isaac Lot VI, 508
Holms, Jesse IV, 820
Holms, Jesse IV, 824
Holms, Joseph VI, 508
Holms, Margaret II, 134
Holms, Martha II, 137
Holms, Mary Ann VI, 508
Holms, Mary D. I, 242
Holms, May V, 339
Holms, Rebecca IV, 820
Holms, Rebecca IV, 824
Holms, Rebecca Hanna IV, 824
Holms, Rosa V, 339
Holms, Samuel II, 137
Holms, Sarah II, 137
Holms, William V, 339
Holms, William VI, 508
Holoday, Angeline V, 401
Holoday, Ann V, 400
Holoday, Anna D. V, 372
Holoday, Anna D. V, 400
Holoday, Anna Osborn V, 683
Holoday, Asa V, 401
Holoday, Bessie V, 683
Holoday, Betsey V, 400
Holoday, Charles V, 401
Holoday, David V, 400
Holoday, Elwood V, 843
Holoday, Enoch V, 400
Holoday, Frederick Samuel V, 683
Holoday, Gold Arrosmith V, 683
Holoday, Jennie V, 859
Holoday, Jesse F. V, 396
Holoday, John V, 843
Holoday, John Henry V, 400
Holoday, Joseph V, 843
Holoday, Joseph M. V, 843
Holoday, Louiza V, 400
Holoday, Maggie V, 843
Holoday, Nancy V, 683
Holoday, Nancy J. V, 683
Holoday, Raleigh V, 401
Holoday, Robert V, 683
Holoday, Ruth V, 396
Holoday, Ruth V, 397
Holoday, Ruth V, 683
Holoday, Ruth V, 686
Holoday, Ruth V, 843
Holoday, Susie V, 683
Holoday, William V, 576
Holoway, Amos V, 402
Holoway, Amy IV, 354
Holoway, Ann IV, 1062
Holoway, David IV, 1062
Holoway, Eleanor V, 421
Holoway, Elizabeth V, 402
Holoway, Francis Elmer IV, 1062
Holoway, Isaac V, 446
Holoway, Louvicy V, 446
Holoway, Mary V, 401
Holoway, Mary Jane V, 402
Holoway, Pleasant V, 446
Holoway, Rachel V, 421
Holoway, Samuel IV, 354
Holoway, Timothy V, 402
Holowell, Esther I, 54
Holowell, John IV, 459
Holowell, Lydia IV, 459
Holowell, Mary Jane I, 54
Holowell, Rachel I, 54
Holowell, Sarah I, 143
Holowell, Sarah I, 167
Holowell, Thomas I, 143
Holowell, Thomas I, 167
Holschoth, Lydia V, 76
Holson, Amy P. IV, 1211
Holson, James IV, 1211
Holson, John IV, 1211
Holson, Juliann IV, 1211
Holson, Mary Ann IV, 1211
Holson, Mary C. IV, 1211
Holson, Phebe V. IV, 1211
Holson, Silvester IV, 1211
Holson, Unity J. IV, 1211
Holsoyd, Hannah V, 911
Holsoyd, Hannah V, 937
Holstead, Benny F. IV, 224
Holston, Daniel II, 444
Holstone, John II, 531
Holstone, John II, 551
Holt, Alan W. II, 877
Holt, Alan W. II, 938
Holt, Allan Wood II, 800
Holt, Alma I, 213
Holt, Ann II, 444
Holt, Ann E. VI, 921
Holt, Asa VI, 826
Holt, Benjamin II, 444
Holt, Bertha II, 877
Holt, Betsy VI, 839
Holt, Betty VI, 983
Holt, Blanch C. VI, 804
Holt, Branch W. VI, 826
Holt, Caleb VI, 822
Holt, Calvin H. VI, 826
Holt, Caroline VI, 826
Holt, Caspar II, 551
Holt, Catharine VI, 935
Holt, Catharine W. VI, 826
Holt, Cavil R. VI, 826
Holt, Chakley II, 800
Holt, Chalkley II, 877
Holt, Charles L. VI, 934
Holt, Christian VI, 934
Holt, Coleman VI, 826
Holt, Colonel John W. VI, 921
Holt, Cordelia II, 800
Holt, Dread VI, 934
Holt, Dredd VI, 880
Holt, Drew VI, 68
Holt, Drew VI, 69
Holt, Edmund VI, 826
Holt, Edna A. VI, 934
Holt, Eleanor VI, 826
Holt, Eliza VI, 950
Holt, Eliza Jane I, 614
Holt, Elizabeth II, 505
Holt, Elizabeth II, 551
Holt, Elizabeth VI, 812
Holt, Elizabeth VI, 822
Holt, Elizabeth VI, 826
Holt, Elizabeth VI, 934
Holt, Elizabeth A. VI, 934
Holt, Elizabeth F. VI, 823
Holt, Elizabeth P. VI, 911
Holt, Elizabeth P. VI, 934
Holt, Ella Jane VI, 934
Holt, Ella K. II, 877
Holt, Ellen II, 800
Holt, Ellen K. II, 877
Holt, Ellen K. II, 938
Holt, Elvira VI, 826
Holt, Elvira P. VI, 893
Holt, Embrow VI, 826
Holt, Embrow F. VI, 804
Holt, F. Smith VI, 934
Holt, Frances A. VI, 826
Holt, Frances J. VI, 897
Holt, Francis VI, 839
Holt, George VI, 856
Holt, Hannah II, 551
Holt, Hannah II, 599
Holt, Hannah Ann II, 803
Holt, Helen II, 877
Holt, Henry VI, 817
Holt, Henry VI, 821
Holt, Henry H. VI, 826
Holt, James VI, 812
Holt, James VI, 826
Holt, James VI, 839
Holt, James VI, 934
Holt, James F. VI, 826
Holt, James F. VI, 839
Holt, James H. VI, 826
Holt, James R. VI, 934
Holt, Jane II, 139
Holt, Jane II, 375
Holt, Jane VI, 983
Holt, Jane D. VI, 887
Holt, Jane S. II, 800
Holt, Jane S. II, 877
Holt, Jane S. II, 938
Holt, Jennie IV, 1254
Holt, Jno. W. VI, 869
Holt, Jno. W. VI, 870
Holt, Jno. W. VI, 897
Holt, Jno. W. VI, 902
Holt, Jno. W. VI, 906
Holt, Jno. W. VI, 918
Holt, Jno. W. VI, 922
Holt, Jno. W. VI, 939
Holt, Jno. W. VI, 987
Holt, Jno. W. VI, 1007
Holt, John II, 139
Holt, John VI, 821
Holt, John VI, 826
Holt, John VI, 879
Holt, John VI, 934
Holt, John VI, 1005
Holt, John W. VI, 886
Holt, John W. VI, 1019
Holt, John W., Jr. VI, 934
Holt, John White VI, 876
Holt, Joseph VI, 934
Holt, Joseph VI, 989
Holt, Joseph VI, 1007
Holt, Joshua II, 551
Holt, Joshua II, 599
Holt, Josiah VI, 837
Holt, Josiah VI, 934
Holt, Josiah J. VI, 813
Holt, Josiah T. VI, 812
Holt, Josiah W. VI, 883
Holt, Josie VI, 55
Holt, Josie VI, 69
Holt, Judith VI, 826
Holt, Kitty F. VI, 856
Holt, Ledia VI, 826
Holt, Leonard VI, 826
Holt, Leonard VI, 854
Holt, Leonard VI, 864
Holt, Levina VI, 68
Holt, Levina VI, 69
Holt, Ligan VI, 826
Holt, Ligon VI, 804
Holt, Lucy VI, 934
Holt, Lucy VI, 1007
Holt, Mabey VI, 917
Holt, Mammie I, 635
Holt, Maria VI, 940
Holt, Martha II, 505
Holt, Martha II, 551
Holt, Martha T. VI, 917
Holt, Martin II, 444
Holt, Mary VI, 68
Holt, Mary VI, 69
Holt, Mary VI, 826
Holt, Mary VI, 839
Holt, Mary VI, 856
Holt, Mary VI, 880
Holt, Mary Ann VI, 897
Holt, Mary E. I, 619
Holt, Mary F. VI, 821
Holt, Nancy VI, 863
Holt, Nancy VI, 934
Holt, Nancy VI, 1009
Holt, Nancy A. VI, 839
Holt, Nathaniel VI, 934
Holt, Obadiah II, 375
Holt, Obadiah II, 505
Holt, Obadiah II, 551
Holt, Parthena C. VI, 826
Holt, Patsey VI, 1007
Holt, Peggy VI, 940
Holt, Polly VI, 826
Holt, Polly VI, 950
Holt, Polly S. VI, 826
Holt, Rachel R. II, 800
Holt, Rachel R. II, 877
Holt, Rachel S. II, 139
Holt, Reaves S. VI, 934
Holt, Rebecca II, 800
Holt, Robert VI, 810
Holt, Robert VI, 812
Holt, Robert VI, 823
Holt, Robert VI, 826
Holt, Robert VI, 839
Holt, Robert VI, 863
Holt, Robert D. VI, 826
Holt, Robert F. VI, 817
Holt, Robert F. VI, 826
Holt, Robt. VI, 934
Holt, Sally VI, 934
Holt, Sally P. VI, 934
Holt, Saml. VI, 994
Holt, Samuel VI, 887
Holt, Samuel VI, 934
Holt, Samuel VI, 940
Holt, Samuel VI, 1004
Holt, Samuel P. VI, 934
Holt, Sarah VI, 810
Holt, Sarah VI, 812
Holt, Sarah VI, 822
Holt, Sarah VI, 826
Holt, Sarah A. VI, 826
Holt, Sarah J. VI, 826
Holt, Seth II, 800
Holt, Spradley VI, 880
Holt, Susan Ann Temperance VI, 817
Holt, Susan S. S. VI, 923
Holt, Susanna VI, 826
Holt, Susanna C. VI, 821
Holt, Susannah VI, 812
Holt, Susannah VI, 934
Holt, Tabitha VI, 837
Holt, Thomas VI, 812
Holt, Thomas VI, 826
Holt, Thomas VI, 837
Holt, Thomas Edgar VI, 893
Holt, Thomas H. VI, 811
Holt, Thomas H. VI, 826
Holt, Thomas R. VI, 826
Holt, William I, 399
Holt, William VI, 822
Holt, William VI, 897
Holt, William VI, 934
Holt, William D. I, 399
Holt, William J. VI, 934
Holt, Zebedia VI, 826
Holten, Arthur II, 376
Holten, Elizabeth II, 376
Holten, George II, 376
Holter, Walter V, 1002
Holton, Alfred I, 436
Holton, Alfred I, 448
Holton, Arthur II, 375
Holton, Arthur II, 376
Holton, Arthur II, 538
Holton, Arthur II, 551
Holton, Celia I, 886
Holton, Celia A. I, 886
Holton, David II, 376
Holton, David II, 551
Holton, Elisabeth II, 551
Holton, Elizabeth II, 375
Holton, Elizabeth II, 376
Holton, Elizabeth II, 538
Holton, Elizabeth II, 551
Holton, Elizabeth II, 644
Holton, Estella Custis V, 684
Holton, Fannie A. I, 886
Holton, Fanny I, 886
Holton, George II, 376
Holton, George E. V, 743
Holton, Irena I, 943
Holton, James M. I, 448
Holton, James Manly I, 436
Holton, Jehu I, 886
Holton, Jesse I, 436
Holton, John II, 376
Holton, John II, 551
Holton, Kezia I, 886
Holton, Louise I, 943
Holton, Lydia II, 551
Holton, Lydia II, 681
Holton, Martha I, 448
Holton, Martha I, 449
Holton, Martha II, 376
Holton, Mary I, 436
Holton, Mary I, 448
Holton, Mary I, 449
Holton, Mary II, 376
Holton, Mary II, 551
Holton, Mary II, 558
Holton, Mary T. I, 436
Holton, Mary T. I, 448
Holton, Nancy I, 886
Holton, Nancy J. I, 448
Holton, Nancy Jane I, 436
Holton, Rachel II, 376
Holton, Rachel IV, 404
Holton, Rachel IV, 411
Holton, Samuel II, 376
Holton, Sarah II, 376
Holton, Sarah IV, 1254
Holton, Susanah I, 436
Holton, Susanah I, 448
Holton, Thomas II, 552
Holton, William II, 376
Holton, Wm. II, 551
Holtry, Elizabeth V, 1002
Holtry, Lettie V, 1002
Holtry, Lovey V, 1002
Holtry, Maggie V, 1002
Holtry, Marvin V, 1002
Holtry, Mary V, 1002
Holtry, William V, 1002
Holway, George N. V, 76
Holway, George Willet V, 76
Holway, Jane II, 370
Holway, Margaret II, 370
Holway, Maria V, 76
Holway, Maria A. V, 76
Holway, Thos. II, 370
Holwell, John D. V, 1002
Holy, Emma V, 1001
Holy, Jno. W. VI, 899
Homan, Aaron V, 743
Homan, Betsy V, 743
Homan, Edward H. IV, 1254
Homan, Jane V, 743
Homan, Lucinda V, 626
Homan, Mark VI, 934
Homan, Mary IV, 1254
Homan, Matthew VI, 934
Homan, Mrs. J. F. IV, 1321
Homan, Nancy VI, 934
Homan, Patty VI, 934
Homan, Ralph VI, 879
Homan, William Jacob V, 402
Hombray, Joseph II, 552
Homel, Mary Nan V, 1002
Homel, Sarah V, 1002
Homer, Elizabeth V, 179
Homer, Hester II, 1002
Homer, Hester II, 1009
Homer, Jacob V, 95
Homer, Lydia V, 95
Homer, Maria V, 1002
Homer, Walker V, 179
Homes, Amasa W. VI, 934
Homes, Archibald I, 195
Homes, Edith I, 713
Homes, Edith I, 721
Homes, Emily VI, 934
Homes, George VI, 934
Homes, Hannah VI, 314
Homes, Jas. VI, 934
Homes, Margaret VI, 502
Homes, Polly VI, 934
Homes, Sarah VI, 314
Homes, Sarah VI, 508
Homey, Edna V, 1002
Hommedien, Charlotte L. III, 170
Honacre, Eleanor VI, 363
Honacre, Eleanor VI, 403
Honeycrout, Mary II, 552
Honeycrout, Mary II, 667
Honeycut, Mary V, 402
Honeycutt, D. M. I, 624
Honeycutt, Deborah IV, 149
Honeycutt, John P. V, 474
Honeycutt, John P. V, 503
Honeycutt, Mary J. I, 624
Honeycutt, Miriam IV, 149
Honeycutt, Ovella I, 624
Honeycutt, Sarah IV, 149
Honeycutt, Susannah V, 474
Honeycutt, Susannah V, 503
Honeycutt, Susannah H. V, 503
Honeycutt, Thomas IV, 149
Honeyman, Callie V, 743
Honeyman, Iris V, 743
Honeyman, Margaret V, 743
Honeyman, Ralph V, 743
Honeyman, Richard V, 743
Honeywell, Phebe III, 170
Honeywell, Wd. James III, 170
Honlacher, Florence Haycock V, 179
Honstett, Adam V, 684
Honycut, Thomas I, 400
Hood, Abigail II, 376
Hood, Abigail II, 679
Hood, Abram II, 376
Hood, Adelaide V. II, 877
Hood, Adelaide Y. II, 800
Hood, Alexander VI, 826
Hood, Ann II, 376
Hood, Anney VI, 807
Hood, Brinton II, 801
Hood, Brinton II, 877
Hood, C. Walton II, 800
Hood, Carrie I, 337
Hood, Chalkley Walton II, 877
Hood, Channing II, 801
Hood, Channing II, 877
Hood, Charles Wesley IV, 477
Hood, Christian F. VI, 821
Hood, Deborah II, 552
Hood, Deborah II, 566
Hood, Edward I, 337
Hood, Eliza A. VI, 840
Hood, Elizabeth II, 376
Hood, Elizabeth II, 552
Hood, Elizabeth II, 575
Hood, Elizabeth III, 310
Hood, Elizabeth VI, 840
Hood, Florence B. II, 877
Hood, Florence V. II, 801

Hood, Hannah May II, 877
Hood, Hannah May II, 903
Hood, Hobson VI, 821
Hood, Hobson VI, 866
Hood, James II, 552
Hood, James II, 800
Hood, James II, 877
Hood, Jane VI, 826
Hood, John II, 376
Hood, John II, 552
Hood, John II, 558
Hood, John II, 656
Hood, John VI, 357
Hood, John VI, 807
Hood, John VI, 826
Hood, John, Sr. II, 376
Hood, Jonathan II, 376
Hood, Jonathan II, 552
Hood, Joseph II, 376
Hood, Joseph II, 473
Hood, Joseph II, 552
Hood, Joseph II, 875
Hood, Joseph II, 877
Hood, Joseph W. II, 800
Hood, Joseph W. II, 877
Hood, Lamartine II, 877
Hood, Lamertine II, 800
Hood, Lamertine II, 877
Hood, Lucy VI, 826
Hood, Margaret II, 800
Hood, Margaret A. II, 875
Hood, Margaret A. II, 877
Hood, Margaret Ann II, 877
Hood, Martha II, 552
Hood, Mary II, 376
Hood, Mary II, 487
Hood, Mary II, 552
Hood, Mary II, 558
Hood, Mary II, 656
Hood, Mary E. VI, 826
Hood, Mary Ella II, 877
Hood, Mrs. Louella V, 743
Hood, Murial I, 337
Hood, Nancy VI, 826
Hood, Nathaniel H. VI, 826
Hood, Philena Belle II, 800
Hood, Philena Belle II, 877
Hood, Philena C. II, 800
Hood, Polly VI, 826
Hood, Rebecca II, 376
Hood, Rebecca II, 507
Hood, Rebecca II, 552
Hood, Rebecca II, 651
Hood, Rebecca B. II, 875
Hood, Rebecca B. II, 877
Hood, Richard VI, 826
Hood, Ruth L. II, 800
Hood, Ruth L. II, 877
Hood, Samuel II, 552
Hood, Samuel II, 558
Hood, Sarah II, 198
Hood, Sarah II, 233
Hood, Sarah II, 376
Hood, Sarah II, 454
Hood, Sarah II, 473
Hood, Sarah II, 543
Hood, Sarah II, 552
Hood, Sarah VI, 866
Hood, Seymour II, 552
Hood, Thomas II, 198
Hood, Thomas II, 233
Hood, Thomas II, 376
Hood, Thomas II, 487
Hood, Thomas II, 552
Hood, Thos. II, 800
Hood, Wd. Abigail II, 552
Hood, William II, 376
Hood, William VI, 826
Hood, William B. VI, 821
Hood, Willie I, 337
Hood, Wilson B. VI, 840
Hood, Wm. II, 552
Hood, Wm. R. II, 877
Hoods, Joseph II, 376
Hoodt, Caspar II, 376
Hoodt, Caspar II, 491
Hoodt, Caspar II, 552
Hoodt, Daniel II, 376
Hoodt, Daniel II, 552
Hoodt, Daniel II, 610
Hoodt, Daniell II, 376
Hoodt, Deborah II, 552
Hoodt, Elisabeth II, 552
Hoodt, Elisabeth II, 670
Hoodt, Esther II, 552
Hoodt, Esther II, 610
Hoodt, Esther, Jr. II, 376
Hoodt, Hester II, 376
Hoodt, Joseph II, 376
Hoodt, Mary II, 549
Hoodt, Mary II, 552
Hoodt, Mary II, 653
Hoodt, Sarah II, 376
Hoodt, Sarah II, 454
Hoodt, Sarah II, 491
Hoodt, Sarah II, 552
Hoodt, Thomas II, 376
Hoodt, Thomas II, 454
Hoodt, Thomas II, 552
Hoof, Charles Rapley VI, 749
Hoof, Charles Rapley VI, 753
Hoof, Eliza Maria VI, 749
Hoof, Janney VI, 749
Hoof, Lewis VI, 749
Hoof, Mary VI, 749
Hoof, Rebecca VI, 749
Hoof, Rebecca VI, 753
Hoofman, Sarah II, 375
Hoofman, Sarah V, 73
Hoogland, Caroline III, 167
Hoogland, Elbert III, 420
Hoogland, Elbert III, 450
Hoogland, Maria III, 420
Hoogland, Maria III, 450
Hoogland, Willemptje III, 420
Hoogland, Willemptje III, 450
Hook, Ann IV, 34
Hook, Ann IV, 39
Hook, Betty VI, 934
Hook, Caroline Revelle V, 576
Hook, Cidna C. IV, 940
Hook, Cidna C. IV, 966
Hook, Dorothy Evonne V, 576
Hook, Earl V, 576
Hook, Esther V, 576
Hook, Frank V, 576
Hook, Frank, Jr. V, 576
Hook, Harold V, 576
Hook, I. C. V, 402
Hook, Israel C. V, 402
Hook, John VI, 870
Hook, John VI, 934
Hook, John VI, 955
Hook, John Melville V, 576
Hook, Lewis V, 1002
Hook, Lucile V, 576
Hook, Markors II, 207
Hook, Martha Maria VI, 934
Hook, Mary Elizabeth V, 576
Hook, Nancie Jane V, 1002
Hook, Nancy J. V, 1002
Hook, Nellie L. V, 576
Hook, Nellie Revelle V, 576
Hook, R. Wilkinson VI, 934
Hook, Rease V, 1002
Hook, Reece V, 1002
Hook, Robert VI, 934
Hook, Stephen VI, 931
Hook, Susanna VI, 934
Hook, William, Sr. VI, 934
Hooker, Edward I, 1032
Hooker, Edward I Sup 1, 11
Hooker, Hannah I, 1032
Hooker, Hannah VI, 509
Hooker, John I, 1032
Hooker, Judith I, 1032
Hooker, Mary I, 1032
Hooker, Thomas VI, 509
Hooker, Uriah VI, 948
Hooker, William I, 1032
Hookes, Elise VI, 7
Hookes, Elizabeth I, 289
Hookes, Ruffin I, 289
Hookes, William L. I, 289
Hooks, Aileen I, 635
Hooks, Alice I, 635
Hooks, Allen I, 625
Hooks, Amanda M. I, 305
Hooks, Amanda M. I, 309
Hooks, Bernice I, 635
Hooks, Bernice Bonnilyn I, 619
Hooks, Bernice Newman I, 627
Hooks, Elizabeth I, 309
Hooks, Herbert I, 337
Hooks, J. C. I, 309
Hooks, James E. I, 309
Hooks, James O. I, 309
Hooks, Julia I, 619
Hooks, Julia I, 625
Hooks, Julia I, 627
Hooks, Julia H. I, 620
Hooks, Julia Hodgin I, 635
Hooks, Lillie I, 631
Hooks, Lillie I, 635
Hooks, Lillie Hunter I, 619
Hooks, Lizzie I, 309
Hooks, Mary I, 337
Hooks, Nellie I, 635
Hooks, Vera I, 635
Hooks, Vera Louella I, 619
Hooks, Vera Luella I, 620
Hooks, W. G. I, 620
Hooks, William I, 309
Hooks, William G. I, 619
Hooks, William G. I, 627
Hooks, William R. I, 309
Hooks, Wm. G. I, 625
Hoole, Chas. VI, 911
Hoole, David VI, 911
Hoole, Jonah VI, 933
Hoole, Nancy VI, 933
Hoole, Rebeckah VI, 911
Hoolt, Spradley VI, 917
Hoop, Bell V, 684
Hoop, Eleanor II, 1002
Hoop, Elizabeth D. II, 746
Hoop, George M. II, 746
Hoop, Isabella II, 552
Hoop, Isabella II, 681
Hoop, Marie J. V, 684
Hoop, Shirley Maude V, 684
Hoop, Shirley Maude V, 716
Hoop, Zora V, 684
Hoopas, Calvin C. V, 1002
Hoope, John II, 552
Hooper, Abraham II, 376
Hooper, Abraham II, 444
Hooper, Anna II, 901
Hooper, Clarence IV, 224
Hooper, Clyde IV, 224
Hooper, Edward II, 901
Hooper, Ella Viola IV, 224
Hooper, Elmir H. IV, 224
Hooper, Emma IV, 224
Hooper, Euphemia IV, 477
Hooper, Euphemia F. IV, 224
Hooper, Isaac II, 444
Hooper, Isaac T. II, 901
Hooper, John IV, 477
Hooper, John B. IV, 477
Hooper, John E. IV, 477
Hooper, Kate IV, 477
Hooper, Lillie May IV, 477
Hooper, Mary May IV, 224
Hooper, Minnie IV, 477
Hooper, Olive IV, 477
Hooper, Pearl Euphemia IV, 224
Hooper, Phillis II, 376
Hooper, Phillis II, 444
Hooper, Sarah II, 901
Hooper, Sarah IV, 477
Hoopes, Aaron II, 548
Hoopes, Aaron II, 552
Hoopes, Abigail II, 822
Hoopes, Abigail II, 1022
Hoopes, Abigail IV, 825
Hoopes, Abigail IV, 857
Hoopes, Abner II, 877
Hoopes, Abner II, 891
Hoopes, Abner IV, 918
Hoopes, Abner, Jr. II, 877
Hoopes, Albert IV, 966
Hoopes, Albert IV, 967
Hoopes, Albert J. IV, 966
Hoopes, Albert William VI, 657
Hoopes, Albert Wm. VI, 618
Hoopes, Albert Wm. VI, 619
Hoopes, Alfaretta IV, 825
Hoopes, Alfred II, 801
Hoopes, Alfred II, 877
Hoopes, Alfred IV, 966
Hoopes, Alfred IV, 967
Hoopes, Amy A. II, 877
Hoopes, Amy Ann II, 801
Hoopes, Ann II, 548
Hoopes, Ann II, 552
Hoopes, Ann II, 801
Hoopes, Ann II, 877
Hoopes, Ann II, 942
Hoopes, Ann IV, 273
Hoopes, Ann IV, 304
Hoopes, Ann IV, 681
Hoopes, Ann IV, 724
Hoopes, Ann Jr. IV, 681
Hoopes, Ann, Jr. IV, 724
Hoopes, Anna IV, 558
Hoopes, Anna L. IV, 918
Hoopes, Anna Mary II, 788
Hoopes, Anna T. II, 877
Hoopes, Annie IV, 676
Hoopes, Annie IV, 724
Hoopes, Arlan Walter IV, 966
Hoopes, Arthur IV, 918
Hoopes, Arwilda IV, 966
Hoopes, B. Tevis II, 877
Hoopes, Barton II, 801
Hoopes, Barton II, 877
Hoopes, Barton II, 901
Hoopes, Barton, Jr. II, 877
Hoopes, Barton, Jr. II, 901
Hoopes, Benjamin II, 708
Hoopes, Benjamin II, 746
Hoopes, Benjamin P. II, 177
Hoopes, Benjamin P. II, 292
Hoopes, Benjamin P. II, 708
Hoopes, Benjamin P. II, 746
Hoopes, Blanch IV, 967
Hoopes, Blanch Briggs IV, 724
Hoopes, Blanche IV, 966
Hoopes, Byron IV, 967
Hoopes, Byron R. IV, 966
Hoopes, Caleb II, 708
Hoopes, Carrie Lucile IV, 966
Hoopes, Charity IV, 825
Hoopes, Charity IV, 829
Hoopes, Charity IV, 966
Hoopes, Charity IV, 967
Hoopes, Charity Elizabeth IV, 967
Hoopes, Clara IV, 918
Hoopes, Clarence IV, 966
Hoopes, Clarence B. IV, 966
Hoopes, Clarence B. IV, 967
Hoopes, Clarence Lee IV, 966
Hoopes, Clement R. II, 877
Hoopes, Cora IV, 918
Hoopes, Cynthia IV, 636
Hoopes, Daniel II, 1002
Hoopes, Daniel II, 1035
Hoopes, Daniel IV, 304
Hoopes, Daniel IV, 825
Hoopes, David II, 552
Hoopes, David II, 801
Hoopes, David II, 877
Hoopes, David II, 942
Hoopes, Dawson II, 877
Hoopes, Dawson II, 879
Hoopes, Debby IV, 588
Hoopes, Donald Julian IV, 966
Hoopes, Doris Naomi IV, 966
Hoopes, Edith B. II, 877
Hoopes, Edward II, 801
Hoopes, Edward II, 877
Hoopes, Edward II, 942
Hoopes, Edward IV, 636
Hoopes, Edward IV, 918
Hoopes, Eleanor II, 1002
Hoopes, Elizabeth IV, 303
Hoopes, Elizabeth IV, 806
Hoopes, Elizabeth IV, 825
Hoopes, Elizabeth IV, 857
Hoopes, Elizabeth IV, 966
Hoopes, Elizabeth IV, 1063
Hoopes, Elizabeth C. IV, 825
Hoopes, Elizabeth Jane IV, 825
Hoopes, Elizabeth Steele II, 795
Hoopes, Elizabeth, Jr. IV, 1063
Hoopes, Ellen IV, 649
Hoopes, Ellen C. IV, 636
Hoopes, Ellen C. IV, 649
Hoopes, Elma II, 877
Hoopes, Elsie IV, 918
Hoopes, Elsie Grace IV, 966
Hoopes, Elsie Myra IV, 966
Hoopes, Emelina IV, 825
Hoopes, Emelina IV, 849
Hoopes, Emma IV, 924
Hoopes, Emma IV, 966
Hoopes, Emma V. IV, 966
Hoopes, Emma V. IV, 967
Hoopes, Erving T. IV, 967
Hoopes, Esther IV, 924
Hoopes, Esther B. IV, 966
Hoopes, Esther B. IV, 967
Hoopes, Eva May IV, 966
Hoopes, Eva May IV, 967
Hoopes, Ezra II, 552
Hoopes, Ezra II, 877
Hoopes, Florence IV, 825
Hoopes, Floyd IV, 966
Hoopes, Francis IV, 636
Hoopes, Francis Pratt II, 822
Hoopes, Garretson IV, 825
Hoopes, George IV, 825
Hoopes, Gladys IV, 966
Hoopes, Glen Eugene IV, 966
Hoopes, Grace IV, 584
Hoopes, Granville Hoopes VI, 657
Hoopes, Gulielma M. II, 877
Hoopes, Gulielma Maria II, 801
Hoopes, Hannah II, 548
Hoopes, Hannah II, 552
Hoopes, Hannah II, 801
Hoopes, Harold IV, 966
Hoopes, Helen IV, 918
Hoopes, Helen E. II, 877
Hoopes, Helen E. II, 901
Hoopes, Helen W. II, 877
Hoopes, Helen W. II, 911
Hoopes, Herman II, 877
Hoopes, Howard II, 877
Hoopes, Howard J. IV, 918
Hoopes, Irving Leroy IV, 932
Hoopes, Irving Leroy IV, 966
Hoopes, Irving Leroy IV, 967
Hoopes, Irving Leroy IV, 1004
Hoopes, Irving T. IV, 966
Hoopes, Isaac N. IV, 637
Hoopes, Isabella II, 552
Hoopes, J. Wilmer IV, 967
Hoopes, James IV, 966
Hoopes, James C. IV, 924
Hoopes, James C. IV, 966
Hoopes, James, Jr. IV, 825
Hoopes, James, Jr. IV, 857
Hoopes, Jane II, 1002
Hoopes, Jane II, 1035
Hoopes, Jane IV, 304
Hoopes, Jane IV, 967
Hoopes, Jane G. IV, 967
Hoopes, Jasper II, 801
Hoopes, John II, 552
Hoopes, John IV, 304
Hoopes, John IV, 825
Hoopes, John IV, 1063
Hoopes, John Henry IV, 966
Hoopes, John Henry IV, 967
Hoopes, John Wilson IV, 636
Hoopes, John, Jr. II, 552
Hoopes, Joseph II, 877
Hoopes, Joseph IV, 304
Hoopes, Joseph IV, 825
Hoopes, Joseph IV, 966
Hoopes, Joseph IV, 1102
Hoopes, Joseph T. II, 877
Hoopes, Joseph T. II, 911
Hoopes, Joseph T. VI, 749
Hoopes, Joseph T. VI, 785
Hoopes, Joshua II, 552
Hoopes, Joshua II, 961
Hoopes, Joshua II, 1002
Hoopes, Joshua II, 1020
Hoopes, Joshua II, 1022
Hoopes, Judith VI, 749
Hoopes, Judith VI, 785
Hoopes, Judith P. II, 877
Hoopes, Judith P. II, 911
Hoopes, Julia L. II, 292
Hoopes, Julia T. II, 177
Hoopes, Julia T. II, 292
Hoopes, Julia T. II, 708
Hoopes, Julia T. II, 746
Hoopes, Katie E. II, 877
Hoopes, Katie E. II, 879
Hoopes, Kenneth Earl IV, 966
Hoopes, Kennett II, 292
Hoopes, Laura G. II, 877
Hoopes, Laura G. II, 942
Hoopes, Leatha Willie IV, 967
Hoopes, Lemuel IV, 825
Hoopes, Lena Irena IV, 1004
Hoopes, Leslie Willard IV, 966
Hoopes, Lester Willard IV, 967
Hoopes, Letha Wilhelmina IV, 966
Hoopes, Lewis IV, 966
Hoopes, Lewis J. IV, 966
Hoopes, Lewis J. IV, 967
Hoopes, Lewis W. IV, 800
Hoopes, Lewis W. IV, 825
Hoopes, Lewis W. IV, 927
Hoopes, Lewis W. IV, 966
Hoopes, Lewis W. IV, 967
Hoopes, Linden IV, 967
Hoopes, Louis J. IV, 966
Hoopes, Louis J. IV, 1016
Hoopes, Louis John IV, 966
Hoopes, Louis John IV, 967
Hoopes, Lucinda IV, 966
Hoopes, Lucinda IV, 967
Hoopes, Lucinda C. IV, 966
Hoopes, Lydia IV, 712
Hoopes, Lydia IV, 724
Hoopes, Lydia IV, 817
Hoopes, Lydia IV, 825
Hoopes, Lydia IV, 854
Hoopes, Lydia Ann IV, 825
Hoopes, Lydia G. IV, 724
Hoopes, Lynden Roy IV, 966
Hoopes, Malcolm IV, 967
Hoopes, Malcolm C. IV, 966
Hoopes, Malinda M. II, 877
Hoopes, Malinda M. II, 891
Hoopes, Margaret IV, 966
Hoopes, Margaret Melba IV, 967
Hoopes, Marietta IV, 966
Hoopes, Marietta IV, 967
Hoopes, Marshal B. IV, 966
Hoopes, Marshall B. IV, 967
Hoopes, Martha Parry II, 877
Hoopes, Martha Parry II, 891
Hoopes, Martha S. IV, 304
Hoopes, Mary II, 552
Hoopes, Mary II, 708
Hoopes, Mary II, 788

Hoopes, Mary II, 808
Hoopes, Mary IV, 304
Hoopes, Mary IV, 918
Hoopes, Mary IV, 966
Hoopes, Mary IV, 1016
Hoopes, Mary IV, 1089
Hoopes, Mary IV, 1102
Hoopes, Mary Ann IV, 806
Hoopes, Mary Ann IV, 825
Hoopes, Mary Eliza IV, 304
Hoopes, Mary Emma IV, 966
Hoopes, Mary Emma IV, 967
Hoopes, Mary Eva VI, 657
Hoopes, Mary J. II, 877
Hoopes, Mary Jones II, 801
Hoopes, Mary R. IV, 966
Hoopes, Mary R. IV, 967
Hoopes, Mercy IV, 1063
Hoopes, Mifflin IV, 649
Hoopes, Mildred Leora IV, 932
Hoopes, Myra IV, 967
Hoopes, Myra E. IV, 966
Hoopes, Myra E. IV, 967
Hoopes, Myrtle IV, 932
Hoopes, Myrtle IV, 1004
Hoopes, Myrtle M. IV, 918
Hoopes, Myrtle May IV, 966
Hoopes, Nathan IV, 303
Hoopes, Nathan IV, 304
Hoopes, Nathan IV, 1063
Hoopes, Neil II, 788
Hoopes, Oscar IV, 918
Hoopes, Pauline Elizabeth IV, 966
Hoopes, Pauline Elizabeth IV, 967
Hoopes, Phebe II, 708
Hoopes, Phebe IV, 800
Hoopes, Phebe IV, 825
Hoopes, Phebe IV, 857
Hoopes, Phebe IV, 973
Hoopes, Phebe Abb IV, 967
Hoopes, Phebe Ann IV, 946
Hoopes, Phebe Ann IV, 947
Hoopes, Phebe Ann IV, 966
Hoopes, Phebe Ann IV, 967
Hoopes, Phineas IV, 966
Hoopes, Phineas IV, 967
Hoopes, Rachel P. II, 177
Hoopes, Rachel P. II, 292
Hoopes, Rachel P. II, 708
Hoopes, Rachel P. II, 746
Hoopes, Rachel Trimble VI, 749
Hoopes, Rachel Trimble VI, 785
Hoopes, Rachel Trimbles VI, 786
Hoopes, Raynor IV, 966
Hoopes, Rebecca IV, 825
Hoopes, Rebecca IV, 857
Hoopes, Rebecca Mary VI, 618
Hoopes, Rebecca Mary VI, 619
Hoopes, Rebecca Mary VI, 657
Hoopes, Richard Wendell IV, 967
Hoopes, Robert IV, 825
Hoopes, Roy Linden IV, 967
Hoopes, Russel E. IV, 966
Hoopes, Russell E. IV, 967
Hoopes, Ruth Anna II, 877
Hoopes, Ruthanna II, 801
Hoopes, Ruthanna II, 877
Hoopes, Ruthanna II, 901
Hoopes, Sarah II, 552
Hoopes, Sarah II, 708
Hoopes, Sarah II, 822
Hoopes, Sarah IV, 224
Hoopes, Sarah IV, 303
Hoopes, Sarah IV, 304
Hoopes, Sarah IV, 820
Hoopes, Sarah IV, 825
Hoopes, Sarah IV, 840
Hoopes, Sarah Ann IV, 800
Hoopes, Sarah Ann IV, 825
Hoopes, Sarah Ann IV, 927
Hoopes, Sarah Ann IV, 966
Hoopes, Sarah Ann IV, 967
Hoopes, Sarah Ann IV, 1063
Hoopes, Sarah Ann IV, 1093
Hoopes, Sarah Ann IV, 1102
Hoopes, Sarah J. IV, 825
Hoopes, Sidney II, 877
Hoopes, Sidney IV, 411
Hoopes, Sidney IV, 419
Hoopes, Susan L. IV, 1000
Hoopes, Susannah IV, 804
Hoopes, Susannah IV, 825
Hoopes, Tevis II, 877
Hoopes, Thomas IV, 304
Hoopes, Thomas IV, 825
Hoopes, Thomas IV, 829
Hoopes, Thomas IV, 966
Hoopes, Thomas P. II, 746
Hoopes, Thos. II, 552
Hoopes, Vera V. IV, 966
Hoopes, Viola IV, 966
Hoopes, Viola IV, 967
Hoopes, Viola Mae IV, 966
Hoopes, Wain IV, 966
Hoopes, Walter J. IV, 967
Hoopes, Walter M. IV, 966
Hoopes, Wd. Laura II, 801
Hoopes, Wilford Carl IV, 966
Hoopes, William IV, 304
Hoopes, William IV, 966
Hoopes, William A. IV, 966
Hoopes, Wilma Marie IV, 966
Hoopes, Wilmer J. IV, 966
Hoopes, Wilmer P. II, 877
Hoopes, Wilmer P. II, 911
Hoopes, Wilmer Worthington II, 877
Hoopes, Wilmer Worthington II, 891
Hoopes, Wm. II, 877
Hoopes, Wm. IV, 681
Hoopes, Wm. IV, 825
Hoopes, Wm. IV, 857
Hoopes, Wm. A. IV, 825
Hoopes, Wm. A. IV, 966
Hoopes, Wm. A. IV, 967
Hoopes, Wm. Warner II, 877
Hoops, Abigail IV, 142
Hoops, Abigail IV, 143
Hoops, Abigail IV, 149
Hoops, Abigail IV, 824
Hoops, Abigail IV, 825
Hoops, Abner II, 877
Hoops, Albert IV, 967
Hoops, Albert J. IV, 825
Hoops, Albert J. IV, 966
Hoops, Alfaretta IV, 825
Hoops, Alfred IV, 967
Hoops, Ann IV, 208
Hoops, Ann IV, 224
Hoops, Ann IV, 637
Hoops, Ann IV, 643
Hoops, Ann IV, 824
Hoops, Ann E. IV, 143
Hoops, Ann L. IV, 636
Hoops, Annie M. IV, 825
Hoops, Arminta IV, 824
Hoops, Arminta IV, 825
Hoops, Armintha IV, 825
Hoops, Armintha IV, 834
Hoops, Blanch IV, 967
Hoops, Byron IV, 967
Hoops, Caleb IV, 143
Hoops, Caleb H. IV, 143
Hoops, Caroline IV, 636
Hoops, Caroline IV, 637
Hoops, Caroline IV, 656
Hoops, Charity IV, 824
Hoops, Charity IV, 825
Hoops, Charity IV, 928
Hoops, Charity IV, 967
Hoops, Charity E. IV, 928
Hoops, Charity Elizabeth IV, 967
Hoops, Charles IV, 143
Hoops, Charles IV, 636
Hoops, Charles IV, 637
Hoops, Clara II, 833
Hoops, Clara II, 838
Hoops, Clarence B. IV, 967
Hoops, Cynthia IV, 636
Hoops, Cynthia IV, 637
Hoops, Cynthia T. IV, 636
Hoops, Cynthia T. IV, 637
Hoops, Cynthia T. IV, 642
Hoops, Daniel IV, 824
Hoops, Daniel IV, 825
Hoops, David II, 552
Hoops, David IV, 636
Hoops, David IV, 637
Hoops, David, Jr. IV, 637
Hoops, Deborah IV, 825
Hoops, Deborah IV, 848
Hoops, Deborah W. IV, 224
Hoops, Deborah W. IV, 637
Hoops, Edward IV, 636
Hoops, Edward IV, 637
Hoops, Eleanor IV, 636
Hoops, Elias IV, 143
Hoops, Elisha IV, 824
Hoops, Elisha IV, 825
Hoops, Elizabeth IV, 206
Hoops, Elizabeth IV, 224
Hoops, Elizabeth IV, 584
Hoops, Elizabeth IV, 636
Hoops, Elizabeth IV, 637
Hoops, Elizabeth IV, 663
Hoops, Elizabeth IV, 824
Hoops, Elizabeth IV, 825
Hoops, Elizabeth IV, 868
Hoops, Elizabeth IV, 873
Hoops, Elizabeth IV, 1063
Hoops, Elizabeth IV, 1102
Hoops, Elizabeth C. IV, 825
Hoops, Elizabeth Jane IV, 825
Hoops, Elizabeth, Jr. IV, 224
Hoops, Elizabeth, Jr. IV, 1063
Hoops, Elizabeth, Jr. IV, 1102
Hoops, Ellen IV, 636
Hoops, Ellen C. IV, 614
Hoops, Ellen C. IV, 636
Hoops, Ellen C. IV, 637
Hoops, Ellis IV, 584
Hoops, Ellis, Jr. IV, 578
Hoops, Ellis, Jr. IV, 584
Hoops, Elma IV, 637
Hoops, Emaline IV, 824
Hoops, Emma V. IV, 967
Hoops, Emmaline IV, 143
Hoops, Erving T. IV, 967
Hoops, Esther IV, 40
Hoops, Esther IV, 636
Hoops, Esther IV, 637
Hoops, Esther IV, 659
Hoops, Esther IV, 825
Hoops, Esther B. IV, 967
Hoops, Evan IV, 636
Hoops, Evan IV, 637
Hoops, Florence IV, 825
Hoops, Francis IV, 636
Hoops, Francis IV, 637
Hoops, Franklin IV, 636
Hoops, Franklin IV, 637
Hoops, Garfield IV, 825
Hoops, Garretson IV, 824
Hoops, Garretson IV, 825
Hoops, George IV, 824
Hoops, George IV, 825
Hoops, George, Jr. IV, 143
Hoops, Grace IV, 578
Hoops, Grace IV, 584
Hoops, Hambleton IV, 636
Hoops, Hannah IV, 143
Hoops, Henry IV, 636
Hoops, Henry Ellen IV, 637
Hoops, Isaac IV, 40
Hoops, Isaac IV, 419
Hoops, Isaac IV, 636
Hoops, Isaac N. IV, 637
Hoops, Isabella II, 552
Hoops, Israel IV, 1254
Hoops, J. Wilmer IV, 967
Hoops, Jacob IV, 824
Hoops, James IV, 143
Hoops, James IV, 206
Hoops, James IV, 224
Hoops, James IV, 824
Hoops, James IV, 825
Hoops, James IV, 1063
Hoops, James IV, 1102
Hoops, James D. IV, 824
Hoops, James, Jr. IV, 825
Hoops, Jane IV, 143
Hoops, Jane IV, 636
Hoops, Jane IV, 824
Hoops, Jane IV, 921
Hoops, Jane IV, 967
Hoops, Jane VI, 368
Hoops, Jane VI, 403
Hoops, Jesse IV, 40
Hoops, Jesse IV, 636
Hoops, Jesse IV, 637
Hoops, Jesther IV, 873
Hoops, John IV, 40
Hoops, John IV, 224
Hoops, John IV, 824
Hoops, John IV, 825
Hoops, John IV, 1063
Hoops, John G. IV, 1063
Hoops, John Henry IV, 824
Hoops, John Henry IV, 967
Hoops, John J. IV, 824
Hoops, John R. IV, 636
Hoops, John R. IV, 637
Hoops, John Wilson IV, 636
Hoops, John, Jr. II, 552
Hoops, Joseph IV, 637
Hoops, Joseph IV, 825
Hoops, Joseph IV, 873
Hoops, Joseph IV, 1102
Hoops, Joseph L. IV, 824
Hoops, Joseph L. IV, 825
Hoops, Joseph L. IV, 850
Hoops, Joseph Leech IV, 824
Hoops, Joseph Leech IV, 825
Hoops, Joseph Leech IV, 869
Hoops, Joshua II, 552
Hoops, Joshua IV, 143
Hoops, Joshua IV, 636
Hoops, Lemuel IV, 825
Hoops, Lewes IV, 824
Hoops, Lewis IV, 636
Hoops, Lewis IV, 637
Hoops, Lewis IV, 928
Hoops, Lewis J. IV, 967
Hoops, Lewis W. IV, 825
Hoops, Lewis W. IV, 967
Hoops, Linden IV, 825
Hoops, Linden IV, 967
Hoops, Lucinda IV, 810
Hoops, Lucinda IV, 825
Hoops, Lucinda IV, 967
Hoops, Lucinda C. IV, 825
Hoops, Lucinda C. IV, 966
Hoops, Lydia IV, 636
Hoops, Lydia IV, 825
Hoops, Lydia IV, 850
Hoops, Lydia IV, 869
Hoops, Lydia IV, 873
Hoops, Lydia Ann IV, 824
Hoops, Lydia Ann IV, 825
Hoops, Lydia G. IV, 636
Hoops, Lydia G. IV, 724
Hoops, Lydia George IV, 825
Hoops, Lydia George IV, 873
Hoops, Lynden Roy IV, 966
Hoops, Malcolm IV, 967
Hoops, Malcolm C. IV, 825
Hoops, Malcolm C. IV, 966
Hoops, Marcolm IV, 825
Hoops, Margaret IV, 584
Hoops, Maria IV, 627
Hoops, Maria IV, 636
Hoops, Mariah IV, 636
Hoops, Marietta IV, 825
Hoops, Marietta IV, 966
Hoops, Marietta IV, 967
Hoops, Mary II, 552
Hoops, Mary IV, 419
Hoops, Mary IV, 615
Hoops, Mary IV, 636
Hoops, Mary IV, 637
Hoops, Mary IV, 642
Hoops, Mary IV, 643
Hoops, Mary IV, 824
Hoops, Mary IV, 825
Hoops, Mary IV, 829
Hoops, Mary IV, 1102
Hoops, Mary Ann IV, 824
Hoops, Mary Ann IV, 825
Hoops, Mary M. IV, 1102
Hoops, Mary, Sr. IV, 636
Hoops, Maryetta IV, 825
Hoops, Mercy IV, 1063
Hoops, Mercy IV, 1064
Hoops, Myra E. IV, 967
Hoops, Nathan IV, 143
Hoops, Nathan IV, 224
Hoops, Nathan IV, 1063
Hoops, Nathan IV, 1102
Hoops, Pamela IV, 637
Hoops, Pamelia IV, 636
Hoops, Phebe II, 809
Hoops, Phebe IV, 824
Hoops, Priscilla IV, 1063
Hoops, Priscilla IV, 1102
Hoops, Priscilla VI, 403
Hoops, R. Emmett IV, 637
Hoops, Rachel IV, 636
Hoops, Rebecca IV, 609
Hoops, Rebecca IV, 636
Hoops, Rebecca IV, 637
Hoops, Rebecca IV, 643
Hoops, Rebecca IV, 824
Hoops, Rebecca IV, 825
Hoops, Rebekah IV, 636
Hoops, Robert IV, 824
Hoops, Robert IV, 825
Hoops, Robert E. IV, 636
Hoops, Russell E. IV, 967
Hoops, Samuel G. IV, 636
Hoops, Samuel Lewis IV, 1102
Hoops, Sarah II, 376
Hoops, Sarah IV, 40
Hoops, Sarah IV, 224
Hoops, Sarah IV, 584
Hoops, Sarah IV, 612
Hoops, Sarah IV, 636
Hoops, Sarah IV, 637
Hoops, Sarah IV, 824
Hoops, Sarah IV, 825
Hoops, Sarah Ann IV, 224
Hoops, Sarah Ann IV, 824
Hoops, Sarah Ann IV, 825
Hoops, Sarah Ann IV, 928
Hoops, Sarah Ann IV, 967
Hoops, Sarah Ann IV, 1063
Hoops, Sarah Elma IV, 636
Hoops, Sarah J. IV, 825
Hoops, Sarahann IV, 224
Hoops, Sarahann IV, 1063
Hoops, Sidney IV, 411
Hoops, Sidney IV, 419
Hoops, Susan IV, 1102
Hoops, Susanna IV, 636
Hoops, Susanna IV, 642
Hoops, Susanna IV, 824
Hoops, Susanna IV, 825
Hoops, Susanna IV, 1102
Hoops, Susannah IV, 636
Hoops, Susannah IV, 642
Hoops, Susannah IV, 824
Hoops, Susannah IV, 825
Hoops, Thomas IV, 636
Hoops, Thomas IV, 637
Hoops, Thomas IV, 642
Hoops, Thomas IV, 643
Hoops, Thomas IV, 824
Hoops, Thomas IV, 825
Hoops, Thomas IV, 1063
Hoops, Thomas IV, 1102
Hoops, Thomas Barby IV, 824
Hoops, Viola IV, 967
Hoops, Walter IV, 825
Hoops, Walter J. IV, 967
Hoops, Walter M. IV, 825
Hoops, Walter M. IV, 966
Hoops, William IV, 824
Hoops, Wilson IV, 40
Hoops, Wilson IV, 637
Hoops, Wm. IV, 825
Hoops, Wm. IV, 928
Hoops, Wm. A. IV, 825
Hoops, Wm. A. IV, 966
Hoops, Wm. A. IV, 967
Hoops, Wm. P. IV, 636
Hoorine, Mattie V, 744
Hoot, Caspar II, 376
Hoot, Catharine II, 376
Hoot, Elizabeth II, 376
Hoot, Elizabeth II, 552
Hoot, Jacob II, 376
Hooten, Ann II, 553
Hooten, Benjamin II, 376
Hooten, Cressa Mildred V, 684
Hooten, Cressie Mildred V, 576
Hooten, Cressie Mildred V, 684
Hooten, Elisabeth II, 658
Hooten, Elizabeth II, 376
Hooten, Elizabeth II, 553
Hooten, Elizabeth II, 641
Hooten, Elizabeth VI, 6
Hooten, Ellen V, 684
Hooten, Esther II, 376
Hooten, Hannah II, 376
Hooten, James II, 552
Hooten, John II, 376
Hooten, Joseph II, 376
Hooten, Joseph VI, 181
Hooten, Lydia II, 552
Hooten, Margaret V, 576
Hooten, Margrett II, 376
Hooten, Martha II, 553
Hooten, Mary II, 376
Hooten, Priscilla Ann II, 553
Hooten, Priscilla Ann II, 746
Hooten, Rebecca II, 376
Hooten, Samuel VI, 181
Hooten, Samuel C. VI, 181
Hooten, Sarah II, 376
Hooten, Sarah II, 553
Hooten, Stephen II, 376
Hooten, Susanna II, 376
Hooten, Thomas II, 376
Hooten, Thomas, Jr. II, 552
Hooten, Thomas, Jr. II, 658
Hootin, Cressie Mildred V, 664
Hooton, ??? III, 420
Hooton, ??? III, 429
Hooton, Ann II, 553
Hooton, Ann C. II, 708
Hooton, Ann C. II, 746
Hooton, Benj. II, 497
Hooton, Benj. II, 552
Hooton, Benj. II, 670
Hooton, Benjamin II, 498
Hooton, Benjamin II, 546
Hooton, Benjamin II, 552
Hooton, Benjamin II, 553
Hooton, Benjamin II, 678
Hooton, Benjamin Head II, 233
Hooton, Benjamin Head II, 552
Hooton, Eliza II, 351
Hooton, Elizabeth II, 233
Hooton, Elizabeth II, 376
Hooton, Elizabeth II, 552
Hooton, Elizabeth II, 553
Hooton, Esther II, 233
Hooton, Esther II, 553
Hooton, Hannah II, 233
Hooton, Hannah II, 274
Hooton, Hannah II, 376
Hooton, Hannah II, 497
Hooton, Hannah II, 498

Hooton, Hannah II, 546
Hooton, Hannah II, 552
Hooton, Hannah II, 670
Hooton, Hannah II, 678
Hooton, James II, 552
Hooton, Jane II, 233
Hooton, Jane II, 552
Hooton, John II, 233
Hooton, John II, 274
Hooton, John II, 498
Hooton, John II, 552
Hooton, Joseph II, 233
Hooton, Joseph II, 552
Hooton, Lydia II, 552
Hooton, Martha II, 552
Hooton, Martha II, 553
Hooton, Martha II, 678
Hooton, Martha II, 708
Hooton, Mary II, 233
Hooton, Mary II, 552
Hooton, Priscilla Ann II, 553
Hooton, Priscilla Ann II, 746
Hooton, Rachel III, 420
Hooton, Rachel III, 429
Hooton, Rebecca II, 233
Hooton, Rebecca II, 552
Hooton, Robert Coe II, 233
Hooton, Robert Coe II, 552
Hooton, Samuel II, 233
Hooton, Samuel II, 552
Hooton, Samuel II, 553
Hooton, Samuel C. II, 553
Hooton, Sarah II, 351
Hooton, Sarah II, 497
Hooton, Sarah II, 552
Hooton, Sarah II, 553
Hooton, Susannah II, 552
Hooton, Susannah II, 670
Hooton, Thomas II, 546
Hooton, Thomas II, 552
Hooton, Thomas, Jr. II, 552
Hooton, Thos. II, 34
Hooton, William II, 233
Hooton, Wm. II, 553
Hooven, Jacob VI, 880
Hooven, Sarah VI, 880
Hoover, Abraham V, 744
Hoover, Absalom V, 744
Hoover, Absalom V, 774
Hoover, Aldis Joel I, 886
Hoover, Alford Marsh I, 702
Hoover, Alfred I, 722
Hoover, Alfred M. I, 702
Hoover, Alice M. V, 626
Hoover, Allen V, 744
Hoover, Alvada V, 699
Hoover, Amanda V, 626
Hoover, Amelia IV, 337
Hoover, Amelia IV, 524
Hoover, Amelia IV, 536
Hoover, Andrew I, 659
Hoover, Andrew I, 695
Hoover, Andrew I, 721
Hoover, Andrew IV, 40
Hoover, Andrew V, 17
Hoover, Andrew V, 76
Hoover, Andrew V, 744
Hoover, Andrew V, 774
Hoover, Andrew, Jr. I, 721
Hoover, Ann I, 721
Hoover, Ann I, 726
Hoover, Anna IV, 1321
Hoover, Anna K. IV, 1321
Hoover, Anna K. IV, 1322
Hoover, Anna Maria I, 886
Hoover, Arvada V, 684
Hoover, Barnabas I, 722
Hoover, Barnia I, 702
Hoover, Benajah V, 744
Hoover, Bertha Laura I, 886
Hoover, Briles I, 702
Hoover, Briles I, 722
Hoover, Caroline I, 702
Hoover, Caroline I, 721
Hoover, Caroline I, 726
Hoover, Catharine I, 702
Hoover, Catharine I, 712
Hoover, Catharine I, 721
Hoover, Catharine V, 816
Hoover, Catherine I, 722
Hoover, Catherine IV, 40
Hoover, Catherine V, 76
Hoover, Catherine V, 145
Hoover, Catherine V, 743
Hoover, Celia V, 774
Hoover, Celia Edna V, 810
Hoover, Charles Edgar V, 810
Hoover, Charles Edwin I, 886
Hoover, Chas. V, 626
Hoover, Clara V, 626
Hoover, Clara C. V, 626
Hoover, Clondy L. I, 702
Hoover, Daniel V, 764
Hoover, David I, 659
Hoover, David I, 721
Hoover, David V, 76
Hoover, Davis. J. V, 744
Hoover, Deborah V, 744
Hoover, Deborah V, 774
Hoover, Deborah V, 810
Hoover, Debrah L. I, 702
Hoover, Delilah V, 744
Hoover, Eleazar I, 702
Hoover, Eleazar I, 721
Hoover, Eleazar I, 722
Hoover, Eleazer I, 721
Hoover, Eli V, 735
Hoover, Eli V, 744
Hoover, Elizabeth I, 659
Hoover, Elizabeth I, 695
Hoover, Elizabeth I, 702
Hoover, Elizabeth I, 710
Hoover, Elizabeth I, 721
Hoover, Elizabeth I, 722
Hoover, Elizabeth I, 731
Hoover, Elizabeth I, 736
Hoover, Elizabeth I, 932
Hoover, Elizabeth IV, 40
Hoover, Elizabeth V, 76
Hoover, Elizabeth V, 743
Hoover, Elizabeth V, 744
Hoover, Elizabeth V, 755
Hoover, Elizabeth V, 810
Hoover, Elizabeth Ann I, 886
Hoover, Elizann V, 782
Hoover, Elizann V, 788
Hoover, Ella V, 626
Hoover, Ella V, 684
Hoover, Ellis S. I, 702
Hoover, Elma M. I, 702
Hoover, Elmer I, 702
Hoover, Ema Caroline V, 810
Hoover, Emma V, 626
Hoover, Emma Elizabeth V, 744
Hoover, Enos V, 744
Hoover, Enos V, 774
Hoover, Esther V, 744
Hoover, Esther V, 810
Hoover, Eunice V, 744
Hoover, F. Y. V, 810
Hoover, Flora I, 722
Hoover, Flora A. I, 702
Hoover, Florence A. V, 810
Hoover, Frank V, 626
Hoover, Franklin I, 722
Hoover, Franklin H. I, 702
Hoover, Fred V, 744
Hoover, Frederic V, 774
Hoover, Frederick I, 659
Hoover, Frederick V, 54
Hoover, Frederick V, 76
Hoover, Frederick V, 744
Hoover, Frederick V, 810
Hoover, Frederick C. V, 744
Hoover, Frederick Henry IV, 40
Hoover, George Fox I, 702
Hoover, George Fox I, 722
Hoover, George W. I, 702
Hoover, George W. I, 722
Hoover, Grover V, 699
Hoover, Grover E. V, 626
Hoover, Grover E. V, 684
Hoover, Gulielma M. I, 932
Hoover, Gulielma Maria I, 722
Hoover, Gulielma Maria I, 732
Hoover, Gulielma Mariah I, 702
Hoover, Hannah I, 717
Hoover, Hannah I, 721
Hoover, Hannah V, 764
Hoover, Harris I, 722
Hoover, Henry V, 743
Hoover, Henry V, 1002
Hoover, Henry Davis V, 744
Hoover, Hervert VI, 227
Hoover, Jacob V, 810
Hoover, Jacob T. V, 810
Hoover, James I, 721
Hoover, James V, 410
Hoover, Jane M. I, 721
Hoover, Jason V, 744
Hoover, Jesse V, 744
Hoover, Jesse V, 746
Hoover, Jesse V, 755
Hoover, Jesse Clark V, 744
Hoover, Jessie V, 626
Hoover, John I, 702
Hoover, John I, 721
Hoover, John I, 722
Hoover, John I, 932
Hoover, John IV, 40
Hoover, John V, 723
Hoover, John V, 744
Hoover, John V, 762
Hoover, John C. V, 744
Hoover, John C. V, 810
Hoover, John G. V, 744
Hoover, John T. I, 702
Hoover, John Y. I, 886
Hoover, John, Jr. I, 721
Hoover, John, Jr. V, 744
Hoover, John, Sr. V, 743
Hoover, John, Sr. V, 744
Hoover, Jonas I, 695
Hoover, Jonas I, 702
Hoover, Jonas I, 721
Hoover, Jonas, Jr. I, 721
Hoover, Joseph V, 744
Hoover, Laura Mahala V, 810
Hoover, Leah V, 410
Hoover, Leander V, 626
Hoover, Lewis Henry IV, 337
Hoover, Lewis S. V, 626
Hoover, Lorna V, 658
Hoover, Lorna V, 684
Hoover, Mahala V, 744
Hoover, Mahala V, 746
Hoover, Mahala V, 774
Hoover, Manerva Jane V, 810
Hoover, Margaret S. V, 744
Hoover, Margaret S. V, 757
Hoover, Martha IV, 322
Hoover, Martha IV, 337
Hoover, Martha V, 810
Hoover, Martha E. V, 626
Hoover, Mary I, 659
Hoover, Mary I, 721
Hoover, Mary I, 722
Hoover, Mary I, 728
Hoover, Mary I, 736
Hoover, Mary V, 626
Hoover, Mary V, 735
Hoover, Mary V, 744
Hoover, Mary V, 749
Hoover, Mary V, 755
Hoover, Mary V, 762
Hoover, Mary V, 764
Hoover, Mary V, 774
Hoover, Mary V, 780
Hoover, Mary V, 782
Hoover, Mary V, 810
Hoover, Mary V, 817
Hoover, Mary Ann V, 410
Hoover, Mary E. IV, 1321
Hoover, Mary E. V, 626
Hoover, Mary Evaline V, 810
Hoover, Mary J. I, 702
Hoover, Mary J. I, 886
Hoover, Mary J. V, 810
Hoover, Mary P. IV, 825
Hoover, Mary P. IV, 837
Hoover, Michael V, 746
Hoover, Michael Elizabeth V, 810
Hoover, Michal V, 744
Hoover, Michal V, 774
Hoover, Michal V, 810
Hoover, Milicent I, 702
Hoover, Milicent I, 721
Hoover, Millacent I, 702
Hoover, Milton V, 626
Hoover, Milton V, 684
Hoover, Nancy I, 722
Hoover, Nancy I, 731
Hoover, Nancy M. I, 702
Hoover, Noah V, 744
Hoover, Noah V, 746
Hoover, Noah V, 773
Hoover, Noah V, 774
Hoover, Noah V, 810
Hoover, Olive E. V, 744
Hoover, Olive Emeline V, 744
Hoover, Olive Mary I, 886
Hoover, Purlie B. I, 702
Hoover, Rachel I, 702
Hoover, Rachel I, 713
Hoover, Rachel I, 715
Hoover, Rachel I, 721
Hoover, Rebecca IV, 40
Hoover, Rebecca V, 76
Hoover, Rebecca V, 744
Hoover, Rebecca V, 746
Hoover, Rebecca V, 755
Hoover, Rebecca V, 794
Hoover, Rebecca Catharine V, 744
Hoover, Rebecca J. V, 744
Hoover, Rebekah I, 1116
Hoover, Rebekah I, 1122
Hoover, Rhodenia I, 702
Hoover, Romulous R. I, 702
Hoover, Ruth I, 702
Hoover, Samuel A. I, 702
Hoover, Sarah I, 702
Hoover, Sarah III, 168
Hoover, Sarah III, 170
Hoover, Sarah IV, 40
Hoover, Sarah V, 76
Hoover, Sarah V, 743
Hoover, Sarah V, 744
Hoover, Sarah V, 746
Hoover, Sarah V, 774
Hoover, Sarah V, 810
Hoover, Sarah V, 812
Hoover, Sarah Ellen V, 744
Hoover, Sarah M. I, 702
Hoover, Sarah M. I, 722
Hoover, Solomon V, 744
Hoover, Solomon V, 757
Hoover, Solomon G. V, 744
Hoover, Solomon Y. V, 744
Hoover, Susan I, 764
Hoover, Susanna I, 659
Hoover, Susanna IV, 40
Hoover, Susannah I, 764
Hoover, Susannah V, 76
Hoover, Susannah V, 144
Hoover, Susannah V, 743
Hoover, Susannah J. I, 749
Hoover, Tamar V, 54
Hoover, Tamar V, 76
Hoover, Thomas I, 722
Hoover, Thomas I, 749
Hoover, Thomas I, 764
Hoover, Thomas IV, 1282
Hoover, William Arthur V, 744
Hoover, Wincie I, 722
Hoover, Winey Ann I, 702
Hoover, Winsa A. I, 702
Hoover, Wm. Arthur V, 744
Hoover, Wm. Jason V, 774
Hoover, Wm. Miles, Jr. V, 810
Hope Doeg, Alfred III, 373
Hope Doeg, Amelia III, 373
Hope Doeg, Amelia C. III, 170
Hope Doeg, Jno. III, 170
Hope Doeg, Phebe III, 170
Hope, Apharacia VI, 332
Hope, Priscilla I, 560
Hopert, Sadie L. V, 684
Hopert, Sadie S. V, 684
Hopewell, Joseph II, 376
Hopewell, Joseph II, 553
Hopewell, Sarah II, 376
Hopewell, Sarah II, 553
Hopewell, Stephen VI, 372
Hopkin, Elizabeth II, 262
Hopkin, Robert, Jr. II, 262
Hopkins, ??? V, 911
Hopkins, Abigail III, 171
Hopkins, Abraham II, 376
Hopkins, Alex. III, 409
Hopkins, Alex. III, 420
Hopkins, Alexander V, 911
Hopkins, Alfred III, 170
Hopkins, Alice II, 1085
Hopkins, Alice V, 105
Hopkins, Alice V, 911
Hopkins, Alice H. V, 912
Hopkins, Amanda P. VI, 1003
Hopkins, Amey III, 450
Hopkins, Amy III, 402
Hopkins, Amy III, 420
Hopkins, Amy III, 421
Hopkins, Amy III, 430
Hopkins, Ann II, 376
Hopkins, Ann II, 522
Hopkins, Ann II, 553
Hopkins, Ann II, 554
Hopkins, Ann II, 671
Hopkins, Ann III, 170
Hopkins, Ann III, 171
Hopkins, Ann IV, 40
Hopkins, Ann IV, 93
Hopkins, Ann IV, 112
Hopkins, Ann V, 52
Hopkins, Ann V, 76
Hopkins, Ann V, 77
Hopkins, Ann V, 883
Hopkins, Ann V, 911
Hopkins, Ann V, 912
Hopkins, Ann H. III, 325
Hopkins, Anna II, 553
Hopkins, Anna III, 325
Hopkins, Anna III, 420
Hopkins, Anna VI, 884
Hopkins, Anna Adelia III, 404
Hopkins, Anna Adelia III, 420
Hopkins, Anna Belle V, 911
Hopkins, Anna Belle V, 912
Hopkins, Anne II, 554
Hopkins, Anne III, 403
Hopkins, Anne III, 404
Hopkins, Anne III, 420
Hopkins, Anne III, 454
Hopkins, Anne IV, 40
Hopkins, Anne B. V, 77
Hopkins, Anne-Arundel II, 535
Hopkins, Anne-Arundel II, 553
Hopkins, Arthur F. VI, 935
Hopkins, Basil B. VI, 749
Hopkins, Benj, Jr. V, 912
Hopkins, Benj. V, 912
Hopkins, Benj. E. V, 912
Hopkins, Benj. W. V, 912
Hopkins, Benjamin V, 76
Hopkins, Benjamin V, 889
Hopkins, Benjamin V, 911
Hopkins, Benjamin E. V, 911
Hopkins, Betsey VI, 948
Hopkins, Betty Ann II, 310
Hopkins, Beulah V, 23
Hopkins, Beulah V, 76
Hopkins, Beulah V, 77
Hopkins, Carrie III, 170
Hopkins, Catharine II, 376
Hopkins, Catharine II, 499
Hopkins, Catharine II, 522
Hopkins, Catharine II, 553
Hopkins, Catharine II, 554
Hopkins, Catharine III, 54
Hopkins, Catharine III, 170
Hopkins, Catharine III, 171
Hopkins, Catharine III, 300
Hopkins, Charles II, 376
Hopkins, Charles V, 77
Hopkins, Charles A. V, 911
Hopkins, Charles E. II, 320
Hopkins, Charles E. II, 321
Hopkins, Charles E. II, 877
Hopkins, Charles E. II, 878
Hopkins, Charles F. III, 170
Hopkins, Charles F. V, 146
Hopkins, Charlotte VI, 1018
Hopkins, Chas. V, 912
Hopkins, Chas. E. II, 801
Hopkins, Chas. F. III, 44
Hopkins, Chas. F. III, 171
Hopkins, Chas. F. V, 903
Hopkins, Chas. F. V, 912
Hopkins, Chas. H. V, 912
Hopkins, Chas. Henderson V, 912
Hopkins, Chas. T. III, 291
Hopkins, Christiana II, 553
Hopkins, Christina II, 654
Hopkins, Clarence II, 134
Hopkins, Coles III, 420
Hopkins, Coles III, 454
Hopkins, Cornelia A. III, 413
Hopkins, Cornelia A. III, 420
Hopkins, Crisson V, 76
Hopkins, Daniel III, 170
Hopkins, Daniel III, 402
Hopkins, Daniel III, 412
Hopkins, Daniel III, 420
Hopkins, Daniel III, 421
Hopkins, Daniel III, 430
Hopkins, Daniel III, 450
Hopkins, Daniel III, 460
Hopkins, Daniel L. III, 420
Hopkins, Daniel M. III, 420
Hopkins, David II, 376
Hopkins, David V, 911
Hopkins, David VI, 509
Hopkins, David C. II, 554
Hopkins, Deborah II, 376
Hopkins, Deborah II, 522
Hopkins, Deborah II, 554
Hopkins, Deborah VI, 749
Hopkins, Dinah II, 233
Hopkins, Dinah II, 255
Hopkins, Dinah II, 267
Hopkins, Dinah III, 402
Hopkins, Dinah III, 420
Hopkins, Dora III, 409
Hopkins, Dora III, 420
Hopkins, Dora III, 446
Hopkins, Dora Flournoy III, 409
Hopkins, Dora Flournoy III, 420
Hopkins, Dorothy VI, 474
Hopkins, Ebenezer II, 350
Hopkins, Ebenezer II, 351
Hopkins, Ebenezer II, 553
Hopkins, Ebenezer V, 911
Hopkins, Edgar III, 171
Hopkins, Edith Dixon II, 801
Hopkins, Edna III, 291
Hopkins, Edna V, 912
Hopkins, Edna D. III, 170
Hopkins, Edward II, 233
Hopkins, Edward II, 235
Hopkins, Edward II, 376
Hopkins, Edward T. P. VI, 935
Hopkins, Edwin III, 170
Hopkins, Edwin III, 171
Hopkins, Edwin III, 420
Hopkins, Edwin III, 431

opkins, Edwin III, 442
opkins, Edwin III, 496
opkins, Edwin A. III, 413
opkins, Edwin A. III, 420
opkins, Edwin A. III, 421
opkins, Edwin A. III, 466
opkins, Elemer II, 553
opkins, Elisabeth II, 553
opkins, Elisha VI, 749
opkins, Elisha VI, 756
opkins, Eliza VI, 236
opkins, Eliza VI, 237
opkins, Eliza VI, 509
opkins, Eliza A. VI, 981
opkins, Elizabeth II, 233
opkins, Elizabeth II, 535
opkins, Elizabeth II, 553
opkins, Elizabeth II, 554
opkins, Elizabeth II, 557
opkins, Elizabeth II, 560
opkins, Elizabeth III, 170
opkins, Elizabeth III, 396
opkins, Elizabeth III, 420
opkins, Elizabeth III, 431
opkins, Elizabeth V, 77
opkins, Elizabeth VI, 403
opkins, Elizabeth VI, 441
opkins, Elizabeth VI, 474
opkins, Elizabeth VI, 509
opkins, Elizabeth VI, 519
opkins, Elizabeth VI, 520
opkins, Elizabeth VI, 521
opkins, Elizabeth VI, 664
opkins, Elizabeth VI, 668
opkins, Elizabeth VI, 749
opkins, Elizabeth VI, 754
opkins, Elizabeth VI, 756
opkins, Elizabeth VI, 757
opkins, Elizabeth VI, 764
opkins, Elizabeth VI, 788
opkins, Elizabeth VI, 789
opkins, Elizabeth VI, 935
opkins, Elizabeth A. II, 801
opkins, Elizabeth A. II, 878
opkins, Elizabeth B. V, 77
opkins, Elizabeth E. II, 320
opkins, Elizabeth E. II, 321
opkins, Elizabeth E. II, 327
Hopkins, Elizabeth F. VI, 948
Hopkins, Elizabeth G. II, 310
Hopkins, Elizabeth G. II, 321
Hopkins, Elizabeth G. II, 877
Hopkins, Elizabeth G. II, 878
Hopkins, Elizabeth G. II, 925
Hopkins, Elizabeth G. III, 420
Hopkins, Elizabeth Howell VI, 521
Hopkins, Elizabeth Howell VI, 749
Hopkins, Elizabeth Howell VI, 751
Hopkins, Elizabeth Howell VI, 755
Hopkins, Elizabeth Howell VI, 756
Hopkins, Elizabeth R. VI, 917
Hopkins, Elizabeth S. VI, 403
Hopkins, Ella IV, 1102
Hopkins, Ella C. II, 801
Hopkins, Ella M. IV, 1095
Hopkins, Ella M. IV, 1102
Hopkins, Elwood II, 321
Hopkins, Elwood E. II, 320
Hopkins, Elwood E. II, 877
Hopkins, Elwood E. II, 878
Hopkins, Emily V, 76
Hopkins, Emily V, 77
Hopkins, Emily V, 882
Hopkins, Emily V, 883
Hopkins, Emily Ann V, 883
Hopkins, Emily W. VI, 749
Hopkins, Emily W. VI, 772
Hopkins, Emma II, 1085
Hopkins, Emma IV, 1237
Hopkins, Esther S. II, 746
Hopkins, Ezekiel II, 553
Hopkins, Fanny VI, 948
Hopkins, Florence V, 883
Hopkins, Florence VI, 749
Hopkins, Florence VI, 772
Hopkins, Florence VI, 792
Hopkins, Frances III, 170
Hopkins, Frances III, 171
Hopkins, Frances III, 172
Hopkins, Frances E. VI, 935
Hopkins, Frances G. VI, 917
Hopkins, Frances G. VI, 935
Hopkins, Frances G. VI, 1003
Hopkins, Francis VI, 948
Hopkins, Francis VI, 1010
Hopkins, Frank C. III, 171
Hopkins, Frank Stanton II, 801
Hopkins, Franklin V, 911
Hopkins, Franklin V, 912
Hopkins, G. G. V, 912
Hopkins, Garred II, 553
Hopkins, George II, 320
Hopkins, George II, 321
Hopkins, George II, 948
Hopkins, George II, 1085
Hopkins, George III, 170
Hopkins, George III, 420
Hopkins, George III, 460
Hopkins, George V, 911
Hopkins, Georgina III, 44
Hopkins, Georgina III, 170
Hopkins, Georgina III, 171
Hopkins, Georgina III, 291
Hopkins, Georgina V, 903
Hopkins, Georgina V, 912
Hopkins, Gerard III, 170
Hopkins, Gerard III, 325
Hopkins, Gerard VI, 403
Hopkins, Gerard VI, 474
Hopkins, Gerard VI, 509
Hopkins, Gerrard II, 535
Hopkins, Gerrard VI, 403
Hopkins, Gerrard, Jr. II, 553
Hopkins, Hannah II, 376
Hopkins, Hannah II, 553
Hopkins, Hannah II, 560
Hopkins, Hannah II, 689
Hopkins, Hannah II, 1085
Hopkins, Hannah III, 171
Hopkins, Hannah III, 300
Hopkins, Hannah V, 21
Hopkins, Hannah V, 76
Hopkins, Hannah V, 77
Hopkins, Hannah V, 140
Hopkins, Hannah V, 402
Hopkins, Hannah V, 432
Hopkins, Hannah V, 883
Hopkins, Hannah VI, 403
Hopkins, Hannah VI, 509
Hopkins, Hannah VI, 519
Hopkins, Hannah VI, 521
Hopkins, Hannah VI, 749
Hopkins, Hannah VI, 750
Hopkins, Hannah VI, 755
Hopkins, Hannah VI, 756
Hopkins, Hannah VI, 757
Hopkins, Hannah VI, 758
Hopkins, Hannah E. II, 1085
Hopkins, Hannah Howell VI, 521
Hopkins, Hannah Howell VI, 749
Hopkins, Hannah L. V, 77
Hopkins, Hannah M. II, 1088
Hopkins, Hannah S. V, 76
Hopkins, Hannah W. V, 77
Hopkins, Harriet B. VI, 878
Hopkins, Hazel IV, 971
Hopkins, Hazel Jones IV, 967
Hopkins, Helen II, 884
Hopkins, Helen III, 21
Hopkins, Helen A. II, 310
Hopkins, Helen A. II, 321
Hopkins, Helen A. II, 878
Hopkins, Helen Elizabeth II, 132
Hopkins, Helen Lee II, 878
Hopkins, Helen Lee II, 884
Hopkins, Henry II, 267
Hopkins, Henry W. V, 744
Hopkins, Hester B. V, 77
Hopkins, Hettie A. II, 878
Hopkins, Hettie A. II, 925
Hopkins, Hettie Ann II, 784
Hopkins, Hettie Ann II, 801
Hopkins, Hetty II, 321
Hopkins, Hetty A. II, 320
Hopkins, Hetty A. II, 321
Hopkins, Hetty A. II, 801
Hopkins, Hetty A. II, 878
Hopkins, Hetty A. II, 884
Hopkins, Hetty Ann II, 310
Hopkins, Hetty Ann II, 321
Hopkins, Hetty Ann II, 801
Hopkins, Hetty Ann II, 877
Hopkins, Hezekiah V, 76
Hopkins, Hezekiah V, 77
Hopkins, Hiram VI, 935
Hopkins, Horace IV, 1369
Hopkins, Horace V, 76
Hopkins, Horace V, 77
Hopkins, Horace V, 146
Hopkins, Horace V, 883
Hopkins, Horace L. V, 77
Hopkins, Howell II, 554
Hopkins, Ichabod III, 420
Hopkins, Isaac II, 233
Hopkins, Isaac II, 255
Hopkins, Isaac II, 376
Hopkins, Isaac II, 553
Hopkins, Isaac F. II, 878
Hopkins, Isaac Francis II, 310
Hopkins, Isaac Francis II, 321
Hopkins, Isaac Francis II, 801
Hopkins, Isaac Francis II, 878
Hopkins, Isaac Francis II, 884
Hopkins, Isaac R. III, 171
Hopkins, Isaiah VI, 749
Hopkins, James II, 376
Hopkins, James II, 553
Hopkins, James V, 77
Hopkins, James VI, 935
Hopkins, James Dixon II, 801
Hopkins, James H. VI, 808
Hopkins, James H. VI, 935
Hopkins, James S. VI, 935
Hopkins, James T. VI, 935
Hopkins, James W. V, 76
Hopkins, James W. V, 883
Hopkins, James Williamson II, 134
Hopkins, Jane III, 171
Hopkins, Jennie V, 744
Hopkins, Jesse V, 107
Hopkins, Jesse Fremont V, 912
Hopkins, Jesse L. VI, 1022
Hopkins, Jesse M. II, 1085
Hopkins, Jesse T. VI, 935
Hopkins, Jessie F. V, 911
Hopkins, John I, 1032
Hopkins, John II, 553
Hopkins, John II, 554
Hopkins, John II, 1085
Hopkins, John II, 1088
Hopkins, John III, 171
Hopkins, John IV, 1102
Hopkins, John VI, 169
Hopkins, John VI, 174
Hopkins, John VI, 175
Hopkins, John VI, 181
Hopkins, John VI, 187
Hopkins, John VI, 474
Hopkins, John VI, 749
Hopkins, John VI, 935
Hopkins, John VI, 952
Hopkins, John C. VI, 935
Hopkins, John Chandlee III, 171
Hopkins, John E. V, 912
Hopkins, John Estaugh V, 911
Hopkins, John L. VI, 509
Hopkins, John M. II, 553
Hopkins, John O. VI, 935
Hopkins, John O. VI, 948
Hopkins, John, Jr. II, 554
Hopkins, Johns II, 553
Hopkins, Johns VI, 509
Hopkins, Johns VI, 519
Hopkins, Johns VI, 520
Hopkins, Johns VI, 521
Hopkins, Johns VI, 749
Hopkins, Johns VI, 756
Hopkins, Johns, Jr. II, 553
Hopkins, Jonathan V, 76
Hopkins, Jonathan V, 77
Hopkins, Jonathan C. V, 77
Hopkins, Jonathan C. V, 883
Hopkins, Joseph II, 376
Hopkins, Joseph II, 535
Hopkins, Joseph II, 553
Hopkins, Joseph II, 554
Hopkins, Joseph III, 54
Hopkins, Joseph III, 171
Hopkins, Joseph V, 45
Hopkins, Joseph V, 76
Hopkins, Joseph V, 77
Hopkins, Joseph V, 883
Hopkins, Joseph VI, 441
Hopkins, Joseph J. VI, 403
Hopkins, Joseph Janney VI, 509
Hopkins, Joseph Richardson II, 554
Hopkins, Joseph S. VI, 403
Hopkins, Julia II, 784
Hopkins, Julia G. III, 420
Hopkins, Julia G. III, 466
Hopkins, Katharine II, 553
Hopkins, Laura Jane III, 171
Hopkins, Lawrence III, 171
Hopkins, Lawrence H. VI, 749
Hopkins, Lawrence H. VI, 772
Hopkins, Leornard III, 171
Hopkins, Lewis VI, 403
Hopkins, Lillie Setty V, 248
Hopkins, Lot III, 171
Hopkins, Louisa III, 420
Hopkins, Lucy I, 615
Hopkins, Lucy E. VI, 935
Hopkins, Lydia II, 1085
Hopkins, Lydia V, 76
Hopkins, Lydia V, 912
Hopkins, Lydia V, 913
Hopkins, Lydia A. IV, 1038
Hopkins, Lydia Ann IV, 967
Hopkins, Lydia R. V, 912
Hopkins, Lydia Roach V, 911
Hopkins, M. Virginia II, 877
Hopkins, Mahlon VI, 509
Hopkins, Margaret II, 233
Hopkins, Margaret II, 255
Hopkins, Margaret II, 376
Hopkins, Margaret II, 501
Hopkins, Margaret II, 502
Hopkins, Margaret II, 553
Hopkins, Margaret VI, 509
Hopkins, Margaret VI, 756
Hopkins, Margaret VI, 787
Hopkins, Margaret D. VI, 796
Hopkins, Margaret D. VI, 872
Hopkins, Maria L. VI, 1014
Hopkins, Maria M. VI, 935
Hopkins, Martha I, 382
Hopkins, Martha I, 399
Hopkins, Martha II, 321
Hopkins, Martha III, 408
Hopkins, Martha IV, 1102
Hopkins, Martha V, 76
Hopkins, Martha V, 248
Hopkins, Martha V, 272
Hopkins, Martha J. VI, 917
Hopkins, Martha M. II, 320
Hopkins, Martha M. II, 877
Hopkins, Martha V. II, 320
Hopkins, Martha Van Winkle V, 248
Hopkins, Mary II, 233
Hopkins, Mary II, 235
Hopkins, Mary II, 351
Hopkins, Mary II, 376
Hopkins, Mary II, 553
Hopkins, Mary II, 563
Hopkins, Mary II, 595
Hopkins, Mary III, 171
Hopkins, Mary III, 410
Hopkins, Mary III, 420
Hopkins, Mary III, 421
Hopkins, Mary III, 442
Hopkins, Mary III, 460
Hopkins, Mary III, 496
Hopkins, Mary V, 76
Hopkins, Mary V, 912
Hopkins, Mary VI, 509
Hopkins, Mary VI, 749
Hopkins, Mary VI, 755
Hopkins, Mary VI, 807
Hopkins, Mary VI, 981
Hopkins, Mary A. III, 420
Hopkins, Mary A. III, 442
Hopkins, Mary A. V, 912
Hopkins, Mary Ann III, 420
Hopkins, Mary Ann V, 77
Hopkins, Mary Ann V, 119
Hopkins, Mary Atmore III, 496
Hopkins, Mary B. II, 801
Hopkins, Mary Catherine V, 77
Hopkins, Mary Cresson V, 911
Hopkins, Mary Eliza V, 911
Hopkins, Mary Eliza V, 912
Hopkins, Mary H. III, 420
Hopkins, Mary H. III, 431
Hopkins, Mary H. III, 466
Hopkins, Mary Hall II, 134
Hopkins, Mary J. VI, 958
Hopkins, Mary L. E. VI, 975
Hopkins, Mary M. V, 883
Hopkins, Mary O. VI, 1001
Hopkins, Mary P. IV, 1212
Hopkins, Mary W. III, 420
Hopkins, Mary W. III, 451
Hopkins, Mary W. V, 45
Hopkins, Mary W. V, 76
Hopkins, Mary W. V, 77
Hopkins, Mary W. V, 883
Hopkins, Mary W. V, 888
Hopkins, Merrill Clark III, 170
Hopkins, Milly VI, 935
Hopkins, Milton III, 420
Hopkins, Milton F. VI, 935
Hopkins, Milton F. VI, 1018
Hopkins, Miriam V, 912
Hopkins, Miriam D. III, 170
Hopkins, Nancy VI, 935
Hopkins, Neill VI, 403
Hopkins, Nicholas II, 376
Hopkins, Nicholas II, 554
Hopkins, Pamelia VI, 935
Hopkins, Parker V, 76
Hopkins, Patsey VI, 1010
Hopkins, Persis II, 1085
Hopkins, Phebe III, 171
Hopkins, Phebe III, 412
Hopkins, Phebe III, 420
Hopkins, Philip II, 553
Hopkins, Philip VI, 509
Hopkins, Philip VI, 749
Hopkins, Philip VI, 755
Hopkins, Pine III, 171
Hopkins, Polly VI, 826
Hopkins, Polly VI, 935
Hopkins, Price VI, 884
Hopkins, Price VI, 917
Hopkins, Price VI, 935
Hopkins, Price VI, 1010
Hopkins, Price W. VI, 1003
Hopkins, Pricilla V, 77
Hopkins, Priscilla V, 76
Hopkins, Priscilla V, 503
Hopkins, Prisilla V, 77
Hopkins, Rachel II, 376
Hopkins, Rachel III, 420
Hopkins, Rachel III, 460
Hopkins, Rachel V, 912
Hopkins, Rachel A. V, 905
Hopkins, Rachel A. V, 912
Hopkins, Rachel H. V, 77
Hopkins, Raper II, 553
Hopkins, Rebecca II, 132
Hopkins, Rebecca II, 376
Hopkins, Rebecca II, 499
Hopkins, Rebecca II, 522
Hopkins, Rebecca II, 553
Hopkins, Rebecca II, 554
Hopkins, Rebecca II, 614
Hopkins, Rebecca II, 708
Hopkins, Rebecca III, 44
Hopkins, Rebecca III, 170
Hopkins, Rebecca III, 171
Hopkins, Rebecca V, 76
Hopkins, Rebecca V, 911
Hopkins, Rebecca V, 912
Hopkins, Rebecca, Sr. V, 912
Hopkins, Reid VI, 23
Hopkins, Richard II, 376
Hopkins, Richard II, 499
Hopkins, Richard II, 522
Hopkins, Richard II, 553
Hopkins, Richard II, 554
Hopkins, Richard II, 614
Hopkins, Richard III, 171
Hopkins, Richard V, 76
Hopkins, Richard V, 77
Hopkins, Richard V, 140
Hopkins, Richard V, 883
Hopkins, Richard S. VI, 749
Hopkins, Richard, Jr. II, 553
Hopkins, Rickard V, 77
Hopkins, Ried VI, 30
Hopkins, Robert II, 233
Hopkins, Robert II, 255
Hopkins, Robert II, 267
Hopkins, Robert II, 376
Hopkins, Robert II, 444
Hopkins, Robert II, 529
Hopkins, Robert II, 553
Hopkins, Robert G. II, 310
Hopkins, Robert G. II, 321
Hopkins, Robert G. II, 877
Hopkins, Robert G. II, 878
Hopkins, Robert G. II, 884
Hopkins, Robert G. II, 925
Hopkins, Robert George II, 784
Hopkins, Robert George II, 801
Hopkins, Robert, Jr. II, 376
Hopkins, Robert, Jr. II, 553
Hopkins, Robt. G. II, 801
Hopkins, Rowland III, 171
Hopkins, Sally VI, 1010
Hopkins, Samuel II, 376
Hopkins, Samuel II, 553
Hopkins, Samuel II, 560
Hopkins, Samuel II, 689
Hopkins, Samuel III, 170
Hopkins, Samuel VI, 403
Hopkins, Samuel VI, 509
Hopkins, Samuel VI, 519
Hopkins, Samuel VI, 521
Hopkins, Samuel VI, 726
Hopkins, Samuel VI, 750
Hopkins, Samuel VI, 758
Hopkins, Samuel VI, 764
Hopkins, Samuel VI, 935
Hopkins, Samuel, Jr. II, 553
Hopkins, Samuel, Jr. II, 689
Hopkins, Samuel, Jr. III, 171
Hopkins, Sarah II, 350
Hopkins, Sarah II, 351
Hopkins, Sarah II, 376
Hopkins, Sarah II, 529
Hopkins, Sarah II, 553
Hopkins, Sarah II, 614
Hopkins, Sarah III, 171
Hopkins, Sarah III, 209
Hopkins, Sarah III, 222
Hopkins, Sarah III, 289

Hopkins, Sarah III, 300
Hopkins, Sarah III, 420
Hopkins, Sarah III, 430
Hopkins, Sarah V, 76
Hopkins, Sarah V, 894
Hopkins, Sarah V, 911
Hopkins, Sarah V, 912
Hopkins, Sarah V, 943
Hopkins, Sarah VI, 475
Hopkins, Sarah VI, 509
Hopkins, Sarah B. III, 171
Hopkins, Sarah J. VI, 661
Hopkins, Sarah J. VI, 935
Hopkins, Sarah Jane VI, 758
Hopkins, Sarah Janney VI, 750
Hopkins, Sarah Janney VI, 752
Hopkins, Sarah L. VI, 952
Hopkins, Sarah P. V, 77
Hopkins, Saul Alley III, 170
Hopkins, Sidney W. III, 170
Hopkins, Sophia IV, 527
Hopkins, Sophia IV, 536
Hopkins, Sue III, 420
Hopkins, Susan III, 420
Hopkins, Susan III, 460
Hopkins, Susanna E. II, 310
Hopkins, Susanna E. II, 316
Hopkins, Susanna E. II, 321
Hopkins, Susannah III, 420
Hopkins, Susannah III, 460
Hopkins, Susannah Edmondson II, 784
Hopkins, Temperance III, 420
Hopkins, Temperance III, 421
Hopkins, Temperance III, 450
Hopkins, Thomas II, 320
Hopkins, Thomas II, 376
Hopkins, Thomas II, 529
Hopkins, Thomas II, 553
Hopkins, Thomas III, 171
Hopkins, Thomas VI, 509
Hopkins, Thomas E. II, 1085
Hopkins, Thos. II, 801
Hopkins, Thos. VI, 935
Hopkins, Virginia II, 926
Hopkins, Virginia M. II, 321
Hopkins, W. VI, 1014
Hopkins, Walter II, 746
Hopkins, Walter L. VI, 917
Hopkins, Wd. Margaret II, 376
Hopkins, Wd. Martha M. II, 801
Hopkins, William II, 376
Hopkins, William III, 171
Hopkins, William III, 403
Hopkins, William III, 420
Hopkins, William V, 76
Hopkins, William V, 77
Hopkins, William VI, 750
Hopkins, William VI, 826
Hopkins, William VI, 935
Hopkins, William VI, 1010
Hopkins, William VI, 1018
Hopkins, William D. III, 420
Hopkins, William D. V, 911
Hopkins, William L. G. VI, 878
Hopkins, William M. VI, 935
Hopkins, William M. VI, 937
Hopkins, William M. VI, 1018
Hopkins, William T. II, 321
Hopkins, William Thomas II, 320
Hopkins, Wm. II, 553
Hopkins, Wm. III, 171
Hopkins, Wm. III, 420
Hopkins, Wm. Dunlap V, 912
Hopkins, Wm. J. II, 132
Hopkins, Wm. J. III, 171
Hopkins, Yarnall Lee II, 784
Hopkinson, Mary II, 233
Hopman, Elizabeth II, 53
Hopman, Elizabeth II, 79
Hopman, John II, 79
Hopman, Mary II, 79
Hopper, Abby III, 234
Hopper, Abigail II, 795
Hopper, Abigail II, 878
Hopper, Abigail III, 110
Hopper, Abigail III, 133
Hopper, Abigail III, 171
Hopper, Anna II, 801
Hopper, Anna II, 878
Hopper, C. H. V, 1002
Hopper, Chas. V, 1002
Hopper, Edward II, 801
Hopper, Edward II, 878
Hopper, Edward III, 171
Hopper, Eliz. III, 171
Hopper, Elizabeth II, 878
Hopper, Elizabeth III, 171
Hopper, Emily IV, 1166
Hopper, George II, 376
Hopper, George A. II, 801
Hopper, Hannah II, 801
Hopper, Hannah II, 878
Hopper, Hannah III, 171
Hopper, Hannah A. III, 420
Hopper, Hannah A. III, 421
Hopper, Hannah T. II, 878
Hopper, Isaac II, 554
Hopper, Isaac III, 171
Hopper, Isaac T. II, 878
Hopper, Isaac T. III, 49
Hopper, Isaac T. III, 171
Hopper, Isaac T. III, 420
Hopper, Isaac T. III, 421
Hopper, Isaac Tatem II, 801
Hopper, Isaac Tatem II, 878
Hopper, Isaac Tatem III, 171
Hopper, Isaac Tatum II, 812
Hopper, James Mott II, 801
Hopper, Jane VI, 826
Hopper, John II, 878
Hopper, John III, 171
Hopper, John Rowlett II, 801
Hopper, Joseph VI, 935
Hopper, Josiah II, 878
Hopper, Josiah III, 82
Hopper, Josiah III, 171
Hopper, Joyce II, 376
Hopper, Leroy IV, 1166
Hopper, Lizzie IV, 1166
Hopper, Lucretia Mott II, 801
Hopper, Margery II, 917
Hopper, Margery M. II, 878
Hopper, Margery Mickle II, 801
Hopper, Margery Mickle II, 818
Hopper, Maria II, 801
Hopper, Marjorie M. II, 878
Hopper, Martha III, 82
Hopper, Martha III, 171
Hopper, Mary II, 818
Hopper, Mary II, 878
Hopper, Mary III, 171
Hopper, Mary III, 243
Hopper, Mary III, 420
Hopper, Mary III, 421
Hopper, Mary VI, 935
Hopper, Mattie V, 1002
Hopper, Nathan III, 171
Hopper, Rachel II, 878
Hopper, Rachel III, 49
Hopper, Rachel III, 171
Hopper, Richard G. VI, 826
Hopper, Sarah II, 812
Hopper, Sarah II, 829
Hopper, Sarah III, 49
Hopper, Sarah III, 133
Hopper, Sarah III, 171
Hopper, Sarah III, 245
Hopper, Susanna III, 171
Hopper, Susannah II, 878
Hopper, Susannah Isaac II, 878
Hopper, Thomas II, 878
Hopper, Thomas III, 171
Hopper, Thos. II, 801
Hopper, Wm. II, 818
Hoppis, Ann I, 988
Hops, Mary II, 552
Hops, Mary II, 554
Hops, Mary II, 649
Hops, Mary II, 651
Hopson, Benjamin VI, 954
Hopson, Catharine I, 481
Hopson, Lyda I, 721
Hopson, Mariam I, 308
Hopson, Miriam I, 308
Hopson, Monallen VI, 403
Hopson, Nancy VI, 954
Hopson, William VI, 403
Hopston, Eliza IV, 939
Hopton, Abigail II, 376
Hopton, Abigail II, 444
Hopton, Abigall II, 444
Hopton, Hannah II, 444
Hopton, Jeremiah II, 444
Hopton, Sarah IV, 32
Hopton, Sarah IV, 40
Hopwood, Fanny VI, 826
Hopwood, John VI, 826
Hopwood, Samuel I, 102
Hord, John II, 377
Hord, Samuel II, 377
Hore, Edward VI, 898
Hore, Edward VI, 963
Hore, Edward VI, 1000
Hore, Edward VI, 1015
Hore, Elizabeth VI, 898
Hore, Hannah VI, 963
Hore, Mary VI, 1000
Horefield, Deborah III, 457
Horefield, Israel III, 457
Horine, Mattie V, 744
Horisfelt, Harmon V, 179
Hormal, Mehitable V, 146
Hormell, Clarence V, 596
Hormell, Freda Emly V, 596
Hormell, Frieda Emily V, 596
Hormell, Lelia V, 596
Hormell, Mary Ellen V, 596
Hormell, Mildred V, 596
Hormell, Mildred Grace V, 596
Hormell, Robert V, 684
Hormell, Roy V, 684
Horn, Abel I, 217
Horn, Abel I, 290
Horn, Abel I, 309
Horn, Abel I, 313
Horn, Ann I, 242
Horn, Ann I, 290
Horn, Ann I, 309
Horn, Ann I, 314
Horn, Ann IV, 873
Horn, Anne I, 54
Horn, Benjamin II, 377
Horn, Betsy I, 290
Horn, Betsy VI, 935
Horn, Caleb H. II, 878
Horn, Catherine VI, 883
Horn, Celia I, 54
Horn, Celia I, 70
Horn, Celia I, 290
Horn, Charity I, 290
Horn, Charity Battle I, 242
Horn, Charles VI, 883
Horn, Christian I, 290
Horn, Christian VI, 935
Horn, Christopher VI, 954
Horn, Cielia I, 242
Horn, Cielia I, 259
Horn, Clarky I, 308
Horn, Clarky I, 309
Horn, Cornelius VI, 877
Horn, Cornelius VI, 913
Horn, Damaries I, 217
Horn, Damaris I, 300
Horn, Damaris I, 309
Horn, Demaris I, 290
Horn, Eady I, 216
Horn, Edward II, 377
Horn, Edward II, 554
Horn, Edward II, 615
Horn, Edward IV, 873
Horn, Edward IV, 874
Horn, Edward IV, 880
Horn, Elce I, 242
Horn, Eliza IV, 825
Horn, Eliza IV, 873
Horn, Eliza IV, 874
Horn, Elizabeth I, 290
Horn, Elizabeth I, 299
Horn, Elizabeth I, 309
Horn, Elizabeth I, 313
Horn, Elizabeth I, 501
Horn, Elizabeth I, 548
Horn, Elizabeth I, 562
Horn, Elizabeth I, 964
Horn, Elizabeth II, 377
Horn, Elizabeth II, 554
Horn, Elizabeth II, 615
Horn, Elizabeth II, 746
Horn, Elizabeth II, 878
Horn, Elizabeth IV, 873
Horn, Elizabeth IV, 874
Horn, Elizabeth IV, 880
Horn, Elizabeth VI, 947
Horn, Elizabeth E. II, 878
Horn, Elizabeth E. II, 884
Horn, Esther I, 54
Horn, Esther I, 71
Horn, George VI, 935
Horn, Henrietta II, 746
Horn, Henrietta M. II, 878
Horn, Henry I, 54
Horn, Henry I, 242
Horn, Henry I, 290
Horn, Henry I, 309
Horn, Henry P. VI, 935
Horn, Henry, Jr. I, 242
Horn, Hiram IV, 873
Horn, Isaac I, 216
Horn, Isaac I, 242
Horn, Jacob I, 242
Horn, Jacob I, 309
Horn, Jeremiah I, 242
Horn, Jeremiah I, 290
Horn, Jeremiah I, 309
Horn, Jeremiah I, 315
Horn, Jeremiah I, 501
Horn, Jeremiah I, 548
Horn, Jeremiah I, 578
Horn, Jeremiah I, 579
Horn, Jeremiah I, 964
Horn, Jeremiah I, 1101
Horn, Jeremiah I Sup 1, 9
Horn, Jesse I, 290
Horn, Jesse I, 306
Horn, Jesse I, 309
Horn, Joel I, 290
Horn, Joel Horn I, 242
Horn, John I, 501
Horn, John I, 548
Horn, John I, 964
Horn, John I, 1122
Horn, John VI, 913
Horn, John VI, 935
Horn, John VI, 968
Horn, John VI, 985
Horn, John VI, 993
Horn, John Thomas I, 242
Horn, Josee I, 309
Horn, Judith I, 501
Horn, Judith I, 548
Horn, Judith I, 579
Horn, Judith I, 964
Horn, Judith I, 1101
Horn, Judith I Sup 1, 9
Horn, Judith Unthank I, 578
Horn, Kitty VI, 935
Horn, Lindley IV, 874
Horn, Louisa IV, 874
Horn, Mahala I, 290
Horn, Mahalia I, 309
Horn, Mahalia I, 312
Horn, Mary I, 217
Horn, Mary I, 290
Horn, Mary I, 299
Horn, Mary I, 309
Horn, Mary I, 399
Horn, Mary I, 402
Horn, Mary I, 501
Horn, Mary I, 548
Horn, Mary I, 964
Horn, Mary V, 953
Horn, Mary VI, 968
Horn, Mourning I, 242
Horn, Nancy I, 217
Horn, Nancy VI, 984
Horn, Nathan I, 217
Horn, Nathan I, 290
Horn, Nathaniel I, 399
Horn, Nathaniel I, 548
Horn, Obadiah VI, 935
Horn, Orpha I, 290
Horn, Orpha I, 309
Horn, Peggy I, 290
Horn, Peter VI, 935
Horn, Peter VI, 984
Horn, Phebe I, 290
Horn, Phebe Ricks I, 242
Horn, Pheraba I, 309
Horn, Pheriba I, 290
Horn, Pheriba I, 309
Horn, Pheriba I, 315
Horn, Philena IV, 874
Horn, Piety I, 290
Horn, Piety I, 306
Horn, Piety I, 309
Horn, Pinninah I, 306
Horn, Pinninah I, 309
Horn, Polly VI, 968
Horn, Priscilla I, 217
Horn, Priscilla VI, 954
Horn, Prudence I, 501
Horn, Prudence I, 548
Horn, Prudence I, 964
Horn, Rebecca I, 290
Horn, Rebecca I, 309
Horn, Rebecca I, 311
Horn, Rix I, 290
Horn, Rose I, 242
Horn, Salley VI, 954
Horn, Sally VI, 935
Horn, Sally VI, 985
Horn, Sally G. VI, 935
Horn, Sarah I, 290
Horn, Sarah I, 306
Horn, Sarah I, 309
Horn, Sarah IV, 873
Horn, Sela I, 242
Horn, Selah I, 217
Horn, Selia I, 309
Horn, Sidney I, 290
Horn, Soloame V, 953
Horn, Sophia VI, 935
Horn, Stephen IV, 873
Horn, Susannah I, 399
Horn, Thomas I, 217
Horn, Thomas I, 242
Horn, Thomas I, 259
Horn, Thomas I, 290
Horn, Thomas I, 309
Horn, Vincent P. IV, 874
Horn, William I, 54
Horn, William I, 70
Horn, William I, 206
Horn, William I, 217
Horn, William I, 242
Horn, William IV, 873
Horn, Wilson I, 309
Horn, Wm. II, 80
Horn, Wm. IV, 873
Horn, Wm. D. IV, 825
Hornada, Anna V, 626
Hornada, Annie E. V, 626
Hornada, Annie Elizabeth V, 626
Hornada, D. Allen V, 626
Hornada, Elizabeth V, 495
Hornada, Elizabeth V, 503
Hornada, Elizabeth V, 626
Hornada, Ezekial V, 503
Hornada, Ezekiel V, 495
Hornada, Ezekiel V, 626
Hornada, John V, 626
Hornada, John V, 651
Hornada, John W. V, 626
Hornada, Mary V, 626
Hornada, Mary V, 651
Hornaday, Albert V, 577
Hornaday, Albert V, 684
Hornaday, Alfred I, 399
Hornaday, Allen V, 577
Hornaday, Allen V, 684
Hornaday, Ann Elizabeth V, 577
Hornaday, Anna I, 399
Hornaday, Anna E. V, 577
Hornaday, Anna E. V, 684
Hornaday, Anna Elizabeth V, 577
Hornaday, Baalam I, 399
Hornaday, Catharine I, 448
Hornaday, Daniel Allen V, 577
Hornaday, Daniel Allen V, 684
Hornaday, Delitha E. V, 577
Hornaday, Dinah I, 373
Hornaday, Dinah I, 399
Hornaday, E. Albert V, 684
Hornaday, Elam K. V, 577
Hornaday, Eleanor V, 577
Hornaday, Eli V, 577
Hornaday, Elizabeth V, 77
Hornaday, Elizabeth V, 576
Hornaday, Elizabeth V, 684
Hornaday, Ellen V, 577
Hornaday, Esther I, 399
Hornaday, Ezekiel V, 77
Hornaday, Ezekiel V, 576
Hornaday, Ezekiel V, 585
Hornaday, Ezekiel V, 684
Hornaday, Ezekiel Albert V, 577
Hornaday, George V, 684
Hornaday, George Kalita V, 577
Hornaday, Hannah V, 577
Hornaday, Hannah V, 585
Hornaday, Hannah V, 859
Hornaday, Hannah Clark V, 684
Hornaday, Hester I, 399
Hornaday, Isaac V, 577
Hornaday, Isaiah V, 576
Hornaday, Isaiah V, 577
Hornaday, Isaiah V, 684
Hornaday, Isaiah F. V, 577
Hornaday, Jane V, 576
Hornaday, Jehu V, 576
Hornaday, Jemima I, 399
Hornaday, John I, 399
Hornaday, John V, 77
Hornaday, John V, 89
Hornaday, John V, 576
Hornaday, John V, 577
Hornaday, John V, 580
Hornaday, John V, 684
Hornaday, John W. V, 577
Hornaday, John W. V, 684
Hornaday, Josiah Forster V, 577
Hornaday, Julia Ann V, 577
Hornaday, Lewis I, 357
Hornaday, Lewis I, 373
Hornaday, Lewis I, 399
Hornaday, Louisa V, 547
Hornaday, Louisa V, 577
Hornaday, Lydia V, 577
Hornaday, Lydia V, 843
Hornaday, Lydia V, 849
Hornaday, Margaret V, 859
Hornaday, Martha V, 77
Hornaday, Martha V, 89
Hornaday, Martha V, 577
Hornaday, Martha V, 580
Hornaday, Martha V, 684
Hornaday, Mary I, 385
Hornaday, Mary I, 399
Hornaday, Mary V, 248
Hornaday, Mary V, 339
Hornaday, Mary V, 576
Hornaday, Mary V, 577
Hornaday, Mary V, 584
Hornaday, Mary V, 684

rnaday, Mary V, 843
rnaday, Mary V, 846
rnaday, Mary J. V, 577
rnaday, Mary Jane V, 577
rnaday, Mary Jane V, 684
rnaday, Nancy V, 843
rnaday, Nelson V, 859
rnaday, Rachel I, 399
rnaday, Rachel I, 448
rnaday, Rebecca I, 357
rnaday, Rebecca I, 372
rnaday, Rebecca I, 395
rnaday, Rebecca I, 399
rnaday, Ruth I, 399
rnaday, Ruth I, 414
rnaday, Ruth V, 77
rnaday, Ruth V, 843
rnaday, Ruth Eleanor I, 399
rnaday, Ruth Eleanor I, 400
rnaday, Sally I, 399
rnaday, Sally I, 430
rnaday, Sarah I, 399
rnaday, Simon I, 399
rnaday, Simon V, 577
rnaday, William I, 399
rnaday, William V, 577
rnaday, Wm. I, 399
rnaday, Wm. E. Mendenhall V, 577
rnaday, Zachariah I, 399
rnady, Ezekiel I, 357
rnady, Lewis I, 357
rnbeck, Josephine IV, 1254
rnby, Ellen II, 139
rnby, Margaret II, 139
rnby, Robert II, 139
rnby, Thomas II, 377
rne, Amanda M. II, 779
rne, Ann I, 216
rne, Ann IV, 873
rne, Anna Mary II, 801
rne, Anne II, 803
rne, Anne IV, 825
rne, Bryn Mawr II, 801
rne, Caleb H. II, 878
rne, Caleb Henry II, 801
rne, Charity I, 216
rne, Demarias I, 216
rne, Edward II, 554
rne, Edward II, 801
rne, Edward IV, 873
rne, Edward IV, 893
rne, Elce I, 257
rne, Elisabeth II, 501
rne, Elisabeth II, 554
rne, Eliza IV, 825
rne, Eliza IV, 873
rne, Elizabeth II, 554
rne, Elizabeth II, 746
rne, Elizabeth II, 878
rne, Elizabeth IV, 893
rne, Elizabeth E. II, 746
rne, Elizabeth Evans II, 803
rne, Elizabeth P. IV, 893
orne, Esther I, 216
orne, Henrietta II, 746
orne, Henrietta M. II, 744
orne, Henrietta M. II, 746
orne, Henrietta M. II, 871
orne, Henrietta M. II, 878
orne, Henry I, 216
orne, Henry H. II, 803
orne, Henry, Jr. I, 216
orne, Hiram IV, 825
orne, Hiram IV, 873
orne, Isaac I, 216
orne, Isaac I, 242
orne, Isaac I, 257
orne, Isaac II, 817
orne, Jacob I, 216
orne, Jacob, Jr. II, 554
orne, Jeremiah I, 216
orne, Joel I, 216
orne, Joseph I, 594
orne, Mary II, 554
orne, Mary II, 801
orne, Mary II, 817
orne, Mary II, 878
orne, Mary Belinda II, 801
orne, Mary C. II, 878
orne, Mournin I, 216
orne, Phebe I, 216
orne, Phebe II, 554
orne, Phebe II, 801
orne, Phebe II, 878
orne, Salome II, 878
orne, Salome Warner II, 817
orne, Sarah IV, 825
orne, Sarah IV, 873
orne, Selah I, 216
orne, Sermon II, 801
Horne, Sermon II, 878
Horne, Simeon II, 554
Horne, Stephen IV, 825
Horne, Stephen IV, 873
Horne, Thomas I, 216
Horne, Vincent P. IV, 893
Horne, William I, 216
Horne, William I, 242
Horne, William IV, 873
Horne, William, Sr. V, 179
Horne, Wm. II, 554
Horne, Wm. D. IV, 825
Horneday, Annie Elizabeth V, 626
Horneday, Daniel Allen V, 577
Horneday, Elizabeth V, 503
Horneday, Ezekial V, 503
Horneday, Ezekiel V, 503
Horneday, Ezekiel Albert V, 577
Horneday, John V, 577
Horneday, John W. V, 626
Horneday, Mary V, 626
Horneday, Ruth I, 399
Hornell, Hattie V, 77
Hornell, Meribah W. V, 77
Hornell, Rosa M. V, 77
Hornell, Roy V, 684
Horner, ??? II, 791
Horner, ??? V, 965
Horner, Achsah II, 815
Horner, Acsah II, 233
Horner, Acsah II, 235
Horner, Alfred W. VI, 836
Horner, Amos IV, 337
Horner, Amos V, 77
Horner, Amos C. V, 971
Horner, Amos F. IV, 724
Horner, Amy II, 377
Horner, Amy II, 554
Horner, Ann I, 1032
Horner, Ann II, 743
Horner, Ann IV, 40
Horner, Ann V, 17
Horner, Ann V, 70
Horner, Ann V, 77
Horner, Ann V, 99
Horner, Ann V, 179
Horner, Ann V, 971
Horner, Ann V, 979
Horner, Ann VI, 403
Horner, Anna V, 971
Horner, Bartholomew II, 233
Horner, Bartholomew II, 273
Horner, Benj. II, 377
Horner, Benj. II, 554
Horner, Benjamin II, 377
Horner, Benjamin II, 554
Horner, Benjamin II, 687
Horner, Benjamin C. II, 554
Horner, Benjamin Fawcett IV, 411
Horner, Benjamin, Jr. II, 204
Horner, Benjamin, Jr. II, 233
Horner, Benjamin, Jr. II, 377
Horner, Benjamin, Jr. II, 489
Horner, Benjamin, Jr. II, 554
Horner, Betsy IV, 363
Horner, Betsy IV, 411
Horner, Charles V, 179
Horner, David V, 77
Horner, David V, 108
Horner, David V, 179
Horner, David V, 971
Horner, Deliverance II, 233
Horner, Deliverance II, 265
Horner, Deliverance III, 171
Horner, Druzilla IV, 337
Horner, Druzilla IV, 358
Horner, Eber V, 971
Horner, Eber V, 979
Horner, Eleanor II, 554
Horner, Eleonor III, 171
Horner, Elizabeth II, 233
Horner, Elizabeth II, 273
Horner, Elizabeth II, 377
Horner, Elizabeth III, 145
Horner, Elizabeth IV, 337
Horner, Elizabeth V, 40
Horner, Elizabeth V, 77
Horner, Elizabeth V, 179
Horner, Elizabeth V, 971
Horner, Elizabeth VI, 750
Horner, Elizabeth Haines II, 810
Horner, Elizabeth Lippincott II, 828
Horner, Esther IV, 724
Horner, Esther IV, 773
Horner, Esther B. IV, 724
Horner, Ethel Henley V, 503
Horner, Eunice IV, 334
Horner, Eunice IV, 337
Horner, Eunice V, 971
Horner, Everette V, 979
Horner, Ezekiel VI, 832
Horner, Fannie V, 971
Horner, Fanny V, 179
Horner, Frances V, 179
Horner, Geo. V, 971
Horner, George V, 77
Horner, Hannah II, 233
Horner, Hannah II, 241
Horner, Hannah II, 930
Horner, Henry V, 971
Horner, Isaac II, 163
Horner, Isaac II, 233
Horner, Isaac II, 273
Horner, Isaac II, 554
Horner, Isaac II, 930
Horner, Isaac III, 13
Horner, Isaac III, 171
Horner, Isaac III, 370
Horner, Isaac III, 391
Horner, Isaac IV, 337
Horner, Isaac VI, 750
Horner, Jacob II, 494
Horner, Jacob II, 554
Horner, Jacob V, 77
Horner, Jacob V, 179
Horner, Jacob V, 186
Horner, Jacob V, 971
Horner, James V, 77
Horner, James V, 971
Horner, Jane II, 554
Horner, Jane II, 687
Horner, Jeffery V, 979
Horner, Jeffrey V, 971
Horner, Jennie V, 179
Horner, Joanna II, 793
Horner, John II, 377
Horner, John IV, 329
Horner, John IV, 334
Horner, John IV, 337
Horner, John IV, 724
Horner, John V, 40
Horner, John V, 77
Horner, John V, 971
Horner, John VI, 741
Horner, John VI, 750
Horner, John, Jr. IV, 337
Horner, Jonathan II, 377
Horner, Jonathan V, 971
Horner, Joseph II, 233
Horner, Joseph II, 257
Horner, Joseph II, 554
Horner, Joseph V, 77
Horner, Joseph V, 971
Horner, Joseph V, 979
Horner, Joseph P. II, 377
Horner, Joseph P. II, 554
Horner, Joshua V, 77
Horner, Levi V, 77
Horner, Levi V, 971
Horner, Lillian II, 326
Horner, Lillie V, 179
Horner, Lydia III, 171
Horner, Lydia III, 370
Horner, Lydia IV, 329
Horner, Lydia IV, 334
Horner, Lydia IV, 337
Horner, Lydia IV, 392
Horner, Lydia IV, 411
Horner, Lydia IV, 724
Horner, Lydia V, 77
Horner, Lydia V, 179
Horner, Lydia V, 186
Horner, Lydia V, 744
Horner, Lydia V, 971
Horner, Lydia VI, 598
Horner, Lydia VI, 741
Horner, Lydia VI, 750
Horner, Lydia Ann IV, 329
Horner, Lydia Ann IV, 337
Horner, Lydia Ann VI, 750
Horner, Lydia W. II, 948
Horner, Lydia W. II, 949
Horner, Marcia VI, 832
Horner, Margaret IV, 724
Horner, Margaret T. II, 308
Horner, Margaret Wilson IV, 724
Horner, Margery V, 70
Horner, Margery V, 77
Horner, Margery V, 176
Horner, Margery V, 179
Horner, Margery V, 971
Horner, Mark II, 743
Horner, Martha II, 520
Horner, Martha IV, 411
Horner, Martha Ann II, 554
Horner, Martha B. IV, 337
Horner, Martha B. VI, 750
Horner, Mary II, 377
Horner, Mary II, 489
Horner, Mary II, 494
Horner, Mary II, 554
Horner, Mary V, 971
Horner, Mary V, 979
Horner, Mary Ann IV, 337
Horner, Mary Ann IV, 724
Horner, Mary Ann IV, 773
Horner, Mary Jane IV, 321
Horner, Mary Jane IV, 337
Horner, Mary W. II, 743
Horner, Maryann IV, 337
Horner, Maryann IV, 345
Horner, Merriam V, 77
Horner, Milo V, 179
Horner, Miriam V, 971
Horner, Miriam V, 979
Horner, Newton V, 971
Horner, Newton V, 979
Horner, Phebe IV, 354
Horner, Phebe VI, 482
Horner, Phebe VI, 509
Horner, Phebe VI, 750
Horner, Phebe Ellen IV, 337
Horner, Rachel II, 233
Horner, Rachel II, 234
Horner, Rachel V, 77
Horner, Rachel V, 971
Horner, Rebecca II, 233
Horner, Rebecca II, 377
Horner, Rebecca II, 554
Horner, Rebecca V, 77
Horner, Rebecca V, 971
Horner, Rebeckah II, 204
Horner, Rebeckah II, 233
Horner, Ruth V, 971
Horner, Sally I, 1056
Horner, Sally V, 77
Horner, Sally V, 159
Horner, Sally V, 179
Horner, Sally V, 971
Horner, Samuel IV, 1321
Horner, Samuel V, 77
Horner, Samuel V, 971
Horner, Samuel H. IV, 1321
Horner, Sarah II, 233
Horner, Sarah II, 257
Horner, Sarah II, 292
Horner, Sarah II, 377
Horner, Sarah II, 554
Horner, Sarah II, 878
Horner, Sarah V, 77
Horner, Sarah V, 99
Horner, Sarah V, 108
Horner, Sarah V, 971
Horner, Sarah C. II, 878
Horner, Sarah H. II, 930
Horner, Stella V, 179
Horner, Thomas I, 1032
Horner, Thomas IV, 40
Horner, Thomas IV, 724
Horner, Thomas V, 70
Horner, Thomas V, 77
Horner, Thomas V, 99
Horner, Thomas V, 179
Horner, Thomas V, 971
Horner, Thomas F. IV, 337
Horner, Thomas F. IV, 724
Horner, Thomas F. IV, 773
Horner, Thomas F. VI, 750
Horner, Thos. F. IV, 345
Horner, Walker V, 179
Horner, Wd. Jane II, 554
Horner, Wd. Joanna H. II, 791
Horner, William V, 77
Horner, William V, 179
Horner, Winfield III, 145
Horner, Winifield G. III, 145
Horner, Wm. I, 1056
Horner, Wm. V, 159
Hornes, Cora V, 458
Hornes, Frank J. V, 1002
Hornes, Isaac II, 241
Hornes, M. C. V, 458
Hornes, Rebecca V, 1002
Hornet, Anna III, 171
Hornett, Anna III, 151
Horney, Ada I, 943
Horney, Ada I, 946
Horney, Albenah I, 783
Horney, Albenia I, 818
Horney, Alfred I, 818
Horney, Ann I, 448
Horney, Ann I, 783
Horney, Ann I, 818
Horney, Ann V, 77
Horney, Ann V, 97
Horney, Ann M. V, 78
Horney, Carter H. V, 78
Horney, Catharine I, 783
Horney, Celia I, 784
Horney, Celia I, 818
Horney, Celia I, 844
Horney, Charles P. I, 818
Horney, Cleopatra H. I, 818
Horney, Cornelia I, 818
Horney, Cornelious I, 784
Horney, Cornelius F. I, 818
Horney, David I, 783
Horney, David I, 818
Horney, David S. V, 77
Horney, David S. V, 97
Horney, Deborah I, 783
Horney, Eli I, 784
Horney, Eli I, 818
Horney, Eli J. I, 818
Horney, Eli Junius I, 818
Horney, Eli P. I, 818
Horney, Elizabeth I, 588
Horney, Elizabeth I, 594
Horney, Elizabeth I, 783
Horney, Elizabeth I, 784
Horney, Elizabeth I, 815
Horney, Elizabeth I, 818
Horney, Elizabeth I, 836
Horney, Elizabeth I, 844
Horney, Elizabeth V, 77
Horney, Elizabeth V, 78
Horney, Emely E. I, 818
Horney, Finly G. I, 818
Horney, Francis J. I, 933
Horney, Francis Jasper I, 928
Horney, Hannah I, 783
Horney, Hannah I, 809
Horney, Hannah I, 818
Horney, Henry I, 784
Horney, Henry I, 818
Horney, Ila A. I, 801
Horney, Ila M. I, 943
Horney, Jabez I, 783
Horney, James I, 589
Horney, James M. I, 783
Horney, Jane I, 588
Horney, Jane I, 593
Horney, Jane I, 594
Horney, Jane I, 783
Horney, Jane I, 817
Horney, Jane I, 818
Horney, Jeffery I, 783
Horney, Jeffery I, 818
Horney, Jeffery I, 924
Horney, Jeffery C. I, 928
Horney, Jeffrey I, 818
Horney, Jeffry I, 594
Horney, Jefrey I, 818
Horney, Jefry I, 784
Horney, Joel V, 78
Horney, John I, 588
Horney, John I, 594
Horney, John I, 596
Horney, John I, 783
Horney, John I, 818
Horney, Jonathan I, 588
Horney, Jonathan I, 783
Horney, Jonathan I, 818
Horney, Jonathan I, 828
Horney, Jonathan I, 844
Horney, Jonathan V, 78
Horney, Jonathan V, 97
Horney, Joseph I, 589
Horney, Joseph D. V, 78
Horney, Julia I, 933
Horney, Julia A. I, 818
Horney, Julia Ann I, 928
Horney, Julia Ann I, 943
Horney, Julia Antoinette I, 818
Horney, Katharine I, 818
Horney, Katharine I, 834
Horney, Kezia I, 807
Horney, Kezia I, 818
Horney, Kezia I, 924
Horney, Kezia I, 928
Horney, Levi B. I, 783
Horney, Levi B. I, 818
Horney, Lucy L. I, 818
Horney, Lydia I, 783
Horney, Lydia I, 818
Horney, Lydia I, 844
Horney, Malinda V, 78
Horney, Mariam M. I, 818
Horney, Mariam M. I, 822
Horney, Mary I, 783
Horney, Mary I, 818
Horney, Mary I, 828
Horney, Mary A. I, 818
Horney, Mary J. I, 818
Horney, Mary Jane I, 815
Horney, Mary Jane I, 818
Horney, Miles V, 78
Horney, Miriam I, 783
Horney, Moses I, 783
Horney, Nancy I, 817
Horney, Nancy I, 818
Horney, Norine I, 943

Horney, Octavia S. I, 924
Horney, Paul S. I, 928
Horney, Phebe J. I, 818
Horney, Prudence I, 588
Horney, Prudence I, 594
Horney, Prudence I, 596
Horney, Prudence I, 818
Horney, Ralto O. I, 818
Horney, Rebecca I, 594
Horney, Rebecca V, 844
Horney, Rebecca Ann V, 78
Horney, Rebeccah I, 589
Horney, Ruby K. I, 933
Horney, Ruby Kate I, 928
Horney, Ruby Kate I, 943
Horney, Ruth I, 783
Horney, Sarah B. V, 78
Horney, Solomon I, 783
Horney, Solomon I, 818
Horney, Solomon I, 836
Horney, Solomon V, 77
Horney, Solomon V, 78
Horney, Stephen I, 783
Horney, Stephen I, 784
Horney, Stephen I, 818
Horney, Susan G. I, 818
Horney, Susan G. I, 829
Horney, Susan L. V, 577
Horney, Susanna L. V, 78
Horney, Susanna L. V, 97
Horney, Susannah L. V, 78
Horney, Will L. I, 943
Horney, William I, 589
Horney, William I, 594
Hornida, Hester I, 399
Hornida, Hesther I, 370
Horniday, Ezekiel V, 179
Horniday, George Halita V, 179
Horniday, Isaiah V, 179
Horniday, Isaiah V, 577
Horniday, Isaiah F. V, 577
Horniday, John W. V, 179
Horniday, Lemuel V, 179
Horniday, Mary I, 399
Horniday, Mary V, 179
Horniday, Mary J. V, 577
Horniday, Mary Jane V, 179
Horniday, Ruth I, 399
Horniman, Annie Smith III, 171
Horniman, Henry V, 912
Hornor, Amy II, 489
Hornor, Amy II, 554
Hornor, Ann II, 747
Hornor, Benj. II, 489
Hornor, Benj. II, 554
Hornor, Benjamin II, 554
Hornor, Benjamin II, 696
Hornor, Benjamin C. II, 747
Hornor, Deliverance II, 177
Hornor, Isaac II, 177
Hornor, Jane II, 554
Hornor, Joseph II, 554
Hornor, Joseph P. II, 554
Hornor, Lydia II, 177
Hornor, Mark II, 747
Hornor, Mary II, 554
Hornor, Mary II, 696
Hornor, Mary II, 747
Hornor, Mary W. II, 747
Hornor, Rebecca II, 489
Hornor, Rebecca II, 554
Hornor, Rebecca II, 696
Hornor, Sarah II, 554
Hornor, Sarah II, 747
Horon, Jeremiah I, 964
Horr, Mabel V, 248
Horr, Mamie V, 248
Horr, Wm. V, 248
Horsefall, Edmon VI, 110
Horsefall, Edmond VI, 110
Horsefall, Mary VI, 110
Horsefall, Mary VI, 135
Horsefalls, Mary VI, 135
Horseman, Alice V, 684
Horseman, Bessie V, 248
Horseman, Charles VI, 403
Horseman, David VI, 404
Horseman, Elizabeth VI, 403
Horseman, Everett V, 684
Horseman, Fanny V, 248
Horseman, George E. V, 684
Horseman, Hannah V, 248
Horseman, Hannah V, 293
Horseman, Jessie V, 248
Horseman, John VI, 404
Horseman, John E. V, 684
Horseman, Joseph V, 248
Horseman, Joseph VI, 404
Horseman, Lewis V, 684
Horseman, Lydia V, 248
Horseman, Lydia VI, 404
Horseman, Marcy VI, 404
Horseman, Mary VI, 403
Horseman, Mercy VI, 404
Horseman, Mercy VI, 418
Horseman, Russel V, 684
Horseman, Ruth VI, 404
Horseman, Ruth VI, 451
Horseman, Silas V, 248
Horseman, Susanna V, 684
Horseman, William VI, 403
Horseman, William VI, 404
Horser, Azariah I, 367
Horser, Deborah I, 367
Horser, Mary I, 367
Horsey, Stephen VI, 11
Horsfall, Edmon VI, 110
Horsfall, Edmond VI, 110
Horsfall, Mary VI, 110
Horskins, Jane III, 172
Horsley, Edmund W. VI, 935
Horsley, Elizabeth VI, 935
Horsley, Henderson VI, 935
Horsley, James, Jr. VI, 888
Horsley, Lucy VI, 935
Horsley, Lucy M. VI, 935
Horsley, Mary J. VI, 935
Horsley, Nancy VI, 935
Horsley, Peter N. III, 172
Horsley, Polly VI, 935
Horsley, Rowland VI, 935
Horsman, Charles VI, 403
Horsman, Charles VI, 598
Horsman, David VI, 460
Horsman, Elizabeth VI, 403
Horsman, Fanny V, 248
Horsman, John VI, 404
Horsman, Joseph V, 248
Horsman, Joseph VI, 598
Horsman, Lewis V, 684
Horsman, Lydia VI, 417
Horsman, Marcy VI, 416
Horsman, Mary IV, 337
Horsman, Mary VI, 403
Horsman, Mary VI, 598
Horsman, Prudence V, 59
Horsman, Prudence V, 78
Horsman, Ruth VI, 404
Horsman, Ruth VI, 460
Horsman, William VI, 403
Horsman, William VI, 416
Horsman, William VI, 598
Horsnal, Annie G. III, 172
Horstman, Elizabeth W. II, 878
Horstman, Elizabeth W. II, 938
Horten, Edith D. IV, 224
Horten, John IV, 40
Horten, Joseph H. IV, 337
Horton, ??? III, 314
Horton, ??? J. III, 510
Horton, Aaron IV, 1269
Horton, Abraham I, 548
Horton, Abraham I, 957
Horton, Adaline M. VI, 750
Horton, Agnes II, 878
Horton, Agnes IV, 224
Horton, Agnes IV, 337
Horton, Agness IV, 150
Horton, Agnus IV, 224
Horton, Alfred II, 747
Horton, Alfred G. VI, 820
Horton, Alfred G. VI, 826
Horton, Alfred Jones II, 747
Horton, Alice W. II, 878
Horton, Alice W. II, 909
Horton, Ann I, 548
Horton, Ann I, 956
Horton, Ann I, 964
Horton, Ann III, 265
Horton, Ann J. VI, 826
Horton, Anna III, 172
Horton, Anna V, 248
Horton, Betsey VI, 1016
Horton, Catherine T. IV, 150
Horton, Catherine T. IV, 163
Horton, Charity Ann V, 249
Horton, Crewes VI, 843
Horton, Cynthia IV, 224
Horton, Cynthia IV, 337
Horton, Cynthia Horton IV, 40
Horton, Cynthia Horton IV, 893
Horton, David V, 248
Horton, Delila VI, 826
Horton, Edith D. IV, 224
Horton, Edward III, 172
Horton, Elisabeth I, 46
Horton, Eliz. III, 506
Horton, Elizabeth I, 54
Horton, Elizabeth II, 878
Horton, Elizabeth IV, 150
Horton, Elizabeth IV, 224
Horton, Elizabeth IV, 337
Horton, Frances I, 271
Horton, Frances A. B. VI, 833
Horton, Freelove III, 485
Horton, George III, 172
Horton, George V, 684
Horton, Howard IV, 137
Horton, Howard V, 248
Horton, Jacob I, 502
Horton, Jacob I, 818
Horton, Jacob I, 964
Horton, Jacob V, 248
Horton, Jacob V, 249
Horton, James I, 501
Horton, James I, 502
Horton, James I, 525
Horton, James I, 548
Horton, James I, 964
Horton, James V, 244
Horton, James V, 248
Horton, James J. V, 249
Horton, Jane III, 485
Horton, Jane III, 495
Horton, Jane VI, 843
Horton, Jesse V, 248
Horton, John I, 548
Horton, John I, 956
Horton, John I, 964
Horton, John II, 554
Horton, John II, 708
Horton, John II, 747
Horton, John IV, 40
Horton, John IV, 224
Horton, John IV, 312
Horton, John IV, 337
Horton, John IV, 893
Horton, John VI, 181
Horton, John Horton IV, 40
Horton, Jonathan Street IV, 150
Horton, Joseph I, 964
Horton, Joseph II, 878
Horton, Joseph III, 172
Horton, Joseph III, 485
Horton, Joseph III, 495
Horton, Joseph IV, 150
Horton, Joseph IV, 224
Horton, Joseph IV, 337
Horton, Joseph H. II, 878
Horton, Joseph H. IV, 150
Horton, Joseph H. IV, 224
Horton, Joseph H. IV, 337
Horton, Joseph Malin IV, 150
Horton, Kesiah VI, 826
Horton, Lawrence A. VI, 826
Horton, Leah I, 956
Horton, Leah I, 963
Horton, Leah I, 964
Horton, Lewis V, 249
Horton, Lewis Horton V, 249
Horton, Lucinda VI, 823
Horton, Lucinda VI, 846
Horton, M. W. II, 708
Horton, Mahlon IV, 337
Horton, Malin IV, 150
Horton, Malin IV, 163
Horton, Malinda V, 248
Horton, Malinda V, 249
Horton, Malinda V, 255
Horton, Malinda Terrell V, 249
Horton, Margaret I, 501
Horton, Margaret I, 502
Horton, Margaret I, 525
Horton, Margaret I, 548
Horton, Margaret I, 964
Horton, Margaret V, 248
Horton, Margaret VI, 826
Horton, Maria II, 747
Horton, Martha I, 955
Horton, Martha I, 961
Horton, Martha I, 964
Horton, Mary III, 277
Horton, Mary IV, 22
Horton, Mary IV, 40
Horton, Mary IV, 893
Horton, Mary V, 248
Horton, Mary VI, 1016
Horton, Mary Ann II, 878
Horton, Mary Ann II, 909
Horton, Mary H. IV, 337
Horton, Mary H. IV, 351
Horton, Mary H. VI, 826
Horton, Mary J. IV, 312
Horton, Mary J. IV, 337
Horton, Mary J. IV, 893
Horton, Mary Jane IV, 224
Horton, Pamelia III, 172
Horton, Parmelia III, 314
Horton, Phebe III, 172
Horton, Phebe V, 249
Horton, Phebe M. IV, 1102
Horton, Phebe M. IV, 1106
Horton, Priscilla I, 525
Horton, Priscilla I, 548
Horton, Rachel I, 501
Horton, Rachel IV, 40
Horton, Rachel IV, 42
Horton, Rachel IV, 44
Horton, Rachel IV, 224
Horton, Rachel IV, 312
Horton, Rachel IV, 337
Horton, Rachel IV, 893
Horton, Rachel V, 248
Horton, Rachel V, 503
Horton, Rebecca IV, 150
Horton, Rebecca IV, 337
Horton, Ruth I, 964
Horton, Samuel V, 249
Horton, Samuel C. Terrell V, 249
Horton, Sarah V, 244
Horton, Sarah V, 248
Horton, Sarah V. V, 249
Horton, Thomas II, 878
Horton, Thomas IV, 150
Horton, Thomas IV, 224
Horton, Thomas IV, 337
Horton, Thos. II, 878
Horton, Thos. IV, 337
Horton, Thos. H. II, 878
Horton, Thos. H. II, 909
Horton, William I, 955
Horton, William III, 172
Horton, William V, 248
Horton, William H. VI, 804
Horton, William H. VI, 826
Horton, Winnafd I, 955
Horton, Winnafd I, 964
Horton, Wm. I, 964
Horton, Wm. H. VI, 823
Horton, Wm. Henry III, 172
Hosack, Myrtle May IV, 1015
Hoser, Lewis I, 722
Hoser, Mary I, 722
Hoser, Milicent I, 722
Hoser, Millisent I, 708
Hoser, Millisent I, 722
Hoser, William I, 722
Hosey, Ann I, 552
Hosey, Ann I, 574
Hosford, James III, 172
Hosher, Hannah II, 64
Hosher, Hannah II, 80
Hosher, Henry II, 64
Hosher, Henry II, 80
Hosher, Jane III, 241
Hosier, Abigail III, 142
Hosier, Abigail III, 172
Hosier, Abigail III, 278
Hosier, Ann III, 172
Hosier, Ann Eliza III, 172
Hosier, Benjamin B. III, 172
Hosier, Catharine III, 172
Hosier, Catharine B. III, 172
Hosier, Edward Hicks III, 172
Hosier, Edward T. IV, 259
Hosier, Elizabeth I, 1010
Hosier, Elizabeth III, 172
Hosier, Elizabeth IV, 259
Hosier, Emily V, 179
Hosier, Francis V, 179
Hosier, George V, 179
Hosier, Hannah III, 55
Hosier, Hannah III, 172
Hosier, Hannah III, 244
Hosier, Hannah IV, 224
Hosier, Hannah IV, 259
Hosier, Hannah IV, 337
Hosier, Harry V, 179
Hosier, Jane III, 172
Hosier, Jane III, 241
Hosier, John III, 142
Hosier, John III, 172
Hosier, John III, 278
Hosier, John Burling III, 172
Hosier, Lydia III, 394
Hosier, Lydia III, 453
Hosier, Lydia T. III, 18
Hosier, Lydia T. III, 318
Hosier, Margaret III, 172
Hosier, Maria III, 172
Hosier, Maria IV, 224
Hosier, Maria IV, 337
Hosier, Mariah IV, 536
Hosier, Mary III, 172
Hosier, Mary V, 179
Hosier, Mary H. III, 142
Hosier, Mary H. III, 172
Hosier, Samuel III, 394
Hosier, Samuel III, 453
Hosier, Samuel III, 454
Hosier, Samuel B. III, 172
Hosier, Samuel P. III, 18
Hosier, Samuel P. III, 172
Hosier, Samuel P. III, 318
Hosier, Susan Amelia III, 172
Hosier, Susan Amelia III, 278
Hosier, William Bowne III, 172
Hosier, Wilson Merritt III, 172
Hoskens, Ardillia V, 249
Hoskens, Estelle V, 249
Hoskens, Joseph V, 249
Hoskens, Moses V, 249
Hoskens, Rebecca V, 249
Hosking, Maud V, 249
Hoskins, Aaron VI, 181
Hoskins, Abigail II, 177
Hoskins, Abigail II, 226
Hoskins, Abigail II, 233
Hoskins, Abigail II, 377
Hoskins, Abigail II, 555
Hoskins, Acenath V, 339
Hoskins, Ada V, 458
Hoskins, Alfred I, 549
Hoskins, Alma V, 339
Hoskins, Amy I, 549
Hoskins, Ann II, 344
Hoskins, Ann V, 249
Hoskins, Ann V, 912
Hoskins, Ann M. I, 549
Hoskins, Anna V, 338
Hoskins, Anna V, 339
Hoskins, Anna V, 402
Hoskins, Anna V, 404
Hoskins, Anna V, 627
Hoskins, Anna V, 629
Hoskins, Anna V, 684
Hoskins, Anne I, 549
Hoskins, Anne I, 563
Hoskins, Anne II, 482
Hoskins, Anne II, 554
Hoskins, Anne V, 912
Hoskins, Ardillia V, 249
Hoskins, Aron VI, 177
Hoskins, Asenath V, 339
Hoskins, Asenith V, 339
Hoskins, Asenith V, 340
Hoskins, Betsy VI, 826
Hoskins, Caleb II, 177
Hoskins, Caleb II, 233
Hoskins, Caleb II, 377
Hoskins, Caroline B. I, 549
Hoskins, Charles I, 549
Hoskins, Charles E. I, 549
Hoskins, Clarence V, 627
Hoskins, Clarence V, 684
Hoskins, Clarence V, 685
Hoskins, Clyde V, 341
Hoskins, Daniel I, 549
Hoskins, David V, 339
Hoskins, David M. V, 339
Hoskins, Eleanor II, 377
Hoskins, Eleanor II, 554
Hoskins, Eleanor II, 708
Hoskins, Eli V, 249
Hoskins, Eli V, 446
Hoskins, Eli V, 503
Hoskins, Elijah V, 627
Hoskins, Elijah V, 684
Hoskins, Eliza A. V, 627
Hoskins, Elizabeth I, 548
Hoskins, Elizabeth II, 377
Hoskins, Elizabeth V, 249
Hoskins, Elizabeth V, 339
Hoskins, Elizabeth V, 351
Hoskins, Ellis V, 249
Hoskins, Ellis N. I, 549
Hoskins, Elma I, 549
Hoskins, Elmina J. I, 549
Hoskins, Emily V, 622
Hoskins, Emily V, 627
Hoskins, Emily S. V, 339
Hoskins, Estelle V, 249
Hoskins, Esther II, 377
Hoskins, Eugene I, 549
Hoskins, Fraizer V, 627
Hoskins, Geo. V, 339
Hoskins, George I, 502
Hoskins, George I, 548
Hoskins, George I, 549
Hoskins, George V, 249
Hoskins, George V, 339
Hoskins, George V, 446
Hoskins, Gertrude V, 627
Hoskins, Gertrude V, 684
Hoskins, Graham II, 377
Hoskins, Graham II, 555
Hoskins, Guli Elma Meriah I, 549
Hoskins, Hannah I, 502
Hoskins, Hannah I, 548
Hoskins, Hannah V, 249
Hoskins, Hannah V, 339
Hoskins, Hannah V, 345
Hoskins, Hannah V, 402
Hoskins, Hannah V, 503

kins, Hannah Mary V, 627
kins, Harley Roy V, 339
kins, Harriett E. I, 549
kins, Henrietta II, 377
kins, Henrietta II, 555
kins, Henrietta II, 708
kins, Henrietta II, 747
kins, Henry II, 377
kins, Henry II, 555
kins, Hester II, 377
kins, Horace E. V, 684
kins, Horace Everest V, 627
kins, Horace Everett V, 627
kins, Ida M. V, 339
kins, Isaac V, 249
kins, Isaac V, 339
kins, Isaac V, 402
kins, Isaac V, 404
kins, Isaac V, 446
kins, Isaac V, 626
kins, Isaac V, 627
kins, Isaac V, 629
kins, Isaac V, 684
kins, Isaac A. V, 339
kins, Isaac Albert V, 339
kins, Isaac Albert V, 627
kins, Isaac Russell V, 684
kins, Isabella V, 894
kins, Isabelle V, 894
kins, Isabelle V, 912
kins, J. W. V, 339
kins, James V, 341
kins, Jane V, 249
kins, Jane V, 339
kins, Jane V, 402
kins, Jane V, 627
kins, Jane Emily V, 319
kins, Jane Emily V, 339
kins, Jennie V, 339
kins, Joel V, 249
kins, Joel V, 331
kins, Joel V, 339
kins, Joel V, 402
kins, Joel V, 621
kins, Joel V, 626
kins, Joel V, 627
kins, John I, 502
kins, John I, 548
kins, John I, 549
kins, John II, 177
kins, John II, 198
kins, John II, 233
kins, John II, 245
kins, John II, 252
kins, John II, 555
kins, John V, 249
kins, John V, 339
kins, John V, 345
kins, John V, 402
kins, John E. I, 549
kins, John G. II, 377
kins, John G. II, 747
kins, John, Jr. II, 233
kins, Jonathan I, 502
kins, Jonathan V, 503
kins, Joseph I, 502
kins, Joseph I, 549
kins, Joseph II, 177
kins, Joseph II, 233
kins, Joseph IV, 1321
kins, Joseph V, 249
kins, Joseph V, 339
kins, Joseph V, 402
kins, Joseph V, 446
kins, Joseph V, 458
kins, Joseph V, 503
kins, Joseph Richardson, Jr. II, 554
kins, Joseph W. I, 549
kins, Joseph W. I, 563
kins, Josephas V, 627
kins, Josephine V, 627
kins, Josephus V, 249
kins, Josephus V, 339
kins, Josephus V, 402
kins, Josephus V, 627
kins, Josiah V, 249
kins, Josiah V, 339
kins, Josiah V, 627
kins, Josiah V, 684
kins, Lela Rebecca V, 458
kins, Lelia I, 549
kins, Louella V, 627
kins, Lydia I, 399
kins, Lydia I, 401
kins, Lydia I, 549
kins, Lydia II, 177
kins, Lydia II, 233
kins, Lydia V, 249
kins, Lydia V, 318
kins, Lydia V, 339
Hoskins, Lydia V, 402
Hoskins, Lydia V, 501
Hoskins, Lydia V, 503
Hoskins, Lydia V, 625
Hoskins, Lydia V, 627
Hoskins, Lydia B. V, 339
Hoskins, Lydia P. V, 331
Hoskins, Lydia P. V, 339
Hoskins, Lydia P. V, 402
Hoskins, Lydia P. V, 621
Hoskins, Lydia P. V, 626
Hoskins, Lydia P. V, 627
Hoskins, Malinda V, 249
Hoskins, Malinda V, 284
Hoskins, Malinda V, 339
Hoskins, Marcy II, 636
Hoskins, Maria J. V, 339
Hoskins, Martha II, 487
Hoskins, Martha II, 554
Hoskins, Martha V, 249
Hoskins, Martha V, 339
Hoskins, Martha V, 625
Hoskins, Martha V, 627
Hoskins, Martha V, 684
Hoskins, Martha A. V, 627
Hoskins, Martha A. V, 684
Hoskins, Martha L. I, 549
Hoskins, Mary I, 399
Hoskins, Mary I, 401
Hoskins, Mary I, 502
Hoskins, Mary I, 549
Hoskins, Mary II, 80
Hoskins, Mary II, 177
Hoskins, Mary II, 198
Hoskins, Mary II, 233
Hoskins, Mary II, 245
Hoskins, Mary II, 252
Hoskins, Mary II, 554
Hoskins, Mary II, 611
Hoskins, Mary II, 678
Hoskins, Mary V, 249
Hoskins, Mary V, 339
Hoskins, Mary V, 486
Hoskins, Mary V, 503
Hoskins, Mary Ann V, 339
Hoskins, Mary B. V, 685
Hoskins, Mary C. V, 339
Hoskins, Mary Elizabeth V, 685
Hoskins, Mary J. I, 549
Hoskins, Mary Jane I, 549
Hoskins, Mary Jane I, 583
Hoskins, Mary Jane V, 339
Hoskins, Mary M. I, 549
Hoskins, Mary Newbold II, 198
Hoskins, Maud IV, 1321
Hoskins, Maud V, 249
Hoskins, Maud V, 339
Hoskins, Maud V, 458
Hoskins, Maud M. V, 458
Hoskins, Maud Milner IV, 1321
Hoskins, Maud Milner V, 339
Hoskins, Maude V, 458
Hoskins, Mildred V, 685
Hoskins, Milicent II, 377
Hoskins, Minnie V, 249
Hoskins, Minnie V, 339
Hoskins, Minnie Blanche V, 339
Hoskins, Moses I, 502
Hoskins, Moses I, 546
Hoskins, Moses I, 548
Hoskins, Moses V, 249
Hoskins, Moses V, 339
Hoskins, Moses V, 446
Hoskins, Moses V, 458
Hoskins, Moses V, 503
Hoskins, Moses V, 626
Hoskins, Moses F. V, 339
Hoskins, Moses F. V, 402
Hoskins, Moses Frazier V, 402
Hoskins, Moses, Jr. I, 548
Hoskins, Moses, Jr. V, 249
Hoskins, Moses, Jr. V, 339
Hoskins, Moses, Jr. V, 446
Hoskins, Nancy Jane V, 341
Hoskins, Nellie Curl V, 577
Hoskins, Nellie Curl V, 627
Hoskins, Nettie V, 627
Hoskins, Nettie V, 684
Hoskins, Nettie K. V, 627
Hoskins, Nettie K. V, 685
Hoskins, Newton I, 549
Hoskins, Newton C. I, 549
Hoskins, Orelius II, 377
Hoskins, P. P. I, 818
Hoskins, Phebe P. I, 818
Hoskins, Phebe P. I, 829
Hoskins, Polly I, 502
Hoskins, Rachel II, 177
Hoskins, Rachel V, 249
Hoskins, Rachel V, 280
Hoskins, Rachel V, 339
Hoskins, Rachel V, 626
Hoskins, Rachel Alma V, 249
Hoskins, Rachel E. V, 458
Hoskins, Raper II, 177
Hoskins, Raper II, 233
Hoskins, Raper II, 377
Hoskins, Raper II, 554
Hoskins, Raymond Reed V, 339
Hoskins, Rebecca V, 249
Hoskins, Richard II, 377
Hoskins, Richard II, 482
Hoskins, Richard II, 487
Hoskins, Richard II, 554
Hoskins, Richard II, 611
Hoskins, Richard II, 636
Hoskins, Richard V, 912
Hoskins, Robert II, 377
Hoskins, Robert Eugene I, 549
Hoskins, Russell V, 684
Hoskins, Ruth I, 502
Hoskins, Ruth I, 546
Hoskins, Ruth I, 548
Hoskins, Ruth I, 549
Hoskins, Ruth II, 177
Hoskins, Ruth II, 233
Hoskins, Ruth II, 252
Hoskins, Ruth II, 554
Hoskins, Ruth II, 634
Hoskins, Ruth V, 233
Hoskins, Ruth V, 249
Hoskins, Ruth V, 503
Hoskins, Sallie I, 549
Hoskins, Sallie E. I, 527
Hoskins, Sallie E. I, 549
Hoskins, Sarah I, 549
Hoskins, Sarah I, 576
Hoskins, Sarah II, 177
Hoskins, Sarah II, 233
Hoskins, Sarah II, 257
Hoskins, Sarah II, 554
Hoskins, Sarah Ann V, 338
Hoskins, Sarah Ann V, 339
Hoskins, Sarah Rebecca V, 341
Hoskins, Susan I, 549
Hoskins, Susan I, 620
Hoskins, Susanna I, 549
Hoskins, Thomas I, 549
Hoskins, Thomas II, 177
Hoskins, Thomas II, 233
Hoskins, Thomas VI, 826
Hoskins, Thomas F. I, 549
Hoskins, Walter I, 635
Hoskins, Walter I, 943
Hoskins, Walter V, 249
Hoskins, Walter Joshua I, 943
Hoskins, Widow Maria I, 549
Hoskins, William I, 502
Hoskins, William I, 549
Hoskins, William V, 249
Hoskins, William V, 339
Hoskins, William V, 503
Hoskins, William E. V, 627
Hoskins, Wm. Arthur V, 627
Hoskins, Wyatt II, 377
Hoskins, Wyatt II, 555
Hosmer, Susanna IV, 866
Hosser, Lewis I, 722
Hosteter, Zalinda IV, 820
Hosteter, Zalinda IV, 825
Hostetter, Elenor V, 627
Hostetter, Mary V, 1002
Hostetter, Samuel V, 627
Hotblach, Mary III, 172
Hotcher, Birch V, 458
Hotchkiss, Agnes III, 172
Hotchkiss, Agnes III, 203
Hotchkiss, Elizabeth IV, 1321
Hotchkiss, H. C. IV, 1321
Hotchkiss, Henry C. IV, 1321
Hotchkiss, Joseph J. IV, 1321
Hotchkiss, Livingston IV, 1321
Hotchkiss, Martha IV, 1321
Hotchkiss, Mathilda IV, 1321
Hotchkiss, Matilda K. IV, 1321
Hotchkiss, Willis IV, 1321
Hotson, John Hastie III, 172
Hotson, John Leslie III, 172
Hotson, John Leslie III, 249
Hotson, Lillie III, 172
Hotson, Mary May III, 172
Hotson, Mary May III, 249
Hott, Eleanor VI, 404
Hottell, Lena VI, 658
Hottell, Naaman VI, 658
Hottell, Naaman VI, 681
Hottell, Ruth N. VI, 658
Houch, Margaret II, 555
Houck, Anna V, 1002
Houck, Annie E. V, 1002
Houck, Barbara V, 1002
Houck, Barbary V, 1002
Houck, Barbra V, 1002
Houck, Camille IV, 967
Houck, Clara IV, 967
Houck, Elisabeth II, 555
Houck, Elizabeth II, 555
Houck, Elizabeth II, 691
Houck, Felty VI, 935
Houck, Geo. V, 1002
Houck, George V, 1002
Houck, Hamson V, 1002
Houck, Hannah II, 555
Houck, Harrison V, 1002
Houck, Isabella IV, 967
Houck, James V, 1002
Houck, Lavina V, 1002
Houck, Lydia E. IV, 967
Houck, Mahlon IV, 967
Houck, Mahlon V, 1002
Houck, Mahlon A. IV, 967
Houck, Margaret II, 555
Houck, Margaret II, 691
Houck, Mary II, 555
Houck, Mary IV, 967
Houck, Nancy V, 1002
Houck, Nona V, 1002
Houck, Nora V, 1002
Houck, Richard S. VI, 404
Houck, Susan V, 1002
Houck, Susanna VI, 935
Houck, Wm. II, 555
Houck, Wm. II, 691
Houck, Wm. V, 1002
Houcke, Elizabeth II, 555
Houcke, Hannah II, 555
Houel, Rebeck II, 80
Houey, Sarah IV, 224
Houge, Jane VI, 511
Houge, John VI, 511
Houge, John, Jr. VI, 511
Houge, Jonah VI, 511
Houge, Lydia VI, 511
Houge, Pleasant VI, 511
Houge, Samuel VI, 511
Houge, Sarah VI, 511
Hough, Alfred I, 976
Hough, Alice VI, 510
Hough, Amasa VI, 472
Hough, Amasa VI, 491
Hough, Amasa VI, 509
Hough, Amasa VI, 510
Hough, Amasa VI, 512
Hough, Amasa VI, 566
Hough, Amasa VI, 567
Hough, Amasa VI, 617
Hough, Amasa VI, 658
Hough, Amasa, Jr. VI, 509
Hough, Amasa, Jr. VI, 567
Hough, Amassa VI, 471
Hough, Amassa VI, 510
Hough, Amassa VI, 617
Hough, Amelia VI, 482
Hough, Amelia VI, 483
Hough, Amelia VI, 509
Hough, Amelia VI, 649
Hough, Amelia VI, 736
Hough, Amelia VI, 750
Hough, Amelis VI, 511
Hough, Amos IV, 17
Hough, Amos IV, 40
Hough, Amos IV, 69
Hough, Amos IV, 93
Hough, Amos IV, 150
Hough, Amos VI, 509
Hough, Amos VI, 512
Hough, Amos VI, 582
Hough, Ann I, 399
Hough, Ann I, 549
Hough, Ann IV, 40
Hough, Ann IV, 69
Hough, Ann IV, 93
Hough, Ann IV, 94
Hough, Ann VI, 404
Hough, Ann VI, 480
Hough, Ann VI, 509
Hough, Ann VI, 510
Hough, Ann VI, 512
Hough, Ann VI, 565
Hough, Ann VI, 780
Hough, Ann Deroza VI, 512
Hough, Ann Derozo VI, 543
Hough, Ann Derozzo VI, 543
Hough, Ann Derroza VI, 512
Hough, Ann Derrozo VI, 509
Hough, Ann Derrozo VI, 513
Hough, Ann Derrozo VI, 542
Hough, Ann E. VI, 471
Hough, Ann E. VI, 472
Hough, Ann E. VI, 491
Hough, Ann E. VI, 509
Hough, Ann E. VI, 510
Hough, Ann E. VI, 512
Hough, Ann E. VI, 566
Hough, Ann E. VI, 567
Hough, Ann E. VI, 617
Hough, Ann E. VI, 658
Hough, Ann Eliza VI, 509
Hough, Ann H. VI, 509
Hough, Ann H. VI, 512
Hough, Ann H. VI, 573
Hough, Anna Maria IV, 93
Hough, Anna Maria IV, 724
Hough, Anne I, 818
Hough, Annie E. VI, 512
Hough, B. VI, 512
Hough, Barnard VI, 511
Hough, Barnett VI, 509
Hough, Benjamin II, 377
Hough, Benjamin II, 555
Hough, Benjamin II, 682
Hough, Benjamin II, 961
Hough, Benjamin II, 1003
Hough, Benjamin IV, 40
Hough, Benjamin IV, 150
Hough, Benjamin IV, 224
Hough, Benjamin VI, 509
Hough, Benjamin VI, 510
Hough, Benjamin VI, 513
Hough, Benjamin VI, 580
Hough, Benjamin F. VI, 510
Hough, Bernard II, 961
Hough, Bernard II, 1003
Hough, Bertha F. VI, 512
Hough, Catharine IV, 150
Hough, Catherine IV, 40
Hough, Catherine IV, 1237
Hough, Catherine VI, 750
Hough, Charity I, 819
Hough, Charlotte I, 784
Hough, Charlotte I, 800
Hough, Charlotte I, 818
Hough, Charlotte I, 819
Hough, Charlotte II, 292
Hough, Daniel I, 818
Hough, Daniel I, 819
Hough, Daniel II, 961
Hough, Daniel V, 339
Hough, Dari Chanlot VI, 513
Hough, David V, 250
Hough, David VI, 510
Hough, David E. B. VI, 471
Hough, David E. B. VI, 473
Hough, David E. B. VI, 513
Hough, David E. B. VI, 658
Hough, David Walter VI, 510
Hough, Deborah II, 538
Hough, Deborah II, 555
Hough, Deborah II, 961
Hough, Deborah II, 998
Hough, Deborah II, 1003
Hough, Deborah VI, 471
Hough, Deborah B. VI, 509
Hough, Deborah B. VI, 510
Hough, Deborah B. VI, 617
Hough, Deborah B. VI, 618
Hough, Deborah B. VI, 658
Hough, Deborah B. VI, 675
Hough, Dezio Chaulette VI, 513
Hough, Edgar VI, 510
Hough, Edgar C. VI, 512
Hough, Edgar Stanley VI, 510
Hough, Edward VI, 510
Hough, Edward S. VI, 750
Hough, Eleanor VI, 472
Hough, Eleanor VI, 475
Hough, Eleanor VI, 481
Hough, Eleanor VI, 505
Hough, Eleanor VI, 509
Hough, Eleanor VI, 510
Hough, Eleanor VI, 512
Hough, Eleanor VI, 543
Hough, Eleanor VI, 556
Hough, Eleanor VI, 565
Hough, Eleanor VI, 568
Hough, Eleanor VI, 573
Hough, Eleanor H. VI, 510
Hough, Eleanor H. VI, 512
Hough, Elinor II, 1003
Hough, Elisabeth II, 555
Hough, Elisabeth VI, 510
Hough, Eliza M. IV, 224
Hough, Eliza M. IV, 241
Hough, Eliza N. VI, 471
Hough, Eliza N. VI, 473
Hough, Eliza N. VI, 475
Hough, Eliza N. VI, 510
Hough, Eliza N. VI, 512
Hough, Eliza P. IV, 93
Hough, Eliza P. IV, 98
Hough, Elizabeth I, 812
Hough, Elizabeth I, 818
Hough, Elizabeth I, 819
Hough, Elizabeth I, 976

Hough, Elizabeth I, 988
Hough, Elizabeth II, 292
Hough, Elizabeth II, 377
Hough, Elizabeth II, 555
Hough, Elizabeth II, 682
Hough, Elizabeth II, 691
Hough, Elizabeth II, 961
Hough, Elizabeth II, 1003
Hough, Elizabeth II, 1031
Hough, Elizabeth II, 1032
Hough, Elizabeth IV, 34
Hough, Elizabeth IV, 40
Hough, Elizabeth IV, 69
Hough, Elizabeth IV, 150
Hough, Elizabeth IV, 337
Hough, Elizabeth V, 339
Hough, Elizabeth V, 782
Hough, Elizabeth V, 787
Hough, Elizabeth VI, 472
Hough, Elizabeth VI, 480
Hough, Elizabeth VI, 487
Hough, Elizabeth VI, 488
Hough, Elizabeth VI, 509
Hough, Elizabeth VI, 510
Hough, Elizabeth VI, 511
Hough, Elizabeth VI, 512
Hough, Elizabeth VI, 513
Hough, Elizabeth VI, 539
Hough, Elizabeth VI, 555
Hough, Elizabeth VI, 556
Hough, Elizabeth VI, 561
Hough, Elizabeth VI, 565
Hough, Elizabeth VI, 572
Hough, Elizabeth VI, 579
Hough, Elizabeth VI, 583
Hough, Elizabeth M. VI, 509
Hough, Elizabeth M. VI, 567
Hough, Elizabeth S. VI, 510
Hough, Ellen H. VI, 509
Hough, Ellen I. VI, 404
Hough, Ellen I. VI, 416
Hough, Esther VI, 404
Hough, Eunice V, 250
Hough, Eunice V, 285
Hough, Fannie VI, 510
Hough, Fannie VI, 513
Hough, Fannie VI, 553
Hough, Fenton D. VI, 543
Hough, Franklin B. VI, 513
Hough, George S. VI, 510
Hough, George S. VI, 511
Hough, George S. VI, 727
Hough, George S. VI, 735
Hough, George S. VI, 746
Hough, George S. VI, 750
Hough, George S., Jr. VI, 750
Hough, Gulielma I, 988
Hough, Gulielma I, 989
Hough, Gulielma V, 953
Hough, Hannah II, 961
Hough, Hannah II, 975
Hough, Hannah II, 1003
Hough, Hannah IV, 337
Hough, Hannah IV, 355
Hough, Hannah VI, 510
Hough, Hannah VI, 511
Hough, Hannah VI, 513
Hough, Hannah VI, 553
Hough, Hannah VI, 554
Hough, Hannah VI, 580
Hough, Hannah Ann VI, 511
Hough, Harriet A. I, 943
Hough, Harriett Almina I, 928
Hough, Harrison V, 1002
Hough, Harrison VI, 750
Hough, Henrietta VI, 510
Hough, Henrietta VI, 512
Hough, Henrietta VI, 543
Hough, Henrietta C. VI, 512
Hough, Henrietta Chalmers VI, 510
Hough, Henrietta Chalmers VI, 513
Hough, Henrietta Chalmers VI, 543
Hough, Henry II, 961
Hough, Henry II, 1003
Hough, Henry II, 1024
Hough, Henry II, 1035
Hough, Henry C. VI, 510
Hough, Hester II, 961
Hough, Hester II, 981
Hough, Hiram V, 953
Hough, Hiram V, 954
Hough, Ida VI, 510
Hough, Ira I, 784
Hough, Ira I, 812
Hough, Ira I, 819
Hough, Ira I, 976
Hough, Ira I, 988
Hough, Isaac II, 961
Hough, Isaac VI, 510
Hough, Isaac VI, 543
Hough, Isaac S. VI, 510
Hough, Isaac S. VI, 512
Hough, Isaac S. VI, 543
Hough, Isabella VI, 416
Hough, Isaiah I, 976
Hough, Israel I, 784
Hough, Israel I, 818
Hough, Israel I, 971
Hough, Israel I, 988
Hough, Israel IV, 337
Hough, Israel IV, 411
Hough, Israel VI, 658
Hough, Israel J. VI, 658
Hough, Israel Janney VI, 510
Hough, Israel Janney VI, 511
Hough, Israel Janney VI, 658
Hough, Ivy Boyd VI, 510
Hough, James I, 928
Hough, James IV, 40
Hough, James IV, 338
Hough, James VI, 511
Hough, James Chalmers VI, 513
Hough, James M. VI, 658
Hough, Jane II, 207
Hough, Jane II, 233
Hough, Jane II, 258
Hough, Jane II, 292
Hough, Jane II, 377
Hough, Jane II, 450
Hough, Jane II, 555
Hough, Jane II, 991
Hough, Jane II, 1002
Hough, Jane VI, 511
Hough, Jane C. II, 878
Hough, Janney VI, 511
Hough, Jas. VI, 658
Hough, Jas. M. VI, 658
Hough, Jefferson II, 555
Hough, Jefferson VI, 510
Hough, Jemima I, 818
Hough, Jemima I, 819
Hough, Jennet II, 1003
Hough, Jesse I, 818
Hough, Jesse II, 961
Hough, Jesse II, 1003
Hough, Jesse II, 1023
Hough, Jesse V, 339
Hough, John I, 784
Hough, John I, 818
Hough, John I, 819
Hough, John I, 976
Hough, John I, 988
Hough, John II, 450
Hough, John II, 555
Hough, John II, 682
Hough, John II, 691
Hough, John II, 961
Hough, John II, 1003
Hough, John II, 1005
Hough, John II, 1031
Hough, John IV, 40
Hough, John IV, 337
Hough, John V, 339
Hough, John VI, 172
Hough, John VI, 181
Hough, John VI, 268
Hough, John VI, 404
Hough, John VI, 464
Hough, John VI, 500
Hough, John VI, 505
Hough, John VI, 507
Hough, John VI, 509
Hough, John VI, 510
Hough, John VI, 512
Hough, John VI, 564
Hough, John VI, 582
Hough, John VI, 645
Hough, John VI, 658
Hough, John C. VI, 511
Hough, John L. II, 801
Hough, John W. VI, 511
Hough, John, Jr. II, 1003
Hough, John, Jr. VI, 507
Hough, Jonah IV, 337
Hough, Jonah VI, 500
Hough, Jonah VI, 510
Hough, Jonah VI, 511
Hough, Jonah VI, 645
Hough, Jonah VI, 658
Hough, Jonathan I, 784
Hough, Jonathan I, 818
Hough, Jonathan I, 988
Hough, Jonathan I, 989
Hough, Jonathan II, 233
Hough, Jonathan II, 801
Hough, Jonathan V, 953
Hough, Jos. B. VI, 512
Hough, Jos., Jr. VI, 511
Hough, Joseph II, 555
Hough, Joseph II, 961
Hough, Joseph II, 1003
Hough, Joseph IV, 40
Hough, Joseph IV, 93
Hough, Joseph V, 78
Hough, Joseph V, 339
Hough, Joseph VI, 509
Hough, Joseph VI, 511
Hough, Joseph VI, 512
Hough, Joseph VI, 587
Hough, Joseph B. VI, 510
Hough, Joseph B. VI, 511
Hough, Joseph Elam VI, 181
Hough, Joseph N. II, 292
Hough, Joseph William IV, 93
Hough, Joseph William VI, 510
Hough, Keziah I, 818
Hough, Leticia II, 983
Hough, Leticia II, 1003
Hough, Lidia II, 1003
Hough, Louisa Richards II, 827
Hough, Lydia II, 555
Hough, Lydia VI, 507
Hough, Lydia VI, 511
Hough, Lydia VI, 587
Hough, Lydia Ann II, 801
Hough, Lydia Ann II, 832
Hough, Lydia Ann II, 878
Hough, Mahlon VI, 482
Hough, Mahlon VI, 509
Hough, Mahlon VI, 510
Hough, Mahlon VI, 511
Hough, Mahlon VI, 564
Hough, Mahlon VI, 736
Hough, Mahlon VI, 750
Hough, Mahlon VI, 780
Hough, Marcy II, 1003
Hough, Mare E. VI, 512
Hough, Margaret II, 878
Hough, Margery II, 961
Hough, Margery II, 989
Hough, Margery II, 1002
Hough, Maria IV, 89
Hough, Maria IV, 93
Hough, Maria IV, 98
Hough, Maria IV, 1237
Hough, Maria G. IV, 93
Hough, Maria G. IV, 105
Hough, Mariah IV, 1237
Hough, Mariam V, 339
Hough, Marietta VI, 509
Hough, Martha I, 818
Hough, Martha I, 928
Hough, Martha I, 988
Hough, Martha I, 989
Hough, Mary I, 784
Hough, Mary I, 818
Hough, Mary I, 819
Hough, Mary I, 971
Hough, Mary I, 976
Hough, Mary I, 985
Hough, Mary I, 988
Hough, Mary II, 212
Hough, Mary II, 233
Hough, Mary II, 377
Hough, Mary II, 555
Hough, Mary II, 691
Hough, Mary II, 829
Hough, Mary II, 961
Hough, Mary II, 975
Hough, Mary II, 1002
Hough, Mary II, 1003
Hough, Mary II, 1005
Hough, Mary II, 1035
Hough, Mary II, 1042
Hough, Mary IV, 40
Hough, Mary IV, 93
Hough, Mary IV, 95
Hough, Mary V, 339
Hough, Mary VI, 404
Hough, Mary VI, 442
Hough, Mary VI, 476
Hough, Mary VI, 480
Hough, Mary VI, 482
Hough, Mary VI, 509
Hough, Mary VI, 510
Hough, Mary VI, 511
Hough, Mary VI, 543
Hough, Mary VI, 558
Hough, Mary VI, 564
Hough, Mary VI, 736
Hough, Mary VI, 750
Hough, Mary VI, 780
Hough, Mary Ann VI, 473
Hough, Mary Ann VI, 481
Hough, Mary Ann VI, 492
Hough, Mary Ann VI, 509
Hough, Mary Ann VI, 510
Hough, Mary Ann VI, 511
Hough, Mary Ann VI, 512
Hough, Mary Ann VI, 513
Hough, Mary Ann VI, 542
Hough, Mary Ann VI, 543
Hough, Mary I. VI, 509
Hough, Mary I. VI, 567
Hough, Mary Isabel VI, 566
Hough, Mary J. V, 43
Hough, Mary J. V, 78
Hough, Mary Jane VI, 510
Hough, Mary Jane VI, 511
Hough, Mary Jane VI, 512
Hough, Mary Jane VI, 543
Hough, Mary M. VI, 511
Hough, Mary M. VI, 512
Hough, Mary Mills I, 988
Hough, Maryc Ann VI, 511
Hough, Mercy II, 961
Hough, Mercy II, 1003
Hough, Mercy II, 1023
Hough, Mical I, 549
Hough, Michal I, 549
Hough, Miriam V, 339
Hough, Miriam H. IV, 224
Hough, Nancy VI, 512
Hough, Oliver II, 803
Hough, Oliver II, 987
Hough, Oliver II, 1003
Hough, Oliver II, 1032
Hough, Olover II, 1052
Hough, Phebe II, 803
Hough, Phebe II, 987
Hough, Phebe II, 1003
Hough, Phebe II, 1023
Hough, Phebe II, 1052
Hough, Phebe Eleanor VI, 510
Hough, Phebe Eleanor VI, 511
Hough, Phebe Eleanor VI, 512
Hough, Phebe Eleanor VI, 513
Hough, Phebe S. VI, 512
Hough, Pheby II, 1032
Hough, Pleasant IV, 322
Hough, Pleasant IV, 337
Hough, Pleasant IV, 338
Hough, Pleasant VI, 500
Hough, Pleasant VI, 510
Hough, Pleasant VI, 645
Hough, Pleasant VI, 658
Hough, R. Clayton VI, 511
Hough, Rachel II, 961
Hough, Rachel IV, 40
Hough, Rachel IV, 150
Hough, Rachel V, 339
Hough, Rachel VI, 511
Hough, Rachel VI, 515
Hough, Rachel VI, 543
Hough, Rachel Ann VI, 492
Hough, Rachel Ann VI, 511
Hough, Rachel Ann VI, 512
Hough, Rachel Ann VI, 513
Hough, Rebecca II, 878
Hough, Rebecca II, 961
Hough, Rebecca II, 975
Hough, Rebecca II, 1003
Hough, Rebecca V, 339
Hough, Rebecca A. II, 878
Hough, Rebecca Jarrett II, 803
Hough, Rebeckah II, 961
Hough, Rebekah I, 818
Hough, Rebekah I, 843
Hough, Rebekah II, 1003
Hough, Rebekah II, 1024
Hough, Richard II, 538
Hough, Richard II, 555
Hough, Richard II, 961
Hough, Richard II, 975
Hough, Richard II, 981
Hough, Richard II, 989
Hough, Richard II, 998
Hough, Richard II, 1002
Hough, Richard II, 1003
Hough, Robert VI, 511
Hough, Robert VI, 512
Hough, Robert B. VI, 510
Hough, Robert B. VI, 512
Hough, Robert B. VI, 543
Hough, Robinson VI, 512
Hough, Robinson VI, 750
Hough, Rosa E. VI, 512
Hough, Ruth IV, 40
Hough, Ruth IV, 93
Hough, Ruth IV, 107
Hough, Ruth V, 339
Hough, Ruth VI, 509
Hough, Samuel II, 233
Hough, Samuel VI, 512
Hough, Samuel VI, 563
Hough, Samuel VI, 780
Hough, Samuel McPherson VI, 513
Hough, Samuel S. VI, 512
Hough, Samuel, Jr. VI, 512
Hough, Sarah I, 784
Hough, Sarah I, 818
Hough, Sarah I, 819
Hough, Sarah I, 820
Hough, Sarah II, 961
Hough, Sarah II, 975
Hough, Sarah II, 1002
Hough, Sarah II, 1003
Hough, Sarah II, 1035
Hough, Sarah IV, 30
Hough, Sarah IV, 40
Hough, Sarah V, 339
Hough, Sarah VI, 500
Hough, Sarah VI, 505
Hough, Sarah VI, 507
Hough, Sarah VI, 509
Hough, Sarah VI, 510
Hough, Sarah VI, 512
Hough, Sarah VI, 513
Hough, Sarah VI, 531
Hough, Sarah VI, 539
Hough, Sarah VI, 540
Hough, Sarah VI, 564
Hough, Sarah VI, 568
Hough, Sarah VI, 582
Hough, Sarah VI, 645
Hough, Sarah VI, 658
Hough, Sarah E. VI, 473
Hough, Sarah E. VI, 513
Hough, Sarah Elizabeth VI, 5
Hough, Sarah I. V, 953
Hough, Sarah I. V, 954
Hough, Sarah Jane IV, 411
Hough, Sarah Jane IV, 423
Hough, Sarah Louisa IV, 89
Hough, Sarah Louisa IV, 93
Hough, Sarah Louisa IV, 724
Hough, Sarah Louiza IV, 93
Hough, Sarah Louiza IV, 724
Hough, Sarah W. VI, 471
Hough, Sarah W. VI, 473
Hough, Sarah W. VI, 510
Hough, Sarah W. VI, 512
Hough, Sarah W. VI, 513
Hough, Sarah W. VI, 658
Hough, Sarah, Jr. VI, 568
Hough, Septimus II, 377
Hough, Septimus II, 961
Hough, Sophia VI, 750
Hough, Sophia VI, 771
Hough, Stacy VI, 512
Hough, Susan II, 720
Hough, Susan IV, 93
Hough, Susan IV, 96
Hough, Susan B. VI, 510
Hough, Susan B. VI, 746
Hough, Susanna IV, 40
Hough, Susanna IV, 93
Hough, Susannah IV, 93
Hough, Susannah VI, 512
Hough, Susannah B. VI, 750
Hough, Susannah M. VI, 491
Hough, Susannah M. VI, 512
Hough, Sydnor Hiram VI, 510
Hough, Sylvester IV, 1237
Hough, Thomas II, 233
Hough, Thomas II, 377
Hough, Thomas II, 450
Hough, Thomas II, 555
Hough, Thomas II, 691
Hough, Thomas II, 961
Hough, Thomas II, 991
Hough, Thomas II, 1002
Hough, Thomas II, 1003
Hough, Thomas IV, 40
Hough, Thomas IV, 337
Hough, Thomas VI, 416
Hough, Thomas VI, 509
Hough, Thomas VI, 511
Hough, Thomas VI, 512
Hough, Thos. IV, 355
Hough, W. H. VI, 511
Hough, W. H. VI, 512
Hough, Warrick C. VI, 512
Hough, Warwick VI, 512
Hough, Warwick C. VI, 491
Hough, Washington IV, 89
Hough, Washington IV, 93
Hough, Washington IV, 98
Hough, Washington IV, 105
Hough, Washington IV, 404
Hough, Washington VI, 512
Hough, Wd. Jane Chapman II, 801
Hough, Wd. Lydia II, 1003
Hough, Wd. Susannah B. VI,
Hough, Widow Deborah B. VI, 621
Hough, Widow Lydia VI, 512
Hough, Widow Mary I, 988
Hough, Widow Mary M. Scott VI, 511

ough, Widow Susannah B. VI, 511
ough, William I, 784
ough, William I, 818
ough, William I, 819
ough, William I, 971
ough, William I, 976
ough, William I, 988
ough, William II, 961
ough, William IV, 40
ough, William VI, 472
ough, William VI, 505
ough, William VI, 509
Hough, William VI, 511
Hough, William VI, 512
ough, William VI, 553
ough, William VI, 565
ough, William VI, 573
Hough, William H. VI, 475
Hough, William H. VI, 481
Hough, William H. VI, 510
Hough, William H. VI, 513
Hough, William H. VI, 565
Hough, William H., Jr. VI, 513
Hough, William III VI, 512
Hough, William S. VI, 750
Hough, William T. VI, 509
Hough, William T. VI, 513
Hough, William, Jr. VI, 512
Hough, Wm. VI, 475
Hough, Wm. VI, 481
Hough, Wm. VI, 499
Hough, Wm. VI, 500
Hough, Wm. VI, 510
Hough, Wm. VI, 512
Hough, Wm. VI, 543
Hough, Wm. VI, 556
Hough, Wm. VI, 568
Hough, Wm. H. VI, 471
Hough, Wm. H. VI, 473
Hough, Wm. H. VI, 492
Hough, Wm. H. VI, 509
Hough, Wm. H. VI, 511
Hough, Wm. H. VI, 512
Hough, Wm. H. VI, 513
Hough, Wm. H. VI, 542
Hough, Wm. H. VI, 543
Hough, Wm. H. VI, 580
Hough, Wm. H. VI, 658
Hough, Wm. H., Jr. VI, 473
Hough, Wm. Ogborn VI, 512
Hough, Zeri IV, 224
Hough, Zeri V, 339
Houghey, Barnett V, 503
Houghey, Elizabeth Ann V, 503
Houghey, John V, 503
Houghey, Margaret V, 503
Houghley, Alice I, 549
Houghton, Clementine III, 211
Houghton, Eliza III, 172
Houghton, Eliza L. III, 172
Houghton, Elwood V, 334
Houghton, Hugo III, 211
Houghton, Hugo H. III, 211
Houghton, John II, 555
Houghton, Lucy V, 78
Houghton, Lucy V, 334
Houghton, Lucy J. III, 211
Houghton, Martha E. S. III, 211
Houghton, Nestor III, 172
Houghton, Richard V, 334
Houghton, Richard E. V, 78
Houghton, Sally V, 78
Houghton, Sally V, 334
Houghton, Sarah V, 78
Houghton, William V, 78
Houghton, William A. III, 172
Houghton, Wm. V, 334
Hougland, Eleanor II, 220
Hougland, Eleanor II, 233
Houk, Clara IV, 967
Houk, Mary II, 555
Houke, Wm. II, 555
Houlton, David II, 376
Houlton, David II, 551
Houlton, John II, 551
Houlton, Mary II, 376
Houlton, William II, 376
Houltry, Elizabeth V, 1002
Houp, Daniel V, 685
Houp, Daniel M. V, 577
Houp, Gracie L. V, 577
Houp, Kate V, 685
Houp, Kate C. V, 577
Houp, Katie C. V, 577
Hourenton, Eliza I, 606
Hourenton, Eliza I, 607
Hous, George II, 377
Hous, Nathan II, 80
House, Ann II, 540
House, Ann II, 555
House, Bangor VI, 13
House, C. H. VI, 513
House, C. H. VI, 548
House, C. H. VI, 688
House, Elisabeth II, 524
House, Elisabeth II, 555
House, Elizabeth II, 377
House, Emma E. IV, 1321
House, Esther II, 377
House, Esther II, 555
House, Esther II, 677
House, Esther, Jr. II, 619
House, Eugene IV, 1321
House, Eugene E. IV, 1321
House, Evaline IV, 724
House, Evaline IV, 730
House, Frances II, 134
House, Francis II, 377
House, Francis II, 444
House, George II, 377
House, George II, 555
House, George II, 677
House, Henry W. IV, 224
House, Jacob II, 134
House, Jacob II, 151
House, Jonathan II, 134
House, Joseph II, 377
House, Joseph II, 555
House, Joseph II, 619
House, Martha II, 781
House, Martha D. II, 698
House, Mary II, 377
House, Mary II, 555
House, Mary II, 601
House, Mary VI, 109
House, Mary VI, 110
House, Mary E. VI, 658
House, Mrs. Emma IV, 1321
House, Nathan II, 80
House, Phebe II, 698
House, Phebe II, 801
House, Rachel II, 555
House, Rachel S. II, 708
House, Rebecca II, 524
House, Rebecca II, 555
House, Samuel II, 377
House, Samuel II, 555
House, Sarah VI, 513
House, Sarah VI, 548
House, Sarah VI, 658
House, Sarah R. VI, 513
House, Sarah R. VI, 548
House, Sarah R. VI, 688
House, Susanna II, 747
House, Susanna II, 801
House, Susannah II, 799
House, William II, 698
House, Wm. II, 801
Housefelt, Harman A. V, 179
Housefelt, Harmon V, 179
Housefelt, Sarah V, 78
Houseman, Margaret C. VI, 404
Houseman, Margaret E. VI, 367
Houser, Sarah V, 905
Houser, Sarah V, 912
Houskins, Ann V, 249
Houskins, Elizabeth V, 249
Houskins, Hannah V, 249
Housman, Mary II, 79
Housman, Mary II, 80
Houstead, Adam V, 1002
Houstead, Jennie V, 1002
Houstead, Rebecca V, 1002
Houstead, Samuel V, 1002
Houstead, Wm. V, 1002
Housted, Jennie V, 1002
Housted, Samuel V, 1002
Housted, William V, 340
Housted, Wm. V, 1002
Housted, Wm. A. V, 340
Houstet, Adam V, 685
Houston, Ardella V, 503
Houston, Daniel III, 370
Houston, Eleonor III, 172
Houston, Elizabeth III, 170
Houston, Elizabeth III, 171
Houston, Elizabeth III, 172
Houston, Elizabeth III, 274
Houston, Elizabethport III, 172
Houston, Ellsworth IV, 1166
Houston, Elsie III, 172
Houston, Frances III, 171
Houston, Frances III, 172
Houston, Lewis III, 370
Houston, Mary III, 172
Houston, Mary F. III, 370
Houston, Mathew V, 180
Houston, Moses B. III, 158
Houston, Moses B. III, 421
Houston, Rebecca V, 503
Houston, Robert V, 79
Hout, Caspar II, 376
Hout, Elizabeth II, 376
Hout, Jacob II, 376
Houton, Elizabeth II, 376
Houton, Thomas II, 444
Houts, Bell V, 1002
Houts, Belle V, 1002
Houts, Eliza IV, 724
Houts, Titus V, 1002
Houtzer, Ellen V, 1002
Houtzer, John C. V, 1002
Houtzer, Lydia V, 1002
Hover, Andrew IV, 40
Hover, Catherine IV, 40
Hover, Elizabeth IV, 40
Hover, Elizabeth V, 810
Hover, Elizabeth V, 817
Hover, Frederick V, 810
Hover, Frederick Henry IV, 40
Hover, John I, 721
Hover, John I, 737
Hover, John C. V, 810
Hover, Milicent I, 711
Hover, Milicent I, 721
Hover, Milicent I, 737
Hover, Rebecca IV, 40
Hover, Sarah IV, 40
Hover, Susanna IV, 40
Hovey, Elizabeth Hunt III, 172
Hovey, Isaac II, 80
Hovey, Ray C. IV, 1254
Hovey, Roy C. IV, 1254
Hovey, Sarah IV, 200
Hovey, Sarah IV, 224
How, Anna II, 177
Howard, ??? III, 316
Howard, ??? VI, 39
Howard, Abigail IV, 224
Howard, Abigail IV, 225
Howard, Abigail IV, 245
Howard, Abigail IV, 536
Howard, Abraham VI, 935
Howard, Ada V, 577
Howard, Adam V, 577
Howard, Alfred V, 577
Howard, Alice IV, 1166
Howard, Alice Naomi IV, 1166
Howard, Amanda V, 577
Howard, Amanda Mary V, 577
Howard, Ann II, 377
Howard, Ann II, 555
Howard, Ann IV, 150
Howard, Ann IV, 338
Howard, Ann IV, 1166
Howard, Ann VI, 504
Howard, Ann VI, 691
Howard, Ann C. II, 842
Howard, Anna I, 272
Howard, Anna I, 273
Howard, Anna IV, 536
Howard, Arthur IV, 1166
Howard, Asa III, 172
Howard, Asa IV, 224
Howard, Avis I, 271
Howard, Bartholomew I, 271
Howard, Bartholomew I, 272
Howard, Bartholomew IV, 150
Howard, Ben VI, 316
Howard, Ben VI, 888
Howard, Benjamin II, 377
Howard, Benjamin III, 172
Howard, Betsy VI, 935
Howard, Caleb II, 80
Howard, Callie I, 1154
Howard, Caroline A. VI, 935
Howard, Catharine III, 317
Howard, Catharine IV, 1177
Howard, Catharine VI, 935
Howard, Charles II, 377
Howard, Charles II, 555
Howard, Charles IV, 224
Howard, Charles IV, 536
Howard, Charles V, 577
Howard, Charles Fleming VI, 181
Howard, Cherry IV, 143
Howard, Cherry IV, 150
Howard, Cherry IV, 169
Howard, Cherry IV, 174
Howard, Cherry IV, 224
Howard, Cherry IV, 225
Howard, Cherry IV, 899
Howard, Cherry IV, 902
Howard, Chester Lester IV, 1166
Howard, Christopher VI, 935
Howard, Clark IV, 1282
Howard, Clem V, 577
Howard, Cleopatra VI, 935
Howard, Cordelia O. I, 1154
Howard, Cornelia O. I, 1142
Howard, David VI, 908
Howard, David VI, 935
Howard, David VI, 1017
Howard, Deborah II, 555
Howard, Deborah II, 589
Howard, Della V, 577
Howard, Delpha VI, 918
Howard, Dr. Samuel VI, 935
Howard, Edith II, 377
Howard, Edith II, 555
Howard, Edward II, 444
Howard, Edward V, 1002
Howard, Effa IV, 1321
Howard, Effa L. IV, 225
Howard, Effie IV, 225
Howard, Eleanor III, 66
Howard, Eleanor III, 148
Howard, Eli V, 577
Howard, Elisha IV, 224
Howard, Eliza A. VI, 860
Howard, Eliza Ann VI, 935
Howard, Eliza B. II, 377
Howard, Elizabeth II, 377
Howard, Elizabeth II, 444
Howard, Elizabeth II, 484
Howard, Elizabeth II, 555
Howard, Elizabeth II, 1003
Howard, Elizabeth II, 1005
Howard, Elizabeth VI, 911
Howard, Elizabeth VI, 935
Howard, Elizabeth S. VI, 898
Howard, Elma III, 172
Howard, Elma III, 364
Howard, Eva V, 577
Howard, Fannie Gordon III, 225
Howard, Florence S. II, 134
Howard, Florence S. W. II, 152
Howard, Florence T. W. II, 134
Howard, Frances VI, 826
Howard, Frances L. VI, 935
Howard, Francis I, 271
Howard, Frank V, 577
Howard, Frank V, 627
Howard, George V, 577
Howard, Grace Hickson IV, 1212
Howard, Gracie III, 510
Howard, Grover V, 577
Howard, Hannah I, 399
Howard, Hannah II, 50
Howard, Hannah II, 377
Howard, Hannah IV, 150
Howard, Hannah IV, 158
Howard, Hannah IV, 224
Howard, Hannah IV, 266
Howard, Hannah IV, 295
Howard, Hannah IV, 338
Howard, Hannah IV, 536
Howard, Hannah IV, 1166
Howard, Hannah Allen II, 80
Howard, Hannah, Jr. IV, 1166
Howard, Harold John V, 577
Howard, Harriet VI, 821
Howard, Harriet F. VI, 979
Howard, Harvey IV, 224
Howard, Henrietta IV, 1166
Howard, Henry I, 272
Howard, Henry II, 484
Howard, Henry II, 555
Howard, Henry II, 627
Howard, Henry IV, 40
Howard, Henry IV, 150
Howard, Henry VI, 216
Howard, Hester I, 1154
Howard, Hester A. I, 1142
Howard, Horton I, 269
Howard, Horton I, 271
Howard, Horton I, 272
Howard, Horton I, 273
Howard, Horton IV, 40
Howard, Horton IV, 150
Howard, Horton IV, 224
Howard, Horton IV, 338
Howard, Horton IV, 1166
Howard, Horton J. IV, 174
Howard, Horton J. IV, 224
Howard, Horton J. IV, 338
Howard, Horton, Jr. IV, 338
Howard, Hugh B. III, 172
Howard, Hugh B. III, 364
Howard, I Howard III, 510
Howard, Ida V, 577
Howard, Irene VI, 826
Howard, Isaac IV, 224
Howard, Isaac IV, 536
Howard, Isaac Ivins II, 1003
Howard, Isabella II, 827
Howard, J. C. VI, 826
Howard, Jacob VI, 826
Howard, James II, 842
Howard, James IV, 224
Howard, James IV, 536
Howard, James V, 577
Howard, James V, 1002
Howard, James V, 1003
Howard, James VI, 8
Howard, James VI, 13
Howard, James VI, 30
Howard, James VI, 148
Howard, James VI, 164
Howard, James VI, 166
Howard, James VI, 181
Howard, James VI, 216
Howard, James VI, 824
Howard, James VI, 935
Howard, James VI, 1018
Howard, James A. I, 1142
Howard, James C. VI, 826
Howard, James C. VI, 916
Howard, James R. IV, 225
Howard, Jane IV, 224
Howard, Jane IV, 295
Howard, Jane IV, 536
Howard, Jemima VI, 824
Howard, Jemima VI, 935
Howard, Jenett VI, 1019
Howard, John I, 271
Howard, John I, 272
Howard, John II, 377
Howard, John II, 555
Howard, John II, 633
Howard, John IV, 143
Howard, John IV, 150
Howard, John IV, 158
Howard, John IV, 174
Howard, John IV, 224
Howard, John IV, 266
Howard, John IV, 295
Howard, John IV, 338
Howard, John IV, 536
Howard, John IV, 899
Howard, John IV, 902
Howard, John IV, 1166
Howard, John VI, 935
Howard, John VI, 986
Howard, John B. VI, 935
Howard, John Bunting II, 555
Howard, John G. III, 172
Howard, John Gibbins, Jr. II, 555
Howard, John Jacob VI, 1017
Howard, John W. VI, 935
Howard, John, Jr. II, 555
Howard, Jones I, 271
Howard, Joseph I, 272
Howard, Joseph IV, 40
Howard, Joseph IV, 150
Howard, Joseph IV, 224
Howard, Joseph IV, 260
Howard, Joseph IV, 338
Howard, Joseph IV, 536
Howard, Joseph IV, 1166
Howard, Joseph VI, 750
Howard, Joseph Brown Cooper II, 555
Howard, Joseph T. D. II, 134
Howard, Josephine T. II, 134
Howard, Joshua II, 842
Howard, Joshua IV, 477
Howard, Judith VI, 994
Howard, Julia F. V, 577
Howard, Julia O. III, 172
Howard, Kate IV, 1147
Howard, Laura T. I, 1142
Howard, Laura T. I, 1154
Howard, Lester IV, 1166
Howard, Lester E. IV, 1166
Howard, Lester Eugene IV, 1166
Howard, Lillie V, 627
Howard, Louisa VI, 826
Howard, Lucy IV, 1166
Howard, Lucy VI, 1017
Howard, Luke II, 555
Howard, Luther Folger IV, 1166
Howard, M. A. G. VI, 826
Howard, Major VI, 935
Howard, Marcy VI, 182
Howard, Martha VI, 1018
Howard, Martha E. I, 1142
Howard, Martha Evelin I, 1154
Howard, Martha J. V, 46
Howard, Martha J. V, 78
Howard, Martha J. V, 577
Howard, Martha Jane V, 485
Howard, Martha Jane V, 503
Howard, Mary I, 268
Howard, Mary I, 269
Howard, Mary I, 271
Howard, Mary I, 272
Howard, Mary I, 936
Howard, Mary II, 80
Howard, Mary II, 233
Howard, Mary II, 240
Howard, Mary II, 377
Howard, Mary II, 444

Howard, Mary IV, 40
Howard, Mary IV, 150
Howard, Mary IV, 224
Howard, Mary IV, 225
Howard, Mary IV, 237
Howard, Mary IV, 338
Howard, Mary IV, 1166
Howard, Mary IV, 1171
Howard, Mary VI, 148
Howard, Mary VI, 164
Howard, Mary VI, 170
Howard, Mary VI, 576
Howard, Mary VI, 935
Howard, Mary VI, 967
Howard, Mary M. IV, 174
Howard, Mattie C. V, 340
Howard, May V, 577
Howard, Mead IV, 1166
Howard, Milley VI, 1018
Howard, Milley J. I, 1142
Howard, Milly I. I, 1154
Howard, Mordecai Bruce VI, 1000
Howard, Mrs. Effie IV, 1321
Howard, Nancy VI, 866
Howard, Nancy VI, 934
Howard, Nancy VI, 935
Howard, Nancy VI, 951
Howard, Nathaniel IV, 1282
Howard, Nicholas II, 444
Howard, Nina V, 577
Howard, Nina B. V, 577
Howard, Oliver II, 842
Howard, P. C. VI, 826
Howard, Peter II, 377
Howard, Peter II, 484
Howard, Peter II, 555
Howard, Peter II, 627
Howard, Pharaby IV, 221
Howard, Pharaby IV, 224
Howard, Pharaby IV, 536
Howard, Pharaby IV, 1166
Howard, Pharaby J. IV, 224
Howard, Pharaby J. IV, 260
Howard, Pharoby IV, 536
Howard, Pheraba IV, 225
Howard, Pleasant VI, 935
Howard, Pleasant VI, 994
Howard, Pleasant VI, 1017
Howard, Pleasant C. VI, 828
Howard, Pleasant C. VI, 831
Howard, Pleasant W. VI, 989
Howard, Pleasant W. VI, 1017
Howard, Pleasant W. VI, 1018
Howard, Polly VI, 935
Howard, Rachel I, 343
Howard, Rachel IV, 224
Howard, Rachel IV, 225
Howard, Rachel IV, 285
Howard, Rachel IV, 338
Howard, Rachel IV, 536
Howard, Rachel IV, 1163
Howard, Rachel IV, 1166
Howard, Rachel VI, 935
Howard, Raymond V, 577
Howard, Raymond B. V, 577
Howard, Rebecca II, 555
Howard, Rebecca II, 633
Howard, Richard II, 555
Howard, Robert II, 80
Howard, Robert VI, 935
Howard, Robert Wander II, 134
Howard, Ruth I, 271
Howard, Ruth I, 272
Howard, Ruth IV, 150
Howard, Ruth IV, 224
Howard, Ruth IV, 902
Howard, Ruth IV, 918
Howard, Sally VI, 935
Howard, Sally VI, 972
Howard, Sally VI, 1017
Howard, Samuel J. VI, 1006
Howard, Sarah I, 1142
Howard, Sarah II, 377
Howard, Sarah II, 530
Howard, Sarah II, 546
Howard, Sarah II, 555
Howard, Sarah III, 317
Howard, Sarah IV, 150
Howard, Sarah IV, 224
Howard, Sarah IV, 338
Howard, Sarah IV, 725
Howard, Sarah IV, 1159
Howard, Sarah IV, 1166
Howard, Sarah V, 1003
Howard, Sarah VI, 750
Howard, Sarah A. VI, 826
Howard, Sarah Crispe VI, 181
Howard, Sarah D. IV, 174
Howard, Sarah D. VI, 224
Howard, Sarah D. IV, 899
Howard, Sarah E. I, 1154
Howard, Sarah Elizabeth VI, 1017
Howard, Sarah L. IV, 629
Howard, Sarah L. IV, 637
Howard, Sarah M. III, 316
Howard, Sarah P. II, 494
Howard, Sarah P. II, 555
Howard, Shadrack VI, 866
Howard, Silvanus VI, 898
Howard, Silvanus VI, 908
Howard, Silvanus VI, 935
Howard, Susan VI, 994
Howard, Susan M. V, 577
Howard, Susie III, 510
Howard, Sylvanus VI, 935
Howard, Sylvanus VI, 979
Howard, Thomas II, 377
Howard, Thomas II, 555
Howard, Thomas IV, 725
Howard, Thomas VI, 826
Howard, Thomas VI, 865
Howard, Thos. III, 317
Howard, Vila IV, 208
Howard, Vila IV, 225
Howard, Viley IV, 224
Howard, W. E., Jr. I, 1142
Howard, W. H. III, 510
Howard, Waldo V, 627
Howard, William II, 377
Howard, William III, 317
Howard, William IV, 821
Howard, William VI, 892
Howard, William VI, 951
Howard, William D. VI, 797
Howard, William E. I, 1142
Howard, William E. I, 1154
Howard, William T. VI, 826
Howard, Wm. V, 577
Howard, Wm. E. I, 1154
Howarth, Henry I, 578
Howarth, Margaret I, 578
Howder, Adaline IV, 1369
Howe, Alta V, 180
Howe, Alta Wright V, 180
Howe, Amanda V, 744
Howe, Amanda M. II, 830
Howe, Amanda M. II, 878
Howe, Caroline M. III, 297
Howe, Ed V, 180
Howe, Edward V, 180
Howe, Elijah V, 180
Howe, Elnora V, 744
Howe, Estella V, 744
Howe, Fannie V, 180
Howe, Fannie S. II, 878
Howe, Frances II, 830
Howe, Jedediah II, 830
Howe, Jedediah II, 878
Howe, Jesse Bell V, 180
Howe, Lucy Leona V, 180
Howe, Lucy Leone V, 180
Howe, Mariah V, 577
Howe, Molly V, 744
Howe, Phebe II, 80
Howe, Phebe II, 95
Howe, Reva V, 180
Howe, Sarah W. II, 878
Howe, Thomas G. V, 78
Howe, William V, 577
Howe, Wm. P. II, 152
Howel, ??? IV, 725
Howel, Aaron V, 577
Howel, Alice I, 549
Howel, Alice I, 552
Howel, Alice I, 819
Howel, Ann I, 389
Howel, Ann I, 399
Howel, Ann VI, 404
Howel, Ann E. II, 295
Howel, Anna E. IV, 725
Howel, Anna Elma IV, 725
Howel, Anne I, 399
Howel, Annie E. IV, 725
Howel, Cosmelia VI, 404
Howel, Daisy V, 685
Howel, Deborah IV, 159
Howel, Dorcas IV, 524
Howel, Dorcas IV, 536
Howel, Elizabeth V, 577
Howel, Elma IV, 687
Howel, Elma IV, 725
Howel, Elma IV, 1197
Howel, Ephraim II, 1003
Howel, Esther I, 819
Howel, Frankey VI, 934
Howel, Hannah I, 819
Howel, Hannah VI, 404
Howel, Isabella V, 577
Howel, Jane IV, 909
Howel, Jane Rebecca IV, 909
Howel, John I, 819
Howel, John VI, 404
Howel, John VI, 934
Howel, John K. V, 685
Howel, John, Jr. I, 819
Howel, John, Sr. I, 819
Howel, Jonathan I, 549
Howel, Levice VI, 901
Howel, Louisa V, 577
Howel, Luther J. IV, 725
Howel, Luther Jonah IV, 725
Howel, Margaret A. I, 242
Howel, Martha I, 234
Howel, Martha I, 242
Howel, Martha V, 953
Howel, Mary I, 819
Howel, Mary I, 831
Howel, Mary II, 556
Howel, Mary II, 688
Howel, Mary II, 1003
Howel, Mary IV, 536
Howel, Mary IV, 549
Howel, Mary IV, 725
Howel, Mary VI, 404
Howel, Mary VI, 497
Howel, Mary D. VI, 404
Howel, Mary E. II, 292
Howel, Minerva IV, 1367
Howel, Rachel I, 722
Howel, Rachel I, 724
Howel, Rebecca I, 798
Howel, Rebecca I, 819
Howel, Rebecca IV, 159
Howel, Rebecca Jane VI, 404
Howel, Rebeck II, 80
Howel, Rebeckah VI, 500
Howel, Ruth VI, 424
Howel, Ruth H. VI, 404
Howel, Sallie V, 685
Howel, Saly VI, 871
Howel, Samuel VI, 404
Howel, Samuel D. II, 292
Howel, Sarah VI, 373
Howel, Sarah VI, 404
Howel, Sarah Ellen V, 591
Howel, Susanna II, 556
Howel, Thomas I, 819
Howel, Timothy IV, 159
Howel, Timothy IV, 909
Howel, Virginia VI, 404
Howel, William VI, 404
Howel, William T. I, 242
Howell, Aaron V, 577
Howell, Aaron V, 685
Howell, Abi I, 309
Howell, Abigail II, 377
Howell, Abigail II, 556
Howell, Abner VI, 936
Howell, Abraham II, 377
Howell, Abraham II, 378
Howell, Abraham II, 508
Howell, Abraham II, 556
Howell, Abraham VI, 925
Howell, Abram VI, 925
Howell, Aby I, 309
Howell, Adala Ann II, 734
Howell, Adala Ann II, 747
Howell, Adaline V, 577
Howell, Adelia Ann II, 557
Howell, Alexander VI, 936
Howell, Alice I, 549
Howell, Alice I, 784
Howell, Alice I, 819
Howell, Alice II, 556
Howell, Alice E. I, 337
Howell, Alice Eliza I, 337
Howell, Altha Ann IV, 1369
Howell, Altheann IV, 1369
Howell, Altheann IV, 1375
Howell, Ann I, 1122
Howell, Ann I, 1123
Howell, Ann II, 377
Howell, Ann II, 378
Howell, Ann II, 454
Howell, Ann II, 481
Howell, Ann II, 546
Howell, Ann II, 556
Howell, Ann II, 557
Howell, Ann II, 655
Howell, Ann II, 1074
Howell, Ann V, 953
Howell, Ann VI, 404
Howell, Ann VI, 658
Howell, Ann VI, 719
Howell, Ann VI, 875
Howell, Ann E. II, 292
Howell, Ann Emlen II, 378
Howell, Ann Emlen II, 557
Howell, Ann Emlin II, 292
Howell, Ann M. VI, 750
Howell, Ann W. II, 1074
Howell, Ann W. II, 1082
Howell, Anna E. IV, 725
Howell, Anna Elma IV, 1166
Howell, Anne II, 557
Howell, Annie Elma IV, 1166
Howell, Aquila VI, 750
Howell, Arthur II, 377
Howell, Arthur II, 378
Howell, Arthur II, 556
Howell, Arthur II, 557
Howell, Arthur II, 604
Howell, Arthur IV, 1166
Howell, Arthur IV, 1282
Howell, Arthur E. IV, 1166
Howell, Arthur W. V, 577
Howell, Asher M. II, 557
Howell, Asher Mott II, 377
Howell, Benjamin V, 577
Howell, Benjamin G. IV, 1369
Howell, Benjamin L. V, 685
Howell, Benjamin S. V, 78
Howell, Benjamin S. V, 577
Howell, Benjamin S. V, 578
Howell, Beulah II, 557
Howell, Blanch V, 503
Howell, Caleb II, 377
Howell, Caleb II, 378
Howell, Caleb II, 557
Howell, Caleb Scattergood II, 233
Howell, Caroline II, 292
Howell, Caroline II, 747
Howell, Caroline VI, 750
Howell, Catharine II, 377
Howell, Catharine II, 557
Howell, Catherine II, 556
Howell, Catherine II, 678
Howell, Charles II, 556
Howell, Charles II, 708
Howell, Charles E. V, 577
Howell, Charles H. V, 578
Howell, Charles H. V, 685
Howell, Charles W. V, 577
Howell, Charlott IV, 1369
Howell, Charlotte IV, 1369
Howell, Charlotte A. IV, 1177
Howell, Charlotte Ann IV, 1166
Howell, Charlotte C. VI, 750
Howell, Chester II, 556
Howell, Clarence IV, 1166
Howell, Clary VI, 935
Howell, Cornelia V, 953
Howell, Cornelia V, 958
Howell, Cornelia VI, 404
Howell, Cosmelia V, 953
Howell, Cosmelia VI, 404
Howell, Cosmelia VI, 750
Howell, Daisy V, 685
Howell, Daisy Dean V, 577
Howell, Daniel VI, 517
Howell, Daniel G. I, 337
Howell, Darius C. II, 557
Howell, Darius C. II, 747
Howell, David VI, 404
Howell, David VI, 661
Howell, David VI, 750
Howell, David VI, 753
Howell, David VI, 755
Howell, David VI, 901
Howell, David VI, 935
Howell, David VI, 936
Howell, David VI, 947
Howell, David VI, 997
Howell, David VI, 1021
Howell, David E. I, 337
Howell, David J. IV, 967
Howell, David, Jr. VI, 404
Howell, Dean V, 78
Howell, Deborah II, 377
Howell, Deborah II, 556
Howell, Deborah II, 557
Howell, Deborah II, 708
Howell, Deborah IV, 150
Howell, Deborah VI, 658
Howell, Deborah T. II, 708
Howell, Drury VI, 936
Howell, Drury O. VI, 936
Howell, E??? II, 377
Howell, Edey VI, 1000
Howell, Edward Warner II, 557
Howell, Elijah VI, 936
Howell, Elizabeth I, 549
Howell, Elizabeth I, 773
Howell, Elizabeth I, 784
Howell, Elizabeth II, 292
Howell, Elizabeth II, 377
Howell, Elizabeth II, 378
Howell, Elizabeth II, 454
Howell, Elizabeth II, 501
Howell, Elizabeth II, 554
Howell, Elizabeth II, 556
Howell, Elizabeth II, 557
Howell, Elizabeth II, 585
Howell, Elizabeth II, 678
Howell, Elizabeth II, 708
Howell, Elizabeth III, 173
Howell, Elizabeth III, 327
Howell, Elizabeth V, 577
Howell, Elizabeth VI, 875
Howell, Elizabeth VI, 933
Howell, Elizabeth VI, 935
Howell, Elizabeth VI, 936
Howell, Elizabeth VI, 997
Howell, Elizabeth VI, 1000
Howell, Elizabeth King VI, 968
Howell, Elizabeth R. II, 557
Howell, Elizabeth S. II, 292
Howell, Elizabeth S. II, 747
Howell, Elizabeth Smith II, 378
Howell, Elizabeth Smith II, 557
Howell, Ellen VI, 949
Howell, Elma IV, 1166
Howell, Emaline M. V, 578
Howell, Emeline II, 557
Howell, Emeline V, 912
Howell, Emeline M. V, 577
Howell, Emeline M. V, 685
Howell, Esther I, 784
Howell, Esther I, 819
Howell, Esther II, 556
Howell, Etta May V, 577
Howell, Eunice VI, 936
Howell, Everett C. V, 685
Howell, Everette C. V, 578
Howell, Fanny VI, 1019
Howell, Flora V, 577
Howell, Flora E. V, 577
Howell, Flora E. V, 578
Howell, Flora E. V, 685
Howell, Florence V, 78
Howell, Florentine VI, 936
Howell, Frances II, 556
Howell, Frances IV, 1282
Howell, Francis IV, 1166
Howell, Francis B. V, 577
Howell, Francis B. V, 578
Howell, Francis B. V, 685
Howell, Francis E. IV, 1166
Howell, Frank I, 337
Howell, Franky VI, 901
Howell, Geitar I, 337
Howell, Geo. IV, 1166
Howell, Geo. IV, 1177
Howell, George II, 177
Howell, George II, 292
Howell, George II, 377
Howell, George II, 378
Howell, George II, 556
Howell, George II, 557
Howell, George II, 747
Howell, George IV, 1166
Howell, George C. I, 337
Howell, George Christopher I, 337
Howell, George F. II, 878
Howell, George F. IV, 1166
Howell, George F. Jr III, 173
Howell, George Francis IV, 1166
Howell, George T. III, 173
Howell, George T. III, 306
Howell, Grace M. IV, 1166
Howell, Hannah I, 549
Howell, Hannah I, 554
Howell, Hannah I, 784
Howell, Hannah I, 819
Howell, Hannah II, 131
Howell, Hannah II, 377
Howell, Hannah II, 378
Howell, Hannah II, 546
Howell, Hannah II, 556
Howell, Hannah II, 557
Howell, Hannah II, 558
Howell, Hannah II, 585
Howell, Hannah II, 604
Howell, Hannah V, 953
Howell, Hannah V, 958
Howell, Hannah VI, 404
Howell, Hannah VI, 407
Howell, Hannah VI, 502
Howell, Hannah VI, 513
Howell, Hannah VI, 517
Howell, Hannah VI, 749
Howell, Hannah VI, 750
Howell, Hannah VI, 753
Howell, Hannah VI, 756
Howell, Hannah Dellis VI, 936
Howell, Hannah L. II, 478
Howell, Hannah L. II, 557
Howell, Hannah M. VI, 404
Howell, Hannah M. VI, 750
Howell, Hannah M. VI, 755
Howell, Hannah McPherson VI, 661

well, Hannah McPherson VI, 753
well, Hannah S. IV, 1369
well, Hannah W. II, 708
well, Henry C. VI, 772
well, Hopewell VI, 404
well, Hugh II, 377
well, Hugh II, 546
well, Hugh II, 556
well, Hugh II, 557
well, Hugh II, 585
well, Huldah I, 86
well, Isaac II, 378
well, Isaac II, 535
well, Isaac II, 556
well, Isaac II, 557
well, Isaac Q. III, 173
well, Isabel IV, 949
well, Isabella V, 577
well, Isabella V, 685
well, Isabelle V, 577
well, Israel II, 377
well, Israel II, 378
well, Israel II, 556
well, Israel II, 557
well, Israel VI, 617
well, Israel VI, 658
well, Israel VI, 704
well, Israel R. VI, 517
well, Israel Richardson VI, 517
well, Jacob I, 784
well, Jacob I, 819
well, Jacob II, 377
well, Jacob II, 378
well, Jacob II, 481
well, Jacob II, 518
well, Jacob II, 556
well, Jacob II, 557
well, Jacob II, 558
well, Jacob R. II, 378
well, Jacob Roberts II, 557
well, Jacob, Jr. II, 556
well, Jacob, Jr. II, 663
well, Jaines VI, 826
well, James I, 819
well, James II, 378
well, James VI, 826
well, James VI, 935
well, James Emlen II, 378
well, James Emlen II, 557
well, James Weaver I, 337
well, Jane II, 378
well, Jane II, 555
well, Jane II, 557
well, Jane II, 587
well, Jane VI, 658
well, Jane VI, 690
owell, Jared R. IV, 1369
owell, Jemima VI, 925
owell, Jesse VI, 871
owell, John I, 549
owell, John I, 554
owell, John I, 784
owell, John I, 819
owell, John II, 378
owell, John II, 556
owell, John III, 327
owell, John V, 953
owell, John VI, 404
owell, John VI, 750
owell, John VI, 906
owell, John VI, 935
owell, John VI, 968
owell, John VI, 1021
owell, John A. II, 557
owell, John A. II, 747
owell, John B. II, 557
owell, John B. II, 708
owell, John B. III, 193
owell, John Brazier III, 173
owell, John C. II, 747
owell, John K. V, 577
owell, John K. V, 627
owell, John K. V, 685
owell, John Ladd II, 378
owell, John Littler II, 556
owell, John M. VI, 404
owell, John, Jr. I, 819
owell, John, Sr. I, 819
owell, Jonathan I, 549
owell, Jonathan I, 773
owell, Jonathan I, 784
owell, Jonathan I, 819
owell, Jonathan II, 556
owell, Joseph II, 377
owell, Joseph II, 378
owell, Joseph II, 454
owell, Joseph II, 518
owell, Joseph II, 556
owell, Joseph II, 557
Howell, Joseph II, 558
Howell, Joseph II, 562
Howell, Joseph II, 604
Howell, Joseph II, 708
Howell, Joseph II, 1074
Howell, Joseph VI, 935
Howell, Joseph B. III, 173
Howell, Joseph E. II, 557
Howell, Joseph, Jr. II, 378
Howell, Joseph, Jr. II, 556
Howell, Joseph, Sr. II, 378
Howell, Joshua II, 377
Howell, Joshua II, 378
Howell, Joshua II, 556
Howell, Joshua II, 678
Howell, Joshua Emlen II, 292
Howell, Joshua Emlen II, 708
Howell, Joshua Emlen II, 747
Howell, Josiah I, 242
Howell, Judith VI, 997
Howell, Katharine II, 557
Howell, Katherine II, 556
Howell, Laviney VI, 935
Howell, Lemuel II, 131
Howell, Lewis II, 49
Howell, Lewis II, 80
Howell, Lewis II, 444
Howell, Lida IV, 1282
Howell, Lloyd II, 444
Howell, Lou I, 337
Howell, Lou I, 340
Howell, Louisa V, 577
Howell, Louisa V, 685
Howell, Lucretia VI, 842
Howell, Lucrettia VI, 1000
Howell, Lucy VI, 935
Howell, Lucy A. VI, 1008
Howell, Luther Jonah IV, 1166
Howell, Lutie A. V, 577
Howell, Lutie A. V, 578
Howell, Lutie A. V, 685
Howell, Lydia II, 378
Howell, Lydia II, 1074
Howell, Lydia II, 1076
Howell, Lydia VI, 404
Howell, Lydia VI, 497
Howell, Lydia VI, 513
Howell, Lydia VI, 658
Howell, Lydia E. IV, 1369
Howell, Lydia Patience I, 337
Howell, Mackaria VI, 896
Howell, Mahlon VI, 658
Howell, Margaret I, 784
Howell, Margaret II, 378
Howell, Margaret II, 503
Howell, Margaret II, 516
Howell, Margaret II, 527
Howell, Margaret II, 556
Howell, Margaret II, 557
Howell, Margaret II, 642
Howell, Margaret II, 655
Howell, Margaret A. I, 242
Howell, Margaret Ann II, 378
Howell, Margaret Ann II, 557
Howell, Margaret Louisa I, 337
Howell, Margaret-Ann II, 557
Howell, Margareta II, 557
Howell, Margareta II, 570
Howell, Margarett I, 819
Howell, Margarett I, 823
Howell, Margarett II, 697
Howell, Mariah G. IV, 1369
Howell, Martha I, 242
Howell, Martha V, 953
Howell, Martha VI, 750
Howell, Martha Caroline I, 337
Howell, Martha W. V, 953
Howell, Mary I, 242
Howell, Mary I, 784
Howell, Mary I, 819
Howell, Mary II, 177
Howell, Mary II, 377
Howell, Mary II, 378
Howell, Mary II, 481
Howell, Mary II, 508
Howell, Mary II, 555
Howell, Mary II, 556
Howell, Mary II, 557
Howell, Mary II, 570
Howell, Mary II, 604
Howell, Mary II, 662
Howell, Mary II, 663
Howell, Mary II, 677
Howell, Mary II, 706
Howell, Mary II, 827
Howell, Mary II, 1003
Howell, Mary III, 173
Howell, Mary IV, 967
Howell, Mary V, 953
Howell, Mary VI, 404
Howell, Mary VI, 513
Howell, Mary VI, 617
Howell, Mary VI, 658
Howell, Mary VI, 704
Howell, Mary VI, 750
Howell, Mary VI, 925
Howell, Mary VI, 936
Howell, Mary A. V, 577
Howell, Mary A. V, 578
Howell, Mary A. V, 685
Howell, Mary Ann VI, 517
Howell, Mary Ann VI, 750
Howell, Mary D. VI, 404
Howell, Mary Dawes II, 378
Howell, Mary Dawes II, 557
Howell, Mary E. II, 292
Howell, Mary E. VI, 517
Howell, Mary Eliza IV, 1166
Howell, Mary Elizabeth I, 337
Howell, Mary Elizabeth II, 557
Howell, Mary G. IV, 1369
Howell, Mary Mott II, 557
Howell, Mary Richardson VI, 750
Howell, Mary S. II, 878
Howell, Mary S. VI, 712
Howell, Mary S. VI, 714
Howell, Mary Sutton III, 173
Howell, Mary W. II, 292
Howell, Mary W. II, 378
Howell, Mary W. II, 708
Howell, Mary W. II, 747
Howell, Mary Whitlock II, 503
Howell, Mary Whitlock II, 557
Howell, Merdith VI, 936
Howell, Moses VI, 936
Howell, Mynerva C. IV, 1369
Howell, Nancy VI, 936
Howell, Naomi VI, 936
Howell, Nathan VI, 404
Howell, Obediah VI, 936
Howell, Ora B. VI, 936
Howell, Patience II, 556
Howell, Patience II, 557
Howell, Patsey VI, 886
Howell, Patsy VI, 936
Howell, Paul VI, 936
Howell, Paul P. I, 337
Howell, Paul Pearson I, 337
Howell, Phebe II, 557
Howell, Phebe II, 747
Howell, Phebe IV, 1166
Howell, Phebe IV, 1177
Howell, Phebe VI, 658
Howell, Phebe C. IV, 1183
Howell, Phebe Catherine IV, 1166
Howell, Phebe H. II, 878
Howell, Phebe H. III, 173
Howell, Phebe H. III, 306
Howell, Philip II, 377
Howell, Philip II, 555
Howell, Philip II, 587
Howell, Phillie IV, 1166
Howell, Phillip II, 444
Howell, Pleasant VI, 936
Howell, Polley VI, 877
Howell, Polly VI, 826
Howell, Polly VI, 972
Howell, Rachel I, 242
Howell, Rachel II, 378
Howell, Rachel II, 557
Howell, Rachel II, 633
Howell, Rachel II, 1065
Howell, Rachel II, 1074
Howell, Rachel II, 1083
Howell, Rachel V, 960
Howell, Rachel VI, 750
Howell, Rebecca I, 819
Howell, Rebecca II, 49
Howell, Rebecca II, 80
Howell, Rebecca II, 378
Howell, Rebecca II, 454
Howell, Rebecca II, 463
Howell, Rebecca II, 556
Howell, Rebecca II, 557
Howell, Rebecca VI, 404
Howell, Rebecca VI, 517
Howell, Rebecca VI, 658
Howell, Rebecca VI, 901
Howell, Rebecca Jane V, 953
Howell, Rebecca Jane VI, 404
Howell, Rebecca Jane VI, 750
Howell, Rebecca Jane VI, 751
Howell, Rebeck II, 80
Howell, Rebecka VI, 1021
Howell, Rebeckah VI, 517
Howell, Rebekah VI, 513
Howell, Rebekah VI, 658
Howell, Rebekah VI, 690
Howell, Reece II, 501
Howell, Richard II, 377
Howell, Robert II, 378
Howell, Rosa V, 685
Howell, Ruhannah II, 444
Howell, Ruth III, 173
Howell, Ruth VI, 404
Howell, Ruth H. VI, 404
Howell, Sallie I, 337
Howell, Sallie V, 577
Howell, Sallie V, 685
Howell, Sallie A. V, 577
Howell, Sallie Peele I, 337
Howell, Sally IV, 1369
Howell, Sally VI, 871
Howell, Sally VI, 947
Howell, Sally A. IV, 1369
Howell, Sally A. IV, 1383
Howell, Samuel II, 377
Howell, Samuel II, 378
Howell, Samuel II, 454
Howell, Samuel II, 481
Howell, Samuel II, 503
Howell, Samuel II, 527
Howell, Samuel II, 546
Howell, Samuel II, 556
Howell, Samuel II, 557
Howell, Samuel II, 570
Howell, Samuel II, 655
Howell, Samuel II, 661
Howell, Samuel V, 953
Howell, Samuel V, 958
Howell, Samuel VI, 404
Howell, Samuel VI, 407
Howell, Samuel VI, 750
Howell, Samuel VI, 753
Howell, Samuel C. V, 953
Howell, Samuel C. V, 960
Howell, Samuel D. II, 292
Howell, Samuel D. II, 557
Howell, Samuel Dawes II, 378
Howell, Samuel Dawes II, 557
Howell, Samuel Daws II, 557
Howell, Samuel E. II, 177
Howell, Samuel E. II, 292
Howell, Samuel E. II, 378
Howell, Samuel E. II, 503
Howell, Samuel E. II, 557
Howell, Samuel, Jr. II, 516
Howell, Samuel, Jr. II, 556
Howell, Samuel, Jr. II, 557
Howell, Sarah I, 549
Howell, Sarah I, 561
Howell, Sarah I, 784
Howell, Sarah I, 819
Howell, Sarah II, 292
Howell, Sarah II, 378
Howell, Sarah II, 495
Howell, Sarah II, 527
Howell, Sarah II, 556
Howell, Sarah II, 557
Howell, Sarah II, 657
Howell, Sarah II, 661
Howell, Sarah II, 827
Howell, Sarah V, 577
Howell, Sarah VI, 397
Howell, Sarah VI, 404
Howell, Sarah VI, 617
Howell, Sarah VI, 618
Howell, Sarah VI, 623
Howell, Sarah VI, 658
Howell, Sarah VI, 704
Howell, Sarah VI, 705
Howell, Sarah VI, 750
Howell, Sarah VI, 936
Howell, Sarah VI, 971
Howell, Sarah Ann VI, 658
Howell, Sarah Ellen V, 577
Howell, Sarah F. II, 292
Howell, Sarah F. II, 747
Howell, Selina VI, 936
Howell, Sidney II, 378
Howell, Sidney II, 556
Howell, Sidney II, 557
Howell, Sidney II, 561
Howell, Sidney II, 562
Howell, Spicer VI, 936
Howell, Spicer VI, 950
Howell, Spicer VI, 971
Howell, Spicer VI, 1000
Howell, Spicy VI, 936
Howell, Stephen I, 549
Howell, Stephen II, 556
Howell, Stephen VI, 658
Howell, Stephen VI, 704
Howell, Stephen VI, 935
Howell, Susan VI, 826
Howell, Susanna II, 521
Howell, Susanna II, 557
Howell, Susanna II, 668
Howell, Susannah II, 378
Howell, Susannah II, 556
Howell, Sydna II, 518
Howell, Sydna II, 556
Howell, Thomas I, 242
Howell, Thomas I, 784
Howell, Thomas I, 819
Howell, Thomas II, 378
Howell, Thomas II, 444
Howell, Thomas II, 495
Howell, Thomas II, 555
Howell, Thomas II, 556
Howell, Thomas II, 573
Howell, Thomas VI, 935
Howell, Thomas VI, 936
Howell, Thomas VI, 971
Howell, Timothy VI, 658
Howell, Timothy VI, 690
Howell, Verna II, 131
Howell, Vincent VI, 936
Howell, Virginia V, 953
Howell, Virginia VI, 404
Howell, Virginia VI, 751
Howell, Washington VI, 875
Howell, Washington VI, 960
Howell, Wd. Hannah II, 556
Howell, Wd. Patience II, 535
Howell, Wd. Ruth VI, 517
Howell, William I, 264
Howell, William II, 377
Howell, William II, 378
Howell, William IV, 1166
Howell, William VI, 404
Howell, William VI, 901
Howell, William VI, 936
Howell, William VI, 1008
Howell, William VI, 1019
Howell, William R. II, 292
Howell, William Rumford II, 292
Howell, William T. I, 242
Howell, Willie Denmark I, 337
Howell, Wm. II, 555
Howell, Wm. II, 557
Howell, Wm. II, 747
Howell, Wm. II, 1074
Howell, Wm. IV, 1166
Howell, Wm. IV, 1282
Howell, Wm. V, 953
Howell, Wm. C. V, 577
Howell, Wm. Douglas VI, 750
Howell, Wm. Rawle II, 557
Howell, Wm. W. II, 557
Howell, Zophar C. II, 557
Howell, Zophar C. II, 747
Hower, Joseph V, 1003
Hower, Maria V, 1003
Howerton, Elizabeth VI, 826
Howerton, Elizabeth VI, 853
Howerton, Elizabeth VI, 995
Howerton, George VI, 826
Howerton, Grief VI, 833
Howerton, Heritage VI, 826
Howerton, Heritage VI, 846
Howerton, Hermitage VI, 811
Howerton, Joseph VI, 811
Howerton, Joseph VI, 827
Howerton, Lucy VI, 995
Howerton, Martha Lester VI, 827
Howerton, Mary VI, 826
Howerton, Nancy VI, 846
Howerton, Penelope VI, 826
Howerton, Susan VI, 811
Howerton, Thomas VI, 826
Howerton, Willmerth VI, 833
Howes, Edgar J. II, 907
Howes, Henry Wilmer IV, 225
Howes, Sarah W. II, 907
Howes, Wm. P. II, 152
Howeth, Elizabeth VI, 820
Howett, Mary C. V, 78
Howey, Abigail II, 80
Howey, Alfred III, 173
Howey, Ann IV, 708
Howey, Benjamin II, 80
Howey, Benjamin II, 557
Howey, Deborah II, 80
Howey, Eliz. T. III, 173
Howey, Isaac II, 80
Howey, Jacob III, 173
Howey, Jacob C. II, 120
Howey, Joshua II, 80
Howey, Mary II, 80
Howey, Naomi II, 62
Howey, Naomi II, 80
Howey, Rebecca II, 32
Howey, Rebecca L. II, 120
Howey, Robert, Jr. II, 62
Howey, Robert, Jr. II, 80
Howey, Sibyl T. II, 120
Howey, Wm. II, 80
Howgan, Barba Mary II, 444
Howgan, Thomas II, 444
Howison, Ebenezer III, 173
Howit, Francis II, 449
Howit, John II, 449
Howit, Sarah II, 449

Howitt, Thomas III, 173
Howland, Abram VI, 751
Howland, Algermon Sydney III, 173
Howland, Allen III, 173
Howland, Ann Eliza III, 173
Howland, Barnabas V, 503
Howland, Barnabas V, 578
Howland, Benjamin V, 78
Howland, Benjamin V, 180
Howland, Bennie V, 180
Howland, Catharine II, 790
Howland, Catharine II, 848
Howland, Catharine II, 878
Howland, Charles H. III, 173
Howland, Chas. Adams II, 847
Howland, Chas. S. V, 912
Howland, Chas. S. V, 931
Howland, Chas. W. V, 912
Howland, Elcy V, 94
Howland, Eliza III, 173
Howland, Eliza H. III, 173
Howland, Elizabeth III, 101
Howland, Emma III, 173
Howland, Euphamia V, 78
Howland, Euphamia V, 180
Howland, Euphenia V, 78
Howland, Fannie V, 180
Howland, Geo. V, 180
Howland, George II, 292
Howland, George II, 301
Howland, George II, 847
Howland, George B. V, 78
Howland, George B. V, 180
Howland, Gideon III, 173
Howland, Gideon VI, 182
Howland, Gilbert Jr III, 173
Howland, Gulielma V, 912
Howland, Hannah III, 173
Howland, Hannah H. III, 173
Howland, Harriett V, 78
Howland, Henry J. III, 173
Howland, I. III, 173
Howland, Isaac III, 173
Howland, John II, 878
Howland, John III, 101
Howland, John H. III, 111
Howland, John H. III, 173
Howland, John Jr III, 173
Howland, Jos. Brown III, 173
Howland, Joseph T. III, 173
Howland, Laura V, 180
Howland, Louisa V, 180
Howland, Louisa V, 627
Howland, Lydia V, 503
Howland, Lydia V, 578
Howland, Martha A. III, 173
Howland, Martha Hazard III, 173
Howland, Mary II, 779
Howland, Mary V, 503
Howland, Mary V, 578
Howland, Mary C. V, 912
Howland, Mary C. V, 931
Howland, Mary H. Delano III, 173
Howland, Mary R. III, 173
Howland, Mary Rodman III, 173
Howland, Mary S. V, 912
Howland, Matthew II, 292
Howland, Matthew II, 301
Howland, Murray S. V, 912
Howland, Oren Clark V, 180
Howland, Owen V, 180
Howland, Owen Clark V, 78
Howland, Pontius III, 173
Howland, Rachel C. II, 292
Howland, Rachel C. II, 301
Howland, Rachel S. II, 292
Howland, Richard G. III, 173
Howland, Robert Bowne III, 173
Howland, Ruth E. Williams V, 578
Howland, Sarah III, 111
Howland, Sarah III, 134
Howland, Sarah III, 173
Howland, Sarah III, 252
Howland, Sarah R. III, 111
Howland, Sarah R. III, 173
Howland, Susan II, 292
Howland, Susan II, 301
Howland, Susannah II, 878
Howland, Tenta III, 173
Howland, Thomas C. III, 173
Howland, Thomas H. VI, 751
Howland, Wd. Frances II, 847
Howland, William H. III, 173
Howland, William Hazard III, 173
Howland, William W. III, 173
Howland, Wm. P. III, 173
Howland, Wm. W. Jr III, 173
Howle, Martha VI, 182
Howle, Martha VI, 208
Howley, Henry III, 173
Howley, Jane III, 173
Howley, John IV, 967
Hownks, Franziska III, 173
Hownks, Franziska III, 243
Hownks, Walter III, 173
Hownks, Walter III, 243
Howood, Barba Mary II, 444
Howood, Edward II, 444
Howood, Elizabeth II, 444
Howood, Mary II, 444
Howry, Catherine VI, 936
Howry, John VI, 936
Howser, Elizabeth VI, 936
Howser, Thos. VI, 936
Howser, W. VI, 936
Howser, William B. VI, 936
Howwell, John I, 272
Hoxey, Betsey IV, 1370
Hoxey, Chas. V, 627
Hoxey, Chas. E. V, 627
Hoxey, Howard A. V, 627
Hoxey, Louisa V, 627
Hoxey, Lydia IV, 1370
Hoxey, Lydia IV, 1371
Hoxey, Rhoda E. V, 627
Hoxey, Susannah A. V, 627
Hoxie, Abigail IV, 1370
Hoxie, Chas. V, 627
Hoxie, Chas. E. V, 627
Hoxie, Christopher III, 173
Hoxie, Edward V, 627
Hoxie, Edward E. V, 627
Hoxie, Ellen III, 173
Hoxie, Ellen III, 297
Hoxie, Ellen H. III, 297
Hoxie, Ezra IV, 1370
Hoxie, Hannah III, 173
Hoxie, Hannah III, 297
Hoxie, Henry N. IV, 1088
Hoxie, Henry N. IV, 1102
Hoxie, Howard A. V, 627
Hoxie, Isaac Upton III, 173
Hoxie, Isaac Upton III, 297
Hoxie, Joseph IV, 1102
Hoxie, Lenard P. IV, 1370
Hoxie, Louisa V, 627
Hoxie, Louisa G. V, 627
Hoxie, Louisa J. V, 627
Hoxie, Mary IV, 1102
Hoxie, Mary IV, 1370
Hoxie, Mary IV, 1383
Hoxie, Phebe IV, 1370
Hoxie, Rhoda E. V, 627
Hoxie, Sarah B. IV, 1088
Hoxie, Sarah B. IV, 1102
Hoxie, Susan A. V, 627
Hoxie, Susannah A. V, 627
Hoxsey, Betsey IV, 1370
Hoxsey, Eliza IV, 1370
Hoxsey, Ezra IV, 1370
Hoxsey, Jane IV, 1370
Hoxsey, John IV, 1370
Hoxsey, Leonard IV, 1370
Hoxsey, Lydia IV, 1370
Hoxsey, Orren IV, 1370
Hoxsey, Phebe IV, 1370
Hoxsey, S. Horrace IV, 1370
Hoxsie, ??? III, 71
Hoxsie, Abigail IV, 1370
Hoxsie, Betsey IV, 1370
Hoxsie, Dorcas III, 15
Hoxsie, Dorcas III, 173
Hoxsie, Eliza IV, 1370
Hoxsie, Ezra IV, 1370
Hoxsie, Harris P. IV, 1370
Hoxsie, Horace S. IV, 1370
Hoxsie, Jane IV, 1370
Hoxsie, John IV, 1369
Hoxsie, John IV, 1370
Hoxsie, Lenard P. IV, 1370
Hoxsie, Leonard IV, 1370
Hoxsie, Leonard S. IV, 1370
Hoxsie, Lodowick III, 15
Hoxsie, Lodowick III, 173
Hoxsie, Lydia IV, 1370
Hoxsie, Martha IV, 1370
Hoxsie, Mary III, 71
Hoxsie, Mary III, 173
Hoxsie, Mary IV, 1370
Hoxsie, Orren IV, 1370
Hoxsie, Orrin IV, 1370
Hoxsie, Phebe IV, 1370
Hoxsie, S. Horrace IV, 1370
Hoxsie, Sarah III, 173
Hoxsie, Zebulon III, 173
Hoxsley, Eliza C. III, 173
Hoy, Mary II, 493
Hoy, Ralph II, 493
Hoy, Ralph II, 557
Hoy, Rebecah II, 493
Hoy, Rebeccah II, 557
Hoy, Wm. II, 493
Hoyce, Elmira I, 5
Hoyce, Josiah I, 5
Hoyes, Alice E. V, 1003
Hoyl, Edith IV, 150
Hoyl, Edith IV, 155
Hoyl, John IV, 150
Hoyl, Sarah IV, 150
Hoyl, William IV, 150
Hoyl, William IV, 155
Hoyland, Eliza III, 94
Hoyland, Elizabeth III, 173
Hoyland, James III, 174
Hoyland, Jane III, 174
Hoyland, Jane III, 224
Hoyland, John III, 174
Hoyland, Mary III, 173
Hoyland, Mary III, 174
Hoyland, Mary III, 224
Hoyland, Wm. III, 173
Hoyland, Wm. III, 174
Hoyland, Wm. III, 224
Hoyle, Albertus IV, 411
Hoyle, Albertus IV, 558
Hoyle, Albertus C. IV, 412
Hoyle, Albertus C. IV, 457
Hoyle, Albertus L. II, 708
Hoyle, Albertus L. II, 747
Hoyle, Albertus L. III, 421
Hoyle, Albertus L. IV, 412
Hoyle, Alburtus L. IV, 536
Hoyle, Alice Cary IV, 412
Hoyle, Amie IV, 478
Hoyle, Amos B. IV, 225
Hoyle, Amos B. IV, 478
Hoyle, Ann IV, 400
Hoyle, Ann IV, 412
Hoyle, Ann IV, 478
Hoyle, Ann IV, 497
Hoyle, Ann Shelitta IV, 478
Hoyle, Ann Shiletto IV, 478
Hoyle, Anna IV, 412
Hoyle, Annie IV, 225
Hoyle, Annie W. IV, 225
Hoyle, Annie W. IV, 478
Hoyle, Benj. IV, 438
Hoyle, Benj. IV, 473
Hoyle, Benj. IV, 478
Hoyle, Benj. IV, 504
Hoyle, Benj. Gilliann IV, 225
Hoyle, Benj. W. III, 421
Hoyle, Benjamin IV, 225
Hoyle, Benjamin IV, 255
Hoyle, Benjamin IV, 304
Hoyle, Benjamin IV, 411
Hoyle, Benjamin IV, 412
Hoyle, Benjamin IV, 421
Hoyle, Benjamin IV, 441
Hoyle, Benjamin IV, 477
Hoyle, Benjamin IV, 478
Hoyle, Benjamin W. II, 708
Hoyle, Benjamin, Jr. IV, 225
Hoyle, Benjamin, Jr. IV, 411
Hoyle, Charles, Jr. VI, 851
Hoyle, Clara P. IV, 412
Hoyle, Clarence P. IV, 412
Hoyle, Clinton III, 421
Hoyle, Deborah IV, 225
Hoyle, Deborah T. IV, 536
Hoyle, Deborah T. IV, 550
Hoyle, Dorathy II, 708
Hoyle, Dorothy IV, 225
Hoyle, Dorothy IV, 478
Hoyle, Dorothy IV, 480
Hoyle, Dorothy IV, 825
Hoyle, Dorothy IV, 828
Hoyle, Dorothy J. IV, 825
Hoyle, Dorothy Johnson IV, 825
Hoyle, Edith IV, 150
Hoyle, Edith IV, 478
Hoyle, Edward IV, 477
Hoyle, Eleanore Mary II, 708
Hoyle, Elizabeth IV, 225
Hoyle, Elizabeth IV, 374
Hoyle, Elizabeth IV, 411
Hoyle, Elizabeth IV, 412
Hoyle, Elizabeth IV, 469
Hoyle, Elizabeth IV, 478
Hoyle, Elizabeth IV, 808
Hoyle, Elizabeth IV, 825
Hoyle, Elizabeth V, 477
Hoyle, Elizabeth V, 503
Hoyle, Elizabeth Morris IV, 478
Hoyle, Elizabeth P. IV, 478
Hoyle, Ellis IV, 225
Hoyle, Ellis IV, 478
Hoyle, Ellis J. IV, 225
Hoyle, Elma IV, 225
Hoyle, Elma IV, 282
Hoyle, Elma C. IV, 478
Hoyle, Elma S. IV, 225
Hoyle, Elmer R. IV, 412
Hoyle, Elmira IV, 478
Hoyle, Elmira IV, 504
Hoyle, Elvira II, 747
Hoyle, Elvira IV, 225
Hoyle, Emery D. IV, 412
Hoyle, Emory D. IV, 412
Hoyle, Ezekiel IV, 225
Hoyle, Ezekiel IV, 412
Hoyle, Ezekiel B. IV, 400
Hoyle, Ezekiel B. IV, 411
Hoyle, Ezekiel B. IV, 412
Hoyle, Frances Clinton III, 421
Hoyle, Frederick IV, 411
Hoyle, Frederick C. IV, 179
Hoyle, Frederick C. IV, 225
Hoyle, Frederick C. IV, 371
Hoyle, Frederick C. IV, 412
Hoyle, Guli Ann IV, 304
Hoyle, Gulia Ann IV, 255
Hoyle, Gulian IV, 225
Hoyle, Guliann IV, 478
Hoyle, Guliann IV, 504
Hoyle, Hammah W. IV, 411
Hoyle, Hannah II, 708
Hoyle, Hannah IV, 170
Hoyle, Hannah IV, 225
Hoyle, Hannah IV, 338
Hoyle, Hannah IV, 364
Hoyle, Hannah IV, 411
Hoyle, Hannah IV, 412
Hoyle, Hannah IV, 438
Hoyle, Hannah IV, 477
Hoyle, Hannah IV, 478
Hoyle, Hannah IV, 497
Hoyle, Hannah IV, 536
Hoyle, Hannah IV, 673
Hoyle, Hannah IV, 825
Hoyle, Hannah M. Hammond IV, 478
Hoyle, Hannah V. IV, 338
Hoyle, Hannah V. IV, 478
Hoyle, Hannah W. IV, 431
Hoyle, Harriet III, 421
Hoyle, Helen IV, 412
Hoyle, Howard E. IV, 225
Hoyle, Howard E. IV, 282
Hoyle, Jane IV, 469
Hoyle, Jane IV, 478
Hoyle, Jane IV, 797
Hoyle, Jane IV, 808
Hoyle, Jane IV, 825
Hoyle, Jane IV, 943
Hoyle, Jane IV, 1012
Hoyle, Jane IV, 1016
Hoyle, Jno. L. VI, 827
Hoyle, John IV, 150
Hoyle, John IV, 225
Hoyle, John IV, 395
Hoyle, John IV, 411
Hoyle, John IV, 469
Hoyle, John IV, 473
Hoyle, John IV, 477
Hoyle, John IV, 478
Hoyle, John IV, 497
Hoyle, John IV, 501
Hoyle, John IV, 808
Hoyle, John IV, 825
Hoyle, John G. IV, 225
Hoyle, John G. IV, 374
Hoyle, John G. IV, 411
Hoyle, John G. IV, 412
Hoyle, John Willets IV, 225
Hoyle, John, Jr. IV, 478
Hoyle, John, Jr. IV, 480
Hoyle, John, Jr. IV, 825
Hoyle, John, Jr. IV, 828
Hoyle, John, Sr. IV, 225
Hoyle, John, Sr. IV, 478
Hoyle, Jos. IV, 502
Hoyle, Joseph IV, 150
Hoyle, Joseph IV, 155
Hoyle, Joseph IV, 225
Hoyle, Joseph IV, 475
Hoyle, Joseph IV, 477
Hoyle, Joseph IV, 478
Hoyle, Joseph IV, 825
Hoyle, Joseph L. IV, 536
Hoyle, Joseph L. IV, 550
Hoyle, Joseph Lindley IV, 225
Hoyle, Joseph Lindley IV, 338
Hoyle, Joseph Lindley IV, 412
Hoyle, Joseph Lindley IV, 478
Hoyle, Joshua Coppock IV, 825
Hoyle, Josiah IV, 411
Hoyle, Josiah IV, 477
Hoyle, Julian IV, 478
Hoyle, Juliann IV, 225
Hoyle, Laura Josephine IV, 411
Hoyle, Lindley IV, 225
Hoyle, Lindley IV, 478
Hoyle, Louisa IV, 478
Hoyle, Lucy IV, 478
Hoyle, Lydia IV, 225
Hoyle, Lydia IV, 255
Hoyle, Mabel II, 708
Hoyle, Mabel B. II, 747
Hoyle, Mabel B. III, 421
Hoyle, Mabel B. IV, 412
Hoyle, Mabel B. IV, 457
Hoyle, Mabel B. IV, 536
Hoyle, Mabel B. IV, 558
Hoyle, Mabel H. IV, 388
Hoyle, Mabel H. IV, 412
Hoyle, Mabel Jane IV, 411
Hoyle, Martha IV, 412
Hoyle, Martha A. Camp. VI, 827
Hoyle, Martha B. IV, 225
Hoyle, Martha B. IV, 412
Hoyle, Martha H. IV, 179
Hoyle, Martha H. IV, 225
Hoyle, Martha H. IV, 371
Hoyle, Martha H. IV, 412
Hoyle, Mary IV, 225
Hoyle, Mary IV, 411
Hoyle, Mary IV, 412
Hoyle, Mary IV, 421
Hoyle, Mary IV, 438
Hoyle, Mary IV, 478
Hoyle, Mary IV, 501
Hoyle, Mary IV, 536
Hoyle, Mary Ann IV, 477
Hoyle, Mary E. IV, 557
Hoyle, Mary Eliza IV, 225
Hoyle, Mary Eliza IV, 304
Hoyle, Mary H. IV, 387
Hoyle, Mary H. IV, 411
Hoyle, Mary H. IV, 412
Hoyle, Matthew W. IV, 478
Hoyle, Matthew Watson IV, 478
Hoyle, Mildred IV, 412
Hoyle, Morris J. IV, 478
Hoyle, Nathan A. IV, 412
Hoyle, Nathan B. IV, 411
Hoyle, Nathan H. IV, 412
Hoyle, Pauline III, 421
Hoyle, Phebe IV, 225
Hoyle, Phebe IV, 475
Hoyle, Phebe IV, 478
Hoyle, Pheby IV, 502
Hoyle, Prudence IV, 225
Hoyle, Prudence IV, 478
Hoyle, Prudence IV, 488
Hoyle, Rachel II, 706
Hoyle, Rachel IV, 225
Hoyle, Rachel IV, 395
Hoyle, Rachel IV, 399
Hoyle, Rachel IV, 427
Hoyle, Rachel IV, 444
Hoyle, Rachel IV, 473
Hoyle, Rachel IV, 478
Hoyle, Richard Wilson III, 421
Hoyle, Robert Bracken IV, 412
Hoyle, Ruth IV, 150
Hoyle, Ruth IV, 155
Hoyle, Ruth IV, 477
Hoyle, Ruth IV, 478
Hoyle, Sabina IV, 477
Hoyle, Sabina IV, 478
Hoyle, Sabina IV, 488
Hoyle, Sarah IV, 150
Hoyle, Sarah IV, 225
Hoyle, Sarah IV, 375
Hoyle, Sarah IV, 382
Hoyle, Sarah IV, 395
Hoyle, Sarah IV, 411
Hoyle, Sarah IV, 441
Hoyle, Sarah IV, 473
Hoyle, Sarah IV, 477
Hoyle, Sarah IV, 478
Hoyle, Sarah IV, 497
Hoyle, Simeon IV, 225
Hoyle, Simeon IV, 411
Hoyle, Simeon IV, 412
Hoyle, Simeon S. IV, 387
Hoyle, Simeon S. IV, 411
Hoyle, Tabitha IV, 374
Hoyle, Tabitha IV, 411
Hoyle, Tabitha IV, 412
Hoyle, Tabitha IV, 441
Hoyle, Tabitha IV, 473
Hoyle, Tabitha IV, 477
Hoyle, Tabitha IV, 478
Hoyle, Thomas IV, 225
Hoyle, Thomas IV, 338
Hoyle, Thomas IV, 412
Hoyle, Thomas IV, 478
Hoyle, Thomas IV, 536

le, Thomas IV, 825
le, Thomas L. VI, 827
le, Webster B. IV, 412
le, William II, 708
le, William IV, 150
le, William IV, 225
le, William IV, 411
le, William IV, 477
le, William IV, 478
le, William C. IV, 338
le, William G. IV, 338
le, William G. IV, 412
le, William L. IV, 225
le, William Wilson II, 708
le, Wm. II, 747
le, Wm. IV, 225
le, Wm. IV, 412
le, Wm. IV, 431
le, Wm. IV, 536
le, Wm. G. IV, 825
t, Edith III, 328
t, Edith III, 330
t, Edith III, 331
t, Edith Lilian III, 174
t, Emeline III, 58
t, Emeline III, 174
t, Emeline III, 331
t, Emily F. VI, 732
t, Emily F. VI, 774
t, Fred IV, 1321
t, Fred R. IV, 1321
t, Geo. A. III, 58
t, George III, 174
t, George A. III, 174
t, George A. III, 331
t, Georgia III, 174
t, Georgia III, 251
t, Georgiana III, 251
t, Georgina III, 174
t, Ida IV, 1321
t, Ida H. IV, 1321
t, Lyda Imogene III, 174
t, Mabel M. III, 58
t, Mabel M. III, 174
t, Matilda IV, 1321
t, Matilda L. IV, 1321
t, S. Olivia III, 174
t, Samuel III, 375
t, Wd. Emeline III, 174
t, Wd. Emeline III, 224
zer, Elizabeth V, 78
zer, Lewis I, 722
zer, Lewis V, 78
zer, Mary V, 78
zer, Nathan V, 78
zer, Nathan V, 744
zer, William I, 722
zer, William V, 78
zer, William V, 744
zier, Elizabeth V, 78
zier, Hannah VI, 751
zier, James M. VI, 751
zier, Maria IV, 536
zier, Maria VI, 751
bard, Edith I, 242
bard, George VI, 167
bard, George VI, 182
bard, Jacob I, 448
bard, Jacob I, 549
bard, Joseph I, 272
bard, Joseph I, 448
bard, Judith VI, 182
bard, Martha H. VI, 936
bard, Stephen VI, 936
bbard, A. H. IV, 227
bbard, Abbie L. III, 30
bbard, Abbie L. III, 174
bbard, Abigail I, 784
bbard, Abigail I, 805
bbard, Abigail I, 819
bbard, Abigail IV, 225
ubbard, Abigail S. III, 174
ubbard, Abram. VI, 936
ubbard, Achsa VI, 229
ubbard, Achsah I, 533
ubbard, Achsah I, 549
ubbard, Agnes VI, 233
ubbard, Agnes VI, 249
ubbard, Agnes VI, 285
ubbard, Agnes VI, 286
ubbard, Agness VI, 233
ubbard, Alice VI, 315
ubbard, Amos L. VI, 182
ubbard, Ann I, 549
ubbard, Ann I, 784
ubbard, Ann I, 814
ubbard, Ann I, 819
ubbard, Anna I, 549
ubbard, Anna I, 784
ubbard, Anna I, 819
ubbard, Anna Grace I, 549
Hubbard, Anna K. IV, 1321
Hubbard, Anna K. IV, 1322
Hubbard, Anna L. IV, 227
Hubbard, Anne I, 511
Hubbard, Anne I, 819
Hubbard, Ashsa VI, 249
Hubbard, Bathsheba V, 340
Hubbard, Bathsheba V, 358
Hubbard, Benjamin I, 784
Hubbard, Benjamin VI, 314
Hubbard, Benjamin VI, 315
Hubbard, Benjamin VI, 827
Hubbard, Benjamin G. VI, 865
Hubbard, Bessie IV, 1322
Hubbard, Bessie L. D. IV, 1322
Hubbard, Bessie L. D. IV, 1344
Hubbard, Betsy VI, 913
Hubbard, Burr Garland VI, 936
Hubbard, Butler I, 602
Hubbard, Butler I, 606
Hubbard, Butler I, 819
Hubbard, Caroline A. VI, 827
Hubbard, Celia I, 602
Hubbard, Celia I, 606
Hubbard, Charles A. IV, 227
Hubbard, Charles C. I, 619
Hubbard, Charles C. I, 749
Hubbard, Charles F. III, 174
Hubbard, Charles S. F. III, 174
Hubbard, Charles Stephen VI, 983
Hubbard, Charlotte S. VI, 936
Hubbard, Chas. IV, 1321
Hubbard, Chas. IV, 1322
Hubbard, Chas. C. IV, 1344
Hubbard, Chas. E. IV, 1322
Hubbard, Clarence III, 174
Hubbard, Clarence III, 242
Hubbard, Clemsey VI, 936
Hubbard, Clifton Travis III, 174
Hubbard, Cornelius VI, 836
Hubbard, David I, 272
Hubbard, Delila Carolus I, 602
Hubbard, Doris V, 1003
Hubbard, Dorothy I, 619
Hubbard, Dorothy I, 749
Hubbard, Edmund VI, 936
Hubbard, Edw. A. III, 174
Hubbard, Edward VI, 936
Hubbard, Edward A. III, 96
Hubbard, Edward A. III, 174
Hubbard, Elias I, 549
Hubbard, Eliza I, 602
Hubbard, Eliza I, 784
Hubbard, Eliza I, 819
Hubbard, Eliza I, 838
Hubbard, Elizabeth I, 784
Hubbard, Elizabeth I, 812
Hubbard, Elizabeth I, 819
Hubbard, Elizabeth VI, 182
Hubbard, Elizabeth VI, 191
Hubbard, Elizabeth VI, 195
Hubbard, Elizabeth VI, 827
Hubbard, Elizabeth VI, 836
Hubbard, Elizabeth VI, 936
Hubbard, Elizabeth VI, 949
Hubbard, Elizabeth A. VI, 827
Hubbard, Elizabeth B. IV, 227
Hubbard, Elizabeth D. VI, 182
Hubbard, Elizabeth D. VI, 215
Hubbard, Emily A. I, 549
Hubbard, Eunice Emily I, 602
Hubbard, Exum VI, 182
Hubbard, Exum Amos VI, 182
Hubbard, Exum S. VI, 182
Hubbard, F. III, 174
Hubbard, F. III, 306
Hubbard, Frances P. I, 749
Hubbard, Frances Walker I, 619
Hubbard, Francis VI, 936
Hubbard, Frank III, 174
Hubbard, Frank H. III, 174
Hubbard, Frank W. III, 174
Hubbard, Frank W. III, 189
Hubbard, Frederick VI, 182
Hubbard, George I, 549
Hubbard, George I, 784
Hubbard, George I, 819
Hubbard, George VI, 165
Hubbard, George VI, 178
Hubbard, George VI, 182
Hubbard, George VI, 190
Hubbard, George VI, 191
Hubbard, George VI, 194
Hubbard, George VI, 195
Hubbard, George VI, 215
Hubbard, George VI, 249
Hubbard, George VI, 936
Hubbard, George M. I, 549
Hubbard, George W. VI, 873
Hubbard, Grace III, 174
Hubbard, Grace W. III, 189
Hubbard, Gretta III, 96
Hubbard, Gretta III, 174
Hubbard, H. VI, 182
Hubbard, Hanna H. IV, 1322
Hubbard, Hannah Reid VI, 827
Hubbard, Hardy I, 549
Hubbard, Harold III, 174
Hubbard, Harold James III, 174
Hubbard, Helen L. III, 71
Hubbard, Helen L. III, 174
Hubbard, Henry I, 549
Hubbard, Hope I, 749
Hubbard, Isabelle III, 174
Hubbard, Jacob I, 448
Hubbard, Jacob I, 549
Hubbard, Jacob I, 576
Hubbard, James V, 180
Hubbard, James V, 627
Hubbard, James VI, 182
Hubbard, James VI, 257
Hubbard, James VI, 827
Hubbard, James VI, 936
Hubbard, Jane I, 784
Hubbard, Jane I, 814
Hubbard, Jane I, 819
Hubbard, Jane VI, 838
Hubbard, Jehiel L. V, 578
Hubbard, Jemima I, 784
Hubbard, Jemima I, 819
Hubbard, Jemima I, 842
Hubbard, Jeremiah I, 602
Hubbard, Jeremiah I, 784
Hubbard, Jeremiah I, 819
Hubbard, Jeremiah I, 907
Hubbard, Jeremiah IV, 225
Hubbard, Jeremiah VI, 132
Hubbard, Jeremiah VI, 135
Hubbard, Jeremiah VI, 163
Hubbard, Jeremiah VI, 182
Hubbard, Jesse I, 309
Hubbard, John I, 549
Hubbard, John I, 784
Hubbard, John I, 805
Hubbard, John I, 819
Hubbard, John I, 833
Hubbard, John IV, 225
Hubbard, John VI, 182
Hubbard, John VI, 249
Hubbard, John VI, 275
Hubbard, John VI, 820
Hubbard, John VI, 827
Hubbard, John VI, 838
Hubbard, John VI, 936
Hubbard, John B. IV, 1254
Hubbard, John B. IV, 1321
Hubbard, John H. VI, 827
Hubbard, John K. VI, 182
Hubbard, John Pleasants VI, 182
Hubbard, John R. I, 549
Hubbard, John R. VI, 229
Hubbard, John R. VI, 249
Hubbard, Jonathan I, 309
Hubbard, Joseph I, 272
Hubbard, Joseph I, 448
Hubbard, Joseph I, 533
Hubbard, Joseph I, 549
Hubbard, Joseph VI, 182
Hubbard, Joseph VI, 229
Hubbard, Joseph VI, 249
Hubbard, Joseph VI, 936
Hubbard, Joseph VI, 950
Hubbard, Joseph B. I, 784
Hubbard, Joseph, Jr. I, 549
Hubbard, Josephine H. III, 174
Hubbard, Josephine H. III, 242
Hubbard, Josiah VI, 827
Hubbard, Judith I, 784
Hubbard, Judith I, 819
Hubbard, Judith I, 834
Hubbard, Judith VI, 165
Hubbard, Judith VI, 182
Hubbard, Judith VI, 186
Hubbard, Juliet VI, 936
Hubbard, Laura V. III, 174
Hubbard, Louisa VI, 827
Hubbard, Lucy VI, 827
Hubbard, Lydia IV, 225
Hubbard, Lydia IV, 227
Hubbard, Lydia V, 340
Hubbard, Lydia V, 342
Hubbard, Lydia V, 976
Hubbard, Lydia E. VI, 936
Hubbard, Lydia H. V, 340
Hubbard, M. A. III, 71
Hubbard, M. A. III, 174
Hubbard, Margaret I, 448
Hubbard, Margaret I, 602
Hubbard, Margaret I, 784
Hubbard, Margaret I, 819
Hubbard, Margaret IV, 1321
Hubbard, Margaret VI, 132
Hubbard, Margaret VI, 135
Hubbard, Margaret VI, 1017
Hubbard, Margaret C. III, 96
Hubbard, Margaret C. III, 174
Hubbard, Margaret E. V, 1003
Hubbard, Margaret R. IV, 1254
Hubbard, Margret I, 448
Hubbard, Mariah VI, 182
Hubbard, Martha I, 549
Hubbard, Martha I, 784
Hubbard, Martha I, 819
Hubbard, Martha I, 835
Hubbard, Martha IV, 225
Hubbard, Martha VI, 163
Hubbard, Martha VI, 182
Hubbard, Martha A. VI, 827
Hubbard, Martha Ann VI, 182
Hubbard, Martha H. VI, 936
Hubbard, Martha I. VI, 815
Hubbard, Mary I, 272
Hubbard, Mary I, 549
Hubbard, Mary I, 784
Hubbard, Mary I, 819
Hubbard, Mary VI, 827
Hubbard, Mary VI, 936
Hubbard, Mary A. VI, 827
Hubbard, Mary Ann II, 878
Hubbard, Mary Ann III, 30
Hubbard, Mary Ann III, 174
Hubbard, Mary Ann III, 306
Hubbard, Mary Ann VI, 178
Hubbard, Mary Ann VI, 179
Hubbard, Mary Ann VI, 182
Hubbard, Mary E. III, 174
Hubbard, Mary J. VI, 841
Hubbard, Mary Jane I, 272
Hubbard, Melissa IV, 1254
Hubbard, Micajah VI, 838
Hubbard, Michael VI, 827
Hubbard, Michael VI, 936
Hubbard, Milton III, 174
Hubbard, Miriam I, 784
Hubbard, Miriam I, 819
Hubbard, Mrs. M. M. IV, 1322
Hubbard, Nancy VI, 852
Hubbard, Nancy A. VI, 908
Hubbard, Nathan I, 784
Hubbard, Nathaniel VI, 827
Hubbard, Nicolas Stone VI, 249
Hubbard, Paul IV, 1322
Hubbard, Penrose IV, 225
Hubbard, Penrose IV, 1254
Hubbard, Penrose V, 340
Hubbard, Penrose H. IV, 1321
Hubbard, Pervilla Bell III, 174
Hubbard, Peter VI, 233
Hubbard, Peter VI, 249
Hubbard, Peter VI, 285
Hubbard, Peter VI, 286
Hubbard, Phebe I, 549
Hubbard, Phebe I, 576
Hubbard, Phebe I, 784
Hubbard, Polly VI, 827
Hubbard, Priscilla VI, 178
Hubbard, Priscilla VI, 182
Hubbard, Priscilla VI, 190
Hubbard, Priscilla VI, 194
Hubbard, Priscilla VI, 215
Hubbard, Rebecca U. IV, 227
Hubbard, Rhoda I, 448
Hubbard, Rhoda I, 784
Hubbard, Rhoda I, 819
Hubbard, Richard I, 784
Hubbard, Richard I, 819
Hubbard, Robert VI, 182
Hubbard, Roda W. I, 799
Hubbard, Roda W. I, 819
Hubbard, Ruth III, 174
Hubbard, Ruth Marie III, 174
Hubbard, Sally VI, 827
Hubbard, Sally VI, 950
Hubbard, Sam'l. VI, 913
Hubbard, Samuel VI, 830
Hubbard, Samuel Delon I, 784
Hubbard, Samuel H. VI, 827
Hubbard, Sarah I, 549
Hubbard, Sarah I, 784
Hubbard, Sarah I, 800
Hubbard, Sarah I, 819
Hubbard, Sarah I, 833
Hubbard, Sarah VI, 182
Hubbard, Sarah VI, 936
Hubbard, Sarah Ann VI, 936
Hubbard, Sarah E. III, 174
Hubbard, Sarah H. VI, 30
Hubbard, Sarah H. VI, 178
Hubbard, Sarah H. VI, 179
Hubbard, Sarah H. VI, 182
Hubbard, Sarah Hix VI, 827
Hubbard, Simeon I, 549
Hubbard, Solomon I, 272
Hubbard, Stephen VI, 182
Hubbard, Stephen VI, 905
Hubbard, Stephen VI, 936
Hubbard, Stephen VI, 973
Hubbard, Stephen VI, 1017
Hubbard, Susan I, 819
Hubbard, Susan VI, 950
Hubbard, Susana I, 549
Hubbard, Susanna I, 784
Hubbard, Susanna I, 814
Hubbard, Susanna I, 819
Hubbard, Susanna F. I, 549
Hubbard, Susanna F. VI, 249
Hubbard, Susannah R. VI, 229
Hubbard, Sylvester III, 30
Hubbard, Sylvester III, 174
Hubbard, Sylvester S. III, 174
Hubbard, Sylvester S. III, 306
Hubbard, T. Chalkley I, 549
Hubbard, Taliaferro VI, 879
Hubbard, Taliaferro VI, 936
Hubbard, Taliaferro G. VI, 936
Hubbard, Taliaferro G. VI, 950
Hubbard, Taliaferro G. VI, 979
Hubbard, Thomas I, 784
Hubbard, Thomas VI, 827
Hubbard, Thomas D. IV, 1254
Hubbard, Unity VI, 257
Hubbard, W. G. IV, 1254
Hubbard, Walter V, 340
Hubbard, Walter E. III, 174
Hubbard, Walter Harper III, 174
Hubbard, William I, 272
Hubbard, William I, 549
Hubbard, William III, 174
Hubbard, William VI, 182
Hubbard, William VI, 827
Hubbard, William Echols, Jr. VI, 314
Hubbard, William G. IV, 225
Hubbard, William H. III, 174
Hubbard, William L. VI, 827
Hubbard, William S. I, 272
Hubbard, William S. VI, 836
Hubbard, Wm. V, 340
Hubbard, Wm. B. IV, 1254
Hubbard, Wm. B. IV, 1321
Hubbard, Wm. B. IV, 1322
Hubbard, Wm. G. IV, 225
Hubbard, Wm. G. IV, 227
Hubbard, Wm. G. IV, 1254
Hubbard, Wm. G. IV, 1321
Hubbard, Wm. G. IV, 1322
Hubbard, Wm. G. V, 340
Hubbard, Wm. G. V, 342
Hubbard, Wm. J. IV, 1254
Hubbard, Woodson I, 549
Hubbart, Abram. VI, 936
Hubbart, Clemsey VI, 936
Hubbart, John VI, 936
Hubbell, Hannah IV, 1166
Hubbell, Hannah IV, 1172
Hubberts, Ann I, 784
Hubberts, Elizabeth I, 784
Hubberts, George I, 784
Hubberts, Jane I, 784
Hubberts, John I, 784
Hubberts, Judith I, 784
Hubberts, Martha I, 784
Hubberts, Susanna I, 784
Hubbick, George Wm. III, 107
Hubbick, Mary III, 107
Hubbs, ??? III, 439
Hubbs, ??? III, 479
Hubbs, Amaziah III, 174
Hubbs, Amos III, 174
Hubbs, Amy III, 174
Hubbs, Anna B. II, 747
Hubbs, Arden III, 485
Hubbs, Beth III, 485
Hubbs, Beulah II, 120
Hubbs, Charity III, 174
Hubbs, Charity III, 230
Hubbs, Charles III, 174
Hubbs, Charles F. III, 174
Hubbs, Chas. II, 58
Hubbs, Chas. II, 80
Hubbs, Christopher III, 174
Hubbs, Christopher III, 230
Hubbs, David III, 174
Hubbs, Deborah III, 485
Hubbs, Elias III, 485
Hubbs, Elizabeth W. III, 485
Hubbs, Esther III, 421
Hubbs, Esther III, 439
Hubbs, Esther P. III, 485
Hubbs, Esther P. III, 495
Hubbs, Fanny III, 174
Hubbs, Hannah III, 485
Hubbs, Hannah III, 486

Hubbs, Hannah III, 494
Hubbs, Hannah C. III, 421
Hubbs, Hannah C. III, 439
Hubbs, Hannah C. III, 485
Hubbs, Hannah C. III, 496
Hubbs, Hiram III, 485
Hubbs, Hyman III, 485
Hubbs, Jacob III, 421
Hubbs, Jacob III, 485
Hubbs, James III, 394
Hubbs, James III, 421
Hubbs, James III, 485
Hubbs, Jane II, 557
Hubbs, Jane III, 485
Hubbs, Jeddiah III, 421
Hubbs, Jediah III, 434
Hubbs, Jefferson III, 485
Hubbs, Jemima III, 485
Hubbs, Jericho III, 485
Hubbs, John III, 485
Hubbs, John D. III, 174
Hubbs, John P. III, 495
Hubbs, John R. III, 421
Hubbs, John R. III, 439
Hubbs, John R. III, 485
Hubbs, Joseph III, 174
Hubbs, Joseph III, 421
Hubbs, Joseph III, 485
Hubbs, Joshua III, 485
Hubbs, Leah III, 129
Hubbs, Leah III, 174
Hubbs, Leah III, 230
Hubbs, Margarett II, 115
Hubbs, Margarett II, 120
Hubbs, Margery III, 485
Hubbs, Martha III, 394
Hubbs, Martha III, 421
Hubbs, Martha III, 479
Hubbs, Martha III, 485
Hubbs, Mary III, 174
Hubbs, Mary III, 421
Hubbs, Mary III, 434
Hubbs, Mary III, 479
Hubbs, Mary III, 485
Hubbs, Mary III, 494
Hubbs, Mary B. III, 174
Hubbs, Mary B. III, 178
Hubbs, Mary B. III, 485
Hubbs, Mary F. III, 174
Hubbs, Mary Jane III, 486
Hubbs, Mercy III, 421
Hubbs, Mercy III, 485
Hubbs, Paul II, 58
Hubbs, Paul II, 80
Hubbs, Paul C. II, 557
Hubbs, Phebe Ann III, 485
Hubbs, Phila II, 58
Hubbs, Platt III, 485
Hubbs, Rebecca II, 32
Hubbs, Rebecca II, 58
Hubbs, Rebecca II, 80
Hubbs, Rebecca H. II, 120
Hubbs, Rebecca H. II, 747
Hubbs, Rebecca H. II, 756
Hubbs, Richard III, 485
Hubbs, Richard C. III, 485
Hubbs, Richard C. III, 486
Hubbs, Richard C. III, 496
Hubbs, Robert III, 174
Hubbs, Robert III, 421
Hubbs, Samuel II, 557
Hubbs, Samuel III, 485
Hubbs, Sarah E. III, 485
Hubbs, Sarah E. III, 496
Hubbs, Selah III, 485
Hubbs, Selah III, 494
Hubbs, Thomas III, 485
Hubbs, Thomas B. III, 485
Hubbs, Thomas Franklin III, 485
Hubbs, Thomas Jefferson III, 485
Hubbs, Valentine III, 485
Hubbs, Wd. Elizabeth P. III, 421
Hubert, George I, 819
Hubert, John I, 819
Hubert, Margret I, 448
Hubert, Nancy IV, 92
Hubert, Nancy IV, 93
Hubert, Nancy IV, 112
Hubert, Susan Grant I, 337
Huberty, Mildred IV, 725
Hubley, Mary II, 519
Hubley, Mary II, 557
Hubson, Elizabeth Anna Ethel III, 191
Hubson, Russell B. III, 191
Huchens, Ann I, 809
Huchens, Ann I, 820
Huchens, Darius I, 976
Huchens, Ede VI, 250
Huchens, Ede VI, 268
Huchens, Gideon I, 989
Huchens, Hezekiah I, 976
Huchens, James I, 976
Huchens, Josiah V, 745
Huchens, Kezia I, 976
Huchens, Mary I, 976
Huchens, Nicholas VI, 251
Huchens, Sarah I, 976
Hucherson, Nancy VI, 858
Hucherson, Thomas II, 380
Huchings, Elizabeth I, 803
Huchings, Elizabeth I, 820
Huchings, Strangeman VI, 251
Huchins, Annie Gertrude V, 402
Huchins, Elizabeth Margaret V, 402
Huchins, John II, 379
Huchins, Mary Ann V, 402
Huchins, Rebecca V, 745
Huchins, William V, 402
Huck, Charlotte VI, 404
Huck, Charlotte VI, 405
Huck, Charlotte VI, 410
Huck, Frances S. VI, 405
Huck, Harriet S. VI, 405
Huck, Harriet S. VI, 751
Huck, Joseph Neill VI, 751
Huck, Lewis N. VI, 405
Huck, Lewis N. VI, 751
Huck, Lydia N. VI, 405
Huck, Mary VI, 404
Huck, Mary VI, 405
Huck, Mary VI, 751
Huck, Mary Neill VI, 769
Huck, Michael VI, 751
Huck, Rebecca VI, 405
Huck, Rebecca Neill VI, 751
Huck, Richard VI, 405
Huck, Richard S. VI, 405
Huck, Richard S. VI, 751
Huck, Richard S. VI, 781
Huck, Richard S. VI, 782
Huck, Richard, Jr. VI, 405
Huck, Sarah VI, 751
Huck, Sarah VI, 781
Huck, Sarah VI, 782
Huck, Sarah S. VI, 405
Huck, Thomas V. VI, 404
Huck, Thomas V. VI, 405
Huck, Thomas V. VI, 751
Huck, Thomas V. VI, 769
Huckabay, Patsy VI, 934
Huckeby, Frankey VI, 936
Huckeby, John VI, 885
Huckeby, John VI, 936
Huckeby, Laurence VI, 936
Huckeby, Lewis I, 1070
Huckeby, Lewis Thomas I, 1070
Huckeby, Molly VI, 885
Huckeby, Thomas VI, 885
Huckerby, Patty VI, 869
Huckings, Achsah II, 32
Huckings, Barbery Barber II, 80
Huckings, David Davis II, 80
Huckings, Elizabeth II, 32
Huckings, Elizabeth II, 80
Huckings, Hannah II, 32
Huckings, Hannah II, 80
Huckings, Hindrance II, 32
Huckings, Huldah II, 32
Huckings, Huldah II, 80
Huckings, Jacob Davis II, 80
Huckings, John II, 32
Huckings, Joseph II, 80
Huckings, Martha II, 80
Huckings, Mary II, 32
Huckings, Mary II, 80
Huckings, Mercy II, 80
Huckings, Patience Lowderback II, 80
Huckings, Roger II, 17
Huckings, Roger II, 32
Huckings, Samuel II, 80
Huckings, Samuel Coles II, 80
Huckings, Samuel Huckins II, 80
Huckings, Sarah II, 32
Huckings, Sarah II, 80
Huckings, Susannah II, 32
Huckings, Thomas II, 32
Huckings, Thomas II, 80
Huckins, Barbery II, 53
Huckins, Barbery Barber II, 80
Huckins, Hannah II, 53
Huckins, Hannah II, 80
Huckins, Samuel II, 65
Huckney, James L. V, 685
Hudd, Wm. II, 991
Huddle, Charles Sumner V, 249
Huddleson, Susannah V, 844
Huddleston, Abraham VI, 870
Huddleston, Abraham VI, 936
Huddleston, Abram S. VI, 883
Huddleston, Abram. VI, 936
Huddleston, Abram. S. VI, 934
Huddleston, Aggie VI, 936
Huddleston, Barnet VI, 936
Huddleston, Blanchey A. VI, 936
Huddleston, Catharine VI, 936
Huddleston, Catherine VI, 936
Huddleston, Daniel VI, 936
Huddleston, Dannel VI, 936
Huddleston, David VI, 936
Huddleston, Elijah VI, 936
Huddleston, Elizabeth VI, 890
Huddleston, Elizabeth VI, 910
Huddleston, Eney VI, 998
Huddleston, Fanny VI, 951
Huddleston, Frances VI, 875
Huddleston, Frances VI, 936
Huddleston, George VI, 883
Huddleston, George VI, 936
Huddleston, Hannah VI, 936
Huddleston, Henrietta VI, 856
Huddleston, Henry VI, 870
Huddleston, Henry VI, 890
Huddleston, Henry VI, 905
Huddleston, Henry VI, 910
Huddleston, Henry VI, 934
Huddleston, Henry VI, 936
Huddleston, Henry VI, 950
Huddleston, Henry VI, 964
Huddleston, Henry VI, 969
Huddleston, Henry VI, 981
Huddleston, Henry VI, 994
Huddleston, Henry, Jr. VI, 936
Huddleston, Isham VI, 890
Huddleston, Isham VI, 905
Huddleston, Isham VI, 936
Huddleston, Isham VI, 981
Huddleston, Isham VI, 1003
Huddleston, Joel VI, 936
Huddleston, John VI, 936
Huddleston, John VI, 951
Huddleston, Jonathan I, 819
Huddleston, Jonathan V, 844
Huddleston, Jos. VI, 951
Huddleston, Joseph VI, 897
Huddleston, Joseph VI, 936
Huddleston, Joseph VI, 986
Huddleston, Joseph VI, 998
Huddleston, Joshua VI, 994
Huddleston, Juda VI, 994
Huddleston, Martha VI, 981
Huddleston, Martha VI, 1022
Huddleston, Martha Ann VI, 936
Huddleston, Mary I, 801
Huddleston, Mary VI, 870
Huddleston, Mary VI, 910
Huddleston, Mary VI, 936
Huddleston, Mary VI, 994
Huddleston, Mary E. VI, 936
Huddleston, Miram VI, 883
Huddleston, Nancey VI, 994
Huddleston, Nancy VI, 981
Huddleston, Patty VI, 936
Huddleston, Permelia VI, 1022
Huddleston, Peter VI, 936
Huddleston, Phebe I, 819
Huddleston, Phebe V, 844
Huddleston, Polly VI, 950
Huddleston, Rachel I, 808
Huddleston, Rachel VI, 886
Huddleston, Rachel VI, 936
Huddleston, Rhoda VI, 897
Huddleston, Sally VI, 936
Huddleston, Sally Ann VI, 936
Huddleston, Saml. VI, 936
Huddleston, Samuel VI, 936
Huddleston, Sarah I, 509
Huddleston, Sarah I, 819
Huddleston, Sarah VI, 870
Huddleston, Sarah VI, 936
Huddleston, Sarah VI, 969
Huddleston, Susanna V, 844
Huddleston, Susanna V, 855
Huddleston, Susanna VI, 936
Huddleston, Susannah V, 844
Huddleston, Susannah VI, 936
Huddleston, Thomas VI, 875
Huddleston, Thomas VI, 886
Huddleston, Thomas VI, 936
Huddleston, William V, 844
Huddleston, William V, 855
Huddleston, William VI, 936
Huddleston, William VI, 1008
Huddlestone, Abigail I, 1120
Huddlestone, Abigail I, 1122
Huddlestone, Anna I, 784
Huddlestone, David I, 784
Huddlestone, Elizabeth I, 784
Huddlestone, Elizabeth I, 819
Huddlestone, Hannah I, 784
Huddlestone, Hannah I, 819
Huddlestone, Hannah I, 824
Huddlestone, Jesse I, 784
Huddlestone, John I, 784
Huddlestone, Jonathan I, 784
Huddlestone, Jonathan I, 810
Huddlestone, Jonathan I, 819
Huddlestone, Levina I, 784
Huddlestone, Levina I, 820
Huddlestone, Levinah I, 819
Huddlestone, Lydia I, 784
Huddlestone, Lydia I, 819
Huddlestone, Lydia I, 820
Huddlestone, Mary I, 784
Huddlestone, Mary I, 819
Huddlestone, Phebe I, 784
Huddlestone, Phebe I, 810
Huddlestone, Phebe I, 819
Huddlestone, Rachel I, 784
Huddlestone, Rachel I, 819
Huddlestone, Sarah I, 784
Huddlestone, Sarah I, 819
Huddlestone, Sarah I, 825
Huddlestone, Seth I, 784
Huddlestone, Seth I, 819
Huddlestone, William I, 784
Huddleton, Jonathan V, 883
Huddy, Agnes II, 80
Huddy, Daniel II, 32
Huddy, Daniel II, 52
Huddy, Daniel II, 80
Huddy, Daniel II, 89
Huddy, Daniel II, 110
Huddy, Daniel, Jr. II, 80
Huddy, Elizabeth II, 32
Huddy, Elizabeth II, 80
Huddy, Elizabeth II, 110
Huddy, John II, 378
Huddy, Joshua II, 32
Huddy, Joshua II, 80
Huddy, Martha II, 32
Huddy, Martha II, 64
Huddy, Martha II, 80
Huddy, Martha II, 558
Huddy, Naomi II, 32
Huddy, Naomi II, 52
Huddy, Naomi II, 80
Huddy, Rachel II, 80
Huddy, Rachel II, 89
Hudelson, Ester IV, 1238
Hudelson, Ester W. IV, 1237
Hudelson, J. L. IV, 1237
Hudge, Ellis V, 503
Hudgel, Almira V, 180
Hudgel, Cora A. V, 180
Hudgel, Cora Bell V, 180
Hudgel, Elizabeth V, 402
Hudgel, Elmina V, 180
Hudgel, Ethel May V, 402
Hudgel, Fannie V, 402
Hudgel, John V, 402
Hudgel, Joseph V, 402
Hudgel, Louisa M. V, 402
Hudgel, Marcelina V, 402
Hudgel, Newton V, 503
Hudgell, Almira V, 180
Hudgens, Eliza IV, 225
Hudgens, John T. IV, 225
Hudgins, Elizabeth I, 817
Hudgins, Elizabeth I, 837
Hudgins, Josephine Sarah IV, 968
Hudler, Elizabeth IV, 225
Hudler, Samuel IV, 225
Hudnal, Mary VI, 937
Hudnal, Richard VI, 937
Hudnall, Betsy VI, 911
Hudnall, Cena VI, 928
Hudnall, Elizabeth VI, 827
Hudnall, Elizabeth VI, 937
Hudnall, Elizabeth VI, 943
Hudnall, Franky VI, 869
Hudnall, Jabez VI, 943
Hudnall, Jabez L. VI, 827
Hudnall, Jno. VI, 911
Hudnall, Jno. VI, 923
Hudnall, Jno. VI, 928
Hudnall, Jno. VI, 955
Hudnall, Jno. VI, 970
Hudnall, Joannah VI, 993
Hudnall, John VI, 932
Hudnall, John VI, 936
Hudnall, John VI, 1010
Hudnall, John VI, 1021
Hudnall, John, Jr. VI, 937
Hudnall, Julian VI, 937
Hudnall, Kitty VI, 942
Hudnall, Mary VI, 932
Hudnall, Mary VI, 937
Hudnall, Nancey VI, 904
Hudnall, Nancy VI, 935
Hudnall, Nancy VI, 937
Hudnall, Nancy VI, 970
Hudnall, Nancy VI, 1012
Hudnall, Nancy VI, 1014
Hudnall, Nimrod VI, 936
Hudnall, Patsey VI, 936
Hudnall, Polly VI, 971
Hudnall, Rhoda VI, 937
Hudnall, Rich. VI, 1018
Hudnall, Richard VI, 937
Hudnall, Richard VI, 1012
Hudnall, Sally S. VI, 1021
Hudnall, Saml. W. VI, 932
Hudnall, Samuel VI, 937
Hudnall, Sophia E. VI, 893
Hudnall, Susanna R. VI, 955
Hudnall, Thomas VI, 937
Hudnall, Thomas S. VI, 1014
Hudnall, Thomas Smith VI, 93
Hudnall, Thos. S. VI, 891
Hudnall, W. VI, 869
Hudnall, William VI, 937
Hudnall, William VI, 943
Hudnall, William VI, 971
Hudnall, William C. A. V. VI, 8
Hudnall, William H. VI, 1014
Hudnall, William, Jr. VI, 937
Hudnall, Wm. VI, 942
Hudnut, Harvey Shaw II, 801
Hudnut, Mercy II, 801
Hudnut, Peter Moore II, 801
Hudnut, Sarah Smith II, 801
Hudnutt, Harvey S. II, 878
Hudson, Abigail II, 378
Hudson, Abigail II, 558
Hudson, Abigail II, 652
Hudson, Achsah I, 817
Hudson, Adeline II, 849
Hudson, Alce II, 378
Hudson, Alex VI, 937
Hudson, Amy VI, 751
Hudson, Ann II, 378
Hudson, Ann II, 558
Hudson, Ann II, 680
Hudson, Ann M. VI, 1019
Hudson, Anna VI, 658
Hudson, Anna VI, 699
Hudson, Anna VI, 700
Hudson, Anna E. VI, 658
Hudson, Anna E. VI, 699
Hudson, Benjamin II, 961
Hudson, Bertha VI, 742
Hudson, Bertha VI, 743
Hudson, Bertha VI, 751
Hudson, Bertha VI, 759
Hudson, Bertha VI, 763
Hudson, Burchy M. VI, 937
Hudson, Burton V, 458
Hudson, Caleb II, 849
Hudson, Carrie Ellen V, 685
Hudson, Clarey VI, 959
Hudson, Daniel II, 976
Hudson, Daniel II, 1003
Hudson, David VI, 937
Hudson, Deborah II, 378
Hudson, Deborah II, 558
Hudson, Deborah II, 627
Hudson, Deborah II, 961
Hudson, Deborah II, 1003
Hudson, Deborah II, 1033
Hudson, Dinah V, 20
Hudson, Ealse II, 1003
Hudson, Edith VI, 658
Hudson, Edith VI, 700
Hudson, Eleanor II, 378
Hudson, Eleanor G. III, 175
Hudson, Elinor II, 378
Hudson, Elisabeth I, 54
Hudson, Elisabeth I, 66
Hudson, Elisabeth II, 558
Hudson, Elizabeth I, 659
Hudson, Elizabeth II, 66
Hudson, Elizabeth II, 80
Hudson, Elizabeth II, 378
Hudson, Elizabeth II, 499
Hudson, Elizabeth II, 558
Hudson, Elizabeth II, 567
Hudson, Elizabeth II, 602
Hudson, Elizabeth II, 639
Hudson, Elizabeth II, 849
Hudson, Elizabeth VI, 827
Hudson, Elizabeth VI, 937
Hudson, Elvira VI, 937
Hudson, Esther VI, 598
Hudson, Fannie IV, 1166
Hudson, Florence IV, 1322
Hudson, Frances VI, 827
Hudson, George VI, 858
Hudson, Georgiana V, 682
Hudson, Georgiana V, 685
Hudson, Hannah II, 378
Hudson, Hannah II, 556

dson, Hannah II, 558
dson, Hannah II, 595
dson, Hannah II, 630
dson, Hannah V, 20
dson, Hannah V, 78
dson, Hannah Ann VI, 751
dson, Hannah, Jr. II, 558
dson, Harold V, 458
dson, Helen V, 685
dson, Helen Louise V, 685
dson, Helen Ruth V, 458
dson, Henrietta III, 145
dson, Henrietta III, 175
dson, Henry II, 378
dson, Henry II, 558
dson, Homer IV, 1322
dson, Howard V, 682
dson, Howard V, 685
dson, Hur I, 817
dson, Isabella E. VI, 937
dson, Jacob M. I, 722
dson, James II, 378
dson, James II, 849
dson, James VI, 937
dson, James E. VI, 937
dson, Jane II, 378
dson, Jane II, 558
dson, Jesse I, 659
dson, John II, 233
dson, John II, 265
dson, John II, 378
dson, John II, 558
dson, John II, 652
dson, John II, 848
dson, John II, 878
dson, John II, 961
dson, John II, 1003
dson, John VI, 11
dson, John VI, 751
dson, John VI, 835
dson, John VI, 891
dson, John VI, 934
dson, John VI, 966
dson, John B. VI, 827
dson, John Newby VI, 937
udson, Joseph II, 878
udson, Leander I, 722
udson, Levi VI, 959
udson, Louisa VI, 937
udson, Louisa VI, 1014
udson, Lucy VI, 937
udson, Lucy T. VI, 798
udson, Lydia I, 722
udson, Madison VI, 827
udson, Maggie IV, 1166
udson, Mahala VI, 937
udson, Margaret I, 1122
udson, Margaret VI, 827
udson, Margrett II, 378
udson, Martha I, 722
udson, Martha II, 378
udson, Martha II, 558
udson, Martha II, 583
udson, Martha V, 78
udson, Martha V, 83
udson, Martha VI, 825
udson, Martha R. VI, 937
udson, Mary I, 343
udson, Mary I, 398
udson, Mary I, 817
udson, Mary II, 80
udson, Mary II, 219
udson, Mary II, 233
ludson, Mary II, 234
ludson, Mary II, 265
ludson, Mary II, 359
ludson, Mary II, 378
ludson, Mary II, 493
ludson, Mary II, 515
ludson, Mary II, 546
ludson, Mary II, 551
ludson, Mary II, 552
ludson, Mary II, 558
Iudson, Mary II, 633
Iudson, Mary VI, 742
Iudson, Mary VI, 819
Iudson, Mary VI, 955
Iudson, Mary E. III, 66
Iudson, Mary E. IV, 1166
Iudson, Mary M. IV, 1166
Iudson, Matilda M. VI, 961
Iudson, Melvine V, 458
Iudson, Micajah VI, 937
Iudson, Milley VI, 959
Hudson, Nancy VI, 937
Hudson, Nathan I, 722
Hudson, Peggy VI, 937
Hudson, Peter VI, 937
Hudson, Phebe V, 685
Hudson, Phinehas Pemberton II, 1003
Hudson, Priscilla II, 961
Hudson, Rachel I, 659
Hudson, Rachel II, 378
Hudson, Rachel II, 516
Hudson, Rachel II, 558
Hudson, Rachel II, 571
Hudson, Rachel IV, 1212
Hudson, Rachel V, 20
Hudson, Rachel P. IV, 1212
Hudson, Rebecca I, 659
Hudson, Rebecca II, 378
Hudson, Rebekah II, 378
Hudson, Richard I, 722
Hudson, Richard I, 1122
Hudson, Richard VI, 937
Hudson, Robert I, 659
Hudson, Robert II, 378
Hudson, Robert II, 478
Hudson, Robert VI, 751
Hudson, Robert VI, 959
Hudson, Robert Lee V, 458
Hudson, Ruth IV, 385
Hudson, Ruth IV, 412
Hudson, Sally VI, 858
Hudson, Sally VI, 937
Hudson, Samuel II, 378
Hudson, Samuel II, 546
Hudson, Samuel II, 551
Hudson, Samuel II, 556
Hudson, Samuel II, 558
Hudson, Samuel II, 567
Hudson, Samuel II, 583
Hudson, Samuel V, 20
Hudson, Samuel VI, 1019
Hudson, Samuel L. VI, 937
Hudson, Sarah I, 722
Hudson, Sarah I, 1122
Hudson, Sarah II, 378
Hudson, Sarah II, 558
Hudson, Sarah II, 576
Hudson, Sarah II, 961
Hudson, Sarah II, 976
Hudson, Sarah II, 1003
Hudson, Sarah III, 175
Hudson, Sarah VI, 955
Hudson, Sarah VI, 1014
Hudson, Sarah J. V, 458
Hudson, Sarah, Sr. II, 482
Hudson, Sarah, Sr. II, 558
Hudson, Simon VI, 937
Hudson, Susan II, 878
Hudson, Susan VI, 825
Hudson, Susanna II, 558
Hudson, Susanna II, 611
Hudson, Susannah II, 378
Hudson, Susannah II, 558
Hudson, Susannah II, 788
Hudson, Susannah II, 848
Hudson, Susannah II, 878
Hudson, Thomas I, 659
Hudson, Thomas VI, 827
Hudson, Thos. A. III, 175
Hudson, Timothy II, 378
Hudson, Timothy II, 558
Hudson, Wd. Susanna II, 611
Hudson, William II, 378
Hudson, William II, 961
Hudson, William VI, 826
Hudson, William VI, 937
Hudson, William VI, 969
Hudson, William T. VI, 937
Hudson, William, Jr. II, 378
Hudson, Wm. II, 441
Hudson, Wm. II, 478
Hudson, Wm. II, 516
Hudson, Wm. II, 558
Hudson, Wm. II, 583
Hudson, Wm. II, 611
Hudson, Wm. II, 633
Hudson, Wm. II, 639
Hudson, Wm. II, 680
Hudson, Wm. V, 458
Hudson, Wm. V, 1003
Hudson, Wm. J. D. III, 175
Hudson, Wyatt VI, 1014
Hudson, Zetta V, 458
Hudspeth, Bulah V, 1003
Hueford, John IV, 226
Hueford, Rachel IV, 226
Hueford, Sarah IV, 226
Hues, Hannah II, 444
Hues, Howard IV, 725
Hues, Hugh II, 444
Hues, Isaac II, 379
Hues, Joan II, 444
Hues, Moses II, 379
Hues, Rebecca II, 444
Hues, Sarah II, 379
Hues, Sarah III, 175
Huested, Moses II, 231
Huestes, Esther IV, 815
Huestes, Isaac IV, 815
Huestes, Sarah IV, 815
Huestis, ??? III, 175
Huestis, Aaron IV, 584
Huestis, Aaron IV, 637
Huestis, Aaron IV, 874
Huestis, Aaron IV, 882
Huestis, Aaron IV, 1102
Huestis, Amanda J. IV, 1103
Huestis, Amanda J. IV, 1121
Huestis, Amanda Jane IV, 1103
Huestis, Ann II, 995
Huestis, Ann II, 1003
Huestis, Aron II, 995
Huestis, Aron II, 1003
Huestis, Bezaleel II, 231
Huestis, Carpenter III, 163
Huestis, David III, 163
Huestis, Edward C. IV, 637
Huestis, Elizabeth III, 163
Huestis, Elizabeth IV, 637
Huestis, Elizabeth IV, 874
Huestis, Elizabeth IV, 882
Huestis, Elizabeth IV, 967
Huestis, Elizabeth IV, 989
Huestis, Elizabeth IV, 1103
Huestis, Elizabeth IV, 1104
Huestis, Emma IV, 874
Huestis, Emmer IV, 874
Huestis, Esther II, 995
Huestis, Esther II, 1003
Huestis, Esther IV, 584
Huestis, Esther IV, 637
Huestis, Esther IV, 874
Huestis, Esther IV, 882
Huestis, Esther IV, 1098
Huestis, Esther IV, 1102
Huestis, Esther IV, 1103
Huestis, Esther C. II, 703
Huestis, Esther C. IV, 1103
Huestis, Esther C. IV, 1104
Huestis, Isaac II, 703
Huestis, Isaac IV, 576
Huestis, Isaac IV, 584
Huestis, Isaac IV, 874
Huestis, Isaac IV, 1063
Huestis, Isaac IV, 1097
Huestis, Isaac IV, 1098
Huestis, Isaac IV, 1102
Huestis, Isaac IV, 1103
Huestis, Isaac IV, 1104
Huestis, Isadora IV, 874
Huestis, James III, 163
Huestis, Jesse IV, 1102
Huestis, Jesse IV, 1103
Huestis, Jesse IV, 1121
Huestis, Job IV, 637
Huestis, Job IV, 874
Huestis, Jonathan III, 163
Huestis, Joseph II, 231
Huestis, Mary III, 163
Huestis, Mary IV, 1097
Huestis, Mary IV, 1102
Huestis, Mary IV, 1103
Huestis, Mary Ann IV, 874
Huestis, Moses II, 995
Huestis, Moses II, 1003
Huestis, Moses IV, 874
Huestis, Rachel IV, 637
Huestis, Rebecca II, 703
Huestis, Rebecca IV, 637
Huestis, Rebecca IV, 874
Huestis, Rebecca IV, 1054
Huestis, Rebecca IV, 1063
Huestis, Rebecca IV, 1103
Huestis, Robert III, 163
Huestis, Robert III, 180
Huestis, Samantha IV, 874
Huestis, Sarah IV, 576
Huestis, Sarah IV, 584
Huestis, Sarah IV, 1097
Huestis, Sarah IV, 1098
Huestis, Sarah IV, 1102
Huestis, Sarah IV, 1103
Huestis, Thomas IV, 1102
Huestis, Thomas IV, 1103
Hueston, Margaret A. V, 912
Huet, Sarah II, 445
Huett, Hannah II, 444
Huett, Sarah II, 444
Huey, James II, 801
Huey, James II, 878
Huey, James Thomas II, 801
Huey, James Thomas II, 878
Huey, James Thomas II, 879
Huey, John II, 879
Huey, Lydia II, 801
Huey, Rachel M. II, 878
Huey, Rachel Mott II, 801
Huey, Russel V, 458
Huey, Russell V, 458
Huey, Sarah II, 801
Huey, Sarah A. II, 879
Huey, Sarah A. II, 886
Huey, Thos. II, 879
Huey, Thos. II, 886
Huey, Wm. II, 801
Huey, Wm. G. II, 878
Huey, Wm. G. II, 879
Huff, Aaron V, 250
Huff, Adda V, 250
Huff, Alice V, 458
Huff, Alice M. V, 250
Huff, Alice M. V, 458
Huff, Allie J. V, 250
Huff, Ameala I, 976
Huff, Ann I, 773
Huff, Ann I, 981
Huff, Ann I, 988
Huff, Anna I, 784
Huff, Anna V, 507
Huff, Anna Grace V, 250
Huff, Anne I, 818
Huff, Aquilla C. I, 976
Huff, Austin Terrell V, 250
Huff, Charity I, 796
Huff, Charity I, 819
Huff, Christie V, 912
Huff, Cristie I, 976
Huff, Curtis Elton V, 250
Huff, Daniel I, 358
Huff, Daniel I, 784
Huff, Daniel I, 803
Huff, Daniel I, 818
Huff, Daniel I, 819
Huff, Daniel I, 964
Huff, Daniel I, 971
Huff, Daniel I, 976
Huff, Daniel I, 987
Huff, Daniel I, 988
Huff, Daniel IV, 1322
Huff, Daniel V, 215
Huff, Daniel V, 223
Huff, Daniel V, 224
Huff, Daniel V, 241
Huff, Daniel V, 243
Huff, Daniel V, 249
Huff, Daniel V, 261
Huff, Daniel V, 276
Huff, Daniel V, 315
Huff, Daniel V, 339
Huff, Daniel V, 374
Huff, Daniel V, 402
Huff, Daniel, Jr. I, 784
Huff, Daniel, Jr. I, 971
Huff, Daniel, Jr. I, 976
Huff, Daniel, Jr. V, 250
Huff, Daniel, Jr. V, 304
Huff, Daniel, Sr. I, 988
Huff, David I, 976
Huff, David V, 250
Huff, David Anderson I, 976
Huff, Dinah I, 976
Huff, Dinah I, 987
Huff, Dinah I, 988
Huff, Elizabeth I, 784
Huff, Elizabeth I, 814
Huff, Elizabeth I, 818
Huff, Elizabeth I, 819
Huff, Elizabeth I, 971
Huff, Elizabeth I, 976
Huff, Elizabeth I, 982
Huff, Elizabeth I, 983
Huff, Elizabeth I, 984
Huff, Elizabeth I, 988
Huff, Elizabeth V, 241
Huff, Elizabeth V, 248
Huff, Elizabeth V, 249
Huff, Elizabeth V, 250
Huff, Elizabeth V, 339
Huff, Ella V, 249
Huff, Ella V, 250
Huff, Eunice V, 249
Huff, Eunice V, 250
Huff, Francis L. V, 250
Huff, Francis Linley V, 249
Huff, Frank V, 458
Huff, Frank L. V, 250
Huff, Frank L. V, 458
Huff, Geo. Wm. V, 250
Huff, George I, 976
Huff, Gladys Marguerite V, 250
Huff, Grace V, 250
Huff, Grace Elizabeth V, 248
Huff, Grace Elizabeth V, 250
Huff, Gracie B. V, 578
Huff, Gracie Elizabeth V, 250
Huff, Gulielma I, 988
Huff, Haines V, 250
Huff, Hannah I, 987
Huff, Hannah I, 988
Huff, Hannah V, 249
Huff, Hannah Matilda I, 976
Huff, Hannah P. I, 988
Huff, Henry Harrison V, 250
Huff, Hester V, 250
Huff, Hester Phebe V, 250
Huff, Ira I, 988
Huff, Israel I, 988
Huff, J. Guy V, 250
Huff, James I, 976
Huff, James V, 250
Huff, James V, 282
Huff, James V, 292
Huff, James M. V, 249
Huff, Jamima I, 784
Huff, Jemima I, 358
Huff, Jemima I, 818
Huff, Jemima I, 819
Huff, Jemima I, 826
Huff, Jesse I, 784
Huff, Jesse I, 818
Huff, Jesse I, 983
Huff, Jesse I, 988
Huff, Jesse V, 249
Huff, Jesse V, 250
Huff, Jesse V, 339
Huff, Jesse Martin I, 976
Huff, Jmmes V, 249
Huff, John I, 784
Huff, John I, 818
Huff, John I, 819
Huff, John I, 976
Huff, John I, 983
Huff, John I, 988
Huff, John V, 249
Huff, John V, 250
Huff, John V, 304
Huff, John V, 339
Huff, John D. I, 976
Huff, John I. IV, 1322
Huff, Jonathan I, 988
Huff, Joseph V, 339
Huff, Joshua I, 784
Huff, Joshua I, 976
Huff, Joshua I, 988
Huff, Joshua I, 990
Huff, Joshua C. I, 976
Huff, Joshua Christy I, 976
Huff, Juliet V, 249
Huff, Juliet V, 250
Huff, Juliet V, 267
Huff, Juliet V, 304
Huff, Kezia I, 784
Huff, Keziah I, 818
Huff, Keziah I, 988
Huff, Lydia I, 784
Huff, Lydia I, 976
Huff, Lydia V, 223
Huff, Lydia V, 249
Huff, Lydia V, 374
Huff, Lydia V, 402
Huff, Lydia Eliza V, 249
Huff, Maggie V, 249
Huff, Maggie V, 250
Huff, Mahlon V, 250
Huff, Mahlon V, 304
Huff, Margaret I, 964
Huff, Margaret I, 976
Huff, Margaret I, 988
Huff, Margaret I, 999
Huff, Margaret V, 249
Huff, Margaret V, 250
Huff, Margaret V, 304
Huff, Margaret V, 310
Huff, Margret I, 784
Huff, Margret I, 976
Huff, Martha I, 784
Huff, Martha I, 818
Huff, Martha I, 886
Huff, Martha I, 988
Huff, Mary I, 358
Huff, Mary I, 784
Huff, Mary I, 800
Huff, Mary I, 818
Huff, Mary I, 819
Huff, Mary I, 976
Huff, Mary I, 988
Huff, Mary V, 224
Huff, Mary V, 249
Huff, Mary V, 250
Huff, Mary V, 259
Huff, Mary V, 276
Huff, Mary V, 304
Huff, Mary V, 313
Huff, Mary V, 339
Huff, Mary Ann V, 249
Huff, Mary Ann V, 250
Huff, Mary B. V, 250
Huff, Mary B. V, 258
Huff, Mary Jane V, 249
Huff, Mary Jane V, 250
Huff, Mary Jane V, 627

Huff, Mary Jane V, 650
Huff, Mary Mills I, 988
Huff, Matilda I, 976
Huff, May V, 250
Huff, Mead IV, 1212
Huff, Michal I, 549
Huff, Nancy V, 250
Huff, Nancy V, 304
Huff, Nannie V, 507
Huff, Nannie E. V, 627
Huff, Patience I, 976
Huff, Peter VI, 937
Huff, Phebe J. V, 249
Huff, Phebe J. V, 250
Huff, Phebe J. V, 283
Huff, Rachel I, 976
Huff, Rachel I, 988
Huff, Rachel IV, 366
Huff, Rachel V, 249
Huff, Rachel V, 250
Huff, Rachel V, 339
Huff, Rachel J. V, 627
Huff, Ralph V, 458
Huff, Rebecah V, 249
Huff, Rebecca I, 976
Huff, Rebecca V, 250
Huff, Rebecca V, 276
Huff, Rebecca V, 339
Huff, Rebecca E. V, 627
Huff, Rebecca Mae V, 250
Huff, Richland V, 249
Huff, Rufus V, 250
Huff, Russell V, 250
Huff, Ruth V, 249
Huff, Ruth V, 261
Huff, Ruth V, 276
Huff, Ruth V, 339
Huff, Ruth V, 359
Huff, Ruth Ann V, 249
Huff, Ruth E. V, 250
Huff, Ruth Mildred V, 250
Huff, Samuel VI, 937
Huff, Sarah I, 803
Huff, Sarah I, 971
Huff, Sarah I, 976
Huff, Sarah I, 988
Huff, Sarah V, 223
Huff, Sarah V, 224
Huff, Sarah V, 241
Huff, Sarah V, 243
Huff, Sarah V, 249
Huff, Sarah V, 250
Huff, Sarah V, 276
Huff, Sarah V, 304
Huff, Sarah V, 339
Huff, Sarah V, 374
Huff, Sarah V, 390
Huff, Sarah V, 402
Huff, Sarah VI, 937
Huff, Sarah A. IV, 513
Huff, Sarah A. IV, 536
Huff, Sarah A. V, 299
Huff, Sarah A. V, 304
Huff, Sarah Cordelia V, 249
Huff, Sidney V, 249
Huff, Sidney V, 250
Huff, Sidney V, 282
Huff, Sidney V, 292
Huff, Sidney H. V, 249
Huff, Sidney H. V, 282
Huff, Simon I, 976
Huff, Simon I, 988
Huff, Susanna I, 976
Huff, Susanna I, 988
Huff, Susanna I, 990
Huff, Susannah V, 871
Huff, Terrell Chalmers V, 250
Huff, Wheeler V, 250
Huff, Widow Mary I, 988
Huff, William I, 818
Huff, William I, 971
Huff, William I, 988
Huff, William V, 250
Huff, William S. Hutchings V, 250
Huff, William W. H. V, 249
Huff, William W. H. V, 250
Huffine, Harry V, 1003
Huffine, Hiram V, 1003
Huffines, Emma I, 886
Huffington, Benny W. IV, 226
Huffins, Hattie Mickles I, 943
Huffman, Amanda V, 503
Huffman, Amos IV, 1237
Huffman, Amos V, 578
Huffman, Amos V, 685
Huffman, Angie Amanda V, 503
Huffman, Christopher V, 503
Huffman, Christopher V, 685
Huffman, Christopher C. V, 503
Huffman, Clara B. V, 180
Huffman, Clement V, 503
Huffman, Cora Esther V, 627
Huffman, Dellis Elmer Francis Marion V, 503
Huffman, Elizabeth IV, 1237
Huffman, Ella V, 503
Huffman, Emma V, 503
Huffman, Emma Hendershot V, 180
Huffman, Emma Hendershot V, 503
Huffman, Emma Jane V, 503
Huffman, Emma R. V, 180
Huffman, Ethel V, 627
Huffman, Eva V, 744
Huffman, George W. V, 503
Huffman, Grace B. V, 685
Huffman, Gracie V, 578
Huffman, Hariet A. V, 503
Huffman, Harriett V, 503
Huffman, Harriett V, 685
Huffman, Herbert VI, 924
Huffman, Herbert VI, 937
Huffman, John IV, 1237
Huffman, Kate V, 578
Huffman, Kate V, 685
Huffman, Kate W. V, 578
Huffman, Kate W. V, 685
Huffman, Lee Otis V, 627
Huffman, Levina V, 180
Huffman, Lloyd C. I, 337
Huffman, Lucy M. V, 180
Huffman, Lydia VI, 405
Huffman, Lydia VI, 443
Huffman, Margaret V, 503
Huffman, Mary V, 578
Huffman, Mary M. V, 73
Huffman, Maude V, 503
Huffman, Millie V, 578
Huffman, Minnie V, 655
Huffman, Minnie V, 685
Huffman, Nancy V, 180
Huffman, Nancy V, 503
Huffman, Nellie S. VI, 405
Huffman, Nellie S. VI, 460
Huffman, Oliver Alvie V, 503
Huffman, Pauline VI, 405
Huffman, Renna A. V, 180
Huffman, Sarah D. VI, 937
Huffman, Virginia VI, 405
Huffman, Warren V, 744
Huffman, Warren G. V, 744
Huffman, Wilber VI, 405
Huffman, Wilber VI, 460
Huffman, Wilbur VI, 460
Huffman, William V, 685
Huffman, Willie V, 578
Huffman, Willie V, 685
Hufford, Belle Keetch IV, 1322
Hufford, Mary IV, 1322
Hufford, Wilbur IV, 1038
Hufman, Elizabeth I, 1010
Hufman, Elizabeth I, 1012
Hufman, Lidia V, 146
Hufman, Lydia V, 131
Hufman, Merser V, 131
Hufman, Susanna V, 131
Hug, Priscilla II, 234
Huges, George VI, 874
Hugg, Ann E. II, 378
Hugg, Elias II, 234
Hugg, Elias II, 272
Hugg, Elias II, 378
Hugg, Elias II, 1038
Hugg, Elisabeth II, 234
Hugg, Elisabeth II, 272
Hugg, Elizabeth II, 234
Hugg, Elizabeth II, 558
Hugg, Elizabeth II, 1003
Hugg, Elizabeth II, 1038
Hugg, Hannah II, 234
Hugg, Hope II, 234
Hugg, John II, 234
Hugg, John II, 242
Hugg, John II, 272
Hugg, Marcy II, 234
Hugg, Marcy II, 238
Hugg, Margaret II, 378
Hugg, Margaret VI, 405
Hugg, Mary II, 234
Hugg, Mary II, 272
Hugg, Mary II, 558
Hugg, Mary II, 638
Hugg, Mercy II, 234
Hugg, Mercy II, 242
Hugg, Priscilla II, 234
Hugg, Sarah II, 234
Hugg, Sarah II, 247
Huggens, Charles Wright I, 325
Huggens, Sarah I, 325
Huggins, Elizabeth II, 78
Huggins, Elizabeth II, 80
Huggins, Huldah II, 80
Huggins, Huldah II, 110
Huggins, Martha II, 379
Huggins, Mary II, 80
Huggins, Mercy II, 65
Huggins, Mercy II, 80
Huggins, Patience II, 85
Huggins, Patience Lowderback II, 80
Huggins, Rose II, 444
Huggins, Samuel II, 80
Huggins, Samuel II, 104
Huggins, Sarah II, 80
Huggins, Sarah II, 104
Huggins, Thomas II, 65
Huggins, Thomas II, 80
Hugh, Abigail II, 379
Hugh, Anna Maria IV, 93
Hugh, Elizabeth I, 819
Hugh, Hugh II, 275
Hugh, Ira I, 988
Hugh, Martha I, 988
Hugh, Mary II, 275
Hugh, Matthew, Jr. II, 1003
Hughes, ??? VI, 154
Hughes, ??? VI, 742
Hughes, ??? VI, 748
Hughes, Aaron II, 234
Hughes, Aaron II, 271
Hughes, Aaron II, 379
Hughes, Aaron II, 558
Hughes, Aaron II, 559
Hughes, Aaron, Jr. VI, 183
Hughes, Abigail II, 379
Hughes, Adrienne VI, 742
Hughes, Adrienne Gillingham VI, 748
Hughes, Alan Marple III, 79
Hughes, Alan Marple III, 175
Hughes, Alice II, 379
Hughes, Alice II, 558
Hughes, Alice III, 103
Hughes, Alice VI, 985
Hughes, Amelia II, 379
Hughes, Amey II, 559
Hughes, Amey II, 580
Hughes, Amey, Jr. II, 559
Hughes, Amos VI, 658
Hughes, Amos VI, 659
Hughes, Amos VI, 663
Hughes, Amos VI, 666
Hughes, Amy II, 558
Hughes, Ann II, 444
Hughes, Ann VI, 557
Hughes, Ann VI, 819
Hughes, Anna C. VI, 659
Hughes, Anna Neill VI, 658
Hughes, Anne VI, 937
Hughes, Anselm VI, 937
Hughes, Archabel II, 32
Hughes, Archibald VI, 937
Hughes, B. VI, 937
Hughes, Belle V, 627
Hughes, Ben VI, 985
Hughes, Benj. VI, 857
Hughes, Benjamin II, 31
Hughes, Benjamin II, 78
Hughes, Benjamin VI, 748
Hughes, Benjamin VI, 755
Hughes, Benjamin VI, 850
Hughes, Benjamin VI, 864
Hughes, Benjamin VI, 937
Hughes, Benjamin J. VI, 827
Hughes, Blackmore VI, 937
Hughes, Caleb II, 379
Hughes, Caleb II, 558
Hughes, Cana VI, 899
Hughes, Carrie IV, 1254
Hughes, Catharine VI, 1010
Hughes, Catherine VI, 850
Hughes, Causmelia VI, 405
Hughes, Celia III, 175
Hughes, Charles II, 379
Hughes, Charles Pennel II, 747
Hughes, Charles Pennell II, 747
Hughes, Chas. V, 971
Hughes, Chas. C. III, 175
Hughes, Christiana VI, 748
Hughes, Clara V. VI, 651
Hughes, Clara V. VI, 654
Hughes, Clara V. VI, 658
Hughes, Clara V. VI, 659
Hughes, Clara V. VI, 749
Hughes, Constantine VI, 513
Hughes, Constantine VI, 518
Hughes, Constantine VI, 630
Hughes, Constantine VI, 659
Hughes, Cosmelia VI, 405
Hughes, Cosmelia VI, 408
Hughes, Cosmelia VI, 658
Hughes, Cosmelia VI, 659
Hughes, Cosmelia VI, 666
Hughes, Cosmelia J. VI, 659
Hughes, Cosmelia Janney VI, 621
Hughes, Cosmelia Janney VI, 658
Hughes, Daniel II, 379
Hughes, Daniel McPherson VI, 621
Hughes, Daniel McPherson VI, 658
Hughes, Daniel McPherson VI, 659
Hughes, David II, 379
Hughes, David II, 558
Hughes, David VI, 827
Hughes, David VI, 914
Hughes, David VI, 930
Hughes, David VI, 944
Hughes, Donald McPherson VI, 658
Hughes, Doroth??? II, 379
Hughes, Dorothea M. VI, 778
Hughes, Dorothea Murray VI, 748
Hughes, Dorothy II, 558
Hughes, Edis VI, 887
Hughes, Edith II, 31
Hughes, Edith IV, 826
Hughes, Edw. III, 163
Hughes, Edward II, 31
Hughes, Edward II, 53
Hughes, Edward II, 78
Hughes, Edward II, 558
Hughes, Edward VI, 182
Hughes, Edward VI, 183
Hughes, Edward VI, 658
Hughes, Edward VI, 827
Hughes, Edward W. V, 685
Hughes, Edwin IV, 412
Hughes, Edwin IV, 826
Hughes, Eleanor II, 559
Hughes, Eleanor V, 971
Hughes, Elias II, 234
Hughes, Elias VI, 621
Hughes, Elias VI, 651
Hughes, Elias VI, 658
Hughes, Elias VI, 659
Hughes, Elias VI, 681
Hughes, Elias VI, 685
Hughes, Elihu II, 31
Hughes, Elisha VI, 659
Hughes, Eliz. R. III, 175
Hughes, Eliza F. VI, 819
Hughes, Elizabeth II, 31
Hughes, Elizabeth II, 32
Hughes, Elizabeth II, 234
Hughes, Elizabeth II, 379
Hughes, Elizabeth IV, 510
Hughes, Elizabeth IV, 536
Hughes, Elizabeth VI, 518
Hughes, Elizabeth VI, 557
Hughes, Elizabeth VI, 621
Hughes, Elizabeth VI, 630
Hughes, Elizabeth VI, 659
Hughes, Elizabeth VI, 748
Hughes, Elizabeth VI, 755
Hughes, Elizabeth VI, 827
Hughes, Elizabeth VI, 867
Hughes, Elizabeth VI, 937
Hughes, Elizabeth H. VI, 659
Hughes, Elizabeth H. VI, 669
Hughes, Elizabeth Hughes VI, 513
Hughes, Elizabeth R. VI, 981
Hughes, Ellis IV, 412
Hughes, Ellis IV, 725
Hughes, Ellis IV, 826
Hughes, Elvira VI, 827
Hughes, Emariah VI, 937
Hughes, Emma III, 175
Hughes, Emory VI, 827
Hughes, Emory VI, 876
Hughes, Emory L. VI, 866
Hughes, Enoch II, 379
Hughes, Ethel Pidgeon V, 627
Hughes, Ethel Pidgeon V, 685
Hughes, Ezekiah II, 31
Hughes, Fanny VI, 864
Hughes, Frances Ann VI, 937
Hughes, Frances G. VI, 937
Hughes, Gabriella VI, 827
Hughes, Geo. T. V, 1003
Hughes, George VI, 899
Hughes, George VI, 937
Hughes, George VI, 978
Hughes, George Chalkley Gillingham VI, 748
Hughes, George T. IV, 1212
Hughes, George T. V, 1003
Hughes, Gideon IV, 825
Hughes, Gideon IV, 826
Hughes, Gideon V, 971
Hughes, Gideon, Jr. IV, 826
Hughes, Grace II, 796
Hughes, Gwen II, 558
Hughes, Gwen II, 578
Hughes, H. V, 1003
Hughes, H. T. VI, 956
Hughes, Hannah II, 31
Hughes, Hannah II, 32
Hughes, Hannah II, 53
Hughes, Hannah II, 78
Hughes, Hannah II, 83
Hughes, Hannah IV, 826
Hughes, Hannah V, 968
Hughes, Hannah V, 971
Hughes, Hannah VI, 491
Hughes, Hannah VI, 621
Hughes, Hannah VI, 659
Hughes, Hannah G. II, 801
Hughes, Hannah G. II, 879
Hughes, Harrison VI, 937
Hughes, Henry II, 558
Hughes, Hezekiah II, 78
Hughes, Hiram II, 31
Hughes, Hopkins VI, 809
Hughes, Hopkins VI, 827
Hughes, Howard IV, 725
Hughes, Hugh VI, 659
Hughes, Isaac II, 31
Hughes, Isaac II, 379
Hughes, Isaiah III, 175
Hughes, Isaiah B. VI, 748
Hughes, J. Elza V, 685
Hughes, Jacob II, 558
Hughes, Jacob II, 559
Hughes, James II, 32
Hughes, James V, 883
Hughes, James V, 971
Hughes, Jancey VI, 882
Hughes, Jane II, 31
Hughes, Jane II, 32
Hughes, Jane II, 78
Hughes, Jane II, 234
Hughes, Jane II, 271
Hughes, Jane II, 379
Hughes, Jemima II, 32
Hughes, Jemima II, 379
Hughes, Jemimah II, 558
Hughes, Jennie II, 877
Hughes, Jennie II, 879
Hughes, John II, 32
Hughes, John II, 379
Hughes, John II, 558
Hughes, John II, 708
Hughes, John II, 877
Hughes, John II, 879
Hughes, John V, 627
Hughes, John V, 883
Hughes, John V, 968
Hughes, John V, 971
Hughes, John VI, 659
Hughes, John VI, 795
Hughes, John VI, 807
Hughes, John VI, 821
Hughes, John VI, 827
Hughes, John VI, 867
Hughes, John VI, 877
Hughes, John VI, 882
Hughes, John VI, 915
Hughes, John VI, 937
Hughes, John VI, 981
Hughes, John VI, 986
Hughes, John VI, 999
Hughes, John C. VI, 937
Hughes, John G. II, 747
Hughes, John Peter III, 175
Hughes, Jonathan II, 708
Hughes, Jos. II, 708
Hughes, Joseph I, 624
Hughes, Joseph II, 78
Hughes, Joseph II, 708
Hughes, Joseph M. V, 1003
Hughes, Josiah II, 379
Hughes, Josiah VI, 844
Hughes, Katherine V, 685
Hughes, Katie E. II, 877
Hughes, Katie E. II, 879
Hughes, Lawrence VI, 827
Hughes, Lee VI, 937
Hughes, Lee VI, 959
Hughes, Littleberry VI, 827
Hughes, Littleberry VI, 857
Hughes, Littleberry VI, 859
Hughes, Littleberry VI, 865
Hughes, Lou I, 624
Hughes, Lucy VI, 965
Hughes, Lucy VI, 983
Hughes, Lucy Ann VI, 863
Hughes, Lucy Gardner VI, 915

ghes, Lucy Maria VI, 912
ghes, Lydia II, 379
ghes, Lydia II, 559
ghes, Lydia VI, 659
ghes, Lydia VI, 686
ghes, Lydia Canby VI, 658
ghes, M. H. VI, 658
ghes, Margaret I, 624
ghes, Margaret II, 558
ghes, Margaret II, 708
ghes, Margaret V, 1003
ghes, Margaret VI, 734
ghes, Margaret VI, 737
ghes, Margaret VI, 748
ghes, Margaret R. IV, 1212
ghes, Margaret R. V, 1003
ghes, Margery Janney VI, 658
ghes, Mariah VI, 659
ghes, Marion III, 175
ghes, Martha II, 78
ghes, Martha II, 379
ghes, Martha II, 558
ghes, Martha II, 563
ghes, Martha II, 674
ghes, Martha VI, 405
ghes, Martha VI, 630
ghes, Martha VI, 658
ghes, Martha VI, 659
ghes, Martha VI, 663
ghes, Martha VI, 666
ghes, Martha VI, 685
ghes, Martha VI, 902
ghes, Martha VI, 937
ghes, Martha R. VI, 748
ghes, Mary II, 32
ghes, Mary II, 156
ghes, Mary II, 379
ghes, Mary II, 559
ghes, Mary II, 708
ghes, Mary II, 747
ghes, Mary V, 627
ghes, Mary VI, 630
ghes, Mary VI, 645
ghes, Mary VI, 659
ghes, Mary VI, 821
ghes, Mary VI, 827
ghes, Mary VI, 937
ghes, Mary VI, 965
ghes, Mary Ann II, 747
ghes, Mary Bracney V, 685
ghes, Mary Christiana VI, 737
ghes, Mary E. IV, 1212
ghes, Mary E. V, 1003
ghes, Mary E. VI, 808
ghes, Mary Elizabeth VI, 659
ghes, Mary Elizabeth VI, 988
ghes, Mary Rowley II, 150
ghes, Mathew VI, 659
ghes, Matthew VI, 513
ghes, Matthew VI, 518
ghes, Matthew VI, 557
ghes, Mattie V, 627
ghes, Michael VI, 819
ghes, Mildred M. III, 175
ghes, Moses II, 379
ghes, Moses II, 558
ghes, Moses IV, 412
ghes, Moses IV, 826
ghes, Nanch VI, 634
ughes, Nancy VI, 619
ughes, Nancy VI, 633
ughes, Nancy VI, 659
ughes, Nancy VI, 737
ughes, Nancy VI, 738
ughes, Nancy VI, 748
ughes, Nancy VI, 857
ughes, Nancy VI, 887
ughes, Nancy VI, 915
ughes, Nancy VI, 937
ughes, Pamela VI, 914
ughes, Patsey VI, 890
ughes, Paulina S. IV, 725
ughes, Peggy VI, 857
ughes, Penelope VI, 1000
ughes, Phebe V, 883
ughes, Phebe V, 971
ughes, Polly VI, 827
ughes, Polly VI, 937
ughes, Powell VI, 827
ughes, Pratt VI, 944
ughes, Rachel II, 558
ughes, Rachel VI, 148
ughes, Rachel VI, 183
ughes, Rachel VI, 582
ughes, Reb. III, 163
ughes, Rebecca I, 934
ughes, Rebecca II, 32
ughes, Rebecca II, 234
ughes, Rebecca II, 559
ughes, Rebecca IV, 825
ughes, Rebecca IV, 826
Hughes, Rebecca VI, 827
Hughes, Rebecca C. III, 163
Hughes, Rebeckah II, 234
Hughes, Rebekah II, 379
Hughes, Rese VI, 965
Hughes, Reubin VI, 937
Hughes, Rice VI, 147
Hughes, Rice VI, 182
Hughes, Rice VI, 915
Hughes, Rice VI, 937
Hughes, Rice VI, 981
Hughes, Rice VI, 988
Hughes, Rice VI, 997
Hughes, Richard II, 708
Hughes, Robert II, 379
Hughes, Robert VI, 8
Hughes, Robert VI, 16
Hughes, Robert VI, 147
Hughes, Robert VI, 154
Hughes, Robert VI, 182
Hughes, Robert VI, 183
Hughes, Robert VI, 808
Hughes, Robert VI, 937
Hughes, Robert L. VI, 937
Hughes, Robert, Jr. VI, 183
Hughes, Robert, Sr. VI, 183
Hughes, Ruth II, 53
Hughes, Ruth II, 78
Hughes, Ruth VI, 557
Hughes, Sally VI, 827
Hughes, Sally VI, 926
Hughes, Sally VI, 937
Hughes, Samuel II, 32
Hughes, Samuel II, 379
Hughes, Samuel II, 558
Hughes, Samuel II, 559
Hughes, Samuel II, 747
Hughes, Samuel VI, 582
Hughes, Samuel VI, 659
Hughes, Samuel VI, 937
Hughes, Samuel, Senr. VI, 557
Hughes, Sarah II, 379
Hughes, Sarah II, 558
Hughes, Sarah II, 559
Hughes, Sarah II, 708
Hughes, Sarah II, 801
Hughes, Sarah II, 826
Hughes, Sarah III, 175
Hughes, Sarah VI, 513
Hughes, Sarah VI, 557
Hughes, Sarah VI, 748
Hughes, Sarah VI, 874
Hughes, Sarah A. VI, 795
Hughes, Sarah Ann II, 747
Hughes, Sarah Ann VI, 997
Hughes, Sarah L. VI, 912
Hughes, Sarah L. VI, 937
Hughes, Sarah M. VI, 827
Hughes, Sarah Powers II, 747
Hughes, Sarah, Jr. VI, 154
Hughes, Sarah, Jr. VI, 183
Hughes, Sarah, Sr. VI, 183
Hughes, Stephen VI, 183
Hughes, Stephen VI, 887
Hughes, Stephen C. IV, 1212
Hughes, Stephen C. V, 1003
Hughes, Susan N. VI, 859
Hughes, Susanna VI, 844
Hughes, Susannah II, 32
Hughes, Tabitha II, 31
Hughes, Tabitha VI, 930
Hughes, Theodore V, 627
Hughes, Thomas II, 31
Hughes, Thomas II, 32
Hughes, Thomas II, 558
Hughes, Thomas II, 879
Hughes, Thomas VI, 405
Hughes, Thomas VI, 513
Hughes, Thomas VI, 557
Hughes, Thomas VI, 630
Hughes, Thomas VI, 658
Hughes, Thomas VI, 659
Hughes, Thomas VI, 663
Hughes, Thomas VI, 666
Hughes, Thomas VI, 685
Hughes, Thomas VI, 827
Hughes, Thos. II, 801
Hughes, Virginia J. VI, 621
Hughes, Virginia J. VI, 651
Hughes, Virginia J. VI, 658
Hughes, Virginia J. VI, 659
Hughes, Virginia J. VI, 681
Hughes, Virginia J. VI, 685
Hughes, Wd. Elizabeth VI, 513
Hughes, Wd. Elizabeth Nichols VI, 518
Hughes, Wd. Phebe VI, 557
Hughes, William II, 379
Hughes, William J. VI, 737
Hughes, Wm. II, 444
Hughes, Wm. II, 558
Hughes, Wm. II, 559
Hughes, Wm. II, 580
Hughes, Wm. V, 1003
Hughes, Wm. VI, 491
Hughes, Wm. C. V, 685
Hughes, Wm. Clifford V, 685
Hughes, Wm. H. IV, 1212
Hughes, Wm. H. V, 1003
Hughes, Wm. Hastings VI, 748
Hughes, Wm. J. VI, 748
Hughes, Wm. L. IV, 1212
Hughes, Wm. L. V, 1003
Hughey, Russel V, 458
Hughie, Wm. Clifford V, 685
Hughs, Aaron II, 379
Hughs, Aaron VI, 405
Hughs, Aaron VI, 513
Hughs, Abner VI, 405
Hughs, Amelia II, 379
Hughs, Amos VI, 658
Hughs, Amy II, 558
Hughs, Ann II, 78
Hughs, Anne VI, 405
Hughs, Causmelia VI, 405
Hughs, Charles V, 78
Hughs, Cosmelia VI, 405
Hughs, David II, 379
Hughs, David VI, 405
Hughs, David VI, 513
Hughs, Deborah II, 67
Hughs, Deborah II, 78
Hughs, Doroth??? II, 379
Hughs, Edith IV, 637
Hughs, Edith IV, 826
Hughs, Edward VI, 405
Hughs, Edwin IV, 826
Hughs, Elenor Star V, 78
Hughs, Elizabeth II, 379
Hughs, Elizabeth IV, 637
Hughs, Elizabeth IV, 666
Hughs, Elizabeth IV, 667
Hughs, Ellis IV, 637
Hughs, Ellis IV, 826
Hughs, Ethel V, 578
Hughs, Frank V, 578
Hughs, Geo. T. V, 1003
Hughs, Gideon IV, 637
Hughs, Gideon IV, 825
Hughs, Gideon IV, 826
Hughs, Gideon IV, 859
Hughs, H. V, 1003
Hughs, Hannah II, 61
Hughs, Hannah II, 78
Hughs, Hannah IV, 826
Hughs, Hannah G. II, 801
Hughs, Hezekiah II, 1003
Hughs, Isaac VI, 405
Hughs, Isabel IV, 666
Hughs, James IV, 666
Hughs, James V, 78
Hughs, Jane II, 78
Hughs, Jane II, 1003
Hughs, John V, 78
Hughs, John VI, 748
Hughs, John Pearson V, 78
Hughs, Jonathan II, 61
Hughs, Jonathan II, 78
Hughs, Joseph M. V, 1003
Hughs, Lydia II, 379
Hughs, Lydia VI, 405
Hughs, Lydia VI, 513
Hughs, Margaret II, 558
Hughs, Margaret II, 615
Hughs, Margaret R. V, 1003
Hughs, Martha VI, 405
Hughs, Mary II, 379
Hughs, Mary VI, 405
Hughs, Mary VI, 513
Hughs, Mary E. V, 1003
Hughs, Matthew, Jr. II, 1003
Hughs, Moses II, 467
Hughs, Moses II, 558
Hughs, Moses IV, 826
Hughs, Paulina S. IV, 684
Hughs, Paulina S. IV, 725
Hughs, Phebe V, 78
Hughs, Rachel II, 78
Hughs, Rebecca IV, 637
Hughs, Rebecca IV, 825
Hughs, Rebecca IV, 826
Hughs, Rebeckah II, 234
Hughs, Ruth VI, 513
Hughs, Sarah II, 379
Hughs, Sarah II, 467
Hughs, Sarah II, 558
Hughs, Sarah II, 801
Hughs, Sarah V, 578
Hughs, Sarah VI, 405
Hughs, Sarah VI, 513
Hughs, Stephen C. V, 1003
Hughs, Susanna V, 78
Hughs, Thomas II, 879
Hughs, Thomas II, 1033
Hughs, Thomas VI, 405
Hughs, Thos. II, 801
Hughs, William II, 379
Hughs, Wm. V, 1003
Hughs, Wm. L. V, 1003
Hughston, Mary II, 379
Hugings, Strangeman VI, 250
Hugings, Strangeman VI, 251
Huhn, Chloreta IV, 1254
Huhn, David S. IV, 1254
Huhn, Davis IV, 1254
Huhn, Edward IV, 1254
Huhn, Elben IV, 1254
Huhn, Ella IV, 1254
Huhn, Fred IV, 1254
Huhn, Lillian IV, 1254
Huhn, Ruth E. IV, 1254
Huhter, Nancy VI, 957
Huin, Ella IV, 1254
Huin, Laura IV, 1254
Huist, Arminda V, 1003
Huitt, Gregory II, 444
Huitt, John II, 444
Huitt, Sarah II, 444
Hulbert, Mary E. III, 19
Hulet, Sarah V, 78
Hulett, Sarah Corlies V, 250
Hulford, Evan IV, 265
Hulford, Samuel, Jr. VI, 598
Hulford, Sarah IV, 226
Hulford, Sarah IV, 265
Hulie, Benjamin III, 421
Hulie, Benjamin III, 429
Hulie, Sarah III, 421
Hulie, Sarah III, 429
Huling, Mary Ann VI, 422
Hulings, Abraham II, 231
Hulings, Honor II, 61
Hulings, Honor II, 80
Hulins, John II, 231
Hulit, Sarah V, 304
Hull, ??? III, 17
Hull, Abigail III, 175
Hull, Alfred C. III, 176
Hull, Alice IV, 1212
Hull, Alice L. III, 254
Hull, Amy III, 89
Hull, Amy III, 156
Hull, Amy III, 175
Hull, Amy III, 176
Hull, Amy III, 177
Hull, Ann III, 176
Hull, Ann IV, 412
Hull, Ann IV, 478
Hull, Ann IV, 496
Hull, Ann C. III, 177
Hull, Anna III, 148
Hull, Anna III, 176
Hull, Anna III, 177
Hull, Anna E. III, 60
Hull, Anna E. III, 175
Hull, Anna J. IV, 1212
Hull, Anna M. F. III, 176
Hull, Anna M. F. III, 268
Hull, Annie A. II, 864
Hull, Annie A. II, 879
Hull, Archy V, 503
Hull, Arnold IV, 1212
Hull, Bertha V, 1003
Hull, Caroline III, 176
Hull, Caroline III, 177
Hull, Caroline C. III, 175
Hull, Caroline C. III, 176
Hull, Caroline E. III, 107
Hull, Caroline E. III, 175
Hull, Caroline E. III, 176
Hull, Caroline E. III, 253
Hull, Carrie Louisa III, 175
Hull, Carrie Louise III, 175
Hull, Carrie Louise III, 253
Hull, Catharine III, 71
Hull, Catharine III, 135
Hull, Catharine III, 175
Hull, Catharine III, 176
Hull, Catharine Field III, 176
Hull, Charles V, 503
Hull, Charles Edward III, 175
Hull, Charles W. III, 175
Hull, Charles Wager III, 175
Hull, Charles Wager III, 176
Hull, Clarence V, 458
Hull, Claud IV, 1212
Hull, Cornelia III, 107
Hull, Cornelia B. III, 175
Hull, Damaris III, 175
Hull, Damaris III, 176
Hull, David III, 175
Hull, David A. III, 175
Hull, David H. IV, 947
Hull, Demaris III, 177
Hull, Dr. James R. V, 250
Hull, Edward III, 175
Hull, Edward III, 176
Hull, Effingham B. III, 176
Hull, Eliz. III, 175
Hull, Eliza V, 340
Hull, Eliza C. III, 133
Hull, Eliza E. III, 175
Hull, Eliza. C. III, 364
Hull, Elizabeth III, 60
Hull, Elizabeth III, 64
Hull, Elizabeth III, 175
Hull, Elizabeth III, 176
Hull, Elizabeth III, 177
Hull, Elizabeth III, 204
Hull, Elizabeth IV, 1166
Hull, Elizabeth V, 340
Hull, Emilie L. III, 279
Hull, Emily III, 177
Hull, Emily L. III, 176
Hull, Emily L. III, 177
Hull, Emily L. III, 302
Hull, Emma L. III, 254
Hull, Emma T. III, 175
Hull, Esther K. III, 175
Hull, Eugene Foster III, 176
Hull, Eugenia III, 175
Hull, Eugenia III, 277
Hull, Franklin III, 104
Hull, Frederic III, 176
Hull, Freelove III, 175
Hull, Freelove III, 176
Hull, Freelove III, 218
Hull, George III, 177
Hull, George IV, 1212
Hull, George D. III, 175
Hull, Georgiana III, 176
Hull, Gertrude IV, 1212
Hull, Hannah III, 175
Hull, Hannah III, 176
Hull, Hannah III, 216
Hull, Hannah IV, 40
Hull, Hannah IV, 55
Hull, Hannah VI, 755
Hull, Hannah Ann VI, 751
Hull, Hannah Ann VI, 756
Hull, Hannah C. II, 879
Hull, Hannah Hallowell II, 849
Hull, Hannah Hollowell II, 879
Hull, Harriet II, 801
Hull, Harriet III, 175
Hull, Harriett IV, 1212
Hull, Helen IV, 1212
Hull, Henrietta III, 55
Hull, Henrietta III, 89
Hull, Henrietta III, 175
Hull, Henrietta III, 176
Hull, Henry III, 177
Hull, Henry IV, 1166
Hull, Henry VI, 465
Hull, Henry C. III, 175
Hull, Henry C. III, 372
Hull, Henry Cohn III, 175
Hull, Henry Cohu III, 177
Hull, Henry Cohu III, 277
Hull, Ida V, 503
Hull, Iris IV, 1212
Hull, Isaac, Jr. III, 254
Hull, Jacob III, 175
Hull, Jacob III, 176
Hull, James III, 175
Hull, James III, 176
Hull, James C. III, 107
Hull, James C. III, 175
Hull, James C. III, 176
Hull, James C. III, 253
Hull, James F. III, 175
Hull, James Frank III, 175
Hull, Jas. C. III, 175
Hull, Jas. C. III, 176
Hull, Jerusha IV, 947
Hull, John III, 89
Hull, John III, 148
Hull, John III, 156
Hull, John III, 175
Hull, John III, 176
Hull, John III, 177
Hull, John IV, 1166
Hull, John C. III, 175
Hull, John C. III, 176
Hull, John C. III, 177
Hull, John Cox III, 176
Hull, John Cox III, 177
Hull, John F. III, 176
Hull, John Jr III, 176
Hull, John W. III, 176
Hull, John Y. III, 176
Hull, Johnna IV, 1212
Hull, Jos. III, 175
Hull, Joseph III, 175

Hull, Joseph III, 176
Hull, Joseph III, 218
Hull, Joseph III, 265
Hull, Julia V, 503
Hull, Keziah III, 155
Hull, Keziah III, 176
Hull, Liddeman III, 17
Hull, Liddeman Jr III, 176
Hull, Lydia III, 175
Hull, Lydia E. III, 177
Hull, Lydia L. III, 78
Hull, Lydia L. III, 176
Hull, Lydia Ruth V, 250
Hull, Martha IV, 1166
Hull, Mary III, 157
Hull, Mary III, 175
Hull, Mary III, 176
Hull, Mary IV, 1212
Hull, Mary Ann III, 176
Hull, Mary C. IV, 947
Hull, Mary Catharine III, 104
Hull, Mary Catharine III, 176
Hull, Mary D. II, 849
Hull, Mary D. II, 879
Hull, Mary E. II, 879
Hull, Mary Elizabeth II, 801
Hull, Mary Ella III, 107
Hull, Mary Ella III, 175
Hull, Mary Ella III, 176
Hull, Mary Ella III, 257
Hull, Mary Emily III, 234
Hull, Mary Emily III, 254
Hull, Mary Florence III, 176
Hull, Mary Florence III, 177
Hull, Mary H. III, 155
Hull, Oliver III, 55
Hull, Oliver III, 175
Hull, Oliver III, 176
Hull, Oliver C. III, 107
Hull, Oliver C. III, 175
Hull, Oliver C. III, 176
Hull, Oliver C. III, 177
Hull, Oliver Jr III, 176
Hull, Oliver, Jr. II, 559
Hull, Penelope III, 55
Hull, Penelope III, 175
Hull, Penelope III, 176
Hull, Penelope III, 177
Hull, Phebe III, 175
Hull, Phebe III, 176
Hull, Phebe III, 177
Hull, Phebe III, 218
Hull, Phebe III, 265
Hull, Phebe Ann III, 148
Hull, Phebe Ann III, 176
Hull, Phebe Anna III, 176
Hull, Phebe B. III, 175
Hull, Phebe B. III, 372
Hull, Phebe C. III, 176
Hull, Phebe C. III, 177
Hull, Phebe H. III, 364
Hull, Phebe Jr III, 176
Hull, Rachel IV, 1166
Hull, Rebecca III, 153
Hull, Rebecca III, 155
Hull, Rebecca III, 156
Hull, Rebecca III, 176
Hull, Rebecca III, 312
Hull, Retha IV, 1212
Hull, Richard Cooper III, 176
Hull, Richard Randolph III, 176
Hull, Richard Randolph III, 268
Hull, Robert III, 175
Hull, Robert III, 176
Hull, Robert VI, 755
Hull, Robert VI, 756
Hull, Robert Bowne III, 176
Hull, Robert Franklin III, 176
Hull, Robert Franklin III, 177
Hull, Robert W. III, 78
Hull, Robert W. III, 175
Hull, Robert W. III, 176
Hull, Robert W. III, 177
Hull, Robt. W. III, 175
Hull, Robt. W. III, 176
Hull, Ruth III, 177
Hull, Ruth IV, 1166
Hull, Ruth IV, 1185
Hull, Sam'l G. III, 64
Hull, Samuel IV, 1166
Hull, Samuel B. III, 60
Hull, Samuel G. III, 175
Hull, Samuel G. III, 177
Hull, Sarah III, 17
Hull, Sarah III, 110
Hull, Sarah III, 175
Hull, Sarah III, 176
Hull, Sarah III, 177
Hull, Sarah III, 204
Hull, Sarah III, 255
Hull, Sarah III, 263
Hull, Sarah Ann III, 176
Hull, Sarah C. III, 205
Hull, Sarah Frances III, 64
Hull, Sarah Frances III, 177
Hull, Sarah J. III, 16
Hull, Sarah J. III, 109
Hull, Solomon III, 177
Hull, Solomon IV, 1166
Hull, Stephen III, 176
Hull, Susan III, 177
Hull, T. Burling II, 849
Hull, T. Burling II, 879
Hull, Theodore G. III, 175
Hull, Thos. Jackson II, 801
Hull, Tiddeman III, 177
Hull, Tiddeman, Jr. III, 177
Hull, Vila IV, 194
Hull, Vila IV, 226
Hull, Wager III, 175
Hull, Wager III, 176
Hull, Wager III, 177
Hull, Wager III, 205
Hull, Wager III, 364
Hull, Wager Jr III, 176
Hull, Wager, Jr. III, 155
Hull, Walter W. IV, 1212
Hull, William III, 177
Hull, William E. III, 302
Hull, William F. III, 177
Hull, William F. III, 279
Hull, William L. III, 176
Hull, Wm. F. III, 176
Hull, Wm. Isaac II, 849
Hull, Wm. Isaac II, 879
Hullinger, Ada V, 1003
Hullinger, C. E. V, 1003
Hullinger, Eli V, 1003
Hulls, Gertrude Elizabeth V, 685
Hulls, Samuel W. V, 685
Hulls, Vesta Mildred V, 685
Hulm, Chloreta IV, 1254
Hulm, David S. IV, 1254
Hulm, Davis IV, 1254
Hulm, Edward IV, 1254
Hulm, Elben IV, 1254
Hulm, Ella IV, 1254
Hulm, Fred IV, 1254
Hulm, Lillian IV, 1254
Hulm, Ruth E. IV, 1254
Hulme, Ann II, 559
Hulme, Benjamin II, 1003
Hulme, Benjamin II, 1004
Hulme, Charles II, 177
Hulme, Edward S. II, 961
Hulme, Edward S. II, 1052
Hulme, Eliza II, 293
Hulme, Eliza II, 820
Hulme, Elizabeth II, 1003
Hulme, Elizabeth K. II, 961
Hulme, Elizabeth K. II, 1046
Hulme, Elizabeth K. II, 1052
Hulme, Emily II, 1052
Hulme, Emily S. II, 961
Hulme, Frederick G. II, 708
Hulme, George II, 234
Hulme, George II, 559
Hulme, George II, 1003
Hulme, George II, 1018
Hulme, George, Jr. II, 293
Hulme, Hannah II, 292
Hulme, Isaac II, 1003
Hulme, J. Kirkbride II, 1052
Hulme, James II, 292
Hulme, John II, 234
Hulme, John II, 559
Hulme, John II, 1003
Hulme, John K. II, 708
Hulme, John K. II, 961
Hulme, John K. II, 1052
Hulme, John, Jr. II, 234
Hulme, John, Jr. II, 559
Hulme, John, Jr. II, 1003
Hulme, Joseph II, 1003
Hulme, Joseph II, 1004
Hulme, Julia II, 310
Hulme, Julia II, 321
Hulme, Julia II, 322
Hulme, Margaret II, 559
Hulme, Margaret II, 1003
Hulme, Maria II, 293
Hulme, Martha II, 234
Hulme, Mary II, 559
Hulme, Mary II, 961
Hulme, Mary II, 999
Hulme, Mary II, 1003
Hulme, Mary II, 1052
Hulme, Mary II, 1054
Hulme, Naomi II, 1003
Hulme, Naomi II, 1018
Hulme, Rachel II, 559
Hulme, Rachel II, 961
Hulme, Rachel II, 1003
Hulme, Rachel II, 1004
Hulme, Rachel S. II, 708
Hulme, Rachel S. II, 1046
Hulme, Rachel S. II, 1052
Hulme, Rachel S. II, 1054
Hulme, Rebecca II, 1003
Hulme, Rebecca Ann II, 292
Hulme, Rebecca F. II, 708
Hulme, Rebeckah II, 1003
Hulme, Robert R. II, 708
Hulme, Robert R. II, 961
Hulme, Robert R. II, 1052
Hulme, Ruth II, 1003
Hulme, Ruth II, 1018
Hulme, Samuel II, 708
Hulme, Samuel II, 961
Hulme, Samuel II, 1003
Hulme, Samuel II, 1046
Hulme, Samuel II, 1052
Hulme, Samuel II, 1054
Hulme, Samuel, Jr. II, 1052
Hulme, Sarah II, 292
Hulme, Sarah B. II, 294
Hulme, Sarah B. Levis II, 292
Hulme, T. Kirkbride II, 961
Hulme, Thomas II, 379
Hulme, Thomas II, 1003
Hulme, William II, 1004
Hulme, Wm. II, 1003
Hulmes, John II, 1003
Hulmes, John II, 1015
Hulmes, John, Jr. II, 234
Hulmes, John, Jr. II, 559
Hulmes, John, Jr. II, 1003
Hulmes, John, Jr. II, 1015
Hulmes, Margaret II, 1003
Hulmes, Margaret II, 1018
Hulmes, Rebeckah II, 1003
Hulmes, Rebeckah II, 1015
Huls, Blanch V, 685
Huls, E. Ella V, 685
Huls, Ella V, 685
Huls, Gertrude Elizabeth V, 685
Huls, James G. V, 685
Huls, Jane G. V, 685
Huls, Samuel W. V, 685
Huls, Vesta Mildred V, 685
Hulse, Ann V, 578
Hulse, Jane G. V, 685
Hults, Lydia V, 78
Hults, Lydia V, 118
Hults, Sarah V, 180
Hultz, Catherine V, 180
Hultz, Catherine L. V, 180
Hultz, Esthel S. V, 180
Hultz, Joseph V, 180
Hultz, Sarah V, 180
Hultz, Walter V, 180
Hultz, Wm. P. V, 180
Humann, Herman III, 177
Humber, Anna II, 1043
Humber, Wd. Sarah II, 1043
Humbles, Jane II, 43
Humbles, Lee VI, 827
Humbles, Mary A. VI, 827
Humbles, Thomas II, 43
Humbleton, James VI, 830
Humbleton, Susanna VI, 830
Humburg, Elizabeth II, 869
Humburg, Elizabeth II, 879
Hume, Sophia II, 559
Humerichehouse, Annie V, 1003
Humerichehouse, Lydia V, 1003
Humerichouse, Elias V, 1003
Humerickhouse, Annie V, 1003
Humerickhouse, Elias V, 1003
Humerickhouse, Lydia V, 1003
Humerickhouse, Sarah V, 1003
Humes, Ida I, 1154
Humes, Lydia VI, 405
Humes, Lydia VI, 440
Humes, Sarah VI, 405
Humes, Thomas VI, 440
Hummel, George Edgar II, 708
Hummel, Martha II, 708
Hummell, Arthur W. VI, 732
Hummell, Arthur W. VI, 751
Hummell, Caroline VI, 751
Hummell, Ruth VI, 732
Hummell, Ruth VI, 751
Hummell, William F. VI, 751
Hummer, Ann II, 1004
Hummiel, Emma V, 1003
Hummiel, Mary Ann V, 1003
Hummiel, Sarah V, 1003
Humpheres, Increece II, 234
Humpheres, Increece II, 238
Humpheres, Joshua II, 234
Humpheres, Joshua II, 238
Humpheries, Anna II, 234
Humpheries, Elizabeth II, 234
Humpheries, Increase II, 234
Humpheries, Increece II, 234
Humpheries, Isaac II, 234
Humpheries, Jonathan II, 215
Humpheries, Jonathan II, 234
Humpheries, Joshua II, 234
Humpheries, Joshua II, 273
Humpheries, Rachel II, 234
Humpheries, Sarah II, 215
Humpheries, Sarah II, 234
Humpheries, Wd. Elizabeth II, 220
Humpheries, Wd. Elizabeth II, 234
Humphrevile, Edra IV, 226
Humphrevile, Mary IV, 226
Humphrevile, Mildred IV, 226
Humphreville, Sarah IV, 194
Humphreville, Sarah IV, 226
Humphreville, William IV, 226
Humphrey, Ada V, 627
Humphrey, Benj. III, 177
Humphrey, Benjamin II, 527
Humphrey, Bertha V, 402
Humphrey, Bertha V, 627
Humphrey, Bertha V, 672
Humphrey, Bertha V, 685
Humphrey, Betsey VI, 937
Humphrey, Charlie V, 627
Humphrey, Chas. L. V, 685
Humphrey, Cora B. V, 402
Humphrey, Daniel IV, 1282
Humphrey, David III, 122
Humphrey, David III, 177
Humphrey, David IV, 1282
Humphrey, David VI, 937
Humphrey, Dennis J. V, 402
Humphrey, Dennis J. V, 627
Humphrey, Dora V, 78
Humphrey, Dora B. V, 627
Humphrey, Elizabeth III, 122
Humphrey, Elizabeth III, 177
Humphrey, Elsworth III, 177
Humphrey, Ester II, 379
Humphrey, Esther V, 250
Humphrey, Frank V, 627
Humphrey, Freda V, 627
Humphrey, Freda N. V, 685
Humphrey, Goldie V, 78
Humphrey, Goldie V, 627
Humphrey, Goldie Ronia V, 402
Humphrey, Hannah II, 80
Humphrey, Hannah II, 854
Humphrey, Hannah VI, 937
Humphrey, Henry V, 627
Humphrey, James IV, 637
Humphrey, Jehua M. V, 685
Humphrey, Joan II, 379
Humphrey, John II, 379
Humphrey, John II, 487
Humphrey, John II, 747
Humphrey, John IV, 637
Humphrey, John VI, 875
Humphrey, John VI, 937
Humphrey, Jonathan II, 527
Humphrey, Joshua II, 379
Humphrey, Laura V, 305
Humphrey, Leala V, 402
Humphrey, Leola V, 627
Humphrey, Leonard Donald V, 402
Humphrey, Leonard Donald V, 627
Humphrey, Lewis VI, 937
Humphrey, Lewis VI, 946
Humphrey, Lewis VI, 1015
Humphrey, Mabel V, 627
Humphrey, Margaret VI, 937
Humphrey, Martha IV, 637
Humphrey, Mary II, 527
Humphrey, Mary II, 560
Humphrey, Mary II, 689
Humphrey, Mary II, 747
Humphrey, Mary IV, 725
Humphrey, Mary IV, 874
Humphrey, Mary Jane IV, 1282
Humphrey, Mildred V, 402
Humphrey, Mildred V, 627
Humphrey, Mildred Leala V, 627
Humphrey, Murrey II, 379
Humphrey, Nancy VI, 937
Humphrey, Nancy VI, 974
Humphrey, Narcissa IV, 873
Humphrey, Narcissa IV, 874
Humphrey, Netty V, 305
Humphrey, Ora V, 78
Humphrey, Ora V, 402
Humphrey, Ora V, 627
Humphrey, Polly VI, 983
Humphrey, Randolph VI, 937
Humphrey, Raymond V, 78
Humphrey, Raymond V, 402
Humphrey, Raymond V, 627
Humphrey, Rebecca II, 487
Humphrey, Rebecca II, 747
Humphrey, Richard II, 379
Humphrey, Richard V. II, 1004
Humphrey, Roma V, 78
Humphrey, Roma V, 627
Humphrey, Sally VI, 910
Humphrey, Sally VI, 937
Humphrey, Saml. H. VI, 910
Humphrey, Samuel III, 177
Humphrey, Sarah II, 560
Humphrey, Sarah V, 627
Humphrey, Sarah V, 685
Humphrey, Sarah W. IV, 725
Humphrey, Sophia VI, 875
Humphrey, Stella IV, 1282
Humphrey, Suckey VI, 1015
Humphrey, Thomas II, 560
Humphrey, Thomas III, 177
Humphrey, W. H. V, 685
Humphrey, Walter V, 627
Humphrey, Walter J. V, 685
Humphrey, Westley V, 305
Humphrey, Will V, 627
Humphrey, William VI, 937
Humphrey, William VI, 1015
Humphrey, Wm. V, 627
Humphrey, Zelma V, 627
Humphreys, Abigail II, 460
Humphreys, Abigail II, 559
Humphreys, Amie II, 559
Humphreys, Amy II, 379
Humphreys, Amy II, 560
Humphreys, Anderson I, 1154
Humphreys, Ann II, 129
Humphreys, Ann II, 351
Humphreys, Ann II, 497
Humphreys, Ann II, 559
Humphreys, Ann II, 560
Humphreys, Ann II, 602
Humphreys, Ann II, 1004
Humphreys, Ann VI, 581
Humphreys, Anna Maria II, 37
Humphreys, Asa II, 379
Humphreys, Benjamin II, 379
Humphreys, Benjamin II, 511
Humphreys, Benjamin II, 559
Humphreys, Clement II, 460
Humphreys, Clement II, 559
Humphreys, Daniel II, 559
Humphreys, David L. V, 578
Humphreys, Deborah II, 379
Humphreys, Dinah II, 379
Humphreys, Dinah II, 559
Humphreys, Edward II, 379
Humphreys, Elioner II, 379
Humphreys, Elizabeth II, 379
Humphreys, Elizabeth II, 451
Humphreys, Elizabeth II, 530
Humphreys, Elizabeth II, 559
Humphreys, Elizabeth II, 560
Humphreys, Elizabeth II, 708
Humphreys, Elizabeth II, 747
Humphreys, Emma V, 578
Humphreys, Emma F. V, 578
Humphreys, Ester II, 379
Humphreys, Esther II, 559
Humphreys, Gulielma II, 379
Humphreys, Gulielma W. II, 74
Humphreys, Gulielma W. II, 74
Humphreys, Hannah II, 351
Humphreys, Hannah II, 379
Humphreys, Hannah II, 497
Humphreys, Hannah II, 514
Humphreys, Hannah II, 559
Humphreys, Hannah II, 560
Humphreys, Hannah II, 673
Humphreys, Hannah VI, 937
Humphreys, Hester II, 560
Humphreys, Increase II, 234
Humphreys, J. II, 894
Humphreys, James V, 578
Humphreys, James Lewis II, 56
Humphreys, Jane II, 559
Humphreys, Jane E. V, 578
Humphreys, Jennie M. V, 578
Humphreys, Joan II, 379
Humphreys, Joan II, 559
Humphreys, John II, 379
Humphreys, John II, 519
Humphreys, John II, 560
Humphreys, John II, 580
Humphreys, John II, 708
Humphreys, John II, 742
Humphreys, John II, 747
Humphreys, John VI, 937
Humphreys, John H. II, 497
Humphreys, John, Jr. II, 379

umphreys, John, Jr. II, 560
umphreys, Jonathan II, 379
umphreys, Jonathan II, 559
umphreys, Joshua II, 379
umphreys, Joshua II, 559
umphreys, Julia Ann II, 879
umphreys, Lizzie A. V, 578
umphreys, Margaret II, 379
umphreys, Margaret VI, 937
umphreys, Martha II, 379
umphreys, Martha II, 559
umphreys, Martha VI, 513
umphreys, Mary II, 379
umphreys, Mary II, 519
umphreys, Mary II, 559
umphreys, Mary II, 560
umphreys, Mary II, 644
umphreys, Mary II, 747
umphreys, Mary IV, 725
umphreys, Mathew Irwin II, 379
umphreys, Mentie V, 578
umphreys, Minnie V, 578
umphreys, Murrey II, 379
umphreys, Phebe II, 559
umphreys, Randolph VI, 937
umphreys, Rebecca II, 366
umphreys, Rebecca II, 708
umphreys, Rebecca II, 747
umphreys, Richard II, 80
umphreys, Richard II, 379
umphreys, Richard II, 430
umphreys, Richard II, 497
umphreys, Richard II, 514
umphreys, Richard II, 519
umphreys, Richard II, 530
umphreys, Richard II, 559
umphreys, Richard II, 560
umphreys, Richard II, 602
umphreys, Richard II, 708
umphreys, Richard II, 879
umphreys, Richard V. II, 801
umphreys, Richard V. II, 879
umphreys, Richard, Jr. II, 559
umphreys, Samuel Jones II, 801
umphreys, Sarah II, 379
umphreys, Sarah II, 486
umphreys, Sarah II, 514
umphreys, Sarah II, 559
umphreys, Sarah II, 560
umphreys, Sarah II, 602
umphreys, Sarah II, 742
umphreys, Sarah II, 747
umphreys, Sarah W. IV, 725
umphreys, Solomon II, 129
umphreys, Solomon II, 560
umphreys, Stella IV, 1282
umphreys, Susan M. II, 129
umphreys, Susan W. II, 379
umphreys, Susanna II, 708
umphreys, Tacy II, 559
umphreys, Tacy II, 560
Humphreys, Thomas II, 379
Humphreys, Thomas II, 486
Humphreys, Thomas II, 514
Humphreys, Thomas II, 559
Humphreys, Thomas II, 560
Humphreys, Thomas II, 602
Humphreys, Wd. Juliann II, 801
Humphreys, Whitehead II, 379
Humphreys, Whitehead II, 559
Humphreys, William H. V, 578
Humphreys, William W. II, 379
Humphreys, Wm. II, 560
Humphreys, Wm. L. II, 560
Humphreys, Wm. W. II, 747
Humphrie, Joshua II, 233
Humphrie, Joshua II, 234
Humphrie, Rachel II, 233
Humphrie, Rachel II, 234
Humphries, Abraham II, 80
Humphries, Abraham II, 98
Humphries, Ann II, 530
Humphries, Ann II, 1004
Humphries, Anna II, 234
Humphries, Asa II, 379
Humphries, Elioner II, 379
Humphries, Elizabeth II, 559
Humphries, Hannah II, 80
Humphries, Hannah II, 98
Humphries, Hester I, 1030
Humphries, Hester I, 1032
Humphries, Increase II, 234
Humphries, Isaac II, 234
Humphries, John, Jr. II, 560
Humphries, Joshua II, 234
Humphries, Joshua II, 379
Humphries, Mary II, 80
Humphries, Mary IV, 725
Humphries, May IV, 1322
Humphries, Powell II, 177
Humphries, Raymond V, 78
Humphries, Richard II, 80
Humphries, Richard II, 379
Humphries, Richard II, 530
Humphries, Richard II, 559
Humphries, Richard V. II, 1004
Humphries, Sarah II, 234
Humphries, Sarah II, 992
Humphries, Sarah II, 1004
Humphries, Susannah II, 808
Humphries, Tacy II, 530
Humphries, Thomas II, 177
Humphries, Thomas II, 560
Humphries, Thomas II, 992
Humphries, Thomas II, 1004
Humphries, Wm. II, 560
Humphries, Wm. II, 1004
Humphris, Benjamin II, 559
Humphris, Benjamin II, 678
Humphris, Elizabeth II, 562
Humphris, Esther II, 559
Humphris, Esther II, 678
Humphris, Mary II, 379
Humphris, Richard II, 379
Humphris, Sarah II, 1004
Humphris, Thomas II, 1004
Humphry, Ada V, 627
Humphry, Bertha V, 402
Humphry, Cora B. V, 402
Humphry, Dennis J. V, 402
Humphry, Frank V, 627
Humphry, Goldie Ronia V, 402
Humphry, Leala V, 402
Humphry, Leonard Donald V, 402
Humphry, Mildred V, 402
Humphry, Ora V, 402
Humphry, Raymond V, 402
Humphry, Sarah V, 627
Humphry, Will V, 627
Humphrys, Amie II, 559
Humphrys, Ann II, 559
Humphrys, Ann II, 1004
Humphrys, Elizabeth II, 559
Humphrys, Esther II, 559
Humphrys, Jonathan II, 559
Humpreys, Martha VI, 580
Humpston, Anna V, 503
Humpston, Anna D. V, 503
Humpston, Asa B. V, 503
Humpston, Harriett V, 503
Humpston, John A. V, 503
Humpston, John E. V, 503
Humpton, Elizabeth II, 560
Hums, Sarah VI, 405
Humston, Glenn V, 578
Humston, Halleck V, 578
Humston, Hartzell W. V, 180
Humston, Mattie J. V, 180
Humston, Ruth Gertrude V, 180
Humwell, Richard K. IV, 226
Humwell, Sarah C. IV, 226
Hun, Priscilla II, 560
Hun, Priscilla II, 676
Hundley, Amos VI, 938
Hundley, Archibald VI, 937
Hundley, Betsey VI, 937
Hundley, Betsy VI, 937
Hundley, Elizabeth VI, 837
Hundley, George W. VI, 938
Hundley, Hannah VI, 938
Hundley, Hiram VI, 938
Hundley, Jane VI, 795
Hundley, Janetta VI, 941
Hundley, Jemima VI, 809
Hundley, John VI, 812
Hundley, John VI, 837
Hundley, John VI, 867
Hundley, Jordan VI, 937
Hundley, Lydia VI, 812
Hundley, Martha W. VI, 938
Hundley, Mary VI, 809
Hundley, Mildred VI, 938
Hundley, Nancy VI, 866
Hundley, Nancy VI, 867
Hundley, Nehemiah VI, 937
Hundley, Polley VI, 937
Hundley, Polly VI, 938
Hundley, Sarah VI, 827
Hundley, Thomas VI, 807
Hundley, Thomas VI, 817
Hundley, Thomas VI, 827
Hundley, William VI, 938
Hundley, Wm. VI, 941
Hundred, Christiana VI, 485
Hundred, Christiana VI, 495
Hungary, Hannah II, 814
Hungary, Hannah II, 827
Hungerford, Oliver V, 458
Hunicut, Peter VI, 183
Hunley, Betsy VI, 937
Hunley, Frances VI, 801
Hunley, Jordan VI, 937
Hunley, Milly VI, 801
Hunn, Ann II, 879
Hunn, Anna E. II, 879
Hunn, Anna Eliza II, 879
Hunn, Betty J. II, 879
Hunn, Charles Sharpless II, 879
Hunn, Edward W. Jenkins II, 879
Hunn, Eliza II, 879
Hunn, Eliza III, 177
Hunn, Eliza J. III, 89
Hunn, Eliza J. III, 177
Hunn, Elizabeth II, 879
Hunn, Elizabeth A. II, 879
Hunn, Emily II, 798
Hunn, Ezekial, Jr. II, 747
Hunn, Ezekiel II, 747
Hunn, Ezekiel II, 765
Hunn, Ezekiel II, 798
Hunn, Ezekiel II, 879
Hunn, Ezekiel II, 899
Hunn, Ezekiel, Jr. II, 879
Hunn, Ezekiel, Jr. II, 899
Hunn, Florence II, 879
Hunn, Florence II, 899
Hunn, Gulielma II, 879
Hunn, Gulielma M. II, 879
Hunn, Gulielma Maria II, 798
Hunn, Hannah A. II, 879
Hunn, Hannah E. II, 879
Hunn, Hannah E. II, 899
Hunn, Jacob W. III, 177
Hunn, John II, 379
Hunn, John II, 747
Hunn, John II, 879
Hunn, John III, 89
Hunn, John III, 177
Hunn, Jonathan III, 177
Hunn, Joseph II, 798
Hunn, Lydia J. II, 747
Hunn, Lydia Jones II, 747
Hunn, Lydia Jones II, 765
Hunn, Lydia M. II, 879
Hunn, Martha W. III, 177
Hunn, Mary II, 879
Hunn, Mary Elizabeth II, 798
Hunn, Mary S. II, 747
Hunn, Nathaniel II, 379
Hunn, Patience II, 803
Hunn, Sarah III, 177
Hunn, Susan III, 177
Hunn, Susannah III, 177
Hunn, Tabitha II, 747
Hunn, Tabitha II, 765
Hunn, Tabitha II, 798
Hunn, Townsend S. II, 747
Hunn, Wm. Rowland II, 879
Hunnabuss, Henry VI, 938
Hunnabuss, Martha E. VI, 938
Hunnecut, Thomas I, 399
Hunneycut, Robert VI, 183
Hunnicut, Micajah V, 649
Hunnicut, Mike I, 140
Hunnicut, Mike I, 143
Hunnicut, Sarah I, 140
Hunnicut, Sarah I, 143
Hunnicut, Sarah V, 649
Hunnicut, Susannah H. V, 503
Hunnicutt, ??? VI, 16
Hunnicutt, ??? VI, 95
Hunnicutt, ??? VI, 144
Hunnicutt, Able V, 628
Hunnicutt, Agnes VI, 104
Hunnicutt, Agness VI, 104
Hunnicutt, Agness VI, 111
Hunnicutt, Amy VI, 112
Hunnicutt, Ann IV, 178
Hunnicutt, Ann IV, 226
Hunnicutt, Ann V, 628
Hunnicutt, Ann VI, 16
Hunnicutt, Ann VI, 97
Hunnicutt, Ann VI, 98
Hunnicutt, Ann VI, 100
Hunnicutt, Ann VI, 107
Hunnicutt, Ann VI, 108
Hunnicutt, Ann VI, 110
Hunnicutt, Ann VI, 111
Hunnicutt, Ann VI, 112
Hunnicutt, Ann VI, 113
Hunnicutt, Ann VI, 120
Hunnicutt, Ann VI, 133
Hunnicutt, Ann VI, 135
Hunnicutt, Ann VI, 250
Hunnicutt, Ann Eliza V, 628
Hunnicutt, Ann Linton V, 685
Hunnicutt, Anna VI, 144
Hunnicutt, Anna E. V, 685
Hunnicutt, Anna P. V, 685
Hunnicutt, Annaky VI, 112
Hunnicutt, Anne VI, 113
Hunnicutt, Anselm VI, 111
Hunnicutt, Ben VI, 112
Hunnicutt, Benjamin VI, 112
Hunnicutt, Benjamin T. IV, 478
Hunnicutt, Benjamin Thomas IV, 478
Hunnicutt, Benjamin Thomas VI, 184
Hunnicutt, Bett VI, 112
Hunnicutt, Burwell IV, 412
Hunnicutt, Burwell IV, 1063
Hunnicutt, Burwell IV, 1103
Hunnicutt, Burwell V, 628
Hunnicutt, Callie Nordyke V, 340
Hunnicutt, Cate VI, 112
Hunnicutt, Catharine V, 628
Hunnicutt, Catharine V, 648
Hunnicutt, Catherine V, 685
Hunnicutt, Chappel V, 628
Hunnicutt, Charles V, 628
Hunnicutt, Charles VI, 112
Hunnicutt, Charles E. V, 685
Hunnicutt, Charley V, 628
Hunnicutt, Charlot VI, 112
Hunnicutt, Daniel VI, 110
Hunnicutt, Daniel VI, 130
Hunnicutt, Daniel VI, 135
Hunnicutt, Daniel VI, 136
Hunnicutt, Daniel VI, 142
Hunnicutt, Daniel B. V, 628
Hunnicutt, David I, 928
Hunnicutt, David V, 628
Hunnicutt, David VI, 136
Hunnicutt, David B. V, 628
Hunnicutt, Davie VI, 112
Hunnicutt, Deborah IV, 412
Hunnicutt, Deborah IV, 457
Hunnicutt, Deborah VI, 111
Hunnicutt, Deborah VI, 144
Hunnicutt, Delena V, 628
Hunnicutt, Delena V, 685
Hunnicutt, Delitha V, 971
Hunnicutt, Delitha VI, 99
Hunnicutt, Delitha VI, 111
Hunnicutt, Delitha VI, 136
Hunnicutt, Delitha Ann V, 971
Hunnicutt, Delitha Ann VI, 136
Hunnicutt, Delitha Bailey VI, 113
Hunnicutt, Dick VI, 111
Hunnicutt, Duke VI, 112
Hunnicutt, Edna IV, 412
Hunnicutt, Edna IV, 1063
Hunnicutt, Edna IV, 1103
Hunnicutt, Edna V, 627
Hunnicutt, Edna V, 628
Hunnicutt, Edna V, 971
Hunnicutt, Edna VI, 136
Hunnicutt, Edna VI, 139
Hunnicutt, Edney V, 628
Hunnicutt, Edward VI, 110
Hunnicutt, Edward VI, 135
Hunnicutt, Edward T. V, 628
Hunnicutt, Eleanor Kathryn V, 685
Hunnicutt, Elijah VI, 144
Hunnicutt, Eliza V, 971
Hunnicutt, Eliza V, 979
Hunnicutt, Eliza VI, 69
Hunnicutt, Eliza VI, 133
Hunnicutt, Eliza VI, 136
Hunnicutt, Elizabeth V, 628
Hunnicutt, Elizabeth V, 637
Hunnicutt, Elizabeth V, 639
Hunnicutt, Elizabeth V, 971
Hunnicutt, Elizabeth VI, 100
Hunnicutt, Elizabeth VI, 102
Hunnicutt, Elizabeth VI, 103
Hunnicutt, Elizabeth VI, 110
Hunnicutt, Elizabeth VI, 111
Hunnicutt, Elizabeth VI, 113
Hunnicutt, Elizabeth VI, 129
Hunnicutt, Elizabeth VI, 136
Hunnicutt, Elizabeth VI, 138
Hunnicutt, Elizabeth VI, 340
Hunnicutt, Elizabeth Ann V, 628
Hunnicutt, Elizabeth Ann VI, 69
Hunnicutt, Elizabeth Jane V, 628
Hunnicutt, Elizabeth, Sr. VI, 136
Hunnicutt, Emily Jane VI, 69
Hunnicutt, Ephraim V, 628
Hunnicutt, Ephraim V, 642
Hunnicutt, Ephraim VI, 69
Hunnicutt, Ephraim VI, 110
Hunnicutt, Ephraim VI, 113
Hunnicutt, Ephraim VI, 135
Hunnicutt, Ephraim VI, 136
Hunnicutt, Ephraim VI, 138
Hunnicutt, Fortune VI, 112
Hunnicutt, Frank V, 628
Hunnicutt, Franklin V, 685
Hunnicutt, Gabral VI, 112
Hunnicutt, Geo. E. V, 628
Hunnicutt, George Edward VI, 136
Hunnicutt, Glaister VI, 110
Hunnicutt, Glaister VI, 111
Hunnicutt, Glaister VI, 112
Hunnicutt, Grace VI, 112
Hunnicutt, Hannah IV, 967
Hunnicutt, Hannah VI, 106
Hunnicutt, Hannah VI, 112
Hunnicutt, Hannah VI, 113
Hunnicutt, Hannah VI, 135
Hunnicutt, Hannah VI, 136
Hunnicutt, Harley D. V, 685
Hunnicutt, Harley E. V, 685
Hunnicutt, Huldah VI, 183
Hunnicutt, Huldah VI, 200
Hunnicutt, Huldah VI, 203
Hunnicutt, Irene I, 928
Hunnicutt, Irene I, 943
Hunnicutt, Irene V, 628
Hunnicutt, Irina V, 628
Hunnicutt, Isaac VI, 112
Hunnicutt, Isabella VI, 183
Hunnicutt, Isabella VI, 191
Hunnicutt, Isabella VI, 195
Hunnicutt, Isabella VI, 250
Hunnicutt, James V, 971
Hunnicutt, James VI, 16
Hunnicutt, James VI, 99
Hunnicutt, James VI, 110
Hunnicutt, James VI, 111
Hunnicutt, James VI, 113
Hunnicutt, James VI, 118
Hunnicutt, James VI, 135
Hunnicutt, James VI, 136
Hunnicutt, James VI, 142
Hunnicutt, James VI, 183
Hunnicutt, James VI, 220
Hunnicutt, James VI, 221
Hunnicutt, James VI, 250
Hunnicutt, James VI, 262
Hunnicutt, James VI, 274
Hunnicutt, James B. V, 971
Hunnicutt, James B. VI, 136
Hunnicutt, James Benj. V, 971
Hunnicutt, James Benjamin VI, 136
Hunnicutt, Jane VI, 97
Hunnicutt, Jane VI, 109
Hunnicutt, Jane VI, 110
Hunnicutt, Jane VI, 112
Hunnicutt, Jane VI, 113
Hunnicutt, Jane VI, 136
Hunnicutt, Jane VI, 142
Hunnicutt, Jane VI, 183
Hunnicutt, Jane II VI, 110
Hunnicutt, Janny VI, 112
Hunnicutt, Jeams VI, 112
Hunnicutt, Jemima W. VI, 136
Hunnicutt, Jemmy VI, 111
Hunnicutt, Jenny VI, 112
Hunnicutt, Jesse VI, 112
Hunnicutt, Jesse VI, 135
Hunnicutt, Jesse VI, 136
Hunnicutt, Jesse VI, 139
Hunnicutt, Joan VI, 112
Hunnicutt, Joe VI, 112
Hunnicutt, John V, 628
Hunnicutt, John VI, 69
Hunnicutt, John VI, 96
Hunnicutt, John VI, 100
Hunnicutt, John VI, 102
Hunnicutt, John VI, 111
Hunnicutt, John VI, 112
Hunnicutt, John VI, 118
Hunnicutt, John VI, 135
Hunnicutt, John VI, 141
Hunnicutt, John VI, 252
Hunnicutt, John Andrew VI, 69
Hunnicutt, John M. VI, 250
Hunnicutt, John Murdaugh VI, 250
Hunnicutt, John Oliver V, 628
Hunnicutt, John P. V, 549
Hunnicutt, John P. V, 578
Hunnicutt, John P. V, 628
Hunnicutt, John P. VI, 136
Hunnicutt, John Pearson VI, 111
Hunnicutt, John T. V, 628
Hunnicutt, John T. VI, 136
Hunnicutt, Joseph IV, 226
Hunnicutt, Joseph IV, 478
Hunnicutt, Joseph VI, 184
Hunnicutt, Joseph W. VI, 250
Hunnicutt, Joshua B. V, 971
Hunnicutt, Joshua B. V, 979
Hunnicutt, Joshua B. VI, 133
Hunnicutt, Joshua B. VI, 136
Hunnicutt, Joshua Bailey V, 971

Hunnicutt, Joshua Bailey VI, 111
Hunnicutt, Joshua P. VI, 250
Hunnicutt, Judy VI, 111
Hunnicutt, Julie VI, 144
Hunnicutt, Laura V, 628
Hunnicutt, Lemuel VI, 110
Hunnicutt, Lemuel VI, 111
Hunnicutt, Lemuel VI, 135
Hunnicutt, Lemuel VI, 136
Hunnicutt, Leslie V, 628
Hunnicutt, Leslie Thomas V, 685
Hunnicutt, Lidia VI, 144
Hunnicutt, Linton V, 685
Hunnicutt, Lura V, 628
Hunnicutt, Lura V, 685
Hunnicutt, Lura T. V, 685
Hunnicutt, Lyddy VI, 112
Hunnicutt, Lydia VI, 144
Hunnicutt, Mahlon V, 628
Hunnicutt, Marey VI, 144
Hunnicutt, Margaret IV, 1063
Hunnicutt, Margaret IV, 1087
Hunnicutt, Margaret IV, 1103
Hunnicutt, Margaret V, 628
Hunnicutt, Margaret V, 642
Hunnicutt, Margaret V, 685
Hunnicutt, Margaret VI, 105
Hunnicutt, Margaret VI, 110
Hunnicutt, Margaret VI, 111
Hunnicutt, Margaret VI, 135
Hunnicutt, Margaret VI, 138
Hunnicutt, Margaret VI, 162
Hunnicutt, Margaret VI, 183
Hunnicutt, Margaret VI, 274
Hunnicutt, Margaret VI, 276
Hunnicutt, Margeritt VI, 162
Hunnicutt, Margeritt VI, 183
Hunnicutt, Margery V, 685
Hunnicutt, Margory Jean V, 685
Hunnicutt, Mark VI, 110
Hunnicutt, Mark VI, 142
Hunnicutt, Mark VI, 144
Hunnicutt, Martha V, 402
Hunnicutt, Martha V, 628
Hunnicutt, Martha VI, 69
Hunnicutt, Martha VI, 100
Hunnicutt, Martha VI, 110
Hunnicutt, Martha VI, 111
Hunnicutt, Martha VI, 130
Hunnicutt, Martha VI, 135
Hunnicutt, Martha A. I, 928
Hunnicutt, Martha Ann V, 628
Hunnicutt, Martha Ann V, 642
Hunnicutt, Martha J. V, 628
Hunnicutt, Martha J. V, 637
Hunnicutt, Martha Jane V, 628
Hunnicutt, Martha Jane VI, 136
Hunnicutt, Mary IV, 1103
Hunnicutt, Mary IV, 1108
Hunnicutt, Mary V, 628
Hunnicutt, Mary V, 685
Hunnicutt, Mary V, 971
Hunnicutt, Mary VI, 16
Hunnicutt, Mary VI, 98
Hunnicutt, Mary VI, 99
Hunnicutt, Mary VI, 100
Hunnicutt, Mary VI, 101
Hunnicutt, Mary VI, 102
Hunnicutt, Mary VI, 110
Hunnicutt, Mary VI, 111
Hunnicutt, Mary VI, 112
Hunnicutt, Mary VI, 113
Hunnicutt, Mary VI, 114
Hunnicutt, Mary VI, 129
Hunnicutt, Mary VI, 130
Hunnicutt, Mary VI, 131
Hunnicutt, Mary VI, 135
Hunnicutt, Mary VI, 136
Hunnicutt, Mary VI, 183
Hunnicutt, Mary VI, 200
Hunnicutt, Mary Ann V, 628
Hunnicutt, Mary Ann V, 639
Hunnicutt, Mary Ann V, 971
Hunnicutt, Mary Ann V, 975
Hunnicutt, Mary Ann VI, 136
Hunnicutt, Mary Ann VI, 250
Hunnicutt, Mary B. V, 628
Hunnicutt, Mary B. VI, 136
Hunnicutt, Mary E. V, 628
Hunnicutt, Mary E. V, 642
Hunnicutt, Mary E. V, 644
Hunnicutt, Mary E. V, 979
Hunnicutt, Mary Elizabeth V, 628
Hunnicutt, Mary Elizabeth V, 971
Hunnicutt, Mary Elizabeth VI, 69
Hunnicutt, Mary Emily V, 628
Hunnicutt, Mary L. V, 685
Hunnicutt, Mary Linn VI, 111
Hunnicutt, Mary Pauline V, 628
Hunnicutt, Mary Pauline V, 685
Hunnicutt, Micajah V, 628
Hunnicutt, Micajah VI, 136
Hunnicutt, Milly VI, 112
Hunnicutt, Miriam VI, 98
Hunnicutt, Miriam VI, 102
Hunnicutt, Miriam VI, 111
Hunnicutt, Miriam VI, 118
Hunnicutt, Miriam VI, 183
Hunnicutt, Miriam VI, 276
Hunnicutt, Miriam Murdaugh VI, 250
Hunnicutt, Miriam Murdaugh VI, 274
Hunnicutt, Miriam Murdock VI, 250
Hunnicutt, Mordecai V, 628
Hunnicutt, Mordecai P. IV, 412
Hunnicutt, Mordecai P. V, 628
Hunnicutt, Mordecia Peebles VI, 113
Hunnicutt, Mordica P. VI, 136
Hunnicutt, Moses VI, 112
Hunnicutt, Nancy VI, 252
Hunnicutt, Nancy VI, 255
Hunnicutt, Nathan VI, 112
Hunnicutt, Ned VI, 111
Hunnicutt, Orville B. V, 685
Hunnicutt, Peter I Sup 1, 4
Hunnicutt, Peter VI, 16
Hunnicutt, Peter VI, 110
Hunnicutt, Peter VI, 111
Hunnicutt, Peter VI, 112
Hunnicutt, Peter VI, 183
Hunnicutt, Pharaby VI, 102
Hunnicutt, Phebe V, 628
Hunnicutt, Phebe VI, 112
Hunnicutt, Phebe Ann V, 578
Hunnicutt, Phebe Ann V, 628
Hunnicutt, Pheraby Brock VI, 113
Hunnicutt, Phereby VI, 183
Hunnicutt, Pleasant VI, 69
Hunnicutt, Pleasant VI, 136
Hunnicutt, Pleasant VI, 143
Hunnicutt, Pleasants VI, 110
Hunnicutt, Pleasants VI, 112
Hunnicutt, Priscilla V, 628
Hunnicutt, Priscilla VI, 100
Hunnicutt, Priscilla VI, 110
Hunnicutt, Priscilla VI, 111
Hunnicutt, Priscilla VI, 113
Hunnicutt, Priscilla M. V, 685
Hunnicutt, Rachel IV, 478
Hunnicutt, Rachel VI, 136
Hunnicutt, Rachel VI, 183
Hunnicutt, Rachel VI, 184
Hunnicutt, Rachel VI, 220
Hunnicutt, Rachel VI, 221
Hunnicutt, Rebecca VI, 250
Hunnicutt, Rebeckah VI, 111
Hunnicutt, Rebeckah VI, 118
Hunnicutt, Robert V, 628
Hunnicutt, Robert V, 685
Hunnicutt, Robert VI, 16
Hunnicutt, Robert VI, 69
Hunnicutt, Robert VI, 94
Hunnicutt, Robert VI, 95
Hunnicutt, Robert VI, 100
Hunnicutt, Robert VI, 102
Hunnicutt, Robert VI, 104
Hunnicutt, Robert VI, 105
Hunnicutt, Robert VI, 110
Hunnicutt, Robert VI, 111
Hunnicutt, Robert VI, 112
Hunnicutt, Robert VI, 114
Hunnicutt, Robert VI, 129
Hunnicutt, Robert VI, 130
Hunnicutt, Robert VI, 135
Hunnicutt, Robert VI, 136
Hunnicutt, Robert VI, 162
Hunnicutt, Robert VI, 183
Hunnicutt, Robert VI, 191
Hunnicutt, Robert VI, 195
Hunnicutt, Robert VI, 199
Hunnicutt, Robert VI, 200
Hunnicutt, Robert B. V, 628
Hunnicutt, Robert Edwin VI, 69
Hunnicutt, Robert II VI, 110
Hunnicutt, Robert Wyke VI, 100
Hunnicutt, Robert Wyke VI, 110
Hunnicutt, Robert Wyke VI, 111
Hunnicutt, Robert Wyke VI, 183
Hunnicutt, Robert, Jr. VI, 111
Hunnicutt, Robert, Jr. VI, 121
Hunnicutt, Robert, Jr. VI, 189
Hunnicutt, Robert, Sr. VI, 104
Hunnicutt, Robert, Sr. VI, 111
Hunnicutt, Robert, Sr. VI, 112
Hunnicutt, Robert, Sr. VI, 183
Hunnicutt, Ruth VI, 98
Hunnicutt, Ruth VI, 110
Hunnicutt, Ruth VI, 111
Hunnicutt, Ruth Bailey VI, 112
Hunnicutt, Sam VI, 112
Hunnicutt, Samuel V, 628
Hunnicutt, Samuel VI, 69
Hunnicutt, Samuel VI, 102
Hunnicutt, Samuel VI, 113
Hunnicutt, Samuel VI, 136
Hunnicutt, Samuel VI, 183
Hunnicutt, Samuel VI, 184
Hunnicutt, Samuel Bailey VI, 111
Hunnicutt, Sarah IV, 366
Hunnicutt, Sarah IV, 412
Hunnicutt, Sarah V, 628
Hunnicutt, Sarah VI, 16
Hunnicutt, Sarah VI, 42
Hunnicutt, Sarah VI, 97
Hunnicutt, Sarah VI, 98
Hunnicutt, Sarah VI, 110
Hunnicutt, Sarah VI, 111
Hunnicutt, Sarah VI, 112
Hunnicutt, Sarah VI, 113
Hunnicutt, Sarah VI, 114
Hunnicutt, Sarah VI, 183
Hunnicutt, Sarah VI, 189
Hunnicutt, Sarah VI, 191
Hunnicutt, Sarah Ann VI, 69
Hunnicutt, Sarah Elizabeth IV, 173
Hunnicutt, Sarah Elizabeth IV, 226
Hunnicutt, Sarah Elizabeth IV, 478
Hunnicutt, Sarah Elizabeth VI, 184
Hunnicutt, Sarah Lead VI, 183
Hunnicutt, Sarah Nixon VI, 113
Hunnicutt, Sarah Priscilla V, 628
Hunnicutt, Sarah, Sr. V, 628
Hunnicutt, Silla VI, 112
Hunnicutt, Silviah Bailey VI, 136
Hunnicutt, Susanna V, 685
Hunnicutt, Susanna VI, 110
Hunnicutt, Susannah V, 610
Hunnicutt, Susannah V, 628
Hunnicutt, Susannah V, 644
Hunnicutt, Susannah VI, 69
Hunnicutt, Susannah H. V, 549
Hunnicutt, Susannah H. V, 578
Hunnicutt, Susannah H. V, 628
Hunnicutt, Tabitha VI, 99
Hunnicutt, Tabitha VI, 110
Hunnicutt, Tabitha VI, 113
Hunnicutt, Tabitha VI, 129
Hunnicutt, Tabitha VI, 135
Hunnicutt, Thomas I, 399
Hunnicutt, Thomas I, 400
Hunnicutt, Thomas IV, 226
Hunnicutt, Thomas IV, 412
Hunnicutt, Thomas V, 628
Hunnicutt, Thomas V, 637
Hunnicutt, Thomas V, 639
Hunnicutt, Thomas V, 644
Hunnicutt, Thomas VI, 16
Hunnicutt, Thomas VI, 98
Hunnicutt, Thomas VI, 110
Hunnicutt, Thomas VI, 111
Hunnicutt, Thomas VI, 112
Hunnicutt, Thomas VI, 135
Hunnicutt, Thomas VI, 136
Hunnicutt, Thomas VI, 183
Hunnicutt, Thomas VI, 191
Hunnicutt, Thomas VI, 195
Hunnicutt, Thomas VI, 250
Hunnicutt, Thomas Dick V, 685
Hunnicutt, Thomas E. V, 685
Hunnicutt, Thos. V, 610
Hunnicutt, Thos. V, 628
Hunnicutt, Tom VI, 112
Hunnicutt, Walter V, 628
Hunnicutt, Walter V, 685
Hunnicutt, Wd. Priscilla VI, 100
Hunnicutt, Wd. Priscilla Hunnicutt VI, 111
Hunnicutt, Wike VI, 183
Hunnicutt, William VI, 16
Hunnicutt, William VI, 100
Hunnicutt, William VI, 102
Hunnicutt, William VI, 111
Hunnicutt, William VI, 112
Hunnicutt, William VI, 120
Hunnicutt, William VI, 135
Hunnicutt, William VI, 136
Hunnicutt, William VI, 139
Hunnicutt, William VI, 315
Hunnicutt, William H. V, 628
Hunnicutt, William P. IV, 412
Hunnicutt, William P. V, 627
Hunnicutt, William P. V, 685
Hunnicutt, William P. V, 979
Hunnicutt, William P. VI, 136
Hunnicutt, William, Jr. VI, 113
Hunnicutt, Wilson V, 628
Hunnicutt, Wilson V, 685
Hunnicutt, Wm. VI, 102
Hunnicutt, Wm. VI, 113
Hunnicutt, Wm. VI, 141
Hunnicutt, Wm. VI, 144
Hunnicutt, Wm. H. V, 628
Hunnicutt, Wm. P. IV, 412
Hunnicutt, Wm. P. IV, 1063
Hunnicutt, Wm. P. IV, 1103
Hunnicutt, Wm. P. V, 628
Hunnicutt, Wm. P. V, 685
Hunnicutt, Wm. P. V, 971
Hunnicutt, Wm. Pearson V, 971
Hunnicutt, Wyke VI, 16
Hunnicutt, Wyke VI, 97
Hunnicutt, Wyke VI, 98
Hunnicutt, Wyke VI, 100
Hunnicutt, Wyke VI, 110
Hunnicutt, Wyke VI, 111
Hunnicutt, Wyke VI, 112
Hunnicutt, Wyke VI, 113
Hunnicutt, Wyke VI, 135
Hunnicutt, Wyke VI, 136
Hunnicutt, Wyke VI, 162
Hunnicutt, Wyke's VI, 183
Hunnicutt, Wyke, Jr. VI, 110
Hunnicutt, Wyke, Jr. VI, 111
Hunninghaus, Ida III, 415
Hunninghaus, Ida III, 421
Hunstead, Anna V, 1003
Hunstead, Estella V. V, 1003
Hunstead, Fred V, 1003
Hunstead, Jennie V, 1003
Hunstead, Mertle V, 1003
Hunt, ??? III, 160
Hunt, ??? III, 178
Hunt, ??? III, 299
Hunt, ??? IV, 725
Hunt, Aaron I, 659
Hunt, Aaron I, 722
Hunt, Aaron II, 553
Hunt, Aaron II, 560
Hunt, Aaron III, 177
Hunt, Aaron V, 78
Hunt, Aaron V, 215
Hunt, Aaron V, 250
Hunt, Aaron V, 265
Hunt, Aaron V, 403
Hunt, Aaron V, 404
Hunt, Aaron V, 405
Hunt, Aaron V, 629
Hunt, Aaron B. V, 250
Hunt, Aaron B. V, 393
Hunt, Aaron B. V, 403
Hunt, Aaron B. V, 405
Hunt, Aaron Betts V, 402
Hunt, Aaron Betts V, 404
Hunt, Aaron L. V, 251
Hunt, Abbie Mary IV, 1282
Hunt, Abel V, 440
Hunt, Abigail I, 552
Hunt, Abigail I, 857
Hunt, Abigail I, 886
Hunt, Abigail I, 901
Hunt, Abigail II, 1004
Hunt, Abigail II, 1019
Hunt, Abigail III, 178
Hunt, Abigail IV, 40
Hunt, Abigail IV, 94
Hunt, Abigail IV, 226
Hunt, Abigail IV, 637
Hunt, Abigail IV, 725
Hunt, Abigail IV, 1282
Hunt, Abigail IV, 1370
Hunt, Abigail VI, 405
Hunt, Abigail VI, 598
Hunt, Abigail VI, 599
Hunt, Abigail VI, 602
Hunt, Abigail H. I, 668
Hunt, Abigail May V, 405
Hunt, Abigail P. I, 850
Hunt, Abigail P. I, 851
Hunt, Abigail P. I, 857
Hunt, Abigail P. I, 871
Hunt, Abigail P. I, 887
Hunt, Abigail, Jr. IV, 94
Hunt, Abigail, Jr. VI, 599
Hunt, Abner I, 502
Hunt, Abner I, 549
Hunt, Abner I, 550
Hunt, Abner I, 551
Hunt, Abner I, 567
Hunt, Abner I, 568
Hunt, Abner I, 582
Hunt, Abner I, 773
Hunt, Abner I, 820
Hunt, Abner I, 964
Hunt, Abner I, 1010
Hunt, Abner V, 245
Hunt, Abner V, 250
Hunt, Abner V, 251
Hunt, Abner V, 340
Hunt, Abner V, 403
Hunt, Abraham I, 1021
Hunt, Abraham V, 768
Hunt, Abraham Gibbons II, 80
Hunt, Abraham R. III, 485
Hunt, Absolam I, 537
Hunt, Absolam I, 551
Hunt, Acenith I, 857
Hunt, Achsah I, 857
Hunt, Adela I, 857
Hunt, Adella I, 876
Hunt, Adella I, 887
Hunt, Adrianna M. II, 310
Hunt, Adrianna M. II, 321
Hunt, Ahira I, 503
Hunt, Albert I, 857
Hunt, Albert V, 403
Hunt, Albert V, 912
Hunt, Alfred I, 502
Hunt, Alfred I, 551
Hunt, Alfred IV, 93
Hunt, Alfred IV, 94
Hunt, Alfred V, 340
Hunt, Alfred V, 405
Hunt, Alice V, 504
Hunt, Alice G. V, 403
Hunt, Allen I, 502
Hunt, Allen I, 551
Hunt, Allen I, 886
Hunt, Allen IV, 1282
Hunt, Allen V, 628
Hunt, Allen V, 629
Hunt, Almeda V, 628
Hunt, Almeda V, 629
Hunt, Almeida V, 629
Hunt, Almina I, 502
Hunt, Almira V, 403
Hunt, Almira V, 418
Hunt, Alsop III, 177
Hunt, Alvaretta V, 405
Hunt, Alverett V, 404
Hunt, Alvin G. V, 844
Hunt, Amiel I, 502
Hunt, Amos I, 1005
Hunt, Amos V, 402
Hunt, Amos V, 403
Hunt, Amos V, 404
Hunt, Amos V, 405
Hunt, Amos V, 416
Hunt, Angelina I, 502
Hunt, Angelina T. V, 844
Hunt, Angelina T. V, 871
Hunt, Angeline V, 844
Hunt, Angeline V, 870
Hunt, Ann I, 343
Hunt, Ann I, 489
Hunt, Ann I, 502
Hunt, Ann I, 503
Hunt, Ann I, 523
Hunt, Ann I, 528
Hunt, Ann I, 550
Hunt, Ann I, 551
Hunt, Ann I, 563
Hunt, Ann I, 564
Hunt, Ann I, 568
Hunt, Ann I, 569
Hunt, Ann I, 594
Hunt, Ann I, 682
Hunt, Ann I, 685
Hunt, Ann I, 722
Hunt, Ann I, 964
Hunt, Ann I, 1007
Hunt, Ann I, 1010
Hunt, Ann II, 81
Hunt, Ann II, 104
Hunt, Ann II, 201
Hunt, Ann II, 234
Hunt, Ann II, 849
Hunt, Ann II, 879
Hunt, Ann IV, 94
Hunt, Ann IV, 127
Hunt, Ann IV, 148
Hunt, Ann IV, 676
Hunt, Ann IV, 691
Hunt, Ann IV, 725
Hunt, Ann IV, 784
Hunt, Ann IV, 1282
Hunt, Ann V, 79
Hunt, Ann V, 340
Hunt, Ann V, 365
Hunt, Ann V, 393
Hunt, Ann V, 405
Hunt, Ann V, 578
Hunt, Ann V, 844
Hunt, Ann V, 883

Hunt, Ann VI, 938
Hunt, Ann C. V, 839
Hunt, Ann C. V, 844
Hunt, Ann E. V, 844
Hunt, Ann E. V, 883
Hunt, Ann H. V, 404
Hunt, Ann H. V, 405
Hunt, Ann S. II, 879
Hunt, Ann W. IV, 609
Hunt, Ann W. IV, 637
Hunt, Ann W. IV, 676
Hunt, Ann W. IV, 725
Hunt, Anna I, 550
Hunt, Anna I, 552
Hunt, Anna I, 579
Hunt, Anna I, 785
Hunt, Anna I, 857
Hunt, Anna I, 886
Hunt, Anna I, 887
Hunt, Anna II, 234
Hunt, Anna II, 813
Hunt, Anna II, 879
Hunt, Anna II, 906
Hunt, Anna V, 402
Hunt, Anna V, 403
Hunt, Anna V, 404
Hunt, Anna V, 416
Hunt, Anna V, 458
Hunt, Anna V, 627
Hunt, Anna V, 629
Hunt, Anna V, 768
Hunt, Anna B. V, 404
Hunt, Anna D. II, 880
Hunt, Anna M. II, 879
Hunt, Anna M. II, 880
Hunt, Anna M. II, 939
Hunt, Anna Maria II, 801
Hunt, Anne R. IV, 1009
Hunt, Anne S. II, 849
Hunt, Anne S. II, 879
Hunt, Anne S. II, 940
Hunt, Anne Smith II, 788
Hunt, Annie II, 801
Hunt, Annie E. V, 405
Hunt, Anselm I, 551
Hunt, Anslam I, 964
Hunt, Artemesa V, 629
Hunt, Arthur V, 405
Hunt, Arthur V, 686
Hunt, Asa I, 502
Hunt, Asa I, 503
Hunt, Asa I, 532
Hunt, Asa I, 550
Hunt, Asa I, 551
Hunt, Asa I, 606
Hunt, Asa I, 811
Hunt, Asa I, 820
Hunt, Asa V, 79
Hunt, Asa V, 251
Hunt, Asa V, 337
Hunt, Asa V, 340
Hunt, Asa V, 343
Hunt, Asa V, 403
Hunt, Asa V, 430
Hunt, Asa B. V, 405
Hunt, Asa J. I, 552
Hunt, Asael I, 551
Hunt, Asael I, 552
Hunt, Asael I, 555
Hunt, Asahel I, 502
Hunt, Asenath I, 503
Hunt, Asenath I, 550
Hunt, Asenath I, 875
Hunt, Asenath I, 886
Hunt, Asenath I, 887
Hunt, Asenath IV, 725
Hunt, Asenath IV, 726
Hunt, Asenith IV, 726
Hunt, Asenith V, 305
Hunt, Asenith V, 339
Hunt, Asenith V, 340
Hunt, Asher I, 502
Hunt, Asher I, 551
Hunt, Bailey V, 250
Hunt, Balinda T. IV, 1204
Hunt, Balinda T. IV, 1212
Hunt, Barbary V, 844
Hunt, Barbary V, 849
Hunt, Barnabas I, 785
Hunt, Barnabas V, 79
Hunt, Barnabas V, 251
Hunt, Barnabas V, 340
Hunt, Barnabas V, 345
Hunt, Bartlett Y. I, 887
Hunt, Barton V, 628
Hunt, Barton V, 629
Hunt, Belinda IV, 1212
Hunt, Belinda T. IV, 1212
Hunt, Benj. V, 912
Hunt, Benj. Lawrence III, 177
Hunt, Benj. Lawrence III, 213
Hunt, Benjamin II, 801
Hunt, Benjamin II, 879
Hunt, Benjamin IV, 967
Hunt, Benjamin IV, 1370
Hunt, Benjamin V, 79
Hunt, Benjamin V, 844
Hunt, Benjamin V, 883
Hunt, Benjamin VI, 827
Hunt, Benjamin VI, 938
Hunt, Benjamin T. VI, 797
Hunt, Benjamin T. VI, 938
Hunt, Benjamin W. III, 177
Hunt, Benjamin W. III, 260
Hunt, Benton I, 503
Hunt, Bernard T. V, 504
Hunt, Beulah I, 502
Hunt, Beulah I, 551
Hunt, Beulah I, 552
Hunt, Briton V, 629
Hunt, Bula V, 340
Hunt, Bulah I, 503
Hunt, Buly I, 550
Hunt, Buly I, 564
Hunt, Burton V, 629
Hunt, C. E. V, 404
Hunt, Caleb II, 560
Hunt, Caleb III, 147
Hunt, Caleb III, 177
Hunt, Caleb III, 178
Hunt, Caleb III, 414
Hunt, Caleb III, 421
Hunt, Caleb IV, 40
Hunt, Caleb IV, 93
Hunt, Caleb IV, 94
Hunt, Caleb IV, 127
Hunt, Caleb IV, 725
Hunt, Caleb IV, 726
Hunt, Caleb IV, 760
Hunt, Caleb VI, 513
Hunt, Caleb VI, 576
Hunt, Caleb VI, 659
Hunt, Caleb VI, 717
Hunt, Caleb S. II, 289
Hunt, Caleb S. II, 293
Hunt, Caleb S. II, 379
Hunt, Caleb S. II, 725
Hunt, Caleb S. II, 747
Hunt, Camm Thomas V, 78
Hunt, Caroline II, 311
Hunt, Caroline II, 880
Hunt, Caroline W. II, 321
Hunt, Caroline W. II, 879
Hunt, Cath. M. III, 177
Hunt, Catharine I, 363
Hunt, Catharine I, 381
Hunt, Catharine I, 400
Hunt, Catharine I, 502
Hunt, Catharine I, 527
Hunt, Catharine I, 535
Hunt, Catharine I, 538
Hunt, Catharine I, 549
Hunt, Catharine I, 550
Hunt, Catharine I, 551
Hunt, Catharine I, 659
Hunt, Catharine I, 722
Hunt, Catharine I, 820
Hunt, Catharine III, 177
Hunt, Catharine III, 178
Hunt, Catharine A. VI, 938
Hunt, Catherine I, 682
Hunt, Catherine V, 78
Hunt, Caty VI, 938
Hunt, Cela I, 503
Hunt, Cela I, 602
Hunt, Celia I, 602
Hunt, Charles I, 502
Hunt, Charles IV, 412
Hunt, Charles IV, 536
Hunt, Charles VI, 938
Hunt, Charles Albert V, 954
Hunt, Charles E. V, 403
Hunt, Charles Edwin V, 403
Hunt, Charles Edwin V, 404
Hunt, Charles Edwin V, 405
Hunt, Charles Howland III, 177
Hunt, Charles T. I, 857
Hunt, Charles T. I, 887
Hunt, Charlotte I, 589
Hunt, Charlotte I, 594
Hunt, Charlotte I, 597
Hunt, Charlotte III, 63
Hunt, Charlotte III, 178
Hunt, Charlotte III, 290
Hunt, Charlotte III, 305
Hunt, Charlotte III, 406
Hunt, Charlotte V, 835
Hunt, Charlotte V, 844
Hunt, Charlotte V, 872
Hunt, Charlotte T. V, 735
Hunt, Charlotte T. V, 744
Hunt, Charlotte T. V, 844
Hunt, Chas. E. V, 629
Hunt, Chas. Edwin V, 629
Hunt, Chas. H. III, 178
Hunt, Chas. Lindley III, 177
Hunt, Chizia VI, 978
Hunt, Christian Wharton II, 1040
Hunt, Christiana V, 78
Hunt, Christiana V, 79
Hunt, Christianna I, 1021
Hunt, Clara V, 404
Hunt, Clarissa V, 613
Hunt, Clarissa V, 628
Hunt, Clarissa V, 629
Hunt, Clark N. V, 405
Hunt, Clarkson V, 405
Hunt, Clarkson V, 912
Hunt, Clarkson A. V, 912
Hunt, Clarkson N. V, 404
Hunt, Claton V, 629
Hunt, Clayton II, 234
Hunt, Clayton II, 293
Hunt, Clayton V, 79
Hunt, Clayton V, 629
Hunt, Clayton V, 844
Hunt, Clayton V, 883
Hunt, Cliffton H. V, 404
Hunt, Clifton V, 405
Hunt, Clinton V, 404
Hunt, Clinton V, 405
Hunt, Clyde V, 405
Hunt, Comfort I, 503
Hunt, Crispin VI, 978
Hunt, Cynthia I, 857
Hunt, Cynthia I, 887
Hunt, Cynthia I, 905
Hunt, Cyrus I, 502
Hunt, Cyrus I, 551
Hunt, Cyrus V, 404
Hunt, Cyrus V, 578
Hunt, Cyrus L. V, 404
Hunt, Cyrus L. V, 405
Hunt, Cyrus L. V, 578
Hunt, Daniel IV, 1370
Hunt, Daniel V, 250
Hunt, Daniel V, 402
Hunt, Daniel V, 404
Hunt, Daniel Huff V, 404
Hunt, Daniel S. I, 589
Hunt, David I, 964
Hunt, David III, 178
Hunt, David IV, 93
Hunt, David IV, 94
Hunt, David IV, 226
Hunt, David IV, 338
Hunt, David IV, 412
Hunt, David IV, 536
Hunt, David IV, 1204
Hunt, David IV, 1212
Hunt, David IV, 1282
Hunt, David IV, 1286
Hunt, David IV, 1299
Hunt, David V, 250
Hunt, David B. V, 404
Hunt, David Bailey V, 251
Hunt, David Bailey V, 403
Hunt, David Bailey V, 404
Hunt, David W. I, 857
Hunt, David W. I, 887
Hunt, David Wright V, 251
Hunt, Deborah Ann V, 629
Hunt, Delaplain II, 880
Hunt, Delaplaine II, 801
Hunt, Delaplane II, 310
Hunt, Delaplane II, 321
Hunt, Delila I, 503
Hunt, Delila I, 551
Hunt, Delila I, 602
Hunt, Delitha Ann V, 628
Hunt, Delitha Ann V, 629
Hunt, Della V, 629
Hunt, Delphina V, 953
Hunt, Diana I, 502
Hunt, Diana I, 551
Hunt, Diana I, 552
Hunt, Diana I, 573
Hunt, Diana IV, 478
Hunt, Diana IV, 561
Hunt, Dillwyn IV, 94
Hunt, Dillwyn IV, 127
Hunt, Dinah V, 79
Hunt, Dorcas I, 502
Hunt, Dorcas I, 551
Hunt, Dorcas I, 572
Hunt, Dorothea II, 560
Hunt, Dorothy V, 686
Hunt, Dorris V, 504
Hunt, Dr. J. Gibbons II, 880
Hunt, Dr. J. Gibbons II, 938
Hunt, Dr. J. Gibbons II, 939
Hunt, Eber I, 502
Hunt, Eber V, 340
Hunt, Edith IV, 1282
Hunt, Edith IV, 1299
Hunt, Edith V, 578
Hunt, Edith H. V, 840
Hunt, Edith H. V, 844
Hunt, Edith S. V, 578
Hunt, Edith S. V, 844
Hunt, Edmund IV, 94
Hunt, Edmund L. III, 177
Hunt, Edmund L. III, 178
Hunt, Edward I, 1021
Hunt, Edward II, 560
Hunt, Edward II, 571
Hunt, Edward P. II, 801
Hunt, Edward P. II, 879
Hunt, Edward S. V, 953
Hunt, Elam I, 503
Hunt, Elam I, 551
Hunt, Elam I, 602
Hunt, Elam I, 606
Hunt, Eleanor V, 305
Hunt, Eleanor V, 340
Hunt, Eleanor V, 351
Hunt, Eleasor I, 722
Hunt, Eleazar I, 343
Hunt, Eleazar I, 363
Hunt, Eleazar I, 381
Hunt, Eleazar I, 400
Hunt, Eleazar I, 487
Hunt, Eleazar I, 502
Hunt, Eleazar I, 503
Hunt, Eleazar I, 535
Hunt, Eleazar I, 549
Hunt, Eleazar I, 550
Hunt, Eleazar I, 551
Hunt, Eleazar I, 552
Hunt, Eleazar I, 564
Hunt, Eleazar I, 583
Hunt, Eleazar I, 682
Hunt, Eleazar I, 685
Hunt, Eleazar I, 820
Hunt, Eleazar IV, 1282
Hunt, Eleazer I, 343
Hunt, Eleazer I, 551
Hunt, Eleazer I, 594
Hunt, Eleazer V, 251
Hunt, Eleazer VI, 513
Hunt, Elen Prudence I, 857
Hunt, Elias W. IV, 1282
Hunt, Eliona V, 340
Hunt, Elisa Jane V, 629
Hunt, Elisabeth I, 804
Hunt, Elisabeth I, 820
Hunt, Elisabeth II, 217
Hunt, Elisabeth II, 234
Hunt, Elisha IV, 40
Hunt, Elisha IV, 93
Hunt, Elisha IV, 94
Hunt, Elisha IV, 725
Hunt, Elisha IV, 726
Hunt, Elisha F. IV, 93
Hunt, Eliza IV, 93
Hunt, Eliza IV, 94
Hunt, Eliza V, 403
Hunt, Eliza V, 404
Hunt, Eliza V, 405
Hunt, Eliza V, 438
Hunt, Eliza V, 768
Hunt, Eliza VI, 513
Hunt, Eliza VI, 538
Hunt, Eliza VI, 544
Hunt, Eliza VI, 576
Hunt, Eliza VI, 577
Hunt, Eliza VI, 659
Hunt, Eliza VI, 677
Hunt, Eliza VI, 717
Hunt, Eliza A. I, 857
Hunt, Eliza A. II, 934
Hunt, Eliza A. V, 437
Hunt, Eliza Ann V, 403
Hunt, Eliza Jane IV, 536
Hunt, Eliza Jane V, 628
Hunt, Eliza Jane Crew IV, 542
Hunt, Eliza K. I, 552
Hunt, Eliza K. I, 857
Hunt, Eliza K. V, 404
Hunt, Eliza M. VI, 827
Hunt, Elizabeth I, 502
Hunt, Elizabeth I, 503
Hunt, Elizabeth I, 528
Hunt, Elizabeth I, 537
Hunt, Elizabeth I, 539
Hunt, Elizabeth I, 548
Hunt, Elizabeth I, 550
Hunt, Elizabeth I, 551
Hunt, Elizabeth I, 552
Hunt, Elizabeth I, 567
Hunt, Elizabeth I, 659
Hunt, Elizabeth I, 682
Hunt, Elizabeth I, 695
Hunt, Elizabeth I, 722
Hunt, Elizabeth I, 820
Hunt, Elizabeth I, 857
Hunt, Elizabeth I, 886
Hunt, Elizabeth I, 887
Hunt, Elizabeth I, 903
Hunt, Elizabeth I, 932
Hunt, Elizabeth I, 964
Hunt, Elizabeth I, 1010
Hunt, Elizabeth II, 81
Hunt, Elizabeth II, 105
Hunt, Elizabeth II, 217
Hunt, Elizabeth II, 230
Hunt, Elizabeth II, 234
Hunt, Elizabeth II, 247
Hunt, Elizabeth II, 289
Hunt, Elizabeth II, 293
Hunt, Elizabeth II, 310
Hunt, Elizabeth II, 311
Hunt, Elizabeth II, 321
Hunt, Elizabeth II, 379
Hunt, Elizabeth II, 553
Hunt, Elizabeth II, 560
Hunt, Elizabeth II, 725
Hunt, Elizabeth II, 747
Hunt, Elizabeth II, 801
Hunt, Elizabeth II, 812
Hunt, Elizabeth II, 879
Hunt, Elizabeth II, 880
Hunt, Elizabeth II, 906
Hunt, Elizabeth II, 912
Hunt, Elizabeth II, 928
Hunt, Elizabeth III, 178
Hunt, Elizabeth III, 257
Hunt, Elizabeth IV, 412
Hunt, Elizabeth IV, 447
Hunt, Elizabeth IV, 725
Hunt, Elizabeth IV, 726
Hunt, Elizabeth IV, 1212
Hunt, Elizabeth IV, 1282
Hunt, Elizabeth V, 65
Hunt, Elizabeth V, 78
Hunt, Elizabeth V, 79
Hunt, Elizabeth V, 218
Hunt, Elizabeth V, 246
Hunt, Elizabeth V, 250
Hunt, Elizabeth V, 251
Hunt, Elizabeth V, 340
Hunt, Elizabeth V, 578
Hunt, Elizabeth V, 628
Hunt, Elizabeth V, 629
Hunt, Elizabeth V, 650
Hunt, Elizabeth V, 844
Hunt, Elizabeth VI, 870
Hunt, Elizabeth VI, 952
Hunt, Elizabeth Ann V, 570
Hunt, Elizabeth Ann V, 578
Hunt, Elizabeth M. V, 578
Hunt, Elizabeth M. V, 601
Hunt, Elizabeth W. II, 879
Hunt, Elizabeth Wyatt II, 560
Hunt, Elizabeth Wyatt II, 683
Hunt, Elizabeth, Jr. II, 321
Hunt, Elizabeth, Jr. II, 879
Hunt, Elizabeth, Sr. II, 321
Hunt, Ella M. II, 879
Hunt, Ella M. V, 404
Hunt, Ellen I, 552
Hunt, Elma B. IV, 1282
Hunt, Elma Ethaleen V, 404
Hunt, Elmina I, 602
Hunt, Elmira V, 403
Hunt, Elva V, 404
Hunt, Elva V, 405
Hunt, Elvirah I, 551
Hunt, Elwood V, 404
Hunt, Emily II, 880
Hunt, Emily II, 928
Hunt, Emily III, 178
Hunt, Emily IV, 1282
Hunt, Emily V, 404
Hunt, Emily V, 405
Hunt, Emily G. II, 879
Hunt, Emma II, 801
Hunt, Emma II, 879
Hunt, Emma V, 391
Hunt, Emma V, 404
Hunt, Emma V, 405
Hunt, Emma V, 409
Hunt, Emma V, 434
Hunt, Emmor IV, 93
Hunt, Emmor IV, 94
Hunt, Emmor IV, 725
Hunt, Emund IV, 93
Hunt, Enoch IV, 40
Hunt, Enoch IV, 93
Hunt, Enoch IV, 94
Hunt, Enoch IV, 127
Hunt, Enoch IV, 725
Hunt, Enoch IV, 726
Hunt, Erasnus I, 887

Hunt, Esther I, 502
Hunt, Esther I, 532
Hunt, Esther I, 550
Hunt, Esther II, 234
Hunt, Esther III, 178
Hunt, Esther IV, 40
Hunt, Esther IV, 71
Hunt, Esther IV, 94
Hunt, Esther IV, 117
Hunt, Esther IV, 127
Hunt, Esther IV, 637
Hunt, Esther IV, 697
Hunt, Esther IV, 725
Hunt, Esther IV, 726
Hunt, Esther IV, 874
Hunt, Esther IV, 881
Hunt, Esther V, 867
Hunt, Esther Collins IV, 94
Hunt, Esther D. IV, 752
Hunt, Esther G. III, 178
Hunt, Esther J. II, 879
Hunt, Esther S. II, 801
Hunt, Esther S. II, 879
Hunt, Esther T. V, 578
Hunt, Esther T. V, 844
Hunt, Esther T. V, 865
Hunt, Esther W. V, 79
Hunt, Esther W. V, 844
Hunt, Esther W. V, 883
Hunt, Esther W. V, 885
Hunt, Ethaleen V, 405
Hunt, Ethelda I, 619
Hunt, Ethelda Elmore I, 616
Hunt, Eunice I, 503
Hunt, Eunice I, 602
Hunt, Eunice V, 329
Hunt, Eunice V, 340
Hunt, Eva I. V, 404
Hunt, Eva J. V, 405
Hunt, Ezra V, 79
Hunt, Ezra V, 251
Hunt, Ezra V, 305
Hunt, Ezra V, 317
Hunt, Ezra V, 340
Hunt, Fannie III, 177
Hunt, Fannie III, 213
Hunt, Felix I, 400
Hunt, Felix I, 857
Hunt, Felix I, 887
Hunt, Fidelia V, 615
Hunt, Fidelia V, 628
Hunt, Fidelia V, 629
Hunt, Florence B. II, 880
Hunt, Florence E. V, 404
Hunt, Florence R. II, 880
Hunt, Frances VI, 938
Hunt, Francis I, 91
Hunt, Francis Orvine V, 403
Hunt, Francis Orvine V, 405
Hunt, Gennett IV, 1370
Hunt, Geo. IV, 148
Hunt, Geo. A. III, 213
Hunt, George I, 502
Hunt, George I, 503
Hunt, George I, 550
Hunt, George I, 551
Hunt, George I, 552
Hunt, George I, 568
Hunt, George I, 572
Hunt, George IV, 94
Hunt, George IV, 127
Hunt, George IV, 725
Hunt, George IV, 726
Hunt, George A. II, 293
Hunt, George Abbott II, 293
Hunt, George Dillwyn IV, 93
Hunt, George Hunt I, 594
Hunt, George M. V, 578
Hunt, George M. V, 844
Hunt, George M. V, 870
Hunt, Gertrude V, 404
Hunt, Gibbons II, 854
Hunt, Gibbons II, 879
Hunt, Gilbert I, 589
Hunt, Gilbert I, 594
Hunt, Gilbert I, 597
Hunt, Gladdis May V, 405
Hunt, Gladis May V, 404
Hunt, Grace V, 79
Hunt, Granville V, 628
Hunt, Gulielma V, 404
Hunt, Gulielma Mariah V, 403
Hunt, Gurney L. V, 404
Hunt, Hamuel V, 79
Hunt, Hanah V, 340
Hunt, Hannah I, 386
Hunt, Hannah I, 400
Hunt, Hannah I, 502
Hunt, Hannah I, 503
Hunt, Hannah I, 528
Hunt, Hannah I, 537
Hunt, Hannah I, 550
Hunt, Hannah I, 551
Hunt, Hannah I, 566
Hunt, Hannah I, 604
Hunt, Hannah I, 796
Hunt, Hannah I, 820
Hunt, Hannah I, 886
Hunt, Hannah I, 887
Hunt, Hannah I, 1016
Hunt, Hannah II, 234
Hunt, Hannah II, 260
Hunt, Hannah II, 795
Hunt, Hannah II, 802
Hunt, Hannah II, 804
Hunt, Hannah II, 807
Hunt, Hannah III, 178
Hunt, Hannah IV, 725
Hunt, Hannah IV, 726
Hunt, Hannah IV, 730
Hunt, Hannah IV, 740
Hunt, Hannah IV, 1204
Hunt, Hannah IV, 1212
Hunt, Hannah IV, 1370
Hunt, Hannah V, 79
Hunt, Hannah V, 250
Hunt, Hannah V, 251
Hunt, Hannah V, 265
Hunt, Hannah V, 337
Hunt, Hannah V, 338
Hunt, Hannah V, 340
Hunt, Hannah V, 345
Hunt, Hannah V, 398
Hunt, Hannah V, 403
Hunt, Hannah V, 404
Hunt, Hannah V, 405
Hunt, Hannah V, 416
Hunt, Hannah V, 446
Hunt, Hannah VI, 513
Hunt, Hannah VI, 524
Hunt, Hannah B. V, 404
Hunt, Hannah Backhouse I, 857
Hunt, Hannah C. IV, 726
Hunt, Hannah G. II, 310
Hunt, Hannah G. II, 321
Hunt, Hannah G. II, 327
Hunt, Hannah Perkins I, 551
Hunt, Hannah R. I, 552
Hunt, Hanuel V, 251
Hunt, Hanuel V, 305
Hunt, Hanuel V, 340
Hunt, Hanuel V, 351
Hunt, Harrie V, 405
Hunt, Harriet V, 340
Hunt, Harriet Ellen V, 403
Hunt, Harry H. V, 404
Hunt, Hattie V, 629
Hunt, Hattie E. V, 405
Hunt, Hattie E. V, 407
Hunt, Hattie Emma V, 404
Hunt, Helen IV, 1009
Hunt, Helen C. V, 686
Hunt, Helen Pauline V, 180
Hunt, Helen T. III, 178
Hunt, Helen T. III, 222
Hunt, Henry I, 552
Hunt, Henry I, 857
Hunt, Henry V, 402
Hunt, Henry V, 578
Hunt, Henry V, 628
Hunt, Henry V, 844
Hunt, Henry H. V, 578
Hunt, Henry H. V, 844
Hunt, Henry M. IV, 1282
Hunt, Herbert Bailey V, 404
Hunt, Herbert Bailey V, 405
Hunt, Hester III, 336
Hunt, Hester G. III, 87
Hunt, Hester G. III, 178
Hunt, Hezekiah V, 628
Hunt, Hezekiah V, 629
Hunt, Hiram I, 502
Hunt, Hiram I, 534
Hunt, Hiram I, 551
Hunt, Hiram I, 552
Hunt, Hiram H. V, 628
Hunt, Howard Abbott II, 177
Hunt, Howard Abbott II, 293
Hunt, Hulda V, 340
Hunt, Huldah I, 551
Hunt, Ira I, 785
Hunt, Ira IV, 94
Hunt, Ira IV, 127
Hunt, Ira IV, 725
Hunt, Ira IV, 726
Hunt, Ira IV, 730
Hunt, Ira V, 340
Hunt, Irvin L. V, 844
Hunt, Isaac III, 178
Hunt, Isaac V, 340
Hunt, Isaac V, 343
Hunt, Isabella IV, 148
Hunt, Isabella IV, 150
Hunt, Isaiah I, 502
Hunt, Isaiah I, 503
Hunt, Isaiah I, 539
Hunt, Isaiah I, 550
Hunt, Isaiah I, 551
Hunt, Isaiah I, 682
Hunt, Isaiah I, 1021
Hunt, Isaiah V, 403
Hunt, Isaiah V, 405
Hunt, Isaiah V, 629
Hunt, Isaiah, Jr. I, 551
Hunt, Isam I, 550
Hunt, Isam I, 563
Hunt, Isam I, 710
Hunt, Isam I, 722
Hunt, Ishaam I, 886
Hunt, Isham I, 552
Hunt, Isom I, 502
Hunt, Isom I, 503
Hunt, Isom I, 550
Hunt, Isom I, 551
Hunt, Isom I, 702
Hunt, Isom I, 722
Hunt, Ithamar I, 502
Hunt, Iva E. V, 404
Hunt, Iva E. V, 405
Hunt, J. Eberly V, 79
Hunt, Jabez I, 503
Hunt, Jabez I, 857
Hunt, Jabez I, 875
Hunt, Jabez I, 886
Hunt, Jabez V, 403
Hunt, Jabez V, 404
Hunt, Jabez V, 405
Hunt, Jabez Hunt I, 886
Hunt, Jacob I, 502
Hunt, Jacob I, 503
Hunt, Jacob I, 528
Hunt, Jacob I, 550
Hunt, Jacob I, 551
Hunt, Jacob I, 602
Hunt, Jacob I, 604
Hunt, Jacob I, 820
Hunt, Jacob I, 847
Hunt, Jacob I, 962
Hunt, Jacob I, 964
Hunt, Jacob I, 971
Hunt, Jacob I, 1005
Hunt, Jacob I, 1010
Hunt, Jacob I, 1101
Hunt, Jacob III, 175
Hunt, Jacob III, 178
Hunt, Jacob V, 249
Hunt, Jacob V, 250
Hunt, Jacob V, 340
Hunt, Jacob V, 369
Hunt, Jacob V, 388
Hunt, Jacob V, 396
Hunt, Jacob V, 402
Hunt, Jacob V, 403
Hunt, Jacob V, 440
Hunt, Jacob V, 468
Hunt, Jacob V, 629
Hunt, Jacob VI, 938
Hunt, Jacob B. V, 404
Hunt, Jacob G. V, 250
Hunt, Jacob G. V, 251
Hunt, Jacob G. V, 404
Hunt, Jacob G. V, 405
Hunt, Jacob G. V, 406
Hunt, Jacob G. V, 686
Hunt, Jacob Green V, 402
Hunt, Jacob W. II, 849
Hunt, Jacob W. II, 879
Hunt, Jacob, Jr. V, 404
Hunt, James I, 551
Hunt, James II, 310
Hunt, James II, 321
Hunt, James II, 379
Hunt, James II, 795
Hunt, James III, 177
Hunt, James III, 178
Hunt, James IV, 1282
Hunt, James V, 250
Hunt, James V, 251
Hunt, James V, 340
Hunt, James V, 402
Hunt, James V, 405
Hunt, James V, 835
Hunt, James Clemmons I, 503
Hunt, James E. V, 403
Hunt, James E. V, 404
Hunt, James E. V, 405
Hunt, James E. V, 409
Hunt, James J. II, 801
Hunt, James J. II, 879
Hunt, James M. II, 934
Hunt, James M. V, 391
Hunt, James M. V, 405
Hunt, James R. V, 403
Hunt, James R. V, 404
Hunt, James W. III, 178
Hunt, James W. III, 222
Hunt, Jane I, 551
Hunt, Jane I, 594
Hunt, Jane II, 1040
Hunt, Jane V, 337
Hunt, Jane V, 340
Hunt, Jane V, 396
Hunt, Jane V, 403
Hunt, Jane V, 404
Hunt, Jane V, 405
Hunt, Jane VI, 870
Hunt, Jean I, 551
Hunt, Jefferson T. V, 629
Hunt, Jemima I, 502
Hunt, Jemima I, 549
Hunt, Jemima I, 579
Hunt, Jemima I, 964
Hunt, Jemima I, 1010
Hunt, Jemima III, 467
Hunt, Jemimah I, 1009
Hunt, Jericho III, 178
Hunt, Jesse I, 502
Hunt, Jesse I, 503
Hunt, Jesse I, 550
Hunt, Jesse I, 551
Hunt, Jesse I, 682
Hunt, Jesse I, 692
Hunt, Jesse I, 886
Hunt, Jesse I, 1005
Hunt, Jesse V, 250
Hunt, Jesse V, 251
Hunt, Jesse V, 340
Hunt, Jesse V, 369
Hunt, Jesse V, 402
Hunt, Jesse V, 403
Hunt, Jesse V, 404
Hunt, Jesse V, 416
Hunt, Jesse V, 628
Hunt, Jesse V, 629
Hunt, Jesse M. V, 405
Hunt, Jesse Milton V, 403
Hunt, Joana V, 405
Hunt, Joanna I, 1021
Hunt, Joanna I, 1060
Hunt, Joanna I, 1061
Hunt, Joanna V, 403
Hunt, Joel I, 502
Hunt, Joel I, 551
Hunt, Joel I, 574
Hunt, Joel I, 586
Hunt, Joel I, 589
Hunt, Joel I, 594
Hunt, Joel II, 1040
Hunt, Joel V, 628
Hunt, Joel V, 629
Hunt, Joel, Jr. V, 628
Hunt, Joel, Jr. V, 629
Hunt, John I, 502
Hunt, John I, 503
Hunt, John I, 550
Hunt, John I, 551
Hunt, John I, 552
Hunt, John I, 602
Hunt, John I, 606
Hunt, John I, 784
Hunt, John I, 814
Hunt, John I, 820
Hunt, John I, 964
Hunt, John I, 1005
Hunt, John I, 1021
Hunt, John I, 1032
Hunt, John II, 81
Hunt, John II, 234
Hunt, John II, 310
Hunt, John II, 311
Hunt, John II, 321
Hunt, John II, 379
Hunt, John II, 544
Hunt, John II, 560
Hunt, John II, 571
Hunt, John II, 683
Hunt, John II, 801
Hunt, John II, 807
Hunt, John II, 854
Hunt, John II, 879
Hunt, John II, 880
Hunt, John II, 928
Hunt, John IV, 40
Hunt, John IV, 94
Hunt, John IV, 226
Hunt, John IV, 338
Hunt, John IV, 412
Hunt, John IV, 536
Hunt, John IV, 637
Hunt, John V, 78
Hunt, John V, 79
Hunt, John V, 215
Hunt, John V, 251
Hunt, John V, 340
Hunt, John V, 380
Hunt, John V, 402
Hunt, John V, 407
Hunt, John V, 435
Hunt, John V, 437
Hunt, John V, 504
Hunt, John V, 538
Hunt, John V, 844
Hunt, John VI, 113
Hunt, John VI, 184
Hunt, John VI, 206
Hunt, John VI, 250
Hunt, John VI, 405
Hunt, John VI, 513
Hunt, John VI, 599
Hunt, John VI, 827
Hunt, John VI, 938
Hunt, John Eberlee V, 78
Hunt, John Eberly IV, 412
Hunt, John Eberly V, 79
Hunt, John G. II, 879
Hunt, John Gibbons II, 801
Hunt, John I. II, 879
Hunt, John I. II, 940
Hunt, John J. II, 879
Hunt, John L. V, 629
Hunt, John Lawrence III, 178
Hunt, John Milton V, 403
Hunt, John Robert I, 619
Hunt, John S. I, 606
Hunt, John T. V, 578
Hunt, John, Jr. II, 201
Hunt, John, Jr. II, 234
Hunt, John, Jr. II, 560
Hunt, John, Jr. V, 340
Hunt, Jonathan I, 503
Hunt, Jonathan I, 551
Hunt, Jonathan I, 785
Hunt, Jonathan I, 820
Hunt, Jonathan I, 857
Hunt, Jonathan I, 1005
Hunt, Jonathan IV, 94
Hunt, Jonathan IV, 226
Hunt, Jonathan IV, 338
Hunt, Jonathan IV, 412
Hunt, Jonathan IV, 536
Hunt, Jonathan V, 251
Hunt, Jonathan V, 340
Hunt, Jonathan V, 390
Hunt, Jonathan V, 402
Hunt, Jonathan V, 403
Hunt, Jonathan V, 404
Hunt, Jonathan V, 405
Hunt, Jonathan V, 418
Hunt, Jonathan L. V, 403
Hunt, Jonathan T. Rogers IV, 40
Hunt, Jonothan V, 79
Hunt, Joseph I, 503
Hunt, Joseph I, 550
Hunt, Joseph I, 579
Hunt, Joseph I, 857
Hunt, Joseph I, 886
Hunt, Joseph I, 887
Hunt, Joseph I, 907
Hunt, Joseph II, 321
Hunt, Joseph II, 560
Hunt, Joseph II, 809
Hunt, Joseph III, 178
Hunt, Joseph V, 340
Hunt, Joseph V, 404
Hunt, Joseph V, 405
Hunt, Joseph VI, 599
Hunt, Joseph B. V, 79
Hunt, Joseph B. V, 839
Hunt, Joseph B. V, 844
Hunt, Joseph B. V, 883
Hunt, Joseph Bartlett IV, 94
Hunt, Joseph G. III, 178
Hunt, Joseph M. V, 403
Hunt, Joseph M. V, 405
Hunt, Joshua IV, 93
Hunt, Joshua IV, 94
Hunt, Joshua IV, 150
Hunt, Joshua IV, 185
Hunt, Joshua IV, 226
Hunt, Joshua IV, 338
Hunt, Joshua IV, 412
Hunt, Joshua IV, 536
Hunt, Joshua IV, 637
Hunt, Joshua IV, 725
Hunt, Joshua V, 78
Hunt, Joshua VI, 405
Hunt, Joshua VI, 440
Hunt, Joshua VI, 599
Hunt, Joshua Hunt IV, 40
Hunt, Josiah I, 550
Hunt, Josiah I, 964
Hunt, Josiah III, 177
Hunt, Josiah III, 178
Hunt, Josiah V, 231
Hunt, Josiah V, 250

unt, Josiah V, 251
unt, Josiah V, 268
unt, Josiah V, 340
unt, Josiah V, 404
unt, Josiah D. III, 178
unt, Julia M. IV, 1370
unt, Katherine III, 177
unt, Katherine V, 246
unt, Katherine V, 250
unt, Katy VI, 953
unt, Ketura V, 953
unt, Keturah V, 953
unt, Keturah V, 957
unt, Laura A. I, 552
unt, Laurena V, 404
unt, Laurenna V, 385
unt, Laurenna V, 405
unt, Lavina V, 250
unt, Lavina V, 251
unt, Lavina V, 268
unt, Lawrence Alexander III, 177
unt, Lenna V, 405
unt, Lenora V, 372
unt, Lenora R. V, 404
unt, Leuiza Jane V, 403
unt, Levi III, 75
unt, Levi III, 178
unt, Levina I, 502
unt, Levina V, 340
unt, Levina V, 352
unt, Lewellyn IV, 1282
unt, Lewis I, 589
unt, Lewis III, 178
unt, Lewis V, 615
unt, Lewis V, 628
unt, Lewis V, 629
unt, Lewis Clark V, 628
unt, Lewis P. III, 63
unt, Lewis P. III, 178
unt, Libney V, 337
unt, Libney V, 340
unt, Libni I, 502
unt, Libni V, 79
unt, Libni V, 251
unt, Libni V, 340
unt, Lidiah III, 178
unt, Linton D. V, 405
unt, Lizzie V, 440
unt, Lorenzo IV, 1282
unt, Lot III, 87
unt, Lot III, 178
unt, Lott G. III, 178
unt, Lottie Alma V, 844
unt, Louisa III, 178
unt, Louise III, 177
unt, Louise III, 260
unt, Louiza J. V, 405
unt, Lucinda V, 383
unt, Lucinda V, 404
unt, Luke III, 178
unt, Luther M. V, 405
unt, Luther M. V, 686
unt, Luther N. V, 404
unt, Luzena I, 502
unt, Luzena I, 551
Hunt, Luzena I, 552
Hunt, Lydda I, 962
Hunt, Lydda I, 964
Hunt, Lydia I, 502
Hunt, Lydia I, 503
Hunt, Lydia I, 544
Hunt, Lydia I, 547
Hunt, Lydia I, 550
Hunt, Lydia I, 551
Hunt, Lydia I, 552
Hunt, Lydia I, 583
Hunt, Lydia I, 606
Hunt, Lydia I, 682
Hunt, Lydia I, 692
Hunt, Lydia I, 1005
Hunt, Lydia I, 1010
Hunt, Lydia III, 178
Hunt, Lydia III, 200
Hunt, Lydia IV, 1370
Hunt, Lydia V, 250
Hunt, Lydia V, 340
Hunt, Lydia V, 360
Hunt, Lydia V, 369
Hunt, Lydia V, 388
Hunt, Lydia V, 396
Hunt, Lydia V, 402
Hunt, Lydia V, 403
Hunt, Lydia V, 440
Hunt, Lydia V, 468
Hunt, Lydia V, 578
Hunt, Lydia V, 629
Hunt, Lydia V, 844
Hunt, Lydia Ann V, 250
Hunt, Lydia Ann V, 251
Hunt, Lydia Ann V, 403
Hunt, Lydia Ann V, 404
Hunt, Lydia Ann V, 844
Hunt, Lydia C. V, 578
Hunt, Lydia E. IV, 1370
Hunt, Lydia F. V, 79
Hunt, Lydia S. V, 79
Hunt, Lydia S. V, 141
Hunt, Maggie V, 180
Hunt, Maggie M. V, 180
Hunt, Mahala I, 604
Hunt, Major VI, 513
Hunt, Mandy E. V, 629
Hunt, Margaret I, 502
Hunt, Margaret I, 503
Hunt, Margaret I, 550
Hunt, Margaret I, 551
Hunt, Margaret I, 555
Hunt, Margaret I, 702
Hunt, Margaret I, 722
Hunt, Margaret I, 816
Hunt, Margaret I, 820
Hunt, Margaret I, 880
Hunt, Margaret I, 886
Hunt, Margaret I, 1032
Hunt, Margaret I, 1038
Hunt, Margaret I, 1053
Hunt, Margaret II, 249
Hunt, Margaret II, 379
Hunt, Margaret II, 518
Hunt, Margaret II, 560
Hunt, Margaret II, 879
Hunt, Margaret III, 178
Hunt, Margaret III, 299
Hunt, Margaret IV, 1271
Hunt, Margaret IV, 1282
Hunt, Margaret V, 78
Hunt, Margaret V, 79
Hunt, Margaret V, 251
Hunt, Margaret V, 340
Hunt, Margaret V, 390
Hunt, Margaret V, 403
Hunt, Margaret V, 404
Hunt, Margaret V, 418
Hunt, Margaret V, 629
Hunt, Margaret VI, 965
Hunt, Margaret Ann V, 404
Hunt, Margaret Ann V, 578
Hunt, Margaret C. V, 405
Hunt, Margaret Jane V, 629
Hunt, Margaret P. I, 552
Hunt, Margaret S. II, 906
Hunt, Margaret S. III, 247
Hunt, Margaret S. V, 629
Hunt, Margaret Shreve II, 812
Hunt, Margery I, 722
Hunt, Margery IV, 1282
Hunt, Margery IV, 1286
Hunt, Marget I, 710
Hunt, Marget I, 722
Hunt, Margrat I, 785
Hunt, Margret I, 551
Hunt, Margret I, 857
Hunt, Maria V, 629
Hunt, Maria V, 643
Hunt, Maria E. V, 405
Hunt, Maria Elizabeth V, 403
Hunt, Mariah V, 628
Hunt, Marian I, 804
Hunt, Marian I, 820
Hunt, Marian III, 178
Hunt, Mariana IV, 967
Hunt, Marianna IV, 967
Hunt, Marianna V, 404
Hunt, Marianna V, 405
Hunt, Marianna Bailey V, 629
Hunt, Marianna H. IV, 970
Hunt, Mark II, 1074
Hunt, Martha I, 503
Hunt, Martha I, 550
Hunt, Martha I, 569
Hunt, Martha I, 857
Hunt, Martha I, 865
Hunt, Martha I, 876
Hunt, Martha I, 885
Hunt, Martha I, 886
Hunt, Martha I, 887
Hunt, Martha I, 903
Hunt, Martha II, 1074
Hunt, Martha IV, 412
Hunt, Martha IV, 1282
Hunt, Martha V, 79
Hunt, Martha V, 403
Hunt, Martha V, 404
Hunt, Martha V, 405
Hunt, Martha V, 430
Hunt, Martha V, 441
Hunt, Martha Bye V, 78
Hunt, Martha Bye V, 79
Hunt, Martha Elma V, 629
Hunt, Martha J. V, 380
Hunt, Martha Jane IV, 164
Hunt, Martha Jane IV, 165
Hunt, Martha Jane IV, 726
Hunt, Martha Jane V, 403
Hunt, Martha Jane V, 405
Hunt, Martha L. II, 1074
Hunt, Martha L. II, 1083
Hunt, Martha Mariah IV, 1282
Hunt, Martha T. IV, 536
Hunt, Martha T. IV, 548
Hunt, Mary I, 502
Hunt, Mary I, 503
Hunt, Mary I, 537
Hunt, Mary I, 549
Hunt, Mary I, 550
Hunt, Mary I, 551
Hunt, Mary I, 552
Hunt, Mary I, 567
Hunt, Mary I, 568
Hunt, Mary I, 569
Hunt, Mary I, 574
Hunt, Mary I, 581
Hunt, Mary I, 586
Hunt, Mary I, 589
Hunt, Mary I, 594
Hunt, Mary I, 722
Hunt, Mary I, 820
Hunt, Mary I, 857
Hunt, Mary I, 879
Hunt, Mary I, 886
Hunt, Mary I, 887
Hunt, Mary I, 912
Hunt, Mary I, 964
Hunt, Mary I, 1005
Hunt, Mary I, 1010
Hunt, Mary I, 1021
Hunt, Mary I, 1032
Hunt, Mary I, 1036
Hunt, Mary I, 1060
Hunt, Mary I, 1061
Hunt, Mary II, 60
Hunt, Mary II, 81
Hunt, Mary II, 234
Hunt, Mary II, 260
Hunt, Mary II, 275
Hunt, Mary II, 379
Hunt, Mary II, 560
Hunt, Mary II, 879
Hunt, Mary II, 1004
Hunt, Mary II, 1019
Hunt, Mary II, 1040
Hunt, Mary III, 87
Hunt, Mary III, 177
Hunt, Mary III, 178
Hunt, Mary III, 289
Hunt, Mary IV, 40
Hunt, Mary IV, 57
Hunt, Mary IV, 93
Hunt, Mary IV, 94
Hunt, Mary IV, 185
Hunt, Mary IV, 226
Hunt, Mary IV, 725
Hunt, Mary IV, 726
Hunt, Mary IV, 1282
Hunt, Mary V, 78
Hunt, Mary V, 79
Hunt, Mary V, 231
Hunt, Mary V, 245
Hunt, Mary V, 250
Hunt, Mary V, 251
Hunt, Mary V, 268
Hunt, Mary V, 332
Hunt, Mary V, 340
Hunt, Mary V, 402
Hunt, Mary V, 403
Hunt, Mary V, 404
Hunt, Mary V, 405
Hunt, Mary V, 431
Hunt, Mary V, 481
Hunt, Mary V, 504
Hunt, Mary V, 578
Hunt, Mary V, 601
Hunt, Mary V, 622
Hunt, Mary V, 628
Hunt, Mary V, 629
Hunt, Mary V, 844
Hunt, Mary V, 867
Hunt, Mary V, 912
Hunt, Mary VI, 513
Hunt, Mary VI, 524
Hunt, Mary VI, 598
Hunt, Mary VI, 599
Hunt, Mary VI, 602
Hunt, Mary VI, 937
Hunt, Mary A. II, 879
Hunt, Mary A. II, 940
Hunt, Mary A. V, 180
Hunt, Mary A. V, 628
Hunt, Mary Abba V, 629
Hunt, Mary Adaline IV, 165
Hunt, Mary Almeda V, 403
Hunt, Mary Almedia V, 405
Hunt, Mary Ann I, 857
Hunt, Mary Ann I, 887
Hunt, Mary Ann I, 897
Hunt, Mary Ann II, 879
Hunt, Mary Ann IV, 725
Hunt, Mary Ann IV, 760
Hunt, Mary Ann IV, 1370
Hunt, Mary Ann V, 251
Hunt, Mary Ann V, 402
Hunt, Mary Ann V, 403
Hunt, Mary Ann V, 628
Hunt, Mary Ann V, 629
Hunt, Mary Ann V, 639
Hunt, Mary Anna V, 611
Hunt, Mary B. III, 174
Hunt, Mary B. III, 178
Hunt, Mary B. III, 485
Hunt, Mary E. V, 404
Hunt, Mary E. V, 405
Hunt, Mary E. V, 686
Hunt, Mary Elizabeth V, 403
Hunt, Mary Elizabeth V, 405
Hunt, Mary Elizabeth V, 439
Hunt, Mary J. III, 213
Hunt, Mary J. V, 403
Hunt, Mary J. V, 404
Hunt, Mary J. L. I, 552
Hunt, Mary Jane I, 621
Hunt, Mary Jane V, 396
Hunt, Mary Jane V, 405
Hunt, Mary S. II, 854
Hunt, Mary S. II, 879
Hunt, Mary S. II, 1074
Hunt, Mary S. II, 1083
Hunt, Mary Wyatt II, 795
Hunt, Mary, Jr. I, 551
Hunt, Mary, Sr. I, 551
Hunt, Maryann V, 953
Hunt, Massey II, 801
Hunt, Massey II, 879
Hunt, Mathew Hodgson V, 446
Hunt, Matilda C. V, 403
Hunt, Maud V, 405
Hunt, Mella V, 405
Hunt, Melvina I, 594
Hunt, Mercy III, 160
Hunt, Mercy III, 175
Hunt, Mercy IV, 1370
Hunt, Merriam V, 79
Hunt, Mildred Marie V, 180
Hunt, Milton IV, 93
Hunt, Milton IV, 94
Hunt, Milton IV, 725
Hunt, Milton IV, 726
Hunt, Milton V, 404
Hunt, Milton V, 628
Hunt, Milton V, 629
Hunt, Milton L. V, 403
Hunt, Milton L. V, 405
Hunt, Miriam I, 502
Hunt, Miriam I, 503
Hunt, Miriam I, 551
Hunt, Miriam I, 804
Hunt, Miriam I, 820
Hunt, Miriam I, 845
Hunt, Miriam V, 251
Hunt, Miriam V, 340
Hunt, Miriam V, 343
Hunt, Miriam Claiton I, 820
Hunt, Mordecai M. IV, 93
Hunt, Mordecai M. IV, 94
Hunt, Moses III, 178
Hunt, Moses IV, 412
Hunt, Moses Starbuck V, 628
Hunt, Mournin I, 682
Hunt, Mourning I, 503
Hunt, Mourning I, 692
Hunt, Mrs. Anna V, 744
Hunt, Myrta Elma V, 844
Hunt, Nancy I, 503
Hunt, Nancy I, 551
Hunt, Nancy I, 702
Hunt, Nancy I, 857
Hunt, Nancy I, 886
Hunt, Nancy V, 340
Hunt, Nancy VI, 938
Hunt, Nancy Ann I, 551
Hunt, Nancy D. I, 552
Hunt, Nancy D. I, 886
Hunt, Nancy D. I, 912
Hunt, Nancy D. I, 914
Hunt, Nancy D. V, 404
Hunt, Nancy Jane V, 340
Hunt, Naomi B. II, 321
Hunt, Naomi P. II, 310
Hunt, Naomi P. II, 321
Hunt, Naomi P. II, 879
Hunt, Naomi P. II, 880
Hunt, Naomi P. II, 930
Hunt, Naomi Passmore II, 783
Hunt, Naomi Passmore II, 815
Hunt, Nathan I, 503
Hunt, Nathan I, 550
Hunt, Nathan I, 551
Hunt, Nathan I, 569
Hunt, Nathan I, 578
Hunt, Nathan I, 785
Hunt, Nathan I, 847
Hunt, Nathan I, 857
Hunt, Nathan I, 865
Hunt, Nathan I, 886
Hunt, Nathan I, 887
Hunt, Nathan I, 912
Hunt, Nathan I, 1005
Hunt, Nathan I, 1101
Hunt, Nathan IV, 40
Hunt, Nathan IV, 94
Hunt, Nathan IV, 127
Hunt, Nathan IV, 226
Hunt, Nathan IV, 338
Hunt, Nathan IV, 412
Hunt, Nathan IV, 536
Hunt, Nathan IV, 676
Hunt, Nathan IV, 691
Hunt, Nathan IV, 697
Hunt, Nathan IV, 725
Hunt, Nathan IV, 760
Hunt, Nathan IV, 784
Hunt, Nathan V, 74
Hunt, Nathan V, 79
Hunt, Nathan V, 250
Hunt, Nathan V, 251
Hunt, Nathan V, 340
Hunt, Nathan V, 369
Hunt, Nathan V, 402
Hunt, Nathan V, 403
Hunt, Nathan V, 404
Hunt, Nathan V, 578
Hunt, Nathan V, 610
Hunt, Nathan V, 629
Hunt, Nathan V, 844
Hunt, Nathan V, 865
Hunt, Nathan V, 867
Hunt, Nathan VI, 405
Hunt, Nathan Allen I, 857
Hunt, Nathan, Jr. I, 886
Hunt, Nathan, Jr. I, 887
Hunt, Nathan, Jr. I, 912
Hunt, Nathan, Jr. I, 914
Hunt, Nathan, Jr. IV, 726
Hunt, Nehemiah IV, 1370
Hunt, Newby I, 502
Hunt, Newby I, 594
Hunt, Newby I, 596
Hunt, Nicholas V, 251
Hunt, Obediah VI, 938
Hunt, Obediah VI, 973
Hunt, Ohizia VI, 978
Hunt, Olaver V, 403
Hunt, Oliver V, 405
Hunt, Oliver G. IV, 1282
Hunt, Oliver W. V, 404
Hunt, Oliver W. V, 578
Hunt, Orien V, 1003
Hunt, Orin V, 1003
Hunt, Ottie C. V, 629
Hunt, Palmer Nathan V, 405
Hunt, Patience V, 953
Hunt, Patric H. I, 552
Hunt, Patsy IV, 1282
Hunt, Patsy IV, 1286
Hunt, Patsy VI, 938
Hunt, Paul H. I, 616
Hunt, Paul H. I, 619
Hunt, Percival III, 178
Hunt, Peter I, 503
Hunt, Peter I, 528
Hunt, Peter I, 551
Hunt, Phanuel I, 503
Hunt, Pharaba V, 504
Hunt, Phareby V, 504
Hunt, Phebah I, 550
Hunt, Phebe I, 503
Hunt, Phebe I, 785
Hunt, Phebe I, 820
Hunt, Phebe II, 809
Hunt, Phebe III, 75
Hunt, Phebe III, 175
Hunt, Phebe III, 178
Hunt, Phebe IV, 94
Hunt, Phebe IV, 637
Hunt, Phebe V, 79
Hunt, Phebe V, 251
Hunt, Phebe V, 340
Hunt, Phebe V, 380
Hunt, Phebe V, 393
Hunt, Phebe V, 403
Hunt, Phebe V, 404
Hunt, Phebe V, 405
Hunt, Phebe V, 407
Hunt, Phebe V, 435
Hunt, Phebe V, 437

Hunt, Phebe V, 629
Hunt, Phebe VI, 599
Hunt, Phebe VI, 953
Hunt, Phebe Ann III, 175
Hunt, Phebe F. V, 504
Hunt, Phebe F. V, 538
Hunt, Phebe H. III, 63
Hunt, Phebe H. III, 178
Hunt, Phebe Jane III, 178
Hunt, Phebe Jane IV, 725
Hunt, Pheriba V, 578
Hunt, Pheriba V, 597
Hunt, Phidelia V, 629
Hunt, Phila. III, 178
Hunt, Philena III, 178
Hunt, Phineas I, 550
Hunt, Phineas IV, 1212
Hunt, Phineas IV, 1282
Hunt, Phineas V, 78
Hunt, Phinehas I, 502
Hunt, Phinehas I, 550
Hunt, Phinehas I, 567
Hunt, Phinehas I, 659
Hunt, Phinehas I, 695
Hunt, Phinehas I, 722
Hunt, Phinehas V, 215
Hunt, Phinehas V, 218
Hunt, Phinehas V, 246
Hunt, Phinehas V, 250
Hunt, Pleasant I, 503
Hunt, Pleasant I, 551
Hunt, Pleasant V, 340
Hunt, Pleasant V, 365
Hunt, Polly VI, 938
Hunt, Polly VI, 952
Hunt, Priscilla I, 502
Hunt, Priscilla I, 503
Hunt, Priscilla I, 532
Hunt, Priscilla I, 550
Hunt, Priscilla I, 875
Hunt, Priscilla I, 886
Hunt, Priscilla I, 963
Hunt, Priscilla I, 964
Hunt, Priscilla IV, 127
Hunt, Priscilla IV, 691
Hunt, Priscilla IV, 725
Hunt, Priscilla IV, 726
Hunt, Priscilla IV, 730
Hunt, Priscilla V, 340
Hunt, Priscilla V, 343
Hunt, Priscilla W. IV, 725
Hunt, Priscilla W. IV, 726
Hunt, Prudence I, 503
Hunt, Prudence I, 550
Hunt, Prudence I, 578
Hunt, Prudence I, 594
Hunt, Prudence I, 847
Hunt, Prudence I, 857
Hunt, Prudence I, 886
Hunt, Prudence I, 912
Hunt, Rachel I, 502
Hunt, Rachel I, 503
Hunt, Rachel I, 526
Hunt, Rachel I, 550
Hunt, Rachel I, 551
Hunt, Rachel I, 784
Hunt, Rachel I, 785
Hunt, Rachel I, 814
Hunt, Rachel I, 820
Hunt, Rachel I, 1005
Hunt, Rachel I, 1021
Hunt, Rachel I, 1032
Hunt, Rachel I, 1061
Hunt, Rachel I, 1062
Hunt, Rachel II, 560
Hunt, Rachel II, 571
Hunt, Rachel II, 806
Hunt, Rachel II, 807
Hunt, Rachel II, 854
Hunt, Rachel II, 879
Hunt, Rachel III, 178
Hunt, Rachel IV, 93
Hunt, Rachel IV, 94
Hunt, Rachel IV, 127
Hunt, Rachel IV, 185
Hunt, Rachel IV, 226
Hunt, Rachel IV, 338
Hunt, Rachel IV, 412
Hunt, Rachel IV, 536
Hunt, Rachel IV, 701
Hunt, Rachel IV, 725
Hunt, Rachel IV, 726
Hunt, Rachel V, 78
Hunt, Rachel V, 79
Hunt, Rachel V, 138
Hunt, Rachel V, 215
Hunt, Rachel V, 249
Hunt, Rachel V, 250
Hunt, Rachel V, 251
Hunt, Rachel V, 315
Hunt, Rachel V, 340
Hunt, Rachel V, 369
Hunt, Rachel V, 388
Hunt, Rachel V, 402
Hunt, Rachel V, 404
Hunt, Rachel V, 578
Hunt, Rachel V, 629
Hunt, Rachel V, 844
Hunt, Rachel VI, 405
Hunt, Rachel VI, 440
Hunt, Rachel VI, 599
Hunt, Rachel G. II, 321
Hunt, Rachel G. V, 578
Hunt, Rachel G. V, 844
Hunt, Rachel L. V, 628
Hunt, Ralph I, 1021
Hunt, Ralph I, 1032
Hunt, Ralph I, 1060
Hunt, Ralph I, 1061
Hunt, Rebecah I, 502
Hunt, Rebecca I, 363
Hunt, Rebecca I, 503
Hunt, Rebecca I, 594
Hunt, Rebecca II, 310
Hunt, Rebecca II, 321
Hunt, Rebecca II, 553
Hunt, Rebecca II, 560
Hunt, Rebecca II, 708
Hunt, Rebecca III, 177
Hunt, Rebecca III, 178
Hunt, Rebecca III, 191
Hunt, Rebecca IV, 93
Hunt, Rebecca IV, 94
Hunt, Rebecca IV, 100
Hunt, Rebecca IV, 127
Hunt, Rebecca IV, 637
Hunt, Rebecca IV, 645
Hunt, Rebecca IV, 725
Hunt, Rebecca IV, 752
Hunt, Rebecca IV, 760
Hunt, Rebecca V, 180
Hunt, Rebecca V, 245
Hunt, Rebecca V, 250
Hunt, Rebecca V, 317
Hunt, Rebecca V, 340
Hunt, Rebecca V, 369
Hunt, Rebecca V, 393
Hunt, Rebecca V, 396
Hunt, Rebecca V, 402
Hunt, Rebecca V, 403
Hunt, Rebecca V, 404
Hunt, Rebecca V, 405
Hunt, Rebecca V, 409
Hunt, Rebecca V, 440
Hunt, Rebecca V, 441
Hunt, Rebecca V, 615
Hunt, Rebecca V, 628
Hunt, Rebecca V, 629
Hunt, Rebecca V, 953
Hunt, Rebecca VI, 938
Hunt, Rebecca A. II, 289
Hunt, Rebecca A. II, 293
Hunt, Rebecca Ann II, 177
Hunt, Rebecca Ann II, 293
Hunt, Rebecca Ann II, 725
Hunt, Rebecca Ann II, 747
Hunt, Rebecca J. V, 403
Hunt, Rebecca Jane V, 390
Hunt, Rebecca Jane V, 405
Hunt, Rebecca Jane V, 628
Hunt, Rebecca Jane V, 629
Hunt, Rebecca P. II, 879
Hunt, Rebecca Price II, 747
Hunt, Rebecca S. II, 879
Hunt, Rebecca S. II, 880
Hunt, Rebecca S. II, 938
Hunt, Rebecca T. II, 879
Hunt, Rebecca T. II, 912
Hunt, Rebeckah I, 502
Hunt, Rebeckah I, 549
Hunt, Rebeckah I, 567
Hunt, Rebeckah III, 178
Hunt, Rebeckah V, 251
Hunt, Rebekah I, 400
Hunt, Rebekah I, 413
Hunt, Rebekah I, 503
Hunt, Rebekah I, 524
Hunt, Rebekah I, 550
Hunt, Rebekah I, 1005
Hunt, Rebekah II, 533
Hunt, Rebekah II, 560
Hunt, Rebekah III, 178
Hunt, Reid V, 404
Hunt, Reuben V, 340
Hunt, Reuben V, 393
Hunt, Reuben V, 402
Hunt, Reuben V, 403
Hunt, Reuben V, 404
Hunt, Reuben V, 629
Hunt, Reuben G. V, 398
Hunt, Reuben G. V, 404
Hunt, Reuben G. V, 405
Hunt, Rhoda I, 503
Hunt, Rhoda I, 857
Hunt, Rhoda IV, 93
Hunt, Rhoda IV, 94
Hunt, Rhoda VI, 513
Hunt, Rhoda VI, 576
Hunt, Rhoda VI, 659
Hunt, Rhoda VI, 717
Hunt, Rhoda M. IV, 94
Hunt, Richard III, 178
Hunt, Richard L. III, 178
Hunt, Richard L. III, 191
Hunt, Riley Davis V, 744
Hunt, Robert I, 1005
Hunt, Robert II, 217
Hunt, Robert II, 234
Hunt, Robert II, 247
Hunt, Robert II, 1004
Hunt, Robert II, 1019
Hunt, Robert IV, 40
Hunt, Robert IV, 94
Hunt, Robert IV, 637
Hunt, Robert V, 340
Hunt, Robert V, 369
Hunt, Robert V, 402
Hunt, Robert V, 404
Hunt, Robert V, 412
Hunt, Robert V, 578
Hunt, Robert V, 844
Hunt, Robert VI, 405
Hunt, Robert VI, 598
Hunt, Robert VI, 599
Hunt, Robert VI, 602
Hunt, Robert VI, 604
Hunt, Robert Edgar V, 405
Hunt, Robert S. V, 404
Hunt, Roger II, 553
Hunt, Roger II, 560
Hunt, Roger III, 178
Hunt, Rohda M. IV, 94
Hunt, Rosanna V, 835
Hunt, Roswel I, 887
Hunt, Ruben V, 369
Hunt, Ruth I, 502
Hunt, Ruth I, 503
Hunt, Ruth I, 549
Hunt, Ruth I, 550
Hunt, Ruth I, 551
Hunt, Ruth I, 577
Hunt, Ruth I, 964
Hunt, Ruth I, 1005
Hunt, Ruth V, 251
Hunt, Ruth V, 293
Hunt, Ruth V, 340
Hunt, Ruth V, 369
Hunt, Ruth V, 402
Hunt, Ruth V, 403
Hunt, Ruth V, 404
Hunt, Ruth V, 412
Hunt, Ruth V, 440
Hunt, Ruth V, 468
Hunt, Ruth V, 578
Hunt, Ruth V, 844
Hunt, Ruth Ann IV, 93
Hunt, Ruth Ann IV, 94
Hunt, Ruth Ann V, 79
Hunt, Ruth Ann VI, 751
Hunt, Ruth Ann VI, 774
Hunt, Ruth Anna V, 79
Hunt, Ruth Anna V, 912
Hunt, Ruth Anne V, 927
Hunt, Ruth Emaly V, 405
Hunt, Ruth Emly V, 403
Hunt, Ruth S. V, 578
Hunt, Ruth S. V, 844
Hunt, Ruthanna V, 74
Hunt, S. Emma V, 403
Hunt, Sally I, 534
Hunt, Sally I, 537
Hunt, Sally I, 551
Hunt, Sally I, 589
Hunt, Sally I, 606
Hunt, Sally I, 857
Hunt, Sally V, 622
Hunt, Sally V, 628
Hunt, Sally V, 629
Hunt, Sally VI, 827
Hunt, Sally VI, 938
Hunt, Sally VI, 973
Hunt, Sally A. I, 602
Hunt, Sally B. I, 886
Hunt, Sally B. I, 887
Hunt, Sally B. I, 912
Hunt, Sally B. I, 914
Hunt, Samira I, 886
Hunt, Samuel I, 503
Hunt, Samuel I, 550
Hunt, Samuel I, 857
Hunt, Samuel I, 886
Hunt, Samuel I, 887
Hunt, Samuel I, 1021
Hunt, Samuel I, 1032
Hunt, Samuel I, 1038
Hunt, Samuel II, 223
Hunt, Samuel II, 234
Hunt, Samuel II, 1040
Hunt, Samuel IV, 94
Hunt, Samuel IV, 226
Hunt, Samuel IV, 338
Hunt, Samuel IV, 412
Hunt, Samuel IV, 536
Hunt, Samuel V, 78
Hunt, Samuel V, 79
Hunt, Samuel VI, 599
Hunt, Samuel B. I, 857
Hunt, Samuel H. B. II, 801
Hunt, Samuel P. IV, 412
Hunt, Samuel P. IV, 447
Hunt, Samuel P. V, 79
Hunt, Sarah I, 400
Hunt, Sarah I, 409
Hunt, Sarah I, 503
Hunt, Sarah I, 549
Hunt, Sarah I, 550
Hunt, Sarah I, 551
Hunt, Sarah I, 572
Hunt, Sarah I, 579
Hunt, Sarah I, 594
Hunt, Sarah I, 596
Hunt, Sarah I, 600
Hunt, Sarah I, 602
Hunt, Sarah I, 606
Hunt, Sarah I, 659
Hunt, Sarah I, 722
Hunt, Sarah I, 811
Hunt, Sarah I, 820
Hunt, Sarah I, 865
Hunt, Sarah I, 880
Hunt, Sarah I, 886
Hunt, Sarah II, 32
Hunt, Sarah II, 81
Hunt, Sarah II, 225
Hunt, Sarah II, 234
Hunt, Sarah II, 560
Hunt, Sarah II, 879
Hunt, Sarah II, 894
Hunt, Sarah II, 1004
Hunt, Sarah III, 147
Hunt, Sarah III, 177
Hunt, Sarah III, 178
Hunt, Sarah III, 414
Hunt, Sarah III, 421
Hunt, Sarah IV, 226
Hunt, Sarah IV, 249
Hunt, Sarah IV, 967
Hunt, Sarah IV, 1282
Hunt, Sarah IV, 1322
Hunt, Sarah V, 78
Hunt, Sarah V, 79
Hunt, Sarah V, 215
Hunt, Sarah V, 250
Hunt, Sarah V, 251
Hunt, Sarah V, 305
Hunt, Sarah V, 337
Hunt, Sarah V, 340
Hunt, Sarah V, 402
Hunt, Sarah V, 403
Hunt, Sarah V, 610
Hunt, Sarah V, 629
Hunt, Sarah V, 912
Hunt, Sarah Ann IV, 1322
Hunt, Sarah Asenith V, 340
Hunt, Sarah E. V, 404
Hunt, Sarah E. V, 405
Hunt, Sarah Elen V, 403
Hunt, Sarah Ellen IV, 1282
Hunt, Sarah Ellen V, 405
Hunt, Sarah F. V, 404
Hunt, Sarah F. V, 405
Hunt, Sarah F. V, 406
Hunt, Sarah Frances III, 178
Hunt, Sarah Jr. IV, 1286
Hunt, Sarah L. V, 665
Hunt, Sarah Lydia V, 403
Hunt, Sarah R. V, 404
Hunt, Sarah R. V, 405
Hunt, Sarah Rebecca V, 405
Hunt, Sarah T. V, 686
Hunt, Sarah, Jr. IV, 1282
Hunt, Sarahann IV, 1204
Hunt, Sarahann IV, 1212
Hunt, Sary I, 820
Hunt, Selah I, 551
Hunt, Semira I, 502
Hunt, Seth IV, 40
Hunt, Seth IV, 94
Hunt, Seth IV, 226
Hunt, Seth IV, 637
Hunt, Seth IV, 725
Hunt, Seth VI, 599
Hunt, Sidney V, 410
Hunt, Sidney E. V, 403
Hunt, Silas I, 932
Hunt, Silas I, 964
Hunt, Silis V, 251
Hunt, Soloman I, 857
Hunt, Solomon I, 551
Hunt, Solomon I, 964
Hunt, Solomon II, 1004
Hunt, Solomon II, 1019
Hunt, Solomon III, 178
Hunt, Solomon V, 912
Hunt, Sopha VI, 938
Hunt, Stacy IV, 40
Hunt, Stacy IV, 93
Hunt, Stacy IV, 94
Hunt, Stacy IV, 100
Hunt, Stacy IV, 127
Hunt, Stacy IV, 637
Hunt, Stacy IV, 645
Hunt, Stacy IV, 725
Hunt, Stacy IV, 726
Hunt, Stacy IV, 752
Hunt, Stafford V, 404
Hunt, Stephanes V, 251
Hunt, Stephanus I, 785
Hunt, Stephanus I, 820
Hunt, Stephanus III, 200
Hunt, Stephanus V, 79
Hunt, Stephen I, 502
Hunt, Stephen I, 551
Hunt, Stephen I, 552
Hunt, Stephen V, 629
Hunt, Stephen VI, 937
Hunt, Stephen VI, 938
Hunt, Stephen VI, 953
Hunt, Stephen VI, 965
Hunt, Stephen F. V, 628
Hunt, Stephen W. V, 744
Hunt, Stephen, Jr. VI, 938
Hunt, Stephen, Sr. VI, 938
Hunt, Stephen, Sr. VI, 973
Hunt, Stevenus III, 178
Hunt, Strafford V, 404
Hunt, Stuart I, 820
Hunt, Sue A. V, 411
Hunt, Susan V, 403
Hunt, Susan V, 405
Hunt, Susan V, 411
Hunt, Susan V, 844
Hunt, Susan V, 859
Hunt, Susan Amelia V, 403
Hunt, Susan Elizabeth V, 402
Hunt, Susanna I, 550
Hunt, Susanna I, 551
Hunt, Susanna I, 552
Hunt, Susanna I, 582
Hunt, Susanna I, 1005
Hunt, Susanna I, 1009
Hunt, Susanna I, 1010
Hunt, Susanna V, 402
Hunt, Susanna V, 883
Hunt, Susanna V, 885
Hunt, Susanna B. V, 844
Hunt, Susannah I, 551
Hunt, Susannah V, 78
Hunt, Susannah V, 79
Hunt, Susannah V, 403
Hunt, Susannah V, 431
Hunt, Susannah B. V, 883
Hunt, Susannah E. V, 629
Hunt, Susannah Elizabeth V, 405
Hunt, Susannah G. V, 403
Hunt, Sylvia V, 383
Hunt, Sylvia V, 403
Hunt, Sylvia V, 405
Hunt, Sylvia Belle V, 844
Hunt, T. Clarkson V, 405
Hunt, T. E. V, 686
Hunt, Tabitha III, 178
Hunt, Theodore V, 440
Hunt, Thomas I, 321
Hunt, Thomas I, 343
Hunt, Thomas I, 344
Hunt, Thomas I, 502
Hunt, Thomas I, 503
Hunt, Thomas I, 549
Hunt, Thomas I, 550
Hunt, Thomas I, 552
Hunt, Thomas I, 600
Hunt, Thomas I, 602
Hunt, Thomas I, 606
Hunt, Thomas I, 682
Hunt, Thomas I, 692
Hunt, Thomas I, 722
Hunt, Thomas I, 886
Hunt, Thomas I, 964
Hunt, Thomas I, 1005
Hunt, Thomas I, 1009
Hunt, Thomas I, 1010
Hunt, Thomas II, 32
Hunt, Thomas III, 175
Hunt, Thomas IV, 412

unt, Thomas IV, 1370
unt, Thomas V, 79
unt, Thomas V, 340
unt, Thomas V, 369
unt, Thomas V, 396
unt, Thomas V, 402
unt, Thomas V, 403
unt, Thomas V, 404
unt, Thomas V, 405
unt, Thomas V, 431
unt, Thomas V, 578
unt, Thomas VI, 513
unt, Thomas VI, 938
unt, Thomas Camm V, 79
unt, Thomas Clarkson V, 403
unt, Thomas Clarkson V, 404
unt, Thomas E. V, 403
unt, Thomas Elwood V, 405
unt, Thomas Elwood V, 629
unt, Thomas Ensley V, 404
unt, Thomas French IV, 40
unt, Thomas I. V, 405
unt, Thomas I. V, 686
unt, Thomas J. V, 403
unt, Thomas J. V, 405
unt, Thomas P. V, 404
unt, Thomas T. I, 552
unt, Thomas T. I, 857
unt, Thomas T. I, 887
unt, Thomas T. I, 912
unt, Thomas T. I, 914
unt, Thomas T. V, 404
unt, Thomas, II I, 551
unt, Thomas, Jr. V, 404
unt, Thos. I, 502
unt, Thos. Elwood V, 629
unt, Timothy V, 404
unt, Uriah I, 503
unt, Uriah I, 550
unt, Uriah I, 551
unt, Uriah I, 785
unt, Uriah I, 820
unt, Uriah II, 379
unt, Uriah II, 560
unt, Uriah II, 725
unt, Uriah II, 747
unt, Uriah II, 812
unt, Uriah II, 879
unt, Uriah II, 906
unt, Uriah II, 912
unt, Uriah V, 78
unt, Uriah V, 251
unt, Valeria M. II, 880
unt, Valeria Maud II, 801
unt, W. P. IV, 1269
unt, Walker II, 809
unt, Walter D. V, 404
unt, Wd. Elizabeth II, 801
unt, Wd. Lot III, 178
unt, Widow Miriam I, 820
unt, Will V, 404
unt, Willet H. II, 311
unt, Willet H. II, 321
unt, William I, 343
unt, William I, 400
unt, William I, 409
unt, William I, 487
unt, William I, 502
unt, William I, 503
unt, William I, 550
unt, William I, 551
unt, William I, 552
unt, William I, 820
unt, William I, 847
unt, William I, 887
unt, William II, 32
unt, William II, 234
unt, William II, 249
unt, William II, 379
unt, William II, 708
unt, William IV, 93
unt, William IV, 94
unt, William IV, 127
unt, William IV, 412
unt, William IV, 725
unt, William V, 403
unt, William V, 405
unt, William VI, 250
unt, William VI, 405
unt, William VI, 524
unt, William VI, 599
unt, William B. I, 552
unt, William C. I, 602
unt, William H. V, 405
unt, William Henry V, 403
unt, William L. III, 178
unt, William L. III, 257
unt, William Lindley V, 403
unt, William S. V, 402
unt, William S. V, 403
unt, William S. V, 404
Hunt, William Sewel I, 1005
Hunt, William Sewel V, 404
Hunt, William T. V, 405
Hunt, William, II I, 550
Hunt, William, III I, 550
Hunt, William, Jr. I, 550
Hunt, Wilson I, 503
Hunt, Wilson V, 629
Hunt, Wilson A. V, 405
Hunt, Wilson A. V, 629
Hunt, Wilson H. V, 404
Hunt, Wm. I, 503
Hunt, Wm. I, 568
Hunt, Wm. II, 81
Hunt, Wm. II, 275
Hunt, Wm. II, 560
Hunt, Wm. II, 879
Hunt, Wm. II, 912
Hunt, Wm. II, 1004
Hunt, Wm. II, 1040
Hunt, Wm. IV, 127
Hunt, Wm. IV, 725
Hunt, Wm. V, 396
Hunt, Wm. V, 629
Hunt, Wm. VI, 513
Hunt, Wm. C. II, 879
Hunt, Wm. Henry V, 405
Hunt, Wm. L. III, 178
Hunt, Wm. L. V, 629
Hunt, Wm. P. IV, 1282
Hunt, Wm. P. IV, 1286
Hunt, Wm. S. V, 393
Hunt, Wm., Jr. II, 879
Hunt, Wright V, 404
Hunt, Zebalond I, 857
Hunt, Zebulon I, 503
Hunt, Zebulon I, 886
Hunt, Zimri I, 502
Hunt, Zimri I, 503
Hunt, Zimri I, 537
Hunt, Zimri I, 550
Hunt, Zimri I, 551
Hunt, Zodack I, 502
Hunte, Elezabeath I, 91
Hunte, Francis I, 91
Hunte, Jeams I, 91
Hunte, John I, 91
Hunter, ??? I, 11
Hunter, ??? III, 63
Hunter, A. W. VI, 936
Hunter, A. W. VI, 944
Hunter, Abraham VI, 977
Hunter, Absalom VI, 915
Hunter, Absalom VI, 938
Hunter, Adaline VI, 805
Hunter, Aeneas VI, 938
Hunter, Alexander VI, 827
Hunter, Alexander VI, 830
Hunter, Alexander VI, 838
Hunter, Alexr. VI, 938
Hunter, Alice VI, 827
Hunter, Amy III, 179
Hunter, Andrew VI, 880
Hunter, Andrew VI, 967
Hunter, Andrew VI, 978
Hunter, Andrew VI, 983
Hunter, Andrew VI, 989
Hunter, Ann II, 560
Hunter, Ann Wilson VI, 811
Hunter, Anna III, 178
Hunter, Anna III, 223
Hunter, Austin W. VI, 960
Hunter, Barbara IV, 726
Hunter, Ben. VI, 833
Hunter, Benj. VI, 805
Hunter, Benjamin VI, 813
Hunter, Benjamin VI, 814
Hunter, Benjamin VI, 823
Hunter, Benjamin VI, 827
Hunter, Benjamin VI, 838
Hunter, Benjamin VI, 866
Hunter, Betsy VI, 827
Hunter, Catharine VI, 855
Hunter, Charlotte S. VI, 936
Hunter, Deborah III, 178
Hunter, Delphia VI, 339
Hunter, Delphia VI, 997
Hunter, Dr. John VI, 827
Hunter, Edney VI, 827
Hunter, Edward VI, 827
Hunter, Edward VI, 833
Hunter, Edward VI, 938
Hunter, Eileen IV, 726
Hunter, Elisabeth I, 11
Hunter, Elisabeth I, 54
Hunter, Elisabeth I, 69
Hunter, Eliz. III, 37
Hunter, Eliza Ann VI, 938
Hunter, Eliza M. VI, 815
Hunter, Elizabeth I, 54
Hunter, Elizabeth III, 178
Hunter, Elizabeth III, 223
Hunter, Elizabeth IV, 40
Hunter, Elizabeth IV, 150
Hunter, Elizabeth IV, 726
Hunter, Elizabeth V, 1003
Hunter, Elizabeth VI, 659
Hunter, Elizabeth VI, 823
Hunter, Elizabeth VI, 835
Hunter, Elizabeth VI, 959
Hunter, Elizabeth VI, 1017
Hunter, Elizabeth T. VI, 970
Hunter, Ellis VI, 825
Hunter, Ellis VI, 827
Hunter, Ellis VI, 851
Hunter, Elmer IV, 726
Hunter, Elsa VI, 893
Hunter, Elvira VI, 838
Hunter, Emily II, 786
Hunter, Frances E. III, 356
Hunter, Francis VI, 893
Hunter, Francis VI, 927
Hunter, Francis VI, 938
Hunter, Francis VI, 960
Hunter, Francis VI, 1017
Hunter, Francis VI, 1021
Hunter, Frank V, 341
Hunter, George II, 379
Hunter, George III, 179
Hunter, George VI, 835
Hunter, Grace IV, 726
Hunter, Gulielma III, 178
Hunter, Gulielma III, 179
Hunter, Hannah III, 178
Hunter, Harieta VI, 813
Hunter, Harriett V, 405
Hunter, Harry V, 745
Hunter, Henry III, 178
Hunter, Henry L. III, 179
Hunter, Hugh IV, 40
Hunter, Hugh IV, 150
Hunter, Hugh VI, 659
Hunter, Ida Rebecca I, 54
Hunter, Isabella II, 293
Hunter, Isabella III, 178
Hunter, Isabella III, 179
Hunter, James II, 880
Hunter, James III, 178
Hunter, James III, 179
Hunter, James VI, 751
Hunter, James VI, 827
Hunter, James VI, 835
Hunter, James Ellsberry I, 54
Hunter, James H. I, 54
Hunter, James T. VI, 751
Hunter, James, Jr. VI, 751
Hunter, James, Jr. VI, 786
Hunter, James, Jr. VI, 787
Hunter, Jane V, 1003
Hunter, Jane VI, 827
Hunter, Jane VI, 938
Hunter, Jane M. VI, 834
Hunter, Jane S. VI, 851
Hunter, Jemima H. VI, 827
Hunter, Jerome A. VI, 930
Hunter, Jno. II, 747
Hunter, John II, 560
Hunter, John III, 148
Hunter, John III, 179
Hunter, John III, 223
Hunter, John VI, 816
Hunter, John VI, 827
Hunter, John VI, 830
Hunter, John VI, 938
Hunter, John VI, 959
Hunter, John J. VI, 827
Hunter, John J. VI, 834
Hunter, John L. I, 54
Hunter, John Lucius I, 54
Hunter, John R. II, 801
Hunter, John R. II, 880
Hunter, John, Jr. VI, 959
Hunter, Jonathan III, 179
Hunter, Joseph III, 179
Hunter, Joseph Henry Riddick I, 54
Hunter, Louisa J. VI, 806
Hunter, Louise VI, 827
Hunter, Lucy VI, 938
Hunter, Lucy W. VI, 940
Hunter, Malinda W. VI, 827
Hunter, Margaret VI, 814
Hunter, Margaret D. II, 880
Hunter, Margaret Divine II, 880
Hunter, Margaret F. VI, 830
Hunter, Marshall C. III, 291
Hunter, Martha VI, 751
Hunter, Martha VI, 938
Hunter, Mary I, 400
Hunter, Mary I, 618
Hunter, Mary I, 1028
Hunter, Mary I, 1032
Hunter, Mary II, 293
Hunter, Mary III, 148
Hunter, Mary III, 178
Hunter, Mary III, 179
Hunter, Mary III, 272
Hunter, Mary V, 303
Hunter, Mary V, 305
Hunter, Mary VI, 811
Hunter, Mary VI, 827
Hunter, Mary VI, 838
Hunter, Mary VI, 1021
Hunter, Mary A. Y. VI, 836
Hunter, Mary Isadore I, 54
Hunter, Mary J. I, 54
Hunter, Mary J. I, 58
Hunter, Mary Jane I, 11
Hunter, Mary Jane I, 54
Hunter, Mary Jane VI, 938
Hunter, Mary, Jr. II, 293
Hunter, Mary, Jr. III, 179
Hunter, Matilda III, 179
Hunter, Matilda VI, 833
Hunter, Miss ??? VI, 938
Hunter, Nancy IV, 1103
Hunter, Nancy IV, 1106
Hunter, Nancy VI, 798
Hunter, Nancy VI, 823
Hunter, Nancy VI, 827
Hunter, Nancy VI, 830
Hunter, Nancy VI, 961
Hunter, Nancy C. VI, 960
Hunter, Nancy J. VI, 830
Hunter, Orin IV, 726
Hunter, Orrin Alex IV, 726
Hunter, Pamelia VI, 927
Hunter, Paulina A. VI, 827
Hunter, Peggy VI, 870
Hunter, Peter III, 291
Hunter, Peter VI, 339
Hunter, Peter VI, 827
Hunter, Peter VI, 870
Hunter, Peter VI, 938
Hunter, Peter VI, 940
Hunter, Peter VI, 961
Hunter, Peter VI, 970
Hunter, Peter VI, 997
Hunter, Peter VI, 1021
Hunter, Peter, Jr. VI, 938
Hunter, Phebe II, 379
Hunter, Priestly II, 379
Hunter, Rachel VI, 816
Hunter, Rachel VI, 827
Hunter, Rachel VI, 866
Hunter, Rachel D. III, 63
Hunter, Rachel D. III, 179
Hunter, Rachel D. III, 257
Hunter, Rebecca I, 54
Hunter, Rebecca VI, 751
Hunter, Rebecca VI, 786
Hunter, Rebecca VI, 787
Hunter, Rebekah II, 53
Hunter, Rebekah II, 81
Hunter, Ro. VI, 829
Hunter, Robert VI, 798
Hunter, Robert VI, 827
Hunter, Robert VI, 851
Hunter, Robert VI, 855
Hunter, Robert Freeling I, 54
Hunter, Robert, Jr. VI, 795
Hunter, Sally VI, 938
Hunter, Sally Lewis VI, 827
Hunter, Samuel VI, 1017
Hunter, Sarah II, 560
Hunter, Sarah II, 651
Hunter, Sarah III, 148
Hunter, Sarah VI, 827
Hunter, Sarah VI, 1017
Hunter, Sarah A. B. VI, 827
Hunter, Sarah E. VI, 751
Hunter, Sarah M. VI, 827
Hunter, Selina VI, 829
Hunter, Selina M. VI, 820
Hunter, Stephen VI, 898
Hunter, Stephen VI, 938
Hunter, Susan II, 293
Hunter, Susan VI, 938
Hunter, Susan M. VI, 827
Hunter, Susanna II, 293
Hunter, Susanna III, 179
Hunter, Susanna VI, 938
Hunter, Sussana III, 291
Hunter, Tamar III, 148
Hunter, Tamar III, 179
Hunter, Thomas III, 178
Hunter, Thomas VI, 815
Hunter, Thomas VI, 820
Hunter, Thomas VI, 827
Hunter, Thomas VI, 830
Hunter, Thos. VI, 806
Hunter, Thos. E. VI, 830
Hunter, Virginia Eileen IV, 726
Hunter, Washington VI, 820
Hunter, Washington VI, 822
Hunter, Washington VI, 823
Hunter, Wd. Mary III, 179
Hunter, William II, 379
Hunter, William III, 178
Hunter, William III, 179
Hunter, William VI, 805
Hunter, William VI, 834
Hunter, William VI, 836
Hunter, William Harvey I, 54
Hunter, Wm. II, 560
Hunter, Wm. V, 1003
Hunter, Wm. H. V, 1003
Huntington, Alice G. IV, 1370
Huntington, Allice G. IV, 1370
Huntington, Anna IV, 1354
Huntington, Anna IV, 1370
Huntington, Anna IV, 1371
Huntington, Anna H. IV, 1370
Huntington, Benjamin Boyce IV, 1371
Huntington, Catharine IV, 1371
Huntington, Eunice III, 179
Huntington, Francis C. III, 179
Huntington, Mary R. III, 353
Huntington, Prescott B. III, 179
Huntington, Prescott B. III, 258
Huntington, Sarah III, 179
Huntington, Sarah H. III, 179
Huntington, Sarah H. III, 258
Huntington, Susan Louisa III, 179
Huntley, Elijah V, 912
Huntley, Eva A. IV, 633
Huntley, Eva A. IV, 637
Huntley, Margaret IV, 826
Huntley, Margaret IV, 844
Huntley, Margaret R. IV, 826
Huntley, Margaret Steer IV, 826
Huntley, Mary C. IV, 826
Huntley, Ralph T. IV, 826
Huntley, Wilson J. IV, 826
Huntsman, Deborah II, 379
Huntsman, John II, 379
Huntsman, Mary V, 733
Huntsman, Susannah II, 445
Hupp, Phebe IV, 40
Hupp, Phebe IV, 42
Hurd, Albert IV, 967
Hurd, Hannah II, 560
Hurd, James II, 560
Hurd, Kate IV, 967
Hurd, Patsey VI, 859
Hurd, Robert V, 79
Hurd, Rosamond V, 79
Hurd, Susannah II, 560
Hurdle, Susanna VI, 751
Hurdle, Susanna VI, 764
Hurfley, Edith V, 504
Hurfley, Ethel V, 504
Hurfley, Howard Noah V, 504
Hurfley, Ida V, 504
Hurfley, Jerema D. V, 504
Hurfley, Vella V, 504
Hurford, Alonzo R. IV, 226
Hurford, Amy IV, 208
Hurford, Amy IV, 226
Hurford, Ann IV, 226
Hurford, Ann IV, 299
Hurford, Ann IV, 555
Hurford, Ann VI, 599
Hurford, Anna Jane IV, 226
Hurford, Anna Jane IV, 263
Hurford, Anne J. IV, 226
Hurford, Annie J. IV, 226
Hurford, Aquilla IV, 226
Hurford, Aquilla IV, 249
Hurford, Benjamin VI, 599
Hurford, Catharine VI, 599
Hurford, Catherine VI, 599
Hurford, Catherine VI, 601
Hurford, Christiana IV, 218
Hurford, Christiana IV, 226
Hurford, Edgar B. IV, 226
Hurford, Edgar J. IV, 226
Hurford, Elizabeth VI, 599
Hurford, Evan IV, 212
Hurford, Evan IV, 218
Hurford, Evan IV, 226
Hurford, Evan IV, 272
Hurford, Hannah II, 379
Hurford, Hannah II, 560
Hurford, Hannah IV, 214
Hurford, Hannah IV, 226
Hurford, Hannah VI, 592
Hurford, Hannah VI, 599
Hurford, Hannah VI, 603
Hurford, Hannah VI, 660
Hurford, Hannah VI, 690
Hurford, Hannah B. IV, 266

Hurford, Isaac VI, 405
Hurford, Joel IV, 726
Hurford, John II, 550
Hurford, John II, 560
Hurford, John II, 1004
Hurford, John IV, 173
Hurford, John IV, 226
Hurford, John IV, 264
Hurford, John IV, 299
Hurford, John VI, 599
Hurford, John H. IV, 208
Hurford, John H. IV, 226
Hurford, John R. IV, 226
Hurford, John, Jr. II, 560
Hurford, Joseph VI, 599
Hurford, Joseph VI, 603
Hurford, Joseph VI, 660
Hurford, Joseph VI, 690
Hurford, July Ann II, 550
Hurford, July Ann II, 560
Hurford, K. IV, 226
Hurford, Keziah IV, 226
Hurford, Mary IV, 173
Hurford, Mary IV, 226
Hurford, Mary IV, 510
Hurford, Mary IV, 536
Hurford, Mary A. IV, 226
Hurford, Mary Ann IV, 272
Hurford, Naomi VI, 592
Hurford, Naomi VI, 599
Hurford, Naomi VI, 603
Hurford, Naomi VI, 690
Hurford, Nathan VI, 599
Hurford, Rachel IV, 150
Hurford, Rachel IV, 226
Hurford, Rachel IV, 249
Hurford, Rachel IV, 253
Hurford, Rachel IV, 264
Hurford, Rachel IV, 338
Hurford, Rachel IV, 346
Hurford, Rachel VI, 599
Hurford, Rachel Elizabeth VI, 599
Hurford, Rachel T. IV, 226
Hurford, Ruth IV, 150
Hurford, Ruth IV, 160
Hurford, Ruth VI, 599
Hurford, Samuel II, 379
Hurford, Samuel II, 560
Hurford, Samuel IV, 226
Hurford, Samuel IV, 266
Hurford, Samuel VI, 352
Hurford, Samuel VI, 405
Hurford, Samuel VI, 592
Hurford, Samuel VI, 599
Hurford, Sarah IV, 150
Hurford, Sarah IV, 173
Hurford, Sarah IV, 200
Hurford, Sarah IV, 212
Hurford, Sarah IV, 218
Hurford, Sarah IV, 226
Hurford, Sarah IV, 264
Hurford, Sarah IV, 272
Hurford, Sarah IV, 299
Hurford, Sarah IV, 478
Hurford, Sarah IV, 494
Hurford, Sarah VI, 599
Hurford, Sarah Ann IV, 226
Hurford, Sarah Ann IV, 274
Hurford, Susannah II, 560
Hurford, Thomas VI, 599
Hurford, Wd. Naomi VI, 592
Hurford, William VI, 599
Hurl, John IV, 478
Hurl, John G. IV, 226
Hurlburt, Anna R. III, 112
Hurlburt, Anna R. III, 179
Hurlburt, Beulah E. III, 179
Hurlburt, Hiram III, 179
Hurlburt, Lawrence III, 112
Hurlburt, Lawrence III, 179
Hurlburt, M. Antoinette III, 179
Hurlburt, Utica III, 179
Hurley, ??? IV, 1166
Hurley, Aaron A. II, 812
Hurley, Arthur V, 180
Hurley, Arthur W. V, 180
Hurley, Benjamin V, 180
Hurley, Carrie V, 180
Hurley, Charles V, 180
Hurley, Chas. A. V, 180
Hurley, Chatta IV, 1167
Hurley, Chattie IV, 1167
Hurley, Cleo May IV, 1282
Hurley, Cleo May V, 180
Hurley, Cory W. V, 180
Hurley, Derward IV, 1167
Hurley, Donald Herbert V, 180
Hurley, Donald Hubert IV, 1282
Hurley, Durward IV, 1166
Hurley, Durward IV, 1167
Hurley, Durward O. IV, 1167
Hurley, Edgar V, 180
Hurley, Edgar V, 686
Hurley, Elizabeth V, 504
Hurley, Elizabeth B. II, 812
Hurley, Ella V, 213
Hurley, Ernest E. V, 213
Hurley, Evaline Edith IV, 1282
Hurley, Evelyn Edith V, 180
Hurley, Florence IV, 1282
Hurley, Francis V, 180
Hurley, Francis W. V, 180
Hurley, Frank M. IV, 1167
Hurley, George V, 180
Hurley, George S. V, 180
Hurley, Glenna S. V, 180
Hurley, Harriet IV, 1166
Hurley, Harriet IV, 1167
Hurley, Harriett IV, 1167
Hurley, Henry II, 81
Hurley, Henry II, 92
Hurley, Henry V, 180
Hurley, Henry M. V, 180
Hurley, Henry T. I, 928
Hurley, Hortense V, 180
Hurley, James II, 802
Hurley, James C. V, 180
Hurley, Jennie V, 213
Hurley, Kenneth IV, 1282
Hurley, Kenneth J. V, 180
Hurley, Laura E. V, 180
Hurley, Lauretta V, 180
Hurley, Lenna IV, 1282
Hurley, Lucy II, 802
Hurley, Maggie D. V, 180
Hurley, Mamie V, 180
Hurley, Margaret II, 841
Hurley, Mary II, 81
Hurley, Mary II, 92
Hurley, Mary II, 812
Hurley, Mary V, 180
Hurley, Mary L. V, 180
Hurley, Pauline IV, 1282
Hurley, Pauline Florence V, 180
Hurley, Ralph V, 504
Hurley, Raymond IV, 1282
Hurley, Raymond V, 180
Hurley, Robert IV, 1167
Hurley, Robert B. IV, 1167
Hurley, Rosa A. V, 180
Hurley, Ruhanna I, 928
Hurley, Russell V, 180
Hurley, Ruth Alma IV, 1282
Hurley, Ruth Elma V, 180
Hurley, Sarah II, 802
Hurley, Sarah V, 180
Hurley, Viola IV, 1282
Hurley, Viola V, 180
Hurley, William I, 943
Hurley, William V, 180
Hurley, William W. I, 928
Hurley, Wm. H. I, 943
Hurley, Wm. H. V, 180
Hurlinger, Eli V, 1003
Hurlow, Martha Adelia IV, 1167
Hurman, Deborah II, 293
Hurshman, Angelina V, 1003
Hurshman, James V, 1003
Hurst, Abigail II, 1074
Hurst, Abigail II, 1083
Hurst, Ann IV, 221
Hurst, Asenath IV, 221
Hurst, David IV, 221
Hurst, Elinor II, 379
Hurst, Elinor II, 445
Hurst, Elizabeth J. IV, 1282
Hurst, Esther H. IV, 530
Hurst, Hannah IV, 335
Hurst, Hannah IV, 340
Hurst, Israel IV, 221
Hurst, Israel Wilson IV, 530
Hurst, John IV, 221
Hurst, John IV, 530
Hurst, Lidia II, 1003
Hurst, Lidia II, 1004
Hurst, Lydia VI, 511
Hurst, Lydia VI, 587
Hurst, Martha II, 379
Hurst, Mary IV, 221
Hurst, Miriah IV, 530
Hurst, Phebe IV, 358
Hurst, Rachel IV, 221
Hurst, Sarah II, 560
Hurst, Smith IV, 221
Hurst, Thomas II, 379
Hurst, Thomas II, 445
Hurst, Thomas IV, 221
Hurst, Thomas VI, 599
Hurst, William II, 379
Hurt, Ann Matilda VI, 914
Hurt, Anna VI, 914
Hurt, Betsy Ann VI, 938
Hurt, Catey VI, 918
Hurt, Catharine P. VI, 828
Hurt, Catherine VI, 969
Hurt, Charles VI, 938
Hurt, Charlotte VI, 938
Hurt, Colby VI, 938
Hurt, Colby VI, 954
Hurt, Coleby VI, 935
Hurt, Elijah VI, 895
Hurt, Elijah VI, 906
Hurt, Elijah VI, 938
Hurt, Elijah VI, 952
Hurt, Elijah VI, 954
Hurt, Elijah VI, 980
Hurt, Elijah VI, 1015
Hurt, Elisha VI, 938
Hurt, Elisha VI, 980
Hurt, Elisha VI, 1000
Hurt, Elisha VI, 1007
Hurt, Eliza B. VI, 1003
Hurt, Elizabeth VI, 809
Hurt, Elizabeth VI, 828
Hurt, Elizabeth VI, 938
Hurt, Elizabeth W. VI, 967
Hurt, Elvira VI, 962
Hurt, Florentine M. VI, 929
Hurt, Fountain G. VI, 939
Hurt, Frances III, 54
Hurt, Frances VI, 938
Hurt, Frances Amanda VI, 939
Hurt, Garland VI, 828
Hurt, Garland VI, 904
Hurt, Garland VI, 918
Hurt, Garland VI, 1006
Hurt, George VI, 1007
Hurt, George W. VI, 828
Hurt, Ginny VI, 995
Hurt, Hastings H. III, 54
Hurt, Henry VI, 938
Hurt, Henry VI, 972
Hurt, Ira VI, 954
Hurt, J. VI, 910
Hurt, James VI, 795
Hurt, James VI, 803
Hurt, James VI, 806
Hurt, James VI, 836
Hurt, James VI, 837
Hurt, James VI, 845
Hurt, James VI, 889
Hurt, James VI, 904
Hurt, James VI, 914
Hurt, James VI, 938
Hurt, James VI, 947
Hurt, James VI, 954
Hurt, James VI, 999
Hurt, James T. VI, 806
Hurt, Jane VI, 939
Hurt, Jenny VI, 938
Hurt, Joel VI, 938
Hurt, Joel L. VI, 939
Hurt, John VI, 806
Hurt, John VI, 809
Hurt, John VI, 828
Hurt, John VI, 924
Hurt, John VI, 938
Hurt, John VI, 969
Hurt, John VI, 985
Hurt, John VI, 999
Hurt, John P. VI, 939
Hurt, John W. VI, 889
Hurt, John W. VI, 929
Hurt, Josephus VI, 938
Hurt, Joshua C. VI, 939
Hurt, Joshua C. VI, 985
Hurt, Joshua C. VI, 999
Hurt, Josiah VI, 938
Hurt, Judith G. VI, 939
Hurt, Laura III, 54
Hurt, Lawson VI, 938
Hurt, Lawson S. VI, 970
Hurt, Littleberry VI, 954
Hurt, Locky L. VI, 939
Hurt, Lucinda VI, 938
Hurt, Lucy VI, 935
Hurt, Lucy O. VI, 938
Hurt, Marcia VI, 828
Hurt, Mariah Frances VI, 939
Hurt, Martha A. VI, 806
Hurt, Mary VI, 845
Hurt, Mary VI, 938
Hurt, Mary VI, 939
Hurt, Mary A. VI, 973
Hurt, Mary Ann VI, 999
Hurt, Matilda VI, 806
Hurt, Mildred VI, 968
Hurt, Mildred Jane VI, 879
Hurt, Mildred S. VI, 889
Hurt, Mille VI, 914
Hurt, Milley VI, 995
Hurt, Milley VI, 1007
Hurt, Nancy VI, 923
Hurt, Nancy VI, 929
Hurt, Nancy VI, 938
Hurt, Nancy VI, 999
Hurt, Narcissa VI, 939
Hurt, Obedience VI, 902
Hurt, Obedience VI, 904
Hurt, Patience VI, 836
Hurt, Polly VI, 859
Hurt, Polly VI, 938
Hurt, Polly VI, 954
Hurt, Polly VI, 1000
Hurt, Polly VI, 1013
Hurt, Polly H. VI, 837
Hurt, Polly J. VI, 938
Hurt, Rhoda VI, 938
Hurt, Robert VI, 828
Hurt, Robert B. VI, 938
Hurt, Ruth VI, 315
Hurt, Ruth VI, 972
Hurt, Sally VI, 980
Hurt, Sally VI, 1006
Hurt, Sarah VI, 939
Hurt, Sarah VI, 985
Hurt, Sarah M. VI, 953
Hurt, Senah VI, 938
Hurt, Sophia Jane VI, 924
Hurt, Stephen C. VI, 939
Hurt, Stephen S. VI, 939
Hurt, Susan Jane VI, 938
Hurt, Tabitha I. VI, 910
Hurt, Tempe VI, 889
Hurt, Temperance VI, 975
Hurt, Thomas VI, 909
Hurt, Thomas VI, 939
Hurt, Thomas VI, 968
Hurt, Thomas VI, 973
Hurt, William VI, 879
Hurt, William VI, 938
Hurt, William VI, 953
Hurt, William VI, 995
Hurt, William VI, 1000
Hurt, William C. VI, 837
Hurt, William O. VI, 938
Hurt, William O. VI, 939
Hurt, Wm. O. VI, 918
Hurt, Wm. O. VI, 1020
Hurt, Wm. S. VI, 929
Hurvey, Charles III, 64
Hurvey, Charles III, 179
Hurvey, Sarah Ann III, 64
Hurvey, Sarah Ann III, 179
Hurvis, Hannah E. IV, 1167
Husband, Abigail II, 880
Husband, Anna II, 810
Husband, Anna II, 880
Husband, Edward II, 880
Husband, Hannah II, 802
Husband, Hannah III, 179
Husband, Hannah III, 277
Husband, Hannah III, 282
Husband, Hannah Ann II, 880
Husband, Hannah R. II, 880
Husband, Herman I, 400
Husband, Herman I Sup 1, 9
Husband, John Finnister II, 880
Husband, John, Jr. II, 880
Husband, Joseph P. II, 880
Husband, Margaret I. II, 880
Husband, Margaret J. II, 802
Husband, Mary II, 802
Husband, Mary II, 880
Husband, Mary R. II, 880
Husband, Mary R. III, 179
Husband, Mary R. III, 282
Husband, Sarah W. II, 880
Husband, Thomas J. II, 802
Husband, Thos J. III, 282
Husband, Thos. J. II, 880
Husband, Thos. J. III, 179
Husband, William I, 400
Husband, Wm. Savery II, 880
Husbands, Amy I, 370
Husbands, Amy I, 400
Husbands, Emy I, 370
Husbands, Emy I, 400
Husbands, Herman I, 400
Husbands, Herman I, 416
Husbands, Mary I, 400
Husbands, Mary I, 416
Husbands, William I, 400
Huse, Alice II, 558
Huse, Henry II, 558
Huse, Littleberry VI, 828
Huse, Rachel II, 78
Huse, Sarah II, 78
Huse, Winney VI, 828
Husey, Drucilla V, 305
Husey, George IV, 637
Husey, John II, 802
Husker, William II, 230
Huskins, Anna M. V, 627
Huskins, Eli V, 249
Huskins, Hannah V, 249
Huskins, Isaac V, 249
Huskins, Jane V, 614
Huskins, John V, 249
Huskins, Joseph V, 249
Huskins, Moses V, 249
Huskins, Moses, Jr. V, 249
Huskins, Ruth V, 249
Huskins, William V, 249
Hussaack, Mary II, 511
Hussaack, Mary II, 561
Hussack, Mary II, 561
Hussea, Martha I, 400
Hussea, Sarah I, 400
Hussey, Abby H. III, 179
Hussey, Adaline V, 342
Hussey, Adaline V, 351
Hussey, Adison V, 341
Hussey, Adison V, 810
Hussey, Agatha I, 717
Hussey, Agatha I, 722
Hussey, Alexander T. IV, 726
Hussey, Alfred V, 341
Hussey, Alfred V, 810
Hussey, Alonzo V, 341
Hussey, Alonzo V, 810
Hussey, Amos V, 79
Hussey, Angeline IV, 227
Hussey, Ann I, 348
Hussey, Ann I, 400
Hussey, Ann I, 504
Hussey, Ann I, 552
Hussey, Ann L. IV, 288
Hussey, Anna II, 1085
Hussey, Anna II, 1087
Hussey, Anna II, 1088
Hussey, Anna M. IV, 227
Hussey, Anna R. V, 342
Hussey, Anne I, 1058
Hussey, Annie II, 948
Hussey, Annie V, 342
Hussey, Asael IV, 478
Hussey, Asahel IV, 227
Hussey, Asahel IV, 479
Hussey, Asahel H. IV, 227
Hussey, Asahel H. IV, 256
Hussey, Barzilla III, 127
Hussey, Barzilla III, 180
Hussey, Benj. B. III, 367
Hussey, Benjamin B. III, 179
Hussey, Benjamin B. III, 180
Hussey, Benjamin S. IV, 188
Hussey, Bethiah III, 179
Hussey, Betsy I, 552
Hussey, Betsy V, 341
Hussey, Beulah I, 551
Hussey, Beulah I, 552
Hussey, Catharine I, 552
Hussey, Charles V, 341
Hussey, Charles V, 810
Hussey, Charlotte B. IV, 726
Hussey, Charlotte M. IV, 794
Hussey, Chas. A. V, 810
Hussey, Christopher I, 348
Hussey, Christopher I, 400
Hussey, Christopher I, 504
Hussey, Christopher IV, 176
Hussey, Christopher IV, 260
Hussey, Christopher IV, 263
Hussey, Christopher IV, 288
Hussey, Christopher IV, 478
Hussey, Christopher V, 79
Hussey, Christopher V, 180
Hussey, Christopher V, 251
Hussey, Christopher V, 289
Hussey, Christopher V, 320
Hussey, Christopher V, 332
Hussey, Christopher V, 341
Hussey, Christopher V, 345
Hussey, Christopher V, 899
Hussey, Christopher V, 901
Hussey, Christopher VI, 513
Hussey, Christopher, Jr. V, 341
Hussey, Cornelia III, 80
Hussey, Curtis IV, 227
Hussey, Curtis G. IV, 227
Hussey, Cyrus V, 341
Hussey, Cyrus V, 810
Hussey, Daniel I, 651
Hussey, Daniel IV, 227
Hussey, David C. III, 179
Hussey, Drucilla V, 322
Hussey, Drucilla V, 341
Hussey, Drusilla V, 299
Hussey, Drusilla V, 341
Hussey, Earl V, 251
Hussey, Edith II, 561
Hussey, Edith II, 687
Hussey, Edith L. IV, 794

ussey, Edmee A. III, 179
ussey, Edmee Alcine III, 85
ussey, Edward III, 179
ussey, Edwin V, 341
ussey, Eli I, 552
ussey, Eli I, 722
ussey, Elisha V, 79
ussey, Eliza I, 912
ussey, Eliza IV, 227
ussey, Eliza V, 251
ussey, Eliza V, 342
ussey, Eliza M. IV, 75
ussey, Eliza M. IV, 94
ussey, Eliza M. IV, 176
ussey, Eliza M. IV, 226
ussey, Elizabeth I, 348
ussey, Elizabeth I, 381
ussey, Elizabeth I, 400
ussey, Elizabeth I, 504
ussey, Elizabeth III, 179
ussey, Elizabeth Ann V, 341
ussey, Ella V, 342
ussey, Elma IV, 726
ussey, Elwood V, 79
ussey, Emanuel I, 504
ussey, Emanuel I, 912
ussey, Emily Ann II, 561
ussey, Emily Ann II, 708
ussey, Emily C. IV, 726
ussey, Emily C. IV, 729
ussey, Erastus IV, 1370
ussey, Esther II, 493
ussey, Esther II, 561
ussey, Esther N. V, 341
ussey, Esther N. V, 810
ussey, Eunice V, 341
ussey, Eunice V, 363
ussey, Frank V, 342
ussey, Frank E. V, 342
ussey, Geo. III, 180
ussey, Geo. F. III, 180
ussey, Geo. T. III, 70
ussey, George III, 179
ussey, George B. III, 180
ussey, George Enion III, 179
ussey, George F. III, 179
ussey, George F. III, 238
ussey, George, Jr. III, 179
ussey, Gertrude Colden III, 179
ussey, Gertrude Colden III, 238
ussey, Graham II, 1087
ussey, Graham II, 1088
ussey, Hannah I, 504
ussey, Hannah I, 552
ussey, Hannah I, 820
ussey, Hannah I, 825
ussey, Hannah I, 912
ussey, Hannah IV, 227
ussey, Hannah G. IV, 226
ussey, Hannah G. IV, 263
ussey, Hannah Webb II, 561
ussey, Helen J. IV, 227
ussey, Hepsabah V, 180
ussey, Hepseba V, 341
ussey, Hepsibah V, 167
ussey, Hepsibath V, 180
ussey, Hester IV, 227
ussey, Hester G. IV, 226
ussey, Hester G. IV, 288
ussey, Hetty III, 179
ussey, Hetty H. III, 180
ussey, Hiram V, 341
ussey, Homer V, 342
ussey, Ida V, 251
ussey, Isaac V, 79
ussey, Isaac V, 341
ussey, Isaac V, 342
ussey, Isaac F. V, 342
ussey, Isaac T. V, 341
ussey, James III, 179
ussey, James V, 342
ussey, Jane IV, 227
ussey, Jane V, 79
ussey, Jane V, 166
ussey, Jane V, 180
ussey, Jane V, 329
ussey, Jane V, 341
ussey, Jane V, 560
ussey, Jane V, 578
ussey, Jane V, 810
ussey, Jane D. V, 341
ussey, Jane Edwards V, 180
ussey, Jane R. IV, 226
ussey, Jane R. IV, 263
ussey, Jane R. IV, 967
ussey, Jane R. IV, 986
ussey, Jane W. V, 317
ussey, Jane W. V, 341
ussey, Jedediah II, 561
ussey, Jediah I, 552
ussey, Jediah I, 722
Hussey, Jedidah I, 503
Hussey, Jedidiah II, 493
Hussey, Jennie V, 342
Hussey, Jesse I, 504
Hussey, Jesse I, 722
Hussey, John I, 400
Hussey, John I, 401
Hussey, John I, 503
Hussey, John I, 504
Hussey, John I, 552
Hussey, John I, 722
Hussey, John I, 820
Hussey, John II, 561
Hussey, John II, 680
Hussey, John II, 681
Hussey, John IV, 227
Hussey, John IV, 412
Hussey, John V, 79
Hussey, John V, 251
Hussey, John V, 341
Hussey, John V, 560
Hussey, John V, 578
Hussey, John B. III, 179
Hussey, John C. IV, 1254
Hussey, John G. IV, 227
Hussey, John M. V, 341
Hussey, John M. V, 342
Hussey, John M. V, 810
Hussey, John Milton V, 341
Hussey, John Milton V, 810
Hussey, John U. III, 85
Hussey, John U. III, 179
Hussey, John, Jr. I, 400
Hussey, Jonathan I, 820
Hussey, Joseph I, 552
Hussey, Joseph II, 681
Hussey, Joseph IV, 227
Hussey, Joseph V, 341
Hussey, Joseph G. IV, 227
Hussey, Joshua I, 382
Hussey, Joshua I, 400
Hussey, Joshua V, 251
Hussey, Joshua V, 322
Hussey, Joshua V, 341
Hussey, Joshua V, 342
Hussey, Joshua, Jr. V, 341
Hussey, Judiah I, 717
Hussey, Judiah I, 722
Hussey, Julia V, 342
Hussey, Julia V, 629
Hussey, Julia A. V, 341
Hussey, Julia A. V, 629
Hussey, Julia A. V, 635
Hussey, Katharine V, 341
Hussey, Katharine V, 365
Hussey, Katharine M. III, 180
Hussey, Kerenhapock V, 341
Hussey, Kerenhapock V, 343
Hussey, Kerenhappoch V, 341
Hussey, Louisa V, 629
Hussey, Lydia I, 503
Hussey, Lydia I, 534
Hussey, Lydia I, 552
Hussey, Lydia I, 722
Hussey, Lydia I, 729
Hussey, Lydia II, 1087
Hussey, Lydia II, 1088
Hussey, Lydia IV, 176
Hussey, Lydia IV, 217
Hussey, Lydia IV, 225
Hussey, Lydia IV, 226
Hussey, Lydia IV, 227
Hussey, Lydia IV, 260
Hussey, Lydia IV, 263
Hussey, Lydia IV, 288
Hussey, Lydia IV, 478
Hussey, Lydia IV, 479
Hussey, Lydia IV, 726
Hussey, Lydia V, 79
Hussey, Lydia V, 340
Hussey, Lydia V, 341
Hussey, Lydia V, 342
Hussey, Lydia V, 350
Hussey, Lydia V, 899
Hussey, Lydia V, 901
Hussey, Lydia C. IV, 726
Hussey, Lydia E. V, 330
Hussey, Lydia E. V, 342
Hussey, M. J. IV, 188
Hussey, Margaret III, 70
Hussey, Margaret III, 179
Hussey, Margaret III, 180
Hussey, Margaret IV, 479
Hussey, Margaret W. IV, 227
Hussey, Margaret W. IV, 267
Hussey, Maria Louisa IV, 726
Hussey, Martha I, 378
Hussey, Martha I, 400
Hussey, Martha I, 552
Hussey, Martha III, 180
Hussey, Martha V, 251
Hussey, Martha V, 286
Hussey, Martha V, 341
Hussey, Martha A. V, 341
Hussey, Martha Ann V, 336
Hussey, Martha Ann V, 341
Hussey, Martha Ann V, 342
Hussey, Martha Ann V, 911
Hussey, Martha Ann V, 912
Hussey, Martha Lydia V, 810
Hussey, Martha P. IV, 227
Hussey, Martha P. IV, 256
Hussey, Mary I, 400
Hussey, Mary I, 401
Hussey, Mary I, 503
Hussey, Mary I, 504
Hussey, Mary I, 523
Hussey, Mary I, 551
Hussey, Mary I, 552
Hussey, Mary I, 711
Hussey, Mary I, 722
Hussey, Mary I, 733
Hussey, Mary I, 820
Hussey, Mary I, 1010
Hussey, Mary I, 1012
Hussey, Mary II, 681
Hussey, Mary II, 792
Hussey, Mary III, 180
Hussey, Mary IV, 94
Hussey, Mary V, 39
Hussey, Mary V, 66
Hussey, Mary V, 79
Hussey, Mary V, 251
Hussey, Mary V, 320
Hussey, Mary V, 341
Hussey, Mary V, 342
Hussey, Mary Ann IV, 226
Hussey, Mary Ann IV, 227
Hussey, Mary Ann IV, 260
Hussey, Mary Ann IV, 472
Hussey, Mary Ann IV, 479
Hussey, Mary Ann V, 79
Hussey, Mary B. III, 179
Hussey, Mary B. III, 180
Hussey, Mary D. III, 179
Hussey, Mary D. III, 180
Hussey, Mary D. III, 367
Hussey, Mary Jane IV, 188
Hussey, Mary Jane IV, 227
Hussey, Mary W. III, 180
Hussey, Matthew W. IV, 288
Hussey, Melvin V, 342
Hussey, Milton IV, 227
Hussey, Milton IV, 479
Hussey, Milton I. IV, 188
Hussey, Milton L. IV, 227
Hussey, Minnie McGill IV, 188
Hussey, Miriam IV, 94
Hussey, Murray III, 179
Hussey, Nancy I, 711
Hussey, Nancy I, 722
Hussey, Nancy V, 635
Hussey, Nathan II, 561
Hussey, Nathan II, 680
Hussey, Nathan IV, 227
Hussey, Nathan IV, 479
Hussey, Nathan IV, 490
Hussey, Nathan V, 341
Hussey, Nathan W. IV, 227
Hussey, Nathan W. IV, 478
Hussey, Nathan W. IV, 479
Hussey, Obed III, 180
Hussey, Obed V, 912
Hussey, Ottie V, 342
Hussey, Patience II, 747
Hussey, Penrose IV, 225
Hussey, Penrose IV, 227
Hussey, Penrose IV, 267
Hussey, Penrose IV, 306
Hussey, Penrose IV, 478
Hussey, Penrose IV, 479
Hussey, Penrose IV, 505
Hussey, Phebe II, 708
Hussey, Phebe II, 747
Hussey, Phebe II, 792
Hussey, Phebe V, 341
Hussey, Phebe V, 363
Hussey, Phebe V, 906
Hussey, Phebe V, 912
Hussey, Phebe W. V, 341
Hussey, Priscilla V, 251
Hussey, Priscilla V, 306
Hussey, Priscilla V, 341
Hussey, Priscilla V, 345
Hussey, Rachel II, 1088
Hussey, Rachel II, 1089
Hussey, Rachel V, 332
Hussey, Rachel V, 341
Hussey, Rachel V, 362
Hussey, Rachel V, 446
Hussey, Rachel V, 448
Hussey, Rachel V, 810
Hussey, Rachel B. V, 336
Hussey, Rachel B. V, 341
Hussey, Rachel B. V, 342
Hussey, Rachel W. IV, 794
Hussey, Ray C. V, 251
Hussey, Rebecca I, 528
Hussey, Rebecca I, 552
Hussey, Rebecca I, 578
Hussey, Rebecca I, 715
Hussey, Rebecca I, 722
Hussey, Rebeckah I, 504
Hussey, Rebekah I, 552
Hussey, Richard IV, 726
Hussey, Robert V, 251
Hussey, Robert V, 341
Hussey, Robert W. V, 341
Hussey, Ruth IV, 227
Hussey, Ruth IV, 490
Hussey, Sally V, 899
Hussey, Samuel II, 1088
Hussey, Samuel II, 1089
Hussey, Samuel III, 179
Hussey, Samuel B. II, 948
Hussey, Samuel B. II, 1085
Hussey, Samuel B. II, 1087
Hussey, Samuel B. II, 1088
Hussey, Samuel B. IV, 794
Hussey, Sarah I, 382
Hussey, Sarah I, 400
Hussey, Sarah I, 503
Hussey, Sarah I, 533
Hussey, Sarah I, 552
Hussey, Sarah I, 651
Hussey, Sarah V, 251
Hussey, Sarah V, 289
Hussey, Sarah V, 312
Hussey, Sarah V, 320
Hussey, Sarah V, 322
Hussey, Sarah V, 341
Hussey, Sarah V, 345
Hussey, Sarah V, 359
Hussey, Sarah A. V, 66
Hussey, Sarah A. V, 79
Hussey, Sarah Ann V, 79
Hussey, Sarah E. IV, 1370
Hussey, Sarah H. III, 179
Hussey, Sarah J. IV, 490
Hussey, Sarah Webb II, 561
Hussey, Sarah, Jr. V, 341
Hussey, Selena Jane I, 928
Hussey, Selina I, 944
Hussey, Sephen V, 341
Hussey, Silas V, 341
Hussey, Stacy B. III, 180
Hussey, Stephen I, 378
Hussey, Stephen I, 400
Hussey, Stephen I, 504
Hussey, Stephen I, 552
Hussey, Stephen V, 251
Hussey, Stephen V, 336
Hussey, Stephen V, 341
Hussey, Stephen V, 362
Hussey, Stephen V, 365
Hussey, Stephen V, 446
Hussey, Stephen V, 448
Hussey, Stephen, Jr. I, 552
Hussey, Susan III, 179
Hussey, Susan IV, 227
Hussey, Susan IV, 1370
Hussey, Susanna III, 127
Hussey, Susanna III, 180
Hussey, Susanna IV, 227
Hussey, Susanna IV, 267
Hussey, Susanna IV, 478
Hussey, Susanna IV, 505
Hussey, Susannah IV, 225
Hussey, Susannah IV, 227
Hussey, Susannah IV, 306
Hussey, Susannah IV, 479
Hussey, Thomas I, 504
Hussey, Thomas I, 552
Hussey, Thomas I, 722
Hussey, Thomas I, 820
Hussey, Thomas I, 825
Hussey, Thomas V, 251
Hussey, Thomas V, 341
Hussey, Thomas V, 635
Hussey, Thos. I, 503
Hussey, Thos. V, 317
Hussey, Thos. V, 810
Hussey, Uriel II, 792
Hussey, Walter J. IV, 227
Hussey, Wd. Edith II, 561
Hussey, Wd. Edith II, 680
Hussey, William I, 400
Hussey, William I, 551
Hussey, William I, 552
Hussey, William V, 180
Hussey, William V, 251
Hussey, William V, 329
Hussey, William V, 341
Hussey, William V, 342
Hussey, William H. III, 179
Hussey, William Henry V, 341
Hussey, William Henry V, 810
Hussey, Wm. V, 166
Hussey, Wm. V, 341
Hussey, Wm. V, 810
Hussey, Wm. H. III, 80
Hussey, Wm. H. III, 180
Husson, ??? III, 285
Husson, Hannah III, 285
Husson, Hannah Louisa III, 180
Husson, John III, 180
Husson, Wd. Hannah B. III, 180
Hussong, Ann Eliza V, 850
Hussong, Emma IV, 1322
Hussy, Christopher IV, 912
Hussy, Hannah I, 820
Hussy, Hannah Z. IV, 912
Hussy, Lydia IV, 912
Hussy, Mary I, 400
Hust, Elinor II, 379
Hust, Lidia II, 1004
Hust, Thomas II, 379
Hustead, Mary II, 231
Hustead, Mary II, 232
Husted, Robert III, 180
Husten, Hannah V, 79
Hustes, ??? III, 175
Hustes, Carpenter III, 163
Hustes, David III, 163
Hustes, Elizabeth III, 163
Hustes, James III, 163
Hustes, Job IV, 726
Hustes, Jonathan III, 163
Hustes, Mary III, 163
Hustes, Rebecca IV, 726
Hustes, Robert III, 163
Hustis, Aaron IV, 637
Hustis, Carpenter III, 163
Hustis, David III, 163
Hustis, Edward C. IV, 637
Hustis, Elizabeth III, 163
Hustis, Esther IV, 637
Hustis, Esther C. IV, 1093
Hustis, Isaac IV, 1093
Hustis, James III, 163
Hustis, Job IV, 637
Hustis, Jonathan III, 163
Hustis, Mary III, 163
Hustis, Rachel IV, 637
Hustis, Rebecca IV, 1093
Hustis, Robert III, 163
Hustler, Ann IV, 338
Hustler, Ann IV, 342
Hustler, Anna IV, 338
Hustler, Elizabeth IV, 324
Hustler, Elizabeth IV, 338
Hustler, Hannah IV, 412
Hustler, Jeremiah, Jr. IV, 412
Hustler, John II, 787
Hustler, John IV, 324
Hustler, Mary II, 787
Hustler, Mary IV, 324
Hustler, Mary IV, 338
Hustler, Sarah II, 787
Hustler, Sarah IV, 412
Huston, Agnes VI, 955
Huston, Charles II, 561
Huston, Charles II, 748
Huston, Elizabeth II, 561
Huston, Elizabeth II, 748
Huston, Elsworth IV, 1167
Huston, Hannah II, 561
Huston, Hannah II, 708
Huston, Hannah II, 748
Huston, Hannah V, 79
Huston, Hannah West II, 748
Huston, Henry II, 708
Huston, Henry II, 748
Huston, Henry VI, 828
Huston, James VI, 955
Huston, James Poultney Perot II, 748
Huston, Joseph II, 379
Huston, Keziah VI, 828
Huston, Letitia Perot II, 748
Huston, Margaret II, 234
Huston, Mary II, 379
Huston, Mary II, 708
Huston, Mary II, 748
Huston, Mary V, 251
Huston, Mary VI, 955
Huston, Mary Perot II, 748
Huston, Matthew VI, 939
Huston, Nathaniel VI, 955
Huston, Patience I, 981
Huston, Patience I, 988
Huston, Polly VI, 955
Huston, Robert V, 79
Huston, Robert M. II, 561

Huston, Robert M. II, 708
Huston, Robert M. II, 748
Huston, Robert W. II, 748
Huston, Sally S. II, 708
Huston, Samuel II, 561
Huston, Samuel II, 748
Huston, Samuel West II, 748
Huston, Sophia VI, 939
Huston, Thomas VI, 955
Huston, William II, 708
Huston, Wm. II, 748
Huston, Wm. P. II, 748
Husy, Julia V, 629
Hutch, Neva V, 686
Hutchason, Strangeman VI, 250
Hutchen, Jonathan I, 989
Hutchen, Nancy V, 790
Hutchens, Agathy I, 820
Hutchens, Alice I, 820
Hutchens, Alice VI, 251
Hutchens, Alice VI, 268
Hutchens, Alice VI, 269
Hutchens, Alse I, 820
Hutchens, Amos I, 989
Hutchens, Amy I, 977
Hutchens, Amy I, 989
Hutchens, Amy I, 993
Hutchens, Anderson I, 820
Hutchens, Anderson I, 976
Hutchens, Anderson I, 988
Hutchens, Anderson I, 989
Hutchens, Anderson V, 783
Hutchens, Anderson V, 810
Hutchens, Ann I, 820
Hutchens, Ann I, 989
Hutchens, Ann V, 794
Hutchens, Ann V, 844
Hutchens, Anna I, 977
Hutchens, Anna I, 982
Hutchens, Anna I, 989
Hutchens, Anne I, 989
Hutchens, Archelaus I, 820
Hutchens, Benjamin I, 785
Hutchens, Benjamin I, 820
Hutchens, Benjamin I, 971
Hutchens, Benjamin I, 976
Hutchens, Benjamin I, 988
Hutchens, Benjamin I, 989
Hutchens, Benjamin J. I, 989
Hutchens, Benjamin, Jr. I, 989
Hutchens, Caroline V, 830
Hutchens, Caroline V, 844
Hutchens, Charles I, 977
Hutchens, Charles I, 989
Hutchens, Charles I, 999
Hutchens, Clarey V, 794
Hutchens, Clary I, 989
Hutchens, Clary I, 997
Hutchens, Clere I, 989
Hutchens, Daniel I, 976
Hutchens, Daniel I, 989
Hutchens, Daniel Huff I, 989
Hutchens, David I, 988
Hutchens, David I, 989
Hutchens, David I. V, 783
Hutchens, Delila Ann V, 810
Hutchens, Denson I, 989
Hutchens, Dorcas V, 745
Hutchens, Dorcas V, 755
Hutchens, Doritha I, 785
Hutchens, Doritha I, 976
Hutchens, Dorothy V, 745
Hutchens, Eliza V, 783
Hutchens, Elizabeth I, 785
Hutchens, Elizabeth I, 820
Hutchens, Elizabeth I, 976
Hutchens, Elizabeth I, 977
Hutchens, Elizabeth I, 988
Hutchens, Elizabeth I, 989
Hutchens, Elizabeth I, 998
Hutchens, Elizabeth V, 745
Hutchens, Elizabeth V, 794
Hutchens, Elizabeth V, 810
Hutchens, Ermina V, 810
Hutchens, George I, 989
Hutchens, Gideon I, 989
Hutchens, Gulielma I, 820
Hutchens, Gulielma I, 971
Hutchens, Gulielma I, 988
Hutchens, Gulielma I, 989
Hutchens, Hannah I, 989
Hutchens, Hannah I, 997
Hutchens, Henry V, 844
Hutchens, Hezekiah I, 989
Hutchens, Hezekiah I, 997
Hutchens, Isaac I, 785
Hutchens, Isaac I, 976
Hutchens, Isaac I, 977
Hutchens, Isaac I, 989
Hutchens, Isaac V, 844
Hutchens, Isaac, Jr. V, 783
Hutchens, James I, 785
Hutchens, James I, 819
Hutchens, James I, 820
Hutchens, James I, 989
Hutchens, Jesse I, 976
Hutchens, Jesse I, 989
Hutchens, Joel I, 989
Hutchens, Joel G. V, 830
Hutchens, John I, 785
Hutchens, John I, 820
Hutchens, John I, 976
Hutchens, John I, 977
Hutchens, John I, 982
Hutchens, John I, 989
Hutchens, John I, 998
Hutchens, John V, 783
Hutchens, John VI, 251
Hutchens, John VI, 268
Hutchens, John VI, 269
Hutchens, John B. I, 989
Hutchens, Jonathan I, 989
Hutchens, Josel I, 989
Hutchens, Joshua B. V, 810
Hutchens, Josiah I, 820
Hutchens, Josiah I, 988
Hutchens, Josiah I, 989
Hutchens, Josiah V, 783
Hutchens, Judith I, 785
Hutchens, Judith I, 820
Hutchens, Judith I, 932
Hutchens, Judith I, 971
Hutchens, Judith I, 976
Hutchens, Judith I, 977
Hutchens, Judith I, 988
Hutchens, Judith I, 989
Hutchens, Judith I, 995
Hutchens, Judith V, 745
Hutchens, Keziah I, 976
Hutchens, Keziah I, 988
Hutchens, Lydia I, 976
Hutchens, Lydia I, 989
Hutchens, Lydia I, 999
Hutchens, Lydia V, 745
Hutchens, Mahala A. I, 989
Hutchens, Margaret I, 989
Hutchens, Margret I, 988
Hutchens, Marideth I, 988
Hutchens, Martha I, 976
Hutchens, Martha I, 988
Hutchens, Martha I, 989
Hutchens, Mary I, 785
Hutchens, Mary I, 820
Hutchens, Mary I, 821
Hutchens, Mary I, 982
Hutchens, Mary I, 986
Hutchens, Mary I, 988
Hutchens, Mary I, 989
Hutchens, Mary V, 783
Hutchens, Mary V, 794
Hutchens, Mary V, 810
Hutchens, Mary A. V, 805
Hutchens, Mary A. V, 810
Hutchens, Mary E. I, 989
Hutchens, Mary E. I, 997
Hutchens, Mary Jane V, 810
Hutchens, Meredith I, 820
Hutchens, Meredith V, 810
Hutchens, Meriditth V, 783
Hutchens, Nancy V, 783
Hutchens, Nancy V, 844
Hutchens, Nicholas I, 820
Hutchens, Nicholas I, 971
Hutchens, Nicholas I, 977
Hutchens, Nicholas I, 989
Hutchens, Nicolas I, 785
Hutchens, Patrick I, 820
Hutchens, Patrick I, 988
Hutchens, Patte VI, 251
Hutchens, Phebe I, 989
Hutchens, Rachel I, 976
Hutchens, Rachel I, 989
Hutchens, Rachel I, 992
Hutchens, Rachel I, 997
Hutchens, Rachel V, 79
Hutchens, Rachel V, 121
Hutchens, Rachel V, 830
Hutchens, Rebecca I, 984
Hutchens, Rebecca I, 989
Hutchens, Rebecca I, 992
Hutchens, Rebeccah I, 989
Hutchens, Rhoda I, 977
Hutchens, Rhoda I, 982
Hutchens, Rhoda I, 989
Hutchens, Rhoda Ann I, 989
Hutchens, Rhoda M. I, 989
Hutchens, Sally V, 810
Hutchens, Sarah I, 785
Hutchens, Sarah I, 819
Hutchens, Sarah I, 820
Hutchens, Sarah I, 971
Hutchens, Sarah I, 977
Hutchens, Sarah I, 987
Hutchens, Sarah I, 989
Hutchens, Sarah V, 794
Hutchens, Sarah Stephens II, 825
Hutchens, Sarrah I, 980
Hutchens, Sarrah I, 989
Hutchens, Sophronia I, 989
Hutchens, Sophronia I, 993
Hutchens, Strangeman I, 785
Hutchens, Strangeman I, 820
Hutchens, Strangeman I, 971
Hutchens, Strangeman I, 976
Hutchens, Strangeman I, 988
Hutchens, Strangeman VI, 250
Hutchens, Strangeman VI, 251
Hutchens, Strangeman, II I, 976
Hutchens, Susanna I, 800
Hutchens, Susanna I, 820
Hutchens, Susanna I, 971
Hutchens, Susanna I, 988
Hutchens, Susanna I, 989
Hutchens, Susanna VI, 184
Hutchens, Susanna VI, 193
Hutchens, Susannah I, 820
Hutchens, Susannah I, 989
Hutchens, Thomas I, 820
Hutchens, Thomas I, 971
Hutchens, Thomas I, 988
Hutchens, Thomas I, 989
Hutchens, Thomas VI, 184
Hutchens, Thomas VI, 193
Hutchens, Thomas VI, 251
Hutchens, Thomas J. I, 988
Hutchens, Thompson I, 977
Hutchens, Thompson I, 989
Hutchens, Vestal I, 977
Hutchens, Vestal I, 989
Hutchens, Widow Rebecca I, 989
Hutchens, William I, 820
Hutchens, William I, 976
Hutchens, William I, 988
Hutchens, William I, 989
Hutchens, William H. V, 810
Hutchens, Zachariah I, 989
Hutchens, Zachary I, 977
Hutchenson, Ann II, 961
Hutchenson, Ella I, 944
Hutchenson, James II, 561
Hutchenson, Margery II, 1019
Hutchenson, Michael II, 961
Hutchenson, Michael II, 1019
Hutchenson, Robert II, 561
Hutcherson, Elizabeth I, 1117
Hutcherson, Elizabeth I, 1122
Hutcherson, Hannah VI, 828
Hutcherson, Hannah B. VI, 836
Hutcherson, James A. VI, 821
Hutcherson, John VI, 828
Hutcherson, John VI, 838
Hutcherson, Mary VI, 858
Hutcherson, Polly VI, 828
Hutcherson, Polly VI, 858
Hutcherson, William VI, 828
Hutcheson, George II, 445
Hutcheson, Robert II, 624
Hutcheson, Sarah II, 561
Hutcheson, Sarah II, 624
Hutchin, Ann II, 1004
Hutchin, Ann V, 844
Hutchin, Caroline V, 844
Hutchin, Charles II, 234
Hutchin, Charles II, 561
Hutchin, Charles II, 1004
Hutchin, Elizabeth II, 234
Hutchin, Elizabeth W. II, 708
Hutchin, Elizabeth W. II, 748
Hutchin, Gainar II, 1004
Hutchin, Gainer II, 1004
Hutchin, Henry V, 844
Hutchin, Henry W. V, 844
Hutchin, Isaac II, 234
Hutchin, Isaac II, 748
Hutchin, Isaac II, 772
Hutchin, Isaac V, 844
Hutchin, Jacob II, 1004
Hutchin, James V, 844
Hutchin, James T. V, 844
Hutchin, Jane II, 748
Hutchin, Jane II, 772
Hutchin, Joel V, 844
Hutchin, Joel G. V, 844
Hutchin, Joel G. V, 872
Hutchin, John II, 234
Hutchin, John II, 561
Hutchin, John II, 1004
Hutchin, Mary III, 180
Hutchin, Mary V, 844
Hutchin, Mary Ann IV, 27
Hutchin, Mary Ann IV, 40
Hutchin, Mary B. II, 748
Hutchin, Mary B. II, 772
Hutchin, Mary C. V, 844
Hutchin, Mary T. V, 844
Hutchin, Mary T. V, 872
Hutchin, Mary, II, 561
Hutchin, Nancy V, 844
Hutchin, Nathan II, 1004
Hutchin, Raceel V, 844
Hutchin, Rachel V, 844
Hutchin, Rachel H. V, 844
Hutchin, Rachel H. V, 872
Hutchin, Sarah II, 234
Hutchin, William II, 234
Hutchin, William III, 180
Hutchin, Wm. II, 748
Hutchin, Wm. II, 772
Hutchings, Anderson I, 820
Hutchings, Ann III, 421
Hutchings, Anne I, 989
Hutchings, B. R. IV, 1332
Hutchings, Benjamin I, 820
Hutchings, Drury VI, 823
Hutchings, Elizabeth III, 180
Hutchings, Elizabeth W. III, 180
Hutchings, John I, 820
Hutchings, Joshua III, 180
Hutchings, Josiah I, 820
Hutchings, Kate IV, 1332
Hutchings, Lucy III, 180
Hutchings, Martha VI, 250
Hutchings, Martha VI, 269
Hutchings, Marthy VI, 250
Hutchings, Marthy VI, 268
Hutchings, Mary I, 800
Hutchings, Mary I, 820
Hutchings, Mary III, 180
Hutchings, Mary VI, 179
Hutchings, Mary VI, 184
Hutchings, Mattie I, 944
Hutchings, Meredith I, 820
Hutchings, Nicholas VI, 179
Hutchings, Nicholas VI, 184
Hutchings, Nicholas VI, 192
Hutchings, Rebekah I, 552
Hutchings, Rebekah I, 557
Hutchings, Sarah VI, 192
Hutchings, Strangeman I, 820
Hutchings, Strangeman VI, 250
Hutchings, Susan IV, 1332
Hutchings, Susannah VI, 823
Hutchings, Thomas VI, 251
Hutchings, William III, 180
Hutchings, William III, 421
Hutchings, William S. V, 251
Hutchingson, Barclay H. III, 180
Hutchingson, E. Eliza III, 180
Hutchingson, Elsie Margarita III, 180
Hutchingson, Jno. Wm. III, 180
Hutchins, ??? VI, 39
Hutchins, Abigail V, 745
Hutchins, Abijah V, 745
Hutchins, Agatha VI, 250
Hutchins, Agathy I, 817
Hutchins, Agathy I, 820
Hutchins, Alice VI, 250
Hutchins, Alice VI, 251
Hutchins, Alice M. V, 745
Hutchins, Allen V, 783
Hutchins, Alonzo VI, 653
Hutchins, Alonzo VI, 660
Hutchins, Alse I, 820
Hutchins, Anderson V, 782
Hutchins, Anderson V, 783
Hutchins, Anderson Thompson V, 782
Hutchins, Andrew J. V, 783
Hutchins, Ann II, 1004
Hutchins, Ann II, 1029
Hutchins, Ann V, 782
Hutchins, Ann V, 783
Hutchins, Ann V, 837
Hutchins, Anna V, 783
Hutchins, Anna V, 787
Hutchins, Auston V, 783
Hutchins, Benj. V, 782
Hutchins, Benj. V, 783
Hutchins, Benj. V, 786
Hutchins, Benjamin V, 745
Hutchins, Benjamin VI, 251
Hutchins, Benjamin VI, 259
Hutchins, Benjamin H. V, 783
Hutchins, Benjamin J. I, 989
Hutchins, Benjamin Xenia V, 782
Hutchins, Benjamin, Jr. V, 782
Hutchins, Benjamin, Sr. V, 782
Hutchins, Branson V, 783
Hutchins, Branston V, 782
Hutchins, Catherine VI, 184
Hutchins, Catherine VI, 213
Hutchins, Charles II, 234
Hutchins, Charles II, 961
Hutchins, Charles E. V, 745
Hutchins, Clarey V, 794
Hutchins, Daniel V, 732
Hutchins, Daniel V, 745
Hutchins, Daniel V, 748
Hutchins, Daniel V, 750
Hutchins, Daniel V, 782
Hutchins, Daniel V, 783
Hutchins, Daniel V, 787
Hutchins, Daniel H. V, 745
Hutchins, Daniel H. V, 783
Hutchins, Daniel H. V, 787
Hutchins, Daniel Huff V, 251
Hutchins, Darius V, 745
Hutchins, Darius V, 783
Hutchins, David V, 782
Hutchins, David I. V, 783
Hutchins, Davis V, 782
Hutchins, Decylvia V, 782
Hutchins, Delilah Ann V, 783
Hutchins, Dorcas V, 732
Hutchins, Dorcas V, 745
Hutchins, Dorcas V, 748
Hutchins, Dorcas V, 750
Hutchins, Dorcas V, 755
Hutchins, Dorcas V, 782
Hutchins, Dorcas V, 783
Hutchins, Dorcas V, 787
Hutchins, Dorothy V, 745
Hutchins, Ede VI, 250
Hutchins, Edey VI, 250
Hutchins, Edey VI, 269
Hutchins, Eli V, 782
Hutchins, Elisabeth V, 779
Hutchins, Eliza V, 783
Hutchins, Elizabeth I, 820
Hutchins, Elizabeth V, 745
Hutchins, Elizabeth V, 782
Hutchins, Elizabeth V, 783
Hutchins, Elizabeth V, 794
Hutchins, Elizabeth VI, 228
Hutchins, Elizabeth VI, 250
Hutchins, Elizabeth VI, 251
Hutchins, Elizabeth Z. V, 782
Hutchins, Elizabeth Z. V, 783
Hutchins, Ella VI, 660
Hutchins, Ffrancis VI, 48
Hutchins, Fidelia V, 782
Hutchins, Fidelia V, 783
Hutchins, Fidelia V, 787
Hutchins, Frances Malinda V, 779
Hutchins, Frances Malinda V, 783
Hutchins, Francis VI, 30
Hutchins, Francis VI, 48
Hutchins, Frs VI, 30
Hutchins, Gainer II, 961
Hutchins, Hannah V, 782
Hutchins, Hannah V, 783
Hutchins, Harrietann V, 783
Hutchins, Harris V, 745
Hutchins, Harris V, 747
Hutchins, Harris V, 782
Hutchins, Harris V, 783
Hutchins, Henry VI, 184
Hutchins, Irenia V, 782
Hutchins, Irenia V, 783
Hutchins, Irenia V, 787
Hutchins, Isaac V, 740
Hutchins, Isaac V, 745
Hutchins, Isaac V, 780
Hutchins, Isaac V, 782
Hutchins, Isaac V, 783
Hutchins, Isaac V, 787
Hutchins, Isaac V, 793
Hutchins, Isaac J. V, 745
Hutchins, Isaac J. V, 783
Hutchins, Isaac, Jr. V, 783
Hutchins, James V, 745
Hutchins, James V, 782
Hutchins, Jane VI, 228
Hutchins, Jane VI, 251
Hutchins, Jemima V, 745
Hutchins, Jemima V, 747
Hutchins, Jemima V, 783
Hutchins, Jemima V, 787
Hutchins, Jemima Jane V, 782
Hutchins, Jemima Jane V, 783
Hutchins, Jesse V, 745
Hutchins, Jesse V, 782
Hutchins, Jesse V, 783
Hutchins, Jesse V, 787
Hutchins, Jesse, Jr. V, 783
Hutchins, Joel G. V, 837
Hutchins, John II, 379
Hutchins, John II, 501
Hutchins, John II, 561
Hutchins, John II, 1004
Hutchins, John II, 1029

Hutchins, John V, 779
Hutchins, John V, 782
Hutchins, John V, 783
Hutchins, John VI, 251
Hutchins, Jonathan VI, 250
Hutchins, Jonathan VI, 251
Hutchins, Joshua III, 180
Hutchins, Josiah V, 745
Hutchins, Josiah V, 782
Hutchins, Josiah V, 783
Hutchins, Judith V, 745
Hutchins, Judith V, 782
Hutchins, Judith V, 786
Hutchins, Judith V, 793
Hutchins, Judith VI, 251
Hutchins, Judith VI, 259
Hutchins, Lillia May V, 745
Hutchins, Lydia V, 745
Hutchins, Lydia V, 782
Hutchins, Lydia V, 786
Hutchins, Lydia VI, 250
Hutchins, Lydia VI, 251
Hutchins, Lydia VI, 252
Hutchins, Lydia VI, 254
Hutchins, Mahala V, 782
Hutchins, Maria Alice V, 504
Hutchins, Mariann V, 782
Hutchins, Martha VI, 250
Hutchins, Marthy VI, 250
Hutchins, Mary I, 820
Hutchins, Mary II, 501
Hutchins, Mary V, 782
Hutchins, Mary V, 783
Hutchins, Mary V, 786
Hutchins, Mary V, 794
Hutchins, Mary VI, 184
Hutchins, Mary VI, 216
Hutchins, Mary VI, 231
Hutchins, Mary VI, 250
Hutchins, Mary VI, 251
Hutchins, Mary A. VI, 653
Hutchins, Mary A. VI, 660
Hutchins, Mary Alice V, 745
Hutchins, Mary B. II, 748
Hutchins, Mary Elizabeth V, 745
Hutchins, Mary Ellen VI, 652
Hutchins, Mary Ellen VI, 660
Hutchins, Mary Jane V, 782
Hutchins, Mary T. IV, 227
Hutchins, Mary T. IV, 288
Hutchins, Mary Virginia V, 745
Hutchins, Mary, II, 561
Hutchins, Maryann V, 780
Hutchins, Maryann V, 783
Hutchins, Matilda Jane V, 783
Hutchins, Meredith V, 779
Hutchins, Meredith V, 782
Hutchins, Meredith V, 783
Hutchins, Meridith V, 783
Hutchins, Milley VI, 251
Hutchins, Myrtle C. V, 745
Hutchins, Myrtle L. V, 745
Hutchins, Nancy V, 782
Hutchins, Nancy V, 783
Hutchins, Nathan II, 961
Hutchins, Nicho VI, 184
Hutchins, Nicho. VI, 148
Hutchins, Nicholas VI, 184
Hutchins, Nicholas VI, 204
Hutchins, Nicholas VI, 213
Hutchins, Nicholas VI, 216
Hutchins, Nicholas VI, 251
Hutchins, Owen E. V, 745
Hutchins, Owen Edgar V, 745
Hutchins, Patrick VI, 250
Hutchins, Patte VI, 233
Hutchins, Patte VI, 251
Hutchins, Phebe V, 740
Hutchins, Rachel V, 740
Hutchins, Rachel V, 782
Hutchins, Rachel H. V, 745
Hutchins, Rachel H. V, 837
Hutchins, Rebecca V, 745
Hutchins, Rebecca V, 783
Hutchins, Rebecca V, 787
Hutchins, Rebecca V, 793
Hutchins, Rebeccah V, 780
Hutchins, Rebeckah V, 782
Hutchins, Rhoda V, 782
Hutchins, Richard VI, 48
Hutchins, Sarah V, 782
Hutchins, Sarah VI, 184
Hutchins, Sarah F. V, 745
Hutchins, Sarah J. V, 732
Hutchins, Sarah J. V, 745
Hutchins, Stanley VI, 652
Hutchins, Stanley VI, 653
Hutchins, Stanley VI, 660
Hutchins, Strangeman V, 782
Hutchins, Strangeman VI, 184
Hutchins, Strangeman VI, 250
Hutchins, Strangeman VI, 251
Hutchins, Strangeman VI, 252
Hutchins, Streingmen's VI, 184
Hutchins, Susanna I, 820
Hutchins, Susanna VI, 184
Hutchins, Susannah I, 989
Hutchins, Susannah VI, 250
Hutchins, Susannah VI, 251
Hutchins, T. Vestal V, 783
Hutchins, Tamer V, 782
Hutchins, Tamer V, 787
Hutchins, Thomas VI, 184
Hutchins, Thomas VI, 233
Hutchins, Thomas VI, 250
Hutchins, Thomas VI, 251
Hutchins, Thomas Pleasants VI, 251
Hutchins, Tommy V, 782
Hutchins, Tommy V, 783
Hutchins, Tommy V, 787
Hutchins, Vestal V, 783
Hutchins, Vestel V, 782
Hutchins, William V, 251
Hutchins, William V, 782
Hutchins, William VI, 250
Hutchins, William S. V, 251
Hutchins, Wm. V, 783
Hutchins, Zelinda V, 782
Hutchins, Zelinda V, 783
Hutchins, Zelinda V, 787
Hutchinson, ??? VI, 726
Hutchinson, Abigail I, 272
Hutchinson, Abigail II, 234
Hutchinson, Abigail II, 250
Hutchinson, Abigail II, 708
Hutchinson, Abigail II, 880
Hutchinson, Abigail B. II, 234
Hutchinson, Alan Bahler III, 180
Hutchinson, Alfred W. III, 180
Hutchinson, Alice II, 445
Hutchinson, Ann II, 379
Hutchinson, Ann II, 547
Hutchinson, Ann II, 561
Hutchinson, Ann II, 961
Hutchinson, Ann II, 962
Hutchinson, Ann II, 989
Hutchinson, Ann II, 1004
Hutchinson, Ann II, 1005
Hutchinson, Ann II, 1012
Hutchinson, Ann II, 1043
Hutchinson, Ann Louise III, 70
Hutchinson, Ann Louise III, 180
Hutchinson, Anna II, 802
Hutchinson, Anna III, 180
Hutchinson, Anna IV, 227
Hutchinson, Anna C. III, 180
Hutchinson, Anna C. III, 371
Hutchinson, Barclay H. III, 22
Hutchinson, Barclay H. III, 180
Hutchinson, Becca IV, 412
Hutchinson, Benjamin II, 380
Hutchinson, Benjamin II, 561
Hutchinson, Benjamin V, 686
Hutchinson, Bennett VI, 848
Hutchinson, Billie IV, 1038
Hutchinson, Daniel L. II, 962
Hutchinson, Daniel L. II, 1053
Hutchinson, David II, 1053
Hutchinson, Dr. ??? II, 379
Hutchinson, Duke IV, 227
Hutchinson, E. Eliza III, 83
Hutchinson, E. Eliza III, 130
Hutchinson, E. Eliza III, 181
Hutchinson, E. Eliza III, 279
Hutchinson, E. Eliza III, 371
Hutchinson, Edgar Snowden I, 944
Hutchinson, Edith IV, 1254
Hutchinson, Edith IV, 1255
Hutchinson, Edith C. III, 151
Hutchinson, Edith C. III, 180
Hutchinson, Edward II, 802
Hutchinson, Edward II, 1043
Hutchinson, Edward D. III, 180
Hutchinson, Edwin Dutton III, 180
Hutchinson, Eliz. D. III, 130
Hutchinson, Eliza II, 962
Hutchinson, Eliza II, 1004
Hutchinson, Eliza II, 1012
Hutchinson, Eliza II, 1074
Hutchinson, Eliza III, 151
Hutchinson, Eliza III, 180
Hutchinson, Eliza E. H. VI, 846
Hutchinson, Eliza E. H. VI, 848
Hutchinson, Eliza L. II, 1053
Hutchinson, Eliza. III, 180
Hutchinson, Elizabeth II, 234
Hutchinson, Elizabeth II, 523
Hutchinson, Elizabeth II, 561
Hutchinson, Elizabeth II, 708
Hutchinson, Elizabeth II, 962
Hutchinson, Elizabeth II, 1000
Hutchinson, Elizabeth II, 1002
Hutchinson, Elizabeth II, 1004
Hutchinson, Elizabeth II, 1005
Hutchinson, Elizabeth II, 1038
Hutchinson, Elizabeth II, 1053
Hutchinson, Elizabeth III, 180
Hutchinson, Elizabeth V, 686
Hutchinson, Elizabeth VI, 854
Hutchinson, Elizabeth D. III, 180
Hutchinson, Elizabeth K. II, 708
Hutchinson, Elizabeth, Jr. II, 986
Hutchinson, Elizabeth, Jr. II, 1004
Hutchinson, Ella I, 944
Hutchinson, Elsie M. III, 180
Hutchinson, Elsie Margarita III, 22
Hutchinson, Emma III, 180
Hutchinson, Emma Eliza III, 180
Hutchinson, Emma Eliza VI, 488
Hutchinson, Emma Eliza VI, 513
Hutchinson, Emma S. III, 83
Hutchinson, Emma S. III, 180
Hutchinson, Esther II, 1004
Hutchinson, Esther II, 1029
Hutchinson, Esther II, 1053
Hutchinson, Etta IV, 1254
Hutchinson, Etta IV, 1255
Hutchinson, Fanny V, 686
Hutchinson, Ferona IV, 1282
Hutchinson, George II, 234
Hutchinson, George II, 445
Hutchinson, George II, 658
Hutchinson, George V, 686
Hutchinson, George C. III, 180
Hutchinson, Grace I, 944
Hutchinson, Hannah II, 234
Hutchinson, Hannah II, 708
Hutchinson, Hannah II, 961
Hutchinson, Hannah II, 1004
Hutchinson, Hannah II, 1010
Hutchinson, Hannah II, 1022
Hutchinson, Hannah III, 180
Hutchinson, Hannah IV, 227
Hutchinson, Hannah Ann II, 802
Hutchinson, Hannah Ann II, 962
Hutchinson, Hannah Ann L. II, 1053
Hutchinson, Hester II, 961
Hutchinson, Hester II, 962
Hutchinson, Isaac II, 802
Hutchinson, Isabella III, 21
Hutchinson, Isabella III, 218
Hutchinson, James I, 272
Hutchinson, James II, 379
Hutchinson, James II, 380
Hutchinson, James II, 561
Hutchinson, James II, 802
Hutchinson, James II, 880
Hutchinson, James II, 962
Hutchinson, James III, 180
Hutchinson, Jane II, 802
Hutchinson, Jane II, 880
Hutchinson, Jane II, 962
Hutchinson, Jane IV, 227
Hutchinson, Jessie III, 180
Hutchinson, John II, 234
Hutchinson, John II, 249
Hutchinson, John II, 379
Hutchinson, John II, 380
Hutchinson, John II, 523
Hutchinson, John II, 561
Hutchinson, John II, 708
Hutchinson, John II, 802
Hutchinson, John II, 894
Hutchinson, John II, 961
Hutchinson, John II, 962
Hutchinson, John II, 985
Hutchinson, John II, 989
Hutchinson, John II, 1002
Hutchinson, John II, 1004
Hutchinson, John II, 1005
Hutchinson, John II, 1007
Hutchinson, John II, 1043
Hutchinson, John III, 180
Hutchinson, John III, 421
Hutchinson, John D'Espau III, 180
Hutchinson, John Fimister II, 748
Hutchinson, John Fimister Hutchinson II, 880
Hutchinson, John Finister II, 379
Hutchinson, John Finister III, 180
Hutchinson, John Finnister III, 180
Hutchinson, John P. II, 748
Hutchinson, John P. II, 962
Hutchinson, John P. II, 1053
Hutchinson, John Palmer II, 379
Hutchinson, John Palmer II, 708
Hutchinson, John W. III, 180
Hutchinson, John William, Jr. III, 180
Hutchinson, John Wm. III, 83
Hutchinson, John Wm. III, 130
Hutchinson, John Wm. III, 151
Hutchinson, John Wm. III, 180
Hutchinson, John Wm. III, 181
Hutchinson, John Wm. III, 279
Hutchinson, John Wm. III, 371
Hutchinson, John Wm., Jr. III, 70
Hutchinson, John Wm., Jr. III, 180
Hutchinson, John, Jr. II, 234
Hutchinson, John, Jr. II, 249
Hutchinson, John, Jr. II, 561
Hutchinson, John, Jr. II, 748
Hutchinson, John, Jr. II, 802
Hutchinson, John, Jr. II, 880
Hutchinson, John, Jr. III, 180
Hutchinson, Joseph II, 234
Hutchinson, Joseph II, 961
Hutchinson, Joseph II, 962
Hutchinson, Joseph II, 981
Hutchinson, Joseph II, 994
Hutchinson, Joseph II, 1004
Hutchinson, Joseph II, 1005
Hutchinson, Joseph II, 1010
Hutchinson, Joseph II, 1029
Hutchinson, Joseph II, 1043
Hutchinson, Joseph B. II, 234
Hutchinson, Joseph B. II, 250
Hutchinson, Joseph Peirce II, 379
Hutchinson, Joseph Peirce II, 748
Hutchinson, Joseph Pierce II, 802
Hutchinson, Joseph Pierce II, 880
Hutchinson, Joseph Pierce III, 180
Hutchinson, Katherine II, 379
Hutchinson, Katherine II, 962
Hutchinson, Katherine II, 1004
Hutchinson, Katherine II, 1015
Hutchinson, Katherine II, 1023
Hutchinson, Lydia II, 379
Hutchinson, Macdonald Hough III, 180
Hutchinson, Mahlon II, 379
Hutchinson, Mahlon II, 380
Hutchinson, Mahlon II, 561
Hutchinson, Mahlon II, 571
Hutchinson, Mahlon II, 708
Hutchinson, Mahlon II, 962
Hutchinson, Mahlon II, 1004
Hutchinson, Mahlon II, 1012
Hutchinson, Mahlon II, 1019
Hutchinson, Mahlon II, 1053
Hutchinson, Mahlon II, 1074
Hutchinson, Mahlon, Jr. II, 561
Hutchinson, Mahlon, Jr. II, 1005
Hutchinson, Margaret II, 234
Hutchinson, Margaret II, 249
Hutchinson, Margaret II, 523
Hutchinson, Margaret II, 561
Hutchinson, Margaret II, 708
Hutchinson, Margaret II, 802
Hutchinson, Margaret II, 880
Hutchinson, Margaret II, 894
Hutchinson, Margaret II, 1004
Hutchinson, Margaret II, 1005
Hutchinson, Margaret F. II, 561
Hutchinson, Margery II, 988
Hutchinson, Margery II, 1004
Hutchinson, Martha II, 561
Hutchinson, Martha II, 961
Hutchinson, Martin Hite III, 180
Hutchinson, Mary II, 234
Hutchinson, Mary II, 561
Hutchinson, Mary II, 658
Hutchinson, Mary II, 880
Hutchinson, Mary II, 961
Hutchinson, Mary II, 962
Hutchinson, Mary II, 981
Hutchinson, Mary II, 1004
Hutchinson, Mary II, 1005
Hutchinson, Mary II, 1023
Hutchinson, Mary II, 1043
Hutchinson, Mary III, 180
Hutchinson, Mary III, 240
Hutchinson, Mary Ann IV, 227
Hutchinson, Mary E. III, 181
Hutchinson, Mary Eliz. III, 279
Hutchinson, Mary Elizabeth III, 180
Hutchinson, Mary Ellen V, 574
Hutchinson, Mary Louise II, 802
Hutchinson, Mary Peirce II, 379
Hutchinson, Mary Peirce II, 748
Hutchinson, Mary Pierce III, 181
Hutchinson, Mathias II, 1004
Hutchinson, Matthias II, 962
Hutchinson, Matthias II, 986
Hutchinson, Matthias II, 1004
Hutchinson, Melva IV, 1254
Hutchinson, Melva IV, 1322
Hutchinson, Mercy II, 961
Hutchinson, Michael II, 961
Hutchinson, Michael II, 962
Hutchinson, Michael II, 1004
Hutchinson, Michael II, 1012
Hutchinson, Nehemiah II, 961
Hutchinson, Oscar V, 578
Hutchinson, Oscar V, 686
Hutchinson, Phebe II, 961
Hutchinson, Phebe II, 962
Hutchinson, Phebe II, 1004
Hutchinson, Phebe II, 1007
Hutchinson, Phebe Jane II, 962
Hutchinson, Phebe Jane II, 1053
Hutchinson, Priscilla II, 961
Hutchinson, Priscilla II, 989
Hutchinson, Priscilla II, 1004
Hutchinson, Rachel II, 802
Hutchinson, Rachel II, 880
Hutchinson, Rachel II, 894
Hutchinson, Randal II, 561
Hutchinson, Randal II, 1000
Hutchinson, Randal II, 1004
Hutchinson, Randall II, 380
Hutchinson, Randall II, 962
Hutchinson, Randall II, 1004
Hutchinson, Randall II, 1023
Hutchinson, Randle II, 1004
Hutchinson, Randle II, 1019
Hutchinson, Rebecca II, 1004
Hutchinson, Rebecca II, 1005
Hutchinson, Rebecca II, 1014
Hutchinson, Rebecca II, 1053
Hutchinson, Robert II, 379
Hutchinson, Robert II, 380
Hutchinson, Robert II, 561
Hutchinson, Robert VI, 11
Hutchinson, Roy Cadmus III, 180
Hutchinson, Samuel II, 802
Hutchinson, Samuel II, 880
Hutchinson, Samuel II, 894
Hutchinson, Samuel II, 961
Hutchinson, Samuel II, 1004
Hutchinson, Samuel VI, 752
Hutchinson, Samuel VI, 854
Hutchinson, Sarah I, 268
Hutchinson, Sarah I, 272
Hutchinson, Sarah II, 379
Hutchinson, Sarah II, 380
Hutchinson, Sarah II, 561
Hutchinson, Sarah II, 571
Hutchinson, Sarah II, 802
Hutchinson, Sarah II, 880
Hutchinson, Sarah II, 961
Hutchinson, Sarah II, 962
Hutchinson, Sarah II, 985
Hutchinson, Sarah II, 994
Hutchinson, Sarah II, 1004
Hutchinson, Sarah II, 1005
Hutchinson, Sarah II, 1012
Hutchinson, Sarah II, 1019
Hutchinson, Sarah II, 1053
Hutchinson, Sarah III, 180
Hutchinson, Sarah III, 181
Hutchinson, Sarah V, 686
Hutchinson, Sarah P. III, 181
Hutchinson, Sarah W. II, 234
Hutchinson, Sarah W. II, 249
Hutchinson, Sarah W. II, 561
Hutchinson, Sarah W. II, 748
Hutchinson, Sarah W. II, 802
Hutchinson, Sarah W. II, 880
Hutchinson, Sarah W. III, 180
Hutchinson, Sarah, Jr. II, 1004
Hutchinson, Sidney II, 557
Hutchinson, Sidney II, 561
Hutchinson, Thomas II, 380
Hutchinson, Thomas II, 561
Hutchinson, Thomas II, 708
Hutchinson, Thomas II, 961
Hutchinson, Thomas II, 1002
Hutchinson, Thomas II, 1004
Hutchinson, Thomas II, 1043
Hutchinson, Thomas III, 181
Hutchinson, Walter IV, 227
Hutchinson, Wd. Ann II, 379
Hutchinson, Wd. Sarah II, 1012
Hutchinson, Welmer IV, 1255
Hutchinson, William II, 380
Hutchinson, William IV, 227

Hutchinson, William V, 578
Hutchinson, William V, 686
Hutchinson, William Savory II, 802
Hutchinson, William Savory III, 180
Hutchinson, William Savory III, 181
Hutchinson, Wilmer IV, 1254
Hutchinson, Wm. II, 1053
Hutchinson, Wm. VI, 488
Hutchinson, Wm. VI, 513
Hutchison, E. S. I, 928
Hutchison, Edgar Snowden I, 928
Hutchison, Ella Burton I, 928
Hutchison, Ellen Elizabeth I, 928
Hutchison, Grace I, 944
Hutchison, Hannah Priscilla IV, 321
Hutchison, Hannah Priscilla IV, 338
Hutchison, Isaac II, 192
Hutchison, Jessie III, 31
Hutchison, John II, 192
Hutchison, John II, 234
Hutchison, John W. III, 31
Hutchison, Julia Fitzhugh VI, 733
Hutchison, Julia Fitzhugh VI, 741
Hutchison, Mary II, 192
Hutchison, Mary II, 234
Hutchison, Mary II, 561
Hutchisson, Hannah V, 79
Hutchisson, Hannah V, 127
Hutchon, Joel G. V, 844
Hutnut, Ann II, 380
Hutnut, Hannah II, 380
Hutnut, William II, 380
Huton, Susanna IV, 41
Hutso, Wm. H. VI, 845
Hutson, Betsy V, 305
Hutson, Betsy VI, 828
Hutson, Charlotte VI, 989
Hutson, Curtis V, 305
Hutson, Edmund VI, 930
Hutson, Elizabeth II, 80
Hutson, Etta IV, 686
Hutson, James H. VI, 825
Hutson, James H. VI, 828
Hutson, Joel VI, 1000
Hutson, Levinia VI, 859
Hutson, Lydia I, 722
Hutson, Lydia I, 731
Hutson, Lydia V, 305
Hutson, Mabel IV, 1322
Hutson, Margaret V, 251
Hutson, Margaret V, 342
Hutson, Margaret V, 405
Hutson, Margaret V, 428
Hutson, Martha I, 722
Hutson, Martha I, 723
Hutson, Nancy W. VI, 864
Hutson, Nathan I, 722
Hutson, Nathan I, 731
Hutson, Patty VI, 1000
Hutson, Phebe V, 305
Hutson, Phebe V, 313
Hutson, Rachel VI, 845
Hutson, Rachel VI, 846
Hutson, Richard I, 722
Hutson, Richard I, 1122
Hutson, Robert VI, 1000
Hutson, Ruth V, 305
Hutson, Sarah I, 399
Hutson, Susan B. VI, 930
Hutson, Susanna A. VI, 828
Hutson, Thomas W. VI, 828
Hutson, William VI, 828
Hutson, William H. VI, 859
Hutson, Wm. VI, 864
Hutt, Daniel II, 380
Hutt, Ester II, 380
Hutt, Sarah II, 380
Hutter, Edward S. VI, 939
Hutter, Emma W. VI, 939
Hutton, Abel IV, 40
Hutton, Abel IV, 41
Hutton, Abel VI, 514
Hutton, Addison II, 748
Hutton, Addison IV, 94
Hutton, Addison IV, 128
Hutton, Adison IV, 128
Hutton, Adison IV, 1134
Hutton, Agnes IV, 750
Hutton, Agnes v. IV, 726
Hutton, Agnes V. IV, 726
Hutton, Agnes V. IV, 826
Hutton, Agnes V. IV, 1103
Hutton, Agnes V. IV, 1106
Hutton, Alice II, 1057
Hutton, Alice H. II, 966
Hutton, Amos IV, 40
Hutton, Amos IV, 41
Hutton, Amos IV, 69
Hutton, Amos IV, 227
Hutton, Amos VI, 514
Hutton, Amy IV, 891
Hutton, Amy IV, 893
Hutton, Amy VI, 480
Hutton, Ann I, 666
Hutton, Ann I, 667
Hutton, Ann IV, 94
Hutton, Ann IV, 126
Hutton, Ann IV, 128
Hutton, Ann IV, 135
Hutton, Ann IV, 227
Hutton, Ann IV, 479
Hutton, Ann IV, 503
Hutton, Ann IV, 726
Hutton, Ann IV, 750
Hutton, Ann IV, 817
Hutton, Ann IV, 826
Hutton, Ann IV, 1103
Hutton, Ann IV, 1134
Hutton, Ann W. IV, 479
Hutton, Ann W. IV, 485
Hutton, Anna IV, 826
Hutton, Anna IV, 841
Hutton, Anne IV, 128
Hutton, Anne IV, 130
Hutton, Annie IV, 94
Hutton, Annie IV, 135
Hutton, Annie IV, 826
Hutton, Arthur W. II, 708
Hutton, Asabel IV, 40
Hutton, Asael VI, 514
Hutton, Asahel VI, 514
Hutton, Benjamin IV, 637
Hutton, Benjamin IV, 726
Hutton, Benjamin IV, 891
Hutton, Benjamin IV, 893
Hutton, Benjamin VI, 514
Hutton, Betty V, 954
Hutton, Betty V, 957
Hutton, Beulah IV, 41
Hutton, Beulah IV, 44
Hutton, Beulah IV, 69
Hutton, Beulah IV, 227
Hutton, Catharine IV, 227
Hutton, Chas. Wetherill IV, 412
Hutton, David I, 436
Hutton, David I, 448
Hutton, Debora IV, 126
Hutton, Debora IV, 128
Hutton, Deborah IV, 88
Hutton, Deborah IV, 94
Hutton, Deborah IV, 128
Hutton, Deborah IV, 129
Hutton, Deborah IV, 227
Hutton, Deborah IV, 479
Hutton, Deborah IV, 817
Hutton, Deborah IV, 823
Hutton, Deborah IV, 1134
Hutton, Deborah S. IV, 128
Hutton, Elisa Ann I, 448
Hutton, Eliza IV, 227
Hutton, Eliza IV, 303
Hutton, Eliza IV, 691
Hutton, Eliza An I, 436
Hutton, Eliza G. IV, 726
Hutton, Eliza W. IV, 227
Hutton, Eliza W. IV, 826
Hutton, Elizabeth II, 708
Hutton, Elizabeth II, 880
Hutton, Elizabeth IV, 40
Hutton, Elizabeth IV, 54
Hutton, Elizabeth IV, 94
Hutton, Elizabeth IV, 227
Hutton, Elizabeth IV, 412
Hutton, Elizabeth IV, 479
Hutton, Elizabeth IV, 480
Hutton, Elizabeth VI, 480
Hutton, Elizabeth VI, 514
Hutton, Elizabeth P. II, 748
Hutton, Elizabeth R. IV, 412
Hutton, Elizabeth R. V, 251
Hutton, Ellen IV, 413
Hutton, Ellen C. IV, 412
Hutton, Ellen C. IV, 826
Hutton, Ellen S. II, 708
Hutton, Ellen S. II, 966
Hutton, Ellen S. IV, 380
Hutton, Ellen S. IV, 413
Hutton, Ellen S. IV, 807
Hutton, Ellen S. IV, 826
Hutton, Elma G. IV, 691
Hutton, Elma G. IV, 726
Hutton, Elma G. IV, 826
Hutton, Elma G. IV, 941
Hutton, Elma G. IV, 967
Hutton, Epaminondas V, 954
Hutton, Ephraim VI, 514
Hutton, Epimonondas V, 251
Hutton, Epimonondus V, 954
Hutton, Findley IV, 1134
Hutton, Finley IV, 94
Hutton, Finley IV, 128
Hutton, Finley IV, 227
Hutton, Finley IV, 303
Hutton, Finley IV, 691
Hutton, Finley IV, 726
Hutton, Finley IV, 750
Hutton, Finley IV, 826
Hutton, Finley IV, 1103
Hutton, Finley IV, 1106
Hutton, Finley M. IV, 135
Hutton, Finley, Jr. IV, 726
Hutton, Finley, Jr. IV, 826
Hutton, George V, 79
Hutton, George S. II, 708
Hutton, George S. II, 966
Hutton, George Smedley II, 748
Hutton, George Smedley II, 758
Hutton, Guli Elma IV, 967
Hutton, Guli Elma IV, 1011
Hutton, Gulielma IV, 637
Hutton, Gulielma IV, 726
Hutton, Gulielma IV, 774
Hutton, Hannah I, 436
Hutton, Hannah II, 380
Hutton, Hannah II, 470
Hutton, Hannah II, 481
Hutton, Hannah II, 561
Hutton, Hannah IV, 637
Hutton, Hannah IV, 686
Hutton, Hannah IV, 726
Hutton, Hannah VI, 361
Hutton, Hannah VI, 405
Hutton, Harmon Linnaeus IV, 135
Hutton, J. IV, 637
Hutton, J. Wetherhill IV, 826
Hutton, J. Wetherill IV, 380
Hutton, J. Wetherill IV, 412
Hutton, J. Wetherill IV, 807
Hutton, James II, 380
Hutton, James II, 481
Hutton, James II, 561
Hutton, James IV, 94
Hutton, James IV, 128
Hutton, James IV, 227
Hutton, James IV, 479
Hutton, James IV, 637
Hutton, James IV, 726
Hutton, Jane IV, 40
Hutton, Jane IV, 53
Hutton, Jane IV, 631
Hutton, Jane IV, 874
Hutton, Jane VI, 405
Hutton, Jane VI, 480
Hutton, Jesse VI, 480
Hutton, Jno. VI, 514
Hutton, Joel IV, 94
Hutton, Joel IV, 126
Hutton, Joel IV, 128
Hutton, Joel IV, 227
Hutton, Joel IV, 466
Hutton, Joel IV, 479
Hutton, Joel IV, 485
Hutton, Joel IV, 536
Hutton, Joel IV, 817
Hutton, Joel IV, 826
Hutton, Joel VI, 514
Hutton, Joel A. IV, 826
Hutton, Joel W. IV, 128
Hutton, Joel W. IV, 135
Hutton, Joel W. IV, 227
Hutton, Joel W. IV, 479
Hutton, Joel W. IV, 726
Hutton, Joel W. IV, 750
Hutton, Joel W. IV, 826
Hutton, Joel W. IV, 1103
Hutton, Joel W. IV, 1134
Hutton, Joel Willets IV, 726
Hutton, Joel, Jr. IV, 128
Hutton, Joel, Jr. IV, 479
Hutton, John I, 1032
Hutton, John II, 380
Hutton, John II, 561
Hutton, John IV, 40
Hutton, John IV, 41
Hutton, John IV, 53
Hutton, John IV, 631
Hutton, John IV, 637
Hutton, John IV, 638
Hutton, John IV, 726
Hutton, John IV, 874
Hutton, John IV, 886
Hutton, John IV, 893
Hutton, John IV, 967
Hutton, John V, 251
Hutton, John V, 290
Hutton, John V, 954
Hutton, John VI, 514
Hutton, John D. II, 880
Hutton, John M. IV, 479
Hutton, John McGrew IV, 479
Hutton, John, Jr. IV, 41
Hutton, John, Jr. IV, 637
Hutton, John, Jr. IV, 638
Hutton, John, Jr. IV, 874
Hutton, John, Sr. IV, 637
Hutton, Jonah VI, 315
Hutton, Jonah VI, 480
Hutton, Jonah VI, 514
Hutton, Jonathan VI, 514
Hutton, Jordan L. V, 251
Hutton, Jordon V, 954
Hutton, Joseph IV, 40
Hutton, Joseph IV, 41
Hutton, Joseph IV, 69
Hutton, Joseph IV, 150
Hutton, Joseph IV, 227
Hutton, Joseph IV, 479
Hutton, Joseph VI, 405
Hutton, Joseph VI, 480
Hutton, Joseph VI, 514
Hutton, Joseph VI, 522
Hutton, Joseph VI, 585
Hutton, Joshua IV, 150
Hutton, Julia Adelaide III, 421
Hutton, Lavina IV, 41
Hutton, Lavina IV, 479
Hutton, Lavinah IV, 479
Hutton, Levi V, 251
Hutton, Levi V, 257
Hutton, Levi V, 954
Hutton, Levi VI, 514
Hutton, Levina IV, 41
Hutton, Levina IV, 227
Hutton, Levina IV, 479
Hutton, Linnaeus IV, 128
Hutton, Linneus IV, 94
Hutton, Lydia II, 380
Hutton, Lydia II, 481
Hutton, Lydia II, 561
Hutton, Lydia IV, 893
Hutton, Lydia IV, 894
Hutton, Margaret II, 708
Hutton, Margaret II, 748
Hutton, Margaret II, 758
Hutton, Margaret IV, 40
Hutton, Margaret IV, 41
Hutton, Margaret Jane IV, 637
Hutton, Margaret Jane IV, 638
Hutton, Margaret Jane IV, 726
Hutton, Margaret Jane IV, 874
Hutton, Margaret Jane IV, 967
Hutton, Maria II, 380
Hutton, Maria II, 561
Hutton, Martha I, 436
Hutton, Martha I, 448
Hutton, Martha V, 504
Hutton, Martha D. V, 501
Hutton, Martha D. V, 504
Hutton, Mary II, 748
Hutton, Mary IV, 30
Hutton, Mary IV, 38
Hutton, Mary IV, 40
Hutton, Mary IV, 41
Hutton, Mary IV, 94
Hutton, Mary IV, 128
Hutton, Mary IV, 135
Hutton, Mary IV, 227
Hutton, Mary IV, 466
Hutton, Mary IV, 479
Hutton, Mary IV, 485
Hutton, Mary IV, 536
Hutton, Mary IV, 637
Hutton, Mary IV, 709
Hutton, Mary IV, 726
Hutton, Mary IV, 815
Hutton, Mary IV, 823
Hutton, Mary IV, 1134
Hutton, Mary V, 290
Hutton, Mary V, 954
Hutton, Mary VI, 405
Hutton, Mary VI, 434
Hutton, Mary VI, 468
Hutton, Mary VI, 479
Hutton, Mary VI, 480
Hutton, Mary VI, 514
Hutton, Mary VI, 551
Hutton, Mary VI, 585
Hutton, Mary Ann II, 380
Hutton, Mary Ann IV, 726
Hutton, Mary Jane IV, 951
Hutton, Mary Jane IV, 967
Hutton, Massey IV, 726
Hutton, Massey IV, 893
Hutton, Matilda IV, 479
Hutton, Matilda IV, 503
Hutton, Mercy IV, 637
Hutton, Mercy V, 251
Hutton, Moses VI, 480
Hutton, Moses Cadwalader VI, 315
Hutton, Moses, Jr. VI, 479
Hutton, Nancy V, 954
Hutton, Nathan IV, 94
Hutton, Nathan IV, 128
Hutton, Nathan IV, 479
Hutton, Nehemiah VI, 514
Hutton, Phebe II, 748
Hutton, Phebe II, 758
Hutton, Phebe IV, 38
Hutton, Phebe IV, 40
Hutton, Phebe VI, 405
Hutton, Phoebe II, 708
Hutton, Polly IV, 637
Hutton, R. IV, 637
Hutton, Rachel IV, 94
Hutton, Rachel IV, 125
Hutton, Rachel IV, 128
Hutton, Rachel IV, 637
Hutton, Rachel IV, 638
Hutton, Rachel IV, 726
Hutton, Rachel IV, 874
Hutton, Rachel IV, 886
Hutton, Rachel IV, 967
Hutton, Rachel VI, 514
Hutton, Rachel F. II, 880
Hutton, Rachel S. VI, 514
Hutton, Rebecca IV, 94
Hutton, Rebecca IV, 128
Hutton, Rebecca IV, 135
Hutton, Rebecca IV, 136
Hutton, Rebecca IV, 227
Hutton, Rebecca IV, 479
Hutton, Rebecca IV, 486
Hutton, Rebecca IV, 499
Hutton, Rebecca IV, 750
Hutton, Rebecca IV, 1134
Hutton, Rebecca V, 251
Hutton, Rebecca V, 257
Hutton, Rebecca V, 954
Hutton, Rebecca A. II, 880
Hutton, Rebecca S. II, 748
Hutton, Rebecca S. IV, 726
Hutton, Rebecca S. IV, 826
Hutton, Rebecca S., Jr. IV, 726
Hutton, Rebecca Savry IV, 750
Hutton, Richard IV, 412
Hutton, Ruth II, 708
Hutton, Ruth II, 748
Hutton, Ruth VI, 479
Hutton, Saml. VI, 514
Hutton, Samuel II, 880
Hutton, Samuel IV, 128
Hutton, Samuel IV, 479
Hutton, Samuel VI, 479
Hutton, Samuel VI, 514
Hutton, Samuel VI, 585
Hutton, Samuel VI, 629
Hutton, Samuel W. IV, 637
Hutton, Samuel W. IV, 638
Hutton, Samuel W. IV, 726
Hutton, Samuel W. IV, 874
Hutton, Samuel W. IV, 967
Hutton, Samuel, Jr. II, 880
Hutton, Sarah I, 400
Hutton, Sarah II, 380
Hutton, Sarah II, 561
Hutton, Sarah IV, 40
Hutton, Sarah IV, 41
Hutton, Sarah IV, 69
Hutton, Sarah IV, 150
Hutton, Sarah IV, 227
Hutton, Sarah IV, 479
Hutton, Sarah IV, 481
Hutton, Sarah IV, 637
Hutton, Sarah IV, 726
Hutton, Sarah V, 251
Hutton, Sarah V, 290
Hutton, Sarah VI, 296
Hutton, Sarah VI, 297
Hutton, Sarah VI, 315
Hutton, Sarah VI, 405
Hutton, Sarah VI, 451
Hutton, Sarah VI, 479
Hutton, Sarah VI, 514
Hutton, Sarah VI, 522
Hutton, Sarah VI, 629
Hutton, Susan IV, 94
Hutton, Susan IV, 128
Hutton, Susan IV, 1134
Hutton, Susan G. IV, 726
Hutton, Susan G. IV, 750
Hutton, Susanna II, 380
Hutton, Susanna IV, 41
Hutton, Susanna IV, 94
Hutton, Susanna IV, 631
Hutton, Susanna VI, 514
Hutton, Susannah IV, 128

Hutton, Susannah IV, 129
Hutton, Susannah IV, 637
Hutton, Thomas IV, 30
Hutton, Thomas IV, 38
Hutton, Thomas IV, 40
Hutton, Thomas IV, 41
Hutton, Thomas IV, 94
Hutton, Thomas VI, 405
Hutton, Thomas VI, 434
Hutton, Thomas VI, 480
Hutton, Thomas VI, 514
Hutton, Thomas Y. II, 708
Hutton, Thomas Y. II, 748
Hutton, Thomas Y. II, 758
Hutton, Thomas, Jr. IV, 41
Hutton, Thomas, Jr. IV, 94
Hutton, Thos. VI, 514
Hutton, Velma Kelley IV, 726
Hutton, Walter P. II, 708
Hutton, Walter P. II, 748
Hutton, Walter P., Jr. II, 748
Hutton, Wd. Sarah VI, 480
Hutton, Widow Sarah VI, 497
Hutton, William II, 380
Hutton, William IV, 41
Hutton, William IV, 94
Hutton, William IV, 479
Hutton, William IV, 637
Hutton, William IV, 638
Hutton, William IV, 726
Hutton, William IV, 967
Hutton, William VI, 514
Hutton, William H. IV, 638
Hutton, William H. IV, 967
Hutton, William P. II, 708
Hutton, Wm. IV, 637
Hutton, Wm. IV, 686
Hutton, Wm. IV, 726
Hutton, Wm. Paxson II, 748
Hutts, Anna VI, 828
Hutts, Anne VI, 828
Hutts, Betsy VI, 939
Hutts, Jacob VI, 828
Hutts, Leonard VI, 828
Hutts, Leonard VI, 939
Hutts, Michael VI, 828
Hutts, Owen VI, 939
Hutts, Peggy VI, 939
Hutts, Rhoda VI, 939
Hutts, Rhoda VI, 967
Hutts, Sally VI, 828
Hutts, Susanna VI, 828
Hutts, William VI, 828
Huxtable, Mary F. V, 686
Huyett, Beatrice VI, 366
Huyett, Beatrice VI, 405
Huyett, Elizabeth VI, 376
Huyett, Elizabeth VI, 405
Huyett, Ella B. VI, 405
Huyett, Ellen VI, 405
Huyett, Florence E. VI, 405
Huyett, Gwendolin VI, 405
Huyett, Gwendolin VI, 415
Huyett, Hattie VI, 376
Huyett, Hattie VI, 377
Huyett, Hattie VI, 405
Huyett, Hattie VI, 415
Huyett, Hattie C. VI, 405
Huyett, Hattie Clevenger VI, 366
Huyett, Jas. Fenton VI, 405
Huyett, Luther A. VI, 405
Huyett, William S. VI, 366
Huyett, William S. VI, 405
Huyett, William Stephenson VI, 376
Huyett, William Stephenson VI, 377
Huyett, William Stephenson VI, 405
Huyett, William Stephenson, Jr. VI, 405
Huyett, Wm. S. VI, 405
Huyett, Wm. S., Jr. VI, 405
Huyett, Wm. Stephenson VI, 405
Huyett, Wm. Stephenson VI, 415
Huyghes, Edward VI, 183
Huyghes, Rachel VI, 183
Huyghes, Robert VI, 182
Huyghes, Robert VI, 183
Huyghes, Robert, Jr. VI, 183
Huyghes, Robert, Sr. VI, 183
Huyghes, Sarah, Jr. VI, 183
Huyghes, Sarah, Sr. VI, 183
Huyghes, Stephen VI, 183
Huyghs, Edward VI, 148
Huyghs, Edward VI, 182
Huyghs, Rice VI, 182
Huzza, Christopher V, 251
Huzza, Eliza I, 912
Huzza, Hannah I, 912
Huzza, John V, 251
Huzza, Jonathan I, 820
Huzza, Joshua V, 251
Huzza, Mary V, 251
Huzza, Priscilla V, 251
Huzza, Sarah V, 251
Huzza, Stephen V, 251
Huzza, Thomas V, 251
Huzza, William V, 251
Huzzah, Eli I, 722
Huzzea, Beulah I, 552
Huzzee, William I, 400
Huzzey, Mary Ann V, 79
Huzzey, Mary Ann V, 91
Huzzy, Ann I, 400
Hyat, Daniel Matthews VI, 504
Hyat, Eliza V, 1003
Hyat, George VI, 504
Hyat, Jennie V, 1003
Hyat, Jonathan Williams VI, 504
Hyat, Lydia VI, 504
Hyat, Martha VI, 504
Hyat, Martha VI, 505
Hyat, Niah V, 1003
Hyatt, ??? III, 54
Hyatt, Abraham III, 181
Hyatt, Adam III, 181
Hyatt, Alice VI, 399
Hyatt, Alice VI, 451
Hyatt, Alvan III, 181
Hyatt, Alvan III, 408
Hyatt, Alvan III, 421
Hyatt, Alvan III, 455
Hyatt, Alvin III, 181
Hyatt, Alvin III, 453
Hyatt, Amy V, 1003
Hyatt, Ann VI, 434
Hyatt, Annie V, 1003
Hyatt, Caroline V, 336
Hyatt, Carpenter III, 181
Hyatt, Charles V, 501
Hyatt, Chloe III, 89
Hyatt, David III, 181
Hyatt, David M. III, 89
Hyatt, Elihu V, 501
Hyatt, Eliz. III, 181
Hyatt, Eliza III, 181
Hyatt, Eliza V, 1003
Hyatt, Eliza Emily V, 1003
Hyatt, Elizabeth VI, 399
Hyatt, Elizabeth VI, 451
Hyatt, Elizabeth R. V, 1003
Hyatt, Ella III, 140
Hyatt, Ella III, 181
Hyatt, Frances Emma III, 34
Hyatt, Frances Emma III, 213
Hyatt, George I, 487
Hyatt, George I, 544
Hyatt, George VI, 400
Hyatt, Isaac III, 181
Hyatt, Isaac III, 421
Hyatt, James B. III, 106
Hyatt, James B. III, 181
Hyatt, James H. III, 181
Hyatt, Jane VI, 449
Hyatt, Jemima III, 140
Hyatt, Jemima III, 181
Hyatt, Jennie V, 1003
Hyatt, Jesse V, 500
Hyatt, John III, 408
Hyatt, Latitia III, 421
Hyatt, Letitia III, 181
Hyatt, Martha IV, 1165
Hyatt, Martha V, 501
Hyatt, Mary II, 709
Hyatt, Mary III, 54
Hyatt, Mary III, 106
Hyatt, Mary III, 181
Hyatt, Mary V, 501
Hyatt, Mary Eva I, 938
Hyatt, Mary Eva I, 943
Hyatt, Milton III, 140
Hyatt, Milton III, 181
Hyatt, Morgan III, 181
Hyatt, Niah V, 1003
Hyatt, Noah V, 1003
Hyatt, Noah H. V, 1003
Hyatt, R. Ida V, 575
Hyatt, Reuben V, 501
Hyatt, Samuel M. V, 501
Hyatt, Sarah III, 89
Hyatt, Sarah III, 106
Hyatt, Sarah III, 181
Hyatt, Sarah III, 408
Hyatt, Sarah III, 421
Hyatt, Sarah III, 453
Hyatt, Sarah III, 455
Hyatt, Sarah V, 500
Hyatt, Stephen III, 181
Hyatt, Stephen V, 501
Hyatt, Thomas III, 181
Hyatt, Thos. III, 181
Hyatt, Wd. Sarah III, 408
Hyatt, William VI, 399
Hyatt, William VI, 451
Hyde, Anna G. III, 181
Hyde, Anna G. III, 338
Hyde, Barnabas B. III, 155
Hyde, Barnabas B. III, 181
Hyde, Cath. A. III, 155
Hyde, Cath. A. III, 181
Hyde, Charle III, 337
Hyde, Charles III, 181
Hyde, Dr. Clinton J. III, 156
Hyde, Dr. Clinton J. III, 181
Hyde, Geo. P. III, 338
Hyde, George V, 578
Hyde, George P. III, 181
Hyde, Hannah III, 114
Hyde, Hannah III, 256
Hyde, Johanna III, 181
Hyde, Jos. Von. Hoegler III, 181
Hyde, Kate L. III, 155
Hyde, Kate L. III, 181
Hyde, Louise III, 181
Hyde, Louise III, 337
Hyde, Lydia II, 380
Hyde, Lydia III, 181
Hyde, Nellie Elma III, 156
Hyde, Nellie Elma III, 181
Hyde, Sarah II, 380
Hyde, Sarah II, 549
Hyde, Sarah II, 561
Hyers, Letha V, 459
Hyerton, Elizabeth II, 234
Hyerton, Elizabeth II, 277
Hyerton, Obediah II, 234
Hyerton, Obediah II, 277
Hykes, Velma IV, 726
Hyland, Austin IV, 1282
Hyland, Essie IV, 1282
Hyland, Oscar IV, 1282
Hyle, Helen IV, 412
Hyler, Catherine IV, 479
Hyler, Catherine IV, 484
Hylton, Charlotte VI, 1009
Hylton, Jeremiah VI, 1009
Hylton, John VI, 869
Hylton, Lucy VI, 1001
Hylton, Lucy E. VI, 839
Hylton, Roberson VI, 874
Hylton, Susanna VI, 874
Hylton, Susannah VI, 888
Hynard, Benj. F. III, 181
Hynard, Eliza T. III, 181
Hynes, Fred IV, 1322
Hynes, Fred C. IV, 1322
Hynson, Bowers VI, 69
Hynson, Harry VI, 69
Hyot, Mary II, 1005
Hypes, Martha IV, 1322
Hypes, Myrtle IV, 1322
Hyre, Gertrude V, 745
Hysell, Eugene IV, 1255
Hyslopp, Rebecca M. I, 721
Hyslopp, Rebecca M. I, 722
Hyte, Sarah IV, 1152
Hyte, Sarah IV, 1167

Iarns, Samuel V, 80
Ibeson, William II, 380
Ibirson, Robert II, 380
Ibison, Margaret II, 380
Ibison, Robert II, 380
Ibison, Robert II, 561
Ibison, William II, 380
Ibison, Wm. II, 561
Ible, Edward II, 380
Ible, Eliza II, 234
Ible, Elizabeth II, 380
Ible, Elizabeth II, 453
Ible, Elizabeth II, 561
Ible, Nathaniel II, 234
Ible, Nathaniel II, 380
Ible, Nathaniel II, 453
Ible, Nathaniel II, 561
Icehouer, Mary IV, 30
Icehouer, Mary IV, 41
Icehower, Charles V, 181
Icenhour, Ann IV, 622
Icenhour, Ann IV, 638
Icenhour, Ann IV, 726
Icenhour, Ann IV, 968
Icenhour, David IV, 726
Icenhour, David IV, 968
Icenhour, David Allen IV, 638
Icenhour, Elizabeth IV, 726
Icenhour, Elizabeth IV, 968
Icenhour, Gulielma IV, 622
Icenhour, Gulielma IV, 638
Icenhour, Gulielma IV, 726
Icenhour, Gulielma IV, 968
Icenhour, Hannah IV, 726
Icenhour, Hannah IV, 922
Icenhour, Hannah IV, 968
Icenhour, John IV, 638
Icenhour, John IV, 726
Icenhour, John IV, 968
Icenhour, John E. IV, 638
Icenhour, John E. IV, 726
Icenhour, John E. IV, 968
Icenhour, Mary IV, 41
Icenhour, Mary IV, 638
Icenhour, Mary IV, 664
Icenhour, Mary IV, 726
Icenhour, Mary IV, 968
Icenhour, Mary, Jr. IV, 638
Icenhour, Mary, Jr. IV, 968
Icenhour, Sarah IV, 726
Icenhour, Sarah IV, 968
Icenhour, Sarah K. IV, 638
Icenhour, Sarah K. IV, 968
Icenhour, Susanna IV, 922
Icenhour, Susanna IV, 968
Icenhour, Susannah IV, 726
Icenhower, Charles V, 181
Icenhower, Charles A. V, 181
Icenhower, John Albert V, 181
Icenhower, Laura V, 180
Icenhower, Laura V, 181
Icenhower, Lenna V. V, 181
Icenhower, Luella V, 181
Icenhower, Marion V, 180
Icenhower, Marion V, 181
Icenhower, Mary V, 181
Icenhower, Minnie F. V, 160
Icenhower, Minnie F. V, 181
Icenhower, Minnie Florence V, 181
Icenhower, Nancy J. V, 180
Icenhower, Nancy J. V, 181
Icenhower, Rachel V, 180
Icenhower, Rachel V, 181
Icenhower, William V, 181
Icenhower, William H. V, 181
Icenhower, Wm. Henry V, 181
Icenhower, Wm. M. V, 180
Icenhower, Wm., Jr. V, 181
Idding, Caleb II, 561
Iddings, ??? V, 795
Iddings, ??? V, 811
Iddings, Alexander V, 783
Iddings, Alice I, 549
Iddings, Alice I, 552
Iddings, Alice I, 785
Iddings, Alice I, 821
Iddings, Ann II, 703
Iddings, Ann II, 791
Iddings, Benj. V, 820
Iddings, Benjamin I, 820
Iddings, Benjamin I, 821
Iddings, Benjamin I, 957
Iddings, Benjamin I, 964
Iddings, Benjamin I, 1077
Iddings, Benjamin I, 1085
Iddings, Benjamin I, 1094
Iddings, Benjamin V, 79
Iddings, Benjamin V, 723
Iddings, Benjamin V, 745
Iddings, Benjamin V, 773
Iddings, Benjamin V, 783
Iddings, Benjamin V, 810
Iddings, Benjamin V, 811
Iddings, Benjamin V, 820
Iddings, Bradford I, 552
Iddings, Caleb II, 561
Iddings, Caleb P. II, 880
Iddings, Caleb P. II, 896
Iddings, Chester I, 552
Iddings, Chister I, 552
Iddings, Clara V, 811
Iddings, Daniel V, 783
Iddings, Davis V, 811
Iddings, Della V, 811
Iddings, Edith Maria V, 811
Iddings, Elihu IV, 908
Iddings, Elisha I, 785
Iddings, Eliza IV, 908
Iddings, Elsie V, 811
Iddings, Elwood IV, 826
Iddings, Elwood IV, 908
Iddings, Frances Harrison II, 880
Iddings, Frances Harrison II, 896
Iddings, Frances Harrison III, 181
Iddings, Francis Harrison II, 880
Iddings, Hannah I, 785
Iddings, Hannah I, 804
Iddings, Hannah I, 821
Iddings, Hannah I, 1085
Iddings, Hannah II, 896
Iddings, Hannah IV, 826
Iddings, Hannah IV, 908
Iddings, Hannah V, 79
Iddings, Harriet II, 880
Iddings, Harriet II, 896
Iddings, Henry V, 783
Iddings, Ida V, 811
Iddings, J. L. V, 79
Iddings, J. Willis II, 896
Iddings, James I, 785
Iddings, James I, 821
Iddings, James II, 380
Iddings, James II, 703
Iddings, James II, 880
Iddings, James II, 896
Iddings, James VI, 184
Iddings, James L. V, 79
Iddings, James L. V, 745
Iddings, Jennetta V, 79
Iddings, Jennette V, 745
Iddings, John IV, 227
Iddings, John V, 811
Iddings, Johnettie V, 79
Iddings, Jonathan I, 785
Iddings, Jonathan I, 821
Iddings, Jonathan Ray I, 552
Iddings, Joseph I, 549
Iddings, Joseph I, 552
Iddings, Joseph I, 785
Iddings, Joseph I, 820
Iddings, Joseph I, 821
Iddings, Joseph I, 957
Iddings, Joseph I, 964
Iddings, Joseph I, 1085
Iddings, Joseph V, 79
Iddings, Joseph V, 734
Iddings, Joseph V, 745
Iddings, Joseph VI, 184
Iddings, Katharine Ann V, 783
Iddings, Katherine Ann V, 781
Iddings, Lawson J. V, 745
Iddings, Maggie V, 811
Iddings, Malvina R. II, 896
Iddings, Maria I, 785
Iddings, Maria I, 821
Iddings, Mark I, 785
Iddings, Mark I, 821
Iddings, Mary I, 821
Iddings, Mary I, 957
Iddings, Mary I, 964
Iddings, Mary I, 1085
Iddings, Mary II, 703
Iddings, Mary II, 849
Iddings, Mary II, 896
Iddings, Mary V, 734
Iddings, Mary V, 745
Iddings, Maryan V, 794
Iddings, Mille I, 957
Iddings, Mille I, 1085
Iddings, Mills V, 79
Iddings, Milly V, 745
Iddings, Milly V, 797
Iddings, Milly V, 820
Iddings, Percilla V, 79
Iddings, Phebe I, 820
Iddings, Phebe I, 821
Iddings, Phebe I, 838
Iddings, Phebe I, 957
Iddings, Phebe I, 964
Iddings, Phebe I, 1085
Iddings, Phebe I, 1094
Iddings, Phebe V, 79
Iddings, Phebe V, 723
Iddings, Phebe V, 745
Iddings, Phebe V, 820
Iddings, Pheby I, 821
Iddings, Priscilla V, 79
Iddings, Priscilla V, 745
Iddings, Rachel I, 820
Iddings, Rachel I, 821
Iddings, Rachel I, 957
Iddings, Rachel I, 964
Iddings, Rachel I, 1085
Iddings, Rachel I, 1094
Iddings, Rachel I, 1096
Iddings, Ruth I, 820
Iddings, Ruth I, 821
Iddings, Ruth I, 957
Iddings, Ruth I, 964
Iddings, Ruth I, 1085
Iddings, Ruth V, 810
Iddings, Ruth V, 811
Iddings, Ruth V, 820
Iddings, Sally V, 783
Iddings, Samuel IV, 826
Iddings, Samuel IV, 908
Iddings, Sarah I, 785
Iddings, Sarah I, 821
Iddings, Sarah V, 745
Iddings, Sarah V, 773
Iddings, Sarah V, 794
Iddings, Sarah V, 811
Iddings, Talbert I, 1094

Iddings, Talbot I, 820
Iddings, Talbot I, 957
Iddings, Talbot I, 964
Iddings, Talbot I, 1085
Iddings, Thomas IV, 908
Iddings, Townsend IV, 908
Iddings, William I, 552
Iddings, William I, 785
Iddings, William I, 821
Iddings, William I, 957
Iddings, William I, 1085
Iddings, William IV, 908
Iddings, William V, 79
Iddings, Wm. V, 783
Iddings, Wm. V, 811
Iddings, Wm. Townsend IV, 826
Iddins, Benjamin I, 964
Iddins, Benjamin VI, 315
Iddins, Joseph I, 964
Iddins, Mary I, 964
Iddins, Phebe I, 964
Iddins, Rachel I, 964
Iddins, Ruth I, 964
Iddins, Talbot I, 964
Idelett, Rebecca I, 523
Iden, Dorithy II, 1005
Iden, Dorothy II, 1029
Iden, Elizabeth II, 380
Iden, Elizabeth V, 912
Iden, G. II, 880
Iden, George II, 802
Iden, Hannah II, 380
Iden, Hannah II, 561
Iden, Hannah II, 880
Iden, Hannah II, 1005
Iden, Hannah V, 912
Iden, Jacob II, 380
Iden, Jacob II, 562
Iden, Jacob II, 671
Iden, John II, 380
Iden, John II, 561
Iden, John II, 671
Iden, John II, 1005
Iden, John V, 912
Iden, John, Jr. II, 562
Iden, Margaret II, 962
Iden, Margaret II, 998
Iden, Margaret II, 1005
Iden, Mary II, 534
Iden, Mary II, 562
Iden, Mary II, 671
Iden, Mary V, 912
Iden, Mary Ellen V, 912
Iden, Randal II, 962
Iden, Randal II, 1005
Iden, Randel II, 998
Iden, Rosamond II, 1005
Iden, Samuel V, 912
Iden, Sarah II, 380
Iden, Sarah II, 962
Iden, Sarah V, 912
Iden, Thomas G. IV, 638
Iden, Thomas J. IV, 638
Iden, Thos. II, 880
Iden, Wd. Hannah II, 802
Iden, Wm. V, 912
Idings, Benjamin VI, 315
Idings, Elihu IV, 908
Idings, Eliza IV, 908
Idings, Elwood IV, 908
Idings, Hannah IV, 908
Idings, James VI, 184
Idings, James VI, 194
Idings, Mary VI, 315
Idings, Phebe VI, 315
Idings, Rachel Ruth VI, 315
Idings, Samuel IV, 908
Idings, Thomas IV, 908
Idings, Townsend IV, 908
Idings, William IV, 908
Idlette, Jemmima I, 523
Idloitt, Rebecca I, 523
Idol, Rebecca I, 552
Idon, Hannah II, 380
Idon, John II, 380
Idons, Elizabeth II, 380
Idons, Jacob II, 380
Iford, Mary A. V, 954
Iford, Mary A. V, 957
Ignew, Mary VI, 514
Ihrie, Annie L. II, 780
Iler, Eldon IV, 726
Iler, Eliza IV, 968
Iler, Everett IV, 968
Iler, Harry IV, 726
Iler, Helen IV, 726
Iler, Mary IV, 726
Iler, Mary Jane IV, 968
Iler, Nettie IV, 726
Iler, Pearl IV, 726
Iler, Roy IV, 726
Iler, Roy IV, 968
Iler, William IV, 479
Iles, Richard II, 445
Iles, William II, 445
Iliff, Lucile IV, 1282
Iliphant, ??? VI, 348
Imbody, Chas. V, 1003
Imbody, Wm. V, 1003
Imlay, Acsah II, 233
Imlay, Acsah II, 235
Imlay, Maria II, 293
Imlay, Maria III, 181
Imlay, Maria IV, 150
Imlay, Richard IV, 150
Imly, John C. V, 837
Imo, Bida IV, 1194
Indicott, Hannah II, 235
Inez, Joanna V, 401
Inez, Susan M. V, 401
Ing, William III, 181
Inge, Claibourn VI, 861
Inge, Elizabeth VI, 828
Inge, Emily M. VI, 828
Inge, Jane VI, 861
Inge, Joel VI, 828
Inge, Joel W. VI, 939
Inge, Keziah VI, 828
Inge, Mary A. VI, 939
Inge, Mary F. VI, 828
Inge, Merrit VI, 828
Inge, Nancy VI, 861
Inge, Ned VI, 828
Inge, Willis VI, 828
Ingels, Eleanor II, 534
Ingels, James II, 534
Inger, William II, 380
Ingham, Anna II, 1005
Ingham, Anna V, 971
Ingham, Anna Simpson II, 1005
Ingham, Deborah II, 1005
Ingham, Deborah V, 23
Ingham, Deborah V, 79
Ingham, Deborah V, 251
Ingham, Deborah V, 745
Ingham, Deborah K. II, 75
Ingham, Deborah K. II, 81
Ingham, Hezekiah V, 251
Ingham, Isiah V, 251
Ingham, John Simpson II, 1005
Ingham, Joseph II, 235
Ingham, Mary II, 1005
Ingham, Mary V, 79
Ingham, Mary V, 80
Ingham, Mary V, 107
Ingham, Mary V, 251
Ingham, Mary V, 745
Ingham, Mary V, 970
Ingham, Mary V, 971
Ingham, Olive IV, 1273
Ingham, Olive IV, 1282
Ingle, A. S. I, 928
Ingle, Amelia V, 80
Ingle, Caleb II, 177
Ingle, Elizabeth II, 177
Ingle, Floy I, 928
Ingle, J. C. V, 745
Ingle, John V, 838
Ingle, John Calvin V, 745
Ingle, Manda V, 745
Ingle, Mary V, 80
Ingle, Mary V, 794
Ingle, Mercy II, 177
Ingle, Mr. J. C. V, 745
Ingle, Mrs. ??? V, 745
Ingle, Nellie V, 745
Ingle, Ruth V, 745
Ingle, Stacy V, 405
Ingledew, Hannah II, 1005
Ingledew, Mary IV, 829
Ingledew, Sarah VI, 503
Ingledue, ??? VI, 352
Ingledue, Ann IV, 638
Ingledue, Ann IV, 646
Ingledue, Blackston VI, 933
Ingledue, Blackstone VI, 514
Ingledue, Blackstone VI, 660
Ingledue, Blackstone VI, 939
Ingledue, Blackstone VI, 997
Ingledue, Blanton II, 380
Ingledue, Catharine IV, 727
Ingledue, Edward IV, 658
Ingledue, Emma IV, 727
Ingledue, Hannah II, 562
Ingledue, Hannah VI, 493
Ingledue, Hannah VI, 496
Ingledue, Hannah VI, 497
Ingledue, Hannah VI, 500
Ingledue, Hannah VI, 508
Ingledue, Hannah VI, 514
Ingledue, Hannah VI, 517
Ingledue, Hannah VI, 518
Ingledue, Hannah VI, 519
Ingledue, Hannah VI, 520
Ingledue, Hannah VI, 521
Ingledue, Hannah VI, 522
Ingledue, Hannah VI, 530
Ingledue, Hannah VI, 539
Ingledue, Hannah VI, 545
Ingledue, Hannah VI, 579
Ingledue, Hannah VI, 640
Ingledue, Hannah VI, 642
Ingledue, Hannah VI, 644
Ingledue, Hannah VI, 660
Ingledue, Hannah VI, 664
Ingledue, Hannah VI, 665
Ingledue, Hannah VI, 666
Ingledue, Hannah VI, 668
Ingledue, Hannah VI, 673
Ingledue, Hannah VI, 674
Ingledue, Hannah VI, 714
Ingledue, Hannah VI, 720
Ingledue, Hannah VI, 753
Ingledue, Hannah VI, 754
Ingledue, Idella IV, 727
Ingledue, Jacob VI, 519
Ingledue, Magdalene IV, 638
Ingledue, Magdalene IV, 646
Ingledue, Magdalene IV, 658
Ingledue, Magdalene VI, 315
Ingledue, Magdaline VI, 315
Ingledue, Margaret VI, 514
Ingledue, Mary IV, 638
Ingledue, Mary IV, 658
Ingledue, Mary IV, 826
Ingledue, Mary IV, 829
Ingledue, Nellie IV, 727
Ingledue, Nelly VI, 939
Ingledue, Rachel IV, 638
Ingledue, Rachel IV, 893
Ingledue, Raymond IV, 727
Ingledue, Sarah VI, 514
Ingledue, Sarah VI, 616
Ingledue, Sarah VI, 649
Ingledue, Sarah VI, 704
Ingledue, Triphenia IV, 638
Ingledue, Triphenia IV, 666
Ingledue, William II, 380
Ingledue, William IV, 646
Ingledue, William IV, 658
Ingledue, William VI, 315
Ingledue, William VI, 1014
Ingles, Eleanor II, 562
Ingles, James II, 562
Ingles, John II, 380
Inglesdue, Blakestone II, 1005
Inglesdue, Hannah II, 1005
Ingleton, Lulu IV, 1322
Ingley, John II, 235
Ingley, John II, 269
Ingley, Rachel II, 235
Ingley, Rachel II, 269
Ingley, Robert II, 235
Ingley, Robert II, 269
Inglidue, Blackstone VI, 939
Inglidue, Magdalen VI, 939
Inglidue, Nelly VI, 939
Inglidue, William VI, 939
Ingling, Esther IV, 698
Ingling, Esther IV, 727
Inglish, Ann II, 217
Ingludue, Sarah VI, 648
Ingmire, Flora V, 1003
Ingold, Mammie I, 635
Ingold, Ruth Eleanor I, 399
Ingold, Ruth Eleanor I, 400
Ingold, Sallie I, 399
Ingraham, Andrew III, 181
Ingraham, Anna E. III, 78
Ingraham, Anna E. III, 181
Ingraham, Clymene III, 181
Ingraham, Edward III, 181
Ingraham, Edward III, 257
Ingraham, Elsie III, 181
Ingraham, Elsie III, 257
Ingraham, Hudson III, 181
Ingraham, Mary E. III, 181
Ingraham, Timothy M. III, 78
Ingrain, Susan IV, 839
Ingram, ??? III, 288
Ingram, Albin IV, 826
Ingram, Alexander R. II, 790
Ingram, Alice G. III, 181
Ingram, Ann II, 380
Ingram, Ann II, 445
Ingram, Ann IV, 1063
Ingram, Anna Eliza IV, 727
Ingram, Annie E. II, 880
Ingram, Aurelius IV, 792
Ingram, Charles IV, 727
Ingram, Charles O. IV, 727
Ingram, Chas. O. IV, 826
Ingram, Edith IV, 968
Ingram, Edith IV, 985
Ingram, Edith Josephine IV, 968
Ingram, Elizabeth II, 445
Ingram, Ellen E. II, 880
Ingram, Elmore IV, 985
Ingram, Elmore J. IV, 968
Ingram, Emily J. II, 880
Ingram, Emily Jane II, 880
Ingram, Emily W. II, 880
Ingram, Frank IV, 826
Ingram, Hannah IV, 413
Ingram, Hannah IV, 826
Ingram, Hannah IV, 1063
Ingram, Hannah V, 954
Ingram, Harlan IV, 413
Ingram, Harlan IV, 1063
Ingram, Harlan V, 954
Ingram, Harlen IV, 413
Ingram, Henry T. III, 181
Ingram, Jane II, 880
Ingram, Jane IV, 727
Ingram, Jeremiah VI, 828
Ingram, Jesse IV, 713
Ingram, Jesse IV, 727
Ingram, Jessie IV, 826
Ingram, John II, 380
Ingram, John II, 445
Ingram, John IV, 727
Ingram, Joseph IV, 727
Ingram, Joseph IV, 730
Ingram, Joseph IV, 777
Ingram, Joseph IV, 785
Ingram, Joseph IV, 792
Ingram, Joseph IV, 826
Ingram, Joseph, Jr. IV, 826
Ingram, Josephine IV, 727
Ingram, Josephine IV, 785
Ingram, Lillie IV, 826
Ingram, Lydia IV, 826
Ingram, Maria J. V, 954
Ingram, Martha IV, 727
Ingram, Martha IV, 730
Ingram, Martha IV, 792
Ingram, Martha IV, 1063
Ingram, Martha Ann V, 954
Ingram, Mary II, 790
Ingram, Mary IV, 413
Ingram, Mary IV, 727
Ingram, Mary IV, 810
Ingram, Mary IV, 826
Ingram, Mary IV, 1063
Ingram, Mary V, 954
Ingram, Mary V, 974
Ingram, Mary B. IV, 810
Ingram, Mary B. IV, 826
Ingram, Mary C. IV, 713
Ingram, Mary C. IV, 727
Ingram, Mary Caroline IV, 826
Ingram, Mary I. IV, 968
Ingram, Mary Mattis II, 790
Ingram, Mary Titus III, 181
Ingram, Mary Titus III, 288
Ingram, Matilda IV, 713
Ingram, Matilda IV, 727
Ingram, Nancy VI, 828
Ingram, Phebe IV, 727
Ingram, Phebe IV, 777
Ingram, Phebe IV, 785
Ingram, Rachel II, 380
Ingram, Raymond IV, 727
Ingram, Raymond IV, 826
Ingram, Robert IV, 413
Ingram, Robert IV, 727
Ingram, Robert IV, 826
Ingram, Robert IV, 1063
Ingram, Robert V, 954
Ingram, Robert, Jr. V, 954
Ingram, Ruth I, 713
Ingram, Ruth I, 722
Ingram, Ruth IV, 727
Ingram, Samuel V, 954
Ingram, Sarah II, 380
Ingram, Sarah E. IV, 826
Ingram, Susan IV, 752
Ingram, Susan IV, 792
Ingram, Susan IV, 826
Ingram, Susan IV, 839
Ingram, Tillie IV, 826
Ingram, Vida IV, 727
Ingram, William IV, 826
Ingram, Wm. II, 880
Ingram, Wm. F. IV, 826
Ingram, Wm. Shannon II, 880
Ingrim, Margaret Ann IV, 128
Ingrim, Margaret Ann IV, 130
Inguire, Lafayette IV, 1255
Inguire, Sylvester W. IV, 1255
Inks, George V, 686
Inks, George V, 697
Inks, Vesta Eleanor V, 686
Inks, Vesta Eleanor V, 697
Inks, Vesta Miller V, 686
Inlow, Rena Hurley V, 629
Inman, ??? V, 756
Inman, Aaron V, 811
Inman, Amelia V, 181
Inman, Amelia V, 811
Inman, Asa V, 811
Inman, Benjamin V, 811
Inman, David V, 811
Inman, Drusilla V, 811
Inman, Eli V, 804
Inman, Eli V, 811
Inman, Elizabeth V, 745
Inman, Elizabeth V, 756
Inman, Elizabeth V, 811
Inman, Fanny V, 811
Inman, Hannah VI, 113
Inman, Hannah VI, 123
Inman, Jane V, 804
Inman, Jane V, 811
Inman, John V, 811
Inman, Joseph VI, 251
Inman, Levi V, 811
Inman, Mary I, 1028
Inman, Mary I, 1032
Inman, Mary V, 811
Inman, Nancy VI, 939
Inman, Polly VI, 965
Inman, Rebecca V, 811
Inman, Rena VI, 251
Inman, Samuel V, 811
Inman, Samuel Warren VI, 113
Inman, Sarah VI, 964
Inman, Susanna VI, 964
Inman, Susannah V, 804
Inman, Susannah V, 811
Inman, William V, 811
Inman, William VI, 939
Inman, William VI, 964
Inman, William VI, 965
Inman, William P. VI, 251
Inmon, Benjamin I, 1021
Innes, El Nettie V, 912
Innes, Elizabeth VI, 939
Innes, Elnetta V, 912
Innes, Harry VI, 939
Innes, Mary IV, 94
Innes, Robert IV, 94
Innis, Emily IV, 536
Innis, Emily IV, 553
Innis, Emla IV, 338
Innis, Harry VI, 911
Innis, Imlah IV, 536
Innis, Isabella IV, 338
Innis, Isabella IV, 536
Innis, Mary IV, 94
Innis, Mary IV, 128
Innis, Mary IV, 689
Innis, Mary IV, 727
Innis, Robert IV, 338
Innis, Robert IV, 536
Innis, Robert IV, 689
Inquire, Lafayette IV, 1255
Inquire, Sylvester IV, 1255
Inquire, Sylvester W. IV, 1255
Insco, Abel I, 1021
Insco, Abel I, 1032
Insco, Abel V, 80
Insco, Abel V, 783
Insco, Able I, 1032
Insco, Ann I, 1032
Insco, Ann V, 80
Insco, Ann V, 745
Insco, Ann V, 783
Insco, Beuley V, 745
Insco, Isabel V, 745
Insco, James I, 1021
Insco, James I, 1032
Insco, James V, 745
Insco, James V, 783
Insco, Joanna I, 1021
Insco, Joanna V, 745
Insco, John I, 1032
Insco, Lydia V, 745
Insco, Mary I, 1032
Insco, Thomas V, 783
Inskeep, Abraham II, 462
Inskeep, Abraham II, 562
Inskeep, Coleman IV, 1282
Inskeep, Deborah VI, 592
Inskeep, Eliza J. IV, 1276
Inskeep, Eliza J. IV, 1282
Inskeep, Hope VI, 592
Inskeep, Hope VI, 599
Inskeep, Jacob Bennett II, 524
Inskeep, James VI, 592
Inskeep, James VI, 599
Inskeep, Joseph II, 380
Inskeep, Joseph II, 462
Inskeep, Joseph II, 562
Inskeep, Lewis IV, 1322

skeep, Lewis M. IV, 1322
skeep, Lily IV, 1322
skeep, Margaret VI, 599
skeep, Miranda IV, 1282
skeep, Rachel VI, 592
skeep, Rachel VI, 599
skeep, Rebecca II, 114
skeep, Rebecca II, 120
skeep, Sarah II, 462
skeep, Sarah II, 562
skeep, Sarah II, 821
skeep, Susannah II, 462
skeep, Susannah II, 524
skeep, Susannah II, 562
skeep, Thomas II, 709
skip, Coleman IV, 1282
skip, Eliza IV, 1276
skip, Eliza IV, 1282
skip, Eliza J. IV, 1282
skip, Margaret VI, 405
skip, Miranda IV, 1282
skip, Pearl IV, 1276
skip, Pearl IV, 1282
skip, Rachel VI, 405
skip, Rachel VI, 592
skipp, Margaret VI, 599
sminger, Jane V, 504
son, Rachel Williams VI, 410
villiers, Chas. E. II, 880
villiers, Chas. E. II, 889
villiers, Mary A. II, 880
villiers, Mary A. II, 889
villiers, Mary A. D. II, 880
villiers, Mary A. D. II, 889
wood, Ashley V, 683
wood, Ashley V, 686
wood, Catharine V, 1003
wood, Hattie Marie IV, 1322
wood, Lucile IV, 1322
wood, Ruth V, 683
wood, Ruth V, 686
wood, Ruth H. V, 686
wood, Wm. V, 1003
yard, Allen V, 1003
yard, Jane V, 1003
ne, Evelyn IV, 1253
rns, Samuel V, 80
a, Elizabeth IV, 727
a, Elizabeth IV, 742
by, Capt. ??? VI, 291
by, Douglass VI, 939
by, Hannah VI, 939
by, Littlebury VI, 184
by, Nancy VI, 828
by, Samuel VI, 828
edell, Charles II, 562
edell, Edith II, 827
edell, Edward II, 562
edell, Edward II, 748
edell, Hannah II, 562
edell, Hannah II, 796
edell, Hannah II, 819
edell, Joseph II, 562
edell, Rachel II, 880
edell, Rachel II, 943
edell, Rachel N. II, 880
edell, Rachel, Jr. II, 880
edell, Rebeckah II, 562
edell, Rebeckah II, 686
edell, Robert II, 827
edell, Samuel Ellis II, 562
edell, Samuel Ellis II, 748
edell, Seth II, 492
edell, Susan II, 827
edell, Thomas II, 562
edell, Thomas II, 686
edell, Wd. Rachel, Sr. II, 802
edell, Wm. II, 793
ego, Rachel II, 1005
ego, Rachel II, 1031
ego, Rebeckah II, 1005
ego, Rebeckah II, 1031
ego, Wm. II, 1005
ego, Wm. II, 1031
elan, Benjamin II, 134
elan, Richard II, 134
elan, Susannah II, 134
eland, Alice V, 629
eland, Annie V, 1003
eland, Bertha V, 1003
eland, Birtha V, 1003
eland, C. S. V, 1003
eland, Christian V, 1003
eland, Christian S. V, 1003
eland, Eliza A. V, 36
eland, Eliza A. V, 80
eland, Elizabeth II, 559
eland, Elizabeth II, 562
eland, Elizabeth V, 1003
eland, Estella V, 686
eland, Eva V, 1003
Ireland, Hertha V, 1003
Ireland, Isaac B. V, 1003
Ireland, Jane II, 562
Ireland, Jane V, 686
Ireland, Jerry V, 1003
Ireland, Jerusha III, 423
Ireland, John III, 398
Ireland, John V, 1003
Ireland, Mabel Alice V, 677
Ireland, Mabel Alice V, 686
Ireland, Mary II, 81
Ireland, Mary II, 380
Ireland, Nicholas II, 559
Ireland, Nicholas II, 562
Ireland, Orven V, 1003
Ireland, Phebe III, 421
Ireland, Prudence II, 52
Ireland, Prudence II, 81
Ireland, Richard II, 152
Ireland, Sarah III, 398
Ireland, Sarah III, 421
Ireland, Thomas III, 421
Ireland, Thos. III, 423
Ireland, U. S. V, 677
Ireland, U. S. V, 686
Ireland, Wilber V, 1003
Ireland, Wilbur D. V, 1003
Irelon, Mary II, 81
Ireson, Benjamin II, 380
Ireson, Dorcas II, 380
Ireson, Elizabeth II, 380
Ireson, Hannah II, 445
Ireson, Jane II, 526
Ireson, Jane II, 562
Ireson, John II, 380
Ireson, John II, 445
Ireson, Joseph II, 380
Ireson, Letitia II, 380
Ireson, Richard II, 445
Ireson, Richard II, 562
Ireson, Richard VI, 405
Ireson, Sarah II, 380
Ireson, Sarah II, 445
Ireson, Sarah II, 562
Ireson, Sarah VI, 405
Ireson, William II, 380
Irey, Ann IV, 826
Irey, Dawson IV, 826
Irey, Hannah IV, 41
Irey, Hannah IV, 826
Irey, Hiram IV, 826
Irey, Isaac IV, 826
Irey, Jane IV, 826
Irey, Margaret IV, 826
Irey, Martha IV, 826
Irey, Martha IV, 854
Irey, Mary IV, 826
Irey, Rachel IV, 826
Irey, Rachel IV, 837
Irey, Rachel IV, 908
Irey, Rebecca IV, 823
Irey, Rebecca IV, 826
Irey, Rebecca IV, 901
Irey, Rebecca IV, 908
Irey, Sarah IV, 826
Irey, Sarah IV, 839
Irick, Emaline II, 281
Irick, Emaline II, 293
Irins, Georgia V, 80
Irish, Allen IV, 1167
Irish, Ann III, 322
Irish, Ann L. VI, 752
Irish, Avis Jane IV, 1212
Irish, Avis Jane IV, 1221
Irish, Bessie III, 107
Irish, Bessie III, 181
Irish, Caroline M. III, 181
Irish, Charles III, 181
Irish, Dallas IV, 826
Irish, Dallas C. IV, 638
Irish, Edmund III, 181
Irish, Edward L. VI, 406
Irish, Edward L. VI, 660
Irish, Elias H. IV, 638
Irish, Eliza III, 181
Irish, Elizabeth III, 181
Irish, Enoch IV, 1167
Irish, Enoch IV, 1212
Irish, Esther III, 181
Irish, Esther III, 192
Irish, Esther III, 337
Irish, Esther III, 341
Irish, Esther IV, 1167
Irish, Esther IV, 1212
Irish, Esther V, 852
Irish, Eugene III, 181
Irish, Eugene V. III, 107
Irish, Eugene V. III, 181
Irish, Franklin IV, 94
Irish, Franklin IV, 638
Irish, Franklin IV, 826
Irish, Franklin Elias H. IV, 826
Irish, Frederick III, 181
Irish, Hannah IV, 78
Irish, Hannah IV, 94
Irish, Hannah IV, 1167
Irish, Hannah IV, 1182
Irish, Israel IV, 1167
Irish, Israel IV, 1212
Irish, Israel A. IV, 1167
Irish, Israel A. IV, 1212
Irish, Israel Allen IV, 1212
Irish, Israel, Jr. IV, 1167
Irish, Joel IV, 1212
Irish, Joel S. IV, 1167
Irish, Joel S. IV, 1212
Irish, Joel T. IV, 1167
Irish, Joseph III, 181
Irish, Lucy III, 181
Irish, Lydia IV, 78
Irish, Lydia IV, 94
Irish, Lydia IV, 613
Irish, Lydia IV, 638
Irish, Lydia IV, 826
Irish, Lydia IV, 1167
Irish, Lydia VI, 660
Irish, Lydia M. IV, 1167
Irish, Lydia W. VI, 406
Irish, Lydia W. VI, 660
Irish, Martha VI, 514
Irish, Martin VI, 406
Irish, Martin VI, 660
Irish, Martin VI, 673
Irish, Martin VI, 752
Irish, Mary III, 181
Irish, Mary VI, 752
Irish, Mary Ann VI, 406
Irish, Mary Ann VI, 514
Irish, Mary Ann VI, 660
Irish, Mary Ann VI, 673
Irish, Mary Ann VI, 752
Irish, Mary Ann L. VI, 752
Irish, Mary W. VI, 406
Irish, Mary W. VI, 417
Irish, Mary W. VI, 529
Irish, Mary W. VI, 660
Irish, Mary W. VI, 703
Irish, Mary W. VI, 752
Irish, Nathaniel IV, 94
Irish, Nathaniel W. IV, 638
Irish, Rachel VI, 705
Irish, Rachel L. VI, 703
Irish, Rachel S. VI, 406
Irish, Rachel S. VI, 514
Irish, Rachel S. VI, 660
Irish, Rachel S. VI, 670
Irish, Rachel S. VI, 702
Irish, Rachel S. VI, 703
Irish, Rachel Steer VI, 514
Irish, Rachel W. IV, 1167
Irish, Ruth III, 181
Irish, Samuel IV, 1167
Irish, Samuel IV, 1212
Irish, Samuel IV, 1221
Irish, Stephen IV, 1212
Irish, Thomas III, 181
Irish, Washington IV, 94
Irish, Wd. Mary W. VI, 514
Irish, William VI, 514
Irish, William B. IV, 78
Irish, William B. IV, 94
Irish, William B. IV, 613
Irish, William B. IV, 638
Irish, William H. VI, 406
Irish, William H. VI, 529
Irish, William H. VI, 752
Irish, William L. VI, 406
Irish, William L. VI, 417
Irish, William L. VI, 752
Irish, Willis VI, 752
Irish, Wm. A. III, 181
Irish, Wm. B. IV, 826
Irish, Wm. H. VI, 660
Irish, Wm. H. VI, 673
Irish, Wm. L. VI, 406
Irish, Wm. L. VI, 660
Irish, Wm. L. VI, 703
Ironmonger, Harriet IV, 1237
Ironmonger, John II, 445
Ironmonger, John IV, 1237
Ironmonger, John IV, 1238
Irons, Arthur V, 80
Irons, Ella V, 686
Irons, Georgia V, 80
Irons, Lena V, 80
Irons, Lena V, 181
Irons, Margaret S. V, 80
Irons, Rebecca V, 80
Irons, Ross V, 181
Irons, Ross Clayton V, 80
Irons, Samuel V, 80
Irvin, Abigail VI, 515
Irvin, Alexander C. IV, 968
Irvin, Alexr. VI, 904
Irvin, Anna IV, 227
Irvin, Augustus V, 883
Irvin, Eldora V, 405
Irvin, Eldora V, 686
Irvin, Eldora McMillan V, 686
Irvin, Elizabeth V, 80
Irvin, Elizabeth V, 681
Irvin, Elizabeth VI, 515
Irvin, Elizabeth A. V, 80
Irvin, Ella M. IV, 1038
Irvin, George V, 686
Irvin, George B. V, 686
Irvin, Hannah VI, 906
Irvin, Irwin VI, 515
Irvin, James VI, 515
Irvin, Jane VI, 515
Irvin, Jenny Clampet IV, 968
Irvin, Jesse IV, 227
Irvin, John VI, 799
Irvin, John VI, 954
Irvin, Jonas VI, 906
Irvin, Lester IV, 968
Irvin, Lillie IV, 1038
Irvin, Loyal V, 686
Irvin, Magdalane VI, 515
Irvin, Margaret VI, 954
Irvin, Mary VI, 515
Irvin, Mary VI, 939
Irvin, Mary V. IV, 1038
Irvin, Mary Viola IV, 968
Irvin, May IV, 968
Irvin, May V. IV, 1038
Irvin, Minnie Jane IV, 1282
Irvin, O. C. IV, 968
Irvin, R. A. IV, 1038
Irvin, Rachel A. IV, 968
Irvin, Reuben A. IV, 1038
Irvin, Robert VI, 939
Irvin, Robert VI, 954
Irvin, Sibyl IV, 968
Irvin, Susannah VI, 515
Irvin, Thomas VI, 515
Irvin, William VI, 871
Irvine, Abraham VI, 828
Irvine, Alexander VI, 939
Irvine, Amelia VI, 825
Irvine, Ann VI, 816
Irvine, Anna VI, 986
Irvine, Anne VI, 844
Irvine, Anne Maria VI, 925
Irvine, Benjamin VI, 939
Irvine, Betsey VI, 985
Irvine, Betsy VI, 1011
Irvine, Catharine VI, 825
Irvine, Catharine VI, 828
Irvine, Catharine P. VI, 828
Irvine, Christopher VI, 844
Irvine, David VI, 820
Irvine, David VI, 825
Irvine, David VI, 844
Irvine, David VI, 848
Irvine, David VI, 852
Irvine, David VI, 869
Irvine, David VI, 929
Irvine, David VI, 1001
Irvine, David VI, 1017
Irvine, Edmund VI, 888
Irvine, Eliza VI, 810
Irvine, Elizabeth VI, 828
Irvine, Elizabeth VI, 896
Irvine, Elizabeth VI, 904
Irvine, Elizabeth VI, 1001
Irvine, Elizabeth Cowan VI, 990
Irvine, Frances VI, 852
Irvine, James VI, 315
Irvine, James VI, 828
Irvine, Jane VI, 315
Irvine, Jane VI, 809
Irvine, Jane VI, 828
Irvine, Jane VI, 939
Irvine, Jesse VI, 811
Irvine, Jesse VI, 816
Irvine, John VI, 805
Irvine, John VI, 827
Irvine, John VI, 828
Irvine, John VI, 839
Irvine, John VI, 857
Irvine, John R. VI, 939
Irvine, John, Jr. VI, 810
Irvine, Joseph VI, 828
Irvine, Katherine P. VI, 815
Irvine, Locky VI, 939
Irvine, Louise VI, 827
Irvine, Lucretia VI, 815
Irvine, Lucretia VI, 857
Irvine, Lucy VI, 939
Irvine, Magdalene VI, 315
Irvine, Magdaline VI, 315
Irvine, Magdeline VI, 848
Irvine, Margaret VI, 844
Irvine, Margaret VI, 1000
Irvine, Mariam VI, 1011
Irvine, Mary VI, 315
Irvine, Mary VI, 869
Irvine, Mary VI, 961
Irvine, Mary A. VI, 805
Irvine, Mary A. VI, 825
Irvine, Mary A. VI, 828
Irvine, Mary A. R. VI, 807
Irvine, Mary B. VI, 888
Irvine, Mathew VI, 807
Irvine, Mathew D. VI, 828
Irvine, Matthew VI, 828
Irvine, May IV, 968
Irvine, Nancy VI, 820
Irvine, Nancy VI, 828
Irvine, Nancy VI, 839
Irvine, Nancy VI, 966
Irvine, Paschal VI, 825
Irvine, Patsey VI, 828
Irvine, Polly VI, 939
Irvine, Robert VI, 820
Irvine, Robert VI, 825
Irvine, Robert VI, 852
Irvine, Robert VI, 939
Irvine, Robt. VI, 935
Irvine, Rosana VI, 904
Irvine, Sally VI, 811
Irvine, Sally VI, 820
Irvine, Sally VI, 922
Irvine, Samuel VI, 314
Irvine, Samuel VI, 315
Irvine, Sarah VI, 314
Irvine, Sarah VI, 315
Irvine, Sarah VI, 882
Irvine, Sophia A. VI, 844
Irvine, Susanna VI, 828
Irvine, Susannah VI, 315
Irvine, William VI, 828
Irvine, William VI, 882
Irvine, William VI, 886
Irvine, William VI, 887
Irvine, William VI, 888
Irvine, William VI, 990
Irvine, William T. VI, 828
Irvine, Wm., Jr. VI, 990
Irwin, Abigail VI, 515
Irwin, Abigail VI, 518
Irwin, Abigail VI, 752
Irwin, Abigail VI, 754
Irwin, Alice II, 562
Irwin, Ann VI, 752
Irwin, Ann Douglas VI, 752
Irwin, Anna Head VI, 735
Irwin, Anna Head VI, 752
Irwin, Eleanor VI, 752
Irwin, Elizabeth II, 313
Irwin, Elizabeth VI, 515
Irwin, Elizabeth VI, 518
Irwin, Elizabeth VI, 519
Irwin, Elizabeth VI, 521
Irwin, Elizabeth VI, 735
Irwin, Elizabeth VI, 752
Irwin, Elizabeth VI, 754
Irwin, Elizabeth VI, 791
Irwin, Ellen VI, 519
Irwin, Ellis Passmore II, 802
Irwin, Esther Boone VI, 519
Irwin, George VI, 519
Irwin, George VI, 754
Irwin, George, Jr. VI, 519
Irwin, Hannah VI, 752
Irwin, Hannah VI, 791
Irwin, Hannah K. II, 880
Irwin, Ida M. IV, 826
Irwin, Isaiah Boone VI, 519
Irwin, Jacob VI, 519
Irwin, James VI, 752
Irwin, John VI, 752
Irwin, John VI, 754
Irwin, Lester IV, 968
Irwin, Magdalene VI, 315
Irwin, Mary I, 872
Irwin, Mary II, 802
Irwin, Mary II, 880
Irwin, Mary VI, 752
Irwin, Nancy VI, 752
Irwin, Ruth Hannah VI, 519
Irwin, Samuel III, 181
Irwin, Samuel McPherson VI, 754
Irwin, Sarah VI, 752
Irwin, Sarah A. VI, 518
Irwin, Sarah A. VI, 754
Irwin, Susanna VI, 519
Irwin, Susannah VI, 754
Irwin, Susannah Boone VI, 519
Irwin, Thomas II, 562
Irwin, Thomas VI, 515
Irwin, Thomas VI, 518

Irwin, Thomas VI, 521
Irwin, Thomas VI, 735
Irwin, Thomas VI, 752
Irwin, Thomas VI, 754
Irwin, Thomas VI, 791
Irwin, Wd. Hannah II, 802
Irwin, Wm. Henry VI, 752
Iry, Ann IV, 826
Iry, Ann IV, 855
Iry, Elizabeth IV, 727
Iry, Hannah IV, 727
Iry, Rachel IV, 826
Isaac, Elizabeth II, 380
Isaac, Katherine II, 380
Isaac, Samuel II, 380
Isaac, Susanna II, 562
Isaac, William II, 380
Isaac, Wm. II, 562
Isaacs, Frank IV, 1167
Isaacs, Frank R. IV, 1167
Isaacs, Susanna II, 631
Isabell, Hannah IV, 1272
Isabell, Irena V, 555
Isamar, Rosa Fredricka IV, 1322
Isamar, Rose IV, 1322
Isbel, Edwin W. I, 1154
Isbel, F. W. VI, 844
Isbel, William Edwin I, 1154
Isbell, Frederick VI, 828
Isbell, Rebecca VI, 828
Isbill, William Edwin I, 1154
Isceriott, Ester II, 380
Isceriott, James II, 380
Isel, Daisy Viola IV, 1255
Isel, Ida IV, 1255
Isel, Margaret IV, 1255
Isel, Marguarite IV, 1255
Isel, Minnie IV, 1255
Isel, Mr. ??? IV, 1255
Isel, Nicholas IV, 1255
Isel, Winona IV, 1255
Isel, Wynona IV, 1255
Isenhour, Ann IV, 638
Isenhour, Elizabeth IV, 690
Isenhour, Gulielma IV, 638
Isenhour, John IV, 638
Isenhour, John IV, 690
Isenhour, John IV, 922
Isenhour, Mary IV, 638
Isenhour, Mary IV, 690
Isenhour, Mary IV, 922
Isenhour, Sarah K. IV, 606
Isenhour, Sarah K. IV, 638
Isenhour, Sarah K. IV, 922
Isenhour, Sarah K. IV, 968
Isensce, Friederike II, 713
Ish, Catherine V, 252
Ish, Mary V, 252
Ishane, Chas. V, 1003
Ishom, Alice A. III, 167
Ishom, Alice Ada III, 311
Isles, Sarah Ellen V, 844
Isley, Eula A. I, 400
Isley, John A. I, 400
Isley, John W. I, 400
Ison, Bessie VI, 752
Ison, Bessie Bridges VI, 765
Ison, Grace VI, 752
Ison, Grace VI, 765
Ison, Joseph VI, 752
Ison, Joseph VI, 765
Israel, Benj. IV, 968
Israel, Blanche E. IV, 968
Israel, Dewie C. IV, 968
Israel, Dinah III, 250
Israel, Hannah IV, 1063
Israel, Hannah IV, 1065
Israel, Henry IV, 968
Israel, Herbert IV, 968
Israel, Jennet IV, 968
Israel, Mary A. IV, 968
Israel, Mary Ann IV, 968
Israel, Rosa IV, 968
Israel, Rose Barber IV, 968
Israel, Susanna II, 562
Israel, Susanna II, 629
Issenberry, Jacob VI, 809
Issenberry, Mary VI, 809
Iszard, Clarence Moon II, 709
Iszard, Grace II, 709
Itch, Alice II, 380
Itkinson, Clara A. D. VI, 615
Ittner, Bernice IV, 1000
Ittner, Emma IV, 1000
Ittner, Godfrey IV, 1000
Iurns, Rebecca V, 80
Ivans, Aaron B. II, 152
Ivans, Anna L. II, 152
Ivans, Betsey I, 337
Ivans, Hosea I, 337
Ivens, Abigail II, 562
Ivens, Allen II, 120
Ivens, Ann II, 562
Ivens, Deborah II, 562
Ivens, Isaac II, 233
Ivens, Isaac II, 235
Ivens, Isaac, Jr. II, 233
Ivens, Joshua II, 562
Ivens, Mary II, 233
Ivens, Mary II, 235
Ivens, Mary II, 562
Ivens, Moses II, 562
Ivens, Rebecca S. II, 880
Ivens, Samuel II, 562
Ivens, Sarah II, 562
Ivers, ??? III, 182
Ivers, Amelia III, 182
Ivers, Charles III, 182
Ivers, Hannah V, 844
Ivers, Hannah V, 856
Ives, Adaline III, 182
Ives, Ann II, 380
Ives, Anne II, 562
Ives, Benjamin II, 380
Ives, Benjamin Cathrall II, 562
Ives, Catharin H. III, 312
Ives, Catharine H. III, 182
Ives, David III, 182
Ives, Elizabeth II, 281
Ives, Hannah II, 572
Ives, John II, 380
Ives, John II, 562
Ives, Joseph Harlan II, 562
Ives, Joseph Harlan II, 572
Ives, Pamela II, 562
Ives, Pamela II, 572
Ives, Samuel II, 380
Ives, Samuel II, 562
Ives, Wd. Elizabeth III, 182
Iveson, Anna IV, 1370
Iveson, Benjamin IV, 1370
Iveson, James IV, 1370
Iveson, John III, 182
Iveson, John IV, 1370
Ivey, Mary C. VI, 828
Ivey, Sarah I, 143
Ivey, Thadeus H. VI, 828
Ivins, Aaron II, 984
Ivins, Aaron II, 990
Ivins, Aaron II, 1005
Ivins, Aaron II, 1053
Ivins, Aaron II, 1072
Ivins, Aaron II, 1074
Ivins, Aaron B. II, 152
Ivins, Aaron B. II, 802
Ivins, Aaron B. II, 880
Ivins, Aaron B. II, 1053
Ivins, Aaron B. II, 1074
Ivins, Aaron Buckman II, 802
Ivins, Aaron Henry II, 880
Ivins, Aaron R. II, 1065
Ivins, Aaron R. II, 1074
Ivins, Aaron, Jr. II, 1005
Ivins, Abigail II, 562
Ivins, Allen II, 120
Ivins, Ann II, 81
Ivins, Ann II, 562
Ivins, Ann II, 990
Ivins, Ann II, 1005
Ivins, Ann II, 1023
Ivins, Ann II, 1053
Ivins, Ann II, 1072
Ivins, Ann II, 1074
Ivins, Ann B. II, 134
Ivins, Ann I. II, 1072
Ivins, Ann I. II, 1074
Ivins, Anna II, 134
Ivins, Anna Foulke II, 802
Ivins, Anna L. II, 152
Ivins, Anna L. II, 880
Ivins, Arthur C. II, 1065
Ivins, Arthur C. II, 1074
Ivins, Barclay II, 802
Ivins, Barclay II, 816
Ivins, Barclay II, 1005
Ivins, Barclay II, 1053
Ivins, Barclay II, 1074
Ivins, Barclay II, 1078
Ivins, Barzillai II, 81
Ivins, Caleb II, 824
Ivins, Deborah II, 562
Ivins, Edward II, 134
Ivins, Edward II, 1074
Ivins, Edward A. II, 152
Ivins, Edward A. II, 1053
Ivins, Edward A. II, 1065
Ivins, Edward A. II, 1074
Ivins, Edward Hicks II, 962
Ivins, Edward Hicks II, 1053
Ivins, Elizabeth II, 81
Ivins, Elizabeth II, 1005
Ivins, Elizabeth II, 1053
Ivins, Elizabeth II, 1074
Ivins, Elizabeth Ann II, 117
Ivins, Elizabeth Ann II, 120
Ivins, Emma II, 880
Ivins, Emma I. II, 857
Ivins, Emma I. II, 880
Ivins, George II, 1005
Ivins, George II, 1053
Ivins, George F. II, 1065
Ivins, George F. II, 1074
Ivins, George Lester II, 152
Ivins, George Lester II, 802
Ivins, George M. II, 802
Ivins, George M. II, 962
Ivins, George M. II, 984
Ivins, George M. II, 1005
Ivins, George M. II, 1053
Ivins, George M. II, 1074
Ivins, Hannah II, 81
Ivins, Hannah II, 562
Ivins, Hannah II, 606
Ivins, Hannah II, 1072
Ivins, Hannah II, 1074
Ivins, Hector II, 1005
Ivins, Hector C. II, 1053
Ivins, Hector C. II, 1074
Ivins, Hope II, 1005
Ivins, Hope II, 1053
Ivins, Howard II, 1053
Ivins, Howard II, 1074
Ivins, Huldah I, 40
Ivins, Huldah Chappel I, 48
Ivins, Isaac II, 81
Ivins, Isaac II, 120
Ivins, Isaac II, 235
Ivins, Isaac II, 1005
Ivins, Isaac II, 1053
Ivins, Isaac, Jr. II, 1005
Ivins, Isaac, Jr. II, 1074
Ivins, James II, 1053
Ivins, James Robert II, 1074
Ivins, Jane II, 1005
Ivins, John II, 120
Ivins, Joshua II, 562
Ivins, Joshua II, 1053
Ivins, Joshua II, 1074
Ivins, Lydia II, 1074
Ivins, Mahlon K. II, 1005
Ivins, Margaret II, 81
Ivins, Margaret Ann II, 81
Ivins, Margaret H. II, 1074
Ivins, Martha S. II, 1053
Ivins, Martha S. T. II, 1074
Ivins, Mary II, 81
Ivins, Mary II, 235
Ivins, Mary II, 562
Ivins, Mary II, 802
Ivins, Mary II, 816
Ivins, Mary II, 990
Ivins, Mary II, 1005
Ivins, Mary II, 1053
Ivins, Mary II, 1059
Ivins, Mary II, 1072
Ivins, Mary II, 1074
Ivins, Mary II, 1078
Ivins, Mary I. II, 1078
Ivins, Mary Louisa II, 152
Ivins, Mary Louisa II, 802
Ivins, Mary Louisa II, 880
Ivins, Mary R. II, 1074
Ivins, Mary T. II, 1074
Ivins, Meriam II, 1005
Ivins, Meriam II, 1074
Ivins, Miriam II, 984
Ivins, Miriam II, 990
Ivins, Miriam II, 1005
Ivins, Moses II, 562
Ivins, Nancy T. II, 1074
Ivins, Patience II, 1005
Ivins, Patience II, 1053
Ivins, Rebecca S. II, 880
Ivins, Robert II, 1053
Ivins, Robert B. II, 880
Ivins, Robert B. II, 1065
Ivins, Robert B. II, 1074
Ivins, Robert Barclay II, 802
Ivins, Rosanna II, 782
Ivins, Rosanna II, 816
Ivins, Rosanna II, 1053
Ivins, Rosanna II, 1059
Ivins, Rosanna II, 1074
Ivins, Rosanna II, 1078
Ivins, Samuel II, 562
Ivins, Samuel II, 1005
Ivins, Samuel II, 1023
Ivins, Sarah II, 824
Ivins, Sarah II, 962
Ivins, Sarah II, 1053
Ivins, Sarah II, 1070
Ivins, Sarah II, 1074
Ivins, Sarah B. II, 1074
Ivins, Sarah, Jr. II, 984
Ivins, Sarah, Jr. II, 1005
Ivins, Sidney II, 562
Ivins, Stephen W. II, 1065
Ivins, Stephen W. II, 1074
Ivins, Stephen Woolston II, 1074
Ivins, Theodosia II, 808
Ivins, Theodosia II, 824
Ivins, Thomas II, 81
Ivins, Thomas II, 120
Ivins, Thomas C. II, 1065
Ivins, Thomas C. II, 1074
Ivins, Wd. Sarah Burroughs II, 802
Ivins, Wilhelmina B. II, 881
Ivins, William II, 880
Ivins, William Henry II, 1065
Ivins, Wm. H. II, 880
Ivins, Wm. H. II, 1074
Ivison, Mary II, 562
Ivison, Mary II, 652
Ivy, Sarah I, 143
Ivy, Sarah I, 166
Iyliff, Elizabeth II, 562
Izzard, Mary V, 405
Izzard, Mary V, 419
Izzards, Mary V, 578

Jack, Franky VI, 939
Jack, George VI, 156
Jack, George VI, 184
Jack, Jack VI, 939
Jack, Rachel T. VI, 721
Jackman, Albert V, 1003
Jackman, Eleanor II, 547
Jackman, Eleanor II, 562
Jackman, Ellinor II, 1001
Jackman, Ellinor II, 1005
Jackman, Florence V, 1003
Jackman, Harriet V, 1003
Jackman, Harriett V, 1003
Jackman, James V, 1003
Jackman, James E. V, 1003
Jackman, Lillie V, 1003
Jackman, Lillie M. V, 1003
Jackman, Mary II, 380
Jackman, Ruth IV, 41
Jackman, Ruth IV, 45
Jackman, Thomas II, 380
Jacks, Celia V, 629
Jacks, Claud V, 504
Jacks, Daniel V, 629
Jacks, Leona V, 504
Jacks, Lizzie V, 686
Jacks, Mani V, 504
Jacks, Mary I, 594
Jacks, Mary J. I, 594
Jacks, William V, 629
Jacks, Wm. V, 629
Jacks, Wm. V, 686
Jacksheimer, Rev. David III, 398
Jackson, ??? III, 509
Jackson, ??? V, 315
Jackson, ??? V, 443
Jackson, Aaron I, 1094
Jackson, Abbie III, 485
Jackson, Abbie III, 486
Jackson, Abbie Jane V, 181
Jackson, Abel IV, 727
Jackson, Abel IV, 827
Jackson, Abel VI, 388
Jackson, Abel VI, 406
Jackson, Abel VI, 407
Jackson, Abel VI, 411
Jackson, Abel VI, 515
Jackson, Abel VI, 942
Jackson, Abigail III, 422
Jackson, Abigail III, 485
Jackson, Able VI, 879
Jackson, Abraham IV, 1167
Jackson, Abraham IV, 1212
Jackson, Abraham IV, 1213
Jackson, Abraham M. IV, 827
Jackson, Absolam I, 1048
Jackson, Absolem I, 400
Jackson, Absolom I, 400
Jackson, Agis Isaac IV, 1212
Jackson, Agnes L. II, 748
Jackson, Agnes L. II, 753
Jackson, Agnes L. II, 881
Jackson, Agnes L. II, 890
Jackson, Albert S. VI, 752
Jackson, Albert S. VI, 779
Jackson, Alfred P. V, 342
Jackson, Alice IV, 827
Jackson, Alice IV, 844
Jackson, Alice IV, 908
Jackson, Alice V, 678
Jackson, Alice Johnson V, 919
Jackson, Alice Morris V, 919
Jackson, Allen V, 342
Jackson, Almy III, 486
Jackson, Amanda IV, 95
Jackson, Amanda V, 913
Jackson, Amanda VI, 854
Jackson, Amelia IV, 1204
Jackson, Amer I, 504
Jackson, Amer I, 964
Jackson, Amer V, 252
Jackson, Amon V, 80
Jackson, Amos II, 293
Jackson, Amos IV, 95
Jackson, Amos IV, 1370
Jackson, Amos V, 181
Jackson, Amos V, 913
Jackson, Amos B. V, 181
Jackson, Amos S. II, 881
Jackson, Amos Smith II, 802
Jackson, Amra V, 305
Jackson, Ancel III, 485
Jackson, Ancel T. III, 485
Jackson, Ancel T. III, 486
Jackson, Andrew I, 887
Jackson, Angeline VI, 828
Jackson, Ann I, 387
Jackson, Ann I, 401
Jackson, Ann I, 504
Jackson, Ann I, 525
Jackson, Ann I, 552
Jackson, Ann I, 578
Jackson, Ann I, 821
Jackson, Ann I, 964
Jackson, Ann II, 293
Jackson, Ann II, 380
Jackson, Ann II, 541
Jackson, Ann II, 563
Jackson, Ann II, 781
Jackson, Ann III, 149
Jackson, Ann III, 182
Jackson, Ann III, 510
Jackson, Ann IV, 40
Jackson, Ann IV, 41
Jackson, Ann IV, 69
Jackson, Ann IV, 93
Jackson, Ann IV, 94
Jackson, Ann IV, 95
Jackson, Ann IV, 727
Jackson, Ann IV, 805
Jackson, Ann IV, 826
Jackson, Ann IV, 827
Jackson, Ann IV, 903
Jackson, Ann IV, 968
Jackson, Ann IV, 1167
Jackson, Ann IV, 1174
Jackson, Ann IV, 1211
Jackson, Ann IV, 1212
Jackson, Ann IV, 1213
Jackson, Ann IV, 1214
Jackson, Ann V, 80
Jackson, Ann V, 181
Jackson, Ann V, 215
Jackson, Ann V, 284
Jackson, Ann V, 305
Jackson, Ann V, 337
Jackson, Ann V, 341
Jackson, Ann V, 342
Jackson, Ann V, 369
Jackson, Ann V, 405
Jackson, Ann V, 406
Jackson, Ann V, 439
Jackson, Ann V, 783
Jackson, Ann VI, 388
Jackson, Ann VI, 406
Jackson, Ann VI, 418
Jackson, Ann VI, 491
Jackson, Ann VI, 567
Jackson, Ann VI, 637
Jackson, Ann VI, 638
Jackson, Ann VI, 660
Jackson, Ann VI, 709
Jackson, Ann VI, 940
Jackson, Ann Elizabeth VI, 377
Jackson, Ann Elizabeth VI, 406
Jackson, Ann M. V, 181
Jackson, Anna III, 182
Jackson, Anna IV, 908
Jackson, Anna IV, 916
Jackson, Anna IV, 1038
Jackson, Anna IV, 1039
Jackson, Anna V, 80
Jackson, Anna V, 142
Jackson, Anna V, 342
Jackson, Anna V, 913
Jackson, Anna VI, 783
Jackson, Anna B. V, 342
Jackson, Anna Belle IV, 1038
Jackson, Anna J. V, 504
Jackson, Anna M. III, 45
Jackson, Anna M. III, 96
Jackson, Anna M. III, 182
Jackson, Anna M. III, 214

ckson, Anna M. V, 919
ckson, Anne V, 913
ckson, Annetta H. V, 406
ckson, Annie III, 486
ckson, Annie III, 495
ckson, Annie III, 500
ckson, Annie III, 508
ckson, Annie VI, 435
ckson, Annie VI, 772
ckson, Annie E. V, 181
ckson, Annie R. VI, 436
ckson, Annie T. III, 485
ckson, Annie T. III, 486
ckson, Ansalem IV, 1212
ckson, Ansalem IV, 1213
ckson, Arena IV, 1212
ckson, Arlina Cox I, 635
ckson, Arthur C. II, 881
ckson, Arthur C. III, 421
ckson, Arthur C. III, 441
ckson, Asenath V, 305
ckson, Asenath V, 342
ckson, Asenath V, 405
ckson, Asenith V, 342
ckson, Atticus L. V, 342
ckson, Atticus S. V, 342
ckson, Benjamin I, 400
ckson, Benjamin I, 1041
ckson, Benjamin I, 1043
ckson, Benjamin II, 380
ckson, Benjamin II, 381
ckson, Bertha IV, 1038
ckson, Bertha V, 1004
ckson, Betsey VI, 925
ckson, Betsy V, 405
ckson, Beulah IV, 1212
ckson, Beulah IV, 1213
ckson, Blanche V, 406
ckson, Bowater I, 504
ckson, Bowater I, 821
ckson, Bowater I, 964
ckson, Bridget II, 464
ckson, Bridget II, 562
ckson, Caleb II, 563
ckson, Carmelite Hernandex VI, 752
ckson, Carmelite Hernandez VI, 779
ckson, Caroline II, 802
ckson, Caroline II, 881
ckson, Caroline III, 486
ckson, Caroline III, 495
ckson, Caroline V, 374
ckson, Caroline V, 406
ckson, Caroline V, 913
ckson, Caroline A. III, 421
ckson, Caroline A. III, 441
ckson, Caroline H. II, 152
ckson, Caroline H. III, 182
ckson, Caroline R. III, 486
ckson, Caroline U. III, 484
ckson, Caroline U. III, 485
ckson, Caroline U. III, 486
ckson, Caroline V. III, 418
ckson, Caroline V. III, 421
ckson, Caroline W. IV, 827
ckson, Carolyn Louise III, 486
ckson, Carolyn Louise III, 508
ckson, Catharine I, 444
ckson, Catharine I, 448
ckson, Catharine I, 453
ckson, Catharine I, 504
ckson, Catharine I, 552
ckson, Catharine I, 659
ckson, Catharine I, 764
ckson, Charity I, 964
ckson, Charity III, 421
ckson, Charity III, 486
ckson, Charity III, 501
ckson, Charity V, 80
ckson, Charity V, 239
ckson, Charity V, 252
ckson, Charles II, 380
ckson, Charles II, 381
ckson, Charles III, 421
ckson, Charles III, 466
ckson, Charles III, 480
ckson, Charles III, 485
ckson, Charles III, 486
ckson, Charles III, 504
ckson, Charles IV, 1213
ckson, Charlotte VI, 939
ckson, Chas. IV, 1213
ckson, Chas. IV, 1282
ckson, Chas. Cowper II, 802
ckson, Chas. Lincoln III, 182
ckson, Chas. Lincoln III, 341
ckson, Chester A. IV, 1238
ckson, Clara V, 406
ckson, Clarence I, 619
ckson, Congrave VI, 996
Jackson, Constance III, 182
Jackson, Constance III, 341
Jackson, Cora I, 619
Jackson, Cora I, 635
Jackson, Cora IV, 1167
Jackson, Cora IV, 1213
Jackson, Cora C. I, 635
Jackson, Cora O. IV, 1167
Jackson, Cora O. IV, 1213
Jackson, Cornelia I, 887
Jackson, Crawford I, 619
Jackson, Curtis I, 504
Jackson, Curtis I, 525
Jackson, Curtis I, 552
Jackson, Curtis I, 821
Jackson, Curtis I, 953
Jackson, Curtis I, 957
Jackson, Curtis I, 964
Jackson, Curtis I, 1094
Jackson, Curtis V, 80
Jackson, Curtis V, 305
Jackson, Curtis V, 342
Jackson, Curtis V, 406
Jackson, Curtis V, 407
Jackson, Curtis V, 439
Jackson, Curtis, Jr. I, 821
Jackson, Cynthia VI, 406
Jackson, Dabney VI, 939
Jackson, Daniel II, 380
Jackson, Daniel II, 1005
Jackson, Daniel III, 421
Jackson, Daniel III, 452
Jackson, Davan V, 919
Jackson, David I, 722
Jackson, David III, 421
Jackson, David III, 465
Jackson, David III, 486
Jackson, David III, 503
Jackson, David V, 181
Jackson, David VI, 406
Jackson, David VI, 407
Jackson, David VI, 444
Jackson, David VI, 515
Jackson, David Smith VI, 406
Jackson, Deborah I, 400
Jackson, Deborah I, 405
Jackson, Deborah I, 1048
Jackson, Deborah I, 1049
Jackson, Deborah III, 486
Jackson, Deborah III, 497
Jackson, Deborah IV, 38
Jackson, Deborah IV, 41
Jackson, Deborah V, 342
Jackson, Deborah S. V, 342
Jackson, Dillin H. V, 342
Jackson, Dinah I, 667
Jackson, Dinah II, 562
Jackson, Dinah II, 658
Jackson, Dora A. V, 504
Jackson, Dora Ann V, 504
Jackson, Doris V, 1004
Jackson, Dorotha V, 406
Jackson, Dorothy V, 406
Jackson, Edgar III, 486
Jackson, Edith I, 803
Jackson, Edith I, 821
Jackson, Edith IV, 701
Jackson, Edith B. IV, 1213
Jackson, Edith Bell IV, 1212
Jackson, Edith Elnora IV, 968
Jackson, Edith Mildred I, 635
Jackson, Edith Nichols IV, 128
Jackson, Edith W. III, 421
Jackson, Edith W. III, 441
Jackson, Edward III, 182
Jackson, Edward III, 183
Jackson, Edward IV, 1322
Jackson, Edward C. II, 802
Jackson, Edward S. II, 881
Jackson, Edwin III, 84
Jackson, Edwin A. III, 182
Jackson, Edwin A. III, 206
Jackson, Edwin Atlee II, 802
Jackson, Edwin Atlee II, 881
Jackson, Edwin L. III, 182
Jackson, Eleanor VI, 1004
Jackson, Eli I, 964
Jackson, Eliab I, 659
Jackson, Eliab I, 764
Jackson, Elihu I, 964
Jackson, Elihu I, 965
Jackson, Elijah I, 964
Jackson, Eliz. III, 53
Jackson, Eliz. III, 421
Jackson, Eliza III, 182
Jackson, Eliza III, 245
Jackson, Eliza Eachus II, 881
Jackson, Elizabeth I, 343
Jackson, Elizabeth I, 357
Jackson, Elizabeth I, 400
Jackson, Elizabeth I, 401
Jackson, Elizabeth I, 413
Jackson, Elizabeth I, 448
Jackson, Elizabeth I, 453
Jackson, Elizabeth I, 504
Jackson, Elizabeth I, 552
Jackson, Elizabeth I, 571
Jackson, Elizabeth I, 964
Jackson, Elizabeth II, 380
Jackson, Elizabeth II, 381
Jackson, Elizabeth II, 457
Jackson, Elizabeth II, 541
Jackson, Elizabeth II, 562
Jackson, Elizabeth II, 563
Jackson, Elizabeth II, 634
Jackson, Elizabeth II, 802
Jackson, Elizabeth II, 881
Jackson, Elizabeth III, 94
Jackson, Elizabeth III, 119
Jackson, Elizabeth III, 182
Jackson, Elizabeth III, 393
Jackson, Elizabeth III, 396
Jackson, Elizabeth III, 421
Jackson, Elizabeth III, 435
Jackson, Elizabeth III, 454
Jackson, Elizabeth III, 486
Jackson, Elizabeth III, 510
Jackson, Elizabeth IV, 38
Jackson, Elizabeth IV, 41
Jackson, Elizabeth IV, 95
Jackson, Elizabeth IV, 108
Jackson, Elizabeth IV, 128
Jackson, Elizabeth IV, 1213
Jackson, Elizabeth V, 80
Jackson, Elizabeth V, 252
Jackson, Elizabeth V, 275
Jackson, Elizabeth V, 305
Jackson, Elizabeth V, 913
Jackson, Elizabeth V, 928
Jackson, Elizabeth VI, 828
Jackson, Elizabeth VI, 852
Jackson, Elizabeth A. III, 182
Jackson, Elizabeth A. III, 327
Jackson, Elizabeth A. III, 381
Jackson, Elizabeth A. III, 389
Jackson, Elizabeth C. II, 881
Jackson, Elizabeth C. III, 182
Jackson, Elizabeth Clapp II, 802
Jackson, Elizabeth E. II, 881
Jackson, Elizabeth Jones II, 802
Jackson, Elizabeth Jones II, 881
Jackson, Ella III, 479
Jackson, Ella III, 486
Jackson, Ella III, 487
Jackson, Ella III, 495
Jackson, Ella A. III, 486
Jackson, Ella A. III, 505
Jackson, Ella L. III, 53
Jackson, Ella L. III, 182
Jackson, Elma IV, 95
Jackson, Elma IV, 126
Jackson, Elma IV, 128
Jackson, Elvira IV, 1212
Jackson, Elvira IV, 1213
Jackson, Elwood IV, 968
Jackson, Emily I, 887
Jackson, Emily III, 432
Jackson, Emily III, 449
Jackson, Emily B. III, 486
Jackson, Emily B. III, 500
Jackson, Emma III, 486
Jackson, Emma III, 500
Jackson, Emma V, 252
Jackson, Emma Jane IV, 227
Jackson, Enos V, 913
Jackson, Erastus V, 406
Jackson, Estelle II, 881
Jackson, Estelle II, 918
Jackson, Esther III, 421
Jackson, Esther III, 422
Jackson, Esther III, 465
Jackson, Esther III, 485
Jackson, Esther III, 486
Jackson, Esther III, 499
Jackson, Esther III, 503
Jackson, Esther IV, 41
Jackson, Esther V, 342
Jackson, Esther L. III, 484
Jackson, Esther L. III, 485
Jackson, Esther L. III, 486
Jackson, Esther L. III, 493
Jackson, Eugene III, 486
Jackson, Eunice III, 182
Jackson, Evan H. V, 629
Jackson, F. Lesley IV, 1212
Jackson, Fanny III, 183
Jackson, Fanny VI, 828
Jackson, Fanny VI, 939
Jackson, Fanny H. III, 22
Jackson, Fanny H. III, 182
Jackson, Fenton VI, 377
Jackson, Feraby I, 722
Jackson, Floren B. V, 406
Jackson, Florence III, 421
Jackson, Florence III, 469
Jackson, Florence III, 486
Jackson, Florence III, 505
Jackson, Florence L. III, 182
Jackson, Florence L. III, 207
Jackson, Florence L. III, 214
Jackson, Flushing III, 182
Jackson, France III, 245
Jackson, Frances IV, 413
Jackson, Frances T. IV, 1228
Jackson, Francis III, 182
Jackson, Francis VI, 818
Jackson, Francis A. II, 748
Jackson, Francis Arestides II, 748
Jackson, Francis H. II, 802
Jackson, Francis H. II, 881
Jackson, Francis T. IV, 1212
Jackson, Francis T. IV, 1213
Jackson, Frank V, 406
Jackson, Frederick J. III, 435
Jackson, Geo. III, 421
Jackson, Geo. III, 435
Jackson, Geo. E. IV, 227
Jackson, Geo. E. IV, 263
Jackson, George III, 182
Jackson, George III, 327
Jackson, George IV, 968
Jackson, George IV, 1212
Jackson, George IV, 1322
Jackson, George VI, 184
Jackson, George A. III, 485
Jackson, George Bement III, 183
Jackson, George E. IV, 1212
Jackson, George E. IV, 1213
Jackson, George E. IV, 1220
Jackson, George R. IV, 227
Jackson, George Ross IV, 227
Jackson, Gertrude III, 485
Jackson, Gilbert III, 182
Jackson, Gilead V, 811
Jackson, Glen V, 1004
Jackson, Glenn V, 1004
Jackson, Grace IV, 826
Jackson, Grace IV, 827
Jackson, Grace IV, 940
Jackson, Grace IV, 968
Jackson, Grace IV, 1167
Jackson, Grace IV, 1204
Jackson, Grace IV, 1212
Jackson, Grace VI, 406
Jackson, Grace VI, 515
Jackson, Grace Anna III, 486
Jackson, Grace Anna III, 508
Jackson, Griffith L. IV, 1212
Jackson, Grifith L. IV, 1212
Jackson, H. F. V, 504
Jackson, Halliday III, 182
Jackson, Hannah I, 504
Jackson, Hannah I, 961
Jackson, Hannah I, 964
Jackson, Hannah II, 380
Jackson, Hannah II, 563
Jackson, Hannah II, 676
Jackson, Hannah II, 802
Jackson, Hannah II, 816
Jackson, Hannah III, 182
Jackson, Hannah III, 422
Jackson, Hannah III, 435
Jackson, Hannah III, 443
Jackson, Hannah IV, 811
Jackson, Hannah IV, 816
Jackson, Hannah IV, 826
Jackson, Hannah IV, 827
Jackson, Hannah IV, 903
Jackson, Hannah IV, 923
Jackson, Hannah IV, 968
Jackson, Hannah IV, 1201
Jackson, Hannah IV, 1212
Jackson, Hannah IV, 1213
Jackson, Hannah V, 47
Jackson, Hannah V, 80
Jackson, Hannah V, 136
Jackson, Hannah V, 301
Jackson, Hannah V, 304
Jackson, Hannah V, 305
Jackson, Hannah V, 383
Jackson, Hannah V, 406
Jackson, Hannah VI, 406
Jackson, Hannah VI, 453
Jackson, Hannah VI, 549
Jackson, Hannah VI, 752
Jackson, Hannah Amelia III, 421
Jackson, Hannah Cobb VI, 942
Jackson, Hannah, Jr. III, 421
Jackson, Hanney VI, 879
Jackson, Harold III, 486
Jackson, Harold A. III, 486
Jackson, Harold A. III, 508
Jackson, Harriet IV, 1370
Jackson, Harriet H. II, 1050
Jackson, Harriet H. II, 1053
Jackson, Harriet M. III, 182
Jackson, Harriette M. III, 245
Jackson, Harry IV, 227
Jackson, Harvey F. V, 504
Jackson, Hazel IV, 968
Jackson, Helen H. II, 881
Jackson, Helena V, 305
Jackson, Helena V, 313
Jackson, Helena V, 406
Jackson, Helena V, 438
Jackson, Helena W. V, 406
Jackson, Hellena V, 406
Jackson, Hellena V, 438
Jackson, Henrietta II, 881
Jackson, Henry III, 182
Jackson, Henry III, 347
Jackson, Henry Vroman IV, 1238
Jackson, Henry W. III, 409
Jackson, Henry W. III, 421
Jackson, Henry W. III, 486
Jackson, Herbert Worth II, 802
Jackson, Herbert Worth II, 881
Jackson, Hester IV, 1282
Jackson, Hester V, 342
Jackson, Hezekiah VI, 818
Jackson, Hezekiah VI, 828
Jackson, Hezekiah VI, 851
Jackson, Hezekiah VI, 939
Jackson, Hiram IV, 1370
Jackson, Holiday II, 152
Jackson, Holliday II, 152
Jackson, Hope I, 957
Jackson, Hope I, 964
Jackson, Hope I, 965
Jackson, Horace II, 918
Jackson, Horace H. II, 881
Jackson, Howard IV, 968
Jackson, Hugh III, 149
Jackson, Hugh III, 182
Jackson, Inez Leora V, 1004
Jackson, Irena IV, 1212
Jackson, Irena IV, 1213
Jackson, Irvin H. V, 629
Jackson, Isaac I, 343
Jackson, Isaac I, 357
Jackson, Isaac I, 400
Jackson, Isaac I, 401
Jackson, Isaac I, 413
Jackson, Isaac I, 448
Jackson, Isaac IV, 38
Jackson, Isaac IV, 40
Jackson, Isaac IV, 41
Jackson, Isaac IV, 94
Jackson, Isaac IV, 727
Jackson, Isaac IV, 826
Jackson, Isaac IV, 827
Jackson, Isaac IV, 903
Jackson, Isaac IV, 968
Jackson, Isaac IV, 1167
Jackson, Isaac IV, 1174
Jackson, Isaac IV, 1201
Jackson, Isaac IV, 1204
Jackson, Isaac IV, 1211
Jackson, Isaac IV, 1212
Jackson, Isaac IV, 1213
Jackson, Isaac IV, 1214
Jackson, Isaac IV, 1370
Jackson, Isaac V, 782
Jackson, Isaac V, 783
Jackson, Isaac VI, 406
Jackson, Isaac VI, 418
Jackson, Isaac VI, 549
Jackson, Isaac VI, 807
Jackson, Isaac VI, 862
Jackson, Isaac W. IV, 1370
Jackson, Isaac, Jr. I, 400
Jackson, Isaac, Jr. IV, 923
Jackson, Isaac, Jr. IV, 968
Jackson, Isaac, Jr. IV, 1207
Jackson, Isaac, Jr. VI, 752
Jackson, Isaac, Sr. IV, 827
Jackson, Israel II, 881
Jackson, Israel II, 944
Jackson, Israel Ernest IV, 413
Jackson, J. A. IV, 1213
Jackson, J. D. IV, 1213
Jackson, J. Fenton VI, 394
Jackson, J. Fenton VI, 406
Jackson, J. W. IV, 1213
Jackson, J. Wesley IV, 1167
Jackson, J. Wesley IV, 1212
Jackson, Jacob I, 357
Jackson, Jacob I, 400
Jackson, Jacob I, 401
Jackson, Jacob I, 504
Jackson, Jacob I, 525
Jackson, Jacob I, 552
Jackson, Jacob I, 659

Jackson, Jacob I, 682
Jackson, Jacob I, 690
Jackson, Jacob I, 764
Jackson, Jacob I, 887
Jackson, Jacob I, 953
Jackson, Jacob I, 964
Jackson, Jacob I, 1094
Jackson, Jacob III, 393
Jackson, Jacob III, 409
Jackson, Jacob III, 421
Jackson, Jacob III, 449
Jackson, Jacob III, 482
Jackson, Jacob III, 486
Jackson, Jacob III, 487
Jackson, Jacob III, 500
Jackson, Jacob V, 80
Jackson, Jacob V, 215
Jackson, Jacob V, 284
Jackson, Jacob V, 305
Jackson, Jacob V, 342
Jackson, Jacob V, 369
Jackson, Jacob V, 405
Jackson, Jacob V, 406
Jackson, Jacob V, 469
Jackson, Jacob W. III, 479
Jackson, Jacob W. III, 486
Jackson, Jacob W. III, 487
Jackson, Jacob W. III, 495
Jackson, Jacob, Jr. V, 305
Jackson, James I, 357
Jackson, James I, 400
Jackson, James I, 413
Jackson, James I, 448
Jackson, James II, 380
Jackson, James III, 119
Jackson, James III, 121
Jackson, James III, 148
Jackson, James III, 182
Jackson, James III, 314
Jackson, James III, 360
Jackson, James III, 457
Jackson, James III, 486
Jackson, James IV, 227
Jackson, James IV, 721
Jackson, James IV, 727
Jackson, James IV, 827
Jackson, James IV, 1167
Jackson, James IV, 1210
Jackson, James IV, 1212
Jackson, James IV, 1213
Jackson, James IV, 1214
Jackson, James VI, 828
Jackson, James A. III, 182
Jackson, James Alvin IV, 1212
Jackson, James Ellwood II, 802
Jackson, James Ellwood II, 881
Jackson, James J. III, 421
Jackson, James J., Jr. III, 399
Jackson, James K. III, 486
Jackson, James K. III, 500
Jackson, James M. II, 563
Jackson, James M. II, 748
Jackson, James M. II, 802
Jackson, James M. II, 881
Jackson, James Sylvester IV, 968
Jackson, James Titus IV, 1212
Jackson, James Wm. IV, 227
Jackson, James, Sr. III, 182
Jackson, Jane II, 829
Jackson, Jane III, 182
Jackson, Jane III, 206
Jackson, Jane III, 421
Jackson, Jane III, 446
Jackson, Jane III, 452
Jackson, Jane IV, 908
Jackson, Jane IV, 1282
Jackson, Jane VI, 828
Jackson, Jane E. II, 881
Jackson, Jane E. III, 182
Jackson, Jane E. III, 480
Jackson, Jane E. III, 486
Jackson, Jane Elizabeth III, 510
Jackson, Jane L. III, 182
Jackson, Jane T. II, 881
Jackson, Jane T. II, 944
Jackson, Jarvis III, 381
Jackson, Jarvis III, 421
Jackson, Jarvis III, 486
Jackson, Jarvis III, 504
Jackson, Jarvis VI, 902
Jackson, Jarvis VI, 1004
Jackson, Jas. III, 421
Jackson, Jas. J. III, 421
Jackson, Jas. J., Jr. III, 399
Jackson, Jas. M. III, 182
Jackson, Jay Dwight IV, 1213
Jackson, Jeannetta II, 802
Jackson, Jehu I, 504
Jackson, Jehu I, 957
Jackson, Jehu I, 964
Jackson, Jehu I, 965
Jackson, Jemima III, 486
Jackson, Jemima V, 745
Jackson, Jemima VI, 902
Jackson, Jennie E. II, 881
Jackson, Jennie Eachus II, 881
Jackson, Jennie Isabel II, 881
Jackson, Jennie Isabella II, 802
Jackson, Jennie Thompson II, 802
Jackson, Jeremiah B. III, 486
Jackson, Jeremiah B. III, 510
Jackson, Jerusha III, 510
Jackson, Jesse I, 1085
Jackson, Jesse I, 1094
Jackson, Jesse IV, 41
Jackson, Jesse IV, 95
Jackson, Jesse IV, 128
Jackson, Jesse IV, 1212
Jackson, Jesse IV, 1370
Jackson, Jesse V, 80
Jackson, Jesse V, 305
Jackson, Jesse V, 337
Jackson, Jesse V, 342
Jackson, Jesse V, 405
Jackson, Jesse V, 406
Jackson, Jesse V, 446
Jackson, Jesse VI, 828
Jackson, Job I, 964
Jackson, Joel I, 964
Jackson, John I, 525
Jackson, John I, 552
Jackson, John I, 953
Jackson, John I, 964
Jackson, John I, 1075
Jackson, John I, 1085
Jackson, John I, 1094
Jackson, John II, 381
Jackson, John II, 445
Jackson, John II, 802
Jackson, John II, 881
Jackson, John III, 454
Jackson, John III, 486
Jackson, John III, 501
Jackson, John IV, 40
Jackson, John IV, 69
Jackson, John IV, 93
Jackson, John IV, 94
Jackson, John IV, 95
Jackson, John V, 80
Jackson, John V, 342
Jackson, John V, 406
Jackson, John V, 459
Jackson, John V, 913
Jackson, John VI, 515
Jackson, John VI, 828
Jackson, John VI, 939
Jackson, John VI, 956
Jackson, John VI, 966
Jackson, John D. III, 183
Jackson, John Fenton VI, 407
Jackson, John H. IV, 1212
Jackson, John H. IV, 1213
Jackson, John W. V, 305
Jackson, John, Jr. VI, 828
Jackson, John, Sr. VI, 828
Jackson, Jonas VI, 11
Jackson, Jonathan IV, 95
Jackson, Jonathan IV, 128
Jackson, Jonathan VI, 406
Jackson, Jonathan VI, 407
Jackson, Jonathan VI, 515
Jackson, Jonathan H. V, 342
Jackson, Jonathan L. I, 448
Jackson, Jonathan S. IV, 128
Jackson, Jonathan Sharpless IV, 95
Jackson, Jonathan Sharpless IV, 128
Jackson, Joseph I, 400
Jackson, Joseph I, 504
Jackson, Joseph I, 635
Jackson, Joseph I, 953
Jackson, Joseph I, 964
Jackson, Joseph I, 965
Jackson, Joseph I, 1038
Jackson, Joseph I Sup 1, 11
Jackson, Joseph II, 881
Jackson, Joseph II, 1005
Jackson, Joseph IV, 41
Jackson, Joseph IV, 128
Jackson, Joseph V, 305
Jackson, Joseph V, 405
Jackson, Joseph V, 913
Jackson, Joseph VI, 406
Jackson, Joseph VI, 407
Jackson, Joseph S. VI, 368
Jackson, Joseph S. VI, 406
Jackson, Joseph S. VI, 407
Jackson, Joseph S. VI, 416
Jackson, Joseph S. VI, 435
Jackson, Joseph T. II, 881
Jackson, Josephine III, 421
Jackson, Josephine III, 486
Jackson, Josephine III, 495
Jackson, Josephine V, 388
Jackson, Josephine V, 406
Jackson, Josiah I, 1094
Jackson, Josiah IV, 95
Jackson, Josiah IV, 827
Jackson, Josiah IV, 1167
Jackson, Josiah V, 80
Jackson, Josiah V, 304
Jackson, Josiah V, 305
Jackson, Josiah V, 394
Jackson, Josiah V, 406
Jackson, Josiah VI, 371
Jackson, Josiah VI, 406
Jackson, Josiah VI, 407
Jackson, Josiah VI, 428
Jackson, Josiah VI, 453
Jackson, Josiah VI, 515
Jackson, Josiah VI, 850
Jackson, Jr. Elizabeth IV, 1212
Jackson, Jr. Isaac IV, 1212
Jackson, Julia III, 486
Jackson, Julia III, 495
Jackson, Julia IV, 1322
Jackson, Julia C. III, 486
Jackson, Julia C. III, 500
Jackson, Jury V, 406
Jackson, Jury T. V, 80
Jackson, Jury T. V, 305
Jackson, Jury T. V, 406
Jackson, Katharine I, 400
Jackson, Katharine I, 409
Jackson, Katharine I, 821
Jackson, Katharine III, 422
Jackson, Katharine King III, 183
Jackson, Katherine VI, 549
Jackson, Kela IV, 1322
Jackson, Kesiah V, 217
Jackson, Kesiah V, 252
Jackson, Keturah IV, 1207
Jackson, Keturah IV, 1211
Jackson, Keturah IV, 1212
Jackson, Keturah V, 782
Jackson, Keturah V, 783
Jackson, Kezia III, 480
Jackson, Kezia III, 485
Jackson, Kezia III, 486
Jackson, Keziah I, 964
Jackson, Keziah III, 486
Jackson, Keziah V, 80
Jackson, Keziah VI, 828
Jackson, Keziah VI, 852
Jackson, Larkin VI, 800
Jackson, Larkin VI, 828
Jackson, Lesley IV, 1213
Jackson, Leslie T. III, 182
Jackson, Levi I, 357
Jackson, Levi I, 400
Jackson, Levi I, 448
Jackson, Levi I, 453
Jackson, Levi IV, 1370
Jackson, Levi V, 397
Jackson, Levi C. V, 342
Jackson, Lewis VI, 846
Jackson, Lewis W. VI, 406
Jackson, Lewis Walker VI, 406
Jackson, Lieut. H. P. III, 510
Jackson, Lilia VI, 488
Jackson, Lilia VI, 575
Jackson, Lilia VI, 635
Jackson, Lilia VI, 717
Jackson, Lillian IV, 968
Jackson, Lillian Irene III, 486
Jackson, Lillie III, 485
Jackson, Lindley H. V, 342
Jackson, Lindley M. V, 342
Jackson, Little Belle III, 435
Jackson, Llewellyn VI, 406
Jackson, Llewellyn VI, 422
Jackson, Lonnie III, 486
Jackson, Louis Irena IV, 1238
Jackson, Louisa V, 80
Jackson, Louisa V, 85
Jackson, Louisa V, 407
Jackson, Louisa Emmaline VI, 752
Jackson, Louisa Emmaline VI, 779
Jackson, Lucinda V, 80
Jackson, Lucinda V, 304
Jackson, Lucinda V, 305
Jackson, Lucinda V, 397
Jackson, Lucinda V, 406
Jackson, Luckey VI, 811
Jackson, Lucretia V, 629
Jackson, Lucretia V, 981
Jackson, Lucretia V, 1004
Jackson, Lucy V, 745
Jackson, Luke VI, 828
Jackson, Luly M. IV, 1238
Jackson, Lydia II, 881
Jackson, Lydia IV, 1212
Jackson, Lydia IV, 1213
Jackson, Lydia V, 80
Jackson, Lydia V, 284
Jackson, Lydia V, 305
Jackson, Lydia V, 342
Jackson, Lydia V, 406
Jackson, Lydia V, 407
Jackson, Lydia V, 439
Jackson, Lydia J. V, 406
Jackson, Lydia Jane V, 406
Jackson, Lydia M. V, 406
Jackson, Lydia, Jr. V, 80
Jackson, Lydia, Sr. V, 80
Jackson, M. Franklin III, 485
Jackson, Mabel Asche III, 30
Jackson, Mabel Asche III, 182
Jackson, Mack VI, 828
Jackson, Malinda V, 80
Jackson, Malinda V, 305
Jackson, Malinda V, 342
Jackson, Malinda V, 405
Jackson, Margaret II, 235
Jackson, Margaret II, 657
Jackson, Margaret II, 1005
Jackson, Margaret III, 486
Jackson, Margaret III, 509
Jackson, Margaret IV, 40
Jackson, Margaret IV, 41
Jackson, Margaret IV, 827
Jackson, Margaret IV, 1167
Jackson, Margaret IV, 1213
Jackson, Margaret VI, 406
Jackson, Margaret VI, 439
Jackson, Margaret C. V, 406
Jackson, Margery I, 722
Jackson, Mari Frances IV, 413
Jackson, Maria V, 619
Jackson, Maria V, 629
Jackson, Maria L. III, 421
Jackson, Marianna I, 635
Jackson, Marion F. III, 486
Jackson, Marion Frances III, 486
Jackson, Martha I, 659
Jackson, Martha I, 682
Jackson, Martha I, 690
Jackson, Martha I, 764
Jackson, Martha II, 381
Jackson, Martha II, 558
Jackson, Martha III, 30
Jackson, Martha III, 182
Jackson, Martha III, 341
Jackson, Martha III, 393
Jackson, Martha III, 409
Jackson, Martha III, 421
Jackson, Martha III, 451
Jackson, Martha III, 454
Jackson, Martha III, 486
Jackson, Martha III, 487
Jackson, Martha III, 494
Jackson, Martha III, 505
Jackson, Martha III, 506
Jackson, Martha VI, 823
Jackson, Martha VI, 828
Jackson, Martha B. III, 486
Jackson, Martha M. V, 406
Jackson, Martha R. V, 181
Jackson, Martha W. IV, 227
Jackson, Mary I, 344
Jackson, Mary I, 357
Jackson, Mary I, 376
Jackson, Mary I, 379
Jackson, Mary I, 400
Jackson, Mary I, 401
Jackson, Mary I, 404
Jackson, Mary I, 413
Jackson, Mary I, 431
Jackson, Mary I, 448
Jackson, Mary I, 453
Jackson, Mary I, 504
Jackson, Mary I, 887
Jackson, Mary I, 964
Jackson, Mary I, 965
Jackson, Mary I, 1085
Jackson, Mary I, 1094
Jackson, Mary I, 1095
Jackson, Mary II, 381
Jackson, Mary II, 553
Jackson, Mary II, 629
Jackson, Mary III, 182
Jackson, Mary III, 360
Jackson, Mary III, 381
Jackson, Mary III, 410
Jackson, Mary III, 421
Jackson, Mary III, 422
Jackson, Mary III, 423
Jackson, Mary III, 430
Jackson, Mary III, 436
Jackson, Mary III, 444
Jackson, Mary III, 445
Jackson, Mary III, 446
Jackson, Mary III, 455
Jackson, Mary III, 457
Jackson, Mary III, 468
Jackson, Mary III, 473
Jackson, Mary III, 485
Jackson, Mary III, 486
Jackson, Mary III, 487
Jackson, Mary III, 501
Jackson, Mary III, 503
Jackson, Mary III, 504
Jackson, Mary III, 506
Jackson, Mary IV, 93
Jackson, Mary IV, 95
Jackson, Mary IV, 128
Jackson, Mary IV, 130
Jackson, Mary IV, 701
Jackson, Mary IV, 827
Jackson, Mary IV, 1167
Jackson, Mary IV, 1174
Jackson, Mary IV, 1212
Jackson, Mary IV, 1213
Jackson, Mary IV, 1220
Jackson, Mary IV, 1238
Jackson, Mary IV, 1370
Jackson, Mary V, 80
Jackson, Mary V, 181
Jackson, Mary V, 446
Jackson, Mary V, 686
Jackson, Mary V, 913
Jackson, Mary VI, 42
Jackson, Mary VI, 251
Jackson, Mary VI, 371
Jackson, Mary VI, 377
Jackson, Mary VI, 406
Jackson, Mary VI, 476
Jackson, Mary VI, 477
Jackson, Mary VI, 511
Jackson, Mary VI, 555
Jackson, Mary VI, 556
Jackson, Mary VI, 558
Jackson, Mary VI, 827
Jackson, Mary VI, 881
Jackson, Mary A. III, 182
Jackson, Mary Alice I, 635
Jackson, Mary Alice IV, 950
Jackson, Mary Ann II, 563
Jackson, Mary Ann II, 748
Jackson, Mary Ann II, 802
Jackson, Mary Ann II, 881
Jackson, Mary Ann III, 182
Jackson, Mary Ann IV, 633
Jackson, Mary Ann IV, 638
Jackson, Mary Ann IV, 721
Jackson, Mary Ann IV, 727
Jackson, Mary Ann IV, 1212
Jackson, Mary Ann IV, 1213
Jackson, Mary Anna III, 182
Jackson, Mary B. IV, 827
Jackson, Mary Burhaus IV, 132
Jackson, Mary C. II, 881
Jackson, Mary C. III, 72
Jackson, Mary C. III, 223
Jackson, Mary C. IV, 227
Jackson, Mary C. IV, 263
Jackson, Mary C. IV, 1213
Jackson, Mary Clapp II, 788
Jackson, Mary Clapp II, 802
Jackson, Mary D. VI, 380
Jackson, Mary D. VI, 406
Jackson, Mary D. VI, 407
Jackson, Mary D. VI, 416
Jackson, Mary D. VI, 435
Jackson, Mary D. VI, 444
Jackson, Mary E. VI, 407
Jackson, Mary Elizabeth VI, 37
Jackson, Mary Elizabeth VI, 39
Jackson, Mary Elizabeth VI, 40
Jackson, Mary Ella IV, 227
Jackson, Mary Ellen I, 887
Jackson, Mary H. II, 802
Jackson, Mary H. II, 881
Jackson, Mary H. III, 139
Jackson, Mary J. III, 486
Jackson, Mary Jane III, 486
Jackson, Mary Jane IV, 968
Jackson, Mary Jane VI, 406
Jackson, Mary L. IV, 95
Jackson, Mary L. VI, 380
Jackson, Mary L. VI, 407
Jackson, Mary Reiff II, 802
Jackson, Mary S. III, 486
Jackson, Mary S. III, 510
Jackson, Mary S. IV, 95
Jackson, Mary S. IV, 128
Jackson, Mary Scott II, 293
Jackson, Maryann IV, 1210
Jackson, Massey L. V, 181
Jackson, Matilda II, 812
Jackson, Matthew VI, 1007

son, Matthew Franklin III, 486
son, Maude E. IV, 1322
son, Melicent I, 195
son, Melicent I, 200
son, Melva Gertrude II, 1050
son, Melva Gertrude II, 1053
son, Mercy IV, 41
son, Mercy IV, 814
son, Mercy IV, 827
son, Mercy IV, 1370
son, Meribah II, 802
son, Michael I, 957
son, Michal I, 964
son, Michal I, 965
son, Milinda V, 342
son, Milton P. IV, 1212
son, Milton P. IV, 1213
son, Minerva IV, 1358
son, Minerva VI, 1001
son, Morris II, 293
son, Morris II, 802
son, Morris III, 182
son, Morris Bacon III, 182
son, Moses III, 183
son, Nancy IV, 123
son, Nancy IV, 128
son, Nancy IV, 227
son, Nancy V, 80
son, Nancy VI, 827
son, Nancy VI, 828
son, Nancy VI, 829
son, Nannie I, 925
son, Naomi IV, 968
son, Nathan I, 504
son, Nathan I, 821
son, Nathan V, 305
son, Nathan V, 405
son, Nathan VI, 406
son, Nellie E. V, 504
son, Nelson IV, 1282
son, Nettie H. V, 252
son, Newel I, 964
son, Nicey VI, 939
son, Noah III, 480
son, Noah III, 486
son, Noah III, 510
son, Noah A. IV, 227
son, Obadiah III, 420
son, Obadiah III, 422
son, Obadiah III, 486
son, Obadiah III, 501
son, Obadiah III, 502
son, Ora IV, 727
son, Oscar V, 406
son, Osie V, 629
son, Pamelia VI, 828
son, Parmenus III, 396
son, Parmenus III, 486
son, Patience VI, 879
son, Pearlee IV, 968
son, Peter III, 182
son, Phebe I, 400
son, Phebe I, 401
son, Phebe I, 504
son, Phebe I, 525
son, Phebe I, 552
son, Phebe I, 957
son, Phebe I, 964
son, Phebe I, 965
son, Phebe I, 1094
son, Phebe III, 121
son, Phebe III, 393
son, Phebe III, 409
son, Phebe III, 421
son, Phebe III, 422
son, Phebe III, 449
son, Phebe III, 466
son, Phebe III, 482
son, Phebe III, 486
son, Phebe III, 487
son, Phebe III, 500
son, Phebe IV, 94
son, Phebe IV, 638
son, Phebe IV, 881
son, Phebe IV, 887
son, Phebe V, 80
son, Phebe V, 305
son, Phebe V, 342
son, Phebe V, 502
son, Phebe V, 504
son, Polly III, 487
son, Polly VI, 826
son, Polly VI, 828
son, Polly VI, 922
son, Priscilla I, 964
son, Priscilla I, 965
son, Rachel I, 357
son, Rachel I, 448
son, Rachel I, 504
son, Rachel I, 989
Jackson, Rachel II, 381
Jackson, Rachel III, 486
Jackson, Rachel III, 501
Jackson, Rachel III, 502
Jackson, Rachel V, 297
Jackson, Rachel V, 305
Jackson, Rachel V, 317
Jackson, Rachel V, 342
Jackson, Rachel VI, 406
Jackson, Rachel VI, 411
Jackson, Rachel VI, 453
Jackson, Rachel Annie VI, 406
Jackson, Rachel Annie, Sr. VI, 435
Jackson, Rachel T. II, 881
Jackson, Rachel Thomas II, 802
Jackson, Rachel Wilkinson VI, 388
Jackson, Rahway I, 401
Jackson, Ralph II, 380
Jackson, Ralph II, 381
Jackson, Ralph II, 507
Jackson, Ralph II, 541
Jackson, Ralph II, 562
Jackson, Ralph II, 634
Jackson, Reba S. III, 421
Jackson, Rebecca I, 887
Jackson, Rebecca II, 698
Jackson, Rebecca II, 748
Jackson, Rebecca II, 881
Jackson, Rebecca III, 119
Jackson, Rebecca III, 149
Jackson, Rebecca III, 182
Jackson, Rebecca III, 421
Jackson, Rebecca III, 457
Jackson, Rebecca IV, 17
Jackson, Rebecca IV, 69
Jackson, Rebecca IV, 71
Jackson, Rebecca IV, 73
Jackson, Rebecca IV, 95
Jackson, Rebecca IV, 127
Jackson, Rebecca IV, 128
Jackson, Rebecca IV, 227
Jackson, Rebecca IV, 1212
Jackson, Rebecca IV, 1214
Jackson, Rebecca V, 913
Jackson, Rebecca VI, 406
Jackson, Rebecca B. III, 148
Jackson, Rebecca B. III, 182
Jackson, Rebecca H. IV, 1212
Jackson, Reuben IV, 1212
Jackson, Reuben IV, 1213
Jackson, Reubin VI, 828
Jackson, Rev. C. L. III, 30
Jackson, Rev. C. L. III, 182
Jackson, Richard II, 748
Jackson, Richard II, 802
Jackson, Richard II, 812
Jackson, Richard II, 881
Jackson, Richard VI, 42
Jackson, Richland III, 182
Jackson, Robert VI, 818
Jackson, Robert VI, 827
Jackson, Robert B. III, 510
Jackson, Robert H. IV, 227
Jackson, Robert Walker II, 1050
Jackson, Robert Walker II, 1053
Jackson, Ruth I, 357
Jackson, Ruth I, 374
Jackson, Ruth I, 400
Jackson, Ruth I, 409
Jackson, Ruth I, 448
Jackson, Ruth I, 453
Jackson, Ruth I, 504
Jackson, Ruth I, 525
Jackson, Ruth I, 552
Jackson, Ruth I, 755
Jackson, Ruth I, 764
Jackson, Ruth I, 809
Jackson, Ruth I, 821
Jackson, Ruth I, 957
Jackson, Ruth I, 964
Jackson, Ruth II, 563
Jackson, Ruth III, 486
Jackson, Ruth IV, 84
Jackson, Ruth IV, 95
Jackson, Ruth IV, 826
Jackson, Ruth IV, 827
Jackson, Ruth IV, 1167
Jackson, Ruth IV, 1212
Jackson, Ruth IV, 1370
Jackson, Ruth V, 304
Jackson, Ruth V, 305
Jackson, Ruth V, 394
Jackson, Ruth V, 406
Jackson, Ruth VI, 371
Jackson, Ruth VI, 406
Jackson, Ruth VI, 407
Jackson, Ruth VI, 411
Jackson, Ruth VI, 453
Jackson, Ruth L. V, 504
Jackson, Ruth T. III, 420
Jackson, Ruth T. III, 422
Jackson, Sally III, 487
Jackson, Sally IV, 1370
Jackson, Sally VI, 807
Jackson, Sally VI, 966
Jackson, Sam'l. III, 182
Jackson, Samuel I, 504
Jackson, Samuel I, 552
Jackson, Samuel I, 964
Jackson, Samuel II, 381
Jackson, Samuel II, 748
Jackson, Samuel III, 182
Jackson, Samuel III, 422
Jackson, Samuel III, 486
Jackson, Samuel III, 487
Jackson, Samuel III, 497
Jackson, Samuel IV, 17
Jackson, Samuel IV, 41
Jackson, Samuel IV, 69
Jackson, Samuel IV, 71
Jackson, Samuel IV, 128
Jackson, Samuel IV, 816
Jackson, Samuel IV, 827
Jackson, Samuel V, 913
Jackson, Samuel VI, 406
Jackson, Samuel K. III, 53
Jackson, Samuel K. III, 94
Jackson, Samuel K. III, 182
Jackson, Samuel King II, 802
Jackson, Samuel King II, 881
Jackson, Samuel, Jr. IV, 128
Jackson, Sarah I, 357
Jackson, Sarah I, 400
Jackson, Sarah I, 401
Jackson, Sarah I, 413
Jackson, Sarah I, 414
Jackson, Sarah I, 445
Jackson, Sarah I, 448
Jackson, Sarah I, 504
Jackson, Sarah I, 682
Jackson, Sarah I, 957
Jackson, Sarah I, 964
Jackson, Sarah I, 965
Jackson, Sarah II, 507
Jackson, Sarah II, 562
Jackson, Sarah II, 748
Jackson, Sarah II, 802
Jackson, Sarah II, 812
Jackson, Sarah II, 881
Jackson, Sarah II, 944
Jackson, Sarah III, 182
Jackson, Sarah III, 314
Jackson, Sarah III, 420
Jackson, Sarah III, 421
Jackson, Sarah III, 422
Jackson, Sarah III, 466
Jackson, Sarah III, 480
Jackson, Sarah III, 485
Jackson, Sarah III, 486
Jackson, Sarah III, 504
Jackson, Sarah IV, 41
Jackson, Sarah IV, 827
Jackson, Sarah V, 80
Jackson, Sarah V, 229
Jackson, Sarah V, 252
Jackson, Sarah V, 305
Jackson, Sarah V, 342
Jackson, Sarah V, 437
Jackson, Sarah VI, 406
Jackson, Sarah Ann II, 807
Jackson, Sarah Ann IV, 1212
Jackson, Sarah Ann IV, 1213
Jackson, Sarah Ann Hicklen IV, 727
Jackson, Sarah B. V, 971
Jackson, Sarah Bell V, 979
Jackson, Sarah C. IV, 727
Jackson, Sarah C. IV, 732
Jackson, Sarah Fisher II, 802
Jackson, Sarah Fisher II, 881
Jackson, Sarah Jane VI, 407
Jackson, Sarah Smith III, 182
Jackson, Sarah W. VI, 406
Jackson, Sidney IV, 827
Jackson, Sidney VI, 362
Jackson, Sidney VI, 406
Jackson, Sidney VI, 407
Jackson, Sidney U. III, 495
Jackson, Sidney W. III, 486
Jackson, Sol. S. III, 510
Jackson, Solomon III, 493
Jackson, Solomon III, 500
Jackson, Solomon S. III, 422
Jackson, Solomon S. III, 484
Jackson, Solomon S. III, 485
Jackson, Solomon S. III, 486
Jackson, Solomon S. III, 495
Jackson, Solomon S. III, 508
Jackson, Stephen II, 380
Jackson, Stephen II, 381
Jackson, Stephen II, 488
Jackson, Stephen II, 562
Jackson, Stephen III, 486
Jackson, Stephen IV, 413
Jackson, Stephen IV, 827
Jackson, Stephen IV, 1167
Jackson, Stephen IV, 1213
Jackson, Stephen IV, 1228
Jackson, Stephen F. III, 486
Jackson, Susan B. III, 182
Jackson, Susan P. III, 347
Jackson, Susanna I, 400
Jackson, Susanna I, 404
Jackson, Susanna I, 525
Jackson, Susanna I, 552
Jackson, Susanna II, 563
Jackson, Susanna IV, 94
Jackson, Susanna IV, 113
Jackson, Susannah I, 957
Jackson, Susannah I, 964
Jackson, Susannah I, 965
Jackson, Susannah VI, 406
Jackson, Sussannah II, 595
Jackson, Sydney IV, 41
Jackson, Sylvester IV, 701
Jackson, Sylvester IV, 968
Jackson, Tacy E. III, 399
Jackson, Tacy E. III, 421
Jackson, Thadeus III, 182
Jackson, Theodore VI, 828
Jackson, Thomas I, 400
Jackson, Thomas I, 1048
Jackson, Thomas I Sup 1, 11
Jackson, Thomas III, 421
Jackson, Thomas III, 422
Jackson, Thomas III, 423
Jackson, Thomas III, 444
Jackson, Thomas III, 445
Jackson, Thomas III, 446
Jackson, Thomas III, 473
Jackson, Thomas III, 485
Jackson, Thomas III, 487
Jackson, Thomas IV, 95
Jackson, Thomas V, 305
Jackson, Thomas VI, 828
Jackson, Thomas VI, 925
Jackson, Thomas H. II, 152
Jackson, Thomas H. III, 182
Jackson, Thomas L. V, 305
Jackson, Thomas S. II, 748
Jackson, Thomas S. V, 80
Jackson, Thos. III, 422
Jackson, Thos. V, 913
Jackson, Thos. S. II, 881
Jackson, Townie III, 421
Jackson, Townsend III, 486
Jackson, Townsend III, 487
Jackson, Townsend III, 505
Jackson, Townsend III, 506
Jackson, Uriah I, 964
Jackson, Uriah I, 1094
Jackson, Uriah V, 80
Jackson, Uriah V, 252
Jackson, Uriah S. V, 181
Jackson, Velma M. IV, 968
Jackson, Verna IV, 968
Jackson, Victorine E. II, 717
Jackson, W. C. I, 635
Jackson, W. Elmore IV, 1167
Jackson, Walter I, 379
Jackson, Walter I, 400
Jackson, Walter I, 1032
Jackson, Walter I, 1041
Jackson, Walter I, 1048
Jackson, Warner II, 802
Jackson, Warner II, 881
Jackson, Warner A. IV, 1212
Jackson, Warner A. IV, 1213
Jackson, Washington VI, 922
Jackson, Washington VI, 939
Jackson, Wd. Catharine II, 816
Jackson, Wd. Elizabeth II, 488
Jackson, Wd. Elizabeth II, 562
Jackson, Wd. Mary D. VI, 406
Jackson, Wd. Milly VI, 862
Jackson, Wd. Nena VI, 422
Jackson, Wd. Nena Mattison VI, 406
Jackson, Wd. Sarah II, 381
Jackson, Wd. Sarah II, 562
Jackson, Wd. Susan P. III, 182
Jackson, Wesley Elmon IV, 1213
Jackson, Wesley Elmore IV, 1167
Jackson, Widow Elizabeth I, 1043
Jackson, William I, 400
Jackson, William I, 401
Jackson, William I, 448
Jackson, William I, 504
Jackson, William I, 659
Jackson, William I, 682
Jackson, William I, 964
Jackson, William I, 965
Jackson, William I, 989
Jackson, William I, 1094
Jackson, William II, 802
Jackson, William III, 182
Jackson, William III, 443
Jackson, William III, 487
Jackson, William IV, 41
Jackson, William IV, 1212
Jackson, William V, 80
Jackson, William V, 305
Jackson, William V, 397
Jackson, William VI, 251
Jackson, William VI, 807
Jackson, William VI, 811
Jackson, William VI, 823
Jackson, William VI, 827
Jackson, William VI, 828
Jackson, William VI, 939
Jackson, William B. VI, 840
Jackson, William C. F. III, 183
Jackson, William F. V, 181
Jackson, William H. IV, 1370
Jackson, William M. III, 96
Jackson, William Morris III, 182
Jackson, William W. III, 182
Jackson, William W. V, 406
Jackson, William Walter III, 182
Jackson, William, Jr. VI, 515
Jackson, Wm. I, 400
Jackson, Wm. I, 413
Jackson, Wm. II, 595
Jackson, Wm. II, 881
Jackson, Wm. II, 1005
Jackson, Wm. III, 422
Jackson, Wm. III, 480
Jackson, Wm. III, 510
Jackson, Wm. IV, 1212
Jackson, Wm. IV, 1213
Jackson, Wm. V, 181
Jackson, Wm. V, 446
Jackson, Wm. V, 1004
Jackson, Wm. VI, 515
Jackson, Wm. A. II, 748
Jackson, Wm. Arthur II, 748
Jackson, Wm. Hayward II, 802
Jackson, Wm. M. III, 214
Jackson, Wm. Morris II, 802
Jackson, Wm. Morris II, 881
Jackson, Wm. P. II, 1050
Jackson, Wm. P. II, 1053
Jackson, Wm. S. IV, 1322
Jackson, Wm. W. III, 22
Jackson, Wm. W. III, 183
Jackson, Wm., Jr. VI, 515
Jackson, Wm., Sr. VI, 515
Jackson, Zebulun III, 486
Jackson, Zelma V, 1004
Jackson, Zipporah III, 183
Jackson, Zodoc I, 964
Jacob, ??? III, 183
Jacob, A. Gertrude III, 183
Jacob, Ann II, 532
Jacob, Ann II, 563
Jacob, Anna II, 709
Jacob, Caleb II, 381
Jacob, Caleb II, 563
Jacob, Edith Gertrude III, 183
Jacob, Edna III, 183
Jacob, Elizabeth II, 381
Jacob, Elizabeth II, 532
Jacob, Elizabeth II, 675
Jacob, Elizabeth II, 709
Jacob, Elizabeth II, 748
Jacob, Emma III, 183
Jacob, Emma L. III, 183
Jacob, Hannah VI, 407
Jacob, Hildegarde V, 671
Jacob, Hildegarde V, 686
Jacob, James I, 722
Jacob, James V, 745
Jacob, James C. III, 183
Jacob, Joseph II, 675
Jacob, Joseph P. II, 709
Jacob, Joshua II, 381
Jacob, Joshua II, 709
Jacob, Lois Antoinette III, 183
Jacob, Louis III, 183
Jacob, Mabelle J. III, 183
Jacob, R. Hildegarde V, 686
Jacob, Samuel II, 532
Jacob, Samuel II, 563
Jacob, Thomas II, 381
Jacob, Walter S. III, 183
Jacobs, Addie M. IV, 1322
Jacobs, Albert IV, 1282
Jacobs, Alen VI, 939
Jacobs, Alta IV, 1283
Jacobs, Amanda IV, 727
Jacobs, Amanda IV, 827
Jacobs, Ann II, 563

Jacobs, Ann II, 709
Jacobs, Anna B. II, 748
Jacobs, Anna W. II, 802
Jacobs, Barclay Abner IV, 968
Jacobs, Bertha I, 633
Jacobs, Bertha I, 635
Jacobs, Beulah II, 489
Jacobs, Beulah II, 563
Jacobs, Caleb II, 381
Jacobs, Caleb II, 563
Jacobs, Caleb II, 685
Jacobs, Caroline IV, 827
Jacobs, Caroline H. IV, 968
Jacobs, Caroline H. IV, 1018
Jacobs, Caroline W. IV, 727
Jacobs, Caroline W. IV, 968
Jacobs, Catharine II, 802
Jacobs, Catharine II, 881
Jacobs, Catherine W. II, 802
Jacobs, Charles II, 802
Jacobs, Don Edwin V, 745
Jacobs, Earl V, 745
Jacobs, Edmon I, 217
Jacobs, Edmund I, 242
Jacobs, Elisabeth I, 52
Jacobs, Elisabeth I, 54
Jacobs, Elisabeth I, 242
Jacobs, Elisha C. VI, 939
Jacobs, Elishabe II, 563
Jacobs, Elizabeth II, 381
Jacobs, Elizabeth II, 563
Jacobs, Elizabeth II, 748
Jacobs, Elizabeth M. II, 791
Jacobs, Emma L. III, 97
Jacobs, Emma L. III, 201
Jacobs, Eva IV, 1283
Jacobs, Eva R. IV, 1283
Jacobs, Florence J. II, 843
Jacobs, Florence J. II, 881
Jacobs, Franklin II, 802
Jacobs, Hannah II, 563
Jacobs, Hannah IV, 95
Jacobs, Hannah IV, 109
Jacobs, Hannah VI, 407
Jacobs, Henry V, 1004
Jacobs, Henry L. II, 802
Jacobs, Henry L. II, 843
Jacobs, Henry L. II, 881
Jacobs, Isaac IV, 1282
Jacobs, Israel, Jr. II, 563
Jacobs, J. R. IV, 1283
Jacobs, Jacob I, 52
Jacobs, Jacob I, 54
Jacobs, Jacob I, 217
Jacobs, Jacob I, 242
Jacobs, Jacob, Jr. I, 242
Jacobs, James I, 242
Jacobs, James I, 722
Jacobs, James II, 445
Jacobs, James V, 745
Jacobs, James C. III, 97
Jacobs, James C. III, 201
Jacobs, James N. IV, 1322
Jacobs, Jenie V, 1004
Jacobs, Jennie IV, 1282
Jacobs, Jennie IV, 1283
Jacobs, Jesse II, 563
Jacobs, John II, 802
Jacobs, John II, 881
Jacobs, John II, 930
Jacobs, John Brownlow II, 709
Jacobs, John Clark VI, 407
Jacobs, John Williams II, 802
Jacobs, Joseph II, 563
Jacobs, Joseph P. II, 748
Jacobs, Joshua II, 381
Jacobs, Joshua R. IV, 1283
Jacobs, Keziah VI, 939
Jacobs, Lydia II, 563
Jacobs, Lydia V, 912
Jacobs, Lydia V, 913
Jacobs, Mabelle J. III, 97
Jacobs, Marvin Earl V, 745
Jacobs, Mary I, 242
Jacobs, Mary II, 381
Jacobs, Mary II, 563
Jacobs, Mary II, 685
Jacobs, Mary III, 422
Jacobs, Mary V, 1004
Jacobs, Mary F. VI, 939
Jacobs, Mathew K. B. III, 201
Jacobs, Mearl Lester V, 745
Jacobs, Nancy V, 1004
Jacobs, Nelva IV, 1039
Jacobs, Nettie C. II, 870
Jacobs, Nettie C. II, 881
Jacobs, Omar IV, 1039
Jacobs, Omar IV, 1322
Jacobs, Patience I, 217
Jacobs, Patience I, 242
Jacobs, Patience I, 250
Jacobs, Phebe Brinton II, 804
Jacobs, Rebecca II, 802
Jacobs, Rebecca III, 254
Jacobs, Rebecca W. II, 881
Jacobs, Rebecca W. II, 930
Jacobs, Rebecca Willson II, 802
Jacobs, Rena L. V, 745
Jacobs, Richard IV, 727
Jacobs, Richard IV, 827
Jacobs, Robert IV, 1282
Jacobs, Rose V, 745
Jacobs, Ross V, 745
Jacobs, Ruth E. V, 745
Jacobs, Ruth Jane IV, 1282
Jacobs, Samuel I, 242
Jacobs, Samuel II, 381
Jacobs, Samuel II, 445
Jacobs, Samuel II, 563
Jacobs, Samuel II, 802
Jacobs, Samuel II, 881
Jacobs, Samuel W. II, 914
Jacobs, Samuel W. II, 930
Jacobs, Samuel W. II, 931
Jacobs, Samuel Willson II, 802
Jacobs, Sarah II, 445
Jacobs, Sarah VI, 377
Jacobs, Sarah VI, 407
Jacobs, Sidney II, 698
Jacobs, Thomas II, 381
Jacobs, Vinnie V, 745
Jacobs, Viola IV, 1282
Jacobs, Viola IV, 1283
Jacobs, Walter IV, 1283
Jacobs, William I, 217
Jacobs, William I, 242
Jacobs, William I, 250
Jacobs, William H. VI, 927
Jacobs, William H. VI, 939
Jacobs, William R. IV, 727
Jacobs, William S. II, 802
Jacobs, Wm. II, 748
Jacobs, Wm. Omar IV, 1322
Jacobs, Wm. R. IV, 727
Jacobs, Wm. R. IV, 827
Jacobs, Wm. R. IV, 968
Jacobs, Wm. R. IV, 1018
Jacobs, Wm. S. II, 870
Jacobs, Wm. S. II, 881
Jacobson, Egbert G. III, 100
Jacobson, Egbert G. III, 183
Jacobson, Franc III, 183
Jacobson, Gustav III, 183
Jacobson, Matilda III, 183
Jacobus, Cath. III, 183
Jacobus, Mary III, 183
Jacobus, Mary III, 224
Jacobus, Samuel III, 183
Jacoby, Beatrice III, 183
Jacoby, Catharine III, 183
Jacoby, Catharine III, 238
Jacoby, Dr. Eugen III, 183
Jacoby, Elaine III, 183
Jacoby, Henrietta III, 183
Jacoby, Herman Murray III, 183
Jacoby, Herman Murray III, 238
Jacocks, George III, 183
Jacocks, Thomas R. III, 183
Jacocks, William T. III, 183
Jacson, Elizabeth Jr. IV, 1221
Jacson, Stephen IV, 1221
Jaffray, Jane II, 372
Jaggar, David III, 487
Jaggar, Margaret S. III, 487
Jaggar, Margaret S. III, 488
Jaggar, Maria III, 487
Jaggar, William III, 488
Jaggar, William, Jr. III, 487
Jaggard, Mary II, 779
Jagger, John III, 183
Jagger, John III, 226
Jagger, Louise M. III, 183
Jagger, Louise M. III, 226
Jagger, Mary E. III, 510
Jagger, Sarah E. III, 183
Jagger, Sarah E. III, 226
Jaggers, Hazel IV, 1213
Jaggers, Mary IV, 1213
Jaggers, N. H. IV, 1213
Jaggers, Nichodemus IV, 1213
Jaggers, Rachel IV, 827
Jalding, Jacob VI, 867
James, ??? IV, 727
James, ??? V, 686
James, Aaron II, 381
James, Abel II, 381
James, Abel II, 484
James, Abel II, 563
James, Abel III, 183
James, Abel IV, 626
James, Abel IV, 638
James, Abel IV, 639
James, Abel IV, 727
James, Abel IV, 968
James, Abigail II, 81
James, Abigail II, 563
James, Abigail III, 183
James, Able II, 381
James, Adeline F. VI, 940
James, Agness VI, 940
James, Alfred P. V, 252
James, Alfred P. V, 406
James, Alfred R. V, 252
James, Alice II, 563
James, Alice II, 639
James, Alice II, 803
James, Alice II, 881
James, Alice III, 183
James, Alice L. M III, 183
James, Alice L. M??? III, 183
James, Allen IV, 874
James, Allen IV, 1283
James, Allie Bell IV, 1283
James, Alsinda VI, 1018
James, Amy R. IV, 413
James, Andrew III, 183
James, Angelina VI, 940
James, Ann II, 445
James, Ann II, 509
James, Ann II, 564
James, Ann II, 612
James, Ann III, 183
James, Ann IV, 630
James, Ann IV, 638
James, Ann IV, 874
James, Ann IV, 883
James, Ann IV, 1283
James, Ann C. V, 686
James, Anna II, 709
James, Anna II, 802
James, Anna II, 881
James, Anna IV, 228
James, Anna V, 583
James, Anna VI, 1012
James, Anna B. V, 406
James, Anna I. II, 783
James, Anna I. II, 839
James, Anna I. II, 881
James, Anna Lena IV, 1039
James, Anna Lizetta IV, 1039
James, Anna McFadden V, 578
James, Anna Walton II, 738
James, Anna Walton II, 748
James, Anne IV, 41
James, Aten Parker IV, 874
James, Aticus S. V, 252
James, Atticus III, 183
James, Atticus S. V, 252
James, Atticus S. V, 406
James, Benj. IV, 638
James, Benjamin IV, 41
James, Benjamin IV, 479
James, Benjamin IV, 874
James, Benjamin VI, 315
James, Bertha G. IV, 1039
James, Betsy VI, 921
James, Byrens VI, 315
James, Caleb IV, 413
James, Catharine IV, 631
James, Catharine IV, 638
James, Catharine IV, 1039
James, Catherine IV, 41
James, Catherine VI, 293
James, Catherine VI, 315
James, Celia E. VI, 995
James, Chalkley III, 183
James, Chalkley IV, 150
James, Cheney II, 748
James, Cheyney II, 748
James, Christiana VI, 991
James, Cloey VI, 1020
James, Curtis IV, 413
James, Curtis Hoops IV, 413
James, Daniel II, 381
James, Daniel IV, 874
James, Daniel VI, 921
James, Daniel VI, 939
James, Daniel VI, 1012
James, Daniel, Jr. VI, 921
James, David II, 563
James, David III, 497
James, David IV, 228
James, David IV, 536
James, David IV, 584
James, David IV, 638
James, David IV, 874
James, David IV, 908
James, David IV, 1255
James, David V, 252
James, David V, 342
James, David V, 352
James, David V, 360
James, David V, 404
James, David V, 406
James, David V, 686
James, Deborah IV, 150
James, Deborah IV, 228
James, Deborah V, 342
James, Deborah V, 360
James, Deborah V, 406
James, Deborah V, 686
James, Deborah S. V, 686
James, Deborah T. V, 406
James, Dillen H. V, 252
James, Dillon H. V, 252
James, Dillon H. V, 406
James, Dinah III, 183
James, Dock Wheeler IV, 968
James, Dr. Thomas C. II, 381
James, Edgar V, 459
James, Edith IV, 228
James, Edith IV, 536
James, Edith IV, 584
James, Edward II, 81
James, Edward II, 95
James, Edward II, 381
James, Edward II, 445
James, Edward II, 563
James, Edward II, 639
James, Edward V, 459
James, Edwin IV, 150
James, Edwin IV, 228
James, Eleanor II, 519
James, Eleanor II, 563
James, Eli IV, 874
James, Elias VI, 940
James, Elias VI, 995
James, Eliza Ann IV, 874
James, Eliza S. IV, 874
James, Elizabeth II, 381
James, Elizabeth II, 798
James, Elizabeth IV, 41
James, Elizabeth IV, 228
James, Elizabeth IV, 413
James, Elizabeth IV, 536
James, Elizabeth IV, 584
James, Elizabeth IV, 605
James, Elizabeth IV, 620
James, Elizabeth IV, 638
James, Elizabeth IV, 639
James, Elizabeth IV, 727
James, Elizabeth IV, 827
James, Elizabeth IV, 867
James, Elizabeth IV, 874
James, Elizabeth IV, 875
James, Elizabeth IV, 876
James, Elizabeth IV, 883
James, Elizabeth IV, 908
James, Elizabeth IV, 1090
James, Elizabeth IV, 1103
James, Elizabeth IV, 1107
James, Elizabeth VI, 293
James, Elizabeth VI, 315
James, Elizabeth VI, 936
James, Elizabeth VI, 939
James, Elizabeth VI, 940
James, Elizabeth VI, 1018
James, Elizabeth Alice V, 46
James, Elizabeth Alice V, 80
James, Elizabeth H. V, 772
James, Elizabeth Leech IV, 639
James, Elizabeth M. IV, 727
James, Elizabeth M. IV, 827
James, Elizabeth Morris II, 381
James, Elizabeth Morris II, 564
James, Elizabeth R. II, 881
James, Elizzbeth VI, 939
James, Ella V, 578
James, Ella N. V, 406
James, Elsa VI, 997
James, Elsa Margaret V, 459
James, Elva H. V, 406
James, Elva H. V, 686
James, Elvie H. V, 504
James, Elvin H. V, 686
James, Emaline IV, 639
James, Emaline IV, 968
James, Emeline I, 1122
James, Emeline IV, 638
James, Emily Chesterson VI, 940
James, Enoch V, 745
James, Enoch V, 772
James, Esther II, 381
James, Esther II, 563
James, Esther II, 649
James, Esther IV, 638
James, Esther IV, 653
James, Esther IV, 874
James, Esther IV, 908
James, Esther V, 305
James, Esther Ann V, 686
James, Ethel III, 183
James, Ethel M. III, 183
James, Ethel M. V, 406
James, Ethel Mae III, 183
James, Ethel Mae III, 298
James, Eunice Ann V, 745
James, Eunice Ann V, 772
James, Eva Rachel IV, 413
James, Evan IV, 41
James, Evan IV, 150
James, Evan IV, 156
James, Evan IV, 228
James, Evan IV, 264
James, Evan IV, 338
James, Evan IV, 536
James, Evan V, 504
James, Ezekiel IV, 150
James, Geo. IV, 173
James, Geo. IV, 1107
James, George II, 381
James, George II, 484
James, George II, 563
James, George IV, 41
James, George IV, 228
James, George IV, 536
James, George IV, 584
James, George K. II, 881
James, George W. VI, 940
James, Gladys IV, 1039
James, Hannah II, 81
James, Hannah II, 108
James, Hannah II, 381
James, Hannah II, 563
James, Hannah II, 680
James, Hannah III, 183
James, Hannah III, 184
James, Hannah IV, 41
James, Hannah IV, 150
James, Hannah IV, 228
James, Hannah IV, 268
James, Hannah IV, 338
James, Hannah IV, 536
James, Hannah IV, 540
James, Hannah IV, 584
James, Hannah IV, 626
James, Hannah IV, 638
James, Hannah IV, 639
James, Hannah IV, 827
James, Hannah IV, 840
James, Hannah IV, 908
James, Hannah IV, 910
James, Hannah IV, 968
James, Hannah V, 80
James, Hannah VI, 481
James, Hannah VI, 515
James, Hannah VI, 562
James, Hannah VI, 968
James, Hannah VI, 997
James, Hannah Pheby IV, 228
James, Harriet Catharine IV, 1039
James, Harriet R. III, 183
James, Harvey IV, 150
James, Henry I, 887
James, Henry III, 183
James, Henry III, 298
James, Henry III, 484
James, Henry P. III, 487
James, Hugh II, 381
James, Humphrey IV, 638
James, Imo IV, 1213
James, Imo Wright IV, 1213
James, Isaac IV, 41
James, Isaac IV, 150
James, Isaac IV, 156
James, Isaac IV, 228
James, Isaac IV, 413
James, Isaac IV, 620
James, Isaac IV, 630
James, Isaac IV, 631
James, Isaac IV, 638
James, Isaac IV, 656
James, Isaac IV, 727
James, Isaac IV, 785
James, Isaac IV, 874
James, Isaac IV, 908
James, Isaac V, 80
James, Isaac V, 342
James, Isaac VI, 293
James, Isaac VI, 310
James, Isaac VI, 315
James, Isaac VI, 341
James, Isaac VI, 344
James, Isaac VI, 936
James, Isaac VI, 939
James, Isaac VI, 977
James, Isaac VI, 1012
James, Isaac VI, 1021
James, Isaac H. IV, 727
James, Isaac H. IV, 874
James, Isaac L. VI, 917
James, Isaac P. IV, 874
James, Isaac, Jr. VI, 940
James, Isaac, Sr. IV, 1283

es, Isaiah V, 745
es, Israel IV, 228
es, J. Edwin II, 738
es, J. Edwin II, 748
es, Jacob VI, 939
es, James II, 81
es, James II, 381
es, James IV, 150
es, James IV, 228
es, James IV, 638
es, James VI, 939
es, James Morris II, 381
es, James Morris II, 564
es, Jane II, 790
es, Jane V, 406
es, Jane VI, 515
es, Jane VI, 584
es, Jesse II, 795
es, Jesse II, 804
es, Jesse IV, 228
es, Jesse IV, 413
es, Jesse IV, 536
es, Jesse IV, 638
es, Jesse IV, 867
es, Jesse IV, 874
es, Jesse IV, 883
es, Jesse IV, 908
es, Jesse James IV, 639
es, Joel L. VI, 940
es, John II, 381
es, John II, 509
es, John II, 564
es, John III, 183
es, John IV, 41
es, John IV, 228
es, John IV, 613
es, John IV, 638
es, John IV, 639
es, John IV, 653
es, John IV, 687
es, John IV, 727
es, John IV, 827
es, John IV, 874
es, John IV, 908
es, John IV, 968
es, John IV, 1039
es, John V, 305
es, John V, 406
es, John VI, 293
es, John VI, 297
es, John VI, 315
es, John VI, 884
es, John VI, 932
es, John VI, 940
es, John VI, 991
es, John, Jr. II, 564
es, Johnson VI, 876
es, Johnson VI, 939
es, Jonas IV, 228
es, Jonas IV, 338
es, Jonas IV, 536
es, Jonathan IV, 874
es, Jonathan IV, 908
es, Jonathan V, 430
es, Jonathan V, 504
es, Jonathan V, 528
es, Jonathan V, 686
es, Jonathan VI, 940
es, Jonathan VI, 943
es, Jonathan H. V, 252
es, Jonathan H. V, 406
es, Jonathan H. V, 686
es, Joseph II, 381
es, Joseph II, 445
es, Joseph III, 183
es, Joseph IV, 41
es, Joseph IV, 227
es, Joseph IV, 630
es, Joseph IV, 638
es, Joseph IV, 874
es, Joseph IV, 883
es, Joseph VI, 293
es, Joseph VI, 315
es, Joseph VI, 939
es, Joseph D. IV, 874
es, Joseph P. IV, 874
es, Joseph Smith IV, 874
es, Joseph Smith IV, 908
es, Josephine Sarah IV, 968
es, Joshua IV, 41
es, Joshua IV, 143
es, Joshua IV, 150
es, Joshua IV, 227
es, Joshua IV, 228
es, Joshua P. IV, 228
es, Joshua P. IV, 536
es, Joshua R. II, 881
es, Josiah IV, 41
es, Josiah IV, 150
es, Josiah VI, 293
es, Josiah Carr IV, 1039
James, Judith R. VI, 940
James, Keziah IV, 150
James, Lany IV, 214
James, Lany IV, 228
James, Lany IV, 968
James, Lawrence VI, 936
James, Leah IV, 727
James, Leah IV, 785
James, Leah IV, 874
James, Leroy C. VI, 917
James, Leroy R. VI, 940
James, Levi IV, 874
James, Levi C. V, 252
James, Levi C. V, 406
James, Lewis IV, 874
James, Lindley M. V, 252
James, Lindley M. V, 406
James, Linton V, 504
James, Lorenzo IV, 413
James, Lucy IV, 638
James, Lucy VI, 700
James, Lydia IV, 150
James, Lydia IV, 151
James, Lydia IV, 219
James, Lydia IV, 228
James, Lydia IV, 874
James, Lydia V, 406
James, Lydia A. II, 881
James, Lydia Ann IV, 150
James, Lydia Ann IV, 638
James, Lydia Ann IV, 639
James, Lydia Ann IV, 968
James, Lydia Frances V, 406
James, Lydia Frances V, 686
James, Lydia H. II, 881
James, Lydia Webb IV, 727
James, Lydia Webb IV, 785
James, Lydia Webb IV, 874
James, Margaret II, 381
James, Margaret IV, 41
James, Margaret IV, 228
James, Margaret IV, 265
James, Marie V, 686
James, Martha II, 381
James, Martha IV, 41
James, Martha IV, 80
James, Martha IV, 95
James, Martha IV, 150
James, Martha IV, 163
James, Martha IV, 228
James, Martha IV, 613
James, Martha IV, 638
James, Martha IV, 639
James, Martha IV, 687
James, Martha IV, 727
James, Martha IV, 874
James, Martha IV, 908
James, Martha IV, 968
James, Martha VI, 297
James, Martha VI, 315
James, Martha Ruth IV, 1039
James, Mary II, 77
James, Mary II, 81
James, Mary II, 381
James, Mary II, 509
James, Mary II, 513
James, Mary II, 563
James, Mary II, 564
James, Mary II, 881
James, Mary III, 183
James, Mary IV, 41
James, Mary IV, 228
James, Mary IV, 536
James, Mary IV, 630
James, Mary IV, 638
James, Mary IV, 639
James, Mary IV, 727
James, Mary IV, 771
James, Mary IV, 874
James, Mary IV, 908
James, Mary IV, 917
James, Mary IV, 968
James, Mary IV, 1039
James, Mary V, 252
James, Mary V, 352
James, Mary V, 404
James, Mary V, 406
James, Mary V, 686
James, Mary VI, 293
James, Mary VI, 315
James, Mary VI, 939
James, Mary Ann IV, 228
James, Mary Ann IV, 277
James, Mary Ann IV, 413
James, Mary Ann VI, 940
James, Mary C. II, 738
James, Mary C. II, 748
James, Mary Catharine IV, 413
James, Mary Catharine IV, 639
James, Mary Elizabeth III, 183
James, Mary H. V, 252
James, Mary H. V, 342
James, Mary H. V, 352
James, Mary J. V, 406
James, Mary J. V, 686
James, Mary Jane V, 406
James, Mary Jane V, 430
James, Mary Jane V, 504
James, Mary Jane V, 528
James, Mary Jane V, 686
James, Mary Katharine IV, 874
James, Mary L. IV, 1039
James, Matson VI, 940
James, Miriam IV, 638
James, Miriam IV, 827
James, Miriam IV, 842
James, Miriam IV, 874
James, Miriam IV, 883
James, Mrs. Elizabeth VI, 888
James, Nancy IV, 228
James, Nancy IV, 277
James, Nancy VI, 939
James, Nancy VI, 940
James, Naomi V, 686
James, Nathan IV, 228
James, Nettie IV, 1255
James, Oliver IV, 228
James, Olivia VI, 634
James, Olivia VI, 663
James, Olivia VI, 680
James, Olivia VI, 684
James, Olivia M. VI, 660
James, Peninah IV, 727
James, Peninah IV, 785
James, Peninah IV, 874
James, Penrose II, 381
James, Phebe II, 790
James, Phebe II, 795
James, Phebe II, 804
James, Phebe IV, 228
James, Phebe IV, 338
James, Phebe IV, 406
James, Phebe IV, 413
James, Phebe IV, 536
James, Phebe IV, 638
James, Phebe IV, 639
James, Phebe IV, 665
James, Phebe IV, 968
James, Phebe V, 80
James, Phebe S. IV, 867
James, Phebe S. IV, 874
James, Phebe S. IV, 908
James, Philip II, 381
James, Philip II, 445
James, Phillip II, 445
James, Polly VI, 918
James, Polly VI, 939
James, Polly VI, 986
James, Rachel II, 381
James, Rachel II, 839
James, Rachel IV, 150
James, Rachel IV, 162
James, Rachel IV, 228
James, Rachel IV, 297
James, Rachel IV, 338
James, Rachel IV, 517
James, Rachel IV, 536
James, Rachel IV, 584
James, Rachel IV, 638
James, Rachel IV, 639
James, Rachel IV, 727
James, Rachel IV, 873
James, Rachel IV, 874
James, Rachel IV, 908
James, Rachel IV, 968
James, Rachel IV, 1103
James, Rachel VI, 311
James, Rachel VI, 315
James, Rachel VI, 511
James, Rachel VI, 515
James, Rachel VI, 752
James, Rachel W. IV, 874
James, Raymond V, 686
James, Rebecca II, 381
James, Rebecca II, 484
James, Rebecca II, 563
James, Rebecca II, 1053
James, Rebecca III, 183
James, Rebecca IV, 150
James, Rebecca IV, 156
James, Rebecca IV, 228
James, Rebecca IV, 264
James, Rebecca IV, 278
James, Rebecca IV, 338
James, Rebecca IV, 536
James, Rebecca IV, 1103
James, Rebecca Chalkley II, 381
James, Rebecca D. IV, 1103
James, Rebeccah II, 381
James, Rebeckah II, 81
James, Rebeckah II, 95
James, Rebeckah IV, 338
James, Rebekah II, 563
James, Richard II, 381
James, Richard B. VI, 897
James, Ruth II, 381
James, Ruth IV, 150
James, Ruth IV, 874
James, Ruth VI, 752
James, Ruth VI, 761
James, Ruth Ann IV, 874
James, Ruth Ann IV, 908
James, Ruthann IV, 874
James, Sally VI, 1020
James, Samuel II, 381
James, Samuel II, 564
James, Samuel II, 790
James, Samuel III, 183
James, Samuel IV, 41
James, Samuel IV, 137
James, Samuel IV, 150
James, Samuel IV, 228
James, Samuel IV, 584
James, Samuel IV, 874
James, Samuel IV, 968
James, Samuel IV, 1039
James, Samuel B. IV, 536
James, Samuel B. IV, 1103
James, Samuel E. IV, 228
James, Samuel, Jr. IV, 228
James, Sarah II, 81
James, Sarah II, 96
James, Sarah II, 381
James, Sarah II, 445
James, Sarah II, 467
James, Sarah II, 563
James, Sarah III, 183
James, Sarah IV, 41
James, Sarah IV, 150
James, Sarah IV, 156
James, Sarah IV, 173
James, Sarah IV, 228
James, Sarah IV, 379
James, Sarah IV, 413
James, Sarah IV, 536
James, Sarah IV, 584
James, Sarah IV, 614
James, Sarah IV, 620
James, Sarah IV, 630
James, Sarah IV, 631
James, Sarah IV, 638
James, Sarah IV, 639
James, Sarah IV, 656
James, Sarah IV, 687
James, Sarah IV, 727
James, Sarah IV, 874
James, Sarah IV, 908
James, Sarah IV, 1103
James, Sarah IV, 1107
James, Sarah V, 80
James, Sarah V, 252
James, Sarah V, 342
James, Sarah V, 406
James, Sarah VI, 293
James, Sarah VI, 315
James, Sarah VI, 1012
James, Sarah Ann IV, 874
James, Sarah Cornelia III, 484
James, Sarah Cornelia III, 487
James, Sarah E. V, 459
James, Sarah F. V, 404
James, Sarah F. V, 406
James, Sarah J. IV, 613
James, Sarah Jr. IV, 638
James, Sidney IV, 228
James, Smith IV, 874
James, Susan VI, 943
James, Susan VI, 1021
James, Susanna IV, 143
James, Susanna IV, 227
James, Susanna IV, 228
James, Susanna IV, 471
James, Susanna IV, 479
James, Susannah II, 381
James, Susannah IV, 150
James, Susannah IV, 874
James, Susannah VI, 939
James, Tace IV, 968
James, Tacy IV, 638
James, Tacy IV, 639
James, Tacy IV, 727
James, Tacy IV, 968
James, Tacy IV, 1012
James, Thomas II, 381
James, Thomas II, 680
James, Thomas IV, 41
James, Thomas IV, 638
James, Thomas IV, 908
James, Thomas IV, 1269
James, Thomas V, 80
James, Thomas V, 745
James, Thomas VI, 311
James, Thomas VI, 315
James, Thomas C. II, 381
James, Thomas C. II, 564
James, Thomas Chalkey II, 564
James, Thomas, Jr. II, 563
James, Thos. IV, 638
James, Thos. IV, 727
James, Umphrey IV, 638
James, Walters S. IV, 413
James, Wd. Ann II, 381
James, Wd. Joanna II, 795
James, William II, 445
James, William IV, 150
James, William IV, 228
James, William IV, 874
James, William V, 504
James, William Carson IV, 413
James, William L. V, 686
James, Wm. II, 839
James, Wm. II, 881
James, Wm. VI, 515
James, Wm. Carson IV, 413
James, Wm. Cope II, 709
James, Wm. Cope II, 738
James, Wm. Cope II, 748
James, Wm. H. II, 881
James, Wm. T. IV, 1039
Jameson, Caleb II, 381
Jameson, David II, 381
Jameson, Elizabeth I, 1122
Jameson, Mary II, 381
Jameson, Mary II, 564
Jameson, William II, 381
Jamieson, Mary Jane IV, 639
Jamison, Allen S. II, 881
Jamison, Chas. R. II, 881
Jamison, Chas. R. II, 886
Jamison, Eliz. M. III, 183
Jamison, Elizabeth I, 887
Jamison, Elizabeth II, 881
Jamison, Elizabeth II, 886
Jamison, Ella B. II, 881
Jamison, Florence B. II, 881
Jamison, Helen L. III, 183
Jamison, Mary S. II, 881
Jamison, Mary S. II, 886
Jamison, Wm. S. II, 881
Jamison, Wm. S. II, 886
Jamison, Wm. S. III, 183
Janden, Susanna V, 913
Janden, Susannah V, 917
Jane, Elizabeth I, 552
Jane, Mary V, 502
Jane, Tucker VI, 146
Janes, David VI, 876
Janeway, Susanna I, 1120
Janeway, Susanna I, 1122
Janey, Frances II, 1006
Janey, Jacob II, 1006
Janey, Jeanette V, 677
Janey, John II, 1006
Janey, John Lea II, 1006
Janey, Martha II, 1006
Janey, Mary II, 1006
Janey, Richard II, 1006
Janey, Ruth Hannah VI, 668
Janey, Ruthanna VI, 668
Janey, Sarah II, 1006
Janey, Stephen II, 1006
Janney, ??? VI, 515
Janney, ??? VI, 516
Janney, ??? VI, 520
Janney, ??? VI, 661
Janney, ??? VI, 667
Janney, Aaron VI, 521
Janney, Aaron VI, 661
Janney, Abel II, 381
Janney, Abel II, 962
Janney, Abel II, 975
Janney, Abel II, 1005
Janney, Abel II, 1006
Janney, Abel II, 1029
Janney, Abel V, 81
Janney, Abel V, 954
Janney, Abel VI, 184
Janney, Abel VI, 204
Janney, Abel VI, 208
Janney, Abel VI, 407
Janney, Abel VI, 408
Janney, Abel VI, 467
Janney, Abel VI, 493
Janney, Abel VI, 499
Janney, Abel VI, 500
Janney, Abel VI, 514
Janney, Abel VI, 516
Janney, Abel VI, 517
Janney, Abel VI, 519
Janney, Abel VI, 520
Janney, Abel VI, 521
Janney, Abel VI, 522
Janney, Abel VI, 523
Janney, Abel VI, 529

Janney, Abel VI, 538
Janney, Abel VI, 545
Janney, Abel VI, 586
Janney, Abel VI, 599
Janney, Abel VI, 660
Janney, Abel VI, 661
Janney, Abel VI, 665
Janney, Abel VI, 666
Janney, Abel VI, 668
Janney, Abel VI, 673
Janney, Abel VI, 676
Janney, Abel VI, 735
Janney, Abel VI, 753
Janney, Abel VI, 758
Janney, Abijah VI, 407
Janney, Abijah VI, 421
Janney, Abijah VI, 500
Janney, Abijah VI, 517
Janney, Abijah VI, 519
Janney, Abijah VI, 645
Janney, Abijah VI, 654
Janney, Abijah VI, 661
Janney, Abijah VI, 662
Janney, Abijah VI, 664
Janney, Abijah VI, 667
Janney, Abijah VI, 668
Janney, Abijah VI, 674
Janney, Abijah VI, 714
Janney, Abijah VI, 739
Janney, Abijah VI, 749
Janney, Abijah VI, 750
Janney, Abijah VI, 752
Janney, Abijah VI, 753
Janney, Abijah VI, 755
Janney, Abijah VI, 756
Janney, Abijah VI, 758
Janney, Abijah VI, 759
Janney, Abijah VI, 763
Janney, Abijah VI, 767
Janney, Abijah, Jr. VI, 662
Janney, Abijah, Jr. VI, 753
Janney, Abinah VI, 516
Janney, Ada VI, 668
Janney, Ada E. VI, 667
Janney, Alabama VI, 663
Janney, Albert VI, 667
Janney, Albert VI, 668
Janney, Albert Blackstone VI, 664
Janney, Albert H. VI, 662
Janney, Albert H. VI, 663
Janney, Albert H. VI, 667
Janney, Albert H. VI, 681
Janney, Albert H. VI, 685
Janney, Albina VI, 496
Janney, Albina VI, 519
Janney, Albina Gregg VI, 664
Janney, Albinah VI, 494
Janney, Albinah VI, 518
Janney, Albinah VI, 522
Janney, Albinah VI, 569
Janney, Albinah VI, 642
Janney, Albinah VI, 661
Janney, Albinah VI, 664
Janney, Albinah VI, 744
Janney, Albinah VI, 754
Janney, Albinah VI, 758
Janney, Albinah Summers VI, 518
Janney, Alcinda VI, 518
Janney, Alcinda Marmaduke VI, 754
Janney, Alexandria VI, 661
Janney, Alfred A. VI, 663
Janney, Alfred A., Jr. VI, 663
Janney, Alice VI, 663
Janney, Alice VI, 668
Janney, Alice M. VI, 667
Janney, Alma F. V, 407
Janney, Alyce Moore VI, 667
Janney, Amanda E. II, 1072
Janney, Amanda E. II, 1074
Janney, Amos II, 1005
Janney, Amos II, 1006
Janney, Amos II, 1041
Janney, Amos IV, 338
Janney, Amos IV, 727
Janney, Amos IV, 827
Janney, Amos VI, 358
Janney, Amos VI, 407
Janney, Amos VI, 463
Janney, Amos VI, 464
Janney, Amos VI, 474
Janney, Amos VI, 493
Janney, Amos VI, 515
Janney, Amos VI, 516
Janney, Amos VI, 517
Janney, Amos VI, 519
Janney, Amos VI, 521
Janney, Amos VI, 522
Janney, Amos VI, 586
Janney, Amos VI, 599
Janney, Amos VI, 609
Janney, Amos VI, 660
Janney, Amos VI, 661
Janney, Amos VI, 662
Janney, Amos VI, 663
Janney, Amy VI, 661
Janney, Ann II, 955
Janney, Ann II, 1006
Janney, Ann VI, 517
Janney, Ann VI, 518
Janney, Ann VI, 579
Janney, Ann VI, 645
Janney, Ann VI, 661
Janney, Ann VI, 663
Janney, Ann VI, 665
Janney, Ann VI, 667
Janney, Ann VI, 674
Janney, Ann VI, 676
Janney, Ann VI, 755
Janney, Ann VI, 756
Janney, Ann VI, 777
Janney, Ann Elizabeth VI, 685
Janney, Ann S. VI, 756
Janney, Ann W. II, 748
Janney, Ann Warder VI, 519
Janney, Ann Warder VI, 755
Janney, Anna V, 81
Janney, Anna V, 143
Janney, Anna VI, 407
Janney, Anna VI, 408
Janney, Anna VI, 417
Janney, Anna VI, 517
Janney, Anna VI, 519
Janney, Anna VI, 535
Janney, Anna VI, 661
Janney, Anna VI, 663
Janney, Anna VI, 667
Janney, Anna VI, 668
Janney, Anna VI, 740
Janney, Anna VI, 745
Janney, Anna VI, 752
Janney, Anna VI, 753
Janney, Anna VI, 754
Janney, Anna VI, 756
Janney, Anna VI, 763
Janney, Anna VI, 765
Janney, Anna VI, 766
Janney, Anna VI, 772
Janney, Anna Canby II, 802
Janney, Anna Canby II, 881
Janney, Anna Canby II, 924
Janney, Anna E. VI, 662
Janney, Anna E. VI, 678
Janney, Anna Eugenia VI, 664
Janney, Anna M. II, 806
Janney, Anna M. II, 882
Janney, Anna M. II, 890
Janney, Anna Maria VI, 642
Janney, Anna Maria VI, 662
Janney, Anna Maria VI, 663
Janney, Anna Mary VI, 755
Janney, Anna Mason VI, 667
Janney, Anna Miller VI, 520
Janney, Anna Naria VI, 663
Janney, Anna P. V, 80
Janney, Anne VI, 517
Janney, Anne VI, 756
Janney, Anne B. II, 882
Janney, Anne B. II, 937
Janney, Anne W. II, 882
Janney, Annie VI, 620
Janney, Annie VI, 664
Janney, Annie VI, 665
Janney, Annie VI, 667
Janney, Annie VI, 674
Janney, Annie Elizabeth VI, 662
Janney, Annie Elizabeth VI, 678
Janney, Annie Laura VI, 662
Janney, Annie Laura VI, 733
Janney, Annie Laura VI, 753
Janney, Annie Laura VI, 755
Janney, Annie Laura VI, 757
Janney, Annie Laura VI, 764
Janney, Annie Lauria VI, 621
Janney, Annie Laurie VI, 662
Janney, Anthony B. VI, 668
Janney, Anthony Benezet VI, 758
Janney, Aquella VI, 407
Janney, Aquila V, 954
Janney, Aquila VI, 404
Janney, Aquila VI, 407
Janney, Aquila VI, 421
Janney, Aquila VI, 519
Janney, Aquila VI, 621
Janney, Aquila VI, 660
Janney, Aquila VI, 661
Janney, Aquila VI, 662
Janney, Aquila VI, 663
Janney, Aquila VI, 683
Janney, Aquila VI, 701
Janney, Aquila VI, 710
Janney, Aquila VI, 725
Janney, Aquila VI, 750
Janney, Aquila VI, 753
Janney, Aquila VI, 754
Janney, Aquila VI, 764
Janney, Aquila Janney VI, 754
Janney, Aquilla VI, 407
Janney, Aquilla VI, 408
Janney, Aquilla VI, 422
Janney, Aquilla VI, 517
Janney, Aquilla VI, 518
Janney, Aquilla VI, 521
Janney, Aquilla VI, 530
Janney, Aquilla VI, 534
Janney, Aquilla VI, 572
Janney, Aquilla VI, 662
Janney, Aquilla VI, 667
Janney, Aquilla VI, 712
Janney, Army VI, 668
Janney, Arthur V, 80
Janney, Asa VI, 408
Janney, Asa VI, 664
Janney, Asa M. VI, 396
Janney, Asa M. VI, 407
Janney, Asa M. VI, 517
Janney, Asa M. VI, 518
Janney, Asa M. VI, 645
Janney, Asa M. VI, 661
Janney, Asa M. VI, 662
Janney, Asa M. VI, 664
Janney, Asa M. VI, 667
Janney, Asa M. VI, 668
Janney, Asa Moore VI, 500
Janney, Asa Moore VI, 517
Janney, Asa Moore VI, 518
Janney, Asa Moore VI, 615
Janney, Asa Moore VI, 661
Janney, Asa Moore VI, 662
Janney, Asa Moore VI, 745
Janney, Asa Moore VI, 752
Janney, Asa Moore VI, 753
Janney, Asa Moore, Jr. VI, 662
Janney, Asbury VI, 662
Janney, Asbury VI, 678
Janney, Asbury VI, 685
Janney, Benjamin VI, 757
Janney, Benjamin F. II, 1074
Janney, Benjamin Say II, 564
Janney, Benjamin T. II, 1074
Janney, Bernard VI, 517
Janney, Bernard T. VI, 662
Janney, Bernard T. VI, 663
Janney, Bernard T. VI, 727
Janney, Bernard Taykor VI, 753
Janney, Bernard Taylor VI, 621
Janney, Bernard Taylor VI, 662
Janney, Bernard Taylor VI, 701
Janney, Bernard Taylor VI, 733
Janney, Bernard Taylor VI, 755
Janney, Bernard Taylor VI, 757
Janney, Bernard Taylor VI, 764
Janney, Bernard Taylor VI, 779
Janney, Bernard Taylor VI, 780
Janney, Bessie VI, 664
Janney, Beulah VI, 408
Janney, Beulah VI, 757
Janney, Blackstone VI, 518
Janney, Blackstone VI, 519
Janney, Blackstone VI, 572
Janney, Blackstone VI, 587
Janney, Blackstone VI, 627
Janney, Blackstone VI, 660
Janney, Blackstone VI, 661
Janney, Blackstone VI, 664
Janney, Blackstone VI, 665
Janney, Blackstone VI, 669
Janney, Blackstone VI, 713
Janney, Blackstone, Jr. VI, 661
Janney, Blakestone VI, 519
Janney, Blakstone VI, 667
Janney, Blandina Ellen VI, 664
Janney, Blandina Ellen Lutz VI, 615
Janney, Blandina Ellen Lutz VI, 662
Janney, Camelia VI, 407
Janney, Caroline IV, 827
Janney, Caroline V, 374
Janney, Caroline V, 406
Janney, Caroline VI, 519
Janney, Caroline VI, 667
Janney, Caroline VI, 755
Janney, Caroline W. II, 748
Janney, Caroline W. VI, 755
Janney, Caroline Winslow VI, 754
Janney, Causmelia VI, 408
Janney, Charles II, 1006
Janney, Charles VI, 519
Janney, Charles L. V, 80
Janney, Charles L. V, 81
Janney, Charles L. VI, 665
Janney, Charles Phillips VI, 518
Janney, Charles Phillips VI, 520
Janney, Charles Phillips VI, 754
Janney, Charles W. VI, 755
Janney, Charlotte II, 962
Janney, Charlotte II, 1046
Janney, Charlotte II, 1053
Janney, Chas Heaton VI, 663
Janney, Chas. Hamilton VI, 664
Janney, Clara VI, 758
Janney, Clara C. VI, 631
Janney, Clara C. VI, 668
Janney, Clara Louise II, 882
Janney, Clarence VI, 668
Janney, Clarissa VI, 666
Janney, Cornelia VI, 408
Janney, Cornelia VI, 517
Janney, Cornelia VI, 518
Janney, Cornelia VI, 663
Janney, Cornelia VI, 664
Janney, Cornelia VI, 668
Janney, Cornelia VI, 754
Janney, Cornelia VI, 758
Janney, Cornelia VI, 765
Janney, Cornelia G. VI, 662
Janney, Cornelia G. VI, 663
Janney, Cornelia G. VI, 680
Janney, Cornelia G. VI, 683
Janney, Cosmelia V, 80
Janney, Cosmelia VI, 405
Janney, Cosmelia VI, 408
Janney, Cosmelia VI, 658
Janney, Cosmelia VI, 659
Janney, Cosmelia VI, 662
Janney, Cosmelia VI, 663
Janney, Cosmelia VI, 666
Janney, Cosmelia VI, 753
Janney, Cosmelia J. VI, 652
Janney, Cosmelia Janney VI, 664
Janney, Daniel VI, 396
Janney, Daniel VI, 407
Janney, Daniel VI, 422
Janney, Daniel VI, 519
Janney, Daniel VI, 642
Janney, Daniel VI, 645
Janney, Daniel VI, 661
Janney, Daniel VI, 662
Janney, Daniel VI, 663
Janney, Daniel VI, 664
Janney, Daniel VI, 667
Janney, Daniel VI, 668
Janney, Daniel VI, 681
Janney, Daniel Silver VI, 663
Janney, Daniel, Jr. VI, 408
Janney, Daniel, Jr. VI, 663
Janney, David VI, 407
Janney, David VI, 518
Janney, David VI, 519
Janney, David VI, 520
Janney, David VI, 535
Janney, David VI, 536
Janney, David VI, 661
Janney, David VI, 663
Janney, David VI, 676
Janney, David VI, 756
Janney, David VI, 757
Janney, David VI, 766
Janney, David VI, 772
Janney, David B. II, 882
Janney, David B. II, 1074
Janney, Deborah VI, 517
Janney, Deborah VI, 519
Janney, Deborah VI, 662
Janney, Deborah Anne VI, 757
Janney, Dinah VI, 661
Janney, Dorcas V, 80
Janney, Dorcas E. V, 120
Janney, Dr. Edgar VI, 754
Janney, Dr. Thamasin VI, 753
Janney, Dr. Wm. S. II, 881
Janney, Edgar VI, 662
Janney, Edgar VI, 663
Janney, Edgar VI, 664
Janney, Edgar VI, 764
Janney, Edward II, 882
Janney, Edward II, 1053
Janney, Edward IV, 827
Janney, Edward V, 80
Janney, Edward V, 81
Janney, Edward VI, 663
Janney, Edward VI, 665
Janney, Edward VI, 733
Janney, Edward A. VI, 518
Janney, Edward A. VI, 521
Janney, Edward A. VI, 528
Janney, Edward A. VI, 587
Janney, Edward A. VI, 668
Janney, Edward A. VI, 754
Janney, Edward A. VI, 757
Janney, Edward Abijah VI, 75
Janney, Edward Abijah VI, 75
Janney, Edward H. VI, 755
Janney, Edward Taylor II, 80
Janney, Edwin Lewis VI, 663
Janney, Edwin McBeth VI, 66
Janney, Eleanor IV, 827
Janney, Eleanor VI, 662
Janney, Eleanor VI, 757
Janney, Eleanor Wilson II, 80
Janney, Eli VI, 518
Janney, Eli VI, 661
Janney, Eli VI, 664
Janney, Eli H. VI, 664
Janney, Eli Hamilton VI, 663
Janney, Eli Hamilton VI, 664
Janney, Elijah Coffin VI, 408
Janney, Elinor VI, 755
Janney, Elinor Wilson II, 882
Janney, Elisabeth II, 1005
Janney, Elisabeth VI, 518
Janney, Elisha VI, 493
Janney, Elisha VI, 494
Janney, Elisha VI, 496
Janney, Elisha VI, 516
Janney, Elisha VI, 517
Janney, Elisha VI, 518
Janney, Elisha VI, 519
Janney, Elisha VI, 520
Janney, Elisha VI, 535
Janney, Elisha VI, 569
Janney, Elisha VI, 572
Janney, Elisha VI, 576
Janney, Elisha VI, 640
Janney, Elisha VI, 642
Janney, Elisha VI, 649
Janney, Elisha VI, 660
Janney, Elisha VI, 661
Janney, Elisha VI, 664
Janney, Elisha VI, 666
Janney, Elisha VI, 667
Janney, Elisha VI, 668
Janney, Elisha VI, 704
Janney, Elisha VI, 712
Janney, Elisha VI, 725
Janney, Elisha VI, 742
Janney, Elisha VI, 744
Janney, Elisha VI, 754
Janney, Elisha VI, 758
Janney, Elisha VI, 766
Janney, Elisha Joseph VI, 75
Janney, Elisha, Jr. VI, 518
Janney, Eliza V, 954
Janney, Eliza VI, 263
Janney, Eliza VI, 518
Janney, Eliza VI, 652
Janney, Eliza VI, 662
Janney, Eliza VI, 753
Janney, Eliza VI, 758
Janney, Eliza F. III, 183
Janney, Eliza F. VI, 631
Janney, Eliza F. VI, 666
Janney, Eliza F. VI, 668
Janney, Eliza F. VI, 693
Janney, Eliza F. Coffin VI, 66
Janney, Eliza M. II, 748
Janney, Eliza Morris VI, 519
Janney, Eliza Pleasant VI, 65
Janney, Eliza Pleasant VI, 65
Janney, Eliza Pleasant VI, 65
Janney, Eliza Pleasant VI, 66
Janney, Eliza Pleasant VI, 66
Janney, Eliza Pleasant VI, 71
Janney, Eliza Pleasant VI, 74
Janney, Eliza Pleasant VI, 78
Janney, Eliza Pleasants VI, 6
Janney, Elizabeth II, 564
Janney, Elizabeth II, 664
Janney, Elizabeth II, 962
Janney, Elizabeth II, 1005
Janney, Elizabeth II, 1006
Janney, Elizabeth II, 1016
Janney, Elizabeth II, 1023
Janney, Elizabeth II, 1028
Janney, Elizabeth II, 1074
Janney, Elizabeth IV, 827
Janney, Elizabeth V, 372
Janney, Elizabeth V, 374
Janney, Elizabeth V, 380
Janney, Elizabeth V, 406
Janney, Elizabeth V, 417
Janney, Elizabeth VI, 408
Janney, Elizabeth VI, 452
Janney, Elizabeth VI, 475
Janney, Elizabeth VI, 509
Janney, Elizabeth VI, 513
Janney, Elizabeth VI, 515
Janney, Elizabeth VI, 516
Janney, Elizabeth VI, 518
Janney, Elizabeth VI, 519
Janney, Elizabeth VI, 520

ney, Elizabeth VI, 521
ney, Elizabeth VI, 522
ney, Elizabeth VI, 535
ney, Elizabeth VI, 536
ney, Elizabeth VI, 538
ney, Elizabeth VI, 586
ney, Elizabeth VI, 631
ney, Elizabeth VI, 661
ney, Elizabeth VI, 663
ney, Elizabeth VI, 664
ney, Elizabeth VI, 666
ney, Elizabeth VI, 667
ney, Elizabeth VI, 668
ney, Elizabeth VI, 674
ney, Elizabeth VI, 676
ney, Elizabeth VI, 700
ney, Elizabeth VI, 709
ney, Elizabeth VI, 735
ney, Elizabeth VI, 748
ney, Elizabeth VI, 749
ney, Elizabeth VI, 752
ney, Elizabeth VI, 753
ney, Elizabeth VI, 754
ney, Elizabeth VI, 755
ney, Elizabeth VI, 756
ney, Elizabeth VI, 757
ney, Elizabeth VI, 758
ney, Elizabeth VI, 763
ney, Elizabeth VI, 766
ney, Elizabeth VI, 772
ney, Elizabeth VI, 789
ney, Elizabeth A. VI, 396
ney, Elizabeth A. VI, 407
ney, Elizabeth A. VI, 662
ney, Elizabeth A. VI, 667
ney, Elizabeth A. VI, 668
ney, Elizabeth A. VI, 681
ney, Elizabeth Ann VI, 663
ney, Elizabeth Ann VI, 763
ney, Elizabeth Avis VI, 642
ney, Elizabeth Avis VI, 645
ney, Elizabeth Avis VI, 663
ney, Elizabeth Avis VI, 664
ney, Elizabeth Brinton II, 882
ney, Elizabeth Howard VI, 668
ney, Elizabeth Howell VI, 521
ney, Elizabeth Howell VI, 749
ney, Elizabeth Howell VI, 751
ney, Elizabeth Howell VI, 755
ney, Elizabeth Howell VI, 756
ney, Elizabeth Howell VI, 757
ney, Elizabeth Morris VI, 755
ney, Elizabeth T. II, 882
ney, Elizabeth Taylor II, 802
ney, Elizha VI, 520
ney, Ella V, 80
ney, Ella VI, 408
ney, Ella VI, 755
ney, Ellen II, 882
ney, Ellen III, 228
ney, Ellen III, 341
ney, Ellen IV, 727
ney, Ellen V, 913
ney, Ellen VI, 408
ney, Ellen VI, 472
ney, Ellen VI, 662
ney, Ellen VI, 664
ney, Ellen VI, 668
ney, Ellen VI, 703
ney, Ellen VI, 755
ney, Ellen VI, 758
ney, Ellen B. II, 881
ney, Ellen Belle VI, 663
ney, Ellen E. II, 881
ney, Ellen E. VI, 755
ney, Ellen Haines VI, 662
ney, Ellen Haines VI, 664
ney, Ellen Haines VI, 753
ney, Ellen M. V, 913
ney, Elouisa V, 80
ney, Elouisa VI, 666
ney, Elouisa D. V, 81
ney, Elouisa D. V, 954
ney, Elvira VI, 666
ney, Emily II, 748
ney, Emily II, 803
ney, Emily V, 380
ney, Emily V, 406
ney, Emily V, 407
ney, Emily VI, 519
ney, Emily VI, 755
ney, Emily B. II, 882
ney, Emily B. II, 924
ney, Emily Betts II, 803
ney, Emily Catharine VI, 652
ney, Emily Catharine VI, 662
ney, Emily Catharine VI, 664
ney, Emily Catharine VI, 665
ney, Emily Catharine VI, 667
ney, Emily Catharine VI, 674
Janney, Emily Catharine VI, 714
Janney, Emily Catherine VI, 615
Janney, Emily Catherine VI, 753
Janney, Emily Florence VI, 663
Janney, Emily Stokes II, 311
Janney, Emma VI, 667
Janney, Emma VI, 756
Janney, Emma L. II, 1074
Janney, Emma L. II, 1082
Janney, Emmor K. II, 881
Janney, Emmor K. II, 882
Janney, Emmor K. III, 183
Janney, Emmor Kimber II, 802
Janney, Emor K. III, 77
Janney, Ernest F. II, 311
Janney, Esther II, 1053
Janney, Esther VI, 520
Janney, Esther VI, 522
Janney, Esther VI, 664
Janney, Esther VI, 666
Janney, Esther VI, 667
Janney, Esther VI, 697
Janney, Esther Boone VI, 754
Janney, Esther L. VI, 620
Janney, Esther L. VI, 665
Janney, Esther L. VI, 667
Janney, Ethel V, 80
Janney, Ethel Hyams VI, 667
Janney, Ethel Warner VI, 757
Janney, Eva V, 80
Janney, Eva L. V, 81
Janney, Evalina VI, 753
Janney, Evelina VI, 407
Janney, Evelina VI, 417
Janney, F. Lamar VI, 667
Janney, Fannie II, 1074
Janney, Fannie II, 1075
Janney, Fanny II, 1074
Janney, Florence A. II, 882
Janney, Florence A. II, 937
Janney, Frances II, 381
Janney, Frances II, 802
Janney, Frances II, 1006
Janney, Frances II, 1053
Janney, Frances III, 183
Janney, Frances VI, 663
Janney, Frances J. III, 46
Janney, Frances Martin VI, 667
Janney, Frances Martin VI, 756
Janney, Francis II, 381
Janney, Francis VI, 519
Janney, Francis VI, 755
Janney, Francis B. II, 311
Janney, Francis Hague VI, 615
Janney, Francis Hague VI, 652
Janney, Francis Hague VI, 662
Janney, Francis Hague VI, 664
Janney, Francis Hague VI, 665
Janney, Francis Hague VI, 674
Janney, Francis Hague VI, 714
Janney, Francis Hague VI, 753
Janney, Francis Haque VI, 667
Janney, Francis Lamar VI, 620
Janney, Francis Lamar VI, 665
Janney, Francis Lamar VI, 667
Janney, Francis McIlvain II, 311
Janney, Francis Miller VI, 662
Janney, Franzin S. VI, 663
Janney, Frederick VI, 662
Janney, Frederick Emery VI, 757
Janney, Geo. VI, 473
Janney, Geo. VI, 661
Janney, George V, 374
Janney, George V, 406
Janney, George VI, 407
Janney, George VI, 410
Janney, George VI, 520
Janney, George VI, 619
Janney, George VI, 663
Janney, George VI, 665
Janney, George VI, 666
Janney, George VI, 668
Janney, George VI, 732
Janney, George Fox VI, 757
Janney, George Mason Long VI, 667
Janney, George Wright VI, 663
Janney, George, Jr. VI, 668
Janney, George, Jr. VI, 755
Janney, Gertrude Kimber II, 802
Janney, Gertrude M. VI, 753
Janney, Gertrude M. VI, 755
Janney, Gertrude M. VI, 764
Janney, Grace McPherson VI, 754
Janney, Hannah II, 979
Janney, Hannah II, 1005
Janney, Hannah V, 81
Janney, Hannah VI, 404
Janney, Hannah VI, 407
Janney, Hannah VI, 416
Janney, Hannah VI, 417
Janney, Hannah VI, 474
Janney, Hannah VI, 475
Janney, Hannah VI, 481
Janney, Hannah VI, 493
Janney, Hannah VI, 496
Janney, Hannah VI, 497
Janney, Hannah VI, 500
Janney, Hannah VI, 501
Janney, Hannah VI, 502
Janney, Hannah VI, 508
Janney, Hannah VI, 509
Janney, Hannah VI, 514
Janney, Hannah VI, 515
Janney, Hannah VI, 517
Janney, Hannah VI, 518
Janney, Hannah VI, 519
Janney, Hannah VI, 520
Janney, Hannah VI, 521
Janney, Hannah VI, 522
Janney, Hannah VI, 523
Janney, Hannah VI, 530
Janney, Hannah VI, 545
Janney, Hannah VI, 553
Janney, Hannah VI, 554
Janney, Hannah VI, 571
Janney, Hannah VI, 572
Janney, Hannah VI, 579
Janney, Hannah VI, 587
Janney, Hannah VI, 622
Janney, Hannah VI, 624
Janney, Hannah VI, 627
Janney, Hannah VI, 640
Janney, Hannah VI, 642
Janney, Hannah VI, 644
Janney, Hannah VI, 650
Janney, Hannah VI, 651
Janney, Hannah VI, 653
Janney, Hannah VI, 660
Janney, Hannah VI, 661
Janney, Hannah VI, 662
Janney, Hannah VI, 664
Janney, Hannah VI, 665
Janney, Hannah VI, 666
Janney, Hannah VI, 667
Janney, Hannah VI, 668
Janney, Hannah VI, 673
Janney, Hannah VI, 674
Janney, Hannah VI, 685
Janney, Hannah VI, 697
Janney, Hannah VI, 711
Janney, Hannah VI, 712
Janney, Hannah VI, 720
Janney, Hannah VI, 749
Janney, Hannah VI, 750
Janney, Hannah VI, 751
Janney, Hannah VI, 752
Janney, Hannah VI, 753
Janney, Hannah VI, 754
Janney, Hannah VI, 755
Janney, Hannah VI, 756
Janney, Hannah VI, 757
Janney, Hannah VI, 758
Janney, Hannah VI, 774
Janney, Hannah VI, 775
Janney, Hannah Ann VI, 751
Janney, Hannah Ann VI, 756
Janney, Hannah B. II, 1053
Janney, Hannah Howell VI, 521
Janney, Hannah M. VI, 404
Janney, Hannah M. VI, 750
Janney, Hannah M. VI, 755
Janney, Hannah McPherson VI, 661
Janney, Hannah McPherson VI, 753
Janney, Hannah R. II, 882
Janney, Hannah R. II, 937
Janney, Hannah R. IV, 827
Janney, Hannah R. VI, 667
Janney, Hannah R. VI, 702
Janney, Hannah R. VI, 755
Janney, Hannah Russell VI, 755
Janney, Hannah Russell VI, 776
Janney, Hanney VI, 571
Janney, Harriet J. III, 46
Janney, Harriet Laura VI, 662
Janney, Harriet, Jr. III, 183
Janney, Harriett VI, 662
Janney, Harriett Isabelle VI, 737
Janney, Harriett Isabelle VI, 753
Janney, Harriett Isabelle VI, 757
Janney, Harriett Laura VI, 757
Janney, Harry Canby VI, 667
Janney, Helen VI, 782
Janney, Helen VI, 790
Janney, Helen Bowne VI, 662
Janney, Helen Bowne VI, 753
Janney, Helen Bowne VI, 755
Janney, Helen Bowne VI, 780
Janney, Helen Bowne VI, 781
Janney, Helen Bowne VI, 782
Janney, Helen MacPherson II, 802
Janney, Henry II, 882
Janney, Henry II, 937
Janney, Henry IV, 827
Janney, Henry VI, 663
Janney, Henry VI, 667
Janney, Henry VI, 702
Janney, Henry VI, 727
Janney, Henry VI, 753
Janney, Henry VI, 755
Janney, Henry VI, 776
Janney, Henry T. VI, 652
Janney, Henry Thornton VI, 652
Janney, Henry Thornton VI, 664
Janney, Henry Thornton VI, 665
Janney, Hester B. VI, 665
Janney, Hester B. VI, 670
Janney, Howard J. VI, 755
Janney, Hugh VI, 665
Janney, Hugh Neill VI, 753
Janney, Hugh S. VI, 662
Janney, Hugh S. VI, 663
Janney, Isaac II, 1006
Janney, Isaac VI, 519
Janney, Isaac VI, 662
Janney, Isaac McPherson VI, 667
Janney, Isaac McPherson VI, 756
Janney, Isaac R. VI, 517
Janney, Isaac R. VI, 521
Janney, Isaac R. VI, 661
Janney, Isaac R. VI, 757
Janney, Isaac Richardson VI, 753
Janney, Isabella VI, 662
Janney, Isabella VI, 701
Janney, Isabelle VI, 753
Janney, Isabelle VI, 755
Janney, Isabelle VI, 779
Janney, Isabelle VI, 780
Janney, Isaiah B. VI, 665
Janney, Isaiah Boone VI, 754
Janney, Isaiah Boone Hughes VI, 755
Janney, Israel VI, 407
Janney, Israel VI, 417
Janney, Israel VI, 499
Janney, Israel VI, 500
Janney, Israel VI, 518
Janney, Israel VI, 519
Janney, Israel VI, 522
Janney, Israel VI, 529
Janney, Israel VI, 645
Janney, Israel VI, 650
Janney, Israel VI, 660
Janney, Israel VI, 661
Janney, Israel VI, 663
Janney, Israel VI, 665
Janney, Israel VI, 667
Janney, Israel VI, 668
Janney, Israel VI, 673
Janney, Israel VI, 674
Janney, Israel VI, 676
Janney, Israel VI, 725
Janney, Israel VI, 752
Janney, Israel VI, 755
Janney, Israel VI, 756
Janney, Israel VI, 757
Janney, Israel Ann VI, 536
Janney, Israel Heaton VI, 518
Janney, Israel Heaton VI, 520
Janney, Israel Heaton VI, 663
Janney, Israel Heaton VI, 756
Janney, Israel Pennock VI, 757
Janney, Israel R. VI, 408
Janney, Israel Richardson VI, 753
Janney, Israel, Jr. VI, 519
Janney, Israel, Jr. VI, 661
Janney, Israel, Jr. VI, 665
Janney, Israel, Jr. VI, 755
Janney, Israel, Jr. VI, 789
Janney, J. Edwin V, 80
Janney, Jackob VI, 520
Janney, Jacob II, 802
Janney, Jacob II, 882
Janney, Jacob II, 962
Janney, Jacob II, 1002
Janney, Jacob II, 1005
Janney, Jacob II, 1006
Janney, Jacob II, 1053
Janney, Jacob IV, 727
Janney, Jacob IV, 827
Janney, Jacob V, 913
Janney, Jacob VI, 407
Janney, Jacob VI, 464
Janney, Jacob VI, 493
Janney, Jacob VI, 495
Janney, Jacob VI, 496
Janney, Jacob VI, 497
Janney, Jacob VI, 500
Janney, Jacob VI, 502
Janney, Jacob VI, 508
Janney, Jacob VI, 514
Janney, Jacob VI, 517
Janney, Jacob VI, 518
Janney, Jacob VI, 519
Janney, Jacob VI, 520
Janney, Jacob VI, 521
Janney, Jacob VI, 522
Janney, Jacob VI, 526
Janney, Jacob VI, 530
Janney, Jacob VI, 533
Janney, Jacob VI, 563
Janney, Jacob VI, 579
Janney, Jacob VI, 609
Janney, Jacob VI, 640
Janney, Jacob VI, 641
Janney, Jacob VI, 642
Janney, Jacob VI, 644
Janney, Jacob VI, 660
Janney, Jacob VI, 661
Janney, Jacob VI, 664
Janney, Jacob VI, 665
Janney, Jacob VI, 666
Janney, Jacob VI, 668
Janney, Jacob VI, 673
Janney, Jacob VI, 674
Janney, Jacob VI, 720
Janney, Jacob VI, 727
Janney, Jacob VI, 744
Janney, Jacob VI, 748
Janney, Jacob VI, 749
Janney, Jacob VI, 753
Janney, Jacob VI, 754
Janney, Jacob VI, 755
Janney, Jacob VI, 757
Janney, Jacob, Jr. VI, 519
Janney, James V, 80
Janney, James V, 954
Janney, James VI, 407
Janney, James VI, 534
Janney, James VI, 661
Janney, James VI, 663
Janney, James C. II, 881
Janney, James C. II, 882
Janney, James C. II, 890
Janney, James C. II, 924
Janney, James C. II, 937
Janney, James C. II, 940
Janney, James Craik II, 803
Janney, James Craik VI, 518
Janney, James Craik VI, 520
Janney, James Craik VI, 576
Janney, James Craik VI, 666
Janney, James E. V, 81
Janney, James Fenton IV, 827
Janney, James Fenton VI, 755
Janney, James M. V, 81
Janney, James M. VI, 408
Janney, James M. VI, 518
Janney, James M. VI, 520
Janney, James M. VI, 529
Janney, James M. VI, 565
Janney, James M. VI, 665
Janney, James M. VI, 666
Janney, James M. VI, 673
Janney, James Mendenhall VI, 520
Janney, James Mendenhall VI, 529
Janney, James Moore VI, 518
Janney, James Moore VI, 520
Janney, James Moore VI, 756
Janney, James Moore, Jr. VI, 663
Janney, James Ruth VI, 408
Janney, James W. II, 881
Janney, James W. II, 882
Janney, James W. II, 924
Janney, James W. II, 1053
Janney, James W. VI, 681
Janney, James Walker II, 802
Janney, James Walker VI, 520
Janney, James Walker VI, 666
Janney, James Walker VI, 667
Janney, Jane V, 393
Janney, Jane V, 406
Janney, Jane V, 407
Janney, Jane VI, 407
Janney, Jane VI, 421
Janney, Jane VI, 500
Janney, Jane VI, 517
Janney, Jane VI, 519
Janney, Jane VI, 645
Janney, Jane VI, 661
Janney, Jane VI, 663
Janney, Jane VI, 664
Janney, Jane VI, 666
Janney, Jane VI, 667
Janney, Jane VI, 668
Janney, Jane VI, 674
Janney, Jane VI, 750

Janney, Jane VI, 752
Janney, Jane VI, 753
Janney, Jane VI, 755
Janney, Jane VI, 756
Janney, Jane VI, 758
Janney, Jane VI, 763
Janney, Jane VI, 781
Janney, Jane VI, 782
Janney, Jane Eliza VI, 668
Janney, Jane Eliza VI, 758
Janney, Jane Elizabeth VI, 667
Janney, Jane Elizabeth VI, 756
Janney, Jane McPherson VI, 756
Janney, Jane Wilson VI, 664
Janney, Janet VI, 733
Janney, Janney VI, 667
Janney, Janney, Asa M. VI, 627
Janney, Jeanette V, 81
Janney, Jeanette V, 686
Janney, Jesse VI, 661
Janney, Jesse VI, 666
Janney, Jesse VI, 669
Janney, John II, 882
Janney, John II, 937
Janney, John II, 1006
Janney, John III, 183
Janney, John VI, 509
Janney, John VI, 518
Janney, John VI, 520
Janney, John VI, 521
Janney, John VI, 631
Janney, John VI, 663
Janney, John VI, 666
Janney, John VI, 668
Janney, John VI, 693
Janney, John VI, 725
Janney, John VI, 742
Janney, John VI, 749
Janney, John VI, 754
Janney, John VI, 756
Janney, John VI, 757
Janney, John VI, 777
Janney, John Craig II, 803
Janney, John Edward VI, 663
Janney, John Hopkins VI, 787
Janney, John Jay VI, 666
Janney, John Joseph VI, 663
Janney, John L. II, 1053
Janney, John Lea II, 1006
Janney, John Thomas VI, 667
Janney, John Thomas VI, 756
Janney, John W. II, 748
Janney, John Warder VI, 519
Janney, John Warder VI, 755
Janney, John, Jr. VI, 758
Janney, Johns Hopkins VI, 756
Janney, Jonah Sands VI, 407
Janney, Jonas V, 65
Janney, Jonas V, 80
Janney, Jonas V, 81
Janney, Jonas V, 954
Janney, Jonas VI, 407
Janney, Jonas VI, 408
Janney, Jonas VI, 433
Janney, Jonas VI, 519
Janney, Jonas VI, 520
Janney, Jonas VI, 522
Janney, Jonas VI, 619
Janney, Jonas VI, 653
Janney, Jonas VI, 658
Janney, Jonas VI, 660
Janney, Jonas VI, 661
Janney, Jonas VI, 663
Janney, Jonas VI, 664
Janney, Jonas VI, 665
Janney, Jonas VI, 666
Janney, Jonas VI, 668
Janney, Jonas VI, 669
Janney, Jonas VI, 676
Janney, Jonas VI, 697
Janney, Jonas VI, 704
Janney, Jonas VI, 705
Janney, Jonas VI, 707
Janney, Jonas, Jr. VI, 397
Janney, Jonas, Jr. VI, 407
Janney, Jonas, Jr. VI, 408
Janney, Jonas, Jr. VI, 520
Janney, Jonas, Jr. VI, 661
Janney, Jonas, Jr. VI, 666
Janney, Jonas, Jr. VI, 667
Janney, Jonas, Jr. VI, 705
Janney, Jonas, Sr. V, 80
Janney, Jonas, Sr. VI, 407
Janney, Jonathan VI, 519
Janney, Jonathan VI, 661
Janney, Jonathan VI, 667
Janney, Jonathan VI, 674
Janney, Jonathan VI, 756
Janney, Jonathan VI, 763
Janney, Jonathan, Jr. VI, 667
Janney, Jonathan, Jr. VI, 756
Janney, Joseph II, 802
Janney, Joseph II, 882
Janney, Joseph II, 975
Janney, Joseph II, 979
Janney, Joseph II, 1005
Janney, Joseph II, 1053
Janney, Joseph II, 1074
Janney, Joseph II, 1082
Janney, Joseph V, 372
Janney, Joseph V, 374
Janney, Joseph V, 380
Janney, Joseph V, 406
Janney, Joseph V, 417
Janney, Joseph VI, 387
Janney, Joseph VI, 408
Janney, Joseph VI, 416
Janney, Joseph VI, 464
Janney, Joseph VI, 499
Janney, Joseph VI, 501
Janney, Joseph VI, 509
Janney, Joseph VI, 514
Janney, Joseph VI, 515
Janney, Joseph VI, 517
Janney, Joseph VI, 518
Janney, Joseph VI, 519
Janney, Joseph VI, 520
Janney, Joseph VI, 521
Janney, Joseph VI, 522
Janney, Joseph VI, 523
Janney, Joseph VI, 553
Janney, Joseph VI, 554
Janney, Joseph VI, 637
Janney, Joseph VI, 660
Janney, Joseph VI, 661
Janney, Joseph VI, 665
Janney, Joseph VI, 667
Janney, Joseph VI, 668
Janney, Joseph VI, 669
Janney, Joseph VI, 673
Janney, Joseph VI, 691
Janney, Joseph VI, 712
Janney, Joseph VI, 749
Janney, Joseph VI, 751
Janney, Joseph VI, 752
Janney, Joseph VI, 754
Janney, Joseph VI, 755
Janney, Joseph VI, 756
Janney, Joseph VI, 757
Janney, Joseph VI, 774
Janney, Joseph VI, 775
Janney, Joseph Abijah VI, 763
Janney, Joseph B. VI, 408
Janney, Joseph Elisha VI, 756
Janney, Joseph J. VI, 757
Janney, Joseph Jacob VI, 755
Janney, Joseph W. II, 882
Janney, Joseph W. II, 1074
Janney, Joseph, Jr. VI, 508
Janney, Joseph, Jr. VI, 521
Janney, Joseph, Jr. VI, 667
Janney, Joseph, Sr. V, 81
Janney, Judith VI, 518
Janney, Judith VI, 522
Janney, Judith VI, 528
Janney, Judith VI, 579
Janney, Judith VI, 587
Janney, Judith VI, 754
Janney, Laurence VI, 753
Janney, Laurence Aquila VI, 662
Janney, Laurence Aquila VI, 737
Janney, Laurence Aquila VI, 757
Janney, Laurence Aquila VI, 773
Janney, Lawrence VI, 780
Janney, Leatitia VI, 667
Janney, Leatitia VI, 668
Janney, Leatitia VI, 669
Janney, Leatitia VI, 681
Janney, Leatitia VI, 712
Janney, Leticia VI, 521
Janney, Letitia VI, 522
Janney, Letitia VI, 579
Janney, Letitia VI, 650
Janney, Letitia VI, 665
Janney, Letitia VI, 669
Janney, Levis VI, 757
Janney, Levis VI, 770
Janney, Lewis II, 381
Janney, Lewis V, 80
Janney, Lewis V, 120
Janney, Lewis VI, 665
Janney, Lewis VI, 755
Janney, Lewis VI, 757
Janney, Lewis Lamar VI, 665
Janney, Lightfoot VI, 184
Janney, Lightfoot VI, 251
Janney, Lightfoot VI, 516
Janney, Lightfoot VI, 599
Janney, Lightfoot VI, 667
Janney, Lilly VI, 663
Janney, Lot V, 406
Janney, Lot Tavener VI, 519
Janney, Louis V, 80
Janney, Louisa V, 80
Janney, Louisa VI, 666
Janney, Louisa J. V, 81
Janney, Louisa J. V, 145
Janney, Lt. Frederick E. VI, 757
Janney, Lucy A. II, 802
Janney, Lucy A. VI, 666
Janney, Lucy A. VI, 667
Janney, Lucy Ann VI, 663
Janney, Lucy N. II, 882
Janney, Lydia V, 81
Janney, Lydia V, 407
Janney, Lydia V, 439
Janney, Lydia V, 954
Janney, Lydia VI, 407
Janney, Lydia VI, 408
Janney, Lydia VI, 518
Janney, Lydia VI, 520
Janney, Lydia VI, 521
Janney, Lydia VI, 529
Janney, Lydia VI, 649
Janney, Lydia VI, 652
Janney, Lydia VI, 661
Janney, Lydia VI, 664
Janney, Lydia VI, 665
Janney, Lydia VI, 666
Janney, Lydia VI, 668
Janney, Lydia VI, 673
Janney, Lydia VI, 676
Janney, Lydia VI, 704
Janney, Lydia VI, 757
Janney, Lydia Ann VI, 662
Janney, Lydia Ann VI, 663
Janney, Lydia Ann VI, 681
Janney, Lydia Ann VI, 685
Janney, Lydia Jane VI, 663
Janney, Lydia Jane VI, 668
Janney, Lydia M. V, 954
Janney, Lydia N. VI, 396
Janney, Lydia N. VI, 407
Janney, Lydia N. VI, 518
Janney, Lydia N. VI, 621
Janney, Lydia N. VI, 626
Janney, Lydia N. VI, 627
Janney, Lydia N. VI, 645
Janney, Lydia N. VI, 661
Janney, Lydia N. VI, 662
Janney, Lydia N. VI, 664
Janney, Lydia N. VI, 667
Janney, Lydia Neill VI, 500
Janney, Lydia Neill VI, 518
Janney, Lydia Neill VI, 662
Janney, Lydia Neill VI, 733
Janney, Lydia Neill VI, 745
Janney, Lydia Neill VI, 752
Janney, Lydia Neill VI, 753
Janney, M. H. VI, 518
Janney, M. H. VI, 658
Janney, M. H. VI, 663
Janney, M. H. VI, 667
Janney, M. H. VI, 668
Janney, Madeline VI, 668
Janney, Madison V, 406
Janney, Mahlon II, 962
Janney, Mahlon II, 1053
Janney, Mahlon VI, 268
Janney, Mahlon VI, 499
Janney, Mahlon VI, 516
Janney, Mahlon VI, 517
Janney, Mahlon VI, 521
Janney, Mahlon VI, 522
Janney, Mahlon VI, 564
Janney, Mahlon VI, 669
Janney, Mahlon B. II, 1053
Janney, Mahlon B. II, 1064
Janney, Mahlon H. VI, 660
Janney, Mahlon H. VI, 664
Janney, Mahlon, Jr. VI, 521
Janney, Margaret II, 311
Janney, Margaret VI, 184
Janney, Margaret VI, 204
Janney, Margaret VI, 208
Janney, Margaret VI, 516
Janney, Margaret VI, 545
Janney, Margaret VI, 667
Janney, Margaret VI, 735
Janney, Margaret VI, 754
Janney, Margaret VI, 756
Janney, Margaret E. III, 183
Janney, Margaret E. III, 230
Janney, Margaret Elgar VI, 666
Janney, Margaret Marshall VI, 667
Janney, Maria A. VI, 663
Janney, Maria W. VI, 408
Janney, Maria W. VI, 517
Janney, Maria W. VI, 663
Janney, Maria W. VI, 667
Janney, Maria W. VI, 754
Janney, Maria Wilson VI, 518
Janney, Maria Wilson VI, 572
Janney, Maria Wilson VI, 621
Janney, Maria Wilson VI, 662
Janney, Maria Wilson VI, 683
Janney, Maria Wilson VI, 701
Janney, Maria Wilson VI, 710
Janney, Maria Wilson VI, 712
Janney, Maria Wilson VI, 753
Janney, Maria Wilson VI, 754
Janney, Marian VI, 662
Janney, Marianna II, 802
Janney, Marion VI, 757
Janney, Marion VI, 773
Janney, Marion Elizabeth VI, 755
Janney, Marion Robbins VI, 753
Janney, Marjorie VI, 662
Janney, Marjorie VI, 757
Janney, Martha II, 1006
Janney, Martha III, 290
Janney, Martha III, 292
Janney, Martha IV, 179
Janney, Martha IV, 228
Janney, Martha VI, 663
Janney, Martha VI, 666
Janney, Martha Ann VI, 755
Janney, Martha Ann VI, 757
Janney, Martha B. IV, 179
Janney, Martha B. IV, 228
Janney, Martha Susan VI, 663
Janney, Martha Susan VI, 667
Janney, Mary II, 508
Janney, Mary II, 564
Janney, Mary II, 962
Janney, Mary II, 996
Janney, Mary II, 1002
Janney, Mary II, 1005
Janney, Mary II, 1006
Janney, Mary II, 1024
Janney, Mary II, 1041
Janney, Mary V, 65
Janney, Mary V, 80
Janney, Mary V, 372
Janney, Mary V, 406
Janney, Mary VI, 387
Janney, Mary VI, 397
Janney, Mary VI, 407
Janney, Mary VI, 408
Janney, Mary VI, 414
Janney, Mary VI, 418
Janney, Mary VI, 422
Janney, Mary VI, 464
Janney, Mary VI, 467
Janney, Mary VI, 474
Janney, Mary VI, 479
Janney, Mary VI, 493
Janney, Mary VI, 508
Janney, Mary VI, 515
Janney, Mary VI, 516
Janney, Mary VI, 517
Janney, Mary VI, 518
Janney, Mary VI, 519
Janney, Mary VI, 520
Janney, Mary VI, 521
Janney, Mary VI, 522
Janney, Mary VI, 535
Janney, Mary VI, 553
Janney, Mary VI, 569
Janney, Mary VI, 572
Janney, Mary VI, 576
Janney, Mary VI, 586
Janney, Mary VI, 587
Janney, Mary VI, 624
Janney, Mary VI, 626
Janney, Mary VI, 627
Janney, Mary VI, 634
Janney, Mary VI, 637
Janney, Mary VI, 644
Janney, Mary VI, 646
Janney, Mary VI, 654
Janney, Mary VI, 657
Janney, Mary VI, 661
Janney, Mary VI, 662
Janney, Mary VI, 663
Janney, Mary VI, 664
Janney, Mary VI, 665
Janney, Mary VI, 666
Janney, Mary VI, 667
Janney, Mary VI, 668
Janney, Mary VI, 669
Janney, Mary VI, 673
Janney, Mary VI, 678
Janney, Mary VI, 680
Janney, Mary VI, 681
Janney, Mary VI, 683
Janney, Mary VI, 684
Janney, Mary VI, 685
Janney, Mary VI, 691
Janney, Mary VI, 692
Janney, Mary VI, 710
Janney, Mary VI, 712
Janney, Mary VI, 713
Janney, Mary VI, 714
Janney, Mary VI, 735
Janney, Mary VI, 742
Janney, Mary VI, 749
Janney, Mary VI, 754
Janney, Mary VI, 755
Janney, Mary VI, 756
Janney, Mary VI, 757
Janney, Mary VI, 758
Janney, Mary VI, 759
Janney, Mary VI, 766
Janney, Mary VI, 770
Janney, Mary VI, 774
Janney, Mary A. V, 954
Janney, Mary A. V, 971
Janney, Mary A. V, 972
Janney, Mary A. VI, 518
Janney, Mary A. VI, 521
Janney, Mary A. VI, 528
Janney, Mary A. VI, 587
Janney, Mary A. VI, 754
Janney, Mary A. VI, 757
Janney, Mary Ann II, 802
Janney, Mary Ann II, 882
Janney, Mary Ann II, 1053
Janney, Mary Ann II, 1061
Janney, Mary Ann II, 1074
Janney, Mary Ann II, 1082
Janney, Mary Ann VI, 407
Janney, Mary Ann VI, 408
Janney, Mary Ann VI, 521
Janney, Mary Ann VI, 534
Janney, Mary Ann VI, 661
Janney, Mary Ann VI, 667
Janney, Mary Ann VI, 668
Janney, Mary Ann VI, 700
Janney, Mary Ann VI, 753
Janney, Mary Ann VI, 758
Janney, Mary Anna II, 1074
Janney, Mary Anna VI, 663
Janney, Mary Anna M. II, 882
Janney, Mary Brown VI, 754
Janney, Mary Brown VI, 764
Janney, Mary C. II, 881
Janney, Mary C. II, 882
Janney, Mary E. V, 80
Janney, Mary E. V, 81
Janney, Mary E. VI, 408
Janney, Mary E. VI, 666
Janney, Mary Elizabeth V, 28
Janney, Mary Elizabeth VI, 66
Janney, Mary Ellen V, 954
Janney, Mary Eva VI, 407
Janney, Mary Eva VI, 417
Janney, Mary Gibson VI, 599
Janney, Mary H. V, 80
Janney, Mary Jane VI, 408
Janney, Mary Jane VI, 519
Janney, Mary Jane VI, 521
Janney, Mary Jane VI, 583
Janney, Mary Jane VI, 662
Janney, Mary Jane VI, 663
Janney, Mary Jane VI, 667
Janney, Mary Jane VI, 753
Janney, Mary Jane VI, 755
Janney, Mary K. III, 183
Janney, Mary Lee VI, 663
Janney, Mary McPherson VI, 4
Janney, Mary R. II, 802
Janney, Mary R. III, 77
Janney, Mary R. III, 183
Janney, Mary S. VI, 561
Janney, Mary S. VI, 575
Janney, Mary S. VI, 667
Janney, Mary S. VI, 668
Janney, Mary S. VI, 702
Janney, Mary S. VI, 717
Janney, Mary Scholfield VI, 75
Janney, Mary Talbot II, 803
Janney, Mary, Jr. VI, 667
Janney, Mary, Jr. VI, 669
Janney, Matilda E. II, 882
Janney, Mayo C. Walkins VI, 6
Janney, Mayo C. Wilkinz VI, 6
Janney, Millard VI, 667
Janney, Millard Fillmore VI, 6
Janney, Millard Fillmore VI, 6
Janney, Millard Fillmore VI, 6
Janney, Millard Fillmore VI, 6
Janney, Millard Fillmore VI, 6
Janney, Milliard Fillmore VI, 6
Janney, Moses VI, 408
Janney, Moses VI, 518
Janney, Moses VI, 519
Janney, Moses VI, 521
Janney, Moses VI, 522
Janney, Moses VI, 526
Janney, Moses VI, 528
Janney, Moses VI, 533
Janney, Moses VI, 563
Janney, Moses VI, 579

ney, Moses VI, 587
ney, Moses VI, 641
ney, Moses VI, 757
ney, Moses VI, 760
ney, Moses VI, 779
ney, Moses Janney VI, 754
ney, N. VI, 627
ney, Nancy VI, 407
ney, Nancy VI, 408
ney, Nancy VI, 518
ney, Nancy VI, 661
ney, Nancy VI, 664
ney, Nancy VI, 668
ney, Nancy C. V, 81
ney, Nancy E. V, 954
ney, Nannie VI, 664
ney, Nannie C. V, 80
ney, Nannie C. V, 81
ney, Nathan Haines VI, 663
ney, Nathan Haines VI, 667
ney, Nathan Haines VI, 668
ney, Nathaniel E. II, 881
ney, Nathaniel Ellicott II, 802
ney, Nathaniel Ellicott VI, 518
ney, Nathaniel Ellicott VI, 520
ney, Nathaniel Ellicott VI, 754
ney, Nathaniel Elliott II, 881
ney, Nathaniel Elliott II, 924
ney, O. Edward II, 937
ney, Oliver VI, 668
ney, Oliver VI, 669
ney, Oliver Edward VI, 755
ney, Oliver S. II, 881
ney, Oliver Spencer VI, 521
ney, Oliver Spencer VI, 522
ney, Oliver Spencer VI, 757
ney, Oscar V, 80
ney, Patience V, 324
ney, Patience V, 342
ney, Patience V, 380
ney, Patience V, 406
ney, Patience VI, 668
ney, Paulina V, 407
ney, Paulina Ann V, 406
ney, Pelena V, 407
ney, Pelena V, 433
ney, Pemberton VI, 519
ney, Pemberton VI, 755
ney, Phebe VI, 518
ney, Phebe VI, 519
ney, Phebe VI, 522
ney, Phebe VI, 627
ney, Phebe VI, 660
ney, Phebe VI, 661
ney, Phebe VI, 663
ney, Phebe Ann VI, 518
ney, Phebe Ann VI, 522
ney, Phebe Ann VI, 535
ney, Phebe Ann VI, 663
ney, Phebe Ann VI, 757
ney, Phebe Ann VI, 766
ney, Philip Hopkins VI, 755
ney, Phineas VI, 407
ney, Phineas VI, 518
ney, Phineas VI, 519
ney, Phineas VI, 624
ney, Phineas VI, 631
ney, Phineas VI, 661
ney, Phineas VI, 663
ney, Phineas VI, 667
ney, Phineas VI, 673
ney, Phineas VI, 727
ney, Phineas VI, 756
ney, Phineas VI, 758
ney, Phineas Albert VI, 662
ney, Phineas Moore VI, 663
ney, Phineas Stewart VI, 663
ney, Phineas, Jr. VI, 522
ney, Phinneas VI, 416
ney, Phinneas VI, 492
ney, Phinneas VI, 522
ney, Phinneas VI, 529
ney, Phinneas VI, 668
ney, Phinneas VI, 746
ney, Phinneas VI, 757
ney, Phinneas VI, 763
ney, Pleasand VI, 519
ney, Pleasant V, 80
ney, Pleasant VI, 407
ney, Pleasant VI, 408
ney, Pleasant VI, 499
ney, Pleasant VI, 500
ney, Pleasant VI, 519
ney, Pleasant VI, 520
ney, Pleasant VI, 522
ney, Pleasant VI, 529
ney, Pleasant VI, 658
ney, Pleasant VI, 661
Janney, Pleasant VI, 663
Janney, Pleasant VI, 666
Janney, Pleasant VI, 668
Janney, Pleasant VI, 673
Janney, Pleasant VI, 705
Janney, Pleasant VI, 752
Janney, Pleasant VI, 757
Janney, Pleasant Sarah VI, 668
Janney, Rachel II, 803
Janney, Rachel II, 955
Janney, Rachel VI, 408
Janney, Rachel VI, 425
Janney, Rachel VI, 521
Janney, Rachel VI, 522
Janney, Rachel VI, 538
Janney, Rachel VI, 581
Janney, Rachel VI, 622
Janney, Rachel VI, 651
Janney, Rachel VI, 652
Janney, Rachel VI, 654
Janney, Rachel VI, 658
Janney, Rachel VI, 661
Janney, Rachel VI, 668
Janney, Rachel VI, 669
Janney, Rachel VI, 755
Janney, Rachel Ellicott VI, 749
Janney, Rachel Ellicott VI, 758
Janney, Rachell Ellicott VI, 753
Janney, Randal II, 381
Janney, Randal II, 635
Janney, Randall II, 381
Janney, Randall II, 564
Janney, Randolph II, 564
Janney, Rebecca II, 890
Janney, Rebecca II, 940
Janney, Rebecca V, 406
Janney, Rebecca V, 417
Janney, Rebecca VI, 387
Janney, Rebecca VI, 407
Janney, Rebecca VI, 408
Janney, Rebecca VI, 497
Janney, Rebecca VI, 519
Janney, Rebecca VI, 520
Janney, Rebecca VI, 521
Janney, Rebecca VI, 522
Janney, Rebecca VI, 527
Janney, Rebecca VI, 561
Janney, Rebecca VI, 637
Janney, Rebecca VI, 642
Janney, Rebecca VI, 643
Janney, Rebecca VI, 644
Janney, Rebecca VI, 656
Janney, Rebecca VI, 660
Janney, Rebecca VI, 661
Janney, Rebecca VI, 668
Janney, Rebecca VI, 669
Janney, Rebecca VI, 701
Janney, Rebecca VI, 715
Janney, Rebecca VI, 749
Janney, Rebecca VI, 753
Janney, Rebecca VI, 757
Janney, Rebecca VI, 758
Janney, Rebecca A. V, 374
Janney, Rebecca A. V, 406
Janney, Rebecca A. V, 686
Janney, Rebecca Ann V, 407
Janney, Rebecca Ann V, 686
Janney, Rebecca J. II, 881
Janney, Rebecca J. II, 882
Janney, Rebecca J. II, 924
Janney, Rebecca J. II, 937
Janney, Rebecca Jane VI, 518
Janney, Rebecca Jane VI, 520
Janney, Rebecca Jane VI, 576
Janney, Rebecca Jane VI, 666
Janney, Rebecca T. II, 882
Janney, Rebecca T. II, 929
Janney, Rebecca T. II, 940
Janney, Rebecca Talbott VI, 520
Janney, Rebeckah II, 979
Janney, Rebeckah II, 1005
Janney, Rebeckah VI, 514
Janney, Rebeckah VI, 519
Janney, Rebeckah VI, 522
Janney, Rebeckah VI, 637
Janney, Rebeckah VI, 661
Janney, Rebekah VI, 407
Janney, Rebekah VI, 497
Janney, Rebekah VI, 517
Janney, Rebekah VI, 521
Janney, Rebekah VI, 534
Janney, Rebekah VI, 660
Janney, Rebekah VI, 701
Janney, Reynold V, 406
Janney, Reynold V, 407
Janney, Reynolds V, 686
Janney, Ricahard Mott VI, 668
Janney, Richard II, 1006
Janney, Richard VI, 516
Janney, Richard VI, 599
Janney, Richard VI, 663
Janney, Richard VI, 758
Janney, Richard M. VI, 522
Janney, Richard Mott VI, 661
Janney, Richard Mott VI, 750
Janney, Richard Mott VI, 752
Janney, Richard Mott VI, 758
Janney, Richard R. VI, 763
Janney, Richard Tunis VI, 667
Janney, Richard Tunis VI, 756
Janney, Richard Worth II, 803
Janney, Robert VI, 668
Janney, Robert Edward Lee VI, 664
Janney, Robert M. II, 881
Janney, Robert M. II, 882
Janney, Robert M. II, 924
Janney, Robert Miller II, 803
Janney, Robert Miller VI, 520
Janney, Rodney Purcell VI, 668
Janney, Ruath Hannah VI, 702
Janney, Ruth V, 80
Janney, Ruth V, 81
Janney, Ruth V, 112
Janney, Ruth V, 954
Janney, Ruth VI, 404
Janney, Ruth VI, 407
Janney, Ruth VI, 416
Janney, Ruth VI, 421
Janney, Ruth VI, 422
Janney, Ruth VI, 433
Janney, Ruth VI, 493
Janney, Ruth VI, 517
Janney, Ruth VI, 518
Janney, Ruth VI, 519
Janney, Ruth VI, 520
Janney, Ruth VI, 521
Janney, Ruth VI, 522
Janney, Ruth VI, 529
Janney, Ruth VI, 530
Janney, Ruth VI, 619
Janney, Ruth VI, 639
Janney, Ruth VI, 640
Janney, Ruth VI, 653
Janney, Ruth VI, 656
Janney, Ruth VI, 661
Janney, Ruth VI, 662
Janney, Ruth VI, 664
Janney, Ruth VI, 665
Janney, Ruth VI, 666
Janney, Ruth VI, 668
Janney, Ruth VI, 669
Janney, Ruth VI, 673
Janney, Ruth VI, 676
Janney, Ruth VI, 691
Janney, Ruth VI, 697
Janney, Ruth VI, 704
Janney, Ruth VI, 705
Janney, Ruth VI, 707
Janney, Ruth VI, 714
Janney, Ruth VI, 742
Janney, Ruth VI, 750
Janney, Ruth VI, 753
Janney, Ruth VI, 754
Janney, Ruth VI, 757
Janney, Ruth VI, 763
Janney, Ruth VI, 764
Janney, Ruth Albinah VI, 754
Janney, Ruth Anna VI, 649
Janney, Ruth Anna VI, 664
Janney, Ruth Bartlett II, 311
Janney, Ruth D. V, 81
Janney, Ruth D. V, 954
Janney, Ruth Hannah VI, 617
Janney, Ruth Hannah VI, 622
Janney, Ruth Hannah VI, 624
Janney, Ruth Hannah VI, 625
Janney, Ruth Hannah VI, 645
Janney, Ruth Hannah VI, 649
Janney, Ruth Hannah VI, 664
Janney, Ruth Hannah VI, 667
Janney, Ruth Hannah VI, 668
Janney, Ruth Hannah VI, 696
Janney, Ruth Hannah VI, 703
Janney, Ruth Hannah VI, 706
Janney, Ruth Hannah VI, 707
Janney, Ruth Hannah VI, 754
Janney, Samuel V, 954
Janney, Samuel VI, 661
Janney, Samuel VI, 668
Janney, Samuel VI, 758
Janney, Samuel VI, 766
Janney, Samuel Hopkins VI, 756
Janney, Samuel Hopkins VI, 758
Janney, Samuel James II, 311
Janney, Samuel M. III, 183
Janney, Samuel M. III, 230
Janney, Samuel M. VI, 516
Janney, Samuel M. VI, 631
Janney, Samuel M. VI, 661
Janney, Samuel M. VI, 663
Janney, Samuel M. VI, 664
Janney, Samuel M. VI, 668
Janney, Samuel M. VI, 700
Janney, Samuel M. VI, 727
Janney, Samuel McPherson VI, 631
Janney, Samuel McPherson VI, 666
Janney, Samuel McPherson VI, 667
Janney, Samuel McPherson VI, 668
Janney, Samuel McPherson VI, 752
Janney, Samuel McPherson VI, 756
Janney, Samuel S. II, 1074
Janney, Samuel S. V, 80
Janney, Samuel S. VI, 665
Janney, Sara VI, 599
Janney, Sarah II, 975
Janney, Sarah II, 1005
Janney, Sarah II, 1006
Janney, Sarah II, 1022
Janney, Sarah V, 954
Janney, Sarah VI, 407
Janney, Sarah VI, 408
Janney, Sarah VI, 419
Janney, Sarah VI, 467
Janney, Sarah VI, 494
Janney, Sarah VI, 495
Janney, Sarah VI, 501
Janney, Sarah VI, 502
Janney, Sarah VI, 514
Janney, Sarah VI, 516
Janney, Sarah VI, 517
Janney, Sarah VI, 518
Janney, Sarah VI, 519
Janney, Sarah VI, 520
Janney, Sarah VI, 521
Janney, Sarah VI, 522
Janney, Sarah VI, 523
Janney, Sarah VI, 526
Janney, Sarah VI, 533
Janney, Sarah VI, 538
Janney, Sarah VI, 563
Janney, Sarah VI, 641
Janney, Sarah VI, 661
Janney, Sarah VI, 666
Janney, Sarah VI, 667
Janney, Sarah VI, 668
Janney, Sarah VI, 669
Janney, Sarah VI, 697
Janney, Sarah VI, 735
Janney, Sarah VI, 744
Janney, Sarah VI, 754
Janney, Sarah VI, 755
Janney, Sarah VI, 757
Janney, Sarah VI, 758
Janney, Sarah A. VI, 408
Janney, Sarah A. VI, 518
Janney, Sarah A. VI, 754
Janney, Sarah Ann V, 80
Janney, Sarah Ann VI, 408
Janney, Sarah Ann VI, 518
Janney, Sarah Ann VI, 520
Janney, Sarah Ann VI, 529
Janney, Sarah Ann VI, 565
Janney, Sarah Ann VI, 654
Janney, Sarah Ann VI, 664
Janney, Sarah Ann VI, 665
Janney, Sarah Ann VI, 666
Janney, Sarah Ann VI, 669
Janney, Sarah Ann VI, 673
Janney, Sarah E. VI, 407
Janney, Sarah E. VI, 410
Janney, Sarah E. VI, 411
Janney, Sarah E. VI, 521
Janney, Sarah Elizabeth VI, 755
Janney, Sarah Ellen II, 803
Janney, Sarah Emily II, 311
Janney, Sarah G. VI, 521
Janney, Sarah G. VI, 522
Janney, Sarah G. VI, 579
Janney, Sarah J. VI, 661
Janney, Sarah Jane VI, 520
Janney, Sarah Jane VI, 663
Janney, Sarah Jane VI, 756
Janney, Sarah Jane VI, 758
Janney, Sarah Jane VI, 772
Janney, Sarah Janney VI, 750
Janney, Sarah Janney VI, 752
Janney, Sarah Marshall VI, 780
Janney, Sarah Miller II, 803
Janney, Sarah S. VI, 757
Janney, Sarah Saunders VI, 519
Janney, Sarah Saunders VI, 668
Janney, Sarah Saunders VI, 746
Janney, Sarahann V, 81
Janney, Sinah VI, 667
Janney, Sinah VI, 756
Janney, Stacy VI, 475
Janney, Stacy VI, 520
Janney, Stacy VI, 522
Janney, Stacy VI, 664
Janney, Stacy VI, 666
Janney, Stacy VI, 667
Janney, Stacy VI, 685
Janney, Stacy VI, 697
Janney, Stephen II, 1006
Janney, Stephen II, 1053
Janney, Stephen V, 406
Janney, Stephen VI, 521
Janney, Stephen VI, 650
Janney, Stephen VI, 661
Janney, Stephen VI, 665
Janney, Stephen VI, 667
Janney, Stephen VI, 668
Janney, Stephen VI, 669
Janney, Stephen VI, 712
Janney, Stephen T. III, 46
Janney, Stephen T. III, 183
Janney, Susan VI, 407
Janney, Susan Boyd VI, 733
Janney, Susan J. II, 955
Janney, Susan Vaux VI, 519
Janney, Susan Vaux VI, 755
Janney, Susan W. II, 882
Janney, Susan Walker VI, 520
Janney, Susanna VI, 473
Janney, Susanna VI, 665
Janney, Susanna VI, 669
Janney, Susanna B. VI, 669
Janney, Susanna B. VI, 724
Janney, Susanna Boone VI, 754
Janney, Susannah VI, 520
Janney, Susannah VI, 521
Janney, Susannah VI, 522
Janney, Susannah VI, 554
Janney, Susannah VI, 619
Janney, Susannah VI, 668
Janney, Susannah VI, 703
Janney, Susannah VI, 732
Janney, Susannah VI, 758
Janney, Susannah VI, 775
Janney, Suzan VI, 410
Janney, Tabitha II, 381
Janney, Tabitha II, 523
Janney, Tabitha II, 564
Janney, Tacy Mitchell VI, 753
Janney, Tacy Mitchell VI, 759
Janney, Tamzin VI, 661
Janney, Tamzin VI, 668
Janney, Thamasin VI, 662
Janney, Thamsin VI, 753
Janney, Thomas II, 381
Janney, Thomas II, 564
Janney, Thomas II, 802
Janney, Thomas II, 803
Janney, Thomas II, 962
Janney, Thomas II, 979
Janney, Thomas II, 1005
Janney, Thomas II, 1022
Janney, Thomas II, 1053
Janney, Thomas VI, 516
Janney, Thomas VI, 517
Janney, Thomas VI, 520
Janney, Thomas VI, 521
Janney, Thomas VI, 523
Janney, Thomas VI, 660
Janney, Thomas VI, 661
Janney, Thomas VI, 662
Janney, Thomas VI, 667
Janney, Thomas VI, 669
Janney, Thomas VI, 706
Janney, Thomas VI, 713
Janney, Thomas Gregg VI, 661
Janney, Thomas Jefferson VI, 518
Janney, Thomas Jefferson VI, 661
Janney, Thomas R. VI, 662
Janney, Thomas Richard VI, 662
Janney, Thomas Richard VI, 667
Janney, Thomas, Jr. II, 1006
Janney, Thomasin VI, 662
Janney, Thos. II, 882
Janney, Thos. III, 183
Janney, Thos. Benton VI, 663
Janney, Thos. Lacy VI, 663
Janney, Walter Coggeshall II, 802
Janney, Warner McKown VI, 663
Janney, Wd. Elizabeth VI, 513
Janney, Wd. Elizabeth Nichols VI, 518
Janney, Wd. Judith VI, 521
Janney, Wd. Judith VI, 563
Janney, Wd. Judith VI, 760
Janney, Wd. Judith Spencer VI, 757
Janney, Wd. Mary VI, 519
Janney, Wd. Mary VI, 713
Janney, Wd. Rebecca Jane II, 803

Janney, Wd. Ruth VI, 407
Janney, Wd. Ruth VI, 422
Janney, Wd. Ruth VI, 753
Janney, Werner Lutz VI, 662
Janney, Widow Beulah VI, 521
Janney, Widow Eliza F. VI, 693
Janney, Widow Elizabeth VI, 538
Janney, Widow Lydia Ann VI, 667
Janney, Widow Mary Mitchell VI, 662
Janney, Widow Rebeckah VI, 674
Janney, Widow Rebeckah Gregg VI, 668
Janney, Widow Rebekah VI, 644
Janney, Widow Ruth VI, 534
Janney, Widow Ruth VI, 661
Janney, Widow Ruth Hannah VI, 633
Janney, Widow Ruth Hannah VI, 705
Janney, Widow Sarah VI, 495
Janney, Widow Sarah VI, 522
Janney, William II, 381
Janney, William II, 564
Janney, William II, 1006
Janney, William V, 28
Janney, William V, 80
Janney, William V, 81
Janney, William V, 406
Janney, William VI, 407
Janney, William VI, 408
Janney, William VI, 475
Janney, William VI, 517
Janney, William VI, 519
Janney, William VI, 521
Janney, William VI, 522
Janney, William VI, 523
Janney, William VI, 538
Janney, William VI, 661
Janney, William VI, 757
Janney, William J., Jr. VI, 408
Janney, William P. V, 80
Janney, William P. V, 81
Janney, William P. VI, 665
Janney, William P. VI, 666
Janney, Wm, Jr. VI, 523
Janney, Wm. II, 1005
Janney, Wm. II, 1006
Janney, Wm. II, 1016
Janney, Wm. II, 1053
Janney, Wm. VI, 513
Janney, Wm. VI, 518
Janney, Wm. VI, 519
Janney, Wm. VI, 520
Janney, Wm. VI, 534
Janney, Wm. VI, 579
Janney, Wm. Smith II, 803
Janney, Wm. Warder VI, 519
Janney, Wm. Warder VI, 755
Janney-Gregg, Rebeckah VI, 674
Janny, Abel VI, 422
Janny, Ann II, 1006
Janny, James M. V, 81
Janny, Lydia VI, 422
Janny, Thomas II, 1005
Janny, William II, 1006
Janny, William V, 80
Janson, Nancy VI, 895
January, Anna Linton V, 686
January, Clara Padget V, 686
January, Clara Pagett V, 629
January, David II, 381
January, Elizabeth II, 482
January, Elizabeth II, 564
January, Elma P. IV, 513
January, Elma P. IV, 537
January, Garnet V, 686
January, Garnett P. V, 629
January, Garnett P. V, 686
January, Mae II, 1050
January, Mae II, 1053
January, Maw V, 629
January, Robert P. V, 629
January, William II, 381
Jaques, ??? III, 184
Jaques, Charles A. III, 184
Jaques, E. III, 184
Jaques, Elias III, 184
Jaques, Elizabeth II, 381
Jaques, Elizabeth III, 184
Jaques, Gideon III, 184
Jaques, Julia Anna III, 184
Jaques, Margaret III, 184
Jaques, Moses III, 184
Jaques, Thomas II, 381
Jared, Chloa IV, 1255
Jared, Joel VI, 877
Jared, John VI, 877
Jared, Rachel VI, 877
Jared, Sarah VI, 877
Jared, Thomas VI, 1006
Jared, Thomas B. VI, 954
Jaret, Thomas VI, 877
Jarman, Edward II, 456
Jarman, Edward II, 565
Jarman, Mary II, 456
Jarman, Mary II, 565
Jarosch, Dr. Martha H. IV, 1322
Jarosh, Dr. Martha H. IV, 1322
Jarosh, Martha H. IV, 1322
Jarrad, John VI, 979
Jarrad, Nicholas VI, 113
Jarrard, Mary VI, 136
Jarratt, Mary Anna II, 948
Jarratt, Polly VI, 940
Jarratt, Thomas VI, 940
Jarred, Betsey VI, 940
Jarred, Elizabeth VI, 877
Jarred, Elizabeth VI, 940
Jarred, Israel VI, 933
Jarred, Israel VI, 940
Jarred, Israel VI, 954
Jarred, Israel VI, 993
Jarred, Joel VI, 940
Jarred, John VI, 877
Jarred, John VI, 940
Jarred, Joseph VI, 940
Jarred, Nicholas VI, 113
Jarred, Polly VI, 940
Jarred, Rachel VI, 979
Jarrel, Amy VI, 985
Jarrel, David VI, 985
Jarrell, Addison I, 626
Jarrell, Anna I, 615
Jarrell, Annie Luella I, 626
Jarrell, Ella A. I, 944
Jarrell, Ellen A. I, 928
Jarrell, Emily I, 626
Jarrell, Eugene I, 944
Jarrell, J. B. I, 944
Jarrell, Ruth I, 944
Jarrell, Wm. I, 944
Jarret, Hannah IV, 584
Jarret, Hannah IV, 586
Jarret, Joana's VI, 185
Jarret, Rebecca II, 1006
Jarret, Rebecca II, 1053
Jarrett, Aggy VI, 940
Jarrett, Ann II, 313
Jarrett, Barclay II, 1088
Jarrett, Barclay II, 1089
Jarrett, Billy Lowe I, 944
Jarrett, Elizabeth II, 717
Jarrett, Ephraim I, 932
Jarrett, Eugene H. I, 944
Jarrett, Eva IV, 1322
Jarrett, Eva V. IV, 1322
Jarrett, Geo. IV, 1322
Jarrett, Hannah VI, 523
Jarrett, Israel VI, 1006
Jarrett, Joseph VI, 940
Jarrett, Laura IV, 1322
Jarrett, Lena I, 945
Jarrett, Lena Lowe I, 944
Jarrett, Lillian Gertrude IV, 1322
Jarrett, Lucy Davis I, 944
Jarrett, Martha I, 944
Jarrett, Martha VI, 940
Jarrett, Mary I, 932
Jarrett, Mary II, 813
Jarrett, Mary Anna II, 948
Jarrett, Mary Anna II, 949
Jarrett, Mary Anna II, 1088
Jarrett, Mary Anna II, 1089
Jarrett, Nellie I, 935
Jarrett, Nettie F. I, 932
Jarrett, Ollin E. I, 944
Jarrett, Polly VI, 940
Jarrett, Sarah L. II, 1088
Jarrett, Sarah L. II, 1089
Jarrett, Tacy II, 313
Jarrett, Thomas VI, 940
Jarrett, Thomas B. VI, 940
Jarrett, William II, 313
Jarrot, Nicholas VI, 96
Jarrot, Nicholas VI, 113
Jarvis, Abigail III, 417
Jarvis, Abigail III, 422
Jarvis, Charles II, 381
Jarvis, David III, 487
Jarvis, Deborah III, 487
Jarvis, Deborah III, 503
Jarvis, Elizabeth II, 381
Jarvis, Elizabeth II, 564
Jarvis, Emma E. III, 417
Jarvis, Emma E. III, 422
Jarvis, Emma E. III, 484
Jarvis, Jane III, 487
Jarvis, Jemima III, 466
Jarvis, John II, 381
Jarvis, John II, 564
Jarvis, John III, 487
Jarvis, John VI, 924
Jarvis, John, Jr. II, 564
Jarvis, Jonathan III, 487
Jarvis, Jonathan III, 503
Jarvis, Lizzie M. V, 252
Jarvis, Lorenzo T. III, 417
Jarvis, Lorenzo T. III, 422
Jarvis, Martin III, 422
Jarvis, Mary I, 984
Jarvis, Mary I, 989
Jarvis, Mary II, 235
Jarvis, Mary II, 381
Jarvis, Mary III, 419
Jarvis, Mary III, 422
Jarvis, Nancy VI, 924
Jarvis, Olive IV, 1322
Jarvis, Olive Ballard V, 686
Jarvis, Rebecca II, 381
Jarvis, Robert III, 487
Jarvis, Samuel II, 381
Jarvis, Samuel II, 564
Jarvis, Sarah III, 487
Jarvis, Sarah A. IV, 1322
Jarvis, Sophia III, 487
Jarvis, Susannah III, 487
Jarvis, Susannah III, 491
Jarvis, Whitson III, 487
Jarvis, Whitson III, 491
Jarvis, Wm. III, 466
Jasper, Celina F. VI, 857
Jasper, Clyde V, 629
Jasper, Daniel VI, 828
Jasper, Elizabeth VI, 828
Jasper, Elizabeth VI, 829
Jasper, Elizabeth H. VI, 801
Jasper, George D. VI, 828
Jasper, Mary C. VI, 828
Jasper, Richard V, 181
Jasper, Richard S. V, 181
Javens, Levi IV, 727
Javens, Margaret Rambo IV, 727
Javens, Mary Viola IV, 727
Jay, ??? V, 746
Jay, A. V, 746
Jay, Abiather Davis V, 799
Jay, Abigail I, 1032
Jay, Abigail IV, 41
Jay, Abigail V, 182
Jay, Abigail V, 811
Jay, Abigail V, 812
Jay, Abijah E. V, 784
Jay, Adaline V, 181
Jay, Adaline V, 182
Jay, Adena S. V, 181
Jay, Alexander I, 553
Jay, Alexander I, 1016
Jay, Alford V, 812
Jay, Alfred V, 811
Jay, Alfred V, 812
Jay, Alice V, 74
Jay, Alice V, 81
Jay, Alice H. V, 81
Jay, Alice W. V, 687
Jay, Allen I, 887
Jay, Allen V, 784
Jay, Allen E. V, 181
Jay, Allen E. V, 182
Jay, Allen E. V, 407
Jay, Amelia V, 811
Jay, Amos V, 160
Jay, Amos V, 181
Jay, Amos V, 182
Jay, Ann I, 1021
Jay, Ann I, 1032
Jay, Ann I, 1036
Jay, Ann V, 163
Jay, Ann V, 168
Jay, Ann V, 181
Jay, Ann V, 182
Jay, Ann V, 746
Jay, Ann V, 748
Jay, Ann V, 783
Jay, Ann V, 784
Jay, Ann V, 785
Jay, Ann V, 812
Jay, Ann Eliza V, 811
Jay, Anna I, 552
Jay, Anna I, 566
Jay, Anna V, 182
Jay, Anna V, 746
Jay, Anna V, 748
Jay, Anna V, 750
Jay, Anna V, 784
Jay, Anna V, 785
Jay, Anna V, 787
Jay, Anna V, 821
Jay, Anna M. V, 811
Jay, Anna Marie V, 746
Jay, Anne I, 1032
Jay, Anne V, 811
Jay, Anne V, 815
Jay, Annie E. V, 812
Jay, Anny V, 803
Jay, Arabel C. V, 181
Jay, Arrena V, 407
Jay, Arrena M. V, 182
Jay, Bathsheba V, 81
Jay, Bathsheba V, 745
Jay, Bathsheba V, 746
Jay, Bathsheba V, 784
Jay, Bathsheba V, 785
Jay, Bathsheba V, 786
Jay, Benjamin V, 799
Jay, Benjamin D. V, 181
Jay, Bershaba V, 81
Jay, Bersheba V, 81
Jay, Bersheba V, 112
Jay, Bersheba V, 794
Jay, Betty I, 1032
Jay, Betty I, 1036
Jay, Betty V, 81
Jay, Betty V, 733
Jay, Betty V, 746
Jay, Betty V, 780
Jay, Betty V, 784
Jay, Betty V, 788
Jay, Betty V, 811
Jay, Cassius M. V, 407
Jay, Charity V, 784
Jay, Charlotte I, 1032
Jay, Charlotte IV, 41
Jay, Charlotte V, 181
Jay, Charlotte V, 812
Jay, Cherry Grove V, 81
Jay, Clara Frances V, 746
Jay, Cordelia V, 812
Jay, D. Russell V, 181
Jay, D. Russell V, 182
Jay, D. Russell V, 407
Jay, Daniel V, 785
Jay, Daniel Webster V, 746
Jay, David I, 553
Jay, David I, 1016
Jay, David I, 1021
Jay, David I, 1032
Jay, David I, 1057
Jay, David V, 81
Jay, David V, 168
Jay, David V, 175
Jay, David V, 176
Jay, David V, 181
Jay, David V, 182
Jay, David V, 194
Jay, David V, 407
Jay, David V, 745
Jay, David V, 746
Jay, David V, 748
Jay, David V, 784
Jay, David V, 785
Jay, David V, 787
Jay, David V, 811
Jay, David V, 812
Jay, David Augustus V, 784
Jay, David H. V, 181
Jay, David H. V, 182
Jay, David H. V, 407
Jay, Deborah V, 160
Jay, Deborah V, 181
Jay, Deborah V, 182
Jay, Delila V, 799
Jay, Dempsey I, 553
Jay, Dempsey I, 1016
Jay, Dempsey V, 182
Jay, Dennis V, 746
Jay, Denny V, 81
Jay, Denny V, 745
Jay, Denny V, 746
Jay, Denny V, 748
Jay, Denny V, 784
Jay, Denny V, 785
Jay, Denny V, 787
Jay, Denny, Jr. V, 785
Jay, Donny V, 746
Jay, Dora M. V, 407
Jay, Drucilla V, 812
Jay, Ed V, 182
Jay, Ede I, 553
Jay, Ede I, 1016
Jay, Edith I, 1016
Jay, Edith V, 81
Jay, Edith V, 100
Jay, Edna V, 812
Jay, Edward I, 887
Jay, Edwin I, 887
Jay, Edwin J. V, 812
Jay, Eli I, 887
Jay, Eli V, 181
Jay, Eli V, 182
Jay, Eli V, 746
Jay, Eli V, 784
Jay, Eli V, 785
Jay, Eli V, 792
Jay, Eli V, 811
Jay, Eli V, 819
Jay, Elijah V, 181
Jay, Elijah V, 182
Jay, Elijah V, 746
Jay, Elijah V, 811
Jay, Elijah V, 812
Jay, Elijah V, 815
Jay, Elijah A. V, 812
Jay, Elisa V, 182
Jay, Elisabeth V, 748
Jay, Elisha V, 733
Jay, Elisha V, 784
Jay, Elisha B. V, 784
Jay, Elisha J. V, 784
Jay, Eliza V, 181
Jay, Eliza V, 182
Jay, Eliza V, 407
Jay, Eliza V, 784
Jay, Eliza V, 785
Jay, Elizabeth I, 1021
Jay, Elizabeth I, 1032
Jay, Elizabeth I, 1035
Jay, Elizabeth IV, 41
Jay, Elizabeth V, 181
Jay, Elizabeth V, 182
Jay, Elizabeth V, 204
Jay, Elizabeth V, 746
Jay, Elizabeth V, 783
Jay, Elizabeth V, 784
Jay, Elizabeth V, 785
Jay, Elizabeth V, 794
Jay, Elizabeth V, 799
Jay, Elizabeth V, 811
Jay, Elizabeth V, 812
Jay, Ella V, 407
Jay, Elma V, 181
Jay, Elma V, 182
Jay, Elvirah V, 784
Jay, Elwood V, 785
Jay, Emily IV, 1322
Jay, Emma V, 181
Jay, Emma V, 182
Jay, Emma V, 812
Jay, Enoch V, 784
Jay, Enoch V, 785
Jay, Enos E. V, 811
Jay, Esther V, 744
Jay, Esther V, 785
Jay, Esther V, 811
Jay, Esther V, 812
Jay, Esther P. V, 812
Jay, Ethel A. V, 812
Jay, Eunice V, 181
Jay, Eva C. V, 181
Jay, Eva C. V, 182
Jay, Eva C. V, 407
Jay, Frank Preston V, 812
Jay, Furnice V, 746
Jay, Gordon V, 182
Jay, Guliann V, 746
Jay, Hannah V, 784
Jay, Harold M. V, 407
Jay, Harry M. V, 812
Jay, Hattie V, 407
Jay, Hattie E. V, 181
Jay, Hattie E. V, 182
Jay, Hattie E. V, 407
Jay, Henery V, 81
Jay, Henry V, 74
Jay, Henry V, 81
Jay, Henry V, 181
Jay, Henry V, 784
Jay, Henry V, 785
Jay, Henry Russell V, 812
Jay, Herman V, 812
Jay, Hery V, 811
Jay, Hugh V, 812
Jay, Insco V, 811
Jay, Insco V, 812
Jay, Insco V, 815
Jay, Isaac I, 553
Jay, Isaac I, 887
Jay, Isaac I, 1016
Jay, Isaac V, 182
Jay, Isaac V, 746
Jay, Isaac V, 780
Jay, Isaac V, 784
Jay, Isaac V, 785
Jay, J. Edwin V, 687
Jay, James I, 552
Jay, James I, 553
Jay, James I, 1016
Jay, James I, 1032
Jay, James I, 1035
Jay, James IV, 41
Jay, James V, 81
Jay, James V, 181
Jay, James V, 182
Jay, James V, 195

James V, 407
James V, 746
James V, 749
James V, 784
James V, 785
James V, 788
James V, 811
James V, 812
James C. V, 182
James C. V, 746
James C. V, 785
James Wilbur V, 407
James, Jr. V, 785
Jane V, 81
Jane V, 746
Jane V, 784
Jane V, 785
Jane V, 788
Jane V, 799
Jane V, 804
Jane V, 806
Jane V, 807
Jane V, 811
Jane V, 812
Jehu V, 182
Jemima I, 1032
Jemima I, 1035
Jemima V, 181
Jemima V, 182
Jemima V, 195
Jemimah I, 552
Jemimah I, 1016
Jenny V, 784
Jesse I, 1032
Jesse V, 81
Jesse V, 745
Jesse V, 746
Jesse V, 783
Jesse V, 784
Jesse V, 785
Jesse V, 811
Jessy I, 1021
Jessy I, 1026
Jessy I, 1032
Jno. V, 746
Job P. V, 732
Job P. V, 746
Job P. V, 784
Job P. V, 785
Job Pugh V, 784
Job T. V, 779
Job T. V, 785
John I, 1021
John I, 1032
John I, 1036
John I, 1055
John IV, 41
John V, 81
John V, 125
John V, 159
John V, 163
John V, 181
John V, 182
John V, 191
John V, 204
John V, 407
John V, 733
John V, 744
John V, 745
John V, 746
John V, 756
John V, 780
John V, 783
John V, 784
John V, 785
John V, 787
John V, 788
John V, 811
John V, 812
John Edwin V, 812
John Pemberton V, 811
John R. V, 746
John, Jr. V, 81
John, Jr. V, 746
John, Jr. V, 784
John, Jr. V, 785
Jonathan V, 746
Jonathan V, 748
Jonathan V, 784
Jonathan V, 785
Jonathan V, 787
Jonathan V, 811
Jonathan V, 812
Jonathan M. V, 812
Joseph I, 401
Joseph V, 785
Joseph V, 799
Joseph V, 806
Joseph V, 811
Joseph V, 812
Joseph F. V, 799
Jay, Joseph F. V, 804
Jay, Joseph F. V, 811
Jay, Joseph F. V, 812
Jay, Josie E. V, 181
Jay, Josie E. V, 182
Jay, Josie E. V, 407
Jay, Juliann V, 746
Jay, Keturah I, 1058
Jay, Keturah V, 155
Jay, Keturah V, 181
Jay, Keturah V, 182
Jay, Keturah V, 746
Jay, Keturah V, 784
Jay, Keturah V, 787
Jay, Keturah V, 794
Jay, Keziah V, 809
Jay, Keziah V, 812
Jay, L. V, 812
Jay, Layton I, 553
Jay, Layton I, 1016
Jay, Layton I, 1032
Jay, Layton I, 1035
Jay, Layton IV, 41
Jay, Layton V, 155
Jay, Layton V, 181
Jay, Layton V, 182
Jay, Layton V, 504
Jay, Layton V, 746
Jay, Layton V, 811
Jay, Layton V, 812
Jay, Leona S. V, 578
Jay, Levi V, 784
Jay, Levi V, 785
Jay, Levina V, 794
Jay, Linnie Alice V, 812
Jay, Lucinda V, 155
Jay, Lucinda V, 182
Jay, Lyddia V, 746
Jay, Lydia I, 1021
Jay, Lydia I, 1055
Jay, Lydia V, 81
Jay, Lydia V, 95
Jay, Lydia V, 159
Jay, Lydia V, 163
Jay, Lydia V, 181
Jay, Lydia V, 182
Jay, Lydia V, 191
Jay, Lydia V, 204
Jay, Lydia V, 407
Jay, Lydia V, 733
Jay, Lydia V, 745
Jay, Lydia V, 746
Jay, Lydia V, 780
Jay, Lydia V, 784
Jay, Lydia V, 785
Jay, Lydia V, 794
Jay, Lydia V, 799
Jay, Lydia V, 803
Jay, Lydia V, 804
Jay, Lydia Ann V, 181
Jay, Macy V, 784
Jay, Madison V, 182
Jay, Mahala I, 887
Jay, Mahala V, 744
Jay, Mahala V, 746
Jay, Mahala V, 792
Jay, Mahala V, 811
Jay, Mahala V, 819
Jay, Mahala Emma V, 746
Jay, Mahalah V, 785
Jay, Marcy V, 81
Jay, Margaret V, 792
Jay, Margaret V, 807
Jay, Margaret V, 811
Jay, Margaret V, 812
Jay, Margaret V, 820
Jay, Margaret Fidella V, 812
Jay, Marmaduke V, 799
Jay, Martha I, 887
Jay, Martha V, 81
Jay, Martha V, 163
Jay, Martha V, 176
Jay, Martha V, 181
Jay, Martha V, 182
Jay, Martha V, 407
Jay, Martha V, 746
Jay, Martha V, 784
Jay, Martha V, 785
Jay, Martha V, 811
Jay, Martha C. V, 807
Jay, Martha E. V, 812
Jay, Martha Elizabeth V, 182
Jay, Martha Ellen Crull V, 811
Jay, Martha H. V, 407
Jay, Martha Louella V, 812
Jay, Martha S. V, 181
Jay, Mary I, 553
Jay, Mary I, 1016
Jay, Mary I, 1021
Jay, Mary I, 1032
Jay, Mary I, 1035
Jay, Mary I, 1036
Jay, Mary V, 47
Jay, Mary V, 81
Jay, Mary V, 125
Jay, Mary V, 181
Jay, Mary V, 182
Jay, Mary V, 191
Jay, Mary V, 739
Jay, Mary V, 746
Jay, Mary V, 748
Jay, Mary V, 782
Jay, Mary V, 783
Jay, Mary V, 784
Jay, Mary V, 785
Jay, Mary V, 786
Jay, Mary V, 787
Jay, Mary V, 789
Jay, Mary V, 799
Jay, Mary V, 803
Jay, Mary V, 804
Jay, Mary V, 806
Jay, Mary V, 811
Jay, Mary V, 812
Jay, Mary V, 815
Jay, Mary VI, 408
Jay, Mary VI, 453
Jay, Mary Ann V, 181
Jay, Mary Ann V, 182
Jay, Mary Ann V, 812
Jay, Mary Elizabeth V, 746
Jay, Mary Elizabeth V, 784
Jay, Mary Ethel V, 407
Jay, Mary Ethel Green V, 407
Jay, Mary Ethel Green V, 686
Jay, Mary Jay I, 1032
Jay, Mary Jay V, 81
Jay, Mary Macy V, 746
Jay, Mary P. V, 811
Jay, Mary P. V, 812
Jay, Mary Pearson V, 745
Jay, Merlin V, 812
Jay, Mertie M. V, 746
Jay, Mills I, 552
Jay, Mills I, 1016
Jay, Mills I, 1032
Jay, Milton V, 784
Jay, Miriam Madeline V, 407
Jay, Moses V, 784
Jay, Moses V, 785
Jay, Moses V, 792
Jay, Moses V, 807
Jay, Moses V, 811
Jay, Moses V, 812
Jay, Moses V, 820
Jay, Moses C. V, 812
Jay, Mrs. Samuel IV, 1322
Jay, Nerlinda V, 81
Jay, Oliver V, 746
Jay, Orlinda V, 784
Jay, Orlistus V, 746
Jay, Patience I, 1032
Jay, Patience IV, 41
Jay, Patience V, 181
Jay, Patience V, 812
Jay, Phama V, 182
Jay, Phama V, 407
Jay, Phamy V, 176
Jay, Phamy V, 181
Jay, Phebe V, 784
Jay, Phebe V, 785
Jay, Prudence V, 811
Jay, Prudence H. V, 811
Jay, Rachel I, 1021
Jay, Rachel I, 1032
Jay, Rachel V, 81
Jay, Rachel V, 100
Jay, Rachel V, 732
Jay, Rachel V, 746
Jay, Rachel V, 779
Jay, Rachel V, 784
Jay, Rachel V, 785
Jay, Rachel V, 786
Jay, Rachel V, 794
Jay, Rachel Arnold V, 81
Jay, Rebecca I, 1057
Jay, Rebecca V, 168
Jay, Rebecca V, 181
Jay, Rebecca V, 194
Jay, Rebecca V, 733
Jay, Rebecca V, 746
Jay, Rebecca V, 756
Jay, Rebecca V, 784
Jay, Rebecca V, 789
Jay, Rebecca V, 811
Jay, Rebecca V, 812
Jay, Rebecca V, 815
Jay, Rebecca V, 817
Jay, Rebecca Ella V, 746
Jay, Rebeckah V, 175
Jay, Rebeckah V, 181
Jay, Rebeckah V, 784
Jay, Reuben I, 552
Jay, Rhoda I, 553
Jay, Rhoda I, 1016
Jay, Rhoda V, 181
Jay, Rhoda V, 182
Jay, Rhoda V, 195
Jay, Rhoda V, 780
Jay, Rhoda V, 784
Jay, Rhoda B. V, 746
Jay, Richard V, 746
Jay, Rollin C. V, 812
Jay, Russell V, 407
Jay, Russell D. V, 407
Jay, Ruth V, 181
Jay, Ruth V, 194
Jay, Ruth V, 748
Jay, Sally V, 745
Jay, Sally V, 811
Jay, Samuel I, 1021
Jay, Samuel IV, 1322
Jay, Samuel V, 81
Jay, Samuel V, 112
Jay, Samuel V, 182
Jay, Samuel V, 744
Jay, Samuel V, 745
Jay, Samuel V, 746
Jay, Samuel V, 783
Jay, Samuel V, 784
Jay, Samuel V, 785
Jay, Samuel V, 786
Jay, Samuel V, 794
Jay, Samuel V, 810
Jay, Samuel V, 811
Jay, Samuel V, 812
Jay, Samuel Gordon V, 181
Jay, Samuel S. V, 176
Jay, Samuel S. V, 182
Jay, Samuel S. V, 407
Jay, Samuel Spray V, 181
Jay, Samuel, Jr. V, 746
Jay, Samuel, Jr. V, 785
Jay, Sarah I, 553
Jay, Sarah I, 1016
Jay, Sarah I, 1026
Jay, Sarah I, 1032
Jay, Sarah V, 81
Jay, Sarah V, 181
Jay, Sarah V, 182
Jay, Sarah V, 744
Jay, Sarah V, 745
Jay, Sarah V, 746
Jay, Sarah V, 748
Jay, Sarah V, 784
Jay, Sarah V, 785
Jay, Sarah V, 787
Jay, Sarah V, 794
Jay, Sarah V, 810
Jay, Sarah V, 812
Jay, Sarah V, 815
Jay, Sarah F. V, 803
Jay, Sarah F. V, 811
Jay, Sarah Jane V, 799
Jay, Sarah Martha V, 811
Jay, Sarah T. V, 181
Jay, Sary V, 784
Jay, Sherman Carl V, 812
Jay, Solomon V, 812
Jay, Stacy V, 812
Jay, Susana V, 812
Jay, Susanna V, 182
Jay, Susanna V, 805
Jay, Susanna V, 807
Jay, Susannah I, 1028
Jay, Susannah I, 1032
Jay, Susannah V, 733
Jay, Susannah V, 736
Jay, Susannah V, 746
Jay, Susannah V, 749
Jay, Susannah V, 784
Jay, Susannah V, 785
Jay, Susannah V, 788
Jay, Susannah V, 803
Jay, Susannah V, 804
Jay, Susannah V, 812
Jay, T. V, 812
Jay, Thomas I, 1021
Jay, Thomas I, 1032
Jay, Thomas I, 1036
Jay, Thomas V, 81
Jay, Thomas V, 746
Jay, Thomas V, 783
Jay, Thomas V, 784
Jay, Thomas V, 789
Jay, Thomas V, 799
Jay, Thomas V, 811
Jay, Thomas V, 815
Jay, Thomas Alert V, 812
Jay, Thomas C. V, 811
Jay, Thomas C. V, 812
Jay, Thomas Elwood V, 784
Jay, Thomas, Jr. V, 785
Jay, Thomas, Jr. V, 812
Jay, Thos. V, 785
Jay, Thos. V, 794
Jay, Verlinda V, 784
Jay, Verlinda V, 786
Jay, Verlinda V, 794
Jay, Vielinda V, 746
Jay, Virlinda V, 784
Jay, W. T. V, 407
Jay, Wade F. V, 812
Jay, Walter V, 81
Jay, Walter D. V, 746
Jay, Walter D. V, 748
Jay, Walter D. V, 784
Jay, Walter D. V, 811
Jay, Walter Denny V, 81
Jay, Walter Denny V, 746
Jay, Walter Denny V, 783
Jay, Walton G. V, 407
Jay, William I, 401
Jay, William I, 887
Jay, William I, 1021
Jay, William I, 1032
Jay, William IV, 41
Jay, William V, 81
Jay, William V, 182
Jay, William V, 739
Jay, William V, 745
Jay, William V, 746
Jay, William V, 783
Jay, William V, 784
Jay, William V, 811
Jay, William V, 812
Jay, William C. I, 887
Jay, William Elwood V, 811
Jay, William, Jr. I, 1032
Jay, Wilson T. V, 181
Jay, Wilson T. V, 182
Jay, Wilson T. V, 407
Jay, Wm. V, 783
Jay, Wm. V, 784
Jay, Wm. V, 785
Jay, Wm. V, 799
Jay, Wm. V, 803
Jay, Wm. V, 811
Jay, Wm. V, 812
Jay, Wm. Denny V, 784
Jay, Wm. Foster V, 811
Jay, Wm., Jr. V, 812
Jaycox, Mrs. E. A. IV, 1167
Jaycox, W. W. IV, 1167
JayJohn, Eliza V, 252
Jean, William VI, 973
Jean, William VI, 1002
Jeanes, Ann II, 564
Jeanes, Anna II, 666
Jeanes, Anna C. II, 863
Jeanes, Anna C. II, 882
Jeanes, Caroline Margaretta II, 803
Jeanes, Humphrey II, 882
Jeanes, Isaac II, 803
Jeanes, Isaiah II, 564
Jeanes, Isaiah II, 666
Jeanes, Jacob II, 564
Jeanes, Jacob II, 666
Jeanes, Joseph II, 882
Jeanes, Keziah II, 803
Jeanes, Keziah II, 882
Jeanes, Leah II, 564
Jeanes, Leah II, 666
Jeanes, Martha II, 803
Jeanes, Mary Jane I, 821
Jeanes, Polly I, 821
Jeanes, Rebecca II, 800
Jeanes, Samuel II, 882
Jeanes, Thomas II, 803
Jeanes, Thomas II, 882
Jeanes, William II, 803
Jeanes, Wm. II, 882
Jeanis, Hannah VI, 828
Jeanis, Tyra VI, 828
Jeans, Ann II, 81
Jeans, Ann II, 103
Jeans, Isaiah II, 564
Jeans, Joseph II, 882
Jeans, Samuel II, 882
Jeepeys, Charles III, 279
Jeepeys, Louisa J. III, 279
Jeepeys, Mary Anna III, 279
Jeffaries, Joab V, 504
Jeffer, Ella K. V, 81
Jefferas, Abraham V, 504
Jefferas, Darlington V, 504
Jefferes, Elizabeth V, 478
Jefferes, Elizabeth V, 504
Jefferes, Hannah S. V, 579
Jefferies, Amos IV, 41
Jefferies, Asa II, 81
Jefferies, Barzillai II, 81
Jefferies, Billie IV, 728

Jefferies, Caleb IV, 41
Jefferies, Claire Marion IV, 728
Jefferies, Constantine II, 81
Jefferies, Darlington VI, 408
Jefferies, Edwin IV, 719
Jefferies, Elijah W. II, 120
Jefferies, Emmor IV, 41
Jefferies, Gulielma II, 81
Jefferies, Hannah II, 81
Jefferies, Hannah VI, 408
Jefferies, Job V, 81
Jefferies, Job VI, 408
Jefferies, Job, Jr. V, 504
Jefferies, Jobe VI, 408
Jefferies, Joshua II, 81
Jefferies, Leatitia II, 81
Jefferies, Lida IV, 719
Jefferies, Lydia C. V, 504
Jefferies, Mamie IV, 719
Jefferies, Martha W. III, 302
Jefferies, Mary II, 748
Jefferies, Mercy II, 81
Jefferies, Mercy, Jr. II, 81
Jefferies, Pamela VI, 858
Jefferies, Patience II, 81
Jefferies, Phebe IV, 41
Jefferies, Raymond IV, 728
Jefferies, Rebecca II, 81
Jefferies, Rebecca VI, 408
Jefferies, Rebekah VI, 408
Jefferies, Rhoda IV, 41
Jefferies, Richard Ware II, 81
Jefferies, Sarah II, 81
Jefferies, Sarah L. VI, 858
Jefferies, William VI, 408
Jefferies, Wilma IV, 728
Jefferis, Abraham V, 504
Jefferis, Ann II, 81
Jefferis, Ann II, 102
Jefferis, Ann Mary V, 504
Jefferis, Anna May V, 658
Jefferis, Asa II, 74
Jefferis, Asa II, 81
Jefferis, Barzillai II, 81
Jefferis, Benjamin G. II, 120
Jefferis, Catherine V, 137
Jefferis, Constantine II, 81
Jefferis, Darlington V, 504
Jefferis, Elijah II, 74
Jefferis, Elijah II, 81
Jefferis, Elijah W. II, 120
Jefferis, Elizabeth II, 74
Jefferis, Elizabeth II, 81
Jefferis, Elizabeth II, 882
Jefferis, Elizabeth V, 504
Jefferis, Eulalia V, 504
Jefferis, Gulielma II, 67
Jefferis, Gulielma II, 81
Jefferis, Hannah II, 32
Jefferis, Hannah II, 81
Jefferis, Hannah V, 81
Jefferis, Hannah V, 504
Jefferis, Hannah S. V, 504
Jefferis, Harriet V, 504
Jefferis, Harriet M. V, 504
Jefferis, Harriett V, 504
Jefferis, Isaac J. V, 504
Jefferis, Jean II, 81
Jefferis, Jeremiah V, 504
Jefferis, Joab V, 504
Jefferis, Job V, 137
Jefferis, Job V, 504
Jefferis, Job VI, 408
Jefferis, Job VI, 414
Jefferis, Job E. V, 504
Jefferis, Job, Jr. V, 504
Jefferis, John II, 32
Jefferis, Joseph II, 120
Jefferis, Joshua II, 32
Jefferis, Joshua II, 81
Jefferis, Joshua V, 504
Jefferis, Joshua M. V, 504
Jefferis, Julianna V, 687
Jefferis, Leatitia II, 81
Jefferis, Leslie V, 687
Jefferis, Leslie D. V, 667
Jefferis, Luther V, 504
Jefferis, Lydia V, 504
Jefferis, Lydia C. V, 504
Jefferis, Martha V, 81
Jefferis, Martha W. V, 81
Jefferis, Mary II, 74
Jefferis, Mary II, 81
Jefferis, Mary II, 882
Jefferis, Mary Belle V, 504
Jefferis, Massey II, 32
Jefferis, Maynard V, 687
Jefferis, Mercy II, 81
Jefferis, Mercy, Jr. II, 81
Jefferis, Nancy Ann V, 504
Jefferis, Norma V, 687
Jefferis, Patience II, 81
Jefferis, Preston V, 504
Jefferis, Rachel V, 483
Jefferis, Rachel V, 504
Jefferis, Rebecca II, 32
Jefferis, Rebecca II, 81
Jefferis, Rebecca V, 504
Jefferis, Rebecca V, 574
Jefferis, Rebecca V, 579
Jefferis, Rebecca B. V, 504
Jefferis, Rebecca H. V, 504
Jefferis, Rebekah II, 57
Jefferis, Rebekah II, 81
Jefferis, Rebekah V, 137
Jefferis, Rebekah VI, 414
Jefferis, Richard II, 81
Jefferis, Richard Ware II, 32
Jefferis, Richard Ware II, 81
Jefferis, Russell V, 504
Jefferis, Sarah II, 32
Jefferis, Sarah II, 72
Jefferis, Sarah II, 81
Jefferis, T. J. V, 504
Jefferis, Taylor II, 882
Jefferis, Verna V, 667
Jefferis, Verna D. V, 687
Jefferis, Wayne V, 504
Jefferis, William Preston V, 504
Jeffers, Caleb IV, 338
Jeffers, Chas. IV, 1322
Jeffers, Edna Lois IV, 1322
Jeffers, Elizabeth II, 882
Jeffers, Ella V, 182
Jeffers, Ella R. V, 182
Jeffers, Emmer IV, 338
Jeffers, Emmor IV, 338
Jeffers, Guy IV, 479
Jeffers, Guy IV, 1322
Jeffers, Guy V. IV, 1322
Jeffers, Guy V. IV, 1325
Jeffers, Job V, 81
Jeffers, Job V, 504
Jeffers, Miriam IV, 479
Jeffers, Miriam IV, 1322
Jeffers, Miriam May IV, 1322
Jeffers, Miriam May IV, 1325
Jeffers, Myriam IV, 479
Jeffers, Myrtle IV, 1322
Jeffers, Phebe IV, 338
Jeffers, Rebecca V, 794
Jeffers, Rhoda IV, 338
Jeffers, Sarah I, 240
Jeffers, Sarah I, 242
Jeffers, Velma V, 182
Jefferson, Campbell VI, 828
Jefferson, Charles A. IV, 1039
Jefferson, Cora I, 611
Jefferson, Cora I, 619
Jefferson, Cora Walker I, 635
Jefferson, Edward II, 564
Jefferson, Eliza V, 954
Jefferson, Elizabeth VI, 828
Jefferson, Jane III, 184
Jefferson, Josiah Cook VI, 113
Jefferson, Mary II, 564
Jefferson, Mary D. II, 748
Jefferson, Nellie I, 619
Jefferson, Nellie I, 635
Jefferson, Pet VI, 185
Jefferson, Pet. VI, 205
Jefferson, Peter VI, 205
Jefferson, Samuel VI, 105
Jefferson, Samuel VI, 113
Jefferson, Thomas III, 184
Jefferson, Thomas VI, 185
Jefferson, Thomas VI, 204
Jefferson, Virginia I, 611
Jefferson, Virginia I, 635
Jefferson, Virginia Maie I, 619
Jefferson, Walter I, 611
Jefferson, Walter Cabot I, 619
Jeffery, Gertrude II, 32
Jeffery, Jane II, 32
Jeffery, Jean II, 81
Jeffery, Jean II, 88
Jeffery, John II, 32
Jeffrey, Velma V, 182
Jeffreys, Charles III, 184
Jeffreys, Hannah V, 81
Jeffreys, Job V, 504
Jeffreys, Louisa J. III, 184
Jeffreys, Mary Anna III, 184
Jeffries, Addie III, 422
Jeffries, Alice V, 629
Jeffries, Anderson V, 342
Jeffries, Anna M. V, 687
Jeffries, Billie IV, 728
Jeffries, Blanch L. V, 579
Jeffries, Bland V, 579
Jeffries, Caleb IV, 1167
Jeffries, Caleb V, 954
Jeffries, Catherine IV, 95
Jeffries, Catherine V, 81
Jeffries, Claire Marion IV, 728
Jeffries, Clare IV, 727
Jeffries, Darlington IV, 95
Jeffries, Darlington V, 81
Jeffries, Edwin IV, 727
Jeffries, Eliza V, 342
Jeffries, Eliza VI, 828
Jeffries, Elizabeth V, 504
Jeffries, Ella K. V, 81
Jeffries, Eulalia P. V, 687
Jeffries, F. L. III, 422
Jeffries, George V, 579
Jeffries, Hannah V, 81
Jeffries, Hannah V, 504
Jeffries, Hannah S. V, 579
Jeffries, Harriett M. V, 579
Jeffries, I. J. V, 687
Jeffries, Jane IV, 95
Jeffries, Jane IV, 109
Jeffries, Jeremiah V, 504
Jeffries, Jessie III, 422
Jeffries, Job IV, 95
Jeffries, Job V, 81
Jeffries, Job E. V, 504
Jeffries, Joseph II, 120
Jeffries, Joseph VI, 819
Jeffries, Joseph W. VI, 828
Jeffries, Joshua V, 687
Jeffries, Julian V, 687
Jeffries, Julianna V, 687
Jeffries, Leslie V, 687
Jeffries, Leslie D. V, 687
Jeffries, Luther V, 687
Jeffries, Lydia IV, 727
Jeffries, Lydia V, 687
Jeffries, Martha V, 81
Jeffries, Martha W. V, 81
Jeffries, Mary II, 882
Jeffries, Mary Burnett IV, 95
Jeffries, Mary C. VI, 759
Jeffries, Mary C. VI, 781
Jeffries, Mary Ellen V, 579
Jeffries, Maynard V, 687
Jeffries, Norma V, 687
Jeffries, Peytan V, 687
Jeffries, Phebe IV, 413
Jeffries, Preston V, 504
Jeffries, Preston V, 687
Jeffries, Rachel IV, 95
Jeffries, Rachel V, 504
Jeffries, Raymond IV, 728
Jeffries, Rebecca IV, 95
Jeffries, Rebecca V, 498
Jeffries, Rebecca V, 504
Jeffries, Rebecca V, 579
Jeffries, Rebecca V, 812
Jeffries, Rebecca B. V, 504
Jeffries, Rebecca H. V, 579
Jeffries, Rhoda IV, 413
Jeffries, Robert III, 422
Jeffries, Roper V, 629
Jeffries, Sadie V, 342
Jeffries, Sarah II, 564
Jeffries, Sarah IV, 95
Jeffries, Sarah IV, 101
Jeffries, Sarah V, 342
Jeffries, Sarah J. III, 422
Jeffries, Taylor II, 882
Jeffries, Verna V, 687
Jeffries, Verna D. V, 687
Jeffries, Wayne V, 687
Jeffries, Wayne W. V, 687
Jeffries, Wd Rebecca IV, 95
Jeffries, Widower Job IV, 95
Jeffries, Wilma IV, 727
Jeffries, Wilma IV, 728
Jeffries, Wright III, 422
Jeffris, Russell V, 504
Jefris, Job IV, 77
Jefris, Job IV, 117
Jefris, Rebecca IV, 77
Jefris, Rebecca IV, 117
Jefris, Wd Rebecca IV, 95
Jefris, Widower Job IV, 95
Jehu, Emeline IV, 969
Jeisure, Alice V, 1004
Jelks, Charlotte IV, 95
Jelks, Charlotte IV, 104
Jelks, Lydia IV, 151
Jelks, Lydia IV, 160
Jelks, Lydia IV, 479
Jelks, Lydia IV, 498
Jelks, Mary IV, 41
Jelks, Mary IV, 60
Jelks, Mary IV, 95
Jelks, Priscilla IV, 41
Jelks, Priscilla IV, 95
Jelks, Priscilla IV, 104
Jelks, Priscilla IV, 479
Jelks, Priscilla IV, 486
Jelks, Priscilla Jelks IV, 95
Jelks, Richard IV, 41
Jelks, Richard IV, 95
Jelks, Richard IV, 104
Jelks, Richard IV, 151
Jelks, Richard IV, 160
Jelks, Richard IV, 479
Jelks, Richard IV, 497
Jelks, Rick I, 272
Jelson, Jane II, 381
Jemieson, Mary Jane IV, 641
Jenet, Jane C. II, 1062
Jenet, Jane C. II, 1074
Jening, Ann II, 177
Jening, Elizabeth II, 177
Jening, Joyce II, 177
Jening, Mercy II, 177
Jening, Samuel II, 177
Jenings, Ann II, 235
Jenings, Ann II, 264
Jenings, Ann II, 381
Jenings, Anne II, 235
Jenings, Chas. II, 565
Jenings, Henry II, 381
Jenings, Isaac Marriott II, 235
Jenings, Jacob, Jr. II, 565
Jenings, John II, 381
Jenings, Joyce II, 235
Jenings, Joyse II, 381
Jenings, Mercy II, 235
Jenings, Mercy II, 264
Jenings, Richard II, 235
Jenings, Samuel II, 235
Jenings, Samuel II, 241
Jenings, Samuel II, 246
Jenings, Samuel II, 381
Jenings, Sarah II, 235
Jenings, Sarah II, 249
Jenings, Thomas II, 235
Jenings, Wd. Margrett II, 381
Jenings, William II, 381
Jenings, William Stevenson II, 235
Jenkenson, Ann IV, 95
Jenkenson, Elizabeth IV, 95
Jenkenson, Isaac II, 469
Jenkenson, Isaac II, 565
Jenkenson, Isaac IV, 95
Jenkenson, John II, 469
Jenkenson, John II, 565
Jenkenson, John IV, 95
Jenkenson, Mary II, 469
Jenkenson, Mary II, 565
Jenkenson, Mary IV, 95
Jenkenson, Rebecca IV, 95
Jenkenson, Sarah IV, 95
Jenkings, Mary II, 779
Jenkings, Thos. II, 779
Jenkins, ??? II, 382
Jenkins, ??? IV, 137
Jenkins, ??? V, 747
Jenkins, A. Margaret IV, 969
Jenkins, A. Margaret IV, 1039
Jenkins, A. Margaret IV, 1322
Jenkins, Abigail II, 235
Jenkins, Abigail II, 381
Jenkins, Abigail II, 382
Jenkins, Abigail II, 564
Jenkins, Abijah V, 747
Jenkins, Abijah V, 786
Jenkins, Abijah Milton V, 786
Jenkins, Abraham VI, 940
Jenkins, Ada IV, 1039
Jenkins, Adelia III, 184
Jenkins, Adila V, 779
Jenkins, Adila V, 786
Jenkins, Adila V, 800
Jenkins, Adila V, 802
Jenkins, Adila V, 812
Jenkins, Adilah V, 801
Jenkins, Alfred I, 1155
Jenkins, Alvina IV, 229
Jenkins, Alvina IV, 279
Jenkins, Alvina IV, 969
Jenkins, Alvina IV, 999
Jenkins, Alvina L. IV, 229
Jenkins, Alvina S. IV, 229
Jenkins, Alvina S. IV, 969
Jenkins, Alvine H. V, 747
Jenkins, Amasa I, 619
Jenkins, Amasa V, 747
Jenkins, Amasa M. V, 747
Jenkins, Amey VI, 829
Jenkins, Amos I, 1021
Jenkins, Amos I, 1033
Jenkins, Amos I, 1037
Jenkins, Amos V, 607
Jenkins, Amos V, 785
Jenkins, Amos V, 786
Jenkins, Amos V, 791
Jenkins, Amos V, 819
Jenkins, Amos VI, 940
Jenkins, Amy VI, 408
Jenkins, Amy VI, 449
Jenkins, Anderson V, 786
Jenkins, Anderson H. V, 786
Jenkins, Ann I, 553
Jenkins, Ann I, 659
Jenkins, Ann III, 184
Jenkins, Ann III, 185
Jenkins, Ann IV, 41
Jenkins, Ann IV, 95
Jenkins, Ann IV, 151
Jenkins, Ann IV, 165
Jenkins, Ann IV, 228
Jenkins, Ann IV, 229
Jenkins, Ann IV, 292
Jenkins, Ann V, 629
Jenkins, Ann V, 745
Jenkins, Ann V, 747
Jenkins, Ann V, 763
Jenkins, Ann V, 766
Jenkins, Ann V, 785
Jenkins, Ann V, 786
Jenkins, Ann V, 791
Jenkins, Ann V, 883
Jenkins, Ann VI, 408
Jenkins, Ann VI, 409
Jenkins, Ann VI, 940
Jenkins, Ann Eliza II, 882
Jenkins, Ann K. III, 185
Jenkins, Ann P. II, 565
Jenkins, Ann W. II, 882
Jenkins, Ann W. V, 954
Jenkins, Anna II, 872
Jenkins, Anna III, 353
Jenkins, Anna IV, 228
Jenkins, Anna V, 241
Jenkins, Anna V, 675
Jenkins, Anna V, 687
Jenkins, Anna V, 747
Jenkins, Anna V, 881
Jenkins, Anna VI, 408
Jenkins, Anna VI, 940
Jenkins, Anna Margaret IV, 96
Jenkins, Anne IV, 151
Jenkins, Annie V, 687
Jenkins, Arthur IV, 1039
Jenkins, Augusta III, 338
Jenkins, Augustine S. V, 687
Jenkins, Avis III, 185
Jenkins, Barbara VI, 809
Jenkins, Bathsheba V, 780
Jenkins, Bathsheba V, 786
Jenkins, Benitt VI, 1003
Jenkins, Benjamin V, 786
Jenkins, Bernice Kinsey IV, 96
Jenkins, Betty IV, 151
Jenkins, Betty VI, 409
Jenkins, Bevan V, 182
Jenkins, Bevan V, 213
Jenkins, Bevan V, 687
Jenkins, Bevan V, 719
Jenkins, Beven V, 687
Jenkins, Caleb J. III, 184
Jenkins, Caroline III, 184
Jenkins, Caroline III, 185
Jenkins, Caroline III, 192
Jenkins, Caroline K. III, 27
Jenkins, Caroline K. III, 184
Jenkins, Caroline K. III, 185
Jenkins, Caroline K. III, 319
Jenkins, Cary VI, 829
Jenkins, Cary E. IV, 969
Jenkins, Catharine IV, 338
Jenkins, Catharine D. III, 184
Jenkins, Catharine D. III, 195
Jenkins, Catherine VI, 862
Jenkins, Caty IV, 151
Jenkins, Caty VI, 409
Jenkins, Charity IV, 33
Jenkins, Charity IV, 41
Jenkins, Charles II, 381
Jenkins, Charles II, 382
Jenkins, Charles II, 535
Jenkins, Charles II, 564
Jenkins, Charles III, 184
Jenkins, Charles Alexander III, 184
Jenkins, Charles Henry IV, 22
Jenkins, Charles L. III, 184
Jenkins, Charles M. V, 747
Jenkins, Chas. E. II, 883
Jenkins, Chas. M. V, 687
Jenkins, Chas. M. V, 747
Jenkins, Child III, 185
Jenkins, Clary V, 630
Jenkins, Clement C. V, 747
Jenkins, Cora E. IV, 1039
Jenkins, Cornelia II, 811
Jenkins, Cornelia II, 882

ins, Cornelia II, 903
ins, Cornelia II, 943
ins, Cornelia VI, 538
ins, Cornelia VI, 577
ins, Cornelia VI, 677
ins, Cornelia VI, 717
ins, Daniel V, 687
ins, David I, 401
ins, David I, 1015
ins, David I, 1021
ins, David I, 1029
ins, David I, 1032
ins, David I, 1033
ins, David IV, 228
ins, David IV, 229
ins, David V, 687
ins, David V, 747
ins, David V, 763
ins, David V, 781
ins, David V, 785
ins, David V, 786
ins, David V, 790
ins, David V, 791
ins, David V, 913
ins, David VI, 940
ins, David C. V, 785
ins, David C. V, 786
ins, David H. V, 747
ins, David Harry V, 786
ins, David Harvey V, 505
ins, David Lindley V, 786
ins, David P. V, 913
ins, David Updegraff IV, 228
ins, David, Jr. V, 786
ins, David, Sr. I, 1033
ins, Deborah III, 184
ins, Deborah T. V, 505
ins, Delia III, 184
ins, Dinah V, 182
ins, Dinah V, 183
ins, Dinah V, 198
ins, Dinah V, 252
ins, Dinah V, 255
ins, Dora IV, 229
ins, Dorothy V, 786
ins, Edith VI, 409
ins, Edith P. IV, 827
ins, Edward III, 46
ins, Edward IV, 728
ins, Edward IV, 787
ins, Edward IV, 827
ins, Edward IV, 969
ins, Edward VI, 883
ins, Edward W. III, 185
ins, Edward Y. III, 184
ins, Edwin IV, 827
ins, Eleanor III, 84
ins, Eleanor III, 184
ins, Eleanor III, 234
ins, Elen V, 182
ins, Eli I, 1033
ins, Eli V, 786
ins, Elisa Ann V, 786
ins, Elisha V, 785
ins, Elisha V, 786
ins, Eliza III, 184
ins, Eliza III, 185
ins, Eliza A. II, 811
ins, Eliza A. II, 882
ins, Eliza Ann II, 803
ins, Eliza Ann II, 811
ins, Eliza Ann II, 882
ins, Eliza L. III, 144
ins, Eliza L. III, 184
ins, Eliza L. III, 185
ins, Eliza L. III, 215
ins, Eliza L. III, 217
ins, Elizabeth I, 401
ins, Elizabeth I, 1021
ins, Elizabeth I, 1032
ins, Elizabeth I, 1033
ins, Elizabeth I, 1037
ins, Elizabeth II, 565
kins, Elizabeth II, 748
kins, Elizabeth II, 794
kins, Elizabeth II, 803
kins, Elizabeth II, 853
kins, Elizabeth II, 862
kins, Elizabeth II, 872
kins, Elizabeth II, 882
kins, Elizabeth III, 184
kins, Elizabeth IV, 41
kins, Elizabeth IV, 143
kins, Elizabeth IV, 151
kins, Elizabeth IV, 192
kins, Elizabeth IV, 228
kins, Elizabeth IV, 229
kins, Elizabeth IV, 292
kins, Elizabeth IV, 338
kins, Elizabeth IV, 339
kins, Elizabeth IV, 537
Jenkins, Elizabeth IV, 728
Jenkins, Elizabeth IV, 787
Jenkins, Elizabeth IV, 933
Jenkins, Elizabeth IV, 969
Jenkins, Elizabeth IV, 1039
Jenkins, Elizabeth V, 747
Jenkins, Elizabeth V, 785
Jenkins, Elizabeth V, 786
Jenkins, Elizabeth V, 791
Jenkins, Elizabeth V, 794
Jenkins, Elizabeth V, 812
Jenkins, Elizabeth V, 819
Jenkins, Elizabeth VI, 379
Jenkins, Elizabeth VI, 400
Jenkins, Elizabeth VI, 408
Jenkins, Elizabeth VI, 409
Jenkins, Elizabeth VI, 413
Jenkins, Elizabeth VI, 829
Jenkins, Elizabeth VI, 940
Jenkins, Elizabeth C. II, 882
Jenkins, Elizabeth H. III, 184
Jenkins, Elizabeth H. III, 234
Jenkins, Elizabeth H. IV, 192
Jenkins, Elizabeth H. IV, 228
Jenkins, Elizabeth Haviland III, 184
Jenkins, Elizabeth M. IV, 827
Jenkins, Elizabeth M. IV, 969
Jenkins, Ella IV, 827
Jenkins, Ella IV, 969
Jenkins, Ella IV, 1039
Jenkins, Elmer IV, 1167
Jenkins, Elmore L. IV, 1167
Jenkins, Elsie IV, 1039
Jenkins, Ely V, 81
Jenkins, Emaline A. V, 786
Jenkins, Emaline A. V, 788
Jenkins, Emeline V, 747
Jenkins, Enoch I, 1021
Jenkins, Enoch I, 1033
Jenkins, Enoch V, 786
Jenkins, Enoch V, 792
Jenkins, Enoch Pearson V, 747
Jenkins, Ephraim II, 382
Jenkins, Estelle B. III, 184
Jenkins, Estelle B. III, 209
Jenkins, Esther IV, 221
Jenkins, Esther IV, 228
Jenkins, Esther IV, 229
Jenkins, Esther V, 781
Jenkins, Esther V, 786
Jenkins, Esther V, 794
Jenkins, Esther F. IV, 969
Jenkins, Esther H. IV, 969
Jenkins, Ethel IV, 1039
Jenkins, Evan IV, 151
Jenkins, Evan IV, 338
Jenkins, Evan V, 504
Jenkins, Evan V, 786
Jenkins, Evan VI, 379
Jenkins, Evan VI, 408
Jenkins, Evan VI, 409
Jenkins, Evan H. V, 505
Jenkins, Evan H. V, 528
Jenkins, Evans V, 747
Jenkins, Evans H. V, 747
Jenkins, Evans H. V, 786
Jenkins, Evans H. V, 788
Jenkins, Evans H. V, 792
Jenkins, Ezekiel II, 565
Jenkins, Fanie I, 1155
Jenkins, Fanny V, 505
Jenkins, Fanny VI, 829
Jenkins, Fanny B. VI, 829
Jenkins, Fansie L. IV, 827
Jenkins, Florence E. IV, 192
Jenkins, Florence E. IV, 229
Jenkins, Florence L. IV, 229
Jenkins, Florence Loretta IV, 229
Jenkins, Florence M. II, 883
Jenkins, Florence M. II, 893
Jenkins, Florence May II, 807
Jenkins, Frances III, 102
Jenkins, Frances V, 687
Jenkins, Frances V, 719
Jenkins, Frances A. VI, 829
Jenkins, Frances E. V, 182
Jenkins, Frances E. V, 213
Jenkins, Francis II, 803
Jenkins, Francis III, 184
Jenkins, Francis VI, 829
Jenkins, Frederick Z. III, 185
Jenkins, Geo. R. IV, 228
Jenkins, Geo. R. IV, 296
Jenkins, George II, 794
Jenkins, George II, 803
Jenkins, George II, 862
Jenkins, George II, 882
Jenkins, George III, 102
Jenkins, George III, 184
Jenkins, George IV, 229
Jenkins, George IV, 338
Jenkins, George V, 687
Jenkins, George Edward III, 184
Jenkins, George Francis II, 803
Jenkins, George Francis II, 882
Jenkins, George Francis III, 184
Jenkins, George Francis IV, 228
Jenkins, George K. IV, 228
Jenkins, George K. IV, 229
Jenkins, Gracy VI, 940
Jenkins, Gulielma Atlee II, 883
Jenkins, Gulielma Atlee II, 939
Jenkins, Halladay, Jr. II, 709
Jenkins, Hallie V, 687
Jenkins, Hannah I, 1033
Jenkins, Hannah I, 1037
Jenkins, Hannah II, 382
Jenkins, Hannah II, 564
Jenkins, Hannah II, 572
Jenkins, Hannah II, 685
Jenkins, Hannah II, 697
Jenkins, Hannah III, 98
Jenkins, Hannah III, 184
Jenkins, Hannah III, 185
Jenkins, Hannah III, 203
Jenkins, Hannah III, 217
Jenkins, Hannah IV, 28
Jenkins, Hannah IV, 41
Jenkins, Hannah IV, 228
Jenkins, Hannah IV, 229
Jenkins, Hannah IV, 827
Jenkins, Hannah V, 610
Jenkins, Hannah V, 629
Jenkins, Hannah V, 747
Jenkins, Hannah V, 785
Jenkins, Hannah V, 786
Jenkins, Hannah V, 791
Jenkins, Hannah V, 792
Jenkins, Hannah VI, 390
Jenkins, Hannah VI, 408
Jenkins, Hannah VI, 409
Jenkins, Hannah Allston II, 803
Jenkins, Hannah Allston II, 883
Jenkins, Hannah Ann II, 803
Jenkins, Hannah J. II, 862
Jenkins, Hannah J. II, 882
Jenkins, Hannah James II, 794
Jenkins, Hannah James II, 803
Jenkins, Hannah L. II, 882
Jenkins, Hannah L. II, 900
Jenkins, Hannah L. IV, 827
Jenkins, Hannah S. IV, 728
Jenkins, Hannah S. IV, 787
Jenkins, Hannah Sawyer IV, 728
Jenkins, Hariot V, 794
Jenkins, Henry III, 184
Jenkins, Henry VI, 829
Jenkins, Henry VI, 940
Jenkins, Henry C. III, 84
Jenkins, Henry C. III, 184
Jenkins, Henry C. III, 185
Jenkins, Henry C. III, 209
Jenkins, Henry C. III, 234
Jenkins, Hepsibah V, 812
Jenkins, Hicks III, 173
Jenkins, Hunn II, 803
Jenkins, Hunn II, 811
Jenkins, Hunn II, 882
Jenkins, Isaac I, 553
Jenkins, Isaac I, 887
Jenkins, Isaac I, 1016
Jenkins, Isaac I, 1021
Jenkins, Isaac I, 1030
Jenkins, Isaac I, 1032
Jenkins, Isaac II, 470
Jenkins, Isaac II, 564
Jenkins, Isaac IV, 41
Jenkins, Isaac IV, 728
Jenkins, Isaac V, 747
Jenkins, Isaac V, 784
Jenkins, Isaac V, 785
Jenkins, Isaac V, 786
Jenkins, Isaac V, 812
Jenkins, Isaac VI, 409
Jenkins, Isaac Kirk I, 553
Jenkins, Isaac M. Johnson V, 252
Jenkins, Israel IV, 95
Jenkins, Israel IV, 116
Jenkins, Israel IV, 192
Jenkins, Israel IV, 228
Jenkins, Israel IV, 229
Jenkins, Israel IV, 292
Jenkins, Israel IV, 304
Jenkins, Israel IV, 969
Jenkins, Israel V, 629
Jenkins, Israel VI, 408
Jenkins, Israel VI, 409
Jenkins, Israel W. IV, 229
Jenkins, Israel W. IV, 279
Jenkins, Israel W. IV, 969
Jenkins, Israel W. IV, 999
Jenkins, Issachar V, 786
Jenkins, J. T. V, 1004
Jenkins, Jabez II, 382
Jenkins, Jabez II, 565
Jenkins, Jabez II, 803
Jenkins, Jabez II, 900
Jenkins, Jabez H. II, 803
Jenkins, Jabez H. II, 882
Jenkins, Jabez H. II, 883
Jenkins, Jabez, Jr. II, 565
Jenkins, Jacob IV, 151
Jenkins, Jacob IV, 228
Jenkins, Jacob V, 610
Jenkins, Jacob VI, 390
Jenkins, Jacob VI, 400
Jenkins, Jacob VI, 408
Jenkins, Jacob VI, 409
Jenkins, Jacob VI, 523
Jenkins, Jacob VI, 940
Jenkins, Jacob, Jr. VI, 409
Jenkins, James II, 382
Jenkins, James II, 564
Jenkins, James III, 106
Jenkins, James III, 184
Jenkins, James III, 316
Jenkins, James IV, 151
Jenkins, James IV, 338
Jenkins, James IV, 728
Jenkins, James V, 182
Jenkins, James V, 747
Jenkins, James V, 812
Jenkins, James VI, 409
Jenkins, James VI, 940
Jenkins, James J. III, 144
Jenkins, James L. VI, 940
Jenkins, James, Jr. III, 184
Jenkins, James, Jr. III, 185
Jenkins, James, Jr. III, 246
Jenkins, Jane II, 564
Jenkins, Jane IV, 151
Jenkins, Jane V, 504
Jenkins, Jane VI, 409
Jenkins, Jane VI, 426
Jenkins, Jas., Jr. III, 184
Jenkins, Jemima II, 467
Jenkins, Jemima II, 565
Jenkins, Jemima V, 745
Jenkins, Jemima V, 747
Jenkins, Jemima V, 779
Jenkins, Jemima V, 786
Jenkins, Jemima V, 787
Jenkins, Jemima V, 800
Jenkins, Jesse I, 1021
Jenkins, Jesse I, 1033
Jenkins, Jesse I, 1037
Jenkins, Jesse V, 785
Jenkins, Jesse V, 786
Jenkins, Jesse V, 791
Jenkins, Joel IV, 95
Jenkins, Joel IV, 229
Jenkins, Joel IV, 304
Jenkins, Johannah I, 1
Jenkins, John I, 553
Jenkins, John I, 659
Jenkins, John II, 382
Jenkins, John IV, 41
Jenkins, John IV, 151
Jenkins, John IV, 229
Jenkins, John IV, 338
Jenkins, John IV, 728
Jenkins, John IV, 969
Jenkins, John IV, 1322
Jenkins, John V, 252
Jenkins, John V, 504
Jenkins, John V, 687
Jenkins, John V, 747
Jenkins, John V, 786
Jenkins, John V, 812
Jenkins, John V, 1004
Jenkins, John VI, 409
Jenkins, John E. IV, 827
Jenkins, John H. IV, 1039
Jenkins, John K. IV, 969
Jenkins, John K. IV, 1039
Jenkins, John K. IV, 1322
Jenkins, John L. V, 687
Jenkins, John R. IV, 969
Jenkins, John W. IV, 728
Jenkins, Jonathan II, 803
Jenkins, Jonathan II, 882
Jenkins, Jonathan III, 184
Jenkins, Jonathan III, 185
Jenkins, Jonathan IV, 95
Jenkins, Jonathan IV, 228
Jenkins, Jonathan IV, 229
Jenkins, Jonathan VI, 408
Jenkins, Jonathan VI, 409
Jenkins, Jos. S. III, 184
Jenkins, Joseph I, 1155
Jenkins, Joseph IV, 969
Jenkins, Joseph VI, 828
Jenkins, Joseph VI, 829
Jenkins, Joseph VI, 850
Jenkins, Joseph E. IV, 827
Jenkins, Joseph E. IV, 969
Jenkins, Joseph Edward IV, 728
Jenkins, Joseph Edward IV, 827
Jenkins, Joseph William V, 747
Jenkins, Josephine V, 687
Jenkins, Joshua III, 184
Jenkins, Joshua IV, 95
Jenkins, Joshua IV, 728
Jenkins, Joshua IV, 827
Jenkins, Joshua C. II, 565
Jenkins, Joshua C. II, 748
Jenkins, Joshua C. II, 882
Jenkins, Joshua C. II, 900
Jenkins, Josie V, 747
Jenkins, Judith III, 184
Jenkins, Judith III, 228
Jenkins, Judith B. III, 184
Jenkins, Judith Ella IV, 969
Jenkins, L. Mildred IV, 969
Jenkins, L. Mildred IV, 1322
Jenkins, Lafayette IV, 229
Jenkins, Laura B. V, 747
Jenkins, Laura J. IV, 827
Jenkins, Laura P. II, 854
Jenkins, Laura P. II, 883
Jenkins, Laura Paxson II, 803
Jenkins, Leah V, 397
Jenkins, Leah V, 407
Jenkins, Lettice I, 659
Jenkins, Lettuce I, 660
Jenkins, Lewis VI, 940
Jenkins, Lewiss II, 382
Jenkins, Lida V, 182
Jenkins, Linney I, 659
Jenkins, Littleberry W. VI, 940
Jenkins, Lloyd M. IV, 969
Jenkins, Lloyd M. IV, 1039
Jenkins, Lloyd M. IV, 1322
Jenkins, Lloyd Miller IV, 969
Jenkins, Lottie IV, 1039
Jenkins, Lucia II, 537
Jenkins, Lucia II, 564
Jenkins, Lucinda V, 747
Jenkins, Lucinda V, 786
Jenkins, Lucinda J. V, 747
Jenkins, Lucy II, 564
Jenkins, Lucy Jane VI, 940
Jenkins, Lydia I, 553
Jenkins, Lydia III, 316
Jenkins, Lydia IV, 95
Jenkins, Lydia IV, 101
Jenkins, Lydia IV, 116
Jenkins, Lydia IV, 151
Jenkins, Lydia IV, 229
Jenkins, Lydia IV, 304
Jenkins, Lydia IV, 338
Jenkins, Lydia IV, 346
Jenkins, Lydia IV, 827
Jenkins, Lydia IV, 969
Jenkins, Lydia V, 782
Jenkins, Lydia V, 786
Jenkins, Lydia VI, 409
Jenkins, Lydia Ann IV, 969
Jenkins, Lydia M. IV, 95
Jenkins, Lydia M. IV, 827
Jenkins, Lydia M. IV, 969
Jenkins, Lydia Mildred IV, 969
Jenkins, Lydia N. IV, 229
Jenkins, Lydia W. III, 184
Jenkins, Lynn III, 185
Jenkins, Margaret V, 182
Jenkins, Margaret L. IV, 229
Jenkins, Margaret L. IV, 235
Jenkins, Margaret L. IV, 969
Jenkins, Margaret L. IV, 1322
Jenkins, Margaret S. IV, 1039
Jenkins, Margery V, 786
Jenkins, Maria V, 81
Jenkins, Maria V, 781
Jenkins, Marian I, 635
Jenkins, Maris I, 1030
Jenkins, Maris I, 1032
Jenkins, Marry VI, 829
Jenkins, Martha I, 659
Jenkins, Martha I, 660
Jenkins, Martha I, 682
Jenkins, Martha I, 1029
Jenkins, Martha I, 1033
Jenkins, Martha II, 565
Jenkins, Martha V, 504
Jenkins, Martha V, 505
Jenkins, Martha V, 528
Jenkins, Martha V, 630
Jenkins, Martha V, 687
Jenkins, Martha V, 747
Jenkins, Martha V, 781
Jenkins, Martha V, 785
Jenkins, Martha V, 786

Jenkins, Martha V, 790
Jenkins, Martha V, 791
Jenkins, Martha V, 792
Jenkins, Martha V, 800
Jenkins, Martha Ann VI, 940
Jenkins, Martha J. V, 687
Jenkins, Martha L. V, 505
Jenkins, Martha N. II, 748
Jenkins, Martha S. V, 505
Jenkins, Mary I, 682
Jenkins, Mary I, 1021
Jenkins, Mary II, 382
Jenkins, Mary II, 535
Jenkins, Mary II, 564
Jenkins, Mary II, 607
Jenkins, Mary II, 696
Jenkins, Mary II, 748
Jenkins, Mary III, 46
Jenkins, Mary III, 106
Jenkins, Mary III, 144
Jenkins, Mary III, 184
Jenkins, Mary III, 185
Jenkins, Mary III, 246
Jenkins, Mary III, 316
Jenkins, Mary IV, 41
Jenkins, Mary IV, 67
Jenkins, Mary IV, 95
Jenkins, Mary IV, 228
Jenkins, Mary IV, 229
Jenkins, Mary IV, 287
Jenkins, Mary IV, 531
Jenkins, Mary IV, 969
Jenkins, Mary V, 183
Jenkins, Mary V, 610
Jenkins, Mary V, 629
Jenkins, Mary V, 747
Jenkins, Mary V, 781
Jenkins, Mary V, 782
Jenkins, Mary V, 784
Jenkins, Mary V, 785
Jenkins, Mary V, 786
Jenkins, Mary V, 794
Jenkins, Mary V, 808
Jenkins, Mary V, 812
Jenkins, Mary VI, 400
Jenkins, Mary VI, 408
Jenkins, Mary VI, 409
Jenkins, Mary VI, 506
Jenkins, Mary VI, 828
Jenkins, Mary Ann I, 619
Jenkins, Mary Ann V, 747
Jenkins, Mary E. IV, 969
Jenkins, Mary Elizabeth IV, 228
Jenkins, Mary Elizabeth IV, 229
Jenkins, Mary Elizabeth V, 504
Jenkins, Mary Elizabeth V, 505
Jenkins, Mary Elizabeth V, 747
Jenkins, Mary Elizabeth V, 786
Jenkins, Mary F. VI, 829
Jenkins, Mary Frances III, 184
Jenkins, Mary Frances III, 185
Jenkins, Mary Jane III, 486
Jenkins, Mary Jane VI, 940
Jenkins, Mary K. III, 27
Jenkins, Mary K. III, 184
Jenkins, Mary K. III, 185
Jenkins, Mary W. II, 803
Jenkins, Mary Wm. II, 883
Jenkins, Mason VI, 940
Jenkins, Matthew III, 184
Jenkins, Mehetable IV, 808
Jenkins, Mehetable IV, 827
Jenkins, Michael V, 786
Jenkins, Michael VI, 408
Jenkins, Michael VI, 433
Jenkins, Mildred IV, 1322
Jenkins, Mildred V. V, 687
Jenkins, Minor V, 812
Jenkins, Misael IV, 151
Jenkins, Mishael IV, 228
Jenkins, Mishael IV, 233
Jenkins, Mishael IV, 248
Jenkins, Mishael IV, 287
Jenkins, Mishael IV, 339
Jenkins, Mishael IV, 346
Jenkins, Mishael VI, 409
Jenkins, Mishael, Jr. IV, 151
Jenkins, Mishael, Sr. IV, 151
Jenkins, Mishal, Jr. IV, 151
Jenkins, N. S. III, 192
Jenkins, Nancy III, 185
Jenkins, Nancy V, 780
Jenkins, Nancy V, 812
Jenkins, Nancy VI, 829
Jenkins, Nancy VI, 940
Jenkins, Nathaniel II, 564
Jenkins, Nathaniel Newlin II, 382
Jenkins, Nathaniel Newlin II, 565
Jenkins, Newton V, 747
Jenkins, Obediah H. VI, 883
Jenkins, Obediah H. VI, 940
Jenkins, Olive I, 635
Jenkins, Olive V, 785
Jenkins, Olive V, 786
Jenkins, Olive VI, 829
Jenkins, Olive J. I, 619
Jenkins, Oliver C. III, 184
Jenkins, Omer E. V, 687
Jenkins, Patience II, 803
Jenkins, Patience H. II, 811
Jenkins, Patience H. II, 882
Jenkins, Patience H. II, 903
Jenkins, Patience Hunn II, 882
Jenkins, Pearl IV, 1039
Jenkins, Peggy VI, 940
Jenkins, Phebann V, 786
Jenkins, Phebe I, 553
Jenkins, Phebe II, 803
Jenkins, Phebe III, 106
Jenkins, Phebe III, 184
Jenkins, Phebe III, 185
Jenkins, Phebe III, 254
Jenkins, Phebe III, 288
Jenkins, Phebe V, 504
Jenkins, Phebe Ann III, 184
Jenkins, Phebe Ellen IV, 827
Jenkins, Phebe Ellen IV, 854
Jenkins, Phineas II, 564
Jenkins, Phinehas V, 785
Jenkins, Phinihas V, 747
Jenkins, Pugh IV, 151
Jenkins, Pugh VI, 409
Jenkins, Rachel I, 659
Jenkins, Rachel I, 660
Jenkins, Rachel IV, 151
Jenkins, Rachel IV, 153
Jenkins, Rachel IV, 228
Jenkins, Rachel IV, 229
Jenkins, Rachel IV, 248
Jenkins, Rachel IV, 339
Jenkins, Rachel IV, 346
Jenkins, Rachel V, 779
Jenkins, Rachel V, 784
Jenkins, Rachel V, 786
Jenkins, Rachel V, 800
Jenkins, Rachel V, 802
Jenkins, Rachel VI, 408
Jenkins, Rachel VI, 409
Jenkins, Rachel VI, 433
Jenkins, Rachel Mary IV, 338
Jenkins, Reason V, 183
Jenkins, Reba IV, 827
Jenkins, Reba IV, 1322
Jenkins, Reba E. IV, 827
Jenkins, Rebecah I, 1030
Jenkins, Rebecah I, 1032
Jenkins, Rebecca I, 887
Jenkins, Rebecca I, 890
Jenkins, Rebecca I, 1016
Jenkins, Rebecca IV, 41
Jenkins, Rebecca V, 747
Jenkins, Rebecca V, 786
Jenkins, Rebecca V, 790
Jenkins, Rebecca A. IV, 229
Jenkins, Rebecca Ann IV, 228
Jenkins, Rebecka I, 887
Jenkins, Rebeckah V, 785
Jenkins, Rebekah I, 553
Jenkins, Rhoda IV, 728
Jenkins, Rhoda E. IV, 827
Jenkins, Rhoda Elisabeth IV, 728
Jenkins, Rhoda Elizabeth IV, 728
Jenkins, Rhoda Elizabeth IV, 827
Jenkins, Robert V, 745
Jenkins, Robert V, 747
Jenkins, Robert V, 766
Jenkins, Robert V, 779
Jenkins, Robert V, 780
Jenkins, Robert V, 784
Jenkins, Robert V, 785
Jenkins, Robert V, 786
Jenkins, Robert V, 787
Jenkins, Robert V, 791
Jenkins, Robert V, 800
Jenkins, Robert A. V, 747
Jenkins, Robert L. I, 1155
Jenkins, Robert Lindley V, 786
Jenkins, Robt. V, 800
Jenkins, Rosanna V, 785
Jenkins, Rosannah V, 785
Jenkins, Ruth I, 659
Jenkins, Ruth I, 682
Jenkins, Ruth IV, 151
Jenkins, Ruth IV, 228
Jenkins, Ruth IV, 229
Jenkins, Ruth IV, 338
Jenkins, Ruth IV, 358
Jenkins, Ruth V, 81
Jenkins, Ruth V, 182
Jenkins, Ruth V, 785
Jenkins, Ruth VI, 408
Jenkins, Ruth VI, 409
Jenkins, S. Mildred IV, 1039
Jenkins, Salathiel V, 687
Jenkins, Samuel V, 780
Jenkins, Samuel V, 784
Jenkins, Samuel V, 785
Jenkins, Samuel V, 786
Jenkins, Samuel V, 792
Jenkins, Samuel Addison V, 786
Jenkins, Samuel H. Hodgin I, 635
Jenkins, Samuel H., Jr. I, 635
Jenkins, Samuel R. V, 785
Jenkins, Samuel R. V, 786
Jenkins, Sarah II, 542
Jenkins, Sarah II, 565
Jenkins, Sarah III, 185
Jenkins, Sarah III, 319
Jenkins, Sarah IV, 41
Jenkins, Sarah IV, 151
Jenkins, Sarah IV, 228
Jenkins, Sarah IV, 229
Jenkins, Sarah IV, 233
Jenkins, Sarah IV, 248
Jenkins, Sarah IV, 287
Jenkins, Sarah IV, 296
Jenkins, Sarah IV, 338
Jenkins, Sarah IV, 722
Jenkins, Sarah IV, 728
Jenkins, Sarah V, 747
Jenkins, Sarah V, 781
Jenkins, Sarah V, 785
Jenkins, Sarah V, 786
Jenkins, Sarah V, 790
Jenkins, Sarah V, 792
Jenkins, Sarah VI, 365
Jenkins, Sarah VI, 390
Jenkins, Sarah VI, 408
Jenkins, Sarah VI, 409
Jenkins, Sarah E. IV, 229
Jenkins, Sarah Jane V, 505
Jenkins, Sarah Matilda II, 748
Jenkins, Sarah T. III, 184
Jenkins, Sarah T. III, 185
Jenkins, Sarah T. III, 246
Jenkins, Seth Smith III, 184
Jenkins, Seth Smith III, 185
Jenkins, Sibbel IV, 95
Jenkins, Silas N. V, 747
Jenkins, Silas Newton V, 786
Jenkins, Siles Newton V, 505
Jenkins, Silvanus III, 184
Jenkins, Silvanus III, 185
Jenkins, Silvanus F. III, 184
Jenkins, Silvanus F. III, 185
Jenkins, Silvanus F. III, 217
Jenkins, Silvanus J. III, 184
Jenkins, Silvanus T. III, 203
Jenkins, Silvanus Waterman III, 184
Jenkins, Silvanus, Jr. III, 185
Jenkins, Simeon III, 185
Jenkins, Stephen II, 382
Jenkins, Stephen II, 535
Jenkins, Stephen II, 564
Jenkins, Stephen II, 685
Jenkins, Stephen II, 696
Jenkins, Stephen II, 1006
Jenkins, Stephen II, 1021
Jenkins, Stephen, Jr. II, 564
Jenkins, Susan II, 966
Jenkins, Susan IV, 304
Jenkins, Susan Willis IV, 95
Jenkins, Susan Willis IV, 229
Jenkins, Susanna V, 812
Jenkins, Susannah V, 786
Jenkins, Susannah V, 791
Jenkins, Susannah V, 819
Jenkins, Susannah VI, 398
Jenkins, Susannah VI, 409
Jenkins, Sylvanus F. III, 338
Jenkins, Tabitha II, 565
Jenkins, Tabitha II, 748
Jenkins, Tabitha II, 882
Jenkins, Tabitha II, 900
Jenkins, Tabitha VI, 940
Jenkins, Thomas I, 553
Jenkins, Thomas I, 659
Jenkins, Thomas I, 660
Jenkins, Thomas I, 682
Jenkins, Thomas I, 1021
Jenkins, Thomas I, 1030
Jenkins, Thomas I, 1032
Jenkins, Thomas I, 1033
Jenkins, Thomas V, 81
Jenkins, Thomas V, 786
Jenkins, Thomas Pugh IV, 338
Jenkins, Thomas W. III, 185
Jenkins, Thomas W. III, 192
Jenkins, Thomas W. III, 353
Jenkins, Thomas W., Jr. III, 185
Jenkins, Thomas, Jr. III, 185
Jenkins, Thos. V, 781
Jenkins, Thos. C. II, 803
Jenkins, Thos. W. III, 184
Jenkins, Thos. W. III, 185
Jenkins, Thos. W. III, 319
Jenkins, Thurza Ann P. VI, 883
Jenkins, Verlinda V, 747
Jenkins, Verlinda V, 766
Jenkins, Verlinda V, 779
Jenkins, Verlinda V, 780
Jenkins, Verlinda V, 784
Jenkins, Verlinda V, 786
Jenkins, Verlinda V, 800
Jenkins, Viola IV, 969
Jenkins, Wd. Hanah II, 565
Jenkins, Wd. Mary II, 382
Jenkins, Wd. Mary R. II, 854
Jenkins, Wd. Sarah III, 184
Jenkins, Wd. Tabitha II, 803
Jenkins, Widow Rebekah I, 1033
Jenkins, William I, 1021
Jenkins, William I, 1032
Jenkins, William I, 1033
Jenkins, William IV, 95
Jenkins, William IV, 101
Jenkins, William IV, 728
Jenkins, William IV, 827
Jenkins, William IV, 969
Jenkins, William V, 747
Jenkins, William V, 785
Jenkins, William V, 786
Jenkins, William VI, 408
Jenkins, William VI, 409
Jenkins, William VI, 829
Jenkins, William VI, 940
Jenkins, William A. V, 182
Jenkins, William A. VI, 829
Jenkins, William B. III, 184
Jenkins, William B. III, 185
Jenkins, William Dolby II, 803
Jenkins, William H. III, 185
Jenkins, William L. III, 185
Jenkins, William L. III, 288
Jenkins, William Levitt III, 185
Jenkins, William M. III, 185
Jenkins, William Miller IV, 969
Jenkins, William R. VI, 829
Jenkins, Willis IV, 969
Jenkins, Willis H. IV, 1039
Jenkins, Wm. II, 564
Jenkins, Wm. II, 1006
Jenkins, Wm. IV, 827
Jenkins, Wm. IV, 834
Jenkins, Wm. IV, 969
Jenkins, Wm. IV, 1039
Jenkins, Wm. V, 781
Jenkins, Wm. V, 782
Jenkins, Wm. V, 786
Jenkins, Wm. A. V, 182
Jenkins, Wm. D. II, 882
Jenkins, Wm. Dolby II, 882
Jenkins, Wm. Leggett III, 185
Jenkins, Wm. M. IV, 969
Jenkins, Zachariah IV, 728
Jenkins, Zachariah, Jr. IV, 728
Jenkinson, Ann IV, 22
Jenkinson, Ann IV, 41
Jenkinson, Ann IV, 95
Jenkinson, Ann IV, 229
Jenkinson, Ann IV, 479
Jenkinson, Ann VI, 409
Jenkinson, Charles II, 883
Jenkinson, Charles Edward II, 883
Jenkinson, Chas. E. II, 883
Jenkinson, Eliza Ann II, 785
Jenkinson, Eliza Ann II, 883
Jenkinson, Eliza H. II, 718
Jenkinson, Elizabeth II, 785
Jenkinson, Elizabeth II, 803
Jenkinson, Elizabeth II, 843
Jenkinson, Elizabeth II, 883
Jenkinson, Elizabeth IV, 95
Jenkinson, Elizabeth IV, 229
Jenkinson, Elizabeth IV, 479
Jenkinson, Elizabeth VI, 409
Jenkinson, Elizabeth A. II, 883
Jenkinson, Ephraim II, 565
Jenkinson, Hannah II, 565
Jenkinson, Henry VI, 409
Jenkinson, Isaac II, 382
Jenkinson, Isaac II, 565
Jenkinson, Isaac IV, 17
Jenkinson, Isaac IV, 95
Jenkinson, Isaac IV, 479
Jenkinson, Isaac VI, 409
Jenkinson, Isaac C. II, 803
Jenkinson, Isaac Cox II, 785
Jenkinson, John II, 565
Jenkinson, John II, 803
Jenkinson, John IV, 17
Jenkinson, John IV, 95
Jenkinson, John IV, 229
Jenkinson, John IV, 479
Jenkinson, John VI, 409
Jenkinson, John Francis II, 8
Jenkinson, John Philip II, 80
Jenkinson, Joseph II, 565
Jenkinson, M. IV, 479
Jenkinson, Mary II, 382
Jenkinson, Mary II, 472
Jenkinson, Mary II, 565
Jenkinson, Mary II, 648
Jenkinson, Mary IV, 41
Jenkinson, Mary IV, 54
Jenkinson, Mary IV, 69
Jenkinson, Mary IV, 90
Jenkinson, Mary IV, 95
Jenkinson, Mary IV, 229
Jenkinson, Mary IV, 479
Jenkinson, Mary IV, 1107
Jenkinson, Mary VI, 409
Jenkinson, Rebecca IV, 95
Jenkinson, Rebecca IV, 229
Jenkinson, Rebecca IV, 479
Jenkinson, Rebecca IV, 500
Jenkinson, Rebeckah IV, 479
Jenkinson, Ruth Ann II, 883
Jenkinson, Ruthann II, 883
Jenkinson, Ruthanna II, 803
Jenkinson, Sarah II, 565
Jenkinson, Sarah II, 803
Jenkinson, Sarah II, 883
Jenkinson, Sarah IV, 95
Jenkinson, Sarah IV, 229
Jenkinson, Sarah IV, 479
Jenkinson, Susan E. II, 803
Jenkinson, Susan E. II, 883
Jenkinson, Susan Elizabeth II, 803
Jenkinson, Wd. Eliza Ann II,
Jenkinson, William II, 803
Jenkinson, Wm. II, 883
Jenks, Ann II, 733
Jenks, Ann II, 738
Jenks, Ann II, 748
Jenks, Ann E. II, 709
Jenks, Anna V, 579
Jenks, Barton L. III, 19
Jenks, Barton Loag III, 185
Jenks, Bertha III, 71
Jenks, Bertha III, 185
Jenks, Bertha C. III, 70
Jenks, Bertha C. III, 342
Jenks, Claudie V, 579
Jenks, David V, 579
Jenks, Dorothy Lucile V, 687
Jenks, Edward VI, 836
Jenks, Eliz. III, 70
Jenks, Eliza II, 565
Jenks, Elizabeth II, 565
Jenks, Elizabeth II, 1006
Jenks, Elizabeth II, 1053
Jenks, Elizabeth V, 579
Jenks, Elizabeth VI, 829
Jenks, Elizabeth H. III, 19
Jenks, Elizabeth H. III, 185
Jenks, Elizabeth Storey III, 7
Jenks, Elizabeth Storey III, 1
Jenks, Elizabeth Story III, 71
Jenks, Emily V, 579
Jenks, Emma III, 185
Jenks, Geo. V, 579
Jenks, George V, 579
Jenks, Hannah E. V, 579
Jenks, Hannah W. II, 733
Jenks, Hannah W. II, 748
Jenks, Harriet V, 713
Jenks, Jedida Ann V, 687
Jenks, Joseph II, 1006
Jenks, Joseph II, 1085
Jenks, Joseph O. V, 579
Jenks, Joseph R. II, 565
Jenks, Joseph R. II, 709
Jenks, Joseph R. II, 733
Jenks, Joseph R. II, 738
Jenks, Joseph R. II, 748
Jenks, Joseph Richardson II,
Jenks, Josephine J. III, 342
Jenks, Josephine, Jr. III, 185
Jenks, Llewellyn H. III, 185
Jenks, Loran A. V, 579
Jenks, Loren V, 579
Jenks, Lorenzo V, 687
Jenks, Lydia Ann II, 709
Jenks, Maria V, 579
Jenks, Mariah V, 687
Jenks, Mary II, 1006
Jenks, Mary II, 1046
Jenks, Mary II, 1053

ks, Mercy II, 790
ks, Michael H. II, 709
ks, Michael H. II, 1006
ks, Rebecca II, 507
ks, Rebecca II, 565
ks, Rebecca II, 705
ks, Rebecca II, 738
ks, Rebecca II, 748
ks, Rebecca II, 1006
ks, Rebecca V, 747
ks, Rebecca V, 813
ks, Rebecca H. V, 747
ks, Rebecca H. V, 813
ks, Rodney V, 579
ks, Ruth II, 507
ks, Ruth II, 565
ks, Sarah II, 382
ks, Sarah II, 565
ks, Tamzin II, 1006
ks, Tamzin II, 1033
ks, Thomas II, 507
ks, Thomas II, 565
ks, Thomas II, 738
ks, Thomas II, 748
ks, Watson II, 565
ks, Wd. Elizabeth II, 1085
ks, William II, 709
ks, William II, 1006
ks, William M. VI, 829
ks, Wm. J. II, 709
ks, Wm. J. II, 748
ks, Wm. J. II, 749
ks, Wm. J. II, 883
ks, Wm. P. III, 70
ks, Wm. P. III, 71
ks, Wm. P. III, 185
ks, Wm. P. III, 342
mins, Hannah II, 564
ner, Edward III, 185
ner, Elizabeth III, 185
ner, Margaret III, 344
ner, Mary Elizabeth III, 185
ner, Phebe Maria III, 185
ner, Sarah III, 185
ner, Solomon III, 185
ner, Solomon III, 344
ner, Wd. Margaret III, 185
ner, William III, 185
ness, Abby B. II, 293
ness, Abby B. II, 303
ness, Elizabeth M. II, 293
ness, Elizabeth M. II, 305
ness, Elizabeth M. II, 749
ness, Elizabeth Meader II, 293
ness, Elizabeth Meader II, 709
ness, Harriett II, 293
ness, Mark II, 120
ness, Mark II, 124
ness, Mark II, 177
ness, Mark II, 293
ness, Mark II, 709
ness, Mark II, 749
ness, Mark II, 776
ness, Mary H. II, 177
ness, Mary H. II, 293
ness, Mary H. II, 709
ness, Mary H. II, 749
ness, Mary H. II, 776
ness, Mehette II, 120
ness, Mehette II, 124
ness, Mehittee II, 293
ness, Mehittee II, 303
ness, Mehittee II, 749
ness, Mehittee II, 776
ness, Paul II, 120
ness, Paul II, 124
ness, Paul II, 177
ness, Paul II, 293
ness, Paul II, 303
ness, Paul II, 749
ness, Paul II, 776
ness, Sarah A. II, 120
ness, Sarah A. II, 124
ness, William S. II, 293
ness, William Smith II, 293
ness, William Smith II, 709
ness, Wm. Smith II, 749
net, John II, 565
net, John II, 614
net, Priscilla II, 614
net, Sarah II, 565
net, Sarah II, 614
nett, Abby I, 290
nett, Abigail P. I, 219
nett, Ann I, 290
nett, Ann I, 327
nett, Ashberry I, 290
nett, B. C. I, 944
nett, Barney C. I, 682
Jennett, Barney C. I, 944
Jennett, David I, 290
Jennett, David I, 327
Jennett, Elsberry I, 290
Jennett, Esther II, 565
Jennett, Esther II, 657
Jennett, Hollen E. I, 682
Jennett, Joab I, 290
Jennett, Joash I, 219
Jennett, John II, 382
Jennett, John II, 565
Jennett, Joseph I, 290
Jennett, Joseph T. I, 290
Jennett, Lilian L. I, 682
Jennett, Lucetta I, 682
Jennett, Lucetta R. I, 682
Jennett, Mary A. I, 290
Jennett, Micheel I, 303
Jennett, Micheel I, 309
Jennett, Mildred I, 290
Jennett, Nathan James I, 290
Jennett, Needham I, 290
Jennett, Needham E. I, 290
Jennett, Needham E. I, 682
Jennett, Ora H. I, 682
Jennett, Rachel I, 290
Jennett, Rachel I, 327
Jennett, Robert E. G. I, 682
Jennett, Ruth I, 290
Jennett, Sally I, 290
Jennett, Sarah II, 565
Jennett, Tilitha Ann I, 290
Jennett, Wd. Bridgett II, 382
Jennett, William I, 303
Jennett, William I, 309
Jennett, William S. I, 290
Jenney, Anna VI, 518
Jenney, Aquella VI, 407
Jenney, Aquilla VI, 407
Jenney, Hannah R. IV, 827
Jenney, Isaac II, 1006
Jenney, Mahlor VI, 546
Jenney, Ruth VI, 407
Jenney, Susannah VI, 666
Jennings, ??? III, 186
Jennings, Abel VI, 599
Jennings, Alice I, 989
Jennings, Alice P. V, 666
Jennings, Alice Peele V, 687
Jennings, Allie M. V, 182
Jennings, Alpheus IV, 1322
Jennings, Amanda M. VI, 829
Jennings, Ambrose VI, 926
Jennings, Ambrose VI, 940
Jennings, Amos VI, 599
Jennings, Ann II, 32
Jennings, Ann II, 81
Jennings, Ann II, 235
Jennings, Ann VI, 878
Jennings, Ann VI, 926
Jennings, Ann VI, 940
Jennings, Ann E. VI, 1011
Jennings, Anna II, 81
Jennings, Anna VI, 940
Jennings, Anna S. V, 883
Jennings, Annah VI, 878
Jennings, Archibald VI, 824
Jennings, Archibald VI, 829
Jennings, Cassandra VI, 940
Jennings, Charles II, 749
Jennings, Chas. II, 565
Jennings, Clarkson V, 883
Jennings, Deborah V, 82
Jennings, Deborah V, 101
Jennings, Delany VI, 940
Jennings, Edmond VI, 930
Jennings, Edmond VI, 974
Jennings, Edmond VI, 982
Jennings, Edmond VI, 1011
Jennings, Edmund VI, 1011
Jennings, Edmund B. VI, 940
Jennings, Edward VI, 940
Jennings, Eliza F. VI, 940
Jennings, Elizabeth VI, 839
Jennings, Elizabeth VI, 930
Jennings, Elizabeth L. VI, 940
Jennings, Elizabeth R. VI, 829
Jennings, Emily VI, 974
Jennings, Fanny VI, 829
Jennings, Frances VI, 829
Jennings, Frances VI, 857
Jennings, Gertrude S. III, 186
Jennings, Hannah II, 32
Jennings, Hannah II, 81
Jennings, Harry N. III, 422
Jennings, Henry II, 17
Jennings, Henry II, 32
Jennings, Henry II, 46
Jennings, Jacob, Jr. II, 565
Jennings, James III, 186
Jennings, James VI, 829
Jennings, James VI, 940
Jennings, James C. III, 186
Jennings, James C. VI, 940
Jennings, James C. VI, 1011
Jennings, James E. III, 186
Jennings, Jane VI, 940
Jennings, Jane A. VI, 829
Jennings, Jersey II, 565
Jennings, Job V, 82
Jennings, Job V, 979
Jennings, John II, 32
Jennings, John II, 78
Jennings, John II, 81
Jennings, John II, 95
Jennings, John II, 381
Jennings, John VI, 940
Jennings, John R. VI, 829
Jennings, Kesiah VI, 814
Jennings, Keziah VI, 809
Jennings, Keziah VI, 829
Jennings, Lafayette IV, 1167
Jennings, Leona IV, 1322
Jennings, Levi II, 32
Jennings, Levi II, 81
Jennings, Levi V, 883
Jennings, Lewis VI, 829
Jennings, Lightfoot VI, 599
Jennings, Lucia V, 182
Jennings, Lucy VI, 822
Jennings, Mackay R. B. VI, 863
Jennings, Margaret II, 32
Jennings, Margaret II, 46
Jennings, Margaret C. V, 883
Jennings, Margret II, 17
Jennings, Mariah L. VI, 1011
Jennings, Martha VI, 829
Jennings, Martha A. C. D. VI, 829
Jennings, Mary II, 32
Jennings, Mary II, 81
Jennings, Mary II, 95
Jennings, Mary III, 186
Jennings, Mary VI, 803
Jennings, Mary VI, 857
Jennings, Mary VI, 978
Jennings, Mary Ann II, 32
Jennings, Mary Ann II, 78
Jennings, Mary Ann II, 81
Jennings, Mary Emeline III, 186
Jennings, Mary Gibson VI, 599
Jennings, May C. VI, 803
Jennings, Missouri VI, 814
Jennings, Nancy I, 138
Jennings, Nancy I, 143
Jennings, Nancy I, 172
Jennings, Pamela A. VI, 830
Jennings, Patterson VI, 819
Jennings, Patterson VI, 829
Jennings, Pleasant VI, 829
Jennings, Pleasant VI, 863
Jennings, Polly VI, 829
Jennings, Polly VI, 940
Jennings, Polly VI, 1011
Jennings, Powhatan VI, 830
Jennings, Priscilla VI, 866
Jennings, Rachel II, 81
Jennings, Rachel II, 113
Jennings, Rachel V, 82
Jennings, Rachel V, 883
Jennings, Rachel E. V, 883
Jennings, Rebecca III, 487
Jennings, Rebecca VI, 940
Jennings, Rebeccah II, 81
Jennings, Rebeckah II, 32
Jennings, Richard VI, 599
Jennings, Sally VI, 982
Jennings, Samuel II, 235
Jennings, Samuel II, 565
Jennings, Samuel II, 620
Jennings, Samuel K. VI, 970
Jennings, Samuel K. VI, 1014
Jennings, Sara VI, 599
Jennings, Sarah II, 32
Jennings, Sarah II, 565
Jennings, Sarah II, 620
Jennings, Sarah III, 186
Jennings, Sarah IV, 1283
Jennings, Sarah A. VI, 803
Jennings, Stephen VI, 829
Jennings, Stephen VI, 930
Jennings, Stephen VI, 974
Jennings, Susanna VI, 819
Jennings, Susannah VI, 599
Jennings, Thomas II, 32
Jennings, Thomas II, 81
Jennings, Thomas VI, 803
Jennings, Thomas VI, 829
Jennings, Thomas A. VI, 829
Jennings, William II, 32
Jennings, William VI, 938
Jennings, William D. VI, 829
Jennings, William H. VI, 845
Jennings, William H. VI, 940
Jennings, William H. VI, 1011
Jennings, William L. VI, 829
Jennings, Zachariah VI, 940
Jennings, Zachariah E. VI, 1011
Jennins, Rebeccah II, 81
Jenny, Abel II, 382
Jenny, Abraham IV, 1167
Jenny, Abraham D. IV, 1167
Jenny, Amos II, 382
Jenny, Amos IV, 727
Jenny, Ann II, 382
Jenny, Ann M. IV, 1148
Jenny, Ann M. IV, 1167
Jenny, Ann M. IV, 1238
Jenny, Anna S. IV, 1167
Jenny, Anna S. IV, 1238
Jenny, Anna S. J. IV, 1238
Jenny, Annie S. J. IV, 1236
Jenny, Benj. IV, 1148
Jenny, Benjamin IV, 1167
Jenny, Benjamin IV, 1238
Jenny, Catharine IV, 1191
Jenny, Catherine IV, 1145
Jenny, Catherine IV, 1167
Jenny, Eliza IV, 1167
Jenny, Elizabeth D. IV, 1145
Jenny, Elizabeth D. IV, 1167
Jenny, Elizabeth Jane IV, 1167
Jenny, Jacob IV, 827
Jenny, Joannah IV, 1167
Jenny, Joannah IV, 1238
Jenny, John IV, 1145
Jenny, John IV, 1167
Jenny, John IV, 1191
Jenny, John IV, 1238
Jenny, Lee W. IV, 1238
Jenny, Levi IV, 1167
Jenny, Mary IV, 1167
Jenny, Mary G. IV, 1167
Jenny, Mary G. IV, 1191
Jenny, Mary Ruth IV, 1167
Jenny, Nicholas D. IV, 1167
Jenny, Nicholas D. IV, 1238
Jenny, Paulina IV, 1235
Jenny, Pauline IV, 1238
Jenny, Rufus IV, 1238
Jenny, Rufus S. IV, 1238
Jenny, Ruth VI, 407
Jenny, Samuel IV, 1167
Jenny, Sarah IV, 1167
Jenny, Susan IV, 1238
Jenny, Truman IV, 1238
Jenny, William V, 81
Jensen, Marietta S. II, 152
Jensen, Marietta S. II, 161
Jensen, Pearl V. IV, 1322
Jenson, Anna V, 182
Jenson, Annie V, 182
Jenson, Jesse V, 182
Jenson, Loren V, 182
Jenson, W. M. V, 1004
Jent, Sarah IV, 1167
Jeofferies, Sarah II, 564
Jeofferies, Sarah II, 638
Jepson, Elisabeth I, 143
Jepson, Eliza I, 143
Jeremiah, Jeremiah II, 382
Jeremiah, Mary II, 382
Jericho, ??? III, 270
Jerman, Edward II, 382
Jerman, Edward II, 565
Jerman, Edward II, 626
Jerman, Elizabeth II, 382
Jerman, Elizabeth II, 565
Jerman, Elizabeth II, 626
Jerman, Mary II, 382
Jerman, Mary II, 565
Jerman, Sarah II, 452
Jerman, Sarah II, 565
Jerman, Wd. Elizabeth II, 565
Jerman, Wd. Elizabeth II, 631
Jerngen???, Decia I, 628
Jernigan, John J. I, 337
Jernigan, Mary I, 337
Jernigan, Paul I, 262
Jernigan, Paul I, 337
Jernigan, Pearl I, 262
Jernigan, Sudie Matilda I, 337
Jerson, Hannah II, 445
Jerson, John II, 445
Jerusha, Ann III, 172
Jervice, Elizabeth II, 1006
Jervice, John II, 1006
Jervis, Charles II, 382
Jervis, Charles II, 565
Jervis, Elizabeth II, 81
Jervis, Elizabeth II, 382
Jervis, Elizabeth II, 565
Jervis, Elizabeth II, 1006
Jervis, Francis, Jr. II, 382
Jervis, Hannah II, 382
Jervis, John II, 382
Jervis, John II, 565
Jervis, John II, 676
Jervis, John II, 1006
Jervis, John, Jr. II, 382
Jervis, Martin II, 382
Jervis, Martin II, 565
Jervis, Martin II, 642
Jervis, Martin III, 67
Jervis, Martin III, 186
Jervis, Martyn II, 565
Jervis, Martyn II, 676
Jervis, Mary II, 382
Jervis, Mary II, 565
Jervis, Mary III, 67
Jervis, Mary III, 186
Jervis, Mary P. III, 186
Jervis, Michael II, 565
Jervis, Michael II, 676
Jervis, Phebe II, 382
Jervis, Phebe II, 565
Jervis, Rebecca II, 382
Jervis, Rebecca II, 565
Jervis, Rebeccah II, 382
Jervis, Rebeccah II, 676
Jervis, Rebekah II, 382
Jervis, Richard II, 382
Jervis, Sarah II, 480
Jervis, Sarah II, 565
Jervis, Sarah II, 642
Jervis, William II, 382
Jerviss, Elizabeth II, 445
Jerviss, Francis II, 445
Jerviss, Hannah II, 445
Jerviss, John II, 445
Jerviss, Mary II, 382
Jesep, Elizabeth II, 565
Jesep, James II, 565
Jesep, Joseph II, 565
Jesep, Mary II, 565
Jesop, Agness I, 448
Jesop, Andrew II, 565
Jesop, Ann II, 1041
Jesop, Anna I, 990
Jesop, Caleb I, 448
Jesop, Eliza E. I, 54
Jesop, Eliza Elliott I, 54
Jesop, Elizabeth I, 195
Jesop, Hannah II, 81
Jesop, Huldah V, 82
Jesop, Issak B. I, 504
Jesop, Josiah I, 589
Jesop, Mary I, 54
Jesop, Mary I, 195
Jesop, Rebecca V, 82
Jesop, Sarah I, 54
Jesop, Thomas I, 195
Jesoup, Elizabeth II, 177
Jess, Ann II, 82
Jess, Ann II, 116
Jess, Ann II, 120
Jess, Ann II, 146
Jess, Ann II, 152
Jess, Ann II, 235
Jess, Ann II, 260
Jess, Ann II, 565
Jess, Ann II, 709
Jess, Ann II, 749
Jess, Ann II, 759
Jess, Bathsheba II, 235
Jess, Charlotte II, 82
Jess, Charlotte II, 495
Jess, Charlotte II, 565
Jess, David II, 81
Jess, David II, 235
Jess, David II, 260
Jess, David II, 749
Jess, David II, 759
Jess, Gulielma II, 82
Jess, Gulielma II, 110
Jess, Hannah II, 235
Jess, Hannah II, 263
Jess, James II, 81
Jess, James II, 82
Jess, James II, 136
Jess, Jonathan II, 81
Jess, Jonathan II, 235
Jess, Keziah II, 136
Jess, Rachel II, 213
Jess, Rachel II, 235
Jess, Rachel II, 238
Jess, Rachel II, 565
Jess, Rachel II, 749
Jess, Rachel II, 759
Jess, Rebecca II, 235
Jess, Rebecca II, 565
Jess, Rebeckah II, 81
Jess, Rebeckah II, 91
Jess, Ruth II, 81

Jess, Ruth II, 235
Jess, Ruth II, 260
Jess, Ruth II, 565
Jess, Ruth II, 709
Jess, Sarah II, 82
Jess, Sarah II, 92
Jess, Sarah II, 136
Jess, Sarah II, 789
Jess, Sarah II, 814
Jess, Stephen Morris II, 235
Jess, Zachariah II, 81
Jess, Zachariah II, 91
Jess, Zachariah II, 235
Jess, Zachariah II, 263
Jess, Zacharias II, 235
Jess, Zacharias II, 238
Jess, Zacharias II, 260
Jess, Zachary II, 177
Jess, Zachary II, 213
Jess, Zachary II, 235
Jess, Zechariah II, 565
Jesse, Ann II, 235
Jesse, David II, 226
Jesse, David II, 235
Jesse, Hannah II, 226
Jesse, Hannah II, 235
Jesse, Rachel II, 235
Jessop, A. I, 957
Jessop, Abigail I, 505
Jessop, Abigail I, 553
Jessop, Abigail I, 958
Jessop, Abigail I, 965
Jessop, Abigail I, 969
Jessop, Abner I, 965
Jessop, Abner I, 1005
Jessop, Abraham I, 504
Jessop, Abraham I, 553
Jessop, Ada I, 887
Jessop, Agnes I, 504
Jessop, Agnes I, 553
Jessop, Agnes I, 571
Jessop, Agness I, 448
Jessop, Alce V, 73
Jessop, Alice I, 504
Jessop, Alice V, 82
Jessop, Alice V, 83
Jessop, Amelia Jane I, 990
Jessop, Amos V, 182
Jessop, Amos C. V, 82
Jessop, Andrew II, 565
Jessop, Ann I, 10
Jessop, Ann I, 401
Jessop, Ann I, 504
Jessop, Ann I, 505
Jessop, Ann I, 509
Jessop, Ann I, 526
Jessop, Ann I, 539
Jessop, Ann I, 553
Jessop, Ann I, 558
Jessop, Ann I, 582
Jessop, Ann I, 594
Jessop, Ann I, 821
Jessop, Ann I, 957
Jessop, Ann I, 958
Jessop, Ann I, 965
Jessop, Ann I, 967
Jessop, Ann I, 1001
Jessop, Ann I, 1010
Jessop, Ann II, 566
Jessop, Ann II, 1006
Jessop, Ann V, 61
Jessop, Ann V, 82
Jessop, Ann V, 182
Jessop, Ann V, 252
Jessop, Ann V, 305
Jessop, Ann V, 342
Jessop, Ann V, 446
Jessop, Ann, Jr. I, 537
Jessop, Ann, Jr. I, 553
Jessop, Anna I, 184
Jessop, Anna I, 401
Jessop, Anna I, 524
Jessop, Anna I, 594
Jessop, Anna I, 990
Jessop, Anna I, 1005
Jessop, Anna V, 40
Jessop, Anna V, 82
Jessop, Anna V, 252
Jessop, Anna Huldah V, 252
Jessop, Anna Huldah V, 342
Jessop, Anne I, 272
Jessop, Anne I, 606
Jessop, Aris I, 505
Jessop, Aris I, 553
Jessop, Avis I, 553
Jessop, Barshaba I, 504
Jessop, Barthen I, 561
Jessop, Bathena Rebecca I, 887
Jessop, Bethany I, 887
Jessop, Bethany I, 965
Jessop, Betsey I, 965
Jessop, Bette I, 965
Jessop, Bette I, 966
Jessop, Bohel I, 965
Jessop, Borden I, 602
Jessop, Borden I, 606
Jessop, Bordon I, 505
Jessop, Burden I, 553
Jessop, Burden I, 965
Jessop, Caleb I, 504
Jessop, Caleb I, 505
Jessop, Caleb I, 553
Jessop, Caleb I, 571
Jessop, Caleb I, 606
Jessop, Caleb I, 887
Jessop, Caleb I, 965
Jessop, Caleb I, 990
Jessop, Caleb, Jr. I, 553
Jessop, Caleb, Sr. I, 526
Jessop, Camby V, 82
Jessop, Catharine I, 504
Jessop, Catharine I, 553
Jessop, Charety V, 954
Jessop, Charity V, 182
Jessop, Charles V, 182
Jessop, Charles V, 207
Jessop, Charles V, 954
Jessop, Charles D. I, 235
Jessop, Clark V, 83
Jessop, Clark W. V, 82
Jessop, Cleopatra I, 10
Jessop, Cleopatra I, 55
Jessop, Cornelia Ann I, 887
Jessop, Cornely V, 82
Jessop, Daniel I, 505
Jessop, Daniel V, 82
Jessop, Daniel V, 182
Jessop, Daniel V, 214
Jessop, David I, 594
Jessop, Deborah I, 505
Jessop, Delilah I, 965
Jessop, Dinah V, 182
Jessop, Dinah V, 204
Jessop, Edith I, 594
Jessop, Edith I, 965
Jessop, Edith I, 1005
Jessop, Edith I, 1007
Jessop, Edith I, 1010
Jessop, Edith P. V, 183
Jessop, Elam I, 602
Jessop, Elam I, 990
Jessop, Elesabeth I, 48
Jessop, Elesabeth I, 54
Jessop, Eli I, 504
Jessop, Eli I, 965
Jessop, Elias I, 504
Jessop, Elias I, 526
Jessop, Elias I, 553
Jessop, Elijah I, 504
Jessop, Elijah I, 965
Jessop, Elijah V, 630
Jessop, Elisha I, 965
Jessop, Elishai I, 505
Jessop, Eliza I, 10
Jessop, Eliza I, 242
Jessop, Eliza E. I, 54
Jessop, Eliza Elliott I, 54
Jessop, Eliza Elliott I, 81
Jessop, Eliza J. I, 195
Jessop, Elizabeth I, 195
Jessop, Elizabeth I, 505
Jessop, Elizabeth I, 524
Jessop, Elizabeth I, 553
Jessop, Elizabeth I, 594
Jessop, Elizabeth I, 606
Jessop, Elizabeth I, 887
Jessop, Elizabeth I, 965
Jessop, Elizabeth II, 565
Jessop, Elizabeth II, 1006
Jessop, Elizabeth II, 1007
Jessop, Elizabeth II, 1017
Jessop, Elizabeth V, 82
Jessop, Elizabeth V, 102
Jessop, Elizabeth V, 630
Jessop, Elizabeth V, 742
Jessop, Elizabeth V, 747
Jessop, Elizabeth Ann V, 630
Jessop, Elizabeth Ann V, 954
Jessop, Ella G. I, 235
Jessop, Ella G. I, 242
Jessop, Ellen V, 183
Jessop, Emily V, 630
Jessop, Enoch I, 54
Jessop, Enoch I, 195
Jessop, Enoch I, 524
Jessop, Enoch I, 553
Jessop, Esther I, 505
Jessop, Esther I, 957
Jessop, Esther I, 965
Jessop, Esther I, 967
Jessop, Evan I, 504
Jessop, Even I, 553
Jessop, Fannie I, 887
Jessop, Fatima I, 55
Jessop, Fatima I, 85
Jessop, Guli I, 957
Jessop, Gulielma I, 821
Jessop, Hanah I, 553
Jessop, Hannah I, 267
Jessop, Hannah I, 272
Jessop, Hannah I, 274
Jessop, Hannah I, 504
Jessop, Hannah I, 505
Jessop, Hannah I, 553
Jessop, Hannah I, 568
Jessop, Hannah I, 821
Jessop, Hannah I, 953
Jessop, Hannah I, 957
Jessop, Hannah I, 958
Jessop, Hannah I, 965
Jessop, Hannah II, 566
Jessop, Hannah V, 82
Jessop, Hannah V, 182
Jessop, Hannah V, 207
Jessop, Hannah V, 954
Jessop, Hannah Sophia V, 182
Jessop, Hannah Sophia V, 214
Jessop, Hariet M. I, 54
Jessop, Harriet M. VI, 65
Jessop, Harriet M. VI, 92
Jessop, Hezekiah I, 553
Jessop, Hezekiah I, 821
Jessop, Hope I, 504
Jessop, Hope I, 505
Jessop, Hope I, 553
Jessop, Hope I, 581
Jessop, Hope I, 964
Jessop, Hope I, 965
Jessop, Horace V, 182
Jessop, Huldah V, 82
Jessop, Ira I, 944
Jessop, Isaac I, 504
Jessop, Isaac I, 505
Jessop, Isaac V, 82
Jessop, Isaac V, 252
Jessop, Isaac Elmer V, 954
Jessop, Isaraeel I, 821
Jessop, Israel I, 957
Jessop, J. William I, 242
Jessop, Jacob I, 504
Jessop, Jacob I, 505
Jessop, Jacob I, 534
Jessop, Jacob I, 553
Jessop, Jacob I, 965
Jessop, Jacob I, 1005
Jessop, Jacob I, 1010
Jessop, Jacob V, 82
Jessop, Jacob V, 500
Jessop, Jacob V, 505
Jessop, Jacob V, 747
Jessop, Jacob Wanen I, 887
Jessop, James I, 602
Jessop, James I, 785
Jessop, James I, 821
Jessop, James I Sup 1, 10
Jessop, James II, 565
Jessop, James B. I, 606
Jessop, James Canon I, 785
Jessop, James H. I, 242
Jessop, Jane I Sup 1, 4
Jessop, Jane I Sup 1, 5
Jessop, Jane I Sup 1, 8
Jessop, Jane V, 82
Jessop, Jemima I, 579
Jessop, Jennie I, 887
Jessop, Jesse I, 10
Jessop, Jesse I, 54
Jessop, Jesse I, 71
Jessop, Jesse I, 81
Jessop, Jesse I, 82
Jessop, Jesse I, 143
Jessop, Jesse I, 175
Jessop, Jesse I, 184
Jessop, Jesse I, 195
Jessop, Jesse I, 242
Jessop, Jesse V, 82
Jessop, Jesse VI, 65
Jessop, Jesse B. I, 504
Jessop, Jesse C. V, 183
Jessop, Jesse W. I, 235
Jessop, Jesse W. I, 242
Jessop, Jesse W. V, 182
Jessop, Jessie C. V, 183
Jessop, Joel I, 957
Jessop, Joel I, 965
Jessop, John I, 504
Jessop, John I, 505
Jessop, John I, 606
Jessop, John I, 785
Jessop, John I, 821
Jessop, John I, 944
Jessop, John I, 957
Jessop, John I, 965
Jessop, John I, 1005
Jessop, John II, 565
Jessop, John II, 566
Jessop, John II, 1006
Jessop, John V, 305
Jessop, John V, 630
Jessop, John C. I, 821
Jessop, John H. I, 887
Jessop, John W. I, 944
Jessop, Johnathan V, 82
Jessop, Jonathan I, 54
Jessop, Jonathan I, 504
Jessop, Jonathan I, 505
Jessop, Jonathan I, 553
Jessop, Jonathan I, 821
Jessop, Jonathan I, 965
Jessop, Jonathan V, 82
Jessop, Jonathan V, 182
Jessop, Jonathan V, 252
Jessop, Jonathan V, 342
Jessop, Jonathan V, 742
Jessop, Jonathan V, 747
Jessop, Jonathan A. I, 10
Jessop, Jonathan A. I, 184
Jessop, Jonathan J. V, 182
Jessop, Jonathan Y. V, 182
Jessop, Jonithan I, 957
Jessop, Jonothan V, 82
Jessop, Jontthan V, 82
Jessop, Joseph I, 272
Jessop, Joseph I, 504
Jessop, Joseph I, 539
Jessop, Joseph I, 553
Jessop, Joseph I, 785
Jessop, Joseph I, 887
Jessop, Joseph I, 953
Jessop, Joseph I, 965
Jessop, Joseph I, 1005
Jessop, Joseph I, 1010
Jessop, Joseph I Sup 1, 6
Jessop, Joseph II, 382
Jessop, Joseph II, 565
Jessop, Joseph V, 82
Jessop, Joseph V, 83
Jessop, Joseph J. I, 10
Jessop, Joseph P. V, 82
Jessop, Joseph P. V, 83
Jessop, Joseph P. V, 505
Jessop, Joseph P. V, 510
Jessop, Joseph, Jr. I, 965
Jessop, Joseph, Jr. I, 966
Jessop, Josephine V, 630
Jessop, Joshua I, 10
Jessop, Joshua I, 48
Jessop, Joshua I, 54
Jessop, Joshua I, 193
Jessop, Joshua I, 195
Jessop, Joshua I, 505
Jessop, Joshua P. I, 55
Jessop, Josiah I, 505
Jessop, Josiah I, 594
Jessop, Josiah I, 606
Jessop, Josiah I, 965
Jessop, Josiah I, 1007
Jessop, Josiah I, 1010
Jessop, Julia I, 10
Jessop, Juliann I, 990
Jessop, Laura Jane V, 182
Jessop, Lee I, 965
Jessop, Levi I, 965
Jessop, Levi I, 1005
Jessop, Levi V, 82
Jessop, Levi V, 83
Jessop, Levi L. I, 579
Jessop, Levi L. I, 965
Jessop, Lewis I, 957
Jessop, Lewis V, 305
Jessop, Louisa V, 83
Jessop, Lydia I, 553
Jessop, Lydia V, 185
Jessop, Lydia V, 500
Jessop, Lydia V, 505
Jessop, Lydia Ann V, 82
Jessop, Margaret I, 195
Jessop, Margaret I, 199
Jessop, Mariam I, 10
Jessop, Martha I, 184
Jessop, Martha I, 504
Jessop, Martha I, 553
Jessop, Martha I, 558
Jessop, Martha V, 78
Jessop, Martha V, 82
Jessop, Martha V, 83
Jessop, Martha Ann V, 82
Jessop, Martha Ann V, 83
Jessop, Martha E. V, 182
Jessop, Martha M. V, 141
Jessop, Martha Priscilla I, 887
Jessop, Martha R. I, 10
Jessop, Martha R. I, 54
Jessop, Martin I, 887
Jessop, Martin I, 957
Jessop, Martin V, 305
Jessop, Mary I, 10
Jessop, Mary I, 54
Jessop, Mary I, 61
Jessop, Mary I, 143
Jessop, Mary I, 175
Jessop, Mary I, 184
Jessop, Mary I, 195
Jessop, Mary I, 272
Jessop, Mary I, 400
Jessop, Mary I, 401
Jessop, Mary I, 504
Jessop, Mary I, 505
Jessop, Mary I, 525
Jessop, Mary I, 539
Jessop, Mary I, 546
Jessop, Mary I, 553
Jessop, Mary I, 568
Jessop, Mary I, 570
Jessop, Mary I, 594
Jessop, Mary I, 600
Jessop, Mary I, 606
Jessop, Mary I, 785
Jessop, Mary I, 821
Jessop, Mary I, 838
Jessop, Mary I, 887
Jessop, Mary I, 957
Jessop, Mary I, 964
Jessop, Mary I, 965
Jessop, Mary I, 1005
Jessop, Mary I, 1010
Jessop, Mary I Sup 1, 8
Jessop, Mary II, 382
Jessop, Mary II, 565
Jessop, Mary V, 61
Jessop, Mary V, 82
Jessop, Mary V, 252
Jessop, Mary V, 305
Jessop, Mary V, 563
Jessop, Mary V, 579
Jessop, Mary A. I, 231
Jessop, Mary A. I, 242
Jessop, Mary B. V, 82
Jessop, Mary B. V, 83
Jessop, Mary B. V, 505
Jessop, Mary B. V, 510
Jessop, Mary D. V, 183
Jessop, Mary E. I, 10
Jessop, Mary E. I, 54
Jessop, Mary E. I, 83
Jessop, Mary E. I, 887
Jessop, Mary Jane I, 887
Jessop, Mary Jane V, 82
Jessop, Mary Jane V, 83
Jessop, Mary Jr. I, 960
Jessop, Mary Jr. I, 965
Jessop, Mary R. I, 10
Jessop, Mary R. I, 77
Jessop, Mary Russell I, 553
Jessop, Mary Thomas V, 342
Jessop, Micajah V, 82
Jessop, Michael I, 957
Jessop, Michal I, 965
Jessop, Miriam I, 184
Jessop, Nancy Lydia I, 553
Jessop, Nathan I, 505
Jessop, Nathan I, 553
Jessop, Nathan I, 1010
Jessop, Nathan V, 252
Jessop, Patience I, 505
Jessop, Patience I, 957
Jessop, Patience I, 965
Jessop, Patience I, 967
Jessop, Patience V, 82
Jessop, Patience V, 182
Jessop, Patience V, 185
Jessop, Patience V, 342
Jessop, Peninah I, 195
Jessop, Peninah I, 202
Jessop, Phatima Wilder I, 10
Jessop, Phebe I, 504
Jessop, Phebe I, 821
Jessop, Phebe I, 957
Jessop, Phebe I, 964
Jessop, Phebe I, 965
Jessop, Phebe I, 1010
Jessop, Phebe V, 82
Jessop, Phebe V, 252
Jessop, Prat I, 553
Jessop, Prat Wilton I, 553
Jessop, Prat Wilton I, 581
Jessop, Prat Wilton I, 965
Jessop, Pratt W. I, 965
Jessop, Pratt Wilton I, 504
Jessop, Pratt Wilton I, 505
Jessop, Priscilla I, 504
Jessop, Priscilla I, 964
Jessop, Priscilla I, 965
Jessop, Priscilla I, 1005
Jessop, Prudence I, 821

sop, Prudence V, 82
sop, Prudence V, 252
sop, Prudence V, 342
sop, Rachall I, 10
sop, Rachel I, 10
sop, Rachel I, 45
sop, Rachel I, 48
sop, Rachel I, 54
sop, Rachel I, 143
sop, Rachel I, 180
sop, Rachel I, 184
sop, Rachel I, 193
sop, Rachel I, 195
sop, Rachel I, 504
sop, Rachel I, 534
sop, Rachel I, 553
sop, Rachel I, 600
sop, Rachel I, 602
sop, Rachel I, 606
sop, Rachel I, 607
sop, Rachel I, 957
sop, Rachel I, 990
sop, Rachel I, 1010
sop, Rachel V, 82
sop, Rachel V, 305
sop, Rachel V, 747
sop, Rebecca I, 600
sop, Rebecca I, 606
sop, Rebecca V, 82
sop, Rebecca V, 252
sop, Rebecca V, 342
sop, Rebecca V, 505
sop, Rebeckah I, 887
sop, Richard I, 821
sop, Richard V, 82
sop, Richard V, 83
sop, Richard V, 252
sop, Richard V, 342
sop, Richard V, 505
sop, Richard W. V, 82
sop, Richard W. V, 83
sop, Ruben I, 553
sop, Ruth I, 505
sop, Ruth I, 553
sop, Ruth I, 578
sop, Ruth I, 785
sop, Ruth I, 821
sop, Ruth I, 965
sop, Ruth I, 967
sop, Ruth Ann V, 36
sop, Ruth Ann V, 82
sop, Ruth Anna V, 36
sop, Ruth Anna V, 83
sop, Ruth Rolch I, 821
sop, Ruthanna V, 82
sop, Samuel I, 965
sop, Samuel II, 565
sop, Samuel II, 1006
sop, Samuel V, 182
sop, Samuel V, 183
sop, Samuel L. V, 630
sop, Samuel S. V, 182
sop, Samuel S. V, 630
sop, Sarah I, 10
sop, Sarah I, 54
sop, Sarah I, 71
sop, Sarah I, 184
sop, Sarah I, 195
sop, Sarah I, 504
sop, Sarah I, 505
sop, Sarah I, 553
sop, Sarah I, 592
sop, Sarah I, 594
sop, Sarah I, 935
sop, Sarah I, 964
ssop, Sarah I, 965
ssop, Sarah I, 1009
ssop, Sarah I, 1010
ssop, Sarah V, 252
ssop, Sarah V, 305
ssop, Sarah Francis I, 887
ssop, Sarah T. V, 954
ssop, Sarah W. I, 10
ssop, Sarah W. I, 54
ssop, Sarah W. I, 67
ssop, Solomon I, 553
ssop, Susann I, 526
ssop, Susanna I, 504
ssop, Susanna I, 1010
ssop, Susanna V, 82
ssop, Susannah I, 957
ssop, Susannah I, 964
ssop, Susannah I, 965
ssop, Susannah V, 305
ssop, Thomas I, 10
ssop, Thomas I, 45
ssop, Thomas I, 54
ssop, Thomas I, 55
ssop, Thomas I, 65
ssop, Thomas I, 68
ssop, Thomas I, 70
Jessop, Thomas I, 90
Jessop, Thomas I, 143
Jessop, Thomas I, 184
Jessop, Thomas I, 195
Jessop, Thomas I, 267
Jessop, Thomas I, 272
Jessop, Thomas I, 401
Jessop, Thomas I, 504
Jessop, Thomas I, 505
Jessop, Thomas I, 509
Jessop, Thomas I, 525
Jessop, Thomas I, 539
Jessop, Thomas I, 553
Jessop, Thomas I, 821
Jessop, Thomas I, 953
Jessop, Thomas I, 957
Jessop, Thomas I, 965
Jessop, Thomas I, 1010
Jessop, Thomas I Sup 1, 4
Jessop, Thomas I Sup 1, 5
Jessop, Thomas I Sup 1, 8
Jessop, Thomas V, 61
Jessop, Thomas V, 82
Jessop, Thomas V, 83
Jessop, Thomas V, 182
Jessop, Thomas V, 252
Jessop, Thomas V, 342
Jessop, Thomas, Jr. I, 965
Jessop, Thomas, Jr. V, 82
Jessop, Thos. I, 505
Jessop, Thos. I Sup 1, 3
Jessop, Thos. I Sup 1, 4
Jessop, Thos. I Sup 1, 6
Jessop, Thos. Thornbrough I, 553
Jessop, Thos., Jr. I, 505
Jessop, Tiediman I, 553
Jessop, Timmothy I, 505
Jessop, Timmothy I, 553
Jessop, Timothy I, 10
Jessop, Timothy I, 54
Jessop, Timothy I, 83
Jessop, Timothy I, 272
Jessop, Timothy I, 274
Jessop, Timothy I, 401
Jessop, Timothy I, 504
Jessop, Timothy I, 505
Jessop, Timothy I, 553
Jessop, Timothy I, 568
Jessop, Timothy I, 570
Jessop, Timothy I, 785
Jessop, Timothy I, 821
Jessop, Timothy I, 953
Jessop, Timothy I, 957
Jessop, Timothy I, 958
Jessop, Timothy I, 964
Jessop, Timothy I, 965
Jessop, Timothy V, 305
Jessop, Timothy H. I, 957
Jessop, Timothy H. I, 964
Jessop, Timothy H. I, 965
Jessop, Timothy H. V, 305
Jessop, Timothy, Jr. I, 965
Jessop, Timothy, Sr. I, 965
Jessop, Vashti V, 82
Jessop, Vashti V, 83
Jessop, Widow Mary Jordan I, 82
Jessop, Widow Rachel I, 561
Jessop, William I, 55
Jessop, William I, 242
Jessop, William I, 272
Jessop, William I, 504
Jessop, William I, 505
Jessop, William I, 553
Jessop, William I, 578
Jessop, William I, 592
Jessop, William I, 594
Jessop, William I, 602
Jessop, William I, 821
Jessop, William I, 887
Jessop, William I, 953
Jessop, William I, 957
Jessop, William I, 965
Jessop, William I, 1010
Jessop, William V, 182
Jessop, William V, 185
Jessop, William P. I, 606
Jessop, William T. I, 231
Jessop, William T. I, 242
Jessop, William Thomas I, 10
Jessop, William, Jr. I, 553
Jessop, William, Jr. I, 965
Jessop, Wilson C. V, 630
Jessop, Wm. I, 505
Jessop, Wm. I, 568
Jessop, Wm. I, 887
Jessop, Wm. I, 965
Jessop, Wm. V, 182
Jessop, Wm. V, 204
Jessop, Wm. M. I, 887
Jessup, Ada I, 887
Jessup, Alice V, 82
Jessup, Amos V, 407
Jessup, Amos C. V, 407
Jessup, Andrew II, 382
Jessup, Ann V, 82
Jessup, Ann V, 83
Jessup, Ann V, 252
Jessup, Anna V, 82
Jessup, Anna Huldah V, 252
Jessup, Beulah Elma I, 217
Jessup, Charety V, 954
Jessup, Charles V, 954
Jessup, Charles W. V, 407
Jessup, Clarissa III, 356
Jessup, Daniel V, 407
Jessup, Elizabeth II, 293
Jessup, Elizabeth II, 382
Jessup, Elizabeth II, 1006
Jessup, Elizabeth V, 615
Jessup, Elizabeth Ann V, 630
Jessup, Elizabeth Ann V, 954
Jessup, Ella G. I, 211
Jessup, Ella G. I, 217
Jessup, Ethel I, 217
Jessup, Gulie E. V, 1004
Jessup, Hannah V, 954
Jessup, Hannah L. V, 407
Jessup, Hannah Sophia V, 407
Jessup, Harriet M. VI, 69
Jessup, Henry White I, 217
Jessup, Herbert Levi V, 913
Jessup, Huldah V, 82
Jessup, Isaac Elmer V, 954
Jessup, James H. I, 217
Jessup, James H. IV, 701
Jessup, James H. IV, 728
Jessup, James H. IV, 770
Jessup, Jesse I, 15
Jessup, Jesse VI, 69
Jessup, Jesse W. I, 211
Jessup, Jesse William I, 217
Jessup, John V, 615
Jessup, John V, 630
Jessup, Jonathan V, 82
Jessup, Jonathan V, 191
Jessup, Jonathan V, 252
Jessup, Jonothan V, 82
Jessup, Joseph II, 382
Jessup, Joseph P. V, 82
Jessup, Josephine V, 630
Jessup, L. M. V, 913
Jessup, Levi V, 83
Jessup, Lindley M. V, 913
Jessup, Louisa V, 83
Jessup, Luzena I, 926
Jessup, Martha Ann V, 44
Jessup, Martha Ann V, 83
Jessup, Martha D. IV, 701
Jessup, Martha D. IV, 728
Jessup, Martha D. IV, 770
Jessup, Mary I, 15
Jessup, Mary II, 382
Jessup, Mary III, 460
Jessup, Mary V, 82
Jessup, Mary V, 252
Jessup, Mary V, 305
Jessup, Mary A. I, 217
Jessup, Mary A. IV, 728
Jessup, Mary Ann I, 209
Jessup, Mary B. V, 82
Jessup, Mary Emma V, 407
Jessup, Mary Olive I, 217
Jessup, Mattie I, 217
Jessup, Myra S. IV, 701
Jessup, Patience V, 191
Jessup, Patience V, 342
Jessup, Patience V, 346
Jessup, Prudence V, 82
Jessup, Prudence V, 252
Jessup, Rachel V, 310
Jessup, Rebecca V, 82
Jessup, Rebecca V, 83
Jessup, Rebecca V, 252
Jessup, Richard III, 186
Jessup, Richard V, 82
Jessup, Richard V, 252
Jessup, Richard W. V, 83
Jessup, Rosanna V, 954
Jessup, S. E. V, 913
Jessup, Samuel II, 382
Jessup, Samuel S. V, 630
Jessup, Sarah Elma V, 913
Jessup, Sarah Jane I, 211
Jessup, Sarah T. V, 954
Jessup, Sarah W. I, 15
Jessup, Sarah W. IV, 229
Jessup, Sarah W. IV, 295
Jessup, Sibyl Ella I, 217
Jessup, Susan Ann III, 186
Jessup, Thomas III, 186
Jessup, Thomas V, 82
Jessup, Thomas V, 83
Jessup, Thomas V, 101
Jessup, Thomas V, 252
Jessup, Timothy V, 305
Jessup, Vashti V, 101
Jessup, Wd. Mary III, 103
Jessup, Wd. Mary III, 186
Jessup, William I, 217
Jessup, William T. I, 209
Jessup, William T. I, 217
Jessup, Wm. T. IV, 728
Jester, Ann V, 747
Jester, Ann V, 786
Jester, Elizabeth I, 1005
Jester, Elizabeth V, 747
Jester, Elizabeth V, 768
Jester, Francis II, 969
Jester, Hiram V, 747
Jester, Jemima I, 887
Jester, John I, 1005
Jester, Lemuel F. V, 747
Jester, Lemuel F. V, 786
Jester, Lemuel F. V, 791
Jester, Lemuel F. V, 813
Jester, Martha V, 813
Jester, Martha Ellen V, 747
Jester, Martha Ellen V, 813
Jester, Mary I, 990
Jester, Mary V, 747
Jester, Mary V, 786
Jester, Mary V, 791
Jester, Mary V, 813
Jester, P. C. III, 186
Jester, Peggy I, 881
Jester, Peggy I, 887
Jester, Rachel I, 977
Jester, Rachel I, 980
Jester, Rachel I, 990
Jester, Rachel I, 1005
Jester, Rachel III, 186
Jester, Simeon Van Trump III, 186
Jester, William P. V, 747
Jester, Wm. V, 747
Jester, Wm. P. V, 813
Jester, Wm. S. V, 786
Jestin, Elizabeth I, 722
Jestin, Elizabeth I, 739
Jesup, Josiah I, 592
Jesup, Sarah I, 592
Jeter, Allen P. VI, 941
Jeter, Allison VI, 940
Jeter, Allison M. VI, 941
Jeter, Allison M. VI, 970
Jeter, Ann Eliza VI, 970
Jeter, Ann V. VI, 940
Jeter, Betsy VI, 929
Jeter, Beverly R. VI, 941
Jeter, C. VI, 972
Jeter, Catharine P. VI, 972
Jeter, Charlotte E. VI, 941
Jeter, Chilnesse VI, 940
Jeter, Eliza J. VI, 940
Jeter, Elizabeth VI, 880
Jeter, Elizabeth A. VI, 941
Jeter, Elizabeth B. VI, 991
Jeter, Elizabeth R. VI, 941
Jeter, Elliott VI, 940
Jeter, Elliott VI, 941
Jeter, Ellott VI, 975
Jeter, Emeline P. VI, 940
Jeter, Fielden H. VI, 941
Jeter, Fielder H. VI, 1007
Jeter, Fielding H. VI, 940
Jeter, Frances VI, 941
Jeter, Henry VI, 894
Jeter, Henry VI, 929
Jeter, Henry VI, 950
Jeter, Henry VI, 969
Jeter, Henry VI, 978
Jeter, Henry E. VI, 940
Jeter, James M. VI, 940
Jeter, James W. VI, 941
Jeter, Jency VI, 950
Jeter, Jenny VI, 940
Jeter, Jeremiah B. VI, 941
Jeter, Jesse VI, 940
Jeter, Jesse VI, 941
Jeter, Jesse VI, 970
Jeter, Jesse R. VI, 941
Jeter, John VI, 880
Jeter, John VI, 882
Jeter, John VI, 894
Jeter, John VI, 938
Jeter, John VI, 940
Jeter, Julia Ann VI, 1010
Jeter, Lucy W. VI, 940
Jeter, Margaret VI, 991
Jeter, Margaret H. VI, 882
Jeter, Martha A. J. VI, 941
Jeter, Mary VI, 941
Jeter, Nancy VI, 940
Jeter, Nancy VI, 978
Jeter, Patsey H. VI, 940
Jeter, Pleasant VI, 940
Jeter, Pleasant VI, 950
Jeter, Pleasant VI, 991
Jeter, Polly VI, 940
Jeter, Ransom VI, 940
Jeter, Ransom VI, 972
Jeter, Samuel VI, 941
Jeter, Sarah Ann VI, 941
Jeter, Sarah J. VI, 894
Jeter, Sarah W. VI, 975
Jeter, Sovereign VI, 962
Jeter, Sovrin VI, 940
Jeter, Sovrin VI, 1010
Jeter, Sovrin H. VI, 975
Jeter, Susan VI, 938
Jeter, Susan VI, 940
Jeter, Susan M. VI, 941
Jeter, Thomas E. VI, 982
Jeter, William VI, 940
Jeter, William A. VI, 940
Jeter, Williamm VI, 930
Jett, Joseph H. VI, 887
Jewel, Patience IV, 41
Jewel, Patience IV, 95
Jewel, Patience IV, 639
Jeweland, Margery V, 83
Jeweland, Margery V, 95
Jewell, Ann Eliza IV, 728
Jewell, Elizabeth VI, 941
Jewell, George II, 566
Jewell, I. B. V, 1004
Jewell, John IV, 1283
Jewell, Joseph II, 382
Jewell, Lucretia V, 1004
Jewell, Lucretia A. IV, 479
Jewell, Lucretia A. V, 1004
Jewell, Lucretia Ann V, 1004
Jewell, Mary II, 566
Jewell, Mary Ann IV, 413
Jewell, Nellie IV, 1283
Jewell, S. V. IV, 479
Jewell, Samuel V, 1004
Jewell, Sarah II, 382
Jewell, Thomas, Jr. VI, 941
Jewet, Jane II, 1075
Jewet, Mary James II, 1075
Jewett, Belle II, 797
Jewett, James J. III, 186
Jewett, Jane II, 1075
Jewett, Jane II, 1081
Jewett, Jane S. VI, 669
Jewett, John VI, 759
Jewett, Joseph H. VI, 753
Jewett, Joseph H. VI, 758
Jewett, Joseph H. VI, 759
Jewett, Mary Ann IV, 413
Jewett, Mary James II, 1075
Jewett, Mary James VI, 669
Jewett, Susannah VI, 759
Jewett, Tacy VI, 758
Jewett, Tacy Mitchell VI, 753
Jewett, Tacy Mitchell VI, 759
Jewett, Thomas L. III, 186
Jewlin, Margery V, 83
Jewry, Enos V, 256
Jhons, Charles VI, 930
Jiberg, Amelia IV, 1322
Jiberg, Blanche IV, 1323
Jiberg, Caroline IV, 1323
Jiberg, John IV, 1322
Jibson, Elisabeth I, 143
Jimmie, James VI, 55
Jinkens, Ann VI, 390
Jinkens, Ann VI, 408
Jinkens, Ann VI, 409
Jinkens, Anna VI, 408
Jinkens, Elizabeth VI, 408
Jinkens, Evan VI, 408
Jinkens, Israel VI, 408
Jinkens, Jacob VI, 408
Jinkens, Jacob, Jr. VI, 409
Jinkens, Jonathan VI, 408
Jinkens, Mary VI, 408
Jinkens, Michael VI, 408
Jinkens, Rachel VI, 421
Jinkens, Ruth VI, 408
Jinkens, Susannah VI, 409
Jinkens, William IV, 728
Jinkenson, Sarah IV, 497
Jinkings, Rhoda IV, 728
Jinkings, Sarah IV, 728
Jinkings, Zachariah IV, 728
Jinkins, Ann VI, 450
Jinkins, David V, 913
Jinkins, Edward VI, 900
Jinkins, Edward G. VI, 900
Jinkins, Ely V, 81
Jinkins, Ely V, 98
Jinkins, Jacob VI, 408

Jinkins, Jonathan VI, 450
Jinkins, Mary I, 682
Jinkins, Mary I, 684
Jinkins, Mary VI, 408
Jinkins, Mary VI, 450
Jinkins, Millissa C. VI, 900
Jinkins, Rachel VI, 409
Jinkins, Rebekah I, 1033
Jinkins, Ruth I, 681
Jinkins, Ruth I, 682
Jinkins, Ruth V, 98
Jinkins, Ruth VI, 401
Jinkins, Widow Rebekah I, 1033
Jinkinson, Ann VI, 409
Jinkinson, Elizabeth VI, 409
Jinkinson, Isaac VI, 409
Jinkinson, Mary VI, 409
Jinks, Emily V, 579
Jinks, Emily V, 601
Jinks, Jesse V, 602
Jinks, Jesse, Jr. V, 602
Jinnett, ??? I, 325
Jinnett, Abbie I, 242
Jinnett, Abbie I, 254
Jinnett, Abbie Ann I, 329
Jinnett, Abbigail Peele I, 325
Jinnett, Abby I, 325
Jinnett, Abby A. I, 325
Jinnett, Abby P. I, 325
Jinnett, Abigail I, 309
Jinnett, Abigail I, 312
Jinnett, Abigail P. I, 329
Jinnett, Abigail P. I, 330
Jinnett, Albert J. I, 325
Jinnett, Allen Jay I, 635
Jinnett, Ann I, 309
Jinnett, Ann I, 325
Jinnett, Ann Davis I, 325
Jinnett, Ashberry I, 309
Jinnett, B. C. I, 944
Jinnett, Barnaby Cox I, 325
Jinnett, Barney I, 309
Jinnett, Barney C. I, 329
Jinnett, Barney C. I, 682
Jinnett, Barney C. I, 688
Jinnett, Barney C. I, 944
Jinnett, Barney C. I, 946
Jinnett, Barney Cox I, 928
Jinnett, Barny C. I, 329
Jinnett, Carolina I, 309
Jinnett, Charity I, 325
Jinnett, David I, 309
Jinnett, David I, 325
Jinnett, David H. I, 325
Jinnett, Edny I, 309
Jinnett, Elijah C. Stanton I, 325
Jinnett, Eliza I, 309
Jinnett, Eliza I, 928
Jinnett, Elizabeth I, 309
Jinnett, Ellsbery L. I, 309
Jinnett, Esther Lois I, 635
Jinnett, Frances I, 944
Jinnett, Frances I, 946
Jinnett, Ginnett, Joseph I, 309
Jinnett, Henry Thos. I, 325
Jinnett, Hollan I, 325
Jinnett, Holland I, 329
Jinnett, Holland E. I, 325
Jinnett, Hollen E. I, 682
Jinnett, Ida L. I, 325
Jinnett, James I, 623
Jinnett, James Wenlock I, 325
Jinnett, Joab I, 303
Jinnett, Joab I, 309
Jinnett, Joab I, 321
Jinnett, Joab I, 325
Jinnett, Joab I, 329
Jinnett, Joab A. I, 325
Jinnett, John C. I, 635
Jinnett, John Carson I, 325
Jinnett, Joseph I, 309
Jinnett, Joseph I, 325
Jinnett, Joseph Gurney I, 325
Jinnett, Joseph Thomas I, 325
Jinnett, Judith I, 309
Jinnett, Juneus E. I, 325
Jinnett, Lillian I, 944
Jinnett, Lillian C. I, 635
Jinnett, Lillian Lenora I, 928
Jinnett, Lucetta I, 682
Jinnett, Lucetta I, 688
Jinnett, Lucetta R. I, 944
Jinnett, Lucetta Reynolds I, 928
Jinnett, Mahetta A. I, 328
Jinnett, Mahetta A. I, 329
Jinnett, Mahitable I, 325
Jinnett, Mary A. I, 325
Jinnett, Mary Davis I, 325
Jinnett, Mary Dorothy I, 635
Jinnett, Maryan I, 309
Jinnett, Michael I, 309
Jinnett, Micheel I, 309
Jinnett, Mildred I, 303
Jinnett, Mildred I, 309
Jinnett, Mildred I, 325
Jinnett, Mildred I, 329
Jinnett, Mildred E. I, 325
Jinnett, Miriam Bishop I, 325
Jinnett, Nathan I, 309
Jinnett, Nathan I, 325
Jinnett, Nathan J. I, 328
Jinnett, Nathan James I, 325
Jinnett, Needham I, 321
Jinnett, Needham I, 325
Jinnett, Needham I, 329
Jinnett, Needham E. I, 325
Jinnett, Needham E. I, 329
Jinnett, Needham E. I, 682
Jinnett, Needham E. I, 928
Jinnett, Needham Everett I, 325
Jinnett, Orianna I, 635
Jinnett, Rachel I, 325
Jinnett, Robert I, 242
Jinnett, Ruth I, 325
Jinnett, Sally I, 309
Jinnett, Sarah I, 303
Jinnett, Sarah I, 309
Jinnett, Sarah I, 623
Jinnett, Sarah E. I, 325
Jinnett, Sarah E. I, 328
Jinnett, Sarah J. I, 309
Jinnett, Sarah J. I, 325
Jinnett, Sarrah E. I, 325
Jinnett, Smithy I, 309
Jinnett, Sophrnia P. I, 325
Jinnett, Sophronia I, 623
Jinnett, Tabitha A. I, 325
Jinnett, Tabitha A. I, 328
Jinnett, Tabitha A. I, 329
Jinnett, Tabitha Ann I, 325
Jinnett, William I, 309
Jinnett, William Jay I, 325
Jinnett, William S. I, 325
Jinnett, William S. I, 328
Jinnett, William S. I, 329
Jinnett, William Sanders I, 325
Jinnett, Zilpha I, 309
Jinnett, Zilpha Davis I, 325
Jinnette, Allen Jay I, 619
Jinnette, Barney I, 934
Jinnette, Barney C. I, 887
Jinnette, Esther Lons I, 619
Jinnette, Ina Fay I, 619
Jinnette, James I, 619
Jinnette, James V. I, 619
Jinnette, John C. I, 619
Jinnette, Lillian I, 619
Jinnette, Lillian I, 939
Jinnette, Lillian I, 944
Jinnette, Lillian L. I, 887
Jinnette, Lucetta I, 934
Jinnette, Lucretta I, 887
Jinnette, Marjory I, 619
Jinnette, Mary Dorothy I, 619
Jinnette, Ora H. I, 887
Jinnette, Ora Helena I, 934
Jinnette, Orianna I, 619
Jinnette, Robert E. G. I, 887
Jinnette, Sarah I, 619
Jinnitt, Ellsbery L. I, 309
Jintle, John IV, 229
Jintle, Stephen IV, 229
Jipson, Elizabeth I, 101
Jipson, Elizabeth I, 117
Jirherg, Blanche IV, 1323
Jirherg, Caroline IV, 1323
Job, Allen IV, 151
Job, Allen IV, 229
Job, Allen IV, 479
Job, Andrew V, 687
Job, Ann Hannah IV, 151
Job, Ann Hannah IV, 229
Job, Archabald V, 459
Job, Archibald V, 252
Job, Asenath IV, 151
Job, Asenith IV, 229
Job, Bert IV, 1323
Job, Caroline V. V, 252
Job, Charity VI, 409
Job, Clara V, 687
Job, Daniel IV, 151
Job, Daniel IV, 229
Job, Elbert V, 687
Job, Eliza Ann IV, 175
Job, Eliza Ann IV, 229
Job, Eliza Ann IV, 338
Job, Eliza Ann W. IV, 151
Job, Elizabeth IV, 229
Job, Elizabeth IV, 479
Job, Elizanna IV, 151
Job, Ella Florence V, 252
Job, Ellen V, 252
Job, Enoch VI, 409
Job, Ethel I, 641
Job, Ethel Stout I, 635
Job, Hannah Elizabeth IV, 151
Job, Hannah Elizabeth IV, 338
Job, Julianna IV, 229
Job, Lydia II, 566
Job, Lydia II, 669
Job, Lydia V, 158
Job, Lydia V, 183
Job, Lydia A. II, 709
Job, Martha V, 240
Job, Martha V, 687
Job, Mary I, 371
Job, Mary IV, 229
Job, Mary IV, 479
Job, Mary Ann IV, 151
Job, Mary Ann IV, 338
Job, Minnie V, 1004
Job, Moses VI, 409
Job, Patience VI, 497
Job, Patience VI, 522
Job, Patience VI, 644
Job, Patience VI, 661
Job, Patience VI, 668
Job, Rachel IV, 151
Job, Rachel Ann IV, 151
Job, Rachel Ann IV, 338
Job, Rebecca IV, 151
Job, Rebecca IV, 229
Job, Rebecca IV, 479
Job, Rebecca V, 687
Job, Rufus E. V, 252
Job, Russell Orville V, 252
Job, Ruth IV, 229
Job, Ruth IV, 247
Job, Ruth IV, 312
Job, Ruth IV, 313
Job, Ruth IV, 479
Job, Sally V, 252
Job, Samuel IV, 151
Job, Samuel IV, 229
Job, Samuel IV, 338
Job, Samuel IV, 479
Job, Samuel F. IV, 151
Job, Sarah E. V, 252
Job, Susanna IV, 229
Job, Thomas I, 635
Job, Thomas I, 641
Job, Thomas P. V, 252
Jobe, Asenath IV, 140
Jobe, Frank V, 579
Jobe, Hannah V, 183
Jobe, John V, 579
Jobe, Lydia V, 183
Jobe, Martha V, 687
Jobe, Mary Ann IV, 338
Jobe, Mary E. V, 164
Jobe, Mary E. V, 183
Jobe, Mary J. E. V, 183
Jobe, Rebecca IV, 229
Jobes, Dinah I, 401
Jobes, Mary IV, 955
Jobes, Mary IV, 969
Jobes, Sarah T. IV, 969
Jobs, Janepher II, 1006
Jobs, Janepher II, 1013
Jobs, Minnie V, 1004
Jobson, Ann II, 382
Jobson, Anne II, 382
Jobson, Charles II, 477
Jobson, Charles II, 566
Jobson, Elizabeth II, 477
Jobson, Elizabeth II, 566
Jobson, Isaac II, 382
Jobson, James II, 382
Jobson, James II, 803
Jobson, Michael II, 382
Jobson, Rebecca II, 477
Jobson, Rebecca II, 566
Jobson, Samuel II, 382
Jobson, Samuel II, 477
Jobson, Samuel II, 566
Jobson, Sarah II, 382
Jobson, Sarah II, 803
Jobson, Sarah II, 883
Jobson, Thomas II, 445
Johansen, Catherine IV, 1319
Johansen, Haus IV, 1319
Johansen, Sofia IV, 1319
John, ??? VI, 591
John, Aaron IV, 65
John, Abel IV, 22
John, Abel IV, 42
John, Abel John IV, 42
John, Abigail IV, 728
John, Abigail IV, 908
John, Abigail IV, 914
John, Abigail IV, 918
John, Abner IV, 728
John, Abner IV, 827
John, Abner IV, 840
John, Abner IV, 908
John, Albina IV, 34
John, Albina IV, 42
John, Alice IV, 42
John, Alice IV, 1103
John, Almira IV, 39
John, Almira IV, 42
John, Alva B. IV, 584
John, Amy IV, 584
John, Amy IV, 639
John, Amy IV, 647
John, Amy IV, 728
John, Amy IV, 742
John, Amy IV, 905
John, Amy IV, 908
John, Amy IV, 909
John, Amy IV, 1092
John, Amy IV, 1103
John, Ann IV, 22
John, Ann IV, 42
John, Ann IV, 229
John, Ann IV, 584
John, Ann IV, 827
John, Ann IV, 851
John, Ann IV, 908
John, Ann IV, 914
John, Ann IV, 1063
John, Ann IV, 1113
John, Ann IV, 1123
John, Ann J. IV, 42
John, Anna V, 83
John, Asenath IV, 42
John, Austin IV, 908
John, Benjamin IV, 728
John, Benjamin IV, 827
John, Benjamin IV, 856
John, Benjamin IV, 908
John, Betsey IV, 828
John, Bulahann IV, 828
John, Caleb Carlton IV, 828
John, Clementine G. II, 917
John, Daniel IV, 95
John, Daniel IV, 128
John, David IV, 42
John, Dorothy Mae IV, 584
John, Ebanezar I, 965
John, Ebanezer V, 305
John, Ebenazar V, 342
John, Ebeneezer V, 252
John, Ebeneezer V, 407
John, Ebenezar I, 554
John, Ebenezar V, 407
John, Ebenezer I, 1122
John, Ebenezer V, 83
John, Ebenezer VI, 409
John, Edith IV, 1103
John, Elizabeth IV, 30
John, Elizabeth IV, 42
John, Elizabeth IV, 56
John, Elizabeth IV, 65
John, Elizabeth IV, 95
John, Elizabeth IV, 639
John, Elizabeth V, 407
John, Elizabeth C. IV, 584
John, Ellen IV, 42
John, Emma IV, 42
John, Ernest H. IV, 1255
John, Florina I, 944
John, Florina I, 951
John, George IV, 229
John, George IV, 566
John, George IV, 584
John, George IV, 1103
John, Gideon IV, 42
John, Griffith IV, 690
John, Griffith IV, 728
John, Griffith IV, 742
John, Griffith IV, 901
John, Griffith IV, 903
John, Griffith IV, 908
John, Hannah IV, 38
John, Hannah IV, 42
John, Hannah IV, 151
John, Hannah IV, 229
John, Hannah IV, 479
John, Hannah IV, 827
John, Hannah IV, 840
John, Hannah IV, 856
John, Hannah IV, 908
John, Hannah IV, 913
John, Hannah IV, 1103
John, Hannah VI, 464
John, Hannah VI, 523
John, Hannah VI, 532
John, Hannah T. IV, 479
John, Hannah T. IV, 498
John, Harry IV, 1103
John, Harvey IV, 1103
John, Herman IV, 1255
John, Imo IV, 1213
John, Isaiah IV, 827
John, Isaiah IV, 859
John, Jane IV, 95
John, Jane VI, 464
John, Jane VI, 483
John, Jane VI, 523
John, Jeremiah IV, 42
John, Jeremiah IV, 95
John, Jesse IV, 229
John, Jesse IV, 584
John, Jesse IV, 703
John, Jesse IV, 1092
John, Jesse IV, 1103
John, Jesse V, 407
John, Jesse T. IV, 229
John, John IV, 42
John, John IV, 639
John, Jonathan V, 407
John, Joseph IV, 30
John, Joseph IV, 31
John, Joseph IV, 35
John, Joseph IV, 38
John, Joseph IV, 42
John, Joseph IV, 65
John, Joseph, Jr. IV, 42
John, Joseph, Jr. IV, 56
John, Joseph, Jr. IV, 95
John, Josiah IV, 34
John, Josiah IV, 42
John, Kenneth Wm. IV, 584
John, Levi IV, 728
John, Levi IV, 908
John, Lewis IV, 908
John, Lizzie C. IV, 584
John, Lydia IV, 151
John, Lydia IV, 229
John, Lydia V, 846
John, Maribah IV, 728
John, Martha IV, 42
John, Martha IV, 65
John, Martha IV, 827
John, Martha IV, 859
John, Mary IV, 30
John, Mary IV, 31
John, Mary IV, 35
John, Mary IV, 38
John, Mary IV, 42
John, Mary IV, 95
John, Mary IV, 111
John, Mary IV, 827
John, Mary IV, 828
John, Mary Ann IV, 42
John, Mary Ann IV, 62
John, Mary Ann IV, 312
John, Mary Ann IV, 314
John, Mary John IV, 42
John, Meribah IV, 908
John, Mordecai IV, 95
John, Mordecai IV, 128
John, Nathan IV, 42
John, Nathan IV, 95
John, Nathan IV, 639
John, Nathan IV, 728
John, Nathan IV, 823
John, Nathan IV, 827
John, Nathan IV, 828
John, Nathan IV, 859
John, Nathan IV, 908
John, Nathan, Jr. IV, 42
John, Nina IV, 1255
John, Phebe II, 803
John, Phebe II, 883
John, Phebe IV, 42
John, Phebe IV, 639
John, Phebe IV, 905
John, Phebe IV, 908
John, Phebe IV, 909
John, Priscilla V, 407
John, Rachel IV, 40
John, Rachel IV, 42
John, Rachel IV, 95
John, Rachel IV, 229
John, Rachel IV, 479
John, Rachel IV, 584
John, Rachel IV, 639
John, Rachel IV, 728
John, Rachel IV, 810
John, Rachel IV, 827
John, Rachel IV, 903
John, Rachel VI, 523
John, Rebecca IV, 35
John, Rebecca IV, 42
John, Rebecca IV, 908
John, Rebecca VI, 409
John, Richard IV, 42
John, Richard IV, 639
John, Richard IV, 828
John, Ruth Fisher IV, 42
John, Samuel IV, 42
John, Samuel IV, 95
John, Samuel IV, 128

n, Samuel IV, 639
n, Samuel IV, 728
n, Samuel IV, 828
n, Samuel IV, 908
n, Samuel V, 407
n, Sara IV, 584
n, Sarah IV, 31
n, Sarah IV, 42
n, Sarah IV, 95
n, Sarah IV, 229
n, Sarah IV, 240
n, Sarah IV, 288
n, Sarah IV, 498
n, Sarah IV, 584
n, Sarah IV, 639
n, Sarah IV, 690
n, Sarah IV, 703
n, Sarah IV, 728
n, Sarah IV, 742
n, Sarah IV, 823
n, Sarah IV, 827
n, Sarah IV, 828
n, Sarah IV, 848
n, Sarah IV, 901
n, Sarah IV, 903
n, Sarah IV, 908
n, Sarah IV, 969
n, Sarah IV, 1103
n, Sarah VI, 591
n, Sarah Jr. IV, 908
n, Sina IV, 566
n, Sina IV, 584
n, Sina IV, 1103
n, Sinah IV, 584
n, Susanna IV, 95
n, Susanna IV, 229
n, Susannah IV, 95
n, Susannah IV, 111
n, Susannah IV, 828
n, Taylor IV, 42
n, Thomas VI, 523
n, Verna C. IV, 584
n, Wd Ann IV, 65
n, William IV, 229
n, William IV, 908
n, William IV, 969
n, William IV, 1103
n, Wm. IV, 229
n, Wm. IV, 288
n, Wm. IV, 498
n, Wm. IV, 1103
n, Wm. Leroy IV, 584
n, Wm. W. IV, 969
n, Young III, 206
ns, Anderson V, 1004
ns, Ann II, 566
ns, Ann II, 569
ns, Ann IV, 42
ns, Ann IV, 50
ns, Ann IV, 875
ns, Ann IV, 881
ns, Ann VI, 862
ns, Anna V, 83
ns, Benjamin IV, 46
ns, Betty IV, 875
hns, Beula Ann IV, 875
hns, Beulah Ann IV, 875
hns, Caleb Carolton IV, 875
hns, Celissa V, 1004
hns, Charles VI, 941
hns, Charles VI, 975
hns, Charles VI, 991
hns, Clementine G. II, 883
hns, Cynthia VI, 801
hns, Daniel Offley II, 566
hns, Edmund VI, 801
hns, Edmund VI, 806
hns, Edmund VI, 822
hns, Edmund VI, 829
hns, Edmund VI, 845
hns, Edmund VI, 863
hns, Edward VI, 805
hns, Edwin Atlee II, 803
hns, Edwin Atlee II, 883
hns, Elizabeth II, 566
hns, Elizabeth II, 811
hns, Elizabeth IV, 42
hns, Elizabeth IV, 46
hns, Elizabeth IV, 639
hns, Elizabeth IV, 875
hns, Elizabeth IV, 883
hns, Elizabeth VI, 886
hns, Elizabeth M. VI, 807
hns, Florence IV, 1323
hns, George IV, 229
hns, Gertrude IV, 1323
hns, Hannah II, 82
hns, Hannah II, 803
hns, Hannah II, 883
hns, Hannah IV, 908
hns, Henry VI, 806
Johns, Imo IV, 1213
Johns, Isaac II, 566
Johns, James VI, 95
Johns, James VI, 147
Johns, James VI, 855
Johns, Jeremiah IV, 95
Johns, Jesse VI, 802
Johns, Jesse VI, 838
Johns, Jesse VI, 862
Johns, Jesse VI, 941
Johns, John IV, 42
Johns, John IV, 639
Johns, John IV, 875
Johns, Joseph II, 566
Johns, Joseph T. II, 883
Johns, Joseph Thorn II, 883
Johns, Josephine IV, 1323
Johns, Judith VI, 806
Johns, Lewis V, 1004
Johns, Lizzie C. IV, 584
Johns, Lockey VI, 838
Johns, Lydia IV, 229
Johns, Magdaleen VI, 830
Johns, Maleroy VI, 842
Johns, Mallery, Jr. VI, 842
Johns, Margaret II, 440
Johns, Margaret II, 566
Johns, Margaret IV, 95
Johns, Margaret IV, 114
Johns, Martha II, 486
Johns, Martha II, 488
Johns, Martha II, 566
Johns, Martha VI, 805
Johns, Martha Garrigues II, 883
Johns, Mary II, 497
Johns, Mary II, 566
Johns, Mary IV, 42
Johns, Mary IV, 827
Johns, Mary IV, 828
Johns, Mary IV, 851
Johns, Mary IV, 875
Johns, Mary A. VI, 829
Johns, Mary Ann II, 803
Johns, Mary Ann II, 883
Johns, Myrtle IV, 1323
Johns, Nancy VI, 822
Johns, Nancy VI, 855
Johns, Nancy P. VI, 806
Johns, Nathan IV, 42
Johns, Nathan IV, 96
Johns, Nathan IV, 639
Johns, Nathan IV, 848
Johns, Nathan IV, 875
Johns, Nathan IV, 881
Johns, Nathan IV, 884
Johns, Nathan, Jr. IV, 42
Johns, Nathan, Jr. IV, 875
Johns, Paulette VI, 806
Johns, Pheba V, 1004
Johns, Phebe II, 803
Johns, Phebe II, 883
Johns, Phebe IV, 639
Johns, Phebe Ann IV, 875
Johns, Phebe Ann IV, 877
Johns, Pleasant VI, 806
Johns, Polly VI, 829
Johns, Polly B. VI, 845
Johns, Priscilla II, 566
Johns, Rachel II, 566
Johns, Rachel IV, 42
Johns, Rachel IV, 95
Johns, Rachel IV, 96
Johns, Rachel IV, 467
Johns, Rachel IV, 479
Johns, Rachel IV, 639
Johns, Rachel IV, 875
Johns, Rachel IV, 884
Johns, Richard II, 382
Johns, Richard II, 486
Johns, Richard II, 488
Johns, Richard II, 566
Johns, Richard IV, 42
Johns, Richard IV, 69
Johns, Richard IV, 639
Johns, Richard IV, 828
Johns, Richard IV, 875
Johns, Richard T. IV, 875
Johns, Sally VI, 806
Johns, Sally VI, 830
Johns, Sally VI, 941
Johns, Samuel II, 382
Johns, Samuel IV, 42
Johns, Samuel IV, 639
Johns, Samuel IV, 875
Johns, Samuel IV, 877
Johns, Samuel V, 1004
Johns, Sarah II, 82
Johns, Sarah II, 566
Johns, Sarah IV, 42
Johns, Sarah IV, 46
Johns, Sarah IV, 69
Johns, Sarah IV, 639
Johns, Sarah IV, 827
Johns, Sarah IV, 848
Johns, Sarah IV, 875
Johns, Sarah IV, 884
Johns, Sarah VI, 801
Johns, Sarah VI, 829
Johns, Sarah VI, 830
Johns, Sarah VI, 842
Johns, Sarah VI, 862
Johns, Sarah T. II, 803
Johns, Sillei VI, 847
Johns, Stephen VI, 829
Johns, Susan VI, 806
Johns, Susanna VI, 829
Johns, Susannah IV, 875
Johns, Verna C. IV, 581
Johns, William II, 803
Johns, William IV, 229
Johns, William VI, 829
Johns, William VI, 830
Johns, William VI, 849
Johns, William VI, 855
Johns, William P. VI, 805
Johns, Wm. II, 566
Johns, Wm. II, 803
Johns, Wm. II, 883
Johns, Wm. IV, 1213
Johns, Wm. L. IV, 581
Johns, Wm. Leroy IV, 584
Johnson, ??? III, 56
Johnson, ??? III, 185
Johnson, ??? III, 186
Johnson, ??? III, 187
Johnson, ??? III, 273
Johnson, ??? III, 344
Johnson, ??? III, 422
Johnson, ??? IV, 310
Johnson, ??? VI, 39
Johnson, ??? VI, 48
Johnson, ??? VI, 66
Johnson, ??? VI, 223
Johnson, ??? VI, 293
Johnson, A. J. V, 253
Johnson, A. J. V, 1004
Johnson, A. L. V, 631
Johnson, Aaron I, 401
Johnson, Aaron I, 505
Johnson, Aaron I, 785
Johnson, Aaron I, 858
Johnson, Abel VI, 70
Johnson, Abel VI, 71
Johnson, Abi V, 221
Johnson, Abi V, 253
Johnson, Abi V, 255
Johnson, Abi V, 343
Johnson, Abi V, 451
Johnson, Abi Sibil V, 343
Johnson, Abigail I, 505
Johnson, Abigail I, 1085
Johnson, Abigail I, 1094
Johnson, Abigail II, 177
Johnson, Abigail II, 235
Johnson, Abigail III, 186
Johnson, Abigail III, 187
Johnson, Abigail IV, 195
Johnson, Abigail IV, 970
Johnson, Abigail IV, 1213
Johnson, Abigail V, 630
Johnson, Abigail VI, 829
Johnson, Abigail K. IV, 1167
Johnson, Abigail K. IV, 1168
Johnson, Abijah V, 21
Johnson, Abijah V, 83
Johnson, Abijah V, 84
Johnson, Abijah V, 85
Johnson, Abijah V, 610
Johnson, Abijah V, 630
Johnson, Abijah V, 972
Johnson, Abijah V, 979
Johnson, Abijah H. V, 85
Johnson, Abira V, 505
Johnson, Able IV, 1283
Johnson, Abner V, 84
Johnson, Abner V, 254
Johnson, Abner V, 255
Johnson, Abner V, 305
Johnson, Abner V, 312
Johnson, Abner V, 446
Johnson, Abner V, 447
Johnson, Abner VI, 317
Johnson, Abner VI, 325
Johnson, Abraham II, 567
Johnson, Achiles V, 505
Johnson, Achiles VI, 317
Johnson, Achiles Douglas IV, 230
Johnson, Achilla V, 774
Johnson, Achilles V, 505
Johnson, Achilles VI, 301
Johnson, Achilles VI, 319
Johnson, Achilles VI, 326
Johnson, Achilles VI, 327
Johnson, Achilles VI, 810
Johnson, Achilles VI, 830
Johnson, Achilles Clark VI, 317
Johnson, Achilles D. IV, 230
Johnson, Achilles D. IV, 242
Johnson, Achilles D. VI, 237
Johnson, Achilles D. VI, 256
Johnson, Achilles D. VI, 275
Johnson, Achilles D. VI, 277
Johnson, Achilles D. VI, 302
Johnson, Achilles D. VI, 327
Johnson, Adaline V, 252
Johnson, Adaline V, 253
Johnson, Adaliza VI, 325
Johnson, Addaline C. VI, 941
Johnson, Addison V, 253
Johnson, Addison V, 265
Johnson, Addison V, 305
Johnson, Addison V, 306
Johnson, Addison V, 307
Johnson, Adeliza VI, 318
Johnson, Aderson I, 990
Johnson, Adila I, 857
Johnson, Affrica V, 254
Johnson, Africa V, 505
Johnson, Agatha I, 821
Johnson, Agatha V, 84
Johnson, Agatha V, 252
Johnson, Agatha V, 253
Johnson, Agatha V, 254
Johnson, Agatha V, 265
Johnson, Agatha V, 266
Johnson, Agatha V, 286
Johnson, Agatha VI, 182
Johnson, Agatha VI, 217
Johnson, Agatha VI, 251
Johnson, Agatha VI, 252
Johnson, Agatha VI, 253
Johnson, Agatha VI, 254
Johnson, Agatha VI, 255
Johnson, Agatha VI, 260
Johnson, Agatha VI, 268
Johnson, Agatha VI, 317
Johnson, Agatha VI, 318
Johnson, Agatha VI, 319
Johnson, Agatha VI, 322
Johnson, Agatha VI, 323
Johnson, Agatha VI, 325
Johnson, Agatha VI, 332
Johnson, Agatha VI, 333
Johnson, Agathy I, 821
Johnson, Agathy VI, 165
Johnson, Agathy VI, 167
Johnson, Agathy VI, 185
Johnson, Agathy VI, 186
Johnson, Aggatha I, 980
Johnson, Aggatha I, 990
Johnson, Agnes II, 1006
Johnson, Agnes V, 84
Johnson, Agnes V, 254
Johnson, Agnes VI, 185
Johnson, Agnes VI, 232
Johnson, Agnes VI, 251
Johnson, Agnes VI, 252
Johnson, Agnes VI, 253
Johnson, Agnes VI, 255
Johnson, Agnes VI, 260
Johnson, Agnes VI, 286
Johnson, Agnes VI, 316
Johnson, Agnes VI, 317
Johnson, Agnes VI, 324
Johnson, Agnes VI, 352
Johnson, Agness V, 253
Johnson, Agness V, 255
Johnson, Agness V, 287
Johnson, Agness VI, 172
Johnson, Agness VI, 173
Johnson, Agness VI, 253
Johnson, Agness VI, 316
Johnson, Agness VI, 321
Johnson, Agness VI, 352
Johnson, Agness VI, 941
Johnson, Ahairah V, 506
Johnson, Ahariah V, 522
Johnson, Ahira V, 630
Johnson, Ahira V, 638
Johnson, Ahirah V, 505
Johnson, Alan III, 101
Johnson, Alan III, 186
Johnson, Alan Dilliston III, 186
Johnson, Alba Flanders VI, 941
Johnson, Albert IV, 413
Johnson, Albert IV, 1255
Johnson, Albert V, 183
Johnson, Albert V, 256
Johnson, Albert VI, 829
Johnson, Albert C. V, 85
Johnson, Albert C. V, 913
Johnson, Albert E. IV, 230
Johnson, Albert E. V, 343
Johnson, Albert H. II, 803
Johnson, Albert H. II, 883
Johnson, Albert H. II, 919
Johnson, Albertia A. V, 343
Johnson, Alcy Anna IV, 729
Johnson, Alexander Nelson I, 55
Johnson, Aley Anna IV, 728
Johnson, Alfred IV, 1255
Johnson, Alfred V, 83
Johnson, Alfred V, 84
Johnson, Alfred V, 132
Johnson, Alfred V, 343
Johnson, Alfred V, 505
Johnson, Alfred V, 506
Johnson, Alfred V, 630
Johnson, Alfred V, 687
Johnson, Alfred V, 913
Johnson, Alfred C. V, 579
Johnson, Alfred C. Hale V, 85
Johnson, Alfred Carel VI, 326
Johnson, Alfred Carrell V, 254
Johnson, Alfred Carroll VI, 319
Johnson, Alfred Carroll VI, 326
Johnson, Alfred Evan V, 630
Johnson, Alfred L. I, 888
Johnson, Alfretta J. V, 579
Johnson, Alice II, 517
Johnson, Alice II, 562
Johnson, Alice II, 566
Johnson, Alice II, 803
Johnson, Alice II, 881
Johnson, Alice IV, 177
Johnson, Alice IV, 181
Johnson, Alice IV, 230
Johnson, Alice IV, 235
Johnson, Alice IV, 1283
Johnson, Alice V, 41
Johnson, Alice V, 85
Johnson, Alice Ann IV, 1283
Johnson, Alice Doan V, 675
Johnson, Alice Doan V, 687
Johnson, Alice E. IV, 230
Johnson, Alice Kinsey IV, 230
Johnson, Alice M. V, 183
Johnson, Alice M. V, 255
Johnson, Alice M. V, 913
Johnson, Alice May V, 631
Johnson, Alice Morris V, 913
Johnson, Alice R. V, 85
Johnson, Alice S. V, 183
Johnson, Allen V, 83
Johnson, Allen V, 459
Johnson, Allen VI, 829
Johnson, Allen VI, 855
Johnson, Allen Clifford V, 579
Johnson, Allen H. V, 255
Johnson, Allen Nelson IV, 413
Johnson, Allen T. V, 459
Johnson, Allen T. V, 631
Johnson, Alma Eugenie III, 50
Johnson, Almeda V, 183
Johnson, Almeda V, 253
Johnson, Almeda V, 579
Johnson, Almeda M. V, 211
Johnson, Almedia V, 255
Johnson, Almedia VI, 71
Johnson, Alvin V, 253
Johnson, Alzada IV, 970
Johnson, Alzada IV, 1039
Johnson, Alzada C. IV, 970
Johnson, Amanda VI, 829
Johnson, Amasa V, 85
Johnson, Amealy I, 554
Johnson, Amelia VI, 186
Johnson, Amelia VI, 227
Johnson, Amelia VI, 252
Johnson, Amelia VI, 253
Johnson, Amelia VI, 254
Johnson, Amelia VI, 255
Johnson, Amelia PM VI, 255
Johnson, Amelia T. VI, 941
Johnson, Ammiel Sophia IV, 230
Johnson, Amos V, 505
Johnson, Amos V, 506
Johnson, Amos V, 630
Johnson, Amos VI, 71
Johnson, Amy I, 482
Johnson, Amy III, 186
Johnson, Amy V, 83
Johnson, Amy V, 85
Johnson, Amy V, 183
Johnson, Amy V, 231
Johnson, Amy V, 256
Johnson, Amy Ann IV, 969
Johnson, Anderson I, 505
Johnson, Anderson I, 785
Johnson, Anderson I, 801
Johnson, Anderson I, 822
Johnson, Anderson I, 976
Johnson, Anderson I, 977
Johnson, Andrew I, 325

Johnson, Andrew VI, 252
Johnson, Andrew VI, 315
Johnson, Andrew VI, 316
Johnson, Andrew VI, 321
Johnson, Angness VI, 894
Johnson, Ann I, 812
Johnson, Ann I, 822
Johnson, Ann I, 913
Johnson, Ann I, 965
Johnson, Ann I, 1010
Johnson, Ann II, 281
Johnson, Ann II, 293
Johnson, Ann II, 382
Johnson, Ann II, 567
Johnson, Ann II, 625
Johnson, Ann II, 803
Johnson, Ann III, 63
Johnson, Ann IV, 151
Johnson, Ann IV, 367
Johnson, Ann IV, 413
Johnson, Ann IV, 708
Johnson, Ann IV, 728
Johnson, Ann IV, 729
Johnson, Ann IV, 905
Johnson, Ann IV, 969
Johnson, Ann IV, 970
Johnson, Ann V, 65
Johnson, Ann V, 83
Johnson, Ann V, 84
Johnson, Ann V, 85
Johnson, Ann V, 121
Johnson, Ann V, 253
Johnson, Ann V, 506
Johnson, Ann V, 520
Johnson, Ann V, 536
Johnson, Ann V, 570
Johnson, Ann V, 579
Johnson, Ann V, 630
Johnson, Ann V, 845
Johnson, Ann V, 861
Johnson, Ann VI, 16
Johnson, Ann VI, 71
Johnson, Ann VI, 136
Johnson, Ann VI, 185
Johnson, Ann VI, 196
Johnson, Ann VI, 255
Johnson, Ann VI, 256
Johnson, Ann VI, 299
Johnson, Ann VI, 316
Johnson, Ann VI, 317
Johnson, Ann VI, 318
Johnson, Ann VI, 321
Johnson, Ann VI, 829
Johnson, Ann VI, 843
Johnson, Ann VI, 845
Johnson, Ann VI, 941
Johnson, Ann Blocksom V, 253
Johnson, Ann E. II, 883
Johnson, Ann E. II, 921
Johnson, Ann E. VI, 829
Johnson, Ann R. II, 859
Johnson, Ann R. II, 883
Johnson, Anna I, 379
Johnson, Anna I, 401
Johnson, Anna I, 505
Johnson, Anna I, 718
Johnson, Anna I, 722
Johnson, Anna I, 822
Johnson, Anna I, 909
Johnson, Anna I, 990
Johnson, Anna III, 186
Johnson, Anna III, 187
Johnson, Anna III, 219
Johnson, Anna III, 258
Johnson, Anna III, 422
Johnson, Anna IV, 230
Johnson, Anna IV, 705
Johnson, Anna IV, 729
Johnson, Anna IV, 1168
Johnson, Anna V, 84
Johnson, Anna V, 254
Johnson, Anna V, 288
Johnson, Anna V, 505
Johnson, Anna V, 579
Johnson, Anna V, 687
Johnson, Anna VI, 324
Johnson, Anna C. II, 803
Johnson, Anna C. II, 864
Johnson, Anna C. II, 883
Johnson, Anna Eliza I, 337
Johnson, Anna H. V, 914
Johnson, Anna Jane IV, 480
Johnson, Anna Jane IV, 828
Johnson, Anna Jane V, 845
Johnson, Anna Jane V, 857
Johnson, Anna L. IV, 828
Johnson, Anna L. V, 913
Johnson, Anna Louisa IV, 828
Johnson, Anna M. I, 888
Johnson, Anna M. IV, 230
Johnson, Anna M. V, 83
Johnson, Anna M. V, 85
Johnson, Anna M. V, 132
Johnson, Anna M. V, 343
Johnson, Anna M. V, 687
Johnson, Anna M. V, 913
Johnson, Anna M. V, 938
Johnson, Anna Maria V, 939
Johnson, Anna Mary V, 343
Johnson, Anna Mary V, 687
Johnson, Annas Mat IV, 230
Johnson, Anne I, 1005
Johnson, Anne V, 254
Johnson, Anne VI, 69
Johnson, Anne VI, 113
Johnson, Anne VI, 251
Johnson, Anne VI, 323
Johnson, Anne VI, 325
Johnson, Anne Jane IV, 230
Johnson, Anne M. V, 913
Johnson, Annie III, 426
Johnson, Annie V, 631
Johnson, Annie J. IV, 479
Johnson, Annie Jane IV, 480
Johnson, Annie M. V, 343
Johnson, Annie Smith V, 343
Johnson, Ansalon D. V, 913
Johnson, Anselem VI, 308
Johnson, Anselem VI, 326
Johnson, Anselm VI, 302
Johnson, Anselm VI, 308
Johnson, Anselm VI, 317
Johnson, Anselm VI, 319
Johnson, Anselm D. VI, 327
Johnson, Anselum Robert VI, 71
Johnson, Anslem D. V, 897
Johnson, Anslem D. V, 913
Johnson, Anthony V, 84
Johnson, Anthony V, 183
Johnson, Anthony V, 241
Johnson, Anthony V, 252
Johnson, Anthony V, 253
Johnson, Anthony V, 254
Johnson, Anthony V, 260
Johnson, Anthony V, 287
Johnson, Anthony VI, 352
Johnson, Apharacia V, 486
Johnson, Apharacia V, 505
Johnson, Apharacia V, 506
Johnson, Apharacia V, 519
Johnson, Apharacia V, 630
Johnson, Aquilla IV, 970
Johnson, Araminta VI, 799
Johnson, Archaleus I, 977
Johnson, Archelaus I, 785
Johnson, Archelaus I, 820
Johnson, Archelaus I, 821
Johnson, Archeleus I, 990
Johnson, Archelus I, 505
Johnson, Archelus I, 785
Johnson, Archillus VI, 242
Johnson, Ariadna I, 990
Johnson, Arthur IV, 1323
Johnson, Arthur V, 256
Johnson, Arthur V, 505
Johnson, Arthur V, 506
Johnson, Arthur C. IV, 970
Johnson, Arthur H. IV, 1323
Johnson, Arthur Seal II, 803
Johnson, Arzilla V, 254
Johnson, Arzilla V, 630
Johnson, Arzilli V, 630
Johnson, Arzilli V, 650
Johnson, Asa I, 1094
Johnson, Asa III, 186
Johnson, Asael I, 555
Johnson, Asenath I, 401
Johnson, Asenath V, 434
Johnson, Ashby V, 954
Johnson, Asheley, Jr. VI, 231
Johnson, Ashely VI, 252
Johnson, Ashle V, 253
Johnson, Ashle VI, 186
Johnson, Ashley I, 554
Johnson, Ashley I, 555
Johnson, Ashley I, 785
Johnson, Ashley I, 821
Johnson, Ashley I, 909
Johnson, Ashley I, 977
Johnson, Ashley I, 990
Johnson, Ashley IV, 229
Johnson, Ashley IV, 269
Johnson, Ashley IV, 413
Johnson, Ashley V, 84
Johnson, Ashley V, 215
Johnson, Ashley V, 252
Johnson, Ashley V, 253
Johnson, Ashley V, 292
Johnson, Ashley VI, 185
Johnson, Ashley VI, 186
Johnson, Ashley VI, 220
Johnson, Ashley VI, 251
Johnson, Ashley VI, 252
Johnson, Ashley VI, 253
Johnson, Ashley VI, 255
Johnson, Ashley VI, 256
Johnson, Ashley VI, 268
Johnson, Ashley VI, 269
Johnson, Ashley VI, 274
Johnson, Ashley VI, 279
Johnson, Ashley VI, 286
Johnson, Ashley VI, 317
Johnson, Ashley VI, 318
Johnson, Ashley VI, 322
Johnson, Ashley VI, 323
Johnson, Ashley VI, 324
Johnson, Ashley VI, 325
Johnson, Ashley VI, 330
Johnson, Ashley VI, 335
Johnson, Ashley VI, 845
Johnson, Ashley M. V, 235
Johnson, Ashley M. V, 253
Johnson, Ashley M. V, 254
Johnson, Ashley M. V, 954
Johnson, Ashley, Jr. V, 254
Johnson, Ashley, Jr. VI, 253
Johnson, Ashley, Jr. VI, 254
Johnson, Ashley, Sr. VI, 253
Johnson, Ashley, Sr. VI, 323
Johnson, Ashley, Sr. VI, 324
Johnson, Ashly I, 822
Johnson, Ashly VI, 316
Johnson, Ashly, Jr. I, 822
Johnson, Asley, Sr. VI, 253
Johnson, Atlanta V, 85
Johnson, Augusta Geise IV, 1168
Johnson, Azalia M. V, 343
Johnson, B. H. VI, 887
Johnson, B. H. VI, 895
Johnson, B. H. VI, 940
Johnson, B. H. VI, 965
Johnson, B. H. VI, 968
Johnson, B. H. VI, 975
Johnson, B. H. VI, 996
Johnson, B. H. VI, 998
Johnson, B. H. VI, 1003
Johnson, B. H. VI, 1022
Johnson, Bailey VI, 185
Johnson, Bailey VI, 187
Johnson, Barbara VI, 54
Johnson, Barbara VI, 69
Johnson, Barbara VI, 71
Johnson, Barbara VI, 72
Johnson, Barclay V, 253
Johnson, Barclay V, 255
Johnson, Barclay V, 298
Johnson, Barclay V, 305
Johnson, Barclay VI, 254
Johnson, Barclay VI, 317
Johnson, Barclay VI, 326
Johnson, Barter I, 1094
Johnson, Bartlett V, 254
Johnson, Bartlett VI, 254
Johnson, Bartlett VI, 326
Johnson, Barton I, 1094
Johnson, Belle V, 631
Johnson, Belle V, 774
Johnson, Belle V, 845
Johnson, Belle Cherry IV, 1323
Johnson, Belva V, 1004
Johnson, Benj. I, 505
Johnson, Benj. V, 297
Johnson, Benj. V, 799
Johnson, Benj. VI, 251
Johnson, Benj. VI, 260
Johnson, Benj. VI, 855
Johnson, Benjamin I, 526
Johnson, Benjamin I, 554
Johnson, Benjamin I, 555
Johnson, Benjamin I, 580
Johnson, Benjamin I, 785
Johnson, Benjamin I, 821
Johnson, Benjamin I, 990
Johnson, Benjamin I, 1094
Johnson, Benjamin II, 382
Johnson, Benjamin II, 567
Johnson, Benjamin IV, 729
Johnson, Benjamin IV, 818
Johnson, Benjamin IV, 828
Johnson, Benjamin IV, 905
Johnson, Benjamin IV, 958
Johnson, Benjamin IV, 969
Johnson, Benjamin IV, 970
Johnson, Benjamin V, 22
Johnson, Benjamin V, 83
Johnson, Benjamin V, 84
Johnson, Benjamin V, 85
Johnson, Benjamin V, 305
Johnson, Benjamin V, 505
Johnson, Benjamin V, 616
Johnson, Benjamin VI, 16
Johnson, Benjamin VI, 113
Johnson, Benjamin VI, 118
Johnson, Benjamin VI, 136
Johnson, Benjamin VI, 154
Johnson, Benjamin VI, 185
Johnson, Benjamin VI, 186
Johnson, Benjamin VI, 187
Johnson, Benjamin VI, 214
Johnson, Benjamin VI, 220
Johnson, Benjamin VI, 244
Johnson, Benjamin VI, 251
Johnson, Benjamin VI, 252
Johnson, Benjamin VI, 253
Johnson, Benjamin VI, 254
Johnson, Benjamin VI, 255
Johnson, Benjamin VI, 256
Johnson, Benjamin VI, 260
Johnson, Benjamin VI, 277
Johnson, Benjamin VI, 286
Johnson, Benjamin VI, 311
Johnson, Benjamin VI, 315
Johnson, Benjamin VI, 316
Johnson, Benjamin VI, 317
Johnson, Benjamin VI, 319
Johnson, Benjamin VI, 320
Johnson, Benjamin VI, 321
Johnson, Benjamin VI, 322
Johnson, Benjamin VI, 323
Johnson, Benjamin VI, 324
Johnson, Benjamin VI, 325
Johnson, Benjamin VI, 343
Johnson, Benjamin VI, 863
Johnson, Benjamin VI, 864
Johnson, Benjamin VI, 870
Johnson, Benjamin VI, 941
Johnson, Benjamin B. V, 83
Johnson, Benjamin B. V, 84
Johnson, Benjamin B. V, 85
Johnson, Benjamin B. VI, 327
Johnson, Benjamin Bradshaw VI, 71
Johnson, Benjamin D. II, 382
Johnson, Benjamin Drew VI, 71
Johnson, Benjamin F. V, 407
Johnson, Benjamin F. V, 408
Johnson, Benjamin F. VI, 942
Johnson, Benjamin W. V, 255
Johnson, Benjamin Watkins V, 254
Johnson, Benjamin, Sr. VI, 255
Johnson, Bennet VI, 137
Johnson, Berneice Geraldine IV, 1323
Johnson, Bernice V, 85
Johnson, Bertha M. V, 579
Johnson, Betsey V, 305
Johnson, Betsey VI, 324
Johnson, Betsey VI, 844
Johnson, Betsey VI, 901
Johnson, Betsey VI, 941
Johnson, Betsy V, 83
Johnson, Betsy V, 84
Johnson, Betsy VI, 252
Johnson, Betsy VI, 256
Johnson, Betsy VI, 279
Johnson, Betsy VI, 297
Johnson, Betsy VI, 317
Johnson, Betsy VI, 318
Johnson, Betsy VI, 319
Johnson, Betsy VI, 322
Johnson, Betsy VI, 325
Johnson, Betsy VI, 326
Johnson, Betsy VI, 327
Johnson, Betsy VI, 333
Johnson, Betsy VI, 334
Johnson, Betsy VI, 352
Johnson, Betsy VI, 823
Johnson, Betsy VI, 941
Johnson, Betty IV, 42
Johnson, Betty VI, 286
Johnson, Betty VI, 287
Johnson, Betty VI, 316
Johnson, Betty VI, 320
Johnson, Betty VI, 323
Johnson, Betty VI, 332
Johnson, Betty VI, 333
Johnson, Betty Elizabeth VI, 317
Johnson, Beverly V, 255
Johnson, Beverly B. V, 253
Johnson, Bill V, 1004
Johnson, Bolin Anthony V, 254
Johnson, Bolling A. V, 255
Johnson, Brian Hare VI, 71
Johnson, Brooks V, 31
Johnson, Brooks V, 83
Johnson, Brooks V, 84
Johnson, Brooks V, 85
Johnson, Brooks V, 479
Johnson, Brooks V, 505
Johnson, Brooks V, 506
Johnson, Brooks V, 913
Johnson, Brooks V, 972
Johnson, Brooks V, 977
Johnson, Brooks V, 979
Johnson, Caleb I, 505
Johnson, Caleb I, 555
Johnson, Caleb I, 568
Johnson, Caleb I, 857
Johnson, Caleb I, 888
Johnson, Caleb I, 889
Johnson, Caleb I, 1085
Johnson, Caleb I, 1094
Johnson, Caleb II, 382
Johnson, Caleb II, 567
Johnson, Caleb II, 647
Johnson, Caleb II, 669
Johnson, Caleb II, 793
Johnson, Caleb IV, 42
Johnson, Caleb IV, 95
Johnson, Caleb VI, 318
Johnson, Caleb VI, 326
Johnson, Caleb VI, 829
Johnson, Caleb VI, 941
Johnson, Calvin I, 401
Johnson, Calvin C. V, 85
Johnson, Calvin C. V, 579
Johnson, Caroline I, 554
Johnson, Caroline IV, 230
Johnson, Caroline V, 252
Johnson, Caroline V, 254
Johnson, Caroline V, 579
Johnson, Caroline VI, 326
Johnson, Caroline Agnes V, 25
Johnson, Caroline Agnes V, 25
Johnson, Caroline Agnes V, 63
Johnson, Caroline Agnes VI, 3
Johnson, Caroline Agness V, 2
Johnson, Caroline M. VI, 941
Johnson, Caroline T. IV, 1370
Johnson, Carrie L. V, 183
Johnson, Carrie L. V, 506
Johnson, Carshall V, 506
Johnson, Castleton VI, 912
Johnson, Catharine II, 803
Johnson, Catharine IV, 69
Johnson, Catharine V, 897
Johnson, Catharine V, 913
Johnson, Catharine VI, 823
Johnson, Catharine C. V, 85
Johnson, Catharine C. V, 913
Johnson, Catherine IV, 42
Johnson, Catherine IV, 95
Johnson, Catherine IV, 116
Johnson, Catherine V, 35
Johnson, Catherine V, 85
Johnson, Catherine V, 579
Johnson, Catherine VI, 318
Johnson, Catherine C. V, 85
Johnson, Catherine C. V, 579
Johnson, Catherine Matilda VI, 318
Johnson, Catherine Matilda VI, 327
Johnson, Caty VI, 318
Johnson, Caty VI, 326
Johnson, Caty VI, 327
Johnson, Caty VI, 351
Johnson, Caty VI, 352
Johnson, Caty Terrell VI, 196
Johnson, Cecile VI, 220
Johnson, Cecilia I, 821
Johnson, Cecilia V, 787
Johnson, Cecilia VI, 242
Johnson, Cecilia VI, 251
Johnson, Cecilia VI, 252
Johnson, Chalkley Thos. V, 63
Johnson, Chapman VI, 924
Johnson, Charity I, 357
Johnson, Charity V, 232
Johnson, Charity V, 255
Johnson, Charity E. I, 296
Johnson, Charles I, 554
Johnson, Charles I, 785
Johnson, Charles I, 821
Johnson, Charles I, 822
Johnson, Charles I, 858
Johnson, Charles I, 887
Johnson, Charles I, 1033
Johnson, Charles IV, 828
Johnson, Charles IV, 1283
Johnson, Charles V, 84
Johnson, Charles V, 85
Johnson, Charles V, 253
Johnson, Charles V, 256
Johnson, Charles V, 343
Johnson, Charles V, 459
Johnson, Charles V, 506
Johnson, Charles V, 631
Johnson, Charles V, 687
Johnson, Charles VI, 167
Johnson, Charles VI, 185
Johnson, Charles VI, 186
Johnson, Charles VI, 187
Johnson, Charles VI, 197

nson, Charles VI, 252
nson, Charles VI, 253
nson, Charles VI, 254
nson, Charles VI, 255
nson, Charles VI, 299
nson, Charles VI, 302
nson, Charles VI, 316
nson, Charles VI, 317
nson, Charles VI, 322
nson, Charles VI, 323
nson, Charles VI, 324
nson, Charles VI, 325
nson, Charles VI, 326
nson, Charles VI, 327
nson, Charles VI, 332
nson, Charles VI, 333
nson, Charles VI, 342
nson, Charles VI, 797
nson, Charles VI, 829
nson, Charles VI, 847
nson, Charles VI, 862
nson, Charles Albert V, 85
nson, Charles Albert V, 579
nson, Charles Edward V, 913
nson, Charles F. IV, 970
nson, Charles F. V, 343
nson, Charles F. V, 687
nson, Charles Lynch VI, 316
nson, Charles M. V, 255
nson, Charles M. V, 499
nson, Charles O. IV, 1168
nson, Charles W. V, 256
nson, Charlie V, 774
nson, Charlie F. V, 687
nson, Charlotte V, 300
nson, Charlotte V, 305
nson, Charlotte W. VI, 941
nson, Chas. III, 50
nson, Chas. IV, 828
nson, Chas. V, 774
nson, Chas. V, 913
nson, Chas. V, 1004
nson, Chas. Albert V, 579
nson, Chas. F. IV, 1039
nson, Chas. F. V, 343
nson, Chas. M. V, 630
nson, Chas. S. C. V, 914
nson, Chatham I, 401
nson, Chester I, 554
nson, Chester N. IV, 585
nson, Chiles VI, 317
nson, Chillis T. V, 183
nson, Christian VI, 45
nson, Christian VI, 71
nson, Christian VI, 78
nson, Christianna VI, 71
nson, Christopher V, 84
nson, Christopher V, 118
nson, Christopher V, 254
nson, Christopher V, 282
nson, Christopher V, 407
nson, Christopher V, 459
nson, Christopher V, 505
nson, Christopher V, 630
nson, Christopher VI, 244
nson, Christopher VI, 251
nson, Christopher VI, 252
nson, Christopher VI, 254
nson, Christopher VI, 255
nson, Christopher VI, 260
nson, Christopher VI, 286
nson, Christopher VI, 287
nson, Christopher VI, 316
nson, Christopher VI, 317
nson, Christopher VI, 318
nson, Christopher VI, 320
nson, Christopher VI, 321
nson, Christopher VI, 322
nson, Christopher VI, 323
nson, Christopher VI, 324
nson, Christopher VI, 325
nson, Christopher VI, 330
nson, Christopher VI, 332
nson, Christopher VI, 334
nson, Christopher VI, 343
nson, Christopher VI, 351
nson, Christopher VI, 352
nson, Christopher VI, 829
nson, Christopher VI, 842
nson, Christopher VI, 859
nson, Christopher VI, 941
nson, Christopher VI, 1005
nson, Christopher A. V, 913
nson, Christopher Anthony V, 84
nson, Christopher Anthony VI, 327
nson, Christopher Anthony VI, 352
nson, Christopher C. VI, 800
nson, Christopher C. VI, 941
Johnson, Christopher E. V, 505
Johnson, Christopher H. V, 255
Johnson, Christopher H. V, 407
Johnson, Christopher H. V, 409
Johnson, Christopher, Jr. VI, 252
Johnson, Christopher, Jr. VI, 319
Johnson, Christopher, Jr. VI, 322
Johnson, Christopher, Jr. VI, 323
Johnson, Christopher, Jr. VI, 324
Johnson, Christopher, Sr. VI, 316
Johnson, Christopher, Sr. VI, 326
Johnson, Cibil V, 253
Johnson, Cibil V, 255
Johnson, Cicile VI, 185
Johnson, Cicile VI, 186
Johnson, Cicilia I, 554
Johnson, Cicilia I, 562
Johnson, Cicilia I, 785
Johnson, Cicily VI, 256
Johnson, Cicley VI, 253
Johnson, Cislah VI, 242
Johnson, Cisley V, 794
Johnson, Cisley VI, 242
Johnson, Cisley VI, 252
Johnson, Cissily I, 909
Johnson, Clara IV, 1283
Johnson, Clara V, 183
Johnson, Clara V, 688
Johnson, Clara A. V, 255
Johnson, Clara L. A. E. Bailey IV, 1168
Johnson, Clara Lucile IV, 1323
Johnson, Clarence I, 944
Johnson, Clarence IV, 230
Johnson, Clarence IV, 1323
Johnson, Clarence Russell IV, 1323
Johnson, Clark V, 252
Johnson, Clark V, 254
Johnson, Clark VI, 318
Johnson, Clark Newton IV, 970
Johnson, Clarke V, 506
Johnson, Clayton F. IV, 729
Johnson, Clemmons I, 888
Johnson, Clemmons J. I, 857
Johnson, Clinton V, 459
Johnson, Clyde V, 342
Johnson, Clyde V, 347
Johnson, Collings VI, 251
Johnson, Collings VI, 286
Johnson, Collins I, 1033
Johnson, Collins VI, 316
Johnson, Collis VI, 253
Johnson, Comfort I, 505
Johnson, Comfort I, 555
Johnson, Comfort I, 580
Johnson, Comfort I, 990
Johnson, Comfort V, 254
Johnson, Comfort V, 260
Johnson, Comfort V, 631
Johnson, Comfort VI, 251
Johnson, Constantia VI, 185
Johnson, Constantia VI, 187
Johnson, Constatia VI, 186
Johnson, Cora IV, 1255
Johnson, Cora E. V, 343
Johnson, Cora V. VI, 830
Johnson, Cornelius I, 401
Johnson, Corrine V, 170
Johnson, Corrinne V, 183
Johnson, Curtis Marion V, 631
Johnson, Cynthia V, 256
Johnson, Cynthia A. V, 146
Johnson, Cynthia A. V, 506
Johnson, Cynthia Ann IV, 970
Johnson, Cynthia Ann IV, 971
Johnson, Cynthia Green II, 803
Johnson, Cynthiann V, 83
Johnson, Cyrus V, 254
Johnson, Cyrus V, 255
Johnson, Cyrus A. V, 83
Johnson, Cyrus C. V, 255
Johnson, Cyrus Clarkson V, 252
Johnson, Daniel I, 55
Johnson, Daniel I, 81
Johnson, Daniel I, 857
Johnson, Daniel I, 888
Johnson, Daniel V, 84
Johnson, Daniel V, 254
Johnson, Daniel V, 631
Johnson, Daniel V, 913
Johnson, Daniel VI, 71
Johnson, Daniel VI, 325
Johnson, Daniel VI, 829
Johnson, David I, 555
Johnson, David I, 990
Johnson, David I, 1033
Johnson, David II, 235
Johnson, David II, 382
Johnson, David II, 625
Johnson, David II, 803
Johnson, David II, 1006
Johnson, David III, 186
Johnson, David III, 187
Johnson, David IV, 828
Johnson, David V, 84
Johnson, David V, 254
Johnson, David V, 343
Johnson, David V, 505
Johnson, David V, 787
Johnson, David VI, 113
Johnson, David VI, 154
Johnson, David VI, 163
Johnson, David VI, 171
Johnson, David VI, 179
Johnson, David VI, 185
Johnson, David VI, 187
Johnson, David VI, 211
Johnson, David VI, 220
Johnson, David VI, 251
Johnson, David VI, 252
Johnson, David VI, 254
Johnson, David VI, 255
Johnson, David VI, 299
Johnson, David VI, 316
Johnson, David VI, 322
Johnson, David VI, 324
Johnson, David VI, 325
Johnson, David VI, 327
Johnson, David VI, 349
Johnson, David VI, 352
Johnson, David VI, 829
Johnson, David VI, 941
Johnson, David B. I, 990
Johnson, David B. V, 255
Johnson, David B. V, 630
Johnson, David Brooks I, 977
Johnson, David F. V, 35
Johnson, David F. V, 83
Johnson, David F. V, 84
Johnson, David F. V, 85
Johnson, David F. V, 506
Johnson, David F. V, 579
Johnson, David F. V, 897
Johnson, David F. V, 913
Johnson, David, Jr. VI, 186
Johnson, David, Jr. VI, 187
Johnson, David, Sr. VI, 325
Johnson, Davis V, 252
Johnson, Davis V, 255
Johnson, Davis V, 459
Johnson, Deborah I, 448
Johnson, Deborah I, 451
Johnson, Deborah II, 382
Johnson, Deborah II, 552
Johnson, Deborah II, 566
Johnson, Deborah IV, 230
Johnson, Deborah IV, 242
Johnson, Deborah IV, 828
Johnson, Deborah V, 83
Johnson, Deborah V, 84
Johnson, Deborah V, 85
Johnson, Deborah V, 87
Johnson, Deborah V, 183
Johnson, Deborah V, 209
Johnson, Deborah V, 252
Johnson, Deborah V, 253
Johnson, Deborah V, 287
Johnson, Deborah V, 482
Johnson, Deborah V, 505
Johnson, Deborah VI, 56
Johnson, Deborah VI, 70
Johnson, Deborah VI, 91
Johnson, Deborah VI, 253
Johnson, Deborah VI, 301
Johnson, Deborah VI, 302
Johnson, Deborah VI, 308
Johnson, Deborah VI, 319
Johnson, Deborah VI, 326
Johnson, Deborah VI, 327
Johnson, Deborah A. V, 85
Johnson, Deborah Butler V, 913
Johnson, Deborah Judith IV, 230
Johnson, Delilah I, 990
Johnson, Delilah VI, 319
Johnson, Delilah Albertine V, 254
Johnson, Delilah Albertine V, 630
Johnson, Della V, 342
Johnson, Della V, 347
Johnson, Dellila VI, 829
Johnson, Demcey IV, 219
Johnson, Demcey IV, 229
Johnson, Demcey IV, 728
Johnson, Dempsey VI, 70
Johnson, Dempsey VI, 71
Johnson, Dempsey VI, 91
Johnson, Demsey VI, 56
Johnson, Demsey VI, 59
Johnson, Demsey VI, 66
Johnson, Demsey VI, 70
Johnson, Demsey VI, 71
Johnson, Demsey VI, 78
Johnson, Demsy VI, 70
Johnson, Denson S. V, 85
Johnson, Dinah V, 182
Johnson, Dinah V, 183
Johnson, Dinah V, 255
Johnson, Dora V, 687
Johnson, Dora V, 688
Johnson, Dorcas IV, 1167
Johnson, Dorcas VI, 941
Johnson, Dorinda V, 883
Johnson, Dorotha V, 85
Johnson, Dorothy IV, 478
Johnson, Dorothy IV, 480
Johnson, Dorothy IV, 825
Johnson, Dorothy IV, 828
Johnson, Dorothy IV, 859
Johnson, Dorothy IV, 969
Johnson, Dorothy VI, 239
Johnson, Dorothy VI, 252
Johnson, Dorothy VI, 256
Johnson, Dosha V, 630
Johnson, Dosha VI, 318
Johnson, Dosha G. V, 630
Johnson, Dr. L. V. J. VI, 318
Johnson, Dr. Leonard V. VI, 321
Johnson, Dr. Samuel John III, 186
Johnson, Drewellen VI, 964
Johnson, Drury H. VI, 942
Johnson, Druscilla VI, 251
Johnson, Drusilla VI, 255
Johnson, Drusilla VI, 323
Johnson, Drusilla VI, 324
Johnson, Duelah V, 407
Johnson, Edgar R. V, 343
Johnson, Edith I, 977
Johnson, Edith I, 990
Johnson, Edith II, 803
Johnson, Edith IV, 230
Johnson, Edith V, 84
Johnson, Edith V, 253
Johnson, Edith V, 451
Johnson, Edith V, 506
Johnson, Edith VI, 252
Johnson, Edith VI, 255
Johnson, Edith VI, 323
Johnson, Edith VI, 324
Johnson, Edith Dillingham IV, 1168
Johnson, Edith Mildred I, 944
Johnson, Edith Rebecca IV, 413
Johnson, Edith V. V, 630
Johnson, Edmund VI, 317
Johnson, Edna IV, 230
Johnson, Edna IV, 310
Johnson, Edna IV, 970
Johnson, Edna V, 232
Johnson, Edna V, 253
Johnson, Edna V, 255
Johnson, Edna V, 256
Johnson, Edna VI, 185
Johnson, Edna VI, 187
Johnson, Edna VI, 195
Johnson, Edna VI, 327
Johnson, Edna L. IV, 302
Johnson, Edna L. IV, 310
Johnson, Edna L. VI, 327
Johnson, Edward I, 822
Johnson, Edward III, 186
Johnson, Edward III, 187
Johnson, Edward IV, 828
Johnson, Edward VI, 71
Johnson, Edward VI, 251
Johnson, Edward VI, 286
Johnson, Edward VI, 812
Johnson, Edward I. IV, 1168
Johnson, Edward Irvin IV, 1168
Johnson, Edward L. VI, 327
Johnson, Edward Lynch VI, 319
Johnson, Edward S. V, 408
Johnson, Edwin II, 803
Johnson, Edwin II, 883
Johnson, Edwin II, 921
Johnson, Edwin V, 83
Johnson, Edwin V, 84
Johnson, Edwin V, 85
Johnson, Edwin V, 128
Johnson, Edwin V, 913
Johnson, Edwin V, 971
Johnson, Edwin V, 972
Johnson, Edwin V, 977
Johnson, Edwin C. V, 630
Johnson, Edwin E. V, 254
Johnson, Edwin E. V, 505
Johnson, Edwin James II, 803
Johnson, Effie V, 343
Johnson, Elam V, 787
Johnson, Eleanor I, 505
Johnson, Eleanor I, 554
Johnson, Eleanor I, 581
Johnson, Eleanor II, 382
Johnson, Eleanor V, 687
Johnson, Eleanor V, 703
Johnson, Eleanor V, 914
Johnson, Eleanor B. V, 913
Johnson, Elenor I, 990
Johnson, Eli V, 40
Johnson, Eli V, 83
Johnson, Eli V, 84
Johnson, Eli V, 85
Johnson, Eli V, 183
Johnson, Eli V, 506
Johnson, Eli V, 913
Johnson, Eli J. V, 253
Johnson, Eli J. V, 255
Johnson, Eli L. IV, 729
Johnson, Eli M. V, 85
Johnson, Eli M. V, 579
Johnson, Eli P. V, 255
Johnson, Eli P. V, 630
Johnson, Elias V, 252
Johnson, Elias V, 253
Johnson, Elias V, 255
Johnson, Elias P. V, 253
Johnson, Elihu I, 357
Johnson, Elija V, 254
Johnson, Elijah I, 785
Johnson, Elijah I, 822
Johnson, Elijah I, 977
Johnson, Elijah III, 186
Johnson, Elijah IV, 229
Johnson, Elijah IV, 728
Johnson, Elijah IV, 1167
Johnson, Elijah IV, 1283
Johnson, Elijah V, 83
Johnson, Elijah V, 233
Johnson, Elijah V, 254
Johnson, Elijah V, 782
Johnson, Elijah V, 787
Johnson, Elijah V, 972
Johnson, Elijah VI, 69
Johnson, Elijah VI, 70
Johnson, Elijah VI, 71
Johnson, Elijah VI, 78
Johnson, Elijah VI, 90
Johnson, Elijah VI, 252
Johnson, Elijah VI, 255
Johnson, Elijah VI, 256
Johnson, Elijah VI, 279
Johnson, Elijah VI, 317
Johnson, Elijah VI, 324
Johnson, Elijah Peoples VI, 71
Johnson, Elijah W. V, 787
Johnson, Eliphalet IV, 729
Johnson, Elisabeth I, 812
Johnson, Elisabeth I, 822
Johnson, Elisabeth II, 566
Johnson, Elisabeth IV, 729
Johnson, Elisha I, 505
Johnson, Elisha I, 785
Johnson, Elisha I, 821
Johnson, Elisha I, 977
Johnson, Elisha V, 342
Johnson, Elisha V, 621
Johnson, Elisha VI, 71
Johnson, Elisha VI, 104
Johnson, Elisha VI, 113
Johnson, Elisha VI, 252
Johnson, Elisha VI, 255
Johnson, Elisha S. V, 845
Johnson, Eliz. III, 186
Johnson, Eliz. III, 187
Johnson, Eliz. III, 347
Johnson, Eliz. Margaret III, 187
Johnson, Eliza II, 82
Johnson, Eliza IV, 230
Johnson, Eliza IV, 1283
Johnson, Eliza V, 85
Johnson, Eliza V, 913
Johnson, Eliza V, 972
Johnson, Eliza VI, 71
Johnson, Eliza Ann V, 254
Johnson, Eliza Ann V, 630
Johnson, Eliza Ann VI, 941
Johnson, Eliza D. V, 84
Johnson, Eliza D. V, 128
Johnson, Eliza D. V, 972
Johnson, Eliza D. V, 977
Johnson, Eliza Ellen V, 252
Johnson, Eliza Ellen V, 253
Johnson, Eliza Jane IV, 1283
Johnson, Eliza L. V, 914
Johnson, Eliza M. IV, 970
Johnson, Eliza Mary IV, 970
Johnson, Eliza Mary IV, 1213
Johnson, Eliza Mary IV, 1228
Johnson, Eliza P. V, 85
Johnson, Eliza S. V, 913
Johnson, Eliza S. V, 914
Johnson, Elizabeth I, 296
Johnson, Elizabeth I, 301
Johnson, Elizabeth I, 309

Johnson, Elizabeth I, 357
Johnson, Elizabeth I, 378
Johnson, Elizabeth I, 401
Johnson, Elizabeth I, 424
Johnson, Elizabeth I, 505
Johnson, Elizabeth I, 555
Johnson, Elizabeth I, 568
Johnson, Elizabeth I, 785
Johnson, Elizabeth I, 821
Johnson, Elizabeth I, 822
Johnson, Elizabeth I, 858
Johnson, Elizabeth I, 907
Johnson, Elizabeth I, 909
Johnson, Elizabeth I, 912
Johnson, Elizabeth I, 965
Johnson, Elizabeth I, 966
Johnson, Elizabeth I, 990
Johnson, Elizabeth I, 1005
Johnson, Elizabeth I, 1085
Johnson, Elizabeth I, 1094
Johnson, Elizabeth I, 1097
Johnson, Elizabeth II, 177
Johnson, Elizabeth II, 566
Johnson, Elizabeth II, 567
Johnson, Elizabeth II, 647
Johnson, Elizabeth III, 186
Johnson, Elizabeth III, 187
Johnson, Elizabeth III, 303
Johnson, Elizabeth IV, 42
Johnson, Elizabeth IV, 229
Johnson, Elizabeth IV, 230
Johnson, Elizabeth IV, 241
Johnson, Elizabeth IV, 480
Johnson, Elizabeth IV, 728
Johnson, Elizabeth IV, 729
Johnson, Elizabeth IV, 765
Johnson, Elizabeth IV, 969
Johnson, Elizabeth IV, 970
Johnson, Elizabeth IV, 1155
Johnson, Elizabeth IV, 1167
Johnson, Elizabeth IV, 1168
Johnson, Elizabeth IV, 1213
Johnson, Elizabeth IV, 1238
Johnson, Elizabeth V, 21
Johnson, Elizabeth V, 32
Johnson, Elizabeth V, 83
Johnson, Elizabeth V, 84
Johnson, Elizabeth V, 85
Johnson, Elizabeth V, 86
Johnson, Elizabeth V, 101
Johnson, Elizabeth V, 183
Johnson, Elizabeth V, 187
Johnson, Elizabeth V, 233
Johnson, Elizabeth V, 253
Johnson, Elizabeth V, 254
Johnson, Elizabeth V, 265
Johnson, Elizabeth V, 293
Johnson, Elizabeth V, 330
Johnson, Elizabeth V, 343
Johnson, Elizabeth V, 494
Johnson, Elizabeth V, 505
Johnson, Elizabeth V, 506
Johnson, Elizabeth V, 518
Johnson, Elizabeth V, 579
Johnson, Elizabeth V, 610
Johnson, Elizabeth V, 611
Johnson, Elizabeth V, 630
Johnson, Elizabeth V, 648
Johnson, Elizabeth V, 782
Johnson, Elizabeth V, 787
Johnson, Elizabeth V, 845
Johnson, Elizabeth V, 852
Johnson, Elizabeth V, 883
Johnson, Elizabeth V, 884
Johnson, Elizabeth V, 913
Johnson, Elizabeth V, 972
Johnson, Elizabeth VI, 70
Johnson, Elizabeth VI, 71
Johnson, Elizabeth VI, 88
Johnson, Elizabeth VI, 104
Johnson, Elizabeth VI, 113
Johnson, Elizabeth VI, 136
Johnson, Elizabeth VI, 172
Johnson, Elizabeth VI, 173
Johnson, Elizabeth VI, 185
Johnson, Elizabeth VI, 186
Johnson, Elizabeth VI, 187
Johnson, Elizabeth VI, 196
Johnson, Elizabeth VI, 235
Johnson, Elizabeth VI, 242
Johnson, Elizabeth VI, 251
Johnson, Elizabeth VI, 252
Johnson, Elizabeth VI, 253
Johnson, Elizabeth VI, 255
Johnson, Elizabeth VI, 256
Johnson, Elizabeth VI, 260
Johnson, Elizabeth VI, 261
Johnson, Elizabeth VI, 279
Johnson, Elizabeth VI, 299
Johnson, Elizabeth VI, 301
Johnson, Elizabeth VI, 311
Johnson, Elizabeth VI, 316
Johnson, Elizabeth VI, 317
Johnson, Elizabeth VI, 318
Johnson, Elizabeth VI, 319
Johnson, Elizabeth VI, 321
Johnson, Elizabeth VI, 322
Johnson, Elizabeth VI, 323
Johnson, Elizabeth VI, 325
Johnson, Elizabeth VI, 327
Johnson, Elizabeth VI, 332
Johnson, Elizabeth VI, 333
Johnson, Elizabeth VI, 352
Johnson, Elizabeth VI, 409
Johnson, Elizabeth VI, 797
Johnson, Elizabeth VI, 829
Johnson, Elizabeth VI, 830
Johnson, Elizabeth VI, 837
Johnson, Elizabeth VI, 838
Johnson, Elizabeth VI, 859
Johnson, Elizabeth VI, 864
Johnson, Elizabeth VI, 865
Johnson, Elizabeth VI, 870
Johnson, Elizabeth VI, 886
Johnson, Elizabeth VI, 925
Johnson, Elizabeth VI, 941
Johnson, Elizabeth A. V, 255
Johnson, Elizabeth Ann IV, 230
Johnson, Elizabeth Ann IV, 273
Johnson, Elizabeth Ann IV, 310
Johnson, Elizabeth Anthony VI, 324
Johnson, Elizabeth B. V, 85
Johnson, Elizabeth B. V, 87
Johnson, Elizabeth B. V, 630
Johnson, Elizabeth B. V, 979
Johnson, Elizabeth Betty VI, 316
Johnson, Elizabeth Butler VI, 113
Johnson, Elizabeth D. IV, 230
Johnson, Elizabeth Douglas IV, 230
Johnson, Elizabeth Edith II, 803
Johnson, Elizabeth H. IV, 413
Johnson, Elizabeth H. V, 253
Johnson, Elizabeth Jane VI, 923
Johnson, Elizabeth L. II, 883
Johnson, Elizabeth L. V, 253
Johnson, Elizabeth L. V, 256
Johnson, Elizabeth L. V, 505
Johnson, Elizabeth M. III, 31
Johnson, Elizabeth M. IV, 828
Johnson, Elizabeth M. IV, 926
Johnson, Elizabeth M. IV, 970
Johnson, Elizabeth Margaret III, 186
Johnson, Elizabeth O. IV, 217
Johnson, Elizabeth Olive V, 255
Johnson, Elizabeth Olive V, 407
Johnson, Elizabeth P. VI, 829
Johnson, Elizabeth Pleasant V, 914
Johnson, Elizabeth Q. II, 883
Johnson, Elizabeth Q. II, 919
Johnson, Elizabeth R. II, 864
Johnson, Elizabeth R. II, 883
Johnson, Elizabeth R. II, 1075
Johnson, Elizabeth R. II, 1077
Johnson, Elizabeth Rich II, 803
Johnson, Elizabeth Walker I, 909
Johnson, Elizabeth, Sr. IV, 230
Johnson, Elizamary IV, 1213
Johnson, Elizaqbeth VI, 941
Johnson, Elizar I, 990
Johnson, Ella IV, 1255
Johnson, Ella V, 1004
Johnson, Ella Kanoy I, 944
Johnson, Ellen V, 183
Johnson, Ellen V, 1004
Johnson, Ellen H. IV, 230
Johnson, Ellen R. VI, 829
Johnson, Ellis V, 687
Johnson, Ellwood II, 749
Johnson, Ellwood II, 843
Johnson, Ellwood V, 255
Johnson, Elmer F. V, 687
Johnson, Elmer F. V, 705
Johnson, Elmina V, 73
Johnson, Elmina V, 83
Johnson, Elmina V, 85
Johnson, Elmina L. V, 85
Johnson, Elva IV, 970
Johnson, Elvira IV, 230
Johnson, Elvira V, 254
Johnson, Elvira V, 883
Johnson, Elvira VI, 326
Johnson, Elvy V, 253
Johnson, Elvy VI, 318
Johnson, Elwood I, 822
Johnson, Elwood II, 883
Johnson, Elwood IV, 1323
Johnson, Elwood V, 883
Johnson, Emaline I, 888
Johnson, Emaline I, 901
Johnson, Emeline III, 369
Johnson, Emely I, 325
Johnson, Emely I, 822
Johnson, Emily I, 329
Johnson, Emily I, 505
Johnson, Emily I, 822
Johnson, Emily I, 888
Johnson, Emily V, 63
Johnson, Emily V, 83
Johnson, Emily V, 252
Johnson, Emily V, 253
Johnson, Emily V, 255
Johnson, Emily V, 265
Johnson, Emily V, 305
Johnson, Emily V, 307
Johnson, Emily V, 567
Johnson, Emily V, 579
Johnson, Emily V, 913
Johnson, Emily V, 914
Johnson, Emily V, 954
Johnson, Emily V, 959
Johnson, Emily VI, 829
Johnson, Emily H. V, 913
Johnson, Emily Jane V, 631
Johnson, Emma I, 309
Johnson, Emma I, 886
Johnson, Emma III, 186
Johnson, Emma IV, 413
Johnson, Emma IV, 970
Johnson, Emma V, 256
Johnson, Emma V, 343
Johnson, Emma V, 408
Johnson, Emma V, 913
Johnson, Emma A. I, 944
Johnson, Emma E. V, 255
Johnson, Emma Huffines I, 888
Johnson, Emma L. IV, 413
Johnson, Emma L. IV, 585
Johnson, Emma Laura IV, 579
Johnson, Emma Laura IV, 585
Johnson, Emma R. V, 506
Johnson, Emma S. V, 343
Johnson, Emma Teresa III, 186
Johnson, Emma Teresa III, 187
Johnson, Emma W. III, 186
Johnson, Emme V, 408
Johnson, Emmor D. V, 21
Johnson, Enos I, 1085
Johnson, Enos I, 1094
Johnson, Enos V, 85
Johnson, Esther IV, 389
Johnson, Esther IV, 413
Johnson, Esther IV, 729
Johnson, Esther IV, 893
Johnson, Esther E. IV, 413
Johnson, Ethel V, 687
Johnson, Eunice I, 357
Johnson, Eunice I, 366
Johnson, Eunice I, 401
Johnson, Eunice I, 422
Johnson, Eunice I, 448
Johnson, Eunice V, 913
Johnson, Eunice VI, 298
Johnson, Eunice VI, 325
Johnson, Eunice VI, 807
Johnson, Eunice VI, 808
Johnson, Eunice VI, 829
Johnson, Eunice VI, 862
Johnson, Eunice Angeline I, 437
Johnson, Euphemy IV, 822
Johnson, Euphemy IV, 828
Johnson, Eva E. V, 913
Johnson, Eva Eunice V, 913
Johnson, Eva Wiles V, 1004
Johnson, Evan V, 505
Johnson, Evan B. I, 401
Johnson, Evan L. V, 83
Johnson, Evan L. V, 84
Johnson, Evan L. V, 630
Johnson, Evan L. V, 913
Johnson, Evan Lewis V, 85
Johnson, Evan Lewis V, 506
Johnson, Evan Lewis V, 913
Johnson, Evan Lewis V, 938
Johnson, Evan Lewis V, 939
Johnson, Evan R. IV, 729
Johnson, Everett V, 343
Johnson, Everett M. V, 256
Johnson, Exum IV, 729
Johnson, Exum IV, 1155
Johnson, Exum IV, 1167
Johnson, Exum IV, 1168
Johnson, Exum VI, 59
Johnson, Exum VI, 70
Johnson, Exum VI, 71
Johnson, Ezekiel II, 382
Johnson, Fam V, 21
Johnson, Fannie K. I, 309
Johnson, Fanny VI, 884
Johnson, Fayette VI, 829
Johnson, Fletcher V, 687
Johnson, Florence A. V, 913
Johnson, Florence Anthony V, 939
Johnson, Florence M. IV, 302
Johnson, Florence R. II, 803
Johnson, Florence R. II, 883
Johnson, Florence R. II, 919
Johnson, Florency Anthony V, 913
Johnson, Floy Hall IV, 230
Johnson, Floy J. IV, 230
Johnson, Floyd V, 1004
Johnson, Frances III, 186
Johnson, Frances IV, 585
Johnson, Frances VI, 941
Johnson, Frances A. IV, 413
Johnson, Frances A. IV, 585
Johnson, Frances Boykin VI, 71
Johnson, Frances M. V, 408
Johnson, Francis VI, 941
Johnson, Francis VI, 942
Johnson, Francis M. V, 255
Johnson, Francis M. V, 408
Johnson, Frank V, 630
Johnson, Frank C. V, 1004
Johnson, Frank S. IV, 230
Johnson, Franklin III, 186
Johnson, Franklin IV, 230
Johnson, Franklin IV, 828
Johnson, Freddie IV, 1323
Johnson, Frederick IV, 1323
Johnson, Fruzanah I, 990
Johnson, Garland V, 254
Johnson, Garland VI, 256
Johnson, Garland VI, 318
Johnson, Garland VI, 326
Johnson, Garland VI, 327
Johnson, Garland VI, 829
Johnson, Garland VI, 896
Johnson, Garrard VI, 255
Johnson, Garrard Moreman V, 505
Johnson, Garrerd I, 990
Johnson, Garretson IV, 729
Johnson, Garrett VI, 253
Johnson, Garrett VI, 279
Johnson, Garvis I, 243
Johnson, Gearrard I, 990
Johnson, Gedion I, 977
Johnson, Genito VI, 256
Johnson, Geo. W. V, 1004
Johnson, George II, 803
Johnson, George II, 921
Johnson, George III, 186
Johnson, George III, 503
Johnson, George V, 343
Johnson, George V, 407
Johnson, George V, 505
Johnson, George VI, 11
Johnson, George VI, 251
Johnson, George VI, 318
Johnson, George VI, 326
Johnson, George VI, 409
Johnson, George VI, 823
Johnson, George VI, 901
Johnson, George VI, 941
Johnson, George VI, 942
Johnson, George Clarence II, 803
Johnson, George K. II, 864
Johnson, George K. II, 883
Johnson, George K., Jr. II, 883
Johnson, George Knorr II, 803
Johnson, George S. V, 21
Johnson, George T. VI, 327
Johnson, George T. VI, 829
Johnson, George W. III, 487
Johnson, George W. V, 506
Johnson, George W. V, 519
Johnson, George W. V, 630
Johnson, Gerard VI, 251
Johnson, Gerard VI, 252
Johnson, Gerard VI, 254
Johnson, Gerard VI, 316
Johnson, Gerard VI, 317
Johnson, Gerard VI, 327
Johnson, Gerard M. V, 324
Johnson, Gerard M. V, 342
Johnson, Gerard Moorman V, 254
Johnson, Gerard Moorman VI, 326
Johnson, Gerrad VI, 341
Johnson, Gerrard V, 231
Johnson, Gerrard VI, 255
Johnson, Gerrard VI, 318
Johnson, Gerrard VI, 334
Johnson, Gerrard E. VI, 319
Johnson, Gerrard M. V, 230
Johnson, Gerrard M. V, 253
Johnson, Gerrard M. V, 255
Johnson, Gertrude III, 50
Johnson, Gerves L. V, 254
Johnson, Gervis I, 61
Johnson, Gervis VI, 327
Johnson, Gervis VI, 352
Johnson, Gervis VI, 829
Johnson, Gervis Johnson I, 55
Johnson, Gervis W. II, 567
Johnson, Gideon IV, 151
Johnson, Gideon V, 183
Johnson, Gideon V, 254
Johnson, Gideon VI, 186
Johnson, Gideon VI, 253
Johnson, Gideon VI, 318
Johnson, Gideon VI, 325
Johnson, Gideon Johnson V, 25
Johnson, Gideon Johnson VI, 2
Johnson, Gidion Nicholes V, 25
Johnson, Glen Edwin IV, 1255
Johnson, Glenn V, 343
Johnson, Goshen IV, 1283
Johnson, Grace II, 625
Johnson, Grace V, 241
Johnson, Grace V, 252
Johnson, Grace V, 253
Johnson, Grace V, 631
Johnson, Gracy Amy V, 913
Johnson, Granville M. VI, 980
Johnson, Greeta II, 445
Johnson, Griffin VI, 318
Johnson, Griffin VI, 327
Johnson, Griffith Edwards, Jr. II, 567
Johnson, Gulielma IV, 1283
Johnson, Gulielma W. II, 883
Johnson, H. L. I, 635
Johnson, Hadley I, 401
Johnson, Hadley IV, 42
Johnson, Hanna IV, 512
Johnson, Hanna V, 845
Johnson, Hannah I, 357
Johnson, Hannah I, 359
Johnson, Hannah I, 391
Johnson, Hannah I, 401
Johnson, Hannah I, 402
Johnson, Hannah I, 406
Johnson, Hannah I, 505
Johnson, Hannah I, 549
Johnson, Hannah I, 554
Johnson, Hannah I, 785
Johnson, Hannah I, 857
Johnson, Hannah I, 884
Johnson, Hannah I, 887
Johnson, Hannah I, 990
Johnson, Hannah I, 999
Johnson, Hannah I, 1085
Johnson, Hannah II, 382
Johnson, Hannah II, 566
Johnson, Hannah II, 567
Johnson, Hannah II, 669
Johnson, Hannah II, 709
Johnson, Hannah II, 713
Johnson, Hannah II, 806
Johnson, Hannah IV, 20
Johnson, Hannah IV, 42
Johnson, Hannah IV, 338
Johnson, Hannah IV, 680
Johnson, Hannah IV, 683
Johnson, Hannah IV, 728
Johnson, Hannah IV, 729
Johnson, Hannah IV, 749
Johnson, Hannah IV, 765
Johnson, Hannah V, 84
Johnson, Hannah V, 235
Johnson, Hannah V, 253
Johnson, Hannah V, 255
Johnson, Hannah V, 305
Johnson, Hannah V, 308
Johnson, Hannah V, 312
Johnson, Hannah V, 447
Johnson, Hannah V, 844
Johnson, Hannah V, 845
Johnson, Hannah V, 852
Johnson, Hannah V, 857
Johnson, Hannah V, 883
Johnson, Hannah V, 954
Johnson, Hannah VI, 324
Johnson, Hannah VI, 327
Johnson, Hannah VI, 349
Johnson, Hannah VI, 350
Johnson, Hannah VI, 351
Johnson, Hannah VI, 352
Johnson, Hannah VI, 845
Johnson, Hannah E. V, 506
Johnson, Hannah Ellen V, 183
Johnson, Hannah Ellen V, 236
Johnson, Hannah Ellen V, 253
Johnson, Hannah Ellen V, 255
Johnson, Hannah M. V, 83
Johnson, Hannah M. V, 85
Johnson, Hannah M. V, 183

Johnson, Hannah M. V, 255
Johnson, Hannah Maria V, 84
Johnson, Hannah Maria V, 506
Johnson, Hannah Maria V, 630
Johnson, Hannah Mariah V, 505
Johnson, Hannah P. V, 505
Johnson, Hannah S. II, 567
Johnson, Hannah S. II, 749
Johnson, Hannah S. II, 771
Johnson, Hannah T. II, 567
Johnson, Hannah T. II, 883
Johnson, Hannah T. II, 943
Johnson, Hannahmariah V, 506
Johnson, Hardy I, 337
Johnson, Harley V, 408
Johnson, Harold V, 506
Johnson, Harriet III, 487
Johnson, Harriet III, 503
Johnson, Harriet V, 954
Johnson, Harriet VI, 327
Johnson, Harriet VI, 334
Johnson, Harriet E. VI, 942
Johnson, Harriet Templeton IV, 828
Johnson, Harriett V, 254
Johnson, Harriett W. V, 254
Johnson, Harriett W. V, 972
Johnson, Harrison VI, 137
Johnson, Harry IV, 230
Johnson, Harry V, 459
Johnson, Harry V, 630
Johnson, Harvey IV, 230
Johnson, Harvey V, 253
Johnson, Haseltine I, 448
Johnson, Hattie E. V, 253
Johnson, Hebe III, 414
Johnson, Hebe III, 422
Johnson, Helen III, 186
Johnson, Helen B. III, 101
Johnson, Helen B. III, 186
Johnson, Helen Wright V, 687
Johnson, Helen Wright V, 711
Johnson, Henrietta III, 186
Johnson, Henrietta III, 363
Johnson, Henrietta A. V, 183
Johnson, Henrietta A. V, 253
Johnson, Henrietta A. V, 255
Johnson, Henry II, 445
Johnson, Henry III, 186
Johnson, Henry V, 83
Johnson, Henry V, 343
Johnson, Henry V, 407
Johnson, Henry VI, 884
Johnson, Henry C. III, 186
Johnson, Henry C. V, 85
Johnson, Henry H. V, 845
Johnson, Henry Hair VI, 70
Johnson, Henry R. V, 1004
Johnson, Hephzibah II, 962
Johnson, Hephzibah II, 1006
Johnson, Herbert E. I, 621
Johnson, Herbert E. I, 944
Johnson, Herman II, 445
Johnson, Hervey V, 255
Johnson, Hervy V, 343
Johnson, Hezekiah I, 912
Johnson, Hezekiah S. I, 990
Johnson, Hibbard V, 774
Johnson, Hibberd V, 774
Johnson, Hiram I, 401
Johnson, Hiram I, 448
Johnson, Hiram I, 812
Johnson, Hiram I, 822
Johnson, Hiram IV, 728
Johnson, Howard C. II, 883
Johnson, Howard Cooper II, 803
Johnson, Howard Cooper II, 883
Johnson, Hulda Ann IV, 495
Johnson, Icy V, 687
Johnson, Ida III, 186
Johnson, Ida IV, 230
Johnson, Ida IV, 1256
Johnson, Ida Caroline V, 85
Johnson, Imo IV, 1213
Johnson, Ira I, 857
Johnson, Ira I, 888
Johnson, Ira I, 904
Johnson, Ira I, 928
Johnson, Irena I, 857
Johnson, Irena I, 888
Johnson, Irena I, 904
Johnson, Irena V, 505
Johnson, Irena M. V, 256
Johnson, Irene I, 928
Johnson, Irven H. V, 631
Johnson, Irvin V, 579
Johnson, Irvin H. V, 579
Johnson, Irvin H. V, 687
Johnson, Isaac I, 357
Johnson, Isaac I, 401
Johnson, Isaac I, 424
Johnson, Isaac I, 1094
Johnson, Isaac II, 382
Johnson, Isaac IV, 42
Johnson, Isaac IV, 69
Johnson, Isaac IV, 479
Johnson, Isaac IV, 828
Johnson, Isaac IV, 970
Johnson, Isaac V, 505
Johnson, Isaac V, 913
Johnson, Isaac VI, 321
Johnson, Isaac VI, 829
Johnson, Isaac F. V, 343
Johnson, Isaac H. I, 1085
Johnson, Isaac Jones V, 85
Johnson, Isaac M. V, 182
Johnson, Isaac M. V, 183
Johnson, Isaac M. V, 255
Johnson, Isaac McPherson V, 252
Johnson, Isaac T. V, 343
Johnson, Isaac T. V, 687
Johnson, Isaac T. V, 913
Johnson, Isaac Thorn V, 687
Johnson, Isaac W. IV, 479
Johnson, Isaac W. IV, 502
Johnson, Isaac W. IV, 828
Johnson, Isaac Wm. IV, 230
Johnson, Isaac, Jr. IV, 42
Johnson, Isabella II, 382
Johnson, Isabella II, 806
Johnson, Isabelle II, 567
Johnson, Isabelle V, 579
Johnson, Isaiah II, 968
Johnson, Israel H. II, 709
Johnson, Israel H. II, 749
Johnson, Israel H. II, 883
Johnson, Israel H., Jr. II, 883
Johnson, Iva Nellie IV, 230
Johnson, J. C. V, 256
Johnson, J. L. V, 687
Johnson, J. Will V, 343
Johnson, J. Will V, 687
Johnson, Jack VI, 995
Johnson, Jacob I, 928
Johnson, Jacob I, 944
Johnson, Jacob II, 382
Johnson, Jacob II, 383
Johnson, Jacob II, 567
Johnson, Jacob II, 669
Johnson, Jacob II, 806
Johnson, Jacob II, 883
Johnson, Jacob II, 943
Johnson, Jacob VI, 45
Johnson, Jacob VI, 70
Johnson, Jacob Lindley II, 382
Johnson, Jacob Lindley II, 567
Johnson, James I, 437
Johnson, James I, 448
Johnson, James I, 505
Johnson, James I, 534
Johnson, James I, 540
Johnson, James I, 554
Johnson, James I, 555
Johnson, James I, 785
Johnson, James I, 821
Johnson, James I, 822
Johnson, James I, 829
Johnson, James I, 831
Johnson, James I, 928
Johnson, James I, 977
Johnson, James I, 1033
Johnson, James I, 1085
Johnson, James I, 1094
Johnson, James IV, 729
Johnson, James IV, 828
Johnson, James IV, 969
Johnson, James IV, 970
Johnson, James IV, 1010
Johnson, James IV, 1168
Johnson, James IV, 1283
Johnson, James V, 83
Johnson, James V, 84
Johnson, James V, 85
Johnson, James V, 101
Johnson, James V, 215
Johnson, James V, 225
Johnson, James V, 253
Johnson, James V, 254
Johnson, James V, 260
Johnson, James V, 265
Johnson, James V, 343
Johnson, James V, 494
Johnson, James V, 505
Johnson, James V, 506
Johnson, James V, 630
Johnson, James V, 774
Johnson, James V, 787
Johnson, James V, 913
Johnson, James VI, 11
Johnson, James VI, 137
Johnson, James VI, 186
Johnson, James VI, 232
Johnson, James VI, 252
Johnson, James VI, 253
Johnson, James VI, 254
Johnson, James VI, 255
Johnson, James VI, 256
Johnson, James VI, 260
Johnson, James VI, 274
Johnson, James VI, 286
Johnson, James VI, 300
Johnson, James VI, 316
Johnson, James VI, 317
Johnson, James VI, 318
Johnson, James VI, 321
Johnson, James VI, 322
Johnson, James VI, 324
Johnson, James VI, 325
Johnson, James VI, 326
Johnson, James VI, 332
Johnson, James VI, 333
Johnson, James VI, 352
Johnson, James VI, 801
Johnson, James VI, 810
Johnson, James VI, 817
Johnson, James VI, 829
Johnson, James VI, 865
Johnson, James VI, 941
Johnson, James A. IV, 230
Johnson, James A. V, 82
Johnson, James A. V, 83
Johnson, James A. V, 84
Johnson, James A. V, 85
Johnson, James A. V, 183
Johnson, James A. V, 253
Johnson, James A. V, 254
Johnson, James A. V, 255
Johnson, James A. V, 506
Johnson, James A. VI, 830
Johnson, James Allen V, 252
Johnson, James Anthony V, 83
Johnson, James Arthur V, 253
Johnson, James B. III, 186
Johnson, James B. V, 107
Johnson, James B. V, 254
Johnson, James B. V, 343
Johnson, James B. V, 687
Johnson, James B. V, 913
Johnson, James B. V, 972
Johnson, James Brooks V, 83
Johnson, James Brooks V, 85
Johnson, James Brooks V, 687
Johnson, James Brooks V, 913
Johnson, James C. V, 254
Johnson, James Chiles VI, 242
Johnson, James D. V, 83
Johnson, James D. V, 84
Johnson, James D. V, 85
Johnson, James D. VI, 327
Johnson, James Dempsey VI, 91
Johnson, James E. IV, 1255
Johnson, James E. V, 252
Johnson, James E. V, 254
Johnson, James E. V, 343
Johnson, James E. VI, 69
Johnson, James E. VI, 71
Johnson, James Ellison V, 254
Johnson, James F. VI, 911
Johnson, James F. VI, 972
Johnson, James H. V, 631
Johnson, James H. VI, 942
Johnson, James Harvey V, 85
Johnson, James L. VI, 829
Johnson, James M. V, 252
Johnson, James M. V, 253
Johnson, James M. VI, 830
Johnson, James M. VI, 831
Johnson, James M. VI, 942
Johnson, James Oliver IV, 828
Johnson, James P. V, 254
Johnson, James P. VI, 318
Johnson, James R. II, 134
Johnson, James R. VI, 69
Johnson, James R. VI, 71
Johnson, James S. V, 631
Johnson, James W. V, 630
Johnson, James W. VI, 941
Johnson, James, II I, 555
Johnson, James, Jr. VI, 352
Johnson, James, Sr. V, 787
Johnson, Jamy V, 252
Johnson, Jamy V, 253
Johnson, Jane I, 401
Johnson, Jane I, 482
Johnson, Jane I, 801
Johnson, Jane I, 821
Johnson, Jane I, 907
Johnson, Jane I, 912
Johnson, Jane I, 977
Johnson, Jane I, 990
Johnson, Jane II, 382
Johnson, Jane II, 485
Johnson, Jane II, 567
Johnson, Jane II, 815
Johnson, Jane III, 187
Johnson, Jane IV, 480
Johnson, Jane IV, 502
Johnson, Jane V, 407
Johnson, Jane V, 408
Johnson, Jane V, 621
Johnson, Jane VI, 68
Johnson, Jane VI, 69
Johnson, Jane VI, 251
Johnson, Jane VI, 252
Johnson, Jane VI, 255
Johnson, Jane VI, 318
Johnson, Jane VI, 324
Johnson, Jane VI, 341
Johnson, Jane VI, 342
Johnson, Jane VI, 855
Johnson, Jane Frusanna Malissa I, 990
Johnson, Jane L. I, 983
Johnson, Jane L. I, 990
Johnson, Janetta VI, 941
Johnson, Jarad M. V, 451
Johnson, Jarad M. V, 459
Johnson, Jared I, 555
Johnson, Jared L. V, 687
Johnson, Jarrad VI, 352
Johnson, Jarvis L. V, 255
Johnson, Jarvis L. V, 630
Johnson, Jas. IV, 479
Johnson, Jeams I, 965
Johnson, Jean VI, 65
Johnson, Jean VI, 70
Johnson, Jean VI, 341
Johnson, Jehu V, 630
Johnson, Jemima I, 821
Johnson, Jemima I, 833
Johnson, Jemima I, 971
Johnson, Jemima I, 977
Johnson, Jemima I, 990
Johnson, Jemima I, 995
Johnson, Jemima V, 231
Johnson, Jemima V, 253
Johnson, Jemima VI, 71
Johnson, Jemima VI, 163
Johnson, Jemima VI, 185
Johnson, Jemima VI, 187
Johnson, Jemima VI, 220
Johnson, Jemima VI, 254
Johnson, Jenette III, 186
Johnson, Jennett II, 709
Johnson, Jennett II, 843
Johnson, Jennett II, 883
Johnson, Jennette Carle IV, 728
Johnson, Jennie III, 187
Johnson, Jennie IV, 585
Johnson, Jennie V, 631
Johnson, Jephtha V, 183
Johnson, Jephtha V, 959
Johnson, Jephthah V, 252
Johnson, Jephthah V, 278
Johnson, Jephthan V, 254
Johnson, Jeptha V, 84
Johnson, Jeptha V, 945
Johnson, Jeptha VI, 317
Johnson, Jeptha VI, 325
Johnson, Jerdan V, 253
Johnson, Jeremiah I, 357
Johnson, Jeremiah I, 401
Johnson, Jerusha IV, 151
Johnson, Jerusha V, 252
Johnson, Jerusha V, 253
Johnson, Jerusha V, 285
Johnson, Jerusha VI, 299
Johnson, Jerusha VI, 318
Johnson, Jervis V, 630
Johnson, Jervis VI, 71
Johnson, Jervis L. V, 255
Johnson, Jervis L. V, 505
Johnson, Jesse I, 357
Johnson, Jesse I, 378
Johnson, Jesse I, 391
Johnson, Jesse I, 401
Johnson, Jesse I, 505
Johnson, Jesse I, 672
Johnson, Jesse I, 785
Johnson, Jesse I, 822
Johnson, Jesse I, 912
Johnson, Jesse I, 965
Johnson, Jesse I, 990
Johnson, Jesse IV, 970
Johnson, Jesse V, 84
Johnson, Jesse V, 183
Johnson, Jesse V, 253
Johnson, Jesse V, 254
Johnson, Jesse V, 255
Johnson, Jesse V, 343
Johnson, Jesse V, 844
Johnson, Jesse VI, 16
Johnson, Jesse VI, 69
Johnson, Jesse VI, 70
Johnson, Jesse VI, 91
Johnson, Jesse VI, 252
Johnson, Jesse VI, 253
Johnson, Jesse VI, 254
Johnson, Jesse VI, 255
Johnson, Jesse VI, 256
Johnson, Jesse VI, 279
Johnson, Jesse VI, 321
Johnson, Jesse VI, 327
Johnson, Jesse VI, 352
Johnson, Jesse C. V, 255
Johnson, Jesse Clark V, 254
Johnson, Jesse Faulkner V, 630
Johnson, Jesse K. V, 343
Johnson, Jesse S. V, 183
Johnson, Jesse, Jr. I, 401
Johnson, Jessy VI, 318
Johnson, Jno. II, 237
Johnson, Joakin VI, 71
Johnson, Joana IV, 1213
Johnson, Joanna IV, 938
Johnson, Joanna IV, 969
Johnson, Joanna IV, 970
Johnson, Joanna IV, 1213
Johnson, Joanna VI, 318
Johnson, Joanna VI, 327
Johnson, Joanna C. IV, 970
Johnson, Joanna C. IV, 1213
Johnson, Joanna T. V, 506
Johnson, Joanna T. V, 522
Johnson, Joannah VI, 941
Johnson, Job I, 357
Johnson, Joel I, 243
Johnson, Joel II, 1006
Johnson, Joel II, 1053
Johnson, Joel V, 630
Johnson, Joel VI, 69
Johnson, Joel VI, 71
Johnson, Joel VI, 86
Johnson, Joel VI, 91
Johnson, Joel Cook VI, 71
Johnson, Joel W. V, 83
Johnson, Joel W. V, 84
Johnson, Joel W. V, 85
Johnson, Joel W. V, 505
Johnson, Joel W. V, 506
Johnson, Joel W. V, 579
Johnson, Johanna II, 382
Johnson, Johanna II, 383
Johnson, John I, 1
Johnson, John I, 357
Johnson, John I, 359
Johnson, John I, 366
Johnson, John I, 401
Johnson, John I, 430
Johnson, John I, 505
Johnson, John I, 554
Johnson, John I, 785
Johnson, John I, 821
Johnson, John I, 833
Johnson, John I, 959
Johnson, John I, 965
Johnson, John I, 971
Johnson, John I, 977
Johnson, John I, 990
Johnson, John I, 1005
Johnson, John I, 1010
Johnson, John I, 1085
Johnson, John I, 1094
Johnson, John II, 177
Johnson, John II, 205
Johnson, John II, 235
Johnson, John II, 382
Johnson, John II, 383
Johnson, John II, 445
Johnson, John II, 566
Johnson, John II, 567
Johnson, John II, 625
Johnson, John II, 862
Johnson, John II, 883
Johnson, John II, 1006
Johnson, John III, 187
Johnson, John IV, 468
Johnson, John IV, 512
Johnson, John IV, 728
Johnson, John IV, 828
Johnson, John IV, 847
Johnson, John IV, 859
Johnson, John IV, 969
Johnson, John IV, 970
Johnson, John IV, 1167
Johnson, John IV, 1168
Johnson, John V, 40
Johnson, John V, 83
Johnson, John V, 85
Johnson, John V, 255
Johnson, John V, 305
Johnson, John V, 343
Johnson, John V, 490
Johnson, John V, 505
Johnson, John V, 506

Johnson, John V, 579
Johnson, John V, 611
Johnson, John V, 630
Johnson, John V, 631
Johnson, John V, 687
Johnson, John V, 844
Johnson, John V, 845
Johnson, John V, 883
Johnson, John V, 913
Johnson, John V, 972
Johnson, John VI, 11
Johnson, John VI, 12
Johnson, John VI, 16
Johnson, John VI, 69
Johnson, John VI, 70
Johnson, John VI, 71
Johnson, John VI, 119
Johnson, John VI, 147
Johnson, John VI, 164
Johnson, John VI, 172
Johnson, John VI, 173
Johnson, John VI, 185
Johnson, John VI, 227
Johnson, John VI, 239
Johnson, John VI, 245
Johnson, John VI, 250
Johnson, John VI, 251
Johnson, John VI, 252
Johnson, John VI, 253
Johnson, John VI, 254
Johnson, John VI, 255
Johnson, John VI, 256
Johnson, John VI, 279
Johnson, John VI, 283
Johnson, John VI, 285
Johnson, John VI, 291
Johnson, John VI, 315
Johnson, John VI, 316
Johnson, John VI, 317
Johnson, John VI, 318
Johnson, John VI, 321
Johnson, John VI, 322
Johnson, John VI, 323
Johnson, John VI, 324
Johnson, John VI, 325
Johnson, John VI, 326
Johnson, John VI, 330
Johnson, John VI, 332
Johnson, John VI, 345
Johnson, John VI, 800
Johnson, John VI, 823
Johnson, John VI, 829
Johnson, John VI, 831
Johnson, John VI, 844
Johnson, John VI, 845
Johnson, John VI, 851
Johnson, John VI, 862
Johnson, John VI, 901
Johnson, John VI, 912
Johnson, John VI, 941
Johnson, John VI, 1015
Johnson, John A. III, 186
Johnson, John Bryan, Jr. VI, 322
Johnson, John Bryan, Jr. VI, 324
Johnson, John C. V, 255
Johnson, John C. VI, 941
Johnson, John Christopher V, 407
Johnson, John Edward V, 85
Johnson, John Edward V, 913
Johnson, John Edward V, 972
Johnson, John Edward V, 979
Johnson, John G. V, 83
Johnson, John G. V, 84
Johnson, John G. V, 85
Johnson, John G. V, 630
Johnson, John G. V, 774
Johnson, John G. V, 813
Johnson, John G. V, 972
Johnson, John Griffith V, 505
Johnson, John Griffith V, 506
Johnson, John Griffith V, 630
Johnson, John H. I, 909
Johnson, John H. I, 990
Johnson, John H. I, 999
Johnson, John H. IV, 683
Johnson, John H. IV, 749
Johnson, John H. IV, 765
Johnson, John H. IV, 828
Johnson, John H. IV, 970
Johnson, John H. IV, 1283
Johnson, John H. V, 254
Johnson, John H. V, 407
Johnson, John H. V, 408
Johnson, John H. V, 579
Johnson, John H. V, 687
Johnson, John Howard V, 70
Johnson, John Howard V, 83
Johnson, John Howard V, 85
Johnson, John Howard V, 574
Johnson, John Howard V, 579
Johnson, John J. V, 256
Johnson, John K. V, 83
Johnson, John K. V, 85
Johnson, John Kelley V, 979
Johnson, John Kelly V, 83
Johnson, John Kelly V, 85
Johnson, John Kelly V, 630
Johnson, John L. V, 506
Johnson, John Linch V, 505
Johnson, John Lynch V, 254
Johnson, John Lynd V, 254
Johnson, John Milton V, 505
Johnson, John Milton VI, 317
Johnson, John Milton VI, 326
Johnson, John Pleasants VI, 113
Johnson, John Reyneer II, 383
Johnson, John T. VI, 942
Johnson, John Van Pelt V, 255
Johnson, John W. IV, 708
Johnson, John W. IV, 728
Johnson, John W. IV, 729
Johnson, John W. V, 254
Johnson, John W. V, 255
Johnson, John W. V, 342
Johnson, John W. V, 343
Johnson, John W. V, 407
Johnson, John W. V, 408
Johnson, John W. V, 505
Johnson, John W. V, 687
Johnson, John W. VI, 326
Johnson, John W. VI, 829
Johnson, John Watkins VI, 252
Johnson, John Watkins VI, 255
Johnson, John William V, 687
Johnson, John Wm. V, 913
Johnson, John, Jr. I, 990
Johnson, John, Jr. IV, 729
Johnson, John, Jr. VI, 174
Johnson, John, Jr. VI, 186
Johnson, John, Jr. VI, 255
Johnson, John, Jr. VI, 318
Johnson, John, Jr. VI, 324
Johnson, John, Jr. VI, 325
Johnson, John, Jr. VI, 333
Johnson, John, Jr. VI, 829
Johnson, John, Jr. VI, 844
Johnson, John, Sr. VI, 186
Johnson, John, Sr. VI, 254
Johnson, John, Sr. VI, 319
Johnson, Johnl, Jr. VI, 185
Johnson, Joiakim VI, 69
Johnson, Joiakim VI, 72
Johnson, Jonah IV, 230
Johnson, Jonathan I, 357
Johnson, Jonathan I, 401
Johnson, Jonathan I, 402
Johnson, Jonathan I, 821
Johnson, Jonathan I, 977
Johnson, Jonathan I, 990
Johnson, Jonathan II, 625
Johnson, Jonathan IV, 42
Johnson, Jonathan IV, 217
Johnson, Jonathan IV, 229
Johnson, Jonathan IV, 230
Johnson, Jonathan IV, 242
Johnson, Jonathan IV, 310
Johnson, Jonathan IV, 969
Johnson, Jonathan IV, 1213
Johnson, Jonathan V, 84
Johnson, Jonathan V, 183
Johnson, Jonathan V, 253
Johnson, Jonathan V, 254
Johnson, Jonathan V, 844
Johnson, Jonathan V, 845
Johnson, Jonathan V, 852
Johnson, Jonathan V, 857
Johnson, Jonathan V, 883
Johnson, Jonathan VI, 185
Johnson, Jonathan VI, 252
Johnson, Jonathan VI, 308
Johnson, Jonathan VI, 317
Johnson, Jonathan VI, 319
Johnson, Jonathan VI, 325
Johnson, Jonathan VI, 327
Johnson, Jonathan Hadley V, 844
Johnson, Jonathan Hadley V, 845
Johnson, Jonathan, Jr. IV, 230
Johnson, Jones I, 722
Johnson, Jonothan V, 84
Johnson, Jordan V, 255
Johnson, Jos. VI, 256
Johnson, Joseph I, 857
Johnson, Joseph I, 888
Johnson, Joseph I, 977
Johnson, Joseph I, 990
Johnson, Joseph I, 1094
Johnson, Joseph II, 383
Johnson, Joseph II, 566
Johnson, Joseph II, 625
Johnson, Joseph II, 803
Johnson, Joseph II, 1006
Johnson, Joseph II, 1007
Johnson, Joseph III, 186
Johnson, Joseph III, 422
Johnson, Joseph IV, 828
Johnson, Joseph V, 83
Johnson, Joseph V, 84
Johnson, Joseph V, 85
Johnson, Joseph V, 236
Johnson, Joseph V, 252
Johnson, Joseph V, 253
Johnson, Joseph V, 254
Johnson, Joseph V, 255
Johnson, Joseph V, 265
Johnson, Joseph V, 305
Johnson, Joseph V, 505
Johnson, Joseph V, 506
Johnson, Joseph V, 630
Johnson, Joseph V, 631
Johnson, Joseph V, 1004
Johnson, Joseph VI, 69
Johnson, Joseph VI, 86
Johnson, Joseph VI, 137
Johnson, Joseph VI, 196
Johnson, Joseph VI, 245
Johnson, Joseph VI, 252
Johnson, Joseph VI, 255
Johnson, Joseph VI, 297
Johnson, Joseph VI, 300
Johnson, Joseph VI, 318
Johnson, Joseph VI, 321
Johnson, Joseph VI, 322
Johnson, Joseph VI, 323
Johnson, Joseph VI, 325
Johnson, Joseph VI, 326
Johnson, Joseph VI, 332
Johnson, Joseph VI, 352
Johnson, Joseph VI, 409
Johnson, Joseph VI, 861
Johnson, Joseph VI, 941
Johnson, Joseph A. V, 253
Johnson, Joseph A. V, 255
Johnson, Joseph A. V, 459
Johnson, Joseph Anthony V, 183
Johnson, Joseph Anthony V, 253
Johnson, Joseph Anthony V, 255
Johnson, Joseph B. II, 864
Johnson, Joseph Barclay II, 803
Johnson, Joseph Barclay II, 883
Johnson, Joseph C. II, 1007
Johnson, Joseph C. V, 73
Johnson, Joseph C. V, 83
Johnson, Joseph C. V, 84
Johnson, Joseph C. V, 85
Johnson, Joseph Clark V, 84
Johnson, Joseph G. IV, 828
Johnson, Joseph G. IV, 970
Johnson, Joseph G. IV, 1039
Johnson, Joseph H. IV, 828
Johnson, Joseph H. IV, 970
Johnson, Joseph H. IV, 1147
Johnson, Joseph H. IV, 1168
Johnson, Joseph John V, 253
Johnson, Joseph Marshall III, 187
Johnson, Joseph N. IV, 1168
Johnson, Joseph Newton V, 255
Johnson, Joseph R. V, 505
Johnson, Joseph R. V, 579
Johnson, Joseph R. V, 687
Johnson, Joseph T. I, 818
Johnson, Joseph T. I, 822
Johnson, Joseph T. I, 888
Johnson, Joseph Warner II, 883
Johnson, Joseph Warner II, 943
Johnson, Joseph, Jr. V, 505
Johnson, Joseph, Jr. VI, 70
Johnson, Joseph, Jr. VI, 326
Johnson, Joseph, Sr. VI, 70
Johnson, Joshau I, 785
Johnson, Joshua I, 401
Johnson, Joshua I, 505
Johnson, Joshua I, 543
Johnson, Joshua I, 554
Johnson, Joshua I, 555
Johnson, Joshua I, 811
Johnson, Joshua I, 822
Johnson, Joshua I, 857
Johnson, Joshua I, 887
Johnson, Joshua I, 888
Johnson, Joshua II, 382
Johnson, Joshua II, 383
Johnson, Joshua II, 566
Johnson, Joshua II, 642
Johnson, Joshua IV, 69
Johnson, Joshua IV, 195
Johnson, Joshua IV, 970
Johnson, Joshua V, 84
Johnson, Joshua V, 121
Johnson, Joshua V, 183
Johnson, Joshua VI, 119
Johnson, Joshua VI, 196
Johnson, Joshua VI, 390
Johnson, Joshua VI, 391
Johnson, Joshua VI, 409
Johnson, Joshua J. I, 822
Johnson, Joshua R. II, 883
Johnson, Joshua Rowland, Jr. II, 803
Johnson, Josiah I, 785
Johnson, Josiah I, 822
Johnson, Josiah II, 567
Johnson, Josiah II, 749
Johnson, Josiah II, 883
Johnson, Josiah VI, 69
Johnson, Joy Dilliston III, 186
Johnson, Judah VI, 1006
Johnson, Judith I, 773
Johnson, Judith I, 785
Johnson, Judith I, 822
Johnson, Judith I, 835
Johnson, Judith I, 977
Johnson, Judith I, 1033
Johnson, Judith IV, 217
Johnson, Judith IV, 229
Johnson, Judith IV, 230
Johnson, Judith IV, 242
Johnson, Judith IV, 310
Johnson, Judith IV, 828
Johnson, Judith IV, 850
Johnson, Judith V, 40
Johnson, Judith V, 83
Johnson, Judith V, 84
Johnson, Judith V, 253
Johnson, Judith V, 254
Johnson, Judith V, 490
Johnson, Judith V, 505
Johnson, Judith V, 506
Johnson, Judith V, 794
Johnson, Judith V, 913
Johnson, Judith V, 972
Johnson, Judith VI, 185
Johnson, Judith VI, 187
Johnson, Judith VI, 220
Johnson, Judith VI, 227
Johnson, Judith VI, 251
Johnson, Judith VI, 252
Johnson, Judith VI, 253
Johnson, Judith VI, 254
Johnson, Judith VI, 255
Johnson, Judith VI, 256
Johnson, Judith VI, 279
Johnson, Judith VI, 303
Johnson, Judith VI, 308
Johnson, Judith VI, 318
Johnson, Judith VI, 319
Johnson, Judith VI, 321
Johnson, Judith VI, 325
Johnson, Judith VI, 327
Johnson, Judith VI, 334
Johnson, Judith VI, 341
Johnson, Judith VI, 352
Johnson, Judith VI, 994
Johnson, Judith C. IV, 230
Johnson, Judith C. IV, 310
Johnson, Judith C. IV, 970
Johnson, Judith C. IV, 999
Johnson, Judith C. VI, 862
Johnson, Judith D. IV, 230
Johnson, Judith D. VI, 327
Johnson, Judith Douglas IV, 230
Johnson, Judith H. VI, 912
Johnson, Judith J. IV, 302
Johnson, Judith J. D. IV, 302
Johnson, Judy VI, 914
Johnson, Juleann V, 630
Johnson, Julia V, 914
Johnson, Julia Ann V, 254
Johnson, Julia Ann V, 630
Johnson, Julia Ann V, 972
Johnson, Julia Dean V, 913
Johnson, Julian V, 255
Johnson, Julian V, 262
Johnson, Julian V, 787
Johnson, Julian H. IV, 512
Johnson, Julian H. IV, 683
Johnson, Julian H. IV, 728
Johnson, Juliann IV, 728
Johnson, Juliann V, 253
Johnson, Juliann V, 506
Johnson, Juliann V, 630
Johnson, Juliann H. II, 700
Johnson, Juliet V, 226
Johnson, Juliet V, 255
Johnson, Juliett V, 299
Johnson, Juliett V, 306
Johnson, Julius Vestal I, 928
Johnson, July Ann V, 969
Johnson, July Ann V, 972
Johnson, Junius V, 343
Johnson, Junius V, 687
Johnson, Junius E. V, 687
Johnson, Jurusha VI, 325
Johnson, Katherine II, 383
Johnson, Kesiah V, 845
Johnson, Keziah II, 235
Johnson, Keziah III, 186
Johnson, Keziah V, 857
Johnson, Kitty V, 254
Johnson, Kitty Winston VI, 318
Johnson, Kitty Winston VI, 326
Johnson, Kitty Winstone V, 253
Johnson, Kitty Winstone V, 265
Johnson, Knoris VI, 71
Johnson, Knoriss VI, 71
Johnson, L. H. VI, 951
Johnson, L. V. VI, 321
Johnson, Laban VI, 70
Johnson, Laban VI, 71
Johnson, Laetitia II, 567
Johnson, Laetitia II, 749
Johnson, Lafayette VI, 827
Johnson, Lafayette VI, 942
Johnson, Lamont IV, 579
Johnson, Larkin V, 972
Johnson, Larkin Fauster V, 630
Johnson, Larkin Foster V, 972
Johnson, Laura V, 631
Johnson, Laura E. V, 913
Johnson, Laura W. III, 60
Johnson, Laurance II, 1006
Johnson, Lawrence II, 445
Johnson, Lawrence IV, 1323
Johnson, Lazarous VI, 45
Johnson, Lazarus VI, 16
Johnson, Lazarus VI, 70
Johnson, Lazarus VI, 71
Johnson, Lazarus VI, 78
Johnson, Lazarus VI, 112
Johnson, Lazarus VI, 113
Johnson, Lazaruss VI, 70
Johnson, Leah V, 255
Johnson, Leander IV, 1283
Johnson, Leander T. IV, 1283
Johnson, Leatitia II, 82
Johnson, Leatitia II, 87
Johnson, Leauraney VI, 829
Johnson, Ledy VI, 253
Johnson, Ledy VI, 279
Johnson, Lemuel VI, 70
Johnson, Lemuel VI, 317
Johnson, Lemuel VI, 325
Johnson, Lemuel VI, 896
Johnson, Lemuel VI, 1009
Johnson, Lemuel Anselm VI, 31
Johnson, Lemuel John VI, 70
Johnson, Leona IV, 1213
Johnson, Leonard V, 343
Johnson, Leslie V, 579
Johnson, Leslie Earl V, 579
Johnson, Leta V, 253
Johnson, Letie Hazletine I, 437
Johnson, Levi E. I, 888
Johnson, Levi Emory I, 857
Johnson, Levi M. V, 255
Johnson, Leviah D. IV, 1168
Johnson, Levina V, 220
Johnson, Levina VI, 843
Johnson, Lewis IV, 42
Johnson, Lewis V, 475
Johnson, Lewis V, 505
Johnson, Lewis V, 506
Johnson, Lewis V, 531
Johnson, Lewis V, 630
Johnson, Lewis V, 813
Johnson, Lewis VI, 318
Johnson, Lewis VI, 326
Johnson, Lewis Thatcher Stratton V, 630
Johnson, Lewis, Jr. V, 630
Johnson, Lida IV, 729
Johnson, Lida Judith IV, 230
Johnson, Lidia VI, 255
Johnson, Lidia VI, 319
Johnson, Lidia VI, 323
Johnson, Lidia VI, 333
Johnson, Lilbun VI, 301
Johnson, Lilburn VI, 318
Johnson, Lilburn VI, 319
Johnson, Lillbun VI, 302
Johnson, Lillbun VI, 325
Johnson, Lillbun VI, 327
Johnson, Lillian Maud V, 253
Johnson, Lindley IV, 1283
Johnson, Lindley H. I, 401
Johnson, Lindley H. I, 857
Johnson, Lindley H. IV, 1283
Johnson, Linton V, 255
Johnson, Livius A. IV, 1168
Johnson, Lizzie M. V, 256
Johnson, Lizzie T. V, 85
Johnson, Locky VI, 1012
Johnson, Lola V, 183
Johnson, Lorain D. IV, 230

hnson, Lorana VI, 254
hnson, Lorena V, 256
hnson, Lorena V, 343
hnson, Lorena H. V, 328
hnson, Lorinda V, 1004
hnson, Lottie J. V, 255
hnson, Louie I, 935
hnson, Louisa V, 80
hnson, Louisa V, 85
hnson, Louisa V, 255
hnson, Louisa V, 305
hnson, Louisa V, 407
hnson, Louisa V, 408
hnson, Louisa V, 447
hnson, Louisa Grace III, 186
hnson, Louise I, 635
hnson, Louissa Grace III, 186
hnson, Louiza I, 888
hnson, Louiza I, 895
hnson, Lovina VI, 67
hnson, Lovina VI, 71
hnson, Lucetta IV, 1278
hnson, Lucetta IV, 1283
hnson, Lucile IV, 1323
hnson, Lucinda VI, 316
hnson, Lucinda VI, 327
hnson, Lucinda VI, 344
hnson, Lucinda VI, 941
hnson, Lucinda H. VI, 1009
hnson, Lucretia IV, 338
hnson, Lucretia VI, 251
hnson, Lucy I, 1033
hnson, Lucy IV, 1167
hnson, Lucy IV, 1323
hnson, Lucy V, 616
hnson, Lucy VI, 186
hnson, Lucy VI, 253
hnson, Lucy VI, 256
hnson, Lucy VI, 260
hnson, Lucy VI, 275
hnson, Lucy VI, 277
hnson, Lucy VI, 321
hnson, Lucy VI, 322
hnson, Lucy VI, 327
hnson, Lucy VI, 800
hnson, Lucy VI, 829
hnson, Lucy VI, 941
hnson, Lucy VI, 945
hnson, Lucy A. VI, 867
hnson, Lucy A. P. VI, 807
hnson, Lucy B. V, 85
hnson, Lucy B. V, 913
hnson, Lucy B. V, 972
hnson, Lucy B. V, 979
hnson, Lucy B. VI, 829
hnson, Lucy D. IV, 1323
hnson, Lucy T. VI, 256
hnson, Lucy W. VI, 941
hnson, Luetta I, 928
hnson, Lunettie J. V, 631
hnson, Luraney VI, 843
hnson, Lutitia I, 764
hnson, Lututia I, 771
hnson, Lydea VI, 252
hnson, Lydea VI, 279
hnson, Lydia I, 357
hnson, Lydia I, 399
hnson, Lydia I, 401
hnson, Lydia I, 785
hnson, Lydia I, 821
hnson, Lydia I, 857
hnson, Lydia I, 888
hnson, Lydia I, 959
hnson, Lydia I, 965
hnson, Lydia I, 990
hnson, Lydia I, 1005
hnson, Lydia I, 1010
hnson, Lydia I, 1114
hnson, Lydia I, 1122
hnson, Lydia IV, 42
hnson, Lydia IV, 55
hnson, Lydia IV, 69
hnson, Lydia IV, 79
hnson, Lydia IV, 95
hnson, Lydia IV, 174
hnson, Lydia IV, 229
hnson, Lydia IV, 230
hnson, Lydia IV, 269
hnson, Lydia IV, 729
hnson, Lydia V, 31
hnson, Lydia V, 84
hnson, Lydia V, 85
hnson, Lydia V, 252
hnson, Lydia V, 254
hnson, Lydia V, 305
hnson, Lydia V, 479
hnson, Lydia V, 505
hnson, Lydia V, 506
hnson, Lydia V, 579
hnson, Lydia V, 617
hnson, Lydia V, 630
Johnson, Lydia V, 844
Johnson, Lydia V, 845
Johnson, Lydia V, 883
Johnson, Lydia V, 979
Johnson, Lydia VI, 70
Johnson, Lydia VI, 91
Johnson, Lydia VI, 250
Johnson, Lydia VI, 251
Johnson, Lydia VI, 252
Johnson, Lydia VI, 254
Johnson, Lydia VI, 317
Johnson, Lydia VI, 318
Johnson, Lydia VI, 319
Johnson, Lydia VI, 324
Johnson, Lydia VI, 325
Johnson, Lydia VI, 326
Johnson, Lydia VI, 334
Johnson, Lydia VI, 341
Johnson, Lydia VI, 390
Johnson, Lydia VI, 391
Johnson, Lydia VI, 409
Johnson, Lydia VI, 1001
Johnson, Lydia B. V, 506
Johnson, Lydia B. V, 972
Johnson, Lydia B. V, 979
Johnson, Lydia E. V, 51
Johnson, Lydia E. V, 85
Johnson, Lydia L. IV, 1147
Johnson, Lydia L. IV, 1168
Johnson, Lydia S. IV, 1168
Johnson, Lydia S. V, 490
Johnson, Lydia S. V, 506
Johnson, Lydia Susanna Nancy V, 254
Johnson, Lynch A. V, 255
Johnson, M. A. IV, 468
Johnson, M. Belle V, 631
Johnson, M. J. V, 253
Johnson, Macal VI, 186
Johnson, Mahala V, 85
Johnson, Mahala V, 93
Johnson, Mahala V, 211
Johnson, Mahala V, 225
Johnson, Mahala V, 253
Johnson, Mahala V, 459
Johnson, Mahala V, 631
Johnson, Mahala VI, 327
Johnson, Mahala C. V, 43
Johnson, Mahala C. V, 84
Johnson, Mahala C. V, 85
Johnson, Mahala I. J. V, 84
Johnson, Mahala I. J. V, 93
Johnson, Mahala J. V, 459
Johnson, Mahala S. VI, 823
Johnson, Mahalah C. V, 83
Johnson, Mahalah Jane I, 1085
Johnson, Mahalon IV, 1283
Johnson, Mahlon V, 225
Johnson, Mahlon V, 252
Johnson, Mahlon V, 253
Johnson, Mahlon V, 255
Johnson, Mahlon VI, 71
Johnson, Mahlon P. IV, 1283
Johnson, Malan VI, 71
Johnson, Malen V, 211
Johnson, Malinda IV, 495
Johnson, Malinda V, 248
Johnson, Malinda V, 255
Johnson, Malinda V, 459
Johnson, Malisant VI, 818
Johnson, Mannah Mariah V, 630
Johnson, Marcy II, 1006
Johnson, Margaret I, 505
Johnson, Margaret I, 531
Johnson, Margaret I, 534
Johnson, Margaret I, 550
Johnson, Margaret I, 554
Johnson, Margaret I, 555
Johnson, Margaret I, 822
Johnson, Margaret I, 857
Johnson, Margaret I, 858
Johnson, Margaret I, 888
Johnson, Margaret I, 889
Johnson, Margaret I, 890
Johnson, Margaret II, 566
Johnson, Margaret II, 793
Johnson, Margaret III, 167
Johnson, Margaret IV, 219
Johnson, Margaret IV, 229
Johnson, Margaret IV, 230
Johnson, Margaret IV, 805
Johnson, Margaret IV, 828
Johnson, Margaret IV, 1283
Johnson, Margaret V, 83
Johnson, Margaret V, 84
Johnson, Margaret V, 121
Johnson, Margaret V, 949
Johnson, Margaret V, 954
Johnson, Margaret VI, 185
Johnson, Margaret VI, 187
Johnson, Margaret VI, 220
Johnson, Margaret VI, 281
Johnson, Margaret VI, 286
Johnson, Margaret VI, 318
Johnson, Margaret A. V, 506
Johnson, Margaret A. V, 687
Johnson, Margaret Ann V, 505
Johnson, Margaret Ann V, 506
Johnson, Margaret Ann V, 630
Johnson, Margaret Ann V, 638
Johnson, Margaret Elisabeth I, 621
Johnson, Margaret H. V, 506
Johnson, Margaret H. H. III, 186
Johnson, Margaret M. I, 944
Johnson, Margaret R. IV, 230
Johnson, Margaret V. IV, 230
Johnson, Margery VI, 186
Johnson, Margret I, 785
Johnson, Maria I, 55
Johnson, Maria I, 81
Johnson, Maria III, 186
Johnson, Maria VI, 71
Johnson, Maria A. III, 186
Johnson, Maria E. V, 343
Johnson, Mariah I, 401
Johnson, Mariam I, 785
Johnson, Mariam I, 857
Johnson, Mariam I, 888
Johnson, Mariam M. I, 818
Johnson, Mariam M. I, 822
Johnson, Mariam M. I, 888
Johnson, Mariam M. I, 903
Johnson, Marianna I, 944
Johnson, Marianna IV, 967
Johnson, Marianna H. IV, 970
Johnson, Martha I, 785
Johnson, Martha I, 821
Johnson, Martha I, 832
Johnson, Martha I, 990
Johnson, Martha I, 997
Johnson, Martha I, 1155
Johnson, Martha II, 383
Johnson, Martha II, 566
Johnson, Martha II, 567
Johnson, Martha II, 647
Johnson, Martha II, 669
Johnson, Martha II, 883
Johnson, Martha II, 920
Johnson, Martha II, 1006
Johnson, Martha III, 422
Johnson, Martha IV, 338
Johnson, Martha IV, 354
Johnson, Martha IV, 692
Johnson, Martha IV, 728
Johnson, Martha IV, 729
Johnson, Martha IV, 818
Johnson, Martha IV, 828
Johnson, Martha IV, 850
Johnson, Martha IV, 864
Johnson, Martha IV, 875
Johnson, Martha IV, 926
Johnson, Martha IV, 958
Johnson, Martha IV, 970
Johnson, Martha V, 84
Johnson, Martha V, 240
Johnson, Martha V, 253
Johnson, Martha V, 254
Johnson, Martha V, 292
Johnson, Martha V, 505
Johnson, Martha V, 506
Johnson, Martha V, 630
Johnson, Martha V, 883
Johnson, Martha V, 972
Johnson, Martha VI, 45
Johnson, Martha VI, 56
Johnson, Martha VI, 58
Johnson, Martha VI, 69
Johnson, Martha VI, 70
Johnson, Martha VI, 71
Johnson, Martha VI, 81
Johnson, Martha VI, 91
Johnson, Martha VI, 137
Johnson, Martha VI, 185
Johnson, Martha VI, 186
Johnson, Martha VI, 187
Johnson, Martha VI, 211
Johnson, Martha VI, 220
Johnson, Martha VI, 244
Johnson, Martha VI, 251
Johnson, Martha VI, 252
Johnson, Martha VI, 253
Johnson, Martha VI, 255
Johnson, Martha VI, 256
Johnson, Martha VI, 274
Johnson, Martha VI, 300
Johnson, Martha VI, 317
Johnson, Martha VI, 318
Johnson, Martha VI, 319
Johnson, Martha VI, 322
Johnson, Martha VI, 323
Johnson, Martha VI, 325
Johnson, Martha VI, 326
Johnson, Martha VI, 825
Johnson, Martha VI, 829
Johnson, Martha VI, 851
Johnson, Martha VI, 855
Johnson, Martha A. I, 212
Johnson, Martha A. V, 183
Johnson, Martha A. V, 255
Johnson, Martha A. V, 343
Johnson, Martha A. V, 1004
Johnson, Martha A. VI, 92
Johnson, Martha A. VI, 830
Johnson, Martha Ann II, 382
Johnson, Martha Ann V, 253
Johnson, Martha Ann V, 254
Johnson, Martha Ann V, 630
Johnson, Martha Ann V, 648
Johnson, Martha C. VI, 69
Johnson, Martha C. VI, 81
Johnson, Martha G. IV, 828
Johnson, Martha G. IV, 970
Johnson, Martha H. V, 1004
Johnson, Martha Hale V, 85
Johnson, Martha Jane V, 954
Johnson, Martha Leone V, 318
Johnson, Martha Leone V, 342
Johnson, Martha M. V, 83
Johnson, Martha M. V, 90
Johnson, Martha Mary V, 83
Johnson, Martha P. VI, 942
Johnson, Martha S. V, 83
Johnson, Martha, Jr. II, 566
Johnson, Marticia E. I, 888
Johnson, Martin VI, 886
Johnson, Martin VI, 914
Johnson, Martin VI, 945
Johnson, Martin VI, 1006
Johnson, Martitia I, 822
Johnson, Martitia E. I, 822
Johnson, Mary I, 357
Johnson, Mary I, 399
Johnson, Mary I, 401
Johnson, Mary I, 437
Johnson, Mary I, 505
Johnson, Mary I, 540
Johnson, Mary I, 543
Johnson, Mary I, 545
Johnson, Mary I, 555
Johnson, Mary I, 722
Johnson, Mary I, 785
Johnson, Mary I, 812
Johnson, Mary I, 820
Johnson, Mary I, 821
Johnson, Mary I, 822
Johnson, Mary I, 857
Johnson, Mary I, 858
Johnson, Mary I, 887
Johnson, Mary I, 888
Johnson, Mary I, 904
Johnson, Mary I, 928
Johnson, Mary I, 977
Johnson, Mary I, 990
Johnson, Mary I, 1005
Johnson, Mary I, 1061
Johnson, Mary I, 1085
Johnson, Mary II, 82
Johnson, Mary II, 92
Johnson, Mary II, 235
Johnson, Mary II, 245
Johnson, Mary II, 311
Johnson, Mary II, 383
Johnson, Mary II, 445
Johnson, Mary II, 567
Johnson, Mary II, 709
Johnson, Mary II, 749
Johnson, Mary II, 792
Johnson, Mary II, 803
Johnson, Mary II, 883
Johnson, Mary II, 921
Johnson, Mary II, 968
Johnson, Mary II, 1006
Johnson, Mary III, 186
Johnson, Mary III, 187
Johnson, Mary III, 273
Johnson, Mary III, 422
Johnson, Mary IV, 229
Johnson, Mary IV, 230
Johnson, Mary IV, 705
Johnson, Mary IV, 718
Johnson, Mary IV, 728
Johnson, Mary IV, 729
Johnson, Mary IV, 828
Johnson, Mary IV, 955
Johnson, Mary IV, 970
Johnson, Mary IV, 1283
Johnson, Mary V, 40
Johnson, Mary V, 84
Johnson, Mary V, 85
Johnson, Mary V, 183
Johnson, Mary V, 227
Johnson, Mary V, 228
Johnson, Mary V, 230
Johnson, Mary V, 241
Johnson, Mary V, 252
Johnson, Mary V, 253
Johnson, Mary V, 254
Johnson, Mary V, 255
Johnson, Mary V, 256
Johnson, Mary V, 260
Johnson, Mary V, 287
Johnson, Mary V, 324
Johnson, Mary V, 342
Johnson, Mary V, 343
Johnson, Mary V, 407
Johnson, Mary V, 408
Johnson, Mary V, 459
Johnson, Mary V, 475
Johnson, Mary V, 490
Johnson, Mary V, 505
Johnson, Mary V, 506
Johnson, Mary V, 579
Johnson, Mary V, 616
Johnson, Mary V, 621
Johnson, Mary V, 625
Johnson, Mary V, 630
Johnson, Mary V, 631
Johnson, Mary V, 774
Johnson, Mary V, 787
Johnson, Mary V, 794
Johnson, Mary V, 799
Johnson, Mary V, 804
Johnson, Mary V, 813
Johnson, Mary V, 816
Johnson, Mary V, 844
Johnson, Mary V, 845
Johnson, Mary V, 883
Johnson, Mary V, 913
Johnson, Mary V, 952
Johnson, Mary V, 954
Johnson, Mary VI, 11
Johnson, Mary VI, 45
Johnson, Mary VI, 58
Johnson, Mary VI, 69
Johnson, Mary VI, 70
Johnson, Mary VI, 71
Johnson, Mary VI, 90
Johnson, Mary VI, 91
Johnson, Mary VI, 112
Johnson, Mary VI, 113
Johnson, Mary VI, 119
Johnson, Mary VI, 171
Johnson, Mary VI, 185
Johnson, Mary VI, 187
Johnson, Mary VI, 196
Johnson, Mary VI, 220
Johnson, Mary VI, 242
Johnson, Mary VI, 244
Johnson, Mary VI, 251
Johnson, Mary VI, 252
Johnson, Mary VI, 253
Johnson, Mary VI, 254
Johnson, Mary VI, 255
Johnson, Mary VI, 256
Johnson, Mary VI, 274
Johnson, Mary VI, 276
Johnson, Mary VI, 286
Johnson, Mary VI, 299
Johnson, Mary VI, 315
Johnson, Mary VI, 316
Johnson, Mary VI, 317
Johnson, Mary VI, 319
Johnson, Mary VI, 320
Johnson, Mary VI, 321
Johnson, Mary VI, 322
Johnson, Mary VI, 323
Johnson, Mary VI, 324
Johnson, Mary VI, 331
Johnson, Mary VI, 333
Johnson, Mary VI, 342
Johnson, Mary VI, 343
Johnson, Mary VI, 351
Johnson, Mary VI, 352
Johnson, Mary VI, 375
Johnson, Mary VI, 409
Johnson, Mary VI, 808
Johnson, Mary VI, 829
Johnson, Mary VI, 863
Johnson, Mary VI, 903
Johnson, Mary VI, 941
Johnson, Mary VI, 961
Johnson, Mary A. I, 944
Johnson, Mary A. V, 579
Johnson, Mary A. V, 971
Johnson, Mary A. V, 972
Johnson, Mary A. VI, 817
Johnson, Mary Alice I, 944
Johnson, Mary Amanda V, 343
Johnson, Mary Ann I, 822
Johnson, Mary Ann III, 56
Johnson, Mary Ann IV, 34
Johnson, Mary Ann IV, 42
Johnson, Mary Ann IV, 230

Johnson, Mary Ann IV, 310
Johnson, Mary Ann V, 631
Johnson, Mary Ann V, 787
Johnson, Mary Ann V, 883
Johnson, Mary Ann V, 972
Johnson, Mary Ann VI, 318
Johnson, Mary Ann VI, 319
Johnson, Mary Ann VI, 327
Johnson, Mary Anna V, 579
Johnson, Mary B. V, 83
Johnson, Mary B. V, 85
Johnson, Mary B. V, 505
Johnson, Mary B. V, 506
Johnson, Mary B. V, 813
Johnson, Mary B. VI, 214
Johnson, Mary Bailey VI, 187
Johnson, Mary Bailey VI, 215
Johnson, Mary Bailey VI, 274
Johnson, Mary C. II, 883
Johnson, Mary C. V, 85
Johnson, Mary C. V, 183
Johnson, Mary C. V, 231
Johnson, Mary C. V, 255
Johnson, Mary C. V, 343
Johnson, Mary C. V, 451
Johnson, Mary C. V, 774
Johnson, Mary C. V, 913
Johnson, Mary Catharine Price V, 687
Johnson, Mary Cooper II, 803
Johnson, Mary Cordelia V, 253
Johnson, Mary E. V, 183
Johnson, Mary E. V, 343
Johnson, Mary E. V, 630
Johnson, Mary E. V, 972
Johnson, Mary E. VI, 942
Johnson, Mary E. VI, 951
Johnson, Mary Eliza I, 990
Johnson, Mary Elizabeth V, 687
Johnson, Mary Elizabeth VI, 942
Johnson, Mary Evans V, 630
Johnson, Mary F. VI, 802
Johnson, Mary G. V, 687
Johnson, Mary G. VI, 327
Johnson, Mary Hunnicutt VI, 113
Johnson, Mary J. I, 984
Johnson, Mary J. I, 990
Johnson, Mary J. II, 883
Johnson, Mary J. II, 943
Johnson, Mary Jane I, 619
Johnson, Mary Jane V, 237
Johnson, Mary Jane V, 255
Johnson, Mary K. V, 913
Johnson, Mary K. V, 914
Johnson, Mary K. V, 940
Johnson, Mary L. III, 83
Johnson, Mary L. VI, 829
Johnson, Mary M. V, 407
Johnson, Mary M. V, 409
Johnson, Mary Mildred V, 255
Johnson, Mary Mildred V, 407
Johnson, Mary Molly VI, 317
Johnson, Mary P. V, 85
Johnson, Mary P. V, 972
Johnson, Mary P. V, 977
Johnson, Mary R. VI, 409
Johnson, Mary S. V, 85
Johnson, Mary S. V, 913
Johnson, Mary T. II, 843
Johnson, Mary T. II, 883
Johnson, Mary T. IV, 310
Johnson, Mary T. VI, 196
Johnson, Mary Taylor V, 913
Johnson, Mary V. I, 990
Johnson, Mary V. IV, 828
Johnson, Mary V. IV, 970
Johnson, Mary V. V, 913
Johnson, Mary V. VI, 844
Johnson, Mary Viva II, 968
Johnson, Mary W. II, 883
Johnson, Mary, Jr. VI, 70
Johnson, Mary, Sr. IV, 828
Johnson, Mary, Sr. VI, 70
Johnson, Mary, Sr. VI, 71
Johnson, Maryanna I, 944
Johnson, Massey VI, 164
Johnson, Massey VI, 166
Johnson, Massey VI, 185
Johnson, Massey VI, 255
Johnson, Matilda I, 1085
Johnson, Matilda IV, 728
Johnson, Matilda V, 255
Johnson, Matilda V, 256
Johnson, Matilda V, 263
Johnson, Matilda VI, 301
Johnson, Matilda VI, 316
Johnson, Matilda VI, 326
Johnson, Matilda VI, 494
Johnson, Matilda VI, 543
Johnson, Matilda VI, 641
Johnson, Matilda VI, 687
Johnson, Matilda Ann IV, 729
Johnson, Matilda M. IV, 810
Johnson, Matilda M. IV, 828
Johnson, Matilda Polly VI, 317
Johnson, Matthew W. IV, 479
Johnson, Maude V, 1004
Johnson, May IV, 1283
Johnson, May V, 256
Johnson, Mehala Jinnet V, 83
Johnson, Melissa I, 990
Johnson, Melissa I, 991
Johnson, Melissa V, 255
Johnson, Melissa VI, 71
Johnson, Melissa Johnson VI, 71
Johnson, Melly V, 254
Johnson, Melvina V, 254
Johnson, Melvina V, 630
Johnson, Mercy II, 830
Johnson, Mercy II, 883
Johnson, Mercy II, 1007
Johnson, Mercy K. II, 883
Johnson, Meriah VI, 299
Johnson, Micah VI, 186
Johnson, Micah VI, 187
Johnson, Micaja V, 254
Johnson, Micajah IV, 302
Johnson, Micajah IV, 310
Johnson, Micajah V, 31
Johnson, Micajah V, 63
Johnson, Micajah V, 65
Johnson, Micajah V, 83
Johnson, Micajah V, 84
Johnson, Micajah V, 85
Johnson, Micajah V, 90
Johnson, Micajah V, 107
Johnson, Micajah V, 253
Johnson, Micajah V, 254
Johnson, Micajah V, 505
Johnson, Micajah V, 570
Johnson, Micajah V, 579
Johnson, Micajah V, 630
Johnson, Micajah V, 971
Johnson, Micajah VI, 187
Johnson, Micajah VI, 188
Johnson, Micajah VI, 317
Johnson, Micajah VI, 318
Johnson, Micajah VI, 322
Johnson, Micajah VI, 324
Johnson, Micajah VI, 325
Johnson, Micajah VI, 332
Johnson, Micajah VI, 829
Johnson, Micajah D. V, 85
Johnson, Micajah D. V, 630
Johnson, Micajah T. IV, 230
Johnson, Micajah T. IV, 310
Johnson, Micajah T. IV, 970
Johnson, Micajah T. VI, 185
Johnson, Micajah T. VI, 187
Johnson, Micajah T. VI, 195
Johnson, Micajah T. VI, 327
Johnson, Micajah Terrel VI, 316
Johnson, Micajah Terrell VI, 319
Johnson, Michael V, 253
Johnson, Michal V, 255
Johnson, Michal VI, 131
Johnson, Michal VI, 137
Johnson, Michel VI, 137
Johnson, Mildred I, 857
Johnson, Mildred II, 134
Johnson, Mildred IV, 1323
Johnson, Mildred IV, 1342
Johnson, Mildred V, 118
Johnson, Mildred V, 252
Johnson, Mildred V, 253
Johnson, Mildred V, 254
Johnson, Mildred V, 505
Johnson, Mildred V, 630
Johnson, Mildred VI, 187
Johnson, Mildred VI, 252
Johnson, Mildred VI, 253
Johnson, Mildred VI, 260
Johnson, Mildred VI, 316
Johnson, Mildred VI, 318
Johnson, Mildred VI, 319
Johnson, Mildred VI, 325
Johnson, Mildred VI, 327
Johnson, Mildred A. IV, 1323
Johnson, Mildred C. IV, 1323
Johnson, Mildred Tyree IV, 230
Johnson, Mildred W. VI, 942
Johnson, Milisant VI, 818
Johnson, Milisant VI, 827
Johnson, Miller V, 306
Johnson, Miller VI, 409
Johnson, Milley V, 342
Johnson, Milley V, 505
Johnson, Milley VI, 252
Johnson, Milley VI, 255
Johnson, Milley VI, 317
Johnson, Milley VI, 322
Johnson, Milley VI, 323
Johnson, Milley VI, 324
Johnson, Milley VI, 325
Johnson, Milley VI, 326
Johnson, Milley VI, 332
Johnson, Millicent VI, 245
Johnson, Millicent VI, 251
Johnson, Millicent VI, 255
Johnson, Millicent VI, 345
Johnson, Millicent VI, 851
Johnson, Millie I, 337
Johnson, Milly IV, 728
Johnson, Milly IV, 729
Johnson, Milly IV, 765
Johnson, Milly V, 84
Johnson, Milly V, 252
Johnson, Milly V, 253
Johnson, Milly V, 254
Johnson, Milly V, 292
Johnson, Milly V, 407
Johnson, Milly V, 434
Johnson, Milly V, 505
Johnson, Milly VI, 317
Johnson, Milly VI, 318
Johnson, Milly VI, 322
Johnson, Milly VI, 323
Johnson, Milly VI, 324
Johnson, Milly VI, 326
Johnson, Milly VI, 333
Johnson, Milly VI, 829
Johnson, Milly VI, 941
Johnson, Milly W. V, 255
Johnson, Milly W. V, 263
Johnson, Milo V, 883
Johnson, Milton B. IV, 230
Johnson, Miner VI, 318
Johnson, Minerva V, 68
Johnson, Minerva V, 85
Johnson, Minerva V, 306
Johnson, Minerva I. V, 579
Johnson, Minerva Isabel V, 687
Johnson, Minnie V, 408
Johnson, Minnie B. V, 256
Johnson, Minnie Smith V, 687
Johnson, Minor VI, 327
Johnson, Miriam I, 505
Johnson, Miriam I, 822
Johnson, Miriam I, 858
Johnson, Miriam I, 965
Johnson, Miriam M. I, 822
Johnson, Missouri L. IV, 970
Johnson, Missouri L. IV, 971
Johnson, Molissa VI, 942
Johnson, Molly VI, 173
Johnson, Molly VI, 174
Johnson, Molly VI, 185
Johnson, Molly VI, 299
Johnson, Molly VI, 322
Johnson, Molly VI, 332
Johnson, Molly VI, 343
Johnson, Moorman I, 1033
Johnson, Moorman V, 84
Johnson, Moorman V, 252
Johnson, Moorman V, 253
Johnson, Moorman V, 305
Johnson, Moorman VI, 254
Johnson, Moorman VI, 255
Johnson, Moorman VI, 317
Johnson, Moorman VI, 321
Johnson, Moorman VI, 322
Johnson, Moorman VI, 323
Johnson, Moorman VI, 324
Johnson, Moorman VI, 325
Johnson, Moorman VI, 332
Johnson, Moorman VI, 829
Johnson, Moorman VI, 941
Johnson, Mordecai III, 186
Johnson, Moreman V, 505
Johnson, Moreman VI, 252
Johnson, Morgan I, 912
Johnson, Morgan I, 913
Johnson, Morman V, 254
Johnson, Morris L. V, 913
Johnson, Morris L. V, 914
Johnson, Morris Lewis V, 913
Johnson, Moses I, 505
Johnson, Moses I, 785
Johnson, Moses I, 858
Johnson, Mourin VI, 316
Johnson, Mourning IV, 728
Johnson, Mourning VI, 324
Johnson, Mourning VI, 343
Johnson, Mourning VI, 1005
Johnson, Mrs. ??? VI, 11
Johnson, Mrs. E. V, 687
Johnson, Mrs. Joseph VI, 12
Johnson, Myra V, 687
Johnson, Myra V, 705
Johnson, Myron Roy IV, 413
Johnson, N. IV, 468
Johnson, N. VI, 825
Johnson, Nancey VI, 1006
Johnson, Nancie V, 631
Johnson, Nancy V, 84
Johnson, Nancy V, 223
Johnson, Nancy V, 252
Johnson, Nancy V, 253
Johnson, Nancy V, 254
Johnson, Nancy V, 255
Johnson, Nancy V, 256
Johnson, Nancy V, 266
Johnson, Nancy V, 505
Johnson, Nancy V, 630
Johnson, Nancy V, 787
Johnson, Nancy V, 792
Johnson, Nancy V, 1004
Johnson, Nancy VI, 16
Johnson, Nancy VI, 70
Johnson, Nancy VI, 113
Johnson, Nancy VI, 187
Johnson, Nancy VI, 250
Johnson, Nancy VI, 252
Johnson, Nancy VI, 255
Johnson, Nancy VI, 256
Johnson, Nancy VI, 299
Johnson, Nancy VI, 301
Johnson, Nancy VI, 305
Johnson, Nancy VI, 317
Johnson, Nancy VI, 318
Johnson, Nancy VI, 319
Johnson, Nancy VI, 320
Johnson, Nancy VI, 325
Johnson, Nancy VI, 326
Johnson, Nancy VI, 333
Johnson, Nancy VI, 334
Johnson, Nancy VI, 345
Johnson, Nancy VI, 352
Johnson, Nancy VI, 356
Johnson, Nancy VI, 829
Johnson, Nancy VI, 851
Johnson, Nancy VI, 896
Johnson, Nancy VI, 941
Johnson, Nancy VI, 942
Johnson, Nancy VI, 947
Johnson, Nancy A. V, 256
Johnson, Nancy A. V, 1004
Johnson, Nancy A. VI, 69
Johnson, Nancy A. VI, 86
Johnson, Nancy A. VI, 91
Johnson, Nancy B. VI, 824
Johnson, Nancy G. V, 630
Johnson, Nancy G. V, 644
Johnson, Nancy R. VI, 54
Johnson, Nancy R. VI, 69
Johnson, Nancy R. VI, 72
Johnson, Nannie I, 928
Johnson, Nannie Josie V, 774
Johnson, Nanthan VI, 54
Johnson, Naomi I, 505
Johnson, Naomi I, 822
Johnson, Naomi I, 839
Johnson, Nathan I, 722
Johnson, Nathan I, 785
Johnson, Nathan I, 812
Johnson, Nathan I, 822
Johnson, Nathan I, 857
Johnson, Nathan I, 858
Johnson, Nathan I, 887
Johnson, Nathan I, 888
Johnson, Nathan IV, 729
Johnson, Nathan VI, 69
Johnson, Nathan VI, 71
Johnson, Nathan VI, 72
Johnson, Nathan VI, 167
Johnson, Nathan VI, 173
Johnson, Nathan VI, 185
Johnson, Nathan VI, 186
Johnson, Nathan VI, 187
Johnson, Nathan VI, 220
Johnson, Nathan W. IV, 495
Johnson, Nellie V, 631
Johnson, Nellie V, 913
Johnson, Nellie V, 940
Johnson, Nellie Johnson Watts V, 914
Johnson, Nelson IV, 1283
Johnson, Neva IV, 230
Johnson, Newby VI, 308
Johnson, Newby VI, 324
Johnson, Newby VI, 326
Johnson, Newby VI, 327
Johnson, Nicah VI, 186
Johnson, Nicholas V, 787
Johnson, Nicholas VI, 244
Johnson, Nicholas VI, 252
Johnson, Nicholas VI, 255
Johnson, Nicholas VI, 308
Johnson, Nicholas VI, 318
Johnson, Nicholas VI, 322
Johnson, Nicholas VI, 323
Johnson, Nicholas VI, 326
Johnson, Nicholas VI, 327
Johnson, Nicholas VI, 351
Johnson, Nicholas VI, 352
Johnson, Nicholas VI, 896
Johnson, Nicholas Betty VI, 31
Johnson, Nona E. V, 256
Johnson, Nora Rebecca IV, 103
Johnson, Norborn M. VI, 910
Johnson, Noris VI, 71
Johnson, Norris VI, 69
Johnson, Norris VI, 71
Johnson, Norris VI, 137
Johnson, Notra I, 619
Johnson, Notra I, 944
Johnson, Notra M. I, 635
Johnson, Notra M. I, 928
Johnson, Notra M. I, 944
Johnson, Nubey VI, 317
Johnson, Obadiah IV, 151
Johnson, Obediah IV, 151
Johnson, Obediah VI, 318
Johnson, Obediah VI, 325
Johnson, Obidiah VI, 299
Johnson, Olin M. IV, 1039
Johnson, Olive V. IV, 230
Johnson, Oliver V, 630
Johnson, Oliver H. V, 408
Johnson, Ora Anna V, 505
Johnson, Orpa V, 255
Johnson, Orpah V, 343
Johnson, Orpha V, 255
Johnson, Orpha V, 459
Johnson, Orpha V, 774
Johnson, Orville IV, 1238
Johnson, Orville C. IV, 1238
Johnson, Overton V, 254
Johnson, Overton V, 972
Johnson, Overton A. V, 85
Johnson, Pamela V, 253
Johnson, Pamela VI, 941
Johnson, Pamelia V, 252
Johnson, Patrick VI, 867
Johnson, Patsey VI, 252
Johnson, Patsey VI, 318
Johnson, Patsy VI, 964
Johnson, Patty VI, 256
Johnson, Patty VI, 274
Johnson, Patty VI, 276
Johnson, Paulina P. V, 254
Johnson, Paulina P. V, 505
Johnson, Paulina P. V, 623
Johnson, Paulina P. V, 630
Johnson, Pauline V, 1004
Johnson, Payton V, 254
Johnson, Pearl M. V, 21
Johnson, Peggy VI, 829
Johnson, Penelepy VI, 253
Johnson, Penelope I, 923
Johnson, Penelope IV, 821
Johnson, Penelope IV, 828
Johnson, Penelope IV, 970
Johnson, Penelope IV, 1147
Johnson, Penelope IV, 1148
Johnson, Penelope IV, 1168
Johnson, Penelope V, 60
Johnson, Penelope V, 83
Johnson, Penelope V, 84
Johnson, Penelope V, 118
Johnson, Penelope V, 225
Johnson, Penelope V, 239
Johnson, Penelope V, 252
Johnson, Penelope V, 253
Johnson, Penelope V, 254
Johnson, Penelope V, 255
Johnson, Penelope V, 260
Johnson, Penelope VI, 251
Johnson, Penelope VI, 252
Johnson, Penelope VI, 256
Johnson, Penelope VI, 286
Johnson, Penelope VI, 318
Johnson, Penelope VI, 319
Johnson, Penelope VI, 321
Johnson, Penelope VI, 325
Johnson, Penelope VI, 328
Johnson, Penelope VI, 352
Johnson, Penelope VI, 353
Johnson, Penelope C. V, 253
Johnson, Penninah I, 325
Johnson, Penniniah I, 329
Johnson, Permillia VI, 865
Johnson, Peter IV, 1283
Johnson, Peter V, 255
Johnson, Peter V, 631
Johnson, Peyton V, 255
Johnson, Peyton VI, 829
Johnson, Pharaby VI, 69
Johnson, Pharaby VI, 71
Johnson, Phebe I, 722
Johnson, Phebe I, 785
Johnson, Phebe I, 857
Johnson, Phebe I, 858
Johnson, Phebe I, 888
Johnson, Phebe I, 890

Johnson, Phebe III, 125
Johnson, Phebe III, 187
Johnson, Phebe III, 422
Johnson, Phebe IV, 40
Johnson, Phebe IV, 42
Johnson, Phebe V, 83
Johnson, Phebe V, 84
Johnson, Phebe V, 85
Johnson, Phebe V, 255
Johnson, Phebe V, 499
Johnson, Phebe V, 505
Johnson, Phebe V, 506
Johnson, Phebe V, 630
Johnson, Phebe VI, 969
Johnson, Phebe Jane III, 63
Johnson, Phebe Jane III, 186
Johnson, Pherebe IV, 728
Johnson, Pheriba IV, 1167
Johnson, Pheriba VI, 70
Johnson, Phila IV, 1167
Johnson, Phila IV, 1168
Johnson, Philia Ann IV, 1168
Johnson, Philip IV, 728
Johnson, Philip VI, 829
Johnson, Philip VI, 867
Johnson, Phillip I, 822
Johnson, Phillip I, 909
Johnson, Phillis Louise I, 635
Johnson, Pleasant IV, 1213
Johnson, Pleasant IV, 1238
Johnson, Pleasant V, 84
Johnson, Pleasant V, 254
Johnson, Pleasant V, 505
Johnson, Pleasant V, 630
Johnson, Pleasant V, 883
Johnson, Pleasant VI, 298
Johnson, Pleasant VI, 317
Johnson, Pleasant VI, 323
Johnson, Pleasant VI, 325
Johnson, Pleasant VI, 327
Johnson, Pleasant VI, 334
Johnson, Pleasant VI, 829
Johnson, Pleasant Irvin V, 407
Johnson, Pleasant T. IV, 969
Johnson, Pleasant T. IV, 970
Johnson, Pleasant T. IV, 1213
Johnson, Pleasant T. IV, 1238
Johnson, Pleasants VI, 252
Johnson, Pleasants VI, 255
Johnson, Polly I, 888
Johnson, Polly V, 84
Johnson, Polly V, 85
Johnson, Polly V, 254
Johnson, Polly V, 305
Johnson, Polly V, 307
Johnson, Polly V, 343
Johnson, Polly V, 407
Johnson, Polly VI, 59
Johnson, Polly VI, 302
Johnson, Polly VI, 316
Johnson, Polly VI, 317
Johnson, Polly VI, 318
Johnson, Polly VI, 325
Johnson, Polly VI, 326
Johnson, Polly VI, 327
Johnson, Polly VI, 810
Johnson, Polly VI, 829
Johnson, Polly VI, 847
Johnson, Polly VI, 862
Johnson, Polly VI, 870
Johnson, Polly VI, 941
Johnson, Polly VI, 995
Johnson, Polly VI, 1008
Johnson, Polly Sally V, 84
Johnson, Priscilla I, 822
Johnson, Priscilla I, 909
Johnson, Priscilla II, 205
Johnson, Priscilla II, 235
Johnson, Priscilla II, 237
Johnson, Priscilla II, 240
Johnson, Priscilla III, 186
Johnson, Priscilla III, 344
Johnson, Priscilla V, 774
Johnson, Priscilla VI, 86
Johnson, Priscilla Sheperd VI, 71
Johnson, Prisilla II, 235
Johnson, Prudence I, 785
Johnson, Prusanna I, 990
Johnson, R. W. VI, 865
Johnson, Rachel I, 401
Johnson, Rachel I, 505
Johnson, Rachel I, 551
Johnson, Rachel I, 555
Johnson, Rachel I, 606
Johnson, Rachel I, 785
Johnson, Rachel I, 858
Johnson, Rachel I, 965
Johnson, Rachel I, 990
Johnson, Rachel I, 1010
Johnson, Rachel I, 1012
Johnson, Rachel II, 382
Johnson, Rachel II, 794
Johnson, Rachel II, 862
Johnson, Rachel II, 883
Johnson, Rachel II, 1006
Johnson, Rachel IV, 42
Johnson, Rachel IV, 338
Johnson, Rachel IV, 413
Johnson, Rachel IV, 828
Johnson, Rachel IV, 970
Johnson, Rachel V, 84
Johnson, Rachel V, 85
Johnson, Rachel V, 228
Johnson, Rachel V, 241
Johnson, Rachel V, 252
Johnson, Rachel V, 253
Johnson, Rachel V, 254
Johnson, Rachel V, 255
Johnson, Rachel V, 260
Johnson, Rachel V, 278
Johnson, Rachel V, 342
Johnson, Rachel V, 343
Johnson, Rachel V, 505
Johnson, Rachel V, 506
Johnson, Rachel V, 526
Johnson, Rachel V, 531
Johnson, Rachel V, 630
Johnson, Rachel VI, 187
Johnson, Rachel VI, 245
Johnson, Rachel VI, 252
Johnson, Rachel VI, 255
Johnson, Rachel VI, 316
Johnson, Rachel VI, 317
Johnson, Rachel VI, 319
Johnson, Rachel VI, 321
Johnson, Rachel VI, 322
Johnson, Rachel VI, 323
Johnson, Rachel VI, 324
Johnson, Rachel VI, 325
Johnson, Rachel VI, 332
Johnson, Rachel VI, 333
Johnson, Rachel VI, 334
Johnson, Rachel VI, 352
Johnson, Rachel VI, 409
Johnson, Rachel VI, 669
Johnson, Rachel VI, 707
Johnson, Rachel VI, 840
Johnson, Rachel A. V, 83
Johnson, Rachel A. V, 84
Johnson, Rachel A. V, 506
Johnson, Rachel B. V, 84
Johnson, Rachel Ballard V, 83
Johnson, Rachel Reneer II, 383
Johnson, Ralph V, 675
Johnson, Ralph V, 687
Johnson, Ralph V, 688
Johnson, Raymond A. V, 256
Johnson, Reah V, 774
Johnson, Rebecca I, 822
Johnson, Rebecca I, 888
Johnson, Rebecca I, 965
Johnson, Rebecca I, 990
Johnson, Rebecca I, 999
Johnson, Rebecca II, 512
Johnson, Rebecca II, 567
Johnson, Rebecca II, 792
Johnson, Rebecca II, 883
Johnson, Rebecca II, 1006
Johnson, Rebecca IV, 970
Johnson, Rebecca IV, 1039
Johnson, Rebecca IV, 1213
Johnson, Rebecca IV, 1283
Johnson, Rebecca V, 31
Johnson, Rebecca V, 63
Johnson, Rebecca V, 82
Johnson, Rebecca V, 83
Johnson, Rebecca V, 85
Johnson, Rebecca V, 90
Johnson, Rebecca V, 107
Johnson, Rebecca V, 506
Johnson, Rebecca V, 971
Johnson, Rebecca VI, 113
Johnson, Rebecca VI, 118
Johnson, Rebecca VI, 179
Johnson, Rebecca VI, 185
Johnson, Rebecca VI, 186
Johnson, Rebecca VI, 187
Johnson, Rebecca VI, 256
Johnson, Rebecca VI, 321
Johnson, Rebecca VI, 831
Johnson, Rebecca VI, 941
Johnson, Rebecca VI, 942
Johnson, Rebecca D. V, 85
Johnson, Rebecca J. II, 567
Johnson, Rebecca Jarrett II, 803
Johnson, Rebecca M. V, 506
Johnson, Rebecca N. V, 83
Johnson, Rebecca N. V, 85
Johnson, Rebecca W. IV, 1283
Johnson, Rebeccah I, 357
Johnson, Rebecka II, 445
Johnson, Rebeckah I, 505
Johnson, Rebeckah I, 887
Johnson, Rebeckah I, 1085
Johnson, Rebeckah VI, 71
Johnson, Rebeckah VI, 113
Johnson, Rebeckah VI, 118
Johnson, Rebeckah VI, 187
Johnson, Rebeckah VI, 214
Johnson, Rebeckah VI, 829
Johnson, Rebekah I, 857
Johnson, Rebekah I, 858
Johnson, Rebekah I, 1010
Johnson, Rebekah I, 1012
Johnson, Redic I, 296
Johnson, Rees Evan VI, 300
Johnson, Reitzel I, 944
Johnson, Rena V. V, 256
Johnson, Reneer II, 383
Johnson, Reuben IV, 42
Johnson, Reuel IV, 42
Johnson, Reyneer II, 383
Johnson, Rhoda I, 401
Johnson, Rhoda I, 672
Johnson, Rhoda I, 812
Johnson, Rhoda I, 822
Johnson, Rhoda I, 888
Johnson, Rhoda I, 894
Johnson, Rhoda I, 1005
Johnson, Rhoda V, 31
Johnson, Rhoda V, 83
Johnson, Rhoda V, 84
Johnson, Rhoda V, 107
Johnson, Rhoda V, 305
Johnson, Rhoda V, 505
Johnson, Rhoda V, 506
Johnson, Rhoda V, 535
Johnson, Rhoda V, 968
Johnson, Rhoda V, 972
Johnson, Rhoda VI, 300
Johnson, Rhoda VI, 317
Johnson, Rhoda VI, 318
Johnson, Rhoda VI, 323
Johnson, Rhoda VI, 325
Johnson, Rhoda VI, 326
Johnson, Rhoda VI, 332
Johnson, Rhoda VI, 333
Johnson, Rhoda VI, 801
Johnson, Rhoda VI, 865
Johnson, Rhoda Ann V, 83
Johnson, Rhoda Ann V, 84
Johnson, Rhoda Ann V, 101
Johnson, Rhoda Ann V, 505
Johnson, Rhoda Ann V, 630
Johnson, Rhoda J. I, 401
Johnson, Rhoda J. I, 822
Johnson, Rhoda M. V, 40
Johnson, Rhoda M. V, 83
Johnson, Rhoda M. V, 84
Johnson, Rhoda M. V, 506
Johnson, Rhody Ann V, 506
Johnson, Rich A. III, 347
Johnson, Rich. A. III, 186
Johnson, Richard II, 382
Johnson, Richard II, 566
Johnson, Richard II, 567
Johnson, Richard III, 186
Johnson, Richard III, 344
Johnson, Richard IV, 42
Johnson, Richard IV, 151
Johnson, Richard IV, 230
Johnson, Richard V, 343
Johnson, Richard VI, 71
Johnson, Richard VI, 299
Johnson, Richard VI, 318
Johnson, Richard VI, 325
Johnson, Richard VI, 830
Johnson, Richard Bloxom V, 183
Johnson, Richard Bloxsom V, 253
Johnson, Richard Bloxsom V, 254
Johnson, Richard Obidiah V, 253
Johnson, Richards II, 567
Johnson, Richards IV, 42
Johnson, Robert I, 505
Johnson, Robert I, 554
Johnson, Robert I, 773
Johnson, Robert I, 785
Johnson, Robert I, 821
Johnson, Robert I, 822
Johnson, Robert I, 977
Johnson, Robert II, 567
Johnson, Robert IV, 42
Johnson, Robert IV, 229
Johnson, Robert IV, 230
Johnson, Robert IV, 294
Johnson, Robert IV, 728
Johnson, Robert IV, 729
Johnson, Robert IV, 765
Johnson, Robert IV, 1167
Johnson, Robert IV, 1168
Johnson, Robert V, 84
Johnson, Robert V, 318
Johnson, Robert V, 342
Johnson, Robert V, 343
Johnson, Robert V, 434
Johnson, Robert VI, 16
Johnson, Robert VI, 45
Johnson, Robert VI, 66
Johnson, Robert VI, 69
Johnson, Robert VI, 70
Johnson, Robert VI, 71
Johnson, Robert VI, 91
Johnson, Robert VI, 172
Johnson, Robert VI, 174
Johnson, Robert VI, 185
Johnson, Robert VI, 186
Johnson, Robert VI, 187
Johnson, Robert VI, 196
Johnson, Robert VI, 242
Johnson, Robert VI, 251
Johnson, Robert VI, 252
Johnson, Robert VI, 253
Johnson, Robert VI, 254
Johnson, Robert VI, 281
Johnson, Robert VI, 286
Johnson, Robert VI, 317
Johnson, Robert VI, 319
Johnson, Robert VI, 326
Johnson, Robert VI, 331
Johnson, Robert VI, 829
Johnson, Robert VI, 837
Johnson, Robert VI, 840
Johnson, Robert VI, 942
Johnson, Robert Barclay V, 407
Johnson, Robert L. IV, 310
Johnson, Robert M. IV, 230
Johnson, Robert M. VI, 327
Johnson, Robert Pleasants VI, 196
Johnson, Robert W. VI, 865
Johnson, Robert, Jr. VI, 70
Johnson, Robert, Sr. VI, 70
Johnson, Robt. VI, 45
Johnson, Rosa V, 774
Johnson, Rosa Eunice V, 183
Johnson, Rosana IV, 1323
Johnson, Rose V, 631
Johnson, Rosellie V, 408
Johnson, Rowland III, 186
Johnson, Rowland III, 363
Johnson, Rowland, Jr. II, 803
Johnson, Roxie F. IV, 828
Johnson, Roy IV, 413
Johnson, Roy L. IV, 585
Johnson, Roy Lamont IV, 413
Johnson, Roy Lamont IV, 585
Johnson, Ruel IV, 42
Johnson, Ruel H. IV, 230
Johnson, Ruel M. IV, 230
Johnson, Rufus V, 631
Johnson, Russell Parrish VI, 316
Johnson, Ruth I, 357
Johnson, Ruth I, 785
Johnson, Ruth I, 821
Johnson, Ruth I, 822
Johnson, Ruth I, 829
Johnson, Ruth I, 858
Johnson, Ruth I, 887
Johnson, Ruth I, 888
Johnson, Ruth I, 894
Johnson, Ruth I, 1075
Johnson, Ruth II, 566
Johnson, Ruth II, 624
Johnson, Ruth II, 625
Johnson, Ruth IV, 230
Johnson, Ruth V, 183
Johnson, Ruth V, 252
Johnson, Ruth V, 254
Johnson, Ruth V, 278
Johnson, Ruth V, 407
Johnson, Ruth V, 420
Johnson, Ruth V, 506
Johnson, Ruth V, 512
Johnson, Ruth V, 959
Johnson, Ruth VI, 317
Johnson, Ruth VI, 318
Johnson, Ruth VI, 323
Johnson, Ruth VI, 331
Johnson, Ruth VI, 523
Johnson, Ruth VI, 532
Johnson, Ruth VI, 840
Johnson, Ruth Ann VI, 942
Johnson, Ruth L. V, 506
Johnson, Ryth II, 566
Johnson, Salley VI, 71
Johnson, Salley VI, 252
Johnson, Salley VI, 318
Johnson, Salley VI, 879
Johnson, Sallie K. II, 883
Johnson, Sallie Kaighn II, 803
Johnson, Sally I, 857
Johnson, Sally I, 977
Johnson, Sally V, 47
Johnson, Sally V, 233
Johnson, Sally V, 253
Johnson, Sally V, 343
Johnson, Sally V, 363
Johnson, Sally VI, 324
Johnson, Sally VI, 325
Johnson, Sally VI, 327
Johnson, Sally VI, 823
Johnson, Sally VI, 829
Johnson, Sally VI, 912
Johnson, Sally VI, 941
Johnson, Sally VI, 1001
Johnson, Sally H. V, 254
Johnson, Sally H. V, 268
Johnson, Sally M. VI, 865
Johnson, Samantha Jane IV, 230
Johnson, Samira V, 255
Johnson, Samira V, 343
Johnson, Samuel I, 965
Johnson, Samuel II, 566
Johnson, Samuel II, 709
Johnson, Samuel II, 843
Johnson, Samuel II, 883
Johnson, Samuel II, 1006
Johnson, Samuel III, 186
Johnson, Samuel V, 505
Johnson, Samuel V, 630
Johnson, Samuel V, 972
Johnson, Samuel V, 979
Johnson, Samuel VI, 119
Johnson, Samuel VI, 185
Johnson, Samuel VI, 187
Johnson, Samuel VI, 245
Johnson, Samuel VI, 252
Johnson, Samuel VI, 255
Johnson, Samuel VI, 256
Johnson, Samuel VI, 298
Johnson, Samuel VI, 316
Johnson, Samuel VI, 321
Johnson, Samuel VI, 322
Johnson, Samuel VI, 325
Johnson, Samuel VI, 326
Johnson, Samuel VI, 332
Johnson, Samuel VI, 333
Johnson, Samuel VI, 798
Johnson, Samuel VI, 829
Johnson, Samuel VI, 941
Johnson, Samuel Cary VI, 324
Johnson, Samuel Hargrave VI, 318
Johnson, Samuel John III, 187
Johnson, Samuel P. V, 972
Johnson, Samuel Pleasant V, 630
Johnson, Samuel Pleasant V, 972
Johnson, Samuel T. IV, 230
Johnson, Samuel Whitfield VI, 196
Johnson, Samuella III, 186
Johnson, Sarah I, 143
Johnson, Sarah I, 357
Johnson, Sarah I, 359
Johnson, Sarah I, 366
Johnson, Sarah I, 401
Johnson, Sarah I, 430
Johnson, Sarah I, 437
Johnson, Sarah I, 448
Johnson, Sarah I, 505
Johnson, Sarah I, 526
Johnson, Sarah I, 554
Johnson, Sarah I, 555
Johnson, Sarah I, 562
Johnson, Sarah I, 626
Johnson, Sarah I, 674
Johnson, Sarah I, 682
Johnson, Sarah I, 785
Johnson, Sarah I, 801
Johnson, Sarah I, 811
Johnson, Sarah I, 821
Johnson, Sarah I, 822
Johnson, Sarah I, 831
Johnson, Sarah I, 836
Johnson, Sarah I, 847
Johnson, Sarah I, 857
Johnson, Sarah I, 858
Johnson, Sarah I, 884
Johnson, Sarah I, 887
Johnson, Sarah I, 902
Johnson, Sarah I, 905
Johnson, Sarah I, 976
Johnson, Sarah I, 977
Johnson, Sarah I, 980
Johnson, Sarah I, 990
Johnson, Sarah I, 998
Johnson, Sarah I, 1000
Johnson, Sarah I, 1033
Johnson, Sarah II, 235
Johnson, Sarah II, 566
Johnson, Sarah II, 567
Johnson, Sarah II, 625
Johnson, Sarah II, 642
Johnson, Sarah II, 1006
Johnson, Sarah II, 1022

Johnson, Sarah III, 185
Johnson, Sarah III, 187
Johnson, Sarah IV, 38
Johnson, Sarah IV, 42
Johnson, Sarah IV, 84
Johnson, Sarah IV, 95
Johnson, Sarah IV, 151
Johnson, Sarah IV, 230
Johnson, Sarah IV, 232
Johnson, Sarah IV, 245
Johnson, Sarah IV, 338
Johnson, Sarah IV, 377
Johnson, Sarah IV, 639
Johnson, Sarah IV, 645
Johnson, Sarah IV, 680
Johnson, Sarah IV, 692
Johnson, Sarah IV, 728
Johnson, Sarah IV, 729
Johnson, Sarah IV, 805
Johnson, Sarah IV, 828
Johnson, Sarah IV, 909
Johnson, Sarah IV, 969
Johnson, Sarah IV, 970
Johnson, Sarah IV, 1010
Johnson, Sarah IV, 1093
Johnson, Sarah IV, 1103
Johnson, Sarah IV, 1106
Johnson, Sarah IV, 1127
Johnson, Sarah IV, 1134
Johnson, Sarah V, 84
Johnson, Sarah V, 85
Johnson, Sarah V, 183
Johnson, Sarah V, 215
Johnson, Sarah V, 252
Johnson, Sarah V, 253
Johnson, Sarah V, 254
Johnson, Sarah V, 255
Johnson, Sarah V, 258
Johnson, Sarah V, 285
Johnson, Sarah V, 298
Johnson, Sarah V, 305
Johnson, Sarah V, 342
Johnson, Sarah V, 343
Johnson, Sarah V, 739
Johnson, Sarah V, 774
Johnson, Sarah V, 883
Johnson, Sarah VI, 69
Johnson, Sarah VI, 70
Johnson, Sarah VI, 71
Johnson, Sarah VI, 172
Johnson, Sarah VI, 174
Johnson, Sarah VI, 185
Johnson, Sarah VI, 186
Johnson, Sarah VI, 187
Johnson, Sarah VI, 244
Johnson, Sarah VI, 251
Johnson, Sarah VI, 252
Johnson, Sarah VI, 254
Johnson, Sarah VI, 255
Johnson, Sarah VI, 256
Johnson, Sarah VI, 281
Johnson, Sarah VI, 286
Johnson, Sarah VI, 287
Johnson, Sarah VI, 299
Johnson, Sarah VI, 308
Johnson, Sarah VI, 316
Johnson, Sarah VI, 317
Johnson, Sarah VI, 318
Johnson, Sarah VI, 319
Johnson, Sarah VI, 321
Johnson, Sarah VI, 322
Johnson, Sarah VI, 323
Johnson, Sarah VI, 324
Johnson, Sarah VI, 325
Johnson, Sarah VI, 329
Johnson, Sarah VI, 352
Johnson, Sarah VI, 409
Johnson, Sarah VI, 523
Johnson, Sarah VI, 531
Johnson, Sarah VI, 532
Johnson, Sarah VI, 867
Johnson, Sarah VI, 933
Johnson, Sarah VI, 941
Johnson, Sarah VI, 949
Johnson, Sarah A. V, 954
Johnson, Sarah A. V, 956
Johnson, Sarah Ann I, 448
Johnson, Sarah Ann IV, 477
Johnson, Sarah Ann IV, 480
Johnson, Sarah Ann IV, 823
Johnson, Sarah Ann IV, 828
Johnson, Sarah Ann V, 505
Johnson, Sarah Ann V, 506
Johnson, Sarah Ann V, 579
Johnson, Sarah Ann VI, 942
Johnson, Sarah Ann Lucinda I, 990
Johnson, Sarah B. V, 774
Johnson, Sarah C. IV, 828
Johnson, Sarah C. VI, 63
Johnson, Sarah C. VI, 69
Johnson, Sarah Christopher VI, 286
Johnson, Sarah Dillingham IV, 1168
Johnson, Sarah E. IV, 230
Johnson, Sarah E. V, 408
Johnson, Sarah E. V, 506
Johnson, Sarah E. VI, 942
Johnson, Sarah Elizabeth IV, 239
Johnson, Sarah Ellen V, 408
Johnson, Sarah Ellen V, 687
Johnson, Sarah H. IV, 230
Johnson, Sarah H. V, 70
Johnson, Sarah H. V, 85
Johnson, Sarah H. V, 579
Johnson, Sarah H. VI, 92
Johnson, Sarah Jane IV, 805
Johnson, Sarah Jane IV, 828
Johnson, Sarah K. IV, 229
Johnson, Sarah K. IV, 294
Johnson, Sarah L. VI, 368
Johnson, Sarah L. VI, 409
Johnson, Sarah M. III, 186
Johnson, Sarah M. III, 258
Johnson, Sarah M. V, 343
Johnson, Sarah M. V, 687
Johnson, Sarah M. VI, 827
Johnson, Sarah N. IV, 970
Johnson, Sarah N. V, 574
Johnson, Sarah N. V, 579
Johnson, Sarah P. IV, 970
Johnson, Sarah P. IV, 1039
Johnson, Sarah R. IV, 302
Johnson, Sarah R. VI, 942
Johnson, Sarah Rebecca III, 186
Johnson, Sarah Rebecca III, 187
Johnson, Sarah Rebecca III, 347
Johnson, Sarah S. II, 567
Johnson, Sarah S. II, 883
Johnson, Sarah T. IV, 230
Johnson, Sarah T. IV, 242
Johnson, Sarah Trithena I, 437
Johnson, Sarah V. IV, 479
Johnson, Sarah V. IV, 828
Johnson, Sarah V. IV, 1168
Johnson, Sarah W. IV, 69
Johnson, Sarah Warner II, 382
Johnson, Sarah Warner II, 829
Johnson, Sarah Wathrald I, 990
Johnson, Scisley VI, 256
Johnson, Seicily I, 822
Johnson, Seisley I, 821
Johnson, Selina III, 186
Johnson, Selina VI, 829
Johnson, Semira V, 253
Johnson, Semira V, 343
Johnson, Seneca VI, 325
Johnson, Seth S. V, 954
Johnson, Sevier D. IV, 1167
Johnson, Sevies D. IV, 1168
Johnson, Seymour R. IV, 1167
Johnson, Seymour R. IV, 1168
Johnson, Shadrac VI, 58
Johnson, Shadrac VI, 69
Johnson, Shadrach VI, 81
Johnson, Shepherd V, 459
Johnson, Sibel V, 255
Johnson, Sicily V, 255
Johnson, Sicily V, 407
Johnson, Sidney V, 255
Johnson, Silas IV, 1213
Johnson, Silas V, 84
Johnson, Silas V, 183
Johnson, Silas C. IV, 1213
Johnson, Silas H. V, 255
Johnson, Silas Heston V, 252
Johnson, Silvester V, 883
Johnson, Silviah B. V, 85
Johnson, Silviah B. V, 630
Johnson, Simeon V, 252
Johnson, Simeon V, 254
Johnson, Simeon VI, 318
Johnson, Simeon VI, 325
Johnson, Simeon VI, 326
Johnson, Simeon VI, 829
Johnson, Simion VI, 319
Johnson, Simon I, 357
Johnson, Simon I, 401
Johnson, Simon V, 630
Johnson, Sinah VI, 667
Johnson, Sinah VI, 756
Johnson, Sisely V, 409
Johnson, Sisley V, 407
Johnson, Sisley VI, 230
Johnson, Sisley VI, 253
Johnson, Sisley A. V, 255
Johnson, Sisley A. V, 282
Johnson, Sisley Ann V, 407
Johnson, Solomon I, 505
Johnson, Solomon I, 554
Johnson, Solomon V, 506
Johnson, Solomon V, 630
Johnson, Solomon F. V, 505
Johnson, Sopha V, 1004
Johnson, Sophia II, 454
Johnson, Sophia II, 566
Johnson, Squire VI, 165
Johnson, Squire VI, 167
Johnson, Squire VI, 185
Johnson, Squire VI, 186
Johnson, Stanley L. V, 687
Johnson, Stanley L. V, 711
Johnson, Stephen I, 990
Johnson, Stephen M. V, 913
Johnson, Strangeman I, 821
Johnson, Strangeman I, 990
Johnson, Strangeman VI, 252
Johnson, Suckey VI, 113
Johnson, Suckey VI, 941
Johnson, Sukey VI, 71
Johnson, Sukey VI, 125
Johnson, Sukey Wrenn VI, 113
Johnson, Susan I, 401
Johnson, Susan VI, 941
Johnson, Susan H. VI, 830
Johnson, Susan J. IV, 186
Johnson, Susan J. IV, 230
Johnson, Susana VI, 255
Johnson, Susanah I, 505
Johnson, Susanah VI, 252
Johnson, Susanna I, 525
Johnson, Susanna I, 554
Johnson, Susanna I, 965
Johnson, Susanna I, 976
Johnson, Susanna I, 988
Johnson, Susanna I, 990
Johnson, Susanna I, 1005
Johnson, Susanna I, 1010
Johnson, Susanna I, 1012
Johnson, Susanna IV, 230
Johnson, Susanna IV, 1213
Johnson, Susanna V, 22
Johnson, Susanna V, 85
Johnson, Susanna V, 253
Johnson, Susanna V, 254
Johnson, Susanna V, 505
Johnson, Susanna V, 579
Johnson, Susanna VI, 187
Johnson, Susanna VI, 251
Johnson, Susanna VI, 316
Johnson, Susanna VI, 317
Johnson, Susanna VI, 318
Johnson, Susanna VI, 319
Johnson, Susanna VI, 321
Johnson, Susanna VI, 322
Johnson, Susanna VI, 323
Johnson, Susanna VI, 324
Johnson, Susanna VI, 325
Johnson, Susanna VI, 326
Johnson, Susanna VI, 327
Johnson, Susanna VI, 329
Johnson, Susanna VI, 332
Johnson, Susanna VI, 333
Johnson, Susanna VI, 334
Johnson, Susanna VI, 342
Johnson, Susanna VI, 345
Johnson, Susanna VI, 829
Johnson, Susanna VI, 830
Johnson, Susanna VI, 842
Johnson, Susanna VI, 941
Johnson, Susanna VI, 965
Johnson, Susanna VI, 1015
Johnson, Susanna Micajah Penelope VI, 324
Johnson, Susanna V. II, 567
Johnson, Susannah I, 909
Johnson, Susannah I, 1049
Johnson, Susannah V, 84
Johnson, Susannah V, 85
Johnson, Susannah V, 253
Johnson, Susannah V, 254
Johnson, Susannah V, 255
Johnson, Susannah V, 297
Johnson, Susannah V, 305
Johnson, Susannah V, 306
Johnson, Susannah V, 505
Johnson, Susannah V, 506
Johnson, Susannah V, 611
Johnson, Susannah V, 630
Johnson, Susannah V, 972
Johnson, Susannah VI, 185
Johnson, Susannah VI, 252
Johnson, Susannah VI, 253
Johnson, Susannah VI, 317
Johnson, Susannah VI, 318
Johnson, Susannah VI, 321
Johnson, Susannah VI, 322
Johnson, Susannah VI, 326
Johnson, Susie II, 134
Johnson, Sylvanus V, 83
Johnson, Sylvanus V, 85
Johnson, Sylvia V, 630
Johnson, Sylvia V, 972
Johnson, Sylvia VI, 66
Johnson, Sylvia VI, 70
Johnson, Sylvia B. V, 979
Johnson, Sylvie B. V, 85
Johnson, Synthia V, 787
Johnson, Sysley I, 505
Johnson, Tabitha VI, 285
Johnson, Tabitha VI, 941
Johnson, Tace VI, 71
Johnson, Tacy IV, 728
Johnson, Tacy IV, 729
Johnson, Tacy V, 83
Johnson, Tacy VI, 69
Johnson, Tacy VI, 71
Johnson, Tacy B. V, 306
Johnson, Tacy L. IV, 719
Johnson, Tacy L. IV, 729
Johnson, Talbot V, 631
Johnson, Talton VI, 254
Johnson, Tarlton I, 505
Johnson, Tarlton I, 554
Johnson, Tarlton I, 562
Johnson, Tarlton I, 773
Johnson, Tarlton I, 785
Johnson, Tarlton I, 822
Johnson, Tarlton I, 857
Johnson, Tarlton I, 858
Johnson, Tarlton I, 887
Johnson, Temperance V, 631
Johnson, Teresa III, 187
Johnson, Tertullian II, 382
Johnson, Tertullian II, 383
Johnson, Tharessa G. IV, 1039
Johnson, Thatcher V, 84
Johnson, Thatcher V, 913
Johnson, Thatcher V, 914
Johnson, Thatcher V, 940
Johnson, Thatcher L. V, 505
Johnson, Thatcher S. V, 83
Johnson, Thatcher S. V, 84
Johnson, Thatcher S. V, 85
Johnson, Thatcher S. V, 630
Johnson, Thatcher-Stratton V, 506
Johnson, Theresa IV, 1039
Johnson, Theron A. IV, 1370
Johnson, Thomas I, 785
Johnson, Thomas I, 821
Johnson, Thomas I, 822
Johnson, Thomas I, 887
Johnson, Thomas I, 888
Johnson, Thomas I, 928
Johnson, Thomas I, 965
Johnson, Thomas I, 977
Johnson, Thomas I, 990
Johnson, Thomas I, 1005
Johnson, Thomas I, 1010
Johnson, Thomas II, 235
Johnson, Thomas II, 566
Johnson, Thomas II, 1006
Johnson, Thomas III, 186
Johnson, Thomas III, 187
Johnson, Thomas IV, 230
Johnson, Thomas IV, 729
Johnson, Thomas IV, 828
Johnson, Thomas IV, 926
Johnson, Thomas IV, 969
Johnson, Thomas IV, 970
Johnson, Thomas V, 84
Johnson, Thomas V, 343
Johnson, Thomas V, 407
Johnson, Thomas V, 490
Johnson, Thomas V, 505
Johnson, Thomas V, 506
Johnson, Thomas V, 579
Johnson, Thomas VI, 119
Johnson, Thomas VI, 185
Johnson, Thomas VI, 186
Johnson, Thomas VI, 187
Johnson, Thomas VI, 245
Johnson, Thomas VI, 252
Johnson, Thomas VI, 254
Johnson, Thomas VI, 255
Johnson, Thomas VI, 256
Johnson, Thomas VI, 301
Johnson, Thomas VI, 305
Johnson, Thomas VI, 316
Johnson, Thomas VI, 317
Johnson, Thomas VI, 318
Johnson, Thomas VI, 319
Johnson, Thomas VI, 321
Johnson, Thomas VI, 322
Johnson, Thomas VI, 323
Johnson, Thomas VI, 324
Johnson, Thomas VI, 325
Johnson, Thomas VI, 823
Johnson, Thomas VI, 843
Johnson, Thomas VI, 851
Johnson, Thomas VI, 864
Johnson, Thomas VI, 870
Johnson, Thomas VI, 923
Johnson, Thomas VI, 941
Johnson, Thomas VI, 942
Johnson, Thomas VI, 964
Johnson, Thomas VI, 967
Johnson, Thomas B. V, 407
Johnson, Thomas B. V, 408
Johnson, Thomas C. IV, 969
Johnson, Thomas Chiles VI, 31
Johnson, Thomas E. IV, 230
Johnson, Thomas E. V, 254
Johnson, Thomas E. V, 255
Johnson, Thomas Elwood IV, 31
Johnson, Thomas G. V, 254
Johnson, Thomas Garland VI, 252
Johnson, Thomas H. V, 407
Johnson, Thomas L. VI, 830
Johnson, Thomas M. IV, 1283
Johnson, Thomas M. V, 254
Johnson, Thomas M. V, 505
Johnson, Thomas Moorman I, 785
Johnson, Thomas Morman I, 55
Johnson, Thomas Potts II, 566
Johnson, Thomas Potts II, 567
Johnson, Thomas W. I, 990
Johnson, Thomas W. VI, 324
Johnson, Thomas Watkins I, 97
Johnson, Thomas Watkins VI, 252
Johnson, Thomas Watkins VI, 255
Johnson, Thomas Watkins VI, 323
Johnson, Thomas, Jr. VI, 187
Johnson, Thomas, Jr. VI, 829
Johnson, Thomas, Sr. VI, 187
Johnson, Thomas, Sr. VI, 324
Johnson, Thompson L. I, 619
Johnson, Thorne V, 913
Johnson, Thos. IV, 728
Johnson, Thos. V, 21
Johnson, Thos. V, 630
Johnson, Thos. VI, 823
Johnson, Thos. E. V, 972
Johnson, Thos. Elwood V, 972
Johnson, Thos. M. V, 630
Johnson, Thos. M. V, 972
Johnson, Tiberias II, 445
Johnson, Timothy V, 883
Johnson, Timothy VI, 70
Johnson, Timothy VI, 71
Johnson, Timothy VI, 137
Johnson, Timothy VI, 316
Johnson, Timothy VI, 319
Johnson, Timothy VI, 324
Johnson, Timothy VI, 829
Johnson, Timothy B. VI, 824
Johnson, Timothy D. VI, 131
Johnson, Timothy D. VI, 137
Johnson, Tolbert V, 631
Johnson, Topliff II, 382
Johnson, Topliff II, 567
Johnson, Tyson I, 401
Johnson, Ulysses N. V, 255
Johnson, Ulysses N. V, 459
Johnson, Unitis IV, 828
Johnson, Unity IV, 151
Johnson, Unity IV, 477
Johnson, Unity IV, 480
Johnson, Unity IV, 509
Johnson, Unity IV, 823
Johnson, Unity IV, 828
Johnson, Unity V, 254
Johnson, Unity VI, 253
Johnson, Unity VI, 256
Johnson, Unity VI, 299
Johnson, Unity VI, 318
Johnson, Unity VI, 325
Johnson, Uriah D. V, 255
Johnson, Ursulah VI, 185
Johnson, Vera M. IV, 970
Johnson, Vernie E. IV, 230
Johnson, Vienna V, 845
Johnson, Vienna V, 857
Johnson, Vienna C. V, 845
Johnson, Viola Ann IV, 230
Johnson, Virgie Wilson V, 1004
Johnson, Virgil H. V, 254
Johnson, Virginia Cicilia VI, 25
Johnson, Viva II, 1060
Johnson, W. Clarence I, 944
Johnson, Walter James II, 803
Johnson, Warner II, 567
Johnson, Warren V, 85
Johnson, Warren V, 253
Johnson, Warren V, 255
Johnson, Warren V, 256
Johnson, Warren V, 343
Johnson, Warren V, 459

Johnson, Watkins V, 253
Johnson, Watkins V, 254
Johnson, Watkins V, 265
Johnson, Watkins VI, 252
Johnson, Watkins VI, 256
Johnson, Watkins VI, 318
Johnson, Watkins VI, 326
Johnson, Wd. Agatha VI, 186
Johnson, Wd. Anna III, 422
Johnson, Wd. Jane II, 566
Johnson, Wd. Jane VI, 112
Johnson, Wd. Mary VI, 962
Johnson, Willard B. III, 63
Johnson, Willard B. III, 186
Johnson, William I, 401
Johnson, William I, 554
Johnson, William I, 555
Johnson, William I, 785
Johnson, William I, 821
Johnson, William I, 822
Johnson, William I, 888
Johnson, William I, 909
Johnson, William I, 912
Johnson, William I, 990
Johnson, William I, 1085
Johnson, William I, 1094
Johnson, William I, 1097
Johnson, William II, 382
Johnson, William II, 383
Johnson, William III, 31
Johnson, William III, 125
Johnson, William III, 186
Johnson, William III, 187
Johnson, William III, 422
Johnson, William IV, 42
Johnson, William IV, 230
Johnson, William IV, 338
Johnson, William IV, 413
Johnson, William IV, 729
Johnson, William IV, 828
Johnson, William IV, 970
Johnson, William IV, 1283
Johnson, William V, 84
Johnson, William V, 252
Johnson, William V, 253
Johnson, William V, 254
Johnson, William V, 255
Johnson, William V, 285
Johnson, William V, 343
Johnson, William V, 407
Johnson, William V, 630
Johnson, William V, 787
Johnson, William VI, 137
Johnson, William VI, 147
Johnson, William VI, 251
Johnson, William VI, 252
Johnson, William VI, 253
Johnson, William VI, 254
Johnson, William VI, 255
Johnson, William VI, 256
Johnson, William VI, 260
Johnson, William VI, 286
Johnson, William VI, 291
Johnson, William VI, 299
Johnson, William VI, 301
Johnson, William VI, 302
Johnson, William VI, 304
Johnson, William VI, 316
Johnson, William VI, 317
Johnson, William VI, 320
Johnson, William VI, 321
Johnson, William VI, 323
Johnson, William VI, 324
Johnson, William VI, 325
Johnson, William VI, 329
Johnson, William VI, 330
Johnson, William VI, 331
Johnson, William VI, 333
Johnson, William VI, 335
Johnson, William VI, 532
Johnson, William VI, 819
Johnson, William VI, 829
Johnson, William VI, 831
Johnson, William VI, 869
Johnson, William VI, 872
Johnson, William VI, 876
Johnson, William VI, 878
Johnson, William VI, 879
Johnson, William VI, 882
Johnson, William VI, 883
Johnson, William VI, 884
Johnson, William VI, 888
Johnson, William VI, 902
Johnson, William VI, 903
Johnson, William VI, 904
Johnson, William VI, 906
Johnson, William VI, 907
Johnson, William VI, 912
Johnson, William VI, 914
Johnson, William VI, 915
Johnson, William VI, 916
Johnson, William VI, 918
Johnson, William VI, 924
Johnson, William VI, 926
Johnson, William VI, 930
Johnson, William VI, 931
Johnson, William VI, 932
Johnson, William VI, 935
Johnson, William VI, 936
Johnson, William VI, 937
Johnson, William VI, 941
Johnson, William VI, 944
Johnson, William VI, 946
Johnson, William VI, 947
Johnson, William VI, 949
Johnson, William VI, 955
Johnson, William VI, 965
Johnson, William VI, 967
Johnson, William VI, 980
Johnson, William VI, 1007
Johnson, William VI, 1013
Johnson, William A. I, 888
Johnson, William A. IV, 230
Johnson, William A. VI, 941
Johnson, William B. IV, 970
Johnson, William C. IV, 310
Johnson, William C. V, 254
Johnson, William C. V, 505
Johnson, William Douglas VI, 319
Johnson, William E. VI, 256
Johnson, William Elonzo I, 857
Johnson, William Elwood I, 888
Johnson, William Elwood VI, 256
Johnson, William F. I, 990
Johnson, William G. I, 822
Johnson, William G. I, 857
Johnson, William G. I, 888
Johnson, William H. V, 506
Johnson, William H. VI, 942
Johnson, William H. VI, 951
Johnson, William H. VI, 1011
Johnson, William Henry III, 187
Johnson, William Henry H. V, 845
Johnson, William Johnson, Jr. VI, 299
Johnson, William Johnson, Jr. VI, 325
Johnson, William L. IV, 729
Johnson, William Marshall III, 187
Johnson, William P. IV, 413
Johnson, William Savery II, 382
Johnson, William W. V, 183
Johnson, William W. VI, 942
Johnson, William, Jr. III, 187
Johnson, William, Jr. V, 254
Johnson, William, Jr. VI, 324
Johnson, William, Jr. VI, 325
Johnson, William, Jr. VI, 326
Johnson, William, Sr. VI, 1012
Johnson, Willis T. IV, 970
Johnson, Willis Thornton I, 722
Johnson, Windsor VI, 69
Johnson, Winston V, 254
Johnson, Wm. I, 1075
Johnson, Wm. II, 803
Johnson, Wm. II, 883
Johnson, Wm. II, 919
Johnson, Wm. II, 1006
Johnson, Wm. III, 186
Johnson, Wm. III, 187
Johnson, Wm. III, 219
Johnson, Wm. III, 258
Johnson, Wm. III, 303
Johnson, Wm. III, 426
Johnson, Wm. IV, 151
Johnson, Wm. IV, 229
Johnson, Wm. IV, 680
Johnson, Wm. IV, 692
Johnson, Wm. IV, 728
Johnson, Wm. IV, 828
Johnson, Wm. IV, 1283
Johnson, Wm. V, 343
Johnson, Wm. V, 407
Johnson, Wm. V, 459
Johnson, Wm. V, 688
Johnson, Wm. V, 1004
Johnson, Wm. VI, 112
Johnson, Wm. VI, 252
Johnson, Wm. VI, 283
Johnson, Wm. VI, 317
Johnson, Wm. VI, 318
Johnson, Wm. VI, 319
Johnson, Wm. VI, 523
Johnson, Wm. VI, 1008
Johnson, Wm. C. IV, 230
Johnson, Wm. C. IV, 970
Johnson, Wm. C. IV, 999
Johnson, Wm. C. V, 630
Johnson, Wm. G. V, 972
Johnson, Wm. G. V, 979
Johnson, Wm. H. IV, 828
Johnson, Wm. L. V, 972
Johnson, Wm. Lewis V, 630
Johnson, Wm. Lewis V, 972
Johnson, Wm. M. III, 187
Johnson, Wm. P. IV, 389
Johnson, Wm. P. IV, 828
Johnson, Wm. Porter VI, 71
Johnson, Wm. W. V, 170
Johnson, Wm., Jr. II, 566
Johnson, Wm., Jr. VI, 299
Johnson, Zachariah I, 243
Johnson, Zachariah V, 83
Johnson, Zachariah V, 84
Johnson, Zachariah VI, 70
Johnson, Zachariah VI, 113
Johnson, Zachariah VI, 125
Johnson, Zachariah VI, 252
Johnson, Zachariah VI, 253
Johnson, Zachariah VI, 286
Johnson, Zachariah VI, 317
Johnson, Zachariah VI, 323
Johnson, Zachariah VI, 327
Johnson, Zachariah M. V, 84
Johnson, Zachariah M. V, 85
Johnson, Zachariah M. VI, 326
Johnson, Zachariah M. VI, 327
Johnson, Zachariah M. VI, 829
Johnson, Zachariah Robert VI, 70
Johnson, Zacharias VI, 70
Johnson, Zacheriah VI, 253
Johnson, Zack VI, 55
Johnson, Zack VI, 70
Johnson, Zalinda VI, 318
Johnson, Zalinda VI, 325
Johnson, Zalinda VI, 327
Johnson, Zalinda L. VI, 829
Johnson, Zebulon II, 625
Johnson, Zebulun II, 625
Johnson, Zilinda E. D. IV, 230
Johnson, Zillah IV, 42
Johnson, Zillah IV, 95
Johnston, Agnes II, 1006
Johnston, Agnes II, 1028
Johnston, Albert T. III, 187
Johnston, Alfred V, 913
Johnston, Anna Eliza I, 337
Johnston, Anna Jane IV, 480
Johnston, Anna M. V, 913
Johnston, Benjamin VI, 1005
Johnston, Brooks V, 913
Johnston, Catherine IV, 42
Johnston, Charles III, 187
Johnston, Charles VI, 292
Johnston, Charles VI, 327
Johnston, Charles VI, 795
Johnston, Charles F. V, 687
Johnston, Charles L. III, 29
Johnston, Charles L. III, 187
Johnston, Charles Lindley III, 187
Johnston, Charles Lindley, Jr. III, 187
Johnston, Chas. V, 913
Johnston, Chas. L. III, 187
Johnston, Chas. S. C. V, 914
Johnston, Clara V, 688
Johnston, Cornelius I, 401
Johnston, David II, 1006
Johnston, Dora V, 687
Johnston, Dora V, 688
Johnston, Edward O. VI, 759
Johnston, Edwin V, 913
Johnston, Eleanor V, 914
Johnston, Eliza III, 187
Johnston, Eliza L. V, 914
Johnston, Eliza S. V, 913
Johnston, Eliza S. V, 914
Johnston, Elizabeth VI, 113
Johnston, Elizabeth VI, 363
Johnston, Elizabeth VI, 409
Johnston, Elizabeth VI, 941
Johnston, Ellen V, 183
Johnston, Ellis V, 687
Johnston, Emily V, 914
Johnston, Emily H. V, 913
Johnston, Emma V, 913
Johnston, Ethel V, 687
Johnston, Eva E. V, 913
Johnston, Fletcher V, 687
Johnston, Grace L. III, 187
Johnston, Hadley IV, 42
Johnston, Hephzibah II, 988
Johnston, Hephzibah II, 1006
Johnston, Hibberd V, 774
Johnston, Icy V, 687
Johnston, Isaac IV, 42
Johnston, Isaac V, 913
Johnston, Isaac T. V, 913
Johnston, J. Will V, 687
Johnston, James I, 1094
Johnston, James B. V, 913
Johnston, James Brooks V, 913
Johnston, James W. III, 187
Johnston, Jane III, 187
Johnston, Joanna IV, 33
Johnston, Joanna IV, 42
Johnston, John II, 1006
Johnston, John V, 687
Johnston, John VI, 941
Johnston, John Edward V, 913
Johnston, John H. V, 687
Johnston, John Wm. V, 913
Johnston, Jonathan IV, 42
Johnston, Joseph II, 962
Johnston, Joseph II, 1036
Johnston, Joseph R. V, 687
Johnston, Joshua VI, 599
Johnston, Judith J. IV, 230
Johnston, Judith J. IV, 302
Johnston, Julia V, 914
Johnston, Junius E. V, 687
Johnston, Laurance II, 1006
Johnston, Lemuel VI, 113
Johnston, Leroi VI, 830
Johnston, Lucy B. V, 913
Johnston, Lucy H. VI, 795
Johnston, Lydia IV, 42
Johnston, Margaret A. V, 687
Johnston, Martha II, 566
Johnston, Martha II, 977
Johnston, Martha II, 1006
Johnston, Mary I, 722
Johnston, Mary I, 821
Johnston, Mary II, 977
Johnston, Mary II, 1006
Johnston, Mary II, 1036
Johnston, Mary IV, 514
Johnston, Mary IV, 537
Johnston, Mary IV, 993
Johnston, Mary V, 913
Johnston, Mary Ann IV, 34
Johnston, Mary Ann IV, 42
Johnston, Mary Catharine Price V, 687
Johnston, Mary K. V, 913
Johnston, Mary K. V, 914
Johnston, Minerva V, 303
Johnston, Minnie Smith V, 687
Johnston, Molly VI, 1005
Johnston, Morris L. V, 913
Johnston, Morris L. V, 914
Johnston, Mrs. E. V, 687
Johnston, Mrs. Flonna IV, 1316
Johnston, Nellie V, 913
Johnston, Nellie Johnson Watts V, 914
Johnston, Phebe I, 722
Johnston, Polly VI, 830
Johnston, Priscilla II, 1006
Johnston, Priscilla II, 1023
Johnston, Priscilla V, 774
Johnston, Rachel II, 962
Johnston, Rachel VI, 409
Johnston, Rachel VI, 599
Johnston, Ralph V, 688
Johnston, Rebecca II, 984
Johnston, Rebecca II, 1006
Johnston, Reuben IV, 42
Johnston, Reuel IV, 42
Johnston, Richard III, 187
Johnston, Robert IV, 230
Johnston, Ruel IV, 42
Johnston, Ruth III, 187
Johnston, Ruth A. III, 187
Johnston, Ruth H. III, 29
Johnston, Sally VI, 967
Johnston, Samuel II, 1006
Johnston, Sarah II, 1006
Johnston, Sarah II, 1032
Johnston, Sarah IV, 230
Johnston, Sarah M. V, 687
Johnston, Susanna IV, 1213
Johnston, Susanna IV, 1226
Johnston, Tamar VI, 759
Johnston, Thatcher V, 913
Johnston, Thatcher V, 914
Johnston, Thomas Elmer III, 187
Johnston, Thomas Potts II, 567
Johnston, Thomas S. IV, 230
Johnston, Thorne V, 913
Johnston, Thos. VI, 999
Johnston, Thos. VI, 1011
Johnston, William IV, 42
Johnston, Wm. II, 977
Johnston, Wm. II, 1006
Johnston, Wm. V, 688
Johnston, Wm. VI, 759
Johnston, Zillah IV, 42
Johnstone, Jessie Jack VI, 759
Johnstone, John VI, 759
Johnstone, Katharine VI, 759
Johnstone, Margaret VI, 747
Johnstone, Margaret VI, 759
Johnstone, Martha Ellen VI, 735
Johnstone, Martha Ellen VI, 747
Johnstone, Martha Ellen VI, 759
Johnstone, Mary Ellen III, 187
Johnstone, Mary Ellen III, 253
Johnstone, Sarah IV, 230
Johnstone, William James VI, 735
Johnstone, Wm. VI, 759
Johnstone, Wm. James VI, 747
Johnstone, Wm. James VI, 759
Johson, Edna VI, 191
Johson, Micajah T. VI, 191
Joice, Cora A. I, 888
Joice, Elizabeth I, 888
Joice, J. Thomas I, 888
Joice, James R. I, 888
Joice, Mary A. I, 888
Joice, Reid P. I, 888
Joice, Thomas A. P. I, 888
Joice, William I, 888
Joiner, Elizabeth VI, 813
Joiner, James H. VI, 815
Joiner, James H. VI, 817
Joiner, John VI, 899
Joiner, John VI, 997
Joiner, Joseph B. I, 243
Joiner, Lillie I, 243
Joiner, Mary Jane VI, 899
Joiner, Milly VI, 814
Joiner, Nelson VI, 830
Joiner, Patsy VI, 830
Joiner, Peter VI, 813
Joiner, Peter VI, 830
Joiner, Polly VI, 830
Joiner, Sarah VI, 997
Joiner, Tinsie I, 243
Joiner, William VI, 830
Joiners, Elizabeth II, 383
Joiners, John II, 383
Joliff, Rachel W. VI, 723
Jolley, Andrew II, 383
Jolley, Elizabeth IV, 413
Jolley, Malachi I, 272
Jolley, Malachi I, 274
Jolley, Malachi IV, 413
Jolley, Malachi IV, 423
Jolley, Susannah IV, 413
Jolley, Susannah IV, 423
Jollife, John VI, 411
Jollifee, Charlotte VI, 404
Jollifee, George J. VI, 404
Jollifee, Joseph L. VI, 439
Jollifee, Laura A. VI, 439
Jolliff, James VI, 410
Jolliff, John E. I, 26
Jolliff, Mary F. I, 26
Jolliff, Susan F. I, 26
Jolliff, William VI, 410
Jolliffe, Alice VI, 410
Jolliffe, Amos VI, 410
Jolliffe, Amos VI, 523
Jolliffe, Charlotte VI, 410
Jolliffe, Edith VI, 411
Jolliffe, Edith M. VI, 410
Jolliffe, Edmund VI, 410
Jolliffe, Edward C. VI, 410
Jolliffe, Edward C. VI, 411
Jolliffe, Elizabeth VI, 410
Jolliffe, Elizabeth VI, 411
Jolliffe, Elizabeth VI, 443
Jolliffe, Elizabeth VI, 453
Jolliffe, Elizabeth VI, 523
Jolliffe, Elizabeth VI, 759
Jolliffe, Elizabeth Ann VI, 411
Jolliffe, Elizabeth H. VI, 411
Jolliffe, Elizabeth J. VI, 411
Jolliffe, Fannie VI, 410
Jolliffe, Fannie VI, 411
Jolliffe, Frank VI, 410
Jolliffe, Frank VI, 411
Jolliffe, Frank Helemer VI, 411
Jolliffe, Gabriel VI, 410
Jolliffe, George J. VI, 410
Jolliffe, George J. VI, 411
Jolliffe, George Janney VI, 410
Jolliffe, Gulielma VI, 410
Jolliffe, J. VI, 410
Jolliffe, J. John VI, 411
Jolliffe, James VI, 410
Jolliffe, John VI, 410
Jolliffe, John VI, 411
Jolliffe, John VI, 759
Jolliffe, John J. VI, 410
Jolliffe, John R. I, 28
Jolliffe, John W. VI, 410
Jolliffe, John W. VI, 425
Jolliffe, Joseph VI, 411

Jolliffe, Joseph VI, 759
Jolliffe, Joseph John VI, 410
Jolliffe, Joseph John VI, 417
Jolliffe, Joseph L. VI, 410
Jolliffe, Joseph N. VI, 401
Jolliffe, Joseph N. VI, 407
Jolliffe, Joseph N. VI, 410
Jolliffe, Joseph N. VI, 411
Jolliffe, Joseph Neill VI, 755
Jolliffe, Laura A. VI, 410
Jolliffe, Laura Alice VI, 410
Jolliffe, Lelia Manola I, 28
Jolliffe, Lillie VI, 410
Jolliffe, Lucy VI, 410
Jolliffe, Lucy VI, 425
Jolliffe, Lydia VI, 374
Jolliffe, Lydia VI, 410
Jolliffe, Margaret VI, 411
Jolliffe, Margaret H. VI, 410
Jolliffe, Margaret H. VI, 411
Jolliffe, Margarette H. VI, 411
Jolliffe, Marie VI, 410
Jolliffe, Marie VI, 411
Jolliffe, Mary I, 28
Jolliffe, Mary VI, 400
Jolliffe, Mary VI, 410
Jolliffe, Mary VI, 411
Jolliffe, Mary VI, 523
Jolliffe, Mary VI, 759
Jolliffe, Mary Ann VI, 410
Jolliffe, Mary Ann VI, 411
Jolliffe, Merideth H. VI, 410
Jolliffe, Merideth H. VI, 411
Jolliffe, Neill W. VI, 410
Jolliffe, Niell VI, 411
Jolliffe, Phebe VI, 410
Jolliffe, Phebe VI, 462
Jolliffe, Rachel A. VI, 411
Jolliffe, Rachel W. VI, 410
Jolliffe, Rachel W. VI, 438
Jolliffe, Rachel W. VI, 695
Jolliffe, Rachel Williams VI, 410
Jolliffe, Rebecca VI, 410
Jolliffe, Rebecca VI, 411
Jolliffe, Rebecca VI, 443
Jolliffe, Rebecca VI, 462
Jolliffe, Rebecca VI, 538
Jolliffe, Rebecca VI, 755
Jolliffe, Rebecca VI, 759
Jolliffe, Rebeckah VI, 411
Jolliffe, Rebekah VI, 410
Jolliffe, Sallie VI, 410
Jolliffe, Sallie J. VI, 411
Jolliffe, Samuel B. Wright VI, 411
Jolliffe, Sarah VI, 410
Jolliffe, Sarah E. VI, 407
Jolliffe, Sarah E. VI, 410
Jolliffe, Sarah E. VI, 411
Jolliffe, Sarah Elizabeth VI, 755
Jolliffe, Sarah G. VI, 410
Jolliffe, Sarah J. VI, 410
Jolliffe, Sarah J. VI, 411
Jolliffe, Sarah J. VI, 417
Jolliffe, Sarah Jane VI, 410
Jolliffe, Sarah John VI, 410
Jolliffe, Susan B. VI, 400
Jolliffe, Susan B. VI, 402
Jolliffe, Susan B. VI, 410
Jolliffe, Susana B. VI, 410
Jolliffe, Thomas H. VI, 410
Jolliffe, Thomas H. VI, 411
Jolliffe, Townsend VI, 411
Jolliffe, Townsend S. VI, 410
Jolliffe, W. Neill VI, 411
Jolliffe, Wd. Lydia Hollingsworth VI, 409
Jolliffe, William VI, 410
Jolliffe, William VI, 411
Jolliffe, William VI, 443
Jolliffe, William VI, 462
Jolliffe, William VI, 538
Jolliffe, William VI, 759
Jolliffe, William H. VI, 411
Jolliffe, William, Jr. VI, 409
Jolliffe, William, Jr. VI, 411
Jolliffe, William, Jr. VI, 453
Jolliffe, Wm. VI, 755
Jolliffe, Wm., Jr. VI, 359
Jolliffe, Wm., Jr. VI, 410
Jolly, Catherine IV, 43
Jolly, Edna IV, 1323
Jolly, Elizabeth IV, 480
Jolly, Elizabeth V, 845
Jolly, Eunice IV, 480
Jolly, Eunice IV, 501
Jolly, Hannah IV, 142
Jolly, Hannah IV, 151
Jolly, Hannah IV, 480
Jolly, Huldy Bogue IV, 43
Jolly, John IV, 43
Jolly, John IV, 231
Jolly, Joseph A. IV, 1323
Jolly, Malachi I, 272
Jolly, Malachi IV, 43
Jolly, Malachi IV, 137
Jolly, Malachi IV, 480
Jolly, Malachi Jolly IV, 43
Jolly, Mary IV, 43
Jolly, Mary IV, 137
Jolly, Mary IV, 1323
Jolly, Miriam IV, 43
Jolly, Phebe II, 1007
Jolly, Philip IV, 43
Jolly, Philip IV, 480
Jolly, Philip IV, 1323
Jolly, Ruth IV, 1323
Jolly, Ruth E. IV, 1323
Jolly, Susanna IV, 480
Jolly, Susannah IV, 480
Jolly, Thomas C. II, 709
Jonah, Susanna II, 445
Jondgs, Mary II, 82
Jone, Elizabeth II, 567
Jone, John II, 567
Jones, ??? II, 384
Jones, ??? II, 445
Jones, ??? III, 187
Jones, ??? III, 188
Jones, ??? III, 286
Jones, ??? III, 391
Jones, ??? V, 85
Jones, ??? V, 86
Jones, ??? V, 756
Jones, ??? V, 770
Jones, ??? V, 965
Jones, ??? VI, 39
Jones, A. B. V, 1004
Jones, A. Lindley V, 750
Jones, A. R. V, 183
Jones, Aaron I, 343
Jones, Aaron I, 357
Jones, Aaron I, 379
Jones, Aaron I, 401
Jones, Aaron I, 402
Jones, Aaron I, 506
Jones, Aaron I, 965
Jones, Aaron I, 1094
Jones, Aaron I, 1143
Jones, Aaron I, 1156
Jones, Aaron VI, 411
Jones, Aaron Hackney I, 1144
Jones, Aaron Morris IV, 413
Jones, Abagil I, 1142
Jones, Abi M. V, 87
Jones, Abigail I, 888
Jones, Abigail I, 1010
Jones, Abigail I, 1012
Jones, Abigail II, 321
Jones, Abigail III, 422
Jones, Abigail III, 472
Jones, Abigail III, 487
Jones, Abigail III, 507
Jones, Abigail IV, 480
Jones, Abigail IV, 537
Jones, Abigail V, 256
Jones, Abigail V, 408
Jones, Abigail V, 447
Jones, Abigail V, 506
Jones, Abigail V, 525
Jones, Abigail VI, 756
Jones, Abigail VI, 777
Jones, Abijah I, 358
Jones, Abijah I, 786
Jones, Abijah I, 813
Jones, Abijah I, 822
Jones, Abijah I, 990
Jones, Abijah V, 86
Jones, Abijah V, 749
Jones, Abijah V, 782
Jones, Abijah V, 786
Jones, Abijah V, 787
Jones, Abijah V, 789
Jones, Abijah F. V, 787
Jones, Abner I, 1107
Jones, Abner IV, 413
Jones, Abner IV, 875
Jones, Abner VI, 669
Jones, Abraham II, 383
Jones, Abraham II, 384
Jones, Abraham II, 498
Jones, Abraham II, 569
Jones, Abraham II, 570
Jones, Abraham II, 962
Jones, Abraham V, 750
Jones, Abraham VI, 943
Jones, Abraham N. VI, 918
Jones, Abram I, 1144
Jones, Abram II, 709
Jones, Abram H. II, 1053
Jones, Abram N. VI, 1000
Jones, Achsah I, 555
Jones, Achsah I, 888
Jones, Achsah I, 928
Jones, Achsah P. I, 635
Jones, Ada V, 256
Jones, Adaline I, 1123
Jones, Addie IV, 1168
Jones, Addie Minerva V, 183
Jones, Adelia III, 510
Jones, Adeline S. VI, 948
Jones, Adilia H. IV, 1255
Jones, Agga VI, 830
Jones, Agnes I, 448
Jones, Agnes IV, 1323
Jones, Agnes VI, 830
Jones, Agness VI, 950
Jones, Agness W. VI, 801
Jones, Aileen I, 928
Jones, Albert I, 1142
Jones, Albert I, 1156
Jones, Albert IV, 231
Jones, Albert V, 813
Jones, Albert V, 914
Jones, Albert VI, 943
Jones, Albert C. I, 928
Jones, Albert C. I, 944
Jones, Albert Carl I, 928
Jones, Albert R. V, 183
Jones, Albert S. V, 914
Jones, Alcinda IV, 875
Jones, Alcinda VI, 669
Jones, Alex. V, 812
Jones, Alex. V, 818
Jones, Alexander V, 813
Jones, Alexander V, 814
Jones, Alexander V, 822
Jones, Alfred I, 1156
Jones, Alfred IV, 96
Jones, Alfred IV, 1283
Jones, Alfred B. II, 749
Jones, Alfred H. V, 579
Jones, Alice II, 235
Jones, Alice II, 263
Jones, Alice II, 383
Jones, Alice II, 476
Jones, Alice II, 568
Jones, Alice II, 569
Jones, Alice IV, 188
Jones, Alice IV, 1168
Jones, Alice Ann V, 748
Jones, Alice Cynthia III, 187
Jones, Alice Cynthia III, 279
Jones, Alice D. V, 27
Jones, Alice D. V, 87
Jones, Alice H. V, 256
Jones, Alice L. IV, 1308
Jones, Alice L. IV, 1323
Jones, Alice R. IV, 231
Jones, Alizabeth I, 1048
Jones, Allen I, 231
Jones, Allen I, 233
Jones, Allen I, 241
Jones, Allen V, 747
Jones, Allen V, 749
Jones, Allen VI, 940
Jones, Allen Picketting V, 750
Jones, Allen White I, 944
Jones, Allie D. V, 1004
Jones, Alma III, 510
Jones, Almira I, 1123
Jones, Almira IV, 875
Jones, Almy III, 487
Jones, Almy III, 497
Jones, Almy III, 510
Jones, Alvin V, 814
Jones, Alvin V, 822
Jones, Alvira A. IV, 953
Jones, Alvira A. IV, 971
Jones, Amanda IV, 231
Jones, Amanda IV, 1168
Jones, Amanda V, 750
Jones, Amanda VI, 844
Jones, Amanda Jane V, 813
Jones, Amanda Jane V, 814
Jones, Amanda Jane V, 818
Jones, Amanda M. V, 748
Jones, Ambrose VI, 942
Jones, Amelia III, 403
Jones, Amelia III, 480
Jones, Amelia III, 487
Jones, Amelia V, 748
Jones, Amelia V, 749
Jones, Amelia V, 750
Jones, Amey II, 568
Jones, Amey II, 638
Jones, Amey III, 399
Jones, Amoreen I, 1156
Jones, Amy II, 567
Jones, Amy II, 568
Jones, Amy II, 569
Jones, Amy II, 1052
Jones, Amy II, 1053
Jones, Amy III, 170
Jones, Amy IV, 96
Jones, Amy IV, 480
Jones, Amy IV, 537
Jones, Amy V, 846
Jones, Amy V, 868
Jones, Amy VI, 390
Jones, Amy VI, 411
Jones, Amy Howard IV, 1255
Jones, Amy J. III, 187
Jones, Anderson I, 823
Jones, Anderson W. I, 823
Jones, Andrew I, 1156
Jones, Andrew II, 445
Jones, Andrew II, 570
Jones, Andrew II, 571
Jones, Andrew M. II, 883
Jones, Angeline VI, 943
Jones, Ann I, 116
Jones, Ann I, 402
Jones, Ann I, 411
Jones, Ann I, 448
Jones, Ann I, 450
Jones, Ann I, 1044
Jones, Ann I, 1049
Jones, Ann I, 1107
Jones, Ann I, 1122
Jones, Ann I, 1137
Jones, Ann I, 1142
Jones, Ann I, 1144
Jones, Ann I, 1155
Jones, Ann I, 1160
Jones, Ann II, 135
Jones, Ann II, 383
Jones, Ann II, 384
Jones, Ann II, 456
Jones, Ann II, 462
Jones, Ann II, 474
Jones, Ann II, 525
Jones, Ann II, 529
Jones, Ann II, 567
Jones, Ann II, 568
Jones, Ann II, 569
Jones, Ann II, 570
Jones, Ann II, 577
Jones, Ann II, 612
Jones, Ann II, 628
Jones, Ann II, 1007
Jones, Ann IV, 43
Jones, Ann IV, 49
Jones, Ann IV, 970
Jones, Ann V, 306
Jones, Ann V, 309
Jones, Ann V, 746
Jones, Ann V, 747
Jones, Ann V, 748
Jones, Ann V, 756
Jones, Ann V, 787
Jones, Ann V, 790
Jones, Ann V, 845
Jones, Ann V, 863
Jones, Ann V, 914
Jones, Ann VI, 16
Jones, Ann VI, 228
Jones, Ann VI, 256
Jones, Ann VI, 523
Jones, Ann VI, 593
Jones, Ann VI, 599
Jones, Ann VI, 824
Jones, Ann VI, 924
Jones, Ann VI, 973
Jones, Ann Booker VI, 943
Jones, Ann Eliza VI, 979
Jones, Ann Emlen II, 383
Jones, Ann L. II, 293
Jones, Ann Lawrence VI, 72
Jones, Ann M. II, 878
Jones, Ann M. II, 884
Jones, Ann M. III, 157
Jones, Ann M. III, 187
Jones, Ann P. VI, 943
Jones, Anna I, 1107
Jones, Anna II, 383
Jones, Anna II, 568
Jones, Anna II, 569
Jones, Anna II, 570
Jones, Anna II, 584
Jones, Anna IV, 480
Jones, Anna V, 183
Jones, Anna V, 343
Jones, Anna V, 408
Jones, Anna V, 746
Jones, Anna V, 748
Jones, Anna V, 750
Jones, Anna V, 758
Jones, Anna V, 783
Jones, Anna V, 784
Jones, Anna V, 785
Jones, Anna V, 787
Jones, Anna V, 794
Jones, Anna V, 812
Jones, Anna V, 813
Jones, Anna V, 814
Jones, Anna V, 818
Jones, Anna V, 827
Jones, Anna V, 845
Jones, Anna V, 846
Jones, Anna VI, 798
Jones, Anna VI, 982
Jones, Anna Alice V, 748
Jones, Anna E. IV, 231
Jones, Anna Elsie V, 846
Jones, Anna Gause V, 87
Jones, Anna Lee II, 311
Jones, Anna Lucile IV, 971
Jones, Anna M. V, 86
Jones, Anna May V, 579
Jones, Anna May V, 688
Jones, Anna R. V, 59
Jones, Anna R. V, 86
Jones, Anna Ruth IV, 1255
Jones, Anna S. I, 635
Jones, Anna T. I, 555
Jones, Anna T. I, 635
Jones, Anna T. I, 888
Jones, Anna T. I, 944
Jones, Anna Thomas I, 928
Jones, Anne I, 51
Jones, Anne I, 55
Jones, Anne I Sup 1, 4
Jones, Anne II, 477
Jones, Anne II, 567
Jones, Anne VI, 12
Jones, Anne Emlen II, 571
Jones, Anne M. VI, 256
Jones, Annie II, 793
Jones, Annie V, 343
Jones, Annie VI, 249
Jones, Annie E. II, 804
Jones, Annie J. VI, 383
Jones, Annie J. VI, 411
Jones, Annie M. V, 87
Jones, Annie M. VI, 249
Jones, Annie M. VI, 256
Jones, Annie Mary V, 688
Jones, Annie S. IV, 231
Jones, Anvard Bevan Beathworth V, 1004
Jones, Aquila II, 568
Jones, Aquila II, 569
Jones, Aquila II, 681
Jones, Aquila VI, 669
Jones, Aquilla II, 383
Jones, Aquilla II, 384
Jones, Aquilla II, 568
Jones, Aquilla II, 569
Jones, Aquilla II, 570
Jones, Aquilla II, 571
Jones, Aquilla II, 684
Jones, Aquilla II, 749
Jones, Aquilla III, 187
Jones, Aquilla IV, 96
Jones, Aquilla IV, 357
Jones, Aquilla IV, 413
Jones, Aquilla IV, 454
Jones, Aquilla IV, 875
Jones, Aquilla V, 914
Jones, Aquilla VI, 669
Jones, Archor I, 1144
Jones, Arthur I Sup 1, 4
Jones, Arthur I Sup 1, 5
Jones, Arthur I Sup 1, 6
Jones, Arthur V, 688
Jones, Asa IV, 537
Jones, Asa IV, 1370
Jones, Asa V, 86
Jones, Asa V, 747
Jones, Asa V, 749
Jones, Asa V, 805
Jones, Asa V, 813
Jones, Asa Potter I, 1155
Jones, Asenath I, 1142
Jones, Asenath I, 1151
Jones, Asenath I, 1155
Jones, Asenath I, 1156
Jones, Athy VI, 72
Jones, Augustin II, 569
Jones, Augustine II, 569
Jones, Augustis Hicks II, 569
Jones, Austin II, 383
Jones, Austin V, 688
Jones, B. E. V, 1004
Jones, B. F. V, 183
Jones, Barbadoes II, 567
Jones, Barbara II, 383
Jones, Barbara II, 567
Jones, Barbara II, 618
Jones, Barbarah II, 383
Jones, Barclay II, 965
Jones, Barton Elwynn V, 1004
Jones, Barton H. V, 813
Jones, Barton K. V, 1004

nes, Bateman V, 972
nes, Benjamin I, 1144
nes, Benjamin II, 177
nes, Benjamin II, 194
nes, Benjamin II, 206
nes, Benjamin II, 235
nes, Benjamin II, 311
nes, Benjamin II, 383
nes, Benjamin II, 557
nes, Benjamin II, 571
nes, Benjamin II, 1007
nes, Benjamin III, 187
nes, Benjamin IV, 231
nes, Benjamin IV, 729
nes, Benjamin IV, 970
nes, Benjamin IV, 971
nes, Benjamin V, 146
nes, Benjamin V, 506
nes, Benjamin V, 507
nes, Benjamin V, 748
nes, Benjamin V, 814
nes, Benjamin VI, 256
nes, Benjamin VI, 798
nes, Benjamin VI, 800
nes, Benjamin VI, 829
nes, Benjamin VI, 943
nes, Benjamin Franklin IV, 970
nes, Benjamin L. IV, 480
nes, Benjamin P. III, 188
nes, Benjamin S. II, 749
nes, Benjamin Smith II, 383
nes, Benjamin W. IV, 231
nes, Benjamin W. IV, 480
nes, Benjamin, Jr. II, 235
nes, Bersheba II, 235
nes, Bert L. V, 688
nes, Bertha V, 688
nes, Bertrand L. V, 688
nes, Betsey V, 814
nes, Betsey VI, 942
nes, Betsy V, 735
nes, Betsy V, 749
nes, Betsy V, 806
nes, Betsy V, 814
nes, Betsy VI, 830
nes, Betsy VI, 856
nes, Betsy Davis V, 742
nes, Betty IV, 34
nes, Betty IV, 43
nes, Betty IV, 95
nes, Betty IV, 96
nes, Betty IV, 106
nes, Billy I, 1144
nes, Blaithwite II, 383
nes, Blath II, 384
nes, Blathwait II, 384
nes, Brantson V, 750
nes, Burwell P. VI, 943
nes, Byron V, 750
nes, C. Rollin V, 748
nes, C. Virginia II, 717
nes, Caleb I, 1142
nes, Caleb II, 383
nes, Caleb II, 529
nes, Caleb II, 569
nes, Caleb IV, 729
nes, Caleb IV, 970
nes, Caleb IV, 971
nes, Calvin I, 749
nes, Calvin I, 764
nes, Calvin I, 869
nes, Calvin I, 888
nes, Capt. Henry VI, 948
nes, Capt. William R. VI, 929
nes, Captola I, 1144
nes, Carl G. V, 183
nes, Carl White I, 928
nes, Carlton Ellis V, 749
nes, Caroline II, 717
nes, Caroline II, 803
nes, Caroline II, 884
nes, Caroline III, 187
nes, Caroline III, 251
nes, Caroline VI, 1008
nes, Caroline L. III, 188
nes, Caroline L. III, 286
nes, Caroline M. III, 187
nes, Caroline Virginia II, 700
nes, Caroline Virginia II, 717
nes, Carrie Emily II, 851
nes, Carrie Emily II, 884
nes, Carrie S. V, 1004
nes, Carrie T. V, 1004
nes, Carrolyn Whittier I, 928
nes, Carry T. V, 1004
nes, Cartlet IV, 971
nes, Cary VI, 854
nes, Catharine I, 506
nes, Catharine I, 1156
nes, Catharine II, 568
nes, Catharine II, 569
Jones, Catharine II, 570
Jones, Catharine II, 584
Jones, Catharine II, 692
Jones, Catharine III, 187
Jones, Catharine III, 466
Jones, Catharine VI, 822
Jones, Catharine VI, 830
Jones, Catharine J. II, 884
Jones, Catherine II, 567
Jones, Catherine II, 568
Jones, Catherine II, 569
Jones, Catherine V, 256
Jones, Catherine VI, 830
Jones, Catherine J. II, 920
Jones, Cathern Lawrence VI, 72
Jones, Cathrine II, 383
Jones, Catlet IV, 729
Jones, Catlet IV, 938
Jones, Catlet IV, 970
Jones, Catlet IV, 971
Jones, Catlett IV, 919
Jones, Catlett IV, 970
Jones, Catlett VI, 133
Jones, Catlett VI, 137
Jones, Catlett VI, 228
Jones, Catlett VI, 256
Jones, Catlett VI, 411
Jones, Catlett, Sr. IV, 970
Jones, Catlit IV, 729
Jones, Catlit V, 506
Jones, Catlitt VI, 16
Jones, Catlitt VI, 256
Jones, Caty VI, 860
Jones, Ceborn V, 749
Jones, Cecil G. V, 183
Jones, Celia V, 87
Jones, Celia B. IV, 1323
Jones, Cena VI, 942
Jones, Chalkley L. II, 884
Jones, Charety II, 445
Jones, Charity I, 1143
Jones, Charity I, 1155
Jones, Charity II, 193
Jones, Charity II, 235
Jones, Charity II, 383
Jones, Charity II, 445
Jones, Charity II, 567
Jones, Charity II, 569
Jones, Charity II, 594
Jones, Charity V, 86
Jones, Charity V, 87
Jones, Charity V, 747
Jones, Charity V, 748
Jones, Charity V, 749
Jones, Charity V, 750
Jones, Charity J. V, 757
Jones, Charles I, 28
Jones, Charles I, 143
Jones, Charles I, 185
Jones, Charles I, 195
Jones, Charles I, 201
Jones, Charles I, 611
Jones, Charles II, 135
Jones, Charles II, 236
Jones, Charles II, 293
Jones, Charles II, 383
Jones, Charles II, 384
Jones, Charles II, 548
Jones, Charles II, 567
Jones, Charles II, 568
Jones, Charles II, 570
Jones, Charles II, 571
Jones, Charles III, 187
Jones, Charles IV, 970
Jones, Charles IV, 1283
Jones, Charles V, 87
Jones, Charles V, 408
Jones, Charles V, 750
Jones, Charles V, 846
Jones, Charles VI, 72
Jones, Charles VI, 942
Jones, Charles VI, 952
Jones, Charles VI, 1018
Jones, Charles A. II, 884
Jones, Charles Attmore II, 803
Jones, Charles E. V, 87
Jones, Charles E. V, 408
Jones, Charles F. V, 813
Jones, Charles M. VI, 830
Jones, Charles N. IV, 1255
Jones, Charles Rowland II, 884
Jones, Charles S. VI, 943
Jones, Charles T. VI, 830
Jones, Charles W. IV, 1370
Jones, Charles W. V, 86
Jones, Charles W. V, 87
Jones, Charles W. V, 579
Jones, Charles W. V, 688
Jones, Charles Walker IV, 537
Jones, Chas. II, 878
Jones, Chas. II, 884
Jones, Chas. V, 579
Jones, Chas. Attmore, Jr. II, 803
Jones, Chas. N. IV, 1283
Jones, Chas. Wm. V, 688
Jones, Chloe Theodosia IV, 971
Jones, Christianna VI, 824
Jones, Christopher II, 962
Jones, Christopher H. II, 1053
Jones, Christopher L. VI, 851
Jones, Clara Crew IV, 947
Jones, Clara Crew IV, 971
Jones, Clarence E. V, 1004
Jones, Clarkson IV, 96
Jones, Claudius Galen IV, 970
Jones, Clement II, 804
Jones, Clinton V, 688
Jones, Clinton A. V, 183
Jones, Col. Allen I, 229
Jones, Col. Allen I, 230
Jones, Col. Allen I, 233
Jones, Col. Allen I, 237
Jones, Col. Allen I, 239
Jones, Col. Allen I, 240
Jones, Col. Allen I, 242
Jones, Col. Allen I, 243
Jones, Col. Allen I, 244
Jones, Col. Allen I, 245
Jones, Col. Allen I, 246
Jones, Col. Allen I, 248
Jones, Col. Allen I, 250
Jones, Col. Allen I, 252
Jones, Col. Allen I, 254
Jones, Col. Allen I, 256
Jones, Col. Allen I, 260
Jones, Collin V, 748
Jones, Colonel Allen I, 243
Jones, Cora V, 183
Jones, Cora E. IV, 1103
Jones, Cora E. IV, 1113
Jones, Cora V. V, 846
Jones, Cordelia V, 812
Jones, Cordelia B. V, 813
Jones, Cordelia P. V, 814
Jones, Cornelia I, 935
Jones, Cornelia Annie I, 924
Jones, Crafford I, 506
Jones, Crawford I, 1094
Jones, Cynthia V, 688
Jones, Cynthia A. IV, 970
Jones, Cynthia A. IV, 971
Jones, Cynthia A. V, 87
Jones, Cynthia A. V, 146
Jones, Cynthia A. V, 506
Jones, Cynthia A. V, 507
Jones, Cynthia A. J. IV, 961
Jones, Cynthia A. J. IV, 971
Jones, Cynthia Ann IV, 231
Jones, Cynthia Ann IV, 970
Jones, Cynthia Ann IV, 971
Jones, Cyrenia V, 814
Jones, D. V, 749
Jones, D. VI, 141
Jones, Daniel I, 358
Jones, Daniel I, 786
Jones, Daniel I, 797
Jones, Daniel I, 822
Jones, Daniel I, 965
Jones, Daniel I, 971
Jones, Daniel I, 990
Jones, Daniel I, 991
Jones, Daniel II, 383
Jones, Daniel II, 384
Jones, Daniel II, 445
Jones, Daniel II, 570
Jones, Daniel IV, 1168
Jones, Daniel IV, 1323
Jones, Daniel V, 28
Jones, Daniel V, 85
Jones, Daniel V, 86
Jones, Daniel V, 87
Jones, Daniel V, 98
Jones, Daniel V, 343
Jones, Daniel V, 408
Jones, Daniel V, 506
Jones, Daniel V, 515
Jones, Daniel V, 749
Jones, Daniel V, 783
Jones, Daniel V, 787
Jones, Daniel V, 788
Jones, Daniel V, 954
Jones, Daniel VI, 815
Jones, Daniel VI, 824
Jones, Daniel VI, 830
Jones, Daniel VI, 849
Jones, Daniel VI, 942
Jones, Daniel B. V, 86
Jones, Daniel B. V, 87
Jones, Daniel D. IV, 1323
Jones, Daniel H. V, 688
Jones, Daniel H. V, 748
Jones, Daniel H. V, 750
Jones, Daniel H. V, 787
Jones, Daniel Henry V, 408
Jones, Daniel Henry V, 688
Jones, Daniel P. VI, 913
Jones, Daniel P. VI, 943
Jones, Daniel P. VI, 978
Jones, David I, 506
Jones, David I, 888
Jones, David I, 928
Jones, David I, 1044
Jones, David I, 1085
Jones, David I, 1142
Jones, David I, 1155
Jones, David I, 1156
Jones, David II, 445
Jones, David II, 570
Jones, David II, 803
Jones, David II, 884
Jones, David III, 487
Jones, David III, 510
Jones, David IV, 480
Jones, David V, 86
Jones, David V, 723
Jones, David V, 747
Jones, David V, 748
Jones, David V, 749
Jones, David V, 787
Jones, David VI, 795
Jones, David VI, 816
Jones, David VI, 825
Jones, David VI, 860
Jones, David VI, 870
Jones, David VI, 893
Jones, David VI, 929
Jones, David VI, 942
Jones, David VI, 973
Jones, David VI, 1000
Jones, David H. I, 823
Jones, David H. V, 787
Jones, David Morgan I, 1143
Jones, David P. II, 884
Jones, David Powell II, 884
Jones, David Winston V, 787
Jones, David, Jr. V, 749
Jones, David, Jr. VI, 897
Jones, David, Jr. VI, 938
Jones, David, Jr. VI, 943
Jones, David, Sr. VI, 918
Jones, Davis W. V, 750
Jones, Debby Ann IV, 639
Jones, Deborah I, 749
Jones, Deborah I, 760
Jones, Deborah I, 764
Jones, Deborah I, 811
Jones, Deborah I, 822
Jones, Deborah I, 823
Jones, Deborah I, 1043
Jones, Deborah II, 383
Jones, Deborah II, 567
Jones, Deborah II, 651
Jones, Deborah IV, 96
Jones, Deborah IV, 182
Jones, Deborah V, 85
Jones, Deborah V, 86
Jones, Deborah V, 87
Jones, Deborah V, 306
Jones, Deborah V, 748
Jones, Deborah V, 749
Jones, Deborah V, 757
Jones, Deborah V, 814
Jones, Deborah A. V, 86
Jones, Deborah Alice V, 86
Jones, Deborah Ann V, 841
Jones, Deborah Ann V, 845
Jones, Deborah B. V, 86
Jones, Deborah F. II, 884
Jones, Deborah F. IV, 639
Jones, Deborah L. V, 813
Jones, Deborah Luella I, 749
Jones, Deborah M. IV, 770
Jones, Deborah M. IV, 931
Jones, Deborah M. IV, 970
Jones, Deborah M. IV, 971
Jones, Deborah M. IV, 1012
Jones, Delany VI, 940
Jones, Delila I, 1143
Jones, Delilah V, 1004
Jones, Delilah Ann III, 187
Jones, Della Downing V, 87
Jones, Dellila VI, 830
Jones, Delos H. II, 851
Jones, Delos H. II, 884
Jones, Delphina T. IV, 971
Jones, Dicey VI, 819
Jones, Dillwyn P. IV, 231
Jones, Docie IV, 1213
Jones, Dolly VI, 820
Jones, Dolly VI, 830
Jones, Dolly VI, 894
Jones, Dorcas I, 722
Jones, Dorcas I, 723
Jones, Dorcas I, 733
Jones, Dorcas I, 1044
Jones, Dorcas III, 73
Jones, Dorcas III, 188
Jones, Dorcas V, 86
Jones, Dorcas V, 734
Jones, Dorcas V, 745
Jones, Dorcas V, 747
Jones, Dorcas V, 748
Jones, Dorcas V, 750
Jones, Dorcas V, 753
Jones, Dorcas V, 760
Jones, Dorcas V, 783
Jones, Dorcas V, 787
Jones, Dorcas V, 813
Jones, Dorcus VI, 842
Jones, Dorkis V, 46
Jones, Dorkis V, 86
Jones, Dorkis V, 749
Jones, Dorothy V, 688
Jones, Dorothy W. III, 187
Jones, Dorothy W. VI, 759
Jones, Doughty II, 383
Jones, Doughty II, 384
Jones, Doughty II, 568
Jones, Dr. E. T. V, 183
Jones, Dr. John II, 383
Jones, Dr. S. L. I, 1156
Jones, Drusilla V, 914
Jones, Dudley VI, 955
Jones, Dynisia VI, 1002
Jones, E. I, 614
Jones, E. A. I, 1156
Jones, E. Everett IV, 971
Jones, E. Harold V, 688
Jones, E. M. V, 1004
Jones, E. Townsend V, 183
Jones, E. Townsend V, 507
Jones, E. Townsend V, 688
Jones, Earnest IV, 1168
Jones, Eathel IV, 729
Jones, Edith IV, 96
Jones, Edith V, 688
Jones, Edith Harris VI, 256
Jones, Edith S. III, 242
Jones, Edith T. IV, 96
Jones, Edna I, 614
Jones, Edna I, 636
Jones, Edna VI, 830
Jones, Edna H. IV, 402
Jones, Edna H. IV, 414
Jones, Edward II, 82
Jones, Edward II, 383
Jones, Edward II, 476
Jones, Edward II, 568
Jones, Edward II, 681
Jones, Edward III, 187
Jones, Edward IV, 231
Jones, Edward VI, 15
Jones, Edward VI, 22
Jones, Edward VI, 29
Jones, Edward VI, 31
Jones, Edward VI, 41
Jones, Edward VI, 72
Jones, Edward VI, 830
Jones, Edward VI, 942
Jones, Edward VI, 948
Jones, Edward B. II, 293
Jones, Edward C. II, 709
Jones, Edward C. II, 749
Jones, Edward C. VI, 894
Jones, Edward C. VI, 943
Jones, Edward D. VI, 849
Jones, Edward Everett IV, 971
Jones, Edward Jones V, 459
Jones, Edward P. IV, 231
Jones, Edward S. IV, 681
Jones, Edward W. IV, 231
Jones, Edward W. IV, 480
Jones, Edward Wood VI, 817
Jones, Edward, Jr. II, 567
Jones, Edward, Jr. III, 170
Jones, Edward, Jr. III, 187
Jones, Edwd VI, 894
Jones, EdWd VI, 990
Jones, Edwin VI, 948
Jones, Edwin N. VI, 796
Jones, Effa Pearl IV, 971
Jones, Effie Pearl IV, 971
Jones, Eithel IV, 729
Jones, Elbert III, 510
Jones, Elbert L. Maupine I, 1155
Jones, Eleaner C. V, 750
Jones, Eleanor I, 723
Jones, Eleanor I, 749
Jones, Eleanor I, 760
Jones, Eleanor I, 764
Jones, Eleanor II, 467
Jones, Eleanor II, 567
Jones, Eleanor II, 569
Jones, Eleanor III, 510

Jones, Eleanor IV, 96
Jones, Eleanor V, 688
Jones, Eleanor C. V, 735
Jones, Eleanor C. V, 748
Jones, Eleanor C. V, 750
Jones, Elener I, 448
Jones, Elener I, 1043
Jones, Elenor I, 764
Jones, Elenor V, 506
Jones, Elenor V, 542
Jones, Elenor V, 845
Jones, Eli I, 965
Jones, Eli I, 1143
Jones, Eli I, 1155
Jones, Eli IV, 480
Jones, Eli IV, 537
Jones, Eli IV, 541
Jones, Eli V, 749
Jones, Eli V, 863
Jones, Eli C. I, 1144
Jones, Eli Clarkson I, 1155
Jones, Elinder I, 357
Jones, Elinder I, 358
Jones, Eling II, 198
Jones, Elisabeth I, 35
Jones, Elisabeth I, 55
Jones, Elisabeth I, 77
Jones, Elisabeth I, 87
Jones, Elisabeth I, 133
Jones, Elisabeth I, 143
Jones, Elisabeth I, 168
Jones, Elisabeth I, 177
Jones, Elisabeth I, 243
Jones, Elisabeth II, 177
Jones, Elisabeth II, 206
Jones, Elisabeth II, 235
Jones, Elisabeth II, 568
Jones, Elisebeth I, 1107
Jones, Elisha I, 1033
Jones, Elisha I, 1143
Jones, Elisha V, 74
Jones, Elisha V, 86
Jones, Elisha V, 743
Jones, Elisha V, 745
Jones, Elisha V, 746
Jones, Elisha V, 747
Jones, Elisha V, 749
Jones, Elisha V, 750
Jones, Elisha V, 757
Jones, Elisha V, 766
Jones, Elisha V, 784
Jones, Elisha V, 787
Jones, Elisha V, 790
Jones, Elisha V, 813
Jones, Elisha A. I, 1143
Jones, Elisha A. I, 1156
Jones, Elisha Absalum I, 1155
Jones, Elisha Benson V, 748
Jones, Elisha C. I, 1143
Jones, Elisha D. I, 1156
Jones, Elisha Henry I, 1142
Jones, Elisha Rufus I, 1142
Jones, Eliz. III, 155
Jones, Eliz. III, 487
Jones, Eliz. S. III, 93
Jones, Eliz. S. III, 222
Jones, Eliz. S. III, 361
Jones, Eliza I, 1142
Jones, Eliza I, 1156
Jones, Eliza III, 187
Jones, Eliza III, 229
Jones, Eliza V, 256
Jones, Eliza V, 787
Jones, Eliza VI, 931
Jones, Eliza VI, 943
Jones, Eliza VI, 992
Jones, Eliza A. VI, 851
Jones, Eliza Ann IV, 1134
Jones, Eliza B. VI, 820
Jones, Eliza E. VI, 967
Jones, Eliza F. III, 187
Jones, Eliza J. VI, 943
Jones, Eliza Jane V, 662
Jones, Eliza Jane VI, 958
Jones, Eliza M. V, 86
Jones, Eliza M. V, 87
Jones, Eliza S. IV, 971
Jones, Eliza S. V, 506
Jones, Eliza S. V, 507
Jones, Eliza W. VI, 830
Jones, Elizabeth I, 28
Jones, Elizabeth I, 184
Jones, Elizabeth I, 358
Jones, Elizabeth I, 402
Jones, Elizabeth I, 422
Jones, Elizabeth I, 448
Jones, Elizabeth I, 506
Jones, Elizabeth I, 555
Jones, Elizabeth I, 594
Jones, Elizabeth I, 786
Jones, Elizabeth I, 822
Jones, Elizabeth I, 928
Jones, Elizabeth I, 957
Jones, Elizabeth I, 990
Jones, Elizabeth I, 994
Jones, Elizabeth I, 1010
Jones, Elizabeth I, 1033
Jones, Elizabeth I, 1044
Jones, Elizabeth I, 1049
Jones, Elizabeth I, 1095
Jones, Elizabeth I, 1122
Jones, Elizabeth I, 1142
Jones, Elizabeth I, 1143
Jones, Elizabeth I, 1144
Jones, Elizabeth I, 1152
Jones, Elizabeth I, 1155
Jones, Elizabeth I, 1156
Jones, Elizabeth I Sup 1, 7
Jones, Elizabeth II, 127
Jones, Elizabeth II, 134
Jones, Elizabeth II, 152
Jones, Elizabeth II, 160
Jones, Elizabeth II, 177
Jones, Elizabeth II, 194
Jones, Elizabeth II, 235
Jones, Elizabeth II, 236
Jones, Elizabeth II, 250
Jones, Elizabeth II, 383
Jones, Elizabeth II, 384
Jones, Elizabeth II, 421
Jones, Elizabeth II, 456
Jones, Elizabeth II, 527
Jones, Elizabeth II, 529
Jones, Elizabeth II, 558
Jones, Elizabeth II, 567
Jones, Elizabeth II, 569
Jones, Elizabeth II, 570
Jones, Elizabeth II, 583
Jones, Elizabeth II, 592
Jones, Elizabeth II, 653
Jones, Elizabeth II, 684
Jones, Elizabeth II, 734
Jones, Elizabeth II, 749
Jones, Elizabeth II, 763
Jones, Elizabeth II, 769
Jones, Elizabeth II, 787
Jones, Elizabeth II, 803
Jones, Elizabeth II, 804
Jones, Elizabeth II, 807
Jones, Elizabeth II, 821
Jones, Elizabeth II, 884
Jones, Elizabeth III, 188
Jones, Elizabeth III, 422
Jones, Elizabeth III, 487
Jones, Elizabeth III, 497
Jones, Elizabeth III, 510
Jones, Elizabeth IV, 96
Jones, Elizabeth IV, 231
Jones, Elizabeth IV, 291
Jones, Elizabeth IV, 300
Jones, Elizabeth IV, 357
Jones, Elizabeth IV, 480
Jones, Elizabeth IV, 494
Jones, Elizabeth IV, 503
Jones, Elizabeth IV, 639
Jones, Elizabeth IV, 680
Jones, Elizabeth IV, 681
Jones, Elizabeth IV, 947
Jones, Elizabeth IV, 971
Jones, Elizabeth IV, 1063
Jones, Elizabeth IV, 1078
Jones, Elizabeth IV, 1283
Jones, Elizabeth IV, 1323
Jones, Elizabeth V, 28
Jones, Elizabeth V, 85
Jones, Elizabeth V, 86
Jones, Elizabeth V, 87
Jones, Elizabeth V, 140
Jones, Elizabeth V, 256
Jones, Elizabeth V, 408
Jones, Elizabeth V, 579
Jones, Elizabeth V, 631
Jones, Elizabeth V, 747
Jones, Elizabeth V, 748
Jones, Elizabeth V, 749
Jones, Elizabeth V, 750
Jones, Elizabeth V, 768
Jones, Elizabeth V, 794
Jones, Elizabeth V, 813
Jones, Elizabeth V, 814
Jones, Elizabeth V, 914
Jones, Elizabeth V, 954
Jones, Elizabeth VI, 72
Jones, Elizabeth VI, 188
Jones, Elizabeth VI, 202
Jones, Elizabeth VI, 802
Jones, Elizabeth VI, 805
Jones, Elizabeth VI, 814
Jones, Elizabeth VI, 817
Jones, Elizabeth VI, 824
Jones, Elizabeth VI, 830
Jones, Elizabeth VI, 854
Jones, Elizabeth VI, 870
Jones, Elizabeth VI, 872
Jones, Elizabeth VI, 876
Jones, Elizabeth VI, 877
Jones, Elizabeth VI, 882
Jones, Elizabeth VI, 901
Jones, Elizabeth VI, 929
Jones, Elizabeth VI, 942
Jones, Elizabeth VI, 943
Jones, Elizabeth VI, 967
Jones, Elizabeth Ann II, 804
Jones, Elizabeth Ann II, 884
Jones, Elizabeth Ann VI, 943
Jones, Elizabeth B. V, 87
Jones, Elizabeth C. II, 152
Jones, Elizabeth E. II, 878
Jones, Elizabeth E. II, 884
Jones, Elizabeth Evans II, 803
Jones, Elizabeth F. VI, 905
Jones, Elizabeth H. III, 157
Jones, Elizabeth H. III, 187
Jones, Elizabeth H. V, 748
Jones, Elizabeth H. VI, 659
Jones, Elizabeth H. VI, 669
Jones, Elizabeth J. I, 1142
Jones, Elizabeth J. I, 1143
Jones, Elizabeth J. II, 749
Jones, Elizabeth J. II, 766
Jones, Elizabeth J. II, 884
Jones, Elizabeth J. II, 921
Jones, Elizabeth J. IV, 211
Jones, Elizabeth J. IV, 681
Jones, Elizabeth Jane I, 1143
Jones, Elizabeth Jane V, 813
Jones, Elizabeth Jane Beryl V, 750
Jones, Elizabeth L. II, 884
Jones, Elizabeth L. IV, 231
Jones, Elizabeth L. IV, 480
Jones, Elizabeth L. IV, 499
Jones, Elizabeth L. IV, 500
Jones, Elizabeth L. IV, 970
Jones, Elizabeth L. IV, 971
Jones, Elizabeth L. IV, 988
Jones, Elizabeth Ladd IV, 231
Jones, Elizabeth Ladd IV, 480
Jones, Elizabeth M. IV, 729
Jones, Elizabeth M. V, 63
Jones, Elizabeth M. V, 86
Jones, Elizabeth M. V, 568
Jones, Elizabeth M. V, 748
Jones, Elizabeth P. IV, 231
Jones, Elizabeth P. VI, 943
Jones, Elizabeth R. V, 28
Jones, Elizabeth R. V, 86
Jones, Elizabeth R. V, 478
Jones, Elizabeth R. V, 507
Jones, Elizabeth R. VI, 942
Jones, Elizabeth S. I, 555
Jones, Elizabeth S. II, 749
Jones, Elizabeth W. II, 805
Jones, Elizabeth W. VI, 848
Jones, Elizabeth, Jr. II, 709
Jones, Ella I, 823
Jones, Ella V, 579
Jones, Ella F. IV, 1323
Jones, Ella M. III, 188
Jones, Ellen A. III, 510
Jones, Ellen K. VI, 943
Jones, Elliman I, 1033
Jones, Elliott I, 55
Jones, Elliott I, 65
Jones, Ellis II, 383
Jones, Ellis II, 567
Jones, Ellis A. IV, 1255
Jones, Ellis E. IV, 1255
Jones, Ellis N. IV, 1255
Jones, Elma I, 1156
Jones, Elma V, 631
Jones, Elma V, 750
Jones, Elma B. I, 1156
Jones, Elmer R. V, 183
Jones, Elmina Adaline I, 1107
Jones, Elmira C. VI, 965
Jones, Elsie V, 183
Jones, Elva III, 123
Jones, Elva III, 310
Jones, Elvira Olinsha III, 187
Jones, Elwood IV, 971
Jones, Elwood VI, 669
Jones, Emaline H. V, 183
Jones, Emiline V, 846
Jones, Emily II, 821
Jones, Emily II, 884
Jones, Emily IV, 339
Jones, Emily IV, 970
Jones, Emily IV, 971
Jones, Emily V, 506
Jones, Emily VI, 830
Jones, Emily VI, 919
Jones, Emily Clara III, 187
Jones, Emily R. VI, 986
Jones, Emily Samira I, 1107
Jones, Emma I, 1156
Jones, Emma III, 445
Jones, Emma V, 688
Jones, Emmaline I, 1156
Jones, Emury A. IV, 1349
Jones, Emury A. IV, 1370
Jones, Endsley I, 965
Jones, Enoch I, 357
Jones, Enoch V, 740
Jones, Enoch V, 748
Jones, Enoch V, 750
Jones, Enoch V, 785
Jones, Enoch V, 787
Jones, Enoch V, 813
Jones, Enoch P. V, 787
Jones, Enos V, 749
Jones, Enos V, 813
Jones, Enos V, 863
Jones, Enos P. V, 749
Jones, Enos P. V, 750
Jones, Enos T. V, 750
Jones, Ephraim Guilford I, 1144
Jones, Ephraim Lee I, 1143
Jones, Ephraim M. V, 813
Jones, Erasmus VI, 808
Jones, Erastus S. I, 823
Jones, Erman Irene IV, 971
Jones, Ernest IV, 1168
Jones, Estella V, 408
Jones, Ester IV, 480
Jones, Ester IV, 483
Jones, Esther I, 506
Jones, Esther I, 555
Jones, Esther I, 564
Jones, Esther I, 1101
Jones, Esther I, 1107
Jones, Esther I, 1122
Jones, Esther I, 1144
Jones, Esther I, 1156
Jones, Esther II, 236
Jones, Esther II, 568
Jones, Esther II, 571
Jones, Esther II, 654
Jones, Esther II, 749
Jones, Esther III, 188
Jones, Esther III, 487
Jones, Esther V, 28
Jones, Esther V, 86
Jones, Esther V, 748
Jones, Esther V, 750
Jones, Esther V, 801
Jones, Esther V, 813
Jones, Esther V, 814
Jones, Esther E. IV, 1255
Jones, Esther T. V, 863
Jones, Esther, Sr. I, 1107
Jones, Esther, Sr. I Sup 1, 11
Jones, Ethel V, 183
Jones, Ethel C. V, 507
Jones, Ethel Curry V, 183
Jones, Ethelbert V, 579
Jones, Ethelbert V, 688
Jones, Eugene B. IV, 231
Jones, Eugene H. V, 688
Jones, Euin I, 55
Jones, Euin I, 77
Jones, Eunice I, 749
Jones, Eunice I, 760
Jones, Eunice I, 764
Jones, Eunice V, 748
Jones, Eunice V, 749
Jones, Eunice V, 822
Jones, Eunice Ann V, 813
Jones, Eunice Ann V, 816
Jones, Eva V, 256
Jones, Evan I, 358
Jones, Evan I, 383
Jones, Evan I, 401
Jones, Evan I, 965
Jones, Evan I, 1077
Jones, Evan I, 1085
Jones, Evan I, 1094
Jones, Evan I, 1142
Jones, Evan I, 1155
Jones, Evan II, 515
Jones, Evan II, 571
Jones, Evan III, 187
Jones, Evan V, 506
Jones, Evan B. II, 290
Jones, Evan, Jr. I, 1094
Jones, Eveline VI, 856
Jones, Even I, 506
Jones, Ezekiel II, 568
Jones, Ezra II, 290
Jones, Ezra II, 383
Jones, Ezra II, 384
Jones, Ezra II, 569
Jones, Ezra II, 571
Jones, Ezraetta II, 965
Jones, Ezraetta II, 1053
Jones, Ezraetta II, 1056
Jones, F. A. I, 1156
Jones, Fanny VI, 879
Jones, Fanny VI, 942
Jones, Farwell VI, 943
Jones, Fayette W. VI, 848
Jones, Fidelia V, 783
Jones, Fidelia V, 787
Jones, Flora V, 688
Jones, Flora Jane I, 749
Jones, Flora V. I, 611
Jones, Florie Leonard V, 688
Jones, Frances I, 1033
Jones, Frances VI, 942
Jones, Frances VI, 943
Jones, Frances VI, 1010
Jones, Frances A. III, 295
Jones, Frances Conner IV, 231
Jones, Frances Conner IV, 480
Jones, Frances G. VI, 946
Jones, Frances N. II, 129
Jones, Frances S. VI, 908
Jones, Francies I, 357
Jones, Francis I, 55
Jones, Francis I, 79
Jones, Francis I, 401
Jones, Francis I, 402
Jones, Francis I, 448
Jones, Francis I, 555
Jones, Francis I, 1033
Jones, Francis I, 1041
Jones, Francis I, 1043
Jones, Francis I, 1044
Jones, Francis I, 1107
Jones, Francis I, 1122
Jones, Francis I, 1137
Jones, Francis I, 1142
Jones, Francis I, 1144
Jones, Francis I, 1155
Jones, Francis I, 1156
Jones, Francis I, 1157
Jones, Francis I Sup 1, 5
Jones, Francis II, 383
Jones, Francis II, 384
Jones, Francis II, 567
Jones, Francis IV, 480
Jones, Francis V, 86
Jones, Francis V, 747
Jones, Francis V, 750
Jones, Francis V, 768
Jones, Francis V, 787
Jones, Francis VI, 830
Jones, Francis A. I, 1143
Jones, Francis A. I, 1155
Jones, Francis Alcwin I, 1142
Jones, Francis P. IV, 231
Jones, Francis Pendleton IV, 23
Jones, Francis, Jr. I, 1041
Jones, Francis, Jr. I, 1044
Jones, Francis, Jr. I, 1049
Jones, Francis, Jr. I, 1142
Jones, Francis, Jr. V, 749
Jones, Francis, Sr. I, 1043
Jones, Francis, Sr. V, 747
Jones, Francis, Sr. V, 748
Jones, Frank V, 343
Jones, Frank V, 408
Jones, Frank V, 688
Jones, Franklin II, 293
Jones, Franklin IV, 96
Jones, Franklin V, 579
Jones, Franklin V, 688
Jones, Franklin C. II, 749
Jones, Franklin Cooper II, 571
Jones, Gabl. VI, 986
Jones, Gainer II, 384
Jones, Galen C. IV, 971
Jones, Genevieve IV, 971
Jones, Genevieve W. IV, 960
Jones, Geo. C. V, 688
Jones, Georbe V, 845
Jones, George I, 337
Jones, George I, 402
Jones, George I, 448
Jones, George I, 1033
Jones, George I, 1044
Jones, George I, 1049
Jones, George I, 1144
Jones, George II, 569
Jones, George II, 570
Jones, George IV, 1370
Jones, George V, 86
Jones, George V, 183
Jones, George V, 506
Jones, George V, 827
Jones, George V, 840
Jones, George V, 845
Jones, George V, 846
Jones, George V, 872
Jones, George VI, 819

nes, George VI, 829
nes, George VI, 830
nes, George VI, 919
nes, George VI, 942
nes, George VI, 965
nes, George VI, 979
nes, George Ashbridge II, 569
nes, George C. V, 507
nes, George C. V, 688
nes, George D. II, 383
nes, George D. II, 570
nes, George D. II, 571
nes, George D. II, 709
nes, George D. II, 734
nes, George D. II, 749
nes, George D. V, 845
nes, George Dillwyn II, 383
nes, George Dillwyn II, 709
nes, George Dillwyn II, 734
nes, George Dillwyn II, 749
nes, George M. VI, 943
nes, George Parker IV, 413
nes, George W. II, 383
nes, George W. VI, 830
nes, George W. VI, 851
nes, Gertrude I, 1142
nes, Gertrude V, 86
nes, Gertrude V, 87
nes, Gertrude E. V, 183
nes, Gideon III, 487
nes, Ginerva IV, 970
nes, Grace III, 188
nes, Grace IV, 320
nes, Grace IV, 336
nes, Grace V, 846
nes, Grace Anderson IV, 1323
nes, Grace Eastburn II, 1054
nes, Granville W. II, 290
nes, Gray VI, 899
nes, Gray VI, 942
nes, Gray VI, 982
nes, Gray VI, 1016
nes, Griffith II, 383
nes, Griffith II, 445
nes, Griffith II, 474
nes, Griffith II, 529
nes, Griffith II, 558
nes, Griffith II, 567
nes, Griffith II, 568
nes, Griffith II, 569
nes, Gulia E. V, 1004
nes, Gulielma II, 913
nes, Gulielma IV, 1255
nes, Gulielma VI, 256
nes, Gulielma M. II, 709
nes, Gulielma M. II, 734
nes, Gulielma M. II, 922
nes, Gulielma M. S. P. II, 749
nes, Gwendoline I, 944
nes, Gwendolyn I, 928
nes, H. M. V, 1004
nes, H. T. I, 1156
nes, Haden VI, 830
nes, Hallet III, 487
nes, Hannah I, 357
nes, Hannah I, 379
nes, Hannah I, 401
nes, Hannah I, 402
nes, Hannah I, 431
nes, Hannah I, 437
nes, Hannah I, 506
nes, Hannah I, 764
nes, Hannah I, 869
nes, Hannah I, 876
nes, Hannah I, 888
nes, Hannah I, 1010
nes, Hannah I, 1013
nes, Hannah I, 1033
nes, Hannah I, 1043
nes, Hannah I, 1048
nes, Hannah I, 1049
nes, Hannah I, 1093
nes, Hannah I, 1095
nes, Hannah I, 1101
nes, Hannah I, 1107
nes, Hannah I, 1111
nes, Hannah I, 1115
nes, Hannah I, 1122
nes, Hannah I, 1123
nes, Hannah I, 1142
nes, Hannah I, 1143
nes, Hannah I, 1155
nes, Hannah I, 1156
nes, Hannah I, 1157
nes, Hannah II, 383
nes, Hannah II, 384
nes, Hannah II, 526
nes, Hannah II, 540
nes, Hannah II, 548
nes, Hannah II, 557
nes, Hannah II, 568
Jones, Hannah II, 569
Jones, Hannah II, 570
Jones, Hannah II, 571
Jones, Hannah II, 597
Jones, Hannah II, 691
Jones, Hannah II, 692
Jones, Hannah II, 749
Jones, Hannah II, 763
Jones, Hannah II, 801
Jones, Hannah II, 884
Jones, Hannah II, 990
Jones, Hannah II, 1007
Jones, Hannah II, 1050
Jones, Hannah II, 1053
Jones, Hannah III, 484
Jones, Hannah III, 487
Jones, Hannah III, 498
Jones, Hannah IV, 96
Jones, Hannah IV, 336
Jones, Hannah IV, 338
Jones, Hannah IV, 357
Jones, Hannah IV, 413
Jones, Hannah IV, 525
Jones, Hannah IV, 537
Jones, Hannah IV, 538
Jones, Hannah IV, 704
Jones, Hannah IV, 729
Jones, Hannah IV, 970
Jones, Hannah IV, 971
Jones, Hannah IV, 981
Jones, Hannah IV, 1213
Jones, Hannah V, 31
Jones, Hannah V, 85
Jones, Hannah V, 86
Jones, Hannah V, 87
Jones, Hannah V, 183
Jones, Hannah V, 343
Jones, Hannah V, 506
Jones, Hannah V, 515
Jones, Hannah V, 750
Jones, Hannah V, 840
Jones, Hannah V, 844
Jones, Hannah V, 845
Jones, Hannah V, 914
Jones, Hannah V, 941
Jones, Hannah VI, 501
Jones, Hannah VI, 509
Jones, Hannah VI, 515
Jones, Hannah VI, 518
Jones, Hannah VI, 519
Jones, Hannah VI, 520
Jones, Hannah VI, 521
Jones, Hannah VI, 522
Jones, Hannah VI, 523
Jones, Hannah VI, 553
Jones, Hannah VI, 554
Jones, Hannah VI, 573
Jones, Hannah VI, 752
Jones, Hannah VI, 754
Jones, Hannah VI, 756
Jones, Hannah VI, 757
Jones, Hannah VI, 758
Jones, Hannah VI, 774
Jones, Hannah VI, 775
Jones, Hannah VI, 942
Jones, Hannah B. V, 51
Jones, Hannah B. V, 86
Jones, Hannah B. V, 914
Jones, Hannah B. V, 972
Jones, Hannah Cobb VI, 942
Jones, Hannah Eliza II, 383
Jones, Hannah Eliza J. II, 749
Jones, Hannah Eliza J. II, 767
Jones, Hannah F. IV, 680
Jones, Hannah H. V, 87
Jones, Hannah H. V, 98
Jones, Hannah J. V, 87
Jones, Hannah M. V, 506
Jones, Hannah Miriam I, 1143
Jones, Hannah R. II, 749
Jones, Hannah R. II, 763
Jones, Hannah Roberts II, 749
Jones, Hannah T. V, 86
Jones, Hannah, Jr. I, 448
Jones, Harold J. V, 688
Jones, Harold Joshua V, 688
Jones, Harriet II, 749
Jones, Harriet V, 86
Jones, Harriet V, 113
Jones, Harriet M. II, 707
Jones, Harriet M. II, 715
Jones, Harry Raymond III, 187
Jones, Harvey V, 814
Jones, Harvey V, 822
Jones, Harvey D. III, 187
Jones, Harvey D. III, 279
Jones, Hattie C. V, 579
Jones, Hattie C. V, 688
Jones, Hattie Clifford V, 579
Jones, Hattie Clifford V, 688
Jones, Hazel IV, 971
Jones, Hazel Marie IV, 971
Jones, Helen C. II, 884
Jones, Helen Elizabeth V, 688
Jones, Helen H. IV, 537
Jones, Helen Lee II, 878
Jones, Helen Lee II, 884
Jones, Helen Maris I, 928
Jones, Helena Elizabeth V, 688
Jones, Henrietta V, 408
Jones, Henrietta L. II, 709
Jones, Henry I, 357
Jones, Henry I, 402
Jones, Henry I, 448
Jones, Henry I, 450
Jones, Henry I, 1033
Jones, Henry I, 1041
Jones, Henry I, 1043
Jones, Henry I, 1044
Jones, Henry I, 1048
Jones, Henry I, 1049
Jones, Henry I Sup 1, 9
Jones, Henry II, 383
Jones, Henry II, 384
Jones, Henry II, 567
Jones, Henry II, 568
Jones, Henry II, 676
Jones, Henry II, 997
Jones, Henry II, 1007
Jones, Henry III, 187
Jones, Henry III, 230
Jones, Henry IV, 231
Jones, Henry V, 70
Jones, Henry V, 688
Jones, Henry V, 747
Jones, Henry V, 748
Jones, Henry V, 750
Jones, Henry V, 813
Jones, Henry V, 827
Jones, Henry V, 844
Jones, Henry V, 845
Jones, Henry VI, 879
Jones, Henry VI, 894
Jones, Henry VI, 942
Jones, Henry D. IV, 971
Jones, Henry H. II, 884
Jones, Henry H. V, 688
Jones, Henry J. II, 920
Jones, Henry M. II, 749
Jones, Henry M. II, 763
Jones, Henry P. V, 688
Jones, Henry R. III, 187
Jones, Henry R. III, 188
Jones, Henry R. III, 229
Jones, Henry T. I, 1156
Jones, Henry Thornburgh I, 1125
Jones, Henry Tolbert I, 1156
Jones, Henry W. IV, 211
Jones, Henry W. V, 1004
Jones, Henry Warren V, 813
Jones, Henry, Jr. V, 845
Jones, Henry, Sr. V, 845
Jones, Herman F. V, 183
Jones, Hester V, 749
Jones, Hester V, 805
Jones, Hester V, 813
Jones, Hester E. I, 1142
Jones, Hezekiah I, 1090
Jones, Hezekiah I, 1095
Jones, Hezekiah I, 1142
Jones, Hezekiah I, 1155
Jones, Hezekiah II, 227
Jones, Hezekiah II, 235
Jones, Hezekiah II, 259
Jones, Hiatt I, 1156
Jones, Hirah IV, 537
Jones, Hiram IV, 537
Jones, Hiram V, 748
Jones, Hiram V, 750
Jones, Hiram V, 863
Jones, Holton II, 569
Jones, Honora V, 183
Jones, Howard T. IV, 611
Jones, Howard T. IV, 639
Jones, Hugh I, 965
Jones, Hugh II, 445
Jones, Hugh S. I, 1142
Jones, Huldah I, 143
Jones, Huldah I, 182
Jones, Huldah I, 184
Jones, Huldah I, 195
Jones, Huldah I, 1123
Jones, Huldah I, 1132
Jones, Huldah V, 506
Jones, Huldah V, 534
Jones, Huldah Bundy I, 185
Jones, Hulday I, 133
Jones, Huldy I, 143
Jones, Humphrey VI, 246
Jones, Humphry VI, 256
Jones, I. L. I, 1156
Jones, I. Lindley I, 1156
Jones, I. Newton V, 748
Jones, Ichsah VI, 849
Jones, Ignatious I, 1144
Jones, Ignatious I, 1156
Jones, Ignatius I, 1156
Jones, Inez V, 750
Jones, Inez D. V, 749
Jones, Irenia V, 783
Jones, Irenia V, 787
Jones, Irving Byron IV, 971
Jones, Isaac I, 10
Jones, Isaac I, 357
Jones, Isaac I, 358
Jones, Isaac I, 402
Jones, Isaac I, 506
Jones, Isaac I, 555
Jones, Isaac I, 645
Jones, Isaac I, 822
Jones, Isaac I, 888
Jones, Isaac I, 953
Jones, Isaac I, 957
Jones, Isaac I, 1010
Jones, Isaac I, 1085
Jones, Isaac I, 1094
Jones, Isaac I, 1101
Jones, Isaac I, 1107
Jones, Isaac I, 1122
Jones, Isaac I, 1123
Jones, Isaac I, 1127
Jones, Isaac I, 1142
Jones, Isaac I, 1143
Jones, Isaac I, 1155
Jones, Isaac II, 208
Jones, Isaac II, 235
Jones, Isaac II, 236
Jones, Isaac II, 271
Jones, Isaac II, 383
Jones, Isaac II, 498
Jones, Isaac II, 568
Jones, Isaac II, 569
Jones, Isaac II, 680
Jones, Isaac II, 962
Jones, Isaac II, 1052
Jones, Isaac II, 1053
Jones, Isaac IV, 480
Jones, Isaac IV, 537
Jones, Isaac V, 23
Jones, Isaac V, 86
Jones, Isaac V, 87
Jones, Isaac V, 89
Jones, Isaac V, 506
Jones, Isaac C. II, 383
Jones, Isaac C. II, 709
Jones, Isaac C. V, 863
Jones, Isaac C., Jr. II, 749
Jones, Isaac Cooper II, 383
Jones, Isaac Cooper II, 570
Jones, Isaac Cooper II, 571
Jones, Isaac E. V, 914
Jones, Isaac E. V, 972
Jones, Isaac Eli I, 749
Jones, Isaac Lindley I, 1107
Jones, Isaac M. IV, 537
Jones, Isaac N. I, 1156
Jones, Isaac Stout I, 1122
Jones, Isaac Thomas IV, 231
Jones, Isaac W. V, 85
Jones, Isaac, Jr. I, 1155
Jones, Isaac, Sr. I, 1107
Jones, Isabel Mary II, 709
Jones, Isabella I, 823
Jones, Isabella IV, 231
Jones, Isabella IV, 480
Jones, Isabella IV, 482
Jones, Isabella IV, 499
Jones, Isabella L. IV, 231
Jones, Isabella L. IV, 475
Jones, Isabella L. IV, 480
Jones, Isaiah I, 506
Jones, Isaiah I, 965
Jones, Isaiah II, 570
Jones, Israel II, 383
Jones, Israel II, 568
Jones, Israel II, 569
Jones, Israel II, 570
Jones, Israel III, 510
Jones, Israel V, 85
Jones, Israel V, 87
Jones, Israel V, 914
Jones, Israel S. III, 422
Jones, Israel S. III, 458
Jones, Israel S. III, 510
Jones, Iva IV, 971
Jones, Iva M. IV, 971
Jones, Iva Mary IV, 971
Jones, Iva Roberts V, 750
Jones, J. V, 816
Jones, J. Byron V, 748
Jones, J. C. II, 841
Jones, J. C. II, 920
Jones, J. C. IV, 503
Jones, J. Huston I, 1156
Jones, J. I. I, 310
Jones, J. J. I, 309
Jones, J. Lindley V, 631
Jones, J. M. I, 930
Jones, J. Murray IV, 971
Jones, Jack VI, 843
Jones, Jackson M. I, 823
Jones, Jacob I, 1142
Jones, Jacob I, 1144
Jones, Jacob I, 1155
Jones, Jacob II, 383
Jones, Jacob II, 384
Jones, Jacob II, 421
Jones, Jacob II, 567
Jones, Jacob II, 568
Jones, Jacob II, 571
Jones, Jacob II, 749
Jones, Jacob II, 803
Jones, Jacob II, 884
Jones, Jacob IV, 491
Jones, Jacob V, 256
Jones, Jacob VI, 799
Jones, Jacob VI, 803
Jones, Jacob Comely II, 571
Jones, Jacob Comly II, 571
Jones, Jacob P. II, 571
Jones, Jacob Paul II, 383
Jones, Jacob Paul II, 570
Jones, Jamaica III, 187
Jones, James I, 506
Jones, James I, 555
Jones, James I, 1085
Jones, James I, 1094
Jones, James I, 1095
Jones, James I, 1107
Jones, James I, 1122
Jones, James I, 1123
Jones, James I, 1128
Jones, James I, 1137
Jones, James I, 1142
Jones, James I, 1143
Jones, James I, 1144
Jones, James I, 1155
Jones, James I, 1156
Jones, James I, 1159
Jones, James II, 235
Jones, James II, 271
Jones, James II, 383
Jones, James II, 384
Jones, James II, 569
Jones, James II, 571
Jones, James II, 667
Jones, James III, 188
Jones, James III, 487
Jones, James IV, 320
Jones, James IV, 336
Jones, James IV, 480
Jones, James IV, 537
Jones, James V, 408
Jones, James V, 506
Jones, James V, 787
Jones, James V, 846
Jones, James VI, 11
Jones, James VI, 113
Jones, James VI, 801
Jones, James VI, 807
Jones, James VI, 817
Jones, James VI, 830
Jones, James VI, 842
Jones, James VI, 851
Jones, James VI, 857
Jones, James VI, 942
Jones, James VI, 992
Jones, James VI, 996
Jones, James Alford I, 1143
Jones, James B. V, 87
Jones, James B. VI, 830
Jones, James Blunt I, 1143
Jones, James Brantson V, 748
Jones, James H. V, 787
Jones, James H. VI, 383
Jones, James H. VI, 411
Jones, James Jordan Scott VI, 72
Jones, James L. VI, 825
Jones, James Nereus I, 1142
Jones, James R. I, 555
Jones, James R. I, 635
Jones, James R. I, 888
Jones, James R. I, 928
Jones, James R. VI, 844
Jones, James S. VI, 820
Jones, James S. VI, 838
Jones, James S. VI, 851
Jones, James W. VI, 69
Jones, James W. VI, 72
Jones, James William V, 846
Jones, James, Jr. II, 569
Jones, James, Jr. II, 570
Jones, Jamima I, 786
Jones, Jamima I, 797

Jones, Jamima I, 822
Jones, Jamima I, 990
Jones, Jamima I, 991
Jones, Jamima V, 256
Jones, Jane I, 34
Jones, Jane I, 55
Jones, Jane I, 357
Jones, Jane I, 358
Jones, Jane I, 448
Jones, Jane I, 1033
Jones, Jane I, 1043
Jones, Jane I, 1049
Jones, Jane I, 1050
Jones, Jane I, 1107
Jones, Jane I, 1122
Jones, Jane I, 1123
Jones, Jane I, 1127
Jones, Jane I, 1142
Jones, Jane I, 1143
Jones, Jane I, 1144
Jones, Jane I, 1155
Jones, Jane II, 82
Jones, Jane II, 94
Jones, Jane II, 194
Jones, Jane II, 235
Jones, Jane II, 383
Jones, Jane II, 384
Jones, Jane II, 515
Jones, Jane II, 526
Jones, Jane II, 567
Jones, Jane II, 568
Jones, Jane II, 570
Jones, Jane II, 571
Jones, Jane II, 601
Jones, Jane II, 638
Jones, Jane III, 449
Jones, Jane IV, 585
Jones, Jane V, 343
Jones, Jane V, 367
Jones, Jane V, 408
Jones, Jane V, 805
Jones, Jane V, 813
Jones, Jane V, 822
Jones, Jane V, 845
Jones, Jane V, 846
Jones, Jane VI, 830
Jones, Jane VI, 840
Jones, Jane B. VI, 815
Jones, Jane C. B. IV, 537
Jones, Jane L. II, 884
Jones, Jane P. II, 709
Jones, Jane P. II, 749
Jones, Jane Pennell II, 749
Jones, Jane S. III, 187
Jones, Jane, Jr. I, 1143
Jones, Jean I, 506
Jones, Jean VI, 411
Jones, Jeane I, 36
Jones, Jeane I, 55
Jones, Jefferson I, 823
Jones, Jefferson I, 944
Jones, Jefferson I, 1156
Jones, Jemima I, 358
Jones, Jemima I, 401
Jones, Jemima I, 402
Jones, Jemima I, 431
Jones, Jemima I, 448
Jones, Jemima I, 773
Jones, Jemima I, 822
Jones, Jemima I, 829
Jones, Jemima I, 830
Jones, Jemima I, 888
Jones, Jemima I, 990
Jones, Jemima V, 86
Jones, Jemima V, 256
Jones, Jemima V, 749
Jones, Jemima V, 783
Jones, Jemima V, 786
Jones, Jemima V, 787
Jones, Jemima V, 794
Jones, Jemima V, 800
Jones, Jemima VI, 920
Jones, Jemima Ann V, 787
Jones, Jemima D. II, 749
Jones, Jemima D. II, 765
Jones, Jemima Jane V, 408
Jones, Jemima Jane V, 688
Jones, Jemimah I, 357
Jones, Jemimah I, 991
Jones, Jency VI, 830
Jones, Jennie V, 183
Jones, Jennie V, 657
Jones, Jenny VI, 910
Jones, Jeremiah II, 571
Jones, Jerusha I, 1090
Jones, Jerusha I, 1095
Jones, Jerusha I, 1142
Jones, Jesse I, 358
Jones, Jesse I, 506
Jones, Jesse I, 965
Jones, Jesse I, 1044
Jones, Jesse I, 1101
Jones, Jesse I, 1107
Jones, Jesse I, 1122
Jones, Jesse I, 1125
Jones, Jesse I, 1144
Jones, Jesse II, 177
Jones, Jesse II, 236
Jones, Jesse II, 568
Jones, Jesse II, 569
Jones, Jesse II, 803
Jones, Jesse II, 962
Jones, Jesse II, 1046
Jones, Jesse II, 1053
Jones, Jesse V, 31
Jones, Jesse V, 85
Jones, Jesse V, 87
Jones, Jesse V, 735
Jones, Jesse V, 742
Jones, Jesse V, 747
Jones, Jesse V, 749
Jones, Jesse V, 750
Jones, Jesse V, 805
Jones, Jesse V, 806
Jones, Jesse V, 809
Jones, Jesse V, 813
Jones, Jesse V, 814
Jones, Jesse V, 822
Jones, Jesse VI, 819
Jones, Jesse VI, 827
Jones, Jesse VI, 830
Jones, Jesse VI, 856
Jones, Jesse VI, 858
Jones, Jesse VI, 905
Jones, Jesse VI, 931
Jones, Jesse VI, 942
Jones, Jesse VI, 943
Jones, Jesse B. II, 884
Jones, Jesse J. I, 1144
Jones, Jesse James I, 1155
Jones, Jesse O. V, 85
Jones, Jesse O. V, 87
Jones, Jesse, Jr. V, 85
Jones, Jesse, Jr. VI, 830
Jones, Jessie B. IV, 639
Jones, Jessie H. IV, 611
Jones, Jessie H. IV, 639
Jones, Jessop H. I, 1156
Jones, Joan II, 383
Jones, Joana I, 1155
Jones, Joanna I, 1113
Jones, Joanna I, 1122
Jones, Joanna I, 1143
Jones, Joanna I, 1144
Jones, Joanna B. IV, 893
Jones, Job II, 293
Jones, Job II, 803
Jones, Job II, 884
Jones, Job Mendenhall I, 482
Jones, Job Mendenhall I, 764
Jones, Job R. I, 888
Jones, Joel II, 570
Jones, Joel IV, 537
Jones, Joel VI, 830
Jones, Joel VI, 943
Jones, Joel VI, 998
Jones, Joel A. T. VI, 942
Jones, Joel A. T. VI, 982
Jones, Joel A. T. VI, 1016
Jones, Joel W. VI, 801
Jones, Joel W. VI, 830
Jones, John I, 55
Jones, John I, 64
Jones, John I, 343
Jones, John I, 357
Jones, John I, 401
Jones, John I, 402
Jones, John I, 411
Jones, John I, 506
Jones, John I, 555
Jones, John I, 1015
Jones, John I, 1033
Jones, John I, 1041
Jones, John I, 1043
Jones, John I, 1044
Jones, John I, 1049
Jones, John I, 1085
Jones, John I, 1094
Jones, John I, 1142
Jones, John I, 1155
Jones, John I Sup 1, 11
Jones, John II, 72
Jones, John II, 82
Jones, John II, 134
Jones, John II, 293
Jones, John II, 300
Jones, John II, 383
Jones, John II, 384
Jones, John II, 445
Jones, John II, 465
Jones, John II, 474
Jones, John II, 525
Jones, John II, 527
Jones, John II, 546
Jones, John II, 548
Jones, John II, 558
Jones, John II, 567
Jones, John II, 568
Jones, John II, 569
Jones, John II, 570
Jones, John II, 571
Jones, John II, 583
Jones, John II, 592
Jones, John II, 596
Jones, John II, 597
Jones, John II, 628
Jones, John II, 629
Jones, John II, 651
Jones, John II, 679
Jones, John II, 749
Jones, John II, 763
Jones, John II, 835
Jones, John II, 884
Jones, John II, 962
Jones, John II, 1046
Jones, John II, 1053
Jones, John III, 187
Jones, John III, 251
Jones, John III, 275
Jones, John III, 484
Jones, John III, 487
Jones, John IV, 34
Jones, John IV, 43
Jones, John IV, 95
Jones, John IV, 96
Jones, John IV, 480
Jones, John IV, 1323
Jones, John V, 86
Jones, John V, 87
Jones, John V, 256
Jones, John V, 306
Jones, John V, 459
Jones, John V, 506
Jones, John V, 507
Jones, John V, 745
Jones, John V, 747
Jones, John V, 748
Jones, John V, 750
Jones, John V, 755
Jones, John V, 757
Jones, John V, 770
Jones, John V, 783
Jones, John V, 787
Jones, John V, 788
Jones, John V, 800
Jones, John V, 813
Jones, John V, 814
Jones, John VI, 72
Jones, John VI, 327
Jones, John VI, 411
Jones, John VI, 521
Jones, John VI, 523
Jones, John VI, 808
Jones, John VI, 816
Jones, John VI, 830
Jones, John VI, 870
Jones, John A. V, 86
Jones, John A. V, 87
Jones, John Albert V, 408
Jones, John Albert V, 688
Jones, John Amos V, 306
Jones, John B. II, 1053
Jones, John B. III, 187
Jones, John Barclay II, 878
Jones, John Barclay II, 884
Jones, John Bartley I, 1142
Jones, John Bolter II, 384
Jones, John Brown V, 507
Jones, John C. I, 944
Jones, John C. I, 1107
Jones, John C. I, 1123
Jones, John Calvin I, 1142
Jones, John Calvin I, 1155
Jones, John D. I, 1143
Jones, John D. I, 1156
Jones, John Elias IV, 1323
Jones, John H. I, 1123
Jones, John Howard V, 506
Jones, John Howard V, 507
Jones, John Howard V, 688
Jones, John L. IV, 1255
Jones, John Luther I, 1107
Jones, John M. I, 1107
Jones, John M. II, 384
Jones, John M. II, 709
Jones, John M. VI, 800
Jones, John M. VI, 830
Jones, John M. VI, 844
Jones, John Marshall V, 408
Jones, John N. IV, 480
Jones, John R. VI, 943
Jones, John S. VI, 830
Jones, John W. V, 579
Jones, John W. V, 813
Jones, John Wm. VI, 948
Jones, John, Jr. I, 1049
Jones, John, Jr. I Sup 1, 11
Jones, John, Jr. II, 567
Jones, John, Jr. II, 569
Jones, John, Sr. IV, 480
Jones, Johnson I, 1143
Jones, Johnston I, 1137
Jones, Johnston I, 1143
Jones, Johnston I, 1155
Jones, Johnston I, 1156
Jones, Johnston Jones I, 1123
Jones, Johnstone I, 1156
Jones, Jonas VI, 943
Jones, Jonathan I, 764
Jones, Jonathan I, 1044
Jones, Jonathan I, 1049
Jones, Jonathan I, 1093
Jones, Jonathan I, 1095
Jones, Jonathan I, 1143
Jones, Jonathan I, 1144
Jones, Jonathan I, 1155
Jones, Jonathan I Sup 1, 11
Jones, Jonathan II, 134
Jones, Jonathan II, 177
Jones, Jonathan II, 235
Jones, Jonathan II, 236
Jones, Jonathan II, 384
Jones, Jonathan II, 568
Jones, Jonathan II, 569
Jones, Jonathan II, 570
Jones, Jonathan II, 597
Jones, Jonathan II, 625
Jones, Jonathan II, 803
Jones, Jonathan II, 884
Jones, Jonathan II, 962
Jones, Jonathan II, 990
Jones, Jonathan II, 1007
Jones, Jonathan IV, 96
Jones, Jonathan IV, 480
Jones, Jonathan IV, 537
Jones, Jonathan V, 85
Jones, Jonathan V, 86
Jones, Jonathan V, 87
Jones, Jonathan V, 747
Jones, Jonathan V, 748
Jones, Jonathan V, 749
Jones, Jonathan V, 750
Jones, Jonathan V, 813
Jones, Jonathan V, 814
Jones, Jonathan V, 845
Jones, Jonathan VI, 411
Jones, Jonathan C. II, 1007
Jones, Jonathan H. V, 787
Jones, Jonathan T. II, 749
Jones, Jos. IV, 499
Jones, Joseph I, 55
Jones, Joseph I, 143
Jones, Joseph I, 157
Jones, Joseph I, 162
Jones, Joseph I, 182
Jones, Joseph I, 184
Jones, Joseph I, 185
Jones, Joseph I, 195
Jones, Joseph I, 358
Jones, Joseph I, 1033
Jones, Joseph I, 1038
Jones, Joseph I, 1044
Jones, Joseph I, 1049
Jones, Joseph I, 1095
Jones, Joseph I, 1122
Jones, Joseph I, 1143
Jones, Joseph I, 1155
Jones, Joseph I, 1156
Jones, Joseph II, 383
Jones, Joseph II, 384
Jones, Joseph II, 557
Jones, Joseph II, 567
Jones, Joseph II, 568
Jones, Joseph II, 569
Jones, Joseph II, 570
Jones, Joseph II, 577
Jones, Joseph II, 597
Jones, Joseph III, 187
Jones, Joseph IV, 151
Jones, Joseph IV, 231
Jones, Joseph IV, 391
Jones, Joseph IV, 413
Jones, Joseph IV, 475
Jones, Joseph IV, 480
Jones, Joseph IV, 482
Jones, Joseph IV, 537
Jones, Joseph IV, 680
Jones, Joseph IV, 729
Jones, Joseph IV, 828
Jones, Joseph IV, 970
Jones, Joseph IV, 1206
Jones, Joseph IV, 1213
Jones, Joseph IV, 1323
Jones, Joseph V, 86
Jones, Joseph V, 845
Jones, Joseph VI, 72
Jones, Joseph VI, 113
Jones, Joseph VI, 523
Jones, Joseph VI, 942
Jones, Joseph B. IV, 971
Jones, Joseph Charles IV, 971
Jones, Joseph Denson VI, 72
Jones, Joseph E. V, 507
Jones, Joseph E. V, 688
Jones, Joseph Edward IV, 681
Jones, Joseph Edwin V, 506
Jones, Joseph Francis IV, 500
Jones, Joseph H. VI, 830
Jones, Joseph H. VI, 943
Jones, Joseph Henry I, 1107
Jones, Joseph Jones IV, 681
Jones, Joseph Morgan I, 1143
Jones, Joseph P. I, 1156
Jones, Joseph Powell II, 763
Jones, Joseph R. IV, 1323
Jones, Joseph R. V, 86
Jones, Joseph S. II, 384
Jones, Joseph T. V, 87
Jones, Joseph T. V, 408
Jones, Joseph Tompkins V, 306
Jones, Joseph Warner II, 709
Jones, Joseph Warner II, 749
Jones, Josephine V, 1004
Jones, Josephine J. V, 813
Jones, Joshen I, 10
Jones, Joshua I, 36
Jones, Joshua I, 55
Jones, Joshua I, 185
Jones, Joshua I, 193
Jones, Joshua I, 195
Jones, Joshua I, 888
Jones, Joshua II, 568
Jones, Joshua IV, 182
Jones, Joshua IV, 494
Jones, Joshua IV, 729
Jones, Joshua IV, 909
Jones, Joshua IV, 911
Jones, Joshua IV, 970
Jones, Joshua IV, 971
Jones, Joshua IV, 980
Jones, Joshua IV, 1134
Jones, Joshua V, 256
Jones, Joshua V, 814
Jones, Joshua VI, 940
Jones, Joshua VI, 942
Jones, Joshua Byron IV, 970
Jones, Joshua R. II, 884
Jones, Joshua Sharpless II, 749
Jones, Joshua Sharpless II, 884
Jones, Joshua Sharpless III, 18
Jones, Josiah II, 570
Jones, Josiah IV, 231
Jones, Josiah VI, 830
Jones, Josiah A. II, 1050
Jones, Josiah A. II, 1053
Jones, Josiah F. II, 749
Jones, Josiah F. II, 763
Jones, Josiah F. II, 1050
Jones, Josiah F. II, 1053
Jones, Judith VI, 808
Jones, Judith VI, 851
Jones, Julia V, 846
Jones, Julia E. I, 944
Jones, Julia Eleanor I, 928
Jones, Julius VI, 883
Jones, Julius VI, 910
Jones, Julius VI, 942
Jones, Julius VI, 974
Jones, Julus VI, 874
Jones, Kate IV, 1283
Jones, Kate V, 579
Jones, Kate V, 583
Jones, Kate V, 688
Jones, Katharine I, 764
Jones, Katharine I, 766
Jones, Katharine VI, 411
Jones, Katherine II, 568
Jones, Kersey IV, 96
Jones, Kesiah V, 844
Jones, Keturah II, 283
Jones, Keturah II, 293
Jones, Kezia I, 358
Jones, Kezia I, 390
Jones, Kezia I, 402
Jones, Kezia I, 528
Jones, Kezia I, 555
Jones, Kezia I, 786
Jones, Kezia I, 1044
Jones, Keziah I, 402
Jones, Keziah I, 1044
Jones, Keziah I, 1049
Jones, Keziah I, 1055
Jones, Keziah V, 70
Jones, Keziah V, 845
Jones, Keziah V, 863

es, Keziah V, 864
es, Keziah VI, 872
es, Kitty VI, 942
es, L. B. IV, 555
es, Laban J. V, 1004
es, Laban Jenks V, 813
es, Lain VI, 946
es, Lambert M. V, 813
es, Lambert W. V, 1004
es, Laura D. I, 823
es, Laura E. IV, 480
es, Laura E. V, 317
es, Laura E. V, 343
es, Laura W. IV, 1323
es, LaVan P. V, 1004
es, Lavina I, 1143
es, Lavinia II, 235
es, Lavinia II, 259
es, Le Roy II, 749
es, Leahorn V, 747
es, Lee IV, 1103
es, Lemuel I, 116
es, Lemuel IV, 231
es, Lemuel IV, 298
es, Lemuel V, 408
es, Lemuel VI, 16
es, Lemuel VI, 72
es, Lemuel O. IV, 231
es, Leon V, 688
es, Leonard V, 688
es, Leroy II, 709
es, Leroy A. V, 183
es, Letitia II, 884
es, Levi Miller IV, 970
es, Levi T. I, 1144
es, Lewallen VI, 814
es, Lewellen VI, 824
es, Lewis I, 702
es, Lewis I, 714
es, Lewis I, 723
es, Lewis I, 764
es, Lewis II, 384
es, Lewis II, 568
es, Lewis VI, 942
es, Lewis W. IV, 176
es, Lewis W. IV, 231
es, Lewis, Jr. I, 764
es, Lida I, 1156
es, Lida V, 631
es, Lida Frances II, 129
es, Lillian II, 709
es, Lillian II, 1050
es, Lillian II, 1054
es, Lillian E. II, 959
es, Lillian H. I, 614
es, Lillian H. II, 1050
es, Lillian H. II, 1053
es, Linda III, 187
es, Linda Cary III, 187
es, Linda L. III, 157
es, Lindley V, 631
es, Lindley M. IV, 971
es, Lindley M. V, 750
es, Lindley M. V, 813
es, Lindley M. V, 814
es, Lindley M. H. I, 1143
es, Lindley Murray IV, 970
es, Lindley Sebohm V, 579
es, Lizzie IV, 1168
es, Lloyd II, 801
es, Lloyd II, 803
es, Lloyd II, 884
es, Lloyd Balderston IV, 537
es, Lockey VI, 807
es, Lockey VI, 997
es, Lois Emily V, 750
es, Loranzo B. I, 1156
es, Loretta IV, 1168
es, Loretta E. VI, 998
es, Lottie Leigh I, 620
es, Lottie Leigh I, 636
es, Louella C. V, 688
es, Louella K. V, 693
es, Louella Kate V, 579
es, Louis V, 688
es, Louis C. II, 571
es, Louis C. II, 691
es, Louis T. V, 688
es, Louis T. V, 694
es, Louisa III, 187
nes, Louisa III, 230
nes, Louisa IV, 480
nes, Louisa VI, 72
nes, Louisa A. V, 846
nes, Louisa E. I, 714
nes, Louisa E. I, 723
nes, Louisa W. VI, 825
nes, Louiza J. IV, 971
nes, Louiza J. IV, 1002
nes, Louiza Jane IV, 970
nes, Lowry II, 384
Jones, Lucile V, 408
Jones, Lucile May V, 408
Jones, Lucinda I, 1142
Jones, Lucinda I, 1143
Jones, Lucinda I, 1156
Jones, Lucinda Elizabeth I, 1156
Jones, Lucretia Bailey V, 688
Jones, Lucretia Bell V, 656
Jones, Lucretia Bell V, 721
Jones, Lucy VI, 113
Jones, Lucy VI, 806
Jones, Lucy VI, 942
Jones, Lucy VI, 1005
Jones, Lucy VI, 1018
Jones, Lucy A. VI, 830
Jones, Lucy A. VI, 857
Jones, Luella V, 688
Jones, Luella V, 845
Jones, Luella V, 846
Jones, Luella Letitia IV, 537
Jones, Luella Letitia IV, 555
Jones, Luella Walker IV, 537
Jones, Luellen V, 579
Jones, Luke Jones I, 1123
Jones, Luke Thomas V, 813
Jones, Lula I, 1148
Jones, Lula I, 1156
Jones, Lula V, 688
Jones, Lula V, 709
Jones, Lula A. I, 1156
Jones, Lulu V, 688
Jones, Lutetia I, 1156
Jones, Lutitia I, 1142
Jones, Luvenia V, 741
Jones, Luvenia V, 748
Jones, Luzena I, 1144
Jones, Lyda V, 845
Jones, Lydia I, 786
Jones, Lydia I, 888
Jones, Lydia I, 1107
Jones, Lydia I, 1122
Jones, Lydia I, 1125
Jones, Lydia I, 1144
Jones, Lydia II, 570
Jones, Lydia II, 571
Jones, Lydia II, 609
Jones, Lydia II, 648
Jones, Lydia II, 684
Jones, Lydia II, 691
Jones, Lydia II, 749
Jones, Lydia II, 803
Jones, Lydia II, 884
Jones, Lydia II, 1052
Jones, Lydia II, 1053
Jones, Lydia III, 487
Jones, Lydia IV, 150
Jones, Lydia IV, 151
Jones, Lydia V, 31
Jones, Lydia V, 85
Jones, Lydia V, 87
Jones, Lydia V, 506
Jones, Lydia V, 747
Jones, Lydia V, 748
Jones, Lydia V, 749
Jones, Lydia V, 814
Jones, Lydia V, 840
Jones, Lydia V, 845
Jones, Lydia V, 846
Jones, Lydia V, 872
Jones, Lydia A. V, 813
Jones, Lydia Ann IV, 875
Jones, Lydia ann IV, 875
Jones, Lydia Ann V, 740
Jones, Lydia Ann V, 750
Jones, Lydia Ann V, 787
Jones, Lydia Ann VI, 669
Jones, Lydia C. IV, 1255
Jones, Lydia E. V, 45
Jones, Lydia E. V, 87
Jones, Lydia F. II, 571
Jones, Lydia H. II, 709
Jones, Lydia L. II, 749
Jones, Lydia L. II, 763
Jones, Lydia L. II, 769
Jones, Lydia L. II, 804
Jones, Lydia L. II, 884
Jones, Lydia S. II, 236
Jones, Lydia S. II, 749
Jones, Lydia S. II, 763
Jones, Lydia, Sr. V, 845
Jones, Lyman W. V, 820
Jones, M. Captolia I, 1156
Jones, M. E. I, 1156
Jones, M. Oliver IV, 96
Jones, Mabel Catherine V, 688
Jones, Mabel Paine V, 688
Jones, Madison VI, 830
Jones, Magdaleen VI, 830
Jones, Malachi I, 55
Jones, Malachi I, 74
Jones, Mamie I, 635
Jones, Manson VI, 830
Jones, Margarata VI, 942
Jones, Margaret I, 55
Jones, Margaret I, 134
Jones, Margaret I, 143
Jones, Margaret I, 402
Jones, Margaret I, 407
Jones, Margaret I, 482
Jones, Margaret I, 749
Jones, Margaret I, 764
Jones, Margaret I, 1033
Jones, Margaret I, 1122
Jones, Margaret I, 1123
Jones, Margaret I, 1137
Jones, Margaret I, 1155
Jones, Margaret II, 227
Jones, Margaret II, 235
Jones, Margaret II, 236
Jones, Margaret II, 293
Jones, Margaret II, 311
Jones, Margaret II, 321
Jones, Margaret II, 383
Jones, Margaret II, 384
Jones, Margaret II, 511
Jones, Margaret II, 567
Jones, Margaret II, 568
Jones, Margaret II, 570
Jones, Margaret II, 571
Jones, Margaret II, 679
Jones, Margaret II, 708
Jones, Margaret II, 749
Jones, Margaret II, 804
Jones, Margaret II, 826
Jones, Margaret III, 416
Jones, Margaret III, 422
Jones, Margaret IV, 480
Jones, Margaret IV, 487
Jones, Margaret V, 70
Jones, Margaret V, 86
Jones, Margaret V, 87
Jones, Margaret V, 506
Jones, Margaret V, 507
Jones, Margaret V, 512
Jones, Margaret V, 747
Jones, Margaret V, 748
Jones, Margaret V, 787
Jones, Margaret V, 813
Jones, Margaret VI, 256
Jones, Margaret Ann V, 914
Jones, Margaret B. VI, 249
Jones, Margaret B. VI, 256
Jones, Margaret C. IV, 74
Jones, Margaret C. IV, 96
Jones, Margaret Cynthia III, 187
Jones, Margaret Louisa V, 408
Jones, Margaret M. I, 888
Jones, Margaret M. IV, 537
Jones, Margaret M. IV, 639
Jones, Margaret M. IV, 656
Jones, Margaret, Jr. I, 55
Jones, Margarett I, 819
Jones, Margarett I, 823
Jones, Margaretta II, 571
Jones, Margarette II, 383
Jones, Margret I, 184
Jones, Margret I, 1143
Jones, Margret I, 1155
Jones, Margret Jane I, 1144
Jones, Maria IV, 74
Jones, Maria IV, 95
Jones, Maria IV, 96
Jones, Maria IV, 231
Jones, Maria IV, 291
Jones, Maria IV, 413
Jones, Maria VI, 72
Jones, Maria P. IV, 43
Jones, Maria W. IV, 231
Jones, Maria W. IV, 480
Jones, Mariah IV, 413
Jones, Mariah IV, 448
Jones, Mariah L. VI, 830
Jones, Mariam I, 722
Jones, Mariam I, 731
Jones, Mariam I, 1123
Jones, Mariam, Jr. I, 195
Jones, Marie IV, 231
Jones, Marie VI, 410
Jones, Marie VI, 411
Jones, Marietta III, 422
Jones, Marietta III, 458
Jones, Marium I, 195
Jones, Mark V, 787
Jones, Mark V, 822
Jones, Mark C. V, 813
Jones, Mark C. V, 814
Jones, Marshal B. VI, 830
Jones, Marshall II, 569
Jones, Marshall II, 570
Jones, Martha I, 555
Jones, Martha I, 801
Jones, Martha I, 822
Jones, Martha I, 1107
Jones, Martha I, 1122
Jones, Martha I, 1125
Jones, Martha I, 1143
Jones, Martha I, 1144
Jones, Martha I, 1150
Jones, Martha I, 1155
Jones, Martha I Sup 1, 12
Jones, Martha II, 177
Jones, Martha II, 236
Jones, Martha II, 383
Jones, Martha II, 384
Jones, Martha II, 445
Jones, Martha II, 465
Jones, Martha II, 568
Jones, Martha II, 569
Jones, Martha II, 570
Jones, Martha II, 571
Jones, Martha II, 709
Jones, Martha II, 884
Jones, Martha III, 466
Jones, Martha IV, 43
Jones, Martha IV, 96
Jones, Martha IV, 231
Jones, Martha IV, 1370
Jones, Martha V, 63
Jones, Martha V, 86
Jones, Martha V, 343
Jones, Martha V, 408
Jones, Martha V, 748
Jones, Martha V, 749
Jones, Martha V, 766
Jones, Martha V, 788
Jones, Martha V, 793
Jones, Martha V, 845
Jones, Martha V, 872
Jones, Martha V, 883
Jones, Martha V, 887
Jones, Martha V, 914
Jones, Martha VI, 30
Jones, Martha VI, 35
Jones, Martha VI, 72
Jones, Martha VI, 669
Jones, Martha VI, 759
Jones, Martha VI, 765
Jones, Martha VI, 807
Jones, Martha VI, 810
Jones, Martha VI, 814
Jones, Martha VI, 830
Jones, Martha VI, 866
Jones, Martha VI, 943
Jones, Martha VI, 1016
Jones, Martha A. III, 510
Jones, Martha A. V, 183
Jones, Martha A. V, 846
Jones, Martha A. VI, 830
Jones, Martha Ann I, 1143
Jones, Martha Ann IV, 211
Jones, Martha Ann IV, 231
Jones, Martha Ann V, 506
Jones, Martha Ann V, 787
Jones, Martha Ann VI, 943
Jones, Martha Eliza I, 723
Jones, Martha Elizabeth I, 1142
Jones, Martha Estella V, 408
Jones, Martha Estella V, 688
Jones, Martha J. V, 910
Jones, Martha J. V, 914
Jones, Martha J. VI, 830
Jones, Martha L. II, 884
Jones, Martha L. II, 911
Jones, Martha L. V, 97
Jones, Martha L. VI, 819
Jones, Martha M. IV, 1370
Jones, Martha N. I, 1156
Jones, Martha P. VI, 901
Jones, Martha R. V, 183
Jones, Martha U. I, 1144
Jones, Marthasa I, 1144
Jones, Martin VI, 830
Jones, Martin VI, 866
Jones, Martin VI, 889
Jones, Martin VI, 942
Jones, Marvin V, 750
Jones, Marvin H. V, 631
Jones, Marvin Hatcher V, 750
Jones, Mary I, 10
Jones, Mary I, 46
Jones, Mary I, 50
Jones, Mary I, 53
Jones, Mary I, 55
Jones, Mary I, 63
Jones, Mary I, 65
Jones, Mary I, 74
Jones, Mary I, 76
Jones, Mary I, 79
Jones, Mary I, 81
Jones, Mary I, 143
Jones, Mary I, 157
Jones, Mary I, 180
Jones, Mary I, 182
Jones, Mary I, 184
Jones, Mary I, 185
Jones, Mary I, 195
Jones, Mary I, 202
Jones, Mary I, 358
Jones, Mary I, 382
Jones, Mary I, 383
Jones, Mary I, 385
Jones, Mary I, 401
Jones, Mary I, 402
Jones, Mary I, 506
Jones, Mary I, 555
Jones, Mary I, 702
Jones, Mary I, 711
Jones, Mary I, 713
Jones, Mary I, 714
Jones, Mary I, 723
Jones, Mary I, 764
Jones, Mary I, 786
Jones, Mary I, 888
Jones, Mary I, 1033
Jones, Mary I, 1038
Jones, Mary I, 1043
Jones, Mary I, 1044
Jones, Mary I, 1049
Jones, Mary I, 1051
Jones, Mary I, 1085
Jones, Mary I, 1091
Jones, Mary I, 1095
Jones, Mary I, 1107
Jones, Mary I, 1123
Jones, Mary I, 1142
Jones, Mary I, 1143
Jones, Mary I, 1144
Jones, Mary I, 1147
Jones, Mary I, 1155
Jones, Mary I, 1163
Jones, Mary I Sup 1, 4
Jones, Mary I Sup 1, 5
Jones, Mary I Sup 1, 7
Jones, Mary I Sup 1, 8
Jones, Mary II, 72
Jones, Mary II, 82
Jones, Mary II, 134
Jones, Mary II, 177
Jones, Mary II, 208
Jones, Mary II, 235
Jones, Mary II, 236
Jones, Mary II, 266
Jones, Mary II, 271
Jones, Mary II, 282
Jones, Mary II, 293
Jones, Mary II, 300
Jones, Mary II, 321
Jones, Mary II, 368
Jones, Mary II, 383
Jones, Mary II, 384
Jones, Mary II, 402
Jones, Mary II, 445
Jones, Mary II, 522
Jones, Mary II, 557
Jones, Mary II, 567
Jones, Mary II, 568
Jones, Mary II, 569
Jones, Mary II, 570
Jones, Mary II, 571
Jones, Mary II, 601
Jones, Mary II, 602
Jones, Mary II, 629
Jones, Mary II, 674
Jones, Mary II, 680
Jones, Mary II, 803
Jones, Mary II, 884
Jones, Mary II, 962
Jones, Mary II, 990
Jones, Mary II, 1007
Jones, Mary III, 127
Jones, Mary III, 187
Jones, Mary III, 188
Jones, Mary III, 422
Jones, Mary III, 457
Jones, Mary III, 487
Jones, Mary III, 501
Jones, Mary IV, 43
Jones, Mary IV, 49
Jones, Mary IV, 57
Jones, Mary IV, 73
Jones, Mary IV, 96
Jones, Mary IV, 151
Jones, Mary IV, 231
Jones, Mary IV, 289
Jones, Mary IV, 413
Jones, Mary IV, 414
Jones, Mary IV, 480
Jones, Mary IV, 537
Jones, Mary IV, 639
Jones, Mary IV, 971
Jones, Mary IV, 1206
Jones, Mary IV, 1213
Jones, Mary IV, 1370
Jones, Mary V, 46

Jones, Mary V, 85
Jones, Mary V, 86
Jones, Mary V, 87
Jones, Mary V, 183
Jones, Mary V, 408
Jones, Mary V, 579
Jones, Mary V, 723
Jones, Mary V, 736
Jones, Mary V, 744
Jones, Mary V, 746
Jones, Mary V, 747
Jones, Mary V, 748
Jones, Mary V, 749
Jones, Mary V, 750
Jones, Mary V, 765
Jones, Mary V, 783
Jones, Mary V, 785
Jones, Mary V, 787
Jones, Mary V, 789
Jones, Mary V, 794
Jones, Mary V, 800
Jones, Mary V, 801
Jones, Mary V, 807
Jones, Mary V, 809
Jones, Mary V, 813
Jones, Mary V, 814
Jones, Mary V, 822
Jones, Mary V, 827
Jones, Mary V, 843
Jones, Mary V, 845
Jones, Mary V, 846
Jones, Mary V, 972
Jones, Mary V, 973
Jones, Mary VI, 411
Jones, Mary VI, 523
Jones, Mary VI, 573
Jones, Mary VI, 803
Jones, Mary VI, 820
Jones, Mary VI, 830
Jones, Mary VI, 849
Jones, Mary VI, 877
Jones, Mary VI, 942
Jones, Mary VI, 954
Jones, Mary VI, 968
Jones, Mary VI, 1019
Jones, Mary A. I, 926
Jones, Mary A. I, 933
Jones, Mary A. II, 804
Jones, Mary A. II, 873
Jones, Mary A. II, 884
Jones, Mary A. IV, 298
Jones, Mary A. IV, 938
Jones, Mary A. IV, 970
Jones, Mary A. IV, 971
Jones, Mary A. V, 86
Jones, Mary Adalade V, 579
Jones, Mary Ann I, 1142
Jones, Mary Ann I, 1144
Jones, Mary Ann I, 1156
Jones, Mary Ann II, 290
Jones, Mary Ann II, 293
Jones, Mary Ann II, 804
Jones, Mary Ann IV, 231
Jones, Mary Ann IV, 537
Jones, Mary Ann IV, 875
Jones, Mary Ann V, 506
Jones, Mary Ann V, 747
Jones, Mary Ann V, 749
Jones, Mary Ann V, 880
Jones, Mary Ann V, 883
Jones, Mary Ann V, 884
Jones, Mary Ann V, 1004
Jones, Mary Ann VI, 669
Jones, Mary Ann VI, 838
Jones, Mary Ann Longstreth IV, 639
Jones, Mary Anna II, 884
Jones, Mary Anna II, 885
Jones, Mary Anna L. IV, 639
Jones, Mary B. II, 383
Jones, Mary B. II, 571
Jones, Mary B. II, 1053
Jones, Mary Beals I, 1145
Jones, Mary C. I, 723
Jones, Mary C. I, 1156
Jones, Mary C. IV, 96
Jones, Mary C. IV, 107
Jones, Mary C. IV, 970
Jones, Mary C. IV, 971
Jones, Mary C. IV, 1002
Jones, Mary C. IV, 1255
Jones, Mary C. V, 813
Jones, Mary Carpenter II, 571
Jones, Mary D. V, 688
Jones, Mary E. II, 804
Jones, Mary E. III, 188
Jones, Mary E. IV, 1213
Jones, Mary E. V, 183
Jones, Mary E. V, 408
Jones, Mary E. V, 688
Jones, Mary E. VI, 894
Jones, Mary E. VI, 942
Jones, Mary Edna IV, 1255
Jones, Mary Eleanor V, 748
Jones, Mary Eliza IV, 1370
Jones, Mary Eliza V, 750
Jones, Mary Elizabeth II, 709
Jones, Mary Elizabeth II, 749
Jones, Mary Elizabeth IV, 231
Jones, Mary Elizabeth V, 408
Jones, Mary Elizabeth V, 688
Jones, Mary Elizabeth V, 846
Jones, Mary Ellen V, 408
Jones, Mary Elmy II, 289
Jones, Mary Elmy II, 293
Jones, Mary Emaline V, 846
Jones, Mary Emily II, 821
Jones, Mary Emma V, 750
Jones, Mary Eveline I, 1143
Jones, Mary F. I, 635
Jones, Mary F. I, 888
Jones, Mary F. IV, 1168
Jones, Mary F. D. VI, 943
Jones, Mary Frances Ann Maria VI, 977
Jones, Mary G. II, 835
Jones, Mary G. II, 884
Jones, Mary H. II, 319
Jones, Mary H. II, 321
Jones, Mary H. V, 183
Jones, Mary J. II, 885
Jones, Mary J. II, 1047
Jones, Mary J. II, 1053
Jones, Mary J. III, 510
Jones, Mary Jane I, 241
Jones, Mary Jane I, 243
Jones, Mary Jane I, 329
Jones, Mary K. II, 884
Jones, Mary Kirk II, 803
Jones, Mary L. II, 884
Jones, Mary L. II, 911
Jones, Mary L. VI, 913
Jones, Mary Lizzie IV, 231
Jones, Mary M. II, 851
Jones, Mary M. II, 884
Jones, Mary M. V, 813
Jones, Mary M. VI, 943
Jones, Mary P. II, 384
Jones, Mary P. III, 487
Jones, Mary P. IV, 176
Jones, Mary P. IV, 231
Jones, Mary P. V, 87
Jones, Mary P. V, 914
Jones, Mary Potter V, 183
Jones, Mary Powel II, 569
Jones, Mary Powel II, 625
Jones, Mary Price V, 86
Jones, Mary R. V, 579
Jones, Mary S. VI, 842
Jones, Mary Susannah I, 749
Jones, Mary T. I, 555
Jones, Mary T. IV, 231
Jones, Mary T. IV, 1213
Jones, Mary T. IV, 1255
Jones, Mary Turner V, 459
Jones, Mary Vanetta IV, 480
Jones, Mary W. VI, 830
Jones, Mary W. VI, 878
Jones, Mary, Jr. IV, 537
Jones, Maryann II, 884
Jones, Maryann IV, 537
Jones, Maryann V, 787
Jones, Mason V, 256
Jones, Massey II, 801
Jones, Mathew II, 603
Jones, Mathew IV, 231
Jones, Mathew Oliver IV, 96
Jones, Matthew VI, 62
Jones, Matthew VI, 72
Jones, Matthew VI, 113
Jones, Matthew Oliver IV, 231
Jones, Matthew Oliver IV, 729
Jones, Mattie I, 930
Jones, Mattie V, 183
Jones, Mattie V, 367
Jones, Mattie V, 750
Jones, Maud M. V, 408
Jones, Maurice V, 750
Jones, Maurice Motta V, 749
Jones, May V, 459
Jones, Mercy II, 1052
Jones, Mercy II, 1053
Jones, Meriam I, 377
Jones, Meriam I, 401
Jones, Meriam III, 187
Jones, Meriam III, 188
Jones, Merideth E. I, 1156
Jones, Micaj I, 1010
Jones, Micajah I, 506
Jones, Micajah I, 822
Jones, Micajah V, 507
Jones, Micajah I. V, 506
Jones, Micajah J. IV, 971
Jones, Micajah J. V, 507
Jones, Micajah Johnson IV, 970
Jones, Micajah, Jr. V, 688
Jones, Milas I, 1143
Jones, Milas I, 1155
Jones, Milborn V, 747
Jones, Mildred IV, 231
Jones, Mildred V, 659
Jones, Mildred V, 688
Jones, Mildred V, 721
Jones, Mildred Ann VI, 1019
Jones, Milicent I, 723
Jones, Milicent I, 729
Jones, Milient I, 723
Jones, Millie I, 1156
Jones, Millisent I, 764
Jones, Mills I, 1142
Jones, Milly V, 749
Jones, Milly VI, 942
Jones, Milly W. VI, 942
Jones, Milton IV, 1323
Jones, Milton V, 688
Jones, Milton V, 846
Jones, Milton I. VI, 871
Jones, Milton J. VI, 871
Jones, Milton J. VI, 938
Jones, Milton J. VI, 941
Jones, Milton S. IV, 1323
Jones, Mina V, 846
Jones, Mina V, 857
Jones, Minerva VI, 918
Jones, Minnie I, 922
Jones, Minnie V, 408
Jones, Minnie A. IV, 1255
Jones, Minnie B. IV, 1255
Jones, Minnie Belle I, 930
Jones, Miriam I, 143
Jones, Miriam I, 184
Jones, Miriam I, 195
Jones, Miriam I, 198
Jones, Miriam I, 357
Jones, Miriam I, 358
Jones, Miriam I, 401
Jones, Miriam I, 402
Jones, Miriam I, 506
Jones, Miriam I, 786
Jones, Miriam I, 965
Jones, Miriam I, 1090
Jones, Miriam I, 1094
Jones, Miriam I, 1143
Jones, Miriam V, 506
Jones, Miriam Ann I, 1143
Jones, Miriam Samantha Jane I, 1107
Jones, Missouri IV, 970
Jones, Missouri L. IV, 970
Jones, Missouri L. IV, 971
Jones, Mordecai II, 570
Jones, Morgan V, 86
Jones, Morgan V, 87
Jones, Morris II, 445
Jones, Mrs. Ann VI, 11
Jones, Murray IV, 971
Jones, Murry J. IV, 971
Jones, Mzrtha II, 570
Jones, Nancy I, 28
Jones, Nancy I, 191
Jones, Nancy I, 195
Jones, Nancy I, 201
Jones, Nancy I, 1123
Jones, Nancy I, 1142
Jones, Nancy I, 1156
Jones, Nancy IV, 624
Jones, Nancy IV, 639
Jones, Nancy IV, 729
Jones, Nancy V, 787
Jones, Nancy VI, 820
Jones, Nancy VI, 823
Jones, Nancy VI, 824
Jones, Nancy VI, 827
Jones, Nancy VI, 830
Jones, Nancy VI, 856
Jones, Nancy VI, 858
Jones, Nancy VI, 872
Jones, Nancy VI, 889
Jones, Nancy VI, 890
Jones, Nancy VI, 893
Jones, Nancy VI, 920
Jones, Nancy VI, 924
Jones, Nancy VI, 942
Jones, Nancy C. VI, 842
Jones, Nancy Elizabeth I, 1143
Jones, Nancy J. VI, 830
Jones, Nancy L. VI, 942
Jones, Nancy Lora III, 187
Jones, Nancy T. I, 1143
Jones, Naomi V, 748
Jones, Naomi V, 749
Jones, Naomi V, 750
Jones, Naomi V, 770
Jones, Naomi V, 813
Jones, Naomi V, 822
Jones, Naomy V, 845
Jones, Narcissa I, 1142
Jones, Narcissa V, 87
Jones, Narcissa V, 579
Jones, Nathan I, 555
Jones, Nathan I, 1049
Jones, Nathan V, 86
Jones, Nathan V, 787
Jones, Nathan V, 845
Jones, Nathan V, 863
Jones, Nathaniel II, 749
Jones, Nathaniel II, 1053
Jones, Nathaniel VI, 815
Jones, Nathaniel VI, 830
Jones, Nathaniel VI, 856
Jones, Nathaniel B. II, 709
Jones, Nathaniel B. II, 1052
Jones, Nathaniel B. II, 1053
Jones, Nathaniel H. II, 709
Jones, Nell M. I, 611
Jones, Nellie E. IV, 971
Jones, Nellie L. I, 555
Jones, Nellie L. I, 635
Jones, Nellie L. I, 888
Jones, Nellie Ruthanna B. IV, 1168
Jones, Nelson VI, 1008
Jones, Nettie IV, 1168
Jones, Newell P. V, 846
Jones, Newton I, 1143
Jones, Newton I, 1156
Jones, Newton V, 86
Jones, Newton V, 750
Jones, Newton V, 845
Jones, Nicolis VI, 1005
Jones, Nila Cleona IV, 875
Jones, Noah II, 82
Jones, Nora Solota V, 813
Jones, Norman V, 750
Jones, Norris II, 383
Jones, Norris II, 384
Jones, Norris II, 569
Jones, Norris II, 570
Jones, Oakley VI, 830
Jones, Obadiah I, 990
Jones, Obadiah I, 1142
Jones, Obadiah I, 1143
Jones, Obadiah I, 1150
Jones, Obadiah V, 749
Jones, Obadiah V, 787
Jones, Obadiah V, 790
Jones, Obidiah V, 86
Jones, Oela Bell I, 1156
Jones, Olive E. V, 408
Jones, Oliver III, 187
Jones, Oliver III, 188
Jones, Oliver IV, 970
Jones, Oliver H. II, 803
Jones, Oliver H. II, 884
Jones, Oliver H. IV, 639
Jones, Oliver W. III, 188
Jones, Oliver W. IV, 231
Jones, Olivia II, 384
Jones, Olivia W. VI, 817
Jones, Ora Anna V, 813
Jones, Oren Edward IV, 971
Jones, Orenda VI, 806
Jones, Orender VI, 830
Jones, Orval S. V, 408
Jones, Oscar V, 183
Jones, Oscar V, 688
Jones, Owen II, 127
Jones, Owen II, 134
Jones, Owen II, 152
Jones, Owen II, 177
Jones, Owen II, 236
Jones, Owen II, 384
Jones, Owen II, 526
Jones, Owen II, 567
Jones, Owen II, 568
Jones, Owen II, 569
Jones, Owen II, 570
Jones, Owen II, 605
Jones, Owen II, 625
Jones, Owen II, 642
Jones, Owen II, 803
Jones, Owen II, 884
Jones, Owen V, 85
Jones, Owen V, 87
Jones, Owen L. II, 134
Jones, Owen L. II, 152
Jones, Owen S. II, 152
Jones, Owen, Jr. II, 569
Jones, Palmyra I, 1143
Jones, Pamela A. VI, 830
Jones, Pastor James R. I, 635
Jones, Patience II, 384
Jones, Patry VI, 1002
Jones, Patsey VI, 942
Jones, Patsy V, 845
Jones, Patsy VI, 815
Jones, Patty VI, 256
Jones, Patty VI, 327
Jones, Paul VI, 832
Jones, Paul G. II, 803
Jones, Paul M. IV, 639
Jones, Paulina VI, 998
Jones, Paulina M. VI, 830
Jones, Pauline V, 667
Jones, Pauline V, 688
Jones, Pauline E. VI, 800
Jones, Pauline E. VI, 830
Jones, Pearl Elizabeth IV, 231
Jones, Pearson V, 747
Jones, Peggy VI, 860
Jones, Peggy VI, 874
Jones, Perling VI, 819
Jones, Peter I, 10
Jones, Peter I, 55
Jones, Peter I, 73
Jones, Peter I Sup 1, 4
Jones, Peter I Sup 1, 5
Jones, Peter I Sup 1, 7
Jones, Peter I Sup 1, 8
Jones, Peter II, 384
Jones, Peter II, 568
Jones, Peter II, 569
Jones, Peter II, 584
Jones, Peter VI, 188
Jones, Peter VI, 199
Jones, Peter, Jr. I, 10
Jones, Peter, Jr. I Sup 1, 7
Jones, Peter, Sr. I, 55
Jones, Peter, Sr. I, 73
Jones, Pethena I, 143
Jones, Phebe II, 290
Jones, Phebe II, 321
Jones, Phebe II, 384
Jones, Phebe III, 187
Jones, Phebe III, 416
Jones, Phebe III, 422
Jones, Phebe III, 487
Jones, Phebe V, 506
Jones, Phebe V, 507
Jones, Phebe V, 527
Jones, Phebe V, 747
Jones, Phebe V, 749
Jones, Phebe Ann V, 813
Jones, Phebe J. I, 1143
Jones, Phebe L. III, 188
Jones, Phebee V, 506
Jones, Philadelphia I, 555
Jones, Philemon V, 747
Jones, Philemon V, 748
Jones, Philemon V, 770
Jones, Philemon V, 801
Jones, Philemon V, 813
Jones, Philemon V, 814
Jones, Philemon P. V, 813
Jones, Philip II, 568
Jones, Phillamoh V, 749
Jones, Phillipinia I, 401
Jones, Phillipinia I, 419
Jones, Pleasant I, 193
Jones, Pleasant I, 195
Jones, Pleasant I, 1143
Jones, Pleasant M. I, 1123
Jones, Pleasant M. I, 1129
Jones, Pleasant M. I, 1143
Jones, Pleasant M. I, 1155
Jones, Pleasant M. I, 1156
Jones, Polly VI, 809
Jones, Polly VI, 942
Jones, Polly Anna I, 965
Jones, Polly M. VI, 854
Jones, Prescious Ann I, 1156
Jones, Priscilla I, 555
Jones, Priscilla II, 568
Jones, Priscilla II, 569
Jones, Priscilla II, 693
Jones, Priscilla II, 705
Jones, Priscilla V, 914
Jones, Priscilla VI, 899
Jones, Priscilla T. V, 914
Jones, Prisela I, 90
Jones, Prudence I, 402
Jones, Prudence I, 448
Jones, Prudence I Sup 1, 9
Jones, Prudence V, 86
Jones, Prudence V, 748
Jones, Prudence V, 755
Jones, Prudence V, 814
Jones, Prudence V, 816
Jones, Prudence V, 817
Jones, Prudence V, 827
Jones, Prudence V, 845
Jones, Prudence VI, 830
Jones, Publins VI, 830
Jones, Publius VI, 805
Jones, Publius VI, 807

es, Publius VI, 813
es, Publius VI, 824
es, Publius VI, 830
es, R. IV, 494
es, R. E. VI, 998
es, R. Frank V, 343
es, R. M. II, 15
es, Rabacah I, 990
es, Rachel I, 55
es, Rachel I, 79
es, Rachel I, 357
es, Rachel I, 813
es, Rachel I, 822
es, Rachel I, 888
es, Rachel I, 990
es, Rachel I, 1033
es, Rachel I, 1035
es, Rachel I, 1043
es, Rachel I, 1044
es, Rachel I, 1049
es, Rachel I, 1085
es, Rachel I, 1093
es, Rachel I, 1094
es, Rachel I, 1107
es, Rachel I, 1122
es, Rachel I, 1123
es, Rachel I, 1142
es, Rachel I, 1143
es, Rachel I, 1144
es, Rachel I Sup 1, 3
es, Rachel I Sup 1, 4
es, Rachel I Sup 1, 6
es, Rachel II, 567
es, Rachel II, 569
es, Rachel II, 709
es, Rachel II, 824
es, Rachel II, 884
es, Rachel IV, 95
es, Rachel IV, 96
es, Rachel IV, 151
es, Rachel IV, 413
es, Rachel IV, 425
es, Rachel IV, 639
es, Rachel IV, 828
es, Rachel IV, 836
es, Rachel IV, 1283
es, Rachel V, 22
es, Rachel V, 23
es, Rachel V, 70
es, Rachel V, 85
es, Rachel V, 86
es, Rachel V, 507
es, Rachel V, 688
es, Rachel V, 736
es, Rachel V, 747
es, Rachel V, 748
es, Rachel V, 749
es, Rachel V, 750
es, Rachel V, 758
es, Rachel V, 760
es, Rachel V, 768
es, Rachel V, 782
es, Rachel V, 786
es, Rachel V, 787
es, Rachel V, 789
es, Rachel V, 813
es, Rachel V, 863
es, Rachel V, 953
es, Rachel VI, 411
es, Rachel VI, 821
es, Rachel VI, 942
es, Rachel A. V, 87
es, Rachel A. V, 183
es, Rachel Ann IV, 231
es, Rachel Ann V, 86
es, Rachel B. V, 972
es, Rachel Foster II, 803
es, Rachel H. II, 884
es, Rachel H. V, 745
es, Rachel H. V, 813
es, Rachel Jane I, 1144
es, Rachel Jesse Wallace V, 845
es, Rachel K. V, 183
es, Rachel Moorman VI, 256
es, Rachel P. VI, 830
es, Rahcel I Sup 1, 4
es, Ramson P. I, 1156
es, Ranson P. I, 1142
es, Ratchel I, 990
es, Raymond L. III, 127
es, Raymond T. III, 188
es, Reachel I, 1107
es, Reason IV, 480
es, Rebecca I, 1123
es, Rebecca I, 1128
es, Rebecca I, 1129
es, Rebecca I, 1142
es, Rebecca I, 1143
es, Rebecca I, 1155
es, Rebecca II, 82
Jones, Rebecca II, 384
Jones, Rebecca II, 421
Jones, Rebecca II, 474
Jones, Rebecca II, 546
Jones, Rebecca II, 567
Jones, Rebecca II, 568
Jones, Rebecca II, 569
Jones, Rebecca II, 570
Jones, Rebecca II, 571
Jones, Rebecca II, 622
Jones, Rebecca II, 653
Jones, Rebecca II, 667
Jones, Rebecca II, 803
Jones, Rebecca II, 884
Jones, Rebecca IV, 182
Jones, Rebecca IV, 413
Jones, Rebecca IV, 480
Jones, Rebecca IV, 490
Jones, Rebecca IV, 909
Jones, Rebecca IV, 911
Jones, Rebecca IV, 970
Jones, Rebecca IV, 971
Jones, Rebecca IV, 980
Jones, Rebecca IV, 1283
Jones, Rebecca V, 86
Jones, Rebecca V, 89
Jones, Rebecca V, 506
Jones, Rebecca V, 733
Jones, Rebecca V, 747
Jones, Rebecca V, 748
Jones, Rebecca V, 749
Jones, Rebecca V, 750
Jones, Rebecca V, 766
Jones, Rebecca V, 787
Jones, Rebecca V, 790
Jones, Rebecca V, 794
Jones, Rebecca V, 813
Jones, Rebecca VI, 69
Jones, Rebecca VI, 72
Jones, Rebecca VI, 521
Jones, Rebecca VI, 523
Jones, Rebecca VI, 830
Jones, Rebecca VI, 997
Jones, Rebecca Ann I, 1142
Jones, Rebecca E. IV, 971
Jones, Rebecca E. V, 507
Jones, Rebecca E. V, 688
Jones, Rebecca Emily IV, 971
Jones, Rebecca G. II, 884
Jones, Rebecca J. I, 1156
Jones, Rebecca J. I, 1159
Jones, Rebecca P. I, 1142
Jones, Rebecca P. I, 1143
Jones, Rebecca P. I, 1155
Jones, Rebecca S. II, 290
Jones, Rebecca, Jr. I, 1123
Jones, Rebeccah I, 1123
Jones, Rebecka II, 384
Jones, Rebeckah I, 1095
Jones, Rebeckah V, 782
Jones, Rebeckah VI, 829
Jones, Rebeckah VI, 837
Jones, Rebekah I, 1044
Jones, Rebekah I, 1061
Jones, Rebekah I, 1062
Jones, Rebekah II, 567
Jones, Rebekah II, 568
Jones, Rebekah II, 597
Jones, Rebekah II, 681
Jones, Rees III, 399
Jones, Rees IV, 95
Jones, Reese II, 570
Jones, Reese IV, 96
Jones, Reuben V, 183
Jones, Reuben V, 631
Jones, Reuben E. V, 183
Jones, Rezin IV, 480
Jones, Rhoda V, 748
Jones, Rhoda V, 800
Jones, Rhoda V, 813
Jones, Rhoda V, 1004
Jones, Rhoda VI, 856
Jones, Rhoda VI, 942
Jones, Rhoda Ann VI, 881
Jones, Rhoda C. V, 748
Jones, Richard I, 357
Jones, Richard I, 358
Jones, Richard I, 401
Jones, Richard I, 402
Jones, Richard I, 555
Jones, Richard I, 773
Jones, Richard I, 786
Jones, Richard I, 822
Jones, Richard I, 830
Jones, Richard I, 990
Jones, Richard I, 1055
Jones, Richard II, 383
Jones, Richard II, 384
Jones, Richard II, 569
Jones, Richard II, 570
Jones, Richard II, 571
Jones, Richard II, 667
Jones, Richard II, 803
Jones, Richard III, 73
Jones, Richard III, 188
Jones, Richard III, 487
Jones, Richard V, 183
Jones, Richard V, 256
Jones, Richard V, 408
Jones, Richard V, 688
Jones, Richard V, 787
Jones, Richard VI, 12
Jones, Richard VI, 411
Jones, Richard VI, 830
Jones, Richard VI, 942
Jones, Richard C. II, 570
Jones, Richard M. V, 86
Jones, Richard S. VI, 801
Jones, Richard T. I, 1123
Jones, Richard T. I, 1155
Jones, Richard T. I, 1156
Jones, Richard T., Jr. I, 1143
Jones, Richard Thompson I, 1143
Jones, Richard, Sr. I, 991
Jones, Robert I, 555
Jones, Robert I, 924
Jones, Robert I, 1033
Jones, Robert II, 445
Jones, Robert II, 462
Jones, Robert II, 567
Jones, Robert II, 568
Jones, Robert II, 569
Jones, Robert II, 570
Jones, Robert II, 594
Jones, Robert IV, 231
Jones, Robert IV, 681
Jones, Robert V, 86
Jones, Robert VI, 30
Jones, Robert VI, 35
Jones, Robert VI, 72
Jones, Robert VI, 177
Jones, Robert VI, 188
Jones, Robert VI, 948
Jones, Robert A. IV, 1323
Jones, Robert B. IV, 231
Jones, Robert B. V, 787
Jones, Robert Barclay II, 884
Jones, Robert Clarkson I, 702
Jones, Robert Clarkson I, 723
Jones, Robert, Jr. II, 569
Jones, Roberta IV, 971
Jones, Roberta Eleanor IV, 971
Jones, Robt. E. VI, 890
Jones, Robt. E. VI, 998
Jones, Roda V, 1004
Jones, Roella Jane I, 823
Jones, Rollin V, 750
Jones, Rosanna V, 813
Jones, Roswell B. V, 813
Jones, Rowland II, 177
Jones, Rowland II, 236
Jones, Rowland II, 293
Jones, Rowland II, 300
Jones, Rozia V, 845
Jones, Rubie V, 750
Jones, Ruby V, 750
Jones, Ruby E. V, 749
Jones, Ruby Virginia V, 846
Jones, Rufus M. II, 15
Jones, Russell IV, 971
Jones, Russell Stanley IV, 971
Jones, Ruth I, 358
Jones, Ruth I, 723
Jones, Ruth I, 738
Jones, Ruth I, 1117
Jones, Ruth I, 1122
Jones, Ruth I, 1123
Jones, Ruth I, 1143
Jones, Ruth I, 1144
Jones, Ruth I, 1155
Jones, Ruth I, 1157
Jones, Ruth III, 487
Jones, Ruth IV, 74
Jones, Ruth IV, 77
Jones, Ruth IV, 95
Jones, Ruth IV, 96
Jones, Ruth IV, 1134
Jones, Ruth IV, 1255
Jones, Ruth V, 491
Jones, Ruth V, 506
Jones, Ruth V, 749
Jones, Ruth V, 760
Jones, Ruth V, 845
Jones, Ruth V, 872
Jones, Ruth V, 887
Jones, Ruth VI, 406
Jones, Ruth VI, 411
Jones, Ruth VI, 635
Jones, Ruth M. I, 1142
Jones, Ruth Naomi IV, 1255
Jones, Ruth, Sr. I, 1156
Jones, Ruthanna IV, 96
Jones, Ruthanna V, 87
Jones, S. C. V, 1004
Jones, S. L. I, 1156
Jones, S. Lydia V, 749
Jones, S. Morris IV, 537
Jones, Sadie V, 749
Jones, Salley VI, 942
Jones, Sally VI, 825
Jones, Sally VI, 830
Jones, Sally VI, 864
Jones, Sally VI, 942
Jones, Sally VI, 982
Jones, Sally B. VI, 926
Jones, Sally P. VI, 929
Jones, Sam I, 1123
Jones, Sam'l I, 1142
Jones, Sam'l I, 1143
Jones, Sam'l I, 1155
Jones, Saml. J. VI, 884
Jones, Samuel I, 55
Jones, Samuel I, 357
Jones, Samuel I, 1033
Jones, Samuel I, 1043
Jones, Samuel I, 1044
Jones, Samuel I, 1049
Jones, Samuel I, 1085
Jones, Samuel I, 1115
Jones, Samuel I, 1123
Jones, Samuel I, 1142
Jones, Samuel I, 1143
Jones, Samuel I, 1145
Jones, Samuel I, 1155
Jones, Samuel I, 1156
Jones, Samuel II, 236
Jones, Samuel II, 383
Jones, Samuel II, 384
Jones, Samuel II, 456
Jones, Samuel II, 567
Jones, Samuel II, 568
Jones, Samuel II, 569
Jones, Samuel II, 570
Jones, Samuel II, 571
Jones, Samuel II, 577
Jones, Samuel II, 584
Jones, Samuel II, 597
Jones, Samuel II, 709
Jones, Samuel II, 804
Jones, Samuel III, 188
Jones, Samuel III, 422
Jones, Samuel III, 472
Jones, Samuel III, 487
Jones, Samuel III, 507
Jones, Samuel IV, 43
Jones, Samuel IV, 74
Jones, Samuel IV, 77
Jones, Samuel IV, 95
Jones, Samuel IV, 96
Jones, Samuel IV, 211
Jones, Samuel IV, 231
Jones, Samuel IV, 291
Jones, Samuel IV, 480
Jones, Samuel V, 46
Jones, Samuel V, 59
Jones, Samuel V, 63
Jones, Samuel V, 86
Jones, Samuel V, 87
Jones, Samuel V, 97
Jones, Samuel V, 132
Jones, Samuel V, 183
Jones, Samuel V, 343
Jones, Samuel V, 367
Jones, Samuel V, 506
Jones, Samuel V, 531
Jones, Samuel V, 723
Jones, Samuel V, 734
Jones, Samuel V, 746
Jones, Samuel V, 747
Jones, Samuel V, 748
Jones, Samuel V, 749
Jones, Samuel V, 750
Jones, Samuel V, 784
Jones, Samuel V, 787
Jones, Samuel V, 813
Jones, Samuel V, 822
Jones, Samuel V, 954
Jones, Samuel V, 960
Jones, Samuel VI, 16
Jones, Samuel VI, 61
Jones, Samuel VI, 72
Jones, Samuel VI, 80
Jones, Samuel VI, 256
Jones, Samuel VI, 411
Jones, Samuel VI, 890
Jones, Samuel VI, 942
Jones, Samuel VI, 998
Jones, Samuel A. I, 1156
Jones, Samuel A. II, 835
Jones, Samuel A. II, 884
Jones, Samuel A. II, 885
Jones, Samuel A. IV, 231
Jones, Samuel A. IV, 289
Jones, Samuel A. V, 343
Jones, Samuel B. V, 748
Jones, Samuel B. V, 800
Jones, Samuel B. V, 813
Jones, Samuel B. V, 1004
Jones, Samuel C. V, 750
Jones, Samuel C. V, 813
Jones, Samuel C. V, 1004
Jones, Samuel D. IV, 639
Jones, Samuel G. II, 570
Jones, Samuel H. IV, 231
Jones, Samuel H. IV, 1255
Jones, Samuel H. VI, 249
Jones, Samuel H. VI, 256
Jones, Samuel Howard IV, 96
Jones, Samuel Huston I, 1144
Jones, Samuel J. VI, 943
Jones, Samuel Jun. I, 1155
Jones, Samuel L. I, 1156
Jones, Samuel Lafayette I, 1144
Jones, Samuel N. V, 183
Jones, Samuel N. V, 408
Jones, Samuel N. V, 845
Jones, Samuel N. V, 846
Jones, Samuel P. IV, 231
Jones, Samuel Pendleton IV, 231
Jones, Samuel Pendleton IV, 480
Jones, Samuel Rufus V, 748
Jones, Samuel Tonkin II, 571
Jones, Samuel Tonkin II, 749
Jones, Samuel W. II, 236
Jones, Samuel Wetherill II, 208
Jones, Samuel Wetherill II, 236
Jones, Samuel, Jr. I, 1155
Jones, Samuel, Jr. V, 749
Jones, Sara VI, 11
Jones, Sarah I, 42
Jones, Sarah I, 55
Jones, Sarah I, 64
Jones, Sarah I, 70
Jones, Sarah I, 73
Jones, Sarah I, 184
Jones, Sarah I, 272
Jones, Sarah I, 357
Jones, Sarah I, 358
Jones, Sarah I, 384
Jones, Sarah I, 401
Jones, Sarah I, 402
Jones, Sarah I, 411
Jones, Sarah I, 448
Jones, Sarah I, 506
Jones, Sarah I, 555
Jones, Sarah I, 786
Jones, Sarah I, 822
Jones, Sarah I, 823
Jones, Sarah I, 888
Jones, Sarah I, 924
Jones, Sarah I, 928
Jones, Sarah I, 1010
Jones, Sarah I, 1033
Jones, Sarah I, 1043
Jones, Sarah I, 1044
Jones, Sarah I, 1049
Jones, Sarah I, 1085
Jones, Sarah I, 1107
Jones, Sarah I, 1122
Jones, Sarah I, 1142
Jones, Sarah I, 1143
Jones, Sarah I, 1144
Jones, Sarah I, 1155
Jones, Sarah II, 75
Jones, Sarah II, 82
Jones, Sarah II, 127
Jones, Sarah II, 134
Jones, Sarah II, 177
Jones, Sarah II, 235
Jones, Sarah II, 236
Jones, Sarah II, 242
Jones, Sarah II, 269
Jones, Sarah II, 293
Jones, Sarah II, 300
Jones, Sarah II, 383
Jones, Sarah II, 384
Jones, Sarah II, 476
Jones, Sarah II, 498
Jones, Sarah II, 515
Jones, Sarah II, 568
Jones, Sarah II, 569
Jones, Sarah II, 570
Jones, Sarah II, 571
Jones, Sarah II, 596
Jones, Sarah II, 625
Jones, Sarah II, 642
Jones, Sarah II, 668
Jones, Sarah II, 734
Jones, Sarah II, 749
Jones, Sarah II, 807
Jones, Sarah II, 815
Jones, Sarah II, 826
Jones, Sarah II, 962
Jones, Sarah II, 997

Jones, Sarah II, 1007
Jones, Sarah II, 1046
Jones, Sarah II, 1053
Jones, Sarah III, 89
Jones, Sarah III, 213
Jones, Sarah IV, 320
Jones, Sarah IV, 338
Jones, Sarah IV, 413
Jones, Sarah IV, 414
Jones, Sarah IV, 454
Jones, Sarah IV, 503
Jones, Sarah IV, 537
Jones, Sarah IV, 541
Jones, Sarah IV, 681
Jones, Sarah IV, 729
Jones, Sarah IV, 970
Jones, Sarah V, 86
Jones, Sarah V, 87
Jones, Sarah V, 132
Jones, Sarah V, 506
Jones, Sarah V, 631
Jones, Sarah V, 688
Jones, Sarah V, 725
Jones, Sarah V, 741
Jones, Sarah V, 745
Jones, Sarah V, 747
Jones, Sarah V, 748
Jones, Sarah V, 750
Jones, Sarah V, 755
Jones, Sarah V, 757
Jones, Sarah V, 765
Jones, Sarah V, 770
Jones, Sarah V, 784
Jones, Sarah V, 785
Jones, Sarah V, 787
Jones, Sarah V, 800
Jones, Sarah V, 813
Jones, Sarah V, 816
Jones, Sarah V, 830
Jones, Sarah V, 840
Jones, Sarah V, 845
Jones, Sarah V, 846
Jones, Sarah V, 872
Jones, Sarah V, 883
Jones, Sarah V, 887
Jones, Sarah V, 954
Jones, Sarah V, 960
Jones, Sarah VI, 133
Jones, Sarah VI, 137
Jones, Sarah VI, 256
Jones, Sarah VI, 411
Jones, Sarah VI, 426
Jones, Sarah VI, 801
Jones, Sarah VI, 830
Jones, Sarah VI, 842
Jones, Sarah VI, 1000
Jones, Sarah A. IV, 964
Jones, Sarah A. IV, 971
Jones, Sarah A. IV, 1349
Jones, Sarah A. IV, 1370
Jones, Sarah A. V, 579
Jones, Sarah A. V, 688
Jones, Sarah A. VI, 830
Jones, Sarah Alice V, 87
Jones, Sarah Ann II, 962
Jones, Sarah Ann II, 1046
Jones, Sarah Ann II, 1053
Jones, Sarah Ann IV, 970
Jones, Sarah Ann IV, 971
Jones, Sarah Ann V, 749
Jones, Sarah Ann VI, 943
Jones, Sarah B. V, 86
Jones, Sarah C. III, 110
Jones, Sarah C. III, 122
Jones, Sarah C. IV, 971
Jones, Sarah C. V, 506
Jones, Sarah C. V, 507
Jones, Sarah Crew IV, 970
Jones, Sarah E. I, 1144
Jones, Sarah E. V, 86
Jones, Sarah E. V, 408
Jones, Sarah E. V, 409
Jones, Sarah Eleanor I, 749
Jones, Sarah Elizabeth II, 1053
Jones, Sarah Elizabeth II, 1054
Jones, Sarah Elizabeth VI, 926
Jones, Sarah Elma V, 748
Jones, Sarah F. VI, 948
Jones, Sarah G. VI, 830
Jones, Sarah H. II, 1053
Jones, Sarah H. V, 408
Jones, Sarah H. V, 914
Jones, Sarah I. I, 1143
Jones, Sarah I. V, 953
Jones, Sarah I. V, 954
Jones, Sarah Jane I, 1142
Jones, Sarah Jane IV, 1039
Jones, Sarah Lydia V, 737
Jones, Sarah Lydia V, 750
Jones, Sarah M. II, 1053
Jones, Sarah M. II, 1055
Jones, Sarah M. V, 579
Jones, Sarah M. VI, 943
Jones, Sarah S. III, 187
Jones, Sarah T. V, 87
Jones, Sarah T. V, 954
Jones, Sarah Wilson I, 928
Jones, Sarah Y. II, 884
Jones, Saray Ann V, 748
Jones, Sealy VI, 830
Jones, Seaney VI, 972
Jones, Seborn V, 749
Jones, Seth II, 804
Jones, Sidney I, 1123
Jones, Sidney Ann IV, 681
Jones, Sidney Monga I, 1107
Jones, Silas IV, 1370
Jones, Silvanus II, 384
Jones, Simon I, 723
Jones, Simon I, 729
Jones, Simon I, 764
Jones, Simon II, 384
Jones, Simpson V, 787
Jones, Sinai E. V, 750
Jones, Solomon II, 571
Jones, Solomon II, 962
Jones, Solomon II, 990
Jones, Solomon II, 1007
Jones, Solomon VI, 942
Jones, Sophia V, 256
Jones, Sophia VI, 850
Jones, Sophia VI, 942
Jones, Sophia VI, 943
Jones, Sophia E. V, 256
Jones, Sophia W. VI, 840
Jones, Spotsford VI, 810
Jones, Spotswood VI, 830
Jones, Stephen I, 358
Jones, Stephen I, 786
Jones, Stephen I, 990
Jones, Stephen V, 783
Jones, Stephen V, 787
Jones, Stephen V, 788
Jones, Stephen VI, 942
Jones, Stephen VI, 1002
Jones, Stephen Alfred V, 579
Jones, Sterling VI, 847
Jones, Steven VI, 1002
Jones, Stokes II, 290
Jones, Susan I, 888
Jones, Susan I, 1123
Jones, Susan I, 1144
Jones, Susan II, 135
Jones, Susan II, 288
Jones, Susan II, 293
Jones, Susan II, 803
Jones, Susan III, 95
Jones, Susan III, 156
Jones, Susan IV, 95
Jones, Susan IV, 639
Jones, Susan V, 816
Jones, Susan V, 845
Jones, Susan E. VI, 830
Jones, Susan J. V, 864
Jones, Susan L. V, 87
Jones, Susan L. V, 103
Jones, Susan M. VI, 1014
Jones, Susan N. II, 835
Jones, Susan N. II, 884
Jones, Susan N. II, 885
Jones, Susan T. I, 1156
Jones, Susan W. II, 822
Jones, Susan W. III, 310
Jones, Susana IV, 1283
Jones, Susanna I, 764
Jones, Susanna I, 965
Jones, Susanna I, 1155
Jones, Susanna II, 384
Jones, Susanna II, 526
Jones, Susanna II, 568
Jones, Susanna II, 569
Jones, Susanna II, 570
Jones, Susanna II, 605
Jones, Susanna II, 625
Jones, Susanna II, 642
Jones, Susanna IV, 96
Jones, Susanna IV, 103
Jones, Susanna V, 74
Jones, Susanna V, 86
Jones, Susanna V, 459
Jones, Susanna V, 746
Jones, Susanna V, 757
Jones, Susanna V, 784
Jones, Susanna V, 814
Jones, Susanna V, 817
Jones, Susanna VI, 669
Jones, Susanna VI, 822
Jones, Susanna VI, 830
Jones, Susanna VI, 942
Jones, Susanna VI, 1005
Jones, Susanna Buffington IV, 96
Jones, Susanna D. IV, 639
Jones, Susanna E. V, 813
Jones, Susanna J. IV, 414
Jones, Susanna J. IV, 432
Jones, Susanna L. V, 86
Jones, Susannah I, 309
Jones, Susannah I, 749
Jones, Susannah I, 764
Jones, Susannah I, 1143
Jones, Susannah II, 82
Jones, Susannah II, 90
Jones, Susannah II, 567
Jones, Susannah IV, 413
Jones, Susannah IV, 414
Jones, Susannah IV, 458
Jones, Susannah IV, 875
Jones, Susannah IV, 1283
Jones, Susannah V, 745
Jones, Susannah V, 746
Jones, Susannah V, 747
Jones, Susannah V, 748
Jones, Susannah V, 749
Jones, Susannah V, 755
Jones, Susannah V, 788
Jones, Susannah VI, 669
Jones, Susannah B. V, 86
Jones, Susannah B. V, 144
Jones, Susannah E. V, 750
Jones, Susannah E. V, 813
Jones, Susannah J. I, 749
Jones, Susie III, 97
Jones, T. M. I, 1156
Jones, Tabitha I, 506
Jones, Tabitha V, 845
Jones, Tabitha V, 863
Jones, Tabitha V, 864
Jones, Tabitha VI, 830
Jones, Tacy II, 177
Jones, Tacy Ann II, 236
Jones, Tacy B. V, 86
Jones, Tacy B. V, 306
Jones, Tacy B. V, 343
Jones, Tacy Burgess V, 306
Jones, Tandy K. VI, 930
Jones, Tarlton VI, 810
Jones, Tarlton VI, 830
Jones, Thelma Elizabeth IV, 1103
Jones, Theodore IV, 1283
Jones, Thomas I, 10
Jones, Thomas I, 55
Jones, Thomas I, 76
Jones, Thomas I, 87
Jones, Thomas I, 357
Jones, Thomas I, 448
Jones, Thomas I, 482
Jones, Thomas I, 483
Jones, Thomas I, 749
Jones, Thomas I, 760
Jones, Thomas I, 764
Jones, Thomas I, 888
Jones, Thomas I, 928
Jones, Thomas I, 1033
Jones, Thomas I, 1043
Jones, Thomas I, 1044
Jones, Thomas I, 1091
Jones, Thomas I, 1094
Jones, Thomas I, 1095
Jones, Thomas I, 1107
Jones, Thomas I, 1122
Jones, Thomas I, 1123
Jones, Thomas I, 1137
Jones, Thomas I, 1142
Jones, Thomas I, 1155
Jones, Thomas I, 1156
Jones, Thomas I, 1159
Jones, Thomas I, 1163
Jones, Thomas II, 384
Jones, Thomas II, 546
Jones, Thomas II, 567
Jones, Thomas II, 692
Jones, Thomas II, 962
Jones, Thomas II, 1053
Jones, Thomas III, 187
Jones, Thomas III, 466
Jones, Thomas IV, 43
Jones, Thomas V, 86
Jones, Thomas V, 87
Jones, Thomas V, 579
Jones, Thomas V, 749
Jones, Thomas V, 785
Jones, Thomas V, 863
Jones, Thomas VI, 134
Jones, Thomas VI, 137
Jones, Thomas VI, 141
Jones, Thomas VI, 142
Jones, Thomas VI, 327
Jones, Thomas VI, 809
Jones, Thomas VI, 811
Jones, Thomas VI, 812
Jones, Thomas VI, 815
Jones, Thomas VI, 819
Jones, Thomas VI, 820
Jones, Thomas VI, 821
Jones, Thomas VI, 822
Jones, Thomas VI, 830
Jones, Thomas VI, 842
Jones, Thomas VI, 856
Jones, Thomas VI, 860
Jones, Thomas VI, 866
Jones, Thomas VI, 867
Jones, Thomas VI, 900
Jones, Thomas VI, 923
Jones, Thomas VI, 942
Jones, Thomas VI, 1015
Jones, Thomas C. II, 884
Jones, Thomas D. VI, 137
Jones, Thomas D. W. F. Maupine I, 1155
Jones, Thomas Elwood IV, 970
Jones, Thomas Elwood IV, 971
Jones, Thomas H. VI, 830
Jones, Thomas Jefferson I, 928
Jones, Thomas Jefferson I, 944
Jones, Thomas Jones I, 764
Jones, Thomas Jun. I, 1143
Jones, Thomas M. I, 1156
Jones, Thomas M. VI, 932
Jones, Thomas M. VI, 943
Jones, Thomas Newton I, 749
Jones, Thomas R. V, 86
Jones, Thomas S. VI, 132
Jones, Thomas S. VI, 141
Jones, Thomas V. VI, 943
Jones, Thomas W. VI, 863
Jones, Thomas, Jr. I, 1122
Jones, Thomas, Sr. VI, 827
Jones, Thos. I, 1142
Jones, Thos. IV, 681
Jones, Thos. V, 741
Jones, Thos. V, 747
Jones, Thos. C. II, 803
Jones, Thos. M. I, 1144
Jones, Thos. Rowland II, 804
Jones, Thos. S. VI, 141
Jones, Townsend III, 422
Jones, Townsend III, 487
Jones, Townsend III, 497
Jones, Townsend III, 498
Jones, Townsend III, 510
Jones, Truman W. IV, 729
Jones, Van Buran I, 723
Jones, Victor IV, 1255
Jones, Victor W. IV, 1255
Jones, Victor W. V, 750
Jones, Vinson VI, 876
Jones, Viola V, 408
Jones, Viola V, 688
Jones, Viola V, 694
Jones, Virginia J. VI, 830
Jones, W. C. IV, 971
Jones, W. H. V, 656
Jones, W. H. V, 721
Jones, W. Rufus I, 1144
Jones, Wallace V, 747
Jones, Wallace V, 748
Jones, Wallace V, 749
Jones, Wallace V, 750
Jones, Wallace V, 760
Jones, Wallace V, 813
Jones, Wallce V, 736
Jones, Walter II, 749
Jones, Walter II, 763
Jones, Walter IV, 480
Jones, Walter C. V, 183
Jones, Walter D. V, 748
Jones, Walter D. V, 785
Jones, Walter J. IV, 1370
Jones, Walter Moore II, 570
Jones, Walter Moore II, 571
Jones, Walter Ray V, 846
Jones, Warren V, 813
Jones, Watson VI, 836
Jones, Wd. Abigail III, 498
Jones, Wd. Amelia III, 422
Jones, Wd. Amelia III, 423
Jones, Wd. Ann V, 820
Jones, Wd. Betsy V, 813
Jones, Wd. Caroline III, 275
Jones, Wd. Elizabeth II, 583
Jones, Wd. Elizabeth III, 487
Jones, Wd. Hannah II, 569
Jones, Wd. Hannah II, 660
Jones, Wd. Jean II, 383
Jones, Wd. Letitia II, 803
Jones, Wd. Margrett II, 384
Jones, Wd. Martha II, 803
Jones, Wd. Martha VI, 327
Jones, Wd. Mary II, 384
Jones, Wd. Mary II, 498
Jones, Wd. Mary II, 803
Jones, Wd. Naomi V, 813
Jones, Wd. Rachel II, 384
Jones, Wd. Rachel II, 803
Jones, Wd. Rebecca Good II, 8
Jones, Wd. Sarah II, 569
Jones, Wesley IV, 1168
Jones, Wetherton IV, 1370
Jones, Whitehead II, 383
Jones, Whitehead II, 569
Jones, Widow Jane I, 1085
Jones, Widow Margaret I, 55
Jones, Widow Margaret I, 76
Jones, Widow Miriam I, 162
Jones, Wilbur V, 688
Jones, Wiley V, 747
Jones, Wiley V, 749
Jones, Wiley VI, 942
Jones, Wiley B. V, 408
Jones, Wiley B. V, 845
Jones, Wiley B. V, 846
Jones, Wiley B. VI, 942
Jones, Will E. IV, 1255
Jones, Willaim Alfred IV, 231
Jones, Willam Allen V, 749
Jones, Willborn V, 749
Jones, Willey R. VI, 990
Jones, William I, 34
Jones, William I, 50
Jones, William I, 55
Jones, William I, 90
Jones, William I, 358
Jones, William I, 402
Jones, William I, 741
Jones, William I, 749
Jones, William I, 760
Jones, William I, 764
Jones, William I, 965
Jones, William I, 1033
Jones, William I, 1044
Jones, William I, 1049
Jones, William I, 1107
Jones, William I, 1122
Jones, William I, 1123
Jones, William I, 1132
Jones, William I, 1142
Jones, William I, 1143
Jones, William I, 1144
Jones, William I, 1156
Jones, William I, 1157
Jones, William II, 177
Jones, William II, 194
Jones, William II, 235
Jones, William II, 236
Jones, William II, 250
Jones, William II, 368
Jones, William II, 383
Jones, William II, 709
Jones, William II, 804
Jones, William III, 188
Jones, William III, 403
Jones, William III, 422
Jones, William III, 423
Jones, William III, 457
Jones, William III, 480
Jones, William III, 487
Jones, William III, 501
Jones, William IV, 231
Jones, William IV, 500
Jones, William IV, 537
Jones, William V, 85
Jones, William V, 86
Jones, William V, 87
Jones, William V, 343
Jones, William V, 748
Jones, William V, 750
Jones, William V, 787
Jones, William V, 822
Jones, William V, 841
Jones, William V, 845
Jones, William V, 863
Jones, William V, 864
Jones, William VI, 72
Jones, William VI, 406
Jones, William VI, 411
Jones, William VI, 523
Jones, William VI, 821
Jones, William VI, 823
Jones, William VI, 830
Jones, William VI, 848
Jones, William VI, 857
Jones, William VI, 880
Jones, William VI, 920
Jones, William VI, 942
Jones, William VI, 943
Jones, William VI, 957
Jones, William A. I, 1143
Jones, William A. V, 750
Jones, William Albert I, 749
Jones, William Alfred VI, 256
Jones, William Arthur V, 408
Jones, William B. VI, 807
Jones, William B. VI, 830
Jones, William Burrus I, 928
Jones, William Catlett IV, 970

Jones, William Charles I, 1107
Jones, William Crawford I, 1156
Jones, William D. III, 487
Jones, William D. III, 497
Jones, William E. I, 1142
Jones, William Foster II, 803
Jones, William H. III, 187
Jones, William H. VI, 830
Jones, William Henderson I, 1107
Jones, William Henry V, 408
Jones, William Howell II, 383
Jones, William I. Hackney
I, 1156
Jones, William Johnson I, 1155
Jones, William Johnston I, 1144
Jones, William L. I, 1156
Jones, William Lee I, 1144
Jones, William M. I, 823
Jones, William M. VI, 830
Jones, William Macy I, 928
Jones, William Martin VI, 940
Jones, William N. VI, 942
Jones, William P. IV, 639
Jones, William Pennell II, 709
Jones, William R. I, 1143
Jones, William R. VI, 953
Jones, William S. VI, 830
Jones, William, Jr. I, 55
Jones, Willie VI, 942
Jones, Willis VI, 943
Jones, Winfield VI, 942
Jones, Winfield VI, 1014
Jones, Wingfield VI, 878
Jones, Wingfield VI, 899
Jones, Wm. I, 1156
Jones, Wm. II, 235
Jones, Wm. II, 445
Jones, Wm. II, 569
Jones, Wm. II, 570
Jones, Wm. II, 571
Jones, Wm. II, 653
Jones, Wm. II, 717
Jones, Wm. II, 749
Jones, Wm. II, 769
Jones, Wm. II, 803
Jones, Wm. II, 821
Jones, Wm. II, 884
Jones, Wm. II, 911
Jones, Wm. II, 1053
Jones, Wm. III, 359
Jones, Wm. III, 416
Jones, Wm. III, 422
Jones, Wm. III, 487
Jones, Wm. V, 306
Jones, Wm. V, 579
Jones, Wm. V, 688
Jones, Wm. V, 845
Jones, Wm. V, 953
Jones, Wm. VI, 840
Jones, Wm. VI, 856
Jones, Wm. VI, 858
Jones, Wm. VI, 877
Jones, Wm. Alfred IV, 1255
Jones, Wm. Arthur V, 408
Jones, Wm. B. V, 914
Jones, Wm. Bateman V, 914
Jones, Wm. C. II, 571
Jones, Wm. C. VI, 895
Jones, Wm. D. III, 510
Jones, Wm. D. V, 783
Jones, Wm. D. V, 787
Jones, Wm. F. II, 749
Jones, Wm. F. II, 884
Jones, Wm. F. VI, 808
Jones, Wm. Firth II, 571
Jones, Wm. Foster II, 884
Jones, Wm. H. II, 129
Jones, Wm. H. III, 187
Jones, Wm. H. III, 510
Jones, Wm. H. V, 408
Jones, Wm. Howell II, 571
Jones, Wm. L. I, 1156
Jones, Wm. Lee I, 1142
Jones, Wm. M. I, 1143
Jones, Wm. Pennell II, 749
Jones, Wm. R. I, 1156
Jones, Wm. R. V, 814
Jones, Wm. R. VI, 913
Jones, Wm. R. VI, 958
Jones, Wm. R. VI, 1019
Jones, Wood VI, 829
Jones, Wood VI, 830
Jones, Wood VI, 860
Jones, Yearsley IV, 413
Jones, Yearsley IV, 414
Jones, Yearsley IV, 875
Jones, Yearsley VI, 669
Jones, Yearsley, Jr. VI, 669
Jones, Yearsly VI, 669
Jones, Zachariah I, 55
Jones, Zelinda V, 783
Jones, Zelinda V, 787
Jones, Zephaniah I, 51
Jones, Zephaniah I, 55
Jones, Zephaniah I, 70
Jones, Zilla II, 571
Jones, Zilpah V, 748
Jonhson, Lydia VI, 297
Jonhson, Mary Jane V, 223
Jonhson, Phebe V, 223
Jonhson, Timothy VI, 297
Jons, Laura D. I, 814
Jons, Laura D. I, 823
Jonson, Ann VI, 16
Jonson, Anna I, 822
Jonson, Archeleus I, 990
Jonson, Ashly, Jr. I, 822
Jonson, David II, 1038
Jonson, Eliza II, 82
Jonson, Eliza IV, 909
Jonson, Eliza IV, 914
Jonson, Elizabeth V, 845
Jonson, Elizabeth V, 853
Jonson, Elwood I, 822
Jonson, Emely I, 822
Jonson, Emily I, 822
Jonson, Hiram I, 822
Jonson, James I, 554
Jonson, Joana IV, 1213
Jonson, John VI, 253
Jonson, Jonathan IV, 1213
Jonson, Joseph II, 566
Jonson, Joseph II, 1038
Jonson, Joseph T. I, 822
Jonson, Joshua II, 383
Jonson, Marcy II, 1038
Jonson, Margaret I, 870
Jonson, Margaret I, 888
Jonson, Maria I, 55
Jonson, Mariam M. I, 822
Jonson, Martha II, 566
Jonson, Martha IV, 338
Jonson, Martitia I, 822
Jonson, Martitia E. I, 822
Jonson, Mary I, 888
Jonson, Mary Ann I, 822
Jonson, Miriam M. I, 822
Jonson, Polly I, 888
Jonson, Rachel I, 606
Jonson, Rebecca I, 822
Jonson, Rhoda I, 822
Jonson, Rhoda J. I, 822
Jonson, Ruth I, 822
Jonson, Sarah I, 822
Jonson, Sarah IV, 909
Jonson, Silas IV, 1213
Jonson, Thomas II, 235
Jonson, William G. I, 822
Jonston, Achiles Douglas IV, 230
Jonston, Deborah Judith IV, 230
Jonston, Elizabeth Douglas
IV, 230
Jonston, Jonathan IV, 230
Jonston, Judith IV, 230
Jonston, Mary Ann IV, 230
Jonston, Mildred Tyree IV, 230
Jonston, Susanna IV, 230
Jopling, Frances Amanda VI, 939
Jopling, James VI, 939
Jopling, James VI, 943
Jopling, James VI, 970
Jopling, James VI, 979
Jopling, James VI, 1010
Jopling, James VI, 1013
Jopling, James W. VI, 872
Jopling, James W. VI, 979
Jopling, James, Sr. VI, 943
Jopling, Jesse VI, 943
Jopling, Jesse VI, 979
Jopling, Julia Ann VI, 943
Jopling, Louisa R. VI, 979
Jopling, Maria Ann B. VI, 970
Jopling, Martha M. VI, 1013
Jopling, Nancy J. M. VI, 1010
Jopling, Polly M. VI, 943
Jopling, Sally Ware VI, 979
Jopling, Sarah VI, 943
Jopling, Susan VI, 943
Jopling, Thomas VI, 943
Jopling, Thomas B. VI, 1013
Jopling, William W. VI, 943
Jordan, ??? I, 29
Jordan, ??? I, 33
Jordan, ??? VI, 39
Jordan, ??? VI, 40
Jordan, ??? VI, 48
Jordan, Aaron Morris, Jr. I, 144
Jordan, Abigal VI, 31
Jordan, Abraham I, 55
Jordan, Absalom VI, 917
Jordan, Absolam VI, 1010
Jordan, Absolem VI, 905
Jordan, Alex VI, 891
Jordan, Alexander VI, 943
Jordan, Alice III, 141
Jordan, Alice III, 188
Jordan, Amanda VI, 1021
Jordan, Amarilla VI, 989
Jordan, Andrew II, 384
Jordan, Ann VI, 31
Jordan, Ann VI, 45
Jordan, Ann VI, 73
Jordan, Ann VI, 77
Jordan, Ann E. M. VI, 863
Jordan, Ann E. R. VI, 924
Jordan, Ann Luthisha VI, 114
Jordan, Ann M. VI, 831
Jordan, Anna I, 101
Jordan, Anna I, 913
Jordan, Anne I, 55
Jordan, Anne I, 74
Jordan, Anne VI, 31
Jordan, Archibald A. VI, 893
Jordan, Augustus M. VI, 943
Jordan, Bellson VI, 31
Jordan, Benj., Jr. VI, 203
Jordan, Benjamin I, 243
Jordan, Benjamin VI, 17
Jordan, Benjamin VI, 73
Jordan, Benjamin VI, 155
Jordan, Benjamin VI, 188
Jordan, Benjamin VI, 193
Jordan, Benjamin VI, 205
Jordan, Benjamin VI, 257
Jordan, Benjamin H. VI, 74
Jordan, Benjamin H. VI, 257
Jordan, Benjamin Harris IV, 480
Jordan, Benjamin Harris VI, 257
Jordan, Benjamin, Jr. VI, 188
Jordan, Benjamin, Sr. VI, 188
Jordan, Benjamine VI, 31
Jordan, Betsy VI, 943
Jordan, Betsy A. VI, 943
Jordan, Bolling VI, 852
Jordan, Carrol R. IV, 1168
Jordan, Cassandria VI, 865
Jordan, Catharine I, 237
Jordan, Catharine I, 243
Jordan, Catharine White I, 243
Jordan, Charles I, 38
Jordan, Charles I, 39
Jordan, Charles I, 55
Jordan, Charles Clary VI, 73
Jordan, Charles L. VI, 815
Jordan, Charles L. VI, 943
Jordan, Charles, Jr. I, 55
Jordan, Charles, Sr. I, 55
Jordan, Chlolilda I, 82
Jordan, Christian I, 243
Jordan, Christian VI, 31
Jordan, Christian VI, 32
Jordan, Christian VI, 33
Jordan, Christian VI, 36
Jordan, Christian VI, 37
Jordan, Christian VI, 73
Jordan, Christian VI, 74
Jordan, Christian VI, 78
Jordan, Christopher VI, 72
Jordan, Christopher Anthony
VI, 114
Jordan, Clement VI, 828
Jordan, Clement VI, 835
Jordan, Clement VI, 865
Jordan, Clotilda I, 23
Jordan, Compton IV, 1168
Jordan, Daisy Miller IV, 1168
Jordan, Daniel VI, 943
Jordan, David VI, 73
Jordan, David VI, 74
Jordan, Deborah VI, 74
Jordan, Deborah Ann IV, 480
Jordan, Deborah Ann IV, 498
Jordan, Deborah Ann VI, 74
Jordan, Deborah Ann VI, 257
Jordan, Delilah I, 10
Jordan, Dorethy I, 55
Jordan, Dorethy I, 69
Jordan, Dorotha I, 144
Jordan, Dorothy I, 56
Jordan, Dorothy I, 77
Jordan, Dorothy I, 101
Jordan, Dorothy I, 144
Jordan, Dorothy IV, 1168
Jordan, Dorothy VI, 188
Jordan, Dorothy VI, 203
Jordan, Dorothy VI, 206
Jordan, Dorrithy VI, 27
Jordan, Edmond VI, 15
Jordan, Edmond VI, 17
Jordan, Edmond VI, 31
Jordan, Edmund I, 154
Jordan, Edmund VI, 62
Jordan, Edmund VI, 72
Jordan, Edmund VI, 73
Jordan, Edmund H. VI, 831
Jordan, Edna Pretlow VI, 73
Jordan, Edward T. VI, 74
Jordan, Edward T. VI, 257
Jordan, Edward Thomas IV, 480
Jordan, Edward Thomas VI, 257
Jordan, Elias Albertson I, 144
Jordan, Elijah VI, 78
Jordan, Elisabeth I, 55
Jordan, Elisabeth I, 56
Jordan, Elisabeth I, 62
Jordan, Elisabeth I, 78
Jordan, Elisabeth I, 143
Jordan, Elisabeth I, 160
Jordan, Elisabeth I, 195
Jordan, Elisabeth I, 243
Jordan, Elisabeth J. VI, 943
Jordan, Elisha R. VI, 831
Jordan, Eliza Jane VI, 943
Jordan, Elizabeth I, 101
Jordan, Elizabeth I, 134
Jordan, Elizabeth I, 144
Jordan, Elizabeth I, 243
Jordan, Elizabeth II, 709
Jordan, Elizabeth VI, 17
Jordan, Elizabeth VI, 28
Jordan, Elizabeth VI, 31
Jordan, Elizabeth VI, 34
Jordan, Elizabeth VI, 63
Jordan, Elizabeth VI, 73
Jordan, Elizabeth VI, 148
Jordan, Elizabeth VI, 176
Jordan, Elizabeth VI, 188
Jordan, Elizabeth VI, 203
Jordan, Elizabeth VI, 206
Jordan, Elizabeth VI, 831
Jordan, Elizabeth VI, 849
Jordan, Elizabeth VI, 853
Jordan, Elizabeth VI, 857
Jordan, Elizabeth VI, 875
Jordan, Elizabeth VI, 888
Jordan, Elizabeth VI, 943
Jordan, Elizabeth Ann VI, 999
Jordan, Elizabeth Burleigh
VI, 17
Jordan, Elizabeth C. H. VI, 849
Jordan, Elizabeth H. VI, 943
Jordan, Elizabeth M. VI, 943
Jordan, Elizabeth T. VI, 831
Jordan, Elsberry I, 7
Jordan, Elsberry I, 10
Jordan, Emeline V, 846
Jordan, Enos IV, 1168
Jordan, Eroscoe V, 631
Jordan, Florence I, 56
Jordan, Florence I, 84
Jordan, Francis VI, 830
Jordan, George VI, 896
Jordan, George VI, 943
Jordan, George VI, 976
Jordan, George J. VI, 831
Jordan, German VI, 831
Jordan, German VI, 840
Jordan, German VI, 850
Jordan, Glaister VI, 114
Jordan, Granville VI, 797
Jordan, Granville VI, 809
Jordan, Granville VI, 836
Jordan, Hannah II, 384
Jordan, Hannah IV, 43
Jordan, Hannah VI, 155
Jordan, Hannah VI, 188
Jordan, Hannah Jordan VI, 73
Jordan, Hattie J. I, 56
Jordan, Hermit VI, 835
Jordan, Hez'r. VI, 853
Jordan, Hezeciah VI, 72
Jordan, Hezekiah VI, 73
Jordan, Hezekiah T. VI, 943
Jordan, Ida Beatrice I, 29
Jordan, Isaac I, 56
Jordan, Isaac I, 144
Jordan, J. S. VI, 73
Jordan, Jacob I, 55
Jordan, Jacob I, 56
Jordan, Jacob I, 74
Jordan, Jacob I, 243
Jordan, Jacob VI, 73
Jordan, Jacob VI, 74
Jordan, Jacobus VI, 943
Jordan, James I, 55
Jordan, James I, 74
Jordan, James I, 144
Jordan, James VI, 8
Jordan, James VI, 17
Jordan, James VI, 31
Jordan, James VI, 32
Jordan, James VI, 34
Jordan, James VI, 943
Jordan, James A. VI, 831
Jordan, James Denson VI, 72
Jordan, James T. VI, 831
Jordan, James T. VI, 853
Jordan, Jane I, 10
Jordan, Jane I, 55
Jordan, Jane I, 144
Jordan, Jane II, 709
Jordan, Jane VI, 74
Jordan, Jane VI, 90
Jordan, Jane VI, 669
Jordan, Jane VI, 692
Jordan, Jane Pleasants VI, 114
Jordan, Jean I, 144
Jordan, Jeremiah VI, 889
Jordan, Jeremiah VI, 943
Jordan, Jeremiah VI, 989
Jordan, Jeremiah R. VI, 807
Jordan, Jeremiah Symons, Jr.
I, 143
Jordan, Jesse VI, 523
Jordan, Joel VI, 943
Jordan, John I, 101
Jordan, John II, 709
Jordan, John VI, 8
Jordan, John VI, 17
Jordan, John VI, 27
Jordan, John VI, 28
Jordan, John VI, 31
Jordan, John VI, 41
Jordan, John VI, 72
Jordan, John VI, 73
Jordan, John E. VI, 943
Jordan, John F. VI, 846
Jordan, John F. VI, 855
Jordan, John Morris I, 101
Jordan, John Price I, 144
Jordan, John S. Sadler VI, 73
Jordan, John, Jr. II, 709
Jordan, John, Jr. VI, 72
Jordan, John, Senior VI, 72
Jordan, Jonas VI, 997
Jordan, Jonathan I, 56
Jordan, Jonathan Price I, 144
Jordan, Jordan Clary VI, 73
Jordan, Joseph I, 55
Jordan, Joseph I, 56
Jordan, Joseph I, 74
Jordan, Joseph I, 91
Jordan, Joseph I, 92
Jordan, Joseph I, 101
Jordan, Joseph I, 121
Jordan, Joseph I, 143
Jordan, Joseph I, 144
Jordan, Joseph I, 166
Jordan, Joseph I, 168
Jordan, Joseph I, 243
Jordan, Joseph II, 384
Jordan, Joseph IV, 480
Jordan, Joseph V, 846
Jordan, Joseph VI, 17
Jordan, Joseph VI, 31
Jordan, Joseph VI, 35
Jordan, Joseph VI, 72
Jordan, Joseph VI, 73
Jordan, Joseph VI, 74
Jordan, Joseph VI, 246
Jordan, Joseph VI, 257
Jordan, Joseph Henley I, 144
Jordan, Joseph Prichard VI, 72
Jordan, Joseph, Jr. I, 56
Jordan, Joseph, Jr. I, 143
Jordan, Joseph, Jr. I, 160
Jordan, Joseph, Jr. VI, 72
Jordan, Joseph, Sr. I, 101
Jordan, Joshua VI, 31
Jordan, Joshua VI, 32
Jordan, Joshua VI, 33
Jordan, Joshua VI, 37
Jordan, Josiah I, 46
Jordan, Josiah I, 56
Jordan, Josiah I, 62
Jordan, Josiah I, 144
Jordan, Josiah VI, 23
Jordan, Josiah VI, 45
Jordan, Josiah VI, 46
Jordan, Josiah VI, 63
Jordan, Josiah VI, 72
Jordan, Josiah VI, 73
Jordan, Josiah VI, 112
Jordan, Josiah, Jr. VI, 111
Jordan, Josiah, Jr. VI, 113
Jordan, Jubal VI, 924
Jordan, Jubal VI, 943
Jordan, Jubal VI, 969
Jordan, Keziah VI, 828
Jordan, Leah I, 37
Jordan, Leah I, 46
Jordan, Leah I, 55
Jordan, Leah I, 56
Jordan, Leah I, 74
Jordan, Leroy VI, 938

Jordan, Leroy VI, 943
Jordan, Leroy VI, 1021
Jordan, Lucie Ann VI, 943
Jordan, Lucy VI, 880
Jordan, Lucy VI, 943
Jordan, Lucy VI, 969
Jordan, Lydia I, 243
Jordan, Lydia II, 1041
Jordan, Lydia VI, 188
Jordan, Lydia VI, 203
Jordan, Lydia VI, 205
Jordan, Lydia VI, 943
Jordan, M. Florence I, 19
Jordan, Malinda J. VI, 1012
Jordan, Margaret I, 56
Jordan, Margaret I, 101
Jordan, Margaret I, 104
Jordan, Margaret I, 115
Jordan, Margaret I, 121
Jordan, Margaret I, 144
Jordan, Margaret I, 163
Jordan, Margaret I, 170
Jordan, Margaret III, 141
Jordan, Margaret III, 188
Jordan, Margaret VI, 28
Jordan, Margaret VI, 31
Jordan, Margaret VI, 40
Jordan, Margaret VI, 45
Jordan, Margaret VI, 46
Jordan, Margaret VI, 64
Jordan, Margaret VI, 73
Jordan, Margaret VI, 188
Jordan, Margaret VI, 831
Jordan, Margarett VI, 27
Jordan, Margarett VI, 29
Jordan, Margarett VI, 32
Jordan, Margreat VI, 31
Jordan, Margret, Senior VI, 32
Jordan, Margrett VI, 31
Jordan, Maria IV, 43
Jordan, Maria VI, 133
Jordan, Maria VI, 137
Jordan, Maria Elizabeth VI, 943
Jordan, Martha VI, 31
Jordan, Martha VI, 74
Jordan, Martha VI, 85
Jordan, Martha Ann VI, 993
Jordan, Martha Gertrude I, 33
Jordan, Martha Lawrence VI, 73
Jordan, Martha R. VI, 863
Jordan, Mary I, 23
Jordan, Mary I, 55
Jordan, Mary I, 56
Jordan, Mary I, 101
Jordan, Mary I, 136
Jordan, Mary I, 142
Jordan, Mary I, 143
Jordan, Mary I, 144
Jordan, Mary I, 154
Jordan, Mary I, 243
Jordan, Mary I, 247
Jordan, Mary II, 384
Jordan, Mary II, 571
Jordan, Mary VI, 15
Jordan, Mary VI, 27
Jordan, Mary VI, 31
Jordan, Mary VI, 35
Jordan, Mary VI, 45
Jordan, Mary VI, 73
Jordan, Mary VI, 89
Jordan, Mary VI, 97
Jordan, Mary VI, 114
Jordan, Mary VI, 173
Jordan, Mary VI, 174
Jordan, Mary VI, 188
Jordan, Mary VI, 203
Jordan, Mary VI, 805
Jordan, Mary C. VI, 815
Jordan, Mary F. VI, 943
Jordan, Mary P. VI, 893
Jordan, Mary Pretlow VI, 73
Jordan, Mathew VI, 27
Jordan, Mathew VI, 31
Jordan, Mathew VI, 45
Jordan, Mathew VI, 843
Jordan, Mathew VI, 857
Jordan, Mathew VI, 861
Jordan, Mathias I, 143
Jordan, Matilda VI, 943
Jordan, Matilda J. IV, 1323
Jordan, Matthew I, 23
Jordan, Matthew I, 82
Jordan, Matthew I, 144
Jordan, Matthew I, 195
Jordan, Matthew VI, 8
Jordan, Matthew VI, 17
Jordan, Matthew VI, 31
Jordan, Matthew VI, 45
Jordan, Matthew VI, 72
Jordan, Matthew VI, 73
Jordan, Matthew VI, 848
Jordan, Matthew, Jr. VI, 72
Jordan, Matthias I, 143
Jordan, Matthias I, 144
Jordan, Matthias I, 160
Jordan, Matthias VI, 113
Jordan, Mattw VI, 291
Jordan, Melville M. I, 19
Jordan, Melville M. I, 56
Jordan, Micah I, 154
Jordan, Micajah I, 144
Jordan, Micajah I, 237
Jordan, Micajah I, 243
Jordan, Michael I, 144
Jordan, Mildred VI, 861
Jordan, Miriam I, 42
Jordan, Miriam I, 56
Jordan, Miriam I, 143
Jordan, Miriam I, 152
Jordan, Morning VI, 45
Jordan, Morning VI, 46
Jordan, Mournen I, 243
Jordan, Mourning I, 243
Jordan, Mourning VI, 73
Jordan, Mourning VI, 257
Jordan, Mr. ??? VI, 42
Jordan, Nancy VI, 848
Jordan, Nancy VI, 917
Jordan, Nancy VI, 943
Jordan, Naomi I, 101
Jordan, Naomi I, 144
Jordan, Naomy I, 144
Jordan, Naomy I, 154
Jordan, Nathaniel VI, 166
Jordan, Nathaniel VI, 182
Jordan, Nathaniel VI, 188
Jordan, Nathaniel VI, 191
Jordan, Nellie IV, 1283
Jordan, Oney VI, 917
Jordan, Oney VI, 1010
Jordan, P. VI, 900
Jordan, Panthea F. VI, 852
Jordan, Parkey VI, 835
Jordan, Patience I, 46
Jordan, Patience I, 55
Jordan, Patience I, 56
Jordan, Patience I, 74
Jordan, Patience I, 243
Jordan, Patience VI, 45
Jordan, Patience VI, 73
Jordan, Patience VI, 88
Jordan, Patience VI, 114
Jordan, Patsey VI, 943
Jordan, Pearl V, 631
Jordan, Penelope I, 143
Jordan, Penelope I, 160
Jordan, Penelope VI, 976
Jordan, Pharaby I, 243
Jordan, Pharaby I, 260
Jordan, Phariby I, 243
Jordan, Pleasant I, 195
Jordan, Pleasants VI, 45
Jordan, Pleasants VI, 72
Jordan, Pleasants VI, 188
Jordan, Pleasants VI, 203
Jordan, Polly VI, 843
Jordan, Polly VI, 889
Jordan, Polly VI, 988
Jordan, Priscilla VI, 943
Jordan, Quiller VI, 943
Jordan, Rachel I, 46
Jordan, Rachel I, 55
Jordan, Rachel I, 56
Jordan, Rachel I, 74
Jordan, Rachel I, 78
Jordan, Rachel VI, 31
Jordan, Rachel VI, 37
Jordan, Rebecca IV, 414
Jordan, Rebecca IV, 443
Jordan, Rebecca IV, 480
Jordan, Rebecca VI, 31
Jordan, Rebecca VI, 34
Jordan, Rebecca VI, 246
Jordan, Rebecca VI, 257
Jordan, Rebecca VI, 831
Jordan, Rebecca VI, 840
Jordan, Rebecca H. VI, 73
Jordan, Rebeckah VI, 73
Jordan, Rebeckah VI, 74
Jordan, Rebeckah VI, 76
Jordan, Rhoda I, 243
Jordan, Rhoda VI, 943
Jordan, Rhoda VI, 976
Jordan, Richard I, 243
Jordan, Richard II, 384
Jordan, Richard VI, 31
Jordan, Richard VI, 34
Jordan, Richard VI, 72
Jordan, Richard VI, 73
Jordan, Richard VI, 74
Jordan, Richard VI, 114
Jordan, Richard VI, 333
Jordan, Ro Lawrence VI, 73
Jordan, Robert I, 55
Jordan, Robert I, 56
Jordan, Robert I, 73
Jordan, Robert I, 78
Jordan, Robert I, 117
Jordan, Robert I, 134
Jordan, Robert I, 144
Jordan, Robert I, 243
Jordan, Robert II, 384
Jordan, Robert II, 549
Jordan, Robert II, 571
Jordan, Robert III, 188
Jordan, Robert VI, 8
Jordan, Robert VI, 17
Jordan, Robert VI, 22
Jordan, Robert VI, 23
Jordan, Robert VI, 27
Jordan, Robert VI, 31
Jordan, Robert VI, 32
Jordan, Robert VI, 33
Jordan, Robert VI, 37
Jordan, Robert VI, 59
Jordan, Robert VI, 173
Jordan, Robert VI, 174
Jordan, Robert VI, 188
Jordan, Robert's VI, 72
Jordan, Robert, Jr. VI, 73
Jordan, Robert, Sr. I, 56
Jordan, Robert, Sr. I, 73
Jordan, Robert, Sr. VI, 64
Jordan, Robert, Sr. VI, 73
Jordan, Robert, Sr. VI, 188
Jordan, Robert, Sr. VI, 204
Jordan, Roscoe H. V, 631
Jordan, Roseanna VI, 905
Jordan, Salley VI, 943
Jordan, Sallie S. I, 44
Jordan, Sallie S. I, 56
Jordan, Sally VI, 938
Jordan, Sam VI, 188
Jordan, Samuel I, 101
Jordan, Samuel II, 384
Jordan, Samuel VI, 8
Jordan, Samuel VI, 17
Jordan, Samuel VI, 31
Jordan, Samuel VI, 73
Jordan, Samuel VI, 154
Jordan, Samuel VI, 155
Jordan, Samuel VI, 176
Jordan, Samuel VI, 188
Jordan, Samuel VI, 809
Jordan, Samuel VI, 815
Jordan, Samuel VI, 817
Jordan, Samuel VI, 831
Jordan, Samuel VI, 843
Jordan, Samuel VI, 852
Jordan, Samuel VI, 943
Jordan, Samuel Copeland VI, 73
Jordan, Samuel Pretlow VI, 73
Jordan, Samuell VI, 31
Jordan, Sarah I, 38
Jordan, Sarah I, 55
Jordan, Sarah I, 56
Jordan, Sarah I, 73
Jordan, Sarah I, 74
Jordan, Sarah I, 79
Jordan, Sarah I, 101
Jordan, Sarah I, 106
Jordan, Sarah I, 144
Jordan, Sarah I, 150
Jordan, Sarah I, 168
Jordan, Sarah I, 174
Jordan, Sarah VI, 31
Jordan, Sarah VI, 62
Jordan, Sarah VI, 73
Jordan, Sarah VI, 89
Jordan, Sarah VI, 111
Jordan, Sarah VI, 112
Jordan, Sarah VI, 114
Jordan, Sarah VI, 155
Jordan, Sarah VI, 188
Jordan, Sarah VI, 831
Jordan, Sarah VI, 888
Jordan, Sarah Isabella IV, 480
Jordan, Sarah Isabella VI, 74
Jordan, Sarah Isabella VI, 257
Jordan, Sarah Isabelle VI, 257
Jordan, Sarah S. I, 7
Jordan, Sarah S. I, 10
Jordan, Sashwell VI, 943
Jordan, Sitnah I, 243
Jordan, Skinner V, 846
Jordan, Stanbury II, 384
Jordan, Susan IV, 971
Jordan, Susan IV, 992
Jordan, Susan VI, 809
Jordan, Susan VI, 943
Jordan, Susanna VI, 31
Jordan, Susanna VI, 64
Jordan, Susanna VI, 74
Jordan, Susanna VI, 831
Jordan, Susannah I, 101
Jordan, Susannah I, 144
Jordan, Sydna VI, 74
Jordan, T. VI, 73
Jordan, Tamsey VI, 896
Jordan, Thomas I, 56
Jordan, Thomas I, 101
Jordan, Thomas I, 104
Jordan, Thomas I, 106
Jordan, Thomas I, 115
Jordan, Thomas I, 127
Jordan, Thomas I, 144
Jordan, Thomas I, 243
Jordan, Thomas VI, 7
Jordan, Thomas VI, 9
Jordan, Thomas VI, 21
Jordan, Thomas VI, 22
Jordan, Thomas VI, 23
Jordan, Thomas VI, 24
Jordan, Thomas VI, 25
Jordan, Thomas VI, 27
Jordan, Thomas VI, 28
Jordan, Thomas VI, 29
Jordan, Thomas VI, 31
Jordan, Thomas VI, 32
Jordan, Thomas VI, 40
Jordan, Thomas VI, 41
Jordan, Thomas VI, 73
Jordan, Thomas VI, 174
Jordan, Thomas VI, 188
Jordan, Thomas Fanning VI, 73
Jordan, Thomas Jordan I, 144
Jordan, Thomas Newby I, 101
Jordan, Thomas Symons I, 101
Jordan, Thomas, Jr. I, 144
Jordan, Vinson VI, 938
Jordan, Virginia VI, 831
Jordan, Wd. Dorothy VI, 45
Jordan, Wd. Dorothy VI, 204
Jordan, Wd. Dorrithy VI, 31
Jordan, Wd. Elizabeth VI, 31
Jordan, Wd. Mary II, 549
Jordan, Wd. Mary II, 571
Jordan, Wd. Mary II, 619
Jordan, Wd. Susanna VI, 27
Jordan, Widow Elisabeth I, 144
Jordan, Widow Elisabeth I, 166
Jordan, Widow Elizabeth I, 117
Jordan, Widow Jane I, 101
Jordan, Widow Jane I, 140
Jordan, Widow Jane I, 144
Jordan, Widow Mary I, 101
Jordan, Widow Sarah I, 56
Jordan, Widow Sarah I, 73
Jordan, William I, 10
Jordan, William I, 56
Jordan, William VI, 72
Jordan, William VI, 73
Jordan, William VI, 828
Jordan, William VI, 831
Jordan, William VI, 856
Jordan, William VI, 880
Jordan, William VI, 897
Jordan, William VI, 943
Jordan, William VI, 976
Jordan, William VI, 988
Jordan, William VI, 993
Jordan, William VI, 999
Jordan, William VI, 1012
Jordan, William Forster VI, 257
Jordan, William Foster IV, 480
Jordan, William Foster VI, 74
Jordan, William H. I, 10
Jordan, William H. I, 56
Jordan, William, Jr. VI, 830
Jordan, Willie IV, 1283
Jordan, Winney VI, 828
Jordan, Winston VI, 943
Jordan, Wm. VI, 993
Jordan, Wm. VI, 1012
Jordan, Wm. VI, 1013
Jordan, Wm. H. III, 141
Jordan, Wm. H. III, 188
Jordan, Wm. William T. VI, 849
Jordan, Woodson VI, 858
Jorden, Margaret I, 144
Jorden, Margaret I, 148
Jorden, Naomi I, 888
Jorden, Naomi I, 903
Jorden, Neomi I, 888
Jorden, Neomi I, 903
Jorden, Thomas I, 144
Jorden, Thomas I, 148
Jordin, Rebecca H. I, 997
Jording, George VI, 891
Jordon, Benjamin I, 217
Jordon, Carrol R. IV, 1168
Jordon, Charity, Sr. VI, 411
Jordon, Daisy Miller IV, 1168
Jordon, Dorotha I, 144
Jordon, Dorothy IV, 1168
Jordon, Elizabeth I, 217
Jordon, Elizabeth I, 243
Jordon, Elizabeth I, 257
Jordon, Isaac I, 144
Jordon, Jacob I, 217
Jordon, James I, 144
Jordon, James I, 217
Jordon, John I, 217
Jordon, John I, 254
Jordon, Joseph I, 217
Jordon, Joseph II, 571
Jordon, Joseph, Jr. I, 217
Jordon, Josiah VI, 599
Jordon, Margaret VI, 180
Jordon, Mary I, 162
Jordon, Mary I, 217
Jordon, Mary I, 243
Jordon, Mary II, 571
Jordon, Mary V, 938
Jordon, Massey VI, 411
Jordon, Matt I, 217
Jordon, Matthew I, 217
Jordon, Mercy VI, 411
Jordon, Mourning I, 217
Jordon, Patience I, 217
Jordon, Pharaby I, 244
Jordon, Pharby I, 217
Jordon, Polly VI, 891
Jordon, Rachel II, 571
Jordon, Richard I, 217
Jordon, Richard I, 243
Jordon, Richard I, 244
Jordon, Robert I, 243
Jordon, Robert I, 254
Jordon, Robert II, 571
Jordon, Situah I, 217
Jordon, Wd. Mary II, 571
Jordon, Wm. Hudson II, 571
Jordwin, Anne VI, 31
Jordwin, Anne VI, 36
Jordwin, James VI, 31
Jordwin, James VI, 36
Jorgenson, James P. Wallon VI, 257
Jorgenson, Laura L. VI, 257
Jorgenson, Louis P. VI, 257
Jory, Rachel II, 558
Jory, Rachel II, 560
Jory, Rachel II, 571
Jory, Wm. Hudson II, 560
Jos, John Dieterick VI, 944
Jos, Mary VI, 944
Joseph, Elma V, 408
Joseph, Gertrude V, 408
Joseph, Hazel V, 408
Joseph, Rachel V, 1004
Joseph, Ray V, 408
Joseph, Raymond V, 408
Joseph, Rebecca IV, 438
Joseph, Thomas V, 408
Joslin, Mary IV, 339
Joslin, Mary IV, 347
Joslyn, Newton IV, 1283
Jouett, Annie B. III, 396
Jouett, Annie B. III, 422
Jouett, Isaac W. III, 396
Jouett, Isaac W. III, 422
Jouett, Jean Gertrude III, 396
Jouett, Jean Gertrude III, 422
Jouett, Sallie III, 323
Jourdan, Charity IV, 37
Jourdan, Hannah IV, 37
Jourdan, Hannah IV, 43
Jourdan, James IV, 37
Jourdan, Joseph VI, 248
Jourdan, Leroy VI, 900
Jourdan, Massey VI, 411
Jourdan, Rebecca VI, 248
Jourdan, Susanna VI, 900
Jourdan, William VI, 921
Jowett, ??? III, 209
Jowett, Sarah III, 188
Jowett, Sarah III, 209
Joy, Alex. III, 188
Joy, Alexander III, 188
Joy, Gordon V, 87
Joy, Levi III, 188
Joy, Margaret III, 188
Joy, Maria III, 188
Joy, Martha Elizabeth V, 87
Joy, Mary I, 553
Joy, Reuben III, 188
Joy, Robert VI, 831
Joy, Sallie V, 87
Joy, Sally III, 188
Joy, Sally VI, 831
Joy, Sarah III, 188
Joyce, Chester III, 188
Joyce, Deborah IV, 96
Joyce, Elizabeth III, 128

yce, Florence Estelle III, 188
yce, Frank III, 128
yce, Frank III, 188
yce, Hamilton M. I, 636
yce, Hannah K. II, 293
yce, Ida V. III, 128
yce, Ida V. III, 188
yce, Jane Susanna III, 188
yce, Lewes III, 188
yce, Thomas IV, 96
yce, Willard Creighton III, 188
yner, Alek VI, 74
yner, Alex VI, 63
yner, Alexander VI, 63
yner, Alexander VI, 74
yner, Alice C. VI, 74
yner, Ann II, 445
yner, Annie VI, 56
yner, Annie VI, 74
yner, Baker VI, 56
yner, Disy VI, 74
yner, Diza VI, 74
yner, Effie J. VI, 58
yner, Effie J. VI, 74
yner, Elijah VI, 64
yner, Elijah VI, 74
yner, Eliza VI, 74
yner, Elizabeth VI, 53
yner, Elizabeth VI, 64
yner, Elizabeth VI, 65
yner, Elizabeth VI, 74
yner, Ella VI, 64
yner, Fannie E. VI, 74
yner, Franklin VI, 74
yner, Geneva VI, 74
yner, Grace VI, 74
yner, Henry C. VI, 74
yner, Jack VI, 74
yner, James Eley VI, 74
yner, James W. VI, 64
yner, James W., Jr. VI, 64
yner, James W., Sr. VI, 64
yner, Jane II, 445
yner, Jemima A. VI, 855
yner, John II, 445
yner, John VI, 53
yner, John VI, 64
yner, John VI, 74
yner, John Ernest VI, 74
yner, John Jones II, 571
yner, John T. VI, 74
yner, Joseph B. I, 243
yner, Leonard VI, 58
yner, Leonard VI, 74
yner, Lillie I, 237
yner, Lillie I, 243
yner, Lilly VI, 74
yner, Lindley VI, 74
yner, Margaret II, 571
yner, Martha VI, 74
yner, Martha A. VI, 53
yner, Martha A. VI, 74
yner, Martha C. VI, 63
yner, Martha C. VI, 74
yner, Martha J. VI, 56
yner, Mary VI, 74
yner, Mason VI, 74
yner, Moses VI, 74
yner, Polly VI, 64
yner, Polly VI, 74
yner, Rebecca I. VI, 74
yner, Ruth VI, 74
yner, Sarah VI, 74
yner, Thomas VI, 74
yner, Tinsie I, 237
yner, Tinsie I, 243
yner, Wilbur VI, 74
yner, William VI, 74
yner, William VI, 855
yner, William A. Geneva VI, 74
yner, Winnie VI, 74
yner, Winnie E. VI, 74
yner, Winny VI, 74
yners, Elizabeth II, 383
yners, John II, 383
ynex, James VI, 189
ube, Mary A. III, 64
ube, Mary A. III, 231
ucely, Anna I, 243
ucely, Anne I, 243
ucely, Anne I, 256
uctice, Elizabeth II, 1007
uctice, John II, 1007
uctice, William II, 1007
ude, Elizabeth VI, 831
ude, Geo. VI, 812
ude, George VI, 831
ude, George VI, 863
ude, George, Jr. VI, 831
ude, Lucy VI, 863
ude, Mary Ann VI, 812
Jude, Sally W. VI, 846
Judge, Hannah III, 188
Judge, Hester III, 188
Judge, Hugh III, 188
Judge, Hugh IV, 339
Judge, Hugh IV, 414
Judge, Hugh IV, 436
Judge, Hugh IV, 447
Judge, Hugh VI, 733
Judge, Hugh VI, 759
Judge, Margaret III, 188
Judge, Margaret VI, 733
Judge, Margaret VI, 759
Judge, Phebe III, 188
Judge, Phebe IV, 339
Judge, Phebe IV, 414
Judge, Phebe IV, 447
Judge, Rachel III, 188
Judge, Rachel VI, 759
Judge, Rachel VI, 789
Judge, Rebecca III, 188
Judge, Rebecca IV, 339
Judge, Rebecca Y. IV, 414
Judge, Rebecca Y. IV, 436
Judge, Rebeckah Y. IV, 414
Judge, Susanna III, 188
Judge, Susannah III, 188
Judge, Susannah IV, 339
Judge, Susannah IV, 414
Judge, Susannah IV, 436
Judge, Susannah IV, 447
Judge, Susannah VI, 733
Judge, Susannah VI, 759
Judge, Susannah, Jr. III, 188
Judge, Thomas III, 188
Judkin, Carolus I, 244
Judkin, Carolus I, 254
Judkin, Charity I, 244
Judkin, Charity I, 254
Judkin, James I, 243
Judkin, Joel I, 243
Judkin, Nicholas I, 243
Judkins, ??? V, 408
Judkins, Abigail I, 217
Judkins, Abigail I, 244
Judkins, Abigail I, 250
Judkins, Abigail IV, 231
Judkins, Anderson I, 217
Judkins, Anderson IV, 231
Judkins, Anderson IV, 414
Judkins, Anderson IV, 466
Judkins, Anderson IV, 480
Judkins, Anderson IV, 481
Judkins, Ann IV, 481
Judkins, Ann IV, 487
Judkins, Ann F. IV, 197
Judkins, Ann F. IV, 232
Judkins, Anna IV, 231
Judkins, Anna M. V, 914
Judkins, Anna M. V, 930
Judkins, Carlois I, 555
Judkins, Carolas I, 555
Judkins, Carolas I, 566
Judkins, Carolies I, 555
Judkins, Carolius IV, 414
Judkins, Carolus I, 244
Judkins, Carolus IV, 414
Judkins, Catharine IV, 339
Judkins, Catharine IV, 344
Judkins, Catharine IV, 466
Judkins, Catharine IV, 480
Judkins, Catherine IV, 480
Judkins, Catherine IV, 481
Judkins, Charity I, 217
Judkins, Charity I, 244
Judkins, Charity I, 555
Judkins, Charity I, 566
Judkins, Charity IV, 414
Judkins, Charity VI, 858
Judkins, Charles IV, 231
Judkins, Charles P. V, 87
Judkins, Chas. Palmer V, 914
Judkins, Cornelius I, 217
Judkins, Cornelius I, 243
Judkins, David IV, 231
Judkins, David IV, 232
Judkins, David IV, 480
Judkins, David IV, 481
Judkins, David IV, 485
Judkins, David V, 914
Judkins, David Judkins V, 919
Judkins, David S. V, 914
Judkins, Dr. Wm. V, 914
Judkins, Edith V, 87
Judkins, Edith V, 914
Judkins, Elisabeth I, 244
Judkins, Elizabeth I, 555
Judkins, Elizabeth IV, 367
Judkins, Elizabeth IV, 414
Judkins, Elizabeth IV, 448
Judkins, Elizabeth IV, 479
Judkins, Elizabeth IV, 480
Judkins, Elizabeth IV, 481
Judkins, Elizabeth VI, 124
Judkins, Emma Gertrude IV, 531
Judkins, Faith I, 244
Judkins, Faith I, 250
Judkins, Fanny V, 914
Judkins, Francis V, 914
Judkins, Helen W. V, 914
Judkins, Hiram IV, 339
Judkins, Isaac IV, 231
Judkins, Isaac P. IV, 231
Judkins, James I, 217
Judkins, James I, 243
Judkins, James I, 244
Judkins, James I, 250
Judkins, James IV, 195
Judkins, James IV, 231
Judkins, James IV, 232
Judkins, James IV, 414
Judkins, James IV, 537
Judkins, James VI, 114
Judkins, James VI, 122
Judkins, James, Jr. IV, 185
Judkins, James, Jr. IV, 231
Judkins, James, Jr. IV, 339
Judkins, James, Jr. IV, 480
Judkins, James, Jr. IV, 537
Judkins, Jas. IV, 480
Judkins, Jesse IV, 231
Judkins, Jesse IV, 232
Judkins, Jesse IV, 414
Judkins, Jesse P. V, 914
Judkins, Joel I, 243
Judkins, Joel I, 244
Judkins, Joel I, 555
Judkins, Joel IV, 332
Judkins, Joel IV, 339
Judkins, Joel IV, 396
Judkins, Joel IV, 414
Judkins, Joel IV, 448
Judkins, Joel VI, 114
Judkins, Joel VI, 122
Judkins, Joel VI, 858
Judkins, John I, 217
Judkins, John I, 232
Judkins, John I, 244
Judkins, Jonathan IV, 151
Judkins, Jonathan IV, 231
Judkins, Jonathan IV, 232
Judkins, Jonathan IV, 339
Judkins, Jonathan IV, 480
Judkins, Jonathan IV, 537
Judkins, Lucy I, 243
Judkins, Lucy I, 244
Judkins, Lucy I, 555
Judkins, Lucy IV, 414
Judkins, Lucy IV, 448
Judkins, Lucy VI, 122
Judkins, Lucy Stanton VI, 114
Judkins, Madora V, 408
Judkins, Margaret I, 244
Judkins, Margaret I, 250
Judkins, Maria IV, 232
Judkins, Maria IV, 339
Judkins, Maria IV, 396
Judkins, Maria IV, 414
Judkins, Maria IV, 537
Judkins, Maria Louisa IV, 481
Judkins, Mariah IV, 332
Judkins, Mariah IV, 339
Judkins, Mariah IV, 414
Judkins, Mariah IV, 537
Judkins, Martha I, 217
Judkins, Martha I, 243
Judkins, Martha IV, 151
Judkins, Martha IV, 195
Judkins, Martha IV, 231
Judkins, Martha IV, 232
Judkins, Martha IV, 339
Judkins, Martha IV, 414
Judkins, Martha IV, 437
Judkins, Martha IV, 480
Judkins, Martha IV, 481
Judkins, Martha IV, 537
Judkins, Martha V, 914
Judkins, Martha VI, 114
Judkins, Martha VI, 122
Judkins, Martha A. V, 900
Judkins, Martha Ann IV, 231
Judkins, Martha Ann IV, 232
Judkins, Martha Ann IV, 481
Judkins, Martha Ann V, 914
Judkins, Mary I, 217
Judkins, Mary I, 232
Judkins, Mary I, 243
Judkins, Mary I, 244
Judkins, Mary IV, 151
Judkins, Mary IV, 174
Judkins, Mary IV, 232
Judkins, Mary IV, 339
Judkins, Mary IV, 377
Judkins, Mary IV, 414
Judkins, Mary IV, 537
Judkins, Mary V, 87
Judkins, Mary V, 914
Judkins, Mary Ann V, 914
Judkins, Mary H. IV, 536
Judkins, Mary H. IV, 537
Judkins, Mary P. V, 87
Judkins, Mary W. IV, 464
Judkins, Mary W. IV, 481
Judkins, Nicholas I, 243
Judkins, Nicholas I, 244
Judkins, Nicholas I, 555
Judkins, Nicholas IV, 339
Judkins, Nicholas IV, 414
Judkins, Rachel IV, 231
Judkins, Rachel IV, 232
Judkins, Rachel IV, 281
Judkins, Rachel IV, 414
Judkins, Rachel IV, 480
Judkins, Rachel IV, 481
Judkins, Rachel V, 914
Judkins, Ray D. IV, 531
Judkins, Rebecca IV, 494
Judkins, Rebecca E. V, 87
Judkins, Rebecca E. V, 914
Judkins, Rebecca Elma V, 914
Judkins, Rebeckah VI, 858
Judkins, Robert IV, 231
Judkins, Robert IV, 232
Judkins, Sarah I, 217
Judkins, Sarah IV, 151
Judkins, Sarah IV, 169
Judkins, Sarah IV, 230
Judkins, Sarah IV, 231
Judkins, Sarah IV, 232
Judkins, Sarah IV, 480
Judkins, Sarah IV, 481
Judkins, Sarah IV, 537
Judkins, Sarah V, 914
Judkins, Sarah R. V, 900
Judkins, Sarah R. V, 914
Judkins, Stanton I, 217
Judkins, Stanton IV, 231
Judkins, Stanton IV, 480
Judkins, Stanton IV, 481
Judkins, Stanton B. V, 408
Judkins, Susa IV, 232
Judkins, Susan IV, 232
Judkins, Susan V, 914
Judkins, Susan P. IV, 480
Judkins, Susan P. IV, 481
Judkins, Susan P. IV, 485
Judkins, Susan P. V, 914
Judkins, Susan P. V, 919
Judkins, Susan R. V, 914
Judkins, Susanna IV, 151
Judkins, Susanna IV, 185
Judkins, Susanna IV, 231
Judkins, Susanna IV, 232
Judkins, Susanna IV, 339
Judkins, Susanna IV, 480
Judkins, Susanna IV, 537
Judkins, Susannah IV, 414
Judkins, Susannah IV, 480
Judkins, Susannah IV, 537
Judkins, Thomas I, 217
Judkins, Thomas I, 244
Judkins, Thomas I, 555
Judkins, Thomas IV, 414
Judkins, William I, 217
Judkins, William IV, 231
Judkins, William IV, 232
Judkins, William IV, 480
Judkins, William V, 87
Judkins, William V, 914
Judkins, William A. IV, 232
Judkins, William A. IV, 481
Judkins, William H. VI, 75
Judkins, William N. V, 87
Judkins, William, Jr. V, 914
Judkins, Wm. IV, 281
Judkins, Wm. IV, 480
Judkins, Wm. IV, 481
Judkins, Wm. V, 914
Judkins, Wm. VI, 858
Judkins, Wm. Tyson V, 914
Judson, Edith III, 334
Judson, Florence E. IV, 1323
Judson, Grace IV, 1323
Judson, Grace R. IV, 1323
Judson, Laura Donelly IV, 971
Judson, Mrs. J. E. IV, 1323
Judy, Lydia A. V, 87
Jueely, Anna I, 243
Juland, Jane I, 764
Julean, Alfred I, 764
Julian, Alfred I, 764
Julian, Azariah V, 788
Julian, Charlotte I, 1033
Julian, Charlotte V, 788
Julian, Charlotte V, 794
Julian, David C. I, 682
Julian, David C. I, 686
Julian, Eliza Jane I, 932
Julian, Elizabeth I, 682
Julian, Elizabeth I, 749
Julian, Elizabeth I, 764
Julian, James IV, 1283
Julian, John R. IV, 1283
Julian, Marjery V, 794
Julian, Susanna I, 1033
Julian, William Osborne I, 682
Julien, Susanna I, 1030
Julien, Susanna I, 1033
Julin, Azariah V, 788
Julin, Elizabeth I, 682
Jump, Eunice IV, 1168
Jump, Eunice IV, 1185
Jump, Eunice IV, 1213
Jump, Eunice IV, 1223
Jump, Mary II, 816
Jung, Elizabeth Hier Ruht III, 487
Jungkairth, Charles IV, 1255
Junkens, J. V, 1004
Junkins, Alice Ann IV, 639
Junkins, Alice Ann IV, 661
Junkins, Joel VI, 858
Jurder, Deida I, 888
Jurder, Deida I, 905
Jurey, Elizabeth V, 238
Jurey, Margaret VI, 411
Jurey, William V, 238
Jury, Abner V, 256
Jury, Clarkson Wright V, 256
Jury, Eleanor V, 256
Jury, Elizabeth V, 220
Jury, Elizabeth V, 256
Jury, Elizabeth V, 451
Jury, Elizabeth V, 459
Jury, Ellen V, 459
Jury, Enos V, 256
Jury, Ezra V, 256
Jury, Isaac V, 256
Jury, Jane V, 237
Jury, Jane V, 256
Jury, John M. V, 256
Jury, Lewis V, 256
Jury, Margaret V, 256
Jury, Melicent V, 220
Jury, Milicent V, 256
Jury, Millicent V, 451
Jury, Milton V, 256
Jury, Milton V, 459
Jury, Sidney V, 256
Jury, Sidney V, 293
Jury, William V, 220
Jury, William V, 256
Jury, Wm. V, 451
Jury, Wm. V, 459
Juson, Jain I, 1010
Justice, Alfred B. II, 884
Justice, Alfred B. II, 894
Justice, Alfred Bunting II, 384
Justice, Alfred Bunting II, 571
Justice, Alfred Bunting II, 804
Justice, Alfred Rudolph II, 804
Justice, Ann I, 764
Justice, Ann I, 765
Justice, Anna II, 1075
Justice, Anna Vaughn II, 804
Justice, Anna Vaughn II, 884
Justice, Anna Vaughn II, 902
Justice, Annie E. II, 1075
Justice, Benjamin V, 750
Justice, Chalkley M. II, 884
Justice, Edith D. II, 1065
Justice, Elizabeth I, 449
Justice, Elizabeth II, 962
Justice, Elizabeth II, 1007
Justice, Elizabeth II, 1054
Justice, Elizabeth V, 750
Justice, Esther II, 384
Justice, Esther B. II, 1065
Justice, Esther B. II, 1075
Justice, Esther S. II, 571
Justice, Esther S. II, 884
Justice, Esther S. II, 894
Justice, Esther Syng II, 804
Justice, F. Millwood II, 884
Justice, Florence Millwood II, 804
Justice, Geo. Middleton II, 804
Justice, George II, 236
Justice, George II, 384
Justice, George II, 1066
Justice, George II, 1075
Justice, George M. II, 384
Justice, George M. II, 571
Justice, George M. II, 884

Justice, George M. II, 894
Justice, George Middleton II, 804
Justice, Hannah I, 444
Justice, Hannah I, 449
Justice, Hannah I, 764
Justice, Hannah II, 384
Justice, Hannah II, 1007
Justice, Hannah II, 1009
Justice, Henry I, 437
Justice, Henry I, 444
Justice, Henry I, 449
Justice, Henry I, 764
Justice, Henry V, 914
Justice, Herbert McIlvain II, 804
Justice, Hilda II, 804
Justice, Huldah II, 884
Justice, Huldah II, 902
Justice, James II, 1007
Justice, James II, 1009
Justice, John I, 449
Justice, John II, 571
Justice, John II, 962
Justice, John II, 1007
Justice, John II, 1009
Justice, John II, 1075
Justice, John V, 750
Justice, Jonathan V, 750
Justice, Joseph II, 884
Justice, Laura F. II, 1075
Justice, Laura G. II, 1066
Justice, Laura G. II, 1075
Justice, Mariah IV, 639
Justice, Mariah IV, 653
Justice, Martha II, 962
Justice, Martha II, 1007
Justice, Martha II, 1009
Justice, Martha II, 1075
Justice, Mary V, 750
Justice, Mary F. II, 885
Justice, Mary Fletcher II, 804
Justice, Mary Sophia II, 804
Justice, Nancy I, 449
Justice, Rebecca II, 810
Justice, Rebecca II, 814
Justice, Sarah II, 384
Justice, Sarah V, 750
Justice, Sarah Jane V, 914
Justice, Susan II, 1075
Justice, Susan G. II, 1075
Justice, Susan H. II, 884
Justice, Susan H. II, 894
Justice, Susan Hunt II, 804
Justice, Theodore II, 804
Justice, Theodore II, 884
Justice, Theodore II, 902
Justice, Thomas II, 384
Justice, Warner II, 884
Justice, Warner II, 902
Justice, William II, 1007
Justice, William G. II, 1066
Justice, William G. II, 1075
Justice, Wm. II, 1007
Justice, Wm. G. II, 1075
Justice, Wm. Warner II, 804
Justin, Ellen V, 914
Justin, Erwin V, 914
Justis, Elizabeth I, 449
Justis, Elizabeth V, 750
Justis, Hannah I, 449
Justis, Hannah I, 741
Justis, Hannah I, 764
Justis, Henry I, 449
Justis, John I, 449
Justis, Mary V, 750
Justis, Nancy I, 447
Justis, Nancy I, 449
Justis, Sarah V, 750
Justiss, Jacob II, 445
Justiss, Rebeckah II, 445
Jylife, Elizabeth II, 562
Jyliff, Elizabeth II, 685

Kabler, Catharine VI, 944
Kabler, Charles S. VI, 813
Kabler, Frederick VI, 877
Kabler, Frederick VI, 881
Kabler, Frederick VI, 883
Kabler, Frederick VI, 887
Kabler, Frederick VI, 889
Kabler, Frederick VI, 893
Kabler, Frederick VI, 894
Kabler, Frederick VI, 895
Kabler, Frederick VI, 896
Kabler, Frederick VI, 903
Kabler, Frederick VI, 912
Kabler, Frederick VI, 914
Kabler, Frederick VI, 921
Kabler, Frederick VI, 922
Kabler, Frederick VI, 930
Kabler, Frederick VI, 934
Kabler, Frederick VI, 935
Kabler, Frederick VI, 936
Kabler, Frederick VI, 939
Kabler, Frederick VI, 941
Kabler, Frederick VI, 944
Kabler, Frederick VI, 955
Kabler, Frederick VI, 956
Kabler, Frederick VI, 963
Kabler, Frederick VI, 965
Kabler, Frederick VI, 968
Kabler, Frederick VI, 974
Kabler, Frederick VI, 983
Kabler, Frederick VI, 988
Kabler, Frederick VI, 1001
Kabler, Frederick VI, 1010
Kabler, Frederick VI, 1011
Kabler, Frederick VI, 1013
Kabler, Frederick VI, 1014
Kabler, Frederick VI, 1017
Kabler, Frederick VI, 1020
Kabler, Harvey VI, 944
Kabler, Mary VI, 831
Kabler, Mary E. VI, 813
Kabler, Nancy VI, 944
Kabler, Nicholas Chilton VI, 944
Kabler, Sarah VI, 944
Kabler, Sarah L. VI, 944
Kabler, Thaddeus VI, 813
Kabler, Thaddeus VI, 831
Kabler, Thaddeus VI, 944
Kahill, Hiram V, 988
Kahl, Olive IV, 1323
Kahn, Hattie III, 132
Kahn, Hattie III, 188
Kahn, I. Robert III, 132
Kahn, I. Robert III, 188
Kahn, Mildred III, 132
Kahn, Mildred III, 188
Kaighin, Elizabeth II, 236
Kaighin, John II, 273
Kaighn, Ann II, 709
Kaighn, Anna II, 885
Kaighn, Bartram II, 737
Kaighn, Bartram II, 749
Kaighn, Charles II, 885
Kaighn, Chas. II, 804
Kaighn, Edward II, 749
Kaighn, Edward B. II, 709
Kaighn, Elizabeth II, 385
Kaighn, Elizabeth II, 571
Kaighn, Elizabeth II, 708
Kaighn, Elizabeth II, 709
Kaighn, Elizabeth II, 737
Kaighn, Elizabeth II, 749
Kaighn, Elizabeth II, 753
Kaighn, Elizabeth B. II, 709
Kaighn, Elizabeth B. II, 711
Kaighn, Elizabeth Bartram II, 385
Kaighn, Elizabeth Bartram II, 571
Kaighn, Elizabeth Bartram II, 726
Kaighn, Elizabeth Bartram II, 749
Kaighn, Hannah II, 708
Kaighn, Hannah E. II, 709
Kaighn, Hannah E. II, 726
Kaighn, Hannah E. II, 749
Kaighn, Hannah E. II, 753
Kaighn, Hannah E. II, 754
Kaighn, Hannah, Jr. II, 571
Kaighn, James E. II, 385
Kaighn, James E. II, 571
Kaighn, James E. II, 709
Kaighn, James E. II, 726
Kaighn, James E. II, 749
Kaighn, James E. II, 753
Kaighn, James E. II, 754
Kaighn, John II, 385
Kaighn, John II, 571
Kaighn, John II, 708
Kaighn, John II, 737
Kaighn, John II, 749
Kaighn, John II, 753
Kaighn, Joseph II, 804
Kaighn, Joseph II, 885
Kaighn, Mary II, 709
Kaighn, Mary II, 804
Kaighn, Mary Ann II, 737
Kaighn, Mary Ann II, 749
Kaighn, Mary Anna II, 709
Kaighn, Mary Anna II, 749
Kaighn, Mary Anna II, 754
Kaighn, Mary C. II, 885
Kaighn, Mary M. II, 885
Kaighn, Moses II, 385
Kaighn, Moses Bartram II, 385
Kaighn, Rebecca II, 709
Kaighn, Robert II, 885
Kaighn, Sally Ann II, 749
Kaighn, Sally C. II, 885
Kaighn, Sarah II, 804
Kailer, Geneva IV, 1245
Kailer, Geneva IV, 1255
Kailer, J. B. IV, 1255
Kailer, Joseph V. IV, 1255
Kaine, Katie I, 627
Kaine, Rose IV, 1339
Kaine, Rose Stemple IV, 1323
Kaiser, ??? VI, 742
Kaiser, Esther VI, 742
Kaiser, Esther Scott VI, 742
Kaiser, Esther Scott VI, 759
Kaiser, Judith IV, 406
Kaiser, Julia II, 711
Kaiser, Julia IV, 406
Kalb, Charles L. IV, 1255
Kalbruner, Geo. IV, 1323
Kalbruner, George IV, 1323
Kalbruner, Howard IV, 1323
Kalbruner, May IV, 1323
Kalbruner, Miss Emma IV, 1323
Kalbruner, Mrs. May IV, 1323
Kalbruner, Mrs. Ruth IV, 1323
Kale, Elizabeth IV, 729
Kale, George IV, 729
Kaler, Anna M. II, 885
Kaler, Bert R. II, 885
Kaler, Elizabeth M. II, 885
Kaler, Geneva IV, 1255
Kaler, James Llewellyn II, 885
Kaler, John Elwood II, 885
Kaler, Joseph V. IV, 1255
Kaler, Llewellyn II, 885
Kallock, Ann II, 823
Kalmt, Henrietta E. III, 194
Kalve, John II, 385
Kalve, Mary II, 385
Kamester, John II, 82
Kaminski, Anna IV, 481
Kaminski, Annie IV, 481
Kammerer, Henry II, 779
Kammerer, Marjorie II, 779
Kammerer, Martha II, 779
Kamp, ??? III, 188
Kamp, Augustus Helm III, 188
Kamp, John Helm III, 188
Kamp, Thomas III, 188
Kanada, Charles VI, 480
Kanada, Wd. Phebe VI, 480
Kanady, Cornelia I, 944
Kanady, Erastus I, 944
Kanady, Lettie I, 944
Kanady, Margaret II, 480
Kandler, Rachel VI, 890
Kandler, Zedekiah VI, 890
Kane, Cassie IV, 475
Kane, Francis V, 688
Kane, Mary V, 688
Kane, Simon V, 688
Kanguesser, Jean Joseph IV, 232
Kannada, Charles I, 493
Kannada, John I, 493
Kannada, Phebe I, 493
Kanoy, C. E. I, 944
Kanoy, Charles I, 888
Kanoy, Charles I, 944
Kanoy, Charles E. I, 928
Kanoy, Cynthia I, 888
Kanoy, Cynthia I, 928
Kanoy, Etta I, 944
Kanoy, Job I, 888
Kanoy, John I, 888
Kanoy, John I, 928
Kanoy, Joseph Elwood I, 888
Kanoy, Sarah J. I, 944
Kanoy, Sarah Jane I, 928
Kanupp, Ira Lee I, 928
Kanupp, Ira Lee I, 929
Kanupp, Mary Sibyl I, 928
Kaphaelian, Arden III, 188
Kaphaelian, Melkis III, 188
Kaphaelian, Sarkis III, 188
Kaphaelian, Vargin III, 188
Kaphaelian, Vargin M. III, 28
Kappack, William II, 385
Kapper, Sallie Belle VI, 759
Kapper, Sallie Belle VI, 787
Karlis, Basil IV, 729
Karlis, George IV, 729
Karlis, John IV, 729
Karlis, Mary IV, 729
Karlis, Mary Katherine IV, 729
Karlis, Paul IV, 729
Karlis, Percy IV, 729
Karlis, Vivian IV, 729
Karn, Abraham VI, 892
Karn, Abraham VI, 944
Karn, Ann VI, 944
Karn, Betsey VI, 944
Karn, Elizabeth VI, 892
Karn, John J. VI, 944
Karn, Michael VI, 944
Karn, Michel VI, 944
Karn, Moses VI, 944
Karn, Nancy VI, 944
Karn, Sarah VI, 944
Karn, William VI, 944
Karnes, Abraham VI, 896
Karnes, Abraham VI, 957
Karnes, Abraham VI, 1020
Karnes, Ann VI, 944
Karnes, Blanch V, 306
Karnes, Caroline IV, 1238
Karnes, Clarence V, 306
Karnes, Clyde V, 306
Karnes, Demarius VI, 945
Karnes, Elizabeth VI, 1020
Karnes, George V, 306
Karnes, Gertrude V, 306
Karnes, Harry O. V, 306
Karnes, Jacob VI, 950
Karnes, John J. VI, 944
Karnes, Joseph V, 306
Karnes, Loren Elwood V, 306
Karnes, Michel VI, 944
Karnes, Minnie Grace V, 183
Karnes, Moses VI, 944
Karnes, Moses VI, 1005
Karnes, Moses VI, 1020
Karnes, Nancy VI, 944
Karnes, Phebe VI, 950
Karnes, Polly VI, 881
Karnes, Rosa IV, 1238
Karnes, Sampson VI, 871
Karnes, Sampson VI, 893
Karnes, Sampson VI, 945
Karnes, Sarah VI, 944
Karnes, William VI, 944
Karns, Carey M. V, 459
Karns, George V, 459
Karns, Isaac V, 459
Karns, Jennie V, 459
Karns, Joseph V, 459
Karns, Louella V, 459
Karns, Marie V, 459
Karns, Michal VI, 1019
Karns, Moses VI, 1015
Karns, Susanna VI, 1019
Kasby, Edward II, 32
Kasby, Elizabeth II, 32
Kasby, Mary II, 32
Kasby, Mather II, 32
Kasby, Susannah II, 32
Kaseman, Katharine III, 420
Kasey, A., Jr. VI, 940
Kasey, Alex. VI, 944
Kasey, Alexander VI, 944
Kasey, Alexander VI, 957
Kasey, Alexander, Jr. VI, 944
Kasey, Ann VI, 991
Kasey, Elvira F. VI, 944
Kasey, Florentine VI, 989
Kasey, Francis VI, 944
Kasey, George VI, 944
Kasey, George, Sr. VI, 939
Kasey, Hannah VI, 944
Kasey, Hannah A. V. VI, 1022
Kasey, James VI, 939
Kasey, James VI, 944
Kasey, James VI, 957
Kasey, James VI, 991
Kasey, James C. VI, 944
Kasey, James C. VI, 989
Kasey, James S. VI, 944
Kasey, James S. VI, 965
Kasey, Jane VI, 944
Kasey, Jas. L. VI, 944
Kasey, Jemima VI, 1018
Kasey, John VI, 944
Kasey, John VI, 946
Kasey, John VI, 965
Kasey, John VI, 989
Kasey, John G. VI, 944
Kasey, John, Jr. VI, 943
Kasey, Juliana Jane VI, 965
Kasey, Marion M. VI, 944
Kasey, Mary VI, 939
Kasey, Mary VI, 944
Kasey, Mary VI, 957
Kasey, Mary Ann VI, 989
Kasey, Mary Frances VI, 944
Kasey, Mary J. VI, 944
Kasey, Mary L. VI, 944
Kasey, Mary W. VI, 944
Kasey, Nancy VI, 944
Kasey, Newlon VI, 944
Kasey, Newlon VI, 958
Kasey, Newlon VI, 989
Kasey, Peggy VI, 944
Kasey, Polly VI, 918
Kasey, Richard VI, 944
Kasey, Sally VI, 944
Kasey, Singleton VI, 944
Kasey, Susannah VI, 944
Kasey, Thomas VI, 944
Kasey, Thomas VI, 989
Kasey, Thomas VI, 1018
Kasey, Thomas A. VI, 922
Kasey, W. C. VI, 958
Kasey, W. C. VI, 1022
Kasey, W. G. VI, 989
Kasey, William VI, 944
Kasey, William VI, 956
Kasey, William C. VI, 944
Kashat, Thomas I, 377
Kashow, Abraham III, 188
Kashow, Eleanor III, 403
Kashow, George D. III, 188
Kashow, Jacob III, 403
Kashow, Lena III, 403
Kashow, Mary III, 188
Kates, Anna Lippincott VI, 759
Kates, Anna Lippincott VI, 786
Kates, E. R. VI, 786
Kates, Ewalt R. VI, 759
Kates, Ewalt R. VI, 786
Kates, Morris Thorne VI, 759
Kathcart, Priscilla V, 788
Kathcart, Priscilla V, 793
Kauffman, Clemenda III, 189
Kauffman, Emanuel III, 189
Kauffman, Emma L. III, 189
Kauffman, Joseph H. III, 189
Kauffman, Nellie IV, 875
Kaufman, A. N. IV, 1255
Kaufman, Clemenda III, 189
Kaufman, Ellis IV, 1255
Kaufman, Ellis S. IV, 1255
Kaufman, Emanuel III, 189
Kaufman, Emma L. III, 189
Kaufman, Harriet G. III, 189
Kaufman, Helen III, 188
Kaufman, Helen III, 275
Kaufman, Joseph H. III, 189
Kaufman, Lola L. IV, 1255
Kaufman, Lola Lucinda IV, 1255
Kaufman, Newton IV, 1255
Kaufman, Olive IV, 1255
Kaufman, Olive E. IV, 1168
Kaufman, Olive E. IV, 1255
Kaufman, Vilas IV, 1255
Kaufman, Vilas Summer IV, 1255
Kaugh, Andrew V, 1004
Kaugh, Maria V, 1004
Kaughman, May V, 1004
Kaulfuss, Ettiel W. III, 189
Kaulfuss, Ettiel W. III, 219
Kay, Albert II, 134
Kay, Albert II, 152
Kay, Ann II, 33
Kay, Ann II, 82
Kay, Ann II, 105
Kay, Ann II, 133
Kay, Ann II, 810
Kay, Ann T. II, 810
Kay, Anna Branch VI, 669
Kay, Anna Branch VI, 678
Kay, Betsey VI, 882
Kay, Buford VI, 944
Kay, Buford H. VI, 960
Kay, Bulah II, 321
Kay, Bulah II, 322
Kay, Charles R. II, 750
Kay, Charles Rogers II, 385
Kay, Charles Rogers II, 572
Kay, Clement II, 82
Kay, Clement II, 154
Kay, Clement H. II, 152
Kay, Clement H. II, 572
Kay, Deborah II, 572
Kay, Deborah E. II, 572
Kay, Edith II, 152
Kay, Edith II, 154
Kay, Eliza Ann II, 385
Kay, Ellen II, 152
Kay, Ellen II, 155
Kay, Ellen T. II, 134
Kay, Elwood II, 134
Kay, Elwood II, 152
Kay, Elwood II, 154
Kay, Frances VI, 944
Kay, Hannah II, 120
Kay, Hannah II, 121
Kay, Hannah II, 134
Kay, Hannah II, 152
Kay, Hannah II, 154
Kay, Hannah II, 236
Kay, Hannah II, 259
Kay, Hannah II, 561
Kay, Hannah II, 571
Kay, Hannah II, 676
Kay, Herbert II, 152

Hope II, 572
Hope II, 818
Isaac II, 33
Isaac II, 82
Isaac II, 236
Isaac II, 259
Isaac II, 561
Isaac II, 571
Isaac II, 572
James II, 152
James VI, 944
James VI, 1005
James Hutchinson II, 385
James Hutchinson II, 572
James Hutchinson II, 750
John II, 481
John II, 571
John Palmer Hutchinson
II, 385
Joseph II, 33
Joseph II, 82
Joseph II, 105
Joseph II, 385
Joseph II, 571
Joseph II, 572
Josiah II, 33
Josiah II, 82
Josiah II, 571
Josiah S. II, 385
Josiah S. II, 561
Josiah S. II, 571
Josiah S. II, 572
Josiah S. II, 709
Mahlon Hutchinson II, 385
Martha Ann VI, 882
Mary II, 481
Mary II, 571
Mary VI, 944
Rebecca Edith II, 134
Rebecca Edith II, 152
Rebecka II, 75
Rebeckah II, 33
Rebeckah II, 82
Rebekah II, 82
Sarah II, 385
Sarah II, 561
Sarah II, 571
Sarah II, 572
Sarah V, 749
Sarah Ann II, 385
Sarah Ann II, 737
Sarah Ann II, 750
Sarah H. II, 750
Thomas VI, 669
Thomas VI, 678
Wellington Wellesley II, 385
Willington Willesly II, 385
Wm. E. II, 572
ler, Albert A. IV, 729
ler, Bell IV, 729
ler, Effie May IV, 729
lor, Effie IV, 829
lor, Effie May IV, 729
lor, Maggie IV, 1323
lor, Sarah Jane IV, 749
s, Joseph I, 362
s, Rebecca I, 362
ch, Rachel V, 87
ch, Rachel V, 145
s, Nathan II, 33
ly, Abraham II, 236
ly, Rachel II, 236
n, David IV, 1039
n, Jacob B. I, 310
ndall, Chas. N. III, 292
ndall, Mary Mae III, 292
ndall, Winifred E. III, 292
ne, Barnado VI, 29
nly, Hannah II, 572
r, Elias V, 1004
r, Elsie V, 1004
r, Iva V, 1004
r, John V, 1004
r, Laura V, 1004
rn, Elizabeth VI, 473
rne, Barnado VI, 29
rne, Widow Elizabeth VI, 523
rnes, Dorothy Hubbard I, 636
rnes, Nancy P. I, 716
rnes, Nancy P. I, 723
rney, ??? II, 385
rney, Edmond II, 385
rney, Edmund II, 385
rney, Elizabeth II, 572
rney, J. Briscoe VI, 729
rney, James II, 385
rney, Johanna II, 385
rney, John Briscoe VI, 729
rney, John Briscoe VI, 759
rney, Mary II, 572
rney, Mary II, 573
Kearney, Philip II, 572
Kearney, Philip II, 573
Kearney, Philip II, 611
Kearney, Philip II, 624
Kearney, Rebecca II, 385
Kearney, Rebecca II, 572
Kearney, Rebecca II, 624
Kearney, Sarah VI, 729
Kearney, Sarah VI, 759
Kearney, Susanna II, 572
Kearney, Susanna II, 611
Kearneys, ??? II, 385
Kearneys, Edmond II, 385
Kearns, Alfred V, 631
Kearns, Alfred T. V, 631
Kearns, Anna V, 459
Kearns, Blanche V, 459
Kearns, C. Ebbert I, 636
Kearns, Carey M. V, 459
Kearns, Catharine Ragan I, 944
Kearns, Charles V, 343
Kearns, Chas. V, 343
Kearns, Clarence V, 459
Kearns, Colier Elbert I, 619
Kearns, Dickinson V, 459
Kearns, Dorothy I, 619
Kearns, Dorothy Hubbard I, 636
Kearns, Edith I, 944
Kearns, Edna III, 51
Kearns, Edna III, 189
Kearns, Edna Marie V, 459
Kearns, Eliza V, 459
Kearns, Emily V, 631
Kearns, George V, 459
Kearns, Gertrude V, 459
Kearns, Henrietta III, 189
Kearns, Isaac V, 459
Kearns, J. H. I, 619
Kearns, James V, 256
Kearns, Jennie V, 459
Kearns, Jessie H. V, 256
Kearns, Jessie Ila I, 944
Kearns, John V, 631
Kearns, John E. V, 631
Kearns, John P. III, 189
Kearns, Joseph V, 459
Kearns, Juliana Miller V, 459
Kearns, Katharine I, 929
Kearns, Louella V, 459
Kearns, Louisa I, 723
Kearns, Louisa I, 738
Kearns, Luella May V, 459
Kearns, Marie V, 459
Kearns, Mary I, 723
Kearns, Mary I, 734
Kearns, Matthew I, 723
Kearns, Myrtle I, 619
Kearns, Nancy P. I, 723
Kearns, Serena Buckman III, 189
Kearns, Susan I, 714
Kearns, Susan I, 723
Kearns, Wd. Elizabeth III, 40
Kearns, Wd. Elizabeth III, 189
Kearns, Wilma D. III, 189
Kearns, Wilmer III, 189
Kearns, Wilmer R. III, 51
Kearns, Wilmer R. III, 189
Kearny, Elizabeth II, 572
Kearny, Elizabeth II, 601
Keas, Nathan II, 82
Keasbey, Bradway II, 33
Keasbey, Jane II, 33
Keasbey, Sarah II, 33
Keasby, Anne Thompson II, 145
Keasby, Anne Thompson II, 152
Keasby, Bradway II, 33
Keasby, Bradway II, 82
Keasby, Bradway II, 96
Keasby, Bradway II, 108
Keasby, Edward II, 33
Keasby, Edward II, 56
Keasby, Edward II, 82
Keasby, Edward II, 98
Keasby, Elizabeth II, 33
Keasby, Elizabeth II, 56
Keasby, Elizabeth II, 69
Keasby, Elizabeth II, 82
Keasby, Elizabeth II, 98
Keasby, Elizabeth II, 109
Keasby, Emma II, 145
Keasby, Emma II, 152
Keasby, Hannah II, 58
Keasby, Hannah II, 82
Keasby, Howard Buzby II, 145
Keasby, Howard Buzby II, 152
Keasby, Jane II, 33
Keasby, Jane II, 82
Keasby, Jane II, 108
Keasby, John II, 33
Keasby, Lydia II, 151
Keasby, Lydia II, 153
Keasby, Mary II, 33
Keasby, Matthew II, 33
Keasby, Prudence II, 33
Keasby, Prudence II, 82
Keasby, Prudence II, 96
Keasby, Quinton II, 145
Keasby, Quinton II, 152
Keasby, Sarah II, 33
Keasby, Sarah II, 82
Keasby, Sarah II, 94
Kease, Alice II, 573
Kease, Wm. II, 573
Keasey, Edward VI, 831
Keasey, Mary VI, 831
Keates, Harry III, 189
Keates, William, Jr. III, 189
Keath, Adeline VI, 930
Keath, Catharine M. V, 1004
Keath, Susan VI, 930
Keath, Wm. V, 1004
Keath, Wm., Sr. V, 1004
Keaton, Ann I, 144
Keaton, Elisabeth I, 144
Keaton, Elisabeth I, 165
Keaton, Elizabeth I, 131
Keaton, Elizabeth I, 144
Keaton, Henry I, 92
Keaton, Henry I, 144
Keaton, Henry I, 165
Keaton, Martha I, 144
Keaton, Martha I, 159
Keaton, Miriam I, 144
Keaton, Miriam I, 172
Keaton, Ruth I, 144
Keaton, Ruth I, 172
Keaton, Sarah I, 144
Keats, C. D. VI, 801
Keats, Deborah IV, 1097
Keats, Deborah IV, 1103
Keatts, Louisa Coal V, 459
Keatts, Lucinda V, 579
Kebbett, Elizabeth II, 445
Keck, Christopher V, 750
Keck, George C. V, 750
Keck, Lola V, 750
Keck, Louisa V, 750
Keck, Mrs. ??? IV, 1323
Keech, Ann IV, 514
Keech, Ann IV, 537
Keefe, Ella B. I, 617
Keefer, David H. III, 216
Keefer, David Holcomb III, 189
Keefer, David Holcomb III, 278
Keefer, Grace III, 189
Keefer, Grace III, 216
Keefer, Grace III, 278
Keefer, Helen III, 189
Keefer, Jacob VI, 411
Keefer, Jacob J. VI, 411
Keefer, Jane VI, 411
Keefer, Jane M. V, 87
Keefer, Mary V, 87
Keefer, Mary Sidney M. V, 87
Keefer, Wm. III, 189
Keegan, Elizabeth II, 782
Keegan, Hannah II, 709
Keeler, Carrie IV, 1213
Keeler, Eleanor III, 189
Keeler, Eleanor Caroline III, 189
Keeler, Eleanor Caroline III, 303
Keeler, Emilia III, 189
Keeler, Emilia III, 303
Keeler, Hannah III, 62
Keeler, Hannah III, 189
Keeler, Henry W. III, 189
Keeler, Henry W. III, 303
Keeler, Mary II, 572
Keeler, Richard III, 62
Keeley, John III, 157
Keeley, John III, 189
Keeley, Josephine III, 157
Keeley, Josephine III, 189
Keeley, Mary J. III, 157
Keeley, Mary J. III, 189
Keeling, Helen Allen V, 914
Keely, Beulah E. IV, 639
Keely, Esther IV, 639
Keely, Esther S. IV, 639
Keely, Geo. IV, 639
Keely, George A. IV, 639
Keely, George S. IV, 639
Keely, Louisa Jane IV, 639
Keely, Mary E. IV, 639
Keemhle, Margaret II, 709
Keen, Ada IV, 1168
Keen, Aquilla IV, 971
Keen, Aquilla P. IV, 971
Keen, Berdetta C. IV, 971
Keen, Elizabeth II, 82
Keen, Elizabeth VI, 844
Keen, Elizabeth L. II, 733
Keen, Elizabeth L. II, 750
Keen, Esek Hermon IV, 971
Keen, Frances A. VI, 851
Keen, Francis III, 422
Keen, Francis III, 437
Keen, Hannah II, 885
Keen, Hannah II, 894
Keen, Hattie IV, 1168
Keen, Henry VI, 831
Keen, Homer IV, 971
Keen, Homer A. IV, 971
Keen, I. Sidney II, 894
Keen, Ida IV, 1168
Keen, Jane IV, 979
Keen, Jeremiah VI, 831
Keen, John H. VI, 844
Keen, John M. V, 256
Keen, Joseph IV, 1168
Keen, Lester L. IV, 971
Keen, Martha III, 422
Keen, Martha III, 437
Keen, Martha IV, 971
Keen, Martha IV, 1009
Keen, Martha IV, 1028
Keen, Martha IV, 1031
Keen, Martha M. VI, 858
Keen, Mary III, 422
Keen, Mary III, 435
Keen, Mary V, 256
Keen, Mary E. IV, 971
Keen, Patsey VI, 831
Keen, Rebecca VI, 831
Keen, Samuel IV, 971
Keen, Samuel IV, 979
Keen, Samuel S. IV, 971
Keen, Sarah IV, 971
Keen, Sarah IV, 979
Keene, Amanda VI, 652
Keene, Amanda VI, 670
Keene, Anna III, 57
Keene, Anna III, 189
Keene, Charles F. VI, 652
Keene, Charles F. VI, 653
Keene, Charles F. VI, 670
Keene, Elizabeth J. VI, 652
Keene, Elizabeth J. VI, 653
Keene, Elizabeth J. VI, 670
Keene, John VI, 652
Keene, John VI, 670
Keene, Josiah I, 244
Keene, Mary Ellen VI, 652
Keene, Nora E. III, 57
Keene, Nora E. III, 189
Keene, Rebecca J. III, 189
Keene, Rebecca, Jr. III, 57
Keene, Samuel III, 57
Keene, Samuel III, 189
Keenes, Josiah I, 244
Keeney, Caleb R. II, 884
Keeney, Caleb R. II, 885
Keeney, Caleb R. II, 900
Keeney, Mary VI, 944
Keeney, Mary A. II, 804
Keeney, Mary A. II, 885
Keeney, Mary Anna II, 884
Keeney, Mary Anna II, 885
Keeney, Mary E. II, 885
Keeney, Mary E. II, 900
Keeney, Mary Ella II, 810
Keeney, Mary Ellen II, 885
Keeney, Mary P. II, 884
Keeney, Mary P. II, 885
Keeney, Mary P. II, 900
Keeney, Susan Dorothea II, 804
Keeney, Thomas VI, 944
Keeney, Virginia Drysdale II, 804
Keeney, William R. II, 804
Keeney, Wm. R. II, 884
Keeney, Wm. R. II, 885
Keenum, Elizabeth VI, 896
Keenum, Elizabeth VI, 918
Keenum, Elizabeth VI, 944
Keenum, Elizabeth VI, 982
Keenum, Fanny VI, 1011
Keenum, Frances L. VI, 952
Keenum, James VI, 944
Keenum, Nancy VI, 944
Keenum, Peggy M. VI, 896
Keenum, Rhoda Mason VI, 918
Keenum, Richard VI, 896
Keenum, Richard VI, 944
Keenum, Richard VI, 952
Keenum, Richard VI, 1011
Keenum, Richd. VI, 896
Keenwicker, Katie IV, 1168
Keeny, Mary P. II, 885
Keer, Clifford IV, 972
Keer, Clifford Baylis IV, 972
Keer, Delilah IV, 972
Keer, Eldon IV, 972
Keer, Eldon Barnard IV, 972
Keer, Ercy C. IV, 972
Keer, Jeanette IV, 972
Keer, John IV, 972
Keer, Lela Leona IV, 972
Keer, Margaret IV, 972
Keer, Margaret Elizabeth IV, 972
Keer, Maud F. IV, 972
Keer, Maud S. IV, 972
Keer, Neil Monroe IV, 972
Keer, Nil IV, 972
Keer, Russell Neil IV, 972
Keer, W. Rufus IV, 972
Keerns, Anna V, 459
Kees, Cynthia Eliza Lenore
IV, 1213
Kees, Gulielma IV, 1213
Kees, Isaac Witford IV, 1213
Kees, Richard IV, 1213
Kees, Samuel John IV, 1213
Kees, Sarah IV, 175
Kees, Sarah IV, 232
Kees, Sarah Evelyn IV, 1213
Kees, Willets Hanson IV, 1213
Keese, Amy A. III, 422
Keese, Ann Eliza IV, 1168
Keese, Ann Eliza IV, 1207
Keese, Ann Eliza IV, 1213
Keese, Anna III, 189
Keese, C. E. Lenore IV, 1168
Keese, C. E. Lenore IV, 1214
Keese, Caroline III, 189
Keese, Caroline M. III, 189
Keese, Catherine III, 189
Keese, Catherine III, 337
Keese, Cynthia Eliza Lenore
IV, 1213
Keese, Eliza Ann III, 285
Keese, Eliza H. III, 189
Keese, Elizabeth III, 189
Keese, Elizabeth III, 281
Keese, Elizabeth III, 422
Keese, Elizabeth III, 443
Keese, Elizabeth III, 451
Keese, Emma D. IV, 1255
Keese, Esther IV, 1168
Keese, Eunice M. V, 87
Keese, Eva IV, 1214
Keese, George M. III, 189
Keese, Gilbert III, 281
Keese, Grace III, 174
Keese, Grace W. III, 189
Keese, Grace Waldron III, 189
Keese, Gula Elma IV, 1168
Keese, Guli Elma IV, 1168
Keese, Guli Elma IV, 1214
Keese, Gulia Elma IV, 1214
Keese, Gulielma IV, 1168
Keese, Gulielma IV, 1197
Keese, Gulielma IV, 1198
Keese, Gulielma IV, 1213
Keese, Gulielma A. IV, 1213
Keese, Hannah III, 422
Keese, Hannah III, 469
Keese, Hannah III, 471
Keese, Hannah IV, 1205
Keese, Hannah IV, 1213
Keese, Herman Bancroft III, 189
Keese, Isaac Wilford IV, 1168
Keese, Isaac Witford IV, 1213
Keese, James Albert IV, 1255
Keese, Jemima III, 189
Keese, Johanna III, 422
Keese, Johanna III, 471
Keese, John III, 41
Keese, John III, 189
Keese, John III, 422
Keese, John III, 451
Keese, John III, 471
Keese, John IV, 1168
Keese, John IV, 1213
Keese, John, Jr. III, 189
Keese, Lenore IV, 1168
Keese, Lydia IV, 1168
Keese, Lydia IV, 1212
Keese, Lydia IV, 1213
Keese, Martha IV, 1168
Keese, Martha IV, 1212
Keese, Martha IV, 1214
Keese, Martha W. IV, 1210
Keese, Mary III, 41
Keese, Mary III, 189
Keese, Mary III, 281
Keese, Mary III, 422
Keese, Mary III, 443
Keese, Mary S. IV, 1168
Keese, Mary S. IV, 1210
Keese, Mary S. IV, 1213
Keese, Mary T. III, 189
Keese, Mildred VI, 207
Keese, Mira IV, 1214
Keese, Nora IV, 1214

Keese, Oliver IV, 1168
Keese, Oliver IV, 1213
Keese, Pamela III, 17
Keese, Pamela III, 189
Keese, Pamelia III, 189
Keese, Paul Dewitt IV, 1255
Keese, Pauline Stoddard III, 189
Keese, Peter III, 189
Keese, Phebe III, 163
Keese, Phebe III, 189
Keese, Phebe B. III, 227
Keese, Phebe F. III, 189
Keese, Phebe M. III, 174
Keese, Rachel III, 443
Keese, Rich. P. III, 189
Keese, Richard IV, 1168
Keese, Richard IV, 1213
Keese, Richard IV, 1214
Keese, Sam'l T. III, 189
Keese, Samuel III, 422
Keese, Samuel IV, 1213
Keese, Samuel John IV, 1168
Keese, Samuel John IV, 1213
Keese, Samuel John IV, 1214
Keese, Samuel T. III, 163
Keese, Samuel T. III, 174
Keese, Samuel T. III, 189
Keese, Samuel T. III, 227
Keese, Samuel T. IV, 1168
Keese, Sarah IV, 1168
Keese, Sarah IV, 1213
Keese, Sarah Ann IV, 1168
Keese, Sarah Evelyn IV, 1168
Keese, Sarah Evelyn IV, 1213
Keese, Sarah Evelyn IV, 1214
Keese, Stephen IV, 1168
Keese, Stephen R. IV, 1168
Keese, Stephen R. V, 89
Keese, Titus IV, 1168
Keese, Titus IV, 1210
Keese, Titus IV, 1212
Keese, Titus IV, 1213
Keese, Wilfred J. IV, 1168
Keese, Wilfred J. IV, 1214
Keese, Willets Hanson IV, 1213
Keese, William III, 189
Keese, William III, 422
Keese, William III, 443
Keese, William Merritt III, 189
Keese, Willits Hansen IV, 1168
Keese, Willits Hanson IV, 1214
Keese, Willots Hanson IV, 1168
Keese, Wm. III, 189
Keese, Wm. III, 281
Keese, Wm. B. III, 189
Keese, Y. III, 189
Keese, Zaydee B. III, 163
Keese, Zaydee Bancroft III, 189
Keesee, Ann VI, 189
Keesee, Avery VI, 831
Keesee, Charles VI, 189
Keesee, Charles VI, 220
Keesee, Elizabeth VI, 189
Keesee, George VI, 189
Keesee, Jenny VI, 831
Keesee, John VI, 189
Keesee, Mary VI, 189
Keesee, Mildred VI, 189
Keesee, Mildred VI, 198
Keesee, Mildred, Jr. VI, 189
Keesee, Thomas VI, 189
Keetch, Arabella IV, 1323
Keetch, Daisy IV, 1323
Keetch, Geo. T. IV, 1323
Keetch, George IV, 1323
Keetch, Joey IV, 1323
Keetch, Josephine IV, 1323
Keetch, Rose Elizabeth IV, 1309
Keetch, Rose Elizabeth IV, 1323
Keetch, Thomas IV, 1323
Keetch, Thos. IV, 1323
Keetch, Violet IV, 1323
Keetch, Violet IV, 1338
Keeth, Collin B. VI, 944
Keeth, Eliza Jane VI, 944
Keeth, Elizabeth VI, 902
Keeth, Nancy VI, 902
Keever, Edward V, 87
Keever, Ida W. V, 87
Keever, Jane V, 87
Keever, Miriam Margaret V, 87
Keever, S. Wynne V, 87
Keever, Stanley Wynne V, 87
Keever, Wynne V, 87
Kegan, George II, 385
Keggle, Mahala I, 1157
Kehbel, Carl IV, 232
Kehbel, Clara IV, 232
Kehbel, Elizabeth IV, 232
Kehbel, Ella IV, 232
Kehbel, Ida IV, 232
Kehrwicker, Katie IV, 1168
Kehrwicker, S. E. IV, 1168
Keiffer, Mary V, 62
Keiffer, Mary V, 87
Keil, Charles III, 487
Keil, Charles G. III, 487
Keil, Francis III, 487
Keil, Julia Francis III, 487
Keim, Esther De Benneville II, 828
Keim, Maud IV, 481
Keintz, Edith H. IV, 688
Keister, Amelia IV, 782
Keister, Daniel IV, 782
Keister, Sarah IV, 782
Keister, William IV, 1255
Keith, Anna IV, 358
Keith, Archibald IV, 232
Keith, Arline V, 256
Keith, Arthur V, 256
Keith, Bessie V, 408
Keith, Blanche V, 256
Keith, Caleb II, 572
Keith, Caleb II, 750
Keith, Cordelia B. V, 256
Keith, Dorris Marie IV, 232
Keith, Eli V, 256
Keith, Elisha V, 408
Keith, Elizabeth V, 256
Keith, Elizabeth Frances V, 256
Keith, Emily I, 883
Keith, Emily I, 888
Keith, George II, 329
Keith, Henrietta V, 915
Keith, Henrietta V, 917
Keith, Henrietta L. V, 915
Keith, Jeremiah V, 256
Keith, Jeremiah A. V, 256
Keith, Jerry V, 256
Keith, Jesse V, 408
Keith, Jesse Lemoyne IV, 232
Keith, Lloyd IV, 358
Keith, Louisa V, 408
Keith, Margaret IV, 232
Keith, Margery II, 572
Keith, Martha V, 256
Keith, Mary IV, 232
Keith, Mary Ann IV, 339
Keith, Mary Ann IV, 358
Keith, Mary E. IV, 232
Keith, Minnie B. V, 408
Keith, Nicholas VI, 886
Keith, Russell Delbert V, 256
Keith, Sarah V, 256
Keith, Sarah Alice V, 256
Keith, Walter V, 408
Keith, Wd. Mary Emma II, 814
Kell, Ann II, 572
Kell, Hannah II, 806
Kell, John II, 806
Kell, Wd. Esther Smith II, 806
Kellar, Katharine V, 688
Kelle, Mary Anne II, 139
Kelleay, Mary Ann VI, 944
Kelleay, Rev. Daniel VI, 944
Kellem, Sarah IV, 481
Keller, Caroline E. V, 852
Keller, Carrie E. V, 846
Keller, Charlotte V, 688
Keller, Delilah V, 853
Keller, Edith IV, 1323
Keller, Edwin C. V, 853
Keller, Elizabeth V, 853
Keller, Eva H. G. II, 152
Keller, George V, 852
Keller, Gulielma I, 911
Keller, Gulielma I, 913
Keller, Hattie V, 853
Keller, Iva V, 853
Keller, Joseph L. V, 853
Keller, Karl V, 688
Keller, Katharine V, 688
Keller, Katharine Pauline V, 688
Keller, Marmaduke V, 853
Keller, Nathan S. V, 853
Keller, Orion Curtis V, 853
Kellers, Alice M. IV, 494
Kellers, Bohl III, 190
Kellers, Bohl III, 342
Kellers, Harriet III, 342
Kellers, Harriet H. III, 190
Kellers, Harriet H. III, 342
Kellers, Hattie Lavinia III, 190
Kellers, Hattie Lavinia III, 342
Kellers, Margaret IV, 494
Kellers, Wm. IV, 494
Kellett, Albert Edmund II, 962
Kellett, Alice II, 962
Kellett, Amelia II, 962
Kellett, Chester Holden II, 962
Kellett, Eleanore May II, 962
Kellett, Elsie Marie II, 962
Kellett, Harold Drewry II, 962
Kellett, Jessie Darbyshire II, 962
Kellett, John II, 962
Kellett, Nancy II, 962
Kellett, William James II, 962
Kelley, Abbie H. IV, 729
Kelley, Abigail IV, 729
Kelley, Abraham II, 236
Kelley, Agnes IV, 729
Kelley, Agnes Bell IV, 829
Kelley, Agnes Belle IV, 729
Kelley, Alfred D. IV, 729
Kelley, Ann VI, 831
Kelley, Benjamin VI, 831
Kelley, Bertha V, 343
Kelley, Charity IV, 829
Kelley, Charles V, 751
Kelley, Claiborn VI, 831
Kelley, David VI, 944
Kelley, Dennis VI, 831
Kelley, Donald Eugene IV, 729
Kelley, Donald Eugene IV, 829
Kelley, Edward A. IV, 729
Kelley, Edwin C. IV, 729
Kelley, Elizabeth II, 572
Kelley, Elizabeth II, 617
Kelley, Elizabeth II, 626
Kelley, Elizabeth IV, 909
Kelley, Elizabeth VI, 831
Kelley, Elvin Chas. IV, 729
Kelley, Emily V, 343
Kelley, Emily C. IV, 726
Kelley, Emily C. IV, 729
Kelley, Ethan V, 88
Kelley, Ethen V, 88
Kelley, Evey VI, 988
Kelley, Hannah IV, 829
Kelley, Harriet III, 298
Kelley, Harriet III, 334
Kelley, Hazel Leora IV, 729
Kelley, Hazel Leora IV, 829
Kelley, Herbert A. IV, 729
Kelley, Hilda IV, 729
Kelley, Hilda Rose IV, 829
Kelley, Hubert Austin IV, 729
Kelley, James VI, 831
Kelley, James VI, 944
Kelley, Jane VI, 831
Kelley, Jessie V, 343
Kelley, Joanna II, 572
Kelley, Joanna II, 595
Kelley, John VI, 831
Kelley, John W. IV, 1371
Kelley, Kenneth IV, 729
Kelley, Kenneth Ray IV, 729
Kelley, Kenneth Ray IV, 829
Kelley, Laura V, 343
Kelley, Leroy V, 343
Kelley, Liddy VI, 944
Kelley, Marianna II, 385
Kelley, Martha A. V, 343
Kelley, Martha A. C. D. VI, 829
Kelley, Mary II, 385
Kelley, Mary V, 343
Kelley, Mary V, 750
Kelley, Mary VI, 831
Kelley, Mary Alice IV, 729
Kelley, Mrs. Russell IV, 729
Kelley, Nancy VI, 831
Kelley, Nancy VI, 918
Kelley, Nancy VI, 988
Kelley, Nancy A. III, 136
Kelley, Nancy S. III, 349
Kelley, Nathe VI, 831
Kelley, Neal VI, 831
Kelley, Olive IV, 729
Kelley, Rachel II, 236
Kelley, Rachel A. IV, 1006
Kelley, Radford VI, 829
Kelley, Ralph IV, 729
Kelley, Ralph Earnest IV, 729
Kelley, Ralph Ernest IV, 829
Kelley, Rebecca IV, 729
Kelley, Rebecca V, 1005
Kelley, Samantha A. IV, 729
Kelley, Samanthan Alverda IV, 829
Kelley, Samuel V, 88
Kelley, Samuel V, 111
Kelley, Samuel V, 750
Kelley, Samuel V, 1005
Kelley, Sarah V, 88
Kelley, Sarah V, 111
Kelley, Sarah V, 115
Kelley, Sarah VI, 831
Kelley, Sarah VI, 944
Kelley, Seth V, 750
Kelley, Seth, Jr. V, 750
Kelley, Susan A. IV, 729
Kelley, Thomas Russell IV, 729
Kelley, Thomas Russell IV, 829
Kelley, Velma IV, 726
Kelley, Velma Odessa IV, 729
Kelley, Velma Odessa IV, 829
Kelley, Walter IV, 729
Kelley, Walter V, 343
Kelley, Walter S. IV, 729
Kelley, William II, 385
Kelley, William V, 343
Kelley, William VI, 831
Kelley, William A. IV, 729
Kelley, Wm. II, 572
Kelley, Wm. II, 595
Kelley, Wm. II, 617
Kelley, Wm. A. IV, 829
Kelley, Wm. Alvaro IV, 829
Kellis, Catharine E. V, 408
Kellis, Eliza V, 688
Kellis, Emma Z. V, 408
Kellis, Frank E. V, 408
Kellis, Frank V. V, 408
Kellis, Howard V, 408
Kellis, John V, 408
Kellis, John W. V, 408
Kellis, Laura L. V, 408
Kellison, James II, 236
Kellogg, B. P. V, 751
Kellogg, Charles W. Arthur V, 751
Kellogg, Edward P. V, 751
Kellogg, George N. V, 751
Kellogg, Maria V, 751
Kellogg, Merton E. V, 751
Kellogg, Retta V, 751
Kellogg, Retta V, 772
Kellogg, Rhetta V, 751
Kellogg, Wait Ann IV, 729
Kells, Ann II, 572
Kellum, Aaron I, 602
Kellum, Abitney I, 602
Kellum, Amiel I, 602
Kellum, Amos I, 858
Kellum, Amos V, 408
Kellum, Ann I, 533
Kellum, Ann I, 555
Kellum, Ann I, 888
Kellum, Ann V, 183
Kellum, Ann V, 408
Kellum, Anna I, 888
Kellum, Anna V, 837
Kellum, Asenath I, 858
Kellum, Asenath I, 888
Kellum, Asenith V, 408
Kellum, Asher I, 858
Kellum, Asher V, 408
Kellum, Bulah I, 888
Kellum, Bulah V, 183
Kellum, Buly V, 408
Kellum, Charles I, 606
Kellum, Charles C. I, 602
Kellum, Christopher I, 858
Kellum, Christopher I, 888
Kellum, Christopher V, 408
Kellum, Christopher V, 579
Kellum, Deborah V, 846
Kellum, Elijah I, 1044
Kellum, Elijah IV, 151
Kellum, Elijah IV, 481
Kellum, Elijah V, 846
Kellum, Elizabeth I, 272
Kellum, Elizabeth I, 602
Kellum, Elizabeth I, 1044
Kellum, Elizabeth IV, 151
Kellum, Elizabeth IV, 481
Kellum, Elizabeth V, 408
Kellum, Elizabeth V, 579
Kellum, Elizabeth V, 580
Kellum, Elizabeth V, 585
Kellum, Elizabeth V, 846
Kellum, Ester I, 888
Kellum, Esther I, 545
Kellum, Esther I, 555
Kellum, Esther I, 858
Kellum, Esther V, 408
Kellum, Geo. V, 579
Kellum, Hannah I, 602
Kellum, Hannah I, 606
Kellum, James I, 602
Kellum, Jesse I, 858
Kellum, Jesse V, 408
Kellum, John I, 272
Kellum, John I, 1044
Kellum, John IV, 151
Kellum, John IV, 232
Kellum, Joseph I, 1044
Kellum, Joseph IV, 151
Kellum, Joseph IV, 481
Kellum, Joseph V, 846
Kellum, Judith Merideth I, 606
Kellum, Keziah V, 827
Kellum, Lindley V, 183
Kellum, Lindley V, 408
Kellum, Lydia I, 858
Kellum, Lydia I, 888
Kellum, Lydia I, 903
Kellum, Mary V, 579
Kellum, Mary V, 834
Kellum, Mary Ann I, 602
Kellum, Mial I, 555
Kellum, Mitney I, 602
Kellum, Nancy I, 602
Kellum, Nancy I, 606
Kellum, Nathan I, 555
Kellum, Nathan I, 602
Kellum, Nathan I, 606
Kellum, Nathaniel I, 272
Kellum, Nathaniel I, 1044
Kellum, Nathaniel IV, 151
Kellum, Nathaniel IV, 481
Kellum, Nathaniel V, 846
Kellum, Noah I, 545
Kellum, Noah I, 555
Kellum, Noah I, 858
Kellum, Noah I, 888
Kellum, Noah V, 408
Kellum, Samuel I, 533
Kellum, Samuel I, 555
Kellum, Samuel I, 858
Kellum, Samuel I, 888
Kellum, Samuel V, 183
Kellum, Samuel V, 408
Kellum, Sarah I, 272
Kellum, Sarah I, 1044
Kellum, Sarah IV, 151
Kellum, Sarah IV, 481
Kellum, Sarah V, 845
Kellum, Sarah V, 846
Kellum, Susanna I, 1044
Kellum, Susanna IV, 481
Kellum, Susannah IV, 151
Kellum, Susannah V, 846
Kellum, William I, 272
Kellum, William I, 602
Kellum, William I, 1044
Kellum, William V, 846
Kelly, ??? II, 236
Kelly, A. D. IV, 1238
Kelly, Abagale V, 88
Kelly, Abbe H. IV, 1238
Kelly, Abby Hannah IV, 1238
Kelly, Abigail I, 1021
Kelly, Abigail I, 1030
Kelly, Abigail IV, 1238
Kelly, Abigail V, 88
Kelly, Abigail V, 117
Kelly, Abigal I, 1033
Kelly, Abijah O'Neal V, 17
Kelly, Abraham II, 236
Kelly, Achsah V, 88
Kelly, Achsah V, 128
Kelly, Adaline IV, 1323
Kelly, Adeline IV, 1323
Kelly, Alfred V, 954
Kelly, Alfred D. IV, 1238
Kelly, Alice Hortense V, 88
Kelly, Alicia V, 88
Kelly, Amelia V, 750
Kelly, Amelia V, 774
Kelly, Andre Lorraine III, 190
Kelly, Ann I, 1021
Kelly, Ann I, 1033
Kelly, Ann I, 1035
Kelly, Ann V, 69
Kelly, Ann V, 70
Kelly, Ann V, 88
Kelly, Ann V, 814
Kelly, Ann V, 816
Kelly, Ann VI, 831
Kelly, Ann Etta V, 88
Kelly, Anna IV, 1238
Kelly, Anna V, 17
Kelly, Anna V, 88
Kelly, Anna V, 107
Kelly, Anna V, 750
Kelly, Anna V, 814
Kelly, Anna V, 815
Kelly, Anna V, 816
Kelly, Anna Mabel V, 88
Kelly, Anne V, 88
Kelly, Annie C. IV, 1238
Kelly, Augusta L. III, 190
Kelly, Avis V, 88
Kelly, Avis V, 121
Kelly, Avis V, 954
Kelly, Avis V, 959
Kelly, Barbara II, 572
Kelly, Barton H. V, 88
Kelly, Barton Hooper V, 88
Kelly, Barton Hoops V, 88
Kelly, Benjamin IV, 1370
Kelly, Benjamin V, 88
Kelly, Betty A. VI, 867

y, Caroline V, 788
y, Caroline V, 793
y, Caroline B. III, 190
y, Charity I, 555
y, Charity IV, 829
y, Charles V, 751
y, Charles Paty IV, 43
y, Chas. V, 183
y, Christen I, 1061
y, Christine Leona V, 88
y, Content IV, 1370
y, Danis VI, 854
y, David VI, 944
y, Deborah IV, 1370
y, Dennis VI, 826
y, Dennis VI, 845
y, Dennis VI, 860
y, Dewain V, 751
y, Dollie M. V, 1004
y, Donald V, 751
y, Dora E. V, 689
y, Edith IV, 972
y, Edward G. III, 190
y, Edwin IV, 1370
y, Effie V, 459
y, Elanor Ann II, 152
y, Eleanor Ann II, 152
y, Elizabeth I, 1029
y, Elizabeth I, 1033
y, Elizabeth I, 1034
y, Elizabeth II, 385
y, Elizabeth II, 486
y, Elizabeth II, 487
y, Elizabeth II, 572
y, Elizabeth VI, 831
y, Elizabeth VI, 944
y, Ella V, 751
y, Ellen IV, 1370
y, Elvin Chas. IV, 729
y, Emily A. VI, 857
y, Erma IV, 232
y, Esther V, 750
y, Esther V, 814
y, Ethan V, 88
y, Ethan E. V, 88
y, Ethen V, 88
y, Eunice V, 184
y, Eunice V, 214
y, Eva Janet V, 751
y, Fanny VI, 867
y, Florence III, 190
y, Florence E. V, 459
y, Florence Rebecca II, 321
y, Gulielma V, 751
y, Hannah I, 555
y, Hannah I, 1016
y, Hannah I, 1021
y, Hannah I, 1033
y, Hannah I, 1036
y, Hannah IV, 43
y, Hannah IV, 957
y, Hannah IV, 972
y, Hannah V, 17
y, Hannah V, 88
y, Hannah V, 140
y, Hannah V, 954
y, Harriet V, 88
y, Harriet C. V, 88
y, Harriet F. IV, 1371
y, Helen III, 29
y, Helen III, 190
y, Hephsiba II, 54
y, Hephsiba II, 82
y, Hicks II, 572
y, Hubert Austin IV, 729
y, Isaac I, 1033
y, Isaac IV, 43
y, Isaac V, 88
y, Isaac V, 184
y, Isabella II, 962
y, Isabella II, 1007
y, Isabella II, 1075
y, James VI, 831
y, James VI, 920
y, James VI, 944
y, Jane IV, 43
y, Jane IV, 49
y, Jane V, 88
y, Jane V, 954
y, Jane S. V, 88
y, Joan II, 385
y, Joanna II, 572
y, Job II, 54
y, Job II, 82
y, Job II, 236
y, John I, 555
y, John I, 1016
y, John I, 1019
y, John I, 1021
y, John I, 1033
y, John III, 190
Kelly, John IV, 43
Kelly, John IV, 232
Kelly, John V, 88
Kelly, John V, 183
Kelly, John V, 750
Kelly, John V, 814
Kelly, John VI, 831
Kelly, John E. III, 190
Kelly, John E. III, 312
Kelly, John W. IV, 1370
Kelly, John W. IV, 1371
Kelly, Joseph V, 751
Kelly, Joseph T. V, 814
Kelly, Joseph Teague V, 750
Kelly, Joseph Teague V, 814
Kelly, Katie V, 557
Kelly, Lael V, 688
Kelly, Lael V, 695
Kelly, Laura May V, 751
Kelly, Leona Christine V, 88
Kelly, Levi V, 88
Kelly, Levi L. V, 88
Kelly, Libni IV, 1370
Kelly, Libni IV, 1371
Kelly, Libnit IV, 1370
Kelly, Liddy VI, 944
Kelly, Lucretia V, 751
Kelly, Luly IV, 1214
Kelly, Lydia IV, 1370
Kelly, Lydia IV, 1371
Kelly, Madora V, 688
Kelly, Madora V, 691
Kelly, Madora E. V, 88
Kelly, Mahala V, 750
Kelly, Mahala V, 773
Kelly, Margaret V, 88
Kelly, Margaret V, 1004
Kelly, Mariam V, 688
Kelly, Mariam V, 689
Kelly, Marianna II, 385
Kelly, Martha VI, 813
Kelly, Martha Ellen V, 751
Kelly, Mary I, 823
Kelly, Mary I, 1019
Kelly, Mary I, 1030
Kelly, Mary I, 1033
Kelly, Mary I, 1038
Kelly, Mary II, 385
Kelly, Mary II, 1007
Kelly, Mary II, 1028
Kelly, Mary IV, 43
Kelly, Mary V, 88
Kelly, Mary V, 140
Kelly, Mary V, 153
Kelly, Mary V, 183
Kelly, Mary V, 343
Kelly, Mary V, 671
Kelly, Mary V, 750
Kelly, Mary V, 799
Kelly, Mary V, 814
Kelly, Mary V, 815
Kelly, Mary VI, 861
Kelly, Mary VI, 944
Kelly, Mary Alice IV, 1238
Kelly, Mary Ann IV, 1370
Kelly, Mary Ann IV, 1371
Kelly, Mary Ann V, 954
Kelly, Mary Ann VI, 944
Kelly, Mary E. V, 689
Kelly, Mary Engliah I, 1033
Kelly, Mary Evelyn V, 671
Kelly, Mary Evelyn V, 688
Kelly, Mary Jane IV, 1370
Kelly, Mary S. V, 88
Kelly, Mary Victoria V, 751
Kelly, Masie V, 663
Kelly, Masie V, 688
Kelly, Maude III, 190
Kelly, Maude III, 312
Kelly, Max V, 750
Kelly, Meriana II, 572
Kelly, Meriana II, 673
Kelly, Michael VI, 944
Kelly, Milly V, 750
Kelly, Milly V, 773
Kelly, Miriam II, 385
Kelly, Mirianna II, 385
Kelly, Moses I, 1033
Kelly, Moses I, 1038
Kelly, Moses IV, 43
Kelly, Moses V, 69
Kelly, Moses V, 88
Kelly, Moses V, 117
Kelly, Moses V, 723
Kelly, Moses V, 750
Kelly, Moses V, 799
Kelly, Moses V, 814
Kelly, Moses V, 815
Kelly, Myrtle IV, 232
Kelly, Myrtle IV, 932
Kelly, Myrtle IV, 1004
Kelly, Myrtle V, 688
Kelly, Myrtle V, 689
Kelly, Myrtle V, 712
Kelly, Myrtle May IV, 966
Kelly, Nancy V, 1005
Kelly, Nancy VI, 814
Kelly, Nancy VI, 831
Kelly, Nathaniel VI, 814
Kelly, Neal IV, 1323
Kelly, Neal VI, 831
Kelly, Neal C. VI, 809
Kelly, Neal C. VI, 842
Kelly, Neal C. VI, 857
Kelly, Neil IV, 1323
Kelly, Nicholas III, 190
Kelly, Peter VI, 944
Kelly, Phebe II, 962
Kelly, Phebe II, 982
Kelly, Phebe II, 1007
Kelly, Presilla II, 1075
Kelly, Priscilla II, 962
Kelly, Priscilla II, 1007
Kelly, Rachel I, 1061
Kelly, Rachel I, 1062
Kelly, Rachel II, 236
Kelly, Rachel V, 814
Kelly, Rebecca I, 1029
Kelly, Rebecca I, 1033
Kelly, Rebecca V, 750
Kelly, Rebecca V, 814
Kelly, Rebecca V, 1005
Kelly, Rebeckah I, 1021
Kelly, Rev. Daniel VI, 944
Kelly, Rhoda V, 814
Kelly, Robert I, 1033
Kelly, Robert I, 1035
Kelly, Robert IV, 43
Kelly, Robert V, 153
Kelly, Robert V, 184
Kelly, Robert V, 751
Kelly, Robert V, 814
Kelly, Rose Marie III, 190
Kelly, Rufus IV, 1370
Kelly, Russell V, 688
Kelly, Russell V, 712
Kelly, Ruth IV, 972
Kelly, Ruthanna V, 59
Kelly, Ruthanna V, 88
Kelly, Samantha IV, 966
Kelly, Samuel I, 1015
Kelly, Samuel I, 1021
Kelly, Samuel I, 1033
Kelly, Samuel I, 1034
Kelly, Samuel I, 1038
Kelly, Samuel IV, 43
Kelly, Samuel IV, 232
Kelly, Samuel V, 17
Kelly, Samuel V, 59
Kelly, Samuel V, 88
Kelly, Samuel V, 140
Kelly, Samuel V, 750
Kelly, Samuel V, 773
Kelly, Samuel V, 799
Kelly, Samuel V, 814
Kelly, Samuel V, 954
Kelly, Samuel V, 1004
Kelly, Samuel V, 1005
Kelly, Samuel, Jr. I, 1033
Kelly, Samuel, Jr. I, 1036
Kelly, Samuel, Jr. V, 88
Kelly, Samuel, Jr. V, 128
Kelly, Samuel, Sr. I, 1021
Kelly, Sarah I, 1033
Kelly, Sarah I, 1035
Kelly, Sarah II, 77
Kelly, Sarah II, 82
Kelly, Sarah II, 385
Kelly, Sarah IV, 43
Kelly, Sarah IV, 1025
Kelly, Sarah IV, 1028
Kelly, Sarah V, 88
Kelly, Sarah V, 153
Kelly, Sarah V, 165
Kelly, Sarah V, 184
Kelly, Sarah V, 580
Kelly, Sarah V, 750
Kelly, Sarah VI, 831
Kelly, Sarah VI, 944
Kelly, Sarah B. II, 321
Kelly, Sarah B. II, 325
Kelly, Sarah L. V, 88
Kelly, Sarah M. IV, 1371
Kelly, Seth V, 750
Kelly, Seth V, 773
Kelly, Seth, Jr. V, 750
Kelly, Suckey VI, 984
Kelly, Susan VI, 944
Kelly, Susan A. IV, 1238
Kelly, Susanna II, 885
Kelly, Thimothy V, 88
Kelly, Thomas R. V, 688
Kelly, Thomas R. V, 689
Kelly, Thomas R. V, 695
Kelly, Timothy IV, 43
Kelly, Timothy V, 88
Kelly, Timothy V, 121
Kelly, Timothy V, 954
Kelly, Timothy V, 959
Kelly, Walter S. IV, 729
Kelly, Widow Mary I, 1033
Kelly, William II, 385
Kelly, William IV, 232
Kelly, William VI, 831
Kelly, William P. IV, 232
Kelly, Wm. II, 572
Kelly, Wm. II, 673
Kelly, Wm. A. IV, 966
Kelly, Wm. D. III, 190
Kelly, Wm. H. V, 1005
Kelly, Zeno IV, 1370
Kelly, Zeno IV, 1371
Kelsall, Amelia II, 962
Kelsall, Caroline II, 1086
Kelsall, Caroline II, 1088
Kelsall, Joshua II, 1086
Kelsall, Joshua II, 1088
Kelsall, Margaret II, 1088
Kelse, Mary IV, 339
Kelse, Mary IV, 341
Kelsel, Lucile IV, 583
Kelsel, Lucile IV, 585
Kelsey, Alma Louise V, 688
Kelsey, Anna V, 97
Kelsey, Anna L. I, 944
Kelsey, Anna L. V, 688
Kelsey, David Culver V, 688
Kelsey, Dora III, 190
Kelsey, Dorothea III, 190
Kelsey, Edward L. III, 422
Kelsey, Edwin V, 688
Kelsey, Elizabeth V, 88
Kelsey, Elizabeth M. V, 88
Kelsey, Elizabeth M. V, 97
Kelsey, Ethan V, 97
Kelsey, Hadley V, 688
Kelsey, Hadley H. I, 944
Kelsey, Huldah R. I, 944
Kelsey, Jesse P. III, 422
Kelsey, John II, 163
Kelsey, Lewis V, 688
Kelsey, Lillie V, 97
Kelsey, Luman P. III, 190
Kelsey, Luman P. III, 301
Kelsey, Mead A. I, 944
Kelsey, Rebecca V, 256
Kelsey, Robert V, 688
Kelsey, Robert M. V, 688
Kelsey, Rollo E. III, 190
Kelsey, Ruth V, 688
Kelsey, Ruth V, 707
Kelsey, Sarah A. I, 944
Kelsey, Sarah P. III, 422
Kelsey, Stella V, 688
Kelsey, William V, 97
Kelso, ??? III, 190
Kelso, ??? III, 336
Kelso, Abner Jane V, 408
Kelso, Ayner Jane V, 408
Kelso, Daniel Orland V, 408
Kelso, Diantha V, 408
Kelso, Diantha V, 420
Kelso, Harriet V, 954
Kelso, Hiram Edwin V, 408
Kelso, James Andrew V, 408
Kelso, John Riley V, 408
Kelso, Joseph Marion V, 408
Kelso, Mary Ann V, 408
Kelso, Peter V, 688
Kelso, Rachel V, 688
Kelso, Robert N. VI, 980
Kelso, Robert N. VI, 1003
Kelso, Sarah III, 190
Kelso, Sarah III, 336
Kelso, William G. V, 408
Kelso, William J. V, 408
Kelson, Robert N. VI, 966
Keltner, Jennie V, 1005
Keltner, Robert V, 1005
Keltner, Sarah V, 1005
Kelton, Hannah II, 385
Kelton, Jane II, 962
Kelton, John II, 962
Kelton, Robert II, 962
Kelty, Alvina B. IV, 730
Kelty, Clement II, 152
Kelty, Clement II, 158
Kelty, Hannah IV, 1025
Kelty, Hannah IV, 1028
Kelty, Hannah B. II, 152
Kelty, Hannah Bullock II, 152
Kelty, Hannah Bullock II, 158
Kelty, James W. IV, 730
Kelty, Kate B. II, 152
Kelty, Kate B. II, 158
Keltz, Ellen IV, 232
Kelvey, Kerenhapock V, 341
Kelvey, Kerenhapock V, 343
Kemball, Hannah II, 236
Kemball, Hannah II, 257
Kemball, Priscilla I, 764
Kemble, Abigail II, 227
Kemble, Abigail II, 236
Kemble, Ann II, 445
Kemble, Ann III, 190
Kemble, Hannah II, 236
Kemble, John II, 445
Kemble, Martha II, 236
Kemble, Mary II, 236
Kemble, Matilda II, 445
Kemble, Rachael II, 177
Kemble, Rachel II, 236
Kemble, Ruth II, 236
Kemble, Ruth IV, 639
Kemble, Samuel II, 177
Kemble, Samuel II, 236
Kemble, Thomas II, 236
Kemble, William II, 236
Kembrough, Sarah I, 888
Kemerly, Thomas I, 1075
Kemmerling, Grace IV, 232
Kemmerling, Mary IV, 232
Kemmerling, Mrs. S. B. IV, 232
Kemmerling, Sadie IV, 232
Kemp, Amelia Jane I, 358
Kemp, Amy I, 468
Kemp, Amy I, 682
Kemp, Amy I, 688
Kemp, Amy E. I, 468
Kemp, Amy R. I, 482
Kemp, Anis S. I, 468
Kemp, Ann I, 358
Kemp, Ann I, 383
Kemp, Ann I, 402
Kemp, Ann II, 792
Kemp, Ann E. I, 465
Kemp, Ann M. VI, 626
Kemp, Anna M. VI, 670
Kemp, Benjamin I, 402
Kemp, Benjamin II, 792
Kemp, Bethel I, 482
Kemp, Daniel I, 402
Kemp, Dinah I, 355
Kemp, Dinah I, 358
Kemp, Dinah I, 402
Kemp, Dinah I, 410
Kemp, Dorcas I, 377
Kemp, Dorcas I, 402
Kemp, Eli J. I, 468
Kemp, Elizabeth I, 358
Kemp, Elizabeth I, 386
Kemp, Elizabeth I, 402
Kemp, Ella I, 402
Kemp, Ella I, 406
Kemp, George VI, 7
Kemp, George VI, 22
Kemp, George VI, 32
Kemp, Guliaelma M. I, 402
Kemp, Guliaelma M. I, 423
Kemp, Gulielma M. I, 358
Kemp, Hannah IV, 1024
Kemp, Jacob I, 358
Kemp, Jacob I, 468
Kemp, Jeremiah I, 468
Kemp, Jeremiah I, 482
Kemp, Jeremiah I, 682
Kemp, Jeremiah I, 688
Kemp, Jesse I, 468
Kemp, Jesse I, 482
Kemp, Jesse I, 723
Kemp, Joab I, 358
Kemp, Joab I, 386
Kemp, Joab I, 402
Kemp, Joab I, 468
Kemp, Joab I, 482
Kemp, Joab S. I, 402
Kemp, Joab Sewel I, 358
Kemp, John I, 391
Kemp, John I, 402
Kemp, John I, 457
Kemp, John I, 468
Kemp, John I, 482
Kemp, John I, 682
Kemp, John I, 723
Kemp, John H. III, 27
Kemp, John William I, 468
Kemp, John William I, 482
Kemp, Joseph I, 358
Kemp, Joseph I, 394
Kemp, Joseph I, 398
Kemp, Joseph I, 402
Kemp, Joseph I, 415
Kemp, Joseph I, 468
Kemp, Joseph, Jr. I, 402

Kemp, Joshia I, 358
Kemp, Joshua I, 358
Kemp, Joshua I, 402
Kemp, Joshua D. I, 468
Kemp, Joshua F. I, 402
Kemp, Josiah I, 355
Kemp, Josiah I, 358
Kemp, Josiah I, 402
Kemp, Josiah I, 410
Kemp, Louanna R. I, 468
Kemp, Margaret II, 572
Kemp, Margaret II, 589
Kemp, Margery I, 354
Kemp, Margery I, 395
Kemp, Margery I, 402
Kemp, Martha I, 358
Kemp, Martha A. I, 402
Kemp, Martha A. I, 424
Kemp, Mary I, 399
Kemp, Mary I, 402
Kemp, Mary Kezia I, 468
Kemp, O. P. V, 88
Kemp, Patience I, 391
Kemp, Patience I, 402
Kemp, Patience I, 468
Kemp, Patience I, 482
Kemp, Patience I, 682
Kemp, Patience I, 723
Kemp, Phebe I, 358
Kemp, Phebe I, 389
Kemp, Phebe I, 402
Kemp, Phebe I, 415
Kemp, Prudence I, 358
Kemp, Rachel I, 358
Kemp, Rachel I, 368
Kemp, Rachel I, 377
Kemp, Rachel I, 397
Kemp, Rachel I, 402
Kemp, Rachel I, 429
Kemp, Rachel I, 1112
Kemp, Richard I, 354
Kemp, Richard I, 358
Kemp, Richard I, 368
Kemp, Richard I, 399
Kemp, Richard I, 402
Kemp, Richard I, 1095
Kemp, Richard VI, 464
Kemp, Richard VI, 523
Kemp, Ruth I, 355
Kemp, Ruth I, 358
Kemp, Ruth I, 398
Kemp, Ruth I, 402
Kemp, Ruth Hannah VI, 625
Kemp, Ruth Hannah VI, 626
Kemp, Ruth Hannah VI, 670
Kemp, Sally II, 799
Kemp, Samira Ann I, 468
Kemp, Samuel Yearnell II, 885
Kemp, Sarah I, 358
Kemp, Sarah I, 402
Kemp, Sarah II, 803
Kemp, Sarah J. I, 482
Kemp, Sarah Jane I, 468
Kemp, Simeon I, 358
Kemp, Simon D. I, 358
Kemp, Sophronia Page I, 358
Kemp, Susahhan VI, 523
Kemp, Susanna I, 354
Kemp, Susanna I, 358
Kemp, Susanna I, 368
Kemp, Susanna I, 402
Kemp, Susanna I, 409
Kemp, Susanna I, 429
Kemp, Susannah I, 358
Kemp, Susannah I, 468
Kemp, Susannah I, 482
Kemp, Susannah II, 792
Kemp, Susannah VI, 582
Kemp, Thomas III, 190
Kemp, Walter E. VI, 626
Kemp, Walter Edward, Jr. VI, 625
Kemp, Walter Edward, Jr. VI, 626
Kemp, Walter Edward, Jr. VI, 670
Kemp, Walter Edward, Sr. VI, 670
Kemp, Wellmet I, 402
Kemp, Wellmet I, 468
Kemp, Welmet I, 371
Kemp, Welmet I, 402
Kemp, Welmet I, 459
Kemp, Welmett I, 358
Kemp, Welmett I, 377
Kemp, Welmett I, 394
Kemp, Welmett I, 402
Kemp, William III, 190
Kemp, William T. III, 190
Kemp, Wilmet I, 402
Kemp, Wilmett I, 358
Kemp., Prudence VI, 904
Kempton, ??? III, 190
Kempton, Aaron W. IV, 1371
Kempton, Caleb IV, 1371
Kempton, Jane I. IV, 1371
Kempton, Jane T. IV, 1371
Kempton, John III, 190
Kempton, Joseph II, 385
Kempton, William II, 385
Kempton, William W. III, 190
Kenada, Walter I, 756
Kenaday, Mary IV, 79
Kenaday, Mary IV, 96
Kenady, R. E. Conelia I, 858
Kenady, Rachel E. I, 858
Kenady, Sarah E. I, 858
Kenady, Sarah J. I, 858
Kenall, Elizabeth V, 88
Kenall, Enion V, 88
Kenall, Isaac V, 88
Kenall, Joseph V, 88
Kenall, William V, 88
Kenan, Phebe IV, 402
Kenan, Phebe IV, 414
Kenard, Ann IV, 151
Kenard, Ann IV, 232
Kenard, Ann IV, 294
Kenard, Eli IV, 1063
Kenard, Elizabeth IV, 144
Kenard, Elizabeth IV, 151
Kenard, Emily IV, 339
Kenard, Levi IV, 151
Kenard, Levi IV, 294
Kenard, Levi, Jr. IV, 151
Kenard, Mary IV, 151
Kenard, Mary IV, 1063
Kenard, Samuel II, 82
Kenard, Sarah IV, 339
Kenard, Sarah IV, 357
Kenby, Henry VI, 327
Kenby, Mary VI, 327
Kenby, Opha VI, 327
Kendal, Benj. I, 506
Kendal, Benj. I, 847
Kendal, Benjamin I, 555
Kendal, Benjamin II, 572
Kendal, Elizabeth I, 506
Kendal, Elizabeth I, 823
Kendal, Elizabeth I, 889
Kendal, Elizabeth V, 256
Kendal, Ezekal I, 888
Kendal, Hannah I, 823
Kendal, Hannah II, 82
Kendal, Hannah II, 85
Kendal, Isaac V, 256
Kendal, John I, 506
Kendal, Joseph II, 572
Kendal, Lydai I, 823
Kendal, Lydai I, 843
Kendal, Margaret I, 506
Kendal, Mary I, 555
Kendal, Mary I, 561
Kendal, Mary II, 572
Kendal, Nathan I, 723
Kendal, Nathan I, 823
Kendal, Nathan I, 889
Kendal, Sally I, 889
Kendal, Thomas I, 555
Kendal, Thos. I, 506
Kendal, William I, 506
Kendale, Ann I, 858
Kendale, Benjamin I, 858
Kendale, Benjamin F. I, 858
Kendale, Job I, 858
Kendale, John I, 858
Kendale, Martha I, 858
Kendale, Mary I, 858
Kendale, Ruth I, 858
Kendale, Solomon I, 858
Kendale, Susanna I, 858
Kendall, ??? II, 385
Kendall, ??? V, 754
Kendall, Ahimaz I, 858
Kendall, Albert V, 751
Kendall, Ann I, 823
Kendall, Ann I, 858
Kendall, Ann I, 889
Kendall, Ann I, 900
Kendall, Ann II, 453
Kendall, Ann II, 572
Kendall, Ann Ross I, 889
Kendall, Asenath I, 858
Kendall, Asenath I, 874
Kendall, Benjamin I, 555
Kendall, Benjamin I, 823
Kendall, Benjamin I, 888
Kendall, Benjamin I, 889
Kendall, Benjamin II, 385
Kendall, Benjamin II, 453
Kendall, Benjamin II, 572
Kendall, Benjamin II, 618
Kendall, Benjamin, Jr. I, 889
Kendall, Betsey I, 889
Kendall, Betty I, 889
Kendall, Chas. H. III, 190
Kendall, Edward H. III, 190
Kendall, Edward H. III, 363
Kendall, Eliza V, 884
Kendall, Eliza V, 885
Kendall, Elizabeth I, 682
Kendall, Elizabeth I, 692
Kendall, Elizabeth I, 716
Kendall, Elizabeth I, 723
Kendall, Elizabeth I, 786
Kendall, Elizabeth I, 823
Kendall, Elizabeth I, 842
Kendall, Elizabeth I, 858
Kendall, Elizabeth I, 889
Kendall, Elizabeth I, 892
Kendall, Elizabeth V, 88
Kendall, Elizabeth V, 256
Kendall, Elizabeth V, 507
Kendall, Elvira I, 858
Kendall, Enion I, 858
Kendall, Enion V, 88
Kendall, Enion V, 256
Kendall, Ennion V, 256
Kendall, Eunice V, 751
Kendall, Eunice V, 754
Kendall, Ezekal I, 888
Kendall, Ezekiel I, 858
Kendall, Giley Elmy I, 858
Kendall, Hannah I, 823
Kendall, Hannah I, 858
Kendall, Hannah I, 877
Kendall, Hannah I, 889
Kendall, Hannah II, 385
Kendall, Harold V, 751
Kendall, Harry V, 751
Kendall, Henry III, 190
Kendall, Hira I, 858
Kendall, Isaac I, 858
Kendall, Isaac V, 88
Kendall, Isaac V, 256
Kendall, Isaac V, 507
Kendall, James I, 858
Kendall, James I, 889
Kendall, James D. I, 870
Kendall, James D. I, 889
Kendall, James G. I, 889
Kendall, James G. I, 893
Kendall, Jesse II, 572
Kendall, Jesse II, 591
Kendall, Job I, 889
Kendall, John I, 823
Kendall, John I, 858
Kendall, John I, 888
Kendall, John I, 889
Kendall, John II, 572
Kendall, John II, 591
Kendall, John V, 751
Kendall, Joseph I, 786
Kendall, Joseph I, 858
Kendall, Joseph II, 572
Kendall, Joseph V, 88
Kendall, Joseph V, 256
Kendall, Joseph V, 751
Kendall, Lydai I, 823
Kendall, Lydia I, 858
Kendall, Lydia I, 889
Kendall, Lydia III, 190
Kendall, Lydia III, 363
Kendall, Margaret I, 888
Kendall, Margaret I, 889
Kendall, Margrid I, 858
Kendall, Marie V, 751
Kendall, Martha I, 858
Kendall, Martha I, 878
Kendall, Martha I, 886
Kendall, Martha I, 889
Kendall, Martha I, 928
Kendall, Martha Huff I, 889
Kendall, Mary I, 889
Kendall, Mary I, 897
Kendall, Mary II, 572
Kendall, Mary II, 591
Kendall, Mary Louisa II, 816
Kendall, Myra Mae III, 190
Kendall, Nancy I, 858
Kendall, Nancy I, 874
Kendall, Nancy I, 889
Kendall, Nathan I, 723
Kendall, Nathan I, 823
Kendall, Nathan I, 858
Kendall, Nathan I, 889
Kendall, Orilla V, 751
Kendall, Rachel I, 889
Kendall, Rachel I, 904
Kendall, Rachel V, 751
Kendall, Rebecca II, 385
Kendall, Rebecca V, 751
Kendall, Ruth I, 858
Kendall, Ruth I, 880
Kendall, Ruth I, 881
Kendall, Ruth I, 889
Kendall, Sallie D. I, 870
Kendall, Sallie D. I, 889
Kendall, Sally I, 889
Kendall, Sarah I, 827
Kendall, Sarah I, 858
Kendall, Solomon I, 858
Kendall, Solomon I, 888
Kendall, Solomon I, 889
Kendall, Susanna I, 889
Kendall, Susannah I, 889
Kendall, Susannah J. I, 886
Kendall, Susannah J. I, 889
Kendall, Syntha I, 889
Kendall, Syntha I, 893
Kendall, Thomas I, 823
Kendall, Thomas I, 858
Kendall, Thomas I, 889
Kendall, Thomas Pedrick II, 572
Kendall, William I, 682
Kendall, William I, 786
Kendall, William I, 823
Kendall, William I, 858
Kendall, William I, 889
Kendall, William V, 88
Kendall, William V, 256
Kendall, Winifred E. III, 190
Kendall, Wlliam I, 692
Kendel, Ann I, 847
Kenderdin, Rebecca Rakestraw II, 816
Kenderdine, Annette T. II, 804
Kenderdine, Christiana II, 572
Kenderdine, E. Maude II, 885
Kenderdine, Elisabeth II, 572
Kenderdine, Elisabeth II, 629
Kenderdine, Elizabeth II, 572
Kenderdine, Elizabeth II, 594
Kenderdine, Elizabeth H. II, 836
Kenderdine, Elizabeth H. II, 885
Kenderdine, Emma C. II, 885
Kenderdine, Frank II, 804
Kenderdine, Frank II, 885
Kenderdine, Isaiah II, 885
Kenderdine, Laura II, 804
Kenderdine, Louis R. II, 836
Kenderdine, Louis R. II, 885
Kenderdine, M. Ella II, 885
Kenderdine, Mary II, 572
Kenderdine, Mary II, 885
Kenderdine, Mary H. II, 804
Kenderdine, Maude II, 836
Kenderdine, Maude B. II, 885
Kenderdine, Sarah II, 572
Kenderdine, Thaddeus S. II, 163
Kenderdine, Thaddeus S. II, 836
Kenderdine, Thaddeus S. II, 885
Kendle, Benjamin I, 555
Kendley, Daniel V, 90
Kendley, Edward V, 90
Kendley, Frederick V, 90
Kendrick, Patience V, 23
Kendrick, Patience V, 88
Kendrix, Mary I, 402
Kenedy, Bell IV, 1238
Kenedy, Benjamin VI, 957
Kenedy, Betsey VI, 1012
Kenedy, Deborah D. I, 244
Kenedy, Doratha Estella IV, 1283
Kenedy, Easter VI, 1012
Kenedy, Jane I, 874
Kenedy, Mary Jane IV, 1371
Kenedy, W. H. I, 337
Kenerly, Joseph VI, 32
Kenerly, Joseph VI, 34
Kenerly, Samuel L. VI, 945
Kenerly, Sara VI, 32
Kenerly, Sara VI, 34
Kenerly, Sarah Ann E. VI, 945
Kenesee, Matilda II, 385
Kenesell, George E. IV, 232
Kenesell, George Edward IV, 232
Kenesell, H. Slagle IV, 232
Kenesell, Henry IV, 232
Kenesell, Henry E. IV, 232
Kenesell, John Milburn IV, 232
Kenesell, John Welburn IV, 232
Kenesell, Kate P. IV, 232
Kenesell, Lemuel Cornelius IV, 232
Keney, Carolina VI, 32
Keney, Catherine VI, 32
Keney, John VI, 32
Kenhaway, Job I, 888
Kenidy, Elizabeth I, 310
Kenisell, George E. IV, 232
Kenisell, Henry IV, 232
Kenisell, Henry E. IV, 232
Kenisell, Kate P. IV, 232
Kenley, Edward I, 695
Kenley, Hannah II, 564
Kenley, Hannah II, 572
Kenley, William VI, 291
Kenly, Hannah II, 385
Kenly, John V, 90
Kenly, William VI, 327
Kenn, Elisha VI, 801
Kenn, Joseph IV, 310
Kennada, Sarah I, 873
Kennady, Elias James I, 330
Kennady, Elizabeth I, 264
Kennady, Elizabeth I, 290
Kennady, John I, 290
Kennady, John VI, 824
Kennady, John VI, 831
Kennady, Mary VI, 831
Kennady, Mary VI, 957
Kennady, Rebeckah VI, 874
Kennady, Robert D. I, 310
Kennady, Susanna VI, 831
Kennady, Thomas I, 290
Kennady, Thomas J. I, 329
Kennady, William VI, 831
Kennady, William G. VI, 831
Kennard, ??? IV, 1047
Kennard, Aaron IV, 414
Kennard, Abbey W. IV, 414
Kennard, Abby IV, 414
Kennard, Abby W. IV, 414
Kennard, Abigail IV, 232
Kennard, Alfred E. II, 709
Kennard, Alfred E. II, 715
Kennard, Alfred E. II, 750
Kennard, Alfred E. IV, 414
Kennard, Alfred E. IV, 415
Kennard, Amanda IV, 151
Kennard, Ann IV, 151
Kennard, Ann IV, 232
Kennard, Ann IV, 339
Kennard, Anna IV, 414
Kennard, Anna IV, 585
Kennard, Anna D. IV, 414
Kennard, Anne IV, 232
Kennard, Annie IV, 415
Kennard, Annie C. IV, 414
Kennard, Annie D. II, 709
Kennard, Annie D. II, 715
Kennard, Annie D. II, 750
Kennard, Annie D. IV, 415
Kennard, Anthony IV, 339
Kennard, Betsy Kennard IV, 2
Kennard, Catharine IV, 232
Kennard, Catharine IV, 292
Kennard, Catharine IV, 414
Kennard, Catharine IV, 1049
Kennard, Catharine IV, 1063
Kennard, Catherine IV, 1063
Kennard, David IV, 1063
Kennard, David Thompson IV, 232
Kennard, Delila IV, 151
Kennard, Delilah IV, 151
Kennard, Delilah Ann IV, 165
Kennard, Eli II, 709
Kennard, Eli IV, 232
Kennard, Eli IV, 339
Kennard, Eli IV, 414
Kennard, Eli IV, 576
Kennard, Eli IV, 585
Kennard, Eli IV, 1063
Kennard, Eli, Jr. IV, 585
Kennard, Elizabeth II, 709
Kennard, Elizabeth II, 750
Kennard, Elizabeth IV, 151
Kennard, Elizabeth IV, 232
Kennard, Elizabeth IV, 338
Kennard, Elizabeth IV, 339
Kennard, Elizabeth IV, 414
Kennard, Elizabeth IV, 415
Kennard, Elizabeth IV, 561
Kennard, Elizabeth IV, 585
Kennard, Elizabeth IV, 1063
Kennard, Elizabeth IV, 1067
Kennard, Elizabeth R. IV, 393
Kennard, Elizabeth R. IV, 414
Kennard, Elizabeth R. IV, 585
Kennard, Elizabeth Roberts IV, 414
Kennard, Elizajane IV, 151
Kennard, Ellen Jane IV, 151
Kennard, Emily IV, 339
Kennard, Esther IV, 232
Kennard, Esther IV, 414
Kennard, Esther IV, 1063
Kennard, Esther IV, 1064
Kennard, Hannah IV, 232
Kennard, Hannah IV, 291
Kennard, Hannah IV, 414
Kennard, Hannah IV, 596
Kennard, Hannah IV, 1063

nard, Hannah Amanda IV, 151
nard, Henry P. IV, 339
nard, Henry P. IV, 561
nard, Henry Preston IV, 232
nard, Henry Preston IV, 339
nard, Henry Preston IV, 414
nard, Jacob IV, 339
nard, Jacob IV, 414
nard, Jacob IV, 561
nard, Jemima IV, 151
nard, Jenkins IV, 339
nard, Jenkins IV, 414
nard, Jenkins IV, 561
nard, Jesse IV, 232
nard, Jesse IV, 415
nard, Jesse IV, 585
nard, John IV, 151
nard, John IV, 339
nard, John IV, 414
nard, John IV, 561
nard, John B. IV, 414
nard, Joseph IV, 232
nard, Joseph IV, 291
nard, Joseph IV, 414
nard, Joseph IV, 415
nard, Joseph IV, 561
nard, Joseph IV, 585
nard, Joseph IV, 596
nard, Joseph IV, 1063
nard, Joseph Walton IV, 1063
nard, Levi IV, 151
nard, Levi IV, 232
nard, Levi IV, 339
nard, Levi IV, 414
nard, Levi IV, 561
nard, Levi, Jr. IV, 151
nard, Lizzie IV, 414
nard, Mary II, 709
nard, Mary IV, 151
nard, Mary IV, 232
nard, Mary IV, 335
nard, Mary IV, 339
nard, Mary IV, 414
nard, Mary IV, 576
nard, Mary IV, 585
nard, Mary IV, 596
nard, Mary IV, 1063
nard, Mary E. II, 709
nard, Mary E. II, 750
nard, Mary E. IV, 414
nard, Mary E. IV, 415
nard, Mary Eleanor Bulger IV, 414
nard, Mary Elizabeth IV, 414
nard, Mary Elizabeth IV, 415
nard, Mary Vilenda IV, 151
nard, Mary, Jr. IV, 232
nard, Mishael IV, 561
nard, Preston IV, 151
nard, Rachel IV, 232
nard, Rachel IV, 339
nard, Rachel IV, 414
nard, Rachel IV, 561
nard, Rachel IV, 585
nard, Ruth II, 709
nard, Ruth A. II, 750
nard, Ruth K. II, 715
nard, Ruthanna IV, 521
nard, Ruthanna IV, 537
nard, Sarah IV, 232
nard, Sarah IV, 339
nard, Sarah IV, 349
nard, Sarah IV, 393
nard, Sarah IV, 585
nard, Sarah J. II, 709
nard, Sarah J. II, 750
nard, Sarah J. IV, 414
nard, Sarah J. IV, 415
nard, Tacy IV, 232
nard, Tacy IV, 414
nard, Tacy IV, 1063
nard, Thomas II, 572
nard, Thomas IV, 232
nard, Thomas IV, 339
nard, Thomas IV, 414
nard, Thomas IV, 561
nard, Thos. IV, 338
nard, William IV, 232
nard, William IV, 393
nard, William IV, 414
nard, William IV, 415
nard, William IV, 585
nard, Wm. IV, 339
nard, Wm. IV, 349
nard, Wm. IV, 414
nard, Wm. IV, 585
nard, Wm. IV, 1063
nneda, Margaret II, 613
nneday, Aletha I, 924
nnedy, ??? I, 889
Kennedy, ??? III, 190
Kennedy, Abigail I, 310
Kennedy, Achsah I, 310
Kennedy, Achsah I, 317
Kennedy, Achsah I, 326
Kennedy, Achsah I, 329
Kennedy, Alexander III, 16
Kennedy, Alexander III, 190
Kennedy, Alexander, Jr. III, 190
Kennedy, Ann M. I, 329
Kennedy, Archie IV, 1323
Kennedy, Arthur III, 488
Kennedy, Bertha IV, 875
Kennedy, Cath A. III, 190
Kennedy, Catharine III, 422
Kennedy, Catharine III, 447
Kennedy, Charity III, 190
Kennedy, Charity III, 334
Kennedy, Christiana Warner VI, 945
Kennedy, Cornelia I, 944
Kennedy, Cornelia IV, 1323
Kennedy, Deborah D. I, 244
Kennedy, Deborah D. I, 248
Kennedy, Deborah D. I, 329
Kennedy, Deborah D. I, 330
Kennedy, Doratha Estella IV, 1283
Kennedy, E. J. I, 325
Kennedy, E. L. I, 944
Kennedy, E. S. I, 944
Kennedy, Edwin Craft III, 190
Kennedy, Effie I, 933
Kennedy, Eleanor IV, 875
Kennedy, Eleanor IV, 880
Kennedy, Elias James I, 330
Kennedy, Elisabeth I, 290
Kennedy, Elisabeth I, 325
Kennedy, Elizabeth I, 144
Kennedy, Elizabeth I, 244
Kennedy, Elizabeth I, 271
Kennedy, Elizabeth I, 272
Kennedy, Elizabeth I, 290
Kennedy, Elizabeth I, 310
Kennedy, Elizabeth I, 313
Kennedy, Elizabeth I, 329
Kennedy, Elizabeth I, 932
Kennedy, Elizabeth A. I, 290
Kennedy, Elizabeth Ann I, 326
Kennedy, Elizabeth C. III, 190
Kennedy, Elizabeth M. III, 190
Kennedy, Elma Colene I, 929
Kennedy, Erastus I, 944
Kennedy, Erastus L. I, 929
Kennedy, Esabella I, 144
Kennedy, Estella IV, 1283
Kennedy, Esther VI, 929
Kennedy, Eugene Lindley I, 929
Kennedy, Exum I, 329
Kennedy, Florence Omega I, 613
Kennedy, Franklin Wm. III, 190
Kennedy, George VI, 945
Kennedy, George F. I, 330
Kennedy, George Fox I, 326
Kennedy, Grace IV, 1323
Kennedy, Grace IV, 1324
Kennedy, Henry C. III, 190
Kennedy, Isabella I, 144
Kennedy, Isabella I, 329
Kennedy, Isabella I, 330
Kennedy, Izbell VI, 946
Kennedy, J. C. I, 928
Kennedy, James I, 325
Kennedy, James III, 190
Kennedy, James III, 334
Kennedy, James III, 488
Kennedy, Jane I, 144
Kennedy, Jennie IV, 1324
Kennedy, Jessie III, 16
Kennedy, Jessie III, 190
Kennedy, John I, 144
Kennedy, John I, 272
Kennedy, John I, 279
Kennedy, John I, 290
Kennedy, John I, 302
Kennedy, John I, 310
Kennedy, John I, 313
Kennedy, John I, 321
Kennedy, John I, 325
Kennedy, John I, 329
Kennedy, John III, 190
Kennedy, John III, 488
Kennedy, John IV, 1324
Kennedy, John B. I, 244
Kennedy, John B. I, 290
Kennedy, John B. I, 321
Kennedy, John B. I, 329
Kennedy, John Brian I, 244
Kennedy, John Brian I, 248
Kennedy, John Brian I, 325
Kennedy, John M. I, 325
Kennedy, John Neil III, 190
Kennedy, L. L. I, 944
Kennedy, Laura L. IV, 232
Kennedy, Leathia I, 929
Kennedy, Lettie I, 944
Kennedy, Lizzie Dora I, 325
Kennedy, Margaret Stoddard III, 190
Kennedy, Maria A. III, 190
Kennedy, Maria A. III, 334
Kennedy, Martha III, 488
Kennedy, Martha H. III, 190
Kennedy, Mary I, 290
Kennedy, Mary I, 302
Kennedy, Mary I, 310
Kennedy, Mary I, 325
Kennedy, Mary I, 328
Kennedy, Mary I, 329
Kennedy, Mary I, 337
Kennedy, Mary III, 488
Kennedy, Mary IV, 96
Kennedy, Mary IV, 875
Kennedy, Mary IV, 880
Kennedy, Mary VI, 831
Kennedy, Mary C. II, 1075
Kennedy, Mary C. II, 1081
Kennedy, Mary C. III, 190
Kennedy, Maud V. I, 929
Kennedy, Micajah Thomas I, 613
Kennedy, Minney Etter I, 325
Kennedy, Miriam I, 329
Kennedy, Miriam I, 873
Kennedy, Miriam I, 883
Kennedy, Mrs. Jennie IV, 1324
Kennedy, Nancy I, 927
Kennedy, Nancy I, 929
Kennedy, Nancy I, 930
Kennedy, Patsy R. VI, 945
Kennedy, Rachel I, 310
Kennedy, Rebeckah VI, 873
Kennedy, Rhoaah I, 310
Kennedy, Richard VI, 945
Kennedy, Robert I, 310
Kennedy, Robert D. I, 310
Kennedy, Sam'l W. III, 190
Kennedy, Sarah I, 280
Kennedy, Sarah I, 290
Kennedy, Sarah I, 302
Kennedy, Sarah I, 310
Kennedy, Sarah I, 325
Kennedy, Sarah I, 326
Kennedy, Sarah I, 329
Kennedy, Sarah I, 928
Kennedy, Sarah J. I, 928
Kennedy, Sarah Jane I, 928
Kennedy, Sarah Lonelm I, 325
Kennedy, Sibyl IV, 730
Kennedy, Sibyl IV, 780
Kennedy, Smytha Augusta I, 613
Kennedy, Thomas I, 139
Kennedy, Thomas I, 144
Kennedy, Thomas I, 244
Kennedy, Thomas I, 271
Kennedy, Thomas I, 272
Kennedy, Thomas I, 290
Kennedy, Thomas I, 310
Kennedy, Thomas I, 317
Kennedy, Thomas I, 321
Kennedy, Thomas I, 325
Kennedy, Thomas I, 326
Kennedy, Thomas I, 329
Kennedy, Thomas J. I, 329
Kennedy, Thomas John I, 326
Kennedy, Thomas John I, 330
Kennedy, W. B. A. I, 325
Kennedy, W. H. I, 337
Kennedy, Walter I, 325
Kennedy, Widow Esabella I, 139
Kennedy, William VI, 946
Kennedy, William B. I, 337
Kennedy, William G. VI, 831
Kennedy, Zelma Carene I, 929
Kenner, Anna E. III, 190
Kenner, Augustus IV, 1214
Kenner, Emanuel IV, 1214
Kenner, Emma IV, 1214
Kenner, Esther R. D. III, 190
Kenner, Harry IV, 1214
Kenner, Henry L. IV, 1214
Kenner, Lydia IV, 1169
Kenner, Lydia IV, 1214
Kenner, Rebecca II, 236
Kenner, Rebecca II, 271
Kenner, Wm. IV, 1214
Kennerley, Joseph VI, 812
Kennerly, Joseph VI, 8
Kennerly, Sarah VI, 8
Kennerly, Susan VI, 342
Kennet, Ella V, 256
Kennet, Evaline IV, 724
Kennet, Joshua VI, 945
Kennet, Martha IV, 727
Kennet, Mary Ann IV, 797
Kennet, Mary Ann Bailey IV, 829
Kennet, Miriam IV, 727
Kennet, Ruth Ann IV, 782
Kennet, Wesley V, 689
Kennet, Wm. IV, 727
Kenneth, Joshua VI, 969
Kennett, Agness VI, 945
Kennett, Apphia VI, 945
Kennett, Blanch V, 689
Kennett, Burchey VI, 945
Kennett, Burchy VI, 937
Kennett, Catharan VI, 945
Kennett, Davis IV, 829
Kennett, Elizabeth VI, 904
Kennett, Evaline IV, 730
Kennett, Evaline IV, 829
Kennett, Eveline IV, 730
Kennett, Eveline IV, 829
Kennett, Florentine VI, 936
Kennett, Frances I, 620
Kennett, Frances VI, 503
Kennett, Frankey VI, 945
Kennett, Hannah VI, 902
Kennett, Hulda VI, 962
Kennett, Isabelle VI, 902
Kennett, Izabell VI, 945
Kennett, James F. VI, 945
Kennett, John VI, 904
Kennett, John VI, 945
Kennett, John M. VI, 945
Kennett, Joseph VI, 945
Kennett, Joseph B. VI, 945
Kennett, Joseph B. VI, 962
Kennett, Joseph L. VI, 945
Kennett, Joshua VI, 945
Kennett, Kendal IV, 829
Kennett, Kendall IV, 730
Kennett, Kendall IV, 829
Kennett, Leah IV, 730
Kennett, Lemuel D. VI, 942
Kennett, Lemuel D. VI, 1001
Kennett, Lewis IV, 829
Kennett, Lucy VI, 945
Kennett, Luraner VI, 945
Kennett, Margaret V, 689
Kennett, Margaret Ann V, 689
Kennett, Martha IV, 719
Kennett, Martha IV, 730
Kennett, Martha IV, 792
Kennett, Martha IV, 822
Kennett, Martha IV, 829
Kennett, Mary V, 689
Kennett, Mary VI, 491
Kennett, Mary VI, 1006
Kennett, Mary Ann Bailey IV, 829
Kennett, Mary F. VI, 939
Kennett, Mary Hunter I, 612
Kennett, Maryann IV, 829
Kennett, Mildred VI, 945
Kennett, Milly VI, 945
Kennett, Nancy VI, 945
Kennett, Nehemiah VI, 945
Kennett, Newark VI, 491
Kennett, Ora B. VI, 939
Kennett, Ora B. VI, 945
Kennett, Peter VI, 945
Kennett, Rebecca VI, 945
Kennett, Ruth Ann IV, 730
Kennett, Ruth Anna IV, 730
Kennett, Ruthanna IV, 829
Kennett, Sally VI, 945
Kennett, Samantha V, 689
Kennett, Sary VI, 945
Kennett, Thomas IV, 730
Kennett, Thomas IV, 829
Kennett, Thomas VI, 945
Kennett, Unity VI, 945
Kennett, Wesley V, 689
Kennett, Wm. IV, 719
Kennett, Wm. IV, 730
Kennett, Wm. IV, 822
Kennett, Wm. IV, 829
Kennett, Wm. L. IV, 829
Kennett, Zachariah VI, 945
Kennett, Zachariah VI, 1006
Kenney, Abie IV, 1283
Kenney, Alice L. IV, 1283
Kenney, Alta V, 507
Kenney, Anna V, 507
Kenney, Bessie IV, 1169
Kenney, Carl IV, 1283
Kenney, David IV, 1169
Kenney, Edward V, 507
Kenney, Effie V, 507
Kenney, Etha V, 507
Kenney, Grace L. IV, 1169
Kenney, Hannah VI, 845
Kenney, James VI, 798
Kenney, James VI, 845
Kenney, James VI, 965
Kenney, James VI, 1004
Kenney, James VI, 1015
Kenney, James T. III, 71
Kenney, Johnnie IV, 1169
Kenney, Louella V, 507
Kenney, Louetta V, 507
Kenney, Louisa IV, 1169
Kenney, Maxwell III, 191
Kenney, Nannie V, 507
Kenney, Robert V, 507
Kenney, Robert S. V, 507
Kenney, Sally VI, 798
Kenney, Sarah R. III, 71
Kennisell, H. Slagle IV, 232
Kennit, Aggy VI, 996
Kennott, Elizabeth VI, 904
Kennott, John VI, 904
Kenny, ??? III, 190
Kenny, Alice IV, 339
Kenny, Anna Eliza IV, 233
Kenny, Anna F. II, 885
Kenny, Annie D. II, 885
Kenny, Daniel III, 190
Kenny, Daniel III, 266
Kenny, Daniel IV, 233
Kenny, David III, 190
Kenny, David III, 191
Kenny, David III, 339
Kenny, Edith II, 885
Kenny, Edith T. II, 885
Kenny, Eleanor II, 885
Kenny, Eleanor III, 190
Kenny, Eleanor III, 266
Kenny, Eleanor Ann II, 817
Kenny, Eleanor Ann III, 190
Kenny, Eleanor Ann III, 266
Kenny, Elenor II, 885
Kenny, Eleqnor II, 885
Kenny, Ellen Maxwell III, 190
Kenny, Ellen Richard III, 191
Kenny, Frank G. V, 184
Kenny, Isabella C. III, 190
Kenny, James II, 572
Kenny, James F. II, 885
Kenny, James F. III, 190
Kenny, James F. III, 191
Kenny, Jane III, 190
Kenny, Jane III, 222
Kenny, Jane IV, 151
Kenny, Jane IV, 351
Kenny, Jane IV, 415
Kenny, Jane IV, 437
Kenny, Jane A. III, 190
Kenny, Jane A. III, 191
Kenny, Jas. T. III, 190
Kenny, Margaret II, 572
Kenny, Margaret II, 635
Kenny, Margaret IV, 339
Kenny, Mary II, 572
Kenny, Mary IV, 151
Kenny, Mary IV, 437
Kenny, Matthias III, 191
Kenny, Maxwell II, 804
Kenny, Maxwell II, 885
Kenny, Maxwell III, 190
Kenny, Maxwell III, 191
Kenny, Phebe IV, 233
Kenny, Rebecca II, 572
Kenny, Richard IV, 151
Kenny, Richard IV, 218
Kenny, Richard IV, 233
Kenny, Richard IV, 415
Kenny, Richard IV, 437
Kenny, Richard IV, 1061
Kenny, Richard IV, 1063
Kenny, Richards IV, 415
Kenny, Robert IV, 233
Kenny, Robert H. IV, 233
Kenny, Sarah III, 191
Kenny, Sarah Ann III, 191
Kenny, Sarah Ann III, 339
Kenny, Sarah Glover III, 190
Kenny, Sarah R. III, 191
Kenny, Sarah W. III, 190
Kenny, Susanna IV, 218
Kenny, Susanna IV, 233
Kenny, Susanna IV, 415
Kenny, Susanna IV, 1061
Kenny, Susanna IV, 1063
Kenny, Susannah IV, 415
Kenny, William IV, 233
Kennyon, Benja. I, 160
Kennyon, Mary I, 160
Kenoy, Charles I, 928
Kenoy, Luetta I, 928
Kenoy, Sarah J. I, 928
Kensel, Anna II, 804
Kensel, John Hamer II, 804
Kensel, Maurice W. II, 804

Kensel, Susan II, 804
Kensel, Wd. Susan II, 804
Kensell, Anna S. II, 885
Kenset, Charlotte II, 321
Kensitt, Charlotte II, 311
Kenszey, Samuel II, 1007
Kent, Alice M. III, 191
Kent, Alice M. III, 265
Kent, Alicia VI, 945
Kent, Amey VI, 945
Kent, Ann II, 82
Kent, Ann A. VI, 853
Kent, Ann H. II, 885
Kent, Anne VI, 1000
Kent, Arther IV, 730
Kent, Arthur IV, 1214
Kent, Arthur Thomas IV, 233
Kent, Benj. Lundy III, 191
Kent, Benj. Lundy III, 265
Kent, Charlotte II, 311
Kent, Daniel II, 562
Kent, Daniel II, 572
Kent, Dora IV, 1255
Kent, Edgar C. II, 885
Kent, Edward IV, 1255
Kent, Eleanor G. IV, 730
Kent, Elinor G. IV, 1214
Kent, Elizabeth I Sup 1, 3
Kent, Elizabeth I Sup 1, 4
Kent, Elizabeth II, 82
Kent, Elizabeth II, 90
Kent, Elizabeth VI, 946
Kent, Emma I, 611
Kent, Emma IV, 1255
Kent, Emma C. II, 885
Kent, Emma C. II, 901
Kent, Flora V, 343
Kent, Frances VI, 958
Kent, Frances Cornelia II, 885
Kent, G. E. IV, 1214
Kent, George IV, 1214
Kent, George VI, 881
Kent, George VI, 887
Kent, George VI, 891
Kent, George VI, 945
Kent, George VI, 958
Kent, George E. IV, 233
Kent, George E. IV, 730
Kent, George E. IV, 1214
Kent, George Ernest IV, 233
Kent, Howard IV, 1214
Kent, Isaac VI, 945
Kent, Jacob VI, 945
Kent, Jessie M. II, 796
Kent, John VI, 911
Kent, John VI, 945
Kent, John VI, 946
Kent, John VI, 986
Kent, John VI, 1000
Kent, John Maddocks II, 82
Kent, Joseph II, 885
Kent, Joseph II, 901
Kent, Joseph IV, 96
Kent, Joseph VI, 853
Kent, Lilliam Elizbeth VI, 383
Kent, Luke VI, 945
Kent, M. Elizabeth VI, 759
Kent, Malcolm Foote VI, 383
Kent, Margaret II, 572
Kent, Margreat II, 82
Kent, Margreat II, 85
Kent, Maria J. II, 885
Kent, Maria J. II, 901
Kent, Martha VI, 891
Kent, Mary III, 191
Kent, Mary VI, 911
Kent, Mary VI, 945
Kent, Nancy VI, 831
Kent, Nellie G. IV, 233
Kent, Olive IV, 1255
Kent, Pamela II, 562
Kent, Pamela II, 572
Kent, Pauline E. VI, 830
Kent, Polly VI, 807
Kent, Polly M. VI, 945
Kent, Rebecca VI, 887
Kent, Robert II, 385
Kent, Robert II, 572
Kent, Robert II, 667
Kent, Robert VI, 831
Kent, Robert Downard IV, 233
Kent, Robert E. VI, 830
Kent, Robert Howard IV, 730
Kent, Robert Howard IV, 1214
Kent, Sally VI, 831
Kent, Samuel C. II, 885
Kent, Samuel C. II, 901
Kent, Sarah III, 191
Kent, Sarah A. III, 265
Kent, Smith VI, 799
Kent, Smith VI, 831
Kent, Wd. Ann II, 804
Kent, William VI, 945
Kent, Wm. II, 804
Kente, John VI, 189
Kentee, William II, 385
Kentin, Mary II, 62
Kentin, Mary II, 82
Kentin, Wm. II, 62
Kentin, Wm. II, 82
Kenton, ??? II, 385
Kenton, Catherine A. VI, 831
Kenton, James I. VI, 831
Kenton, John II, 385
Kenton, Joseph II, 33
Kenton, Mary II, 33
Kenton, Mary II, 82
Kenton, Mary II, 87
Kenton, Phebe V, 22
Kenton, Phebe V, 88
Kenton, William II, 33
Kentral, Susanna I, 1123
Kentral, Susanna I, 1131
Kenway, Gawen Pearse III, 191
Kenway, Peter III, 191
Kenway, Sophia III, 191
Kenworhty, Ruth IV, 43
Kenworthy, ??? V, 823
Kenworthy, ??? V, 847
Kenworthy, ??? V, 965
Kenworthy, Abigail IV, 972
Kenworthy, Alice V, 88
Kenworthy, Alice V, 825
Kenworthy, Alice V, 846
Kenworthy, Alice Gertrude V, 847
Kenworthy, Alma V, 847
Kenworthy, Almira V, 847
Kenworthy, Alpheus V, 847
Kenworthy, Alvan Lindley V, 846
Kenworthy, Alvin L. V, 847
Kenworthy, Amos IV, 43
Kenworthy, Amos IV, 49
Kenworthy, Amos IV, 96
Kenworthy, Amos IV, 101
Kenworthy, Amos IV, 1255
Kenworthy, Amos V, 89
Kenworthy, Amos V, 846
Kenworthy, Amos V, 847
Kenworthy, Amos V, 972
Kenworthy, Amos V, 979
Kenworthy, Amos M. V, 972
Kenworthy, Amos M. V, 979
Kenworthy, Amy Ella V, 846
Kenworthy, Ann I, 1060
Kenworthy, Ann I, 1062
Kenworthy, Ann V, 89
Kenworthy, Ann V, 184
Kenworthy, Ann V, 408
Kenworthy, Ann V, 428
Kenworthy, Ann V, 751
Kenworthy, Ann V, 847
Kenworthy, Ann V, 849
Kenworthy, Ann V, 915
Kenworthy, Ann V, 944
Kenworthy, Ann V, 972
Kenworthy, Ann V, 979
Kenworthy, Anna E. V, 846
Kenworthy, Anna E. V, 847
Kenworthy, Anna Louise III, 78
Kenworthy, Anna Louise III, 191
Kenworthy, Arthur William III, 191
Kenworthy, Arthur Wm. III, 78
Kenworthy, Asa V, 343
Kenworthy, Asa L. V, 847
Kenworthy, Barclay V, 847
Kenworthy, Betty V, 88
Kenworthy, Betty V, 184
Kenworthy, Carol V, 915
Kenworthy, Carol V, 919
Kenworthy, Caroline V, 847
Kenworthy, Carroll B. V, 689
Kenworthy, Carroll H. V, 689
Kenworthy, Catharine I, 1157
Kenworthy, Catharine IV, 972
Kenworthy, Cecil A. V, 847
Kenworthy, Celestia V, 847
Kenworthy, Charles IV, 1255
Kenworthy, Charles E. V, 839
Kenworthy, Charles E. V, 847
Kenworthy, Daniel V, 846
Kenworthy, Daniel V, 847
Kenworthy, Daniel L. V, 847
Kenworthy, Daniel Linden V, 847
Kenworthy, David I, 403
Kenworthy, David I, 1060
Kenworthy, David I, 1062
Kenworthy, David V, 88
Kenworthy, David V, 184
Kenworthy, David V, 230
Kenworthy, David V, 343
Kenworthy, David V, 846
Kenworthy, David V, 851
Kenworthy, David Milton V, 847
Kenworthy, David, Jr. V, 847
Kenworthy, Dianah V, 184
Kenworthy, Dinah I, 1060
Kenworthy, Dinah I, 1062
Kenworthy, Dinah V, 88
Kenworthy, Dinah V, 184
Kenworthy, Dinah V, 230
Kenworthy, Dinah V, 256
Kenworthy, Dinah V, 846
Kenworthy, Dorcus E. I, 1157
Kenworthy, Edna IV, 972
Kenworthy, Eli V, 846
Kenworthy, Eli V, 847
Kenworthy, Elihu V, 846
Kenworthy, Elisha I, 382
Kenworthy, Elisha I, 403
Kenworthy, Elisha V, 89
Kenworthy, Elisha V, 215
Kenworthy, Elisha V, 256
Kenworthy, Elisha V, 335
Kenworthy, Elisha V, 343
Kenworthy, Elisha V, 344
Kenworthy, Elisha V, 349
Kenworthy, Elizabeth III, 191
Kenworthy, Elizabeth V, 846
Kenworthy, Ella V, 847
Kenworthy, Elmira V, 847
Kenworthy, Emma T. I, 1157
Kenworthy, Enoch I, 1157
Kenworthy, Esley I, 1157
Kenworthy, Eunice IV, 972
Kenworthy, Eunice E. IV, 972
Kenworthy, Flora Ellen V, 875
Kenworthy, Hannah IV, 43
Kenworthy, Hannah IV, 49
Kenworthy, Hannah H. IV, 20
Kenworthy, Hannah H. IV, 43
Kenworthy, Harriet V, 846
Kenworthy, Harriet V, 847
Kenworthy, Helen IV, 972
Kenworthy, Helen Rowe V, 306
Kenworthy, Henry V, 846
Kenworthy, Henry V, 847
Kenworthy, Henry I. V, 847
Kenworthy, Ira V, 343
Kenworthy, Ira V, 344
Kenworthy, Isaac I, 1058
Kenworthy, Isaac IV, 43
Kenworthy, Isaac IV, 972
Kenworthy, Isaac V, 88
Kenworthy, Isaac V, 184
Kenworthy, Isaac V, 340
Kenworthy, Isaac V, 343
Kenworthy, Isaac V, 351
Kenworthy, Isaac V, 846
Kenworthy, Isaac F. V, 972
Kenworthy, Isaac F. V, 979
Kenworthy, Isabel IV, 972
Kenworthy, Jabez V, 846
Kenworthy, Jabez H. V, 841
Kenworthy, Jabez J. V, 847
Kenworthy, James K. III, 191
Kenworthy, Jehu V, 256
Kenworthy, Jess I, 403
Kenworthy, Jesse I, 1060
Kenworthy, Jesse I, 1062
Kenworthy, Jesse IV, 43
Kenworthy, Jesse IV, 49
Kenworthy, Jesse V, 88
Kenworthy, Jesse V, 343
Kenworthy, Jesse V, 344
Kenworthy, Jesse V, 828
Kenworthy, Jesse V, 846
Kenworthy, Jesse V, 865
Kenworthy, Jesse V, 915
Kenworthy, Jesse V, 972
Kenworthy, Jesse V, 979
Kenworthy, Jesse G. V, 846
Kenworthy, Jesse J. V, 52
Kenworthy, Jesse J. V, 88
Kenworthy, Jesse J. V, 847
Kenworthy, Jesse, Jr. V, 849
Kenworthy, Joel V, 972
Kenworthy, Joel V, 979
Kenworthy, John I, 1058
Kenworthy, John I, 1060
Kenworthy, John I, 1062
Kenworthy, John V, 88
Kenworthy, John V, 89
Kenworthy, John V, 184
Kenworthy, John V, 344
Kenworthy, John V, 845
Kenworthy, John V, 846
Kenworthy, John V, 849
Kenworthy, John R. V, 846
Kenworthy, John R. V, 847
Kenworthy, Joseph V, 846
Kenworthy, Joshua I, 403
Kenworthy, Joshua I, 1057
Kenworthy, Joshua I, 1058
Kenworthy, Joshua I, 1062
Kenworthy, Joshua V, 88
Kenworthy, Joshua V, 344
Kenworthy, Lenora V, 689
Kenworthy, Leonard V, 689
Kenworthy, Lillian V, 847
Kenworthy, Lucy A. V, 847
Kenworthy, Lucy Angie V, 847
Kenworthy, Lydia I, 1157
Kenworthy, Lydia V, 343
Kenworthy, Lydia V, 344
Kenworthy, Lydia V, 845
Kenworthy, Lydia V, 846
Kenworthy, Lydia V, 847
Kenworthy, Lydia V, 849
Kenworthy, M. J. V, 846
Kenworthy, Margaret V, 408
Kenworthy, Margaret V, 428
Kenworthy, Margaret V, 751
Kenworthy, Margaret V, 847
Kenworthy, Margaret V, 853
Kenworthy, Margaret V, 884
Kenworthy, Mariam V, 351
Kenworthy, Marianna IV, 972
Kenworthy, Martha I, 1057
Kenworthy, Martha I, 1061
Kenworthy, Martha I, 1062
Kenworthy, Martha V, 846
Kenworthy, Martha V, 851
Kenworthy, Martha A. V, 847
Kenworthy, Martha Ann V, 875
Kenworthy, Mary I, 382
Kenworthy, Mary I, 403
Kenworthy, Mary I, 1057
Kenworthy, Mary I, 1058
Kenworthy, Mary I, 1062
Kenworthy, Mary IV, 43
Kenworthy, Mary IV, 49
Kenworthy, Mary IV, 96
Kenworthy, Mary IV, 101
Kenworthy, Mary IV, 972
Kenworthy, Mary V, 88
Kenworthy, Mary V, 89
Kenworthy, Mary V, 184
Kenworthy, Mary V, 256
Kenworthy, Mary V, 257
Kenworthy, Mary V, 315
Kenworthy, Mary V, 335
Kenworthy, Mary V, 343
Kenworthy, Mary V, 344
Kenworthy, Mary V, 349
Kenworthy, Mary V, 351
Kenworthy, Mary V, 828
Kenworthy, Mary V, 846
Kenworthy, Mary V, 847
Kenworthy, Mary V, 849
Kenworthy, Mary V, 865
Kenworthy, Mary V, 875
Kenworthy, Mary V, 915
Kenworthy, Mary V, 919
Kenworthy, Mary V, 965
Kenworthy, Mary V, 972
Kenworthy, Mary V, 979
Kenworthy, Mary VI, 523
Kenworthy, Mary VI, 653
Kenworthy, Mary VI, 670
Kenworthy, Mary VI, 759
Kenworthy, Mary Ann IV, 233
Kenworthy, Mary Ann V, 846
Kenworthy, Mary Ann V, 847
Kenworthy, Mary Ann V, 849
Kenworthy, Mary Ann V, 915
Kenworthy, Mary Anna IV, 972
Kenworthy, Mary B. V, 839
Kenworthy, Mary B. V, 847
Kenworthy, Mary E. V, 89
Kenworthy, Mary H. V, 846
Kenworthy, Mary Jane V, 846
Kenworthy, Mary Jane V, 847
Kenworthy, Mary M. IV, 233
Kenworthy, Mary M. IV, 278
Kenworthy, Mary P. V, 52
Kenworthy, Mary P. V, 88
Kenworthy, Milton V, 846
Kenworthy, Miriam V, 340
Kenworthy, Miriam V, 343
Kenworthy, Murray V, 689
Kenworthy, Murray S. V, 689
Kenworthy, Nancy VI, 945
Kenworthy, Olivar V, 89
Kenworthy, Olive I, 1058
Kenworthy, Olive V, 184
Kenworthy, Orlando I, 1157
Kenworthy, Peggy V, 884
Kenworthy, Phebe IV, 1255
Kenworthy, Rachel I, 1060
Kenworthy, Rachel I, 1062
Kenworthy, Rachel IV, 43
Kenworthy, Rachel IV, 96
Kenworthy, Rachel IV, 1255
Kenworthy, Rachel V, 88
Kenworthy, Rachel V, 89
Kenworthy, Rachel V, 257
Kenworthy, Rachel V, 343
Kenworthy, Rachel V, 349
Kenworthy, Rachel V, 828
Kenworthy, Rachel V, 846
Kenworthy, Rachel V, 847
Kenworthy, Rachel V, 853
Kenworthy, Rachel V, 915
Kenworthy, Rachel V, 972
Kenworthy, Rachel C. V, 846
Kenworthy, Rachel C. V, 865
Kenworthy, Rachel H. V, 847
Kenworthy, Rachel H. V, 867
Kenworthy, Rebecca I, 1058
Kenworthy, Rebecca V, 89
Kenworthy, Rebecca V, 184
Kenworthy, Rebecca VI, 523
Kenworthy, Rebecca VI, 524
Kenworthy, Rebecca VI, 653
Kenworthy, Rebecca VI, 670
Kenworthy, Rebecca J. V, 846
Kenworthy, Rebecca J. V, 847
Kenworthy, Rebekah I, 402
Kenworthy, Rebekah I, 403
Kenworthy, Rebekah I, 1060
Kenworthy, Rebekah I, 1062
Kenworthy, Rebekah VI, 506
Kenworthy, Rebekah VI, 654
Kenworthy, Rebekah VI, 670
Kenworthy, Rebekah VI, 749
Kenworthy, Rebekah VI, 759
Kenworthy, Rettie H. V, 847
Kenworthy, Rhoda V, 846
Kenworthy, Rhoda E. V, 847
Kenworthy, Richard P. IV, 972
Kenworthy, Robert IV, 43
Kenworthy, Robert V, 89
Kenworthy, Robert V, 847
Kenworthy, Robert V, 972
Kenworthy, Robert V, 979
Kenworthy, Robert B. V, 847
Kenworthy, Ruth IV, 43
Kenworthy, Ruth IV, 59
Kenworthy, Sally V, 846
Kenworthy, Sarah I, 1057
Kenworthy, Sarah I, 1061
Kenworthy, Sarah I, 1062
Kenworthy, Sarah IV, 59
Kenworthy, Sarah V, 88
Kenworthy, Sarah V, 89
Kenworthy, Sarah V, 184
Kenworthy, Sarah V, 257
Kenworthy, Sarah V, 335
Kenworthy, Sarah V, 343
Kenworthy, Sarah A. V, 847
Kenworthy, Sarah Ellen V, 846
Kenworthy, Sarah Elma V, 847
Kenworthy, Sarah Martha I, 4C
Kenworthy, Silas V, 89
Kenworthy, Silas V, 344
Kenworthy, Silas V, 846
Kenworthy, Silis V, 256
Kenworthy, Sina V, 915
Kenworthy, Susan V, 846
Kenworthy, Susan V, 865
Kenworthy, Susan H. V, 847
Kenworthy, Susan H. V, 867
Kenworthy, Tamar I, 403
Kenworthy, Tamar I, 1058
Kenworthy, Tamar V, 88
Kenworthy, Tamar V, 89
Kenworthy, Tamar V, 184
Kenworthy, Tamer I, 403
Kenworthy, Tamer I, 1062
Kenworthy, Tamer V, 343
Kenworthy, Tamer Lillian V, 84
Kenworthy, Thamar V, 257
Kenworthy, Thamer V, 215
Kenworthy, Thamer V, 230
Kenworthy, Thomas V, 256
Kenworthy, Thomas V, 344
Kenworthy, Thomas VI, 945
Kenworthy, Truman C. IV, 972
Kenworthy, Truman S. IV, 972
Kenworthy, Valearia V, 841
Kenworthy, Valeria V, 841
Kenworthy, Valerie V, 846
Kenworthy, Velerie V, 847
Kenworthy, Wayne V, 88
Kenworthy, Widow Rebecca VI, 670
Kenworthy, William I, 402
Kenworthy, William I, 1058
Kenworthy, William IV, 43
Kenworthy, William IV, 59
Kenworthy, William IV, 96
Kenworthy, William V, 88
Kenworthy, William V, 89
Kenworthy, William V, 184

nworthy, William V, 257
nworthy, William V, 825
nworthy, William V, 846
nworthy, William V, 875
nworthy, William V, 979
nworthy, William VI, 523
nworthy, William VI, 653
nworthy, William VI, 670
nworthy, William VI, 759
nworthy, William H. V, 846
nworthy, William, Jr. VI, 523
nworthy, William, Jr. VI, 524
nworthy, William, Jr. VI, 749
nworthy, Willis V, 972
nworthy, Willis V, 979
nworthy, Wilmer V, 689
nworthy, Wm, Sr. VI, 523
nworthy, Wm. V, 915
nworthy, Wm. V, 944
nworthy, Wm. V, 972
nworthy, Wm. VI, 524
nworthy, Wm. VI, 759
nworthy, Wm., Jr. VI, 506
nworthy, Wm., Jr. VI, 654
nworthy, Zimri V, 846
nworthy, Zimri V, 847
nworty, Jabez H. V, 857
nworty, Rhida E. V, 857
nyon, Abigail III, 191
nyon, Benja. I, 144
nyon, David III, 191
nyon, Elisabeth I, 36
nyon, Elisabeth I, 56
nyon, Elizabeth I, 56
nyon, Hannah I, 140
nyon, Hannah I, 144
nyon, James III, 191
nyon, Levi I, 144
nyon, Margaret I, 36
nyon, Margaret I, 56
nyon, Margaret I, 195
nyon, Mary I, 144
nyon, Mialma R. IV, 949
nyon, Phebe Ann IV, 1371
nyon, Rebecca IV, 985
nyon, Roger I, 36
nyon, Roger I, 56
nyon, Samuel III, 191
nyon, Sarah I, 56
nyon, Sarah I, 71
nyon, William I, 195
nyon, William III, 191
okenhour, Rosa V, 1005
phart, Clara V, 915
phart, Ella Gardner VI, 670
phart, Ella Gardner VI, 702
phart, Harry V, 184
phart, Leslie V, 915
phart, Neil V, 915
phart, Thos. J. V, 915
pke, Minnie E. IV, 1324
plar, Sarah I, 924
pler, Eva May IV, 1255
pler, W. R. IV, 1255
pler, Wm. R. IV, 1255
plinger, Ann V, 865
pp, Margaret VI, 759
pple, Deborah II, 385
pple, John II, 385
pple, John Lynn II, 385
pple, Martha II, 573
pple, Martha II, 588
pport, Elizabeth IV, 233
pport, Elizabeth IV, 234
rbride, Joseph II, 979
rbride, Joseph II, 1007
rby, Ann I, 195
rby, Ann I, 196
rby, Archibald VI, 327
rby, Elizabeth VI, 295
rby, Elizabeth VI, 328
rby, Esther VI, 327
rby, Ezekiah VI, 327
rby, Henry VI, 295
rby, Henry VI, 327
rby, Jeremiah VI, 327
rby, John VI, 295
rby, Judith VI, 328
rby, Mary IV, 43
rby, Mary IV, 47
rby, Mary VI, 295
rby, Mary VI, 327
rby, Obediah VI, 327
rby, Orpha VI, 295
rby, Orpha VI, 327
rby, Pauling VI, 295
rby, Paxwood VI, 295
rby, Rachel VI, 295
rby, Richard VI, 295
rby, Richard VI, 328
rby, Richard, Jr. VI, 328
Kerby, Ruth V, 257
Kerby, Sarah V, 954
Kerby, Sarah VI, 327
Kerby, William VI, 295
Kerchgessner, John IV, 829
Kerell, Thomas II, 573
Keric, Ada M. V, 184
Kerk, Caleb V, 631
Kerk, Daniel V, 631
Kerk, James E. V, 631
Kerk, Susanna V, 631
Kerk, Susannah V, 631
Kerkhide, Eliza P. I, 817
Kerkindoll, Ella V, 1005
Kerkpatrick, Roxannah I, 890
Kerl, Katherine II, 1007
Kerl, Katherine II, 1039
Kerlin, Ann II, 573
Kerlin, Ann II, 655
Kerlin, David II, 573
Kerlin, Davis II, 573
Kerlin, Elizabeth II, 177
Kerlin, Elizabeth II, 178
Kerlin, Elizabeth II, 573
Kerlin, Jemima II, 573
Kerlin, Jemimah II, 385
Kerlin, John II, 385
Kerlin, John II, 573
Kerlin, Mary II, 486
Kerlin, Mary II, 573
Kerlin, Matthias II, 178
Kerlin, Matthias II, 236
Kerlin, Sarah II, 178
Kerlin, Sarah II, 236
Kerlin, Sarah II, 573
Kerlin, Sarah II, 1007
Kerlin, Wm. II, 573
Kerlin, Wm. II, 1007
Kerling, Hannah II, 445
Kerling, John II, 445
Kermish, Elizabeth IV, 1324
Kermish, F. W. IV, 1324
Kern, Abraham VI, 944
Kern, Ann VI, 944
Kern, Anna IV, 758
Kern, Anna VI, 945
Kern, Barbara VI, 945
Kern, Betsey VI, 944
Kern, Charles VI, 945
Kern, Elizabeth VI, 945
Kern, George VI, 945
Kern, Hannah VI, 945
Kern, Jane IV, 758
Kern, Jessie IV, 1238
Kern, John VI, 945
Kern, John J. VI, 944
Kern, Lucinda IV, 678
Kern, Lucinda IV, 1246
Kern, Martha IV, 678
Kern, Martha V, 153
Kern, Michael VI, 945
Kern, Michael VI, 995
Kern, Samuel IV, 758
Kern, Seth IV, 678
Kern, Seth IV, 1246
Kern, Thomas VI, 945
Kerner, Alice Mary I, 620
Kerner, Judith I, 912
Kerner, Judith I, 913
Kerner, Margorite C. I, 636
Kerner, Marguerite I, 613
Kerner, Marguerite I, 620
Kerner, Marguerite C. I, 636
Kerner, Marguerite Cartland I, 620
Kerner, Mary Alice I, 636
Kerner, Percy I, 620
Kerner, Percy D. I, 613
Kernes, Alfred T. V, 631
Kernes, Chas. V, 343
Kernes, George Carns. VI, 1017
Kernes, Jacob VI, 907
Kernes, John VI, 945
Kernes, Polly VI, 945
Kernes, Sally VI, 1017
Kerney, Johanna II, 385
Kerney, Mary II, 572
Kerney, Mary II, 573
Kernney, Rhoda V, 1005
Kernodle, Fannie I, 626
Kerns, Abraham VI, 872
Kerns, Abraham VI, 945
Kerns, Adaline VI, 1012
Kerns, Alfred V, 631
Kerns, Anna VI, 945
Kerns, Anna VI, 993
Kerns, B. A. VI, 870
Kerns, Barbara VI, 945
Kerns, Barbara Ann VI, 870
Kerns, Catherine VI, 945
Kerns, Charles VI, 945
Kerns, Demarius VI, 945
Kerns, Doshia VI, 872
Kerns, Edith L. IV, 736
Kerns, Elizabeth II, 885
Kerns, Elizabeth VI, 945
Kerns, Elizabeth P. II, 804
Kerns, Emily V, 631
Kerns, Geo. VI, 872
Kerns, George VI, 945
Kerns, Hannah VI, 945
Kerns, Horatio Sprague II, 804
Kerns, Ida IV, 233
Kerns, Jacob VI, 872
Kerns, Jesse R. V, 751
Kerns, Job VI, 945
Kerns, John VI, 870
Kerns, John VI, 871
Kerns, John VI, 945
Kerns, John E. V, 631
Kerns, Katy VI, 983
Kerns, Lucy VI, 875
Kerns, Lydia VI, 872
Kerns, Maria IV, 829
Kerns, Martha Gertrude V, 344
Kerns, Mary VI, 1005
Kerns, Mary VI, 1008
Kerns, Mary Jane VI, 870
Kerns, Michael VI, 870
Kerns, Michael VI, 945
Kerns, Michael, Jr. VI, 945
Kerns, Michel VI, 944
Kerns, Minnie IV, 736
Kerns, Minnie IV, 829
Kerns, Minnie V, 344
Kerns, Moses VI, 944
Kerns, Nelly VI, 953
Kerns, Orin IV, 736
Kerns, Phebe VI, 945
Kerns, Polly VI, 945
Kerns, Polly VI, 992
Kerns, Rebecca VI, 1008
Kerns, Rebecca VI, 1015
Kerns, Reubin VI, 945
Kerns, Reubin VI, 1012
Kerns, Sampson VI, 945
Kerns, Sarah VI, 944
Kerns, Susanna VI, 935
Kerns, William IV, 639
Kerns, William VI, 870
Kerr, ??? VI, 714
Kerr, Alexander VI, 945
Kerr, Betty VI, 831
Kerr, Catharine VI, 978
Kerr, Charles VI, 945
Kerr, Charles VI, 981
Kerr, Charles B. VI, 889
Kerr, Cornelia III, 178
Kerr, Cornelia III, 191
Kerr, David VI, 1020
Kerr, Edithy VI, 945
Kerr, Eliz. A. III, 168
Kerr, Elizabeth II, 385
Kerr, Elizabeth VI, 946
Kerr, Elizabeth Anna Ethel III, 191
Kerr, Elizabeth Ann Ethel III, 168
Kerr, Frances VI, 953
Kerr, Frances VI, 1020
Kerr, Hannah J. VI, 714
Kerr, Harriett IV, 401
Kerr, Isham VI, 945
Kerr, Isham VI, 978
Kerr, James VI, 945
Kerr, James VI, 946
Kerr, James VI, 975
Kerr, Jane III, 191
Kerr, John VI, 831
Kerr, John VI, 981
Kerr, Katharine VI, 945
Kerr, Laura F. I, 1157
Kerr, Lilla F. I, 1157
Kerr, Lucy VI, 874
Kerr, Lucy VI, 1020
Kerr, Lurany VI, 1020
Kerr, Lurena VI, 945
Kerr, Martha VI, 945
Kerr, Mary VI, 945
Kerr, Nancy VI, 978
Kerr, Nathaniel VI, 945
Kerr, Ortense IV, 1371
Kerr, Rebecca III, 178
Kerr, Rebecca III, 191
Kerr, Rebecca VI, 945
Kerr, Rebecca T. IV, 1214
Kerr, Ruth II, 707
Kerr, Ruth VI, 945
Kerr, Sally VI, 981
Kerr, Sarah IV, 1156
Kerr, Sarah IV, 1169
Kerr, Tabitha VI, 946
Kerr, Thomas VI, 945
Kerr, Thomas VI, 946
Kerr, Thomas VI, 975
Kerr, William III, 178
Kerr, William III, 191
Kerr, William VI, 874
Kerr, William VI, 945
Kerr, William VI, 953
Kerr, William VI, 1020
Kerr, William, Jr. VI, 1020
Kerr, Wm. VI, 945
Kerrick, Adra M. V, 89
Kerrick, James V, 89
Kersen, Jane I, 890
Kersey, Abigail I, 859
Kersey, Abigail I, 890
Kersey, Abigail I, 905
Kersey, Abigail M. I, 890
Kersey, Alice I, 871
Kersey, Alice I, 889
Kersey, Alvira I, 613
Kersey, Amos I, 506
Kersey, Amos I, 660
Kersey, Amos I, 674
Kersey, Amos I, 682
Kersey, Amos I, 786
Kersey, Amos I, 823
Kersey, Amos I, 847
Kersey, Amos I, 858
Kersey, Amos I, 889
Kersey, Amos I, 890
Kersey, Amos V, 631
Kersey, Amos W. I, 859
Kersey, Amos W. I, 890
Kersey, Amos W. V, 631
Kersey, Ann I, 682
Kersey, Ann I, 686
Kersey, Ann I, 859
Kersey, Ann I, 872
Kersey, Ann I, 889
Kersey, Ann IV, 730
Kersey, Ann V, 507
Kersey, Ann V, 580
Kersey, Ann H. IV, 730
Kersey, Ann H. IV, 752
Kersey, Anna I, 859
Kersey, Anna I, 872
Kersey, Anna I, 889
Kersey, Anna V, 77
Kersey, Anna V, 86
Kersey, Anna V, 89
Kersey, Anna V, 126
Kersey, Anna V, 774
Kersey, Anna Mary V, 89
Kersey, Arena V, 89
Kersey, Arena E. V, 89
Kersey, Arena E. V, 757
Kersey, Arena E. V, 774
Kersey, Arena Ellen V, 89
Kersey, Arthur V, 459
Kersey, Arthur C. V, 459
Kersey, Asenath I, 859
Kersey, Asenath I, 890
Kersey, Asenath I, 899
Kersey, Asher I, 859
Kersey, Ayles I, 889
Kersey, Beaulah I, 859
Kersey, Benjamin I, 682
Kersey, Benjamin I, 686
Kersey, Benjamin I, 786
Kersey, Benjamin I, 858
Kersey, Benjamin I, 889
Kersey, Beulah I, 890
Kersey, Beulah I, 896
Kersey, Carter V, 507
Kersey, Carter V, 580
Kersey, Charity W. I, 890
Kersey, Daniel I, 377
Kersey, Daniel I, 403
Kersey, Daniel I, 506
Kersey, Daniel I, 555
Kersey, Daniel I, 723
Kersey, Daniel I, 786
Kersey, Daniel I, 823
Kersey, Daniel I, 847
Kersey, Daniel I, 872
Kersey, Daniel I, 889
Kersey, Daniel V, 89
Kersey, Daniel V, 580
Kersey, David I, 859
Kersey, David I, 890
Kersey, David E. I, 890
Kersey, Dinah I, 660
Kersey, Dinah I, 674
Kersey, Dinah I, 682
Kersey, Dinah I, 786
Kersey, Dinah I, 823
Kersey, Dinah I, 858
Kersey, Dr. Joshua II, 804
Kersey, Eleazar I, 506
Kersey, Eleazar I, 823
Kersey, Eleazar I, 858
Kersey, Eleazar I, 889
Kersey, Eleazar I, 890
Kersey, Eleazar V, 89
Kersey, Elen I, 890
Kersey, Elen I, 905
Kersey, Eli I, 859
Kersey, Eli I, 890
Kersey, Eliezer I, 889
Kersey, Elizabeth I, 506
Kersey, Elizabeth I, 786
Kersey, Elizabeth I, 858
Kersey, Elizabeth I, 859
Kersey, Elizabeth I, 870
Kersey, Elizabeth I, 875
Kersey, Elizabeth I, 883
Kersey, Elizabeth I, 884
Kersey, Elizabeth I, 889
Kersey, Elizabeth I, 890
Kersey, Elizabeth IV, 716
Kersey, Elizabeth V, 89
Kersey, Elizabeth V, 507
Kersey, Elizabeth VI, 524
Kersey, Elizabeth F. I, 859
Kersey, Ellen I, 890
Kersey, Ellen I, 906
Kersey, Emily I, 882
Kersey, Emily I, 890
Kersey, Emily V, 972
Kersey, Emily L. I, 859
Kersey, Emma II, 885
Kersey, Emma W. II, 870
Kersey, Emma W. II, 885
Kersey, Enoch I, 889
Kersey, Enoch I, 890
Kersey, Esther I, 889
Kersey, Esther I, 890
Kersey, Esther I, 906
Kersey, Ezra I, 858
Kersey, Ezra I, 859
Kersey, Ezra I, 889
Kersey, Ezra I, 890
Kersey, Ezra Allen I, 859
Kersey, Fanny Helen V, 89
Kersey, Franklin Smith I, 890
Kersey, George I, 890
Kersey, George A., Jr. I, 944
Kersey, George M. I, 859
Kersey, Gertrude Von Hill V, 89
Kersey, Guli E. I, 859
Kersey, Gulia I, 873
Kersey, Gulia I, 890
Kersey, Hannah I, 403
Kersey, Hannah I, 506
Kersey, Hannah I, 682
Kersey, Hannah I, 723
Kersey, Hannah I, 773
Kersey, Hannah I, 786
Kersey, Hannah I, 823
Kersey, Hannah I, 847
Kersey, Hannah I, 889
Kersey, Hannah I, 897
Kersey, Hannah V, 580
Kersey, Hannah VI, 513
Kersey, Hannah VI, 524
Kersey, Henry I, 859
Kersey, Henry I, 883
Kersey, Henry I, 890
Kersey, Henry V, 89
Kersey, Henry V, 146
Kersey, Henry J. I, 859
Kersey, Henry J. I, 890
Kersey, Isaac I, 786
Kersey, Isaac I, 858
Kersey, Isaac I, 859
Kersey, Isaac I, 889
Kersey, Isaac I, 890
Kersey, Isabel I, 858
Kersey, Isabel I, 889
Kersey, Isabel I, 896
Kersey, James I, 858
Kersey, James I, 859
Kersey, James I, 889
Kersey, James C. I, 884
Kersey, James C. I, 890
Kersey, Jane I, 859
Kersey, Jane I, 883
Kersey, Jane I, 890
Kersey, Jane I, 891
Kersey, Jemima I, 889
Kersey, Jesse I, 506
Kersey, Jesse I, 814
Kersey, Jesse I, 823
Kersey, Jesse I, 859
Kersey, Jesse I, 889
Kersey, Jesse I, 890
Kersey, Jesse V, 506
Kersey, Jesse VI, 599
Kersey, Jessee I, 890
Kersey, John I, 786
Kersey, John I, 859
Kersey, John V, 77

Kersey, John V, 86
Kersey, John V, 89
Kersey, John V, 507
Kersey, John V, 580
Kersey, John V, 689
Kersey, John V, 774
Kersey, John I. II, 797
Kersey, John I. II, 870
Kersey, John I. II, 885
Kersey, John J. II, 885
Kersey, John Jacobs II, 804
Kersey, John P. I, 859
Kersey, John P. I, 890
Kersey, Letitia V, 44
Kersey, Letitia V, 89
Kersey, Letitia V, 580
Kersey, Letitia V, 670
Kersey, Letitia V, 689
Kersey, Lettitia V, 89
Kersey, Lititia V, 557
Kersey, Lois I, 858
Kersey, Lois I, 859
Kersey, Lois I, 873
Kersey, Lois I, 889
Kersey, Lois I, 890
Kersey, Lois I, 898
Kersey, Louisa I, 890
Kersey, Lowiza I, 859
Kersey, Lydia I, 878
Kersey, Lydia I, 890
Kersey, Madora Elizabeth V, 89
Kersey, Mahlon I, 859
Kersey, Malinda I, 889
Kersey, Mariah I, 859
Kersey, Martha I, 859
Kersey, Martha I, 890
Kersey, Martha I, 894
Kersey, Martha V, 77
Kersey, Martha V, 89
Kersey, Martha V, 550
Kersey, Martha V, 577
Kersey, Martha V, 580
Kersey, Martha V, 684
Kersey, Martha Jane I, 859
Kersey, Mary I, 377
Kersey, Mary I, 403
Kersey, Mary I, 555
Kersey, Mary I, 786
Kersey, Mary I, 823
Kersey, Mary V, 459
Kersey, Mary V, 586
Kersey, Mary VI, 524
Kersey, Mary C. I, 823
Kersey, Mary C. I, 889
Kersey, Mary Ellen I, 859
Kersey, Mary Emily V, 968
Kersey, Mary Emily V, 972
Kersey, Melinda I, 889
Kersey, Melissa J. I, 823
Kersey, Miriam I, 889
Kersey, Moses I, 823
Kersey, Moses I, 859
Kersey, Moses I, 889
Kersey, Moses I, 890
Kersey, Moses V, 847
Kersey, Nancy I, 889
Kersey, Nancy Alvira I, 620
Kersey, Nereus I, 823
Kersey, Phebe I, 859
Kersey, Phebe I, 888
Kersey, Phebe I, 890
Kersey, Phebe Brinton II, 804
Kersey, Rachel I, 545
Kersey, Rachel I, 555
Kersey, Rachel I, 814
Kersey, Rachel I, 823
Kersey, Rachel I, 859
Kersey, Rachel I, 889
Kersey, Rachel I, 890
Kersey, Rachel V, 972
Kersey, Rebecca I, 377
Kersey, Rebecca I, 403
Kersey, Rebecca I, 786
Kersey, Rebecca I, 847
Kersey, Rebecca II, 780
Kersey, Rebecca V, 86
Kersey, Rebecca V, 89
Kersey, Rebecca V, 507
Kersey, Rebecca V, 580
Kersey, Rebecca, Jr. V, 507
Kersey, Rebeckah I, 889
Kersey, Rebekah I, 403
Kersey, Rebekah I, 823
Kersey, Rebekah I, 859
Kersey, Rebekah V, 89
Kersey, Robert V, 459
Kersey, Robert M. V, 459
Kersey, Ruth H. I, 859
Kersey, Sally I, 859
Kersey, Samuel I, 859
Kersey, Samuel V, 89
Kersey, Samuel V, 757
Kersey, Samuel V, 774
Kersey, Sarah I, 823
Kersey, Sarah I, 859
Kersey, Sarah I, 889
Kersey, Sarah I, 890
Kersey, Sarah II, 797
Kersey, Sarah II, 804
Kersey, Sarah II, 885
Kersey, Sarah II, 934
Kersey, Sarah V, 631
Kersey, Sarah E. I, 859
Kersey, Sarah E. I, 890
Kersey, Sarah M. I, 859
Kersey, Sarah W. II, 870
Kersey, Sarah W. II, 885
Kersey, Shubal C. I, 859
Kersey, Shubal C. I, 890
Kersey, Stephanas I, 859
Kersey, Stephanus I, 859
Kersey, Stephanus I, 888
Kersey, Stephanus I, 890
Kersey, Stephen I, 889
Kersey, Stephen I, 890
Kersey, Thomas I, 377
Kersey, Thomas I, 403
Kersey, Thomas I, 506
Kersey, Thomas I, 786
Kersey, Thomas I, 823
Kersey, Thomas I, 859
Kersey, Thomas I, 889
Kersey, Thomas V, 44
Kersey, Thomas V, 89
Kersey, Thomas V, 507
Kersey, Thomas V, 557
Kersey, Thomas V, 580
Kersey, Thomas V, 689
Kersey, Thomas C. V, 89
Kersey, Thomas, Jr. V, 580
Kersey, Thomas, Sr. V, 580
Kersey, Vierling I, 859
Kersey, Vierling V, 968
Kersey, Vierling V, 972
Kersey, Virgil V, 459
Kersey, William I, 506
Kersey, William I, 545
Kersey, William I, 555
Kersey, William I, 682
Kersey, William I, 786
Kersey, William I, 823
Kersey, William I, 859
Kersey, William I, 889
Kersey, William I, 890
Kersey, William V, 580
Kersey, William VI, 513
Kersey, William VI, 524
Kersey, William J. I, 859
Kersey, William Rufus V, 89
Kersey, William, Jr. I, 889
Kersey, William, Jr. VI, 524
Kersey, Wm. I, 403
Kersey, Wm. V, 972
Kersey, Wm. VI, 524
Kersey, Zebidee I, 859
Kershaw, Florence A. IV, 1255
Kershaw, Mable IV, 1255
Kershaw, Mary A. IV, 1255
Kershaw, Paul IV, 1255
Kershaw, Will IV, 1255
Kershaw, Wm. IV, 1255
Kershner, Hayden V, 673
Kershner, Hayden V, 689
Kershner, John V, 689
Kershner, Mary V, 673
Kershner, Mary V, 689
Kershow, Abraham III, 188
Kershow, George D. III, 188
Kershow, Mary III, 188
Kersy, Elizabeth I, 890
Kersy, Mary C. I, 823
Kersy, Melissa J. I, 823
Kersy, Moses I, 823
Kersy, Nereus I, 823
Kersy, Rachel I, 823
Kersy, Sarah I, 823
Kertice, Jane V, 631
Kerton, Elma V, 954
Kervode, Ann IV, 96
Kervode, Ann IV, 113
Kerwein, Edith Anne III, 191
Kerwein, Henrietta III, 191
Kerwein, John R. III, 191
Kerwoo, Ann IV, 96
Kerwoo, Ann IV, 113
Kesay, Ruth V, 707
Kesice, Samuel V, 1005
Kesler, Abraham VI, 994
Kesler, Barnabas VI, 946
Kesler, Barnett VI, 946
Kesler, Barnett VI, 971
Kesler, Benjamin VI, 946
Kesler, Bruce IV, 1324
Kesler, Bruce Harrison IV, 1324
Kesler, David VI, 932
Kesler, Dolly VI, 932
Kesler, Eliza Ann VI, 946
Kesler, Florence IV, 1324
Kesler, Hannah V, 1005
Kesler, Herman IV, 1324
Kesler, Jacob VI, 946
Kesler, John V, 981
Kesler, John V, 1005
Kesler, Luisa V, 1005
Kesler, Martha Ann V, 1005
Kesler, Martha Ann VI, 946
Kesler, Martin V, 631
Kesler, Mary VI, 946
Kesler, Minerva Ann VI, 946
Kesler, Peter V, 1005
Kesler, Ruth V, 788
Kesley, Josephine III, 150
Kessler, Arden P. V, 751
Kessler, Benjamin VI, 946
Kessler, Dr. Arden V, 814
Kessler, Eliza Ann VI, 946
Kessler, Elizabeth V, 770
Kesson, David VI, 946
Kesson, Elizabeth VI, 946
Kester, Aaron IV, 339
Kester, Aaron IV, 415
Kester, Abi IV, 415
Kester, Ada V, 257
Kester, Ada V, 409
Kester, Alonzo V, 955
Kester, Alvin V, 955
Kester, Amy Ann V, 955
Kester, Ann I, 823
Kester, Ann I, 965
Kester, Ann IV, 339
Kester, Ann IV, 345
Kester, Ann IV, 415
Kester, Ann IV, 453
Kester, Ann V, 497
Kester, Ann V, 507
Kester, Ann V, 954
Kester, Anna V, 392
Kester, Anna V, 408
Kester, Anna V, 409
Kester, Ansalem I, 890
Kester, Ansalem A. I, 859
Kester, Arcada I, 859
Kester, Benjamin IV, 339
Kester, Benjamin IV, 405
Kester, Benjamin IV, 415
Kester, Carey D. V, 257
Kester, Carey D. V, 408
Kester, Carey D. V, 409
Kester, Charity IV, 415
Kester, Charles V, 954
Kester, Clara D. IV, 233
Kester, Clemmie E. V, 409
Kester, Cora V, 344
Kester, D. M. V, 409
Kester, Daniel V, 377
Kester, Daniel V, 392
Kester, Daniel V, 408
Kester, Daniel V, 409
Kester, Daniel V, 411
Kester, Daniel V, 507
Kester, Daniel O. V, 409
Kester, Daniel Samuel V, 409
Kester, David IV, 339
Kester, David IV, 345
Kester, David IV, 415
Kester, David V, 322
Kester, David V, 344
Kester, David V, 954
Kester, Deborah I, 823
Kester, Deborah I, 890
Kester, Delilah E. V, 409
Kester, Delilah Ettie V, 409
Kester, Dillwyn P. II, 885
Kester, Donald V, 409
Kester, Edith I, 823
Kester, Edith I, 965
Kester, Edith I, 1010
Kester, Edith I, 1012
Kester, Edith V, 184
Kester, Edith V, 397
Kester, Edith V, 409
Kester, Elijah II, 949
Kester, Elizabeth IV, 339
Kester, Elizabeth IV, 415
Kester, Elizabeth IV, 1087
Kester, Elizabeth IV, 1103
Kester, Elizabeth V, 322
Kester, Elizabeth V, 344
Kester, Elizabeth V, 377
Kester, Elizabeth V, 392
Kester, Elizabeth V, 408
Kester, Elizabeth V, 409
Kester, Elizabeth V, 410
Kester, Elizabeth V, 411
Kester, Elizabeth A. IV, 1283
Kester, Elizabeth L. V, 955
Kester, Elwood V, 409
Kester, Emma V, 409
Kester, Emma A. V, 409
Kester, Emmy Ann IV, 1283
Kester, Ephraim W. IV, 415
Kester, Ephraim Williams IV, 415
Kester, Eva Elizabeth V, 409
Kester, Geo. V, 409
Kester, George V, 409
Kester, Gilla I, 890
Kester, Gilla I, 913
Kester, Gilly I, 913
Kester, Guilla I, 890
Kester, Guylla I, 859
Kester, Guylla I, 870
Kester, Guylla I, 890
Kester, Gylla I, 890
Kester, Hannah IV, 415
Kester, Hannah V, 184
Kester, Hannah V, 344
Kester, Hannah V, 383
Kester, Hannah V, 408
Kester, Hannah V, 409
Kester, Hannah V, 507
Kester, Hannah V, 547
Kester, Hannah V, 580
Kester, Harmon V, 409
Kester, Harmon V, 507
Kester, Harmon V, 580
Kester, Harmon Kester V, 184
Kester, Harmon Kester V, 507
Kester, Harrison IV, 1214
Kester, Harry IV, 1214
Kester, Hartley IV, 339
Kester, Henry V, 954
Kester, Ida A. V, 409
Kester, Isaac I, 890
Kester, James I, 823
Kester, James IV, 415
Kester, James Kitely IV, 339
Kester, James Kitely IV, 415
Kester, Jane V, 408
Kester, Jane V, 409
Kester, Jason I, 859
Kester, Jason I, 890
Kester, Jason V, 954
Kester, Jason V, 955
Kester, Jesse IV, 339
Kester, Jesse IV, 415
Kester, Jesse V, 409
Kester, John I, 823
Kester, John I, 859
Kester, John I, 870
Kester, John I, 890
Kester, John I, 913
Kester, John I, 965
Kester, John IV, 339
Kester, John IV, 415
Kester, John V, 407
Kester, John V, 408
Kester, John V, 409
Kester, John V, 507
Kester, John V, 580
Kester, John B. IV, 339
Kester, John B. IV, 415
Kester, John, Jr. IV, 415
Kester, Jonathan IV, 339
Kester, Jonathan V, 955
Kester, Jonathan H. IV, 415
Kester, Jonathan Hartley IV, 415
Kester, Jonathan L. IV, 1283
Kester, Josiah Albertson V, 184
Kester, Kennett II, 885
Kester, Lavina IV, 339
Kester, Lavinia IV, 415
Kester, Lena IV, 1214
Kester, Lenna V, 409
Kester, Leroy V, 257
Kester, Louisa I, 859
Kester, Louisa V, 955
Kester, Louiza I, 890
Kester, Lovina IV, 415
Kester, Luisa I, 890
Kester, Mahlon IV, 415
Kester, Malinda IV, 405
Kester, Malinda IV, 406
Kester, Malinda IV, 415
Kester, Manser V, 954
Kester, Margaret V, 954
Kester, Martha I, 555
Kester, Martha I, 589
Kester, Martha I, 594
Kester, Martha I, 823
Kester, Martha I, 913
Kester, Martha IV, 339
Kester, Martha IV, 415
Kester, Mary I, 589
Kester, Mary I, 594
Kester, Mary I, 823
Kester, Mary I, 890
Kester, Mary I, 892
Kester, Mary I, 913
Kester, Mary I, 965
Kester, Mary IV, 339
Kester, Mary IV, 415
Kester, Mary IV, 1103
Kester, Mary IV, 1214
Kester, Mary V, 409
Kester, Mary V, 411
Kester, Mary V, 507
Kester, Mary V, 955
Kester, Mary Ann IV, 406
Kester, Mary Ann IV, 415
Kester, Mary Ann V, 955
Kester, Mary F. V, 344
Kester, Mary F. V, 409
Kester, Mary Jane IV, 415
Kester, Mary M. V, 407
Kester, Mary M. V, 409
Kester, Mary M. V, 441
Kester, Maryan I, 890
Kester, Melinda IV, 415
Kester, Melissa IV, 415
Kester, Miles V, 344
Kester, Miles V, 408
Kester, Miles V, 409
Kester, Milton V, 257
Kester, Milton L. V, 344
Kester, Milton Leroy V, 409
Kester, Minnie L. V, 409
Kester, Mollie Scales I, 636
Kester, Morgan I, 890
Kester, Moses H. I, 859
Kester, Nancy I, 890
Kester, Nancy J. V, 257
Kester, Nancy J. V, 409
Kester, Nancy Jane V, 409
Kester, Nathan Harold V, 507
Kester, Olive E. V, 409
Kester, Orland W. V, 409
Kester, Pearl V, 344
Kester, Peter I, 823
Kester, Peter I, 965
Kester, Peter V, 344
Kester, Peter V, 408
Kester, Phebe I, 823
Kester, Phebe I, 890
Kester, Phebe I, 898
Kester, Phebe I, 965
Kester, Phebe V, 954
Kester, Phebe Ann IV, 415
Kester, Rachel V, 408
Kester, Richard I, 823
Kester, Richard I, 833
Kester, Richard I, 890
Kester, Richard I, 913
Kester, Richard I, 965
Kester, Robert IV, 339
Kester, Robert IV, 415
Kester, Ruth IV, 339
Kester, Ruth IV, 415
Kester, Ruth Anna IV, 415
Kester, Sabina V, 955
Kester, Sarah I, 822
Kester, Sarah I, 823
Kester, Sarah I, 833
Kester, Sarah I, 890
Kester, Sarah I, 913
Kester, Sarah I, 965
Kester, Sarah IV, 410
Kester, Sarah IV, 415
Kester, Sarah IV, 1283
Kester, Sarah V, 409
Kester, Sarah V, 411
Kester, Sarah E. IV, 339
Kester, Sarah E. IV, 415
Kester, Sarah E. V, 408
Kester, Sarah E. V, 409
Kester, Sarah L. V, 955
Kester, Stanley V, 409
Kester, Stephen D. V, 955
Kester, Susan E. II, 714
Kester, Susanna W. II, 949
Kester, Sylvia V, 409
Kester, Tamer E. V, 409
Kester, Thomas II, 1007
Kester, Thomas V, 507
Kester, Warren W. V, 409
Kester, William I, 822
Kester, William I, 823
Kester, William I, 890
Kester, William I, 892
Kester, William I, 913
Kester, William IV, 339
Kester, William IV, 415
Kester, William V, 954
Kester, William H. I, 859
Kester, Wm. II, 573
Kester, Wm. II, 750

Kester, Wm. IV, 415
Kester, Wm. IV, 1103
Ketcham, ??? III, 191
Ketcham, ??? III, 491
Ketcham, A. III, 191
Ketcham, Adelaide III, 488
Ketcham, Alanson III, 488
Ketcham, Almira III, 488
Ketcham, Catharine III, 423
Ketcham, Charity III, 488
Ketcham, David III, 191
Ketcham, David III, 346
Ketcham, David III, 422
Ketcham, David III, 423
Ketcham, David III, 444
Ketcham, David III, 483
Ketcham, David III, 488
Ketcham, David III, 498
Ketcham, David III, 506
Ketcham, Dorcas S. III, 191
Ketcham, Ebenezer III, 488
Ketcham, Edna III, 488
Ketcham, Edward III, 488
Ketcham, Emma III, 488
Ketcham, Ester III, 422
Ketcham, Esther III, 423
Ketcham, Esther III, 488
Ketcham, Esther III, 499
Ketcham, Eugene A. III, 423
Ketcham, Frederick W. III, 423
Ketcham, Geo. D. III, 422
Ketcham, Geo. W. III, 423
Ketcham, Geo. W. III, 440
Ketcham, George III, 422
Ketcham, George D. III, 423
Ketcham, Gulielma III, 423
Ketcham, Gulielma III, 440
Ketcham, Hannah III, 191
Ketcham, Hannah Ann III, 488
Ketcham, Hannah Ann III, 494
Ketcham, Ida A. III, 488
Ketcham, Isaac III, 488
Ketcham, Isaac S. III, 488
Ketcham, Isaac S. III, 490
Ketcham, Israel III, 422
Ketcham, Israel III, 423
Ketcham, Israel III, 488
Ketcham, Israel III, 499
Ketcham, James III, 191
Ketcham, James Sand III, 191
Ketcham, Jane III, 422
Ketcham, Jane III, 444
Ketcham, Jane III, 488
Ketcham, Jane III, 498
Ketcham, John III, 483
Ketcham, John III, 487
Ketcham, John III, 488
Ketcham, John III, 499
Ketcham, John T. III, 488
Ketcham, Joseph III, 191
Ketcham, Latitia III, 491
Ketcham, Margaret III, 423
Ketcham, Margaret III, 488
Ketcham, Margaret J. III, 440
Ketcham, Margaret S. III, 487
Ketcham, Margaret S. III, 488
Ketcham, Martha III, 488
Ketcham, Martha S. III, 483
Ketcham, Martha S. III, 488
Ketcham, Martha T. III, 483
Ketcham, Martha T. III, 488
Ketcham, Martin III, 488
Ketcham, Mary III, 191
Ketcham, Mary III, 423
Ketcham, Mary A. F. III, 488
Ketcham, Mary Ann III, 191
Ketcham, Mary Elizabeth III, 488
Ketcham, Mary L. III, 422
Ketcham, Melissa III, 488
Ketcham, Nathaniel III, 488
Ketcham, Peter V. III, 488
Ketcham, Phebe III, 191
Ketcham, Phebe III, 423
Ketcham, Phebe III, 483
Ketcham, Phebe III, 488
Ketcham, Phebe III, 506
Ketcham, Phebe H. III, 488
Ketcham, Phebe H. III, 490
Ketcham, Phebe Jane III, 191
Ketcham, Phebe Jane III, 346
Ketcham, Phebe P. III, 191
Ketcham, Phebe S. III, 191
Ketcham, Philetus III, 423
Ketcham, Philip III, 488
Ketcham, Rebecca III, 483
Ketcham, Rebecca III, 487
Ketcham, Rebecca III, 488
Ketcham, Rebecca III, 499
Ketcham, Ruth III, 488
Ketcham, Ruth H. III, 488
Ketcham, Samuel III, 191
Ketcham, Sarah III, 191
Ketcham, Sarah III, 488
Ketcham, Sarah III, 490
Ketcham, Sarah Ann III, 191
Ketcham, Sarah M. III, 488
Ketcham, Sarah P. III, 191
Ketcham, Susie III, 488
Ketcham, Sybil P. III, 488
Ketcham, Terry III, 488
Ketcham, Thomas III, 191
Ketcham, William III, 488
Ketcham, William A. III, 488
Ketcher, Rachel H. III, 255
Ketcher, Rachel H. III, 362
Ketchin, J. Brinton III, 134
Ketchin, Mina III, 134
Ketchum, ??? III, 191
Ketchum, Samuel III, 191
Keton, Ann I, 131
Keton, Ann I, 144
Keton, Henry I, 91
Keton, Sarah I, 144
Keton, Sarah I, 172
Kettell, Hope II, 236
Kettell, Jane II, 236
Kettell, Rachel II, 236
Kettle, Hope II, 236
Kettle, Jane II, 236
Kettle, Rachel II, 236
Ketzel, Ida Schoonover V, 689
Keutch, Viola V, 1005
Kevil, Mary VI, 820
Kevode, Ann IV, 96
Kevode, Ann IV, 113
Key, Abigail II, 385
Key, Alice II, 573
Key, Ann II, 30
Key, Ann Elizabeth VI, 878
Key, Anna I, 1157
Key, Barberry VI, 918
Key, Betsy VI, 831
Key, Charles H. VI, 946
Key, Docia VI, 946
Key, Dora I, 1157
Key, Doshia VI, 1007
Key, Eliza J. VI, 946
Key, Elizabeth I, 1157
Key, Elizabeth II, 573
Key, Elizabeth VI, 815
Key, Elizabeth VI, 831
Key, Elizabeth P. VI, 1007
Key, Elnora G. VI, 882
Key, Enoch I, 1157
Key, Frances G. VI, 946
Key, Frankey VI, 857
Key, George VI, 946
Key, George VI, 1007
Key, Izbell VI, 946
Key, J. C. I, 1157
Key, Jacob VI, 800
Key, Jacob VI, 815
Key, Jacob VI, 835
Key, Jacob VI, 857
Key, Jacob VI, 874
Key, James C. I, 1157
Key, John II, 385
Key, John II, 573
Key, John VI, 878
Key, John VI, 886
Key, John VI, 946
Key, John VI, 963
Key, John, Jr. II, 573
Key, Joseph I, 1157
Key, Joseph II, 30
Key, Josiah II, 82
Key, Judith VI, 963
Key, Lenora IV, 1214
Key, Lou Emma I, 1157
Key, Lucy VI, 800
Key, Malinda VI, 968
Key, Malinda A. I, 1157
Key, Martin VI, 951
Key, Mary II, 481
Key, Mary II, 571
Key, Mary VI, 806
Key, Mary VI, 815
Key, Mary VI, 946
Key, Mildred F. VI, 946
Key, Mildred P. VI, 951
Key, Milly VI, 835
Key, Nancy VI, 946
Key, Nelson J. VI, 968
Key, Pelina VI, 946
Key, Pleasant VI, 831
Key, Pleasant VI, 867
Key, Rebecca II, 30
Key, Rebecka II, 385
Key, Robert VI, 806
Key, Sally VI, 867
Key, Sally VI, 946
Key, Sarah II, 385
Key, Sarah II, 573
Key, Stanfield VI, 946
Key, Suckey VI, 946
Key, Thomas VI, 831
Key, Thomas VI, 835
Key, Thomas VI, 946
Key, Thomas W. B. VI, 946
Key, Tilman VI, 946
Key, Uriah VI, 946
Key, William I, 1157
Key, William VI, 806
Key, William VI, 831
Key, William VI, 867
Key, Winney Caudle VI, 886
Key, Wm. II, 573
Keyes, Ames III, 110
Keyes, Elizabeth II, 1007
Keys, Benjamin I, 977
Keys, Benjamin P. I, 981
Keys, Benjamin P. I, 991
Keys, Benjamin S. I, 991
Keys, Daniel I, 977
Keys, Elizabeth I, 977
Keys, Elizabeth I, 981
Keys, Elizabeth I, 991
Keys, Elizabeth I, 997
Keys, Emma M. V, 31
Keys, Emma M. V, 89
Keys, Frances G. VI, 946
Keys, Hannah I, 977
Keys, Hannah I, 991
Keys, Hannah I, 998
Keys, Henry M. VI, 882
Keys, Ida V, 459
Keys, Ida M. V, 257
Keys, J. C. I, 1157
Keys, J. Milton V, 89
Keys, James C. I, 1140
Keys, James C. I, 1144
Keys, John I, 977
Keys, John VI, 946
Keys, Joseph I, 403
Keys, Joseph I, 414
Keys, Joseph I, 823
Keys, Joseph I, 977
Keys, Joseph I, 991
Keys, Joseph I, 993
Keys, Joseph, Jr. I, 971
Keys, Joseph, Jr. I, 977
Keys, Joseph, Jr. I, 991
Keys, Joseph, Sr. I, 977
Keys, Joseph, Sr. I, 991
Keys, Lydia I, 823
Keys, Lydia I, 971
Keys, Lydia I, 991
Keys, Martha D. VI, 892
Keys, Mary I, 403
Keys, Mary I, 414
Keys, Mary I, 977
Keys, Mary I, 991
Keys, Pelina VI, 946
Keys, Rachel IV, 481
Keys, Rachel IV, 504
Keys, Rebecah I, 983
Keys, Rebecah I, 991
Keys, Rebecca I, 403
Keys, Rebecca I, 977
Keys, Rebekah I, 823
Keys, Ruth I, 977
Keys, Ruth I, 991
Keys, Ruth I, 993
Keys, Sarah II, 573
Keys, Sarah II, 686
Keys, Stanfield VI, 946
Keys, Stephen R. V, 89
Keys, Thomas IV, 481
Keys, Thomas VI, 892
Keys, Tilman VI, 892
Keys, Warren V, 89
Keyser, Alta L. IV, 1324
Keyser, Andrew Dirck II, 820
Keyser, Anna II, 885
Keyser, Catharine II, 885
Keyser, Catharine II, 901
Keyser, Chas. II, 804
Keyser, Chas. II, 885
Keyser, Cley IV, 1238
Keyser, Ella IV, 730
Keyser, Ella IV, 1238
Keyser, Henry IV, 730
Keyser, Ira IV, 1324
Keyser, Jane W. II, 885
Keyser, Jane Wood II, 885
Keyser, Jerusha S. III, 402
Keyser, Mary IV, 730
Keyser, Rebecca II, 820
Keyser, Solomon IV, 730
Keyser, Susanna II, 885
Keyser, Susannah II, 885
Keyser, Wd. Catharine II, 804
Keyser, Wd. Rebecca Jane II, 820
Keysor, Mary V, 1005
Kheemle, Margaret II, 573
Kibby, Ambrose V, 507
Kibby, Ambrose V, 689
Kibby, Effie V, 507
Kibby, Laura V, 507
Kibby, Laura V, 689
Kibby, Lillie V, 689
Kibby, Lily V, 689
Kibby, Louisa V, 507
Kibby, Louisa V, 689
Kibby, Louisa C. V, 689
Kibby, Mary E. V, 689
Kibby, Norah B. V, 689
Kibby, Oren V, 689
Kibby, Orin V, 689
Kibby, Oscar V, 507
Kibby, Thomas E. V, 409
Kiber, Martin IV, 1283
Kibly, Thomas E. V, 409
Kicherer, Alice III, 191
Kicherer, John C. III, 191
Kid, Isabel II, 72
Kid, Isabel II, 82
Kidd, Ann M. VI, 831
Kidd, Annie E. I, 403
Kidd, Arnold VI, 831
Kidd, Delia VI, 831
Kidd, Elizabeth VI, 946
Kidd, Henry VI, 831
Kidd, Henry D. VI, 831
Kidd, Henry D. VI, 946
Kidd, Isabel II, 82
Kidd, John VI, 833
Kidd, John A. VI, 946
Kidd, John W. VI, 831
Kidd, Lewis B. VI, 831
Kidd, Marth II, 82
Kidd, Martha II, 82
Kidd, Martha II, 108
Kidd, Mary II, 385
Kidd, Mary VI, 831
Kidd, Mary C. VI, 946
Kidd, Nancy M. I, 403
Kidd, Obediah VI, 833
Kidd, Patsey VI, 831
Kidd, Polly VI, 833
Kidd, Samuel III, 191
Kidd, Sarah I, 403
Kidd, William I, 403
Kidd, William II, 385
Kidd, William H. VI, 831
Kidley, Thomas VI, 74
Kidney, Aurilla IV, 1214
Kidney, Aurilla IV, 1221
Kidney, George IV, 1221
Kidney, Helen A. IV, 1214
Kidney, Helen A. IV, 1221
Kiedd, Marth II, 82
Kiefer, Jane VI, 505
Kiefer, Jane VI, 524
Kieffer, Clara III, 227
Kieffer, Geo. III, 423
Kieffer, Jennie III, 423
Kieffer, Reginald III, 423
Kiehl, Anna Maria IV, 1134
Kiehl, Anna Maria IV, 1135
Kieht, George VI, 13
Kier, Francis M. V, 344
Kier, Mary E. V, 257
Kier, Mary E. V, 344
Kiger, Huldah V, 89
Kiger, Lillian R. II, 132
Kiger, Minnie V, 631
Kiger, Vina V, 409
Kiggins, Albert V, 1005
Kight, Hannah II, 386
Kight, James II, 386
Kight, James, Jr. II, 386
Kight, John II, 386
Kight, Mary II, 574
Kiker, Elizabeth III, 191
Kilborn, Frances II, 573
Kilborn, Frances II, 679
Kilborn, John II, 573
Kilborn, John II, 679
Kilborn, Rachel II, 573
Kilborn, Rachel II, 679
Kilbreath, Katharine L. IV, 639
Kilbreath, Katharine L. IV, 641
Kilbreath, Sarah I, 606
Kilby, Robert V, 469
Kilcop, John II, 573
Kilcup, Elizabeth II, 556
Kilcup, Elizabeth II, 573
Kilcup, John II, 573
Kilcup, Mary II, 573
Kilcup, Mary II, 635
Kilden, John II, 573
Kilden, John, Jr. II, 573
Kildon, Allen V, 507
Kildon, Azel V, 507
Kildow, Allen V, 507
Kildow, Azel V, 507
Kildow, Eber Azel V, 507
Kildow, Eliza Jane V, 507
Kildow, Eunice Lewvenia V, 507
Kildow, Eunice Louvenia V, 507
Kildow, Harvey Allen V, 507
Kildow, James V, 689
Kildow, Joseph V, 689
Kildow, Joseph A. V, 507
Kildow, Joseph Abraham V, 507
Kildow, Margaret Ann V, 507
Kildow, Michael V, 507
Kildow, Michael L. V, 507
Kildow, Viola V, 507
Kile, Michell II, 385
Kilham, Elijah IV, 481
Kilham, Elizabeth IV, 481
Kilham, Joseph IV, 481
Kilham, Nathaniel IV, 481
Kilham, Sarah IV, 481
Kilham, Susanna IV, 481
Killcrece, Birdie L. IV, 730
Killcrece, Sarah E. IV, 730
Killcrece, William H. IV, 730
Kille, ??? II, 236
Kille, Abraham II, 194
Kille, Abraham II, 236
Kille, Alpharetta IV, 972
Kille, Ann IV, 972
Kille, Ann IV, 979
Kille, Anna Gaunt II, 134
Kille, Anna Gaunt II, 152
Kille, Anna M. IV, 972
Kille, Benjamin IV, 972
Kille, Benjamin A. IV, 972
Kille, Charles W. IV, 972
Kille, Chas. Omar IV, 972
Kille, Chas. W. IV, 972
Kille, Clayton IV, 96
Kille, Clayton IV, 694
Kille, Clayton IV, 933
Kille, Clayton IV, 972
Kille, Clayton IV, 992
Kille, Clayton IV, 996
Kille, Edith IV, 972
Kille, Edmund IV, 941
Kille, Eleanor Caroline II, 134
Kille, Eleanor Caroline II, 152
Kille, Eli IV, 972
Kille, Eli S. IV, 972
Kille, Elizabeth IV, 972
Kille, Elizabeth IV, 987
Kille, Elizabeth IV, 992
Kille, Elizabeth IV, 996
Kille, Elizabeth P. IV, 972
Kille, Elmer B. IV, 972
Kille, Emma Alter IV, 972
Kille, Eva H. II, 134
Kille, Eva H. G. II, 152
Kille, Florence Rebecca II, 321
Kille, Hannah IV, 972
Kille, Helen Noreen II, 134
Kille, Helen Noreen II, 152
Kille, Horace Fillmore II, 134
Kille, Horace Fillmore II, 152
Kille, Isaac IV, 972
Kille, Isaac C. IV, 972
Kille, Isaac Clever IV, 972
Kille, Isaac E. IV, 972
Kille, Isaac E. IV, 987
Kille, Jane IV, 96
Kille, Jane IV, 101
Kille, Jane IV, 972
Kille, Jane M. IV, 959
Kille, Jane M. IV, 972
Kille, Jemima IV, 972
Kille, Jemima IV, 1018
Kille, Job II, 236
Kille, John II, 194
Kille, John II, 236
Kille, John IV, 96
Kille, John IV, 101
Kille, John IV, 972
Kille, Leeward IV, 972
Kille, Martha J. IV, 972
Kille, Martha Jane IV, 941
Kille, Martha Jane IV, 972
Kille, Mary IV, 933
Kille, Mary IV, 972
Kille, Mary IV, 996
Kille, Mary IV, 1209
Kille, Mary IV, 1214
Kille, Mary Emma IV, 972
Kille, Omer IV, 972
Kille, Rachel II, 194
Kille, Rachel II, 236
Kille, Rebecca IV, 96
Kille, Rebecca IV, 694

Kille, Rebecca IV, 959
Kille, Rebecca IV, 972
Kille, Ruth IV, 972
Kille, Sarah II, 82
Kille, Sarah IV, 941
Kille, Sarah B. II, 321
Kille, Seward J. IV, 972
Kille, Thomas IV, 972
Kille, William IV, 972
Kille, Wilmore II, 134
Kille, Wilmore B. II, 152
Kille, Wm. IV, 959
Kille, Wm. IV, 972
Killee, Martha J. IV, 972
Killee, Martha J. IV, 976
Killem, Ann I, 555
Killen, Alice VI, 510
Killett, Alice II, 1054
Killett, Chester Holden II, 1054
Killett, Elbert Edmund II, 1054
Killett, Elinor May II, 1054
Killett, Elsie Marie II, 1054
Killett, Harrold Drewey II, 1054
Killett, Jesse Derbyshire II, 1054
Killett, Nancy II, 1054
Killett, Wm. II, 1054
Killey, Charity I, 555
Killey, Charity I, 1016
Killey, Margaret II, 794
Killie, Ann IV, 972
Killie, Clayton IV, 730
Killie, Clayton IV, 972
Killie, Elizabeth IV, 972
Killie, Isaac IV, 730
Killie, Isaac Clever IV, 972
Killie, Jemima IV, 972
Killie, John IV, 972
Killie, Martha IV, 730
Killie, Mary IV, 972
Killie, Rebecca IV, 730
Killie, Rebecca IV, 972
Killie, Thomas IV, 972
Killie, William IV, 972
Killum, Esther I, 555
Killum, Noah I, 555
Killum, Noah I, 888
Killy, Hannah IV, 829
Killy, Hannah IV, 853
Kilpatrick, Sarah III, 191
Kilsey, ??? III, 404
Kilsey, ??? III, 423
Kilsey, Lorette III, 404
Kilsey, Lorrette III, 423
Kimbal, Phebe II, 977
Kimbal, Phebe II, 1007
Kimbal, Rachel II, 573
Kimbal, Ruth IV, 639
Kimbal, Thomas Bayly II, 1007
Kimball, Blanche L. III, 191
Kimball, David N. I, 764
Kimball, Evaline P. III, 58
Kimball, Evaline P. III, 106
Kimball, Florence III, 191
Kimball, Florence Chevy III, 191
Kimball, Florence Chevy III, 294
Kimball, Florence M. III, 294
Kimball, Francis W. III, 191
Kimball, Francis W. III, 294
Kimball, John III, 231
Kimball, L. P. IV, 1255
Kimball, Martha III, 191
Kimball, Martha P. III, 191
Kimball, Martha R. III, 231
Kimball, Pauline III, 421
Kimball, Percival C. III, 294
Kimball, Priscilla I, 756
Kimball, Priscilla I, 764
Kimball, Sarah III, 231
Kimball, Wm. C. III, 191
Kimball, Wm. L. III, 270
Kimball, Wm. Lockwood III, 191
Kimbeau, Polly VI, 942
Kimbel, David N. I, 764
Kimbell, Georgia H. I, 929
Kimber, Amie M. III, 192
Kimber, Ann III, 192
Kimber, Anna II, 385
Kimber, Anna II, 573
Kimber, Anna II, 809
Kimber, Anna III, 192
Kimber, Anna III, 381
Kimber, Anna M. III, 192
Kimber, Anthony M. IV, 233
Kimber, Edward H. II, 886
Kimber, Edward Hicks II, 385
Kimber, Edward Hicks II, 750
Kimber, Elizabeth V, 575
Kimber, Elizabeth V, 580
Kimber, Elizabeth D. II, 227
Kimber, Ellwood W. II, 886
Kimber, Ellwood Walter II, 750
Kimber, Ellwood Walter II, 804
Kimber, Elward H. II, 886
Kimber, Elwood W. II, 886
Kimber, Elwood Walter II, 573
Kimber, Emmer, Jr. II, 750
Kimber, Emmor J. II, 885
Kimber, Emmor, Jr. II, 385
Kimber, Emmor, Jr. II, 573
Kimber, Emmor, Jr. II, 750
Kimber, Emmor, Jr. II, 798
Kimber, Emmor, Jr. II, 804
Kimber, Emmor, Jr. II, 885
Kimber, Emmor, Jr. II, 886
Kimber, Emmor, Sr. II, 809
Kimber, Geo. D. III, 192
Kimber, George III, 381
Kimber, George D. III, 192
Kimber, H. III, 192
Kimber, Harriet A. III, 192
Kimber, Harriet A. III, 296
Kimber, Harriet A. III, 365
Kimber, Harriet Ann III, 192
Kimber, Joshua II, 227
Kimber, Joshua II, 236
Kimber, Joshua II, 385
Kimber, Joshua II, 573
Kimber, Joshua III, 192
Kimber, Joshua III, 271
Kimber, Joshua III, 381
Kimber, Joshua, Jr. III, 192
Kimber, Louisa III, 192
Kimber, Lydia II, 385
Kimber, Lydia II, 573
Kimber, Lydia II, 750
Kimber, Lydia II, 798
Kimber, Lydia II, 804
Kimber, Lydia II, 885
Kimber, Lydia II, 886
Kimber, Lydia G. III, 192
Kimber, Lydia G. III, 381
Kimber, Margaret C. IV, 233
Kimber, Marmaduke C. V, 689
Kimber, Mary A. III, 192
Kimber, Mary Louisa II, 804
Kimber, Mary S. III, 286
Kimber, Phebe M. III, 70
Kimber, Phebe M. III, 192
Kimber, Rachel II, 385
Kimber, Rachel III, 192
Kimber, Rachel III, 271
Kimber, Rachel I. II, 227
Kimber, Rachel I. II, 236
Kimber, Rachel J. II, 236
Kimber, Rachel J. II, 573
Kimber, Rachel J. III, 381
Kimber, Richard II, 227
Kimber, Richard II, 236
Kimber, Richard H. II, 886
Kimber, Richard R. II, 886
Kimber, Samuel Gummere II, 385
Kimber, Samuel R. II, 227
Kimber, Sarah II, 825
Kimber, Sarah III, 192
Kimber, Sarah III, 271
Kimber, Susan II, 573
Kimber, Susan IV, 93
Kimber, Susan IV, 96
Kimber, Susanna II, 227
Kimber, Susanna II, 236
Kimber, Susanna II, 573
Kimber, Susanna II, 809
Kimber, Taressa I. II, 886
Kimber, Taressa J. II, 885
Kimber, Teressa J. II, 573
Kimber, Theresa II, 797
Kimber, Theresa II, 798
Kimber, Theresa G. II, 750
Kimber, Thomas III, 192
Kimber, Thomas III, 286
Kimber, William III, 192
Kimber, William G. III, 192
Kimber, William G. III, 381
Kimberley, Elizabeth IV, 30
Kimberley, Elizabeth IV, 43
Kimberlick, Amy V, 89
Kimberlin, Elsie IV, 1324
Kimberling, Louisa IV, 481
Kimberly, ??? III, 99
Kimberly, Amos E. IV, 730
Kimberly, Elizabeth IV, 730
Kimberly, Ellen IV, 972
Kimberly, Esther III, 181
Kimberly, Esther III, 192
Kimberly, Isabell I, 1076
Kimberly, Iseabel I, 1075
Kimberly, Jane IV, 730
Kimberly, John IV, 730
Kimberly, Louisa IV, 481
Kimberly, Mary IV, 233
Kimberly, Mrs. Samuel IV, 233
Kimberly, Samuel IV, 730
Kimberly, Thomas I, 1076
Kimberly, Wm. IV, 730
Kimbert, Geo. D. III, 192
Kimbert, Harriet Ann III, 192
Kimble, Jane IV, 635
Kimble, Jane IV, 639
Kimble, Martha II, 236
Kimble, Rachel II, 236
Kimble, Ruth II, 236
Kimble, Ruth IV, 639
Kimble, Susan S. II, 321
Kimble, Susan S. II, 323
Kimble, William II, 236
Kimbro, Elizabeth V, 566
Kimbro, Jeremiah V, 915
Kimbro, Lula L. V, 915
Kimbro, Rhoda V, 915
Kimbro, Susanna V, 566
Kimbro, Thomas V, 566
Kimbro, Willard V, 580
Kimbro, Willard V, 915
Kimbrough, Anna V, 580
Kimbrough, Anna B. V, 580
Kimbrough, Anna B. V, 689
Kimbrough, Caroline V, 89
Kimbrough, Charity V, 507
Kimbrough, Charity V, 575
Kimbrough, Charity V, 580
Kimbrough, Clark V, 689
Kimbrough, Clifford V, 580
Kimbrough, Clifford E. V, 580
Kimbrough, Clifford E. V, 689
Kimbrough, D. V, 580
Kimbrough, Demas V, 689
Kimbrough, Demetrius V, 580
Kimbrough, Demetrius V, 689
Kimbrough, Dennice V, 580
Kimbrough, Eddie V, 580
Kimbrough, Edith V, 696
Kimbrough, Edward J. IV, 1255
Kimbrough, Elizabeth IV, 1255
Kimbrough, Elizabeth V, 566
Kimbrough, Elizabeth V, 580
Kimbrough, Elizabeth V, 679
Kimbrough, Elizabeth V, 689
Kimbrough, Elizabeth V, 721
Kimbrough, Ellen IV, 933
Kimbrough, Ellen V, 675
Kimbrough, Ellsworth V, 580
Kimbrough, Elva V, 580
Kimbrough, Elva M. V, 689
Kimbrough, Estella E. V, 580
Kimbrough, Ester V, 580
Kimbrough, Esther V, 574
Kimbrough, Esther V, 580
Kimbrough, Esther V, 689
Kimbrough, Esther C. V, 580
Kimbrough, Esther C. V, 689
Kimbrough, Esther E. V, 689
Kimbrough, Ethel V, 580
Kimbrough, Ethel M. V, 689
Kimbrough, J. Eddie V, 689
Kimbrough, J. Edward IV, 1255
Kimbrough, J. Omar V, 689
Kimbrough, Jeremiah V, 507
Kimbrough, Jeremiah V, 568
Kimbrough, Jeremiah V, 580
Kimbrough, Jeremiah V, 689
Kimbrough, Jeremiah J. V, 574
Kimbrough, Jeremiah J. V, 580
Kimbrough, John V, 689
Kimbrough, Lawson V, 580
Kimbrough, Lawson V, 689
Kimbrough, Lewis Hiatt V, 507
Kimbrough, Lizzie IV, 1255
Kimbrough, Louisa V, 557
Kimbrough, Louisa V, 580
Kimbrough, Louise V, 689
Kimbrough, Lulu V, 580
Kimbrough, Lulu L. V, 689
Kimbrough, Lulu S. V, 580
Kimbrough, Mary V, 663
Kimbrough, Nancy V, 689
Kimbrough, Nancy E. V, 563
Kimbrough, Nancy E. V, 580
Kimbrough, Nancy Emily V, 580
Kimbrough, Ora V, 580
Kimbrough, Orah M. V, 580
Kimbrough, Orah M. V, 689
Kimbrough, Pamela V, 580
Kimbrough, Permelia V, 89
Kimbrough, Permelia V, 580
Kimbrough, Permelia V, 606
Kimbrough, Raymond J. V, 580
Kimbrough, Raymond J. V, 689
Kimbrough, Rhoda V, 580
Kimbrough, Rhoda Ann V, 568
Kimbrough, Rhoda Ann V, 580
Kimbrough, Rhoda E. V, 580
Kimbrough, Rhoda E. V, 689
Kimbrough, Sarah, Jr. V, 580
Kimbrough, Susanna V, 580
Kimbrough, Susannah V, 568
Kimbrough, Susannah V, 676
Kimbrough, Thomas V, 689
Kimbrough, Timothy V, 580
Kimbrough, Timothy C. V, 563
Kimbrough, Timothy C. V, 689
Kimbrough, Willard V, 580
Kimbrough, Willard T. V, 580
Kimbrough, Willard T. V, 689
Kime, Bertha IV, 1039
Kime, Ray IV, 1039
Kime, Sarah IV, 1039
Kimell, Daniel II, 385
Kimell, Jacob II, 385
Kimell, Susanna II, 385
Kimmer, Homer V, 580
Kimmer, Jane V, 580
Kimmer, Mary Alice V, 580
Kimmer, Samuel V, 580
Kimmey, Mary J. II, 698
Kimmins, Elizabeth I, 535
Kimmins, Elizabeth I, 583
Kimnsey, Hope II, 206
Kimnsey, Hope II, 237
Kimsey, Sarah II, 152
Kimsey, Sarah II, 160
Kincade, Constance VI, 831
Kincade, Robert VI, 831
Kincaid, Flora Pier V, 184
Kincaid, Hannah P. II, 886
Kincaid, Hannah P. II, 929
Kinchn, Catherine IV, 1283
Kinchn, Newsom IV, 1283
Kinchn, Ortice IV, 1283
Kinchn, Tabitha IV, 1283
Kinck, C. M. V, 184
Kinck, Elbert V, 184
Kinck, Mary E. V, 184
Kinckle, William H. VI, 901
Kinckle, William H. VI, 981
Kind, Robert V, 1005
Kindell, Phebe II, 385
Kinder, Arthur IV, 233
Kinder, Bertha IV, 233
Kinder, Ida H. IV, 233
Kinder, Margeretta IV, 233
Kinder, Mary IV, 233
Kinderdine, M. Ella II, 885
Kinderdine, Mary II, 572
Kinderdine, Sarah II, 572
Kinding, John II, 445
Kindley, Ann V, 90
Kindley, Asa V, 89
Kindley, Asa V, 90
Kindley, Bette V, 90
Kindley, Betty V, 89
Kindley, Betty V, 544
Kindley, Betty V, 794
Kindley, Cornelia V, 90
Kindley, Cornelius V, 89
Kindley, Daniel V, 89
Kindley, Daniel V, 90
Kindley, Daniel V, 884
Kindley, Daniel, Jr. V, 884
Kindley, David V, 89
Kindley, Davis V, 89
Kindley, Davis V, 90
Kindley, Dinah V, 57
Kindley, Dinah V, 89
Kindley, Dinah V, 171
Kindley, Dinah V, 184
Kindley, Edward V, 57
Kindley, Edward V, 67
Kindley, Edward V, 89
Kindley, Edward V, 90
Kindley, Edward V, 113
Kindley, Edward V, 884
Kindley, Edward V, 955
Kindley, Eliza V, 90
Kindley, Elizabeth V, 89
Kindley, Elizabeth V, 794
Kindley, Emily V, 90
Kindley, Emily V, 884
Kindley, Emma V, 89
Kindley, Emma V, 90
Kindley, Enoch V, 89
Kindley, Enoch V, 90
Kindley, Enoch V, 884
Kindley, Frederic V, 54
Kindley, Frederic V, 90
Kindley, Frederick V, 89
Kindley, Frederick V, 90
Kindley, Frederick V, 951
Kindley, Frederick V, 955
Kindley, Isaac V, 89
Kindley, Isaac V, 90
Kindley, Jane V, 90
Kindley, Joel V, 89
Kindley, John V, 89
Kindley, John V, 90
Kindley, John V, 544
Kindley, John V, 794
Kindley, Jonathan V, 89
Kindley, Margaret I, 723
Kindley, Margaret V, 57
Kindley, Margaret V, 67
Kindley, Margaret V, 89
Kindley, Margaret V, 90
Kindley, Margaret V, 113
Kindley, Margaret V, 884
Kindley, Margaret V, 886
Kindley, Margaret V, 955
Kindley, Margaret Jane V, 89
Kindley, Margaret Jane V, 884
Kindley, Mary V, 89
Kindley, Mary V, 90
Kindley, Mary V, 113
Kindley, Mary V, 951
Kindley, Mary V, 955
Kindley, Mary, Jr. V, 54
Kindley, Mary, Jr. V, 90
Kindley, Maryann V, 89
Kindley, Priscilla V, 879
Kindley, Priscilla V, 884
Kindley, Rachel V, 89
Kindley, Rebecca V, 89
Kindley, Rebekah V, 67
Kindley, Rebekah V, 89
Kindley, Ruth V, 89
Kindley, Ruth V, 794
Kindley, Sarah V, 89
Kindley, Sarah V, 90
Kindley, Sarah V, 794
Kindley, Sarah V, 884
Kindley, Sarah V, 886
Kindley, Sarah E. V, 89
Kindley, Sarah Eliza V, 884
Kindley, Susan V, 89
Kindley, Susan V, 90
Kindley, Susan V, 884
Kindley, Susan E. V, 884
Kindley, Susanna V, 884
Kindly, Daniel V, 887
Kindly, Isaac V, 90
Kindly, Susan V, 887
Kineon, Margaret I, 195
Kinesly, Charles II, 386
Kiney, William I, 310
King, ??? III, 193
King, ??? IV, 730
King, ??? IV, 1047
King, ??? V, 751
King, Abel IV, 415
King, Abel IV, 1064
King, Abigail II, 236
King, Abigail II, 294
King, Abigail II, 304
King, Abigail II, 386
King, Abigail II, 573
King, Abigail III, 193
King, Abraham VI, 946
King, Abraham VI, 962
King, Abram L. V, 90
King, Adella IV, 1016
King, Alfred II, 886
King, Alfred IV, 1063
King, Alfred IV, 1064
King, Alice I, 556
King, Alice II, 445
King, Alice IV, 1214
King, Alice R. I, 890
King, Alice R. I, 929
King, Allen V, 507
King, Almyra V, 507
King, Alta Florence III, 192
King, Ambrose VI, 946
King, Amos IV, 1064
King, Amos V, 580
King, Andrew M. IV, 1324
King, Ann II, 178
King, Ann II, 573
King, Ann II, 689
King, Ann III, 192
King, Ann III, 227
King, Ann III, 315
King, Ann III, 381
King, Ann IV, 151
King, Ann IV, 339
King, Ann IV, 382
King, Ann IV, 415
King, Ann IV, 1063
King, Ann VI, 832
King, Ann VI, 946
King, Ann K. III, 81
King, Anna II, 178
King, Anna II, 236
King, Anna II, 288
King, Anna II, 291
King, Anna II, 293
King, Anna II, 294

ing, Anna II, 301
ing, Anna II, 386
ing, Anna II, 573
ing, Anna II, 689
ing, Anna III, 193
ing, Anna IV, 585
ing, Anna IV, 591
ing, Anna IV, 1064
ing, Anna Anabe V, 184
ing, Anna E. II, 294
ing, Anna R. IV, 233
ing, Anna Wilson II, 178
ing, Annabella II, 385
ing, Annabella II, 709
ing, Annabella II, 750
ing, Anne II, 294
ing, Anne II, 304
ing, Anne II, 573
ing, Anne IV, 1064
ing, Anne IV, 1071
ing, Arthur V, 580
ing, Avary VI, 946
ing, Avery VI, 946
ing, Avery VI, 962
ing, Avra VI, 947
ing, Benjamin II, 385
ing, Benjamin VI, 946
ing, Bessie V, 184
ing, Bettie VI, 75
ing, Bettie C. VI, 92
ing, Betty VI, 946
ing, Bryant VI, 946
ing, C. W. I, 620
ing, Caleb VI, 946
ing, Calvin V, 507
ing, Caroline III, 185
ing, Caroline III, 192
ing, Caroline III, 193
ing, Caroline III, 227
ing, Caroline IV, 151
ing, Caroline IV, 339
ing, Caroline IV, 1063
ing, Caroline IV, 1064
ing, Carrie IV, 233
ing, Catharine II, 712
ing, Catharine III, 192
ing, Catharine IV, 151
ing, Catharine IV, 1064
ing, Catharine VI, 831
ing, Catharine Murray IV, 151
ng, Catharine Murry IV, 339
ing, Catherine V, 580
ng, Charles VI, 831
ng, Charles VI, 946
ng, Charles D. III, 381
ing, Charles E. V, 90
ing, Chloe V, 257
ng, Chloe V, 278
ing, Chooe V, 257
ing, Christine Lois III, 192
ing, Clarissa V, 507
ng, Clarissa V, 915
ng, Claudine V, 751
ng, Content IV, 415
ng, Content IV, 450
ng, Content IV, 1063
ng, Content IV, 1064
ng, Cora IV, 829
ng, Cordelia I, 935
ng, Cordelia I, 944
ng, Cordelia I, 950
ng, Curtis IV, 782
ng, Cyrus IV, 1064
ng, David V, 580
ng, David Sands III, 192
ng, Dean V, 90
ng, Dean V, 480
ng, Dean V, 507
ng, Dean V, 915
ng, Dean V, 972
ng, Dearman W. IV, 1064
ng, Deborah IV, 415
ng, Deborah IV, 1063
ng, Deborah IV, 1064
ng, Deborah IV, 1078
ng, Deerman IV, 1064
ng, Della I, 1157
ng, Dorothy III, 192
ng, Dorris IV, 730
ng, Druella V, 751
ng, Edith IV, 1324
ng, Edward V, 507
ng, Edward F. IV, 233
ng, Edward Joshua III, 192
ng, Edward S. I, 944
ng, Edward Skull I, 929
ng, Edward Skull I, 944
ng, Eleaner II, 386
ng, Eleanor II, 236
ng, Eleanor II, 293
ng, Eleanor II, 301
King, Eleanor II, 573
King, Eleanor III, 192
King, Eleanor III, 193
King, Eleanor III, 315
King, Elender VI, 946
King, Eli IV, 1064
King, Elias III, 192
King, Elijah V, 409
King, Elisha I, 1157
King, Eliza III, 192
King, Eliza III, 193
King, Eliza IV, 1063
King, Eliza VI, 946
King, Elizabeth I, 931
King, Elizabeth II, 178
King, Elizabeth II, 231
King, Elizabeth II, 236
King, Elizabeth II, 1007
King, Elizabeth II, 1015
King, Elizabeth III, 192
King, Elizabeth IV, 151
King, Elizabeth IV, 161
King, Elizabeth IV, 233
King, Elizabeth IV, 339
King, Elizabeth IV, 1063
King, Elizabeth IV, 1064
King, Elizabeth IV, 1214
King, Elizabeth V, 90
King, Elizabeth V, 507
King, Elizabeth V, 948
King, Elizabeth V, 955
King, Elizabeth VI, 524
King, Elizabeth VI, 577
King, Elizabeth VI, 832
King, Elizabeth VI, 918
King, Elizabeth VI, 1009
King, Elizabeth G. II, 294
King, Elizabeth L. V, 253
King, Elizabeth Rogers V, 689
King, Elizabeth Rogers V, 692
King, Elizabeth T. III, 364
King, Ellen III, 51
King, Ellen III, 192
King, Ellwood IV, 1064
King, Emily V, 253
King, Emma III, 137
King, Emma V, 580
King, Emma Gurney I, 556
King, Emma Gurney I, 890
King, Estella IV, 1324
King, Esther V, 480
King, Esther V, 507
King, Esther B. VI, 75
King, Eurity V, 915
King, Everett W. IV, 1324
King, Ezra IV, 1063
King, Ezra IV, 1064
King, Fanny III, 193
King, Florence E. IV, 1283
King, Francis I, 636
King, Frank IV, 973
King, Frank L. IV, 972
King, Frank L. IV, 973
King, Franklin F. V, 409
King, Fred IV, 481
King, George C. II, 178
King, George G. II, 294
King, Gill VI, 937
King, Gillam VI, 983
King, Gilliam VI, 946
King, Grace IV, 1064
King, Grace IV, 1070
King, Grace T. IV, 1056
King, Grace T. IV, 1058
King, Grace T. IV, 1064
King, Gurney, Jr. I, 944
King, Hannah II, 236
King, Hannah II, 263
King, Hannah II, 385
King, Hannah III, 192
King, Hannah III, 227
King, Hannah IV, 151
King, Hannah IV, 339
King, Hannah IV, 415
King, Hannah IV, 455
King, Hannah IV, 585
King, Hannah IV, 1063
King, Hannah IV, 1064
King, Hannah IV, 1076
King, Hannah IV, 1103
King, Hannah V, 507
King, Hannay IV, 1064
King, Harmans III, 192
King, Harmon IV, 415
King, Harriet III, 192
King, Harriet Fox II, 294
King, Harry IV, 233
King, Henry V, 507
King, Henry D. V, 90
King, Henry D. V, 972
King, Hiram IV, 1238
King, Howard IV, 233
King, Howard K. II, 886
King, Hyram IV, 1064
King, Ida W. IV, 1324
King, Iden IV, 233
King, Iris VI, 946
King, Irving III, 192
King, Isaac IV, 151
King, Isaac IV, 382
King, Isaac IV, 415
King, Isaac L. IV, 233
King, Isaac L. V, 915
King, Isabell IV, 395
King, Isabell IV, 415
King, Isabella IV, 151
King, Isabella E. IV, 925
King, Israel V, 507
King, J. J. IV, 829
King, Jacob IV, 151
King, Jacob IV, 415
King, Jacob IV, 1064
King, James III, 488
King, James III, 495
King, James IV, 415
King, James IV, 1063
King, James IV, 1064
King, James V, 580
King, James VI, 831
King, James VI, 946
King, James J. IV, 829
King, James L. I, 890
King, James M. V, 580
King, James W. IV, 972
King, James W. IV, 1064
King, James, Jr. III, 192
King, James, Jr. IV, 1064
King, Jane I, 538
King, Jane I, 555
King, Jane III, 192
King, Jane IV, 151
King, Jane IV, 161
King, Jane IV, 339
King, Jane IV, 537
King, Jane IV, 554
King, Jane IV, 1169
King, Jane IV, 1182
King, Jane H. VI, 862
King, Jenny VI, 946
King, Jephtha IV, 1064
King, Jeptha IV, 415
King, Jeptha IV, 1064
King, Jesse VI, 831
King, Jesse W. VI, 831
King, Jno. VI, 844
King, John II, 385
King, John II, 445
King, John III, 51
King, John III, 81
King, John III, 185
King, John III, 192
King, John III, 227
King, John III, 364
King, John IV, 151
King, John IV, 339
King, John V, 253
King, John V, 915
King, John VI, 32
King, John VI, 36
King, John VI, 801
King, John VI, 931
King, John VI, 946
King, John A. V, 90
King, John Bowne III, 192
King, John Bowne IV, 339
King, John Brown IV, 151
King, John Paul II, 294
King, John T. V, 90
King, John T. V, 972
King, John W. VI, 831
King, John W. VI, 862
King, Joseph II, 178
King, Joseph II, 236
King, Joseph II, 385
King, Joseph II, 386
King, Joseph II, 573
King, Joseph II, 689
King, Joseph III, 105
King, Joseph III, 192
King, Joseph III, 238
King, Joseph III, 315
King, Joseph III, 381
King, Joseph IV, 151
King, Joseph IV, 415
King, Joseph IV, 422
King, Joseph IV, 585
King, Joseph IV, 591
King, Joseph IV, 1063
King, Joseph IV, 1064
King, Joseph IV, 1071
King, Joseph IV, 1076
King, Joseph IV, 1103
King, Joseph VI, 63
King, Joseph VI, 75
King, Joseph B. III, 193
King, Joseph H. III, 193
King, Joseph R. II, 174
King, Joseph R. II, 178
King, Joseph R. II, 236
King, Joseph R. II, 288
King, Joseph R. II, 293
King, Joseph R. II, 294
King, Joseph R. II, 573
King, Joseph, Jr. III, 193
King, Joseph, Jr. III, 381
King, Joshua IV, 1283
King, Josiah VI, 75
King, Judah VI, 983
King, Julyann IV, 1064
King, Katharine III, 193
King, Katharine IV, 151
King, Katharine J. III, 193
King, Katie I, 337
King, Killis E. VI, 931
King, Killis E. VI, 946
King, L. VI, 832
King, L. VI, 844
King, Lackville VI, 862
King, Laura I, 926
King, Laura III, 62
King, Laura III, 193
King, Laura IV, 1324
King, Lavina IV, 1063
King, Lavina IV, 1064
King, Lavina IV, 1092
King, Lavina IV, 1103
King, Leola IV, 1256
King, Leroy IV, 1039
King, Levina V, 915
King, Levinus V, 507
King, Levynas V, 915
King, Lewis IV, 1063
King, Lewis IV, 1064
King, Link I, 1157
King, Lottie IV, 730
King, Lottie IV, 972
King, Louella I, 636
King, Louetta I, 636
King, Louisa V, 507
King, Louisa VI, 946
King, Lubie I, 337
King, Lucinda IV, 1103
King, Lucy II, 291
King, Lucy II, 294
King, Lula IV, 1256
King, Lydia IV, 1064
King, Lydia Jane IV, 1064
King, Lydia Lane IV, 1062
King, Lydia M. IV, 1256
King, Mae Osborn V, 689
King, Magdalena V, 915
King, Maggie V, 580
King, Margaret Ann I, 615
King, Mariam IV, 1063
King, Martha IV, 415
King, Martha IV, 1064
King, Martha V, 90
King, Martha VI, 803
King, Martha VI, 1009
King, Martha E. V, 90
King, Martha E. V, 184
King, Martha T. IV, 1064
King, Martha W. VI, 804
King, Martin VI, 977
King, Martin VI, 1009
King, Martin, Jr. VI, 946
King, Mary I, 636
King, Mary I, 929
King, Mary I, 935
King, Mary I, 1049
King, Mary I, 1050
King, Mary II, 174
King, Mary II, 178
King, Mary II, 231
King, Mary II, 236
King, Mary II, 288
King, Mary II, 293
King, Mary II, 573
King, Mary II, 672
King, Mary III, 105
King, Mary III, 192
King, Mary III, 225
King, Mary III, 227
King, Mary III, 238
King, Mary III, 381
King, Mary IV, 151
King, Mary IV, 233
King, Mary IV, 339
King, Mary IV, 415
King, Mary IV, 422
King, Mary IV, 1063
King, Mary IV, 1064
King, Mary IV, 1076
King, Mary IV, 1078
King, Mary IV, 1103
King, Mary V, 507
King, Mary V, 891
King, Mary V, 915
King, Mary VI, 831
King, Mary A. III, 182
King, Mary A. VI, 801
King, Mary A. VI, 863
King, Mary Adel IV, 233
King, Mary Alice IV, 1064
King, Mary Ann III, 182
King, Mary Ann III, 193
King, Mary Ann III, 227
King, Mary Ann III, 238
King, Mary Ann V, 409
King, Mary Ann V, 507
King, Mary Ann VI, 962
King, Mary Cornelia I, 929
King, Mary E. I, 636
King, Mary E. V, 90
King, Mary E. V, 972
King, Mary G. II, 178
King, Mary J. VI, 820
King, Mary Jane IV, 193
King, Mary Jane IV, 233
King, Mary R. III, 51
King, Mary R. III, 81
King, Mary R. III, 185
King, Mary R. III, 192
King, Mary R. III, 193
King, Mary R. III, 227
King, Mary R. III, 364
King, Mary S. IV, 1058
King, Mary S. IV, 1064
King, Mary, Jr. II, 236
King, Mary, Jr. II, 1001
King, Mary, Jr. II, 1007
King, May V, 689
King, May V, 702
King, Melissa A. V, 90
King, Mercy IV, 233
King, Mercy IV, 415
King, Mercy IV, 1063
King, Mercy IV, 1064
King, Mercy Ann V, 507
King, Mercy Ann V, 522
King, Michael IV, 151
King, Michael IV, 415
King, Michael IV, 455
King, Michael IV, 585
King, Michael IV, 1063
King, Michael IV, 1064
King, Michael IV, 1092
King, Michael IV, 1103
King, Miles II, 236
King, Millie IV, 782
King, Milly VI, 946
King, Miram VI, 960
King, Miranda IV, 782
King, Mrs. Gurney I, 944
King, Murry J. IV, 829
King, Nancy VI, 937
King, Nancy VI, 946
King, Nancy VI, 947
King, Nancy VI, 1006
King, Nancy E. V, 409
King, Nancy Ellen V, 409
King, Nancy L. VI, 946
King, Nany VI, 946
King, Naomi V, 507
King, Nathan IV, 233
King, Obed IV, 415
King, Obed IV, 1063
King, Obed IV, 1064
King, Olive IV, 973
King, Olive VI, 75
King, Olive V. VI, 92
King, Phebe III, 192
King, Phebe III, 227
King, Phebe IV, 415
King, Phebe IV, 416
King, Phebe IV, 455
King, Phebe IV, 1064
King, Phebe IV, 1070
King, Phebe V, 915
King, Phebe Ann IV, 1169
King, Philip III, 192
King, Philip Burk III, 192
King, Phineas L. V, 915
King, Polly VI, 818
King, Polly VI, 844
King, Polly VI, 946
King, Priscilla IV, 730
King, Quincy V, 90
King, R. P. I, 556
King, Rachel III, 192
King, Rachel IV, 1103
King, Rachel IV, 1116
King, Rachel V, 257
King, Rachel V, 265

King, Rachel V, 507
King, Reay II, 178
King, Reay II, 236
King, Reay II, 288
King, Reay II, 291
King, Reay II, 293
King, Reay II, 294
King, Reay II, 301
King, Reay II, 304
King, Reay II, 386
King, Reay II, 573
King, Reay II, 689
King, Reay III, 192
King, Reay III, 193
King, Rebecca II, 573
King, Rebecca IV, 218
King, Rebecca IV, 233
King, Rebecca IV, 415
King, Rebecca IV, 1063
King, Rebecca IV, 1064
King, Rebecca IV, 1066
King, Rebecca E. I, 682
King, Rebecca E. I, 692
King, Rebecca W. II, 294
King, Rebeckah IV, 151
King, Rebekah IV, 415
King, Rebekah IV, 455
King, Rhoda Ann V, 90
King, Richard II, 445
King, Robert I, 1157
King, Robert IV, 1063
King, Robert IV, 1064
King, Robert E. III, 192
King, Rosana I, 555
King, Rosanna I, 555
King, Rufus P. I, 890
King, Rufus P. I, 929
King, Russell V, 580
King, Ruth IV, 1049
King, Ruth IV, 1063
King, Ruth IV, 1064
King, Ruth IV, 1076
King, Ruth A. I, 587
King, Ruth Anna IV, 1214
King, Sackville VI, 804
King, Sackville VI, 852
King, Sally V, 90
King, Sally V, 915
King, Sally V, 972
King, Sally VI, 977
King, Samuel II, 236
King, Samuel II, 445
King, Samuel III, 192
King, Samuel IV, 151
King, Samuel IV, 339
King, Samuel IV, 415
King, Samuel IV, 450
King, Samuel IV, 455
King, Samuel IV, 1056
King, Samuel IV, 1058
King, Samuel IV, 1063
King, Samuel IV, 1064
King, Samuel IV, 1078
King, Sara Ann IV, 1058
King, Sarah II, 178
King, Sarah II, 236
King, Sarah II, 293
King, Sarah II, 294
King, Sarah II, 321
King, Sarah II, 801
King, Sarah III, 192
King, Sarah III, 193
King, Sarah III, 323
King, Sarah IV, 415
King, Sarah IV, 1063
King, Sarah IV, 1064
King, Sarah IV, 1084
King, Sarah V, 90
King, Sarah V, 116
King, Sarah V, 507
King, Sarah V, 915
King, Sarah A. II, 879
King, Sarah A. II, 886
King, Sarah Ann IV, 1064
King, Sarah E. C. VI, 63
King, Sarah E. C. VI, 75
King, Sarah J. III, 367
King, Sarah King IV, 1064
King, Sarah M. IV, 1064
King, Seckville VI, 825
King, Sinea VI, 946
King, Stephen III, 193
King, Susan VI, 411
King, Susan G. VI, 397
King, Susanah II, 82
King, Susannah II, 82
King, Susannah II, 526
King, Susannah II, 573
King, Theodotia VI, 906
King, Thomas II, 385
King, Thomas II, 386
King, Thomas II, 445
King, Thomas II, 573
King, Thomas III, 381
King, Thomas III, 389
King, Thomas IV, 161
King, Thomas V, 90
King, Thomas V, 507
King, Thomas Clarkson V, 507
King, Thomas J. III, 227
King, Thomas W. V, 90
King, Thomas W. V, 915
King, Thomas W. V, 972
King, Thos. Ellwood II, 886
King, Thos. L. II, 886
King, Thos. W. V, 972
King, Uretta V, 915
King, Uritta V, 915
King, Uritta V, 924
King, Vera Luella I, 620
King, Violetta IV, 1059
King, Violetta IV, 1064
King, W. C. Wells I, 944
King, Walter III, 192
King, Wd. Lucy II, 178
King, Wilbur V, 580
King, William I, 682
King, William IV, 1063
King, William IV, 1064
King, William V, 257
King, William V, 689
King, William V, 702
King, William V, 751
King, William VI, 803
King, William VI, 820
King, William VI, 832
King, William VI, 906
King, William VI, 946
King, William Anthony I, 929
King, William Anthony I, 935
King, William G. II, 178
King, William G. IV, 233
King, William Henry III, 227
King, William Nelson III, 193
King, William S. III, 193
King, William W. II, 294
King, William Wilson II, 178
King, William Wilson II, 236
King, William Wilson II, 291
King, William Wilson II, 386
King, William Wilton II, 294
King, Wilson II, 573
King, Winnie L. I, 1157
King, Wm. II, 526
King, Wm. II, 573
King, Wm. IV, 730
King, Wm. IV, 1049
King, Wm. IV, 1064
King, Wm. Irving IV, 233
King, Wm. Nelson III, 193
King, Wm. S. III, 173
King, Wm. Sutcliff III, 193
King, Zilpha IV, 401
King, Zilpha IV, 402
King, Zilpha IV, 415
King, Zilpha IV, 416
Kingery, Ada V, 631
Kingh, Andrew I, 556
Kingh, Andrew I, 574
Kingh, Ruth I, 556
Kingh, Ruth I, 574
Kingkade, Jesse IV, 836
Kingkade, John IV, 836
Kingkade, Mary Jane IV, 829
Kingkade, Mary Jane IV, 835
Kingman, O. F. IV, 1169
Kingman, Sarah IV, 1210
Kingman, Sarah IV, 1214
Kingsberry, Abey Sally IV, 730
Kingsland, ??? III, 193
Kingsland, ??? III, 306
Kingsland, Daniel III, 193
Kingsland, Eliza L. III, 193
Kingsland, Henry III, 193
Kingsland, Mary I. III, 193
Kingsland, Mary J. III, 193
Kingsland, Mary J. III, 216
Kingsland, Mary Jane III, 193
Kingsland, Wm. H. III, 193
Kingsland, Wm. M. III, 193
Kingsland, Wm. M. III, 216
Kingsley, Ann II, 573
Kingsley, Ann II, 665
Kingsley, Esther II, 573
Kingsley, Gladys IV, 730
Kingsley, John IV, 730
Kingsley, Lillian Shaffer IV, 730
Kingsley, Wd. Isabella III, 193
Kingsley, Zephania III, 193
Kingsmith, Elsie E. III, 275
Kingston, Kathleen III, 21
Kingston, Kathleen III, 117
Kingun, Polly VI, 945
Kinkead, Amy T. III, 143
Kinkead, Amy T. III, 193
Kinkead, Amy T. III, 279
Kinkead, Cath. J. III, 193
Kinkead, Dorothy III, 143
Kinkead, Dorothy III, 193
Kinkead, Edward Maxwell III, 193
Kinkead, Maxwell III, 193
Kinkead, Wm. L. III, 143
Kinkead, Wm. L. III, 193
Kinkead, Wm. Lloyd III, 193
Kinkead, Wm. Lloyd III, 279
Kinley, Ann V, 306
Kinley, Betty V, 508
Kinley, Betty V, 543
Kinley, Dan IV, 43
Kinley, Davis IV, 43
Kinley, Edward I, 723
Kinley, Edward IV, 43
Kinley, Edward V, 17
Kinley, Elizabeth I, 709
Kinley, Elizabeth I, 723
Kinley, Frederick IV, 43
Kinley, Isaac IV, 43
Kinley, John IV, 43
Kinley, John V, 508
Kinley, John V, 543
Kinley, Margaret I, 695
Kinley, Margaret I, 723
Kinley, Margaret IV, 43
Kinley, Margaret V, 17
Kinley, Marget I, 723
Kinley, Rebecca IV, 43
Kinley, Rebeckah I, 723
Kinly, Daniel II, 386
Kinly, William II, 386
Kinnard, Elizabeth II, 386
Kinnard, Margaret Leslie II, 785
Kinnard, Margaret Leslie II, 813
Kinnard, Margaret Leslie II, 816
Kinnard, Tacy II, 798
Kinneon, Hannah I, 140
Kinneon, Hannah I, 144
Kinnet, John VI, 1006
Kinnet, Katy VI, 1006
Kinnet, Polly VI, 869
Kinnett, Burchy M. VI, 937
Kinnett, James F. VI, 945
Kinnett, Mildred VI, 945
Kinnett, Sary VI, 945
Kinney, ??? III, 193
Kinney, Abie IV, 1283
Kinney, Alice IV, 345
Kinney, Alice L. IV, 1283
Kinney, Anna V, 507
Kinney, Anna F. II, 885
Kinney, Annie D. II, 885
Kinney, Carl IV, 1283
Kinney, David IV, 1169
Kinney, Edith II, 885
Kinney, Edith T. II, 885
Kinney, James F. III, 193
Kinney, James M. I, 965
Kinney, Lillian Wynn IV, 1283
Kinney, Louisa IV, 1214
Kinney, Nannie V, 507
Kinney, Naomi Huff V, 631
Kinney, Rebecca II, 572
Kinney, Rebecca II, 639
Kinney, Richard IV, 233
Kinnier, Andrew VI, 831
Kinnier, Ann E. VI, 831
Kinnings, Robert V, 508
Kinnion, Benjamin I, 56
Kinnion, Hannah I, 50
Kinnion, Hannah I, 56
Kinnison, Elizabeth II, 573
Kinnison, Joseph II, 573
Kinnison, Sarah IV, 128
Kinnison, Sarah IV, 134
Kinnison, Sarah IV, 135
Kinnit, Nancy VI, 945
Kinnit, Thomas VI, 945
Kinny, ??? III, 193
Kinny, Arabella C. III, 193
Kinny, David III, 193
Kinny, Helen Eliza III, 193
Kinny, James F. III, 193
Kinny, Sadie R. IV, 481
Kinny, Sarah Ann III, 193
Kinsell, John Milburn IV, 232
Kinsell, Lemuel Cornelius IV, 232
Kinser, Catharine VI, 961
Kinsey, ??? V, 184
Kinsey, ??? VI, 738
Kinsey, Aaron IV, 96
Kinsey, Aaron IV, 185
Kinsey, Aaron IV, 233
Kinsey, Aaron IV, 234
Kinsey, Aaron IV, 416
Kinsey, Aaron IV, 1064
Kinsey, Abi IV, 416
Kinsey, Abi IV, 1064
Kinsey, Abraham V, 915
Kinsey, Abram V, 915
Kinsey, Absalam IV, 339
Kinsey, Absalom IV, 339
Kinsey, Absalom IV, 481
Kinsey, Absalom IV, 537
Kinsey, Absalom V, 649
Kinsey, Absolam IV, 537
Kinsey, Absolom IV, 96
Kinsey, Absolom IV, 234
Kinsey, Absolom IV, 481
Kinsey, Addie V, 184
Kinsey, Alcesta II, 978
Kinsey, Alcesta II, 1007
Kinsey, Alcesta II, 1020
Kinsey, Alfred IV, 233
Kinsey, Alice IV, 235
Kinsey, Alice E. IV, 235
Kinsey, Amos E. IV, 234
Kinsey, Amos G. IV, 233
Kinsey, Ann I, 310
Kinsey, Ann II, 237
Kinsey, Ann II, 271
Kinsey, Ann II, 750
Kinsey, Ann IV, 233
Kinsey, Ann IV, 234
Kinsey, Ann IV, 241
Kinsey, Ann IV, 296
Kinsey, Ann IV, 305
Kinsey, Ann IV, 307
Kinsey, Ann IV, 481
Kinsey, Ann IV, 537
Kinsey, Ann V, 52
Kinsey, Ann V, 90
Kinsey, Ann V, 649
Kinsey, Ann C. V, 904
Kinsey, Ann C. V, 915
Kinsey, Ann E. V, 90
Kinsey, Ann E. V, 915
Kinsey, Ann Lucy IV, 234
Kinsey, Anna IV, 233
Kinsey, Anna IV, 251
Kinsey, Anna IV, 481
Kinsey, Anna IV, 490
Kinsey, Anna IV, 973
Kinsey, Anna V, 1005
Kinsey, Anna L. IV, 234
Kinsey, Anna R. IV, 1039
Kinsey, Anne II, 178
Kinsey, Anne R. IV, 1039
Kinsey, Annie E. IV, 973
Kinsey, Annie R. IV, 235
Kinsey, Anny I, 303
Kinsey, Anny I, 310
Kinsey, Benjamin II, 1007
Kinsey, Benjamin II, 1020
Kinsey, Benjamin II, 1037
Kinsey, Benjamin IV, 96
Kinsey, Benjamin IV, 152
Kinsey, Benjamin IV, 416
Kinsey, Benjamin IV, 481
Kinsey, Benjamin IV, 1064
Kinsey, C. B. V, 184
Kinsey, Caleb IV, 233
Kinsey, Caleb B. IV, 234
Kinsey, Caroline E. IV, 234
Kinsey, Cassandra IV, 234
Kinsey, Cassandra IV, 235
Kinsey, Cassandra IV, 248
Kinsey, Catharine II, 779
Kinsey, Charles II, 178
Kinsey, Charles II, 237
Kinsey, Charles II, 386
Kinsey, Charles II, 573
Kinsey, Charles IV, 75
Kinsey, Charles IV, 96
Kinsey, Charles IV, 233
Kinsey, Charles IV, 234
Kinsey, Charles IV, 537
Kinsey, Charles IV, 538
Kinsey, Charles V, 184
Kinsey, Chas. IV, 177
Kinsey, Chas. IV, 213
Kinsey, Chas. IV, 234
Kinsey, Chas. IV, 279
Kinsey, Chas. IV, 307
Kinsey, Christopher IV, 96
Kinsey, Christopher IV, 234
Kinsey, Christopher IV, 339
Kinsey, Christopher IV, 481
Kinsey, Christopher IV, 537
Kinsey, Christopher IV, 538
Kinsey, Christopher V, 184
Kinsey, Christopher V, 508
Kinsey, Claudius IV, 538
Kinsey, Cyrus V, 915
Kinsey, Cyrus G. V, 915
Kinsey, Daniel IV, 538
Kinsey, Daniel D. IV, 537
Kinsey, David II, 386
Kinsey, David II, 573
Kinsey, David II, 574
Kinsey, David, Jr. II, 573
Kinsey, Deborah IV, 233
Kinsey, Dr. John II, 804
Kinsey, Dwight Hillis V, 1005
Kinsey, Edith IV, 234
Kinsey, Edith IV, 235
Kinsey, Edith IV, 973
Kinsey, Edith E. IV, 235
Kinsey, Edith E. C. IV, 235
Kinsey, Edith E. C. IV, 730
Kinsey, Edmond II, 386
Kinsey, Edmond IV, 234
Kinsey, Edmond IV, 339
Kinsey, Edmond IV, 481
Kinsey, Edmond, Jr. II, 386
Kinsey, Edmund II, 574
Kinsey, Edmund II, 709
Kinsey, Edmund II, 1007
Kinsey, Edmund II, 1037
Kinsey, Edmund IV, 152
Kinsey, Edmund IV, 234
Kinsey, Edmund IV, 537
Kinsey, Edmund IV, 538
Kinsey, Edmund V, 508
Kinsey, Edward F. IV, 1039
Kinsey, Edward T. IV, 235
Kinsey, Edwards F. IV, 1039
Kinsey, Eleanor II, 573
Kinsey, Eleanor IV, 511
Kinsey, Eleanor IV, 537
Kinsey, Eleanor IV, 538
Kinsey, Elenor V, 508
Kinsey, Eliz. III, 132
Kinsey, Eliz. M. III, 183
Kinsey, Eliza IV, 538
Kinsey, Eliza IV, 546
Kinsey, Eliza Ann IV, 43
Kinsey, Elizabeth I Sup 1, 4
Kinsey, Elizabeth II, 219
Kinsey, Elizabeth II, 220
Kinsey, Elizabeth II, 237
Kinsey, Elizabeth II, 386
Kinsey, Elizabeth II, 804
Kinsey, Elizabeth II, 881
Kinsey, Elizabeth II, 886
Kinsey, Elizabeth II, 946
Kinsey, Elizabeth II, 949
Kinsey, Elizabeth IV, 43
Kinsey, Elizabeth IV, 233
Kinsey, Elizabeth IV, 234
Kinsey, Elizabeth IV, 307
Kinsey, Elizabeth IV, 481
Kinsey, Elizabeth IV, 503
Kinsey, Elizabeth IV, 538
Kinsey, Elizabeth IV, 540
Kinsey, Elizabeth IV, 1064
Kinsey, Elizabeth VI, 759
Kinsey, Elizabeth Ann V, 631
Kinsey, Elizabeth D. IV, 233
Kinsey, Elizabeth E. IV, 234
Kinsey, Elizabeth E. IV, 538
Kinsey, Elizabeth L. IV, 221
Kinsey, Elizabeth L. IV, 234
Kinsey, Elizabeth L. IV, 235
Kinsey, Elizabeth L. IV, 476
Kinsey, Elizabeth L. IV, 481
Kinsey, Elizabeth L. IV, 505
Kinsey, Elizabeth M. II, 881
Kinsey, Elizabeth M. II, 886
Kinsey, Ella V, 184
Kinsey, Emma II, 835
Kinsey, Emma II, 886
Kinsey, Esther II, 1007
Kinsey, Esther IV, 1063
Kinsey, Esther IV, 1064
Kinsey, Evaline IV, 234
Kinsey, Ezra IV, 233
Kinsey, Ezra IV, 234
Kinsey, Ezra V, 915
Kinsey, Ezra VI, 524
Kinsey, Ezra VI, 760
Kinsey, Fanney V, 184
Kinsey, Fanney H. V, 508
Kinsey, Fanny IV, 537
Kinsey, Fanny IV, 538
Kinsey, Fanny V, 184
Kinsey, Fanny H. V, 184
Kinsey, Francis Lowell V, 1005
Kinsey, Frank E. V, 1005
Kinsey, Geo IV, 295
Kinsey, Geo. IV, 233
Kinsey, Geo. IV, 234
Kinsey, Geo. IV, 251
Kinsey, Geo. IV, 296
Kinsey, Geo. IV, 537

sey, Geo. VI, 759
sey, George II, 1007
sey, George IV, 228
sey, George IV, 233
sey, George IV, 234
sey, George IV, 416
sey, George IV, 537
sey, George IV, 538
sey, George B. IV, 234
sey, George B. IV, 973
sey, George B. IV, 1039
sey, George Wm. IV, 234
sey, George, Jr. IV, 234
sey, George, Jr. IV, 416
sey, Gillingham W. IV, 234
sey, Gillingham W. IV, 537
sey, Gulingham IV, 233
sey, Hannah II, 178
sey, Hannah II, 237
sey, Hannah IV, 234
sey, Hannah V, 90
sey, Hannah V, 915
sey, Hannah V, 920
sey, Hannah Ann V, 344
sey, Hannah Ann V, 915
sey, Hannah Ann V, 916
sey, Hannah, Jr. II, 214
sey, Harrison M. IV, 235
sey, Harrison M. V, 344
sey, Harry M. V, 344
sey, Harry Raymond V, 1005
sey, Hirah IV, 234
sey, Hiram IV, 152
sey, Hiram IV, 233
sey, Hope II, 237
sey, Irene V, 184
sey, Isaac II, 1007
sey, Isaac IV, 233
sey, Isaac IV, 730
sey, Isaac V, 915
sey, Isaac V, 916
sey, Isaac L. IV, 235
sey, Isaac L. IV, 730
sey, Isaac L. IV, 973
sey, Isabella V, 184
sey, Isabella Anna V, 184
sey, Jacob IV, 481
sey, James II, 83
sey, James II, 178
sey, James II, 214
sey, James II, 237
sey, James II, 386
sey, James II, 573
sey, James II, 574
sey, James IV, 152
sey, James IV, 233
sey, James IV, 234
sey, James IV, 241
sey, James IV, 305
sey, James D. IV, 234
sey, James D. IV, 235
sey, James G. IV, 233
sey, James G. IV, 234
sey, James G. IV, 307
sey, James G. IV, 481
sey, James G. IV, 505
sey, James, Jr. II, 83
sey, James, Jr. II, 237
sey, James, Jr. IV, 234
nsey, Jane II, 1007
nsey, Jane IV, 152
nsey, Jane IV, 233
nsey, Jane IV, 235
nsey, Jane V, 344
nsey, Jane G. V, 915
nsey, Jane G. V, 920
nsey, Jane M. V, 915
nsey, Jane M. V, 916
nsey, Jas. IV, 481
nsey, Jephtha IV, 233
nsey, Jesse IV, 43
nsey, Jesse IV, 96
nsey, Jesse IV, 339
nsey, Jesse IV, 481
nsey, Jesse IV, 523
nsey, Jesse IV, 537
nsey, Jesse IV, 538
nsey, Jesse H. IV, 561
nsey, John I Sup 1, 4
nsey, John I Sup 1, 5
nsey, John II, 163
nsey, John II, 178
nsey, John II, 237
nsey, John II, 386
nsey, John II, 572
nsey, John II, 573
nsey, John II, 660
nsey, John II, 835
nsey, John II, 842
insey, John II, 886
insey, John IV, 96
Kinsey, John IV, 152
Kinsey, John IV, 222
Kinsey, John IV, 233
Kinsey, John IV, 234
Kinsey, John IV, 268
Kinsey, John IV, 339
Kinsey, John IV, 481
Kinsey, John IV, 511
Kinsey, John IV, 537
Kinsey, John IV, 538
Kinsey, John V, 508
Kinsey, John B. IV, 538
Kinsey, John Gaylord V, 1005
Kinsey, John L. IV, 233
Kinsey, John, Jr. II, 573
Kinsey, Jonathan II, 83
Kinsey, Jonathan II, 574
Kinsey, Jonathan B. IV, 537
Kinsey, Jonathan B. V, 508
Kinsey, Joseph II, 386
Kinsey, Joseph II, 574
Kinsey, Joseph IV, 43
Kinsey, Joseph V, 915
Kinsey, Joseph V, 916
Kinsey, Josephine V, 915
Kinsey, Julia E. IV, 537
Kinsey, Kersey II, 178
Kinsey, Kersey W. IV, 233
Kinsey, Kinsey IV, 234
Kinsey, Kinsey IV, 537
Kinsey, Laura M. V, 847
Kinsey, Lemuel IV, 233
Kinsey, Leo B. IV, 1039
Kinsey, Letitia II, 783
Kinsey, Lewis I, 310
Kinsey, Lewis IV, 481
Kinsey, Lewis V, 508
Kinsey, Louisa IV, 1214
Kinsey, Louisa IV, 1226
Kinsey, Louisa V, 508
Kinsey, Lucinda IV, 233
Kinsey, Lucinda IV, 234
Kinsey, Lucinda IV, 538
Kinsey, Lucy IV, 476
Kinsey, Lydia IV, 234
Kinsey, Lydia IV, 538
Kinsey, Lydia Ann IV, 152
Kinsey, Lydia Ann IV, 233
Kinsey, Lydia Ann IV, 234
Kinsey, Lydia Ann IV, 295
Kinsey, Lydia W. IV, 234
Kinsey, Lydia W. IV, 538
Kinsey, Macy V, 508
Kinsey, Margaret II, 835
Kinsey, Margaret II, 842
Kinsey, Margaret II, 886
Kinsey, Margaret IV, 234
Kinsey, Margaret V, 649
Kinsey, Margaret V, 915
Kinsey, Margaret B. IV, 234
Kinsey, Margaret B. IV, 279
Kinsey, Margaret B. IV, 973
Kinsey, Margaret B. IV, 999
Kinsey, Margaret B. IV, 1000
Kinsey, Margaret B. IV, 1002
Kinsey, Margaret Elizabeth V, 1005
Kinsey, Margaret L. IV, 229
Kinsey, Margaret L. IV, 234
Kinsey, Margaret L. IV, 235
Kinsey, Margaret L. IV, 969
Kinsey, Margaret L. IV, 1039
Kinsey, Margaret L. V, 916
Kinsey, Maria IV, 43
Kinsey, Maria IV, 47
Kinsey, Maria IV, 234
Kinsey, Maria IV, 481
Kinsey, Martha II, 1007
Kinsey, Martha II, 1037
Kinsey, Martha IV, 416
Kinsey, Martha IV, 1064
Kinsey, Martha E. IV, 537
Kinsey, Martha Eliza IV, 538
Kinsey, Mary I, 303
Kinsey, Mary I, 310
Kinsey, Mary II, 178
Kinsey, Mary II, 237
Kinsey, Mary II, 386
Kinsey, Mary II, 572
Kinsey, Mary II, 573
Kinsey, Mary IV, 96
Kinsey, Mary IV, 152
Kinsey, Mary IV, 194
Kinsey, Mary IV, 222
Kinsey, Mary IV, 228
Kinsey, Mary IV, 233
Kinsey, Mary IV, 234
Kinsey, Mary IV, 251
Kinsey, Mary IV, 268
Kinsey, Mary IV, 295
Kinsey, Mary IV, 339
Kinsey, Mary IV, 537
Kinsey, Mary IV, 538
Kinsey, Mary V, 184
Kinsey, Mary V, 344
Kinsey, Mary V, 916
Kinsey, Mary V, 918
Kinsey, Mary A. V, 344
Kinsey, Mary A. V, 916
Kinsey, Mary Ann IV, 233
Kinsey, Mary Ann IV, 234
Kinsey, Mary Ann IV, 235
Kinsey, Mary Ann IV, 481
Kinsey, Mary Ann IV, 538
Kinsey, Mary Ann V, 344
Kinsey, Mary Ann V, 508
Kinsey, Mary Ann V, 513
Kinsey, Mary Anne IV, 537
Kinsey, Mary D. IV, 233
Kinsey, Mary E. IV, 235
Kinsey, Mary E. IV, 1039
Kinsey, Mary Eliza IV, 213
Kinsey, Mary Eliza IV, 234
Kinsey, Mary Elizabeth IV, 481
Kinsey, Mary L. V, 916
Kinsey, Mary P. V, 915
Kinsey, Mary S. II, 717
Kinsey, Mary S. IV, 234
Kinsey, Mary S. IV, 538
Kinsey, Mary T. IV, 234
Kinsey, Matilda V, 508
Kinsey, Mercy IV, 233
Kinsey, Mercy IV, 234
Kinsey, Mercy IV, 241
Kinsey, Mercy IV, 305
Kinsey, Mercy IV, 969
Kinsey, Mercy L. IV, 234
Kinsey, Mercy L. IV, 235
Kinsey, Mercy L. IV, 1039
Kinsey, Mercy L. V, 916
Kinsey, Meriman IV, 233
Kinsey, Milton V, 508
Kinsey, Miriam IV, 152
Kinsey, Miriam IV, 233
Kinsey, Miriam IV, 268
Kinsey, Mootry III, 193
Kinsey, Nancy IV, 339
Kinsey, Nancy IV, 481
Kinsey, Nancy IV, 522
Kinsey, Nancy IV, 537
Kinsey, Naomi IV, 523
Kinsey, Naomi IV, 537
Kinsey, Naomi IV, 538
Kinsey, Naomi IV, 561
Kinsey, Nathan IV, 96
Kinsey, Nathan IV, 234
Kinsey, Nathan IV, 339
Kinsey, Nathan IV, 481
Kinsey, Nathan IV, 537
Kinsey, Nathan J. IV, 234
Kinsey, Nathan L. V, 508
Kinsey, Nathaniel II, 886
Kinsey, Nathaniel V, 90
Kinsey, Nathaniel V, 915
Kinsey, Nathaniel V, 916
Kinsey, Nathaniel V, 920
Kinsey, Nathaniel F. II, 881
Kinsey, Nathaniel, Jr. V, 916
Kinsey, Oliver IV, 339
Kinsey, Oliver IV, 538
Kinsey, Oliver V, 915
Kinsey, Oliver V, 916
Kinsey, Oliver C. IV, 234
Kinsey, Oliver C. IV, 538
Kinsey, Oliver J. IV, 233
Kinsey, Pearson V, 915
Kinsey, Phebe IV, 234
Kinsey, Phebe IV, 248
Kinsey, Phebe IV, 538
Kinsey, Phebe Anna II, 717
Kinsey, Phebe M. IV, 234
Kinsey, Phebe M. IV, 538
Kinsey, Philip II, 178
Kinsey, Philip II, 386
Kinsey, Philip II, 574
Kinsey, Piersen V, 915
Kinsey, Priscilla I Sup 1, 4
Kinsey, Priscilla I Sup 1, 5
Kinsey, Priscilla I Sup 1, 6
Kinsey, Rachel IV, 339
Kinsey, Rachel IV, 481
Kinsey, Rachel IV, 537
Kinsey, Rachel IV, 538
Kinsey, Rachel V, 90
Kinsey, Rachel V, 478
Kinsey, Rachel V, 508
Kinsey, Rachel V, 915
Kinsey, Rachel C. V, 90
Kinsey, Rachel C. V, 915
Kinsey, Rachel C. V, 916
Kinsey, Rachel Ella V, 344
Kinsey, Rachel Ella V, 915
Kinsey, Rachel Ella V, 916
Kinsey, Rachel G. V, 344
Kinsey, Rachel G. V, 915
Kinsey, Rachel G. V, 916
Kinsey, Rease IV, 538
Kinsey, Rebecca IV, 481
Kinsey, Rebecca IV, 487
Kinsey, Rebecca VI, 524
Kinsey, Rebecca VI, 526
Kinsey, Rebecca VI, 760
Kinsey, Rebecca VI, 761
Kinsey, Rees IV, 537
Kinsey, Rhoda IV, 43
Kinsey, Rhoda IV, 96
Kinsey, Rhoda IV, 339
Kinsey, Rhoda IV, 481
Kinsey, Rhoda Emeline IV, 538
Kinsey, Richard IV, 43
Kinsey, Richard IV, 96
Kinsey, Richard IV, 152
Kinsey, Richard IV, 326
Kinsey, Richard IV, 339
Kinsey, Richard IV, 481
Kinsey, Richard IV, 537
Kinsey, Richard IV, 538
Kinsey, Ridley IV, 339
Kinsey, Ridley IV, 481
Kinsey, Robert Cooper IV, 43
Kinsey, Ruth IV, 339
Kinsey, Ruth IV, 481
Kinsey, Ruth IV, 537
Kinsey, Ruth IV, 538
Kinsey, Ruth V, 508
Kinsey, Ruth V, 542
Kinsey, Ruth VI, 759
Kinsey, Ruth Ann IV, 234
Kinsey, Ruth Ann IV, 467
Kinsey, Ruth Ann IV, 481
Kinsey, Ruth Anna IV, 234
Kinsey, Ruthann IV, 481
Kinsey, Ruthanna IV, 233
Kinsey, Ruthanna IV, 234
Kinsey, Sallie E. V, 915
Kinsey, Sallie E. V, 916
Kinsey, Samuel II, 1007
Kinsey, Samuel IV, 233
Kinsey, Samuel IV, 235
Kinsey, Samuel IV, 476
Kinsey, Samuel V, 344
Kinsey, Samuel A. IV, 235
Kinsey, Samuel A. IV, 1039
Kinsey, Samuel B. IV, 234
Kinsey, Samuel B. IV, 537
Kinsey, Samuel B. IV, 538
Kinsey, Samuel B. V, 344
Kinsey, Samuel B. V, 508
Kinsey, Samuel B. V, 915
Kinsey, Samuel B. V, 916
Kinsey, Samuel B., Jr. V, 344
Kinsey, Samuel, Jr. V, 344
Kinsey, Sarah II, 178
Kinsey, Sarah II, 386
Kinsey, Sarah II, 573
Kinsey, Sarah II, 660
Kinsey, Sarah II, 842
Kinsey, Sarah II, 886
Kinsey, Sarah II, 1007
Kinsey, Sarah II, 1037
Kinsey, Sarah IV, 75
Kinsey, Sarah IV, 96
Kinsey, Sarah IV, 177
Kinsey, Sarah IV, 185
Kinsey, Sarah IV, 213
Kinsey, Sarah IV, 228
Kinsey, Sarah IV, 233
Kinsey, Sarah IV, 234
Kinsey, Sarah IV, 279
Kinsey, Sarah IV, 326
Kinsey, Sarah IV, 339
Kinsey, Sarah IV, 342
Kinsey, Sarah IV, 537
Kinsey, Sarah IV, 538
Kinsey, Sarah IV, 639
Kinsey, Sarah IV, 657
Kinsey, Sarah IV, 875
Kinsey, Sarah V, 915
Kinsey, Sarah A. IV, 234
Kinsey, Sarah Ann IV, 234
Kinsey, Sarah Ann IV, 538
Kinsey, Sarah B. IV, 96
Kinsey, Sarah B. IV, 234
Kinsey, Sarah B. IV, 1039
Kinsey, Sarah E. IV, 235
Kinsey, Sarah E. V, 90
Kinsey, Sarah M. IV, 312
Kinsey, Sarah M. IV, 313
Kinsey, Simeon IV, 537
Kinsey, Stephen IV, 96
Kinsey, Stephen IV, 152
Kinsey, Stephen IV, 481
Kinsey, Stephen IV, 490
Kinsey, Stephen IV, 537
Kinsey, Susan V, 916
Kinsey, Susana IV, 233
Kinsey, Susana IV, 295
Kinsey, Susanna IV, 152
Kinsey, Susanna IV, 233
Kinsey, Susanna IV, 234
Kinsey, Susanna IV, 481
Kinsey, Susanna IV, 538
Kinsey, Susannah I, 302
Kinsey, Susannah I, 310
Kinsey, Susannah IV, 234
Kinsey, Susannah IV, 336
Kinsey, Susannah IV, 339
Kinsey, Susannah IV, 537
Kinsey, Susannah V, 508
Kinsey, Susannah V, 532
Kinsey, Susie E. V, 1005
Kinsey, Sussanah IV, 222
Kinsey, Tacy IV, 416
Kinsey, Tacy IV, 1064
Kinsey, Thomas II, 178
Kinsey, Thomas II, 237
Kinsey, Thomas II, 574
Kinsey, Thomas IV, 43
Kinsey, Thomas Fairman II, 386
Kinsey, Thomas Theodore V, 1005
Kinsey, Thomas W. V, 90
Kinsey, Thomas W. V, 915
Kinsey, Thomas, Jr. II, 574
Kinsey, Thos. V, 916
Kinsey, Thos. Theodore V, 1005
Kinsey, Wd. Margaret II, 804
Kinsey, William I, 310
Kinsey, William II, 717
Kinsey, William IV, 43
Kinsey, William IV, 234
Kinsey, William G. IV, 233
Kinsey, William G. IV, 234
Kinsey, William G. IV, 235
Kinsey, William G. V, 52
Kinsey, William G. V, 90
Kinsey, William G. V, 915
Kinsey, William Irving IV, 234
Kinsey, William Irwin IV, 234
Kinsey, Wilma IV, 235
Kinsey, Wilma IV, 730
Kinsey, Wilma IV, 994
Kinsey, Wilma V. IV, 730
Kinsey, Wm. IV, 969
Kinsey, Wm. IV, 973
Kinsey, Wm. E. IV, 1039
Kinsey, Wm. G. IV, 234
Kinsey, Wm. G. IV, 241
Kinsey, Wm. G. IV, 1039
Kinsey, Wm. G. V, 904
Kinsey, Wm. G. V, 915
Kinsey, Wm. G. V, 916
Kinsey, Wm. G. V, 918
Kinsey, Wm. H. M. V, 916
Kinsey, Wm. H. Malone V, 915
Kinsey, Wm. Irving V, 916
Kinsie, Matilda V, 474
Kinsie, Matilda V, 508
Kinsley, Ann II, 386
Kinsley, Charles II, 386
Kinsley, Elisabeth I Sup 1, 3
Kinsolvin, O. A. VI, 874
Kinsolvin, O. A. VI, 898
Kinsolvin, O. A. VI, 923
Kinsolvin, O. A. VI, 965
Kinsolvin, O. A. VI, 980
Kinsolvin, O. A. VI, 986
Kinsolvin, O. A. VI, 988
Kinsolvin, O. A. VI, 989
Kinsolvin, O. A. VI, 1000
Kinsolvin, O. A. VI, 1006
Kinsolving, O. A. VI, 893
Kinsolving, O. A. VI, 911
Kinsolving, O. A. VI, 944
Kinson, Florence I, 310
Kinson, Victoria I, 310
Kinsy, Edmund II, 962
Kinsy, Elizabeth II, 962
Kinsy, Sarah II, 962
Kintz, Edith H. IV, 730
Kinweorthy, Joshua I, 403
Kinworthy, Ann V, 751
Kinworthy, Betty V, 184
Kinworthy, David V, 184
Kinworthy, David V, 230
Kinworthy, Dianah V, 184
Kinworthy, Dinah V, 184
Kinworthy, Mary I, 403
Kinworthy, Mary V, 184
Kinworthy, Mary V, 230
Kinworthy, Mary V, 256
Kinworthy, Mary V, 257
Kinworthy, Mary Ann V, 849
Kinworthy, Rachel V, 257
Kinworthy, Rachel V, 447

Kinworthy, Rebekah I, 402
Kinworthy, Rebekah I, 403
Kinworthy, Sarah V, 184
Kinworthy, Sarah V, 257
Kinworthy, Tamer I, 403
Kinworthy, Tamer Kinworthy I, 380
Kinworthy, Thamar V, 257
Kinworthy, Thamer V, 230
Kinworthy, William I, 402
Kinyan, Benjamin I, 56
Kinyon, Benjamin I, 56
Kinyon, Elisabeth I, 56
Kinyon, Elizabeth I, 56
Kinyon, Hannah I, 56
Kinyon, Joab I, 56
Kinyon, Joseph I, 56
Kinyon, Levi I, 144
Kinyon, Margaret I, 56
Kinyon, Margaret I, 185
Kinyon, Mary I, 185
Kinyon, Miriam I, 185
Kinyon, Rachel I, 52
Kinyon, Rachel I, 56
Kinyon, Rachel I, 185
Kinyon, Roger I, 56
Kinyon, Thomas I, 52
Kinyon, Thomas I, 56
Kinyon, Thomas I, 185
Kinzee, Mary V, 336
Kinzel, Dr. ??? V, 656
Kinzel, Dr. ??? V, 689
Kinzel, Elsie V, 656
Kinzel, Elsie V, 689
Kinzer, Adam VI, 946
Kinzer, Cathrine VI, 918
Kinzer, Christina VI, 946
Kinzer, Daniel V, 257
Kinzer, Daniel V, 344
Kinzer, Elizabeth VI, 946
Kinzer, Ella V, 257
Kinzer, George VI, 946
Kinzer, Henry VI, 946
Kinzer, Jane V, 344
Kinzer, John VI, 918
Kinzer, John VI, 946
Kinzer, Luella V, 257
Kinzer, Mary V, 257
Kinzer, Mary V, 344
Kinzer, Myrtie V, 344
Kinzer, Polly VI, 946
Kinzer, Robert V, 344
Kinzer, Sally VI, 946
Kinzer, Sarah Jane V, 344
Kinzor, Adam VI, 946
Kinzy, Hannah Ann V, 344
Kinzy, Hannah Ann V, 360
Kiphart, Clara V, 915
Kiphart, Katharine Hanrietta V, 915
Kiphart, Leslie V, 915
Kiphart, Neil V, 915
Kiphart, Peninah V, 896
Kiphart, Peninnah V, 915
Kiphart, Thos. J. V, 915
Kiphart, Vincent William V, 915
Kiphart, Viola V, 915
Kipp, ??? III, 83
Kipp, ??? III, 193
Kipp, ??? III, 194
Kipp, Abigail III, 194
Kipp, Abraham III, 193
Kipp, Abraham H. III, 334
Kipp, Amy III, 193
Kipp, Anne III, 423
Kipp, Caleb III, 193
Kipp, Cora IV, 1256
Kipp, Eden III, 193
Kipp, Eliz. III, 73
Kipp, Eliza III, 193
Kipp, Emma J. III, 193
Kipp, Emma Jane III, 194
Kipp, Ethel III, 73
Kipp, Ethel III, 193
Kipp, Ethel IV, 1256
Kipp, Griffanna III, 193
Kipp, Hanna S. III, 212
Kipp, Hannah S. III, 95
Kipp, Isaac III, 193
Kipp, Isaac III, 194
Kipp, Jane III, 193
Kipp, Jane III, 291
Kipp, Josiah F. III, 193
Kipp, Leonard IV, 1256
Kipp, Mary III, 403
Kipp, Mary III, 423
Kipp, Mary M. III, 193
Kipp, Mary M. III, 334
Kipp, Nora IV, 1256
Kipp, Phebe III, 83
Kipp, Phebe III, 193
Kipp, Phebe H. III, 193
Kipp, Rachel I. III, 193
Kipp, Ruth IV, 1256
Kipp, Samuel III, 193
Kipp, Thomas III, 193
Kipp, Thomas III, 194
Kipp, Thomas III, 423
Kipp, Wm. De Graw III, 193
Kipp, Wm. DeGraw III, 73
Kirbey, ??? III, 423
Kirbey, ??? III, 462
Kirbey, Chalkley II, 120
Kirbey, Jacob II, 120
Kirbey, Mary III, 423
Kirbey, Mary III, 462
Kirbitt, Mary II, 197
Kirbitt, Mary II, 237
Kirby, ??? II, 33
Kirby, ??? III, 423
Kirby, ??? VI, 293
Kirby, Abigail II, 33
Kirby, Abigail T. IV, 730
Kirby, Alice V, 257
Kirby, Alice M. IV, 481
Kirby, Alice M. IV, 1256
Kirby, Amos II, 74
Kirby, Amos II, 83
Kirby, Amy III, 423
Kirby, Amy III, 443
Kirby, Amy III, 488
Kirby, Amy III, 489
Kirby, Amy III, 492
Kirby, Ann II, 74
Kirby, Ann II, 83
Kirby, Ann III, 423
Kirby, Ann III, 429
Kirby, Ann III, 449
Kirby, Ann IV, 481
Kirby, Ann IV, 1065
Kirby, Ann W. V, 90
Kirby, Ann W. V, 127
Kirby, Anna III, 429
Kirby, Anna E. III, 194
Kirby, Anna Ross III, 113
Kirby, Anna S. II, 886
Kirby, Anna Simmons II, 872
Kirby, Anna Simmons II, 886
Kirby, Anne III, 423
Kirby, Archibald VI, 327
Kirby, Arnold II, 120
Kirby, Asa II, 33
Kirby, Asa II, 83
Kirby, Asa II, 87
Kirby, Benjamin II, 33
Kirby, Benjamin II, 83
Kirby, Bessie V, 344
Kirby, Beulah III, 194
Kirby, Beulah E. III, 112
Kirby, Beulah E. III, 194
Kirby, Beulahelma Twining III, 194
Kirby, Caroline Louisa III, 113
Kirby, Caroline M. V, 344
Kirby, Catharine III, 113
Kirby, Catharine Hicks III, 113
Kirby, Chalkley II, 120
Kirby, Chalkley II, 152
Kirby, Chalkley II, 886
Kirby, Chalkley, Jr. II, 152
Kirby, Chalkley, Jr. II, 160
Kirby, Chalkley, Jr. II, 804
Kirby, Clement S. II, 886
Kirby, Deborah III, 194
Kirby, Ebenezer II, 33
Kirby, Ebenezer II, 120
Kirby, Edgar II, 886
Kirby, Edith IV, 1039
Kirby, Edith VI, 295
Kirby, Edith VI, 328
Kirby, Edmond III, 112
Kirby, Edmond III, 194
Kirby, Edmond III, 489
Kirby, Edmund III, 134
Kirby, Edmund III, 194
Kirby, Edmund III, 209
Kirby, Edmund III, 348
Kirby, Edmund III, 355
Kirby, Edmund III, 381
Kirby, Edmund III, 423
Kirby, Edmund III, 488
Kirby, Edmund III, 506
Kirby, Edward III, 194
Kirby, Edward Augustus III, 113
Kirby, Eleanor IV, 481
Kirby, Eleanor IV, 1059
Kirby, Eleanor IV, 1064
Kirby, Eleanor IV, 1065
Kirby, Eliz. III, 194
Kirby, Eliz. III, 428
Kirby, Eliza V, 344
Kirby, Eliza Jane V, 344
Kirby, Elizabeth II, 66
Kirby, Elizabeth II, 83
Kirby, Elizabeth III, 423
Kirby, Elizabeth III, 428
Kirby, Elizabeth III, 450
Kirby, Elizabeth III, 488
Kirby, Elizabeth III, 489
Kirby, Elizabeth III, 491
Kirby, Elizabeth IV, 1064
Kirby, Elizabeth IV, 1065
Kirby, Elizabeth IV, 1083
Kirby, Elizabeth IV, 1103
Kirby, Elizabeth IV, 1122
Kirby, Elizabeth VI, 328
Kirby, Elizabeth Ann II, 120
Kirby, Elizabeth Farquhar IV, 481
Kirby, Elmy T. III, 194
Kirby, Emma L. II, 152
Kirby, Emma L. II, 160
Kirby, Emma L. II, 886
Kirby, Emma Louisa II, 804
Kirby, Esther VI, 327
Kirby, Esther VI, 328
Kirby, Eveline V, 90
Kirby, Eveline V, 118
Kirby, Ezekiah VI, 327
Kirby, Farquhar IV, 1065
Kirby, George III, 113
Kirby, Gilbert R. III, 194
Kirby, Granville Wilson II, 804
Kirby, Hannah II, 33
Kirby, Hannah II, 62
Kirby, Hannah II, 83
Kirby, Hannah II, 87
Kirby, Hannah III, 194
Kirby, Hannah III, 423
Kirby, Hannah III, 434
Kirby, Hannah III, 451
Kirby, Hannah III, 452
Kirby, Hannah III, 480
Kirby, Hannah III, 488
Kirby, Hannah III, 489
Kirby, Hannah III, 493
Kirby, Hannah III, 497
Kirby, Hannah IV, 481
Kirby, Hannah IV, 1063
Kirby, Hannah IV, 1064
Kirby, Hannah IV, 1065
Kirby, Hannah VI, 328
Kirby, Harrison III, 113
Kirby, Henry III, 194
Kirby, Henry VI, 295
Kirby, Henry VI, 327
Kirby, Henry VI, 328
Kirby, Henry S. II, 831
Kirby, Henry S. II, 852
Kirby, Henry S. II, 872
Kirby, Henry S. II, 886
Kirby, Henry, Jr. VI, 328
Kirby, Ila Marshall I, 944
Kirby, Ira B. I, 930
Kirby, Isaac III, 423
Kirby, Isaac IV, 481
Kirby, Isaac IV, 1064
Kirby, Isaac IV, 1065
Kirby, Isaac IV, 1083
Kirby, Isaac IV, 1103
Kirby, Isaac IV, 1122
Kirby, Jacob II, 120
Kirby, Jacob II, 152
Kirby, Jacob II, 160
Kirby, Jacob III, 194
Kirby, Jacob III, 423
Kirby, Jacob III, 428
Kirby, Jacob III, 434
Kirby, Jacob III, 443
Kirby, Jacob III, 483
Kirby, Jacob III, 488
Kirby, Jacob III, 489
Kirby, Jacob III, 491
Kirby, Jacob III, 493
Kirby, Jacob III, 498
Kirby, Jacob III, 507
Kirby, James II, 237
Kirby, James II, 241
Kirby, James V, 257
Kirby, James V, 344
Kirby, James Jackson II, 824
Kirby, Jas. Jackson III, 194
Kirby, Jennie IV, 1324
Kirby, Jennie E. IV, 1324
Kirby, Jeremiah VI, 327
Kirby, Jeremiah VI, 328
Kirby, Jericho Mary III, 488
Kirby, Job II, 237
Kirby, Job II, 241
Kirby, Job II, 321
Kirby, Job II, 886
Kirby, Johana VI, 328
Kirby, Johanna VI, 328
Kirby, John VI, 328
Kirby, Jonathan II, 33
Kirby, Jonathan II, 83
Kirby, Jonathan II, 84
Kirby, Jonathan II, 108
Kirby, Jonathan IV, 1065
Kirby, Jonathan IV, 1083
Kirby, Joseph II, 120
Kirby, Joseph III, 423
Kirby, Joseph III, 429
Kirby, Joseph V, 90
Kirby, Joseph VI, 328
Kirby, Joseph M. II, 886
Kirby, Joseph Mason III, 194
Kirby, Judith VI, 309
Kirby, Judith VI, 328
Kirby, Ketturah IV, 1064
Kirby, Keturah IV, 1065
Kirby, Keturah IV, 1067
Kirby, Kiturah IV, 481
Kirby, Letitia III, 367
Kirby, Lidya II, 83
Kirby, Louisa IV, 533
Kirby, Lydia II, 33
Kirby, Lydia II, 83
Kirby, Lydia II, 108
Kirby, Mahala VI, 815
Kirby, Marcy II, 83
Kirby, Maria II, 804
Kirby, Maria II, 852
Kirby, Maria II, 886
Kirby, Maria III, 194
Kirby, Maria III, 269
Kirby, Maria III, 348
Kirby, Martha II, 83
Kirby, Martha II, 120
Kirby, Martha II, 124
Kirby, Martha II, 886
Kirby, Martha II, 928
Kirby, Martha VI, 815
Kirby, Mary II, 237
Kirby, Mary II, 241
Kirby, Mary II, 824
Kirby, Mary II, 886
Kirby, Mary II, 931
Kirby, Mary III, 194
Kirby, Mary III, 421
Kirby, Mary III, 423
Kirby, Mary III, 428
Kirby, Mary III, 434
Kirby, Mary III, 444
Kirby, Mary III, 483
Kirby, Mary III, 488
Kirby, Mary III, 489
Kirby, Mary III, 491
Kirby, Mary III, 493
Kirby, Mary III, 498
Kirby, Mary III, 506
Kirby, Mary III, 507
Kirby, Mary IV, 235
Kirby, Mary V, 49
Kirby, Mary V, 90
Kirby, Mary VI, 246
Kirby, Mary VI, 295
Kirby, Mary VI, 327
Kirby, Mary VI, 328
Kirby, Mary A. II, 152
Kirby, Mary A. II, 160
Kirby, Mary A. III, 489
Kirby, Mary B. II, 886
Kirby, Mary B. II, 934
Kirby, Mary H. II, 831
Kirby, Mary H. II, 852
Kirby, Mary H. II, 872
Kirby, Mary H. II, 886
Kirby, Mary R. III, 488
Kirby, Mary W. III, 488
Kirby, Mary W. III, 489
Kirby, Mary W. III, 507
Kirby, Matilda III, 489
Kirby, Mercy II, 33
Kirby, Mercy II, 83
Kirby, Mercy II, 84
Kirby, Nancy V, 344
Kirby, Obadiah III, 194
Kirby, Obediah VI, 327
Kirby, Obediah VI, 328
Kirby, Orpha VI, 327
Kirby, Perry III, 194
Kirby, Phebe III, 423
Kirby, Phebe III, 480
Kirby, Phebe III, 489
Kirby, Phebe IV, 1134
Kirby, Rachel IV, 470
Kirby, Rachel IV, 481
Kirby, Rachel IV, 1059
Kirby, Rachel IV, 1065
Kirby, Rachel VI, 328
Kirby, Rebecca IV, 481
Kirby, Rebecca IV, 1059
Kirby, Rebecca IV, 1064
Kirby, Rebecca IV, 1065
Kirby, Rebecca IV, 1103
Kirby, Rebecca Ann IV, 1064
Kirby, Rebecca Ann IV, 1065
Kirby, Rebecca Ann IV, 1067
Kirby, Rebeccaa IV, 470
Kirby, Ricaard V, 409
Kirby, Richard II, 83
Kirby, Richard III, 423
Kirby, Richard V, 409
Kirby, Richard VI, 309
Kirby, Richard VI, 328
Kirby, Richard, Jr. II, 120
Kirby, Richard, Jr. VI, 328
Kirby, Robert II, 804
Kirby, Robert II, 852
Kirby, Robert II, 886
Kirby, Robert J. II, 886
Kirby, Robert Jackson II, 804
Kirby, Ruth IV, 1058
Kirby, Ruth IV, 1065
Kirby, Ruth V, 257
Kirby, Ruth V, 344
Kirby, Ruth VI, 313
Kirby, Ruth VI, 328
Kirby, Sallie A. II, 804
Kirby, Sallie C. II, 886
Kirby, Samuel II, 33
Kirby, Samuel II, 83
Kirby, Samuel IV, 533
Kirby, Samuel IV, 1065
Kirby, Samuel, Jr. IV, 1065
Kirby, Sarah II, 83
Kirby, Sarah III, 112
Kirby, Sarah III, 194
Kirby, Sarah III, 209
Kirby, Sarah III, 423
Kirby, Sarah III, 470
Kirby, Sarah III, 473
Kirby, Sarah III, 489
Kirby, Sarah III, 497
Kirby, Sarah III, 507
Kirby, Sarah IV, 1065
Kirby, Sarah IV, 1069
Kirby, Sarah V, 90
Kirby, Sarah V, 104
Kirby, Sarah VI, 327
Kirby, Sarah Ann II, 237
Kirby, Sarah Ann II, 241
Kirby, Sarah Ann II, 824
Kirby, Sarah Ann III, 76
Kirby, Sarah Ann III, 112
Kirby, Sarah Ann III, 194
Kirby, Sarah Ann V, 409
Kirby, Sarah C. II, 886
Kirby, Sarah Conrow II, 831
Kirby, Sarah Conrow II, 886
Kirby, Sarah L. III, 483
Kirby, Sarah L. III, 489
Kirby, Theodore IV, 1324
Kirby, Thomas III, 113
Kirby, Thomas IV, 470
Kirby, Thomas IV, 481
Kirby, Thomas IV, 1059
Kirby, Thomas IV, 1064
Kirby, Thomas IV, 1065
Kirby, Thomas IV, 1103
Kirby, Valentine, Jr. III, 113
Kirby, Wd. Mary III, 423
Kirby, Willet III, 194
Kirby, Willet III, 452
Kirby, Willet III, 489
Kirby, Willet III, 497
Kirby, Willet T. III, 194
Kirby, Willets III, 421
Kirby, Willets III, 423
Kirby, Willets III, 444
Kirby, Willets III, 451
Kirby, Willets III, 480
Kirby, Willets III, 488
Kirby, Willets III, 489
Kirby, William III, 194
Kirby, William III, 423
Kirby, William III, 488
Kirby, William III, 489
Kirby, William IV, 1256
Kirby, William Henry III, 113
Kirby, William S. III, 194
Kirby, Wm. III, 470
Kirby, Wm. IV, 1256
Kirby, Wm. IV, 1324
Kircher, Effie Belle II, 722
Kirchgesener, Elvin IV, 829
Kirchgesener, Elvin E. IV, 829
Kirchgesener, John IV, 829
Kirchgesener, Myrtle M. IV, 82
Kirchgesener, Nellie IV, 829
Kirchgesener, Nellie M. IV, 829
Kirchoff, Regina Henrietta III, 1
Kirchoff, Regina Henrietta III, 3
Kirk, ??? II, 445

rk, ??? IV, 235
rk, A. Lincoln V, 508
k, Abigail III, 413
k, Abigail III, 423
rk, Abigail III, 424
rk, Abigail V, 508
rk, Abigail V, 509
k, Abigail V, 536
rk, Abigail V, 541
rk, Abraham B. IV, 1169
rk, Adam IV, 43
k, Adam IV, 96
rk, Adam IV, 97
rk, Adam VI, 524
rk, Addie I, 927
k, Albert IV, 1214
k, Albert IV, 1215
rk, Albertus T. IV, 482
rk, Alice Ann IV, 1214
rk, Alice Ann IV, 1215
k, Alice C. IV, 639
rk, Alice C. IV, 640
rk, Alice C. IV, 731
rk, Alice M. S. IV, 235
k, Alice Mary IV, 235
rk, Alice Mary IV, 282
rk, Alice Mary IV, 640
rk, Alice May IV, 657
k, Alice T. IV, 973
rk, Allen V, 508
k, Allice Ann IV, 1214
k, Almira IV, 340
rk, Almira V, 580
k, Alvertas IV, 416
k, Amanda IV, 1214
k, Amelia IV, 340
rk, Amelia IV, 354
rk, Amelia IV, 829
rk, Amey III, 423
rk, Amy III, 407
rk, Amy III, 423
rk, Amy III, 459
rk, Amy E. IV, 1214
rk, Amy Etta IV, 1215
rk, Amy T. IV, 482
rk, Amy T. IV, 936
rk, Amy T. IV, 973
rk, Amyetta IV, 973
rk, Amyetta IV, 993
rk, Angelina V, 509
rk, Angeline V, 509
rk, Angeline V, 689
rk, Angeline V, 690
rk, Ann II, 574
rk, Ann II, 610
rk, Ann III, 333
rk, Ann III, 423
rk, Ann IV, 43
rk, Ann IV, 92
rk, Ann IV, 96
rk, Ann IV, 97
rk, Ann IV, 116
rk, Ann IV, 416
rk, Ann IV, 1169
rk, Ann IV, 1211
rk, Ann IV, 1212
rk, Ann IV, 1214
rk, Ann V, 508
rk, Ann VI, 524
rk, Ann Eliza IV, 731
rk, Ann Eliza IV, 829
rk, Ann Jenkins I, 556
rk, Ann Jenkins I, 1016
k, Ann N. III, 413
rk, Anna III, 222
rk, Anna III, 333
rk, Anna III, 334
rk, Anna III, 423
rk, Anna III, 462
rk, Anna IV, 482
rk, Anna C. IV, 639
rk, Anna K. III, 333
rk, Anna M. II, 750
rk, Anna M. IV, 973
rk, Anna Mary IV, 973
rk, Anna V. III, 423
rk, Anne III, 423
rk, Anne III, 424
rk, Anne III, 444
rk, Annyetta IV, 973
rk, Aquilla IV, 482
rk, Aquilla N. IV, 482
rk, Armella IV, 482
rk, Armella IV, 814
rk, Armella IV, 829
rk, Armelle IV, 482
rk, Arter G. IV, 973
rk, Arthur III, 423
rk, Arthur III, 444
rk, Arthur G. IV, 973
rk, Augustus S. IV, 416
Kirk, Badok P. IV, 973
Kirk, Benjamin III, 403
Kirk, Benjamin III, 422
Kirk, Benjamin III, 423
Kirk, Benjamin IV, 96
Kirk, Benjamin IV, 97
Kirk, Benjamin IV, 1169
Kirk, Benjamin VI, 524
Kirk, Benjamin C. III, 423
Kirk, Benjamin, Jr. IV, 1169
Kirk, Betsy IV, 1169
Kirk, Betta IV, 481
Kirk, Betty IV, 43
Kirk, Betty IV, 495
Kirk, Betty VI, 670
Kirk, Beulah IV, 97
Kirk, Beulah IV, 204
Kirk, Beulah IV, 235
Kirk, Beulah IV, 482
Kirk, Caleb IV, 43
Kirk, Caleb IV, 146
Kirk, Caleb IV, 152
Kirk, Caleb IV, 299
Kirk, Caleb IV, 481
Kirk, Caleb IV, 482
Kirk, Caleb IV, 829
Kirk, Caleb IV, 832
Kirk, Caleb IV, 1169
Kirk, Caleb IV, 1214
Kirk, Caleb IV, 1215
Kirk, Caleb IV, 1220
Kirk, Caleb IV, 1221
Kirk, Caleb V, 473
Kirk, Caleb V, 508
Kirk, Caleb V, 631
Kirk, Caleb VI, 670
Kirk, Caleb L. IV, 1169
Kirk, Caleb Lewis IV, 1214
Kirk, Carel IV, 973
Kirk, Caroline Adelaide VI, 760
Kirk, Caroline B. II, 709
Kirk, Carrel Evan IV, 973
Kirk, Carroll E. IV, 973
Kirk, Catharine IV, 482
Kirk, Catharine B. V, 536
Kirk, Catharine S. IV, 482
Kirk, Catharine S. IV, 497
Kirk, Catherine IV, 829
Kirk, Catherna IV, 482
Kirk, Cecil V, 509
Kirk, Chalkley IV, 482
Kirk, Chalkley H. IV, 482
Kirk, Chalkley H. IV, 973
Kirk, Charity IV, 97
Kirk, Charity IV, 152
Kirk, Charity IV, 235
Kirk, Charity IV, 730
Kirk, Charity IV, 731
Kirk, Charity IV, 825
Kirk, Charity IV, 829
Kirk, Charles II, 886
Kirk, Charles D. IV, 235
Kirk, Charles D. IV, 236
Kirk, Charles D. IV, 629
Kirk, Charles D. IV, 640
Kirk, Charles H. V, 502
Kirk, Charles H. V, 508
Kirk, Charles H. V, 509
Kirk, Chas. II, 886
Kirk, Chas. II, 926
Kirk, Chas. D. IV, 214
Kirk, Chas. D. IV, 235
Kirk, Chas. D. IV, 639
Kirk, Chas. D. IV, 640
Kirk, Chas. P. Willis II, 886
Kirk, Christiana IV, 212
Kirk, Christiana IV, 235
Kirk, Christiana IV, 639
Kirk, Christianna IV, 235
Kirk, Christianna IV, 802
Kirk, Christianna IV, 829
Kirk, Christine IV, 235
Kirk, Clarinda V, 689
Kirk, Cleo E. V, 509
Kirk, Clorena V, 689
Kirk, Comly IV, 731
Kirk, Daniel III, 333
Kirk, Daniel III, 423
Kirk, Daniel III, 426
Kirk, Daniel III, 459
Kirk, Daniel III, 462
Kirk, Daniel V, 508
Kirk, Daniel V, 631
Kirk, Daton H. V, 536
Kirk, Dayton H. V, 536
Kirk, Deborah II, 134
Kirk, Deborah II, 152
Kirk, Deborah II, 802
Kirk, Deborah II, 886
Kirk, Deborah II, 940
Kirk, Deborah III, 423
Kirk, Deborah IV, 43
Kirk, Deborah IV, 85
Kirk, Deborah IV, 96
Kirk, Deborah IV, 219
Kirk, Deborah IV, 235
Kirk, Dorothy IV, 235
Kirk, Dorothy M. IV, 236
Kirk, Dorothy M. IV, 640
Kirk, Dorothy Mary IV, 235
Kirk, Ebenezer VI, 412
Kirk, Edith IV, 97
Kirk, Edith IV, 248
Kirk, Edith IV, 339
Kirk, Edith IV, 481
Kirk, Edith IV, 482
Kirk, Edith IV, 497
Kirk, Edith IV, 538
Kirk, Edith IV, 550
Kirk, Edith C. IV, 1324
Kirk, Edith L. IV, 639
Kirk, Edith L. IV, 724
Kirk, Edith L. IV, 731
Kirk, Edith L. IV, 824
Kirk, Edith Lydia IV, 635
Kirk, Edith Lydia IV, 640
Kirk, Edith Lydia IV, 723
Kirk, Edmund IV, 1169
Kirk, Edmund IV, 1214
Kirk, Edward N. IV, 639
Kirk, Edwin V, 508
Kirk, Edwin V, 509
Kirk, Edwin VI, 760
Kirk, Edwin VI, 785
Kirk, Edwin Whinery V, 509
Kirk, Elbert J. V, 508
Kirk, Elbert J. V, 509
Kirk, Eleanor V, 581
Kirk, Eli IV, 235
Kirk, Eli IV, 248
Kirk, Eli IV, 339
Kirk, Eli IV, 416
Kirk, Eli V, 581
Kirk, Elisha IV, 212
Kirk, Elisha IV, 219
Kirk, Elisha IV, 235
Kirk, Elisha IV, 525
Kirk, Elisha IV, 538
Kirk, Elisha IV, 639
Kirk, Elisha IV, 731
Kirk, Elisha IV, 802
Kirk, Elisha IV, 829
Kirk, Elisha V, 580
Kirk, Elisha T. IV, 235
Kirk, Elisha T. IV, 282
Kirk, Elisha T. IV, 639
Kirk, Elisha T. IV, 640
Kirk, Elisha T. IV, 657
Kirk, Eliza VI, 760
Kirk, Eliza Anna IV, 416
Kirk, Elizabeth II, 574
Kirk, Elizabeth II, 750
Kirk, Elizabeth IV, 43
Kirk, Elizabeth IV, 213
Kirk, Elizabeth IV, 235
Kirk, Elizabeth IV, 340
Kirk, Elizabeth IV, 481
Kirk, Elizabeth IV, 482
Kirk, Elizabeth IV, 490
Kirk, Elizabeth IV, 538
Kirk, Elizabeth IV, 548
Kirk, Elizabeth IV, 731
Kirk, Elizabeth IV, 829
Kirk, Elizabeth IV, 931
Kirk, Elizabeth IV, 973
Kirk, Elizabeth IV, 1169
Kirk, Elizabeth IV, 1210
Kirk, Elizabeth IV, 1214
Kirk, Elizabeth V, 508
Kirk, Elizabeth V, 689
Kirk, Elizabeth V, 690
Kirk, Elizabeth VI, 412
Kirk, Elizabeth VI, 415
Kirk, Elizabeth Alice IV, 618
Kirk, Elizabeth Alice IV, 640
Kirk, Elizabeth Alice IV, 693
Kirk, Elizabeth Alice IV, 730
Kirk, Elizabeth Ann V, 509
Kirk, Elizabeth Ann V, 689
Kirk, Elizabeth B. IV, 973
Kirk, Elizabeth C. V, 508
Kirk, Elizabeth E. V, 508
Kirk, Elizabeth Mary IV, 973
Kirk, Elizabeth May IV, 973
Kirk, Elizabeth N. IV, 482
Kirk, Elizabeth P. V, 482
Kirk, Elizabeth P. V, 508
Kirk, Elizabeth P. V, 509
Kirk, Elizabeth R. II, 886
Kirk, Elizabeth Virginia IV, 731
Kirk, Elmer IV, 1028
Kirk, Elmina IV, 482
Kirk, Elmina IV, 506
Kirk, Elmira IV, 482
Kirk, Elmor IV, 416
Kirk, Elvira R. IV, 547
Kirk, Emaline IV, 1215
Kirk, Emaline R. IV, 1214
Kirk, Emilie II, 886
Kirk, Emilie II, 940
Kirk, Emily IV, 416
Kirk, Emily V, 184
Kirk, Emily V, 502
Kirk, Emily V, 508
Kirk, Emily V, 581
Kirk, Emma III, 423
Kirk, Emmeline IV, 1214
Kirk, Emory V, 690
Kirk, Enid M. III, 266
Kirk, Enid Mary III, 194
Kirk, Erastus IV, 235
Kirk, Erastus W. IV, 416
Kirk, Esther IV, 43
Kirk, Esther IV, 96
Kirk, Esther IV, 97
Kirk, Esther IV, 340
Kirk, Esther V, 581
Kirk, Esther V, 602
Kirk, Esther VI, 524
Kirk, Eunice Elizabeth IV, 1169
Kirk, Ezekial V, 508
Kirk, Ezekiel V, 508
Kirk, Ezekiel N. V, 482
Kirk, Ezekiel N. V, 509
Kirk, Florence III, 423
Kirk, Florence J. IV, 639
Kirk, Francis III, 267
Kirk, George III, 423
Kirk, Gertrude P. III, 194
Kirk, Gertrude Townsend III, 423
Kirk, Gilbert Mahlon V, 508
Kirk, Grace V, 712
Kirk, Grace Anna IV, 1169
Kirk, H. Alma I, 927
Kirk, Hannah III, 264
Kirk, Hannah III, 400
Kirk, Hannah III, 423
Kirk, Hannah III, 426
Kirk, Hannah IV, 96
Kirk, Hannah IV, 97
Kirk, Hannah IV, 114
Kirk, Hannah IV, 829
Kirk, Hannah IV, 832
Kirk, Hannah IV, 1169
Kirk, Hannah IV, 1189
Kirk, Hannah IV, 1214
Kirk, Hannah IV, 1220
Kirk, Hannah IV, 1221
Kirk, Hannah V, 508
Kirk, Hannah V, 518
Kirk, Hannah V, 536
Kirk, Hannah VI, 411
Kirk, Hannah VI, 412
Kirk, Hannah VI, 435
Kirk, Hannah VI, 524
Kirk, Hannah A. IV, 1214
Kirk, Hannah A. IV, 1220
Kirk, Hannah L. II, 886
Kirk, Hannah Rhoda IV, 1215
Kirk, Hannah T. V, 508
Kirk, Hannah, Sr. V, 508
Kirk, Hanuel I, 927
Kirk, Harriet V, 580
Kirk, Harriet E. II, 886
Kirk, Harriet E. II, 926
Kirk, Henry II, 134
Kirk, Henry IV, 416
Kirk, Henry C. IV, 416
Kirk, Henry C. IV, 481
Kirk, Henry C. IV, 482
Kirk, Henry C. IV, 487
Kirk, Henry E. III, 194
Kirk, Henry Ecroyd III, 194
Kirk, Henry Ecroyd III, 266
Kirk, Hester V, 135
Kirk, Hester V, 581
Kirk, Howard A. IV, 1169
Kirk, Ida V, 509
Kirk, Isaac I, 556
Kirk, Isaac I, 1015
Kirk, Isaac I, 1016
Kirk, Isaac I, 1033
Kirk, Isaac IV, 482
Kirk, Isaac IV, 829
Kirk, Isaac IV, 1214
Kirk, Isaac V, 508
Kirk, Isaac Jenkins I, 556
Kirk, Isaac Jenkins I, 1016
Kirk, Isaah IV, 1169
Kirk, Isaiah II, 709
Kirk, Isaiah IV, 96
Kirk, Isaiah IV, 97
Kirk, Isaiah IV, 1169
Kirk, Isaiah V, 508
Kirk, Isaiah VI, 524
Kirk, Israel V, 508
Kirk, Jacob II, 886
Kirk, Jacob II, 926
Kirk, Jacob V, 508
Kirk, James II, 386
Kirk, James II, 445
Kirk, James III, 423
Kirk, James B. IV, 538
Kirk, James E. V, 631
Kirk, James Edwin V, 508
Kirk, James V. IV, 1214
Kirk, Jemima III, 424
Kirk, Jerusha III, 423
Kirk, Jesse IV, 213
Kirk, Jesse IV, 235
Kirk, Jesse V, 508
Kirk, Jesse V, 509
Kirk, Jesse V, 689
Kirk, Jesse H. V, 509
Kirk, Joel IV, 235
Kirk, Joel IV, 481
Kirk, Joel IV, 482
Kirk, Joel IV, 497
Kirk, Joel IV, 538
Kirk, Joel IV, 550
Kirk, Joel IV, 930
Kirk, Joel IV, 936
Kirk, Joel IV, 973
Kirk, Joel T. IV, 482
Kirk, Joel T. IV, 538
Kirk, John I, 1033
Kirk, John II, 386
Kirk, John II, 574
Kirk, John II, 802
Kirk, John III, 194
Kirk, John III, 423
Kirk, John IV, 482
Kirk, John IV, 973
Kirk, John IV, 1212
Kirk, John IV, 1214
Kirk, John V, 508
Kirk, John V, 509
Kirk, John V, 955
Kirk, John D. III, 423
Kirk, John K. IV, 1169
Kirk, John L. II, 886
Kirk, John M. V, 689
Kirk, John W. V, 689
Kirk, John, Jr. II, 574
Kirk, John, Jr. III, 194
Kirk, Jonah H. V, 536
Kirk, Joseph IV, 26
Kirk, Joseph IV, 43
Kirk, Joseph IV, 85
Kirk, Joseph IV, 109
Kirk, Joseph IV, 235
Kirk, Joseph IV, 481
Kirk, Joseph IV, 482
Kirk, Joseph IV, 538
Kirk, Joseph IV, 550
Kirk, Joseph IV, 1169
Kirk, Joseph IV, 1214
Kirk, Joseph IV, 1215
Kirk, Joseph G. IV, 830
Kirk, Joseph P. V, 508
Kirk, Joseph P. V, 509
Kirk, Joshua III, 400
Kirk, Joshua III, 423
Kirk, Joshua IV, 97
Kirk, Joshua IV, 152
Kirk, Joshua IV, 235
Kirk, Joshua IV, 731
Kirk, Joshua IV, 829
Kirk, Josiah V, 581
Kirk, Josiah M. V, 536
Kirk, Judith IV, 43
Kirk, Judith IV, 85
Kirk, Judith IV, 96
Kirk, Judith IV, 109
Kirk, Judith IV, 128
Kirk, Judith IV, 132
Kirk, Levi V, 581
Kirk, Lewis H. II, 886
Kirk, Lewis H. II, 940
Kirk, Lewis J. IV, 618
Kirk, Lewis J. IV, 640
Kirk, Lewis T. IV, 1169
Kirk, Lindley IV, 640
Kirk, Lindley IV, 829
Kirk, Lindley M. IV, 482
Kirk, Lindley M. IV, 931
Kirk, Lindley M. IV, 973
Kirk, Lindley W. IV, 482
Kirk, Lorena IV, 973
Kirk, Lorenzo IV, 1214
Kirk, Lorenzo IV, 1215
Kirk, Louis IV, 639
Kirk, Louis J. IV, 639
Kirk, Louis J. IV, 640

Kirk, Louis J. IV, 693
Kirk, Louis J. IV, 730
Kirk, Louisa IV, 340
Kirk, Lurena T. IV, 973
Kirk, Lydia IV, 416
Kirk, Lydia IV, 481
Kirk, Lydia IV, 482
Kirk, Lydia IV, 730
Kirk, Lydia IV, 731
Kirk, Lydia IV, 748
Kirk, Lydia IV, 973
Kirk, Lydia IV, 1169
Kirk, Lydia IV, 1186
Kirk, Lydia V, 581
Kirk, Lydia V, 598
Kirk, Lydia Ann IV, 482
Kirk, Lydia Jane IV, 731
Kirk, Lydia Jenkins I, 556
Kirk, Lydia Jenkins I, 1016
Kirk, Mahlon IV, 481
Kirk, Mahlon IV, 482
Kirk, Mahlon V, 501
Kirk, Mahlon V, 508
Kirk, Mahlon VI, 760
Kirk, Malissa V, 581
Kirk, Malon V, 508
Kirk, Margaret IV, 481
Kirk, Margaret IV, 482
Kirk, Margaret IV, 487
Kirk, Margaret V, 509
Kirk, Margaret VI, 524
Kirk, Margaret W. II, 709
Kirk, Margaret W. II, 750
Kirk, Margaretta IV, 416
Kirk, Maria IV, 235
Kirk, Maria IV, 416
Kirk, Maria IV, 1104
Kirk, Maria V, 689
Kirk, Maria V, 847
Kirk, Mariah IV, 416
Kirk, Martha IV, 235
Kirk, Martha IV, 294
Kirk, Martha IV, 465
Kirk, Martha IV, 481
Kirk, Martha IV, 482
Kirk, Martha IV, 490
Kirk, Martha IV, 497
Kirk, Martha IV, 538
Kirk, Martha IV, 973
Kirk, Martha C. IV, 1214
Kirk, Martha T. IV, 930
Kirk, Martha T. IV, 973
Kirk, Martha T. IV, 1019
Kirk, Mary I, 521
Kirk, Mary II, 386
Kirk, Mary II, 496
Kirk, Mary II, 574
Kirk, Mary II, 1007
Kirk, Mary III, 423
Kirk, Mary III, 426
Kirk, Mary III, 459
Kirk, Mary IV, 43
Kirk, Mary IV, 96
Kirk, Mary IV, 97
Kirk, Mary IV, 111
Kirk, Mary IV, 152
Kirk, Mary IV, 235
Kirk, Mary IV, 299
Kirk, Mary IV, 340
Kirk, Mary IV, 417
Kirk, Mary IV, 481
Kirk, Mary IV, 482
Kirk, Mary IV, 489
Kirk, Mary IV, 538
Kirk, Mary IV, 635
Kirk, Mary IV, 639
Kirk, Mary IV, 730
Kirk, Mary IV, 731
Kirk, Mary IV, 824
Kirk, Mary IV, 825
Kirk, Mary IV, 826
Kirk, Mary IV, 829
Kirk, Mary IV, 973
Kirk, Mary IV, 1169
Kirk, Mary IV, 1208
Kirk, Mary IV, 1214
Kirk, Mary IV, 1215
Kirk, Mary V, 689
Kirk, Mary A. III, 423
Kirk, Mary Amanda IV, 1201
Kirk, Mary Ann III, 423
Kirk, Mary Ann IV, 416
Kirk, Mary Ann IV, 482
Kirk, Mary Ann IV, 497
Kirk, Mary Ann IV, 538
Kirk, Mary Ann IV, 550
Kirk, Mary Ann IV, 829
Kirk, Mary Ann IV, 930
Kirk, Mary Ann IV, 936
Kirk, Mary Ann IV, 973
Kirk, Mary Ann V, 508
Kirk, Mary Byram V, 508
Kirk, Mary Elma IV, 1214
Kirk, Mary Emily V, 689
Kirk, Mary Emma V, 689
Kirk, Mary Evaline IV, 235
Kirk, Mary Evalyn IV, 235
Kirk, Mary F. IV, 647
Kirk, Mary F. IV, 723
Kirk, Mary F. IV, 830
Kirk, Mary G. IV, 482
Kirk, Mary G. IV, 731
Kirk, Mary G. IV, 909
Kirk, Mary Ida IV, 748
Kirk, Mary M. IV, 235
Kirk, Mary M. IV, 639
Kirk, Mary M. IV, 640
Kirk, Mary M. IV, 641
Kirk, Mary M. IV, 730
Kirk, Mary M. IV, 803
Kirk, Mary M. IV, 829
Kirk, Mary M. IV, 830
Kirk, Mary Mann Page VI, 760
Kirk, Mary Morlan IV, 802
Kirk, Mary T. III, 333
Kirk, Mary T. III, 423
Kirk, Mary T. III, 462
Kirk, Mary Willis VI, 740
Kirk, Mary Willis VI, 760
Kirk, Mary, Jr. II, 574
Kirk, Maryan IV, 973
Kirk, Matilda IV, 1028
Kirk, Milton McMillan V, 508
Kirk, Morris IV, 639
Kirk, Mrs. Lydia IV, 731
Kirk, Nancy VI, 946
Kirk, Naomi V, 508
Kirk, Nathan IV, 235
Kirk, Nathan IV, 339
Kirk, Nathan IV, 340
Kirk, Nathan IV, 354
Kirk, Nathan IV, 417
Kirk, Nathan IV, 635
Kirk, Nathan IV, 639
Kirk, Nathan IV, 640
Kirk, Nathan IV, 641
Kirk, Nathan IV, 647
Kirk, Nathan IV, 723
Kirk, Nathan IV, 730
Kirk, Nathan IV, 802
Kirk, Nathan IV, 824
Kirk, Nathan IV, 829
Kirk, Nathan IV, 830
Kirk, Nathan V, 508
Kirk, Nathan V, 509
Kirk, Nathan V, 541
Kirk, Nathan Allen VI, 760
Kirk, Nathaniel IV, 641
Kirk, New Sharon IV, 1215
Kirk, Newton G. IV, 973
Kirk, Nora V, 90
Kirk, Nuton IV, 973
Kirk, Oliver IV, 416
Kirk, Oliver James IV, 235
Kirk, Page VI, 760
Kirk, Page VI, 785
Kirk, Phebe I, 553
Kirk, Phebe I, 890
Kirk, Phebe I, 892
Kirk, Phebe I, 1016
Kirk, Phebe IV, 43
Kirk, Phebe IV, 97
Kirk, Phebe IV, 235
Kirk, Phebe IV, 340
Kirk, Phebe IV, 346
Kirk, Phebe IV, 538
Kirk, Phebe IV, 550
Kirk, Phebe IV, 561
Kirk, Phebe IV, 731
Kirk, Phebe IV, 804
Kirk, Phebe IV, 829
Kirk, Phebe Ann III, 459
Kirk, Phebe Kirk I, 556
Kirk, Philena IV, 416
Kirk, Priscilla II, 823
Kirk, Rachel IV, 43
Kirk, Rachel IV, 75
Kirk, Rachel IV, 97
Kirk, Rachel IV, 146
Kirk, Rachel IV, 152
Kirk, Rachel IV, 235
Kirk, Rachel IV, 340
Kirk, Rachel IV, 378
Kirk, Rachel IV, 416
Kirk, Rachel IV, 417
Kirk, Rachel IV, 418
Kirk, Rachel IV, 465
Kirk, Rachel IV, 472
Kirk, Rachel IV, 481
Kirk, Rachel IV, 482
Kirk, Rachel IV, 495
Kirk, Rachel IV, 525
Kirk, Rachel IV, 538
Kirk, Rachel IV, 802
Kirk, Rachel IV, 803
Kirk, Rachel IV, 829
Kirk, Rachel IV, 830
Kirk, Rachel IV, 973
Kirk, Rachel IV, 1169
Kirk, Rachel V, 502
Kirk, Rachel V, 508
Kirk, Rachel V, 509
Kirk, Rachel V, 542
Kirk, Rachel V, 690
Kirk, Rachel VI, 524
Kirk, Rachel VI, 670
Kirk, Rachel A. V, 508
Kirk, Rachel B. IV, 973
Kirk, Rachel C. IV, 1169
Kirk, Rachel C. IV, 1214
Kirk, Rachel C. IV, 1221
Kirk, Rachel Elizabeth Roberts IV, 1214
Kirk, Rachel G. IV, 482
Kirk, Rachel K. IV, 802
Kirk, Rachel K. IV, 973
Kirk, Rachel Roberts IV, 1214
Kirk, Rachel S. IV, 639
Kirk, Rachel S. IV, 641
Kirk, Rachel W. V, 508
Kirk, Ralph V, 509
Kirk, Rebecca II, 886
Kirk, Rebecca II, 926
Kirk, Rebecca IV, 96
Kirk, Rebecca IV, 97
Kirk, Rebecca IV, 482
Kirk, Rebecca IV, 1169
Kirk, Rebecca IV, 1212
Kirk, Rebecca IV, 1214
Kirk, Rebecca V, 508
Kirk, Rebecca VI, 524
Kirk, Rebecca T. IV, 1214
Kirk, Rebecca T. IV, 1215
Kirk, Rebecca T. IV, 1225
Kirk, Rebeckah III, 267
Kirk, Rebeckah, Jr. III, 267
Kirk, Rebekah I, 556
Kirk, Rebekah I, 890
Kirk, Rebekah I, 1016
Kirk, Rebekah I, 1033
Kirk, Rebekah VI, 524
Kirk, Rebekah Jenkins I, 556
Kirk, Rebekah Jenkins I, 1016
Kirk, Reuben Thos. IV, 1169
Kirk, Rhoda Emaline IV, 1214
Kirk, Rhoda H. IV, 829
Kirk, Richard III, 413
Kirk, Richard III, 423
Kirk, Richard III, 424
Kirk, Richard S. VI, 740
Kirk, Richard S. VI, 760
Kirk, Robert IV, 639
Kirk, Robert V, 581
Kirk, Robert V, 916
Kirk, Robert VI, 435
Kirk, Roger IV, 1169
Kirk, Roger V, 955
Kirk, Roger VI, 411
Kirk, Roger Edwin VI, 760
Kirk, Roger H. II, 886
Kirk, Roger H. II, 940
Kirk, Rolen W. IV, 973
Kirk, Rollen W. IV, 973
Kirk, Rollin W. IV, 973
Kirk, Rollo S. V, 509
Kirk, Rosetta III, 423
Kirk, Ruth II, 816
Kirk, Samuel IV, 1169
Kirk, Samuel IV, 1214
Kirk, Samuel VI, 524
Kirk, Samuel R. II, 750
Kirk, Sara S. IV, 1215
Kirk, Sarah II, 700
Kirk, Sarah II, 886
Kirk, Sarah IV, 26
Kirk, Sarah IV, 43
Kirk, Sarah IV, 146
Kirk, Sarah IV, 152
Kirk, Sarah IV, 235
Kirk, Sarah IV, 299
Kirk, Sarah IV, 481
Kirk, Sarah IV, 482
Kirk, Sarah IV, 802
Kirk, Sarah IV, 803
Kirk, Sarah IV, 829
Kirk, Sarah IV, 830
Kirk, Sarah IV, 1169
Kirk, Sarah IV, 1214
Kirk, Sarah IV, 1215
Kirk, Sarah V, 501
Kirk, Sarah V, 508
Kirk, Sarah V, 689
Kirk, Sarah V, 690
Kirk, Sarah VI, 670
Kirk, Sarah VI, 733
Kirk, Sarah VI, 791
Kirk, Sarah Ann IV, 481
Kirk, Sarah Ann IV, 482
Kirk, Sarah Ann IV, 1151
Kirk, Sarah Ann IV, 1169
Kirk, Sarah Ann IV, 1214
Kirk, Sarah Elizabeth IV, 1169
Kirk, Sarah H. VI, 760
Kirk, Sarah H. VI, 791
Kirk, Sarah R. III, 423
Kirk, Sarah S. II, 709
Kirk, Sarah S. II, 750
Kirk, Sarah S. IV, 1214
Kirk, Sarah W. V, 508
Kirk, Sidwell IV, 235
Kirk, Sidwell IV, 731
Kirk, Sidwell IV, 829
Kirk, Silas III, 423
Kirk, Stanley V, 690
Kirk, Stephen IV, 1169
Kirk, Stephen IV, 1214
Kirk, Susan IV, 97
Kirk, Susan IV, 235
Kirk, Susan IV, 731
Kirk, Susan IV, 829
Kirk, Susan IV, 830
Kirk, Susan IV, 856
Kirk, Susan Lindley IV, 731
Kirk, Susanna IV, 43
Kirk, Susanna IV, 75
Kirk, Susanna IV, 97
Kirk, Susanna IV, 235
Kirk, Susanna IV, 248
Kirk, Susanna IV, 481
Kirk, Susanna IV, 482
Kirk, Susanna IV, 487
Kirk, Susanna IV, 495
Kirk, Susanna IV, 497
Kirk, Susanna IV, 1169
Kirk, Susanna IV, 1212
Kirk, Susanna IV, 1214
Kirk, Susanna IV, 1221
Kirk, Susanna V, 631
Kirk, Susanna P. II, 709
Kirk, Susannah IV, 482
Kirk, Susannah IV, 1151
Kirk, Susannah IV, 1169
Kirk, Susannah V, 473
Kirk, Susannah V, 508
Kirk, Susannah V, 631
Kirk, Susannah Jemima IV, 1169
Kirk, Tacy Lenox II, 785
Kirk, Tacy M. IV, 214
Kirk, Tacy M. IV, 235
Kirk, Tacy M. IV, 236
Kirk, Tacy M. IV, 629
Kirk, Tacy M. IV, 640
Kirk, Tamer II, 574
Kirk, Temperance III, 423
Kirk, Thamar II, 574
Kirk, Theodore J. IV, 1169
Kirk, Theophilus IV, 802
Kirk, Thomas II, 1007
Kirk, Thomas V, 508
Kirk, Thomas Clarkson V, 508
Kirk, Timothy IV, 43
Kirk, Timothy IV, 97
Kirk, Timothy IV, 152
Kirk, Timothy IV, 235
Kirk, Timothy IV, 481
Kirk, Timothy IV, 482
Kirk, Timothy IV, 495
Kirk, Timothy IV, 730
Kirk, Timothy IV, 731
Kirk, Timothy IV, 825
Kirk, Timothy IV, 829
Kirk, Timothy IV, 1169
Kirk, Timothy IV, 1189
Kirk, Timothy IV, 1212
Kirk, Timothy V, 508
Kirk, Timothy V, 536
Kirk, Timothy V, 580
Kirk, Timothy VI, 670
Kirk, Valentine III, 423
Kirk, Walter S. IV, 235
Kirk, Walter S. IV, 236
Kirk, Walter S. IV, 640
Kirk, Warren V, 690
Kirk, Wd. Lydia T. IV, 802
Kirk, Wd. Mary VI, 524
Kirk, Widow Rebekah I, 1033
Kirk, Wilbur V, 509
Kirk, Wilford N. IV, 640
Kirk, Willard B. IV, 973
Kirk, William III, 423
Kirk, William IV, 43
Kirk, William IV, 97
Kirk, William IV, 137
Kirk, William IV, 416
Kirk, William IV, 481
Kirk, William IV, 538
Kirk, William IV, 731
Kirk, William IV, 1169
Kirk, William V, 508
Kirk, William V, 542
Kirk, William VI, 464
Kirk, William VI, 476
Kirk, William VI, 524
Kirk, William VI, 670
Kirk, William VI, 946
Kirk, William H. IV, 482
Kirk, William J. IV, 236
Kirk, William J. IV, 640
Kirk, William J. IV, 829
Kirk, Willis V, 508
Kirk, Willis V, 509
Kirk, Wilmer B. V, 689
Kirk, Wilson F. V, 508
Kirk, Wilson T. V, 508
Kirk, Wm. I, 521
Kirk, Wm. IV, 146
Kirk, Wm. IV, 152
Kirk, Wm. IV, 235
Kirk, Wm. IV, 294
Kirk, Wm. IV, 465
Kirk, Wm. IV, 481
Kirk, Wm. IV, 490
Kirk, Wm. IV, 495
Kirk, Wm. IV, 497
Kirk, Wm. IV, 538
Kirk, Wm. IV, 748
Kirk, Wm. IV, 829
Kirk, Wm. IV, 973
Kirk, Wm. IV, 1169
Kirk, Wm. VI, 477
Kirk, Wm. VI, 524
Kirk, Wm. A. IV, 1169
Kirk, Wm. Allen IV, 1169
Kirk, Wm. Allen IV, 1186
Kirk, Wm. B. IV, 1214
Kirk, Wm. B. IV, 1215
Kirk, Wm. B. IV, 1225
Kirk, Wm. Joshua IV, 235
Kirk, Wm. R. IV, 1169
Kirk, Wm. S. II, 750
Kirk, Zadock P. IV, 482
Kirk, Zadock P. IV, 973
Kirk, Zadok IV, 482
Kirk, Zadok IV, 973
Kirk, Zeno IV, 1201
Kirk, Zeno IV, 1214
Kirk, Zeno IV, 1215
Kirkbride, Abijah VI, 571
Kirkbride, Ambrose VI, 571
Kirkbride, Ann II, 963
Kirkbride, Ann II, 1008
Kirkbride, Ann II, 1054
Kirkbride, Ann Eliza II, 294
Kirkbride, Ann J. II, 710
Kirkbride, Ann J. II, 750
Kirkbride, Ann W. II, 710
Kirkbride, Ann W. II, 750
Kirkbride, Ann, Jr. II, 1008
Kirkbride, Ann, Jr. II, 1023
Kirkbride, Anna II, 962
Kirkbride, Anna II, 1032
Kirkbride, Annie B. II, 963
Kirkbride, Annie B. II, 1054
Kirkbride, Asher IV, 1028
Kirkbride, Benjamin Franklin IV, 731
Kirkbride, David II, 963
Kirkbride, Edith II, 1007
Kirkbride, Edith II, 1018
Kirkbride, Elisabeth II, 1008
Kirkbride, Eliza Ann IV, 973
Kirkbride, Eliza Ann IV, 982
Kirkbride, Eliza P. I, 547
Kirkbride, Elizabeth II, 746
Kirkbride, Elizabeth II, 750
Kirkbride, Elizabeth II, 961
Kirkbride, Elizabeth II, 962
Kirkbride, Elizabeth II, 963
Kirkbride, Elizabeth II, 992
Kirkbride, Elizabeth II, 1007
Kirkbride, Elizabeth II, 1008
Kirkbride, Elizabeth II, 1030
Kirkbride, Elizabeth II, 1032
Kirkbride, Elizabeth II, 1035
Kirkbride, Elizabeth II, 1048
Kirkbride, Elizabeth II, 1052
Kirkbride, Elizabeth II, 1054
Kirkbride, Elizabeth II, 1075
Kirkbride, Elizabeth H. II, 750
Kirkbride, Elizabeth, Jr. II, 10
Kirkbride, Ellen II, 294
Kirkbride, Ellen II, 304
Kirkbride, Esther IV, 973
Kirkbride, Esther IV, 1011
Kirkbride, Ferdinand IV, 731

Kirkbride, Frances II, 963
Kirkbride, Frances II, 1008
Kirkbride, Frances Maria II, 814
Kirkbride, Frances Maria II, 819
Kirkbride, Francis II, 962
Kirkbride, Francis Maria VI, 524
Kirkbride, George B. II, 294
Kirkbride, Grace II, 574
Kirkbride, Grace II, 963
Kirkbride, Grace II, 1007
Kirkbride, Grace II, 1008
Kirkbride, Grace II, 1040
Kirkbride, Grace II, 1054
Kirkbride, Hannah II, 962
Kirkbride, Hannah II, 963
Kirkbride, Hannah II, 979
Kirkbride, Hannah II, 1007
Kirkbride, Hannah II, 1008
Kirkbride, Hannah II, 1024
Kirkbride, Hannah II, 1071
Kirkbride, Hannah II, 1075
Kirkbride, Hannah Emma II, 1066
Kirkbride, Harriet II, 294
Kirkbride, James S. IV, 731
Kirkbride, Jane II, 184
Kirkbride, Jane II, 294
Kirkbride, Jane II, 307
Kirkbride, Jane II, 321
Kirkbride, Jane II, 962
Kirkbride, Jane II, 1007
Kirkbride, Jane II, 1027
Kirkbride, Jane R. II, 321
Kirkbride, Jane R. II, 327
Kirkbride, Jno. II, 294
Kirkbride, John II, 321
Kirkbride, John II, 327
Kirkbride, John II, 961
Kirkbride, John II, 962
Kirkbride, John II, 1007
Kirkbride, John II, 1008
Kirkbride, John II, 1018
Kirkbride, John II, 1030
Kirkbride, John II, 1040
Kirkbride, John II, 1048
Kirkbride, John II, 1052
Kirkbride, John II, 1054
Kirkbride, John II, 1075
Kirkbride, John Paul VI, 524
Kirkbride, Jonathan II, 962
Kirkbride, Jonathan II, 963
Kirkbride, Jonathan II, 992
Kirkbride, Jonathan II, 1008
Kirkbride, Jonathan II, 1032
Kirkbride, Jonathan II, 1035
Kirkbride, Jonathan II, 1054
Kirkbride, Jonathan II, 1071
Kirkbride, Jonathan II, 1075
Kirkbride, Jonathan II, 1082
Kirkbride, Jonathan, Jr. II, 1075
Kirkbride, Joseph II, 184
Kirkbride, Joseph II, 962
Kirkbride, Joseph II, 963
Kirkbride, Joseph II, 1007
Kirkbride, Joseph II, 1008
Kirkbride, Joseph II, 1021
Kirkbride, Joseph II, 1024
Kirkbride, Joseph II, 1027
Kirkbride, Joseph II, 1041
Kirkbride, Joseph VI, 524
Kirkbride, Joseph Ann II, 710
Kirkbride, Joseph John II, 750
Kirkbride, Joseph, Jr. II, 1007
Kirkbride, Julia C. II, 294
Kirkbride, Julia C. II, 304
Kirkbride, Julia Clark II, 294
Kirkbride, Latitia II, 1008
Kirkbride, Latitia II, 1031
Kirkbride, Letitia II, 962
Kirkbride, Letitia II, 963
Kirkbride, Letitia VI, 563
Kirkbride, Letitia VI, 570
Kirkbride, Letitia VI, 571
Kirkbride, Letitia VI, 697
Kirkbride, Letitia VI, 705
Kirkbride, Letitia VI, 710
Kirkbride, Letitia VI, 711
Kirkbride, Lydia II, 321
Kirkbride, Lydia II, 327
Kirkbride, Mahlon II, 746
Kirkbride, Mahlon II, 750
Kirkbride, Mahlon II, 962
Kirkbride, Mahlon II, 963
Kirkbride, Mahlon II, 1007
Kirkbride, Mahlon II, 1008
Kirkbride, Mahlon II, 1023
Kirkbride, Mahlon II, 1024
Kirkbride, Mahlon II, 1031
Kirkbride, Mahlon II, 1035
Kirkbride, Mahlon II, 1042
Kirkbride, Mahlon II, 1052
Kirkbride, Mahlon II, 1054
Kirkbride, Mahlon II, 1075
Kirkbride, Mahlon IV, 973
Kirkbride, Mahlon IV, 1028
Kirkbride, Mahlon IV, 1039
Kirkbride, Mahlon VI, 570
Kirkbride, Mahlon S. II, 962
Kirkbride, Mahlon S. II, 963
Kirkbride, Mahlon S. II, 1054
Kirkbride, Mahlon S. II, 1086
Kirkbride, Mahlon, Jr. II, 1008
Kirkbride, Mahlon, Jr. II, 1023
Kirkbride, Margery II, 1008
Kirkbride, Margery II, 1040
Kirkbride, Marianna II, 1079
Kirkbride, Marianna T. II, 1075
Kirkbride, Marianna T. II, 1079
Kirkbride, Martha II, 1007
Kirkbride, Martha II, 1013
Kirkbride, Mary II, 804
Kirkbride, Mary II, 886
Kirkbride, Mary II, 962
Kirkbride, Mary II, 963
Kirkbride, Mary II, 971
Kirkbride, Mary II, 1007
Kirkbride, Mary II, 1008
Kirkbride, Mary II, 1021
Kirkbride, Mary II, 1024
Kirkbride, Mary II, 1031
Kirkbride, Mary II, 1035
Kirkbride, Mary II, 1041
Kirkbride, Mary II, 1075
Kirkbride, Mary IV, 731
Kirkbride, Mary IV, 1028
Kirkbride, Mary IV, 1029
Kirkbride, Mary VI, 524
Kirkbride, Mary VI, 571
Kirkbride, Mary A. IV, 986
Kirkbride, Mary Ann VI, 524
Kirkbride, Mary Anna T. II, 1066
Kirkbride, Mary B. II, 746
Kirkbride, Mary B. II, 750
Kirkbride, Mary B. II, 1054
Kirkbride, Mary Ella II, 963
Kirkbride, Mary Ella II, 1054
Kirkbride, Mary Esther IV, 973
Kirkbride, Mary W. II, 963
Kirkbride, Mary W. II, 1054
Kirkbride, Mathew II, 963
Kirkbride, Matthew II, 963
Kirkbride, Nancy IV, 731
Kirkbride, Nancy IV, 1028
Kirkbride, Nancy IV, 1029
Kirkbride, Paul II, 294
Kirkbride, Phebe II, 962
Kirkbride, Phebe II, 1004
Kirkbride, Phebe II, 1007
Kirkbride, Phebe II, 1008
Kirkbride, Phebe II, 1014
Kirkbride, Phebe Ann II, 963
Kirkbride, Phebe Ann II, 1052
Kirkbride, Phebe Ann II, 1054
Kirkbride, Phebe Ann II, 1086
Kirkbride, Prudence II, 963
Kirkbride, Prudence II, 1008
Kirkbride, Prudence II, 1032
Kirkbride, R. Estella II, 1075
Kirkbride, R. Estella II, 1079
Kirkbride, Rachel II, 961
Kirkbride, Rachel II, 962
Kirkbride, Rachel II, 1071
Kirkbride, Rachel II, 1075
Kirkbride, Rachel C. II, 1075
Kirkbride, Rachel C. II, 1082
Kirkbride, Rachel S. II, 708
Kirkbride, Rachel S. II, 1052
Kirkbride, Rachel S. II, 1054
Kirkbride, Rebecca II, 962
Kirkbride, Rebecca II, 963
Kirkbride, Rebecca Estella II, 1075
Kirkbride, Rebecca Estella II, 1082
Kirkbride, Rebecca W. II, 281
Kirkbride, Rebecca W. II, 294
Kirkbride, Rebecca W. II, 710
Kirkbride, Richard II, 304
Kirkbride, Richard M. II, 178
Kirkbride, Richard M. II, 294
Kirkbride, Richard M. II, 1054
Kirkbride, Robert II, 962
Kirkbride, Robert II, 963
Kirkbride, Robert II, 979
Kirkbride, Robert II, 1008
Kirkbride, Robert IV, 1028
Kirkbride, Robert Twining II, 1066
Kirkbride, Roberta S. IV, 973
Kirkbride, Ruth II, 963
Kirkbride, Samuel II, 963
Kirkbride, Sarah II, 810
Kirkbride, Sarah II, 829
Kirkbride, Sarah II, 962
Kirkbride, Sarah II, 963
Kirkbride, Sarah II, 983
Kirkbride, Sarah II, 1007
Kirkbride, Sarah II, 1008
Kirkbride, Sarah II, 1021
Kirkbride, Sarah II, 1042
Kirkbride, Sarah IV, 731
Kirkbride, Sarah IV, 1028
Kirkbride, Sarah, Jr. II, 1007
Kirkbride, Stacy II, 962
Kirkbride, Stacy II, 963
Kirkbride, Stacy II, 983
Kirkbride, Stacy II, 1008
Kirkbride, Stacy II, 1021
Kirkbride, Thomas II, 386
Kirkbride, Thomas II, 710
Kirkbride, Thomas II, 962
Kirkbride, Thomas II, 963
Kirkbride, Thomas II, 992
Kirkbride, Thomas II, 1007
Kirkbride, Thomas II, 1040
Kirkbride, Thomas S. II, 750
Kirkbride, Thomas S. II, 962
Kirkbride, Thomas S. II, 1054
Kirkbride, Watson IV, 731
Kirkbride, Wd. Elizabeth II, 992
Kirkbride, William II, 962
Kirkbride, William B. II, 963
Kirkbride, William C. II, 1066
Kirkbride, Wm. B. II, 746
Kirkbride, Wm. B. II, 750
Kirkbride, Wm. B. II, 1054
Kirkbride, Wm. C. II, 1075
Kirkbride, Wm. C. II, 1079
Kirkbride, Wm. C. II, 1082
Kirkbridge, Joseph II, 1029
Kirkbridge, Sarah II, 1029
Kirke, Elizabeth V, 508
Kirke, Elizabeth V, 514
Kirke, Thomas II, 1007
Kirkham, Cora Celesta May V, 581
Kirkham, Cora M. V, 581
Kirkland, Dolly VI, 844
Kirkland, George VI, 844
Kirkman, Adaline I, 682
Kirkman, Adaline I, 689
Kirkman, Alfred Andrew I, 620
Kirkman, Alice I, 823
Kirkman, Alice R. I, 621
Kirkman, Alpheus A. I, 636
Kirkman, Andrew M. I, 620
Kirkman, Andrew M. I, 621
Kirkman, Bernard I, 636
Kirkman, Bernard Worth I, 620
Kirkman, Cyrus I, 823
Kirkman, Effie Myrtle I, 636
Kirkman, Elizabeth I, 928
Kirkman, Emily I, 682
Kirkman, Emily Ann I, 682
Kirkman, Emily Ann I, 685
Kirkman, Emily Ann I, 690
Kirkman, George Lindsey I, 682
Kirkman, Herman Peel I, 620
Kirkman, James I, 682
Kirkman, James Elzeran I, 682
Kirkman, Jane I, 620
Kirkman, Jane I, 621
Kirkman, Jane I, 636
Kirkman, John W. I, 556
Kirkman, Joseph Albert I, 620
Kirkman, Julia A. I, 387
Kirkman, Julia A. I, 403
Kirkman, Louisa I, 620
Kirkman, Louisa L. I, 636
Kirkman, Margaret I, 934
Kirkman, Martha I, 618
Kirkman, Martha A. I, 682
Kirkman, Mary I, 556
Kirkman, Mary I, 636
Kirkman, Mary I, 640
Kirkman, Mary Hinton I, 620
Kirkman, Mary J. I, 675
Kirkman, Mary J. I, 682
Kirkman, Maud E. I, 618
Kirkman, Myrtle E. I, 631
Kirkman, Myrtle E. I, 636
Kirkman, Myrtle Effie I, 620
Kirkman, Nora I, 682
Kirkman, Nora I, 689
Kirkman, Peter Alphonso I, 682
Kirkman, W. F. I, 618
Kirkman, William O. I, 387
Kirkman, William O. I, 403
Kirkman, William O. I, 682
Kirkman, William Oliver I, 682
Kirkman, Wm. V, 916
Kirkner, Jacob II, 796
Kirkner, Martha II, 796
Kirkner, Sarah II, 796
Kirkpatric, Fronie IV, 1169
Kirkpatrick, Anna III, 194
Kirkpatrick, Daniel III, 111
Kirkpatrick, Daniel III, 194
Kirkpatrick, Daniel III, 371
Kirkpatrick, Dinah III, 194
Kirkpatrick, Dinah III, 371
Kirkpatrick, Dorcas III, 111
Kirkpatrick, Dorcas III, 194
Kirkpatrick, Ida IV, 236
Kirkpatrick, John W. H. I, 859
Kirkpatrick, Roxanna I, 859
Kirkpatrick, Roxannah I, 890
Kirkpatrick, Rufus I, 859
Kirkpatrick, Rufus I, 890
Kirkpatrick, Samuel III, 194
Kirkpatrick, Sarah III, 194
Kirkpatrick, Susanna II, 386
Kirkpatrick, Thomas VI, 976
Kirkwood, John IV, 236
Kirkwood, Mary II, 712
Kirkwood, Mary II, 713
Kirkwood, Mary IV, 741
Kirkwood, Rebecca Ann II, 702
Kirlin, Ann II, 573
Kirlin, David II, 573
Kirlin, Elizabeth II, 573
Kirlin, Jemima II, 573
Kirlin, John II, 573
Kirlin, Mary II, 573
Kirlin, Sarah II, 573
Kirling, Elizabeth II, 237
Kirll, John II, 386
Kirll, John II, 445
Kirll, Joseph II, 386
Kirll, Joseph II, 445
Kirll, Joseph II, 471
Kirll, Joseph II, 574
Kirll, Margaret II, 445
Kirll, Mary II, 386
Kirll, Mary II, 471
Kirll, Mary II, 574
Kirscht, Amelia C. II, 710
Kirscht, August C. II, 710
Kirscht, Charles W. II, 710
Kirscht, Charles W. II, 750
Kirsey, John V, 507
Kirshaw, Sidney IV, 1324
Kirtley, Lottie H. V, 690
Kirtley, Lottie H. V, 693
Kirtly, Jeremiah VI, 946
Kirtly, Keziah VI, 946
Kirts, Ann IV, 822
Kirts, Ann IV, 830
Kirvey, Edmund II, 386
Kirvey, Philip II, 386
Kirwan, John J. III, 130
Kirwan, John J. III, 194
Kirwan, Marie III, 194
Kirwan, Mary Louise III, 130
Kirwan, Mary Louise III, 194
Kiser, Armilda V, 581
Kiser, Byron V, 1005
Kiser, Elizabeth C. V, 184
Kiser, Francis M. V, 344
Kiser, Jacob V, 581
Kiser, Mary V, 1005
Kiser, R. M. V, 1005
Kiser, Sarah J. V, 1005
Kisling, Charles IV, 1215
Kisling, Charles H. IV, 1215
Kisling, Chas. H. IV, 1215
Kisling, Eunice Juanita V, 306
Kisling, Gladys E. V, 306
Kisling, John F. V, 306
Kisling, John G. V, 306
Kisling, Lusetta IV, 1215
Kisling, Mary Ellen V, 306
Kisling, Mary J. V, 306
Kissam, Albert W. III, 194
Kissam, Albert W. III, 280
Kissam, Albert W. III, 367
Kissam, Benj. III, 194
Kissam, Emeline III, 489
Kissam, Emeline S. III, 501
Kissam, Jane III, 158
Kissam, Jane III, 194
Kissam, Jane VI, 747
Kissam, Jane VI, 760
Kissam, Margaret III, 194
Kissam, Margaret III, 280
Kissam, Margaret III, 367
Kissam, Margaret III, 381
Kissam, Margaret III, 389
Kissam, Margaret C. III, 194
Kissam, Marie III, 299
Kissam, Natilie W. III, 194
Kissam, Natilie W. III, 280
Kissam, Natilie Wardell III, 194
Kissam, Oscar III, 489
Kissam, Oscar III, 501
Kissam, Sarah S. III, 194
Kissan, Levine III, 400
Kitcham, Ebenezer III, 503
Kitcham, Sarah III, 503
Kitcham, Susie III, 503
Kitchen, ??? VI, 95
Kitchen, Ann V, 35
Kitchen, Ann V, 90
Kitchen, Hannah L. II, 294
Kitchen, Lydia VI, 106
Kitchen, Lydia VI, 114
Kitchen, Martha VI, 98
Kitchen, Martha VI, 114
Kitchen, Mary II, 574
Kitchen, Mary II, 683
Kitchen, Mary IV, 1030
Kitchen, Nancy VI, 831
Kitchen, Nelle Collins V, 1005
Kitchen, Nellie B. IV, 1324
Kitchen, Nellie V. IV, 1324
Kitchen, Samuel VI, 845
Kitchen, Samuel C. II, 750
Kitchen, Thomas II, 574
Kitchen, Thomas VI, 831
Kitchen, Thomas VI, 852
Kitchen, Tyral Bailey VI, 114
Kitchens, Bales I, 1157
Kitchens, Nancy I, 1157
Kitchin, J. Brinton III, 194
Kitchin, Jennie C. III, 194
Kitchin, Martha T. III, 194
Kitchin, Mary II, 589
Kitchin, Mina III, 194
Kitchin, Sam'l Carey III, 194
Kitchin, Samuel II, 750
Kitchin, Samuel C. II, 750
Kitchin, Samuel C. III, 194
Kitchin, Thomas II, 589
Kitching, Matthew VI, 75
Kitching, Pennington III, 194
Kite, ??? II, 386
Kite, Abbie III, 194
Kite, Abi II, 386
Kite, Abi II, 574
Kite, Abi II, 676
Kite, Abi II, 721
Kite, Abraham II, 471
Kite, Abraham II, 574
Kite, Abraham II, 621
Kite, Anna V, 916
Kite, Anna Elizabeth V, 916
Kite, Anna H. II, 702
Kite, Anna M. II, 750
Kite, Annie S. II, 710
Kite, Annie S. II, 750
Kite, Annie S. IV, 1065
Kite, Benjamin II, 386
Kite, Benjamin II, 574
Kite, Benjamin II, 676
Kite, Benjamin II, 710
Kite, Benjamin II, 750
Kite, Benjamin II, 773
Kite, Benjamin IV, 830
Kite, Benjamin IV, 973
Kite, Benjamin, Jr. II, 574
Kite, Charles IV, 971
Kite, Charlotta IV, 973
Kite, Charlotte IV, 973
Kite, Charlotte IV, 998
Kite, Daisy V, 184
Kite, Deborah II, 386
Kite, Deborah II, 574
Kite, Deborah II, 622
Kite, Deborah II, 815
Kite, Dora II, 710
Kite, Edith II, 386
Kite, Edith II, 574
Kite, Edith II, 710
Kite, Edith II, 730
Kite, Edith II, 750
Kite, Edith V, 916
Kite, Eliza II, 750
Kite, Eliza Ann II, 386
Kite, Elizabeth II, 386
Kite, Elizabeth II, 574
Kite, Elizabeth II, 579
Kite, Elizabeth II, 750
Kite, Elizabeth II, 765
Kite, Elizabeth L. II, 294
Kite, Elizabeth L. II, 300
Kite, Ellen IV, 973
Kite, Ellen B. IV, 951
Kite, Ellen B. IV, 973
Kite, Esther II, 750
Kite, Grissel II, 574
Kite, Grissell II, 574
Kite, Grissell II, 579
Kite, Hannah II, 386
Kite, Hannah II, 574
Kite, Hannah II, 710

Kite, Hannah II, 750
Kite, Isaac II, 386
Kite, J. Alban II, 294
Kite, J. Alban II, 300
Kite, James II, 294
Kite, James II, 300
Kite, James II, 386
Kite, James II, 574
Kite, James II, 710
Kite, James II, 750
Kite, James II, 1088
Kite, James IV, 416
Kite, James R. II, 710
Kite, James R. II, 750
Kite, James R. IV, 416
Kite, James R. IV, 421
Kite, James R. IV, 1065
Kite, James Rodman II, 750
Kite, James, Jr. II, 386
Kite, Jehu L. IV, 951
Kite, Jehu L. IV, 971
Kite, Jehu L. IV, 973
Kite, Jehu L. IV, 998
Kite, Jehu Lord IV, 731
Kite, Jehu Lord IV, 973
Kite, Jehu Lord IV, 976
Kite, John II, 386
Kite, John IV, 973
Kite, John C. IV, 794
Kite, John L. II, 574
Kite, John L. II, 710
Kite, John L. II, 1088
Kite, John L. IV, 830
Kite, John Letchworth II, 386
Kite, John P. V, 184
Kite, Jonathan II, 386
Kite, Jonathan II, 574
Kite, Joseph II, 386
Kite, Joseph II, 574
Kite, Joseph II, 710
Kite, Joseph II, 750
Kite, Joseph II, 773
Kite, Joseph, Jr. II, 574
Kite, Joseph, Jr. II, 750
Kite, Joshua II, 386
Kite, Joshua II, 710
Kite, Lydia II, 710
Kite, Lydia IV, 416
Kite, Lydia B. II, 710
Kite, Lydia B. II, 750
Kite, Lydia B. IV, 1065
Kite, Margaret V, 895
Kite, Margaret V, 916
Kite, Margarite V, 916
Kite, Martha II, 490
Kite, Martha II, 574
Kite, Mary II, 386
Kite, Mary II, 471
Kite, Mary II, 574
Kite, Mary II, 579
Kite, Mary II, 621
Kite, Mary II, 750
Kite, Mary II, 1088
Kite, Mary IV, 794
Kite, Mary IV, 830
Kite, Mary IV, 973
Kite, Mary Anna II, 294
Kite, Mary Anna II, 300
Kite, Mary Burden II, 574
Kite, Mary F. II, 750
Kite, Mary L. II, 1088
Kite, Mary M. II, 710
Kite, Mary M. II, 750
Kite, Mary M. IV, 1065
Kite, Mary T. II, 710
Kite, Nathan II, 386
Kite, Nathan II, 710
Kite, Nathan II, 750
Kite, Nathan II, 751
Kite, Rebecca II, 386
Kite, Rebecca II, 574
Kite, Rebecca II, 676
Kite, Rebecca II, 710
Kite, Rebecca II, 730
Kite, Rebecca II, 750
Kite, Rebecca II, 773
Kite, Rebecca IV, 731
Kite, Rebecca W. II, 750
Kite, Ruth II, 710
Kite, Ruth IV, 416
Kite, Ruth IV, 421
Kite, Ruth IV, 1065
Kite, Ruth M. IV, 1065
Kite, Samuel II, 710
Kite, Sarah II, 386
Kite, Sarah II, 574
Kite, Susanna II, 386
Kite, Susanna II, 574
Kite, Susanna II, 710
Kite, Susanna II, 718
Kite, Susanna II, 750
Kite, Susanna II, 765
Kite, Susanna S. II, 710
Kite, Susannah II, 495
Kite, Susannah II, 574
Kite, Thomas II, 386
Kite, Thomas II, 471
Kite, Thomas II, 574
Kite, Thomas II, 579
Kite, Thomas II, 622
Kite, Thomas II, 710
Kite, Thomas II, 730
Kite, Thomas II, 750
Kite, Thomas II, 765
Kite, Thomas V, 916
Kite, Thomas, Jr. II, 750
Kite, Thomas, Jr. V, 916
Kite, Thomas, Sr. II, 386
Kite, Thos. V, 895
Kite, Thos. V, 916
Kite, Thos., Jr. V, 916
Kite, William II, 386
Kite, William II, 710
Kite, William Henry V, 916
Kite, Wm. II, 710
Kite, Wm. II, 750
Kite, Wm. H. V, 916
Kitely, Elizabeth II, 712
Kitely, Joseph II, 712
Kitely, Mary II, 711
Kitely, Mary II, 712
Kithcart, Allen II, 386
Kithcart, William II, 386
Kithkart, Jane N. IV, 236
Kithkart, Jennie N. IV, 236
Kitner, George II, 386
Kitselman, Raymond IV, 875
Kitson, Albert IV, 1324
Kitson, Alfred II, 867
Kitson, Alfred Ernest II, 886
Kitson, Eliza II, 710
Kitson, Eliza II, 714
Kitson, Elsie IV, 1324
Kitson, Eva IV, 1324
Kitson, James II, 867
Kitson, James II, 886
Kitson, Lizzie IV, 1324
Kitson, Nelle Collins V, 1005
Kitson, Sarah V, 1005
Kitson, Sarah Elizabeth II, 867
Kitson, Sarah Elizabeth II, 886
Kitson, Susannah Woolston II, 867
Kitson, Susannah Woolston II, 886
Kitte, John II, 386
Kitte, Joseph II, 386
Kittel, Geo. W. IV, 1324
Kitteringham, Walter IV, 1324
Kittle, Geo. W. IV, 1324
Kittrell, Cora H. V, 916
Kittrell, John V, 690
Kittrell, John L. I, 1157
Kittrell, Mollie I, 1157
Kitts, Helen P. II, 751
Kitts, Helen P. II, 761
Kitzmiller, Chas. V, 1005
Kitzmiller, Henry V, 1005
Kitzmiller, Maggie Gilbert V, 1005
Kivel, Patsey VI, 799
Kivet, Hannah I, 403
Kivett, Bertie Elmore I, 615
Kivett, Rhoda I, 615
Kivett, S. W. I, 615
Kivette, Frances I, 636
Kivette, Francis Virginia I, 627
Kivette, Rhoda I, 627
Kivette, S. W. I, 627
Kizer, Byron V, 1005
Kizer, Elizabeth C. V, 184
Kizer, Louisa V, 257
Kizer, Mary V, 257
Kizer, Mary V, 277
Kizser, Joanna W. IV, 322
Kizser, Johanna W. IV, 340
Klain, John Eberly V, 90
Klamt, ??? III, 317
Klamt, Harvey III, 194
Klamt, Harvey Leeson III, 194
Klamt, Henrietta E. III, 317
Klamt, Henry E. III, 194
Klamt, Henry E. III, 317
Klaphaak, David Roberts VI, 760
Klaphaak, Johannus Clara VI, 760
Klaphaak, Mary VI, 760
Klaphaak, Mary VI, 773
Klaphaak, Patrus J. VI, 760
Klaphaak, Peter John VI, 760
Klaphaak, Peter John VI, 773
Klaphaak, Peter John, Jr. VI, 760
Klapp, Anna II, 574
Klapp, Anna II, 598
Klause, Ralph C. IV, 1324
Klein, Bertha W. IV, 1310
Klein, Dr. M. C. VI, 754
Klein, Esther Boone VI, 754
Klein, Hester V, 90
Klein, Hester B. VI, 665
Klein, Hester B. VI, 670
Klein, John E. V, 83
Klein, John E. V, 90
Klein, John Eberly V, 90
Klein, Madison V, 90
Klein, Martha M. V, 83
Klein, Martha M. V, 90
Klein, Mrs. H. E. IV, 482
Klenke, Pauline II, 127
Klepinger, Eleon Dale V, 751
Klepinger, Glenna V, 751
Klepinger, Harold V, 751
Klepinger, Juanita V, 751
Klepinger, Nolan Wayne V, 751
Klieves, Dr. F. A. IV, 482
Klieves, Dr. Frank A. IV, 482
Kline, Bertha Walker IV, 1324
Kline, Frederick Ludwig II, 804
Kline, Hannah VI, 412
Kline, Ida V, 847
Kline, Ida P. II, 804
Kline, John E. VI, 412
Kline, John Eberle VI, 412
Kline, John Eberley VI, 412
Kline, Madison VI, 412
Kline, Mary V, 257
Kline, Mary V, 690
Kline, Phebe R. II, 886
Kline, Sarah C. II, 886
Kline, Sarah Catherine II, 804
Kline, Sarah Cowgill II, 804
Kline, Thelma V, 690
Kline, Walter Lyon II, 804
Kline, Wd. Sarah Cowgill II, 804
Klingsmith, Elsie E. III, 17
Klippard, William V, 581
Klise, Mollie V, 690
Klise, Mollie V, 706
Klopp, Elizabeth F. III, 84
Klopp, Elizabeth F. III, 194
Klopper, John V, 90
Klug, Modesta V, 916
Knabley, John II, 575
Knabley, Sarah II, 575
Knapp, Anna IV, 1371
Knapp, Elsie III, 179
Knapp, Elsie III, 194
Knapp, Elsie III, 195
Knapp, Elsie III, 258
Knapp, Elsie III, 259
Knapp, Emma III, 194
Knapp, Emma III, 259
Knapp, Fannie M. III, 195
Knapp, Fannie M. III, 214
Knapp, Gertrude III, 195
Knapp, Gertrude III, 263
Knapp, Gertrude VI, 693
Knapp, Milton III, 195
Knapp, Milton III, 263
Knapp, Orlando IV, 1238
Knapp, Paula III, 195
Knapp, Paula III, 263
Knapp, Seth IV, 1371
Knapp, Shepherd III, 194
Knapp, Shepherd III, 259
Knapton, Ann II, 33
Knapton, Ann II, 76
Knapton, Ann II, 83
Knapton, Benjamin II, 33
Knapton, Benjamin II, 76
Knapton, Benjamin II, 83
Knapton, Phebe II, 33
Knapton, Phebe II, 83
Knapton, Phebe II, 95
Kneadler, Bell V, 356
Kneadler, Belle V, 344
Knealer, Edith V, 459
Knee, Annie V, 184
Knee, Lola V, 184
Knee, Lorena V, 184
Knee, William V, 184
Knee, Wm. V, 184
Kneed, Elanora V, 833
Kneed, Rebecca V, 833
Kneel, Charles VI, 335
Kneisley, Rena Vansant V, 344
Knick, Blanch V, 631
Knick, Charles V, 631
Knick, Elbert V, 631
Knick, Mary V, 631
Knick, Myrtle V, 631
Kniffen, A. Sidney III, 277
Kniffen, Algernon Sidney III, 195
Kniffen, Algernon Sidney III, 267
Kniffen, Edgar III, 195
Kniffen, Eliz. C. III, 195
Kniffen, Eliz. C. III, 277
Kniffen, Ella III, 195
Kniffen, Ella III, 267
Kniffen, Emalane C. III, 195
Kniffen, Emelane C. III, 277
Kniffen, Sarah Ann III, 195
Kniffin, Alfred IV, 1238
Kniffin, Daniel IV, 1238
Kniffin, Dolly IV, 1238
Kniffin, Elizabeth III, 510
Kniffin, Ida IV, 1238
Kniffin, J. M. III, 510
Kniffin, Kittie IV, 1238
Kniffin, Kitty IV, 1238
Kniffin, Lucy IV, 1238
Kniffin, Lucy A. IV, 1238
Kniffin, Lula IV, 1238
Kniffin, Lulu IV, 1238
Kniffin, Mary III, 510
Kniffin, Mary IV, 1238
Kniffin, Minda IV, 1238
Kniffin, Sarah IV, 1169
Kniffin, Sarah IV, 1177
Knight, ??? III, 195
Knight, Abel I, 506
Knight, Abel I, 534
Knight, Abel I, 556
Knight, Abel I, 823
Knight, Abel I, 824
Knight, Abel I, 847
Knight, Abel II, 386
Knight, Abel II, 575
Knight, Abel II, 710
Knight, Abel II, 751
Knight, Abel IV, 43
Knight, Abel IV, 44
Knight, Abel IV, 49
Knight, Abel IV, 66
Knight, Abel IV, 731
Knight, Abel VI, 412
Knight, Abel, Jr. I, 556
Knight, Abigail II, 453
Knight, Abigail II, 574
Knight, Abigail II, 575
Knight, Abijah IV, 538
Knight, Able I, 343
Knight, Able I, 403
Knight, Able I, 506
Knight, Able I, 556
Knight, Able, II I, 506
Knight, Abraham I, 594
Knight, Abraham I, 823
Knight, Abram I, 824
Knight, Absalem I, 506
Knight, Absalom I, 928
Knight, Absalom I, 929
Knight, Absalom I, 945
Knight, Absalom II, 1008
Knight, Absilla I, 244
Knight, Absilla I, 260
Knight, Absle I, 244
Knight, Absolam I, 10
Knight, Absoley I, 244
Knight, Absoley I, 260
Knight, Absolum II, 1008
Knight, Absolum II, 1040
Knight, Aletha I, 556
Knight, Aletha I, 627
Knight, Alexander II, 792
Knight, Alexander II, 875
Knight, Alexander II, 887
Knight, Alexander, Jr. II, 805
Knight, Amos Peasley IV, 561
Knight, Andrew I, 506
Knight, Andrew I, 556
Knight, Andrew I, 574
Knight, Ann I, 506
Knight, Ann I, 556
Knight, Ann I, 570
Knight, Ann II, 956
Knight, Ann II, 957
Knight, Ann II, 1008
Knight, Ann II, 1040
Knight, Ann IV, 38
Knight, Ann IV, 43
Knight, Ann IV, 44
Knight, Ann IV, 49
Knight, Ann IV, 66
Knight, Ann IV, 97
Knight, Ann IV, 125
Knight, Ann IV, 128
Knight, Ann IV, 1283
Knight, Ann P. II, 701
Knight, Ann P. II, 986
Knight, Ann P. II, 1008
Knight, Ann, Sr. IV, 44
Knight, Anna I, 594
Knight, Anna I, 823
Knight, Anna I, 824
Knight, Anna III, 45
Knight, Anna V, 916
Knight, Anna K. III, 195
Knight, Anna K. V, 916
Knight, Anna W. II, 710
Knight, Anna W. II, 751
Knight, Anne II, 992
Knight, Anne III, 195
Knight, Anne VI, 311
Knight, Anne K. V, 916
Knight, Annie K. III, 195
Knight, Armela I, 556
Knight, Armiger I, 260
Knight, Arthur Percival V, 916
Knight, Asa I, 627
Knight, Azariah I, 506
Knight, Benajah I, 10
Knight, Benajah I, 929
Knight, Benedict II, 792
Knight, Benj. I, 506
Knight, Benjamin I, 1067
Knight, Benjamin IV, 1283
Knight, Benjamin Ansell IV, 128
Knight, Bushrod W. II, 804
Knight, Bushrod W. II, 886
Knight, Bushrod Washington II, 886
Knight, Bushrod Washington II, 887
Knight, Bushrod Washington II, 941
Knight, Caleb II, 790
Knight, Caroline II, 386
Knight, Caroline II, 751
Knight, Caroline R. II, 887
Knight, Caroline R. II, 900
Knight, Catharine I, 506
Knight, Catharine IV, 538
Knight, Catharine C. II, 887
Knight, Catharine Canby II, 804
Knight, Catharine, Jr. IV, 538
Knight, Charity Ellen III, 195
Knight, Charity Ellen III, 222
Knight, Charles II, 575
Knight, Charles Burton II, 1008
Knight, Charles D. II, 751
Knight, Charles F. IV, 1283
Knight, Charles W. II, 575
Knight, Charles Wilson II, 804
Knight, Charles, Jr. II, 887
Knight, Charley IV, 1283
Knight, Chas. Wilson II, 887
Knight, Christan I, 1067
Knight, Christan I, 1071
Knight, Christan Thomas I, 107(
Knight, Clara Alice IV, 1283
Knight, Clifford IV, 1238
Knight, Cooper D. III, 195
Knight, Cornelius I, 556
Knight, Cornelius I, 620
Knight, Cynthia I, 506
Knight, Daniel II, 804
Knight, David II, 805
Knight, David II, 869
Knight, David II, 887
Knight, David IV, 44
Knight, Deborah Ann I, 682
Knight, Delilah I, 10
Knight, Delilah I, 929
Knight, Dora I, 928
Knight, Dora I, 929
Knight, Dora I, 945
Knight, Dora W. I, 10
Knight, Dorothy III, 195
Knight, Dorothy III, 222
Knight, Dorothy IV, 44
Knight, Dorothy IV, 49
Knight, Dubre II, 294
Knight, Dubree II, 237
Knight, Ebenezer II, 804
Knight, Ebenezer II, 887
Knight, Edith M. II, 887
Knight, Edith M. II, 900
Knight, Edna II, 386
Knight, Edna II, 575
Knight, Edna III, 195
Knight, Edward D. II, 887
Knight, Edward Duffield II, 805
Knight, Edward H. V, 916
Knight, Edward Henry V, 916
Knight, Edward K. II, 887
Knight, Edward Samuel IV, 1283
Knight, Edwin II, 386
Knight, Eleanor II, 751
Knight, Elias I, 506
Knight, Elias I, 556
Knight, Elias I, 1008
Knight, Elias I, 1010
Knight, Elisabeth I, 231
Knight, Elisabeth I, 244

ight, Eliza IV, 1283
ight, Eliza Ann V, 90
ight, Elizabeth I, 506
ight, Elizabeth I, 556
ight, Elizabeth I, 567
ight, Elizabeth I, 1070
ight, Elizabeth II, 83
ight, Elizabeth II, 89
ight, Elizabeth II, 386
ight, Elizabeth II, 575
ight, Elizabeth II, 688
ight, Elizabeth II, 710
ight, Elizabeth II, 751
ight, Elizabeth II, 792
ight, Elizabeth II, 823
ight, Elizabeth II, 886
ight, Elizabeth II, 941
ight, Elizabeth II, 982
ight, Elizabeth II, 1008
ight, Elizabeth II, 1045
ight, Elizabeth II, 1054
ight, Elizabeth IV, 44
ight, Elizabeth IV, 46
ight, Elizabeth IV, 236
ight, Elizabeth IV, 538
ight, Elizabeth IV, 548
ight, Elizabeth C. II, 1044
ight, Elizabeth C. II, 1054
ight, Elizabeth C. V, 90
ight, Elizabeth C. V, 126
ight, Elizabeth Cooper II, 805
ight, Elizabeth H. II, 386
ight, Elizabeth H. II, 751
ight, Elizabeth H. II, 760
ight, Elizabeth J. II, 751
ight, Elizabeth J. II, 760
ight, Elizabeth Jane IV, 1283
ight, Elizabeth Jones II, 386
ight, Elizabeth Jones II, 751
ight, Elizabeth L. II, 1054
ight, Elizabeth L. Antrim III, 195
ight, Elizabeth P. II, 800
ight, Elizabeth P. II, 803
ight, Ella I, 620
ight, Ellen II, 710
ight, Ellen II, 751
ight, Ellen II, 929
ight, Emmor III, 195
ight, Emmor III, 352
ight, Emmor IV, 538
ight, Eva Helen III, 195
ight, Evan II, 804
ight, Evan II, 887
ight, Ezekiel Hunn III, 195
ight, Ezra Croasdale II, 804
ight, Fannie IV, 1283
ight, Gainer II, 886
ight, Gainer II, 887
night, Gainor II, 321
night, Gaynor II, 237
night, Gaynor II, 294
night, Geo H. V, 916
night, Geo, Jr. V, 916
night, Geo. V, 916
night, Geo. Henry III, 45
ight, Geo. Henry III, 195
ight, Geo. Henry V, 916
night, George III, 195
night, George IV, 1283
ight, George V, 916
ight, George VI, 760
night, George Edward II, 805
night, George Edward II, 869
night, George Edward II, 887
night, George Harris IV, 1283
night, George Henry III, 195
night, George Henry V, 916
night, George Henry, Jr. III, 195
night, George Palmer III, 195
night, Giles II, 805
night, Gyles II, 575
night, Hamilton IV, 1283
night, Hannah I, 506
night, Hannah I, 556
night, Hannah II, 386
night, Hannah II, 387
night, Hannah II, 457
night, Hannah II, 532
night, Hannah II, 575
night, Hannah IV, 32
night, Hannah IV, 44
night, Hannah IV, 97
night, Hannah IV, 128
night, Hannah IV, 537
night, Hannah IV, 538
night, Hannah C. II, 575
night, Harriet A. II, 805
night, Harriet Elizabeth III, 195
Knight, Harry K. III, 195
Knight, Harry P. III, 195
Knight, Harry P. III, 222
Knight, Harry Palmer III, 195
Knight, Harry S. III, 195
Knight, Hazel Starbuck V, 690
Knight, Helen VI, 412
Knight, Helen VI, 417
Knight, Henrietta I, 556
Knight, Henrietta I, 614
Knight, Henrietta I, 627
Knight, Henry II, 386
Knight, Henry II, 575
Knight, Henry II, 887
Knight, Henry II, 900
Knight, Henry III, 195
Knight, Henry IV, 44
Knight, Henry R. II, 887
Knight, Henry R. II, 900
Knight, Henry Ridgway II, 887
Knight, Henry S. IV, 97
Knight, Hilda IV, 1256
Knight, Hiram IV, 538
Knight, Hulday I, 556
Knight, Immer IV, 538
Knight, Immor IV, 561
Knight, Ira I, 556
Knight, Ira Lee I, 929
Knight, Isaac I, 506
Knight, Isaac I, 556
Knight, Isaac D. II, 575
Knight, Isaac D. II, 751
Knight, Israel II, 575
Knight, Israel II, 751
Knight, Israel II, 887
Knight, Jacob II, 321
Knight, Jacob III, 195
Knight, James II, 386
Knight, James E. IV, 1283
Knight, James Edwards IV, 1283
Knight, Jane II, 790
Knight, Jane D. II, 575
Knight, Jane D. II, 751
Knight, Jane Knight II, 804
Knight, John I, 506
Knight, John I, 556
Knight, John I, 620
Knight, John I, 1067
Knight, John II, 33
Knight, John II, 83
Knight, John II, 386
Knight, John II, 387
Knight, John II, 457
Knight, John II, 574
Knight, John II, 575
Knight, John II, 661
Knight, John II, 805
Knight, John IV, 538
Knight, John IV, 1283
Knight, John VI, 13
Knight, John B. IV, 538
Knight, John B. IV, 561
Knight, John Brown IV, 538
Knight, John F. IV, 128
Knight, John Fisher IV, 97
Knight, Jonathan I, 506
Knight, Jonathan I, 556
Knight, Jonathan II, 1008
Knight, Jonathan II, 1040
Knight, Jonathan IV, 38
Knight, Jonathan IV, 43
Knight, Jonathan IV, 44
Knight, Jonathan IV, 97
Knight, Jonathan Paul II, 575
Knight, Jonathan, Jr. I, 556
Knight, Jonathan, Jr. I, 586
Knight, Jonathan, Jr. I, 594
Knight, Jonathan, Jr. IV, 26
Knight, Jonathan, Jr. IV, 44
Knight, Jonathan, Sr. I, 589
Knight, Joseph I, 506
Knight, Joseph II, 386
Knight, Joseph II, 445
Knight, Joseph II, 453
Knight, Joseph II, 574
Knight, Joseph II, 575
Knight, Joseph IV, 538
Knight, Joseph IV, 561
Knight, Joshua III, 195
Knight, Josiah Stokes II, 886
Knight, Julius I, 556
Knight, Katharine IV, 538
Knight, Kerenhappuck V, 788
Knight, Lewis II, 886
Knight, Lewis II, 887
Knight, Loretta I, 620
Knight, Louetta I, 636
Knight, Luella I, 937
Knight, Luella I, 945
Knight, Luetta I, 636
Knight, Lydia I, 800
Knight, Lydia I, 823
Knight, Lydia II, 575
Knight, Lydia II, 661
Knight, Lydia IV, 44
Knight, Lydia IV, 538
Knight, Lydia IV, 561
Knight, Margaret II, 492
Knight, Margaret II, 575
Knight, Margaret IV, 1283
Knight, Margaret S. II, 575
Knight, Martha I, 506
Knight, Martha I, 556
Knight, Martha I, 1016
Knight, Martha I, 1033
Knight, Martha II, 887
Knight, Martha B. II, 294
Knight, Martha J. II, 751
Knight, Martha J. II, 767
Knight, Martha James II, 386
Knight, Martha James II, 751
Knight, Mary I, 823
Knight, Mary I, 839
Knight, Mary II, 294
Knight, Mary II, 299
Knight, Mary II, 574
Knight, Mary II, 575
Knight, Mary II, 600
Knight, Mary II, 790
Knight, Mary II, 792
Knight, Mary II, 805
Knight, Mary II, 875
Knight, Mary II, 886
Knight, Mary II, 887
Knight, Mary II, 956
Knight, Mary II, 968
Knight, Mary II, 969
Knight, Mary II, 1045
Knight, Mary II, 1054
Knight, Mary III, 45
Knight, Mary III, 352
Knight, Mary IV, 1283
Knight, Mary V, 379
Knight, Mary V, 409
Knight, Mary Ann II, 804
Knight, Mary Ann II, 822
Knight, Mary Ann II, 886
Knight, Mary Ann II, 887
Knight, Mary Ann II, 941
Knight, Mary Ann IV, 340
Knight, Mary Ann IV, 355
Knight, Mary E. III, 195
Knight, Mary E. V, 916
Knight, Mary Eliza IV, 1273
Knight, Mary Eliza IV, 1283
Knight, Mary Estelle III, 45
Knight, Mary Estelle V, 916
Knight, Mary Esther III, 195
Knight, Mary Hannah IV, 97
Knight, Mary Hannah IV, 128
Knight, Mary Sibyl I, 928
Knight, Mary W. III, 195
Knight, Milton I, 556
Knight, Nancy I, 556
Knight, Nathan Tyson II, 822
Knight, Neadham IV, 561
Knight, Needham IV, 538
Knight, Nereus I, 556
Knight, Octavius V, 916
Knight, Oliver IV, 44
Knight, Oliver G. II, 710
Knight, Oliver George II, 751
Knight, Paul II, 886
Knight, Paul II, 941
Knight, Phebe I, 506
Knight, Phebe Lucy IV, 1283
Knight, Priscilla III, 195
Knight, Prudence I, 556
Knight, Rachel I, 506
Knight, Rachel I, 556
Knight, Rachel I, 561
Knight, Rachel I, 577
Knight, Rachel I, 1070
Knight, Rachel I, 1071
Knight, Rachel II, 804
Knight, Rachel II, 1008
Knight, Rachel II, 1054
Knight, Rachel IV, 1324
Knight, Rachel S. IV, 1324
Knight, Rebecca II, 321
Knight, Rebecca P. II, 887
Knight, Rebeckah P. II, 875
Knight, Rebeckah P. II, 887
Knight, Rebekah II, 575
Knight, Roxana I, 556
Knight, Ruth I, 534
Knight, Ruth I, 556
Knight, Ruth I, 574
Knight, Ruth I, 594
Knight, Ruth I, 823
Knight, Ruth I, 824
Knight, Ruth IV, 26
Knight, Ruth IV, 44
Knight, Ruth C. IV, 44
Knight, Sallie II, 805
Knight, Sallie B. II, 869
Knight, Sallie B. II, 887
Knight, Sallie R. II, 869
Knight, Sallie R. II, 887
Knight, Sallie Rebecca II, 805
Knight, Samuel I, 506
Knight, Samuel I, 556
Knight, Samuel II, 386
Knight, Samuel II, 575
Knight, Samuel II, 710
Knight, Samuel II, 751
Knight, Samuel V, 184
Knight, Samuel Dark II, 1008
Knight, Samuel W. II, 710
Knight, Samuel W. II, 751
Knight, Sarah I, 506
Knight, Sarah I, 556
Knight, Sarah I, 890
Knight, Sarah I, 893
Knight, Sarah I, 1008
Knight, Sarah I, 1010
Knight, Sarah I, 1070
Knight, Sarah II, 33
Knight, Sarah II, 83
Knight, Sarah II, 89
Knight, Sarah II, 386
Knight, Sarah II, 387
Knight, Sarah II, 488
Knight, Sarah II, 575
Knight, Sarah II, 648
Knight, Sarah II, 688
Knight, Sarah II, 710
Knight, Sarah II, 751
Knight, Sarah III, 195
Knight, Sarah V, 916
Knight, Sarah Ann II, 710
Knight, Sarah Ann II, 751
Knight, Sarah Ann IV, 1283
Knight, Sarah Eliza II, 963
Knight, Sarah Elizabeth II, 1053
Knight, Sarah Elizabeth II, 1054
Knight, Sarah Haydock II, 792
Knight, Sibyl I, 929
Knight, Sibyl I, 945
Knight, Solomon I, 506
Knight, Solomon I, 556
Knight, Solomon I, 1067
Knight, Solomon I, 1070
Knight, Solomon VI, 412
Knight, Stephen II, 1045
Knight, Stephen II, 1054
Knight, Stephen III, 195
Knight, Susan I, 620
Knight, Susanna II, 387
Knight, Susannah II, 575
Knight, Susannah II, 792
Knight, Tacy II, 887
Knight, Tacy M. II, 575
Knight, Tacy M. II, 751
Knight, Tacy M. II, 754
Knight, Thomas I, 506
Knight, Thomas I, 556
Knight, Thomas I, 567
Knight, Thomas I, 1067
Knight, Thomas I, 1070
Knight, Thomas I, 1071
Knight, Thomas II, 387
Knight, Thomas II, 488
Knight, Thomas II, 574
Knight, Thomas II, 575
Knight, Thomas II, 710
Knight, Thomas II, 751
Knight, Thomas II, 956
Knight, Thomas II, 1045
Knight, Thomas II, 1054
Knight, Thomas Brown II, 1008
Knight, Thomas, Jr. I, 556
Knight, Thomas, Jr. II, 575
Knight, Wd. Esther II, 805
Knight, Wd. Martha II, 804
Knight, Wd. Mary II, 805
Knight, Wd. Mary Elizabeth II, 822
Knight, Widow Ann II, 1008
Knight, Widow Elizabeth I, 556
Knight, William II, 387
Knight, William IV, 32
Knight, William IV, 44
Knight, William IV, 97
Knight, William IV, 538
Knight, William F. IV, 97
Knight, William H. II, 710
Knight, William Henry II, 710
Knight, William Paul II, 804
Knight, Wm. II, 575
Knight, Wm. II, 688
Knight, Wm. II, 792
Knight, Wm. IV, 128
Knight, Wm. Benjamin IV, 1283
Knight, Wm. H. II, 751
Knight, Wm. Hulme II, 1008
Knight, Wm. Paul II, 887
Knight, Wm. R. II, 751
Knight, Zephaniah Z. IV, 44
Knight, Zilpah IV, 1298
Knight, Zilpha IV, 1283
Knisely, John W. IV, 718
Knisely, Lucinda M. IV, 718
Knisely, Sarah IV, 718
Knittle, Wm. V, 1005
Knoblock, Adam V, 1005
Knoblock, Minnie V, 1005
Knock, Daniel C. IV, 561
Knock, Ezekiel IV, 561
Knock, Jane IV, 561
Knock, Jane IV, 562
Knock, Phebe IV, 522
Knock, Phebe IV, 542
Knock, Rachel IV, 542
Knock, Rachel IV, 561
Knock, Sarah IV, 560
Knock, Sarah Chandler IV, 561
Knock, William IV, 561
Knoll, Hannah II, 826
Knoll, Zella IV, 236
Knorr, Catharine II, 803
Knorr, Charles II, 387
Knorr, Elizabeth II, 805
Knorr, George II, 805
Knorr, Jacob II, 387
Knorr, Jacob II, 575
Knorr, Jemima II, 575
Knorr, Mary II, 792
Knorr, Wd. Mary II, 805
Knorr, William II, 387
Knott, Anna V, 410
Knott, Annie V, 409
Knott, Helen V, 409
Knott, Helen M. V, 409
Knott, Mary P. V, 409
Knott, Oliver V. V, 410
Knott, Robert V, 344
Knotts, James W. V, 344
Knotts, Milton V, 344
Knotts, Robert V, 344
Knowlan, Esto V, 410
Knowlan, Joseph H. V, 410
Knowlan, Mary A. V, 410
Knowland, Esto V, 410
Knowland, Joseph V, 410
Knowland, Joseph H. V, 410
Knowland, Mary A. V, 410
Knowland, Mary Alice V, 410
Knowles, ??? II, 387
Knowles, Abigail III, 59
Knowles, Abigail III, 195
Knowles, Abram IV, 1371
Knowles, Abram A. IV, 1371
Knowles, Abram H. IV, 1371
Knowles, Adaline II, 1054
Knowles, Albert II, 1054
Knowles, Alice II, 1009
Knowles, Alice II, 1020
Knowles, Alice G. IV, 1371
Knowles, Ann II, 387
Knowles, Ann II, 575
Knowles, Ann II, 1008
Knowles, Ann II, 1009
Knowles, Ann Eliza II, 1054
Knowles, Anna IV, 1370
Knowles, Anna IV, 1371
Knowles, Anna H. IV, 1370
Knowles, Anna H. IV, 1371
Knowles, Anna T. II, 1054
Knowles, Banner II, 1000
Knowles, Banner II, 1008
Knowles, Banner, Jr. II, 1054
Knowles, Benjamin II, 1054
Knowles, Benjamin IV, 1370
Knowles, Benjamin IV, 1371
Knowles, Benjamin L. II, 887
Knowles, Benjamin Lacy II, 805
Knowles, Bertha VI, 748
Knowles, Bertha L. II, 887
Knowles, Bertha Longshore II, 805
Knowles, Catharine D. III, 184
Knowles, Catharine D. III, 195
Knowles, Charles II, 1054
Knowles, Charles III, 195
Knowles, Charles B. II, 1054
Knowles, Charles B. II, 1057
Knowles, Charles S. III, 184
Knowles, Charles S. III, 195
Knowles, Clarinda II, 1054
Knowles, David II, 805
Knowles, David II, 887
Knowles, David E. V, 916
Knowles, Dr. William III, 195

Knowles, Edmund Kinsey II, 805
Knowles, Edward II, 805
Knowles, Edward II, 887
Knowles, Eliza D. IV, 1371
Knowles, Eliza W. II, 805
Knowles, Elizabeth II, 387
Knowles, Elizabeth II, 536
Knowles, Elizabeth II, 575
Knowles, Elizabeth II, 805
Knowles, Elizabeth II, 1000
Knowles, Elizabeth II, 1008
Knowles, Elizabeth II, 1054
Knowles, Esther II, 1054
Knowles, Esther II, 1064
Knowles, Eunice III, 195
Knowles, Eunice E. III, 195
Knowles, Frances II, 387
Knowles, Francis II, 387
Knowles, Francis II, 575
Knowles, Francis II, 578
Knowles, Hannah II, 387
Knowles, Hannah II, 532
Knowles, Hannah II, 575
Knowles, Hannah II, 1008
Knowles, Hannah II, 1009
Knowles, Hannah II, 1033
Knowles, Henry IV, 1371
Knowles, Henry A. IV, 1371
Knowles, Jacob II, 805
Knowles, Jacob II, 983
Knowles, Jacob II, 1008
Knowles, Jacob II, 1054
Knowles, John II, 387
Knowles, John II, 575
Knowles, John II, 805
Knowles, John II, 963
Knowles, John II, 983
Knowles, John II, 994
Knowles, John II, 1008
Knowles, John II, 1009
Knowles, John II, 1012
Knowles, John II, 1020
Knowles, John II, 1031
Knowles, John II, 1054
Knowles, Joseph II, 963
Knowles, Joseph II, 1008
Knowles, Joseph II, 1054
Knowles, Joseph, Jr. II, 1054
Knowles, Juliann II, 1054
Knowles, Latitia II, 1008
Knowles, Latitia II, 1020
Knowles, Letitia II, 1008
Knowles, Mahlon K. II, 1054
Knowles, Marcy II, 1008
Knowles, Marcy II, 1031
Knowles, Margaret P. II, 1054
Knowles, Margaret P. II, 1057
Knowles, Maria A. II, 716
Knowles, Martha II, 387
Knowles, Martha M. IV, 1371
Knowles, Mary II, 387
Knowles, Mary II, 983
Knowles, Mary II, 1008
Knowles, Mary II, 1009
Knowles, Mary II, 1012
Knowles, Mary II, 1020
Knowles, Mary II, 1028
Knowles, Mary II, 1032
Knowles, Mary II, 1054
Knowles, Mary III, 195
Knowles, Mary III, 361
Knowles, Mary Ann II, 805
Knowles, Mary Ann II, 1054
Knowles, Mary C. IV, 1371
Knowles, Mary P. II, 1009
Knowles, Mary P. II, 1028
Knowles, Mary R. VI, 748
Knowles, Mary, Jr. II, 1054
Knowles, Murray IV, 1371
Knowles, Nathaniel IV, 1371
Knowles, Rachel II, 805
Knowles, Rachel II, 983
Knowles, Rachel II, 994
Knowles, Rachel II, 1008
Knowles, Rachel II, 1054
Knowles, Rebecca II, 805
Knowles, Rebecca II, 1008
Knowles, Rebecca II, 1032
Knowles, Rhoda Ann II, 805
Knowles, Rhoda Ann II, 887
Knowles, Rhoda Ann II, 896
Knowles, Rhoda K. II, 887
Knowles, Rhoda K. II, 892
Knowles, Rhoda Longshore II, 805
Knowles, Robert II, 1008
Knowles, Robert II, 1009
Knowles, Robert II, 1028
Knowles, Robert II, 1032
Knowles, Robert II, 1054
Knowles, Ruth II, 1054
Knowles, Sarah II, 387
Knowles, Sarah II, 575
Knowles, Sarah II, 578
Knowles, Sarah II, 963
Knowles, Sarah II, 1008
Knowles, Sarah III, 295
Knowles, Sarah IV, 385
Knowles, Sarah IV, 388
Knowles, Sarah IV, 417
Knowles, Sarah IV, 421
Knowles, Sarah IV, 435
Knowles, Sarah D. III, 195
Knowles, Smyrna IV, 1371
Knowles, Susan III, 100
Knowles, Susan III, 195
Knowles, Susan IV, 1371
Knowles, Susan L. IV, 1256
Knowles, Susanna II, 1054
Knowles, Susanna III, 195
Knowles, Tabitha III, 195
Knowles, Wm. II, 1008
Knowlin, Moses II, 387
Knowllton, Robt. III, 195
Knowllton, Sarah III, 195
Knowls, John II, 963
Knowls, John II, 1008
Knowls, John II, 1015
Knowls, Mariah IV, 841
Knowls, Sarah II, 963
Knowls, Sarah II, 1008
Knowls, Sarah II, 1015
Knowlton, ??? III, 44
Knowlton, ??? III, 195
Knowlton, Cynthia A. III, 195
Knowlton, Elizabeth III, 195
Knowlton, Elizabeth III, 196
Knowlton, Elizabeth III, 284
Knowlton, Jane V, 1005
Knowlton, Julia A. V, 581
Knowlton, Julia Ann V, 581
Knowlton, Julia Ann V, 631
Knowlton, Julia Ann V, 916
Knowlton, Maria Amelia III, 44
Knowlton, Maria Amelia III, 195
Knowlton, Mary E. III, 65
Knowlton, Phyllis III, 195
Knowlton, Robt. III, 195
Knowlton, Samuel V, 916
Knowlton, Sarah A. M. III, 195
Knowlton, Theodore V, 1005
Knox, Abigail I, 244
Knox, Abigal I, 217
Knox, Charity I, 244
Knox, Christia I, 206
Knox, Christian I, 217
Knox, Christian I, 259
Knox, Clariba I, 206
Knox, Dennis VI, 946
Knox, Elisabeth I, 45
Knox, Elisabeth I, 56
Knox, Elisabeth I, 260
Knox, Elisabeth White I, 244
Knox, Elizabeth I, 217
Knox, Elizabeth VI, 485
Knox, Ella IV, 1324
Knox, George III, 195
Knox, Hannah IV, 538
Knox, Hannah IV, 548
Knox, Henry I, 79
Knox, Isaac I, 217
Knox, Isaac I, 244
Knox, John I, 217
Knox, John I, 241
Knox, John I, 244
Knox, John I, 247
Knox, John, Jr. I, 244
Knox, Joseph I, 217
Knox, Joseph I, 244
Knox, Keziah VI, 946
Knox, Lemuel I, 244
Knox, Lidia I, 244
Knox, Lois IV, 1324
Knox, Lydia I, 206
Knox, Lydia I, 217
Knox, Margaret I, 10
Knox, Margaret I, 56
Knox, Margaret I, 78
Knox, Margaret I, 79
Knox, Margaret I, 244
Knox, Margaret I, 260
Knox, Marium I, 217
Knox, Mary I, 79
Knox, Mary I, 217
Knox, Mary I, 233
Knox, Mary I, 244
Knox, Mary I, 259
Knox, Meriam I, 244
Knox, Meriam I, 253
Knox, Pharaby I, 217
Knox, Pharaby I, 243
Knox, Pharaby I, 244
Knox, Pharaby I, 247
Knox, Ruth I, 217
Knox, Ruth IV, 1324
Knox, Samuel I, 217
Knox, Sarah II, 710
Knox, Sarah II, 751
Knox, Sarah III, 195
Knox, Thomas I, 56
Knox, Thomas I, 78
Knox, Thomas I, 217
Knox, Thomas I, 244
Knox, Widow Margaret I, 56
Knox, William IV, 1269
Knox, William VI, 11
Knox, Wm. IV, 1324
Knox, Wm. A. IV, 1324
Knubley, John II, 575
Knubley, John II, 643
Knubley, Sarah II, 575
Knubley, Sarah II, 643
Knubly, Jane II, 550
Knubly, Jane II, 575
Knubly, John II, 575
Knubly, Sarah II, 575
Knupp, Ira Lee I, 945
Kobbe, Dorothea F. III, 132
Kobbe, E. Dorothea III, 195
Koch, James B. IV, 1215
Kochler, Asenath V, 344
Kochler, Asenath V, 346
Kochsperger, Sarah A. II, 887
Koehler, Mathilda IV, 1321
Koepke, Chas. IV, 1324
Koepke, Mabel IV, 1324
Koester, Henry IV, 1324
Koester, Henry J. IV, 1324
Koesting, Charles C. III, 195
Koesting, Chas. E. III, 51
Koesting, Elizabeth III, 195
Koesting, Helen III, 195
Koesting, Helen C. III, 51
Koesting, Helen C. III, 195
Kohlenkamp, Emma J. II, 825
Kohler, Caroline Margaretta II, 803
Kohler, Fred A. IV, 1324
Kohler, Henry IV, 1324
Kohr, Amanda E. IV, 1371
Kohr, Maria A. IV, 1371
Koile, Elizabeth II, 387
Koile, Michael II, 387
Kolb, Charles L. IV, 1256
Koll, ??? IV, 768
Koll, Benj. IV, 640
Koll, Benj. C. IV, 731
Koll, Benj. S. IV, 731
Koll, Benjamin IV, 640
Koll, Benjamin IV, 731
Koll, Benjamin S. IV, 731
Koll, Charles IV, 731
Koll, Charles IV, 794
Koll, Daniel II, 711
Koll, Daniel II, 946
Koll, Daniel II, 1086
Koll, Daniel II, 1088
Koll, Daniel II, 1089
Koll, Daniel IV, 640
Koll, Daniel IV, 655
Koll, Daniel IV, 731
Koll, Daniel IV, 794
Koll, Esther IV, 640
Koll, Esther IV, 731
Koll, Esther IV, 778
Koll, Joseph IV, 640
Koll, Joseph IV, 731
Koll, Julia II, 711
Koll, Julia II, 1088
Koll, Julia II, 1089
Koll, Julia IV, 640
Koll, Julia IV, 655
Koll, Julia IV, 731
Koll, Julia IV, 734
Koll, Julie IV, 640
Koll, Karl Daniel IV, 734
Koll, Lydia II, 711
Koll, Lydia IV, 640
Koll, Lydia IV, 731
Koll, Lydia IV, 734
Koll, Lydia Esther IV, 731
Koll, Martha II, 949
Koll, Martha II, 1088
Koll, Martha II, 1089
Koll, Martha IV, 731
Koll, Martha K. IV, 731
Koll, Martha K. IV, 747
Koll, Mary IV, 731
Koll, Mary J. IV, 705
Koll, Mary J. IV, 731
Koll, Mary J. IV, 794
Koll, Wd. Mary J. II, 1086
Koll, William IV, 731
Koll, Wm. IV, 731
Koll, Wm. IV, 794
Kollar, Harvey Willard IV, 1324
Kollar, Isole IV, 1324
Kollar, Joseph IV, 1324
Kollar, M. L. IV, 1324
Kollar, Nellie IV, 1324
Koller, Betty Lou IV, 1324
Koller, Lionel LeMar IV, 1324
Koller, Mabel IV, 1324
Kolling, Benjamin IV, 1104
Kolling, Daniel IV, 1104
Kolling, Elizabeth IV, 236
Kolling, Elizabeth IV, 640
Kolling, Elizabeth IV, 1104
Kolling, Elizabeth, Jr. IV, 640
Kolling, Elizabeth, Jr. IV, 1104
Kolling, Ernest IV, 1104
Kolling, Ernest, Jr. IV, 1104
Kolling, Hannah IV, 1104
Kolling, John IV, 1104
Kolling, Louisa IV, 640
Kolling, Louisa IV, 646
Kolling, Louiza IV, 640
Kolling, Mary IV, 1104
Kollings, Benjamin IV, 1104
Kollings, Daniel IV, 1104
Kollings, Elizabeth IV, 1104
Kollings, Ernest IV, 1104
Kollings, Hannah IV, 1104
Kollings, John IV, 1104
Kollings, Louiza IV, 640
Kollings, Mary IV, 1104
Kolwoord, Vera V, 90
Komori, Elizabeth III, 195
Komori, Elizabeth III, 196
Komori, Elizabeth III, 284
Komori, Maurice A. III, 196
Komori, Norie III, 195
Komori, Norie III, 196
Komori, Norie III, 284
Komori, Phyllis III, 196
Komori, Phyllis III, 284
Konigmacher, Adam II, 387
Konigmacher, Elizabeth II, 575
Konigmaker, Elizabeth II, 1009
Konigmaker, Elizabeth II, 1042
Konkle, Edward IV, 1256
Koogler, Louisa V, 90
Koogler, Wm. H. V, 90
Koon, Arlie V. IV, 1324
Koon, Austin V, 990
Koon, Harold IV, 1324
Koon, Harry S. IV, 1324
Koon, Mr. ??? IV, 1324
Koon, Mrs. H. S. IV, 1324
Koone, Davolt I, 712
Koone, George I, 712
Koons, Abigaail V, 751
Koons, Arland IV, 1284
Koons, George IV, 1284
Koons, Hannah V, 751
Koons, Henry V, 751
Koons, Jasper I, 712
Koons, Jasper V, 751
Koons, Jeremiah V, 751
Koons, John V, 751
Koons, Nathan V, 751
Koons, Orville IV, 1284
Koons, Samuel V, 751
Koons, William V, 751
Koonse, Mary I, 310
Koonts, Sarah V, 839
Koontz, Elizabeth IV, 585
Koontz, Elizabeth IV, 600
Koping, Maria C. III, 149
Korey, Francina IV, 538
Korey, Francina IV, 552
Kormawer, Dorothea II, 132
Kormawer, Margaret II, 132
Kormawer, Simon II, 132
Koser, Elizabeth Howard VI, 668
Koser, Wilmer, J. VI, 668
Koster, Arnold II, 575
Koster, Benjamin II, 387
Koster, Elizabeth II, 387
Koster, Elizabeth II, 552
Koster, Elizabeth II, 575
Koster, John II, 387
Koster, John II, 552
Koster, John II, 575
Koster, Rachel II, 387
Koster, Rachel II, 575
Koster, William II, 387
Koster, Wm. II, 575
Kouts, Norma V, 1005
Koutsman, Mary IV, 1284
Kowlinski, Marie H. III, 367
Kraemer, Elizabeth V, 916
Kraemer, Geo. E. V, 916
Kramer, Alva V, 459
Kramer, Alva V, 690
Kramer, Annie V, 1005
Kramer, Charles V, 459
Kramer, Charles V, 690
Kramer, Dell IV, 1324
Kramer, Ellen IV, 1324
Kramer, Florence M. IV, 1324
Kramer, Frederick III, 107
Kramer, Frederick VI, 488
Kramer, Frederick VI, 524
Kramer, Mary J. V, 344
Kramer, Melissa M. III, 107
Kramer, Melissa Madeline III, 107
Kramer, Melissa Madeline VI, 488
Kramer, Melissa Madeline VI, 524
Kramer, Sarah L. III, 107
Kramer, Sarah L. VI, 488
Kramer, Sarah L. VI, 524
Kranse, Charles VI, 947
Kranse, Elimiah VI, 947
Krants, Sally VI, 947
Krants, Thomas VI, 947
Krantz, Abraham VI, 947
Krantz, Abraham L. VI, 947
Krantz, Abram VI, 947
Krantz, Barbara VI, 947
Krantz, Charles VI, 947
Krantz, David VI, 918
Krantz, David VI, 947
Krantz, Delilah VI, 816
Krantz, Elimiah VI, 947
Krantz, Eliza VI, 918
Krantz, Eliza VI, 1008
Krantz, Elizabeth VI, 901
Krantz, Elizabeth VI, 946
Krantz, Jacob VI, 946
Krantz, Joseph VI, 947
Krantz, Lucy VI, 947
Krantz, Margaret VI, 906
Krantz, Mariah F. VI, 947
Krantz, Mary VI, 901
Krantz, Mary VI, 998
Krantz, Michael VI, 947
Krantz, Michael VI, 1016
Krantz, Nancy VI, 947
Krantz, Patience VI, 946
Krantz, Polly VI, 947
Krantz, Rebecca VI, 947
Krantz, Rhoda J. VI, 947
Krantz, Sally VI, 947
Krantz, Sarah VI, 946
Krantz, Susan VI, 947
Krantz, Thomas VI, 906
Krantz, Thomas VI, 946
Krantz, Thomas VI, 947
Krantz, William VI, 901
Krantz, William VI, 946
Krantz, William VI, 947
Kratz, Bertha Virginia II, 887
Kratz, Bertha Virginia II, 940
Kratz, Harvey II, 887
Kratz, Harvey II, 940
Kratz, Sarah R. II, 887
Kratz, Sarah R. II, 940
Krause, Kate IV, 1324
Krecker, R. Hoffman III, 196
Kreider, Bertha V, 1005
Kreider, Harry M. V, 1005
Kreider, Hattie V, 1005
Kreider, John V, 1005
Kreider, Mary V, 1005
Kreis, Hazel IV, 1204
Kreis, Hazel Casto IV, 1215
Kreitzer, Alice V, 751
Kreitzer, George F. V, 751
Krekel, Madge Barrett IV, 1324
Krekler, Marion V, 847
Kremer, Carrie IV, 1325
Kremer, Carrie T. IV, 1325
Kremer, Christian II, 387
Kremer, David II, 387
Kremer, Pearl IV, 1325
Kremer, Phares S. IV, 1325
Kremer, Pharez IV, 1325
Kreps, Hannah VI, 412
Kreps, Hannah VI, 461
Kress, Clara V, 90
Kresson, A. G. V, 1005
Kresson, D. A. V, 1005
Kresson, Sarah E. V, 1005
Kreugar, Sophia IV, 869
Kreugar, Sophia IV, 875
Krider, Mary V, 1005
Kriggin, Mary II, 575
Krikana, Frank IV, 1325
Kring, Albert V, 1005
Kring, Elizabeth V, 1005
Kring, Wm. V, 1005

ripner, Elizabeth II, 387
ripner, Elizabeth II, 575
ripner, Elizabeth II, 673
ripner, Paul II, 387
ripner, Paul II, 546
ripner, Paul II, 575
ripner, Paul II, 673
ripner, Paulus II, 575
ripner, Susanna II, 546
ripner, Susanna II, 575
roll, Carl III, 196
roll, Carl III, 215
roll, Margaretha III, 196
roll, Margaretha Magdalena III, 196
roll, Margaretta III, 215
roll, Margaretta Magdalena III, 215
royter, Rebecca Lea II, 575
rueger, Cecelia III, 233
rueger, Cecelie III, 196
rueger, Karl III, 196
rueger, Sophia III, 196
rueger, Theodore H. III, 196
rueger, Theodore H. III, 233
ruger, Alfred P. III, 196
ruger, Cecelie III, 196
ruger, Christian IV, 640
ruger, Christian IV, 875
ruger, Helena III, 196
ruger, Helena III, 328
ruger, Karl III, 196
ruger, Karl A. III, 196
ruger, Sophia III, 196
ruger, Sophia IV, 875
ruger, Theodore H. III, 196
runel, Katherine II, 971
ruzeman, Alvin V, 916
ruzeman, Florence V, 916
ruzeman, John, Jr. V, 916
ruzeman, John, Sr. V, 916
ubler, Herman III, 196
ubler, Louise III, 196
ubler, William H. III, 196
uch, Alice V, 848
uch, Henry V, 848
Kucheremund, Anna Louise IV, 731
Kuchnel, Edward W. IV, 1215
Kuchnel, Esther Mae IV, 1215
Kuchnel, Mary IV, 1215
Kuehnel, Edward IV, 875
Kuehnel, Edward H. IV, 1310
Kuehnel, Edward H. IV, 1325
Kuehnel, Esther IV, 875
Kuehnel, Esther Mae IV, 875
Kuehnel, Mary IV, 875
Kuehnel, Mary E. IV, 1310
Kuehnel, Mary E. IV, 1325
Kuehnel, Ruth IV, 1313
Kuelmel, Earl Wm. IV, 1325
Kuelmel, Edward H. IV, 1325
Kuelmel, Emma IV, 1325
Kuelmel, Faith IV, 1325
Kuelmel, Margaretta IV, 1325
Kuelmel, Mary IV, 1325
Kuelmel, Mary E. IV, 1325
Kuelmel, Ruth IV, 1325
Kuelmel, William IV, 1325
Kuelmel, Wm. IV, 1325
Kuelmel, Wm. E. IV, 1325
Kuelmel, Wm. Edward IV, 1325
Kuelmell, William IV, 1325
Kugelmann, Eliz. III, 196
Kugelmann, Wilhelm III, 196
Kugelmann, Wilhelmine III, 196
Kugh, Mary IV, 236
Kuhlman, Earl Wm. IV, 1329
Kuhlman, Faith IV, 1329
Kuhn, Brenda III, 196
Kuhn, Harold IV, 1324
Kuhn, Ida Virginia II, 822
Kuhn, Jesse V, 990
Kuhn, Maria IV, 1215
Kuhn, Maria IV, 1219
Kuhn, Vera III, 196
Kuhn, Walt III, 196
Kuhnamond, ??? IV, 731
Kuhnamond, Anna Louise IV, 731
Kuhns, Dorothy IV, 731
Kuhns, Elmer IV, 731
Kuhns, Harrison IV, 731
Kuhns, Vernon IV, 731
Kuhns, Willetta IV, 731
Kuirljian, Sarkis T. III, 196
Kukuk, Mabel V, 916
Kulsch, Nella V, 1005
Kumhall, Anastacia IV, 1325
Kumhall, Anastasia IV, 1325
Kunkle, George II, 387
Kunkle, Henry II, 387
Kunkle, Henry II, 710
Kunkle, Margaret II, 387
Kunkle, Susanna II, 575
Kunkles, Henry II, 387
Kunkles, Margaret II, 387
Kuntz, Catherine IV, 1215
Kuntz, John V, 184
Kuntz, Minnie IV, 875
Kuntz, Sarah IV, 401
Kuntz, Sarah IV, 416
Kuntzman, Louisa IV, 966
Kuntzman, Mary IV, 966
Kuntzman, Mary IV, 1016
Kuntzman, Mary Emma IV, 966
Kuntzman, Robert IV, 966
Kunz, Caroline III, 196
Kunz, Christine Lois III, 196
Kunz, Edith T. III, 196
Kunz, Jacob III, 196
Kurtholz, Chas. IV, 1256
Kurtholz, Ella IV, 1256
Kurtholz, Emerson IV, 1256
Kurtholz, Henry IV, 1256
Kurtholz, Kitty IV, 1256
Kurtholz, Mary Binns IV, 1256
Kurtz, Daniel VI, 760
Kurtzholt, Chas. IV, 1256
Kurtzholt, Ella IV, 1256
Kurtzholt, Henry IV, 1256
Kurtzholz, Emerson IV, 1256
Kusch, John G. III, 424
Kushmane, Henry V, 1005
Kushmane, Samuel V, 1005
Kushmaul, Henry V, 1005
Kushmaul, Samuel V, 1005
Kutch, Maggie V, 1005
Kutch, Stella V, 1005
Kutz, Malissa IV, 402
Kutz, Malissa IV, 416
Kuy, Caleb VI, 937
Kyle, Ann Lucy V, 916
Kyle, Ann M. VI, 831
Kyle, David VI, 947
Kyle, John VI, 803
Kyle, John VI, 831
Kyle, John VI, 832
Kyle, Judy VI, 803
Kyle, Julia I, 592
Kyle, Julia I, 595
Kyle, Juliann I, 587
Kyle, Juliann VI, 947
Kyle, Lucy Ann V, 916
Kyle, Mary VI, 832
Kynett, Anna IV, 731
Kynett, Samuel IV, 731
Kynett, Sarah Hutchinson IV, 731

L'Hommedier, Kenneth Edw. III, 440
L'Hommedier, Nancy III, 440
L'Hommedieu, Kenneth Edw. III, 425
L'Hommedieu, Nancy III, 425
L???, Martha III, 157
L???, Martha III, 362
La Losette, ??? III, 197
La Losette, Paul III, 197
La Mar, Martha Ann V, 848
La Mar, William V, 848
La Mont, Elizabeth III, 197
La Mont, Laura J. III, 206
La Mont, Lewis P. III, 206
La Mont, Louis R. III, 84
La Mont, Louis R. III, 197
La Mont, Louis R. III, 344
La Mont, Wd. Elizabeth III, 206
La Rich, Sarah II, 576
La Rich, Sarah II, 589
La Rue, ??? II, 1066
La Rue, Emma Cecelia II, 1066
La Rue, Florence II, 1066
La Rue, George II, 1066
La Rue, Headley II, 1066
La Rue, Mary Yardley II, 1066
Labareacre, Elizabeth VI, 795
Labeck, Jno. V, 1006
Lace, Abner VI, 832
Lace, Susannah VI, 832
Lacey, Ailce I, 56
Lacey, Alice I, 52
Lacey, Alice I, 56
Lacey, Anestasia II, 801
Lacey, Ann I, 196
Lacey, Anne V, 802
Lacey, Anne V, 814
Lacey, Burley VI, 947
Lacey, Curtis VI, 947
Lacey, Elisabeth I, 57
Lacey, Elisabeth I, 195
Lacey, Elisabeth I, 196
Lacey, Elizabeth I, 185
Lacey, Elizabeth I, 193
Lacey, Elizabeth I, 195
Lacey, Elizabeth I, 196
Lacey, Elizabeth VI, 896
Lacey, Elizabeth VI, 947
Lacey, Ephraim IV, 152
Lacey, Esther VI, 475
Lacey, Esther VI, 524
Lacey, Esther VI, 538
Lacey, Esther VI, 555
Lacey, Esther VI, 556
Lacey, Esther VI, 697
Lacey, Evan I, 196
Lacey, Evens I, 185
Lacey, Florence Ruth III, 196
Lacey, Florence Ruth III, 267
Lacey, Henry I, 185
Lacey, Isaac I, 185
Lacey, Israel Uphamy Tacy Elias VI, 412
Lacey, James I, 185
Lacey, James I, 196
Lacey, Jane I, 56
Lacey, Jean I, 56
Lacey, Jemima I, 52
Lacey, Jemima I, 56
Lacey, John I, 56
Lacey, John I, 144
Lacey, John I, 702
Lacey, John II, 801
Lacey, Joseph I, 56
Lacey, Joseph I, 57
Lacey, Joseph I, 67
Lacey, Joseph I, 68
Lacey, Joseph I, 86
Lacey, Joseph I, 185
Lacey, Joseph I, 192
Lacey, Joseph I, 193
Lacey, Joseph I, 195
Lacey, Joseph I, 196
Lacey, Joseph I, 723
Lacey, Joseph, Jr. I, 56
Lacey, Josiah I, 57
Lacey, Josiah I, 144
Lacey, Josiah I, 702
Lacey, Judith VI, 947
Lacey, Leroy III, 196
Lacey, Leroy III, 267
Lacey, Liddia I, 56
Lacey, Liddia I, 68
Lacey, Lydia I, 57
Lacey, Margaret I, 196
Lacey, Martha I, 185
Lacey, Martha I, 195
Lacey, Mary I, 48
Lacey, Mary I, 57
Lacey, Mary I, 144
Lacey, Mary I, 185
Lacey, Mary I Sup 1, 4
Lacey, Mary III, 196
Lacey, Mary III, 267
Lacey, Mary VI, 993
Lacey, Mary D. V, 581
Lacey, Mashach VI, 412
Lacey, Miles I, 196
Lacey, Miriam I, 56
Lacey, Miriam I, 57
Lacey, Miriam I, 86
Lacey, Miriam I, 185
Lacey, Miriam I, 195
Lacey, Nancy I, 196
Lacey, Nancy VI, 993
Lacey, Nathan I, 48
Lacey, Nathan I, 57
Lacey, Nathan I, 185
Lacey, Nathan I, 195
Lacey, Nathan I, 196
Lacey, Pearson I, 702
Lacey, Penninah I, 192
Lacey, Penninah I, 196
Lacey, Peter I, 57
Lacey, Peter I, 144
Lacey, Peter I, 702
Lacey, Peter I, 723
Lacey, Peter I, 732
Lacey, Petery I, 162
Lacey, Phebe I, 144
Lacey, Phebe I, 702
Lacey, Robert I, 185
Lacey, Robert I, 196
Lacey, Ruth I, 196
Lacey, Ruth I, 702
Lacey, Ruth C. V, 549
Lacey, Ruth C. V, 581
Lacey, Sarah I, 56
Lacey, Sarah I, 67
Lacey, Sarah I, 185
Lacey, Sarah I, 195
Lacey, Sarah I, 196
Lacey, Sarah I, 198
Lacey, Sary VI, 993
Lacey, Susanna I, 723
Lacey, Susanna I, 732
Lacey, Susannah I, 144
Lacey, Susannah I, 162
Lacey, Susannah I, 702
Lacey, Thomas I, 56
Lacey, Thomas VI, 556
Lacey, Wd. Jane Chapman II, 801
Lacey, William I, 57
Lacey, William I, 144
Lacey, William I, 185
Lacey, William I, 195
Lachem, Howard V, 91
Lachem, Martin Howard V, 91
Lachem, Mary H. V, 90
Lachey, Macy I, 144
Lachner, Clyde C. V, 751
Lacie, ??? VI, 39
Lacie, Robert VI, 41
Lack, Benjamin VI, 832
Lack, John I, 403
Lack, Mary Ann VI, 832
Lack, William VI, 832
Lackes, James L. VI, 947
Lackes, Lucinda VI, 947
Lackey, Ann I, 403
Lackey, Elizabeth I, 403
Lackey, Elizabeth VI, 525
Lackey, Elizabeth VI, 835
Lackey, Florence N. IV, 694
Lackey, Florence N. IV, 731
Lackey, Francis I, 403
Lackey, James I, 403
Lackey, James I, 991
Lackey, John I, 403
Lackey, Leota V, 631
Lackey, Lyle G. V, 184
Lackey, Macy I, 144
Lackey, Mary I, 144
Lackey, Mayner I, 403
Lackey, Mayner I, 824
Lackey, Nancy H. VI, 947
Lackey, Polly VI, 795
Lackey, Sarah IV, 91
Lackey, Sarah IV, 97
Lackey, Sarah VI, 831
Lackey, Susanna I, 403
Lackey, Susannah I, 824
Lackey, Thos. S. IV, 731
Lackey, William I, 403
Lackey, William VI, 525
Lackey, William VI, 835
Lackey, William VI, 947
Lackey, Wm. I, 403
Lackey, Wm. VI, 525
Lackey, Wm. VI, 835
Lackland, Wm. M. VI, 959
Lacks, Benjamin VI, 947
Lacks, Benjamin VI, 1021
Lacks, Elizabeth VI, 947
Lacks, Elizabeth VI, 974
Lacks, Elizabeth D. VI, 947
Lacks, Garland VI, 947
Lacks, Mary Jane VI, 1021
Lacks, Nancy VI, 922
Lacks, William VI, 922
Lacks, Wm. VI, 974
Lacky, John I Sup 1, 9
Lacky, Mary I, 144
Lacky, William I Sup 1, 9
Lacock, Naomi IV, 236
Lacock, Naomi IV, 340
Lacy, Abigail I Sup 1, 4
Lacy, Abigail I Sup 1, 6
Lacy, Ailce I, 56
Lacy, Alice I, 45
Lacy, Amos IV, 236
Lacy, Ann I, 195
Lacy, Ann I, 196
Lacy, Archibald VI, 832
Lacy, Arthur V, 690
Lacy, Barbara II, 1009
Lacy, Barbara II, 1032
Lacy, Benjamin VI, 524
Lacy, Charles V, 690
Lacy, David VI, 524
Lacy, Elias VI, 412
Lacy, Elias VI, 524
Lacy, Elias VI, 670
Lacy, Elisabeth I, 196
Lacy, Elizabeth II, 963
Lacy, Elizabeth II, 1009
Lacy, Elizabeth IV, 1238
Lacy, Elizabeth V, 184
Lacy, Elizabeth V, 205
Lacy, Ephraim IV, 236
Lacy, Ephraim VI, 524
Lacy, Esther VI, 524
Lacy, Esther VI, 525
Lacy, Esther VI, 555
Lacy, Esther VI, 622
Lacy, Evan I, 196
Lacy, Helen V, 690
Lacy, Helen P. V, 690
Lacy, Israel VI, 412
Lacy, Israel VI, 524
Lacy, Israel VI, 525
Lacy, Israel VI, 670
Lacy, Israel Uphamy Tacy Elias VI, 412
Lacy, James I, 196
Lacy, James VI, 525
Lacy, Jane I, 49
Lacy, Jane I, 56
Lacy, Jane I, 1049
Lacy, Jean I, 56
Lacy, Jean I, 59
Lacy, Jesse VI, 412
Lacy, John I, 49
Lacy, John I, 56
Lacy, John I, 723
Lacy, John II, 963
Lacy, John II, 1009
Lacy, John V, 184
Lacy, John VI, 865
Lacy, Joseph I, 723
Lacy, Joseph I Sup 1, 4
Lacy, Joseph I Sup 1, 7
Lacy, Joseph VI, 412
Lacy, Joseph H. IV, 1238
Lacy, Juriah VI, 832
Lacy, Lael V, 688
Lacy, Lydia I, 57
Lacy, Lydia I, 75
Lacy, Margaret I, 188
Lacy, Margaret I, 196
Lacy, Mary I, 146
Lacy, Mary I Sup 1, 4
Lacy, Mary II, 387
Lacy, Mary II, 963
Lacy, Mary D. V, 581
Lacy, Mary D. V, 690
Lacy, Mashach VI, 412
Lacy, Mashack VI, 412
Lacy, Mashack VI, 524
Lacy, Meshack VI, 670
Lacy, Nancy I, 194
Lacy, Nancy I, 196
Lacy, Partell II, 1009
Lacy, Peter I, 723
Lacy, Phebe I, 723
Lacy, Phebe I, 737
Lacy, Rachel II, 963
Lacy, Rachel II, 1009
Lacy, Ralph VI, 525
Lacy, Richard V, 690
Lacy, Richard V, 698
Lacy, Robert I, 196
Lacy, Robert VI, 27
Lacy, Robert VI, 93
Lacy, Ruth I, 194
Lacy, Ruth I, 196
Lacy, Sallie I, 935
Lacy, Sarah I, 195
Lacy, Sarah I, 199
Lacy, Sarah A. V, 690
Lacy, Susanna I, 723
Lacy, Susannah I, 144
Lacy, Tacey VI, 524
Lacy, Tacy VI, 412
Lacy, Tacy VI, 670
Lacy, Thomas I, 45
Lacy, Thomas I, 56
Lacy, Thomas I Sup 1, 4
Lacy, Thomas II, 387
Lacy, Thomas II, 445
Lacy, Thomas V, 91
Lacy, Thomas V, 690
Lacy, Thomas VI, 524
Lacy, Thomas VI, 525
Lacy, Thomas, Jr. VI, 525
Lacy, Uphamey VI, 412
Lacy, Uphamy VI, 524
Lacy, Wanda V, 690
Lacy, Wanda V, 698
Lacy, William I, 144
Lacy, William I, 146
Lacy, William I Sup 1, 4
Lacy, William II, 963
Lacy, William VI, 525
Lacy, William, Jr. II, 963
Lacy, Wm. Parcell II, 1009
Lad, Isabell VI, 61
Lad, Isabell Denson VI, 75
Lad, James VI, 61
Lad, James VI, 75
Lad, Samuel II, 575
Lad, William VI, 191
Ladd, ??? IV, 236

Ladd, ??? VI, 95
Ladd, ??? VI, 153
Ladd, ??? VI, 194
Ladd, Abbey V, 344
Ladd, Adney V, 259
Ladd, Agatha VI, 114
Ladd, Agnes VI, 189
Ladd, Agnes VI, 192
Ladd, Agnes VI, 213
Ladd, Agnes VI, 214
Ladd, Alfred V, 257
Ladd, Alfred V, 258
Ladd, Amos VI, 17
Ladd, Amos VI, 114
Ladd, Amos VI, 157
Ladd, Amos VI, 158
Ladd, Amos VI, 159
Ladd, Amos VI, 182
Ladd, Amos VI, 189
Ladd, Amos VI, 190
Ladd, Amos VI, 191
Ladd, Amos VI, 192
Ladd, Amos VI, 193
Ladd, Amos VI, 194
Ladd, Amos VI, 195
Ladd, Amos VI, 196
Ladd, Amos VI, 198
Ladd, Amos VI, 201
Ladd, Amos VI, 214
Ladd, Amos VI, 947
Ladd, Andrew VI, 192
Ladd, Ann III, 148
Ladd, Ann IV, 236
Ladd, Ann IV, 416
Ladd, Ann IV, 438
Ladd, Ann VI, 155
Ladd, Ann VI, 156
Ladd, Ann VI, 158
Ladd, Ann VI, 173
Ladd, Ann VI, 174
Ladd, Ann VI, 189
Ladd, Ann VI, 190
Ladd, Ann VI, 194
Ladd, Ann Maria VI, 195
Ladd, Anna IV, 189
Ladd, Anna IV, 236
Ladd, Anna IV, 248
Ladd, Anna IV, 288
Ladd, Anna IV, 973
Ladd, Anna V, 219
Ladd, Anna V, 257
Ladd, Anna V, 258
Ladd, Anna V, 266
Ladd, Anna VI, 114
Ladd, Anna VI, 137
Ladd, Anna VI, 191
Ladd, Anna B. IV, 236
Ladd, Anna Maria IV, 483
Ladd, Anna Maria IV, 488
Ladd, Anna Maria VI, 190
Ladd, Anna Maria VI, 195
Ladd, Anna Maria VI, 199
Ladd, Anne M. V, 257
Ladd, Anne U. IV, 940
Ladd, Anne U. IV, 974
Ladd, Annie V, 259
Ladd, Annie R. IV, 978
Ladd, Armelia VI, 190
Ladd, Arthur V, 258
Ladd, Arthur V, 459
Ladd, Arthur C. V, 258
Ladd, Arthur C. V, 259
Ladd, Arthur E. V, 258
Ladd, Arthur E. V, 459
Ladd, Arthur G. V, 258
Ladd, Arthur G. V, 259
Ladd, Arthur Langden V, 258
Ladd, Asa V, 257
Ladd, Asa V, 258
Ladd, Asa J. V, 258
Ladd, Asa J. V, 459
Ladd, Asa, Jr. V, 258
Ladd, Asia VI, 137
Ladd, Benj. IV, 468
Ladd, Benj. IV, 480
Ladd, Benj. IV, 482
Ladd, Benj. Franklin VI, 190
Ladd, Benj. Harris VI, 190
Ladd, Benj. W. IV, 473
Ladd, Benj. Whitehead VI, 190
Ladd, Benjamin IV, 236
Ladd, Benjamin IV, 482
Ladd, Benjamin IV, 483
Ladd, Benjamin IV, 504
Ladd, Benjamin VI, 101
Ladd, Benjamin VI, 115
Ladd, Benjamin VI, 137
Ladd, Benjamin VI, 190
Ladd, Benjamin VI, 194
Ladd, Benjamin VI, 195
Ladd, Benjamin Crew VI, 195
Ladd, Benjamin F. VI, 257
Ladd, Benjamin Franklin VI, 190
Ladd, Benjamin Franklin VI, 196
Ladd, Benjamin H. VI, 17
Ladd, Benjamin H. VI, 179
Ladd, Benjamin H. VI, 184
Ladd, Benjamin H. VI, 191
Ladd, Benjamin H. VI, 194
Ladd, Benjamin H. VI, 195
Ladd, Benjamin H. VI, 196
Ladd, Benjamin W. III, 196
Ladd, Benjamin W. IV, 236
Ladd, Benjamin W. IV, 482
Ladd, Benjamin W. IV, 483
Ladd, Benjamin W. IV, 505
Ladd, Benjamin W. VI, 191
Ladd, Benjamin W. VI, 195
Ladd, Betsey B. V, 459
Ladd, Betsy V, 258
Ladd, Betty Kinsey VI, 190
Ladd, Beulah M. V, 257
Ladd, Bulah M. V, 228
Ladd, Bulah M. V, 257
Ladd, Caroline III, 83
Ladd, Caroline III, 196
Ladd, Caroline IV, 482
Ladd, Caroline C. IV, 236
Ladd, Caroline C. IV, 482
Ladd, Caroline C. IV, 483
Ladd, Caroline E. III, 109
Ladd, Caroline E. III, 196
Ladd, Caroline E. IV, 236
Ladd, Caroline E. IV, 483
Ladd, Carolyn III, 145
Ladd, Carrie V, 459
Ladd, Catharine IV, 189
Ladd, Catharine IV, 236
Ladd, Catharine IV, 263
Ladd, Catharine IV, 279
Ladd, Catharine V, 459
Ladd, Catherine V, 258
Ladd, Catherine VI, 166
Ladd, Catherine VI, 170
Ladd, Catherine VI, 191
Ladd, Catherine VI, 195
Ladd, Catherine VI, 196
Ladd, Catherine VI, 214
Ladd, Caty Terrell IV, 236
Ladd, Charles VI, 114
Ladd, Charles VI, 153
Ladd, Charles VI, 154
Ladd, Charles VI, 189
Ladd, Charles Anthony VI, 194
Ladd, Charles C. IV, 236
Ladd, Charles C. VI, 482
Ladd, Charles F. C. IV, 483
Ladd, Charlie Ozborn V, 258
Ladd, Chlotilda VI, 179
Ladd, Chlotilda VI, 190
Ladd, Chlotilda VI, 194
Ladd, Chlotilda VI, 246
Ladd, Clara E. V, 258
Ladd, Clotilde VI, 190
Ladd, Cordelia V, 258
Ladd, Cyrus R. V, 344
Ladd, Daniel V, 266
Ladd, Darahann IV, 236
Ladd, Deborah IV, 236
Ladd, Deborah IV, 290
Ladd, Deborah VI, 189
Ladd, Deborah VI, 190
Ladd, Deborah VI, 194
Ladd, Delilah VI, 194
Ladd, Delilia VI, 190
Ladd, Denson V, 257
Ladd, Denson V, 258
Ladd, Denson V, 459
Ladd, Denson, Jr. V, 258
Ladd, Edith G. IV, 973
Ladd, Edith G. IV, 974
Ladd, Edna IV, 310
Ladd, Edna VI, 185
Ladd, Edna VI, 187
Ladd, Edna VI, 191
Ladd, Edna VI, 195
Ladd, Edna VI, 327
Ladd, Elbert C. V, 259
Ladd, Elbert Clinton V, 258
Ladd, Elisabeth I, 244
Ladd, Elisabeth I, 245
Ladd, Elisabeth I, 256
Ladd, Elisabeth V, 257
Ladd, Eliza V, 258
Ladd, Eliza E. V, 229
Ladd, Eliza Estelle V, 258
Ladd, Elizabeth I, 252
Ladd, Elizabeth II, 68
Ladd, Elizabeth II, 83
Ladd, Elizabeth IV, 236
Ladd, Elizabeth IV, 237
Ladd, Elizabeth IV, 426
Ladd, Elizabeth IV, 427
Ladd, Elizabeth IV, 430
Ladd, Elizabeth IV, 468
Ladd, Elizabeth IV, 472
Ladd, Elizabeth IV, 480
Ladd, Elizabeth IV, 482
Ladd, Elizabeth IV, 483
Ladd, Elizabeth IV, 504
Ladd, Elizabeth IV, 973
Ladd, Elizabeth IV, 974
Ladd, Elizabeth IV, 998
Ladd, Elizabeth V, 219
Ladd, Elizabeth V, 257
Ladd, Elizabeth V, 258
Ladd, Elizabeth V, 274
Ladd, Elizabeth V, 294
Ladd, Elizabeth VI, 114
Ladd, Elizabeth VI, 115
Ladd, Elizabeth VI, 153
Ladd, Elizabeth VI, 158
Ladd, Elizabeth VI, 161
Ladd, Elizabeth VI, 162
Ladd, Elizabeth VI, 166
Ladd, Elizabeth VI, 169
Ladd, Elizabeth VI, 182
Ladd, Elizabeth VI, 189
Ladd, Elizabeth VI, 190
Ladd, Elizabeth VI, 191
Ladd, Elizabeth VI, 192
Ladd, Elizabeth VI, 193
Ladd, Elizabeth VI, 194
Ladd, Elizabeth VI, 195
Ladd, Elizabeth VI, 201
Ladd, Elizabeth VI, 202
Ladd, Elizabeth VI, 213
Ladd, Elizabeth VI, 214
Ladd, Elizabeth VI, 240
Ladd, Elizabeth VI, 349
Ladd, Elizabeth VI, 353
Ladd, Elizabeth A. VI, 934
Ladd, Elizabeth Ann VI, 947
Ladd, Elizabeth Binford VI, 190
Ladd, Elizabeth F. IV, 483
Ladd, Elizabeth P. V, 257
Ladd, Elizabeth P. V, 294
Ladd, Ella Dora IV, 237
Ladd, Ellen V, 344
Ladd, Ellen V, 346
Ladd, Ellen C. III, 83
Ladd, Ellen C. III, 196
Ladd, Ellen C. IV, 236
Ladd, Ellen C. VI, 482
Ladd, Ellen C. IV, 483
Ladd, Ellen R. IV, 236
Ladd, Ellen R. IV, 482
Ladd, Ellwood Grant V, 258
Ladd, Ellwood Oscar V, 258
Ladd, Elsie M. V, 258
Ladd, Elwood V, 257
Ladd, Elwood G. V, 258
Ladd, Emerson B. V, 257
Ladd, Emily IV, 236
Ladd, Emma Jane V, 258
Ladd, Emma Jane V, 410
Ladd, Erba IV, 248
Ladd, Erba IV, 973
Ladd, Erba IV, 974
Ladd, Erba IV, 978
Ladd, Esther V, 226
Ladd, Esther V, 257
Ladd, Esther VI, 114
Ladd, Esther VI, 137
Ladd, Ethel Fransena IV, 974
Ladd, Eunice E. V, 257
Ladd, Evan VI, 190
Ladd, Ezekiel Lewis V, 258
Ladd, Frances II, 556
Ladd, Francina IV, 973
Ladd, Frank V, 258
Ladd, Franklin V, 229
Ladd, Franklin V, 257
Ladd, Franklin V, 258
Ladd, Fransina IV, 1024
Ladd, Fransina IV, 1028
Ladd, G. Jordan V, 258
Ladd, Garrad I, 244
Ladd, Garrard V, 226
Ladd, Garrard VI, 114
Ladd, Geo. V, 258
Ladd, Gerard VI, 17
Ladd, Gerard VI, 137
Ladd, Gerard VI, 192
Ladd, Gerard VI, 193
Ladd, Gerrard V, 228
Ladd, Gerrard V, 257
Ladd, Gerrard V, 258
Ladd, Gerrard V, 268
Ladd, Gerrard VI, 114
Ladd, Gerrard VI, 137
Ladd, Grace V, 257
Ladd, Grace G. V, 917
Ladd, Guli VI, 190
Ladd, Gululma VI, 194
Ladd, Hannah III, 196
Ladd, Hannah IV, 221
Ladd, Hannah IV, 236
Ladd, Hannah IV, 482
Ladd, Hannah V, 916
Ladd, Hannah VI, 114
Ladd, Hannah VI, 137
Ladd, Hannah VI, 193
Ladd, Hannah VI, 194
Ladd, Hannah B. V, 257
Ladd, Hannah G. V, 258
Ladd, Hannah G. V, 261
Ladd, Hannah G. V, 266
Ladd, Hannah P. III, 196
Ladd, Hannah P. IV, 483
Ladd, Hannah P. V, 917
Ladd, Hannah S. IV, 476
Ladd, Hannah S. IV, 482
Ladd, Hannah S. IV, 483
Ladd, Hannah S. IV, 505
Ladd, Hannah T. IV, 473
Ladd, Harmon V, 257
Ladd, Harold V, 257
Ladd, Harriet Viola V, 258
Ladd, Henrietta V, 259
Ladd, Henry VI, 194
Ladd, Henry Adna V, 258
Ladd, Henry C. IV, 973
Ladd, Henry C. IV, 974
Ladd, Henry C. V, 410
Ladd, Hester V, 258
Ladd, Howard J. IV, 973
Ladd, Huldah VI, 114
Ladd, Huldah VI, 116
Ladd, Huldah VI, 117
Ladd, Huldah VI, 121
Ladd, Huldah VI, 165
Ladd, Huldah VI, 189
Ladd, Huldah VI, 190
Ladd, Huldah VI, 192
Ladd, Huldah VI, 193
Ladd, Huldah VI, 203
Ladd, Ida V, 258
Ladd, Ida V, 259
Ladd, Ida M. IV, 966
Ladd, Ida M. IV, 973
Ladd, Ida May IV, 237
Ladd, Ida May IV, 974
Ladd, Isaac VI, 190
Ladd, Isaac G. III, 196
Ladd, Isaac G. V, 916
Ladd, Isaac M. V, 257
Ladd, Isaac Newton VI, 191
Ladd, Isabell VI, 17
Ladd, Isabell VI, 193
Ladd, Isabell Denson VI, 75
Ladd, Isabella IV, 231
Ladd, Isabella IV, 236
Ladd, Isabella IV, 480
Ladd, Isabella IV, 482
Ladd, Isabella IV, 483
Ladd, Isabella VI, 183
Ladd, Isabella VI, 190
Ladd, Isabella VI, 191
Ladd, Isabella VI, 195
Ladd, Isabella VI, 250
Ladd, Isaiah V, 257
Ladd, Isaiah V, 258
Ladd, Isaiah V, 410
Ladd, J. Everett V, 258
Ladd, J. Ollie V, 258
Ladd, J. R. V, 258
Ladd, Jacob I, 217
Ladd, Jacob I, 244
Ladd, Jacob I, 245
Ladd, Jacob I, 246
Ladd, Jacob I, 256
Ladd, Jacob V, 219
Ladd, Jacob V, 251
Ladd, Jacob V, 257
Ladd, Jacob V, 258
Ladd, Jacob V, 261
Ladd, Jacob V, 274
Ladd, Jacob V, 294
Ladd, Jacob VI, 114
Ladd, Jacob VI, 115
Ladd, Jacob VI, 137
Ladd, Jacob VI, 193
Ladd, Jacob P. V, 257
Ladd, Jacob P. V, 258
Ladd, Jacob, Jr. V, 258
Ladd, James IV, 472
Ladd, James IV, 482
Ladd, James IV, 483
Ladd, James VI, 17
Ladd, James VI, 75
Ladd, James VI, 100
Ladd, James VI, 114
Ladd, James VI, 155
Ladd, James VI, 158
Ladd, James VI, 161
Ladd, James VI, 163
Ladd, James VI, 165
Ladd, James VI, 168
Ladd, James VI, 179
Ladd, James VI, 189
Ladd, James VI, 191
Ladd, James VI, 192
Ladd, James VI, 193
Ladd, James VI, 194
Ladd, James VI, 204
Ladd, James VI, 213
Ladd, James Binford VI, 189
Ladd, James D. IV, 236
Ladd, James D. IV, 483
Ladd, James D. VI, 17
Ladd, James D. VI, 106
Ladd, James D. VI, 191
Ladd, James D. VI, 194
Ladd, James D. VI, 195
Ladd, James Denson VI, 114
Ladd, James Denson VI, 190
Ladd, James Denson VI, 194
Ladd, James H. VI, 195
Ladd, James Harris VI, 190
Ladd, James Harris VI, 195
Ladd, James M. VI, 257
Ladd, James Monroe VI, 190
Ladd, James, Jr. VI, 192
Ladd, James, Jr. VI, 193
Ladd, James, Jr. VI, 194
Ladd, Jane VI, 106
Ladd, Jane VI, 114
Ladd, Jane VI, 115
Ladd, Jane VI, 190
Ladd, Jane VI, 191
Ladd, Jane VI, 194
Ladd, Jane Davis V, 257
Ladd, Jane Evans VI, 114
Ladd, Jared V, 257
Ladd, Jarrard I, 245
Ladd, Jarrard VI, 114
Ladd, Jarrot VI, 114
Ladd, Jennie D. V, 258
Ladd, Jeremiah V, 257
Ladd, Jeremiah V, 258
Ladd, Jeremiah VI, 115
Ladd, Jeremiah VI, 137
Ladd, Jesse VI, 45
Ladd, Jesse VI, 46
Ladd, Jesse VI, 154
Ladd, Jesse VI, 166
Ladd, Jesse VI, 191
Ladd, Jesse VI, 192
Ladd, Jesse VI, 194
Ladd, Jesse VI, 195
Ladd, Jesse VI, 196
Ladd, Jesse P. V, 410
Ladd, Jesse, Jr. VI, 194
Ladd, Jessie VI, 193
Ladd, John II, 556
Ladd, John IV, 476
Ladd, John V, 258
Ladd, John VI, 114
Ladd, John VI, 149
Ladd, John VI, 153
Ladd, John VI, 158
Ladd, John VI, 164
Ladd, John VI, 179
Ladd, John VI, 189
Ladd, John VI, 190
Ladd, John VI, 191
Ladd, John VI, 192
Ladd, John VI, 193
Ladd, John VI, 194
Ladd, John VI, 195
Ladd, John VI, 213
Ladd, John VI, 216
Ladd, John VI, 245
Ladd, John VI, 246
Ladd, John VI, 257
Ladd, John A. V, 257
Ladd, John A. V, 258
Ladd, John Andrews VI, 114
Ladd, John Bradley VI, 195
Ladd, John Crew VI, 192
Ladd, John D. VI, 17
Ladd, John Everet V, 258
Ladd, John Kinsey VI, 189
Ladd, John Milton VI, 190
Ladd, John Milton VI, 196
Ladd, John R. V, 257
Ladd, John W. V, 258
Ladd, John, Jr. VI, 114
Ladd, Jonathan V, 258
Ladd, Jonathan V, 259
Ladd, Jonathan V, 459
Ladd, Jonathan B. V, 257
Ladd, Jordan V, 220
Ladd, Jordan V, 257

dd, Jordan V, 459
dd, Jordan VI, 137
dd, Jordon V, 459
dd, Joseph IV, 973
dd, Joseph IV, 974
dd, Joseph VI, 114
dd, Joseph VI, 158
dd, Joseph VI, 159
dd, Joseph VI, 190
dd, Joseph VI, 193
dd, Joseph Jones IV, 236
dd, Josephine V, 258
dd, Joshua II, 556
dd, Joshua IV, 973
dd, Joshua IV, 974
dd, Judith VI, 114
dd, Judith VI, 137
dd, Judith VI, 158
dd, Judith VI, 167
dd, Judith VI, 189
dd, Judith VI, 190
dd, Judith VI, 191
dd, Judith VI, 192
dd, Judith VI, 193
dd, Julian IV, 966
dd, Julian IV, 973
dd, Julian IV, 974
dd, Julian J. IV, 974
dd, Kate E. III, 196
dd, Kate Everit III, 216
dd, Kathryn V, 459
dd, Lancelott VI, 196
dd, Leadbetter VI, 190
dd, Ledbetter VI, 195
dd, Levi V, 257
dd, Levi VI, 190
dd, Levi VI, 195
dd, Levy VI, 194
dd, Lewis V, 257
dd, Lewis V, 459
dd, Louie V, 459
dd, Louis V, 258
dd, Louisa V, 257
dd, Louisa V, 258
dd, Louise V, 258
dd, Louiza V, 258
dd, Lucile V, 459
dd, Lucy VI, 178
dd, Lucy VI, 179
dd, Lucy VI, 191
dd, Lucy VI, 195
dd, Lucy Ann IV, 173
dd, Lucy Ann IV, 236
dd, Lucy Ann VI, 191
dd, Lucy Ann VI, 196
dd, Lydia IV, 236
dd, Lydia IV, 436
dd, Lydia IV, 473
dd, Lydia IV, 476
dd, Lydia IV, 482
dd, Lydia IV, 940
dd, Lydia IV, 973
dd, Lydia IV, 974
dd, Lydia V, 247
dd, Lydia V, 257
dd, Lydia V, 258
dd, Lydia V, 268
dd, Lydia V, 459
dd, Lydia V, 509
dd, Lydia VI, 114
dd, Lydia VI, 137
dd, Lydia VI, 163
dd, Lydia VI, 190
dd, Lydia VI, 192
dd, Lydia VI, 193
dd, Lydia B. V, 258
dd, Maggie V, 258
add, Maggie A. V, 258
add, Mahala J. V, 257
add, Mahala Jane V, 257
add, Mahlon IV, 974
add, Mahlon Leon IV, 974
add, Margaret V, 218
add, Margaret V, 257
add, Margaret V, 258
add, Margaret VI, 45
add, Margaret VI, 46
add, Margaret VI, 137
add, Margaret VI, 158
add, Margaret VI, 160
add, Margaret VI, 165
add, Margaret VI, 168
add, Margaret VI, 190
add, Margaret VI, 191
add, Margaret VI, 193
add, Margaret VI, 194
add, Margaret VI, 195
add, Margaret VI, 216
add, Margaret VI, 238
add, Margaret L. IV, 974
add, Margaret Luella IV, 973
Ladd, Margery V, 218
Ladd, Margery V, 258
Ladd, Mariah IV, 483
Ladd, Marian H. III, 148
Ladd, Marian H. III, 196
Ladd, Mariana C. IV, 482
Ladd, Mariana C. L. III, 196
Ladd, Marianna C. IV, 236
Ladd, Marianna C. IV, 483
Ladd, Marium I, 217
Ladd, Mark V, 258
Ladd, Martha IV, 236
Ladd, Martha A. V, 243
Ladd, Martha Ann V, 257
Ladd, Martha Ann V, 258
Ladd, Martha Ann V, 273
Ladd, Mary IV, 217
Ladd, Mary IV, 236
Ladd, Mary IV, 247
Ladd, Mary IV, 288
Ladd, Mary IV, 482
Ladd, Mary IV, 925
Ladd, Mary V, 257
Ladd, Mary V, 324
Ladd, Mary V, 410
Ladd, Mary VI, 111
Ladd, Mary VI, 157
Ladd, Mary VI, 158
Ladd, Mary VI, 159
Ladd, Mary VI, 160
Ladd, Mary VI, 164
Ladd, Mary VI, 169
Ladd, Mary VI, 178
Ladd, Mary VI, 182
Ladd, Mary VI, 189
Ladd, Mary VI, 190
Ladd, Mary VI, 191
Ladd, Mary VI, 192
Ladd, Mary VI, 193
Ladd, Mary VI, 194
Ladd, Mary VI, 195
Ladd, Mary VI, 199
Ladd, Mary VI, 204
Ladd, Mary VI, 208
Ladd, Mary VI, 213
Ladd, Mary VI, 214
Ladd, Mary VI, 215
Ladd, Mary VI, 216
Ladd, Mary VI, 257
Ladd, Mary VI, 263
Ladd, Mary VI, 274
Ladd, Mary VI, 277
Ladd, Mary A. R. V, 257
Ladd, Mary Ann IV, 468
Ladd, Mary Ann IV, 482
Ladd, Mary Ann Rebecca V, 258
Ladd, Mary B. V, 250
Ladd, Mary B. V, 257
Ladd, Mary B. V, 258
Ladd, Mary B. VI, 214
Ladd, Mary E. IV, 236
Ladd, Mary E. IV, 292
Ladd, Mary E. VI, 191
Ladd, Mary Elizabeth IV, 236
Ladd, Mary Elizabeth IV, 293
Ladd, Mary Elizabeth V, 258
Ladd, Mary Ellen V, 258
Ladd, Mary Ellen V, 410
Ladd, Mary Emily IV, 279
Ladd, Mary Emily IV, 1001
Ladd, Mary Emily VI, 196
Ladd, Mary F. IV, 236
Ladd, Mary Folger IV, 482
Ladd, Mary Hunnicutt VI, 114
Ladd, Mary Luella V, 258
Ladd, Mary T. IV, 236
Ladd, Mary T. VI, 184
Ladd, Mary, Jr. VI, 158
Ladd, Mary, Jr. VI, 160
Ladd, Mary, Jr. VI, 191
Ladd, Mary, Jr. VI, 195
Ladd, Matilda V, 234
Ladd, Matilda V, 257
Ladd, Matilda V, 258
Ladd, Maud Amelia V, 258
Ladd, May F. IV, 483
Ladd, Meredith V, 258
Ladd, Meredith A. V, 259
Ladd, Michael V, 257
Ladd, Michal V, 257
Ladd, Michal VI, 191
Ladd, Michal VI, 195
Ladd, Michal VI, 212
Ladd, Mildred E. V, 258
Ladd, Millicent VI, 193
Ladd, Millie V, 258
Ladd, Minerva Ann V, 410
Ladd, Miriam I, 244
Ladd, Miriam I, 246
Ladd, Mourning VI, 154
Ladd, Mourning VI, 190
Ladd, Mourning VI, 194
Ladd, Myrtie V, 258
Ladd, N. R. V, 229
Ladd, Nancy V, 258
Ladd, Nancy VI, 179
Ladd, Nancy VI, 190
Ladd, Nancy H. VI, 179
Ladd, Nancy H. VI, 191
Ladd, Nancy H. VI, 196
Ladd, Nancy R. V, 258
Ladd, Nathan VI, 191
Ladd, Nathan B. VI, 257
Ladd, Nathan Bell VI, 190
Ladd, Nettie M. V, 258
Ladd, Noble VI, 194
Ladd, Obediah VI, 196
Ladd, Olive C. V, 258
Ladd, Olive C. V, 259
Ladd, Oliver IV, 483
Ladd, Oliver VI, 190
Ladd, Oliver VI, 195
Ladd, Oliver I. IV, 236
Ladd, Oliver M. IV, 236
Ladd, Oliver M. IV, 482
Ladd, Oliver M. IV, 483
Ladd, Oliver T. IV, 237
Ladd, Ora V, 258
Ladd, Ora V, 259
Ladd, Oscar Elwood V, 257
Ladd, Peggy VI, 166
Ladd, Peggy VI, 169
Ladd, Peggy VI, 191
Ladd, Peggy VI, 194
Ladd, Peggy VI, 240
Ladd, Peggy VI, 257
Ladd, Peter IV, 189
Ladd, Peter IV, 217
Ladd, Peter IV, 236
Ladd, Peter IV, 237
Ladd, Peter IV, 263
Ladd, Peter IV, 279
Ladd, Peter VI, 189
Ladd, Peter VI, 190
Ladd, Peter VI, 191
Ladd, Peter VI, 194
Ladd, Peter VI, 195
Ladd, Peter VI, 196
Ladd, Peter, Jr. VI, 166
Ladd, Peter, Jr. VI, 170
Ladd, Peter, Jr. VI, 191
Ladd, Peter, Jr. VI, 195
Ladd, Pleasant IV, 236
Ladd, Pleasant V, 258
Ladd, Priscilla V, 258
Ladd, Priscilla VI, 114
Ladd, Priscilla VI, 137
Ladd, Priscilla VI, 182
Ladd, Priscilla VI, 189
Ladd, Priscilla VI, 190
Ladd, Priscilla VI, 191
Ladd, Priscilla VI, 194
Ladd, Priscilla VI, 213
Ladd, Priscilla VI, 214
Ladd, Priscilla VI, 269
Ladd, Priscilla VI, 272
Ladd, R. V, 257
Ladd, Rachel V, 220
Ladd, Rachel V, 257
Ladd, Rachel V, 459
Ladd, Rachel VI, 190
Ladd, Rachel E. V, 459
Ladd, Randall M. V, 259
Ladd, Rebecca IV, 482
Ladd, Rebecca V, 217
Ladd, Rebecca V, 251
Ladd, Rebecca V, 257
Ladd, Rebecca V, 258
Ladd, Rebecca V, 259
Ladd, Rebecca VI, 189
Ladd, Rebecca VI, 194
Ladd, Rebecca VI, 214
Ladd, Rebecca E. V, 459
Ladd, Rebecca Elmira V, 258
Ladd, Rebeckah V, 258
Ladd, Rebeckah VI, 137
Ladd, Rebeckah VI, 170
Ladd, Rebeckah VI, 190
Ladd, Rebeckah VI, 195
Ladd, Rebeckah VI, 213
Ladd, Rendell McPherson V, 258
Ladd, Robert IV, 236
Ladd, Robert IV, 247
Ladd, Robert IV, 288
Ladd, Robert VI, 178
Ladd, Robert VI, 190
Ladd, Robert VI, 191
Ladd, Robert VI, 195
Ladd, Robert VI, 257
Ladd, Robert VI, 274
Ladd, Robert VI, 277
Ladd, Robert C. VI, 191
Ladd, Robert Crew IV, 236
Ladd, Robert Crew VI, 196
Ladd, Robert P. IV, 236
Ladd, Robert P. IV, 237
Ladd, Robert P. IV, 285
Ladd, Robert P. IV, 289
Ladd, Robert P. IV, 292
Ladd, Robert P. VI, 191
Ladd, Rodman VI, 190
Ladd, Rollin C. IV, 974
Ladd, Ruanna IV, 236
Ladd, Ruanna IV, 289
Ladd, Ruanna T. IV, 285
Ladd, Ruannah T. IV, 217
Ladd, Ruannah T. IV, 236
Ladd, Ruannah T. IV, 292
Ladd, Ruth V, 257
Ladd, Ruth V, 258
Ladd, Ruth V, 278
Ladd, Ruth Alma V, 258
Ladd, S. W. IV, 974
Ladd, Sally Ann IV, 236
Ladd, Samuel IV, 998
Ladd, Samuel V, 257
Ladd, Samuel VI, 158
Ladd, Samuel VI, 166
Ladd, Samuel VI, 169
Ladd, Samuel VI, 190
Ladd, Samuel VI, 191
Ladd, Samuel VI, 195
Ladd, Samuel W. IV, 973
Ladd, Samuel W. IV, 974
Ladd, Samuel Whitefield IV, 974
Ladd, Samuel Whitfield IV, 731
Ladd, Samuel Whitfield IV, 973
Ladd, Samuel Whitfield VI, 191
Ladd, Sarah I, 244
Ladd, Sarah I, 245
Ladd, Sarah I, 253
Ladd, Sarah II, 556
Ladd, Sarah IV, 236
Ladd, Sarah V, 226
Ladd, Sarah V, 255
Ladd, Sarah V, 258
Ladd, Sarah V, 268
Ladd, Sarah VI, 17
Ladd, Sarah VI, 100
Ladd, Sarah VI, 101
Ladd, Sarah VI, 114
Ladd, Sarah VI, 115
Ladd, Sarah VI, 158
Ladd, Sarah VI, 159
Ladd, Sarah VI, 160
Ladd, Sarah VI, 179
Ladd, Sarah VI, 180
Ladd, Sarah VI, 181
Ladd, Sarah VI, 184
Ladd, Sarah VI, 189
Ladd, Sarah VI, 190
Ladd, Sarah VI, 191
Ladd, Sarah VI, 192
Ladd, Sarah VI, 193
Ladd, Sarah VI, 194
Ladd, Sarah VI, 195
Ladd, Sarah VI, 198
Ladd, Sarah VI, 201
Ladd, Sarah VI, 257
Ladd, Sarah VI, 328
Ladd, Sarah VI, 344
Ladd, Sarah Ann IV, 236
Ladd, Sarah Ann IV, 285
Ladd, Sarah Bell VI, 190
Ladd, Sarah Binford VI, 114
Ladd, Sarah Binford VI, 115
Ladd, Sarah Elizabeth VI, 196
Ladd, Sarah Elizabeth VI, 214
Ladd, Sarah G. V, 257
Ladd, Sarah G. V, 274
Ladd, Sarah G. VI, 137
Ladd, Sarah Gilliam VI, 114
Ladd, Sarah L. IV, 236
Ladd, Sarah L. IV, 263
Ladd, Sarah Leadbetter IV, 236
Ladd, Sarah Leadbetter VI, 191
Ladd, Sarah Leadbetter VI, 196
Ladd, Sibelia A. VI, 235
Ladd, Sibelia A. VI, 257
Ladd, Sibelia Ann Joanna VI, 190
Ladd, Sibilla IV, 438
Ladd, Sibyl E. IV, 974
Ladd, Sibyl E. IV, 1039
Ladd, Sidney V, 235
Ladd, Sidney V, 258
Ladd, Sidney H. V, 257
Ladd, Stephen IV, 438
Ladd, Susanna II, 556
Ladd, Susanna VI, 184
Ladd, Susanna VI, 189
Ladd, Susanna VI, 193
Ladd, Sylvia I, 244
Ladd, Tabitha I, 217
Ladd, Thirza IV, 909
Ladd, Thirza IV, 911
Ladd, Thomas IV, 236
Ladd, Thomas IV, 483
Ladd, Thomas V, 459
Ladd, Thomas V, 916
Ladd, Thomas VI, 17
Ladd, Thomas VI, 114
Ladd, Thomas VI, 153
Ladd, Thomas VI, 156
Ladd, Thomas VI, 158
Ladd, Thomas VI, 173
Ladd, Thomas VI, 174
Ladd, Thomas VI, 184
Ladd, Thomas VI, 189
Ladd, Thomas VI, 192
Ladd, Thomas VI, 193
Ladd, Thomas VI, 194
Ladd, Thomas VI, 195
Ladd, Thomas VI, 198
Ladd, Thomas VI, 218
Ladd, Thomas VI, 221
Ladd, Thomas Binford VI, 192
Ladd, Thomas E. V, 258
Ladd, Thomas Ellwood V, 257
Ladd, Thomas Elwood V, 258
Ladd, Thomas Mifflin VI, 190
Ladd, Thomas Mifflin VI, 196
Ladd, Thomas W. III, 196
Ladd, Thomas W. IV, 482
Ladd, Thomas W. IV, 483
Ladd, Thomas W. V, 917
Ladd, Thomas, Sr. VI, 190
Ladd, Thos. E. V, 258
Ladd, Thos. Elwood VI, 191
Ladd, Thos. W. V, 917
Ladd, Timothy Wardwith VI, 114
Ladd, Unity VI, 157
Ladd, Unity VI, 179
Ladd, Unity VI, 180
Ladd, Unity VI, 190
Ladd, Unity VI, 191
Ladd, Unity VI, 193
Ladd, Unity VI, 194
Ladd, Unity VI, 216
Ladd, Unity VI, 245
Ladd, Unity VI, 246
Ladd, Unity VI, 250
Ladd, Unity VI, 257
Ladd, Unity Smith VI, 190
Ladd, Ursley VI, 114
Ladd, Ursly VI, 102
Ladd, Ursly VI, 104
Ladd, Ursly VI, 114
Ladd, Ursula VI, 114
Ladd, Ursula VI, 192
Ladd, Ursula VI, 193
Ladd, Ursulah VI, 172
Ladd, Ursulah VI, 173
Ladd, Ursulah VI, 189
Ladd, Ursulah VI, 191
Ladd, Ursulah VI, 192
Ladd, Vera V. IV, 966
Ladd, Vernon V, 459
Ladd, Victoria V, 257
Ladd, Virginia IV, 236
Ladd, Virginia IV, 237
Ladd, Virginia IV, 482
Ladd, Walter G. III, 216
Ladd, Walter J. III, 196
Ladd, Walter J. V, 917
Ladd, Walter Jay V, 916
Ladd, Warren F. IV, 483
Ladd, Wd. lizabeth VI, 189
Ladd, William IV, 482
Ladd, William V, 258
Ladd, William V, 259
Ladd, William V, 344
Ladd, William VI, 17
Ladd, William VI, 111
Ladd, William VI, 114
Ladd, William VI, 117
Ladd, William VI, 148
Ladd, William VI, 158
Ladd, William VI, 165
Ladd, William VI, 180
Ladd, William VI, 182
Ladd, William VI, 189
Ladd, William VI, 190
Ladd, William VI, 191
Ladd, William VI, 192
Ladd, William VI, 193
Ladd, William VI, 212
Ladd, William VI, 257
Ladd, William C. IV, 236
Ladd, William C. IV, 482
Ladd, William C. IV, 483
Ladd, William C. V, 257
Ladd, William Charles VI, 189
Ladd, William Glenn V, 258

Ladd, William H. IV, 236
Ladd, William H. IV, 482
Ladd, William H. IV, 483
Ladd, William J. III, 148
Ladd, William P. VI, 257
Ladd, William Penn VI, 190
Ladd, William Penn VI, 196
Ladd, William Penn VI, 257
Ladd, William W. V, 257
Ladd, William, Jr. VI, 173
Ladd, William, Jr. VI, 191
Ladd, William, Jr. VI, 192
Ladd, William, Jr. VI, 193
Ladd, William, Sr. VI, 192
Ladd, Wm. IV, 248
Ladd, Wm. VI, 111
Ladd, Wm. VI, 189
Ladd, Wm. E. IV, 973
Ladd, Wm. E. IV, 978
Ladd, Wm. H. III, 83
Ladd, Wm. H. III, 196
Ladd, Wm., Jr. VI, 172
Ladd, Wm., Jr. VI, 173
Ladds, Edward IV, 1325
Ladds, Nora IV, 1325
Laden, Sarah I, 57
Laden, Sarah I, 89
Ladner, David IV, 640
Ladner, Elizabeth IV, 640
Ladner, James Vail IV, 640
Ladner, John IV, 640
Ladner, John V. IV, 640
Ladner, Martha IV, 606
Ladner, Martha IV, 640
Ladner, Mary IV, 640
Ladner, Susan IV, 611
Ladner, Susan IV, 640
Ladner, Susan W. IV, 640
Ladnor, Mary IV, 612
Ladnor, Mary IV, 640
Lafay, John VI, 947
Lafay, Mary VI, 947
Lafayette, Albert M. II, 887
Lafayette, Albert M. II, 938
Lafayette, Reba Emma II, 887
Lafayette, Reba Emma II, 938
Lafetra, ??? III, 196
Lafetra, Amy III, 196
Lafetra, Benjamin V, 146
Lafetra, David III, 196
Lafetra, Elizabeth III, 196
Lafetra, Elizabeth V, 146
Lafetra, George F. III, 196
Lafetra, George W. V, 146
Lafetra, James III, 196
Lafetra, James III, 363
Lafetra, James H. V, 146
Lafetra, Jane T. V, 146
Lafetra, Joseph W. III, 196
Lafetra, Mary III, 196
LaFetra, Mary V, 91
Lafetra, Meribah V, 146
Lafetra, Nathan A. III, 196
Lafetra, Robert V, 146
Lafetra, Samuel III, 196
Lafetra, Sarah III, 170
Lafetra, Sarah III, 196
Lafetra, Sarah L. III, 196
Lafetra, Sarah L. III, 363
Lafetre, Benjamin V, 91
Lafetre, Mary V, 91
Lafetre, Robert V, 91
Lafferty, Dean D. IV, 1325
Lafferty, Dean Dewitt IV, 1325
Lafferty, Dora A. IV, 1325
Lafferty, Edson B. IV, 1325
Lafferty, Edson Brice IV, 1325
Lafferty, L. S. IV, 1325
Lafferty, Lucile IV, 1325
Lafferty, Marion May IV, 1325
Lafferty, Mary E. V, 665
Lafferty, Miriam May IV, 1322
Lafferty, Miriam May IV, 1325
Lafferty, Paul IV, 1325
Lafferty, Paul LeMoine IV, 1325
LaFountain, Wallas IV, 1039
Lafoy, John VI, 947
Lafoy, Lavanny VI, 969
Lafoy, Mary VI, 947
Lafoy, Mary VI, 969
Lagerblom, Joseph N. III, 196
LaGorughe, Helen III, 58
LaGrane, Fred IV, 1039
LaGrane, Fred W. IV, 1039
Lague, Francis II, 1009
Lagues, ??? III, 196
Lagues, ??? III, 207
Lagues, Wilhelmina III, 196
Lagues, Wilhelmina III, 207
Lahmon, James E. V, 1006
Lahue, Edward E. V, 1006
Lahue, Emma B. V, 1006
Lahue, Kitty V, 1006
Laiky, James I, 403
Laiky, John I, 403
Laiky, John I Sup 1, 9
Laiky, William I Sup 1, 9
Lain, Ann I, 404
Lain, Betsy VI, 826
Lain, Jacob I, 58
Lain, Jane VI, 826
Lain, Jane VI, 832
Lain, Joel VI, 824
Lain, John I, 58
Lain, Majory VI, 257
Lain, Mordicai VI, 257
Lain, Rebecca VI, 832
Lain, Sarah I, 542
Lain, Sarah Hencock I, 557
Lain, Thomas VI, 257
Lain, Thomas VI, 832
Lain, William VI, 257
Lain, William T. VI, 832
Laine, Alex VI, 832
Laine, Barnet II, 221
Laine, Barnet II, 237
Laine, Daniel VI, 257
Laine, Jane VI, 832
Laine, John VI, 832
Laine, Rebecca VI, 832
Laine, Sally VI, 832
Laine, Sally VI, 848
Laine, Sarah II, 221
Laine, Sarah II, 237
Laine, Thomas VI, 257
Laine, Thomas VI, 832
Laine, Thomas H. VI, 831
Laine, William VI, 257
Laine, William T. VI, 832
Laing, ??? III, 150
Laing, ??? III, 252
Laing, Aaron G. III, 197
Laing, Abbey IV, 1368
Laing, Abbey IV, 1371
Laing, Abbey IV, 1372
Laing, Abby IV, 1361
Laing, Abby IV, 1364
Laing, Abby IV, 1371
Laing, Albert III, 197
Laing, Albert D. III, 197
Laing, Alec Edgar III, 197
Laing, Alfred D. III, 197
Laing, Alva E. II, 887
Laing, Alva E. III, 197
Laing, Alva Edgar II, 805
Laing, Alva Edgar II, 887
Laing, Alva Edgar III, 197
Laing, Alve E. II, 887
Laing, Amy IV, 1361
Laing, Amy IV, 1371
Laing, Ann Elisa II, 887
Laing, Ann Eliza II, 805
Laing, Ann Eliza II, 887
Laing, Ann Eliza III, 138
Laing, Ann Eliza III, 197
Laing, Ann Eliza III, 326
Laing, Anna II, 805
Laing, Anna II, 887
Laing, Anna II, 924
Laing, Anna II, 932
Laing, Annie Roberts II, 805
Laing, Benjamin IV, 1371
Laing, Benjamin Davids III, 197
Laing, Benjamin P. IV, 1371
Laing, Benjamin T. IV, 1371
Laing, Catharine III, 197
Laing, Catharine Moore II, 924
Laing, Catharine R. II, 887
Laing, Catharine Randolph II, 805
Laing, Catherine Moore II, 805
Laing, Catherine R. II, 932
Laing, Charles II, 805
Laing, Charles II, 887
Laing, Daniel III, 197
Laing, David IV, 97
Laing, David IV, 340
Laing, Edgar III, 326
Laing, Emma Louisa II, 805
Laing, George II, 887
Laing, George T. II, 887
Laing, George Truman II, 805
Laing, George Truman II, 887
Laing, George Truman II, 924
Laing, Hannah IV, 1368
Laing, Hannah IV, 1371
Laing, Helen II, 887
Laing, Helen III, 197
Laing, Helen L. III, 197
Laing, Henry M. II, 887
Laing, Henry M. II, 924
Laing, Henry M. II, 932
Laing, Henry Moore II, 805
Laing, Howard II, 887
Laing, Howard E. II, 805
Laing, Howard E. III, 197
Laing, Hugh III, 197
Laing, John Freeman II, 575
Laing, John Freeman II, 751
Laing, Joseph IV, 1371
Laing, Joseph Smith IV, 1371
Laing, Katharine Moore II, 821
Laing, Louise III, 197
Laing, Louise III, 252
Laing, Margaret II, 792
Laing, Margaret B. III, 197
Laing, Martha III, 197
Laing, Mary IV, 1371
Laing, Mary S. IV, 1371
Laing, Mary Truman II, 805
Laing, Phebe II, 798
Laing, Phebe Ann IV, 1371
Laing, Phebe Ann IV, 1372
Laing, Rebecca II, 823
Laing, Sarah III, 197
Laing, Sarah A. III, 197
Laing, Sarah Maria IV, 1364
Laing, Sarah Maria IV, 1371
Laing, Silvanus III, 197
Laing, Smith IV, 1361
Laing, Smith IV, 1364
Laing, Smith IV, 1368
Laing, Smith IV, 1371
Laing, Smith IV, 1372
Laing, Webster A. IV, 1371
Laing, William II, 805
Laing, William III, 197
Laing, Wm. II, 805
Laing, Wm. II, 887
Laing, Wm. II, 932
Lair, Mary C. II, 887
Lair, Rosa V, 751
Laird, Carrie W. V, 173
Laird, Carrie W. V, 1006
Laird, Catharine IV, 1325
Laird, Charles V, 173
Laird, Chas. F. V, 1006
Laird, Edith V, 173
Laird, Geo A. V, 1006
Laird, Louise Conarroe V, 848
Laird, M. E. V, 1006
Laird, Sarah R. V, 848
Laird, Sarah R. V, 1006
Laish, Hugh II, 445
Lake, Ann II, 710
Lake, Ann II, 751
Lake, Ann II, 756
Lake, Camden II, 751
Lake, Daniel II, 710
Lake, Daniel II, 751
Lake, Daniel II, 756
Lake, David II, 387
Lake, Dinah Ann II, 751
Lake, Dinah Ann II, 756
Lake, Elizabeth II, 387
Lake, Elizabeth II, 575
Lake, Joseph III, 424
Lake, Lewis V, 1006
Lake, Lucinda II, 710
Lake, Lucinda II, 751
Lake, Park V, 91
Lake, Priscilla Ann II, 751
Lake, Rebecca I, 887
Lake, Rebecca I, 890
Lake, Rebecca II, 710
Lake, Sarah III, 424
Lake, Sarah III, 444
Lake, William II, 387
Lakey, Ann I, 403
Lakey, Ann I, 991
Lakey, Elizabeth I, 310
Lakey, Elizabeth I, 403
Lakey, Elizabeth I, 824
Lakey, Francis I, 824
Lakey, Francis I, 991
Lakey, James I, 824
Lakey, James I, 991
Lakey, Mayner I, 824
Lakey, Ruth I, 991
Lakey, Susanna I, 403
Lakey, Susanna I, 824
Lakey, Susannah I, 824
Lakin, Ann II, 575
Lakin, Ann II, 578
Lakin, Henry II, 575
Lakin, Henry II, 578
Lakin, Rachel II, 445
Laky, Elizabeth I, 343
Laky, Elizabeth I, 403
Laky, Ruth I, 985
Laky, Ruth I, 991
Lam, Darcas I, 144
Lam, Israel A. I, 58
Lam, Jemimah I, 445
Lam, Jemimah I, 449
Lam, Josiah I, 1070
Lam, Kesiah V, 848
Lam, Kesiah V, 854
Lam, Martha P. I, 58
Lam, Rebecca V, 631
Lam, Rebecca V, 639
Lam, Reuben I, 695
Laman, Daniel VI, 934
Lamar, Greenville V, 848
Lamar, Hannah V, 509
Lamar, Ida V, 848
Lamar, Iva V, 848
Lamar, Iva C. V, 848
Lamar, Leila III, 140
Lamar, Leila III, 197
Lamar, Leona V, 848
Lamar, Leona May V, 848
Lamar, Martha A. V, 848
Lamar, Martha Ann V, 848
Lamar, Mary V, 486
Lamar, Mary V, 509
Lamar, Mattie A. V, 848
Lamar, Nathan Dennis V, 509
Lamar, Osborn V, 509
Lamar, Ruth V, 509
Lamar, Samuel V, 509
Lamar, William V, 848
Lamb, Abigail I, 10
Lamb, Abigail I, 683
Lamb, Abigail I, 765
Lamb, Abigail B. I, 683
Lamb, Abigail B. I, 765
Lamb, Abigail B. I, 766
Lamb, Abigale I, 40
Lamb, Abigale I, 57
Lamb, Abner I, 749
Lamb, Abner I, 764
Lamb, Abner I, 765
Lamb, Abner B. I, 403
Lamb, Abner B. I, 415
Lamb, Achsa I, 57
Lamb, Adaline I, 403
Lamb, Adeline I, 683
Lamb, Agaron I, 58
Lamb, Ageron B. I, 11
Lamb, Agron I, 58
Lamb, Albert I, 403
Lamb, Albert I, 660
Lamb, Albert I, 683
Lamb, Albert I, 723
Lamb, Albert B. I, 403
Lamb, Alce I, 1021
Lamb, Alce I, 1062
Lamb, Alfred I, 403
Lamb, Alice VI, 525
Lamb, Alva N. I, 11
Lamb, Alvah N. III, 309
Lamb, Alvah Newby III, 197
Lamb, Amelia O. VI, 832
Lamb, Amijah I, 196
Lamb, Anderson I, 683
Lamb, Anderson L. I, 765
Lamb, Andrew J. I, 58
Lamb, Ann I, 683
Lamb, Ann I, 687
Lamb, Ann II, 238
Lamb, Ann Leeds II, 237
Lamb, Anna I, 683
Lamb, Anna II, 237
Lamb, Anna II, 244
Lamb, Anna III, 197
Lamb, Anna V, 848
Lamb, Anna A. III, 309
Lamb, Anna Alice III, 197
Lamb, Annas I, 677
Lamb, Annas I, 683
Lamb, Archibald VI, 994
Lamb, Arlando B. I, 403
Lamb, Arlando B. I, 683
Lamb, Armajah I, 10
Lamb, Armajah I, 35
Lamb, Armajah I, 57
Lamb, Armajah I, 196
Lamb, Armejah I, 189
Lamb, Armejah I, 196
Lamb, Armella Ann I, 749
Lamb, Armiger I, 57
Lamb, Asenath I, 683
Lamb, Barbara L. I, 683
Lamb, Barbara Luzena I, 683
Lamb, Barbary L. I, 403
Lamb, Barnabe I, 57
Lamb, Beatrice I, 11
Lamb, Benjamin I, 10
Lamb, Benjamin I, 57
Lamb, Benjamin I, 58
Lamb, Benjamin I, 145
Lamb, Benjamin I, 660
Lamb, Benjamin I, 764
Lamb, Benjamin I, 765
Lamb, Benjamin B. I, 101
Lamb, Benjamin Craig I, 11
Lamb, Benjamin F. I, 11
Lamb, Benjamin F. I, 58
Lamb, Benjamin Ridgway II, 29
Lamb, Benjamine I, 58
Lamb, Bethia I, 526
Lamb, Bethia I, 556
Lamb, Betsy I, 11
Lamb, Betsy VI, 1016
Lamb, Beulah II, 294
Lamb, Caleb I, 11
Lamb, Caleb I, 57
Lamb, Caleb I, 101
Lamb, Caleb I, 145
Lamb, Caleb I, 196
Lamb, Caleb I, 198
Lamb, Caleb I, 660
Lamb, Caleb I, 723
Lamb, Caleb I, 764
Lamb, Caroline I, 371
Lamb, Caroline I, 403
Lamb, Carolyn Elisabeth I, 11
Lamb, Carrie IV, 1325
Lamb, Casper Scott I, 11
Lamb, Catharine I, 22
Lamb, Catharine I, 58
Lamb, Catharine I, 82
Lamb, Catharine I, 660
Lamb, Catharine I, 678
Lamb, Catharine I, 682
Lamb, Catharine V, 631
Lamb, Catherine I, 58
Lamb, Centre I, 556
Lamb, Chalkley I, 11
Lamb, Chalkley I, 660
Lamb, Charity I, 660
Lamb, Charles E. I, 11
Lamb, Charlotte I, 764
Lamb, Charlotte II, 237
Lamb, Charlotte II, 250
Lamb, Chas. II, 887
Lamb, Christian I, 660
Lamb, Christiana II, 825
Lamb, Clarence IV, 1325
Lamb, Clarence H. IV, 1325
Lamb, Cyrus Rinaldon I, 403
Lamb, Daniel I, 10
Lamb, Daniel I, 57
Lamb, Daniel I, 58
Lamb, Daniel IV, 97
Lamb, Daniel V, 848
Lamb, Daniel V, 1006
Lamb, Daniel S. IV, 128
Lamb, Daniel S. IV, 152
Lamb, Darcas I, 144
Lamb, David I, 101
Lamb, David I, 196
Lamb, David I, 1021
Lamb, David V. VI, 832
Lamb, Delila VI, 832
Lamb, Dorcas I, 101
Lamb, Dorcas I, 673
Lamb, Dorcas I, 682
Lamb, Dorithy I, 11
Lamb, Dorothy I, 10
Lamb, Dorothy I, 11
Lamb, Dorothy I, 57
Lamb, Dorothy I, 74
Lamb, Dr. B. F. I, 58
Lamb, Dr. Benjamin F. I, 58
Lamb, Edee I, 660
Lamb, Edeth I, 651
Lamb, Edith I, 675
Lamb, Edith I, 683
Lamb, Edmond I, 683
Lamb, Edmund I, 101
Lamb, Edmund I, 196
Lamb, Edward I, 683
Lamb, Edward VI, 525
Lamb, Edward David I, 145
Lamb, Eleanor I, 683
Lamb, Eleanor I, 688
Lamb, Eli I, 403
Lamb, Elijah I, 403
Lamb, Elinor VI, 525
Lamb, Elisabeth I, 8
Lamb, Elisabeth I, 10
Lamb, Elisabeth I, 11
Lamb, Elisabeth I, 43
Lamb, Elisabeth I, 57
Lamb, Elisabeth I, 62
Lamb, Elisabeth I, 65
Lamb, Elisabeth I, 67
Lamb, Elisabeth I, 69
Lamb, Elisabeth I, 144
Lamb, Elisabeth I. I, 58
Lamb, Elisabeth J. I, 7
Lamb, Eliza IV, 128
Lamb, Eliza Ann IV, 97

b, Elizabeth I, 101
b, Elizabeth I, 403
b, Elizabeth I, 506
b, Elizabeth I, 556
b, Elizabeth I, 565
b, Elizabeth I, 660
b, Elizabeth I, 682
b, Elizabeth I, 683
b, Elizabeth I, 691
b, Elizabeth I, 765
b, Elizabeth I, 1021
b, Elizabeth II, 237
b, Elizabeth II, 250
b, Elizabeth A. I, 660
b, Elizabeth White II, 799
b, Elwood E. I, 683
b, Emariah B. V, 631
b, Enoch I, 749
b, Eri I, 57
b, Eri V, 631
b, Esau I, 57
b, Esau I, 62
b, Esau I, 144
b, Esau I, 660
b, Esau I, 682
b, Esau I, 786
b, Esau I, 824
b, Esau I, 1123
b, Esaue I, 101
b, Esom V, 91
b, Esther I, 10
b, Esther I, 58
b, Esther I, 403
b, Esther I, 416
b, Esther I, 681
b, Esther I, 682
b, Esther I, 683
b, Esther I, 749
b, Esther I, 764
b, Esther I, 765
b, Esther E. I, 611
b, Esther Eliza I, 749
b, Eunice I, 764
b, Flora Melissa Allice I, 403
b, Flossie IV, 1325
b, Frances I, 526
b, Frances I, 556
b, Frances I, 620
b, Frances I, 660
b, Frederick I, 556
b, Frederick VI, 525
b, Galen I, 11
b, Galen I, 58
b, Genn I, 764
b, Geo. V, 631
b, George I, 11
b, George IV, 97
b, George IV, 128
b, Green I, 765
b, Gulielma I, 6
b, Gulielma I, 11
b, Gulielma I, 41
b, Gulielma I, 48
b, Gulielma I, 57
b, Gulielma I, 58
b, Gulielma J. I, 5
b, Gwin I, 890
b, Gwin I, 899
b, Hannah I, 611
b, Hannah I, 674
b, Hannah I, 676
b, Hannah I, 682
b, Hannah I, 683
b, Hannah I, 749
b, Hannah I, 786
b, Hannah I, 1123
b, Hannah II, 387
b, Hannah IV, 88
b, Hannah IV, 97
b, Hannah IV, 99
b, Hannah IV, 128
b, Hannah IV, 152
b, Hannah IV, 237
b, Hannah V, 91
b, Hannah V, 631
b, Hannah H. I, 683
b, Hannah H. I, 765
b, Hannah M. I, 765
b, Henrietta V, 631
b, Henry I, 5
b, Henry I, 10
b, Henry I, 11
b, Henry I, 57
b, Henry I, 71
b, Henry I, 81
b, Henry I, 556
b, Henry I, 660
b, Henry I, 683
b, Hosea I, 57
b, Huldah I, 41
b, Huldah I, 58
Lamb, Huldah I, 403
Lamb, Huldah I, 660
Lamb, Huldah I, 683
Lamb, Huldah I, 686
Lamb, Huldath I, 449
Lamb, Irene I, 11
Lamb, Irene Gertrude I, 11
Lamb, Isaac I, 10
Lamb, Isaac I, 11
Lamb, Isaac I, 22
Lamb, Isaac I, 57
Lamb, Isaac I, 58
Lamb, Isaac I, 65
Lamb, Isaac I, 82
Lamb, Isaac I, 196
Lamb, Isaac I, 786
Lamb, Isaac I, 824
Lamb, Isaac V, 625
Lamb, Isaac V, 631
Lamb, Isabel I, 824
Lamb, Isabella I, 786
Lamb, Israel A. I, 58
Lamb, J. Howard I, 620
Lamb, Jacob I, 11
Lamb, Jacob I, 57
Lamb, Jacob I, 58
Lamb, Jacob I, 63
Lamb, Jacob I, 64
Lamb, Jacob I, 556
Lamb, Jacob I, 575
Lamb, Jacob I, 660
Lamb, Jacob I, 682
Lamb, Jacob I, 683
Lamb, Jacob I, 764
Lamb, Jacob I, 765
Lamb, Jacob I, 991
Lamb, Jacob II, 227
Lamb, Jacob II, 237
Lamb, Jacob II, 238
Lamb, Jacob, Jr. I, 57
Lamb, Jacob, Jr. V, 848
Lamb, James I, 764
Lamb, James I, 1021
Lamb, James IV, 128
Lamb, James V, 917
Lamb, James E. I, 58
Lamb, James H. V, 1006
Lamb, James L. IV, 97
Lamb, James L. V, 917
Lamb, James T. I, 58
Lamb, Jamimah I, 449
Lamb, Jane I, 57
Lamb, Jane I, 683
Lamb, Jehu B. V, 631
Lamb, Jemima I, 57
Lamb, Jemima I, 77
Lamb, Jemima I, 403
Lamb, Jemima I, 415
Lamb, Jemima I Sup 1, 9
Lamb, Jeremiah I, 660
Lamb, Jesse I, 660
Lamb, Joab I, 660
Lamb, Joab I, 683
Lamb, Joab I, 765
Lamb, John I, 11
Lamb, John I, 57
Lamb, John I, 58
Lamb, John I, 69
Lamb, John I, 74
Lamb, John I, 145
Lamb, John I, 660
Lamb, John I, 683
Lamb, John I, 684
Lamb, John I, 764
Lamb, John I, 765
Lamb, John I, 786
Lamb, John I, 824
Lamb, John I, 1021
Lamb, John I, 1123
Lamb, John IV, 88
Lamb, John IV, 97
Lamb, John IV, 128
Lamb, John IV, 152
Lamb, John V, 91
Lamb, John V, 631
Lamb, John V, 848
Lamb, John A. I, 101
Lamb, John Anderson I, 145
Lamb, John Anderson I, 196
Lamb, John B. I, 403
Lamb, John C. I, 403
Lamb, John C. I, 683
Lamb, John C. VI, 833
Lamb, John Evan V, 751
Lamb, John Gibson IV, 97
Lamb, John J. I, 620
Lamb, John N. I, 11
Lamb, John T. I, 11
Lamb, John T. I, 58
Lamb, John W. V, 631
Lamb, John, Jr. I, 57
Lamb, Johnathan I, 1123
Lamb, Jonathan I, 101
Lamb, Jonathan I, 145
Lamb, Jonathan I, 786
Lamb, Jonathan V, 751
Lamb, Jonothan V, 91
Lamb, Joseph I, 10
Lamb, Joseph I, 57
Lamb, Joseph I, 74
Lamb, Joseph I, 101
Lamb, Joseph I, 145
Lamb, Joseph I, 526
Lamb, Joseph I, 556
Lamb, Joseph I, 660
Lamb, Joseph I, 683
Lamb, Joseph I, 1021
Lamb, Joseph II, 237
Lamb, Joseph M. I, 683
Lamb, Joshua I, 403
Lamb, Joshua I, 556
Lamb, Joshua I, 567
Lamb, Joshua I, 645
Lamb, Joshua I, 660
Lamb, Joshua IV, 152
Lamb, Joshua G. IV, 97
Lamb, Joshua G. IV, 128
Lamb, Joshua G. V, 917
Lamb, Josiah I, 11
Lamb, Josiah I, 41
Lamb, Josiah I, 57
Lamb, Josiah I, 58
Lamb, Josiah I, 74
Lamb, Josiah I, 786
Lamb, Josiah I, 824
Lamb, Josiah I, 1066
Lamb, Josiah I, 1123
Lamb, Josiah V, 91
Lamb, Josiah V, 751
Lamb, Josiah V, 794
Lamb, Julia E. I, 683
Lamb, Katurah I, 58
Lamb, Kendall I, 683
Lamb, Kezia I, 57
Lamb, Kezia I, 86
Lamb, Keziah I, 11
Lamb, Lathan G. VI, 832
Lamb, Leah I, 58
Lamb, Leah I, 64
Lamb, Leah McCollum I, 723
Lamb, Lelia B. VI, 823
Lamb, Lettice II, 237
Lamb, Littleton P. VI, 806
Lamb, Littleton P. VI, 823
Lamb, Longshore I, 1033
Lamb, Louisa I, 924
Lamb, Louisa Jane I, 923
Lamb, Lovey I, 57
Lamb, Lovey I, 74
Lamb, Low I, 683
Lamb, Lucy I, 929
Lamb, Luzena I, 683
Lamb, Luzena I, 684
Lamb, Luzena C. I, 660
Lamb, Lydia I, 58
Lamb, Lydia I, 660
Lamb, Lydia I, 683
Lamb, Lydia I, 786
Lamb, Lydia I, 812
Lamb, Lydia I, 824
Lamb, Lydia II, 227
Lamb, Lydia II, 237
Lamb, Lydia IV, 97
Lamb, Lydia VI, 832
Lamb, Mahala I, 683
Lamb, Malinda I, 765
Lamb, Manson VI, 832
Lamb, Margaret I, 11
Lamb, Margaret I, 18
Lamb, Margaret I, 101
Lamb, Margaret I, 145
Lamb, Margaret I, 506
Lamb, Margaret I, 888
Lamb, Margaret I, 890
Lamb, Margaret Hester I, 660
Lamb, Margaret J. I, 11
Lamb, Margaret J. I, 58
Lamb, Mariah IV, 711
Lamb, Mariah IV, 732
Lamb, Marie IV, 237
Lamb, Martha I, 38
Lamb, Martha I, 57
Lamb, Martha I, 58
Lamb, Martha I, 60
Lamb, Martha I, 310
Lamb, Martha I, 380
Lamb, Martha I, 403
Lamb, Martha I, 449
Lamb, Martha I, 722
Lamb, Martha I, 723
Lamb, Martha I, 1058
Lamb, Martha V, 184
Lamb, Martha VI, 832
Lamb, Martha P. I, 58
Lamb, Mary I, 7
Lamb, Mary I, 10
Lamb, Mary I, 11
Lamb, Mary I, 37
Lamb, Mary I, 53
Lamb, Mary I, 57
Lamb, Mary I, 58
Lamb, Mary I, 64
Lamb, Mary I, 71
Lamb, Mary I, 81
Lamb, Mary I, 144
Lamb, Mary I, 145
Lamb, Mary I, 160
Lamb, Mary I, 184
Lamb, Mary I, 387
Lamb, Mary I, 403
Lamb, Mary I, 651
Lamb, Mary I, 660
Lamb, Mary I, 679
Lamb, Mary I, 682
Lamb, Mary I, 683
Lamb, Mary I, 687
Lamb, Mary I, 730
Lamb, Mary I, 749
Lamb, Mary I, 810
Lamb, Mary I, 824
Lamb, Mary I, 1021
Lamb, Mary I, 1062
Lamb, Mary II, 294
Lamb, Mary IV, 957
Lamb, Mary V, 625
Lamb, Mary V, 631
Lamb, Mary V, 848
Lamb, Mary A. I, 11
Lamb, Mary A. I, 58
Lamb, Mary A. I, 89
Lamb, Mary A. III, 197
Lamb, Mary Ann I, 32
Lamb, Mary Ann I, 683
Lamb, Mary Ann IV, 97
Lamb, Mary Ann IV, 128
Lamb, Mary Ann IV, 152
Lamb, Mary E. I, 403
Lamb, Mary E. I, 683
Lamb, Mary Elizabeth I, 683
Lamb, Mary Emily I, 403
Lamb, Mary J. I, 54
Lamb, Mary J. I, 58
Lamb, Mary Jane I, 11
Lamb, Mary Pearson I, 723
Lamb, Mary Pike I, 660
Lamb, Mary Ruth I, 11
Lamb, Massy I, 683
Lamb, Matilda IV, 1371
Lamb, Matilda IV, 1379
Lamb, Meriam I, 11
Lamb, Meriam I, 57
Lamb, Meriam I, 62
Lamb, Merieb I, 449
Lamb, Micajah I, 660
Lamb, Michael IV, 97
Lamb, Michel IV, 97
Lamb, Miles I, 57
Lamb, Miles I, 683
Lamb, Milicent I, 7
Lamb, Milicent I, 11
Lamb, Milicent I, 57
Lamb, Milicent I, 87
Lamb, Milisent I, 57
Lamb, Milisent Elisabeth I, 58
Lamb, Miriam I, 9
Lamb, Miriam I, 10
Lamb, Miriam I, 43
Lamb, Miriam I, 46
Lamb, Miriam I, 51
Lamb, Miriam I, 57
Lamb, Miriam I, 58
Lamb, Miriam I, 67
Lamb, Miriam I, 101
Lamb, Miriam I, 403
Lamb, Miriam I, 556
Lamb, Miriam I, 567
Lamb, Miriam I, 660
Lamb, Mordacai I, 765
Lamb, Mordecai I, 611
Lamb, Mordecai I, 676
Lamb, Mordecai I, 683
Lamb, Mordecai I, 749
Lamb, Mordecai I, 764
Lamb, Mordecai I, 765
Lamb, Mordicai I, 403
Lamb, Mordicai I, 416
Lamb, Mourning I, 683
Lamb, Myrtle A. I, 11
Lamb, Nancy I, 764
Lamb, Nancy V, 751
Lamb, Nancy VI, 823
Lamb, Nancy VI, 832
Lamb, Nancy VI, 842
Lamb, Nancy I. I, 683
Lamb, Nancy W. VI, 832
Lamb, Naomi I, 403
Lamb, Naomi I, 723
Lamb, Naomi I, 749
Lamb, Naomi I, 765
Lamb, Naomi I, 786
Lamb, Naomi I, 824
Lamb, Naomi I, 1123
Lamb, Naomi V, 91
Lamb, Naomi V, 751
Lamb, Naomy I, 723
Lamb, Nathan I, 651
Lamb, Nathan I, 660
Lamb, Nathan I, 683
Lamb, Nehemiah II, 237
Lamb, Nora I, 18
Lamb, Nora V. I, 11
Lamb, Obed I, 683
Lamb, Octavia I, 10
Lamb, Octavo I, 58
Lamb, Patrick VI, 832
Lamb, Penn I, 660
Lamb, Penninah I, 11
Lamb, Penninah I, 58
Lamb, Penninah I, 82
Lamb, Phebe I, 683
Lamb, Phebe I, 684
Lamb, Phebe I, 1062
Lamb, Phebe G. IV, 128
Lamb, Phebe G. IV, 152
Lamb, Phineas I, 8
Lamb, Phineas I, 10
Lamb, Phineas I, 11
Lamb, Phineas I, 57
Lamb, Phinehas I, 57
Lamb, Phinehas I, 58
Lamb, Polly I, 57
Lamb, Polly T. VI, 842
Lamb, Rachel I, 52
Lamb, Rachel I, 57
Lamb, Rachel I, 403
Lamb, Rachel I, 506
Lamb, Rachel I, 556
Lamb, Rachel I, 576
Lamb, Rachel I, 660
Lamb, Rachel I, 682
Lamb, Rachel I, 683
Lamb, Rachel I, 723
Lamb, Rachel I, 727
Lamb, Rachel I, 749
Lamb, Rachel I, 764
Lamb, Rachel I, 765
Lamb, Rachel I, 768
Lamb, Rachel I, 786
Lamb, Rachel I, 802
Lamb, Rachel I, 824
Lamb, Ralph W. I, 11
Lamb, Raymond Carlton I, 11
Lamb, Rebecah I, 723
Lamb, Rebecca I, 58
Lamb, Rebecca I, 674
Lamb, Rebecca I, 683
Lamb, Rebecca I, 749
Lamb, Rebecca I, 765
Lamb, Rebecca I, 991
Lamb, Rebecca IV, 97
Lamb, Rebecca IV, 128
Lamb, Rebecca IV, 152
Lamb, Rebecca V, 631
Lamb, Rebecca J. I, 723
Lamb, Rebecca J. I, 765
Lamb, Rebecca Jane I, 683
Lamb, Rebecca Merritt II, 294
Lamb, Rebecca Merritt II, 305
Lamb, Rebeccah I, 660
Lamb, Rebekah I, 991
Lamb, Rebekah I, 996
Lamb, Rengamon I, 196
Lamb, Restore I, 7
Lamb, Restore I, 11
Lamb, Restore I, 57
Lamb, Restore I, 87
Lamb, Restore II, 294
Lamb, Reuben I, 10
Lamb, Reuben I, 57
Lamb, Reuben I, 58
Lamb, Reuben I, 60
Lamb, Reuben I, 556
Lamb, Reuben I, 723
Lamb, Reuben I, 1123
Lamb, Reuben V, 91
Lamb, Reuben V, 848
Lamb, Richard I, 660
Lamb, Robert I, 403
Lamb, Robert I, 506
Lamb, Robert I, 556
Lamb, Robert I, 576
Lamb, Robert I, 645
Lamb, Robert I, 660
Lamb, Robert I, 682

Lamb, Robert I, 683
Lamb, Robert I, 786
Lamb, Robert I, 824
Lamb, Robert I, 1021
Lamb, Robert I, 1033
Lamb, Robert VI, 832
Lamb, Robert B. I, 11
Lamb, Ruth I, 101
Lamb, Ruth I, 765
Lamb, Ruth I, 1123
Lamb, Ruth V, 91
Lamb, Ruth V, 751
Lamb, Salem I, 765
Lamb, Samuel I, 506
Lamb, Samuel I, 674
Lamb, Samuel I, 682
Lamb, Samuel I, 786
Lamb, Samuel I, 824
Lamb, Sarah I, 10
Lamb, Sarah I, 11
Lamb, Sarah I, 35
Lamb, Sarah I, 41
Lamb, Sarah I, 57
Lamb, Sarah I, 58
Lamb, Sarah I, 60
Lamb, Sarah I, 69
Lamb, Sarah I, 74
Lamb, Sarah I, 101
Lamb, Sarah I, 145
Lamb, Sarah I, 189
Lamb, Sarah I, 196
Lamb, Sarah I, 198
Lamb, Sarah I, 403
Lamb, Sarah I, 449
Lamb, Sarah I, 556
Lamb, Sarah I, 575
Lamb, Sarah I, 660
Lamb, Sarah I, 682
Lamb, Sarah I, 683
Lamb, Sarah I, 991
Lamb, Sarah I, 1021
Lamb, Sarah I, 1053
Lamb, Sarah I, 1058
Lamb, Sarah I, 1062
Lamb, Sarah II, 227
Lamb, Sarah II, 237
Lamb, Sarah IV, 97
Lamb, Sarah IV, 105
Lamb, Sarah IV, 128
Lamb, Sarah IV, 132
Lamb, Sarah V, 185
Lamb, Sarah V, 631
Lamb, Sarah V, 1006
Lamb, Sarah A. I, 11
Lamb, Sarah A. E. I, 5
Lamb, Sarah A. E. I, 7
Lamb, Sarah A. E. I, 11
Lamb, Sarah J. I, 683
Lamb, Sarah R. I, 11
Lamb, Sarah R. I, 58
Lamb, Silas Benjamin I, 11
Lamb, Silas Benjamin I, 58
Lamb, Simeon I, 660
Lamb, Simeon I, 682
Lamb, Simeon I, 687
Lamb, Sophia VI, 525
Lamb, Sophia VI, 825
Lamb, Sophia VI, 832
Lamb, Stanton I, 57
Lamb, Stephen I, 11
Lamb, Stephen I, 43
Lamb, Stephen I, 57
Lamb, Stephen I, 58
Lamb, Susan Alice I, 11
Lamb, Susan Alice I, 58
Lamb, Susanna I, 660
Lamb, Susanna I, 683
Lamb, Susanna IV, 97
Lamb, Susannah I, 403
Lamb, Susannah IV, 97
Lamb, Susannah IV, 128
Lamb, Thomas I, 11
Lamb, Thomas I, 57
Lamb, Thomas I, 58
Lamb, Thomas I, 60
Lamb, Thomas I, 403
Lamb, Thomas I, 556
Lamb, Thomas I, 660
Lamb, Thomas I, 683
Lamb, Thomas I, 1021
Lamb, Thomas I, 1033
Lamb, Thomas I, 1058
Lamb, Thomas V, 91
Lamb, Thomas V, 185
Lamb, Thomas V, 848
Lamb, Thomas VI, 257
Lamb, Thomas VI, 525
Lamb, Thomas C. I, 683
Lamb, Thomas C. I, 749
Lamb, Thomas C. I, 765
Lamb, Thomas E. I, 11
Lamb, Thomas E. I, 18
Lamb, Thomas E. I, 58
Lamb, Thomas G. IV, 97
Lamb, Thomas G. IV, 128
Lamb, Thomas O. I, 11
Lamb, Thomas O. I, 58
Lamb, Thomas Oscar I, 58
Lamb, Thomas Troy I, 11
Lamb, Thomas W. I, 11
Lamb, Thomas, Jr. I, 1033
Lamb, Thomas, Jr. VI, 525
Lamb, Thyele I, 11
Lamb, Thyele I, 58
Lamb, Timothy I, 58
Lamb, Townsend I, 5
Lamb, Townsend I, 7
Lamb, Townsend I, 11
Lamb, Townsend I, 58
Lamb, Townsend E. I, 11
Lamb, Uriah F. I, 403
Lamb, Uriah F. I, 683
Lamb, Vashti I, 11
Lamb, Vashti I, 58
Lamb, Velna R. I, 681
Lamb, Velna R. I, 683
Lamb, W. Haywood I, 11
Lamb, Wayne I, 57
Lamb, Widow Hannah I, 58
Lamb, Widow Hannah I, 69
Lamb, Widow Leah I, 57
Lamb, Widow Leah I, 63
Lamb, Widow Sarah I, 52
Lamb, Widow Sarah I, 57
Lamb, William I, 11
Lamb, William I, 57
Lamb, William I, 62
Lamb, William I, 764
Lamb, William I, 1021
Lamb, William I, 1033
Lamb, William VI, 832
Lamb, William A. I, 403
Lamb, William A. I, 660
Lamb, William A. I, 683
Lamb, William A. VI, 832
Lamb, William C. I, 683
Lamb, William H. I, 11
Lamb, William H. I, 42
Lamb, William H. I, 58
Lamb, William P. I, 765
Lamb, William Penn I, 683
Lamb, William Penn I, 749
Lamb, Willis I, 11
Lamb, Willis I, 57
Lamb, Willis I, 58
Lamb, Willis I, 64
Lamb, Willis I, 82
Lamb, Willis V, 631
Lamb, Willis H. I, 11
Lamb, Willis H. I, 58
Lamb, Willis Henry I, 11
Lamb, Wm. I, 32
Lamb, Wm. H. I, 11
Lamb, Wm. H. III, 197
Lamb, Yancy I, 683
Lamb, Zachariah I, 51
Lamb, Zachariah I, 57
Lamb, Zecheriah I, 11
Lambe, Esther I, 621
Lambe, Laura I, 614
Lambern, Clayton IV, 732
Lambern, Isaac IV, 732
Lambern, Isaac VI, 412
Lambert, Abigail I, 507
Lambert, Abigail I, 556
Lambert, Abigail I, 583
Lambert, Abigail I, 600
Lambert, Abigail L. I, 522
Lambert, Abigail, II I, 507
Lambert, Abner IV, 44
Lambert, Abner IV, 97
Lambert, Abner IV, 137
Lambert, Abner IV, 143
Lambert, Abner IV, 145
Lambert, Abner IV, 152
Lambert, Abner, Jr. IV, 152
Lambert, Abnere I, 272
Lambert, Albert IV, 44
Lambert, Albert IV, 97
Lambert, Albert IV, 152
Lambert, Albert IV, 585
Lambert, Albert IV, 1055
Lambert, Albert IV, 1065
Lambert, Albert IV, 1104
Lambert, Albert IV, 1134
Lambert, Albert IV, 1139
Lambert, Ann I, 507
Lambert, Ann I, 543
Lambert, Ann I, 556
Lambert, Ann II, 237
Lambert, Ann II, 264
Lambert, Ann II, 387
Lambert, Ann II, 575
Lambert, Ann IV, 1088
Lambert, Ann IV, 1104
Lambert, Anna IV, 44
Lambert, Anna IV, 97
Lambert, Ansel IV, 1371
Lambert, Asenath IV, 1095
Lambert, Asenath IV, 1104
Lambert, Benjamin IV, 44
Lambert, Benjamin IV, 97
Lambert, Benjamin IV, 152
Lambert, Catharine V, 632
Lambert, Catharine B. VI, 970
Lambert, Daniel IV, 44
Lambert, Daniel IV, 97
Lambert, Daniel IV, 237
Lambert, Deborah IV, 1056
Lambert, Deborah IV, 1065
Lambert, Dinah VI, 890
Lambert, Edward Newman I, 556
Lambert, Edward W. III, 197
Lambert, Eli B. I, 482
Lambert, Elizabeth II, 178
Lambert, Elizabeth II, 979
Lambert, Elizabeth II, 1009
Lambert, Elizabeth III, 197
Lambert, Elizabeth III, 353
Lambert, Elizabeth IV, 44
Lambert, Elizabeth IV, 97
Lambert, Elizabeth IV, 152
Lambert, Elizabeth IV, 416
Lambert, Elizabeth IV, 442
Lambert, Elizabeth IV, 585
Lambert, Elizabeth IV, 1055
Lambert, Elizabeth IV, 1065
Lambert, Elizabeth IV, 1103
Lambert, Elizabeth IV, 1104
Lambert, Elizabeth IV, 1134
Lambert, Elizabeth IV, 1139
Lambert, Elizabeth H. IV, 1104
Lambert, Emeline III, 197
Lambert, Geo. VI, 966
Lambert, George VI, 890
Lambert, George VI, 947
Lambert, George VI, 964
Lambert, George VI, 970
Lambert, George VI, 1007
Lambert, Hannah II, 237
Lambert, Hannah II, 257
Lambert, Hannah II, 387
Lambert, James D. IV, 1134
Lambert, John I, 404
Lambert, John II, 387
Lambert, John II, 445
Lambert, John II, 575
Lambert, John II, 989
Lambert, John II, 1009
Lambert, John IV, 585
Lambert, John IV, 1104
Lambert, John IV, 1134
Lambert, John IV, 1371
Lambert, John V, 788
Lambert, John Biles II, 1009
Lambert, John C. I, 991
Lambert, John C. I, 995
Lambert, John Scott II, 237
Lambert, Joseph IV, 44
Lambert, Joseph IV, 97
Lambert, Judith I, 482
Lambert, Lemira J. VI, 995
Lambert, Luce II, 445
Lambert, Lucetta S. VI, 1007
Lambert, Lucie II, 445
Lambert, Margaret I, 556
Lambert, Margaret II, 237
Lambert, Margaret II, 257
Lambert, Margery I, 506
Lambert, Margery I, 507
Lambert, Margery I, 522
Lambert, Margery I, 556
Lambert, Margrett II, 445
Lambert, Martha IV, 1092
Lambert, Martha IV, 1104
Lambert, Martha IV, 1134
Lambert, Martha W. III, 197
Lambert, Mary I, 391
Lambert, Mary I, 404
Lambert, Mary I, 507
Lambert, Mary II, 178
Lambert, Mary II, 222
Lambert, Mary II, 237
Lambert, Mary II, 979
Lambert, Mary II, 1009
Lambert, Mary IV, 44
Lambert, Mary IV, 97
Lambert, Mary IV, 143
Lambert, Mary IV, 152
Lambert, Mary IV, 1134
Lambert, Mary IV, 1138
Lambert, Mary IV, 1371
Lambert, Mary D. IV, 1104
Lambert, Mary E. I, 479
Lambert, Mary E. I, 482
Lambert, Mary M. VI, 1007
Lambert, Mrs. Susan W. VI, 893
Lambert, Olive I, 891
Lambert, Phebe IV, 1134
Lambert, Rachel IV, 585
Lambert, Rachel IV, 1104
Lambert, Rachel E. IV, 1134
Lambert, Rachel E. IV, 1139
Lambert, Rebeckah II, 989
Lambert, Sally Ann VI, 964
Lambert, Samuel II, 178
Lambert, Samuel II, 387
Lambert, Samuel W. III, 197
Lambert, Samuel W. III, 353
Lambert, Sarah II, 575
Lambert, Sarah II, 635
Lambert, Sarah II, 1044
Lambert, Sarah II, 1054
Lambert, Sarah IV, 585
Lambert, Sarah IV, 589
Lambert, Sarah IV, 1065
Lambert, Sarah IV, 1134
Lambert, Sarah IV, 1139
Lambert, Sarah IV, 1284
Lambert, Sarah IV, 1371
Lambert, Sarah V, 1006
Lambert, Sarah A. V, 1006
Lambert, Sarah Ann VI, 893
Lambert, Sarah C. IV, 1104
Lambert, Susanna IV, 145
Lambert, Susanna IV, 152
Lambert, Susanna IV, 237
Lambert, Susanna VI, 947
Lambert, Thomas II, 178
Lambert, Thomas II, 222
Lambert, Thomas II, 237
Lambert, Thomas II, 255
Lambert, Thomas II, 257
Lambert, Thomas II, 264
Lambert, Thomas II, 979
Lambert, Thomas II, 1009
Lambert, Thomas Biles II, 1009
Lambert, William I, 506
Lambert, William I, 507
Lambert, William I, 522
Lambert, William I, 556
Lambert, Winifred IV, 44
Lambert, Winneford IV, 97
Lambert, Winneford IV, 143
Lambert, Wm. M. VI, 983
Lambert, Zilpha IV, 1104
Lambeth, Angeline G. VI, 832
Lambeth, Caroline VI, 863
Lambeth, Dr. Wm. L. VI, 858
Lambeth, Elizabeth VI, 813
Lambeth, Elizabeth VI, 832
Lambeth, George VI, 832
Lambeth, John P. VI, 813
Lambeth, Marcia VI, 832
Lambeth, Martha B. VI, 798
Lambeth, Meredith VI, 806
Lambeth, Meredith VI, 813
Lambeth, Meredith VI, 832
Lambeth, Meredith VI, 844
Lambeth, Meredith VI, 857
Lambeth, Samuel M. VI, 832
Lambeth, Sarah L. VI, 844
Lambeth, Susan VI, 832
Lambeth, Susan H. VI, 832
Lambeth, Washington VI, 832
Lambeth, Washington VI, 961
Lambeth, William L. VI, 832
Lambhorn, Phebe IV, 754
Lambhorn, Wm. W. IV, 754
Lambis, Nancy VI, 825
Lambis, Peter VI, 825
Lamborn, Albert IV, 830
Lamborn, Alice IV, 1028
Lamborn, Amos P. IV, 1028
Lamborn, Ann IV, 732
Lamborn, Ann IV, 775
Lamborn, Ann IV, 1028
Lamborn, Ann H. IV, 732
Lamborn, Ann H. IV, 786
Lamborn, Ann J. IV, 732
Lamborn, Ann J. IV, 775
Lamborn, Ann P. IV, 1025
Lamborn, Ann P. IV, 1028
Lamborn, Anna IV, 732
Lamborn, Anna IV, 830
Lamborn, Anna IV, 974
Lamborn, Anna IV, 1028
Lamborn, Anna VI, 525
Lamborn, Anna Lee Dora IV, 1028
Lamborn, Anna R. II, 887
Lamborn, Carey Lee II, 835
Lamborn, Carey Lee II, 887
Lamborn, Clarence Larwell IV, 830
Lamborn, Clayton IV, 732
Lamborn, Clayton IV, 775
Lamborn, Clayton IV, 830
Lamborn, David IV, 1028
Lamborn, Debbie IV, 830
Lamborn, Deborah IV, 830
Lamborn, Dinah II, 71
Lamborn, Dinah II, 83
Lamborn, Dinah IV, 732
Lamborn, Dinah IV, 822
Lamborn, Dinah IV, 830
Lamborn, Dinah IV, 974
Lamborn, Dinah VI, 525
Lamborn, Dinah VI, 580
Lamborn, Edith IV, 830
Lamborn, Edward IV, 1028
Lamborn, Edward VI, 525
Lamborn, Edward H. IV, 732
Lamborn, Elizabeth IV, 44
Lamborn, Elizabeth IV, 732
Lamborn, Elizabeth IV, 792
Lamborn, Elizabeth IV, 798
Lamborn, Elizabeth IV, 830
Lamborn, Elizabeth IV, 974
Lamborn, Elizabeth IV, 982
Lamborn, Elizabeth IV, 1028
Lamborn, Elizabeth IV, 1029
Lamborn, Elizabeth VI, 525
Lamborn, Elwood IV, 1028
Lamborn, Emma IV, 676
Lamborn, Emma IV, 798
Lamborn, Emma IV, 830
Lamborn, Esther IV, 732
Lamborn, Esther IV, 974
Lamborn, Esther IV, 1006
Lamborn, Esther IV, 1028
Lamborn, Ezra II, 1088
Lamborn, Franklin IV, 1028
Lamborn, Gladys Emma IV, 1
Lamborn, Hannah IV, 686
Lamborn, Hannah IV, 732
Lamborn, Hannah IV, 775
Lamborn, Hannah IV, 830
Lamborn, Hannah IV, 974
Lamborn, Hannah IV, 1028
Lamborn, Hannah VI, 525
Lamborn, Hannah VI, 526
Lamborn, Hannah VI, 580
Lamborn, Hannah VI, 582
Lamborn, Hannah M. IV, 732
Lamborn, Henrietta II, 835
Lamborn, Henrietta II, 887
Lamborn, Hobson II, 710
Lamborn, Hobson II, 1088
Lamborn, Isaac II, 887
Lamborn, Isaac IV, 732
Lamborn, Isaac IV, 830
Lamborn, Isaac IV, 974
Lamborn, Isaac VI, 412
Lamborn, Isaac VI, 525
Lamborn, Jane B. IV, 732
Lamborn, Job IV, 732
Lamborn, Job IV, 1006
Lamborn, Job IV, 1028
Lamborn, Job IV, 1029
Lamborn, John IV, 974
Lamborn, John F. IV, 1028
Lamborn, Jonathan II, 805
Lamborn, Jonathan II, 822
Lamborn, Joseph A. IV, 1028
Lamborn, Joseph Allen IV, 10
Lamborn, Lemuel IV, 830
Lamborn, Lemuel F. IV, 830
Lamborn, Lemuel T. IV, 732
Lamborn, Lemuel T. IV, 798
Lamborn, Lemuel T. IV, 830
Lamborn, Levi L. IV, 732
Lamborn, Lydia IV, 732
Lamborn, Lydia IV, 830
Lamborn, Lydia IV, 974
Lamborn, Lydia IV, 1028
Lamborn, Lydia IV, 1029
Lamborn, Lydia B. IV, 689
Lamborn, Lydia B. IV, 732
Lamborn, Lydia P. IV, 732
Lamborn, Lydia W. IV, 1028
Lamborn, Margaret Emma IV, 820
Lamborn, Margaret Emma IV, 830
Lamborn, Marhta II, 710
Lamborn, Martha II, 805
Lamborn, Martha II, 822
Lamborn, Martha II, 1088
Lamborn, Martha IV, 830
Lamborn, Martha Emma IV, 7
Lamborn, Martha Emma IV, 8
Lamborn, Martha S. IV, 732
Lamborn, Martha S. IV, 830
Lamborn, Mary II, 83
Lamborn, Mary IV, 732

born, Mary IV, 830
born, Mary IV, 974
born, Mary IV, 1028
born, Mary VI, 525
born, Mary Emily IV, 1023
born, Mary Emily IV, 1028
born, Mary Hill II, 835
born, Mary Hill II, 887
born, Meriam VI, 525
born, Miriam IV, 686
born, Miriam IV, 732
born, Miriam IV, 804
born, Miriam IV, 830
born, Miriam IV, 974
born, Nancy IV, 830
born, Nancy C. IV, 798
born, Nancy C. IV, 830
born, Parmenas IV, 686
born, Parmenas IV, 732
born, Parmenas IV, 974
born, Parmenas IV, 1028
born, Parmenas VI, 525
born, Parmenas VI, 526
born, Parmenus IV, 830
born, Parmenus VI, 580
born, Parmenus VI, 582
born, Permanas IV, 830
born, Phebe II, 71
born, Phebe II, 83
born, Phebe IV, 732
born, Phebe IV, 1028
born, Phebe H. II, 1088
born, Phebe R. IV, 1021
born, Phebe R. IV, 1028
born, Philena IV, 732
born, Philena IV, 974
born, Philena IV, 1006
born, Rachel A. II, 887
born, Rachel Anna II, 805
born, Raymond Ellwood IV, 1028
born, Rebecca II, 710
born, Richard II, 71
born, Richard II, 83
born, Sarah II, 826
born, Sarah A. IV, 1028
born, Sarah Ann IV, 1026
born, Sarah Ann IV, 1028
born, Sarah C. IV, 727
born, Sarah C. IV, 732
born, Sarah C. IV, 974
born, Sarah C. IV, 1028
born, Susanna M. IV, 732
born, Susannah M. IV, 732
born, Thomas VI, 525
born, Thomas VI, 580
born, Thomas E. IV, 1025
born, Thomas E. IV, 1028
born, Thomas Elwood IV, 732
born, Thomas Elwood IV, 974
born, Thos. II, 71
born, Thos. II, 83
born, Thos. Ellwood IV, 732
born, Townsend II, 575
born, Townsend II, 576
born, Townsend IV, 732
born, Townsend IV, 775
born, W. C. IV, 1028
born, Wd. Priscilla II, 822
born, William IV, 732
born, William IV, 830
born, William IV, 974
born, William IV, 1028
born, William VI, 525
born, William C. IV, 732
born, William C. IV, 1028
born, William W. IV, 1021
born, William W. IV, 1028
born, Wm. IV, 732
born, Wm. IV, 830
born, Wm. C. IV, 732
born, Wm. C. IV, 974
born, Wm. W. IV, 732
born, Wm. W. IV, 830
born, Ziba II, 835
born, Ziba II, 887
borne, Ann IV, 732
bourn, Ann IV, 732
bourn, Ann IV, 772
bourn, Clayton IV, 732
bourn, Clayton IV, 830
bourn, Edward H. IV, 732
bourn, Elizabeth IV, 732
bourn, Esther IV, 732
bourn, Hannah IV, 732
bourn, Isaac VI, 412
bourn, Isaac VI, 793
bourn, Job IV, 732
bourn, Permanas IV, 830
Lambourn, Philena IV, 732
Lambourn, Susanna M. IV, 732
Lambourn, Thos. Ellwood IV, 732
Lambourn, Townsend IV, 732
Lambourn, Wm. C. IV, 732
Lambreth, Annie I, 227
Lambreth, John I, 227
Lamburn, Anna IV, 732
Lamburn, Dinah IV, 732
Lamburn, Elizabeth IV, 675
Lamburn, Elizabeth IV, 732
Lamburn, Elizabeth IV, 792
Lamburn, Hannah IV, 732
Lamburn, Hannah VI, 412
Lamburn, Isaac IV, 732
Lamburn, Isaac V, 509
Lamburn, Isaac VI, 412
Lamburn, Miriam IV, 732
Lamburn, Parmenas IV, 732
Lamburn, Parmenas VI, 412
Lamburn, Richard II, 83
Lamburn, William IV, 732
Lamd, Thomas I, 403
Lame, Ann II, 237
Lamer, Anna I, 723
Lamer, Frank S. V, 690
Lamer, Franklin S. V, 690
Lamer, Miriam V, 690
Lamer, Richmond V, 690
Lamer, Zitella V, 690
Lamhorn, Anna M. IV, 215
Lamhorn, Anna M. IV, 237
Lamm, Amajah V, 848
Lamm, Anna V, 848
Lamm, Annie V, 848
Lamm, Bethena V, 862
Lamm, Betty I, 310
Lamm, Caleb I, 723
Lamm, Caleb V, 848
Lamm, Daniel V, 848
Lamm, Eli I, 403
Lamm, Elizabeth V, 829
Lamm, Elizabeth V, 834
Lamm, Elizabeth V, 842
Lamm, Elizabeth V, 848
Lamm, Elizabeth V, 870
Lamm, Emma V, 848
Lamm, Flossie IV, 1325
Lamm, George V, 848
Lamm, Henry V, 834
Lamm, Henry V, 848
Lamm, Huldah I, 310
Lamm, Jacob V, 848
Lamm, Jacob, Jr. V, 848
Lamm, Jeanette V, 848
Lamm, Jemima I, 310
Lamm, John V, 829
Lamm, John V, 848
Lamm, John V, 870
Lamm, John R. V, 848
Lamm, John, Jr. V, 848
Lamm, Joseph V, 848
Lamm, Joseph F. V, 848
Lamm, Joseph Franklin V, 848
Lamm, Joshua I, 310
Lamm, Kesiah V, 848
Lamm, Keziah V, 829
Lamm, Keziah V, 836
Lamm, Keziah V, 848
Lamm, Leah I, 310
Lamm, Leah I, 725
Lamm, Leah McCollum I, 723
Lamm, Lovey I, 57
Lamm, Lydia V, 848
Lamm, Martha I, 304
Lamm, Martha I, 310
Lamm, Martha V, 848
Lamm, Martha V, 870
Lamm, Martha Mary I, 310
Lamm, Mary V, 848
Lamm, Milton V, 848
Lamm, Miriam I, 310
Lamm, Naomi I, 723
Lamm, Naomi I, 735
Lamm, Nathan C. V, 848
Lamm, Phineas V, 848
Lamm, Phines V, 848
Lamm, Rachel I, 723
Lamm, Rebecca V, 848
Lamm, Reuben I, 310
Lamm, Reuben V, 836
Lamm, Reuben V, 848
Lamm, Sarah I, 57
Lamm, Sarah I, 196
Lamm, Sarah V, 848
Lamm, Thomas V, 848
Lamm, William C. V, 848
Lamn, Thomas I, 403
Lamond, Carolina Augusta III, 199
Lamond, Wm. III, 199
Lamont, Louis R. VI, 736
LaMont, Louis R. VI, 790
Lamont, Wd. Elizabeth D. VI, 736
Lamoreaux, Clarinda IV, 1325
Lamphrey, Carrie Thompson IV, 237
Lamplew, Phebe II, 751
Lamprecht, Louisa IV, 1325
Lampson, Alfred V, 1006
Lamson, Martha V. B. III, 197
Lan, Yung III, 197
Lancaster, Aaron I, 269
Lancaster, Aaron I, 272
Lancaster, Aaron I, 276
Lancaster, Aaron I, 290
Lancaster, Aaron I, 310
Lancaster, Aaron III, 197
Lancaster, Aaron III, 424
Lancaster, Adaline V, 581
Lancaster, Addie V, 581
Lancaster, Alice Sears V, 632
Lancaster, Allie V, 581
Lancaster, Ann I, 206
Lancaster, Ann I, 218
Lancaster, Ann I, 245
Lancaster, Ann I, 247
Lancaster, Ann I, 290
Lancaster, Ann I, 309
Lancaster, Ann I, 310
Lancaster, Ann II, 178
Lancaster, Ann II, 313
Lancaster, Ann II, 1008
Lancaster, Ann II, 1009
Lancaster, Anna VI, 1003
Lancaster, Arcada I, 310
Lancaster, Benj. I, 620
Lancaster, Benjamin V, 848
Lancaster, Benjamin F. I, 636
Lancaster, Benjamin Franklin I, 620
Lancaster, Benjamin Lancaster V, 848
Lancaster, Catharine I, 290
Lancaster, Catharine I, 308
Lancaster, Catharine I, 310
Lancaster, David II, 387
Lancaster, David V, 581
Lancaster, Deborah V, 581
Lancaster, Edgar Burkhart V, 91
Lancaster, Edward V, 581
Lancaster, Eleanor II, 1007
Lancaster, Eleanor II, 1009
Lancaster, Elizabeth I, 217
Lancaster, Elizabeth I, 218
Lancaster, Elizabeth I, 290
Lancaster, Elizabeth I, 300
Lancaster, Elizabeth I, 310
Lancaster, Elizabeth I, 318
Lancaster, Elizabeth II, 313
Lancaster, Elizabeth III, 197
Lancaster, Elizabeth VI, 832
Lancaster, Elizabeth VI, 972
Lancaster, Elizabeth Ann I, 272
Lancaster, Elizabeth Ann I, 290
Lancaster, Elizabeth Ann I, 310
Lancaster, Elizabeth Mary I, 330
Lancaster, Hannah II, 178
Lancaster, Hannah II, 237
Lancaster, Hannah II, 274
Lancaster, Hannah V, 185
Lancaster, Hannah V, 214
Lancaster, Hannah V, 581
Lancaster, Harriet II, 237
Lancaster, Harriet A. II, 237
Lancaster, Henry Davis I, 272
Lancaster, Huldah I, 272
Lancaster, Huldah I, 310
Lancaster, Isaac II, 387
Lancaster, Isaac II, 576
Lancaster, Israel II, 178
Lancaster, Israel II, 237
Lancaster, Jacob II, 237
Lancaster, Jacob II, 274
Lancaster, Jacob II, 974
Lancaster, Jacob II, 976
Lancaster, Jacob II, 1009
Lancaster, Jacob II, 1043
Lancaster, James V, 581
Lancaster, James VI, 832
Lancaster, Jane II, 387
Lancaster, Jane II, 1009
Lancaster, Jane II, 1041
Lancaster, Jesse V, 581
Lancaster, John II, 237
Lancaster, John II, 274
Lancaster, John II, 313
Lancaster, John II, 387
Lancaster, John II, 471
Lancaster, John II, 576
Lancaster, John II, 1007
Lancaster, John II, 1009
Lancaster, John II, 1043
Lancaster, John V, 581
Lancaster, John VI, 947
Lancaster, John VI, 956
Lancaster, John C. V, 632
Lancaster, Jonathan II, 387
Lancaster, Joseph II, 387
Lancaster, Joseph II, 576
Lancaster, Joseph III, 197
Lancaster, Josiah VI, 921
Lancaster, Judith I, 310
Lancaster, Levi I, 217
Lancaster, Levi I, 300
Lancaster, Levi I, 310
Lancaster, Levi I, 330
Lancaster, Levy I, 290
Lancaster, Lewis VI, 947
Lancaster, Lewis VI, 988
Lancaster, Louisa I, 217
Lancaster, Louisa I, 290
Lancaster, Louisa VI, 703
Lancaster, Lourie I, 302
Lancaster, Lourie I, 310
Lancaster, Lydia II, 576
Lancaster, Maggie Marie V, 581
Lancaster, Margaret I, 326
Lancaster, Mariam I, 272
Lancaster, Mariam I, 276
Lancaster, Marie Shank V, 581
Lancaster, Martha I, 595
Lancaster, Martha II, 1007
Lancaster, Martha II, 1009
Lancaster, Martha II, 1041
Lancaster, Martha VI, 947
Lancaster, Mary I, 101
Lancaster, Mary I, 145
Lancaster, Mary I, 272
Lancaster, Mary I, 290
Lancaster, Mary I, 310
Lancaster, Mary I, 315
Lancaster, Mary VI, 582
Lancaster, Mary Cordelia I, 326
Lancaster, Mary J. V, 690
Lancaster, Miriam I, 272
Lancaster, Miriam I, 290
Lancaster, Miriam I, 310
Lancaster, Morris II, 237
Lancaster, Moses II, 576
Lancaster, Nancy VI, 947
Lancaster, Nancy VI, 956
Lancaster, Parris I, 326
Lancaster, Pharaba I, 308
Lancaster, Pharabe I, 310
Lancaster, Phebe III, 197
Lancaster, Phebe V, 91
Lancaster, Phebe V, 581
Lancaster, Phoebe V, 581
Lancaster, Polly VI, 1012
Lancaster, Rachel I, 272
Lancaster, Rachel I, 290
Lancaster, Rachel I, 299
Lancaster, Rachel I, 310
Lancaster, Rachel V, 91
Lancaster, Rachel V, 509
Lancaster, Rachel V, 581
Lancaster, Rachel V, 751
Lancaster, Rebecca I, 600
Lancaster, Rebecca I, 620
Lancaster, Rebecca II, 237
Lancaster, Rebecca II, 274
Lancaster, Rebecca II, 976
Lancaster, Rebecca II, 1009
Lancaster, Rebeckah I, 556
Lancaster, Robert VI, 917
Lancaster, Robert VI, 918
Lancaster, Robert VI, 947
Lancaster, Robert VI, 972
Lancaster, Robert VI, 1003
Lancaster, Robert VI, 1012
Lancaster, Sallie V, 632
Lancaster, Samuel I, 217
Lancaster, Samuel I, 290
Lancaster, Samuel Carney I, 326
Lancaster, Samuel N. II, 178
Lancaster, Samuel N. II, 237
Lancaster, Sarah I, 217
Lancaster, Sarah I, 290
Lancaster, Sarah I, 302
Lancaster, Sarah I, 310
Lancaster, Sarah II, 387
Lancaster, Sarah II, 471
Lancaster, Sarah II, 576
Lancaster, Sarah II, 974
Lancaster, Sarah II, 1009
Lancaster, Sarah V, 848
Lancaster, Susan VI, 947
Lancaster, Thomas I, 290
Lancaster, Thomas II, 387
Lancaster, Thomas II, 576
Lancaster, Thomas II, 1009
Lancaster, Thomas II, 1041
Lancaster, Thomas VI, 947
Lancaster, Thomas, Jr. II, 1008
Lancaster, Thomas, Jr. II, 1009
Lancaster, Thos. VI, 838
Lancaster, William I, 217
Lancaster, William I, 245
Lancaster, William I, 247
Lancaster, William I, 272
Lancaster, William I, 290
Lancaster, William I, 310
Lancaster, William II, 237
Lancaster, William VI, 947
Lancaster, William O. I, 310
Lancaster, William Olan I, 310
Lancaster, William Owen I, 272
Lancaster, William Owen I, 310
Lancaster, William Owin I, 290
Lancaster, William S. I, 290
Lancaster, William Sanders I, 217
Lancaster, Wright I, 290
Lancaster, Wryght I, 217
Lancaster, Zilpha I, 303
Lancaster, Zilpha I, 310
Lancaster, Zilphia I, 290
Lance, Christina VI, 947
Lance, Henry L. VI, 947
Lancelet, Martin II, 980
Lancelet, Wd. Mary II, 980
Lanchester, Rachel I, 1033
Lanckaster, Joshuah I, 1075
Lancroft, Cornelia III, 197
Lancroft, Cornelia III, 315
Lancroft, Henry S. III, 197
Lancroft, Henry S. III, 315
Lancroft, Mabel III, 197
Lancroft, Mabel L. III, 315
Land, John VI, 832
Land, Martha VI, 832
Land, Nathan S. VI, 832
Land, Sally VI, 832
Landale, Jane II, 387
Landale, John II, 387
Landcaster, Catharine I, 324
Lander, Mary II, 387
Landerman, Rose V, 917
Landers, Anny VI, 825
Landers, Christina VI, 861
Landers, Christopher VI, 861
Landers, Henry VI, 825
Landers, Henry VI, 880
Landers, Mary VI, 880
Landers, Peter VI, 947
Landers, Polly VI, 947
Landers, Sally VI, 850
Landery, Rebeckah II, 963
Landery, Robert II, 963
Landes, Christopher VI, 947
Landes, Elizabeth VI, 947
Landes, Henry VI, 974
Landes, Samuel VI, 947
Landgraff, Juliana III, 111
Landies, Louisa IV, 97
Landis, Elizabeth VI, 817
Landis, Louisa IV, 97
Landis, Louisa C. II, 284
Landis, Louisa C. II, 294
Landis, Louisa C. IV, 97
Landonia, Edmund VI, 894
Landonia, Lucy Henry VI, 894
Landres, Jas. P. I, 945
Landreth, Mary I, 628
Landrum, John VI, 832
Landrum, Susanna VI, 832
Lands, Louisa Marie VI, 417
Landsdown, Joel VI, 947
Landsdown, Nancy VI, 947
Landus, Emasett IV, 1256
Landus, Geo. W. IV, 1256
Landwer, Adda Rose IV, 732
Landwert, Adda Rose IV, 732
Landwert, Anna M. IV, 732
Landwert, Eliza IV, 732
Landwert, Henry IV, 732
Landwert, J. H. IV, 732
Landwert, John H. IV, 732
Landwert, Mr. Henry IV, 732
Landwert, Mrs. ??? IV, 732
Landwert, Nancy IV, 732
Landwert, Nancy J. IV, 732
Landwert, Orville IV, 732
Landwert, Orville F. IV, 732
Landwert, Thomas Lutton IV, 732
Landwerth, Henry IV, 732
Landworth, Mr. Henry IV, 732
Landworth, Mrs. ??? IV, 732
Landy, Rachel I, 989
Landy, Rachel I, 992
Lane, ??? I, 7

Lane, Aaron VI, 832
Lane, Abigail V, 873
Lane, Addison I, 11
Lane, Addison I, 59
Lane, Albert V, 849
Lane, Alberta I, 12
Lane, Alcora Susan I, 12
Lane, Alex. III, 197
Lane, Alfred L. III, 417
Lane, Alfred L. III, 424
Lane, Alfred William I, 12
Lane, Alfred William I, 59
Lane, Alice I, 44
Lane, Alice I, 59
Lane, Allen Henry I, 12
Lane, Allie V, 849
Lane, Amy W. III, 417
Lane, Amy W. III, 424
Lane, Ann I, 404
Lane, Ann I, 557
Lane, Ann I Sup 1, 9
Lane, Ann II, 887
Lane, Ann II, 928
Lane, Ann V, 847
Lane, Ann V, 848
Lane, Ann V, 849
Lane, Ann VI, 257
Lane, Ann T. V, 917
Lane, Anna V, 849
Lane, Anna J. I, 59
Lane, Anna May I, 12
Lane, Anne VI, 164
Lane, Anne VI, 196
Lane, Annie J. I, 11
Lane, Annuel V, 848
Lane, Annuel V, 849
Lane, Archer R. VI, 832
Lane, Armistead VI, 832
Lane, Aron VI, 832
Lane, Asenath Elizabeth I, 12
Lane, Baker V, 848
Lane, Baker V, 849
Lane, Barbary V, 844
Lane, Barbary V, 849
Lane, Barnard II, 178
Lane, Barnard II, 210
Lane, Barnard II, 237
Lane, Barnet II, 237
Lane, Bartholomew II, 445
Lane, Benjamin VI, 832
Lane, Benjamin VI, 852
Lane, Charles V, 848
Lane, Charles R. I, 12
Lane, Charles R. I, 42
Lane, Charles Robert I, 12
Lane, Charles Walton I, 12
Lane, Chas. III, 197
Lane, Christopher C. I, 1157
Lane, Claude Lee IV, 1325
Lane, Clinton V, 849
Lane, Clinton F. V, 849
Lane, Columbus I, 12
Lane, Columbus I, 21
Lane, Columbus I, 24
Lane, Columbus I, 58
Lane, Cyrus I, 1157
Lane, Daniel I, 556
Lane, Daniel I, 557
Lane, Daniel VI, 257
Lane, David I, 11
Lane, David V, 847
Lane, David VI, 832
Lane, David VI, 837
Lane, David VI, 908
Lane, David H. III, 197
Lane, Deborah III, 197
Lane, Deborah IV, 1065
Lane, Dempsey Sidney I, 12
Lane, Doris Mayhew I, 12
Lane, Ebenezer III, 197
Lane, Edward VI, 947
Lane, Elenor II, 178
Lane, Eli P. I, 404
Lane, Elias VI, 832
Lane, Elisabeth E. I, 24
Lane, Elisabeth P. I, 12
Lane, Eliza VI, 947
Lane, Elizabeth I, 1157
Lane, Elizabeth V, 848
Lane, Elizabeth V, 849
Lane, Elizabeth V, 853
Lane, Elizabeth V, 857
Lane, Elizabeth VI, 837
Lane, Ellen H. I, 58
Lane, Ellsberry I, 58
Lane, Ellsberry E. I, 58
Lane, Elmer V, 690
Lane, Elmer E. V, 690
Lane, Eloise W. III, 424
Lane, Eloise Wentworth III, 417
Lane, Elsan I, 12
Lane, Elsberry I, 12
Lane, Elsberry I, 26
Lane, Elsberry A. I, 12
Lane, Elsberry E. I, 12
Lane, Elsberry E. I, 59
Lane, Elson I, 59
Lane, Elson A. I, 58
Lane, Elvira R. V, 849
Lane, Emily I, 12
Lane, Emily I, 44
Lane, Emily I, 59
Lane, Emily S. I, 12
Lane, Emily S. I, 44
Lane, Emily S. I, 59
Lane, Emily Squires I, 58
Lane, Enos R. V, 849
Lane, Enos. B. V, 849
Lane, Estella Elizabeth V, 849
Lane, Esther III, 99
Lane, Esther III, 197
Lane, Esther V, 849
Lane, Esther Rebecca I, 12
Lane, Etty I, 1157
Lane, Evanda I, 1157
Lane, Exum I, 31
Lane, Farriss VI, 947
Lane, Francis B. V, 849
Lane, Francis Mariam V, 849
Lane, George H. V, 849
Lane, Gilbert III, 197
Lane, Hannah I, 819
Lane, Hannah I, 824
Lane, Hannah IV, 44
Lane, Hannah IV, 86
Lane, Hannah IV, 97
Lane, Hannah V, 91
Lane, Hannah V, 825
Lane, Hannah V, 834
Lane, Hannah V, 848
Lane, Hannah V, 849
Lane, Hannah V, 864
Lane, Hannah V, 873
Lane, Hannah D. V, 632
Lane, Harmon I, 12
Lane, Hempsted Harbor III, 197
Lane, Henby I, 89
Lane, Henry I, 58
Lane, Henry I, 1157
Lane, Henry V, 846
Lane, Henry V, 849
Lane, Henry VI, 988
Lane, Henry A. VI, 908
Lane, Henry D. V, 344
Lane, Henry D. V, 632
Lane, Henry J. V, 849
Lane, Henry, Jr. VI, 947
Lane, Henry, Jr. VI, 1007
Lane, Henry, Sr. VI, 947
Lane, Herman I, 6
Lane, Hiram V, 848
Lane, Hiram V, 849
Lane, Ira V, 834
Lane, Ira V, 848
Lane, Ira V, 849
Lane, Isaac V, 849
Lane, Isabella Anna I, 12
Lane, Israel A. I, 12
Lane, Israel A. I, 41
Lane, Israel A. I, 44
Lane, Israel A. I, 59
Lane, Israel Aaron I, 58
Lane, Jabez H. V, 847
Lane, Jacob I, 58
Lane, Jacob VI, 799
Lane, Jacob VI, 832
Lane, James I, 12
Lane, James V, 632
Lane, James V, 848
Lane, James V, 849
Lane, James C. I, 59
Lane, James E. I, 59
Lane, James Ellsberry I, 58
Lane, James Elsberry I, 12
Lane, James LaFayette I, 12
Lane, Jane I, 10
Lane, Jemima I, 37
Lane, Jemima I, 58
Lane, Jenet II, 178
Lane, Jennitt II, 210
Lane, Jennitt II, 237
Lane, Jesse I, 12
Lane, Jesse I, 556
Lane, Jesse I, 557
Lane, Jesse I Sup 1, 9
Lane, Jesse V, 825
Lane, Jesse V, 847
Lane, Jesse V, 848
Lane, Jesse V, 849
Lane, Jesse V, 864
Lane, Jesse V, 873
Lane, Jesse VI, 832
Lane, Jesse E. I, 44
Lane, Jesse E. I, 59
Lane, Jesse E. I, 235
Lane, Jesse E. I, 245
Lane, Jesse Elsberry I, 12
Lane, Jesse, Jr. V, 849
Lane, Jno. VI, 843
Lane, John I, 12
Lane, John I, 58
Lane, John I, 330
Lane, John V, 846
Lane, John V, 849
Lane, John VI, 832
Lane, John VI, 947
Lane, John VI, 1000
Lane, John A. I, 32
Lane, John Alf. I, 18
Lane, John D. I, 11
Lane, John D. I, 59
Lane, John L. I, 12
Lane, John L. I, 33
Lane, John Timothy I, 12
Lane, Jonathan V, 849
Lane, Joseph S. V, 344
Lane, Joseph S. V, 632
Lane, Julia M. I, 12
Lane, Julianna I, 12
Lane, Julianna I, 42
Lane, Julianna E. I, 12
Lane, Julius V, 848
Lane, Julius V, 849
Lane, Julius V, 857
Lane, Lela IV, 875
Lane, Leonidas Lee I, 12
Lane, Levi V, 848
Lane, Levi V, 849
Lane, Lidia V, 849
Lane, Lillie V, 185
Lane, Lillie Mae I, 18
Lane, Littleberry VI, 832
Lane, Louella V, 632
Lane, Louis R. IV, 1169
Lane, Louisa VI, 852
Lane, Lucind I, 59
Lane, Lucinda I, 12
Lane, Lucinda I, 59
Lane, Lucinda E. I, 59
Lane, Lucinda E. I, 89
Lane, Lucius I, 31
Lane, Lucy May I, 12
Lane, Luella V, 632
Lane, Lydia I, 6
Lane, Lydia I, 12
Lane, Lydia V, 843
Lane, Lydia V, 848
Lane, Lydia V, 849
Lane, M. J. V, 846
Lane, Majory VI, 257
Lane, Maltby G. III, 197
Lane, Margaret Ann I, 12
Lane, Margaret Ann I, 58
Lane, Margaret J. I, 12
Lane, Margaret Jane I, 58
Lane, Marjory I, 556
Lane, Martha I, 18
Lane, Martha I, 26
Lane, Martha V, 847
Lane, Martha V, 849
Lane, Martha VI, 852
Lane, Martha VI, 947
Lane, Martha A. I, 58
Lane, Martha E. I, 12
Lane, Martha G. III, 96
Lane, Martha L. I, 12
Lane, Martha P. I, 12
Lane, Martha P. I, 41
Lane, Martha P. I, 59
Lane, Mary I, 3
Lane, Mary I, 12
Lane, Mary I, 21
Lane, Mary I, 24
Lane, Mary I, 145
Lane, Mary II, 178
Lane, Mary III, 197
Lane, Mary IV, 97
Lane, Mary V, 848
Lane, Mary V, 849
Lane, Mary V, 862
Lane, Mary VI, 803
Lane, Mary VI, 832
Lane, Mary VI, 988
Lane, Mary A. I, 41
Lane, Mary A. I, 58
Lane, Mary Ann I, 58
Lane, Mary Ann V, 846
Lane, Mary Ann V, 847
Lane, Mary Ann V, 849
Lane, Mary Ann Elisabeth I, 12
Lane, Mary Anna I, 12
Lane, Mary D. IV, 97
Lane, Mary D. IV, 640
Lane, Mary Dix IV, 44
Lane, Mary E. I, 12
Lane, Mary E. I, 31
Lane, Mary E. I, 42
Lane, Mary E. I, 58
Lane, Mary E. I, 59
Lane, Mary Eliza I, 58
Lane, Mary Eliza I, 77
Lane, Mary J. I, 12
Lane, Mary J. I, 21
Lane, Mary J. I, 59
Lane, Mary J. I, 84
Lane, Mary J. V, 690
Lane, Mary Jane I, 58
Lane, Mary Jane I, 330
Lane, Mary Jane V, 846
Lane, Mary Louisa V, 852
Lane, Mary Verna I, 12
Lane, Mary Vernon I, 26
Lane, Millie I, 44
Lane, Millie I, 59
Lane, Miriam C. I, 12
Lane, Miriam C. I, 59
Lane, Miriam R. I, 235
Lane, Miriam R. I, 245
Lane, Mordecai I, 556
Lane, Mordecai I, 824
Lane, Mordecai VI, 257
Lane, Mordicai VI, 257
Lane, Nancy VI, 826
Lane, Nancy VI, 832
Lane, Nancy VI, 947
Lane, Nancy A. I, 31
Lane, Nancy L. I, 59
Lane, Nancy N. I, 330
Lane, Nellie I, 12
Lane, Nellie I, 59
Lane, Oliver I, 59
Lane, Oliver C. I, 12
Lane, Oliver Edward I, 12
Lane, Opal V, 670
Lane, Opal V, 690
Lane, Orie IV, 1325
Lane, Park H. III, 197
Lane, Patsy VI, 832
Lane, Peachey VI, 843
Lane, Peter III, 197
Lane, Phebe V, 825
Lane, Phebe V, 848
Lane, Phebe V, 849
Lane, Phebe A. III, 197
Lane, Pleasant V, 852
Lane, Priscilla II, 237
Lane, Rachel V, 848
Lane, Rachel V, 849
Lane, Rachel V, 864
Lane, Rebecca II, 178
Lane, Rebecca VI, 947
Lane, Rhoda V, 848
Lane, Rhoda V, 849
Lane, Rhoda V, 873
Lane, Rollo Alva I, 12
Lane, Rosanna V, 849
Lane, Ruth Alice I, 32
Lane, Sallie I, 12
Lane, Sallie I, 59
Lane, Sallie A. I, 59
Lane, Sallie Ann I, 12
Lane, Sallie Ann I, 58
Lane, Sally I, 12
Lane, Sarah I, 3
Lane, Sarah I, 12
Lane, Sarah I, 41
Lane, Sarah I, 58
Lane, Sarah I, 80
Lane, Sarah I, 556
Lane, Sarah II, 178
Lane, Sarah II, 237
Lane, Sarah V, 120
Lane, Sarah V, 846
Lane, Sarah V, 848
Lane, Sarah V, 849
Lane, Sarah V, 850
Lane, Sarah VI, 832
Lane, Sarah VI, 1007
Lane, Sarah A. I, 33
Lane, Sarah A. I, 59
Lane, Sarah Ann I, 404
Lane, Sarah Ann V, 849
Lane, Sarah B. VI, 832
Lane, Sarah E. I, 245
Lane, Sarah E. I, 1157
Lane, Sarah Elisabeth I, 58
Lane, Sarah Elisabeth I, 89
Lane, Sarah Elizabeth I, 29
Lane, Sarah Frances I, 58
Lane, Sarah Hencock I, 557
Lane, Sarah J. I, 12
Lane, Sarah Jane I, 12
Lane, Sarah Jane III, 197
Lane, Sarah Matilda I, 12
Lane, Seny Elizabeth I, 58
Lane, Susan III, 197
Lane, Susan III, 331
Lane, Susan VI, 832
Lane, Susan A. III, 197
Lane, Susan U. III, 197
Lane, Susanna I, 797
Lane, Susanna I, 824
Lane, Susannah V, 831
Lane, Susannah V, 848
Lane, Susannah V, 849
Lane, Susannah VI, 947
Lane, Theodate M. IV, 416
Lane, Thomas I, 556
Lane, Thomas I, 1157
Lane, Thomas VI, 196
Lane, Thomas VI, 257
Lane, Thomas VI, 947
Lane, Thompson H. VI, 947
Lane, Valearia V, 847
Lane, Victoria I, 310
Lane, W. Henby I, 3
Lane, W. Henby I, 59
Lane, W. J. III, 197
Lane, Walter VI, 11
Lane, Webster III, 197
Lane, Willard Eugene V, 690
Lane, William I, 556
Lane, William V, 849
Lane, William VI, 164
Lane, William VI, 196
Lane, William VI, 257
Lane, William H. I, 12
Lane, William H. I, 59
Lane, William H. I, 89
Lane, William H. I, 245
Lane, William Henby I, 12
Lane, William Henby I, 58
Lane, William, Jr. I, 557
Lane, William, Sr. I, 557
Lane, Winslow Earle I, 12
Lane, Wm. III, 197
Lane, Wm. Henby I, 29
Lane, Wm. J. III, 197
Lane, Wm. J. III, 331
Lanehart, Cata VI, 907
Lanehart, Caty VI, 907
Lanes, Jonathan II, 576
Lanes, Jonathan II, 648
Lanes, Mary II, 576
Lanes, Mary II, 648
Lanfasty, Martha II, 576
Lanfertey, Priscilla II, 834
Lanfesty, Priscilla II, 887
Lang, Clementina VI, 847
Lang, Eliza H. III, 212
Lang, Elizabeth VI, 832
Lang, Mary III, 197
Lang, Mary III, 200
Lang, Peter VI, 832
Langdale, Alice II, 387
Langdale, Alice II, 489
Langdale, Alice II, 576
Langdale, Ann II, 387
Langdale, Elizabeth II, 458
Langdale, Elizabeth II, 576
Langdale, Jane II, 387
Langdale, Jane II, 576
Langdale, Jane II, 613
Langdale, John II, 387
Langdale, John II, 458
Langdale, John II, 576
Langdale, John, Jr. II, 387
Langdale, John, Jr. II, 576
Langdale, Josiah II, 347
Langdale, Josiah II, 489
Langdale, Josiah II, 576
Langdale, Josiah II, 603
Langdale, Lydia II, 387
Langdale, Margaret II, 347
Langdale, Margaret II, 387
Langdale, Margaret II, 576
Langdale, Margrett II, 387
Langdale, Mary II, 347
Langdale, Mary II, 489
Langdale, Mary II, 576
Langdale, Rachel II, 387
Langdale, Rachel II, 576
Langdale, Ruth II, 387
Langdale, Samuel II, 576
Langdale, Sarah II, 387
Langdale, Sarah II, 458
Langdale, Sarah II, 558
Langdale, Sarah II, 576
Langdale, Thomas II, 387
Langdale, Wd Margaret II, 6[illegible]
Langdale, Wd. Margaret II, 5[illegible]
Langdale, Wd. Margrett II, 3[illegible]
Langdale, William II, 387
Langdale, Wm. II, 576
Langdall, John II, 387

Langdall, Margrett II, 387
Langdall, William II, 387
Langden, Lucinda IV, 1169
Langden, Lucinda IV, 1180
Langdon, Abigail III, 70
Langdon, Abigail III, 197
Langdon, Chloe Ann IV, 1202
Langdon, Chloe Ann IV, 1215
Langdon, Elmore IV, 1256
Langdon, Ethel IV, 1256
Langdon, Hannah III, 424
Langdon, John III, 198
Langdon, Lucinda IV, 1202
Langdon, Lucinda IV, 1215
Langdon, Lucinda V, 1006
Langdon, Martha III, 198
Langdon, Mary Mills V, 690
Langdon, Mary P. IV, 1215
Langdon, Mercy III, 198
Langdon, Mercy III, 360
Langdon, Mercy III, 470
Langdon, Minna V, 1006
Langdon, Minnie Allen V, 1006
Langdon, Nancy V, 1006
Langdon, Paul Russell IV, 1256
Langdon, Rachel III, 198
Langdon, Samuel P. IV, 1215
Langdon, W. E. IV, 1256
Langdon, W. F. V, 1006
Langdon, W. L. V, 1006
Langdon, Washington F. V, 1006
Langdon, Wm. IV, 1202
Lange, Edith III, 122
Lange, Edward III, 198
Lange, Edward III, 263
Lange, Kate III, 198
Lange, Kate III, 263
Lange, Susan III, 198
Lange, Susan III, 263
Langfasty, Martha II, 710
Langford, Anna Elizabeth V, 849
Langford, Craig V, 849
Langford, Dora VI, 75
Langford, Fannie V, 849
Langford, Fannie V, 862
Langford, Fanny V, 849
Langford, Franklin VI, 75
Langford, Hattie V, 849
Langford, Isaac E. V, 849
Langford, Jesse S. V, 849
Langford, Martha VI, 75
Langford, Mary V, 849
Langford, Stephen VI, 75
Langford, Stephen R. V, 849
Langford, Walter J. V, 849
Langford, Wiley VI, 75
Langhorn, G. W. VI, 953
Langhorn, Grace II, 979
Langhorn, Grace II, 1009
Langhorn, Sarah II, 979
Langhorn, Sarah II, 1009
Langhorne, Amos VI, 832
Langhorne, Ardelia E. VI, 832
Langhorne, Elizabeth VI, 832
Langhorne, Frances VI, 832
Langhorne, Henry VI, 832
Langhorne, John VI, 832
Langhorne, Lewis VI, 832
Langhorne, Parmelia VI, 832
Langley, Eliza VI, 115
Langley, Elizabeth VI, 115
Langley, Elizabeth VI, 196
Langley, Elizabeth VI, 203
Langley, Elizabeth VI, 205
Langley, George III, 198
Langley, James I, 557
Langley, James II, 576
Langley, John VI, 17
Langley, John VI, 196
Langley, John Walker VI, 115
Langley, Margaret VI, 115
Langley, Robert VI, 115
Langley, Robert VI, 121
Langley, Robert VI, 196
Langley, Robert VI, 203
Langley, Robert VI, 205
Langley, Robt. VI, 291
Langley, Wm. II, 576
Langraven, Charles IV, 1284
Langraven, Nettie IV, 1284
Langsdon, Lucy VI, 961
Langstaff, Ann IV, 391
Langstaff, Ann IV, 416
Langstaff, Ann IV, 523
Langstaff, Ann IV, 538
Langstaff, Ann IV, 702
Langstaff, Ann IV, 733
Langstaff, Ann IV, 952
Langstaff, Ann IV, 974
Langstaff, Ann IV, 975
Langstaff, Ann S. V, 917
Langstaff, Benj. V, 917
Langstaff, Benjamin IV, 733
Langstaff, Benjamin IV, 847
Langstaff, Benjamin V, 410
Langstaff, Benjamin V, 917
Langstaff, Benjamin P. IV, 733
Langstaff, Benjamin P. IV, 974
Langstaff, Benjamin P. IV, 975
Langstaff, Benjamin P. IV, 989
Langstaff, Benjamin P. IV, 1104
Langstaff, Benjamin P. V, 410
Langstaff, Benjamin P. V, 917
Langstaff, Catharine IV, 733
Langstaff, Catharine IV, 974
Langstaff, Catharine IV, 975
Langstaff, Catharine IV, 989
Langstaff, Catharine IV, 1104
Langstaff, Catharine V, 410
Langstaff, Catharine V, 917
Langstaff, Catherine IV, 1104
Langstaff, Catherine V, 410
Langstaff, David R. IV, 974
Langstaff, Drucilla IV, 847
Langstaff, Drusilla II, 959
Langstaff, Drusilla II, 967
Langstaff, Drusilla IV, 672
Langstaff, Drusilla IV, 733
Langstaff, Drusilla IV, 775
Langstaff, Drusilla IV, 830
Langstaff, Drusilla IV, 847
Langstaff, Drusilla IV, 974
Langstaff, Drusilla IV, 975
Langstaff, E. Anetta IV, 733
Langstaff, Edgar IV, 974
Langstaff, Edgar IV, 975
Langstaff, Edgar IV, 1039
Langstaff, Elisabeth IV, 733
Langstaff, Elizabeth IV, 733
Langstaff, Elizabeth IV, 830
Langstaff, Elizabeth IV, 940
Langstaff, Elizabeth IV, 974
Langstaff, Elizabeth IV, 975
Langstaff, Elizabeth V, 917
Langstaff, Elizabeth Dole IV, 733
Langstaff, Elizabeth P. IV, 938
Langstaff, Elizabeth P. IV, 940
Langstaff, Elizabeth P. IV, 975
Langstaff, Ella IV, 974
Langstaff, Ellen IV, 1134
Langstaff, Ellen M. IV, 1134
Langstaff, Ellnathan IV, 1104
Langstaff, Elma IV, 1039
Langstaff, Elmor IV, 1039
Langstaff, Elmore IV, 974
Langstaff, Elmore IV, 975
Langstaff, Elmore IV, 1039
Langstaff, Elnathan IV, 416
Langstaff, Elnathan IV, 1104
Langstaff, Elnathan IV, 1134
Langstaff, Elnathan V, 917
Langstaff, Elnathen V, 917
Langstaff, Emily IV, 847
Langstaff, Emmet D. IV, 847
Langstaff, Enoch IV, 416
Langstaff, Enoch IV, 1104
Langstaff, Enoch IV, 1134
Langstaff, Enoch V, 917
Langstaff, Evan IV, 733
Langstaff, Evan IV, 974
Langstaff, Evan IV, 975
Langstaff, Evan IV, 1009
Langstaff, Evan IV, 1039
Langstaff, Even IV, 1039
Langstaff, Fannie Belle V, 917
Langstaff, Gertrude Landon V, 917
Langstaff, Hannah IV, 416
Langstaff, Hannah IV, 732
Langstaff, Hannah IV, 733
Langstaff, Hannah IV, 938
Langstaff, Hannah IV, 974
Langstaff, Hannah IV, 975
Langstaff, Hannah IV, 994
Langstaff, Hannah IV, 1065
Langstaff, Hannah IV, 1104
Langstaff, Hannah IV, 1134
Langstaff, Hannah V, 917
Langstaff, Hannah L. IV, 1134
Langstaff, Henrietta V, 917
Langstaff, Henry IV, 1134
Langstaff, Henry H. IV, 1104
Langstaff, Henry H. IV, 1134
Langstaff, Henry H. V, 917
Langstaff, Henry Hall V, 917
Langstaff, Ida V, 344
Langstaff, Ida V, 917
Langstaff, Ida M. V, 344
Langstaff, Ida M. V, 917
Langstaff, James IV, 483
Langstaff, James IV, 732
Langstaff, James IV, 733
Langstaff, James IV, 830
Langstaff, James IV, 974
Langstaff, James V, 917
Langstaff, James, Jr. IV, 483
Langstaff, James, Jr. IV, 733
Langstaff, James, Jr. IV, 974
Langstaff, Jennie Warren V, 917
Langstaff, John V, 917
Langstaff, John W. IV, 733
Langstaff, John W. IV, 974
Langstaff, Joseph IV, 538
Langstaff, Joseph IV, 733
Langstaff, Laban IV, 975
Langstaff, Laban IV, 1104
Langstaff, Laban V, 410
Langstaff, Laban V, 917
Langstaff, Laben IV, 1104
Langstaff, Lemuel IV, 847
Langstaff, Levi V, 917
Langstaff, Lewis T. IV, 974
Langstaff, Lewis T. IV, 975
Langstaff, Lewis T. IV, 1039
Langstaff, Lindley T. IV, 1134
Langstaff, Louis T. IV, 975
Langstaff, Lydia IV, 909
Langstaff, Lydia IV, 912
Langstaff, Lydia V, 917
Langstaff, Lydia E. V, 917
Langstaff, Martha IV, 847
Langstaff, Mary IV, 733
Langstaff, Mary IV, 974
Langstaff, Mary V, 917
Langstaff, Mary A. V, 917
Langstaff, Mary Ann V, 917
Langstaff, Mary Ann V, 921
Langstaff, Mary D. IV, 974
Langstaff, Mary D. IV, 975
Langstaff, Mary D. IV, 1009
Langstaff, Mary D. IV, 1039
Langstaff, Mary J. IV, 733
Langstaff, Mary Jane V, 917
Langstaff, Mary Jones IV, 416
Langstaff, Mira IV, 974
Langstaff, Mira H. IV, 975
Langstaff, Mira H. IV, 1039
Langstaff, Priscilla IV, 733
Langstaff, Rachel IV, 538
Langstaff, Rachel IV, 733
Langstaff, Rhoda IV, 416
Langstaff, Rhoda IV, 732
Langstaff, Rhoda IV, 733
Langstaff, Rhoda IV, 974
Langstaff, Rhoda IV, 975
Langstaff, Rhoda IV, 1104
Langstaff, Rhoda IV, 1134
Langstaff, Rhoda V, 917
Langstaff, Robert William IV, 733
Langstaff, Rodah IV, 1104
Langstaff, Sallie IV, 847
Langstaff, Samuel IV, 732
Langstaff, Samuel IV, 733
Langstaff, Samuel IV, 847
Langstaff, Samuel IV, 938
Langstaff, Samuel IV, 974
Langstaff, Samuel V, 917
Langstaff, Samuel Willis V, 917
Langstaff, Samuel, Jr. IV, 775
Langstaff, Samuel, Jr. IV, 952
Langstaff, Samuel, Jr. IV, 974
Langstaff, Samuel, Sr. IV, 974
Langstaff, Sarah IV, 1039
Langstaff, Sarah V, 917
Langstaff, Sarah V, 926
Langstaff, Sarah B. IV, 733
Langstaff, Sarah B. V, 917
Langstaff, Sarah E. IV, 975
Langstaff, Sarah Elma IV, 1039
Langstaff, Sarah Pennington V, 917
Langstaff, Susanna IV, 538
Langstaff, Susannah IV, 733
Langstaff, Tabitha IV, 538
Langstaff, Tabitha IV, 733
Langstaff, Tabitha IV, 775
Langstaff, Tabitha IV, 847
Langstaff, Tabitha IV, 952
Langstaff, Tabitha IV, 974
Langstaff, Taylor IV, 975
Langstaff, Taylor V, 917
Langstaff, Taylor F. IV, 672
Langstaff, Taylor F. IV, 733
Langstaff, Taylor F. IV, 847
Langstaff, Taylor F. IV, 974
Langstaff, Taylor F. V, 917
Langstaff, Taylor Frankin V, 917
Langstaff, Thomas IV, 416
Langstaff, Thomas IV, 523
Langstaff, Thomas IV, 538
Langstaff, Thomas IV, 702
Langstaff, Thomas IV, 732
Langstaff, Thomas IV, 733
Langstaff, Thomas IV, 952
Langstaff, Thomas IV, 974
Langstaff, Thomas IV, 975
Langstaff, Thomas V, 917
Langstaff, Thomas D. IV, 416
Langstaff, Thomas D. IV, 733
Langstaff, Thomas D. IV, 974
Langstaff, Thomas D. IV, 975
Langstaff, Thomas D. IV, 1065
Langstaff, Thomas D. IV, 1104
Langstaff, Thomas D. IV, 1134
Langstaff, Thomas Farmer IV, 733
Langstaff, Thos. V, 917
Langstaff, Thos. D. IV, 994
Langstaff, Thos. D. IV, 1134
Langstaff, Thos. D. V, 917
Langstaff, William IV, 416
Langstaff, William IV, 847
Langstaff, William IV, 1134
Langstaff, William V, 917
Langstaff, Willis V, 917
Langstaff, Wm. IV, 416
Langstaff, Wm. IV, 1104
Langstaff, Wm. IV, 1134
Langston, Charity V, 849
Langston, David L. I, 310
Langston, Hannah V, 849
Langston, Hannah V, 850
Langston, Hannah V, 852
Langston, Jonathan V, 849
Langston, Jonathan V, 850
Langston, Jonathan V, 852
Langston, Luke V, 846
Langston, Luke V, 849
Langston, Luke V, 850
Langston, Mary V, 846
Langston, Mary V, 849
Langston, Rebecca V, 846
Langston, Rebecca V, 849
Langston, Sarah II, 576
Langston, Sarah II, 674
Langston, Sarah, Jr. II, 576
Langston, Thomas II, 387
Langston, William W. I, 245
Langstone, Luke V, 858
Langstone, Rebecca V, 858
Langstreath, Wm. V, 788
Langstreth, Mary II, 576
Langstroth, Ella M. II, 887
Langstroth, Ella M. II, 928
Langstroth, George II, 576
Langstroth, Huson II, 387
Langstroth, Huson II, 576
Langstroth, James F. II, 887
Langstroth, James F. II, 928
Langstroth, Mary II, 507
Langstroth, Mary II, 576
Langstroth, Samuel II, 387
Langthorne, Francis IV, 1325
Langton, Kitty IV, 1325
Langtree, Emmolada IV, 1131
Langtree, Emmolada IV, 1134
Langwerthy, Sarah I, 145
Langworthy, Eliza Collings II, 782
Langworthy, Jonathan I, 101
Langworthy, Jonathan I, 145
Langworthy, Sarah I, 145
Lanham, Clarence VI, 633
Lanier, Anna G. I, 749
Lanier, Charles F. H. I, 749
Lanier, Deborah I, 760
Lanier, Deborah I, 765
Lanier, Deborah I, 928
Lanier, Deborah Ann I, 749
Lanier, Elijah I, 749
Lanier, Elijah I, 765
Lanier, Elijah I, 928
Lanier, Emma Theodosia I, 749
Lanier, Julia Eleanor I, 928
Lanier, Julia Ella I, 749
Lanier, Mary A. I, 749
Lanier, William Hanner I, 749
Lanin, Hannah II, 212
Lanin, Hannah II, 237
Laning, Ann Eliza II, 998
Laning, Ann Eliza II, 1009
Laning, Isaac II, 576
Laning, Martha IV, 44
Laning, Martha IV, 47
Laninger, Anna V, 1006
Lankford, Ann VI, 162
Lankford, Cordelia VI, 163
Lankford, Cordelia VI, 196
Lankford, Martha VI, 196
Lankford, Martha VI, 217
Lankford, Matha VI, 217
Lankford, Michal VI, 185
Lankford, Susannah VI, 989
Lankford, Thomas VI, 8
Lankford, Thomas VI, 17
Lankford, Thomas VI, 162
Lankford, Thomas VI, 185
Lankford, Thomas VI, 196
Lankford, Thomas VI, 217
Lankhant, Eliz. III, 196
Lankister, Lidia VI, 209
Lanner, Mary I, 310
Lannin, Hannah IV, 733
Lannin, Hannah IV, 771
Lanning, Hannah II, 576
Lanning, Isaac II, 576
Lanning, John II, 83
Lanning, Rachel IV, 185
Lanning, Rachel IV, 237
Lannings, Hannah II, 576
Lansbil, Hannah I, 404
Lansdale, Thomas II, 387
Lansdale, Wd. Margrett II, 387
Lansdall, Ruth II, 387
Lansdown, Johnson VI, 960
Lansdown, Polly VI, 960
Lansing, Carrie A. III, 112
Lansing, Carrie A. III, 198
Lansing, Durck C. III, 112
Lansing, Durck C. III, 198
Lansing, Elizabeth III, 424
Lansing, Elizabeth III, 433
Lansing, Gulian III, 424
Lansing, Gulian III, 433
Lansing, Isabella III, 424
Lansing, Jos. Mc C. III, 424
Lansing, Susan F. III, 112
Lansing, Susan F. III, 198
Lanston, Sarah, Jr. II, 576
Lantas, Mahalah Elizabeth V, 850
Lanthrop, Joseph IV, 1039
Lantis, David V, 850
Lantis, Eliza V, 826
Lantis, Eliza V, 850
Lantis, Eliza Jane V, 850
Lantis, Elizabeth V, 850
Lantis, Hannah V, 850
Lantis, Mahalah V, 850
Lantis, Mahalah Elizabeth V, 826
Lantis, Mahalah Elizabeth V, 850
Lantis, Samuel V, 826
Lantis, Samuel V, 850
Lantis, William V, 850
Lantz, Charles IV, 733
Lantz, Charlotte V, 259
Lantz, Chas., Jr. IV, 733
Lantz, Christina VI, 947
Lantz, Elizabeth S. VI, 934
Lantz, Emily V, 259
Lantz, Henry L. VI, 917
Lantz, Henry L. VI, 934
Lantz, Henry L. VI, 947
Lantz, Junior IV, 733
Lantz, Lillian IV, 875
Lantz, Mary V, 259
Lantz, Mary Magdeline V, 259
Lantz, Matilda R. VI, 934
Lantz, Neta Charlotte IV, 733
Lantz, Neva IV, 733
Lantz, Neva Edna IV, 733
Lanum, Bathsheba V, 460
Lanum, Mary V, 460
Lanum, Robert E. V, 460
Lapham, Abraham IV, 1372
Lapham, Adrian IV, 1372
Lapham, Alfred IV, 1372
Lapham, Amelia IV, 1284
Lapham, Amelia V, 955
Lapham, Ann W. III, 424
Lapham, Anna III, 198
Lapham, Anna III, 424
Lapham, Anna III, 467
Lapham, Anna D. III, 198
Lapham, Anna L. III, 469
Lapham, Annie III, 198
Lapham, Annie Ann III, 353
Lapham, Annie Ann III, 355
Lapham, Annie Willets III, 424
Lapham, Anson III, 198
Lapham, Anson III, 356
Lapham, Arden B. III, 424
Lapham, Asa IV, 1372
Lapham, Cynthia IV, 1372
Lapham, Daniel IV, 1372
Lapham, Darius IV, 1372
Lapham, David IV, 1372
Lapham, Deborah IV, 1372
Lapham, Deborah B. IV, 1372
Lapham, Edw. M. III, 424
Lapham, Edw. M. III, 469
Lapham, Edw. Morgan III, 424
Lapham, Edw. Morgan III, 467
Lapham, Edw. Morgan, Jr. III, 424

Lapham, Edward III, 424
Lapham, Edwin M., Jr. III, 424
Lapham, Edwin Morgan, Jr. III, 433
Lapham, Eli IV, 1372
Lapham, Elizabeth III, 198
Lapham, Elizabeth IV, 1169
Lapham, Elizabeth IV, 1215
Lapham, Elizabeth A. III, 198
Lapham, Ethan IV, 1372
Lapham, Ethan A. IV, 1372
Lapham, Ethen IV, 1372
Lapham, Ethen A. IV, 1372
Lapham, Ezra IV, 1372
Lapham, Grace W. III, 399
Lapham, Grace W. III, 424
Lapham, Hannah IV, 1372
Lapham, Hannah D. III, 198
Lapham, Henry G. III, 198
Lapham, Henry G. III, 332
Lapham, Huldah IV, 1372
Lapham, Humphrey IV, 1169
Lapham, James III, 424
Lapham, James H. IV, 1372
Lapham, James Pollock III, 424
Lapham, James R. IV, 1372
Lapham, Jesse III, 198
Lapham, John IV, 1215
Lapham, John P. IV, 1169
Lapham, Joseph IV, 1169
Lapham, Joseph IV, 1215
Lapham, Lavina IV, 1372
Lapham, Leon A., Jr. III, 399
Lapham, Logan IV, 1284
Lapham, Lorana V, 955
Lapham, Luther IV, 1372
Lapham, Mabel Rose IV, 1325
Lapham, Margaret IV, 1372
Lapham, Margaret P. IV, 1372
Lapham, Mary III, 424
Lapham, Milla IV, 1372
Lapham, Milly IV, 1372
Lapham, Mrs. Mabel IV, 1325
Lapham, Nancy V, 489
Lapham, Nancy V, 509
Lapham, Nancy V, 917
Lapham, Nancy L. V, 509
Lapham, Nancy L. V, 917
Lapham, Norton P. IV, 1372
Lapham, Peggy Ann III, 424
Lapham, Phebe III, 424
Lapham, Phebe IV, 1169
Lapham, Phebe IV, 1215
Lapham, Phebe Anna III, 198
Lapham, Phebe Greer III, 424
Lapham, Phebe M. III, 353
Lapham, Philip III, 353
Lapham, Rachel IV, 1284
Lapham, Rachel IV, 1372
Lapham, Rachel R. IV, 1372
Lapham, Robert A. IV, 1169
Lapham, Ruth Isabella III, 433
Lapham, Ruth Isabelle III, 424
Lapham, Samuel T. III, 198
Lapham, Semantha III, 198
Lapham, Semantha III, 332
Lapham, Stephen III, 198
Lapham, Stephen IV, 1169
Lapham, Stephen IV, 1215
Lapham, Stephen IV, 1372
Lapham, Susanna III, 353
Lapham, Thomas W. III, 424
Lapham, Thomas Willets III, 424
Lapham, Wd. Ann F. III, 198
Lapham, William Hannah IV, 1284
Lapham, Wm. V, 955
Laport, Sarah J. IV, 1284
Laport, Ziphaniah IV, 1284
Lappan, Sarah IV, 483
Lappan, Sarah IV, 484
Lappe, John V, 690
Lappe, Mary V, 690
Lappum, Elizabeth IV, 1215
Lappy, Mary V, 690
Lapsly, Elizabeth VI, 328
Lapsly, Elizabeth VI, 342
Larabee, Ellen F. III, 199
Laraby, Hannah III, 284
Larance, Abigail I, 404
Larance, Mary I, 404
Larance, Peter I, 404
Larar, Ann I, 991
Larar, Mary I, 991
Lare, Joel II, 887
Lare, Joel II, 935
Lare, Leonard II, 887
Lare, Leonard II, 935
Lare, Mary C. II, 887
Lare, Mary C. II, 935
Lare, Sarah II, 887
Lare, Sarah II, 935
Larew, Ann VI, 353
Larew, Hannah VI, 328
Larew, Lewis VI, 353
Larew, Richard VI, 328
Large, Dorothy II, 178
Large, Dorothy II, 197
Large, Dorothy II, 237
Large, Dorothy II, 387
Large, Dorothy II, 576
Large, Ebenasar II, 963
Large, Ebeneezer II, 387
Large, Ebeneezer II, 576
Large, Ebenezar II, 197
Large, Ebenezar II, 237
Large, Ebenezer II, 168
Large, Ebenezer II, 178
Large, Ebenezer II, 237
Large, Ebenezer II, 387
Large, Ebenezer II, 576
Large, Ebenezer II, 1008
Large, Ebenezer II, 1009
Large, Ebenezer II, 1011
Large, Edith III, 299
Large, Eliz. C. III, 291
Large, Elizabeth II, 178
Large, Elizabeth II, 461
Large, Elizabeth II, 576
Large, Elizabeth II, 963
Large, Elizabeth II, 974
Large, Elizabeth II, 1009
Large, Elizabeth II, 1012
Large, Elizabeth II, 1030
Large, Elizabeth III, 198
Large, Elizabeth C. III, 198
Large, Hannah II, 387
Large, Hannah II, 1008
Large, Hannah II, 1009
Large, Henry II, 963
Large, Hester II, 1002
Large, Hester II, 1009
Large, Hester II, 1022
Large, Jacob II, 1008
Large, Jacob II, 1009
Large, James II, 387
Large, James II, 576
Large, Jane II, 203
Large, Jane II, 237
Large, Jane II, 963
Large, Jane II, 1000
Large, Jane II, 1001
Large, Jane II, 1009
Large, Jemima II, 1009
Large, Jemima II, 1025
Large, John II, 576
Large, John II, 963
Large, John II, 991
Large, John II, 1009
Large, John B. II, 387
Large, John Baldwin II, 576
Large, Jonathan II, 963
Large, Joseph II, 178
Large, Joseph II, 963
Large, Joseph II, 1009
Large, Joseph II, 1024
Large, Lidia II, 963
Large, Margrett II, 387
Large, Martha II, 387
Large, Mary II, 237
Large, Mary II, 251
Large, Mary II, 387
Large, Mary II, 576
Large, Mary II, 963
Large, Mary II, 1009
Large, Mary II, 1011
Large, Mary II, 1024
Large, Mary III, 291
Large, Mary H. III, 198
Large, Minnie IV, 1325
Large, Mrs. Minnie IV, 1325
Large, Rachel II, 387
Large, Rebecca II, 387
Large, Rebecca II, 576
Large, Rebecca II, 963
Large, Richard II, 1002
Large, Richard II, 1009
Large, Robert H. II, 576
Large, Samuel III, 198
Large, Samuel III, 291
Large, Sarah II, 387
Large, Sarah II, 576
Large, Sarah II, 597
Large, Sarah II, 963
Large, Sarah II, 991
Large, Sarah II, 1009
Large, Sarah II, 1038
Large, Sarah IV, 237
Large, Sarah, Jr. IV, 237
Large, Susan H. II, 387
Large, Wd. Jane II, 168
Large, William II, 963
Large, Wm. II, 1000
Large, Wm. II, 1009
Largent, Elizabeth V, 884
Largent, Jonah V, 884
Largent, Jonathan V, 884
Larick, Bertha V, 344
Larick, Chas. V, 690
Larick, Chas. Clinton V, 344
Larick, Ella V, 690
Larick, Floyd Charles V, 690
Larick, Ida V, 344
Larick, Lora V, 344
Larick, Maud V, 690
Larick, Ocie V, 344
Larick, Olive V, 410
Larick, Wm. V, 690
Larison, Elizabeth II, 821
Lark, Beulah II, 521
Lark, Beulah II, 576
Lark, Elizabeth II, 521
Lark, Elizabeth II, 576
Lark, Lucy IV, 483
Lark, Lucy IV, 504
Lark, Lucy L. IV, 483
Lark, Lucy L. IV, 504
Lark, Tenison IV, 504
Lark, Wm. II, 521
Lark, Wm. II, 576
Larken, Isaac V, 306
Larken, John S. V, 306
Larken, Mary IV, 225
Larken, Mary Ann V, 306
Larken, Sarah V, 306
Larkens, Agnes V, 306
Larkens, Ann V, 306
Larkens, Charles V, 306
Larkens, John V, 306
Larkens, Joseph V, 306
Larkens, Joseph W. V, 306
Larkens, Joseph W. V, 314
Larkens, Margaret V, 306
Larkens, Margaret V, 314
Larkens, Rachel V, 306
Larkens, Reece V, 306
Larkin, ??? IV, 237
Larkin, A. Claire V, 91
Larkin, Agnes V, 306
Larkin, Agness IV, 237
Larkin, Agness IV, 270
Larkin, Alice V, 344
Larkin, Alonsa V, 91
Larkin, Alonzo V, 91
Larkin, Alonzo V, 344
Larkin, Alonzo E. V, 259
Larkin, Alonzo M. V, 306
Larkin, Alonzo M. V, 344
Larkin, Alonzo M. V, 345
Larkin, Ann IV, 237
Larkin, Ann V, 297
Larkin, Ann V, 306
Larkin, Charles IV, 237
Larkin, Charles V, 306
Larkin, Chas. V, 306
Larkin, Elijah V, 91
Larkin, Elizabeth II, 713
Larkin, Elizabeth II, 722
Larkin, Elizabeth V, 91
Larkin, Elizabeth V, 259
Larkin, Elizabeth V, 345
Larkin, Ezekiel R. IV, 237
Larkin, Hepsibah V, 344
Larkin, Isaac IV, 237
Larkin, Isaac V, 91
Larkin, Isaac V, 306
Larkin, Jesse V, 91
Larkin, Jesse F. V, 91
Larkin, Jesse F. V, 306
Larkin, Jesse H. V, 91
Larkin, John IV, 237
Larkin, John IV, 312
Larkin, John IV, 315
Larkin, John V, 91
Larkin, John V, 306
Larkin, John S. IV, 237
Larkin, John S. V, 91
Larkin, John S. V, 306
Larkin, Joseph IV, 237
Larkin, Joseph V, 91
Larkin, Joseph V, 306
Larkin, Joseph V, 344
Larkin, Joseph W. IV, 237
Larkin, Joseph W. IV, 313
Larkin, Joseph W. IV, 315
Larkin, Joseph W. V, 306
Larkin, Joseph William IV, 237
Larkin, Joseph, Jr. IV, 237
Larkin, Lavina V, 344
Larkin, Lydia IV, 483
Larkin, Lydia IV, 497
Larkin, Lydia E. IV, 1088
Larkin, Lydia E. IV, 1104
Larkin, Mannie V, 632
Larkin, Margaret IV, 237
Larkin, Margaret IV, 313
Larkin, Margaret IV, 315
Larkin, Margaret V, 91
Larkin, Margaret V, 306
Larkin, Margaret V, 344
Larkin, Margaret V, 349
Larkin, Margaret Edna V, 91
Larkin, Martha V, 91
Larkin, Martha Ann V, 91
Larkin, Mary IV, 237
Larkin, Mary V, 91
Larkin, Mary V, 344
Larkin, Mary Ann IV, 237
Larkin, Mary Ann V, 91
Larkin, Mary Ann V, 306
Larkin, Mary F. V, 91
Larkin, Mary F. V, 344
Larkin, Nathan V, 91
Larkin, Paul V, 632
Larkin, Pearl A. V, 459
Larkin, Pearl Anderson V, 459
Larkin, Rachel IV, 237
Larkin, Rachel V, 91
Larkin, Rachel V, 306
Larkin, Rachel Ann IV, 237
Larkin, Rachel S. V, 91
Larkin, Rachel, Sr. V, 91
Larkin, Reece V, 306
Larkin, Rees IV, 237
Larkin, Rees IV, 270
Larkin, Reese IV, 237
Larkin, Richard V, 459
Larkin, S. V, 91
Larkin, Salkeld V, 91
Larkin, Sarah IV, 237
Larkin, Sarah IV, 312
Larkin, Sarah IV, 315
Larkin, Sarah V, 91
Larkin, Sarah V, 306
Larkin, Sarah Margarette V, 344
Larkin, Townsend T. IV, 237
Larkin, Willard E. V, 459
Larkin, William V, 91
Larkins, Alonzo V, 259
Larkins, Alonzo E. V, 259
Larkins, Alonzo M. V, 344
Larkins, Asa V, 632
Larkins, Eli V, 632
Larkins, Elizabeth V, 259
Larkins, Isaac James V, 632
Larkins, John V, 632
Larkins, John W. V, 632
Larkins, John Wm. V, 632
Larkins, Joseph V, 259
Larkins, Joseph W. V, 259
Larkins, Lavina V, 259
Larkins, Levina V, 259
Larkins, Mannie V, 632
Larkins, Mary V, 955
Larkins, Mary V, 961
Larkins, Mary Ann V, 79
Larkins, Mary Ann V, 91
Larkins, Nancy M. V, 632
Larkins, Paul V, 632
Larkins, Sarah Margaret V, 259
Larkins, Thos. V, 632
Larou, Jesse I, 965
Larou, Joel I, 965
Larou, Lewis I, 965
Larou, Richard I, 965
Larow, Anna VI, 353
Larow, Hannah VI, 353
Larow, Jesse VI, 353
Larow, Joel VI, 353
Larow, Lewis VI, 353
Larow, Mary VI, 353
Larow, Richard VI, 353
Larowe, Ann VI, 353
Larowe, Anna VI, 353
Larowe, Hannah VI, 353
Larowe, Hannah VI, 527
Larowe, Jesse VI, 353
Larowe, Joel VI, 353
Larowe, Lewis VI, 353
Larowe, Mary VI, 353
Larowe, Richard VI, 353
Larowe, Richard VI, 527
Larrabee, Ama III, 198
Larrabee, Ama. Anna III, 198
Larrabee, Ann III, 198
Larrabee, Anna III, 198
Larrabee, Daniel III, 198
Larrance, Abigail I, 358
Larrance, Abigail I, 457
Larrance, Abigail I, 469
Larrance, Abigail I, 482
Larrance, Betsey I, 469
Larrance, David I, 1107
Larrance, David I, 1123
Larrance, Elizabeth I, 459
Larrance, Elizabeth I, 473
Larrance, Elizabeth I, 482
Larrance, George II, 78
Larrance, George II, 83
Larrance, Isaac I, 469
Larrance, Isaac I, 482
Larrance, Isaac V, 917
Larrance, Jane I, 1107
Larrance, Jane I, 1123
Larrance, Jesse I, 469
Larrance, John I, 469
Larrance, John I, 482
Larrance, John I, 1107
Larrance, John I, 1123
Larrance, Johnathan I, 1123
Larrance, Jonathan I, 469
Larrance, Jonathan I, 482
Larrance, Jonathan I, 1107
Larrance, Mary I, 469
Larrance, Mary I, 482
Larrance, Mary II, 78
Larrance, Nancy I, 469
Larrance, Nancy I, 480
Larrance, Nancy I, 482
Larrance, Nancy I, 1107
Larrance, Nathan I, 469
Larrance, Nathan I, 482
Larrance, Patsey I, 469
Larrance, Peter I, 457
Larrance, Peter I, 469
Larrance, Peter I, 482
Larrance, Pinny I, 469
Larrance, Rebecca I, 469
Larrance, Rebecca C. II, 1075
Larrance, Richard I, 1107
Larrance, Richard I, 1123
Larrance, Ruth I, 469
Larrance, Ruth I, 480
Larrance, Ruth I, 482
Larrance, Sarah I, 469
Larrance, Sarah I, 482
Larrance, Sarah I, 1107
Larrance, Stephen I, 469
Larrance, Susanna I, 457
Larrance, Susanna I, 471
Larrance, Susannah I, 469
Larrance, Susannah I, 482
Larrance, Susannah I, 485
Larrance, Thomas H. I, 469
Larrance, William I, 469
Larrance, Winney I, 469
Larrence, Abigail I, 396
Larrence, Abigail I, 404
Larrence, Ann I, 404
Larrence, Ann I, 1122
Larrence, Ann I, 1123
Larrence, David I, 1123
Larrence, Frankey VI, 836
Larrence, Jane I, 1123
Larrence, Jean I, 716
Larrence, Jean I, 723
Larrence, John I, 404
Larrence, John I, 1123
Larrence, Johnathan I, 1123
Larrence, Peter I, 396
Larrence, Peter I, 404
Larrence, Peter I, 762
Larrence, Peter I, 765
Larrence, Richard I, 1123
Larrence, Ruth I, 1123
Larrence, Ruth I, 1127
Larrence, Sarah I, 762
Larrence, Sarah I, 1123
Larrence, Sarah I, 1127
Larrick, Amelia VI, 412
Larrick, Amelia VI, 427
Larrick, Etta V, 259
Larrick, Ida M. V, 259
Larrick, Nancy V, 259
Larrick, Nancy V, 509
Larrick, William V, 259
Larrick, William V, 509
Larrieck, Nancy V, 509
Larrieck, William V, 509
Larronce, Mary I, 1008
Larronce, Mary I, 1010
Larrowe, Anna I, 977
Larrowe, Anna VI, 353
Larrowe, Elizabeth I, 991
Larrowe, Elizabeth I, 994
Larrowe, Elnathan I, 977
Larrowe, Hannah I, 977
Larrowe, Hannah VI, 353
Larrowe, Hannah VI, 526
Larrowe, James I, 1006
Larrowe, Janney I, 977
Larrowe, Jesse I, 1006
Larrowe, Jesse VI, 353
Larrowe, Joel I, 977
Larrowe, Joel I, 980

arrowe, Joel I, 991
arrowe, Joel I, 1010
arrowe, Joel VI, 353
arrowe, John I, 1006
arrowe, Jonathan I, 977
arrowe, Lewis VI, 353
arrowe, Luzzena I, 1010
arrowe, Mary I, 991
arrowe, Mary I, 1006
arrowe, Mary V, 410
arrowe, Mary V, 421
arrowe, Mary VI, 353
arrowe, Mary Ann I, 991
arrowe, Mary Ann I, 994
arrowe, Matilda I, 977
arrowe, Matilda I, 991
arrowe, Richard VI, 353
arrowe, Richard VI, 526
arrowe, Sarah I, 982
arrowe, Sarah I, 991
arrowe, Susanna I, 977
arrowe, Susanna I, 991
arrowe, Susannah I, 980
arrowe, Susannah I, 991
arrowe, William I, 977
arsh, Bertha Commons V, 850
arsh, Eleanor V, 850
arsh, Elizabeth V, 850
arsh, Emily V, 850
arson, Bertha IV, 375
arson, Bertha IV, 416
arson, Bertha R. IV, 416
arson, Elezabeath I, 91
arson, Lindley C. IV, 375
arson, Lindley C. IV, 416
arson, Lydia IV, 416
arson, Nicholas IV, 416
arson, William I, 91
aRue, Hannah VI, 526
arue, Hannah VI, 527
arue, Hannah VI, 671
arue, Mary II, 821
aRue, Richard VI, 526
arue, Richard VI, 527
arue, Richard VI, 671
arupe, Saddie V, 1006
ary, Mary VI, 412
arzalere, Sallie A. II, 804
arzelere, Charles T. III, 198
arzelere, Ida III, 198
arzelere, Nicholas H. III, 198
asell, Mary Ann II, 751
asell, Mary Ann II, 762
asenbee, Mary V, 91
asey, Elisabeth I, 195
asey, Elisabeth I, 199
asey, John I, 56
asey, Martha I, 195
asey, Miriam I, 195
asey, Sarah I, 196
asey, Sarah I, 200
asey, William I, 195
ash, Edward IV, 1325
ashbrook, Mrs. ??? IV, 1325
ashbrook, Mrs. C. IV, 1325
ashell, Lydia VI, 412
ashells, Lydia VI, 818
asher, Amanda Melvina II, 800
ashley, Alfred V, 91
ashley, Alfred V, 581
ashley, Charity I, 404
ashley, Florence Emma V, 91
ashley, Isadora Belle V, 185
ashley, Robert V, 91
ashley, Robert B. V, 91
ashley, Robert Boon V, 91
ashley, Robert Boone V, 581
ashley, Sarah J. V, 91
ashley, William V, 91
ashly, Ruth I, 448
ashly, Ruth I, 449
ashmit, Hazeltine I, 933
ashmit, John I, 933
ashmit, Pauline I, 933
asley, Elizabeth VI, 832
asley, Ellen K. VI, 943
asley, John VI, 832
asley, John VI, 847
assater, Meriam I, 710
assater, Meriam I, 723
assing, Peter G. IV, 1372
assiter, Ada May I, 724
assiter, Anna Florence I, 724
assiter, Chloie Lee I, 724
assiter, Eleanor I, 628
assiter, Eleanor I, 927
assiter, Eliza Jane I, 724
assiter, Elizabeth M. I, 724
assiter, Elmer Cartland I, 12
assiter, Harold Roundtree I, 12
assiter, Helen VI, 257
Lassiter, Henry J. I, 724
Lassiter, J. Hal I, 620
Lassiter, J. Hal I, 636
Lassiter, James I, 12
Lassiter, Jane I, 936
Lassiter, John I, 12
Lassiter, John I, 29
Lassiter, Josiah T. I, 724
Lassiter, Kenneth R. I, 245
Lassiter, Kennith R. I, 245
Lassiter, Lillie Adelia I, 724
Lassiter, Lydia I, 718
Lassiter, Lydia I, 723
Lassiter, Mattie I, 12
Lassiter, Mattie I, 29
Lassiter, Mattie J. I, 620
Lassiter, Meriam I, 723
Lassiter, Micajah H. I, 724
Lassiter, Miles I, 723
Lassiter, Miriam I, 615
Lassiter, Nancy G. I, 723
Lassiter, Robert Franklin I, 724
Lassiter, Sallie I, 620
Lassiter, Sampson C. I, 724
Lassiter, W. W. I, 620
Lassiter, William W. I, 723
Lassitor, Eleanor I, 618
Latchmore, Edwin III, 198
Latey, Gilbod IV, 106
Latham, Abigail III, 198
Latham, Abigail III, 274
Latham, Amy III, 424
Latham, Amy III, 427
Latham, Ann III, 162
Latham, Ann III, 198
Latham, Benjamin III, 198
Latham, Caroline A. VI, 935
Latham, Daniel II, 577
Latham, Daniel III, 162
Latham, Daniel III, 198
Latham, Daniel, Jr. III, 198
Latham, David III, 198
Latham, Delia III, 198
Latham, Eleanor G. VI, 1013
Latham, Elizabeth III, 198
Latham, George III, 198
Latham, Hannah III, 198
Latham, Henry VI, 935
Latham, Hope D. III, 198
Latham, Isabella III, 224
Latham, James III, 198
Latham, Jane III, 198
Latham, Jane III, 396
Latham, Jane III, 416
Latham, Jane III, 424
Latham, Jane III, 432
Latham, John III, 198
Latham, John III, 405
Latham, John III, 424
Latham, Joseph III, 42
Latham, Joseph III, 198
Latham, Joseph III, 396
Latham, Joseph III, 424
Latham, Joseph III, 432
Latham, Lucinda J. VI, 947
Latham, Margaret III, 42
Latham, Margaret III, 198
Latham, Margaret III, 396
Latham, Mary III, 198
Latham, Mary III, 405
Latham, Mary III, 424
Latham, Mary III, 427
Latham, Mary III, 432
Latham, Mary VI, 971
Latham, Mary A. VI, 929
Latham, Mary B. VI, 1013
Latham, Phebe III, 351
Latham, Sarah III, 198
Latham, Sarah III, 424
Latham, Sarah III, 427
Latham, Silas G. VI, 909
Latham, Silas G. VI, 947
Latham, Stephen III, 198
Latham, Thomas II, 576
Latham, Thomas III, 198
Latham, William III, 198
Latham, William III, 424
Latham, William III, 427
Latham, Wm. III, 424
Lathbury, Hannah II, 388
Lathorn, Elizabeth VI, 832
Lathorn, John VI, 832
Lathram, Frances Ann IV, 237
Lathrop, Emily V, 91
Lathrop, Emily VI, 708
Lathrop, Emily VI, 721
Lathrop, Jonathan V, 72
Lathrop, Rebecca V, 72
Lathrop, Rebecca V, 91
Lathrop, Rebecca V, 144
Lathrop, Rebecca Hill V, 91
Lathrop, Rebekah V, 91
Lathrop, Susanna V, 72
Latimer, Florence IV, 1325
Latimer, Florence, Jr. IV, 1325
Latimer, May IV, 1325
Laton, Joseph I, 824
Latourette, ??? III, 198
Latta, Mary I, 389
Latta, Mary I, 400
Latta, Mary I, 404
Latta, Susanna I, 400
Latta, Susanna I, 404
Lattimer, Mabel W. III, 123
Lattimer, Mabel W. III, 199
Lattimer, Margaret III, 123
Lattimer, Margaret III, 199
Lattimer, Thos. Henry III, 123
Lattimer, Thos. Henry III, 199
Lattimore, Ellen F. III, 199
Lattimore, Florence III, 199
Lattimore, Samuel III, 199
Lattin, Catharine V, 917
Lattin, Catharine V, 929
Lattin, Mary III, 199
Latting, Amy III, 489
Latting, Attell III, 489
Latting, Charles G. III, 489
Latting, Daniel III, 424
Latting, Deborah Jane III, 489
Latting, Ella T. III, 489
Latting, Emily III, 489
Latting, Ethelinda III, 489
Latting, Ethelinda III, 502
Latting, George III, 489
Latting, Henry III, 489
Latting, Isaac III, 424
Latting, Joseph III, 489
Latting, Joseph H. III, 489
Latting, Julia III, 489
Latting, Martha III, 424
Latting, Mary III, 199
Latting, Mary III, 489
Latting, Susannah III, 489
Latting, Wm. H. III, 489
Latty, Rebecca IV, 975
Latty, Rebecca S. IV, 1005
Lauck, Florence J. VI, 412
Lauck, Florence J. VI, 438
Lauck, Julia Florence VI, 439
Lauderbach, Ella V. II, 887
Lauderback, Ella V. II, 944
Lauderman, Rose V, 917
Laughlin, Alexander C. I, 750
Laughlin, Alexander C. I, 765
Laughlin, Anna Livezey II, 887
Laughlin, Franklin I, 750
Laughlin, Franklin I, 765
Laughlin, Franklin V, 1006
Laughlin, Franklin W. I, 750
Laughlin, Franklin W. I, 765
Laughlin, Hannah L. I, 750
Laughlin, Hannah Loretta I, 765
Laughlin, Hugh I, 343
Laughlin, Hugh I, 369
Laughlin, James L. I, 750
Laughlin, James L. I, 765
Laughlin, Jane I, 921
Laughlin, Levenia I, 750
Laughlin, Lillie V, 1006
Laughlin, Lovena I, 616
Laughlin, Luvenia I, 765
Laughlin, Mahla I, 763
Laughlin, Mahla I, 765
Laughlin, Mary I, 343
Laughlin, Mary I, 369
Laughlin, Nancy I, 750
Laughlin, Nancy I, 765
Laughlin, Ranson F. IV, 1238
Laughlin, Rebecca I, 625
Laughlin, Rebecca R. I, 750
Laughlin, Rebecca Roellen I, 765
Laughlin, Rhoda IV, 416
Laughlin, Rhoda IV, 443
Laughlin, Robert I, 750
Laughlin, Robert I, 765
Laughlin, Sarah I, 750
Laughlin, Sarah I, 765
Laughlin, Sarah IV, 1238
Laughlin, Seth I, 750
Laughlin, Seth I, 765
Laughlin, Seth W. I, 750
Laughlin, Seth W. I, 765
Laughlin, Susanna Jane I, 765
Laughlin, Susannah I, 750
Laughlin, William I, 750
Laughlin, William I, 765
Laughman, Ella IV, 1256
Laughon, Abner VI, 948
Laughon, Betsy VI, 993
Laughon, Daniel VI, 993
Laughon, Isham VI, 1014
Laughon, Isham, Jr. VI, 948
Laughon, Joshua VI, 1014
Laughon, Margaret VI, 948
Laughon, Mary J. VI, 948
Laughon, Mary Jane VI, 948
Laughon, Susan VI, 1014
Laughon, William VI, 948
Laughorn, Daniel VI, 1009
Laughorn, Polly VI, 948
Laughorn, Thomas VI, 948
Laughton, Kittie Cowley IV, 1325
Laughton, Sarah G. IV, 513
Laughton, Sarah G. IV, 538
Lauk, Everet S. VI, 762
Lauk, Everett Staunton VI, 762
Lauk, Everett Staunton VI, 793
Lauk, Myra Elizabeth VI, 762
Lauk, Myra Elizabeth VI, 793
Laur, Robert VI, 7
Laur, Robert VI, 32
Laurance, Hannah W. II, 152
Laurance, Jane I, 1033
Laurance, Jane I, 1038
Laurance, Margaret I, 76
Laurance, Mary Elizabeth II, 152
Laurance, Sarah I, 482
Laurance, Widow Margaret I, 59
Laurence, Abigail I, 394
Laurence, Abigail I, 404
Laurence, Ann I, 218
Laurence, Ann W. II, 887
Laurence, Ann W. II, 893
Laurence, Benjamin VI, 526
Laurence, Captain ??? VI, 526
Laurence, Catharine R. I, 218
Laurence, Daniel W. I, 1157
Laurence, David I, 218
Laurence, Deborah I, 218
Laurence, Duke I, 218
Laurence, Exum I, 218
Laurence, George II, 78
Laurence, George II, 83
Laurence, George VI, 526
Laurence, Hannah II, 78
Laurence, Hannah W. II, 888
Laurence, James Coffin VI, 526
Laurence, Jane V, 1006
Laurence, Janne I Sup 1, 4
Laurence, Jedidah VI, 526
Laurence, John I, 218
Laurence, John I, 245
Laurence, John I Sup 1, 4
Laurence, John J. I, 218
Laurence, Jonathan I, 218
Laurence, Josephas Duke William I, 218
Laurence, Judith VI, 526
Laurence, Lydia T. II, 152
Laurence, Margaret I, 59
Laurence, Margaret I, 218
Laurence, Margaret I Sup 1, 4
Laurence, Margaret I Sup 1, 7
Laurence, Margaret IV, 830
Laurence, Martha II, 600
Laurence, Martha Elizabeth I, 218
Laurence, Mary I, 218
Laurence, Mary II, 823
Laurence, Mary E. II, 116
Laurence, Mordecai II, 577
Laurence, Nancy I, 218
Laurence, Patsy I, 218
Laurence, Philip IV, 1215
Laurence, Phillip W. IV, 1215
Laurence, Piety E. I, 1157
Laurence, Polly I, 218
Laurence, Rebeca I. I, 245
Laurence, Rebecca II, 321
Laurence, Rebecca T. I, 218
Laurence, Rebecca T. II, 321
Laurence, Ricks I, 218
Laurence, Robert VI, 17
Laurence, Robert VI, 22
Laurence, Robt. I, 245
Laurence, Ruth I, 480
Laurence, Ruth I, 482
Laurence, Sally VI, 526
Laurence, Sarah I, 218
Laurence, Thomas R. II, 321
Laurence, Widow Judith VI, 526
Laurence, William I, 59
Laurence, William I, 218
Laurence, William I Sup 1, 4
Laurence, William VI, 526
Laurence, Wm. S. II, 152
Laurens, James V, 185
Laurens, Josephine V, 185
Laurens, Milly V, 185
Laurie, Abigail II, 751
Laurie, Ann II, 539
Laurie, Ann II, 577
Laurie, Annie III, 489
Laurie, Annie III, 502
Laurie, Charity III, 502
Laurie, Charles II, 710
Laurie, David III, 502
Laurie, Deborah II, 710
Laurie, Fannie III, 510
Laurie, Frances III, 498
Laurie, Frances F. III, 489
Laurie, Frances F. III, 502
Laurie, Francis III, 445
Laurie, George B. II, 751
Laurie, Helena A. II, 710
Laurie, James II, 120
Laurie, Jane II, 751
Laurie, Margaret J. III, 489
Laurie, Margaret J. III, 498
Laurie, Margaret L. III, 445
Laurie, Mary III, 489
Laurie, Mary III, 502
Laurie, Mary III, 510
Laurie, Patrick III, 489
Laurie, Thomas II, 539
Laurie, Thomas II, 577
Laurie, William W. III, 489
Laurie, Wm. III, 510
Laurie, Wm. W. III, 445
Laurie, Wm. W. III, 489
Laurie, Wm. W. III, 498
Laurie, Wm. W. III, 502
Laurrance, Mary I, 481
Laurrance, Mary I, 482
Lausenby, Mary V, 304
Lausenby, Mary V, 306
Lauton, Rachel VI, 670
Lauton, Rachel VI, 703
Lauton, Rachel VI, 705
Laux, Mrs. L. IV, 1325
Lavander, Sarah R. III, 359
Lavander, Thomas III, 359
Lavelle, Alice IV, 1215
Lavender, Jane III, 199
Lavender, Sarah R. III, 199
Lavender, Thomas III, 199
Lavender, Wm. III, 199
Lavinder, Elizabeth VI, 947
Lavinder, John VI, 947
Lavinder, John VI, 948
Lavinder, Mary VI, 948
Lavinder, Robert VI, 948
Law, Agnes IV, 975
Law, Beulah I, 1076
Law, Bulah I, 1076
Law, Mary Rytha IV, 1325
Law, Sarah V, 562
Law, Sarah V, 581
Law, Thomas IV, 975
Law, William IV, 975
Law, Wm. IV, 975
Lawallan, Deborah IV, 47
Lawallan, Margaret IV, 44
Lawallan, Margaret IV, 47
Lawallan, Shadrach IV, 47
Lawallen, Deborah, Jr. IV, 44
Lawerence, Deborah Ann III, 389
Lawerence, Elizabeth W. III, 389
Lawerence, Isabella VI, 257
Lawerence, Milicent VI, 257
Lawerence, Robert VI, 257
Lawerence, Thomas VI, 257
Lawes, Elijah, Jr. II, 805
Lawes, Herbert V, 690
Lawhead, Eliza Jane V, 1006
Lawhead, Emma V, 1006
Lawhead, George V, 1006
Lawhead, Millie V, 1006
Lawhorn, Abner VI, 948
Lawhorn, Daniel VI, 948
Lawhorn, Elizabeth VI, 930
Lawhorn, Gincy VI, 1010
Lawhorn, Harriet VI, 948
Lawhorn, Henry VI, 948
Lawhorn, Isham VI, 948
Lawhorn, Isham, Jr. VI, 948
Lawhorn, Lawson VI, 916
Lawhorn, Lawson VI, 924
Lawhorn, Lorsan VI, 948
Lawhorn, Lucinda VI, 924
Lawhorn, Lucinda VI, 948
Lawhorn, Lydia A. VI, 948
Lawhorn, Margaret VI, 948
Lawhorn, Martha VI, 923
Lawhorn, Mary J. VI, 948
Lawhorn, Mary Jane VI, 948
Lawhorn, Nancy VI, 948
Lawhorn, Polly VI, 948
Lawhorn, Rhoda VI, 890
Lawhorn, Rodah VI, 948
Lawhorn, Sally VI, 948
Lawhorn, Sarah VI, 884
Lawhorn, Sarah VI, 948

Lawhorn, Thomas VI, 948
Lawhorn, Willey Ann VI, 948
Lawhorn, William VI, 923
Lawhorn, William VI, 930
Lawhorn, William VI, 948
Lawhorn, William VI, 1010
Lawhorn, William VI, 1013
Lawhorne, Henry VI, 884
Lawhorne, Lucinda VI, 948
Lawhorne, Willey Ann VI, 948
Lawhorne, William VI, 948
Lawless, Catharine P. VI, 1012
Lawless, Elizabeth VI, 930
Lawless, Elizabeth VI, 948
Lawless, Elizabeth Ann VI, 948
Lawless, James R. VI, 948
Lawless, Laland VI, 1012
Lawless, Leland VI, 930
Lawless, Leland VI, 1012
Lawless, Wiatt VI, 895
Lawless, Wiatt VI, 948
Lawrance, Abigail I, 404
Lawrance, Ann I, 404
Lawrance, Ann II, 568
Lawrance, Ann II, 577
Lawrance, Elizabeth II, 577
Lawrance, Hannah II, 83
Lawrance, Hannah II, 577
Lawrance, Isaac I, 404
Lawrance, John I, 145
Lawrance, John I, 245
Lawrance, John I, 404
Lawrance, John I, 482
Lawrance, Jonathan I, 404
Lawrance, Joshua II, 568
Lawrance, Joshua II, 577
Lawrance, Peter I, 404
Lawrance, Peter I, 482
Lawrance, Thomas II, 577
Lawrence, ??? III, 134
Lawrence, ??? III, 201
Lawrence, ??? III, 218
Lawrence, ??? III, 240
Lawrence, ??? III, 381
Lawrence, ??? VI, 39
Lawrence, ??? VI, 48
Lawrence, Abigail I, 404
Lawrence, Abigail I, 699
Lawrence, Abigail M. IV, 237
Lawrence, Abigail M. IV, 312
Lawrence, Abigail M. IV, 313
Lawrence, Abigail M. V, 955
Lawrence, Abraham B. III, 489
Lawrence, Agnes C. III, 278
Lawrence, Albert III, 199
Lawrence, Alfred IV, 640
Lawrence, Alfred N. III, 199
Lawrence, Alfred N. III, 200
Lawrence, Alice III, 27
Lawrence, Alice III, 199
Lawrence, Alice III, 200
Lawrence, Alice III, 329
Lawrence, Alletta Bement III, 199
Lawrence, Amelia III, 60
Lawrence, Amelia III, 64
Lawrence, Amelia III, 199
Lawrence, Amey II, 577
Lawrence, Amos III, 40
Lawrence, Amos III, 199
Lawrence, Amy II, 388
Lawrence, Amy II, 577
Lawrence, Amy II, 581
Lawrence, Amy III, 40
Lawrence, Amy III, 201
Lawrence, Amy III, 381
Lawrence, Amy III, 383
Lawrence, Amy III, 384
Lawrence, Ann I, 245
Lawrence, Ann I, 257
Lawrence, Ann I, 765
Lawrence, Ann II, 388
Lawrence, Ann II, 577
Lawrence, Ann II, 992
Lawrence, Ann II, 1009
Lawrence, Ann III, 51
Lawrence, Ann III, 54
Lawrence, Ann III, 122
Lawrence, Ann III, 199
Lawrence, Ann III, 200
Lawrence, Ann III, 208
Lawrence, Ann III, 334
Lawrence, Ann III, 381
Lawrence, Ann VI, 75
Lawrence, Ann D. IV, 237
Lawrence, Ann D. IV, 288
Lawrence, Ann D. IV, 733
Lawrence, Ann D. IV, 775
Lawrence, Ann D. IV, 847
Lawrence, Ann D. VI, 75
Lawrence, Ann Scott VI, 75
Lawrence, Anna III, 51
Lawrence, Anna III, 199
Lawrence, Anna III, 200
Lawrence, Anna III, 381
Lawrence, Anna III, 382
Lawrence, Anne, Jr. II, 1009
Lawrence, Anne, Jr. II, 1019
Lawrence, Annie III, 199
Lawrence, Annie W. III, 134
Lawrence, Antoinette III, 489
Lawrence, Benjamin VI, 760
Lawrence, Benjamin VI, 794
Lawrence, Benjamin Bates IV, 237
Lawrence, Burt V, 1006
Lawrence, Caleb II, 388
Lawrence, Caleb III, 55
Lawrence, Caleb III, 199
Lawrence, Caleb III, 200
Lawrence, Caleb III, 201
Lawrence, Capt. Geo. VI, 563
Lawrence, Capt. Geo. VI, 760
Lawrence, Capt. Geo. VI, 779
Lawrence, Capt. Geo. VI, 794
Lawrence, Capt. Geo., Jr. VI, 521
Lawrence, Capt. Geo., Jr. VI, 757
Lawrence, Captain ??? VI, 526
Lawrence, Carolina Augusta III, 199
Lawrence, Caroline III, 199
Lawrence, Caroline III, 200
Lawrence, Caroline III, 348
Lawrence, Caroline V, 917
Lawrence, Caroline Augusta III, 200
Lawrence, Caroline B. V, 91
Lawrence, Catharine III, 200
Lawrence, Catherin I, 245
Lawrence, Catherin I, 247
Lawrence, Cathern VI, 75
Lawrence, Charles III, 201
Lawrence, Charles IV, 313
Lawrence, Charles IV, 733
Lawrence, Charles D. III, 381
Lawrence, Charles Spencer VI, 760
Lawrence, Charles Spencer VI, 794
Lawrence, Charles W. III, 199
Lawrence, Charlotte III, 199
Lawrence, Charlotte III, 381
Lawrence, Clariss IV, 640
Lawrence, Clarissa IV, 640
Lawrence, Clement II, 577
Lawrence, Cornelia III, 200
Lawrence, Cornelius III, 164
Lawrence, Cornelius III, 199
Lawrence, Daniel I, 625
Lawrence, Daniel II, 237
Lawrence, Daniel II, 577
Lawrence, Daniel III, 200
Lawrence, Daniel III, 313
Lawrence, Daniel IV, 1372
Lawrence, Daniel V, 955
Lawrence, Daniel V, 960
Lawrence, Daniel Test IV, 733
Lawrence, David I, 245
Lawrence, David II, 388
Lawrence, David II, 1009
Lawrence, David VI, 75
Lawrence, David VI, 80
Lawrence, Deborah III, 199
Lawrence, Deborah III, 201
Lawrence, Deborah III, 360
Lawrence, Deborah IV, 201
Lawrence, Deborah IV, 219
Lawrence, Deborah IV, 237
Lawrence, Deborah VI, 80
Lawrence, Deborah Ann III, 381
Lawrence, Deborah Pretlow VI, 75
Lawrence, Deborah R. IV, 219
Lawrence, Deborah R. IV, 237
Lawrence, Deborah Ricks IV, 237
Lawrence, Deborah Rix VI, 75
Lawrence, Demcy I, 245
Lawrence, Derimon IV, 640
Lawrence, Edith II, 710
Lawrence, Edith II, 714
Lawrence, Edith II, 751
Lawrence, Edward III, 199
Lawrence, Edward B. III, 200
Lawrence, Edward M. IV, 237
Lawrence, Edward N. III, 199
Lawrence, Edward N. III, 200
Lawrence, Edward S. II, 134
Lawrence, Effingham III, 200
Lawrence, Effingham III, 381
Lawrence, Effingham W. III, 199
Lawrence, Effingham W. III, 381
Lawrence, Elijah IV, 313
Lawrence, Eliz. III, 354
Lawrence, Eliz. III, 444
Lawrence, Eliza I, 245
Lawrence, Eliza II, 710
Lawrence, Eliza II, 714
Lawrence, Eliza III, 199
Lawrence, Elizabeth II, 223
Lawrence, Elizabeth II, 237
Lawrence, Elizabeth II, 388
Lawrence, Elizabeth II, 577
Lawrence, Elizabeth II, 679
Lawrence, Elizabeth III, 41
Lawrence, Elizabeth III, 199
Lawrence, Elizabeth III, 300
Lawrence, Elizabeth III, 381
Lawrence, Elizabeth III, 385
Lawrence, Elizabeth IV, 847
Lawrence, Elizabeth V, 917
Lawrence, Elizabeth W. II, 577
Lawrence, Elizabeth W. III, 381
Lawrence, Elizabeth W. III, 382
Lawrence, Elizabeth W. III, 389
Lawrence, Emeline III, 61
Lawrence, Emmet IV, 237
Lawrence, Esther III, 70
Lawrence, Esther III, 199
Lawrence, Esther III, 381
Lawrence, Esther III, 383
Lawrence, Esther III, 389
Lawrence, Esther III, 434
Lawrence, Esther P. III, 381
Lawrence, Esther P. III, 384
Lawrence, Euphemia V, 893
Lawrence, Euphemia V, 917
Lawrence, Euphemia Baily V, 917
Lawrence, Evan IV, 313
Lawrence, Exum I, 245
Lawrence, Francis II, 1019
Lawrence, Frank V, 1006
Lawrence, Gelia I, 865
Lawrence, George II, 83
Lawrence, George II, 710
Lawrence, George II, 714
Lawrence, George III, 199
Lawrence, George VI, 760
Lawrence, George VI, 791
Lawrence, George VI, 794
Lawrence, George C. II, 1084
Lawrence, George N. III, 199
Lawrence, George N. III, 200
Lawrence, Gilbert III, 381
Lawrence, Gilbert III, 383
Lawrence, H. H. V, 893
Lawrence, Hannah I, 625
Lawrence, Hannah II, 83
Lawrence, Hannah II, 148
Lawrence, Hannah II, 152
Lawrence, Hannah II, 525
Lawrence, Hannah II, 540
Lawrence, Hannah II, 577
Lawrence, Hannah III, 40
Lawrence, Hannah III, 122
Lawrence, Hannah III, 159
Lawrence, Hannah III, 199
Lawrence, Hannah III, 200
Lawrence, Hannah III, 237
Lawrence, Hannah III, 328
Lawrence, Hannah III, 329
Lawrence, Hannah III, 339
Lawrence, Hannah V, 960
Lawrence, Hannah H. III, 199
Lawrence, Hannah L. III, 339
Lawrence, Hannah N. III, 199
Lawrence, Hannah N. III, 200
Lawrence, Hannah W. II, 152
Lawrence, Harriet III, 201
Lawrence, Helen II, 134
Lawrence, Helen II, 152
Lawrence, Henry II, 388
Lawrence, Henry II, 577
Lawrence, Henry III, 199
Lawrence, Henry III, 200
Lawrence, Henry III, 348
Lawrence, Henry III, 381
Lawrence, Henry III, 383
Lawrence, Henry III, 384
Lawrence, Henry V, 917
Lawrence, Henry VI, 32
Lawrence, Henry VI, 33
Lawrence, Henry H. II, 525
Lawrence, Henry H. II, 577
Lawrence, Henry H. III, 199
Lawrence, Henry Haydock V, 917
Lawrence, Henry, Jr. II, 577
Lawrence, Hervey, Jr. II, 577
Lawrence, Hester III, 199
Lawrence, Isaac II, 577
Lawrence, Isaac III, 61
Lawrence, Isaac V, 917
Lawrence, Isaac T. IV, 640
Lawrence, Isabell VI, 32
Lawrence, Isabell VI, 33
Lawrence, Isabella IV, 237
Lawrence, Isabella IV, 483
Lawrence, Isabella VI, 75
Lawrence, Isabella VI, 246
Lawrence, Isabella VI, 248
Lawrence, Israel F. III, 200
Lawrence, Jacent II, 577
Lawrence, Jacob III, 200
Lawrence, James II, 1071
Lawrence, James II, 1075
Lawrence, James III, 201
Lawrence, James V, 259
Lawrence, James V, 581
Lawrence, James C. VI, 760
Lawrence, James C. VI, 794
Lawrence, James Coffin VI, 760
Lawrence, James Coffin VI, 794
Lawrence, Jane III, 200
Lawrence, Jane V, 1006
Lawrence, Jane H. III, 200
Lawrence, Jarvis W. III, 489
Lawrence, Jason II, 577
Lawrence, Jedediah VI, 760
Lawrence, Jedediah VI, 794
Lawrence, Jedidah VI, 760
Lawrence, Jedidah VI, 794
Lawrence, Jesse II, 1019
Lawrence, Jesse IV, 313
Lawrence, Joane VI, 32
Lawrence, John I, 145
Lawrence, John I, 156
Lawrence, John I, 237
Lawrence, John I, 245
Lawrence, John I, 765
Lawrence, John II, 83
Lawrence, John II, 388
Lawrence, John II, 577
Lawrence, John III, 51
Lawrence, John III, 54
Lawrence, John III, 199
Lawrence, John III, 200
Lawrence, John III, 201
Lawrence, John III, 208
Lawrence, John IV, 1256
Lawrence, John VI, 45
Lawrence, John VI, 46
Lawrence, John VI, 75
Lawrence, John B. III, 199
Lawrence, John B. III, 200
Lawrence, John F. III, 199
Lawrence, John F. III, 201
Lawrence, John N. III, 200
Lawrence, John, Jr. I, 245
Lawrence, John, Jr. VI, 75
Lawrence, Jonathan I, 245
Lawrence, Jonathan III, 200
Lawrence, Jonathan VI, 75
Lawrence, Joseph II, 388
Lawrence, Joseph III, 41
Lawrence, Joseph III, 381
Lawrence, Joseph III, 424
Lawrence, Joseph III, 457
Lawrence, Joseph IV, 312
Lawrence, Joseph IV, 313
Lawrence, Joseph Denson VI, 75
Lawrence, Joshua II, 388
Lawrence, Joshua II, 577
Lawrence, Joshua II, 581
Lawrence, Joshua Duke William I, 245
Lawrence, Josiah II, 33
Lawrence, Judith VI, 757
Lawrence, Judith VI, 760
Lawrence, Judith VI, 794
Lawrence, Julia Ann IV, 237
Lawrence, Julia Ann IV, 985
Lawrence, Julia Ann W. IV, 237
Lawrence, Julian Wilkinson IV, 237
Lawrence, July Ann Wilkinson VI, 75
Lawrence, Lanselot III, 201
Lawrence, Lemuell Jones VI, 75
Lawrence, Leonard III, 104
Lawrence, Leonard III, 200
Lawrence, Leonard III, 201
Lawrence, Leonard III, 381
Lawrence, Lillian C. II, 134
Lawrence, Louisa II, 1084
Lawrence, Lulu V, 259
Lawrence, Lydia II, 129
Lawrence, Lydia II, 483
Lawrence, Lydia II, 577
Lawrence, Lydia III, 178
Lawrence, Lydia III, 200
Lawrence, Lydia IV, 313
Lawrence, Lydia VI, 760
Lawrence, Lydia VI, 794
Lawrence, Lydia T. II, 134
Lawrence, Lydia T. II, 144
Lawrence, Lydia T. II, 152
Lawrence, Marcy II, 388
Lawrence, Margaret I, 145
Lawrence, Margaret I, 156
Lawrence, Margaret I, 245
Lawrence, Margaret III, 104
Lawrence, Margaret III, 200
Lawrence, Margaret III, 381
Lawrence, Margaret I. IV, 219
Lawrence, Margaret I. IV, 237
Lawrence, Margaret J. IV, 237
Lawrence, Maria C. III, 381
Lawrence, Marion II, 134
Lawrence, Mark II, 1084
Lawrence, Marsha R. VI, 75
Lawrence, Marsha R. VI, 86
Lawrence, Martha I, 13
Lawrence, Martha I, 245
Lawrence, Martha II, 388
Lawrence, Martha II, 546
Lawrence, Martha II, 577
Lawrence, Martha III, 105
Lawrence, Martha III, 489
Lawrence, Martha IV, 237
Lawrence, Martha IV, 313
Lawrence, Martha VI, 45
Lawrence, Martha VI, 46
Lawrence, Martha VI, 75
Lawrence, Martha VI, 77
Lawrence, Martha Jane IV, 125(
Lawrence, Martha Murry IV, 23
Lawrence, Martha Nixon VI, 75
Lawrence, Mary I, 145
Lawrence, Mary I, 237
Lawrence, Mary I, 245
Lawrence, Mary I, 404
Lawrence, Mary I, 625
Lawrence, Mary I, 1010
Lawrence, Mary II, 83
Lawrence, Mary II, 178
Lawrence, Mary II, 388
Lawrence, Mary II, 525
Lawrence, Mary II, 577
Lawrence, Mary II, 598
Lawrence, Mary II, 685
Lawrence, Mary III, 27
Lawrence, Mary III, 41
Lawrence, Mary III, 110
Lawrence, Mary III, 197
Lawrence, Mary III, 199
Lawrence, Mary III, 200
Lawrence, Mary III, 201
Lawrence, Mary III, 221
Lawrence, Mary III, 313
Lawrence, Mary III, 381
Lawrence, Mary III, 385
Lawrence, Mary IV, 237
Lawrence, Mary IV, 733
Lawrence, Mary V, 1006
Lawrence, Mary VI, 32
Lawrence, Mary VI, 75
Lawrence, Mary VI, 77
Lawrence, Mary VI, 760
Lawrence, Mary VI, 791
Lawrence, Mary VI, 794
Lawrence, Mary Ann III, 78
Lawrence, Mary Ann III, 240
Lawrence, Mary Ann IV, 201
Lawrence, Mary Ann IV, 237
Lawrence, Mary E. II, 134
Lawrence, Mary Elizabeth II, 15
Lawrence, Mary Ellen V, 581
Lawrence, Mary Isabella IV, 237
Lawrence, Mary L. III, 201
Lawrence, Mary Louise III, 20
Lawrence, Mary Louise III, 201
Lawrence, Mary T. II, 577
Lawrence, Mary, Jr. I, 245
Lawrence, Mary, Jr. IV, 313
Lawrence, Matilda III, 199
Lawrence, Matilda VI, 880
Lawrence, Matthew Jones VI, 75
Lawrence, Milicent IV, 285
Lawrence, Milisent I, 233
Lawrence, Milisent I, 245
Lawrence, Millicent I, 245
Lawrence, Milly V, 185
Lawrence, Milly V, 208
Lawrence, Mordecai II, 388
Lawrence, Mordecai II, 577
Lawrence, Mordecai II, 751
Lawrence, Naomi III, 199
Lawrence, Newbold III, 200
Lawrence, Norris III, 199
Lawrence, Norris III, 200
Lawrence, Norris III, 221
Lawrence, Obadiah III, 41
Lawrence, Obadiah III, 200
Lawrence, Obed IV, 640
Lawrence, Oliver VI, 757

wrence, Oliver VI, 760
wrence, Pauline III, 61
wrence, Pennel II, 577
wrence, Peter I, 404
wrence, Peter I, 699
wrence, Peter I, 765
wrence, Peter V, 955
wrence, Phebe III, 200
wrence, Phebe III, 381
wrence, Phebe III, 424
wrence, Phebe III, 457
wrence, Phebe V, 917
wrence, Phebe L. V, 917
wrence, Phebe L. V, 939
wrence, Philadelphia II, 577
wrence, Philip IV, 1215
wrence, Rachel Ann III, 164
wrence, Rachel Ann III, 199
wrence, Ralph S. IV, 1325
wrence, Rebeca I. I, 245
wrence, Rebecca II, 129
wrence, Rebecca II, 388
wrence, Rebecca II, 1071
wrence, Rebecca II, 1075
wrence, Rebecca IV, 313
wrence, Rebecca Ann II, 1075
wrence, Rebecca Ann II, 1083
wrence, Rebecca C. II, 1075
wrence, Rebecca S. II, 144
wrence, Rebecca S. II, 152
wrence, Rich. R. III, 199
wrence, Richard III, 27
wrence, Richard III, 40
wrence, Richard III, 159
wrence, Richard III, 199
wrence, Richard III, 200
wrence, Richard E. III, 122
wrence, Richard R. II, 525
wrence, Richard R. II, 577
wrence, Richard R. III, 199
wrence, Richard R. III, 253
wrence, Richard R. III, 329
wrence, Ricks I, 245
wrence, Robert I, 233
wrence, Robert I, 245
wrence, Robert III, 381
wrence, Robert III, 389
wrence, Robert IV, 237
wrence, Robert IV, 847
wrence, Robert VI, 7
wrence, Robert VI, 22
wrence, Robert VI, 32
wrence, Robert VI, 75
wrence, Robert B. IV, 174
wrence, Robert B. IV, 237
wrence, Robert B. IV, 483
wrence, Robert Barclay IV, 237
wrence, Robert Barclay Thomas VI, 75
wrence, Robert H. IV, 237
wrence, Robert R. III, 339
wrence, Robert W. III, 278
wrence, Robt. I, 245
wrence, Robt. VI, 25
wrence, Robt. B. IV, 464
wrence, Robt. L. III, 199
wrence, Ruth I, 699
wrence, Ruth B. III, 199
wrence, Sally VI, 760
wrence, Sally VI, 794
wrence, Samuel I, 245
wrence, Samuel II, 237
wrence, Samuel II, 577
wrence, Samuel III, 105
wrence, Samuel III, 199
wrence, Samuel III, 201
wrence, Samuel III, 360
wrence, Samuel, Jr. II, 577
wrence, Samuell VI, 75
wrence, Sarah I, 245
wrence, Sarah I, 765
wrence, Sarah II, 577
wrence, Sarah II, 626
wrence, Sarah III, 41
wrence, Sarah III, 55
wrence, Sarah III, 138
wrence, Sarah III, 199
wrence, Sarah III, 201
wrence, Sarah III, 218
wrence, Sarah III, 240
wrence, Sarah III, 273
wrence, Sarah V, 955
wrence, Sarah M. IV, 985
wrence, Smith III, 201
wrence, Sophia Pretlow VI, 75
wrence, Sophia S. VI, 75
wrence, Sophia S. VI, 80
wrence, Stephen III, 40
wrence, Stephen III, 201
wrence, Stephen IV, 985
wrence, Summerset III, 201
Lawrence, Susan F. III, 199
Lawrence, Susanna I, 404
Lawrence, Susanna II, 237
Lawrence, Susanna II, 388
Lawrence, Susannah II, 577
Lawrence, Susannah II, 1071
Lawrence, Susannah II, 1075
Lawrence, Susannah II, 1083
Lawrence, Tace B. IV, 483
Lawrence, Tacy IV, 174
Lawrence, Tacy IV, 237
Lawrence, Tacy IV, 464
Lawrence, Tacy IV, 483
Lawrence, Tacy B. IV, 237
Lawrence, Tamar III, 201
Lawrence, Thamar III, 201
Lawrence, Theron III, 20
Lawrence, Theron III, 201
Lawrence, Thomas I, 245
Lawrence, Thomas II, 237
Lawrence, Thomas II, 388
Lawrence, Thomas II, 540
Lawrence, Thomas II, 577
Lawrence, Thomas II, 1009
Lawrence, Thomas II, 1019
Lawrence, Thomas IV, 237
Lawrence, Thomas VI, 75
Lawrence, Thomas VI, 80
Lawrence, Thomas VI, 248
Lawrence, Thomas D. II, 388
Lawrence, Thomas Dell II, 577
Lawrence, Thomas Duke I, 245
Lawrence, Thomas Gay VI, 32
Lawrence, Thomas N. III, 200
Lawrence, Thomas, Jr. II, 1009
Lawrence, Thomas, Jr. II, 1019
Lawrence, Thos. IV, 201
Lawrence, Thos. IV, 219
Lawrence, Thos. IV, 483
Lawrence, Thos. VI, 246
Lawrence, Walter II, 1071
Lawrence, Walter II, 1075
Lawrence, Walter II, 1083
Lawrence, Walter III, 201
Lawrence, Wd. Judith VI, 521
Lawrence, Wd. Judith VI, 563
Lawrence, Wd. Judith VI, 779
Lawrence, Wd. Judith VI, 794
Lawrence, Wd. Judith Spencer VI, 757
Lawrence, Wd. Sarah III, 201
Lawrence, Widow Judith VI, 526
Lawrence, Willet III, 201
Lawrence, Willet, Jr. III, 424
Lawrence, William II, 388
Lawrence, William III, 201
Lawrence, William III, 381
Lawrence, William VI, 760
Lawrence, William VI, 794
Lawrence, William Bates IV, 237
Lawrence, William Henry III, 199
Lawrence, William P. II, 388
Lawrence, Wm. II, 129
Lawrence, Wm. II, 134
Lawrence, Wm. II, 150
Lawrence, Wm. II, 152
Lawrence, Wm. II, 157
Lawrence, Wm. II, 546
Lawrence, Wm. II, 577
Lawrence, Wm. II, 685
Lawrence, Wm. III, 389
Lawrence, Wm. C. II, 1075
Lawrence, Wm. C. II, 1083
Lawrence, Wm. E. II, 134
Lawrence, Wm. P. II, 577
Lawrence, Wm. S. II, 134
Lawrence, Wm. S. II, 144
Lawrence, Wm. S. II, 152
Lawrence, Zipporah III, 381
Lawrens, James V, 185
Lawrens, Josephine V, 185
Lawrie, ??? III, 234
Lawrie, Abigail II, 33
Lawrie, Abigail II, 120
Lawrie, Abigail II, 751
Lawrie, Abigail III, 70
Lawrie, Abigail III, 201
Lawrie, Achsah II, 237
Lawrie, Achsah II, 243
Lawrie, Ann II, 33
Lawrie, Ann II, 120
Lawrie, Ann II, 123
Lawrie, Ann II, 577
Lawrie, Ann II, 797
Lawrie, Benjamin II, 797
Lawrie, Caroline H. III, 201
Lawrie, Charles II, 294
Lawrie, Deborah II, 120
Lawrie, Edith II, 178
Lawrie, Edith II, 294
Lawrie, Edith, Jr. II, 294
Lawrie, Francis III, 424
Lawrie, George B. II, 751
Lawrie, George G. II, 751
Lawrie, George G. III, 201
Lawrie, James II, 120
Lawrie, James II, 294
Lawrie, Jane II, 120
Lawrie, Jane II, 123
Lawrie, Jane II, 751
Lawrie, John II, 237
Lawrie, John II, 243
Lawrie, John III, 70
Lawrie, John III, 201
Lawrie, Joseph M. II, 178
Lawrie, Joseph M. II, 294
Lawrie, Lucy Ann II, 178
Lawrie, Lucy Ann II, 294
Lawrie, Margaret J. III, 424
Lawrie, Martha III, 234
Lawrie, Martha M. II, 237
Lawrie, Martha M. II, 243
Lawrie, Martha M. III, 70
Lawrie, Martha M. III, 201
Lawrie, Thomas II, 33
Lawrie, Thomas II, 237
Lawrie, Thomas II, 243
Lawrie, Thomas II, 577
Lawrie, Thos. II, 120
Lawrie, Thos. II, 123
Lawrie, Wm. W. III, 424
Lawronce, Mary I, 1010
Lawronce, Mary I, 1012
Lawry, Jane II, 120
Laws, Ann II, 577
Laws, Anna III, 201
Laws, Anne II, 577
Laws, Clement II, 388
Laws, Clement II, 577
Laws, Clement II, 785
Laws, Daniel II, 577
Laws, Elijah II, 577
Laws, Elijah, Jr. II, 577
Laws, Elijah, Jr. II, 888
Laws, Elizabeth II, 577
Laws, Esq. John II, 880
Laws, George W. II, 577
Laws, George Washington II, 577
Laws, James II, 888
Laws, John II, 577
Laws, John M. II, 577
Laws, John May II, 577
Laws, Ludowick II, 577
Laws, Ludowick III, 201
Laws, Ludwick II, 577
Laws, Lydia II, 388
Laws, Lydia II, 577
Laws, Mary II, 388
Laws, Mary II, 577
Laws, Mary II, 785
Laws, Mary II, 818
Laws, Mary II, 844
Laws, Mary II, 917
Laws, Mary Ann III, 201
Laws, Melsom II, 751
Laws, Melson II, 577
Laws, Phebe H. III, 201
Laws, Phebe H. III, 218
Laws, Thomas II, 577
Laws, Thomas III, 201
Laws, Thomas III, 218
Laws, Wm. II, 577
Lawson, ??? III, 34
Lawson, ??? III, 37
Lawson, Agnes IV, 948
Lawson, Alfred IV, 640
Lawson, Caroline IV, 640
Lawson, Catharine V, 690
Lawson, Cornelius IV, 640
Lawson, Elizabeth III, 183
Lawson, Elizabeth VI, 328
Lawson, Elizabeth VI, 335
Lawson, Elizabeth M. III, 37
Lawson, Emma III, 183
Lawson, Emma V, 1006
Lawson, Emma L. III, 201
Lawson, Frances VI, 328
Lawson, Harvey IV, 640
Lawson, Jesse I, 942
Lawson, Jesse I, 945
Lawson, John II, 577
Lawson, John IV, 948
Lawson, John VI, 328
Lawson, Kate V, 690
Lawson, Keziah VI, 946
Lawson, Lettie I, 942
Lawson, Lettie I, 945
Lawson, Lillie H. I, 929
Lawson, Lydia IV, 1372
Lawson, Lydia IV, 1379
Lawson, Mary II, 517
Lawson, Mary II, 577
Lawson, Mary IV, 948
Lawson, Matthew U. B. III, 183
Lawson, Patty Ann IV, 640
Lawson, Wd. ??? III, 201
Lawson, Wd. Elizabeth W. III, 201
Lawson, William IV, 640
Lawton, Abigail III, 114
Lawton, Abigail III, 201
Lawton, Abraham III, 76
Lawton, Abraham III, 96
Lawton, Abraham III, 202
Lawton, Abraham A. III, 201
Lawton, Albert III, 201
Lawton, Albert VI, 721
Lawton, Albert R. III, 201
Lawton, Albert R. III, 202
Lawton, Albert R. III, 361
Lawton, Albert R. III, 365
Lawton, Alfred III, 201
Lawton, Amelia III, 201
Lawton, Augustus III, 201
Lawton, Catharine III, 201
Lawton, Charles III, 102
Lawton, Charles III, 201
Lawton, Charles III, 202
Lawton, Charles Haviland IV, 1372
Lawton, Charles, Jr. III, 201
Lawton, Chas. III, 202
Lawton, Eliza B. III, 353
Lawton, Eliza W. III, 424
Lawton, Elizabeth III, 201
Lawton, Elizabeth III, 202
Lawton, Elizabeth III, 353
Lawton, Elizabeth III, 361
Lawton, Elizabeth III, 365
Lawton, Elizabeth A. D. VI, 832
Lawton, Elizabeth C. III, 202
Lawton, Emily E. VI, 721
Lawton, Emily W. III, 201
Lawton, Emily W. III, 202
Lawton, Emily W. III, 365
Lawton, Emily W. VI, 670
Lawton, Esther III, 76
Lawton, Esther III, 202
Lawton, George III, 202
Lawton, James IV, 44
Lawton, James IV, 371
Lawton, James IV, 538
Lawton, James IV, 1065
Lawton, James IV, 1372
Lawton, Jane III, 167
Lawton, Jane III, 352
Lawton, Jesse IV, 44
Lawton, Jesse IV, 1065
Lawton, Jesse S. III, 201
Lawton, John II, 388
Lawton, John II, 578
Lawton, John W. III, 201
Lawton, John W. III, 202
Lawton, Joseph G. III, 201
Lawton, Louise M. III, 201
Lawton, Louise Marie III, 202
Lawton, Martha IV, 1372
Lawton, Mary II, 388
Lawton, Mary III, 201
Lawton, Matilda III, 201
Lawton, Naomi II, 791
Lawton, Naomi II, 856
Lawton, Naomi III, 96
Lawton, Naomi III, 202
Lawton, Nicholas II, 578
Lawton, Nicholas Easton II, 578
Lawton, Phebe III, 44
Lawton, Phebe III, 202
Lawton, Phebe P. III, 201
Lawton, Phila IV, 1372
Lawton, Rebecca IV, 44
Lawton, Rebecca IV, 1059
Lawton, Rebecca IV, 1065
Lawton, Rebecca D. III, 201
Lawton, Ruth III, 202
Lawton, Ruth III, 362
Lawton, Sarah II, 237
Lawton, Sarah III, 76
Lawton, Sarah III, 96
Lawton, Sarah III, 202
Lawton, Sarah G. IV, 371
Lawton, Sarah G. IV, 416
Lawton, Sarah H. III, 201
Lawton, Sarah L. IV, 1372
Lawton, Simeon IV, 44
Lawton, Simeon IV, 1065
Lawton, Sophia III, 201
Lawton, Sophia III, 202
Lawton, Susanna IV, 44
Lawton, Susanna IV, 371
Lawton, Susanna IV, 1065
Lawton, Susannah IV, 538
Lawton, Thomas VI, 832
Lawton, Walter III, 201
Lawton, William II, 445
Lawton, William III, 201
Lawton, William III, 202
Lawton, William T. III, 353
Lawton, William T. III, 424
Lawton, Wm. IV, 1372
Lax, Abner VI, 833
Lax, Susanna VI, 833
Lay, Adam IV, 581
Lay, Benjamin II, 578
Lay, Caty VI, 832
Lay, Dora M. IV, 581
Lay, Gideon VI, 258
Lay, Harriet Ann IV, 581
Lay, James II, 578
Lay, Mary II, 578
Lay, Sarah II, 578
Lay, Thomas VI, 832
Lay, William I, 1049
Lay, William IV, 152
Lay, William IV, 416
Laycock, Charles L. II, 783
Laycock, Eliza Hunt II, 783
Laycock, Elizabeth VI, 616
Laycock, Elizabeth VI, 671
Laycock, Gwen II, 558
Laycock, Gwen II, 578
Laycock, John II, 1009
Laycock, Joseph II, 388
Laycock, Mary II, 783
Laycock, Mary II, 785
Laycock, Mary Wyatt II, 783
Laycock, Naomi Passmore II, 783
Laycock, Sarah W. II, 783
Laycock, Thomas II, 783
Laycock, Thomas Vincent II, 783
Laycock, William II, 388
Laycock, William II, 783
Laycock, Wm. II, 558
Laycock, Wm. II, 578
Laycock, Wm. Carpenter II, 783
Laycork, Mary Ann IV, 1169
Layden, ??? I, 29
Layden, John I, 13
Layden, John I, 28
Layden, John W. I, 32
Layden, Luna I, 29
Layden, Nora A. I, 32
Layden, Sarah I, 13
Layden, Sarah E. I, 28
Layden, Sarah E. I, 32
Layman, Alice V, 1006
Layman, Elizabeth V, 1006
Layman, Meriam IV, 733
Layman, Meriam IV, 791
Layman, Miriam IV, 733
Layman, Miriam IV, 791
Laymon, Nellie V, 325
Laymon, Nellie V, 345
Laymon, Stanley R. V, 325
Laymon, Stanley R. V, 345
Layn, Edward P. VI, 932
Layn, Thompson H. VI, 947
Layne, Amanda VI, 838
Layne, Amanda VI, 839
Layne, Ann VI, 832
Layne, Ann G. VI, 838
Layne, Asberry VI, 832
Layne, Carolyn VI, 810
Layne, Cornelius Organ VI, 839
Layne, Curtis VI, 832
Layne, Curtis VI, 859
Layne, David VI, 833
Layne, David VI, 838
Layne, Edward VI, 947
Layne, Elizabeth VI, 833
Layne, Elizabeth VI, 988
Layne, Faris VI, 912
Layne, Faris VI, 963
Layne, Farriss VI, 947
Layne, Harriet VI, 862
Layne, James VI, 832
Layne, James VI, 833
Layne, James VI, 837
Layne, Jane M. VI, 832
Layne, John VI, 833
Layne, John W. VI, 839
Layne, Littleberry VI, 810
Layne, Louisa V. VI, 862
Layne, Ludwell E. VI, 832
Layne, Mahala VI, 833
Layne, Martha VI, 947
Layne, Martha A. VI, 832
Layne, Martha H. VI, 838
Layne, Mary VI, 832
Layne, Mary VI, 850
Layne, Mordecai VI, 257
Layne, Oreson V. VI, 832
Layne, Polly VI, 963

Layne, Rebecca VI, 912
Layne, Rebecca VI, 947
Layne, Sarah A. VI, 832
Layne, Susanna VI, 837
Layrowe, Susannah I, 991
Layton, Albert III, 489
Layton, Baby III, 489
Layton, David III, 403
Layton, David III, 424
Layton, Davie III, 489
Layton, Elbert III, 489
Layton, Ellen M. III, 403
Layton, Ellen M. III, 424
Layton, Emma Leona I, 617
Layton, Hannah III, 489
Layton, Harriet III, 489
Layton, Henrietta III, 489
Layton, Leona I, 620
Layton, Leona I, 633
Layton, Leona I, 636
Layton, Maria III, 489
Layton, Roscoe I, 633
Layton, Roscoe I, 636
Layton, Roy I, 617
Layton, Roy I, 620
Layton, Sarah III, 403
Layton, Sarah III, 424
Layton, Sarah A. III, 489
Layton, Willet III, 489
Lazader, Leah IV, 39
Lazader, Leah IV, 44
Lazarelere, Nicholas Henry III, 198
Lazelere, Charles T. III, 224
Lazelere, Frances W. III, 224
Lazenby, Alex, Jr. VI, 948
Lazenby, Alexander VI, 948
Lazenby, Alexander VI, 958
Lazenby, Annis E. VI, 948
Lazenby, Caroline M. VI, 948
Lazenby, Edward VI, 948
Lazenby, Eliza VI, 1017
Lazenby, Elizabeth F. VI, 948
Lazenby, Frances VI, 948
Lazenby, Geo. W. VI, 901
Lazenby, Geo. W. VI, 973
Lazenby, John VI, 886
Lazenby, John VI, 942
Lazenby, John VI, 948
Lazenby, John VI, 967
Lazenby, Joshua VI, 927
Lazenby, Joshua VI, 948
Lazenby, Joshua VI, 984
Lazenby, Joshua VI, 1012
Lazenby, Keziah VI, 927
Lazenby, Lizzie V, 259
Lazenby, Lucy VI, 948
Lazenby, Lucy VI, 967
Lazenby, Lucy Ann Mary VI, 1003
Lazenby, Mary V, 91
Lazenby, Mary V, 394
Lazenby, Mary V, 410
Lazenby, Mary VI, 989
Lazenby, Mary M. V, 72
Lazenby, Mary M. V, 91
Lazenby, Permelia VI, 948
Lazenby, Rebecca VI, 942
Lazenby, Reizen VI, 948
Lazenby, Rezin VI, 873
Lazenby, Rezin VI, 1003
Lazenby, Robert VI, 989
Lazenby, Ruth VI, 948
Lazenby, Sarah E. V, 259
Lazenby, William R. VI, 948
Le Comte, Julia III, 309
Le Duc, Alex. N. III, 202
Le Duc, John Spencer III, 202
Le Duc, Lewin Bell III, 202
Le Duc, Nannie III, 202
Lea, Ada I, 636
Lea, Ada Elliott I, 636
Lea, Agnes VI, 833
Lea, Alexander III, 202
Lea, Ann II, 575
Lea, Ann II, 578
Lea, Ann II, 790
Lea, Ann V, 259
Lea, Ann V, 345
Lea, Ann VI, 328
Lea, Ann Robeson II, 888
Lea, Anna II, 833
Lea, Anna II, 888
Lea, Anna Massey II, 888
Lea, Anne VI, 328
Lea, Anne Lea VI, 328
Lea, Barbara I, 921
Lea, Byrom VI, 328
Lea, Catharine M. II, 871
Lea, Catharine M. II, 888
Lea, Catharine Moore II, 888
Lea, David Wilson II, 805
Lea, David Wilson II, 888
Lea, Edith Helen III, 202
Lea, Eleanor VI, 328
Lea, Eleanor R. II, 805
Lea, Elender VI, 810
Lea, Elizabeth II, 888
Lea, Elizabeth IV, 97
Lea, Elizabeth V, 259
Lea, Elizabeth V, 345
Lea, Elizabeth V, 917
Lea, Elizabeth VI, 328
Lea, Elizabeth VI, 760
Lea, Elizabeth VI, 782
Lea, Elizabeth H. II, 888
Lea, Elizabeth R. II, 888
Lea, Elizabeth Robeson II, 888
Lea, Elizabeth Starbuck III, 202
Lea, Elizabeth W. II, 888
Lea, Ellen II, 888
Lea, Elvira B. IV, 180
Lea, Elvira B. IV, 237
Lea, Florence II, 805
Lea, Florence Lea II, 888
Lea, Frances II, 888
Lea, Frances Ann VI, 494
Lea, Gideon VI, 328
Lea, Gideon VI, 810
Lea, Gideon VI, 832
Lea, Gideon, Jr. VI, 833
Lea, Hannah II, 578
Lea, Hannah II, 609
Lea, Helen III, 202
Lea, Helen III, 335
Lea, Henry IV, 97
Lea, Henry V, 917
Lea, Henry V, 918
Lea, Henry Tyson III, 202
Lea, I. Gurney V, 345
Lea, Isaac II, 888
Lea, Isaac Elwood I, 245
Lea, James IV, 97
Lea, James V, 917
Lea, Jane I, 245
Lea, Jane P. II, 857
Lea, Jane P. II, 888
Lea, Jane Preston II, 888
Lea, John II, 578
Lea, John III, 202
Lea, John Bentley III, 202
Lea, John Bentley III, 335
Lea, Jonathan G. I, 245
Lea, Joseph II, 578
Lea, Joseph II, 805
Lea, Joseph II, 857
Lea, Joseph II, 888
Lea, Joseph II, 900
Lea, Joseph VI, 801
Lea, Joseph VI, 832
Lea, Joseph VI, 833
Lea, Joseph John Gurney I, 245
Lea, Joseph, Jr. II, 751
Lea, Joseph, Jr. II, 888
Lea, Margery II, 888
Lea, Martha L. II, 840
Lea, Martha L. II, 888
Lea, Martha R. II, 805
Lea, Mary II, 578
Lea, Mary II, 682
Lea, Mary II, 888
Lea, Mary II, 899
Lea, Mary VI, 760
Lea, Mary VI, 781
Lea, Mary VI, 782
Lea, Mary VI, 801
Lea, Mary Ann II, 888
Lea, Mary J. I, 245
Lea, Mary Louisa II, 294
Lea, Milicent I, 245
Lea, Nancy Ann I, 245
Lea, Nathan II, 805
Lea, Nathan II, 888
Lea, Phebe VI, 833
Lea, Rebecca II, 578
Lea, Rebekah II, 578
Lea, Robeson II, 888
Lea, Samuel II, 294
Lea, Samuel II, 578
Lea, Sarah II, 578
Lea, Sarah II, 684
Lea, Sarah II, 810
Lea, Sarah II, 818
Lea, Sarah II, 888
Lea, Sarah II, 900
Lea, Sarah III, 233
Lea, Sarah VI, 832
Lea, Sarah A. II, 857
Lea, Sarah A. II, 888
Lea, Sarah A. II, 900
Lea, Sarah Ann II, 805
Lea, Sarah Ann II, 888
Lea, Sarah L. II, 888
Lea, Susan VI, 832
Lea, Susan M. II, 888
Lea, Susanna II, 578
Lea, Susanna IV, 97
Lea, Susanna V, 913
Lea, Susanna VI, 328
Lea, Susanna Massey II, 888
Lea, Susannah I, 245
Lea, Susannah II, 578
Lea, Susannah II, 805
Lea, Susannah V, 917
Lea, Tatnall II, 888
Lea, Thomas VI, 760
Lea, Thomas G. IV, 97
Lea, Thomas J. VI, 494
Lea, Thos. II, 888
Lea, Thos. T. II, 888
Lea, Uree II, 805
Lea, Uree II, 888
Lea, William I, 404
Lea, William Exum I, 245
Lea, Wm. II, 888
Leach, ??? III, 102
Leach, ??? III, 111
Leach, Achsah E. IV, 733
Leach, Achsah E. IV, 736
Leach, Alice III, 202
Leach, Alice Mary III, 102
Leach, Alice Mary III, 202
Leach, Alonzo H. IV, 733
Leach, Ann II, 445
Leach, Ann V, 509
Leach, Annie L. VI, 670
Leach, Caleb VI, 905
Leach, Caleb VI, 924
Leach, Carra IV, 1256
Leach, Charles IV, 416
Leach, Charles IV, 733
Leach, Charlotte III, 202
Leach, Cornelius IV, 733
Leach, Cush V, 509
Leach, Deborah IV, 416
Leach, Deborah Jane IV, 733
Leach, Della IV, 1256
Leach, Eleanor IV, 733
Leach, Eliza I, 925
Leach, Elizabeth IV, 416
Leach, Emma V, 185
Leach, Emma V, 210
Leach, Eva V, 509
Leach, Frances A. B. VI, 833
Leach, Frances G. VI, 851
Leach, Grace III, 104
Leach, Grace III, 176
Leach, Grant V, 581
Leach, Hannah V, 509
Leach, Hannah Maria IV, 733
Leach, Henry H. VI, 833
Leach, Hugh I, 824
Leach, James A. IV, 733
Leach, James M. III, 202
Leach, Jane IV, 416
Leach, Jane L. IV, 716
Leach, Jane L. IV, 733
Leach, Jeanne H. VI, 819
Leach, John IV, 416
Leach, John IV, 733
Leach, John V, 509
Leach, John B. VI, 670
Leach, John B. VI, 679
Leach, Joseph V, 509
Leach, Lewis IV, 416
Leach, Lewis IV, 733
Leach, Mary IV, 733
Leach, Mary VI, 679
Leach, Mary E. IV, 718
Leach, Mary E. IV, 733
Leach, Mary Frances III, 111
Leach, Mary Frances III, 202
Leach, Mary Jane III, 202
Leach, Merritt III, 202
Leach, Merritt III, 227
Leach, Rebecca IV, 733
Leach, Rosanna I, 891
Leach, Rosanna I, 892
Leach, Ross IV, 416
Leach, Ross IV, 733
Leach, Samuel Y. IV, 733
Leach, Sanford C. IV, 733
Leach, Sarah IV, 733
Leach, Sarah IV, 882
Leach, Sarah VI, 670
Leach, Sarah VI, 679
Leach, Sarah Jane V, 509
Leach, Susan W. III, 202
Leach, Susan W. III, 227
Leach, Susannah IV, 825
Leach, Thomas II, 445
Leach, Thomas IV, 416
Leach, Thomas IV, 733
Leach, Thomas V, 581
Leach, Thomas H. IV, 733
Leach, William III, 202
Leach, William VI, 851
Leach, Wm. IV, 1256
Leach, Wm. N. IV, 1256
Leacock, Godfrey II, 388
Lead, Elizabeth VI, 172
Lead, Elizabeth VI, 173
Lead, Elizabeth VI, 189
Lead, Elizabeth VI, 192
Lead, Huldah VI, 158
Lead, Huldah VI, 189
Lead, James VI, 172
Lead, James VI, 173
Lead, James VI, 174
Lead, James VI, 189
Lead, James VI, 191
Lead, James VI, 192
Lead, James VI, 213
Lead, Jesse VI, 192
Lead, John VI, 149
Lead, John VI, 166
Lead, John VI, 189
Lead, John VI, 191
Lead, John VI, 192
Lead, Judith VI, 159
Lead, Judith VI, 172
Lead, Judith VI, 173
Lead, Judith VI, 189
Lead, Judith VI, 191
Lead, Judith VI, 192
Lead, Lydia VI, 165
Lead, Lydia VI, 167
Lead, Mary VI, 166
Lead, Mary VI, 189
Lead, Mary VI, 191
Lead, Mary VI, 197
Lead, Sarah VI, 183
Lead, Sarah VI, 189
Lead, Ursulah VI, 192
Lead, William VI, 148
Lead, William VI, 159
Lead, William VI, 165
Lead, William VI, 166
Lead, William VI, 172
Lead, William VI, 183
Lead, William VI, 191
Lead, William VI, 192
Lead, William VI, 197
Lead, William Charles VI, 189
Lead, William, Jr. VI, 174
Lead, William, Jr. VI, 191
Lead, William, Jr. VI, 192
Lead, William, Sr. VI, 192
Lead, Wm. VI, 158
Lead, Wm. VI, 189
Lead, Wm. VI, 212
Leadbeater, Agnes III, 202
Leadbeater, Alice VI, 760
Leadbeater, Alice VI, 761
Leadbeater, Anna VI, 747
Leadbeater, Anna VI, 760
Leadbeater, Anna VI, 761
Leadbeater, Edward S. VI, 760
Leadbeater, Elizabeth VI, 169
Leadbeater, John VI, 747
Leadbeater, John VI, 760
Leadbeater, Lucy VI, 760
Leadbeater, Lucy VI, 761
Leadbeater, Mary VI, 760
Leadbeater, Mary P. VI, 747
Leadbeater, Mary P. VI, 760
Leadbeater, Mary P. VI, 779
Leadbeater, Peter III, 202
Leadbeater, Thomas VI, 761
Leadbeater, William VI, 761
Leadbetter, Elizabeth VI, 165
Leadbetter, Elizabeth VI, 196
Leadbetter, Henry VI, 196
Leadbetter, Isaac VI, 196
Leadbetter, Isaac VI, 258
Leadbetter, Jacob VI, 196
Leadbetter, Jacob VI, 258
Leadbetter, Mary VI, 196
Leadbetter, Peter VI, 132
Leadbetter, Sarah IV, 237
Leadge, Addie I, 891
Leadge, Georgia I, 891
Leadom, Ann II, 1010
Leadom, Ann II, 1042
Leadom, Edward II, 578
Leadom, Jesse II, 578
Leadom, Mary II, 578
Leads, Susan II, 294
Leaf, Anna S. V, 918
Leaf, Anna Shearman V, 918
Leaf, Joseph V, 918
Leaf, Joseph Tucker V, 918
Leaf, Lula IV, 733
Leaf, Sarah V, 918
Leaf, Shearman V, 918
League, Ann V, 410
League, Ann V, 429
League, Rebecca I, 1056
League, Sam'l I, 1056
Leahy, Dennis III, 139
Leahy, Dennis III, 202
Leahy, Katharine III, 121
Leahy, Katharine III, 257
Leahy, Mary A. III, 139
Leahy, Minnie Victoria III, 139
Leahy, Minnie Victoria III, 202
Leak, C. Park V, 92
Leak, Cammie I, 621
Leak, David S. I, 929
Leak, Davie S. I, 945
Leak, Elmer I, 621
Leak, J. H. I, 929
Leak, J. Van I, 929
Leak, J. Van I, 945
Leak, M. A. I, 929
Leak, Verda I, 945
Leak, Verna I, 929
Leak, Virginia A. I, 945
Leak, Virginia C. I, 929
Leaka, Alpheus V, 345
Leaka, Elizabeth V, 345
Leaka, Harvey V, 345
Leaka, Jonathan V, 345
Leaka, Lucinda V, 345
Leaka, Lucinda B. V, 345
Leaka, Martha E. V, 345
Leaka, Mary V, 345
Leaka, Milton V, 345
Leaka, Sarah V, 345
Leaka, Sylvanus V, 345
Leake, Mary I, 595
Leake, Mary I, 596
Leakey, Ann I, 394
Leakey, Ann I, 403
Leakey, Elizabeth I, 403
Leakey, Francis I, 991
Leakey, Wm. I, 403
Leaky, Elizabeth V, 259
Leaky, Elizabeth V, 345
Leaming, Edna V, 185
Leaming, Helen V, 185
Leaming, James V, 690
Leaming, Lydia V, 690
Leaming, Lydia H. V, 690
Leaming, Lydia H. V, 918
Leaming, Margaret V, 185
Leaming, Ralph V, 185
Leaming, Samuel V, 690
Leaming, Sarah V, 185
Leamon, Levina V, 509
Leamon, Levina V, 529
Lean, Elizabeth II, 388
Lean, Mary II, 388
Lean, Robert II, 388
Leaper, Emma IV, 1039
Leaper, Ida IV, 1039
Leaper, William IV, 1039
Lear, Elizabeth A. VI, 994
Lear, Joseph II, 949
Lear, Joseph VI, 891
Lear, Joseph VI, 927
Lear, Joseph VI, 958
Lear, Joseph VI, 965
Lear, Joseph VI, 994
Lear, Low V, 410
Lear, Winnie V, 410
Lear, Zimri V, 410
Learning, Joseph S. V, 185
Learning, Mary V, 185
Learning, Ralph P. V, 185
Learning, Ralph S. V, 185
Lease, Anna V, 770
Lease, Calvin V, 770
Lease, Clyde Henry V, 770
Lease, Cora V, 770
Lease, David V, 770
Lease, Edward V, 770
Lease, Edward, Sr. V, 770
Lease, Elwood C. V, 770
Lease, Esther Ann V, 770
Lease, Jemima Cox V, 770
Lease, Laura E. V, 770
Lease, Lindley V, 770
Lease, Louisa V, 751
Lease, Louisa V, 769
Lease, Martha M. V, 770
Lease, Mary V, 770
Lease, Merle V, 770
Lease, Minerva V, 770
Lease, Minnie V, 770
Lease, Nora E. V, 770
Lease, Reuben V, 770
Lease, Rhoda J. V, 770
Lease, Susan M. V, 770
Leaser, Hattie Inwood IV, 1325

aser, Wm. V, 1006
ash, Anna VI, 904
ash, Jacob VI, 904
asley, David II, 237
ason, Mary VI, 849
asure, Alonzo V, 459
asure, James V, 1006
atherberry, Jacob IV, 733
atherberry, Neva IV, 733
atherberry, Rosa IV, 733
atherbury, Thomas VI, 11
atus, Daniel I Sup 1, 7
avens, Emuel V, 1006
aver, Hannah II, 178
aver, Hannah II, 279
aver, Hannah II, 294
aver, Lucy Ann II, 279
aver, Lucy Ann II, 294
aver, William II, 279
aver, William II, 294
avering, Esther L. IV, 1202
avering, Esther L. IV, 1215
avering, Griffith IV, 1202
avering, Griffith IV, 1215
avering, Rachel Ann IV, 1215
avering, Thomas IV, 1215
averton, Alice V, 459
averton, Edgar E. V, 259
averton, Ella V, 259
averton, Eva V, 259
averton, George W. V, 345
averton, Grace V, 459
averton, Hattie V, 345
averton, Helen Louise V, 259
averton, Hubert V, 259
averton, Jessie V, 259
averton, John V, 259
averton, John V, 345
averton, Joseph V, 259
averton, Lavina V, 459
averton, Lavinia M. V, 459
averton, Mamie V, 259
averton, Mamie Ridgeway V, 345
averton, Mary V, 259
averton, Mrs. Jessie V, 259
averton, Stanley V, 259
avey, Bertha C. III, 202
avey, Bertha C. III, 367
avey, Rose III, 202
avey, Rose III, 367
avey, Samuel III, 202
avey, Samuel III, 367
avitt, ??? III, 356
avitt, Amelia III, 382
avitt, G. Howland III, 382
avitt, Sarah E. III, 202
avitt, Sarah E. III, 356
avitt, Sarah H. III, 382
aware, John III, 367
er, Alma III, 33
er, Alma III, 202
er, Edward III, 202
er, Gertrude IV, 733
er, Lilla Christiana IV, 1325
er, Mathilde C. III, 202
er, Robert Edward III, 33
er, Robert Edward III, 202
lanc, Louise III, 99
lanc, Louise III, 238
aust, ??? III, 202
kee, William VI, 795
kenby, Alfred B. I, 557
kenby, Alfred B. VI, 258
kie, Ann VI, 823
kie, Clarissa L. L. VI, 817
kie, Elizabeth S. VI, 833
kie, Sarah VI, 826
kie, Susan VI, 826
kie, William VI, 823
kie, William VI, 826
kie, William VI, 833
olie, Adam Lewis II, 578
olie, Mary II, 578
better, A. E. I, 636
better, Albion I, 636
better, Alice I, 636
better, Alice I, 642
better, Alice Cordelia I, 620
better, Alice Cordelia I, 824
better, Alice L. I, 627
better, Alvira I, 613
better, Anna I, 824
better, Anna I, 826
better, Arthur A. I, 824
better, Arthur Albion I, 620
better, Arthur Albion I, 824
better, Arthur E. I, 627
better, Arthur E. I, 808
better, Arthur E. I, 824
better, Arthur Erastus I, 620
Ledbetter, Coleman VI, 803
Ledbetter, Cordelia I, 636
Ledbetter, Erastis A. I, 824
Ledbetter, Erastus A. I, 613
Ledbetter, Erastus Adams I, 620
Ledbetter, Florence Elliott I, 620
Ledbetter, Florence Elliott I, 824
Ledbetter, Harriet W. VI, 833
Ledbetter, Joseph VI, 803
Ledbetter, Joseph VI, 851
Ledbetter, Joseph VI, 948
Ledbetter, Judith VI, 803
Ledbetter, Laurra Alice I, 613
Ledbetter, Lottie Leigh I, 620
Ledbetter, Lottie Leigh I, 636
Ledbetter, Luraney VI, 803
Ledbetter, Martha VI, 864
Ledbetter, Mary A. VI, 833
Ledbetter, Mary R. VI, 819
Ledbetter, Merbert W. VI, 833
Ledbetter, N. Alvira I, 824
Ledbetter, Nancy VI, 851
Ledbetter, Nancy Alvira I, 620
Ledbetter, Peter VI, 137
Ledbetter, Phebe I, 824
Ledbetter, Phebe I, 921
Ledbetter, R. Cordelia I, 627
Ledbetter, R. Cordelia I, 636
Ledbetter, R. Cordelia I, 808
Ledbetter, R. Cordelia I, 824
Ledbetter, Rhoda C. I, 824
Ledbetter, Rhoda Cordelia I, 620
Ledbetter, Rufus VI, 913
Ledbetter, Rufus VI, 918
Ledbetter, Rufus VI, 928
Ledbetter, Rufus VI, 937
Ledbetter, Rufus VI, 978
Ledbetter, Rufus VI, 992
Ledbetter, Rufus VI, 1013
Ledbetter, Samuel W. VI, 833
Ledbetter, Susanna VI, 948
Leddon, Abraham II, 388
Leddon, Elizabeth II, 350
Leddon, James II, 350
Leddon, Mary II, 350
Lederer, John VI, 289
Ledford, Elizabeth I, 912
Ledford, Elizabeth I, 913
Ledom, Jeese II, 578
Ledom, Mary II, 578
Ledwell, Benjamin C. I, 724
Ledwell, Elizabeth I, 717
Ledwell, Elizabeth I, 724
Ledwell, Elwood I, 724
Lee, ??? I, 1139
Lee, Abbie IV, 1039
Lee, Abel T. IV, 734
Lee, Abel T. IV, 975
Lee, Abet T. IV, 734
Lee, Abigail I, 358
Lee, Abigail I, 383
Lee, Abigail I, 404
Lee, Abigail I, 724
Lee, Abigail I, 765
Lee, Abigail VI, 412
Lee, Abraham B. III, 424
Lee, Achsa M. I, 750
Lee, Ada I, 620
Lee, Ada I, 626
Lee, Ada I, 636
Lee, Ada E. I, 636
Lee, Ada E. I, 1157
Lee, Ada Elliott I, 636
Lee, Ada Elliott I, 1144
Lee, Ada Elliott V, 690
Lee, Adeline S. VI, 948
Lee, Agness VI, 881
Lee, Albert IV, 1284
Lee, Alexander VI, 833
Lee, Alexander VI, 957
Lee, Alexander VI, 1016
Lee, Allen IV, 909
Lee, Allen IV, 1104
Lee, Allen T. IV, 530
Lee, Allen T. IV, 538
Lee, Allen T. IV, 576
Lee, Allen T. IV, 585
Lee, Allen T. IV, 1101
Lee, Allen T. IV, 1104
Lee, Allen Thomas IV, 1104
Lee, Almary C. VI, 948
Lee, Almira IV, 1215
Lee, Alva W. IV, 975
Lee, Alvah W. IV, 734
Lee, Amanda IV, 530
Lee, Amanda IV, 538
Lee, Amanda IV, 909
Lee, Amanda IV, 1101
Lee, Amanda IV, 1104
Lee, Amanda H. IV, 909
Lee, Amanda H. IV, 1104
Lee, Amanda H. VI, 948
Lee, Amanda R. IV, 734
Lee, Amanda R. IV, 975
Lee, Amanda T. IV, 538
Lee, Amelia VI, 948
Lee, Amy II, 995
Lee, Amy II, 1009
Lee, Amy IV, 186
Lee, Amy S. III, 424
Lee, Andrew VI, 833
Lee, Angaline IV, 733
Lee, Angelina IV, 734
Lee, Angelina IV, 760
Lee, Angelina C. VI, 796
Lee, Angeline IV, 734
Lee, Ann I, 449
Lee, Ann I, 675
Lee, Ann I, 683
Lee, Ann I, 750
Lee, Ann I, 765
Lee, Ann I, 1157
Lee, Ann II, 388
Lee, Ann II, 578
Lee, Ann II, 677
Lee, Ann VI, 807
Lee, Ann VI, 825
Lee, Anna I, 702
Lee, Anna I, 724
Lee, Anna I, 1158
Lee, Anna IV, 734
Lee, Anna IV, 1284
Lee, Anna C. IV, 1091
Lee, Anna C. IV, 1104
Lee, Anna Jenette IV, 1039
Lee, Anna M. IV, 733
Lee, Anne I, 358
Lee, Anne I, 449
Lee, Annie I, 929
Lee, Annie I, 945
Lee, Annie IV, 734
Lee, Annie VI, 60
Lee, Annie VI, 75
Lee, Anthony VI, 385
Lee, Anthony VI, 412
Lee, Anthony, Jr. VI, 412
Lee, Armella I, 750
Lee, Avey VI, 932
Lee, Avey VI, 980
Lee, Barnett, Jr. VI, 830
Lee, Bernice III, 32
Lee, Bessie I, 1158
Lee, Betsy VI, 833
Lee, Beverley VI, 948
Lee, Beverly VI, 932
Lee, Bricely O. IV, 1039
Lee, Bridget I, 683
Lee, Bridget I, 750
Lee, Bridget I, 755
Lee, Bridget B. I, 755
Lee, Bridget B. I, 765
Lee, Bridget B. I, 869
Lee, Bridget B. I, 891
Lee, Burwel VI, 796
Lee, Burwel VI, 809
Lee, Burwel VI, 832
Lee, Burwel, Sr. VI, 796
Lee, Burwell VI, 805
Lee, Burwell VI, 833
Lee, Burwell VI, 865
Lee, Burwell VI, 866
Lee, Burwell VI, 948
Lee, C. F. I, 1158
Lee, Caroline A. III, 424
Lee, Catharine II, 710
Lee, Celia VI, 833
Lee, Charles I, 945
Lee, Charles II, 578
Lee, Charles II, 710
Lee, Charles M. VI, 1016
Lee, Charles O. I, 1157
Lee, Charlotte VI, 948
Lee, Chas. F. I, 1158
Lee, Chas. Fredric I, 1144
Lee, Chas. M. II, 784
Lee, Christina I, 891
Lee, Corda I, 1157
Lee, Cordelia Belle I, 1152
Lee, Cordelia Belle I, 1157
Lee, Cordie Bell I, 1144
Lee, Cynthia IV, 538
Lee, Cynthia IV, 585
Lee, Cynthia IV, 901
Lee, Cynthia IV, 1065
Lee, Cynthia IV, 1103
Lee, Cynthia IV, 1104
Lee, Daniel II, 975
Lee, Daniel II, 983
Lee, Daniel II, 1009
Lee, Daniel B. Anderson I, 891
Lee, David Wilson II, 888
Lee, David Wilson IV, 1169
Lee, Debby VI, 412
Lee, Debby VI, 452
Lee, Deborah II, 963
Lee, Deborah III, 454
Lee, Deborah VI, 412
Lee, Deborah VI, 456
Lee, Deborah Susan M. VI, 412
Lee, Deborah T. III, 202
Lee, Delila VI, 833
Lee, Delilah I, 477
Lee, Delilah I, 482
Lee, Delilah I, 750
Lee, Delilah I, 765
Lee, Dorothy B. IV, 1372
Lee, Edward III, 202
Lee, Edward P. VI, 833
Lee, Effie I, 1157
Lee, Eleanor II, 751
Lee, Eleanor VI, 412
Lee, Elen VI, 412
Lee, Elias H. I, 1144
Lee, Elias H. I, 1157
Lee, Elihu M. I, 1144
Lee, Elihu M. I, 1157
Lee, Eliza J. IV, 416
Lee, Eliza J. IV, 1170
Lee, Eliza Jane IV, 416
Lee, Eliza Jane IV, 417
Lee, Eliza Jane IV, 448
Lee, Eliza Jane IV, 1169
Lee, Elizabeth I, 445
Lee, Elizabeth I, 449
Lee, Elizabeth I, 683
Lee, Elizabeth I, 687
Lee, Elizabeth I, 724
Lee, Elizabeth I, 765
Lee, Elizabeth I, 1123
Lee, Elizabeth I, 1157
Lee, Elizabeth II, 491
Lee, Elizabeth II, 578
Lee, Elizabeth II, 1009
Lee, Elizabeth III, 202
Lee, Elizabeth III, 272
Lee, Elizabeth IV, 416
Lee, Elizabeth IV, 901
Lee, Elizabeth IV, 1169
Lee, Elizabeth V, 827
Lee, Elizabeth V, 850
Lee, Elizabeth VI, 412
Lee, Elizabeth VI, 420
Lee, Elizabeth VI, 760
Lee, Elizabeth VI, 832
Lee, Elizabeth VI, 833
Lee, Elizabeth VI, 1020
Lee, Elizabeth A. IV, 1091
Lee, Elizabeth A. IV, 1104
Lee, Elizabeth Ann IV, 1065
Lee, Elizabeth B. IV, 416
Lee, Elizabeth B. IV, 1169
Lee, Elizabeth B. IV, 1170
Lee, Elizabeth E. II, 710
Lee, Elizabeth H. II, 888
Lee, Elizabeth H. II, 890
Lee, Elizabeth N. VI, 893
Lee, Elizabeth S. III, 482
Lee, Elizabeth S. III, 489
Lee, Elizabeth S. VI, 948
Lee, Elizabeth U. II, 710
Lee, Elizabeth W. II, 888
Lee, Elizabeth W. IV, 1169
Lee, Ellen I, 677
Lee, Ellen I, 683
Lee, Ellen IV, 777
Lee, Ellen VI, 366
Lee, Ellen VI, 412
Lee, Ellen C. I, 683
Lee, Ellen Christena I, 750
Lee, Ellen Dodge IV, 1326
Lee, Ellis P. IV, 416
Lee, Ellis P. IV, 417
Lee, Elma IV, 959
Lee, Elma IV, 975
Lee, Elma E. IV, 734
Lee, Elma E. IV, 975
Lee, Elma Elizabeth IV, 1104
Lee, Elmira Jane IV, 733
Lee, Elmira Jane IV, 734
Lee, Elvira VI, 948
Lee, Elvira B. IV, 237
Lee, Elvira B. IV, 483
Lee, Emily C. I, 765
Lee, Emily C. I, 824
Lee, Emily Corrinna I, 750
Lee, Emma E. IV, 1104
Lee, Ephragm I, 765
Lee, Ephraim I, 358
Lee, Ephraim I, 683
Lee, Ephraim I, 750
Lee, Ephraim I, 765
Lee, Ephraim I, 869
Lee, Ephraim I, 870
Lee, Ephraim I, 891
Lee, Ephraim I, 1121
Lee, Ephraim I, 1123
Lee, Ephraim I, 1144
Lee, Ephraim I, 1157
Lee, Ephraim I, 1158
Lee, Ephraim I, 1163
Lee, Ephraim P. I, 1157
Lee, Ephraim Penrose IV, 734
Lee, Ephraim Perry I, 1144
Lee, Ephraim W. I, 1157
Lee, Ephraim Wayne I, 1144
Lee, Ephraim, Jr. I, 1144
Lee, Ephraim, Jr. I, 1157
Lee, Ephriam I, 1137
Lee, Esther I, 557
Lee, Esther IV, 1065
Lee, Esther C. II, 703
Lee, Esther C. IV, 1103
Lee, Esther C. IV, 1104
Lee, Eugenia III, 489
Lee, Eva IV, 1284
Lee, Evelyn IV, 237
Lee, Ezra H. I, 1144
Lee, Ezra Rodolphus I, 1157
Lee, F. L. VI, 863
Lee, Frances C. VI, 1016
Lee, Frances S. J. VI, 948
Lee, Frances T. VI, 796
Lee, Francis VI, 948
Lee, Francis L. VI, 948
Lee, Francis L. VI, 964
Lee, Franklin I, 1144
Lee, Fred V, 1006
Lee, Frederick III, 489
Lee, Garnet VI, 833
Lee, Garnett VI, 881
Lee, Garnett VI, 948
Lee, Garnett VI, 975
Lee, George VI, 833
Lee, George W. III, 202
Lee, George W. III, 315
Lee, George W. III, 482
Lee, George W. III, 489
Lee, George W. VI, 795
Lee, Glenn V, 1006
Lee, Gomery Williams I, 1157
Lee, Grace IV, 1256
Lee, Greenville S. I, 1144
Lee, Gurney IV, 1256
Lee, Gurney J. IV, 1256
Lee, Guy VI, 833
Lee, Hannah I, 1144
Lee, Hannah I, 1155
Lee, Hannah I, 1157
Lee, Hannah II, 388
Lee, Hannah II, 578
Lee, Hannah II, 710
Lee, Hannah IV, 682
Lee, Hannah IV, 733
Lee, Hannah IV, 734
Lee, Hannah Boon IV, 733
Lee, Hannah Boone IV, 734
Lee, Hannah G. IV, 734
Lee, Hannah M. IV, 734
Lee, Harriet Ann IV, 416
Lee, Harriet Ann IV, 1169
Lee, Harriet E. VI, 821
Lee, Harriett Ann IV, 1163
Lee, Harriett Ann IV, 1169
Lee, Harriett Ann IV, 1170
Lee, Helen III, 202
Lee, Helen III, 315
Lee, Henry H. III, 424
Lee, Henry M. IV, 734
Lee, Henry S. III, 424
Lee, Hetty A. I, 1157
Lee, I. G. IV, 1215
Lee, I. Gurney IV, 1039
Lee, I. Gurney V, 345
Lee, Ida IV, 1256
Lee, Ida J. IV, 1215
Lee, Ida Johnson IV, 1039
Lee, Isaac I, 358
Lee, Isaac I, 404
Lee, Isaac I, 477
Lee, Isaac I, 482
Lee, Isaac I, 667
Lee, Isaac I, 683
Lee, Isaac I, 724
Lee, Isaac I, 750
Lee, Isaac I, 765
Lee, Isaac I, 891
Lee, Isaac II, 888
Lee, Isaac IV, 1169
Lee, Isaac VI, 412
Lee, Isaac Elwood I, 245
Lee, Isaac G. I, 750
Lee, Isaac W. IV, 1104
Lee, Isaac, Jr. I, 724
Lee, Iscoh I, 750

Lee, Israel IV, 734
Lee, Jacob I, 750
Lee, Jacob??? I, 750
Lee, James II, 710
Lee, James IV, 1065
Lee, James IV, 1104
Lee, James VI, 807
Lee, James G. VI, 881
Lee, James G. VI, 943
Lee, James G. VI, 949
Lee, James Oliver I, 1144
Lee, Jane I, 245
Lee, Jane I, 358
Lee, Jane I, 404
Lee, Jane I, 449
Lee, Jane I, 452
Lee, Jane IV, 1169
Lee, Jane VI, 866
Lee, Jane C. II, 281
Lee, Jane C. II, 294
Lee, Jeptha W. I, 1144
Lee, Jeremiah IV, 734
Lee, Jesse IV, 734
Lee, Joan II, 388
Lee, Joan II, 445
Lee, John I, 358
Lee, John I, 702
Lee, John I, 724
Lee, John I, 1123
Lee, John I, 1144
Lee, John I, 1157
Lee, John I, 1158
Lee, John II, 388
Lee, John II, 578
Lee, John II, 677
Lee, John II, 983
Lee, John II, 988
Lee, John II, 1009
Lee, John III, 202
Lee, John IV, 1169
Lee, John VI, 412
Lee, John VI, 805
Lee, John VI, 809
Lee, John VI, 825
Lee, John VI, 832
Lee, John VI, 833
Lee, John E. IV, 416
Lee, John E. IV, 1169
Lee, John E. IV, 1170
Lee, John Ezra I, 1157
Lee, John Hackney I, 1158
Lee, John Preston IV, 734
Lee, John S. I, 1144
Lee, John Wesley I, 750
Lee, John, II I, 358
Lee, Jonathan I, 218
Lee, Jonathan I, 765
Lee, Jonathan I, 1144
Lee, Jonathan IV, 585
Lee, Jonathan G. I, 218
Lee, Jonathan G. I, 245
Lee, Jonathan G. I, 750
Lee, Jonathan G. I, 765
Lee, Joseph I, 482
Lee, Joseph I, 675
Lee, Joseph I, 683
Lee, Joseph I, 724
Lee, Joseph I, 750
Lee, Joseph I, 765
Lee, Joseph II, 578
Lee, Joseph III, 202
Lee, Joseph III, 454
Lee, Joseph John Gurney I, 218
Lee, Joseph John Gurney I, 245
Lee, Joseph Moore I, 750
Lee, Joseph, Jr. II, 751
Lee, Joshua Boon IV, 733
Lee, Joshua Boone IV, 734
Lee, Josiah IV, 733
Lee, Josiah IV, 734
Lee, Joyce VI, 760
Lee, Judith A. VI, 833
Lee, Keziah I, 750
Lee, Keziah I, 765
Lee, Lafayett VI, 948
Lee, Lawrence II, 388
Lee, Leah H. VI, 412
Lee, Leah H. VI, 452
Lee, Levi VI, 833
Lee, Levi VI, 837
Lee, Levi B. IV, 416
Lee, Levi B. IV, 1169
Lee, Lewis Orlando I, 1157
Lee, Liberty VI, 833
Lee, Louisa L. I, 765
Lee, Lucella Wilson IV, 1169
Lee, Lucella Wilson IV, 1174
Lee, Lucinda I, 1144
Lee, Lucinda I, 1157
Lee, Lucinda I, 1160
Lee, Lucy VI, 865
Lee, Lucy Wilson IV, 1169
Lee, Luther B. III, 482
Lee, Luther B. III, 489
Lee, Lydia II, 710
Lee, Lydia IV, 416
Lee, Lydia IV, 435
Lee, Lydia IV, 585
Lee, Lydia IV, 734
Lee, Lydia A. VI, 833
Lee, Lydia C. IV, 1104
Lee, Lydia Emma IV, 734
Lee, Lydia Jane I, 750
Lee, M. Ada E. I, 824
Lee, M. Ada Elliot I, 1157
Lee, Mabel I, 1158
Lee, Margaret I, 702
Lee, Margaret II, 710
Lee, Margaret II, 983
Lee, Margaret II, 1009
Lee, Margaret IV, 416
Lee, Margaret IV, 585
Lee, Margaret IV, 734
Lee, Margaret C. III, 489
Lee, Margaret Chrisman IV, 733
Lee, Margaret E. III, 482
Lee, Margaret E. IV, 734
Lee, Margery II, 888
Lee, Martha I, 358
Lee, Martha II, 578
Lee, Martha II, 710
Lee, Martha Aleson IV, 733
Lee, Martha E. IV, 416
Lee, Martha E. IV, 1169
Lee, Martha E. IV, 1170
Lee, Martitia I, 750
Lee, Martitia E. I, 683
Lee, Mary I, 404
Lee, Mary I, 702
Lee, Mary I, 713
Lee, Mary I, 724
Lee, Mary II, 578
Lee, Mary II, 963
Lee, Mary II, 975
Lee, Mary II, 1009
Lee, Mary III, 202
Lee, Mary III, 424
Lee, Mary IV, 237
Lee, Mary IV, 576
Lee, Mary IV, 585
Lee, Mary IV, 682
Lee, Mary IV, 734
Lee, Mary IV, 923
Lee, Mary IV, 975
Lee, Mary IV, 1053
Lee, Mary IV, 1104
Lee, Mary VI, 412
Lee, Mary VI, 437
Lee, Mary VI, 760
Lee, Mary VI, 840
Lee, Mary A. VI, 833
Lee, Mary Ann I, 1144
Lee, Mary Ann II, 888
Lee, Mary Ann IV, 1169
Lee, Mary B. III, 424
Lee, Mary B. VI, 948
Lee, Mary C. E. VI, 948
Lee, Mary E. IV, 585
Lee, Mary E. IV, 1104
Lee, Mary Elizabeth IV, 733
Lee, Mary Elizabeth IV, 734
Lee, Mary Ella I, 750
Lee, Mary J. I, 245
Lee, Mary J. I, 249
Lee, Mary Jane I, 218
Lee, Mary Jane VI, 865
Lee, Mary L. II, 281
Lee, Mary L. II, 294
Lee, Mary Louisa II, 294
Lee, Mary P. II, 710
Lee, Mary P. IV, 734
Lee, Mary R. IV, 734
Lee, Mary R. IV, 975
Lee, Mary Susanna I, 218
Lee, Mary W. IV, 1170
Lee, Mary W. IV, 1215
Lee, Matilda VI, 825
Lee, Matilda VI, 833
Lee, Maud I, 945
Lee, Michael I, 358
Lee, Mildred VI, 833
Lee, Mildred A. VI, 881
Lee, Milicent I, 218
Lee, Milicent I, 245
Lee, Milison I, 765
Lee, Miller VI, 833
Lee, Millicen I, 765
Lee, Mollie IV, 1238
Lee, Mordecai IV, 734
Lee, Mordica IV, 975
Lee, Moses A. VI, 833
Lee, Mylercent I, 234
Lee, Mylercent I, 245
Lee, Nancy I, 482
Lee, Nancy I, 750
Lee, Nancy I, 765
Lee, Nancy I, 1157
Lee, Nancy VI, 871
Lee, Nancy VI, 948
Lee, Nancy VI, 980
Lee, Nancy Ann I, 218
Lee, Nancy Ann I, 245
Lee, Nancy Ann I, 765
Lee, Nancy E. VI, 863
Lee, Nancy E. VI, 864
Lee, Nancy G. I, 750
Lee, Nancy L. I, 765
Lee, Nannie I, 1157
Lee, Nannie Effie I, 1157
Lee, Naomi I, 765
Lee, Nathan I, 358
Lee, Nathan I, 702
Lee, Nathan I, 1123
Lee, Nathan I, 1157
Lee, Nathan II, 888
Lee, Nathan IV, 1169
Lee, Nathaniel IV, 975
Lee, Norman III, 202
Lee, Omar S. IV, 734
Lee, Omar S. IV, 975
Lee, Omer S. IV, 975
Lee, P. F. Stanley I, 636
Lee, Pamelia VI, 809
Lee, Patience I, 404
Lee, Patience I, 449
Lee, Patience I, 667
Lee, Patience I, 683
Lee, Patience I, 724
Lee, Patience I, 750
Lee, Patience I, 765
Lee, Patsey VI, 957
Lee, Peggy VI, 833
Lee, Phebe I, 460
Lee, Phebe I, 750
Lee, Phebe I, 755
Lee, Phebe I, 765
Lee, Phebe E. IV, 416
Lee, Phebe E. IV, 1169
Lee, Phebe E. IV, 1170
Lee, Polly VI, 833
Lee, Polly VI, 948
Lee, Preston IV, 733
Lee, Rachel I, 683
Lee, Rachel I, 702
Lee, Rachel I, 719
Lee, Rachel I, 724
Lee, Rachel I, 765
Lee, Rachel I, 1123
Lee, Rachel Ann I, 683
Lee, Rachel Ann I, 750
Lee, Rachel N. IV, 416
Lee, Rachel N. IV, 1169
Lee, Rachel N. IV, 1170
Lee, Rachel R. II, 294
Lee, Rachel R. II, 302
Lee, Ralph II, 995
Lee, Ralph II, 1009
Lee, Rebecca II, 578
Lee, Rebecca II, 713
Lee, Rebecca II, 995
Lee, Rebecca II, 1009
Lee, Rebecca IV, 734
Lee, Rebecca IV, 776
Lee, Rebecca IV, 778
Lee, Rebecca VI, 412
Lee, Rebecca VI, 948
Lee, Rebecca J. IV, 733
Lee, Rebecka II, 445
Lee, Rebekah II, 578
Lee, Richard VI, 825
Lee, Richard VI, 926
Lee, Richard VI, 948
Lee, Richard VI, 1020
Lee, Richard H. VI, 833
Lee, Riley Wilson I, 1144
Lee, Robert A. I, 1158
Lee, Rosa E. I, 1158
Lee, Rosa Ethel I, 1144
Lee, Ruth I, 702
Lee, Ruth I, 1121
Lee, Ruth I, 1123
Lee, Ruth I, 1139
Lee, Ruth I, 1144
Lee, Ruth I, 1155
Lee, Ruth I, 1157
Lee, Ruth IV, 416
Lee, Ruth IV, 451
Lee, Ruth Ann IV, 711
Lee, Ruth Ann IV, 734
Lee, Sabella A. IV, 416
Lee, Sabella R. IV, 416
Lee, Salem I, 765
Lee, Sally VI, 948
Lee, Samuel I, 358
Lee, Samuel I, 702
Lee, Samuel I, 724
Lee, Samuel I, 1121
Lee, Samuel I, 1123
Lee, Samuel I, 1157
Lee, Samuel II, 281
Lee, Samuel II, 294
Lee, Samuel II, 388
Lee, Samuel II, 578
Lee, Samuel II, 710
Lee, Samuel II, 963
Lee, Samuel IV, 538
Lee, Samuel IV, 585
Lee, Samuel IV, 901
Lee, Samuel IV, 1065
Lee, Samuel IV, 1103
Lee, Samuel IV, 1104
Lee, Samuel VI, 412
Lee, Samuel G. I, 750
Lee, Sarah I, 1121
Lee, Sarah I, 1123
Lee, Sarah I, 1144
Lee, Sarah I, 1157
Lee, Sarah II, 388
Lee, Sarah II, 445
Lee, Sarah II, 575
Lee, Sarah II, 578
Lee, Sarah II, 988
Lee, Sarah II, 1009
Lee, Sarah III, 202
Lee, Sarah VI, 412
Lee, Sarah Boone II, 707
Lee, Sarah E. I, 1144
Lee, Sarah Ellen IV, 734
Lee, Sarah Ellen IV, 760
Lee, Sarah G. VI, 833
Lee, Sarah J. V, 955
Lee, Sarah J. V, 958
Lee, Sarah L. I, 750
Lee, Sarah P. IV, 416
Lee, Sarah P. IV, 1170
Lee, Sebela A. IV, 1169
Lee, Sebela A. IV, 1170
Lee, Shelley VI, 840
Lee, Silas II, 995
Lee, Silas II, 1009
Lee, Silas W. VI, 833
Lee, Sophia III, 215
Lee, Stephen VI, 825
Lee, Susan L. VI, 833
Lee, Susanna I, 358
Lee, Susanna I, 404
Lee, Susanna I, 415
Lee, Susanna I, 431
Lee, Susanna I, 445
Lee, Susanna I, 449
Lee, Susanna I, 724
Lee, Susanna I, 755
Lee, Susanna I, 765
Lee, Susanna I, 768
Lee, Susanna I, 1123
Lee, Susanna I, 1157
Lee, Susanna II, 578
Lee, Susanna G. VI, 957
Lee, Susannah I, 245
Lee, Susannah I, 667
Lee, Susannah I, 750
Lee, Susannah I, 765
Lee, Susannah II, 578
Lee, Susannah IV, 734
Lee, Susannah IV, 776
Lee, Susannah VI, 805
Lee, Susannah G. VI, 796
Lee, Susie May IV, 1326
Lee, T. B. I, 1158
Lee, T. R. I, 1157
Lee, T. Riley I, 1157
Lee, Tabitha VI, 807
Lee, Tabitha VI, 926
Lee, Theophilus Beesly I, 1144
Lee, Thomas II, 294
Lee, Thomas II, 578
Lee, Thomas II, 710
Lee, Thomas II, 1010
Lee, Thomas IV, 44
Lee, Thomas VI, 412
Lee, Thomas VI, 452
Lee, Thomas VI, 760
Lee, Thomas VI, 807
Lee, Thomas Allen IV, 1104
Lee, Thomas B. IV, 1169
Lee, Thomas Boon IV, 1169
Lee, Thomas J. IV, 1104
Lee, Thomas N. VI, 948
Lee, Thomas Parvin IV, 734
Lee, Thomas R. I, 1157
Lee, Thomas Riley I, 1144
Lee, Thos. Parvin IV, 734
Lee, Thos. R. I, 1144
Lee, Uree II, 888
Lee, Uree Ann IV, 1143
Lee, Uree Ann IV, 1170
Lee, Ury IV, 1169
Lee, Ury Ann IV, 1169
Lee, Vernon III, 32
Lee, Walter IV, 1215
Lee, Walter IV, 1256
Lee, Walter Pinckham IV, 1256
Lee, Wiatt VI, 948
Lee, Widow Bridget B. I, 869
Lee, Widow Bridget B. Anderson I, 870
Lee, William I, 358
Lee, William I, 404
Lee, William I, 415
Lee, William I, 695
Lee, William I, 702
Lee, William I, 724
Lee, William I, 1144
Lee, William I, 1157
Lee, William II, 388
Lee, William II, 445
Lee, William III, 202
Lee, William VI, 796
Lee, William VI, 833
Lee, William VI, 948
Lee, William A. VI, 796
Lee, William A. VI, 833
Lee, William Allen I, 1144
Lee, William Branson I, 750
Lee, William Exum I, 218
Lee, William Exum I, 245
Lee, William G. VI, 918
Lee, William H. VI, 948
Lee, William K. VI, 821
Lee, William Southby II, 388
Lee, William T. I, 1157
Lee, Wm. I, 358
Lee, Wm. I, 404
Lee, Wm. I, 724
Lee, Wm. II, 445
Lee, Wm. II, 578
Lee, Wm. B. I, 683
Lee, Wm. Chandler IV, 1065
Lee, Wm. Forster I, 1144
Lee, Wm. Kendall VI, 865
Lee, Wm. Scarlot IV, 1169
Leech, Alonzo H. IV, 733
Leech, Ann I, 557
Leech, Ann IV, 640
Leech, Ann IV, 876
Leech, Charles IV, 640
Leech, Charles IV, 876
Leech, Cornelius IV, 640
Leech, Cornelius IV, 733
Leech, Cornelius IV, 870
Leech, Cornelius IV, 875
Leech, Cornelius IV, 876
Leech, Deborah IV, 640
Leech, Deborah Jane IV, 876
Leech, Eleanor IV, 733
Leech, Elizabeth IV, 640
Leech, Elizabeth IV, 875
Leech, Elizabeth IV, 876
Leech, Ellan IV, 876
Leech, Ellen IV, 876
Leech, Ellen IV, 909
Leech, Ellen IV, 916
Leech, Ellon IV, 876
Leech, Hambleton IV, 875
Leech, Hannah IV, 640
Leech, Hannah IV, 875
Leech, Hannah IV, 876
Leech, Hannah IV, 886
Leech, Hannah Maria IV, 733
Leech, Hugh I, 557
Leech, Hugh I, 891
Leech, James I, 557
Leech, Jane IV, 608
Leech, Jane IV, 640
Leech, Jane IV, 647
Leech, Jane IV, 656
Leech, Jane IV, 693
Leech, Jane IV, 863
Leech, Jane IV, 873
Leech, Jane IV, 875
Leech, Jane IV, 876
Leech, Jane, Jr. IV, 875
Leech, Jesse James IV, 640
Leech, John I, 557
Leech, John I, 891
Leech, John IV, 640
Leech, John IV, 876
Leech, Lewis J. IV, 876
Leech, Mahlon IV, 640
Leech, Mahlon Hollingsworth IV, 876
Leech, Margaret IV, 635
Leech, Margaret IV, 640
Leech, Margaret IV, 693
Leech, Margaret IV, 873

ech, Margaret IV, 875
ech, Maria IV, 875
ech, Maria IV, 876
ech, Maria IV, 884
ech, Mariah IV, 640
ech, Mary I, 557
ech, Mary II, 388
ech, Mary Catharine IV, 640
ech, Phebe IV, 635
ech, Phebe IV, 640
ech, Phebe IV, 873
ech, Phebe IV, 875
ech, Phebe IV, 876
ech, Phebe IV, 886
ech, Phebe Y. IV, 876
ech, Rachel IV, 876
ech, Rebecca IV, 640
ech, Rebecca IV, 875
ech, Rebecca IV, 876
ech, Rebecca IV, 882
ech, Rosanna I, 891
ech, Rosannah I, 891
ech, Ross IV, 640
ech, Ross IV, 876
ech, Samuel IV, 876
ech, Sanford C. IV, 733
ech, Sarah II, 388
ech, Sarah IV, 640
ech, Sarah IV, 733
ech, Sarah IV, 875
ech, Sarah IV, 876
ech, Sarah IV, 882
ech, Sarah L. IV, 870
ech, Sarah L. IV, 875
ech, Susannah IV, 824
ech, Thomas II, 388
ech, Thomas IV, 640
ech, Thomas IV, 875
ech, Thomas IV, 876
ech, Thomas IV, 909
ech, Thomas IV, 916
ech, Thomas H. IV, 733
ech, William IV, 635
ech, William IV, 640
ech, William IV, 873
ech, William IV, 875
ech, Wm. IV, 608
ech, Wm. IV, 635
ech, Wm. IV, 640
ech, Wm. IV, 863
ech, Wm. IV, 873
ech, Wm. IV, 876
ed, Margaret I, 929
edom, Alice II, 1010
edom, Ann II, 1010
edom, Anna C. E. II, 963
edom, Benjamin II, 983
edom, Benjamin II, 1010
edom, Benjamin I. II, 834
edom, Benjamin I. II, 888
edom, Benjamin J. II, 888
edom, Benjamin J. III, 202
edom, Benjamin Jones II, 805
edom, Benjamin, Jr. II, 1010
edom, Charles II, 888
edom, Charles II, 1054
edom, Charles V, 918
edom, Chas. V, 918
edom, Clara II, 836
edom, Clara II, 888
edom, Clara V, 918
edom, David II, 1054
edom, David R. II, 1054
edom, Edward II, 578
edom, Edward II, 1054
edom, Elijah II, 1010
edom, Elijah II, 1054
edom, Elizabeth II, 850
edom, Elizabeth II, 888
edom, Elizabeth II, 1044
edom, Elizabeth II, 1054
edom, Elizabeth III, 202
edom, Elvira M. II, 888
edom, George F. II, 963
edom, Giles Carolton II, 963
edom, Grace II, 1010
edom, Hannah II, 850
edom, Hannah II, 888
edom, Hannah V, 918
edom, Hannah A. II, 836
edom, Hannah A. II, 888
edom, Hannah A. V, 918
edom, Hannah B. II, 888
edom, Hannah B. III, 202
edom, Hannah Ballinger II, 805
edom, Hayes II, 805
edom, Helen II, 963
edom, Helen II, 1054
edom, Jeese II, 578
edom, Jesse II, 578
Leedom, Jesse II, 1054
Leedom, Jesse T. II, 1054
Leedom, John II, 786
Leedom, John II, 850
Leedom, John II, 888
Leedom, John Moore II, 805
Leedom, John Moore II, 888
Leedom, John Moore III, 202
Leedom, Jonathan II, 578
Leedom, Jonathan II, 710
Leedom, Jonathan II, 834
Leedom, Jonathan II, 888
Leedom, Lewis II, 1054
Leedom, Louis C. II, 963
Leedom, Louis C. II, 1054
Leedom, Lucy II, 1054
Leedom, Lydia II, 578
Leedom, Lydia II, 710
Leedom, Lydia II, 1054
Leedom, Mary II, 578
Leedom, Mary II, 1054
Leedom, Mary W. II, 963
Leedom, Priscilla II, 805
Leedom, Priscilla II, 834
Leedom, Priscilla II, 888
Leedom, Priscilla B. II, 888
Leedom, Priscilla B. III, 202
Leedom, Rachel II, 786
Leedom, Rachel II, 1054
Leedom, Rachel B. II, 823
Leedom, Samuel II, 850
Leedom, Samuel II, 888
Leedom, Sarah II, 710
Leedom, Sarah II, 834
Leedom, Sarah II, 888
Leedom, Sarah III, 46
Leedom, Sarah Coates II, 805
Leedom, Sarah E. II, 805
Leedom, Sarah Jones II, 819
Leedom, Sarah Jones II, 888
Leedom, Susannah II, 983
Leedom, Susannah II, 1010
Leedom, Thomas II, 1054
Leedom, Thomas V, 918
Leedom, Thomas L. II, 888
Leedom, Thos. L. II, 805
Leedom, Thos. L. II, 836
Leedom, Wd. Elvira Matilda II, 805
Leedom, Wd. Ruth Anna II, 786
Leeds, ??? III, 113
Leeds, ??? V, 965
Leeds, Abel II, 311
Leeds, Abigail II, 311
Leeds, Ann II, 137
Leeds, Ann II, 153
Leeds, Ann II, 178
Leeds, Ann II, 238
Leeds, Ann II, 263
Leeds, Ann II, 710
Leeds, Ann II, 888
Leeds, Ann IV, 1372
Leeds, Ann V, 92
Leeds, Ann V, 972
Leeds, Ann C. II, 578
Leeds, Ann C. V, 92
Leeds, Ann C. V, 972
Leeds, Ann E. V, 92
Leeds, Ann E. V, 972
Leeds, Ann L. II, 578
Leeds, Ann L. II, 888
Leeds, Ann L. V, 92
Leeds, Anna V, 91
Leeds, Anna V, 972
Leeds, Anne L. V, 972
Leeds, Augustus V, 92
Leeds, Barclay R. II, 710
Leeds, Benjamin S. VI, 258
Leeds, Beulah VI, 258
Leeds, Caroline H. II, 311
Leeds, Charles II, 388
Leeds, Charles IV, 417
Leeds, Charles H. IV, 1372
Leeds, Charles W. II, 710
Leeds, Charles W. II, 751
Leeds, Craig V, 972
Leeds, Daniel II, 178
Leeds, Daniel II, 238
Leeds, Daniel II, 263
Leeds, Daniel II, 710
Leeds, Deborah III, 202
Leeds, Deborah A. VI, 258
Leeds, Deborah Ann VI, 236
Leeds, Deborah Ann VI, 237
Leeds, Deborah Ann VI, 258
Leeds, Edith R. II, 710
Leeds, Edwin II, 751
Leeds, Eliza IV, 417
Leeds, Eliza T. IV, 417
Leeds, Elizabeth II, 308
Leeds, Elizabeth IV, 639
Leeds, Elizabeth IV, 1372
Leeds, Elizabeth IV, 1386
Leeds, Elizabeth V, 91
Leeds, Elizabeth V, 92
Leeds, Elizabeth B. V, 23
Leeds, Elizabeth B. V, 91
Leeds, Elizabeth B. V, 92
Leeds, Elizabeth B. V, 972
Leeds, Elizabeth H. II, 311
Leeds, Elizabeth H. II, 321
Leeds, Elizabeth L. II, 311
Leeds, Elizabeth L. II, 317
Leeds, Elizabeth L. II, 321
Leeds, Elizabeth L. H. II, 311
Leeds, Elizabeth S. II, 701
Leeds, Elizabeth S. II, 949
Leeds, Ellen II, 294
Leeds, Ellen IV, 929
Leeds, Ellen IV, 975
Leeds, Eugenia H. II, 311
Leeds, Gertrude H. II, 309
Leeds, Gertrude H. II, 311
Leeds, Gideon II, 751
Leeds, Gideon Howard II, 751
Leeds, Granville II, 309
Leeds, Granville II, 311
Leeds, Granville W. II, 311
Leeds, Granville W. II, 321
Leeds, Hannah II, 238
Leeds, Hannah II, 264
Leeds, Hannah II, 888
Leeds, Hannah II, 919
Leeds, Hannah IV, 1372
Leeds, Henry IV, 1372
Leeds, Henry IV, 1385
Leeds, Henry B. IV, 417
Leeds, Henry B. IV, 929
Leeds, Henry B. IV, 975
Leeds, Henry Brown IV, 417
Leeds, Henry H. II, 311
Leeds, Henry H. II, 321
Leeds, J. H. VI, 236
Leeds, Jacob II, 308
Leeds, Jacob II, 311
Leeds, Jacob H. II, 311
Leeds, Jacob H. II, 321
Leeds, Jacob H. II, 327
Leeds, John C. IV, 1372
Leeds, Josiah VI, 237
Leeds, Josiah W. VI, 237
Leeds, Josiah W. VI, 258
Leeds, Josiah Woodward VI, 258
Leeds, Justice Howell II, 710
Leeds, Laetitia Craig II, 578
Leeds, Letitia V, 972
Leeds, Letitia C. V, 972
Leeds, Letitia Craig V, 92
Leeds, Lettitia Craig V, 92
Leeds, Lovisa II, 53
Leeds, Lovisa II, 83
Leeds, Margaret II, 209
Leeds, Margaret II, 238
Leeds, Margaret II, 308
Leeds, Margaret II, 311
Leeds, Margaret II, 388
Leeds, Margaret L. II, 311
Leeds, Margaret L. II, 321
Leeds, Margaret L. II, 327
Leeds, Margaret W. II, 308
Leeds, Margaret W. II, 311
Leeds, Margarit II, 163
Leeds, Margery Ann II, 699
Leeds, Maria III, 415
Leeds, Maria IV, 1372
Leeds, Maria IV, 1385
Leeds, Maria M. III, 113
Leeds, Maria W. VI, 747
Leeds, Maria W. VI, 761
Leeds, Mariana Priscilla IV, 417
Leeds, Mary II, 710
Leeds, Mary B. II, 716
Leeds, Mary H. II, 311
Leeds, Mary H. II, 751
Leeds, Mary L. II, 311
Leeds, Mary L. II, 317
Leeds, Mary L. II, 321
Leeds, Mary M. II, 311
Leeds, Nancie M. II, 321
Leeds, Nancy II, 309
Leeds, Nancy M. II, 311
Leeds, Noah II, 134
Leeds, Noah II, 137
Leeds, Noah II, 153
Leeds, Noah II, 578
Leeds, Noah II, 751
Leeds, Noah II, 888
Leeds, Noah V, 972
Leeds, Noah L. V, 972
Leeds, Phebe II, 321
Leeds, Phebe Ann IV, 1371
Leeds, Phebe Ann IV, 1372
Leeds, Phebe W. II, 311
Leeds, Rebecca II, 710
Leeds, Rebecca S. II, 698
Leeds, Ruth II, 698
Leeds, Ruth IV, 1372
Leeds, Samuel II, 53
Leeds, Samuel II, 83
Leeds, Samuel II, 698
Leeds, Samuel IV, 1372
Leeds, Samuel IV, 1386
Leeds, Samuel T. IV, 1372
Leeds, Samuel, Jr. IV, 1371
Leeds, Samuel, Jr. IV, 1372
Leeds, Sarah II, 238
Leeds, Sarah II, 698
Leeds, Susan II, 294
Leeds, Susanna R. II, 710
Leeds, Susanna R. IV, 417
Leeds, Susannah II, 294
Leeds, Thomas II, 163
Leeds, Thomas II, 209
Leeds, Thomas II, 238
Leeds, Vincent II, 238
Leeds, Vincent II, 264
Leeds, Vincent IV, 830
Leeds, Vincent V, 92
Leeds, Vincent Augustus II, 578
Leeds, Vincent Augustus V, 92
Leeds, Vincent Augustus V, 972
Leeds, Warner V, 92
Leeds, Warner M. V, 91
Leeds, Warner M. V, 92
Leeds, Warner M. V, 972
Leeds, William B. III, 202
Leeds, William B. III, 203
Leeds, William C. V, 92
Leeds, William D. II, 311
Leeds, William W. IV, 1372
Leeds, Wm. II, 751
Leeds, Wm. V, 972
Leeds, Wm. B. V, 972
Leeds, Wm. C. II, 751
Leeds, Wm. Craig II, 888
Leek, Catharine V, 918
Leek, Catherine VI, 526
Leek, Elizabeth IV, 147
Leek, Elizabeth IV, 152
Leek, Elizabeth IV, 1065
Leek, Hannah V, 918
Leek, Hannah Ann IV, 1065
Leek, Hannah M. VI, 526
Leek, Hannah M. VI, 529
Leek, Henry V, 918
Leek, James E. V, 918
Leek, Maria IV, 152
Leek, Philip III, 424
Leek, Philip W. IV, 1065
Leek, Richard V, 918
Leek, Richard VI, 526
Leek, Richard VI, 529
Leek, Sarah B. III, 424
Leek, Wm. V, 918
Leeka, Ada M. V, 690
Leeka, Ada M. V, 721
Leeka, Ernest V, 690
Leeka, Ernest V, 721
Leeka, Martha E. V, 345
Leeka, Martha E. V, 351
Leeka, Mary V, 337
Leeke, Ann IV, 417
Leeke, Ann IV, 434
Leeke, C. Park V, 92
Leeke, Elizabeth IV, 538
Leeke, Elizabeth IV, 539
Leeke, Elizabeth IV, 561
Leeke, Elizabeth IV, 1104
Leeke, Elizabeth D. IV, 1104
Leeke, Elizabeth L. IV, 1118
Leeke, Hannah Ann IV, 538
Leeke, Hannah Ann IV, 1104
Leeke, Hannah Ann IV, 1118
Leeke, Hannah M. V, 92
Leeke, Joseph IV, 417
Leeke, Juliann IV, 530
Leeke, Mariah IV, 434
Leeke, Martha IV, 417
Leeke, Martha IV, 455
Leeke, Philip W. IV, 538
Leeke, Philip W. IV, 539
Leeke, Philip W. IV, 1104
Leeke, Philip W. IV, 1118
Leeke, Rebecca IV, 561
Leeke, Samuel IV, 417
Leeke, Samuel IV, 434
Leeke, Samuel IV, 455
Leeke, Samuel IV, 561
Leeke, Sarah J. V, 92
Leeky, Ruth V, 632
Leeky, Ruth V, 647
Leeming, Geo. L. III, 424
Leeming, Geo. L. III, 471
Leeming, Laura G. F. III, 424
Leeming, Laura G. F. III, 471
Leeming, Laura L. III, 424
Leeming, Laura L. III, 471
Leeper, Anna IV, 1019
Leer, Elizabeth II, 1010
Leera, Sarah V, 345
Lees, Ann III, 203
Lees, Anna III, 203
Lees, Elizabeth II, 578
Lees, Elizabeth II, 805
Lees, Elizabeth II, 888
Lees, Elizabeth IV, 97
Lees, Elizabeth VI, 412
Lees, Joseph II, 578
Lees, Sarah II, 578
Lees, Sarah IV, 238
Lees, Sarah IV, 249
Leese, Mrs. Gertrude IV, 1326
Leese, Sarah IV, 238
Leeson, Betsy VI, 833
Leeson, Michael VI, 833
Leeson, Nancy VI, 809
Leet, Mary III, 33
Leetch, Ann I, 824
Leetch, Hugh I, 824
Leetch, Hugh I, 891
Leetch, James I, 786
Leetch, Jane I, 786
Leetch, John I, 891
Leetch, Mary I, 786
Leetch, Mary I, 824
Leete, Daniel II, 238
Leeth, George VI, 420
Leeth, Rachel VI, 412
Leeth, Rachel VI, 420
Leeworthy, Bessie IV, 1326
Lefeaver, Hannah II, 445
Lefeaver, Hipolitus II, 445
Lefevre, Mary Ann IV, 1372
Lefevre, Sarah III, 203
Lefevre, Thomas III, 203
Leff, Janet III, 203
Leff, Janet III, 285
Leff, Ralph III, 285
Leff, Susan III, 285
Leff, Viola Susan III, 203
Leff, Wm. III, 203
Leff, Wm. III, 285
Leffert, Ann III, 72
Lefferts, Aaron III, 203
Lefferts, Abby L. III, 203
Lefferts, Anna III, 489
Lefferts, Hope III, 89
Lefferts, Hope III, 203
Lefferts, Jericho III, 203
Lefferts, John III, 89
Lefferts, John III, 203
Lefferts, Joseph III, 203
Lefferts, Julia III, 415
Lefferts, Julia III, 424
Lefferts, Leffert III, 203
Lefferts, Martha III, 203
Lefferts, Mary III, 203
Lefferts, Miriam III, 203
Lefferts, Samuel III, 203
Lefferts, Samuel III, 489
Lefferts, Sarah T. III, 203
Lefferts, Thomas III, 203
Lefferts, Wd. Anna III, 203
Leffingwell, Hanson V, 1006
Leffingwell, Weodocia V, 1006
Lefler, Aron VI, 948
Lefler, J. P. VI, 948
Lefler, Milly VI, 948
Leftwich, Alex VI, 871
Leftwich, Alex VI, 949
Leftwich, Alexander VI, 995
Leftwich, America VI, 971
Leftwich, America W. VI, 949
Leftwich, Ann VI, 949
Leftwich, Ann VI, 981
Leftwich, Ann M. VI, 923
Leftwich, Augt. VI, 910
Leftwich, Augustine VI, 948
Leftwich, Augustine VI, 949
Leftwich, Augustine VI, 989
Leftwich, Augustine VI, 999
Leftwich, Augustine, Jr. VI, 948
Leftwich, Augustine, Jr. VI, 949
Leftwich, B. S. VI, 900
Leftwich, B. S. VI, 982
Leftwich, Betsy VI, 909
Leftwich, Bird S. VI, 900
Leftwich, Bird S. VI, 901
Leftwich, Bird S. VI, 949
Leftwich, Burd L. VI, 873
Leftwich, Burwell VI, 925
Leftwich, Catharine VI, 949
Leftwich, Catharine VI, 1019
Leftwich, Catharine VI, 1021

Leftwich, Catherine VI, 842
Leftwich, Cealy VI, 908
Leftwich, Charlotte VI, 893
Leftwich, Cindarilla VI, 975
Leftwich, Delilah VI, 949
Leftwich, Dolly R. VI, 949
Leftwich, Doshia VI, 949
Leftwich, Doss, Azariah VI, 908
Leftwich, Eglentine VI, 895
Leftwich, Eleanor J. VI, 950
Leftwich, Eliza Ann VI, 927
Leftwich, Eliza J. VI, 892
Leftwich, Eliza Jane VI, 949
Leftwich, Elizabeth VI, 260
Leftwich, Elizabeth VI, 878
Leftwich, Elizabeth VI, 887
Leftwich, Elizabeth VI, 948
Leftwich, Elizabeth VI, 949
Leftwich, Elizabeth VI, 982
Leftwich, Elizabeth VI, 998
Leftwich, Elizabeth VI, 1000
Leftwich, Elizabeth L. VI, 949
Leftwich, Elizabeth S. VI, 951
Leftwich, Ellen VI, 949
Leftwich, Ellis VI, 995
Leftwich, Emelia VI, 871
Leftwich, Emily S. VI, 917
Leftwich, Etchison G. VI, 916
Leftwich, Etchison G. VI, 937
Leftwich, Etchison G. VI, 949
Leftwich, Ethelinda L. VI, 970
Leftwich, Eveline VI, 949
Leftwich, Fanny VI, 948
Leftwich, Frances VI, 883
Leftwich, Frances VI, 949
Leftwich, Frances M. C. VI, 972
Leftwich, Frankey VI, 949
Leftwich, G. W. VI, 949
Leftwich, Geo. W. VI, 918
Leftwich, Geo. W. VI, 949
Leftwich, Geo. W. VI, 975
Leftwich, George W. VI, 977
Leftwich, Granderson VI, 950
Leftwich, Hariet VI, 1012
Leftwich, Harston VI, 949
Leftwich, Huldy VI, 949
Leftwich, Jabez VI, 906
Leftwich, Jabez VI, 949
Leftwich, Jabez VI, 961
Leftwich, Jabez VI, 973
Leftwich, Jabez, Jr. VI, 949
Leftwich, Jabez, Jr. VI, 952
Leftwich, Jack VI, 923
Leftwich, Jack VI, 949
Leftwich, Jack H. VI, 895
Leftwich, Jack H. VI, 949
Leftwich, Jacky VI, 906
Leftwich, Jacky VI, 909
Leftwich, Jacky VI, 973
Leftwich, James VI, 869
Leftwich, James VI, 870
Leftwich, James VI, 873
Leftwich, James VI, 878
Leftwich, James VI, 879
Leftwich, James VI, 882
Leftwich, James VI, 886
Leftwich, James VI, 887
Leftwich, James VI, 888
Leftwich, James VI, 889
Leftwich, James VI, 892
Leftwich, James VI, 893
Leftwich, James VI, 894
Leftwich, James VI, 897
Leftwich, James VI, 898
Leftwich, James VI, 899
Leftwich, James VI, 900
Leftwich, James VI, 901
Leftwich, James VI, 905
Leftwich, James VI, 909
Leftwich, James VI, 910
Leftwich, James VI, 915
Leftwich, James VI, 916
Leftwich, James VI, 917
Leftwich, James VI, 918
Leftwich, James VI, 919
Leftwich, James VI, 920
Leftwich, James VI, 921
Leftwich, James VI, 922
Leftwich, James VI, 923
Leftwich, James VI, 927
Leftwich, James VI, 928
Leftwich, James VI, 929
Leftwich, James VI, 930
Leftwich, James VI, 933
Leftwich, James VI, 934
Leftwich, James VI, 935
Leftwich, James VI, 936
Leftwich, James VI, 939
Leftwich, James VI, 943
Leftwich, James VI, 948
Leftwich, James VI, 949
Leftwich, James VI, 952
Leftwich, James VI, 953
Leftwich, James VI, 954
Leftwich, James VI, 955
Leftwich, James VI, 958
Leftwich, James VI, 959
Leftwich, James VI, 960
Leftwich, James VI, 962
Leftwich, James VI, 963
Leftwich, James VI, 968
Leftwich, James VI, 970
Leftwich, James VI, 973
Leftwich, James VI, 975
Leftwich, James VI, 976
Leftwich, James VI, 977
Leftwich, James VI, 979
Leftwich, James VI, 981
Leftwich, James VI, 983
Leftwich, James VI, 992
Leftwich, James VI, 994
Leftwich, James VI, 995
Leftwich, James VI, 997
Leftwich, James VI, 999
Leftwich, James VI, 1000
Leftwich, James VI, 1001
Leftwich, James VI, 1003
Leftwich, James VI, 1004
Leftwich, James VI, 1007
Leftwich, James VI, 1008
Leftwich, James VI, 1009
Leftwich, James VI, 1011
Leftwich, James VI, 1012
Leftwich, James VI, 1021
Leftwich, James VI, 1022
Leftwich, James R. H. VI, 893
Leftwich, James T. VI, 949
Leftwich, James, Jr. VI, 887
Leftwich, James, Jr. VI, 898
Leftwich, James, Jr. VI, 900
Leftwich, James, Jr. VI, 914
Leftwich, James, Jr. VI, 917
Leftwich, James, Jr. VI, 934
Leftwich, James, Jr. VI, 938
Leftwich, James, Jr. VI, 943
Leftwich, James, Jr. VI, 948
Leftwich, James, Jr. VI, 949
Leftwich, James, Jr. VI, 957
Leftwich, James, Jr. VI, 960
Leftwich, James, Jr. VI, 970
Leftwich, James, Jr. VI, 975
Leftwich, James, Jr. VI, 984
Leftwich, James, Jr. VI, 988
Leftwich, James, Jr. VI, 991
Leftwich, James, Jr. VI, 998
Leftwich, James, Jr. VI, 1007
Leftwich, James, Jr. VI, 1021
Leftwich, Jane VI, 884
Leftwich, Jane VI, 925
Leftwich, Jane VI, 948
Leftwich, Jas. VI, 1021
Leftwich, Jennet VI, 949
Leftwich, Jenny VI, 949
Leftwich, Jesse VI, 949
Leftwich, Jesse VI, 951
Leftwich, Jesse VI, 981
Leftwich, Jno. VI, 873
Leftwich, Jno. VI, 943
Leftwich, Jno. VI, 1019
Leftwich, Joel VI, 917
Leftwich, Joel VI, 948
Leftwich, Joel VI, 949
Leftwich, Joel VI, 962
Leftwich, Joel VI, 1003
Leftwich, Joel B. VI, 833
Leftwich, John VI, 301
Leftwich, John VI, 311
Leftwich, John VI, 326
Leftwich, John VI, 928
Leftwich, John VI, 938
Leftwich, John VI, 948
Leftwich, John VI, 949
Leftwich, John VI, 959
Leftwich, John L. VI, 889
Leftwich, John O. VI, 949
Leftwich, John Q. VI, 915
Leftwich, John Q. VI, 949
Leftwich, John Q. VI, 965
Leftwich, John T. VI, 949
Leftwich, Judith VI, 949
Leftwich, Juliet VI, 936
Leftwich, Libry VI, 999
Leftwich, Lilbourn W. VI, 833
Leftwich, Littleberry VI, 870
Leftwich, Littleberry VI, 895
Leftwich, Littleberry VI, 938
Leftwich, Littleberry VI, 948
Leftwich, Littleberry VI, 949
Leftwich, Littleberry VI, 964
Leftwich, Littleton VI, 820
Leftwich, Littleton VI, 836
Leftwich, Littleton VI, 851
Leftwich, Littleton VI, 949
Leftwich, Lock VI, 893
Leftwich, Lockey VI, 989
Leftwich, Locky VI, 917
Leftwich, Lucinda W. VI, 984
Leftwich, Lucy A. VI, 950
Leftwich, Lucy F. VI, 833
Leftwich, Lynch A. VI, 915
Leftwich, Lynch A. VI, 949
Leftwich, Lynch A. VI, 971
Leftwich, Major ??? VI, 1007
Leftwich, Major William, Jr. VI, 949
Leftwich, Mariah B. VI, 833
Leftwich, Martha VI, 915
Leftwich, Martha Jones VI, 949
Leftwich, Mary VI, 874
Leftwich, Mary VI, 910
Leftwich, Mary VI, 948
Leftwich, Mary VI, 949
Leftwich, Mary VI, 994
Leftwich, Mary VI, 1010
Leftwich, Mary E. VI, 818
Leftwich, Mary E. VI, 949
Leftwich, Mary L. VI, 949
Leftwich, Marzel L. VI, 950
Leftwich, Massy Ann VI, 949
Leftwich, Matilda VI, 949
Leftwich, Matilda VI, 973
Leftwich, Matilda E. VI, 949
Leftwich, Mildred VI, 971
Leftwich, Mildred A. VI, 915
Leftwich, Mildred Ann VI, 949
Leftwich, Mildred O. VI, 949
Leftwich, Mildred S. VI, 900
Leftwich, Milley VI, 949
Leftwich, Milly VI, 949
Leftwich, Milton VI, 842
Leftwich, Minerva L. VI, 949
Leftwich, Mrs. Charlotte C. VI, 949
Leftwich, Nancy VI, 874
Leftwich, Nancy VI, 948
Leftwich, Nancy VI, 973
Leftwich, Nancy VI, 982
Leftwich, Naomi VI, 936
Leftwich, Nichodemus VI, 874
Leftwich, Nichodemus VI, 936
Leftwich, Nichodemus VI, 962
Leftwich, Nichodomus VI, 915
Leftwich, Nicodemus VI, 949
Leftwich, Nicodemus VI, 962
Leftwich, Nicodemus VI, 971
Leftwich, Orphey VI, 886
Leftwich, Pamelia VI, 906
Leftwich, Paulina VI, 995
Leftwich, Payton VI, 973
Leftwich, Peggy VI, 949
Leftwich, Peyton VI, 842
Leftwich, Peyton VI, 949
Leftwich, Polley VI, 910
Leftwich, Polley VI, 966
Leftwich, Polly VI, 922
Leftwich, Polly VI, 949
Leftwich, Polly VI, 957
Leftwich, Polly VI, 969
Leftwich, Rebecca C. VI, 932
Leftwich, Robert VI, 949
Leftwich, Ruth VI, 949
Leftwich, Sally VI, 925
Leftwich, Sally VI, 949
Leftwich, Sally VI, 999
Leftwich, Sally VI, 1007
Leftwich, Sally S. C. VI, 995
Leftwich, Sarah VI, 873
Leftwich, Sarah VI, 936
Leftwich, Sarah VI, 949
Leftwich, Sarah VI, 962
Leftwich, Sarah C. VI, 904
Leftwich, Sarah J. VI, 950
Leftwich, Sarah Jane VI, 871
Leftwich, Sarah Povall VI, 949
Leftwich, Sina A. VI, 962
Leftwich, Sophia VI, 906
Leftwich, Susan C. VI, 995
Leftwich, Susanna VI, 949
Leftwich, Susannah VI, 949
Leftwich, Thomas VI, 862
Leftwich, Thomas VI, 933
Leftwich, Thomas VI, 949
Leftwich, Thomas VI, 1000
Leftwich, Thomas L. VI, 878
Leftwich, Thomas L. VI, 949
Leftwich, Thomas W. VI, 950
Leftwich, Thomas W. VI, 964
Leftwich, Thos VI, 925
Leftwich, Thos. VI, 871
Leftwich, Thos. VI, 893
Leftwich, Thos. VI, 906
Leftwich, Thos. L. VI, 984
Leftwich, Uriah VI, 966
Leftwich, Uriah VI, 1005
Leftwich, Uriah VI, 1007
Leftwich, Uriah, Jr. VI, 966
Leftwich, V. K. VI, 883
Leftwich, V. K. VI, 932
Leftwich, Valentine VI, 873
Leftwich, Valentine VI, 887
Leftwich, Valentine VI, 903
Leftwich, Valentine VI, 923
Leftwich, Valentine VI, 949
Leftwich, Valentine VI, 953
Leftwich, Valentine VI, 972
Leftwich, Valentine VI, 1001
Leftwich, Valentine K. VI, 883
Leftwich, Valentine K. VI, 910
Leftwich, Valentine K. VI, 943
Leftwich, Valentine K. VI, 949
Leftwich, Valentine K. VI, 994
Leftwich, Valenyine K. VI, 949
Leftwich, W. VI, 887
Leftwich, W. VI, 949
Leftwich, W. VI, 971
Leftwich, W. VI, 978
Leftwich, W. VI, 1010
Leftwich, Walter VI, 949
Leftwich, William VI, 869
Leftwich, William VI, 870
Leftwich, William VI, 871
Leftwich, William VI, 872
Leftwich, William VI, 874
Leftwich, William VI, 875
Leftwich, William VI, 877
Leftwich, William VI, 878
Leftwich, William VI, 879
Leftwich, William VI, 880
Leftwich, William VI, 881
Leftwich, William VI, 884
Leftwich, William VI, 886
Leftwich, William VI, 891
Leftwich, William VI, 892
Leftwich, William VI, 893
Leftwich, William VI, 900
Leftwich, William VI, 901
Leftwich, William VI, 902
Leftwich, William VI, 903
Leftwich, William VI, 904
Leftwich, William VI, 905
Leftwich, William VI, 906
Leftwich, William VI, 908
Leftwich, William VI, 909
Leftwich, William VI, 910
Leftwich, William VI, 912
Leftwich, William VI, 914
Leftwich, William VI, 916
Leftwich, William VI, 917
Leftwich, William VI, 918
Leftwich, William VI, 919
Leftwich, William VI, 920
Leftwich, William VI, 921
Leftwich, William VI, 922
Leftwich, William VI, 923
Leftwich, William VI, 924
Leftwich, William VI, 926
Leftwich, William VI, 928
Leftwich, William VI, 929
Leftwich, William VI, 933
Leftwich, William VI, 934
Leftwich, William VI, 935
Leftwich, William VI, 936
Leftwich, William VI, 937
Leftwich, William VI, 939
Leftwich, William VI, 944
Leftwich, William VI, 945
Leftwich, William VI, 946
Leftwich, William VI, 947
Leftwich, William VI, 949
Leftwich, William VI, 950
Leftwich, William VI, 951
Leftwich, William VI, 958
Leftwich, William VI, 963
Leftwich, William VI, 964
Leftwich, William VI, 966
Leftwich, William VI, 967
Leftwich, William VI, 968
Leftwich, William VI, 971
Leftwich, William VI, 972
Leftwich, William VI, 974
Leftwich, William VI, 977
Leftwich, William VI, 979
Leftwich, William VI, 980
Leftwich, William VI, 981
Leftwich, William VI, 984
Leftwich, William VI, 985
Leftwich, William VI, 986
Leftwich, William VI, 988
Leftwich, William VI, 989
Leftwich, William VI, 992
Leftwich, William VI, 993
Leftwich, William VI, 994
Leftwich, William VI, 995
Leftwich, William VI, 996
Leftwich, William VI, 997
Leftwich, William VI, 998
Leftwich, William VI, 999
Leftwich, William VI, 1000
Leftwich, William VI, 1001
Leftwich, William VI, 1004
Leftwich, William VI, 1007
Leftwich, William VI, 1008
Leftwich, William VI, 1009
Leftwich, William VI, 1010
Leftwich, William VI, 1012
Leftwich, William VI, 1013
Leftwich, William VI, 1014
Leftwich, William VI, 1015
Leftwich, William VI, 1016
Leftwich, William VI, 1017
Leftwich, William VI, 1018
Leftwich, William VI, 1019
Leftwich, William VI, 1020
Leftwich, William VI, 1021
Leftwich, William A. VI, 949
Leftwich, William B. H. VI, 949
Leftwich, William C. VI, 949
Leftwich, William, Jr. VI, 949
Leftwich, Williamm VI, 932
Leftwich, Wilmoth VI, 904
Leftwich, Wlliam VI, 1004
Leftwich, Wm. VI, 898
Leftwich, Wm. VI, 914
Leftwich, Wm. VI, 917
Leftwich, Wm. VI, 928
Leftwich, Wm. VI, 942
Leftwich, Wm. VI, 949
Leftwich, Wm. VI, 984
Leftwich, Wm. VI, 987
Leftwich, Wm. VI, 1014
Leftwich, Wm. B. VI, 901
Leftwich, Wm. B. VI, 906
Leftwich, Wm. B. VI, 968
Leftwich, Wm. B. VI, 990
Leftwich, Wm. B. VI, 999
Leftwich, Wm. B. VI, 1008
Leftwich, Wm. C. VI, 981
Leftwich, Wm., Jr. VI, 1009
Leftwich, Zilopha VI, 968
Leftwick, James VI, 947
Lefwich, James VI, 1018
Lefwich, John VI, 336
Legett, Jacob V, 345
Legg, Albert IV, 1170
Legg, Bertha IV, 1170
Legg, Martha IV, 1170
Legget, Ann III, 236
Legget, Leander IV, 238
Legget, Leroy H. IV, 238
Legget, Mary E. IV, 238
Leggett, ??? III, 205
Leggett, ??? III, 281
Leggett, Aaron III, 203
Leggett, Abm. W. III, 52
Leggett, Abraham III, 204
Leggett, Abraham W. III, 203
Leggett, Agnes III, 172
Leggett, Agnes III, 203
Leggett, Alfred III, 204
Leggett, Ann III, 203
Leggett, Ann III, 204
Leggett, Ann III, 205
Leggett, Ann III, 248
Leggett, Ann III, 379
Leggett, Ann III, 382
Leggett, Ann Farrington III, 204
Leggett, Ann Maria III, 204
Leggett, Ann Maria III, 243
Leggett, Anna III, 203
Leggett, Anna F. III, 204
Leggett, Anna F. III, 316
Leggett, Anna F. III, 382
Leggett, Anne III, 380
Leggett, Annie Sands III, 205
Leggett, Augustus III, 424
Leggett, Avis III, 382
Leggett, Avis J. III, 204
Leggett, Avis J. III, 205
Leggett, Avis L. III, 380
Leggett, Avis. III, 382
Leggett, Caroline III, 203
Leggett, Caroline III, 205
Leggett, Caroline III, 382
Leggett, Caroline III, 389
Leggett, Caroline V, 345
Leggett, Caroline H. III, 203
Leggett, Caroline H. III, 204
Leggett, Caroline H. III, 205
Leggett, Caroline H. III, 382
Leggett, Catharine T. III, 203
Leggett, Catharine T. III, 382
Leggett, Charles V, 345
Leggett, Charles P. III, 382
Leggett, Charles Pleasants III, 205

ggett, Charlotte III, 125
ggett, Charlotte III, 203
ggett, Charlotte III, 204
ggett, Charlotte F. III, 204
ggett, Charlotte F. III, 382
ggett, Charlotte L. III, 203
ggett, Charlotte L. III, 215
ggett, Charlotte M. III, 315
ggett, Charlotte S. III, 205
ggett, Chas. III, 382
ggett, Clayton N. III, 205
ggett, Dr. Valentine III, 203
ggett, Eliza III, 88
ggett, Eliza III, 203
ggett, Eliza III, 204
ggett, Eliza III, 281
ggett, Eliza III, 379
ggett, Eliza III, 382
ggett, Eliza III, 424
ggett, Eliza P. III, 382
ggett, Elizabeth III, 203
ggett, Elizabeth III, 204
ggett, Elizabeth A. III, 203
ggett, Elizabeth H. III, 203
ggett, Elizabeth H. III, 205
ggett, Elva V, 345
ggett, Esther III, 86
ggett, Esther III, 140
ggett, Esther III, 203
ggett, Esther III, 204
ggett, Esther III, 230
ggett, Frances III, 204
ggett, Frances III, 382
ggett, Frances Chase III, 203
ggett, Frances Pleasants III, 205
ggett, Frances V. II, 578
ggett, Frances V. II, 623
ggett, Frances V. III, 205
ggett, Frances V. III, 380
ggett, Frances V. III, 382
ggett, Francis III, 382
ggett, Francis V. III, 382
ggett, Francis Vant III, 126
ggett, Geo. F. III, 204
ggett, Geo. F. III, 315
ggett, George F. III, 203
ggett, George F. III, 215
ggett, Hannah III, 185
ggett, Hannah III, 203
ggett, Hannah III, 205
ggett, Hannah III, 217
ggett, Hannah H. III, 167
ggett, Hannah H. III, 203
ggett, Hannah H. III, 205
ggett, Henry III, 203
ggett, Henry Atkins III, 203
ggett, Isaac III, 52
ggett, Isaac III, 204
ggett, Isaac G. III, 203
ggett, Jacob V, 345
ggett, Jacob Henry V, 345
ggett, James F. III, 204
ggett, James Kent III, 203
ggett, James S. III, 203
ggett, James Shaw III, 203
ggett, Jesse V, 345
ggett, John III, 203
ggett, John III, 304
ggett, Joseph II, 578
ggett, Joseph II, 623
ggett, Joseph III, 86
ggett, Joseph III, 125
ggett, Joseph III, 185
ggett, Joseph III, 203
ggett, Joseph R. III, 203
ggett, Joseph S. III, 172
ggett, Joseph S. III, 203
ggett, Joseph Samuel III, 204
ggett, Judith III, 52
ggett, Judith III, 204
ggett, Katharine T. III, 204
eggett, Lela I, 262
ggett, Lindley Hoag III, 34
ggett, Lindley Hoag III, 203
ggett, Lindley Hoag III, 205
eggett, Lizzie IV, 1039
eggett, Lizzie M. IV, 1039
eggett, Louisa III, 204
eggett, Louisa III, 262
eggett, Louisa III, 263
eggett, Louise III, 205
eggett, Margaret III, 203
eggett, Margaret III, 204
eggett, Margaret III, 205
eggett, Margaret III, 382
eggett, Margaret III, 389
eggett, Maria A. III, 203
eggett, Marion III, 86
eggett, Martha III, 204
eggett, Martha III, 379
Leggett, Martha III, 382
Leggett, Martha P. III, 382
Leggett, Mary II, 874
Leggett, Mary II, 888
Leggett, Mary III, 125
Leggett, Mary III, 140
Leggett, Mary III, 203
Leggett, Mary III, 204
Leggett, Mary III, 205
Leggett, Mary III, 236
Leggett, Mary III, 248
Leggett, Mary III, 304
Leggett, Mary III, 382
Leggett, Mary III, 424
Leggett, Mary III, 459
Leggett, Mary B. III, 203
Leggett, Mary E. II, 797
Leggett, Mary E. III, 88
Leggett, Mary E. III, 140
Leggett, Mary E. III, 204
Leggett, Mary F. III, 382
Leggett, Mary Haight III, 203
Leggett, Mary L. III, 251
Leggett, Mary M. III, 49
Leggett, Mary M. III, 149
Leggett, Mary M. III, 204
Leggett, Miriam II, 578
Leggett, Miriam II, 623
Leggett, Miriam III, 125
Leggett, Miriam III, 203
Leggett, Miriam III, 205
Leggett, Miriam III, 380
Leggett, Miriam III, 382
Leggett, Miriam L. III, 126
Leggett, Miriam L. III, 204
Leggett, Mirriam III, 185
Leggett, Nancy III, 382
Leggett, Nancy Emlen III, 205
Leggett, Nancy Emlen III, 382
Leggett, Nantucket III, 204
Leggett, Patience II, 874
Leggett, Patience II, 888
Leggett, Patience H. II, 888
Leggett, Patience H. III, 382
Leggett, Patience H. III, 383
Leggett, Pemberton III, 205
Leggett, Pemberton III, 382
Leggett, Phebe III, 203
Leggett, Phebe Ann III, 47
Leggett, Phebe Ann III, 49
Leggett, Phebe Ann III, 204
Leggett, Phebe B. III, 203
Leggett, Phebe G. III, 52
Leggett, Phebe G. III, 204
Leggett, Pleasants III, 382
Leggett, Rebecca F. III, 204
Leggett, Reuben III, 49
Leggett, Reuben III, 140
Leggett, Reuben III, 203
Leggett, Reuben III, 204
Leggett, Reuben III, 243
Leggett, Rosanna F. III, 164
Leggett, Rosanna F. III, 204
Leggett, Rose Anna III, 47
Leggett, Ruth M. IV, 1039
Leggett, Sally Ann III, 203
Leggett, Samuel II, 888
Leggett, Samuel III, 88
Leggett, Samuel III, 204
Leggett, Samuel III, 205
Leggett, Samuel III, 379
Leggett, Samuel III, 382
Leggett, Samuel III, 389
Leggett, Samuel, Jr. III, 204
Leggett, Samuel, Jr. III, 382
Leggett, Sara III, 204
Leggett, Sara F. III, 203
Leggett, Sara F. III, 204
Leggett, Sara F. III, 315
Leggett, Sarah II, 888
Leggett, Sarah III, 110
Leggett, Sarah III, 203
Leggett, Sarah III, 204
Leggett, Sarah III, 232
Leggett, Sarah III, 263
Leggett, Sarah III, 304
Leggett, Sarah III, 382
Leggett, Sarah C. III, 205
Leggett, Sarah C. III, 231
Leggett, Sarah F. III, 204
Leggett, Sarah H. III, 205
Leggett, Sarah H. III, 262
Leggett, Sarah Hull III, 110
Leggett, Sarah Hull III, 204
Leggett, Silvanus J. III, 204
Leggett, Silvanus Jenkins III, 204
Leggett, Sophia III, 203
Leggett, Susan H. III, 204
Leggett, Susan H. III, 382
Leggett, Thomas III, 125
Leggett, Thomas III, 203
Leggett, Thomas III, 204
Leggett, Thomas III, 205
Leggett, Thomas III, 236
Leggett, Thomas III, 248
Leggett, Thomas III, 389
Leggett, Thomas III, 424
Leggett, Thomas III, 459
Leggett, Thomas H. II, 578
Leggett, Thomas H. II, 623
Leggett, Thomas H. III, 205
Leggett, Thomas H., Jr. III, 205
Leggett, Thomas H., Jr. III, 382
Leggett, Thomas, Jr. III, 203
Leggett, Thomas, Jr. III, 204
Leggett, Thomas, Jr. III, 205
Leggett, Thomas, Jr. III, 379
Leggett, Thomas, Jr. III, 382
Leggett, Thos. II, 874
Leggett, Thos. III, 380
Leggett, Thos. III, 424
Leggett, Thos. H. III, 126
Leggett, Thos. H. III, 204
Leggett, Thos. H. III, 380
Leggett, Thos. H. III, 382
Leggett, Thos. H., Jr. III, 167
Leggett, Thos. H., Jr. III, 203
Leggett, Thos., Jr. II, 874
Leggett, Thos., Jr. II, 888
Leggett, Thos., Jr. III, 204
Leggett, Thos., Jr. III, 382
Leggett, Tripp III, 205
Leggett, W. H. IV, 1039
Leggett, Wager III, 204
Leggett, Walter F. III, 205
Leggett, Walter Farrington III, 204
Leggett, William F. III, 204
Leggett, William F. III, 205
Leggett, William F., Jr. III, 205
Leggett, William H. III, 205
Leggett, William Jenkins III, 203
Leggett, Wm. F. III, 110
Leggett, Wm. F. III, 204
Leggett, Wm. F. III, 262
Leggett, Wm. F. III, 263
Leggett, Wm. H., Jr. III, 205
Leggett, Wm. Haight III, 204
Leggett, Wm. Penn III, 205
Leggett, Wm. W. IV, 1039
Leggitt, Leander IV, 238
Leggot, Mary Louisa IV, 975
Legion, Rachel VI, 526
Legion, William VI, 526
LeGraen, Fred W. IV, 1039
LeGrand, Arch. A. VI, 833
Legrand, Ethelbert VI, 797
LeGrand, Ethelbert VI, 826
LeGrand, Ethelbert VI, 833
LeGrand, Lucy D. VI, 833
LeGrand, Matilda VI, 833
Lehew, Edward E. V, 1006
Lehew, Emma B. V, 1006
Lehew, Rosa L. V, 1006
Lehew, Thos. M. V, 1006
Lehman, Hannah V, 509
Lehman, James III, 136
Lehman, James III, 205
Lehman, Levina V, 509
Lehman, Mary V, 509
Lehman, Minnie Catharine IV, 581
Lehman, Osborn V, 509
Lehman, Paulina III, 136
Lehman, Pauline L. III, 205
Lehman, Ruth V, 509
Lehman, Samuel V, 509
Lehman, Sarah IV, 1256
Lehman, Sarah E. II, 745
Lehman, Sarah E. II, 751
Lehr, Louise III, 438
Leibert, Sidney II, 578
Leibert, Sidney II, 583
Leiby, Harry Nathan III, 381
Leiby, Harry Nathan III, 382
Leiby, Jonathan III, 382
Leiby, Mary Elizabeth III, 381
Leiby, Mary Elizabeth III, 382
Leiby, Sarah III, 382
Leicester, Mary III, 205
Leicester, Stephen III, 205
Leicester, Thomas III, 205
Leichty, Matilda V, 1006
Leichty, Van Buren V, 1006
Leigh, Catharine V, 690
Leigh, Cecelia VI, 616
Leigh, Cecilia VI, 670
Leigh, Elizabeth II, 1086
Leigh, Elizabeth F. II, 1086
Leigh, Elizabeth F. II, 1088
Leigh, Florence III, 205
Leigh, Florence III, 251
Leigh, George VI, 833
Leigh, Howard VI, 616
Leigh, Howard VI, 670
Leigh, John II, 1086
Leigh, Mary II, 578
Leigh, Mary II, 657
Leigh, Paulina II, 1086
Leigh, Pauline II, 1086
Leigh, Thomas II, 963
Leigh, Thomas II, 1010
Leigh, Thomas II, 1075
Leigh, Thomas II, 1086
Leigh, Thomas II, 1088
Leigh, Willmerth VI, 833
Leighthizer, George V, 186
Leinbach, Rebecca Jane II, 714
Leirck, Sophronie E. IV, 1326
Leister, Abel IV, 1170
Leister, Abel IV, 1183
Leister, Andrew VI, 88
Leister, Benj. Wm. IV, 1170
Leister, Jane II, 998
Leister, Jeremiah IV, 1170
Leister, Margaret W. IV, 1170
Leister, Mary Margaret IV, 1170
Leister, Maurice II, 998
Leister, Maurice II, 1010
Leister, Samuel IV, 1170
Leister, Sarah IV, 1170
Leister, Wm. Howard IV, 1170
Leisure, Addie J. V, 1006
Leisure, Eliza V, 1006
Leisure, Ella V, 1006
Leisure, Wm. V, 1006
Leithen, Hannah II, 388
Leivzey, David II, 583
Lely, Daniel II, 238
Lely, Martha II, 238
Lely, Martha II, 261
Lely, Rachel II, 238
Lely, Rachel II, 261
Lemar, Alvie E. V, 185
Lemar, Elizabeth V, 185
Lemar, Ettie F. V, 185
Lemar, Hannah V, 509
Lemar, John A. V, 185
Lemar, John S. V, 185
Lemar, Kenton V, 185
Lemar, Mary V, 185
Lemar, Mary V, 509
Lemar, Mary E. V, 185
Lemar, Nathan Dennis V, 509
Lemar, Osborn V, 509
Lemar, Raymond R. V, 185
Lemar, Rolla V, 185
Lemar, Ruth V, 509
Lemar, Samuel V, 509
Lemar, Samuel Kenton V, 185
Lemaster, Belle IV, 483
Lemaster, Belvia IV, 483
Lemerick, Nettie V, 1006
Lemert, Anna VI, 526
Lemert, Anna VI, 635
Lemert, Elizabeth VI, 526
Lemert, Elizabeth VI, 530
Lemert, Elizabeth VI, 645
Lemert, Elizabeth VI, 670
Lemert, George VI, 526
Lemert, Henry VI, 635
Lemert, Jacob VI, 526
Lemert, Joseph VI, 635
Lemert, Joshua VI, 671
Lemert, Lewis VI, 526
Lemert, Lewis VI, 635
Lemert, Lewis VI, 670
Lemert, Lewis, Jr. VI, 671
Lemert, Mary VI, 526
Lemert, Mary VI, 649
Lemert, Mary VI, 671
Lemert, Mary VI, 931
Lemert, Solomon, Jr. VI, 635
Lemert, Stephan VI, 635
Lemert, Widow Anna VI, 670
Lemlie, Jessie V, 460
Lemmon, Carrie V, 632
Lemmon, George H. VI, 833
Lemmon, Janet VI, 833
Lemmon, Jennette E. VI, 833
Lemmon, Lillie V, 632
Lemmon, Robert T. VI, 833
Lemmond, Frankey VI, 833
Lemmond, William VI, 833
Lemon, Bertha V, 690
Lemon, Bertha V, 696
Lemon, Forest V, 690
Lemon, Forest V, 696
Lemon, George A. IV, 238
Lemon, George E. IV, 238
Lemon, George G. IV, 483
Lemon, Gulia IV, 1284
Lemon, John H. VI, 950
Lemon, Margaret IV, 483
Lemon, Mary IV, 1284
Lemon, Narcissas VI, 950
Lemon, Phebe IV, 334
Lemon, Phebe IV, 340
Lemons, Carrie V, 632
Lemons, George A. IV, 238
Lemons, Jasper V, 632
Lemons, Lillie V, 632
Lenair, Anna I, 724
Lenair, Anna I, 734
Lenard, Abigail I, 660
Lenard, Abigail I, 661
Lenard, Eleanor I, 660
Lenard, Eleanor I, 683
Lenard, Eleanor I, 690
Lenard, Ezekiel I, 507
Lenard, Ezekiel I, 660
Lenard, George I, 660
Lenard, Hannah I, 660
Lenard, John I, 660
Lenard, Joseph I, 660
Lenard, Lydia I, 660
Lenard, Mary I, 507
Lenard, Mary I, 660
Lenard, Pheniah I, 660
Lenard, Rebekah I, 507
Lenard, Sarah I, 661
Lenard, Selinah I, 660
Lenard, Thomas I, 507
Lenear, William VI, 115
Lenfesty, Sarah Ann IV, 539
Lenfesty, Sarah Ann IV, 545
Lenhart, Lenora M. IV, 648
Lenhart, Leonora M. IV, 640
Lenies, Charles V, 460
Lenies, Harry V, 460
Lenies, Sallie V, 460
Lennard, Hannah II, 83
Lennard, Robert VI, 833
Lennard, Susan VI, 833
Lenninger, Rhena C. V, 690
Lennon, Ann II, 578
Lennox, Tacy II, 578
Lennox, Tacy II, 587
Lenoir, Ann II, 1010
Lenoir, Ann II, 1036
Lenoir, Isaac II, 388
Lenoir, Lewis II, 1010
Lenoir, Lewis II, 1036
Lenoir, Mary II, 388
Lenoir, Mary II, 1010
Lenoire, Isaac II, 495
Lenoire, Isaac II, 578
Lenoire, Mary II, 495
Lenoire, Mary II, 578
LeNorman, Cora IV, 1326
Lenox, ??? III, 265
Lenox, Christiana III, 205
Lenox, Christina III, 276
Lenox, David III, 205
Lenox, David III, 314
Lenox, Hannah R. III, 205
Lenox, Hugh III, 205
Lenox, Hugh W. III, 205
Lenox, James II, 1010
Lenox, James R. III, 205
Lenox, James R. III, 276
Lenox, James R., Jr. III, 205
Lenox, Joseph III, 205
Lenox, Leontine J. III, 205
Lenox, Leontine J. III, 208
Lenox, Leontine J. III, 265
Lenox, Lydia III, 205
Lenox, Lydia III, 314
Lenox, Margaret III, 205
Lenox, Mary J. III, 205
Lenox, Mary J. III, 208
Lenox, Narcisse III, 205
Lenox, Narcisse Remond III, 208
Lenox, Susanna III, 205
Lenox, Susannah III, 205
Lenox, Susannah III, 314
Lenoyer, Isaac II, 388
Lent, ??? III, 106
Lent, ??? III, 205
Lent, Elizabeth IV, 417
Lent, Elizabeth IV, 437
Lent, Lucy M. III, 106
Lent, Lucy M. III, 205
Lenton, Wm. II, 578
Lentz, John V, 581
Lentz, John J. V, 581
Lenwire, Ann II, 1010
Lenwire, Ann II, 1025
Lenzler, Helen IV, 1326
Leonard, Abbie V, 509
Leonard, Abigail I, 557
Leonard, Abigail I, 661
Leonard, Abigail I, 683

Leonard, Abigail V, 92
Leonard, Abigail V, 469
Leonard, Abigail V, 509
Leonard, Addison I, 636
Leonard, Albert G. V, 509
Leonard, Alfred I, 683
Leonard, Alpheus I, 660
Leonard, Alta Dell V, 509
Leonard, Amanda Jane I, 891
Leonard, Amanda Jane I, 901
Leonard, Andrew I, 891
Leonard, Andrew F. I, 859
Leonard, Anna I, 660
Leonard, Anna I, 683
Leonard, Anna I, 693
Leonard, Annie I, 613
Leonard, Annie B. I, 620
Leonard, Annie Blanch I, 636
Leonard, Arthur C. V, 509
Leonard, Asenath I, 882
Leonard, Asenath I, 891
Leonard, Asnath I, 859
Leonard, Barzillai V, 509
Leonard, Bezillar V, 509
Leonard, Brazille V, 509
Leonard, C. B. V, 389
Leonard, C. B. V, 509
Leonard, Calvin B. V, 509
Leonard, Calvin B. V, 690
Leonard, Catharine II, 827
Leonard, Charles I, 660
Leonard, Charles S. I, 660
Leonard, Charles S. I, 683
Leonard, Charles S. I, 693
Leonard, Colbert B. I, 620
Leonard, Colbert Blair I, 636
Leonard, Colvin B. V, 509
Leonard, Cora P. V, 509
Leonard, Cordelia I, 613
Leonard, Cordelia I, 891
Leonard, Cordelia I, 899
Leonard, Cordelia B. I, 615
Leonard, Cordelia B. I, 620
Leonard, Cordelia B. I, 636
Leonard, Cordelia B. I, 684
Leonard, Cyrus I, 891
Leonard, Cyrus W. I, 859
Leonard, Cyrus W. C. I, 891
Leonard, Daniel S. VI, 833
Leonard, David I, 824
Leonard, De Ella V, 509
Leonard, Della M. V, 509
Leonard, Dicie Jane I, 404
Leonard, Drucella V, 713
Leonard, Edgar S. V, 509
Leonard, Edward I, 636
Leonard, Edward C. I, 620
Leonard, Edward C. I, 636
Leonard, Edward Charles I, 636
Leonard, Eleanor I, 683
Leonard, Eleanor V, 481
Leonard, Eleanor V, 509
Leonard, Eli I, 859
Leonard, Eli I, 891
Leonard, Eli L. M. I, 859
Leonard, Elizabeth VI, 401
Leonard, Elizabeth VI, 412
Leonard, Emma V, 509
Leonard, Emma V, 690
Leonard, Emma A. V, 509
Leonard, Emma E. V, 509
Leonard, Ernest D. I, 620
Leonard, Ernest DeLong I, 636
Leonard, Esther VI, 526
Leonard, Eunice I, 615
Leonard, Eunice I, 620
Leonard, Eunice I, 632
Leonard, Eunice I, 636
Leonard, Eunice I, 683
Leonard, Eunice I, 691
Leonard, Eunice Abigail I, 660
Leonard, Eunice L. I, 750
Leonard, Eunice Louezar I, 765
Leonard, Ezekiel I, 507
Leonard, Ezekiel I, 547
Leonard, Ezekiel I, 557
Leonard, Ezekiel V, 92
Leonard, Ezekiel V, 509
Leonard, Frances II, 238
Leonard, Franklin I, 660
Leonard, Franklin I, 891
Leonard, Hannah II, 49
Leonard, Hannah II, 83
Leonard, Hannah V, 92
Leonard, Hannah V, 501
Leonard, Hannah V, 509
Leonard, Isaac VI, 526
Leonard, J. A. I, 615
Leonard, Jack D. VI, 258
Leonard, James I, 859
Leonard, James I, 891
Leonard, James A. I, 613
Leonard, James A. V, 1006
Leonard, James Addison I, 620
Leonard, James M. I, 765
Leonard, James Madison I, 750
Leonard, Jesse L. I, 765
Leonard, Jesse Lafayette I, 750
Leonard, Job W. I, 683
Leonard, Job Worth I, 660
Leonard, John I, 404
Leonard, John I, 557
Leonard, John I, 661
Leonard, John I, 683
Leonard, John V, 92
Leonard, John V, 453
Leonard, John V, 509
Leonard, John C. I, 620
Leonard, John Chester I, 636
Leonard, John Milton I, 660
Leonard, Jonathan I, 683
Leonard, Joseph I, 557
Leonard, Joseph I, 574
Leonard, Joseph I, 620
Leonard, Joseph I, 636
Leonard, Joseph I, 660
Leonard, Joseph I, 661
Leonard, Joseph I, 683
Leonard, Joseph I, 684
Leonard, Joseph V, 509
Leonard, Joseph A. I, 636
Leonard, Joseph A. I, 765
Leonard, Joseph Addison I, 660
Leonard, Joseph Addison I, 750
Leonard, Josie I, 891
Leonard, Josie I, 899
Leonard, Lafayette IV, 1170
Leonard, Lafe IV, 1170
Leonard, Laffa IV, 1170
Leonard, Leslie I, 636
Leonard, Leslie A. I, 620
Leonard, Leslie Augustine I, 636
Leonard, Lina L. I, 859
Leonard, Lottie IV, 972
Leonard, Lucinda V, 509
Leonard, Lydia I, 557
Leonard, Lydia I, 574
Leonard, Lydia I, 680
Leonard, Lydia I, 683
Leonard, Lydia V, 453
Leonard, Lydia VI, 493
Leonard, Lydia VI, 526
Leonard, Lydia VI, 640
Leonard, Lydia VI, 700
Leonard, Malinda V, 453
Leonard, Mamie I, 636
Leonard, Margaret III, 79
Leonard, Margaret III, 175
Leonard, Martha I, 636
Leonard, Martha J. I, 859
Leonard, Martha Jane I, 891
Leonard, Mary I, 683
Leonard, Mary V, 92
Leonard, Mary V, 389
Leonard, Mary V, 500
Leonard, Mary V, 509
Leonard, Mary VI, 883
Leonard, Mary A. I, 859
Leonard, Mary C. I, 620
Leonard, Mary Catharine I, 750
Leonard, Mary Catharine I, 765
Leonard, Mary Cordelia I, 636
Leonard, Mary E. V, 509
Leonard, Mary L. V, 389
Leonard, Mary L. A. I, 891
Leonard, Myrtle VI, 622
Leonard, Myrtle VI, 628
Leonard, Myrtle VI, 671
Leonard, Nancy A. C. V, 185
Leonard, Nancy A. C. V, 509
Leonard, Nancy A. C. V, 690
Leonard, Nellie V, 520
Leonard, Parintha C. I, 683
Leonard, Parintha C. I, 684
Leonard, Parintha Caroline I, 660
Leonard, Parmelia V, 509
Leonard, Phebe I, 661
Leonard, Phebe I, 683
Leonard, Phebe I, 684
Leonard, Pheniah V, 523
Leonard, Phiniah I, 683
Leonard, Phiniah I, 686
Leonard, Rachel I, 557
Leonard, Rachel I, 574
Leonard, Rachel I, 660
Leonard, Rachel I, 661
Leonard, Rachel I, 683
Leonard, Rachel V, 481
Leonard, Rachel V, 509
Leonard, Rachel Ana I, 765
Leonard, Rachel Ann I, 750
Leonard, Rachel S. I, 683
Leonard, Rachel S. I, 689
Leonard, Rebecca I, 547
Leonard, Rebecca I, 557
Leonard, Rebecca V, 92
Leonard, Rebecca V, 509
Leonard, Rebecca M. V, 509
Leonard, Rebekah I, 390
Leonard, Rebekah I, 404
Leonard, Rebekah I, 557
Leonard, Rhoda Jane I, 750
Leonard, Rhoda Jane I, 765
Leonard, Roxanna V. I, 859
Leonard, Roxanna Victoria I, 891
Leonard, Ruth V, 509
Leonard, Salathiel I, 750
Leonard, Salathiel I, 765
Leonard, Saline V, 517
Leonard, Sallie I, 921
Leonard, Sally VI, 833
Leonard, Sarah I, 661
Leonard, Sarah I, 683
Leonard, Sarah I, 690
Leonard, Sarah I, 750
Leonard, Sarah I, 765
Leonard, Sarah II, 27
Leonard, Sarah V, 509
Leonard, Sarah V, 524
Leonard, Sarah Derinda I, 750
Leonard, Silvanus I, 661
Leonard, Solina I, 683
Leonard, Solina I, 685
Leonard, Susan V, 92
Leonard, Susan H. V, 92
Leonard, Susan H. V, 509
Leonard, Susanna I, 661
Leonard, Susanna I, 683
Leonard, Susanna I, 690
Leonard, Susannah V, 509
Leonard, Thomas V, 92
Leonard, Thomas V, 509
Leonard, Thos. II, 27
Leonard, Victory I, 882
Leonard, Victory I, 891
Leonard, Walter E. V, 509
Leonard, Wd. Priscilla III, 205
Leonard, William I, 750
Leptcut, Mary II, 84
Lerenberry, Charles IV, 238
Lerenberry, Patsy IV, 238
Lerow, Hannah I, 1001
Leroy, Benjamin III, 205
Leroy, Catharine III, 205
LeRoy, Franklin IV, 1256
LeRoy, Martha IV, 1256
Lertwich, William VI, 920
Lervis, Mary IV, 1256
Lesh, Dora V, 185
Leslie, Elizabeth IV, 238
Leslie, Elizabeth IV, 340
Leslie, Elizabeth IV, 417
Leslie, Elizabeth IV, 483
Leslie, Elizabeth IV, 585
Leslie, Elizabeth IV, 588
Leslie, Elizabeth V, 1006
Leslie, Elizabeth VI, 833
Leslie, James VI, 950
Leslie, John VI, 833
Leslie, Johnson IV, 238
Leslie, Johnson IV, 340
Leslie, Johnson IV, 417
Leslie, Johnson IV, 483
Leslie, Johnson IV, 585
Leslie, Levi IV, 238
Leslie, Levi IV, 340
Leslie, Levi IV, 483
Leslie, Levi IV, 585
Leslie, Levi L. IV, 417
Leslie, Margaret IV, 238
Leslie, Margaret IV, 340
Leslie, Margaret IV, 341
Leslie, Margaret IV, 483
Leslie, Margaret V, 850
Leslie, Mary IV, 238
Leslie, Mary IV, 340
Leslie, Mary IV, 417
Leslie, Mary IV, 483
Leslie, Mary IV, 585
Leslie, Mary IV, 594
Leslie, Mary Jane VI, 950
Leslie, Montana Evans V, 1006
Leslie, Rachel IV, 238
Leslie, Rachel IV, 340
Leslie, Rachel IV, 341
Leslie, Rachel IV, 417
Leslie, Rachel IV, 483
Leslie, Rachel IV, 585
Leslie, Rachel IV, 588
Leslie, Rachel IV, 594
Leslie, Rachel IV, 601
Leslie, Rebecca VI, 524
Leslie, Rebecca VI, 526
Leslie, Rebecca VI, 760
Leslie, Rebecca VI, 761
Leslie, Rilla IV, 1256
Leslie, Robert IV, 238
Leslie, Robert IV, 340
Leslie, Robert IV, 341
Leslie, Robert IV, 417
Leslie, Robert IV, 483
Leslie, Robert IV, 585
Leslie, Robert IV, 588
Leslie, Robert IV, 594
Leslie, Robert IV, 601
Leslie, Sarah IV, 238
Leslie, Sarah IV, 340
Leslie, Sarah IV, 417
Leslie, Sarah IV, 483
Leslie, Sarah IV, 585
Leslie, Sarah IV, 596
Leslie, Sarah IV, 601
Leslie, Thomas IV, 238
Leslie, Thomas IV, 340
Leslie, Thomas IV, 417
Leslie, Thomas IV, 483
Leslie, Thomas IV, 585
Leslie, Wm. J. V, 1006
Lesly, Margaret V, 850
Lessly, Menoah VI, 828
Lessly, Polly VI, 828
Lester, ??? III, 205
Lester, Abel IV, 1170
Lester, Alice E. IV, 1326
Lester, Angeline V, 509
Lester, Anna II, 238
Lester, Anna Foulke II, 802
Lester, Benj. Wm. IV, 1170
Lester, Bertha May IV, 1170
Lester, Bertha May Crawford IV, 1170
Lester, Catherine VI, 671
Lester, Eastman III, 424
Lester, Eastman III, 427
Lester, Eleanor IV, 31
Lester, Eleanor IV, 44
Lester, Elizabeth II, 445
Lester, Elizabeth III, 205
Lester, Elizabeth III, 207
Lester, Elizabeth IV, 44
Lester, Elizabeth VI, 833
Lester, Ellen IV, 1326
Lester, Emanuel III, 205
Lester, Ester II, 445
Lester, Eunice V, 509
Lester, Evan Jones II, 888
Lester, Geo. W. III, 424
Lester, George II, 445
Lester, Gerald, Jr. III, 425
Lester, Gertrude III, 205
Lester, Gertrude E. III, 275
Lester, Hannah IV, 44
Lester, Harry IV, 1326
Lester, Hester II, 445
Lester, Ida Maria III, 205
Lester, James VI, 833
Lester, James VI, 835
Lester, Jedediah III, 205
Lester, Jennie III, 424
Lester, Jeremiah IV, 1170
Lester, John III, 425
Lester, John IV, 44
Lester, John M. III, 425
Lester, John Merritt III, 425
Lester, Joshua VI, 833
Lester, Joshua VI, 848
Lester, Lucy VI, 833
Lester, Margaret II, 805
Lester, Margaret IV, 1170
Lester, Margaret F. II, 888
Lester, Margaret W. IV, 1170
Lester, Martha Ellen V, 509
Lester, Mary II, 805
Lester, Mary IV, 44
Lester, Mary IV, 1170
Lester, Mary VI, 833
Lester, Mary C. IV, 1170
Lester, Mary C. IV, 1191
Lester, Mary E. V, 955
Lester, Mary Margaret IV, 1170
Lester, Mildred VI, 833
Lester, Miles VI, 810
Lester, Miles VI, 833
Lester, Mrs. Ellen W. IV, 1326
Lester, Nancy VI, 833
Lester, Patsy VI, 810
Lester, Peter II, 805
Lester, Peter II, 888
Lester, Phebe III, 205
Lester, Polly VI, 818
Lester, Rebecca VI, 833
Lester, Rose VI, 800
Lester, Sally VI, 833
Lester, Samuel IV, 1170
Lester, Samuel V. IV, 1170
Lester, Sarah IV, 1170
Lester, Sarah Crawford IV, 117
Lester, Selah VI, 833
Lester, Susanna VI, 848
Lester, Thos. II, 805
Lester, Vincent VI, 833
Lester, Violet III, 425
Lester, Violet III, 427
Lester, Walter H. V, 509
Lester, Wilhelmina III, 207
Lester, William V, 509
Lester, William VI, 827
Lester, William VI, 833
Lester, William VI, 848
Lester, Wm. IV, 1170
Lester, Wm. Howard IV, 1170
Lesueur, Fell VI, 893
Lesueur, Frances VI, 893
Lesueur, John C. VI, 950
Lesueur, Susanna P. VI, 950
Letchworth, Albert S. II, 850
Letchworth, Albert S. II, 884
Letchworth, Albert S. II, 910
Letchworth, Albert S. II, 916
Letchworth, Albert S. II, 927
Letchworth, Albert Stepney II, 751
Letchworth, Ann II, 229
Letchworth, Ann II, 238
Letchworth, Anna II, 578
Letchworth, Diana II, 574
Letchworth, Diana II, 578
Letchworth, Dinah II, 578
Letchworth, Eliza S. II, 238
Letchworth, Elizabeth II, 388
Letchworth, Elizabeth II, 574
Letchworth, Elizabeth II, 578
Letchworth, Elizabeth II, 579
Letchworth, Elizabeth II, 710
Letchworth, Elizabeth II, 751
Letchworth, Elizana II, 578
Letchworth, Hannah II, 294
Letchworth, Hannah II, 297
Letchworth, Hannah II, 388
Letchworth, Hannah II, 579
Letchworth, Hannah II, 790
Letchworth, Hannah D. II, 238
Letchworth, John II, 388
Letchworth, John II, 574
Letchworth, John II, 578
Letchworth, John II, 579
Letchworth, John II, 751
Letchworth, Joseph II, 388
Letchworth, Joseph II, 579
Letchworth, Josiah II, 229
Letchworth, Josiah II, 238
Letchworth, Josiah II, 388
Letchworth, Mary II, 178
Letchworth, Mary II, 180
Letchworth, Mary II, 229
Letchworth, Mary II, 238
Letchworth, Mary II, 245
Letchworth, Mary II, 388
Letchworth, Mary II, 579
Letchworth, Mary II, 710
Letchworth, Mary II, 751
Letchworth, Mary Ann II, 238
Letchworth, Mary P. II, 287
Letchworth, Mary P. II, 294
Letchworth, Robert II, 578
Letchworth, Robert II, 579
Letchworth, Robert II, 710
Letchworth, Robert II, 751
Letchworth, Sarah Ann II, 238
Letchworth, Sarah Ann II, 245
Letchworth, Sarah Hayes II, 751
Letchworth, Susan L. II, 180
Letchworth, Susanna II, 388
Letchworth, Susanna II, 578
Letchworth, Susanna II, 579
Letchworth, Susannah II, 294
Letchworth, Susannah II, 298
Letchworth, Thomas II, 245
Letchworth, Thomas II, 294
Letchworth, Thomas II, 388
Letchworth, Thomas II, 579
Letchworth, William II, 178
Letchworth, William II, 180
Letchworth, William II, 229
Letchworth, William II, 238
Letchworth, William II, 245
Letchworth, William II, 294
Letchworth, William II, 388
Letchworth, William P. III, 205
Letchworth, William R., Jr. II, 294
Letchworth, Wm. II, 578
Letchworth, Wm. II, 579
Letner, Alice I, 1123

Letsinger, Ann VI, 950
Letsinger, Philip VI, 950
Lettrell, Chloa V, 692
Lettrell, R. H. V, 692
Lettrell, Ulyssis V, 692
Leur, Henry I, 337
Leuszler, Helen IV, 1326
Leval, Amos F. V, 850
Leval, Mary V, 850
Levan, C. O. IV, 1170
Levan, Lucina IV, 1170
Levan, Margaret Allman IV, 1284
Levan, Sarah IV, 711
Levan, Sarah IV, 734
LeVaser, Louisa V, 918
LeVaser, Louisa V, 938
Leveller, John II, 225
Leveller, John II, 238
Leveller, Sarah II, 225
Leveller, Sarah II, 238
Levenberry, Patsy IV, 238
Lever, Abiel V, 581
Lever, Eliza V, 581
Lever, Frank V, 581
Lever, Hannah V, 581
Lever, Iva V, 581
Lever, McClane V, 581
Leveridge, Sarah IV, 830
Leveridge, Sarah IV, 841
Levering, ??? VI, 726
Levering, Arthur Rollin IV, 1170
Levering, Charles IV, 238
Levering, Clara M. IV, 1170
Levering, Clara Maria IV, 1170
Levering, Elizabeth I, 636
Levering, Elizabeth Berta I, 636
Levering, Elizabeth Bertha I, 620
Levering, Elma C. IV, 1170
Levering, Elma Catharine IV, 1170
Levering, Emely Rebecca I, 636
Levering, Emily Rebecca I, 620
Levering, Emily Rebecca I, 636
Levering, Emily Virginia I, 620
Levering, Emily Virginia I, 636
Levering, Esther IV, 1170
Levering, Esther L. IV, 1170
Levering, Esther L. IV, 1189
Levering, Fanny Esther IV, 1170
Levering, Frances Margaret I, 620
Levering, George C. I, 636
Levering, George Canby I, 620
Levering, George Canby IV, 1170
Levering, Griffith IV, 1170
Levering, Griffith IV, 1189
Levering, Griffith VI, 761
Levering, Hannah IV, 1170
Levering, Jannie IV, 1170
Levering, Jennie Eva IV, 1170
Levering, Joseph VI, 761
Levering, Laura IV, 1183
Levering, Laura Letitia IV, 1170
Levering, Lydia Francine IV, 1170
Levering, Margaret I, 636
Levering, Mary VI, 761
Levering, Mary Alice IV, 1170
Levering, Mary E. IV, 1170
Levering, Mary Elizabeth IV, 1170
Levering, Patsy IV, 238
Levering, Phebe IV, 1170
Levering, Phebe R. IV, 1164
Levering, Phebe R. IV, 1170
Levering, Phebe R. IV, 1236
Levering, Phebe R. IV, 1238
Levering, Phoebe R. I, 620
Levering, R. Ella IV, 1170
Levering, Rachel A. VI, 761
Levering, Rachel Ann II, 579
Levering, Rachel Ann II, 751
Levering, Rachel Ann IV, 1170
Levering, Rachel Ann VI, 761
Levering, Rachel Ann VI, 776
Levering, Rachel Annet IV, 1170
Levering, Rachel Annet IV, 1189
Levering, Rachel Annette IV, 1170
Levering, Rachel Ella IV, 1170
Levering, Ralph Griffith IV, 1170
Levering, Ruth I, 636
Levering, Ruth Ella I, 620
Levering, Samuel I, 620
Levering, Samuel II, 751
Levering, Samuel IV, 1164
Levering, Samuel IV, 1170
Levering, Samuel IV, 1236
Levering, Samuel IV, 1238
Levering, Samuel VI, 761
Levering, Susanna IV, 1170
Levering, Susannah M. IV, 1170
Levering, Thomas II, 579
Levering, Thomas II, 751
Levering, Thomas IV, 1170
Levering, Thomas VI, 761
Levering, Thomas VI, 776
Levering, Thomas H. IV, 1170
Levering, Thomas Henry IV, 1170
Leverton, Alice V, 459
Leverton, Anna V, 185
Leverton, Eliza V, 345
Leverton, Emma E. V, 345
Leverton, Etta Cora V, 345
Leverton, Frank V, 345
Leverton, George W. V, 345
Leverton, Hattie V, 345
Leverton, James V, 185
Leverton, John V, 345
Leverton, John T. V, 345
Leverton, Joseph V. V, 345
Leverton, Lelia A. V, 345
Leverton, Mamie Ridgeway V, 345
Leverton, Mary A. V, 345
Leverton, Milton V, 345
Leverton, Minnie J. V, 345
Levester, Duncan VI, 833
Levester, Matilda VI, 833
Levey, Mary V, 237
Levey, Mary V, 259
Levi, Abigail III, 425
Levi, Edward III, 425
Levick, A. Lucille II, 889
Levick, Alice Bullock II, 805
Levick, Anna E. II, 805
Levick, Anna E. II, 889
Levick, Anna L. II, 889
Levick, Charles M. II, 888
Levick, Charles M. II, 889
Levick, Chas. M. II, 888
Levick, Chas. M. II, 889
Levick, Deborah II, 579
Levick, Deborah D. II, 579
Levick, Deborah D. II, 752
Levick, Ebenezer II, 805
Levick, Elizabeth B. II, 752
Levick, Elizabeth W. II, 805
Levick, Ellen III, 182
Levick, Ellen III, 206
Levick, Esther D. II, 752
Levick, Florence II, 889
Levick, Jane III, 206
Levick, Jane F. II, 888
Levick, Jane L. III, 182
Levick, Lewis J. II, 880
Levick, Lewis J. II, 888
Levick, Lewis J. II, 889
Levick, Martha A. II, 888
Levick, Martha A. II, 889
Levick, Mary II, 579
Levick, Mary A. II, 880
Levick, Mary A. II, 889
Levick, Peter S. II, 579
Levick, Peter S. II, 752
Levick, Rebecca II, 579
Levick, Rebecca II, 752
Levick, Richard II, 579
Levick, Richard II, 752
Levick, Richard II, 888
Levick, Robert R. II, 579
Levick, Robert R. II, 752
Levick, Sally W. II, 752
Levick, Samuel J. II, 888
Levick, Samuel J. II, 889
Levick, Samuel J. III, 182
Levick, Samuel J. III, 206
Levick, Samuel J., Jr. II, 889
Levick, Samuel Jones II, 805
Levick, Samuel Jones, Jr. II, 805
Levick, Sarah W. II, 752
Levick, Susan II, 579
Levick, Susanna II, 727
Levick, Susanna II, 752
Levick, Susanna M. II, 888
Levick, Susannah II, 888
Levick, Susannah M. II, 805
Levick, Susannah M. II, 889
Levick, Susannah Morris II, 805
Levick, Thomas B. II, 752
Levick, Wd. Jane III, 84
Levick, Wm. II, 579
Levick, Wm. II, 752
Levick, Wm. V, 955
Levick, Wm. E. II, 888
Levick, Wm. E. II, 889
Levick, Wm. Ebenezer II, 805
Levick, Wm. M. II, 805
Levingston, James V, 850
Levingstone, James V, 972
Levington, Alfred P. II, 805
Levining, David II, 1010
Levining, Rachel II, 1010
Levining, Rachel II, 1036
Levis, Alfred Conrow II, 805
Levis, Alfred Conrow II, 889
Levis, Ann II, 579
Levis, Anna Alida II, 805
Levis, Anna Alida II, 889
Levis, Anna Conrow II, 805
Levis, Anna Conrow II, 889
Levis, Anne II, 579
Levis, Charles II, 805
Levis, Charles II, 889
Levis, Chas. II, 889
Levis, Chas. Raymond II, 805
Levis, Chas. Raymond II, 889
Levis, Cyrus II, 579
Levis, Elizabeth II, 579
Levis, Elizabeth VI, 757
Levis, Elizabeth M. II, 889
Levis, Evan Evans II, 752
Levis, Evans II, 752
Levis, Hannah II, 579
Levis, Hannah Rhoads II, 784
Levis, Henrietta R. II, 752
Levis, Henrietta R. II, 763
Levis, Isaac II, 579
Levis, Joseph II, 388
Levis, Joseph II, 579
Levis, Joseph II, 675
Levis, Joseph II, 752
Levis, Mary II, 388
Levis, Mary II, 752
Levis, Mary Deb II, 763
Levis, Pancoast II, 294
Levis, Pancoast S. II, 294
Levis, Raymond II, 889
Levis, Rebecca II, 710
Levis, Rebecca II, 752
Levis, Rebecca O. II, 889
Levis, Rebecca Owen II, 805
Levis, Richard II, 579
Levis, Robert J. II, 752
Levis, S. J. II, 710
Levis, Saloma II, 294
Levis, Saloma W. II, 294
Levis, Samuel II, 294
Levis, Samuel II, 579
Levis, Samuel F. II, 294
Levis, Samuel F. II, 295
Levis, Sarah II, 388
Levis, Sarah II, 498
Levis, Sarah II, 579
Levis, Sarah II, 823
Levis, Sarah B. II, 294
Levis, Susanna II, 579
Levis, Susanna II, 675
Levis, Susannah II, 579
Levis, Susannah II, 675
Levisley, Tacy II, 1010
Leviss, Ann II, 579
Leviss, Ann II, 583
Leviss, Anne II, 579
Leviss, Richard II, 579
Leviss, Sarah II, 579
Leviss, Susanna II, 579
Levizley, Lacy II, 977
Levizley, Tacy II, 1010
Levizley, Wm. Bayly II, 1010
Lewallan, John VI, 858
Lewallen, Edith I, 724
Lewallen, Emery Eugene I, 724
Lewallen, Hattie I, 724
Lewallen, Henderson I, 724
Lewallen, Henry I, 724
Lewallen, Jane I, 724
Lewallen, John I, 724
Lewallen, Lula I, 724
Lewallen, Mary Ada I, 724
Lewallen, Mesheck I, 724
Lewallen, Rebecca V, 258
Lewallen, Rebecca V, 259
Lewallen, Sarah I, 724
Lewallen, Sarah J. I, 724
Lewallen, Seth I, 724
Lewallen, William I, 724
Lewallen, Zimri A. I, 724
Lewalling, Sarah I, 721
Lewalling, Sarah I, 724
Lewden, Rebeckah II, 83
Lewellan, John VI, 839
Lewellen, Ann VI, 526
Lewellen, Charles VI, 950
Lewellen, Deborah VI, 526
Lewellen, Edgar V, 691
Lewellen, Elizabeth VI, 820
Lewellen, George V, 691
Lewellen, Hannah VI, 526
Lewellen, Henry V, 691
Lewellen, Isaac VI, 526
Lewellen, James T. VI, 822
Lewellen, John VI, 799
Lewellen, Keziah VI, 950
Lewellen, Margaret VI, 526
Lewellen, Mary VI, 526
Lewellen, Mary VI, 629
Lewellen, Mary VI, 671
Lewellen, Meshach VI, 671
Lewellen, Meshek VI, 526
Lewellen, Polly VI, 820
Lewellen, Rachel VI, 504
Lewellen, Rachel VI, 526
Lewellen, Rhoda IV, 876
Lewellen, Rhoda IV, 884
Lewellen, Sarah IV, 64
Lewellen, Sarah VI, 526
Lewellen, Shadrach VI, 526
Lewellen, Shadrach, Jr. VI, 526
Lewellen, William A. VI, 887
Lewellin, Alfred VI, 834
Lewellin, Ann IV, 44
Lewellin, Ann VI, 526
Lewellin, Ann E. VI, 822
Lewellin, Anne VI, 526
Lewellin, Asa VI, 922
Lewellin, Asa VI, 950
Lewellin, Catherine II, 440
Lewellin, Catherine VI, 795
Lewellin, Charles VI, 833
Lewellin, Charles VI, 950
Lewellin, Deborah IV, 44
Lewellin, Deborah VI, 526
Lewellin, Deborah, Jr. IV, 44
Lewellin, Elizabeth VI, 834
Lewellin, Elizabeth VI, 859
Lewellin, Elizabeth A. VI, 833
Lewellin, Frances VI, 950
Lewellin, Francis VI, 834
Lewellin, Green B. VI, 833
Lewellin, Green B. VI, 1017
Lewellin, Hannah IV, 44
Lewellin, Hannah VI, 526
Lewellin, Isaac IV, 44
Lewellin, Isaac VI, 526
Lewellin, James VI, 820
Lewellin, James VI, 834
Lewellin, James VI, 859
Lewellin, John VI, 834
Lewellin, Keziah VI, 950
Lewellin, Lucinda VI, 950
Lewellin, Marcus VI, 834
Lewellin, Margaret IV, 44
Lewellin, Margaret IV, 47
Lewellin, Margaret VI, 526
Lewellin, Mary IV, 44
Lewellin, Mary VI, 526
Lewellin, Mary VI, 833
Lewellin, Meshek VI, 526
Lewellin, Rachel VI, 526
Lewellin, Sally VI, 834
Lewellin, Sally VI, 859
Lewellin, Sarah IV, 44
Lewellin, Sarah VI, 526
Lewellin, Sarah VI, 834
Lewellin, Shadrach VI, 526
Lewellin, Shadrach, Jr. VI, 526
Lewellin, Shadrack IV, 44
Lewellin, Susannah VI, 950
Lewellin, William VI, 950
Lewellin, William J. VI, 950
Lewellyn, Abigail S. IV, 831
Lewellyn, Anna V, 411
Lewellyn, Anna Elizabeth V, 411
Lewellyn, Betsy H. VI, 798
Lewellyn, Charles B. IV, 831
Lewellyn, Elisha IV, 831
Lewellyn, Elisha IV, 845
Lewellyn, Elizabeth VI, 798
Lewellyn, Harold V, 411
Lewellyn, John V, 411
Lewellyn, Mabel E. IV, 831
Lewellyn, Martha Hannah V, 411
Lewellyn, Mary Alice V, 411
Lewellyn, Shadrach VI, 478
Lewellyn, Wm. T. IV, 831
Lewen, Clarinda V, 1006
Lewen, Emil V, 1006
Lewes, Alice II, 580
Lewes, Ann II, 580
Lewes, Ellis II, 579
Lewes, Hannah II, 579
Lewes, Henry VI, 413
Lewes, Jale II, 88
Lewes, John II, 83
Lewes, John II, 88
Lewes, John II, 238
Lewes, John II, 580
Lewes, Mary II, 580
Lewes, Nathaniel II, 580
Lewes, Phebe II, 580
Lewes, Robert II, 580
Lewes, Susanna II, 580
Lewes, Wm. II, 580
Lewillen, Ann VI, 413
Lewillen, Margaret VI, 413
Lewin, Mary III, 311
Lewis, ??? III, 206
Lewis, ??? III, 319
Lewis, ??? III, 464
Lewis, ??? IV, 238
Lewis, ??? V, 147
Lewis, ??? VI, 348
Lewis, A. F. V, 691
Lewis, A. H. IV, 1326
Lewis, Aaron IV, 539
Lewis, Aaron V, 182
Lewis, Aaron V, 185
Lewis, Aaron V, 306
Lewis, Aaron V, 346
Lewis, Abel IV, 239
Lewis, Abel IV, 240
Lewis, Abel IV, 332
Lewis, Abel IV, 340
Lewis, Abel IV, 417
Lewis, Abel IV, 530
Lewis, Abel IV, 539
Lewis, Abigail II, 534
Lewis, Abigail II, 580
Lewis, Abigail II, 694
Lewis, Able IV, 335
Lewis, Able IV, 340
Lewis, Able IV, 417
Lewis, Abner V, 185
Lewis, Abner V, 346
Lewis, Abner VI, 353
Lewis, Adam II, 388
Lewis, Adam II, 389
Lewis, Adam II, 579
Lewis, Adam II, 679
Lewis, Adda V, 185
Lewis, Addie Lewis V, 185
Lewis, Adelaide Hall VI, 762
Lewis, Adna IV, 1171
Lewis, Adna IV, 1197
Lewis, Adnah IV, 1171
Lewis, Adoni IV, 239
Lewis, Adoni IV, 539
Lewis, Adoni IV, 559
Lewis, Adoni IV, 1171
Lewis, Agnes VI, 353
Lewis, Agness VI, 847
Lewis, Agness VI, 950
Lewis, Albert III, 485
Lewis, Albert III, 489
Lewis, Albert V, 306
Lewis, Albert H. IV, 1326
Lewis, Albert N. V, 918
Lewis, Alexander III, 206
Lewis, Alice I, 636
Lewis, Alice II, 548
Lewis, Alice II, 579
Lewis, Alice II, 580
Lewis, Alice V, 259
Lewis, Alice VI, 328
Lewis, Alice VI, 355
Lewis, Alice VI, 526
Lewis, Alice VI, 527
Lewis, Alice VI, 613
Lewis, Alice VI, 633
Lewis, Alice VI, 671
Lewis, Alice J. V, 1007
Lewis, Alice Jay V, 1007
Lewis, Alinza V, 185
Lewis, Alistus V, 185
Lewis, Allen IV, 240
Lewis, Allis Loyed I, 326
Lewis, Almira IV, 1171
Lewis, Almira IV, 1182
Lewis, Alvah V, 306
Lewis, Amanda V, 510
Lewis, Ambrose IV, 1215
Lewis, Amey II, 559
Lewis, Amey II, 580
Lewis, Amos II, 388
Lewis, Amos II, 579
Lewis, Amos IV, 640
Lewis, Amos IV, 876
Lewis, Amos V, 92
Lewis, Amos V, 306
Lewis, Amos V, 318
Lewis, Amos V, 342
Lewis, Amos V, 345
Lewis, Amos V, 346
Lewis, Amos V, 352
Lewis, Amos VI, 353
Lewis, Amos T. V, 346
Lewis, Amy II, 388
Lewis, Amy II, 580
Lewis, Amy G. VI, 834
Lewis, Amy Lee IV, 240
Lewis, Ann I, 449
Lewis, Ann I, 526
Lewis, Ann I, 557
Lewis, Ann I, 1107

Lewis, Ann I, 1123
Lewis, Ann I, 1132
Lewis, Ann I, 1145
Lewis, Ann I, 1158
Lewis, Ann II, 83
Lewis, Ann II, 238
Lewis, Ann II, 388
Lewis, Ann II, 579
Lewis, Ann II, 580
Lewis, Ann II, 581
Lewis, Ann III, 333
Lewis, Ann III, 420
Lewis, Ann III, 425
Lewis, Ann IV, 21
Lewis, Ann IV, 146
Lewis, Ann IV, 152
Lewis, Ann IV, 240
Lewis, Ann IV, 242
Lewis, Ann IV, 340
Lewis, Ann IV, 483
Lewis, Ann IV, 547
Lewis, Ann V, 306
Lewis, Ann V, 334
Lewis, Ann V, 345
Lewis, Ann V, 346
Lewis, Ann V, 573
Lewis, Ann V, 581
Lewis, Ann VI, 329
Lewis, Ann VI, 345
Lewis, Ann VI, 353
Lewis, Ann VI, 413
Lewis, Ann VI, 419
Lewis, Ann VI, 490
Lewis, Ann VI, 498
Lewis, Ann VI, 527
Lewis, Ann VI, 540
Lewis, Ann VI, 565
Lewis, Ann VI, 567
Lewis, Ann VI, 671
Lewis, Ann VI, 1022
Lewis, Ann Elizabeth III, 425
Lewis, Ann Elizabeth III, 461
Lewis, Ann L. VI, 76
Lewis, Ann L. VI, 258
Lewis, Ann L. VI, 275
Lewis, Anna I, 721
Lewis, Anna I, 724
Lewis, Anna IV, 152
Lewis, Anna IV, 239
Lewis, Anna IV, 539
Lewis, Anna IV, 734
Lewis, Anna IV, 1171
Lewis, Anna IV, 1195
Lewis, Anna IV, 1284
Lewis, Anna V, 691
Lewis, Anna B. VI, 258
Lewis, Anna D. IV, 585
Lewis, Anna D. IV, 586
Lewis, Anna G. II, 805
Lewis, Anna L. IV, 239
Lewis, Anna L. V, 918
Lewis, Anna L. VI, 258
Lewis, Anna L. VI, 277
Lewis, Anne IV, 152
Lewis, Anne IV, 483
Lewis, Anne VI, 329
Lewis, Annie III, 206
Lewis, Annie III, 223
Lewis, Annie III, 285
Lewis, Annie III, 332
Lewis, Annie III, 334
Lewis, Annie VI, 733
Lewis, Appleberry V, 185
Lewis, Aquilla V, 345
Lewis, Arthur III, 502
Lewis, Arthur P. IV, 1326
Lewis, Asenath V, 344
Lewis, Asenath V, 346
Lewis, Asenath P. IV, 1104
Lewis, Assenath V, 345
Lewis, Atlantic O. IV, 238
Lewis, Atlantic O. IV, 312
Lewis, Atlantic O. IV, 313
Lewis, Atlantic O. IV, 539
Lewis, Atlanticotion IV, 238
Lewis, Barbara II, 580
Lewis, Barclay L. II, 889
Lewis, Barclay Z. II, 889
Lewis, Beaulah IV, 63
Lewis, Benj. V, 918
Lewis, Benjamin II, 388
Lewis, Benjamin III, 115
Lewis, Benjamin III, 206
Lewis, Benjamin III, 313
Lewis, Benjamin III, 314
Lewis, Benjamin V, 918
Lewis, Benjamin S. IV, 240
Lewis, Betsey I, 1011
Lewis, Betsey V, 92
Lewis, Betsey V, 346
Lewis, Betsey Ann I, 1145
Lewis, Betsy V, 92
Lewis, Betsy V, 306
Lewis, Betsy V, 313
Lewis, Betsy V, 346
Lewis, Betsy VI, 353
Lewis, Beulah IV, 44
Lewis, Beulah IV, 69
Lewis, Beulah IV, 239
Lewis, Bulah VI, 413
Lewis, Burlough VI, 413
Lewis, C. H. V, 1007
Lewis, Cabel I, 1034
Lewis, Caleb I, 1028
Lewis, Caleb I, 1034
Lewis, Caleb V, 92
Lewis, Caleb V, 185
Lewis, Caleb V, 345
Lewis, Caleb V, 460
Lewis, Caleb V, 581
Lewis, Caleb V, 955
Lewis, Caleb V, 956
Lewis, Caleb H. V, 61
Lewis, Caleb H. V, 92
Lewis, Caleb H. V, 185
Lewis, Caleb H. V, 691
Lewis, Caleb H. V, 1007
Lewis, Calvin I, 1085
Lewis, Calvin I, 1145
Lewis, Calvin T. I, 1093
Lewis, Calvin T. I, 1095
Lewis, Calvin T. I, 1144
Lewis, Calvin T. I, 1158
Lewis, Capt. Ezra III, 425
Lewis, Carol V, 581
Lewis, Caroline I, 1082
Lewis, Caroline I, 1092
Lewis, Caroline I, 1095
Lewis, Caroline I, 1145
Lewis, Caroline V, 259
Lewis, Caroline V, 345
Lewis, Caroline Babb V, 691
Lewis, Caroline E. IV, 1104
Lewis, Caroline E. V, 346
Lewis, Caroline Eliza IV, 1104
Lewis, Carrie V, 185
Lewis, Carrie J. III, 502
Lewis, Catharine III, 425
Lewis, Catharine III, 460
Lewis, Catharine IV, 69
Lewis, Catharine IV, 152
Lewis, Catharine IV, 207
Lewis, Catharine IV, 238
Lewis, Catharine IV, 239
Lewis, Catharine IV, 340
Lewis, Catharine V, 346
Lewis, Catharine V, 691
Lewis, Catharine VI, 366
Lewis, Catharine VI, 386
Lewis, Catharine VI, 413
Lewis, Catharine B. I, 1145
Lewis, Catharine S. III, 425
Lewis, Catharine S. III, 461
Lewis, Catherine I, 1095
Lewis, Catherine II, 889
Lewis, Catherine IV, 44
Lewis, Catherine IV, 98
Lewis, Catherine V, 259
Lewis, Catherine V, 691
Lewis, Catherine VI, 56
Lewis, Catherine VI, 76
Lewis, Catherine A. I, 1124
Lewis, Catherine L. VI, 76
Lewis, Cathrine IV, 98
Lewis, Celah Sirilla I, 724
Lewis, Celia Cerille I, 702
Lewis, Chalkley IV, 1104
Lewis, Charity V, 92
Lewis, Charity V, 162
Lewis, Charity V, 185
Lewis, Charity V, 955
Lewis, Charity V, 956
Lewis, Charles II, 388
Lewis, Charles II, 580
Lewis, Charles II, 603
Lewis, Charles III, 206
Lewis, Charles IV, 45
Lewis, Charles IV, 152
Lewis, Charles IV, 240
Lewis, Charles IV, 340
Lewis, Charles IV, 734
Lewis, Charles IV, 1215
Lewis, Charles V, 306
Lewis, Charles V, 691
Lewis, Charles VI, 961
Lewis, Charles Evan V, 346
Lewis, Charles H. I, 945
Lewis, Charles Harvey I, 929
Lewis, Charles K. VI, 75
Lewis, Charles K. VI, 76
Lewis, Charles M. V, 259
Lewis, Charles R. V, 691
Lewis, Charles S. VI, 827
Lewis, Charles Smith III, 206
Lewis, Charles W. IV, 45
Lewis, Charley Pearce I, 326
Lewis, Charlotte II, 865
Lewis, Charlotte II, 889
Lewis, Charlotte IV, 734
Lewis, Charlotte Maud II, 805
Lewis, Charlotte S. II, 889
Lewis, Charlotte S. II, 930
Lewis, Charlotte Smith II, 805
Lewis, Chas. IV, 332
Lewis, Chas. V, 691
Lewis, Christopher V, 92
Lewis, Christopher V, 306
Lewis, Christopher V, 312
Lewis, Clara IV, 1215
Lewis, Clarissa III, 109
Lewis, Clarissa III, 206
Lewis, Clarissa III, 319
Lewis, Clarissa III, 328
Lewis, Clarissa L. III, 206
Lewis, Clark II, 83
Lewis, Clark V, 92
Lewis, Clark V, 306
Lewis, Clark V, 345
Lewis, Clark E. IV, 240
Lewis, Clark E. V, 92
Lewis, Clinton V, 259
Lewis, Clovis VI, 258
Lewis, Clyde V, 581
Lewis, Cora M. V, 691
Lewis, Coral V, 581
Lewis, Corbin VI, 834
Lewis, Corbin VI, 863
Lewis, Corbin VI, 916
Lewis, Cordelia A. I, 1124
Lewis, Cynthia IV, 239
Lewis, Cynthia IV, 1171
Lewis, Cynthia IV, 1193
Lewis, Cynthia V, 185
Lewis, Cynthia V, 955
Lewis, Dalton H. V, 1007
Lewis, Dan'l III, 420
Lewis, Daniel I, 330
Lewis, Daniel I, 1095
Lewis, Daniel I, 1145
Lewis, Daniel II, 445
Lewis, Daniel V, 92
Lewis, Daniel V, 185
Lewis, Daniel V, 306
Lewis, Daniel V, 341
Lewis, Daniel V, 345
Lewis, Daniel V, 346
Lewis, Daniel V, 505
Lewis, Daniel VI, 329
Lewis, Daniel VI, 353
Lewis, Daniel B. I, 1085
Lewis, Daniel W. IV, 1171
Lewis, Davan V, 919
Lewis, David I, 330
Lewis, David I, 337
Lewis, David I, 1085
Lewis, David I, 1095
Lewis, David II, 559
Lewis, David II, 580
Lewis, David II, 752
Lewis, David III, 206
Lewis, David IV, 238
Lewis, David IV, 239
Lewis, David IV, 242
Lewis, David IV, 417
Lewis, David IV, 975
Lewis, David VI, 413
Lewis, David A. IV, 975
Lewis, David D. IV, 975
Lewis, David E. I, 326
Lewis, David J. IV, 240
Lewis, David J. IV, 830
Lewis, David James I, 330
Lewis, David Levis II, 889
Lewis, David Stanton IV, 238
Lewis, David Z. IV, 240
Lewis, Delitha IV, 1104
Lewis, Dewitt Clinton V, 259
Lewis, Dillwyn II, 889
Lewis, Dillwyn P. II, 889
Lewis, Dorcas Corinna I, 724
Lewis, Dorcus Corenna I, 702
Lewis, Dorothy III, 206
Lewis, Dorothy Ann IV, 240
Lewis, E. D. I, 724
Lewis, Edmund II, 805
Lewis, Edmund II, 889
Lewis, Edmund P. III, 425
Lewis, Edward II, 889
Lewis, Edward III, 206
Lewis, Edward III, 489
Lewis, Edward J. II, 752
Lewis, Edward M. IV, 539
Lewis, Eileen VI, 76
Lewis, Elander I, 1011
Lewis, Eleanor I, 1008
Lewis, Eleanor I, 1011
Lewis, Eleanor I, 1107
Lewis, Eleanor I, 1113
Lewis, Eleanor I, 1123
Lewis, Eleanor II, 580
Lewis, Eleanor V, 92
Lewis, Eleanor V, 306
Lewis, Eleanor V, 345
Lewis, Eleanor V, 346
Lewis, Eleanor VI, 353
Lewis, Eleanor VI, 413
Lewis, Eleanor VI, 419
Lewis, Elesebeth VI, 847
Lewis, Eli V, 185
Lewis, Eli V, 955
Lewis, Elias III, 425
Lewis, Elias III, 502
Lewis, Elias, Jr. III, 206
Lewis, Elias, Jr. III, 329
Lewis, Elias, Jr. III, 334
Lewis, Elias, Jr. III, 425
Lewis, Elias, Jr. III, 434
Lewis, Elias, Jr. III, 459
Lewis, Elias, Jr. III, 460
Lewis, Elijah IV, 152
Lewis, Elijah IV, 238
Lewis, Elijah Fletcher V, 346
Lewis, Elinor VI, 353
Lewis, Elisabeth II, 579
Lewis, Elisha IV, 217
Lewis, Elisha IV, 1171
Lewis, Elisha VI, 76
Lewis, Elisha VI, 258
Lewis, Eliz. F. III, 223
Lewis, Eliza I, 702
Lewis, Eliza I, 724
Lewis, Eliza II, 793
Lewis, Eliza II, 805
Lewis, Eliza IV, 185
Lewis, Eliza IV, 239
Lewis, Eliza IV, 417
Lewis, Eliza IV, 439
Lewis, Eliza IV, 483
Lewis, Eliza IV, 1065
Lewis, Eliza IV, 1104
Lewis, Eliza IV, 1107
Lewis, Eliza V, 345
Lewis, Eliza J. V, 1006
Lewis, Eliza N. III, 425
Lewis, Elizabeth I, 1034
Lewis, Elizabeth I, 1107
Lewis, Elizabeth I, 1124
Lewis, Elizabeth II, 388
Lewis, Elizabeth II, 533
Lewis, Elizabeth II, 579
Lewis, Elizabeth II, 580
Lewis, Elizabeth II, 581
Lewis, Elizabeth II, 601
Lewis, Elizabeth II, 630
Lewis, Elizabeth II, 655
Lewis, Elizabeth II, 752
Lewis, Elizabeth II, 889
Lewis, Elizabeth II, 1074
Lewis, Elizabeth II, 1075
Lewis, Elizabeth III, 206
Lewis, Elizabeth III, 461
Lewis, Elizabeth IV, 44
Lewis, Elizabeth IV, 45
Lewis, Elizabeth IV, 51
Lewis, Elizabeth IV, 217
Lewis, Elizabeth IV, 238
Lewis, Elizabeth IV, 239
Lewis, Elizabeth IV, 266
Lewis, Elizabeth IV, 300
Lewis, Elizabeth IV, 396
Lewis, Elizabeth IV, 417
Lewis, Elizabeth IV, 1065
Lewis, Elizabeth IV, 1171
Lewis, Elizabeth V, 92
Lewis, Elizabeth V, 185
Lewis, Elizabeth V, 306
Lewis, Elizabeth V, 345
Lewis, Elizabeth V, 346
Lewis, Elizabeth V, 510
Lewis, Elizabeth V, 918
Lewis, Elizabeth V, 955
Lewis, Elizabeth V, 956
Lewis, Elizabeth VI, 76
Lewis, Elizabeth VI, 258
Lewis, Elizabeth VI, 350
Lewis, Elizabeth VI, 353
Lewis, Elizabeth VI, 409
Lewis, Elizabeth VI, 413
Lewis, Elizabeth VI, 415
Lewis, Elizabeth VI, 527
Lewis, Elizabeth VI, 834
Lewis, Elizabeth VI, 851
Lewis, Elizabeth A. I, 1154
Lewis, Elizabeth A. I, 1158
Lewis, Elizabeth Ann IV, 1104
Lewis, Elizabeth Coleman II, 80
Lewis, Elizabeth F. II, 823
Lewis, Elizabeth F. II, 889
Lewis, Elizabeth F. II, 931
Lewis, Elizabeth F. III, 321
Lewis, Elizabeth H. V, 92
Lewis, Elizabeth S. VI, 833
Lewis, Elizabeth Shelton VI, 25
Lewis, Elizabeth Steele II, 795
Lewis, Elizabeth T. III, 425
Lewis, Elizabeth T. IV, 397
Lewis, Elizabeth T. IV, 417
Lewis, Elizana IV, 483
Lewis, Elizana IV, 491
Lewis, Ella H. IV, 240
Lewis, Ella H. J. IV, 830
Lewis, Ella N. J. IV, 240
Lewis, Ellen II, 580
Lewis, Ellen V, 259
Lewis, Ellen Brumfield II, 805
Lewis, Ellender I, 1011
Lewis, Ellinor VI, 413
Lewis, Ellinor VI, 527
Lewis, Ellis II, 388
Lewis, Ellis II, 579
Lewis, Ellis II, 580
Lewis, Ellis II, 976
Lewis, Ellis II, 1010
Lewis, Ellis V, 259
Lewis, Ellis A. V, 345
Lewis, Ellis A. V, 346
Lewis, Ellis A. V, 691
Lewis, Elma IV, 313
Lewis, Elmer IV, 975
Lewis, Elmer G. IV, 975
Lewis, Elsie I, 620
Lewis, Elsie V, 510
Lewis, Elvira IV, 1171
Lewis, Elvira IV, 1284
Lewis, Elwood IV, 1104
Lewis, Emala IV, 29
Lewis, Emala IV, 45
Lewis, Emaline A. V, 786
Lewis, Emaline A. V, 788
Lewis, Emeline IV, 1171
Lewis, Emery IV, 239
Lewis, Emery IV, 372
Lewis, Emery IV, 417
Lewis, Emery IV, 539
Lewis, Emily V, 345
Lewis, Emily C. II, 889
Lewis, Emily H. V, 581
Lewis, Emily H. V, 691
Lewis, Emlin IV, 1171
Lewis, Emly IV, 239
Lewis, Emma III, 206
Lewis, Emma B. IV, 240
Lewis, Emma C. V, 346
Lewis, Emma E. B. IV, 240
Lewis, Emma K. VI, 742
Lewis, Emma K. VI, 743
Lewis, Emma K. VI, 762
Lewis, Emma Kezia II, 889
Lewis, Emma Keziah II, 868
Lewis, Emor IV, 417
Lewis, Emory IV, 239
Lewis, Emrey IV, 238
Lewis, Emry IV, 238
Lewis, Emry IV, 288
Lewis, Endsley IV, 239
Lewis, Enoch II, 752
Lewis, Enoch II, 805
Lewis, Enoch II, 865
Lewis, Enoch II, 889
Lewis, Enoch II, 930
Lewis, Enoch III, 206
Lewis, Enoch IV, 1171
Lewis, Enoch V, 92
Lewis, Enoch V, 306
Lewis, Enoch V, 330
Lewis, Enoch V, 345
Lewis, Enoch V, 346
Lewis, Enoch V, 363
Lewis, Enoch V, 510
Lewis, Enoch VI, 350
Lewis, Enoch VI, 353
Lewis, Enoch, Jr. II, 805
Lewis, Enos IV, 238
Lewis, Enos IV, 239
Lewis, Enos IV, 818
Lewis, Enos IV, 830
Lewis, Enos IV, 859
Lewis, Enos V, 185
Lewis, Enos M. II, 805
Lewis, Ensley IV, 238
Lewis, Ensley IV, 239
Lewis, Ester II, 83
Lewis, Ester IV, 1238
Lewis, Esther I, 1034
Lewis, Esther II, 33

Lewis, Esther II, 83
Lewis, Esther II, 84
Lewis, Esther II, 388
Lewis, Esther II, 537
Lewis, Esther II, 580
Lewis, Esther II, 581
Lewis, Esther II, 603
Lewis, Esther IV, 45
Lewis, Esther IV, 152
Lewis, Esther IV, 238
Lewis, Esther IV, 243
Lewis, Esther V, 306
Lewis, Esther V, 469
Lewis, Esther V, 510
Lewis, Esther V, 525
Lewis, Esther VI, 413
Lewis, Esther B. IV, 240
Lewis, Esther L. IV, 1284
Lewis, Esther Lundy IV, 1104
Lewis, Estor II, 83
Lewis, Ethel Ines I, 929
Lewis, Ethel Inez I, 945
Lewis, Eugene V, 1007
Lewis, Eugene C. V, 92
Lewis, Eva V, 581
Lewis, Eva V, 632
Lewis, Eva V, 691
Lewis, Eva O. V, 581
Lewis, Evan I, 557
Lewis, Evan I, 966
Lewis, Evan I, 1101
Lewis, Evan I, 1107
Lewis, Evan I, 1123
Lewis, Evan I, 1124
Lewis, Evan II, 471
Lewis, Evan II, 579
Lewis, Evan II, 711
Lewis, Evan II, 805
Lewis, Evan II, 889
Lewis, Evan II, 930
Lewis, Evan III, 206
Lewis, Evan IV, 152
Lewis, Evan IV, 239
Lewis, Evan V, 185
Lewis, Evan V, 334
Lewis, Evan V, 340
Lewis, Evan V, 345
Lewis, Evan V, 346
Lewis, Evan VI, 328
Lewis, Evan VI, 329
Lewis, Evan VI, 341
Lewis, Evan VI, 353
Lewis, Evan VI, 413
Lewis, Evan VI, 527
Lewis, Evan VI, 671
Lewis, Evan John IV, 240
Lewis, Evelyn V, 1007
Lewis, Even I, 507
Lewis, Even I, 557
Lewis, Even I, 563
Lewis, Even V, 345
Lewis, Evin VI, 328
Lewis, Evin VI, 526
Lewis, Fam V, 92
Lewis, Fannie III, 206
Lewis, Fanny III, 206
Lewis, Farly I, 724
Lewis, Fleming B. IV, 1171
Lewis, Flemming IV, 1171
Lewis, Florence IV, 734
Lewis, Frances III, 206
Lewis, Frank IV, 585
Lewis, Frank V, 185
Lewis, Franklin Spencer VI, 762
Lewis, Fred B. III, 206
Lewis, G. C. IV, 1171
Lewis, Geneva Moon V, 410
Lewis, Genevra IV, 975
Lewis, George V, 259
Lewis, George V, 306
Lewis, George VI, 328
Lewis, George VI, 329
Lewis, George VI, 353
Lewis, George VI, 671
Lewis, George VI, 892
Lewis, George VI, 950
Lewis, George D. II, 889
Lewis, George E. I, 337
Lewis, George Edgar I, 326
Lewis, George H. V, 92
Lewis, George H. V, 306
Lewis, George Harrison II, 889
Lewis, Gertrude Maxton VI, 258
Lewis, Gilbert III, 206
Lewis, Giles II, 388
Lewis, Giles II, 389
Lewis, Giles II, 580
Lewis, Giles II, 666
Lewis, Giles VI, 527
Lewis, Ginerva IV, 975
Lewis, Grace Anna II, 889
Lewis, Grace W. VI, 731
Lewis, Grace Winder VI, 730
Lewis, Grace Winder VI, 762
Lewis, Grace Winder VI, 769
Lewis, Grace Winder VI, 794
Lewis, Grant V, 92
Lewis, Griffin VI, 817
Lewis, Griffin VI, 827
Lewis, Griffin VI, 828
Lewis, Griffin VI, 830
Lewis, Griffin VI, 834
Lewis, Griffin VI, 849
Lewis, Griffin VI, 851
Lewis, Griffin VI, 865
Lewis, Griffin, Jr. VI, 833
Lewis, Griffin, Jr. VI, 834
Lewis, Griffith IV, 239
Lewis, Griffith IV, 1171
Lewis, Griffith IV, 1195
Lewis, Griffith IV, 1284
Lewis, Grissell II, 574
Lewis, Grissell II, 579
Lewis, Guiney VI, 959
Lewis, Halanah IV, 1104
Lewis, Hannah I, 763
Lewis, Hannah I, 765
Lewis, Hannah II, 83
Lewis, Hannah II, 238
Lewis, Hannah II, 295
Lewis, Hannah II, 388
Lewis, Hannah II, 389
Lewis, Hannah II, 579
Lewis, Hannah II, 580
Lewis, Hannah II, 643
Lewis, Hannah II, 655
Lewis, Hannah II, 667
Lewis, Hannah II, 679
Lewis, Hannah II, 710
Lewis, Hannah II, 752
Lewis, Hannah III, 206
Lewis, Hannah IV, 98
Lewis, Hannah IV, 107
Lewis, Hannah IV, 128
Lewis, Hannah IV, 152
Lewis, Hannah IV, 208
Lewis, Hannah IV, 220
Lewis, Hannah IV, 238
Lewis, Hannah IV, 239
Lewis, Hannah IV, 242
Lewis, Hannah IV, 312
Lewis, Hannah IV, 313
Lewis, Hannah IV, 335
Lewis, Hannah IV, 340
Lewis, Hannah IV, 417
Lewis, Hannah IV, 525
Lewis, Hannah IV, 530
Lewis, Hannah IV, 539
Lewis, Hannah IV, 1171
Lewis, Hannah IV, 1197
Lewis, Hannah V, 92
Lewis, Hannah V, 146
Lewis, Hannah V, 185
Lewis, Hannah V, 339
Lewis, Hannah V, 340
Lewis, Hannah V, 345
Lewis, Hannah V, 346
Lewis, Hannah V, 410
Lewis, Hannah V, 411
Lewis, Hannah V, 573
Lewis, Hannah V, 581
Lewis, Hannah V, 955
Lewis, Hannah VI, 353
Lewis, Hannah VI, 526
Lewis, Hannah VI, 527
Lewis, Hannah VI, 671
Lewis, Hannah A. II, 889
Lewis, Hannah Abbott II, 388
Lewis, Hannah Addah IV, 1104
Lewis, Hannah Ann V, 345
Lewis, Hannah E. II, 805
Lewis, Hannah E. II, 866
Lewis, Hannah E. II, 889
Lewis, Hannah J. I, 1145
Lewis, Hannah M. IV, 539
Lewis, Hannah McCune IV, 417
Lewis, Harriet V, 346
Lewis, Harriett V, 345
Lewis, Harvey IV, 238
Lewis, Helen G. II, 805
Lewis, Helen G. II, 889
Lewis, Helen M. IV, 45
Lewis, Helena IV, 1104
Lewis, Helena IV, 1105
Lewis, Helena IV, 1112
Lewis, Henery IV, 239
Lewis, Henrietta II, 529
Lewis, Henrietta II, 580
Lewis, Henry I, 1082
Lewis, Henry I, 1084
Lewis, Henry I, 1085
Lewis, Henry I, 1095
Lewis, Henry I, 1107
Lewis, Henry I, 1124
Lewis, Henry I, 1145
Lewis, Henry I, 1158
Lewis, Henry II, 388
Lewis, Henry II, 579
Lewis, Henry II, 580
Lewis, Henry II, 597
Lewis, Henry III, 206
Lewis, Henry III, 290
Lewis, Henry III, 425
Lewis, Henry IV, 45
Lewis, Henry IV, 152
Lewis, Henry IV, 167
Lewis, Henry IV, 238
Lewis, Henry IV, 243
Lewis, Henry IV, 585
Lewis, Henry IV, 1104
Lewis, Henry VI, 362
Lewis, Henry VI, 413
Lewis, Henry VI, 419
Lewis, Henry VI, 527
Lewis, Henry C. IV, 585
Lewis, Henry C. IV, 586
Lewis, Henry J. II, 752
Lewis, Henry J. IV, 734
Lewis, Henry, Jr. IV, 238
Lewis, Henry, Jr. VI, 413
Lewis, Herbert Spencer VI, 730
Lewis, Herbert Spencer VI, 734
Lewis, Herbert Spencer VI, 762
Lewis, Herbert Spencer VI, 769
Lewis, Herbert Spencer VI, 794
Lewis, Hester V, 92
Lewis, Hiram H. IV, 586
Lewis, Hiram P. IV, 585
Lewis, Howel VI, 943
Lewis, Howel VI, 948
Lewis, Howel VI, 950
Lewis, Howell VI, 842
Lewis, I. Curis I, 326
Lewis, Ida V, 691
Lewis, Ira IV, 238
Lewis, Ira IV, 239
Lewis, Ira IV, 340
Lewis, Ira IV, 417
Lewis, Ira IV, 561
Lewis, Isaac I, 1145
Lewis, Isaac II, 388
Lewis, Isaac II, 580
Lewis, Isaac IV, 44
Lewis, Isaac IV, 45
Lewis, Isaac IV, 238
Lewis, Isaac IV, 340
Lewis, Isaac IV, 483
Lewis, Isaac IV, 1065
Lewis, Isaac IV, 1104
Lewis, Isaac V, 92
Lewis, Isaac V, 156
Lewis, Isaac V, 185
Lewis, Isaac V, 339
Lewis, Isaac V, 345
Lewis, Isaac V, 356
Lewis, Isaac V, 691
Lewis, Isaac V, 955
Lewis, Isaac V, 1006
Lewis, Isaac VI, 413
Lewis, Isaac Buck III, 425
Lewis, Isaac Buck III, 460
Lewis, Isaac Buck III, 461
Lewis, Isaac N. V, 259
Lewis, Isaac N. V, 346
Lewis, Isaiah V, 346
Lewis, Israel II, 579
Lewis, Israel II, 601
Lewis, Iva Jane IV, 975
Lewis, J. Allen IV, 240
Lewis, J. Curtis I, 337
Lewis, J. Edgar I, 945
Lewis, J. L. IV, 1238
Lewis, Jacob II, 83
Lewis, Jacob II, 178
Lewis, Jacob II, 238
Lewis, Jacob II, 388
Lewis, Jacob II, 389
Lewis, Jacob II, 579
Lewis, Jacob II, 580
Lewis, Jacob II, 597
Lewis, Jacob IV, 44
Lewis, Jacob IV, 76
Lewis, Jacob IV, 98
Lewis, Jacob IV, 152
Lewis, Jacob IV, 167
Lewis, Jacob IV, 208
Lewis, Jacob IV, 239
Lewis, Jacob IV, 340
Lewis, Jacob IV, 417
Lewis, Jacob IV, 539
Lewis, Jacob V, 510
Lewis, Jacob VI, 413
Lewis, Jacob VI, 527
Lewis, Jacob, Jr. II, 580
Lewis, Jail II, 83
Lewis, Jale II, 83
Lewis, James I, 630
Lewis, James I, 631
Lewis, James I, 636
Lewis, James II, 33
Lewis, James II, 83
Lewis, James II, 84
Lewis, James II, 388
Lewis, James II, 389
Lewis, James II, 579
Lewis, James II, 581
Lewis, James II, 603
Lewis, James II, 694
Lewis, James II, 889
Lewis, James III, 206
Lewis, James V, 185
Lewis, James V, 581
Lewis, James VI, 803
Lewis, James Edgar I, 929
Lewis, James G. I, 620
Lewis, James G., Jr. I, 620
Lewis, James L. III, 63
Lewis, James L. III, 206
Lewis, James Monroe I, 702
Lewis, James Monroe I, 724
Lewis, James P. A. V, 955
Lewis, James S. III, 206
Lewis, James Smith II, 580
Lewis, James Smith II, 581
Lewis, James T. I, 1124
Lewis, James W. VI, 950
Lewis, James Wm. II, 752
Lewis, Jane I, 1085
Lewis, Jane I, 1093
Lewis, Jane I, 1095
Lewis, Jane I, 1144
Lewis, Jane I, 1158
Lewis, Jane II, 388
Lewis, Jane II, 579
Lewis, Jane II, 678
Lewis, Jane II, 795
Lewis, Jane II, 805
Lewis, Jane IV, 539
Lewis, Jane IV, 547
Lewis, Jane IV, 640
Lewis, Jane IV, 646
Lewis, Jane IV, 1171
Lewis, Jane IV, 1182
Lewis, Jane IV, 1197
Lewis, Jane V, 259
Lewis, Jane V, 1006
Lewis, Jane VI, 351
Lewis, Jane VI, 353
Lewis, Jane C. II, 740
Lewis, Jane C. II, 752
Lewis, Jane R. IV, 1284
Lewis, Jane W. IV, 1152
Lewis, Jane W. IV, 1171
Lewis, Janetta Davis V, 691
Lewis, Japhett II, 445
Lewis, Jas. G. I, 636
Lewis, Jas. Smith III, 206
Lewis, Jason IV, 640
Lewis, Jason IV, 1152
Lewis, Jason IV, 1171
Lewis, Jason IV, 1196
Lewis, Jason IV, 1284
Lewis, Jason VI, 353
Lewis, Jefferson I, 1123
Lewis, Jefferson IV, 63
Lewis, Jehu IV, 44
Lewis, Jehu IV, 50
Lewis, Jehu IV, 239
Lewis, Jehu IV, 525
Lewis, Jehu IV, 539
Lewis, Jehu IV, 1171
Lewis, Jehu V, 92
Lewis, Jehu V, 306
Lewis, Jehu V, 345
Lewis, Jehu V, 346
Lewis, Jehu VI, 328
Lewis, Jehu VI, 350
Lewis, Jehu VI, 353
Lewis, Jehu VI, 355
Lewis, Jehu VI, 413
Lewis, Jehu VI, 526
Lewis, Jehu VI, 527
Lewis, Jehu VI, 613
Lewis, Jehu VI, 633
Lewis, Jehu VI, 671
Lewis, Jehu F. IV, 45
Lewis, Jemima IV, 258
Lewis, Jenkins II, 389
Lewis, Jeptha II, 580
Lewis, Jerusha III, 425
Lewis, Jerusha III, 464
Lewis, Jesse IV, 152
Lewis, Jesse IV, 641
Lewis, Jesse IV, 646
Lewis, Jesse V, 92
Lewis, Jesse V, 185
Lewis, Jesse V, 345
Lewis, Jesse V, 346
Lewis, Jesse V, 573
Lewis, Jesse V, 581
Lewis, Jesse VI, 328
Lewis, Jesse VI, 329
Lewis, Jesse VI, 334
Lewis, Jesse VI, 345
Lewis, Jesse VI, 351
Lewis, Jesse VI, 353
Lewis, Jesse VI, 671
Lewis, Jessie IV, 1215
Lewis, Jessie E. IV, 240
Lewis, Joanna I, 1145
Lewis, Job II, 805
Lewis, Job II, 889
Lewis, Job II, 931
Lewis, Job III, 206
Lewis, Job III, 321
Lewis, Job W. II, 889
Lewis, Joel II, 559
Lewis, Joel II, 580
Lewis, Joel V, 92
Lewis, Joel V, 306
Lewis, Joel V, 345
Lewis, Joel V, 346
Lewis, Joel VI, 328
Lewis, Joel VI, 329
Lewis, Joel VI, 349
Lewis, Joel VI, 353
Lewis, Joel VI, 355
Lewis, Joel VI, 526
Lewis, Joel VI, 613
Lewis, Joel VI, 633
Lewis, Joel VI, 671
Lewis, Johaw I, 1011
Lewis, Johaw??? I, 1011
Lewis, John I, 620
Lewis, John I, 891
Lewis, John II, 83
Lewis, John II, 238
Lewis, John II, 388
Lewis, John II, 579
Lewis, John II, 580
Lewis, John II, 581
Lewis, John II, 752
Lewis, John II, 805
Lewis, John II, 807
Lewis, John II, 889
Lewis, John III, 425
Lewis, John III, 461
Lewis, John IV, 98
Lewis, John IV, 107
Lewis, John IV, 239
Lewis, John IV, 539
Lewis, John IV, 547
Lewis, John IV, 1104
Lewis, John IV, 1171
Lewis, John IV, 1182
Lewis, John V, 185
Lewis, John V, 306
Lewis, John V, 345
Lewis, John V, 346
Lewis, John V, 410
Lewis, John V, 510
Lewis, John V, 955
Lewis, John VI, 328
Lewis, John VI, 348
Lewis, John VI, 409
Lewis, John VI, 413
Lewis, John VI, 527
Lewis, John VI, 834
Lewis, John B. I, 1085
Lewis, John B. I, 1095
Lewis, John B. I, 1124
Lewis, John Barker II, 580
Lewis, John D. II, 581
Lewis, John Edwin I, 620
Lewis, John F. IV, 45
Lewis, John H. VI, 131
Lewis, John H. VI, 137
Lewis, John Henry III, 461
Lewis, John Ira IV, 45
Lewis, John Ira IV, 340
Lewis, John Milton IV, 340
Lewis, John Rease II, 889
Lewis, John Reece II, 838
Lewis, John Reece II, 889
Lewis, John W. III, 206
Lewis, John W. IV, 1171
Lewis, John W. IV, 1197
Lewis, John W. V, 411
Lewis, John, Jr. IV, 1171
Lewis, Johnson Perry, Jr. IV, 1256
Lewis, Jonah V, 92
Lewis, Jonah V, 306
Lewis, Jonah V, 345
Lewis, Jonah V, 346

Lewis, Jonah V, 510
Lewis, Jonah VI, 353
Lewis, Jonathan II, 388
Lewis, Jonathan II, 471
Lewis, Jonathan II, 579
Lewis, Jonathan II, 580
Lewis, Jonathan II, 643
Lewis, Jonathan Butler VI, 76
Lewis, Jonathan S. IV, 1152
Lewis, Josep T. IV, 239
Lewis, Joseph II, 74
Lewis, Joseph II, 83
Lewis, Joseph II, 295
Lewis, Joseph II, 388
Lewis, Joseph II, 533
Lewis, Joseph II, 579
Lewis, Joseph II, 581
Lewis, Joseph II, 795
Lewis, Joseph III, 206
Lewis, Joseph IV, 44
Lewis, Joseph IV, 45
Lewis, Joseph IV, 60
Lewis, Joseph IV, 239
Lewis, Joseph IV, 483
Lewis, Joseph VI, 76
Lewis, Joseph Jr II, 238
Lewis, Joseph M. IV, 239
Lewis, Joseph P. V, 918
Lewis, Joseph P. Jessop V, 92
Lewis, Joseph Smith III, 206
Lewis, Josiah V, 345
Lewis, Judith V, 156
Lewis, Judith V, 185
Lewis, Juhu I, 1008
Lewis, Juhu I, 1011
Lewis, Julia IV, 239
Lewis, Julia IV, 417
Lewis, Julia E. V, 259
Lewis, Juliann IV, 170
Lewis, Juliann IV, 239
Lewis, Juliet IV, 240
Lewis, Juliet C. IV, 340
Lewis, Kate IV, 483
Lewis, Kate V, 346
Lewis, Katey IV, 238
Lewis, Katharine IV, 238
Lewis, Katherine II, 580
Lewis, Katy IV, 239
Lewis, Kezia I, 1080
Lewis, Kezia I, 1085
Lewis, Kezia I, 1158
Lewis, Keziah I, 1082
Lewis, Keziah I, 1084
Lewis, Keziah I, 1095
Lewis, Keziah I, 1145
Lewis, Keziah I, 1147
Lewis, Keziah I, 1158
Lewis, Kizia I, 1145
Lewis, Laura V, 1007
Lewis, Laura Cecilia II, 795
Lewis, Lavina IV, 1152
Lewis, Lavina V, 45
Lewis, Lavina V, 92
Lewis, Lemuel IV, 1171
Lewis, Lemuel V, 339
Lewis, Lemuel V, 345
Lewis, Lemuel V, 346
Lewis, Lemuel V, 410
Lewis, Lena IV, 734
Lewis, Lewella I, 724
Lewis, Lewis IV, 45
Lewis, Lewis IV, 152
Lewis, Lewis IV, 238
Lewis, Lewis IV, 239
Lewis, Lewis IV, 266
Lewis, Lewis IV, 1065
Lewis, Lewis IV, 1104
Lewis, Lewis IV, 1107
Lewis, Lewis V, 259
Lewis, Lewis VI, 413
Lewis, Lewis VI, 834
Lewis, Lewis Adams IV, 1171
Lewis, Lidia II, 559
Lewis, Lidia II, 580
Lewis, Lizzie V, 92
Lewis, Lizzie L. V, 92
Lewis, Lizzie M. VI, 258
Lewis, Lorenzo IV, 238
Lewis, Lorenzo IV, 239
Lewis, Lorenzo IV, 417
Lewis, Lorenzo IV, 539
Lewis, Lorenzo IV, 585
Lewis, Lorenzo D. IV, 239
Lewis, Lorenzo D. IV, 397
Lewis, Lorenzo D. IV, 417
Lewis, Lorenzo D. IV, 585
Lewis, Lottie I, 929
Lewis, Louisa I, 724
Lewis, Louisa I, 725
Lewis, Louisa V, 92
Lewis, Louisa J. III, 425
Lewis, Louisa K. V, 92
Lewis, Louise I, 620
Lewis, Lucina V, 490
Lewis, Lucinda I, 1124
Lewis, Lucinda I, 1145
Lewis, Lucinda I Sup 1, 12
Lewis, Lucinda IV, 238
Lewis, Lucinda IV, 332
Lewis, Lucinda IV, 340
Lewis, Lucinda VI, 834
Lewis, Lucinda Susanna IV, 238
Lewis, Lucy II, 838
Lewis, Lucy II, 889
Lewis, Lucy A. V, 918
Lewis, Lucy B. II, 889
Lewis, Lucy J. IV, 239
Lewis, Lucy J. V, 918
Lewis, Lucy L. VI, 865
Lewis, Lydia II, 533
Lewis, Lydia II, 580
Lewis, Lydia II, 581
Lewis, Lydia IV, 203
Lewis, Lydia IV, 238
Lewis, Lydia IV, 254
Lewis, Lydia IV, 279
Lewis, Lydia IV, 312
Lewis, Lydia IV, 313
Lewis, Lydia IV, 340
Lewis, Lydia IV, 539
Lewis, Lydia IV, 561
Lewis, Lydia IV, 1171
Lewis, Lydia VI, 362
Lewis, Lydia VI, 413
Lewis, Lydia Ann IV, 45
Lewis, Lydia Ann IV, 152
Lewis, Lydia Ann IV, 155
Lewis, Lydia Ann IV, 240
Lewis, Lydia Ann IV, 256
Lewis, Lydia Ann IV, 332
Lewis, Lydia Ann IV, 340
Lewis, Lydia Ann V, 345
Lewis, Lydia E. IV, 239
Lewis, Lynn I, 1095
Lewis, M. Alice I, 631
Lewis, Mahlon I, 1145
Lewis, Mahlon H. I, 1085
Lewis, Mahlon H. I, 1090
Lewis, Mahlon H. I, 1095
Lewis, Margaret II, 889
Lewis, Margaret III, 489
Lewis, Margaret IV, 239
Lewis, Margaret IV, 818
Lewis, Margaret IV, 830
Lewis, Margaret IV, 1238
Lewis, Margaret VI, 76
Lewis, Margaret Ann IV, 239
Lewis, Margaret Ann V, 918
Lewis, Margaret Anna IV, 975
Lewis, Margaret Anne IV, 483
Lewis, Margaret Ellis II, 580
Lewis, Margaret J. IV, 217
Lewis, Margaret J. IV, 239
Lewis, Marguerite IV, 1256
Lewis, Maria IV, 331
Lewis, Maria IV, 340
Lewis, Maria IV, 1028
Lewis, Maria Ann II, 1072
Lewis, Maria Ann II, 1075
Lewis, Maria Ann V, 918
Lewis, Maria B. IV, 892
Lewis, Maria B. IV, 893
Lewis, Maria B. IV, 1028
Lewis, Marion V, 92
Lewis, Martha I, 1034
Lewis, Martha II, 580
Lewis, Martha II, 603
Lewis, Martha III, 425
Lewis, Martha IV, 152
Lewis, Martha IV, 311
Lewis, Martha IV, 313
Lewis, Martha IV, 1171
Lewis, Martha V, 92
Lewis, Martha V, 185
Lewis, Martha V, 345
Lewis, Martha V, 346
Lewis, Martha V, 955
Lewis, Martha Ann IV, 238
Lewis, Martha Ann IV, 239
Lewis, Martha Ann IV, 1059
Lewis, Martha Ann IV, 1065
Lewis, Martha Ann V, 259
Lewis, Martha E. II, 889
Lewis, Martha Ellen II, 805
Lewis, Martha S. VI, 75
Lewis, Martin II, 580
Lewis, Martin II, 581
Lewis, Martin Clarkson Young V, 92
Lewis, Mary I, 507
Lewis, Mary I, 945
Lewis, Mary I, 966
Lewis, Mary I, 1034
Lewis, Mary I, 1107
Lewis, Mary I, 1121
Lewis, Mary I, 1123
Lewis, Mary I, 1145
Lewis, Mary I, 1154
Lewis, Mary II, 74
Lewis, Mary II, 83
Lewis, Mary II, 389
Lewis, Mary II, 463
Lewis, Mary II, 464
Lewis, Mary II, 505
Lewis, Mary II, 579
Lewis, Mary II, 580
Lewis, Mary II, 679
Lewis, Mary II, 976
Lewis, Mary II, 1010
Lewis, Mary III, 196
Lewis, Mary III, 206
Lewis, Mary III, 329
Lewis, Mary III, 334
Lewis, Mary III, 363
Lewis, Mary III, 425
Lewis, Mary III, 434
Lewis, Mary III, 459
Lewis, Mary III, 460
Lewis, Mary III, 502
Lewis, Mary IV, 45
Lewis, Mary IV, 76
Lewis, Mary IV, 98
Lewis, Mary IV, 152
Lewis, Mary IV, 203
Lewis, Mary IV, 207
Lewis, Mary IV, 208
Lewis, Mary IV, 209
Lewis, Mary IV, 238
Lewis, Mary IV, 239
Lewis, Mary IV, 293
Lewis, Mary IV, 319
Lewis, Mary IV, 340
Lewis, Mary IV, 417
Lewis, Mary IV, 539
Lewis, Mary IV, 585
Lewis, Mary IV, 734
Lewis, Mary IV, 1171
Lewis, Mary IV, 1215
Lewis, Mary IV, 1256
Lewis, Mary IV, 1326
Lewis, Mary V, 92
Lewis, Mary V, 306
Lewis, Mary V, 345
Lewis, Mary V, 613
Lewis, Mary VI, 55
Lewis, Mary VI, 75
Lewis, Mary VI, 413
Lewis, Mary VI, 419
Lewis, Mary VI, 527
Lewis, Mary VI, 842
Lewis, Mary VI, 849
Lewis, Mary VI, 961
Lewis, Mary A. I, 929
Lewis, Mary A. I, 945
Lewis, Mary A. III, 420
Lewis, Mary A. IV, 1326
Lewis, Mary Alice I, 620
Lewis, Mary Ann I, 1085
Lewis, Mary Ann I, 1145
Lewis, Mary Ann I, 1158
Lewis, Mary Ann II, 1075
Lewis, Mary Ann III, 420
Lewis, Mary Ann IV, 238
Lewis, Mary Ann IV, 239
Lewis, Mary Ann IV, 372
Lewis, Mary Ann IV, 417
Lewis, Mary Ann IV, 539
Lewis, Mary Ann V, 185
Lewis, Mary Anna III, 425
Lewis, Mary B. V, 82
Lewis, Mary B. V, 83
Lewis, Mary B. V, 92
Lewis, Mary B. V, 505
Lewis, Mary B. V, 510
Lewis, Mary Barker II, 580
Lewis, Mary C. V, 1007
Lewis, Mary D. IV, 1104
Lewis, Mary Delitha IV, 1104
Lewis, Mary E. II, 784
Lewis, Mary E. III, 63
Lewis, Mary E. III, 206
Lewis, Mary E. IV, 1326
Lewis, Mary E. V, 411
Lewis, Mary Esther IV, 734
Lewis, Mary G. II, 740
Lewis, Mary G. II, 752
Lewis, Mary H. IV, 44
Lewis, Mary H. IV, 60
Lewis, Mary J. I, 1124
Lewis, Mary J. III, 502
Lewis, Mary J. V, 356
Lewis, Mary Jane V, 259
Lewis, Mary Jane V, 339
Lewis, Mary Jane V, 345
Lewis, Mary Jane V, 346
Lewis, Mary Jaune V, 691
Lewis, Mary L. IV, 45
Lewis, Mary L. VI, 824
Lewis, Mary S. IV, 45
Lewis, Mary T. II, 865
Lewis, Mary T. II, 889
Lewis, Mary Thorn II, 805
Lewis, Mary U. III, 206
Lewis, Mary W. III, 425
Lewis, Mary, Jr. II, 579
Lewis, Mary, Jr. IV, 238
Lewis, Mary, Jr. IV, 239
Lewis, Maryann IV, 238
Lewis, Mattie I, 630
Lewis, Mattie I, 636
Lewis, Mattie May I, 620
Lewis, Maude IV, 734
Lewis, May IV, 1326
Lewis, Melissa D. VI, 950
Lewis, Metilda IV, 239
Lewis, Mildred III, 138
Lewis, Mildred III, 206
Lewis, Mildred IV, 734
Lewis, Milton V, 259
Lewis, Minnie IV, 701
Lewis, Minnie IV, 734
Lewis, Miriam I, 718
Lewis, Miriam I, 724
Lewis, Monroe I, 724
Lewis, Mordecai II, 503
Lewis, Mordecai II, 534
Lewis, Mordecai II, 580
Lewis, Mordecai II, 643
Lewis, Mordecai II, 655
Lewis, Mordecai II, 667
Lewis, Mordecai II, 838
Lewis, Mordecai II, 889
Lewis, Mordecai III, 206
Lewis, Mordecai D. II, 581
Lewis, Morgan IV, 238
Lewis, Morgan IV, 239
Lewis, Morgan IV, 293
Lewis, Morris IV, 238
Lewis, Moses V, 92
Lewis, Moses V, 306
Lewis, Moses V, 346
Lewis, Mourning V, 306
Lewis, Mourning V, 345
Lewis, Mourning V, 346
Lewis, Mourning V, 363
Lewis, Mrs. Charlotte IV, 734
Lewis, Myra Elizabeth VI, 762
Lewis, Myra Elizabeth VI, 793
Lewis, Myrta VI, 733
Lewis, Myrta VI, 734
Lewis, Nancy I, 1090
Lewis, Nancy I, 1095
Lewis, Nancy I, 1145
Lewis, Nancy I, 1158
Lewis, Nancy III, 425
Lewis, Nancy V, 92
Lewis, Nancy V, 185
Lewis, Nancy V, 346
Lewis, Nancy VI, 903
Lewis, Nancy VI, 950
Lewis, Nancy VI, 959
Lewis, Nancy E. I, 1124
Lewis, Nancy Louisa I, 724
Lewis, Nancy Louiza I, 702
Lewis, Nancy W. VI, 851
Lewis, Naomi I, 1145
Lewis, Narcissa I, 1084
Lewis, Narcissa I, 1145
Lewis, Narcissus I, 1154
Lewis, Narcissus I, 1158
Lewis, Nathan II, 580
Lewis, Nathan II, 581
Lewis, Nathan II, 805
Lewis, Nathan V, 92
Lewis, Nathan V, 345
Lewis, Nathan V, 346
Lewis, Nathan V, 362
Lewis, Nathan V, 918
Lewis, Nathan VI, 353
Lewis, Nathaniel II, 580
Lewis, Nathaniel III, 206
Lewis, Nellie IV, 734
Lewis, Neodore III, 489
Lewis, Nicholas IV, 734
Lewis, Oborn Levis II, 889
Lewis, Olive V, 92
Lewis, Olive L. V, 92
Lewis, Oliver I, 945
Lewis, Oliver Francis I, 929
Lewis, Parker IV, 238
Lewis, Parker IV, 240
Lewis, Patience V, 182
Lewis, Patience V, 185
Lewis, Patience V, 342
Lewis, Patience V, 346
Lewis, Patsy VI, 834
Lewis, Paulina VI, 817
Lewis, Penelope V, 613
Lewis, Phebe II, 580
Lewis, Phebe II, 599
Lewis, Phebe II, 604
Lewis, Phebe II, 807
Lewis, Phebe III, 206
Lewis, Phebe IV, 1284
Lewis, Phebe V, 92
Lewis, Phebe V, 318
Lewis, Phebe V, 345
Lewis, Phebe V, 352
Lewis, Philo III, 206
Lewis, Philo III, 319
Lewis, Polly VI, 834
Lewis, Polly VI, 920
Lewis, Polly VI, 950
Lewis, Preston V, 185
Lewis, Priscilla V, 134
Lewis, Priscilla V, 306
Lewis, Priscilla V, 312
Lewis, Priscilla V, 318
Lewis, Priscilla V, 341
Lewis, Priscilla V, 345
Lewis, Priscilla V, 474
Lewis, Priscilla V, 505
Lewis, Priscilla V, 510
Lewis, Priscilla V, 536
Lewis, Prudence V, 955
Lewis, Rachel I, 1028
Lewis, Rachel I, 1034
Lewis, Rachel I, 1107
Lewis, Rachel I, 1120
Lewis, Rachel I, 1123
Lewis, Rachel II, 388
Lewis, Rachel II, 389
Lewis, Rachel II, 471
Lewis, Rachel II, 579
Lewis, Rachel II, 580
Lewis, Rachel II, 643
Lewis, Rachel II, 666
Lewis, Rachel IV, 44
Lewis, Rachel IV, 50
Lewis, Rachel IV, 216
Lewis, Rachel IV, 238
Lewis, Rachel IV, 239
Lewis, Rachel IV, 288
Lewis, Rachel IV, 330
Lewis, Rachel IV, 340
Lewis, Rachel IV, 372
Lewis, Rachel IV, 417
Lewis, Rachel IV, 539
Lewis, Rachel IV, 1152
Lewis, Rachel IV, 1171
Lewis, Rachel IV, 1196
Lewis, Rachel IV, 1197
Lewis, Rachel IV, 1284
Lewis, Rachel V, 92
Lewis, Rachel V, 147
Lewis, Rachel V, 162
Lewis, Rachel V, 185
Lewis, Rachel V, 306
Lewis, Rachel V, 345
Lewis, Rachel V, 346
Lewis, Rachel V, 362
Lewis, Rachel V, 469
Lewis, Rachel V, 955
Lewis, Rachel VI, 384
Lewis, Rachel VI, 935
Lewis, Rachel O. IV, 45
Lewis, Rachel W. IV, 1152
Lewis, Rachel W. IV, 1171
Lewis, Rebecca I, 1124
Lewis, Rebecca II, 710
Lewis, Rebecca IV, 152
Lewis, Rebecca IV, 238
Lewis, Rebecca IV, 239
Lewis, Rebecca IV, 243
Lewis, Rebecca IV, 258
Lewis, Rebecca IV, 535
Lewis, Rebecca IV, 539
Lewis, Rebecca IV, 640
Lewis, Rebecca IV, 646
Lewis, Rebecca IV, 1171
Lewis, Rebecca V, 185
Lewis, Rebecca V, 955
Lewis, Rebecca VI, 329
Lewis, Rebecca VI, 345
Lewis, Rebecca VI, 353
Lewis, Rebecca C. II, 581
Lewis, Rebecca Chalkley II, 580
Lewis, Rebecca Chalkley II, 667
Lewis, Rebecca H. IV, 539
Lewis, Rebecca H. IV, 1171
Lewis, Rebeckah IV, 539
Lewis, Rebeckah IV, 559
Lewis, Rebeckah VI, 328
Lewis, Rebeckah VI, 334
Lewis, Reeca IV, 240

vis, Reece IV, 340
vis, Reece IV, 417
vis, Rees IV, 239
vis, Reese IV, 340
vis, Rena I, 620
vis, Rena B. I, 636
vis, Reuben L. IV, 547
vis, Reuben Lundy IV, 547
vis, Rhoda I, 1085
vis, Rhoda I, 1090
vis, Rhoda I, 1095
vis, Rhoda V, 460
vis, Rhoda A. V, 691
vis, Rhoda Ann V, 61
vis, Rhoda Ann V, 92
vis, Rhodema V, 185
vis, Richard I, 966
vis, Richard I, 1107
vis, Richard I, 1123
vis, Richard II, 389
vis, Richard II, 579
vis, Richard VI, 258
vis, Richard VI, 413
vis, Robert II, 463
vis, Robert II, 580
vis, Robert II, 604
vis, Robert IV, 734
vis, Robert VI, 258
vis, Robert VI, 824
vis, Robert VI, 834
vis, Robert A. VI, 733
vis, Robert Glenn IV, 734
vis, Robert H. VI, 742
vis, Robert H. VI, 743
vis, Robert H. VI, 762
vis, Robert Hill II, 868
vis, Robert Hill II, 889
vis, Robert J. II, 752
vis, Robert W. III, 489
vis, Robert W. VI, 258
vis, Robert W., Jr. VI, 258
vis, Robert, Jr. II, 580
vis, Ronald V, 581
vis, Roy VI, 258
vis, Ruhamy V, 185
vis, Russell V, 581
vis, Ruth II, 83
vis, Ruth III, 485
vis, Ruth III, 489
vis, Ruth IV, 734
vis, Ruth IV, 1171
vis, Ruth IV, 1189
vis, Ruth IV, 1284
vis, Ruth V, 185
vis, Ruth V, 903
vis, Ruth V, 918
vis, Ruth VI, 567
vis, Ruth Anna VI, 762
vis, Ruth Anna VI, 769
vis, Ruth Mary III, 485
vis, Ruth Mary III, 489
vis, Ruth Stretch II, 581
vis, Ruth T. IV, 1171
vis, Ruthanna V, 185
vis, Sallie I, 326
vis, Sally V, 303
vis, Sally V, 306
vis, Sally V, 345
vis, Sally V, 346
vis, Sally B. VI, 834
vis, Sally P. VI, 950
vis, Sally P. VI, 1004
vis, Sampson B. VI, 892
vis, Sampson B. VI, 903
vis, Sampson B. VI, 920
vis, Sampson B. VI, 923
vis, Sampson B. VI, 950
vis, Samuel I, 966
vis, Samuel I, 1145
vis, Samuel I, 1158
vis, Samuel II, 529
vis, Samuel II, 574
vis, Samuel II, 579
vis, Samuel II, 580
vis, Samuel II, 581
vis, Samuel II, 601
vis, Samuel IV, 44
vis, Samuel IV, 49
vis, Samuel IV, 63
vis, Samuel IV, 69
vis, Samuel IV, 98
vis, Samuel IV, 137
vis, Samuel IV, 152
vis, Samuel IV, 238
vis, Samuel IV, 239
vis, Samuel IV, 340
vis, Samuel VI, 413
vis, Samuel VI, 527
vis, Samuel Bunting II, 889
vis, Samuel E. IV, 586
vis, Samuel Neave II, 580
Lewis, Samuel Neave II, 667
Lewis, Samuel S. IV, 1104
Lewis, Samuel, Jr. IV, 1105
Lewis, Samuel, Jr. VI, 413
Lewis, Samuel, Sr. VI, 413
Lewis, Sarah II, 83
Lewis, Sarah II, 388
Lewis, Sarah II, 389
Lewis, Sarah II, 579
Lewis, Sarah II, 580
Lewis, Sarah II, 597
Lewis, Sarah II, 683
Lewis, Sarah II, 711
Lewis, Sarah II, 752
Lewis, Sarah II, 805
Lewis, Sarah II, 830
Lewis, Sarah II, 889
Lewis, Sarah II, 931
Lewis, Sarah III, 206
Lewis, Sarah III, 290
Lewis, Sarah III, 313
Lewis, Sarah IV, 44
Lewis, Sarah IV, 49
Lewis, Sarah IV, 63
Lewis, Sarah IV, 238
Lewis, Sarah IV, 239
Lewis, Sarah IV, 240
Lewis, Sarah IV, 248
Lewis, Sarah IV, 313
Lewis, Sarah IV, 417
Lewis, Sarah IV, 436
Lewis, Sarah IV, 585
Lewis, Sarah IV, 586
Lewis, Sarah IV, 592
Lewis, Sarah IV, 1171
Lewis, Sarah V, 22
Lewis, Sarah V, 92
Lewis, Sarah V, 185
Lewis, Sarah V, 312
Lewis, Sarah V, 330
Lewis, Sarah V, 334
Lewis, Sarah V, 340
Lewis, Sarah V, 345
Lewis, Sarah V, 346
Lewis, Sarah V, 581
Lewis, Sarah VI, 76
Lewis, Sarah VI, 297
Lewis, Sarah VI, 328
Lewis, Sarah VI, 329
Lewis, Sarah VI, 341
Lewis, Sarah VI, 349
Lewis, Sarah VI, 353
Lewis, Sarah VI, 362
Lewis, Sarah VI, 413
Lewis, Sarah VI, 498
Lewis, Sarah VI, 527
Lewis, Sarah VI, 540
Lewis, Sarah VI, 613
Lewis, Sarah VI, 633
Lewis, Sarah VI, 671
Lewis, Sarah Ann II, 889
Lewis, Sarah Ann II, 901
Lewis, Sarah Ann V, 306
Lewis, Sarah C. IV, 1104
Lewis, Sarah D. III, 115
Lewis, Sarah E. IV, 230
Lewis, Sarah E. IV, 483
Lewis, Sarah E. VI, 258
Lewis, Sarah Elizabeth II, 889
Lewis, Sarah Elizabeth IV, 239
Lewis, Sarah Elizabeth IV, 483
Lewis, Sarah Elizabeth IV, 1171
Lewis, Sarah Elizabeth VI, 258
Lewis, Sarah J. I, 1145
Lewis, Sarah Jane IV, 332
Lewis, Sarah Jane IV, 340
Lewis, Sarah M. IV, 585
Lewis, Sarah M. IV, 586
Lewis, Sarah T. IV, 240
Lewis, Sarah W. II, 838
Lewis, Sarah W. II, 889
Lewis, Sarah Z. III, 321
Lewis, Sarah Zane II, 752
Lewis, Serenda VI, 834
Lewis, Serilla I, 724
Lewis, Serilla I, 725
Lewis, Seth V, 510
Lewis, Seth B. IV, 240
Lewis, Sharon C. II, 889
Lewis, Sharon Hill II, 838
Lewis, Sidney VI, 413
Lewis, Sidney VI, 435
Lewis, Sidney VI, 527
Lewis, Sidney Ann II, 711
Lewis, Sidney Ann II, 752
Lewis, Sidney Ann II, 889
Lewis, Sidney Ann II, 930
Lewis, Sidney Ann III, 206
Lewis, Sirah IV, 238
Lewis, Smithy Jane I, 326
Lewis, Solomon W. II, 84
Lewis, Solomon White II, 83
Lewis, Solomon White II, 580
Lewis, Sophia V, 1006
Lewis, Stephen A. IV, 340
Lewis, Stephen W. VI, 834
Lewis, Steven II, 83
Lewis, Susan IV, 239
Lewis, Susan IV, 293
Lewis, Susan A. D. VI, 834
Lewis, Susan E. VI, 803
Lewis, Susan Frances VI, 892
Lewis, Susan H. IV, 238
Lewis, Susan H. IV, 239
Lewis, Susan H. IV, 1065
Lewis, Susan H. IV, 1104
Lewis, Susan H. IV, 1107
Lewis, Susanah I, 966
Lewis, Susanna I, 507
Lewis, Susanna I, 557
Lewis, Susanna I, 563
Lewis, Susanna I, 1114
Lewis, Susanna I, 1123
Lewis, Susanna I, 1124
Lewis, Susanna II, 579
Lewis, Susanna II, 580
Lewis, Susanna IV, 45
Lewis, Susanna IV, 152
Lewis, Susanna IV, 238
Lewis, Susanna IV, 239
Lewis, Susanna IV, 243
Lewis, Susanna V, 185
Lewis, Susanna VI, 353
Lewis, Susanna VI, 413
Lewis, Susanna W. VI, 842
Lewis, Susannah I, 1028
Lewis, Susannah I, 1034
Lewis, Susannah I, 1101
Lewis, Susannah I, 1107
Lewis, Susannah I, 1123
Lewis, Susannah I, 1145
Lewis, Susannah IV, 152
Lewis, Susannah IV, 633
Lewis, Susannah IV, 640
Lewis, Susannah V, 92
Lewis, Susannah V, 330
Lewis, Susannah V, 345
Lewis, Susannah V, 346
Lewis, Susannah V, 955
Lewis, Susannah V, 956
Lewis, Susannah VI, 353
Lewis, Susannah VI, 401
Lewis, Susannah VI, 413
Lewis, Sydney Ann II, 805
Lewis, Syra IV, 239
Lewis, Syrina V, 345
Lewis, Tabitha IV, 1104
Lewis, Tabitha IV, 1112
Lewis, Tace II, 389
Lewis, Tacy IV, 372
Lewis, Tacy IV, 417
Lewis, Tacy IV, 569
Lewis, Tacy IV, 586
Lewis, Tacy VI, 903
Lewis, Tacy F. IV, 417
Lewis, Tacy T. IV, 239
Lewis, Tacy T. IV, 417
Lewis, Tacy T. IV, 585
Lewis, Tamar II, 807
Lewis, Tennyson V, 1007
Lewis, Theodore J. II, 805
Lewis, Theodore J. II, 889
Lewis, Thomas I, 1028
Lewis, Thomas I, 1033
Lewis, Thomas I, 1034
Lewis, Thomas I, 1145
Lewis, Thomas I, 1158
Lewis, Thomas II, 389
Lewis, Thomas II, 579
Lewis, Thomas II, 580
Lewis, Thomas II, 666
Lewis, Thomas IV, 203
Lewis, Thomas IV, 207
Lewis, Thomas IV, 238
Lewis, Thomas IV, 239
Lewis, Thomas IV, 254
Lewis, Thomas IV, 340
Lewis, Thomas IV, 539
Lewis, Thomas V, 92
Lewis, Thomas V, 162
Lewis, Thomas V, 185
Lewis, Thomas V, 955
Lewis, Thomas VI, 498
Lewis, Thomas VI, 527
Lewis, Thomas VI, 950
Lewis, Thomas E. II, 889
Lewis, Thomas Ellwood II, 805
Lewis, Thomas Ellwood II, 889
Lewis, Thomas, Jr. IV, 239
Lewis, Thomas, Jr. IV, 539
Lewis, Thos. II, 805
Lewis, Thos. IV, 238
Lewis, Thos. IV, 258
Lewis, Thos. E. II, 866
Lewis, Thos. E. II, 889
Lewis, Tracy II, 83
Lewis, Ulysses G. V, 92
Lewis, Uriah V, 306
Lewis, Velma V, 581
Lewis, Vennie V, 581
Lewis, Vernie V, 581
Lewis, Victor I, 620
Lewis, Viola Pearl IV, 1256
Lewis, Virginia J. III, 502
Lewis, Virginia Jones III, 502
Lewis, Waid Barker II, 580
Lewis, Walter V, 691
Lewis, Walter C. V, 691
Lewis, Walter H. V, 92
Lewis, Ward V, 185
Lewis, Wd. Mary II, 389
Lewis, Wd. Sarah II, 580
Lewis, Wd. Sarah III, 314
Lewis, Wesley V, 955
Lewis, Wheeler III, 206
Lewis, Widow Keziah I, 1158
Lewis, Willaby IV, 1215
Lewis, William I, 824
Lewis, William I, 929
Lewis, William I, 1033
Lewis, William I, 1090
Lewis, William I, 1095
Lewis, William I, 1145
Lewis, William I, 1158
Lewis, William II, 389
Lewis, William II, 445
Lewis, William IV, 45
Lewis, William IV, 238
Lewis, William IV, 239
Lewis, William IV, 1171
Lewis, William V, 92
Lewis, William V, 185
Lewis, William V, 955
Lewis, William VI, 75
Lewis, William VI, 76
Lewis, William VI, 362
Lewis, William VI, 413
Lewis, William VI, 950
Lewis, William F. VI, 865
Lewis, William G. III, 502
Lewis, William Gray VI, 847
Lewis, William H. I, 1124
Lewis, William Harvey IV, 45
Lewis, William Henry IV, 239
Lewis, William J. IV, 239
Lewis, William J. VI, 76
Lewis, William J. VI, 258
Lewis, William J. VI, 275
Lewis, William J. VI, 277
Lewis, William J. VI, 834
Lewis, William P. I, 1145
Lewis, William P. I, 1158
Lewis, William R. V, 346
Lewis, William Vurlar I, 326
Lewis, William, Jr. I, 1158
Lewis, Willoughby IV, 1215
Lewis, Wilson IV, 340
Lewis, Wm. II, 83
Lewis, Wm. II, 580
Lewis, Wm. IV, 152
Lewis, Wm. IV, 279
Lewis, Wm. IV, 975
Lewis, Wm. IV, 1104
Lewis, Wm. IV, 1112
Lewis, Wm. V, 185
Lewis, Wm. V, 955
Lewis, Wm. F. IV, 1171
Lewis, Wm. F. IV, 1189
Lewis, Wm. F. IV, 1284
Lewis, Wm. G. II, 752
Lewis, Wm. G. IV, 483
Lewis, Wm. H. II, 889
Lewis, Wm. H. IV, 340
Lewis, Wm. H. IV, 1104
Lewis, Wm. Harvey IV, 340
Lewis, Wm. Henry IV, 238
Lewis, Wm. Henry IV, 1065
Lewis, Wm. J. IV, 239
Lewis, Wm. J. IV, 483
Lewis, Wm. Penn II, 889
Lewis, Wm. West V, 185
Lewis, Zebidee C. I, 724
Lewis, Zebides Calvin I, 702
Lewis, Zimri V, 92
Lewis, Zimri V, 185
Lewis, Zimri V, 955
Lewiss, Adam II, 388
Lewiss, Daniel II, 445
Lewiss, Elizabeth II, 388
Lewiss, Esther II, 388
Lewiss, Evan II, 445
Lewiss, Hannah II, 388
Lewiss, James II, 388
Lewiss, Jane II, 388
Lewiss, Jenkins II, 389
Lewiss, John II, 388
Lewiss, John II, 445
Lewiss, Mary II, 445
Lewiss, Richard II, 389
Lewiss, Sarah II, 388
Lewiss, Sarah II, 389
Lewiss, Thomas II, 389
Lewiss, Thomas II, 445
Lewiss, Wd. Mary II, 389
Lewkins, Elizabeth V, 94
Lewkins, Hannah V, 28
Lewkins, Hannah V, 94
Lewkins, Joseph V, 28
Lewkins, Joseph V, 94
Lewkins, Levi V, 94
Leyburn, Elizabeth W. VI, 950
Leyburn, G. W. VI, 987
Leyburn, G. W. VI, 1011
Leyburn, George VI, 950
Leyffer, Minnie IV, 1171
Libek, Charles IV, 1326
Liber, Ida IV, 830
Liber, Ida IV, 831
Liber, Martha IV, 830
Liberty, Amy II, 577
Liberty, Amy II, 581
Libole, Sarah V, 51
Libole, Sarah V, 92
Lichty, Matilda V, 1007
Lichty, Mose V, 1007
Lichty, Van Buren V, 1007
Lick, Cammie I, 636
Lick, Cammie I, 637
Lick, J. I, 636
Lick, J. Elmer I, 636
Lick, J. Elmer I, 637
Lick, Van Lindley I, 637
Lickes, Nellie A. IV, 1326
Lickliter, Leta V, 185
Lida, Eliza W. IV, 611
Lidbetter, Mary III, 159
Liddell, Agnes III, 206
Liddell, Agnes III, 240
Liddell, Agnes Wilson III, 206
Liddell, Andrew III, 206
Liddell, Elizabeth Lindsay III, 206
Liddell, John Anderson III, 206
Liddell, John Anderson III, 240
Liddell, Kathren M. V, 346
Liddell, Margaret III, 206
Liddell, Raymond Neilson III, 206
Liddle, David P. IV, 240
Liddle, George IV, 240
Liddle, George L. IV, 240
Liddle, Matilda IV, 240
Liddon, Abraham II, 581
Liddon, Elizabeth II, 581
Liddon, Isabella II, 389
Liddon, Isabella II, 581
Liddon, Mary II, 405
Liddon, Mary II, 496
Liddon, Mary II, 581
Liebyer, Edward IV, 735
Liebyer, Nancy IV, 735
Liebyer, Sylvia IV, 735
Liesure, James V, 1006
Liesure, Joseph V, 1006
Liesure, Mary V, 1006
Lieurance, Alva V, 346
Lieurance, Burt V, 1006
Lieurance, Cordelia V, 410
Lieurance, David V, 410
Lieurance, Etta Leota V, 410
Lieurance, Ettie Leota V, 410
Lieurance, Laurenna Maud V, 410
Lieurance, Lourenna Maud V, 410
Lieurance, Mary V, 1006
Lieurance, Piercon V, 410
Lieurance, Pierson V, 410
Lieurance, Rhue D. V, 410
Lieurance, Sidney V, 410
Ligen, Agness VI, 853
Liggat, Mary VI, 329
Liggat, Mary VI, 330
Liggett, Anna Laura V, 581
Liggett, Jacob Henry V, 345
Light, Daniel II, 238
Light, Daniel II, 270
Light, Eliza. II, 238
Light, John V, 918
Light, Mary V, 410
Light, Mary V, 918
Light, Wm. A. V, 632
Light, Wm. A. V, 918
Lightfoot, Abbie II, 711

Lightfoot, Abi II, 711
Lightfoot, Abi II, 752
Lightfoot, Abi II, 772
Lightfoot, Abi W. II, 752
Lightfoot, Addison IV, 593
Lightfoot, Agness IV, 593
Lightfoot, Alice A. IV, 1066
Lightfoot, Alice Ann IV, 1049
Lightfoot, Alice Ann IV, 1065
Lightfoot, Alice Ann IV, 1066
Lightfoot, Ann II, 84
Lightfoot, Ann II, 752
Lightfoot, Ann L. II, 752
Lightfoot, Ann L. II, 770
Lightfoot, Annie E. II, 711
Lightfoot, Annie E. II, 752
Lightfoot, Benjamin II, 581
Lightfoot, Benjamin II, 711
Lightfoot, Benjamin II, 752
Lightfoot, Benjamin IV, 731
Lightfoot, Benjamin H. II, 752
Lightfoot, Benjamin H. II, 773
Lightfoot, Benjamin H. II, 938
Lightfoot, Benjamin H. IV, 734
Lightfoot, Benjamin H. IV, 768
Lightfoot, Catharine II, 581
Lightfoot, Catherine II, 581
Lightfoot, Clarkson IV, 593
Lightfoot, Daniel Ferris II, 711
Lightfoot, David II, 711
Lightfoot, David II, 716
Lightfoot, David II, 721
Lightfoot, David II, 752
Lightfoot, David II, 772
Lightfoot, David II, 773
Lightfoot, David II, 777
Lightfoot, David IV, 734
Lightfoot, David F. II, 752
Lightfoot, David Ferris II, 711
Lightfoot, David Ferris II, 752
Lightfoot, Deborah II, 721
Lightfoot, Elisha B. IV, 240
Lightfoot, Elisha P. IV, 734
Lightfoot, Elizabeth II, 389
Lightfoot, Elizabeth IV, 586
Lightfoot, Ellen II, 752
Lightfoot, Emma IV, 240
Lightfoot, Emma IV, 586
Lightfoot, Emma IV, 593
Lightfoot, Esther II, 723
Lightfoot, Ferris IV, 734
Lightfoot, Florence II, 711
Lightfoot, Foster IV, 240
Lightfoot, Foster IV, 1049
Lightfoot, Foster IV, 1065
Lightfoot, Foster IV, 1066
Lightfoot, Foster IV, 1105
Lightfoot, Foster H. IV, 1066
Lightfoot, Fran II, 752
Lightfoot, Francis II, 711
Lightfoot, Francis II, 752
Lightfoot, Francis II, 772
Lightfoot, Francis Hanson II, 711
Lightfoot, Hannah IV, 240
Lightfoot, Hannah IV, 575
Lightfoot, Hannah IV, 584
Lightfoot, Hannah IV, 586
Lightfoot, Hannah IV, 1066
Lightfoot, Hannah IV, 1072
Lightfoot, Hannah V, 93
Lightfoot, Hannah M. IV, 240
Lightfoot, Hannah M. IV, 262
Lightfoot, Hannah M. IV, 1066
Lightfoot, Harriet IV, 1065
Lightfoot, Harriet B. IV, 1066
Lightfoot, Isaac IV, 240
Lightfoot, Isaac IV, 586
Lightfoot, Isaac IV, 593
Lightfoot, Jane II, 389
Lightfoot, Jane II, 581
Lightfoot, Jane II, 752
Lightfoot, Jane II, 773
Lightfoot, Jane W. II, 711
Lightfoot, Jephtha V, 410
Lightfoot, Jeptha V, 410
Lightfoot, Joseph II, 711
Lightfoot, Joseph IV, 152
Lightfoot, Joseph IV, 153
Lightfoot, Joseph IV, 240
Lightfoot, Joseph IV, 1065
Lightfoot, Joseph IV, 1066
Lightfoot, Joseph IV, 1105
Lightfoot, Julia IV, 768
Lightfoot, Julian IV, 1065
Lightfoot, Juliann D. IV, 1066
Lightfoot, Karl Daniel IV, 768
Lightfoot, Katharine VI, 491
Lightfoot, Katharine VI, 534
Lightfoot, Lawrence IV, 240
Lightfoot, Lindley IV, 593
Lightfoot, Lydia II, 711
Lightfoot, Lydia IV, 731
Lightfoot, Lydia IV, 734
Lightfoot, Lydia IV, 768
Lightfoot, Lydia K. II, 752
Lightfoot, Lydia K. IV, 240
Lightfoot, Lydia K. IV, 283
Lightfoot, Lydia K. IV, 734
Lightfoot, Malinda V, 410
Lightfoot, Margaret II, 711
Lightfoot, Margaret II, 752
Lightfoot, Margaret Jane II, 711
Lightfoot, Martha IV, 240
Lightfoot, Mary II, 238
Lightfoot, Mary II, 261
Lightfoot, Mary II, 581
Lightfoot, Mary II, 711
Lightfoot, Mary IV, 240
Lightfoot, Mary IV, 586
Lightfoot, Melinda V, 410
Lightfoot, Melinda V, 419
Lightfoot, Michael II, 238
Lightfoot, Michael II, 261
Lightfoot, Michael II, 389
Lightfoot, Michael II, 581
Lightfoot, Philip VI, 231
Lightfoot, Rachel IV, 152
Lightfoot, Rachel IV, 153
Lightfoot, Rachel IV, 240
Lightfoot, Rachel IV, 262
Lightfoot, Rachel IV, 340
Lightfoot, Rachel IV, 352
Lightfoot, Rachel IV, 586
Lightfoot, Rachel IV, 1065
Lightfoot, Rachel IV, 1066
Lightfoot, Rachel IV, 1077
Lightfoot, Rachel IV, 1105
Lightfoot, Rachel K. IV, 570
Lightfoot, Rachel K. IV, 586
Lightfoot, Samuel IV, 152
Lightfoot, Samuel IV, 240
Lightfoot, Samuel IV, 262
Lightfoot, Samuel IV, 586
Lightfoot, Samuel IV, 1065
Lightfoot, Samuel IV, 1066
Lightfoot, Samuel IV, 1105
Lightfoot, Sarah II, 84
Lightfoot, Sarah II, 95
Lightfoot, Sarah II, 463
Lightfoot, Sarah II, 581
Lightfoot, Sarah II, 711
Lightfoot, Sarah II, 716
Lightfoot, Sarah II, 721
Lightfoot, Sarah II, 752
Lightfoot, Sarah II, 772
Lightfoot, Sarah II, 773
Lightfoot, Sarah II, 777
Lightfoot, Sarah IV, 240
Lightfoot, Sarah IV, 567
Lightfoot, Sarah IV, 586
Lightfoot, Sarah IV, 734
Lightfoot, Susanna II, 752
Lightfoot, Susanna II, 777
Lightfoot, Susanna IV, 1049
Lightfoot, Susanna IV, 1066
Lightfoot, Susanna IV, 1105
Lightfoot, Susanna VI, 231
Lightfoot, Susannah IV, 1065
Lightfoot, Thomas II, 238
Lightfoot, Thomas II, 261
Lightfoot, Thomas II, 389
Lightfoot, Thomas II, 463
Lightfoot, Thomas II, 581
Lightfoot, Thomas IV, 240
Lightfoot, Thomas IV, 586
Lightfoot, Thomas V, 410
Lightfoot, Thomas VI, 304
Lightfoot, Thos. V, 410
Lightfoot, Wd. Mary II, 389
Lightfoot, William II, 389
Lightfoot, William IV, 240
Lightfoot, William IV, 340
Lightfoot, William IV, 539
Lightfoot, William IV, 734
Lightfoot, William VI, 76
Lightfoot, William John II, 711
Lightfoot, William Joseph IV, 1065
Lightfoot, William K. IV, 586
Lightfoot, Wm. II, 581
Lightfoot, Wm. IV, 586
Lightfoot, Wm. IV, 831
Lightfoot, Wm. V, 972
Lightfoot, Wm. J. II, 752
Lightfoot, Wm. J. IV, 1066
Lightfoot, Wm. John II, 752
Lightfoot, Wm. L. IV, 1066
Lightfoot, Wm. M. IV, 152
Lightheart, Christopher II, 445
Lighthiser, Edward V, 185
Lighthiser, James V, 185
Lighthizer, Clara V, 186
Lighthizer, Edith V, 186
Lighthizer, Edward V, 185
Lighthizer, Edward V, 186
Lighthizer, George V, 186
Lighthizer, Howard V, 186
Lighthizer, James V, 186
Lighthizer, Nellie V, 186
Lightner, Ada V, 691
Lightner, Charley V, 751
Lightner, Ella V, 751
Lightner, Frank V, 691
Lightner, Harvey V, 751
Lightner, Mertie V, 691
Lightner, Roy V, 751
Lightner, S. B. V, 691
Ligon, Agnes VI, 833
Likens, Henrietta II, 810
Likens, Phebe VI, 430
Likins, Phebe VI, 413
Likins, Phebe VI, 430
Lilburn, Ruth II, 790
Lile, James IV, 417
Liles, Peninnah IV, 417
Liley, Elizabeth VI, 834
Liley, John VI, 834
Lillas, William IV, 1021
Lilley, Edmond VI, 286
Lilley, Elizabeth III, 197
Lilley, Elizabeth III, 206
Lilley, Elizabeth III, 344
Lilley, Elizabeth IV, 98
Lilley, Elizabeth IV, 105
Lilley, Ellis IV, 45
Lilley, Ellis IV, 98
Lilley, Ellis IV, 105
Lilley, Ellis IV, 114
Lilley, Ellis N. IV, 45
Lilley, George W. III, 84
Lilley, George W. III, 197
Lilley, George W. III, 206
Lilley, Hannah IV, 98
Lilley, Hannah IV, 116
Lilley, Homer C. IV, 45
Lilley, Honor C. IV, 98
Lilley, Jane IV, 98
Lilley, Laura J. III, 344
Lilley, Lewis P. III, 344
Lilley, Phebe IV, 98
Lilley, Phebe IV, 105
Lilley, Phebe Ann IV, 45
Lilley, Robert IV, 98
Lilley, Ruth I, 46
Lilley, Ruth I, 59
Lilley, Ruth IV, 84
Lilley, Ruth IV, 98
Lilley, Ruth IV, 105
Lilley, Ruth IV, 116
Lilley, Sarah I, 59
Lilley, Sarah I, 62
Lilley, Solomon P. IV, 45
Lilley, Thomas IV, 98
Lilley, Thomas IV, 105
Lilley, Thomas IV, 116
Lilley, Thomas W. IV, 45
Lillian, Ella IV, 772
Lillie, Daniel IV, 1326
Lillie, Dorcas II, 581
Lillie, George W. III, 344
Lillie, George W. VI, 736
Lillie, George W. VI, 790
Lillie, Jefferson J. IV, 1326
Lillie, Lena H. IV, 1326
Lillie, Therisa IV, 1326
Lillie, Wd. Elizabeth D. VI, 736
Lillie, Wd. Elizabeth D. VI, 790
Lilly, Edmond VI, 286
Lilly, Ellis IV, 45
Lilly, Ellis N. IV, 45
Lilly, Hannah IV, 45
Lilly, Harriett V, 725
Lilly, Homer C. IV, 45
Lilly, Jane IV, 45
Lilly, Lucinda V, 725
Lilly, Phebe IV, 45
Lilly, Phebe Ann IV, 45
Lilly, Robert IV, 45
Lilly, Robert IV, 340
Lilly, Robert IV, 539
Lilly, Ruth IV, 41
Lilly, Ruth IV, 45
Lilly, Solomon P. IV, 45
Lilly, Thomas IV, 45
Lilly, Thomas W. IV, 45
Lilly, Wm. V, 725
Lily, Honor C. IV, 734
Lim, Lan III, 206
Limburner, Elizabeth II, 806
Limburner, John II, 806
Limburner, Mary II, 806
Limes, Athaliah V, 259
Limes, Clara V, 460
Limes, Hazel V, 460
Limes, Lenore V, 460
Limes, Mabel IV, 1256
Limes, Sarah IV, 1256
Limes, William V, 259
Liming, Andrew V, 691
Liming, Daisy V, 691
Liming, Eliza V, 93
Liming, Homer V, 93
Lin, Bessie Gloria III, 206
Lin, Evelyn Doris III, 206
Lin, Fannie III, 206
Lin, Helen III, 206
Lin, John III, 206
Lin, Lucy E. B. III, 206
Lin, Ruth III, 206
Lin, Yen III, 206
Lin, Young III, 206
Linagar, Isaac I, 824
Linch, Ann I, 443
Linch, Ann I, 450
Linch, Dennis II, 445
Linch, Esther I, 405
Linch, George Anner I, 290
Linch, George Anner I, 291
Linch, George Henry I, 291
Linch, Haywod I, 290
Linch, Haywod I, 291
Linch, Jesse II, 581
Linch, Marion Justice I, 291
Linch, Patcy VI, 944
Linch, Peter V, 186
Linch, Raffard I, 290
Linch, Rebecca I, 290
Linch, Sarah II, 54
Linch, Sarah II, 84
Linches, Chas VI, 291
Linckhorn, Sarah V, 850
Lincohorn, Sarah V, 849
Lincohorn, Sarah V, 850
Lincoln, Ann IV, 1066
Lincoln, Anna II, 889
Lincoln, Elizabeth Hague IV, 1256
Lincoln, Guli Elma IV, 1053
Lincoln, Guli Elma IV, 1066
Lincoln, Luther, Jr. IV, 1372
Lincoln, Mary II, 581
Lincoln, Robert VI, 732
Lincoln, Ruth Doing VI, 732
Lincoln, Sarah II, 581
Lincoln, Sarah II, 616
Lincoln, Wd. Mary II, 581
Lincon, Mary II, 581
Lincon, Mary II, 639
Lincon, Wd. Mary II, 581
Lincorn, Martha II, 389
Lincorn, Mary II, 389
Lindaman, Mrs. Elma V, 1007
Lindamood, Alta V, 93
Lindamood, Sarah E. V, 93
Lindell, Louisa III, 206
Lindell, Louisa III, 270
Lindell, Louisa M. III, 206
Lindell, William III, 206
Linden, Emily IV, 240
Linden, Florence V, 186
Linden, John A. IV, 240
Linden, Sarah I, 920
Lindenmuth, Bertha D. V, 186
Linder, Caleb V, 186
Linder, Florence V, 186
Lindgard, Mary II, 389
Lindley, A. H. V, 346
Lindley, Aaron I, 359
Lindley, Aaron I, 404
Lindley, Aaron I, 437
Lindley, Aaron I, 438
Lindley, Aaron I, 764
Lindley, Aaron I, 765
Lindley, Aaron I, 766
Lindley, Aaron, Jr. I, 449
Lindley, Adeline I, 438
Lindley, Albert I, 449
Lindley, Albert I, 557
Lindley, Albert G. I, 557
Lindley, Albert N. I, 437
Lindley, Alford I, 438
Lindley, Alford H. I, 437
Lindley, Alfred H. I, 450
Lindley, Alfred H. I, 720
Lindley, Alfred H. I, 724
Lindley, Alfred W. I, 449
Lindley, Ama K. V, 581
Lindley, Amy I, 378
Lindley, Amy I, 404
Lindley, Amy I, 449
Lindley, Ann I, 764
Lindley, Ann I, 765
Lindley, Ann I, 766
Lindley, Anna K. V, 561
Lindley, Anna K. V, 581
Lindley, Anna Lois IV, 1256
Lindley, Anna Maie I, 621
Lindley, Annie M. I, 626
Lindley, Aron I, 449
Lindley, Aron I, 765
Lindley, Asenath I, 684
Lindley, Asenath A. I, 437
Lindley, Asenath C. I, 661
Lindley, Asenath C. I, 684
Lindley, Asenath Cathrin I, 4
Lindley, Asenath O. I, 691
Lindley, Callie D. I, 450
Lindley, Cammie I, 621
Lindley, Cammie I, 636
Lindley, Cammie I, 637
Lindley, Carnelia G. S. I, 437
Lindley, Caroline I, 437
Lindley, Caroline I, 449
Lindley, Caroline I, 450
Lindley, Caroline I, 454
Lindley, Caroline I, 538
Lindley, Caroline I, 557
Lindley, Catharine I, 367
Lindley, Catharine I, 404
Lindley, Catharine I, 428
Lindley, Catharine I, 437
Lindley, Catharine I, 449
Lindley, Charles I, 557
Lindley, Charles G. I, 437
Lindley, Clarkson I, 437
Lindley, Clarkson I, 557
Lindley, Cornelia I, 437
Lindley, Cyrus T. I, 437
Lindley, David I, 359
Lindley, David I, 404
Lindley, David I, 437
Lindley, David I, 438
Lindley, David I, 449
Lindley, Deborah I, 352
Lindley, Deborah I, 358
Lindley, Deborah I, 359
Lindley, Deborah I, 362
Lindley, Deborah I, 404
Lindley, Deborah I, 411
Lindley, Deborah I, 431
Lindley, Deborah I, 449
Lindley, Elbridge M. I, 438
Lindley, Eleanor I, 404
Lindley, Eleanor I, 406
Lindley, Eleanor I, 437
Lindley, Eleanor I, 449
Lindley, Eleanor I, 450
Lindley, Eleanor I, 453
Lindley, Eleanor, Jr. I, 449
Lindley, Elender I, 358
Lindley, Elender I, 359
Lindley, Elenor I, 404
Lindley, Elenor I, 444
Lindley, Elenor I, 449
Lindley, Elinor I, 359
Lindley, Elinor I, 437
Lindley, Eliza I, 720
Lindley, Eliza I, 724
Lindley, Eliza J. I, 437
Lindley, Eliza J. I, 449
Lindley, Eliza J. I, 724
Lindley, Elizabeth I, 359
Lindley, Elizabeth I, 437
Lindley, Elizabeth I, 449
Lindley, Elizabeth II, 389
Lindley, Ella I, 437
Lindley, Ella I, 438
Lindley, Elmina I, 438
Lindley, Elva Jane I, 437
Lindley, Elwood I, 438
Lindley, Elwood I, 450
Lindley, Elwood A. I, 557
Lindley, Emeline I, 449
Lindley, Emily I, 438
Lindley, Emily I, 449
Lindley, Emma L. I, 661
Lindley, Esther IV, 310
Lindley, Eunice I, 438
Lindley, Eva I, 621
Lindley, Feriba I, 684
Lindley, Fowel Buxton I, 437
Lindley, Franklin D. I, 437
Lindley, Grace I, 449
Lindley, Gurney P. I, 437
Lindley, Hannah I, 358
Lindley, Hannah I, 404
Lindley, Hannah I, 437
Lindley, Hannah I, 444
Lindley, Hannah I, 449
Lindley, Hannah II, 389
Lindley, Hannah II, 510
Lindley, Hannah II, 581
Lindley, Hannah II, 604
Lindley, Hannah E. V, 581
Lindley, Harriet E. I, 450

dley, Harriett E. I, 437
dley, Ida M. I, 661
dley, Ida M. I, 684
dley, Ida May I, 437
dley, Isham I, 438
dley, J. Van I, 637
dley, Jabez Ingram I, 437
dley, Jacob, Jr. V, 918
dley, Jain I, 449
dley, James I, 358
dley, James I, 359
dley, James I, 404
dley, James I, 437
dley, James I, 449
dley, James I, 450
dley, James I, 453
dley, James II, 389
dley, James II, 581
dley, James II, 586
dley, James T. I, 438
dley, James T. I, 450
dley, James T. I, 661
dley, James T. I, 684
dley, James T. I, 691
dley, James Thompson I, 437
dley, Jane I, 449
dley, Jesse I, 437
dley, Jesse I, 449
dley, John I, 359
dley, John I, 404
dley, John I, 437
dley, John I, 438
dley, John I, 449
dley, John I, 557
dley, John V. I, 533
dley, John V. I, 557
dley, John Van I, 557
dley, John Van I, 620
dley, John Van I, 621
dley, John W. I, 661
dley, John W. I, 684
dley, Jonathan I, 352
dley, Jonathan I, 358
dley, Jonathan I, 359
dley, Jonathan I, 404
dley, Jonathan I, 437
dley, Jonathan I, 438
dley, Jonathan I, 449
dley, Jonathan V, 245
dley, Jonathan V, 259
dley, Jonathan G. I, 437
dley, Jonathan H. I, 450
dley, Joseph I, 437
dley, Joseph I, 449
dley, Joseph I, 450
dley, Joseph II, 581
dley, Joseph III, 207
dley, Joseph IV, 825
dley, Joseph VI, 196
dley, Joseph M. I, 437
dley, Joshua I, 359
dley, Joshua I, 449
dley, Joshua I, 450
dley, Joshua I, 557
dley, Joshua I, 620
dley, Judith I, 449
dley, Judith I, 620
dley, Julia I, 437
ndley, Kathren I, 358
ndley, Lenora I, 450
ndley, Lilian V, 346
ndley, Lillian V, 346
ndley, Lysandra I, 557
ndley, Mable I, 621
ndley, Mahlon I, 438
ndley, Manly I, 437
ndley, Manly I, 438
ndley, Manly I, 449
ndley, Manly I, 450
ndley, Margarett Pauline IV, 1256
ndley, Margery I, 404
ndley, Margery I, 437
ndley, Margery I, 438
ndley, Margery I, 449
ndley, Mariam V, 346
ndley, Martha I, 437
ndley, Martha I, 438
ndley, Martha I, 446
ndley, Martha I, 448
ndley, Martha I, 449
ndley, Martha I, 450
ndley, Martha I, 454
ndley, Martha V, 245
ndley, Martha V, 259
ndley, Mary I, 359
ndley, Mary I, 404
ndley, Mary I, 437
ndley, Mary I, 438
ndley, Mary I, 448
ndley, Mary I, 449
Lindley, Mary I, 450
Lindley, Mary I, 557
Lindley, Mary I, 724
Lindley, Mary II, 581
Lindley, Mary II, 604
Lindley, Mary IV, 310
Lindley, Mary Ann I, 438
Lindley, Mary B. IV, 1039
Lindley, Mary E. I, 438
Lindley, Mary Esther IV, 1039
Lindley, Mary Esther IV, 1256
Lindley, Mary J. I, 437
Lindley, Mary J. I, 450
Lindley, Mary J. I, 626
Lindley, Mary K. I, 557
Lindley, Mary R. IV, 1256
Lindley, Mary W. I, 533
Lindley, Mary W. I, 557
Lindley, Mary W. I, 620
Lindley, Matilda I, 438
Lindley, Maurice Bertram IV, 1256
Lindley, Melissa I, 990
Lindley, Melissa I, 991
Lindley, Melissa F. I, 991
Lindley, Mergery I, 404
Lindley, Milton I, 404
Lindley, Miriam V, 346
Lindley, Miriam V, 351
Lindley, Nancy I, 437
Lindley, Nancy I, 438
Lindley, Nancy I, 450
Lindley, Nancy I, 661
Lindley, Nancy I, 684
Lindley, Nancy E. I, 437
Lindley, Nannie V, 346
Lindley, Owen I, 359
Lindley, Owen I, 404
Lindley, Owen I, 423
Lindley, Owen I, 437
Lindley, Owen I, 449
Lindley, Owen T. I, 437
Lindley, Owen T. I, 450
Lindley, Owen W. I, 449
Lindley, Owen W. I, 450
Lindley, Paul IV, 310
Lindley, Paul B. IV, 1039
Lindley, Paul B. IV, 1256
Lindley, Paul Cameron I, 621
Lindley, Pearl I, 621
Lindley, Pearl I, 637
Lindley, Pearl I, 641
Lindley, Phebe I, 404
Lindley, Phebe I, 449
Lindley, Phebe I, 450
Lindley, Phebe I, 765
Lindley, Pheby I, 449
Lindley, Pheriba C. I, 661
Lindley, Polly I, 404
Lindley, Rodema E. I, 437
Lindley, Rodema E. I, 450
Lindley, Roxie M. I, 661
Lindley, Ruth I, 352
Lindley, Ruth I, 358
Lindley, Ruth I, 359
Lindley, Ruth I, 362
Lindley, Ruth I, 367
Lindley, Ruth I, 404
Lindley, Ruth I, 445
Lindley, Ruth I, 449
Lindley, Ruth V, 582
Lindley, Ruth V, 587
Lindley, Ruth V, 698
Lindley, Ruth E. I, 438
Lindley, Sallie Donia I, 437
Lindley, Samuel I, 359
Lindley, Samuel I, 557
Lindley, Samuel Hill I, 437
Lindley, Sandia I, 621
Lindley, Sarah I, 359
Lindley, Sarah I, 404
Lindley, Sarah I, 423
Lindley, Sarah I, 431
Lindley, Sarah I, 437
Lindley, Sarah I, 449
Lindley, Sarah I, 450
Lindley, Sarah V, 564
Lindley, Sarah B. V, 582
Lindley, Sarah Lorena I, 437
Lindley, Sibyl I, 438
Lindley, Simon I, 358
Lindley, Sophrona I, 557
Lindley, Sophronia I, 443
Lindley, Sophronia I, 449
Lindley, Sophronia I, 450
Lindley, Sophronia P. I, 438
Lindley, Susan I, 438
Lindley, Susanna II, 581
Lindley, Susanna II, 586
Lindley, Susannah I, 437
Lindley, Susannah I, 449
Lindley, Susannah I, 450
Lindley, Susannah II, 581
Lindley, Susannah III, 207
Lindley, T. Milton I, 438
Lindley, Thomas I, 358
Lindley, Thomas I, 359
Lindley, Thomas I, 362
Lindley, Thomas I, 404
Lindley, Thomas I, 431
Lindley, Thomas I, 437
Lindley, Thomas I, 449
Lindley, Thomas I, 695
Lindley, Thomas I, 724
Lindley, Thomas II, 389
Lindley, Thomas II, 510
Lindley, Thomas II, 581
Lindley, Thomas Hill I, 437
Lindley, Thomas, Jr. I, 404
Lindley, Thomas, Sr. I, 438
Lindley, Thompson I, 449
Lindley, Thos. I, 352
Lindley, Thos. I, 359
Lindley, Thos. I, 367
Lindley, U. Allen I, 661
Lindley, Ulysses Allen I, 437
Lindley, Ulysses Allen I, 684
Lindley, Victoria I, 557
Lindley, Walter O. I, 437
Lindley, Walter O. I, 438
Lindley, William I, 358
Lindley, William I, 359
Lindley, William I, 404
Lindley, William I, 437
Lindley, William I, 449
Lindley, William I, 450
Lindley, William I, 557
Lindley, William I, 661
Lindley, William I, 684
Lindley, William V, 581
Lindley, William V, 751
Lindley, William Isaac I, 437
Lindley, William T. I, 438
Lindley, William T. I, 449
Lindley, William T. I, 450
Lindley, William W. I, 450
Lindley, Wm. I, 359
Lindley, Wm. I, 378
Lindley, Wm. V, 561
Lindley, Zacharias I, 358
Lindley, Zilpha IV, 1326
Lindlow, Frank W. IV, 1326
Lindlow, Frederick D. IV, 1326
Lindlow, Louise E. IV, 1326
Lindly, Aaron I, 404
Lindly, Aaron I, 765
Lindly, Alfred H. I, 450
Lindly, David I, 444
Lindly, David I, 449
Lindly, Deborah I, 404
Lindly, Elenor I, 404
Lindly, Elizabeth I, 449
Lindly, Elizabeth I, 453
Lindly, Grace I, 444
Lindly, Grace I, 449
Lindly, Hannah I, 404
Lindly, Hannah I, 444
Lindly, James I, 392
Lindly, John I, 449
Lindly, John I, 453
Lindly, Jonathan I, 404
Lindly, Manly I, 450
Lindly, Margery I, 376
Lindly, Mary I, 375
Lindly, Mary I, 385
Lindly, Mary I, 404
Lindly, Mary I, 414
Lindly, Mary I, 437
Lindly, Mary I, 449
Lindly, Owen I, 444
Lindly, Owen I, 449
Lindly, Phebe I, 404
Lindly, Polly I, 404
Lindly, Polly I, 405
Lindly, Ruth I, 391
Lindly, Ruth I, 392
Lindly, Ruth I, 404
Lindly, Ruth I, 416
Lindly, Sarah I, 404
Lindly, Sarah I, 405
Lindly, Sarah I, 438
Lindly, Thomas I, 376
Lindly, Thomas I, 414
Lindly, Thomas I, 438
Lindly, William I, 404
Lindly, Wm. I, 405
Lindon, Mary II, 600
Lindsay, Ann L. II, 889
Lindsay, Ann L. II, 890
Lindsay, Brintha J. VI, 950
Lindsay, Charles Sexton III, 31
Lindsay, Chas. S. III, 207
Lindsay, Chas. Seton III, 207
Lindsay, David Henry III, 207
Lindsay, Elizabeth III, 207
Lindsay, Elizabeth VI, 834
Lindsay, Elizabeth VI, 1005
Lindsay, Harvey Bell III, 207
Lindsay, James VI, 801
Lindsay, James VI, 834
Lindsay, James VI, 862
Lindsay, Janet M. VI, 834
Lindsay, Jene L. III, 207
Lindsay, Joseph II, 889
Lindsay, Joseph II, 890
Lindsay, Lewin Seton III, 207
Lindsay, Margaret VI, 801
Lindsay, Margaret VI, 821
Lindsay, Martha VI, 950
Lindsay, Mary A. VI, 834
Lindsay, Mary A. VI, 862
Lindsay, Mary L. III, 207
Lindsay, Mary Lewin III, 31
Lindsay, Mary Lewin III, 207
Lindsay, Mildred VI, 834
Lindsay, Nancy VI, 843
Lindsay, Nancy M. VI, 834
Lindsay, Rebecca II, 890
Lindsay, Rebecca M. II, 889
Lindsay, Robert VI, 821
Lindsay, Robert VI, 834
Lindsay, Robert VI, 843
Lindsay, Robert A. VI, 834
Lindsay, Sally VI, 950
Lindsay, Sarah Ann S. VI, 1005
Lindsay, Solomon VI, 843
Lindsay, Solomon VI, 949
Lindsay, Solomon VI, 950
Lindsay, Solomon VI, 996
Lindsay, Susan VI, 950
Lindsay, Thomas VI, 834
Lindsay, William VI, 834
Lindsay, William VI, 950
Lindsay, Winna I, 991
Lindsay, Wm. III, 207
Lindsay, Wright VI, 950
Lindsey, Ann II, 889
Lindsey, Ann L. II, 889
Lindsey, Ann L. II, 890
Lindsey, Anna I, 939
Lindsey, Anna I, 945
Lindsey, Anna Wilson I, 929
Lindsey, George V, 1007
Lindsey, Hannah II, 389
Lindsey, James V, 93
Lindsey, Jordan I, 994
Lindsey, Joseph II, 806
Lindsey, Joseph II, 889
Lindsey, Joseph II, 890
Lindsey, Joseph, Jr. II, 806
Lindsey, Mahala V, 85
Lindsey, Mahala V, 93
Lindsey, Mahala I. J. V, 84
Lindsey, Mahala I. J. V, 93
Lindsey, Malissa V, 1007
Lindsey, Rebecca II, 889
Lindsey, Rebecca II, 890
Lindsey, Rebecca M. II, 806
Lindsey, Rebecca M. II, 889
Lindsey, Samiry I, 991
Lindsey, Sarah J. I, 933
Lindsey, Thomas II, 389
Lindsey, Wd. Ann II, 806
Lindsey, Winna I, 991
Lindsey, Winny I, 991
Lindsey, Winny I, 994
Lindsey, Wm. II, 806
Lindsey, Wm. II, 889
Lindsey, Wm. V, 1007
Lindzey, Achsah II, 127
Lindzey, Charles II, 127
Lindzey, Sarah II, 127
Line, Amos IV, 641
Line, Bathsheba IV, 641
Line, Bathsheba IV, 656
Line, Charles V, 870
Line, Charles E. IV, 1284
Line, Chas. E. IV, 1284
Line, Harry C. IV, 1284
Line, Isaac IV, 641
Line, Isaac IV, 656
Line, James IV, 641
Line, Joseph IV, 641
Line, Lulu IV, 1284
Line, Mary IV, 641
Line, Mary IV, 657
Line, Mary L. IV, 1284
Line, Phebe IV, 641
Line, Rachel IV, 641
Line, Smith IV, 641
Line, Susan IV, 1284
Line, Susan V. V, 870
Line, Susia V. IV, 1284
Linear, Elijah I, 765
Lineberry, Anna I, 684
Lineberry, Jane I, 374
Lineberry, Jane I, 404
Lineberry, William G. I, 684
Linegar, Elizabeth I, 824
Linegar, Isaac I, 824
Linegar, Isaac I, 1070
Lineham, Margaret II, 588
Lines, Frances E. III, 34
Lines, Susan V, 850
Ling, Robert H. IV, 1326
Lingard, Cornelius II, 389
Lingard, John II, 389
Lingard, Mary II, 389
Lingard, Mary II, 581
Lingard, Sarah II, 389
Lingard, William II, 389
Lingard, Wm. II, 581
Linginfelter, Anna I, 1158
Linginfelter, Fred I, 1158
Linginfelter, Isaac I, 1158
Linginfelter, Josephine I, 1158
Linginfelter, Rachel I, 1158
Linginfelter, Ratie I, 1158
Lingingfelter, Anna I, 1158
Lingingfelter, Isaac I, 1158
Lingingfelter, Ratie I, 1158
Lingo, Mary IV, 371
Lingo, Mary IV, 417
Lingshore, Clarinda IV, 1147
Linhoss, Adam IV, 649
Linhoss, Eva IV, 649
Linhoss, Minnie IV, 649
Liniger, Isaac I, 891
Lininger, A. J. V, 1007
Lininger, Amelia V, 1007
Lininger, Andrew J. V, 1007
Lininger, Lucy V, 1007
Lininger, Malissa V, 1007
Link, Albert J. IV, 1256
Link, Catharine IV, 1256
Link, Charles V, 259
Link, Chas. V, 259
Link, Lafayette V, 259
Link, Laura M. IV, 1256
Link, Lu Nettie IV, 1256
Link, Margaret IV, 1256
Link, Mary Jane V, 259
Link, Maud Barrett V, 259
Linken, Ann IV, 1054
Linkhart, Clara V, 186
Linkhart, Cleo C. V, 346
Linkhart, Dallas V, 510
Linkhart, Dallas E. V, 510
Linkhart, Edith C. V, 691
Linkhart, Edward G. V, 691
Linkhart, Elizabeth V, 346
Linkhart, Elizabeth V, 379
Linkhart, Elizabeth V, 410
Linkhart, Elizabeth V, 510
Linkhart, Elizabeth V, 644
Linkhart, Elizabeth J. V, 510
Linkhart, Elizabeth L. V, 510
Linkhart, George V, 510
Linkhart, George L. V, 510
Linkhart, Harry C. V, 186
Linkhart, Herbert V, 510
Linkhart, Herbert B. V, 510
Linkhart, John V, 346
Linkhart, Joseph V, 186
Linkhart, Luther J. V, 691
Linkhart, Mary V, 510
Linkhart, Mary C. V, 632
Linkhart, Mellia V, 510
Linkhart, Milton V, 510
Linkhart, Milton S. V, 510
Linkhart, Nellie V, 510
Linkhart, Nellie Revelle V, 410
Linkhart, Richard N. V, 691
Linkhart, Robert C. V, 691
Linkhart, Thomas V, 510
Linkheart, Elizabeth V, 510
Linkheart, Nellie V, 510
Linkhorn, Isaac II, 389
Linkhorn, Mary II, 389
Linkhorn, Sarah II, 581
Links, Margaret IV, 1326
Linley, Joseph II, 581
Linley, Mary I, 824
Linley, Mary I, 825
Linley, Pheby I, 449
Linly, Deborah I, 404
Linn, Addie V, 1007
Linn, Alba B. V, 751
Linn, Albert IV, 240
Linn, Charles IV, 240
Linn, Chester IV, 240
Linn, George V, 1007
Linn, Jane Elizabeth V, 751
Linn, John II, 391

Linn, Joseph II, 391
Linn, Martha II, 391
Linn, Mary II, 391
Linn, Mary IV, 240
Linn, Norma IV, 240
Linn, Sallie E. IV, 240
Linn, Sally IV, 240
Linn, Viola IV, 240
Linn, William V, 751
Linn, Wm. Linus V, 751
Linnegar, Isaac I, 824
Linnegar, Isaac I, 1066
Linnegar, Isaac I, 1070
Linnegar, Isac I, 1070
Linnekin, Harold V. III, 65
Linnekin, Harold V. III, 207
Linnekin, Ruth Eleanor III, 65
Linnekin, Ruth Eleanor III, 207
Linnett, Edith K. III, 207
Linnett, John Wm. III, 207
Linnett, Maria Louisa III, 207
Linniard, James V, 186
Linnington, Susanna II, 481
Linnington, Susanna II, 581
Linox, James II, 1010
Linsay, William VI, 985
Linscott, Minerva V, 186
Linse, Lottie V, 751
Linsey, Lottie V, 751
Linsey, Samiry I, 991
Linsey, Wm. V, 1007
Linsh, Ann I, 405
Linsley, George V, 1007
Linsley, Thomas II, 581
Linson, Scott IV, 1284
Linsy, Malissa V, 1007
Linthecum, Zacheus I. I, 891
Linthicum, Cornelius D. VI, 950
Linthicum, Mary Ann VI, 950
Lintner, Mary V, 884
Linto, Mary II, 1010
Linton, Abi V, 489
Linton, Abi V, 510
Linton, Abigail Ann V, 510
Linton, Abigail Ann V, 511
Linton, Ada V, 510
Linton, Ada V, 691
Linton, Agnes II, 999
Linton, Agnes L. II, 881
Linton, Agnes L. II, 890
Linton, Agnes Martin II, 1011
Linton, Albert III, 207
Linton, Albert IV, 483
Linton, Albert IV, 975
Linton, Albert V, 510
Linton, Albert W. III, 136
Linton, Albert W. III, 207
Linton, Albert W. III, 277
Linton, Albert W. III, 340
Linton, Alfred Alonzo V, 582
Linton, Alfred Alonzo V, 691
Linton, Alida C. V, 510
Linton, Allen V, 93
Linton, Alma H. V, 511
Linton, Almira V, 93
Linton, Almira V, 186
Linton, Alonzo A. V, 691
Linton, Amanda V, 510
Linton, Amy V, 186
Linton, Ann IV, 39
Linton, Ann IV, 45
Linton, Ann IV, 46
Linton, Ann M. V, 495
Linton, Ann M. V, 511
Linton, Ann M. V, 567
Linton, Ann M. V, 582
Linton, Anna M. V, 691
Linton, Anna R. V, 918
Linton, Annie V, 186
Linton, Arnold V, 691
Linton, Arnold V, 710
Linton, Arnold Edward V, 691
Linton, Belle IV, 768
Linton, Belle IV, 975
Linton, Benjamin II, 963
Linton, Benjamin II, 964
Linton, Benjamin II, 1004
Linton, Benjamin II, 1010
Linton, Benjamin II, 1011
Linton, Benjamin II, 1017
Linton, Benjamin II, 1024
Linton, Benjamin II, 1030
Linton, Benjamin II, 1032
Linton, Benjamin II, 1037
Linton, Benjamin IV, 45
Linton, Benjamin IV, 46
Linton, Benjamin V, 510
Linton, Benjamin V, 511
Linton, Benjamin L. IV, 46
Linton, Benjamin, Jr. II, 1010
Linton, Benjamin, Jr. II, 1024
Linton, Caroline L. IV, 46
Linton, Caroline L. IV, 48
Linton, Carrie M. V, 691
Linton, Carrie Margaret V, 582
Linton, Cary V, 186
Linton, Charles II, 1055
Linton, Charles J. V, 510
Linton, Charles J. V, 511
Linton, Charles Linton V, 582
Linton, Clarence IV, 831
Linton, Cyrus II, 1055
Linton, Cyrus V, 495
Linton, Cyrus V, 510
Linton, Cyrus V, 511
Linton, Cyrus V, 567
Linton, Cyrus V, 574
Linton, Cyrus V, 582
Linton, Cyrus V, 691
Linton, Daniel II, 963
Linton, Daniel IV, 45
Linton, Daniel IV, 46
Linton, Daniel V, 510
Linton, David II, 1010
Linton, David IV, 45
Linton, David IV, 483
Linton, David V, 93
Linton, David V, 121
Linton, David V, 510
Linton, David V, 511
Linton, David Hector III, 207
Linton, Dorothy Selma III, 207
Linton, Dorothy Selma III, 340
Linton, Edith IV, 768
Linton, Edith IV, 975
Linton, Edith V, 510
Linton, Edith V, 511
Linton, Edith V, 528
Linton, Edward II, 1075
Linton, Edward B. II, 1055
Linton, Edwin C. V, 510
Linton, Edwin C. V, 691
Linton, Effie A. IV, 483
Linton, Effie A. IV, 975
Linton, Effie Amelia IV, 975
Linton, Elanor V, 691
Linton, Eleanor V, 582
Linton, Eliza V, 495
Linton, Eliza V, 511
Linton, Eliza V, 567
Linton, Eliza V, 582
Linton, Eliza V, 691
Linton, Eliza H. V, 691
Linton, Elizabeth II, 581
Linton, Elizabeth II, 963
Linton, Elizabeth II, 964
Linton, Elizabeth II, 1010
Linton, Elizabeth II, 1011
Linton, Elizabeth II, 1028
Linton, Elizabeth II, 1037
Linton, Elizabeth II, 1040
Linton, Elizabeth II, 1075
Linton, Elizabeth IV, 44
Linton, Elizabeth IV, 46
Linton, Elizabeth IV, 483
Linton, Elizabeth V, 32
Linton, Elizabeth V, 93
Linton, Elizabeth V, 117
Linton, Elizabeth V, 161
Linton, Elizabeth V, 186
Linton, Elizabeth V, 479
Linton, Elizabeth V, 510
Linton, Elizabeth V, 526
Linton, Elizabeth V, 534
Linton, Elizabeth B. II, 1075
Linton, Elizabeth F. V, 511
Linton, Eloise B. III, 207
Linton, Eloise Beatrice III, 207
Linton, Elsa V, 511
Linton, Elsa V, 582
Linton, Elsie V, 511
Linton, Elsie V, 691
Linton, Emma II, 1075
Linton, Ester IV, 480
Linton, Ester IV, 483
Linton, Esther II, 713
Linton, Esther IV, 483
Linton, Ethel V, 93
Linton, Ethel V, 186
Linton, Ethel V, 691
Linton, Eunice Ellen V, 186
Linton, Fred V, 691
Linton, Fred W. V, 582
Linton, Fred W. V, 691
Linton, Frederick II, 1055
Linton, Gertrude V, 582
Linton, Gertrude V, 691
Linton, Grace III, 207
Linton, Grace III, 277
Linton, Grace IV, 975
Linton, Guy V, 691
Linton, H. Lawrence IV, 483
Linton, Hannah II, 1004
Linton, Hannah II, 1010
Linton, Hannah II, 1011
Linton, Hannah II, 1024
Linton, Hannah II, 1038
Linton, Hannah II, 1048
Linton, Hannah II, 1054
Linton, Hannah IV, 45
Linton, Hannah IV, 483
Linton, Hannah V, 510
Linton, Hannah V, 918
Linton, Hannah Mary II, 705
Linton, Harriet V, 510
Linton, Harriett IV, 483
Linton, Helen V, 691
Linton, Helen Leroy V, 681
Linton, Helen Leroy V, 691
Linton, Henry II, 1075
Linton, Henry Jehu V, 691
Linton, Hezekiah II, 963
Linton, Hezekiah II, 1010
Linton, Hilles IV, 768
Linton, Hilles IV, 962
Linton, Hilles IV, 975
Linton, Hillis Lawrence IV, 975
Linton, Isaac II, 964
Linton, Isabella III, 136
Linton, Isabella III, 207
Linton, Isabella III, 277
Linton, Isabella III, 340
Linton, Isabella IV, 962
Linton, Isaiah II, 1038
Linton, Isaiah IV, 46
Linton, Isaiah IV, 483
Linton, Isaiah V, 510
Linton, Isaiah V, 918
Linton, Isaiah W. III, 207
Linton, Isiah II, 1011
Linton, Jacob I, 1076
Linton, Jacob II, 581
Linton, Jacob II, 1010
Linton, James II, 1011
Linton, James IV, 45
Linton, James V, 495
Linton, James V, 510
Linton, James V, 511
Linton, James V, 567
Linton, James V, 582
Linton, James M. V, 691
Linton, James Martin II, 1010
Linton, James W. V, 511
Linton, James W. V, 528
Linton, James William V, 93
Linton, James William V, 510
Linton, Jane II, 963
Linton, Jane II, 1010
Linton, Jane II, 1011
Linton, Jane II, 1024
Linton, Jane II, 1054
Linton, Jane IV, 45
Linton, Jane V, 472
Linton, Jane V, 510
Linton, Jeremiah II, 581
Linton, Joan II, 389
Linton, Joan II, 581
Linton, Joan II, 679
Linton, John II, 389
Linton, John II, 581
Linton, John II, 679
Linton, John II, 963
Linton, John II, 964
Linton, John II, 999
Linton, John II, 1010
Linton, John II, 1011
Linton, John II, 1013
Linton, John II, 1017
Linton, John II, 1024
Linton, John II, 1028
Linton, John II, 1030
Linton, John III, 168
Linton, John IV, 483
Linton, John V, 691
Linton, John V, 918
Linton, John Hadley V, 582
Linton, John, Jr. II, 1054
Linton, Jonathan II, 964
Linton, Jonathan V, 511
Linton, Jonathan B. V, 93
Linton, Joseph II, 581
Linton, Joseph II, 964
Linton, Joseph II, 979
Linton, Joseph II, 1010
Linton, Joseph II, 1013
Linton, Joseph II, 1040
Linton, Joseph II, 1075
Linton, Joseph IV, 46
Linton, Joseph IV, 1028
Linton, Joseph V, 582
Linton, Joseph Eli V, 582
Linton, Joseph W. II, 1055
Linton, Joseph W. IV, 1028
Linton, Joshua II, 963
Linton, Joshua II, 1004
Linton, Joshua II, 1010
Linton, Joshua II, 1011
Linton, Joshua IV, 45
Linton, Joshua IV, 46
Linton, Joshua V, 510
Linton, Joshua V, 511
Linton, Joshua V, 582
Linton, Joshua V, 691
Linton, Joshua, Jr. II, 1010
Linton, Joshua, Jr. II, 1011
Linton, Kate D. V, 691
Linton, Kate Eldred V, 691
Linton, Katie V, 691
Linton, Laura IV, 944
Linton, Laura IV, 975
Linton, Laurence IV, 975
Linton, Lavinia II, 964
Linton, Lawrence IV, 975
Linton, Leah V, 952
Linton, Leah V, 955
Linton, Lettitia V, 93
Linton, Lettitia V, 121
Linton, Lidia V, 510
Linton, Loftus W. V, 511
Linton, Loftus Walter V, 511
Linton, Lois IV, 484
Linton, Lois E. IV, 975
Linton, Lois Evangeline IV, 975
Linton, Lucie II, 963
Linton, Lucy II, 1010
Linton, Lucy II, 1032
Linton, Lydia V, 510
Linton, Lydia V, 511
Linton, Lydia V, 574
Linton, Lydia V, 582
Linton, Lydia V, 691
Linton, Madge Osborn V, 691
Linton, Madge Osborn V, 710
Linton, Madora V, 688
Linton, Madora V, 691
Linton, Mahlon IV, 39
Linton, Mahlon IV, 45
Linton, Mahlon IV, 46
Linton, Marg. A. III, 207
Linton, Margaret III, 207
Linton, Margaret IV, 46
Linton, Margaret IV, 52
Linton, Margaret Anne III, 207
Linton, Margaret Anne III, 214
Linton, Maria D. V, 511
Linton, Maria E. V, 510
Linton, Mariah V, 582
Linton, Martha I, 59
Linton, Martha I, 85
Linton, Martha II, 582
Linton, Martha II, 963
Linton, Martha II, 1010
Linton, Martin II, 1011
Linton, Mary II, 389
Linton, Mary II, 445
Linton, Mary II, 581
Linton, Mary II, 963
Linton, Mary II, 964
Linton, Mary II, 979
Linton, Mary II, 999
Linton, Mary II, 1010
Linton, Mary II, 1011
Linton, Mary II, 1013
Linton, Mary II, 1017
Linton, Mary II, 1024
Linton, Mary II, 1028
Linton, Mary II, 1030
Linton, Mary IV, 329
Linton, Mary IV, 340
Linton, Mary IV, 962
Linton, Mary V, 495
Linton, Mary V, 510
Linton, Mary V, 511
Linton, Mary V, 567
Linton, Mary V, 582
Linton, Mary Ann IV, 46
Linton, Mary Ann IV, 62
Linton, Mary Ann V, 582
Linton, Mary Anne IV, 62
Linton, Mary B. V, 33
Linton, Mary B. V, 93
Linton, Mary B. V, 691
Linton, Mary Baker V, 663
Linton, Mary Baker V, 691
Linton, Mary Butterworth V, 93
Linton, Mary Butterworth V, 691
Linton, Mary E. III, 207
Linton, Mary E. IV, 975
Linton, Mary E. V, 582
Linton, Mary Etta V, 691
Linton, Matilda IV, 45
Linton, Matilda IV, 46
Linton, Matilda IV, 61
Linton, Mercy II, 1047
Linton, Mercy II, 1054
Linton, Myra V, 510
Linton, Myra V, 511
Linton, N. M. V, 510
Linton, Nancy V, 510
Linton, Nancy V, 511
Linton, Nancy V, 515
Linton, Naomi IV, 37
Linton, Naomi IV, 46
Linton, Nathan II, 1010
Linton, Nathan IV, 45
Linton, Nathan V, 93
Linton, Nathan V, 122
Linton, Nathan V, 469
Linton, Nathan V, 510
Linton, Nathan V, 511
Linton, Nathan M. V, 510
Linton, Olive V, 510
Linton, Olive V, 511
Linton, Olive V, 568
Linton, Olive V, 582
Linton, Olive V, 691
Linton, Oliver V, 510
Linton, Oliver V, 511
Linton, Phebe II, 964
Linton, Rachel IV, 1284
Linton, Rachel IV, 1295
Linton, Rachel V, 93
Linton, Rachel V, 122
Linton, Rachel V, 510
Linton, Rachel V, 511
Linton, Rachel V, 530
Linton, Rachel V, 918
Linton, Ralph III, 207
Linton, Ralph III, 214
Linton, Rebecca II, 581
Linton, Rebecca II, 1010
Linton, Rebecca II, 1011
Linton, Rebecca II, 1075
Linton, Rebecka II, 581
Linton, Robert V, 93
Linton, Robert V, 186
Linton, Rose V, 691
Linton, Rose V, 710
Linton, Ruth V, 510
Linton, Ruth V, 511
Linton, Ruth V, 541
Linton, Ruth Ida V, 582
Linton, Sally V, 510
Linton, Samuel II, 963
Linton, Samuel II, 1011
Linton, Samuel IV, 45
Linton, Samuel IV, 46
Linton, Samuel IV, 483
Linton, Samuel V, 17
Linton, Samuel V, 93
Linton, Samuel V, 510
Linton, Samuel V, 691
Linton, Samuel B. V, 510
Linton, Samuel S. V, 510
Linton, Samuel S. V, 691
Linton, Sarah II, 581
Linton, Sarah II, 963
Linton, Sarah II, 1010
Linton, Sarah II, 1011
Linton, Sarah II, 1013
Linton, Sarah II, 1024
Linton, Sarah II, 1038
Linton, Sarah IV, 45
Linton, Sarah IV, 46
Linton, Sarah IV, 483
Linton, Sarah V, 918
Linton, Sarah A., Jr. V, 511
Linton, Sarah Ann II, 1054
Linton, Sarah Ann IV, 240
Linton, Sarah Ann V, 510
Linton, Sarah Ann V, 518
Linton, Sarah Ann V, 582
Linton, Sarah Frances V, 511
Linton, Sarah R. V, 511
Linton, Seth V, 510
Linton, Seth V, 518
Linton, Seth V, 582
Linton, Seth H. V, 511
Linton, Seth H. V, 582
Linton, Seth S. V, 93
Linton, Silas II, 1054
Linton, Smith V, 510
Linton, Stella V, 582
Linton, Susanna II, 581
Linton, Thomas II, 1010
Linton, Thomas II, 1011
Linton, Thomas II, 1038
Linton, Thomas II, 1054
Linton, Thomas IV, 483
Linton, Walter V, 510
Linton, Walter V, 511
Linton, Walter V, 582
Linton, Walter V, 688
Linton, Walter V, 691
Linton, Wd. Rebecca II, 1024

ton, William IV, 483
ton, William IV, 1028
ton, William V, 93
ton, William V, 346
ton, William V, 510
ton, William C. V, 582
ton, William H. IV, 45
ton, William H. IV, 46
ton, William H. IV, 61
ton, William, Jr. V, 510
ton, Willie V, 346
ton, Wm. II, 445
ton, Wm. II, 581
ton, Wm. V, 691
ton, Wm. V, 918
ton, Wm. C. V, 582
ton, Wm. H. II, 1055
ville, Alice R. III, 207
ville, Ann IV, 1028
ville, Ann IV, 1284
ville, Asahel W. III, 207
ville, Benj. A. IV, 1284
ville, Eva IV, 1284
ville, Harriet Jane IV, 1284
ville, Jacob H. IV, 1284
ville, Lydia R. III, 207
ville, Quincey IV, 1284
n, ??? III, 212
n, Elizabeth III, 207
n, William III, 207
nes, Rich. III, 132
nes, Sarah III, 132
ur, Emma V, 1007
incot, Darwin IV, 1284
incott, Charles V, 186
incott, Charley V, 186
incott, Hope II, 273
incott, Samuel II, 273
oncot, Hannah II, 84
oncot, Mary II, 84
p, Florence IV, 1305
pencot, Meribah II, 239
pencot, Moses II, 239
pencote, Hannah II, 239
pencott, Abigail II, 964
pencott, Abigail B. II, 964
pencott, Abigail B. V, 93
pencott, Alice II, 304
pencott, Allen II, 964
pencott, Ann II, 120
pencott, Anna II, 219
pencott, Anna II, 238
pencott, Anna II, 269
pencott, Anna Pitfield II, 964
pencott, Beulah II, 239
pencott, Beulah II, 245
pencott, Caleb II, 85
pencott, Caleb II, 120
pencott, Caleb II, 269
pencott, Charles II, 84
pencott, Charles V, 93
pencott, Charles E. II, 84
pencott, David Brown II, 964
pencott, Deborah West II, 582
pencott, Edward II, 244
pencott, Edwin V, 918
pencott, Elisabeth II, 269
pencott, Elizabeth II, 239
pencott, Elizabeth II, 245
pencott, Elizabeth T. II, 304
pencott, George Widdifield
II, 582
pencott, Hannah II, 219
pencott, Hannah II, 238
pencott, Hannah II, 295
pencott, Hannah B. V, 93
pencott, Henry II, 964
pencott, Henry Allen II, 964
pencott, Hope II, 53
pencott, Isaac II, 269
pencott, Isaac II, 582
pencott, Jacob II, 238
pencott, James II, 219
pencott, James II, 238
pencott, John II, 239
pencott, John II, 245
pencott, John H. II, 304
pencott, John H. V, 93
pencott, Joseph K. II, 121
pencott, Lindzey II, 245
pencott, Mary II, 389
pencott, Mary V, 93
pencott, Mary G. V, 93
pencott, Mary Jane II, 153
pencott, Meriba II, 239
pencott, Meribah II, 244
pencott, Moses II, 244
pencott, Oswell V, 93
pencott, Pennington V, 93
pencott, Preston II, 295
pencott, Priscilla M. II, 121
Lippencott, Rachel II, 235
Lippencott, Rachel II, 238
Lippencott, Rebecca Ann V, 93
Lippencott, Restore II, 235
Lippencott, Richard II, 389
Lippencott, Sadie V, 93
Lippencott, Samuel II, 84
Lippencott, Sarah II, 582
Lippencott, Sarah B. II, 964
Lippencott, Sarah E. V, 918
Lippencott, Thomas II, 582
Lippencott, William V, 93
Lippencutt, Charles II, 120
Lippiatt, Charles A. IV, 734
Lippiatt, Charles A. IV, 735
Lippiatt, Elanor IV, 734
Lippiatt, Eleanor IV, 735
Lippiatt, Frederick IV, 734
Lippiatt, Frederick IV, 735
Lippiatt, Jacob IV, 734
Lippiatt, Katheryn IV, 734
Lippiatt, Valda IV, 734
Lippiatt, Valda IV, 735
Lippincoat, Jacob, Jr. II, 84
Lippincoate, Jacob II, 84
Lippincot, Hannah II, 239
Lippincot, Hope II, 239
Lippincot, Jacob, Jr. II, 239
Lippincot, Joseph II, 208
Lippincot, Joseph II, 239
Lippincot, Martha II, 582
Lippincot, Rachel II, 238
Lippincot, Rachel II, 269
Lippincot, Rebecca II, 208
Lippincot, Rebecca II, 224
Lippincot, Rebecca II, 238
Lippincot, Rebecca II, 239
Lippincot, Wallace II, 239
Lippincote, Elizabeth II, 238
Lippincote, Hannah II, 84
Lippincote, Hannah II, 85
Lippincote, Hannah II, 582
Lippincote, Joseph II, 238
Lippincote, Sarah II, 74
Lippincote, Sarah II, 84
Lippincott, ??? II, 176
Lippincott, Aaron II, 33
Lippincott, Aaron II, 74
Lippincott, Aaron II, 84
Lippincott, Aaron II, 120
Lippincott, Aaron II, 134
Lippincott, Aaron II, 239
Lippincott, Aaron II, 890
Lippincott, Aaron II, 917
Lippincott, Aaron S. II, 582
Lippincott, Aaron Y. II, 582
Lippincott, Abigail II, 33
Lippincott, Abigail II, 84
Lippincott, Abigail II, 108
Lippincott, Abigail II, 120
Lippincott, Abigail II, 238
Lippincott, Abigail II, 258
Lippincott, Abigail II, 1045
Lippincott, Abigail II, 1055
Lippincott, Abraham II, 239
Lippincott, Abraham II, 242
Lippincott, Achsah III, 207
Lippincott, Ada II, 890
Lippincott, Ada II, 917
Lippincott, Aden II, 890
Lippincott, Adon II, 890
Lippincott, Alberta Ogden II, 134
Lippincott, Alberta Sherron
II, 153
Lippincott, Alberta Sherron
II, 154
Lippincott, Alice II, 295
Lippincott, Alice II, 304
Lippincott, Alice Matthews
II, 891
Lippincott, Alice Matthews
II, 903
Lippincott, Allen II, 1011
Lippincott, Allen II, 1045
Lippincott, Allen II, 1055
Lippincott, Allen II, 1075
Lippincott, Amey II, 33
Lippincott, Amey II, 54
Lippincott, Amey II, 84
Lippincott, Amy II, 116
Lippincott, Amy II, 120
Lippincott, Andrew T. II, 134
Lippincott, Ann II, 33
Lippincott, Ann II, 84
Lippincott, Ann II, 85
Lippincott, Ann II, 101
Lippincott, Ann II, 106
Lippincott, Ann II, 120
Lippincott, Ann II, 125
Lippincott, Ann II, 134
Lippincott, Ann II, 135
Lippincott, Ann II, 142
Lippincott, Ann II, 153
Lippincott, Ann II, 195
Lippincott, Ann II, 223
Lippincott, Ann II, 238
Lippincott, Ann II, 239
Lippincott, Ann II, 295
Lippincott, Ann II, 306
Lippincott, Ann II, 479
Lippincott, Ann II, 582
Lippincott, Ann II, 890
Lippincott, Ann II, 936
Lippincott, Ann Elizabeth II, 144
Lippincott, Ann T. II, 144
Lippincott, Ann T. II, 153
Lippincott, Ann W. II, 134
Lippincott, Ann W. II, 295
Lippincott, Anna II, 33
Lippincott, Anna II, 120
Lippincott, Anna II, 121
Lippincott, Anna II, 238
Lippincott, Anna II, 239
Lippincott, Anna II, 711
Lippincott, Anna II, 716
Lippincott, Anna II, 817
Lippincott, Anna III, 207
Lippincott, Anna Elizabeth
II, 153
Lippincott, Anna L. II, 740
Lippincott, Anna L. II, 752
Lippincott, Anna M. II, 806
Lippincott, Anna M. II, 882
Lippincott, Anna M. II, 890
Lippincott, Anna Mary II, 1075
Lippincott, Anna T. II, 890
Lippincott, Annie II, 852
Lippincott, Annie II, 891
Lippincott, Annie H. II, 852
Lippincott, Annie H. II, 891
Lippincott, Aquila B. II, 114
Lippincott, Aquila B. II, 121
Lippincott, Aquilla II, 33
Lippincott, Aquilla B. II, 33
Lippincott, Aquilla B. II, 120
Lippincott, Asa II, 310
Lippincott, Asa II, 852
Lippincott, Asa II, 891
Lippincott, Atlantic II, 890
Lippincott, Atlantic II, 936
Lippincott, Barclay II, 120
Lippincott, Barclay II, 856
Lippincott, Barclay II, 890
Lippincott, Barzillai II, 68
Lippincott, Barzillai II, 84
Lippincott, Barzillia II, 84
Lippincott, Benajah B. II, 582
Lippincott, Benjamin II, 33
Lippincott, Benjamin II, 84
Lippincott, Benjamin II, 92
Lippincott, Benjamin II, 238
Lippincott, Benjamin II, 273
Lippincott, Benjamin II, 389
Lippincott, Benjamin VI, 762
Lippincott, Benjamin B. II, 582
Lippincott, Benjamin H. II, 134
Lippincott, Benjamin H. II, 153
Lippincott, Benjamin R. II, 752
Lippincott, Bessie V, 582
Lippincott, Beulah II, 239
Lippincott, Beulah II, 810
Lippincott, Beulah VI, 645
Lippincott, Beulah VI, 707
Lippincott, C. Carroll II, 890
Lippincott, C. Carroll II, 891
Lippincott, Caleb II, 56
Lippincott, Caleb II, 84
Lippincott, Caleb II, 85
Lippincott, Caleb II, 106
Lippincott, Caleb II, 120
Lippincott, Caleb II, 134
Lippincott, Caleb II, 135
Lippincott, Caleb II, 142
Lippincott, Caleb II, 153
Lippincott, Caleb II, 178
Lippincott, Caleb II, 239
Lippincott, Caleb II, 270
Lippincott, Caleb II, 295
Lippincott, Carlton II, 315
Lippincott, Caroline II, 311
Lippincott, Caroline II, 806
Lippincott, Caroline Elizabeth
Cooper II, 795
Lippincott, Catharine B. V, 918
Lippincott, Charles II, 84
Lippincott, Charles II, 120
Lippincott, Charles II, 389
Lippincott, Charles II, 582
Lippincott, Charles II, 752
Lippincott, Charles E. II, 84
Lippincott, Charles E. II, 582
Lippincott, Charles E. III, 207
Lippincott, Chas. II, 84
Lippincott, Christiana II, 56
Lippincott, Christiana II, 84
Lippincott, Christiana II, 153
Lippincott, Clara T. II, 134
Lippincott, Clara T. II, 153
Lippincott, Clarkson II, 134
Lippincott, Clarkson II, 153
Lippincott, Clayton II, 295
Lippincott, Clayton II, 304
Lippincott, Clement II, 153
Lippincott, Clement G. II, 134
Lippincott, Clement G. II, 135
Lippincott, Clement G. II, 153
Lippincott, Cornelia N. II, 903
Lippincott, Cynthia S. II, 890
Lippincott, Cynthia Shoemaker
II, 806
Lippincott, D. Conrow II, 890
Lippincott, D. Conrow II, 917
Lippincott, Daniel II, 33
Lippincott, Daniel II, 120
Lippincott, Daniel II, 238
Lippincott, Daniel II, 311
Lippincott, Darius II, 84
Lippincott, Darling Conrow
II, 806
Lippincott, Darling Conrow
II, 890
Lippincott, David VI, 730
Lippincott, David VI, 762
Lippincott, Deborah II, 33
Lippincott, Deborah II, 120
Lippincott, Deborah II, 123
Lippincott, Deborah II, 582
Lippincott, Deborah C. II, 295
Lippincott, Deborah W. II, 890
Lippincott, Deborah West II, 389
Lippincott, Deborah West II, 582
Lippincott, Debrah S. II, 121
Lippincott, Dorothy II, 809
Lippincott, Edith II, 239
Lippincott, Edith II, 278
Lippincott, Edward II, 389
Lippincott, Edward II, 752
Lippincott, Edward II, 891
Lippincott, Edward II, 903
Lippincott, Edwin V, 918
Lippincott, Edwin Kirk II, 806
Lippincott, Eleanor II, 389
Lippincott, Eleanor II, 582
Lippincott, Eleanor II, 711
Lippincott, Elisabeth II, 238
Lippincott, Elisabeth II, 239
Lippincott, Elisha III, 207
Lippincott, Eliz III, 283
Lippincott, Eliz. III, 280
Lippincott, Eliz. D. III, 207
Lippincott, Eliza S. II, 890
Lippincott, Eliza S. II, 926
Lippincott, Eliza Stow II, 821
Lippincott, Elizabeth II, 33
Lippincott, Elizabeth II, 57
Lippincott, Elizabeth II, 68
Lippincott, Elizabeth II, 84
Lippincott, Elizabeth II, 85
Lippincott, Elizabeth II, 104
Lippincott, Elizabeth II, 113
Lippincott, Elizabeth II, 121
Lippincott, Elizabeth II, 144
Lippincott, Elizabeth II, 193
Lippincott, Elizabeth II, 208
Lippincott, Elizabeth II, 217
Lippincott, Elizabeth II, 238
Lippincott, Elizabeth II, 239
Lippincott, Elizabeth II, 258
Lippincott, Elizabeth II, 259
Lippincott, Elizabeth II, 273
Lippincott, Elizabeth II, 295
Lippincott, Elizabeth II, 304
Lippincott, Elizabeth II, 389
Lippincott, Elizabeth II, 582
Lippincott, Elizabeth II, 813
Lippincott, Elizabeth II, 820
Lippincott, Elizabeth II, 882
Lippincott, Elizabeth II, 890
Lippincott, Elizabeth II, 921
Lippincott, Elizabeth III, 207
Lippincott, Elizabeth III, 255
Lippincott, Elizabeth IV, 675
Lippincott, Elizabeth Acton
II, 116
Lippincott, Elizabeth Acton
II, 121
Lippincott, Elizabeth B. II, 153
Lippincott, Elizabeth B. II, 315
Lippincott, Elizabeth D. II, 153
Lippincott, Elizabeth D. III, 207
Lippincott, Elizabeth E. II, 114
Lippincott, Elizabeth E. II, 120
Lippincott, Elizabeth E. II, 121
Lippincott, Elizabeth H. II, 888
Lippincott, Elizabeth H. II, 890
Lippincott, Elizabeth L. II, 117
Lippincott, Elizabeth L. II, 752
Lippincott, Elizabeth L. II, 764
Lippincott, Elizabeth S. II, 806
Lippincott, Elizabeth Smedley
II, 134
Lippincott, Elizabeth Smedley
II, 153
Lippincott, Elizabeth T. II, 295
Lippincott, Elizabeth T. II, 890
Lippincott, Elizabeth T. II, 909
Lippincott, Elizabeth T., Jr.
II, 890
Lippincott, Elizabeth Tatum
II, 806
Lippincott, Elizabeth White
II, 806
Lippincott, Ella II, 322
Lippincott, Ella III, 207
Lippincott, Ella III, 357
Lippincott, Ella H. II, 322
Lippincott, Ella H. III, 207
Lippincott, Ella Hansell III, 357
Lippincott, Ellwood III, 207
Lippincott, Elma II, 120
Lippincott, Emelie E. II, 295
Lippincott, Emelie E. II, 754
Lippincott, Emily S. II, 890
Lippincott, Emily T. II, 890
Lippincott, Emily T. II, 944
Lippincott, Emma II, 119
Lippincott, Emma II, 153
Lippincott, Emma II, 875
Lippincott, Emma V, 691
Lippincott, Emma Dyer II, 800
Lippincott, Emma Linda II, 134
Lippincott, Emma P. II, 153
Lippincott, Emma T. II, 134
Lippincott, Ezra II, 890
Lippincott, Ezra II, 891
Lippincott, Flora II, 133
Lippincott, Frank Albert II, 806
Lippincott, Freedom II, 33
Lippincott, Freedom II, 178
Lippincott, Freedom II, 213
Lippincott, Freedom II, 238
Lippincott, Freedom II, 273
Lippincott, George II, 806
Lippincott, George H. II, 806
Lippincott, George Ogden II, 134
Lippincott, George P. II, 752
Lippincott, George Pancoast
II, 295
Lippincott, George Pancoast
II, 711
Lippincott, George Pancoast
II, 754
Lippincott, George Pancoast,
Jr. II, 752
Lippincott, George W. II, 890
Lippincott, George W. II, 944
Lippincott, George Widdefield
II, 806
Lippincott, George Widdifield
II, 389
Lippincott, George Widdifield
II, 582
Lippincott, George Wilkins
II, 891
Lippincott, Gertrude II, 116
Lippincott, Gertrude II, 121
Lippincott, Gertrude II, 935
Lippincott, Grace II, 57
Lippincott, Grace II, 84
Lippincott, Hannah II, 33
Lippincott, Hannah II, 56
Lippincott, Hannah II, 84
Lippincott, Hannah II, 85
Lippincott, Hannah II, 113
Lippincott, Hannah II, 120
Lippincott, Hannah II, 134
Lippincott, Hannah II, 208
Lippincott, Hannah II, 210
Lippincott, Hannah II, 238
Lippincott, Hannah II, 239
Lippincott, Hannah II, 268
Lippincott, Hannah II, 270
Lippincott, Hannah II, 295
Lippincott, Hannah II, 315
Lippincott, Hannah II, 389
Lippincott, Hannah II, 582
Lippincott, Hannah II, 806
Lippincott, Hannah II, 890
Lippincott, Hannah III, 207
Lippincott, Hannah A. II, 116
Lippincott, Hannah A. II, 295
Lippincott, Hannah C. II, 135
Lippincott, Hannah D. II, 310
Lippincott, Hannah E. II, 153

Lippincott, Hannah W. II, 120
Lippincott, Hannah W. II, 752
Lippincott, Hazel V, 691
Lippincott, Hazel V, 704
Lippincott, Henry II, 33
Lippincott, Henry II, 153
Lippincott, Henry II, 239
Lippincott, Henry II, 1011
Lippincott, Henry II, 1045
Lippincott, Henry II, 1055
Lippincott, Henry A. II, 120
Lippincott, Henry A. II, 121
Lippincott, Henry C. II, 295
Lippincott, Henry C. II, 754
Lippincott, Henry Cla II, 856
Lippincott, Henry Clay II, 890
Lippincott, Henry H. II, 877
Lippincott, Henry H. II, 890
Lippincott, Henry H. II, 891
Lippincott, Henry H. II, 906
Lippincott, Henry Heulings II, 806
Lippincott, Hephzibah II, 295
Lippincott, Hephzibah II, 306
Lippincott, Hope II, 33
Lippincott, Hope II, 84
Lippincott, Hope II, 210
Lippincott, Hope II, 225
Lippincott, Hope II, 238
Lippincott, Hope II, 239
Lippincott, Hope II, 273
Lippincott, Hope Cowperthwaite II, 239
Lippincott, Horace II, 806
Lippincott, Howard V, 691
Lippincott, Howard W. II, 882
Lippincott, Howard W. II, 890
Lippincott, Howard White II, 806
Lippincott, Increece II, 234
Lippincott, Increece II, 238
Lippincott, Isaac II, 33
Lippincott, Isaac II, 120
Lippincott, Isaac II, 193
Lippincott, Isaac II, 239
Lippincott, Isaac II, 314
Lippincott, Isaac II, 315
Lippincott, Isaac II, 582
Lippincott, Isaac II, 806
Lippincott, Isaac H. II, 120
Lippincott, Isaac H. II, 806
Lippincott, Isabella II, 806
Lippincott, Isabella J. II, 890
Lippincott, Israel II, 890
Lippincott, Israel II, 936
Lippincott, J. Haines II, 891
Lippincott, J. Haines II, 903
Lippincott, Jacob II, 84
Lippincott, Jacob II, 203
Lippincott, Jacob II, 238
Lippincott, Jacob II, 239
Lippincott, Jacob II, 273
Lippincott, Jacob, Jr. II, 84
Lippincott, Jacob, Jr. II, 239
Lippincott, James II, 234
Lippincott, James II, 238
Lippincott, James II, 389
Lippincott, James Janney II, 806
Lippincott, James, Jr. II, 239
Lippincott, Jas. W. II, 134
Lippincott, Jason Evans V, 918
Lippincott, Jehu III, 207
Lippincott, Jehu III, 256
Lippincott, Jehu III, 280
Lippincott, Jehu III, 283
Lippincott, Jemima II, 295
Lippincott, Jesse T. V, 918
Lippincott, Jethro II, 68
Lippincott, Jethro II, 84
Lippincott, Job II, 57
Lippincott, Job II, 84
Lippincott, John II, 33
Lippincott, John II, 238
Lippincott, John II, 239
Lippincott, John II, 389
Lippincott, John II, 752
Lippincott, John III, 207
Lippincott, John H. II, 33
Lippincott, John H. II, 120
Lippincott, John H. II, 121
Lippincott, John H. II, 123
Lippincott, John H. II, 295
Lippincott, John H., Jr. II, 121
Lippincott, John K. II, 120
Lippincott, John K. II, 123
Lippincott, John M. II, 33
Lippincott, John Preston II, 134
Lippincott, John Russell II, 806
Lippincott, John, Jr. II, 120
Lippincott, Jonathan II, 239
Lippincott, Joseph II, 33
Lippincott, Joseph II, 84
Lippincott, Joseph II, 101
Lippincott, Joseph II, 121
Lippincott, Joseph II, 238
Lippincott, Joseph II, 239
Lippincott, Joseph II, 389
Lippincott, Joseph II, 582
Lippincott, Joseph V, 691
Lippincott, Joseph B. II, 295
Lippincott, Joseph B. II, 306
Lippincott, Joseph Davis II, 33
Lippincott, Joseph K. II, 33
Lippincott, Joseph K. II, 116
Lippincott, Joseph K. II, 121
Lippincott, Joseph R. II, 33
Lippincott, Joseph W. II, 295
Lippincott, Joseph W. II, 306
Lippincott, Joseph W. II, 711
Lippincott, Joseph W. II, 716
Lippincott, Joseph Z. II, 153
Lippincott, Josephine C. II, 866
Lippincott, Josephine C. II, 891
Lippincott, Joshua II, 33
Lippincott, Joshua II, 54
Lippincott, Joshua II, 84
Lippincott, Joshua II, 582
Lippincott, Joshua II, 806
Lippincott, Joshua II, 882
Lippincott, Joshua II, 890
Lippincott, Joshua II, 923
Lippincott, Joshua W. II, 806
Lippincott, Joshua W. II, 906
Lippincott, Joshua, Jr. II, 752
Lippincott, Joshua, Jr. II, 806
Lippincott, Joshua, Jr. II, 890
Lippincott, Joshua, Jr. II, 923
Lippincott, Josiah II, 120
Lippincott, Josiah II, 806
Lippincott, Josiah II, 862
Lippincott, Josiah II, 890
Lippincott, Judith II, 178
Lippincott, Julia Anna M. VI, 730
Lippincott, Julia Anna M. VI, 762
Lippincott, Keturah II, 33
Lippincott, Keturah II, 120
Lippincott, Keturah II, 123
Lippincott, Laura M. II, 890
Lippincott, Lenah Ann II, 135
Lippincott, Letticia II, 68
Lippincott, Letticia II, 84
Lippincott, Lidya II, 33
Lippincott, Lizzie A. II, 121
Lippincott, Lucy A. II, 295
Lippincott, Lucy A. H. II, 295
Lippincott, Lucy H. II, 295
Lippincott, Lydia II, 67
Lippincott, Lydia II, 84
Lippincott, Lydia II, 92
Lippincott, Lydia II, 120
Lippincott, Lydia II, 135
Lippincott, Lydia II, 153
Lippincott, Lydia II, 310
Lippincott, Lydia E. II, 890
Lippincott, Lydia E. II, 917
Lippincott, Lydia L. II, 134
Lippincott, Lydia L. II, 135
Lippincott, Lydia L. II, 320
Lippincott, Lydia L. II, 321
Lippincott, Marcy II, 234
Lippincott, Marcy II, 238
Lippincott, Margaret II, 315
Lippincott, Margaret Masters II, 711
Lippincott, Margaret Masters II, 752
Lippincott, Maria C. VI, 759
Lippincott, Maria C. VI, 786
Lippincott, Mark K. II, 295
Lippincott, Martha II, 117
Lippincott, Martha II, 120
Lippincott, Martha II, 135
Lippincott, Martha II, 238
Lippincott, Martha II, 239
Lippincott, Martha II, 582
Lippincott, Martha II, 819
Lippincott, Martha II, 1037
Lippincott, Martha VI, 730
Lippincott, Martha VI, 762
Lippincott, Martha B. II, 135
Lippincott, Martha B. II, 311
Lippincott, Martha B. II, 890
Lippincott, Martha B. II, 921
Lippincott, Martha D. II, 582
Lippincott, Martha D. II, 793
Lippincott, Martha D. II, 862
Lippincott, Martha D. II, 890
Lippincott, Martha F. II, 153
Lippincott, Martha H. II, 806
Lippincott, Martha H. II, 890
Lippincott, Martha H. II, 923
Lippincott, Martha Pancoast II, 134
Lippincott, Martha Pancoast II, 153
Lippincott, Martha Parry II, 806
Lippincott, Martha Parry II, 877
Lippincott, Martha Parry II, 891
Lippincott, Mary II, 33
Lippincott, Mary II, 53
Lippincott, Mary II, 79
Lippincott, Mary II, 84
Lippincott, Mary II, 85
Lippincott, Mary II, 100
Lippincott, Mary II, 101
Lippincott, Mary II, 106
Lippincott, Mary II, 135
Lippincott, Mary II, 158
Lippincott, Mary II, 178
Lippincott, Mary II, 203
Lippincott, Mary II, 213
Lippincott, Mary II, 238
Lippincott, Mary II, 239
Lippincott, Mary II, 243
Lippincott, Mary II, 273
Lippincott, Mary II, 295
Lippincott, Mary II, 389
Lippincott, Mary II, 582
Lippincott, Mary II, 627
Lippincott, Mary II, 645
Lippincott, Mary II, 696
Lippincott, Mary II, 806
Lippincott, Mary II, 890
Lippincott, Mary II, 923
Lippincott, Mary III, 207
Lippincott, Mary III, 230
Lippincott, Mary IV, 675
Lippincott, Mary A. II, 890
Lippincott, Mary A. II, 944
Lippincott, Mary Adaline II, 806
Lippincott, Mary Ann II, 806
Lippincott, Mary B. II, 582
Lippincott, Mary D. II, 153
Lippincott, Mary E. II, 890
Lippincott, Mary E. II, 891
Lippincott, Mary E. II, 903
Lippincott, Mary E. II, 906
Lippincott, Mary Elizabeth II, 806
Lippincott, Mary Ellen III, 207
Lippincott, Mary Ellen III, 280
Lippincott, Mary H. II, 33
Lippincott, Mary H. II, 121
Lippincott, Mary H. II, 153
Lippincott, Mary H. II, 856
Lippincott, Mary H. II, 890
Lippincott, Mary J. II, 856
Lippincott, Mary J. II, 890
Lippincott, Mary Jane II, 134
Lippincott, Mary Jane II, 153
Lippincott, Mary L. II, 153
Lippincott, Mary L. II, 730
Lippincott, Mary L. II, 752
Lippincott, Mary L. III, 207
Lippincott, Mary M. II, 135
Lippincott, Mary O. II, 153
Lippincott, Mary S. II, 717
Lippincott, Mary W. II, 134
Lippincott, Mary W. II, 137
Lippincott, Mary W. II, 153
Lippincott, Mary W. II, 806
Lippincott, Mary W. II, 890
Lippincott, Mary W. II, 906
Lippincott, Mary Woodward II, 806
Lippincott, Mercy II, 33
Lippincott, Mercy II, 83
Lippincott, Mercy II, 84
Lippincott, Mercy II, 238
Lippincott, Meriba II, 239
Lippincott, Meriba II, 273
Lippincott, Meribah II, 239
Lippincott, Moses II, 239
Lippincott, Naomy II, 84
Lippincott, Naomy II, 107
Lippincott, Naomy II, 108
Lippincott, Narcissa E. II, 711
Lippincott, Narcissa E. II, 752
Lippincott, Narcissa Elizabeth II, 295
Lippincott, Narcissa Elizabeth II, 754
Lippincott, Narcissa M. II, 752
Lippincott, Nathan II, 135
Lippincott, Orphy III, 207
Lippincott, Oswel V, 691
Lippincott, Oswell V, 93
Lippincott, Oswell V, 691
Lippincott, Parvin II, 295
Lippincott, Patience II, 221
Lippincott, Patience II, 238
Lippincott, Patience II, 806
Lippincott, Paul S. II, 33
Lippincott, Paul S. II, 121
Lippincott, Phebe II, 68
Lippincott, Phebe II, 84
Lippincott, Phebe II, 239
Lippincott, Phebe II, 582
Lippincott, Phebe II, 752
Lippincott, Phebe W. II, 314
Lippincott, Phebe W. II, 315
Lippincott, Preston II, 295
Lippincott, Priscilla II, 806
Lippincott, Priscilla II, 890
Lippincott, Priscilla II, 906
Lippincott, Priscilla M. II, 33
Lippincott, Priscilla M. II, 120
Lippincott, Priscilla M. II, 121
Lippincott, Priscilla M. II, 752
Lippincott, Priscilla P. II, 877
Lippincott, Priscilla P. II, 891
Lippincott, Rachel II, 119
Lippincott, Rachel II, 120
Lippincott, Rachel II, 213
Lippincott, Rachel II, 238
Lippincott, Rachel II, 239
Lippincott, Rachel II, 243
Lippincott, Rachel II, 261
Lippincott, Rachel II, 582
Lippincott, Rachel II, 823
Lippincott, Rahway II, 239
Lippincott, Rebecca II, 33
Lippincott, Rebecca II, 84
Lippincott, Rebecca II, 85
Lippincott, Rebecca II, 238
Lippincott, Rebecca II, 239
Lippincott, Rebecca II, 242
Lippincott, Rebecca II, 271
Lippincott, Rebecca IV, 975
Lippincott, Rebecca Atmore II, 828
Lippincott, Rebecca L. II, 120
Lippincott, Restore II, 178
Lippincott, Restore II, 214
Lippincott, Restore II, 225
Lippincott, Restore II, 238
Lippincott, Restore II, 239
Lippincott, Restore II, 246
Lippincott, Restore II, 582
Lippincott, Rich. Robt. III, 207
Lippincott, Rich. Robt. III, 357
Lippincott, Richard II, 389
Lippincott, Richard II, 582
Lippincott, Richard II, 645
Lippincott, Richard R. II, 311
Lippincott, Richard R. II, 321
Lippincott, Richard R. II, 322
Lippincott, Robert C. II, 806
Lippincott, Robert C. II, 890
Lippincott, Robert K. II, 890
Lippincott, Ruth II, 1045
Lippincott, Ruth II, 1055
Lippincott, Samuel II, 33
Lippincott, Samuel II, 56
Lippincott, Samuel II, 79
Lippincott, Samuel II, 84
Lippincott, Samuel II, 85
Lippincott, Samuel II, 106
Lippincott, Samuel II, 120
Lippincott, Samuel II, 134
Lippincott, Samuel II, 135
Lippincott, Samuel II, 142
Lippincott, Samuel II, 153
Lippincott, Samuel II, 178
Lippincott, Samuel II, 221
Lippincott, Samuel II, 223
Lippincott, Samuel II, 238
Lippincott, Samuel II, 239
Lippincott, Samuel II, 295
Lippincott, Samuel II, 389
Lippincott, Samuel II, 582
Lippincott, Samuel II, 627
Lippincott, Samuel II, 711
Lippincott, Samuel II, 752
Lippincott, Samuel II, 806
Lippincott, Samuel II, 890
Lippincott, Samuel III, 207
Lippincott, Samuel IV, 675
Lippincott, Samuel B. II, 582
Lippincott, Samuel Parry II, 806
Lippincott, Samuel R. II, 389
Lippincott, Samuel R. II, 752
Lippincott, Samuel R. II, 890
Lippincott, Samuel R. II, 906
Lippincott, Samuel Roberts II, 806
Lippincott, Samuel S. II, 890
Lippincott, Samuel T. II, 134
Lippincott, Samuel T. II, 135
Lippincott, Samuel T. II, 153
Lippincott, Samuel T. III, 230
Lippincott, Samuel, Jr. II, 84
Lippincott, Sarah II, 33
Lippincott, Sarah II, 74
Lippincott, Sarah II, 84
Lippincott, Sarah II, 120
Lippincott, Sarah II, 121
Lippincott, Sarah II, 153
Lippincott, Sarah II, 239
Lippincott, Sarah II, 273
Lippincott, Sarah II, 389
Lippincott, Sarah II, 582
Lippincott, Sarah II, 683
Lippincott, Sarah II, 752
Lippincott, Sarah II, 806
Lippincott, Sarah III, 207
Lippincott, Sarah V, 918
Lippincott, Sarah A. II, 114
Lippincott, Sarah A. II, 121
Lippincott, Sarah Ann II, 153
Lippincott, Sarah Ann II, 890
Lippincott, Sarah E. V, 918
Lippincott, Sarah J. L. II, 153
Lippincott, Sarah Jane II, 135
Lippincott, Sarah Jane II, 142
Lippincott, Sarah Jane II, 153
Lippincott, Sarah Jane III, 230
Lippincott, Sarah M. II, 862
Lippincott, Sarah M. II, 890
Lippincott, Sarah Mickle II, 806
Lippincott, Susan II, 1075
Lippincott, Susan II, 1083
Lippincott, Susan C. II, 176
Lippincott, Susan C. II, 291
Lippincott, Susan C. II, 295
Lippincott, Susan S. II, 1066
Lippincott, Susan S. II, 1075
Lippincott, Susanna W. II, 711
Lippincott, Susanna Wills II, 71
Lippincott, Thomas II, 33
Lippincott, Thomas II, 84
Lippincott, Thomas II, 85
Lippincott, Thomas II, 234
Lippincott, Thomas II, 238
Lippincott, Thomas II, 239
Lippincott, Thomas II, 261
Lippincott, Thomas II, 582
Lippincott, Thomas II, 1011
Lippincott, Thomas Ellwood II, 711
Lippincott, Thomas Elwood II, 752
Lippincott, Thornton Conrow II, 806
Lippincott, Wallace II, 239
Lippincott, Wd. Elizabeth M. II, 890
Lippincott, Wd. Esther Jane II, 806
Lippincott, Wd. Martha II, 246
Lippincott, Wendella III, 207
Lippincott, Wendella III, 283
Lippincott, Wilbur II, 582
Lippincott, Wilbur II, 645
Lippincott, William II, 120
Lippincott, William II, 208
Lippincott, William II, 239
Lippincott, William V, 93
Lippincott, William Folwell II, 3
Lippincott, Wm. II, 57
Lippincott, Wm. II, 84
Lippincott, Wm. II, 85
Lippincott, Wm. II, 113
Lippincott, Wm. II, 153
Lippincott, Wm. II, 582
Lippincott, Wm. II, 627
Lippincott, Wm. II, 819
Lippincott, Wm. II, 890
Lippincott, Wm. II, 903
Lippincott, Wm. II, 921
Lippincott, Wm. II, 936
Lippincott, Wm. F. II, 120
Lippincott, Wm. F. II, 153
Lippincott, Wm. F. II, 752
Lippincott, Wm. F. V, 918
Lippincott, Wm. Henry II, 144
Lippincott, Wm. Henry II, 153
Lippincott, Wm. P. II, 84
Lippincott, Wm. P. II, 85
Lippincott, Wm. P. II, 113
Lippincut, Restore II, 582
Lippincut, Samuel II, 582
Lippincutt, Hannah W. II, 120
Lippincutt, Joshua II, 84
Lippingcoate, Benjamin II, 84
Lippingcott, Freedom II, 238
Lippingcott, Mary II, 238
Lippinkot, Martha II, 582
Lippiot, Frederick IV, 735
Lipponcot, Mary II, 84
Lipscomb, Jane M. VI, 834
Lipscomb, John VI, 834
Lipscomb, Leonard VI, 834
Lipscomb, Nancy VI, 834
Lipscombe, Frances A. VI, 826
Lipscombe, Jane M. VI, 826

psey, ??? IV, 240
psey, Abraham IV, 975
psey, Abraham S. IV, 831
psey, Abraham S. IV, 976
psey, Albert IV, 240
psey, Albert IV, 241
psey, Albert IV, 641
psey, Amara IV, 137
psey, Amasa I, 272
psey, Amasa I, 299
psey, Amasa I, 310
psey, Amasa IV, 42
psey, Amasa IV, 46
psey, Amasa IV, 67
psey, Amasa IV, 98
psey, Amasa IV, 184
psey, Amasa IV, 192
psey, Amasa IV, 229
psey, Amasa IV, 240
psey, Amasa IV, 975
psey, Amy IV, 240
psey, Amy IV, 831
psey, Amy IV, 975
psey, Amy IV, 1009
psey, Ann IV, 184
psey, Ann IV, 240
psey, Ann IV, 539
psey, Ann IV, 641
psey, Ann IV, 659
psey, Ann IV, 735
psey, Ann IV, 1171
psey, Ann Eliza IV, 641
psey, Ann Eliza IV, 662
psey, Ann Eliza IV, 735
psey, Chalkley IV, 641
psey, Chalkley T. IV, 241
psey, Chalkley T. IV, 641
psey, Challkey IV, 240
psey, Edmond IV, 240
psey, Edmund IV, 90
psey, Edmund IV, 98
psey, Edmund IV, 240
psey, Edmund IV, 831
psey, Edmund IV, 965
psey, Edmund IV, 975
psey, Edmund IV, 976
psey, Edmund IV, 1009
psey, Eli IV, 240
psey, Eli IV, 831
psey, Eli H. IV, 240
psey, Eli M. IV, 831
psey, Eli M. IV, 975
psey, Eli M. IV, 976
psey, Eliza IV, 831
psey, Eliza IV, 975
psey, Eliza Ann IV, 641
psey, Eliza M. IV, 975
psey, Ellwood IV, 641
psey, Elvira IV, 641
psey, Elwood IV, 240
psey, Hannah IV, 1171
psey, Hannah IV, 1193
psey, Hannah IV, 1215
psey, Hannah IV, 1227
psey, Hannah W. IV, 1215
psey, Israel IV, 240
psey, Jane IV, 641
psey, Jefferson IV, 46
psey, John IV, 184
psey, John IV, 240
psey, John IV, 539
psey, John IV, 641
psey, John IV, 659
psey, John IV, 735
psey, John IV, 1171
psey, John Alonzo IV, 641
psey, Lemuel IV, 241
psey, Lemuel IV, 641
psey, Lemuel IV, 735
psey, Lemuel J. IV, 641
psey, Lenira H. IV, 1215
psey, Lindley M. IV, 831
psey, Lindley M. IV, 975
psey, Lindley M. IV, 976
psey, Lucius IV, 1215
psey, Lwien W. IV, 1215
psey, Lydia IV, 240
psey, Lydia IV, 831
psey, Lydia H. IV, 240
psey, Lydia H. IV, 831
psey, Lydia H. IV, 965
psey, Lydia H. IV, 975
psey, Lydia H. IV, 976
psey, Martha IV, 184
psey, Martha IV, 240
psey, Martha IV, 831
psey, Martha J. IV, 831
psey, Martha J. IV, 972
psey, Martha J. IV, 976
psey, Martha Jane IV, 240
psey, Martha Jane IV, 975
Lipsey, Martha T. IV, 975
Lipsey, Mary IV, 46
Lipsey, Mary IV, 240
Lipsey, Mary Ann IV, 240
Lipsey, Mary Ann IV, 831
Lipsey, Mary Ann IV, 934
Lipsey, Mary Ann IV, 975
Lipsey, Mary Ann IV, 976
Lipsey, Mary Jane IV, 240
Lipsey, Mary Jane IV, 639
Lipsey, Mary Jane IV, 641
Lipsey, Maryann IV, 831
Lipsey, Mikker IV, 976
Lipsey, Oliva C. IV, 831
Lipsey, Oliva O. IV, 976
Lipsey, Oliver IV, 1215
Lipsey, Oliver J. IV, 1215
Lipsey, Olivia O. IV, 975
Lipsey, Penina I, 272
Lipsey, Peninah I, 299
Lipsey, Peninah I, 310
Lipsey, Peninah IV, 240
Lipsey, Penninah I, 310
Lipsey, Rachel IV, 46
Lipsey, Rachel IV, 67
Lipsey, Rachel IV, 98
Lipsey, Rachel IV, 184
Lipsey, Rachel IV, 240
Lipsey, Rachel Ann IV, 1215
Lipsey, Rasco I, 310
Lipsey, Rasco IV, 46
Lipsey, Rosco IV, 240
Lipsey, Ruth IV, 240
Lipsey, Ruth IV, 831
Lipsey, Ruth IV, 953
Lipsey, Ruth IV, 975
Lipsey, Ruth IV, 976
Lipsey, Ruth Anna IV, 641
Lipsey, Ruth Anna IV, 659
Lipsey, Ruthanna IV, 240
Lipsey, Sarah IV, 42
Lipsey, Sarah IV, 46
Lipsey, Sarah IV, 90
Lipsey, Sarah IV, 98
Lipsey, Sarah IV, 192
Lipsey, Sarah IV, 229
Lipsey, Sarah IV, 240
Lipsey, Sarah IV, 310
Lipsey, Sarah IV, 323
Lipsey, Sarah IV, 340
Lipsey, Sarah IV, 641
Lipsey, Sarah IV, 831
Lipsey, Sarah IV, 941
Lipsey, Sarah IV, 965
Lipsey, Sarah IV, 975
Lipsey, Sarah IV, 976
Lipsey, Sarah IV, 1009
Lipsey, Sarah H. IV, 98
Lipsey, Sarah H. IV, 240
Lipsey, Sarah H. IV, 831
Lipsey, Sarah J. IV, 240
Lipsey, Sarah J. IV, 641
Lipsey, Sarah J. IV, 735
Lipsey, Sarah Josephine IV, 240
Lipsey, Sarah Josephine IV, 608
Lipsey, Sarah Josephine IV, 641
Lipsey, Seneca IV, 1215
Lipsey, Tamer IV, 46
Lipsey, Tamer IV, 240
Lipsey, William B. IV, 240
Lipsey, William B. IV, 641
Lipsey, William D. IV, 539
Lipsey, William M. IV, 975
Lipsey, Wm. IV, 976
Lipsey, Wm. IV, 1215
Lipsey, Wm. B. IV, 641
Lipsey, Wm. B. IV, 1171
Lipsey, Wm. B. IV, 1193
Lipsey, Wm. B. IV, 1215
Lipsey, Wm. B. IV, 1227
Lipsey, Wm. Miller IV, 831
Lipsy, Ann IV, 539
Lipsy, Edmund IV, 976
Lipsy, John IV, 539
Lipton, Mary IV, 503
Lipton, R. IV, 503
Lipton, S. IV, 503
Lisbay, Jennie IV, 241
Lisby, Anna IV, 241
Lisby, Anna M. IV, 241
Lisby, Jennie IV, 241
Lisk, John II, 445
Lisk, Joseph II, 389
Lisk, M??? II, 389
Lisk, Margrett II, 445
Lisle, Elizabeth II, 454
Lisle, Elizabeth II, 582
Lisle, George IV, 417
Lisle, Henry II, 582
Lisle, Henry IV, 417
Lisle, James IV, 385
Lisle, James IV, 417
Lisle, James, Jr. IV, 417
Lisle, John IV, 417
Lisle, Joseph IV, 417
Lisle, Lettice IV, 417
Lisle, Mary II, 392
Lisle, Mary II, 457
Lisle, Mary II, 582
Lisle, Mary IV, 404
Lisle, Mary IV, 417
Lisle, Maurice II, 454
Lisle, Maurice II, 457
Lisle, Maurice II, 582
Lisle, Peninnah IV, 385
Lisle, Peninnah IV, 417
Lisle, Phebe IV, 417
Lisle, Phebe IV, 458
Lisle, William Turner II, 711
List, Pearle V, 1007
List, Raymond V, 1007
Listar, Anne II, 239
Lister, ??? III, 205
Lister, Anna II, 239
Lister, Anne II, 239
Lister, Bevan IV, 560
Lister, Catherine IV, 560
Lister, Elizabeth III, 205
Lister, Elizabeth III, 207
Lister, Emanuel III, 205
Lister, Gertrude III, 205
Lister, Ida Maria III, 205
Lister, Jedediah III, 205
Lister, Jonathan M. IV, 560
Lister, Jonathan, Jr. IV, 560
Lister, Joseph II, 582
Lister, Martha IV, 560
Lister, Mary II, 582
Lister, Peter M. IV, 560
Lister, Phamy IV, 560
Lister, Phebe III, 205
Lister, Sarah IV, 560
Lister, Sarah IV, 561
Lister, Solomon Jehu IV, 560
Lister, Theodore IV, 560
Lister, Thomas II, 582
Lister, Walter V, 511
Lister, Wilhelmina III, 196
Lister, Wilhelmina III, 207
Lister, Wm. V, 511
Listern, Catherine VI, 820
Listern, Caty VI, 820
Listern, Nancy VI, 820
Listern, Susanna VI, 820
Liston, Martha VI, 856
Liston, Raymond IV, 1326
Litchfield, John II, 389
Litchfield, Mary T. E. III, 338
Litchfield, Mary Ten Eyck III, 208
Litchfield, Mary Ten Eyck III, 339
Litchford, Andrew J. VI, 834
Litchford, Arthur VI, 834
Litchford, Austin VI, 834
Litchford, Calista VI, 834
Litchford, Calista H. VI, 818
Litchford, Collins VI, 819
Litchford, Collins VI, 834
Litchford, Eliza VI, 834
Litchford, Eliza VI, 849
Litchford, Elizabeth VI, 834
Litchford, Elizabeth A. VI, 818
Litchford, Emily VI, 819
Litchford, Francis VI, 834
Litchford, Gillian VI, 834
Litchford, James VI, 834
Litchford, John VI, 834
Litchford, Judith A. VI, 833
Litchford, Kessiah VI, 825
Litchford, Lucinda VI, 834
Litchford, Mary VI, 834
Litchford, Milly VI, 834
Litchford, Sally VI, 834
Litchford, Sarah VI, 816
Litchford, Thomas VI, 834
Litchford, Thomas I. VI, 797
Litchford, Thomas J. VI, 825
Litchmins, Mercy II, 239
Litle, Charles VI, 413
Litle, Charles VI, 761
Litle, Charles VI, 769
Litle, Charles William VI, 413
Litle, Charles William VI, 761
Litle, Elizabeth VI, 569
Litle, Elizabeth VI, 570
Litle, Elizabeth VI, 761
Litle, Elizabeth VI, 785
Litle, Hanna VI, 785
Litle, Hannah II, 239
Litle, Hannah II, 583
Litle, Hannah VI, 570
Litle, Hannah VI, 761
Litle, Hannah, Jr. VI, 761
Litle, Hannah, Jr. VI, 785
Litle, Isaac P. IV, 152
Litle, Isaac P. VI, 413
Litle, Isaac P. VI, 761
Litle, James VI, 761
Litle, John II, 295
Litle, John II, 583
Litle, John VI, 761
Litle, John VI, 785
Litle, John Henry Eaton VI, 761
Litle, John I. II, 891
Litle, John J. II, 295
Litle, John J. II, 753
Litle, John James II, 891
Litle, John James VI, 761
Litle, Lydia VI, 413
Litle, Lydia VI, 761
Litle, Lydia VI, 769
Litle, Mary II, 389
Litle, Nathan VI, 413
Litle, Nathan Parkins VI, 761
Litle, Rebecca VI, 761
Litle, Rebecca T. VI, 761
Litle, Richard VI, 570
Litle, Richard VI, 761
Litle, Richard H. VI, 569
Litle, Richard H. VI, 752
Litle, Richard H. VI, 761
Litle, Richard H. VI, 785
Litle, Richard, Jr. VI, 761
Litle, Robert II, 389
Litle, Robert Sinclair VI, 761
Litle, Ruth II, 295
Litle, Ruth II, 891
Litle, Ruth VI, 761
Litle, Samuel B. VI, 761
Litle, Sarah VI, 761
Litle, Sarah Ann VI, 761
Litle, Sidney VI, 413
Litle, Sidney VI, 761
Litle, Sidney P. VI, 413
Litle, Thomas II, 389
Litle, Wd. Lydia VI, 761
Litle, William VI, 413
Litle, William VI, 761
Litler, Albert IV, 1284
Litler, Catharine I, 469
Litler, Catharine I, 724
Litler, Catharine I, 734
Litler, Charles VI, 428
Litler, David VI, 414
Litler, Elias I, 469
Litler, Harriet IV, 1284
Litler, Isaiah VI, 414
Litler, Jehu I, 469
Litler, Jeremiah I, 469
Litler, Jeremiah I, 482
Litler, Jeremiah I, 724
Litler, John I, 724
Litler, Lydia VI, 428
Litler, Mary Ellen V, 958
Litler, Mincher I, 405
Litler, Nancy I, 724
Litler, Nancy I, 733
Litler, Nathan, Jr. VI, 414
Litler, Rachel I, 722
Litler, Rachel I, 724
Litler, Sallie IV, 1285
Litler, Sarah IV, 1284
Litteljohn, Wd. Mary II, 191
LittellJohn, Wd. Mary II, 239
Litter, Henry II, 389
Litter, John II, 389
Litter, Mincher I, 724
Litter, Rachel B. VI, 472
Little, Abot II, 687
Little, Alcina V, 460
Little, Anna V, 1007
Little, Annetta B. V, 410
Little, Annetty B. V, 410
Little, Barnabas VI, 920
Little, Charles III, 208
Little, Charles VI, 527
Little, Charles C. VI, 946
Little, Charles C. VI, 952
Little, Clara V, 1007
Little, D. VI, 808
Little, Daniel II, 687
Little, David III, 208
Little, Davis II, 389
Little, Deborah I, 391
Little, Deborah I, 405
Little, Deborah IV, 1284
Little, Deborah IV, 1287
Little, Delilah V, 410
Little, Dinah II, 389
Little, Edward II, 687
Little, Edward V, 918
Little, Edward P. II, 707
Little, Edy R. II, 707
Little, Elden V, 1007
Little, Elisabeth II, 582
Little, Elizabeth II, 583
Little, Elizabeth II, 658
Little, Elizabeth VI, 106
Little, Elizabeth VI, 115
Little, Elizabeth VI, 841
Little, Ellen V, 1007
Little, Ennion II, 687
Little, Francis II, 445
Little, Francis II, 582
Little, Francis II, 692
Little, Geo. H. IV, 1326
Little, Geo. H. V, 918
Little, Geo. Henry V, 918
Little, George IV, 1256
Little, George E. IV, 1256
Little, George Henry IV, 1326
Little, Hannah II, 239
Little, Hannah II, 583
Little, Hannah II, 673
Little, Hezekiah V, 410
Little, Hezikiah V, 410
Little, Isaac P. IV, 152
Little, Jacob V, 1007
Little, James VI, 816
Little, James VI, 834
Little, James VI, 841
Little, James VI, 842
Little, James H. IV, 1284
Little, Jane II, 687
Little, Jane VI, 834
Little, Jessie IV, 1326
Little, Jessie G. IV, 1326
Little, Jessie M. G. V, 918
Little, John II, 239
Little, John II, 389
Little, John II, 583
Little, John VI, 816
Little, John H. VI, 834
Little, Justin VI, 920
Little, Katy IV, 1284
Little, Luadia V, 410
Little, Luanda V, 410
Little, Lucinda VI, 816
Little, Lucy S. VI, 952
Little, Lustin VI, 834
Little, Lydia VI, 413
Little, M. E. IV, 1284
Little, Margaret V, 632
Little, Martha V, 410
Little, Martha A. VI, 834
Little, Martha V. V, 410
Little, Mary II, 389
Little, Mary II, 501
Little, Mary II, 582
Little, Mary II, 687
Little, Mary II, 692
Little, Mary IV, 1166
Little, Mary IV, 1171
Little, Mary V, 38
Little, Mary V, 93
Little, Mary V, 410
Little, Mary VI, 834
Little, Mary VI, 841
Little, Mary Ann II, 389
Little, Mary Ann V, 410
Little, Mattie V, 1007
Little, Mildred VI, 808
Little, Mildred VI, 834
Little, Minnie IV, 1256
Little, Miriam I, 724
Little, Nathan VI, 413
Little, Permelia VI, 834
Little, Rachel W. II, 707
Little, Rebecca VI, 834
Little, Richard VI, 808
Little, Richard VI, 842
Little, Richard L. VI, 834
Little, Robert II, 389
Little, Robert IV, 152
Little, Robert VI, 834
Little, Sallie A. VI, 834
Little, Samuel VI, 841
Little, Samuel S. VI, 834
Little, Sidney VI, 413
Little, Susanna II, 389
Little, Tacy II, 687
Little, Thomas II, 389
Little, Thomas Denson VI, 115
Little, Violetta VI, 920
Little, Walter V, 1007
Little, Weltha V, 1007
Little, Widow Lydia VI, 527
Little, William VI, 834
LittleJohn, Ann VI, 413
LittleJohn, Elizabeth VI, 414
LittleJohn, James VI, 413
LittleJohn, John VI, 413
LittleJohn, Martha VI, 413

LittleJohn, Mary VI, 414
Littlejohn, Sally V, 814
Littlejohn, Sarah V, 736
Littlejohn, Sarah V, 751
LittleJohn, Sarah VI, 413
LittleJohn, Thomas VI, 413
LittleJohn, William VI, 413
Littlepage, Annie VI, 834
Littlepage, Benjamin VI, 801
Littlepage, Benjamin VI, 834
Littlepage, Francis VI, 834
Littlepage, John VI, 834
Littler, Abigail II, 583
Littler, Ann II, 583
Littler, Ann VI, 472
Littler, Ann VI, 501
Littler, Ann VI, 527
Littler, Ann VI, 536
Littler, Anna I, 469
Littler, Anna I, 471
Littler, Anna I, 482
Littler, Anna I, 485
Littler, Catharine I, 405
Littler, Catharine I, 469
Littler, Catharine I, 482
Littler, Catharine I, 724
Littler, Catharine I, 732
Littler, Catherine VI, 414
Littler, Catherine VI, 457
Littler, Charles VI, 414
Littler, David VI, 414
Littler, Deborah I, 405
Littler, Deborah I, 469
Littler, Deborah I, 724
Littler, Deborah II, 583
Littler, Elias I, 469
Littler, Elizabeth I, 405
Littler, Elizabeth I, 416
Littler, Elizabeth I, 469
Littler, Hannah I, 405
Littler, Hannah I, 416
Littler, Hannah VI, 414
Littler, Hannah Jane I, 469
Littler, Hugh II, 583
Littler, Isaiah VI, 414
Littler, Jacob II, 583
Littler, Jehu I, 469
Littler, Jeremiah I, 469
Littler, Jeremiah I, 482
Littler, Jeremiah I, 724
Littler, Jeremiah Linney I, 469
Littler, Joel I, 469
Littler, Joel I, 482
Littler, John I, 405
Littler, John I, 469
Littler, John I, 474
Littler, John I, 482
Littler, John I, 724
Littler, John I, 732
Littler, John II, 583
Littler, John V, 918
Littler, John VI, 357
Littler, John VI, 414
Littler, John VI, 501
Littler, John VI, 527
Littler, John Oxley I, 469
Littler, John S. VI, 472
Littler, John S. VI, 527
Littler, Joseph I, 724
Littler, Joshua I, 724
Littler, Katharine I, 482
Littler, Katharine VI, 411
Littler, Katharine VI, 414
Littler, Lydia I, 382
Littler, Lydia I, 405
Littler, Lydia I, 463
Littler, Lydia I, 464
Littler, Lydia I, 469
Littler, Lydia I, 478
Littler, Lydia I, 482
Littler, Lydia VI, 414
Littler, Mary I, 382
Littler, Mary I, 405
Littler, Mary I, 469
Littler, Mary II, 497
Littler, Mary II, 583
Littler, Mary V, 93
Littler, Mary V, 122
Littler, Mary V, 955
Littler, Mary V, 958
Littler, Mary VI, 359
Littler, Mary VI, 414
Littler, Mary VI, 437
Littler, Mary Anna I, 482
Littler, Mary Ellen V, 955
Littler, Mincher I, 405
Littler, Mincher I, 469
Littler, Mincher I, 724
Littler, Minshe I, 724
Littler, Nancy I, 724
Littler, Nathan VI, 414
Littler, Nathan VI, 449
Littler, Nathan VI, 457
Littler, Nathan VI, 671
Littler, Nathan VI, 709
Littler, Nathan, Jr. VI, 414
Littler, Rachel I, 724
Littler, Rachel V, 935
Littler, Rachel VI, 414
Littler, Rachel VI, 449
Littler, Rachel VI, 527
Littler, Rachel VI, 569
Littler, Rachel VI, 671
Littler, Rachel VI, 709
Littler, Rachel B. VI, 527
Littler, Rebeca VI, 414
Littler, Rebecca I, 724
Littler, Rebecca VI, 414
Littler, Rebecca VI, 671
Littler, Rebecca VI, 709
Littler, Sallie IV, 1284
Littler, Samuel II, 583
Littler, Samuel VI, 414
Littler, Samuel Howel II, 583
Littler, Sarah II, 803
Littler, Sarah Ann VI, 501
Littler, Sarah Ann VI, 527
Littler, Sarah Ann VI, 536
Littler, Sidney II, 578
Littler, Sidney II, 583
Littler, Tamer I, 469
Littler, Thamer I, 474
Littler, Thamer I, 482
Littler, Thomas V, 186
Littler, Thomas V, 955
Littler, Thomas V, 958
Littler, Thomas VI, 414
Littler, Thomas VI, 437
Littler, Winchester VI, 414
Littleton, Bernard II, 207
Littleton, Bernard II, 239
Littleton, Chancey V, 582
Littleton, Chauncey T. V, 582
Littleton, Chauncy V, 751
Littleton, Ernest V, 751
Littleton, Ernest N. V, 582
Littleton, Mary II, 239
Littleton, Myra V, 751
Littleton, Myrta V, 751
Littleton, Orpha V, 751
Littleton, Orpha A. V, 582
Littleton, Raymond V, 751
Littleton, Wayne V, 751
Littleton, Wayne C. V, 582
Litton, Nancy VI, 977
Litton, Rachel VI, 977
Litty, Catharine Louise IV, 735
Litty, Cordelia R. IV, 792
Litty, Elizabeth IV, 792
Litty, Frederick IV, 792
Litty, Herman P. IV, 792
Litty, Jean IV, 735
Litty, Jean IV, 792
Litty, John IV, 792
Litty, John C. IV, 735
Litty, Myra E. IV, 792
Litz, Birl V, 1007
Litz, Matilda V, 1007
Litz, Rachel V, 1007
Liuthan, Elizabeth IV, 1105
Lively, Acton S. IV, 241
Lively, Elizabeth VI, 1017
Lively, Milley VI, 922
Lively, Orin IV, 241
Lively, Polly VI, 884
Lively, R. J. IV, 241
Lively, William VI, 922
Lively, William VI, 1017
Lively, Willis B. VI, 884
Livesey, ??? III, 200
Livesey, ??? IV, 1085
Livesey, Anna IV, 241
Livesey, Anna IV, 641
Livesey, Charles IV, 241
Livesey, Elizabeth IV, 241
Livesey, Elizabeth IV, 1171
Livesey, Elizabeth W. IV, 241
Livesey, Ezra III, 208
Livesey, Jane III, 200
Livesey, Jane III, 208
Livesey, Jesse IV, 241
Livesey, Jesse K. IV, 241
Livesey, Joseph IV, 241
Livesey, Oliver IV, 1171
Livesey, Sarah Jane IV, 1171
Livesey, Wm. B. IV, 1171
Livezey, ???ward IV, 831
Livezey, Aaron Thomas IV, 276
Livezey, Abraham II, 891
Livezey, Abraham II, 1075
Livezey, Abram II, 891
Livezey, Albert H. IV, 586
Livezey, Albert J. IV, 416
Livezey, Albert J. IV, 417
Livezey, Albert J. IV, 418
Livezey, Albert J. IV, 586
Livezey, Albert J. IV, 641
Livezey, Alberta II, 806
Livezey, Alice R. IV, 800
Livezey, Alice R. IV, 831
Livezey, Alice Rebecca IV, 641
Livezey, Alice Rebecca IV, 831
Livezey, Anna IV, 581
Livezey, Anna IV, 583
Livezey, Anna IV, 586
Livezey, Anna IV, 628
Livezey, Anna IV, 641
Livezey, Anna V, 346
Livezey, Asenath IV, 1105
Livezey, Bertha V, 346
Livezey, Bertha M. IV, 418
Livezey, C. Albert II, 891
Livezey, Charles IV, 417
Livezey, Charles IV, 418
Livezey, Charles IV, 586
Livezey, Charles IV, 641
Livezey, Charles B. II, 891
Livezey, Charles C. II, 583
Livezey, Chas. IV, 276
Livezey, Chas. IV, 641
Livezey, Chas. IV, 831
Livezey, Chas. B. II, 891
Livezey, Cyrus Albert II, 806
Livezey, David II, 583
Livezey, Deborah II, 1011
Livezey, Deborah II, 1070
Livezey, Deborah II, 1075
Livezey, Deborah P. II, 891
Livezey, Donald William IV, 831
Livezey, Donald Wm. IV, 641
Livezey, Donald Wm. IV, 831
Livezey, Dorothy Mary IV, 417
Livezey, Edith II, 891
Livezey, Edith S. II, 806
Livezey, Edith S. II, 843
Livezey, Edith S. II, 891
Livezey, Eleanor IV, 735
Livezey, Elias II, 891
Livezey, Elizabeth II, 788
Livezey, Elizabeth IV, 276
Livezey, Elizabeth IV, 417
Livezey, Elizabeth IV, 418
Livezey, Elizabeth IV, 581
Livezey, Elizabeth IV, 586
Livezey, Elizabeth IV, 591
Livezey, Elizabeth IV, 641
Livezey, Elizabeth IV, 831
Livezey, Elizabeth IV, 1088
Livezey, Elizabeth IV, 1105
Livezey, Elizabeth Baker II, 891
Livezey, Elizabeth M. II, 891
Livezey, Elizabeth W. IV, 276
Livezey, Elizabeth W. IV, 417
Livezey, Elizabeth W. IV, 586
Livezey, Elizabeth W. IV, 641
Livezey, Emma L. IV, 418
Livezey, Emma L. IV, 816
Livezey, Emma L. IV, 831
Livezey, Ezra IV, 1066
Livezey, Felicia R. II, 891
Livezey, Gertrude S. II, 806
Livezey, Glen Charles IV, 831
Livezey, Hannah II, 875
Livezey, Hannah II, 891
Livezey, Hannah Ann IV, 418
Livezey, Hannah Ann IV, 1066
Livezey, Hannah Ann IV, 1105
Livezey, Hannah Ann IV, 1108
Livezey, Hannah Ann IV, 1136
Livezey, Helen Edith IV, 417
Livezey, Jason IV, 735
Livezey, Jeremiah IV, 418
Livezey, Jeremiah IV, 1066
Livezey, Jesse IV, 581
Livezey, Jesse IV, 1066
Livezey, Jesse K. IV, 417
Livezey, Jesse K. IV, 418
Livezey, Jesse K. IV, 586
Livezey, Jesse K. IV, 591
Livezey, Jesse K. IV, 641
Livezey, Jesse K. IV, 800
Livezey, Jesse K. IV, 831
Livezey, Jesse K. IV, 1105
Livezey, Jesse R., Jr. IV, 417
Livezey, John II, 389
Livezey, John II, 711
Livezey, John II, 753
Livezey, John IV, 1136
Livezey, John H. IV, 418
Livezey, John H. IV, 586
Livezey, John H. IV, 1066
Livezey, John H. IV, 1105
Livezey, John H. IV, 1108
Livezey, John H. IV, 1134
Livezey, John P. IV, 586
Livezey, John W. IV, 276
Livezey, John, Jr. II, 583
Livezey, Joseph II, 806
Livezey, Joseph II, 891
Livezey, Joseph Burr II, 806
Livezey, Joseph Burr II, 891
Livezey, Joseph D. II, 891
Livezey, Joseph Dilworth II, 891
Livezey, Joseph Exum IV, 586
Livezey, Joseph R. II, 891
Livezey, Joseph, Jr. II, 843
Livezey, Joseph, Jr. II, 891
Livezey, Lavina IV, 1066
Livezey, Lavina IV, 1088
Livezey, Lavina IV, 1105
Livezey, Lilla C. II, 806
Livezey, Lillia II, 891
Livezey, Lura Mildred IV, 831
Livezey, Lydia II, 799
Livezey, Margaret Rebecca IV, 831
Livezey, Marianna II, 891
Livezey, Marianna D. II, 891
Livezey, Marianna D. II, 938
Livezey, Martha II, 810
Livezey, Mary II, 583
Livezey, Mary II, 711
Livezey, Mary II, 843
Livezey, Mary II, 891
Livezey, Mary V, 346
Livezey, Mary H. S. V, 346
Livezey, Mildred Anna IV, 417
Livezey, Nellie V, 346
Livezey, Oliver IV, 418
Livezey, Oliver IV, 586
Livezey, Oliver IV, 1066
Livezey, Oliver IV, 1088
Livezey, Oliver IV, 1105
Livezey, Paul Albert IV, 418
Livezey, Rachel IV, 276
Livezey, Rachel IV, 416
Livezey, Rachel IV, 417
Livezey, Rachel IV, 418
Livezey, Rachel K. IV, 418
Livezey, Rachel K. IV, 641
Livezey, Rachel S. IV, 641
Livezey, Ralph Arthur IV, 641
Livezey, Ralph Arthur IV, 831
Livezey, Rebecca IV, 1066
Livezey, Robert II, 891
Livezey, Robert S. IV, 417
Livezey, Robert S. IV, 586
Livezey, Ruth Elizabeth IV, 417
Livezey, Samuel II, 843
Livezey, Samuel II, 891
Livezey, Samuel M. II, 583
Livezey, Samuel M. II, 682
Livezey, Sarah II, 753
Livezey, Sarah II, 754
Livezey, Sarah IV, 418
Livezey, Sarah IV, 586
Livezey, Sarah IV, 1066
Livezey, Sarah IV, 1105
Livezey, Sarah IV, 1134
Livezey, Sarah Jane IV, 1105
Livezey, Sarah M. II, 891
Livezey, Stephen IV, 276
Livezey, Theodore II, 891
Livezey, Theodore II, 1075
Livezey, Thos. II, 799
Livezey, Walter IV, 417
Livezey, Walter B. II, 891
Livezey, Walter C. IV, 418
Livezey, Walter C. IV, 586
Livezey, Walter C. IV, 816
Livezey, Walter C. IV, 831
Livezey, Walter E. IV, 586
Livezey, William V, 346
Livezey, William B. IV, 1105
Livezey, William E. IV, 417
Livezey, William Penn II, 806
Livezey, Wm. B. IV, 1105
Livezey, Wm. B. V, 346
Livezey, Wm. P. II, 891
Livezey, Wm. Penn II, 891
Livezy, Alice IV, 641
Livezy, Alice Rebecca IV, 641
Livezy, Ann II, 964
Livezy, Anna II, 964
Livezy, Chas. IV, 641
Livezy, Donald William IV, 641
Livezy, Donald Wm. IV, 641
Livezy, Elizabeth IV, 641
Livezy, Jesse K. IV, 641
Livezy, Ralph Arthur IV, 641
Livezy, Robert II, 964
Livezy, William V, 346
Livingood, A. Frank I, 945
Livingood, Andrew Frank I, 929
Livingood, Beatrice Gertrude I, 929
Livingood, Bernice I, 945
Livingood, Edw. I, 945
Livingood, Edward Verrel I, 92
Livingood, Frank I, 922
Livingood, Franklin I, 945
Livingood, Gertrude I, 922
Livingood, Gertrude I, 938
Livingood, Gertrude I, 945
Livingood, Howard I, 945
Livingood, Howard Franklin I, 929
Livingood, Ione Bernice I, 929
Livingood, J. Frank I, 945
Livingood, Lorenzo I, 929
Livingood, Mary I, 929
Livingood, Mary Janina I, 929
Livingood, Minnie Lee Velna I, 929
Livingood, Nellie I, 939
Livingood, Nellie C. I, 922
Livingood, Nellie Colene I, 929
Livingood, William Harrison I, 929
Livingood, Wm. I, 945
Livingood, Zelma I, 945
Livingood, Zelma Pauline I, 92
Livingston, Ada III, 208
Livingston, Ada A. III, 280
Livingston, Ada L. III, 325
Livingston, Elizabeth III, 208
Livingston, George IV, 241
Livingston, George F. IV, 241
Livingston, Harriet V, 259
Livingston, Harry III, 510
Livingston, Holden V, 259
Livingston, James V, 93
Livingston, James VI, 834
Livingston, Jemima W. VI, 101
Livingston, John VI, 547
Livingston, John VI, 671
Livingston, Lida IV, 241
Livingston, Lida C. IV, 241
Livingston, Pleasant VI, 547
Livingston, Sally VI, 834
Livingston, Tamar V, 93
Livingstone, Elizabeth VI, 548
Livingstone, John VI, 548
Livingstonn, Elizabeth VI, 527
Livingstonn, John VI, 527
Liviret, Robt VI, 291
Livizey, Rebecca IV, 1064
Livtir, William IV, 484
Livzey, Alice IV, 641
Livzey, Donald William IV, 641
Livzey, Jesse K. IV, 641
Livzey, Ralph Arthur IV, 641
Livzey, Wm. B. V, 346
Llewellen, Hannah II, 753
Llewellyn, Abigail II, 711
Llewellyn, Abigail IV, 418
Llewellyn, Abigail IV, 831
Llewellyn, Abigail IV, 1066
Llewellyn, Abigail S. II, 744
Llewellyn, Abigail S. II, 753
Llewellyn, Abigail S. IV, 831
Llewellyn, Abigail S. IV, 1066
Llewellyn, Adriadna II, 786
Llewellyn, Alice V, 410
Llewellyn, Amos IV, 1066
Llewellyn, Anna IV, 241
Llewellyn, Anna IV, 1066
Llewellyn, Anna V, 410
Llewellyn, Anna V, 411
Llewellyn, Anna Elizabeth V, 4
Llewellyn, Anna Elizabeth V, 4
Llewellyn, Anna Kester V, 392
Llewellyn, Anna M. IV, 628
Llewellyn, Anna M. IV, 715
Llewellyn, Anna M. IV, 768
Llewellyn, Anne IV, 1066
Llewellyn, Bailey IV, 1066
Llewellyn, Benjamin F. IV, 241
Llewellyn, Catherine II, 583
Llewellyn, Charles B. II, 711
Llewellyn, Charles B. II, 753
Llewellyn, Charles B. IV, 393
Llewellyn, Charles B. IV, 418
Llewellyn, Charles B. IV, 831
Llewellyn, Charles B. IV, 1066
Llewellyn, Cicely II, 472
Llewellyn, Cicely II, 583
Llewellyn, Daniel IV, 1066
Llewellyn, Daniel W. IV, 1105
Llewellyn, Edgar V, 410
Llewellyn, Edgar V, 411
Llewellyn, Elisha II, 711
Llewellyn, Elisha II, 744
Llewellyn, Elisha II, 753
Llewellyn, Elisha IV, 418

wellyn, Elisha IV, 626
wellyn, Elisha IV, 641
wellyn, Elisha IV, 713
wellyn, Elisha IV, 735
wellyn, Elisha IV, 831
wellyn, Elisha IV, 1066
wellyn, Elisha IV, 1078
wellyn, Elisha IV, 1105
wellyn, Elizabeth IV, 1066
wellyn, Elizabeth IV, 1067
wellyn, Ella II, 711
wellyn, Ella H. II, 744
wellyn, Ella H. II, 753
wellyn, Emily D. II, 711
wellyn, Emily D. II, 753
wellyn, Emily D. IV, 418
wellyn, Emily Dennis IV, 393
wellyn, Emily Dennis IV, 418
wellyn, Esther L. II, 711
wellyn, Eza IV, 1066
wellyn, Ezra IV, 418
wellyn, Ezra IV, 641
wellyn, Ezra IV, 1105
wellyn, Grace IV, 1102
wellyn, Grace IV, 1105
wellyn, Hannah II, 711
wellyn, Hannah II, 753
wellyn, Hannah IV, 1066
wellyn, Harold V, 410
wellyn, Harold V, 411
wellyn, James IV, 1066
wellyn, John IV, 1066
wellyn, John V, 392
wellyn, John V, 410
wellyn, John V, 411
wellyn, Joseph IV, 418
wellyn, Joseph IV, 1066
wellyn, Mabel E. II, 711
wellyn, Mabel E. IV, 831
wellyn, Mabel E. IV, 1066
wellyn, Martha IV, 641
wellyn, Martha IV, 768
wellyn, Martha IV, 831
wellyn, Martha IV, 1066
wellyn, Martha IV, 1105
wellyn, Martha Hanna V, 410
wellyn, Martha Hannah V, 411
wellyn, Martha J. V, 411
wellyn, Mary II, 711
wellyn, Mary IV, 324
wellyn, Mary IV, 340
wellyn, Mary IV, 1066
wellyn, Mary V, 410
wellyn, Mary Alice V, 411
wellyn, Mary B. IV, 1066
wellyn, Morris II, 472
wellyn, Morris II, 583
wellyn, Rachel IV, 636
wellyn, Rachel IV, 641
wellyn, Rachel A. IV, 641
wellyn, Rachel C. IV, 626
wellyn, Rachel C. IV, 627
wellyn, Rachel C. IV, 641
wellyn, Rachel C. IV, 713
wellyn, Rachel C. IV, 735
wellyn, Rachel C. IV, 831
wellyn, Rachel C. IV, 1105
wellyn, Rachel E. IV, 641
wellyn, Rebecca IV, 1066
wellyn, Robert Hall II, 711
wellyn, Ruth II, 711
wellyn, Samuel J. V, 411
wellyn, Samuel Joseph V, 410
wellyn, Sarah IV, 418
wellyn, Sarah IV, 1066
wellyn, Sarah V, 409
wellyn, Sarah V, 410
wellyn, Sarah V, 411
wellyn, Sarah Lydia V, 410
wellyn, Sarah Lydia V, 411
wellyn, Sarah S. IV, 1066
wellyn, Sarah W. IV, 627
wellyn, Thomas IV, 418
wellyn, Thomas IV, 768
wellyn, Thomas IV, 831
wellyn, Thomas IV, 1066
wellyn, Thomas IV, 1105
wellyn, Thos. IV, 641
wellyn, Walter E. II, 711
wellyn, William IV, 340
wellyn, William IV, 418
wellyn, William IV, 1066
wellyn, William F. IV, 831
wellyn, William Frame II, 711
wellyn, William T. II, 711
wellyn, Winona IV, 641
wellyn, Wm. II, 711
wellyn, Wm. IV, 324
wellyn, Wm. IV, 340
wellyn, Wm. IV, 1066
Llewellyn, Wm. V, 410
Llewellyn, Wm. T. II, 744
Llewellyn, Wm. T. II, 753
Llewellyn, Wm. T. IV, 831
Llewellyn, Wm. T. IV, 1066
Llewelyn, Ann L. IV, 1077
Llewelyn, Anna IV, 1077
Llewelyn, Martha IV, 1062
Llewelyn, Martha IV, 1077
Llewelyn, Mary B. IV, 1052
Llewelyn, Rebecca IV, 1076
Llewelyn, Sarah IV, 418
Llewelyn, Sarah M. IV, 1077
Llewelyn, Thomas IV, 418
Llewelyn, Thomas IV, 1077
Llewelyn, Thos. IV, 1062
Llewelyn, William IV, 418
Lloyd, ??? II, 390
Lloyd, Abigail IV, 241
Lloyd, Abigail IV, 242
Lloyd, Albert H. IV, 242
Lloyd, Albert H. IV, 1238
Lloyd, Alice B. V, 691
Lloyd, Ann II, 389
Lloyd, Ann II, 579
Lloyd, Ann II, 583
Lloyd, Ann II, 1011
Lloyd, Ann II, 1042
Lloyd, Ann II, 1055
Lloyd, Ann IV, 241
Lloyd, Ann Elizabeth II, 891
Lloyd, Ann Laura IV, 241
Lloyd, Anna III, 125
Lloyd, Anna III, 208
Lloyd, Anna VI, 768
Lloyd, Anna L. IV, 976
Lloyd, Anna Laura IV, 242
Lloyd, Anna Laura IV, 976
Lloyd, Anna Maria III, 211
Lloyd, Anne II, 583
Lloyd, Anne L. IV, 242
Lloyd, Barclay VI, 615
Lloyd, Barclay VI, 616
Lloyd, Barclay VI, 635
Lloyd, Barclay VI, 671
Lloyd, Barclay VI, 672
Lloyd, Barcley VI, 672
Lloyd, Benjamin II, 806
Lloyd, Benjamin II, 891
Lloyd, Benjamin II, 999
Lloyd, Benjamin II, 1011
Lloyd, Benjamin II, 1042
Lloyd, Benjamin II, 1055
Lloyd, Benjamin II, 1075
Lloyd, Benjamin, Jr. II, 1011
Lloyd, Carrie E. V, 691
Lloyd, Catherine II, 583
Lloyd, Charles II, 891
Lloyd, Charles IV, 241
Lloyd, Charles IV, 418
Lloyd, Chas. II, 891
Lloyd, Chas. H. IV, 242
Lloyd, Chester I. IV, 976
Lloyd, Chester J. IV, 976
Lloyd, Christian II, 512
Lloyd, Christian II, 583
Lloyd, Cicero I, 557
Lloyd, Cyrene I, 557
Lloyd, Daniel II, 584
Lloyd, David I, 557
Lloyd, David II, 390
Lloyd, David II, 537
Lloyd, David II, 583
Lloyd, Deborah II, 389
Lloyd, Deborah II, 583
Lloyd, Deborah II, 600
Lloyd, Deborah V, 186
Lloyd, Deborah J. IV, 242
Lloyd, Deborah J. V, 93
Lloyd, Deborah J. V, 124
Lloyd, Deborah T. IV, 242
Lloyd, Edith IV, 187
Lloyd, Edith IV, 241
Lloyd, Edith IV, 242
Lloyd, Edith IV, 976
Lloyd, Edith IV, 1238
Lloyd, Edward IV, 341
Lloyd, Edward IV, 418
Lloyd, Edward VI, 806
Lloyd, Edward H. IV, 1238
Lloyd, Edward W. IV, 242
Lloyd, Edward Wm. IV, 241
Lloyd, Eleanor II, 1007
Lloyd, Eleanor II, 1009
Lloyd, Eliza IV, 46
Lloyd, Eliza IV, 48
Lloyd, Eliza M. IV, 224
Lloyd, Eliza M. IV, 241
Lloyd, Eliza P. IV, 93
Lloyd, Eliza P. IV, 98
Lloyd, Eliza P. IV, 100
Lloyd, Eliza P. IV, 241
Lloyd, Elizabeth II, 390
Lloyd, Elizabeth II, 569
Lloyd, Elizabeth II, 583
Lloyd, Elizabeth II, 584
Lloyd, Elizabeth II, 668
Lloyd, Elizabeth II, 696
Lloyd, Elizabeth II, 711
Lloyd, Elizabeth II, 713
Lloyd, Elizabeth II, 728
Lloyd, Elizabeth II, 781
Lloyd, Elizabeth II, 806
Lloyd, Elizabeth II, 826
Lloyd, Elizabeth II, 1011
Lloyd, Elizabeth II, 1055
Lloyd, Elizabeth II, 1075
Lloyd, Elizabeth III, 211
Lloyd, Elizabeth IV, 957
Lloyd, Elizabeth B. IV, 242
Lloyd, Elizabeth E. I, 797
Lloyd, Elizabeth E. I, 824
Lloyd, Elizabeth M. IV, 210
Lloyd, Elizabeth M. IV, 241
Lloyd, Elizabeth T. IV, 241
Lloyd, Elizabeth T. IV, 957
Lloyd, Elizabeth T. IV, 976
Lloyd, Elwood A. IV, 242
Lloyd, Emma VI, 615
Lloyd, Emma VI, 616
Lloyd, Emma VI, 671
Lloyd, Emma VI, 672
Lloyd, Esther II, 523
Lloyd, Esther II, 584
Lloyd, Esther C. IV, 241
Lloyd, Florence E. VI, 615
Lloyd, Florence E. VI, 671
Lloyd, Florence E. VI, 672
Lloyd, Grace II, 390
Lloyd, Grace II, 537
Lloyd, Grace II, 583
Lloyd, Guy V, 691
Lloyd, Hannah I, 557
Lloyd, Hannah I, 572
Lloyd, Hannah II, 390
Lloyd, Hannah II, 405
Lloyd, Hannah II, 523
Lloyd, Hannah II, 583
Lloyd, Hannah II, 584
Lloyd, Hannah II, 619
Lloyd, Hannah II, 713
Lloyd, Hannah II, 753
Lloyd, Hannah II, 806
Lloyd, Hannah II, 811
Lloyd, Hannah II, 999
Lloyd, Hannah II, 1011
Lloyd, Hannah II, 1055
Lloyd, Hannah II, 1075
Lloyd, Hannah III, 99
Lloyd, Hannah III, 211
Lloyd, Hannah IV, 976
Lloyd, Hannah VI, 415
Lloyd, Hannah VI, 452
Lloyd, Hannah S. II, 584
Lloyd, Hannah S. II, 728
Lloyd, Hannah W. IV, 242
Lloyd, Hannah W. IV, 976
Lloyd, Henry B. IV, 242
Lloyd, Henry B. IV, 1238
Lloyd, Henry P. II, 891
Lloyd, Humpery I, 507
Lloyd, Humphery I, 507
Lloyd, Humphry I, 557
Lloyd, Humpry I, 507
Lloyd, Isaac II, 584
Lloyd, Isaac II, 711
Lloyd, Isaac II, 713
Lloyd, Isaac II, 728
Lloyd, Isaac IV, 98
Lloyd, Isaac IV, 234
Lloyd, Isaac IV, 241
Lloyd, Isaac IV, 242
Lloyd, Isaac IV, 254
Lloyd, Isaac IV, 418
Lloyd, Isaac IV, 976
Lloyd, Isaac V, 93
Lloyd, Isaac S. III, 211
Lloyd, Isaac, Jr. II, 584
Lloyd, Isaac, Jr. II, 753
Lloyd, Isaac, Jr. IV, 242
Lloyd, Isaac, Sr. IV, 242
Lloyd, James II, 389
Lloyd, James II, 583
Lloyd, James V, 691
Lloyd, Jane I, 557
Lloyd, Jane IV, 341
Lloyd, Jane IV, 418
Lloyd, Jane, Jr. I, 557
Lloyd, Jean I, 557
Lloyd, Jesse II, 806
Lloyd, Jesse II, 1011
Lloyd, Jesse II, 1042
Lloyd, Jesse II, 1055
Lloyd, Jesse IV, 241
Lloyd, Jesse IV, 242
Lloyd, Jesse IV, 976
Lloyd, Jesse IV, 1238
Lloyd, Jesse W. IV, 1238
Lloyd, Jesse, Jr. IV, 242
Lloyd, Jesse, Jr. IV, 976
Lloyd, John II, 389
Lloyd, John II, 583
Lloyd, John II, 658
Lloyd, John II, 753
Lloyd, John IV, 241
Lloyd, John IV, 242
Lloyd, John IV, 340
Lloyd, John IV, 922
Lloyd, John IV, 976
Lloyd, John VI, 521
Lloyd, Jonathan II, 806
Lloyd, Jonathan II, 891
Lloyd, Joseph I, 824
Lloyd, Joseph III, 211
Lloyd, Josephine IV, 242
Lloyd, Josephine Floyd IV, 1238
Lloyd, Joshua IV, 241
Lloyd, Joshua IV, 242
Lloyd, Joshua IV, 337
Lloyd, Joshua IV, 340
Lloyd, Joshua IV, 341
Lloyd, Joshua IV, 418
Lloyd, Joshua IV, 424
Lloyd, Julie A. V, 691
Lloyd, Laura IV, 241
Lloyd, Lewis D. IV, 242
Lloyd, Lewiss II, 445
Lloyd, Lizzie S. V, 691
Lloyd, Lloyd, Mercy IV, 341
Lloyd, Louis D. IV, 242
Lloyd, Luella V, 186
Lloyd, Lydia II, 806
Lloyd, Lydia Y. II, 891
Lloyd, Lyntha I, 824
Lloyd, Marcy IV, 337
Lloyd, Margaret II, 389
Lloyd, Margaret II, 891
Lloyd, Margaret IV, 241
Lloyd, Margaret IV, 242
Lloyd, Margaret IV, 922
Lloyd, Margaret IV, 976
Lloyd, Margaret V, 915
Lloyd, Margaret A. IV, 242
Lloyd, Margaret J. IV, 241
Lloyd, Margaret J. IV, 242
Lloyd, Margaret J. IV, 254
Lloyd, Margaret R. IV, 241
Lloyd, Mark Balderston II, 1011
Lloyd, Martha II, 558
Lloyd, Martha II, 583
Lloyd, Martha II, 584
Lloyd, Martha II, 822
Lloyd, Martha VI, 934
Lloyd, Martha Emma IV, 241
Lloyd, Mary I, 557
Lloyd, Mary II, 389
Lloyd, Mary II, 583
Lloyd, Mary II, 584
Lloyd, Mary II, 608
Lloyd, Mary II, 655
Lloyd, Mary II, 779
Lloyd, Mary II, 793
Lloyd, Mary II, 803
Lloyd, Mary II, 806
Lloyd, Mary II, 891
Lloyd, Mary IV, 81
Lloyd, Mary IV, 98
Lloyd, Mary IV, 241
Lloyd, Mary IV, 337
Lloyd, Mary IV, 340
Lloyd, Mary IV, 341
Lloyd, Mary IV, 418
Lloyd, Mary IV, 424
Lloyd, Mary V, 691
Lloyd, Mary V, 916
Lloyd, Mary Ada IV, 241
Lloyd, Mary Adah IV, 242
Lloyd, Mary Adah IV, 976
Lloyd, Mary Ann II, 584
Lloyd, Mary Caroline IV, 241
Lloyd, Mary Nichols IV, 418
Lloyd, Mercy II, 583
Lloyd, Mercy II, 593
Lloyd, Mercy IV, 234
Lloyd, Mercy IV, 241
Lloyd, Mercy IV, 340
Lloyd, Mercy IV, 341
Lloyd, Mercy IV, 418
Lloyd, Mercy L. V, 915
Lloyd, Minnie M. V, 691
Lloyd, Mordecai II, 389
Lloyd, Mordecai II, 390
Lloyd, Mordecai II, 523
Lloyd, Mordecai II, 583
Lloyd, Mordecai II, 619
Lloyd, Nixon Morris IV, 242
Lloyd, Noralee VI, 672
Lloyd, Oliver II, 1055
Lloyd, Oliver II, 1075
Lloyd, Pascal IV, 735
Lloyd, Patience II, 583
Lloyd, Patience III, 211
Lloyd, Patience III, 301
Lloyd, Patricia VI, 672
Lloyd, Peter II, 389
Lloyd, Peter II, 583
Lloyd, Peter II, 593
Lloyd, Phebe V, 186
Lloyd, Phebe V, 205
Lloyd, Rachel I, 557
Lloyd, Rachel II, 583
Lloyd, Rachel IV, 241
Lloyd, Rachel IV, 341
Lloyd, Rachel IV, 344
Lloyd, Rachel A. II, 744
Lloyd, Rachel A. II, 753
Lloyd, Rebecca VI, 522
Lloyd, Rebecca VI, 527
Lloyd, Rebecca VI, 616
Lloyd, Rebecca VI, 635
Lloyd, Rebecca VI, 671
Lloyd, Rebecca VI, 672
Lloyd, Rebecca VI, 762
Lloyd, Rebecca Elizabeth VI, 671
Lloyd, Rebecca S. III, 211
Lloyd, Rebeckah I, 557
Lloyd, Rebekah I, 552
Lloyd, Rebekah I, 557
Lloyd, Rebekah VI, 521
Lloyd, Reece II, 390
Lloyd, Rees II, 390
Lloyd, Rees II, 496
Lloyd, Rees II, 583
Lloyd, Rees II, 668
Lloyd, Reese II, 389
Lloyd, Reese II, 584
Lloyd, Richard II, 803
Lloyd, Robert I, 557
Lloyd, Robert II, 390
Lloyd, Robert II, 583
Lloyd, Robert II, 584
Lloyd, Robert, Jr. II, 583
Lloyd, Robert, Jr. II, 668
Lloyd, Ruth II, 496
Lloyd, Ruth II, 583
Lloyd, Ruth IV, 98
Lloyd, Ruth IV, 234
Lloyd, Ruth IV, 241
Lloyd, Ruth IV, 242
Lloyd, Ruth IV, 254
Lloyd, Ruth IV, 418
Lloyd, Ruth IV, 976
Lloyd, Ruth V, 93
Lloyd, Ruth H. IV, 242
Lloyd, Ruth, Jr. IV, 242
Lloyd, Samson II, 1033
Lloyd, Samuel I, 557
Lloyd, Samuel II, 390
Lloyd, Samuel II, 584
Lloyd, Samuel IV, 187
Lloyd, Samuel IV, 210
Lloyd, Samuel IV, 241
Lloyd, Samuel IV, 242
Lloyd, Samuel V, 93
Lloyd, Samuel V, 124
Lloyd, Samuel VI, 616
Lloyd, Samuel VI, 632
Lloyd, Samuel VI, 635
Lloyd, Samuel VI, 671
Lloyd, Samuel VI, 672
Lloyd, Samuel A. I, 1158
Lloyd, Samuel A. VI, 671
Lloyd, Samuel S. V, 186
Lloyd, Sarah II, 389
Lloyd, Sarah II, 496
Lloyd, Sarah II, 583
Lloyd, Sarah II, 584
Lloyd, Sarah II, 600
Lloyd, Sarah II, 655
Lloyd, Sarah II, 658
Lloyd, Sarah II, 694
Lloyd, Sarah II, 711
Lloyd, Sarah II, 1011
Lloyd, Sarah II, 1042
Lloyd, Sarah II, 1055
Lloyd, Sarah II, 1075
Lloyd, Sarah VI, 672
Lloyd, Sarah Elma IV, 241
Lloyd, Sarah P. VI, 632
Lloyd, Sarah P. VI, 672
Lloyd, Sirena I, 557
Lloyd, Susan III, 211
Lloyd, Susan IV, 241
Lloyd, Susan IV, 242

Lloyd, Susan IV, 341
Lloyd, Susanna II, 390
Lloyd, Susanna II, 583
Lloyd, Susanna II, 584
Lloyd, Susanna II, 683
Lloyd, Susanna IV, 241
Lloyd, Susannah II, 583
Lloyd, Susannah II, 611
Lloyd, Susannah II, 779
Lloyd, Susannah IV, 241
Lloyd, Sybil T. IV, 241
Lloyd, Thomas I, 507
Lloyd, Thomas I, 557
Lloyd, Thomas II, 390
Lloyd, Thomas II, 496
Lloyd, Thomas II, 504
Lloyd, Thomas II, 523
Lloyd, Thomas II, 551
Lloyd, Thomas II, 583
Lloyd, Thomas II, 584
Lloyd, Thomas II, 600
Lloyd, Thomas II, 608
Lloyd, Thomas II, 611
Lloyd, Thomas II, 655
Lloyd, Thomas II, 781
Lloyd, Thomas II, 1011
Lloyd, Thomas III, 99
Lloyd, Thomas III, 211
Lloyd, Thomas III, 301
Lloyd, Thos. III, 168
Lloyd, Tilman V, 186
Lloyd, Wd. Elizabeth II, 583
Lloyd, Wd. Martha II, 803
Lloyd, Wd. Patience II, 389
Lloyd, Wd. Patience III, 301
Lloyd, William I, 557
Lloyd, William II, 445
Lloyd, William II, 584
Lloyd, William IV, 93
Lloyd, William IV, 98
Lloyd, William IV, 241
Lloyd, William F. IV, 242
Lloyd, William G. IV, 241
Lloyd, William G. IV, 242
Lloyd, William H. I, 797
Lloyd, William H. I, 824
Lloyd, Wm. II, 512
Lloyd, Wm. II, 583
Lloyd, Wm. II, 1055
Lloyd, Wm. IV, 224
Lloyd, Wm. Fleming IV, 241
Lloyd, Wm. G. V, 915
Lloyd, Zachery II, 390
Llyod, Hannah W. IV, 933
Llyod, Isaac IV, 933
Llywellyn, Anna IV, 280
Lo???, Elizabeth II, 134
Loag, Emma III, 185
Loansdale, Thomas II, 391
Lobb, Benjamin II, 445
Lobb, Christopher II, 390
Lobb, Christopher II, 445
Lobb, Edward II, 584
Lobb, Emma Jane IV, 744
Lobb, James IV, 98
Lobb, Jane IV, 648
Lobb, Joel II, 445
Lobb, Matilda K. II, 827
Lobb, Rachel II, 390
Lobb, Rachel II, 445
Lobb, Rebecca II, 390
Lobb, Rebecca II, 447
Lobb, Rebeckah II, 445
Lobb, Rebekah II, 445
Lobb, Sarah II, 584
Lobb, Stephen II, 445
Lobb, William II, 239
Lobbs, James IV, 46
Lobdale, Isaac II, 390
Lobdale, Samuel II, 390
Lobdel, Isaac II, 584
Lobdell, Anna II, 569
Lobdell, Anna II, 584
Lobdell, Elizabeth II, 390
Lobdell, Elizabeth II, 584
Lobdell, Elizabeth II, 618
Lobdell, Ethel III, 208
Lobdell, Ethel III, 281
Lobdell, George G. III, 208
Lobdell, George G. III, 281
Lobdell, Isaac II, 390
Lobdell, Isaac II, 497
Lobdell, Isaac II, 569
Lobdell, Isaac II, 584
Lobdell, Rebecca II, 390
Lobdell, Rebecca II, 569
Lobdell, Rebecca II, 584
Lobdell, Rebekah II, 497
Lobdell, Rebekah II, 584
Lobdell, Samuel II, 390
Lobdell, Samuel II, 584
Lobdell, Sarah II, 390
Loble, Polly VI, 950
Loble, William VI, 950
Loch, Ida III, 198
Loch, Judith F. V, 632
Lochner, Alma C. V, 751
Lochner, Clyde V, 752
Lochner, Clyde C. V, 751
Lochner, May V, 751
Lochner, May V, 752
Lochner, Philip C. V, 751
Locin, James VI, 599
Lock, John II, 390
Lock, John II, 584
Lock, John II, 641
Lock, John IV, 735
Lock, Laura IV, 735
Lock, Lucreacy I, 1124
Lock, Lula May IV, 735
Lock, Maris I, 1124
Lock, Maris I, 1126
Lock, Mary I, 405
Lock, Mary I, 429
Lock, Mary II, 390
Lock, Mary II, 584
Lock, Mary II, 641
Lock, Philip IV, 735
Lock, William I, 1124
Lockard, Delaware VI, 924
Lockard, Delaware VI, 950
Lockard, Elizabeth VI, 950
Lockard, Fleming VI, 924
Lockard, Fleming VI, 950
Lockard, Fleming VI, 993
Lockard, Judith VI, 876
Lockard, Martha Ann VI, 950
Lockard, Mary V, 1007
Lockard, Matilda VI, 962
Lockard, Minerva Ann VI, 924
Lockard, Nancy A. VI, 1002
Lockard, Philip VI, 876
Lockard, Philip VI, 995
Lockard, Phillip VI, 962
Lockard, Phoebe VI, 897
Lockard, Sophia VI, 995
Lockard, William VI, 950
Lockard, Winston VI, 937
Lockart, James C. VI, 950
Lockart, Sarah VI, 950
Locke, Florence Kate III, 208
Locke, Jesse D. V, 752
Locke, John IV, 735
Locke, John V, 632
Locke, Judith F. V, 615
Locke, Judith F. V, 632
Locke, Laura IV, 735
Locke, Lucretia V, 632
Locke, Philip IV, 735
Locke, William V, 632
Locke, Wm. John V, 615
Locker, Ellen IV, 1284
Locker, George IV, 1284
Locker, John F. IV, 1284
Locker, Mariah R. IV, 1284
Lockett, Daniel VI, 924
Lockett, Daniel VI, 950
Lockett, Daniel VI, 955
Lockett, David VI, 880
Lockett, David VI, 932
Lockett, David VI, 950
Lockett, Dosha VI, 957
Lockett, Jency VI, 950
Lockett, Jere. VI, 946
Lockett, Jeremiah VI, 893
Lockett, Jeremiah VI, 950
Lockett, Jeremiah VI, 951
Lockett, Jeremiah VI, 1015
Lockett, Jeremiah VI, 1016
Lockett, Jeremiah, Jr. VI, 950
Lockett, Jeremiah, Sr. VI, 950
Lockett, Jesse VI, 912
Lockett, Jesse VI, 950
Lockett, Jesse VI, 983
Lockett, Jesse VI, 1011
Lockett, Josiah VI, 950
Lockett, Lydia VI, 950
Lockett, Lydia VI, 957
Lockett, Mary VI, 950
Lockett, Nancy VI, 1016
Lockett, Phebe VI, 950
Lockett, Polly VI, 950
Lockett, Rachel VI, 950
Lockett, Rhoda VI, 1015
Lockett, Sally VI, 946
Lockett, Susanna VI, 880
Lockett, Susanna VI, 893
Lockey, John VI, 329
Lockhard, Elathian VI, 993
Lockhard, Martha IV, 241
Lockhard, Samuel IV, 241
Lockhard, Samuel J. IV, 241
Lockhard, Sarah IV, 909
Lockhart, Eliza VI, 907
Lockhart, Frederick IV, 1040
Lockhart, Phyllis IV, 1040
Lockhart, Ralph IV, 1040
Lockhart, Susanna VI, 907
Lockhart, Verna IV, 1040
Lockheart, Fleming VI, 950
Lockheart, James C. VI, 950
Lockheart, Mourning VI, 950
Lockheart, Sarah VI, 950
Lockland, Carson VI, 974
Lockley, John VI, 329
Lockner, Minnie Luella IV, 1326
Lockwood, ??? III, 208
Lockwood, Abraham III, 87
Lockwood, Abraham III, 208
Lockwood, Alberta F. IV, 1284
Lockwood, Alfred Cornell III, 208
Lockwood, Alma L. IV, 1284
Lockwood, Amy III, 20
Lockwood, Amy A. III, 208
Lockwood, Amy, Jr. III, 208
Lockwood, Anna Mary III, 208
Lockwood, Anthony III, 208
Lockwood, Anthony III, 209
Lockwood, Arthur III, 208
Lockwood, Bernard IV, 1326
Lockwood, Carl IV, 1284
Lockwood, Carl P. IV, 1284
Lockwood, Charles III, 306
Lockwood, Charles Penn III, 208
Lockwood, Chas. M. IV, 1284
Lockwood, Clara IV, 1284
Lockwood, Clara A. III, 208
Lockwood, Daniel III, 208
Lockwood, David A. IV, 1284
Lockwood, Della IV, 1284
Lockwood, Edward III, 208
Lockwood, Edward III, 209
Lockwood, Edward Pearsall III, 208
Lockwood, Elias III, 209
Lockwood, Eliza III, 40
Lockwood, Eliza III, 208
Lockwood, Eliza. III, 208
Lockwood, Emily III, 208
Lockwood, Ercile IV, 1284
Lockwood, Evelyn IV, 1284
Lockwood, George Truman III, 208
Lockwood, H. III, 208
Lockwood, H. H. IV, 1284
Lockwood, Hannah C. III, 209
Lockwood, Harrison IV, 1326
Lockwood, Hattie IV, 1284
Lockwood, Hazel IV, 876
Lockwood, Hazel C. IV, 1284
Lockwood, Helen A. III, 296
Lockwood, Helen Augusta III, 208
Lockwood, Herman IV, 876
Lockwood, Herman IV, 1284
Lockwood, Hester III, 208
Lockwood, Hildred IV, 876
Lockwood, J. III, 209
Lockwood, Jane III, 208
Lockwood, Jane Ann III, 128
Lockwood, Jane Ann III, 208
Lockwood, Jane Ann III, 209
Lockwood, Janette IV, 1326
Lockwood, Jennie IV, 1326
Lockwood, John III, 20
Lockwood, John III, 208
Lockwood, John Franklin III, 208
Lockwood, John J. IV, 1284
Lockwood, John, Jr. III, 208
Lockwood, Joseph J. IV, 1284
Lockwood, Joseph W. III, 208
Lockwood, Joseph W. III, 209
Lockwood, Leontine J. III, 205
Lockwood, Leontine J. III, 208
Lockwood, Leontine J. III, 265
Lockwood, Levi A. III, 208
Lockwood, Levi H. III, 208
Lockwood, Levi N. III, 205
Lockwood, Levi N. III, 265
Lockwood, Lloyd IV, 1284
Lockwood, Lydia A. III, 208
Lockwood, Martha III, 208
Lockwood, Martha III, 209
Lockwood, Martha III, 304
Lockwood, Martha IV, 1284
Lockwood, Martha H. III, 128
Lockwood, Martha Jane III, 208
Lockwood, Mary III, 87
Lockwood, Mary III, 208
Lockwood, Mary III, 209
Lockwood, Mary IV, 876
Lockwood, Mary V, 918
Lockwood, Mary H. III, 208
Lockwood, Mildred J. IV, 1284
Lockwood, Mrs. Lewellyn IV, 1284
Lockwood, Nancy IV, 1284
Lockwood, Neely III, 40
Lockwood, Neely III, 208
Lockwood, Neely III, 296
Lockwood, Otis IV, 876
Lockwood, Otis B. IV, 1284
Lockwood, Phebe III, 208
Lockwood, Phebe III, 209
Lockwood, Phebe III, 304
Lockwood, Phebe III, 306
Lockwood, Samuel III, 40
Lockwood, Sarah III, 188
Lockwood, Sarah III, 208
Lockwood, Sarah III, 209
Lockwood, Stephen III, 208
Lockwood, Stephen III, 209
Lockwood, Susannah II, 891
Lockwood, Susannah II, 900
Lockwood, Virginia III, 208
Lockwood, Walter III, 128
Lockwood, Walter III, 208
Lockwood, Walter III, 209
Lockwood, Walter III, 304
Lockwood, Walter IV, 1326
Lockwood, Walter V, 918
Lockwood, Walter Field III, 208
Lockwood, Walter H. III, 209
Lockwood, Walter J. III, 208
Lockwood, Walter, Jr. III, 209
Lockwood, Warren IV, 1284
Lockwood, Wendell IV, 1284
Lockwood, William Abraham III, 208
Lockwood, Wm. IV, 1326
Lockyear, Benjamin II, 390
Locy, Chas. V, 1007
Lode, Matilda V, 48
Lode, Matilda V, 93
Loden, Benjamin IV, 976
Loden, Betsy IV, 976
Loden, Hannah E. IV, 943
Loden, Hannah E. IV, 976
Loden, Hannah E. C. IV, 976
Loden, John IV, 943
Loden, John IV, 976
Lodge, Abel VI, 528
Lodge, Abel VI, 672
Lodge, Abel VI, 834
Lodge, Ann II, 85
Lodge, Ann II, 584
Lodge, Anna M. II, 813
Lodge, Anna M. II, 906
Lodge, Benjamin II, 85
Lodge, Caleb V, 93
Lodge, Caleb VI, 329
Lodge, Catharine VI, 528
Lodge, Catharine VI, 672
Lodge, Catherine VI, 329
Lodge, Catherine VI, 528
Lodge, Celene V, 93
Lodge, Celina VI, 329
Lodge, Celine V, 918
Lodge, Clement II, 806
Lodge, Clement II, 891
Lodge, Elizabeth II, 806
Lodge, Esther VI, 528
Lodge, Esther VI, 672
Lodge, Isaac II, 792
Lodge, Isabel V, 918
Lodge, Jacob VI, 528
Lodge, Jacob VI, 672
Lodge, Jane II, 78
Lodge, Jane II, 85
Lodge, Jane II, 792
Lodge, Jasabad VI, 528
Lodge, Jasabed V, 93
Lodge, Jazabed V, 918
Lodge, Jazabad VI, 329
Lodge, Jonathan VI, 528
Lodge, Jonathan VI, 672
Lodge, Josabad VI, 329
Lodge, Josabed VI, 672
Lodge, Josabed, Jr. VI, 672
Lodge, Jozabad VI, 318
Lodge, Jozabad VI, 323
Lodge, Jozabad VI, 329
Lodge, Jozabad VI, 528
Lodge, Jozabed VI, 528
Lodge, Laban V, 93
Lodge, Laban VI, 329
Lodge, Martha VI, 528
Lodge, Mary II, 792
Lodge, Nathan VI, 528
Lodge, Nathan VI, 672
Lodge, Nelson V, 93
Lodge, Nelson VI, 329
Lodge, Rebecca VI, 414
Lodge, Rebecca VI, 434
Lodge, Rebecca Janney VI, 691
Lodge, Robert II, 85
Lodge, Robert II, 584
Lodge, Sarah V, 93
Lodge, Sarah VI, 318
Lodge, Sarah VI, 323
Lodge, Sarah VI, 329
Lodge, Seline VI, 329
Lodge, Tacy VI, 834
Lodge, Thos. Benton II, 806
Lodge, Tirzah IV, 873
Lodge, Tirzah IV, 876
Lodge, William VI, 414
Lodge, William VI, 528
Lodge, William VI, 672
Lodge, William Esther VI, 528
Lodge, William Johnson V, 93
Lodge, William Johnson VI, 32?
Lodge, Wm. VI, 691
Lodon, Hannah E. C. IV, 976
Loe, Alice II, 539
Loe, Alice II, 586
Loe, Ann V, 752
Loe, George I, 145
Loe, Jane I, 891
Loe, Joshua III, 209
Loe, William V, 752
Loeser, Estelle B. III, 184
Loeser, Estelle B. III, 209
Loeser, Mathilde III, 184
Loeser, Mathilde III, 209
Loffer, Mary IV, 1256
Lofters, John II, 445
Loftis, ??? II, 390
Loftis, Ann II, 390
Loftis, Charles II, 390
Loftis, Elizabeth II, 390
Loftis, Jane II, 390
Loftis, John II, 390
Loftis, Mary II, 1011
Loftis, Mary II, 1024
Loftis, Mathew VI, 834
Loftis, Matthew M. VI, 839
Loftis, Permelia A. VI, 834
Loftis, Ralph II, 390
Loftis, Samuel II, 390
Loftis, Thomas II, 390
Loftis, Wilmouth VI, 839
Loftus, ??? II, 390
Loftus, Jane II, 482
Loftus, Jane II, 584
Loftus, Ralph II, 482
Loftus, Ralph II, 584
Logan, Albanus Charles II, 585
Logan, Alfred VI, 656
Logan, Alfred VI, 672
Logan, Alfred VI, 684
Logan, Algernon Sidney II, 585
Logan, Alice II, 135
Logan, Alice VI, 639
Logan, Alice VI, 672
Logan, Almira M. II, 135
Logan, Ann Eliza VI, 656
Logan, Ann Eliza VI, 672
Logan, Anna Eliza VI, 656
Logan, Anna Eliza VI, 672
Logan, Charles II, 390
Logan, Charles II, 584
Logan, Charles II, 623
Logan, Charles VI, 258
Logan, Debby II, 584
Logan, Debby II, 608
Logan, Deborah II, 585
Logan, Elizabeth II, 891
Logan, Elizabeth A. VI, 950
Logan, Elizabeth Elaine V, 259
Logan, Esther II, 891
Logan, Eugene I, 1158
Logan, Eva V, 259
Logan, Eva V, 260
Logan, George II, 584
Logan, George II, 585
Logan, George II, 608
Logan, Hannah II, 184
Logan, Hannah II, 516
Logan, Hannah II, 524
Logan, Hannah II, 584
Logan, Hannah II, 608
Logan, Hannah II, 623
Logan, Hannah II, 654
Logan, James II, 184
Logan, James II, 390
Logan, James II, 454
Logan, James II, 516
Logan, James II, 584
Logan, James II, 585
Logan, James II, 608
Logan, James II, 630
Logan, James II, 654
Logan, James VI, 258
Logan, James VI, 834

an, James, Jr. II, 584
an, Jasper V, 259
an, Jasper E. V, 260
an, John M. VI, 950
an, John W. VI, 656
an, John W. VI, 672
an, Joseph II, 806
an, Katherine Clodine V, 259
an, Luella V, 259
gan, Margaret IV, 1326
gan, Margaret E. VI, 672
gan, Martha Matilda I, 1158
gan, Mary II, 584
gan, Mary II, 623
gan, Mary II, 1011
gan, Mary II, 1022
gan, Mary VI, 258
gan, Mary VI, 834
gan, Mary Alice VI, 645
gan, Mary Alice VI, 672
gan, Mary Jane I, 1158
gan, Mary W. IV, 484
gan, Paul Robert V, 259
gan, Priscilla II, 454
gan, Priscilla II, 585
gan, Rachel II, 390
gan, Sarah II, 172
gan, Sarah II, 183
gan, Sarah II, 184
gan, Sarah II, 390
gan, Sarah II, 454
gan, Sarah II, 524
gan, Sarah II, 584
gan, Sarah II, 608
gan, Sarah II, 630
gan, Sarah II, 794
gan, Sarah VI, 258
gan, Sarah VI, 656
gan, Sarah VI, 672
gan, Sarah VI, 684
gan, Wd. Esther Smith II, 806
gan, Wd. Hannah II, 390
gan, William II, 390
gan, William, Jr. II, 390
gan, Wm. II, 516
gan, Wm. II, 524
gan, Wm. II, 584
gan, Wm. II, 608
gan, Wm. II, 623
gan, Wm. F. II, 135
gan, Wm., Jr. II, 584
ogg, Bartholomew II, 1011
ogue, Alvin IV, 976
ogue, Charles Willard IV, 976
ogue, Elizabeth IV, 735
ogue, Elizabeth IV, 893
ogue, Elizabeth IV, 895
ogue, Esther IV, 718
ogue, Esther IV, 735
ogue, Frances S. IV, 976
ogue, Francis IV, 976
ogue, Hannah IV, 718
ogue, Hannah IV, 735
ogue, Hannah IV, 895
ogue, Hannah IV, 927
ogue, Hannah IV, 976
ogue, Homer IV, 976
ogue, Howard IV, 976
ogue, Howard W. IV, 976
ogue, Joseph IV, 976
ogue, Lester Kirkland IV, 976
ogue, Louise IV, 976
ogue, Martha IV, 976
ogue, Mary IV, 976
ogue, Mary IV, 994
ogue, Mary B. IV, 976
ogue, Mordecai IV, 976
ogue, Ruth IV, 815
ogue, Ruth IV, 831
ogue, Samuel IV, 735
ogue, Sarah IV, 735
ogue, Sarah IV, 831
ogue, Sarah IV, 851
ogue, Sarah IV, 976
ogue, Sarah W. IV, 735
ogue, Sarah W. IV, 976
ogue, Stephen IV, 718
ogue, Stephen IV, 735
ogue, Stephen IV, 895
Logue, Stephen IV, 976
Logue, Stephen, Jr. IV, 641
Logue, Thomas IV, 976
Logue, Thomas W. IV, 927
Logue, Thomas W. IV, 976
Logue, Thos. IV, 976
Logwood, A. H. VI, 881
Logwood, A. H. VI, 951
Logwood, Alexander H. VI, 893
Logwood, Alexander H. VI, 951
Logwood, Ann VI, 889
Logwood, Burwell VI, 942
Logwood, Burwell VI, 951
Logwood, Catharine VI, 972
Logwood, Edith B. VI, 951
Logwood, Edmond VI, 951
Logwood, Edmond VI, 1013
Logwood, Edmund VI, 951
Logwood, Edmund VI, 953
Logwood, Eliza VI, 893
Logwood, Elizabeth VI, 951
Logwood, Euphan VI, 889
Logwood, Fanny VI, 951
Logwood, Kitty VI, 951
Logwood, Lucinda P. VI, 951
Logwood, Lucy McDaniel VI, 951
Logwood, Margaret VI, 1007
Logwood, Martha VI, 951
Logwood, Martha Hill VI, 885
Logwood, Martha P. VI, 942
Logwood, Mary VI, 881
Logwood, Mary E. VI, 951
Logwood, Mary G. VI, 972
Logwood, Nancy VI, 889
Logwood, Nancy VI, 990
Logwood, Pruey VI, 951
Logwood, R. R. VI, 1007
Logwood, Robert R. VI, 951
Logwood, Sally VI, 1012
Logwood, Sarah Ann VI, 942
Logwood, Theodosia A. VI, 951
Logwood, Thomas VI, 885
Logwood, Thomas VI, 951
Logwood, Thomas VI, 990
Logwood, Thomas VI, 1013
Logwood, Thomas G. VI, 889
Logwood, Thomas G. VI, 951
Lohman, Minnie Catharine IV, 960
Lohman, Minnie Catherine IV, 961
Lohman, Peter IV, 961
Lohman, Susanna IV, 961
Lohnes, Sarah Jane IV, 27
Lohnes, Sarah Jane IV, 46
Lohra, Lewis II, 390
Lohra, Mary II, 498
Lohra, Mary II, 585
Loid, David I, 507
Loid, Hannah I, 507
Loid, Humpry I, 507
Loid, Jane I, 507
Loid, John I, 507
Loid, Mary I, 507
Loid, Rachel I, 557
Loid, Rebekah I, 507
Loid, Samuel I, 507
Loid, Thomas I, 507
Loines, Abigail III, 425
Loines, Adelia III, 209
Loines, Alice III, 52
Loines, Alice III, 209
Loines, Alice A. III, 210
Loines, Ann III, 425
Loines, Anna III, 209
Loines, Anna III, 275
Loines, Anna III, 425
Loines, Anna III, 446
Loines, Anna R. III, 209
Loines, Anne III, 210
Loines, Anne III, 425
Loines, Anne III, 489
Loines, Charles III, 209
Loines, Charles W. III, 209
Loines, Charlotte III, 209
Loines, Clarence III, 209
Loines, Eliz. H. III, 64
Loines, Elizabeth III, 425
Loines, Elizabeth H. III, 209
Loines, Elizabeth L. III, 16
Loines, Elizabeth L. III, 210
Loines, Emma III, 209
Loines, Hannah III, 425
Loines, Harriet III, 209
Loines, Harriet L. III, 209
Loines, Helen A. III, 210
Loines, James III, 209
Loines, James III, 210
Loines, James III, 425
Loines, James III, 489
Loines, James III, 509
Loines, Jericho III, 209
Loines, John III, 52
Loines, John III, 209
Loines, John III, 425
Loines, John III, 444
Loines, John III, 446
Loines, John III, 489
Loines, Jonas III, 209
Loines, Jonas III, 425
Loines, Jonas III, 489
Loines, Jonas P. III, 209
Loines, Joseph III, 209
Loines, Martha III, 425
Loines, Martha III, 489
Loines, Martha III, 506
Loines, Mary III, 52
Loines, Mary III, 166
Loines, Mary III, 209
Loines, Mary III, 425
Loines, Mary Ann III, 209
Loines, Mary B. III, 52
Loines, Mary B. III, 209
Loines, Mary B. III, 222
Loines, Mary Elizabeth III, 63
Loines, Mary Elizabeth III, 209
Loines, Mary M. III, 210
Loines, Phebe III, 209
Loines, Phebe III, 425
Loines, Phebe III, 444
Loines, Phebe III, 446
Loines, Phebe III, 454
Loines, Phebe III, 461
Loines, Phebe III, 489
Loines, Phebe III, 509
Loines, Phebe A. III, 53
Loines, Phebe Lawrence III, 209
Loines, Rebecca III, 209
Loines, Reuben Bunker III, 209
Loines, Rich. III, 209
Loines, Rich. III, 222
Loines, Richard III, 64
Loines, Richard III, 132
Loines, Richard III, 171
Loines, Richard III, 209
Loines, Richard III, 210
Loines, Richard III, 425
Loines, Richard A. III, 63
Loines, Richard A. III, 209
Loines, Richard S. III, 209
Loines, Robert L. III, 209
Loines, Russel Hillard III, 209
Loines, Sarah III, 64
Loines, Sarah III, 132
Loines, Sarah III, 171
Loines, Sarah III, 194
Loines, Sarah III, 209
Loines, Sarah III, 210
Loines, Sarah III, 222
Loines, Sarah III, 275
Loines, Sarah III, 394
Loines, Sarah III, 425
Loines, Sarah III, 489
Loines, Sarah K. III, 132
Loines, Sarah K. III, 209
Loines, Sarah W. III, 425
Loines, Sarah W. III, 510
Loines, Sarah, Sr. III, 210
Loines, Sibbil III, 425
Loines, Simeon III, 425
Loines, Simeon III, 489
Loines, Simeon III, 506
Loines, Step. III, 494
Loines, Stephen III, 166
Loines, Stephen III, 209
Loines, Stephen III, 425
Loines, Stephen III, 454
Loines, Stephen III, 461
Loines, Stephen III, 489
Loines, Stephen III, 494
Loines, Sybel III, 209
Loines, Sybil III, 209
Loines, Sybil III, 425
Loines, Sybil III, 489
Loines, Sybil III, 494
Loines, Thomas III, 425
Loines, Walter III, 209
Loines, William III, 209
Loines, William III, 210
Loines, William III, 425
Loines, William III, 489
Loines, William H. III, 210
Loines, William Hopkins III, 209
Loines, William, Jr. III, 394
Loines, William, Jr. III, 425
Loines, Wm. III, 194
Loines, Wm. III, 209
Loines, Wm. III, 275
Loines, Wm. A. III, 53
Loines, Wm. H. III, 16
Loines, Wm. Haight III, 209
Lokey, Francis VI, 599
Lolfrey, Maria Amelia III, 44
Lolfrey, Wm. III, 44
Lollefeon, Alice L. IV, 1326
Lollis, Leeland VI, 951
Lollis, Prudence VI, 951
Loman, M. E. I, 405
Loman, Mary Elizabeth I, 929
Lomax, Mary I, 724
Lomax, Mary I, 734
Londen, Samuel IV, 1284
London, Sarah I, 981
London, Sarah I, 991
London, Sarah II, 497
London, Sarah II, 585
London, Thomas II, 390
Londy, Abagail V, 512
Londy, Amos I, 966
Londy, Ann I, 966
Londy, Daniel I, 825
Londy, David I, 992
Londy, Ebanezar I, 966
Londy, Ezekiel I, 966
Londy, Isaac I, 966
Londy, Jesse V, 512
Londy, Lot I, 983
Londy, Lot I, 992
Londy, Rachel I, 983
Londy, Rachel I, 992
Londy, Rhoda I, 966
Londy, Richard I, 825
Londy, Richard I, 966
Londy, Susanna I, 992
Londy, Tamer I, 966
Londy, Thomas I, 966
Londy, Thomas, Jr. I, 992
Long, Aimy VI, 414
Long, Albert G. VI, 834
Long, Alexander II, 585
Long, Alphonso W. I, 359
Long, Alphonzo I, 405
Long, Amy VI, 414
Long, Amy VI, 444
Long, Amy VI, 599
Long, Ann I, 359
Long, Ann I, 391
Long, Ann I, 405
Long, Ann I, 824
Long, Ann II, 390
Long, Ann II, 585
Long, Anna VI, 672
Long, Anna VI, 1016
Long, Armstead VI, 834
Long, Barbara G. IV, 1284
Long, Bertha IV, 1326
Long, Bertha M. IV, 1284
Long, Calista VI, 834
Long, Caroline V, 850
Long, Charity VI, 399
Long, Charity VI, 414
Long, Charity VI, 452
Long, Daisy IV, 1215
Long, Eliza V, 511
Long, Elizabeth VI, 414
Long, Elizabeth Tatum V, 919
Long, Ellett IV, 735
Long, Frances Martin VI, 667
Long, Frances Martin VI, 756
Long, G. V, 1007
Long, G. M. Roosa IV, 418
Long, George Mason VI, 667
Long, Guy V, 706
Long, Harper V, 603
Long, Harry V, 1007
Long, Harry C. V, 1007
Long, Henry V, 404
Long, Henry V, 411
Long, Ida Bell V, 603
Long, Israel I, 824
Long, Iva IV, 735
Long, Iva IV, 763
Long, Iva D. IV, 735
Long, J. H. IV, 1284
Long, James I, 359
Long, James IV, 735
Long, Jennie V, 814
Long, John I, 359
Long, John I, 405
Long, John VI, 482
Long, John VI, 528
Long, John VI, 672
Long, John VI, 951
Long, John W. I, 1158
Long, John, Jr. I, 405
Long, John, Sr. I, 405
Long, Jonathan II, 445
Long, Joseph V, 752
Long, Judith IV, 1215
Long, Kezia II, 390
Long, Kezia II, 585
Long, Keziah II, 585
Long, Lewis IV, 735
Long, Lewis IV, 1171
Long, Lewis Ervin IV, 735
Long, Lewis Walker IV, 735
Long, Lewis Walter IV, 735
Long, Lidia VI, 414
Long, Lydia IV, 37
Long, Lydia IV, 46
Long, Lydia VI, 408
Long, Lydia VI, 414
Long, Lydia VI, 444
Long, Margaret Elizabeth VI, 667
Long, Maria VI, 834
Long, Mariam V, 955
Long, Mariam V, 958
Long, Martha I, 824
Long, Martha C. I, 991
Long, Mary I, 359
Long, Mary I, 389
Long, Mary I, 405
Long, Mary I, 557
Long, Mary IV, 735
Long, Mary V, 706
Long, Mary V, 760
Long, Mary VI, 375
Long, Mary VI, 414
Long, Mary VI, 482
Long, Mary VI, 528
Long, Mary VI, 672
Long, Mary VI, 951
Long, Mary A. II, 918
Long, Mary B. III, 210
Long, Mary C. III, 23
Long, Mary Ellen V, 603
Long, Mary W. I, 359
Long, Massay VI, 951
Long, Maud IV, 418
Long, Maud Clark IV, 1326
Long, Mrs. ??? IV, 1256
Long, Nancy I, 359
Long, Owen VI, 408
Long, Owen VI, 414
Long, Owen VI, 444
Long, Owen VI, 452
Long, Polly I, 359
Long, Polly I, 404
Long, Polly I, 405
Long, Rachel I, 359
Long, Rachel I, 824
Long, Rachel II, 390
Long, Rachel II, 585
Long, Rachel V, 404
Long, Rachel V, 411
Long, Rachel VI, 414
Long, Ray IV, 735
Long, Rebecca I, 359
Long, Rebeckah VI, 414
Long, Rebekah I, 405
Long, Rebekah I, 412
Long, Rebekah VI, 408
Long, Rebekah VI, 414
Long, Reuben I, 824
Long, Robert VI, 414
Long, Robert C. IV, 1284
Long, Ruth II, 390
Long, Sarah I, 359
Long, Sarah I, 404
Long, Sarah I, 405
Long, Sarah IV, 98
Long, Sarah IV, 101
Long, Sarah V, 752
Long, Sarah V, 1007
Long, Sylvia IV, 735
Long, Sylvia Jean IV, 735
Long, Thelma IV, 735
Long, Thomas B. III, 23
Long, Thomas H. III, 210
Long, Tobias I, 824
Long, Walter II, 585
Long, Will V, 404
Long, William VI, 951
Longacers, Rachel VI, 414
Longacre, Ann I, 1124
Longacre, Edwin V, 93
Longacre, Edwin B. V, 93
Longacre, Edwin L. V, 93
Longacre, Hannah VI, 414
Longacre, Hannah VI, 595
Longacre, Hannah VI, 599
Longacre, Isaac J. V, 93
Longacre, Joseph VI, 414
Longacre, Lucy Ellen V, 93
Longacre, Martha C. V, 93
Longacre, Martha E. V, 93
Longacre, Rachel VI, 414
Longacre, Rebeckah VI, 599
Longacre, Rebekah VI, 595
Longbotham, ??? III, 128
Longbotham, Edward C. III, 210
Longbotham, Eliz. W. III, 58
Longbotham, Eliz. W. III, 210
Longbotham, Elizabeth III, 128
Longbotham, Elizabeth III, 188
Longbotham, Elizabeth W. III, 128
Longbotham, Elizabeth W. III, 210
Longbotham, James F. III, 210
Longbotham, Joseph C. III, 210
Longbotham, Mary III, 58
Longbotham, Mary III, 210
Longbotham, Sarah Ann III, 210
Longbotham, Wm. G. III, 210

Longbottam, Edward C. III, 230
Longbottam, Sarah Ann III, 230
Longcope, Henry II, 915
Longcope, Jennie Cecilia II, 891
Longcope, Jennie Celia II, 891
Longcope, Jennie Lelia II, 915
Longden, Lucinda IV, 1171
Longshaw, Christian II, 390
Longshaw, Samuel II, 390
Longshaw, Thomas II, 390
Longshore, Abraham II, 806
Longshore, Alfred II, 891
Longshore, Alfred A. II, 892
Longshore, Ann IV, 876
Longshore, Ann IV, 877
Longshore, Barak IV, 641
Longshore, Catharine IV, 609
Longshore, Catharine IV, 641
Longshore, Catharine J. IV, 641
Longshore, Clarinda IV, 1171
Longshore, Clyde I, 557
Longshore, Clyde I, 1016
Longshore, David II, 1011
Longshore, Edward W. II, 892
Longshore, Eleanor V, 582
Longshore, Eleanor V, 597
Longshore, Ellen II, 1055
Longshore, Evelide I, 1034
Longshore, Frances II, 995
Longshore, Frances II, 1011
Longshore, Francis II, 976
Longshore, Francis II, 1011
Longshore, Francis II, 1042
Longshore, Hannah E. II, 806
Longshore, Hannah E. II, 891
Longshore, Hannah E. IV, 831
Longshore, Hannah Elsie II, 806
Longshore, Isaac S. II, 891
Longshore, Isaac S. II, 892
Longshore, James II, 976
Longshore, James II, 995
Longshore, James II, 1011
Longshore, James II, 1042
Longshore, James II, 1055
Longshore, Jane Ashton IV, 641
Longshore, Jolly II, 585
Longshore, Jolly II, 1011
Longshore, Jolly II, 1042
Longshore, Jolly II, 1055
Longshore, Katharine L. IV, 639
Longshore, Katharine L. IV, 641
Longshore, Lucretia M. II, 891
Longshore, Lucretia Mott II, 783
Longshore, Lucretia Mott II, 891
Longshore, Margaret II, 1055
Longshore, Maria II, 806
Longshore, Maria P. II, 892
Longshore, Maria P. IV, 1028
Longshore, Mary II, 891
Longshore, Mary II, 995
Longshore, Mary II, 1011
Longshore, Mary IV, 641
Longshore, Mary IV, 653
Longshore, Mary IV, 735
Longshore, Mary IV, 876
Longshore, Mary IV, 881
Longshore, Mary B. II, 892
Longshore, Mercy II, 1011
Longshore, Mercy II, 1042
Longshore, Mercy II, 1055
Longshore, Permelia II, 1055
Longshore, Permelia II, 1062
Longshore, Phebe II, 976
Longshore, Phebe II, 1011
Longshore, Phebe II, 1027
Longshore, Rachel P. II, 825
Longshore, Rachel P. II, 891
Longshore, Rachel P. II, 892
Longshore, Rachel P. II, 935
Longshore, Rhoda II, 806
Longshore, Rhoda Ann II, 805
Longshore, Rhoda Ann II, 892
Longshore, Rhoda K. II, 887
Longshore, Rhoda K. II, 892
Longshore, Robert II, 1011
Longshore, Robert II, 1055
Longshore, Rudolph P. II, 806
Longshore, Ruth II, 1011
Longshore, Sarah I, 557
Longshore, Sarah I, 1016
Longshore, Sarah I, 1034
Longshore, Sarah II, 1011
Longshore, Sarah IV, 641
Longshore, Sarah IV, 666
Longshore, Sary I, 557
Longshore, Sary I, 1016
Longshore, T. Ellwood II, 891
Longshore, Tamar II, 892
Longshore, Thomas Elwood II, 806
Longshore, Thomas Elwood IV, 831
Longshore, Thos. Elwood II, 806
Longshore, William II, 1011
Longshore, Wm. II, 892
Longshore, Wm. B. II, 892
Longshore, Wm. E. Channing II, 891
Longshore, Wm. E. Channing II, 892
Longshore, Wm. Ellery Channing II, 806
Longstaff, E. Anetta II, 711
Longstaff, Henrietta V, 915
Longstaff, Roberts W. II, 711
Longstaff, Thomas IV, 919
Longston, Elinor VI, 525
Longston, Thomas VI, 525
Longstreet, Margaret III, 489
Longstreth, ??? II, 806
Longstreth, Abby Ann II, 295
Longstreth, Abby Ann II, 303
Longstreth, Ann II, 797
Longstreth, Ann II, 798
Longstreth, Ann L. II, 753
Longstreth, Ann L. II, 777
Longstreth, Ann W. II, 806
Longstreth, Ann W. II, 892
Longstreth, Ann W. II, 897
Longstreth, Ann Williams II, 806
Longstreth, Anna II, 390
Longstreth, Anna II, 585
Longstreth, Anna II, 829
Longstreth, Anna II, 892
Longstreth, Anna II, 943
Longstreth, Benjamin II, 557
Longstreth, Benjamin II, 585
Longstreth, Benjamin V, 511
Longstreth, Charles II, 390
Longstreth, Charles II, 585
Longstreth, Charles II, 753
Longstreth, Charles II, 806
Longstreth, Charles, Jr. II, 753
Longstreth, Charles, Jr. II, 892
Longstreth, Chas. II, 843
Longstreth, Chas. II, 892
Longstreth, Chas. Tyson II, 798
Longstreth, Cresson II, 798
Longstreth, Daniel II, 585
Longstreth, Daniel II, 861
Longstreth, Daniel II, 892
Longstreth, Daniel VI, 414
Longstreth, David II, 390
Longstreth, David II, 585
Longstreth, Deborah II, 209
Longstreth, Edward T. II, 892
Longstreth, Edwin T. II, 892
Longstreth, Elihu II, 711
Longstreth, Elizabeth II, 312
Longstreth, Elizabeth II, 390
Longstreth, Elizabeth II, 557
Longstreth, Elizabeth II, 585
Longstreth, Elizabeth II, 593
Longstreth, Elizabeth II, 794
Longstreth, Elizabeth II, 830
Longstreth, Elizabeth II, 892
Longstreth, Elizabeth V, 96
Longstreth, Elizabeth J. II, 806
Longstreth, Elizabeth J. II, 892
Longstreth, Elizabeth Jackson II, 806
Longstreth, Elizabeth L. II, 861
Longstreth, Elizabeth L. II, 892
Longstreth, Elizabeth W. II, 753
Longstreth, Elizabeth W. II, 892
Longstreth, Emeline II, 892
Longstreth, Emily T. II, 861
Longstreth, Emily T. II, 892
Longstreth, Emily W. II, 843
Longstreth, Emily W. II, 892
Longstreth, Emmeline II, 806
Longstreth, Esther II, 585
Longstreth, Esther II, 1011
Longstreth, Esther Fisher II, 390
Longstreth, Esther Fisher II, 711
Longstreth, Gertrude V, 691
Longstreth, Grace VI, 414
Longstreth, Hannah II, 585
Longstreth, Hannah II, 946
Longstreth, Hannah V, 93
Longstreth, Hannah C. V, 93
Longstreth, Hannah C. V, 582
Longstreth, Hannah L. V, 556
Longstreth, Hannah L. V, 582
Longstreth, Hannah Smith II, 798
Longstreth, Helen II, 390
Longstreth, Helen II, 806
Longstreth, Helen II, 892
Longstreth, Helen II, 906
Longstreth, Helen II, 909
Longstreth, Helen G. II, 753
Longstreth, Henry II, 390
Longstreth, Henry II, 585
Longstreth, Horace V, 691
Longstreth, Howell II, 390
Longstreth, Howell II, 585
Longstreth, Isaac II, 209
Longstreth, Isaac II, 585
Longstreth, Isaac II, 593
Longstreth, Isaac T. II, 209
Longstreth, Isaac T. II, 239
Longstreth, Isaac T. II, 295
Longstreth, Isaac T. II, 303
Longstreth, Isaac T. II, 390
Longstreth, Isaac T. II, 585
Longstreth, Jacob II, 585
Longstreth, Jacob V, 93
Longstreth, Jacob V, 511
Longstreth, John II, 806
Longstreth, John II, 1011
Longstreth, John H. II, 585
Longstreth, John H. II, 753
Longstreth, John H. II, 843
Longstreth, John H. II, 892
Longstreth, John Hunt II, 390
Longstreth, John Hunt II, 892
Longstreth, John L. II, 861
Longstreth, John L. II, 892
Longstreth, John Ogden II, 390
Longstreth, John Ogden II, 585
Longstreth, Jonathan II, 1011
Longstreth, Jonathan VI, 414
Longstreth, Jonathan VI, 435
Longstreth, Joseph II, 390
Longstreth, Joseph II, 493
Longstreth, Joseph II, 585
Longstreth, Joseph II, 797
Longstreth, Joseph II, 806
Longstreth, Joseph II, 897
Longstreth, Joshua II, 390
Longstreth, Joshua II, 585
Longstreth, Joshua II, 628
Longstreth, Joshua II, 668
Longstreth, Joshua II, 711
Longstreth, Joshua II, 753
Longstreth, Joshua II, 779
Longstreth, Joshua II, 798
Longstreth, Joshua II, 806
Longstreth, Joshua II, 892
Longstreth, Joshua II, 946
Longstreth, Lambert V, 93
Longstreth, Letitia II, 1011
Longstreth, Letitia II, 1016
Longstreth, Lydia II, 390
Longstreth, Lydia II, 585
Longstreth, Lydia II, 753
Longstreth, Lydia W. II, 585
Longstreth, Lydia W. II, 628
Longstreth, Lydia Williams II, 708
Longstreth, Lydia Williams II, 812
Longstreth, Lydia Williams II, 816
Longstreth, M. Fisher II, 892
Longstreth, Margaret II, 493
Longstreth, Margaret II, 585
Longstreth, Margaret II, 806
Longstreth, Margaret II, 897
Longstreth, Martha II, 209
Longstreth, Martha II, 390
Longstreth, Martha II, 585
Longstreth, Martha II, 593
Longstreth, Martha II, 822
Longstreth, Martha V, 93
Longstreth, Martha V, 482
Longstreth, Martha V, 511
Longstreth, Martha M. II, 892
Longstreth, Mary II, 209
Longstreth, Mary II, 239
Longstreth, Mary II, 240
Longstreth, Mary II, 295
Longstreth, Mary II, 303
Longstreth, Mary II, 390
Longstreth, Mary II, 585
Longstreth, Mary Ann II, 390
Longstreth, Mary Anna II, 585
Longstreth, Mary Bringhurst II, 806
Longstreth, Mary C. II, 892
Longstreth, Mary Clapp II, 806
Longstreth, Mary E. II, 753
Longstreth, Mary Elizabeth II, 493
Longstreth, Mary Elizabeth II, 585
Longstreth, Mary T. II, 848
Longstreth, Mary T. II, 892
Longstreth, Mary Tyson II, 806
Longstreth, Mary Wooley II, 784
Longstreth, Miers Fisher II, 390
Longstreth, Miers Fisher II, 806
Longstreth, Miers Fisher II, 848
Longstreth, Miers Fisher II, 892
Longstreth, Morris II, 390
Longstreth, Morris II, 493
Longstreth, Morris II, 585
Longstreth, Morris II, 753
Longstreth, Morris Longstreth II, 798
Longstreth, Myers Fisher II, 753
Longstreth, Myra II, 390
Longstreth, Phebe VI, 414
Longstreth, Phebe VI, 435
Longstreth, Preston II, 390
Longstreth, Rachel II, 390
Longstreth, Rachel II, 585
Longstreth, Rachel II, 753
Longstreth, Rachel II, 806
Longstreth, Rachel II, 843
Longstreth, Rachel II, 892
Longstreth, Rachel V, 477
Longstreth, Rachel V, 511
Longstreth, Rachel B. V, 511
Longstreth, Rachel H. II, 728
Longstreth, Rachel H. II, 753
Longstreth, Rachel Hunt II, 390
Longstreth, Rachel Hunt II, 839
Longstreth, Rachel Hunt II, 892
Longstreth, Rachel P. V, 93
Longstreth, Rebecca C. II, 892
Longstreth, Rebecca Clapp II, 806
Longstreth, Richard II, 312
Longstreth, Sally Redwood II, 892
Longstreth, Samuel II, 390
Longstreth, Samuel II, 585
Longstreth, Samuel II, 806
Longstreth, Samuel II, 812
Longstreth, Samuel II, 848
Longstreth, Samuel II, 892
Longstreth, Samuel II, 905
Longstreth, Samuel II, 943
Longstreth, Samuel F. II, 892
Longstreth, Samuel Fisher II, 806
Longstreth, Sarah II, 390
Longstreth, Sarah II, 557
Longstreth, Sarah II, 585
Longstreth, Sarah II, 758
Longstreth, Sarah II, 779
Longstreth, Sarah II, 806
Longstreth, Sarah II, 906
Longstreth, Sarah Cresson II, 798
Longstreth, Sarah K. II, 848
Longstreth, Sarah K. II, 892
Longstreth, Sarah R. II, 390
Longstreth, Sarah R. II, 711
Longstreth, Sarah R. II, 892
Longstreth, Sarah R. II, 905
Longstreth, Sarah R. II, 943
Longstreth, Sarah Redwood II, 390
Longstreth, Sarah Redwood II, 753
Longstreth, Sarah Redwood II, 806
Longstreth, Sarah Redwood II, 812
Longstreth, Sarah W. II, 585
Longstreth, Sarah W. II, 628
Longstreth, Sarah W. II, 668
Longstreth, Sarah W. II, 753
Longstreth, Sarah W. II, 892
Longstreth, Sidney E. II, 390
Longstreth, Sidney E. II, 753
Longstreth, Sidney E. II, 892
Longstreth, Sidney Elizabeth II, 806
Longstreth, Susan II, 390
Longstreth, Susan II, 585
Longstreth, Susan M. II, 585
Longstreth, Susan M. II, 668
Longstreth, Susanna II, 585
Longstreth, Susannah II, 797
Longstreth, Thomas II, 585
Longstreth, Thomas M. II, 711
Longstreth, Thomas M. II, 753
Longstreth, Thos. M. II, 892
Longstreth, Virginia II, 806
Longstreth, Wd. Elizabeth Williams II, 779
Longstreth, Wd. Margaret Bullock II, 806
Longstreth, William II, 390
Longstreth, William V, 93
Longstreth, William V, 482
Longstreth, William V, 511
Longstreth, William V, 582
Longstreth, William C. II, 295
Longstreth, William C. II, 303
Longstreth, William W. II, 390
Longstreth, William Wilson II, 806
Longstreth, Wm. II, 557
Longstreth, Wm. II, 585
Longstreth, Wm. II, 1011
Longstreth, Wm. V, 556
Longstreth, Wm. V, 788
Longstreth, Wm. K. II, 892
Longstreth, Wm. W. II, 892
Longstreth, Wm. W. II, 897
Longten, Catherine IV, 479
Longten, Catherine IV, 484
Longworth, Nicholas V, 889
Lonnon, Hannah II, 390
Lonnon, Joshua II, 390
Lonsdale, John IV, 46
Lonsdale, John IV, 98
Lonsdale, John IV, 128
Lonsdale, Ruth II, 585
Lonsdale, Thomas IV, 98
Lonsdale, Thomas IV, 128
Lonshore, Lucretia M. II, 839
Lonshore, Lucretia M. II, 891
Lont, Hallie V, 632
Lont, John V, 632
Loob, Wm. II, 1011
Loodg, Ann II, 85
Loof, Anthony III, 210
Loof, Mary II, 586
Loofborrow, ??? II, 390
Loofborrow, Nathaniel II, 390
Loofborrow, William II, 390
Loofbourrough, Mr. ??? II, 592
Loofbourrough, Wm. II, 522
Loofbourrough, Wm. II, 586
Loofburgh, Margaret II, 586
Loofburrow, Margaret II, 586
Loofburrow, Mary II, 390
Loofburrow, Mary II, 586
Loofburrow, Nathaniel II, 390
Loofburrow, William II, 390
Loofburrow, Wm. II, 586
Loofbury, ??? III, 211
Loofbury, Abraham III, 210
Looker, Nina III, 337
Looker, Sarah III, 337
Looker, Wm. A. III, 337
Lookes, Judith VI, 258
Looman, Sarah Ann IV, 163
Loomis, Benjamin V, 460
Loomis, Bessie V, 460
Loomis, Charles H. IV, 1256
Loomis, Clark S. IV, 1256
Loomis, Everett V, 460
Loomis, Hannah IV, 1105
Loomis, Hannah IV, 1120
Loomis, Jennie V, 460
Loomis, Jessie V, 460
Loomis, Margaret IV, 1256
Loomis, Oscar V, 460
Loomis, Raymond V, 460
Loop, Elizabeth V, 919
Loop, John IV, 1257
Loop, Lawrence IV, 1257
Loop, Manerva IV, 1257
Loosely, Elizabeth II, 586
Loosely, Robert II, 586
Loper, Hannah II, 823
Loper, Sarah II, 118
Loper, Sarah II, 121
Lopez, Barbara III, 210
Lopez, Barbara A. III, 210
Lopez, Edna Russell III, 210
Lopez, Lila III, 210
Lopez, Virgil G. III, 210
Loramar, Sarah II, 993
Loramar, Thomas II, 993
Loramar, Thomas II, 1011
Loramore, Hannah II, 987
Loramore, Hannah II, 1011
Loramore, Martha II, 1011
Loramore, Mary II, 1011
Loramore, Sarah II, 1011
Loramore, Thomas II, 1011
Lorane, Agnes V, 870
Lord, Ann IV, 976
Lord, Azuba II, 62
Lord, Azuba II, 85
Lord, Cyrus W. V, 632
Lord, David II, 85
Lord, E. Jay IV, 484
Lord, Edwin Jay IV, 484
Lord, Hannah II, 84
Lord, Hannah II, 85
Lord, Jane II, 240
Lord, Jehu IV, 735
Lord, Jehu IV, 976
Lord, Jehu Lord Kite IV, 735
Lord, Jennie V, 1007

, Josephine IV, 484
, Joshua II, 240
, Joshua II, 273
, Joshua, Jr. II, 84
, Joshua, Jr. II, 85
, Kezia II, 85
, Keziah II, 85
, Lydia IV, 718
, Mary C. II, 892
, Nathan II, 62
, Nathan II, 85
, Nathan, Jr. II, 85
, Rebecca IV, 735
, Rebecca IV, 952
, Rebecca IV, 976
, Rebecca IV, 989
, Rebecca S. IV, 976
, Rebecca, Jr. IV, 976
, Robert II, 240
, Ruth II, 62
, Ruth II, 85
, Sarah II, 55
, Sarah II, 85
, Sarah II, 240
, Sarah II, 273
ein, Mamie IV, 1215
ensen, Mr. ??? IV, 1326
ensen, Mrs. ??? IV, 1326
enz, Chas. III, 210
enz, Leocadie B. III, 210
enz, Phebe Anna III, 210
enz, William A. III, 210
enzo, Annie II, 968
enzo, Esther Mary Christine II, 968
enzo, Niss II, 968
ing, Ann IV, 735
ing, Gilbert III, 210
ing, James III, 210
ing, Sarah IV, 735
men, Mary A. I, 612
raine, Jack F. III, 381
raine, Jack F. III, 382
raine, Martha B. III, 381
raine, Martha B. III, 382
ramore, Martha II, 1011
ramore, Sarah II, 1011
ramore, Thomas II, 1011
rimer, A. IV, 1326
rimer, Alexander D. IV, 1326
ton, Amy Eliza III, 210
ton, Eugene V. III, 210
ton, Sarah II, 240
y, Lewis II, 390
chinsky, Joseph Wayne IV, 735
see, Abigail III, 425
see, Caroline III, 425
see, Elias III, 425
see, Emmeline III, 425
see, Isaac III, 425
see, Maria III, 425
see, Oliver III, 425
sey, Chas. V, 1007
sey, Daniel R. V, 1007
sey, James E. V, 1007
sy, A. K. V, 582
sy, Lennie V, 582
th, Anthony V, 1007
th, Sarah E. V, 1007
tham, Elizabeth IV, 1134
tham, Joseph III, 394
threy, Esther IV, 1215
throp, Charles Francis VI, 762
throp, Cornelia L. VI, 762
throp, Elsa Marvel VI, 762
throp, Elsa Marvel VI, 770
throp, Frank B. VI, 762
throp, Guy Cecil VI, 762
throp, James VI, 762
throp, James Norris VI, 762
throp, James Norris, Jr. VI, 762
throp, John Ira VI, 762
throp, Mabel Irma VI, 762
throp, Nellie VI, 741
throp, Nellie VI, 762
throp, Norris VI, 741
throp, Rebecca V, 91
ts, Sarah II, 586
tt, Cornelius III, 425
tt, Cornelius III, 462
tt, Mary III, 425
tt, Mary III, 462
tt, Mary IV, 1257
tt, Susan V, 955
ott, Susan V, 957
ott, William IV, 1257
otten, John II, 391
otten, William II, 391
otton, Elizabeth II, 391
Lotton, John II, 391
Lotton, Sarah II, 391
Lotton, William II, 391
Lotz, Earnest V, 691
Lotz, Erenst V, 93
Lotz, Ernest V, 691
Louallen, Edith I, 724
Louallen, Edith I, 728
Louden, Easther II, 85
Louden, Easther II, 112
Louden, Elizabeth IV, 1105
Louden, Elizabeth IV, 1119
Louden, Esther II, 85
Louden, Jonathan I, 991
Louden, Lenora IV, 1284
Louden, Lovis S. IV, 1284
Louden, Mary IV, 1284
Louden, Renier II, 85
Louden, Renier II, 112
Louden, Samuel I, 991
Louden, Thomas I, 991
Louden, Wm. A. IV, 1284
Loudenback, Nell III, 47
Loudenback, Walter III, 47
Louder, Caleb I, 507
Louder, Caleb I, 557
Louder, Catharine I, 507
Louder, Celia V, 511
Louder, Hannah I, 507
Louder, Hannah I, 557
Louder, Job I, 507
Louder, Job I, 557
Louder, John I, 507
Louder, John I, 557
Louder, Joseph I, 507
Louder, Joseph I, 557
Louder, Joshua I, 507
Louder, Joshua I, 557
Louder, Lawrence IV, 1171
Louder, Mary I, 507
Louder, Mary I, 557
Louder, Nathan I, 507
Louder, Ralph I, 507
Louder, Rebeckah I, 557
Louder, Rebekah I, 507
Louder, Samuel I, 507
Louder, Samuel I, 557
Louder, William I, 507
Louder, William I, 557
Louderback, Andrew J. III, 210
Louderback, Matilda III, 210
Louderback, Nell III, 210
Louderback, Vivian IV, 1326
Louderback, Walter III, 210
Louders, Hannah IV, 292
Loudon, Elizabeth II, 1011
Loudon, Isaac Walker Waterford II, 803
Loudon, Susan II, 803
Loudon, Wd. Rebecca Jane II, 803
Louella, Frances V, 669
Loufburrow, Mary II, 390
Loufburrow, William II, 390
Loughborough, Wm. II, 586
Louhoff, F. C. II, 711
Louhoff, Frank A. IV, 586
Louhoff, Frank Allen IV, 575
Louhoff, Frank Allen IV, 586
Louhoff, Frederic Charles IV, 406
Louhoff, Frederick C. IV, 586
Louhoff, Frederick Charles IV, 586
Louhoff, Judith IV, 406
Louhoff, Julia II, 711
Louhoff, Julia IV, 406
Louhoff, Julia Kaiser IV, 586
Louhoff, Louise E. II, 711
Louhoff, Louise E. II, 753
Louhoff, M. Elizabeth II, 711
Louhoff, M. Elizabeth II, 753
Louhoff, M. Elizabeth IV, 418
Louhoff, Martha Eliza IV, 406
Louhoff, Mary IV, 586
Louhoff, Rosetta B. IV, 575
Louhoff, Rosetta B. IV, 586
Louise, Verna IV, 856
Louks, Marie IV, 1257
Lounds, Emmor IV, 418
Lounes, Anna VI, 197
Lounes, Hannah II, 837
Lounes, James VI, 197
Lounsbury, Phebe III, 210
Lounsdale, Elizabeth II, 391
Lounsdale, Margaret II, 391
Lounsdale, Thomas II, 391
Lousdale, Thomas II, 1011
Lousdale, Thomas IV, 128
Louty, Maude V, 1007
Love, Alfred H. II, 831
Love, Alfred H. II, 892
Love, Ann I, 813
Love, Ann I, 824
Love, Belta G. V, 411
Love, Betty VI, 688
Love, Catharan I, 957
Love, Charity I, 957
Love, Daniel W. VI, 951
Love, David I, 957
Love, David I, 966
Love, Edmund V, 691
Love, Edmund V, 704
Love, Eli VI, 528
Love, Eli A. VI, 579
Love, Elizabeth II, 800
Love, Elizabeth VI, 528
Love, Elizabeth VI, 672
Love, Elizabeth Ellis II, 831
Love, Elizabeth Ellis II, 892
Love, Emaline V, 411
Love, Giles II, 586
Love, Hannah I, 813
Love, Hannah I, 824
Love, Hannah I, 957
Love, Hannah VI, 528
Love, Hannah VI, 547
Love, Hannah VI, 548
Love, Hannah VI, 672
Love, Hannah VI, 688
Love, Harriet VI, 951
Love, Hattie V, 691
Love, Hattie V, 704
Love, Hattie Pond V, 691
Love, Jaboel II, 240
Love, James VI, 528
Love, James VI, 548
Love, James VI, 672
Love, Jane VI, 485
Love, Jane VI, 528
Love, Jane VI, 672
Love, Jas. VI, 528
Love, John I, 957
Love, John I, 966
Love, John VI, 528
Love, Jonathan I, 966
Love, Jonithan I, 957
Love, Juliet VI, 951
Love, Katharine I, 966
Love, Laura III, 54
Love, Laura III, 152
Love, Laura VI, 528
Love, Louisa Jane II, 830
Love, Louisa Jane II, 892
Love, Lydia II, 240
Love, Lydia II, 254
Love, Mabel V, 692
Love, Martha I, 450
Love, Mary R. V, 411
Love, Mattie J. VI, 528
Love, Opal V, 692
Love, Priscilla II, 235
Love, Priscilla II, 240
Love, Rachel II, 892
Love, Rebecah I, 957
Love, Rebecca J. VI, 528
Love, Rebekah I, 966
Love, Richard I, 957
Love, Richard I, 966
Love, Richard II, 235
Love, Richard II, 240
Love, Richard II, 391
Love, Richard II, 586
Love, Richard II, 613
Love, Sadie VI, 620
Love, Sadie VI, 665
Love, Samuel VI, 528
Love, Samuel VI, 672
Love, Sarah I, 957
Love, Sarah I, 966
Love, Sarah VI, 528
Love, Sarah VI, 548
Love, Sarah VI, 672
Love, Sarah Ann IV, 586
Love, Sarah Ann VI, 528
Love, Sarah Ann VI, 579
Love, Sintha I, 957
Love, Susan H. II, 831
Love, Susan H. II, 892
Love, Thomas I, 957
Love, Thomas I, 966
Love, Thomas VI, 528
Love, Thomas VI, 548
Love, Thomas VI, 672
Love, Thomas VI, 951
Love, Wd. Priscilla II, 586
Love, Wm. H. II, 830
Love, Wm. H. II, 892
Loveall, Ethel V, 692
Lovegrove, James II, 892
Lovegrove, Jane II, 892
Lovegrove, Jane G. II, 892
Lovegrove, Jenny VI, 951
Lovegrove, Mary L. II, 892
Lovegrove, Mary S. II, 892
Lovegrove, Mary S. II, 893
Lovegrove, Thomas G. II, 892
Lovegrove, Thomas J. II, 892
Lovegrove, Thos. G. II, 892
Lovegrove, Thos. J. II, 892
Lovegrove, William VI, 951
Lovegrove, Wm. II, 892
Lovegrove, Wm. H. II, 892
Loveit, Dorothy II, 586
Loveit, Mary II, 225
Loveit, Mary II, 240
Loveit, Samuel II, 225
Loveit, Samuel II, 240
Lovejoy, Alfaretta IV, 947
Lovejoy, Alfretta IV, 959
Lovejoy, Clinton III, 421
Lovejoy, Eliza Jane IV, 947
Lovejoy, Harriet III, 421
Lovejoy, Patty IV, 1372
Lovejoy, Pauline III, 421
Lovejoy, Wm. W. IV, 947
Lovel, Adaliza IV, 1133
Lovel, Edmund VI, 866
Lovel, Elizabeth J. VI, 866
Lovel, John VI, 810
Lovel, John VI, 867
Lovel, Marianna IV, 1133
Lovelace, J. P. I, 935
Lovelace, May L. I, 935
Lovelace, Sallie I, 935
Lovelace, Serenda VI, 834
Lovelace, Thomas A. VI, 834
Loveland, Ann Eliza II, 135
Loveland, Ann Eliza II, 295
Loveland, Ann Eliza II, 300
Loveland, Ann Elizabeth II, 153
Loveland, Rebecca II, 295
Loveland, Rebecca II, 300
Lovelin, Lucinda VI, 834
Lovelin, Thomas VI, 834
Lovell, ??? V, 692
Lovell, ??? V, 706
Lovell, Adaliza IV, 1134
Lovell, Anna V, 632
Lovell, Ethel V, 692
Lovell, Ethel V, 706
Lovell, George III, 210
Lovell, Ignatius III, 210
Lovell, John III, 425
Lovell, John III, 475
Lovell, John VI, 834
Lovell, Marcus III, 210
Lovell, Margaret III, 210
Lovell, Marianna IV, 1134
Lovell, Mary Ann IV, 1133
Lovell, Mary Ann IV, 1134
Lovell, Michael II, 391
Lovell, Obedience VI, 834
Lovell, Patience III, 425
Lovell, Patience III, 475
Lovell, Robert III, 210
Lovering, Ann II, 807
Lovering, Ann C. II, 853
Lovering, Ann C. II, 892
Lovering, Ann C. II, 938
Lovering, Anna C. II, 892
Lovering, Anna C. II, 938
Lovering, Anna Corbit II, 807
Lovering, Annie II, 870
Lovering, C. H. IV, 1326
Lovering, Corbit II, 892
Lovering, Edgar Lea II, 807
Lovering, Edgar Lea II, 892
Lovering, Elizabeth C. II, 711
Lovering, Elizabeth Corbit II, 807
Lovering, Gilpin II, 892
Lovering, Joseph II, 853
Lovering, Joseph S. II, 586
Lovering, Joseph S. II, 753
Lovering, Joseph S. II, 853
Lovering, Joseph S. II, 892
Lovering, Joseph S. II, 908
Lovering, Joseph S. II, 938
Lovering, Joseph S., Jr. II, 853
Lovering, Joseph S., Jr. II, 892
Lovering, Joseph Samuel II, 807
Lovering, Joseph Shallcross II, 807
Lovering, Mary II, 807
Lovering, Mary II, 892
Lovering, Mary II, 938
Lovering, Mary B. II, 892
Lovering, Mary B. II, 908
Lovering, Mary B. C. II, 892
Lovering, Mary B. C. II, 908
Lovering, Mary Barrett II, 807
Lovering, Mary S. II, 853
Lovering, May IV, 1326
Lovering, Rachel Ann II, 586
Lovering, Samuel II, 807
Lovering, Samuel II, 892
Lovering, Susan II, 908
Lovering, Susan S. II, 892
Lovering, Thomas II, 586
Lovesee, Edmund VI, 951
Lovesee, Lucy VI, 951
Lovesee, Polly VI, 951
Lovesee, Wiatt VI, 951
Lovesy, Edmund VI, 951
Lovesy, Polly VI, 951
Lovesy, Wyatt VI, 882
Lovet, Ann II, 979
Lovet, Ann VI, 414
Lovet, Ann, Jr. II, 981
Lovet, Daniel II, 981
Lovet, Daniel II, 1011
Lovet, Dorothy II, 240
Lovet, Edmund II, 1009
Lovet, Edmund II, 1011
Lovet, Edmund) II, 1018
Lovet, Elizabeth II, 178
Lovet, Elizabeth II, 1011
Lovet, Elizabeth II, 1027
Lovet, Jonathan II, 178
Lovet, Jonathan II, 233
Lovet, Jonathan II, 240
Lovet, Joseph I, 557
Lovet, Joseph II, 979
Lovet, Joseph II, 1012
Lovet, Mahlon S. VI, 415
Lovet, Mahlon Smith VI, 414
Lovet, Mary I, 536
Lovet, Mary I, 557
Lovet, Mary II, 178
Lovet, Mary II, 240
Lovet, Mary II, 1009
Lovet, Mary II, 1011
Lovet, Mary Ann VI, 414
Lovet, Meriot II, 178
Lovet, Nathan II, 178
Lovet, Phebe II, 1011
Lovet, Pheby V, 1007
Lovet, Rebecca II, 178
Lovet, Samuel II, 178
Lovet, Sarah I, 557
Lovet, Sarah II, 178
Lovet, Susannah II, 1011
Lovet, Susannah II, 1018
Lovet, William I, 245
Lovett, Aaron II, 240
Lovett, Abigail II, 1075
Lovett, Addie M. IV, 1326
Lovett, Amos Ellis II, 1066
Lovett, Amos Ellis II, 1075
Lovett, Ann II, 956
Lovett, Ann II, 964
Lovett, Ann II, 1012
Lovett, Ann II, 1055
Lovett, Ann II, 1075
Lovett, Ann VI, 388
Lovett, Ann VI, 414
Lovett, Ann VI, 599
Lovett, Ann VI, 637
Lovett, Ann VI, 641
Lovett, Ann VI, 672
Lovett, Ann, Sr. II, 1055
Lovett, Anna II, 968
Lovett, Anna VI, 672
Lovett, Anna J. II, 964
Lovett, Anna J. II, 1059
Lovett, Anna M. II, 893
Lovett, Anna Mary II, 1055
Lovett, Anna Mary II, 1075
Lovett, Anna Miller II, 807
Lovett, Aron II, 240
Lovett, Aron II, 270
Lovett, Benj. II, 240
Lovett, Benjamin T. II, 1066
Lovett, Benjamin T. II, 1075
Lovett, Caroline B. II, 1055
Lovett, Caroline B. IV, 735
Lovett, Caroline H. II, 964
Lovett, Caroline Hoagland IV, 679
Lovett, Caroline Hoagland IV, 735
Lovett, Cassandra II, 980
Lovett, Cassandra II, 1012
Lovett, Charles H. II, 1055
Lovett, Daniel II, 955
Lovett, Daniel II, 956
Lovett, Daniel II, 964
Lovett, Daniel II, 982
Lovett, Daniel II, 1004
Lovett, Daniel II, 1011
Lovett, Daniel II, 1012
Lovett, Daniel II, 1046
Lovett, Daniel II, 1055
Lovett, Daniel II, 1075

Lovett, Daniel VI, 496
Lovett, Daniel VI, 528
Lovett, Daniel VI, 641
Lovett, Daniel VI, 672
Lovett, Daniel, Jr. II, 1001
Lovett, Daniel, Jr. II, 1012
Lovett, Daniel, Jr. II, 1055
Lovett, David H. II, 1055
Lovett, David Heston II, 1012
Lovett, Dorothy II, 216
Lovett, Dorothy II, 240
Lovett, Dorothy II, 586
Lovett, Edmund II, 964
Lovett, Edmund II, 998
Lovett, Edmund II, 1011
Lovett, Edmund, Jr. II, 1011
Lovett, Edna Thorp II, 964
Lovett, Edna Thorpe II, 1055
Lovett, Edna W. II, 1055
Lovett, Edwin II, 964
Lovett, Elaline G. II, 893
Lovett, Elisa II, 240
Lovett, Elisa II, 257
Lovett, Eliza II, 1004
Lovett, Eliza II, 1012
Lovett, Elizabeth II, 178
Lovett, Elizabeth II, 240
Lovett, Elizabeth II, 259
Lovett, Elizabeth II, 955
Lovett, Elizabeth II, 964
Lovett, Elizabeth II, 982
Lovett, Elizabeth II, 1004
Lovett, Elizabeth II, 1011
Lovett, Elizabeth II, 1012
Lovett, Elizabeth II, 1055
Lovett, Elizabeth II, 1073
Lovett, Elizabeth II, 1075
Lovett, Elvyra II, 1055
Lovett, Emaline G. II, 930
Lovett, Fannie II, 1074
Lovett, Fannie II, 1075
Lovett, Fanny II, 1066
Lovett, Francis Lucas II, 964
Lovett, George B. II, 964
Lovett, George B. II, 1055
Lovett, Hannah II, 964
Lovett, Hannah II, 991
Lovett, Hannah II, 1012
Lovett, Hannah II, 1075
Lovett, Hannah Ann II, 964
Lovett, Hector T. II, 1066
Lovett, J. S. V, 306
Lovett, James S. II, 964
Lovett, Jane II, 964
Lovett, Jane II, 1075
Lovett, Jesse II, 1012
Lovett, Jesse II, 1055
Lovett, Jesse II, 1075
Lovett, John T. II, 1075
Lovett, Jonathan II, 240
Lovett, Jonathan VI, 388
Lovett, Jonathan VI, 414
Lovett, Jonathan VI, 599
Lovett, Jonathan VI, 637
Lovett, Jonathan VI, 641
Lovett, Jonathan VI, 672
Lovett, Joseph II, 240
Lovett, Joseph II, 586
Lovett, Joseph II, 964
Lovett, Joseph II, 1012
Lovett, Joseph VI, 528
Lovett, Joseph B. II, 1055
Lovett, Joshua VI, 414
Lovett, Laura II, 1055
Lovett, Lydia II, 240
Lovett, Lydia II, 270
Lovett, Magdalene II, 964
Lovett, Magdalene II, 998
Lovett, Magdalene II, 1011
Lovett, Mahlon VI, 414
Lovett, Mahlon L. II, 964
Lovett, Mahlon L. II, 1046
Lovett, Mahlon L. II, 1055
Lovett, Mahlon Lucas II, 1012
Lovett, Mahlon S. VI, 415
Lovett, Mahlon Smith VI, 414
Lovett, Mahlon Smith VI, 672
Lovett, Malcolm II, 1075
Lovett, Margaret II, 1066
Lovett, Martha II, 964
Lovett, Martha II, 1012
Lovett, Martha II, 1046
Lovett, Martha II, 1055
Lovett, Martha VI, 496
Lovett, Martha VI, 528
Lovett, Mary II, 178
Lovett, Mary II, 240
Lovett, Mary II, 273
Lovett, Mary II, 586
Lovett, Mary II, 954
Lovett, Mary II, 964
Lovett, Mary II, 1001
Lovett, Mary II, 1011
Lovett, Mary II, 1012
Lovett, Mary II, 1046
Lovett, Mary II, 1055
Lovett, Mary A. VI, 388
Lovett, Mary A. VI, 414
Lovett, Mary A. VI, 637
Lovett, Mary Ann VI, 414
Lovett, Mary Ann VI, 672
Lovett, Mary C. II, 1062
Lovett, Mary C. II, 1075
Lovett, Mary C. II, 1081
Lovett, Mary Jane II, 964
Lovett, Mary Jane II, 1012
Lovett, Mary Jane II, 1055
Lovett, Mary S. II, 893
Lovett, Mary T. II, 964
Lovett, Mary Tacie II, 1044
Lovett, Mary Tacie II, 1055
Lovett, Mercy II, 1012
Lovett, Mercy II, 1028
Lovett, Mercy II, 1055
Lovett, Meriot II, 178
Lovett, Nancy VI, 414
Lovett, Nancy VI, 599
Lovett, Nancy VI, 672
Lovett, Nathan II, 178
Lovett, Nathan II, 240
Lovett, Nathan II, 273
Lovett, Phebe II, 964
Lovett, Phebe II, 1011
Lovett, Phebe II, 1012
Lovett, Phebe Ann II, 1055
Lovett, Rebecca II, 178
Lovett, Rebecca II, 964
Lovett, Rebecca II, 982
Lovett, Rebecca II, 1012
Lovett, Rebecca II, 1055
Lovett, Reola V, 460
Lovett, Robert B. II, 1055
Lovett, Robert P. II, 954
Lovett, Robert P. II, 964
Lovett, Robert P. II, 982
Lovett, Robert P. II, 1012
Lovett, Robert P. II, 1055
Lovett, Robert P. II, 1059
Lovett, Robert P. II, 1075
Lovett, Robert P. IV, 679
Lovett, Robert P. IV, 735
Lovett, Robert Pittfield II, 964
Lovett, Robert Pittfield II, 1044
Lovett, Robert Pittfield II, 1055
Lovett, Robert Pittfield II, 1059
Lovett, Robert Pittfield IV, 735
Lovett, Sampson V, 460
Lovett, Samuel II, 178
Lovett, Samuel II, 240
Lovett, Samuel II, 257
Lovett, Samuel II, 259
Lovett, Samuel II, 261
Lovett, Samuel II, 270
Lovett, Samuel II, 1012
Lovett, Samuel II, 1055
Lovett, Sarah II, 178
Lovett, Sarah II, 240
Lovett, Sarah II, 261
Lovett, Sarah II, 955
Lovett, Sarah II, 964
Lovett, Sarah II, 982
Lovett, Sarah II, 1012
Lovett, Sarah II, 1055
Lovett, Sarah VI, 414
Lovett, Sarah VI, 599
Lovett, Sarah VI, 641
Lovett, Sarah VI, 672
Lovett, Sarah A. II, 954
Lovett, Sarah A. II, 1055
Lovett, Sarah A. II, 1059
Lovett, Sarah A. IV, 735
Lovett, Sarah B. II, 964
Lovett, Sarah B. II, 1055
Lovett, Sarah B. II, 1058
Lovett, Sarah Charles H. II, 1012
Lovett, Sarah L. II, 964
Lovett, Susannah II, 240
Lovett, Susannah II, 1002
Lovett, Susannah II, 1011
Lovett, Susannah II, 1012
Lovett, Tacy R. II, 1059
Lovett, William James II, 964
Lovett, William Lucas II, 964
Lovett, William S. II, 964
Lovett, Wm. P. II, 893
Lovett, Wm. P. II, 930
Lovett, Wm. Penn II, 807
Lovett, Wm. S. II, 1055
Lovett, Wm., Jr. II, 1012
Lovette, Mary II, 1012
Lovette, Rebecca II, 1055
Lovin, William I, 245
Loving, C. M. VI, 834
Loving, Elizabeth S. VI, 951
Loving, Emma E. VI, 834
Loving, Frederick I, 310
Loving, Frederick I, 314
Loving, John H. VI, 951
Loving, Louisa Semour VI, 951
Loving, Orville VI, 951
Loving, Orville VI, 971
Loving, Peggy VI, 862
Loving, Sarah I, 245
Loving, Sarah I, 310
Loving, Sarah, Jr. I, 310
Loving, Widow Sarah I, 310
Loving, Widow Sarah I, 314
Loving, William I, 245
Loving, William I, 310
Loving, Winnefred I, 310
Lovingfoss, Alice V, 346
Lovingfoss, Jennie V, 346
Lovingfoss, Lewis V, 346
Lovingfoss, Louis V, 346
Lovingfoss, William V, 346
Lovingpass, Alice V, 346
Lovingpass, Louis V, 346
Lovingpass, William V, 346
Lovingston, Duncan VI, 865
Lovit, Sarah I, 557
Lovitt, Addie M. IV, 1326
Lovitt, Sarah A. IV, 1326
Lovless, Doris V, 1007
Low, Aaron I, 101
Low, Aaron I, 145
Low, Abigail I, 703
Low, Abigail Maria I, 703
Low, Abigail S. I, 725
Low, Agnes R. I, 702
Low, Alice II, 586
Low, Allen Ridgeway II, 391
Low, Ann I, 92
Low, Ann I, 557
Low, Ann II, 85
Low, Ann V, 850
Low, Anna I, 703
Low, Barnabe I, 128
Low, Barnabe I, 145
Low, Belinda I, 725
Low, Belinda I, 766
Low, Benj. W. II, 586
Low, Benj. W. II, 641
Low, Benjamin II, 391
Low, Benjamin II, 586
Low, Benjamin W. II, 391
Low, Benjamin W. II, 586
Low, Benjamin Wait II, 391
Low, Benjamin Wait II, 586
Low, Benjamin Waite II, 818
Low, Carrie S. I, 702
Low, Catharine I, 725
Low, Catharine I, 766
Low, Catharine II, 85
Low, Catharine II, 502
Low, Catharine II, 513
Low, Catherine II, 391
Low, Charlotte II, 391
Low, Charlotte II, 586
Low, Charlotte II, 641
Low, Charlotte II, 753
Low, Charlotte II, 818
Low, Charlotte II, 893
Low, Cora J. I, 725
Low, Daniel I, 703
Low, Daniel I, 725
Low, Donnie R. I, 702
Low, Edward H. II, 807
Low, Eli I, 703
Low, Elisabeth I, 128
Low, Elisabeth I, 145
Low, Elisabeth I, 157
Low, Elisabeth II, 664
Low, Elizabeth I, 111
Low, Elizabeth I, 145
Low, Elizabeth II, 586
Low, Elizabeth IV, 28
Low, Elizabeth IV, 46
Low, Elvira G. I, 702
Low, Emaline IV, 401
Low, Emanuel I, 92
Low, Emanuel I, 145
Low, Fanny I, 703
Low, Fanny I, 708
Low, Fanny I, 724
Low, Frederick I, 724
Low, Georg I, 101
Low, George I, 101
Low, George I, 145
Low, Grace I, 703
Low, Grace I, 717
Low, Grace I, 725
Low, Hannah I, 102
Low, Hannah I, 128
Low, Hannah I, 139
Low, Hannah I, 145
Low, Hannah I, 703
Low, Hannah I, 725
Low, Hannah II, 391
Low, Harriet III, 209
Low, Hugh II, 85
Low, Hugh II, 391
Low, Hugh II, 513
Low, Hugh II, 586
Low, James I, 702
Low, James I, 703
Low, James I, 725
Low, James I, 891
Low, Jane I, 145
Low, Jane I, 766
Low, Jane I, 891
Low, Jane Pinnina I, 725
Low, Jehu I, 101
Low, Jemima I, 132
Low, Jemima I, 145
Low, Jesse I, 145
Low, John I, 101
Low, John I, 102
Low, John I, 111
Low, John I, 128
Low, John I, 145
Low, John I, 167
Low, John I, 703
Low, John I, 724
Low, John I, 725
Low, John I, 766
Low, John II, 391
Low, John II, 586
Low, John L. II, 807
Low, John, Jr. I, 102
Low, John, Sr. I, 102
Low, Joseph II, 586
Low, Joseph II, 664
Low, Joseph D. I, 725
Low, Joseph S. I, 725
Low, Katharine I, 766
Low, Kezia I, 145
Low, Keziah I, 101
Low, Levi B. I, 724
Low, Levi B. I, 725
Low, Levi Branson I, 703
Low, Lida I, 145
Low, Lida I, 173
Low, Lilias I, 766
Low, Lillias I, 725
Low, Lillias M. I, 725
Low, Lillie C. I, 725
Low, Lina Iredel I, 725
Low, Louisa I, 724
Low, Louisa I, 725
Low, Lucy II, 85
Low, Lydda I, 102
Low, Margaret I, 145
Low, Margaret I, 151
Low, Margaret I, 725
Low, Margaret D. I, 725
Low, Martha I, 145
Low, Martha I, 147
Low, Martha I, 891
Low, Mary I, 101
Low, Mary I, 128
Low, Mary I, 145
Low, Mary I, 152
Low, Mary I, 457
Low, Mary I, 703
Low, Mary I, 721
Low, Mary I, 724
Low, Mary I, 725
Low, Mary I, 766
Low, Mary I, 891
Low, Mary II, 391
Low, Mary Elizabeth I, 703
Low, Mary L. I, 702
Low, Mary S. I, 684
Low, Mary S. I, 690
Low, Mary S. I, 725
Low, Mattie I, 614
Low, Miriam I, 102
Low, Miriam I, 145
Low, Mollie I, 725
Low, Mollie S. I, 702
Low, Muriel I, 725
Low, Nathan I, 101
Low, Nathan I, 145
Low, Nathan I, 703
Low, Nathan B. I, 725
Low, Nereus M. I, 725
Low, Oliver I, 891
Low, Orpha I, 145
Low, Phebe Ann II, 391
Low, Phebe Ann II, 586
Low, Phebe Ann II, 641
Low, Phebe Ann II, 818
Low, Rebecca I, 725
Low, Rebeckah I, 167
Low, Rebeckah I, 703
Low, Rebekah I, 102
Low, Rebekah I, 145
Low, Rebekah I, 154
Low, Richard II, 586
Low, Robert II, 391
Low, Samira A. I, 725
Low, Samuel I, 725
Low, Sarah I, 101
Low, Sarah I, 145
Low, Sarah I, 162
Low, Sarah I, 166
Low, Sarah I, 167
Low, Sarah I, 703
Low, Sarah Jane I, 703
Low, Serilla I, 725
Low, Sophronia I, 713
Low, Sophronia I, 725
Low, Tamer I, 145
Low, Tempa I, 101
Low, Thamer I, 101
Low, Thamer I, 145
Low, Thomas I, 101
Low, Thomas I, 102
Low, Thomas I, 115
Low, Thomas I, 145
Low, Thomas I, 167
Low, Thomas I, 703
Low, Thomas I, 721
Low, Thomas I, 724
Low, Thomas I, 725
Low, Thomas I, 766
Low, Wd. Anne VI, 924
Low, Wd. Charlotte II, 807
Low, Widow Mary I, 132
Low, Widow Mary I, 145
Low, Widow Rebeckah I, 108
Low, William I, 101
Low, William I, 132
Low, William I, 145
Low, William I, 557
Low, William I, 703
Low, William I, 717
Low, William I, 725
Low, William V, 850
Low, William Forster I, 1158
Low, William Penn I, 703
Lowber, Patience II, 810
Lowden, Alice VI, 399
Lowden, Alice VI, 415
Lowden, John II, 391
Lowden, Joseph I, 991
Lowder, Ann I, 661
Lowder, Ann I, 684
Lowder, Ann I, 685
Lowder, Ann I, 966
Lowder, Betsey I, 991
Lowder, Caleb I, 661
Lowder, Caleb I, 684
Lowder, Caleb I, 685
Lowder, Caleb I, 966
Lowder, Charles I, 966
Lowder, Edeith I, 991
Lowder, Edith I, 991
Lowder, Elizabeth I, 991
Lowder, Hanah I, 991
Lowder, Hannah I, 991
Lowder, Hiram I, 991
Lowder, Jacob II, 391
Lowder, Job I, 966
Lowder, John I, 557
Lowder, John I, 684
Lowder, John I, 966
Lowder, Jonathan I, 991
Lowder, Joseph I, 966
Lowder, Joseph I, 991
Lowder, Joshua I, 966
Lowder, Mary I, 684
Lowder, Mary I, 685
Lowder, Mary II, 547
Lowder, Mary II, 586
Lowder, Matthew I, 661
Lowder, Matthew I, 885
Lowder, Matthew I, 891
Lowder, Matthew I, 966
Lowder, Meriam I, 991
Lowder, Nathan I, 966
Lowder, Phenias I, 991
Lowder, Ralph I, 966
Lowder, Ruth I, 885
Lowder, Ruth I, 891
Lowder, Sabithar I, 966
Lowder, Sally I, 991
Lowdër, Samuel I, 966
Lowder, Samuel I, 991
Lowder, Sarah I, 991
Lowder, Sarah I, 996
Lowder, Thomas I, 991
Lowder, William I, 966
Lowderback, Patience II, 85
Lowdermilk, Emsley I, 466

ermilk, Hannah I, 468
ermilk, Hannah I, 469
ermilk, Hannah I, 482
ermilk, Maary I, 466
ermilk, Marie I, 923
ermilk, Marie I, 930
ermilk, Mary I, 482
ermilk, Mary Jane I, 482
ermilk, Nancy A. I, 466
nes, Annie V, 94
nes, Miriam V, 94
lon, Elizabeth II, 586
lon, Esther II, 586
lon, Hugh II, 586
lon, John II, 391
lon, Robert II, 391
lon, Wd. Rachel II, 391
e, Agnes I, 931
e, Agnes I, 945
e, Agnes I, 947
e, Alice Ione I, 945
e, Ann I, 101
e, Barbara I, 926
e, Barneby I, 101
e, Billy I, 945
e, C. Fred I, 621
e, Carrie I, 945
e, Carrie Stanton I, 929
e, Cornelius V, 692
e, Effie O. VI, 76
e, Eleazar P. I, 703
e, Eliza VI, 76
e, Elizabeth I, 101
e, Elizabeth I, 923
e, Elizabeth II, 586
e, Elizabeth II, 665
e, Emanuel I, 101
e, Fany I, 461
e, Fred I, 637
e, Hannah I, 101
e, Hannah II, 391
e, Harriet IV, 1040
e, Harry C. VI, 76
e, Henry VI, 76
e, Hymen Fox I, 621
e, Ida III, 418
e, Ida III, 425
e, Isabel I, 621
e, J. S. I, 614
e, J. S. I, 621
e, James I, 891
e, James I, 929
e, James I, 931
e, James I. VI, 76
e, James J. VI, 76
e, Jennetta V, 692
e, John I, 621
e, John I, 764
e, John I, 766
e, John C. VI, 64
e, John C. VI, 76
ve, Julius R. I, 703
ve, Katharine I, 764
ve, Keziah I, 145
ve, Keziah I, 164
ve, Laura A. VI, 54
ve, Laura A. VI, 76
ve, Laura Winston I, 750
ve, Lena I, 929
ve, Lena I, 945
ve, Lilias I, 750
ve, Lillias I, 725
ve, Lillias M. I, 725
ve, Linwood VI, 76
ve, Lucy VI, 76
ve, Lulu Mason VI, 76
ve, Lulu Mason VI, 81
ve, Lulu Mason VI, 82
we, Luther VI, 76
we, Lydda I, 101
we, Mabel Allen I, 750
we, Mallory VI, 76
we, Margaret I, 725
we, Martha I, 891
we, Martha E. VI, 76
we, Mary I, 614
we, Mary I, 621
we, Mary A. VI, 518
we, Mary A. VI, 521
we, Mary A. VI, 528
we, Mary A. VI, 587
we, Mary A. VI, 754
we, Mary A. VI, 757
we, Mary Crater I, 614
we, Mary S. I, 725
we, Miriam I, 101
we, Miriel Marriage I, 750
we, Mollie I, 929
we, Mollie I, 931
we, Muriel I, 725
we, Oliver I, 891
Lowe, Ollin E. I, 945
Lowe, Paul S. VI, 76
Lowe, Rebecca I, 703
Lowe, Samuel I, 724
Lowe, Samuel I, 725
Lowe, Samuel H. I, 703
Lowe, Sarah J. VI, 64
Lowe, Sarah J. VI, 76
Lowe, Serilla I, 724
Lowe, Serilla I, 725
Lowe, Thomas I, 703
Lowe, Thomas I, 750
Lowe, Thomas J. VI, 76
Lowe, Virginia VI, 76
Lowe, William VI, 76
Lowe, William VI, 81
Lowe, William Brown I, 750
Lowe, William D. VI, 76
Lowe, William S. VI, 82
Lowe, Wm. VI, 54
Lowell, Anne L. III, 460
Lowell, Annie L. III, 425
Lowell, Charles Frances III, 425
Lowell, Charles P. III, 425
Lowell, Charles P. III, 460
Lowens, Ann II, 587
Lowens, Caleb II, 587
Lowens, Caleb, Jr. II, 587
Lowens, Edward II, 587
Lowens, Edward F. II, 587
Lowens, Ellen II, 587
Lowens, George II, 587
Lowens, Hannah P. II, 587
Lowens, John II, 587
Lowens, Miriam V, 94
Lower, Abraham II, 586
Lower, Beulah S. II, 1075
Lower, Esther II, 1076
Lower, George C. II, 893
Lower, Gertrude IV, 1284
Lower, Mary S. II, 892
Lower, Mary S. II, 893
Lower, Rebecca II, 586
Lower, Rev. O. O. IV, 1284
Lower, Susan, Jr. II, 1071
Lower, Susan, Jr. II, 1075
Lower, Susanna II, 586
Lower, Susannah II, 586
Lowerre, ??? III, 78
Lowerre, A. B. III, 389
Lowerre, Anna M. III, 276
Lowerre, Anna M. III, 331
Lowerre, Arthur H. III, 210
Lowerre, C. P. III, 389
Lowerre, Caroline III, 210
Lowerre, Daniel III, 382
Lowerre, Daniel III, 425
Lowerre, Eliz. S. III, 210
Lowerre, Eliza III, 210
Lowerre, Eliza III, 381
Lowerre, Eliza III, 382
Lowerre, Eliza L. III, 153
Lowerre, Eliza L. III, 210
Lowerre, Elizabeth III, 210
Lowerre, Elizabeth III, 382
Lowerre, Elizabeth III, 389
Lowerre, Elizabeth S. III, 210
Lowerre, Giles H. III, 382
Lowerre, Giles H. III, 389
Lowerre, John III, 382
Lowerre, John III, 389
Lowerre, Joseph III, 210
Lowerre, Josephine III, 210
Lowerre, Lewis III, 382
Lowerre, Lewis III, 389
Lowerre, Mary III, 153
Lowerre, Mary III, 210
Lowerre, Mary III, 381
Lowerre, Mary III, 382
Lowerre, Rachel III, 210
Lowerre, Rachel H. III, 78
Lowerre, Rachel H. III, 210
Lowerre, Sarah III, 210
Lowerre, Sarah W. III, 55
Lowerre, Sarah W. III, 210
Lowerre, Thomas III, 153
Lowerre, Thomas III, 210
Lowerre, Thomas III, 381
Lowerre, Thomas III, 382
Lowerre, Walter III, 210
Lowerre, Walter III, 382
Lowerre, William R. III, 55
Lowerre, William R. III, 210
Lowerre, William W. III, 210
Lowes, Adilla V, 692
Lowes, Cornelius V, 692
Lowes, Herbert V, 692
Lowes, Herbert V, 919
Lowes, Herbert A. V, 919
Lowes, James A. V, 919
Lowes, Jennetta V, 692
Lowes, Martha H. V, 582
Lowes, Martha H. V, 919
Lowes, Mary V, 692
Lowes, Mary V, 915
Lowes, Mary V, 919
Lowes, Rhoda V, 919
Lowman, Abel VI, 951
Lowman, Dorothy I, 145
Lowman, Elizabeth S. VI, 951
Lowman, Ellen V, 344
Lowman, Ellen V, 346
Lowman, Mary E. I, 945
Lowndes, ??? V, 94
Lowndes, Anna V, 94
Lowndes, Miriam V, 94
Lownds, Emor IV, 418
Lownds, Joseph IV, 418
Lowne, David II, 587
Lownes, ??? II, 391
Lownes, ??? V, 94
Lownes, Agnes II, 391
Lownes, Agnes II, 587
Lownes, Agnes II, 596
Lownes, Agness II, 586
Lownes, Alexandria VI, 196
Lownes, Ann II, 586
Lownes, Ann II, 587
Lownes, Ann II, 612
Lownes, Ann II, 639
Lownes, Ann VI, 197
Lownes, Anna V, 94
Lownes, Anna VI, 197
Lownes, Anne VI, 197
Lownes, Annie V, 94
Lownes, Benanuel II, 587
Lownes, Bethula II, 1012
Lownes, Beulah II, 1055
Lownes, Caleb II, 587
Lownes, Caleb VI, 415
Lownes, Caleb VI, 528
Lownes, Caleb VI, 529
Lownes, Caleb VI, 599
Lownes, Caleb, Jr. II, 587
Lownes, Charles II, 1012
Lownes, Charles IV, 241
Lownes, Charles IV, 418
Lownes, Chas. IV, 171
Lownes, Daniel II, 1012
Lownes, David II, 391
Lownes, David II, 587
Lownes, David II, 782
Lownes, David II, 837
Lownes, David II, 893
Lownes, Deborah II, 587
Lownes, Deborah VI, 196
Lownes, Deborah VI, 208
Lownes, Deborah VI, 415
Lownes, Deborah VI, 528
Lownes, Deborah VI, 529
Lownes, Deborah VI, 599
Lownes, Edmund II, 391
Lownes, Edward II, 391
Lownes, Edward II, 587
Lownes, Edward F. II, 587
Lownes, Edward F. II, 753
Lownes, Eleanor II, 391
Lownes, Elias Paxson II, 1055
Lownes, Eliza II, 1055
Lownes, Eliza W. II, 805
Lownes, Elizabeth II, 782
Lownes, Elizabeth II, 837
Lownes, Elizabeth II, 893
Lownes, Elizabeth II, 1055
Lownes, Elizabeth IV, 241
Lownes, Elizabeth IV, 418
Lownes, Elizabeth A. V, 94
Lownes, Elizabeth A. V, 116
Lownes, Elizabeth Jr. IV, 171
Lownes, Elizabeth Jr. IV, 241
Lownes, Ellen II, 587
Lownes, Elmira IV, 418
Lownes, Elmira V, 28
Lownes, Emmor IV, 418
Lownes, Esther II, 587
Lownes, Esther II, 596
Lownes, Esther II, 1055
Lownes, George II, 587
Lownes, Grace II, 587
Lownes, Hannah II, 391
Lownes, Hannah II, 451
Lownes, Hannah II, 586
Lownes, Hannah II, 612
Lownes, Hannah II, 638
Lownes, Hannah II, 1055
Lownes, Hannah Ann II, 391
Lownes, Hannah Ann II, 753
Lownes, Hannah P. II, 587
Lownes, Hugh II, 587
Lownes, Hugh M. II, 753
Lownes, Hyat VI, 415
Lownes, Hyat VI, 528
Lownes, Hyat VI, 529
Lownes, Hyatt II, 587
Lownes, Hyatt VI, 528
Lownes, Hyett VI, 599
Lownes, Isaac II, 650
Lownes, James II, 391
Lownes, James II, 586
Lownes, James II, 587
Lownes, James II, 612
Lownes, James II, 695
Lownes, James II, 978
Lownes, James II, 1012
Lownes, James VI, 196
Lownes, James VI, 197
Lownes, James VI, 218
Lownes, James VI, 415
Lownes, James VI, 528
Lownes, James VI, 529
Lownes, James VI, 541
Lownes, James VI, 599
Lownes, James VI, 762
Lownes, James, Jr. II, 391
Lownes, James, Jr. II, 586
Lownes, James, Jr. VI, 529
Lownes, James, Sr. VI, 529
Lownes, Jane III, 211
Lownes, Jane VI, 599
Lownes, Janes III, 211
Lownes, John II, 391
Lownes, John II, 586
Lownes, John II, 587
Lownes, John II, 596
Lownes, John VI, 415
Lownes, John VI, 528
Lownes, John VI, 529
Lownes, John VI, 599
Lownes, Joseph II, 391
Lownes, Joseph II, 515
Lownes, Joseph II, 581
Lownes, Joseph II, 586
Lownes, Joseph II, 587
Lownes, Joseph II, 596
Lownes, Joseph II, 612
Lownes, Joseph II, 638
Lownes, Joseph II, 649
Lownes, Joseph II, 668
Lownes, Joseph II, 964
Lownes, Joseph II, 978
Lownes, Joseph II, 995
Lownes, Joseph II, 1012
Lownes, Joseph II, 1055
Lownes, Joseph IV, 241
Lownes, Joseph IV, 418
Lownes, Joseph VI, 196
Lownes, Joseph VI, 529
Lownes, Joseph VI, 599
Lownes, Joseph, Jr. II, 391
Lownes, Joseph, Jr. II, 1055
Lownes, Josiah II, 1012
Lownes, Margaret II, 587
Lownes, Marianna II, 893
Lownes, Mary II, 457
Lownes, Mary II, 586
Lownes, Mary II, 587
Lownes, Mary II, 622
Lownes, Mary II, 782
Lownes, Mary II, 837
Lownes, Mary II, 893
Lownes, Mary II, 964
Lownes, Mary II, 1008
Lownes, Mary II, 1012
Lownes, Mary II, 1049
Lownes, Mary II, 1055
Lownes, Mary VI, 415
Lownes, Mary VI, 529
Lownes, Mary VI, 593
Lownes, Mary VI, 599
Lownes, Mercy II, 978
Lownes, Mercy II, 1012
Lownes, Mercy II, 1055
Lownes, Merriam II, 978
Lownes, Merriam II, 1012
Lownes, Miriam II, 1012
Lownes, Miriam IV, 241
Lownes, Miriam V, 94
Lownes, Rachel II, 391
Lownes, Rachel II, 995
Lownes, Rebecca II, 454
Lownes, Rebecca II, 515
Lownes, Rebecca II, 586
Lownes, Rebecca II, 587
Lownes, Rebecca II, 695
Lownes, Rebecca II, 978
Lownes, Rebecca II, 1012
Lownes, Rebecca II, 1055
Lownes, Rebecca IV, 241
Lownes, Rebecca V, 94
Lownes, Rebecca V, 141
Lownes, Ruth Anna II, 779
Lownes, Samuel II, 391
Lownes, Sarah II, 391
Lownes, Sarah II, 586
Lownes, Sarah II, 587
Lownes, Sarah II, 612
Lownes, Sarah II, 649
Lownes, Sarah II, 668
Lownes, Sarah II, 1012
Lownes, Sarah II, 1055
Lownes, Sarah VI, 415
Lownes, Sarah VI, 528
Lownes, Sarah VI, 529
Lownes, Sarah VI, 541
Lownes, Sarah VI, 545
Lownes, Sarah VI, 599
Lownes, Sarah Ann II, 964
Lownes, Sarah Ann II, 1055
Lownes, Sarah Burns II, 753
Lownes, Susan II, 1055
Lownes, Susanna II, 581
Lownes, Susanna II, 586
Lownes, Susanna, Jr. II, 586
Lownes, Susannah II, 391
Lownes, Susannah II, 1012
Lownes, Susannah II, 1030
Lownes, Thomas II, 1055
Lownes, Thomas Betts II, 1055
Lownes, Thomas Burns II, 391
Lownes, William VI, 196
Lownes, William VI, 197
Lownes, William VI, 529
Lownes, William VI, 762
Lownes, Wm. II, 515
Lownes, Wm. II, 586
Lownes, Wm. II, 587
Lownes, Wm. II, 978
Lownes, Wm. II, 995
Lownes, Wm. II, 1012
Lownes, Wm. VI, 529
Lownes, Wm., Jr. II, 1030
Lownes, Wm., Jr. II, 1055
Lownes, Zachariah II, 1012
Lowness, Daniel II, 1012
Lowness, James II, 1012
Lowness, Joseph II, 1012
Lowness, Mary II, 1012
Lowness, Merriam II, 1012
Lowness, Rebecca II, 1012
Lowness, Rebecca II, 1055
Lowness, Sarah II, 1012
Lowness, Susannah II, 1012
Lowness, Wm. II, 1012
Lowns, ??? IV, 418
Lowns, Caleb II, 587
Lowns, Charles IV, 341
Lowns, Charles IV, 418
Lowns, Chas. IV, 418
Lowns, Eliza IV, 418
Lowns, Elizabeth IV, 341
Lowns, Elizabeth IV, 418
Lowns, Elizabeth Ann V, 972
Lowns, Elmira IV, 418
Lowns, Emmor IV, 341
Lowns, Emmor IV, 418
Lowns, Emmor B. IV, 418
Lowns, Emor IV, 418
Lowns, Esther IV, 418
Lowns, Hyatt VI, 528
Lowns, James II, 391
Lowns, James II, 586
Lowns, Joseph IV, 341
Lowns, Joseph IV, 418
Lowns, Miriam V, 972
Lowns, Rachel II, 391
Lowns, Rebecca IV, 418
Lowns, Rebecca H. IV, 341
Lowns, Susanna II, 586
Lowns, Susannah II, 391
Lowns, Wm. V, 972
Lownsberry, Rebeccah II, 85
Lownsbury, Phebe III, 211
Lowramore, Mary II, 1011
Lowree, Daniel III, 425
Lowrey, Hannah II, 20
Lowrie, Ann II, 214
Lowry, Abigail VI, 951
Lowry, Albert M. VI, 888
Lowry, Alfred II, 711
Lowry, Alfred II, 753
Lowry, Ann I, 59
Lowry, Ann I, 145
Lowry, Ann B. VI, 976
Lowry, Anna II, 711
Lowry, Anna M. II, 711
Lowry, Anne B. II, 753
Lowry, Arthur T. II, 753
Lowry, Arthur Tilman II, 711
Lowry, Benjamin II, 711
Lowry, Benjamin H. II, 711
Lowry, Benjamin H. II, 753
Lowry, Charles S. II, 711
Lowry, Deborah II, 705
Lowry, Deborah H. II, 711

Lowry, Deborah H. II, 753
Lowry, Deborah H. II, 759
Lowry, Edward S. II, 705
Lowry, Edward S. II, 711
Lowry, Edward S. II, 753
Lowry, Edward S. II, 759
Lowry, Eizabeth S. II, 711
Lowry, Eleanor VI, 970
Lowry, Elizabeth II, 705
Lowry, Elizabeth VI, 951
Lowry, Elizabeth VI, 953
Lowry, Elizabeth B. II, 711
Lowry, Elizabeth C. II, 711
Lowry, Elizabeth C. II, 753
Lowry, Elizabeth C. II, 759
Lowry, Elizabeth Collins II, 711
Lowry, Elliott VI, 951
Lowry, Frances E. VI, 978
Lowry, Gainor II, 711
Lowry, Gowin II, 445
Lowry, Hannah I, 126
Lowry, Howard Lowry VI, 970
Lowry, Isaac II, 711
Lowry, Isaac S. II, 711
Lowry, Isaac S. II, 753
Lowry, John VI, 894
Lowry, John VI, 943
Lowry, John VI, 951
Lowry, John C. II, 711
Lowry, John C. II, 753
Lowry, John S. II, 711
Lowry, John S. II, 753
Lowry, John S. II, 759
Lowry, Joseph II, 779
Lowry, Levina VI, 951
Lowry, Lidia VI, 894
Lowry, Lydia II, 711
Lowry, Lydia C. II, 711
Lowry, Margaret II, 711
Lowry, Mary V, 898
Lowry, Mary VI, 951
Lowry, Mary B. II, 711
Lowry, Mary J. VI, 878
Lowry, Matilda C. VI, 951
Lowry, Mildred P. VI, 951
Lowry, Milton VI, 951
Lowry, Nancy VI, 951
Lowry, Nelson VI, 951
Lowry, Phebe II, 711
Lowry, Phebe P. II, 753
Lowry, Rebecca II, 779
Lowry, Rebecca B. II, 711
Lowry, Rebecca B. II, 753
Lowry, Richard VI, 878
Lowry, Robert P. II, 711
Lowry, Robert Pharo II, 753
Lowry, Sarah IV, 581
Lowry, Sarah IV, 586
Lowry, Sarah VI, 888
Lowry, Sarah VI, 951
Lowry, Sarah C. VI, 951
Lowry, Thomas II, 391
Lowry, Thomas VI, 918
Lowry, Thomas VI, 944
Lowry, Thomas VI, 951
Lowry, Triplett E. VI, 929
Lowry, Triplett E. VI, 951
Lowry, Triplett E. VI, 976
Lowry, Tripplett E. VI, 1018
Lowry, Wd. Mary II, 445
Lowry, William II, 391
Lowry, William VI, 911
Lowry, William VI, 951
Lowry, William VI, 967
Lowry, William VI, 970
Lowry, William VI, 978
Lowry, William, Jr. VI, 951
Lowry, Wm. Chalkley II, 711
Lowry, Wm., Sr. VI, 925
Lowth, Elizabeth II, 391
Lowther, Augustus II, 712
Lowther, Catharine II, 712
Lowther, Elizabeth II, 712
Lowther, Jefferson IV, 1171
Lowther, John II, 391
Lowther, Martha II, 391
Lowther, Martha II, 472
Lowther, Martha II, 587
Lowther, Sylvie IV, 1171
Lowthrop, Anastacia B. III, 426
Lowthrop, F. C. III, 469
Lowthrop, Fannie III, 469
Lowthrop, Fannie Amelia III, 426
Lowthrop, Fannie Amelia III, 468
Lowthrop, Francis C. III, 426
Lowthrop, Francis Cowlyn III, 426
Lowthrop, Francis Cowlyn III, 468
Loxley, Benjamin II, 391
Loxley, Benjamin II, 711
Loxley, Mary II, 711
Loxley, Richard II, 711
Loy, Elizabeth VI, 413
Loy, Elizabeth VI, 415
Loy, Gladys IV, 1326
Loy, John I, 405
Loy, Mildred IV, 1041
Loy, Mildred Mottishaw IV, 1040
Loyd, ??? II, 390
Loyd, Ann II, 389
Loyd, Ann IV, 233
Loyd, Ann IV, 241
Loyd, Anna I, 1124
Loyd, Anna Maria II, 295
Loyd, Anna Maria III, 211
Loyd, Benjamin, Jr. II, 1011
Loyd, Betsey VI, 1012
Loyd, Christina VI, 947
Loyd, Cicero I, 557
Loyd, David I, 557
Loyd, Deborah II, 389
Loyd, Deborah V, 186
Loyd, Eliza P. IV, 98
Loyd, Elizabeth II, 295
Loyd, Elizabeth II, 976
Loyd, Elizabeth III, 211
Loyd, Elizabeth VI, 848
Loyd, Elizabeth VI, 1003
Loyd, Fanny VI, 951
Loyd, Finetta VI, 951
Loyd, Hannah II, 504
Loyd, Hannah II, 583
Loyd, Hannah II, 1011
Loyd, Hannah III, 211
Loyd, Hannah VI, 415
Loyd, Henry VI, 354
Loyd, Henry VI, 936
Loyd, Henry VI, 951
Loyd, Henry VI, 960
Loyd, Henry VI, 964
Loyd, Henry VI, 994
Loyd, Henry VI, 1012
Loyd, Henry P. II, 891
Loyd, Isaac IV, 219
Loyd, Isaac IV, 241
Loyd, Isaac S. II, 295
Loyd, Isaac S. III, 211
Loyd, James II, 389
Loyd, Janetta VI, 890
Loyd, Jesse II, 1011
Loyd, Jesse IV, 241
Loyd, John II, 389
Loyd, John IV, 169
Loyd, John IV, 219
Loyd, John IV, 233
Loyd, John IV, 241
Loyd, John IV, 256
Loyd, John IV, 340
Loyd, John H. VI, 951
Loyd, Joseph II, 295
Loyd, Joseph III, 211
Loyd, Joshua IV, 241
Loyd, Joshua IV, 340
Loyd, Joshua IV, 341
Loyd, Joshua IV, 344
Loyd, Katy VI, 354
Loyd, Katy VI, 964
Loyd, Kennett VI, 415
Loyd, Levi VI, 886
Loyd, Levi VI, 947
Loyd, Levi VI, 951
Loyd, Levi VI, 953
Loyd, Levi VI, 1011
Loyd, Lloyd, Mercy IV, 341
Loyd, Lockey VI, 951
Loyd, Mahala VI, 1004
Loyd, Margaret IV, 169
Loyd, Margaret IV, 241
Loyd, Martha Ann VI, 960
Loyd, Mary II, 389
Loyd, Mary IV, 340
Loyd, Mary IV, 341
Loyd, Mary IV, 344
Loyd, Mary V, 918
Loyd, Mary VI, 832
Loyd, Mary Jane VI, 1011
Loyd, Mary S. VI, 951
Loyd, Mason VI, 951
Loyd, Mercy IV, 219
Loyd, Mercy IV, 233
Loyd, Mercy IV, 241
Loyd, Mercy IV, 256
Loyd, Mercy IV, 340
Loyd, Mordecai II, 389
Loyd, Mordecai II, 390
Loyd, Nancy VI, 951
Loyd, Patience III, 211
Loyd, Patty VI, 936
Loyd, Permelia VI, 951
Loyd, Rachel II, 583
Loyd, Rachel II, 626
Loyd, Rachel IV, 241
Loyd, Rachel IV, 256
Loyd, Rebecca S. III, 211
Loyd, Rebeckah I, 557
Loyd, Reese II, 389
Loyd, Ruth IV, 219
Loyd, Ruth IV, 241
Loyd, Sallie II, 284
Loyd, Samuel I, 557
Loyd, Samuel IV, 241
Loyd, Samuel S. V, 186
Loyd, Sarah II, 389
Loyd, Sarah VI, 994
Loyd, Sarah Ann VI, 953
Loyd, Sarah Frances VI, 951
Loyd, Silas R. VI, 951
Loyd, Sirena I, 557
Loyd, Squires Henry Levi VI, 994
Loyd, Susan II, 295
Loyd, Susan III, 211
Loyd, Susan IV, 219
Loyd, Susan IV, 241
Loyd, Susannah IV, 241
Loyd, Tempy VI, 951
Loyd, Thomas II, 504
Loyd, Thomas II, 583
Loyd, Thomas II, 626
Loyd, Thomas III, 211
Loyd, Tilman V, 186
Loyd, Washington VI, 951
Loyd, Wd. Patience II, 389
Loyd, William I, 557
Loyd, William IV, 241
Loyde, Martha II, 558
Loyde, Martha II, 583
Loyed, Cyrene I, 557
Loyner, Maria V, 831
Loyner, Maria V, 850
Loynsdall, Thomas II, 587
Lualen, Edith I, 724
Lualing, Jane I, 724
Luallin, John VI, 834
Luallin, Sarah L. VI, 834
Lubolt, Arthur E. VI, 679
Lubolt, Mabel Alice VI, 679
Luca, Elizabeth V, 346
Lucado, Lucy VI, 835
Lucado, Thomas VI, 835
Lucas, Ann II, 391
Lucas, Ann II, 961
Lucas, Ann II, 964
Lucas, Ann II, 1004
Lucas, Ann II, 1012
Lucas, Ann Eliza VI, 952
Lucas, Barbara V, 260
Lucas, Barbara V, 692
Lucas, Benjamin II, 964
Lucas, Bridget II, 965
Lucas, Bridget II, 1012
Lucas, Bridget II, 1025
Lucas, Bridgett II, 964
Lucas, Catharine V, 1007
Lucas, Dora V, 692
Lucas, Edith IV, 1257
Lucas, Edward II, 961
Lucas, Edward II, 964
Lucas, Edward II, 965
Lucas, Edward II, 1012
Lucas, Edward II, 1016
Lucas, Edward II, 1025
Lucas, Edward, Jr. II, 1012
Lucas, Elizabeth II, 240
Lucas, Elizabeth II, 257
Lucas, Elizabeth II, 587
Lucas, Elizabeth II, 624
Lucas, Elizabeth II, 964
Lucas, Elizabeth II, 965
Lucas, Elizabeth II, 1012
Lucas, Elizabeth II, 1016
Lucas, Elizabeth II, 1021
Lucas, Elizabeth II, 1025
Lucas, Elizabeth VI, 835
Lucas, Elizabeth VI, 956
Lucas, Ella V, 260
Lucas, Floy Hudson V, 460
Lucas, Frances L. VI, 952
Lucas, Gideon VI, 835
Lucas, Glen IV, 1215
Lucas, Grace II, 964
Lucas, Grace II, 1012
Lucas, Grace II, 1021
Lucas, Hannah II, 240
Lucas, Hannah II, 964
Lucas, Hannah II, 1012
Lucas, Hannah II, 1031
Lucas, Isabel II, 1000
Lucas, Isabel II, 1012
Lucas, Isabel II, 1018
Lucas, Jacob V, 260
Lucas, James VI, 835
Lucas, James VI, 853
Lucas, James VI, 956
Lucas, James Lamar V, 460
Lucas, Jane V, 260
Lucas, Jeane VI, 852
Lucas, Jesse IV, 1215
Lucas, Jessie IV, 1215
Lucas, John II, 964
Lucas, John II, 1000
Lucas, John II, 1012
Lucas, John VI, 952
Lucas, Joseph II, 1012
Lucas, Lucy R. VI, 835
Lucas, Mable II, 964
Lucas, Maggie May V, 260
Lucas, Mahlon II, 964
Lucas, Margaret II, 964
Lucas, Margaret II, 1012
Lucas, Margaret II, 1013
Lucas, Margaret V, 260
Lucas, Mary II, 964
Lucas, Mary II, 1012
Lucas, Mary II, 1013
Lucas, Mary V, 511
Lucas, Mary Elizabeth V, 850
Lucas, Maud V, 260
Lucas, Mercy II, 977
Lucas, Mercy II, 1012
Lucas, Mildred VI, 806
Lucas, Mildred VI, 825
Lucas, Milly VI, 835
Lucas, Minnie V, 260
Lucas, Minnie V, 692
Lucas, Molly VI, 795
Lucas, Nancy VI, 965
Lucas, Nathaniel II, 587
Lucas, Paul Hudson V, 460
Lucas, Presley VI, 965
Lucas, Rebeckah VI, 835
Lucas, Robert II, 240
Lucas, Robert II, 257
Lucas, Robert II, 964
Lucas, Robert II, 1004
Lucas, Robert II, 1012
Lucas, Robert II, 1025
Lucas, Robert II, 1031
Lucas, Robert VI, 952
Lucas, Robert, Jr. II, 240
Lucas, Ruth IV, 1215
Lucas, Ruth A. IV, 1215
Lucas, Sarah II, 964
Lucas, Sarah II, 1004
Lucas, Sarah II, 1012
Lucas, Sarah IV, 1257
Lucas, Sarah Catharine V, 460
Lucas, Sarah, Jr. II, 1012
Lucas, Sarah, Jr. II, 1028
Lucas, Wd. Bridget II, 964
Lucas, Wd. Sarah II, 1012
Lucas, William II, 391
Lucas, William VI, 835
Lucas, Winston H. VI, 956
Lucey, Esther VI, 556
Lucile, Flossie IV, 1324
Lucile, Isole IV, 1324
Luck, Alice V, 325
Luck, Alice V, 346
Luck, Amanda VI, 835
Luck, Catharine V, 325
Luck, Catharine V, 346
Luck, Charles V, 346
Luck, Charles M. V, 346
Luck, Chas. M. V, 325
Luck, David VI, 835
Luck, David VI, 841
Luck, Eliza W. VI, 952
Luck, Elizabeth I, 482
Luck, Elizabeth VI, 835
Luck, Frances A. VI, 835
Luck, George VI, 835
Luck, George P. VI, 952
Luck, George P. VI, 958
Luck, Lucreti E. VI, 895
Luck, Lucy J. VI, 841
Luck, Martin V, 325
Luck, Martin V, 346
Luck, Nancy VI, 952
Luck, Nath. VI, 841
Luck, Nathaniel VI, 895
Luck, Ransom I, 725
Luck, William VI, 835
Lucken, John II, 587
Luckens, Elizabeth VI, 777
Lucker, George IV, 1285
Lucoss, Hannah II, 224
Lucoss, Hannah II, 240
Lucoss, Robert II, 224
Lucoss, Robert II, 240
Lucoss, Susannah II, 224
Lucus, Mary V, 543
Luddington, Daniel V, 692
Luddington, Franklin V, 692
Luddington, George V, 692
Luddington, Harvey V, 692
Luddington, Henry L. V, 692
Luddington, Lewis V, 692
Luddington, Lydia V, 692
Ludgate, John II, 445
Ludgate, Mary II, 445
Ludington, David V, 582
Ludington, Hannah IV, 1372
Ludington, Harrison V, 582
Ludington, Lewis V, 582
Ludington, Lewis V, 692
Ludington, Lydia V, 692
Ludington, Mary V, 582
Ludington, Sarah V, 582
Ludington, Thomas V, 582
Ludlam, Anna II, 117
Ludlam, Anna II, 121
Ludlam, Elizabeth III, 211
Ludlam, Henry II, 823
Ludlam, Henry III, 211
Ludlam, Howland VI, 197
Ludlam, James III, 211
Ludlam, Lewis VI, 182
Ludlam, Lewis VI, 197
Ludlam, Mary II, 823
Ludlam, Sarah III, 211
Ludlam, Sarah W. III, 211
Ludlam, Wd. Hannah Smith II, 823
Ludlow, Anthony II, 391
Ludlow, Geneveive Sprigg II, 8
Ludlow, Genevieve Sprigg II, 8
Ludlow, Jane V, 715
Ludlum, ??? III, 287
Ludlum, Anna II, 121
Ludlum, Anna D. II, 121
Ludlum, Elizabeth III, 287
Ludlum, Sarah W. V, 902
Ludlum, Sarah W. V, 919
Ludlum, Wm. F. V, 692
Ludlum, Wm. T. V, 692
Luella, Elizabeth I, 736
Luella, Margaret I, 903
Luellen, Thos. Albert V, 632
Luellin, Susannah VI, 955
Lues, Estor II, 83
Luff, Elizabeth II, 391
Luff, Elizabeth III, 211
Luff, George III, 211
Luff, Harriet II, 798
Luff, Hue II, 391
Luff, James Neat II, 798
Luff, Rebecca III, 211
Luff, Sarah II, 391
Luffbury, ??? III, 211
Luffe, Edward II, 587
Luffe, Edward II, 653
Luffe, Elizabeth II, 587
Luffe, Elizabeth II, 653
Luffe, Jane II, 555
Luffe, Jane II, 587
Lufton, ??? IV, 137
Luick, Gordon IV, 1326
Luis, Jail II, 83
Luis, Jail II, 86
Luke, Faithful VI, 835
Luke, Jacob II, 587
Luke, John II, 587
Luke, Leoney VI, 835
Luke, Richard II, 445
Luken, Elizabeth V, 117
Luken, Jane II, 391
Luken, Jane IV, 1278
Luken, Jane IV, 1285
Luken, Jane F. IV, 1285
Luken, John II, 391
Luken, Levi V, 117
Luken, Mary II, 391
Luken, Rhoda VI, 952
Luken, Samuel V, 117
Luken, Sarah II, 391
Luken, Sarah Ann V, 117
Luken, William J. VI, 952
Lukens, ??? II, 391
Lukens, ??? IV, 242
Lukens, A. Amos Lewis VI, 762
Lukens, Aaron II, 893
Lukens, Aaron II, 923
Lukens, Abigail II, 587
Lukens, Adele C. II, 807
Lukens, Adele E. II, 893
Lukens, Agnes II, 587
Lukens, Agnes L. II, 748
Lukens, Agnes L. II, 753
Lukens, Alan R. II, 831
Lukens, Alan R. II, 893
Lukens, Alice IV, 484
Lukens, Alice Mullin II, 807
Lukens, Alice P. II, 893
Lukens, Amanda Jane VI, 1001

ens, Amos II, 807
ens, Amos II, 893
ens, Amos II, 929
ens, Amos Lewis VI, 738
ens, Amos Lewis VI, 762
ens, Ann II, 587
ens, Ann II, 804
ens, Ann II, 893
ens, Ann II, 916
ens, Ann IV, 240
ens, Ann IV, 242
ens, Ann B. IV, 242
ens, Ann E. IV, 143
ens, Ann E. IV, 311
ens, Ann E. IV, 313
ens, Ann W. II, 240
ens, Ann W. II, 887
ens, Ann W. II, 893
ens, Anna III, 211
ens, Anna IV, 484
ens, Anna VI, 729
ens, Anna VI, 759
ens, Anna VI, 762
ens, Anna B. IV, 539
ens, Anna E. IV, 152
ens, Anna Jane II, 807
ens, Anna M. II, 893
ens, Anna M. II, 905
ens, Anna M. II, 923
ens, Anna M. J. IV, 243
ens, Anna N. VI, 762
ens, Annie M. II, 893
ens, Annie May II, 807
ens, Arthur Lewis II, 807
ens, Azor II, 85
ens, Barclay Walton II, 807
ens, Benjamin IV, 242
ens, Benjamin IV, 484
ens, Benjamin V, 94
ens, Benjamin V, 117
ens, Benjamin VI, 415
ens, Benjamin VI, 673
ens, Benjamin C. IV, 1171
ens, Bessie Carroll II, 807
ens, Bonnie Edward V, 692
ens, Bulah VI, 415
ens, Bulah VI, 428
ens, Caroline A. II, 926
ens, Carrie A. II, 893
ens, Catharine D. II, 893
ens, Catherine III, 211
ens, Charles II, 587
ens, Charles E. V, 94
ens, Charles Teas VI, 762
ens, Charles Teas VI, 791
ens, Charles W. IV, 242
ens, Chas. II, 587
ens, Chas. K. II, 893
ens, Chas. Kirk II, 807
ens, Chas. Wm. IV, 243
ens, Clarence E. II, 807
ens, Clayton V, 94
ens, Courtland VI, 729
ens, Courtland VI, 762
ens, David II, 240
ens, David II, 276
ens, David II, 807
ens, David II, 893
ens, David II, 1076
ens, David II, 1078
ens, David VI, 763
ens, David VI, 787
ens, David L. II, 893
ens, Deborah II, 587
ens, Deborah II, 588
ens, Deborah IV, 230
ens, Deborah IV, 242
ens, Deborah J. IV, 243
ens, Dr. ??? II, 135
ens, Dr. Israel III, 211
ens, Dr. Israel III, 330
ens, Edith II, 459
ens, Edith II, 587
ens, Edith II, 807
ens, Edith II, 893
ens, Edith Greene V, 411
ens, Edith L. VI, 738
ens, Edith L. VI, 762
ens, Edward II, 753
kens, Edward H. II, 807
kens, Edward H. II, 893
kens, Edward H. II, 944
kens, Edward M. V, 94
kens, Edward S. II, 807
kens, Elcy V, 94
kens, Elcy H. A. V, 146
kens, Eleanor Lee II, 893
kens, Eleanor Lee II, 925
kens, Eliza II, 240
kens, Eliza II, 276
kens, Eliza II, 814
Lukens, Eliza II, 1078
Lukens, Eliza W. II, 240
Lukens, Eliza W. II, 1076
Lukens, Elizabeth II, 240
Lukens, Elizabeth II, 587
Lukens, Elizabeth II, 675
Lukens, Elizabeth II, 753
Lukens, Elizabeth II, 804
Lukens, Elizabeth II, 807
Lukens, Elizabeth II, 814
Lukens, Elizabeth II, 821
Lukens, Elizabeth II, 893
Lukens, Elizabeth IV, 173
Lukens, Elizabeth IV, 230
Lukens, Elizabeth IV, 242
Lukens, Elizabeth IV, 539
Lukens, Elizabeth IV, 891
Lukens, Elizabeth IV, 893
Lukens, Elizabeth V, 69
Lukens, Elizabeth V, 94
Lukens, Elizabeth V, 511
Lukens, Elizabeth VI, 377
Lukens, Elizabeth VI, 415
Lukens, Elizabeth VI, 599
Lukens, Elizabeth VI, 631
Lukens, Elizabeth VI, 673
Lukens, Elizabeth VI, 762
Lukens, Elizabeth VI, 773
Lukens, Elizabeth VI, 777
Lukens, Elizabeth VI, 778
Lukens, Elizabeth VI, 788
Lukens, Elizabeth A. II, 893
Lukens, Elizabeth D. IV, 242
Lukens, Elizabeth D. IV, 243
Lukens, Elizabeth E. II, 893
Lukens, Elizabeth E. II, 929
Lukens, Elizabeth Evans II, 807
Lukens, Elizabeth H. II, 311
Lukens, Elizabeth J. II, 893
Lukens, Elizabeth J. II, 925
Lukens, Elizabeth S. VI, 734
Lukens, Ellen II, 816
Lukens, Ellen VI, 762
Lukens, Ellen T. II, 807
Lukens, Elsie II, 807
Lukens, Emma III, 211
Lukens, Emma L. III, 145
Lukens, Emma L. III, 211
Lukens, Ephraim C. II, 893
Lukens, Ephraim C. II, 905
Lukens, Ephraim C. VI, 762
Lukens, Esther Ann IV, 816
Lukens, Esther Ann IV, 831
Lukens, Eugenia II, 311
Lukens, Ezra II, 893
Lukens, Ezra II, 895
Lukens, Florence M. II, 883
Lukens, Florence M. II, 893
Lukens, Florence May II, 807
Lukens, Gainer II, 587
Lukens, Gainor II, 587
Lukens, Gertrude II, 807
Lukens, Gilbert Ely II, 807
Lukens, Granville W. II, 240
Lukens, Granville W. II, 1076
Lukens, Granville W. II, 1078
Lukens, H. Reeves II, 831
Lukens, Hannah II, 240
Lukens, Hannah IV, 242
Lukens, Hannah IV, 484
Lukens, Hannah IV, 891
Lukens, Hannah IV, 893
Lukens, Hannah IV, 1171
Lukens, Hannah IV, 1172
Lukens, Hannah V, 94
Lukens, Hannah VI, 415
Lukens, Hannah VI, 451
Lukens, Harriet II, 792
Lukens, Harriet III, 327
Lukens, Harriet IV, 242
Lukens, Harriet IV, 243
Lukens, Harriet E. IV, 243
Lukens, Harriet E. IV, 246
Lukens, Harriet Elizabeth IV, 242
Lukens, Harriet L. III, 211
Lukens, Harriet L. III, 330
Lukens, Hattie V, 94
Lukens, Helen II, 807
Lukens, Henry II, 807
Lukens, Henry H. II, 311
Lukens, Henry Reeves II, 893
Lukens, Herman T. II, 807
Lukens, Herman T. II, 893
Lukens, Herman T. II, 925
Lukens, Howard A. II, 807
Lukens, Howard J. II, 883
Lukens, Howard J. II, 893
Lukens, Howard Jones II, 807
Lukens, Israel III, 211
Lukens, Israel L. III, 145
Lukens, J. Atley II, 893
Lukens, J. S. II, 893
Lukens, Jacob II, 807
Lukens, Jacob IV, 484
Lukens, James II, 391
Lukens, James II, 587
Lukens, James II, 893
Lukens, James II, 925
Lukens, James Cope IV, 152
Lukens, James T. II, 893
Lukens, James Tyson II, 807
Lukens, Jane II, 391
Lukens, Jane II, 893
Lukens, Jane F. V, 94
Lukens, Jane W. II, 807
Lukens, Jary Jane II, 893
Lukens, Jesse II, 587
Lukens, Jesse II, 893
Lukens, Jesse VI, 415
Lukens, Jessie V, 692
Lukens, Jessie M. II, 807
Lukens, John II, 391
Lukens, John II, 587
Lukens, John IV, 484
Lukens, John V, 94
Lukens, John VI, 415
Lukens, John VI, 631
Lukens, John VI, 673
Lukens, John Atley II, 807
Lukens, John S. V, 94
Lukens, Johnson II, 391
Lukens, Jonathan VI, 415
Lukens, Jonathan VI, 595
Lukens, Jonathan VI, 599
Lukens, Joseph II, 804
Lukens, Joseph II, 893
Lukens, Joseph IV, 1172
Lukens, Joseph V, 94
Lukens, Joseph V, 511
Lukens, Joseph VI, 415
Lukens, Joseph VI, 673
Lukens, Judah II, 391
Lukens, Judah II, 587
Lukens, Judith J. IV, 242
Lukens, Judith J. IV, 243
Lukens, Latitia II, 1055
Lukens, Latitia II, 1058
Lukens, Lemuel IV, 242
Lukens, Lemuel IV, 539
Lukens, Letitia W. II, 1076
Lukens, Letitia W. II, 1078
Lukens, Levi V, 69
Lukens, Levi V, 94
Lukens, Levi VI, 377
Lukens, Levi VI, 415
Lukens, Levi VI, 599
Lukens, Levi VI, 631
Lukens, Levi VI, 673
Lukens, Lewis V, 94
Lukens, Louisa II, 807
Lukens, Louisa II, 831
Lukens, Louisa II, 893
Lukens, Louisa V, 94
Lukens, Louisa V, 955
Lukens, Louisa A. II, 893
Lukens, Lucy C. VI, 762
Lukens, Lucy C. VI, 791
Lukens, Lydia II, 799
Lukens, Lydia II, 893
Lukens, Lydia IV, 341
Lukens, Lydia IV, 484
Lukens, Lydia IV, 1172
Lukens, Lydia VI, 415
Lukens, Lydia VI, 595
Lukens, Lydia VI, 599
Lukens, Margaret IV, 539
Lukens, Margaret Anna II, 820
Lukens, Margaret Anna II, 893
Lukens, Margaret Anna II, 923
Lukens, Maria II, 753
Lukens, Maria II, 819
Lukens, Maria F. II, 893
Lukens, Maria L. II, 741
Lukens, Maria L. II, 753
Lukens, Marion II, 807
Lukens, Martha II, 699
Lukens, Martha II, 893
Lukens, Martha IV, 242
Lukens, Martha VI, 415
Lukens, Martha VI, 599
Lukens, Martha Elizabeth IV, 1172
Lukens, Martha Elizabeth VI, 415
Lukens, Martha L. IV, 243
Lukens, Martha L. IV, 309
Lukens, Martha S. IV, 242
Lukens, Mary II, 391
Lukens, Mary II, 796
Lukens, Mary II, 825
Lukens, Mary IV, 242
Lukens, Mary IV, 311
Lukens, Mary IV, 313
Lukens, Mary IV, 484
Lukens, Mary IV, 893
Lukens, Mary V, 64
Lukens, Mary V, 94
Lukens, Mary V, 117
Lukens, Mary VI, 729
Lukens, Mary VI, 762
Lukens, Mary VI, 763
Lukens, Mary VI, 787
Lukens, Mary Ann IV, 1172
Lukens, Mary Ann VI, 415
Lukens, Mary B. II, 831
Lukens, Mary C. II, 893
Lukens, Mary C. IV, 242
Lukens, Mary E. IV, 243
Lukens, Mary E. IV, 253
Lukens, Mary Edna IV, 243
Lukens, Mary Ellen IV, 242
Lukens, Mary Emily V, 94
Lukens, Mary Emma V, 94
Lukens, Mary Hurley II, 893
Lukens, Mary Hurley II, 905
Lukens, Mary J. II, 807
Lukens, Mary Jane II, 944
Lukens, Mary L. V, 64
Lukens, Mary L. V, 94
Lukens, Mary P. II, 893
Lukens, Mary S. V, 94
Lukens, Mary T. VI, 762
Lukens, Massy II, 587
Lukens, Mathia II, 535
Lukens, Mathias II, 391
Lukens, Mathias II, 587
Lukens, Mercy II, 535
Lukens, Mercy II, 587
Lukens, Merican IV, 484
Lukens, Merrican IV, 484
Lukens, Miriam V, 511
Lukens, Moses IV, 173
Lukens, Moses IV, 230
Lukens, Moses IV, 242
Lukens, Moses IV, 341
Lukens, Moses IV, 484
Lukens, Moses, Jr. IV, 242
Lukens, Nancy Emily VI, 762
Lukens, Nellie II, 893
Lukens, Pennel IV, 242
Lukens, Peter II, 391
Lukens, Peter II, 587
Lukens, Peter II, 814
Lukens, Peter IV, 1171
Lukens, Peter IV, 1172
Lukens, Peter VI, 415
Lukens, Peter VI, 451
Lukens, Peter VI, 599
Lukens, Phebe II, 807
Lukens, Phebe II, 893
Lukens, Phebe IV, 242
Lukens, Phebe IV, 484
Lukens, Phebe VI, 603
Lukens, Phebe M. II, 893
Lukens, Phebe S. II, 807
Lukens, Priscilla II, 711
Lukens, Priscilla Ann II, 295
Lukens, Priscilla Ann II, 753
Lukens, Rachel II, 391
Lukens, Rachel II, 893
Lukens, Rachel IV, 191
Lukens, Rachel IV, 242
Lukens, Rachel IV, 341
Lukens, Rachel IV, 484
Lukens, Rachel IV, 539
Lukens, Rachel V, 69
Lukens, Rachel V, 94
Lukens, Rachel VI, 415
Lukens, Rachel VI, 442
Lukens, Rachel VI, 673
Lukens, Rachel VI, 763
Lukens, Rachel VI, 787
Lukens, Rebecca II, 814
Lukens, Rebecca IV, 484
Lukens, Reuben II, 807
Lukens, Reuben III, 211
Lukens, Ruth IV, 484
Lukens, Ruth Ann II, 587
Lukens, Ruth Ann II, 753
Lukens, Ruth Ann II, 893
Lukens, Ruth Ann II, 916
Lukens, Salathiel V, 94
Lukens, Salathiel V, 955
Lukens, Salathiel VI, 415
Lukens, Salathiel VI, 673
Lukens, Samuel IV, 891
Lukens, Samuel B. IV, 230
Lukens, Samuel B. IV, 242
Lukens, Samuel B. IV, 243
Lukens, Samuel B. IV, 539
Lukens, Samuel C. II, 893
Lukens, Samuel Conrad II, 807
Lukens, Samuel Conrad, Jr. II, 807
Lukens, Sara V, 692
Lukens, Sarah II, 240
Lukens, Sarah II, 276
Lukens, Sarah II, 295
Lukens, Sarah II, 391
Lukens, Sarah II, 587
Lukens, Sarah II, 807
Lukens, Sarah II, 893
Lukens, Sarah II, 929
Lukens, Sarah III, 211
Lukens, Sarah IV, 242
Lukens, Sarah IV, 341
Lukens, Sarah IV, 484
Lukens, Sarah IV, 539
Lukens, Sarah V, 94
Lukens, Sarah Ann II, 814
Lukens, Sarah Eleanor VI, 762
Lukens, Sarah H. II, 893
Lukens, Sarah Harper II, 807
Lukens, Sarah L. V, 94
Lukens, Sarah Snowden V, 511
Lukens, Sarah T. IV, 230
Lukens, Sarah T. IV, 242
Lukens, Sarah, Jr. IV, 242
Lukens, Solomon II, 946
Lukens, Solomon II, 1086
Lukens, Susan II, 135
Lukens, Susan II, 153
Lukens, Susan II, 861
Lukens, Susan II, 940
Lukens, Susan II, 946
Lukens, Susan III, 211
Lukens, Susan IV, 893
Lukens, Susan J. III, 145
Lukens, Susan J. III, 211
Lukens, Susan J. III, 312
Lukens, Susan J. III, 330
Lukens, Susan J. IV, 243
Lukens, Susan J. V, 511
Lukens, Susan J. C. IV, 242
Lukens, Tace IV, 484
Lukens, Tacy II, 578
Lukens, Tacy II, 587
Lukens, Tacy V, 94
Lukens, Thomas Chalkley II, 587
Lukens, Violetta II, 587
Lukens, Violetta II, 624
Lukens, Walter Lee II, 807
Lukens, Wd. Catharine Davis II, 807
Lukens, Wd. Elizabeth II, 807
Lukens, Wd. Emma L. III, 145
Lukens, William II, 807
Lukens, William IV, 242
Lukens, William IV, 243
Lukens, William IV, 484
Lukens, William V, 94
Lukens, William VI, 415
Lukens, William B. VI, 763
Lukens, William E. IV, 242
Lukens, William E. IV, 243
Lukens, William Ellis IV, 242
Lukens, Wm. II, 807
Lukens, Wm. II, 893
Lukens, Wm. IV, 1172
Lukens, Wm. Brisco II, 905
Lukens, Wm. Courtland VI, 762
Luker, Amy E. V, 260
Luker, David V, 260
Luker, Enoch V, 260
Luker, George V, 260
Luker, George W. V, 260
Luker, Mary Ann V, 260
Luker, Thomas W. V, 260
Luker, William V, 260
Lukin, Cyrus II, 807
Lukin, Edith II, 807
Lukin, Esther II, 807
Lukin, Ezra II, 807
Lukin, George II, 807
Lukin, Mary J. VI, 891
Lukin, Sarah E. VI, 942
Lukin, William J. VI, 891
Lukin, Wm. VI, 942
Lukins, Alice V, 682
Lukins, Alice V, 692
Lukins, Azor II, 85
Lukins, Benjamin IV, 242
Lukins, Bonnie V, 670
Lukins, Bonnie V, 692
Lukins, Bonnie Edward V, 692
Lukins, Carl V, 692
Lukins, Clayton V, 94
Lukins, David II, 240
Lukins, Edith II, 587
Lukins, Eliza W. II, 240
Lukins, Elizabeth V, 94
Lukins, Elizabeth V, 692
Lukins, Granville W. II, 240

Lukins, Hannah II, 240
Lukins, Hannah IV, 238
Lukins, Hannah IV, 242
Lukins, Hannah V, 94
Lukins, Harold V, 692
Lukins, Harold V, 708
Lukins, Hattie V, 94
Lukins, Hattie V, 692
Lukins, Helen V, 692
Lukins, Helen V, 720
Lukins, Henry II, 445
Lukins, Jane II, 391
Lukins, Jane II, 522
Lukins, Jane II, 587
Lukins, Jessie V, 678
Lukins, Jessie V, 692
Lukins, John II, 391
Lukins, John V, 186
Lukins, Joseph V, 94
Lukins, Levi V, 94
Lukins, Louisa V, 94
Lukins, Luther V, 670
Lukins, Luther V, 692
Lukins, Mabel V, 692
Lukins, Margaret IV, 519
Lukins, Margaret IV, 539
Lukins, Mary V, 94
Lukins, Mary Ann IV, 1172
Lukins, Mary Ann IV, 1178
Lukins, Mary E. V, 692
Lukins, Mary Emma V, 186
Lukins, Mary Emma V, 692
Lukins, Mary S. V, 94
Lukins, Miriam V, 511
Lukins, Moses IV, 238
Lukins, Moses IV, 242
Lukins, Nellie V, 692
Lukins, Peter II, 391
Lukins, Phebe IV, 242
Lukins, Rachel IV, 242
Lukins, Rachel V, 692
Lukins, Rebecca IV, 484
Lukins, Rebecca IV, 497
Lukins, Robert Carl V, 692
Lukins, Sara V, 692
Lukins, Sarah II, 240
Lukins, Sarah IV, 238
Lukins, Sarah V, 692
Lukins, Sarah L. V, 69
Lukins, Sarah L. V, 94
Lukins, Sarah Virginia V, 692
Lukins, Tacy V, 65
Lukins, Tacy V, 94
Lukins, Violet V, 692
Lukins, Violet V, 708
Lukins, William IV, 243
Lukins, William V, 94
Lukkens, Mary IV, 313
Lum, Mary VI, 482
Lum, Mary VI, 529
Luman, Dorothea III, 301
Luman, Sarah Ann IV, 152
Luman, Sarah Ann IV, 163
Lumbart, Hazel IV, 1172
Lumbert, Hazel IV, 1172
Lumbey, Addie I, 927
Lumbling, Nancy V, 1007
Lumbling, Obediah V, 1007
Lumbling, Wm. M. V, 1007
Lume, John II, 445
Lumkin, Milly VI, 952
Lumkin, Robert W. VI, 1021
Lumkin, Thomas Moore VI, 952
Lumm, Jane IV, 876
Lumm, Jane IV, 884
Lummas, Henry II, 85
Lummis, Grace II, 85
Lummis, Grace II, 90
Lummis, Henry II, 85
Lummis, Henry II, 90
Lumpkin, Albert J. V, 186
Lumpkin, Amy B. V, 186
Lumpkin, Ann VI, 952
Lumpkin, Ann Mariah VI, 1004
Lumpkin, Audrey III, 426
Lumpkin, Clementina VI, 1012
Lumpkin, Edward R. V, 186
Lumpkin, Elener T. V, 186
Lumpkin, Elizabeth VI, 956
Lumpkin, Elvira F. VI, 944
Lumpkin, Harry III, 426
Lumpkin, Ida R. V, 186
Lumpkin, Laurence L. V, 186
Lumpkin, Lucy VI, 952
Lumpkin, Mabel T. V, 186
Lumpkin, Martha VI, 912
Lumpkin, Martha E. VI, 938
Lumpkin, Maude R. III, 426
Lumpkin, Milly VI, 952
Lumpkin, Robert W. VI, 938
Lumpkin, Robert W. VI, 944
Lumpkin, Robert W. VI, 1004
Lumpkin, Russell M. V, 186
Lumpkin, Sophia VI, 885
Lumpkin, Thomas VI, 885
Lumpkin, Thomas VI, 952
Lumpkin, Thomas VI, 956
Lumpkin, Thomas VI, 1012
Lumpkin, Thomas Moore VI, 952
Lumpkin, Thomas W. VI, 875
Lumpkin, W. H. V, 186
Lumpkin, Wm. H. V, 186
Luna, Robert VI, 357
Lunbeck, Elizabeth V, 949
Lunbeck, Elizabeth V, 955
Lunda, Priscilla I, 960
Lunda, Priscilla I, 966
Lunda, Susannah V, 260
Lunday, James V, 810
Lunday, Sophia V, 810
Lundey, Rhoda I, 985
Lundey, Rhoda I, 992
Lundford, Merryman VI, 877
Lundy, Aaron IV, 1285
Lundy, Aaron V, 306
Lundy, Aaron V, 411
Lundy, Aaron V, 493
Lundy, Aaron V, 511
Lundy, Aaron V, 512
Lundy, Aaron B. V, 512
Lundy, Abagail V, 512
Lundy, Abigail II, 240
Lundy, Abigail II, 295
Lundy, Abigail II, 311
Lundy, Abigail II, 322
Lundy, Abigail II, 327
Lundy, Abigail V, 493
Lundy, Abigail V, 512
Lundy, Abner IV, 1285
Lundy, Alice V, 512
Lundy, Amos I, 824
Lundy, Amos I, 825
Lundy, Amos I, 966
Lundy, Amos I, 1011
Lundy, Amos IV, 418
Lundy, Amos V, 260
Lundy, Amos V, 390
Lundy, Amos V, 511
Lundy, Amos V, 512
Lundy, Amos, Jr. IV, 152
Lundy, Amy V, 512
Lundy, Ann I, 825
Lundy, Ann I, 966
Lundy, Ann I, 1011
Lundy, Ann V, 260
Lundy, Ann V, 512
Lundy, Ann E. II, 311
Lundy, Anna V, 511
Lundy, Anna V, 582
Lundy, Anna E. II, 311
Lundy, Anne V, 260
Lundy, Asenath V, 512
Lundy, Asenith V, 511
Lundy, Asenith V, 512
Lundy, Asenith V, 520
Lundy, Asenith V, 582
Lundy, Azariah I, 1006
Lundy, Benjamin II, 311
Lundy, Benjamin II, 781
Lundy, Benjamin IV, 152
Lundy, Benjamin IV, 238
Lundy, Benjamin IV, 243
Lundy, Benjamin IV, 341
Lundy, Calvin V, 512
Lundy, Calvin J. V, 512
Lundy, Charles II, 311
Lundy, Charles II, 322
Lundy, Charles III, 211
Lundy, Charles L. IV, 243
Lundy, Charles T. II, 295
Lundy, Charles T. II, 322
Lundy, Charles T. IV, 341
Lundy, Charles Talmadge II, 311
Lundy, Charlotte V, 493
Lundy, Charlotte V, 511
Lundy, Charlotte V, 512
Lundy, Chas. T. I, 1095
Lundy, Chas. T. II, 240
Lundy, Christian II, 982
Lundy, Christian Brown II, 1013
Lundy, Cyrus V, 511
Lundy, Cyrus V, 1007
Lundy, Daniel I, 825
Lundy, David I, 991
Lundy, David I, 992
Lundy, Deborah II, 240
Lundy, Deborah II, 295
Lundy, Deborah II, 311
Lundy, Deborah II, 322
Lundy, Demcy V, 512
Lundy, Dempsey V, 411
Lundy, Dempsey V, 511
Lundy, Dempsey V, 512
Lundy, Ebanezar I, 824
Lundy, Ebanezar I, 966
Lundy, Ebenezer II, 976
Lundy, Ebenezer II, 982
Lundy, Ebenezer II, 1012
Lundy, Ebenezer II, 1013
Lundy, Ebenezer III, 211
Lundy, Edith M. II, 311
Lundy, Edith M. II, 322
Lundy, Edith M. II, 327
Lundy, Eleazer II, 1013
Lundy, Eleazer III, 211
Lundy, Eleazor II, 1012
Lundy, Eli V, 260
Lundy, Elijah I, 825
Lundy, Elijah I, 966
Lundy, Elijah I, 991
Lundy, Eliza A. V, 562
Lundy, Eliza A. V, 582
Lundy, Eliza Ann V, 582
Lundy, Eliza S. II, 322
Lundy, Elizabeth I, 825
Lundy, Elizabeth I, 965
Lundy, Elizabeth I, 966
Lundy, Elizabeth I, 991
Lundy, Elizabeth I, 1006
Lundy, Elizabeth I, 1008
Lundy, Elizabeth I, 1011
Lundy, Elizabeth II, 240
Lundy, Elizabeth II, 295
Lundy, Elizabeth II, 311
Lundy, Elizabeth II, 1013
Lundy, Elizabeth III, 211
Lundy, Elizabeth III, 224
Lundy, Elizabeth IV, 243
Lundy, Elizabeth IV, 1285
Lundy, Elizabeth V, 260
Lundy, Elizabeth V, 481
Lundy, Elizabeth V, 511
Lundy, Elizabeth V, 512
Lundy, Elizabeth V, 521
Lundy, Elizabeth V, 582
Lundy, Elizabeth V, 701
Lundy, Elizabeth C. IV, 1285
Lundy, Elizabeth S. II, 240
Lundy, Elizabeth S. II, 322
Lundy, Elizabeth S. IV, 243
Lundy, Elizabeth S. IV, 341
Lundy, Elizabeth Shotwell II, 311
Lundy, Elizabeth, Jr. V, 378
Lundy, Elizabeth, Jr. V, 411
Lundy, Ellen II, 311
Lundy, Ellen II, 322
Lundy, Emma IV, 1285
Lundy, Enoch V, 260
Lundy, Enoch V, 493
Lundy, Enoch V, 511
Lundy, Enoch V, 512
Lundy, Enoch V, 582
Lundy, Enoch William V, 260
Lundy, Esther I, 1095
Lundy, Esther II, 311
Lundy, Esther II, 984
Lundy, Esther II, 1012
Lundy, Esther IV, 238
Lundy, Esther IV, 243
Lundy, Esther IV, 341
Lundy, Ezekiel I, 825
Lundy, Ezekiel I, 966
Lundy, Ezekiel I, 991
Lundy, Ezekiel I, 992
Lundy, Ezrah V, 512
Lundy, Frank V, 512
Lundy, Franklin V, 512
Lundy, George W. II, 311
Lundy, George W. II, 322
Lundy, Hannah II, 976
Lundy, Hannah II, 984
Lundy, Hannah II, 1013
Lundy, Hannah III, 211
Lundy, Hannah IV, 1285
Lundy, Hannah Bard II, 1012
Lundy, Hannah M. II, 311
Lundy, Henry IV, 1285
Lundy, Henry Irving V, 512
Lundy, Henry Irwin V, 512
Lundy, Honey Creek V, 512
Lundy, Horace E. V, 512
Lundy, Howard II, 311
Lundy, Howard II, 322
Lundy, Hulda V, 512
Lundy, Hulda V, 529
Lundy, Huldah IV, 1285
Lundy, Huldah V, 512
Lundy, Isaac I, 825
Lundy, Isaac I, 966
Lundy, Isham VI, 942
Lundy, Israel V, 512
Lundy, Israel V, 582
Lundy, J. Wilmer II, 322
Lundy, Jacob II, 784
Lundy, James I, 825
Lundy, James I, 966
Lundy, James I, 1011
Lundy, James IV, 1285
Lundy, James V, 260
Lundy, James V, 502
Lundy, James V, 511
Lundy, James V, 512
Lundy, James V, 527
Lundy, James V, 582
Lundy, Jeams I, 965
Lundy, Jeams I, 966
Lundy, Jemima I, 825
Lundy, Jemima I, 966
Lundy, Jemima I, 1009
Lundy, Jemima I, 1011
Lundy, Jesse V, 260
Lundy, Jesse V, 493
Lundy, Jesse V, 511
Lundy, Jesse V, 512
Lundy, Jesse V, 529
Lundy, Jesse V, 582
Lundy, Joanna III, 426
Lundy, Joanna V, 1007
Lundy, Joannah II, 311
Lundy, John IV, 1285
Lundy, John V, 260
Lundy, John V, 511
Lundy, John V, 512
Lundy, John V, 582
Lundy, Josaphine E. V, 512
Lundy, Joseph I, 991
Lundy, Joseph I, 992
Lundy, Joseph II, 231
Lundy, Joseph II, 240
Lundy, Joseph II, 295
Lundy, Joseph II, 311
Lundy, Joseph II, 322
Lundy, Joseph II, 781
Lundy, Joseph III, 426
Lundy, Joseph III, 453
Lundy, Joseph IV, 243
Lundy, Joseph W. II, 311
Lundy, Laura II, 311
Lundy, Laura II, 322
Lundy, Laura II, 326
Lundy, Levi IV, 1285
Lundy, Levi V, 260
Lundy, Levi V, 511
Lundy, Levi V, 512
Lundy, Levi V, 542
Lundy, Levi V, 544
Lundy, Levi V, 582
Lundy, Lillian M. V, 186
Lundy, Lillian M. V, 512
Lundy, Lindley V, 512
Lundy, Lindley V, 692
Lundy, Lindley L. V, 692
Lundy, Lindley L. V, 695
Lundy, Lizzie II, 311
Lundy, Lot I, 992
Lundy, Lydia II, 784
Lundy, Lydia S. II, 240
Lundy, Lydia S. II, 295
Lundy, Lydia S. II, 311
Lundy, Lydia S. II, 322
Lundy, Lydia S. II, 326
Lundy, Lydia W. V, 512
Lundy, Margaret V, 512
Lundy, Margaret V, 523
Lundy, Margaret S. V, 512
Lundy, Margarett V, 512
Lundy, Maria Ann V, 512
Lundy, Maria Ann V, 529
Lundy, Maria Ann V, 582
Lundy, Maria H. II, 322
Lundy, Maria R. II, 311
Lundy, Mariah R. II, 322
Lundy, Marian Ann V, 512
Lundy, Marion E. V, 512
Lundy, Mary I, 725
Lundy, Mary I, 813
Lundy, Mary I, 825
Lundy, Mary I, 992
Lundy, Mary I, 1006
Lundy, Mary I, 1011
Lundy, Mary I, 1012
Lundy, Mary II, 231
Lundy, Mary II, 240
Lundy, Mary II, 295
Lundy, Mary II, 311
Lundy, Mary II, 316
Lundy, Mary II, 322
Lundy, Mary II, 781
Lundy, Mary III, 426
Lundy, Mary III, 453
Lundy, Mary V, 306
Lundy, Mary V, 308
Lundy, Mary Ann IV, 1285
Lundy, Mary Ann V, 394
Lundy, Mary Ann V, 411
Lundy, Mary Ann V, 512
Lundy, Mary D. II, 311
Lundy, Mary E. II, 311
Lundy, Mary E. II, 322
Lundy, Mary Elizabeth III, 343
Lundy, Mary G. II, 322
Lundy, Mary W. II, 311
Lundy, Mary W. II, 322
Lundy, Mary, Jr. II, 295
Lundy, Maryann V, 511
Lundy, Maurice II, 311
Lundy, Maurice II, 322
Lundy, Maurice E. II, 311
Lundy, Mercy Ann V, 512
Lundy, Miriam I, 965
Lundy, Nancy I, 981
Lundy, Nancy I, 992
Lundy, Nancy I, 1006
Lundy, Nancy I, 1011
Lundy, Nancy Jane V, 493
Lundy, Nathan I, 824
Lundy, Nathan I, 966
Lundy, Nathan V, 94
Lundy, Nathan V, 260
Lundy, Nathan V, 512
Lundy, Nickolas V, 512
Lundy, Pauline V, 692
Lundy, Pauline V, 695
Lundy, Phebe II, 231
Lundy, Phebe II, 240
Lundy, Phebe II, 311
Lundy, Phebe V, 512
Lundy, Priscilla I, 825
Lundy, Priscilla I, 966
Lundy, Rachel I, 825
Lundy, Rachel I, 959
Lundy, Rachel I, 966
Lundy, Rachel I, 992
Lundy, Rachel III, 211
Lundy, Rachel V, 389
Lundy, Rachel V, 390
Lundy, Rachel V, 411
Lundy, Rachel V, 493
Lundy, Rachel V, 511
Lundy, Rachel V, 512
Lundy, Rachel, Jr. III, 211
Lundy, Rebecca I, 725
Lundy, Rebekah I, 991
Lundy, Rebekah I, 992
Lundy, Reuben II, 984
Lundy, Reuben II, 1012
Lundy, Reubin II, 1012
Lundy, Rhoda I, 825
Lundy, Rhoda I, 966
Lundy, Rhoda C. V, 493
Lundy, Richard I, 825
Lundy, Richard I, 966
Lundy, Richard I, 1006
Lundy, Richard I, 1011
Lundy, Richard II, 240
Lundy, Richard II, 295
Lundy, Richard II, 311
Lundy, Richard II, 322
Lundy, Richard II, 982
Lundy, Richard II, 1012
Lundy, Richard II, 1013
Lundy, Richard McPherson V, 692
Lundy, Richard, Jr. II, 1009
Lundy, Richard, Jr. II, 1012
Lundy, Ruth V, 506
Lundy, Ruth V, 512
Lundy, Ruth V, 582
Lundy, Ruth V, 597
Lundy, Ruth M. V, 512
Lundy, Ruth M. V, 632
Lundy, Sally I, 992
Lundy, Sally I, 1006
Lundy, Sally I, 1008
Lundy, Sally I, 1011
Lundy, Sally Ann III, 211
Lundy, Samuel I, 966
Lundy, Samuel I, 1006
Lundy, Samuel V, 512
Lundy, Samule, Jr. I, 992
Lundy, Sarah I, 1008
Lundy, Sarah I, 1011
Lundy, Sarah II, 1013
Lundy, Sarah IV, 567
Lundy, Sarah IV, 586
Lundy, Sarah V, 511
Lundy, Sarah V, 512
Lundy, Sarah V, 527
Lundy, Sarah V, 542
Lundy, Sarah V, 544
Lundy, Sarah B. V, 582
Lundy, Sarah B. V, 598
Lundy, Sarah M. V, 512
Lundy, Sarah Mary V, 512
Lundy, Sarah N. V, 512

dy, Sarah T. IV, 1285
dy, Sophia V, 502
dy, Sophia V, 511
dy, Sophia V, 512
dy, Susan M. II, 240
dy, Susanna I, 966
dy, Susanna I, 992
dy, Susanna I, 1011
dy, Susanna I, 1012
dy, Susanna V, 260
dy, Susanna V, 582
dy, Susannah I, 825
dy, Susannah I, 991
dy, Susannah V, 260
dy, Susannah V, 276
dy, Susannah V, 390
dy, Susannah V, 496
dy, Susannah V, 511
dy, Susannah V, 512
dy, Susannah M. II, 240
dy, Susannah M. IV, 243
dy, Susannah M. IV, 341
dy, Tamer I, 825
dy, Tamer I, 966
dy, Thomas I, 966
dy, Thomas I, 991
dy, Thomas II, 311
dy, Thomas II, 984
dy, Thomas II, 1012
dy, Thomas II, 1013
dy, Thomas III, 426
dy, Thomas N. V, 512
dy, Thomas, Jr. I, 992
dy, Walter J. V, 512
dy, Wd. Christiana II, 1043
dy, Wd. Mary II, 781
dy, William I, 825
dy, William I, 966
dy, William I, 992
dy, William I, 1006
dy, William V, 260
dy, William V, 511
dy, William V, 529
dy, William V, 582
dy, William Schooly V, 512
dy, Willson IV, 1285
gley, Thomas II, 1013
sford, Alice V, 582
sford, Elizabeth VI, 952
sford, Gwendolin VI, 405
sford, Gwendolin VI, 415
sford, Henry Redi VI, 405
sford, Henry Reid VI, 405
sford, Henry Reid VI, 415
sford, James V, 582
sford, Merryman VI, 869
sford, Merryman VI, 877
sford, Merryman VI, 879
sford, Merryman VI, 882
sford, Merryman VI, 884
sford, Merryman VI, 921
sford, Merryman VI, 933
sford, Merryman VI, 952
sford, Merryman VI, 983
sford, Merryman VI, 990
sford, Merryman VI, 1010
sford, Susan R. VI, 952
sford, Thomas VI, 952
tsford, Rebeckah I, 1085
ulling, Sarah I, 724
inski, Hugo III, 211
inski, Hugo H. III, 355
inski, Martha E. T. III, 355
o, Juliette III, 211
o, Victor A. III, 211
o, Victor E. III, 211
ton, A. Russell IV, 244
ton, Abigail VI, 416
ton, Abigail VI, 600
ton, Abigail VI, 605
ton, Achsa IV, 243
ton, Achsa IV, 260
ton, Achsah IV, 179
ton, Achsah IV, 243
ton, Achsah IV, 254
ton, Achsah IV, 1134
ton, Achsah C. IV, 1134
ton, Achsah E. IV, 244
ton, Achsah E. IV, 733
ton, Achsah E. IV, 735
ton, Achsah E. IV, 736
ton, Achsah E. IV, 831
ton, Achsah Elizabeth IV, 244
ton, Achsah Elizabeth IV, 736
ton, Achsah P. IV, 243
ton, Achsah P. IV, 281
ton, Albert IV, 243
ton, Alexandria VI, 417
ton, Alfred Roberts VI, 417
ton, Allen IV, 152
ton, Allen V, 94
Lupton, Allen V, 252
Lupton, Allen V, 260
Lupton, Allen VI, 417
Lupton, Amos VI, 416
Lupton, Amos VI, 417
Lupton, Amos VI, 418
Lupton, Amos VI, 665
Lupton, Amos VI, 673
Lupton, Ann IV, 243
Lupton, Ann IV, 244
Lupton, Ann IV, 281
Lupton, Ann IV, 341
Lupton, Ann IV, 418
Lupton, Ann IV, 586
Lupton, Ann IV, 587
Lupton, Ann V, 260
Lupton, Ann V, 512
Lupton, Ann V, 972
Lupton, Ann V, 973
Lupton, Ann VI, 406
Lupton, Ann VI, 415
Lupton, Ann VI, 416
Lupton, Ann VI, 417
Lupton, Ann VI, 418
Lupton, Ann VI, 421
Lupton, Ann VI, 435
Lupton, Ann VI, 448
Lupton, Ann VI, 451
Lupton, Ann VI, 529
Lupton, Ann VI, 566
Lupton, Ann VI, 573
Lupton, Ann VI, 600
Lupton, Ann VI, 606
Lupton, Ann VI, 763
Lupton, Ann M. VI, 366
Lupton, Ann M. VI, 367
Lupton, Ann M. VI, 417
Lupton, Anna IV, 243
Lupton, Anna IV, 244
Lupton, Anna IV, 291
Lupton, Anna IV, 735
Lupton, Anna IV, 736
Lupton, Anna IV, 831
Lupton, Anna IV, 1134
Lupton, Anna V, 346
Lupton, Anna V, 352
Lupton, Anna V, 512
Lupton, Anna V, 919
Lupton, Anna V, 923
Lupton, Anna VI, 416
Lupton, Anna VI, 417
Lupton, Anna VI, 418
Lupton, Anna VI, 752
Lupton, Anna VI, 753
Lupton, Anna VI, 763
Lupton, Anna M. VI, 416
Lupton, Anna V. IV, 244
Lupton, Anne IV, 244
Lupton, Annie IV, 244
Lupton, Asa V, 228
Lupton, Asa V, 231
Lupton, Asa VI, 397
Lupton, Asa VI, 415
Lupton, Asa VI, 416
Lupton, Asa VI, 417
Lupton, Asenath IV, 586
Lupton, Axche Elizabeth IV, 831
Lupton, Bathsheba IV, 152
Lupton, Bathsheba V, 17
Lupton, Bathsheba V, 94
Lupton, Bathsheba V, 112
Lupton, Bathsheba V, 116
Lupton, Bathsheba V, 215
Lupton, Bathsheba V, 252
Lupton, Bathsheba V, 260
Lupton, Bathsheba VI, 416
Lupton, Bathsheba VI, 417
Lupton, Bathsheba VI, 421
Lupton, Benjamin C. IV, 243
Lupton, Benjamin C. IV, 244
Lupton, Benjamin T. IV, 1372
Lupton, Betty VI, 361
Lupton, Betty VI, 416
Lupton, Betty VI, 421
Lupton, Caroline Damon VI, 367
Lupton, Caroline Damon VI, 417
Lupton, Carrie D. VI, 417
Lupton, Charles IV, 243
Lupton, Charles E. V, 260
Lupton, Charles L. VI, 416
Lupton, Charles T. IV, 244
Lupton, Charlotte V, 260
Lupton, Chas. V, 260
Lupton, Chas. L. W. VI, 416
Lupton, Clarissa IV, 1009
Lupton, Cordelia E. V, 260
Lupton, Daniel V, 972
Lupton, Daniel VI, 442
Lupton, Daniel W. VI, 416
Lupton, Daniel W. VI, 417
Lupton, Daniel W. VI, 418
Lupton, Daniel W. VI, 426
Lupton, Daniel Walker VI, 437
Lupton, David IV, 243
Lupton, David IV, 244
Lupton, David IV, 285
Lupton, David IV, 340
Lupton, David IV, 341
Lupton, David IV, 484
Lupton, David IV, 574
Lupton, David IV, 586
Lupton, David IV, 587
Lupton, David IV, 735
Lupton, David IV, 736
Lupton, David IV, 831
Lupton, David IV, 1134
Lupton, David V, 260
Lupton, David VI, 402
Lupton, David VI, 406
Lupton, David VI, 407
Lupton, David VI, 415
Lupton, David VI, 417
Lupton, David VI, 418
Lupton, David VI, 419
Lupton, David VI, 507
Lupton, David VI, 522
Lupton, David VI, 529
Lupton, David VI, 600
Lupton, David VI, 668
Lupton, David VI, 673
Lupton, David VI, 725
Lupton, David VI, 727
Lupton, David VI, 757
Lupton, David VI, 763
Lupton, David E. V, 260
Lupton, David P. VI, 416
Lupton, David P. VI, 418
Lupton, David W. V, 972
Lupton, David W. V, 973
Lupton, David W. VI, 418
Lupton, David Walker VI, 417
Lupton, David, Jr. VI, 416
Lupton, David, Jr. VI, 417
Lupton, David, Jr. VI, 421
Lupton, David, Jr. VI, 763
Lupton, Davis IV, 152
Lupton, Davis V, 94
Lupton, Davis VI, 417
Lupton, Deborah IV, 281
Lupton, Deborah Ann IV, 243
Lupton, Deborah Ann IV, 244
Lupton, Deborah Ann IV, 272
Lupton, Deborah Ann IV, 736
Lupton, Deborah Ann R. IV, 735
Lupton, Dorothy Taylor VI, 417
Lupton, Dorothy Taylor VI, 418
Lupton, Dorothy Taylor VI, 442
Lupton, Drucilla IV, 831
Lupton, Drusilla IV, 831
Lupton, Drusilla IV, 1134
Lupton, Drusilla S. IV, 244
Lupton, Drusilla S. IV, 686
Lupton, Drusilla S. IV, 735
Lupton, Drusilla S. IV, 736
Lupton, E. Janney S. VI, 417
Lupton, Edith VI, 417
Lupton, Edward IV, 243
Lupton, Edward IV, 244
Lupton, Edward F. IV, 244
Lupton, Edward Irish VI, 417
Lupton, Edward Janney Sidwell VI, 418
Lupton, Edward W. VI, 407
Lupton, Edward W. VI, 416
Lupton, Edward W. VI, 417
Lupton, Edward W. VI, 418
Lupton, Elias V, 260
Lupton, Eliza VI, 390
Lupton, Eliza VI, 416
Lupton, Elizabeth IV, 179
Lupton, Elizabeth IV, 243
Lupton, Elizabeth IV, 1280
Lupton, Elizabeth IV, 1285
Lupton, Elizabeth V, 260
Lupton, Elizabeth VI, 375
Lupton, Elizabeth VI, 412
Lupton, Elizabeth VI, 415
Lupton, Elizabeth VI, 417
Lupton, Elizabeth VI, 600
Lupton, Elizabeth Ann V, 512
Lupton, Elizabeth Ann VI, 418
Lupton, Elizabeth M. VI, 396
Lupton, Ella B. IV, 243
Lupton, Ellen V, 260
Lupton, Ellen I. VI, 404
Lupton, Ellen I. VI, 416
Lupton, Ellen I. VI, 418
Lupton, Ellen M. IV, 183
Lupton, Ellen M. IV, 243
Lupton, Ellis VI, 417
Lupton, Elwood IV, 243
Lupton, Emmor IV, 243
Lupton, Emmor IV, 976
Lupton, Emmor IV, 977
Lupton, Emmor IV, 988
Lupton, Emor IV, 244
Lupton, Esther V, 972
Lupton, Esther VI, 416
Lupton, Esther VI, 448
Lupton, Esther VI, 454
Lupton, Esther VI, 459
Lupton, Esther VI, 529
Lupton, Esther VI, 566
Lupton, Esther VI, 763
Lupton, Esther Jane V, 512
Lupton, Evaline IV, 976
Lupton, Everett L. V, 260
Lupton, Frances VI, 416
Lupton, Frances VI, 600
Lupton, Francis IV, 243
Lupton, Francis IV, 244
Lupton, Francis VI, 417
Lupton, Frederick VI, 600
Lupton, Gedion VI, 417
Lupton, Geo. IV, 469
Lupton, George IV, 243
Lupton, George IV, 244
Lupton, George IV, 484
Lupton, George IV, 586
Lupton, George IV, 587
Lupton, George VI, 417
Lupton, George A. IV, 243
Lupton, George A. IV, 244
Lupton, Gideon IV, 244
Lupton, Gideon IV, 466
Lupton, Gideon IV, 484
Lupton, Gideon IV, 735
Lupton, Gideon IV, 736
Lupton, Gideon IV, 1352
Lupton, Gideon IV, 1367
Lupton, Gideon IV, 1373
Lupton, Grace IV, 152
Lupton, Grace V, 94
Lupton, Grace V, 112
Lupton, Grace V, 260
Lupton, Grace VI, 371
Lupton, Grace VI, 403
Lupton, Grace VI, 415
Lupton, Grace VI, 416
Lupton, Grace VI, 417
Lupton, Hannah IV, 244
Lupton, Hannah IV, 586
Lupton, Hannah IV, 587
Lupton, Hannah V, 228
Lupton, Hannah V, 231
Lupton, Hannah VI, 407
Lupton, Hannah VI, 415
Lupton, Hannah VI, 416
Lupton, Hannah VI, 417
Lupton, Hannah VI, 418
Lupton, Hannah VI, 594
Lupton, Hannah VI, 600
Lupton, Hannah VI, 665
Lupton, Hannah VI, 673
Lupton, Hannah M. V, 92
Lupton, Hannah M. VI, 418
Lupton, Hannah M. VI, 526
Lupton, Hannah M. VI, 529
Lupton, Hannah W. VI, 416
Lupton, Hannah W. VI, 454
Lupton, Haran IV, 976
Lupton, Harriet A. VI, 566
Lupton, Harvey IV, 244
Lupton, Harvey IV, 587
Lupton, Harvey IV, 1105
Lupton, Helen VI, 412
Lupton, Helen VI, 417
Lupton, Henry IV, 179
Lupton, Henry IV, 243
Lupton, Henry IV, 244
Lupton, Henry IV, 254
Lupton, Henry IV, 260
Lupton, Henry IV, 285
Lupton, Henry IV, 831
Lupton, Henry IV, 845
Lupton, Henry Rees IV, 243
Lupton, Henry W. IV, 244
Lupton, Hugh VI, 416
Lupton, Hugh S. VI, 367
Lupton, Hugh S. VI, 416
Lupton, Hugh S. VI, 417
Lupton, Hugh S. VI, 418
Lupton, Hugh S. VI, 447
Lupton, Hugh S., Jr. VI, 417
Lupton, Hugh S., Jr. VI, 418
Lupton, Hugh Sidwell III VI, 417
Lupton, Hugh Sidwell, Jr. VI, 399
Lupton, Hugh Sidwell, Jr. VI, 417
Lupton, Isaac IV, 152
Lupton, Isaac IV, 201
Lupton, Isaac IV, 243
Lupton, Isaac IV, 244
Lupton, Isaac IV, 1134
Lupton, Isaac V, 94
Lupton, Isaac V, 260
Lupton, Isaac VI, 390
Lupton, Isaac VI, 412
Lupton, Isaac VI, 415
Lupton, Isaac VI, 417
Lupton, Isaac VI, 418
Lupton, Isaac VI, 421
Lupton, Isaac VI, 451
Lupton, Isaac VI, 526
Lupton, Isaac VI, 529
Lupton, Isaac VI, 600
Lupton, Isaac VI, 607
Lupton, Isaac B. IV, 244
Lupton, Isaac B. IV, 587
Lupton, Isaac B. IV, 831
Lupton, Isaac B. IV, 977
Lupton, Isaac D. IV, 587
Lupton, Isaac P. IV, 244
Lupton, Isaac, Jr. VI, 417
Lupton, Isaiah VI, 417
Lupton, Isaiah VI, 600
Lupton, James V, 260
Lupton, James H. IV, 243
Lupton, James H. IV, 244
Lupton, James McSherry VI, 412
Lupton, James McSherry VI, 417
Lupton, James R. VI, 417
Lupton, James Roberts VI, 417
Lupton, James Roberts VI, 438
Lupton, James Roberts, Jr. VI, 417
Lupton, Jane VI, 416
Lupton, Jane VI, 417
Lupton, Jane VI, 451
Lupton, Jane VI, 600
Lupton, Jane VI, 763
Lupton, Jane R. VI, 394
Lupton, Jane R. VI, 418
Lupton, Jas. H. IV, 183
Lupton, Jehu IV, 244
Lupton, Jehu IV, 586
Lupton, Jehu IV, 587
Lupton, Jesse VI, 390
Lupton, Jesse VI, 415
Lupton, Jesse, Jr. VI, 417
Lupton, Joel VI, 396
Lupton, Joel VI, 410
Lupton, Joel VI, 416
Lupton, Joel VI, 417
Lupton, Joel VI, 418
Lupton, Joel, Jr. VI, 404
Lupton, Joel, Jr. VI, 416
Lupton, Joel, Sr. VI, 410
Lupton, Joel, Sr. VI, 416
Lupton, John IV, 189
Lupton, John IV, 243
Lupton, John IV, 244
Lupton, John IV, 341
Lupton, John IV, 484
Lupton, John VI, 375
Lupton, John VI, 390
Lupton, John VI, 415
Lupton, John VI, 418
Lupton, John VI, 435
Lupton, John VI, 600
Lupton, John VI, 603
Lupton, John VI, 605
Lupton, John VI, 607
Lupton, John VI, 763
Lupton, John G. IV, 587
Lupton, John M. VI, 418
Lupton, John S. IV, 243
Lupton, John Shinn VI, 415
Lupton, Jonah VI, 416
Lupton, Jonah VI, 417
Lupton, Jonah VI, 418
Lupton, Jonah VI, 435
Lupton, Jonah H. VI, 367
Lupton, Jonah H. VI, 371
Lupton, Jonah H. VI, 406
Lupton, Jonah H. VI, 416
Lupton, Jonah H. VI, 417
Lupton, Jonah H. VI, 418
Lupton, Jonah H. VI, 444
Lupton, Jonah H. VI, 454
Lupton, Jonah H. VI, 514
Lupton, Jonah H. VI, 529
Lupton, Jonah H. VI, 660
Lupton, Jonah H. VI, 673
Lupton, Jonathan IV, 152
Lupton, Jonathan IV, 221
Lupton, Jonathan IV, 238
Lupton, Jonathan IV, 243
Lupton, Jonathan IV, 244
Lupton, Jonathan IV, 539
Lupton, Jonathan IV, 559
Lupton, Jonathan IV, 586

Lupton, Jonathan IV, 587
Lupton, Jonathan IV, 976
Lupton, Jonathan IV, 977
Lupton, Jonathan IV, 1009
Lupton, Jonathan V, 94
Lupton, Jonathan V, 260
Lupton, Jonathan VI, 387
Lupton, Jonathan VI, 415
Lupton, Jonathan VI, 417
Lupton, Jonathan VI, 418
Lupton, Jonathan VI, 593
Lupton, Jonathan VI, 597
Lupton, Jonathan VI, 598
Lupton, Jonathan VI, 600
Lupton, Jonathan VI, 604
Lupton, Jos. IV, 243
Lupton, Joseph IV, 243
Lupton, Joseph IV, 244
Lupton, Joseph IV, 587
Lupton, Joseph IV, 1105
Lupton, Joseph V, 972
Lupton, Joseph VI, 374
Lupton, Joseph VI, 415
Lupton, Joseph VI, 417
Lupton, Joseph VI, 451
Lupton, Joseph VI, 454
Lupton, Joseph VI, 457
Lupton, Joseph VI, 459
Lupton, Joseph VI, 529
Lupton, Joseph VI, 566
Lupton, Joseph VI, 573
Lupton, Joseph VI, 600
Lupton, Joseph VI, 606
Lupton, Joseph VI, 607
Lupton, Joseph VI, 763
Lupton, Joseph A. V, 260
Lupton, Joseph A. V, 512
Lupton, Joseph Abijah V, 512
Lupton, Joseph Abijah VI, 418
Lupton, Joseph P. IV, 243
Lupton, Joseph P. IV, 281
Lupton, Joseph R. IV, 244
Lupton, Joseph, Sr. VI, 429
Lupton, Joseph, Sr. VI, 453
Lupton, Joshua IV, 243
Lupton, Joshua IV, 244
Lupton, Joshua VI, 415
Lupton, Joshua VI, 416
Lupton, Joshua VI, 418
Lupton, Joshua VI, 600
Lupton, Joshua VI, 604
Lupton, Joshua VI, 607
Lupton, Joshua VI, 665
Lupton, Joshua VI, 673
Lupton, Joshua B. IV, 341
Lupton, Joshua R. VI, 418
Lupton, Josiah IV, 244
Lupton, Josiah IV, 586
Lupton, Julia A. IV, 244
Lupton, Julia A. IV, 267
Lupton, Julia Anna IV, 243
Lupton, Julian V, 260
Lupton, Lane IV, 1037
Lupton, Lansen E. V, 260
Lupton, Laura IV, 243
Lupton, Laura IV, 1040
Lupton, Leah VI, 416
Lupton, Leah VI, 448
Lupton, Leah VI, 453
Lupton, Leah VI, 520
Lupton, Leah VI, 529
Lupton, Leah VI, 565
Lupton, Leah VI, 576
Lupton, Leah VI, 665
Lupton, Leah VI, 673
Lupton, Levi IV, 244
Lupton, Levi IV, 484
Lupton, Levi IV, 586
Lupton, Levi IV, 587
Lupton, Levi IV, 977
Lupton, Levi R. IV, 1040
Lupton, Lewis IV, 243
Lupton, Lewis IV, 586
Lupton, Lewis IV, 587
Lupton, Lewis VI, 396
Lupton, Lewis VI, 397
Lupton, Lewis VI, 415
Lupton, Lewis VI, 417
Lupton, Lewis VI, 418
Lupton, Lewis VI, 421
Lupton, Lewis VI, 445
Lupton, Lewis VI, 448
Lupton, Lewis VI, 529
Lupton, Lidia IV, 244
Lupton, Lucina IV, 243
Lupton, Lucina IV, 244
Lupton, Lucina IV, 296
Lupton, Lucina IV, 736
Lupton, Lucina IV, 935
Lupton, Lucina IV, 976
Lupton, Lucina IV, 977
Lupton, Lucina IV, 1009
Lupton, Lucinda IV, 244
Lupton, Lusina IV, 735
Lupton, Lusina IV, 756
Lupton, Lydia IV, 152
Lupton, Lydia IV, 244
Lupton, Lydia IV, 341
Lupton, Lydia IV, 571
Lupton, Lydia IV, 586
Lupton, Lydia IV, 587
Lupton, Lydia IV, 976
Lupton, Lydia IV, 977
Lupton, Lydia IV, 1271
Lupton, Lydia IV, 1285
Lupton, Lydia V, 94
Lupton, Lydia V, 116
Lupton, Lydia V, 260
Lupton, Lydia VI, 367
Lupton, Lydia VI, 368
Lupton, Lydia VI, 371
Lupton, Lydia VI, 375
Lupton, Lydia VI, 404
Lupton, Lydia VI, 406
Lupton, Lydia VI, 415
Lupton, Lydia VI, 416
Lupton, Lydia VI, 417
Lupton, Lydia VI, 454
Lupton, Lydia VI, 514
Lupton, Lydia VI, 529
Lupton, Lydia VI, 600
Lupton, Lydia VI, 604
Lupton, Lydia VI, 607
Lupton, Lydia VI, 660
Lupton, Lydia VI, 665
Lupton, Lydia VI, 673
Lupton, Lydia Ann IV, 341
Lupton, Lydia Jane IV, 243
Lupton, Lydia R. IV, 243
Lupton, Lydia R. IV, 244
Lupton, Lydia R. IV, 976
Lupton, Lydia R. IV, 988
Lupton, Mahlon IV, 152
Lupton, Mahlon V, 94
Lupton, Mahlon V, 260
Lupton, Mahlon VI, 417
Lupton, Marcy VI, 415
Lupton, Marcy VI, 416
Lupton, Marcy VI, 429
Lupton, Marcy VI, 451
Lupton, Marcy VI, 453
Lupton, Marcy VI, 573
Lupton, Marcy VI, 600
Lupton, Margaret IV, 243
Lupton, Margaret IV, 244
Lupton, Margaret IV, 281
Lupton, Margaret IV, 340
Lupton, Margaret IV, 341
Lupton, Margaret IV, 418
Lupton, Margaret IV, 484
Lupton, Margaret IV, 574
Lupton, Margaret IV, 586
Lupton, Margaret IV, 587
Lupton, Margaret IV, 735
Lupton, Margaret IV, 736
Lupton, Margaret IV, 976
Lupton, Margaret IV, 977
Lupton, Margaret IV, 988
Lupton, Margaret IV, 1276
Lupton, Margaret IV, 1285
Lupton, Margaret IV, 1367
Lupton, Margaret IV, 1373
Lupton, Margaret V, 231
Lupton, Margaret V, 260
Lupton, Margaret VI, 397
Lupton, Margaret VI, 417
Lupton, Margaret VI, 600
Lupton, Margaret VI, 604
Lupton, Margaret H. VI, 418
Lupton, Margaret Harmon VI, 417
Lupton, Margaret Harmon VI, 438
Lupton, Margaret Helen VI, 417
Lupton, Margaret Stone VI, 417
Lupton, Margaret, Jr. IV, 244
Lupton, Marget VI, 600
Lupton, Marget Reese VI, 417
Lupton, Maria VI, 391
Lupton, Maria VI, 418
Lupton, Maria C. VI, 416
Lupton, Martha IV, 243
Lupton, Martha IV, 244
Lupton, Martha IV, 935
Lupton, Martha IV, 976
Lupton, Martha IV, 977
Lupton, Martha VI, 435
Lupton, Martha Ann IV, 244
Lupton, Martha Ann VI, 416
Lupton, Martha Ann VI, 418
Lupton, Martha Ann VI, 444
Lupton, Martha Walker VI, 417
Lupton, Martin IV, 243
Lupton, Martin IV, 244
Lupton, Martin IV, 586
Lupton, Martin IV, 735
Lupton, Martin IV, 756
Lupton, Martin IV, 935
Lupton, Martin IV, 976
Lupton, Martin IV, 977
Lupton, Martin L. IV, 976
Lupton, Mary IV, 152
Lupton, Mary IV, 184
Lupton, Mary IV, 201
Lupton, Mary IV, 243
Lupton, Mary IV, 244
Lupton, Mary IV, 580
Lupton, Mary IV, 587
Lupton, Mary IV, 736
Lupton, Mary IV, 831
Lupton, Mary IV, 1105
Lupton, Mary IV, 1134
Lupton, Mary V, 94
Lupton, Mary V, 252
Lupton, Mary V, 260
Lupton, Mary V, 307
Lupton, Mary VI, 362
Lupton, Mary VI, 368
Lupton, Mary VI, 374
Lupton, Mary VI, 402
Lupton, Mary VI, 403
Lupton, Mary VI, 407
Lupton, Mary VI, 408
Lupton, Mary VI, 415
Lupton, Mary VI, 416
Lupton, Mary VI, 417
Lupton, Mary VI, 418
Lupton, Mary VI, 507
Lupton, Mary VI, 522
Lupton, Mary VI, 529
Lupton, Mary VI, 600
Lupton, Mary VI, 603
Lupton, Mary VI, 604
Lupton, Mary VI, 668
Lupton, Mary VI, 673
Lupton, Mary VI, 757
Lupton, Mary VI, 763
Lupton, Mary B. IV, 244
Lupton, Mary B. IV, 587
Lupton, Mary C. IV, 244
Lupton, Mary D. VI, 406
Lupton, Mary D. VI, 407
Lupton, Mary D. VI, 416
Lupton, Mary D. VI, 418
Lupton, Mary Eva VI, 407
Lupton, Mary Eva VI, 417
Lupton, Mary Eva VI, 418
Lupton, Mary Jane V, 260
Lupton, Mary Jean VI, 417
Lupton, Mary P. IV, 243
Lupton, Mary P. IV, 244
Lupton, Mary P. IV, 254
Lupton, Mary P. IV, 735
Lupton, Mary P. IV, 736
Lupton, Mary P. IV, 831
Lupton, Mary P. IV, 1134
Lupton, Mary P. IV, 1136
Lupton, Mary R. VI, 416
Lupton, Mary R. VI, 417
Lupton, Mary R. VI, 418
Lupton, Mary R. VI, 445
Lupton, Mary R. VI, 446
Lupton, Mary R. VI, 447
Lupton, Mary S. VI, 367
Lupton, Mary S. VI, 417
Lupton, Mary S. VI, 418
Lupton, Mary W. IV, 281
Lupton, Mary W. VI, 406
Lupton, Mary W. VI, 416
Lupton, Mary W. VI, 417
Lupton, Mary W. VI, 529
Lupton, Mary W. VI, 660
Lupton, Mary W. VI, 673
Lupton, Mary W. VI, 703
Lupton, Mary W. VI, 752
Lupton, Mary Winston IV, 243
Lupton, Mary Winston IV, 735
Lupton, Mercy VI, 390
Lupton, Mercy VI, 416
Lupton, Mercy VI, 417
Lupton, Mercy VI, 431
Lupton, Mildred VI, 399
Lupton, Mildred VI, 417
Lupton, Mildred H. VI, 418
Lupton, Morris IV, 244
Lupton, Moses VI, 605
Lupton, Myra B. IV, 243
Lupton, Myra B. IV, 244
Lupton, Nathan IV, 243
Lupton, Nathan IV, 244
Lupton, Nathan IV, 272
Lupton, Nathan IV, 281
Lupton, Nathan IV, 341
Lupton, Nathan IV, 418
Lupton, Nathan IV, 484
Lupton, Nathan IV, 735
Lupton, Nathan IV, 736
Lupton, Nathan IV, 976
Lupton, Nathan IV, 977
Lupton, Nathan IV, 988
Lupton, Nathan VI, 415
Lupton, Nathan VI, 418
Lupton, Nathan VI, 600
Lupton, Nathan VI, 604
Lupton, Nathan VI, 607
Lupton, Nathan, Jr. IV, 244
Lupton, Nathan, Jr. IV, 735
Lupton, Nathan, Jr. IV, 736
Lupton, Norris IV, 244
Lupton, Norris IV, 578
Lupton, Norris IV, 586
Lupton, Norris IV, 587
Lupton, Norris IV, 1105
Lupton, Oliver IV, 586
Lupton, Penelope V, 260
Lupton, Phebe V, 972
Lupton, Phebe VI, 415
Lupton, Phebe VI, 600
Lupton, Phinneas VI, 415
Lupton, Rachel IV, 46
Lupton, Rachel IV, 152
Lupton, Rachel IV, 165
Lupton, Rachel IV, 189
Lupton, Rachel IV, 221
Lupton, Rachel IV, 243
Lupton, Rachel IV, 244
Lupton, Rachel IV, 281
Lupton, Rachel IV, 539
Lupton, Rachel IV, 587
Lupton, Rachel V, 94
Lupton, Rachel V, 252
Lupton, Rachel V, 260
Lupton, Rachel VI, 366
Lupton, Rachel VI, 374
Lupton, Rachel VI, 400
Lupton, Rachel VI, 415
Lupton, Rachel VI, 416
Lupton, Rachel VI, 417
Lupton, Rachel VI, 418
Lupton, Rachel VI, 419
Lupton, Rachel VI, 426
Lupton, Rachel VI, 457
Lupton, Rachel VI, 600
Lupton, Rachel VI, 605
Lupton, Rachel VI, 606
Lupton, Rachel VI, 763
Lupton, Rachel A. VI, 396
Lupton, Rachel Ann IV, 244
Lupton, Rachel Ann IV, 341
Lupton, Rachel Ann IV, 387
Lupton, Rachel Ann IV, 484
Lupton, Rachel Ann IV, 574
Lupton, Rachel Ann IV, 586
Lupton, Rachel Ann IV, 587
Lupton, Rachel Ann VI, 367
Lupton, Rachel Ann VI, 416
Lupton, Rachel Ann VI, 417
Lupton, Rachel Ann VI, 418
Lupton, Rachel Ann VI, 421
Lupton, Rachel Ann VI, 445
Lupton, Rachel II VI, 415
Lupton, Rebecca IV, 238
Lupton, Rebecca IV, 243
Lupton, Rebecca IV, 244
Lupton, Rebecca IV, 578
Lupton, Rebecca IV, 587
Lupton, Rebecca IV, 831
Lupton, Rebecca IV, 977
Lupton, Rebecca IV, 1105
Lupton, Rebecca V, 260
Lupton, Rebecca VI, 390
Lupton, Rebecca VI, 401
Lupton, Rebecca VI, 416
Lupton, Rebecca VI, 417
Lupton, Rebecca VI, 462
Lupton, Rebecca B. IV, 976
Lupton, Rebecca B. IV, 988
Lupton, Rebecca H. VI, 396
Lupton, Rebecca H. VI, 416
Lupton, Rebecca J. III, 47
Lupton, Rebecca J. IV, 1129
Lupton, Rebecca J. IV, 1134
Lupton, Rebecca J. VI, 371
Lupton, Rebecca J. VI, 416
Lupton, Rebecca J. VI, 417
Lupton, Rebecca M. V, 260
Lupton, Rebecca McPherson V, 502
Lupton, Rebeckah VI, 415
Lupton, Rebeckah VI, 600
Lupton, Reese V, 260
Lupton, Rice W. V, 260
Lupton, Richard VI, 418
Lupton, Richard R. V, 512
Lupton, Richard R. VI, 417
Lupton, Richard R. VI, 418
Lupton, Richard R. VI, 752
Lupton, Richard R. VI, 753
Lupton, Richard Ridgeway VI, 763
Lupton, Ruth IV, 189
Lupton, Ruth IV, 243
Lupton, Ruth IV, 244
Lupton, Ruth IV, 518
Lupton, Ruth IV, 539
Lupton, Ruth V, 228
Lupton, Ruth V, 260
Lupton, Ruth VI, 361
Lupton, Ruth VI, 407
Lupton, Ruth VI, 415
Lupton, Ruth VI, 416
Lupton, Ruth VI, 417
Lupton, Ruth VI, 418
Lupton, Ruth VI, 519
Lupton, Ruth VI, 522
Lupton, Ruth VI, 529
Lupton, Ruth VI, 600
Lupton, Ruth VI, 607
Lupton, Ruth VI, 668
Lupton, Ruth VI, 757
Lupton, Ruth VI, 763
Lupton, Samantha IV, 244
Lupton, Samuel VI, 361
Lupton, Samuel VI, 366
Lupton, Samuel VI, 367
Lupton, Samuel VI, 371
Lupton, Samuel VI, 415
Lupton, Samuel VI, 444
Lupton, Samuel VI, 448
Lupton, Samuel VI, 453
Lupton, Samuel VI, 520
Lupton, Samuel VI, 565
Lupton, Samuel VI, 566
Lupton, Samuel VI, 576
Lupton, Samuel VI, 665
Lupton, Samuel VI, 673
Lupton, Sarah IV, 238
Lupton, Sarah IV, 243
Lupton, Sarah IV, 244
Lupton, Sarah IV, 285
Lupton, Sarah IV, 484
Lupton, Sarah IV, 539
Lupton, Sarah IV, 559
Lupton, Sarah IV, 586
Lupton, Sarah IV, 735
Lupton, Sarah IV, 736
Lupton, Sarah IV, 831
Lupton, Sarah IV, 845
Lupton, Sarah IV, 1134
Lupton, Sarah VI, 361
Lupton, Sarah VI, 366
Lupton, Sarah VI, 371
Lupton, Sarah VI, 387
Lupton, Sarah VI, 390
Lupton, Sarah VI, 396
Lupton, Sarah VI, 415
Lupton, Sarah VI, 416
Lupton, Sarah VI, 417
Lupton, Sarah VI, 418
Lupton, Sarah VI, 444
Lupton, Sarah VI, 446
Lupton, Sarah VI, 529
Lupton, Sarah VI, 600
Lupton, Sarah VI, 603
Lupton, Sarah Ann IV, 243
Lupton, Sarah Ann IV, 244
Lupton, Sarah Ann IV, 469
Lupton, Sarah Ann IV, 484
Lupton, Sarah Ann V, 80
Lupton, Sarah Ann VI, 520
Lupton, Sarah Ann VI, 529
Lupton, Sarah Ann VI, 576
Lupton, Sarah Ann VI, 665
Lupton, Sarah Anne VI, 448
Lupton, Sarah C. IV, 484
Lupton, Sarah C. IV, 1352
Lupton, Sarah C. IV, 1373
Lupton, Sarah G. VI, 396
Lupton, Sarah G. VI, 397
Lupton, Sarah G. VI, 416
Lupton, Sarah G. VI, 417
Lupton, Sarah G. VI, 418
Lupton, Sarah J. IV, 923
Lupton, Sarah J. VI, 410
Lupton, Sarah J. VI, 411
Lupton, Sarah J. VI, 417
Lupton, Sarah Jane IV, 976
Lupton, Sarah Jane VI, 410
Lupton, Sarah Jane VI, 416
Lupton, Sarah W. IV, 243
Lupton, Smith IV, 586
Lupton, Solomon IV, 152
Lupton, Solomon IV, 165
Lupton, Solomon IV, 1285
Lupton, Solomon V, 94

pton, Solomon V, 260
pton, Solomon VI, 417
pton, Susanna IV, 244
pton, Susanna IV, 466
pton, Susanna IV, 484
pton, Susanna IV, 736
pton, Susanna IV, 1367
pton, Susanna IV, 1373
pton, Susannah IV, 244
pton, Susannah IV, 484
pton, Susannah IV, 735
pton, Susannah IV, 736
pton, Susannah IV, 1352
pton, Tamsin VI, 529
pton, Tamson VI, 416
pton, Tamson VI, 451
pton, Thamasin M. VI, 416
pton, Thamasin M. VI, 435
pton, Thamizin M. V, 114
pton, Thamsin VI, 416
pton, Thamson VI, 526
pton, Thamzin VI, 416
pton, Thamzin VI, 421
pton, Thomas IV, 244
pton, Thomas IV, 586
pton, Thomas IV, 587
pton, Victoria VI, 417
pton, Victoria VI, 426
pton, Victoria VI, 442
pton, Victoria N. VI, 418
pton, Victoria N. VI, 437
pton, Victoria V. VI, 417
pton, Viola IV, 244
pton, Viola IV, 261
pton, Virginia Noel VI, 417
pton, Virginia Noel VI, 418
pton, Virginia Noel VI, 437
pton, Walter J. IV, 243
pton, Wd. Ann VI, 763
pton, Wd. Leah VI, 565
pton, Wd. Mary VI, 429
pton, Wd. Mary W. VI, 514
pton, Widow Leah VI, 529
pton, William IV, 152
pton, William IV, 244
pton, William IV, 484
pton, William IV, 586
pton, William IV, 736
pton, William V, 94
pton, William V, 112
pton, William V, 116
pton, William V, 215
pton, William V, 260
pton, William V, 346
pton, William VI, 362
pton, William VI, 403
pton, William VI, 415
pton, William VI, 417
pton, William VI, 418
pton, William VI, 421
pton, William VI, 600
pton, William C. IV, 1373
pton, William C. V, 260
pton, William G. VI, 416
pton, William G. VI, 418
pton, William, Jr. VI, 417
pton, William, Sr. VI, 415
pton, Wm. IV, 152
pton, Wm. IV, 735
pton, Wm. V, 252
pton, Wm. V, 307
pton, Wm. V, 352
pton, Wm. S. IV, 244
pton, Wm. Taylor VI, 417
pton, Zacheus IV, 831
se, Roena Berlin V, 692
se, Ronald Wright V, 692
se, Wendell V, 692
sh, Mary VI, 952
sh, William VI, 952
sk, Jane VI, 1013
sk, Lida I, 1158
ster, Barbara VI, 952
ster, Edward VI, 952
ster, Frances VI, 851
ster, Hannah V, 512
ster, James VI, 817
ster, James VI, 835
ster, John VI, 816
ster, John VI, 851
ster, John VI, 866
ster, John, Jr. VI, 835
ster, Leannah VI, 835
ster, Luviner VI, 835
ster, Mildred VI, 835
ster, Parker VI, 835
ster, Sealy VI, 851
ter, Lavina VI, 67
ter, Lavinia VI, 76
ter, Martha VI, 67
tes, Sarah IV, 977
Lutes, Sarah IV, 982
Luther, Charles IV, 1373
Luther, Emily I, 919
Luther, Emily I, 927
Luther, James O. IV, 1321
Luther, Jennie M. IV, 1373
Luther, Mary E. IV, 1321
Luther, Matilda L. IV, 1321
Luton, Amelia V, 919
Luton, Ann V, 919
Luton, Charlotte V, 919
Luton, Daniel V, 919
Luton, Elizabeth Ann V, 919
Luton, Elizabeth Jane V, 919
Luton, Martha V, 919
Luton, Robert II, 391
Luton, Thomas V, 919
Lutpon, Deborah Ann IV, 281
Lutpon, Nathan IV, 281
Lutrell, Chloe E. V, 411
Lutrell, Fannie V, 411
Lutrell, Fanny E. V, 411
Lutrell, Mary V, 411
Lutrell, Mary V, 919
Lutrell, Otto C. V, 919
Lutrell, Robert V, 411
Lutrell, Robert C. V, 919
Lutrell, Robert H. V, 411
Lutrell, Ulissius D. V, 411
Lutteral, Mary V, 409
Lutteral, Mary V, 411
Lutteral, R. H. V, 692
Lutterel, Robert H. V, 692
Lutterell, Robert H. V, 411
Luttle, Cornelia III, 197
Luttle, Daniel IV, 1326
Lutton, Margaret IV, 341
Lutton, Margaret IV, 343
Luttrell, Chloa V, 692
Luttrell, Chloa E. V, 411
Luttrell, Chloe E. V, 411
Luttrell, Clayton V, 347
Luttrell, Fannie V, 411
Luttrell, Fannie V, 432
Luttrell, Fanny E. V, 411
Luttrell, Margaret V, 347
Luttrell, Margaretta V, 260
Luttrell, Margaretta V, 279
Luttrell, Mary V, 411
Luttrell, Mary V, 582
Luttrell, Mary V, 692
Luttrell, O. C. V, 347
Luttrell, Otto Clayton V, 692
Luttrell, R. H. V, 411
Luttrell, R. H. V, 692
Luttrell, Robert V, 411
Luttrell, Robert V, 432
Luttrell, Robert H. V, 411
Luttrell, Robert H. V, 460
Luttrell, Robert H. V, 692
Luttrell, Robert Holland V, 411
Luttrell, Sarah F. V, 432
Luttrell, Ulissius D. V, 411
Luttrell, Ulyssis V, 411
Luttrell, Ulyssis V, 692
Lutz, Anna J. II, 707
Lutz, Blandina Ellen VI, 664
Lutz, Carolina II, 707
Lutz, John M. II, 707
Lutz, Laura V, 94
Lutz, Laura V, 129
Luxford, Florence IV, 1327
Luxford, Miss Florence IV, 1326
Luxford, Mrs. A. E. IV, 1326
Luxford, Mrs. A. E. IV, 1327
Luzena, Margaret V, 507
Luzena, Margaret V, 512
Lybarger, Albert V, 1007
Lybarger, Nellie B. V, 1007
Lybole, James VI, 529
Lybole, Rebeccah VI, 529
Lybolt, Arthur E. VI, 673
Lybolt, Arthur Eugene VI, 673
Lybolt, Arthur Eugene VI, 681
Lybolt, James VI, 529
Lybolt, Mabel Alice VI, 673
Lybolt, Mabel Alice VI, 681
Lybolt, Mortimer Lewis VI, 673
Lybolt, Motimer Lewis VI, 681
Lybolt, Rebeccah VI, 529
Lybolt, Sarah VI, 673
Lybolt, Sarah VI, 681
Lydecker, Frederick A. III, 63
Lydecker, Frederick A. III, 211
Lydecker, H. F. III, 211
Lydecker, Letitia III, 211
Lydecker, Mary III, 63
Lydecker, Mary III, 211
Lydecker, Matilda III, 336
Lyden, Hannah II, 587
Lydig, Catharine M. III, 298
Lydig, Catherine M. III, 212
Lydig, Philip M. III, 212
Lydig, Philip M. III, 298
Lydig, Rosalie III, 212
Lydig, Rosalie III, 298
Lyford, Thomas II, 587
Lyle, Alice Morris V, 913
Lyle, Alice Morris V, 919
Lyle, Benj. Franklin V, 913
Lyle, Benjamin Franklin V, 919
Lyle, Elizabeth II, 391
Lyle, Ella Gaddis V, 692
Lyle, Florence V, 692
Lyle, Florence S. V, 656
Lyle, Florence S. V, 692
Lyle, James, Jr. VI, 197
Lyle, John M. V, 919
Lyle, Mary II, 391
Lyle, Mary V, 919
Lyle, Mary Jane VI, 964
Lyle, Mercy VI, 418
Lyle, Morriss II, 391
Lyle, Sally VI, 197
Lyle, Sally VI, 887
Lyle, Thurman V, 260
Lyles, Anna I, 1124
Lyles, Elizabeth R. VI, 1019
Lyles, Frances VI, 929
Lyles, Francis F. E. I, 1124
Lyles, George VI, 952
Lyles, George VI, 964
Lyles, George VI, 1019
Lyles, James A. VI, 1019
Lyles, James P. B. I, 1124
Lyles, Jane I, 1124
Lyles, Jane O. Y. I, 1124
Lyles, John I, 1124
Lyles, John S. S. I, 1124
Lyles, Judith VI, 952
Lyles, Lucinda VI, 952
Lyles, Malinda VI, 913
Lyles, Martha M. VI, 952
Lyles, Mary F. I, 1124
Lyles, Mercy VI, 418
Lyles, Millar G. I, 1124
Lyles, Robert VI, 952
Lyles, Susanna VI, 952
Lyles, Thomas VI, 929
Lyles, Thomas VI, 952
Lyles, Thomas H. I, 1124
Lyles, William H. VI, 952
Lylife, Elizabeth II, 685
Lyman, Clara G. II, 816
Lyman, Elizabeth VI, 329
Lyman, Elizabeth VI, 338
Lymin, Lucy Mason IV, 587
Lymin, Lucy Mason IV, 596
Lyn, Deborah VI, 418
Lyncan, Ursula IV, 244
Lyncan, Ursula IV, 287
Lynch, ??? VI, 293
Lynch, Angelina B. VI, 809
Lynch, Ann I, 405
Lynch, Ann I, 450
Lynch, Ann IV, 736
Lynch, Ann IV, 808
Lynch, Ann IV, 831
Lynch, Ann IV, 832
Lynch, Ann IV, 943
Lynch, Ann IV, 977
Lynch, Ann V, 898
Lynch, Ann VI, 330
Lynch, Ann VI, 811
Lynch, Ann VI, 952
Lynch, Ann R. VI, 835
Lynch, Anna I, 557
Lynch, Anna I, 577
Lynch, Anna VI, 330
Lynch, Anne V, 36
Lynch, Anne VI, 258
Lynch, Anne VI, 274
Lynch, Anne VI, 275
Lynch, Anselm VI, 329
Lynch, Anselm VI, 330
Lynch, Anselm VI, 840
Lynch, Anselm VI, 863
Lynch, Ascenith IV, 641
Lynch, Asenath IV, 977
Lynch, Asenath IV, 986
Lynch, Asenath E. IV, 641
Lynch, Auselm VI, 799
Lynch, Auselm VI, 835
Lynch, Austin VI, 976
Lynch, Avarilla VI, 835
Lynch, Benjamin Ball IV, 736
Lynch, Charity V, 94
Lynch, Charity V, 919
Lynch, Charity V, 979
Lynch, Charles V, 94
Lynch, Charles VI, 258
Lynch, Charles VI, 274
Lynch, Charles VI, 275
Lynch, Charles VI, 303
Lynch, Charles VI, 304
Lynch, Charles VI, 330
Lynch, Charles VI, 858
Lynch, Charles Clark VI, 329
Lynch, Charles E. V, 95
Lynch, Charles E. V, 919
Lynch, Charles Edward VI, 329
Lynch, Charles H. VI, 852
Lynch, Charles, Jr. VI, 952
Lynch, Charles, Senior VI, 289
Lynch, Chas. E. V, 919
Lynch, Chris. VI, 310
Lynch, Chris. VI, 904
Lynch, Christopher VI, 329
Lynch, Christopher VI, 330
Lynch, Christopher VI, 952
Lynch, Col. Charles VI, 290
Lynch, Edward V, 94
Lynch, Edward V, 919
Lynch, Edward V, 972
Lynch, Edward VI, 329
Lynch, Edward VI, 330
Lynch, Edward VI, 342
Lynch, Edward VI, 345
Lynch, Edward VI, 835
Lynch, Edwin V, 94
Lynch, Edwin C. VI, 844
Lynch, Elijah VI, 813
Lynch, Elijah VI, 835
Lynch, Elijah VI, 841
Lynch, Elizabeth III, 131
Lynch, Elizabeth III, 212
Lynch, Elizabeth IV, 736
Lynch, Elizabeth IV, 831
Lynch, Elizabeth IV, 977
Lynch, Elizabeth VI, 813
Lynch, Elizabeth VI, 875
Lynch, Elizabeth VI, 952
Lynch, Elizabeth VI, 973
Lynch, Elizabeth Ann V, 972
Lynch, Elizabeth Ann VI, 329
Lynch, Elizabeth Ann VI, 330
Lynch, Ella W. II, 893
Lynch, Ella W. II, 929
Lynch, Elvira VI, 835
Lynch, Emma I, 621
Lynch, Emma I, 637
Lynch, Emma I, 639
Lynch, Esther I, 405
Lynch, Eva V, 632
Lynch, George I, 621
Lynch, George I, 637
Lynch, Georgeaner I, 310
Lynch, Georgianna I, 621
Lynch, Hannah III, 131
Lynch, Hannah III, 212
Lynch, Hannah IV, 674
Lynch, Hannah IV, 736
Lynch, Hannah IV, 924
Lynch, Hannah IV, 977
Lynch, Hannah B. VI, 329
Lynch, Hannah Lynch IV, 736
Lynch, Haywood I, 310
Lynch, Haywood I, 621
Lynch, Hester Ann VI, 799
Lynch, Jame IV, 910
Lynch, James II, 893
Lynch, James VI, 870
Lynch, James VI, 875
Lynch, James VI, 952
Lynch, James VI, 961
Lynch, James VI, 963
Lynch, James VI, 976
Lynch, Jane IV, 909
Lynch, Jane IV, 977
Lynch, Jane VI, 976
Lynch, Jennie V, 1007
Lynch, Jno. VI, 822
Lynch, John V, 1007
Lynch, John VI, 290
Lynch, John VI, 329
Lynch, John VI, 330
Lynch, John VI, 835
Lynch, John VI, 952
Lynch, John VI, 973
Lynch, John P. VI, 811
Lynch, John P. VI, 862
Lynch, John, Jr. VI, 329
Lynch, John, Jr. VI, 330
Lynch, John, Jr. VI, 344
Lynch, John, Jr. VI, 861
Lynch, Jonah V, 94
Lynch, Joseph IV, 610
Lynch, Joseph IV, 641
Lynch, Joseph IV, 736
Lynch, Joseph IV, 925
Lynch, Joseph IV, 977
Lynch, Joseph V, 632
Lynch, Joshua IV, 641
Lynch, Joshua IV, 736
Lynch, Joshua IV, 831
Lynch, Joshua IV, 832
Lynch, Joshua IV, 859
Lynch, Joshua IV, 909
Lynch, Joshua IV, 910
Lynch, Joshua IV, 919
Lynch, Joshua IV, 924
Lynch, Joshua IV, 943
Lynch, Joshua IV, 977
Lynch, Josiah VI, 835
Lynch, Lavina V, 94
Lynch, Lydia IV, 98
Lynch, Lydia IV, 117
Lynch, Maggie A. I, 310
Lynch, Malissa V, 632
Lynch, Marion Justice I, 310
Lynch, Martha VI, 875
Lynch, Martha G. VI, 803
Lynch, Mary I, 637
Lynch, Mary IV, 736
Lynch, Mary IV, 831
Lynch, Mary IV, 977
Lynch, Mary V, 94
Lynch, Mary V, 919
Lynch, Mary V, 972
Lynch, Mary VI, 329
Lynch, Mary VI, 330
Lynch, Mary VI, 342
Lynch, Mary VI, 345
Lynch, Mary VI, 742
Lynch, Mary VI, 952
Lynch, Mary VI, 973
Lynch, Mary A. VI, 811
Lynch, Mary Hudson VI, 743
Lynch, Mary Hudson VI, 763
Lynch, Mary J. VI, 952
Lynch, Mary, Jr. V, 95
Lynch, Mary, Jr. V, 919
Lynch, Mary, Jr. V, 973
Lynch, Mary, Jr. VI, 330
Lynch, Mathew VI, 962
Lynch, Matilda VI, 329
Lynch, Matilda VI, 330
Lynch, Matilda VI, 338
Lynch, Matilda VI, 961
Lynch, Melissa V, 632
Lynch, Micajah VI, 330
Lynch, Micajah VI, 806
Lynch, Micajah VI, 835
Lynch, Micajah Terrell VI, 329
Lynch, Nancy VI, 840
Lynch, Nelly VI, 963
Lynch, Pamelia VI, 952
Lynch, Parkey VI, 835
Lynch, Patrick VI, 875
Lynch, Patrick VI, 952
Lynch, Patrick VI, 969
Lynch, Philena C. II, 893
Lynch, Polly VI, 835
Lynch, Rachel IV, 641
Lynch, Rachel IV, 736
Lynch, Rachel IV, 831
Lynch, Rachel IV, 924
Lynch, Rachel IV, 943
Lynch, Rachel IV, 977
Lynch, Raymond VI, 742
Lynch, Raymond VI, 743
Lynch, Raymond VI, 763
Lynch, Rebecca IV, 610
Lynch, Rebecca IV, 641
Lynch, Rebecca IV, 925
Lynch, Rebecca IV, 977
Lynch, Sally V, 94
Lynch, Sally V, 95
Lynch, Sally VI, 841
Lynch, Sally VI, 858
Lynch, Sally VI, 952
Lynch, Samuel Coppock IV, 832
Lynch, Sarah V, 919
Lynch, Sarah V, 972
Lynch, Sarah V, 973
Lynch, Sarah VI, 258
Lynch, Sarah VI, 274
Lynch, Sarah VI, 275
Lynch, Sarah VI, 286
Lynch, Sarah VI, 329
Lynch, Sarah VI, 330
Lynch, Sarah VI, 344
Lynch, Sarah VI, 870
Lynch, Sarah VI, 973
Lynch, Sarah VI, 1010
Lynch, Sarah E. VI, 835
Lynch, Susannah VI, 835
Lynch, Thomas VI, 952
Lynch, Wd. Anna VI, 329
Lynch, Wd. Sarah VI, 330
Lynch, William III, 131
Lynch, William III, 212
Lynch, William VI, 329
Lynch, William VI, 835

Lynch, William C. VI, 809
Lynch, William C. VI, 828
Lynch, William C. VI, 835
Lynch, Wilson J. VI, 870
Lynch, Zalinda VI, 329
Lynch, Zalinda VI, 330
Lynch, Zalinda VI, 345
Lynch, Zalinda VI, 782
Lynch-Terrell, Sarah VI, 290
Lynches, Sarah VI, 291
Lynde, Cornelius VI, 773
Lynde, Marion VI, 773
Lynder, William V, 95
Lyndley, Hannah II, 581
Lynds, Ruth II, 736
Lynes, Anna P. III, 118
Lynes, Anna P. III, 212
Lynes, Caroline S. III, 118
Lynes, Caroline S. III, 212
Lynes, Stephen C. III, 118
Lynes, Stephen C. III, 212
Lynham, John II, 587
Lynham, Margaret II, 588
Lynk, Charles VI, 418
Lynk, Charles VI, 439
Lynk, Effa Steer VI, 418
Lynk, Effa Steer VI, 439
Lynn, Aaron I, 145
Lynn, Abraham Symons I, 145
Lynn, Ann II, 588
Lynn, Ann V, 847
Lynn, Ann Eliza V, 850
Lynn, Anna E. V, 846
Lynn, Anna E. V, 847
Lynn, Charles IV, 240
Lynn, Deborah II, 588
Lynn, Earnest L. V, 847
Lynn, Elisabeth II, 537
Lynn, Elisabeth II, 588
Lynn, Elizabeth II, 588
Lynn, Esther II, 458
Lynn, Esther II, 588
Lynn, Hannah II, 391
Lynn, Hannah V, 347
Lynn, Hannah VI, 673
Lynn, James II, 587
Lynn, James II, 588
Lynn, James VI, 673
Lynn, Jeremiah II, 391
Lynn, Jeremiah II, 588
Lynn, John II, 391
Lynn, John II, 493
Lynn, John II, 588
Lynn, John V, 847
Lynn, John V, 850
Lynn, Joseph II, 391
Lynn, Joseph II, 493
Lynn, Joseph II, 504
Lynn, Joseph II, 520
Lynn, Joseph II, 588
Lynn, Joseph II, 591
Lynn, Joseph, Jr. II, 588
Lynn, Martha II, 391
Lynn, Martha II, 504
Lynn, Martha II, 573
Lynn, Martha II, 588
Lynn, Mary II, 391
Lynn, Mary II, 493
Lynn, Mary II, 588
Lynn, Mary VI, 673
Lynn, Mary Emma II, 782
Lynn, Phebe II, 588
Lynn, Sarah II, 391
Lynn, Sarah II, 520
Lynn, Sarah II, 588
Lynn, Sarah II, 591
Lynn, Sarah V, 850
Lynn, Sarah VI, 673
Lynn, Sarah Ellen V, 847
Lynn, William V, 850
Lyntch, Anna I, 557
Lynton, Mary II, 979
Lynton, Mary II, 1010
Lynton, Matilda IV, 46
Lynton, Matilda IV, 62
Lynum, John II, 391
Lynum, Margaret II, 391
Lynum, Sarah IV, 587
Lynum, Sarah IV, 596
Lyon, ??? III, 212
Lyon, Anna M. III, 212
Lyon, Arthur I, 929
Lyon, Arthur I, 945
Lyon, Caroline III, 393
Lyon, Caroline III, 426
Lyon, Charles II, 391
Lyon, Charles IV, 244
Lyon, Charles W. IV, 244
Lyon, David VI, 952
Lyon, Elijah VI, 952
Lyon, Elisha VI, 952
Lyon, Elizabeth II, 588
Lyon, Elizabeth III, 207
Lyon, Elizabeth III, 212
Lyon, Elizabeth VI, 952
Lyon, Hanna S. III, 212
Lyon, Hannah III, 423
Lyon, Hannah III, 426
Lyon, Hannah K. III, 212
Lyon, Hannah S. III, 95
Lyon, Hannah T. III, 212
Lyon, Henry L. III, 95
Lyon, Henry L. III, 212
Lyon, Hezekiah VI, 921
Lyon, J. R. IV, 245
Lyon, Jane II, 1012
Lyon, Jane II, 1013
Lyon, John R. IV, 244
Lyon, Lydia VI, 838
Lyon, Martha Jane IV, 244
Lyon, Mary II, 391
Lyon, Mary II, 523
Lyon, Mary II, 588
Lyon, Matilda J. IV, 736
Lyon, Matilda J. IV, 785
Lyon, Miriam III, 212
Lyon, Miriam K. III, 95
Lyon, Miriam K. III, 212
Lyon, Myrtle IV, 245
Lyon, Pearl IV, 245
Lyon, Phebe III, 212
Lyon, Rhoda VI, 952
Lyon, Roberta I, 945
Lyon, Roberta I, 950
Lyon, Roberta T. I, 929
Lyon, Rudolph G. III, 212
Lyon, Sally VI, 952
Lyon, Sarah II, 391
Lyon, Sener III, 382
Lyon, Stephen VI, 952
Lyon, Sylvanus III, 212
Lyon, Sylvanus III, 423
Lyon, Sylvanus III, 426
Lyon, Walter S. III, 393
Lyon, Walter S. III, 426
Lyon, William III, 207
Lyon, William III, 212
Lyon, William VI, 921
Lyons, Anna M. III, 212
Lyons, Annie Campbell IV, 1327
Lyons, Bessie III, 489
Lyons, David VI, 952
Lyons, Elizabeth II, 588
Lyons, Elizabeth II, 661
Lyons, Elizabeth III, 489
Lyons, Elizabeth VI, 952
Lyons, George III, 489
Lyons, Joseph IV, 1327
Lyons, Joseph H. IV, 1327
Lyons, Mahala V, 752
Lyons, Mary II, 391
Lyons, Mary V, 411
Lyons, Mary V, 438
Lyons, Rebecca IV, 1238
Lyons, Stephen VI, 952
Lyons, Thomas E. V, 752
Lypes, Archie J. I, 621
Lypes, Pearl I, 621
Lypsey, Amasa IV, 185
Lypsey, Amasa IV, 260
Lypsey, Mary IV, 260
Lypsey, Peninah IV, 260
Lypsey, Penninah IV, 185
Lypsey, Sarah IV, 185
Lypsey, Sarah IV, 310
Lysle, Ann II, 391
Lysle, Elizabeth II, 391
Lysle, Elizabeth II, 392
Lysle, Henry II, 391
Lysle, Henry II, 392
Lysle, Mary II, 391
Lysle, Mary II, 392
Lysle, Maurice II, 392
Lysle, Morriss II, 391
Lysle, Nathaniel II, 392
Lytch, Andrew B. VI, 763
Lytch, Andrew B. VI, 781
Lytch, Elizabeth VI, 763
Lytch, Elizabeth W. VI, 763
Lytch, Elizabeth W. VI, 781
Lytch, Wd. Elizabeth VI, 729
Lytch, Wd. Elizabeth VI, 781
Lytford, Thomas II, 392
Lytle, Albert V, 347
Lytle, Anna II, 753
Lytle, Anna II, 762
Lytle, Anna R. II, 753
Lytle, Charles VI, 527
Lytle, Charles C. VI, 952
Lytle, Cloista Adell IV, 1040
Lytle, Harry V, 186
Lytle, John V, 347
Lytle, John J. II, 753
Lytle, John J. II, 762
Lytle, Julia Maude V, 186
Lytle, Lucy S. VI, 952
Lytle, Lydia VI, 413
Lytle, Mary Ann II, 389
Lytle, Maude V, 186
Lytle, Minnie IV, 245
Lytle, Pearl IV, 245
Lytle, Polly VI, 952
Lytle, Richard H. II, 753
Lytle, Richard H. II, 762
Lytle, Ruth II, 295
Lytle, Ruth II, 753
Lytle, Ruth II, 762
Lytle, Ruth II, 891
Lytle, Ruth IV, 1327
Lytle, Samuel IV, 1040
Lytle, Widow Lydia VI, 527
Lytle, William IV, 245
Lytle, William B. VI, 952
Lytles, Susannah V, 489
Lytles, Susannah V, 512
Lyton, Elizabeth VI, 896
Lyton, Rachel VI, 896
Lyttle, Minnie IV, 245
Lytton, Martha VI, 1008
Lytton, Rachel VI, 1008

M'Cllelan, Sarah VI, 419
M'Connel, Abigail VI, 592
M'Connel, Ann VI, 592
M'Connel, Elizabeth VI, 600
M'Connel, Eunice VI, 592
M'Connel, Isaac VI, 592
M'Connel, Isaiah VI, 592
M'Connel, James VI, 591
M'Connel, James VI, 592
M'Connel, James VI, 600
M'Connel, James VI, 603
M'Connel, Mary VI, 592
M'Connel, Morris VI, 600
M'Connel, Phebe VI, 592
M'Connel, Rachel VI, 591
M'Connel, Rachel VI, 600
M'Connel, Rebekah VI, 592
M'Connel, Rese VI, 592
M'Connell, James VI, 607
M'Coole, Ann VI, 395
M'Coole, Eleanor VI, 413
M'Coole, James VI, 395
M'Coole, John VI, 413
M'Coole, Martha VI, 395
M'Grew, James IV, 110
M'Grew, Jane IV, 110
M'Grew, Mary IV, 110
M'Kay, Abraham VI, 597
M'Kay, Andrew VI, 591
M'Kay, Andrew VI, 592
M'Kay, Andrew VI, 595
M'Kay, Andrew VI, 596
M'Kay, Andrew VI, 600
M'Kay, Andrew VI, 607
M'Kay, Catherine VI, 599
M'Kay, Catherine VI, 601
M'Kay, Hannah VI, 607
M'Kay, Jacob VI, 600
M'Kay, Jacob VI, 602
M'Kay, Jacob VI, 607
M'Kay, Jane VI, 592
M'Kay, Jane VI, 593
M'Kay, Jane VI, 600
M'Kay, Jane VI, 607
M'Kay, Patience VI, 607
M'Kay, Rachel VI, 596
M'Kay, Rachel VI, 597
M'Kay, Rachel VI, 607
M'Kay, Sarah VI, 607
M'Millan, Ruth IV, 312
M'Millan, Ruth IV, 313
M'Pherson, Daniel VI, 421
M'Pherson, Jane VI, 421
M'Pherson, Jonas VI, 421
M'Pherson, Rebekah VI, 421
M'Pherson, William VI, 421
M???, Amanda III, 150
M???, Arena III, 371
M???gnume, Ann I, 367
M???gnume, Elizabeth I, 367
M???gnume, John I, 367
Mabbet, Hannah III, 426
Mabbet, Jonathan III, 426
Mabbet, Joseph III, 426
Mabbet, Mary III, 426
Mabbet, Samuel III, 426
Mabbet, Sarah III, 426
Mabbet, Susanna III, 426
Mabbet, Susannah III, 426
Mabbett, Adlina S. III, 215
Mabbett, Hannah III, 215
Mabbett, Hannah III, 426
Mabbett, Hannah III, 431
Mabbett, Joseph III, 215
Mabbett, Joseph III, 426
Mabbett, Joseph III, 431
Mabbett, Ruth III, 215
Mabbett, Samuel III, 215
Mabbett, Sarah III, 426
Mabbett, Susanna III, 426
Mabbett, Susanna III, 431
Mabbett, Susannah III, 215
Mabbett, Sussannah III, 431
Mabe, James IV, 1257
Mabe, James Isaac IV, 1257
Mabe, Josephine IV, 1257
Mabe, Malissa IV, 1257
Mabe, Nettie IV, 1257
Mabee, Catharine F. V, 515
Mabee, Catharine F. V, 535
Mabee, Deborah V, 515
Mabee, Eliza B. V, 515
Mabee, Hannah H. V, 515
Mabee, John V, 515
Mabee, Susan V, 480
Mabee, Susan V, 515
Maben, ??? V, 1008
Maberry, Agness G. VI, 837
Maberry, Elizabeth VI, 837
Maberry, Elizabeth VI, 867
Maberry, Jesse VI, 837
Maberry, John VI, 867
Maberry, Nancy VI, 843
Maberry, Thomas VI, 837
Mabery, Abednego IV, 1285
Mabery, Abednigo IV, 1285
Mabery, Cordelia IV, 1285
Mabery, Sarah VI, 824
Mabery, Thomas L. IV, 1285
Mabery, Thos. L. IV, 1285
Mabery, William VI, 824
Mabery, Wm. C. IV, 1285
Mabey, Alice Maude VI, 733
Mabey, Alice Maude VI, 743
Mabie, Catharine V, 584
Mabie, Catharine F. V, 515
Mabie, Catherine V, 602
Mabie, Deborah V, 515
Mabie, Eliza B. V, 495
Mabie, Eliza B. V, 515
Mabie, Eliza B. V, 567
Mabie, Eliza B. V, 584
Mabie, Hannah V, 86
Mabie, Hannah V, 506
Mabie, Hannah V, 515
Mabie, Hannah H. V, 515
Mabie, John V, 515
Mabie, John V, 584
Mabie, Susan V, 515
Mac Ann, Elisabeth I, 825
Mac Kenzie, Dudley S. III, 137
Mac Kenzie, Gladys Kinghorn III, 137
Mac Master, Gilbert Lee III, 196
Mac Master, Margaretha Magdalena III, 196
Mac Nicholson, Mercy II, 977
Macadam, Mary I, 145
Macadam, Mary I, 174
MacBride, Elizabeth I Sup 1, 4
Maccann, Elizabeth I, 450
Maccann, Elizabeth I, 455
Maccelvy, Mary II, 392
Maccelvy, Susan II, 392
Macclane, Catharine C. II, 1060
Maccomb, Elizabeth II, 392
Maccomb, Elizabeth II, 445
Maccomb, Hannah II, 372
Maccomb, John II, 372
Maccomb, John II, 392
Maccomb, John II, 445
Maccomb, John, Jr. II, 445
Maccomb, Rebecka II, 445
Maccomb, Samuel II, 445
Maccomb, Thomas II, 445
Maccombs, John II, 392
MacCommac, John VI, 835
MacCommac, Missouri VI, 835
MacCommac, Pleasant L. VI, 835
MacCommac, Susanna L. VI, 835
MacConnell, Andrew VI, 763
MacConnell, Andrew VI, 791
MacConnell, Katherine VI, 763
MacConnell, Katherine VI, 791
MacConnell, Mary Crete Hatch VI, 763
MacConnell-Hatch, Mary Crete VI, 791
Maccord, Deborah I, 981
Maccord, Deborah I, 992
Maccord, Mary I, 981
Maccord, Mary I, 992
Maccoy, William VI, 969
Maccracken, Pricilla I, 450
Maccraken, Martha I, 450
Maccury, Christian I, 558
Maccury, Christian I, 582
Macdonald, Martha II, 588
Mace, Abel I, 265
Mace, Abigail I, 266
Mace, Alice I, 272
Mace, Alice I, 273
Mace, Alice I, 276
Mace, Alice IV, 47
Mace, Anene I, 273
Mace, Ann I, 102
Mace, Ann I, 146
Mace, Ann I, 152
Mace, Ann I, 273
Mace, Anna I, 265
Mace, Anna I, 272
Mace, Anna I, 273
Mace, Anna I, 558
Mace, Anna IV, 47
Mace, Anna IV, 153
Mace, Anna Breathwail I, 273
Mace, Anne I, 146
Mace, Anne I, 266
Mace, Anne I, 273
Mace, Anne I, 276
Mace, Anne B. I, 507
Mace, Anne Thomas I, 273
Mace, Benjamin I, 265
Mace, Benjamin I, 273
Mace, Benjamin I, 276
Mace, Benjamin I, 311
Mace, Benjamin IV, 47
Mace, Betsey Ann I, 311
Mace, Betsy Ann I, 273
Mace, Betsy Ann I, 311
Mace, Betsyan I, 311
Mace, Bety I, 102
Mace, Borden I, 266
Mace, Borden I, 273
Mace, Borden I, 311
Mace, Catharine I, 268
Mace, Catharine I, 273
Mace, David I, 273
Mace, David I, 507
Mace, David I, 558
Mace, David I, 563
Mace, David I, 605
Mace, David I, 606
Mace, David IV, 47
Mace, Doncilla C. I, 558
Mace, Drucilla Catherine I, 507
Mace, Eliza J. I, 558
Mace, Eliza Jane I, 507
Mace, Elizab VI, 23
Mace, Elizabeth VI, 32
Mace, Elizabeth??? VI, 23
Mace, Elwood I, 558
Mace, Enoch I, 265
Mace, Enoch IV, 47
Mace, Eunice C. I, 507
Mace, Ferabah I, 507
Mace, Ferebah I, 273
Mace, Feriba I, 273
Mace, Feribah I, 270
Mace, Feribah I, 273
Mace, Ferybah I, 558
Mace, Frances I, 606
Mace, Francis I, 102
Mace, Francis I, 146
Mace, Francis I, 152
Mace, Francis I, 270
Mace, Francis I, 273
Mace, Francis I, 558
Mace, Francis IV, 47
Mace, Francis Elwood I, 507
Mace, Glenn V, 1008
Mace, Hanna I, 102
Mace, Hannah I, 146
Mace, Hannah I, 265
Mace, Hannah I, 271
Mace, Hannah I, 272
Mace, Hannah I, 273
Mace, Hannah IV, 47
Mace, Hannah IV, 153
Mace, Hannah IV, 247
Mace, Henry I, 311
Mace, Henry A. I, 558
Mace, Henry Alaxandre I, 507
Mace, Hope I, 273
Mace, Isaac I, 265
Mace, Isaac I, 273
Mace, James I, 265
Mace, James I, 273
Mace, James I, 274
Mace, James I, 275
Mace, James IV, 47
Mace, James Emslen I, 507
Mace, James T. I, 273

ace, John I, 102
ace, John I, 146
ace, John I, 265
ace, John I, 272
ace, John I, 273
ace, John IV, 47
ace, John V, 1008
ace, John, Jr. I, 273
ace, John, Sr. I, 273
ace, Jonas I, 273
ace, Jonas IV, 47
ace, Joseph I, 265
ace, Joseph I, 266
ace, Joseph IV, 47
ace, Joseph IV, 153
ace, Joseph D. I, 273
ace, Katharine I, 265
ace, Katherine IV, 153
ace, Laurence V, 656
ace, Laurence V, 695
ace, Lulu V, 656
ace, Lulu V, 695
ace, Mary I, 102
ace, Mary I, 119
ace, Mary I, 146
ace, Mary I, 167
ace, Mary I, 265
ace, Mary I, 271
ace, Mary I, 273
ace, Mary I, 511
ace, Mary I, 558
ace, Mary II, 574
ace, Mary II, 589
ace, Mary IV, 47
ace, Mary J. I, 558
ace, Mary Josephine I, 507
ace, Mary P. I, 507
ace, Mary P. I, 558
ace, Mary P. I, 563
ace, Nathan I, 266
ace, Nathan I, 273
ace, Pharaba IV, 47
ace, Pheriba I, 558
ace, Pheriba I, 606
ace, Pheribe I, 273
ace, Rachel C. I, 558
ace, Rachel L. Carline I, 507
ace, Rhoda I, 269
ace, Rhoda I, 273
ace, Sarah I, 102
ace, Sarah I, 146
ace, Sarah I, 265
ace, Sarah I, 273
ace, Sarah I, 274
ace, Sarah I, 275
ace, Sarah IV, 47
ace, Stephen T. I, 273
ace, Susan A. I, 558
ace, Susan Allice I, 507
ace, Susanah I, 507
ace, Susanah I, 558
ace, Susanna I, 273
ace, Susanna I, 276
ace, Susanna I, 558
ace, Susanna I, 605
ace, Susanna I, 606
ace, Susannah I, 606
ace, Sybeal I, 507
ace, Teriba I, 273
ace, Thomas C. I, 507
ace, Thomas C. I, 558
ace, Thomas Clarkson I, 273
ace, Thomas Elwood I, 273
ace, Widow Sarah I, 273
Mace, William I, 265
Mace, William I, 269
Mace, William I, 272
Mace, William I, 273
Mace, William I, 276
Mace, William I, 311
Mace, William IV, 153
Mace, William IV, 247
Mace, William, Sr. I, 273
Macey, Micajah VI, 331
Macey, Sarah VI, 331
Macey, Uriah I, 560
MacFarland, Alexander II, 847
MacFarland, Alexander II, 894
MacFarland, Allegra V. III, 214
MacFarland, Cassie II, 847
MacFarland, Cassie L. II, 847
MacFarland, Cassie L. II, 894
MacFarland, Catharine II, 847
MacFarland, Catharine II, 894
MacFarland, Elijah P. III, 214
Macfarland, Emma S. II, 876
MacFarland, Evelyn III, 214
Macfarland, John II, 876
Macgahea, Mary VI, 197
Macgahea, Samuel VI, 197
Macgee, Martha VI, 181
Macgee, Martha VI, 197
Macgee, Samuel VI, 181
Macgee, Samuel VI, 197
Macgee, Sarah VI, 268
MacGregor, Sara E. II, 800
Machett, Ruth IV, 1329
Machgeehee, Ann VI, 259
Machgeehee, Milley VI, 259
Macieie, Mary I, 383
Macieie, Mary I, 406
MacIntire, Lucy P. II, 894
Mack, Henry Q. III, 215
Mack, Rachel Y. III, 36
Mack, Rachel Y. III, 215
Mackaney, Alexander VI, 198
MacKay, Abigail VI, 420
Mackay, Alexander VI, 847
MacKay, Andrew VI, 420
MacKay, Andrew VI, 437
MacKay, David VI, 420
MacKay, Enos VI, 420
MacKay, Esther VI, 420
Mackay, Helen VI, 847
MacKay, Jacob VI, 420
MacKay, Jacob II VI, 420
MacKay, Jane VI, 420
MacKay, Jane VI, 437
MacKay, John VI, 420
MacKay, Margaret VI, 420
MacKay, Moses VI, 420
MacKay, Patience VI, 420
MacKay, Rachel VI, 420
MacKay, Robert VI, 420
Mackbride, Elizabeth I Sup 1, 4
Mackbride, John I Sup 1, 4
Mackbride, Margaret I Sup 1, 4
Macke, Martha I, 786
Macke, Rebeccah I, 786
Mackee, Mary I, 144
Mackee, Mary I, 146
MacKellar, Archibald III, 214
MacKellar, Jeannie III, 214
MacKellar, Walter III, 214
Mackelutch, Mary II, 192
Mackelutch, Mary II, 240
Mackeney, Alexander VI, 147
Mackeny, Alexd VI, 198
MacKenzie, Agnes III, 214
MacKenzie, Dudley S. III, 214
MacKenzie, Dudley S., Jr. III, 214
MacKenzie, Dudley Shannon III, 214
MacKenzie, Eleanor T. III, 214
MacKenzie, Florence III, 214
MacKenzie, Gladys Kinghorn III, 214
Mackenzie, Ida J. III, 382
Mackenzie, Ida J. III, 388
MacKenzie, James III, 214
MacKenzie, Jean III, 214
MacKenzie, Thomas III, 214
Mackey, Alexander VI, 853
Mackey, Catharine I, 984
Mackey, Catharine I, 992
Mackey, Elizabeth I, 992
Mackey, Jane VI, 815
Mackey, John I, 992
Mackey, Martha I, 825
Mackey, Mary I, 992
Mackey, Mary VI, 827
Mackey, Mary J. VI, 842
Mackey, Rebeckah I, 878
Mackey, Rebeckah I, 891
Mackey, Vera Brannon I, 637
Mackgecha, Joseph VI, 259
Mackgeehee, Joseph VI, 259
Mackgeehee, Milly VI, 259
Mackgehe, Joseph VI, 233
Mackgehe, Joseph VI, 259
Mackgehe, Mary VI, 233
Mackgehe, Mary VI, 259
Mackhee, Rebecca VI, 197
Mackhee, Rebeckah VI, 168
Mackie, Abigail I, 992
Mackie, Abigail I, 993
Mackie, Ann III, 215
Mackie, Catharine I, 992
Mackie, Elizabeth I, 992
Mackie, Elizabeth F. I, 992
Mackie, Eunice I, 987
Mackie, Eunice I, 992
Mackie, George Wm. III, 215
Mackie, James III, 215
Mackie, James III, 312
Mackie, James, Jr. III, 215
Mackie, Jane I, 992
Mackie, John I, 977
Mackie, John I, 992
Mackie, Maria III, 215
Mackie, Maria III, 312
Mackie, Mary I, 463
Mackie, Mary I, 992
Mackie, Mary I, 996
Mackie, Naomi I, 977
Mackie, Naomi I, 992
Mackie, Naomi, Jr. I, 977
Mackie, Rebecah I, 992
Mackie, Rebecca I, 989
Mackie, Rebecca I, 992
Mackie, Rebekah I, 992
MacKiney, James I, 953
Mackinney, Bette I, 965
MacKinney, Bette I, 966
MacKinney, Byrom I, 966
Mackintosh, Eliza V, 920
Macklane, Anna II, 208
Macklane, Anna II, 240
Macklane, Charles II, 208
Macklane, Charles II, 240
Macklane, Hannah II, 208
Macklane, Hannah II, 240
Mackleray, Rachel II, 85
Macklin, America V, 263
Macklin, Arksah V, 547
Macklin, Arksah V, 584
Macklin, Newton V, 263
Macks, Mary V, 1009
Macky, Ann I, 354
Macky, Jos. I, 354
Macky, Mary I, 406
Macky, Naomi I, 992
Macky, Rebecah I, 992
Macky, Rebecca I, 354
MacLan, Mary V, 95
MacLay, Charles III, 214
MacLay, Emily III, 214
MacLay, Emily C. III, 214
MacLean, George II, 808
MacLean, Mary II, 808
Maclean, Mary B. II, 894
Maclin, Newton V, 263
Maclotche, Amy II, 240
Macmannaway, James VI, 907
MacMaster, Arch. Alex. III, 215
MacMaster, Gilbert Lee III, 215
MacMaster, Margaretta Magdalena III, 215
MacMaster, Sophia III, 215
Macmurtry, Margery II, 523
Macmurtry, Margery II, 589
MacNealy, Jane II, 589
MacNeely, Jane II, 632
MacNees, Charity I, 1095
MacNees, Lydia I, 1095
MacNees, Marmaduke I, 1095
MacNees, Samuel I, 1095
MacNichols, George II, 85
MacNicholson, Mercy II, 1013
MacNight, Rachel I, 1124
Macomber, Abbie J. II, 749
Macomber, Abbie J. II, 754
Macomber, Adaline III, 215
Macomber, Albert IV, 1373
Macomber, Anna B. III, 215
Macomber, Caleb II, 749
Macomber, Caleb II, 754
Macomber, Edward B. II, 750
Macomber, Edwin IV, 1373
Macomber, Elmer Elwood IV, 1373
Macomber, Elmor Elwood IV, 1373
Macomber, Esther IV, 1373
Macomber, George Refine IV, 1373
Macomber, Hannah E. II, 750
Macomber, James E. II, 750
Macomber, Mary Ann II, 754
Macomber, Mary Anna II, 749
Macomber, Mary Anna II, 754
Macomber, Mary Elizabeth IV, 1373
Macomber, Nathaniel G. II, 749
Macomber, Nathaniel G. II, 754
Macomber, Parmelia III, 311
Macomber, Richard R. IV, 1373
Macomber, Sarah Jane IV, 1373
Macomber, William P. IV, 1373
Macomber, Wm. P. IV, 1373
Macon, Abijah I, 469
Macon, Abijah I, 470
Macon, Abijah I, 482
Macon, Alen J. I, 469
Macon, Alfred I, 470
Macon, Alfred I, 483
Macon, Alfred J. I, 483
Macon, Alfred S. I, 483
Macon, Asworth I, 469
Macon, Barbara I, 469
Macon, Barbra I, 483
Macon, Benjamin Franklin I, 469
Macon, Bertie E. I, 469
Macon, Betsy VI, 867
Macon, Carey I, 466
Macon, Cary I, 483
Macon, Charles F. I, 473
Macon, Charles F. I, 483
Macon, Charles T. I, 469
Macon, Charles T. I, 483
Macon, Clarkson I, 469
Macon, Cora Bell I, 469
Macon, Cora Caroline I, 483
Macon, Dinah S. I, 469
Macon, Dinah S. I, 473
Macon, Dinah S. I, 483
Macon, Eli I, 469
Macon, Eli I, 482
Macon, Eli I, 483
Macon, Eli I, 485
Macon, Elias I, 469
Macon, Elias I, 470
Macon, Elias I, 482
Macon, Elias I, 483
Macon, Elmira C. I, 483
Macon, Elta I, 469
Macon, Emily I, 469
Macon, Emily I, 483
Macon, Emily I, 725
Macon, Emily J. I, 469
Macon, Emily J. I, 483
Macon, Etta I, 483
Macon, George T. I, 469
Macon, George Thomas I, 483
Macon, Gideon I, 469
Macon, Gideon I, 483
Macon, Gidion T. I, 483
Macon, Hartwell I, 469
Macon, Hartwell I, 482
Macon, Isah I, 483
Macon, Isaiah I, 466
Macon, Isaiah I, 469
Macon, Isaiah I, 483
Macon, James G. I, 483
Macon, Joab I, 483
Macon, John I, 469
Macon, John I, 482
Macon, John VI, 887
Macon, John C. I, 469
Macon, John D. I, 483
Macon, Josiah I, 471
Macon, K. Elma I, 479
Macon, K. Elma I, 483
Macon, Leah I, 483
Macon, Leah I, 485
Macon, Levi B. I, 469
Macon, Levi B. I, 479
Macon, Levi B. I, 483
Macon, Levi Benet I, 482
Macon, Malinda I, 471
Macon, Malinda I, 483
Macon, Martitia I, 467
Macon, Mary E. I, 469
Macon, Mary E. I, 483
Macon, Mary F. I, 466
Macon, Mary F. I, 478
Macon, Mary F. I, 483
Macon, Mettie Rosanna I, 469
Macon, Molcy I, 469
Macon, Molsey I, 469
Macon, Molsy I, 482
Macon, Molsy I, 483
Macon, Nancy I, 471
Macon, Nancy A. I, 483
Macon, Nancy A. I, 485
Macon, Nathaniel I, 469
Macon, Nathaniel I, 470
Macon, Nathaniel I, 483
Macon, Peggy VI, 887
Macon, Penelope I, 483
Macon, Rebecca I, 468
Macon, Rebecca I, 469
Macon, Rebecca I, 482
Macon, Rosanna I, 469
Macon, Rosanna I, 470
Macon, Rosanna I, 483
Macon, Rosannah I, 469
Macon, Rosannah I, 470
Macon, Rosannah I, 471
Macon, Rosannah I, 483
Macon, Rosannah I, 485
Macon, Rufus Edgar I, 469
Macon, Tacy I, 483
Macon, Thomas I, 469
Macon, Thomas I, 470
Macon, Thomas I, 483
Macon, Thomas G. I, 469
Macon, Thomas Gourney I, 469
Macon, Thomas W. I, 469
Macon, Thomas Walker I, 482
MacPherson, Patience I, 448
MacPherson, Patience I, 450
Macreken, Abigail I, 450
Macreken, Martha I, 450
MacWalters, Hannah II, 894
MacWalters, John L. II, 894
MacWalters, Wm. J. II, 894
Macy, ??? III, 217
Macy, ??? V, 754
Macy, Aaron V, 726
Macy, Aaron V, 753
Macy, Aaron V, 757
Macy, Aaron V, 788
Macy, Aaron V, 789
Macy, Aaron C., Jr. III, 79
Macy, Aaron C., Jr. III, 216
Macy, Abigail I, 507
Macy, Abigail I, 508
Macy, Abigail I, 540
Macy, Abigail I, 558
Macy, Abigail I, 559
Macy, Abigail I, 574
Macy, Abigail I, 725
Macy, Abigail I, 773
Macy, Abigail I, 786
Macy, Abigail I, 804
Macy, Abigail I, 825
Macy, Abigail I, 826
Macy, Abigail V, 815
Macy, Abigail F. V, 96
Macy, Abraham W. III, 215
Macy, Abraham W. III, 336
Macy, Adaline III, 51
Macy, Albert I, 661
Macy, Alfred I, 602
Macy, Alice I, 1124
Macy, Alice I, 1127
Macy, Alvah J. I, 1107
Macy, Amanda V, 753
Macy, Amanda V, 789
Macy, Amanda Laura V, 753
Macy, Amy I, 525
Macy, Amy I, 558
Macy, Ann I, 507
Macy, Ann I, 560
Macy, Ann I, 825
Macy, Ann I, 982
Macy, Ann I, 992
Macy, Ann III, 215
Macy, Ann Eliza III, 215
Macy, Ann Eliza III, 216
Macy, Ann Elizabeth V, 726
Macy, Ann Elizabeth V, 753
Macy, Anna I, 507
Macy, Anna I, 508
Macy, Anna I, 509
Macy, Anna I, 558
Macy, Anna I, 559
Macy, Anna I, 565
Macy, Anna I, 574
Macy, Anna I, 661
Macy, Anna I, 786
Macy, Anna I, 825
Macy, Anna I, 840
Macy, Anna I, 977
Macy, Anna I, 992
Macy, Anna I, 1107
Macy, Anna I, 1124
Macy, Anna I, 1134
Macy, Anna III, 109
Macy, Anna III, 215
Macy, Anna V, 746
Macy, Anna V, 753
Macy, Anna V, 754
Macy, Anna V, 755
Macy, Anna V, 766
Macy, Anna V, 782
Macy, Anna V, 784
Macy, Anna V, 788
Macy, Anna V, 789
Macy, Anna V, 791
Macy, Anna V, 794
Macy, Anna ??? III, 215
Macy, Anna Elizabeth I, 560
Macy, Anna Hussey III, 217
Macy, Anna J. V, 760
Macy, Anna Jane I, 602
Macy, Anna Maria V, 757
Macy, Anne V, 753
Macy, Anns S. V, 753
Macy, Asa I, 508
Macy, Asa I, 559
Macy, Asa I, 786
Macy, Asenath I, 977
Macy, Asia I, 558
Macy, Barachiah I, 507
Macy, Barachiah I, 558
Macy, Barachiah I, 673
Macy, Barachiah I, 684
Macy, Barachiah I, 1107
Macy, Barachiah I, 1124
Macy, Barachiah I, 1135
Macy, Barclay V, 753
Macy, Barnard V, 96

Macy, Bathiah I, 559
Macy, Benedick I, 508
Macy, Benedict I, 602
Macy, Benjamin I, 508
Macy, Benjamin I, 558
Macy, Benjamin III, 52
Macy, Benjamin III, 215
Macy, Benjamin III, 216
Macy, Benjamin III, 299
Macy, Benjamin III, 357
Macy, Benjamin C. III, 215
Macy, Benjamin W. III, 196
Macy, Bennidick D. I, 507
Macy, Bethia I, 558
Macy, Bethiah I, 508
Macy, Bethiah I, 558
Macy, Bethiah I, 825
Macy, Bethiah V, 788
Macy, Betsy An I, 602
Macy, Betty V, 753
Macy, Betty V, 788
Macy, Beulah I, 508
Macy, Beulah V, 753
Macy, Beulah V, 781
Macy, Beulah V, 788
Macy, Beulah V, 789
Macy, Beulah V, 794
Macy, Beulah E. III, 216
Macy, Calvin V, 753
Macy, Carolina V, 263
Macy, Caroline II, 895
Macy, Caroline II, 915
Macy, Caroline III, 45
Macy, Caroline III, 60
Macy, Caroline III, 151
Macy, Caroline III, 196
Macy, Caroline III, 215
Macy, Caroline III, 216
Macy, Caroline III, 217
Macy, Caroline III, 268
Macy, Caroline V, 231
Macy, Caroline VI, 764
Macy, Caroline L. III, 112
Macy, Caroline L. III, 216
Macy, Caroline L. III, 354
Macy, Caroline L. III, 355
Macy, Caroline Louisa III, 196
Macy, Caroline M. V, 96
Macy, Caroline M. V, 136
Macy, Caroline R. II, 895
Macy, Caroline R. III, 221
Macy, Catharine I, 533
Macy, Catharine I, 558
Macy, Catharine I, 559
Macy, Catharine I, 581
Macy, Catharine I, 602
Macy, Catharine I, 977
Macy, Catharine I, 992
Macy, Catharine III, 217
Macy, Catharine III, 257
Macy, Catharine V, 753
Macy, Catharine V, 788
Macy, Catherine I, 600
Macy, Charles I, 786
Macy, Charles I, 992
Macy, Charles III, 215
Macy, Charles A. III, 86
Macy, Charles A. III, 215
Macy, Charles A. III, 216
Macy, Charles A., Jr. III, 215
Macy, Charles B. III, 215
Macy, Charles F. C. III, 196
Macy, Charles Marshall III, 217
Macy, Charles, Jr. III, 216
Macy, Charlotte L. III, 203
Macy, Charlotte L. III, 215
Macy, Chas. A. III, 203
Macy, Cornelia III, 217
Macy, Cornelia M. III, 151
Macy, Cornelia T. III, 215
Macy, Cornelia T. III, 338
Macy, Cornelia Trimble III, 217
Macy, Cornelia W. III, 215
Macy, Daniel V, 788
Macy, David I, 507
Macy, David I, 509
Macy, David I, 537
Macy, David I, 558
Macy, David I, 559
Macy, David I, 581
Macy, David I, 684
Macy, David V, 20
Macy, David V, 96
Macy, David V, 789
Macy, David S. V, 753
Macy, David S. V, 789
Macy, David T. V, 782
Macy, David T. V, 789
Macy, Deborah I, 507
Macy, Deborah I, 508
Macy, Deborah I, 534
MAcy, Deborah I, 534
Macy, Deborah I, 559
Macy, Deborah I, 661
Macy, Deborah I, 684
Macy, Deborah I, 690
Macy, Deborah III, 22
Macy, Deborah III, 215
Macy, Deborah III, 216
Macy, Deborah III, 327
Macy, Deborah V, 789
Macy, Delilah V, 753
Macy, Delilah V, 782
Macy, Delilah V, 789
Macy, Dinah I, 508
Macy, Dinah I, 558
Macy, Dinah I, 559
Macy, Dinah I, 574
Macy, Dinah I, 786
Macy, Edith I, 766
Macy, Edith III, 61
Macy, Edward L. V, 96
Macy, Edward Starbuck III, 217
Macy, Edwin III, 215
Macy, Elbert V, 753
Macy, Eli I, 559
Macy, Eli V, 788
Macy, Eli O. I, 560
Macy, Eli O. V, 753
Macy, Eli O. V, 760
Macy, Eli Oliver V, 753
Macy, Eliab G. V, 850
Macy, Eliah G. V, 850
Macy, Elihu I, 507
Macy, Elihu I, 558
Macy, Elihu I, 1107
Macy, Elihu I, 1124
Macy, Elihu I, 1137
Macy, Elihu C. I, 1107
Macy, Elisa IV, 1373
Macy, Elisabeth I, 826
Macy, Eliz. III, 216
Macy, Eliza III, 217
Macy, Eliza IV, 1373
Macy, Eliza V, 789
Macy, Eliza V, 850
Macy, Eliza Gardner IV, 1373
Macy, Eliza Hudson III, 217
Macy, Eliza L. II, 895
Macy, Eliza L. II, 915
Macy, Eliza L. III, 184
Macy, Eliza L. III, 185
Macy, Eliza L. III, 193
Macy, Eliza L. III, 215
Macy, Eliza L. III, 216
Macy, Eliza L. III, 217
Macy, Eliza L. III, 338
Macy, Elizabeth I, 508
Macy, Elizabeth I, 509
Macy, Elizabeth I, 559
Macy, Elizabeth I, 560
Macy, Elizabeth I, 661
Macy, Elizabeth I, 673
Macy, Elizabeth I, 684
Macy, Elizabeth I, 786
Macy, Elizabeth I, 804
Macy, Elizabeth I, 810
Macy, Elizabeth I, 825
Macy, Elizabeth I, 826
Macy, Elizabeth I, 992
Macy, Elizabeth I, 1124
Macy, Elizabeth III, 215
Macy, Elizabeth V, 96
Macy, Elizabeth V, 748
Macy, Elizabeth V, 753
Macy, Elizabeth V, 766
Macy, Elizabeth V, 781
Macy, Elizabeth V, 788
Macy, Elizabeth V, 789
Macy, Elizabeth V, 905
Macy, Elizabeth V, 920
Macy, Elizabeth VI, 298
Macy, Elizabeth B. III, 215
Macy, Elizabeth Hussey III, 217
Macy, Ella III, 215
Macy, Ella III, 336
Macy, Ellen C. III, 196
Macy, Elmina I, 508
Macy, Elmira V, 753
Macy, Emily V, 753
Macy, Emily V, 789
Macy, Enoch I, 507
Macy, Enoch I, 508
Macy, Enoch I, 558
Macy, Enoch I, 559
Macy, Enoch I, 600
Macy, Enoch I, 602
Macy, Enoch I, 606
Macy, Enoch I, 971
Macy, Enoch I, 992
Macy, Enoch V, 788
Macy, Enoch V, 789
Macy, Esther V, 753
Macy, Esther C. I, 684
Macy, Eunice I, 507
Macy, Eunice I, 508
Macy, Eunice I, 509
Macy, Eunice I, 541
Macy, Eunice I, 558
Macy, Eunice I, 559
Macy, Eunice I, 684
Macy, Eunice I, 1107
Macy, Eunice V, 753
Macy, Eunice V, 781
Macy, Eunice V, 788
Macy, Eunice V, 789
Macy, Eunice V, 791
Macy, Eunice V, 794
Macy, Eunice V, 815
Macy, Eunice V, 819
Macy, Eunice V, 820
Macy, Frances V, 788
Macy, Francis H. III, 22
Macy, Francis H. III, 215
Macy, Francis H. III, 216
Macy, Francis H. III, 240
Macy, Francis H. III, 327
Macy, Francis H., Jr. III, 215
Macy, Franklin E. III, 221
Macy, Frederic I, 661
Macy, Frederick B. III, 215
Macy, Frederick H. I, 684
Macy, Gayar I, 992
Macy, Gayer I, 508
Macy, Gayer I, 786
Macy, Gayer I, 825
Macy, Gayr I, 558
Macy, Geare I, 992
Macy, Geo. V, 905
Macy, Geo. V, 920
Macy, George I, 508
Macy, George I, 558
Macy, George I, 559
Macy, George I, 786
Macy, George I, 809
Macy, George I, 825
Macy, George I, 826
Macy, George III, 215
Macy, George V, 96
Macy, George V, 920
Macy, George H. III, 65
Macy, George Hussey I, 508
Macy, George Hussey I, 559
Macy, George Trimble III, 217
Macy, Gethrow I, 559
Macy, Grace III, 189
Macy, Grace III, 216
Macy, Grace III, 277
Macy, Hannah I, 507
Macy, Hannah I, 508
Macy, Hannah I, 521
Macy, Hannah I, 533
Macy, Hannah I, 558
Macy, Hannah I, 559
Macy, Hannah I, 581
Macy, Hannah I, 661
Macy, Hannah I, 1107
Macy, Hannah I, 1121
Macy, Hannah I, 1124
Macy, Hannah I, 1130
Macy, Hannah III, 145
Macy, Hannah III, 216
Macy, Hannah V, 788
Macy, Hannah C. I, 508
Macy, Harriet H. III, 216
Macy, Harriet H. III, 249
Macy, Henery I, 661
Macy, Henery I, 676
Macy, Henery I, 677
Macy, Henery I, 684
Macy, Henery M. I, 560
Macy, Henry I, 507
Macy, Henry I, 508
Macy, Henry I, 559
Macy, Henry I, 560
Macy, Henry I, 661
Macy, Henry I, 682
Macy, Henry I, 684
Macy, Henry I, 725
Macy, Henry B. III, 215
Macy, Henry M. I, 508
Macy, Henry M. I, 560
Macy, Henry, Jr. I, 559
Macy, Hephzabah I, 558
Macy, Hepsibah V, 779
Macy, Hepsibah V, 789
Macy, Hepzabah I, 508
Macy, Hepzabeth I, 559
Macy, Hepzebah I, 1124
Macy, Hepzebeth I, 825
Macy, Hepzibah I, 508
Macy, Hepzibah I, 509
Macy, Hepzibah F. III, 215
Macy, Hepzibah, Jr. I, 559
Macy, Hepzibah, Sr. I, 559
Macy, Hepzibeth I, 508
Macy, Hepzibeth I, 512
Macy, Hepzibeth I, 558
Macy, Hepzibeth I, 567
Macy, Hepzibeth I, 825
Macy, Hezekiah III, 215
Macy, Hezekiah B. III, 216
Macy, Hiram III, 215
Macy, Howard III, 216
Macy, Hudson III, 215
Macy, Hulda I, 825
Macy, Huldah I, 508
Macy, Huldah I, 509
Macy, Huldah I, 536
Macy, Huldah I, 559
Macy, Huldah I, 797
Macy, Huldah I, 825
Macy, Huldah I, 992
Macy, Huldah I, 998
Macy, Hulday I, 558
Macy, Ida C. V, 850
Macy, Irena V, 850
Macy, Irene V, 851
Macy, Isaac I, 507
Macy, Isaac I, 508
Macy, Isaac I, 558
Macy, Isaac I, 559
Macy, Isaac I, 1107
Macy, Isaac I, 1124
Macy, Isaac III, 215
Macy, Isaac III, 216
Macy, Isaac V, 753
Macy, Isaac V, 788
Macy, Isaac Augustus III, 216
Macy, Isaac Gardner I, 558
Macy, Isaac Hall III, 216
Macy, Isabel III, 216
Macy, Isabella I, 508
Macy, Isabelle I, 559
Macy, Isabelle I, 560
Macy, Isabelle I, 575
Macy, Jabez I, 508
Macy, Jabez I, 559
Macy, Jabez I, 560
Macy, Jabez I, 575
Macy, James I, 509
Macy, James V, 753
Macy, James V, 754
Macy, James C. III, 215
Macy, James Rufus V, 753
Macy, Jamima I, 559
Macy, Jamima I, 580
Macy, Jamma I, 559
Macy, Jane III, 124
Macy, Jane III, 216
Macy, Jane III, 249
Macy, Jane V, 753
Macy, Jane V, 784
Macy, Jane V, 788
Macy, Jane H. III, 51
Macy, Jared III, 216
Macy, Jathro I, 508
Macy, Jedidah I, 508
Macy, Jedidah I, 558
Macy, Jedidah I, 576
Macy, Jemima I, 540
Macy, Jemima I, 558
Macy, Jemima V, 788
Macy, Jemime I, 508
Macy, Jesse I, 602
Macy, Jesse V, 788
Macy, Jesse V, 789
Macy, Jethro I, 509
Macy, Jethro I, 512
Macy, Jethro I, 558
Macy, Jethro I, 786
Macy, Jethro I, 825
Macy, Jethro I, 992
Macy, John I, 508
Macy, John I, 541
Macy, John I, 558
Macy, John I, 559
Macy, John I, 661
Macy, John I, 684
Macy, John I, 977
Macy, John I, 1095
Macy, John I, 1107
Macy, John I, 1124
Macy, John I Sup 1, 9
Macy, John IV, 737
Macy, John V, 753
Macy, John V, 788
Macy, John V, 789
Macy, John V, 850
Macy, John VI, 331
Macy, John G. I, 508
Macy, John G. V, 753
Macy, John G. V, 788
Macy, John G. V, 789
Macy, John H. III, 277
Macy, John H., Jr. III, 189
Macy, John H., Jr. III, 216
Macy, John Hicks III, 20
Macy, John Hicks III, 60
Macy, John Hicks III, 216
Macy, John Hinshaw I, 1107
Macy, John I. III, 124
Macy, John I. III, 216
Macy, John I. III, 249
Macy, John J. III, 51
Macy, John J. III, 216
Macy, John, Jr. I Sup 1, 10
Macy, John, Jr. III, 216
Macy, John, Sr. I, 773
Macy, Johnathan I, 1124
Macy, Jonathan I, 507
Macy, Jonathan I, 1107
Macy, Jonathan II, 589
Macy, Jonathan III, 216
Macy, Jonathan V, 753
Macy, Jonathan V, 788
Macy, Jonathan V, 789
Macy, Jonathan B. I, 1107
Macy, Jonathan W. I, 508
Macy, Joseph I, 558
Macy, Joseph I, 661
Macy, Joseph I, 684
Macy, Joseph I, 691
Macy, Joseph I, 825
Macy, Joseph I, 992
Macy, Joseph I, 1071
Macy, Joseph V, 788
Macy, Joseph W. I, 661
Macy, Josiah III, 215
Macy, Josiah III, 216
Macy, Josiah III, 217
Macy, Josiah G. III, 216
Macy, Josiah J. III, 216
Macy, Josiah J. III, 354
Macy, Josiah M. III, 216
Macy, Josiah, Jr. III, 112
Macy, Josiah, Jr. III, 196
Macy, Josiah, Jr. III, 216
Macy, Josiah, Jr. III, 217
Macy, Josiah, Jr. III, 355
Macy, Josiah, Sr. III, 217
Macy, Judith I, 508
Macy, Judith I, 509
Macy, Judith I, 536
Macy, Judith I, 559
Macy, Judith I, 574
Macy, Judith I, 661
Macy, Judith I, 684
Macy, Judith V, 788
Macy, Kate III, 65
Macy, Kate III, 196
Macy, Kate III, 216
Macy, Kate E. III, 196
Macy, Kate Everit III, 216
Macy, Katharine I, 508
Macy, Kezia B. III, 215
Macy, Laban I, 508
Macy, Laban I, 558
Macy, Lael V, 695
Macy, Laura V, 753
Macy, Laura V, 789
Macy, Lenna V, 753
Macy, Lindley V, 753
Macy, Lindley V, 789
Macy, Louisa III, 22
Macy, Louisa III, 216
Macy, Louisa III, 303
Macy, Louisa Y. III, 79
Macy, Love I, 661
Macy, Lucinda I, 507
Macy, Lucinda I, 558
Macy, Lucinda I, 684
Macy, Lucinda I, 1107
Macy, Lucinda I, 1124
Macy, Lucinda S. I, 661
Macy, Lucinday I, 684
Macy, Lucretia III, 215
Macy, Luzena I, 683
Macy, Luzena I, 684
Macy, Lydia I, 508
Macy, Lydia I, 536
Macy, Lydia I, 558
Macy, Lydia I, 559
Macy, Lydia I, 684
Macy, Lydia I, 786
Macy, Lydia I, 816
Macy, Lydia I, 825
Macy, Lydia I, 920
Macy, Lydia I, 992
Macy, Lydia I, 995
Macy, Lydia I, 1107
Macy, Lydia III, 52
Macy, Lydia III, 215
Macy, Lydia III, 216
Macy, Lydia III, 217

y, Lydia III, 292
y, Lydia IV, 1373
y, Lydia V, 753
y, Lydia V, 781
y, Lydia V, 788
y, Lydia V, 789
y, Lydia V, 794
y, Lydia V, 808
y, Lydia V, 815
y, Lydia V, 819
y, Lydia A. III, 299
y, Lydia Ann V, 753
y, Lydia H. III, 216
y, Lydia Jane I, 977
y, Lydia S. III, 216
y, Lydia S. III, 277
y, Lydia Starbuck III, 217
y, Lydiai I, 509
y, M. Matilda V, 726
y, Margaret V, 96
y, Margaret V, 920
y, Margaret S. III, 215
y, Maria V, 753
y, Mariana C. III, 196
y, Martha I, 684
y, Martha III, 124
y, Martha III, 216
y, Mary I, 507
y, Mary I, 508
y, Mary I, 558
y, Mary I, 559
y, Mary I, 560
y, Mary I, 661
y, Mary I, 682
y, Mary I, 684
y, Mary I, 709
y, Mary I, 725
y, Mary I, 786
y, Mary I, 797
y, Mary I, 804
y, Mary I, 810
y, Mary I, 825
y, Mary I, 826
y, Mary I, 891
y, Mary I, 981
y, Mary I, 983
y, Mary I, 992
y, Mary I, 1071
y, Mary I, 1107
y, Mary I, 1124
y, Mary I, 1125
y, Mary III, 217
y, Mary III, 240
y, Mary V, 746
y, Mary V, 753
y, Mary V, 779
y, Mary V, 784
y, Mary V, 788
y, Mary V, 789
y, Mary V, 791
y, Mary V, 850
y, Mary V, 851
y, Mary V, 905
y, Mary A. I, 677
y, Mary A. I, 684
y, Mary A. III, 216
y, Mary Ann I, 508
y, Mary Ann I, 524
y, Mary Ann I, 560
y, Mary Ann V, 753
y, Mary B. III, 216
y, Mary Barnard I, 825
y, Mary Etta I, 560
y, Mary J. III, 216
y, Mary J. III, 217
y, Mary Jay V, 753
y, Mary K. M. III, 355
y, Mary Kingsland III, 216
y, Mary Kingsland III, 354
y, Mary S. III, 217
y, Maryann V, 789
y, Maryann V, 793
y, Mathew IV, 832
y, Matilda I, 507
y, Matilda I, 508
y, Matilda I, 558
cy, Matilda I, 559
cy, Matilda I, 583
cy, Matilda I, 786
cy, Matilda I, 809
cy, Matilda I, 825
cy, Matilda I, 826
cy, Matilda I, 1107
cy, Matilda I, 1124
cy, Matilda I, 1134
cy, Matilda V, 753
cy, Matilda V, 788
cy, Matilda M. V, 753
cy, Matilda M. V, 757
cy, Matthew I, 508
cy, Matthew I, 558
Macy, Matthew I, 773
Macy, Matthew I, 786
Macy, Matthew I, 825
Macy, Matthew I, 826
Macy, Matthew V, 753
Macy, Matthew V, 788
Macy, Matthew, Jr. I, 825
Macy, Matthew, Jr. I Sup 1, 10
Macy, Merab I, 508
Macy, Merab I, 509
Macy, Merab I, 558
Macy, Merab I, 559
Macy, Meriah I, 559
Macy, Micajah I, 558
Macy, Micajah IV, 737
Macy, Micajah V, 96
Macy, Micajah VI, 311
Macy, Micajah VI, 314
Macy, Micajah VI, 325
Macy, Micajah VI, 331
Macy, Micajah T. V, 96
Macy, Milton V, 96
Macy, Milton T. V, 96
Macy, Milton T. V, 136
Macy, Miriam I, 507
Macy, Miriam I, 530
Macy, Miriam I, 558
Macy, Miriam I, 559
Macy, Miriam I, 600
Macy, Miriam I, 750
Macy, Miriam I, 766
Macy, Miriam I, 786
Macy, Miriam I, 806
Macy, Miriam I, 825
Macy, Miriam I, 913
Macy, Miriam V, 779
Macy, Mirium I, 825
Macy, Mitilda I, 558
Macy, Moses V, 788
Macy, Moses V, 789
Macy, Nancy I, 507
Macy, Nancy I, 559
Macy, Nancy I, 560
Macy, Nancy I, 568
Macy, Nancy I, 579
Macy, Nancy I, 600
Macy, Nancy I, 602
Macy, Nancy I, 977
Macy, Nancy I, 992
Macy, Nathan I, 508
Macy, Nathan I, 509
Macy, Nathan I, 606
Macy, Nathan V, 96
Macy, Nathan V, 788
Macy, Nathan V, 789
Macy, Nathan D. V, 96
Macy, Nathan H. I, 1107
Macy, Nathaniel I, 508
Macy, Nathaniel I, 558
Macy, Nathaniel I, 559
Macy, Nathaniel I, 825
Macy, Nathaniel I Sup 1, 9
Macy, Obed I, 508
Macy, Obed I, 536
Macy, Obed I, 559
Macy, Obed IV, 1373
Macy, Obed V, 753
Macy, Obed V, 788
Macy, Obed V, 789
Macy, Parintha I, 937
Macy, Parintha I, 945
Macy, Parintha C. I, 683
Macy, Parintha C. I, 684
Macy, Paul I, 508
MAcy, Paul I, 534
Macy, Paul I, 558
Macy, Paul I, 559
Macy, Paul I, 825
Macy, Paul I Sup 1, 9
Macy, Paul V, 753
Macy, Paul V, 755
Macy, Paul V, 781
Macy, Paul V, 788
Macy, Paul V, 789
Macy, Paul V, 791
Macy, Paul V, 815
Macy, Paul V, 819
Macy, Paul, Sr. I, 559
Macy, Pauline V, 753
Macy, Pheba V, 789
Macy, Phebe I, 508
Macy, Phebe I, 546
Macy, Phebe I, 559
Macy, Phebe I, 576
Macy, Phebe I, 661
Macy, Phebe I, 683
Macy, Phebe I, 684
Macy, Phebe I, 766
Macy, Phebe I, 786
Macy, Phebe I, 825
Macy, Phebe I, 834
Macy, Phebe I, 992
Macy, Phebe I, 1071
Macy, Phebe III, 215
Macy, Phebe IV, 1373
Macy, Phebe V, 753
Macy, Phebe V, 754
Macy, Phebe V, 788
Macy, Phebe V, 789
Macy, Phebe V, 815
Macy, Phebe C. IV, 1373
Macy, Phebe Coffin IV, 1373
Macy, Phebe S. III, 216
Macy, Phebe S. III, 217
Macy, Phebe S. III, 277
Macy, Pheebe I, 725
Macy, Priscilla I, 508
Macy, Priscilla I, 558
Macy, Priscilla I, 786
Macy, Priscilla I, 825
Macy, Priscilla I, 826
Macy, Rachel I, 508
Macy, Rachel I, 559
Macy, Rachel I, 560
Macy, Rachel I, 661
Macy, Rachel I, 977
Macy, Rachel I, 984
Macy, Rachel I, 992
Macy, Rachel V, 834
Macy, Rachel V, 850
Macy, Rachel E. I, 992
Macy, Rebecah I, 992
Macy, Rebecca I, 558
Macy, Rebecca I, 661
Macy, Rebecca I, 684
Macy, Rebecca I, 980
Macy, Rebecca I, 992
Macy, Rebecca V, 753
Macy, Rebeckah I, 992
Macy, Rebeckah V, 788
Macy, Rebekah I, 559
Macy, Rebekah I, 977
Macy, Reuben I, 558
Macy, Reuben I, 661
Macy, Reuben I, 786
Macy, Reuben I, 826
Macy, Reuben III, 216
Macy, Reuben Folger I, 508
Macy, Rhoada I, 541
Macy, Rhoada I, 558
Macy, Rhoda I, 558
Macy, Rhoda I, 661
Macy, Rhoda I, 684
Macy, Rhoda I, 692
Macy, Rhoda I, 825
Macy, Rhoda I, 992
Macy, Rhoda V, 753
Macy, Rhoda V, 788
Macy, Rhoda V, 850
Macy, Robert I, 508
Macy, Robert I, 558
Macy, Robert I, 559
Macy, Robert V, 753
Macy, Robert B. III, 215
Macy, Robert B. III, 216
Macy, Rose ??? III, 216
Macy, Sally I, 559
Macy, Sally I, 560
Macy, Samiel I, 977
Macy, Samira I, 537
Macy, Samira I, 560
Macy, Samuel I, 983
Macy, Samuel I, 992
Macy, Samuel IV, 737
Macy, Samuel V, 788
Macy, Samuel V, 789
Macy, Samuel VI, 331
Macy, Samuel H. III, 216
Macy, Sarah I, 507
Macy, Sarah I, 508
Macy, Sarah I, 509
Macy, Sarah I, 510
Macy, Sarah I, 521
Macy, Sarah I, 523
Macy, Sarah I, 537
Macy, Sarah I, 558
Macy, Sarah I, 559
Macy, Sarah I, 560
Macy, Sarah I, 661
Macy, Sarah I, 684
Macy, Sarah I, 786
Macy, Sarah I, 819
Macy, Sarah I, 825
Macy, Sarah I, 837
Macy, Sarah I, 992
Macy, Sarah I, 996
Macy, Sarah III, 20
Macy, Sarah III, 216
Macy, Sarah III, 217
Macy, Sarah IV, 737
Macy, Sarah V, 20
Macy, Sarah V, 94
Macy, Sarah V, 96
Macy, Sarah V, 753
Macy, Sarah V, 850
Macy, Sarah V, 920
Macy, Sarah V, 934
Macy, Sarah VI, 311
Macy, Sarah VI, 314
Macy, Sarah VI, 331
Macy, Sarah A. III, 216
Macy, Sarah Emaline I, 977
Macy, Sarah Emaly I, 508
Macy, Sarah G. III, 216
Macy, Sarah H. I, 684
Macy, Sarah Jane I, 508
Macy, Sarah Jane I, 544
Macy, Sarah Jane I, 560
Macy, Sarah Jane V, 753
Macy, Sarah L. III, 86
Macy, Sarah L. III, 203
Macy, Sarah L. III, 215
Macy, Sarah Mary V, 96
Macy, Sarah R. III, 45
Macy, Sarah R. III, 216
Macy, Sarry I, 559
Macy, Sarry I, 561
Macy, Seth I, 559
Macy, Seth V, 753
Macy, Silas III, 215
Macy, Silas III, 216
Macy, Silburn I, 602
Macy, Silvanus I, 509
Macy, Silvanus J. II, 915
Macy, Silvanus J. III, 45
Macy, Silvanus J. III, 151
Macy, Silvanus J. III, 215
Macy, Silvanus J. III, 216
Macy, Silvanus J. III, 217
Macy, Silvanus J. III, 221
Macy, Silvanus J. III, 268
Macy, Solomon I, 508
Macy, Solomon I, 606
Macy, Stephen I, 507
Macy, Stephen I, 508
Macy, Stephen I, 521
Macy, Stephen I, 523
Macy, Stephen I, 558
Macy, Stephen I, 559
Macy, Stephen I, 560
Macy, Stephen I, 977
Macy, Stephen I, 980
Macy, Stephen I, 992
Macy, Stephen V, 753
Macy, Stephen V, 788
Macy, Stephen V, 789
Macy, Stephen V, 850
Macy, Stephen V, 851
Macy, Susan III, 79
Macy, Susan III, 122
Macy, Susanna I, 559
Macy, Susanna I, 661
Macy, Susannah V, 753
Macy, Sylvanus I, 559
Macy, Sylvanus J. II, 895
Macy, Sylvanus J. VI, 764
Macy, Taylor V, 850
Macy, Terrill V, 96
Macy, Thadden I, 602
Macy, Thaddeus I, 508
Macy, Thaddeus I, 558
Macy, Thaddeus I, 559
Macy, Thaddeus I, 581
Macy, Thaddeus I, 600
Macy, Thaddeus, II I, 507
Macy, Thomas I, 508
Macy, Thomas I, 509
Macy, Thomas I, 559
Macy, Thomas I, 661
Macy, Thomas I, 684
Macy, Thomas I, 825
Macy, Thomas I, 840
Macy, Thomas I, 1095
Macy, Thomas III, 216
Macy, Thomas V, 96
Macy, Thomas V, 746
Macy, Thomas V, 753
Macy, Thomas V, 788
Macy, Thomas B. V, 920
Macy, Thomas C. I, 661
Macy, Thomas J. V, 789
Macy, Thomas M. III, 216
Macy, Thomas, Jr. III, 216
Macy, Thos. V, 753
Macy, Thos. V, 766
Macy, Thos. V, 784
Macy, Thos. V, 788
Macy, Thos. V, 791
Macy, Thos. V, 793
Macy, Thos. B. V, 920
Macy, Thos. Webster V, 753
Macy, Timmothy I, 558
Macy, Timothy I, 508
Macy, Timothy I, 509
Macy, Timothy I, 559
Macy, Timothy I, 600
Macy, Tristram I, 786
Macy, Tristram I, 825
Macy, Tristram V, 779
Macy, Tristram D. I, 661
Macy, Unice I, 559
Macy, Uriah I, 560
Macy, Uriah III, 217
Macy, Uriah Baldwin I, 508
Macy, V. Everit III, 216
Macy, Valentine Everit III, 61
Macy, Verlinda V, 850
Macy, Virlinda V, 850
Macy, W. H. III, 175
Macy, Wd. Lydia III, 357
Macy, Widow Dinah I, 507
Macy, Widow Elizabeth I, 676
Macy, Widow Elizabeth I, 1135
Macy, Widow Hannah I, 558
Macy, Widow Mary Way I, 684
Macy, William I, 507
Macy, William I, 508
Macy, William I, 546
Macy, William I, 559
Macy, William I, 560
Macy, William I, 579
Macy, William I, 602
Macy, William I, 661
Macy, William I, 725
Macy, William I, 797
Macy, William I, 825
Macy, William I, 977
Macy, William I, 992
Macy, William I, 1071
Macy, William I, 1107
Macy, William I, 1121
Macy, William I, 1124
Macy, William V, 96
Macy, William V, 753
Macy, William C. III, 196
Macy, William D. V, 96
Macy, William Gayer I, 977
Macy, William H. III, 196
Macy, William H. III, 216
Macy, William H., Jr. III, 216
Macy, William H., Jr. III, 217
Macy, William Henry, Jr. III, 217
Macy, William W. III, 217
Macy, Wm. III, 215
Macy, Wm. V, 753
Macy, Wm. H. II, 895
Macy, Wm. H. II, 915
Macy, Wm. H. III, 184
Macy, Wm. H. III, 215
Macy, Wm. H. III, 216
Macy, Wm. H. III, 217
Macy, Wm. H. III, 338
Macy, Wm. H., Jr. III, 217
Macy, Wm. M. I, 1107
Macy, Wm. W. III, 216
Macy, Wm. W. III, 277
Macy, Zabdiah I, 507
Macy, Zabdiah I, 559
Macy, Zaccheus I, 508
Macy, Zachariah I, 558
Macy, Zacharus I, 509
Macy, Zacheus I, 559
Macy, Zacheus I, 819
Macy, Zacheus I, 825
Macy, Zacheus V, 753
Macy, Zalinda V, 20
Macy, Zalinda V, 96
Macy, Zeris I, 508
Maddans, Ingo III, 217
Maddans, Julia Willets III, 217
Maddans, Paul III, 217
Maddeera, Branch T. VI, 956
Maddeera, Sarah VI, 956
Madden, Alice Jane V, 633
Madden, Alpheus E. V, 584
Madden, Alpheus E. V, 585
Madden, Ann I, 450
Madden, Ann V, 498
Madden, Ann V, 515
Madden, Ann V, 516
Madden, Anna V, 96
Madden, Anna Maria V, 96
Madden, Anna Maria V, 584
Madden, Arthur V, 96
Madden, Arthur V, 584
Madden, Arthur W. V, 96
Madden, Charles V, 96
Madden, Clinton V, 665
Madden, Clinton C. V, 585
Madden, Cora V, 584
Madden, Cora G. V, 550
Madden, Cyrus V, 633
Madden, Cyrus W. V, 584
Madden, Cyrus W. V, 633

Madden, Deborah I, 450
Madden, Deborah V, 516
Madden, Douglas V, 550
Madden, Edith V, 584
Madden, Edith V, 601
Madden, Eli V, 584
Madden, Elizabeth I, 406
Madden, Elizabeth I, 450
Madden, Elizabeth V, 515
Madden, Elizabeth V, 619
Madden, Elizabeth V, 633
Madden, Elizabeth R. V, 633
Madden, Ellen III, 21
Madden, Ellen III, 268
Madden, Geo. V, 633
Madden, George V, 515
Madden, George V, 584
Madden, George V, 585
Madden, George V, 633
Madden, George, Jr. V, 584
Madden, George, Jr. V, 585
Madden, Hannah V, 96
Madden, Hannah V, 515
Madden, Hannah V, 584
Madden, Hannah C. V, 96
Madden, Hannah C. V, 584
Madden, Harlan V, 584
Madden, Henry V, 633
Madden, Hiram V, 96
Madden, Hiram V, 515
Madden, Hiram, Jr. V, 96
Madden, Hiram, Jr. V, 584
Madden, Jane V, 550
Madden, Jehu S. V, 584
Madden, John V, 515
Madden, Joseph G. V, 633
Madden, Lindon F. V, 584
Madden, Margaret V, 584
Madden, Mary I, 450
Madden, Mary V, 515
Madden, Mary V, 584
Madden, Mary Ann V, 633
Madden, Maryann V, 633
Madden, Moses George V, 633
Madden, Nellie C. V, 585
Madden, Nellie S. V, 665
Madden, Rachel V, 585
Madden, Rachel V, 633
Madden, Rebecah I, 450
Madden, Rebecca V, 515
Madden, Rebecca V, 554
Madden, Rebecca V, 584
Madden, Rebecca Ann V, 584
Madden, Ruth V, 404
Madden, Ruth V, 412
Madden, Ruth V, 516
Madden, Ruth V, 585
Madden, Ruth V, 633
Madden, Ruth Shires I, 450
Madden, Sally M. V, 584
Madden, Sarah V, 585
Madden, Solomon V, 515
Madden, Solomon V, 633
Madden, Thomas Elwood V, 585
Madden, William V, 633
Madden, William H. V, 584
Madden, William H. V, 585
Madden, Wm. V, 585
Madden, Wm. H. V, 633
Madder, Dellie IV, 978
Maddera, Branch T. VI, 956
Maddera, John VI, 956
Maddera, Mary M. VI, 956
Maddera, Nancy VI, 956
Maddera, Sarah VI, 956
Maddera, William VI, 956
Maddery, Nancy VI, 969
Maddery, William VI, 890
Maddicks, John II, 85
Maddison, Dolly I, 565
Maddison, Dolly II, 589
Maddison, Dolly II, 668
Maddix, Alice V, 1009
Maddock, ??? V, 756
Maddock, ??? V, 823
Maddock, Absilit V, 851
Maddock, Absillit V, 851
Maddock, Absillit V, 874
Maddock, Alpheus V, 851
Maddock, Alpheus T. V, 851
Maddock, Alvin S. V, 851
Maddock, Ann V, 851
Maddock, Anna II, 392
Maddock, Anna B. V, 852
Maddock, Anna Brummet V, 851
Maddock, Benj. II, 589
Maddock, Benj. II, 600
Maddock, Benjamin I, 1041
Maddock, Benjamin II, 392
Maddock, Benjamin II, 512
Maddock, Benjamin II, 543
Maddock, Benjamin II, 589
Maddock, Benjamin, Jr. II, 589
Maddock, David V, 851
Maddock, Deborah I, 406
Maddock, Deborah I, 422
Maddock, Deborah I, 1044
Maddock, Delilah V, 851
Maddock, Dorcas V, 753
Maddock, Dorcas V, 756
Maddock, Dorcas V, 851
Maddock, Eleanor V, 96
Maddock, Eleanor V, 833
Maddock, Elener I, 1044
Maddock, Elenor V, 42
Maddock, Elenor V, 96
Maddock, Eli V, 851
Maddock, Eli V, 874
Maddock, Eli C. V, 851
Maddock, Elijah V, 851
Maddock, Elisabeth II, 589
Maddock, Eliza H. II, 589
Maddock, Elizabeth II, 512
Maddock, Elizabeth II, 543
Maddock, Elizabeth II, 589
Maddock, Elizabeth II, 600
Maddock, Elizabeth V, 850
Maddock, Elizabeth V, 851
Maddock, Elizabeth H. II, 471
Maddock, Elizabeth H. II, 589
Maddock, Elizabeth Harr II, 392
Maddock, Elizabeth Harr II, 589
Maddock, Elmina V, 851
Maddock, Ezekiah II, 589
Maddock, Ezekiel Edwards II, 589
Maddock, Ezra II, 895
Maddock, Frances I, 1044
Maddock, Frances V, 846
Maddock, Frances V, 850
Maddock, Francis V, 96
Maddock, Francis V, 842
Maddock, Francis V, 851
Maddock, Francis V, 852
Maddock, Francis J. V, 851
Maddock, Frank V, 741
Maddock, Hannah I, 1041
Maddock, Hannah I, 1044
Maddock, Hannah V, 851
Maddock, Hannah V, 852
Maddock, Hannah V, 856
Maddock, Hannah V, 884
Maddock, Henry V, 851
Maddock, Hiram S. V, 851
Maddock, Hiram S. V, 852
Maddock, Hiram S. V, 920
Maddock, Irena V, 850
Maddock, Irena V, 851
Maddock, Irene V, 834
Maddock, Irene V, 851
Maddock, Isaac V, 851
Maddock, Jane II, 392
Maddock, Jane II, 471
Maddock, Jane II, 589
Maddock, Jane II, 600
Maddock, Jane V, 851
Maddock, John I, 1041
Maddock, John I, 1044
Maddock, John II, 572
Maddock, John II, 589
Maddock, John V, 851
Maddock, John V, 852
Maddock, John V, 864
Maddock, John C. V, 851
Maddock, John C. V, 852
Maddock, John C. V, 864
Maddock, John Frasier I, 406
Maddock, Joseph I, 389
Maddock, Joseph I, 406
Maddock, Joseph I, 1044
Maddock, Joseph I, 1049
Maddock, Joseph V, 834
Maddock, Joseph V, 850
Maddock, Joseph V, 851
Maddock, Joseph, Jr. V, 864
Maddock, Joseph, Sr. V, 851
Maddock, Josiah V, 851
Maddock, Lorenzo S. V, 851
Maddock, Lydia V, 851
Maddock, Lydia Ann V, 851
Maddock, Margaret II, 572
Maddock, Margaret II, 589
Maddock, Margaret Day I, 1041
Maddock, Maria F. II, 893
Maddock, Maria F. II, 895
Maddock, Martha V, 96
Maddock, Martha V, 833
Maddock, Martha V, 846
Maddock, Martha V, 851
Maddock, Martha V, 852
Maddock, Martha V, 864
Maddock, Martha Ann V, 851
Maddock, Martha Ellen V, 851
Maddock, Martha Ellen V, 852
Maddock, Martha S. V, 851
Maddock, Mary I, 406
Maddock, Mary V, 741
Maddock, Mary V, 742
Maddock, Mary V, 753
Maddock, Mary V, 842
Maddock, Mary V, 851
Maddock, Mary V, 864
Maddock, Mary Ann V, 851
Maddock, Mary Elizabeth V, 851
Maddock, Mary H. V, 851
Maddock, Mordecai II, 543
Maddock, Mordecai II, 589
Maddock, Nath V, 735
Maddock, Nathan I, 406
Maddock, Nathan I, 1044
Maddock, Nathan V, 96
Maddock, Nathan V, 835
Maddock, Nathan V, 851
Maddock, Nathan V, 852
Maddock, Nathan V, 875
Maddock, Phebe II, 549
Maddock, Phebe II, 589
Maddock, Phebe II, 712
Maddock, Phebe V, 741
Maddock, Phebe V, 830
Maddock, Phebe V, 834
Maddock, Phebe V, 835
Maddock, Phebe V, 842
Maddock, Phebe V, 846
Maddock, Phebe V, 850
Maddock, Phebe V, 851
Maddock, Phebe Ann V, 851
Maddock, Rachel I, 406
Maddock, Rachel I, 1041
Maddock, Rachel I, 1044
Maddock, Rachel I, 1049
Maddock, Rachel V, 42
Maddock, Rachel V, 96
Maddock, Rachel V, 735
Maddock, Rachel V, 753
Maddock, Rachel V, 833
Maddock, Rachel V, 835
Maddock, Rachel V, 851
Maddock, Rachel V, 864
Maddock, Rachel H. V, 851
Maddock, Rachel H. V, 852
Maddock, Randal Mahlon II, 589
Maddock, Randall Malin II, 392
Maddock, Rebekah I, 395
Maddock, Rebekah I, 406
Maddock, Samuel I, 1041
Maddock, Samuel I, 1044
Maddock, Samuel I, 1049
Maddock, Samuel V, 42
Maddock, Samuel V, 96
Maddock, Samuel V, 833
Maddock, Samuel V, 850
Maddock, Samuel V, 851
Maddock, Samuel, Jr. V, 851
Maddock, Sarah I, 1044
Maddock, Sarah V, 835
Maddock, Sarah V, 851
Maddock, Sarah V, 866
Maddock, Sarah Moore II, 392
Maddock, Sarah Moore II, 589
Maddock, Sarah Moore II, 754
Maddock, Sarar V, 851
Maddock, Sue V, 851
Maddock, Tamer V, 851
Maddock, Theodore V, 920
Maddock, Theodore M. V, 920
Maddock, Theodore W. V, 851
Maddock, Theodore W. V, 852
Maddock, Virlanda V, 851
Maddock, Virlinda V, 851
Maddock, Wd. Elijah V, 851
Maddock, William II, 392
Maddock, William V, 851
Maddock, William L. II, 392
Maddock, William P. V, 851
Maddock, William S. V, 851
Maddock, Wm. II, 589
Maddock, Wm. V, 884
Maddock, Wm. L. II, 471
Maddock, Wm. L. II, 589
Maddock, Wm. Lloyd II, 589
Maddock, Wm. Lloyd II, 600
Maddockes, John II, 85
Maddockes, John II, 88
Maddockes, Sisley II, 88
Maddocks, Benjamin II, 392
Maddocks, Elijah V, 884
Maddocks, Elizabeth II, 26
Maddocks, Elizabeth II, 33
Maddocks, Elizabeth II, 34
Maddocks, Elizabeth II, 65
Maddocks, Elizabeth II, 85
Maddocks, Elizabeth V, 884
Maddocks, Hannah V, 884
Maddocks, John II, 26
Maddocks, John II, 33
Maddocks, John II, 85
Maddocks, Joseph V, 884
Maddocks, Margreat II, 85
Maddocks, Mary V, 884
Maddocks, Nathan I, 406
Maddocks, Nathan V, 884
Maddocks, Ralph II, 33
Maddocks, Sisley II, 85
Maddocks, Stacy V, 884
Maddocks, Wd. Elizabeth II, 33
Maddocks, Wm. V, 884
Maddon, Susanna IV, 210
Maddox, Alexander C. VI, 826
Maddox, Alice V, 1009
Maddox, Anna IV, 212
Maddox, Anna IV, 248
Maddox, Anna Mary IV, 247
Maddox, Annie W. IV, 211
Maddox, Caroline Eliza IV, 247
Maddox, Charles V, 585
Maddox, Charles VI, 198
Maddox, Edwin Milton VI, 259
Maddox, Eliza IV, 247
Maddox, Eliza IV, 248
Maddox, Eliza VI, 259
Maddox, Elizabeth II, 589
Maddox, Elizabeth VI, 137
Maddox, Elizabeth VI, 140
Maddox, Elizabeth VI, 198
Maddox, Elizabeth VI, 259
Maddox, Elizabeth VI, 837
Maddox, Elizabeth VI, 853
Maddox, Erba IV, 248
Maddox, Erba IV, 978
Maddox, Erba R. IV, 248
Maddox, Francina IV, 248
Maddox, Genevere V, 585
Maddox, Griffin VI, 259
Maddox, Harriett V, 585
Maddox, Harrison IV, 247
Maddox, Hattie J. V, 585
Maddox, Henrietta IV, 211
Maddox, Henrietta L. IV, 247
Maddox, Henrietta T. IV, 211
Maddox, Henrietta T. IV, 248
Maddox, Henry IV, 247
Maddox, Henry B. V, 1009
Maddox, James VI, 837
Maddox, Jane IV, 247
Maddox, Jane IV, 248
Maddox, Jane VI, 243
Maddox, Jane VI, 259
Maddox, John VI, 137
Maddox, John VI, 140
Maddox, John VI, 189
Maddox, John VI, 198
Maddox, John VI, 837
Maddox, John M. VI, 837
Maddox, John S. VI, 861
Maddox, John Wilson VI, 259
Maddox, John Wilson VI, 353
Maddox, John Wm. Griffin VI, 259
Maddox, Joseph IV, 248
Maddox, Joseph V, 585
Maddox, Joseph T. IV, 248
Maddox, Lawson VI, 812
Maddox, Lucy R. VI, 835
Maddox, Malissa V, 1009
Maddox, Margaret IV, 247
Maddox, Margaret VI, 198
Maddox, Margaret VI, 805
Maddox, Margaret VI, 812
Maddox, Margaret L. IV, 248
Maddox, Margaretta VI, 837
Maddox, Maria VI, 259
Maddox, Maria Ann VI, 259
Maddox, Mariah VI, 259
Maddox, Martha VI, 804
Maddox, Mary IV, 188
Maddox, Mary IV, 236
Maddox, Mary IV, 247
Maddox, Mary IV, 248
Maddox, Mary VI, 146
Maddox, Mary VI, 147
Maddox, Mary VI, 198
Maddox, Mary VI, 247
Maddox, Mary VI, 259
Maddox, Mary VI, 837
Maddox, Mary Jane IV, 188
Maddox, Mary Jane IV, 247
Maddox, Mary Jane IV, 248
Maddox, Mary L. IV, 248
Maddox, Melissa V, 1009
Maddox, Mildred VI, 198
Maddox, Mildred VI, 259
Maddox, Mildred VI, 835
Maddox, Mildred A. VI, 826
Maddox, Mildred, Jr. VI, 189
Maddox, Nathan I, 1034
Maddox, Nathan V, 96
Maddox, Nathaniel VI, 837
Maddox, Polly H. VI, 837
Maddox, Sarah A. VI, 821
Maddox, Sherard VI, 826
Maddox, Shired VI, 821
Maddox, Susan L. VI, 231
Maddox, Susan L. VI, 259
Maddox, Susanna IV, 248
Maddox, Susanna VI, 259
Maddox, Susanna K. VI, 259
Maddox, Susannah Lightfoot VI, 231
Maddox, Thomas IV, 247
Maddox, Thomas IV, 248
Maddox, Thomas VI, 243
Maddox, Thomas VI, 259
Maddox, Thomas VI, 331
Maddox, Thomas VI, 353
Maddox, Thomas Joseph IV, 2
Maddox, Thos. IV, 211
Maddox, Thos. IV, 247
Maddox, Virginia IV, 247
Maddox, William IV, 247
Maddox, William VI, 259
Maddox, William G. VI, 231
Maddox, William G. VI, 259
Maddox, William Garland VI, 198
Maddox, William Garland VI, 259
Maddox, William Griffin VI, 2
Maddox, William Gufing VI, 2
Maddox, William H. IV, 211
Maddox, Wilson IV, 188
Maddox, Wilson IV, 247
Maddox, Wilson IV, 248
Maddox, Wilson VI, 259
Maddox, Wilson H. IV, 248
Maddox, Wilson H. IV, 978
Maddox, Wm. IV, 236
Maddox, Wm. Edward V, 1009
Maddox, Wood IV, 211
Maddra, Branch T. VI, 956
Maddra, Martha VI, 988
Maddra, Martha A. VI, 988
Maddra, Sarah VI, 956
Maddry, John VI, 956
Maddry, Mary M. VI, 956
Maden, Alice V, 584
Maden, Alice Jane V, 559
Maden, Alice Jane V, 584
Maden, Alpheus E. V, 584
Maden, Alpheus E. V, 585
Maden, Ann V, 572
Maden, Anna Maria V, 584
Maden, Arthur V, 584
Maden, C. Clinton V, 695
Maden, Clinton V, 695
Maden, Clinton C. V, 585
Maden, Cora V, 584
Maden, Cyrus V, 584
Maden, Cyrus V, 695
Maden, Cyrus W. V, 584
Maden, Cyrus W. V, 585
Maden, Edith V, 584
Maden, Eleanor V, 695
Maden, Eli V, 584
Maden, Eli V, 695
Maden, Elizabeth I, 450
Maden, Elizabeth V, 584
Maden, Elizabeth V, 591
Maden, Elizabeth Ann V, 584
Maden, Elizabeth R. V, 584
Maden, George V, 584
Maden, George V, 585
Maden, George V, 695
Maden, George, Jr. V, 584
Maden, George, Jr. V, 585
Maden, Hannah V, 515
Maden, Hannah V, 584
Maden, Hannah V, 695
Maden, Hannah C. V, 574
Maden, Hannah C. V, 584
Maden, Harlan V, 584
Maden, Harlan V, 591
Maden, Harlan V, 695
Maden, Hiram V, 584
Maden, Hiram V, 591
Maden, Hiram V, 599
Maden, Hiram, Jr. V, 574
Maden, Hiram, Jr. V, 584
Maden, Jehu V, 584
Maden, Jehu S. V, 584
Maden, Jehu S. V, 605
Maden, John V, 584
Maden, John V, 695
Maden, Leon Doan V, 695
Maden, Lindon F. V, 584

aden, Margaret V, 584
aden, Margaret V, 591
aden, Margaret V, 695
aden, Mary V, 554
aden, Mary V, 573
aden, Mary V, 584
aden, Mary Ann V, 584
aden, Moses V, 584
aden, Moses G. V, 585
aden, Nellie C. V, 585
aden, Nellie C. V, 695
aden, Nellie S. V, 695
aden, Phebe E. V, 695
aden, Rachel V, 584
aden, Rachel V, 585
aden, Rebecca V, 584
aden, Rebecca V, 695
aden, Rebecca Ann V, 584
aden, Rebecca Ann V, 693
aden, Rhoena V, 584
aden, Roena V, 695
aden, Ruth V, 578
aden, Ruth V, 584
aden, Ruth V, 585
aden, Ruth V, 605
aden, Sally M. V, 584
aden, Sally M. V, 695
Maden, Samuel V, 584
Maden, Samuel C. V, 584
Maden, Sarah V, 585
Maden, Solomon V, 584
Maden, Solomon V, 585
Maden, Susanna V, 584
Maden, Susanna V, 585
Maden, Susanna V, 693
Maden, Susannah V, 582
Maden, Susannah V, 584
Maden, Susannah V, 599
Maden, Thomas E. V, 695
Maden, Thomas Elwood V, 584
Maden, Thomas Elwood V, 585
Maden, Thomas Elwood V, 695
Maden, William V, 584
Maden, William H. V, 584
Maden, William H. V, 585
Maden, Wm. V, 585
Maden, Wm. Henry V, 584
Madex, Wm. Edward V, 1009
Madiera, Charles II, 392
Madison, Dolly VI, 466
Madkins, Ann VI, 115
Madkins, Arebella VI, 115
Madkins, Daniel VI, 115
Madkins, Esther VI, 115
Madkins, Huldah VI, 115
Madkins, Jane VI, 115
Madkins, Martha VI, 115
Madkins, Mary VI, 115
Madkins, Ruth VI, 115
Madkins, Sarah VI, 115
Madkins, Thomas VI, 115
Madkins, Thomas Durham VI, 115
Madkins, William VI, 115
Madlin, Elizabeth VI, 956
Madlin, Mial VI, 956
Madon, Elizabeth I, 377
Madon, Elizabeth I, 406
Mador, Francis V, 42
Mador, Francis V, 96
Mador, Phebe V, 42
Mador, Samuel V, 96
Madras, Gertrude L. IV, 1328
Madrin, Reuben I, 146
Madson, Ella V, 516
Maerkt, Amelia IV, 99
Maerkt, Amelia IV, 130
Maerkt, Amelia IV, 737
Maerkt, Amelia IV, 832
Maerkt, Amelia Caroline IV, 737
Maerkt, Amelia Caroline IV, 832
Maerkt, Ann IV, 130
Maerkt, Anna IV, 99
Maerkt, Anna IV, 737
Maerkt, Anna IV, 738
Maerkt, Anna IV, 832
Maerkt, Charlot IV, 832
Maerkt, Charlotte IV, 130
Maerkt, Charlotte D. IV, 130
Maerkt, Charlotte D. IV, 737
Maerkt, Charlotte D. IV, 832
Maerkt, Emelia Caroline IV, 737
Maerkt, Frederick IV, 99
Maerkt, Frederick IV, 130
Maerkt, Frederick IV, 737
Maerkt, Frederick IV, 832
Maerkt, Hanna G. IV, 737
Maerkt, Hannah IV, 832
Maerkt, Hannah C. IV, 99
Maerkt, Hannah G. IV, 99
Maerkt, Hannah G. IV, 130
Maerkt, Hannah G. IV, 737
Maerkt, Hannah G. IV, 738
Maerkt, Jane IV, 99
Maerkt, Jane IV, 737
Maerkt, Jane IV, 832
Maerkt, Jane J. IV, 130
Maerkt, Jane J. IV, 737
Maerkt, Jane J. IV, 738
Maerkt, Jane J. IV, 762
Maerkt, Louisa IV, 130
Maerkt, Louisa IV, 737
Maerkt, Louisa IV, 832
Maerkt, Louiza IV, 737
Maerkt, Wilhelmina IV, 99
Maerkt, Wilhelmina IV, 130
Maerkt, Wilhelmina IV, 683
Maerkt, Wilhelmina IV, 737
Maerkt, Wilhelmina IV, 832
Maerkt, Williamina IV, 99
Maerkt, Williamina IV, 832
Magahe, Huldah VI, 268
Magahe, James VI, 197
Magahe, James VI, 209
Magahe, James VI, 242
Magahe, James VI, 278
Magahe, Mabel VI, 278
Magahe, Mary VI, 189
Magahe, Mary VI, 191
Magahe, Mary VI, 197
Magahe, Rebeckah VI, 197
Magahe, Rebeckah VI, 209
Magahe, Samuel VI, 189
Magahe, Samuel VI, 191
Magahe, Samuel VI, 197
Magahe, William VI, 197
Magahea, Huldah VI, 197
Magahea, Huldah VI, 213
Magahea, Samuel VI, 197
Magahea, Samuel VI, 213
Magahey, James VI, 197
Magahey, James VI, 209
Magahey, Rebeckah VI, 197
Magahey, Rebeckah VI, 209
Magahey, William VI, 197
Magam, Nancy VI, 837
Magam, Pleasant VI, 837
Magan, Ann VI, 1021
Magan, James VI, 960
Magan, Jane VI, 1021
Magan, Wiatt VI, 887
Magann, Archelous VI, 1015
Magann, Elizabeth VI, 835
Magann, James VI, 1003
Magann, John VI, 887
Magann, John VI, 960
Magann, Lewis VI, 956
Magann, Lewis Merrett VI, 835
Magann, Lucinda VI, 956
Magann, Lucy Ann VI, 960
Magann, Martha R. VI, 887
Magann, Nancy VI, 800
Magann, Pleasant VI, 880
Magann, Pleasant VI, 961
Magarge, Ezra II, 946
Magarge, Hannah II, 1086
Magarge, Hannah S. II, 946
Magba, Hannah VI, 331
Magba, Vardry VI, 331
Magba, Vardy VI, 331
Magee, Alice Gertrude V, 412
Magee, Archer V, 412
Magee, Archer James V, 412
Magee, Edith V, 681
Magee, Edith V, 695
Magee, Edith Maria V, 412
Magee, Edith Mariah V, 412
Magee, Elizabeth E. V, 657
Magee, Elizabeth E. V, 695
Magee, James V, 412
Magee, Joseph V, 412
Magee, Lula I, 891
Magee, Missouri V, 412
Magee, Wm. Webster V, 412
Mageehee, Cann VI, 259
Mageehee, Carr VI, 259
Mageehee, Elizabeth VI, 259
Mager, ??? III, 217
Mager, Maria III, 217
Mager, Simeon III, 217
Magers, Dinah VI, 837
Magers, Henry VI, 837
Magers, Nancy VI, 925
Maggee, Lula I, 880
Maghe, Huldah VI, 197
Maghe, Huldah VI, 213
Maghe, Mary VI, 197
Maghe, Samuel VI, 197
Maghe, William VI, 197
Maghehe, Samuel VI, 197
Magill, Allen III, 217
Magill, Allen H. III, 217
Magill, Allen H. III, 367
Magill, Amy II, 1013
Magill, Amy II, 1020
Magill, Anna II, 1055
Magill, Beatrice II, 895
Magill, Carrie II, 831
Magill, Carrie II, 895
Magill, Catharine J. II, 815
Magill, David II, 322
Magill, David II, 895
Magill, Edgar R. III, 217
Magill, Edw. H. III, 217
Magill, Edward H. II, 895
Magill, Edward H. II, 939
Magill, Edward H. III, 131
Magill, Edward H. III, 132
Magill, Edward H. III, 306
Magill, Edward Hicks II, 808
Magill, Edward Hicks II, 895
Magill, Edward W. II, 831
Magill, Edward W. II, 895
Magill, Eudora II, 895
Magill, Frances II, 322
Magill, Frances II, 895
Magill, Francis Gardiner II, 895
Magill, Francis Gardner II, 808
Magill, Gertrude B. II, 895
Magill, Grace III, 217
Magill, Grace III, 367
Magill, Helen II, 895
Magill, Helen II, 939
Magill, Jacob II, 1013
Magill, Jacob II, 1020
Magill, Jacob II, 1036
Magill, Jane II, 1013
Magill, Jane II, 1020
Magill, John II, 1013
Magill, John II, 1020
Magill, Jonathan II, 1013
Magill, Jonathan P. II, 1013
Magill, Jonathan P. II, 1036
Magill, Jonathan P. III, 217
Magill, Katie III, 217
Magill, Marian II, 895
Magill, Mary II, 895
Magill, Mary II, 1013
Magill, Mary II, 1036
Magill, Mary Harvey II, 831
Magill, Mary W. III, 217
Magill, Rachel II, 1013
Magill, Rebecca II, 1013
Magill, Rebecca II, 1036
Magill, Rebeckah II, 1013
Magill, Rebeckah II, 1020
Magill, Robert II, 712
Magill, Robert B. II, 712
Magill, Robert B. II, 754
Magill, Samuel II, 808
Magill, Samuel II, 895
Magill, Sarah II, 895
Magill, Sarah II, 1013
Magill, Sarah E. III, 131
Magill, Sarah Eliz III, 306
Magill, Sarah Eliz. III, 217
Magill, Sarah Elizabeth III, 131
Magill, Sarah G. II, 712
Magill, Sarah G. II, 754
Magill, Sarah G. II, 770
Magill, Sarah M. II, 1053
Magill, Sarah M. II, 1055
Magill, Sarah W. II, 895
Magill, Sarah W. II, 939
Magill, Sarah W. II, 1055
Magill, Sarah Warner II, 808
Magill, Watson P. II, 831
Magill, Watson P. II, 895
Magill, Wm. II, 895
Magill, Wm. II, 1013
Magill, Wm. II, 1020
Magill, Wm., Jr. II, 895
Maginis, Mary Ann III, 217
Maginnis, Mary IV, 248
Magner, ??? I Sup 1, 12
Magner, Ada IV, 1328
Magner, Adah IV, 1328
Magner, Ann I, 359
Magner, Betty I, 359
Magner, Carlton IV, 1328
Magner, Henry I, 359
Magner, Henry I Sup 1, 8
Magner, Jean I, 359
Magner, Jean I Sup 1, 8
Magner, Wm. IV, 1328
Magoon, Albert V, 263
Magoon, Albert V, 460
Magoon, Albert V, 633
Magoon, Alfred V, 220
Magoon, Alfred V, 263
Magoon, Alfred V, 348
Magoon, Alfred V, 460
Magoon, Alfred V, 633
Magoon, Asenath V, 329
Magoon, Asenath V, 348
Magoon, Elizabeth V, 220
Magoon, Elizabeth V, 460
Magoon, Frank V, 460
Magoon, Hiram V, 460
Magoon, Josiah V, 263
Magoon, Josiah V, 460
Magoon, Josiah V, 633
Magoon, Mary V, 263
Magoon, Mary V, 451
Magoon, Mary V, 612
Magoon, Mary V, 633
Magoon, Mary E. V, 220
Magoon, Mary E. V, 263
Magoon, Mary E. V, 633
Magoon, Olive J. V, 263
Magoon, Parthena V, 263
Magoon, Parthena V, 633
Magoon, Parthenia V, 263
Magoon, William V, 263
Magoon, William O. V, 263
Magoon, Wm. V, 633
Magoon, Wm. O. V, 633
Magor, James VI, 958
Magrage, Mrs. G. T. IV, 1328
MaGrew, Mary IV, 832
Magrew, Mary IV, 843
Maguire, John III, 17
Maguire, John III, 217
Maguire, Mary V. D. III, 17
Maguire, Mary V. D. III, 217
Maguire, Rebecca III, 17
Maguire, Rebecca III, 217
Mahaffey, Clarence W. V, 633
Mahaffey, Clarence W. V, 695
Mahaffey, Goldie M. V, 633
Mahaffey, Goldie M. V, 695
Mahaffey, Nathan A. V, 633
Mahaffey, Nathan A. V, 695
Mahaffey, Sarah V, 633
Mahaffey, Sarah A. V, 695
Mahaffy, Clarence V, 633
Mahaffy, Clarence W. V, 633
Mahaffy, George V, 633
Mahaffy, Goldie V, 633
Mahaffy, Goldie M. V, 633
Mahaffy, Irena V, 633
Mahaffy, Nathan V, 633
Mahaffy, Nathan A. V, 633
Mahaffy, Sara Alice V, 633
Mahaffy, Sarah V, 633
Mahaffy, Wesley V, 815
Mahaly, Pritchet Benton I, 621
Mahaly, Willis I, 621
Mahan, Ann II, 1055
Mahan, Ann II, 1076
Mahan, Ann II, 1080
Mahan, Bertelle V, 460
Mahan, John II, 1056
Mahan, John II, 1076
Mahan, John II, 1080
Mahan, Mary II, 1055
Mahan, Ruth II, 1076
Mahan, Ruth II, 1080
Mahan, Zephaniah II, 1076
Mahan, Zephaniah II, 1080
Mahan, Zepheniah II, 1056
Mahane, Pleasant VI, 837
Mahane, Polly VI, 837
Mahaney, William I, 1159
Mahany, Rachel VI, 601
Maharry, Ann II, 392
Maharry, James II, 392
Mahary, James II, 392
Mahew, Alexander VI, 959
Mahew, Lucos VI, 910
Mahew, Madgalena VI, 910
Mahew, Moses VI, 959
Mahew, N. VI, 950
Mahew, Nancy VI, 937
Mahew, Polly VI, 950
Mahew, Sally VI, 1018
Mahler, ??? III, 217
Mahler, Jamima III, 217
Mahlon, Elijah II, 589
Mahlon, Enoch II, 589
Mahlon, Margaret II, 589
Mahlon, Rachel II, 589
Maholin, Edwin F. IV, 540
Maholin, Elizabeth IV, 538
Maholin, Elizabeth IV, 540
Mahon, Ann II, 1055
Mahon, John II, 1056
Mahon, Mary II, 1055
Mahon, Zepheniah II, 1056
Mahone, Barnett VI, 837
Mahone, Catharine VI, 837
Mahone, Daniel VI, 956
Mahone, Dennis VI, 837
Mahone, Elizabeth VI, 956
Mahone, Robert VI, 837
Mahone, Sophia VI, 837
Mahone, Susanna VI, 837
Mahoney, Archabel I, 1159
Mahoney, Elizabeth I, 1124
Mahoney, Elizabeth VI, 421
Mahoney, Harriett I, 1145
Mahoney, J. L. I, 1159
Mahoney, John L. I, 1145
Mahoney, John L. I, 1159
Mahoney, Martha I, 1145
Mahoney, Nancy J. I, 1145
Mahoney, Rachel VI, 421
Mahoney, Rachel VI, 602
Mahoney, Rachel Ann VI, 416
Mahoney, Rachel Ann VI, 417
Mahoney, Rachel Ann VI, 421
Mahoney, Rachel Ann VI, 445
Mahoney, William I, 1095
Mahoney, William I, 1145
Mahoney, William I, 1159
Mahoney, Willie I, 1159
Mahony, William I, 1095
Mai, Shinji I. III, 217
Maibie, Deborah V, 515
Maidlin, Eliza VI, 928
Maids, Ane I, 91
Mailand, Robert III, 21
Mailer, Catharine III, 87
Mailler, Catherine III, 36
Mailor, ??? III, 217
Mailor, Hallock R. III, 217
Mailor, Jamima III, 217
Mailor, Jemima III, 218
Mailor, Mary Ann III, 217
Mailor, William III, 217
Main, Benjamin II, 392
Main, Elizabeth VI, 421
Main, Hannah IV, 1172
Main, Maggie V, 1009
Maine, Elizabeth F. III, 217
Maine, Elizabeth F. III, 275
Maine, Frederick E. III, 68
Maine, Horace S. III, 217
Maine, Jas. C. III, 217
Maine, Josephine F. III, 68
Maine, Malcolm T. III, 147
Maine, Malcolm T. III, 217
Maine, Malcolm T. III, 275
Maine, Minerva B. III, 217
Maine, P. Francena III, 147
Maine, Phebe F. III, 217
Maine, Phebe F. III, 275
Maine, Phebe Francena III, 217
Mains, Ann IV, 130
Mains, Ann IV, 726
Mains, Ann IV, 750
Mains, Anne IV, 128
Mains, Anne IV, 130
Mains, Deborah IV, 130
Mains, Deborah IV, 132
Mains, Dinah IV, 99
Mains, Dinah IV, 100
Mains, Elizabeth IV, 48
Mains, Elma IV, 130
Mains, Elma IV, 133
Mains, Finley IV, 100
Mains, James IV, 130
Mains, James, Jr. IV, 130
Mains, Jane IV, 130
Mains, Jane IV, 133
Mains, John IV, 130
Mains, Margaret IV, 130
Mains, Margaret IV, 131
Mains, Mary IV, 92
Mains, Mary IV, 100
Mains, Rebecca IV, 130
Maiphy, Anna III, 106
Maiphy, Anna III, 218
Maiphy, Anna W. III, 218
Maiphy, Evelyn Jeanne III, 218
Maiphy, Thomas F. III, 218
Maise, Rebecca V, 485
Maise, Rebecca V, 516
Maisterman, Mary II, 593
Maisterman, Thomas II, 592
Maisterman, Thomas II, 593
Maitland, Elizabeth VI, 993
Maitland, Frederick VI, 993
Maitland, Georgia IV, 1328
Maitland, Georgia A. IV, 1328
Maitland, James VI, 956
Maitland, John IV, 1328
Maitland, John Martin III, 218
Maitland, Louise III, 21
Maitland, Louise III, 218
Maitland, Mary III, 218
Maitland, Mary Eleanor III, 218
Maitland, Melinda VI, 956
Maitland, Ralph Waldo III, 218
Maitland, Robert III, 218

Major, Abigal VI, 956
Major, Angelina H. VI, 986
Major, Charles II, 895
Major, Charles Percy II, 895
Major, Charles, Sr. II, 895
Major, Cleopatra Albertine VI, 956
Major, Eleanor S. II, 895
Major, Elizabeth VI, 956
Major, Emily M. VI, 956
Major, Estella II, 895
Major, Frances VI, 914
Major, Harwood VI, 956
Major, Harwood VI, 971
Major, Harwood VI, 986
Major, James VI, 903
Major, James VI, 938
Major, James VI, 956
Major, James VI, 964
Major, John VI, 903
Major, John VI, 956
Major, John VI, 986
Major, Lucretia VI, 956
Major, Lucy T. VI, 903
Major, Mary Ann VI, 956
Major, Mildred VI, 956
Major, Roland VI, 956
Major, Simon VI, 956
Major, William W. VI, 928
Major, William W. VI, 956
Major, William W. VI, 962
Majors, Elizabeth VI, 956
Majors, Henry VI, 837
Majors, Roland VI, 956
Makeel, Susan M. III, 287
Makensey, Alex VI, 198
Makensey, Alexander VI, 198
Makensey, Alexd VI, 198
Makeny, Alex VI, 198
Makepeace, Albert S. VI, 956
Makepeace, Ruhama VI, 956
Makie, Rebekah I, 991
Makie, Rebekah I, 992
Makin, Sarah II, 392
Makin, Sarah II, 576
Makin, Sarah II, 589
Makin, Thomas II, 392
Makin, Thomas II, 576
Makin, Thomas II, 589
Makin, William II, 392
Makins, Sarah II, 392
Makins, Thomas II, 392
Makins, William II, 392
Malachi, Milton V, 1009
Malanger, Mary Jane V, 611
Malanger, Mary Jane V, 633
Malcolm, A. N. V, 754
Malcolm, Alice I, 637
Malcolm, Alice R. I, 621
Malcolm, Annie I, 621
Malcolm, Bettie I, 621
Malcolm, David I, 621
Malcolm, David I, 637
Malcolm, Deborah II, 555
Malcolm, Deborah II, 589
Malcolm, Earnest I, 637
Malcolm, Emery I, 637
Malcolm, Emory I, 621
Malcolm, Ernest I, 621
Malcolm, George I, 621
Malcolm, George I, 637
Malcolm, Hannah W. III, 501
Malcolm, James Arthur III, 501
Malcolm, James Landreth I, 621
Malcolm, Jeannie III, 214
Malcolm, Lena V, 754
Malcolm, Maude I, 621
Malcolm, Maude I, 637
Malcolm, Newton V, 754
Malcom, Deborah II, 589
Malcom, Hannah II, 589
Malcom, Hannah II, 637
Malcom, Isaac II, 589
Malcom, John J. II, 392
Malcomson, Abraham Bell III, 218
Malcomson, John III, 218
Malcum, George I, 637
Malester, Rebecca V, 1009
Malett, Susannah I, 450
Maletta, Susannah I, 450
Maletta, Susannah I, 454
Maley, Mary M. IV, 1106
Malie, Catharine I, 992
Malie, John I, 992
Malie, Naomi I, 992
Malin, Charles II, 712
Malin, David II, 589
Malin, David VI, 421
Malin, Elijah II, 589
Malin, Elizabeth VI, 479
Malin, Elizabeth VI, 530
Malin, Elizabeth VI, 629
Malin, Elizabeth VI, 633
Malin, Elizabeth VI, 675
Malin, Enoch II, 589
Malin, George II, 589
Malin, Gideon II, 476
Malin, Gideon II, 589
Malin, Isaac VI, 361
Malin, Isaac VI, 421
Malin, John II, 589
Malin, Lydia VI, 361
Malin, Lydia VI, 421
Malin, Margaret II, 356
Malin, Margaret II, 589
Malin, Phebe II, 476
Malin, Phebe II, 589
Malin, Rachel II, 589
Malin, Rachel II, 822
Malin, Rachel, Jr. II, 356
Malin, Sarah II, 476
Malin, Sarah II, 589
Malin, Thomas VI, 479
Malin, Thomas VI, 530
Malin, Thomas VI, 629
Malin, Thomas VI, 675
Malkey, Carl IV, 1328
Malkey, Chas. IV, 1328
Malkey, Elizabeth IV, 1328
Mall, Edward IV, 739
Mallanger, Mary J. V, 633
Mallanger, Mary Jane V, 633
Mallcum, Ann II, 1013
Mallcum, Jane Greer II, 1013
Mallee, George IV, 1328
Mallsberry, Jane II, 206
Mallsberry, Jane II, 240
Mallsbury, Sarah H. IV, 738
Mallsby, William I, 1125
Malmesbury, Isabel II, 1076
Malmesbury, Isabel II, 1081
Malmesbury, Isabela T. II, 895
Malmesbury, Isabella II, 895
Malmesbury, Isabella II, 1076
Malmesbury, Mary Anna II, 1076
Malmesbury, Mary L. II, 1076
Malmsberrberry, Benjamin IV, 932
Malmsberrberry, Mary IV, 932
Malmsberry, Adella IV, 978
Malmsberry, Adelza IV, 978
Malmsberry, Arvine C. IV, 978
Malmsberry, Benj. IV, 932
Malmsberry, Benjamin IV, 738
Malmsberry, Benjamin IV, 951
Malmsberry, Benjamin IV, 978
Malmsberry, Benjamin IV, 990
Malmsberry, Benjamin IV, 993
Malmsberry, Benjamin IV, 1014
Malmsberry, Benjamin, Jr. IV, 942
Malmsberry, Edith IV, 942
Malmsberry, Edith IV, 978
Malmsberry, Edith M. IV, 1040
Malmsberry, Elizabeth IV, 738
Malmsberry, Elizabeth IV, 832
Malmsberry, Elizabeth IV, 853
Malmsberry, Elizabeth IV, 978
Malmsberry, Elizabeth IV, 1014
Malmsberry, Emmor IV, 978
Malmsberry, Emmor C. IV, 978
Malmsberry, Fazetta IV, 950
Malmsberry, Fazetta C. IV, 978
Malmsberry, Geo. IV, 950
Malmsberry, George B. IV, 978
Malmsberry, Hannah IV, 738
Malmsberry, Hannah IV, 978
Malmsberry, Hannah IV, 993
Malmsberry, Isaac IV, 738
Malmsberry, Isaac IV, 832
Malmsberry, Isaac IV, 978
Malmsberry, James IV, 738
Malmsberry, James IV, 978
Malmsberry, James IV, 993
Malmsberry, Jane IV, 738
Malmsberry, Jane IV, 932
Malmsberry, Jane IV, 951
Malmsberry, Jane IV, 978
Malmsberry, Jane IV, 990
Malmsberry, Jane IV, 1014
Malmsberry, Jane, Jr. IV, 738
Malmsberry, Margaret IV, 832
Malmsberry, Mary IV, 978
Malmsberry, Rebecca IV, 738
Malmsberry, Rebecca IV, 978
Malmsberry, Rebecca IV, 990
Malmsberry, Sarah IV, 932
Malmsberry, Sarah IV, 978
Malmsberry, Sarah Anna IV, 978
Malmsberry, Sarah H. IV, 832
Malmsberry, Sarah H. IV, 929
Malmsberry, Sarah H. IV, 950
Malmsberry, Sarah H. IV, 978
Malmsberry, Sarah V. IV, 738
Malmsberry, Sarah V. IV, 978
Malmsberry, Tazetta C. IV, 978
Malmsbury, Benjamin IV, 738
Malmsbury, Elizabeth IV, 738
Malmsbury, Hannah IV, 738
Malmsbury, Isaac IV, 738
Malmsbury, Isabella II, 1076
Malmsbury, James IV, 738
Malmsbury, Jane II, 240
Malmsbury, Jane II, 241
Malmsbury, Jane IV, 738
Malmsbury, Jane, Jr. IV, 738
Malmsbury, Margaret IV, 805
Malmsbury, Rebecca IV, 738
Malmsbury, Sarah H. IV, 738
Malmsbury, Sarah V. IV, 738
Malona, Massah I, 725
Malona, Massah I, 731
Malone, ??? IV, 1303
Malone, Alice V, 898
Malone, Alice V, 920
Malone, Alice E. V, 348
Malone, Alice E. V, 361
Malone, Alice E. V, 412
Malone, Alice Elvira V, 412
Malone, Anne F. III, 56
Malone, Anne F. III, 218
Malone, Bessie V, 348
Malone, Bessie V, 695
Malone, Carl V, 695
Malone, Carrie H. IV, 738
Malone, Carroll B. IV, 1328
Malone, Charles E. V, 412
Malone, Charles E. V, 920
Malone, Charles O. IV, 738
Malone, Charles O. V, 412
Malone, Charles Oskar V, 412
Malone, Chas. A. V, 920
Malone, Chas. B. V, 348
Malone, Chas. O. IV, 1328
Malone, Chas. O. V, 348
Malone, Earl IV, 1328
Malone, Edwin Meadow V, 412
Malone, Edwin T. V, 348
Malone, Edwin T. V, 412
Malone, Elizabeth IV, 1328
Malone, Elizabeth Mather IV, 1310
Malone, Elizabeth Mather IV, 1328
Malone, Emma IV, 1308
Malone, Emma IV, 1328
Malone, Emma V, 348
Malone, Emma V, 695
Malone, Esther A. IV, 1328
Malone, Florence IV, 1328
Malone, Frances Emaly V, 412
Malone, Franklin IV, 1328
Malone, Franklin Bye V, 920
Malone, H. P. V, 348
Malone, H. P. V, 412
Malone, Harrison IV, 738
Malone, Harrison IV, 1328
Malone, Harrison V, 348
Malone, Harry IV, 1328
Malone, Harry P. V, 412
Malone, Henry G. V, 348
Malone, Henry G. V, 412
Malone, Hezekiah V, 348
Malone, Hezekiah B. V, 920
Malone, Hezekiah P. V, 412
Malone, Hezekiah P. V, 695
Malone, J. Walter IV, 1308
Malone, J. Walter IV, 1328
Malone, J. Walter, Jr. IV, 1310
Malone, J. Walter, Jr. IV, 1328
Malone, James V, 920
Malone, James S. IV, 738
Malone, James S. V, 348
Malone, James S. V, 412
Malone, James Scott V, 412
Malone, James T. V, 348
Malone, Jane V, 915
Malone, Jane G. V, 915
Malone, Jane G. V, 920
Malone, Jas. E. III, 56
Malone, Jas. Ellias III, 218
Malone, John IV, 1328
Malone, John V, 188
Malone, John V, 348
Malone, John V, 412
Malone, John VI, 956
Malone, John C. IV, 1328
Malone, John C. V, 361
Malone, John Howard V, 920
Malone, John W. V, 348
Malone, John W. V, 412
Malone, John Walter IV, 738
Malone, John Walter V, 412
Malone, Levi H. V, 348
Malone, Levi H. V, 412
Malone, Levi Harison V, 412
Malone, Lizzie J. III, 412
Malone, Lizzie J. III, 426
Malone, Lloyd S. IV, 1328
Malone, Louella V, 188
Malone, Margaret IV, 1312
Malone, Margaret IV, 1328
Malone, Mary II, 824
Malone, Mary V, 695
Malone, Mary A. V, 348
Malone, Mary A. V, 412
Malone, Mary Ann IV, 910
Malone, Mary Ann IV, 912
Malone, Mary Ann IV, 1328
Malone, Mary Ann V, 361
Malone, Mary Ann V, 412
Malone, Mary Ann VI, 956
Malone, May V, 348
Malone, May V, 695
Malone, Mildred Bowder V, 348
Malone, Nathaniel Frankin V, 920
Malone, P. Harrison V, 348
Malone, Rachel Ella V, 920
Malone, Ruth IV, 1328
Malone, Ruth IV, 1332
Malone, Ruth Ann Winifred III, 56
Malone, Ruth Ann Winifred III, 218
Malone, Sarah II, 782
Malone, Sarah IV, 1328
Malone, Sarah V, 920
Malone, Sarah C. IV, 978
Malone, Sarah C. IV, 986
Malone, Walter J. IV, 1328
Malone, William H. V, 920
Malone, William L. V, 412
Malone, Wm. H. V, 695
Malone, Wm. Harrison V, 920
Malone, Wm. L. V, 348
Maloney, Dorothea II, 755
Maloney, Edward J. II, 755
Maloney, Elizabeth F. VI, 837
Maloney, Esther II, 755
Maloney, James F. VI, 837
Maloney, James S. VI, 823
Maloney, Laura B. II, 755
Maloney, Rebecca A. II, 755
Maloney, Wm. L. II, 755
Malory, Lydia IV, 323
Malory, Lydia IV, 341
Malott, Elsa Stewart V, 348
Malott, Hiram IV, 1257
Malott, Hiram V. IV, 1257
Malott, Ida L. IV, 1257
Malott, Ida Lathem IV, 1257
Malott, James V, 1009
Malsbe, John I, 966
Malsberry, Jane IV, 623
Malsberry, Jane IV, 643
Malsby, Ann II, 394
Malsby, Ebenezer VI, 422
Malsby, Eliner VI, 422
Malsby, John I, 560
Malsby, John VI, 422
Malsby, Lydia VI, 422
Malsby, Mary II, 594
Malsmburg, Benjamin IV, 738
Malsmburg, Jane IV, 738
Maltbie, Narcissa IV, 1328
Maltbie, Narcissa E. IV, 1328
Maltby, John II, 394
Maltby, Joseph II, 394
Maltby, Mary II, 394
Maltby, Narcissa E. IV, 1328
Maltby, William II, 394
Man, Aaron V, 263
Man, Benjamin V, 263
Man, Elizabeth V, 263
Man, Hannah V, 852
Man, Jane I, 406
Man, Jane I, 424
Man, John V, 263
Man, Joseph V, 263
Man, Lewis V, 852
Man, Mary V, 852
Man, Rebecca V, 852
Man, Rhoda V, 223
Man, Rhoda V, 263
Man, Richard V, 852
Man, Warner V, 263
Man, William V, 852
Manaloto, Glen III, 376
Mancher, Albert V, 412
Mancher, Grace V, 412
Mandaville, Lydia W. V, 955
Mandeville, Elizabeth III, 218
Mandeville, Elizabeth III, 234
Mandeville, Giles III, 218
Mandeville, Giles III, 234
Mandeville, Giles III, 334
Mandeville, Hannah III, 396
Mandy, Sally A. I, 324
Maner, Betty I, 826
Manerva, Elizabeth V, 647
Manerva, Mary V, 647
Manerva, Mary Jane V, 647
Maness, Sarah A. I, 406
Maness, William I, 406
Maney, James H. III, 218
Manfield, Joseph II, 589
Manfield, Sarah II, 589
Manfield, Stephen II, 589
Manfield, Susanna II, 589
Mangam, Mary T. II, 754
Mangam, Mary T. II, 770
Mangham, ??? III, 218
Mangham, John III, 218
Mangham, Phebe III, 218
Mangham, Ruth III, 218
Manhasset, Cow Neck III, 42
Manifee, Chas. V, 1009
Manifee, Mary V, 1009
Manifold, Samuel V, 263
Manington, Charity V, 19
Manington, Charity V, 96
Manker, Albert V, 412
Manker, Albert N. V, 412
Manker, Alpheus O. V, 412
Manker, Alpheus O. V, 696
Manker, Beryha V, 412
Manker, Estel V, 412
Manker, Frank IV, 1257
Manker, Grace V, 412
Manker, Harley V, 412
Manker, Harley A. V, 412
Manker, Ida A. V, 412
Manker, Lesta V, 412
Manker, Mabel V, 412
Manker, Maryetta V, 412
Manker, Maud Louise V, 412
Manker, Mildred Lucile V, 412
Manker, Rachel VI, 409
Manker, Rachel VI, 421
Manker, Sanford V, 412
Manker, Stanley V, 412
Manker, Tillie V, 696
Mankin, Anne Jane IV, 791
Mankin, Caroline IV, 791
Mankin, Charity IV, 738
Mankin, Charity IV, 790
Mankin, Elizabeth IV, 643
Mankin, Elizabeth IV, 647
Mankin, Elizabeth IV, 791
Mankin, Hannah Miriam IV, 79
Mankin, Henry VI, 530
Mankin, Joseph IV, 791
Mankin, Lydia IV, 791
Mankin, Martha IV, 791
Mankin, Mary Ann IV, 791
Mankin, Rebecca IV, 791
Mankin, Sarah II, 104
Mankin, Sarah A. II, 104
Mankin, Susannah VI, 530
Mankin, Susannah, Jr. VI, 533
Mankin, Wm. II, 104
Mankin, Wm. V. II, 85
Mankin, Wm. V. II, 104
Mankins, Sarah II, 85
Mankins, Sarah A. II, 85
Mankins, Wm. II, 85
Mankins, Wm. V. II, 85
Mankins, Wm., Jr. II, 85
Manley, Amy IV, 173
Manley, Amy IV, 248
Manley, Amy H. IV, 248
Manley, Ancil VI, 849
Manley, Betty IV, 738
Manley, Jane I, 560
Manley, John IV, 248
Manley, Lydia G. V, 188
Manley, William VI, 955
Manley, Wm. F. V, 188
Manley, Wm. T. V, 188
Manlove, Ann V, 348
Manlove, Anna I, 826
Manlove, Anna I, 842
Manlove, Belle V, 696
Manlove, David I, 826
Manlove, Elizabeth I, 826
Manlove, George I, 826
Manlove, Jane V, 337
Manlove, Jane V, 348
Manlove, John I, 826
Manlove, Jonathan I, 826
Manlove, Mary I, 798
Manlove, Mary I, 826
Manlove, Mary I, 891
Manlove, Rachel I, 826

anlove, Rachel V, 348
anlove, Sarah V, 696
anlove, William I, 826
anlove, William, Jr. I, 826
anly, Sarah I, 1124
anly, Wm. VI, 931
ann, Adrian S. III, 218
ann, Agga VI, 830
ann, Alexander VI, 837
ann, Alexander VI, 867
ann, Ally A. VI, 837
ann, Andrew VI, 837
ann, Andrew VI, 841
ann, Andrew VI, 847
ann, Ann VI, 845
ann, Bessie IV, 1216
ann, Betsy VI, 838
ann, Buel H. III, 218
ann, Buel H. III, 362
ann, Caroline III, 97
ann, Charity IV, 643
ann, Charity IV, 647
ann, Charles VI, 814
ann, Charles VI, 1004
ann, Charles A. VI, 837
ann, Charles A. VI, 846
ann, Charles E. VI, 835
ann, Charlotte Marie V, 696
ann, Elanor VI, 837
ann, Eleanor VI, 863
ann, Eliza III, 218
ann, Elizabeth VI, 797
ann, Elizabeth VI, 818
ann, Elizabeth VI, 828
ann, Elizabeth VI, 831
ann, Elizabeth VI, 833
ann, Elizabeth VI, 837
ann, Elizabeth VI, 858
ann, Elizabeth VI, 931
ann, Elizabeth W. VI, 837
ann, Ella B. V, 188
ann, Ella May V, 188
ann, Emma L. V, 188
ann, Emma Luella V, 188
ann, Field VI, 837
ann, Field VI, 890
ann, Fisher VI, 828
ann, Fountain VI, 837
ann, Frances VI, 835
ann, Freelove III, 175
ann, Freelove III, 218
ann, George B. III, 218
ann, George H. III, 218
ann, George M. III, 218
ann, George M. III, 239
ann, Hannah V, 852
ann, Harold V, 188
ann, Harold S. V, 188
ann, Henrietta Boyles III, 218
ann, Horace V, 188
ann, Isaac V, 188
ann, James III, 218
ann, James VI, 797
ann, James VI, 837
ann, James VI, 841
ann, Jane V, 188
ann, Jane VI, 837
ann, Jane VI, 841
ann, Jane VI, 842
ann, Jesse VI, 837
ann, Joel VI, 810
ann, Joel VI, 817
ann, Joel VI, 821
ann, Joel VI, 823
ann, Joel VI, 837
ann, Joel VI, 863
ann, Joel VI, 867
ann, John III, 175
ann, John III, 218
ann, John III, 488
ann, John III, 490
ann, John V, 188
ann, John VI, 837
ann, John VI, 838
ann, John VI, 922
ann, John VI, 956
ann, John VI, 958
ann, John B. VI, 837
ann, John, Jr. III, 218
ann, Joseph III, 218
ann, Joseph J. VI, 817
ann, Joseph J. VI, 837
ann, Kate III, 218
ann, Kate C. III, 239
ann, Keziah V, 188
ann, Kitty VI, 837
ann, Lewis V, 852
ann, Lindsay J. VI, 837
ann, Louise D. III, 218
ann, Louise D. III, 362
ann, Luella V, 1009
Mann, Margaret VI, 817
Mann, Margaret VI, 818
Mann, Margaret VI, 837
Mann, Margaret W. III, 299
Mann, Marindy VI, 837
Mann, Martha VI, 837
Mann, Martha VI, 845
Mann, Martha VI, 849
Mann, Mary IV, 584
Mann, Mary IV, 587
Mann, Mary V, 852
Mann, Mary VI, 799
Mann, Mary VI, 837
Mann, Mary VI, 890
Mann, Mary F. VI, 835
Mann, Matthias III, 218
Mann, Maud Halcyon II, 808
Mann, Maude Halcyon II, 866
Mann, Maude Halcyon II, 895
Mann, Nancey VI, 1004
Mann, Nancy VI, 810
Mann, Nancy Catherine V, 188
Mann, Nathaniel VI, 837
Mann, Nellie V, 188
Mann, Nelly VI, 956
Mann, Patience VI, 838
Mann, Patsey VI, 837
Mann, Patsy VI, 823
Mann, Phebe III, 218
Mann, Phebe III, 488
Mann, Phebe III, 490
Mann, Phebe IV, 587
Mann, Phebe IV, 595
Mann, Phebe H. III, 201
Mann, Phebe H. III, 218
Mann, Phebe L. II, 866
Mann, Phebe L. II, 895
Mann, Philip VI, 837
Mann, Polly VI, 837
Mann, Prudence VI, 837
Mann, Rachel V, 852
Mann, Rachel VI, 984
Mann, Rachel E. V, 188
Mann, Rebecca V, 852
Mann, Rebeckah VI, 837
Mann, Richard V, 852
Mann, Richard VI, 797
Mann, Richard VI, 810
Mann, Richard VI, 818
Mann, Richard VI, 828
Mann, Richard VI, 830
Mann, Richard VI, 831
Mann, Richard VI, 837
Mann, Richard, Sr. VI, 837
Mann, Sally VI, 823
Mann, Sally VI, 837
Mann, Sarah III, 201
Mann, Sarah III, 218
Mann, Sarah III, 488
Mann, Sarah III, 490
Mann, Sarah VI, 837
Mann, Sarah Jane V, 188
Mann, Susan P. III, 218
Mann, Susan P. III, 362
Mann, Tabitha VI, 837
Mann, Thomas VI, 829
Mann, Thomas VI, 837
Mann, Thomas B. VI, 823
Mann, Thurman V, 188
Mann, Victor V, 696
Mann, Wanda Caroline V, 696
Mann, Warner V, 263
Mann, William V, 852
Mann, William VI, 837
Mann, Wm H. II, 866
Mann, Wm. H. II, 808
Mann, Wm. H. II, 895
Mann, Wm. H. H. II, 866
Mann, Wm. H. H. II, 895
Mannalie, Jane VI, 838
Mannalie, Joshua D. VI, 838
Mannen, Elizabeth II, 999
Mannen, Elizabeth II, 1013
Mannen, John Hair II, 1013
Mannin, Charles VI, 956
Mannin, Susanna VI, 956
Manning, Anna M. III, 218
Manning, Catharine III, 426
Manning, Catharine III, 451
Manning, Charles VI, 1014
Manning, Dr. Preston V, 920
Manning, Gladys II, 700
Manning, Gladys II, 754
Manning, Laura Meeker V, 920
Manning, Louisa V, 460
Manning, Mary III, 120
Manning, Mary III, 218
Manning, Mary V, 920
Manning, Mary VI, 52
Manning, Mary VI, 76
Manning, Mary C. III, 120
Manning, Mary C. III, 218
Manning, Mary S. V, 939
Manning, Richard H. III, 120
Manning, Richard H. III, 218
Manning, Sherman Leroy V, 920
Mannington, Charity V, 96
Mannington, John II, 392
Mannington, Lewis F. V, 96
Mannington, Mary II, 392
Mannington, Robert V, 188
Mannington, Susannah II, 392
Mannington, William II, 392
Mannington, Wm. II, 589
Mannuel, Elizabeth VI, 838
Mannuel, Thornton VI, 838
Manny, Benjamin B. III, 218
Manny, John W. III, 218
Manry, Joseph I, 30
Manry, Margaret A. I, 30
Mans, Susan II, 782
Mansfield, Ann I, 59
Mansfield, Ann E. I, 59
Mansfield, Benjamin H. VI, 956
Mansfield, Cassandra IV, 235
Mansfield, Cassandra IV, 248
Mansfield, Cassie IV, 248
Mansfield, Clara Elizabeth IV, 248
Mansfield, David VI, 530
Mansfield, David VI, 572
Mansfield, Edward III, 218
Mansfield, Eliza Ann VI, 941
Mansfield, Elizabeth VI, 956
Mansfield, Henry V, 348
Mansfield, Joseph II, 589
Mansfield, Joseph VI, 956
Mansfield, Margaret E. VI, 956
Mansfield, Nancy VI, 999
Mansfield, Sally VI, 530
Mansfield, Sarah II, 589
Mansfield, Sarah II, 613
Mansfield, Sarah VI, 530
Mansfield, Sarah VI, 572
Mansfield, Stephen II, 589
Mansfield, Susanna II, 589
Mansfield, Wd. Sarah II, 392
Mansfield, Wm. VI, 942
Manson, Addisonia E. D. VI, 889
Manson, Elizabeth VI, 894
Manson, James II, 589
Manson, Lucy W. VI, 895
Manson, Martha L. VI, 961
Manson, Mary VI, 895
Manson, Mary C. E. VI, 948
Manson, Mathew J. VI, 948
Manson, N. C. VI, 889
Manson, Nathaniel VI, 888
Manson, Nathl. I. VI, 895
Manson, Nathl. I. VI, 1009
Manson, Nathl. J. VI, 961
Manson, Natl. I. VI, 889
Manson, Peggy VI, 895
Manson, Sallie IV, 1284
Manson, Sallie IV, 1285
Manspile, Mary Ann VI, 956
Manspile, Michael VI, 956
Manter, David V, 1009
Manter, Lavina V, 1009
Manter, Lavona V, 1009
Manter, Lovana V, 1009
Mantor, Lavina V, 1009
Manual, Ella S. VI, 422
Manual, Ella S. VI, 439
Manuel, Julia A. VI, 822
Manuel, Thornton IV, 822
Manville, Edwin IV, 1172
Manwaring, Mary Ann II, 1076
Many, Cecelia IV, 1328
Many, J. J. IV, 1328
Many, J. L. IV, 1328
Maper, Joseph III, 218
Mapes, Allice V, 1009
Mapes, Jemima III, 218
Mapes, Mary Ann III, 217
Mapes, Mary Ann III, 218
Maple, L. F. IV, 738
Maple, Maria IV, 43
Maple, Maria IV, 47
Mapson, Alice A. III, 469
Maramon, Peter I, 560
Maran, Malinda I, 371
Maran, Malinda I, 406
Marany, Mary I, 826
Marany, Rachel I, 826
Marble, Emma L. V, 696
Marble, Frank V, 696
Marble, John B. III, 490
Marbly, Jacob V, 516
Marbury, J. S. VI, 871
Marbury, J. S. VI, 878
Marbury, J. S. VI, 891
Marbury, J. S. VI, 935
Marbury, J. S. V, 977
Marbury, J. S. VI, 994
Marcelline, ??? III, 218
Marcelline, Edward III, 218
Marcelline, Mary D. III, 218
March, Samuel III, 218
Marchand, Laura IV, 1328
Marchand, Myrtle Estell IV, 1328
Marchand, Myrtle Estelle IV, 1328
Marchant, Dick VI, 838
Marchant, Elizabeth VI, 859
Marchant, Isaac V, 263
Marchant, Priscilla IV, 479
Marchant, Priscilla IV, 486
Marchant, Sally VI, 838
Marchbank, Bessie A. IV, 248
Marchbank, Howard IV, 248
Marchent, Richard VI, 423
Marcheson, John VI, 808
Marcile, Catharine IV, 1311
Marckle, Chas. VI, 887
Marckle, Sarah Adaline VI, 887
Marcline, Caroline III, 219
Marcline, Mary III, 219
Marcline, Wm. T. III, 219
Marcum, Daniel V, 741
Marcum, Eliza V, 741
Marcum, Lucy A. V, 741
Marcy, Patience II, 392
Marcy, Samuel II, 392
Marcy, Sarah II, 392
Mardick, Ann V, 852
Mardick, Elizabeth I, 375
Mardick, Elizabeth I, 406
Mardick, William I, 1125
Mardock, Ann I, 450
Mardock, Ann I, 1125
Mardock, Ann I, 1135
Mardock, Ann V, 852
Mardock, David I, 438
Mardock, David I, 1125
Mardock, Elizabeth I, 406
Mardock, Elizabeth I, 431
Mardock, Elizabeth I, 438
Mardock, Elizabeth I, 450
Mardock, Elizabeth I, 1125
Mardock, Elizabeth I, 1159
Mardock, James I, 406
Mardock, James I, 438
Mardock, James I, 1125
Mardock, James I, 1159
Mardock, Joel I, 438
Mardock, Joel I, 1125
Mardock, John I, 406
Mardock, John I, 438
Mardock, John I, 1125
Mardock, Mary I, 438
Mardock, Mary I, 1125
Mardock, Prudence I, 450
Mardock, Stephen I, 438
Mardock, Stephen I, 1125
Mardock, Stephen I, 1159
Mardock, William I, 406
Mardock, William I, 438
Mardock, William I, 450
Mardock, William I, 1125
Mardock, William I, 1137
Maredith, Margaret IV, 740
Maremoon, Ann IV, 249
Maremoon, Anna IV, 248
Maremoon, Benjamin I, 246
Maremoon, Christian I, 246
Maremoon, David I, 246
Maremoon, Elisabeth I, 246
Maremoon, Elisabeth, Jr. I, 246
Maremoon, Elizabeth IV, 248
Maremoon, Elizabeth IV, 249
Maremoon, Francis I, 246
Maremoon, Hannah I, 246
Maremoon, James IV, 248
Maremoon, James IV, 249
Maremoon, Jehu, Jr. I, 246
Maremoon, Jesse I, 246
Maremoon, John I, 246
Maremoon, John, Jr. I, 246
Maremoon, Joseph I, 246
Maremoon, Kexia I, 248
Maremoon, Kezia I, 246
Maremoon, Letters IV, 248
Maremoon, Lettice IV, 249
Maremoon, Marcy IV, 248
Maremoon, Margaret I, 246
Maremoon, Martha I, 246
Maremoon, Martin I, 246
Maremoon, Martin IV, 248
Maremoon, Martin IV, 249
Maremoon, Mary I, 246
Maremoon, Matilda IV, 248
Maremoon, Matilda IV, 249
Maremoon, Miriam I, 246
Maremoon, Mourning I, 246
Maremoon, Obedience I, 246
Maremoon, Obedience IV, 248
Maremoon, Obedience IV, 249
Maremoon, Paley IV, 248
Maremoon, Patey IV, 249
Maremoon, Peggay I, 246
Maremoon, Peggey I, 246
Maremoon, Peggy IV, 248
Maremoon, Peggy IV, 249
Maremoon, Peter I, 246
Maremoon, Rachel I, 246
Maremoon, Rachel IV, 248
Maremoon, Rachel IV, 249
Maremoon, Rainna I, 246
Maremoon, Raney I, 246
Maremoon, Rebecca IV, 248
Maremoon, Rebecca IV, 249
Maremoon, Rhoda I, 246
Maremoon, Robert I, 246
Maremoon, Robert IV, 248
Maremoon, Robert IV, 249
Maremoon, Samuel I, 246
Maremoon, Samuel IV, 248
Maremoon, Samuel IV, 249
Maremoon, Sarah IV, 249
Maremoon, Susanna IV, 248
Maremoon, Susanna IV, 249
Maremoon, Susannah I, 246
Maremoon, Tabitha I, 246
Maremoon, Thomas I, 246
Maremoon, Watkins IV, 248
Maremoon, Watkins IV, 249
Margaret, Maggie A. VI, 82
Margaret, Mary IV, 516
Margaret, Peggy III, 419
Margarge, Hannah S. II, 946
Margerum, Abraham II, 1012
Margerum, Abraham II, 1013
Margerum, Benjamin II, 1013
Margerum, Edward II, 964
Margerum, Edward II, 1013
Margerum, Hannah II, 1013
Margerum, Hannah II, 1037
Margerum, Henry II, 964
Margerum, Henry II, 1013
Margerum, Isabel II, 964
Margerum, Isabel II, 1013
Margerum, Janepher II, 1006
Margerum, Janepher II, 1013
Margerum, John II, 964
Margerum, John II, 1013
Margerum, Margaret II, 1012
Margerum, Margaret II, 1013
Margerum, Margaret II, 1021
Margerum, Mary II, 964
Margerum, Mary II, 989
Margerum, Mary II, 1012
Margerum, Mary II, 1013
Margerum, Mary II, 1034
Margerum, Mary, Jr. II, 1013
Margerum, Phebe II, 1013
Margerum, Phebe II, 1023
Margerum, Rachel II, 1013
Margerum, Richard II, 964
Margerum, Richard II, 1012
Margerum, Richard II, 1013
Margerum, Richard II, 1037
Margerum, Richard, Jr. II, 1013
Margerum, Robert II, 964
Margerum, Robert II, 1013
Margerum, Samuel II, 1013
Margerum, Wm. II, 1013
Margeson, Darius V, 1009
Margeson, James V, 1009
Margeson, John V, 1009
Margrave, Abigail VI, 601
Margy, Mary VI, 507
Mariand, Jane VI, 808
Maricle, Rachel IV, 75
Maricle, Rachel IV, 99
Marideth, Frank Stanley IV, 1257
Marideth, Jane I, 589
Marideth, Mary I, 589
Marideth, Sarah I, 589
Marideth, Sarah E. IV, 1257
Marideth, William I, 589
Maries, Aaron I, 406
Maries, George I, 406
Maries, John I, 560
Marimon, David I, 992
Marimon, Thomas I, 992
Marimoon, Anna IV, 248
Marimoon, Benjamin I, 218
Marimoon, Benjamin I, 246
Marimoon, Christian I, 218
Marimoon, David I, 218
Marimoon, David I, 246
Marimoon, Dorothy I, 218

Marimoon, Edmond I, 218
Marimoon, Elisabeth, Jr. I, 246
Marimoon, Elizabeth I, 218
Marimoon, Francis I, 218
Marimoon, Francis I, 246
Marimoon, Hannah I, 218
Marimoon, Hannah I, 231
Marimoon, Hannah I, 246
Marimoon, Hannah I, 252
Marimoon, James IV, 248
Marimoon, Jemimah I, 218
Marimoon, Jesse I, 218
Marimoon, Jesse I, 246
Marimoon, John I, 218
Marimoon, John I, 238
Marimoon, John I, 246
Marimoon, Joseph I, 218
Marimoon, Joshua I, 218
Marimoon, Kezia I, 218
Marimoon, Kezia I, 238
Marimoon, Kezia I, 246
Marimoon, Margaret I, 259
Marimoon, Marium I, 218
Marimoon, Martha I, 218
Marimoon, Martin I, 218
Marimoon, Martin IV, 248
Marimoon, Mary I, 246
Marimoon, Miriam I, 218
Marimoon, Miriam I, 244
Marimoon, Miriam I, 246
Marimoon, Mourning I, 218
Marimoon, Obedience I, 218
Marimoon, Paley IV, 248
Marimoon, Peggay I, 241
Marimoon, Peggay I, 246
Marimoon, Peter I, 218
Marimoon, Peter I, 246
Marimoon, Prissilla I, 218
Marimoon, Rachel I, 218
Marimoon, Rachel I, 231
Marimoon, Rachel I, 246
Marimoon, Rhoda I, 218
Marimoon, Rhoda I, 246
Marimoon, Rhoda I, 252
Marimoon, Richmon I, 218
Marimoon, Robert I, 218
Marimoon, Robert I, 246
Marimoon, Robert I, 259
Marimoon, Robert IV, 248
Marimoon, Samuel I, 218
Marimoon, Samuel I, 241
Marimoon, Samuel I, 246
Marimoon, Susanna IV, 248
Marimoon, Tabitha I, 241
Marimoon, Tabitha I, 246
Marimoon, Talitha I, 218
Marimoon, Thomas I, 218
Marimoon, Thomas I, 246
Marimoon, Watkins IV, 248
Marine, Abba I, 1067
Marine, Abba I, 1070
Marine, Abba I, 1071
Marine, Anna I, 311
Marine, Anna I, 1067
Marine, Arlando III, 18
Marine, Arlando III, 70
Marine, Arlando III, 219
Marine, Charles I, 826
Marine, Charles I, 1067
Marine, Charles I, 1070
Marine, Charles I, 1071
Marine, Eleanor Graves III, 18
Marine, Eleanor Graves III, 219
Marine, Elinor Graves III, 219
Marine, Hannah III, 219
Marine, Harriet P. VI, 504
Marine, James Sydney III, 219
Marine, Jesse I, 826
Marine, Jesse I, 1067
Marine, Jesse I, 1070
Marine, Jesse I, 1071
Marine, John I, 661
Marine, John I, 826
Marine, John I, 1066
Marine, John I, 1067
Marine, John I, 1071
Marine, Jonathan I, 826
Marine, Jonathan I, 1066
Marine, Jonathan I, 1067
Marine, Jonathan I, 1071
Marine, Jonathan V, 263
Marine, Mabel Frances III, 70
Marine, Mabel Frances III, 219
Marine, Mary I, 826
Marine, Mary I, 1066
Marine, Mary I, 1067
Marine, Mary I, 1071
Marine, Orland IV, 1328
Marine, Orlando IV, 1328
Marine, Pheba I, 311
Marine, Pheba I, 1067
Marine, Pheba I, 1071
Marine, Phebe I, 311
Marine, Phebe I, 1070
Marine, Pheby I, 1071
Marine, Rachel B. I, 661
Marine, Viola III, 18
Marine, Viola III, 219
Marine, Viola B. III, 70
Marine, William III, 219
Marine, Ziba I, 1067
Marion, Edith IV, 841
Mariot, Isaac II, 241
Mariot, Isaac II, 246
Mariot, Jane II, 590
Mariot, Joyce II, 241
Mariot, Joyce II, 246
Mariot, Mary II, 590
Mariot, Mary II, 643
Mariot, Susannah II, 223
Mariot, Susannah II, 241
Mariott, Thomas L. II, 895
Maris, Aaron I, 359
Maris, Aaron I, 406
Maris, Aaron I, 447
Maris, Aaron I, 450
Maris, Aaron I, 509
Maris, Aaron I, 560
Maris, Abraham IV, 978
Maris, Abraham IV, 979
Maris, Abram IV, 978
Maris, Abram IV, 1040
Maris, Albert B. II, 712
Maris, Albert B. II, 754
Maris, Alfred E. II, 754
Maris, Alfred Edward II, 712
Maris, Alice VI, 527
Maris, Alice VI, 671
Maris, Amy S. IV, 1118
Maris, Amy S. IV, 1123
Maris, Ann I, 509
Maris, Ann I, 546
Maris, Ann I, 560
Maris, Ann II, 536
Maris, Ann II, 589
Maris, Ann II, 590
Maris, Ann II, 826
Maris, Ann IV, 623
Maris, Ann IV, 643
Maris, Ann IV, 738
Maris, Ann IV, 751
Maris, Ann IV, 978
Maris, Ann IV, 979
Maris, Ann IV, 1040
Maris, Ann IV, 1067
Maris, Ann IV, 1080
Maris, Ann P. IV, 978
Maris, Ann P. IV, 979
Maris, Ann P. IV, 1040
Maris, Ann W. IV, 1067
Maris, Anna I, 787
Maris, Anna I, 824
Maris, Anna I, 826
Maris, Anna Belva IV, 978
Maris, Anna Belva IV, 979
Maris, Anna M. II, 808
Maris, Anna W. IV, 1106
Maris, Anna W. IV, 1118
Maris, Anne IV, 738
Maris, Annie M. II, 895
Maris, Aron I, 682
Maris, Aron I, 684
Maris, Arthur S. II, 754
Maris, Arthur Stanley II, 712
Maris, Barclay IV, 738
Maris, Barclay IV, 751
Maris, Barclay IV, 978
Maris, Barclay IV, 1040
Maris, Barkley IV, 738
Maris, Benjamin L. I, 787
Maris, Benjamin L. I, 826
Maris, Beulah IV, 978
Maris, Caleb IV, 486
Maris, Caleb IV, 502
Maris, Caleb IV, 933
Maris, Caleb IV, 978
Maris, Caleb IV, 979
Maris, Catharine I, 450
Maris, Charles IV, 1106
Maris, Cidney IV, 587
Maris, Cidney IV, 1067
Maris, Cidney IV, 1106
Maris, Clare E. IV, 978
Maris, Clark IV, 1106
Maris, Clark T. IV, 1106
Maris, Cora I, 933
Maris, David IV, 248
Maris, David IV, 419
Maris, David IV, 1067
Maris, David IV, 1123
Maris, Deborah IV, 486
Maris, Deborah IV, 487
Maris, Deborah IV, 502
Maris, Deborah IV, 978
Maris, Deborah IV, 979
Maris, Deborah W. IV, 1040
Maris, Earnest IV, 979
Maris, Earnest J. IV, 978
Maris, Edward II, 712
Maris, Edward II, 754
Maris, Edward II, 764
Maris, Edward III, 219
Maris, Edward III, 364
Maris, Edward IV, 979
Maris, Edward B. IV, 1106
Maris, Edward W. IV, 978
Maris, Eleanor I, 404
Maris, Eleanor I, 406
Maris, Eleanor I, 450
Maris, Eleanor II, 712
Maris, Eleanor K. III, 219
Maris, Eleanor K. III, 364
Maris, Eleanor W. II, 754
Maris, Elenor I, 352
Maris, Elenor I, 359
Maris, Elinor I, 359
Maris, Elinor I, 363
Maris, Elinor I, 406
Maris, Elisabeth I, 146
Maris, Elisha IV, 1106
Maris, Elisha Vanlaw IV, 1067
Maris, Elisha Vanlaw IV, 1106
Maris, Elizabeth II, 589
Maris, Elizabeth IV, 933
Maris, Elizabeth IV, 978
Maris, Elizabeth IV, 979
Maris, Elizabeth IV, 1106
Maris, Elizabeth IV, 1122
Maris, Elizabeth Jones II, 826
Maris, Elizabeth T. IV, 933
Maris, Elizabeth T. IV, 978
Maris, Elma II, 712
Maris, Elma B. II, 754
Maris, Elma B. IV, 536
Maris, Elma B. IV, 540
Maris, Ernest J. IV, 978
Maris, Esther I, 826
Maris, Esther IV, 978
Maris, Esther IV, 979
Maris, Esther IV, 1040
Maris, George I, 352
Maris, George I, 359
Maris, George I, 363
Maris, George I, 404
Maris, George I, 406
Maris, George I, 450
Maris, George II, 590
Maris, George IV, 1106
Maris, George VI, 671
Maris, George J. IV, 248
Maris, George J. IV, 1067
Maris, George J. IV, 1106
Maris, George L. II, 895
Maris, George L. II, 906
Maris, George L. II, 938
Maris, George Lewis II, 808
Maris, Hannah I, 509
Maris, Hannah I, 560
Maris, Hannah I, 562
Maris, Hannah IV, 953
Maris, Hannah IV, 979
Maris, Hannah V, 412
Maris, Helen M. II, 895
Maris, Hellen IV, 978
Maris, Henry C. IV, 978
Maris, Herbert L. II, 895
Maris, Howard II, 712
Maris, Howard II, 754
Maris, Isaac IV, 978
Maris, J. Emlen II, 895
Maris, Jain I, 447
Maris, Jain I, 450
Maris, James E. IV, 1106
Maris, Jane I, 450
Maris, Jane I, 495
Maris, Jane I, 509
Maris, Jane I, 560
Maris, Jane I, 684
Maris, Jean I, 146
Maris, Jean I, 509
Maris, Jemima II, 392
Maris, Jemima II, 589
Maris, Jemima II, 590
Maris, Jemima II, 682
Maris, Jennie B. II, 895
Maris, Jennie Bond II, 808
Maris, Jesse I, 786
Maris, Jesse II, 392
Maris, Jesse II, 512
Maris, Jesse II, 536
Maris, Jesse II, 589
Maris, Jesse II, 590
Maris, Jesse IV, 978
Maris, Jesse Emlen II, 754
Maris, Jesse Emlen II, 808
Maris, Jesse I. III, 219
Maris, Jesse J. II, 712
Maris, Jesse J. II, 754
Maris, Jesse J. II, 764
Maris, Jesse J. III, 219
Maris, Jesse, Jr. II, 392
Maris, Jesse, Jr. II, 589
Maris, Job Shreve IV, 978
Maris, John I, 359
Maris, John I, 495
Maris, John I, 509
Maris, John I, 560
Maris, John I, 684
Maris, John I, 786
Maris, John I, 787
Maris, John I, 826
Maris, John I, 830
Maris, John I Sup 1, 4
Maris, Jonathan I, 450
Maris, Jonathan I, 787
Maris, Jonathan IV, 486
Maris, Jonathan IV, 738
Maris, Jonathan IV, 743
Maris, Jonathan IV, 978
Maris, Joseph II, 512
Maris, Joseph II, 589
Maris, Joseph IV, 738
Maris, Joseph IV, 979
Maris, Joseph M. IV, 978
Maris, Joseph P. IV, 1040
Maris, Katharine I, 359
Maris, Katharine I, 363
Maris, Lavina IV, 738
Maris, Lewis IV, 411
Maris, Lewis IV, 419
Maris, Lewis IV, 978
Maris, Louis Thomasson IV, 979
Maris, Louisa Thomason IV, 978
Maris, Louiza T. IV, 979
Maris, Lucy A. II, 895
Maris, Lucy Alice II, 808
Maris, Luiza IV, 979
Maris, Lydia I, 787
Maris, Margaret I, 786
Maris, Margaret II, 392
Maris, Margaret II, 512
Maris, Margaret II, 519
Maris, Margaret II, 536
Maris, Margaret II, 589
Maris, Margaret II, 590
Maris, Margaret II, 1013
Maris, Marianna M. III, 366
Maris, Martha I, 450
Maris, Martha I, 509
Maris, Martha I, 545
Maris, Martha I, 560
Maris, Martha I, 826
Maris, Mary I, 786
Maris, Mary I, 787
Maris, Mary I, 826
Maris, Mary I, 842
Maris, Mary II, 712
Maris, Mary II, 754
Maris, Mary II, 764
Maris, Mary III, 219
Maris, Mary IV, 486
Maris, Mary IV, 487
Maris, Mary IV, 494
Maris, Mary IV, 587
Maris, Mary IV, 1067
Maris, Mary A. IV, 978
Maris, Mary Ann IV, 248
Maris, Mary Anna IV, 248
Maris, Mary Anna IV, 1067
Maris, Mary Anna IV, 1106
Maris, Mary Anna IV, 1111
Maris, Mary C. II, 895
Maris, Mary D. IV, 1067
Maris, Mary D. IV, 1077
Maris, Mary Eleanor II, 712
Maris, Mary Eleanor II, 754
Maris, Michael IV, 248
Maris, Michael J. IV, 1067
Maris, Michal IV, 248
Maris, Mishael IV, 1106
Maris, Norris II, 826
Maris, Owen IV, 153
Maris, Owen IV, 228
Maris, Owen IV, 248
Maris, Owen IV, 1067
Maris, Owen IV, 1080
Maris, Owen IV, 1106
Maris, Owen IV, 1111
Maris, Owen IV, 1112
Maris, Owen IV, 1118
Maris, Owen IV, 1123
Maris, Paul B. IV, 978
Maris, Perigrene I, 146
Maris, Phebe I, 787
Maris, Phebe I, 826
Maris, Phebe IV, 419
Maris, Phebe IV, 587
Maris, Phebe IV, 1067
Maris, Phebe IV, 1106
Maris, Phebe B. IV, 248
Maris, Phebe B. IV, 1067
Maris, Phebe M. IV, 1102
Maris, Phebe M. IV, 1106
Maris, Rachel I, 560
Maris, Rachel I, 787
Maris, Rachel I, 826
Maris, Rachel I, 830
Maris, Rachel II, 590
Maris, Rachel II, 640
Maris, Rachel II, 712
Maris, Rachel II, 754
Maris, Rachel II, 764
Maris, Rachel IV, 153
Maris, Rachel IV, 228
Maris, Rachel IV, 248
Maris, Rachel IV, 419
Maris, Rachel IV, 587
Maris, Rachel IV, 1067
Maris, Rachel IV, 1106
Maris, Rachel IV, 1111
Maris, Rachel IV, 1112
Maris, Rachel H. IV, 1106
Maris, Rebecca IV, 1106
Maris, Richard II, 392
Maris, Richard II, 589
Maris, Richard II, 590
Maris, Robert W. II, 712
Maris, Robert W. II, 754
Maris, Robert Wood II, 712
Maris, Robert Wood IV, 513
Maris, Russell IV, 978
Maris, Ruth I, 352
Maris, Ruth I, 359
Maris, Ruth I, 391
Maris, Ruth I, 406
Maris, Sarah I, 447
Maris, Sarah I, 450
Maris, Sarah I, 787
Maris, Sarah I Sup 1, 4
Maris, Sarah I Sup 1, 5
Maris, Sarah IV, 248
Maris, Sarah IV, 419
Maris, Sarah IV, 1067
Maris, Sarah IV, 1123
Maris, Sarah B. IV, 978
Maris, Sarah B. IV, 979
Maris, Sarah B. IV, 1016
Maris, Sarah B. Williams IV, 9
Maris, Sarah J. IV, 248
Maris, Sarah J. IV, 1067
Maris, Sarah J. IV, 1106
Maris, Sarah J. IV, 1112
Maris, Sarah Pim IV, 978
Maris, Sidney IV, 411
Maris, Sidney IV, 419
Maris, Sidney IV, 587
Maris, Sidney IV, 1106
Maris, Silas I, 509
Maris, Silas I, 545
Maris, Silas I, 560
Maris, Silas I, 826
Maris, Susanna I, 359
Maris, Susanna I, 495
Maris, Susanna I, 509
Maris, Susanna I, 535
Maris, Susanna I, 560
Maris, Susanna I, 682
Maris, Susanna I, 684
Maris, Susanna I, 787
Maris, Susannah I, 450
Maris, Susannah I, 560
Maris, Temple V, 412
Maris, Temple L. I, 826
Maris, Temple S. I, 787
Maris, Thomas I, 359
Maris, Thomas I, 447
Maris, Thomas I, 450
Maris, Thomas Elwood IV, 1106
Maris, Thomason IV, 486
Maris, Thomason IV, 738
Maris, Thomason IV, 743
Maris, Thomason IV, 978
Maris, Thomasson IV, 978
Maris, Thomasson IV, 979
Maris, Thomison IV, 738
Maris, Wd. Amy S. IV, 1106
Maris, Wd. Mary Carr II, 808
Maris, Willard L. II, 895
Maris, Willard Lorraine II, 808
Maris, William I, 359
Maris, William I, 450
Maris, William I, 787
Maris, William I, 826
Maris, William II, 392
Maris, William IV, 978

is, Wm. II, 589
is, Wm. II, 590
is, Wm. IV, 979
ise, Martha I, 450
ise, Martha I, 453
ise, William I, 450
ise, William I, 453
iss, Martha VI, 867
jarim, Martha Esther II, 295
jarim, Martha Esther II, 300
jorum, Rachel II, 1013
k, Amelia Caroline IV, 832
k, Ann Smith VI, 758
k, Ann Smith VI, 764
k, Anna IV, 832
k, Chancy V, 1009
k, Channcy V, 1009
k, Charlot IV, 832
k, Elizabeth VI, 756
k, Elizabeth VI, 758
k, Elizabeth VI, 764
k, Emily III, 219
k, Frederick IV, 832
k, Hannah IV, 832
k, Hannah J. IV, 681
k, Jane IV, 832
k, Lishmins II, 241
k, Louisa IV, 832
k, Lucy V, 1009
k, Samuel VI, 758
k, Samuel VI, 764
k, Williamina IV, 832
kahm, Henry Ann VI, 905
kee, Edith IV, 170
kee, Edith IV, 248
ker, Bertha Priscilla VI, 422
ker, Edwin VI, 422
ker, Edwin VI, 439
kesom, Mary Ann IV, 248
keson, Mary Ann IV, 263
kham, Alice VI, 1012
kham, Ann Eliza VI, 957
kham, Arther VI, 1005
kham, Arthur VI, 956
kham, Catharine VI, 957
kham, Christopher VI, 957
kham, Dosha VI, 957
kham, Edith VI, 957
kham, Elizabeth VI, 813
kham, Elizabeth VI, 956
kham, Elizabeth VI, 957
kham, Elizabeth Catharine VI, 956
kham, Elizabeth Jane VI, 912
kham, Elmira VI, 959
kham, George IV, 1216
kham, Henrietta VI, 957
kham, Henrietta VI, 1003
kham, James VI, 916
kham, James VI, 956
kham, James VI, 959
kham, James E. VI, 984
kham, James E. VI, 1011
kham, James M. VI, 957
kham, James S. VI, 957
kham, Jane VI, 957
kham, Jenney VI, 838
kham, Jesse VI, 957
kham, Jesse F. VI, 957
kham, Jno. P. E. VI, 1011
kham, John VI, 838
kham, John VI, 905
kham, John VI, 946
kham, John VI, 956
kham, John VI, 957
kham, John E. VI, 957
kham, Joseph VI, 957
kham, Josiah VI, 956
kham, Josiah VI, 974
kham, Julia Ann VI, 905
kham, Kesiah VI, 957
kham, Leonard VI, 957
kham, Leonard S. VI, 928
kham, Leonard S. VI, 957
kham, Leonard S. VI, 959
kham, Louisa VI, 946
kham, Lucy VI, 956
kham, Marshall VI, 878
kham, Martha VI, 896
kham, Martha VI, 956
kham, Martha VI, 957
kham, Martha VI, 1005
kham, Martha Jane VI, 896
kham, Mary VI, 957
kham, Mary M. VI, 928
kham, Matilda VI, 984
kham, Nancy VI, 956
kham, Nancy VI, 957
kham, Narcissa E. VI, 878
kham, Nathan VI, 957
Markham, Nathaniel VI, 957
Markham, Nathaniel VI, 984
Markham, Nelly VI, 956
Markham, Olivia A. VI, 957
Markham, Owen VI, 878
Markham, Owen VI, 956
Markham, Paulina A. VI, 1011
Markham, Peggy VI, 956
Markham, Penelope Ann VI, 928
Markham, Polly VI, 956
Markham, Roxa IV, 1216
Markham, Roxy IV, 1216
Markham, Sabrina VI, 956
Markham, Sally VI, 876
Markham, Sally VI, 974
Markham, Sarah VI, 957
Markham, Sarah VI, 1015
Markham, Susan M. VI, 1012
Markham, Susannah VI, 928
Markham, Thomas VI, 323
Markham, Thomas VI, 345
Markham, Thomas VI, 956
Markham, Thomas VI, 957
Markham, Thomas VI, 1012
Markham, Thomas VI, 1015
Markham, Thomas, Sr. VI, 957
Markham, Thos. VI, 905
Markham, Thos., Sr. VI, 957
Markham, Tilghman VI, 890
Markham, Tillman VI, 957
Markham, William VI, 957
Markham, William C. VI, 1012
Markham, William V. VI, 957
Markley, Aaron V, 754
Markley, Callie V, 754
Markley, Elmina V, 754
Markley, Helen V, 754
Markley, John V, 754
Markley, John Jacob V, 754
Markley, Johnnie V, 754
Markley, Joseph V, 754
Markley, Martin V, 754
Markley, Mrs. Lena IV, 248
Markley, Mrs. Rachel V, 754
Markley, Opal V, 754
Markley, Opel V, 754
Markley, Victoria V, 754
Markram, Mary VI, 1005
Markram, Nelly VI, 1005
Markram, Thomas VI, 1005
Markrim, Owen VI, 1005
Marks, Charles VI, 129
Marks, Charles VI, 135
Marks, Charles VI, 138
Marks, Charles H. VI, 140
Marks, Edwd VI, 291
Marks, Nathaniel VI, 130
Marks, Nathaniel VI, 133
Marks, Nathaniel VI, 135
Marks, Nathaniel VI, 138
Marks, Nathaniel VI, 140
Marks, Nathaniel VI, 141
Markum, Arthur VI, 1015
Markum, Sarah VI, 1015
Marl, Jane II, 392
Marl, Jeremiah II, 392
Marl, John II, 392
Marl, John II, 590
Marl, Thomas II, 392
Marlatt, Bertha V, 585
Marlatt, Jacob III, 219
Marlatt, Mary Eliz. III, 219
Marlatt, Mollie Anna Bell V, 585
Marlatt, Rachel III, 219
Marlatt, Rebecca V, 585
Marlatt, Theodore V, 585
Marle, Elisabeth II, 513
Marle, Elisabeth II, 590
Marle, Elizabeth II, 590
Marle, Esther II, 509
Marle, Esther II, 590
Marle, Hannah II, 392
Marle, Hannah II, 590
Marle, Hester II, 590
Marle, Isaac II, 392
Marle, John II, 392
Marle, John II, 513
Marle, John II, 590
Marle, John, Jr. II, 590
Marle, Margaret II, 590
Marle, Rachel II, 590
Marle, Sarah II, 590
Marle, Thomas II, 590
Marles, Elizabeth II, 392
Marles, Hannah II, 392
Marles, Isaac II, 392
Marles, Jane II, 392
Marles, Jeremiah II, 392
Marles, John II, 392
Marles, Thomas II, 392
Marley, Ella I, 402
Marley, Ella I, 406
Marley, Gregory II, 46
Marlin, Elizabeth III, 207
Marlin, Elizabeth III, 255
Marlings, Sarah VI, 534
Marlings, Wm. VI, 534
Marll, Elizabeth VI, 560
Marll, Hannah II, 590
Marll, Hannah II, 651
Marll, Hannah VI, 560
Marll, John II, 612
Marll, John II, 651
Marll, John Marle VI, 560
Marll, Marll VI, 560
Marll, Sarah II, 590
Marll, Sarah II, 612
Marlle, John II, 649
Marlle, Margaret II, 590
Marlle, Margaret II, 649
Marlot, James V, 1009
Marlott, Jacob III, 358
Marlott, Mary Elizabeth III, 358
Marlott, Rachel III, 358
Marlow, Ada IV, 1257
Marlow, Charles W. IV, 1257
Marlow, Chas. F. IV, 1257
Marlow, Chas. W., Jr. IV, 1257
Marlow, Grace IV, 1257
Marlow, James V, 696
Marlow, James F. V, 696
Marlow, Lamond IV, 1257
Marlow, Lamont IV, 1257
Marlow, Martha V, 696
Marlow, Martha A. V, 696
Marlowe, James V, 696
Marmaduke, Alcinda VI, 518
Marman, David V, 102
Marman, Dorothy V, 102
Marman, Elizabeth V, 102
Marman, Lettice V, 463
Marman, Peggy V, 463
Marman, Peter V, 102
Marman, Samuel V, 463
Marmen, Kezia I, 237
Marmen, Kezia I, 246
Marmon, Ann IV, 1286
Marmon, Anna IV, 1275
Marmon, Anna IV, 1285
Marmon, Anna IV, 1286
Marmon, Anna IV, 1289
Marmon, Anna V, 102
Marmon, Annie E. IV, 1286
Marmon, Asa IV, 248
Marmon, Asa IV, 1285
Marmon, Asenath IV, 1285
Marmon, Benjamin I, 678
Marmon, Benjamin I, 684
Marmon, Bessie B. IV, 1286
Marmon, Caleb IV, 1285
Marmon, Caleb IV, 1286
Marmon, Carlile IV, 1285
Marmon, Christian I, 246
Marmon, Christian I, 978
Marmon, Christian I, 992
Marmon, David I, 684
Marmon, David I, 992
Marmon, David IV, 1285
Marmon, David IV, 1286
Marmon, David V, 102
Marmon, Dorothy IV, 1286
Marmon, Dorothy V, 102
Marmon, Edmund IV, 1269
Marmon, Edmund V, 102
Marmon, Elisabeth I, 246
Marmon, Eliza B. IV, 1286
Marmon, Elizabeth I, 684
Marmon, Elizabeth V, 102
Marmon, Elmina IV, 1285
Marmon, Elvira IV, 1285
Marmon, Eva IV, 1286
Marmon, Francis I, 992
Marmon, Gideon IV, 1285
Marmon, Hannah IV, 1273
Marmon, Hannah IV, 1285
Marmon, Hannah IV, 1286
Marmon, Hannah V, 102
Marmon, Hannah Ann IV, 1286
Marmon, Harriett IV, 1286
Marmon, Henry IV, 1285
Marmon, Henry IV, 1286
Marmon, Henry W. IV, 1286
Marmon, Ida IV, 1286
Marmon, Isaiah IV, 1286
Marmon, James IV, 1282
Marmon, James IV, 1286
Marmon, James V, 102
Marmon, James Frederick IV, 1286
Marmon, James W. IV, 1285
Marmon, James W. IV, 1286
Marmon, Jane IV, 1271
Marmon, Jane IV, 1286
Marmon, Jemima I, 992
Marmon, Jesse IV, 1285
Marmon, Jesse IV, 1286
Marmon, Jesse L. IV, 1286
Marmon, John IV, 1271
Marmon, John IV, 1286
Marmon, John H. IV, 1286
Marmon, John M. IV, 1286
Marmon, John Milton IV, 1286
Marmon, Joseph I, 992
Marmon, Joseph IV, 1286
Marmon, Joseph E. IV, 1286
Marmon, Joseph Emmons IV, 1286
Marmon, Joshua IV, 1285
Marmon, Joshua IV, 1286
Marmon, Joshua V, 102
Marmon, Kezia I, 246
Marmon, Kezia I, 248
Marmon, Lanson IV, 1286
Marmon, Lanson C. IV, 1285
Marmon, Laura IV, 1286
Marmon, Letitia IV, 1285
Marmon, Lettice V, 102
Marmon, Louisa Ann IV, 1286
Marmon, Margaret IV, 1285
Marmon, Margaret IV, 1286
Marmon, Margaret IV, 1291
Marmon, Margaret V, 102
Marmon, Margery IV, 1282
Marmon, Margery IV, 1286
Marmon, Martha I, 246
Marmon, Martha V, 102
Marmon, Martin IV, 1285
Marmon, Martin IV, 1286
Marmon, Martin V, 102
Marmon, Mary IV, 1285
Marmon, Mary IV, 1286
Marmon, Mary V, 102
Marmon, Mary A. IV, 1286
Marmon, Matilda IV, 1285
Marmon, Matilda V, 102
Marmon, Melissa IV, 1286
Marmon, Miriam IV, 1274
Marmon, Miriam IV, 1286
Marmon, Mourning I, 246
Marmon, Mourning I, 992
Marmon, Mourning I, 994
Marmon, Nancy Stanton IV, 1286
Marmon, Nathaniel C. IV, 1286
Marmon, Obedience V, 102
Marmon, Patsy IV, 1282
Marmon, Patsy IV, 1286
Marmon, Patsy V, 102
Marmon, Peggy IV, 1286
Marmon, Peggy V, 102
Marmon, Peter I, 246
Marmon, Peter I, 560
Marmon, Peter IV, 1285
Marmon, Peter V, 102
Marmon, Pricilla V, 102
Marmon, Rachel I, 678
Marmon, Rachel I, 684
Marmon, Rachel I, 741
Marmon, Rachel I, 766
Marmon, Rachel V, 102
Marmon, Reames V, 102
Marmon, Rebecca V, 102
Marmon, Richmond IV, 1285
Marmon, Rickman V, 102
Marmon, Robert IV, 1285
Marmon, Robert IV, 1286
Marmon, Robert V, 102
Marmon, Ruth IV, 1286
Marmon, Samuel IV, 1285
Marmon, Samuel IV, 1286
Marmon, Samuel V, 102
Marmon, Samuel Lewis IV, 1286
Marmon, Sarah IV, 1271
Marmon, Sarah IV, 1285
Marmon, Sarah IV, 1286
Marmon, Sarah V, 102
Marmon, Sarah Ann IV, 1286
Marmon, Sarah Jr. IV, 1286
Marmon, Sarah, Jr. IV, 1282
Marmon, Shirley IV, 1286
Marmon, Solomon IV, 1285
Marmon, Stephen IV, 1285
Marmon, Stephen V, 102
Marmon, Susan IV, 1286
Marmon, Susana IV, 1285
Marmon, Susanna IV, 1285
Marmon, Susanna IV, 1286
Marmon, Susannah I, 246
Marmon, Susannah V, 102
Marmon, Thomas I, 992
Marmon, William IV, 1286
Marmon, Zilpah IV, 1285
Marmon, Zilpah IV, 1286
Marmoon, Elisabeth I, 246
Marmoon, Francis I, 241
Marmoon, Francis I, 246
Marmoone, Peggey I, 246
Marmoone, Rainna I, 246
Marona, Sallie I, 595
Marony, Sallie I, 595
Marony, Sally I, 593
Marony, Sally I, 595
Maroone, Raney I, 246
Maros, William I, 450
Marot, Ada Bassett II, 808
Marot, Ann II, 797
Marot, Ann II, 808
Marot, Benjamin Johnson V, 920
Marot, Benjamin T. II, 895
Marot, Charity II, 895
Marot, Charles II, 754
Marot, Charles H. II, 895
Marot, Charles Henry II, 754
Marot, Charles Henry II, 808
Marot, Chas. H. II, 895
Marot, Chas. Henry II, 808
Marot, Davenport II, 895
Marot, Davenport, Jr. II, 808
Marot, Davenport, Jr. II, 895
Marot, Davenport, Sr. II, 808
Marot, Deborah II, 808
Marot, Deborah II, 895
Marot, Devenport II, 590
Marot, Devenport II, 912
Marot, Edward II, 590
Marot, Edward II, 895
Marot, Edward V, 920
Marot, Edward Lewis II, 754
Marot, Edward Lewis V, 920
Marot, Eliza II, 808
Marot, Elizabeth II, 712
Marot, Elizabeth II, 808
Marot, Elizabeth II, 895
Marot, Elizabeth II, 912
Marot, Elizabeth Griscom II, 808
Marot, Emeline G. II, 895
Marot, Emeline G. II, 913
Marot, Emmeline II, 808
Marot, Grace Edna II, 895
Marot, Grace Edna II, 913
Marot, Hannah S. II, 895
Marot, Hannah Stuart II, 808
Marot, Helen II, 808
Marot, Henry II, 712
Marot, Henry II, 754
Marot, Henry II, 895
Marot, Henry V, 920
Marot, Jane J. V, 920
Marot, Jane Johnson II, 808
Marot, Jane Johnson II, 895
Marot, Jane Johnson V, 920
Marot, John Richards II, 808
Marot, John Richards II, 895
Marot, John Richards V, 920
Marot, Jonathan II, 895
Marot, Joseph II, 392
Marot, Joseph II, 590
Marot, Joseph II, 712
Marot, Joseph II, 754
Marot, Joseph II, 808
Marot, Joseph II, 895
Marot, Joseph V, 920
Marot, Joshua II, 895
Marot, Lewis II, 392
Marot, Lewis II, 895
Marot, Lewis V, 920
Marot, Mary II, 392
Marot, Mary II, 590
Marot, Mary II, 712
Marot, Mary II, 754
Marot, Mary II, 808
Marot, Mary II, 895
Marot, Mary V, 920
Marot, Mary Griscom II, 808
Marot, Mary Stuart II, 808
Marot, Peter II, 590
Marot, Philip II, 590
Marot, Philip II, 808
Marot, Philip II, 895
Marot, Philip II, 913
Marot, Rebecca II, 895
Marot, Sabina II, 808
Marot, Samuel II, 590
Marot, Samuel II, 754
Marot, Samuel II, 808
Marot, Samuel II, 895
Marot, Samuel V, 920
Marot, Sarah II, 808
Marot, Sarah II, 895
Marot, Sarah B. II, 754
Marot, Sarah Bassett II, 808
Marot, Sarah Griscom II, 808
Marot, Theodosia, Jr. II, 895
Marot, Thomas L. II, 895
Marot, William II, 808

Marot, William Griscom II, 808
Marot, William, Jr. II, 808
Marot, Wm. II, 754
Marot, Wm. II, 808
Marot, Wm. II, 895
Marot, Wm. II, 913
Marot, Wm. V, 920
Marot, Wm. Henry II, 895
Marot, Wm., Jr. II, 895
Marott, Bertha IV, 1286
Marott, Bessie IV, 1286
Marott, Charles H. II, 895
Marott, Charles Henry II, 754
Marott, Chas. H. II, 895
Marott, Davenport, Jr. II, 895
Marott, Edward II, 895
Marott, Hannah S. II, 895
Marott, Harriet IV, 1286
Marott, Henry II, 895
Marott, Henry IV, 1286
Marott, Henry V, 920
Marott, Jane Johnson II, 895
Marott, Jennie Mayse IV, 1286
Marott, John Richards II, 895
Marott, Joseph II, 895
Marott, Lewis II, 895
Marott, Louise IV, 1286
Marott, Mary II, 590
Marott, Mary II, 637
Marott, Mary II, 895
Marott, Sarah B. II, 754
Marple, Abner B. II, 895
Marple, Elizabeth V, 828
Marple, Elizabeth H. II, 895
Marple, Elizabeth H. II, 896
Marple, Hannah II, 1013
Marple, Isaiah V, 828
Marple, John II, 1013
Marple, John T. II, 895
Marple, Lydia M. II, 895
Marple, Lydia M. II, 896
Marple, Lydia W. II, 948
Marple, Lydia W. II, 949
Marple, Martha T. II, 895
Marple, Mary Ann II, 1013
Marple, Mary Jane II, 712
Marple, Priscilla V, 828
Marple, Sarah II, 1013
Marple, Sibella M. II, 895
Marple, Sibella M. II, 896
Marple, Viola II, 712
Marple, Viola II, 754
Marple, Wm. R. II, 712
Marples, Elizabeth VI, 816
Marples, George VI, 816
Marput, Sarah I, 560
Marquet, Catherine V, 1009
Marquis, D. W. VI, 866
Marquist, Marquis S. V, 1009
Marr, A. R. VI, 957
Marr, Ambrose VI, 957
Marr, Ambrose VI, 1009
Marr, Ambrose R. VI, 853
Marr, Ambrose R. VI, 957
Marr, Caroline VI, 957
Marr, Elizabeth VI, 957
Marr, Elizabeth VI, 1009
Marr, Georgina F. III, 219
Marr, Henry W. II, 322
Marr, James VI, 957
Marr, John VI, 957
Marr, Joshua VI, 957
Marr, Lewis E. V, 920
Marr, Lissie III, 219
Marr, Louis V, 920
Marr, Nancy VI, 957
Marr, Polly VI, 957
Marr, Robert III, 219
Marr, Sarah S. VI, 1009
Marr, William G. III, 219
Marres, Jean I, 131
Marres, Jean I, 146
Marriage, Lilias I, 750
Marriage, Lilias I, 766
Marriage, Lillias I, 725
Marriage, Lillias Lowe I, 725
Marriage, Margaret VI, 67
Marriage, Margaret VI, 68
Marriage, Margaret VI, 76
Marrice, Aaron I, 560
Marriot, Jacob II, 241
Marriot, Joseph II, 241
Marriott, Abraham M. II, 932
Marriott, Abraham, Jr. II, 241
Marriott, Ann II, 392
Marriott, Ann, Jr. II, 932
Marriott, Anna II, 241
Marriott, Anna II, 1020
Marriott, Anna Maria II, 808
Marriott, Benj. Tucker II, 808
Marriott, Benjamin II, 241
Marriott, Benjamin T. II, 895
Marriott, Benjamin Tucker II, 808
Marriott, Caroline Elizabeth II, 808
Marriott, Charity II, 808
Marriott, Charity II, 895
Marriott, Charles III, 86
Marriott, Charles III, 219
Marriott, Charles III, 350
Marriott, Davenport II, 392
Marriott, Davenport II, 590
Marriott, Devenport II, 590
Marriott, Edith II, 977
Marriott, Edward II, 590
Marriott, Elizabeth II, 241
Marriott, Emma Adele II, 808
Marriott, Esther II, 932
Marriott, Hannah II, 241
Marriott, Henry III, 219
Marriott, Henry Chillman II, 808
Marriott, Isaac II, 220
Marriott, Isaac II, 241
Marriott, Isaac II, 590
Marriott, Isaac II, 685
Marriott, Isaac II, 964
Marriott, Jacob II, 241
Marriott, Jane II, 590
Marriott, Jane Marsh II, 590
Marriott, Jonathan II, 808
Marriott, Jonathan II, 895
Marriott, Joseph II, 85
Marriott, Joseph II, 99
Marriott, Joseph II, 241
Marriott, Joseph II, 392
Marriott, Joseph II, 590
Marriott, Joyce II, 241
Marriott, Joyce II, 462
Marriott, Joyce II, 590
Marriott, Joyce II, 964
Marriott, Lewis II, 392
Marriott, Lishmins II, 241
Marriott, Margaret II, 932
Marriott, Margaret III, 219
Marriott, Maria III, 219
Marriott, Martha II, 782
Marriott, Martha II, 964
Marriott, Martha II, 987
Marriott, Martha II, 1007
Marriott, Martha II, 1013
Marriott, Mary II, 85
Marriott, Mary II, 99
Marriott, Mary II, 241
Marriott, Mary II, 392
Marriott, Mary II, 526
Marriott, Mary II, 590
Marriott, Mary II, 685
Marriott, Mary II, 808
Marriott, Mary II, 895
Marriott, Mary II, 932
Marriott, Mary II, 964
Marriott, Mary II, 996
Marriott, Mary II, 1013
Marriott, Mary II, 1026
Marriott, Matthew Owen II, 241
Marriott, Peter II, 590
Marriott, Philip II, 392
Marriott, Philip II, 590
Marriott, Rachel II, 241
Marriott, Richard II, 241
Marriott, Richard II, 590
Marriott, Samuel II, 241
Marriott, Samuel II, 590
Marriott, Samuel II, 685
Marriott, Sarah II, 241
Marriott, Sarah II, 500
Marriott, Sarah II, 590
Marriott, Sarah Owen II, 590
Marriott, Sarah W. III, 86
Marriott, Sarah W. III, 219
Marriott, Sarah, Jr. II, 1043
Marriott, Susanah II, 241
Marriott, Susannah II, 220
Marriott, Susannah II, 241
Marriott, Susannah III, 219
Marriott, Theodosia II, 808
Marriott, Theodosia, Jr. II, 895
Marriott, Theodosia, Jr. II, 932
Marriott, Thomas II, 241
Marriott, Thomas II, 392
Marriott, Thomas II, 526
Marriott, Thomas II, 590
Marriott, Thomas II, 964
Marriott, Thomas II, 987
Marriott, Thomas II, 996
Marriott, Thomas II, 1007
Marriott, Thomas II, 1013
Marriott, Thomas II, 1026
Marriott, Thomas Tucker II, 808
Marriott, Thomasin II, 241
Marriott, Thos. II, 932
Marriott, Wd. Sarah II, 1043
Marriott, Wd. Sarah III, 219
Marriott, Wd. Sarah W. III, 86
Marriott, William II, 808
Marriott, Wm. II, 590
Marriott, Wm. II, 754
Marriott, Wm. II, 895
Marriott, Wm. II, 932
Marriott, Wm. A. Garrigues II, 932
Marriott, Wm. Henry II, 808
Marriott, Wm. Henry II, 895
Marriottt, Anna II, 1013
Marris, Aaron I, 509
Marris, Ann IV, 643
Marris, Anna Pim IV, 832
Marris, Catharine I, 450
Marris, Catharine I, 452
Marris, Esther I, 919
Marris, George I, 509
Marris, George I, 919
Marris, Jane I, 509
Marris, Lydia Cora I, 919
Marris, Rachel I, 509
Marris, Susanah I, 509
Marrot, Davenport II, 590
Marrott, Ann II, 392
Marrott, Bertha IV, 1286
Marrott, Bessie IV, 1286
Marrott, Davenport II, 392
Marrott, Edith Anna IV, 1286
Marrott, Edward Lewis V, 920
Marrott, Emily Clara IV, 1286
Marrott, Harriet IV, 1286
Marrott, Henry IV, 1286
Marrott, Henry V, 920
Marrott, Jane IV, 1286
Marrott, Jennie Mayse IV, 1286
Marrott, Louise IV, 1286
Marrott, Lucy Anna IV, 1286
Marrott, Lucy Mary IV, 1286
Marrott, Lucy Moyce IV, 1286
Marrott, Moyce IV, 1286
Marrs, Henry W. II, 322
Marrs, Henry Webb II, 322
Marrs, Joshua VI, 957
Marrs, Nancy VI, 957
Marryott, Jane II, 590
Marryott, Wd. Jane II, 534
Mars, John VI, 970
Marsbourn, Sarah I, 406
Marsburn, Sarah I, 406
Marsey, Elizabeth II, 550
Marsey, Elizabeth II, 592
Marsh, ??? III, 219
Marsh, Abel II, 295
Marsh, Abraham IV, 487
Marsh, Abraham IV, 540
Marsh, Alfred R. I, 891
Marsh, Almara VI, 859
Marsh, Almira Lora III, 426
Marsh, Amanda IV, 48
Marsh, Amos IV, 99
Marsh, Amos IV, 313
Marsh, Amos IV, 314
Marsh, Amos IV, 643
Marsh, Amos IV, 877
Marsh, Ann III, 219
Marsh, Ann IV, 153
Marsh, Ann IV, 248
Marsh, Ann IV, 385
Marsh, Ann IV, 419
Marsh, Ann IV, 482
Marsh, Ann IV, 487
Marsh, Ann IV, 643
Marsh, Ann IV, 665
Marsh, Ann IV, 877
Marsh, Ann VI, 911
Marsh, Anna S. IV, 531
Marsh, Benj. V. II, 175
Marsh, Benjamin II, 289
Marsh, Benjamin II, 295
Marsh, Benjamin III, 219
Marsh, Benjamin V. II, 178
Marsh, Benjamin V. II, 295
Marsh, Benjamin W. II, 295
Marsh, Catharine III, 143
Marsh, Catharine III, 219
Marsh, Chester S. III, 426
Marsh, Christiana II, 295
Marsh, Cynthia IV, 540
Marsh, Cynthia Ann IV, 487
Marsh, Cynthia Ann IV, 540
Marsh, Cynthia Ann IV, 561
Marsh, Cynthiann IV, 487
Marsh, Davis IV, 738
Marsh, Deborah IV, 135
Marsh, Dillon IV, 487
Marsh, Dinah IV, 99
Marsh, Dinah IV, 100
Marsh, Dinah IV, 130
Marsh, Dr. Van Norton IV, 531
Marsh, E. III, 114
Marsh, Eden III, 219
Marsh, Edgar IV, 487
Marsh, Edgar IV, 540
Marsh, Edith IV, 47
Marsh, Edith IV, 99
Marsh, Edith IV, 643
Marsh, Edith IV, 833
Marsh, Edith IV, 849
Marsh, Edith IV, 870
Marsh, Edith IV, 871
Marsh, Edith IV, 877
Marsh, Edith IV, 885
Marsh, Edith IV, 910
Marsh, Edmund VI, 809
Marsh, Edmund VI, 957
Marsh, Edward VI, 859
Marsh, Eli I, 406
Marsh, Eli R. IV, 47
Marsh, Elias II, 590
Marsh, Elias III, 219
Marsh, Elias IV, 738
Marsh, Elias IV, 833
Marsh, Elias IV, 849
Marsh, Elias IV, 910
Marsh, Elias V, 585
Marsh, Elias V, 591
Marsh, Elisabeth IV, 643
Marsh, Elisha II, 392
Marsh, Eliza II, 811
Marsh, Eliza IV, 35
Marsh, Eliza IV, 47
Marsh, Eliza IV, 48
Marsh, Eliza IV, 877
Marsh, Eliza IV, 883
Marsh, Eliza IV, 910
Marsh, Eliza C. IV, 877
Marsh, Eliza C. IV, 979
Marsh, Eliza C. IV, 1001
Marsh, Eliza G. IV, 47
Marsh, Eliza G. IV, 48
Marsh, Eliza G. IV, 877
Marsh, Elizabeth IV, 153
Marsh, Elizabeth IV, 487
Marsh, Elizabeth IV, 523
Marsh, Elizabeth IV, 540
Marsh, Elizabeth IV, 870
Marsh, Elizabeth IV, 877
Marsh, Elizabeth IV, 910
Marsh, Elizabeth V, 901
Marsh, Elizabeth V, 920
Marsh, Elizabeth VI, 675
Marsh, Elizabeth VI, 838
Marsh, Elizabeth VI, 947
Marsh, Ellen A. I, 928
Marsh, Emily Jane IV, 863
Marsh, Emily Jane IV, 877
Marsh, Emmor B. IV, 47
Marsh, Fanny IV, 833
Marsh, Fanny IV, 849
Marsh, Fanny IV, 910
Marsh, Frances II, 175
Marsh, Frances II, 289
Marsh, Frances II, 295
Marsh, Frances F. I, 766
Marsh, Frances F. I, 891
Marsh, Francis III, 219
Marsh, Fred D. III, 219
Marsh, Gibbons II, 896
Marsh, Glenna V, 96
Marsh, Grissel IV, 738
Marsh, Hannah IV, 738
Marsh, Hannah IV, 877
Marsh, Hannah F. III, 219
Marsh, Hannah G. IV, 48
Marsh, Hannah H. IV, 871
Marsh, Hannah H. IV, 877
Marsh, Harry III, 219
Marsh, Henry IV, 48
Marsh, Henry VI, 911
Marsh, Henry, Senior I, 1085
Marsh, Henry, Sr. I, 1095
Marsh, Hobart V, 96
Marsh, Hugh IV, 487
Marsh, Hugh IV, 540
Marsh, Isaac II, 590
Marsh, Isaac IV, 487
Marsh, Israel IV, 643
Marsh, James IV, 47
Marsh, James IV, 99
Marsh, James IV, 643
Marsh, James IV, 866
Marsh, James IV, 870
Marsh, James IV, 871
Marsh, James IV, 877
Marsh, James IV, 883
Marsh, James IV, 885
Marsh, James VI, 957
Marsh, James D. V, 263
Marsh, James E. VI, 985
Marsh, James E. VI, 1019
Marsh, James R. II, 590
Marsh, James, Jr. IV, 643
Marsh, James, Jr. IV, 877
Marsh, James, Jr. IV, 910
Marsh, Jane I, 890
Marsh, Jane I, 891
Marsh, Jane II, 590
Marsh, Jane III, 115
Marsh, Jane III, 302
Marsh, Jane IV, 643
Marsh, Jane IV, 655
Marsh, Jane IV, 738
Marsh, Jane IV, 833
Marsh, Jane IV, 842
Marsh, Jane V, 920
Marsh, Jane F. III, 219
Marsh, Jane Marriott II, 590
Marsh, Jane T. III, 114
Marsh, Jesse IV, 833
Marsh, Jesse IV, 910
Marsh, John III, 219
Marsh, John IV, 487
Marsh, John IV, 540
Marsh, John IV, 863
Marsh, John IV, 877
Marsh, John VI, 838
Marsh, John VI, 892
Marsh, John VI, 947
Marsh, John G. II, 295
Marsh, John N. IV, 235
Marsh, John N. IV, 248
Marsh, John N. IV, 482
Marsh, John N. IV, 487
Marsh, Jonathan IV, 487
Marsh, Jonathan IV, 540
Marsh, Jonathan IV, 607
Marsh, Jonathan IV, 643
Marsh, Jonathan IV, 665
Marsh, Jonathan IV, 875
Marsh, Jonathan IV, 877
Marsh, Jonathan, Jr. IV, 643
Marsh, Joseph IV, 859
Marsh, Joseph IV, 910
Marsh, Lavina IV, 487
Marsh, Lavina IV, 540
Marsh, Lavina IV, 1067
Marsh, Lillian III, 96
Marsh, Lillian III, 219
Marsh, Lydia IV, 738
Marsh, Lydia IV, 783
Marsh, Lydia IV, 833
Marsh, Lydia IV, 866
Marsh, Lydia IV, 877
Marsh, Lydia IV, 883
Marsh, Lydia IV, 910
Marsh, Lydia Fanny IV, 738
Marsh, Margaret IV, 130
Marsh, Margaret IV, 480
Marsh, Margaret IV, 481
Marsh, Margaret IV, 487
Marsh, Margaret V, 585
Marsh, Margaret V, 591
Marsh, Maria F. III, 219
Marsh, Martha IV, 130
Marsh, Martha IV, 833
Marsh, Martha IV, 910
Marsh, Martha Jane VI, 995
Marsh, Mary I, 717
Marsh, Mary II, 86
Marsh, Mary II, 106
Marsh, Mary II, 590
Marsh, Mary IV, 48
Marsh, Mary IV, 487
Marsh, Mary IV, 491
Marsh, Mary IV, 643
Marsh, Mary IV, 877
Marsh, Mary V, 585
Marsh, Mary VI, 531
Marsh, Mary VI, 646
Marsh, Mary VI, 675
Marsh, Mary Ann II, 867
Marsh, Mary Ann II, 896
Marsh, Mary Ann IV, 35
Marsh, Mary Ann IV, 47
Marsh, Mary Ann IV, 99
Marsh, Mary Ann IV, 487
Marsh, Mary Ann IV, 643
Marsh, Mary Ann IV, 870
Marsh, Mary Ann IV, 877
Marsh, Mary Ann VI, 892
Marsh, Mary B. VI, 957
Marsh, Mary E. III, 426
Marsh, Mary Frances VI, 915
Marsh, Mary H. IV, 48
Marsh, Mary H. IV, 54
Marsh, Mary H. IV, 617
Marsh, Mary H. IV, 643
Marsh, Mary H. IV, 657
Marsh, Mary H. IV, 738
Marsh, Mary H. IV, 767

Marsh, Mary H. IV, 877
Marsh, Mary H. VI, 957
Marsh, Mary Hannah I, 725
Marsh, Michael I, 922
Marsh, Mifflin IV, 153
Marsh, Mifflin IV, 487
Marsh, Milton IV, 35
Marsh, Milton IV, 47
Marsh, Milton IV, 48
Marsh, Milton IV, 870
Marsh, Milton IV, 877
Marsh, Minor IV, 910
Marsh, Miriam IV, 99
Marsh, Miriam IV, 632
Marsh, Miriam IV, 643
Marsh, Miriam IV, 872
Marsh, Miriam IV, 877
Marsh, Myra Ann IV, 540
Marsh, Myraan IV, 561
Marsh, Nancy I, 928
Marsh, Nathan Pusey IV, 48
Marsh, Pamilia VI, 957
Marsh, Patsey VI, 957
Marsh, Pennock, Joseph IV, 738
Marsh, Peter VI, 957
Marsh, Peter VI, 985
Marsh, Phebe IV, 607
Marsh, Phebe IV, 643
Marsh, Phebe IV, 875
Marsh, Phebe IV, 877
Marsh, Phebe Ann IV, 875
Marsh, Phebe ann IV, 877
Marsh, Phebe Ann IV, 877
Marsh, Phebe Ann IV, 877
Marsh, Phebe Ann IV, 910
Marsh, Priscilla III, 219
Marsh, Rachel IV, 371
Marsh, Rachel IV, 419
Marsh, Rebecca I, 922
Marsh, Rebecca IV, 130
Marsh, Rebecca IV, 313
Marsh, Rebecca IV, 314
Marsh, Rebecca IV, 877
Marsh, Rebecca T. IV, 248
Marsh, Rebecca T. IV, 877
Marsh, Rebecca W. IV, 47
Marsh, Richard II, 590
Marsh, Robert IV, 833
Marsh, Robert IV, 910
Marsh, Robert VI, 957
Marsh, Ruth IV, 643
Marsh, Ruth IV, 877
Marsh, Ruth IV, 884
Marsh, Ruth VI, 675
Marsh, Sabina IV, 910
Marsh, Samuel III, 219
Marsh, Samuel IV, 738
Marsh, Samuel IV, 833
Marsh, Sara S. III, 426
Marsh, Sarah II, 876
Marsh, Sarah II, 896
Marsh, Sarah III, 219
Marsh, Sarah IV, 487
Marsh, Sarah IV, 877
Marsh, Sarah IV, 884
Marsh, Sarah IV, 910
Marsh, Sarah V, 263
Marsh, Sarah VI, 997
Marsh, Sarah A. VI, 809
Marsh, Sarah Dillin IV, 540
Marsh, Susan VI, 764
Marsh, Susan Ann VI, 911
Marsh, Susan Ann VI, 985
Marsh, Susanna IV, 235
Marsh, Susanna IV, 248
Marsh, Susanna IV, 487
Marsh, Susanna G. VI, 957
Marsh, Susanna N. IV, 153
Marsh, Susanna, Jr. IV, 487
Marsh, Susannah II, 809
Marsh, Susannah IV, 482
Marsh, Susannah IV, 487
Marsh, Susannah IV, 643
Marsh, Susannah Cope IV, 643
Marsh, Susannah, Sr. IV, 487
Marsh, Tabitha VI, 957
Marsh, Tamer I, 922
Marsh, Thaddeus IV, 487
Marsh, Thaddeus IV, 540
Marsh, Thaddeus Constantine IV, 561
Marsh, Thomas I, 928
Marsh, Thomas IV, 738
Marsh, Thomas VI, 957
Marsh, Thomas Osborn V, 585
Marsh, Victor III, 219
Marsh, William III, 219
Marsh, William IV, 130
Marsh, William IV, 487
Marsh, William IV, 540
Marsh, William IV, 910
Marsh, William VI, 838
Marsh, William VI, 915
Marsh, William VI, 947
Marsh, William VI, 957
Marsh, William VI, 995
Marsh, William H. VI, 911
Marsh, William, Jr. IV, 487
Marsh, Wm. IV, 130
Marsh, Wm. IV, 248
Marsh, Wm. IV, 482
Marsh, Wm. IV, 487
Marsh, Wm. IV, 833
Marsh, Wm. V, 920
Marsh, Wm., Jr. IV, 487
Marsh, Zillah IV, 99
Marsh, Zillah IV, 643
Marsh, Zillah IV, 877
Marsh, Zillah IV, 885
Marshal, Ann I, 1095
Marshal, Benjamin IV, 738
Marshal, Christopher II, 393
Marshal, David I, 891
Marshal, Elizabeth I, 408
Marshal, Elizabeth I, 451
Marshal, Elizabeth II, 64
Marshal, Elmyra IV, 877
Marshal, Emaline I, 438
Marshal, Jane IV, 99
Marshal, Jasa J. I, 438
Marshal, John I, 1095
Marshal, John II, 591
Marshal, Joseph I, 451
Marshal, Joseph IV, 738
Marshal, Joshua I, 966
Marshal, Margaret II, 591
Marshal, Mary I, 1062
Marshal, Miles I, 1095
Marshal, Milly VI, 916
Marshal, Nancy I, 451
Marshal, Rebeccah I, 1125
Marshal, Rebekah I, 1060
Marshal, Rebekah I, 1062
Marshal, Sarah II, 591
Marshal, Susanna I, 725
Marshal, Thomas I, 1095
Marshal, Thomas Newton I, 438
Marshal, William I, 966
Marshal, William I, 1159
Marshall, ??? I, 359
Marshall, ??? I, 406
Marshall, ??? III, 220
Marshall, ??? III, 276
Marshall, ??? IV, 1125
Marshall, ??? VI, 806
Marshall, Aaron I, 408
Marshall, Abigail I, 560
Marshall, Abigail I, 860
Marshall, Abigail II, 478
Marshall, Abigail II, 591
Marshall, Abigail II, 603
Marshall, Abigail II, 691
Marshall, Abigail II, 808
Marshall, Abigail II, 864
Marshall, Abraham I, 59
Marshall, Abraham I, 146
Marshall, Abraham I, 1091
Marshall, Abraham I, 1092
Marshall, Abraham I, 1095
Marshall, Abraham I, 1096
Marshall, Abram I, 1077
Marshall, Abram II, 837
Marshall, Abram II, 896
Marshall, Aggy VI, 973
Marshall, Agness VI, 973
Marshall, Albert E. III, 169
Marshall, Albert E. III, 219
Marshall, Albert E. III, 220
Marshall, Albert E. III, 228
Marshall, Albert E. III, 229
Marshall, Albert E. III, 303
Marshall, Albert E., Jr. III, 189
Marshall, Albert E., Jr. III, 219
Marshall, Alexander VI, 914
Marshall, Alexander VI, 957
Marshall, Alfred II, 808
Marshall, Alfred II, 896
Marshall, Alfred II, 897
Marshall, Alice M. V, 585
Marshall, Allen VI, 957
Marshall, Allie M. V, 412
Marshall, Almira III, 220
Marshall, Andrew III, 219
Marshall, Andrew III, 220
Marshall, Angeline IV, 1257
Marshall, Ann I, 408
Marshall, Ann I, 826
Marshall, Ann II, 393
Marshall, Ann II, 479
Marshall, Ann II, 491
Marshall, Ann II, 511
Marshall, Ann II, 547
Marshall, Ann II, 590
Marshall, Ann II, 591
Marshall, Ann II, 691
Marshall, Ann III, 220
Marshall, Ann IV, 689
Marshall, Ann IV, 738
Marshall, Ann IV, 1106
Marshall, Ann IV, 1107
Marshall, Ann IV, 1133
Marshall, Ann IV, 1135
Marshall, Ann VI, 848
Marshall, Ann VI, 852
Marshall, Ann Douglas VI, 752
Marshall, Ann Eliza III, 219
Marshall, Ann Eliza III, 220
Marshall, Ann M. VI, 957
Marshall, Ann Maria III, 220
Marshall, Ann Mercy IV, 877
Marshall, Anna II, 184
Marshall, Anna II, 590
Marshall, Anna II, 653
Marshall, Anna II, 896
Marshall, Anna III, 187
Marshall, Anna III, 219
Marshall, Anna M. IV, 390
Marshall, Anna M. IV, 1135
Marshall, Anna Maria III, 57
Marshall, Anna Maria III, 220
Marshall, Anna Maria IV, 487
Marshall, Anna Maria IV, 506
Marshall, Anna Maria IV, 1134
Marshall, Anna Maria IV, 1135
Marshall, Anna Mercy IV, 419
Marshall, Anna Mercy IV, 1067
Marshall, Anna Mercy IV, 1106
Marshall, Anna W. I, 1159
Marshall, Annie III, 426
Marshall, Annie E. V, 412
Marshall, Annie E. V, 585
Marshall, Aquilla II, 754
Marshall, Aquilla B. II, 896
Marshall, Aquilla Bolton II, 591
Marshall, Aquilla Bolton II, 896
Marshall, Aquilla Bolton III, 219
Marshall, Aquilla Bolton III, 220
Marshall, Asa III, 219
Marshall, Asa III, 220
Marshall, Asa III, 228
Marshall, Bathana A. I, 891
Marshall, Benj. II, 499
Marshall, Benj. II, 709
Marshall, Benj. II, 712
Marshall, Benjamin I, 684
Marshall, Benjamin II, 393
Marshall, Benjamin II, 499
Marshall, Benjamin II, 508
Marshall, Benjamin II, 530
Marshall, Benjamin II, 588
Marshall, Benjamin II, 590
Marshall, Benjamin III, 220
Marshall, Benjamin III, 221
Marshall, Benjamin IV, 636
Marshall, Benjamin IV, 643
Marshall, Benjamin IV, 689
Marshall, Benjamin IV, 738
Marshall, Benjamin F. I, 891
Marshall, Benjamin G. III, 228
Marshall, Betsey VI, 957
Marshall, Betsy VI, 826
Marshall, Betsy VI, 838
Marshall, Caleb II, 808
Marshall, Caleb II, 864
Marshall, Caleb II, 896
Marshall, Caleb II, 897
Marshall, Caleb IV, 419
Marshall, Caleb IV, 872
Marshall, Caleb IV, 877
Marshall, Caleb IV, 1067
Marshall, Caleb IV, 1106
Marshall, Caleb IV, 1135
Marshall, Carolina S. III, 220
Marshall, Caroline III, 220
Marshall, Cassandra VI, 965
Marshall, Catharine VI, 800
Marshall, Catharine VI, 957
Marshall, Catharine J. VI, 973
Marshall, Charles II, 393
Marshall, Charles II, 591
Marshall, Charles II, 603
Marshall, Charles II, 614
Marshall, Charles II, 672
Marshall, Charles E. III, 220
Marshall, Charles, Jr. II, 591
Marshall, Charlotte I, 891
Marshall, Charlotte III, 220
Marshall, Charlotte J. III, 219
Marshall, Charlotte J. III, 220
Marshall, Charlotte J. III, 229
Marshall, Charlotte J. III, 303
Marshall, Chas. II, 808
Marshall, Christina I, 891
Marshall, Christina I, 922
Marshall, Christina I, 945
Marshall, Christina Elizabeth I, 930
Marshall, Christo II, 393
Marshall, Christopher II, 393
Marshall, Christopher II, 511
Marshall, Christopher II, 588
Marshall, Christopher II, 590
Marshall, Christopher II, 591
Marshall, Christopher II, 614
Marshall, Christopher II, 653
Marshall, Christopher II, 667
Marshall, Christopher II, 754
Marshall, Christopher, Jr. II, 393
Marshall, Christopher, Jr. II, 491
Marshall, Christopher, Jr. II, 508
Marshall, Christopher, Jr. II, 525
Marshall, Christopher, Jr. II, 591
Marshall, Christopher, Jr. II, 691
Marshall, Clarence III, 219
Marshall, Clarence III, 220
Marshall, Clarence Mather II, 808
Marshall, Cora III, 490
Marshall, Cora S. III, 495
Marshall, Daniel III, 220
Marshall, Daniel VI, 813
Marshall, Daniel VI, 838
Marshall, Daniel H. III, 220
Marshall, David I, 560
Marshall, David I, 860
Marshall, David I, 891
Marshall, David III, 220
Marshall, David IV, 1373
Marshall, David VI, 838
Marshall, David VI, 854
Marshall, David VI, 864
Marshall, Deborah II, 547
Marshall, Deborah II, 590
Marshall, Deborah II, 591
Marshall, Deborah II, 799
Marshall, Douglas H. VI, 838
Marshall, Dr. Eugene III, 220
Marshall, Edith VI, 555
Marshall, Edith VI, 764
Marshall, Edith VI, 776
Marshall, Edw. III, 57
Marshall, Edw. III, 220
Marshall, Edward II, 393
Marshall, Edward II, 591
Marshall, Edward III, 368
Marshall, Edward J. III, 220
Marshall, Edward, Jr. III, 57
Marshall, Edward, Jr. III, 220
Marshall, Edwin III, 220
Marshall, Edwin III, 228
Marshall, Edwin III, 230
Marshall, Edythe VI, 764
Marshall, Elender VI, 1008
Marshall, Eli I, 1086
Marshall, Eli I, 1156
Marshall, Eli I, 1159
Marshall, Eli II, 797
Marshall, Elihu III, 220
Marshall, Eliz. W. III, 210
Marshall, Eliza III, 220
Marshall, Eliza Jane III, 220
Marshall, Elizabeth I, 408
Marshall, Elizabeth I, 451
Marshall, Elizabeth I, 560
Marshall, Elizabeth I, 826
Marshall, Elizabeth I, 955
Marshall, Elizabeth I, 959
Marshall, Elizabeth I, 966
Marshall, Elizabeth I, 1034
Marshall, Elizabeth I, 1086
Marshall, Elizabeth II, 64
Marshall, Elizabeth II, 86
Marshall, Elizabeth II, 226
Marshall, Elizabeth II, 241
Marshall, Elizabeth II, 525
Marshall, Elizabeth II, 590
Marshall, Elizabeth II, 591
Marshall, Elizabeth II, 653
Marshall, Elizabeth II, 712
Marshall, Elizabeth II, 814
Marshall, Elizabeth III, 220
Marshall, Elizabeth IV, 99
Marshall, Elizabeth IV, 248
Marshall, Elizabeth IV, 419
Marshall, Elizabeth IV, 1106
Marshall, Elizabeth V, 188
Marshall, Elizabeth VI, 838
Marshall, Elizabeth VI, 978
Marshall, Elizabeth VI, 986
Marshall, Elizabeth Ann II, 712
Marshall, Elizabeth Flower II, 591
Marshall, Elizabeth Flower II, 653
Marshall, Elizabeth G. II, 393
Marshall, Elizabeth G. II, 754
Marshall, Elizabeth L. III, 368
Marshall, Elizabeth Messina I, 1086
Marshall, Elizabeth V. IV, 419
Marshall, Ellan I, 891
Marshall, Ellen I, 611
Marshall, Ellen I, 891
Marshall, Ellen VI, 227
Marshall, Ellen P. III, 245
Marshall, Elmira IV, 872
Marshall, Elmira IV, 877
Marshall, Elmira IV, 1106
Marshall, Elmira IV, 1135
Marshall, Elmyra IV, 877
Marshall, Elvira VI, 838
Marshall, Emma I, 438
Marshall, Emma III, 228
Marshall, Enoch Flower II, 393
Marshall, Esther II, 530
Marshall, Esther II, 591
Marshall, Esther II, 795
Marshall, Ethel II, 808
Marshall, Ettiel W. III, 189
Marshall, Ettiel W. III, 219
Marshall, Eva V, 412
Marshall, Eva V, 696
Marshall, Eva L. V, 412
Marshall, Eva L. V, 585
Marshall, F. P. VI, 1022
Marshall, F. Warren II, 808
Marshall, Florence III, 220
Marshall, Florence Amelia III, 169
Marshall, Florence Amelia III, 219
Marshall, Florence V. II, 896
Marshall, Florence Virginia II, 808
Marshall, Florence Virginia II, 897
Marshall, Francis W. III, 228
Marshall, G. H. VI, 827
Marshall, Gelinda I, 891
Marshall, Geo. III, 220
Marshall, George II, 393
Marshall, George II, 591
Marshall, George III, 25
Marshall, George V, 1009
Marshall, George Lowry VI, 733
Marshall, George Lowry VI, 764
Marshall, Gertrude III, 219
Marshall, Gertrude III, 220
Marshall, Gertrude III, 303
Marshall, Halford V, 1009
Marshall, Hannah I, 408
Marshall, Hannah I, 961
Marshall, Hannah I, 966
Marshall, Hannah I, 1060
Marshall, Hannah I, 1062
Marshall, Hannah I, 1086
Marshall, Hannah I, 1159
Marshall, Hannah II, 241
Marshall, Hannah II, 261
Marshall, Hannah II, 393
Marshall, Hannah II, 445
Marshall, Hannah II, 538
Marshall, Hannah II, 591
Marshall, Hannah II, 754
Marshall, Hannah II, 797
Marshall, Hannah III, 221
Marshall, Hannah III, 276
Marshall, Hannah IV, 99
Marshall, Hannah IV, 248
Marshall, Hannah IV, 419
Marshall, Hannah IV, 892
Marshall, Hannah IV, 893
Marshall, Hannah IV, 894
Marshall, Hannah IV, 1373
Marshall, Hannah V, 956
Marshall, Hannah VI, 828
Marshall, Hannah P. IV, 419
Marshall, Hannah S. VI, 957
Marshall, Harold A. III, 220
Marshall, Harold A. III, 320
Marshall, Harriet IV, 1373
Marshall, Henry G. III, 219
Marshall, Henry G. III, 220
Marshall, Hephsibah I, 684
Marshall, Hephsibah I, 689
Marshall, Hepzibah I, 684
Marshall, Hiram IV, 1373
Marshall, Howard II, 896
Marshall, Huldah I, 611
Marshall, Huldah I, 629
Marshall, Huldah I, 637
Marshall, Huldah Minthorn VI, 227
Marshall, Humphrey II, 42
Marshall, Ira B. I, 930

Marshall, Isaac R. II, 591
Marshall, Isaac Roberts II, 393
Marshall, Isaac S. III, 220
Marshall, Isabel II, 393
Marshall, Isabella II, 591
Marshall, Isabella II, 691
Marshall, Isla B. I, 945
Marshall, Isla Belle I, 930
Marshall, Issabell II, 42
Marshall, J. Elwood I, 945
Marshall, J. Howard II, 808
Marshall, J. Howard II, 864
Marshall, J. Howard II, 896
Marshall, J. W. VI, 986
Marshall, Jacob I, 560
Marshall, Jacob II, 393
Marshall, James II, 179
Marshall, James II, 393
Marshall, James II, 590
Marshall, James II, 837
Marshall, James II, 896
Marshall, James II, 907
Marshall, James IV, 419
Marshall, James IV, 1067
Marshall, James IV, 1106
Marshall, James V, 516
Marshall, James V, 1009
Marshall, James VI, 800
Marshall, James Bateman II, 896
Marshall, James C. IV, 643
Marshall, James C. IV, 738
Marshall, James C. IV, 979
Marshall, James E. IV, 419
Marshall, James Engle IV, 1106
Marshall, Jane IV, 99
Marshall, Jane IV, 248
Marshall, Jane IV, 275
Marshall, Jane VI, 838
Marshall, Jane P. II, 864
Marshall, Jane P. II, 896
Marshall, Jane P. II, 897
Marshall, Jane Peirce II, 808
Marshall, Jemima I, 819
Marshall, Jemima I, 826
Marshall, Jemima I, 992
Marshall, Jesse IV, 406
Marshall, Jesse IV, 1067
Marshall, Jesse IV, 1106
Marshall, Jesse IV, 1135
Marshall, Jesse B. IV, 419
Marshall, Jesse W. I, 1159
Marshall, Joel D. IV, 1373
Marshall, John I, 451
Marshall, John I, 1086
Marshall, John I, 1159
Marshall, John II, 393
Marshall, John II, 445
Marshall, John II, 591
Marshall, John IV, 390
Marshall, John IV, 419
Marshall, John IV, 877
Marshall, John IV, 1067
Marshall, John IV, 1106
Marshall, John IV, 1107
Marshall, John IV, 1133
Marshall, John IV, 1135
Marshall, John VI, 422
Marshall, John VI, 752
Marshall, John VI, 806
Marshall, John VI, 812
Marshall, John VI, 838
Marshall, John VI, 847
Marshall, John VI, 852
Marshall, John VI, 864
Marshall, John B. I, 860
Marshall, John J. V, 412
Marshall, John R. VI, 939
Marshall, John R. VI, 957
Marshall, John S. I, 891
Marshall, John W. IV, 1257
Marshall, John, Jr. III, 490
Marshall, John, Jr. III, 495
Marshall, John, Jr. VI, 76
Marshall, John, Jr. VI, 795
Marshall, Jonathan I, 438
Marshall, Jonathan I, 451
Marshall, Jonathan III, 220
Marshall, Jones Elwood I, 930
Marshall, Jos. III, 187
Marshall, Jos. III, 219
Marshall, Joseph I, 451
Marshall, Joseph I, 826
Marshall, Joseph I, 977
Marshall, Joseph I, 978
Marshall, Joseph I, 1086
Marshall, Joseph II, 393
Marshall, Joseph II, 499
Marshall, Joseph II, 590
Marshall, Joseph II, 591
Marshall, Joseph III, 426
Marshall, Joseph IV, 643
Marshall, Joseph IV, 738
Marshall, Joseph IV, 787
Marshall, Joseph IV, 892
Marshall, Joseph IV, 893
Marshall, Joseph Crukshank II, 393
Marshall, Joseph John I, 1086
Marshall, Joshua I, 966
Marshall, Justus III, 220
Marshall, Laura F. III, 220
Marshall, Laura F. III, 228
Marshall, Laura F. III, 293
Marshall, Leah C. V, 920
Marshall, Leah C. V, 927
Marshall, Letitia V, 1009
Marshall, Lida V, 1009
Marshall, Lottie Belle III, 320
Marshall, Lottiebelle III, 220
Marshall, Louise K. VI, 764
Marshall, Louise K. VI, 792
Marshall, Lucy IV, 1365
Marshall, Lucy IV, 1373
Marshall, Lucy B. VI, 838
Marshall, Lucy R. IV, 1373
Marshall, Lydia IV, 1361
Marshall, Lydia IV, 1373
Marshall, Lydia Ann V, 1009
Marshall, Lydia W. IV, 1373
Marshall, Maggie V, 188
Marshall, Margaret I, 826
Marshall, Margaret II, 393
Marshall, Margaret II, 591
Marshall, Margaret II, 712
Marshall, Margaret II, 896
Marshall, Margret I, 826
Marshall, Marion I, 891
Marshall, Marshall IV, 1373
Marshall, Martha II, 896
Marshall, Martha III, 220
Marshall, Martha IV, 419
Marshall, Martha IV, 1106
Marshall, Martha VI, 859
Marshall, Martha VI, 947
Marshall, Martha Adeline I, 1086
Marshall, Martha E. IV, 1133
Marshall, Martha E. IV, 1135
Marshall, Martha H. II, 907
Marshall, Martha Jay I, 891
Marshall, Mary I, 684
Marshall, Mary I, 689
Marshall, Mary I, 826
Marshall, Mary I, 1053
Marshall, Mary II, 179
Marshall, Mary II, 393
Marshall, Mary II, 499
Marshall, Mary II, 508
Marshall, Mary II, 572
Marshall, Mary II, 590
Marshall, Mary II, 591
Marshall, Mary II, 709
Marshall, Mary II, 712
Marshall, Mary II, 790
Marshall, Mary II, 808
Marshall, Mary II, 837
Marshall, Mary II, 870
Marshall, Mary II, 896
Marshall, Mary III, 38
Marshall, Mary III, 219
Marshall, Mary III, 220
Marshall, Mary IV, 643
Marshall, Mary IV, 738
Marshall, Mary IV, 787
Marshall, Mary IV, 893
Marshall, Mary IV, 1373
Marshall, Mary VI, 555
Marshall, Mary VI, 764
Marshall, Mary VI, 776
Marshall, Mary VI, 838
Marshall, Mary A. III, 220
Marshall, Mary A. III, 230
Marshall, Mary Ann II, 754
Marshall, Mary Ann II, 808
Marshall, Mary Ann II, 896
Marshall, Mary Ann VI, 838
Marshall, Mary B. III, 220
Marshall, Mary B. III, 228
Marshall, Mary C. V, 412
Marshall, Mary C. V, 585
Marshall, Mary Christina I, 891
Marshall, Mary E. III, 220
Marshall, Mary E. V, 412
Marshall, Mary E. VI, 957
Marshall, Mary J. VI, 957
Marshall, Mary Pendora I, 891
Marshall, Mary T. VI, 1022
Marshall, Maryetta IV, 1135
Marshall, Merlin L. I, 611
Marshall, Michael VI, 879
Marshall, Mildred E. H. VI, 862
Marshall, Minnie I, 922
Marshall, Minnie I, 945
Marshall, Minnie B. V, 412
Marshall, Minnie B. V, 585
Marshall, Minnie Belle I, 930
Marshall, Moses III, 220
Marshall, Mrs. Permelia VI, 987
Marshall, Murtin L. I, 891
Marshall, Murtin L. I, 895
Marshall, Myra T. III, 25
Marshall, Myra T. III, 220
Marshall, Myrtle Elizabeth VI, 733
Marshall, Myrtle Elizabeth VI, 764
Marshall, Nancy I, 451
Marshall, Nancy VI, 813
Marshall, Nancy VI, 912
Marshall, Nancy VI, 957
Marshall, Nancy VI, 978
Marshall, Nancy VI, 999
Marshall, Nathan III, 38
Marshall, Nathan III, 219
Marshall, Nathan III, 220
Marshall, Nathan III, 221
Marshall, Nelly VI, 822
Marshall, Newton I, 451
Marshall, Niobe III, 220
Marshall, Nora H. V, 412
Marshall, Nora H. V, 585
Marshall, Norah H. V, 412
Marshall, Obed III, 220
Marshall, Patience I, 966
Marshall, Patience II, 591
Marshall, Patience II, 603
Marshall, Patience II, 614
Marshall, Patience II, 672
Marshall, Patience II, 712
Marshall, Patience II, 808
Marshall, Patience VI, 838
Marshall, Patience Alvina II, 896
Marshall, Patience Alvira II, 896
Marshall, Patience, Jr. II, 591
Marshall, Patience, Jr. II, 672
Marshall, Patsey VI, 837
Marshall, Pemela IV, 48
Marshall, Perdila I, 891
Marshall, Permelia IV, 48
Marshall, Permelia IV, 63
Marshall, Permelia VI, 957
Marshall, Permelia Roy VI, 957
Marshall, Phebe I, 773
Marshall, Phebe II, 393
Marshall, Phebe II, 591
Marshall, Phebe II, 712
Marshall, Phebe II, 754
Marshall, Phebe III, 96
Marshall, Phebe III, 187
Marshall, Phebe III, 219
Marshall, Phebe III, 220
Marshall, Phebe III, 422
Marshall, Phebe III, 426
Marshall, Phebe C. III, 62
Marshall, Phebe C. III, 220
Marshall, Phebe C. III, 228
Marshall, Phebe C. III, 326
Marshall, Phebe W. II, 907
Marshall, Philena II, 909
Marshall, Poindexter C. VI, 957
Marshall, Poindexter C. VI, 973
Marshall, Polly VI, 806
Marshall, Preston II, 808
Marshall, Preston II, 907
Marshall, Priscilla I, 560
Marshall, Priscilla I, 826
Marshall, Rachel II, 179
Marshall, Rachel II, 222
Marshall, Rachel II, 241
Marshall, Rachel II, 247
Marshall, Rachel II, 393
Marshall, Rachel II, 590
Marshall, Rachel II, 591
Marshall, Ralph II, 393
Marshall, Ralph II, 590
Marshall, Ralph II, 591
Marshall, Rebecca I, 408
Marshall, Rebecca I, 826
Marshall, Rebecca II, 787
Marshall, Rebecca II, 819
Marshall, Rebecca II, 896
Marshall, Rebecca II, 915
Marshall, Rebecca IV, 406
Marshall, Rebecca IV, 636
Marshall, Rebecca IV, 643
Marshall, Rebecca J. I, 1156
Marshall, Rebecca J. I, 1159
Marshall, Rebecca Jane I, 1086
Marshall, Rebeccah I, 1122
Marshall, Rebeckah VI, 838
Marshall, Rebekah I, 826
Marshall, Rebekah II, 86
Marshall, Rebekah II, 88
Marshall, Richard II, 64
Marshall, Richard II, 86
Marshall, Richard II, 590
Marshall, Richard K. I, 891
Marshall, Richard K. I, 922
Marshall, Richard K. I, 930
Marshall, Richard Mather II, 808
Marshall, Robert I, 945
Marshall, Robert II, 808
Marshall, Robert VI, 838
Marshall, Robert VI, 957
Marshall, Robert Kassuth I, 930
Marshall, Robert M. VI, 764
Marshall, Rosela J. IV, 406
Marshall, Rosella IV, 406
Marshall, Rosella IV, 583
Marshall, Rosella J. IV, 574
Marshall, Rosella J. IV, 583
Marshall, Ruth I, 812
Marshall, Ruth I, 826
Marshall, Ruth I, 977
Marshall, Ruth I, 978
Marshall, Ruth IV, 1328
Marshall, Ruth VI, 422
Marshall, Salley VI, 957
Marshall, Sallie T. II, 896
Marshall, Sallie Thompson II, 808
Marshall, Sally VI, 1022
Marshall, Samuel I, 560
Marshall, Samuel II, 591
Marshall, Samuel II, 1076
Marshall, Samuel IV, 419
Marshall, Samuel IV, 1106
Marshall, Samuel VI, 957
Marshall, Samuel VI, 978
Marshall, Samuel E. I, 891
Marshall, Samuel Furman II, 808
Marshall, Sarah I, 451
Marshall, Sarah II, 393
Marshall, Sarah II, 499
Marshall, Sarah II, 508
Marshall, Sarah II, 530
Marshall, Sarah II, 588
Marshall, Sarah II, 590
Marshall, Sarah II, 591
Marshall, Sarah II, 603
Marshall, Sarah II, 667
Marshall, Sarah II, 692
Marshall, Sarah II, 712
Marshall, Sarah II, 753
Marshall, Sarah II, 754
Marshall, Sarah II, 810
Marshall, Sarah II, 814
Marshall, Sarah III, 158
Marshall, Sarah III, 220
Marshall, Sarah III, 221
Marshall, Sarah IV, 643
Marshall, Sarah IV, 738
Marshall, Sarah IV, 893
Marshall, Sarah IV, 894
Marshall, Sarah VI, 864
Marshall, Sarah Adelia III, 220
Marshall, Sarah Ann II, 491
Marshall, Sarah Ann II, 591
Marshall, Sarah C. I, 1125
Marshall, Sarah C. II, 896
Marshall, Sarah E. I, 891
Marshall, Sarah Elizabeth III, 220
Marshall, Sarah H. III, 220
Marshall, Sarah H. III, 233
Marshall, Sarah Thompson II, 808
Marshall, Sarah W. II, 837
Marshall, Sarah W. II, 896
Marshall, Shirley III, 220
Marshall, Simon I, 992
Marshall, Sophronia I, 989
Marshall, Sophronia I, 993
Marshall, Susan J. VI, 957
Marshall, Susanna I, 725
Marshall, Susanna II, 393
Marshall, Susanna III, 220
Marshall, Susanna IV, 643
Marshall, Susanna C. III, 220
Marshall, Susanna Nancy I, 891
Marshall, Susannah I, 725
Marshall, Tacy M. II, 751
Marshall, Tacy M. II, 754
Marshall, Thomas I, 826
Marshall, Thomas I, 1102
Marshall, Thomas I, 1125
Marshall, Thomas II, 393
Marshall, Thomas II, 547
Marshall, Thomas II, 591
Marshall, Thomas III, 220
Marshall, Thomas IV, 99
Marshall, Thomas IV, 248
Marshall, Thomas IV, 419
Marshall, Thomas IV, 420
Marshall, Thomas VI, 70
Marshall, Thomas VI, 76
Marshall, Thomas VI, 555
Marshall, Thomas VI, 764
Marshall, Thomas VI, 776
Marshall, Thomas VI, 828
Marshall, Thomas VI, 862
Marshall, Thomas VI, 957
Marshall, Thomas VI, 999
Marshall, Thomas B. VI, 838
Marshall, Thomas J. VI, 838
Marshall, Thomas R. VI, 838
Marshall, Thomasine II, 590
Marshall, Thomasine II, 596
Marshall, Thos. VI, 1008
Marshall, Tomlinson II, 179
Marshall, Ulisses VI, 838
Marshall, Ury Etta IV, 1127
Marshall, Ury Etta IV, 1135
Marshall, Wallace II, 808
Marshall, Wallace II, 896
Marshall, Wallace II, 915
Marshall, Walter W. III, 220
Marshall, Wd. Margaret II, 808
Marshall, Wd. Margaret Hargraves II, 808
Marshall, Wd. Rebecca II, 808
Marshall, Willey VI, 914
Marshall, William I, 407
Marshall, William I, 826
Marshall, William I, 955
Marshall, William I, 966
Marshall, William I, 1159
Marshall, William III, 220
Marshall, William IV, 99
Marshall, William IV, 248
Marshall, William IV, 419
Marshall, William IV, 643
Marshall, William IV, 1373
Marshall, William VI, 813
Marshall, William VI, 826
Marshall, William VI, 837
Marshall, William VI, 879
Marshall, William VI, 912
Marshall, William VI, 957
Marshall, William VI, 965
Marshall, William Henry I, 637
Marshall, William I. VI, 957
Marshall, William P. IV, 419
Marshall, William, Jr. I, 826
Marshall, Wilmer W. II, 896
Marshall, Wm. I, 560
Marshall, Wm. I, 966
Marshall, Wm. II, 572
Marshall, Wm. II, 591
Marshall, Wm. II, 808
Marshall, Wm. IV, 738
Marshall, Wm. IV, 893
Marshall, Wm. VI, 859
Marshall, Wm. C. III, 220
Marshall, Zelinda I, 560
Marshall, Zelinda I, 860
Marshall, Zelinda VI, 92
Marshalle, Nancy VI, 957
Marshalle, Thomas VI, 957
Marshbum, Lydia I, 625
Marshbum, Obed I, 625
Marshbum, Sallie C. M. I, 625
Marshburn, Allen J. I, 407
Marshburn, Alzora E. I, 1159
Marshburn, Alzoria I, 1159
Marshburn, Beulah I, 359
Marshburn, Catharine I, 415
Marshburn, Esther I, 359
Marshburn, Hannah I, 359
Marshburn, Hannah I, 401
Marshburn, Julia I, 386
Marshburn, Malon P. I, 407
Marshburn, Matthew I, 359
Marshburn, Obed I, 359
Marshburn, Obed I, 386
Marshburn, Obed I, 415
Marshburn, Rachel I, 246
Marshburn, Rebecca I, 359
Marshburn, Rebecca I, 407
Marshburn, Rebecca I, 426
Marshburn, Ruth I, 359
Marshburn, Sallie C. I, 407
Marshburn, Sarah I, 359
Marshburn, William I, 1159
Marshburn, William V. I, 407
Marshburn, Wm. I, 359
Marshburn, Wm. I, 401
Marshel, Abram I, 1085
Marshel, Ann I, 1125
Marshel, Eunice I, 438
Marshel, Hannah I, 1085
Marshel, Jacob I, 560
Marshel, Jacob I, 567
Marshel, Jonathan I, 438
Marshel, Joseph I, 438

arshel, Joseph I, 451
arshel, Martha I, 1085
arshel, Priscilla I, 567
arshel, Ruth I, 1125
arshele, Dinah I, 978
arshele, Joseph I, 978
arshele, Joshua I, 978
arshele, Ruth I, 978
arshele, Simon I, 978
arshele, Thomas I, 978
arshell, Joseph I, 978
arshell, Joseph I, 992
arshell, Thomas I, 993
arshil, Jemima I, 992
arshil, Priscilla I, 560
arshil, Priscilla I, 566
arshill, ??? I, 406
arshill, Aaron I, 360
arshill, Aaron I, 408
arshill, Aaron I, 1108
arshill, Abigail I, 354
arshill, Abraham I, 360
arshill, Abraham I, 407
arshill, Abraham I, 1095
arshill, Abraham I, 1107
arshill, Abraham, Jr. I, 1085
arshill, Abram I, 360
arshill, Abram I, 387
arshill, Abram I, 407
arshill, Abram I, 1085
arshill, Abram I, 1086
arshill, Abram I, 1089
arshill, Abram I, 1095
arshill, Abram I, 1096
arshill, Abram I, 1097
arshill, Abram I, 1098
arshill, Abram, Jr. I, 1085
arshill, Abram, Sr. I, 1085
arshill, Alvin I, 360
arshill, Alvin I, 408
arshill, Ann I, 350
arshill, Ann I, 351
arshill, Ann I, 360
arshill, Ann I, 361
arshill, Ann I, 379
arshill, Ann I, 384
arshill, Ann I, 407
arshill, Ann I, 408
arshill, Ann I, 423
arshill, Ann I, 975
arshill, Ann I, 987
arshill, Ann I, 993
arshill, Ann I, 1095
arshill, Ann I, 1101
arshill, Ann I, 1104
arshill, Ann I, 1106
arshill, Ann I, 1108
arshill, Ann I, 1125
arshill, Anne I, 993
arshill, Benj. I, 354
arshill, Benjamin I, 360
arshill, Benjamin I, 407
arshill, David I, 1086
arshill, David I, 1096
arshill, Deborah I, 353
arshill, Deborah I, 356
arshill, Deborah I, 360
arshill, Deborah I, 395
arshill, Deborah I, 407
arshill, Deborah I, 978
arshill, Deborah I, 987
arshill, Deborah I, 992
arshill, Deborah I Sup 1, 10
arshill, Deborah Hinshaw I, 407
arshill, Dinah I, 355
arshill, Dinah I, 360
arshill, Dinah I, 397
arshill, Dinah I, 407
arshill, Dinah I, 408
arshill, Dinah I, 412
arshill, Dinah I, 981
arshill, Dinah I, 993
arshill, Eli I, 1086
arshill, Elizabeth I, 352
arshill, Elizabeth I, 359
arshill, Elizabeth I, 360
arshill, Elizabeth I, 361
arshill, Elizabeth I, 389
arshill, Elizabeth I, 397
arshill, Elizabeth I, 407
arshill, Elizabeth I, 408
arshill, Elizabeth I, 800
arshill, Elizabeth I, 978
arshill, Elizabeth I, 992
arshill, Elizabeth I, 993
arshill, Elizabeth I, 1085
arshill, Elizabeth I, 1091
arshill, Elizabeth I, 1095
arshill, Elizabeth I, 1107
arshill, Emey I, 360
Marshill, Emy I, 355
Marshill, Emy I, 397
Marshill, Emy I, 407
Marshill, Ephraim I, 360
Marshill, Ephraim I, 1107
Marshill, Francis I, 360
Marshill, Francis I, 407
Marshill, Francis I, 408
Marshill, George I, 408
Marshill, Hannah I, 359
Marshill, Hannah I, 360
Marshill, Hannah I, 361
Marshill, Hannah I, 372
Marshill, Hannah I, 407
Marshill, Hannah I, 408
Marshill, Hannah I, 411
Marshill, Hannah I, 417
Marshill, Hannah I, 1085
Marshill, Hannah I, 1086
Marshill, Hannah I, 1089
Marshill, Hannah I, 1095
Marshill, Hannah I, 1107
Marshill, Hannah I, 1125
Marshill, Isaac I, 359
Marshill, Isaac I, 360
Marshill, Isaac I, 387
Marshill, Isaac I, 407
Marshill, Isaac I, 408
Marshill, Isaac I, 1085
Marshill, Isaac I, 1095
Marshill, Isaac I, 1101
Marshill, Isaac I, 1107
Marshill, Isaac I, 1108
Marshill, Isaac I, 1125
Marshill, Jacob I, 352
Marshill, Jacob I, 354
Marshill, Jacob I, 360
Marshill, Jacob I, 372
Marshill, Jacob I, 384
Marshill, Jacob I, 407
Marshill, Jacob I, 408
Marshill, Jacob I, 560
Marshill, Jacob I, 695
Marshill, Jacob I, 1108
Marshill, Jacob I, 1125
Marshill, Jacob, Jr. I, 360
Marshill, Jane I, 1086
Marshill, Jemima I, 978
Marshill, Jemima I, 992
Marshill, Jesse I, 1085
Marshill, Jesse I, 1086
Marshill, Jesse I, 1095
Marshill, Jesse I, 1097
Marshill, John I, 351
Marshill, John I, 359
Marshill, John I, 360
Marshill, John I, 407
Marshill, John I, 975
Marshill, John I, 978
Marshill, John I, 987
Marshill, John I, 992
Marshill, John I, 993
Marshill, John I, 1085
Marshill, John I, 1086
Marshill, John I, 1089
Marshill, John I, 1095
Marshill, John I, 1107
Marshill, John I, 1108
Marshill, John I, 1125
Marshill, John, Jr. I, 407
Marshill, Joseph I, 360
Marshill, Joseph I, 407
Marshill, Joseph I, 826
Marshill, Joseph I, 992
Marshill, Joseph I, 1085
Marshill, Joseph I, 1095
Marshill, Margaret I, 352
Marshill, Margaret I, 354
Marshill, Margaret I, 360
Marshill, Margaret I, 384
Marshill, Margaret I, 402
Marshill, Margaret I, 407
Marshill, Margaret I, 826
Marshill, Margaret I, 1104
Marshill, Margaret I, 1108
Marshill, Margaret I, 1117
Marshill, Margaret I, 1125
Marshill, Margaret I Sup 1, 11
Marshill, Martha I, 360
Marshill, Martha I, 387
Marshill, Martha I, 407
Marshill, Martha I, 1085
Marshill, Martha I, 1086
Marshill, Martha I, 1095
Marshill, Martha I, 1096
Marshill, Martha I, 1108
Marshill, Martha I, 1125
Marshill, Martha, Jr. I, 1086
Marshill, Martha, Sen. I, 1086
Marshill, Mary I, 350
Marshill, Mary I, 354
Marshill, Mary I, 360
Marshill, Mary I, 361
Marshill, Mary I, 395
Marshill, Mary I, 407
Marshill, Mary I, 420
Marshill, Mary I, 425
Marshill, Mary I, 1086
Marshill, Mary I, 1095
Marshill, Mary I, 1097
Marshill, Mary I, 1107
Marshill, Michael I, 407
Marshill, Miles I, 360
Marshill, Miles I, 1095
Marshill, Miles I, 1108
Marshill, Miles I, 1125
Marshill, Miles I Sup 1, 12
Marshill, Patience I, 961
Marshill, Priscilla I, 407
Marshill, Priscilla I, 416
Marshill, Priscilla I, 560
Marshill, Priscilla I, 826
Marshill, Rachel I, 361
Marshill, Rachel I, 407
Marshill, Rachel I, 1085
Marshill, Rachel I, 1086
Marshill, Rebecca I, 350
Marshill, Rebecca I, 353
Marshill, Rebecca I, 354
Marshill, Rebecca I, 355
Marshill, Rebecca I, 356
Marshill, Rebecca I, 359
Marshill, Rebecca I, 360
Marshill, Rebecca I, 407
Marshill, Rebecca I, 408
Marshill, Rebecca I, 978
Marshill, Rebecca I, 1106
Marshill, Rebecca I, 1107
Marshill, Rebecca I, 1108
Marshill, Rebeccah I, 407
Marshill, Rebeckah I, 395
Marshill, Rebeckah I, 407
Marshill, Rebekah I, 407
Marshill, Robert I, 360
Marshill, Robert I, 407
Marshill, Robert I, 408
Marshill, Ruth I, 350
Marshill, Ruth I, 351
Marshill, Ruth I, 352
Marshill, Ruth I, 353
Marshill, Ruth I, 354
Marshill, Ruth I, 359
Marshill, Ruth I, 360
Marshill, Ruth I, 361
Marshill, Ruth I, 386
Marshill, Ruth I, 387
Marshill, Ruth I, 391
Marshill, Ruth I, 395
Marshill, Ruth I, 407
Marshill, Ruth I, 975
Marshill, Ruth I, 991
Marshill, Ruth I, 993
Marshill, Ruth I, 997
Marshill, Ruth I, 1085
Marshill, Ruth I, 1090
Marshill, Ruth I, 1096
Marshill, Ruth I, 1101
Marshill, Ruth I, 1107
Marshill, Ruth I, 1108
Marshill, Ruth I, 1125
Marshill, Sarah I, 360
Marshill, Sarah I, 407
Marshill, Sarah I, 408
Marshill, Sarah I, 1086
Marshill, Sarah C. I, 1125
Marshill, Simon I, 992
Marshill, Simon I, 993
Marshill, Simon I, 1085
Marshill, Simon I, 1096
Marshill, Sophronia I, 993
Marshill, Thomas I, 360
Marshill, Thomas I, 361
Marshill, Thomas I, 379
Marshill, Thomas I, 407
Marshill, Thomas I, 826
Marshill, Thomas I, 993
Marshill, Thomas I, 1085
Marshill, Thomas I, 1095
Marshill, Thomas I, 1096
Marshill, Thomas I, 1101
Marshill, Thomas I, 1104
Marshill, Thomas I, 1106
Marshill, Thomas I, 1108
Marshill, Thomas I, 1125
Marshill, Thomas I, 1137
Marshill, Thomas, Jr. I, 1125
Marshill, Thos. I, 397
Marshill, Thos. I, 407
Marshill, William I, 343
Marshill, William I, 360
Marshill, William I, 361
Marshill, William I, 407
Marshill, William I, 425
Marshill, William I, 800
Marshill, William I, 826
Marshill, William I, 978
Marshill, William I, 992
Marshill, William I, 993
Marshill, William I, 1086
Marshill, William I, 1108
Marshill, William, Jr. I, 407
Marshill, William, Jr. I, 408
Marshill, William, Jr. I, 826
Marshill, Wm. I, 350
Marshill, Wm. I, 353
Marshill, Wm. I, 354
Marshill, Wm. I, 355
Marshill, Wm. I, 356
Marshill, Wm. I, 360
Marshill, Wm. I, 361
Marshill, Wm. I, 407
Marshourn, Sarah I, 425
Marsillac, John II, 591
Marson, Atter I, 264
Mart, Alice V, 96
Mart, Alice W. V, 96
Mart, Carrie Earl V, 96
Mart, Edwin G. V, 96
Mart, Elizabeth V, 96
Mart, Frances Eugene V, 96
Mart, Hannah V, 585
Mart, Harry Leroy V, 96
Mart, Jennie V, 696
Mart, Jennie V, 702
Mart, Laura V, 585
Mart, Moses V, 696
Mart, S. E. V, 96
Mart, Stella Netta V, 585
Mart, Susie C. V, 696
Mart, Sylvester V, 96
Mart, Sylvester V, 696
Mart, Sylvester E. V, 96
Martain, George I, 408
Martain, Henry I, 826
Martain, Luvina I, 993
Martain, Sarah I, 146
Marten, Andrew V, 585
Marten, Chas. V, 585
Marten, Elizabeth II, 591
Marten, Elizabeth II, 652
Marten, Ellener I, 264
Marten, John II, 591
Marten, John II, 652
Marten, Mary I, 993
Martenel, Alexis II, 705
Martenel, Eugenie II, 705
Martenel, Pauline II, 705
Martengale, Rebekah I, 1061
Martengale, Rebekah I, 1062
Martens, Bahne III, 221
Martens, Carl III, 221
Martens, Carl III, 361
Martens, Josephine III, 221
Martens, Josephine III, 361
Martens, Teresa L. III, 361
Martens, Terese L. III, 221
Marthews, Elizabeth VI, 422
Martial, Susannah I, 725
Martig, Elizabeth IV, 1040
Martig, Mrs. Caleb IV, 1040
Martin, ??? I, 218
Martin, ??? II, 393
Martin, ??? III, 329
Martin, ??? VI, 531
Martin, Abbie III, 221
Martin, Abbie III, 263
Martin, Abby B. III, 264
Martin, Abigail I, 146
Martin, Abigail I, 161
Martin, Abigail I, 810
Martin, Abigail I, 827
Martin, Abigail II, 179
Martin, Abigail II, 241
Martin, Abigail II, 592
Martin, Abigail III, 221
Martin, Abigail V, 96
Martin, Abigail V, 131
Martin, Abner VI, 892
Martin, Abner VI, 981
Martin, Abner VI, 1013
Martin, Abraham V, 227
Martin, Adam I, 361
Martin, Adam I, 408
Martin, Agnes II, 999
Martin, Agnes II, 1010
Martin, Agnes IV, 342
Martin, Agnes IV, 420
Martin, Agnes B. III, 221
Martin, Agness II, 1013
Martin, Agness II, 1036
Martin, Agness VI, 634
Martin, Agness VI, 675
Martin, Alfred V, 188
Martin, Alfred V, 696
Martin, Alice II, 1086
Martin, Alice D. II, 1088
Martin, Alice D. IV, 376
Martin, Alice D. IV, 420
Martin, Allen V, 655
Martin, Allen V, 696
Martin, Alvina IV, 1328
Martin, Alvina Rose IV, 1329
Martin, Amanda VI, 838
Martin, Amanda VI, 845
Martin, Amos IV, 588
Martin, Amos G. IV, 248
Martin, Andrew V, 585
Martin, Andrew VI, 838
Martin, Andrew VI, 936
Martin, Andrew C. VI, 838
Martin, Ann I, 408
Martin, Ann I, 426
Martin, Ann II, 393
Martin, Ann II, 520
Martin, Ann II, 592
Martin, Ann III, 221
Martin, Ann VI, 331
Martin, Ann VI, 339
Martin, Ann VI, 531
Martin, Ann VI, 797
Martin, Ann VI, 807
Martin, Ann VI, 838
Martin, Ann VI, 847
Martin, Ann VI, 854
Martin, Ann VI, 1006
Martin, Ann B. VI, 838
Martin, Ann E. V, 633
Martin, Ann E. VI, 846
Martin, Ann Eliza VI, 958
Martin, Ann G. VI, 838
Martin, Ann T. II, 754
Martin, Anna II, 896
Martin, Anna II, 949
Martin, Anna V, 164
Martin, Anna V, 188
Martin, Anna V, 633
Martin, Anna V, 696
Martin, Anna M. III, 221
Martin, Anna M. III, 223
Martin, Anna M. V, 696
Martin, Anna Morris II, 754
Martin, Anna S. A. V, 633
Martin, Anne I, 361
Martin, Anne II, 179
Martin, Anne V, 696
Martin, Anne VI, 844
Martin, Annie V, 633
Martin, Annoca VI, 850
Martin, Aquila I, 993
Martin, Aranah VI, 865
Martin, Azariah VI, 838
Martin, Baley VI, 958
Martin, Belinda I, 978
Martin, Belinda I, 993
Martin, Benjamin II, 782
Martin, Benjamin II, 809
Martin, Benjamin II, 896
Martin, Benjamin IV, 248
Martin, Benjamin IV, 487
Martin, Bertha IV, 1161
Martin, Bertha IV, 1173
Martin, Bertha J. III, 426
Martin, Bessie L. IV, 1173
Martin, Betsey VI, 876
Martin, Beulah W. IV, 248
Martin, Biard IV, 644
Martin, Brice A. VI, 817
Martin, Brice A. VI, 838
Martin, Brice A. VI, 865
Martin, Burling III, 200
Martin, Burling III, 221
Martin, Caroline VI, 958
Martin, Caroline Emily IV, 1328
Martin, Catharine I, 408
Martin, Catharine I, 429
Martin, Catharine III, 221
Martin, Catharine VI, 838
Martin, Catharine VI, 957
Martin, Cecelia VI, 838
Martin, Charles II, 809
Martin, Charles II, 896
Martin, Charles V, 585
Martin, Charles V, 754
Martin, Charles VI, 795
Martin, Charles VI, 830
Martin, Charles VI, 838
Martin, Charles VI, 899
Martin, Charles VI, 958
Martin, Charles VI, 1006
Martin, Charles C. VI, 838
Martin, Charles W. VI, 844
Martin, Charlotte VI, 872
Martin, Charlotte W. VI, 941
Martin, Chas. V, 585

Martin, Chas. Caffery VI, 984
Martin, Chas. L. V, 633
Martin, Clara A. V, 633
Martin, Clifford IV, 1328
Martin, Conrad IV, 1329
Martin, Conrad M. IV, 1328
Martin, Cornelia II, 809
Martin, Cynthia VI, 958
Martin, Cyrus Griffin V, 696
Martin, Dabney VI, 838
Martin, Dabney VI, 958
Martin, Daniel I, 993
Martin, Daniel VI, 958
Martin, Daniel C. IV, 393
Martin, Daniel C. IV, 420
Martin, Daniel C. V, 96
Martin, Daniel H. I, 978
Martin, Daniel H. I, 993
Martin, David IV, 537
Martin, David V, 188
Martin, David VI, 838
Martin, David VI, 849
Martin, David VI, 866
Martin, David VI, 939
Martin, David VI, 958
Martin, David S. VI, 797
Martin, David S. VI, 821
Martin, David, Jr. VI, 849
Martin, David, Sr. VI, 863
Martin, Delaplaine III, 221
Martin, Delila VI, 833
Martin, Delphina Catharine I, 978
Martin, Delphina Katharine I, 993
Martin, Dolly VI, 796
Martin, Dora IV, 1173
Martin, Dorothea II, 132
Martin, Dorothy IV, 1329
Martin, Dorothy Parker IV, 1329
Martin, Drucilla IV, 420
Martin, Dudley VI, 838
Martin, Eady VI, 972
Martin, Edgar IV, 833
Martin, Edgar IV, 1328
Martin, Edgar J. IV, 833
Martin, Edith II, 754
Martin, Edith IV, 48
Martin, Edith IV, 54
Martin, Edith IV, 99
Martin, Edna VI, 830
Martin, Edward IV, 248
Martin, Eleanor VI, 958
Martin, Eleanor Maule II, 1086
Martin, Eley VI, 838
Martin, Elijah V, 696
Martin, Elinder I, 146
Martin, Eliphalet VI, 838
Martin, Eliz. III, 221
Martin, Eliz. Annie IV, 1328
Martin, Eliza III, 34
Martin, Eliza Hough VI, 617
Martin, Eliza Hough VI, 675
Martin, Elizabeth I, 826
Martin, Elizabeth I, 827
Martin, Elizabeth I, 839
Martin, Elizabeth I, 993
Martin, Elizabeth II, 393
Martin, Elizabeth II, 591
Martin, Elizabeth II, 592
Martin, Elizabeth II, 801
Martin, Elizabeth II, 896
Martin, Elizabeth II, 976
Martin, Elizabeth II, 1013
Martin, Elizabeth II, 1014
Martin, Elizabeth II, 1039
Martin, Elizabeth III, 99
Martin, Elizabeth III, 221
Martin, Elizabeth IV, 48
Martin, Elizabeth IV, 537
Martin, Elizabeth IV, 644
Martin, Elizabeth IV, 1173
Martin, Elizabeth V, 227
Martin, Elizabeth V, 263
Martin, Elizabeth V, 585
Martin, Elizabeth V, 696
Martin, Elizabeth V, 923
Martin, Elizabeth V, 944
Martin, Elizabeth VI, 198
Martin, Elizabeth VI, 351
Martin, Elizabeth VI, 353
Martin, Elizabeth VI, 837
Martin, Elizabeth VI, 838
Martin, Elizabeth VI, 841
Martin, Elizabeth VI, 842
Martin, Elizabeth VI, 846
Martin, Elizabeth VI, 849
Martin, Elizabeth VI, 857
Martin, Elizabeth VI, 867
Martin, Elizabeth VI, 888
Martin, Elizabeth VI, 906
Martin, Elizabeth VI, 957
Martin, Elizabeth VI, 958
Martin, Elizabeth VI, 984
Martin, Elizabeth VI, 997
Martin, Elizabeth VI, 1010
Martin, Elizabeth VI, 1012
Martin, Elizabeth C. VI, 802
Martin, Elizabeth J. VI, 817
Martin, Elizabeth J. VI, 838
Martin, Elizabeth J. VI, 958
Martin, Elizabeth M. VI, 958
Martin, Elizabeth W. VI, 958
Martin, Elizabeth W. VI, 1013
Martin, Ella IV, 1216
Martin, Ellas J. I, 247
Martin, Ellener I, 268
Martin, Ellener I, 273
Martin, Elma V, 188
Martin, Emily VI, 958
Martin, Emlen II, 179
Martin, Emlen II, 296
Martin, Emlen II, 949
Martin, Emma IV, 1173
Martin, Emma IV, 1286
Martin, Enoch P. H. II, 896
Martin, Ephraim I, 146
Martin, Ernestine V, 696
Martin, Esther II, 290
Martin, Esther II, 295
Martin, Esther VI, 820
Martin, Eugene IV, 1173
Martin, F. B. VI, 847
Martin, Faith IV, 1325
Martin, Faith IV, 1328
Martin, Faith IV, 1329
Martin, Fanny VI, 851
Martin, Fanny VI, 915
Martin, Flora V, 188
Martin, Frances I, 787
Martin, Frances I, 826
Martin, Frances I, 832
Martin, Frances II, 809
Martin, Frances II, 896
Martin, Frances VI, 946
Martin, Frances VI, 958
Martin, Frances VI, 1006
Martin, Frances A. VI, 797
Martin, Frances H. II, 896
Martin, Frances Harrison II, 880
Martin, Francis Linton V, 696
Martin, Frank IV, 1328
Martin, Frank IV, 1329
Martin, Frank V, 681
Martin, Frank V, 696
Martin, Frank P. IV, 1328
Martin, Frank P. IV, 1329
Martin, Frank P. V, 263
Martin, Frank Percy IV, 1328
Martin, Freeman C. VI, 838
Martin, Geo. VI, 912
Martin, Geo. VI, 941
Martin, Geo. VI, 1013
Martin, George I, 361
Martin, George I, 408
Martin, George II, 754
Martin, George II, 896
Martin, George III, 221
Martin, George Yardley II, 809
Martin, George, Jr. I, 408
Martin, Gracia IV, 1329
Martin, Green B. VI, 958
Martin, Gulielma III, 221
Martin, Hannah I, 361
Martin, Hannah I, 408
Martin, Hannah I, 607
Martin, Hannah I, 787
Martin, Hannah I, 826
Martin, Hannah I, 840
Martin, Hannah II, 393
Martin, Hannah II, 592
Martin, Hannah II, 801
Martin, Hannah II, 809
Martin, Hannah II, 1072
Martin, Hannah II, 1076
Martin, Hannah IV, 536
Martin, Hannah IV, 540
Martin, Hannah VI, 838
Martin, Hannah J. II, 896
Martin, Hannah J. IV, 540
Martin, Harold IV, 1173
Martin, Harold Dwight IV, 1173
Martin, Harold Eugene IV, 1173
Martin, Harold Garfield II, 896
Martin, Hawlet VI, 838
Martin, Henry I, 787
Martin, Henry I, 826
Martin, Henry II, 809
Martin, Henry II, 896
Martin, Henry Macy V, 188
Martin, Howard VI, 838
Martin, Hutson VI, 958
Martin, I. Willis II, 896
Martin, Irene VI, 866
Martin, Isaac II, 592
Martin, Isaac III, 99
Martin, Isaac III, 221
Martin, Isaac III, 288
Martin, Isaac IV, 35
Martin, Isaac IV, 48
Martin, Isaac IV, 54
Martin, Isaac IV, 67
Martin, Isaac IV, 248
Martin, Isaac V, 188
Martin, Isaac, Jr. III, 221
Martin, Isaiah V, 920
Martin, J. B. I, 945
Martin, J. B. I, 947
Martin, J. E. VI, 864
Martin, James I, 787
Martin, James I, 826
Martin, James II, 241
Martin, James II, 592
Martin, James II, 809
Martin, James II, 829
Martin, James II, 880
Martin, James II, 896
Martin, James II, 944
Martin, James II, 976
Martin, James II, 1013
Martin, James II, 1014
Martin, James III, 221
Martin, James IV, 487
Martin, James IV, 644
Martin, James IV, 878
Martin, James VI, 331
Martin, James VI, 802
Martin, James VI, 818
Martin, James VI, 819
Martin, James VI, 838
Martin, James VI, 864
Martin, James VI, 883
Martin, James VI, 913
Martin, James VI, 943
Martin, James VI, 957
Martin, James VI, 971
Martin, James VI, 974
Martin, James VI, 996
Martin, James Albert V, 188
Martin, James F. VI, 958
Martin, James Martin II, 688
Martin, James S. IV, 487
Martin, James, Jr. I, 826
Martin, James, Jr. II, 809
Martin, James, Jr. II, 896
Martin, Jane II, 460
Martin, Jane II, 592
Martin, Jane IV, 342
Martin, Jane IV, 349
Martin, Jane VI, 801
Martin, Jane VI, 850
Martin, Jane VI, 906
Martin, Jane VI, 976
Martin, Jane H. VI, 847
Martin, Jarvis III, 399
Martin, Jas. III, 223
Martin, Jean I, 361
Martin, Jean VI, 838
Martin, Jefferson VI, 617
Martin, Jefferson VI, 675
Martin, Jehu V, 696
Martin, Jemima II, 782
Martin, Jemima II, 809
Martin, Jemima II, 896
Martin, Jemima VI, 969
Martin, Jeremiah II, 591
Martin, Jesse III, 33
Martin, Jesse VI, 838
Martin, Jesse M. VI, 841
Martin, Jesse M. VI, 857
Martin, Jesse M. VI, 965
Martin, Jessie III, 221
Martin, Jno. II, 241
Martin, Job VI, 957
Martin, Job VI, 958
Martin, Job VI, 997
Martin, John I, 361
Martin, John I, 408
Martin, John I, 993
Martin, John I Sup 1, 10
Martin, John II, 393
Martin, John II, 445
Martin, John II, 586
Martin, John II, 591
Martin, John II, 592
Martin, John II, 809
Martin, John II, 1010
Martin, John II, 1013
Martin, John II, 1036
Martin, John II, 1039
Martin, John VI, 644
Martin, John IV, 878
Martin, John IV, 1216
Martin, John V, 263
Martin, John V, 585
Martin, John V, 696
Martin, John VI, 331
Martin, John VI, 339
Martin, John VI, 826
Martin, John VI, 838
Martin, John VI, 848
Martin, John VI, 851
Martin, John VI, 853
Martin, John VI, 854
Martin, John VI, 867
Martin, John VI, 876
Martin, John VI, 879
Martin, John VI, 902
Martin, John VI, 906
Martin, John VI, 957
Martin, John VI, 958
Martin, John VI, 964
Martin, John VI, 976
Martin, John VI, 977
Martin, John VI, 993
Martin, John VI, 1009
Martin, John VI, 1012
Martin, John A. IV, 644
Martin, John A. IV, 878
Martin, John Alexander IV, 878
Martin, John H. VI, 958
Martin, John P. III, 426
Martin, John Thomas IV, 878
Martin, John Thomas VI, 817
Martin, John W. VI, 807
Martin, John W. VI, 838
Martin, John W. VI, 846
Martin, John William II, 809
Martin, John Wm. II, 896
Martin, John, Jr. I, 978
Martin, John, Sr. I, 978
Martin, John, Sr. I Sup 1, 10
Martin, Jonathan VI, 838
Martin, Jonathan VI, 867
Martin, Jonathan VI, 957
Martin, Jonathan Willis II, 809
Martin, Jordan VI, 958
Martin, Joseph II, 592
Martin, Joseph VI, 838
Martin, Joseph VI, 956
Martin, Joseph VI, 957
Martin, Joseph VI, 958
Martin, Joseph VI, 997
Martin, Joseph D. II, 393
Martin, Joseph D. II, 592
Martin, Joseph Delaplaine II, 801
Martin, Joseph L. III, 221
Martin, Joseph R. IV, 644
Martin, Joseph R. IV, 667
Martin, Joseph R. IV, 878
Martin, Josephine III, 426
Martin, Joshua I, 102
Martin, Joshua I, 146
Martin, Josiah VI, 823
Martin, Josiah VI, 849
Martin, Josiah VI, 866
Martin, Judith VI, 838
Martin, Judith A. C. VI, 838
Martin, Julia VI, 996
Martin, Julia Ellen I, 218
Martin, Katharine Penelope I, 993
Martin, Katherine II, 591
Martin, Kathrine I, 361
Martin, Kesiah VI, 826
Martin, Keziah E. VI, 958
Martin, L. J. I, 637
Martin, L. J. I, 945
Martin, Lancelet II, 1013
Martin, Lavina I, 993
Martin, Lemuel I, 945
Martin, Lenna IV, 1173
Martin, Leticia J. D. VI, 818
Martin, Letitia J. VI, 838
Martin, Levina I, 993
Martin, Levira VI, 872
Martin, Lewis Arthur IV, 1328
Martin, Little Mary VI, 873
Martin, Lizzie V, 696
Martin, Lockey VI, 838
Martin, Locy VI, 838
Martin, Loretta IV, 1161
Martin, Loretta IV, 1173
Martin, Lottie IV, 1173
Martin, Louis A. IV, 1328
Martin, Lucile I, 945
Martin, Lucile V, 696
Martin, Lucile V, 718
Martin, Lucile V, 719
Martin, Lucy II, 179
Martin, Lucy II, 290
Martin, Lucy II, 295
Martin, Lucy VI, 838
Martin, Lucy VI, 847
Martin, Lucy VI, 858
Martin, Lucy C. VI, 838
Martin, Lucy D. VI, 838
Martin, Lucy Elvira I, 993
Martin, Lucy H. II, 295
Martin, Lucy H. II, 949
Martin, Lula A. I, 945
Martin, Luna VI, 958
Martin, Luney VI, 879
Martin, Luvina I, 993
Martin, Lydia V, 902
Martin, Lydia V, 920
Martin, Lydia VI, 584
Martin, Lydia VI, 838
Martin, Lydia VI, 958
Martin, Lydia Ann II, 709
Martin, Lydia L. V, 696
Martin, M. L. I, 209
Martin, Maggie V, 1009
Martin, Mahala VI, 958
Martin, Malinda I, 993
Martin, Malvina II, 809
Martin, Mamie L. I, 209
Martin, Marcus D. W. VI, 838
Martin, Margaret I, 345
Martin, Margaret I, 361
Martin, Margaret I, 375
Martin, Margaret I, 408
Martin, Margaret I, 978
Martin, Margaret I Sup 1, 10
Martin, Margaret IV, 248
Martin, Margaret V, 188
Martin, Margaret VI, 957
Martin, Margaret VI, 977
Martin, Margaret E. V, 696
Martin, Margaret H. IV, 393
Martin, Margaret H. IV, 420
Martin, Margaret H. V, 96
Martin, Margaret S. VI, 887
Martin, Margaretta I, 218
Martin, Margit VI, 853
Martin, Margret I, 993
Martin, Maria III, 221
Martin, Maria W. VI, 964
Martin, Martha I, 926
Martin, Martha IV, 48
Martin, Martha IV, 67
Martin, Martha IV, 248
Martin, Martha IV, 342
Martin, Martha IV, 352
Martin, Martha IV, 588
Martin, Martha IV, 1173
Martin, Martha VI, 801
Martin, Martha VI, 838
Martin, Martha A. VI, 823
Martin, Martha D. VI, 838
Martin, Martha F. VI, 922
Martin, Martha G. VI, 958
Martin, Martha H. VI, 838
Martin, Martha J. V, 696
Martin, Martha J. VI, 804
Martin, Mary I, 361
Martin, Mary I, 395
Martin, Mary I, 408
Martin, Mary I, 787
Martin, Mary I, 799
Martin, Mary I, 826
Martin, Mary I, 993
Martin, Mary II, 460
Martin, Mary II, 520
Martin, Mary II, 592
Martin, Mary II, 688
Martin, Mary II, 809
Martin, Mary II, 829
Martin, Mary II, 880
Martin, Mary II, 981
Martin, Mary II, 1010
Martin, Mary II, 1013
Martin, Mary II, 1014
Martin, Mary II, 1018
Martin, Mary III, 33
Martin, Mary III, 200
Martin, Mary III, 221
Martin, Mary III, 288
Martin, Mary III, 399
Martin, Mary IV, 420
Martin, Mary IV, 428
Martin, Mary IV, 1329
Martin, Mary V, 227
Martin, Mary V, 263
Martin, Mary V, 633
Martin, Mary V, 639
Martin, Mary VI, 764
Martin, Mary VI, 792
Martin, Mary VI, 800
Martin, Mary VI, 838
Martin, Mary VI, 848
Martin, Mary VI, 853
Martin, Mary VI, 858
Martin, Mary VI, 861

Martin, Mary VI, 866
Martin, Mary VI, 913
Martin, Mary VI, 957
Martin, Mary VI, 969
Martin, Mary VI, 1006
Martin, Mary Alice V, 188
Martin, Mary Ann I, 993
Martin, Mary Ann III, 221
Martin, Mary Ann III, 329
Martin, Mary Ann VI, 1009
Martin, Mary D. VI, 838
Martin, Mary E. V, 96
Martin, Mary J. III, 56
Martin, Mary J. III, 153
Martin, Mary J. VI, 838
Martin, Mary L. II, 896
Martin, Mary L. II, 944
Martin, Mary Letitia II, 829
Martin, Mary P. II, 896
Martin, Mary Rankin III, 221
Martin, Mary Rankin III, 223
Martin, Mary W. II, 896
Martin, Mary W. II, 944
Martin, Mary, Jr. II, 1013
Martin, Mathew VI, 808
Martin, Mathew VI, 843
Martin, Matilda VI, 957
Martin, Matthew VI, 838
Martin, Matthew VI, 842
Martin, May V, 696
Martin, Mildred M. VI, 974
Martin, Mill VI, 233
Martin, Minnie V, 263
Martin, Minnie V, 696
Martin, Missouri VI, 843
Martin, Modecai II, 1014
Martin, Molly VI, 838
Martin, Mordecai II, 976
Martin, Mordecai II, 1013
Martin, Moses I, 345
Martin, Moses I, 361
Martin, N. I, 218
Martin, Nancy VI, 854
Martin, Nancy VI, 860
Martin, Nancy VI, 904
Martin, Nancy VI, 916
Martin, Nancy VI, 957
Martin, Nancy VI, 984
Martin, Nancy A. VI, 838
Martin, Nancy E. VI, 838
Martin, Nanie IV, 248
Martin, Nannie IV, 248
Martin, Nathan S. II, 754
Martin, Nathaniel I, 102
Martin, Nathaniel I, 146
Martin, Nathaniel I, 157
Martin, Neoma VI, 958
Martin, Nereus Simon I, 978
Martin, Nereus Simon I, 993
Martin, Nettie V, 1009
Martin, Norris Jones II, 393
Martin, Norris Jones II, 754
Martin, Norris L. III, 221
Martin, Norris Lawrence II, 520
Martin, Norris Lawrence II, 592
Martin, Oliver II, 592
Martin, Oliver II, 688
Martin, Oliver II, 754
Martin, Oliver II, 809
Martin, Oliver V, 899
Martin, Oliver V, 920
Martin, Oliver V, 923
Martin, Oliver V, 927
Martin, Oliver W. VI, 958
Martin, Oliver, Jr. V, 902
Martin, Oliver, Jr. V, 920
Martin, Oscar IV, 1173
Martin, Owcar IV, 1173
Martin, Patsy I. VI, 912
Martin, Pearl IV, 1328
Martin, Pearl IV, 1329
Martin, Pearl Clifford IV, 1329
Martin, Pearl E. IV, 1329
Martin, Pearl E. V, 263
Martin, Perlina VI, 836
Martin, Permelia Ann I, 978
Martin, Peter I, 218
Martin, Peter W. I, 247
Martin, Phebe III, 221
Martin, Phebe IV, 234
Martin, Phebe IV, 248
Martin, Phebe IV, 1173
Martin, Phebe IV, 1197
Martin, Phebe H. II, 949
Martin, Phebe Haines II, 179
Martin, Philip IV, 1173
Martin, Philip IV, 1216
Martin, Phillip IV, 1173
Martin, Phillip IV, 1216
Martin, Pleasant VI, 974
Martin, Polly VI, 838
Martin, Polly VI, 860
Martin, Polly VI, 958
Martin, Pryer D. VI, 865
Martin, R. R. IV, 1216
Martin, Rachel I, 361
Martin, Rachel I, 395
Martin, Rachel I, 408
Martin, Rachel II, 1014
Martin, Rachel IV, 537
Martin, Rachel VI, 818
Martin, Rachel VI, 863
Martin, Rachel VI, 984
Martin, Rachel VI, 997
Martin, Rachel C. IV, 537
Martin, Rebecca II, 809
Martin, Rebecca II, 896
Martin, Rebecca IV, 35
Martin, Rebecca IV, 48
Martin, Rebecca IV, 54
Martin, Rebecca IV, 248
Martin, Rebecca IV, 588
Martin, Rebecca IV, 644
Martin, Rebecca IV, 878
Martin, Rebecca D. IV, 537
Martin, Rebekah VI, 531
Martin, Rebekah VI, 534
Martin, Rees VI, 803
Martin, Rees VI, 838
Martin, Reese VI, 838
Martin, Richard II, 591
Martin, Richard V, 1009
Martin, Richard VI, 958
Martin, Robert V, 696
Martin, Robert VI, 838
Martin, Robert VI, 913
Martin, Robert M. V, 696
Martin, Robert W. I, 993
Martin, Robert W. III, 221
Martin, Robt., Jr. VI, 957
Martin, Roxie I, 930
Martin, Roxie I, 945
Martin, Roxie I, 947
Martin, Ruby V, 263
Martin, Russell V, 696
Martin, Ruth I, 993
Martin, Ruth II, 591
Martin, Ruth IV, 1328
Martin, Ruth V, 681
Martin, Ruth V, 696
Martin, Sadie Martha IV, 248
Martin, Sally VI, 339
Martin, Sally VI, 838
Martin, Sally VI, 854
Martin, Sally VI, 892
Martin, Sam VI, 802
Martin, Samantha V, 696
Martin, Samuel IV, 248
Martin, Samuel IV, 420
Martin, Samuel IV, 588
Martin, Samuel VI, 331
Martin, Samuel VI, 338
Martin, Samuel VI, 800
Martin, Samuel VI, 836
Martin, Samuel VI, 838
Martin, Samuel VI, 841
Martin, Samuel VI, 842
Martin, Samuel VI, 843
Martin, Samuel VI, 845
Martin, Samuel VI, 846
Martin, Samuel VI, 852
Martin, Samuel VI, 861
Martin, Samuel VI, 957
Martin, Samuel VI, 958
Martin, Samuel B. IV, 537
Martin, Samuel G. VI, 838
Martin, Samuel G. VI, 867
Martin, Samuel H. VI, 958
Martin, Sarah I, 102
Martin, Sarah I, 146
Martin, Sarah I, 157
Martin, Sarah I, 161
Martin, Sarah I, 273
Martin, Sarah I, 361
Martin, Sarah I, 799
Martin, Sarah I, 827
Martin, Sarah II, 976
Martin, Sarah II, 1013
Martin, Sarah II, 1014
Martin, Sarah II, 1034
Martin, Sarah IV, 239
Martin, Sarah IV, 248
Martin, Sarah IV, 252
Martin, Sarah IV, 313
Martin, Sarah IV, 537
Martin, Sarah IV, 644
Martin, Sarah IV, 878
Martin, Sarah V, 899
Martin, Sarah V, 920
Martin, Sarah V, 944
Martin, Sarah V, 1009
Martin, Sarah VI, 331
Martin, Sarah VI, 338
Martin, Sarah VI, 819
Martin, Sarah VI, 834
Martin, Sarah VI, 838
Martin, Sarah VI, 849
Martin, Sarah VI, 913
Martin, Sarah VI, 916
Martin, Sarah VI, 958
Martin, Sarah A. VI, 887
Martin, Sarah C. I, 986
Martin, Sarah C. I, 993
Martin, Sarah Caroline I, 993
Martin, Sarah Elizabeth V, 696
Martin, Sarah F. IV, 1173
Martin, Sarah L. VI, 834
Martin, Sarah M. V, 927
Martin, Sarah P. II, 896
Martin, Sarah Phipps II, 782
Martin, Sarah S. VI, 958
Martin, Simon I, 993
Martin, Sophia III, 221
Martin, Sophia VI, 958
Martin, Sophia VI, 964
Martin, Sperry IV, 1173
Martin, Sperry Leroy IV, 1173
Martin, Stephen VI, 353
Martin, Stephen VI, 833
Martin, Stephen VI, 850
Martin, Stephen VI, 892
Martin, Stephen VI, 906
Martin, Stephen VI, 957
Martin, Stephen VI, 958
Martin, Stephen VI, 965
Martin, Sterling VI, 958
Martin, Stith VI, 957
Martin, Susan M. VI, 838
Martin, Susan R. VI, 836
Martin, Susanah I, 102
Martin, Susanah VI, 994
Martin, Susanna II, 592
Martin, Susanna II, 688
Martin, Susanna V, 655
Martin, Susanna V, 696
Martin, Susanna VI, 800
Martin, Susanna VI, 838
Martin, Susanna VI, 957
Martin, Susannah I, 146
Martin, Susannah I, 345
Martin, Susannah II, 809
Martin, Susannah V, 920
Martin, Susannah V, 923
Martin, Susannah V, 927
Martin, T. F. VI, 882
Martin, Theodore V, 585
Martin, Thomas I, 993
Martin, Thomas II, 290
Martin, Thomas II, 295
Martin, Thomas II, 592
Martin, Thomas II, 1013
Martin, Thomas IV, 48
Martin, Thomas IV, 248
Martin, Thomas IV, 588
Martin, Thomas IV, 644
Martin, Thomas IV, 878
Martin, Thomas IV, 1216
Martin, Thomas VI, 325
Martin, Thomas VI, 818
Martin, Thomas VI, 823
Martin, Thomas VI, 829
Martin, Thomas VI, 838
Martin, Thomas VI, 849
Martin, Thomas VI, 850
Martin, Thomas VI, 861
Martin, Thomas VI, 873
Martin, Thomas VI, 904
Martin, Thomas VI, 922
Martin, Thomas VI, 957
Martin, Thomas VI, 958
Martin, Thomas VI, 969
Martin, Thomas VI, 984
Martin, Thomas VI, 1006
Martin, Thomas Aquilla I, 978
Martin, Timothy II, 1014
Martin, Valentine VI, 833
Martin, Valentine VI, 838
Martin, Vera Ritchy IV, 738
Martin, Viola Mary V, 585
Martin, Viola May V, 585
Martin, W. Jasper V, 188
Martin, Waller E. V, 696
Martin, Walter V, 696
Martin, Wd Beulah M. IV, 644
Martin, Wd Elizabeth IV, 644
Martin, Wd Elizabeth IV, 667
Martin, Wd. Elizabeth II, 801
Martin, Wd. Sarah V, 920
Martin, Widower Joseph R. IV, 644
Martin, William I, 945
Martin, William II, 179
Martin, William II, 296
Martin, William II, 949
Martin, William II, 1086
Martin, William II, 1088
Martin, William IV, 1173
Martin, William IV, 1258
Martin, William IV, 1286
Martin, William V, 920
Martin, William VI, 801
Martin, William VI, 804
Martin, William VI, 807
Martin, William VI, 819
Martin, William VI, 838
Martin, William VI, 847
Martin, William VI, 848
Martin, William VI, 854
Martin, William VI, 957
Martin, William VI, 958
Martin, William VI, 959
Martin, William VI, 1010
Martin, William C. VI, 836
Martin, William C. VI, 838
Martin, William C. VI, 861
Martin, William C. VI, 958
Martin, William D. VI, 888
Martin, William D. VI, 958
Martin, William F. VI, 838
Martin, William Harold II, 1086
Martin, William L. II, 179
Martin, William L. II, 290
Martin, William L. II, 295
Martin, William L. II, 949
Martin, William P. VI, 859
Martin, William Penn I, 993
Martin, William Peters VI, 865
Martin, William, Jr. VI, 831
Martin, William, Jr. VI, 957
Martin, William, Jr. VI, 958
Martin, Willie I, 637
Martin, Willis VI, 838
Martin, Willis VI, 855
Martin, Willis VI, 866
Martin, Wm. IV, 1161
Martin, Wm. IV, 1173
Martin, Wm. IV, 1216
Martin, Wm. IV, 1286
Martin, Wm. IV, 1328
Martin, Wm. VI, 836
Martin, Wm. VI, 857
Martin, Wm. H. V, 633
Martin, Wm. James VI, 971
Martin, Wm. Logan III, 33
Martin, Wm. Logan III, 221
Martin, Wm. P. VI, 940
Martin, Wm. P. VI, 941
Martin, Wm. P. VI, 986
Martin, Wm. P. VI, 990
Martin, Wm. P. VI, 1010
Martin, Wm. Peters VI, 887
Martin, Wm. Robert V, 696
Martin, Wm. S. VI, 796
Martin, Zeke M. VI, 844
Martindaile, ??? II, 445
Martindaile, John II, 445
Martindale, Ann II, 393
Martindale, Camden II, 896
Martindale, Charles B. II, 896
Martindale, Chas. II, 834
Martindale, Chas. II, 896
Martindale, Elizabeth II, 445
Martindale, Elizabeth V, 754
Martindale, Elizabeth J. II, 834
Martindale, Elizabeth J. II, 896
Martindale, Isaac C. II, 834
Martindale, Isaac C. II, 896
Martindale, James VI, 919
Martindale, John II, 393
Martindale, John II, 445
Martindale, John II, 592
Martindale, John II, 1014
Martindale, John V, 516
Martindale, Joseph II, 1014
Martindale, Joseph C. II, 896
Martindale, Martha II, 1014
Martindale, Mary II, 393
Martindale, Mary II, 445
Martindale, Mary Ann V, 516
Martindale, Phebe II, 834
Martindale, Phebe II, 896
Martindale, Sarah II, 1014
Martindale, Sarah Ann II, 896
Martindale, Strickland II, 1014
Martindale, Thomas II, 1014
Martindale, Vincent V, 516
Martindale, Wallace S. II, 896
Martindale, William II, 393
Martindale, William V, 516
Martindall, John II, 393
Martindall, John II, 592
Martindell, Hannah II, 445
Martindell, John II, 445
Martindell, Joseph II, 1014
Martindell, Martha II, 1014
Martindell, Mary II, 445
Martindell, Sarah II, 1014
Martindill, Elizabeth V, 754
Marting, John II, 1015
Marting, Sarah II, 1015
Marting, Thomas II, 1015
Martingall, ??? II, 445
Martingall, John II, 445
Martingall, Mary II, 445
Martins, John V, 263
Martins, Sarah II, 1013
Martins, Thomas II, 1013
Martinson, Anna IV, 1329
Martinson, Otto IV, 1329
Martion, James VI, 339
Martion, James VI, 854
Marton, Agnes B. III, 221
Marton, Agnes B. III, 222
Marton, Elizabeth II, 393
Marton, Elizabeth III, 221
Marton, Elizabeth III, 222
Marton, George III, 221
Marton, George III, 222
Marts, Chancy V, 1009
Marts, Chaney V, 1009
Marts, Mary V, 1009
Martyndale, John V, 516
Marvel, Josiah P. III, 221
Marvin, Isaac IV, 1173
Marvin, John W. VI, 372
Marvin, John W. VI, 422
Marvin, Matilda V, 255
Marvin, Matilda V, 263
Marvin, Rebecca VI, 372
Marvin, Rebecca VI, 422
Marvin, Rebecca R. VI, 422
Marvin, Sarah IV, 644
Marwick, James III, 45
Marwick, James III, 216
Marwick, James III, 221
Marwick, James VI, 764
Marwick, Sarah R. III, 216
Marwick, Sarah R. VI, 764
Marwick, Wd. Sarah R. III, 221
Marwick, Wd. Sarah R. VI, 764
Mary Ward, Muriel III, 274
Mary, Matilda Polly VI, 317
Maryland, ??? VI, 13
Maryland, Henry VI, 13
Marymoon, Letters IV, 248
Marymoon, Marcy IV, 248
Marymoon, Martin IV, 248
Marymoon, Martin VI, 115
Marymoon, Martin VI, 116
Marymoon, Matilda IV, 248
Marymoon, Peggy IV, 248
Marymoon, Rachel IV, 248
Marymoon, Rebecca IV, 248
Marymoon, Samuel IV, 248
Marys, Edward II, 40
Marys, Susannah II, 40
Masen, Hannah II, 779
Masey, Margaret V, 905
Mash, Joseph II, 393
Mash, Lavina IV, 1067
Mash, Mary II, 86
Mash, Mary II, 393
Mashawn, Sarah IV, 196
Mashawn, Sarah IV, 249
Mashburn, Bula I, 406
Mashburn, Catharine I, 406
Mashburn, Esther I, 406
Mashburn, Hannah I, 406
Mashburn, Julia I, 406
Mashburn, Matthew I, 406
Mashburn, Obed I, 406
Mashburn, Ruth I, 406
Mashburn, Sarah I, 406
Mashburn, William I, 406
Mashburn, Wm. I, 406
Mashman, Mary II, 445
Mason, ??? II, 825
Mason, Aaron II, 34
Mason, Aaron IV, 1216
Mason, Abagail II, 61
Mason, Abagail II, 86
Mason, Abigail II, 34
Mason, Abigail II, 86
Mason, Abigail II, 95
Mason, Abigail II, 241
Mason, Abigel II, 86
Mason, Abner VI, 817
Mason, Abner VI, 828
Mason, Abner VI, 839
Mason, Abner W. VI, 826
Mason, Abner W. VI, 839
Mason, Abraham II, 393
Mason, Abraham II, 592
Mason, Adin VI, 839
Mason, Agnes II, 592

Mason, Agnes II, 675
Mason, Andrew II, 34
Mason, Ann II, 34
Mason, Ann II, 43
Mason, Ann II, 64
Mason, Ann II, 75
Mason, Ann II, 86
Mason, Ann II, 104
Mason, Ann II, 109
Mason, Ann IV, 481
Mason, Ann IV, 487
Mason, Ann V, 137
Mason, Ann VI, 123
Mason, Ann VI, 531
Mason, Ann VI, 533
Mason, Ann H. VI, 839
Mason, Anna II, 241
Mason, Anna II, 311
Mason, Anna IV, 1239
Mason, Anna VI, 115
Mason, Anna M. II, 1066
Mason, Anna M. II, 1076
Mason, Anne II, 193
Mason, Anne II, 241
Mason, Annie A. III, 106
Mason, Annie Augusta III, 221
Mason, Aron II, 86
Mason, Arthur II, 311
Mason, Barrat II, 86
Mason, Barrat II, 101
Mason, Barrett II, 86
Mason, Barrott II, 34
Mason, Benjamin II, 241
Mason, Benjamin II, 393
Mason, Benjamin II, 592
Mason, Benjamin II, 675
Mason, Benjamin VI, 764
Mason, Betsey VI, 958
Mason, Betsy VI, 839
Mason, Beulah II, 296
Mason, Beulah II, 311
Mason, Bulah II, 321
Mason, Bulah II, 322
Mason, Burrell VI, 839
Mason, C. E. I, 621
Mason, Caroline III, 271
Mason, Catharine W. VI, 826
Mason, Caty VI, 958
Mason, Celain VI, 839
Mason, Charles E. VI, 839
Mason, Claiborne B. VI, 839
Mason, Cona VI, 855
Mason, Cora I, 621
Mason, David V, 1009
Mason, David M. V, 188
Mason, David Montgomery V, 188
Mason, David W. V, 188
Mason, Edith V, 696
Mason, Eleanor IV, 249
Mason, Elisa II, 195
Mason, Elisa II, 241
Mason, Elisabeth II, 592
Mason, Elizabeth II, 53
Mason, Elizabeth II, 78
Mason, Elizabeth II, 86
Mason, Elizabeth II, 111
Mason, Elizabeth II, 498
Mason, Elizabeth II, 592
Mason, Elizabeth II, 665
Mason, Elizabeth IV, 87
Mason, Elizabeth IV, 99
Mason, Elizabeth IV, 577
Mason, Elizabeth IV, 588
Mason, Elizabeth V, 516
Mason, Elizabeth V, 648
Mason, Elizabeth VI, 796
Mason, Elizabeth VI, 839
Mason, Elizabeth VI, 840
Mason, Elizabeth VI, 898
Mason, Elizabeth VI, 944
Mason, Elizabeth VI, 982
Mason, Elizabeth C. II, 592
Mason, Elizabeth C. II, 712
Mason, Elizabeth S. III, 296
Mason, Elizabeth Smart III, 221
Mason, Elizabeth, Jr. II, 77
Mason, Ellendar VI, 920
Mason, Elnor IV, 249
Mason, Embro W. VI, 839
Mason, Emily III, 221
Mason, Ervin P. V, 188
Mason, Esther IV, 979
Mason, Fanny VI, 836
Mason, Fanny VI, 839
Mason, Flora V, 188
Mason, Florence IV, 1216
Mason, Frances VI, 822
Mason, Frances VI, 836
Mason, Francis VI, 839
Mason, Frank E. V, 188
Mason, Frank Elvin V, 188
Mason, George E. VI, 839
Mason, George W. VI, 836
Mason, George W. VI, 839
Mason, Grace II, 86
Mason, Grant IV, 1216
Mason, Hannah II, 34
Mason, Hannah II, 60
Mason, Hannah II, 63
Mason, Hannah II, 77
Mason, Hannah II, 86
Mason, Hannah II, 109
Mason, Hannah II, 114
Mason, Hannah II, 121
Mason, Hannah II, 142
Mason, Hannah II, 153
Mason, Hannah IV, 420
Mason, Hannah H. II, 34
Mason, Harriet C. VI, 817
Mason, Henry IV, 249
Mason, Henry VI, 839
Mason, Howard Riehle II, 311
Mason, Ira V, 516
Mason, Irene IV, 1216
Mason, Irwin V, 188
Mason, Iry V, 516
Mason, J. H. III, 221
Mason, Jacob C. VI, 839
Mason, Jail II, 83
Mason, Jail II, 86
Mason, James II, 34
Mason, James II, 86
Mason, James II, 93
Mason, James II, 101
Mason, James II, 204
Mason, James II, 241
Mason, James V, 35
Mason, James VI, 839
Mason, James VI, 848
Mason, James R. VI, 839
Mason, Jane II, 592
Mason, Jane II, 754
Mason, Jane V, 620
Mason, Jane V, 633
Mason, Jane W. VI, 846
Mason, Jean VI, 882
Mason, Jemima VI, 844
Mason, Jenny VI, 839
Mason, Jesse VI, 814
Mason, Jesse VI, 920
Mason, Jesse Hiatt V, 516
Mason, John II, 22
Mason, John II, 34
Mason, John II, 43
Mason, John II, 53
Mason, John II, 55
Mason, John II, 72
Mason, John II, 75
Mason, John II, 77
Mason, John II, 83
Mason, John II, 86
Mason, John II, 99
Mason, John II, 104
Mason, John II, 140
Mason, John II, 311
Mason, John II, 592
Mason, John VI, 813
Mason, John VI, 814
Mason, John VI, 826
Mason, John VI, 839
Mason, John VI, 840
Mason, John VI, 848
Mason, John VI, 866
Mason, John VI, 958
Mason, John B. V, 188
Mason, John F. VI, 817
Mason, John F. VI, 839
Mason, John G. II, 34
Mason, John Goodwin II, 86
Mason, John M. VI, 839
Mason, John M. VI, 855
Mason, John S. VI, 834
Mason, John S. VI, 839
Mason, John W. III, 221
Mason, John W. VI, 813
Mason, John W. VI, 819
Mason, John W. VI, 839
Mason, John W. VI, 862
Mason, John William III, 221
Mason, John Wm. III, 221
Mason, John, Jr. VI, 795
Mason, Jonathan II, 34
Mason, Jonathan V, 516
Mason, Jos. P. III, 221
Mason, Joseph II, 34
Mason, Joseph II, 296
Mason, Joseph II, 311
Mason, Joseph II, 322
Mason, Joseph III, 221
Mason, Joseph C. V, 188
Mason, Joseph P. III, 106
Mason, Joseph P. III, 221
Mason, Joseph P. III, 369
Mason, Joshua VI, 839
Mason, Judith VI, 826
Mason, Katharine W. II, 738
Mason, Katharine W. II, 754
Mason, Katharine Wistar II, 704
Mason, Katherine E. II, 704
Mason, Keese IV, 1216
Mason, Ketha IV, 1216
Mason, Kimble II, 241
Mason, Lawrence VI, 839
Mason, Leatitia II, 34
Mason, Lewis VI, 914
Mason, Lewis VI, 958
Mason, Lewis G. II, 121
Mason, Lewis G. II, 153
Mason, Lidy II, 204
Mason, Lidy II, 241
Mason, Lizzie V, 1009
Mason, Louisa VI, 862
Mason, Lucinda VI, 839
Mason, Lucy VI, 839
Mason, Lucy Ellen VI, 784
Mason, Lulu VI, 83
Mason, Luminar VI, 839
Mason, Maggie IV, 1239
Mason, Mahala VI, 958
Mason, Margaret II, 86
Mason, Margaret II, 101
Mason, Margaret II, 592
Mason, Margaret IV, 1258
Mason, Margaret VI, 805
Mason, Margaret A. VI, 824
Mason, Maria III, 221
Mason, Maria H. III, 221
Mason, Martha II, 34
Mason, Martha IV, 420
Mason, Martha IV, 434
Mason, Martha VI, 810
Mason, Martha VI, 866
Mason, Martha E. I, 827
Mason, Martha E. I, 839
Mason, Martha J. VI, 839
Mason, Martha M. VI, 839
Mason, Martin VI, 796
Mason, Martin VI, 803
Mason, Martin VI, 839
Mason, Martin VI, 844
Mason, Martin VI, 850
Mason, Martin VI, 855
Mason, Martin VI, 888
Mason, Martin C. VI, 839
Mason, Martin C. VI, 866
Mason, Mary II, 22
Mason, Mary II, 34
Mason, Mary II, 55
Mason, Mary II, 60
Mason, Mary II, 86
Mason, Mary II, 93
Mason, Mary II, 95
Mason, Mary II, 99
Mason, Mary II, 140
Mason, Mary II, 285
Mason, Mary II, 296
Mason, Mary II, 317
Mason, Mary II, 322
Mason, Mary II, 393
Mason, Mary II, 484
Mason, Mary II, 498
Mason, Mary II, 592
Mason, Mary II, 787
Mason, Mary II, 828
Mason, Mary III, 221
Mason, Mary IV, 1373
Mason, Mary V, 516
Mason, Mary V, 648
Mason, Mary VI, 810
Mason, Mary VI, 839
Mason, Mary VI, 1017
Mason, Mary A. V, 696
Mason, Mary A. T. VI, 839
Mason, Mary H. VI, 813
Mason, Mary H. VI, 839
Mason, Mary Hannah V, 516
Mason, Mary J. V, 188
Mason, Mary J. VI, 839
Mason, Mary Jane V, 188
Mason, Mary L. VI, 839
Mason, Mary Thompson III, 221
Mason, Mathew II, 592
Mason, Matthew II, 592
Mason, Melissa II, 34
Mason, Melissa II, 86
Mason, Millisant II, 86
Mason, Milly VI, 914
Mason, Mirhartt VI, 11
Mason, Mirhartt VI, 12
Mason, Nancy VI, 839
Mason, Nancy A. VI, 819
Mason, Nancy A. VI, 839
Mason, Nancy E. V, 516
Mason, Nathan V, 516
Mason, Nathan VI, 839
Mason, Nathaniel VI, 824
Mason, Nathaniel VI, 839
Mason, Nathaniel VI, 840
Mason, Obedience VI, 834
Mason, Oliver L. VI, 826
Mason, Oliver L. VI, 839
Mason, Pamelia VI, 828
Mason, Parthenia VI, 839
Mason, Paschal B. VI, 826
Mason, Patsey VI, 841
Mason, Patsey VI, 866
Mason, Paulina W. VI, 836
Mason, Pearl IV, 1216
Mason, Philip VI, 839
Mason, Philip G. VI, 839
Mason, Polly VI, 814
Mason, Polly VI, 839
Mason, Polly VI, 845
Mason, Priscilla VI, 848
Mason, Rachel II, 195
Mason, Rachel II, 237
Mason, Rachel II, 241
Mason, Rachel II, 296
Mason, Rachel II, 311
Mason, Rachel VI, 813
Mason, Rachel C. VI, 839
Mason, Rachel Hiatt V, 516
Mason, Rachel, Jr. II, 296
Mason, Ralph II, 311
Mason, Rebecca II, 34
Mason, Rebecca II, 52
Mason, Rebecca II, 86
Mason, Rebecca II, 101
Mason, Rebecca II, 296
Mason, Rebecca II, 311
Mason, Rebecca II, 322
Mason, Rebecca II, 324
Mason, Rebeckah II, 34
Mason, Rebeckah V, 35
Mason, Reuben VI, 958
Mason, Rhoda Ann II, 887
Mason, Rhoda Ann II, 896
Mason, Richard II, 393
Mason, Richard II, 592
Mason, Royal IV, 1216
Mason, Ruth II, 34
Mason, Ruth II, 86
Mason, Ruth V, 35
Mason, Ruth V, 96
Mason, Ruth V, 516
Mason, Sally VI, 839
Mason, Sally VI, 982
Mason, Samuel II, 34
Mason, Samuel II, 64
Mason, Samuel II, 78
Mason, Samuel II, 86
Mason, Samuel II, 195
Mason, Samuel II, 237
Mason, Samuel II, 241
Mason, Samuel II, 311
Mason, Samuel II, 498
Mason, Samuel II, 592
Mason, Samuel II, 665
Mason, Samuel II, 704
Mason, Samuel II, 754
Mason, Samuel IV, 249
Mason, Samuel P. V, 348
Mason, Samuel, Jr. II, 498
Mason, Samuel, Jr. II, 592
Mason, Sarah II, 34
Mason, Sarah II, 58
Mason, Sarah II, 86
Mason, Sarah II, 95
Mason, Sarah II, 112
Mason, Sarah II, 592
Mason, Sarah II, 667
Mason, Sarah II, 896
Mason, Sarah V, 348
Mason, Sarah V, 516
Mason, Sarah VI, 512
Mason, Sarah VI, 531
Mason, Sarah VI, 826
Mason, Sarah VI, 839
Mason, Sarah Ann II, 237
Mason, Sarah Ann II, 241
Mason, Sarah Ann II, 824
Mason, Sarah E. VI, 839
Mason, Sarah R. III, 221
Mason, Saray II, 99
Mason, Sary VI, 853
Mason, Stacy V, 516
Mason, Stephen V, 516
Mason, Susanah II, 86
Mason, Susanna II, 34
Mason, Susanna II, 43
Mason, Susanna IV, 521
Mason, Susanna IV, 540
Mason, Susanna VI, 751
Mason, Susanna VI, 764
Mason, Susanna VI, 826
Mason, Susanna VI, 830
Mason, Susannah II, 22
Mason, Susannah II, 34
Mason, Susannah II, 55
Mason, Susannah II, 72
Mason, Susannah II, 77
Mason, Susannah II, 86
Mason, Susannah II, 105
Mason, Susannah II, 110
Mason, Susannah II, 140
Mason, Thomas II, 34
Mason, Thomas II, 86
Mason, Thomas VI, 920
Mason, Thos. II, 77
Mason, Thos. II, 86
Mason, Thos. V, 648
Mason, Viney VI, 803
Mason, Virginia II, 311
Mason, William II, 34
Mason, William II, 393
Mason, William III, 221
Mason, William IV, 1239
Mason, William VI, 115
Mason, William VI, 822
Mason, William VI, 826
Mason, William VI, 834
Mason, William VI, 836
Mason, William VI, 839
Mason, William VI, 841
Mason, William VI, 846
Mason, William VI, 851
Mason, William VI, 853
Mason, William R. VI, 839
Mason, William T. I, 637
Mason, Wilmouth VI, 839
Mason, Wm. II, 592
Mason, Wm. F. V, 633
Mason, Wm. P. V, 348
Mason, Wm. Thomas I, 621
Massa, Polly I, 308
Massa, Polly I, 311
Massa, William V, 348
Massacree, Nancy VI, 810
Massee, Jane I, 451
Massee, Sarah VI, 853
Massey, Abigail B. II, 312
Massey, Alice Ann I, 326
Massey, Alvis I, 338
Massey, Ann II, 393
Massey, Anna II, 311
Massey, Anna II, 809
Massey, Anna B. II, 312
Massey, Anna B. II, 322
Massey, Anna K. II, 896
Massey, Anne VI, 198
Massey, Anson L. V, 585
Massey, Avis I, 301
Massey, Avis I, 311
Massey, Avis I, 326
Massey, Avis I, 330
Massey, Avis I, 338
Massey, Avis C. I, 339
Massey, Cecelia VI, 198
Massey, Charles II, 356
Massey, Charles II, 393
Massey, Charles II, 592
Massey, Charles II, 712
Massey, Charles V, 348
Massey, Charles VI, 198
Massey, Charles B. II, 311
Massey, Charles, Jr. II, 393
Massey, Charles, Jr. VI, 198
Massey, Chas. A. V, 348
Massey, Cogdell I, 311
Massey, Cogdell B. I, 311
Massey, Cogdell B. I, 321
Massey, Cogdell B. I, 326
Massey, Ebenezer II, 592
Massey, Edwin V, 348
Massey, Eli V, 585
Massey, Elijah C. I, 213
Massey, Elijah Coleman I, 326
Massey, Elisabeth I, 623
Massey, Elizabeth II, 393
Massey, Elizabeth II, 503
Massey, Elizabeth II, 513
Massey, Elizabeth II, 517
Massey, Elizabeth II, 567
Massey, Elizabeth II, 592
Massey, Elizabeth V, 496
Massey, Elizabeth V, 516
Massey, Elizabeth V, 585
Massey, Elizabeth Ashton II, 312
Massey, Elizabeth C. II, 733
Massey, Elizabeth C. II, 754
Massey, Elwood IV, 979
Massey, Emma Gertrude I, 213
Massey, Enos II, 809
Massey, Enos II, 896

ssey, Ethel E. I, 338
ssey, Ethel Edith I, 326
ssey, George II, 809
ssey, Hannah IV, 979
ssey, Helen C. V, 585
ssey, Henry P. II, 311
ssey, Henry P. II, 312
ssey, Henry P. II, 322
ssey, Isaac II, 592
ssey, Israel IV, 979
ssey, James V, 496
ssey, James V, 516
ssey, James D. V, 516
ssey, James D. V, 585
ssey, James E. V, 348
ssey, Jane I, 330
ssey, Jane I, 338
ssey, Jane I, 451
ssey, Jane V, 516
ssey, Jonathan VI, 552
ssey, Levi I, 311
ssey, Levi I, 326
ssey, Levi I, 338
ssey, Levi I, 339
ssey, Levi H. I, 301
ssey, Levi H. I, 305
ssey, Levi H. I, 311
ssey, Levi H. I, 326
ssey, Levi H. I, 330
ssey, Levi H. I, 338
ssey, Lydia II, 592
ssey, Lydia II, 629
ssey, Margaret V, 920
ssey, Mary I, 451
ssey, Mary I, 1062
ssey, Mary II, 356
ssey, Mary II, 393
ssey, Mary II, 522
ssey, Mary II, 592
ssey, Mary II, 712
ssey, Mary V, 348
ssey, Mary V, 585
ssey, Mary Catharine I, 326
ssey, Massey IV, 979
ssey, Miriam IV, 979
ssey, Parker Louis IV, 979
ssey, Peter VI, 198
ssey, Polley I, 326
ssey, Polly I, 311
ssey, Rachel I, 338
ssey, Rachel Eliza I, 326
ssey, Richard II, 393
ssey, Robert V. II, 896
ssey, Robert Valentine II, 809
ssey, Ruth I, 451
ssey, S. Jane I, 338
ssey, Samuel II, 393
ssey, Samuel II, 567
ssey, Samuel II, 592
ssey, Samuel Emsley V, 585
ssey, Sarah I, 339
ssey, Sarah II, 393
ssey, Sarah II, 592
ssey, Sarah II, 610
ssey, Sarah II, 686
ssey, Sarah IV, 395
ssey, Sarah IV, 420
ssey, Sarah VI, 198
ssey, Sarah Smiley I, 326
ssey, Sidney II, 896
ssey, Smithy Jane I, 326
ssey, Susannah II, 805
ssey, Tabitha I, 305
ssey, Tabitha I, 311
ssey, Tabitha I, 326
ssey, Tabitha I, 330
ssey, Tabitha Cume I, 326
ssey, Theodore Kirby I, 326
ssey, Thomas I, 338
ssey, Thomas II, 312
ssey, Thomas II, 592
ssey, Thomas L. I, 326
ssey, Thomas L. I, 330
ssey, Thomas L. I, 338
ssey, Thomas T. I, 326
ssey, White II, 592
ssey, Wight II, 393
ssey, Wight II, 567
ssey, Wight II, 592
ssey, William IV, 420
ssey, William V, 348
ssey, Wm. IV, 1067
ssey, Wm. V, 348
ssey, Wm. A. V, 348
ssey, Zilpha I, 305
ssey, Zilpha I, 311
ssie, Catharine R. VI, 958
ssie, James D. V, 516
ssie, Jane V, 96
ssie, John VI, 958
ssie, Lucretia VI, 251
Massie, Sarah VI, 198
Massie, Sarah VI, 839
Massie, Theodosia F. VI, 958
Massie, Thomas VI, 799
Massie, Thomas VI, 958
Massie, William VI, 839
Masson, Atter I, 264
Masson, Sarah V, 500
Masson, Sarah V, 516
Masson, Wm. II, 592
Masssey, Aquilla VI, 531
Masssey, Jonathan VI, 531
Massten, Rebecca V, 1009
Massy, Avis I, 338
Massy, Hannah I, 408
Massy, Hannah I, 417
Massy, Jane I, 408
Massy, Jane I, 411
Massy, Mary I, 386
Massy, Mary I, 408
Massy, Mary I, 451
Massy, Mary V, 497
Massy, Mary V, 516
Massy, Ruth I, 385
Massy, Ruth I, 408
Massy, William IV, 420
Mast, Alta V, 754
Mast, Hannah V, 764
Mast, Hattie V, 754
Mast, Herbert V, 754
Mast, Isabel V, 754
Mast, J. B. V, 344
Mast, J. B. V, 349
Mast, John V, 771
Mast, John M. V, 754
Mast, Margaret V, 344
Mast, Margaret V, 349
Mast, Margaret V, 754
Mast, Mary V, 754
Mast, Mary V, 771
Mast, Mrs. Winifred V, 754
Mast, Richard Eugene V, 754
Mast, Susannah V, 754
Master, Agnes II, 593
Master, Ann II, 593
Master, Ann II, 821
Master, Ann II, 896
Master, Ann II, 924
Master, Anna IV, 1067
Master, Barclay D. IV, 1067
Master, Benjamin II, 593
Master, Benjamin II, 754
Master, Catharine H. II, 671
Master, Catharine Hickman II, 805
Master, Catherine H. II, 593
Master, Catherine Hickman II, 824
Master, Daniel IV, 1067
Master, Daniel S. IV, 1067
Master, David II, 897
Master, David IV, 1083
Master, Edith Marie V, 516
Master, Elizabeth III, 273
Master, Esther IV, 1067
Master, James IV, 1067
Master, Jane II, 489
Master, Jane II, 593
Master, Jane C. II, 593
Master, Joseph II, 241
Master, Joseph II, 489
Master, Joseph II, 593
Master, Joseph II, 809
Master, Mary II, 394
Master, Mary II, 593
Master, Mary II, 671
Master, Mary II, 809
Master, Mary II, 821
Master, Mary II, 824
Master, Mary A. IV, 1067
Master, Priscilla IV, 1067
Master, Priscilla IV, 1083
Master, Robert II, 241
Master, Robert II, 593
Master, Samuel II, 394
Master, Sophia II, 809
Master, Stephen H. IV, 1067
Master, Thomas II, 394
Master, Thomas III, 273
Master, William II, 241
Master, William II, 821
Master, William G. II, 296
Master, Wm. II, 593
Master, Wm. II, 671
Master, Wm. II, 809
Master, Wm. II, 824
Masterman, Ann II, 393
Masterman, Earl IV, 1329
Masterman, Earl E. IV, 1329
Masterman, Elizabeth II, 393
Masterman, James II, 393
Masterman, Joseph II, 393
Masterman, Mary II, 393
Masterman, Mary II, 593
Masterman, Mary II, 660
Masterman, Rachel II, 393
Masterman, Thomas II, 393
Masterman, Thomas II, 592
Masterman, Thomas II, 593
Masterman, Thomas II, 660
Masterman, William II, 393
Masters, Agnes II, 393
Masters, Agnes II, 593
Masters, Ann II, 394
Masters, Ann II, 593
Masters, Anna IV, 249
Masters, Anna IV, 277
Masters, Anna IV, 803
Masters, Anna IV, 833
Masters, Anna IV, 855
Masters, Anna IV, 1053
Masters, Anna IV, 1067
Masters, Anne IV, 249
Masters, Arter H. II, 754
Masters, Arthur H. II, 712
Masters, Arthur H. II, 754
Masters, Barclay D. IV, 833
Masters, Benjamin II, 393
Masters, Benjamin II, 593
Masters, Benjamin II, 754
Masters, Burvin IV, 738
Masters, Catharine H. II, 394
Masters, Catherine H. II, 593
Masters, Daniel S. IV, 628
Masters, Daniel S. IV, 644
Masters, Daniel S. IV, 738
Masters, Daniel S. IV, 833
Masters, David II, 712
Masters, David II, 897
Masters, David IV, 249
Masters, David IV, 420
Masters, David IV, 487
Masters, David IV, 1067
Masters, David IV, 1106
Masters, David James IV, 1067
Masters, Deborah E. IV, 756
Masters, Elizabeth II, 393
Masters, Elizabeth III, 221
Masters, Esther II, 700
Masters, Esther IV, 644
Masters, Esther IV, 684
Masters, Esther IV, 738
Masters, Esther IV, 802
Masters, Esther IV, 833
Masters, Esther IV, 846
Masters, Esther IV, 1078
Masters, Esther Thomas V, 188
Masters, Geo. III, 221
Masters, Geo. III, 473
Masters, George II, 393
Masters, George III, 144
Masters, George III, 221
Masters, George III, 357
Masters, George III, 359
Masters, Hannah II, 393
Masters, Hannah II, 505
Masters, Hannah II, 560
Masters, Hannah II, 593
Masters, Hannah II, 821
Masters, Hannah IV, 1067
Masters, Hannah M. IV, 738
Masters, Hannah M. IV, 833
Masters, Hannah Mary IV, 628
Masters, Hannah Mary IV, 644
Masters, Hannah Mary IV, 738
Masters, Hannah Mary IV, 833
Masters, Helen B. III, 221
Masters, Helen B. III, 369
Masters, Isaac IV, 249
Masters, Isaac IV, 487
Masters, Isaac IV, 833
Masters, Isaac IV, 1067
Masters, Isabella II, 394
Masters, James IV, 249
Masters, James IV, 487
Masters, Jane II, 394
Masters, Jane II, 593
Masters, Jane C. II, 394
Masters, Jane C. II, 593
Masters, Jason Kirk IV, 738
Masters, Joseph II, 393
Masters, Joseph II, 593
Masters, Joseph II, 700
Masters, Joseph II, 712
Masters, Joseph II, 754
Masters, Joseph IV, 249
Masters, Joseph IV, 644
Masters, Joseph IV, 684
Masters, Joseph IV, 738
Masters, Joseph IV, 802
Masters, Joseph IV, 823
Masters, Joseph IV, 833
Masters, Joseph IV, 846
Masters, Joseph IV, 1067
Masters, Joseph IV, 1078
Masters, Joseph, Jr. II, 394
Masters, Margaret IV, 194
Masters, Margaret IV, 249
Masters, Margaret P. II, 712
Masters, Margaret P. II, 754
Masters, Margaret Parvin II, 701
Masters, Mark K. II, 754
Masters, Martha IV, 249
Masters, Mary II, 394
Masters, Mary II, 593
Masters, Mary II, 711
Masters, Mary II, 712
Masters, Mary III, 144
Masters, Mary III, 221
Masters, Mary III, 357
Masters, Mary III, 359
Masters, Mary III, 473
Masters, Mary IV, 249
Masters, Mary V, 188
Masters, Mary A. II, 700
Masters, Mary A. IV, 683
Masters, Mary A. IV, 733
Masters, Mary A. IV, 802
Masters, Mary A. IV, 833
Masters, Mary A. Brantingham II, 754
Masters, Mary K. II, 754
Masters, Matilda IV, 738
Masters, Matilda IV, 753
Masters, Matilda M. IV, 756
Masters, Mercy II, 583
Masters, Mercy II, 593
Masters, Naomi II, 712
Masters, Naomi IV, 249
Masters, Naomi IV, 463
Masters, Naomi IV, 487
Masters, Naomi IV, 738
Masters, Naomi IV, 812
Masters, Naomi IV, 833
Masters, Naomi IV, 1053
Masters, Naomi IV, 1067
Masters, Narcissa IV, 738
Masters, Narcissa E. II, 711
Masters, Narcissa E. II, 712
Masters, Narcissa E. II, 752
Masters, Narcissa E. II, 754
Masters, Narcissa Elizabeth II, 295
Masters, Narcissa Elizabeth II, 754
Masters, Parvin II, 711
Masters, Parvin II, 712
Masters, Parvin II, 754
Masters, Parvin IV, 756
Masters, Philadelphia III, 221
Masters, Philadelphia III, 357
Masters, Priscilla IV, 420
Masters, Priscilla IV, 1067
Masters, Richard V, 981
Masters, Robert II, 593
Masters, Ruth Anna IV, 699
Masters, Ruth Anna IV, 812
Masters, Ruthann IV, 1067
Masters, Ruthann IV, 1093
Masters, Ruthann IV, 1106
Masters, Ruthanna IV, 487
Masters, Ruthanna IV, 812
Masters, Ruthanna IV, 948
Masters, Sabella II, 393
Masters, Sabilla II, 394
Masters, Samuel II, 394
Masters, Sara Ann IV, 823
Masters, Sara Ann IV, 833
Masters, Sarah II, 394
Masters, Sarah II, 476
Masters, Sarah II, 593
Masters, Sarah IV, 226
Masters, Sarah IV, 249
Masters, Sarah IV, 487
Masters, Sibella II, 593
Masters, Stephen IV, 1067
Masters, Thomas II, 393
Masters, Thomas II, 394
Masters, Thomas II, 476
Masters, Thomas II, 505
Masters, Thomas II, 560
Masters, Thomas II, 593
Masters, Thomas III, 221
Masters, Thomas IV, 1373
Masters, Thomas Howard IV, 738
Masters, Thomas, Jr. III, 221
Masters, Thos. Howard IV, 738
Masters, Thos. Howard IV, 753
Masters, W. B. V, 188
Masters, William II, 393
Masters, William II, 712
Masters, William IV, 249
Masters, William IV, 420
Masters, William IV, 487
Masters, William IV, 1067
Masters, William G. II, 296
Masters, William K. IV, 249
Masters, Wm. II, 593
Masters, Wm. IV, 463
Masters, Wm. IV, 738
Masters, Wm. IV, 812
Masters, Wm. IV, 833
Masters, Wm. IV, 1053
Masters, Wm. IV, 1067
Masters, Wm. IV, 1106
Masterton, Avis III, 221
Masterton, Avis L. III, 281
Masterton, Mary I, 618
Masterton, Robert M. III, 221
Masterton, Robert M. III, 281
Masterton, Thomas III, 221
Mastin, Elizabeth VI, 926
Mastin, James VI, 932
Mastin, Jane VI, 883
Mastin, Jemima VI, 958
Mastin, Jenny VI, 883
Mastin, John I, 827
Mastin, Peter VI, 958
Mastins, Martha II, 445
Mastins, Mary II, 445
Mastins, Samuel II, 445
Maston, Aletha I, 560
Maston, Elizabeth Stanley I, 909
Maston, John I, 907
Maston, John I, 909
Maston, Rachel IV, 979
Maston, Rachel Pennock IV, 979
Matchet, Eliza IV, 588
Matchett, Alice IV, 1329
Matchett, Cecelia IV, 1329
Matchett, Eliza IV, 597
Matchett, Elizabeth Jane IV, 1329
Matchett, G. H. IV, 1329
Matchett, George IV, 1329
Matchett, Harold IV, 1329
Matchett, Harriett A. IV, 1329
Matchett, Jennie IV, 1329
Matchett, Miss Betty IV, 1329
Mateer, Mercy II, 1014
Matern, Abigail II, 594
Matern, John George II, 594
Mathena, Malissa V, 1009
Mathena, Mary V, 1009
Mathena, Rebecca E. V, 1009
Mather, Abigail II, 896
Mather, Agnes B. III, 221
Mather, Agnes B. III, 222
Mather, Albert H. V, 585
Mather, Albert H. V, 633
Mather, Albert H. V, 696
Mather, Alice Ann IV, 1028
Mather, Alice Mandana IV, 1029
Mather, Allan Stewart III, 398
Mather, Allan Stewart III, 426
Mather, Ann II, 585
Mather, Ann II, 593
Mather, Ann II, 819
Mather, Ann II, 824
Mather, Ann II, 897
Mather, Ann IV, 675
Mather, Ann IV, 739
Mather, Ann IV, 833
Mather, Ann IV, 979
Mather, Ann V, 77
Mather, Ann V, 97
Mather, Ann K. IV, 745
Mather, Ann W. II, 809
Mather, Ann W. II, 892
Mather, Ann W. II, 897
Mather, Ann W. II, 900
Mather, Ann Williams II, 806
Mather, Anna III, 222
Mather, Anna Thomas II, 809
Mather, Anne IV, 833
Mather, Bartholemew V, 921
Mather, Bartholmew T. V, 921
Mather, Bartholomew II, 593
Mather, Bartholomew II, 819
Mather, Bartholomew II, 824
Mather, Benjamin II, 585
Mather, Benjamin II, 593
Mather, Benjamin V, 97
Mather, Benjamin, Jr. II, 317
Mather, Benjamin, Jr. II, 322
Mather, Bertha V, 690
Mather, Bertha V, 696
Mather, Caroline B. V, 696
Mather, Carrie V, 585
Mather, Catahrine IV, 739
Mather, Catharine II, 892
Mather, Catharine IV, 738
Mather, Catharine IV, 833
Mather, Catharine IV, 1028

Mather, Catharine Moore II, 897
Mather, Catherine IV, 893
Mather, Catherine IV, 979
Mather, Catherine IV, 1029
Mather, Catherine Moore II, 809
Mather, Charles II, 897
Mather, Charles V, 97
Mather, Charles Elmer II, 322
Mather, Charles Elmer II, 897
Mather, Charles L. II, 312
Mather, Charles L. II, 322
Mather, Charles L. IV, 739
Mather, Charles L. V, 97
Mather, Charles Sidney II, 312
Mather, Charles Sidney II, 322
Mather, Charles W. V, 585
Mather, Chas. C. II, 897
Mather, Chas. Elmer II, 897
Mather, Chas. L. II, 894
Mather, Chas. L. II, 897
Mather, Christopher VI, 11
Mather, Clara Louise II, 882
Mather, Clara Louise II, 897
Mather, Cynthia Shoemaker II, 806
Mather, Daniel IV, 739
Mather, Daniel IV, 833
Mather, Daniel IV, 979
Mather, Daniel IV, 1021
Mather, Daniel IV, 1028
Mather, Daniel E. IV, 1029
Mather, David IV, 1276
Mather, David IV, 1286
Mather, David V, 70
Mather, David V, 96
Mather, David V, 97
Mather, David V, 125
Mather, David Lindley V, 97
Mather, Edith IV, 979
Mather, Edith IV, 1023
Mather, Edith IV, 1029
Mather, Edith Dell IV, 1024
Mather, Edith Dell IV, 1029
Mather, Eleanor May II, 809
Mather, Eliz. H. III, 242
Mather, Elizabeth II, 312
Mather, Elizabeth II, 322
Mather, Elizabeth II, 585
Mather, Elizabeth II, 593
Mather, Elizabeth II, 821
Mather, Elizabeth II, 894
Mather, Elizabeth II, 897
Mather, Elizabeth III, 242
Mather, Elizabeth IV, 467
Mather, Elizabeth IV, 487
Mather, Elizabeth IV, 745
Mather, Elizabeth IV, 790
Mather, Elizabeth V, 78
Mather, Elizabeth V, 86
Mather, Elizabeth V, 88
Mather, Elizabeth V, 96
Mather, Elizabeth V, 97
Mather, Elizabeth C. V, 97
Mather, Elizabeth M. II, 809
Mather, Elizabeth M. II, 897
Mather, Elizabeth M. V, 97
Mather, Elva IV, 1023
Mather, Elva IV, 1029
Mather, Emily L. II, 897
Mather, Emily Robeson II, 809
Mather, Emily Robinson II, 897
Mather, Emma L. II, 861
Mather, Emma L. II, 897
Mather, Esther L. V, 696
Mather, Esther V. II, 896
Mather, Esther V. II, 897
Mather, Esther V. II, 943
Mather, Esther Virginia II, 322
Mather, Esther Virginia II, 809
Mather, Esther Virginia II, 897
Mather, Ethel E. V, 633
Mather, Eva V, 585
Mather, Eva V, 696
Mather, Fam V, 97
Mather, Florence V. II, 896
Mather, Florence Virginia II, 322
Mather, Florence Virginia II, 808
Mather, Florence Virginia II, 897
Mather, Frances Vergina II, 322
Mather, George II, 593
Mather, George V, 97
Mather, George V, 115
Mather, Hannah II, 821
Mather, Hannah IV, 97
Mather, Hannah IV, 99
Mather, Hannah IV, 739
Mather, Hannah IV, 892
Mather, Hannah IV, 893
Mather, Hannah IV, 1023
Mather, Hannah IV, 1028
Mather, Hannah IV, 1029
Mather, Hannah G. IV, 99
Mather, Harriet Parker II, 809
Mather, Henry V, 97
Mather, Hugh McIlvain II, 312
Mather, Huldah IV, 685
Mather, Irene Adalade II, 322
Mather, Irene Adalaide II, 322
Mather, Irene Adelaide II, 897
Mather, Irene Adelaide II, 943
Mather, Irine Adelaide II, 897
Mather, Isaac II, 593
Mather, Isaac IV, 1029
Mather, Isaac Elwood IV, 1029
Mather, J. Howard II, 896
Mather, James IV, 739
Mather, James IV, 833
Mather, James IV, 979
Mather, Jane II, 897
Mather, Jesse IV, 739
Mather, Jesse IV, 833
Mather, Jesse IV, 979
Mather, John II, 892
Mather, John II, 897
Mather, John IV, 738
Mather, John IV, 739
Mather, John IV, 833
Mather, John IV, 893
Mather, John IV, 979
Mather, John IV, 1023
Mather, John IV, 1029
Mather, John R. V, 97
Mather, John Russell II, 1014
Mather, John, Jr. II, 754
Mather, John, Jr. II, 897
Mather, John, Jr. IV, 739
Mather, John, Jr. IV, 1029
Mather, Jonathan II, 821
Mather, Joseph II, 1014
Mather, Joseph III, 222
Mather, Joseph V, 28
Mather, Joseph V, 97
Mather, Joseph V, 551
Mather, Joseph V, 567
Mather, Joseph V, 585
Mather, Joseph V, 696
Mather, Joseph C. V, 63
Mather, Joseph C. V, 97
Mather, Joseph M. II, 861
Mather, Joseph M. II, 897
Mather, Joseph T. II, 806
Mather, Joseph T. II, 809
Mather, Joseph T. II, 897
Mather, Katharine II, 897
Mather, Lewis Montgomery II, 322
Mather, Lewis Montgomery II, 882
Mather, Lewis Montgomery II, 897
Mather, Longstreth V, 97
Mather, Louisa IV, 1276
Mather, Louisa IV, 1286
Mather, Louisa V, 63
Mather, Louisa V, 97
Mather, Louisa V, 567
Mather, Louisa V, 585
Mather, Louisa A. IV, 1286
Mather, Louisa A. V, 97
Mather, Lucy V, 97
Mather, Lucy V, 140
Mather, Lucy R. V, 921
Mather, Lurana V, 97
Mather, Lurana V, 125
Mather, Lurena V, 70
Mather, Lydia II, 322
Mather, Lydia II, 806
Mather, Lydia IV, 611
Mather, Lydia IV, 644
Mather, Lydia IV, 702
Mather, Lydia IV, 739
Mather, Lydia IV, 766
Mather, Lydia IV, 833
Mather, Lydia IV, 927
Mather, Lydia IV, 979
Mather, Lydia V, 97
Mather, Lydia V, 921
Mather, Lydia B. IV, 979
Mather, Lydia B. IV, 1014
Mather, Lydia H. II, 861
Mather, Lydia H. II, 897
Mather, Lydia M. II, 312
Mather, Lydia M. II, 322
Mather, Margaret III, 426
Mather, Martha II, 457
Mather, Martha II, 593
Mather, Martha V, 86
Mather, Martha V, 97
Mather, Martha L. V, 97
Mather, Mary V, 97
Mather, Mary V, 115
Mather, Mary V, 921
Mather, Mary A. IV, 1023
Mather, Mary A. IV, 1029
Mather, Mary A. V, 696
Mather, Mary A. K. VI, 685
Mather, Mary Ann IV, 1029
Mather, Mary Ann V, 28
Mather, Mary Ann V, 97
Mather, Mary Ann V, 551
Mather, Mary Ann V, 585
Mather, Mary Anna K. IV, 739
Mather, Mary Shoemaker II, 824
Mather, McElvain II, 593
Mather, McIlvaine II, 593
Mather, McIlvaine V, 97
Mather, Naomi M., Jr. II, 312
Mather, Naomi P. II, 312
Mather, Naomi P. II, 322
Mather, Naomi P. II, 894
Mather, Naomi P. II, 897
Mather, Naomi, Jr. II, 322
Mather, Omar B. V, 633
Mather, Omar B. V, 696
Mather, Patience II, 322
Mather, Patience S. II, 317
Mather, Patience S. II, 322
Mather, Penrose II, 806
Mather, Phebe V, 696
Mather, Phebe E. V, 633
Mather, Phebe W. II, 897
Mather, Phineas B. V, 97
Mather, Phineas R. V, 97
Mather, Phineas R. V, 112
Mather, Rachel II, 819
Mather, Rachel IV, 342
Mather, Rachel IV, 1028
Mather, Rachel V, 97
Mather, Rachel C. V, 921
Mather, Rebecca IV, 739
Mather, Rebecca IV, 924
Mather, Rebecca IV, 979
Mather, Rebecca IV, 1028
Mather, Richard II, 296
Mather, Richard II, 322
Mather, Richard II, 585
Mather, Richard II, 593
Mather, Richard II, 809
Mather, Richard II, 894
Mather, Richard II, 896
Mather, Richard II, 897
Mather, Richard II, 943
Mather, Richard V, 28
Mather, Richard V, 78
Mather, Richard V, 86
Mather, Richard V, 96
Mather, Richard V, 97
Mather, Richard V, 921
Mather, Rowland III, 221
Mather, Rowland III, 222
Mather, Ruth III, 398
Mather, Ruth III, 426
Mather, Ruth V, 28
Mather, Ruth V, 97
Mather, Ruth Ann V, 97
Mather, Ruth Ann V, 112
Mather, Samuel IV, 702
Mather, Samuel IV, 738
Mather, Samuel IV, 739
Mather, Samuel V, 97
Mather, Sarah II, 593
Mather, Sarah II, 828
Mather, Sarah IV, 738
Mather, Sarah IV, 739
Mather, Sarah IV, 773
Mather, Sarah IV, 833
Mather, Sarah V, 97
Mather, Sarah V, 921
Mather, Sarah A. V, 921
Mather, Sarah Ann II, 593
Mather, Sarah Ann V, 921
Mather, Sarah B. V, 78
Mather, Sarah B. V, 97
Mather, Sidney II, 322
Mather, Sophia IV, 1029
Mather, Susan V, 70
Mather, Susan V, 97
Mather, Susan V, 575
Mather, Susan V, 585
Mather, Susan V, 921
Mather, Susan L. II, 322
Mather, Susanna II, 312
Mather, Susanna V, 97
Mather, Susanna L. II, 322
Mather, Susanna L. V, 78
Mather, Susanna L. V, 97
Mather, Susannah M. II, 805
Mather, Susannah Morris II, 805
Mather, Thomas II, 593
Mather, Thomas IV, 685
Mather, Thomas IV, 739
Mather, Thomas IV, 745
Mather, Thomas IV, 790
Mather, Thomas IV, 833
Mather, Thomas IV, 927
Mather, Thomas Lorenzo IV, 1029
Mather, Thos. V, 921
Mather, William IV, 739
Mather, William IV, 833
Mather, William IV, 893
Mather, William IV, 979
Mather, Willis Elmer IV, 1029
Mather, Wm. III, 426
Mather, Wm. IV, 739
Mather, Wm. IV, 833
Mathers, Ann IV, 979
Mathers, Benjamin II, 593
Mathers, Catherine IV, 979
Mathers, Charles II, 672
Mathers, Charles Sidney II, 322
Mathers, Daniel IV, 979
Mathers, Edith IV, 924
Mathers, Edith IV, 979
Mathers, James IV, 979
Mathers, Jesse IV, 979
Mathers, John IV, 979
Mathers, Lydia II, 322
Mathers, Lydia IV, 979
Mathers, Mary IV, 649
Mathers, Raymond Chas. IV, 1040
Mathers, Rebecca IV, 675
Mathers, Rebecca IV, 739
Mathers, Richard V, 97
Mathers, Samuel IV, 739
Mathers, Susan V, 921
Mathers, William IV, 979
Mathess, Jesse I, 311
Mathew, Ann F. VI, 839
Mathew, Bartholomew T. II, 593
Mathew, Charles IV, 249
Mathew, Edward VI, 839
Mathew, Elizabeth May IV, 249
Mathew, Lucy V, 921
Mathew, Mary V, 921
Mathew, Rachel V, 921
Mathew, Sarah V, 921
Mathew, Susanna VI, 839
Mathew, William VI, 839
Mathewman, Hannah J. V, 97
Mathewman, Hannah Josephine V, 164
Mathewman, Hannah Josephine V, 188
Mathews, ??? III, 350
Mathews, Albert Frederic III, 222
Mathews, Amos III, 222
Mathews, Ann II, 394
Mathews, Ann III, 222
Mathews, Ann IV, 77
Mathews, Ann V, 97
Mathews, Ann V, 110
Mathews, Ann Eliza III, 178
Mathews, Ann Eliza III, 222
Mathews, Ann Eliza IV, 48
Mathews, Ann Eliza IV, 50
Mathews, Ann V. III, 222
Mathews, Anna III, 222
Mathews, Aquila V, 97
Mathews, Bartholomew T. II, 593
Mathews, Caleb B. II, 593
Mathews, Caleb Bentley II, 394
Mathews, Caleb Bentley II, 593
Mathews, Caroline J. III, 222
Mathews, Caroline Jones III, 222
Mathews, Charles II, 394
Mathews, Charles II, 593
Mathews, Charles III, 222
Mathews, Charles IV, 100
Mathews, Charles Bentley II, 593
Mathews, Clara A. III, 222
Mathews, Daniel VI, 259
Mathews, Edith VI, 839
Mathews, Eliz. S. III, 222
Mathews, Elizabeth III, 222
Mathews, Elizabeth IV, 48
Mathews, Elizabeth IV, 56
Mathews, Elizabeth IV, 1088
Mathews, Elizabeth IV, 1106
Mathews, Elizabeth V, 97
Mathews, Elizabeth VI, 422
Mathews, Elizabeth VI, 831
Mathews, Elizabeth VI, 853
Mathews, Elizabeth S. III, 222
Mathews, Ellen M. III, 222
Mathews, Emily A. III, 222
Mathews, Emme IV, 1239
Mathews, Etta V, 1009
Mathews, Eunice III, 222
Mathews, Eunice III, 426
Mathews, Frederic L. III, 222
Mathews, Frederick III, 222
Mathews, Frederick L. III, 222
Mathews, Frederick L. III, 333
Mathews, George VI, 259
Mathews, Hannah II, 242
Mathews, Helen T. III, 178
Mathews, Helen T. III, 222
Mathews, Henry C. III, 222
Mathews, Jacob III, 178
Mathews, Jacob III, 222
Mathews, James T. III, 222
Mathews, Jane III, 222
Mathews, Joel V, 97
Mathews, John Jones III, 222
Mathews, Jonathan V, 97
Mathews, Jos. B. III, 222
Mathews, Joseph II, 394
Mathews, Joseph A. IV, 1329
Mathews, Joseph C. IV, 1329
Mathews, Joshua VI, 422
Mathews, Juli Ann IV, 833
Mathews, Julia Ann IV, 833
Mathews, Julia Ann IV, 844
Mathews, Lenna IV, 1173
Mathews, Lucy V, 921
Mathews, Luke VI, 831
Mathews, Maggie V, 263
Mathews, Mahlon II, 394
Mathews, Margaret II, 593
Mathews, Martha III, 222
Mathews, Martha VI, 669
Mathews, Martha VI, 861
Mathews, Martha A. VI, 827
Mathews, Martin P. VI, 797
Mathews, Martin P. VI, 803
Mathews, Martin T. VI, 808
Mathews, Mary I, 408
Mathews, Mary I, 1113
Mathews, Mary I, 1125
Mathews, Mary II, 394
Mathews, Mary II, 593
Mathews, Mary IV, 48
Mathews, Mary IV, 487
Mathews, Mary IV, 1025
Mathews, Mary IV, 1029
Mathews, Mary V, 921
Mathews, Mary VI, 422
Mathews, Mary VI, 689
Mathews, Mary Anna III, 222
Mathews, Mary Anna III, 333
Mathews, Mary Anna V. III, 222
Mathews, Mary B. III, 222
Mathews, Mary Ellen III, 222
Mathews, Mary F. III, 222
Mathews, Milton V, 188
Mathews, Miriam IV, 48
Mathews, Miriam IV, 77
Mathews, Miriam IV, 99
Mathews, Miriam IV, 100
Mathews, Mrs. Anna IV, 1329
Mathews, Mrs. E. IV, 1329
Mathews, Oliver II, 593
Mathews, Oliver III, 178
Mathews, Oliver III, 222
Mathews, Oliver IV, 1216
Mathews, Oliver V, 97
Mathews, Oliver B. III, 222
Mathews, Paschal VI, 853
Mathews, Phebe V, 97
Mathews, Rachel V, 921
Mathews, Rachel C. III, 222
Mathews, Rebecca IV, 487
Mathews, Rebecca IV, 833
Mathews, Robert F. III, 222
Mathews, Robert V. III, 222
Mathews, Robert Valentine III, 222
Mathews, Robt. III, 222
Mathews, Ruth Hannah VI, 369
Mathews, Ruth Hannah VI, 422
Mathews, Sam'l. T. III, 222
Mathews, Samuel II, 394
Mathews, Samuel H. VI, 369
Mathews, Samuel H. VI, 422
Mathews, Sarah II, 394
Mathews, Sarah II, 593
Mathews, Sarah IV, 1239
Mathews, Sarah V, 921
Mathews, Sarah Ann III, 222
Mathews, Sarah Ann III, 350
Mathews, Sophia II, 242
Mathews, Susan V, 921
Mathews, Susanna V, 97
Mathews, Teressa Roberta III, 222
Mathews, Thomas II, 242
Mathews, Thomas II, 394
Mathews, Thomas II, 593
Mathews, Thomas J. II, 394
Mathews, Thomas J. II, 593
Mathews, Thomas, Jr. II, 593
Mathews, Thos. VI, 587
Mathews, William II, 394

thews, William III, 222
thews, William V, 97
thews, William VI, 808
thews, William VI, 839
thews, William, Jr. VI, 807
hews, Wm. II, 593
thews, Wm. IV, 77
thiatt, John IV, 130
thiet, Ann IV, 100
thiet, Casandra IV, 100
thiet, Catharine IV, 100
thiet, Elizabeth IV, 83
thiet, Elizabeth IV, 100
thiet, George IV, 100
thiet, Jacob IV, 100
thiet, John IV, 100
thiet, Joshua IV, 100
thiet, Mary IV, 100
thiet, Ruth IV, 100
thiet, Susan IV, 100
thiot, Ann IV, 100
thiot, Casandra IV, 100
thiot, George IV, 100
thiot, John IV, 100
thiot, Joshua IV, 100
thiot, Mary IV, 100
thiot, Ruth IV, 100
thiot, Susan IV, 100
thiott, George IV, 130
thiott, Henry IV, 130
thiott, John IV, 130
thiott, Katharine IV, 130
thiott, Katharine IV, 133
thiott, Mary IV, 130
thiott, Susannah IV, 130
athis, Charles H. II, 312
athis, Eli II, 706
athis, Elizabeth VI, 45
athis, Esther II, 241
athis, Esther II, 706
athis, Judith II, 706
athis, Rebecca B. II, 312
athis, Sarah Kirby II, 897
athis, William B. II, 312
atikan, Mary I, 766
atikan, Sarah C. I, 766
atikan, Tamer D. I, 766
atilda, Caroline VI, 156
atilda, Eliza II, 1023
atilda, Eliza II, 1059
atlac, Martha II, 323
atlac, Sarah R. II, 323
atlach, Mary Ann V, 884
atlack, ??? III, 78
atlack, Aaron II, 394
atlack, Abigail II, 790
atlack, Albert II, 897
atlack, Albina H. II, 312
atlack, Albina H. II, 322
atlack, Ann II, 192
atlack, Ann II, 241
atlack, Ann II, 712
atlack, Ann II, 717
atlack, Ann II, 721
atlack, Anna II, 229
atlack, Anna II, 241
atlack, Anna II, 712
atlack, Anna II, 755
atlack, Armela II, 179
atlack, Armela II, 241
atlack, Armistead G. III, 222
atlack, Armistead G. VI, 765
atlack, Arthur II, 229
atlack, Arthur II, 241
atlack, Arthur II, 296
atlack, Arthur II, 312
atlack, Arthur II, 322
atlack, Atlantic T. II, 322
atlack, Benjamin II, 322
atlack, Benjamin II, 323
atlack, Catharine II, 593
atlack, Catherine II, 594
atlack, Catherine II, 605
atlack, Charles II, 712
atlack, Charles II, 755
atlack, Charles F. II, 712
atlack, Charles F. II, 755
atlack, Charles F. II, 946
atlack, Charles F. II, 1086
atlack, Chas II, 594
atlack, Chas. S. II, 897
atlack, Deborah II, 781
atlack, Deborah G. II, 897
atlack, Deborah G. II, 920
atlack, Dorothy II, 179
atlack, Dorothy II, 241
atlack, Dorothy II, 296
atlack, Dorothy II, 809
atlack, Eleanor II, 593
atlack, Eleanor II, 712
atlack, Eleanor II, 755
Matlack, Elizabeth II, 229
Matlack, Elizabeth II, 241
Matlack, Elizabeth II, 296
Matlack, Elizabeth II, 312
Matlack, Elizabeth II, 322
Matlack, Elizabeth II, 394
Matlack, Elizabeth II, 484
Matlack, Elizabeth II, 572
Matlack, Elizabeth II, 593
Matlack, Elizabeth II, 594
Matlack, Elizabeth II, 605
Matlack, Elizabeth L. II, 241
Matlack, Elizabeth L. II, 296
Matlack, Elizabeth Newlin II, 829
Matlack, Elizabeth R. II, 241
Matlack, Elizabeth R. II, 322
Matlack, Elizabeth S. III, 37
Matlack, Elizabeth S. III, 222
Matlack, Ellen II, 394
Matlack, Ellen II, 593
Matlack, Ellen II, 695
Matlack, Ellen VI, 765
Matlack, Ellen VI, 788
Matlack, Ellen M. II, 897
Matlack, Ellwood II, 897
Matlack, Emily III, 78
Matlack, Emily III, 222
Matlack, Franklin II, 897
Matlack, George II, 86
Matlack, George II, 221
Matlack, George II, 241
Matlack, George II, 712
Matlack, George II, 717
Matlack, Hannah II, 233
Matlack, Hannah II, 241
Matlack, Hannah II, 312
Matlack, Hannah II, 322
Matlack, Hannah II, 394
Matlack, Hannah II, 497
Matlack, Hannah II, 593
Matlack, Hannah II, 594
Matlack, Hannah II, 755
Matlack, Hannah III, 79
Matlack, Hannah III, 222
Matlack, Hannah III, 382
Matlack, Hannah VI, 736
Matlack, Hannah VI, 765
Matlack, Hannah M. II, 712
Matlack, Helena E. II, 897
Matlack, Helena E. II, 901
Matlack, Helena Emma II, 809
Matlack, Hephzibah II, 712
Matlack, Isaac S. II, 322
Matlack, John II, 86
Matlack, John II, 88
Matlack, John II, 179
Matlack, John II, 233
Matlack, John II, 241
Matlack, John II, 394
Matlack, John III, 222
Matlack, John W. II, 897
Matlack, John W. II, 901
Matlack, John Warrington II, 809
Matlack, Joseph II, 229
Matlack, Joseph II, 241
Matlack, Joseph II, 296
Matlack, Joseph II, 312
Matlack, Joseph II, 322
Matlack, Joseph II, 394
Matlack, Joseph II, 497
Matlack, Joseph II, 594
Matlack, Joseph II, 712
Matlack, Joseph II, 755
Matlack, Joseph II, 809
Matlack, Joseph II, 897
Matlack, Joseph Stretch II, 594
Matlack, Joseph, Jr. II, 897
Matlack, Josiah II, 394
Matlack, Josiah II, 593
Matlack, Josiah II, 605
Matlack, Leticia II, 77
Matlack, Letitia II, 86
Matlack, Lettitia II, 86
Matlack, Lettitia II, 88
Matlack, Lettitia Miller II, 86
Matlack, Lydia II, 296
Matlack, Lydia S. II, 322
Matlack, Lydia S. II, 323
Matlack, Margaret II, 394
Matlack, Marion II, 784
Matlack, Marion II, 897
Matlack, Martha II, 296
Matlack, Martha II, 323
Matlack, Martha II, 394
Matlack, Martha II, 476
Matlack, Martha II, 593
Matlack, Martha II, 594
Matlack, Martha II, 809
Matlack, Martha II, 897
Matlack, Martha Atlantic II, 322
Matlack, Mary II, 86
Matlack, Mary II, 221
Matlack, Mary II, 241
Matlack, Mary II, 394
Matlack, Mary II, 497
Matlack, Mary II, 593
Matlack, Mary II, 594
Matlack, Mary II, 651
Matlack, Mary II, 797
Matlack, Mary III, 165
Matlack, Mary III, 222
Matlack, Mary III, 382
Matlack, Mary B. II, 323
Matlack, Mary C. II, 714
Matlack, Mary C. II, 717
Matlack, Mary H. II, 241
Matlack, Mary H. II, 296
Matlack, Mary H. II, 820
Matlack, Mary H. II, 897
Matlack, Mary Hewlings II, 820
Matlack, Mary R. II, 897
Matlack, Mary Roberts II, 809
Matlack, Mary T. II, 312
Matlack, Mary T. II, 322
Matlack, Mary W. III, 79
Matlack, Mary W. III, 222
Matlack, Mary W. VI, 736
Matlack, Mary W. VI, 765
Matlack, Nathan II, 497
Matlack, Nathan II, 594
Matlack, Priscilla II, 593
Matlack, Rachel II, 88
Matlack, Rachel II, 241
Matlack, Rachel II, 821
Matlack, Rachel II, 825
Matlack, Rachel M. II, 319
Matlack, Rachel M. II, 323
Matlack, Rebecca II, 593
Matlack, Rebecca II, 594
Matlack, Rebecca II, 785
Matlack, Rebecca III, 222
Matlack, Reuben II, 296
Matlack, Reuben II, 312
Matlack, Reuben II, 322
Matlack, Reuben II, 394
Matlack, Reuben J. II, 312
Matlack, Reuben J. II, 322
Matlack, Reuben L. II, 322
Matlack, Richard II, 809
Matlack, Richard II, 897
Matlack, Richard II, 901
Matlack, Richard K. II, 897
Matlack, Rosalie H. III, 79
Matlack, Ruth II, 86
Matlack, Ruth II, 88
Matlack, Ruth II, 241
Matlack, Ruth II, 255
Matlack, Samuel II, 809
Matlack, Samuel III, 222
Matlack, Samuel VI, 788
Matlack, Sarah II, 86
Matlack, Sarah II, 394
Matlack, Sarah II, 593
Matlack, Sarah II, 632
Matlack, Sarah II, 809
Matlack, Sarah II, 897
Matlack, Sarah II, 901
Matlack, Sarah VI, 730
Matlack, Sarah VI, 786
Matlack, Sarah VI, 788
Matlack, Sarah VI, 789
Matlack, Sarah Ann II, 241
Matlack, Sarah Ann II, 296
Matlack, Sarah Ann II, 712
Matlack, Sarah Ann II, 755
Matlack, Sarah Ann II, 820
Matlack, Sarah Ann II, 897
Matlack, Sarah C. II, 936
Matlack, Sarah M. II, 323
Matlack, Sarah R. II, 312
Matlack, Sarah R. II, 322
Matlack, Sarah R. II, 323
Matlack, Sarah S. II, 826
Matlack, Sarah S. II, 897
Matlack, Sarah S. VI, 765
Matlack, Sarah S. VI, 790
Matlack, Seth II, 394
Matlack, Seth II, 593
Matlack, Seth II, 594
Matlack, Stacy H. VI, 765
Matlack, Stacy H. VI, 788
Matlack, Sumner G. II, 897
Matlack, Sybel II, 593
Matlack, Sybil II, 493
Matlack, Sybil II, 593
Matlack, Sybil II, 594
Matlack, Sybil II, 662
Matlack, Tacy II, 594
Matlack, Thos. II, 809
Matlack, Timothy II, 394
Matlack, Timothy II, 484
Matlack, Timothy II, 593
Matlack, Timothy II, 605
Matlack, Timothy II, 695
Matlack, Timothy III, 222
Matlack, Timothy III, 382
Matlack, Timothy, Jr. III, 222
Matlack, Titus II, 394
Matlack, Titus II, 593
Matlack, Wd. Martha II, 809
Matlack, Wd. Mary II, 594
Matlack, White II, 394
Matlack, White II, 593
Matlack, White III, 165
Matlack, White III, 222
Matlack, White, Jr. III, 222
Matlack, Willett III, 222
Matlack, William II, 241
Matlack, William II, 394
Matlack, Wm. II, 77
Matlack, Wm. II, 86
Matlack, Wm. II, 192
Matlock, ??? III, 43
Matlock, Elizabeth V, 900
Matlock, Elizabeth V, 921
Matlock, Elizabeth VI, 531
Matlock, George II, 86
Matlock, George VI, 422
Matlock, Hannah II, 241
Matlock, Hannah III, 389
Matlock, John II, 241
Matlock, Martha VI, 422
Matlock, Martha VI, 436
Matlock, Mary VI, 755
Matlock, Mary Ann V, 884
Matlock, Mary Ann V, 886
Matlock, Mercer VI, 755
Matlock, Samuel V, 852
Matlock, Samuel G. V, 884
Matlock, Samuel G. V, 886
Matlock, Sarah II, 86
Matlock, Tacy II, 594
Matlock, Thos. II, 809
Matlock, Timothy III, 389
Matlock, Wd. Martha II, 809
Matlocks, Elizabeth II, 542
Matlocks, Elizabeth II, 593
Matox, William VI, 259
Matreviss, James II, 394
Matson, Alfred S. II, 897
Matson, Catharine H. II, 897
Matson, Chas. H. II, 897
Matson, Chas. Henry II, 897
Matson, David IV, 249
Matson, Eleanor Douglas IV, 249
Matson, Elijah IV, 249
Matson, Elizabeth II, 34
Matson, Elizabeth II, 73
Matson, Elizabeth II, 86
Matson, Ella II, 897
Matson, Elnora IV, 249
Matson, Elnora Douglas IV, 249
Matson, Enoch IV, 207
Matson, Enoch IV, 226
Matson, Enoch IV, 249
Matson, Enoch IV, 291
Matson, Esther IV, 207
Matson, Esther IV, 249
Matson, Hanna Mary IV, 249
Matson, Hephzibah II, 86
Matson, Hepzibah II, 34
Matson, James II, 809
Matson, James II, 897
Matson, John IV, 249
Matson, Mary II, 34
Matson, Mary II, 86
Matson, Mary II, 594
Matson, Mary IV, 249
Matson, Mary IV, 294
Matson, Mathias II, 34
Matson, Mathias II, 86
Matson, Morris IV, 249
Matson, Nehemiah IV, 249
Matson, Nehemiah VI, 422
Matson, Nellie A. IV, 1329
Matson, Phebe II, 809
Matson, Phebe II, 897
Matson, Phebe IV, 249
Matson, Rachel IV, 226
Matson, Rachel IV, 249
Matson, Rachel VI, 422
Matson, Rebecca II, 897
Matson, Samuel II, 897
Matson, Sarah II, 34
Matson, Sarah II, 86
Matson, Sarah II, 241
Matson, Sarah II, 242
Matson, Sarah II, 956
Matson, Sarah II, 985
Matson, Sarah II, 1014
Matson, Sarah IV, 226
Matson, Sarah IV, 238
Matson, Sarah IV, 249
Matson, Sarah IV, 291
Matson, Thomas II, 809
Matson, Walker II, 897
Matson, William IV, 249
Matson, Wm. IV, 249
Mattack, Martha V, 96
Mattacks, Elizabeth I, 1115
Mattacks, Elizabeth I, 1125
Mattern, Abigail II, 463
Mattern, Abigail II, 464
Mattern, Abigail II, 594
Mattern, John George II, 594
Mattern, Owen II, 464
Mattern, Sarah II, 464
Mattern, Wm. II, 464
Mattews, Edith D. VI, 481
Mattews, Martin P. VI, 815
Mattews, Thomas C. VI, 854
Mattheas, Robert VI, 833
Matthes, ??? III, 195
Matthes, ??? III, 222
Matthes, Dorothy III, 195
Matthes, Dorothy III, 222
Matthew, Ann VI, 557
Matthew, Christine D. III, 330
Matthew, George I, 408
Matthew, Jackson I, 891
Matthew, Joel V, 852
Matthew, Jonothan V, 97
Matthew, Marion D. III, 330
Matthew, Mrs. Esther IV, 739
Matthew, Richard I, 560
Matthew, Robt. E. III, 330
Matthew, Susan VI, 859
Matthew, Walter I, 408
Matthews, Acton N. VI, 989
Matthews, Agness VI, 601
Matthews, Amanda I, 621
Matthews, Ann I, 505
Matthews, Ann I, 509
Matthews, Ann V, 97
Matthews, Ann V, 516
Matthews, Ann VI, 499
Matthews, Ann VI, 510
Matthews, Ann VI, 523
Matthews, Ann VI, 531
Matthews, Ann VI, 554
Matthews, Ann VI, 556
Matthews, Ann VI, 617
Matthews, Ann VI, 675
Matthews, Ann VI, 696
Matthews, Ann VI, 697
Matthews, Ann VI, 701
Matthews, Ann Eliza V, 852
Matthews, Ann Eliza VI, 532
Matthews, Ann F. VI, 839
Matthews, Anna E. VI, 531
Matthews, Aquila V, 97
Matthews, Aquilla VI, 765
Matthews, Aquilla VI, 793
Matthews, Betty I, 560
Matthews, Burrel J. VI, 765
Matthews, Caleb B. II, 593
Matthews, Caleb Bentley II, 593
Matthews, Caleb Bentley VI, 765
Matthews, Caroline III, 242
Matthews, Caroline J. III, 222
Matthews, Caroline J. III, 361
Matthews, Caroline Jones III, 222
Matthews, Caroline S. VI, 913
Matthews, Charles II, 593
Matthews, Charles VI, 765
Matthews, Charlette Eileen V, 1009
Matthews, Charlotte A. VI, 958
Matthews, Chas. V, 1009
Matthews, Clara V, 349
Matthews, Clifton VI, 962
Matthews, Clifton J. VI, 958
Matthews, Cora Lee V, 1009
Matthews, Dale V, 1009
Matthews, Dale T. V, 1009
Matthews, Daniel II, 224
Matthews, Daniel II, 242
Matthews, Daniel VI, 259
Matthews, Daniel VI, 469
Matthews, Daniel VI, 499
Matthews, Daniel VI, 523
Matthews, Daniel VI, 531
Matthews, Daniel VI, 532
Matthews, Daniel VI, 554
Matthews, Dora I, 827
Matthews, Earl V, 1009
Matthews, Edith VI, 839
Matthews, Edith B. VI, 532
Matthews, Edith D. VI, 531
Matthews, Edith S. III, 242
Matthews, Edward I, 343
Matthews, Edward I, 408

Matthews, Edward I, 560
Matthews, Edward VI, 531
Matthews, Edward VI, 532
Matthews, Edward VI, 543
Matthews, Edward VI, 552
Matthews, Edward VI, 765
Matthews, Edward VI, 839
Matthews, Edward Y. VI, 495
Matthews, Edward Y. VI, 531
Matthews, Edward Y. VI, 532
Matthews, Edwin VI, 958
Matthews, Eli V, 1009
Matthews, Elias VI, 765
Matthews, Eliz. S. III, 93
Matthews, Eliz. S. III, 222
Matthews, Eliz. S. III, 361
Matthews, Eliza V, 349
Matthews, Eliza V, 352
Matthews, Elizabeth I, 392
Matthews, Elizabeth I, 408
Matthews, Elizabeth I, 560
Matthews, Elizabeth III, 222
Matthews, Elizabeth V, 97
Matthews, Elizabeth V, 516
Matthews, Elizabeth VI, 531
Matthews, Elizabeth VI, 532
Matthews, Elizabeth VI, 623
Matthews, Elizabeth VI, 675
Matthews, Elizabeth VI, 696
Matthews, Elizabeth VI, 859
Matthews, Elizabeth VI, 911
Matthews, Elizabeth A. VI, 989
Matthews, Elizabeth R. VI, 958
Matthews, Elizabeth S. III, 222
Matthews, Ellen M. III, 222
Matthews, Ellen Maxwell III, 190
Matthews, Emily VI, 958
Matthews, Esther V, 956
Matthews, Esther VI, 629
Matthews, Esther VI, 675
Matthews, Etta V, 1009
Matthews, Ettie V, 1009
Matthews, Evelina B. VI, 878
Matthews, Evelyn V, 1009
Matthews, Fannie VI, 765
Matthews, Flora I. I, 621
Matthews, Francis VI, 531
Matthews, Francis, Jr. VI, 499
Matthews, Fred C. V, 349
Matthews, George I, 408
Matthews, George VI, 531
Matthews, George VI, 585
Matthews, Gideon VI, 531
Matthews, Grace VI, 752
Matthews, Grace VI, 765
Matthews, Grace Katherine VI, 765
Matthews, Hannah I, 408
Matthews, Hannah I, 429
Matthews, Hannah II, 222
Matthews, Hannah II, 242
Matthews, Hannah V, 852
Matthews, Hannah V, 884
Matthews, Hannah V, 973
Matthews, Hannah V, 974
Matthews, Hannah VI, 371
Matthews, Hannah VI, 373
Matthews, Hannah VI, 499
Matthews, Hannah VI, 523
Matthews, Hannah VI, 532
Matthews, Hannah VI, 552
Matthews, Harriet VI, 958
Matthews, Harvy I, 560
Matthews, Isaac VI, 499
Matthews, J. Flora I, 637
Matthews, J. R. V, 1009
Matthews, Jackson I, 891
Matthews, James I, 408
Matthews, James M. VI, 958
Matthews, James M. VI, 980
Matthews, James M. VI, 1022
Matthews, James T. III, 222
Matthews, Jane III, 222
Matthews, Joel V, 97
Matthews, Joel V, 516
Matthews, Joel V, 852
Matthews, Joel V, 884
Matthews, Joel V, 973
Matthews, Joel V, 974
Matthews, John I, 247
Matthews, John I, 408
Matthews, John II, 224
Matthews, John II, 242
Matthews, John V, 1009
Matthews, John VI, 499
Matthews, John VI, 629
Matthews, John VI, 675
Matthews, John VI, 839
Matthews, John Jones III, 222
Matthews, John Jones III, 287
Matthews, Jonathan V, 97
Matthews, Jonathan V, 516
Matthews, Jonothan V, 97
Matthews, Jos. B. III, 93
Matthews, Jos. B. III, 222
Matthews, Jos. B. III, 361
Matthews, Joseph B. III, 242
Matthews, Joseph B. VI, 752
Matthews, Joseph Brown VI, 765
Matthews, Joy V, 1009
Matthews, Lucy V, 349
Matthews, Maggie V, 263
Matthews, Malinda VI, 839
Matthews, Margaret II, 674
Matthews, Margaret VI, 532
Matthews, Margaret VI, 765
Matthews, Margaret E. VI, 490
Matthews, Margaret Elizabeth VI, 765
Matthews, Margaret Lamb VI, 793
Matthews, Marinda B. VI, 958
Matthews, Martha III, 299
Matthews, Martha VI, 532
Matthews, Martha VI, 759
Matthews, Martha VI, 765
Matthews, Martin P. VI, 827
Matthews, Martin P. VI, 829
Matthews, Martin P. VI, 866
Matthews, Marvin P. VI, 822
Matthews, Mary I, 343
Matthews, Mary I, 344
Matthews, Mary I, 408
Matthews, Mary I, 410
Matthews, Mary I, 509
Matthews, Mary VI, 474
Matthews, Mary VI, 499
Matthews, Mary VI, 531
Matthews, Mary VI, 532
Matthews, Mary VI, 554
Matthews, Mary VI, 620
Matthews, Mary VI, 675
Matthews, Mary VI, 676
Matthews, Mary VI, 690
Matthews, Mary VI, 765
Matthews, Mary VI, 793
Matthews, Mary B. III, 209
Matthews, Mary J. VI, 958
Matthews, Mary, Jr. VI, 532
Matthews, Melvie V, 1009
Matthews, Mordecai VI, 495
Matthews, Mordecai VI, 531
Matthews, Myrtle V, 263
Matthews, Myrtle V, 1009
Matthews, Nancy VI, 864
Matthews, Nancy VI, 867
Matthews, Nancy VI, 958
Matthews, Ned VI, 958
Matthews, Nellie I, 827
Matthews, Nellie V, 1009
Matthews, O. B. III, 190
Matthews, Olive I, 4
Matthews, Oliver I, 560
Matthews, Oliver V, 97
Matthews, Oliver V, 516
Matthews, Oliver V, 852
Matthews, Oliver VI, 464
Matthews, Oliver VI, 523
Matthews, Oliver VI, 531
Matthews, Oliver VI, 585
Matthews, Ollie I, 827
Matthews, Ollie V, 349
Matthews, Oscar V, 349
Matthews, Paschal VI, 843
Matthews, Patsy VI, 814
Matthews, Paul Gene V, 1009
Matthews, Pharaby I, 244
Matthews, Pharaby I, 247
Matthews, Phareba I, 247
Matthews, Phebe V, 97
Matthews, Phebe V, 516
Matthews, Phebe V, 921
Matthews, Phebe E. V, 633
Matthews, Phebe Lawrence III, 209
Matthews, Philip VI, 867
Matthews, Polly VI, 857
Matthews, Rachel C. III, 222
Matthews, Rachel C. III, 287
Matthews, Rachel H. VI, 765
Matthews, Rebecca IV, 481
Matthews, Rebecca IV, 487
Matthews, Rebecca VI, 499
Matthews, Rebecca VI, 617
Matthews, Rebecca VI, 618
Matthews, Rebecca VI, 619
Matthews, Rebecca VI, 675
Matthews, Rebecca VI, 714
Matthews, Rhoda VI, 513
Matthews, Rhoda VI, 576
Matthews, Rhoda VI, 659
Matthews, Rhoda VI, 717
Matthews, Richard I, 560
Matthews, Richard VI, 531
Matthews, Richard VI, 532
Matthews, Richard David V, 1009
Matthews, Robert Ellis I, 621
Matthews, Robert F. III, 209
Matthews, Rose I, 891
Matthews, Rose I, 899
Matthews, Roy Earl VI, 765
Matthews, Russel V, 1009
Matthews, Ruth IV, 634
Matthews, Ruth IV, 644
Matthews, Ruth VI, 495
Matthews, Ruth Hannah VI, 422
Matthews, Ruth Matthews VI, 531
Matthews, Sally VI, 839
Matthews, Sally VI, 848
Matthews, Samuel V, 852
Matthews, Samuel V, 884
Matthews, Samuel V, 973
Matthews, Samuel VI, 531
Matthews, Samuel VI, 864
Matthews, Samuel N. V, 852
Matthews, Sarah I, 560
Matthews, Sarah II, 593
Matthews, Sarah V, 852
Matthews, Sarah V, 884
Matthews, Sarah V, 973
Matthews, Sarah VI, 499
Matthews, Sarah VI, 523
Matthews, Sarah VI, 531
Matthews, Sarah VI, 532
Matthews, Sarah VI, 765
Matthews, Sarah VI, 848
Matthews, Sarah VI, 859
Matthews, Sarah G. VI, 495
Matthews, Sarah G. VI, 532
Matthews, Sarah H. VI, 495
Matthews, Sarah H. VI, 531
Matthews, Sarah H. VI, 532
Matthews, Sarah R. VI, 765
Matthews, Sophia II, 224
Matthews, Sophia II, 242
Matthews, Sophia VI, 552
Matthews, Sophia H. VI, 765
Matthews, Sukey VI, 862
Matthews, Susan V, 928
Matthews, Susanah I, 1145
Matthews, Susanna V, 97
Matthews, Susanna V, 973
Matthews, Susanna VI, 839
Matthews, Susannah I, 560
Matthews, Susannah V, 97
Matthews, Susannah V, 516
Matthews, Susannah V, 921
Matthews, Susannah VI, 549
Matthews, Susannah VI, 555
Matthews, Susannah VI, 556
Matthews, Susannah VI, 862
Matthews, T. J. I, 637
Matthews, Tandy I, 827
Matthews, Temperance VI, 495
Matthews, Temperance VI, 532
Matthews, Teressa III, 93
Matthews, Teressa Roberta III, 222
Matthews, Thomas I, 560
Matthews, Thomas II, 242
Matthews, Thomas II, 593
Matthews, Thomas II, 712
Matthews, Thomas VI, 499
Matthews, Thomas VI, 523
Matthews, Thomas VI, 531
Matthews, Thomas VI, 532
Matthews, Thomas VI, 617
Matthews, Thomas VI, 675
Matthews, Thomas VI, 696
Matthews, Thomas VI, 725
Matthews, Thomas VI, 765
Matthews, Thomas VI, 839
Matthews, Thomas VI, 878
Matthews, Thomas VI, 911
Matthews, Thomas A. I, 637
Matthews, Thomas C. VI, 862
Matthews, Thomas J. II, 593
Matthews, Thomas, Jr. II, 593
Matthews, Valentine III, 299
Matthews, Walter I, 273
Matthews, Walter I, 408
Matthews, Walter I, 509
Matthews, Walter I, 560
Matthews, Wd. Ann VI, 532
Matthews, Widow Sophia VI, 543
Matthews, William I, 343
Matthews, William I, 408
Matthews, William I, 560
Matthews, William II, 712
Matthews, William III, 222
Matthews, William V, 97
Matthews, William V, 516
Matthews, William VI, 499
Matthews, William VI, 532
Matthews, William VI, 533
Matthews, William VI, 765
Matthews, William VI, 814
Matthews, William VI, 839
Matthews, William VI, 958
Matthews, William H. VI, 948
Matthews, William H. VI, 958
Matthews, William H. VI, 974
Matthews, William H. VI, 985
Matthews, Wilson VI, 946
Matthews, Wilson VI, 958
Matthias, Mary Ann V, 774
Matthiott, George IV, 130
Matthiott, Henry IV, 130
Matthis, Elizabeth VI, 45
Matthis, Lidia VI, 45
Matthis, Mary VI, 852
Matthis, Rebeckah VI, 45
Matthis, Rebeckah VI, 46
Matthis, Richard VI, 45
Matthis, Richard VI, 46
Matthis, William VI, 852
Matti, Charles A. IV, 1040
Matti, Charles A. IV, 1216
Matti, Elsie V. IV, 1216
Mattingly, Elizabeth VI, 765
Mattingly, Elizabeth VI, 787
Mattingly, Levi VI, 765
Mattingly, Raphael VI, 765
Mattingly, Raphael VI, 787
Mattingly, Winafred VI, 787
Mattis, Frederic II, 897
Mattis, Lenora II, 897
Mattis, Mary I. II, 897
Mattis, Mary J. II, 897
Mattison, Don S. VI, 422
Mattison, Don Scott VI, 406
Mattison, Don Scott VI, 422
Mattison, Don Scott VI, 439
Mattison, Jesse VI, 422
Mattison, Joseph S. VI, 422
Mattison, Mary Ann VI, 422
Mattison, Nena VI, 422
Mattison, Nena VI, 439
Mattison, Raymond L. VI, 422
Mattison, Raymond Love VI, 422
Mattison, Rebecca VI, 422
Mattison, Wd. Nena VI, 422
Mattlack, Armistead G. VI, 765
Mattlack, Hannah VI, 765
Mattock, Deborah I, 406
Mattock, Dorcas V, 753
Mattock, Jane IV, 48
Mattock, Jane IV, 58
Mattock, Mary I, 406
Mattock, Mary V, 752
Mattock, Rachel I, 406
Mattock, Rebecca IV, 739
Mattock, Rebecca B. IV, 705
Mattock, Stacy V, 884
Mattocks, Posey VI, 955
Matton, Flora V. I, 611
Mattox, Catherine VI, 839
Mattox, Charlotte C. VI, 958
Mattox, Eliza IV, 191
Mattox, Eliza IV, 248
Mattox, Gabriel VI, 958
Mattox, George H. VI, 839
Mattox, Haley VI, 958
Mattox, Margaret IV, 979
Mattox, Mary VI, 958
Mattox, Mary J. E. VI, 996
Mattox, Mary V. VI, 839
Mattox, Nancy C. VI, 996
Mattox, Polly VI, 808
Mattox, Posey VI, 958
Mattox, Robert P. VI, 958
Mattox, Robert P. VI, 996
Mattox, Sarah B. VI, 874
Mattox, Sherard VI, 839
Mattox, Wesley VI, 874
Mattox, Wesley VI, 945
Mattox, Wesley VI, 996
Mattson, Alfred S. II, 897
Mattson, Alfred Simmons II, 809
Mattson, Catharine II, 828
Mattson, Catherine Hill II, 809
Mattson, Charles Henry II, 809
Mattson, Charles Levi II, 809
Mattson, Chas. H. II, 897
Mattson, Chas. Henry II, 828
Mattson, Chas. Henry II, 897
Mattson, Ella II, 809
Mattson, Ella II, 828
Mattson, Ella II, 897
Mattson, Ella Mattson II, 943
Mattson, James II, 809
Mattson, Levi II, 809
Mattson, Levi II, 822
Mattson, Phebe II, 809
Mattson, Rebecca II, 809
Mattson, Rebecca II, 822
Mattson, Rebecca II, 897
Mattson, Samuel Hewes II, 80
Mattson, Tacy II, 809
Mattson, Thomas II, 809
Mattson, Wd. Sarah II, 822
Matz, Augusta III, 426
Matz, Augusta III, 461
Matz, Frieda III, 426
Matz, Frieda Harriet III, 461
Matz, Henry Fredk III, 461
Matz, Jno. Henry Falk III, 42
Maud, Eva II, 836
Maud, Mary IV, 958
Maude, Ella III, 475
Maude, Emily V, 712
Maudlen, Edmund I, 59
Maudlen, Jean I, 56
Maudlen, Jean I, 59
Maudlen, Joseph I, 56
Maudlen, Joseph I, 59
Maudlin, Ann I, 59
Maudlin, Ann I, 146
Maudlin, Ann I, 725
Maudlin, Anna I, 996
Maudlin, Benjamin I, 196
Maudlin, Benjamin I, 725
Maudlin, Charles I, 59
Maudlin, Charles I, 146
Maudlin, Charles I, 725
Maudlin, Edmund I, 59
Maudlin, Edmund I, 311
Maudlin, Elias I, 726
Maudlin, Elisabeth I, 59
Maudlin, Elisabeth I, 146
Maudlin, Elwood I, 726
Maudlin, George I, 725
Maudlin, George I, 993
Maudlin, George I, 995
Maudlin, Hannah I, 59
Maudlin, Hannah I, 146
Maudlin, Hannah I, 725
Maudlin, Hannah I, 726
Maudlin, Hannah I, 993
Maudlin, James I, 196
Maudlin, James I, 725
Maudlin, Jane I, 59
Maudlin, Jean I, 59
Maudlin, Jesse I, 59
Maudlin, Jesse I, 725
Maudlin, Jessee I, 146
Maudlin, John I, 59
Maudlin, John I, 146
Maudlin, John I, 725
Maudlin, John I, 726
Maudlin, John, Jr. I, 59
Maudlin, Joseph I, 59
Maudlin, Joseph I, 146
Maudlin, Joseph I, 196
Maudlin, Joseph I, 408
Maudlin, Joseph I, 725
Maudlin, Joseph I, 726
Maudlin, Leah I, 302
Maudlin, Leah I, 311
Maudlin, Leah I, 725
Maudlin, Mark I, 725
Maudlin, Mark I, 726
Maudlin, Mary I, 59
Maudlin, Mary I, 62
Maudlin, Mary I, 68
Maudlin, Mary I, 146
Maudlin, Mary I, 725
Maudlin, Mary I, 726
Maudlin, Mourning I, 59
Maudlin, Nancy I, 726
Maudlin, Nathan I, 398
Maudlin, Nathan I, 408
Maudlin, Nathan I, 725
Maudlin, Nathan I, 726
Maudlin, Newby I, 726
Maudlin, Peninah I, 146
Maudlin, Pleasant I, 59
Maudlin, Pleasant I, 146
Maudlin, Pleasant I, 725
Maudlin, Rachel I, 311
Maudlin, Rachel I, 316
Maudlin, Reuben I, 995
Maudlin, Rhoda I, 995
Maudlin, Samuel I, 725
Maudlin, Sarah I, 311
Maudlin, Sarah I, 398
Maudlin, Sarah I, 408
Maudlin, Sarah I, 726
Maudlin, Sarah I, 993
Maudlin, Sarah I, 995
Maudlin, Thomas I, 726
Maudlin, Violet I, 726
Maudlin, Violett I, 726

dlin, Vitt I, 408
dlin, William I, 59
dlin, William I, 146
dlin, William I, 725
dlin, William I, 726
dlin, William I, 993
dlin, William I, 996
dlin, Wright I, 725
dling, Benjamin I, 725
dling, John I, 726
dling, Joseph I, 726
dling, Mark I, 726
dling, Nathan I, 726
dling, Newby I, 726
dling, Samuel I, 725
dling, Thomas I, 726
dling, William I, 726
dling, Wright I, 725
l, Charity II, 594
l, Daniel II, 594
l, Edward IV, 739
l, Elizabeth II, 594
l, Hannah R. IV, 739
l, James E. IV, 739
l, Jane II, 394
l, Joshua II, 848
l, Lydia II, 594
l, Margaret T. IV, 739
l, Mary II, 848
l, Rebecca II, 848
l, Sarah II, 594
l, Thomas II, 594
ldin, Ann I, 59
ldin, Mourning I, 59
lding, Ann I, 146
lding, Joseph I, 725
le, Alice D. II, 946
le, Alice D. II, 949
le, Alice D. II, 1088
le, Ann G. II, 712
le, Ann Jr. IV, 249
le, Ann W. II, 480
le, Ann W. II, 594
le, Asariah L. II, 898
le, Azariah II, 594
le, Azariah II, 755
le, Azariah L. II, 755
le, Benjamin II, 710
le, Caleb VI, 198
le, Caleb J. VI, 198
le, Caroline R. VI, 198
le, Charity II, 394
le, Charity II, 567
le, Charity II, 594
le, Charlotte II, 1086
le, Charlotte W. II, 946
le, Charlotte W. II, 949
le, Charlotte W. II, 1088
le, Cornelia B. II, 755
le, Cornelia Broome II, 755
le, Daniel II, 394
le, Daniel II, 456
le, Daniel II, 480
le, Daniel II, 594
le, Daniel II, 712
le, Daniel II, 755
le, Ebenezer VI, 190
le, Ebenezer VI, 194
le, Ebenezer VI, 198
le, Edith VI, 178
le, Edith VI, 198
le, Edward IV, 249
le, Edward IV, 262
le, Edward IV, 1067
le, Edward IV, 1072
le, Edward IV, 1106
le, Eleanor II, 946
le, Eleanor II, 949
le, Eleanor II, 1086
le, Eleanor II, 1088
le, Elisha II, 755
le, Eliza M. VI, 178
le, Eliza M. VI, 198
le, Elizabeth II, 456
le, Elizabeth II, 480
le, Elizabeth II, 567
le, Elizabeth II, 594
le, Elizabeth II, 755
le, Elizabeth II, 809
le, Elizabeth II, 897
le, Elizabeth II, 898
le, Elizabeth II, 908
le, Elizabeth II, 959
le, Elizabeth VI, 166
le, Elizabeth VI, 170
le, Elizabeth VI, 198
le, Elizabeth A. VI, 198
le, Elizabeth Coleman
I, 805
le, Elizabeth Johnson II, 594
le, Elizabeth M. II, 908
Maule, Elizabeth M. II, 948
Maule, Elizabeth M. II, 949
Maule, Eva II, 755
Maule, Evert Price II, 755
Maule, Hannah II, 394
Maule, Hannah II, 567
Maule, Hannah II, 594
Maule, Hannah II, 755
Maule, Hannah IV, 249
Maule, Hannah IV, 262
Maule, Hannah IV, 1067
Maule, Hannah IV, 1072
Maule, Hannah IV, 1106
Maule, Hannah L. II, 755
Maule, Hannah Lewis II, 809
Maule, Hannah Lewis II, 897
Maule, Hannah R. IV, 704
Maule, Henry IV, 1067
Maule, Henry E. IV, 249
Maule, Israel II, 712
Maule, J. E. II, 947
Maule, Jacob II, 594
Maule, Jacob II, 755
Maule, Jacob II, 809
Maule, Jacob II, 897
Maule, Jacob II, 898
Maule, Jacob IV, 211
Maule, Jacob IV, 249
Maule, Jacob IV, 266
Maule, Jacob W. II, 898
Maule, Jacob, Jr. II, 712
Maule, James IV, 249
Maule, James E. IV, 249
Maule, James E. IV, 704
Maule, James S. IV, 1067
Maule, Jane II, 394
Maule, Jesse IV, 1067
Maule, John II, 394
Maule, John II, 445
Maule, John II, 567
Maule, John II, 594
Maule, John II, 672
Maule, John II, 1086
Maule, John IV, 153
Maule, John C. II, 946
Maule, John C. II, 949
Maule, John C. II, 1086
Maule, John C. II, 1088
Maule, John P. IV, 1067
Maule, Jonathan II, 480
Maule, Jonathan II, 594
Maule, Joseph II, 394
Maule, Joseph II, 594
Maule, Joseph VI, 166
Maule, Joseph VI, 178
Maule, Joseph VI, 198
Maule, Joseph E. II, 949
Maule, Joseph E. II, 959
Maule, Joseph E. II, 1086
Maule, Joseph L. II, 898
Maule, Joseph Lewis II, 594
Maule, Joseph Lewis II, 755
Maule, Joseph, Jr. VI, 166
Maule, Joshua II, 464
Maule, Joshua II, 594
Maule, Joshua II, 898
Maule, Joshua II, 908
Maule, Joshua IV, 249
Maule, Lavinia II, 755
Maule, Lewis VI, 178
Maule, Lewis VI, 198
Maule, Lydia II, 594
Maule, Margaret II, 594
Maule, Margaret II, 710
Maule, Margaret II, 755
Maule, Margaret II, 897
Maule, Margaret II, 898
Maule, Margaret VI, 166
Maule, Margaret VI, 198
Maule, Margaret J. VI, 198
Maule, Martha II, 594
Maule, Martha II, 712
Maule, Mary II, 394
Maule, Mary II, 567
Maule, Mary II, 594
Maule, Mary II, 710
Maule, Mary II, 755
Maule, Mary II, 787
Maule, Mary II, 897
Maule, Mary II, 898
Maule, Mary IV, 211
Maule, Mary IV, 249
Maule, Mary VI, 163
Maule, Mary VI, 166
Maule, Mary VI, 198
Maule, Mary W. II, 949
Maule, Mary W. II, 1087
Maule, Mary W. II, 1088
Maule, Mary Wood II, 946
Maule, Naomy II, 394
Maule, Rachel IV, 249
Maule, Rachel IV, 266
Maule, Rachel VI, 198
Maule, Rachel R. IV, 211
Maule, Rebecca II, 464
Maule, Rebecca II, 594
Maule, Rebecca II, 898
Maule, Rebecca II, 908
Maule, Rebecca J. II, 464
Maule, Rebecca J. II, 567
Maule, Rebecca J. II, 594
Maule, Sarah II, 242
Maule, Sarah II, 394
Maule, Sarah II, 488
Maule, Sarah II, 594
Maule, Sarah II, 946
Maule, Sarah II, 947
Maule, Sarah II, 949
Maule, Sarah II, 959
Maule, Sarah II, 1086
Maule, Sarah II, 1088
Maule, Sarah IV, 249
Maule, Sarah IV, 1067
Maule, Sarah VI, 190
Maule, Sarah VI, 194
Maule, Sarah VI, 198
Maule, Sarah B. II, 594
Maule, Sarah B. II, 672
Maule, Sarah N. IV, 249
Maule, Susan C. II, 948
Maule, Susan C. II, 949
Maule, Susanna II, 394
Maule, Susanna II, 594
Maule, Susanna II, 672
Maule, Susannah II, 394
Maule, Susannah II, 550
Maule, Susannah II, 594
Maule, Thomas II, 394
Maule, Thomas II, 456
Maule, Thomas II, 550
Maule, Thomas II, 567
Maule, Thomas II, 594
Maule, Thomas VI, 166
Maule, Thomas VI, 198
Maule, Walter IV, 1067
Maule, Wd. Sarah II, 594
Maule, Wd. Susan C. II, 1086
Maule, William VI, 198
Maule, William Lewis VI, 198
Maule, Zilla II, 594
Maule, Zillah II, 394
Maule, Zillah II, 456
Maull, Mary II, 394
Maulmsbury, Isabella II, 895
Maulsby, Ann I, 966
Maulsby, Ann I, 1111
Maulsby, Ann II, 394
Maulsby, Ann VI, 422
Maulsby, David I, 1124
Maulsby, David I, 1125
Maulsby, David II, 394
Maulsby, David Williams II, 594
Maulsby, Ebenezar I, 966
Maulsby, Ebenezer VI, 422
Maulsby, Eleanor VI, 422
Maulsby, Elenor I, 966
Maulsby, Eliner VI, 422
Maulsby, Elizabeth II, 394
Maulsby, Hannah II, 594
Maulsby, John I, 966
Maulsby, John I, 1101
Maulsby, John I, 1125
Maulsby, John II, 394
Maulsby, John VI, 422
Maulsby, John, Jr. I, 1125
Maulsby, Joseph II, 394
Maulsby, Lydda I, 966
Maulsby, Lydia I, 1101
Maulsby, Lydia I, 1122
Maulsby, Lydia I, 1125
Maulsby, Lydia VI, 422
Maulsby, Mary I, 1124
Maulsby, Mary I, 1125
Maulsby, Mary II, 394
Maulsby, Mary II, 594
Maulsby, Mary II, 686
Maulsby, Merchant II, 394
Maulsby, Sarah I, 966
Maulsby, Sarah I, 1109
Maulsby, Sarah I, 1125
Maulsby, Sarah I, 1126
Maulsby, Sarah VI, 422
Maulsby, Susannah VI, 422
Maulsby, William I, 966
Maulsby, William I, 1125
Maulsby, William II, 394
Maulsby, William VI, 422
Maulsby, Wm. II, 594
Maultsby, Mary II, 594
Mauney, Josephine I, 891
Maupin, A. L. I, 1159
Maupin, Addison VI, 958
Maupin, Albert I, 1159
Maupin, Albert L. I, 1145
Maupin, Albert L. I, 1159
Maupin, Carr M. VI, 958
Maupin, Elbert L. I, 1159
Maupin, Eliza Jane VI, 958
Maupin, Frances Ann VI, 958
Maupin, Georg. W. I, 1159
Maupin, George I, 1159
Maupin, Ira VI, 958
Maupin, T. D. W. C. I, 1159
Maupin, Thomas D. W. C. I, 1159
Maupin, Thomas D. W. F. I, 1159
Maupine, Elbert L. I, 1159
Maupine, Thomas D. W. F.
I, 1159
Maure, Amy I, 59
Maure, Dora I, 59
Maure, Harriett I, 59
Maure, Joseph I, 59
Maure, Margaret I, 59
Maure, Margaret A. I, 59
Maure, Margaret A. I, 88
Maurice, Camilla III, 222
Maurice, Charles III, 48
Maurice, Charles III, 222
Maurice, Florence III, 48
Maurice, Florence III, 223
Maurice, Sarah E. III, 222
Maurise, Gleen V, 595
Maurise, Mary Louise V, 595
Maury, Amy I, 59
Maury, Dora I, 59
Maury, Harriett I, 59
Maury, Harriett Ellen I, 13
Maury, Joseph I, 13
Maury, Joseph I, 59
Maury, Margaret I, 13
Maury, Margaret I, 59
Maury, Margaret A. I, 59
Mause, Jacob II, 822
Mause, Nancy II, 822
Mause, Susan II, 822
Maverick, Augusta L. III, 190
Maverty, Lydia Ann V, 585
Maverty, Lydia Ann V, 598
Mawfitt, John I, 1128
Maxen, David IV, 100
Maxen, Hannah IV, 100
Maxen, Jesse IV, 100
Maxen, Jesse IV, 130
Maxen, Joel IV, 100
Maxen, John IV, 100
Maxen, Jonathan IV, 100
Maxen, Margaret IV, 100
Maxen, Mary Magdalen IV, 100
Maxen, Nathan IV, 100
Maxen, Rachel IV, 123
Maxen, Rachel IV, 130
Maxen, Stephen IV, 100
Maxen, Stephen IV, 130
Maxen, Stephen, Jr. IV, 130
Maxen, William IV, 100
Maxey, Hiram T. VI, 959
Maxey, Isaac VI, 960
Maxey, James VI, 839
Maxey, James, Jr. VI, 959
Maxey, Jamima VI, 959
Maxey, Milley VI, 959
Maxey, Nancy VI, 839
Maxey, Sarah Ann VI, 960
Maxey, Sarah J. VI, 959
Maxey, Suckey VI, 926
Maxey, Walter VI, 959
Maxfield, Elizabeth II, 472
Maxfield, Elizabeth II, 594
Maxfield, Elizabeth Maxwell
II, 594
Maxfield, James V, 696
Maxfield, Jennie V, 696
Maxfield, Joseph II, 594
Maxfield, Joseph II, 809
Maxfield, Joseph II, 812
Maxfield, Sarah II, 594
Maxfield, Sarah II, 809
Maxfield, Sarah II, 812
Maxfield, Stephen II, 594
Maxfield, Susanna II, 594
Maxfield, Susannah II, 812
Maxfield, Wm. R. II, 594
Maxfield, Wm. R. II, 898
Maxfield, Wm. Rowan II, 809
Maxin, David IV, 100
Maxin, David IV, 342
Maxin, John IV, 100
Maxin, John IV, 342
Maxin, Jonathan IV, 100
Maxin, Jonathan IV, 342
Maxin, Mary Magdalen IV, 100
Maxin, Mary Magdalin IV, 342
Maxin, Nathan IV, 100
Maxin, Nathan IV, 342
Maxin, William IV, 100
Maxin, William IV, 342
Maxon, Adolphus V, 1009
Maxon, Alfred IV, 540
Maxon, Amanda IV, 1305
Maxon, David IV, 342
Maxon, David IV, 540
Maxon, Elmer V, 1009
Maxon, Gertrude V, 1009
Maxon, Hannah IV, 100
Maxon, Hannah IV, 342
Maxon, Hannah IV, 420
Maxon, Ira IV, 540
Maxon, John IV, 342
Maxon, John IV, 540
Maxon, Jonathan IV, 342
Maxon, Jonathan IV, 540
Maxon, Lydia IV, 540
Maxon, Mary IV, 342
Maxon, Mary IV, 540
Maxon, Mary Hannah IV, 540
Maxon, Mary M. IV, 342
Maxon, Mary Magdalin IV, 342
Maxon, Nathan IV, 342
Maxon, Nathan IV, 540
Maxon, Priscilla IV, 540
Maxon, Ruth IV, 540
Maxon, Sarah IV, 342
Maxon, Sarah IV, 540
Maxon, Stephen IV, 130
Maxon, Stephen IV, 540
Maxon, Susanna IV, 540
Maxon, Susannah IV, 342
Maxon, Susannah IV, 540
Maxon, Tacy IV, 48
Maxon, William IV, 342
Maxon, William IV, 540
Maxson, Adolphus V, 1009
Maxson, Bertha V, 1009
Maxson, Catharine W. III, 490
Maxson, Cora V, 1009
Maxson, David IV, 100
Maxson, David IV, 339
Maxson, David IV, 342
Maxson, David V, 1009
Maxson, Doris V, 1009
Maxson, Elmer V, 1009
Maxson, Gertie V, 1009
Maxson, Gertrude V, 1009
Maxson, Hannah IV, 1067
Maxson, Horace Sterman V, 1009
Maxson, Ira IV, 540
Maxson, Jesse IV, 100
Maxson, John III, 490
Maxson, Jonathan IV, 100
Maxson, Jonathan IV, 342
Maxson, Jonathan IV, 540
Maxson, Lizzie V, 1009
Maxson, Margaret IV, 100
Maxson, Margaret Rose V, 1009
Maxson, Mary Hannah IV, 540
Maxson, Mary M. IV, 342
Maxson, Mary Magdalen IV, 100
Maxson, Nathan IV, 100
Maxson, Nathan IV, 540
Maxson, Perl V, 1009
Maxson, Ruth IV, 540
Maxson, Sarah IV, 339
Maxson, Sarah IV, 342
Maxson, Sarah IV, 540
Maxson, Stephen IV, 48
Maxson, Stephen IV, 100
Maxson, Stephen IV, 540
Maxson, Susannah IV, 540
Maxson, Tacy IV, 48
Maxson, Wm. V, 1009
Maxton, Susan II, 898
Maxwell, Albert IV, 588
Maxwell, Allen IV, 576
Maxwell, Allen IV, 588
Maxwell, Allen J. I, 338
Maxwell, Arsinoe IV, 621
Maxwell, Arthur B. IV, 621
Maxwell, Arthur T. V, 815
Maxwell, Bonnie V, 815
Maxwell, Caroline IV, 48
Maxwell, Caroline L. IV, 46
Maxwell, Caroline L. IV, 48
Maxwell, David I, 1108
Maxwell, David V, 882
Maxwell, David V, 884
Maxwell, Dillon I, 1125
Maxwell, Edith III, 223
Maxwell, Electa IV, 1258
Maxwell, Electra IV, 1258
Maxwell, Elizabeth I, 408
Maxwell, Elizabeth I, 1108
Maxwell, Elizabeth I, 1120
Maxwell, Elizabeth I, 1125
Maxwell, Elizabeth II, 87

Maxwell, Elizabeth IV, 1345
Maxwell, Elizabeth V, 98
Maxwell, Ellen M. III, 222
Maxwell, Elsie IV, 621
Maxwell, Elsie IV, 622
Maxwell, Elsie IV, 644
Maxwell, Ester IV, 311
Maxwell, Ester IV, 313
Maxwell, Fern V, 815
Maxwell, Flora V, 815
Maxwell, George II, 808
Maxwell, Hannah I, 1108
Maxwell, Hannah I, 1125
Maxwell, Hannah IV, 730
Maxwell, Hannah V, 882
Maxwell, Hannah V, 884
Maxwell, Hugh I, 408
Maxwell, Hugh I, 1108
Maxwell, Hugh I, 1125
Maxwell, Hugh G. I, 330
Maxwell, Hugh G. I, 338
Maxwell, Jacob I, 1108
Maxwell, Jacob I, 1125
Maxwell, James I, 1125
Maxwell, John I, 1108
Maxwell, John I, 1125
Maxwell, John I, 1159
Maxwell, John II, 34
Maxwell, John III, 223
Maxwell, John J. IV, 1329
Maxwell, John R. III, 223
Maxwell, John Rogers III, 223
Maxwell, John Rogers, Jr. III, 72
Maxwell, John Rogers, Jr. III, 223
Maxwell, Lizzie N. IV, 1329
Maxwell, Lucinda IV, 1051
Maxwell, Lucinda IV, 1067
Maxwell, Lydia I, 1108
Maxwell, Lydia III, 72
Maxwell, Lydia III, 223
Maxwell, Margaret II, 808
Maxwell, Maria IV, 588
Maxwell, Maria Louise III, 223
Maxwell, Mary I, 1108
Maxwell, Mary IV, 937
Maxwell, Matilda I, 1108
Maxwell, Max V, 98
Maxwell, Minor IV, 1216
Maxwell, Morris Clothier III, 223
Maxwell, Nancy S. I, 338
Maxwell, Naomi II, 394
Maxwell, Narcellua V, 815
Maxwell, Nathan Miner IV, 1216
Maxwell, Rachel I, 1108
Maxwell, Richard Hayworth I, 1125
Maxwell, Ruth I, 1108
Maxwell, Sarah II, 594
Maxwell, Sarah T. IV, 576
Maxwell, Sarah T. IV, 588
Maxwell, Thomas I, 1108
Maxwell, Thomas I, 1125
Maxwell, Thomas V, 460
Maxwell, Vernon V, 815
Maxwell, W. J. IV, 1258
Maxwell, Wd. Elizabeth II, 34
Maxwell, Wd. Margaret Hargraves II, 808
Maxwell, Wd. Sarah II, 594
Maxwell, William I, 1108
Maxwell, William I, 1125
Maxwell, William II, 394
Maxwell, William IV, 1258
May, Ada IV, 1329
May, Amanda VI, 877
May, Anna G. III, 249
May, Bertha IV, 1173
May, Charlotte VI, 839
May, Daniel I, 439
May, Daniel I, 451
May, Elizabeth VI, 959
May, Ella L. IV, 618
May, Ella L. IV, 644
May, Floy IV, 1286
May, Hannah II, 445
May, Henry II, 445
May, Jacob II, 445
May, John VI, 839
May, John VI, 959
May, Joseph VI, 839
May, Katy VI, 944
May, Lewis IV, 1329
May, Mary II, 595
May, Mary II, 604
May, Mary A. VI, 839
May, Polly VI, 839
May, Rachel IV, 48
May, Rachel VI, 839
May, Rebecca I, 439
May, Rebecca I, 451
May, Royal VI, 877
May, Sarah II, 445
May, Susanna II, 445
May, Viola I, 937
May, William VI, 839
May, William VI, 959
Maybee, Hannah H. V, 87
Maybee, Hannah H. V, 98
Mayberry, Abraham VI, 959
Mayberry, Ann VI, 959
Mayberry, Barbara VI, 876
Mayberry, Betsey VI, 959
Mayberry, David VI, 839
Mayberry, David VI, 950
Mayberry, David VI, 959
Mayberry, Dosia VI, 988
Mayberry, Edith W. VI, 839
Mayberry, Elizabeth I, 912
Mayberry, Elizabeth I, 913
Mayberry, Elizabeth VI, 824
Mayberry, Elizabeth VI, 946
Mayberry, Elizabeth VI, 959
Mayberry, Elizabeth J. VI, 839
Mayberry, Fred'k VI, 880
Mayberry, Frederick VI, 876
Mayberry, Frederick VI, 959
Mayberry, Henry VI, 945
Mayberry, Henry VI, 946
Mayberry, Henry VI, 959
Mayberry, Henry VI, 977
Mayberry, Henry VI, 988
Mayberry, Henry VI, 993
Mayberry, Isham VI, 839
Mayberry, Jacob VI, 959
Mayberry, Jasteny VI, 824
Mayberry, Jesse VI, 830
Mayberry, Jesse VI, 839
Mayberry, Kathrine VI, 880
Mayberry, Magdalene VI, 959
Mayberry, Mary VI, 919
Mayberry, Michael VI, 959
Mayberry, Nancy VI, 825
Mayberry, Peggy VI, 959
Mayberry, Polly VI, 797
Mayberry, Rachel VI, 876
Mayberry, Rody VI, 959
Mayberry, Susanna VI, 993
Maybry, David VI, 839
Maybry, Elizabeth J. VI, 839
Mayburry, Ann II, 595
Mayburry, Jeremiah II, 595
Mayburry, Lydia II, 595
Mayburry, Mary II, 595
Mayburry, Rebecca II, 595
Mayburry, Rebecca II, 677
Mayburry, Sophia II, 595
Mayburry, Thomas II, 595
Mayburry, Thomas II, 677
Mayburry, Willoughby II, 595
Mayburry, Wm. II, 595
Maybury, Ann II, 595
Maybury, Jeremiah II, 595
Maybury, Lydia II, 595
Maybury, Mary II, 595
Maybury, Rebecca II, 595
Maybury, Sophia II, 595
Maybury, Thomas II, 595
Maybury, Willoughby II, 595
Maybury, Wm. II, 595
Maychim, Sarah Ann III, 300
Maye, Edward I, 313
Maye, Mary I, 313
Mayer, Andrew II, 898
Mayer, Andrew II, 931
Mayer, Andrew III, 223
Mayer, Andrew, Jr. III, 223
Mayer, Andrew, Jr. III, 333
Mayer, August III, 223
Mayer, Augusta III, 223
Mayer, Ella III, 223
Mayer, Ella T. II, 898
Mayer, Ella T. III, 223
Mayer, Ella V. II, 898
Mayer, Emily III, 223
Mayer, Emily III, 359
Mayer, Katharine III, 223
Mayer, Macdonald III, 223
Mayer, MacDonald III, 223
Mayer, Mary A. II, 898
Mayer, Mary A. II, 931
Mayer, Mary A. III, 223
Mayer, Mary L. III, 223
Mayer, Mary L. III, 333
Mayer, Mary Rankin III, 223
Mayer, Mary Virginia III, 223
Mayer, Robert Canfield III, 223
Mayer, Robt. III, 223
Mayer, Wilson Townsend III, 223
Mayers, Ella V. II, 931
Mayes, Ann II, 964
Mayes, Ann II, 1014
Mayes, Ann II, 1028
Mayes, Edward II, 964
Mayes, Edward II, 965
Mayes, Jacob IV, 420
Mayes, Jacob IV, 446
Mayes, Joseph II, 965
Mayes, Mary II, 964
Mayes, Mary IV, 420
Mayes, Rachel B. IV, 446
Mayes, Rebecca B. IV, 420
Mayes, Wm. IV, 420
Mayhew, Alanson VI, 973
Mayhew, Alanson VI, 976
Mayhew, Alex VI, 895
Mayhew, Alexander VI, 959
Mayhew, Catharine J. VI, 999
Mayhew, Charles III, 426
Mayhew, Ellen E. III, 426
Mayhew, Frances VI, 1016
Mayhew, Francis VI, 937
Mayhew, Francis VI, 959
Mayhew, Francis VI, 1018
Mayhew, George VI, 956
Mayhew, George VI, 959
Mayhew, George VI, 1017
Mayhew, Given VI, 973
Mayhew, Grace V, 1009
Mayhew, Guiney VI, 959
Mayhew, James VI, 959
Mayhew, James VI, 976
Mayhew, James VI, 999
Mayhew, John V, 1009
Mayhew, John VI, 959
Mayhew, John VI, 964
Mayhew, Jonah W. III, 426
Mayhew, Lou V, 1009
Mayhew, Lydda VI, 959
Mayhew, Margaret E. VI, 956
Mayhew, Mary VI, 959
Mayhew, Mary Ann III, 426
Mayhew, Mary Ann VI, 976
Mayhew, Moses VI, 959
Mayhew, Moses VI, 1017
Mayhew, Nancey VI, 895
Mayhew, Nancy VI, 895
Mayhew, Nancy VI, 937
Mayhew, Nancy VI, 959
Mayhew, Nancy VI, 973
Mayhew, Nancy, Sr. VI, 959
Mayhew, Pearl V, 1009
Mayhew, Pearle V, 1009
Mayhew, Reason VI, 959
Mayhew, Rebecca VI, 959
Mayhew, Rebecca VI, 1016
Mayhew, Sarah VI, 959
Mayhew, William M. VI, 959
Mayhew, Zora V, 1009
Mayhue, Hannah IV, 1173
Mayhue, Hannah IV, 1191
Mayhugh, John VI, 1017
Maylen, Sarah V, 921
Maylin, Sarah II, 755
Maylin, Sarah IV, 100
Maylin, Thomas II, 755
Maylor, Mattie V, 349
Maylor, Wm. V, 349
Maynard, Charles IV, 739
Maynard, Cornelia III, 223
Maynard, Cornelia III, 349
Maynard, Edwin III, 223
Maynard, Edwin III, 349
Maynard, Henry I, 362
Maynard, Henry VI, 533
Maynard, Lucy E. VI, 839
Maynard, Rachel I, 362
Maynard, Sarah VI, 533
Maynard, Soporah VI, 533
Maynard, Stith VI, 839
Maynard, Susanna I, 362
Maynard, Susannah VI, 533
Maynard, Susannah, Jr. VI, 533
Mayner, ??? I Sup 1, 12
Mayner, Ann I, 408
Mayner, Ann I, 424
Mayner, Betty I, 408
Mayner, Henry I, 344
Mayner, Henry I, 362
Mayner, Henry I, 398
Mayner, Henry I, 408
Mayner, Henry I Sup 1, 8
Mayner, Jane I, 372
Mayner, Jane I, 398
Mayner, Jane I, 408
Mayner, Jane N. VI, 115
Mayner, Jean I Sup 1, 8
Mayner, Mary I, 408
Mayner, Phillip I, 408
Mayner, Rachel I, 344
Mayner, Rachel I, 362
Mayner, Rachel I, 408
Mayner, Susanna I, 362
Mayner, Susanna I, 408
Mayner, Susannah VI, 530
Maynor, Ann I, 366
Maynor, Henry I, 343
Maynor, Henry I, 346
Maynor, Henry I, 366
Maynor, Henry I, 408
Maynor, Henry VI, 464
Maynor, Jane I, 366
Maynor, Mary I, 346
Maynor, Mary I, 374
Maynor, Mary I, 408
Maynor, Rachel I, 408
Maynor, Rachel I, 413
Maynor, Sarah VI, 474
Maynor, Susanna I, 346
Maynor, Susanna I, 408
Maynor, Susannah VI, 530
Mayo, ??? I, 279
Mayo, Ann I, 102
Mayo, Asenath I, 291
Mayo, Asenath C. I, 311
Mayo, Asenath C. I, 316
Mayo, Celia I, 304
Mayo, Celia I, 311
Mayo, Charity I, 291
Mayo, Charity I, 308
Mayo, Charity I, 311
Mayo, Edward I, 92
Mayo, Edward I, 102
Mayo, Edward I, 108
Mayo, Edward I, 146
Mayo, Edward I, 291
Mayo, Edward I, 311
Mayo, Edward I Sup 1, 3
Mayo, Edward I Sup 1, 4
Mayo, Edward I Sup 1, 8
Mayo, Edward S. I, 311
Mayo, Edward, Jr. I, 102
Mayo, Elisabeth I, 13
Mayo, Elisabeth I, 37
Mayo, Elisabeth I, 59
Mayo, Elisabeth I, 62
Mayo, Elizabeth I, 102
Mayo, Elizabeth I Sup 1, 7
Mayo, Ezekiel T. I, 311
Mayo, Hannah II, 242
Mayo, Hannah II, 260
Mayo, Jesse I, 291
Mayo, Jesse I, 304
Mayo, Jesse I, 311
Mayo, Jesse T. I, 291
Mayo, John I, 102
Mayo, John I, 291
Mayo, John I, 311
Mayo, John I, 317
Mayo, John I Sup 1, 8
Mayo, John Exum I, 311
Mayo, Jonathan I, 291
Mayo, Joseph I, 13
Mayo, Joseph I, 54
Mayo, Joseph I, 59
Mayo, Joseph I, 62
Mayo, Joseph I, 66
Mayo, Joseph I, 73
Mayo, Joseph I, 78
Mayo, Joseph I, 102
Mayo, Joseph I Sup 1, 7
Mayo, Joseph, Jr. I, 60
Mayo, Joseph, Sr. I, 59
Mayo, Mary I, 59
Mayo, Mary I, 73
Mayo, Mary I, 102
Mayo, Mary I, 108
Mayo, Mary I, 146
Mayo, Mary I, 165
Mayo, Mary I, 291
Mayo, Mary I, 311
Mayo, Mary I, 317
Mayo, Mary I Sup 1, 3
Mayo, Mary I Sup 1, 4
Mayo, Mary I Sup 1, 8
Mayo, Mary Newby I, 102
Mayo, Orpha I, 46
Mayo, Orpha I, 60
Mayo, Samuel I, 60
Mayo, Sarah I, 102
Mayo, Sarah I, 291
Mayo, Sarah I, 311
Mayo, Sarah I, 320
Mayo, Thomas I, 311
Mayo, Widow Gormack I, 146
Mayors, Elizabeth VI, 857
Mayors, Philip VI, 857
Mays, Agness VI, 871
Mays, Agness VI, 959
Mays, Ballenger VI, 959
Mays, Bingham VI, 996
Mays, Charlotte VI, 839
Mays, Elijah VI, 880
Mays, Elijah VI, 959
Mays, Elizabeth VI, 943
Mays, Elizabeth VI, 959
Mays, Elizabeth VI, 1021
Mays, Elmira VI, 959
Mays, Fletcher H. VI, 959
Mays, James VI, 871
Mays, James VI, 911
Mays, James VI, 1021
Mays, Jesse VI, 959
Mays, John VI, 880
Mays, John VI, 943
Mays, John VI, 959
Mays, John, Senr. VI, 920
Mays, Joseph May VI, 331
Mays, Joseph W. VI, 959
Mays, Joseph W. VI, 1021
Mays, Juggy VI, 959
Mays, Malinda VI, 959
Mays, Mary Ann VI, 331
Mays, Mary Ann VI, 338
Mays, Mrs. Mary L. VI, 959
Mays, Nancy VI, 880
Mays, Nancy VI, 959
Mays, Nancy A. VI, 959
Mays, Patsey VI, 959
Mays, Richard VI, 920
Mays, Richard VI, 933
Mays, Richard VI, 959
Mays, Robert VI, 959
Mays, Samuel VI, 959
Mays, Susan R. VI, 959
Mays, Susannah VI, 920
Mays, William VI, 839
Mays, William VI, 959
Mays, William L. VI, 871
Mays, William L. VI, 959
Mayse, Ballenger VI, 959
Mayse, Elizabeth VI, 959
Mayse, James VI, 886
Mayse, James VI, 891
Mayse, James VI, 905
Mayse, James VI, 909
Mayse, James VI, 1021
Mayse, James D. K. VI, 905
Mayse, Jesse VI, 959
Mayse, John VI, 880
Mayse, John VI, 943
Mayse, Joseph W. VI, 959
Mayse, Martha VI, 891
Mayse, Mary VI, 911
Mayse, Milley VI, 896
Mayse, Permelia VI, 905
Mayse, Polly VI, 911
Mayse, Rhoda VI, 943
Mayse, Salley VI, 880
Mayse, Susanna VI, 880
Mayse, Synthia VI, 1021
Mayse, William VI, 959
Mayse, William L. VI, 959
Maywhere, Richard V, 1010
Maywhere, Sarah Jane V, 1010
Maze, Rebecca V, 485
Maze, Rebecca V, 516
Mazean, Camille III, 223
Mc Afee, Effie D. III, 30
Mc Afee, Helen D. III, 30
Mc Afee, Jas. R. III, 30
Mc Clellan, Emma III, 100
Mc Clellan, Emma P. III, 100
Mc Donnell, John IV, 111
Mc Donnell, Sabina IV, 111
Mc Gee, Sue VI, 643
Mc Taggart, Margaretta A. III, 462
McAaden, James IV, 98
McAbe, Phebe IV, 581
McAbe, Phebe IV, 587
McAdam, Helana I, 102
McAdam, Helena I, 138
McAdam, James I, 102
McAdam, Jeneta I, 102
McAdam, Joseph I, 102
McAdam, Joseph I, 138
McAdam, Mary I, 102
McAdam, Mary V, 260
McAdams, Helena I, 145
McAdams, James I, 145
McAdams, Joseph I, 59
McAdams, Joseph I, 76
McAdams, Joseph I, 145
McAdams, Mary I, 59
McAdams, Mary I, 76
McAdams, Mary I, 145
McAdams, Mary V, 238
McAdams, Mary V, 260
McAdams, Samuel G. IV, 484
McAden, John Wesley I, 661
McAden, Martitia I, 661
McAden, Robert T. I, 661
McAden, Samuel Hugh I, 661
McAfee, Effie D. III, 212

Afee, Effie L. D. V, 95
Afee, Helen D. III, 212
Afee, Jas. R. III, 212
Affee, Annie III, 212
Affee, Archibald III, 212
Affee, Effie III, 212
Affee, Effie L. III, 212
Affee, Helen III, 212
Affee, James III, 212
Affee, Nancy III, 212
Affee, Renwick III, 212
Alexander, Leroy VI, 952
Alexander, Martha VI, 952
Alister, Ann VI, 836
Alister, Chas. VI, 805
Alister, Thomas B. VI, 805
Allester, William IV, 245
Allester, William E. IV, 245
Allister, Daniel VI, 835
Allister, Edna D. VI, 857
Allister, Eliz III, 489
Allister, Elizabeth VI, 410
Allister, Elizabeth VI, 835
Allister, H., Jr. III, 488
Allister, Henry III, 489
Allister, Henry, Jr. III, 488
Allister, Henry, Jr. III, 489
Allister, James VI, 835
Allister, James S. VI, 952
Allister, John VI, 835
Allister, John, Jr. VI, 822
Allister, John, Jr. VI, 835
Allister, Joseph VI, 835
cAllister, Joseph VI, 865
cAllister, Lydia VI, 952
cAllister, Margaret C. VI, 835
Allister, Mary VI, 835
Allister, Phebe H. III, 488
Allister, Phebe H. III, 490
cAllister, Sarah I, 927
Allister, Sarah VI, 835
cAllister, Sarah L. VI, 952
Allister, Sarah M. III, 489
cAllister, Sarah W. VI, 863
cAllister, Thomas B. VI, 804
cAllister, Thomas B. VI, 848
cAllister, William IV, 245
cAllister, William VI, 835
cAllister, William VI, 860
cAllister, William VI, 952
cAllister, William C. VI, 826
cAllister, William C. VI, 835
cAnnally, ??? III, 365
cAnnally, Mary Jane III, 212
cAnnally, Mary Jane III, 365
cArdle, Mary VI, 952
cArdle, Owen VI, 952
cArter, Colin IV, 977
cArter, Etta IV, 977
cArter, Margaret IV, 977
cArthur, Milton IV, 876
cArtor, Achilles IV, 876
cArtor, Colin IV, 977
cArtor, Etta IV, 977
cArtor, James IV, 885
cArtor, Margaret IV, 944
cArtor, Margaret IV, 957
cArtor, Margaret IV, 977
cArtor, Mary IV, 885
IcArtor, Mary Ann IV, 871
IcArtor, Mary Ann IV, 876
IcArtor, Olivia W. IV, 876
IcArtor, Olivia W. IV, 885
ICarty, Sarah A. II, 1089
IcAtee, James C. IV, 1285
IcAtee, Obedience IV, 1285
IcAuley, Catharine IV, 1373
IcAuley, Catherine IV, 1354
IcAuley, Diana IV, 1373
IcAuley, Elizabeth IV, 1373
IcAuley, Jemima IV, 1373
IcAuley, Jemimah IV, 1373
McAuley, John D. IV, 1373
McAuley, Mariah Carnel IV, 1373
McAuley, Sarah IV, 1356
McAuley, Sarah IV, 1373
McAuley, William Henry IV, 1373
McAuley, Wm. Henry IV, 1373
McAuly, John D. IV, 1373
McBain, Louis IV, 1327
McBaine, Lewis IV, 1327
McBaine, Louis IV, 1327
McBane, Ada E. I, 621
McBane, Alfred N. I, 621
McBane, Camillis I, 438
McBane, Carnilis I, 450
McBane, Caroline I, 438
McBane, Caroline I, 450
McBane, Cornelis I, 450
McBane, Edgar I, 637
McBane, Edgar Holt I, 621
McBane, Flora I, 245
McBane, Florence I, 245
McBane, George Grant I, 450
McBane, Lenora I, 450
McBane, Mary I, 922
McBane, Pearl I, 621
McBane, Pearl I, 637
McBane, Pearl I, 643
McBane, Rachel III, 406
McBane, Sarah I, 449
McBane, Sarah I, 450
McBane, Sarah Margaret I, 621
McBane, Sarah Margaret I, 637
McBane, William I, 450
McBane, William M. I, 450
McBane, William Malon I, 438
McBee, Vardry VI, 331
McBeth, Sarah V, 656
McBeth, Sarah V, 692
McBride, ??? IV, 795
McBride, Abisha IV, 642
McBride, Abisha IV, 736
McBride, Abisha IV, 876
McBride, Abishai IV, 642
McBride, Abishai IV, 736
McBride, Abraham IV, 736
McBride, Abraham IV, 832
McBride, Abraham IV, 909
McBride, Abraham VI, 419
McBride, Albert IV, 910
McBride, Albert V, 582
McBride, Albert B. V, 692
McBride, Andrew IV, 736
McBride, Andrew IV, 832
McBride, Andrew IV, 909
McBride, Andrew VI, 419
McBride, Ann IV, 245
McBride, Ann IV, 736
McBride, Ann IV, 859
McBride, Ann IV, 909
McBride, Ann IV, 910
McBride, Ann IV, 1172
McBride, Ann IV, 1181
McBride, Ann IV, 1215
McBride, Ann VI, 406
McBride, Ann VI, 418
McBride, Anna I, 891
McBride, Anna I, 903
McBride, Benjamin IV, 642
McBride, Benjamin IV, 736
McBride, Benjamin IV, 876
McBride, Benjamin IV, 910
McBride, Benjamin IV, 1172
McBride, Benjamin Stanton IV, 484
McBride, Betsy IV, 484
McBride, Betsy IV, 498
McBride, Betsy IV, 832
McBride, Betsy IV, 909
McBride, Betsy IV, 916
McBride, Betty IV, 736
McBride, Betty IV, 909
McBride, Betty VI, 419
McBride, Charity IV, 736
McBride, Charity IV, 756
McBride, Charity IV, 909
McBride, Charity IV, 910
McBride, Charles VI, 953
McBride, Charles VI, 966
McBride, David IV, 910
McBride, David IV, 1172
McBride, David E. IV, 909
McBride, Elihu IV, 642
McBride, Elihu IV, 876
McBride, Elihu IV, 910
McBride, Elihu IV, 1172
McBride, Eliza IV, 1172
McBride, Elizabeth IV, 641
McBride, Elizabeth IV, 642
McBride, Elizabeth IV, 736
McBride, Elizabeth IV, 798
McBride, Elizabeth IV, 832
McBride, Elizabeth IV, 849
McBride, Elizabeth IV, 876
McBride, Elizabeth IV, 909
McBride, Elizabeth IV, 910
McBride, Elizabeth IV, 1172
McBride, Elizabeth VI, 953
McBride, Elvira Ann V, 246
McBride, Elvira Ann V, 260
McBride, Emily VI, 953
McBride, Evan IV, 736
McBride, Evan IV, 832
McBride, Evan IV, 837
McBride, Evan IV, 909
McBride, Evan VI, 419
McBride, Flora V, 1007
McBride, Frances IV, 1040
McBride, Frances VI, 835
McBride, George V, 752
McBride, Gideon IV, 909
McBride, Grace IV, 245
McBride, Grace IV, 258
McBride, Grace IV, 642
McBride, Grace IV, 736
McBride, Grace IV, 876
McBride, Grace IV, 910
McBride, Grace IV, 1172
McBride, Hannah IV, 642
McBride, Hannah IV, 657
McBride, Hannah IV, 736
McBride, Hannah IV, 829
McBride, Hannah IV, 832
McBride, Hannah IV, 859
McBride, Hannah IV, 908
McBride, Hannah IV, 909
McBride, Hannah IV, 910
McBride, Hannah IV, 916
McBride, Hannah IV, 1172
McBride, Hannah VI, 406
McBride, Hannah VI, 418
McBride, Hannah VI, 419
McBride, Hannah VI, 455
McBride, Hannah S. IV, 909
McBride, Isaac IV, 910
McBride, Isaac IV, 1172
McBride, Isaac V. IV, 909
McBride, J. S. V, 1007
McBride, Jacob H. IV, 909
McBride, Jame IV, 910
McBride, James IV, 642
McBride, James IV, 736
McBride, James IV, 798
McBride, James IV, 832
McBride, James IV, 876
McBride, James IV, 909
McBride, James IV, 910
McBride, James IV, 1172
McBride, James VI, 418
McBride, James VI, 953
McBride, James L. VI, 959
McBride, James, Jr. IV, 641
McBride, James, Sr. IV, 641
McBride, Jane IV, 832
McBride, Jane IV, 837
McBride, Jane IV, 909
McBride, Jane IV, 977
McBride, Jane IV, 987
McBride, Jeremiah IV, 736
McBride, Jeremiah IV, 832
McBride, Jeremiah IV, 849
McBride, Jeremiah IV, 909
McBride, Jeremiah IV, 1172
McBride, Jeremiah IV, 1216
McBride, Jeremiah VI, 418
McBride, Jesse IV, 910
McBride, Jesse IV, 1172
McBride, Jesse B. IV, 909
McBride, Jesse B. IV, 910
McBride, John IV, 736
McBride, John IV, 909
McBride, John IV, 910
McBride, John IV, 1172
McBride, John IV, 1181
McBride, John IV, 1215
McBride, John IV, 1257
McBride, John V, 582
McBride, John V, 692
McBride, John V, 752
McBride, John VI, 418
McBride, John VI, 953
McBride, Joseph IV, 977
McBride, Joseph IV, 986
McBride, Joseph IV, 1172
McBride, Joseph IV, 1215
McBride, Joseph VI, 835
McBride, Joseph P. IV, 909
McBride, Joseph P. IV, 977
McBride, Joshua IV, 909
McBride, Joshua IV, 910
McBride, Katy VI, 953
McBride, Lydia IV, 642
McBride, Lydia IV, 736
McBride, Lydia IV, 876
McBride, Lydia IV, 910
McBride, Lydia IV, 1172
McBride, Mahlon IV, 909
McBride, Margaret IV, 909
McBride, Margery IV, 906
McBride, Margery IV, 909
McBride, Margety IV, 910
McBride, Maria IV, 812
McBride, Maria IV, 832
McBride, Maria IV, 909
McBride, Maria IV, 1172
McBride, Maria IV, 1181
McBride, Martha IV, 1257
McBride, Martha V, 582
McBride, Martha V, 692
McBride, Martha A. IV, 1257
McBride, Martha A. V, 582
McBride, Mary IV, 736
McBride, Mary IV, 832
McBride, Mary IV, 838
McBride, Mary IV, 853
McBride, Mary IV, 909
McBride, Mary IV, 910
McBride, Mary IV, 912
McBride, Mary V, 582
McBride, Mary A. IV, 909
McBride, Mary A. IV, 910
McBride, Mary A. IV, 986
McBride, Mary Ann IV, 906
McBride, Mary Ann IV, 909
McBride, Mary C. V, 692
McBride, Mary F. VI, 835
McBride, Mattie V, 582
McBride, Melissa V, 1007
McBride, Mildred R. IV, 909
McBride, Mildred R. IV, 977
McBride, Moses IV, 909
McBride, Nancy VI, 914
McBride, Nancy VI, 938
McBride, Nancy VI, 953
McBride, Obediah VI, 914
McBride, Phebe IV, 622
McBride, Phebe IV, 642
McBride, Phebe VI, 953
McBride, Polly VI, 973
McBride, Rachel IV, 642
McBride, Rachel IV, 736
McBride, Rachel IV, 859
McBride, Rachel IV, 876
McBride, Rachel IV, 908
McBride, Rachel IV, 909
McBride, Rachel IV, 910
McBride, Rebecca IV, 900
McBride, Rebecca IV, 909
McBride, Rebecca IV, 910
McBride, Rebecca IV, 1172
McBride, Rebecca IV, 1215
McBride, Rebecca IV, 1222
McBride, Ruth IV, 736
McBride, Ruth IV, 910
McBride, Ruth IV, 1172
McBride, Samuel IV, 736
McBride, Samuel IV, 832
McBride, Samuel IV, 909
McBride, Samuel VI, 419
McBride, Sarah IV, 909
McBride, Sarah VI, 953
McBride, Sarah J. VI, 959
McBride, Sidney J. IV, 909
McBride, Stephen IV, 736
McBride, Stephen IV, 756
McBride, Stephen IV, 897
McBride, Stephen IV, 909
McBride, Stephen IV, 977
McBride, Stephen IV, 987
McBride, Stephen VI, 406
McBride, Stephen VI, 418
McBride, Stephen VI, 953
McBride, Stephen VI, 959
McBride, Stephen, Jr. IV, 736
McBride, Stephen, Jr. VI, 419
McBride, Susanna IV, 909
McBride, Susanna IV, 977
McBride, Susanna IV, 986
McBride, Thomas VI, 914
McBride, Thomas VI, 953
McBride, Thomas VI, 973
McBride, William VI, 953
McBride, William T. V, 692
McBride, Willie V, 582
McBride, Wm. V, 582
McBride, Zella V, 1007
McBroome, Mary Catharine IV, 418
McBroome, Mary Catharine IV, 449
McCabe, Ann W. VI, 835
McCabe, Catharine VI, 992
McCabe, Cleopatra A. VI, 953
McCabe, Elizabeth VI, 880
McCabe, George W. VI, 953
McCabe, John VI, 880
McCabe, John VI, 937
McCabe, John VI, 953
McCabe, John VI, 992
McCabe, John VI, 997
McCabe, Juliann VI, 953
McCabe, L. Octavia VI, 968
McCabe, Malinda VI, 953
McCabe, Malinda VI, 968
McCabe, Margaret VI, 419
McCabe, Margaret VI, 456
McCabe, Sarah VI, 997
McCabe, Sarah Elizabeth VI, 967
McCabe, Sarah J. VI, 953
McCabe, Susannah VI, 953
McCabe, Thomas VI, 953
McCabe, William VI, 835
McCabe, William VI, 953
McCabe, William VI, 967
McCadden, Ann IV, 98
McCadden, Elizabeth IV, 98
McCadden, James IV, 98
McCadden, John IV, 98
McCaddin, Elizabeth IV, 98
McCaddin, John IV, 98
McCaddon, Elizabeth IV, 46
McCaddon, Elizabeth IV, 58
McCaddon, John IV, 46
McCaddon, John IV, 58
McCaha, Sarah A. VI, 975
McCain, Ann V, 752
McCain, Forister I, 595
McCain, Harrison V, 752
McCain, Rebecca I, 595
McCaine, Ann V, 752
McCaine, Harrison V, 752
McCalahanan, Thomas VI, 945
McCalam, William VI, 982
McCalanaham, William VI, 879
McCalanahan, Frances VI, 889
McCalanahan, Martha VI, 945
McCaleb, Sarah A. VI, 835
McCaleb, William VI, 835
McCall, Alice II, 462
McCall, Alice II, 588
McCall, Alice IV, 30
McCall, Alice IV, 46
McCall, Alice IV, 893
McCall, Anna V, 347
McCall, Della V, 342
McCall, Della V, 347
McCall, Dorcas V, 411
McCall, Eleanor IV, 46
McCall, Elizabeth IV, 46
McCall, Elizabeth IV, 69
McCall, Elizabeth IV, 893
McCall, George IV, 46
McCall, Hannah II, 53
McCall, Hannah II, 85
McCall, Hannah IV, 893
McCall, Jane IV, 46
McCall, John IV, 30
McCall, John IV, 46
McCall, John V, 411
McCall, Josiah IV, 893
McCall, Lucy IV, 1285
McCall, Lydia IV, 868
McCall, Lydia IV, 876
McCall, Margaret V, 411
McCall, Marion V, 847
McCall, Martha Jane IV, 1052
McCall, Martha Jane IV, 1066
McCall, Mary IV, 24
McCall, Mary IV, 46
McCall, Mary IV, 1105
McCall, Mary V, 692
McCall, Mary Ann IV, 1054
McCall, Mary Ann IV, 1066
McCall, Mary Susanna V, 411
McCall, Matilda IV, 46
McCall, Naomi IV, 511
McCall, Naomi IV, 539
McCall, Ruth IV, 30
McCall, Ruth IV, 46
McCall, Ruth IV, 893
McCall, Sarah IV, 30
McCall, Sarah IV, 46
McCall, Solomon IV, 46
McCall, Thomas III, 212
McCall, Thomas IV, 46
McCall, William IV, 46
McCall, William IV, 69
McCall, William V, 411
McCall, William Elliott IV, 46
McCall, Wm. II, 462
McCall, Wm. II, 588
McCall, Wm. IV, 1285
McCallam, Mahala V, 788
McCallester, Polly VI, 835
McCallester, William VI, 835
McCalley, Catharine IV, 1373
McCallister, James VI, 835
McCallister, Mary VI, 835
McCallock, Rachel II, 392
McCallough, Sara II, 588
McCallum, ??? III, 84
McCallum, Anthrina IV, 672
McCallum, Catharine III, 84
McCallum, Duncan IV, 672
McCallum, Pauline IV, 672
McCamish, Ann II, 588
McCamish, Anne VI, 835
McCamish, James VI, 835
McCammish, Carl V, 692
McCammish, Carl V, 700
McCammish, Cordelia V, 692
McCammish, Cordelia V, 700
McCammish, Cordelia Murrell V, 692

McCammon, Bueda IV, 736
McCammon, Edith IV, 736
McCammon, Edith L. IV, 736
McCammon, Jane II, 808
McCammon, Katharine IV, 736
McCammon, Oscar L. IV, 736
McCammon, Richard II, 808
McCammon, Sylvanus IV, 736
McCammon, Wd. Margaret II, 808
McCan, Alta IV, 736
McCan, Betsy VI, 953
McCan, Daniel VI, 905
McCan, Daniel VI, 953
McCan, Daniel VI, 1021
McCan, Ediah VI, 905
McCan, Elisabeth I, 825
McCan, Elizabeth I, 825
McCan, Elizabeth I, 1011
McCan, Elizabeth VI, 905
McCan, John VI, 889
McCan, John VI, 939
McCan, Mary VI, 939
McCan, Sally VI, 889
McCan, Tacy IV, 245
McCan, Tacy IV, 736
McCandry, John VI, 953
McCandry, Michael VI, 953
McCandry, Nelly VI, 953
McCane, Margaret I, 1001
McCane, Sarah IV, 390
McCane, Sarah IV, 418
McCanley, Nara IV, 1040
McCann, Abraham Davis IV, 46
McCann, Anna IV, 1327
McCann, Betsy VI, 953
McCann, Daniel VI, 953
McCann, Danl. VI, 908
McCann, Edward IV, 46
McCann, Elizabeth I, 450
McCann, Elizabeth VI, 953
McCann, Ellis IV, 46
McCann, Estella IV, 977
McCann, Estella IV, 1003
McCann, Hannah IV, 46
McCann, Jennie IV, 1257
McCann, Josie IV, 1257
McCann, Julia IV, 1257
McCann, Lydia VI, 1021
McCann, Martha A. IV, 1257
McCann, Martha Alberta IV, 1257
McCann, Mary IV, 1257
McCann, Myrtle IV, 1327
McCann, Nelson VI, 953
McCann, Phebe IV, 46
McCann, Polly VI, 953
McCann, Rachel IV, 46
McCann, Sarah IV, 1097
McCann, Sarah IV, 1105
McCann, Tacy IV, 28
McCann, Tacy IV, 46
McCann, Tacy IV, 98
McCann, Tacy VI, 485
McCann, Tacy VI, 486
McCann, Tacy VI, 529
McCann, William VI, 953
McCarger, L. E. IV, 1285
McCarger, Leslie E. IV, 1285
McCargo, David VI, 835
McCargo, Hugh VI, 1006
McCargo, Kitty Miller VI, 1006
McCargo, Nancy VI, 835
McCarson, Sara II, 136
McCarta, Hannah VI, 419
McCartae, Elizabeth III, 286
McCartee, Febey VI, 888
McCarter, Atchalus IV, 876
McCarter, Chalkley T. IV, 876
McCarter, Collin B. IV, 876
McCarter, Lena Nelson II, 795
McCarter, Lena Nelson II, 865
McCarter, Mary IV, 876
McCarter, Mary E. IV, 736
McCarter, Olivia IV, 876
McCarter, Stella IV, 876
McCarter, Susannah IV, 876
McCarthey, Pauline VI, 770
McCarthy, Abigail IV, 225
McCarthy, Daniel VI, 1002
McCarthy, Elizabeth VI, 1002
McCarthy, Elizabeth M. P. IV, 1327
McCarthy, Hettie Frame V, 186
McCarthy, Matilda VI, 1002
McCartney, Alphia IV, 245
McCartney, Arnold IV, 245
McCartney, David IV, 245
McCartney, Della IV, 245
McCartney, Edwin IV, 245
McCartney, Elana Eliza IV, 404
McCartney, Elana Eliza IV, 418
McCartney, Ella IV, 245
McCartney, Ellen IV, 245
McCartney, George IV, 245
McCartney, Hazel IV, 245
McCartney, James E. IV, 832
McCartney, Josephine E. V, 582
McCartney, Lota IV, 245
McCartney, Mary V, 632
McCartney, Mary S. IV, 832
McCartney, Ola IV, 245
McCartney, Robert IV, 245
McCartney, Walter T. IV, 245
McCartor, Susanna IV, 883
McCarty, Abigail IV, 245
McCarty, Cynthia II, 946
McCarty, Cynthia II, 948
McCarty, Cynthia II, 949
McCarty, Cynthia II, 1086
McCarty, Cynthia II, 1087
McCarty, Cynthia II, 1088
McCarty, David T. IV, 245
McCarty, Edward II, 946
McCarty, Edwin H. IV, 245
McCarty, Elizabeth II, 712
McCarty, Elizabeth IV, 910
McCarty, Elizabeth A. VI, 882
McCarty, Elmer IV, 245
McCarty, Emily IV, 143
McCarty, Emily IV, 153
McCarty, Estella V, 752
McCarty, Hannah II, 240
McCarty, Hannah II, 588
McCarty, Hannah II, 597
McCarty, Hannah IV, 245
McCarty, James VI, 927
McCarty, James W. IV, 832
McCarty, Jane IV, 832
McCarty, Job IV, 832
McCarty, John T. VI, 953
McCarty, Joseph H. II, 946
McCarty, Joseph P. IV, 832
McCarty, Joseph Paxton IV, 832
McCarty, Joshua P. II, 949
McCarty, Joshua R. II, 946
McCarty, Joshua R. II, 948
McCarty, Joshua R. II, 949
McCarty, Joshua R. II, 1087
McCarty, Joshua R. II, 1088
McCarty, Joshua R. II, 1089
McCarty, Lucy IV, 1257
McCarty, Margaret VI, 953
McCarty, Martha L. IV, 832
McCarty, Mary VI, 835
McCarty, Mary Ann IV, 832
McCarty, Mary Hufford IV, 1327
McCarty, Ola IV, 245
McCarty, Oliver C. IV, 832
McCarty, Peggy VI, 1006
McCarty, Rachel IV, 832
McCarty, Rachel E. IV, 832
McCarty, Samuel II, 946
McCarty, Samuel VI, 882
McCarty, Samuel D. VI, 884
McCarty, Samuel D. VI, 979
McCarty, Sara IV, 832
McCarty, Sarah II, 1087
McCarty, Sarah II, 1088
McCarty, Sarah II, 1089
McCarty, Sarah A. II, 949
McCarty, Sarah A. II, 1088
McCarty, Sarah Ann II, 946
McCarty, Sarah Ann VI, 953
McCarty, Sarah Elizabeth IV, 832
McCarty, Silas II, 1087
McCarty, Silas II, 1088
McCarty, Silas II, 1089
McCarty, Silas T. II, 946
McCarty, Sumner F. II, 946
McCarty, Taylor II, 946
McCarty, Thomas VI, 835
McCarty, Thomas H. IV, 832
McCarty, Thomas Heston IV, 832
McCarty, Walter IV, 245
McCarty, Walton IV, 832
McCarty, William VI, 953
McCaskey, Hannah II, 597
McCasky, Alexander II, 588
McCasky, Hannah II, 588
McCasky, Mary IV, 876
McCasky, Mary IV, 881
McCatts, Hannah II, 85
McCaudle, Angie I, 229
McCaudle, Angie I, 245
McCauley, Caroline V, 95
McCauley, Carrie V, 95
McCauley, Diana IV, 1373
McCauley, Elizabeth IV, 1373
McCauley, Grace VI, 74
McCauley, Jemimah IV, 1373
McCauley, William Henry IV, 1373
McCaulley, Charles III, 200
McCaulley, Charles III, 212
McCaulley, Frances II, 717
McCaulley, Jane III, 200
McCaulley, Jane III, 212
McCaully, Emily J. VI, 363
McCaully, Emily J. VI, 419
McCawley, Edward VI, 835
McCawley, Polly VI, 835
McCay, Ella C. II, 893
McCay, Martha N. V, 95
McCay, Rachel V, 490
McCay, Rachel V, 513
MccFarland, Alexander I, 1158
MccFarland, James I, 1158
MccFarland, John I, 1158
McChere, Maggie V, 1007
McChristie, Jennie V, 1007
McChristre, Jennie V, 1007
McCinne, Bettey I, 557
McCinne, Birim I, 557
McCinne, Frances I, 557
McCinne, James I, 557
McCinne, John I, 557
McCinne, Shdarack I, 557
McCinne, William I, 557
McClain, Cora E. IV, 484
McClain, Creed VI, 953
McClain, Elizabeth VI, 905
McClain, Elizabeth VI, 953
McClain, Frederick F. IV, 977
McClain, Haley VI, 958
McClain, Isabel IV, 484
McClain, Isabella IV, 484
McClain, James VI, 905
McClain, James VI, 951
McClain, James VI, 953
McClain, James VI, 959
McClain, Jesse I, 966
McClain, John I, 966
McClain, John IV, 484
McClain, John VI, 912
McClain, John VI, 953
McClain, John VI, 960
McClain, John W. VI, 953
McClain, Letitia VI, 953
McClain, Lewis I, 966
McClain, Mary V, 260
McClain, Mary V, 275
McClain, Mordecia VI, 927
McClain, Noah C. IV, 484
McClain, Rachel VI, 958
McClain, Rebecca IV, 484
McClain, Rhoda VI, 905
McClain, Saml. VI, 914
McClain, Samuel I, 966
McClain, Sarah F. VI, 953
McClain, Theodate IV, 418
McClain, William IV, 418
McClain, William VI, 905
McClain, William B. IV, 484
McClain, Wm. H. IV, 1257
McClamrock, Dora I, 621
McClamrock, L. E. I, 637
McClamrock, Lemuel D. I, 621
McClamrock, Lemuel E. I, 621
McClanahan, Absalom VI, 890
McClanahan, Adaley Willis VI, 953
McClanahan, Alexander VI, 953
McClanahan, Elijah VI, 953
McClanahan, Eliza VI, 835
McClanahan, Elizabeth VI, 953
McClanahan, Frances VI, 953
McClanahan, Francis Campbell VI, 968
McClanahan, James VI, 835
McClanahan, James VI, 953
McClanahan, Lucinda VI, 968
McClanahan, Mary VI, 890
McClanahan, Rachell VI, 907
McClanahan, Sarah VI, 1011
McClanahan, Sarah M. VI, 953
McClanahan, Thomas VI, 953
McClanahan, Thomas VI, 997
McClanahan, William VI, 953
McClanahan, William, Jr. VI, 953
McClanahan, Wm., Sr. VI, 953
McClane, Catharine C. II, 1055
McClane, Sarah VI, 960
McClane, Wm. H. IV, 1257
McClard, John VI, 953
McClard, Phillis VI, 953
McClaren, Josie V, 347
McClaren, Roy V, 347
McClarey, Catharine VI, 964
McClarey, Eliza IV, 324
McClarey, Eliza IV, 341
McClary, Eliza IV, 380
McClary, Eliza IV, 418
McClary, Elizabeth IV, 1147
McClary, Elizabeth IV, 1172
McClary, Elizabeth VI, 889
McClary, Rachel I, 1124
McClary, Rachel VI, 429
McClaskey, James VI, 953
McClaskey, Mary Ann VI, 953
McClay, Donald III, 212
McClay, Euphemia III, 212
McClay, Sarah IV, 46
McClay, Sarah IV, 69
McClean, Ann II, 240
McClean, Anna II, 240
McClean, Charles II, 240
McClean, Clarence F. IV, 1327
McClean, Clarence G. IV, 1327
McClean, Hannah II, 240
McCleary, Alexander V, 1008
McCleary, Chas. V, 1007
McCleary, James V, 1007
McCleary, James V, 1008
McCleary, Lucy A. V, 1007
McCleary, Rachel I, 1095
McCleary, Rachel I, 1124
McClehan, William VI, 890
McClellan, Emma III, 212
McClellan, Emma P. III, 212
McClellan, Mary B. III, 270
McClelland, George IV, 297
McClelland, Sarah VI, 666
McClelland, Sarah A. VI, 408
McClelland, Wm. B. VI, 666
McClellen, Charlotte Emily III, 426
McClellen, John III, 426
McClellen, John V, 973
McClellen, Phebe Emily III, 426
McClemcey, John W. I, 337
McClenachan, Catharine VI, 1017
McClenachan, John VI, 953
McClenachan, Mary VI, 953
McClenachan, Thomas VI, 1017
McClenney, ??? I, 337
McClenney, Eliza I, 337
McClenney, Eliza Jane I, 337
McClenney, Essie Mildred I, 337
McClenney, Eunice Irene I, 337
McClenney, James W. I, 337
McClenney, John I, 337
McClenney, John E. I, 337
McClenney, Luther Carl I, 337
McClenney, Margaret Alice I, 337
McClenney, Minnie Viola I, 337
McClenney, Sallie I, 337
McClenney, Samuel Festus I, 337
McClenney, Sarah Elizabeth I, 337
McClenny, Eva L. VI, 76
McClenny, Sallie I, 337
McCletche, Amey II, 240
McCletche, James II, 240
McClintock, Ann II, 240
Mcclintock, Ann II, 274
McClintock, Catharine VI, 953
McClintock, Edwin M. V, 347
McClintock, Elizabeth VI, 953
McClintock, Irwin IV, 1327
McClintock, James D. V, 347
McClintock, James N. V, 347
McClintock, John VI, 953
McClintock, Lee VI, 953
McClintock, Mary II, 240
Mcclintock, Mary II, 274
McClintock, Mary Ann II, 240
McClintock, Mary Ann II, 824
McClintock, Maud A. IV, 1327
McClintock, Nellie T. V, 347
McClintock, Phebe Ann III, 26
McClintock, Phebe Ann III, 339
McClintock, Priscilla IV, 1327
McClintock, Rachel V, 347
McClintock, Sarah II, 879
McClintock, Sarah II, 893
McClintock, Sarah II, 894
McClintock, Thomas II, 240
Mcclintock, Thomas II, 274
McClintock, Thos. II, 807
McClintock, Thos. II, 824
McClintock, Wd. Mary Ann II, 807
McClinton, Edwin M. V, 347
McClinton, James D. V, 347
McClinton, James M. V, 347
McClinton, James N. V, 347
McClinton, Kate E. V, 347
McClinton, Nellie T. V, 347
McClinton, Rachel V, 347
McCloskey, Fannie IV, 1327
McCloskey, Will IV, 1327
McCloskey, Wm. IV, 1327
McCloud, Effa C. IV, 1172
McCloud, Effie IV, 1172
McCloud, Elizabeth VI, 835
McCloud, Leona IV, 1257
McCloud, Lulu IV, 1172
McCloud, Lulu IV, 1257
McCloud, Lulu W. IV, 1172
McCloud, Pearl IV, 1172
McCloud, Pearl IV, 1257
McCloud, Pearl B. IV, 1172
McCloud, Robert VI, 835
McCloy, Amelia III, 212
McCloy, Helen W. III, 71
McCloy, Helen W. III, 212
McCloy, Helen W. C., Jr. III, 21
McCloy, Sarah VI, 400
McCloy, Sarah VI, 419
McCloy, Wm. III, 212
McCloy, Wm. C. III, 71
McCloy, Wm. C. III, 212
McCluer, Betsey VI, 987
McCluer, Lydia IV, 695
McCluer, Lydia IV, 736
McCluer, Martha VI, 943
McCluer, William VI, 943
McCluer, William VI, 987
McCluggage, Clara IV, 736
McCluggage, Effie Amelia IV, 9
McCluggage, Enoch IV, 832
McCluggage, Eva IV, 832
McCluggage, Gladys J. IV, 736
McCluggage, Joseph IV, 736
McCluggage, Lawrence IV, 736
McClun Bond, Carrie D. VI, 41
McClun Bond, Walker VI, 417
McClun, Cynthia IV, 605
McClun, Cynthia IV, 642
McClun, Cynthia VI, 674
McClun, David VI, 674
McClun, Elisabeth VI, 419
McClun, Elizabeth IV, 605
McClun, Elizabeth IV, 642
McClun, Elizabeth IV, 662
McClun, Elizabeth VI, 469
McClun, Elizabeth VI, 529
McClun, Elizabeth VI, 674
McClun, Folio VI, 673
McClun, Hannah IV, 605
McClun, Hannah VI, 363
McClun, Hannah VI, 366
McClun, Hannah VI, 419
McClun, Hannah VI, 428
McClun, Hannah VI, 469
McClun, Hannah VI, 529
McClun, Hannah VI, 673
McClun, Hannah VI, 674
McClun, Huldah VI, 673
McClun, Huldah VI, 674
McClun, Isaac VI, 674
McClun, James VI, 624
McClun, James VI, 673
McClun, John IV, 605
McClun, John IV, 642
McClun, John IV, 662
McClun, John VI, 419
McClun, John VI, 469
McClun, John VI, 529
McClun, John VI, 600
McClun, John VI, 674
McClun, Jonathan VI, 419
McClun, Joseph Beal VI, 674
McClun, Lydia VI, 366
McClun, Lydia VI, 419
McClun, Martha VI, 469
McClun, Martha VI, 529
McClun, Martha L. VI, 632
McClun, Martha L. VI, 674
McClun, Mary VI, 363
McClun, Mary VI, 366
McClun, Mary VI, 419
McClun, Mary VI, 600
McClun, Mary VI, 624
McClun, Mary VI, 673
McClun, Mary VI, 674
McClun, Nathan VI, 419
McClun, Rachel IV, 642
McClun, Rachel IV, 662
McClun, Rachel VI, 416
McClun, Rachel VI, 419
McClun, Rachel VI, 674
McClun, Sarah IV, 605
McClun, Sarah VI, 673
McClun, Sarah VI, 674
McClun, Sarah VI, 710
McClun, Sarah VI, 714
McClun, Susan VI, 674
McClun, Susan VI, 723
McClun, Thomas IV, 642
McClun, Thomas VI, 363
McClun, Thomas VI, 366
McClun, Thomas VI, 419
McClun, Thomas VI, 428

Clun, Thomas VI, 469
Clun, Thomas VI, 529
Clun, Thomas VI, 674
Clun, Yarel Benj. VI, 674
Cluney, Isabella VI, 953
Cluney, John VI, 953
Cluney, William VI, 953
Clung, Arminta I, 621
Clung, Arminta A. I, 637
Clung, Arminta Ann I, 611
Clung, Elliott A. I, 611
Clung, Elliott A. I, 621
Clung, Lucile I, 621
Clung, Lucille I, 637
Clung, Matilda I, 637
Clung, Matilda Mae I, 621
Clunn, Cinthia IV, 642
Clunn, Cynthia IV, 642
Clunn, Elizabeth IV, 642
Clunn, Hannah IV, 642
Clunn, Isaac IV, 642
Clunn, John IV, 642
Clunn, Joseph B. IV, 642
Clunn, Joseph Beal IV, 642
Clunn, Mary VI, 600
Clunn, Rachel IV, 642
Clunn, Sarah IV, 642
Clunn, Thomas IV, 642
Clure, ??? III, 212
Clure, Aaron I, 1158
Clure, Abel IV, 876
Clure, Abel T. IV, 539
Clure, Abel T. IV, 642
Clure, Abel T. IV, 876
Clure, Agnes III, 212
Clure, Agnes III, 306
Clure, Alice V, 260
Clure, Allie V, 260
Clure, Ann IV, 47
Clure, Ann VI, 953
Clure, Arthur J. V, 260
Clure, Cynthia T. IV, 637
Clure, Cynthia T. IV, 642
Clure, Daniel IV, 47
Clure, David I, 1158
Clure, Diana V, 1008
Clure, Edith L. I, 1158
Clure, Edna M. III, 212
Clure, Edna M. III, 269
Clure, Edward IV, 47
Clure, Elijah I, 1158
Clure, Eliza H. III, 212
Clure, Ella V, 1008
Clure, Emma V, 1008
Clure, Endley IV, 642
Clure, Endley IV, 876
Clure, Endly IV, 876
Clure, Gertie V, 260
Clure, Gertrude W. V, 260
Clure, Graham III, 212
Clure, Graham T. III, 306
Clure, Graham Traquain III, 212
Clure, Hannah IV, 642
Clure, Hannah V, 1008
Clure, Harry V, 260
Clure, Henneretta V, 1008
Clure, Henrietta V, 1008
Clure, Jacob I, 1034
Clure, James IV, 47
Clure, James VI, 953
Clure, James Graham III, 212
Clure, Jane V, 632
Clure, Jas. T. III, 212
Clure, Jesse IV, 47
Clure, John I, 1034
Clure, John V, 95
Clure, John V, 1008
Clure, John P. V, 1008
Clure, Joseph IV, 642
Clure, Joseph IV, 876
Clure, Joseph V, 260
Clure, Joseph V, 919
Clure, Joseph V, 1008
Clure, Joseph A. V, 260
Clure, Levi IV, 47
Clure, Levi Hackney I, 1158
Clure, Louisa IV, 642
Clure, Louisa IV, 650
Clure, Louisa IV, 651
Clure, Louisa IV, 876
Clure, Louisa IV, 1105
Clure, Louisa IV, 1109
Clure, Louisa V, 1008
Clure, Lovina V, 1008
Clure, Lydia IV, 619
Clure, Lydia IV, 642
Clure, Lydia IV, 876
Clure, Maggie V, 1008
Clure, Malinda J. V, 260
Clure, Margaret I, 1034
McClure, Margery I, 1034
McClure, Margery V, 83
McClure, Margery V, 95
McClure, Margery V, 790
McClure, Marion V, 260
McClure, Marion C. V, 260
McClure, Marjorie V, 760
McClure, Mary I, 1034
McClure, Mary IV, 642
McClure, Mary IV, 650
McClure, Mary IV, 661
McClure, Mary IV, 876
McClure, Mary V, 24
McClure, Mary V, 95
McClure, Mary V, 1008
McClure, Mathew IV, 1105
McClure, Mira S. IV, 642
McClure, Moses V, 1008
McClure, Myra IV, 876
McClure, Myra S. IV, 876
McClure, Nathan V, 1008
McClure, Rachel IV, 47
McClure, Robert I, 1034
McClure, Robert IV, 46
McClure, Robert V, 95
McClure, Robert V, 760
McClure, Robert V, 788
McClure, Robert V, 790
McClure, Robert T. V, 260
McClure, Rosanna V, 95
McClure, Rosanna V, 760
McClure, Rosanna V, 762
McClure, Rosanna V, 794
McClure, Rosannah V, 790
McClure, Rosella A. V, 1008
McClure, Rozella V, 1008
McClure, Sadie V, 260
McClure, Sally VI, 953
McClure, Samuel IV, 637
McClure, Samuel IV, 642
McClure, Samuel IV, 876
McClure, Samuel VI, 953
McClure, Samuel VI, 1003
McClure, Sarah IV, 47
McClure, Sarah V, 260
McClure, Seth IV, 650
McClure, Seth IV, 876
McClure, Seth C. IV, 876
McClure, Seth, Jr. IV, 642
McClure, Seth, Jr. IV, 876
McClure, Sina Ann IV, 876
McClure, Sinah Ann IV, 642
McClure, Sinai Ann IV, 876
McClure, Taylor V, 260
McClure, Thomas T. III, 212
McClure, William VI, 953
McClure, Wm. V, 1008
McClure, Wm. H. V, 1008
McClure, Wm. J. V, 1008
McClutche, Amey II, 240
McClutche, Amy II, 240
McClutche, James II, 240
McClutche, Mary II, 240
McCobb, Charles III, 212
McCobb, Louise R. III, 212
McCoin, Forister I, 595
McCoin, Louzena I, 557
McColgin, Anna V, 347
McColgin, Bell V, 347
McColgin, John V, 347
McCollam, Anthelia III, 212
McColle-Wright, Ann V, 783
McCollin, Allen II, 588
McCollin, Allen II, 663
McCollin, Elizabeth II, 392
McCollin, Frances B. II, 712
McCollin, Hannah E. II, 709
McCollin, Hannah E. II, 749
McCollin, Hannah E. II, 753
McCollin, James G. II, 712
McCollin, John II, 588
McCollin, John II, 663
McCollin, John II, 712
McCollin, John II, 717
McCollin, John II, 753
McCollin, John M. II, 753
McCollin, John M. II, 764
McCollin, John W. II, 749
McCollin, John W. II, 753
McCollin, Margaret II, 712
McCollin, Mary II, 712
McCollin, Mary II, 717
McCollin, Mary II, 753
McCollin, Mary II, 764
McCollin, Rachel II, 588
McCollin, Rachel II, 663
McCollin, Rachel II, 712
McCollin, Rachel II, 717
McCollin, Rachel II, 749
McCollin, Rachel II, 753
McCollin, Rachel II, 764
McCollin, Rebecca II, 588
McCollin, Rebecca II, 663
McCollin, Rebecca II, 712
McCollin, Rebecca II, 753
McCollin, Samuel II, 753
McCollin, Sarah II, 529
McCollin, Sarah II, 588
McCollin, Susanna II, 712
McCollin, Susanna II, 753
McCollin, Thomas II, 392
McCollin, William T. II, 712
McCollin, Wm. T. II, 753
McCollister, Tacy V, 692
McCollock, Bernice IV, 1285
McCollom, Alex. VI, 898
McCollough, E. Leeke IV, 1105
McCollough, Martha IV, 1105
McCollough, Martha L. IV, 1105
McCollough, Philip IV, 1105
McCollum, Abigail B. I, 750
McCollum, Abigail B. I, 765
McCollum, Abigail B. I, 766
McCollum, Anthelia III, 212
McCollum, Chas. V, 1008
McCollum, Clarkson I, 750
McCollum, Elizabeth I, 825
McCollum, Elizabeth I, 838
McCollum, Gertie V, 1008
McCollum, Gertrude V, 1008
McCollum, H. R. V, 1008
McCollum, Hiram V, 1008
McCollum, John H. I, 750
McCollum, John H. I, 766
McCollum, Joseph I, 398
McCollum, Joseph I, 405
McCollum, Joseph I, 750
McCollum, Joseph I, 766
McCollum, Joseph M. I, 766
McCollum, Leah I, 725
McCollum, Lucinda I, 1158
McCollum, Mary I, 398
McCollum, Mary I, 405
McCollum, Mary I, 750
McCollum, Mary I, 766
McCollum, Milton L. I, 750
McCollum, Nancy I, 405
McCollum, Nancy I, 741
McCollum, Nancy I, 750
McCollum, Naomy I, 766
McCollum, Rebecca I, 750
McCollum, Rebecca I, 756
McCollum, Rebecca I, 766
McCollum, Salem I, 766
McCollum, Stephen I, 405
McCollum, Stephen I, 750
McCollum, Stephen I, 766
McCollum, Susannah I, 766
McCollum, William M. I, 750
McCollum, William M. I, 766
McColum, Mary I, 766
McComack, Anderson VI, 890
McComack, Delilah VI, 1021
McComack, Lydia VI, 798
McComack, Missouri VI, 835
McComack, Nancy VI, 890
McComack, Pleasant L. VI, 835
McComas, Eliza V, 95
McComas, Genevieve VI, 377
McComas, John L. VI, 377
McComas, Maggie V, 95
McComas, Maggie V, 186
McComas, Margaretta V, 95
McComb, Elizabeth II, 588
McComb, Elizabeth II, 596
McComb, Grace Stewart II, 712
McComb, Grace Stewart Ewing II, 753
McComb, Hannah II, 543
McComb, Hannah II, 588
McComb, John II, 543
McComb, John II, 588
McComb, John II, 596
McComb, M. Barnett II, 712
McComb, Margaret II, 588
McComb, Meribah II, 588
McCombs, Achilles Douglas IV, 245
McCombs, Elizabeth Ann IV, 245
McCombs, Judith D. IV, 245
McCombs, Margaret II, 588
McCombs, Martha Ellen Johnson IV, 245
McCombs, Samuel Tiry IV, 245
McCombs, Sarah IV, 230
McCombs, Sarah IV, 245
McConaga, Hannah V, 950
McConaga, Hannah V, 955
McConaha, Jane VI, 985
McConaha, Margaret VI, 990
McConaha, Mary VI, 909
McConahey, Hannah IV, 1166
McConahey, Hannah IV, 1172
McConahy, ??? V, 1008
McConahy, Clarence V, 1008
McConahy, Maud V, 1008
McConaley, ??? V, 1008
McConaugh, Eleonor III, 327
McConaughy, ??? III, 22
McConaughy, David III, 212
McConaughy, Eleanor III, 22
McConaughy, Eleanor III, 212
McConaughy, James III, 212
McConaughy, James III, 327
McConaughy, James III, 347
McConaughy, Katharine III, 22
McConaughy, Katherine III, 212
McConaughy, Leana III, 212
McConaughy, Mary III, 212
McConaughy, Mary III, 347
McConehey, Martha VI, 870
McConhey, Thomas IV, 1327
McConihay, Hannah VI, 954
McConihay, John VI, 954
McConihay, Nancy VI, 954
McConihay, Polly VI, 954
McConihay, Saml. VI, 1013
McConihay, Samuel VI, 870
McConihay, Samuel VI, 909
McConihay, Samuel VI, 954
McConihay, Samuel VI, 975
McConihay, William VI, 954
McConiheay, Matilda VI, 1008
McConiheay, Samuel VI, 1008
McConihey, John VI, 954
McConihey, Nancy VI, 954
McConihey, Nancy VI, 959
McConihey, Samuel VI, 990
McConihey, William VI, 954
McConnahey, John VI, 917
McConnal, Ann IV, 519
McConnal, Ann IV, 539
McConnal, James IV, 642
McConnal, Jesse M. IV, 613
McConnal, Jesse M. IV, 642
McConnal, Rachel IV, 613
McConnal, Rachel IV, 642
McConnall, Catharine VI, 835
McConnall, Edward IV, 660
McConnall, Lydia IV, 660
McConnall, Seaborn VI, 835
McConnaughey, Elizabeth V, 692
McConnaughey, Elizabeth V, 706
McConnaughey, Hattie V, 460
McConnaughey, Roy V, 460
McConnaughey, Velma V, 460
McConnehay, John VI, 954
McConnehay, Polly VI, 954
McConnehey, John VI, 870
McConnehey, John VI, 933
McConnehey, Polly VI, 933
McConnel, Adaline IV, 642
McConnel, Adaline IV, 876
McConnel, Adaline IV, 877
McConnel, Adaline IV, 1066
McConnel, Adaline IV, 1105
McConnel, Albert IV, 1105
McConnel, Amos IV, 642
McConnel, Amos IV, 876
McConnel, Amos IV, 877
McConnel, Ann IV, 877
McConnel, Ann E. II, 292
McConnel, Ann E. II, 295
McConnel, Anna IV, 736
McConnel, Austin IV, 632
McConnel, Austin IV, 643
McConnel, Daniel IV, 877
McConnel, David IV, 643
McConnel, Edith IV, 632
McConnel, Edward IV, 642
McConnel, Edward IV, 876
McConnel, Edward IV, 877
McConnel, Edward IV, 1066
McConnel, Edward IV, 1105
McConnel, Edward VI, 600
McConnel, Eliza Ann IV, 877
McConnel, Elizabeth VI, 600
McConnel, Elmira IV, 1105
McConnel, Emeline IV, 612
McConnel, Emeline IV, 643
McConnel, Harriet IV, 877
McConnel, Harriet IV, 884
McConnel, Harriett IV, 877
McConnel, James IV, 642
McConnel, James IV, 863
McConnel, James IV, 876
McConnel, James IV, 877
McConnel, James IV, 1066
McConnel, James IV, 1087
McConnel, James IV, 1105
McConnel, James VI, 600
McConnel, Jesse IV, 642
McConnel, Jesse IV, 877
McConnel, Jesse VI, 600
McConnel, John VI, 952
McConnel, Jonathan IV, 1066
McConnel, Jonathan IV, 1105
McConnel, Levi IV, 642
McConnel, Levi IV, 660
McConnel, Lydia IV, 642
McConnel, Lydia IV, 876
McConnel, Lydia IV, 877
McConnel, Lydia IV, 1066
McConnel, Lydia IV, 1105
McConnel, Mary IV, 863
McConnel, Mary IV, 867
McConnel, Mary IV, 877
McConnel, Mary IV, 886
McConnel, Mary IV, 1087
McConnel, Mary IV, 1105
McConnel, Melissa IV, 877
McConnel, Morris VI, 600
McConnel, Nathan IV, 642
McConnel, Nathan IV, 876
McConnel, Nathan IV, 877
McConnel, Nathan IV, 1066
McConnel, Nathan IV, 1105
McConnel, Nelson IV, 877
McConnel, Orpha IV, 642
McConnel, Orpha IV, 876
McConnel, Orpha IV, 877
McConnel, Orpha IV, 1066
McConnel, Orpha IV, 1105
McConnel, Rachel IV, 877
McConnel, Rachel VI, 600
McConnel, Rachel, Jr. IV, 877
McConnel, Rachel, Sr. IV, 877
McConnel, Ruth IV, 642
McConnel, Ruth IV, 660
McConnel, Ruth IV, 1066
McConnel, Ruth IV, 1105
McConnel, Sarah IV, 877
McConnel, Sarah Jane IV, 877
McConnel, Susan Jane IV, 877
McConnel, Talbert IV, 1105
McConnel, Talbot IV, 642
McConnel, Talbot IV, 877
McConnel, Talbot IV, 1105
McConnel, Talbott IV, 876
McConnel, Townsend IV, 642
McConnel, Townsend IV, 643
McConnel, Townsend IV, 876
McConnel, Townsend IV, 877
McConnell, Abbie I, 1163
McConnell, Adaline IV, 642
McConnell, Adaline IV, 876
McConnell, Adaline IV, 977
McConnell, Adeline IV, 1117
McConnell, Albert IV, 642
McConnell, Albert IV, 977
McConnell, Amelia IV, 643
McConnell, Amos IV, 642
McConnell, Amos IV, 876
McConnell, Anabel IV, 737
McConnell, Ann IV, 539
McConnell, Anna IV, 539
McConnell, Anna IV, 736
McConnell, Anna IV, 737
McConnell, Anna V, 809
McConnell, Annabel IV, 642
McConnell, Annabelle IV, 643
McConnell, Austin IV, 642
McConnell, Austin IV, 643
McConnell, Beryl Whitten IV, 484
McConnell, Charles IV, 643
McConnell, Charles IV, 737
McConnell, Chas. IV, 642
McConnell, David IV, 642
McConnell, David IV, 643
McConnell, Dolo Rose I, 1158
McConnell, Edith IV, 642
McConnell, Edith IV, 643
McConnell, Edith IV, 737
McConnell, Edith M. IV, 643
McConnell, Edward IV, 642
McConnell, Edward IV, 876
McConnell, Edward IV, 977
McConnell, Edward M. IV, 1117
McConnell, Edwin IV, 642
McConnell, Edwin IV, 643
McConnell, Eliza Ann IV, 642
McConnell, Eliza Ann IV, 877
McConnell, Elizabeth V, 733
McConnell, Elizabeth V, 804
McConnell, Emaline IV, 643
McConnell, Emaline IV, 737
McConnell, Emeline IV, 642
McConnell, Emeline IV, 643
McConnell, Emeline IV, 667
McConnell, Emma Lucile I, 1158
McConnell, Emmet IV, 642
McConnell, Emmet IV, 737
McConnell, Emmit IV, 643

McConnell, Hadley IV, 642
McConnell, Hannah VI, 178
McConnell, Hannah VI, 197
McConnell, Harriet IV, 642
McConnell, Harriett IV, 877
McConnell, Henry IV, 643
McConnell, Henry H. IV, 642
McConnell, Hugh Lee I, 1158
McConnell, James IV, 642
McConnell, James IV, 876
McConnell, James IV, 977
McConnell, James V, 186
McConnell, James VI, 600
McConnell, Jane IV, 642
McConnell, Jennie V, 632
McConnell, Jesse IV, 642
McConnell, Jesse IV, 877
McConnell, Jesse M. IV, 642
McConnell, John V, 733
McConnell, John V, 804
McConnell, Jonathan IV, 642
McConnell, Jonathan IV, 977
McConnell, Joseph IV, 642
McConnell, Joseph IV, 643
McConnell, Laura IV, 642
McConnell, Laura IV, 737
McConnell, Levi IV, 636
McConnell, Levi IV, 642
McConnell, Levi IV, 643
McConnell, Levi IV, 667
McConnell, Lewis IV, 643
McConnell, Lydia IV, 642
McConnell, Lydia IV, 876
McConnell, Lydia IV, 977
McConnell, Lydia IV, 1117
McConnell, Mahlon IV, 977
McConnell, Maria V, 733
McConnell, Mary IV, 642
McConnell, Mary IV, 643
McConnell, Mary IV, 667
McConnell, Mary IV, 877
McConnell, Mary Ann IV, 642
McConnell, Mary Ann IV, 643
McConnell, Mary Ann IV, 737
McConnell, Mary H. VI, 178
McConnell, Mary H. VI, 197
McConnell, Melissa IV, 642
McConnell, Melissa IV, 877
McConnell, Minerva IV, 642
McConnell, Minerva IV, 643
McConnell, Moriah V, 804
McConnell, Nathan IV, 642
McConnell, Nathan IV, 876
McConnell, Nathan IV, 977
McConnell, Nelson IV, 642
McConnell, Nelson IV, 877
McConnell, Orpha IV, 642
McConnell, Orpha IV, 876
McConnell, Orpha IV, 977
McConnell, Rachel IV, 642
McConnell, Rachel IV, 877
McConnell, Ruth IV, 642
McConnell, Ruth IV, 667
McConnell, Ruth IV, 977
McConnell, Ruth Ann IV, 642
McConnell, Ruth Ann IV, 643
McConnell, Ruth Elizabeth I, 1158
McConnell, Samuel IV, 245
McConnell, Sarah IV, 614
McConnell, Sarah IV, 642
McConnell, Sarah IV, 643
McConnell, Sarah IV, 877
McConnell, Susan IV, 642
McConnell, Susan IV, 643
McConnell, Susan Jane IV, 877
McConnell, Susanna IV, 636
McConnell, Susanna IV, 642
McConnell, Susannah IV, 636
McConnell, Susannah IV, 642
McConnell, Susannah Elizabeth I, 1158
McConnell, Talbot IV, 642
McConnell, Talbot IV, 977
McConnell, Talbott IV, 876
McConnell, Thomas IV, 642
McConnell, Thomas IV, 643
McConnell, Tolbert IV, 977
McConnell, Townsend IV, 245
McConnell, Townsend IV, 642
McConnell, Townsend IV, 643
McConnell, Townsend IV, 876
McConnell, William IV, 736
McConnell, William C. IV, 643
McConnell, William Edgar I, 1158
McConnell, Wm. IV, 642
McConnelll, Anny V, 803
McConnohey, John VI, 933
McConnol, Anabel IV, 737
McConnol, Charles IV, 737
McConnol, Edith IV, 737
McConnol, Emaline IV, 737
McConnol, Emmet IV, 737
McConnol, Laura IV, 737
McConnol, Mary Ann IV, 737
McConohea, Polly VI, 975
McConohey, Betsy VI, 917
McConohey, Peggy VI, 933
McConohey, Sally VI, 870
McConville, Ann VI, 836
McConville, Mary A. Y. VI, 836
McConville, William VI, 836
McCook, Elizabeth V, 904
McCook, Gabriel V, 904
McCook, Rachel V, 904
McCool, Alisabeth I, 1021
McCool, Ann I, 1021
McCool, Ann I, 1034
McCool, Ann I, 1039
McCool, Ann VI, 382
McCool, Ann VI, 413
McCool, Ann VI, 419
McCool, Ann Pugh I, 1034
McCool, Betsy V, 752
McCool, Betty V, 723
McCool, Betty V, 752
McCool, Catharine VI, 419
McCool, Catherine VI, 382
McCool, Charity V, 794
McCool, Charity VI, 420
McCool, Deborah VI, 419
McCool, Eleanor VI, 419
McCool, Elisha V, 814
McCool, Eliza VI, 420
McCool, Elizann V, 794
McCool, Emma V, 1008
McCool, Esther V, 814
McCool, Gabriel I, 1021
McCool, Gabriel I, 1034
McCool, Gabriel V, 723
McCool, Gabriel, Jr. I, 1034
McCool, Gabril I, 1021
McCool, Grace VI, 362
McCool, Grace VI, 419
McCool, Hester V, 814
McCool, Hester V, 820
McCool, James I, 1021
McCool, James I, 1034
McCool, James VI, 419
McCool, James VI, 420
McCool, James J. V, 1008
McCool, Joaceann V, 794
McCool, John I, 557
McCool, John I, 1021
McCool, John V, 814
McCool, Julia Ann I, 725
McCool, Juliann V, 752
McCool, July Ann I, 725
McCool, Mark V, 814
McCool, Martha I, 1021
McCool, Martha V, 752
McCool, Martha VI, 420
McCool, Martha VI, 455
McCool, Mary I, 1021
McCool, Mary V, 814
McCool, Mary VI, 365
McCool, Mary Ann V, 1008
McCool, Olivia VI, 419
McCool, Olivia VI, 455
McCool, Rachel I, 1021
McCool, Rachel I, 1029
McCool, Rachel I, 1034
McCool, Rachel V, 794
McCool, Rachel VI, 420
McCool, Sarah VI, 382
McCool, Sarah VI, 419
McCool, Thomas I, 725
McCool, Thomas I, 1021
McCool, Thomas I, 1034
McCool, Thomas M. I, 725
McCool, Thomas W. V, 752
McCool, Wells V, 814
McCoole, ??? V, 752
McCoole, Ann VI, 419
McCoole, Betsy V, 752
McCoole, Betty V, 752
McCoole, Charity V, 752
McCoole, Charity V, 788
McCoole, Charity VI, 420
McCoole, Deborah VI, 419
McCoole, Eleanor VI, 419
McCoole, Eleonor VI, 420
McCoole, Elisha V, 752
McCoole, Elisha V, 814
McCoole, Eliza VI, 420
McCoole, Eliza Ann V, 752
McCoole, Elizann V, 782
McCoole, Elizann V, 788
McCoole, Gabriel V, 752
McCoole, Gabriel VI, 419
McCoole, Grace VI, 419
McCoole, Graceann V, 788
McCoole, Hester V, 813
McCoole, Hetty V, 816
McCoole, James V, 752
McCoole, James VI, 419
McCoole, James VI, 420
McCoole, James, Jr. VI, 419
McCoole, John II, 588
McCoole, John V, 752
McCoole, John VI, 419
McCoole, John, Jr. VI, 419
McCoole, John, Sr. VI, 419
McCoole, Julia Ann V, 752
McCoole, Julian V, 752
McCoole, Juliann V, 752
McCoole, Mark V, 814
McCoole, Martha V, 752
McCoole, Martha VI, 419
McCoole, Mary V, 752
McCoole, Mary VI, 419
McCoole, Rachel V, 752
McCoole, Rachel V, 788
McCoole, Rachel VI, 420
McCoole, Sarah VI, 419
McCoole, Thomas V, 813
McCoole, Thomas W. V, 752
McCoole, Thos. V, 752
McCoole, Wells V, 752
McCoole, Wells V, 814
McCoole, William V, 788
McCoole, Wm. II, 588
McCoole, Wm. V, 788
McCord, Anna III, 144
McCord, Anna III, 212
McCord, C. Bertram III, 212
McCord, Charles III, 212
McCord, Charles L. III, 144
McCord, Chas. Luther III, 212
McCord, Grace III, 134
McCord, Grace C. III, 133
McCord, Grace C. III, 212
McCord, Grace C. III, 232
McCord, Grace C. III, 292
McCord, Grace Caroline III, 134
McCord, Grace Caroline III, 212
McCord, Grace Caroline III, 354
McCord, Herbert III, 212
McCord, Hilma Kindlund III, 242
McCord, Jason III, 212
McCord, Willet III, 134
McCord, Willet III, 212
McCord, Willet III, 354
McCord, Wm. Rufus III, 242
McCorkle, Mary J. I, 624
McCormack, Adam VI, 954
McCormack, Agnes VI, 1013
McCormack, Albert V, 460
McCormack, Anderson VI, 954
McCormack, Anderson VI, 964
McCormack, Anderson VI, 1013
McCormack, Anna V, 460
McCormack, Betsey VI, 954
McCormack, Betty VI, 954
McCormack, Charlotte VI, 1013
McCormack, David VI, 836
McCormack, David VI, 839
McCormack, Dennis VI, 910
McCormack, Dennis VI, 954
McCormack, Dennis VI, 1021
McCormack, Doris V, 919
McCormack, Edith W. VI, 839
McCormack, Elizabeth VI, 876
McCormack, Elizabeth VI, 954
McCormack, Evelina VI, 905
McCormack, Fanny VI, 876
McCormack, Frankey VI, 954
McCormack, Green B. VI, 954
McCormack, Henry VI, 836
McCormack, James VI, 954
McCormack, Jesse VI, 954
McCormack, John VI, 954
McCormack, John VI, 1013
McCormack, Joyassa VI, 836
McCormack, Judith VI, 954
McCormack, Locky J. VI, 836
McCormack, Louisa VI, 954
McCormack, Martha VI, 954
McCormack, Mary VI, 905
McCormack, Mary VI, 954
McCormack, Mecager VI, 876
McCormack, Micajah VI, 870
McCormack, Micajah VI, 954
McCormack, Mina VI, 836
McCormack, Nancy VI, 954
McCormack, Nancy VI, 1004
McCormack, Patsy Jane VI, 905
McCormack, Polly VI, 1021
McCormack, Priscilla VI, 977
McCormack, Richard VI, 905
McCormack, Richard VI, 954
McCormack, Richard VI, 977
McCormack, Richd. VI, 1004
McCormack, Sally VI, 834
McCormack, Sarah VI, 954
McCormack, Sukey VI, 1013
McCormack, Thomas VI, 954
McCormack, Unicea VI, 954
McCormack, William VI, 954
McCormack, William M. VI, 836
McCormack, Wm. VI, 834
McCormick, Albert V, 460
McCormick, Ann VI, 530
McCormick, Ann VI, 536
McCormick, Ann VI, 763
McCormick, Ann VI, 768
McCormick, Anna V, 460
McCormick, Annabelle V, 460
McCormick, Blanche L. IV, 1327
McCormick, Catharine II, 712
McCormick, Clara Hayes III, 213
McCormick, Clara Hayes III, 302
McCormick, David VI, 828
McCormick, David VI, 836
McCormick, Dennis VI, 937
McCormick, Eliza VI, 530
McCormick, Eliza VI, 536
McCormick, Eliza VI, 763
McCormick, Eliza VI, 767
McCormick, Eliza VI, 768
McCormick, Elizabeth VI, 536
McCormick, Elizabeth VI, 828
McCormick, Emmett IV, 1257
McCormick, Emmett IV, 1327
McCormick, Emmett A. IV, 1327
McCormick, Ester IV, 311
McCormick, Ester IV, 313
McCormick, Ida IV, 1285
McCormick, Jacob Franklin IV, 1285
McCormick, James VI, 530
McCormick, James VI, 536
McCormick, James VI, 763
McCormick, James VI, 768
McCormick, James VI, 772
McCormick, James VI, 954
McCormick, John IV, 1285
McCormick, Joseph VI, 767
McCormick, Kate M. III, 213
McCormick, Louisa VI, 954
McCormick, Lydia III, 213
McCormick, Maggie J. III, 162
McCormick, Maggie J. III, 213
McCormick, Marey VI, 937
McCormick, Mary VI, 763
McCormick, Mary VI, 772
McCormick, Mina VI, 836
McCormick, Patsy VI, 854
McCormick, Raymond B. II, 712
McCormick, Sally VI, 937
McCornish, Ann II, 392
McCornish, Frances II, 392
McCornish, Hannah II, 392
McCornish, Patrick II, 392
McCortney, Amy IV, 89
McCortney, Amy IV, 98
McCoubrey, Daisy III, 213
McCoubrey, Daisy I. III, 213
McCoubrey, Frances Emma III, 213
McCoubrey, James III, 213
McCoubrey, Lucilla III, 213
McCoubrey, Lucilla Bird III, 213
McCoubrey, William III, 213
McCoughie, Thos. IV, 1327
McCoun, Charles III, 426
McCoun, Charles III, 459
McCoun, Chas. III, 460
McCoun, Mary III, 426
McCoun, Pamela T. III, 502
McCoun, Pamelia III, 459
McCoun, Pamelia III, 460
McCoun, Pamelia P. III, 426
McCoun, Sarah III, 393
McCoun, Sarah III, 426
McCoun, Wm. III, 393
McCoun, Wm. III, 426
McCourbrey, Daisy I. III, 34
McCourbrey, James III, 34
McCourrey, C. Clayton I, 1158
McCourrey, Tessie I, 1158
McCowan, Jane IV, 98
McCowan, Jane IV, 111
McCowan, Maria V, 95
McCowan, Maria V, 513
McCowan, Mariah V, 513
McCowen, Bathsheba I, 1049
McCowen, Mariah V, 513
McCowen, Mariah V, 533
McCowen, Mary Elizabeth IV, 737
McCowen, Mary Elizabeth IV, 751
McCowen, William I, 337
McCown, Theziah VI, 836
McCown, Thomas VI, 836
McCoy, Abigail V, 187
McCoy, Abigail VI, 420
McCoy, Ada Chance V, 261
McCoy, Amos V, 95
McCoy, Amos VI, 420
McCoy, Andrew V, 261
McCoy, Andrew VI, 420
McCoy, Ann V, 411
McCoy, Anna V, 411
McCoy, Anna V, 420
McCoy, Anna VI, 980
McCoy, Archie V, 261
McCoy, Arthur V, 693
McCoy, Arthur H. V, 693
McCoy, Bertha Bell V, 1008
McCoy, Betsy VI, 822
McCoy, Blanch Hartman V, 69
McCoy, Cassandra VI, 420
McCoy, Cassandra VI, 424
McCoy, Catharine VI, 836
McCoy, Charley V, 460
McCoy, Comfort V, 254
McCoy, Comfort V, 260
McCoy, Daniel VI, 822
McCoy, Daniel VI, 839
McCoy, Daniel VI, 861
McCoy, Edmund H. IV, 245
McCoy, Edward M. IV, 245
McCoy, Elizabeth V, 347
McCoy, Elizabeth V, 692
McCoy, Elizabeth V, 814
McCoy, Elizabeth VI, 420
McCoy, Elizabeth VI, 894
McCoy, Elizabeth VI, 985
McCoy, Elizabeth Rogers V, 68
McCoy, Elizabeth Rogers V, 69
McCoy, Ella V, 261
McCoy, Emily VI, 954
McCoy, Ethel V, 261
McCoy, Eva V, 693
McCoy, Eva Thorpe V, 693
McCoy, Filander V, 347
McCoy, Frances VI, 420
McCoy, Francis V, 187
McCoy, Frank Wm. V, 347
McCoy, Geo. J. V, 693
McCoy, George V, 187
McCoy, George VI, 420
McCoy, Gertrude V, 261
McCoy, Haines V, 95
McCoy, Halley IV, 245
McCoy, Hannah V, 261
McCoy, Harry P. V, 347
McCoy, Harvey W. V, 347
McCoy, Helen V, 693
McCoy, Henry V, 261
McCoy, Hugh V, 693
McCoy, Hulda V, 814
McCoy, Huldah V, 794
McCoy, Huldah V, 814
McCoy, Ida May V, 347
McCoy, J. H. V, 261
McCoy, Jacob VI, 420
McCoy, Jane V, 39
McCoy, Jane V, 95
McCoy, Jane VI, 420
McCoy, Jesse V, 261
McCoy, Jesse E. V, 347
McCoy, Jessie V, 261
McCoy, Jno. VI, 985
McCoy, Joanna VI, 925
McCoy, Joanna VI, 954
McCoy, Joanna Oren V, 260
McCoy, John V, 260
McCoy, John V, 261
McCoy, John VI, 836
McCoy, John VI, 871
McCoy, John VI, 875
McCoy, John VI, 876
McCoy, John G. VI, 954
McCoy, John P. VI, 954
McCoy, Jubal VI, 954
McCoy, Jubal VI, 994
McCoy, Laodice V, 814
McCoy, Lavina VI, 836
McCoy, Lenna V, 261
McCoy, Leo J. V, 689
McCoy, Leo J. V, 692
McCoy, Leo J. V, 693
McCoy, Letha VI, 994
McCoy, Levi V, 187
McCoy, Levi VI, 420
McCoy, Lorrihanna V, 260
McCoy, Lucy VI, 871
McCoy, Lydia V, 814
McCoy, Margaret V, 187
McCoy, Margaret V, 693
McCoy, Margaret VI, 420

cCoy, Margaret VI, 980
cCoy, Margaret Barrett V, 693
cCoy, Maria V, 187
cCoy, Maria VI, 420
cCoy, Martha IV, 418
cCoy, Martha E. IV, 453
cCoy, Mary V, 357
cCoy, Mary V, 814
cCoy, Mary VI, 969
cCoy, Mary Ann V, 508
cCoy, Mary Ann V, 513
cCoy, Mary Elsie V, 693
cCoy, Mary Idamay V, 347
cCoy, Mary W. V, 347
cCoy, Matilda V, 382
cCoy, Matilda V, 411
cCoy, Nancy VI, 925
cCoy, Nancy VI, 954
cCoy, Nelly VI, 875
cCoy, Oliver V, 692
cCoy, Oliver R. V, 693
cCoy, Philander V, 347
cCoy, Polly V, 260
cCoy, Polly V, 305
cCoy, Polly V, 307
cCoy, Polly VI, 876
cCoy, Priscilla VI, 954
cCoy, Rachel V, 347
cCoy, Rachel VI, 397
cCoy, Rachel VI, 954
cCoy, Reece V, 261
cCoy, Rees V, 260
cCoy, Richard Hugh V, 692
cCoy, Robert V, 693
cCoy, Robert VI, 420
cCoy, Robert A. V, 261
cCoy, Robert C. V, 347
cCoy, Robert Thorp V, 693
cCoy, Rosa V, 261
cCoy, Ruth V, 347
cCoy, Samuel V, 347
cCoy, Samuel B. VI, 954
cCoy, Sarah V, 187
cCoy, Sarah VI, 420
cCoy, Sarah VI, 871
cCoy, Sarah VI, 875
cCoy, Sarah VI, 876
cCoy, Sarah VI, 894
cCoy, Sarah Ethel V, 671
cCoy, Sarah Ethel V, 693
cCoy, Susan V, 260
cCoy, Tamsey VI, 954
cCoy, Thomas VI, 836
cCoy, Thomas VI, 954
cCoy, Tilden V, 187
cCoy, Tilden VI, 420
cCoy, Virginia V, 187
cCoy, Virginia VI, 420
cCoy, William VI, 891
cCoy, William VI, 954
cCoy, William VI, 969
cCoy, William VI, 985
Coy, Wm. VI, 969
Coy, Wm. VI, 994
Coy, Zilpha VI, 891
Coye, Esther VI, 600
Coye, Grace VI, 600
Coye, Martha VI, 600
Coye, Unis VI, 600
Cracken, Abigail I, 405
Cracken, Abigail I, 438
Cracken, Abigail I, 450
Cracken, Abigail I, 766
Cracken, Alexander I, 405
Cracken, Alexander I, 438
Cracken, Alexander I, 450
Cracken, Ann I, 405
Cracken, Ann I, 428
cracken, Ann I, 431
Cracken, Ann I, 438
Cracken, Ann I, 553
Cracken, Ann I, 558
Cracken, Brice IV, 1216
Cracken, Daniel I, 741
Cracken, David I, 661
Cracken, David I, 684
Cracken, David I, 766
Cracken, Elizabeth I, 438
Cracken, Elizabeth I, 450
Cracken, Elizabeth I, 661
Cracken, Elizabeth I, 766
Cracken, Elizabeth I, 984
Cracken, Elizabeth I, 992
Cracken, Elizabeth IV, 98
Cracken, Elizabeth IV, 112
Cracken, Henry I, 766
Cracken, Jane I, 766
Cracken, Jane H. I, 825
Cracken, Jane M. I, 825
Cracken, John I, 438
Cracken, John I, 450
McCracken, Joseph I, 438
McCracken, Joseph I, 450
McCracken, Lois Evelyn IV, 1216
McCracken, M. Jane I, 825
McCracken, Marth I, 450
McCracken, Martha I, 405
McCracken, Martha I, 426
McCracken, Martha I, 438
McCracken, Martha I, 450
McCracken, Martha I, 553
McCracken, Martha I, 558
McCracken, Martha I, 661
McCracken, Martha I, 684
McCracken, Martha I, 741
McCracken, Martha I, 750
McCracken, Martha I, 766
McCracken, Martha I, 825
McCracken, Mary I, 372
McCracken, Mary I, 405
McCracken, Mary I, 661
McCracken, Mary I, 756
McCracken, Mary I, 766
McCracken, Nathan I, 661
McCracken, Ollie IV, 1216
McCracken, Percila I, 450
McCracken, Phebe II, 1062
McCracken, Pricilla I, 450
McCracken, Priscilla I, 438
McCracken, Prisila I, 450
McCracken, Rebecca I, 1158
McCracken, Rhodah I, 450
McCracken, Robart I, 405
McCracken, Robert I, 405
McCracken, Robert I, 426
McCracken, Robert I, 438
McCracken, Robert I, 661
McCracken, Robert I, 684
McCracken, Robert I, 741
McCracken, Robert I, 750
McCracken, Robert I, 766
McCracken, Robert I, 771
McCracken, Robert I, 825
McCracken, Robert I, 992
McCracken, Robert, Jr. I, 984
McCracken, Robert, Jr. I, 992
McCracken, Ruth I, 405
McCracken, Ruth I, 444
McCracken, Ruth I, 450
McCracken, Samuel I, 405
McCracken, Samuel I, 428
McCracken, Samuel I, 438
McCracken, Samuel I, 450
McCracken, Samuel Vestal I, 766
McCracken, Stephen I, 438
McCracken, Thomas I, 405
McCracken, Thomas I, 438
McCracken, Thomas I, 450
McCracken, Thomas I, 766
McCracken, Thomas I, 825
McCracken, Thomas I, 829
McCracken, William I, 405
McCracken, William I, 438
McCracken, William I, 450
McCracken, William I, 766
McCrackin, William I, 766
McCraight, Edith V, 693
McCraken, Phebe II, 1055
McCrakin, Mary I, 741
McCrakin, William I, 405
McCrary, Anna V, 371
McCrary, Anna V, 411
McCrary, Elma IV, 1285
McCrary, Frances A. V, 371
McCrary, John V, 371
McCrary, John V, 411
McCraw, Aggetha VI, 954
McCraw, Alexander VI, 954
McCraw, Catharine VI, 1018
McCraw, Dancy VI, 801
McCraw, Dancy VI, 826
McCraw, Elizabeth VI, 836
McCraw, Elizabeth VI, 839
McCraw, Elizabeth VI, 945
McCraw, Hilery VI, 836
McCraw, Hugh VI, 954
McCraw, James VI, 836
McCraw, James VI, 877
McCraw, James VI, 954
McCraw, James E. VI, 836
McCraw, James L. VI, 836
McCraw, John VI, 945
McCraw, Martha VI, 836
McCraw, Martha J. VI, 836
McCraw, Mary H. VI, 839
McCraw, Merit VI, 836
McCraw, Merritt VI, 839
McCraw, Nancy VI, 836
McCraw, Nancy VI, 954
McCraw, Paulina W. VI, 836
McCraw, Polly VI, 836
McCraw, Polly S. VI, 826
McCraw, Richard VI, 836
McCraw, Sally P. VI, 801
McCraw, Samuel D. VI, 836
McCraw, Sucky VI, 915
McCraw, Sukey VI, 954
McCraw, Susan VI, 836
McCraw, Susan R. VI, 836
McCraw, William VI, 836
McCray, Amelia V, 460
McCray, Amelia V, 583
McCray, Anna V, 411
McCray, Anna Mary V, 693
McCray, Arthur V, 582
McCray, Arthur L. V, 693
McCray, Arthur William V, 693
McCray, Clayton Harlan V, 693
McCray, Dr. W. F. V, 186
McCray, Joseph V, 460
McCray, Letitia V, 583
McCray, Lettie V, 186
McCray, Lettie V, 583
McCray, Mary V, 582
McCray, Mary Emily V, 582
McCray, Mary Emily V, 591
McCray, Maude Jane V, 582
McCray, Minnie V, 583
McCray, Olive E. V, 693
McCray, Rebecca Ann V, 693
McCray, Susanna V, 693
McCray, Susannah V, 582
McCray, Thomas V, 582
McCray, Thomas V, 693
McCray, Vernon V, 186
McCray, William V, 186
McCray, Wm. V, 583
McCray, Wm. F. V, 583
McCray, Wm. Thomas V, 186
McCrea, Ellen V, 904
McCrea, Ellen V, 919
McCrea, Mary II, 588
McCrea, Mary II, 623
McCreary, George H. VI, 420
McCreary, Mary K. III, 492
McCreary, Sarah Ann III, 492
McCreary, Thos. Amos III, 492
McCreight, Ed V, 693
McCreight, Edith V, 693
McCreight, Edward V, 693
McCreight, Ethel V, 693
McCrew, Anne IV, 977
McCrey, Amelia V, 583
McCrey, Letitia V, 583
McCrey, Lettie V, 583
McCrey, Minnie V, 583
McCrey, Susanna V, 585
McCrey, Susannah V, 582
McCrey, Wm. V, 583
McCrey, Wm. F. V, 583
McCright, Ed V, 693
McCrory, Mabel Packard IV, 1327
McCue, Belle IV, 245
McCue, Gertie IV, 245
McCue, Hobert IV, 245
McCue, Irene IV, 245
McCue, John E. IV, 245
McCue, Lillian M. IV, 245
McCue, Mildred Edna IV, 245
McCue, William IV, 245
McCullah, Robert VI, 674
McCulloch, Elizabeth I, 684
McCullock, Elizabeth I, 661
McCullock, Joseph I, 661
McCullock, Sarah A. IV, 1238
McCullock, Solomon IV, 1238
McCullough, Ann II, 588
McCullough, Ann II, 663
McCullough, Esther II, 528
McCullough, Esther II, 588
McCullough, James II, 528
McCullough, James II, 588
McCullough, James II, 647
McCullough, James II, 663
McCullough, Jane V, 1008
McCullough, Louisa Emmaline VI, 752
McCullough, Louisa Emmaline VI, 779
McCullough, Mary II, 588
McCullough, Mary II, 647
McCullough, Matheny V, 1008
McCullough, Matthew V, 1008
McCullough, Rachel II, 588
McCullough, Rachel II, 605
McCullough, Rachel II, 657
McCullough, Rachel II, 663
McCullough, Sara II, 588
McCullough, Sarah II, 588
McCullow, Agnes IV, 1238
McCullow, Agnes IV, 1242
McCullum, Susan V, 583
McCully, Charles III, 200
McCully, Charles III, 212
McCully, Jane III, 200
McCully, Jane III, 212
McCully, Louisa IV, 1197
McCully, Louisa IV, 1198
McCully, Louisa IV, 1238
McCumber, Nancy A. IV, 1239
McCumber, Nancy Ann IV, 1236
McCumber, Nancy Ann IV, 1239
McCune, Adam VI, 836
McCune, Arthur V, 347
McCune, Clara D. V, 347
McCune, Edger V, 347
McCune, Edward V, 347
McCune, Maggie V, 347
McCune, Margaret V, 347
McCune, Sally VI, 836
McCune, Thomas V, 347
McCune, Thomas VI, 862
McCune, Valeria B. V, 347
McCurdy, Daniel II, 894
McCurdy, Daniel IV, 737
McCurdy, Eleonor VI, 420
McCurdy, Emma IV, 1172
McCurdy, Sarah VI, 420
McCurry, C. Clayton I, 1158
McCurry, Claton I, 1158
McCurry, Lillie IV, 245
McCurry, Lillie Dale IV, 245
McCurry, Mary IV, 245
McCurry, Mary Elva IV, 245
McCurry, Pansy IV, 245
McCurry, Tessie I, 1158
McCurty, Eleanor VI, 419
McCurty, Eleonor VI, 420
McCutchen, Janet K. IV, 1327
McCutchen, Wm. H. IV, 1327
McCutchen, Wm. Henry IV, 1327
McCutcheon, Eliz. III, 248
McDaniel, Abigail I, 703
McDaniel, Abigail I, 725
McDaniel, Abigal I, 725
McDaniel, Agnes C. VI, 836
McDaniel, Albert VI, 954
McDaniel, Albon VI, 836
McDaniel, Alen H. I, 716
McDaniel, Alen H. I, 725
McDaniel, Alexander VI, 331
McDaniel, Alexander VI, 891
McDaniel, Alexander VI, 954
McDaniel, Alexander VI, 985
McDaniel, Alexander VI, 986
McDaniel, Alfred VI, 1014
McDaniel, Alfred M. VI, 995
McDaniel, Balda VI, 891
McDaniel, Balda VI, 899
McDaniel, Balda VI, 932
McDaniel, Balda VI, 954
McDaniel, Benjamin H. VI, 954
McDaniel, Catharine S. VI, 954
McDaniel, Charity I, 405
McDaniel, Cleopatra VI, 880
McDaniel, Dolly R. VI, 949
McDaniel, Eliza Susan VI, 954
McDaniel, Elizabeth I, 405
McDaniel, Elizabeth I, 425
McDaniel, Elizabeth V, 347
McDaniel, Elizabeth V, 367
McDaniel, Elizabeth V, 850
McDaniel, Elizabeth V, 851
McDaniel, Elizabeth VI, 954
McDaniel, Elvira V, 347
McDaniel, Florentine VI, 995
McDaniel, Frank V, 347
McDaniel, George VI, 954
McDaniel, Gideon VI, 954
McDaniel, Hannah I, 703
McDaniel, Hannah I, 725
McDaniel, Harriett VI, 891
McDaniel, Huldah IV, 1235
McDaniel, Huldah IV, 1239
McDaniel, J. F. V, 347
McDaniel, James VI, 836
McDaniel, Jane I, 716
McDaniel, Jane I, 725
McDaniel, Jemima V, 95
McDaniel, Jesse W. VI, 954
McDaniel, Jno. R. VI, 953
McDaniel, Jno. Robin VI, 953
McDaniel, Joanna VI, 954
McDaniel, John I, 703
McDaniel, John I, 725
McDaniel, John VI, 836
McDaniel, John H. I, 703
McDaniel, Juliann VI, 953
McDaniel, L. VI, 953
McDaniel, L. VI, 980
McDaniel, Loderick VI, 954
McDaniel, Loderwick VI, 959
McDaniel, Lodowick VI, 968
McDaniel, Lodowick VI, 987
McDaniel, Lucy V, 347
McDaniel, Lucy V, 367
McDaniel, Lucy VI, 899
McDaniel, Lydia V, 95
McDaniel, Marinda VI, 987
McDaniel, Martha Ann VI, 899
McDaniel, Mary I, 405
McDaniel, Mary I, 419
McDaniel, Mary II, 588
McDaniel, Mary IV, 1257
McDaniel, Mary V, 347
McDaniel, Mary V, 451
McDaniel, Mary V, 693
McDaniel, Mary VI, 258
McDaniel, Mary Ann V, 261
McDaniel, Mary E. VI, 954
McDaniel, Mary F. VI, 954
McDaniel, Mary G. VI, 964
McDaniel, Mary J. V, 186
McDaniel, Mary L. VI, 954
McDaniel, Mary M. VI, 836
McDaniel, Milly VI, 836
McDaniel, Nancy V, 884
McDaniel, Nancy V, 887
McDaniel, Nancy VI, 954
McDaniel, Nannie V, 347
McDaniel, Phebe IV, 1088
McDaniel, Phebe IV, 1105
McDaniel, R. V, 261
McDaniel, Rachel I, 375
McDaniel, Rachel I, 405
McDaniel, Randolph V, 261
McDaniel, Randolph V, 451
McDaniel, Raymond V, 632
McDaniel, Reba May V, 347
McDaniel, Reba May V, 693
McDaniel, Samuel VI, 954
McDaniel, Sarah V, 95
McDaniel, Sarah V, 128
McDaniel, Sarah V, 850
McDaniel, Sarah VI, 836
McDaniel, Sarah VI, 850
McDaniel, Sarah H. VI, 921
McDaniel, Temperance V, 752
McDaniel, Virginia Frances V, 451
McDaniel, William I, 1034
McDaniel, William VI, 836
McDaniel, Wilmena Powell V, 186
McDaniel, Wm. VI, 925
McDaniel, Wm. VI, 1013
McDaniels, Jane E. I, 934
McDaniels, Jane F. IV, 1127
McDaniels, Jane F. IV, 1135
McDaniels, Martha I, 934
McDaniels, Mary J. V, 186
McDaniels, R. V, 261
McDanniel, Jemima V, 95
McDanniel, Lydia V, 95
McDanold, Charles V, 752
McDanold, John V, 752
McDanold, Jos. V, 762
McDanold, Joseph V, 752
McDanold, Mahala V, 762
McDanold, Mark V, 752
McDanold, Phebe V, 747
McDanold, Sarah M. V, 752
McDanold, Temperance V, 762
McDarch, Margaret V, 752
McDarch, Mary Catherine V, 752
McDarch, Nora Frances V, 752
McDarnell, Mary W. V, 884
McDarr, Blanch V, 1008
McDarr, Catharine V, 1008
McDarr, John V, 1008
McDavitt, Anna VI, 954
McDavitt, James VI, 954
McDearman, Frances VI, 808
McDearman, John G. VI, 808
McDearman, Mary VI, 808
McDearman, Sterling VI, 831
McDearmon, Martha VI, 840
McDerman, Fanny VI, 836
McDerman, Thomas, Jr. VI, 836
McDermand, Ada Narcissa II, 789
McDermed, Daniel VI, 954
McDermed, Martha VI, 954
McDerment, Nancy VI, 828
McDermont, Edw. III, 411
McDermont, Jemima III, 411
McDermot, Edward III, 412
McDermot, Jemima III, 412
McDermott, Catharine II, 848
McDermott, Catharine II, 894
McDermott, Edward III, 401
McDermott, James W. III, 166
McDermott, James W. III, 213
McDermott, John II, 848
McDermott, John II, 894

McDermott, Loretta III, 401
McDermott, Maria III, 213
McDermott, Mary II, 848
McDermott, Mary II, 894
McDermott, Mary E. III, 166
McDermott, Mary E. III, 213
McDermott, R. VI, 985
McDermott, Roderick VI, 883
McDermott, Wm. III, 213
McDevitt, Mary Jane IV, 692
McDiarmid, Dorothy VI, 763
McDiarmid, Dorothy VI, 777
McDiarmid, Norman Hugh VI, 763
McDiarmid, Norman Hugh VI, 777
McDoe, Ada I, 1158
McDole, Ada I, 1158
McDole, John W. I, 1158
McDole, Oda I, 1158
McDonal, Joseph I, 1034
McDonal, Lydia IV, 699
McDonald, ??? III, 103
McDonald, ??? V, 754
McDonald, Aaron V, 632
McDonald, Alexander III, 213
McDonald, Alice V, 186
McDonald, Allan I, 725
McDonald, Allen V, 752
McDonald, Allen V, 814
McDonald, Allen V, 815
McDonald, Alvin W. V, 583
McDonald, Ana V, 752
McDonald, Andrew V, 186
McDonald, Anna IV, 1360
McDonald, Anna IV, 1373
McDonald, Anna V, 693
McDonald, Annetta M. V, 693
McDonald, Asenath V, 186
McDonald, Bertha E. IV, 977
McDonald, Bertha Edna V, 186
McDonald, Bertha Elizabeth IV, 977
McDonald, Charity IV, 910
McDonald, Charles V, 693
McDonald, Charles V, 752
McDonald, Charles V, 814
McDonald, Charles V, 815
McDonald, Charles VI, 953
McDonald, Charles Albert V, 186
McDonald, Chas. IV, 977
McDonald, Curtis V, 186
McDonald, Dorcas V, 814
McDonald, Dorcas V, 815
McDonald, Duncan IV, 977
McDonald, Eber V, 186
McDonald, Elizabeth I, 1034
McDonald, Elizabeth I, 1036
McDonald, Elizabeth V, 95
McDonald, Elizabeth V, 723
McDonald, Elizabeth V, 814
McDonald, Elizabeth V, 815
McDonald, Elizabeth VI, 412
McDonald, Elizabeth VI, 420
McDonald, Emily Elton IV, 737
McDonald, Emma D. V, 261
McDonald, Emma D. V, 270
McDonald, Emma Jane I, 627
McDonald, Enos V, 814
McDonald, Enos V, 815
McDonald, Ester V, 693
McDonald, Estes IV, 1373
McDonald, Esther E. IV, 977
McDonald, Estus IV, 1373
McDonald, Fannie V, 693
McDonald, Florence Amelia V, 186
McDonald, Frank V, 513
McDonald, Frank V, 583
McDonald, Frank V, 693
McDonald, Frank L. V, 693
McDonald, Geo. V, 1008
McDonald, Geo. W. V, 1008
McDonald, George V, 513
McDonald, George V, 693
McDonald, George W. VI, 826
McDonald, Gerald Doan V, 693
McDonald, Grace V, 632
McDonald, Grace V, 1008
McDonald, Henrietta V, 752
McDonald, Ida Belle V, 1008
McDonald, Isaac VI, 907
McDonald, J. C. I, 627
McDonald, James III, 406
McDonald, James III, 426
McDonald, James IV, 1360
McDonald, James IV, 1373
McDonald, James V, 513
McDonald, James V, 583
McDonald, James V, 1008
McDonald, James W. V, 583
McDonald, James W. V, 693
McDonald, Jemima I, 1034
McDonald, Jemima I, 1036
McDonald, Jemima V, 179
McDonald, Jerusha IV, 1360
McDonald, John I, 1034
McDonald, John II, 507
McDonald, John IV, 98
McDonald, John V, 752
McDonald, John V, 814
McDonald, John Allen V, 186
McDonald, Jos. V, 760
McDonald, Joseph I, 1034
McDonald, Joseph I, 1036
McDonald, Joseph V, 723
McDonald, Joseph V, 748
McDonald, Joseph V, 752
McDonald, Joseph V, 807
McDonald, Joseph V, 814
McDonald, Joseph Peitsmeyer V, 261
McDonald, Keron V, 752
McDonald, Kitty IV, 737
McDonald, Lecy V, 513
McDonald, Louisa IV, 977
McDonald, Lydia I, 1034
McDonald, Lydia V, 77
McDonald, Lydia V, 95
McDonald, Lydia V, 179
McDonald, Lydia V, 186
McDonald, Lydia V, 752
McDonald, Lydia V, 754
McDonald, Lydia V, 755
McDonald, Lydia V, 815
McDonald, Mabel V, 693
McDonald, Mahala V, 760
McDonald, Mahala V, 768
McDonald, Mark V, 752
McDonald, Mark V, 814
McDonald, Mark V, 815
McDonald, Martha E. V, 347
McDonald, Mary I, 1034
McDonald, Mary II, 507
McDonald, Mary III, 103
McDonald, Mary III, 213
McDonald, Mary IV, 977
McDonald, Mary A. III, 223
McDonald, Mary A. IV, 977
McDonald, Mary Annetta V, 583
McDonald, Mary Dean V, 919
McDonald, Mary Etta V, 186
McDonald, Mordicai V, 1008
McDonald, Nancy B. III, 406
McDonald, Nancy B. III, 426
McDonald, Nathaniel IV, 1373
McDonald, Nettie V, 513
McDonald, Nettie V, 583
McDonald, Pearl I, 642
McDonald, Pearl Olive I, 627
McDonald, Peitsmeyer V, 270
McDonald, Phebe I, 1034
McDonald, Phebe I, 1035
McDonald, Rachel IV, 977
McDonald, Rachel V, 807
McDonald, Rachel M. IV, 977
McDonald, Rebekah VI, 420
McDonald, Richard IV, 737
McDonald, Rose V, 693
McDonald, Russel V, 513
McDonald, Russell V, 513
McDonald, Russell V, 583
McDonald, Russell V, 693
McDonald, Russell T. V, 693
McDonald, Ruth V, 513
McDonald, S. C. V, 95
McDonald, Sabin V, 95
McDonald, Samuel V, 693
McDonald, Sarah I, 146
McDonald, Sarah I, 165
McDonald, Sarah IV, 1373
McDonald, Sarah V, 95
McDonald, Sarah V, 513
McDonald, Sarah V, 583
McDonald, Sarah V, 693
McDonald, Sarah V, 723
McDonald, Sarah V, 752
McDonald, Sarah B. V, 693
McDonald, Sarah M. V, 752
McDonald, Sarah Maria III, 213
McDonald, Susannah IV, 1360
McDonald, Susannah IV, 1373
McDonald, Temperance V, 752
McDonald, Temperance V, 760
McDonald, Temperance V, 807
McDonald, Temperance V, 815
McDonald, Thomas I, 1034
McDonald, Thomas IV, 1373
McDonald, Thomas A. III, 213
McDonald, Thomas Russell V, 693
McDonald, Thos. V, 1008
McDonald, Wd. Mary II, 588
McDonald, William I, 1034
McDonald, William I, 1036
McDonald, William V, 179
McDonald, William V, 752
McDonald, William V, 814
McDonald, Wm. V, 815
McDonald, Wm. Estes V, 693
McDonall, Daniel VI, 863
McDonel, Esther E. IV, 977
McDonnal, Hannah II, 1013
McDonnald, Elizabeth I, 1034
McDonnald, Elizabeth V, 95
McDonnald, Jane F. IV, 1127
McDonnald, Jane F. IV, 1135
McDonnald, Joseph I, 1034
McDonnald, Mary I, 1034
McDonnald, S. C. V, 95
McDonnel, Hannah II, 392
McDonnel, John II, 588
McDonnel, Mary II, 392
McDonnell, John II, 588
McDonnell, John IV, 98
McDonnell, John M. IV, 98
McDonnell, Margaret VI, 197
McDonnell, Margaret VI, 212
McDonnell, Martha II, 588
McDonnell, Mary II, 392
McDonnell, Sabina IV, 98
McDonnell, Sabina T. IV, 98
McDonnell, Sabina T. V, 955
McDonnell, Sebina M. IV, 98
McDonnell, Wd. Mary II, 588
McDonnell, Wm. P. IV, 98
McDonnold, Louisa IV, 927
McDonnold, Louisa IV, 977
McDonnold, Martha II, 588
McDorman, James I, 684
McDorman, James I, 825
McDormick, Mary II, 200
McDormick, Mary II, 240
McDowel, Esther E. IV, 977
McDowel, John IV, 977
McDowell, Alex. III, 57
McDowell, Alex. III, 213
McDowell, Alex. III, 214
McDowell, Alex. H. III, 332
McDowell, Alexander II, 785
McDowell, Alexander III, 213
McDowell, Alexander H. III, 213
McDowell, Ann II, 512
McDowell, Ann II, 588
McDowell, Anna L. III, 149
McDowell, Anna L. III, 273
McDowell, Annie L. III, 213
McDowell, Annie L. III, 214
McDowell, Annie L. III, 301
McDowell, Arthur III, 214
McDowell, Caroline Carpenter III, 213
McDowell, Charles III, 214
Mcdowell, Charlotte Katharine III, 131
McDowell, Charlotte Katharine III, 213
McDowell, Cora III, 213
McDowell, Dr. Charles III, 89
McDowell, Dr. Charles III, 213
McDowell, Edwin Carleton III, 131
McDowell, Edwin Carleton III, 213
McDowell, Edwin Carlton III, 214
McDowell, Egbert G. III, 284
McDowell, Egbert Guernsey III, 214
McDowell, Eliza. Ann III, 57
McDowell, Elizabeth III, 213
McDowell, Elizabeth Ann III, 213
McDowell, Elizabeth Anne II, 785
McDowell, Ella B. III, 213
McDowell, Ella Vail III, 213
McDowell, Fannie III, 177
McDowell, Fannie III, 213
McDowell, Fannie M. III, 195
McDowell, Fannie M. III, 214
McDowell, Frances M. III, 214
McDowell, Frances Mary III, 214
McDowell, Frank III, 214
McDowell, G. A. III, 177
McDowell, Geo. A. III, 62
McDowell, Geo. A. III, 177
McDowell, Geo. A. III, 213
McDowell, Geo. Alexander III, 213
McDowell, George II, 392
McDowell, George A. III, 213
McDowell, George A. III, 284
McDowell, George Alexander III, 213
McDowell, George T. III, 213
McDowell, Harriett III, 89
McDowell, Harriett III, 213
McDowell, Henry M. III, 213
McDowell, Henry W. III, 213
McDowell, Ida III, 214
McDowell, Imogene III, 214
McDowell, Imogene III, 307
McDowell, Isabella III, 214
McDowell, Isabella M. III, 213
McDowell, Isabella M. III, 302
McDowell, James VI, 839
McDowell, James T. III, 213
McDowell, James Vail III, 213
McDowell, Jane III, 53
McDowell, Jane III, 62
McDowell, Jane III, 213
McDowell, Jos. T. III, 213
McDowell, Jos. T. III, 214
McDowell, Joseph III, 149
McDowell, Joseph T. III, 213
McDowell, Joseph T. III, 301
McDowell, Joseph T. III, 302
McDowell, Leona IV, 1327
McDowell, Lilian Josephine III, 214
McDowell, Lillian III, 83
McDowell, Lillian III, 145
McDowell, Lillian J. III, 149
McDowell, Lillian J. III, 214
McDowell, Lillian M. III, 214
McDowell, Lottie IV, 1327
McDowell, Margaret II, 392
McDowell, Mary I, 1124
McDowell, Mary III, 213
McDowell, Mary Ann III, 149
McDowell, Mary Ann III, 214
McDowell, Mary Dell III, 213
McDowell, Mary Dell III, 332
McDowell, Mary E. III, 284
McDowell, Mary J. III, 177
McDowell, Mary J. III, 213
McDowell, Mary Jane III, 213
McDowell, Mary Jane III, 284
McDowell, Mary Stone III, 214
McDowell, Mordecai III, 213
McDowell, Mrs. Sarah A. IV, 1327
McDowell, Naomi I, 1124
McDowell, Phebe Haviland III, 213
McDowell, Sarah II, 785
McDowell, Sarah III, 57
McDowell, Sarah III, 213
McDowell, Sarah III, 214
McDowell, Sarah IV, 330
McDowell, Sarah IV, 341
McDowell, Sarah ??? III, 213
McDowell, Sarah A. IV, 1327
McDowell, Sarah Maria III, 213
McDowell, Tandy VI, 837
McDowell, Theodore III, 145
McDowell, Theodore III, 214
McDowell, Theodore III, 307
McDowell, Theodore L. III, 214
McDowell, Thomas F. III, 213
McDowell, Thomas F. III, 214
McDowell, Thomas Fair III, 195
McDowell, Thos. F. III, 214
McDowell, Walter Thomas III, 214
McDowell, Wilmer Irving III, 213
McDuffie, Maggie Mae I, 219
McDugle, Elizabeth I, 405
McDugle, Elizabeth I, 419
McDurmott, Patrick B. V, 411
McEachin, Eliz. III, 446
McEldowney, Emma IV, 1040
McEldowney, Harry IV, 1040
McEldowney, Paul IV, 1040
McEldowney, Wm. IV, 1040
McEldowny, Emma IV, 1040
McEldowny, Harry IV, 1040
McEldowny, Harry W. IV, 1040
McEldowny, Paul IV, 1040
McEldowny, W. IV, 1040
McEldowny, Wm. IV, 1040
McElhany, Doris IV, 1257
McEliver, Charles E. V, 583
McEliver, Isaac V, 583
McEliver, Rhoda G. V, 583
McElkiney, Henrietta VI, 836
McElkiney, William VI, 836
McElory, James VI, 954
McElory, Margaret VI, 954
McElroy, Agnes IV, 433
McElroy, Agnes A. IV, 433
McElroy, Bell IV, 1285
McElroy, Mary IV, 1285
McElroy, Robert J. F. IV, 433
McElroy, Samuel IV, 1285
McElroy, Zetia V, 186
McElvaine, Jane VI, 872
McElvaine, Saml. VI, 872
McElvane, Alice V, 752
McElwee, Charles V, 583
McElwee, Charles E. V, 693
McElwee, Chas. V, 583
McElwee, Chas. E. V, 693
McElwee, Dana V, 661
McElwee, Elizabeth V, 693
McElwee, Ethbert J. V, 693
McElwee, Ethelbert V, 632
McElwee, Ethelbert J. V, 632
McElwee, Flora V, 583
McElwee, Helen V, 583
McElwee, Isaac R. V, 583
McElwee, Isaac R. V, 693
McElwee, Kate V, 583
McElwee, Kate V, 632
McElwee, Kate V, 693
McElwee, Louella K. V, 693
McElwee, May V, 661
McElwee, May V, 693
McElwee, Minnie V, 693
McElwee, Myrtle V, 613
McElwee, Myrtle V, 632
McElwee, Myrtle Sprague V, 6
McElwee, Rhoda G. V, 693
McElwee, Stella A. V, 693
McElwee, Will V, 583
McElwee, Will V, 632
McElwee, Winifred V, 583
McElwee, Wm. R. V, 583
McFadden, Ann V, 342
McFadden, Anna V, 583
McFadden, Esper Ann V, 583
McFadden, Esper Ann V, 693
McFadden, Eva V, 347
McFadden, James Lucien V, 58
McFadden, John V, 547
McFadden, John V, 583
McFadden, John V, 693
McFadden, John W. V, 693
McFadden, John William V, 58
McFadden, Laura D. V, 693
McFadden, Laura Delila V, 58
McFadden, Lydia A. V, 347
McFadden, Malinda V, 186
McFadden, Martha Jane V, 58
McFadden, Mary V, 693
McFadden, Mary Elizabeth V, 583
McFadden, Mary Elizabeth V, 693
McFadden, Samuel V, 583
McFadden, Samuel V, 693
McFadden, Susannah V, 547
McFadden, Susannah V, 583
McFadden, Susannah V, 693
McFaden, Sopha IV, 1285
McFall, James VI, 954
McFall, Jane VI, 954
McFarlan, Elizabeth III, 214
McFarland, Archie V, 632
McFarland, Benjamin VI, 954
McFarland, Blanch IV, 1257
McFarland, Blanche IV, 1257
McFarland, Charles IV, 1327
McFarland, Dessie IV, 1257
McFarland, Earl J. I, 945
McFarland, Earle J. I, 929
McFarland, George W. I, 929
McFarland, Guy IV, 1257
McFarland, James VI, 954
McFarland, James C. I, 1158
McFarland, John IV, 1257
McFarland, John VI, 954
McFarland, Julia E. I, 929
McFarland, Lewis Paul I, 929
McFarland, Lewis W. I, 929
McFarland, Lewis W. I, 945
McFarland, Margaret VI, 954
McFarland, Mary VI, 954
McFarland, Mrs. Stella M. IV, 1327
McFarland, Paul Lewis I, 945
McFarland, Pearl I, 945
McFarland, Pearl Edna I, 929
McFarland, Robert VI, 954
McFarland, Sabra IV, 1327
McFarland, Stella IV, 1327
McFarland, Thos. IV, 1327
McFarlin, James C. I, 1158
McFarlin, Mary II, 85
McFaul, Mary E. V, 52
McFaul, Mary E. V, 95
McFaul, Mary Elizabeth V, 95
McFee, C. N. I, 1159
McFee, Charles N. I, 1159
McFeeters, Mary IV, 1216
McGaffic, Emma IV, 737

cGaffick, Emma IV, 737
cGaffick, Emma A. IV, 737
cGahea, Elizabeth VI, 167
cGahea, Elizabeth VI, 197
cgahea, Mary VI, 165
cGahea, Mary VI, 167
cGahea, Samuel VI, 157
cGahea, Samuel VI, 197
cGahee, Lydia V, 713
cGahera, Elizabeth VI, 165
cGahera, Samuel VI, 165
cGann, Pleasant VI, 856
cGarr, Arthur IV, 47
cGarr, Rebecca III, 224
cGarr, William IV, 47
cGaskey, Cornelius II, 392
cGaskey, William II, 392
cGavock, ??? VI, 667
cGavock, Alice VI, 668
cGavock, Ann VI, 667
cGavock, Ann VI, 674
cGavock, Annie VI, 620
cGavock, Annie VI, 664
cGavock, Annie VI, 665
cGavock, Annie VI, 667
cGavock, Annie VI, 674
cGavock, John VI, 667
cGavock, John VI, 674
cGeach, Affinity VI, 530
cGeath Hoge, Mary VI, 654
cGeath, Mary VI, 506
cGeath, Mary VI, 551
cGeath, Mary VI, 577
cGeath, Mary VI, 652
cGeath, Mary VI, 653
cGeath, Mary VI, 654
cGeath, Mary VI, 664
Geath, Mary VI, 668
cGeath, Mary VI, 674
cGeath, Mary VI, 713
cGee, Ann VI, 197
gee, Charles VI, 953
cGee, Elizabeth VI, 197
Gee, Herbert I, 616
Gee, Huldah VI, 197
Gee, James VI, 197
Gee, Joel V, 187
Gee, John VI, 197
Gee, Laura I, 616
Gee, Luella V, 261
Gee, Lydia VI, 197
Gee, Maddox Stanley VI, 197
Gee, Martha V, 187
Gee, Martha VI, 197
gee, Martha VI, 953
Gee, Martha C. VI, 836
Gee, Mary I, 558
Gee, Mary VI, 197
Gee, Myrtle I, 616
Gee, Rebecca VI, 197
Gee, Rebeckah VI, 197
Gee, Samuel VI, 197
Gee, Samuel VI, 213
Gee, Sarah VI, 197
Gee, Sarah VI, 213
Gee, Sue VI, 642
Gee, Sue VI, 674
Gee, Wd. Mary VI, 197
Gee, William VI, 197
Gee, William VI, 836
Geehe, Lynch VI, 851
Geehe, Mathew VI, 851
Geehee, Jenny VI, 851
Gehan, Mary IV, 1327
gehee, Ann VI, 233
Gehee, Ann VI, 259
Gehee, Betsey VI, 884
Gehee, Cann VI, 259
Gehee, Carr VI, 259
Gehee, Charlotte VI, 954
Gehee, Elizabeth VI, 259
Gehee, John VI, 954
Gehee, Joseph VI, 259
Gehee, Judith VI, 259
Gehee, Mary I, 945
Gehee, Mary VI, 259
Gehee, Milley VI, 259
Gehee, Milly VI, 259
Gehee, Mourning VI, 954
Gehee, Ruth Hamilton, Jr. I, 945
Gehee, William VI, 954
Genaiss, James IV, 245
Genaiss, Mary IV, 245
Genaiss, Mary M. IV, 245
George, Agness VI, 960
George, Ann Elizabeth VI, 955
George, Edmond VI, 960
George, Edmund VI, 960
George, Elizabeth VI, 864
George, Elizabeth VI, 993

McGeorge, Fanny VI, 905
McGeorge, Law VI, 905
McGeorge, Lawrence VI, 864
McGeorge, Lawrence VI, 955
McGeorge, Lawrence VI, 960
McGeorge, Margaret VI, 923
McGeorge, Marget VI, 1014
McGeorge, Mary VI, 955
McGeorge, Mary VI, 960
McGeorge, Nancy VI, 955
McGeorge, Rhoda VI, 960
McGeorge, Rhoda VI, 1021
McGeorge, Ruthy VI, 955
McGeorge, William VI, 955
McGeorge, Wm. William VI, 1021
McGerr, Ann IV, 47
McGerr, James IV, 47
McGhee, Ann VI, 955
McGhee, Ann Booker VI, 1010
McGhee, Ann Mary VI, 923
McGhee, Charles VI, 954
McGhee, Charlotte VI, 954
McGhee, Elizabeth VI, 920
McGhee, Elizabeth F. H. VI, 988
McGhee, Emily VI, 953
McGhee, Emily VI, 955
McGhee, Frances VI, 938
McGhee, Grace IV, 737
McGhee, James VI, 954
McGhee, James VI, 994
McGhee, James VI, 1010
McGhee, James D. VI, 955
McGhee, John VI, 197
McGhee, John VI, 954
McGhee, John VI, 955
McGhee, Lena I, 920
McGhee, Lewis C. VI, 955
McGhee, Lucinda VI, 955
McGhee, Lucinda VI, 994
McGhee, Martha VI, 938
McGhee, Martha VI, 955
McGhee, Martha N. VI, 920
McGhee, Martha N. VI, 989
McGhee, Mary M. VI, 955
McGhee, Mourning VI, 954
McGhee, Patsey VI, 954
McGhee, Polly VI, 989
McGhee, Rachel VI, 954
McGhee, Saml. H. VI, 1010
McGhee, Samuel H. VI, 955
McGhee, Sopha VI, 938
McGhee, Sophia VI, 964
McGhee, Susanna R. VI, 955
McGhee, William VI, 923
McGhee, William VI, 954
McGhee, William VI, 955
McGhee, William VI, 988
McGhee, William T. VI, 955
McGhehe, Joseph VI, 233
Mcghehe, Joseph VI, 259
McGhehe, Mary VI, 233
Mcghehe, Mary VI, 259
McGhie, Jessie III, 310
McGhie, Viola IV, 245
McGill, Anna II, 1055
McGill, Deborah IV, 245
McGill, Deborah IV, 575
McGill, Deborah E. IV, 575
McGill, Deborah E. IV, 587
McGill, Grace IV, 1257
McGill, Hannah VI, 420
McGill, Minnie IV, 245
McGill, Susanna IV, 568
McGill, Susanna IV, 587
McGill, Wm., Jr. II, 895
McGinnes, Miriam II, 211
McGinnes, Miriam II, 240
McGinnis, Frances VI, 955
McGinnis, Isabel IV, 1257
McGinnis, John III, 214
McGinnis, John VI, 955
McGinnis, Loretta V, 835
McGinnis, Mary VI, 955
McGinnis, Mary Ann III, 214
McGinnis, Miriam II, 240
McGinnis, Nicholas VI, 955
McGinnis, Rev. ??? V, 835
McGinnis, Samuel M. V, 632
McGinnis, William III, 214
McGinns, Miriam II, 208
McGinty, Deborah I, 400
McGinty, Deborah I, 405
McGinty, Deborah I, 1048
McGinty, Deborah I, 1049
McGinty, Joseph I, 1048
McGinty, Joseph I, 1049
McGinty, Joseph Jackson I, 405
McGinty, Thomas I, 405
McGinty, Thomas I, 1048
McGinty, Thomas Jackson I, 1049

McGir, Alexander IV, 893
McGir, Ann IV, 893
McGir, Sarah IV, 893
McGir, Thomas IV, 893
McGirr, ??? IV, 1125
McGirr, Alexander IV, 1105
McGirr, Alexander IV, 1135
McGirr, Alexander C. IV, 419
McGirr, Alexander C. IV, 587
McGirr, Alexcinder C. IV, 1106
McGirr, Ann IV, 47
McGirr, Ann IV, 893
McGirr, Ann IV, 1135
McGirr, Arthur IV, 27
McGirr, Arthur IV, 47
McGirr, Arthur IV, 341
McGirr, Arthur IV, 419
McGirr, Arthur IV, 587
McGirr, Arthur IV, 1105
McGirr, Arthur IV, 1106
McGirr, Benjamin IV, 1040
McGirr, Elisabeth IV, 419
McGirr, Eliza Ann IV, 419
McGirr, Eliza Ann IV, 1106
McGirr, Elizabeth IV, 27
McGirr, Elizabeth IV, 47
McGirr, Elizabeth IV, 341
McGirr, Elizabeth IV, 419
McGirr, Elizabeth IV, 587
McGirr, Elizabeth IV, 1106
McGirr, Elizabeth IV, 1135
McGirr, Frances IV, 341
McGirr, Frances IV, 419
McGirr, Frances IV, 587
McGirr, Frances J. IV, 1106
McGirr, Francis J. IV, 419
McGirr, Francis J. IV, 587
McGirr, Francis J. IV, 1106
McGirr, Harpley IV, 1105
McGirr, Harpley IV, 1135
McGirr, Henry IV, 1105
McGirr, Henry IV, 1135
McGirr, Isaac IV, 47
McGirr, James IV, 47
McGirr, James IV, 566
McGirr, James IV, 587
McGirr, James IV, 1087
McGirr, James IV, 1105
McGirr, James IV, 1127
McGirr, James IV, 1135
McGirr, Jane F. IV, 1135
McGirr, John IV, 977
McGirr, John IV, 1105
McGirr, John IV, 1106
McGirr, Jonah IV, 1105
McGirr, Jonah IV, 1135
McGirr, Latitia IV, 1105
McGirr, Letitia IV, 1135
McGirr, Letitia IV, 1139
McGirr, Levi IV, 1105
McGirr, Lewis H. IV, 1106
McGirr, Lewis Henry IV, 1135
McGirr, Lydia IV, 1087
McGirr, Lydia IV, 1105
McGirr, Mahlon IV, 1105
McGirr, Martha IV, 44
McGirr, Martha IV, 47
McGirr, Mary IV, 977
McGirr, Mary IV, 1093
McGirr, Mary IV, 1105
McGirr, Mary IV, 1106
McGirr, Mary IV, 1135
McGirr, Mary C. IV, 419
McGirr, Mary M. IV, 1106
McGirr, Nancy IV, 47
McGirr, Nancy IV, 341
McGirr, Nancy IV, 419
McGirr, Nancy IV, 1103
McGirr, Nancy IV, 1106
McGirr, Nancy H. IV, 419
McGirr, Nancy H. IV, 587
McGirr, Nancy H. IV, 1106
McGirr, Rachel IV, 566
McGirr, Rachel IV, 587
McGirr, Rachel IV, 1127
McGirr, Rachel IV, 1135
McGirr, Rebecca IV, 35
McGirr, Rebecca IV, 47
McGirr, Rebecca IV, 419
McGirr, Sarah IV, 47
McGirr, Sarah IV, 341
McGirr, Sarah IV, 419
McGirr, Sarah IV, 587
McGirr, Sarah IV, 1040
McGirr, Sarah IV, 1087
McGirr, Sarah IV, 1103
McGirr, Sarah IV, 1105
McGirr, Sarah IV, 1106
McGirr, Sarah IV, 1127
McGirr, Sarah IV, 1135
McGirr, Sarah Ann IV, 1105

McGirr, Sarah C. IV, 419
McGirr, Sarah C. IV, 587
McGirr, Sarah C. IV, 1106
McGirr, Thomas IV, 893
McGirr, Thomas Elwood IV, 1135
McGirr, Walter J. IV, 1106
McGirr, Walter J. IV, 1135
McGirr, William IV, 35
McGirr, William IV, 47
McGirr, William P. IV, 419
McGirr, Wm. IV, 1105
McGirr, Wm. H. IV, 1135
McGladary, Ann V, 513
McGladdery, Ann V, 513
McGladdery, James V, 513
McGladdery, James V, 693
McGladdery, Margaret V, 693
McGladdery, Margaret E. V, 693
McGlade, Robert V, 95
McGlady, Lydia II, 392
McGlasson, Barnet VI, 836
McGlasson, Dosha VI, 955
McGlasson, Jane VI, 955
McGlasson, Joel VI, 955
McGlasson, Matthew VI, 955
McGlasson, Sophia VI, 836
McGlasson, William VI, 955
McGlathery, Elinor Govett II, 392
McGlathery, Hannah II, 392
McGlathery, Lydia II, 392
McGlathry, Eleanor II, 534
McGlathry, Elizabeth II, 534
McGlathry, Lydia II, 534
McGlathry, Lydia II, 589
McGlathry, Wm. II, 534
McGlaughlin, Elizabeth VI, 955
McGlaughlin, Thomas VI, 955
McGlinchrey, Bell IV, 1257
McGlinchrey, Thomas A. IV, 1257
McGlocklin, Charles, Jr. VI, 955
McGlocklin, Chas. VI, 955
McGlocklin, Elizabeth VI, 955
McGlothan, Marley V, 752
McGlother, Ann E. V, 752
McGlother, Anna E. V, 737
McGlothin, Marley V, 752
McGlothin, Verlin V, 752
McGlothlan, John VI, 351
McGlothlan, John VI, 906
McGlothlan, John VI, 957
McGlothlan, Nancy VI, 351
McGlothlan, William VI, 351
McGlothlan, William VI, 888
McGlothlen, John VI, 971
McGlothlen, Mary VI, 971
McGlothlin, Charles, Jr. VI, 955
McGlothlin, Elizabeth VI, 955
McGlothlin, John VI, 955
McGlothlin, Rhoda VI, 955
McGlothlin, Thomas VI, 921
McGlothlin, Thomas VI, 955
McGonigal, Geo. H. IV, 1327
McGonigal, Nancy III, 490
McGonigal, Olive IV, 1327
McGowan, Bertha IV, 737
McGowan, Eugene IV, 737
McGowen, James IV, 910
McGowin, Thomas P. V, 1008
McGrab, Charles VI, 836
McGrab, Frankey VI, 836
McGrail, Alfred IV, 129
McGrail, Alfred IV, 205
McGrail, Alfred IV, 250
McGrail, Alfred IV, 484
McGrail, Alfred IV, 832
McGrail, Alfred H. IV, 832
McGrail, Amey IV, 484
McGrail, Amy IV, 484
McGrail, Amy Ann IV, 129
McGrail, Amy Ann IV, 135
McGrail, Amy Ann IV, 250
McGrail, Amy Ann IV, 832
McGrail, Amy Ann IV, 839
McGrail, Amy Ann McGrail IV, 135
McGrail, Ann IV, 98
McGrail, Ann IV, 484
McGrail, Ann Eliza IV, 832
McGrail, Anna E. IV, 832
McGrail, Annie A. IV, 801
McGrail, Annie A. IV, 832
McGrail, Deborah IV, 98
McGrail, Deborah IV, 129
McGrail, Deborah IV, 484
McGrail, Edith IV, 484
McGrail, Edwin G. IV, 135
McGrail, Edwin G. IV, 832
McGrail, Eliza IV, 484
McGrail, Elizabeth IV, 98
McGrail, Elizabeth IV, 129
McGrail, Elizabeth IV, 135

McGrail, Elizabeth IV, 832
McGrail, Elizabeth A. IV, 484
McGrail, Finley IV, 484
McGrail, Francis Price IV, 135
McGrail, Francis Price IV, 832
McGrail, George G. IV, 129
McGrail, George G. IV, 135
McGrail, George G. IV, 250
McGrail, George G. IV, 832
McGrail, George Gilbert IV, 135
McGrail, Gilbert IV, 484
McGrail, Hannah IV, 135
McGrail, Irving T. IV, 832
McGrail, Isabel IV, 129
McGrail, Isabell IV, 129
McGrail, Isabella IV, 484
McGrail, James IV, 98
McGrail, James IV, 129
McGrail, James IV, 250
McGrail, James IV, 484
McGrail, James W. IV, 484
McGrail, John IV, 98
McGrail, John IV, 128
McGrail, John IV, 129
McGrail, John IV, 484
McGrail, Lamira IV, 250
McGrail, Lydia M. IV, 484
McGrail, Mary IV, 98
McGrail, Mary IV, 128
McGrail, Mary IV, 129
McGrail, Mary IV, 135
McGrail, Mary IV, 250
McGrail, Mary IV, 484
McGrail, Mary A. IV, 832
McGrail, Mary Agnes IV, 832
McGrail, Mary Ann IV, 832
McGrail, Moses IV, 98
McGrail, Rachel IV, 98
McGrail, Rachel IV, 129
McGrail, Rachel IV, 484
McGrail, Rebecca IV, 98
McGrail, Rebecca IV, 129
McGrail, Rebecca IV, 135
McGrail, Rebecca IV, 136
McGrail, Rebecca IV, 205
McGrail, Rebecca IV, 250
McGrail, Rebecca IV, 484
McGrail, Rebecca IV, 832
McGrail, Sarah IV, 98
McGrail, Sarah IV, 100
McGrail, Sarah IV, 129
McGrail, Sarah IV, 135
McGrail, Sarah IV, 483
McGrail, Sarah IV, 484
McGrail, Sarah IV, 1135
McGrail, Sina IV, 832
McGrail, Susan IV, 484
McGrail, Thomas IV, 98
McGrail, Thomas IV, 484
McGrail, Uriah Price IV, 135
McGrail, Uriah Price IV, 832
McGrail, Wd. Rebecca IV, 839
McGrail, William IV, 250
McGraile, Deborah IV, 129
McGraile, Isabel IV, 129
McGraile, John IV, 128
McGraile, John IV, 129
McGraile, Mary IV, 128
McGraile, Mary IV, 129
McGraile, Rachel IV, 129
McGraile, Sarah IV, 129
McGrale, Deborah IV, 129
McGrath, Mary VI, 749
McGraw, Thomas G. VI, 827
McGray, Charles VI, 834
McGray, Mary VI, 530
McGregor, Catharine VI, 955
McGregor, Harriet III, 484
McGregor, Harriet III, 490
McGregor, Maria V, 693
McGregor, Peter III, 484
McGregor, Peter III, 490
McGregor, Spotswood VI, 955
McGreil, Rebecca IV, 129
McGreil, Rebecca IV, 133
McGrew, ??? IV, 531
McGrew, Abner IV, 130
McGrew, Abner Gilbert IV, 129
McGrew, Addison IV, 485
McGrew, Agnes IV, 1067
McGrew, Agnes v. IV, 726
McGrew, Agnes V. IV, 826
McGrew, Agnes V. IV, 1067
McGrew, Agnes V. IV, 1103
McGrew, Agnes V. IV, 1106
McGrew, Aletta IV, 245
McGrew, Aletta IV, 466
McGrew, Aletta IV, 485
McGrew, Aletta IV, 505
McGrew, Alexander IV, 129
McGrew, Almedia IV, 1054

McGrew, Almedia IV, 1066
McGrew, Almedia IV, 1067
McGrew, Althisa IV, 246
McGrew, Alva IV, 1066
McGrew, Amanda IV, 471
McGrew, Amanda IV, 485
McGrew, Amanda IV, 486
McGrew, Anderson H. IV, 1172
McGrew, Anderson J. IV, 485
McGrew, Ann IV, 126
McGrew, Ann IV, 129
McGrew, Ann IV, 246
McGrew, Ann IV, 289
McGrew, Ann IV, 304
McGrew, Ann IV, 480
McGrew, Ann IV, 485
McGrew, Ann IV, 608
McGrew, Ann V, 919
McGrew, Ann C. IV, 245
McGrew, Ann E. IV, 486
McGrew, Ann E. IV, 501
McGrew, Ann G. IV, 129
McGrew, Ann G. IV, 170
McGrew, Ann G. IV, 211
McGrew, Ann G. IV, 246
McGrew, Ann G. IV, 485
McGrew, Ann J. IV, 198
McGrew, Ann J. IV, 246
McGrew, Ann P. IV, 486
McGrew, Ann P. V, 914
McGrew, Ann P. V, 919
McGrew, Ann W. IV, 479
McGrew, Ann W. IV, 485
McGrew, Anna IV, 246
McGrew, Anna IV, 419
McGrew, Anna IV, 539
McGrew, Anna L. IV, 1257
McGrew, Annaletta IV, 486
McGrew, Anne IV, 473
McGrew, Anne IV, 486
McGrew, Anne IV, 539
McGrew, Anne G. IV, 486
McGrew, Archebald B. IV, 129
McGrew, Archibald IV, 129
McGrew, Asa IV, 246
McGrew, Benjamin IV, 129
McGrew, Benjamin IV, 130
McGrew, Benjamin H. IV, 486
McGrew, Benjamin H. IV, 1172
McGrew, Bertha IV, 832
McGrew, Caroline IV, 246
McGrew, Caroline IV, 277
McGrew, Caroline IV, 1172
McGrew, Catherine IV, 129
McGrew, David IV, 485
McGrew, David IV, 486
McGrew, David D. IV, 1172
McGrew, David Davis IV, 1172
McGrew, David Smith IV, 1067
McGrew, Deborah IV, 75
Mcgrew, Deborah IV, 99
McGrew, Deborah IV, 99
McGrew, Deborah IV, 128
McGrew, Deborah IV, 129
McGrew, Deborah IV, 130
McGrew, Deborah IV, 475
McGrew, Deborah IV, 485
McGrew, Deborah IV, 486
McGrew, Deborah IV, 1066
McGrew, Deborah IV, 1172
McGrew, Deborah IV, 1197
McGrew, Deborah Jane IV, 1067
McGrew, Deborah Jane IV, 1073
McGrew, Dinah IV, 47
McGrew, Dinah IV, 99
McGrew, Dinah IV, 129
McGrew, Dinah IV, 341
McGrew, Dinah IV, 485
McGrew, Dinah IV, 539
McGrew, Dinah IV, 557
McGrew, Dinah VI, 420
McGrew, Dorsey IV, 485
McGrew, Dorsey IV, 486
McGrew, Dorsey IV, 1172
McGrew, Ebeneezer IV, 98
McGrew, Ebenezer IV, 99
McGrew, Edgar IV, 813
McGrew, Edgar W. IV, 832
McGrew, Edith IV, 246
McGrew, Edith IV, 277
McGrew, Edith M. IV, 246
McGrew, Edith M. IV, 278
McGrew, Edwar W. IV, 832
McGrew, Eleanor IV, 486
McGrew, Elenor IV, 539
McGrew, Eli IV, 485
McGrew, Eli W. IV, 413
McGrew, Elijah IV, 485
McGrew, Eliza IV, 213
McGrew, Eliza IV, 246
McGrew, Eliza IV, 419
McGrew, Eliza IV, 467
McGrew, Eliza IV, 485
McGrew, Eliza IV, 486
McGrew, Eliza IV, 608
McGrew, Eliza IV, 643
McGrew, Eliza C. IV, 419
McGrew, Eliza C. IV, 444
McGrew, Eliza G. IV, 170
McGrew, Eliza G. IV, 245
McGrew, Eliza G. IV, 608
McGrew, Eliza H. IV, 246
McGrew, Eliza H. IV, 277
McGrew, Eliza H. IV, 280
Mcgrew, Eliza H. IV, 282
McGrew, Eliza J. IV, 413
McGrew, Eliza J. IV, 486
McGrew, Eliza Jane IV, 204
McGrew, Eliza Jane IV, 245
McGrew, Eliza Jane IV, 246
McGrew, Eliza Jane IV, 485
McGrew, Eliza Jane IV, 570
McGrew, Eliza Jane IV, 579
McGrew, Eliza Jane IV, 580
McGrew, Eliza Jane IV, 585
McGrew, Eliza Jane IV, 587
McGrew, Elizabeth IV, 47
McGrew, Elizabeth IV, 99
Mcgrew, Elizabeth IV, 99
McGrew, Elizabeth IV, 104
McGrew, Elizabeth IV, 123
McGrew, Elizabeth IV, 124
McGrew, Elizabeth IV, 129
McGrew, Elizabeth IV, 130
McGrew, Elizabeth IV, 245
McGrew, Elizabeth IV, 246
McGrew, Elizabeth IV, 341
McGrew, Elizabeth IV, 465
McGrew, Elizabeth IV, 470
McGrew, Elizabeth IV, 484
McGrew, Elizabeth IV, 485
McGrew, Elizabeth IV, 486
McGrew, Elizabeth IV, 488
McGrew, Elizabeth IV, 505
McGrew, Elizabeth IV, 521
McGrew, Elizabeth IV, 539
McGrew, Elizabeth IV, 617
McGrew, Elizabeth IV, 693
McGrew, Elizabeth IV, 1076
McGrew, Elizabeth A. IV, 198
McGrew, Elizabeth A. IV, 245
McGrew, Elizabeth A. IV, 949
McGrew, Elizabeth A. IV, 977
McGrew, Elizabeth Ann IV, 485
McGrew, Elizabeth W. IV, 486
McGrew, Elizabeth W. IV, 1257
McGrew, Elma IV, 246
McGrew, Elma IV, 280
McGrew, Elmer IV, 1067
McGrew, Elmer E. IV, 1106
McGrew, Emily IV, 127
McGrew, Emily IV, 129
McGrew, Emly IV, 129
McGrew, Emma L. IV, 413
McGrew, Eulyssus A. IV, 513
McGrew, Eulyssus A. IV, 539
McGrew, Findley IV, 99
McGrew, Findley IV, 246
McGrew, Findley IV, 1172
McGrew, Finely IV, 71
McGrew, Finley I, 558
McGrew, Finley IV, 47
McGrew, Finley IV, 75
McGrew, Finley IV, 99
McGrew, Finley IV, 129
McGrew, Finley IV, 245
McGrew, Finley IV, 341
McGrew, Finley IV, 485
McGrew, Finley IV, 486
McGrew, Finley IV, 539
McGrew, Finley IV, 579
McGrew, Finley IV, 737
McGrew, Finley IV, 1172
McGrew, Finley VI, 420
McGrew, Finley A. IV, 129
McGrew, Finley A. IV, 485
McGrew, Finley A. IV, 486
McGrew, Finley B. IV, 466
McGrew, Finley B. IV, 485
McGrew, Finley B. IV, 505
McGrew, Finley W. IV, 204
McGrew, Finley W. IV, 246
McGrew, Finley W. IV, 486
McGrew, Finley W. IV, 539
McGrew, Finley, Jr. IV, 485
McGrew, Finley, Sr. IV, 129
McGrew, Finly VI, 420
McGrew, Geo. IV, 539
McGrew, George IV, 485
McGrew, George IV, 486
McGrew, Gilbert IV, 213
McGrew, Gilbert IV, 245
McGrew, Gilbert IV, 246
McGrew, Gilbert IV, 277
McGrew, Gilbert IV, 280
McGrew, Gilbert IV, 419
McGrew, Gilbert IV, 444
McGrew, Gilbert IV, 485
McGrew, Harriet IV, 1164
McGrew, Harriet IV, 1172
McGrew, Harriet C. IV, 1172
McGrew, Ida IV, 485
McGrew, Isaac Dewees IV, 1106
McGrew, Isabel IV, 47
Mcgrew, Isabella IV, 99
McGrew, Isabella IV, 129
McGrew, Isabella IV, 130
McGrew, Isabella IV, 477
McGrew, Isabella IV, 485
McGrew, Isabella IV, 486
Mcgrew, Jacob IV, 99
McGrew, Jacob IV, 129
McGrew, Jacob IV, 485
McGrew, Jacob IV, 486
McGrew, Jacob VI, 420
McGrew, Jacob A. IV, 485
McGrew, Jacob A. IV, 486
McGrew, Jacob B. IV, 486
McGrew, Jacob B. IV, 1172
McGrew, Jacob O. IV, 245
McGrew, Jacob O. IV, 246
McGrew, James IV, 47
Mcgrew, James IV, 99
McGrew, James IV, 125
McGrew, James IV, 129
McGrew, James IV, 134
McGrew, James IV, 245
McGrew, James IV, 246
McGrew, James IV, 485
McGrew, James IV, 486
McGrew, James IV, 608
McGrew, James IV, 1066
McGrew, James VI, 420
McGrew, James VI, 530
McGrew, James VI, 552
McGrew, James A. IV, 99
McGrew, James A. IV, 123
McGrew, James A. IV, 129
McGrew, James A. IV, 246
McGrew, James A. IV, 539
McGrew, James A. IV, 832
McGrew, James Addison IV, 485
Mcgrew, James B. IV, 99
McGrew, James B. IV, 129
McGrew, James B. IV, 245
McGrew, James B. IV, 485
McGrew, James B. IV, 486
McGrew, James B. IV, 726
McGrew, James B. IV, 826
McGrew, James B. IV, 1172
McGrew, James C. IV, 98
McGrew, James C. IV, 99
McGrew, James C. IV, 246
McGrew, James C. IV, 485
McGrew, James C. IV, 486
McGrew, James H. IV, 486
McGrew, James M. IV, 246
McGrew, James P. IV, 1103
McGrew, James W. IV, 98
McGrew, James W. IV, 126
McGrew, James W. IV, 129
McGrew, James W. IV, 170
McGrew, James W. IV, 198
McGrew, James W. IV, 211
McGrew, James W. IV, 246
McGrew, James W. IV, 289
McGrew, James W. IV, 473
McGrew, James W. IV, 485
McGrew, James W. IV, 486
McGrew, James, Jr. IV, 47
McGrew, James, Jr. IV, 99
Mcgrew, James, Jr. IV, 99
McGrew, James, Jr. IV, 485
McGrew, James, Sr. IV, 71
McGrew, Jamima IV, 1257
McGrew, Jane IV, 47
McGrew, Jane IV, 99
McGrew, Jane IV, 129
McGrew, Jane IV, 246
McGrew, Jane IV, 477
McGrew, Jane IV, 485
McGrew, Jane IV, 486
McGrew, Jane IV, 488
McGrew, Jane IV, 499
McGrew, Jane VI, 420
McGrew, Jas. IV, 477
McGrew, Jas. IV, 485
McGrew, Jas. A. IV, 550
McGrew, Jas. B. IV, 485
McGrew, Jasper C. IV, 1066
McGrew, Jemima IV, 486
McGrew, Jennie IV, 486
McGrew, Jesse IV, 485
McGrew, John IV, 129
McGrew, John IV, 485
McGrew, John IV, 486
McGrew, John VI, 420
McGrew, John B. IV, 245
McGrew, John B. IV, 485
McGrew, John B. IV, 486
McGrew, John B. IV, 490
McGrew, Joseph IV, 91
Mcgrew, Joseph IV, 99
McGrew, Joseph IV, 216
McGrew, Joseph IV, 245
McGrew, Joseph IV, 485
McGrew, Joseph IV, 486
McGrew, Joseph A. IV, 486
McGrew, Joseph A. V, 919
McGrew, Joseph Addison V, 919
McGrew, Josephine K. IV, 486
McGrew, Josephine K. IV, 1257
McGrew, Julian IV, 485
McGrew, Juliann IV, 465
McGrew, Juliann IV, 486
McGrew, Lemuel IV, 1066
McGrew, Lindley B. IV, 246
McGrew, Lydia IV, 129
McGrew, Lydia IV, 130
McGrew, Lydia IV, 134
McGrew, Lydia B. IV, 211
McGrew, Lydia B. IV, 245
McGrew, Lydia B. IV, 485
McGrew, Lydia V. IV, 1066
McGrew, Lydia V. IV, 1067
McGrew, Lydia V. IV, 1076
McGrew, Margaret IV, 47
McGrew, Margaret IV, 67
McGrew, Margaret IV, 91
Mcgrew, Margaret IV, 99
McGrew, Margaret IV, 129
McGrew, Margaret IV, 130
McGrew, Margaret IV, 134
McGrew, Margaret IV, 216
McGrew, Margaret IV, 245
McGrew, Margaret IV, 246
McGrew, Margaret IV, 485
McGrew, Margaret IV, 726
McGrew, Margaret IV, 1066
McGrew, Margaret IV, 1103
McGrew, Margaret IV, 1135
McGrew, Margaret VI, 420
McGrew, Margaret Ann IV, 128
McGrew, Margaret Ann IV, 129
McGrew, Margaret Ann IV, 130
McGrew, Margaret V. IV, 826
McGrew, Margaret V. IV, 1066
McGrew, Martha IV, 99
McGrew, Martha IV, 129
McGrew, Martha IV, 485
McGrew, Martha IV, 486
McGrew, Martha IV, 1172
McGrew, Martha IV, 1257
McGrew, Martha J. IV, 486
McGrew, Mary IV, 47
McGrew, Mary IV, 99
McGrew, Mary IV, 124
McGrew, Mary IV, 125
McGrew, Mary IV, 129
McGrew, Mary IV, 135
McGrew, Mary IV, 245
McGrew, Mary IV, 246
McGrew, Mary IV, 341
McGrew, Mary IV, 485
McGrew, Mary IV, 486
McGrew, Mary IV, 490
McGrew, Mary IV, 493
McGrew, Mary IV, 503
McGrew, Mary IV, 516
McGrew, Mary IV, 539
McGrew, Mary IV, 737
McGrew, Mary IV, 791
McGrew, Mary IV, 832
McGrew, Mary VI, 420
McGrew, Mary VI, 530
McGrew, Mary VI, 552
McGrew, Mary A. IV, 486
McGrew, Mary Ann IV, 485
McGrew, Mary Emily IV, 485
McGrew, Mary Emily IV, 486
McGrew, Mary H. IV, 485
McGrew, Mary H. IV, 832
McGrew, Mary Jane IV, 129
McGrew, Mary Jane IV, 130
McGrew, Mary Jane IV, 485
McGrew, Mary Rebecca IV, 485
McGrew, Mary T. IV, 282
McGrew, Mary T. IV, 1257
McGrew, Mary Tabitha IV, 486
McGrew, Mary W. IV, 246
McGrew, Mary W. IV, 539
McGrew, Mary W. IV, 550
McGrew, Maurice Austin IV, 246
McGrew, May IV, 485
McGrew, Moses IV, 129
McGrew, Moses IV, 479
McGrew, Moses IV, 485
Mcgrew, Nathan IV, 99
McGrew, Nathan IV, 124
McGrew, Nathan IV, 129
McGrew, Nathan IV, 135
McGrew, Nathan IV, 245
McGrew, Nathan IV, 246
McGrew, Nathan IV, 484
McGrew, Nathan IV, 488
McGrew, Nathan IV, 539
McGrew, Nathan VI, 420
McGrew, Nathan M. IV, 129
McGrew, Oliver IV, 245
McGrew, Oliver IV, 485
McGrew, Phebe IV, 129
McGrew, Phebe Catharine IV, 130
McGrew, Phebe Catharine IV, 132
McGrew, Philena IV, 129
McGrew, Philena W. IV, 126
McGrew, Philena W. IV, 130
McGrew, R. Bertha IV, 813
McGrew, R. Bertha IV, 832
McGrew, Rachel IV, 98
McGrew, Rachel IV, 99
McGrew, Rachel IV, 341
McGrew, Rachel IV, 485
McGrew, Rachel IV, 539
McGrew, Rachel IV, 557
McGrew, Rachel A. IV, 486
McGrew, Rachel P. IV, 477
McGrew, Rachel P. IV, 486
McGrew, Rachel P. IV, 531
McGrew, Rachel P. IV, 532
McGrew, Rachel P. IV, 539
McGrew, Rachel, Jr. IV, 341
McGrew, Rachel, Jr. IV, 485
Mcgrew, Rebecca IV, 99
McGrew, Rebecca IV, 104
McGrew, Rebecca IV, 123
McGrew, Rebecca IV, 125
McGrew, Rebecca IV, 129
McGrew, Rebecca IV, 130
McGrew, Rebecca IV, 245
McGrew, Rebecca IV, 463
McGrew, Rebecca IV, 485
McGrew, Rebecca IV, 486
McGrew, Rebecca IV, 539
McGrew, Rebecca IV, 737
McGrew, Rebecca IV, 1093
McGrew, Rebecca IV, 1106
McGrew, Rebecca VI, 420
McGrew, Rebecca Bertha IV, 832
McGrew, Rebecca D. IV, 204
McGrew, Rebecca D. IV, 246
McGrew, Rebecca D. IV, 579
McGrew, Rebeckah IV, 99
McGrew, Rebeckah IV, 485
McGrew, Reece IV, 737
McGrew, Rees IV, 129
McGrew, Rosanna IV, 99
McGrew, Rosanna IV, 104
McGrew, Rosanna IV, 737
McGrew, Ross IV, 485
McGrew, Ross IV, 486
McGrew, Ross H. IV, 486
McGrew, Ruth IV, 122
McGrew, Ruth IV, 129
Mcgrew, Samuel IV, 99
McGrew, Samuel IV, 129
McGrew, Samuel IV, 485
McGrew, Samuel IV, 532
McGrew, Samuel IV, 539
McGrew, Samuel IV, 1066
McGrew, Samuel IV, 1076
McGrew, Samuel C. IV, 477
McGrew, Samuel C. IV, 486
McGrew, Samuel C. IV, 539
McGrew, Samuel P. IV, 486
McGrew, Samuel, Jr. IV, 130
McGrew, Sarah IV, 485
McGrew, Shepherd IV, 129
Mcgrew, Simeon IV, 99
McGrew, Simeon IV, 485
McGrew, Simon IV, 99
McGrew, Simon B. IV, 129
McGrew, Simon B. IV, 130
McGrew, Simon B. IV, 486
McGrew, Simon O. IV, 124
McGrew, Simon O. IV, 129
McGrew, Simon O. IV, 130
McGrew, Simon O. IV, 135
McGrew, Sinah IV, 99
McGrew, Sinah IV, 341
McGrew, Sinah IV, 485
McGrew, Sinai IV, 518
McGrew, Sinai IV, 539
McGrew, Stephen IV, 99

Grew, Stephen IV, 129
Grew, Susan IV, 99
Grew, Susan IV, 246
Grew, Susan IV, 289
Grew, Susan IV, 643
Grew, Susan IV, 660
Grew, Susan G. IV, 513
Grew, Susan G. IV, 539
Grew, Susan Jane IV, 245
Grew, Susan Jane IV, 485
Grew, Susan P. IV, 480
Grew, Susan P. IV, 485
Grew, Susan P. V, 914
Grew, Susan P. V, 919
Grew, Susanna IV, 129
Grew, Susannah IV, 128
Grew, Susannah IV, 129
Grew, Susannah IV, 135
Grew, T. B. IV, 245
Grew, Thomas IV, 47
grew, Thomas IV, 99
Grew, Thomas IV, 129
Grew, Thomas IV, 485
Grew, Thomas IV, 486
Grew, Thomas B. IV, 485
Grew, Thomas B. IV, 486
Grew, Thomas B. V, 919
Grew, Thomas O. IV, 486
Grew, Thomas O. V, 919
Grew, Thomas P. IV, 485
Grew, Thos. V, 919
Grew, Thos. B. IV, 480
Grew, Thos. B. V, 914
Grew, Thos. B. V, 919
Grew, Walter IV, 246
Grew, Willets IV, 245
Grew, Willett IV, 485
Grew, William IV, 485
Grew, William IV, 737
Grew, William IV, 1257
Grew, William B. IV, 486
Grew, William L. IV, 485
Grew, William Leslie IV, 486
Grew, Wm. IV, 129
Grew, Wm. IV, 282
Griffen, Dr. ??? V, 752
Griffen, Rebecca V, 752
Griffith, Margaret VI, 754
Guilkin, Teresa IV, 99
Guilkin, Teresa IV, 115
Guiness, Hannah Isabel IV, 1257
Guiness, Isabel IV, 1257
Guire, Edna VI, 711
Guire, Edna VI, 716
Guire, George W. IV, 539
Guire, Jennie G. II, 894
Guire, Jennie Graham II, 894
Guire, Joseph VI, 955
Guire, Lawrence VI, 955
Guire, Lawrence VI, 990
Guire, Mary IV, 1327
Guire, Mary VI, 955
Guire, Mary VI, 990
Guire, Rachel V, 560
Guire, Rachel V, 583
Guire, Seth E. VI, 960
Gumery, Jane I, 891
Gumery, Jane I, 905
Gur, Arthur IV, 587
Gur, Elizabeth IV, 587
Gurthy, Martha V, 692
Hahea, Mary VI, 197
Hailing, John VI, 907
Hammon, Elizabeth V, 900
Hammon, Elizabeth V, 919
Haney, Cornelius VI, 836
Haney, Cornelius VI, 861
Haney, Frances VI, 861
Haney, Patience VI, 836
Hatten, Rebecca IV, 479
Hatten, Rebecca IV, 486
Hell, Dula Larbet IV, 978
Hell, Nora IV, 978
Hell, Wm. IV, 978
Henney, George VI, 836
Henney, Phebe VI, 836
Henry, Solomon V, 1008
Hugh, Dennis IV, 246
Hugh, John IV, 246
Ibray, Emily IV, 1285
Ibray, John M. IV, 1285
Iilvaain, Martha II, 782
Iilvain, Anna Mary II, 783
Iilvain, Hannah II, 782
Ilhargy, Sophis II, 706
Ilhenny, A. C. V, 411
Ilhenny, John J. V, 411
Ilhenny, Sue A. V, 411
Ilhenny, Susan V, 411
Illhenry, Susan V, 405
McIllhenry, Susan V, 411
McIllvain, Hannah II, 804
McIllvain, Hugh, Sr. II, 804
McIllvain, Susan Hunt II, 804
McIlvain, Abraham Gibbons II, 894
McIlvain, Abraham R. II, 894
McIlvain, Abraham Robinson II, 807
McIlvain, Ann II, 820
McIlvain, Anna II, 313
McIlvain, Anna II, 314
McIlvain, Anna II, 899
McIlvain, Anna E. II, 322
McIlvain, Anna E. II, 325
McIlvain, Anna E. II, 807
McIlvain, Anna E. II, 894
McIlvain, Anna Mary II, 807
McIlvain, Anna Mary II, 838
McIlvain, Anna Mary II, 894
McIlvain, Anna Mary II, 921
McIlvain, Charles Henry II, 894
McIlvain, Chas. Henry II, 807
McIlvain, Clara II, 322
McIlvain, Clara J. II, 894
McIlvain, Edith S. II, 322
McIlvain, Edith S. II, 894
McIlvain, Edith Sterling II, 311
McIlvain, Edith Sterling II, 807
McIlvain, Edith Weatherby II, 311
McIlvain, Edna Bunting II, 807
McIlvain, Elizabeth M. II, 807
McIlvain, Elizabeth M. II, 808
McIlvain, Elizabeth M. II, 894
McIlvain, Emma II, 807
McIlvain, Emma II, 852
McIlvain, Emma II, 894
McIlvain, George Debble II, 899
McIlvain, Hannah II, 311
McIlvain, Hannah II, 312
McIlvain, Hannah II, 802
McIlvain, Hannah II, 807
McIlvain, Hannah II, 833
McIlvain, Hannah II, 838
McIlvain, Hannah II, 880
McIlvain, Hannah II, 885
McIlvain, Hannah II, 894
McIlvain, Hannah II, 897
McIlvain, Hannah G. II, 894
McIlvain, Helen II, 784
McIlvain, Helen II, 807
McIlvain, Helen II, 842
McIlvain, Helen II, 894
McIlvain, Hugh II, 311
McIlvain, Hugh II, 312
McIlvain, Hugh II, 802
McIlvain, Hugh II, 807
McIlvain, Hugh II, 808
McIlvain, Hugh II, 838
McIlvain, Hugh II, 842
McIlvain, Hugh II, 852
McIlvain, Hugh II, 858
McIlvain, Hugh II, 880
McIlvain, Hugh II, 894
McIlvain, Hugh II, 897
McIlvain, Hugh II, 921
McIlvain, Hugh, Jr. II, 807
McIlvain, J. Gibson II, 894
McIlvain, J. Humphreys II, 894
McIlvain, James II, 311
McIlvain, James II, 313
McIlvain, James II, 322
McIlvain, James II, 807
McIlvain, James II, 894
McIlvain, James Sterling II, 311
McIlvain, James Sterling II, 322
McIlvain, James Sterling II, 807
McIlvain, James Sterling II, 894
McIlvain, James, Jr. II, 322
McIlvain, John Gibson II, 807
McIlvain, John Gibson II, 808
McIlvain, John Gibson, Jr. II, 808
McIlvain, John Humphreys II, 808
McIlvain, John Humphries II, 894
McIlvain, John Hunt II, 807
McIlvain, John Hunt II, 894
McIlvain, Julia II, 321
McIlvain, Julia II, 322
McIlvain, Julia P. II, 322
McIlvain, Julia P. II, 807
McIlvain, Julia P. II, 894
McIlvain, Lucretia II, 807
McIlvain, Lucretia II, 819
McIlvain, Lucretia II, 894
McIlvain, Lucretia II, 921
McIlvain, Lydia II, 807
McIlvain, Lydia II, 894
McIlvain, Lydia M. II, 807
McIlvain, Martha II, 807
McIlvain, Martha II, 808
McIlvain, Martha II, 842
McIlvain, Martha II, 852
McIlvain, Martha II, 858
McIlvain, Martha G. II, 838
McIlvain, Martha G. II, 842
McIlvain, Martha G. II, 858
McIlvain, Martha G. II, 894
McIlvain, Martha G. II, 921
McIlvain, Martha Gibson II, 894
McIlvain, Mary II, 894
McIlvain, Mary Bunting II, 807
McIlvain, Mary Hibberd Tomlinson II, 807
McIlvain, Mary Oakford II, 808
McIlvain, Naomi P. II, 894
McIlvain, Naomi P. II, 897
McIlvain, Rachel II, 802
McIlvain, Rachel II, 880
McIlvain, Rachel II, 894
McIlvain, Rebecca II, 311
McIlvain, Rebecca II, 313
McIlvain, Rebecca B. II, 311
McIlvain, Rebecca B. II, 322
McIlvain, Rebecca B. II, 807
McIlvain, Rebecca B. II, 894
McIlvain, Richard II, 589
McIlvain, Richard II, 808
McIlvain, Richard II, 894
McIlvain, Sarah II, 823
McIlvain, Sarah Ann II, 807
McIlvain, Sarah Gibson II, 807
McIlvain, Susan H. II, 807
McIlvain, Susan H. II, 894
McIlvain, Susannah II, 808
McIlvain, Susannah II, 894
McIlvain, Thomas II, 311
McIlvain, Thomas Sterling II, 311
McIlvain, Thomas Sterling II, 322
McIlvain, Thos. Sterling II, 807
McIlvain, Thos. Sterling II, 894
McIlvain, Walter Biddle II, 808
McIlvain, Wd. Hannah II, 804
McIlvaine, Abraham Gibbons II, 894
McIlvaine, Abraham R. II, 894
McIlvaine, Chas. F. III, 256
McIlvaine, Elizabeth M. II, 894
McIlvaine, Hannah II, 884
McIlvaine, Hannah II, 894
McIlvaine, Hannah G. II, 894
McIlvaine, Hugh II, 884
McIlvaine, Hugh II, 894
McIlvaine, J. Gibson II, 894
McIlvaine, James II, 894
McIlvaine, John Humphries II, 894
McIlvaine, John Hunt II, 894
McIlvaine, Josephine III, 256
McIlvaine, Lulu III, 256
McIlvaine, Lydia II, 894
McIlvaine, Martha G. II, 894
McIlvaine, Naomi P. II, 894
McIlvaine, Rachel II, 894
McIlvaine, Richard II, 894
McIlvaine, Susan H. II, 884
McIlvaine, Susan H. II, 894
McIlvaine, Susannah II, 894
McIlvane, Hugh II, 589
McIlvane, Michael V, 1008
McIlvane, Richard II, 589
McIlwain, Ann IV, 637
McIlwain, Ann IV, 643
McIlwaine, ??? VI, 5
McIlwaine, Richard II, 589
McIntire, Abigail V, 187
McIntire, Anthony VI, 955
McIntire, Dora IV, 246
McIntire, Edith V, 187
McIntire, Eliza VI, 955
McIntire, Frank V, 187
McIntire, Henry V, 187
McIntire, James IV, 246
McIntire, James VI, 955
McIntire, James R. IV, 246
McIntire, John V, 187
McIntire, Lucinda V, 1008
McIntire, Lula IV, 246
McIntire, Lulu IV, 246
McIntire, May Catherine Wilson V, 187
McIntire, Polly VI, 955
McIntire, Rachel IV, 643
McIntire, Susannah VI, 955
McIntire, William VI, 955
McIntosh, Andrew J. III, 182
McIntosh, Andrew J. III, 207
McIntosh, Andrew J. III, 214
McIntosh, Andrew James, Jr. III, 214
McIntosh, Annie I, 405
McIntosh, Deborah II, 589
McIntosh, Deborah II, 681
McIntosh, Florence L. III, 182
McIntosh, Florence L. III, 207
McIntosh, Florence L. III, 214
McIntosh, George W. IV, 246
McIntosh, Harriet III, 214
McIntosh, Harriet T. III, 214
McIntosh, Hector III, 214
McIntosh, Maggie IV, 246
McIntosh, Marg. A. III, 207
McIntosh, Margaret III, 214
McIntosh, Margaret Anne III, 207
McIntosh, Margaret Anne III, 214
McIntosh, Martha Ann III, 214
McIntosh, Susan Stokes III, 214
McIntosh, Whitewater III, 214
McInturf, Elizabeth IV, 1066
McInturf, Elizabeth IV, 1067
McIntyre, Anthony VI, 955
McIntyre, Edith V, 187
McIntyre, Elma V, 669
McIntyre, Polly VI, 955
McIvar, Jane VI, 816
McIvar, Samuel VI, 816
McIver, Catharine VI, 837
McIver, Daniel VI, 836
McIver, Daniel VI, 837
McIver, Elizabeth VI, 796
McIver, Elizabeth VI, 836
McIver, James VI, 796
McIver, James VI, 812
McIver, James VI, 836
McIver, James VI, 837
McIver, James VI, 847
McIver, Margaret VI, 857
McIver, Nancy VI, 836
McIver, Polly VI, 812
McIver, Sally VI, 836
McIver, Sally VI, 847
McIver, William C. VI, 836
McIvor, Elizabeth VI, 815
McIvor, James VI, 799
McIvor, James VI, 807
McIvor, James VI, 815
McIvor, James VI, 816
McIvor, James VI, 836
McIvor, James G. VI, 822
McIvor, John VI, 815
McIvor, Nancy VI, 830
McIvor, Nancy VI, 836
McIwain, Hugh II, 589
McJunkin, Mary Ann IV, 47
McJunkin, Mary Ann IV, 57
McKanan, Rachel IV, 47
McKane, Armelda IV, 246
McKann, Jane IV, 153
McKay, Abigail V, 187
McKay, Abigail VI, 420
McKay, Abigail VI, 600
McKay, Abraham VI, 420
McKay, Ada Turner V, 513
McKay, Ada Turner V, 693
McKay, Allen H. V, 95
McKay, Allen H. V, 632
McKay, Amos VI, 420
McKay, Andrew VI, 420
McKay, Andrew VI, 530
McKay, Andrew VI, 579
McKay, Andrew VI, 600
McKay, Andrew VI, 720
McKay, Ann VI, 445
McKay, Ann VI, 600
McKay, David VI, 420
McKay, Donald III, 48
McKay, Donald III, 214
McKay, Donald S. V, 95
McKay, Donald S. V, 632
McKay, E. Harold V, 95
McKay, E. Harold V, 632
McKay, Edith S. V, 95
McKay, Edith S. V, 513
McKay, Edith S. V, 632
McKay, Edith Starbuck V, 513
McKay, Edith Starbuck V, 632
McKay, Elizabeth VI, 420
McKay, Ella May V, 513
McKay, Enoch VI, 420
McKay, Enos VI, 420
McKay, Enos VI, 600
McKay, Esther VI, 420
McKay, Francis V, 187
McKay, George V, 187
McKay, George Lewis VI, 763
McKay, Haines VI, 420
McKay, Hannah VI, 402
McKay, Hannah VI, 420
McKay, Hannah VI, 600
McKay, Harold V, 513
McKay, Harold V, 632
McKay, Howard V, 513
McKay, Howard F. V, 95
McKay, Howard F. V, 632
McKay, Ida Haworth V, 632
McKay, Ila V, 513
McKay, Ila H. V, 95
McKay, Ila H. V, 632
McKay, Irene Pound VI, 763
McKay, Isaac VI, 420
McKay, Isabel III, 312
McKay, Isabel III, 342
McKay, Jacob IV, 341
McKay, Jacob V, 187
McKay, Jacob VI, 420
McKay, Jacob VI, 437
McKay, Jacob VI, 497
McKay, Jacob VI, 519
McKay, Jacob VI, 522
Mckay, Jacob VI, 593
McKay, Jacob VI, 597
McKay, Jacob VI, 600
McKay, Jacob VI, 605
McKay, Jacob VI, 644
McKay, Jacob VI, 661
McKay, Jacob VI, 674
McKay, Jacob VI, 725
McKay, Jacob II VI, 420
McKay, Jacob, Jr. VI, 600
McKay, James VI, 420
McKay, Jane IV, 99
McKay, Jane IV, 112
McKay, Jane VI, 420
McKay, Jane VI, 530
McKay, Jane VI, 579
McKay, Jane VI, 593
McKay, Jane VI, 597
McKay, Jane VI, 598
McKay, Jane VI, 600
McKay, Jane VI, 601
McKay, Jane VI, 603
McKay, Jane VI, 720
McKay, Jean IV, 1327
McKay, Jene IV, 1327
McKay, Jeremiah VI, 420
McKay, Jesse VI, 420
McKay, Job VI, 420
McKay, John VI, 420
McKay, John VI, 600
McKay, John VI, 837
McKay, Jonas Tilden V, 187
McKay, Kenneth III, 214
McKay, Laviner VI, 837
McKay, Levi V, 187
McKay, Levi D. V, 187
McKay, Lewis Pound VI, 763
McKay, Lida V, 513
McKay, Margaret V, 172
McKay, Margaret V, 187
McKay, Margaret VI, 420
McKay, Margaret VI, 437
McKay, Marget VI, 600
McKay, Maria V, 187
McKay, Martha VI, 600
McKay, Mary III, 48
McKay, Mary III, 214
McKay, Mary VI, 420
McKay, Mary VI, 597
McKay, Mary Ann V, 187
McKay, Mary Elba V, 513
McKay, Mary Elba V, 693
McKay, Mary Manning V, 919
McKay, Maynard V, 693
McKay, Maynard F. V, 513
McKay, Maynard J. V, 513
McKay, Moses VI, 420
McKay, Moses VI, 600
McKay, Patience V, 140
McKay, Patience VI, 420
McKay, Patience VI, 437
McKay, Patience VI, 497
McKay, Patience VI, 522
McKay, Patience VI, 579
McKay, Patience VI, 600
McKay, Patience VI, 644
McKay, Patience VI, 661
McKay, Patience VI, 674
McKay, Patience VI, 720
McKay, Priscilla V, 513
McKay, Priscilla V, 693
McKay, Rachel V, 513
McKay, Rachel VI, 412
McKay, Rachel VI, 420
McKay, Rachel VI, 437
McKay, Rachel VI, 593
McKay, Rachel VI, 600
McKay, Rachel VI, 605
McKay, Rebecca VI, 519

McKay, Rebeccah IV, 341
Mckay, Rebeckah VI, 674
McKay, Rebekah VI, 420
Mckay, Rebekah VI, 674
McKay, Robert V, 513
McKay, Robert V, 632
McKay, Robert VI, 420
McKay, Robert VI, 437
McKay, Robert VI, 497
McKay, Robert VI, 522
McKay, Robert VI, 644
McKay, Robert VI, 661
McKay, Robert VI, 674
McKay, Robert F. V, 95
McKay, Robert F. V, 632
McKay, Robert Franklin V, 513
McKay, Robert, Jr. VI, 420
McKay, Sarah V, 158
McKay, Sarah V, 187
McKay, Sarah VI, 405
McKay, Sarah VI, 420
McKay, Sarah VI, 600
McKay, Susanna V, 714
McKay, Tilden V, 187
McKay, Virginia V, 158
McKay, Virginia V, 187
McKay, Walter VI, 836
McKay, Widow Rebeckah Gregg VI, 668
McKay, Widower Jacob VI, 668
McKay, Zachariah VI, 420
McKaye, Jene IV, 1327
McKeachey, Andrew VI, 955
McKeachey, Sarah VI, 955
McKechnie, John V, 693
McKechnie, John Wm. V, 693
McKechnie, Joseph V, 693
McKechnie, Josiah B. V, 693
McKechnie, Julia V, 693
McKechnie, Lottie H. V, 693
McKecknie, John V, 690
McKecknie, Lottie H. V, 690
McKecney, Julia V, 583
McKee, Ada C. V, 513
McKee, Adda V, 513
McKee, Alma V, 513
McKee, Alma C. V, 513
McKee, Carrie IV, 1327
McKee, Charles V, 513
McKee, Charles O. V, 513
McKee, Charles O. V, 694
McKee, Chas. O. V, 693
McKee, Eli A. V, 513
McKee, Elizabeth V, 513
McKee, Emiline S. V, 187
McKee, Emily Jane V, 513
McKee, Emma J. V, 477
McKee, Evaline L. V, 187
McKee, George V, 693
McKee, Harriet Alice V, 187
McKee, James II, 900
McKee, James H. II, 900
McKee, M. Emily II, 900
McKee, Margaret II, 806
McKee, Martha V, 693
McKee, Martha M. II, 900
McKee, Minerva Ault V, 693
McKee, Rebecca VI, 420
McKee, Rebecca VI, 456
McKee, Sarah V, 757
McKee, Thomas V, 187
McKee, Thomas W. V, 187
McKee, Thos. Woodward V, 187
McKeel, Amy Q. II, 1088
McKeel, Amy Q. II, 1089
McKencie, Julia V, 568
McKencie, Julia V, 583
McKennan, Rachel IV, 21
McKennan, Rachel IV, 47
McKennedy, Ann VI, 65
McKennedy, John VI, 65
McKennedy, Sarah VI, 65
McKenney, Allen V, 187
McKenney, Bessie V, 187
McKenney, Charles V, 187
McKenney, Elisabeth VI, 955
McKenney, Henry J. V, 348
McKenney, Jeams I, 966
McKenney, Jeams I, 967
McKenney, Leannah VI, 800
McKenney, Levinna V, 187
McKenney, Louisa IV, 1186
McKenney, Mary I, 966
McKenney, Mary VI, 836
McKenney, Paul V, 187
McKenney, Robinson VI, 836
McKenney, Sarah I, 966
McKenney, Sarah I, 967
McKenney, Sarah V, 187
McKenney, Wilson VI, 955
McKennon, Daniel IV, 1285
McKennon, Ellen IV, 1285
McKennon, Lillian IV, 1327
McKenny, Alexander V, 583
McKenny, Carrie Bell V, 566
McKenny, Charles S. V, 583
McKenny, Louisa IV, 1172
McKenny, Mary Ann III, 415
McKenny, Mary Ann III, 426
McKenny, Phebe III, 104
McKenny, Phebe III, 214
McKenny, Rebecca Ann V, 583
McKenny, Robert V, 566
McKenny, Sarah VI, 530
McKenny, Sarah VI, 583
McKenny, Sina Almeda V, 583
McKenny, Susan V, 566
McKenzie, Collin II, 795
McKenzie, Ella V, 694
McKenzie, Emma W. II, 745
McKenzie, Emma W. II, 753
McKenzie, James IV, 1327
McKenzie, Lucile V, 513
McKenzie, Mabel IV, 1327
McKenzie, Mrs. ??? IV, 1327
McKenzie, Zella V, 694
McKenzie, Zella A. V, 694
McKeon, Ellen III, 214
McKeon, Ellen III, 276
McKeon, Ellen S. III, 214
McKeon, Ellen Sidney III, 214
McKeon, Maria III, 214
McKeon, Peter Joseph III, 214
McKeon, Peter Joseph III, 276
McKeon, Terence III, 214
McKewen, Mabel Alberta III, 214
McKibben, Amanda V, 187
McKibben, Amanda V, 513
McKibben, Amanda E. V, 632
McKibben, Chemiah V, 632
McKibben, Cheniah V, 187
McKibben, Cheniah V, 513
McKibben, Etta May V, 411
McKibben, Hannah V, 694
McKibben, Hester V, 372
McKibben, Joseph V, 372
McKibben, Joseph V, 411
McKibben, Lou Ella V, 513
McKibben, Louella V, 187
McKibben, Lula V, 694
McKibben, Maggie V, 187
McKibben, Maggie V, 513
McKibben, Maggie V, 632
McKibben, Maud V, 187
McKibben, Maud V, 513
McKibben, Maud V, 632
McKibben, Minnie Pearl V, 513
McKibben, Minnie T. V, 632
McKibben, Nancy V, 372
McKibben, Oliva V, 694
McKibben, Olivia V, 670
McKibben, Olivia V, 694
McKibben, Pearl V, 177
McKibben, Pearl V, 187
McKibben, Phebe V, 411
McKibben, Wm. V, 694
McKibbins, Lydia IV, 1216
McKibbon, Oliva V, 694
McKim, J. Miller III, 214
McKim, Madge Iola IV, 246
McKim, Sarah A. III, 214
McKine, John VI, 819
McKiney, Emma V, 583
McKiney, Jesse V, 583
McKinley, Al IV, 1327
McKinley, Albert IV, 1327
McKinley, Albert IV, 1328
McKinley, Albert Sidney IV, 1327
McKinley, Anna IV, 1327
McKinley, Avilla J. V, 261
McKinley, Bertha B. V, 220
McKinley, Chas. V, 220
McKinley, Cleo V, 850
McKinley, Darrel F. V, 850
McKinley, Dolia Maria V, 850
McKinley, Dorothy Cleo V, 850
McKinley, Elizabeth V, 261
McKinley, Ezra V, 261
McKinley, Frank IV, 1327
McKinley, Grace IV, 1327
McKinley, Henry V, 850
McKinley, Jane IV, 419
McKinley, Levina V, 220
McKinley, Lillie B. IV, 1327
McKinley, Matilda IV, 1327
McKinley, Mrs. Mamie V, 753
McKinley, Pete IV, 1257
McKinley, Tamer VI, 626
Mckinley, Tamer VI, 674
McKinley, Vincent IV, 1328
McKinne, Annie I, 620
McKinney, Adah V, 95
McKinney, Alexander V, 583
McKinney, Alexander V, 694
McKinney, Alfred V, 261
McKinney, Alfred V, 460
McKinney, Alfred V, 468
McKinney, Alfred Allen V, 261
McKinney, Allen V, 187
McKinney, Alonzo V, 719
McKinney, Anderson V, 261
McKinney, Anderson V, 460
McKinney, Anna V, 348
McKinney, Anna B. V, 460
McKinney, Bertha I. V, 261
McKinney, Bessie V, 187
McKinney, Bessie L. V, 197
McKinney, Bessie L. V, 261
McKinney, Bette I, 966
McKinney, Byrom I, 966
McKinney, Callie V, 1008
McKinney, Carl V, 187
McKinney, Carl A. V, 187
McKinney, Carl A. V, 261
McKinney, Caroline V, 1008
McKinney, Charles V, 187
McKinney, Charles V, 261
McKinney, Charles A. V, 261
McKinney, Charles A. V, 460
McKinney, Charles L. V, 694
McKinney, Charles Paul V, 261
McKinney, Charles S. V, 583
McKinney, Charles Wm. V, 694
McKinney, Chas. K. V, 721
McKinney, Chas. Wm. V, 718
McKinney, Clara V, 24
McKinney, Clara V, 95
McKinney, Clara M. V, 24
McKinney, Clara M. V, 95
McKinney, Clyde V, 694
McKinney, Corah V, 95
McKinney, Daniel VI, 828
McKinney, Daniel VI, 836
McKinney, Donald V, 187
McKinney, Earnest V, 583
McKinney, Edward G. VI, 836
McKinney, Eli V, 583
McKinney, Elizabeth V, 187
McKinney, Elizabeth VI, 836
McKinney, Emma V, 583
McKinney, Etha V, 721
McKinney, Ethel V, 719
McKinney, Fanny VI, 836
McKinney, Frde D. V, 187
McKinney, Fred V, 187
McKinney, Fred V, 261
McKinney, Fred D. V, 261
McKinney, Freda V, 187
McKinney, Galen I, 957
McKinney, George VI, 836
McKinney, H. M. V, 583
McKinney, Hannah VI, 828
McKinney, Hannah B. VI, 836
McKinney, Harold V, 187
McKinney, Harvard VI, 820
McKinney, Henry V, 583
McKinney, Henry VI, 827
McKinney, Henry J. V, 348
McKinney, Howard V, 694
McKinney, Ira I, 957
McKinney, J. H. V, 348
McKinney, James Monroe I, 957
McKinney, James W. V, 694
McKinney, Jane V, 606
McKinney, Jeams I, 957
McKinney, Jeams I, 966
McKinney, Jenny VI, 836
McKinney, Jeremiah VI, 836
McKinney, Jesse I, 966
McKinney, Jesse V, 411
McKinney, Jesse V, 583
McKinney, Joel L. I, 957
McKinney, John I, 966
McKinney, John V, 583
McKinney, John VI, 820
McKinney, John VI, 827
McKinney, John VI, 828
McKinney, John VI, 836
McKinney, John C. VI, 836
McKinney, John, Jr. VI, 836
McKinney, Jordan VI, 823
McKinney, Letty VI, 836
McKinney, Levina V, 261
McKinney, Levinna V, 187
McKinney, Lewis V, 694
McKinney, Lucile V, 719
McKinney, Lucy V, 348
McKinney, Martha VI, 800
McKinney, Mary I, 957
McKinney, Mary I, 966
McKinney, Mary V, 95
McKinney, Mary VI, 836
McKinney, Mary A. V, 694
McKinney, Mary A. VI, 827
McKinney, Mary Jane V, 95
McKinney, Mary Jane V, 98
McKinney, May V, 583
McKinney, Melvin IV, 1216
McKinney, Molly R. VI, 836
McKinney, Nancy VI, 847
McKinney, Nancy VI, 865
McKinney, Nathan I, 957
McKinney, Nellie V, 187
McKinney, Nellie J. V, 187
McKinney, Obadiah I, 966
McKinney, Obadiah V, 261
McKinney, Obadiah V, 460
McKinney, Obadiah V, 583
McKinney, Obadiah V, 694
McKinney, Obediah V, 694
McKinney, Ora V, 694
McKinney, Ora V, 721
McKinney, Oscar V, 719
McKinney, Patsy VI, 836
McKinney, Paul V, 187
McKinney, Pearl V, 583
McKinney, Pearl V, 694
McKinney, Perlina VI, 836
McKinney, Phebe V, 261
McKinney, Phebe V, 460
McKinney, Phebe V, 468
McKinney, Phebe VI, 836
McKinney, Polly VI, 836
McKinney, Presley VI, 836
McKinney, Rachel I, 992
McKinney, Rachel V, 583
McKinney, Rachel V, 694
McKinney, Rachel VI, 836
McKinney, Rachel Ann V, 583
McKinney, Rebecca V, 694
McKinney, Rebecca Ann V, 583
McKinney, Rose Towne V, 460
McKinney, Roy V, 719
McKinney, Roy D. V, 719
McKinney, Ruby V, 460
McKinney, Ruth Elizabeth V, 694
McKinney, Ruth Emma V, 583
McKinney, Samuel V, 694
McKinney, Sarah I, 957
McKinney, Sarah I, 966
McKinney, Sarah V, 187
McKinney, Sarah V, 460
McKinney, Sarah V, 694
McKinney, Sarah L. V, 468
McKinney, Sarah Louisa V, 261
McKinney, Sarah Phebe V, 261
McKinney, Shadrack I, 966
McKinney, Sina Almeda V, 583
McKinney, Sophia VI, 836
McKinney, Susanna VI, 836
McKinney, Susie V, 187
McKinney, Thomas VI, 795
McKinney, Thomas VI, 840
McKinney, Thomas. W. VI, 800
McKinney, Tinsley VI, 836
McKinney, Tinsley VI, 859
McKinney, Verna V, 694
McKinney, Verna V, 718
McKinney, Vincent VI, 836
McKinney, William I, 966
McKinney, William V, 261
McKinney, William VI, 836
McKinney, William H. V, 95
McKinney, William R. V, 95
McKinney, Wm. V, 694
McKinney, Wm. VI, 800
McKinney, Wm. D. V, 694
McKinnie, Gertie M. IV, 1172
McKinnie, W. H. IV, 1172
McKinnon, Agnes IV, 1327
McKinnon, Agnes IV, 1345
McKinnon, Alexander III, 214
McKinnon, Clyde IV, 1327
McKinnon, Clyde H. IV, 1327
McKinnon, Elizabeth IV, 1327
McKinnon, Florence IV, 1327
McKinnon, Geo. Yapple IV, 1327
McKinnon, John IV, 1327
McKinnon, John IV, 1337
McKinnon, John C. IV, 1345
McKinnon, Lela IV, 1327
McKinnon, Lela IV, 1337
McKinnon, Lillian IV, 1327
McKinnon, Lottie IV, 1327
McKinnon, Lottie IV, 1343
McKinnon, Mrs. Ruth IV, 1327
McKinnon, Phylis Ileen IV, 1327
McKinnon, Willie IV, 1345
McKinsey, Anna V, 348
McKinsey, Bertha I. V, 261
McKinsey, Bessie L. V, 261
McKinsey, Carl A. V, 261
McKinsey, Charles V, 261
McKinsey, Charley J. V, 411
McKinsey, Cora V, 411
McKinsey, Fred D. V, 261
McKinsey, Gracie Pearl V, 411
McKinsey, Jacob V, 411
McKinsey, John IV, 737
McKinsey, John VI, 76
McKinsey, Karl IV, 737
McKinsey, Laura Elizabeth V, 9
McKinsey, Lesley Howard V, 41
McKinsey, Lucy V, 348
McKinsey, Mary V, 95
McKinsey, Minnie V, 95
McKinsey, Rebecca V, 187
McKinsey, Rebecca V, 205
McKinsey, Rebekah I, 405
McKinsey, Samuel R. V, 411
McKinzie, Ada IV, 737
McKinzie, Armintha Weaver IV, 737
McKinzie, Carl IV, 737
McKinzie, Ella V, 694
McKinzie, Harry IV, 737
McKinzie, John IV, 737
McKinzie, John IV, 1040
McKinzie, Karl IV, 737
McKinzie, Lizzie IV, 737
McKinzie, Milly VI, 819
McKinzie, Russell IV, 737
McKinzie, Zella V, 694
McKinzie, Zella A. V, 694
McKisick, Madeline VI, 668
McKisson, Hannah IV, 333
McKisson, Hannah IV, 341
McKisson, Joanna IV, 322
McKisson, Joanna IV, 341
McKittrick, Maria III, 214
McKnight, Eliza A. V, 95
McKnight, Sarah Amanda IV, 334
McKnight, Sarah Amanda IV, 341
McKnob, Sarah VI, 877
McKowan, James H. IV, 246
McKown, Lucy Ann VI, 663
McKown, Warner VI, 663
McKoy, Jacob VI, 420
McKoy, Jane V, 95
McKoy, Rachel VI, 420
McKurdy, Sarah VI, 420
McKurdy, Sarah VI, 436
McLain, Anney VI, 955
McLain, John, Jr. VI, 955
McLain, Lydia VI, 955
McLain, Mordecai VI, 955
McLain, Theodate IV, 246
McLain, William B. IV, 484
McLane, J. R. VI, 76
McLane, J. R. VI, 85
McLane, James VI, 960
McLane, Martha VI, 960
McLane, Miriam I, 146
McLane, Rebecca VI, 76
McLane, Rebecca VI, 85
McLane, Theodate IV, 418
McLane, Theodate IV, 450
McLane, Theodate IV, 587
McLane, William IV, 418
McLaren, Margaret V, 348
McLaren, Margaret Bell V, 348
McLaren, Roy V, 347
McLaren, Roy V, 348
McLaren, Sarah V, 348
McLaren, Susan V, 348
McLaren, Thomas V, 348
McLaughlin, Ann II, 808
McLaughlin, Anna IV, 1092
McLaughlin, Anna IV, 1106
McLaughlin, Earl IV, 832
McLaughlin, Edith V, 678
McLaughlin, Edith V, 694
McLaughlin, Fanny Floid V, 26
McLaughlin, Genevra IV, 246
McLaughlin, Harriet E. IV, 243
McLaughlin, Harriet E. IV, 246
McLaughlin, J. W. V, 261
McLaughlin, James V, 261
McLaughlin, James W. V, 261
McLaughlin, Joseph V, 261
McLaughlin, Katie IV, 832
McLaughlin, Lida IV, 246
McLaughlin, Mary E. IV, 962
McLaughlin, Minnie IV, 246
McLaughlin, Paul IV, 246
McLaughlin, Pearl IV, 246
McLaughlin, Ralph Mitchel IV, 246
McLaughlin, Sarah V, 261
McLaughlin, Sewell IV, 246
McLaughlin, Thomas VI, 1009
McLaughlin, William V, 261
McLea, Donald III, 214

cLead, Amanda IV, 1172
Lead, Freddie IV, 1172
Lead, Lammie IV, 1172
Lead, Lena IV, 1172
cLean, Alexander IV, 910
cLean, Cora E. IV, 484
Lean, Frederick C. IV, 978
Lean, John I, 1011
cLean, John, Jr. VI, 955
cLean, Lela IV, 1040
Lean, Lydia VI, 955
Lean, Noah C. IV, 484
Lean, Noah C. IV, 1239
Lean, Noah C. IV, 1285
Lean, Noah C. IV, 1328
Lean, Samuel IV, 978
Lean, Sarah IV, 978
Lean, Theodate IV, 587
Lelen, Charlotte V, 850
Lelen, Charlotte V, 855
Lellan, Bessie S. IV, 246
Lellan, Eliza J. IV, 246
Lellan, Ella M. IV, 246
Lellan, Harriet A. IV, 246
Lellan, Harriett IV, 246
Lellan, Paul D. IV, 246
Lennan, Connie E. I, 621
Lennan, D. A. I, 621
Lennan, John Walter I, 621
Lennan, Marietta I, 621
Lennan, Martha Blair I, 621
Lennan, Martha T. M. I, 621
Lennon, Martha Blair I, 637
Lennon, Martha T. I, 622
Lennon, William I, 622
Leod, Mary Ellen I, 945
Lilly, William A. I, 338
lin, America V, 263
Lin, Mary I, 1094
Lin, Mary I, 1095
Linn, Mary V, 411
Lintock, Charity V, 261
Lintock, Charity V, 286
Loemar, Mary J. V, 1008
lure, Gertrude W. V, 260
lure, Joseph A. V, 260
lure, Malinda J. V, 260
lure, Marion C. V, 260
Machen, John IV, 1257
Mahan, Ann IV, 1067
Mahan, Ann IV, 1079
Mahan, John IV, 1040
Mammis, Imelda IV, 246
Man, John IV, 1040
Manama, David VI, 955
Manama, Elizabeth VI, 955
Manama, James VI, 921
Manama, James VI, 955
Manama, Nancy VI, 955
Manama, Pattsy VI, 921
Manama, Paty VI, 876
Manama, Rebecca VI, 876
Manama, Ruth VI, 921
Manaway, Charles H. VI, 955
Manaway, Elizabeth VI, 917
Manaway, Marthew VI, 917
Manaway, Nancy A. VI, 955
Manaway, Thomas VI, 955
Manaway, Uney VI, 955
Manis, Armelda IV, 246
Manis, Cora V, 1008
Manis, Emma R. V, 1008
Manis, Francis V, 1008
Manis, Wm. V, 1008
Manis, Wm. R. V, 1008
Mannaway, Polly VI, 897
Manner, Mary VI, 169
Manners, Mary VI, 165
Manners, Mary VI, 198
Mannis, Anna IV, 246
Mannis, Charles E. IV, 246
Mannis, Clara E. IV, 246
Mannis, Cora IV, 246
Mannis, Elizabeth IV, 246
Mannis, Emma R. V, 1008
Mannis, Grace IV, 246
Mannis, Imelda IV, 246
Mannis, Isaiah IV, 246
Mannis, James IV, 246
Mannis, James V, 261
Mannis, James F. IV, 246
Mannis, Jesse V, 261
Mannis, John IV, 246
Mannis, Kate IV, 246
Mannis, Maria V, 261
Mannis, Martha IV, 246
Mannis, Martha E. IV, 246
Mannis, Mary J. V, 261
Mannis, Orville IV, 246
Mannis, Wilson IV, 246
Mannis, Wm. R. V, 1008
McMannus, Mary VI, 165
McMannus, Mary VI, 169
McManus, James F. IV, 246
McMasters, Ann II, 1055
McMasters, Dinah I, 396
McMasters, Dinah I, 405
McMasters, Elener I, 391
McMasters, Elener I, 405
McMasters, Elizabeth I, 405
McMasters, Elizabeth I, 423
McMasters, Hannah I, 396
McMasters, Hannah I, 405
McMasters, Ida May IV, 246
McMasters, Mary I, 676
McMasters, Mary I, 684
McMasters, Mary I, 925
McMath, Hannah IV, 561
McMellen, Bertha V, 1008
McMellen, Eliza V, 1008
McMellen, Esther V, 1008
McMellen, John V, 1008
McMellen, Leonides V, 1008
McMellen, Wm. V, 973
McMellon, Hannah IV, 341
McMelon, Mary IV, 229
McMennis, James VI, 1006
McMichael, A. J. IV, 1172
McMichael, Ella IV, 1172
McMichael, General ??? IV, 1172
McMichael, Hattie IV, 1172
McMichael, Ida B. V, 1008
McMichael, Ida Bell V, 1008
McMichael, Jane IV, 1172
McMichael, Thomas IV, 1172
McMilan, David J. V, 187
McMilan, Eunice V, 187
McMilan, John Josiah V, 187
McMillain, Jane IV, 313
McMillan, ??? IV, 247
McMillan, Ada V, 515
McMillan, Ada B. V, 514
McMillan, Ada B. V, 694
McMillan, Adaline IV, 247
McMillan, Adelbert V, 95
McMillan, Adelbert V, 515
McMillan, Adelebert V, 515
McMillan, Albert E. IV, 247
McMillan, Albert Earl V, 583
McMillan, Albert Earl V, 584
McMillan, Alfred V, 513
McMillan, Alice IV, 173
McMillan, Alice IV, 247
McMillan, Alice IV, 313
McMillan, Alice IV, 389
McMillan, Alice IV, 419
McMillan, Alice D. V, 583
McMillan, Alice Eleanor IV, 247
McMillan, Alice J. V, 584
McMillan, Alice M. V, 515
McMillan, Ann IV, 876
McMillan, Ann V, 513
McMillan, Ann C. V, 513
McMillan, Ann Maria V, 515
McMillan, Annie IV, 247
McMillan, Blanch V, 662
McMillan, Blanch V, 694
McMillan, Blanch Martha V, 515
McMillan, Blanch Martha V, 694
McMillan, Burritt V, 694
McMillan, Calvin V, 513
McMillan, Calvin M. V, 513
McMillan, Carl V, 411
McMillan, Carl V, 515
McMillan, Carl V, 633
McMillan, Carl L. V, 411
McMillan, Carrie E. V, 694
McMillan, Charles V, 95
McMillan, Charles V, 515
McMillan, Charles V, 633
McMillan, Charles Percy IV, 247
McMillan, Chase Grant V, 514
McMillan, Chase Grant V, 515
McMillan, Clarkson V, 187
McMillan, Clarkson V, 514
McMillan, Clarkson V, 515
McMillan, Clarkson M. V, 513
McMillan, Clifton J. V, 694
McMillan, Clinton V, 514
McMillan, David V, 95
McMillan, David V, 191
McMillan, David V, 469
McMillan, David V, 513
McMillan, David V, 514
McMillan, David V, 632
McMillan, David V, 694
McMillan, David J. V, 187
McMillan, David J. V, 513
McMillan, David R. V, 514
McMillan, David, Jr. V, 480
McMillan, David, Jr. V, 514
McMillan, Deborah IV, 341
McMillan, Deborah V, 95
McMillan, Deborah V, 513
McMillan, Deborah V, 514
McMillan, Deborah V, 533
McMillan, Deborah J. V, 514
McMillan, Deborah J. V, 544
McMillan, Deborah T. V, 498
McMillan, Deborah T. V, 515
McMillan, Dick V, 514
McMillan, Dillen V, 515
McMillan, Dillon V, 95
McMillan, Dillon V, 515
McMillan, Dillon K. V, 584
McMillan, Dillon R. V, 583
McMillan, Dorothea Mae V, 694
McMillan, Edith V, 484
McMillan, Edith V, 514
McMillan, Edith Olga IV, 247
McMillan, Edna V, 515
McMillan, Edna R. V, 514
McMillan, Edna R. V, 694
McMillan, Eldora V, 515
McMillan, Eleanor R. IV, 247
McMillan, Eli IV, 247
McMillan, Eli IV, 313
McMillan, Eli V, 95
McMillan, Eli V, 489
McMillan, Eli V, 513
McMillan, Eli V, 514
McMillan, Eli V, 560
McMillan, Eli V, 583
McMillan, Eli W. F. V, 694
McMillan, Eli, Jr. V, 514
McMillan, Eli, Jr. V, 515
McMillan, Eli, Jr. V, 694
McMillan, Eliza V, 95
McMillan, Eliza V, 514
McMillan, Eliza V, 919
McMillan, Eliza Jane V, 514
McMillan, Elizabeth IV, 47
McMillan, Elizabeth IV, 246
McMillan, Elizabeth IV, 247
McMillan, Elizabeth V, 514
McMillan, Elizabeth V, 694
McMillan, Elizabeth H. V, 515
McMillan, Elizabeth M. V, 513
McMillan, Elizabeth N. V, 514
McMillan, Ella V, 514
McMillan, Elvan L. V, 694
McMillan, Elveron Lewis V, 694
McMillan, Elvira V, 514
McMillan, Emer H. V, 515
McMillan, Emma V, 95
McMillan, Emma V, 513
McMillan, Emma V, 515
McMillan, Emma D. V, 583
McMillan, Emma D. V, 584
McMillan, Emma H. V, 515
McMillan, Emmer V, 514
McMillan, Emmor V, 584
McMillan, Emmor V, 694
McMillan, Emmor H. V, 583
McMillan, Emmor H. V, 601
McMillan, Enoch V, 514
McMillan, Enoch V, 515
McMillan, Enoch W. V, 513
McMillan, Esper V, 515
McMillan, Esther IV, 194
McMillan, Esther IV, 247
McMillan, Esther V, 96
McMillan, Esther V, 261
McMillan, Esther V, 515
McMillan, Esther Carroll V, 411
McMillan, Esther Carroll V, 515
McMillan, Esther Jacob V, 514
McMillan, Ethel Ealora IV, 247
McMillan, Eunice V, 187
McMillan, Eunice V, 191
McMillan, Eva V, 95
McMillan, Eva V, 514
McMillan, Eva V, 515
McMillan, Eva V, 583
McMillan, Eva A. V, 515
McMillan, Eva W. V, 583
McMillan, Eva W. V, 584
McMillan, Evalena V, 515
McMillan, Evalend V, 514
McMillan, Evaline V, 411
McMillan, Ever V, 515
McMillan, Ezra V, 513
McMillan, Fallis V, 694
McMillan, Geo. Addison IV, 247
McMillan, Glenard V, 514
McMillan, Glenora M. V, 515
McMillan, Hannah IV, 313
McMillan, Hannah IV, 341
McMillan, Hannah IV, 350
McMillan, Hannah V, 95
McMillan, Hannah V, 469
McMillan, Hannah V, 513
McMillan, Hannah V, 514
McMillan, Hannah V, 541
McMillan, Hannah V, 632
McMillan, Hannah V, 919
McMillan, Hannah Ann V, 489
McMillan, Hannah Ann V, 513
McMillan, Hannah Ann V, 514
McMillan, Hannah J. V, 513
McMillan, Hannah L. V, 514
McMillan, Hannah M. V, 514
McMillan, Hannah S. V, 919
McMillan, Harriet V, 514
McMillan, Harriet V, 541
McMillan, Harriett V, 515
McMillan, Harriett V, 694
McMillan, Helen V, 694
McMillan, Helen B. V, 694
McMillan, Henry V, 694
McMillan, Henry I. IV, 247
McMillan, Henry Iden IV, 247
McMillan, Herbert V, 95
McMillan, Herbert V, 515
McMillan, Hester Ann V, 514
McMillan, Hondora V, 514
McMillan, Hondora K. V, 515
McMillan, Horace G. V, 514
McMillan, Ina B. IV, 247
McMillan, Ira S. IV, 247
McMillan, Ira Vale IV, 247
McMillan, Isaac V, 511
McMillan, Isaac V, 515
McMillan, Isaac V, 694
McMillan, Isaac C. V, 513
McMillan, Isaac C. V, 514
McMillan, Isaac C. V, 583
McMillan, Isaac C. V, 694
McMillan, Isaac Newton IV, 247
McMillan, Isabella R. V, 514
McMillan, Isabelle Ann V, 583
McMillan, J. Albert V, 584
McMillan, Jacob IV, 247
McMillan, Jacob IV, 313
McMillan, Jacob, Sr. IV, 247
McMillan, James IV, 247
McMillan, James Lincoln V, 583
McMillan, James, Jr. IV, 247
McMillan, Jane IV, 47
McMillan, Jane IV, 246
McMillan, Jane IV, 247
McMillan, Jane IV, 313
McMillan, Jane V, 95
McMillan, Jane V, 514
McMillan, Jane V, 544
McMillan, Jane Ann V, 502
McMillan, Jane Ann V, 514
McMillan, Jediah V, 513
McMillan, Jediah H. V, 694
McMillan, Jesse V, 694
McMillan, Jessie V, 694
McMillan, Joanna IV, 169
McMillan, Joanna IV, 247
McMillan, Joe IV, 247
McMillan, Joel IV, 247
McMillan, John IV, 194
McMillan, John V, 96
McMillan, John V, 187
McMillan, John V, 261
McMillan, John V, 583
McMillan, John Josiah V, 187
McMillan, Jonathan IV, 341
McMillan, Jonathan IV, 350
McMillan, Jonathan V, 411
McMillan, Jonathan V, 491
McMillan, Jonathan V, 513
McMillan, Jonathan V, 514
McMillan, Jonathan V, 542
McMillan, Jonathan V, 544
McMillan, Jonathan V, 621
McMillan, Jonathan V, 632
McMillan, Jonathan V, 919
McMillan, Jonothan V, 95
McMillan, Jos. IV, 247
McMillan, Joseph IV, 246
McMillan, Joseph V, 95
McMillan, Joseph V, 514
McMillan, Joseph V, 515
McMillan, Joseph V, 583
McMillan, Joseph V, 584
McMillan, Joseph Adelbert V, 583
McMillan, Joseph L. V, 583
McMillan, Joseph Lincoln V, 584
McMillan, Joshua V, 411
McMillan, Joshua F. V, 411
McMillan, Joshua F. V, 513
McMillan, Joshua F. V, 514
McMillan, Joshua F. V, 515
McMillan, Joshua F. V, 633
McMillan, Josiah V, 95
McMillan, Josiah V, 187
McMillan, Josiah V, 484
McMillan, Josiah V, 513
McMillan, Josiah V, 514
McMillan, Josiah V, 515
McMillan, Julia A. IV, 247
McMillan, Kirk V, 515
McMillan, Kirk V, 694
McMillan, L. Dora V, 411
McMillan, L. Dora V, 633
McMillan, Lena V, 411
McMillan, Lena V, 633
McMillan, Leroy J. V, 515
McMillan, Leroy J. V. V, 514
McMillan, Lidia V, 485
McMillan, Lidia V, 515
McMillan, Louetta V, 694
McMillan, Lydia V, 81
McMillan, Lydia V, 95
McMillan, Lydia V, 489
McMillan, Lydia V, 514
McMillan, Lydia V, 560
McMillan, Lydia V, 583
McMillan, Lydia Emily V, 513
McMillan, Lydia Emily V, 514
McMillan, Lydia Emily V, 541
McMillan, Mabel V, 95
McMillan, Mabel V, 515
McMillan, Mable V, 515
McMillan, Mable E. V, 583
McMillan, Mable E. V, 584
McMillan, Mahlon IV, 247
McMillan, Mahlon IV, 313
McMillan, Maria IV, 864
McMillan, Maria IV, 877
McMillan, Maria C. V, 694
McMillan, Maria Louisa V, 515
McMillan, Maria M. V, 488
McMillan, Maria M. V, 514
McMillan, Maria S. I, 945
McMillan, Mariah V, 513
McMillan, Mariam V, 514
McMillan, Mark V, 95
McMillan, Mark V, 515
McMillan, Mark E. C. V, 583
McMillan, Mark E. C. V, 584
McMillan, Martha V, 513
McMillan, Martha V, 514
McMillan, Martha Blanch V, 515
McMillan, Mary IV, 247
McMillan, Mary V, 95
McMillan, Mary V, 484
McMillan, Mary V, 513
McMillan, Mary V, 514
McMillan, Mary V, 515
McMillan, Mary V, 583
McMillan, Mary Ann V, 187
McMillan, Mary Ann V, 205
McMillan, Mary Ann V, 515
McMillan, Mary Ann V, 530
McMillan, Mary E. V, 411
McMillan, Mary E. V, 515
McMillan, Mary E. V, 633
McMillan, Mary E. V, 694
McMillan, Mary Elizabeth V, 187
McMillan, Mary Elizabeth V, 514
McMillan, Mary Elizabeth V, 515
McMillan, Mary Emily V, 514
McMillan, Mary Emily V, 528
McMillan, Mary Inez IV, 247
McMillan, Mary Laura IV, 247
McMillan, Mary M. V, 513
McMillan, Mary Probasco V, 515
McMillan, Mary Probasco V, 694
McMillan, Milton V, 513
McMillan, Milton V, 514
McMillan, Moses V, 513
McMillan, Moses V, 694
McMillan, Moses C. V, 515
McMillan, Nancy V, 511
McMillan, Nancy V, 515
McMillan, Nancy V, 694
McMillan, Nancy L. V, 514
McMillan, Nancy L. V, 515
McMillan, Nancy L. V, 694
McMillan, Neomi V, 514
McMillan, Newton V, 95
McMillan, Newton V, 514
McMillan, Newton V, 515
McMillan, Oletha V, 584
McMillan, Oliver M. V, 514
McMillan, Oliver Milton V, 513
McMillan, Orville J. V, 514
McMillan, Parmer A. V, 514
McMillan, Pearl V, 187
McMillan, Pearl V, 583
McMillan, Pearl V, 584
McMillan, Phebe IV, 247
McMillan, Phebe V, 187
McMillan, Phebe V, 208
McMillan, Phebe V, 694
McMillan, Phebe H. V, 187
McMillan, Phebe H. V, 515
McMillan, Phebe H. V, 694
McMillan, Rachel IV, 247

McMillan, Rachel IV, 313
McMillan, Rachel IV, 523
McMillan, Rachel IV, 539
McMillan, Rachel IV, 1328
McMillan, Rachel V, 478
McMillan, Rachel V, 514
McMillan, Rebecca V, 95
McMillan, Rebecca V, 411
McMillan, Rebecca V, 513
McMillan, Rebecca V, 514
McMillan, Rebecca V, 515
McMillan, Rebecca V, 621
McMillan, Rebecca V, 632
McMillan, Rebecca V, 633
McMillan, Rebecca V, 694
McMillan, Rebecca V, 1008
McMillan, Rebecca Ann V, 513
McMillan, Rebecca Ann V, 514
McMillan, Rebecca Ann V, 515
McMillan, Rebecca M. V, 515
McMillan, Rebecca Mary V, 583
McMillan, Rebecca W. V, 584
McMillan, Rex V, 187
McMillan, Rex V, 584
McMillan, Robert V, 95
McMillan, Robert V, 96
McMillan, Robert V, 187
McMillan, Robert V, 515
McMillan, Robert V, 584
McMillan, Robert D. V, 515
McMillan, Robert D. V, 584
McMillan, Robert J. V, 515
McMillan, Robert J. V, 583
McMillan, Ruth IV, 247
McMillan, Ruth IV, 313
McMillan, Ruth IV, 678
McMillan, Ruth V, 95
McMillan, Ruth V, 187
McMillan, Ruth V, 192
McMillan, Ruth V, 515
McMillan, Ruth Ann IV, 313
McMillan, Ruth Ann IV, 737
McMillan, Ruth Elizabeth IV, 313
McMillan, Ruth Emma V, 583
McMillan, Ruth Emma V, 584
McMillan, Ruth Hanna IV, 313
McMillan, Ruth Hannah IV, 315
McMillan, Ruthann IV, 247
McMillan, Ruthanna II, 782
McMillan, Ruthanna IV, 247
McMillan, S. K. V, 662
McMillan, S. K. V, 694
McMillan, Sallie V. IV, 247
McMillan, Sanford V, 514
McMillan, Sanford V, 515
McMillan, Sanford V, 583
McMillan, Sanford V, 584
McMillan, Sanford V, 694
McMillan, Sarah IV, 194
McMillan, Sarah IV, 246
McMillan, Sarah IV, 247
McMillan, Sarah IV, 313
McMillan, Sarah V, 480
McMillan, Sarah V, 513
McMillan, Sarah V, 514
McMillan, Sarah V, 515
McMillan, Sarah V, 694
McMillan, Sarah A. IV, 247
McMillan, Sarah A. V, 514
McMillan, Sarah Ann IV, 247
McMillan, Sarah Ann IV, 313
McMillan, Sarah Ann V, 513
McMillan, Sarah Ellen V, 694
McMillan, Sarah H. V, 514
McMillan, Sarah K. V, 513
McMillan, Sarah L. V, 514
McMillan, Sarah L. V, 515
McMillan, Seth L. V, 514
McMillan, Seth L. V, 515
McMillan, Seth L. V, 694
McMillan, Shipley V, 514
McMillan, Shipley V, 515
McMillan, Shipley V, 694
McMillan, Susan V, 514
McMillan, Susan V, 515
McMillan, Susan V, 583
McMillan, Susan V, 584
McMillan, Susan V, 601
McMillan, Susan V, 694
McMillan, Susan A. V, 583
McMillan, Susan M. V, 514
McMillan, Susan P. V, 187
McMillan, Susanna V, 187
McMillan, Susannah IV, 351
McMillan, Susannah V, 484
McMillan, Susannah V, 513
McMillan, Susannah V, 514
McMillan, Susannah V, 542
McMillan, Susannah H. V, 514
McMillan, Susannah H. V, 544
McMillan, Susannah M. V, 513
McMillan, Taylor IV, 47
McMillan, Thomas IV, 47
McMillan, Thomas IV, 313
McMillan, Thomas V, 513
McMillan, Thomas V, 514
McMillan, Thomas V, 544
McMillan, Thomas Dick V, 515
McMillan, Thomas Dick V, 694
McMillan, Thomas Henry V, 514
McMillan, Thomas Herbert V, 583
McMillan, Thomas M. V, 513
McMillan, Thomas R. IV, 247
McMillan, Thomas W. V, 513
McMillan, Thomas W. V, 514
McMillan, Turner W. V, 514
McMillan, Turner W. V, 583
McMillan, Uriah IV, 247
McMillan, Uriah IV, 523
McMillan, Uriah IV, 539
McMillan, Vera V, 90
McMillan, Vera V, 95
McMillan, Vera A. V, 515
McMillan, Vera Ann V, 515
McMillan, Vera Ann V, 583
McMillan, Vera Ann V, 584
McMillan, Viola V, 514
McMillan, Viola V, 515
McMillan, Viola V, 688
McMillan, Viola V, 694
McMillan, Viola H. V, 411
McMillan, Viola H. V, 633
McMillan, Walter V, 514
McMillan, Walter T. V, 515
McMillan, Walter T. V, 694
McMillan, Warren V, 583
McMillan, William IV, 313
McMillan, William V, 95
McMillan, William V, 514
McMillan, William V, 694
McMillan, Willis V, 95
McMillan, Willis V, 515
McMillan, Willis O. V, 583
McMillan, Willis O. V, 584
McMillan, Wm. IV, 341
McMillan, Wm. V, 583
McMillen, Ann IV, 876
McMillen, Ann IV, 877
McMillen, Ann C. V, 515
McMillen, Ann C. V, 539
McMillen, Bertha V, 1008
McMillen, David V, 514
McMillen, Deborah V, 514
McMillen, Edith V, 514
McMillen, Eli IV, 313
McMillen, Eli V, 514
McMillen, Eliza IV, 877
McMillen, Eliza V, 1008
McMillen, Eliza Ann IV, 877
McMillen, Elizabeth IV, 47
McMillen, Elizabeth IV, 67
McMillen, Elizabeth V, 297
McMillen, Elizabeth V, 307
McMillen, Elizabeth J. IV, 643
McMillen, Elizabeth J. IV, 662
McMillen, Emer H. V, 515
McMillen, Emer H. V, 534
McMillen, Enoch V, 515
McMillen, Enos IV, 877
McMillen, Ephraim M. V, 1008
McMillen, Esther V, 1008
McMillen, Jacob IV, 313
McMillen, Jane IV, 643
McMillen, Jane IV, 867
McMillen, Jane IV, 877
McMillen, Jane V, 514
McMillen, John V, 1008
McMillen, John W. IV, 877
McMillen, Jonathan V, 514
McMillen, Joseph IV, 877
McMillen, Joseph H. IV, 877
McMillen, Josiah V, 515
McMillen, Josiah V, 541
McMillen, Leonides V, 1008
McMillen, Maria IV, 877
McMillen, Mary IV, 153
McMillen, Mary Ann V, 515
McMillen, Mary Ann V, 530
McMillen, Mary Elizabeth V, 515
McMillen, Moses C. V, 515
McMillen, Phebe IV, 303
McMillen, Rebecca V, 515
McMillen, Rebecca V, 1008
McMillen, Rebecca Ann V, 515
McMillen, Rebecca Ann V, 541
McMillen, Ruth V, 517
McMillen, Ruth Ann IV, 737
McMillen, Ruth Elizabeth IV, 313
McMillen, Ruth W. V, 515
McMillen, Ruth W. V, 517
McMillen, Sadie V, 1008
McMillen, Sanford V, 515
McMillen, Sarah IV, 313
McMillen, Sarah Ann IV, 313
McMillen, Sarah H. V, 514
McMillen, Sarah Jane IV, 877
McMillen, Sarah W. IV, 877
McMillen, Susan V, 515
McMillen, Susan V, 534
McMillen, Taylor IV, 643
McMillen, Taylor IV, 877
McMillen, Thomas IV, 643
McMillen, Thomas IV, 877
McMillen, Thomas V, 514
McMillen, Uriah IV, 877
McMillin, Eliza V, 514
McMillin, Eliza Ann IV, 877
McMillin, Enos IV, 877
McMillin, Hannah IV, 313
McMillin, Hannah L. V, 514
McMillin, John W. IV, 877
McMillin, Joseph IV, 877
McMillin, Mahlon IV, 313
McMillin, Rachel IV, 313
McMillin, Rebecca Ann IV, 832
McMillin, Ruth IV, 313
McMillin, Sarah Jane IV, 877
McMillin, Sarah W. IV, 877
McMillin, Taylor IV, 877
McMillin, Thomas IV, 313
McMillin, Uriah IV, 877
McMillin, William IV, 313
McMillon, Jane V, 514
McMinn, Prudence IV, 419
McMinnis, James VI, 955
McMinnis, Mary VI, 955
McMulin, Ann IV, 158
McMulin, Elizabeth IV, 153
McMulin, Elizabeth IV, 158
McMulin, Richard IV, 158
McMullan, Albert Earl V, 584
McMullan, Elizabeth N. V, 471
McMullan, Elizabeth N. V, 514
McMullan, Harriet V, 514
McMullan, Helen V, 658
McMullan, Hester Ann V, 514
McMullan, Isaac V, 658
McMullan, Joseph Lincoln V, 584
McMullan, Mrs. J. E. V, 322
McMullan, Oletha V, 584
McMullan, Rebecca V, 514
McMullan, Samuel II, 392
McMullan, Thomas W. V, 471
McMullan, Thomas W. V, 514
McMullen, Albert Earl V, 583
McMullen, Alice D. V, 583
McMullen, Elizabeth V, 318
McMullen, Elizabeth V, 348
McMullen, Joseph L. V, 583
McMullen, Lulu IV, 737
McMullen, Mary V, 583
McMullen, Matthew VI, 913
McMullen, Olitha V, 586
McMullen, Wilma IV, 419
McMullen, Wilma IV, 434
McMullin, Christopher M. VI, 874
McMullin, Elizabeth VI, 882
McMullin, Hannah IV, 99
McMullin, Hannah IV, 115
McMullin, Margaret VI, 874
McMullin, Margarett VI, 875
McMullin, Mary VI, 877
McMullin, Mary A. VI, 837
McMullin, Matthew VI, 877
McMullin, Samuel VI, 837
McMullins, Elizabeth IV, 153
McMun, Elizabeth I, 558
McMun, John I, 406
McMun, John I, 1049
McMun, Prudence I, 558
McMun, Sarah I, 558
McMunn, Elizabeth V, 753
McMunn, John I, 406
McMunn, Prudence V, 753
McMunn, Sarah V, 753
McMunn, Sarah V, 794
McMurray, James VI, 869
McMurry, Armilla I, 606
McMurtrie, Margery II, 589
McMurtry, Joseph VI, 955
McMurtry, Susanna VI, 955
McNabb, John II, 392
McNabb, Mary II, 392
McNair, Mary P. III, 94
McNairy, Sarah I, 622
McNama, Florence V, 694
McNama, Florence V, 707
McNama, Mary Ann V, 694
McNama, Reba V, 695
McNama, Sarah M. V, 584
McNama, Sarah M. V, 694
McNama, William V, 694
McNama, Wm. V, 707
McNamee, Ann IV, 341
McNamee, Barnabas IV, 17
McNamee, Barnabas IV, 47
McNamee, Barnabas IV, 62
McNamee, Barnabas IV, 486
McNamee, Barnabas VI, 420
McNamee, Cynthia IV, 341
McNamee, Cynthia IV, 540
McNamee, Cynthia Ann IV, 486
McNamee, Cynthia Ann IV, 540
McNamee, Cynthiann IV, 486
McNamee, Cynthiann IV, 487
McNamee, Cynthiann IV, 540
McNamee, Cyrus IV, 47
McNamee, Cyrus IV, 341
McNamee, Cyrus IV, 486
McNamee, Cyrus IV, 540
McNamee, Cyrus IV, 561
McNamee, Cyrus K. IV, 540
McNamee, Elias IV, 47
McNamee, Elias IV, 486
McNamee, Elias VI, 420
McNamee, Elias B. IV, 540
McNamee, Elizabeth IV, 540
McNamee, Gideon VI, 420
McNamee, Helana IV, 486
McNamee, Helen IV, 47
McNamee, Helena IV, 341
McNamee, Helena IV, 486
McNamee, Helena IV, 540
McNamee, Helena IV, 544
McNamee, Hellen A. IV, 540
McNamee, Isaac IV, 44
McNamee, Isaac IV, 47
McNamee, Isaac IV, 341
McNamee, Isaac IV, 486
McNamee, Isaac IV, 540
McNamee, Isaac IV, 561
McNamee, Isaac VI, 420
McNamee, Isaac P. IV, 540
McNamee, Israel IV, 341
McNamee, Jacob VI, 420
McNamee, Margaret IV, 44
McNamee, Margaret IV, 47
McNamee, Margaret IV, 247
McNamee, Margaret IV, 341
McNamee, Margaret IV, 486
McNamee, Margaret IV, 540
McNamee, Margaret VI, 420
McNamee, Mary IV, 43
McNamee, Mary IV, 47
McNamee, Mary IV, 62
McNamee, Mary IV, 486
McNamee, Mary IV, 489
McNamee, Mary VI, 420
McNamee, Mashac IV, 540
McNamee, Mashach IV, 341
McNamee, Mashack IV, 47
McNamee, Meshack IV, 486
McNamee, Rachel Cairy IV, 540
McNamee, Reuben IV, 47
McNamee, Reuben IV, 341
McNamee, Reuben IV, 486
McNamee, Reuben IV, 540
McNamee, Ruben IV, 486
McNamee, Rubin VI, 420
McNamee, Sarah IV, 47
McNamee, Sarah IV, 62
McNamee, Sarah IV, 486
McNamee, Sarah IV, 497
McNamee, Sarah VI, 420
McNamee, Wilhelmina II, 894
McNamee, Wilhelmina W. II, 753
McNamee, Wilhelmina W. II, 776
McNamee, Wilhemina II, 894
McNamee, Wilhemina C. II, 941
McNamee, William IV, 47
McNamee, William IV, 341
McNamee, William IV, 486
McNamee, William IV, 540
McNamee, William J. IV, 540
McNamee, William Marsh, Jr. IV, 486
McNamee, Wm. IV, 540
McNance, Elizabeth S. VI, 837
McNance, James VI, 837
McNary, Susannah V, 948
McNary, Susannah V, 955
McNeal, Ada V, 633
McNeal, Daniel W. V, 460
McNeal, Emily E. V, 466
McNeal, Esther E. II, 295
McNeal, George L. I, 637
McNeal, George L., Jr. I, 637
McNeal, Hannah V, 187
McNeal, Hannah Spray V, 187
McNeal, Hazel V, 633
McNeal, Isaac Lionel V, 187
McNeal, John I, 1044
McNeal, John I, 1046
McNeal, John I, 1124
McNeal, John V, 633
McNeal, John G. V, 187
McNeal, Lee V, 187
McNeal, Lee V, 515
McNeal, Leonidas Lee V, 187
McNeal, Lillian IV, 1040
McNeal, Marjorie Rebecca I, 63
McNeal, Mary I, 1034
McNeal, Mary I, 1039
McNeal, Mary I, 1044
McNeal, Mary I, 1046
McNeal, Mary V, 460
McNeal, Mary V, 466
McNeal, Mary V, 633
McNeal, Mary V, 695
McNeal, Mary H. V, 261
McNeal, Mary Lee V, 187
McNeal, Nello V, 187
McNeal, Samuel W. V, 466
McNeal, Velna I, 637
McNealy, Abigail IV, 643
McNealy, Abigail IV, 832
McNealy, George IV, 832
McNealy, Jane II, 589
McNealy, Lydia IV, 832
McNealy, Mary IV, 832
McNealy, Rachel IV, 832
McNealy, Robert IV, 832
McNealy, Sarah IV, 832
McNealy, Sarah IV, 840
McNealy, William IV, 832
McNeelan, Miriam B. V, 919
McNeeley, Sarah IV, 47
McNeely, Abigail IV, 643
McNeely, Abigail IV, 737
McNeely, Abigail IV, 910
McNeely, Abigail IV, 912
McNeely, Agness VI, 955
McNeely, George IV, 832
McNeely, George IV, 859
McNeely, Jane IV, 859
McNeely, Michael VI, 955
McNeely, Rachel IV, 859
McNees, Charity I, 1085
McNees, Charity I, 1089
McNees, Charity I, 1095
McNees, Edwin I, 1095
McNees, Elihu I, 1095
McNees, Gravener I, 1095
McNees, Gravner I, 1124
McNees, Isaiah I, 1095
McNees, James I, 1095
McNees, Leddra I, 1095
McNees, Lyda I, 1085
McNees, Lydia I, 1095
McNees, Lydia Ann I, 1085
McNees, Marmaduke I, 1085
McNees, Marmaduke I, 1089
McNees, Marmaduke I, 1095
McNees, Samuel I, 1085
McNees, Samuel I, 1089
McNees, Samuel I, 1095
McNees, Samuel I, 1098
McNeese, Gravenor I, 1124
McNeese, Gravner I, 1124
McNeil, Allie V, 633
McNeil, Carlos V, 633
McNeil, Carrie Mabel V, 633
McNeil, Daniel VI, 956
McNeil, Ella V, 633
McNeil, Ella H. IV, 1328
McNeil, Ella Hastings IV, 1328
McNeil, Herburt V, 633
McNeil, Imogene V, 633
McNeil, Isaac Lionel V, 187
McNeil, John VI, 955
McNeil, John G. V, 187
McNeil, Mary VI, 955
McNeil, Mary Lee V, 187
McNeil, Mary M. V, 633
McNeil, Sallie V, 633
McNeil, Sarah VI, 956
McNeil, Thomas V, 633
McNeil, Waller V, 633
McNeile, ??? III, 131
McNeile, Anna III, 215
McNeile, Anna D. W. III, 131
McNeile, Anna Gordon III, 131
McNeill, George L. I, 621
McNeill, George Lynch, Jr. I, 621
McNeill, John S. I, 621
McNeill, Marian Opal I, 621
McNeill, Marjorie Rebecca I, 621
McNeill, Velma H. I, 621
McNely, Abigail IV, 910
McNely, Jane II, 589
McNely, Jane IV, 910
McNely, Lydia IV, 910
McNely, Mary IV, 910

cNely, Rachel IV, 910
cNema, Abraham V, 694
cNema, Florence V, 694
cNema, Lawther V, 694
cNema, Margaret V, 694
cNema, Mary A. V, 694
cNema, Mary Ann V, 694
cNema, Reba V, 695
cNema, Sarah M. V, 694
cNema, William V, 694
cNemar, Donald V, 695
cNichol, George II, 85
cNichol, George II, 105
cNichol, Hannah II, 82
cNichol, Hannah II, 85
cNichol, Leslie V, 261
cNichol, Mary II, 85
cNichol, Phebey II, 62
cNichol, Phebey II, 85
cNichol, Rebekah II, 105
cNichol, Robert V, 261
cNichol, Sarah E. V, 261
cNichols, ??? IV, 587
cNichols, Andrew II, 33
cNichols, Andrew II, 85
cNichols, Benjamin IV, 341
cNichols, Benjamin IV, 419
cNichols, Charity IV, 419
cNichols, Charity IV, 424
cNichols, Cyrus IV, 247
cNichols, Cyrus IV, 419
cNichols, Cyrus IV, 587
cNichols, Daniel II, 33
cNichols, Elizabeth IV, 341
cNichols, Elizabeth IV, 419
cNichols, Esther IV, 419
cNichols, George II, 33
cNichols, George II, 85
cNichols, George IV, 247
cNichols, George IV, 404
cNichols, George IV, 419
cNichols, George IV, 587
cNichols, Hannah II, 33
cNichols, Hannah II, 85
cNichols, Hester IV, 247
cNichols, Isaac W. II, 33
cNichols, Jane IV, 419
cNichols, Jane IV, 587
cNichols, John II, 33
cNichols, John IV, 419
cNichols, John IV, 587
cNichols, John Faucett IV, 419
cNichols, John Fawcett IV, 341
cNichols, John Fawcett IV, 587
cNichols, John, Jr. II, 33
cNichols, Joseph IV, 341
cNichols, Joseph IV, 419
cNichols, Keturah IV, 1067
cNichols, Margaret II, 33
cNichols, Maria IV, 341
cNichols, Maria IV, 392
cNichols, Maria IV, 419
cNichols, Martha IV, 247
cNichols, Martha IV, 341
cNichols, Martha IV, 404
cNichols, Martha IV, 419
cNichols, Martha IV, 456
cNichols, Martha IV, 486
cNichols, Martha IV, 587
cNichols, Martha IV, 599
cNichols, Martha VI, 421
cNichols, Mary II, 33
cNichols, Mary II, 85
cNichols, Mary IV, 247
cNichols, Mary IV, 339
cNichols, Mary IV, 341
cNichols, Mary IV, 419
cNichols, Mary IV, 587
McNichols, Mary IV, 589
McNichols, Nathaniel IV, 419
McNichols, Nathaniel IV, 486
McNichols, Nathaniel IV, 587
McNichols, Nathaniel W. II, 33
McNichols, Nethaniel II, 85
McNichols, Phebe II, 33
McNichols, Phebey II, 85
McNichols, Prudence IV, 404
McNichols, Prudence IV, 419
McNichols, Prudence IV, 587
McNichols, Rachel IV, 328
McNichols, Rachel IV, 341
McNichols, Rachel IV, 350
McNichols, Rachel IV, 419
McNichols, Rachel IV, 486
McNichols, Rachel IV, 587
McNichols, Rachel IV, 599
McNichols, Rebecca II, 84
McNichols, Rebecca II, 85
McNichols, Rebecca Ann IV, 1065
McNichols, Rebecca Ann IV, 1067
McNichols, Rebeckah II, 33
McNichols, Rebekah II, 85
McNichols, Ruth IV, 247
McNichols, Ruth IV, 419
McNichols, Smith IV, 419
McNichols, Smith IV, 587
McNichols, Thomas IV, 419
McNichols, Thomas IV, 587
McNichols, Thomas IV, 599
McNichols, William II, 33
McNichols, William IV, 341
McNichols, William IV, 419
McNichols, William IV, 486
McNichols, Wm. II, 85
McNichols, Wm. IV, 328
McNichols, Wm. IV, 587
McNickel, Sarah E. V, 460
McNickle, Rachel IV, 1328
McNickles, Keturah IV, 1065
McNickles, Keturah IV, 1067
McNickol, John V, 348
McNickolls, George II, 240
McNicles, Mary IV, 424
McNicol, John V, 348
McNiece, Widower Isaiah II, 589
McNight, Abigail I, 1119
McNight, Abigail I, 1124
McNight, Rachel I, 1124
McNod, Sarah VI, 877
McNuly, George IV, 897
McNutt, Hannah IV, 99
McNutty, Patrick VI, 837
McNutty, Susan VI, 837
McPark, Artie IV, 1216
McPark, Bernisa IV, 1216
McPark, Gladys IV, 1216
McPark, Jessie IV, 1216
McPark, Wilford IV, 1216
McPeak, Ernest IV, 1172
McPeak, Laura IV, 1172
McPeak, Rebeckah II, 78
McPeak, Rebeckah II, 85
McPeak, Tobias IV, 1172
McPeek, Artie IV, 1216
McPeek, Benisa IV, 1216
McPeek, Elijah IV, 1216
McPeek, Gladyse IV, 1216
McPeek, Jane IV, 1216
McPeek, Jesse IV, 1216
McPeek, Wilford IV, 1216
McPerson, Jane VI, 500
McPerson, Jean VI, 421
McPhail, Caroline V, 96
McPhail, Caroline V, 695
McPhail, Donald E. V, 695
McPherson, ??? V, 443
McPherson, ??? VI, 348
McPherson, Aaron I, 438
McPherson, Aaron I, 450
McPherson, Abbigail I, 825
McPherson, Abigail I, 359
McPherson, Abigail I, 406
McPherson, Abigail I, 595
McPherson, Abigail I, 786
McPherson, Abigail I, 909
McPherson, Abigail I, 913
McPherson, Alexandria VI, 421
McPherson, Alice I, 406
McPherson, Alice Myrtle IV, 1328
McPherson, Aline VI, 764
McPherson, Almeda V, 262
McPherson, Angeline I, 406
McPherson, Angeline V, 262
McPherson, Angeline R. IV, 1328
McPherson, Angie V, 262
McPherson, Ann I, 595
McPherson, Ann I, 786
McPherson, Ann I, 913
McPherson, Ann V, 96
McPherson, Ann V, 261
McPherson, Ann V, 282
McPherson, Ann VI, 331
McPherson, Ann VI, 406
McPherson, Ann VI, 416
McPherson, Ann VI, 421
McPherson, Ann VI, 424
McPherson, Ann VI, 492
McPherson, Ann VI, 530
McPherson, Ann VI, 549
McPherson, Ann VI, 623
McPherson, Ann VI, 674
McPherson, Ann VI, 675
McPherson, Ann VI, 680
McPherson, Ann VI, 763
McPherson, Ann M. V, 261
McPherson, Anna I, 1011
McPherson, Anna IV, 978
McPherson, Anna V, 230
McPherson, Anna V, 257
McPherson, Anna V, 262
McPherson, Anna V, 266
McPherson, Anna V, 348
McPherson, Anna V, 695
McPherson, Anna VI, 667
McPherson, Anna E. V, 695
McPherson, Anne I, 1008
McPherson, Anne I, 1011
McPherson, Annie V, 262
McPherson, Annie Laura VI, 662
McPherson, Annie M. V, 348
McPherson, Anny VI, 353
McPherson, Arlendo W. I, 406
McPherson, Atlantic V, 261
McPherson, Ava I, 945
McPherson, Ava I, 949
McPherson, Ava L. I, 930
McPherson, Benjamin V, 262
McPherson, Bertha V, 262
McPherson, Betty V, 96
McPherson, Betty V, 261
McPherson, Betty VI, 416
McPherson, Betty VI, 421
McPherson, Blanch V, 460
McPherson, Blanch V, 695
McPherson, Bunyan I, 945
McPherson, Bunyan I, 949
McPherson, C. V, 262
McPherson, Carey V, 262
McPherson, Carey V, 412
McPherson, Carey Ellis V, 262
McPherson, Carey Lee V, 412
McPherson, Caroline V, 412
McPherson, Caroline E. V, 412
McPherson, Catharine IV, 737
McPherson, Catharine A. I, 438
McPherson, Catherine M. V, 262
McPherson, Charity I, 406
McPherson, Charles VI, 763
McPherson, Charles Earle IV, 1257
McPherson, Charlotte V, 262
McPherson, Charlotte V, 447
McPherson, Chase Roe IV, 978
McPherson, Chase Talbott IV, 978
McPherson, Clara V, 412
McPherson, Clarence VI, 668
McPherson, Cleo V, 695
McPherson, Cora Ann V, 262
McPherson, Cornelia I, 406
McPherson, Cosmelia J. VI, 627
McPherson, Daniel I, 1011
McPherson, Daniel V, 249
McPherson, Daniel V, 257
McPherson, Daniel V, 261
McPherson, Daniel V, 262
McPherson, Daniel V, 348
McPherson, Daniel V, 385
McPherson, Daniel V, 412
McPherson, Daniel V, 488
McPherson, Daniel V, 515
McPherson, Daniel VI, 299
McPherson, Daniel VI, 331
McPherson, Daniel VI, 353
McPherson, Daniel VI, 364
McPherson, Daniel VI, 395
McPherson, Daniel VI, 407
McPherson, Daniel VI, 421
McPherson, Daniel VI, 470
McPherson, Daniel VI, 489
McPherson, Daniel VI, 517
McPherson, Daniel VI, 530
McPherson, Daniel VI, 627
McPherson, Daniel VI, 661
McPherson, Daniel VI, 727
McPherson, Daniel VI, 744
McPherson, Daniel VI, 753
McPherson, Daniel VI, 763
McPherson, Daniel VI, 769
McPherson, Daniel VI, 775
McPherson, Daniel VI, 956
McPherson, Daniel, Jr. VI, 421
McPherson, Daniel, Jr. VI, 470
McPherson, Darnie Mae V, 262
McPherson, Deborah I, 450
McPherson, Dora V, 460
McPherson, Dora V, 695
McPherson, Douglas, Jr. VI, 662
McPherson, Duncan VI, 754
McPherson, Duncan VI, 764
McPherson, Earl IV, 1257
McPherson, Edith Emilie I, 406
McPherson, Edna V, 262
McPherson, Edna V, 277
McPherson, Edna V, 283
McPherson, Edna V, 412
McPherson, Edna J. V, 262
McPherson, Edney V, 412
McPherson, Edward VI, 437
McPherson, Edward Everett V, 412
McPherson, Elcie O. V, 262
McPherson, Eli I, 406
McPherson, Elizabeth I, 930
McPherson, Elizabeth I, 1008
McPherson, Elizabeth I, 1011
McPherson, Elizabeth V, 282
McPherson, Elizabeth VI, 331
McPherson, Elizabeth VI, 353
McPherson, Elizabeth VI, 395
McPherson, Elizabeth VI, 421
McPherson, Elizabeth VI, 526
McPherson, Elizabeth VI, 530
McPherson, Elizabeth VI, 553
McPherson, Elizabeth VI, 661
McPherson, Elizabeth VI, 667
McPherson, Elizabeth VI, 674
McPherson, Elizabeth VI, 744
McPherson, Elizabeth VI, 754
McPherson, Elizabeth VI, 756
McPherson, Elizabeth VI, 763
McPherson, Elizabeth VI, 764
McPherson, Elizabeth VI, 769
McPherson, Elizabeth, Jr. VI, 763
McPherson, Ella V, 262
McPherson, Elmer T. V, 695
McPherson, Elmore V, 633
McPherson, Elsie O. V, 262
McPherson, Emaline V, 262
McPherson, Emaline V, 695
McPherson, Emiline V, 262
McPherson, Emily V, 173
McPherson, Emily V, 261
McPherson, Emily V, 496
McPherson, Emily V, 515
McPherson, Emily VI, 763
McPherson, Emily T. V, 243
McPherson, Emily T. V, 261
McPherson, Emma V, 695
McPherson, Esther V, 258
McPherson, Esther V, 262
McPherson, Esther V, 919
McPherson, Esther VI, 764
McPherson, Ethel V, 262
McPherson, Ethel Blanch V, 460
McPherson, Florence V, 412
McPherson, Forest S. IV, 978
McPherson, Frances VI, 764
McPherson, Frances VI, 790
McPherson, Francis M. V, 412
McPherson, Fred V, 695
McPherson, Frederick B. V, 695
McPherson, Geo. V, 695
McPherson, Geo. B. V, 695
McPherson, George III, 215
McPherson, George V, 262
McPherson, George V, 695
McPherson, George B. V, 695
McPherson, George M. I, 786
McPherson, George Myron V, 695
McPherson, George W. V, 187
McPherson, George W. V, 262
McPherson, Gertrude M. VI, 753
McPherson, Gertrude M. VI, 755
McPherson, Gertrude M. VI, 764
McPherson, Grace V, 261
McPherson, Grace V, 262
McPherson, H. D. I, 406
McPherson, Hannah I, 359
McPherson, Hannah I, 786
McPherson, Hannah I, 820
McPherson, Hannah I, 825
McPherson, Hannah V, 412
McPherson, Hannah V, 919
McPherson, Hannah V, 920
McPherson, Hannah VI, 407
McPherson, Hannah VI, 416
McPherson, Hannah VI, 421
McPherson, Hannah VI, 441
McPherson, Hannah VI, 462
McPherson, Hannah VI, 489
McPherson, Hannah VI, 530
McPherson, Hannah VI, 661
McPherson, Hannah VI, 668
McPherson, Hannah VI, 674
McPherson, Hannah VI, 739
McPherson, Hannah VI, 752
McPherson, Hannah VI, 763
McPherson, Hannah VI, 764
McPherson, Hannah VI, 769
McPherson, Hannah VI, 775
McPherson, Hannah B. V, 257
McPherson, Hannah G. V, 261
McPherson, Hannah G. V, 262
McPherson, Harriett I, 406
McPherson, Harrison V, 262
McPherson, Harrison V, 460
McPherson, Harry Maxwell V, 262
McPherson, Hattie V, 695
McPherson, Hattie V, 697
McPherson, Hazel V, 669
McPherson, Hazel V, 695
McPherson, Henrietta V. I, 406
McPherson, Henry C. V, 633
McPherson, Henry C. V, 695
McPherson, Hettie V, 187
McPherson, Hiram IV, 247
McPherson, Hiram V, 412
McPherson, Hugh D. I, 406
McPherson, Ida Jane IV, 978
McPherson, Isaac V, 96
McPherson, Isaac V, 241
McPherson, Isaac V, 261
McPherson, Isaac V, 282
McPherson, Isaac VI, 416
McPherson, Isaac VI, 421
McPherson, Isaac VI, 489
McPherson, Isaac VI, 530
McPherson, Isaac VI, 553
McPherson, Isaac VI, 667
McPherson, Isaac VI, 674
McPherson, Isaac VI, 756
McPherson, Isaac VI, 763
McPherson, Isaac VI, 764
McPherson, Isaac B. V, 262
McPherson, Isaac Bourd V, 262
McPherson, Isabelle V, 262
McPherson, J. Bunyan I, 945
McPherson, Jane I, 786
McPherson, Jane I, 913
McPherson, Jane V, 221
McPherson, Jane V, 261
McPherson, Jane V, 262
McPherson, Jane VI, 374
McPherson, Jane VI, 407
McPherson, Jane VI, 421
McPherson, Jane VI, 437
McPherson, Jane VI, 517
McPherson, Jane VI, 519
McPherson, Jane VI, 645
McPherson, Jane VI, 661
McPherson, Jane VI, 664
McPherson, Jane VI, 668
McPherson, Jane VI, 674
McPherson, Jane VI, 750
McPherson, Jane VI, 752
McPherson, Jane VI, 753
McPherson, Jane VI, 755
McPherson, Jane VI, 758
McPherson, Jane VI, 763
McPherson, Jane VI, 764
McPherson, Jane A. VI, 763
McPherson, Janet VI, 627
McPherson, Janet VI, 733
McPherson, Jean VI, 376
McPherson, Jean VI, 421
McPherson, Jehu I, 786
McPherson, Jehu I, 913
McPherson, Jesse I, 406
McPherson, Jesse IV, 1328
McPherson, Jesse V, 261
McPherson, Jesse V, 262
McPherson, John I, 359
McPherson, John I, 406
McPherson, John I, 786
McPherson, John I, 825
McPherson, John IV, 153
McPherson, John V, 240
McPherson, John V, 261
McPherson, John V, 262
McPherson, John V, 270
McPherson, John V, 412
McPherson, John V, 437
McPherson, John V, 447
McPherson, John VI, 137
McPherson, John VI, 353
McPherson, John VI, 407
McPherson, John VI, 416
McPherson, John VI, 421
McPherson, John VI, 441
McPherson, John VI, 462
McPherson, John VI, 530
McPherson, John VI, 661
McPherson, John VI, 674
McPherson, John VI, 725
McPherson, John VI, 752
McPherson, John VI, 763
McPherson, John VI, 769
McPherson, John VI, 775
McPherson, John VI, 956
McPherson, John Aaron I, 930
McPherson, John D. VI, 763
McPherson, John D. VI, 764
McPherson, John D. VI, 790
McPherson, John Douglas VI, 764
McPherson, John Douglas, Jr. VI, 753
McPherson, John Douglas, Jr. VI, 755
McPherson, John Douglas, Jr. VI, 764
McPherson, John T. I, 406
McPherson, John W. V, 262

McPherson, John, Jr. VI, 530
McPherson, John, Jr. VI, 764
McPherson, Jonas VI, 421
McPherson, Joseph I, 359
McPherson, Joseph I, 406
McPherson, Joseph I, 414
McPherson, Joseph I, 786
McPherson, Joseph I, 825
McPherson, Joseph I, 909
McPherson, Joseph I, 913
McPherson, Joseph V, 262
McPherson, Joseph V, 322
McPherson, Joseph V, 348
McPherson, Joseph V, 412
McPherson, Joseph V, 633
McPherson, Joseph C. V, 262
McPherson, Joseph C. V, 412
McPherson, Joseph David IV, 978
McPherson, Joseph G. VI, 763
McPherson, Joseph H. V, 262
McPherson, Joseph Merrab V, 262
McPherson, Joshiah V, 262
McPherson, Josiah V, 258
McPherson, Josiah V, 261
McPherson, Josiah V, 262
McPherson, Josiah V, 412
McPherson, Julian V, 255
McPherson, Julian V, 262
McPherson, Katharine V, 262
McPherson, Keziah VI, 674
McPherson, Keziah VI, 704
McPherson, Lida E. V, 418
McPherson, Lindley L. V, 692
McPherson, Linley M. V, 262
McPherson, Lola A. I, 406
McPherson, Louisa V, 246
McPherson, Louisa V, 261
McPherson, Louisa V, 262
McPherson, Louise Marie I, 930
McPherson, Lucian A. I, 406
McPherson, Lulu B. V, 695
McPherson, Luther Bunyan I, 930
McPherson, Lydia I, 595
McPherson, Lydia I, 786
McPherson, Lydia I, 913
McPherson, Lydia V, 261
McPherson, Lydia V, 919
McPherson, Lydia V, 920
McPherson, Lydia VI, 675
McPherson, Lydia VI, 764
McPherson, Lydia E. V, 262
McPherson, Lydia E. V, 753
McPherson, Lydia Mariah V, 261
McPherson, Lydia Mary V, 385
McPherson, Lydia Mary V, 412
McPherson, Lydia Mary V, 488
McPherson, Lydia Mary V, 515
McPherson, Major John D. III VI, 764
McPherson, Malinda I, 406
McPherson, Malinda C. V, 261
McPherson, Margaret V, 261
McPherson, Margaret V, 920
McPherson, Margaret VI, 764
McPherson, Margaret Delores VI, 764
McPherson, Maria V, 240
McPherson, Maria V, 261
McPherson, Maria V, 262
McPherson, Maria V, 270
McPherson, Maria V, 412
McPherson, Maria V, 437
McPherson, Mariah V, 262
McPherson, Mariam V, 262
McPherson, Marianna V, 437
McPherson, Marianne VI, 764
McPherson, Marion V, 261
McPherson, Marion V, 262
McPherson, Marion V, 277
McPherson, Martha I, 1008
McPherson, Martha I, 1011
McPherson, Martha V, 919
McPherson, Martha V, 920
McPherson, Martha VI, 331
McPherson, Martha VI, 353
McPherson, Martha VI, 364
McPherson, Martha VI, 421
McPherson, Martha VI, 437
McPherson, Martha VI, 470
McPherson, Martha VI, 530
McPherson, Martha VI, 764
McPherson, Martha B. V, 240
McPherson, Martha B. V, 261
McPherson, Martha B. V, 387
McPherson, Martha B. V, 412
McPherson, Martha Esther V, 262
McPherson, Mary I, 359
McPherson, Mary I, 406
McPherson, Mary I, 786
McPherson, Mary I, 824
McPherson, Mary I, 825
McPherson, Mary I, 1011
McPherson, Mary V, 243
McPherson, Mary V, 249
McPherson, Mary V, 261
McPherson, Mary V, 262
McPherson, Mary V, 270
McPherson, Mary V, 276
McPherson, Mary V, 277
McPherson, Mary V, 348
McPherson, Mary V, 412
McPherson, Mary V, 418
McPherson, Mary V, 447
McPherson, Mary V, 460
McPherson, Mary V, 695
McPherson, Mary V, 719
McPherson, Mary V, 919
McPherson, Mary VI, 299
McPherson, Mary VI, 331
McPherson, Mary VI, 353
McPherson, Mary VI, 376
McPherson, Mary VI, 407
McPherson, Mary VI, 421
McPherson, Mary VI, 422
McPherson, Mary VI, 447
McPherson, Mary VI, 462
McPherson, Mary VI, 470
McPherson, Mary VI, 489
McPherson, Mary VI, 500
McPherson, Mary VI, 517
McPherson, Mary VI, 518
McPherson, Mary VI, 530
McPherson, Mary VI, 565
McPherson, Mary VI, 645
McPherson, Mary VI, 661
McPherson, Mary VI, 662
McPherson, Mary VI, 675
McPherson, Mary VI, 745
McPherson, Mary VI, 753
McPherson, Mary VI, 764
McPherson, Mary VI, 769
McPherson, Mary Amney V, 262
McPherson, Mary Amney V, 288
McPherson, Mary Ann VI, 421
McPherson, Mary Ann VI, 626
McPherson, Mary Ann VI, 659
McPherson, Mary Ann VI, 666
McPherson, Mary Ann VI, 674
McPherson, Mary Ann VI, 681
McPherson, Mary Ann VI, 682
McPherson, Mary Ann VI, 683
McPherson, Mary Ann VI, 685
McPherson, Mary Ann VI, 708
McPherson, Mary Ann VI, 763
McPherson, Mary Ann VI, 764
McPherson, Mary Brown VI, 754
McPherson, Mary Brown VI, 764
McPherson, Mary E. V, 262
McPherson, Mary L. I, 406
McPherson, Mary M. V, 262
McPherson, Mary Margaret V, 348
McPherson, Mary Margaret V, 412
McPherson, Mary Margarett V, 348
McPherson, Maud V, 695
McPherson, Mauda R. V, 695
McPherson, Maxwell V, 262
McPherson, May Lucile I, 930
McPherson, Merab V, 262
McPherson, Minette V, 412
McPherson, Minnie V, 412
McPherson, Morris M. V, 262
McPherson, Nancy Ellen V, 695
McPherson, Nancy Jane V, 262
McPherson, Nancy Leanna I, 406
McPherson, Neil V, 695
McPherson, Neva V, 695
McPherson, Nina V, 695
McPherson, Nina V. V, 515
McPherson, Nina V. V, 695
McPherson, Oio V, 695
McPherson, Olive C. V, 258
McPherson, Oliver I, 406
McPherson, Ollie S. V, 695
McPherson, Patience I, 450
McPherson, Patsy VI, 956
McPherson, Pauline V, 692
McPherson, Pauline V, 695
McPherson, Pauline L. V, 695
McPherson, Phebe I, 406
McPherson, Phebe V, 262
McPherson, Phebe A. V, 262
McPherson, Phebe A. V, 270
McPherson, Phebe A. V, 633
McPherson, Phebe A. V, 640
McPherson, Polly VI, 956
McPherson, Rachel I, 377
McPherson, Rachel I, 406
McPherson, Rachel V, 262
McPherson, Rachel V, 348
McPherson, Rachel V, 445
McPherson, Rachel V, 447
McPherson, Ralph V, 669
McPherson, Ralph V, 695
McPherson, Ralph W. V, 695
McPherson, Raymond V, 412
McPherson, Rebecca V, 919
McPherson, Rebecca VI, 421
McPherson, Rebecca VI, 530
McPherson, Rebecca VI, 751
McPherson, Rebecca VI, 764
McPherson, Rebecca VI, 769
McPherson, Rebecca Jane V, 262
McPherson, Rebecca N. VI, 763
McPherson, Rebecca N. VI, 764
McPherson, Rebecca N. VI, 769
McPherson, Rebekah VI, 421
McPherson, Rebekah VI, 462
McPherson, Rebekah VI, 768
McPherson, Robert Janney VI, 764
McPherson, Roscoe V, 262
McPherson, Ruth I, 786
McPherson, Ruth I, 913
McPherson, Ruth I, 1011
McPherson, Ruth V, 241
McPherson, Ruth V, 249
McPherson, Ruth V, 261
McPherson, Ruth V, 262
McPherson, Ruth V, 322
McPherson, Ruth V, 348
McPherson, Ruth V, 412
McPherson, Ruth V, 423
McPherson, Ruth V, 919
McPherson, Ruth VI, 353
McPherson, Ruth VI, 407
McPherson, Ruth VI, 421
McPherson, Ruth VI, 517
McPherson, Ruth VI, 519
McPherson, Ruth VI, 521
McPherson, Ruth VI, 530
McPherson, Ruth VI, 638
McPherson, Ruth VI, 661
McPherson, Ruth VI, 662
McPherson, Ruth VI, 674
McPherson, Ruth VI, 715
McPherson, Ruth VI, 750
McPherson, Ruth VI, 753
McPherson, Ruth VI, 764
McPherson, Ruth Anna V, 262
McPherson, Ruth Ellen I, 406
McPherson, Ruth G. V, 262
McPherson, Sally VI, 915
McPherson, Sally VI, 956
McPherson, Samuel VI, 421
McPherson, Samuel VI, 447
McPherson, Samuel VI, 530
McPherson, Samuel VI, 565
McPherson, Samuel VI, 661
McPherson, Samuel VI, 758
McPherson, Samuel VI, 763
McPherson, Samuel VI, 764
McPherson, Sarah I, 386
McPherson, Sarah I, 406
McPherson, Sarah I, 411
McPherson, Sarah I, 414
McPherson, Sarah I, 786
McPherson, Sarah I, 825
McPherson, Sarah I, 1011
McPherson, Sarah V, 244
McPherson, Sarah V, 261
McPherson, Sarah V, 262
McPherson, Sarah V, 412
McPherson, Sarah V, 919
McPherson, Sarah VI, 331
McPherson, Sarah VI, 353
McPherson, Sarah VI, 650
McPherson, Sarah VI, 674
McPherson, Sarah VI, 675
McPherson, Sarah VI, 715
McPherson, Sarah VI, 764
McPherson, Sidney V, 261
McPherson, Stella V, 262
McPherson, Stephen I, 786
McPherson, Stephen I, 825
McPherson, Stephen V, 243
McPherson, Stephen V, 261
McPherson, Stephen V, 262
McPherson, Stephen V, 447
McPherson, Stephen VI, 331
McPherson, Stephen VI, 353
McPherson, Stephen VI, 674
McPherson, Stephen VI, 675
McPherson, Stephen VI, 715
McPherson, Stephen VI, 915
McPherson, Stephen VI, 956
McPherson, Stephen VI, 984
McPherson, Stephen, Jr. VI, 530
McPherson, Stephen, Jr. VI, 549
McPherson, Stephen, Jr. VI, 650
McPherson, Stephen, Jr. VI, 674
McPherson, Stephen, Jr. VI, 675
McPherson, Sylvester IV, 737
McPherson, Tacy VI, 530
McPherson, Tacy VI, 764
McPherson, Tamsin VI, 529
McPherson, Thamson VI, 526
McPherson, Thamzin VI, 416
McPherson, Thamzin VI, 421
McPherson, Theresa V, 262
McPherson, Thomas I, 406
McPherson, Thomas VI, 734
McPherson, Thomas N. I, 406
McPherson, Vada M. V, 695
McPherson, Walter V, 262
McPherson, Walter R. V, 262
McPherson, Wd. Mary VI, 752
McPherson, William I, 406
McPherson, William I, 786
McPherson, William I, 825
McPherson, William I, 913
McPherson, William V, 261
McPherson, William V, 262
McPherson, William VI, 376
McPherson, William VI, 397
McPherson, William VI, 421
McPherson, William VI, 764
McPherson, William C. V, 262
McPherson, William P. V, 262
McPherson, Wm. V, 418
McPherson, Wm. VI, 763
McPherson, Zebba V, 1008
McPherson-Janney, Ruth VI, 534
McPhetridge, Jemima I, 825
McPhetridge, Jemima I, 828
McPhillen, Elizabeth II, 240
McQuigan, Mary Elizabeth IV, 1328
McQuilkin, Teresa IV, 99
McQuilkin, Teresa IV, 115
McQuiston, Carlton V, 671
McQuiston, Carlton V, 695
McQuiston, Joan Worth V, 695
McQuiston, Mary Elma V, 695
McQuiston, Rebecca V, 671
McQuiston, Rebecca V, 695
McQuiston, Robert Farquhar V, 695
McQuown, Lydia L. V, 1008
McQuown, Rachel V, 1008
McQuown, Viola V, 1008
McQuown, W. M. V, 1008
McRacken, Abigail I, 748
McRacken, Abigail I, 766
McRacken, Elizabeth I, 741
McRacken, George I, 750
McRacken, Jane I, 750
McRacken, Robert I, 748
McRacken, Thomas I, 450
McRacken, Thomas I, 750
McRae, ??? I, 611
McRae, Effie I, 621
McRae, Effie Barker I, 637
McRae, Effie Margaret I, 611
McRae, O. B. I, 629
McRae, O. B. I, 637
McRay, Mary Ann V, 584
McRay, Mary E. V, 584
McReel, Murphy P. I, 310
McRey, Alexander I, 406
McReynolds, Arch VI, 837
McReynolds, Benjamin VI, 837
McReynolds, Catharine VI, 837
McReynolds, Elizabeth VI, 835
McReynolds, Elizabeth VI, 837
McReynolds, Elizabeth VI, 850
McReynolds, Elva II, 946
McReynolds, Elva II, 949
McReynolds, James VI, 835
McReynolds, Jane VI, 837
McReynolds, Jenny VI, 837
McReynolds, Jessie B. VI, 764
McReynolds, John VI, 803
McReynolds, John VI, 837
McReynolds, John C. VI, 837
McReynolds, Joseph VI, 824
McReynolds, Joseph VI, 837
McReynolds, Joseph VI, 866
McReynolds, Lucy VI, 956
McReynolds, Martha VI, 837
McReynolds, Martha VI, 859
McReynolds, Mary VI, 837
McReynolds, Mary VI, 850
McReynolds, Matthew VI, 846
McReynolds, Mrs. Frederick W. VI, 764
McReynolds, Nellie Cate I, 1159
McReynolds, O. McReynolds VI, 837
McReynolds, Oliver VI, 827
McReynolds, Oliver VI, 837
McReynolds, Polly VI, 866
McReynolds, Robert VI, 835
McReynolds, Sally VI, 832
McReynolds, Sally VI, 837
McReynolds, Samuel VI, 837
McReynolds, Sarah VI, 824
McReynolds, Thomas VI, 956
McReynolds, Thomas VI, 962
McReynolds, William VI, 833
McReynolds, William VI, 837
McReynolds, William Flowers VI, 832
McShane, Betty Larsh V, 850
McVaugh, Alice II, 894
McVaugh, Chas. L. II, 808
McVaugh, Chas. L. II, 894
McVaugh, Eliza II, 805
McVaugh, Frank C. III, 215
McVaugh, Lydia II, 240
McVaugh, Maberry II, 240
McVaugh, Mayberry II, 178
McVaugh, Roy III, 215
McVaugh, Ruth A. III, 215
McVaugh, Wd. Lydia II, 178
McVay, Asa Cadwalader IV, 99
McVay, Elizabeth IV, 47
McVay, Elizabeth IV, 59
McVay, Elizabeth IV, 1063
McVay, Elizabeth IV, 1067
McVay, Jane IV, 47
McVay, Jane IV, 77
McVay, Jane IV, 99
McVeigh, ??? III, 490
McVeigh, Cynthia VI, 406
McVeigh, Frankie III, 490
McVeigh, Hattie III, 490
McVeigh, Josie III, 490
McVeigh, Thomas IV, 1239
McVey, Ada V, 348
McVey, Ada V, 515
McVey, Ada V, 633
McVey, Ada Ollie V, 515
McVey, Adelia V, 348
McVey, Adrian V, 262
McVey, Albert I, 406
McVey, Alcina V, 262
McVey, Alfred V, 348
McVey, Alfred I. V, 263
McVey, Alfred I. V, 695
McVey, Alfred J. V, 262
McVey, Alice V, 348
McVey, Alva V, 263
McVey, Alva V, 348
McVey, Amanda Jackson VI, 956
McVey, Anderson I, 613
McVey, Anita V, 262
McVey, Ardella V, 515
McVey, Ardiela V, 633
McVey, Bessie V, 633
McVey, Bessie M. V, 348
McVey, Bessie M. V, 515
McVey, Bessie M. V, 633
McVey, Burlie D. V, 263
McVey, Caroline I, 613
McVey, Clara E. V, 258
McVey, Clara E. V, 262
McVey, Cora V, 262
McVey, Cora V, 263
McVey, Cora V, 348
McVey, Cora Barrett V, 348
McVey, Cora Barrett V, 460
McVey, Deborah V, 584
McVey, Deborah V, 695
McVey, Della V, 633
McVey, Ed V, 348
McVey, Edmond V, 348
McVey, Elijah V, 348
McVey, F. L. V, 263
McVey, Frank S. V, 262
McVey, Franklin V, 262
McVey, Harold V, 262
McVey, Harold V, 263
McVey, Harold V, 348
McVey, Herbert V, 262
McVey, Ina V, 262
McVey, Irving M. V, 262
McVey, Isaac V, 220
McVey, Isaac V, 240
McVey, Isaac V, 258
McVey, Isaac V, 262
McVey, Isaac V, 263
McVey, Isaac N. V, 262
McVey, Isaac Newman V, 348
McVey, James V, 658
McVey, James V, 695
McVey, James Carl V, 348
McVey, James Carl V, 515
McVey, James Carl V, 633
McVey, James P. V, 263

McVey, John VI, 956
McVey, Josephine V, 262
McVey, Josephine V, 263
McVey, Josephine Barrell V, 460
McVey, Josephine Barrett V, 348
McVey, Kenneth V, 262
McVey, Leroy V, 348
McVey, Leroy V, 515
McVey, Leroy M. V, 633
McVey, Mabel V, 248
McVey, Mabel V, 262
McVey, Mabel E. V, 240
McVey, Martha V, 240
McVey, Martha V, 258
McVey, Martha V, 262
McVey, Martha V, 263
McVey, Martha E. V, 348
McVey, Martha Job V, 220
McVey, Mary V, 658
McVey, Mary V, 695
McVey, Mary B. V, 263
McVey, Mildred V, 263
McVey, Mildred V, 348
McVey, Mildred Helen V, 262
McVey, Minnie M. V, 262
McVey, N. Alva V, 263
McVey, N. R. V, 229
McVey, Neuman Isaac V, 262
McVey, Newman V, 263
McVey, Newman I. V, 263
McVey, Newman I. V, 348
McVey, Noah A. V, 262
McVey, Noah Alva V, 262
McVey, Olive V, 515
McVey, Olive V, 633
McVey, Phebe IV, 419
McVey, Phebe IV, 456
McVey, Rosetta I, 613
McVey, Roy V, 633
McVey, Ruth V, 49
McVey, Ruth V, 96
McVey, Ruth V, 132
McVey, Ruth V, 262
McVey, Ruth V, 263
McVey, Ruth V, 584
McVey, Sarah Eunice V, 220
McVey, Sarah U. V, 262
McVey, Tacy IV, 1162
McVey, Tacy IV, 1172
McVey, Thelma V, 263
McVey, Thelma V, 348
McVey, Turner V, 262
McVey, Vernon V, 263
McVey, Warren V, 263
McVey, William V, 262
McVey, William H. V, 515
McVey, William I. V, 262
McVey, Willie V, 633
McVey, Wm. H. V, 348
McVey, Wm. H. V, 633
McVickers, Myra IV, 1328
McVickers, Myra Mae IV, 1328
McWade, Achsah V, 96
McWaters, Hannah II, 894
McWaters, Wm. J. II, 894
McWhenney, Louisa IV, 1172
McWhenney, Louisa IV, 1186
McWhirk, Hattie IV, 1172
McWhirk, Printie IV, 1216
McWilliams, G. G. IV, 1216
McWilliams, Harry IV, 1216
McWilliams, John V, 348
McWilliams, Rachel IV, 1328
McWirick, Oda V, 1008
Meach, Naomi IV, 516
Meach, Naomi IV, 540
Mead, ??? III, 138
Mead, Aaron W. IV, 342
Mead, Abraham III, 223
Mead, Alonzo IV, 342
Mead, Ann II, 1014
Mead, Ann VI, 531
Mead, Ann VI, 533
Mead, Ann VI, 542
Mead, Ann VI, 657
Mead, Ann VI, 675
Mead, Ann Eliza IV, 342
Mead, Ann R. III, 138
Mead, Anna III, 223
Mead, Aquila VI, 675
Mead, Asenath III, 223
Mead, Asenath VI, 533
Mead, Asenath VI, 644
Mead, Asenath VI, 675
Mead, Benjamin IV, 342
Mead, Benjamin VI, 482
Mead, Benjamin VI, 533
Mead, Benjamin VI, 542
Mead, Benjamin VI, 657
Mead, Benjamin VI, 675
Mead, Benjamin VI, 676
Mead, Benjamin VI, 687
Mead, Benjamin VI, 959
Mead, Bertha III, 223
Mead, Bertha III, 335
Mead, Caroline IV, 739
Mead, Caroline IV, 791
Mead, Ch. L. III, 223
Mead, Charles IV, 420
Mead, Charles Elwood IV, 342
Mead, Charles Elwood IV, 561
Mead, Charles L. III, 223
Mead, Christian VI, 533
Mead, Christiana VI, 675
Mead, Christiana VI, 720
Mead, Clara D. IV, 953
Mead, Daniel Independence III, 223
Mead, Dionitia VI, 1000
Mead, Earl I, 945
Mead, Edy VI, 1005
Mead, Eleanor VI, 481
Mead, Eleanor J. III, 223
Mead, Elhena II, 1014
Mead, Eliz. M. III, 143
Mead, Elizabeth II, 1014
Mead, Elizabeth VI, 533
Mead, Elizabeth VI, 546
Mead, Elizabeth VI, 580
Mead, Elizabeth VI, 941
Mead, Elizabeth VI, 959
Mead, Elizabeth R. IV, 1374
Mead, Elizabeth R. IV, 1381
Mead, Ellen II, 1014
Mead, Elma E. IV, 342
Mead, Elmore I, 726
Mead, Elwood IV, 420
Mead, Emily A. III, 168
Mead, Emily A. III, 223
Mead, Emily Acheson III, 223
Mead, Florence III, 371
Mead, Florence L. III, 223
Mead, Florence Louise III, 223
Mead, Frances VI, 959
Mead, Francis Julian IV, 342
Mead, Geo. Livingston III, 223
Mead, Geo. Livingston III, 335
Mead, Geo. U. III, 223
Mead, Geo. V. III, 223
Mead, Geo. V. III, 371
Mead, George Livingston III, 223
Mead, George V. III, 35
Mead, George V. III, 36
Mead, George V. III, 168
Mead, George V. III, 223
Mead, George V. III, 280
Mead, Guela Elma IV, 342
Mead, Hannah II, 995
Mead, Hannah II, 1014
Mead, Hannah III, 129
Mead, Hannah III, 223
Mead, Hannah IV, 739
Mead, Hannah IV, 791
Mead, Hannah VI, 482
Mead, Hannah VI, 533
Mead, Hannah VI, 551
Mead, Hannah VI, 572
Mead, Harold Hallock III, 223
Mead, Henry III, 143
Mead, Ida III, 32
Mead, Ida May III, 223
Mead, Joanna II, 572
Mead, Joanna II, 595
Mead, John IV, 342
Mead, John VI, 506
Mead, John VI, 653
Mead, John VI, 654
Mead, John VI, 657
Mead, John VI, 675
Mead, John VI, 676
Mead, John VI, 683
Mead, John VI, 889
Mead, John VI, 931
Mead, John VI, 943
Mead, John VI, 956
Mead, John VI, 1013
Mead, John H. IV, 342
Mead, John S. IV, 342
Mead, Jonathan VI, 675
Mead, Jos. IV, 356
Mead, Joseph IV, 342
Mead, Joseph IV, 356
Mead, Joseph IV, 420
Mead, Joseph IV, 561
Mead, Joseph VI, 675
Mead, Joseph VI, 680
Mead, Joseph VI, 683
Mead, Joseph James IV, 342
Mead, Joseph James IV, 561
Mead, Joseph M. IV, 342
Mead, Joseph P. IV, 342
Mead, Joseph Philo IV, 342
Mead, Joseph Philo VI, 676
Mead, Joseph W. IV, 342
Mead, Joshua G. IV, 342
Mead, Joshua R. IV, 342
Mead, Julia A. III, 223
Mead, Lucy J. VI, 1016
Mead, M. Cornelia IV, 342
Mead, M. Cornelia IV, 356
Mead, Margaret II, 87
Mead, Margaret II, 1014
Mead, Margaret VI, 533
Mead, Margaret E. III, 295
Mead, Margaret, Jr. VI, 533
Mead, Maria IV, 342
Mead, Mariah IV, 342
Mead, Marietta III, 223
Mead, Martha II, 1014
Mead, Martha II, 1041
Mead, Martha VI, 533
Mead, Mary II, 993
Mead, Mary II, 1014
Mead, Mary III, 35
Mead, Mary III, 168
Mead, Mary III, 223
Mead, Mary III, 280
Mead, Mary III, 371
Mead, Mary IV, 420
Mead, Mary VI, 533
Mead, Mary VI, 551
Mead, Mary VI, 657
Mead, Mary VI, 675
Mead, Mary VI, 680
Mead, Mary VI, 959
Mead, Mary Ann VI, 683
Mead, Mary B. III, 223
Mead, Mary B. III, 280
Mead, Mary Birdsall III, 223
Mead, Mary E. III, 223
Mead, Mary E. VI, 954
Mead, Mary Emily IV, 334
Mead, Mary Emily IV, 342
Mead, Mary Emily IV, 561
Mead, Mary M. IV, 342
Mead, Mary Winston VI, 959
Mead, Nathan Orville IV, 342
Mead, Nathaniel III, 129
Mead, Nathaniel III, 223
Mead, Nathaniel Earl I, 726
Mead, Nathaniel S. III, 223
Mead, Nicholas VI, 959
Mead, Nicholas VI, 1004
Mead, Nicholas VI, 1016
Mead, Phebe III, 223
Mead, Phebe III, 302
Mead, Phebe IV, 342
Mead, Phebe IV, 356
Mead, Phebe IV, 420
Mead, Phebe IV, 561
Mead, Phebe Alice IV, 342
Mead, Phebe G. IV, 342
Mead, Phebe G. VI, 676
Mead, Phebe G. VI, 680
Mead, Philco IV, 342
Mead, Philo IV, 342
Mead, Philo D. IV, 342
Mead, Phineas Janney VI, 683
Mead, Priscilla VI, 959
Mead, Rachel II, 988
Mead, Rachel II, 1014
Mead, Rachel IV, 878
Mead, Rachel IV, 880
Mead, Rhodes VI, 959
Mead, Richard II, 87
Mead, Richard VI, 533
Mead, Robert VI, 1005
Mead, Ruth II, 62
Mead, Ruth II, 87
Mead, Ruth VI, 533
Mead, Ruth Annah IV, 420
Mead, Ruth Annah IV, 442
Mead, Samantha III, 223
Mead, Saml. VI, 973
Mead, Samuel II, 87
Mead, Samuel II, 993
Mead, Samuel II, 1014
Mead, Samuel VI, 533
Mead, Samuel VI, 676
Mead, Samuel VI, 959
Mead, Samuel, Jr. II, 87
Mead, Samuel, Jr. VI, 533
Mead, Sarah II, 63
Mead, Sarah II, 87
Mead, Sarah VI, 683
Mead, Sarah VI, 1004
Mead, Sarah E. IV, 342
Mead, Sarah E. VI, 347
Mead, Sarah S. III, 36
Mead, Sarah S. IV, 1374
Mead, Semantha Weeks III, 129
Mead, Stella IV, 1329
Mead, Stith VI, 1000
Mead, Thomas IV, 420
Mead, Thomas IV, 561
Mead, Thomas VI, 675
Mead, Thomas VI, 676
Mead, Thomas G. IV, 1357
Mead, Thomas G. IV, 1374
Mead, Thomas G. IV, 1381
Mead, Thomas W. IV, 1374
Mead, Washington III, 223
Mead, Wd. Margaret E. III, 143
Mead, Wd. Mary Holmes VI, 506
Mead, Widow Mary VI, 653
Mead, Widow Mary VI, 654
Mead, Widow Mary VI, 676
Mead, William IV, 342
Mead, William IV, 420
Mead, William IV, 561
Mead, William VI, 331
Mead, William VI, 533
Mead, William VI, 910
Mead, William VI, 954
Mead, William VI, 959
Mead, William E. I, 945
Mead, William Elmore III, 223
Mead, William, Jr. VI, 331
Mead, Wm. II, 1014
Mead, Wm. Elmer I, 945
Mead, Wm., Jr. VI, 533
Meade, Alena Elizabeth I, 726
Meade, Bishop ??? VI, 42
Meade, Elmore I, 726
Meade, Joanna II, 595
Meade, Julia Willets III, 217
Meade, Nathaniel Earl I, 726
Meade, Rhodes VI, 959
Meade, Stella IV, 1329
Meade, William E. I, 945
Meade, Wm. Elmore I, 726
Meader, Albert O. III, 223
Meader, Almon IV, 739
Meader, Bessie I, 891
Meader, Eliza H. IV, 1209
Meader, Eliza H. IV, 1216
Meader, Elizabeth I, 530
Meader, Elizabeth I, 560
Meader, Elizabeth I, 936
Meader, Elizabeth IV, 926
Meader, Elizabeth M. I, 945
Meader, Elizabeth M. I, 950
Meader, Erza M. I, 535
Meader, Eunice I, 45
Meader, Eunice I, 60
Meader, Eunice N. IV, 1173
Meader, Ezra I, 560
Meader, Ezra I, 936
Meader, Ezra M. I, 560
Meader, Gideon IV, 1173
Meader, Herbert E. I, 891
Meader, James IV, 1173
Meader, James E. Cartland I, 891
Meader, Jesse G. Hartley IV, 1216
Meader, Leslie Cartland I, 891
Meader, Levi J. IV, 1173
Meader, Louisa IV, 1173
Meader, Lydia IV, 1173
Meader, Mary E. I, 530
Meader, Mary E. I, 535
Meader, Mary E. I, 560
Meader, Mary E. I, 936
Meader, Micca IV, 1173
Meader, Priscilla H. IV, 1173
Meader, Susan IV, 739
Meader, Webster IV, 739
Meader, Widow Mary E. I, 560
Meader, William F. III, 223
Meador, Abner VI, 960
Meador, Agness VI, 960
Meador, Albert H. VI, 960
Meador, Alsey VI, 913
Meador, Ambrous VI, 909
Meador, Annanias VI, 960
Meador, Ausburn VI, 1003
Meador, Bannister VI, 960
Meador, Benj. VI, 996
Meador, Benjamin VI, 870
Meador, Benjamin VI, 871
Meador, Benjamin VI, 872
Meador, Benjamin VI, 875
Meador, Benjamin VI, 876
Meador, Benjamin VI, 878
Meador, Benjamin VI, 883
Meador, Benjamin VI, 887
Meador, Benjamin VI, 890
Meador, Benjamin VI, 905
Meador, Benjamin VI, 912
Meador, Benjamin VI, 917
Meador, Benjamin VI, 921
Meador, Benjamin VI, 924
Meador, Benjamin VI, 928
Meador, Benjamin VI, 932
Meador, Benjamin VI, 939
Meador, Benjamin VI, 942
Meador, Benjamin VI, 943
Meador, Benjamin VI, 950
Meador, Benjamin VI, 951
Meador, Benjamin VI, 953
Meador, Benjamin VI, 954
Meador, Benjamin VI, 956
Meador, Benjamin VI, 958
Meador, Benjamin VI, 959
Meador, Benjamin VI, 960
Meador, Benjamin VI, 965
Meador, Benjamin VI, 967
Meador, Benjamin VI, 968
Meador, Benjamin VI, 969
Meador, Benjamin VI, 976
Meador, Benjamin VI, 977
Meador, Benjamin VI, 978
Meador, Benjamin VI, 982
Meador, Benjamin VI, 984
Meador, Benjamin VI, 985
Meador, Benjamin VI, 994
Meador, Benjamin VI, 995
Meador, Benjamin VI, 996
Meador, Benjamin VI, 997
Meador, Benjamin VI, 1004
Meador, Benjamin VI, 1011
Meador, Benjamin VI, 1018
Meador, Benjamin VI, 1019
Meador, Benjamin VI, 1021
Meador, Berryman VI, 960
Meador, Betsy VI, 932
Meador, Burwell VI, 960
Meador, Calvert VI, 960
Meador, Caroline VI, 932
Meador, Catharine VI, 960
Meador, Charlotte VI, 964
Meador, Creed VI, 960
Meador, David VI, 960
Meador, Drusilla VI, 913
Meador, Eliza VI, 1020
Meador, Eliza J. VI, 960
Meador, Elizabeth VI, 959
Meador, Elizabeth VI, 1021
Meador, Elizabeth Ann VI, 960
Meador, Elizabeth D. VI, 960
Meador, Elizabeth Frances VI, 912
Meador, Fanny VI, 909
Meador, Fennette Jane VI, 965
Meador, Florentine J. VI, 962
Meador, George VI, 893
Meador, George VI, 960
Meador, Green B. VI, 960
Meador, Green B. VI, 978
Meador, Henrietta VI, 960
Meador, Herbert VI, 958
Meador, Ira VI, 959
Meador, James VI, 877
Meador, James VI, 960
Meador, James G. VI, 960
Meador, Jane VI, 959
Meador, Jason VI, 259
Meador, Jason VI, 905
Meador, Jason VI, 959
Meador, Jason VI, 964
Meador, Jehu VI, 959
Meador, Jeremiah VI, 898
Meador, Jeremiah VI, 909
Meador, Jeremiah VI, 917
Meador, Jeremiah VI, 954
Meador, Jeremiah VI, 959
Meador, Jeremiah VI, 996
Meador, Jeremiah, Jr. VI, 960
Meador, Jeremiah, Sr. VI, 1011
Meador, Job VI, 959
Meador, Joel VI, 259
Meador, Joel VI, 918
Meador, Joel VI, 960
Meador, John VI, 905
Meador, John VI, 912
Meador, John VI, 959
Meador, John VI, 960
Meador, John C. VI, 960
Meador, John W. VI, 912
Meador, John W. VI, 953
Meador, John W. VI, 997
Meador, Jonah VI, 259
Meador, Jonas VI, 960
Meador, Jubal D. VI, 960
Meador, Juda VI, 994
Meador, Leroy VI, 969
Meador, Lucinda VI, 932
Meador, Lucy VI, 876
Meador, Lucy Ann VI, 881
Meador, Mahala VI, 960
Meador, Malinda VI, 960
Meador, Margaret VI, 1019
Meador, Martha VI, 960
Meador, Martha Ann VI, 960

Meador, Mary VI, 912
Meador, Mary VI, 954
Meador, Mary Ann VI, 960
Meador, Mary E. VI, 960
Meador, Mary Jane VI, 960
Meador, Matilda Ann VI, 960
Meador, Melinda VI, 893
Meador, Milly VI, 897
Meador, Miram VI, 960
Meador, Nancy VI, 951
Meador, Nancy VI, 959
Meador, Nancy VI, 960
Meador, Nancy VI, 964
Meador, Nancy VI, 996
Meador, Nancy VI, 1011
Meador, Oney VI, 960
Meador, Osborn VI, 936
Meador, Osborne VI, 897
Meador, Paschal VI, 960
Meador, Pattey VI, 959
Meador, Patty VI, 918
Meador, Pegga VI, 996
Meador, Polly VI, 959
Meador, Polly VI, 960
Meador, Polly VI, 996
Meador, Prudence VI, 996
Meador, Rachel VI, 898
Meador, Rachel VI, 959
Meador, Rhoda VI, 960
Meador, Richard VI, 959
Meador, Richard VI, 960
Meador, Richard VI, 996
Meador, Richard, Sr. VI, 932
Meador, Sally VI, 960
Meador, Sarah VI, 898
Meador, Sarah VI, 932
Meador, Sarah VI, 959
Meador, Sarah VI, 960
Meador, Sarah VI, 996
Meador, Sarah Ann VI, 960
Meador, Sarah Ann VI, 1004
Meador, Sarah J. VI, 960
Meador, Sparnial H. VI, 950
Meador, Sparriel H. VI, 960
Meador, Susan VI, 960
Meador, Tempy VI, 951
Meador, Thomas VI, 913
Meador, Thomas VI, 1019
Meador, Thomas C. VI, 960
Meador, Whitfield VI, 960
Meador, William VI, 890
Meador, William VI, 932
Meador, William VI, 951
Meador, William VI, 959
Meador, William VI, 960
Meador, William VI, 964
Meador, William VI, 965
Meador, William VI, 996
Meador, William G. VI, 960
Meador, Wilson VI, 895
Meador, Wilson VI, 959
Meador, Wilson VI, 962
Meador, Wilson VI, 1004
Meador, Wilson VI, 1020
Meadow, Benjn. VI, 888
Meadow, Caroline VI, 991
Meadow, Elisabeth M. M. I, 21
Meadow, Elizabeth VI, 953
Meadow, Elizabeth VI, 960
Meadow, Ezra I, 21
Meadow, Henrietta VI, 991
Meadow, Jeremiah VI, 953
Meadow, Jeremiah VI, 991
Meadow, Jeremiah VI, 1021
Meadow, Mary E. I, 21
Meadow, Nancy VI, 953
Meadow, Obediah VI, 960
Meadow, Oney VI, 888
Meadow, Polly VI, 996
Meadow, Richard VI, 996
Meadow, Sarah VI, 934
Meadow, Sarah VI, 996
Meadow, William VI, 953
Meadows, Eliza VI, 839
Meadows, John W. VI, 839
Meadows, Obediah VI, 905
Meadows, Polly VI, 905
Meadows, Prudence VI, 905
Meads, Sarah I, 102
Meads, Timothy I, 91
Meads, Timothy I, 102
Meagee, Mary I, 558
Meagee, Mary I, 566
Meaghy, Anna III, 223
Meaghy, Anna Mary III, 223
Meaghy, John III, 223
Meaid, John I, 102
Meaid, Timothy I, 102
Meaids, Ane I, 130
Meaids, Anne I, 91
Meaids, Anne I, 146
Meaids, Timothy I, 91
Meaids, Timothy I, 92
Meaids, Timothy I, 130
Meaids, Timothy I, 146
Meaks, Mourning VI, 797
Meally, Job II, 440
Meals, Bertha Richards V, 1010
Mealy, Ethel III, 224
Mealy, Ethel III, 295
Meander, Joseph V, 516
Means, Deborah IV, 100
Means, Dinah IV, 100
Means, Elizabeth IV, 100
Means, Elizabeth IV, 103
Means, Findley IV, 100
Means, Finley IV, 100
Means, Ida May V, 558
Means, Isabella VI, 840
Means, James IV, 100
Means, Jane IV, 100
Means, Jane VI, 803
Means, John IV, 100
Means, Joseph Francis V, 558
Means, Josie Beryl V, 558
Means, Margaret IV, 100
Means, Mary IV, 100
Means, Rachel VI, 472
Means, Rachel Ann VI, 472
Means, Rachel Ann VI, 533
Means, Rebecca IV, 100
Means, Rebeckah IV, 100
Means, Rebekah IV, 100
Means, Robert VI, 840
Means, Samuel C. VI, 472
Means, Sarah IV, 98
Means, Sarah IV, 100
Mearis, Aaron I, 439
Mearis, Aron I, 439
Mearis, Eleanor I, 406
Mearis, Elener I, 439
Mearis, George I, 406
Mearis, George I, 439
Mearis, Jane I, 439
Mearis, Sarah I, 439
Mearis, William I, 439
Mearis, William I, 826
Mears, Ann VI, 960
Mears, Benj. II, 563
Mears, Benj. II, 595
Mears, Benjamin II, 394
Mears, Benjamin II, 455
Mears, Benjamin II, 595
Mears, Benjamin II, 755
Mears, Benjamin II, 809
Mears, Benjamin, Jr. II, 755
Mears, Charles II, 394
Mears, Charles II, 595
Mears, Cora V, 713
Mears, Ed. Burroughs II, 394
Mears, Edward B. II, 755
Mears, Edward P. II, 755
Mears, Elizabeth II, 394
Mears, Elizabeth II, 755
Mears, Ellwood P. II, 755
Mears, Elwood II, 394
Mears, Hannah II, 595
Mears, Hannah II, 755
Mears, Hannah II, 766
Mears, Henry II, 394
Mears, Henry II, 755
Mears, John II, 394
Mears, John II, 455
Mears, John II, 595
Mears, John II, 669
Mears, John II, 755
Mears, John II, 809
Mears, John II, 898
Mears, John II, 934
Mears, John VI, 960
Mears, Joseph II, 394
Mears, Joseph II, 595
Mears, Marian II, 809
Mears, Marian II, 898
Mears, Marian II, 934
Mears, Martha III, 224
Mears, Mary III, 224
Mears, Rebecca II, 394
Mears, Rebecca II, 755
Mears, Richard III, 224
Mears, Ruth II, 394
Mears, Ruth II, 455
Mears, Ruth II, 563
Mears, Ruth II, 595
Mears, Ruth II, 809
Mears, Susanna II, 563
Mears, Susanna II, 595
Mears, Susanna II, 669
Mears, Susannah II, 455
Mears, Susannah II, 595
Mears, Sussannah II, 595
Mears, William II, 394
Mears, Wm. II, 595
Mears, Wm. II, 669
Mears, Wm. II, 755
Mease, Grace A. IV, 1040
Measure, Sarah J. IV, 1374
Measure, Sarah J. IV, 1379
Mecan, Jane IV, 140
Mecan, Jane IV, 153
Mecan, Tacy IV, 736
Mecca, Phebe I, 684
Mecca, Phebe I, 688
Mechem, Elisha IV, 1286
Mechem, John IV, 1286
Mechem, Joshua IV, 100
Mechem, Lydia V, 956
Mechems, Elisha IV, 1286
Mechend, Joshua IV, 100
Mechracken, Rhodah I, 450
Meckel, Elizabeth V, 864
Meclain, John I, 1011
Mecracken, Marth I, 450
Mecracken, Martha I, 448
Mecraken, David I, 680
Mecraken, David I, 684
Mecraken, Elizabeth I, 680
Mecraken, Elizabeth I, 684
Mecraken, Martha I, 684
Mecraken, Robert I, 684
Mecum, Dorcus II, 87
Medal, Kate IV, 1286
Medal, Kate IV, 1293
Medcalf, Abraham IV, 153
Medcalf, Abraham IV, 342
Medcalf, Abram IV, 153
Medcalf, Adaline IV, 342
Medcalf, Anna M. IV, 979
Medcalf, Asenath IV, 153
Medcalf, Asenath IV, 250
Medcalf, Asenath IV, 342
Medcalf, Asenath IV, 1068
Medcalf, Aseneth IV, 342
Medcalf, Caroline IV, 250
Medcalf, Caroline IV, 342
Medcalf, David IV, 153
Medcalf, David IV, 250
Medcalf, Elizabeth IV, 153
Medcalf, Elizabeth IV, 342
Medcalf, George I, 53
Medcalf, George I, 60
Medcalf, Hannah II, 595
Medcalf, Hannah IV, 153
Medcalf, Hannah IV, 342
Medcalf, Jacob II, 595
Medcalf, Jemima IV, 153
Medcalf, Jemima L. IV, 153
Medcalf, Jemima S. IV, 153
Medcalf, Jeremiah S. IV, 342
Medcalf, Jesse IV, 153
Medcalf, Jesse IV, 250
Medcalf, Jesse IV, 342
Medcalf, Jesse IV, 1068
Medcalf, John IV, 153
Medcalf, John IV, 342
Medcalf, Joseph IV, 153
Medcalf, Joseph IV, 250
Medcalf, Joseph H. IV, 249
Medcalf, Joseph Mead IV, 1068
Medcalf, Joshua IV, 250
Medcalf, Joshua IV, 342
Medcalf, Lewis IV, 1068
Medcalf, Lidea Ann IV, 342
Medcalf, Lydia IV, 249
Medcalf, Lydia Ann IV, 153
Medcalf, Lydia Ann IV, 342
Medcalf, Lydia S. IV, 250
Medcalf, Lydiann IV, 153
Medcalf, Martha IV, 250
Medcalf, Mary IV, 153
Medcalf, Mary IV, 250
Medcalf, Mary IV, 303
Medcalf, Matilda IV, 249
Medcalf, Moses IV, 153
Medcalf, Moses IV, 249
Medcalf, Moses IV, 342
Medcalf, Moses, Jr. IV, 250
Medcalf, Oliver IV, 250
Medcalf, Oliver IV, 342
Medcalf, Rachel II, 595
Medcalf, Rachel IV, 153
Medcalf, Rebecca IV, 153
Medcalf, Sarah I, 53
Medcalf, Sarah I, 60
Medcalf, Sarah M. IV, 312
Medcalf, Sarah M. IV, 313
Medcalf, Stephen IV, 342
Medcalf, Stephen IV, 1068
Medcalf, Susana IV, 153
Medcalf, Susanna IV, 153
Medcalf, Susanna IV, 249
Medcalf, Susanna IV, 250
Medcalf, Susanna IV, 1068
Medcalf, Susannah II, 595
Medcalf, Susannah IV, 153
Medcalf, Susannah IV, 342
Medcalf, William IV, 342
Medcalfe, Jacob II, 683
Medcalfe, Rachel II, 595
Medcalfe, Rachel II, 683
Medcalfe, Susannah II, 595
Medcalfe, Susannah II, 683
Medcalph, Abraham IV, 342
Medcalph, Elizabeth IV, 342
Medcalph, Hannah IV, 342
Medcalph, Jeremiah S. IV, 342
Medcalph, John IV, 342
Medcalph, Lidea Ann IV, 342
Medcalph, Susannah IV, 342
Medcelf, Abraham IV, 153
Medcelf, Abram IV, 153
Medcelf, Asenath IV, 153
Medcelf, Asenath IV, 332
Medcelf, Asenath IV, 342
Medcelf, Elizabeth IV, 153
Medcelf, Hannah II, 595
Medcelf, Hannah IV, 153
Medcelf, Hannah, Jr. II, 558
Medcelf, Jacob II, 558
Medcelf, Jacob II, 595
Medcelf, Jemima IV, 153
Medcelf, Jemima L. IV, 153
Medcelf, Jemima S. IV, 153
Medcelf, Jesse IV, 153
Medcelf, Jesse IV, 332
Medcelf, Jesse IV, 342
Medcelf, John IV, 153
Medcelf, Lydiann IV, 153
Medcelf, Moses IV, 142
Medcelf, Moses IV, 152
Medcelf, Moses IV, 153
Medcelf, Moses IV, 342
Medcelf, Rachel IV, 152
Medcelf, Rebecca IV, 142
Medcelf, Susana IV, 153
Medcelf, Susanna IV, 152
Medcelf, Susanna IV, 153
Medcelf, Susannah IV, 142
Medcelf, Susannah IV, 342
Medheart, Hannah IV, 89
Medheart, Hannah IV, 100
Medkalf, Abraham IV, 342
Medkalf, Elizabeth IV, 342
Medkalf, Hannah IV, 342
Medkalf, Jeremiah S. IV, 342
Medkalf, John IV, 342
Medkalf, Lydia Ann IV, 342
Medkalf, Susannah IV, 342
Medkeff, Abraham IV, 420
Medkeff, Abraham IV, 588
Medkeff, Elizabeth IV, 420
Medkeff, Hannah IV, 420
Medkeff, Jemimah S. IV, 420
Medkeff, John IV, 420
Medkeff, Jos. H. IV, 259
Medkeff, Lydia Ann IV, 420
Medkeff, Lydia Ann IV, 588
Medkeff, Matilda IV, 259
Medkeff, Moses IV, 249
Medkeff, Susanna IV, 1068
Medkeff, Susannah IV, 420
Medkelf, Abraham IV, 153
Medkelf, David IV, 153
Medkelf, Jesse IV, 153
Medkelf, Joseph IV, 153
Medkelf, Mary IV, 153
Medkelf, Moses IV, 153
Medkelf, Rachel IV, 153
Medkelf, Rebecca IV, 153
Medkelf, Susannah IV, 153
Medkiff, Adaline IV, 1068
Medkiff, Asenath IV, 1068
Medkiff, Caroline IV, 1068
Medkiff, Jesse IV, 1068
Medkiff, Joseph IV, 1068
Medkiff, Joshua IV, 1068
Medkiff, Matilda IV, 1068
Medkiff, Oliver IV, 1068
Medkiff, Stephen IV, 1068
Medkiff, Susanna IV, 250
Medkiff, Wm. IV, 1068
Medlar, Cath. III, 183
Medlar, Catharine III, 224
Medlar, Mary III, 224
Medlar, Samuel III, 224
Medlar, Samuel J. III, 224
Medlar, William S. III, 224
Medley, Geo. VI, 981
Medley, George VI, 933
Medley, James M. V, 754
Medley, James W. VI, 960
Medley, Madison V, 754
Medley, Nancy C. VI, 960
Medley, Patsy VI, 982
Medlicott, Daniel II, 595
Medlicott, Daniel II, 697
Medlicott, Martha II, 595
Medlin, George I, 930
Medlin, George I, 946
Medlin, Henry L. VI, 960
Medlin, John VI, 960
Medlin, Julina VI, 960
Medlin, Lucy VI, 960
Medlin, Mamie I, 946
Medlin, Rachel Perdita I, 930
Medlin, Vivian I, 930
Medlin, Vivian I, 946
Medlin, Winefred Mamie I, 930
Medling, Susan VI, 897
Medlock, ??? III, 107
Medlock, ??? III, 224
Medlock, Anna III, 224
Medlock, Anna B. III, 107
Medlock, Anna B. III, 224
Medly, George VI, 879
Meece, John VI, 960
Meece, Katey VI, 960
Meecham, Francis III, 395
Meecham, Francis III, 401
Meecham, Mary III, 395
Meecham, Mary III, 401
Meechum, Elisha J. IV, 420
Meechum, John IV, 420
Meechum, Jonathan E. IV, 420
Meechum, Joshua IV, 420
Meechum, Lydia IV, 420
Meed, Ann Eliza IV, 342
Meed, Ann Eliza IV, 357
Meeds, John V, 381
Meeds, Mariah D. V, 381
Meeds, Mary V, 381
Meeds, Timothy I Sup 1, 5
Meek, Ann IV, 338
Meek, Ann IV, 342
Meek, Love IV, 250
Meek, Mary IV, 1040
Meek, Mary V, 1010
Meek, Mary Jane IV, 250
Meek, William Walker IV, 250
Meeker, Aaron Benedict IV, 1173
Meeker, Alden IV, 1216
Meeker, Alfretta IV, 1216
Meeker, Alpharetta IV, 1216
Meeker, Arlington IV, 1216
Meeker, Benjamin IV, 1216
Meeker, Charlie V, 412
Meeker, Davis IV, 1216
Meeker, Edith Emaline IV, 1216
Meeker, Elizabeth IV, 1173
Meeker, Elizabeth IV, 1174
Meeker, Emaline IV, 1173
Meeker, Emeline IV, 1150
Meeker, Emeline IV, 1173
Meeker, Emeline IV, 1216
Meeker, Eunice IV, 1216
Meeker, Gideon IV, 1216
Meeker, Harriet H. IV, 1173
Meeker, Harriett IV, 1216
Meeker, Harriett H. IV, 1173
Meeker, Jefferson V, 412
Meeker, John Q. V, 412
Meeker, Louisa IV, 1148
Meeker, Louisa IV, 1173
Meeker, Louisa IV, 1216
Meeker, Lydia V, 263
Meeker, Martha V, 412
Meeker, Nellie IV, 1216
Meeker, Phebe IV, 1216
Meeker, Rachel IV, 1173
Meeker, Rachel IV, 1176
Meeker, Rachel IV, 1216
Meeker, Robert IV, 1173
Meeker, Robert IV, 1216
Meeker, Robert B. IV, 1173
Meeker, Robert B. IV, 1329
Meeker, Susan IV, 1173
Meeker, Susan E. IV, 1173
Meeker, Susan Elizabeth IV, 1173
Meeks, Alice Caroline V, 696
Meeks, Alice Caroline V, 707
Meeks, Elwood V, 98
Meeks, Francis VI, 840
Meeks, Henderson VI, 840
Meeks, Horace Wm. V, 696
Meeks, Horace Wm. V, 707
Meeks, Mary V, 1010
Meely, Aaron V, 1010
Meenan, Hugh VI, 929
Meers, George I, 1075
Meers, John II, 595
Meers, Susanna II, 595
Meese, Grace IV, 1329
Mefford, Charles V, 188
Mefford, Julia V, 188
Megan, Catharine VI, 960

Megan, Hudson VI, 960
Megan, James VI, 960
Megan, John VI, 960
Megan, Lucy Ann VI, 960
Megan, Martha W. VI, 960
Megan, Nancy VI, 960
Megan, Robert VI, 960
Megann, John VI, 995
Megann, Sarah VI, 995
Megear, Eliza II, 794
Megear, Thomas J. II, 898
Megear, Thos. J. II, 898
Megecy, Samuel VI, 197
Megecy, Samuel VI, 214
Megee, Polly VI, 830
Megee, Rose VI, 830
Megerity, Deborah I, 400
Megerity, Deborah I, 405
Megginson, Joseph C. VI, 840
Megginson, Sarah VI, 840
Meggs, Agnes Maude III, 157
Meggs, Ann S. III, 157
Meggs, Jos. III, 157
Megill, Amy II, 1013
Megill, Jacob II, 1013
Megill, Jane II, 1013
Megill, John II, 1013
Megill, Jonathan II, 1013
Megill, Jonathan P. II, 1013
Megill, Mary II, 1013
Megill, Rachel II, 1013
Megill, Rebecca II, 1013
Megill, Rebeckah II, 1013
Megill, Sarah II, 1013
Megill, Sarah II, 1026
Megill, Wm. II, 1013
Megill, Wm. II, 1026
Megilton, Elizabeth VI, 422
Megirian, Acabe III, 224
Megirian, Acabe III, 290
Megirian, Acabe III, 299
Megirian, Della Louise III, 224
Megirian, Della Louise III, 371
Megirian, Fareh III, 371
Megirian, Jacob III, 224
Megirian, Jacob III, 290
Megirian, Jacob III, 299
Megirian, John III, 224
Megirian, Joseph III, 224
Megirian, Marian III, 224
Megirian, Rosa III, 224
Megirian, Rosa III, 290
Megirian, Stephen III, 224
Megirian, Zareh III, 224
Megnard, Maurice IV, 1329
Megraiel, James IV, 470
Megraiel, Mary IV, 470
Megrail, Alfred IV, 126
Megrail, Alfred IV, 129
Megrail, Alfred IV, 250
Megrail, Alfred IV, 474
Megrail, Alfred IV, 487
Megrail, Alfred IV, 801
Megrail, Alfred IV, 832
Megrail, Alfred H. IV, 832
Megrail, Amy IV, 250
Megrail, Amy IV, 474
Megrail, Amy IV, 487
Megrail, Amy Ann IV, 250
Megrail, Ann IV, 474
Megrail, Ann IV, 487
Megrail, Ann Eliza IV, 832
Megrail, Annie E. IV, 801
Megrail, Edith IV, 250
Megrail, Edith IV, 487
Megrail, Elmira IV, 250
Megrail, Elmira IV, 487
Megrail, Geo. G. IV, 803
Megrail, George IV, 487
Megrail, George E. IV, 250
Megrail, George E. IV, 487
Megrail, George G. IV, 250
Megrail, George G. IV, 832
Megrail, Irving T. IV, 832
Megrail, Isabella IV, 487
Megrail, Isabella IV, 498
Megrail, James IV, 129
Megrail, James IV, 250
Megrail, James IV, 487
Megrail, John IV, 498
Megrail, John L. IV, 250
Megrail, John L. IV, 487
Megrail, Lamira IV, 250
Megrail, Lindley H. IV, 250
Megrail, Lindley H. IV, 487
Megrail, Mary IV, 129
Megrail, Mary IV, 250
Megrail, Mary IV, 487
Megrail, Mary IV, 498
Megrail, Mary A. IV, 832
Megrail, Mary Agnes IV, 832
Megrail, Mary R. IV, 250
Megrail, Nathan IV, 250
Megrail, Rebecca IV, 126
Megrail, Rebecca IV, 129
Megrail, Rebecca IV, 250
Megrail, Rebecca IV, 474
Megrail, Rebecca IV, 487
Megrail, Rebecca IV, 801
Megrail, Rebecca IV, 832
Megrail, Sina IV, 803
Megrail, Sina IV, 832
Megrail, Thomas IV, 250
Megrail, Thomas IV, 487
Megrail, Thos. IV, 250
Megrail, Thos. IV, 474
Megrail, Thos. IV, 487
Megrail, William IV, 250
Megrail, William P. IV, 250
Megrail, William P. IV, 487
Megregar, Maria V, 516
Megrew, Abner IV, 130
Megrew, Aletta IV, 245
Megrew, Ann IV, 493
Megrew, Ann C. IV, 245
Megrew, Archebald B. IV, 126
Megrew, Elizabeth IV, 245
Megrew, John B. IV, 245
Megrew, Joseph IV, 245
Megrew, Mary IV, 245
Megrew, Nathan IV, 245
Megrew, Oliver IV, 245
Megrew, Rebecca IV, 245
Megrew, Samuel, Jr. IV, 130
Megrew, Sarah V, 918
Megrew, Susannah IV, 126
Megrew, T. B. IV, 245
Megrew, Thos. B. IV, 493
Megrew, Willets IV, 245
Megrin, Margaret IV, 700
Megrue, Mary IV, 737
Megrue, Rebecca IV, 737
Meholin, John IV, 487
Meholin, John W. IV, 487
Mehorney, Andrew VI, 840
Mehorney, Betty VI, 840
Meidner, Hannah I, 709
Meidner, Hannah I, 726
Mein, Andrew II, 595
Mein, Elizabeth White II, 799
Mein, Isaac Pearson II, 799
Mein, Mary Lamb II, 799
Mein, Susanna II, 242
Mein, Susanna II, 595
Meinger, Wm. IV, 1329
Meischlan, Alice M. IV, 215
Meischlan, Alice M. IV, 250
Meiser, Alice B. IV, 612
Meiser, Alice B. IV, 644
MeKay, Zachariah VI, 420
Mekeel, Anna U. III, 224
Mekeel, Caleb III, 224
Mekeel, Emeline III, 224
Mekeel, George III, 174
Mekeel, George III, 224
Mekeel, George A. III, 224
Mekeel, Isaac III, 140
Mekeel, Isaac III, 224
Mekeel, Jacob, Jr. III, 224
Mekeel, Maria III, 224
Mekeel, Mary III, 140
Mekeel, Mary III, 224
Mekeel, Phebe III, 140
Mekeel, Phebe III, 224
Mekeel, Wd. Emeline III, 174
Mekeel, Wd. Emeline III, 224
Mekever, John II, 446
Mekever, Sarah II, 446
Mekever, Susanna II, 446
Mekins, Thomas II, 394
Mekins, Thomas II, 446
Mekins, Thomas, Jr. II, 394
Mekins, Wd. Sarah II, 394
Melbourne, Elizabeth IV, 1329
Melbourne, Elizabeth IV, 1345
Melbourne, George IV, 1329
Melbourne, George IV, 1345
Melbourne, George W. IV, 1329
Melchi, Hazel V, 1010
Melchia, Hazel V, 1010
Melchia, Lucy Pearl V, 1010
Meldrom, Rachel IV, 511
Meldrom, Rachel IV, 540
Meldru, Elizabeth III, 224
Meldrum, Elizabeth III, 211
Melick, Addie III, 224
Melick, Addie III, 311
Melick, Anna H. III, 224
Melick, Annie III, 224
Melick, Annie III, 323
Melick, Elmer Ellsworth III, 224
Melick, Elmer Ellsworth III, 323
Melick, J. M. III, 224
Melick, Virginia A. III, 224
Melick, Virginia A. III, 323
Meligan, John IV, 979
Melin, Daniel II, 394
Melin, Margaret II, 394
Melinger, Mary J. V, 633
Mell, Frances B. VI, 765
Mell, Ross Mell VI, 765
Mellekan, Jess I, 894
Mellen, Ella V, 516
Mellen, Halleck V, 516
Mellen, James V, 516
Mellen, Joseph V, 516
Mellen, Teymiah V, 516
Mellener, Elizabeth V, 758
Mellenger, Daniel IV, 250
Meller, Emma VI, 245
Mellford, Minnie V, 98
Mellichamp, Bertha I, 942
Mellichamp, Bertha I, 946
Mellichamp, Winburn I, 946
Mellichampe, Bertha H. I, 930
Mellick, Addie III, 311
Melligan, Sarah IV, 250
Mellin, George II, 595
Mellinger, Alliance IV, 1329
Mellinger, Clarence IV, 1173
Mellinger, Eva IV, 1329
Mellinger, Fred C. IV, 1329
Mellinger, Fred E. IV, 1329
Mellinger, Rose IV, 1173
Mellinger, Rosetta IV, 1173
Mellis, Catharine III, 224
Mellis, Catharine III, 317
Mellis, Jane III, 174
Mellis, Jane III, 224
Mellis, John III, 224
Mellis, John III, 317
Mellis, Samuel III, 174
Mellis, Samuel III, 224
Mellis, Sarah III, 224
Mellis, Sarah III, 317
Mellor, Alfred III, 224
Mellor, Augustine II, 595
Mellor, Charles VI, 534
Mellor, Chas. II, 809
Mellor, Deborah Wharton II, 835
Mellor, Deborah Wharton II, 898
Mellor, Edward II, 835
Mellor, Edward II, 898
Mellor, Eliz. III, 224
Mellor, Eliz. Wharton III, 224
Mellor, Elizabeth II, 861
Mellor, Elizabeth II, 898
Mellor, Elizabeth III, 224
Mellor, Emma VI, 245
Mellor, George II, 394
Mellor, Isabella III, 224
Mellor, Jacob II, 394
Mellor, Jacob II, 595
Mellor, Jacob VI, 534
Mellor, Jeremiah II, 394
Mellor, Martha II, 791
Mellor, Martha II, 809
Mellor, Martha II, 835
Mellor, Martha II, 861
Mellor, Martha II, 898
Mellor, Martha III, 96
Mellor, Martha III, 224
Mellor, Mary II, 595
Mellor, Mary VI, 534
Mellor, Thomas II, 898
Mellor, Thos. II, 791
Mellor, Thos. II, 809
Mellor, Thos. II, 835
Mellor, Thos. II, 861
Mellor, Thos. II, 898
Mellor, Walter III, 224
Mellson, Martha VI, 389
Mellson, Martha VI, 422
Melon, George II, 595
Melon, Mary II, 553
Melon, Mary II, 595
Melon, Susannah II, 468
Melon, Susannah II, 595
Meloney, Anna G. II, 712
Meloney, Dorothea II, 712
Meloney, Dorothea II, 755
Meloney, Edward J. II, 712
Meloney, Edward J. II, 755
Meloney, Esther II, 712
Meloney, Esther II, 755
Meloney, James II, 712
Meloney, Laura II, 712
Meloney, Laura B. II, 755
Meloney, Laura V. II, 755
Meloney, Rebecca A. II, 755
Meloney, Rebecca Anna II, 712
Meloney, William L. II, 712
Meloney, Wm. L. II, 755
Meloy, Catherine V, 41
Meloy, Catherine V, 98
Melson, Alethea I, 207
Melson, Charles VI, 871
Melson, Elizabeth VI, 960
Melson, Harriet H. VI, 969
Melson, John VI, 960
Melson, John D. VI, 960
Melson, John D. VI, 969
Melson, Mary II, 785
Melson, Mary A. VI, 960
Melson, Polly VI, 960
Melson, Sarah VI, 871
Melson, Sarah B. VI, 886
Melson, Thomas VI, 886
Melson, Thomas VI, 960
Melton, Absalom VI, 935
Melton, Absalom VI, 961
Melton, Absalom VI, 1015
Melton, Allen VI, 961
Melton, Amos IV, 153
Melton, Anderson VI, 961
Melton, Anderson VI, 1015
Melton, Ann IV, 153
Melton, Ann VI, 961
Melton, Anna G. IV, 509
Melton, Anna G. IV, 540
Melton, Armella IV, 540
Melton, Caroline R. III, 426
Melton, Charlotte VI, 928
Melton, Eleanor V, 188
Melton, Ellanor V, 166
Melton, Ellanor V, 188
Melton, Esther I, 273
Melton, Esther IV, 48
Melton, Fanny IV, 100
Melton, Fanny IV, 153
Melton, Fanny IV, 336
Melton, Fanny IV, 343
Melton, Fanny IV, 487
Melton, George A. III, 426
Melton, Henry IV, 153
Melton, John I, 273
Melton, John IV, 540
Melton, Jonathan Bogue IV, 153
Melton, Jonathan Bouge IV, 100
Melton, Joseph IV, 153
Melton, Joseph IV, 250
Melton, Josephine III, 426
Melton, Josiah VI, 961
Melton, Mariah W. VI, 961
Melton, Mary IV, 146
Melton, Mary IV, 153
Melton, Mary VI, 198
Melton, Mary VI, 422
Melton, Mary VI, 676
Melton, Mary VI, 961
Melton, Mary G. IV, 540
Melton, Moses IV, 153
Melton, Moses IV, 487
Melton, Moses IV, 540
Melton, Moses Melton IV, 100
Melton, Nancy VI, 961
Melton, Nelly I, 274
Melton, Nelly I, 276
Melton, Patience IV, 540
Melton, Phebe V, 177
Melton, Phebe V, 188
Melton, Rebecca IV, 1131
Melton, Rebecca IV, 1135
Melton, Rhoda VI, 961
Melton, Richd VI, 198
Melton, Robert III, 426
Melton, Samuel VI, 961
Melton, Sarah IV, 100
Melton, Sarah IV, 153
Melton, Sarah IV, 487
Melton, Sarah IV, 540
Melton, Sarah Bogue IV, 140
Melton, Stafford IV, 48
Melton, Stafford IV, 146
Melton, Stafford IV, 153
Melton, Stafford IV, 561
Melton, Susan VI, 961
Melton, Tamer IV, 153
Melton, Thomas IV, 153
Melton, William I, 274
Melton, William IV, 100
Melton, William IV, 487
Melton, Wm. IV, 153
Melvin, Will V, 633
Mendehall, Annie II, 712
Mendehall, Birkenshaw II, 712
Mendehall, Deborah Ruth II, 712
Mendehall, Helen II, 712
Mendehall, Patricia Ann II, 712
Mendehall, Walter Wm. II, 712
Mendelson, Anna III, 224
Mendelson, Anna W. III, 224
Mendelson, August Lewis III, 224
Mendelson, Dorothy III, 224
Mendelson, Dorothy W. III, 307
Mendelson, Dr. Walter III, 224
Mendelson, Dr. Walter III, 225
Mendelson, Dr. Walter III, 348
Mendelson, Eliz. Wharton III, 224
Mendelson, Elizabeth III, 224
Mendelson, Elizabeth Wharton III, 224
Mendelson, Frances III, 224
Mendelson, Frances W. III, 198
Mendelson, Frances W. III, 224
Mendelson, Lewis III, 224
Mendelson, Mary III, 198
Mendelson, Mary III, 224
Mendelson, Mary III, 225
Mendelson, Mary III, 307
Mendelson, Mary III, 348
Mendelson, Mary W. III, 224
Mendelson, Rebecca III, 224
Mendelson, Simon III, 224
Mendelson, Walter III, 198
Mendelson, Walter III, 224
Mendelson, Walter III, 225
Mendelson, Walter III, 307
Mendemhall, Eliza Ann V, 858
Mendenghal, James VI, 422
Mendenghal, John VI, 422
Mendenghal, Martha VI, 422
Mendenghal, Wd. Ruth VI, 422
Mendenhall, ??? IV, 250
Mendenhall, ??? V, 877
Mendenhall, Aaron I, 509
Mendenhall, Aaron I, 561
Mendenhall, Aaron I, 605
Mendenhall, Aaron I, 607
Mendenhall, Aaron I, 684
Mendenhall, Aaron I, 688
Mendenhall, Aaron I, 787
Mendenhall, Aaron I, 788
Mendenhall, Aaron I, 828
Mendenhall, Aaron I, 860
Mendenhall, Aaron I, 861
Mendenhall, Aaron I, 892
Mendenhall, Aaron I, 1044
Mendenhall, Aaron I, 1108
Mendenhall, Aaron IV, 48
Mendenhall, Aaron IV, 250
Mendenhall, Aaron IV, 251
Mendenhall, Aaron IV, 644
Mendenhall, Aaron IV, 654
Mendenhall, Aaron IV, 833
Mendenhall, Aaron IV, 910
Mendenhall, Aaron IV, 913
Mendenhall, Aaron IV, 1068
Mendenhall, Aaron V, 98
Mendenhall, Aaron V, 188
Mendenhall, Aaron V, 189
Mendenhall, Aaron VI, 470
Mendenhall, Aaron VI, 534
Mendenhall, Aaron, Jr. I, 602
Mendenhall, Abaetta V, 98
Mendenhall, Abia V, 754
Mendenhall, Abigail I, 470
Mendenhall, Abigail I, 483
Mendenhall, Abigail I, 804
Mendenhall, Abigail I, 828
Mendenhall, Abigail I, 1034
Mendenhall, Abigail IV, 48
Mendenhall, Abigail IV, 833
Mendenhall, Abigail IV, 838
Mendenhall, Abigail IV, 913
Mendenhall, Abigail C. I, 483
Mendenhall, Abigail N. I, 720
Mendenhall, Abigail N. I, 726
Mendenhall, Abigail N. I, 787
Mendenhall, Abigail N. I, 829
Mendenhall, Absalom V, 516
Mendenhall, Absalum V, 516
Mendenhall, Absolom V, 516
Mendenhall, Achsah I, 861
Mendenhall, Achsah I, 862
Mendenhall, Achsah I, 893
Mendenhall, Achsah I, 926
Mendenhall, Ada Morgan I, 946
Mendenhall, Adam II, 595
Mendenhall, Adeline I, 930
Mendenhall, Adella Gardner V, 754
Mendenhall, Agnes VI, 400
Mendenhall, Agnes VI, 407
Mendenhall, Agnes VI, 422
Mendenhall, Agnes VI, 423
Mendenhall, Agnes VI, 462
Mendenhall, Agnes VI, 520
Mendenhall, Agnes VI, 661
Mendenhall, Agnes VI, 666
Mendenhall, Agness VI, 423
Mendenhall, Agness VI, 425
Mendenhall, Agness VI, 676
Mendenhall, Ahemar I, 860

Mendenhall, Albert V, 812
Mendenhall, Albert W. V, 815
Mendenhall, Aldus V, 754
Mendenhall, Alexander I, 861
Mendenhall, Alexander V, 307
Mendenhall, Alexander V, 349
Mendenhall, Alice I, 509
Mendenhall, Alice I, 788
Mendenhall, Alice I, 827
Mendenhall, Alice I, 861
Mendenhall, Alice I, 892
Mendenhall, Alice I, 1044
Mendenhall, Alice I, 1047
Mendenhall, Alice I, 1049
Mendenhall, Alice I, 1070
Mendenhall, Alice I, 1071
Mendenhall, Alice I, 1108
Mendenhall, Alice I, 1125
Mendenhall, Alice V, 516
Mendenhall, Alice V, 852
Mendenhall, Alice Carey V, 189
Mendenhall, Alice D. V, 516
Mendenhall, Alice E. V, 189
Mendenhall, Alice E. W. I, 930
Mendenhall, Alice Everett I, 946
Mendenhall, Alice Everett I, 951
Mendenhall, Alice S. V, 189
Mendenhall, Alice Thayer V, 754
Mendenhall, Allen H. V, 853
Mendenhall, Allen Harvey V, 852
Mendenhall, Allen Kelly V, 189
Mendenhall, Alma Jane V, 189
Mendenhall, Alpheus L. I, 621
Mendenhall, Alpheus L. I, 622
Mendenhall, Alpheus L. I, 829
Mendenhall, Alpheus L. I, 862
Mendenhall, Alpheus L. I, 893
Mendenhall, Alpheus Leonadus I, 788
Mendenhall, Alveron P. I, 829
Mendenhall, Alveron Pinchney I, 788
Mendenhall, Amos V, 585
Mendenhall, Amos VI, 422
Mendenhall, Amos VI, 423
Mendenhall, Amos C. V, 189
Mendenhall, Amy B. V, 189
Mendenhall, Andrew IV, 1173
Mendenhall, Andrew V, 852
Mendenhall, Andy IV, 1173
Mendenhall, Ann I, 509
Mendenhall, Ann I, 527
Mendenhall, Ann I, 561
Mendenhall, Ann I, 602
Mendenhall, Ann I, 603
Mendenhall, Ann I, 605
Mendenhall, Ann I, 607
Mendenhall, Ann I, 626
Mendenhall, Ann I, 720
Mendenhall, Ann I, 726
Mendenhall, Ann I, 787
Mendenhall, Ann I, 827
Mendenhall, Ann I, 829
Mendenhall, Ann I, 843
Mendenhall, Ann I, 862
Mendenhall, Ann I, 880
Mendenhall, Ann I, 892
Mendenhall, Ann I, 893
Mendenhall, Ann I, 907
Mendenhall, Ann I, 913
Mendenhall, Ann I, 993
Mendenhall, Ann I, 995
Mendenhall, Ann I, 1016
Mendenhall, Ann II, 394
Mendenhall, Ann II, 595
Mendenhall, Ann IV, 645
Mendenhall, Ann IV, 653
Mendenhall, Ann IV, 1216
Mendenhall, Ann V, 160
Mendenhall, Ann V, 188
Mendenhall, Ann V, 189
Mendenhall, Ann V, 475
Mendenhall, Ann V, 516
Mendenhall, Ann V, 585
Mendenhall, Ann V, 754
Mendenhall, Ann V, 852
Mendenhall, Ann V, 853
Mendenhall, Ann V, 863
Mendenhall, Ann VI, 422
Mendenhall, Ann VI, 423
Mendenhall, Anna I, 483
Mendenhall, Anna I, 726
Mendenhall, Anna I, 748
Mendenhall, Anna I, 787
Mendenhall, Anna I, 816
Mendenhall, Anna I, 828
Mendenhall, Anna I, 829
Mendenhall, Anna I, 861
Mendenhall, Anna II, 716
Mendenhall, Anna IV, 1305
Mendenhall, Anna IV, 1329
Mendenhall, Anna V, 189
Mendenhall, Anna V, 753
Mendenhall, Anna V, 754
Mendenhall, Anna A. IV, 1329
Mendenhall, Anna Armintage IV, 1329
Mendenhall, Anna E. V, 956
Mendenhall, Anna Eliza I, 602
Mendenhall, Anna L. I, 893
Mendenhall, Anna Ledwell I, 622
Mendenhall, Anna R. V, 189
Mendenhall, Anna T. IV, 250
Mendenhall, Anna T. IV, 296
Mendenhall, Anna T. IV, 645
Mendenhall, Anna T. IV, 663
Mendenhall, Annie I, 618
Mendenhall, Annie I, 622
Mendenhall, Annie I, 946
Mendenhall, Annie A. I, 637
Mendenhall, Annie Armitage I, 637
Mendenhall, Annie Jay I, 619
Mendenhall, Annie Jay I, 622
Mendenhall, Annie T. IV, 250
Mendenhall, Aquilla VI, 407
Mendenhall, Aron I, 561
Mendenhall, Aron I, 602
Mendenhall, Aron I, 684
Mendenhall, Aron I, 689
Mendenhall, Aron, Jr. I, 607
Mendenhall, Arthur I, 860
Mendenhall, Arthur I, 893
Mendenhall, Arthur C. V, 853
Mendenhall, Asael I, 862
Mendenhall, Asahel I, 787
Mendenhall, Asceneth IV, 251
Mendenhall, Asenath I, 603
Mendenhall, Asenath I, 626
Mendenhall, Asenath I, 789
Mendenhall, Asenath I, 860
Mendenhall, Asenath IV, 250
Mendenhall, Asenath IV, 251
Mendenhall, Asenath IV, 313
Mendenhall, Asenath IV, 644
Mendenhall, Ashel I, 892
Mendenhall, Aulman I, 893
Mendenhall, Barzillai G. I, 788
Mendenhall, Benjamin I, 561
Mendenhall, Benjamin I, 602
Mendenhall, Benjamin I, 607
Mendenhall, Benjamin I, 788
Mendenhall, Benjamin I, 861
Mendenhall, Benjamin I, 892
Mendenhall, Benjamin I, 993
Mendenhall, Benjamin V, 98
Mendenhall, Benjamin V, 188
Mendenhall, Benjamin V, 189
Mendenhall, Benjamin V, 789
Mendenhall, Benjamin Franklin II, 857
Mendenhall, Benjamin Franklin II, 933
Mendenhall, Berkinshaw IV, 1329
Mendenhall, Betsey I, 1108
Mendenhall, Bettie R. I, 880
Mendenhall, Betty I, 561
Mendenhall, Betty I, 577
Mendenhall, Betty I, 861
Mendenhall, Betty I, 891
Mendenhall, Betty I, 892
Mendenhall, Betty I, 1071
Mendenhall, Betty V, 160
Mendenhall, Betty V, 188
Mendenhall, Betty V, 189
Mendenhall, Betty V, 204
Mendenhall, Betty V, 206
Mendenhall, Betty V, 209
Mendenhall, Betty VI, 422
Mendenhall, Betty VI, 423
Mendenhall, Beulah I, 510
Mendenhall, Beulah I, 788
Mendenhall, Beulah I, 860
Mendenhall, Beulah I, 892
Mendenhall, Beulah I, 893
Mendenhall, Beulah VI, 534
Mendenhall, Birkenshaw I, 637
Mendenhall, Bulah I, 893
Mendenhall, Cabel I, 1049
Mendenhall, Caleb I, 787
Mendenhall, Caleb I, 810
Mendenhall, Caleb I, 827
Mendenhall, Caleb I, 1034
Mendenhall, Caleb IV, 48
Mendenhall, Caleb V, 98
Mendenhall, Caleb V, 723
Mendenhall, Caleb V, 754
Mendenhall, Caleb V, 756
Mendenhall, Caleb V, 767
Mendenhall, Caleb V, 789
Mendenhall, Caleb, Jr. V, 755
Mendenhall, Callie M. V, 862
Mendenhall, Camella J. V, 853
Mendenhall, Carky I, 828
Mendenhall, Caroline E. V, 852
Mendenhall, Caroline M. V, 862
Mendenhall, Cary V, 189
Mendenhall, Catharine I, 483
Mendenhall, Catharine I, 827
Mendenhall, Catharine I, 861
Mendenhall, Catharine I, 892
Mendenhall, Catharine I, 1049
Mendenhall, Catharine I, 1050
Mendenhall, Catharine IV, 153
Mendenhall, Catherine V, 161
Mendenhall, Catherine V, 188
Mendenhall, Catherine V, 189
Mendenhall, Catherine V, 209
Mendenhall, Cathren I, 1049
Mendenhall, Catrin V, 98
Mendenhall, Chariety I, 603
Mendenhall, Charity I, 408
Mendenhall, Charity I, 509
Mendenhall, Charity I, 527
Mendenhall, Charity I, 561
Mendenhall, Charity I, 562
Mendenhall, Charity I, 602
Mendenhall, Charity I, 684
Mendenhall, Charity I, 773
Mendenhall, Charity I, 788
Mendenhall, Charity I, 827
Mendenhall, Charity I, 842
Mendenhall, Charity I, 860
Mendenhall, Charity I, 861
Mendenhall, Charity I, 880
Mendenhall, Charity I, 891
Mendenhall, Charity I, 893
Mendenhall, Charity I, 901
Mendenhall, Charity I, 1109
Mendenhall, Charity I, 1126
Mendenhall, Charity V, 205
Mendenhall, Charity V, 307
Mendenhall, Charity V, 349
Mendenhall, Charity V, 754
Mendenhall, Charity V, 772
Mendenhall, Charity VI, 422
Mendenhall, Charity VI, 423
Mendenhall, Charity VI, 462
Mendenhall, Charles I, 861
Mendenhall, Charles I, 893
Mendenhall, Charles IV, 251
Mendenhall, Charles IV, 1068
Mendenhall, Charles V, 189
Mendenhall, Charles H. I, 860
Mendenhall, Charles H. I, 893
Mendenhall, Charles Hendrix I, 622
Mendenhall, Charles M. I, 621
Mendenhall, Charles S. I, 621
Mendenhall, Charles S. I, 629
Mendenhall, Charles S. I, 637
Mendenhall, Charles Scales I, 622
Mendenhall, Charles Scales I, 637
Mendenhall, Charles W. IV, 1068
Mendenhall, Charles W. IV, 1173
Mendenhall, Chas. B. IV, 1342
Mendenhall, Chas. Berkenshaw IV, 1329
Mendenhall, Chas. Berkinshaw IV, 1329
Mendenhall, Chester I, 560
Mendenhall, Christianna I, 804
Mendenhall, Christianna I, 827
Mendenhall, Christina I, 828
Mendenhall, Clara V, 853
Mendenhall, Clara Lucile IV, 1329
Mendenhall, Claresey I, 862
Mendenhall, Clarissa I, 862
Mendenhall, Clarissa I, 892
Mendenhall, Clarissa I, 893
Mendenhall, Clarkey I, 860
Mendenhall, Clarkson I, 860
Mendenhall, Clarkson I, 893
Mendenhall, Clarkson I, 927
Mendenhall, Clarkson I, 930
Mendenhall, Clarky I, 787
Mendenhall, Clarky I, 829
Mendenhall, Clarky I, 893
Mendenhall, Clasky I, 893
Mendenhall, Clasky I, 906
Mendenhall, Cora Elizabeth V, 754
Mendenhall, Cordelia IV, 251
Mendenhall, Corella V, 853
Mendenhall, Cyntha, Jr. I, 893
Mendenhall, Cynthia I, 621
Mendenhall, Cynthia I, 622
Mendenhall, Cynthia I, 860
Mendenhall, Cynthia I, 893
Mendenhall, Cynthia I, 928
Mendenhall, Cynthia V, 189
Mendenhall, Cyrus I, 788
Mendenhall, Cyrus I, 829
Mendenhall, Cyrus IV, 250
Mendenhall, Cyrus IV, 251
Mendenhall, Cyrus IV, 296
Mendenhall, Cyrus IV, 644
Mendenhall, Cyrus IV, 645
Mendenhall, Cyrus IV, 654
Mendenhall, Cyrus IV, 663
Mendenhall, Cyrus V, 921
Mendenhall, Cyrus P. I, 829
Mendenhall, Cyrus, Jr. II, 242
Mendenhall, Cyrus, Jr. II, 296
Mendenhall, Daidama I, 1126
Mendenhall, Daniel I, 787
Mendenhall, Daniel I, 827
Mendenhall, Daniel I, 828
Mendenhall, Daniel I, 913
Mendenhall, David I, 603
Mendenhall, David I, 787
Mendenhall, David I, 788
Mendenhall, David I, 828
Mendenhall, David I, 830
Mendenhall, David I, 860
Mendenhall, David I, 861
Mendenhall, David I, 892
Mendenhall, David I, 993
Mendenhall, David V, 189
Mendenhall, David V, 197
Mendenhall, David James V, 754
Mendenhall, David Willis I, 930
Mendenhall, Deborah I, 787
Mendenhall, Deborah I, 801
Mendenhall, Deborah I, 828
Mendenhall, Deborah I, 913
Mendenhall, Deborah IV, 250
Mendenhall, Deborah IV, 251
Mendenhall, Deborah IV, 1068
Mendenhall, Deborah V, 98
Mendenhall, Deborah V, 126
Mendenhall, Deborah V, 188
Mendenhall, Deborah V, 189
Mendenhall, Deborah V, 206
Mendenhall, Deborah Brooks I, 913
Mendenhall, Deborah M. I, 637
Mendenhall, Deborah Miriam IV, 1329
Mendenhall, Debroh I, 913
Mendenhall, Deida V, 794
Mendenhall, Deidamia I, 1126
Mendenhall, Delilah V, 852
Mendenhall, Delilah A. V, 853
Mendenhall, Delilah A. V, 859
Mendenhall, Delirga E. V, 585
Mendenhall, Delith M. I, 602
Mendenhall, Delitha V, 585
Mendenhall, Delitha V, 603
Mendenhall, Delphina E. I, 389
Mendenhall, Delphina E. I, 408
Mendenhall, Delphina E. I, 787
Mendenhall, Delphine E. I, 408
Mendenhall, Delphinia E. I, 828
Mendenhall, Demcy B. I, 861
Mendenhall, Dinah I, 509
Mendenhall, Dinah I, 560
Mendenhall, Dinah I, 561
Mendenhall, Dinah I, 563
Mendenhall, Dinah I, 570
Mendenhall, Dinah I, 603
Mendenhall, Dinah I, 773
Mendenhall, Dinah I, 827
Mendenhall, Dinah I, 847
Mendenhall, Dinah I, 860
Mendenhall, Dinah I, 861
Mendenhall, Dinah I, 892
Mendenhall, Dr. Geo. P. I, 389
Mendenhall, Dr. Geo. P. I, 408
Mendenhall, E. V, 862
Mendenhall, E. Clarkson I, 946
Mendenhall, E. Clarkson I, 951
Mendenhall, E. E. I, 637
Mendenhall, E. Jane I, 920
Mendenhall, E. Jane I, 927
Mendenhall, Earl I, 637
Mendenhall, Easter I, 862
Mendenhall, Eddy Jay I, 637
Mendenhall, Edgar Eugene I, 893
Mendenhall, Edith I, 892
Mendenhall, Edith IV, 250
Mendenhall, Edith IV, 251
Mendenhall, Edith IV, 1068
Mendenhall, Edith IV, 1079
Mendenhall, Edith V, 516
Mendenhall, Edith V, 853
Mendenhall, Edith VI, 422
Mendenhall, Edith VI, 423
Mendenhall, Edith A. V, 160
Mendenhall, Edith A. V, 189
Mendenhall, Edith Mildred III, 225
Mendenhall, Edmund Emerson I, 621
Mendenhall, Edward V, 189
Mendenhall, Edward E. I, 621
Mendenhall, Edward E. I, 626
Mendenhall, Edward Emerson I, 637
Mendenhall, Edward Jay I, 622
Mendenhall, Elam K. V, 585
Mendenhall, Elbert IV, 1329
Mendenhall, Eleanor I, 1126
Mendenhall, Eleanor I, 1132
Mendenhall, Eleanor II, 394
Mendenhall, Eleanor II, 595
Mendenhall, Eleazar I, 860
Mendenhall, Eleazar I, 893
Mendenhall, Eli I, 827
Mendenhall, Eli I, 861
Mendenhall, Eli I, 862
Mendenhall, Eli B. I, 862
Mendenhall, Elias I, 788
Mendenhall, Elihu I, 787
Mendenhall, Elihu I, 829
Mendenhall, Elihu Clarkson I, 787
Mendenhall, Elihu E. I, 720
Mendenhall, Elihu E. I, 726
Mendenhall, Elihu E. I, 787
Mendenhall, Elihu E. I, 829
Mendenhall, Elihu P. I, 829
Mendenhall, Elijah I, 555
Mendenhall, Elijah I, 561
Mendenhall, Elijah I, 787
Mendenhall, Elijah I, 805
Mendenhall, Elijah I, 827
Mendenhall, Elijah I, 828
Mendenhall, Elijah I, 1016
Mendenhall, Elijah I, 1044
Mendenhall, Elijah I, 1049
Mendenhall, Elijah V, 98
Mendenhall, Elijah V, 852
Mendenhall, Elijah V, 853
Mendenhall, Elijah V, 858
Mendenhall, Elijah V, 863
Mendenhall, Elijah Joseph V, 85
Mendenhall, Elijtorn I, 891
Mendenhall, Elisha IV, 313
Mendenhall, Eliza I, 788
Mendenhall, Eliza I, 878
Mendenhall, Eliza I, 893
Mendenhall, Eliza A. I, 860
Mendenhall, Eliza Ann V, 852
Mendenhall, Eliza Ann V, 853
Mendenhall, Eliza D. I, 829
Mendenhall, Eliza D. I, 844
Mendenhall, Eliza Delphina I, 788
Mendenhall, Eliza J. I, 860
Mendenhall, Eliza J. I, 893
Mendenhall, Eliza Jane I, 884
Mendenhall, Eliza Jane I, 893
Mendenhall, Eliza Jane I, 927
Mendenhall, Eliza L. I, 816
Mendenhall, Eliza L. I, 829
Mendenhall, Elizabeth I, 470
Mendenhall, Elizabeth I, 483
Mendenhall, Elizabeth I, 510
Mendenhall, Elizabeth I, 561
Mendenhall, Elizabeth I, 569
Mendenhall, Elizabeth I, 577
Mendenhall, Elizabeth I, 600
Mendenhall, Elizabeth I, 602
Mendenhall, Elizabeth I, 788
Mendenhall, Elizabeth I, 827
Mendenhall, Elizabeth I, 828
Mendenhall, Elizabeth I, 840
Mendenhall, Elizabeth I, 843
Mendenhall, Elizabeth I, 847
Mendenhall, Elizabeth I, 860
Mendenhall, Elizabeth I, 861
Mendenhall, Elizabeth I, 862
Mendenhall, Elizabeth I, 889
Mendenhall, Elizabeth I, 892
Mendenhall, Elizabeth I, 893
Mendenhall, Elizabeth I, 898
Mendenhall, Elizabeth I, 907
Mendenhall, Elizabeth I, 913
Mendenhall, Elizabeth I, 928
Mendenhall, Elizabeth I, 993
Mendenhall, Elizabeth I, 1044
Mendenhall, Elizabeth I, 1049
Mendenhall, Elizabeth I, 1050
Mendenhall, Elizabeth I, 1071
Mendenhall, Elizabeth II, 451
Mendenhall, Elizabeth II, 595
Mendenhall, Elizabeth IV, 250
Mendenhall, Elizabeth IV, 251
Mendenhall, Elizabeth IV, 1068

endenhall, Elizabeth IV, 1079
endenhall, Elizabeth V, 516
endenhall, Elizabeth V, 585
endenhall, Elizabeth V, 754
endenhall, Elizabeth V, 833
endenhall, Elizabeth V, 835
endenhall, Elizabeth V, 845
endenhall, Elizabeth V, 849
endenhall, Elizabeth V, 852
endenhall, Elizabeth V, 853
endenhall, Elizabeth V, 858
endenhall, Elizabeth V, 859
endenhall, Elizabeth V, 862
endenhall, Elizabeth V, 883
endenhall, Elizabeth V, 884
endenhall, Elizabeth VI, 423
endenhall, Elizabeth A. V, 516
endenhall, Elizabeth A. V, 853
endenhall, Elizabeth Ann V, 189
endenhall, Elizabeth Ann V, 483
endenhall, Elizabeth Ann V, 516
endenhall, Elizabeth Ann V, 853
endenhall, Elizabeth C. V, 852
endenhall, Elizabeth D. IV, 892
endenhall, Elizabeth D. IV, 893
endenhall, Elizabeth R. V, 755
endenhall, Elizabeth S. I, 828
endenhall, Elizabeth S. I, 837
endenhall, Elizabethann V, 516
endenhall, Ella I, 621
endenhall, Ella I, 622
endenhall, Ella I, 629
endenhall, Ella I, 637
endenhall, Elleanor V, 98
endenhall, Ellen I, 862
endenhall, Ellenor V, 98
endenhall, Elmer V, 852
endenhall, Elmer C. V, 853
endenhall, Elnora V, 835
endenhall, Elnora V, 852
endenhall, Elom T. I, 602
endenhall, Elvira I, 684
endenhall, Ely I, 1071
endenhall, Emeline I, 893
endenhall, Emery P. I, 637
endenhall, Emery P. I, 893
endenhall, Emily I, 602
endenhall, Emily I, 812
endenhall, Emily I, 829
endenhall, Emily I, 860
endenhall, Emily I, 893
endenhall, Emily I, 904
endenhall, Emily E. I, 860
endenhall, Emily J. I, 602
endenhall, Emily Luanda I, 788
endenhall, Emma V, 852
endenhall, Emma L. I, 893
endenhall, Enoch I, 828
endenhall, Enoch I, 840
endenhall, Enoch I, 860
endenhall, Enoch I, 861
endenhall, Enoch I, 893
endenhall, Enoch I, 928
endenhall, Enos I, 789
endenhall, Enos I, 860
endenhall, Enos I, 880
endenhall, Enos I, 892
endenhall, Enos I, 893
endenhall, Enos V, 754
endenhall, Enos T. I, 860
endenhall, Erastas I, 860
endenhall, Erastus W. I, 893
endenhall, Erastus Wm. I, 860
endenhall, Erma V, 189
endenhall, Erma M. V, 214
endenhall, Ester I, 911
endenhall, Ester I, 913
endenhall, Esther I, 470
endenhall, Esther I, 483
endenhall, Esther I, 787
endenhall, Esther I, 828
endenhall, Esther I, 892
endenhall, Esther I, 893
endenhall, Esther I, 911
endenhall, Esther I, 913
endenhall, Esther IV, 644
endenhall, Esther IV, 654
endenhall, Esther V, 852
endenhall, Esther Alma V, 852
endenhall, Estus IV, 1329
endenhall, Ethel I, 930
endenhall, Ethel I, 946
endenhall, Ethel V, 98
endenhall, Ethel M. V, 853
endenhall, Etta I, 622
endenhall, Etta I, 631
Mendenhall, Etta I, 637
Mendenhall, Eunice I, 828
Mendenhall, Eunice V, 160
Mendenhall, Eunice V, 189
Mendenhall, Eunice V, 412
Mendenhall, Eunice V, 751
Mendenhall, Eunice V, 754
Mendenhall, Eva V, 852
Mendenhall, Eva V, 853
Mendenhall, Eva C. I, 893
Mendenhall, Evelyn I, 626
Mendenhall, Evelyn I, 638
Mendenhall, Evelyn I, 642
Mendenhall, Everett J. V, 189
Mendenhall, Everetta F. V, 754
Mendenhall, Evin Penock IV, 1216
Mendenhall, Evon P. IV, 1216
Mendenhall, Ezekiel I, 861
Mendenhall, Ezekiel V, 307
Mendenhall, Ezekiel V, 349
Mendenhall, Fannie IV, 1173
Mendenhall, Fanny I, 876
Mendenhall, Francis I, 861
Mendenhall, Francis I, 892
Mendenhall, Frank I, 946
Mendenhall, Gardner V, 753
Mendenhall, Gardner V, 754
Mendenhall, Gardner V, 789
Mendenhall, George I, 540
Mendenhall, George I, 561
Mendenhall, George I, 787
Mendenhall, George I, 827
Mendenhall, George I, 828
Mendenhall, George II, 394
Mendenhall, George IV, 644
Mendenhall, George IV, 739
Mendenhall, George C. I, 787
Mendenhall, George C. I, 828
Mendenhall, George W. V, 853
Mendenhall, Gertrude W. I, 637
Mendenhall, Gertrude Whittier I, 621
Mendenhall, Gertrude Whittier I, 788
Mendenhall, Gra V, 98
Mendenhall, Grace I, 509
Mendenhall, Grace I, 510
Mendenhall, Grace I, 787
Mendenhall, Grace I, 827
Mendenhall, Grace I, 842
Mendenhall, Grace I, 1034
Mendenhall, Grace I, 1049
Mendenhall, Grace IV, 48
Mendenhall, Grace V, 754
Mendenhall, Grace V, 767
Mendenhall, Griffith I, 787
Mendenhall, Griffith II, 595
Mendenhall, Griffith IV, 48
Mendenhall, Griffith V, 754
Mendenhall, Hannah I, 408
Mendenhall, Hannah I, 444
Mendenhall, Hannah I, 451
Mendenhall, Hannah I, 509
Mendenhall, Hannah I, 532
Mendenhall, Hannah I, 561
Mendenhall, Hannah I, 602
Mendenhall, Hannah I, 603
Mendenhall, Hannah I, 607
Mendenhall, Hannah I, 633
Mendenhall, Hannah I, 637
Mendenhall, Hannah I, 787
Mendenhall, Hannah I, 788
Mendenhall, Hannah I, 796
Mendenhall, Hannah I, 816
Mendenhall, Hannah I, 827
Mendenhall, Hannah I, 828
Mendenhall, Hannah I, 841
Mendenhall, Hannah I, 860
Mendenhall, Hannah I, 861
Mendenhall, Hannah I, 862
Mendenhall, Hannah I, 882
Mendenhall, Hannah I, 892
Mendenhall, Hannah I, 893
Mendenhall, Hannah I, 1044
Mendenhall, Hannah I, 1049
Mendenhall, Hannah I, 1071
Mendenhall, Hannah I, 1101
Mendenhall, Hannah I, 1105
Mendenhall, Hannah I, 1108
Mendenhall, Hannah I, 1121
Mendenhall, Hannah I, 1125
Mendenhall, Hannah I, 1126
Mendenhall, Hannah II, 394
Mendenhall, Hannah II, 595
Mendenhall, Hannah II, 809
Mendenhall, Hannah II, 815
Mendenhall, Hannah II, 898
Mendenhall, Hannah IV, 48
Mendenhall, Hannah IV, 250
Mendenhall, Hannah IV, 251
Mendenhall, Hannah IV, 252
Mendenhall, Hannah IV, 614
Mendenhall, Hannah IV, 644
Mendenhall, Hannah IV, 646
Mendenhall, Hannah IV, 687
Mendenhall, Hannah IV, 805
Mendenhall, Hannah IV, 833
Mendenhall, Hannah IV, 1068
Mendenhall, Hannah IV, 1173
Mendenhall, Hannah V, 188
Mendenhall, Hannah V, 189
Mendenhall, Hannah V, 204
Mendenhall, Hannah V, 413
Mendenhall, Hannah V, 441
Mendenhall, Hannah V, 577
Mendenhall, Hannah V, 585
Mendenhall, Hannah V, 849
Mendenhall, Hannah V, 852
Mendenhall, Hannah V, 853
Mendenhall, Hannah VI, 422
Mendenhall, Hannah VI, 423
Mendenhall, Hannah VI, 487
Mendenhall, Hannah VI, 584
Mendenhall, Hannah Ann V, 852
Mendenhall, Hannah Ann V, 853
Mendenhall, Hannah Ann V, 859
Mendenhall, Hannah C. II, 791
Mendenhall, Hannah Clark V, 684
Mendenhall, Hannah M. V, 412
Mendenhall, Hannah M. VI, 584
Mendenhall, Harriet Emma V, 852
Mendenhall, Harriett Elisabeth I, 622
Mendenhall, Harrison IV, 644
Mendenhall, Harrison IV, 645
Mendenhall, Harvey V, 853
Mendenhall, Hattie B. I, 946
Mendenhall, Hattie E. I, 637
Mendenhall, Hattie G. I, 893
Mendenhall, Hazel III, 150
Mendenhall, Hazel III, 225
Mendenhall, Hazel E. V, 189
Mendenhall, Helen I, 219
Mendenhall, Helen IV, 1329
Mendenhall, Helen H. I, 637
Mendenhall, Helen Hadassa I, 621
Mendenhall, Helen Marguerite IV, 1329
Mendenhall, Helen Marguerite IV, 1342
Mendenhall, Helen Webb IV, 1329
Mendenhall, Henry I, 470
Mendenhall, Henry I, 474
Mendenhall, Henry I, 483
Mendenhall, Henry W. V, 921
Mendenhall, Hester I, 483
Mendenhall, Himelius I, 684
Mendenhall, Himelius I, 787
Mendenhall, Himelius I, 805
Mendenhall, Himelius I, 828
Mendenhall, Hiram V, 516
Mendenhall, Hiram V, 570
Mendenhall, Hiram V, 585
Mendenhall, Horace V, 189
Mendenhall, Hulda I, 828
Mendenhall, Huldah I, 462
Mendenhall, Huldah I, 470
Mendenhall, Huldah I, 477
Mendenhall, Huldah I, 483
Mendenhall, Huldah I, 805
Mendenhall, Huldah I, 828
Mendenhall, Huldah I, 862
Mendenhall, Huldah I, 892
Mendenhall, Ida A. I, 626
Mendenhall, Ida Evelyn I, 621
Mendenhall, Ida Evelyn I, 637
Mendenhall, Ida Martitia I, 621
Mendenhall, Iona May I, 637
Mendenhall, Ionia May I, 639
Mendenhall, Ira I, 470
Mendenhall, Ira I, 483
Mendenhall, Ira I, 787
Mendenhall, Ira I, 860
Mendenhall, Ira I, 861
Mendenhall, Ira I, 993
Mendenhall, Ira V, 151
Mendenhall, Ira V, 188
Mendenhall, Ira V, 189
Mendenhall, Ira W. I, 684
Mendenhall, Ira W. I, 687
Mendenhall, Ira W. I, 893
Mendenhall, Irena V, 349
Mendenhall, Irene I, 861
Mendenhall, Irene V, 307
Mendenhall, Irma I, 637
Mendenhall, Irma Maie I, 622
Mendenhall, Irma May I, 637
Mendenhall, Isaac I, 470
Mendenhall, Isaac I, 483
Mendenhall, Isaac I, 509
Mendenhall, Isaac I, 510
Mendenhall, Isaac I, 561
Mendenhall, Isaac I, 684
Mendenhall, Isaac I, 726
Mendenhall, Isaac I, 787
Mendenhall, Isaac I, 788
Mendenhall, Isaac I, 847
Mendenhall, Isaac I, 860
Mendenhall, Isaac I, 861
Mendenhall, Isaac I, 862
Mendenhall, Isaac I, 889
Mendenhall, Isaac I, 892
Mendenhall, Isaac II, 394
Mendenhall, Isaac IV, 178
Mendenhall, Isaac IV, 250
Mendenhall, Isaac IV, 251
Mendenhall, Isaac IV, 644
Mendenhall, Isaac IV, 1068
Mendenhall, Isaac V, 852
Mendenhall, Isaac V, 853
Mendenhall, Isaac B. IV, 250
Mendenhall, Isaac B. IV, 251
Mendenhall, Isaac B. IV, 1068
Mendenhall, Isaac, Jr. I, 892
Mendenhall, Isaac, Sr. I, 892
Mendenhall, Isaiah I, 804
Mendenhall, Isaiah I, 827
Mendenhall, Isaiah I, 828
Mendenhall, Israel IV, 250
Mendenhall, Israel IV, 251
Mendenhall, Israel IV, 614
Mendenhall, Israel IV, 644
Mendenhall, Israel IV, 645
Mendenhall, Israel IV, 653
Mendenhall, Israel IV, 1216
Mendenhall, Israel B. IV, 250
Mendenhall, Iva A. V, 853
Mendenhall, J. I, 829
Mendenhall, J. F. I, 930
Mendenhall, J. Lindley IV, 420
Mendenhall, J. Lindley V, 98
Mendenhall, J. R. I, 637
Mendenhall, Jabez I, 861
Mendenhall, Jabez I, 862
Mendenhall, Jabez I, 892
Mendenhall, Jabez I, 893
Mendenhall, Jabez R. I, 637
Mendenhall, Jabez R. I, 860
Mendenhall, Jabez R. I, 893
Mendenhall, Jabez R. I, 895
Mendenhall, Jabez R., Jr. I, 621
Mendenhall, Jabez Reddic I, 622
Mendenhall, Jabez Riddick I, 619
Mendenhall, Jacob I, 787
Mendenhall, Jacob I, 860
Mendenhall, Jacob I, 861
Mendenhall, Jacob I, 892
Mendenhall, Jacob I, 893
Mendenhall, Jacob V, 852
Mendenhall, Jacob V, 853
Mendenhall, Jacob V, 884
Mendenhall, Jacob VI, 422
Mendenhall, Jacob VI, 423
Mendenhall, Jacob VI, 521
Mendenhall, Jacob VI, 533
Mendenhall, Jacob VI, 534
Mendenhall, James I, 509
Mendenhall, James I, 561
Mendenhall, James I, 578
Mendenhall, James I, 595
Mendenhall, James I, 602
Mendenhall, James I, 606
Mendenhall, James I, 607
Mendenhall, James I, 726
Mendenhall, James I, 748
Mendenhall, James I, 787
Mendenhall, James I, 805
Mendenhall, James I, 827
Mendenhall, James I, 828
Mendenhall, James I, 829
Mendenhall, James I, 862
Mendenhall, James I, 885
Mendenhall, James I, 891
Mendenhall, James I, 913
Mendenhall, James I, 930
Mendenhall, James I, 1034
Mendenhall, James I, 1044
Mendenhall, James I, 1049
Mendenhall, James II, 800
Mendenhall, James IV, 250
Mendenhall, James IV, 251
Mendenhall, James IV, 644
Mendenhall, James V, 98
Mendenhall, James V, 189
Mendenhall, James V, 852
Mendenhall, James V, 853
Mendenhall, James V, 884
Mendenhall, James VI, 400
Mendenhall, James VI, 407
Mendenhall, James VI, 422
Mendenhall, James VI, 423
Mendenhall, James VI, 462
Mendenhall, James VI, 517
Mendenhall, James VI, 520
Mendenhall, James VI, 530
Mendenhall, James VI, 661
Mendenhall, James VI, 666
Mendenhall, James VI, 725
Mendenhall, James VI, 753
Mendenhall, James VI, 764
Mendenhall, James C. I, 861
Mendenhall, James Clemmons V, 307
Mendenhall, James Clemmons V, 349
Mendenhall, James N. I, 787
Mendenhall, James, Jr. I, 827
Mendenhall, Jane I, 560
Mendenhall, Jane I, 577
Mendenhall, Jane I, 773
Mendenhall, Jane I, 788
Mendenhall, Jane I, 827
Mendenhall, Jane I, 843
Mendenhall, Jane I, 847
Mendenhall, Jane I, 891
Mendenhall, Jane I, 892
Mendenhall, Jane I, 893
Mendenhall, Jane I, 899
Mendenhall, Jane I, 901
Mendenhall, Jane I, 1126
Mendenhall, Jane IV, 100
Mendenhall, Jane IV, 1173
Mendenhall, Jane V, 794
Mendenhall, Jane E. V, 98
Mendenhall, Jane H. I, 825
Mendenhall, Jane H. I, 828
Mendenhall, Jane H. V, 50
Mendenhall, Jane H. V, 98
Mendenhall, Jason I, 860
Mendenhall, Jason I, 883
Mendenhall, Jason I, 892
Mendenhall, Jason I, 893
Mendenhall, Jason V, 98
Mendenhall, Jeams I, 560
Mendenhall, Jeams I, 561
Mendenhall, Jeane I, 510
Mendenhall, Jehu I, 787
Mendenhall, Jemima I, 825
Mendenhall, Jemima I, 828
Mendenhall, Jennie E. V, 189
Mendenhall, Jeremiah I, 470
Mendenhall, Jeremiah I, 483
Mendenhall, Jeremiah I, 861
Mendenhall, Jeremiah I, 892
Mendenhall, Jesse I, 788
Mendenhall, Jesse I, 827
Mendenhall, Jesse IV, 644
Mendenhall, Jesse H. V, 441
Mendenhall, Jesse N. V, 412
Mendenhall, Job I, 470
Mendenhall, Job I, 483
Mendenhall, Job I, 766
Mendenhall, John I, 470
Mendenhall, John I, 483
Mendenhall, John I, 509
Mendenhall, John I, 510
Mendenhall, John I, 561
Mendenhall, John I, 571
Mendenhall, John I, 602
Mendenhall, John I, 603
Mendenhall, John I, 607
Mendenhall, John I, 773
Mendenhall, John I, 787
Mendenhall, John I, 788
Mendenhall, John I, 801
Mendenhall, John I, 827
Mendenhall, John I, 860
Mendenhall, John I, 861
Mendenhall, John I, 862
Mendenhall, John I, 873
Mendenhall, John I, 892
Mendenhall, John I, 893
Mendenhall, John I, 1034
Mendenhall, John I, 1044
Mendenhall, John I, 1049
Mendenhall, John I, 1066
Mendenhall, John I, 1071
Mendenhall, John I, 1108
Mendenhall, John I Sup 1, 10
Mendenhall, John II, 595
Mendenhall, John II, 755
Mendenhall, John IV, 250
Mendenhall, John IV, 251
Mendenhall, John IV, 252
Mendenhall, John IV, 644
Mendenhall, John IV, 646
Mendenhall, John IV, 1068
Mendenhall, John IV, 1173
Mendenhall, John V, 98

Mendenhall, John V, 147
Mendenhall, John V, 151
Mendenhall, John V, 160
Mendenhall, John V, 188
Mendenhall, John V, 189
Mendenhall, John V, 209
Mendenhall, John V, 412
Mendenhall, John V, 789
Mendenhall, John V, 849
Mendenhall, John V, 852
Mendenhall, John V, 853
Mendenhall, John V, 884
Mendenhall, John VI, 422
Mendenhall, John VI, 517
Mendenhall, John Barker I, 483
Mendenhall, John Brooks I, 828
Mendenhall, John C. I, 602
Mendenhall, John G. V, 852
Mendenhall, John H. IV, 833
Mendenhall, John Harold III, 225
Mendenhall, John M. I, 861
Mendenhall, John M. IV, 251
Mendenhall, John Milton V, 307
Mendenhall, John Milton V, 349
Mendenhall, John T. IV, 251
Mendenhall, John Thomas I, 509
Mendenhall, John Tribby IV, 250
Mendenhall, John, Jr. I, 561
Mendenhall, Jonathan I, 787
Mendenhall, Jonathan I, 788
Mendenhall, Jonathan I, 805
Mendenhall, Jonathan I, 827
Mendenhall, Jonathan I, 828
Mendenhall, Jonathan I, 861
Mendenhall, Jonathan I, 907
Mendenhall, Jonathan I, 913
Mendenhall, Jonathan I, 993
Mendenhall, Jonathan I, 995
Mendenhall, Jonathan I, 1044
Mendenhall, Jonathan I, 1049
Mendenhall, Jonathan IV, 644
Mendenhall, Jonathan IV, 660
Mendenhall, Jonathan V, 852
Mendenhall, Jonathan C. Backhouse I, 862
Mendenhall, Joseph I, 787
Mendenhall, Joseph I, 788
Mendenhall, Joseph I, 810
Mendenhall, Joseph I, 827
Mendenhall, Joseph I, 828
Mendenhall, Joseph I, 861
Mendenhall, Joseph I, 892
Mendenhall, Joseph I, 907
Mendenhall, Joseph I, 913
Mendenhall, Joseph I, 993
Mendenhall, Joseph I, 1034
Mendenhall, Joseph I, 1044
Mendenhall, Joseph I, 1049
Mendenhall, Joseph I, 1050
Mendenhall, Joseph I, 1125
Mendenhall, Joseph I, 1126
Mendenhall, Joseph IV, 250
Mendenhall, Joseph IV, 251
Mendenhall, Joseph IV, 1068
Mendenhall, Joseph IV, 1216
Mendenhall, Joseph V, 98
Mendenhall, Joseph V, 188
Mendenhall, Joseph V, 263
Mendenhall, Joseph V, 475
Mendenhall, Joseph V, 516
Mendenhall, Joseph V, 585
Mendenhall, Joseph V, 732
Mendenhall, Joseph V, 753
Mendenhall, Joseph V, 754
Mendenhall, Joseph V, 774
Mendenhall, Joseph V, 789
Mendenhall, Joseph V, 829
Mendenhall, Joseph V, 853
Mendenhall, Joseph B. V, 189
Mendenhall, Joseph L. V, 853
Mendenhall, Joseph Lindley V, 852
Mendenhall, Joseph R. I, 1108
Mendenhall, Joseph, Sr. V, 754
Mendenhall, Joshua IV, 833
Mendenhall, Josiah I, 861
Mendenhall, Judith I, 540
Mendenhall, Judith I, 561
Mendenhall, Judith I, 787
Mendenhall, Judith I, 788
Mendenhall, Judith I, 827
Mendenhall, Judith I, 828
Mendenhall, Judith Ann V, 516
Mendenhall, Judith Genevieve I, 788
Mendenhall, Judith, Jr. I, 828
Mendenhall, Julia Ann V, 551
Mendenhall, Julia Ann V, 585
Mendenhall, Julia Fisk I, 788
Mendenhall, Julia Fisk I, 829
Mendenhall, Julia Fisk I, 831
Mendenhall, Juliann I, 602
Mendenhall, Julius P. I, 893
Mendenhall, Katharine I, 470
Mendenhall, Kelley V, 189
Mendenhall, Kirk V, 754
Mendenhall, Kirk V, 755
Mendenhall, L. Pearl I, 829
Mendenhall, Laura I, 788
Mendenhall, Laura I, 807
Mendenhall, Laura I, 829
Mendenhall, Lena I, 622
Mendenhall, Lena I, 637
Mendenhall, Lena I, 642
Mendenhall, Leurin I, 637
Mendenhall, Levi V, 789
Mendenhall, Levina V, 189
Mendenhall, Lewzene I, 860
Mendenhall, Lidia I, 860
Mendenhall, Lindley V, 98
Mendenhall, Lindley Clarkson V, 852
Mendenhall, Linus V, 754
Mendenhall, Lizette I, 930
Mendenhall, Lizette I, 946
Mendenhall, Louella A. V, 189
Mendenhall, Louisa I, 862
Mendenhall, Lucile IV, 1329
Mendenhall, Lucile Williams IV, 1329
Mendenhall, Lucinda I, 470
Mendenhall, Lucinda I, 483
Mendenhall, Luoren D. I, 622
Mendenhall, Lurence DeLowso I, 893
Mendenhall, Lurin D. I, 637
Mendenhall, Luzena I, 892
Mendenhall, Luzena I, 893
Mendenhall, Luzena I, 904
Mendenhall, Lyda I, 913
Mendenhall, Lydai I, 788
Mendenhall, Lydia I, 408
Mendenhall, Lydia I, 416
Mendenhall, Lydia I, 509
Mendenhall, Lydia I, 561
Mendenhall, Lydia I, 602
Mendenhall, Lydia I, 787
Mendenhall, Lydia I, 828
Mendenhall, Lydia I, 837
Mendenhall, Lydia I, 860
Mendenhall, Lydia I, 861
Mendenhall, Lydia I, 876
Mendenhall, Lydia I, 880
Mendenhall, Lydia I, 892
Mendenhall, Lydia I, 893
Mendenhall, Lydia I, 911
Mendenhall, Lydia I, 913
Mendenhall, Lydia IV, 48
Mendenhall, Lydia IV, 178
Mendenhall, Lydia IV, 250
Mendenhall, Lydia IV, 251
Mendenhall, Lydia IV, 417
Mendenhall, Lydia IV, 644
Mendenhall, Lydia IV, 645
Mendenhall, Lydia IV, 654
Mendenhall, Lydia IV, 660
Mendenhall, Lydia IV, 833
Mendenhall, Lydia IV, 910
Mendenhall, Lydia IV, 913
Mendenhall, Lydia IV, 1068
Mendenhall, Lydia IV, 1082
Mendenhall, Lydia V, 98
Mendenhall, Lydia V, 137
Mendenhall, Lydia V, 188
Mendenhall, Lydia V, 307
Mendenhall, Lydia V, 349
Mendenhall, Lydia V, 752
Mendenhall, Lydia V, 754
Mendenhall, Lydia V, 755
Mendenhall, Lydia VI, 407
Mendenhall, Lydia VI, 422
Mendenhall, Lydia VI, 520
Mendenhall, Lydia VI, 529
Mendenhall, Lydia VI, 661
Mendenhall, Lydia VI, 665
Mendenhall, Lydia VI, 666
Mendenhall, Lydia VI, 673
Mendenhall, Lydia VI, 676
Mendenhall, Lydia Ann IV, 251
Mendenhall, Lydia Ann IV, 1068
Mendenhall, Lydia Ann IV, 1173
Mendenhall, Lydia C. IV, 251
Mendenhall, Lydia D. II, 800
Mendenhall, Lydiann IV, 1068
Mendenhall, M. V, 862
Mendenhall, M. J. V, 862
Mendenhall, M. Milton M. I, 861
Mendenhall, M. Pauline I, 829
Mendenhall, Mabel V, 862
Mendenhall, Magery I, 892
Mendenhall, Margaret I, 470
Mendenhall, Margaret I, 483
Mendenhall, Margaret I, 710
Mendenhall, Margaret I, 726
Mendenhall, Margaret I, 766
Mendenhall, Margaret I, 787
Mendenhall, Margaret I, 788
Mendenhall, Margaret I, 828
Mendenhall, Margaret I, 829
Mendenhall, Margaret I, 830
Mendenhall, Margaret I, 860
Mendenhall, Margaret I, 861
Mendenhall, Margaret I, 892
Mendenhall, Margaret I, 893
Mendenhall, Margaret IV, 644
Mendenhall, Margaret IV, 1329
Mendenhall, Margaret V, 98
Mendenhall, Margaret V, 151
Mendenhall, Margaret V, 188
Mendenhall, Margaret V, 189
Mendenhall, Margaret V, 830
Mendenhall, Margaret V, 847
Mendenhall, Margaret V, 849
Mendenhall, Margaret V, 852
Mendenhall, Margaret V, 853
Mendenhall, Margaret V, 884
Mendenhall, Margaret Elisabeth I, 621
Mendenhall, Margaret Elizabeth I, 637
Mendenhall, Margaret J. I, 862
Mendenhall, Margerry I, 893
Mendenhall, Margery I, 470
Mendenhall, Margery I, 483
Mendenhall, Margery I, 684
Mendenhall, Margery I, 787
Mendenhall, Margery I, 828
Mendenhall, Margery I, 829
Mendenhall, Margery I, 861
Mendenhall, Margery I, 871
Mendenhall, Margery I, 892
Mendenhall, Margery I, 898
Mendenhall, Margery Beard I, 893
Mendenhall, Maria V, 189
Mendenhall, Mariam L. I, 860
Mendenhall, Mariam L. I, 893
Mendenhall, Mariam L. I, 895
Mendenhall, Marian Harland I, 637
Mendenhall, Maries I, 892
Mendenhall, Marietta I, 621
Mendenhall, Marietta I, 622
Mendenhall, Marietta M. I, 637
Mendenhall, Marion I, 637
Mendenhall, Marion I, 642
Mendenhall, Marion Harland I, 621
Mendenhall, Maris I, 509
Mendenhall, Maris I, 510
Mendenhall, Maris I, 788
Mendenhall, Maris I, 862
Mendenhall, Maris I, 881
Mendenhall, Maris I, 892
Mendenhall, Marium I, 829
Mendenhall, Marjary I, 847
Mendenhall, Marjery I, 726
Mendenhall, Marjory I, 860
Mendenhall, Marmaduke I, 561
Mendenhall, Marmaduke I, 787
Mendenhall, Marmaduke I, 827
Mendenhall, Marmaduke I, 1034
Mendenhall, Marmaduke I, 1044
Mendenhall, Marmaduke I, 1047
Mendenhall, Marmaduke I, 1049
Mendenhall, Marmaduke V, 98
Mendenhall, Marmaduke V, 852
Mendenhall, Marmaduke V, 859
Mendenhall, Marmaduke V, 862
Mendenhall, Marmaduke V, 884
Mendenhall, Marmaduke Hudson I, 788
Mendenhall, Marmaduke Hudson I, 829
Mendenhall, Marmaduke, Jr. V, 853
Mendenhall, Marmiduke I, 828
Mendenhall, Martain I, 788
Mendenhall, Martha I, 561
Mendenhall, Martha I, 621
Mendenhall, Martha I, 622
Mendenhall, Martha I, 637
Mendenhall, Martha I, 829
Mendenhall, Martha I, 860
Mendenhall, Martha I, 861
Mendenhall, Martha I, 873
Mendenhall, Martha I, 883
Mendenhall, Martha I, 892
Mendenhall, Martha I, 930
Mendenhall, Martha I, 1016
Mendenhall, Martha IV, 251
Mendenhall, Martha IV, 606
Mendenhall, Martha IV, 644
Mendenhall, Martha IV, 1068
Mendenhall, Martha IV, 1173
Mendenhall, Martha V, 570
Mendenhall, Martha V, 585
Mendenhall, Martha V, 851
Mendenhall, Martha V, 852
Mendenhall, Martha V, 853
Mendenhall, Martha V, 862
Mendenhall, Martha V, 863
Mendenhall, Martha VI, 400
Mendenhall, Martha VI, 422
Mendenhall, Martha VI, 470
Mendenhall, Martha VI, 517
Mendenhall, Martha VI, 534
Mendenhall, Martha VI, 753
Mendenhall, Martha Ann V, 585
Mendenhall, Martha B. I, 637
Mendenhall, Martha D. I, 561
Mendenhall, Martha D. I, 829
Mendenhall, Martha Elma V, 852
Mendenhall, Martha F. I, 829
Mendenhall, Martha Hiatt I, 893
Mendenhall, Martha T. M. I, 621
Mendenhall, Martin I, 827
Mendenhall, Martitia I, 637
Mendenhall, Mary I, 451
Mendenhall, Mary I, 509
Mendenhall, Mary I, 510
Mendenhall, Mary I, 527
Mendenhall, Mary I, 555
Mendenhall, Mary I, 561
Mendenhall, Mary I, 602
Mendenhall, Mary I, 607
Mendenhall, Mary I, 612
Mendenhall, Mary I, 618
Mendenhall, Mary I, 684
Mendenhall, Mary I, 687
Mendenhall, Mary I, 689
Mendenhall, Mary I, 726
Mendenhall, Mary I, 773
Mendenhall, Mary I, 787
Mendenhall, Mary I, 788
Mendenhall, Mary I, 812
Mendenhall, Mary I, 817
Mendenhall, Mary I, 818
Mendenhall, Mary I, 827
Mendenhall, Mary I, 828
Mendenhall, Mary I, 829
Mendenhall, Mary I, 832
Mendenhall, Mary I, 833
Mendenhall, Mary I, 843
Mendenhall, Mary I, 860
Mendenhall, Mary I, 861
Mendenhall, Mary I, 862
Mendenhall, Mary I, 890
Mendenhall, Mary I, 891
Mendenhall, Mary I, 892
Mendenhall, Mary I, 893
Mendenhall, Mary I, 913
Mendenhall, Mary I, 914
Mendenhall, Mary I, 921
Mendenhall, Mary I, 938
Mendenhall, Mary I, 1044
Mendenhall, Mary I, 1049
Mendenhall, Mary I Sup 1, 10
Mendenhall, Mary II, 595
Mendenhall, Mary II, 898
Mendenhall, Mary III, 362
Mendenhall, Mary IV, 250
Mendenhall, Mary V, 98
Mendenhall, Mary V, 188
Mendenhall, Mary V, 189
Mendenhall, Mary V, 754
Mendenhall, Mary V, 829
Mendenhall, Mary V, 852
Mendenhall, Mary V, 853
Mendenhall, Mary V, 862
Mendenhall, Mary V, 884
Mendenhall, Mary VI, 407
Mendenhall, Mary VI, 422
Mendenhall, Mary VI, 423
Mendenhall, Mary VI, 470
Mendenhall, Mary Ann I, 788
Mendenhall, Mary Ann I, 828
Mendenhall, Mary Ann I, 829
Mendenhall, Mary Ann I, 913
Mendenhall, Mary Ann I, 914
Mendenhall, Mary Ann Janney VI, 423
Mendenhall, Mary B. I, 893
Mendenhall, Mary Belle I, 930
Mendenhall, Mary Catharine V, 189
Mendenhall, Mary E. I, 807
Mendenhall, Mary E. I, 829
Mendenhall, Mary E. V, 189
Mendenhall, Mary Eliza I, 787
Mendenhall, Mary Elizabeth V, 98
Mendenhall, Mary J. I, 1108
Mendenhall, Mary Jane I, 828
Mendenhall, Mary Louisa V, 852
Mendenhall, Mary Myrtle I, 930
Mendenhall, Mary Roberts II, 800
Mendenhall, Mary Wilson VI, 517
Mendenhall, Mary, Jr. II, 898
Mendenhall, Maryann V, 189
Mendenhall, Maryann V, 197
Mendenhall, Mattie I, 872
Mendenhall, Mattie I, 893
Mendenhall, Mattie I, 946
Mendenhall, Mattie Gray I, 930
Mendenhall, Maurice V, 853
Mendenhall, Melisent I, 561
Mendenhall, Meriam I, 543
Mendenhall, Meriam I, 561
Mendenhall, Merium I, 466
Mendenhall, Merium I, 891
Mendenhall, Merriam I, 527
Mendenhall, Merriam I, 561
Mendenhall, Mildred I, 787
Mendenhall, Mildred B. I, 811
Mendenhall, Mildred B. I, 829
Mendenhall, Miles I, 710
Mendenhall, Miles I, 726
Mendenhall, Miles I, 860
Mendenhall, Miles I, 861
Mendenhall, Miles I, 893
Mendenhall, Milicent I, 607
Mendenhall, Milicent I, 805
Mendenhall, Milicent I, 828
Mendenhall, Milisent I, 602
Mendenhall, Milly V, 852
Mendenhall, Milly W. V, 255
Mendenhall, Milly W. V, 263
Mendenhall, Milton IV, 250
Mendenhall, Milton IV, 251
Mendenhall, Milton IV, 295
Mendenhall, Milton IV, 644
Mendenhall, Milton M. I, 893
Mendenhall, Minerva I, 788
Mendenhall, Minnie V, 853
Mendenhall, Miriam I, 509
Mendenhall, Miriam I, 561
Mendenhall, Miriam I, 595
Mendenhall, Miriam I, 602
Mendenhall, Miriam I, 619
Mendenhall, Miriam I, 684
Mendenhall, Miriam I, 688
Mendenhall, Miriam I, 726
Mendenhall, Miriam I, 787
Mendenhall, Miriam I, 796
Mendenhall, Miriam I, 827
Mendenhall, Miriam I, 828
Mendenhall, Miriam I, 829
Mendenhall, Miriam I, 835
Mendenhall, Miriam I, 885
Mendenhall, Miriam I, 891
Mendenhall, Miriam I, 913
Mendenhall, Miriam IV, 48
Mendenhall, Miriam IV, 1329
Mendenhall, Miriam V, 754
Mendenhall, Miriam V, 756
Mendenhall, Miriam V, 757
Mendenhall, Miriam C. IV, 1329
Mendenhall, Miriam Launa I, 622
Mendenhall, Miriam M. I, 637
Mendenhall, Mirriam I, 787
Mendenhall, Mordacai I, 408
Mendenhall, Mordacai I, 483
Mendenhall, Mordacai I, 788
Mendenhall, Mordai I, 561
Mendenhall, Mordaycai I, 788
Mendenhall, Mordeca I, 966
Mendenhall, Mordecai I, 343
Mendenhall, Mordecai I, 408
Mendenhall, Mordecai I, 470
Mendenhall, Mordecai I, 483
Mendenhall, Mordecai I, 487
Mendenhall, Mordecai I, 561
Mendenhall, Mordecai I, 684
Mendenhall, Mordecai I, 827
Mendenhall, Mordecai I, 828
Mendenhall, Mordecai I, 861
Mendenhall, Mordecai I, 862
Mendenhall, Mordecai I, 891
Mendenhall, Mordecai I, 892
Mendenhall, Mordecai I, 893
Mendenhall, Mordecai I, 898
Mendenhall, Mordecai I, 1101
Mendenhall, Mordecai I, 1105
Mendenhall, Mordecai I, 1108
Mendenhall, Mordecai I, 1125
Mendenhall, Mordecai I, 1126
Mendenhall, Mordecai I, 1132
Mendenhall, Mordecai V, 98
Mendenhall, Mordecai VI, 422
Mendenhall, Mordecai, Jr. I, 112

denhall, Mordecai, Sr. I, 1126
denhall, Mordica I, 530
denhall, Mordica I, 561
denhall, Mordica I, 726
ndenhall, Mordica I, 892
denhall, Mordicai I, 509
ndenhall, Mordicai I, 510
ndenhall, Mordicai I, 561
ndenhall, Mordicai I, 827
ndenhall, Mordicai I, 860
ndenhall, Mordicai I, 861
ndenhall, Mordicai I, 892
ndenhall, Mordicai I, 1071
ndenhall, Mordicha I, 509
ndenhall, Mordicha I, 560
ndenhall, Mordicha I, 561
ndenhall, Moris V, 516
ndenhall, Morrow W. V, 189
ndenhall, Moses I, 509
ndenhall, Moses I, 549
ndenhall, Moses I, 560
ndenhall, Moses I, 561
ndenhall, Moses I, 570
ndenhall, Moses I, 577
ndenhall, Moses I, 600
ndenhall, Moses I, 602
ndenhall, Moses I, 603
ndenhall, Moses I, 605
ndenhall, Moses I, 607
ndenhall, Moses I, 626
ndenhall, Moses I, 773
ndenhall, Moses I, 787
ndenhall, Moses I, 788
ndenhall, Moses I, 827
ndenhall, Moses I, 828
ndenhall, Moses I, 847
ndenhall, Moses I, 861
ndenhall, Moses I, 892
ndenhall, Moses I, 1071
ndenhall, Moses IV, 644
ndenhall, Moses IV, 1329
ndenhall, Moses V, 263
ndenhall, Moses V, 307
ndenhall, Moses V, 349
ndenhall, Moses VI, 422
ndenhall, Moses VI, 423
ndenhall, Moses Craven I, 509
ndenhall, Moses H. I, 828
ndenhall, Moses H. I, 829
ndenhall, Moses H. I, 913
ndenhall, Moses H. I, 914
ndenhall, Moses T. IV, 1329
ndenhall, Moses, Jr. I, 827
ndenhall, Myrtle A. I, 946
ndenhall, Nancy I, 561
ndenhall, Nancy I, 602
ndenhall, Nancy I, 860
ndenhall, Nancy I, 862
ndenhall, Nancy I, 874
ndenhall, Nancy I, 893
ndenhall, Nancy I, 927
ndenhall, Nancy I, 930
ndenhall, Nancy I, 1108
ndenhall, Nancy I, 1114
ndenhall, Nancy I, 1126
ndenhall, Nancy V, 852
ndenhall, Nancy V, 884
ndenhall, Nancy Carlick I, 892
ndenhall, Nancy J. I, 893
ndenhall, Nancy Jane I, 933
ndenhall, Nancy L. I, 829
ndenhall, Naomi I, 1034
ndenhall, Naomi IV, 250
ndenhall, Naomi IV, 251
ndenhall, Naomi IV, 1052
ndenhall, Naomi IV, 1068
ndenhall, Narciss I, 893
ndenhall, Narcissa I, 893
ndenhall, Narcissa I, 896
ndenhall, Narcissa I, 1108
ndenhall, Nathan I, 321
ndenhall, Nathan I, 510
ndenhall, Nathan I, 788
ndenhall, Nathan I, 792
ndenhall, Nathan I, 814
ndenhall, Nathan I, 827
ndenhall, Nathan I, 828
ndenhall, Nathan I, 860
ndenhall, Nathan I, 862
ndenhall, Nathan I, 880
ndenhall, Nathan I, 892
ndenhall, Nathan II, 595
ndenhall, Nathan V, 188
ndenhall, Nathan V, 189
ndenhall, Nathan V, 516
ndenhall, Nathan V, 585
ndenhall, Nathan V, 833
ndenhall, Nathan C. I, 861
Mendenhall, Nathan Lindley I, 509
Mendenhall, Nathan Marshall I, 788
Mendenhall, Nathan S. V, 835
Mendenhall, Nathan S. V, 852
Mendenhall, Nathaniel I, 860
Mendenhall, Nereus I, 621
Mendenhall, Nereus I, 726
Mendenhall, Nereus I, 737
Mendenhall, Nereus I, 788
Mendenhall, Nereus I, 829
Mendenhall, Nereus Franklin I, 930
Mendenhall, Nereus H. I, 860
Mendenhall, Nettie V, 189
Mendenhall, Obadiah I, 861
Mendenhall, Obadiah I, 993
Mendenhall, Obadiah V, 50
Mendenhall, Obadiah V, 98
Mendenhall, Obadiah V, 188
Mendenhall, Obadiah V, 189
Mendenhall, Obadiah V, 196
Mendenhall, Obediah I, 892
Mendenhall, Obediah V, 98
Mendenhall, Obidiah V, 98
Mendenhall, Olive I, 862
Mendenhall, Olive I, 892
Mendenhall, Olive I, 901
Mendenhall, Olive V, 516
Mendenhall, Olive V, 565
Mendenhall, Olive V, 567
Mendenhall, Olive V, 585
Mendenhall, Omar IV, 1329
Mendenhall, Oriana I, 621
Mendenhall, Oriana I, 788
Mendenhall, Oriana R. I, 829
Mendenhall, Orianna I, 829
Mendenhall, Orianna P. I, 726
Mendenhall, Orianna R. I, 726
Mendenhall, Orianna R. I, 737
Mendenhall, Orpah IV, 644
Mendenhall, Orpha IV, 178
Mendenhall, Orpha IV, 250
Mendenhall, Orval I. V, 189
Mendenhall, Orval J. V, 189
Mendenhall, Ottis I, 946
Mendenhall, Ottis E. I, 946
Mendenhall, Ottis Earl I, 930
Mendenhall, Parhaltha IV, 1173
Mendenhall, Paris I, 828
Mendenhall, Parris I, 827
Mendenhall, Patty S. I, 860
Mendenhall, Pearl L. I, 829
Mendenhall, Pearl L. I, 843
Mendenhall, Peggy V, 852
Mendenhall, Penick IV, 251
Mendenhall, Peninah IV, 251
Mendenhall, Pennell IV, 644
Mendenhall, Pennock IV, 250
Mendenhall, Pennock IV, 644
Mendenhall, Percy Albright I, 893
Mendenhall, Permela I, 860
Mendenhall, Permelia I, 828
Mendenhall, Pernatha IV, 1173
Mendenhall, Peter I, 861
Mendenhall, Peter V, 307
Mendenhall, Peter V, 349
Mendenhall, Pheba V, 789
Mendenhall, Phebe I, 460
Mendenhall, Phebe I, 470
Mendenhall, Phebe I, 474
Mendenhall, Phebe I, 483
Mendenhall, Phebe I, 510
Mendenhall, Phebe I, 530
Mendenhall, Phebe I, 560
Mendenhall, Phebe I, 561
Mendenhall, Phebe I, 570
Mendenhall, Phebe I, 787
Mendenhall, Phebe I, 788
Mendenhall, Phebe I, 792
Mendenhall, Phebe I, 805
Mendenhall, Phebe I, 814
Mendenhall, Phebe I, 827
Mendenhall, Phebe I, 828
Mendenhall, Phebe I, 845
Mendenhall, Phebe I, 847
Mendenhall, Phebe I, 861
Mendenhall, Phebe I, 862
Mendenhall, Phebe I, 878
Mendenhall, Phebe I, 890
Mendenhall, Phebe I, 891
Mendenhall, Phebe I, 892
Mendenhall, Phebe I, 899
Mendenhall, Phebe I, 911
Mendenhall, Phebe I, 913
Mendenhall, Phebe I, 1044
Mendenhall, Phebe I, 1049
Mendenhall, Phebe I, 1101
Mendenhall, Phebe I, 1108
Mendenhall, Phebe I, 1125
Mendenhall, Phebe I, 1126
Mendenhall, Phebe IV, 250
Mendenhall, Phebe IV, 251
Mendenhall, Phebe IV, 644
Mendenhall, Phebe IV, 667
Mendenhall, Phebe V, 98
Mendenhall, Phebe V, 753
Mendenhall, Phebe V, 754
Mendenhall, Phebe V, 755
Mendenhall, Phebe VI, 422
Mendenhall, Phebe VI, 423
Mendenhall, Phebe C. I, 684
Mendenhall, Phebe E. V, 921
Mendenhall, Phebe Fraser I, 893
Mendenhall, Phebe P. I, 818
Mendenhall, Phebe P. I, 829
Mendenhall, Phebe Paulina I, 788
Mendenhall, Philena L. I, 893
Mendenhall, Philip Ham I, 827
Mendenhall, Phineas I, 827
Mendenhall, Phineas I, 1041
Mendenhall, Phineas V, 754
Mendenhall, Phinehas I, 510
Mendenhall, Phinehas I, 561
Mendenhall, Phinehas I, 827
Mendenhall, Phinehas I, 1034
Mendenhall, Phinehas I, 1049
Mendenhall, Polly I, 561
Mendenhall, Polly I, 860
Mendenhall, Polly I, 892
Mendenhall, Polly I, 893
Mendenhall, Polly V, 307
Mendenhall, Polly V, 349
Mendenhall, Polly V, 794
Mendenhall, Porris I, 787
Mendenhall, Priscilla I, 684
Mendenhall, Priscilla I, 805
Mendenhall, Priscilla I, 828
Mendenhall, Prose I, 1044
Mendenhall, R. Elizabeth I, 922
Mendenhall, Rachel I, 470
Mendenhall, Rachel I, 509
Mendenhall, Rachel I, 554
Mendenhall, Rachel I, 561
Mendenhall, Rachel I, 578
Mendenhall, Rachel I, 602
Mendenhall, Rachel I, 605
Mendenhall, Rachel I, 606
Mendenhall, Rachel I, 607
Mendenhall, Rachel I, 622
Mendenhall, Rachel I, 726
Mendenhall, Rachel I, 787
Mendenhall, Rachel I, 788
Mendenhall, Rachel I, 800
Mendenhall, Rachel I, 810
Mendenhall, Rachel I, 827
Mendenhall, Rachel I, 828
Mendenhall, Rachel I, 847
Mendenhall, Rachel I, 860
Mendenhall, Rachel I, 861
Mendenhall, Rachel I, 862
Mendenhall, Rachel I, 873
Mendenhall, Rachel I, 892
Mendenhall, Rachel I, 893
Mendenhall, Rachel IV, 250
Mendenhall, Rachel IV, 251
Mendenhall, Rachel IV, 1068
Mendenhall, Rachel IV, 1069
Mendenhall, Rachel V, 98
Mendenhall, Rachel V, 160
Mendenhall, Rachel V, 161
Mendenhall, Rachel V, 189
Mendenhall, Rachel V, 732
Mendenhall, Rachel V, 751
Mendenhall, Rachel V, 753
Mendenhall, Rachel V, 754
Mendenhall, Rachel V, 774
Mendenhall, Rachel V, 800
Mendenhall, Rachel V, 829
Mendenhall, Rachel E. I, 602
Mendenhall, Rachel E. I, 922
Mendenhall, Raymond III, 225
Mendenhall, Raymond E. III, 150
Mendenhall, Raymond E. III, 225
Mendenhall, Rebeca I, 860
Mendenhall, Rebecca I, 711
Mendenhall, Rebecca I, 726
Mendenhall, Rebecca I, 805
Mendenhall, Rebecca I, 827
Mendenhall, Rebecca I, 828
Mendenhall, Rebecca I, 885
Mendenhall, Rebecca I, 892
Mendenhall, Rebecca I, 893
Mendenhall, Rebecca I, 966
Mendenhall, Rebecca I, 993
Mendenhall, Rebecca I, 1105
Mendenhall, Rebecca IV, 250
Mendenhall, Rebecca IV, 833
Mendenhall, Rebecca IV, 851
Mendenhall, Rebecca V, 98
Mendenhall, Rebecca V, 189
Mendenhall, Rebecca V, 585
Mendenhall, Rebecca Jane I, 621
Mendenhall, Rebecca Menhall I, 843
Mendenhall, Rebeccah I, 788
Mendenhall, Rebeckah I, 509
Mendenhall, Rebeckah I, 788
Mendenhall, Rebeckah I, 861
Mendenhall, Rebeckah I, 862
Mendenhall, Rebeckah I, 892
Mendenhall, Rebeckah V, 188
Mendenhall, Rettie R. I, 893
Mendenhall, Rhoda I, 684
Mendenhall, Rhoda I, 787
Mendenhall, Rhoda I, 788
Mendenhall, Rhoda I, 828
Mendenhall, Rhoda I, 842
Mendenhall, Rhoda I, 860
Mendenhall, Rhoda I, 1108
Mendenhall, Rhoda V, 736
Mendenhall, Rhoda V, 754
Mendenhall, Rhoda C. I, 620
Mendenhall, Rhoda C. I, 808
Mendenhall, Rhoda C. I, 829
Mendenhall, Rhoda Coffin I, 620
Mendenhall, Richard I, 509
Mendenhall, Richard I, 560
Mendenhall, Richard I, 561
Mendenhall, Richard I, 577
Mendenhall, Richard I, 726
Mendenhall, Richard I, 788
Mendenhall, Richard I, 813
Mendenhall, Richard I, 827
Mendenhall, Richard I, 828
Mendenhall, Richard I, 829
Mendenhall, Richard I, 833
Mendenhall, Richard I, 847
Mendenhall, Richard I, 861
Mendenhall, Richard I, 891
Mendenhall, Richard I, 892
Mendenhall, Richard I, 993
Mendenhall, Richard I Sup 1, 10
Mendenhall, Richard V, 98
Mendenhall, Richard V, 188
Mendenhall, Richard V, 189
Mendenhall, Richard V, 307
Mendenhall, Richard V, 349
Mendenhall, Richard V, 469
Mendenhall, Richard V, 516
Mendenhall, Richard V, 789
Mendenhall, Richard Junius I, 788
Mendenhall, Richard Junius I, 829
Mendenhall, Richard L. I, 829
Mendenhall, Richard, Jr. V, 189
Mendenhall, Robert I, 787
Mendenhall, Robert I, 827
Mendenhall, Robert I, 1044
Mendenhall, Robert I, 1049
Mendenhall, Robert I, 1108
Mendenhall, Robert I, 1125
Mendenhall, Robert E. I, 861
Mendenhall, Robert Earl I, 622
Mendenhall, Robert Earl I, 637
Mendenhall, Robert J. V, 189
Mendenhall, Rosanna I, 861
Mendenhall, Rosanna I, 862
Mendenhall, Rosanna I, 891
Mendenhall, Rowena V, 585
Mendenhall, Rudduck I, 861
Mendenhall, Rudduck I, 862
Mendenhall, Rudduck I, 898
Mendenhall, Rudick I, 862
Mendenhall, Rusannah I, 893
Mendenhall, Ruth I, 510
Mendenhall, Ruth I, 593
Mendenhall, Ruth I, 595
Mendenhall, Ruth I, 602
Mendenhall, Ruth I, 621
Mendenhall, Ruth I, 622
Mendenhall, Ruth I, 787
Mendenhall, Ruth I, 788
Mendenhall, Ruth I, 801
Mendenhall, Ruth I, 827
Mendenhall, Ruth I, 828
Mendenhall, Ruth I, 861
Mendenhall, Ruth I, 870
Mendenhall, Ruth I, 874
Mendenhall, Ruth I, 892
Mendenhall, Ruth I, 893
Mendenhall, Ruth I, 1108
Mendenhall, Ruth I, 1126
Mendenhall, Ruth V, 98
Mendenhall, Ruth V, 151
Mendenhall, Ruth V, 188
Mendenhall, Ruth V, 189
Mendenhall, Ruth V, 205
Mendenhall, Ruth V, 209
Mendenhall, Ruth V, 754
Mendenhall, Ruth V, 755
Mendenhall, Ruth V, 774
Mendenhall, Ruth VI, 422
Mendenhall, Ruth VI, 423
Mendenhall, Ruth VI, 534
Mendenhall, Ruth VI, 649
Mendenhall, Ruth VI, 676
Mendenhall, Ruth VI, 679
Mendenhall, Ruth VI, 764
Mendenhall, Ruth Worth I, 637
Mendenhall, S. Willard I, 946
Mendenhall, Sally I, 862
Mendenhall, Samuel I, 726
Mendenhall, Samuel I, 788
Mendenhall, Samuel I, 860
Mendenhall, Samuel I, 861
Mendenhall, Samuel I, 874
Mendenhall, Samuel I, 892
Mendenhall, Samuel I, 893
Mendenhall, Samuel II, 395
Mendenhall, Samuel V, 189
Mendenhall, Samuel VI, 422
Mendenhall, Samuel VI, 423
Mendenhall, Samuel H. I, 787
Mendenhall, Samuel H. I, 829
Mendenhall, Samuel N. I, 829
Mendenhall, Samuel Thompson V, 852
Mendenhall, Sarah I, 509
Mendenhall, Sarah I, 510
Mendenhall, Sarah I, 549
Mendenhall, Sarah I, 561
Mendenhall, Sarah I, 602
Mendenhall, Sarah I, 637
Mendenhall, Sarah I, 787
Mendenhall, Sarah I, 788
Mendenhall, Sarah I, 800
Mendenhall, Sarah I, 812
Mendenhall, Sarah I, 813
Mendenhall, Sarah I, 827
Mendenhall, Sarah I, 828
Mendenhall, Sarah I, 829
Mendenhall, Sarah I, 847
Mendenhall, Sarah I, 861
Mendenhall, Sarah I, 862
Mendenhall, Sarah I, 869
Mendenhall, Sarah I, 890
Mendenhall, Sarah I, 892
Mendenhall, Sarah I, 893
Mendenhall, Sarah I, 896
Mendenhall, Sarah I, 993
Mendenhall, Sarah I, 1108
Mendenhall, Sarah I, 1126
Mendenhall, Sarah I, 1135
Mendenhall, Sarah II, 595
Mendenhall, Sarah IV, 250
Mendenhall, Sarah IV, 251
Mendenhall, Sarah IV, 311
Mendenhall, Sarah IV, 313
Mendenhall, Sarah IV, 614
Mendenhall, Sarah IV, 644
Mendenhall, Sarah IV, 810
Mendenhall, Sarah IV, 833
Mendenhall, Sarah IV, 843
Mendenhall, Sarah V, 98
Mendenhall, Sarah V, 151
Mendenhall, Sarah V, 188
Mendenhall, Sarah V, 189
Mendenhall, Sarah V, 196
Mendenhall, Sarah V, 812
Mendenhall, Sarah V, 815
Mendenhall, Sarah V, 816
Mendenhall, Sarah V, 884
Mendenhall, Sarah A. V, 755
Mendenhall, Sarah Ann IV, 250
Mendenhall, Sarah Annie IV, 251
Mendenhall, Sarah Elizabeth I, 622
Mendenhall, Sarah Eva V, 853
Mendenhall, Sarah J. I, 860
Mendenhall, Sarah J. IV, 295
Mendenhall, Sarah J. V, 516
Mendenhall, Sarah Jane I, 483
Mendenhall, Sarah Jane I, 816
Mendenhall, Sarah Jane I, 828
Mendenhall, Sarah Jane IV, 250
Mendenhall, Sarah Jane IV, 251
Mendenhall, Sarah Jane V, 516
Mendenhall, Sarah Selinah I, 605
Mendenhall, Sarah Selinah I, 607
Mendenhall, Sarahann IV, 644
Mendenhall, Sarry I, 559
Mendenhall, Sarry I, 561
Mendenhall, Semira I, 862
Mendenhall, Semira H. I, 804
Mendenhall, Semira H. I, 829
Mendenhall, Semira Harriet I, 788

Mendenhall, Seth I, 510
Mendenhall, Seth I, 861
Mendenhall, Seth I, 862
Mendenhall, Seth I, 892
Mendenhall, Shirley Nathaniel I, 621
Mendenhall, Shirley Nathaniel I, 637
Mendenhall, Shirley Nathaniel I, 642
Mendenhall, Sidney I, 860
Mendenhall, Sina I, 861
Mendenhall, Sinia I, 893
Mendenhall, Sith I, 788
Mendenhall, Solomon I, 470
Mendenhall, Solomon I, 483
Mendenhall, Solomon I, 862
Mendenhall, Stanton I, 860
Mendenhall, Stanton I, 893
Mendenhall, Stephen I, 509
Mendenhall, Stephen I, 510
Mendenhall, Stephen I, 559
Mendenhall, Stephen I, 560
Mendenhall, Stephen I, 561
Mendenhall, Stephen I, 569
Mendenhall, Stephen I, 773
Mendenhall, Stephen I, 788
Mendenhall, Stephen I, 827
Mendenhall, Stephen I, 828
Mendenhall, Stephen I, 860
Mendenhall, Stephen I, 862
Mendenhall, Stephen I, 892
Mendenhall, Stephen I, 1066
Mendenhall, Stephen I, 1071
Mendenhall, Stephen I, 1096
Mendenhall, Stephen I, 1108
Mendenhall, Stephen I, 1126
Mendenhall, Stephen II, 395
Mendenhall, Stephen IV, 644
Mendenhall, Stephen V, 413
Mendenhall, Stephen V, 516
Mendenhall, Stephen V, 585
Mendenhall, Stephen V, 815
Mendenhall, Stephen D. IV, 644
Mendenhall, Stephen G. I, 828
Mendenhall, Stephen G. I, 869
Mendenhall, Stephen G. I, 892
Mendenhall, Stephen, Jr. I, 1071
Mendenhall, Susan III, 225
Mendenhall, Susan IV, 644
Mendenhall, Susan V, 725
Mendenhall, Susan V, 754
Mendenhall, Susan G. I, 818
Mendenhall, Susan G. I, 829
Mendenhall, Susan Giluann I, 788
Mendenhall, Susan P. IV, 644
Mendenhall, Susana V, 754
Mendenhall, Susanah I, 788
Mendenhall, Susanah I, 892
Mendenhall, Susanna I, 509
Mendenhall, Susanna I, 561
Mendenhall, Susanna I, 571
Mendenhall, Susanna I, 787
Mendenhall, Susanna I, 788
Mendenhall, Susanna I, 810
Mendenhall, Susanna I, 827
Mendenhall, Susanna I, 860
Mendenhall, Susanna I, 874
Mendenhall, Susanna I, 892
Mendenhall, Susanna I, 893
Mendenhall, Susanna I, 1126
Mendenhall, Susanna IV, 48
Mendenhall, Susanna V, 754
Mendenhall, Susanna V, 767
Mendenhall, Susannah I, 861
Mendenhall, Susannah I, 893
Mendenhall, Susannah I, 1108
Mendenhall, Susannah I, 1125
Mendenhall, Susannah V, 723
Mendenhall, Susannah V, 756
Mendenhall, Susannah V, 789
Mendenhall, Susie Withrow V, 853
Mendenhall, Syntha I, 889
Mendenhall, Syntha I, 893
Mendenhall, T. S. V, 853
Mendenhall, Tamar I, 827
Mendenhall, Tamar V, 754
Mendenhall, Tamar V, 767
Mendenhall, Tamer I, 510
Mendenhall, Tamer I, 827
Mendenhall, Tamer V, 98
Mendenhall, Tamer V, 754
Mendenhall, Tamer V, 763
Mendenhall, Temple I, 861
Mendenhall, Temple V, 307
Mendenhall, Temple V, 349
Mendenhall, Thaddeus V, 98
Mendenhall, Thaddeus V, 754
Mendenhall, Thadeus V, 754
Mendenhall, Theodore S. V, 853
Mendenhall, Thirza IV, 250
Mendenhall, Thirza IV, 251
Mendenhall, Thirza IV, 1068
Mendenhall, Thomas I, 509
Mendenhall, Thomas I, 510
Mendenhall, Thomas I, 560
Mendenhall, Thomas I, 711
Mendenhall, Thomas I, 726
Mendenhall, Thomas I, 788
Mendenhall, Thomas I, 827
Mendenhall, Thomas I, 861
Mendenhall, Thomas I, 862
Mendenhall, Thomas I, 891
Mendenhall, Thomas I, 892
Mendenhall, Thomas I, 893
Mendenhall, Thomas II, 394
Mendenhall, Thomas II, 595
Mendenhall, Thomas IV, 1068
Mendenhall, Thomas Jones I, 766
Mendenhall, Thos. I, 570
Mendenhall, Vashti I, 561
Mendenhall, Vashti I, 602
Mendenhall, Vesti I, 607
Mendenhall, W. D. I, 637
Mendenhall, W. W. I, 637
Mendenhall, Walter IV, 1329
Mendenhall, Walter H. IV, 1305
Mendenhall, Walter H. IV, 1329
Mendenhall, Walter Leonidas I, 621
Mendenhall, Walter Leonidus I, 637
Mendenhall, Walter S. V, 921
Mendenhall, Walter W. I, 629
Mendenhall, Walter W. I, 637
Mendenhall, Walter W. IV, 1329
Mendenhall, Walter William I, 622
Mendenhall, Warner I, 470
Mendenhall, Warner I, 483
Mendenhall, Warner I, 862
Mendenhall, Warner I, 892
Mendenhall, Warren Orestes IV, 1329
Mendenhall, Wd. Ruth VI, 407
Mendenhall, Wd. Ruth VI, 422
Mendenhall, Wd. Ruth VI, 753
Mendenhall, Wd. Sarah Eva V, 853
Mendenhall, Wd. Sarah Eva V, 856
Mendenhall, Widow Beulah VI, 521
Mendenhall, Widow Beulah VI, 533
Mendenhall, Widow Deborah I, 828
Mendenhall, Widow Mary I, 571
Mendenhall, Widow Mary I, 827
Mendenhall, Widow Rachel I, 561
Mendenhall, Widow Ruth VI, 534
Mendenhall, Widow Ruth VI, 661
Mendenhall, William I, 787
Mendenhall, William I, 788
Mendenhall, William I, 805
Mendenhall, William I, 827
Mendenhall, William I, 828
Mendenhall, William I, 861
Mendenhall, William I, 862
Mendenhall, William I, 891
Mendenhall, William I, 893
Mendenhall, William I, 966
Mendenhall, William I, 1126
Mendenhall, William IV, 48
Mendenhall, William IV, 251
Mendenhall, William IV, 833
Mendenhall, William IV, 1068
Mendenhall, William IV, 1173
Mendenhall, William V, 98
Mendenhall, William V, 160
Mendenhall, William V, 188
Mendenhall, William V, 189
Mendenhall, William V, 204
Mendenhall, William V, 206
Mendenhall, William V, 263
Mendenhall, William V, 754
Mendenhall, William VI, 470
Mendenhall, William VI, 534
Mendenhall, William A. V, 189
Mendenhall, William Alen I, 787
Mendenhall, William Blair I, 622
Mendenhall, William C. I, 1108
Mendenhall, William D. I, 621
Mendenhall, William D. I, 622
Mendenhall, William D. I, 637
Mendenhall, William D. I, 893
Mendenhall, William Delacy I, 622
Mendenhall, William F. I, 602
Mendenhall, William H. V, 189
Mendenhall, William H. V, 853
Mendenhall, William Hadley V, 852
Mendenhall, William Hadley V, 853
Mendenhall, William Hadley V, 856
Mendenhall, William Ira I, 893
Mendenhall, William J. I, 860
Mendenhall, William P. I, 829
Mendenhall, Willie Blair I, 637
Mendenhall, Wm. II, 595
Mendenhall, Wm. IV, 644
Mendenhall, Wm. IV, 833
Mendenhall, Wm. IV, 851
Mendenhall, Wm. V, 209
Mendenhall, Wm. V, 754
Mendenhall, Wm. A. I, 861
Mendenhall, Wm. Armfield V, 884
Mendenhall, Wm. D. I, 622
Mendenhall, Wm. E. V, 585
Mendenhall, Wm. Franklin I, 621
Mendenhall, Wm. O. V, 696
Mendenhall, Wm. Orville V, 696
Mendenhall, Zadoc I, 470
Mendenhall, Zadoc I, 862
Mendenhall, Zebulon V, 188
Mendenhall, Zebulon V, 189
Mendenhall, Zedok I, 860
Mendenhall, Zenas I, 860
Mendenhall, Zenis R. IV, 1216
Mendenhall, Zenos I, 893
Mendenhall, Ziba I, 861
Mendenhall, Zodack I, 892
Mendenhall, Zodak I, 483
Mendenhall, Zodak I, 787
Mendenhall, Zodak I, 893
Mendenhall, Zodoc I, 470
Mendenhall, Zodoc I, 483
Mendenhall, Zodock I, 483
Mendenyall, Hannah I, 1109
Mendilall, Rebecca I, 962
Mendilall, Rebecca I, 966
Mendinggall, Mordica VI, 390
Mendinghall, Agnes VI, 422
Mendinghall, Alice I, 1125
Mendinghall, Alice I, 1126
Mendinghall, Amos V, 82
Mendinghall, Ann II, 595
Mendinghall, Ann V, 82
Mendinghall, Benjamin I, 102
Mendinghall, Charity I, 408
Mendinghall, Charles W. IV, 1068
Mendinghall, David V, 82
Mendinghall, Denny V, 82
Mendinghall, Edith V, 483
Mendinghall, Edith V, 516
Mendinghall, Eli V, 82
Mendinghall, Elizabeth V, 82
Mendinghall, Elizabeth V, 475
Mendinghall, Elizabeth V, 516
Mendinghall, Enoch V, 82
Mendinghall, Esther V, 82
Mendinghall, George IV, 739
Mendinghall, Griffith II, 595
Mendinghall, Hannah I, 407
Mendinghall, Hannah I, 408
Mendinghall, Hannah II, 595
Mendinghall, Hannah IV, 1068
Mendinghall, Hannah V, 81
Mendinghall, Hannah V, 82
Mendinghall, Harriet V, 82
Mendinghall, Isaac V, 82
Mendinghall, Issachar V, 82
Mendinghall, James VI, 385
Mendinghall, James VI, 422
Mendinghall, Jane IV, 100
Mendinghall, Jesse V, 82
Mendinghall, John IV, 1068
Mendinghall, John VI, 422
Mendinghall, John H. IV, 833
Mendinghall, Joseph V, 789
Mendinghall, Lydia VI, 422
Mendinghall, Lydiann IV, 1068
Mendinghall, Martha IV, 1068
Mendinghall, Martha V, 82
Mendinghall, Martha VI, 422
Mendinghall, Mary V, 82
Mendinghall, Mary VI, 422
Mendinghall, Mordacai I, 407
Mendinghall, Mordacai I, 408
Mendinghall, Mordecai I, 1126
Mendinghall, Mordecai V, 81
Mendinghall, Mordecai, Jr. I, 1125
Mendinghall, Phineas V, 82
Mendinghall, Rebecca V, 82
Mendinghall, Richard V, 475
Mendinghall, Richard V, 516
Mendinghall, Robert V, 82
Mendinghall, Rosanna V, 82
Mendinghall, Ruth V, 81
Mendinghall, Ruth V, 98
Mendinghall, Samuel V, 82
Mendinghall, Sarah I, 993
Mendinghall, Sarah II, 595
Mendinghall, Sarah IV, 833
Mendinghall, Sarah V, 82
Mendinghall, Stephen V, 413
Mendinghall, Thomas II, 595
Mendinghall, Thomas IV, 1068
Mendinghall, Thomas V, 82
Mendinghall, Wm. II, 595
Mendinghall, Zebulum V, 82
Mendingham, Ann V, 516
Mendingham, Edith V, 516
Mendingham, Elizabeth V, 516
Mendingham, Hiram V, 516
Mendingham, Moris V, 516
Mendingham, Nathan V, 516
Mendingham, Olive V, 516
Mendinhall, Amos VI, 423
Mendinhall, Ann VI, 423
Mendinhall, Hannah II, 616
Mendinhall, Jacob VI, 423
Mendinhall, James VI, 423
Mendinhall, Martha VI, 422
Mendinhall, Miriam I, 827
Mendinhall, Moses VI, 422
Mendinhall, Phebe VI, 423
Mendinhall, Samuel VI, 423
Menefee, Immogene V, 1010
Menefee, Mary E. V, 1010
Menefee, Maud V, 1010
Meng, Dorothea II, 811
Menhall, Rebecca I, 827
Mennell, Edward N. III, 117
Mennell, Edward Newman III, 225
Mennell, Henry T. III, 225
Mennell, Mabel L. III, 117
Mennell, Mabel Livingston III, 225
Mennell, Maria B. III, 225
Mennell, Shirley III, 225
Mennis, Frances C. VI, 962
Mennis, Nancey VI, 985
Mente, William V, 349
Mentee, Mary V, 98
Menzies, John VI, 961
Menzies, Mary VI, 961
Meradith, Charity D. I, 894
Meramoon, Benjamin I, 246
Meramoon, Jesse I, 246
Merany, Rachel I, 815
Merany, Rachel I, 826
Mercer, ??? IV, 979
Mercer, Abraham IV, 878
Mercer, Abraham IV, 1173
Mercer, Abraham IV, 1216
Mercer, Agnes Deborah IV, 1040
Mercer, Alice IV, 635
Mercer, Alice IV, 637
Mercer, Alice IV, 645
Mercer, Alice IV, 697
Mercer, Alice IV, 740
Mercer, Andrew II, 712
Mercer, Ann II, 821
Mercer, Ann IV, 605
Mercer, Ann IV, 645
Mercer, Ann VI, 470
Mercer, Ann VI, 524
Mercer, Anna IV, 740
Mercer, Anna V, 263
Mercer, Anna V, 349
Mercer, Anna M. V, 627
Mercer, Anna M. V, 647
Mercer, Anne IV, 629
Mercer, Anne IV, 645
Mercer, Arthur IV, 740
Mercer, B. C. IV, 251
Mercer, Belle Pile IV, 251
Mercer, Beulah IV, 878
Mercer, Caleb IV, 878
Mercer, Caleb VI, 423
Mercer, Catharine V, 349
Mercer, Charity IV, 645
Mercer, Charity IV, 833
Mercer, Charity IV, 878
Mercer, Charity, Jr. IV, 878
Mercer, Charles II, 898
Mercer, Charles H. II, 898
Mercer, Charlie V, 460
Mercer, Chas. II, 809
Mercer, Chas. H. II, 898
Mercer, Cyrus IV, 645
Mercer, Daniel IV, 48
Mercer, Daniel IV, 100
Mercer, Daniel IV, 634
Mercer, Daniel IV, 635
Mercer, Daniel IV, 637
Mercer, Daniel IV, 645
Mercer, Daniel IV, 654
Mercer, Daniel IV, 697
Mercer, Daniel IV, 759
Mercer, Daniel IV, 833
Mercer, Daniel IV, 878
Mercer, David IV, 605
Mercer, David IV, 645
Mercer, David IV, 971
Mercer, David IV, 979
Mercer, Deborah E. IV, 804
Mercer, Deborah E. IV, 833
Mercer, Edward VI, 423
Mercer, Eliphaz II, 712
Mercer, Eliphaz II, 755
Mercer, Elizabeth II, 800
Mercer, Elizabeth II, 809
Mercer, Elizabeth IV, 48
Mercer, Elizabeth IV, 60
Mercer, Elizabeth IV, 342
Mercer, Elizabeth IV, 346
Mercer, Elizabeth R. II, 712
Mercer, Elizabeth R. II, 755
Mercer, Emily IV, 740
Mercer, Emily IV, 759
Mercer, Emily IV, 1106
Mercer, Emily IV, 1110
Mercer, Emley Schooly IV, 645
Mercer, Eunice Emily V, 263
Mercer, Eva E. II, 898
Mercer, Eva M. II, 898
Mercer, Eva M. II, 904
Mercer, Faithful IV, 645
Mercer, Faithful IV, 649
Mercer, Fay V, 460
Mercer, George IV, 645
Mercer, George IV, 833
Mercer, George IV, 878
Mercer, George V, 116
Mercer, Gladys Alberta IV, 104
Mercer, Hannah IV, 100
Mercer, Hannah IV, 130
Mercer, Hannah IV, 645
Mercer, Hannah IV, 649
Mercer, Hannah IV, 654
Mercer, Hannah IV, 660
Mercer, Hannah IV, 726
Mercer, Hannah IV, 740
Mercer, Hannah IV, 957
Mercer, Hannah IV, 971
Mercer, Hannah IV, 979
Mercer, Harvey IV, 979
Mercer, Harvey S. IV, 979
Mercer, Hatton II, 800
Mercer, Hatton II, 809
Mercer, Hazel IV, 740
Mercer, Helen M. II, 800
Mercer, Hepsibah IV, 48
Mercer, Hepsibah IV, 100
Mercer, Hilda V, 349
Mercer, Jane V, 263
Mercer, Jane V, 349
Mercer, Jane V, 460
Mercer, Janie V, 349
Mercer, Jason V, 263
Mercer, Jason V, 349
Mercer, Jason V, 516
Mercer, Jeanette V, 349
Mercer, Jesse Blaine IV, 1040
Mercer, John IV, 48
Mercer, John IV, 100
Mercer, John IV, 645
Mercer, John IV, 833
Mercer, John IV, 878
Mercer, John IV, 1258
Mercer, John V, 460
Mercer, John K. IV, 645
Mercer, John P. IV, 630
Mercer, John P. IV, 645
Mercer, John R. IV, 645
Mercer, John T. IV, 251
Mercer, Joseph IV, 48
Mercer, Joseph IV, 100
Mercer, Joshua VI, 676
Mercer, Kenneth Eli IV, 1040
Mercer, Kennith V, 460
Mercer, Laura IV, 979
Mercer, Laura B. IV, 979
Mercer, Laura E. IV, 251
Mercer, Lemoyne IV, 251
Mercer, Leona V, 460
Mercer, Louella II, 898
Mercer, Louisa V, 116
Mercer, Lucretia IV, 878
Mercer, Lydia IV, 645
Mercer, Lydia IV, 666
Mercer, Lydia VI, 363
Mercer, Lydia VI, 423
Mercer, Martha IV, 633
Mercer, Martha IV, 645

cer, Martha IV, 651
cer, Martha IV, 833
cer, Martha Cheyney II, 809
cer, Mary IV, 645
cer, Mary IV, 720
cer, Mary IV, 739
cer, Mary IV, 740
cer, Mary IV, 833
cer, Mary IV, 1258
cer, Mary V, 98
cer, Mary V, 116
cer, Mary V, 263
cer, Mary V, 349
cer, Mary V, 516
cer, Mary Ann IV, 645
cer, Mary Ann IV, 878
cer, Mary E. IV, 971
cer, Mary Idella IV, 1040
cer, Mathias IV, 100
cer, Matthias IV, 48
cer, Moses VI, 423
cer, Mrs. Ella IV, 740
cer, Myrtle V, 98
cer, Nellie IV, 251
cer, Olive IV, 635
cer, Olive IV, 645
cer, Olive IV, 723
cer, Olive IV, 740
cer, Olive IV, 833
cer, Opal V, 349
cer, Opal V, 351
cer, Pearl IV, 833
cer, Pearl IV, 979
cer, Phebe IV, 645
cer, Phebe IV, 740
cer, Philip IV, 979
cer, Phillip A. IV, 979
cer, Rachel IV, 630
cer, Rachel IV, 631
cer, Rachel IV, 645
cer, Rachel IV, 697
cer, Rachel IV, 740
cer, Rachel IV, 759
cer, Rachel V, 116
cer, Rachel Schooly IV, 645
cer, Rebecca IV, 94
cer, Rebecca IV, 100
cer, Rebecca IV, 107
cer, Rebecca IV, 637
cer, Rebecca IV, 645
cer, Rebecca IV, 740
cer, Ruth IV, 645
cer, Ruth IV, 910
cer, Ruth IV, 918
cer, Ruth VI, 566
cer, Ruth VI, 567
cer, Ruthanna IV, 1101
cer, Ruthanna B. IV, 1106
cer, Sarah II, 712
cer, Sarah II, 800
cer, Sarah IV, 605
cer, Sarah IV, 640
cer, Sarah IV, 642
cer, Sarah IV, 645
cer, Sarah IV, 654
cer, Sarah IV, 660
cer, Sarah IV, 740
cer, Sarah IV, 759
cer, Sarah IV, 979
cer, Sarah J. IV, 979
cer, Sarah, Jr. IV, 645
cer, Sidney VI, 423
cer, Sidney VI, 461
cer, Solomon IV, 48
cer, Solomon IV, 100
cer, Solomon IV, 645
cer, Solomon IV, 740
cer, Solomon IV, 833
cer, Stacy IV, 645
cer, Sylvester V, 263
cer, Tacy IV, 634
cer, Tacy IV, 645
cer, Theodore V, 263
cer, Theodore V, 349
cer, Thomas IV, 629
cer, Thomas IV, 645
cer, Thomas IV, 649
cer, Thomas IV, 654
cer, Thomas IV, 660
cer, Thos. IV, 645
rcer, Virginia V, 460
rcer, Warren C. II, 898
rcer, Wilbur V, 460
rcer, William IV, 251
rcer, William IV, 342
rcer, William IV, 645
rcer, William IV, 833
rcer, William IV, 878
rcer, William, Jr. IV, 878
rcer, Wm. IV, 740
rcer, Wm. IV, 833
Mercer, Wm. IV, 878
Mercer, Wm. C. II, 898
Mercer, Wm. James IV, 1040
Merchant, Anderson VI, 840
Merchant, Ann VI, 961
Merchant, Billy VI, 961
Merchant, Daniel VI, 374
Merchant, Elizabeth VI, 840
Merchant, Iris VI, 946
Merchant, Isaac V, 263
Merchant, Isaac V, 460
Merchant, Jacob VI, 961
Merchant, Jane VI, 840
Merchant, Louisa V, 263
Merchant, Lydia VI, 374
Merchant, Madison VI, 840
Merchant, Margaret VI, 961
Merchant, Mary VI, 374
Merchant, Mary VI, 423
Merchant, Matthew VI, 961
Merchant, Nancy VI, 946
Merchant, Priscilla IV, 540
Merchant, Rebecca II, 395
Merchant, Richard VI, 423
Merchant, Rosannah VI, 423
Merchant, Sarah VI, 374
Merchant, Sarah VI, 423
Merchant, William VI, 946
Merden, Ethelbert H. V, 585
Merden, Susan V, 585
Mereday, Hannah II, 517
Mereday, Hannah II, 595
Meredeth, James I, 561
Meredeth, Martha I, 561
Meredeth, Nathan I, 607
Meredith, A. S. I, 946
Meredith, Ada I, 943
Meredith, Ada I, 946
Meredith, Albert S. I, 946
Meredith, Albert Sylvester I, 930
Meredith, Beulah IV, 740
Meredith, C. M. I, 946
Meredith, Charity D. I, 894
Meredith, Choica I, 930
Meredith, Cornelia Martitia I, 930
Meredith, David I, 586
Meredith, David I, 595
Meredith, David IV, 979
Meredith, David C. IV, 740
Meredith, David K. I, 561
Meredith, Edwin D. VI, 961
Meredith, Eleanor V, 307
Meredith, Eleanor V, 308
Meredith, Elenor V, 98
Meredith, Eliza C. IV, 951
Meredith, Eliza C. IV, 979
Meredith, Elizabeth II, 489
Meredith, Elizabeth II, 595
Meredith, Elizabeth IV, 740
Meredith, Elizabeth IV, 979
Meredith, Elizabeth IV, 980
Meredith, Elizabeth R IV, 740
Meredith, Elizabeth S. IV, 1258
Meredith, Ella II, 796
Meredith, Ella B. V, 98
Meredith, Ellen V, 307
Meredith, Esther L. I, 894
Meredith, Eunice I, 561
Meredith, Frances I, 930
Meredith, Frank S. IV, 1258
Meredith, Henry VI, 832
Meredith, Henry VI, 961
Meredith, Henry H. VI, 961
Meredith, Horace VI, 259
Meredith, Isaac II, 794
Meredith, James I, 595
Meredith, James I, 894
Meredith, Jane II, 805
Meredith, Jane Q. I, 561
Meredith, Jane R. V, 921
Meredith, Jane R. V, 929
Meredith, Jehu I, 595
Meredith, Jesse I, 561
Meredith, John II, 395
Meredith, John II, 595
Meredith, John IV, 979
Meredith, John V, 98
Meredith, John L. IV, 740
Meredith, Jonathan I, 561
Meredith, Joseph I, 930
Meredith, Joseph W. I, 829
Meredith, Laura I, 929
Meredith, Laura A. I, 930
Meredith, Margaret IV, 740
Meredith, Margaret IV, 979
Meredith, Martha II, 395
Meredith, Martha II, 482
Meredith, Martha II, 595
Meredith, Martha Elizabeth I, 946
Meredith, Mary I, 595
Meredith, Mary II, 781
Meredith, Mary II, 785
Meredith, Mary II, 794
Meredith, Mary VI, 961
Meredith, Mary Ann IV, 979
Meredith, Mary Ann IV, 980
Meredith, Mary E. IV, 740
Meredith, Mary Epps VI, 961
Meredith, Mary Jane V, 95
Meredith, Mary Jane V, 98
Meredith, Mary Jane V, 141
Meredith, Mary M. IV, 740
Meredith, Morris I, 930
Meredith, Nelly VI, 961
Meredith, Paul Robert V, 307
Meredith, Rach I, 595
Meredith, Rachel I, 934
Meredith, Rachel II, 395
Meredith, Rachel V, 98
Meredith, Rachel M. I, 561
Meredith, Rebekah I, 993
Meredith, Rebekah I, 994
Meredith, Rebekah II, 595
Meredith, Rebekah II, 685
Meredith, Reece II, 395
Meredith, Rees II, 482
Meredith, Rees II, 595
Meredith, Reese II, 395
Meredith, Reese II, 482
Meredith, Reese II, 595
Meredith, Roxanna I, 946
Meredith, Samuel II, 595
Meredith, Sarah I, 595
Meredith, Sarah IV, 740
Meredith, Sarah IV, 979
Meredith, Sarah Ellen V, 31
Meredith, Sarah Ellen V, 98
Meredith, Seneca V, 98
Meredith, Seneca V, 141
Meredith, Seneca L. V, 98
Meredith, Simon IV, 979
Meredith, Simon C. IV, 740
Meredith, Simon C. IV, 1029
Meredith, Solomon I, 595
Meredith, Sylvester I, 946
Meredith, Tabitha Curris I, 930
Meredith, Telitha I, 894
Meredith, Thamazin II, 794
Meredith, William IV, 740
Meredith, William IV, 979
Meredith, William, Jr. IV, 1029
Meredith, Wm. IV, 979
Merger, Anna M. V, 633
Meriam, Edith Scott VI, 765
Meriam, Elizabeth VI, 765
Meriam, Horatio VI, 765
Meriam, Lewis VI, 765
Meriam, Pink VI, 765
Merice, John I, 826
Meriday, Mary I, 561
Merideth, Abigail I, 600
Merideth, Abigirl I, 510
Merideth, Albert C. I, 904
Merideth, Andrew I, 603
Merideth, Andrew I, 607
Merideth, Ann I, 510
Merideth, Anna V, 461
Merideth, Benjamin V, 461
Merideth, David I, 561
Merideth, David I, 595
Merideth, David I, 638
Merideth, David I, 829
Merideth, Edward V, 461
Merideth, Elisha I, 595
Merideth, Elizabeth I, 510
Merideth, Elizabeth VI, 753
Merideth, Emily Ann I, 607
Merideth, Eunice I, 638
Merideth, Frances L. I, 829
Merideth, Gustavus A. I, 904
Merideth, Hannah I, 600
Merideth, Hannah I, 603
Merideth, James I, 510
Merideth, James I, 595
Merideth, James M. IV, 48
Merideth, Jane I, 595
Merideth, Jehu I, 595
Merideth, Jesse I, 638
Merideth, John I, 595
Merideth, John I, 600
Merideth, John I, 603
Merideth, Jonathan I, 595
Merideth, Joseph W. I, 829
Merideth, Joseph W. E. I, 829
Merideth, Judith I, 603
Merideth, Judith I, 607
Merideth, Leonidas I, 904
Merideth, Leslie V, 461
Merideth, Lindsey I, 904
Merideth, Luzene I, 510
Merideth, Lydia I, 603
Merideth, Lydia I, 607
Merideth, Mabel V, 461
Merideth, Mabel M. V, 461
Merideth, Martha I, 510
Merideth, Martha I, 595
Merideth, Mary I, 510
Merideth, Mary I, 595
Merideth, Mary I, 600
Merideth, Mary I, 603
Merideth, Mary I, 607
Merideth, Minerva Franklin I, 607
Merideth, Nathan I, 603
Merideth, Nathan I, 607
Merideth, Nora I, 638
Merideth, Quincy I, 638
Merideth, Rach I, 595
Merideth, Rachel I, 510
Merideth, Ruth I, 607
Merideth, Sally I, 595
Merideth, Sally I, 597
Merideth, Sarah I, 595
Merideth, Sarah I, 603
Merideth, Sarah I, 807
Merideth, Sarah I, 829
Merideth, Simon IV, 1021
Merideth, Solomon I, 595
Merideth, Telitha I, 894
Merideth, Telitha I, 904
Merideth, William I, 595
Merideth, William I, 904
Merideth, William IV, 1021
Meridith, Abigail I, 561
Meridith, Andrew I, 561
Meridith, Ann I, 561
Meridith, David I, 561
Meridith, David K. I, 561
Meridith, Dover I, 561
Meridith, Eunice I, 561
Meridith, Hannah I, 561
Meridith, Ithamar I, 561
Meridith, James I, 561
Meridith, James I, 586
Meridith, Jane Q. I, 561
Meridith, Jehu I, 561
Meridith, Jesse I, 561
Meridith, John I, 561
Meridith, John II, 395
Meridith, John IV, 782
Meridith, John, II I, 561
Meridith, Jonathan I, 561
Meridith, Jonathan I, 586
Meridith, Martha I, 561
Meridith, Mary I, 561
Meridith, Mary I, 595
Meridith, Mary E. IV, 782
Meridith, Mary M. IV, 740
Meridith, Rachel I, 561
Meridith, Rachel IV, 782
Meridith, Rachel M. I, 561
Meridith, Temperance I, 561
Meridy, Polley VI, 993
Meridy, Rachel I, 556
Meridy, Rachel I, 561
Merier, Elizabeth II, 395
Merimon, Elisabeth I, 246
Merimoon, Ann IV, 249
Merimoon, David I, 246
Merimoon, Elisabeth I, 246
Merimoon, Elizabeth IV, 248
Merimoon, Elizabeth IV, 249
Merimoon, Francis I, 246
Merimoon, Hannah I, 218
Merimoon, Hannah I, 246
Merimoon, James IV, 249
Merimoon, John I, 218
Merimoon, John I, 246
Merimoon, Lettice IV, 249
Merimoon, Martin IV, 249
Merimoon, Matilda IV, 249
Merimoon, Obedience IV, 248
Merimoon, Obedience IV, 249
Merimoon, Patey IV, 249
Merimoon, Peggy IV, 249
Merimoon, Peter I, 246
Merimoon, Rachel IV, 249
Merimoon, Rebecca IV, 249
Merimoon, Robert IV, 249
Merimoon, Samuel IV, 249
Merimoon, Sarah IV, 249
Merimoon, Susanna IV, 249
Merimoon, Watkins IV, 249
Merine, Mary I, 796
Merine, Mary I, 826
Merion, Mamie IV, 1258
Merion, Rebecka II, 87
Merion, Rebecka II, 93
Merion, T. N. IV, 1258
Merion, Thomas II, 87
Merion, Thomas II, 93
Meriot, Anna II, 179
Meriot, Benjamin II, 179
Meriot, Benjamin II, 241
Meriot, Benjamin II, 246
Meriot, Isaac II, 179
Meriot, Isaac II, 241
Meriot, Jacob II, 179
Meriot, Joseph II, 179
Meriot, Joyce II, 179
Meriot, Mary II, 179
Meriot, Mary II, 188
Meriot, Mary II, 241
Meriot, Mary II, 272
Meriot, Matthew II, 246
Meriot, Matthew Owen II, 241
Meriot, Richard II, 179
Meriot, Samuel II, 179
Meriot, Samuel II, 188
Meriot, Samuel II, 241
Meriot, Samuel, Sr. II, 179
Meriot, Sarah II, 179
Meriot, Susanah II, 220
Meriot, Susanah II, 241
Meriot, Susannah II, 179
Meriot, Thomas II, 179
Meriott, Benjamin II, 241
Meriott, Sarah II, 241
Meris, Alma V, 1010
Meris, Jane I, 450
Meris, Susannah I, 449
Meris, Susannah I, 450
Merite, Sabina IV, 488
Meritt, Hannah II, 241
Meritt, Lewis VI, 811
Meritt, Nancy VI, 811
Meritt, Wd. Hannah II, 270
Meriwether, Elizabeth M. VI, 961
Meriwether, Martha L. VI, 961
Meriwether, Mary II, 446
Meriwether, Walker C. VI, 961
Meriwether, William N. VI, 961
Merker, Barbara Jean V, 696
Merker, Charles Edward V, 696
Merker, Clarence V, 663
Merker, Clarence V, 696
Merker, Clarence Edward V, 696
Merker, Clarence G. V, 696
Merker, Mary V, 663
Merker, Mary V, 696
Merker, Ruth Anna V, 696
Merker, Ruthanna V, 696
Merker, Wendell Carey V, 696
Merkle, Carrie E. V, 853
Merling, Sarah VI, 534
Merling, Wm. VI, 534
Mermoon, Joseph I, 992
Mermoon, Thomas I, 992
Meroney, Margaret I, 625
Merrath, Lydia Dougherty II, 786
Merrefield, Amelia II, 596
Merrefield, Hannah II, 538
Merrefield, Hannah II, 596
Merrefield, Joseph II, 538
Merrefield, Joseph II, 596
Merrefield, Mary II, 538
Merrefield, Mary II, 596
Merrel, Mary I, 894
Merrett, Hannah IV, 342
Merrett, Myrtle L. I, 311
Merriam, Lewis VI, 792
Merriam, Pink VI, 792
Merrice, Abraham IV, 978
Merrice, Ann IV, 978
Merrice, Barclay IV, 978
Merrice, Caleb IV, 978
Merrice, Esther IV, 978
Merrice, Isaac IV, 978
Merrice, Jesse IV, 978
Merrice, Job Shreve IV, 978
Merrice, Jonathan IV, 978
Merrice, Joseph M. IV, 978
Merrice, Thomasson IV, 978
Merrice, William IV, 978
Merrick, Abi II, 1076
Merrick, Abi II, 1083
Merrick, Amos II, 1015
Merrick, Ann II, 986
Merrick, Ann II, 1014
Merrick, Ann II, 1015
Merrick, Ann II, 1024
Merrick, Anna II, 965
Merrick, Anna II, 1014
Merrick, Deborah II, 1015
Merrick, Elizabeth II, 1014
Merrick, Elizabeth II, 1015
Merrick, Elizabeth II, 1028
Merrick, Enos II, 965
Merrick, Enos II, 1014
Merrick, Enos II, 1076
Merrick, Enos II, 1083
Merrick, George II, 1008

Merrick, George II, 1014
Merrick, George II, 1034
Merrick, Hannah II, 989
Merrick, Hannah II, 996
Merrick, Hannah II, 1014
Merrick, Hannah II, 1015
Merrick, Hannah II, 1025
Merrick, Henry II, 1014
Merrick, Isaiah II, 1014
Merrick, Jacob II, 1015
Merrick, James III, 306
Merrick, Jane IV, 903
Merrick, Jane IV, 910
Merrick, Jason II, 1014
Merrick, Jesse Hough II, 1014
Merrick, John II, 991
Merrick, John II, 1003
Merrick, John II, 1014
Merrick, John II, 1015
Merrick, John II, 1016
Merrick, John II, 1024
Merrick, John II, 1034
Merrick, John Scot II, 1014
Merrick, John, Jr. II, 1014
Merrick, Joseph II, 1014
Merrick, Joseph II, 1015
Merrick, Joseph II, 1028
Merrick, Joseph II, 1076
Merrick, Joseph II, 1083
Merrick, Leatitia II, 984
Merrick, Letitia II, 1014
Merrick, Letitia II, 1021
Merrick, Marcy II, 1003
Merrick, Marcy II, 1014
Merrick, Martha II, 1014
Merrick, Martha II, 1037
Merrick, Mary II, 989
Merrick, Mary II, 991
Merrick, Mary II, 992
Merrick, Mary II, 1014
Merrick, Mary II, 1015
Merrick, Mary II, 1028
Merrick, Mary II, 1029
Merrick, Mercy II, 1015
Merrick, Mercy II, 1076
Merrick, Mercy II, 1083
Merrick, Naomi II, 1014
Merrick, Phebe II, 1008
Merrick, Phebe II, 1014
Merrick, Phebe II, 1024
Merrick, Phebe Jane III, 225
Merrick, Phebe Jane III, 306
Merrick, Pheby II, 1014
Merrick, Pheby II, 1016
Merrick, Priscilla II, 1014
Merrick, Priscilla II, 1015
Merrick, Rachel II, 595
Merrick, Rachel II, 982
Merrick, Rachel II, 1014
Merrick, Rachel II, 1034
Merrick, Rebecca II, 1004
Merrick, Rebecca II, 1014
Merrick, Robert I, 1015
Merrick, Robert I, 1034
Merrick, Robert II, 965
Merrick, Robert II, 991
Merrick, Robert II, 1014
Merrick, Robert II, 1015
Merrick, Robert, Jr. II, 1014
Merrick, Ruth II, 965
Merrick, Ruth II, 991
Merrick, Ruth II, 1014
Merrick, Samuel II, 1014
Merrick, Sarah II, 993
Merrick, Sarah II, 1014
Merrick, Thomas II, 1014
Merrick, Thomas II, 1037
Merrick, Thomas III, 225
Merrick, Timothy II, 1014
Merrideth, Jane I, 595
Merrideth, John I, 561
Merrideth, Joseph VI, 28
Merrideth, Joseph VI, 32
Merrideth, Samson VI, 32
Merrideth, Sara VI, 28
Merrideth, Sara VI, 32
Merridith, David IV, 979
Merridith, Hervey I, 589
Merridith, James, Jr. I, 589
Merridith, Jefferson I, 589
Merridith, Joanna I, 589
Merridith, Joseph W. E. I, 829
Merridith, Martha I, 595
Merridith, Mary I, 589
Merrifield, Amelia II, 596
Merrifield, Amelia G. II, 395
Merrifield, Elizabeth II, 395
Merrifield, Elizabeth II, 755
Merrifield, Elizabeth V, 921
Merrifield, Hannah II, 596
Merrifield, John G. II, 395
Merrifield, John Guest II, 596
Merrifield, Joseph II, 395
Merrifield, Joseph II, 596
Merrifield, Joseph II, 755
Merrifield, Joseph III, 225
Merrifield, Joseph VI, 757
Merrifield, Mary II, 395
Merrifield, Mary II, 596
Merrifield, Mary II, 755
Merrifield, Rebecca VI, 757
Merrifield, Sarah II, 395
Merrifield, Sarah II, 596
Merrifield, Sarah Anna II, 395
Merrifield, Sarah Anna II, 755
Merrihew, Caroline III, 225
Merrihew, Eliza W. II, 755
Merrihew, Eliza W. II, 758
Merrihew, Frank III, 225
Merrihew, Mary R. II, 755
Merrihew, Mary R. II, 758
Merrihew, Stephen III, 225
Merril, Elizabeth II, 596
Merril, Elizabeth II, 679
Merril, Ferrand S. IV, 833
Merril, Hannah IV, 420
Merril, Hannah IV, 588
Merril, Isaac IV, 420
Merril, Isaac IV, 588
Merril, Jesse IV, 420
Merril, Jesse IV, 588
Merril, Jonathan IV, 420
Merril, Jonathan IV, 588
Merril, Joseph IV, 420
Merril, Joseph IV, 588
Merril, Linneus IV, 833
Merril, Margaret IV, 420
Merril, Margaret IV, 588
Merril, Richard IV, 420
Merril, Sara Etta IV, 833
Merril, Saretta IV, 833
Merril, Saretta IV, 851
Merril, Sina IV, 833
Merril, Stephen IV, 420
Merril, Stephen IV, 588
Merrill, Charles III, 225
Merrill, Charles III, 297
Merrill, Eliza III, 225
Merrill, Eliza III, 297
Merrill, Frances V, 263
Merrill, Hannah IV, 420
Merrill, Henry A. V, 696
Merrill, Isaac IV, 420
Merrill, Jane IV, 561
Merrill, Jane IV, 562
Merrill, Jesse IV, 420
Merrill, Jonathan IV, 420
Merrill, Joseph IV, 420
Merrill, Loatta III, 96
Merrill, Manning II, 395
Merrill, Margaret IV, 420
Merrill, Mary IV, 1099
Merrill, Mary IV, 1106
Merrill, Richard IV, 420
Merrill, Stephen IV, 420
Merrill, William V, 263
Merrill, William J. III, 96
Merrill, Wm. V, 461
Merriman, Alley VI, 920
Merriman, Anna IV, 487
Merriman, Edward VI, 890
Merriman, Kate IV, 1258
Merriman, Lucinda IV, 1173
Merriman, Maude V, 189
Merriman, Patsy VI, 920
Merriman, Susan IV, 1151
Merriman, Susan IV, 1173
Merrimon, Elizabeth VI, 115
Merrimon, Hannah VI, 115
Merrimon, Margaret VI, 115
Merrimon, Martin VI, 116
Merrimon, Obedience VI, 115
Merrimon, Peter VI, 115
Merrimon, Rhoda VI, 115
Merrimon, Robert VI, 115
Merrimon, Susanna VI, 116
Merrimoon, Burle VI, 199
Merrimoon, Burleigh VI, 199
Merrimoon, Christian I, 992
Merrimoon, Hannah VI, 198
Merrimoon, Hannah VI, 199
Merrimoon, John VI, 198
Merrimoon, John VI, 199
Merrimoon, Obedience VI, 199
Merrimoon, Obedience VI, 210
Merrimoon, Peter VI, 199
Merrimoon, Peter VI, 210
Merrimoon, Sarah VI, 199
Merrion, Lidy II, 132
Merriot, Jacob II, 241
Merriot, Mary II, 590
Merriot, Mary II, 611
Merriot, Sarah Owen II, 590
Merriot, Thomasin II, 241
Merriott, Benjamin VI, 105
Merriott, Benjamin VI, 116
Merriott, Caleb Trublood VI, 116
Merriott, Mary VI, 105
Merriott, Mourning VI, 123
Merriott, Mourning Cornwell VI, 116
Merriott, William VI, 105
Merris, Abraham IV, 979
Merriss, Corinna I, 919
Merrit, Abraham II, 296
Merrit, Benj. III, 449
Merrit, Eliza IV, 46
Merrit, Eliza IV, 48
Merrit, Eliza P. IV, 98
Merrit, Eliza P. IV, 100
Merrit, Elizabeth V, 956
Merrit, Elizabeth H. II, 596
Merrit, Hannah IV, 342
Merrit, Hannah IV, 346
Merrit, Hannah E. III, 449
Merrit, Isaac II, 395
Merrit, Isaac IV, 342
Merrit, J. Clement IV, 342
Merrit, Jane II, 296
Merrit, John IV, 342
Merrit, Jonathan II, 596
Merrit, Josiah Edward V, 956
Merrit, Levina VI, 840
Merrit, Lewis VI, 840
Merrit, Margaret M. IV, 342
Merrit, Mary II, 596
Merrit, Mary IV, 342
Merrit, Milton V, 633
Merrit, Rebecca S. IV, 342
Merrit, Sarah IV, 342
Merrit, Sarah V, 52
Merrit, Sarah V, 98
Merrit, Solomon II, 596
Merrit, Thomas II, 296
Merrit, Thomas V, 956
Merrit, Thos. V, 956
Merritt, ??? III, 75
Merritt, ??? III, 225
Merritt, ??? III, 226
Merritt, ??? III, 227
Merritt, ??? III, 481
Merritt, Abraham II, 296
Merritt, Abraham, Jr. II, 296
Merritt, Adaline III, 227
Merritt, Adele III, 226
Merritt, Adele III, 244
Merritt, Adele O. III, 58
Merritt, Adele O. III, 226
Merritt, Albert A. III, 225
Merritt, Alfred III, 225
Merritt, Alfred C. II, 121
Merritt, Alice II, 596
Merritt, Alice III, 225
Merritt, Alice III, 362
Merritt, Allen C. III, 227
Merritt, Almira III, 163
Merritt, Almira III, 226
Merritt, Amanda B. III, 100
Merritt, Amanda B. III, 151
Merritt, Amanda B. III, 162
Merritt, Amelia III, 225
Merritt, Amelia III, 353
Merritt, Amelia C. III, 245
Merritt, Amelia E. III, 225
Merritt, Amelia E. III, 227
Merritt, Amelia H. III, 226
Merritt, Andrew III, 225
Merritt, Ann III, 82
Merritt, Ann III, 226
Merritt, Ann III, 232
Merritt, Ann III, 234
Merritt, Ann III, 490
Merritt, Ann Eliza III, 225
Merritt, Ann Eliza III, 227
Merritt, Anna III, 225
Merritt, Anna III, 227
Merritt, Anna III, 490
Merritt, Anna V, 956
Merritt, Anna V. III, 368
Merritt, Anne III, 225
Merritt, Anne III, 226
Merritt, Anne III, 243
Merritt, Anne III, 426
Merritt, Benj. A. III, 226
Merritt, Benj. A. III, 227
Merritt, Benj. A. III, 293
Merritt, Benj. A. III, 426
Merritt, Benjamin III, 124
Merritt, Benjamin III, 225
Merritt, Benjamin III, 227
Merritt, Benjamin A. III, 449
Merritt, Benjamin A. III, 490
Merritt, Benjamin A. III, 503
Merritt, Caroline III, 227
Merritt, Charles III, 227
Merritt, Charles Edward III, 225
Merritt, Charles Ovington III, 226
Merritt, Clary VI, 899
Merritt, Cornelius VI, 961
Merritt, Daniel III, 225
Merritt, Daniel III, 227
Merritt, Daniel T. III, 225
Merritt, Daniel T. III, 333
Merritt, Daniel V. III, 225
Merritt, Daniel Valentine III, 225
Merritt, Deborah III, 119
Merritt, Deborah III, 225
Merritt, Deborah III, 226
Merritt, Dorothy Weeks III, 490
Merritt, E. III, 245
Merritt, E. Robins III, 234
Merritt, Edward III, 156
Merritt, Edward III, 225
Merritt, Edward III, 226
Merritt, Edward III, 227
Merritt, Edward III, 353
Merritt, Edward V, 956
Merritt, Edward Haviland III, 226
Merritt, Edwin A. II, 121
Merritt, Edwin A. II, 755
Merritt, Edwin S. II, 755
Merritt, Eleanor III, 225
Merritt, Eleanor III, 227
Merritt, Eleanor III, 270
Merritt, Elinor VI, 961
Merritt, Eliz. III, 227
Merritt, Eliz. III, 482
Merritt, Eliza III, 109
Merritt, Eliza III, 225
Merritt, Eliza III, 226
Merritt, Eliza F. III, 225
Merritt, Eliza F. III, 226
Merritt, Eliza H. III, 226
Merritt, Eliza L. III, 124
Merritt, Eliza L. III, 225
Merritt, Eliza T. III, 313
Merritt, Elizabeth II, 34
Merritt, Elizabeth II, 296
Merritt, Elizabeth II, 395
Merritt, Elizabeth II, 596
Merritt, Elizabeth II, 713
Merritt, Elizabeth III, 226
Merritt, Elizabeth III, 227
Merritt, Elizabeth III, 480
Merritt, Elizabeth III, 485
Merritt, Elizabeth III, 490
Merritt, Elizabeth III, 497
Merritt, Elizabeth IV, 251
Merritt, Elizabeth V, 951
Merritt, Elizabeth V, 956
Merritt, Elizabeth V, 961
Merritt, Elizabeth VI, 973
Merritt, Elizabeth Ann II, 395
Merritt, Elizabeth Ann V, 956
Merritt, Elizabeth C. III, 226
Merritt, Elizabeth H. II, 121
Merritt, Elizabeth H. II, 395
Merritt, Elizabeth H. II, 596
Merritt, Elizabeth H. II, 755
Merritt, Elizabeth L. II, 34
Merritt, Elizabeth L. II, 121
Merritt, Elizabeth L. II, 713
Merritt, Elizabeth L. II, 755
Merritt, Elizabeth S. III, 484
Merritt, Elizabeth S. III, 490
Merritt, Ella III, 225
Merritt, Ella III, 333
Merritt, Ellen III, 227
Merritt, Ellen III, 490
Merritt, Ellen III, 495
Merritt, Ellen V, 99
Merritt, Evelyn Helen III, 490
Merritt, Fannie Gordon III, 225
Merritt, Frances III, 227
Merritt, Geo. S. III, 225
Merritt, Geo. S. III, 313
Merritt, George III, 183
Merritt, George III, 226
Merritt, Grace III, 226
Merritt, Gurtie I, 311
Merritt, Hannah II, 1050
Merritt, Hannah II, 1056
Merritt, Hannah II, 1072
Merritt, Hannah II, 1076
Merritt, Hannah III, 192
Merritt, Hannah III, 225
Merritt, Hannah III, 226
Merritt, Hannah III, 227
Merritt, Hannah III, 293
Merritt, Hannah III, 490
Merritt, Hannah III, 503
Merritt, Hannah B. III, 189
Merritt, Hannah B. III, 226
Merritt, Hannah B. III, 227
Merritt, Hannah B. III, 304
Merritt, Hannah E. III, 227
Merritt, Hannah E. III, 426
Merritt, Hannah E. III, 449
Merritt, Harriet III, 225
Merritt, Harriet III, 227
Merritt, Harriet III, 368
Merritt, Harriet F. III, 128
Merritt, Harriet F. III, 368
Merritt, Harriett III, 226
Merritt, Harry G. III, 226
Merritt, Helen M. III, 234
Merritt, Isaac II, 395
Merritt, Isaac III, 120
Merritt, Isaac III, 225
Merritt, Isaac III, 226
Merritt, Isaac III, 227
Merritt, Isaac N. III, 163
Merritt, Isaac N. III, 226
Merritt, Isaiah III, 225
Merritt, J. Clement IV, 330
Merritt, J. Clement IV, 342
Merritt, Jacob II, 296
Merritt, Jacob III, 227
Merritt, Jacob T. III, 226
Merritt, James III, 92
Merritt, James III, 226
Merritt, James III, 490
Merritt, James H. III, 58
Merritt, James H. III, 225
Merritt, James H. III, 226
Merritt, James H. III, 244
Merritt, James N. III, 226
Merritt, James N. III, 227
Merritt, Jane II, 296
Merritt, Jane III, 225
Merritt, Jane III, 226
Merritt, Jane III, 227
Merritt, Jane III, 400
Merritt, Jane III, 426
Merritt, Jane III, 490
Merritt, Jane V, 956
Merritt, Jane V, 961
Merritt, Jane M. III, 75
Merritt, Jesse III, 225
Merritt, Jesse III, 362
Merritt, Jesse III, 405
Merritt, Jesse III, 419
Merritt, Jesse III, 426
Merritt, Jesse III, 485
Merritt, Jesse III, 490
Merritt, Jesse III, 497
Merritt, Jesse III, 507
Merritt, Jesse III, 508
Merritt, Jessica III, 490
Merritt, Jno. C. III, 485
Merritt, John III, 82
Merritt, John III, 119
Merritt, John III, 225
Merritt, John III, 237
Merritt, John III, 400
Merritt, John III, 426
Merritt, John III, 490
Merritt, John IV, 342
Merritt, John VI, 913
Merritt, John VI, 961
Merritt, John VI, 969
Merritt, John VI, 1011
Merritt, John C. III, 226
Merritt, John C. III, 227
Merritt, John C. III, 479
Merritt, John C. III, 482
Merritt, John C. III, 484
Merritt, John C. III, 490
Merritt, John C., Jr. III, 490
Merritt, John I. III, 226
Merritt, John J. III, 189
Merritt, John J. III, 226
Merritt, John M. VI, 864
Merritt, John W. III, 490
Merritt, John W. III, 495
Merritt, John, Jr. III, 227
Merritt, John, Jr. VI, 961
Merritt, Jonathan II, 596
Merritt, Joseph II, 1072
Merritt, Joseph II, 1076
Merritt, Joseph III, 225
Merritt, Joseph III, 226
Merritt, Joseph W. III, 227
Merritt, Josiah IV, 251
Merritt, Josiah V, 956
Merritt, Josiah Clement V, 98
Merritt, Josiah Edward II, 296
Merritt, Josiah Edward V, 956
Merritt, Lavinia II, 596
Merritt, Lemuel III, 226
Merritt, Letitia III, 426
Merritt, Letitia III, 430
Merritt, Lewis VI, 835

rritt, Lewis VI, 841
rritt, Louisa III, 153
rritt, Louisa III, 154
rritt, Louisa III, 226
rritt, Louisa III, 227
rritt, Louise III, 58
rritt, Louise III, 226
rritt, Louise M. III, 183
rritt, Louise M. III, 226
rritt, Lucy VI, 1003
rritt, Mabel III, 490
rritt, Mabel III, 508
rritt, Margaret III, 226
rritt, Margaret III, 227
rritt, Maria III, 227
rritt, Maria V, 956
rritt, Maria B. III, 226
rritt, Marjorie Mae III, 490
rritt, Marjorie Mae III, 508
rritt, Marjory III, 490
rritt, Marshall III, 225
rritt, Martha H. III, 227
rritt, Mary II, 596
rritt, Mary II, 690
rritt, Mary III, 225
rritt, Mary III, 226
rritt, Mary III, 227
rritt, Mary III, 245
rritt, Mary III, 293
rritt, Mary III, 304
rritt, Mary III, 405
rritt, Mary III, 419
rritt, Mary III, 426
rritt, Mary III, 481
rritt, Mary III, 484
rritt, Mary III, 485
rritt, Mary III, 490
rritt, Mary III, 497
rritt, Mary III, 498
rritt, Mary IV, 342
rritt, Mary A. III, 419
rritt, Mary A. III, 426
rritt, Mary Ann III, 193
rritt, Mary Ann III, 225
rritt, Mary Ann III, 227
rritt, Mary Ann III, 485
rritt, Mary Ann III, 490
rritt, Mary B. III, 202
rritt, Mary K. III, 154
rritt, Mary K. III, 225
rritt, Mary K. III, 270
rritt, Mary Louise III, 225
rritt, Mary P. III, 225
rritt, Mary S. III, 227
rritt, Matthew III, 225
rritt, Matthew Franklin III, 227
rritt, Mattie I, 311
rritt, Michael III, 225
rritt, Michael III, 226
rritt, Michael III, 227
rritt, Milton V, 633
rritt, Myrtle L. I, 311
rritt, Nancy VI, 961
rritt, Nanny VI, 1021
rritt, Nathaniel III, 226
rritt, Nathaniel III, 426
rritt, Nathaniel III, 490
rritt, Nathaniel S. III, 154
rritt, Nathaniel S. III, 193
rritt, Nathaniel S. III, 225
rritt, Nathaniel S. III, 226
rritt, Nathaniel S. III, 227
rritt, Nathaniel S. III, 270
rritt, Nehemiah III, 225
rritt, Nehemiah III, 227
rritt, Pauline III, 225
rritt, Pauline III, 362
rritt, Pauline III, 490
rritt, Pauline III, 507
rritt, Pauline W. III, 490
rritt, Pauline W. III, 508
rritt, Peter III, 225
rritt, Phebe II, 1072
rritt, Phebe II, 1076
rritt, Phebe III, 82
rritt, Phebe III, 119
rritt, Phebe III, 163
rritt, Phebe III, 189
rritt, Phebe III, 225
rritt, Phebe III, 226
rritt, Phebe III, 227
rritt, Phebe III, 234
rritt, Phebe III, 237
rritt, Phebe III, 490
rritt, Phebe A. III, 227
rritt, Phebe A. III, 293
rritt, Phebe A. III, 312
rritt, Phebe A. III, 426
rritt, Phebe A. III, 449
rritt, Phebe Alice III, 490
Merritt, Phebe Alice III, 508
Merritt, Phebe Ann III, 225
Merritt, Phebe B. III, 226
Merritt, Phebe B. III, 227
Merritt, Phebe C. III, 225
Merritt, Phebe H. III, 479
Merritt, Phebe H. III, 490
Merritt, Phebe I. III, 226
Merritt, Phebe J. III, 226
Merritt, Phebe J. III, 227
Merritt, Phebe Jane III, 227
Merritt, Phebe M. III, 225
Merritt, Phebe M. III, 227
Merritt, Phebe N. III, 227
Merritt, Philip H. III, 226
Merritt, Philip H. III, 227
Merritt, Polly VI, 913
Merritt, Polly A. VI, 841
Merritt, Rachel III, 226
Merritt, Rebecca II, 296
Merritt, Rebecca V, 98
Merritt, Rebecca H. II, 34
Merritt, Rebecca H. II, 121
Merritt, Rebecca H. II, 713
Merritt, Rebecca H. II, 755
Merritt, Rebecca L. III, 225
Merritt, Rebecca L. III, 313
Merritt, Rebecca S. IV, 330
Merritt, Rebecca S. IV, 342
Merritt, Rebecca S. V, 98
Merritt, Rhoda VI, 961
Merritt, Rich. P. III, 226
Merritt, Richard III, 226
Merritt, Richard III, 227
Merritt, Richard VI, 961
Merritt, Richard P. III, 128
Merritt, Richard P. III, 225
Merritt, Richard P. III, 227
Merritt, Richard P. III, 368
Merritt, Robert III, 227
Merritt, S. Ellen V, 98
Merritt, Samuel VI, 961
Merritt, Sarah II, 596
Merritt, Sarah II, 755
Merritt, Sarah II, 898
Merritt, Sarah III, 91
Merritt, Sarah III, 92
Merritt, Sarah III, 93
Merritt, Sarah III, 226
Merritt, Sarah III, 227
Merritt, Sarah III, 490
Merritt, Sarah IV, 342
Merritt, Sarah V, 951
Merritt, Sarah V, 956
Merritt, Sarah Ann III, 226
Merritt, Sarah Ann III, 400
Merritt, Sarah Ann III, 426
Merritt, Sarah E. V, 99
Merritt, Sarah L. III, 226
Merritt, Sarah S. III, 156
Merritt, Sarah S. III, 226
Merritt, Sarah W. II, 34
Merritt, Sarah W. II, 121
Merritt, Sarah W. II, 713
Merritt, Sarah W. II, 755
Merritt, Solomon II, 121
Merritt, Solomon II, 395
Merritt, Solomon II, 596
Merritt, Solomon II, 713
Merritt, Solomon H. II, 34
Merritt, Solomon H. II, 121
Merritt, Solomon H. II, 395
Merritt, Solomon H. II, 755
Merritt, Susan VI, 961
Merritt, Susan Lee II, 898
Merritt, Susan M. V, 956
Merritt, Susan M. V, 958
Merritt, Susan W. III, 202
Merritt, Susan W. III, 227
Merritt, Susanna VI, 969
Merritt, Susannah III, 120
Merritt, Susannah III, 226
Merritt, Thankful III, 227
Merritt, Thomas II, 296
Merritt, Thomas II, 713
Merritt, Thomas V, 956
Merritt, Thomas V, 961
Merritt, Thomas VI, 899
Merritt, Thomas VI, 961
Merritt, Thomas VI, 969
Merritt, Thomas VI, 973
Merritt, Thos. V, 951
Merritt, Thos. V, 956
Merritt, Thos. U. III, 227
Merritt, Titus III, 227
Merritt, Violet III, 425
Merritt, Violet III, 427
Merritt, Violet III, 490
Merritt, Violet A. III, 482
Merritt, Violet A. III, 490
Merritt, Walter III, 227
Merritt, William III, 227
Merritt, William G. III, 226
Merritt, William T. III, 192
Merritt, William T. III, 227
Merritt, Wilson III, 202
Merritt, Wilson III, 225
Merritt, Wilson III, 226
Merritt, Wilson III, 227
Merritt, Wilson III, 245
Merritt, Wm. II, 1072
Merritt, Wm. II, 1076
Merritt, Wm. Henry III, 227
Merritt, Wm. T. III, 227
Merritte, Sabina IV, 478
Merriwether, Henry Ann VI, 903
Merriwether, John II, 395
Merriwether, Mary II, 395
Merriwether, Richard II, 395
Merriwether, Walker G. VI, 903
Merry, Joseph II, 446
Merry, Sarah I, 829
Merry, Simon II, 446
Merry, Susanna II, 446
Merryman, Anna IV, 487
Merryman, Celia IV, 487
Merryman, Joshua VI, 840
Merryman, Matthias IV, 487
Merryman, Rebecca VI, 840
Merryman, Rosa IV, 487
Merryman, Wm. IV, 487
Merrymond, Eleanor VI, 880
Merrymoon, Amelia VI, 115
Merrymoon, Ann VI, 115
Merrymoon, David VI, 115
Merrymoon, David VI, 116
Merrymoon, David VI, 117
Merrymoon, David Francis VI, 115
Merrymoon, EdWd. VI, 161
Merrymoon, Elizabeth VI, 115
Merrymoon, Elizabeth VI, 116
Merrymoon, Elizabeth VI, 117
Merrymoon, Francis VI, 116
Merrymoon, Hannah VI, 115
Merrymoon, Hannah VI, 119
Merrymoon, Hannah VI, 199
Merrymoon, Hannah VI, 202
Merrymoon, James VI, 115
Merrymoon, John VI, 115
Merrymoon, John VI, 116
Merrymoon, John VI, 119
Merrymoon, John VI, 161
Merrymoon, John VI, 198
Merrymoon, John VI, 199
Merrymoon, John VI, 202
Merrymoon, John VI, 215
Merrymoon, Joseph Butler VI, 117
Merrymoon, Margaret VI, 115
Merrymoon, Margaret VI, 119
Merrymoon, Martin VI, 115
Merrymoon, Martin VI, 116
Merrymoon, Martin VI, 124
Merrymoon, Obedience VI, 115
Merrymoon, Peter I, 246
Merrymoon, Peter VI, 115
Merrymoon, Peter VI, 116
Merrymoon, Rhoda VI, 115
Merrymoon, Robert VI, 115
Merrymoon, Susanna VI, 116
Merrymoon, Susanna VI, 124
Merrymoon, Susannah VI, 115
Merrymoon, Susannah VI, 116
Merryweather, William III, 227
Merschert, Mercy C. II, 1076
Mershon, Theodoshia II, 281
Mershow, Mary Asenath V, 189
Merson, Clara P. V, 516
Merth, Richard II, 596
Merton, Anna IV, 1329
Merton, Anna May IV, 1329
Merton, C. E. IV, 1329
Merton, Chas. C. IV, 1329
Merton, Eddie IV, 1329
Merton, Eddie IV, 1330
Merton, Edward IV, 1329
Merton, George IV, 1329
Merton, George IV, 1330
Merton, John IV, 1329
Merton, John IV, 1330
Merton, Lola IV, 1330
Merton, Lula IV, 1329
Merton, Mabel IV, 1329
Merton, Maggie IV, 1329
Merton, Margaret IV, 1329
Merton, Martha V, 956
Merton, Samuel IV, 1329
Merton, Samuel IV, 1330
Merton, Tracy IV, 1329
Merton, Tracy IV, 1330
Merton, Willis IV, 1329
Merwin, Eliza III, 20
Mesecher, James F. V, 189
Mesecher, John H. V, 189
Mesecher, Mary E. V, 189
Mesecher, William V, 189
Meseimer, Barbara M. I, 993
Meskimen, Frank V, 189
Meskimen, Jemima V, 189
Meskimen, Mary V, 189
Meskimen, Mary E. V, 189
Meskimen, May V, 189
Meskimer, Frank V, 189
Meskimer, Mary V, 189
Meskinner, Jemima V, 189
Meskinner, May V, 189
Messenger, ??? V, 98
Messenger, Charles F. V, 98
Messenger, Dora V, 1010
Messenger, Frank R. V, 98
Messenger, J. Ira V, 696
Messenger, Martha V, 921
Messenger, Martha A. V, 98
Messenger, Martha A. VI, 423
Messenger, Martha A. VI, 436
Messenger, Mary E. V, 1010
Messenger, Walter V, 921
Messenger, Walter C. V, 98
Messer, Charles II, 395
Messer, Della IV, 1258
Messer, Ella IV, 1258
Messer, John IV, 1258
Messer, John A. IV, 1258
Messer, Lena IV, 1330
Messer, Moses VI, 423
Messeroe, ??? III, 226
Messeroe, Mary III, 226
Messeroe, Mary III, 227
Messeroe, Mary S. III, 227
Messeroe, Wilson III, 227
Messersmith, Helen IV, 1330
Messick, Sarah V, 98
Messick, Sarah V, 129
Messinger, ??? V, 921
Messinger, Charles F. V, 921
Messinger, Chas. F. V, 921
Messinger, Frank R. V, 921
Messinger, Martha V, 921
Messinger, Martha A. V, 921
Messinger, Walter V, 921
Messinger, Walter C. V, 921
Messner, Ann IV, 1374
Messner, Charles W. III, 227
Messner, Clara III, 227
Messner, Ellen IV, 1374
Messner, George IV, 1374
Messner, Hannah III, 228
Messner, Hannah III, 341
Messner, Henry L. III, 227
Messner, Henry L. III, 228
Messner, Henry L. III, 341
Messner, Henry L., Jr. III, 228
Messner, Ida III, 227
Messner, John IV, 1374
Messner, Martin A. III, 227
Messner, Mary Elizabeth III, 227
Messner, Rebecca IV, 1374
Messner, Shirley Anne III, 228
Metcalf, Abraham IV, 420
Metcalf, Abraham IV, 588
Metcalf, Abraham IV, 1068
Metcalf, Acenath IV, 420
Metcalf, Adaline IV, 420
Metcalf, Adaline IV, 1068
Metcalf, Asenath IV, 250
Metcalf, Asenath IV, 420
Metcalf, Asenath IV, 1068
Metcalf, Asenath G. IV, 1068
Metcalf, Caroline IV, 250
Metcalf, Caroline IV, 420
Metcalf, Caroline IV, 1068
Metcalf, Caroline IV, 1083
Metcalf, Elizabeth IV, 420
Metcalf, Elizabeth IV, 1068
Metcalf, Elizabeth IV, 1075
Metcalf, Elizabeth E. IV, 588
Metcalf, George I, 60
Metcalf, George I, 146
Metcalf, Hannah II, 395
Metcalf, Hannah IV, 420
Metcalf, Hannah IV, 588
Metcalf, Hannah IV, 1068
Metcalf, Hannah D. IV, 420
Metcalf, Hannah D. IV, 1068
Metcalf, Hannah D. IV, 1075
Metcalf, Hannah D. IV, 1106
Metcalf, Hannah E. IV, 1068
Metcalf, Jacob II, 395
Metcalf, Jehu IV, 1106
Metcalf, Jemima IV, 1068
Metcalf, Jemima IV, 1081
Metcalf, Jemima S. IV, 588
Metcalf, Jemima S. IV, 1068
Metcalf, Jemima Stephenson IV, 588
Metcalf, Jemimah S. IV, 420
Metcalf, Jesse IV, 250
Metcalf, Jesse IV, 420
Metcalf, Jesse IV, 1068
Metcalf, Jesse IV, 1075
Metcalf, Jesse VI, 423
Metcalf, John I, 60
Metcalf, John IV, 420
Metcalf, John IV, 588
Metcalf, John IV, 1068
Metcalf, John B. IV, 588
Metcalf, John B. IV, 1068
Metcalf, Joseph IV, 1068
Metcalf, Joseph Mead IV, 1068
Metcalf, Joshua IV, 250
Metcalf, Joshua IV, 420
Metcalf, Joshua IV, 1068
Metcalf, Joshua Hudson IV, 1068
Metcalf, Lewis IV, 1068
Metcalf, Lydia IV, 249
Metcalf, Lydia Ann IV, 420
Metcalf, Lydia Ann IV, 588
Metcalf, Lydia Ann IV, 1049
Metcalf, Lydia Ann IV, 1068
Metcalf, Mary II, 395
Metcalf, Mathew II, 395
Metcalf, Matilda IV, 420
Metcalf, Matilda IV, 1068
Metcalf, Moses IV, 1068
Metcalf, Oliver IV, 250
Metcalf, Oliver IV, 420
Metcalf, Oliver IV, 1068
Metcalf, Oliver G. IV, 1068
Metcalf, Oliver J. IV, 420
Metcalf, Rachel II, 395
Metcalf, Rachel VI, 423
Metcalf, Sarah I, 60
Metcalf, Sarah I, 146
Metcalf, Sarah II, 395
Metcalf, Stephen IV, 420
Metcalf, Stephen IV, 1068
Metcalf, Susanna II, 395
Metcalf, Susanna IV, 588
Metcalf, Susanna IV, 592
Metcalf, Susanna IV, 1068
Metcalf, Susannah IV, 420
Metcalf, Susannah IV, 1068
Metcalf, William II, 395
Metcalf, Wm. IV, 1068
Metcalfe, Sarah I, 60
Meteer, Joshua II, 1015
Meteer, Mercy II, 1056
Meteer, Sarah II, 1015
Meteer, Thomas II, 1015
Metford, ??? III, 84
Metford, Daniel III, 228
Metford, Francis III, 228
Metford, Phebe III, 228
Metford, Phebe H. III, 84
Metford, Phebe H. III, 228
Metford, Ruth III, 228
Metford, Seymour III, 228
Metford, Thomas Bevan III, 228
Methiatt, Ann IV, 130
Methiatt, Ann IV, 134
Metler, Riley IV, 1216
Meton, Josephine III, 426
Meton, Robert III, 426
Mettler, J. R. IV, 1216
Mettler, Ola IV, 1216
Mettler, Riley IV, 1216
Metts, James R. VI, 961
Metts, Matilda V. VI, 961
Metz, ??? III, 136
Metz, Herman III, 228
Metz, James R. VI, 961
Metz, John VI, 961
Metz, Mary III, 136
Metz, Mary III, 228
Metz, Mary Ann II, 898
Metz, Mary Ann II, 923
Metz, Matilda VI, 961
Metz, Matilda V. VI, 961
Metz, Selma III, 136
Metzgar, Miriam G. IV, 740
Metzgar, Miriam G. IV, 748
Metzger, Geo. S. VI, 685
Metzger, Margery IV, 645
Metzger, Margery IV, 649
Metzger, Margery VI, 423
Metzger, Margery VI, 685
Metzzer, Margery VI, 423
Metzzer, Margery VI, 426
Mevay, Jane IV, 24
Mevay, Jane IV, 47
Mevay, Josiah Haines IV, 24
Meyer, Amelia Louiza II, 755
Meyer, Ellen C. III, 228

Meyer, George III, 228
Meyer, Jacob II, 755
Meyer, Job II, 755
Meyer, Lavinia Robinson II, 789
Meyer, Louisa II, 605
Meyer, Phebe III, 135
Meyer, Phebe III, 228
Meyers, Ambrose Worthington IV, 420
Meyers, Bernice L. IV, 420
Meyers, Bernice L. IV, 421
Meyers, Bernice Lydia IV, 420
Meyers, Catherine V, 697
Meyers, Charles Lionel IV, 420
Meyers, Charles William Henry V, 267
Meyers, Clifford V, 697
Meyers, Cora V, 697
Meyers, David V, 697
Meyers, Elen V, 267
Meyers, Eliza V, 697
Meyers, Elizabeth Ann V, 98
Meyers, Eva G. V, 697
Meyers, Fred V, 697
Meyers, George V, 267
Meyers, Grace Ann IV, 1239
Meyers, Hannah V, 697
Meyers, Harry IV, 1174
Meyers, Harry V, 98
Meyers, Harry S. V, 697
Meyers, Hattie V, 697
Meyers, Henry V, 697
Meyers, Henry B. V, 697
Meyers, Iota V, 461
Meyers, John V, 267
Meyers, John A. IV, 1239
Meyers, Joseph D. IV, 420
Meyers, Joseph E. IV, 393
Meyers, Joseph E. IV, 420
Meyers, Joseph E. IV, 421
Meyers, Joseph E. IV, 459
Meyers, Levi IV, 1239
Meyers, Louisa II, 605
Meyers, Martha Louise V, 697
Meyers, Mary V, 98
Meyers, Mary C. V, 697
Meyers, Mary J. IV, 420
Meyers, Mary J. IV, 459
Meyers, Mary R. IV, 420
Meyers, Mary W. IV, 393
Meyers, Mary W. IV, 420
Meyers, Pearly E. V, 697
Meyers, Ralph V, 697
Meyers, Ralph J. V, 697
Meyers, Samuel V, 697
Meyers, Sarah IV, 420
Meyers, Sarah V, 697
Meyers, Sarah Ann IV, 1239
Meyers, Sylvia V, 697
Meyers, Sylvia Sanders V, 697
Meyers, Thyra Jane IV, 393
Meyers, Thyra Jane IV, 420
Meyers, William D. IV, 420
Meyers, Willie V, 697
Meyers, Wm. B. V, 697
Meyers, Zebedee V, 267
Meyors, Jacob VI, 840
Meyors, Sarah VI, 840
Miars, Abigail V, 516
Miars, Abigail V, 517
Miars, Alice B. V, 517
Miars, Anna V, 517
Miars, Anna V, 586
Miars, Annie V, 517
Miars, Bessie V, 517
Miars, Catharine V, 517
Miars, Catherine V, 697
Miars, Chas. E. V, 634
Miars, Clifford V, 695
Miars, Clifford V, 697
Miars, Clifford D. V, 194
Miars, Cora V, 697
Miars, Cora B. V, 517
Miars, Corwin V, 517
Miars, David V, 517
Miars, David V, 697
Miars, Dora V, 634
Miars, Earl V, 517
Miars, Edith V, 517
Miars, Eliza V, 697
Miars, Elizabeth V, 586
Miars, Elva V, 517
Miars, Emma B. V, 517
Miars, Esther L. V, 634
Miars, Eva C. V, 423
Miars, Eva G. V, 697
Miars, Fred V, 697
Miars, Haines V, 517
Miars, Hannah V, 517
Miars, Hannah V, 697
Miars, Hannah Foster V, 517
Miars, Harry S. V, 697
Miars, Hattie V, 695
Miars, Hattie V, 697
Miars, Henry V, 349
Miars, Henry V, 517
Miars, Henry V, 697
Miars, Henry B. V, 697
Miars, Isaac V, 586
Miars, Isaiah V, 517
Miars, Isaiah F. V, 516
Miars, Isaiah F. V, 517
Miars, James M. V, 517
Miars, James W. V, 516
Miars, James W. V, 517
Miars, Joseph V, 517
Miars, Levicy V, 634
Miars, Lindley V, 517
Miars, Linley John V, 517
Miars, Louella V, 516
Miars, Louella J. V, 517
Miars, Lula V, 517
Miars, Marcia V, 634
Miars, Margaret V, 516
Miars, Margaret J. V, 517
Miars, Martha Louise V, 697
Miars, Martin V, 517
Miars, Mary C. V, 697
Miars, Mary E. V, 517
Miars, Mary Eliza V, 517
Miars, Mary Ellen V, 517
Miars, Matilda V, 516
Miars, Matilda V, 517
Miars, Maud V, 517
Miars, Minnie V, 194
Miars, Minnie M. V, 517
Miars, Mintie V, 586
Miars, Nancy A. V, 517
Miars, Nicholas V, 517
Miars, Nicholas D. V, 517
Miars, Olitha V, 586
Miars, Oliver B. V, 517
Miars, Ollie V, 517
Miars, Orlando V, 634
Miars, Pearly E. V, 697
Miars, Ralph V, 697
Miars, Ralph J. V, 423
Miars, Ralph J. V, 697
Miars, Rebecca V, 516
Miars, Rebecca M. V, 517
Miars, Sallie V, 586
Miars, Sally V, 517
Miars, Samuel V, 517
Miars, Samuel V, 697
Miars, Sarah V, 516
Miars, Sarah V, 517
Miars, Sarah V, 532
Miars, Sarah V, 697
Miars, Sarah S. V, 517
Miars, Sophronia V, 517
Miars, Sophronia A. V, 516
Miars, Sylvia V, 697
Miars, Sylvia Sanders V, 697
Miars, Willie V, 517
Miars, Willie V, 697
Miars, Willie B. V, 517
Miars, Wm. B. V, 697
Mical, Ruth I, 978
Micgehe, Judith VI, 251
Micgehe, Judith VI, 259
Michael, Alma V, 349
Michael, Alva V, 349
Michael, Archibald II, 596
Michael, Archibald II, 680
Michael, Bertie V, 755
Michael, Elizabeth V, 755
Michael, Emily V, 263
Michael, Harold, Jr. V, 263
Michael, John V, 413
Michael, Lucinda V, 317
Michael, Lucinda V, 349
Michael, Lucinda V, 413
Michael, Martha J. V, 697
Michael, Mattie V, 413
Michael, Nina V, 264
Michael, Norah V, 755
Michael, Phoebe V, 263
Michael, Sarah II, 596
Michael, Sarah II, 680
Michael, Sarah Ann V, 319
Michael, Sarah Ann V, 349
Michael, William W. V, 413
Michael, Wm. W. V, 413
Michaels, Alma V, 349
Michaels, Alva V, 349
Michaels, Lillie IV, 1258
Michaels, Phoebe V, 263
Michaels, William W. V, 413
Michal, Hannah VI, 879
Michanar, Mary IV, 265
Michaner, Barak IV, 421
Michaner, Charles IV, 421
Michaner, Elizabeth IV, 421
Michaner, Lydia IV, 421
Michaner, Mary IV, 252
Michaner, Robert Lindley IV, 421
Michel, Mary I, 311
Michel, Stanley IV, 1286
Michell, Capt. William VI, 11
Michels, Mattie V, 413
Michen, Littleberry VI, 840
Michen, Rachel VI, 840
Michen, Samuel VI, 947
Michener, Abi II, 722
Michener, Abigail IV, 251
Michener, Abigail IV, 252
Michener, Abigail IV, 279
Michener, Abigail IV, 1286
Michener, Abigail V, 98
Michener, Abigail V, 956
Michener, Abraham IV, 740
Michener, Ada V, 99
Michener, Alice V, 193
Michener, Amy IV, 421
Michener, Amy IV, 1106
Michener, Amy IV, 1107
Michener, Amy E. IV, 1107
Michener, Amy T. IV, 540
Michener, Ann II, 898
Michener, Ann IV, 540
Michener, Ann IV, 541
Michener, Ann IV, 740
Michener, Ann IV, 941
Michener, Ann IV, 979
Michener, Ann IV, 980
Michener, Ann V, 99
Michener, Ann V, 921
Michener, Ann E. IV, 692
Michener, Ann E. IV, 740
Michener, Anna IV, 233
Michener, Anna IV, 251
Michener, Anna IV, 266
Michener, Anna IV, 421
Michener, Anna IV, 541
Michener, Anna IV, 550
Michener, Anna IV, 1107
Michener, Anna IV, 1110
Michener, Anna V, 99
Michener, Anna Ellen VI, 488
Michener, Anna Ellen VI, 534
Michener, Anne IV, 421
Michener, Anne IV, 540
Michener, Anne IV, 1106
Michener, Asenath IV, 740
Michener, Barach IV, 421
Michener, Barak IV, 251
Michener, Barak IV, 252
Michener, Barak IV, 302
Michener, Barak IV, 342
Michener, Barak IV, 343
Michener, Barak IV, 421
Michener, Barak IV, 541
Michener, Barak IV, 588
Michener, Bareck IV, 252
Michener, Baruch IV, 251
Michener, Baruch, Jr. IV, 252
Michener, Baruck IV, 252
Michener, Benj. IV, 252
Michener, Benjamin IV, 251
Michener, Benjamin IV, 252
Michener, Benjamin IV, 279
Michener, Benjamin IV, 1274
Michener, Benjamin IV, 1286
Michener, Benjamin V, 98
Michener, Benjamin V, 956
Michener, Borak IV, 421
Michener, Catharine S. IV, 540
Michener, Chalkley IV, 588
Michener, Chalkley Thomas IV, 588
Michener, Charles IV, 251
Michener, Charles IV, 252
Michener, Charles IV, 342
Michener, Charles IV, 343
Michener, Charles IV, 421
Michener, Charles IV, 540
Michener, Charles IV, 541
Michener, Charles IV, 588
Michener, Charles A. VI, 488
Michener, Charles A. VI, 534
Michener, Charles C. IV, 645
Michener, Charles E. V, 99
Michener, Charles Edward V, 99
Michener, Charles G. II, 713
Michener, Charles H. II, 898
Michener, Charles K. IV, 421
Michener, Charles K. IV, 540
Michener, Chas. IV, 541
Michener, Chas. IV, 544
Michener, Chas. C. IV, 645
Michener, Chas. H. II, 898
Michener, Chas. R. IV, 541
Michener, Daniel IV, 233
Michener, Daniel IV, 251
Michener, Daniel IV, 252
Michener, Daniel IV, 266
Michener, Daniel IV, 540
Michener, Daniel IV, 541
Michener, Daniel IV, 550
Michener, David IV, 251
Michener, David IV, 252
Michener, David IV, 1068
Michener, David IV, 1286
Michener, David Bidderson VI, 534
Michener, David H. IV, 540
Michener, David H. IV, 541
Michener, David O. IV, 1146
Michener, David O. IV, 1173
Michener, Eber IV, 252
Michener, Eber IV, 421
Michener, Eber IV, 740
Michener, Edwin IV, 251
Michener, Edwin IV, 252
Michener, Edwin IV, 1286
Michener, Edwin IV, 1294
Michener, Edwin V, 99
Michener, Edwin B. V, 98
Michener, Edwin B. V, 99
Michener, Elisha IV, 1286
Michener, Eliza IV, 692
Michener, Eliza IV, 740
Michener, Eliza IV, 979
Michener, Eliza IV, 980
Michener, Eliza IV, 1286
Michener, Eliza IV, 1294
Michener, Elizabeth II, 395
Michener, Elizabeth IV, 251
Michener, Elizabeth IV, 252
Michener, Elizabeth IV, 342
Michener, Elizabeth IV, 343
Michener, Elizabeth IV, 398
Michener, Elizabeth IV, 421
Michener, Elizabeth IV, 588
Michener, Elizabeth IV, 1174
Michener, Elizabeth V, 956
Michener, Elizabeth E. II, 713
Michener, Elizabeth F. IV, 1106
Michener, Elizabeth L. IV, 252
Michener, Ellen V, 99
Michener, Ellsworth IV, 541
Michener, Elma IV, 251
Michener, Elma IV, 252
Michener, Elmir IV, 540
Michener, Elmor IV, 541
Michener, Emelina IV, 1146
Michener, Emeline IV, 1173
Michener, Emma IV, 421
Michener, Esther IV, 48
Michener, Esther IV, 251
Michener, Esther IV, 252
Michener, Esther VI, 531
Michener, Esther, Jr. VI, 534
Michener, Eva H. IV, 645
Michener, Ezra II, 15
Michener, Ezra IV, 540
Michener, Fleming Crew IV, 1107
Michener, Florence V, 193
Michener, Francis IV, 252
Michener, Francis IV, 343
Michener, Francis IV, 588
Michener, Geo. IV, 201
Michener, Geo. IV, 251
Michener, George IV, 251
Michener, George IV, 252
Michener, George IV, 421
Michener, George IV, 1052
Michener, George IV, 1106
Michener, George IV, 1107
Michener, Grace IV, 222
Michener, Grace IV, 251
Michener, Grace IV, 1174
Michener, Hannah II, 395
Michener, Hannah IV, 48
Michener, Hannah IV, 54
Michener, Hannah IV, 188
Michener, Hannah IV, 251
Michener, Hannah IV, 252
Michener, Hannah IV, 302
Michener, Hannah IV, 421
Michener, Hannah VI, 534
Michener, Hannah Emma IV, 252
Michener, Hannah Emma IV, 342
Michener, Harriet IV, 540
Michener, Harriet IV, 541
Michener, Henrietta R. II, 809
Michener, Henrietta R. II, 898
Michener, Henry IV, 251
Michener, Henry IV, 252
Michener, Henry IV, 1286
Michener, Henry IV, 1297
Michener, Henry V, 956
Michener, Henry V, 961
Michener, Horace V, 193
Michener, Isaac II, 809
Michener, Isaac II, 810
Michener, Isaac IV, 251
Michener, Isaac IV, 252
Michener, Isaac IV, 541
Michener, Isaac IV, 1279
Michener, Isaac IV, 1286
Michener, Isaac V, 59
Michener, Isaac V, 98
Michener, Isaac V, 99
Michener, Isaac V, 956
Michener, Israel IV, 252
Michener, Israel IV, 421
Michener, J. William II, 713
Michener, Jacob IV, 251
Michener, Jacob IV, 252
Michener, Jacob IV, 1068
Michener, James IV, 692
Michener, James IV, 740
Michener, James IV, 750
Michener, James IV, 979
Michener, James IV, 980
Michener, James IV, 1029
Michener, James Carlow VI, 5
Michener, Jane IV, 222
Michener, Jane IV, 251
Michener, Jane IV, 252
Michener, Jane IV, 302
Michener, Jane IV, 476
Michener, Jane IV, 488
Michener, Jane IV, 541
Michener, Jesse IV, 252
Michener, Jesse IV, 343
Michener, Jesse IV, 421
Michener, John II, 395
Michener, John II, 784
Michener, John IV, 49
Michener, John IV, 116
Michener, John IV, 188
Michener, John IV, 211
Michener, John IV, 222
Michener, John IV, 251
Michener, John IV, 252
Michener, John IV, 299
Michener, John IV, 331
Michener, John IV, 342
Michener, John IV, 343
Michener, John IV, 421
Michener, John IV, 488
Michener, John IV, 540
Michener, John IV, 541
Michener, John IV, 588
Michener, John IV, 1286
Michener, John VI, 534
Michener, John E. IV, 252
Michener, John E. IV, 421
Michener, John E. IV, 645
Michener, John G. II, 707
Michener, John G. II, 809
Michener, John G. II, 898
Michener, John Henry IV, 128
Michener, John J. IV, 1273
Michener, John J. IV, 1286
Michener, John L. IV, 251
Michener, John L. IV, 252
Michener, John L. IV, 541
Michener, John M. II, 713
Michener, John Staunton VI, 5
Michener, John W. IV, 251
Michener, John W. IV, 252
Michener, John Waterman IV, 541
Michener, John Watterman IV, 252
Michener, John, Sr. IV, 343
Michener, Jonathan IV, 48
Michener, Jonathan IV, 49
Michener, Jonathan IV, 222
Michener, Jonathan IV, 251
Michener, Jonathan IV, 252
Michener, Jonathan IV, 476
Michener, Jonathan IV, 488
Michener, Jonathan VI, 534
Michener, Jonathan E. IV, 128
Michener, Jones II, 898
Michener, Joseph IV, 251
Michener, Joseph IV, 252
Michener, Joseph IV, 421
Michener, Joseph IV, 541
Michener, Joseph IV, 1106
Michener, Joseph IV, 1107
Michener, Joseph V, 264
Michener, Joseph L. IV, 251
Michener, Julia II, 707
Michener, Julia II, 898
Michener, Julia A. II, 898
Michener, Julia Ann II, 809
Michener, Kinsey IV, 251
Michener, Kinsey IV, 252
Michener, Kinsey IV, 540
Michener, Kinsey IV, 541

hener, Kinsey IV, 550
hener, Lawrence V, 192
hener, Levi IV, 251
hener, Levi IV, 252
hener, Levi IV, 1286
hener, Lindley H. IV, 540
hener, Lindley H. IV, 541
hener, Louisa S. II, 898
hener, Lucena H. IV, 633
hener, Lucena H. IV, 645
hener, Luceta IV, 541
hener, Lucina IV, 645
hener, Lydia II, 898
hener, Lydia II, 1074
hener, Lydia II, 1076
hener, Lydia IV, 251
hener, Lydia IV, 252
hener, Lydia IV, 313
hener, Lydia IV, 342
hener, Lydia IV, 343
hener, Lydia IV, 421
hener, Lydia IV, 540
hener, Lydia IV, 541
hener, Lydia IV, 544
hener, Lydia IV, 588
hener, Lydia IV, 1280
hener, Lydia IV, 1286
hener, Lydia IV, 1297
hener, Lydia V, 921
hener, Lydia V, 956
hener, Lydia V, 961
hener, Lydia Ann IV, 421
hener, Lydia Ann IV, 453
hener, Lydia Ann IV, 540
hener, Lydia Ann IV, 541
hener, Lydia B. IV, 421
hener, Lydia P. IV, 588
hener, Lydia R. IV, 421
hener, Lydia S. II, 809
hener, Lydia S. II, 898
hener, Lydia W. IV, 1286
hener, Lydia W. V, 956
hener, Margaret V, 193
hener, Margaretta D. II, 898
hener, Martha II, 784
hener, Martha II, 809
hener, Martha IV, 188
hener, Martha IV, 211
hener, Martha IV, 222
hener, Martha IV, 251
hener, Martha IV, 252
hener, Martha IV, 266
hener, Martha IV, 488
hener, Martha IV, 1068
hener, Martha IV, 1174
hener, Martha IV, 1279
hener, Martha IV, 1286
hener, Martha V, 60
hener, Martha V, 99
hener, Martha V, 921
hener, Martha V, 956
hener, Martha Lucette
IV, 343
hener, Martha P. IV, 1286
hener, Martha P. V, 59
hener, Martha P. V, 99
hener, Martha Parry II, 810
hener, Mary II, 395
hener, Mary IV, 34
hener, Mary IV, 49
hener, Mary IV, 251
hener, Mary IV, 252
hener, Mary IV, 313
hener, Mary IV, 342
hener, Mary IV, 343
hener, Mary IV, 421
hener, Mary IV, 588
hener, Mary IV, 740
hener, Mary IV, 1029
hener, Mary IV, 1068
hener, Mary IV, 1106
hener, Mary IV, 1107
hener, Mary V, 99
hener, Mary A. IV, 251
hener, Mary A. V, 99
hener, Mary Ann II, 779
hener, Mary Ann II, 810
hener, Mary Ann IV, 251
hener, Mary Ann IV, 252
hener, Mary Ann IV, 514
hener, Mary Ann IV, 541
hener, Mary Ann IV, 1068
hener, Mary Ann IV, 1273
hener, Mary Ann IV, 1286
hener, Mary Ann V, 99
hener, Mary C. IV, 541
hener, Mary C. IV, 1052
hener, Mary C. IV, 1068
hener, Mary Cornelia IV, 540
hener, Mary E. IV, 541
hener, Mary Evaline IV, 541
Michener, Mary L. IV, 421
Michener, Mary L. IV, 1092
Michener, Mary L. IV, 1107
Michener, Mercy II, 809
Michener, Miriam IV, 252
Michener, Miriam IV, 343
Michener, Miriam IV, 421
Michener, Mordecai IV, 48
Michener, Mordecai IV, 49
Michener, Mordecai IV, 251
Michener, Mordecai IV, 252
Michener, Mordecai IV, 1173
Michener, Mordecai IV, 1174
Michener, Mordecai VI, 534
Michener, Naomi IV, 49
Michener, Naomi IV, 251
Michener, Naomi IV, 252
Michener, Nathan IV, 514
Michener, Nathan IV, 541
Michener, Nathan S. IV, 540
Michener, Nathan S. IV, 541
Michener, Neomi IV, 116
Michener, Patience II, 898
Michener, Peninah IV, 421
Michener, Peninah IV, 1106
Michener, Peninah IV, 1107
Michener, Peninah F. IV, 1107
Michener, Penninah IV, 1106
Michener, Phebe IV, 740
Michener, Phebe IV, 1029
Michener, Phebe V, 19
Michener, Phebe V, 99
Michener, Phebe H. IV, 740
Michener, Phebe H. V, 99
Michener, Priscilla II, 809
Michener, Priscilla II, 898
Michener, Rachel II, 898
Michener, Rachel IV, 48
Michener, Rachel IV, 211
Michener, Rachel IV, 251
Michener, Rachel IV, 252
Michener, Rachel IV, 540
Michener, Rachel IV, 541
Michener, Rachel IV, 550
Michener, Rachel VI, 534
Michener, Rebecca II, 395
Michener, Rebecca IV, 201
Michener, Rebecca IV, 251
Michener, Rebecca IV, 252
Michener, Rebecca IV, 299
Michener, Rebecca IV, 343
Michener, Rebecca IV, 421
Michener, Rebecca IV, 541
Michener, Rebecca IV, 550
Michener, Rebecca IV, 588
Michener, Rebecca IV, 1052
Michener, Rebecca IV, 1102
Michener, Rebecca IV, 1106
Michener, Rebecca IV, 1107
Michener, Rebecca W. IV, 251
Michener, Rebecca W. IV, 252
Michener, Rebeckah IV, 541
Michener, Rebekah IV, 541
Michener, Rebekah VI, 531
Michener, Rebekah VI, 534
Michener, Reyner II, 809
Michener, Richard V, 99
Michener, Richard J. V, 99
Michener, Richard Jehu V, 99
Michener, Robert Lindley IV, 342
Michener, Robert Lindley IV, 343
Michener, Robert Lindley IV, 421
Michener, Robert Lindley IV, 588
Michener, Robert Linley IV, 342
Michener, Ruth IV, 1174
Michener, Ryner II, 898
Michener, S. Ella M. V, 99
Michener, S. Ellen V, 98
Michener, Samuel K. V, 99
Michener, Samuel Kelly V, 99
Michener, Samuel R. V, 99
Michener, Sarah II, 395
Michener, Sarah IV, 248
Michener, Sarah IV, 251
Michener, Sarah IV, 252
Michener, Sarah IV, 313
Michener, Sarah IV, 315
Michener, Sarah IV, 331
Michener, Sarah IV, 342
Michener, Sarah IV, 343
Michener, Sarah IV, 421
Michener, Sarah IV, 541
Michener, Sarah IV, 1029
Michener, Sarah IV, 1106
Michener, Sarah IV, 1107
Michener, Sarah IV, 1174
Michener, Sarah IV, 1274
Michener, Sarah IV, 1286
Michener, Sarah VI, 534
Michener, Sarah Alice IV, 541
Michener, Sarah B. IV, 1088
Michener, Sarah B. IV, 1107
Michener, Sarah E. IV, 740
Michener, Sarah E. IV, 750
Michener, Sarah E. V, 99
Michener, Seneca IV, 251
Michener, Seneca IV, 252
Michener, Senoca IV, 1068
Michener, Seth IV, 252
Michener, Seth IV, 343
Michener, Seth IV, 421
Michener, Sina S. II, 713
Michener, Susanna IV, 251
Michener, Susanna IV, 252
Michener, Susanna IV, 313
Michener, Susanna IV, 1173
Michener, Susanna IV, 1286
Michener, Susannah II, 784
Michener, Susannah IV, 1174
Michener, Susannah IV, 1273
Michener, Thomas IV, 48
Michener, Thomas IV, 102
Michener, Thomas IV, 252
Michener, Thomas IV, 740
Michener, Thomas IV, 979
Michener, Thomas IV, 980
Michener, Thomas VI, 534
Michener, Thomas Chalkley
IV, 342
Michener, Thompson Chalkley
IV, 343
Michener, Thos. Chalkley IV, 252
Michener, Thurman V, 193
Michener, Virgo V, 193
Michener, Walter V, 193
Michener, Warner V, 956
Michener, William II, 395
Michener, William IV, 49
Michener, William IV, 251
Michener, William IV, 421
Michener, William IV, 541
Michener, William IV, 1106
Michener, William IV, 1107
Michener, William VI, 534
Michener, William H. V, 99
Michener, William Henry V, 99
Michener, William, Sr. VI, 534
Michener, Wilson IV, 252
Michener, Wilson IV, 421
Michener, Wilson IV, 1068
Michener, Wm. II, 755
Michener, Wm. II, 809
Michener, Wm. IV, 541
Michener, Wm. IV, 1068
Michener, Wm. IV, 1106
Michener, Wm. VI, 531
Michener, Wm. VI, 534
Michener, Wm. Arthur IV, 541
Michener, Wm. F. IV, 1107
Michener, Wm. Galon IV, 540
Michener, Wm. J. II, 755
Michener, Wm. R. IV, 740
Michener, Woodrow V, 956
Michener, Zenadie II, 898
Michener, Zenaida II, 707
Michener, Zenaide II, 898
Michenor, Ann II, 898
Michenor, Barak IV, 380
Michenor, Benjamin IV, 252
Michenor, Charles H. II, 898
Michenor, Chas. C. IV, 645
Michenor, Elma IV, 252
Michenor, Louisa S. II, 898
Michenor, Lucina IV, 645
Michenor, Lydia II, 898
Michenor, Lydia V, 921
Michenor, Lydia R. IV, 380
Michenor, Margaretta D. II, 898
Michenor, Rachel II, 898
Michenor, Rebecca II, 599
Michenor, Ryner II, 898
Michenor, Wilson IV, 421
Micherner, John IV, 526
Micherner, Sarah IV, 526
Michie, Frances D. VI, 824
Michie, Jones VI, 824
Michie, Joseph P. VI, 824
Michineer, Hannah II, 551
Michineer, Hannah II, 599
Michineer, John II, 551
Michineer, Sarah II, 551
Michiner, Ann IV, 833
Michiner, Baruch IV, 251
Michiner, Daniel IV, 1173
Michiner, Daniel IV, 1217
Michiner, David O. IV, 1173
Michiner, David O. IV, 1174
Michiner, David O. IV, 1217
Michiner, Edwin IV, 1173
Michiner, Eliza IV, 833
Michiner, Elizabeth IV, 421
Michiner, Elizabeth IV, 1173
Michiner, Elizabeth IV, 1174
Michiner, Emeline IV, 1173
Michiner, Emeline IV, 1174
Michiner, Enos P. IV, 1174
Michiner, Esther IV, 48
Michiner, Grace IV, 1146
Michiner, Grace IV, 1173
Michiner, Grace IV, 1174
Michiner, Hannah IV, 48
Michiner, Jacob L. IV, 1174
Michiner, Jacob Lukens IV, 1173
Michiner, Jacob Lukens IV, 1174
Michiner, James IV, 833
Michiner, Jane II, 965
Michiner, Jane IV, 1173
Michiner, Jane IV, 1217
Michiner, John IV, 251
Michiner, John IV, 1173
Michiner, John IV, 1174
Michiner, John IV, 1179
Michiner, John E. IV, 421
Michiner, Jonathan IV, 48
Michiner, Jonathan IV, 49
Michiner, Josiah II, 965
Michiner, Lydia IV, 1173
Michiner, Lydian IV, 1174
Michiner, Macre W. II, 965
Michiner, Margaret II, 956
Michiner, Martha IV, 251
Michiner, Martha IV, 1168
Michiner, Martha IV, 1173
Michiner, Martha IV, 1174
Michiner, Mordecai IV, 48
Michiner, Mordecai IV, 49
Michiner, Mordecai IV, 1146
Michiner, Mordecai IV, 1173
Michiner, Mordecai IV, 1174
Michiner, Peninah IV, 1122
Michiner, Rachel IV, 1173
Michiner, Rebecca IV, 541
Michiner, Ruth IV, 1173
Michiner, Ruth IV, 1174
Michiner, Sarah IV, 1155
Michiner, Sarah IV, 1173
Michiner, Sarah IV, 1174
Michiner, Susanna IV, 1146
Michiner, Susanna IV, 1173
Michiner, Susanna P. IV, 1174
Michiner, Susanna P. IV, 1179
Michiner, Susannah IV, 1174
Michiner, Thomas IV, 48
Michiner, Thomas IV, 833
Michiner, Titus IV, 1174
Michiner, William IV, 49
Michiner, Wm. IV, 1173
Michinor, Charles IV, 1216
Michinor, Chas. Enoch IV, 1217
Michinor, Daniel IV, 1217
Michinor, David O. IV, 1217
Michinor, Enoch IV, 1216
Michinor, Esther IV, 1216
Michinor, Esther C. IV, 1217
Michinor, Henry P. IV, 1216
Michinor, Henry P. IV, 1217
Michinor, John IV, 1216
Michinor, John IV, 1217
Michinor, Martha IV, 1216
Michinor, Martha H. IV, 1217
Michinor, Rebecca Ann IV, 1216
Michinor, Rebecca Ann IV, 1217
Michinor, Ruth IV, 1203
Michinor, Ruth IV, 1217
Michinor, Susanna IV, 1216
Michinor, Susanna IV, 1217
Michinor, Wm. P. IV, 1217
Michner, Hannah IV, 356
Michner, Mary IV, 1068
Michoner, Daniel IV, 1217
Micholl, Jane VI, 11
Micholl, William VI, 11
Michols, H. S. IV, 1330
Michy, Elmira A. V, 921
Mickel, Annie L. III, 382
Mickel, Annie L. III, 387
Mickinley, William V, 506
Mickle, Amelia VI, 323
Mickle, Ann S. II, 296
Mickle, Ann S. II, 304
Mickle, Anna Amelia II, 179
Mickle, Anna Amelia II, 296
Mickle, Archibald II, 596
Mickle, David II, 242
Mickle, David II, 274
Mickle, David VI, 323
Mickle, Elizabeth II, 364
Mickle, Elizabeth II, 527
Mickle, Elizabeth II, 596
Mickle, Elizabeth V, 755
Mickle, Gerard VI, 323
Mickle, Hannah II, 596
Mickle, Hannah II, 602
Mickle, Howard II, 296
Mickle, Howard A. II, 179
Mickle, Howard A. II, 296
Mickle, Howard A. II, 304
Mickle, Howard Abbott II, 296
Mickle, Jane VI, 323
Mickle, John II, 242
Mickle, John II, 264
Mickle, John II, 296
Mickle, John II, 304
Mickle, John Howard II, 179
Mickle, John Howard II, 296
Mickle, John Watkins VI, 323
Mickle, Judith VI, 323
Mickle, Margaretta II, 296
Mickle, Margaretta II, 304
Mickle, Margaretta T. II, 179
Mickle, Mary II, 242
Mickle, Mary II, 264
Mickle, Mary II, 785
Mickle, Mary II, 852
Mickle, Millicent VI, 323
Mickle, Penelope VI, 323
Mickle, Rachel II, 242
Mickle, Rachel II, 274
Mickle, Robert II, 296
Mickle, Robert VI, 323
Mickle, Robert T. II, 296
Mickle, Robert Thomas II, 179
Mickle, Rooth I, 993
Mickle, Ruth VI, 323
Mickle, Ruth VI, 331
Mickle, Ruth VI, 840
Mickle, Samuel II, 395
Mickle, Samuel II, 527
Mickle, Samuel II, 590
Mickle, Samuel II, 596
Mickle, Samuel II, 602
Mickle, Samuel VI, 323
Mickle, Sarah II, 242
Mickle, Sarah II, 274
Mickle, Sarah II, 596
Mickle, Sarah II, 804
Mickle, Sarah E. P. II, 1056
Mickle, Thomasin II, 395
Mickle, Thomasine II, 590
Mickle, Thomasine II, 596
Mickle, Tomasin II, 395
Mickle, William II, 242
Mickle, William II, 274
Mickle, William VI, 331
Mickle, William VI, 840
Mickles, Alvin G. I, 946
Mickles, Nellie I, 946
Mickoll, Samuel II, 395
Micracken, William I, 766
Midcaff, Joseph IV, 250
Midcaff, Martha IV, 250
Midcelf, Abraham IV, 153
Midcelf, Hannah IV, 153
Midcelf, John IV, 153
Middleberger, Judith III, 228
Middlebrook, ??? III, 282
Middlebrook, Mary Ann III, 228
Middlebrook, Mary Ann III, 282
Middlecott, ??? III, 98
Middlecott, Agnes III, 228
Middlecott, Israel III, 228
Middlecott, Mary Ann III, 98
Middlecott, Mary Ann III, 228
Middlemas, Anna IV, 252
Middlemas, Robert IV, 252
Middlesworth, Andrew J.
IV, 1287
Middleton, ??? II, 809
Middleton, Aaron II, 395
Middleton, Aaron Hewes II, 596
Middleton, Abel II, 587
Middleton, Abel II, 596
Middleton, Alfred H. II, 834
Middleton, Alfred H. II, 898
Middleton, Alfred Harvey II, 809
Middleton, Amelia R. IV, 740
Middleton, Amelia R. IV, 790
Middleton, Amos II, 205
Middleton, Amos II, 242
Middleton, Anna II, 537
Middleton, Anna II, 596
Middleton, Anna P. II, 898
Middleton, Anna Parry II, 809
Middleton, Avis II, 780
Middleton, Bell V, 517
Middleton, Belle V, 517
Middleton, Benjamin II, 596
Middleton, Benjamin Ferguson
II, 596
Middleton, Catharine II, 809
Middleton, Catharine II, 898
Middleton, Catherine IV, 747
Middleton, Chamless II, 242
Middleton, Chamless II, 276

Middleton, Chamliss II, 242
Middleton, Charlotte II, 898
Middleton, Charlotte II, 1015
Middleton, Chas. II, 898
Middleton, Chas. IV, 1040
Middleton, Christiana I, 562
Middleton, Christianna I, 600
Middleton, Christianna I, 607
Middleton, Clara B. II, 809
Middleton, Clara E. II, 813
Middleton, Clara E. II, 898
Middleton, Clara E. II, 906
Middleton, Deborah IV, 645
Middleton, Deborah IV, 646
Middleton, Deborah IV, 680
Middleton, Deborah IV, 704
Middleton, Deborah IV, 740
MIddleton, Deborah IV, 740
Middleton, Deborah IV, 833
Middleton, Deborah IV, 980
Middleton, Deborah V, 349
Middleton, Deborah VI, 597
Middleton, Deborah VI, 601
Middleton, Deborah, Jr. IV, 910
Middleton, Doratha IV, 980
Middleton, Dorothy IV, 645
Middleton, Dorothy IV, 833
Middleton, Dorothy IV, 910
Middleton, Dorothy IV, 980
Middleton, Elisha II, 475
Middleton, Eliza IV, 1040
Middleton, Elizabeth II, 205
Middleton, Elizabeth II, 242
Middleton, Elizabeth II, 450
Middleton, Elizabeth II, 588
Middleton, Elizabeth II, 596
Middleton, Elizabeth IV, 377
Middleton, Elizabeth IV, 421
Middleton, Elizabeth IV, 740
Middleton, Elizabeth IV, 979
Middleton, Elizabeth IV, 980
Middleton, Elizabeth IV, 1040
Middleton, Elizabeth V, 517
Middleton, Elizabeth A. II, 899
Middleton, Elizabeth H. II, 296
Middleton, Elizabeth H. II, 298
Middleton, Elizabeth M. II, 834
Middleton, Elizabeth M. II, 898
Middleton, Elizabeth Marshall II, 809
Middleton, Ella C. II, 809
Middleton, Ellis S. II, 898
Middleton, Ellwood II, 809
Middleton, Ellwood II, 834
Middleton, Ellwood II, 898
Middleton, Enoch II, 793
Middleton, Enoch II, 809
Middleton, Esther II, 587
Middleton, Esther II, 596
Middleton, Esther IV, 980
Middleton, Esther IV, 1008
Middleton, Gabriel II, 852
Middleton, Gabriel II, 898
Middleton, Geo. A. V, 921
Middleton, George, Jr. II, 242
Middleton, Gustavius IV, 790
Middleton, Hannah I, 562
Middleton, Hannah I, 789
Middleton, Hannah I, 829
Middleton, Hannah I, 961
Middleton, Hannah I, 966
Middleton, Hannah I, 1049
Middleton, Hannah II, 296
Middleton, Hannah II, 475
Middleton, Hannah II, 713
Middleton, Hannah II, 755
Middleton, Hannah II, 793
Middleton, Hannah IV, 421
Middleton, Hannah IV, 645
Middleton, Hannah IV, 704
Middleton, Hannah IV, 740
Middleton, Hannah IV, 833
Middleton, Hannah IV, 910
Middleton, Hannah V, 99
Middleton, Hannah Ann II, 809
Middleton, Hannah Ann II, 898
Middleton, Hannah C. II, 296
Middleton, Hannah C. II, 728
Middleton, Hannah C. II, 755
Middleton, Hannah Gill II, 596
Middleton, Hannah L. III, 149
Middleton, Hannah L. III, 228
Middleton, Hannah S. II, 832
Middleton, Hannah S. II, 898
Middleton, Harriett II, 904
Middleton, Harvey M. II, 809
Middleton, Helen Narsau II, 596
Middleton, Hester II, 596
Middleton, Hudson IV, 645
Middleton, Hudson IV, 680
Middleton, Hudson IV, 704
Middleton, Hudson IV, 740
Middleton, Hudson V, 343
Middleton, Hudson V, 349
Middleton, Hudson V, 447
Middleton, Hudson VI, 597
Middleton, Hudson VI, 601
Middleton, Hudson, Jr. IV, 645
Middleton, Hudson, Jr. IV, 740
Middleton, Hugh II, 82
Middleton, Hugh II, 87
Middleton, Ira IV, 645
Middleton, Ira IV, 833
Middleton, Ira IV, 980
Middleton, Ira V, 349
Middleton, Irey IV, 980
Middleton, Isaac IV, 980
Middleton, Isaac Ivins II, 1015
Middleton, J. Raymond V, 517
Middleton, James II, 395
Middleton, James II, 596
Middleton, James Vernon I, 829
Middleton, Jane III, 149
Middleton, Jane III, 228
Middleton, Jehu I, 789
Middleton, Jehu I, 829
Middleton, Jehu I, 830
Middleton, Jehu I, 966
Middleton, Jehu I, 1049
Middleton, Jehu IV, 377
Middleton, Jehu IV, 421
Middleton, Jehu V, 99
Middleton, Joel IV, 980
Middleton, John II, 474
Middleton, John II, 521
Middleton, John II, 596
Middleton, John IV, 153
Middleton, John B. II, 296
Middleton, John B. II, 713
Middleton, John B. II, 755
Middleton, John Beck I, 789
Middleton, John Beck I, 829
Middleton, Joseph I, 789
Middleton, Joseph I, 829
Middleton, Joseph I, 966
Middleton, Joseph I, 1001
Middleton, Joseph I, 1011
Middleton, Joseph I, 1049
Middleton, Joseph II, 780
Middleton, Joseph II, 852
Middleton, Joseph II, 898
Middleton, Joseph IV, 140
Middleton, Joseph IV, 153
Middleton, Joseph IV, 385
Middleton, Joseph IV, 421
Middleton, Joseph V, 99
Middleton, Joseph H. III, 228
Middleton, Joseph Hewes II, 596
Middleton, Joshua IV, 790
Middleton, Josiah Hewes II, 179
Middleton, Josiah Hewes II, 242
Middleton, Levi IV, 645
Middleton, Levi IV, 646
Middleton, Levi IV, 980
Middleton, Levi IV, 1040
Middleton, Levi V, 447
Middleton, Lewis IV, 980
Middleton, Lizzie M. V, 517
Middleton, Luzena I, 562
Middleton, Lydia II, 852
Middleton, Lydia II, 898
Middleton, Lydia IV, 646
Middleton, Lydia IV, 833
Middleton, Lydia IV, 910
Middleton, Lydia IV, 916
Middleton, Lydia V, 921
Middleton, Lydia V, 933
Middleton, Lydia Cooke II, 898
Middleton, Mahlon IV, 980
Middleton, Malon IV, 980
Middleton, Margaret II, 793
Middleton, Margaret II, 852
Middleton, Margaret II, 898
Middleton, Maria II, 804
Middleton, Martha I, 789
Middleton, Martha I, 966
Middleton, Martha II, 795
Middleton, Martha IV, 142
Middleton, Martha IV, 153
Middleton, Martha L. II, 898
Middleton, Mary I, 789
Middleton, Mary I, 829
Middleton, Mary I, 830
Middleton, Mary I, 966
Middleton, Mary II, 82
Middleton, Mary II, 87
Middleton, Mary II, 205
Middleton, Mary II, 242
Middleton, Mary II, 276
Middleton, Mary II, 587
Middleton, Mary II, 596
Middleton, Mary II, 809
Middleton, Mary II, 898
Middleton, Mary IV, 140
Middleton, Mary IV, 153
Middleton, Mary IV, 377
Middleton, Mary IV, 421
Middleton, Mary IV, 645
Middleton, Mary IV, 833
Middleton, Mary IV, 902
Middleton, Mary IV, 910
Middleton, Mary IV, 1040
Middleton, Mary V, 99
Middleton, Mary V, 190
Middleton, Mary VI, 597
Middleton, Mary VI, 601
Middleton, Mary VI, 980
Middleton, Mary Ann II, 290
Middleton, Mary Ann II, 296
Middleton, Mary Ann IV, 979
Middleton, Mary Ann IV, 980
Middleton, Mary Ann V, 99
Middleton, Mary Ann V, 102
Middleton, Mary E. V, 517
Middleton, Mary F. V, 190
Middleton, Mary H. II, 898
Middleton, Mary R. V, 189
Middleton, Mary S. III, 228
Middleton, Mary S. III, 253
Middleton, Mellie E. V, 189
Middleton, Mercy II, 234
Middleton, Mercy II, 242
Middleton, Micajah IV, 980
Middleton, Nancy I, 562
Middleton, Naomi Passmore II, 820
Middleton, Nathan II, 832
Middleton, Nathan II, 898
Middleton, Nathaniel IV, 645
Middleton, Nathaniel IV, 833
Middleton, Nathaniel IV, 910
Middleton, Nathaniel IV, 980
Middleton, Nathaniel VI, 601
Middleton, Nathaniel Gill II, 596
Middleton, Patience II, 1005
Middleton, Phebe I, 408
Middleton, Phebe I, 425
Middleton, Phebe I, 776
Middleton, Phebe I, 789
Middleton, Phebe I, 829
Middleton, Phebe I, 1011
Middleton, Phebe IV, 140
Middleton, Phebe IV, 153
Middleton, Phebe IV, 421
Middleton, Phebe V, 99
Middleton, Rachel II, 242
Middleton, Rachel II, 276
Middleton, Rachel II, 481
Middleton, Rachel II, 596
Middleton, Rachel II, 799
Middleton, Rachel IV, 421
Middleton, Rachel IV, 965
Middleton, Rachel IV, 980
Middleton, Rachel V, 99
Middleton, Rachel V, 343
Middleton, Rachel V, 349
Middleton, Rachel V, 447
Middleton, Rachel W. II, 242
Middleton, Rebecca II, 132
Middleton, Rebecca II, 475
Middleton, Rebecca II, 780
Middleton, Rebecca II, 834
Middleton, Rebecca II, 898
Middleton, Rebecca IV, 951
Middleton, Rebecca IV, 980
Middleton, Rebecca IV, 1040
Middleton, Rebecca Ann II, 809
Middleton, Richard IV, 421
Middleton, Richard V, 99
Middleton, Robert II, 205
Middleton, Robert II, 242
Middleton, Robert II, 276
Middleton, Robert II, 596
Middleton, Samuel I, 562
Middleton, Samuel I, 600
Middleton, Samuel II, 475
Middleton, Samuel II, 832
Middleton, Samuel II, 898
Middleton, Samuel V, 933
Middleton, Samuel B. II, 296
Middleton, Samuel B. II, 755
Middleton, Samuel C. II, 296
Middleton, Samuel H. I, 607
Middleton, Sarah II, 450
Middleton, Sarah II, 475
Middleton, Sarah II, 481
Middleton, Sarah II, 596
Middleton, Sarah II, 605
Middleton, Sarah IV, 421
Middleton, Sarah IV, 588
Middleton, Sarah IV, 639
Middleton, Sarah IV, 645
Middleton, Sarah IV, 833
Middleton, Sarah IV, 980
Middleton, Sarah VI, 601
Middleton, Sarah Jane I, 562
Middleton, Sarah Knowles IV, 385
Middleton, Sarah T. II, 832
Middleton, Sarah T. II, 898
Middleton, Spencer II, 755
Middleton, Spencer II, 898
Middleton, T. J. V, 189
Middleton, Thomas II, 242
Middleton, Thomas II, 296
Middleton, Thomas II, 395
Middleton, Thomas II, 450
Middleton, Thomas II, 481
Middleton, Thomas II, 596
Middleton, Thomas II, 713
Middleton, Thomas II, 755
Middleton, Thomas V, 190
Middleton, Thomas F. II, 296
Middleton, Thomas F. II, 755
Middleton, Wd. Mary Hill II, 809
Middleton, Wd. Miriam II, 809
Middleton, Wd. Sarah Doyle II, 596
Middleton, William IV, 980
Middleton, Wm. II, 475
Middleton, Wm. III, 149
Middleton, Wm. III, 228
Middleton, Wm. IV, 980
Middleton, Wm. IV, 1040
Middletown, George, Jr. II, 242
Midelton, Christianna I, 607
Midleton, Hannah I, 966
Midleton, Jehu I, 966
Midleton, Joseph I, 966
Midleton, Martha I, 966
Midleton, Mary I, 966
Midleton, Mary II, 87
Midleton, Thomas II, 508
Midleton, Thomas II, 596
Midleton, Wd. Sarah II, 508
Midleton, Wd. Sarah Doyle II, 596
Mien, Andrew II, 595
Mien, Susanna II, 595
Miers, Benjamin II, 605
Miers, Elizabeth II, 605
Miers, Henry V, 349
Miers, Levicy V, 622
Miers, Levicy V, 634
Miers, Mary V, 194
Miers, Priscilla V, 379
Miers, Samuel V, 379
Miers, Sarah IV, 420
Miers, Sarah IV, 428
Mierse, Abigail IV, 1287
Mierse, Abigail IV, 1290
Mifflen, Sarah II, 597
Mifflin, ??? II, 395
Mifflin, Ann II, 372
Mifflin, Ann II, 597
Mifflin, Ann, Jr. II, 516
Mifflin, Anne II, 371
Mifflin, Anne II, 395
Mifflin, Anne II, 516
Mifflin, Anne II, 597
Mifflin, Benjamin II, 395
Mifflin, Benjamin II, 596
Mifflin, Benjamin II, 597
Mifflin, Charles II, 395
Mifflin, Daniel II, 396
Mifflin, Daniel II, 516
Mifflin, Daniel II, 597
Mifflin, Deborah II, 395
Mifflin, Deborah Ann II, 242
Mifflin, Edward II, 395
Mifflin, Edward II, 596
Mifflin, Elisabeth II, 596
Mifflin, Elizabeth II, 395
Mifflin, Elizabeth II, 541
Mifflin, Elizabeth II, 596
Mifflin, Elizabeth II, 597
Mifflin, Elizabeth II, 602
Mifflin, Elizabeth II, 811
Mifflin, Ester II, 395
Mifflin, Esther II, 495
Mifflin, Esther II, 596
Mifflin, Esther II, 597
Mifflin, Florence II, 879
Mifflin, Florence II, 899
Mifflin, George II, 495
Mifflin, George II, 596
Mifflin, George II, 597
Mifflin, George II, 602
Mifflin, George, Jr. II, 395
Mifflin, George, Jr. II, 597
Mifflin, Hannah II, 395
Mifflin, Hannah II, 588
Mifflin, Hannah II, 597
Mifflin, Hannah II, 664
Mifflin, Hester II, 395
Mifflin, James II, 242
Mifflin, Jane II, 395
Mifflin, Jane II, 596
Mifflin, Jane II, 675
Mifflin, John II, 395
Mifflin, John II, 396
Mifflin, John II, 523
Mifflin, John II, 541
Mifflin, John II, 596
Mifflin, John II, 602
Mifflin, John II, 664
Mifflin, John Houston II, 242
Mifflin, John Houston II, 756
Mifflin, Jonathan II, 395
Mifflin, Jonathan II, 518
Mifflin, Jonathan II, 568
Mifflin, Jonathan II, 596
Mifflin, Jonathan II, 597
Mifflin, Jonathan II, 602
Mifflin, Jonathan II, 615
Mifflin, Jonathan II, 626
Mifflin, Jonathan II, 638
Mifflin, Joseph II, 242
Mifflin, Joseph II, 395
Mifflin, Lemuel II, 395
Mifflin, Lemuel II, 597
Mifflin, Liddia II, 395
Mifflin, Lloyd II, 597
Mifflin, Martha II, 242
Mifflin, Martha II, 597
Mifflin, Martha II, 602
Mifflin, Mary II, 395
Mifflin, Mary II, 455
Mifflin, Mary II, 516
Mifflin, Mary II, 597
Mifflin, Maude R. II, 879
Mifflin, Maude R. II, 899
Mifflin, Mifflin II, 597
Mifflin, Morris Morris II, 596
Mifflin, Patience II, 395
Mifflin, Patience II, 615
Mifflin, Rebecca II, 818
Mifflin, Rebecca II, 917
Mifflin, Rebecca Rowland II, 8
Mifflin, Rebeccah II, 395
Mifflin, Rebekah II, 512
Mifflin, Samuel II, 395
Mifflin, Samuel II, 512
Mifflin, Samuel E. II, 597
Mifflin, Samuel H. II, 879
Mifflin, Samuel H. II, 899
Mifflin, Sarah II, 395
Mifflin, Sarah II, 396
Mifflin, Sarah II, 523
Mifflin, Sarah II, 568
Mifflin, Sarah II, 576
Mifflin, Sarah II, 596
Mifflin, Sarah II, 597
Mifflin, Sarah II, 602
Mifflin, Sarah II, 638
Mifflin, Sarah II, 811
Mifflin, Sarah L. II, 597
Mifflin, Susanna II, 597
Mifflin, Thomas II, 597
Mifflin, Thomas II, 602
Mifflin, Thomas, Jr. II, 597
Mifflin, Warner II, 395
Mifflin, Warner II, 516
Mifflin, Warner II, 597
Mifflin, Warner II, 811
Mifflin, Wd Sarah II, 626
Mifflin, Wd. Elizabeth II, 395
Mifflin, Wd. Sarah II, 597
Mifflin, William II, 396
Miflin, Elizabeth II, 395
Miflin, George II, 580
Miflin, Jonathan II, 395
Miflin, Mary IV, 76
Miflin, Mary IV, 100
Miflin, Sarah II, 580
Miflin, Sarah II, 597
Mignard, Maurice IV, 1330
Migrange, Girden IV, 1330
Mihuns, Morris I, 146
Mihuns???, Morris I, 146
Mikell, Rogers VI, 11
Mikels, Alvin G. I, 946
Mikels, Amy I, 989
Mikels, Amy I, 993
Mikels, Carrie Marie I, 946
Mikels, David I, 946
Mikels, David Rosco I, 946
Mikels, David Roscoe I, 930
Mikels, Frances I, 944
Mikels, Frances I, 946
Mikels, Hettie Iredell I, 946
Mikels, Ida Ruth I, 930
Mikels, J. Alvia I, 930
Mikels, Junius Allen I, 946
Mikels, Laura A. I, 930

els, Laura A. I, 946
els, Lena E. I, 930
els, Lena Estelle I, 946
els, Lewis P. I, 930
els, Lois I, 930
els, Louis P. I, 946
els, Mary I, 946
els, Mary Frances I, 930
els, Nellie I, 946
els, Nellie Camilla I, 930
els, Nicholas I, 930
els, Raymond Wilson I, 930
els, Rooth I, 993
els, Sarah I, 930
els, Sarah I, 946
els, Sarah Elizabeth I, 930
esell, Adda IV, 252
esell, Catharine IV, 252
le, Mary VI, 991
les, Carrie Marie I, 946
les, Hettie Iredell I, 946
les, Laura I, 929
les, Lena I, 929
les, Lewis I, 929
am, Ann VI, 996
am, Ann VI, 1002
am, Anne VI, 912
am, Anny VI, 961
am, Benjamin VI, 961
am, Benjamin VI, 984
am, Benjamin K. VI, 961
am, Catharine VI, 961
am, Charity VI, 961
am, Deborah VI, 1016
am, Delaney VI, 961
am, Ditsey VI, 961
am, Edy VI, 961
am, Elenor VI, 996
am, Elizabeth VI, 961
am, Elizabeth VI, 1016
am, Frances VI, 912
am, James P. VI, 961
am, Jemima VI, 961
am, Jerusha VI, 885
am, Jerusha Jane VI, 885
am, Joel R. VI, 974
am, John VI, 885
am, John VI, 961
am, John E. VI, 961
am, Joseph VI, 961
am, Liza VI, 961
am, Lucy VI, 961
am, Margarett VI, 961
am, Mary K. VI, 984
am, Matilda M. VI, 961
am, Micajah VI, 961
am, Moses VI, 961
am, Nancy VI, 885
am, Nancy VI, 961
am, Nancy VI, 1000
am, Pettis VI, 961
am, Pettis C. VI, 983
am, Polly VI, 1002
am, Rhoda VI, 961
am, Rush VI, 881
am, Rush VI, 961
am, Rush VI, 1015
am, Ruth VI, 966
am, Salley VI, 885
am, Sally VI, 961
am, Sally VI, 983
am, Solomon VI, 961
am, Solomon VI, 966
am, Solomon VI, 976
am, Susanna VI, 961
am, Thomas VI, 961
am, William VI, 961
am, Zachariah VI, 961
born, Patience VI, 428
bourn, Andrew VI, 331
bourn, Anna IV, 49
bourn, Anna VI, 331
bourn, Anne VI, 331
bourn, Betsy IV, 900
bourn, Betsy IV, 910
bourn, Betty IV, 646
bourn, David IV, 49
bourn, David IV, 834
bourn, David VI, 331
bourn, Jacob IV, 49
bourn, Jacob IV, 834
bourn, Jacob VI, 331
bourn, Jane IV, 809
bourn, Jane IV, 833
bourn, Jane IV, 910
bourn, Jonathan IV, 49
bourn, Jonathan IV, 833
bourn, Jonathan VI, 331
bourn, Jonathan William Jacob
Lot VI, 331
bourn, Lot IV, 49
Milbourn, Lot IV, 834
Milbourn, Lot VI, 331
Milbourn, Lydia IV, 905
Milbourn, Lydia IV, 910
Milbourn, Samuel IV, 49
Milbourn, Samuel IV, 809
Milbourn, Samuel IV, 833
Milbourn, Samuel VI, 331
Milbourn, Sarah IV, 49
Milbourn, Sarah IV, 646
Milbourn, Sarah VI, 331
Milbourn, William IV, 49
Milbourn, William IV, 834
Milbourn, William VI, 331
Milbourn, Zenas Samuel VI, 331
Milbourn, Zenis IV, 49
Milbourn, Zenoss VI, 331
Milbourne, Anna IV, 740
Milbourne, Betsy IV, 740
Milbourne, David IV, 740
Milbourne, Jacob IV, 740
Milbourne, Jonathan IV, 740
Milbourne, Lott IV, 740
Milbourne, Patience VI, 423
Milbourne, Samuel IV, 740
Milbourne, Sarah IV, 740
Milbourne, Sarah VI, 331
Milbourne, William IV, 740
Milburn, Andrew VI, 423
Milburn, Andrew VI, 534
Milburn, Anna VI, 331
Milburn, David VI, 423
Milburn, Frances Olive V, 291
Milburn, Jemima V, 291
Milburn, John VI, 423
Milburn, Jonathan William Jacob
Lot VI, 331
Milburn, Patience VI, 423
Milburn, Robert VI, 374
Milburn, Robert VI, 423
Milburn, Sarah VI, 331
Milburn, Sarah VI, 374
Milburn, Sarah VI, 534
Milburn, Wd. Sarah VI, 423
Milburn, Wesley V, 291
Milburn, William VI, 423
Milburn, Zenas Samuel VI, 331
Mildeberger, ??? III, 228
Mildeberger, Adelia III, 228
Mildeberger, Emeline III, 228
Mildeburger, ??? III, 184
Mildeburger, Judith III, 184
Milegan, Ann IV, 980
Miler, Betsy VI, 882
Miler, Elizabeth VI, 916
Miler, Nancy VI, 877
Miler, Thomas VI, 916
Miles, ??? V, 795
Miles, A. C. V, 816
Miles, Abigail V, 755
Miles, Abijah V, 816
Miles, Abraham N. VI, 838
Miles, Alexander V, 817
Miles, Allen V, 816
Miles, Alma F. IV, 1040
Miles, Alma T. IV, 980
Miles, Amos VI, 423
Miles, Ann V, 816
Miles, Anna V, 814
Miles, Anna V, 815
Miles, Anna V, 816
Miles, Anna V, 817
Miles, Anna Mary V, 816
Miles, Anne V, 755
Miles, Anne V, 811
Miles, Anne V, 815
Miles, Anne V, 816
Miles, Anne V, 822
Miles, Anne Jane V, 816
Miles, Anzinnetta V, 755
Miles, Armstead J. VI, 961
Miles, Benjamin V, 748
Miles, Benjamin V, 755
Miles, Benjamin V, 814
Miles, Benjamin V, 815
Miles, Benjamin V, 816
Miles, Benjamin V, 817
Miles, Branson J. V, 755
Miles, Branston J. V, 816
Miles, Caleb IV, 815
Miles, Caroline IV, 980
Miles, Caroline V, 817
Miles, Carroll IV, 980
Miles, Carroll IV, 1040
Miles, Carroll H. IV, 252
Miles, Carroll H. IV, 397
Miles, Carroll H. IV, 959
Miles, Carroll H. IV, 980
Miles, Carroll H. IV, 1040
Miles, Carroll Hagen IV, 980
Miles, Carroll Hogan IV, 980
Miles, Catharine I, 1021
Miles, Catharine I, 1034
Miles, Catharine C. V, 755
Miles, Catherine V, 853
Miles, Catherine C. V, 816
Miles, Charity V, 816
Miles, Charles F. V, 816
Miles, Charley L. V, 817
Miles, Charlotte VI, 891
Miles, Cora Alice V, 816
Miles, D. V, 816
Miles, David I, 562
Miles, David I, 1016
Miles, David I, 1027
Miles, David I, 1034
Miles, David V, 755
Miles, David V, 789
Miles, David V, 799
Miles, David V, 806
Miles, David V, 815
Miles, David V, 816
Miles, David V, 817
Miles, David V, 822
Miles, David E. V, 816
Miles, David E. V, 817
Miles, David W. V, 748
Miles, David W. V, 755
Miles, David W. V, 814
Miles, David W. V, 817
Miles, Deborah II, 597
Miles, Deborah II, 669
Miles, Dorcas V, 745
Miles, Dorcas V, 755
Miles, Elizabeth I, 1027
Miles, Elizabeth I, 1034
Miles, Elizabeth II, 396
Miles, Elizabeth V, 744
Miles, Elizabeth V, 755
Miles, Elizabeth V, 799
Miles, Elizabeth V, 815
Miles, Elizabeth V, 816
Miles, Elizabeth V, 817
Miles, Elizabeth V, 818
Miles, Elizabeth VI, 961
Miles, Elizabeth Brown V, 817
Miles, Elizabeth C. V, 805
Miles, Elizabeth C. V, 816
Miles, Elizabeth C. V, 817
Miles, Elizabeth H. V, 817
Miles, Ellwood V, 816
Miles, Elma IV, 1040
Miles, Elma F. IV, 980
Miles, Elna IV, 980
Miles, Elwood V, 817
Miles, Emeline V, 817
Miles, Emma V, 586
Miles, Enoch V, 815
Miles, Enoch V, 816
Miles, Enoch P. V, 744
Miles, Enoch P. V, 755
Miles, Enoch P. V, 810
Miles, Enoch P. V, 817
Miles, Enos P. V, 816
Miles, Esther IV, 815
Miles, Esther V, 799
Miles, Esther V, 804
Miles, Esther V, 815
Miles, Esther V, 816
Miles, Esther Martin V, 817
Miles, Eunice V, 815
Miles, Eunice V, 817
Miles, Eunice Ann V, 749
Miles, Eunice Ann V, 813
Miles, Eunice Ann V, 815
Miles, Eunice Ann V, 816
Miles, Francis IV, 980
Miles, Francy E. V, 817
Miles, Geo. IV, 588
Miles, Geo. IV, 980
Miles, George IV, 396
Miles, George IV, 588
Miles, Hannah IV, 154
Miles, Hannah IV, 332
Miles, Hannah IV, 343
Miles, Hannah IV, 396
Miles, Hannah IV, 421
Miles, Hannah IV, 588
Miles, Hannah IV, 980
Miles, Hannah VI, 423
Miles, Hannah J. V, 816
Miles, Hannah, Jr. IV, 343
Miles, Hannah, Jr. IV, 421
Miles, Helen IV, 1040
Miles, Helen Elvira IV, 1000
Miles, Henry V, 815
Miles, Henry V, 816
Miles, Henry V, 817
Miles, Henry VI, 886
Miles, Henry VI, 911
Miles, Henry VI, 959
Miles, Henry VI, 961
Miles, Henry C. V, 817
Miles, Henry F. V, 812
Miles, Henry L. V, 805
Miles, Henry L. V, 817
Miles, Henry W. V, 816
Miles, Henry W. V, 817
Miles, Hester V, 816
Miles, Hester V, 817
Miles, I. Hannah IV, 1040
Miles, I. Hannah IV, 1043
Miles, Ines IV, 1040
Miles, Inez IV, 980
Miles, Inez M. IV, 980
Miles, Inez M. A. IV, 252
Miles, Inez M. A. IV, 980
Miles, Inez M. A. IV, 1040
Miles, Iona H. IV, 980
Miles, Iona Hannah IV, 252
Miles, Ira E. V, 816
Miles, Irena Katy IV, 980
Miles, Irena Katy J. IV, 1040
Miles, Irene K. J. IV, 980
Miles, Irene Katy J. IV, 252
Miles, Isaac Newton V, 816
Miles, Isham VI, 925
Miles, Isham VI, 926
Miles, Isham VI, 941
Miles, Isham VI, 962
Miles, Isham VI, 973
Miles, Israel V, 815
Miles, Israel V, 817
Miles, Jacob V, 817
Miles, Jacob T. V, 816
Miles, James II, 597
Miles, James V, 815
Miles, James V, 816
Miles, James V, 817
Miles, Jane I, 562
Miles, Jane I, 1034
Miles, Jane I, 1038
Miles, Jane V, 755
Miles, Jane V, 789
Miles, Jane V, 815
Miles, Jane V, 816
Miles, Jean V, 799
Miles, Jean V, 815
Miles, Jean V, 822
Miles, Jeremiah V, 815
Miles, Jeremiah V, 816
Miles, Jeremiah V, 817
Miles, Joanna V, 815
Miles, Joanna V, 816
Miles, John IV, 1000
Miles, John IV, 1040
Miles, John IV, 1174
Miles, John V, 745
Miles, John V, 755
Miles, John V, 784
Miles, John V, 789
Miles, John V, 812
Miles, John V, 815
Miles, John V, 816
Miles, John V, 817
Miles, John VI, 949
Miles, John C. V, 816
Miles, John C. VI, 962
Miles, John Edgar V, 816
Miles, John H. V, 817
Miles, John S. IV, 815
Miles, John W. V, 816
Miles, John Webster V, 755
Miles, John, Jr. I, 1034
Miles, John, Sr. I, 1034
Miles, Jonathan I, 966
Miles, Jonathan I, 1034
Miles, Jonathan I, 1036
Miles, Jonathan V, 799
Miles, Jonathan V, 800
Miles, Jonathan V, 811
Miles, Jonathan V, 815
Miles, Jonathan V, 816
Miles, Jonathan V, 817
Miles, Jonathan B. V, 816
Miles, Joseph VI, 961
Miles, Joseph VI, 989
Miles, Joseph VI, 1001
Miles, Joseph F. V, 816
Miles, Joseph I. V, 816
Miles, Joseph R. VI, 959
Miles, Juliann V, 801
Miles, Juliann V, 816
Miles, Katie IV, 1040
Miles, Keturah V, 817
Miles, Laban J. V, 816
Miles, Lambert J. V, 816
Miles, Laura Ellen V, 816
Miles, Leona May III, 169
Miles, Leona May III, 228
Miles, Leroy G. V, 816
Miles, Lindley IV, 1174
Miles, Lindley IV, 1193
Miles, Lindley V, 817
Miles, Linie Jane V, 816
Miles, Linley V, 815
Miles, Lizabeth I, 1021
Miles, Lowry II, 527
Miles, Lowry II, 597
Miles, Lucy VI, 961
Miles, Lyddia VI, 423
Miles, Lydia IV, 153
Miles, Lydia IV, 154
Miles, Lydia IV, 160
Miles, Lydia IV, 343
Miles, Lydia IV, 1174
Miles, Lydia IV, 1193
Miles, Lydia V, 817
Miles, Lydia VI, 423
Miles, Lydia F. V, 816
Miles, Lydia G. IV, 980
Miles, Mabel IV, 1000
Miles, Mabel E. IV, 1040
Miles, Mahala Catherine V, 817
Miles, Malinda W. V, 817
Miles, Margaret V, 815
Miles, Margaret V, 816
Miles, Margaret E. V, 816
Miles, Mark P. V, 816
Miles, Martha E. V, 816
Miles, Martha F. V, 817
Miles, Martha S. V, 816
Miles, Mary I, 1021
Miles, Mary I, 1027
Miles, Mary I, 1034
Miles, Mary I, 1035
Miles, Mary I, 1036
Miles, Mary I, 1038
Miles, Mary IV, 815
Miles, Mary IV, 851
Miles, Mary V, 740
Miles, Mary V, 744
Miles, Mary V, 755
Miles, Mary V, 759
Miles, Mary V, 797
Miles, Mary V, 799
Miles, Mary V, 800
Miles, Mary V, 804
Miles, Mary V, 808
Miles, Mary V, 810
Miles, Mary V, 811
Miles, Mary V, 813
Miles, Mary V, 815
Miles, Mary V, 816
Miles, Mary V, 817
Miles, Mary VI, 959
Miles, Mary VI, 961
Miles, Mary Ann V, 815
Miles, Mary Ann V, 816
Miles, Mary Ann V, 817
Miles, Mary B. V, 816
Miles, Mary E. V, 816
Miles, Mary F. V, 815
Miles, Mary F. V, 816
Miles, Mary F. V, 817
Miles, Mary Iona IV, 980
Miles, Mary J. IV, 1174
Miles, Mary J. IV, 1193
Miles, Mary Jane V, 816
Miles, Mary P. IV, 815
Miles, Mary P. V, 815
Miles, Mary P. V, 817
Miles, Mary R. V, 817
Miles, Mary Sara IV, 815
Miles, Melissa E. V, 815
Miles, Melissa E. V, 817
Miles, Mildred IV, 1040
Miles, Moses IV, 153
Miles, Moses IV, 154
Miles, Moses IV, 343
Miles, Moses V, 808
Miles, Moses V, 815
Miles, Moses V, 816
Miles, Moses VI, 423
Miles, Moses K. V, 801
Miles, Moses K. V, 816
Miles, Moses K. V, 817
Miles, Moses Kelly V, 815
Miles, Nancey VI, 925
Miles, Nancy V, 780
Miles, Nancy V, 789
Miles, Nancy V, 806
Miles, Nancy V, 816
Miles, Nancy V, 817
Miles, Naomi V, 816
Miles, Oral IV, 1040
Miles, Orville E. III, 169
Miles, Orville E. III, 228
Miles, Patience I, 966
Miles, Phebe V, 815
Miles, Phebe V, 816
Miles, Polly VI, 941
Miles, Prudence V, 748
Miles, Prudence V, 755

Miles, Prudence V, 814
Miles, Prudence V, 816
Miles, Prudence V, 817
Miles, Rachel I, 1029
Miles, Rachel I, 1034
Miles, Rachel V, 755
Miles, Rachel V, 789
Miles, Rachel V, 815
Miles, Rachel V, 816
Miles, Rachel V, 819
Miles, Rachel E. V, 815
Miles, Rachel E. V, 817
Miles, Rebecca IV, 1174
Miles, Rebecca V, 725
Miles, Rebecca V, 755
Miles, Rebecca V, 784
Miles, Rebecca V, 789
Miles, Rebecca V, 797
Miles, Rebecca V, 812
Miles, Rebecca V, 815
Miles, Rebecca V, 816
Miles, Rebecca V, 817
Miles, Rebecca V, 956
Miles, Rebecca VI, 959
Miles, Rebecca VI, 973
Miles, Rebecca D. V, 800
Miles, Rebecca D. V, 816
Miles, Rebecca Jane V, 815
Miles, Rebecca K. V, 815
Miles, Rebecca K. V, 817
Miles, Rhoda I, 1021
Miles, Rolen O. V, 816
Miles, Sally V, 755
Miles, Sally VI, 1007
Miles, Samuel I, 1021
Miles, Samuel I, 1034
Miles, Samuel I, 1038
Miles, Samuel II, 597
Miles, Samuel V, 755
Miles, Samuel V, 789
Miles, Samuel V, 814
Miles, Samuel V, 816
Miles, Samuel V, 817
Miles, Samuel V, 818
Miles, Samuel C. V, 780
Miles, Samuel C. V, 806
Miles, Samuel C. V, 816
Miles, Samuel C. V, 817
Miles, Samuel P. V, 817
Miles, Samuel T. V, 817
Miles, Samuel Y. V, 817
Miles, Samuel, Jr. V, 817
Miles, Sarah V, 799
Miles, Sarah V, 804
Miles, Sarah V, 815
Miles, Sarah VI, 423
Miles, Sarah VI, 548
Miles, Sarah VI, 574
Miles, Sarah VI, 962
Miles, Sarah Ann V, 816
Miles, Sarah C. V, 816
Miles, Sarah Jane V, 815
Miles, Sarah Jane V, 816
Miles, Sarah R. V, 816
Miles, Sarah S. IV, 815
Miles, Selma IV, 959
Miles, Selma IV, 980
Miles, Selma IV, 1040
Miles, Selma P. IV, 252
Miles, Selma P. IV, 397
Miles, Selma P. IV, 980
Miles, Sina A. VI, 962
Miles, Susan V, 755
Miles, Susan V, 816
Miles, Susan V, 916
Miles, Susana V, 817
Miles, Susanna IV, 144
Miles, Susanna IV, 154
Miles, Susanna V, 814
Miles, Susanna V, 817
Miles, Susanna VI, 423
Miles, Susanna VI, 926
Miles, Susannah IV, 980
Miles, Susannah V, 748
Miles, Susannah V, 755
Miles, Susannah V, 806
Miles, Susannah V, 812
Miles, Susannah V, 816
Miles, Thomas V, 816
Miles, Thomas F. V, 815
Miles, Thos. V, 956
Miles, Vashti V, 801
Miles, Vashti V, 816
Miles, Wade V, 801
Miles, Wade V, 804
Miles, Wade V, 815
Miles, Wade V, 816
Miles, Wade V, 817
Miles, Wilkinson V, 755
Miles, Wilkinson V, 815
Miles, William I, 562
Miles, William I, 1016
Miles, William I, 1021
Miles, William I, 1029
Miles, William I, 1034
Miles, William I, 1038
Miles, William V, 755
Miles, William V, 759
Miles, William V, 789
Miles, William V, 804
Miles, William V, 815
Miles, William V, 816
Miles, William V, 817
Miles, William VI, 961
Miles, William, Sr. I, 1034
Miles, Wm. IV, 815
Miles, Wm. V, 744
Miles, Wm. V, 797
Miles, Wm. V, 799
Miles, Wm. V, 813
Miles, Wm. V, 815
Miles, Wm. V, 816
Miles, Wm. V, 817
Miles, Wm. Franklin V, 817
Miles, Wm., Jr. V, 817
Miles, Young Samuel V, 815
Miles, Zalo IV, 980
Miles, Zalo C. IV, 980
Miles, Zalo G. IV, 1040
Miles, Zalo George IV, 980
Miles, Zoa C. IV, 980
Miles, Zoa Caroline IV, 252
Miles, Zoa Caroline IV, 397
Miles, Zoa Caroline IV, 959
Miles, Zoa Caroline IV, 980
Milhone, Josephine IV, 253
Milhorn, Alvina IV, 253
Milhorn, Anna IV, 253
Milhorn, Benjamin IV, 253
Milhorn, Elizabeth IV, 253
Milhorn, George A. IV, 253
Milhorn, John IV, 253
Milhorn, John, Jr. IV, 253
Milhorn, Josephine IV, 253
Milhorn, Sabina IV, 253
Milhorn, Sarah IV, 253
Milhorn, William IV, 253
Milhous, Amos Milhous V, 190
Milhous, Ann I, 1058
Milhous, Ann I, 1061
Milhous, Ann V, 190
Milhous, Anna V, 99
Milhous, Anna V, 128
Milhous, Anna V, 190
Milhous, Charity V, 190
Milhous, Dinah I, 1058
Milhous, Dinah I, 1060
Milhous, Dinah I, 1062
Milhous, Dinah V, 171
Milhous, Dinah V, 190
Milhous, Eli Scott V, 190
Milhous, Elizabeth I, 1058
Milhous, Elizabeth V, 99
Milhous, Elizabeth V, 190
Milhous, Henry I, 1058
Milhous, Henry I, 1062
Milhous, Henry V, 77
Milhous, Henry V, 99
Milhous, Henry V, 128
Milhous, Henry V, 190
Milhous, Henry, Jr. V, 190
Milhous, Isaac V, 190
Milhous, Isam V, 190
Milhous, Jean I, 1062
Milhous, John I, 1058
Milhous, John V, 190
Milhous, John V, 191
Milhous, Mary I, 1053
Milhous, Mary I, 1058
Milhous, Mary I, 1062
Milhous, Mary I, 1063
Milhous, Mary V, 190
Milhous, Mary V, 191
Milhous, Rebecca V, 190
Milhous, Rebeckah I, 1058
Milhous, Rebekah I, 1053
Milhous, Rebekah I, 1058
Milhous, Rebekah I, 1060
Milhous, Rebekah I, 1062
Milhous, Robart V, 99
Milhous, Robert I, 1058
Milhous, Robert I, 1062
Milhous, Robert V, 171
Milhous, Robert, Jr. V, 190
Milhous, Ruth II, 710
Milhous, Sally V, 190
Milhous, Sally Nelson I, 1058
Milhous, Samuel I, 1058
Milhous, Samuel V, 190
Milhous, Samuel V, 201
Milhous, Sarah I, 1058
Milhous, Sarah I, 1060
Milhous, Sarah V, 77
Milhous, Sarah V, 190
Milhous, Sarah V, 201
Milhouse, ??? V, 147
Milhouse, Amos V, 190
Milhouse, Amos V, 201
Milhouse, Amos Milhous V, 190
Milhouse, Ann I, 1022
Milhouse, Ann V, 190
Milhouse, Anna IV, 541
Milhouse, Anna IV, 552
Milhouse, Anna IV, 1068
Milhouse, Anna IV, 1069
Milhouse, Anna V, 190
Milhouse, Anna V, 196
Milhouse, Anne V, 469
Milhouse, Catharine I, 409
Milhouse, Charity IV, 1068
Milhouse, Charity IV, 1069
Milhouse, Charity V, 190
Milhouse, Charity V, 201
Milhouse, Daniel I, 1044
Milhouse, Daniel IV, 1062
Milhouse, Daniel IV, 1068
Milhouse, Daniel IV, 1069
Milhouse, Daniel IV, 1080
Milhouse, Dinah V, 190
Milhouse, Dinnah I, 1022
Milhouse, Edith IV, 252
Milhouse, Edith J. IV, 252
Milhouse, Eli V, 201
Milhouse, Eli Scott V, 190
Milhouse, Elizabeth I, 1033
Milhouse, Elizabeth I, 1034
Milhouse, Elizabeth IV, 1068
Milhouse, Elizabeth IV, 1069
Milhouse, Elizabeth V, 190
Milhouse, Elizabeth V, 191
Milhouse, Elizabeth P. IV, 252
Milhouse, Esther IV, 1062
Milhouse, Esther IV, 1068
Milhouse, Esther IV, 1069
Milhouse, Esther IV, 1080
Milhouse, Franklin IV, 252
Milhouse, George V, 196
Milhouse, Hannah IV, 250
Milhouse, Hannah IV, 252
Milhouse, Hannah IV, 1068
Milhouse, Hannah IV, 1069
Milhouse, Hannah IV, 1080
Milhouse, Henry I, 1021
Milhouse, Henry I, 1022
Milhouse, Henry V, 190
Milhouse, Henry V, 201
Milhouse, Henry, Jr. V, 190
Milhouse, Isaac IV, 1068
Milhouse, Isaac IV, 1069
Milhouse, Isaac V, 190
Milhouse, Isaac C. IV, 1069
Milhouse, Isam V, 190
Milhouse, Isam V, 201
Milhouse, Jane I, 1038
Milhouse, Jane IV, 157
Milhouse, Jane IV, 252
Milhouse, Jane IV, 1069
Milhouse, Jesse II, 597
Milhouse, Jesse IV, 252
Milhouse, Jesse G. IV, 252
Milhouse, John V, 190
Milhouse, John V, 201
Milhouse, Joshua V. IV, 252
Milhouse, Katharine I, 400
Milhouse, Katharine I, 409
Milhouse, Lydia IV, 1068
Milhouse, Lydia IV, 1069
Milhouse, Margery V, 190
Milhouse, Martha IV, 250
Milhouse, Martha IV, 252
Milhouse, Martha IV, 1068
Milhouse, Martha IV, 1069
Milhouse, Martha IV, 1080
Milhouse, Mary I, 1022
Milhouse, Mary IV, 438
Milhouse, Mary IV, 1068
Milhouse, Mary IV, 1069
Milhouse, Mary V, 190
Milhouse, Mary V, 201
Milhouse, Mary Elizabeth IV, 1068
Milhouse, Mary Elizabeth IV, 1069
Milhouse, Phebe IV, 252
Milhouse, Rachel IV, 1068
Milhouse, Rachel IV, 1069
Milhouse, Rachel IV, 1080
Milhouse, Rebecca IV, 1068
Milhouse, Rebecca IV, 1069
Milhouse, Rebecca V, 171
Milhouse, Rebecca V, 190
Milhouse, Rebekah I, 1021
Milhouse, Robert I, 1022
Milhouse, Robert I, 1027
Milhouse, Robert I, 1034
Milhouse, Robert I, 1044
Milhouse, Robert IV, 280
Milhouse, Robert IV, 1068
Milhouse, Robert IV, 1069
Milhouse, Robert IV, 1080
Milhouse, Robert V, 190
Milhouse, Robert V, 191
Milhouse, Robert, Jr. V, 190
Milhouse, Ruth IV, 1068
Milhouse, Ruth IV, 1069
Milhouse, Sally V, 190
Milhouse, Sally V, 191
Milhouse, Sally Nelson I, 1027
Milhouse, Samuel I, 400
Milhouse, Samuel I, 409
Milhouse, Samuel I, 1034
Milhouse, Samuel V, 190
Milhouse, Samuel V, 201
Milhouse, Sarah I, 1022
Milhouse, Sarah I, 1044
Milhouse, Sarah IV, 252
Milhouse, Sarah IV, 768
Milhouse, Sarah IV, 1062
Milhouse, Sarah IV, 1068
Milhouse, Sarah IV, 1069
Milhouse, Sarah IV, 1077
Milhouse, Sarah V, 190
Milhouse, Sarah V, 196
Milhouse, Sarah V, 201
Milhouse, Sarah V, 469
Milhouse, Sarah Ann IV, 1068
Milhouse, Sarah Esther IV, 1069
Milhouse, Sarah M. IV, 280
Milhouse, Stephen IV, 541
Milhouse, Thomas IV, 252
Milhouse, Thomas IV, 1069
Milhouse, Thomas V, 190
Milhouse, Vickers IV, 252
Milhouse, Widow Jane I, 1034
Milhouse, William IV, 252
Milhouse, William IV, 1068
Milhouse, William, Jr. IV, 252
Milhouse, Wm. IV, 250
Milhouse, Wm. IV, 1069
Milican, Almedia R. V, 586
Milican, Almedia R. V, 697
Milican, Ann I, 883
Milican, Ann I, 894
Milican, Dorcas I, 767
Milican, Eleazar I, 894
Milican, Eli W. V, 697
Milican, Grace D. I, 894
Milican, Hannah C. V, 586
Milican, Hannah C. V, 697
Milican, Jesse D. F. V, 586
Milican, Jessie D. F. V, 697
Milican, John I, 894
Milican, John V, 586
Milican, John V, 697
Milican, Lydia I, 763
Milican, Lydia I, 766
Milican, Lydia I, 767
Milican, Margaret V, 586
Milican, Margaret C. V, 697
Milican, Margaret E. V, 697
Milican, Margaret Eleanor V, 586
Milican, Martha J. V, 586
Milican, Martha J. V, 697
Milican, Mary E. V, 586
Milican, Mary E. V, 697
Milican, Pamelia A. V, 697
Milican, Priscilla E. V, 586
Milican, Priscilla E. V, 697
Milican, Rachel I, 876
Milican, Rachel I, 894
Milican, Rachel C. V, 697
Milican, Rhoda I, 888
Milican, Rhoda I, 894
Milican, Sarah V, 697
Milican, Sarah J. V, 605
Milican, Sarah J. V, 697
Milican, Thomas N. V, 586
Milican, Thomas N. V, 697
Milican, William I, 894
Milicen, ??? I, 685
Miligan, Ann IV, 979
Miligan, Ann IV, 980
Miligan, Jesse IV, 980
Miligan, John IV, 979
Miligan, John IV, 980
Miligan, Joseph IV, 979
Miligan, Sarah L. IV, 154
Milikan, Almina I, 876
Milikan, Almina I, 894
Milikan, Clark I, 767
Milikan, Eli I, 894
Milikan, Eli V, 586
Milikan, Hannah V, 554
Milikan, Hannah V, 586
Milikan, Mary Ann I, 894
Milikan, Rachel C. V, 586
Milikan, Sarah J. V, 586
Miliken, Eli V, 517
Milikin, Eli V, 517
Milikin, John V, 517
Milikin, Mary V, 517
Milikin, Samuel I, 562
Milikin, William Thomas V, 5
Miliner, Athanissa IV, 343
Miliner, Athanissa IV, 345
Milis, Hiram I, 829
Milison, Elizabeth IV, 343
Milison, Elizabeth IV, 351
Milison, William IV, 343
Mill, John I, 1035
Mill, Jonathan I, 447
Mill, Jonathan I, 451
Mill, Mary I, 1035
Mill, Mary I, 1039
Mill, Sarah I, 447
Millagan, Jesse IV, 666
Millagan, Ruth IV, 666
Millam, Ditsey VI, 961
Millam, John VI, 961
Millam, John VI, 974
Millam, John E. VI, 961
Millam, Lucy VI, 961
Millam, Mary R. VI, 974
Millam, Matilda M. VI, 961
Millam, Nancey VI, 983
Millam, Thomas VI, 961
Millam, Zachariah VI, 983
Millam, Zachariah VI, 1011
Millar, Margaret II, 597
Millar, Rachel II, 597
Millard, ??? III, 185
Millard, Anna II, 1015
Millard, Catharine V, 973
Millard, Catherine V, 99
Millard, David B. IV, 893
Millard, David B. IV, 894
Millard, Elizabeth V, 349
Millard, Joseph II, 1015
Millard, Mary II, 1015
Millard, Mary IV, 893
Millard, Mary IV, 894
Millard, Mary Elizabeth III, 1
Millard, Rebecca IV, 893
Millard, Sarah II, 1015
Millard, Sarah H. IV, 893
Millard, Sarah H. IV, 894
Millard, Wm. II, 1015
Millard, Wm. IV, 893
Millburn, Andrew VI, 423
Millegan, Abigail IV, 50
Millegan, Ann IV, 50
Millegan, Clement IV, 50
Millegan, James IV, 50
Millegan, John IV, 50
Millegan, Joseph IV, 50
Millegan, William IV, 50
Milleger, Abbie IV, 252
Milleger, Dan IV, 252
Millekin, Priscilla V, 697
Millen, George V, 1010
Millener, Beverly VI, 332
Millener, Elizabeth VI, 831
Millenger, Clarence IV, 1173
Millens, Mary VI, 840
Millens, Samuel VI, 840
Millep, Amy Ann VI, 535
Millep, Ann VI, 534
Millep, Anna VI, 534
Millep, Arthur VI, 534
Millep, Elizabeth VI, 535
Millep, Hannah, Jr. VI, 534
Millep, Isaac VI, 534
Millep, James VI, 534
Millep, Katharine VI, 534
Millep, Llewellyn VI, 535
Millep, Mary H. VI, 535
Millep, Mordecai VI, 535
Millep, Rebecca VI, 535
Millep, Warwick VI, 535
Millep, Wm. H. VI, 535
Miller, ??? I, 29
Miller, ??? III, 95
Miller, ??? III, 228
Miller, ??? III, 229
Miller, ??? IV, 137
Miller, A??? V, 752
Miller, Abigail II, 942
Miller, Abigail III, 229
Miller, Abigail IV, 1374
Miller, Abigail M. II, 899
Miller, Abigail M. W. II, 899
Miller, Abm. III, 229
Miller, Abraham II, 34
Miller, Abraham II, 87
Miller, Abraham II, 88

er, Abraham II, 99
er, Abraham II, 899
er, Abraham II, 925
er, Abraham III, 219
er, Abraham III, 228
er, Abraham III, 229
er, Abraham III, 230
er, Abraham C. III, 228
er, Abraham C. III, 229
er, Abraham C. III, 291
er, Abrm. E. III, 187
er, Ada III, 228
er, Ada III, 229
er, Ada IV, 1174
er, Ada Tompt IV, 1330
er, Adaline A. VI, 962
er, Addie V, 1010
er, Agatha C. III, 98
er, Albert III, 427
er, Albert E. III, 228
er, Albert E. III, 293
er, Albert F. V, 1010
er, Alex. III, 229
er, Alexander II, 810
er, Alice V, 349
er, Alice V, 1010
er, Alice VI, 765
er, Alice Thompson II, 135
er, Alice Thompson II, 153
er, Alida E. II, 859
er, Alida E. II, 899
er, Alles V, 1010
er, Allice V, 1010
er, Alvar Edward III, 230
er, Amanda III, 229
er, Amanda V, 979
er, Amanda VI, 962
er, Amanda K. III, 228
er, Amanda K. III, 229
er, Amanda M. II, 135
er, Amaziah III, 228
er, Amie III, 229
er, Amie Jane III, 229
er, Amos IV, 101
er, Amos IV, 541
er, Amy III, 141
er, Amy III, 228
er, Amy III, 230
er, Amy IV, 21
er, Amy IV, 49
er, Amy Ann VI, 535
er, Amy Ann VI, 766
er, Amy Ann VI, 767
er, Amy Ann VI, 770
er, Amy J. III, 230
er, Andrew II, 34
er, Andrew II, 54
er, Andrew II, 87
er, Andrew II, 598
er, Andrew II, 607
er, Andrew II, 713
er, Andrew II, 899
er, Andrew III, 220
er, Andrew VI, 897
er, Andrew VI, 958
er, Andrew VI, 962
er, Andrew R. II, 756
er, Andrew R. II, 810
ler, Ann I, 409
ler, Ann I, 410
ler, Ann II, 62
ler, Ann II, 87
ler, Ann II, 88
ler, Ann II, 121
ler, Ann II, 135
ler, Ann II, 396
ler, Ann II, 502
ler, Ann II, 516
ler, Ann II, 597
ler, Ann II, 598
ler, Ann II, 820
ler, Ann II, 899
ler, Ann II, 929
ler, Ann IV, 49
ler, Ann IV, 93
ler, Ann IV, 100
ler, Ann IV, 101
ler, Ann IV, 740
ler, Ann IV, 834
ler, Ann IV, 850
ler, Ann IV, 873
ler, Ann IV, 878
ler, Ann IV, 905
ler, Ann IV, 907
ler, Ann IV, 911
ler, Ann IV, 965
ler, Ann V, 99
ler, Ann V, 264
ler, Ann V, 851
ler, Ann V, 921
ler, Ann V, 972

Miller, Ann V, 973
Miller, Ann VI, 467
Miller, Ann VI, 490
Miller, Ann VI, 491
Miller, Ann VI, 505
Miller, Ann VI, 585
Miller, Ann VI, 888
Miller, Ann A. III, 228
Miller, Ann C. II, 899
Miller, Ann C. II, 929
Miller, Ann Charlton II, 899
Miller, Ann Eliza III, 187
Miller, Ann Eliza III, 229
Miller, Ann Eliza III, 230
Miller, Ann Eliza III, 249
Miller, Ann Eliza III, 351
Miller, Ann G. V, 921
Miller, Ann H. II, 899
Miller, Ann P. II, 323
Miller, Ann S. VI, 800
Miller, Ann T. II, 323
Miller, Ann, Jr. IV, 911
Miller, Anna II, 699
Miller, Anna II, 708
Miller, Anna II, 714
Miller, Anna II, 717
Miller, Anna II, 728
Miller, Anna II, 756
Miller, Anna II, 783
Miller, Anna II, 794
Miller, Anna II, 810
Miller, Anna II, 838
Miller, Anna II, 899
Miller, Anna II, 1066
Miller, Anna II, 1076
Miller, Anna III, 229
Miller, Anna III, 230
Miller, Anna IV, 343
Miller, Anna IV, 347
Miller, Anna V, 190
Miller, Anna V, 1010
Miller, Anna VI, 517
Miller, Anna VI, 518
Miller, Anna VI, 535
Miller, Anna VI, 740
Miller, Anna VI, 745
Miller, Anna VI, 753
Miller, Anna VI, 754
Miller, Anna VI, 765
Miller, Anna VI, 766
Miller, Anna VI, 772
Miller, Anna Charlton II, 838
Miller, Anna McIlvain II, 838
Miller, Anna McIlvaine II, 899
Miller, Anna P. II, 899
Miller, Anna P. II, 915
Miller, Anna R. II, 810
Miller, Anna R. II, 899
Miller, Anna R. III, 228
Miller, Anna Ware II, 153
Miller, Anne II, 516
Miller, Anne II, 597
Miller, Anne IV, 100
Miller, Anne VI, 332
Miller, Anne P. II, 756
Miller, Anne W. II, 139
Miller, Annie II, 899
Miller, Annie III, 122
Miller, Annie III, 224
Miller, Annie III, 228
Miller, Annie III, 229
Miller, Annie III, 323
Miller, Annie VI, 766
Miller, Annie R. II, 899
Miller, Annie W. II, 135
Miller, Anton M. III, 214
Miller, Arthur II, 899
Miller, Arthur VI, 535
Miller, Arthur VI, 767
Miller, Asa IV, 343
Miller, Asa IV, 488
Miller, Asa IV, 541
Miller, Atlantic Ocean VI, 424
Miller, Atlantic Ocean VI, 454
Miller, Austin V, 349
Miller, Austin V, 413
Miller, Austin V, 921
Miller, Beatrice Maul II, 135
Miller, Bell VI, 316
Miller, Belle IV, 1174
Miller, Benj. C. III, 26
Miller, Benj. C. III, 228
Miller, Benj. C. III, 230
Miller, Benjamin II, 48
Miller, Benjamin II, 396
Miller, Benjamin C. III, 228
Miller, Benjamin C. III, 293
Miller, Bertha Margaret III, 98
Miller, Bessie V, 697
Miller, Bessie A. IV, 253
Miller, Betsey VI, 962

Miller, Bryan V, 1010
Miller, Burlie I, 627
Miller, Burrell V, 190
Miller, Byron V, 1010
Miller, C. III, 229
Miller, C. C. I, 726
Miller, C. H. IV, 980
Miller, Caleb IV, 49
Miller, Caleb IV, 101
Miller, Caleb IV, 106
Miller, Caleb IV, 253
Miller, Caleb V, 969
Miller, Caleb V, 972
Miller, Caleb V, 973
Miller, Caleb VI, 423
Miller, Caleb VI, 601
Miller, Caleb S. VI, 765
Miller, Caleb S. VI, 791
Miller, Caleb Stabler VI, 766
Miller, Carl IV, 1330
Miller, Caroline I, 721
Miller, Caroline I, 726
Miller, Caroline V, 99
Miller, Caroline V, 190
Miller, Caroline VI, 666
Miller, Caroline VI, 745
Miller, Caroline VI, 765
Miller, Caroline VI, 766
Miller, Caroline VI, 767
Miller, Caroline VI, 840
Miller, Caroline VI, 962
Miller, Caroline H. III, 183
Miller, Caroline H. III, 230
Miller, Caroline M. II, 899
Miller, Caroline Macy II, 810
Miller, Caroline S. VI, 740
Miller, Caroline S. VI, 765
Miller, Caroline S. VI, 766
Miller, Caroline S. VI, 782
Miller, Carolyn II, 846
Miller, Carolyn II, 899
Miller, Carolyn V, 190
Miller, Carolyn A. III, 65
Miller, Carolyn A. III, 228
Miller, Carolyn Alice III, 229
Miller, Carrie II, 148
Miller, Casandra IV, 88
Miller, Casandra IV, 95
Miller, Cascius C. I, 726
Miller, Cassander VI, 597
Miller, Cassander VI, 601
Miller, Cassandra IV, 91
Miller, Cassandra IV, 96
Miller, Cassandra IV, 101
Miller, Cassandra VI, 420
Miller, Cassandra VI, 423
Miller, Cassandra VI, 424
Miller, Cassandra VI, 639
Miller, Cassandra VI, 676
Miller, Cassandrew IV, 101
Miller, Cassandria VI, 601
Miller, Catharine II, 455
Miller, Catharine II, 598
Miller, Catharine II, 710
Miller, Catharine III, 94
Miller, Catharine III, 228
Miller, Catharine III, 229
Miller, Catharine IV, 873
Miller, Catharine IV, 878
Miller, Catharine V, 1010
Miller, Catharine H. IV, 911
Miller, Catherine III, 219
Miller, Catherine III, 228
Miller, Catherine IV, 792
Miller, Catherine IV, 1258
Miller, Catherine V, 832
Miller, Catherine VI, 862
Miller, Catherine A. VI, 831
Miller, Celia I, 330
Miller, Celina VI, 1016
Miller, Charity IV, 834
Miller, Charity IV, 837
Miller, Charity V, 349
Miller, Charity V, 413
Miller, Charity V, 955
Miller, Charity V, 956
Miller, Charity VI, 423
Miller, Charity VI, 462
Miller, Charity P. IV, 834
Miller, Charity P. IV, 911
Miller, Charity P. IV, 980
Miller, Charity P. V, 413
Miller, Charles III, 141
Miller, Charles III, 228
Miller, Charles III, 229
Miller, Charles III, 230
Miller, Charles V, 1010
Miller, Charles VI, 765
Miller, Charles VI, 766
Miller, Charles VI, 767
Miller, Charles VI, 768

Miller, Charles C. III, 228
Miller, Charles D. II, 153
Miller, Charles D. III, 229
Miller, Charles Dare II, 135
Miller, Charles Dare II, 153
Miller, Charles E. IV, 488
Miller, Charles Edward III, 229
Miller, Charles F. V, 413
Miller, Charles Miller II, 783
Miller, Charles P. II, 396
Miller, Charles P. II, 756
Miller, Charles W. IV, 1258
Miller, Charley P. IV, 980
Miller, Charlotte III, 229
Miller, Charlotte C. IV, 1287
Miller, Charlotte J. III, 219
Miller, Charlotte J. III, 229
Miller, Chas. III, 134
Miller, Chas. R. II, 899
Miller, Chas. R. II, 942
Miller, Chas. W. IV, 1258
Miller, Chester V, 1010
Miller, Christina II, 34
Miller, Christina V, 752
Miller, Clara III, 228
Miller, Clara III, 229
Miller, Clara III, 291
Miller, Clara V, 190
Miller, Claud V, 349
Miller, Claud V, 586
Miller, Claud V, 697
Miller, Claude V, 697
Miller, Clement II, 783
Miller, Clement Miller II, 783
Miller, Cornelia VI, 766
Miller, Cornelia Janney VI, 766
Miller, Cornelia Janney VI, 781
Miller, Cornelius IV, 980
Miller, Cynthia IV, 1287
Miller, Cynthia IV, 1289
Miller, Cynthia V, 853
Miller, Cynthia V, 1010
Miller, Daniel II, 34
Miller, Daniel II, 87
Miller, Daniel II, 838
Miller, Daniel III, 229
Miller, Daniel III, 230
Miller, Daniel IV, 343
Miller, Daniel C. III, 76
Miller, Daniel C. III, 90
Miller, Daniel C. III, 187
Miller, Daniel C. III, 229
Miller, Daniel C. III, 230
Miller, Daniel C. III, 249
Miller, Daniel H. III, 228
Miller, Daniel H. III, 229
Miller, Daniel L. II, 88
Miller, Daniel L. II, 396
Miller, Daniel L. II, 598
Miller, Daniel L. II, 607
Miller, Daniel L. II, 713
Miller, Daniel L. II, 756
Miller, Daniel L. II, 838
Miller, Daniel L. II, 859
Miller, Daniel L. II, 899
Miller, Daniel L. II, 905
Miller, Daniel L. II, 915
Miller, Daniel L., Jr. II, 756
Miller, Daniel L., Jr. II, 810
Miller, Daniel L., Jr. II, 899
Miller, Daniel Leeds II, 783
Miller, Daniel Leeds II, 810
Miller, Daniel Leeds II, 813
Miller, Daniel Leeds II, 899
Miller, Daniel Leeds, Jr. II, 810
Miller, Darius V, 1010
Miller, David II, 499
Miller, David II, 1015
Miller, David III, 229
Miller, David IV, 49
Miller, David IV, 74
Miller, David IV, 78
Miller, David IV, 85
Miller, David IV, 101
Miller, David IV, 110
Miller, David IV, 130
Miller, David IV, 421
Miller, David IV, 741
Miller, David IV, 765
Miller, David IV, 1069
Miller, David IV, 1287
Miller, David V, 99
Miller, David V, 973
Miller, David VI, 423
Miller, David VI, 601
Miller, David H. III, 229
Miller, David H. V, 99
Miller, David H. V, 973
Miller, David Willson IV, 101
Miller, Debby IV, 911
Miller, Deborah I, 935

Miller, Deborah IV, 49
Miller, Deborah IV, 588
Miller, Deborah IV, 708
Miller, Deborah IV, 834
Miller, Deborah IV, 878
Miller, Deborah IV, 905
Miller, Deborah IV, 910
Miller, Deborah IV, 911
Miller, Deborah IV, 952
Miller, Deborah IV, 980
Miller, Deborah Ann IV, 911
Miller, Deborah Ann V, 413
Miller, Deborah Ann V, 424
Miller, Deborah D. IV, 588
Miller, Dickerson V, 306
Miller, Dora V, 264
Miller, Dorcas V, 560
Miller, Dorcas V, 586
Miller, Dorcas V, 973
Miller, Dorcus V, 979
Miller, Dr. Charles III, 70
Miller, Dr. Charles III, 228
Miller, Dr. Charles III, 229
Miller, Dr. Chas. III, 229
Miller, Drusilla IV, 101
Miller, E. J. V, 1010
Miller, Earnest C. V, 697
Miller, Ebenezer II, 34
Miller, Ebenezer II, 35
Miller, Ebenezer II, 48
Miller, Ebenezer II, 87
Miller, Ebenezer II, 112
Miller, Ebenezer, Jr. II, 48
Miller, Ebenezer, Jr. II, 87
Miller, Ebenezer, Jr. II, 89
Miller, Edgar III, 229
Miller, Edgar VI, 767
Miller, Edith IV, 252
Miller, Edith IV, 541
Miller, Edna IV, 1174
Miller, Edna IV, 1258
Miller, Edna V, 884
Miller, Edna V, 887
Miller, Edna E. IV, 1258
Miller, Edward III, 228
Miller, Edward IV, 1287
Miller, Edward V, 413
Miller, Edward T. II, 783
Miller, Edwin III, 220
Miller, Edwin III, 228
Miller, Eli IV, 343
Miller, Eli IV, 488
Miller, Eli IV, 541
Miller, Elias V, 973
Miller, Elias F. V, 586
Miller, Elias F. V, 973
Miller, Elias F. V, 979
Miller, Elijah IV, 541
Miller, Elijah VI, 322
Miller, Elijah VI, 332
Miller, Elijah VI, 840
Miller, Elisabeth I, 60
Miller, Elisabeth II, 597
Miller, Elisha VI, 766
Miller, Eliz. III, 210
Miller, Eliz. III, 230
Miller, Eliz. Clark III, 229
Miller, Eliz. D. III, 65
Miller, Eliz. D. III, 228
Miller, Eliz. D. III, 229
Miller, Eliz. D. III, 326
Miller, Eliza II, 720
Miller, Eliza III, 187
Miller, Eliza III, 229
Miller, Eliza IV, 708
Miller, Eliza IV, 905
Miller, Eliza IV, 918
Miller, Eliza IV, 955
Miller, Eliza IV, 980
Miller, Eliza V, 484
Miller, Eliza V, 517
Miller, Eliza V, 969
Miller, Eliza V, 973
Miller, Eliza V, 975
Miller, Eliza V, 979
Miller, Eliza H. III, 141
Miller, Eliza Hewes VI, 766
Miller, Eliza Jane III, 220
Miller, Eliza Jane IV, 101
Miller, Eliza Jane V, 99
Miller, Eliza Morgan VI, 765
Miller, Eliza W. II, 119
Miller, Eliza W. II, 121
Miller, Elizabeth II, 19
Miller, Elizabeth II, 34
Miller, Elizabeth II, 35
Miller, Elizabeth II, 48
Miller, Elizabeth II, 49
Miller, Elizabeth II, 87
Miller, Elizabeth II, 88
Miller, Elizabeth II, 96

Miller, Elizabeth II, 99
Miller, Elizabeth II, 133
Miller, Elizabeth II, 153
Miller, Elizabeth II, 179
Miller, Elizabeth II, 226
Miller, Elizabeth II, 242
Miller, Elizabeth II, 396
Miller, Elizabeth II, 493
Miller, Elizabeth II, 597
Miller, Elizabeth II, 598
Miller, Elizabeth II, 691
Miller, Elizabeth II, 713
Miller, Elizabeth II, 756
Miller, Elizabeth II, 793
Miller, Elizabeth II, 795
Miller, Elizabeth II, 899
Miller, Elizabeth II, 905
Miller, Elizabeth II, 925
Miller, Elizabeth II, 1015
Miller, Elizabeth II, 1038
Miller, Elizabeth II, 1056
Miller, Elizabeth II, 1057
Miller, Elizabeth III, 229
Miller, Elizabeth III, 230
Miller, Elizabeth III, 297
Miller, Elizabeth III, 327
Miller, Elizabeth IV, 49
Miller, Elizabeth IV, 74
Miller, Elizabeth IV, 78
Miller, Elizabeth IV, 85
Miller, Elizabeth IV, 101
Miller, Elizabeth IV, 110
Miller, Elizabeth IV, 343
Miller, Elizabeth IV, 703
Miller, Elizabeth IV, 741
Miller, Elizabeth IV, 765
Miller, Elizabeth V, 99
Miller, Elizabeth V, 190
Miller, Elizabeth V, 264
Miller, Elizabeth V, 349
Miller, Elizabeth V, 586
Miller, Elizabeth V, 697
Miller, Elizabeth V, 965
Miller, Elizabeth V, 970
Miller, Elizabeth V, 973
Miller, Elizabeth V, 974
Miller, Elizabeth VI, 423
Miller, Elizabeth VI, 487
Miller, Elizabeth VI, 513
Miller, Elizabeth VI, 535
Miller, Elizabeth VI, 601
Miller, Elizabeth VI, 602
Miller, Elizabeth VI, 663
Miller, Elizabeth VI, 738
Miller, Elizabeth VI, 746
Miller, Elizabeth VI, 766
Miller, Elizabeth VI, 878
Miller, Elizabeth VI, 962
Miller, Elizabeth VI, 972
Miller, Elizabeth A. II, 135
Miller, Elizabeth A. II, 153
Miller, Elizabeth Clark II, 800
Miller, Elizabeth Clark III, 169
Miller, Elizabeth Clark III, 228
Miller, Elizabeth D. III, 229
Miller, Elizabeth H. II, 942
Miller, Elizabeth Hewes VI, 766
Miller, Elizabeth K. III, 229
Miller, Elizabeth M. II, 756
Miller, Elizabeth M. II, 758
Miller, Elizabeth Marion II, 944
Miller, Elizabeth Marion Young II, 899
Miller, Elizabeth P. VI, 785
Miller, Elizabeth Parrish II, 783
Miller, Elizabeth W. II, 114
Miller, Elizabeth W. II, 121
Miller, Elizabeth W. II, 899
Miller, Elizabeth W. V, 682
Miller, Elizabeth W. V, 697
Miller, Elizabeth Wright II, 813
Miller, Ella III, 229
Miller, Ella III, 248
Miller, Ella III, 338
Miller, Ellen III, 230
Miller, Ellen M. VI, 765
Miller, Ellen M. VI, 767
Miller, Ellen M. VI, 768
Miller, Ellis IV, 1287
Miller, Elma IV, 1174
Miller, Elma F. IV, 980
Miller, Elma Miles IV, 980
Miller, Elmer V, 1010
Miller, Elvin Elizabeth V, 697
Miller, Emett V, 1010
Miller, Emily IV, 1287
Miller, Emily V, 99
Miller, Emily V, 246
Miller, Emily V, 264
Miller, Emily V, 349
Miller, Emily V, 399
Miller, Emily V, 413
Miller, Emily V, 973
Miller, Emily H. V, 264
Miller, Emily H. V, 349
Miller, Emily S. V, 461
Miller, Emma II, 147
Miller, Emma II, 153
Miller, Emma II, 717
Miller, Emma III, 229
Miller, Emma V, 99
Miller, Emma V, 973
Miller, Emma V, 1010
Miller, Emma C. II, 135
Miller, Emma Comly II, 810
Miller, Emma H. V, 99
Miller, Emma H. V, 126
Miller, Emma Ruth I, 625
Miller, Emmer H. IV, 101
Miller, Emmet V, 1010
Miller, Emmett Palmer II, 810
Miller, Emmett Palmer II, 899
Miller, Emmor IV, 101
Miller, Ernest Clyde V, 697
Miller, Erwin R. III, 230
Miller, Ester Griffin II, 153
Miller, Esther II, 34
Miller, Esther II, 35
Miller, Esther II, 88
Miller, Esther II, 114
Miller, Esther II, 121
Miller, Esther Cooper II, 34
Miller, Esther Griffen II, 135
Miller, Esther Wintermute II, 899
Miller, Ethel A. III, 229
Miller, Ethel A. III, 232
Miller, Eugene III, 228
Miller, Eugene James V, 697
Miller, Ezekiel III, 228
Miller, Ezekiel III, 229
Miller, Ezekiel H. III, 122
Miller, Ezekiel H. III, 229
Miller, Ezekiel H. III, 230
Miller, Ezekiel H. III, 330
Miller, Ezekiel H. III, 411
Miller, Ezekiel H. III, 427
Miller, Ezekiel H. III, 464
Miller, F. W. IV, 1330
Miller, Fannie V, 99
Miller, Fannie V, 1010
Miller, Farrand Rogers III, 427
Miller, Farrand Rogers III, 448
Miller, Fay V, 1010
Miller, Fay B. V, 1010
Miller, Ferrand Rogers III, 427
Miller, Ferrish II, 783
Miller, Flora E. V, 853
Miller, Flora J. V, 349
Miller, Florence IV, 1174
Miller, Florence V, 973
Miller, Florence V, 979
Miller, Forman W. III, 229
Miller, Frances V, 349
Miller, Frances V, 363
Miller, Frances V, 921
Miller, Frances VI, 911
Miller, Frances C. VI, 962
Miller, Frances Canby II, 783
Miller, Frances P. IV, 49
Miller, Frances Willard IV, 1040
Miller, Francis III, 183
Miller, Francis III, 230
Miller, Francis V, 349
Miller, Francis V, 413
Miller, Francis VI, 666
Miller, Francis VI, 745
Miller, Francis VI, 765
Miller, Francis VI, 766
Miller, Francis P. IV, 911
Miller, Frank V, 1010
Miller, Frank Wildey II, 713
Miller, Frank Wildey II, 756
Miller, Franklin II, 34
Miller, Franklin II, 35
Miller, Franklin II, 114
Miller, Franklin II, 121
Miller, Franklin II, 153
Miller, Franklin IV, 49
Miller, Franklin IV, 911
Miller, Franklin V, 921
Miller, Franklin G. II, 153
Miller, Fred W. IV, 1330
Miller, Freda V, 755
Miller, Frederick III, 228
Miller, Frederick VI, 766
Miller, Geo W. V, 1010
Miller, Geo. V, 1010
Miller, Geo. D. II, 899
Miller, Geo. J. IV, 1330
Miller, George II, 48
Miller, George II, 87
Miller, George II, 810
Miller, George II, 899
Miller, George V, 755
Miller, George V, 1010
Miller, George Bremer II, 899
Miller, George Bremer II, 944
Miller, George Brook VI, 766
Miller, George D. II, 899
Miller, George D. II, 929
Miller, George Deeble II, 838
Miller, George F. W. III, 229
Miller, George W. II, 810
Miller, George W. III, 229
Miller, Gertrude V, 306
Miller, Grace II, 153
Miller, Grace A. II, 135
Miller, Grace A. II, 153
Miller, Grace C. III, 229
Miller, Grace Halsey III, 229
Miller, Grace Robuck V, 697
Miller, Grief VI, 840
Miller, Grief VI, 864
Miller, Guyon VI, 766
Miller, Gwendolyn III, 427
Miller, Gwendolyn III, 448
Miller, H. Griffen III, 297
Miller, Hannah II, 34
Miller, Hannah II, 47
Miller, Hannah II, 48
Miller, Hannah II, 69
Miller, Hannah II, 83
Miller, Hannah II, 87
Miller, Hannah II, 112
Miller, Hannah II, 113
Miller, Hannah II, 396
Miller, Hannah II, 515
Miller, Hannah II, 523
Miller, Hannah II, 597
Miller, Hannah II, 598
Miller, Hannah II, 607
Miller, Hannah II, 713
Miller, Hannah II, 756
Miller, Hannah II, 783
Miller, Hannah II, 810
Miller, Hannah II, 813
Miller, Hannah II, 821
Miller, Hannah II, 838
Miller, Hannah II, 859
Miller, Hannah II, 899
Miller, Hannah II, 905
Miller, Hannah II, 915
Miller, Hannah II, 1015
Miller, Hannah II, 1056
Miller, Hannah II, 1076
Miller, Hannah III, 96
Miller, Hannah III, 220
Miller, Hannah III, 228
Miller, Hannah III, 229
Miller, Hannah III, 230
Miller, Hannah IV, 49
Miller, Hannah IV, 88
Miller, Hannah IV, 101
Miller, Hannah IV, 110
Miller, Hannah IV, 740
Miller, Hannah IV, 741
Miller, Hannah IV, 765
Miller, Hannah IV, 766
Miller, Hannah IV, 834
Miller, Hannah IV, 911
Miller, Hannah IV, 914
Miller, Hannah V, 99
Miller, Hannah VI, 402
Miller, Hannah VI, 423
Miller, Hannah VI, 507
Miller, Hannah VI, 535
Miller, Hannah VI, 601
Miller, Hannah VI, 639
Miller, Hannah VI, 676
Miller, Hannah Edwards II, 821
Miller, Hannah F. V, 586
Miller, Hannah F. V, 973
Miller, Hannah G. IV, 101
Miller, Hannah G. V, 973
Miller, Hannah M. II, 899
Miller, Hannah Miller II, 783
Miller, Hannah N. II, 121
Miller, Hannah N. II, 125
Miller, Hannah N. II, 738
Miller, Hannah N. II, 756
Miller, Hannah N. II, 810
Miller, Hannah N. II, 859
Miller, Hannah N. II, 899
Miller, Hannah Nicholson II, 783
Miller, Hannah W. IV, 343
Miller, Hannah White II, 34
Miller, Hannah, Jr. II, 87
Miller, Hannah, Jr. II, 89
Miller, Hannah, Jr. VI, 573
Miller, Harold IV, 1258
Miller, Harold V, 697
Miller, Harold Acton III, 230
Miller, Harvey IV, 1174
Miller, Helen II, 783
Miller, Helen III, 136
Miller, Helen III, 229
Miller, Helen V, 1010
Miller, Helen A. III, 125
Miller, Helen Adeline III, 229
Miller, Helen G. III, 94
Miller, Helen G. III, 228
Miller, Henrietta II, 810
Miller, Henrietta III, 229
Miller, Henrietta III, 411
Miller, Henrietta III, 427
Miller, Henrietta III, 464
Miller, Henrietta V, 921
Miller, Henry II, 455
Miller, Henry II, 598
Miller, Henry III, 230
Miller, Henry V, 349
Miller, Henry V, 921
Miller, Henry VI, 766
Miller, Henry VI, 962
Miller, Henry Canby II, 783
Miller, Henry Clay V, 349
Miller, Henry Clay V, 413
Miller, Henry Clay V, 921
Miller, Henry Clay VI, 663
Miller, Henry E. V, 517
Miller, Henry G. III, 229
Miller, Henry G. III, 230
Miller, Henry H. III, 94
Miller, Henry H. III, 228
Miller, Henry H. VI, 765
Miller, Henry H. VI, 766
Miller, Henry Oldine V, 517
Miller, Henry Spencer II, 899
Miller, Henry W. III, 65
Miller, Henry W. III, 228
Miller, Henry W. III, 229
Miller, Henry W. III, 327
Miller, Herbert III, 229
Miller, Herbert IV, 1330
Miller, Herbert James III, 229
Miller, Hetty C. II, 117
Miller, Hetty C. II, 121
Miller, Hetty Hall II, 127
Miller, Hezekiah V, 921
Miller, Hezekiah P. IV, 49
Miller, Hezikiah P. IV, 911
Miller, Hiram IV, 101
Miller, Hiram V, 264
Miller, Hiram V, 973
Miller, Hiram V, 979
Miller, Horace V, 973
Miller, Horace G. V, 979
Miller, Horace W. II, 810
Miller, Howard II, 783
Miller, Hulda VI, 962
Miller, Hyman G. III, 229
Miller, Hyman G. III, 271
Miller, I. Newton V, 413
Miller, Ida III, 214
Miller, Ida III, 228
Miller, Ida III, 229
Miller, Ida V, 973
Miller, Ida V, 979
Miller, Irving Underhill III, 229
Miller, Isaac II, 34
Miller, Isaac II, 48
Miller, Isaac II, 87
Miller, Isaac II, 396
Miller, Isaac II, 756
Miller, Isaac II, 1015
Miller, Isaac III, 146
Miller, Isaac III, 229
Miller, Isaac IV, 49
Miller, Isaac IV, 93
Miller, Isaac IV, 834
Miller, Isaac IV, 837
Miller, Isaac IV, 911
Miller, Isaac V, 264
Miller, Isaac V, 413
Miller, Isaac V, 424
Miller, Isaac L. II, 821
Miller, Isaac N. V, 349
Miller, Isaac Newton IV, 911
Miller, Isaac Newton V, 413
Miller, Isaac V. IV, 740
Miller, Isabell VI, 766
Miller, Isabella III, 230
Miller, Isabella III, 312
Miller, Isabella Amanda K. III, 70
Miller, Isabella T. III, 83
Miller, Isabella T. III, 230
Miller, Isabelle V, 264
Miller, Isham VI, 332
Miller, Israel V, 1010
Miller, Israel VI, 663
Miller, Israel VI, 766
Miller, Israel W. V, 1010
Miller, J. V, 1010
Miller, J. Everett V, 349
Miller, J. G. III, 83
Miller, J. M. I, 627
Miller, Jacob III, 228
Miller, Jacob III, 229
Miller, Jacob III, 230
Miller, Jacob V, 1010
Miller, Jacob VI, 962
Miller, Jacob VI, 972
Miller, Jacob A. V, 1010
Miller, Jacob B. II, 899
Miller, Jacob Butz II, 810
Miller, Jacob, Jr. II, 396
Miller, Jame M. IV, 96
Miller, James I, 726
Miller, James II, 48
Miller, James II, 88
Miller, James II, 135
Miller, James II, 396
Miller, James II, 446
Miller, James II, 597
Miller, James III, 312
Miller, James III, 346
Miller, James V, 349
Miller, James V, 586
Miller, James V, 697
Miller, James V, 1010
Miller, James VI, 423
Miller, James VI, 491
Miller, James VI, 535
Miller, James VI, 663
Miller, James VI, 766
Miller, James VI, 951
Miller, James VI, 962
Miller, James VI, 1003
Miller, James E. III, 229
Miller, James E. III, 356
Miller, James H. III, 229
Miller, James H. IV, 980
Miller, James H. VI, 765
Miller, James Harrison IV, 98
Miller, James Harrison V, 413
Miller, James J. V, 1010
Miller, James M. V, 349
Miller, James M. V, 586
Miller, James Madison IV, 49
Miller, James Madison IV, 911
Miller, James Madison V, 413
Miller, James Madison V, 921
Miller, James Moore VI, 663
Miller, James W. IV, 488
Miller, Jane III, 125
Miller, Jane III, 228
Miller, Jane III, 229
Miller, Jane III, 230
Miller, Jane IV, 43
Miller, Jane IV, 49
Miller, Jane IV, 96
Miller, Jane IV, 101
Miller, Jane V, 190
Miller, Jane V, 264
Miller, Jane V, 755
Miller, Jane V, 969
Miller, Jane V, 973
Miller, Jane VI, 423
Miller, Jane VI, 663
Miller, Jane VI, 766
Miller, Janette IV, 1287
Miller, Jean VI, 423
Miller, Jemima III, 229
Miller, Jennie V, 1010
Miller, Jennie A. II, 810
Miller, Jennie E. III, 228
Miller, Jennie E. III, 293
Miller, Jerusha IV, 421
Miller, Jerusha IV, 434
Miller, Jess IV, 1069
Miller, Jesse III, 229
Miller, Jesse IV, 343
Miller, Jesse IV, 421
Miller, Jesse V, 99
Miller, Jesse V, 956
Miller, Jesse VI, 855
Miller, Jesse A. V, 413
Miller, Jessie V, 413
Miller, Jessie V, 435
Miller, Job I, 60
Miller, Job I, 61
Miller, John II, 34
Miller, John II, 35
Miller, John II, 48
Miller, John II, 51
Miller, John II, 86
Miller, John II, 87
Miller, John II, 88
Miller, John II, 133
Miller, John II, 139
Miller, John II, 153
Miller, John II, 396
Miller, John II, 455

r, John II, 597
r, John II, 598
r, John II, 717
r, John II, 868
r, John II, 899
r, John II, 960
r, John II, 965
r, John II, 986
r, John II, 1001
r, John II, 1015
r, John II, 1016
r, John II, 1038
r, John II, 1076
r, John III, 94
r, John III, 146
r, John III, 230
r, John III, 270
r, John IV, 154
r, John IV, 252
r, John IV, 343
r, John IV, 1174
r, John IV, 1258
r, John IV, 1287
r, John V, 190
r, John V, 264
r, John V, 560
r, John V, 586
r, John V, 979
r, John V, 1010
r, John VI, 316
r, John VI, 322
r, John VI, 384
r, John VI, 423
r, John VI, 514
r, John VI, 840
r, John VI, 864
r, John VI, 927
r, John VI, 942
r, John VI, 962
r, John VI, 1009
r, John B. II, 1056
r, John B. II, 1066
r, John B. II, 1076
r, John B. III, 98
r, John E. V, 349
r, John E. V, 413
r, John Miller VI, 332
r, John N. IV, 1258
r, John R. II, 153
r, John S. VI, 535
r, John S. VI, 766
r, John Saunders VI, 766
r, John T. III, 230
r, John T. V, 973
r, John W. IV, 1330
r, John, Jr. II, 965
r, John, Jr. II, 1015
r, John, Jr. II, 1056
r, John, Jr. II, 1076
r, John, Jr. II, 1081
r, Jonah VI, 402
r, Jonas V, 190
r, Jonas V, 755
r, Jonas VI, 423
r, Jonathan V, 190
r, Jonathan V, 517
r, Jonathan V, 755
r, Jonathan VI, 840
r, Jonathan L. V, 1010
r, Jonathan L. V, 517
r, Jonathan N. II, 859
r, Jonathan N. II, 899
r, Jonathan T. V, 190
r, Jones C. I, 726
r, Jos. Richardson III, 229
r, Joseph II, 34
r, Joseph II, 48
r, Joseph II, 86
r, Joseph II, 88
r, Joseph II, 135
r, Joseph II, 153
r, Joseph II, 810
r, Joseph II, 899
r, Joseph II, 1015
r, Joseph II, 1018
r, Joseph III, 96
r, Joseph III, 220
r, Joseph III, 228
r, Joseph III, 230
r, Joseph IV, 49
r, Joseph IV, 101
r, Joseph V, 99
r, Joseph V, 190
r, Joseph V, 586
r, Joseph V, 973
r, Joseph V, 1010
r, Joseph VI, 423
r, Joseph G. III, 83
r, Joseph G. III, 220
er, Joseph G. III, 230
er, Joseph G. III, 312
Miller, Joseph H. IV, 43
Miller, Joseph H. IV, 49
Miller, Joseph H. IV, 87
Miller, Joseph H. IV, 101
Miller, Joseph H. IV, 1258
Miller, Joseph H. V, 970
Miller, Joseph H. V, 973
Miller, Joseph H. VI, 535
Miller, Joseph H. VI, 757
Miller, Joseph H. VI, 766
Miller, Joseph H. VI, 772
Miller, Joseph H., Jr. VI, 663
Miller, Joseph H., Jr. VI, 766
Miller, Joseph Hartshorne VI, 663
Miller, Joseph Hartshorne VI, 766
Miller, Joseph T. II, 949
Miller, Josephine B. III, 129
Miller, Josephine B. III, 230
Miller, Josephine Wyatt W. III, 230
Miller, Joshua IV, 343
Miller, Joshua V, 190
Miller, Joshua V, 264
Miller, Joshua VI, 423
Miller, Josiah II, 34
Miller, Josiah II, 35
Miller, Josiah II, 87
Miller, Josiah II, 88
Miller, Josiah II, 112
Miller, Josiah II, 135
Miller, Josiah II, 153
Miller, Julia Ann V, 752
Miller, Juliana V, 306
Miller, Katharine VI, 491
Miller, Katherine II, 396
Miller, Katherine III, 230
Miller, Katherine III, 270
Miller, Kathleen Osborn V, 586
Miller, Katie V, 697
Miller, L. Emma V, 697
Miller, Latitia II, 87
Miller, Latitia II, 112
Miller, Laura II, 810
Miller, Laura V, 973
Miller, Laura V, 979
Miller, Laura Belle III, 230
Miller, Laura F. III, 220
Miller, Laura F. III, 228
Miller, Laura F. III, 230
Miller, Laura F. III, 293
Miller, Laura F. III, 295
Miller, Leah III, 83
Miller, Leah III, 129
Miller, Leah III, 174
Miller, Leah III, 230
Miller, Leah H. III, 47
Miller, Leah H. III, 83
Miller, Leah H. III, 128
Miller, Leah H. III, 143
Miller, Leah H. III, 230
Miller, Leanna IV, 1374
Miller, Leanna D. IV, 1287
Miller, Leatitia II, 34
Miller, Leatitia II, 35
Miller, Leatitia II, 82
Miller, Leatitia II, 87
Miller, Leona V, 1010
Miller, Leonard Survetus V, 413
Miller, Leora V, 1010
Miller, Letitia II, 48
Miller, Lettitia II, 86
Miller, Lettitia II, 87
Miller, Lettitia II, 88
Miller, Lettitia II, 94
Miller, Lettitia II, 96
Miller, Levi IV, 49
Miller, Levi IV, 343
Miller, Levi IV, 588
Miller, Levi IV, 834
Miller, Levi IV, 859
Miller, Levi IV, 873
Miller, Levi IV, 878
Miller, Levi IV, 897
Miller, Levi IV, 910
Miller, Levi IV, 911
Miller, Levi V, 349
Miller, Levi V, 413
Miller, Levi, Jr. IV, 741
Miller, Levi, Jr. IV, 834
Miller, Levi, Jr. IV, 837
Miller, Levis II, 820
Miller, Levis II, 899
Miller, Levis II, 929
Miller, Lewellyn VI, 535
Miller, Lewis II, 87
Miller, Lewis IV, 101
Miller, Lewis IV, 1174
Miller, Lewis V, 99
Miller, Lewis V, 586
Miller, Lewis V, 1010
Miller, Lewis N. IV, 101
Miller, Lewis N. V, 99
Miller, Lewis N. V, 557
Miller, Lewis N. V, 586
Miller, Lewis N. V, 969
Miller, Lewis N. V, 973
Miller, Lewis N. V, 979
Miller, Lidya II, 87
Miller, Lizzie IV, 741
Miller, Lizzie V, 349
Miller, Lizzie V, 586
Miller, Lizzie V, 697
Miller, Llewellyn VI, 535
Miller, Llewellyn VI, 767
Miller, Lloyd IV, 1287
Miller, Lockey H. VI, 1016
Miller, Locky VI, 962
Miller, Lola H. V, 413
Miller, Lottie F. II, 859
Miller, Lottie F. II, 899
Miller, Loueza I, 409
Miller, Loueza I, 416
Miller, Louis V, 190
Miller, Louis V, 1010
Miller, Louisa III, 187
Miller, Louisa III, 229
Miller, Louisa III, 230
Miller, Louisa IV, 640
Miller, Louisa IV, 646
Miller, Louisa V, 99
Miller, Louisa V, 190
Miller, Louisa V, 685
Miller, Louisa V, 979
Miller, Louisa B. V, 817
Miller, Louisa M. V, 817
Miller, Louise IV, 1287
Miller, Lucinda V, 413
Miller, Lucinda V, 419
Miller, Lucy P. II, 899
Miller, Lucy Pancoast II, 810
Miller, Lydia II, 35
Miller, Lydia IV, 95
Miller, Lydia IV, 100
Miller, Lydia IV, 101
Miller, Lydia IV, 116
Miller, Lydia IV, 252
Miller, Lydia IV, 253
Miller, Lydia IV, 343
Miller, Lydia IV, 390
Miller, Lydia IV, 392
Miller, Lydia IV, 421
Miller, Lydia IV, 541
Miller, Lydia IV, 827
Miller, Lydia IV, 834
Miller, Lydia IV, 1069
Miller, Lydia IV, 1287
Miller, Lydia V, 99
Miller, Lydia V, 391
Miller, Lydia V, 413
Miller, Lydia V, 817
Miller, Lydia V, 956
Miller, Lydia V, 970
Miller, Lydia V, 973
Miller, Lydia V, 1010
Miller, Lydia VI, 601
Miller, Lydia E. IV, 980
Miller, Lydia Elizabeth IV, 980
Miller, Lydia Elizabeth V, 413
Miller, Lydia L. V, 190
Miller, Lydia M. IV, 101
Miller, Lydia W. IV, 85
Miller, Lydia W. IV, 101
Miller, Lydia W. IV, 705
Miller, Lydia W. IV, 741
Miller, Lytha V, 884
Miller, Madison V, 349
Miller, Magdalena IV, 816
Miller, Magdalena IV, 956
Miller, Margaret II, 34
Miller, Margaret II, 86
Miller, Margaret II, 88
Miller, Margaret II, 133
Miller, Margaret II, 541
Miller, Margaret II, 597
Miller, Margaret II, 868
Miller, Margaret II, 899
Miller, Margaret III, 229
Miller, Margaret III, 230
Miller, Margaret III, 270
Miller, Margaret IV, 49
Miller, Margaret IV, 130
Miller, Margaret IV, 132
Miller, Margaret IV, 343
Miller, Margaret IV, 1287
Miller, Margaret V, 190
Miller, Margaret V, 264
Miller, Margaret V, 517
Miller, Margaret VI, 384
Miller, Margaret VI, 423
Miller, Margaret VI, 535
Miller, Margaret VI, 1001
Miller, Margaret A. IV, 1330
Miller, Margaret D. IV, 253
Miller, Margaret D. IV, 305
Miller, Margaret E. III, 183
Miller, Margaret E. III, 230
Miller, Margaret Elgar VI, 666
Miller, Margaret H. VI, 766
Miller, Margaret W. II, 899
Miller, Margaret, Jr. II, 51
Miller, Margaret, Jr. II, 87
Miller, Margareta IV, 834
Miller, Margarett IV, 154
Miller, Margaretta II, 868
Miller, Margaretta II, 899
Miller, Margaretta II, 942
Miller, Margaretta IV, 1287
Miller, Margaretta W. II, 868
Miller, Margaretta W. II, 899
Miller, Margrett II, 396
Miller, Maria I, 329
Miller, Maria I, 330
Miller, Maria IV, 49
Miller, Maria IV, 101
Miller, Maria IV, 911
Miller, Maria V, 413
Miller, Maria V, 921
Miller, Maria P. IV, 49
Miller, Maria P. IV, 78
Miller, Maria P. IV, 101
Miller, Maria P. IV, 911
Miller, Mariah IV, 741
Miller, Mariah IV, 834
Miller, Mariah IV, 837
Miller, Mariah V, 99
Miller, Mariah V, 349
Miller, Mariah V, 413
Miller, Mariah V, 973
Miller, Mariah V, 1010
Miller, Mariah B. V, 349
Miller, Marianna II, 135
Miller, Marianna II, 153
Miller, Marianna VI, 766
Miller, Marjorie J. V, 413
Miller, Marjory Jay V, 413
Miller, Mark II, 34
Miller, Mark II, 35
Miller, Mark II, 47
Miller, Mark II, 62
Miller, Mark II, 87
Miller, Mark II, 112
Miller, Mark, Jr. II, 87
Miller, Martha I, 890
Miller, Martha I, 894
Miller, Martha II, 242
Miller, Martha II, 508
Miller, Martha II, 597
Miller, Martha II, 598
Miller, Martha III, 229
Miller, Martha IV, 84
Miller, Martha IV, 101
Miller, Martha IV, 588
Miller, Martha IV, 834
Miller, Martha IV, 837
Miller, Martha IV, 911
Miller, Martha V, 99
Miller, Martha V, 264
Miller, Martha V, 349
Miller, Martha V, 413
Miller, Martha V, 424
Miller, Martha V, 586
Miller, Martha Canby II, 783
Miller, Martha Catharine III, 231
Miller, Martha J. IV, 980
Miller, Martha Jane IV, 980
Miller, Martha Jane V, 349
Miller, Martha Jane V, 413
Miller, Martha L. V, 1010
Miller, Martha Louise IV, 980
Miller, Martin I, 330
Miller, Mary I, 60
Miller, Mary I, 61
Miller, Mary II, 34
Miller, Mary II, 35
Miller, Mary II, 47
Miller, Mary II, 48
Miller, Mary II, 87
Miller, Mary II, 88
Miller, Mary II, 96
Miller, Mary II, 112
Miller, Mary II, 121
Miller, Mary II, 396
Miller, Mary II, 597
Miller, Mary II, 598
Miller, Mary II, 649
Miller, Mary II, 783
Miller, Mary II, 807
Miller, Mary II, 816
Miller, Mary II, 828
Miller, Mary II, 972
Miller, Mary II, 976
Miller, Mary II, 1015
Miller, Mary II, 1038
Miller, Mary II, 1076
Miller, Mary II, 1081
Miller, Mary II, 1086
Miller, Mary II, 1088
Miller, Mary III, 76
Miller, Mary III, 90
Miller, Mary III, 141
Miller, Mary III, 187
Miller, Mary III, 207
Miller, Mary III, 228
Miller, Mary III, 229
Miller, Mary III, 230
Miller, Mary III, 249
Miller, Mary III, 312
Miller, Mary III, 427
Miller, Mary III, 440
Miller, Mary III, 449
Miller, Mary IV, 43
Miller, Mary IV, 49
Miller, Mary IV, 84
Miller, Mary IV, 96
Miller, Mary IV, 101
Miller, Mary IV, 343
Miller, Mary IV, 488
Miller, Mary IV, 511
Miller, Mary IV, 541
Miller, Mary IV, 581
Miller, Mary IV, 586
Miller, Mary IV, 588
Miller, Mary IV, 740
Miller, Mary IV, 834
Miller, Mary IV, 850
Miller, Mary IV, 906
Miller, Mary IV, 911
Miller, Mary IV, 917
Miller, Mary IV, 965
Miller, Mary V, 99
Miller, Mary V, 118
Miller, Mary V, 264
Miller, Mary V, 413
Miller, Mary V, 420
Miller, Mary V, 755
Miller, Mary V, 972
Miller, Mary V, 973
Miller, Mary V, 1010
Miller, Mary VI, 316
Miller, Mary VI, 320
Miller, Mary VI, 331
Miller, Mary VI, 376
Miller, Mary VI, 423
Miller, Mary VI, 424
Miller, Mary VI, 480
Miller, Mary VI, 514
Miller, Mary VI, 535
Miller, Mary VI, 585
Miller, Mary VI, 601
Miller, Mary VI, 774
Miller, Mary VI, 782
Miller, Mary VI, 823
Miller, Mary VI, 981
Miller, Mary A. III, 220
Miller, Mary A. III, 230
Miller, Mary A. E. VI, 962
Miller, Mary Alice V, 1010
Miller, Mary Ann IV, 49
Miller, Mary Ann IV, 87
Miller, Mary Ann IV, 101
Miller, Mary Ann IV, 343
Miller, Mary Ann IV, 911
Miller, Mary Ann IV, 944
Miller, Mary Ann V, 917
Miller, Mary Ann V, 921
Miller, Mary Ann VI, 543
Miller, Mary Anna VI, 766
Miller, Mary Anna VI, 772
Miller, Mary Betts II, 783
Miller, Mary C. IV, 1174
Miller, Mary C. V, 1010
Miller, Mary C. VI, 978
Miller, Mary E. I, 29
Miller, Mary E. IV, 1258
Miller, Mary E. V, 413
Miller, Mary E. V, 755
Miller, Mary E. VI, 766
Miller, Mary E. VI, 791
Miller, Mary Elizabeth IV, 878
Miller, Mary Emily III, 229
Miller, Mary Emily III, 230
Miller, Mary G. II, 153
Miller, Mary H. IV, 101
Miller, Mary H. IV, 582
Miller, Mary H. IV, 588
Miller, Mary H. IV, 741
Miller, Mary H. IV, 792
Miller, Mary H. IV, 834
Miller, Mary H. V, 970
Miller, Mary H. V, 973
Miller, Mary Hewes VI, 766
Miller, Mary Hewes VI, 767

Miller, Mary J. IV, 733
Miller, Mary J. IV, 741
Miller, Mary Jane IV, 911
Miller, Mary Jane V, 413
Miller, Mary Janet VI, 766
Miller, Mary K. V, 586
Miller, Mary K. V, 970
Miller, Mary K. V, 973
Miller, Mary K. V, 979
Miller, Mary L. II, 88
Miller, Mary L. II, 127
Miller, Mary L. II, 135
Miller, Mary L. III, 140
Miller, Mary L. III, 230
Miller, Mary L. V, 1010
Miller, Mary M. II, 1056
Miller, Mary M. II, 1061
Miller, Mary M. VI, 765
Miller, Mary Moore VI, 766
Miller, Mary O. II, 153
Miller, Mary R. III, 427
Miller, Mary R. V, 817
Miller, Mary Rebecca V, 190
Miller, Mary T III, 170
Miller, Mary T. III, 72
Miller, Mary T. III, 170
Miller, Mary T. III, 230
Miller, Mary Thomas II, 899
Miller, Mary U. III, 230
Miller, Mary Underhill III, 230
Miller, Mary W. II, 899
Miller, Mary W. III, 229
Miller, Mary W. III, 271
Miller, Mary W. III, 297
Miller, Mary W. V, 973
Miller, Mason IV, 49
Miller, Mason IV, 343
Miller, Mason IV, 488
Miller, Mason IV, 541
Miller, Matilda IV, 541
Miller, Matilda IV, 556
Miller, Matilda VI, 962
Miller, Matilda Bracken II, 1015
Miller, Matilda S. III, 214
Miller, Mattie V, 1010
Miller, Maurice IV, 834
Miller, Maurice IV, 850
Miller, Maurice IV, 859
Miller, May III, 291
Miller, Mib IV, 488
Miller, Mildred V, 697
Miller, Mildred Marie V, 697
Miller, Mildred Thorn III, 229
Miller, Milo IV, 1287
Miller, Milton IV, 343
Miller, Milton IV, 1069
Miller, Minnie IV, 1330
Miller, Minnie V, 1010
Miller, Minnie G. IV, 1330
Miller, Miriam II, 597
Miller, Mody III, 230
Miller, Mollie V, 697
Miller, Mordecai IV, 911
Miller, Mordecai V, 413
Miller, Mordecai V, 921
Miller, Mordecai VI, 517
Miller, Mordecai VI, 543
Miller, Mordecai VI, 663
Miller, Mordecai VI, 725
Miller, Mordecai VI, 746
Miller, Mordecai VI, 766
Miller, Mordecai, Jr. VI, 767
Miller, Mordicai IV, 49
Miller, Moriah V, 1010
Miller, Morris IV, 49
Miller, Morris IV, 740
Miller, Morris IV, 834
Miller, Morris IV, 897
Miller, Morris IV, 905
Miller, Morris IV, 907
Miller, Morris IV, 910
Miller, Morris IV, 965
Miller, Morris IV, 980
Miller, Morris M. III, 441
Miller, Morris, Jr. IV, 911
Miller, Moses VI, 962
Miller, Moses VI, 999
Miller, Mrs. Mina V, 755
Miller, Myrtie V, 1010
Miller, Myrtie V. V, 1010
Miller, Nancy VI, 840
Miller, Nancy Ann I, 1159
Miller, Naomi I, 60
Miller, Naomi I, 84
Miller, Nathan II, 1015
Miller, Nathan IV, 343
Miller, Nathan IV, 541
Miller, Nathan IV, 911
Miller, Nathan V, 789
Miller, Nathaniel V, 789
Miller, Nathen IV, 488
Miller, Nellie V, 1010
Miller, Nellie May IV, 1258
Miller, Neoma IV, 1330
Miller, Newton IV, 343
Miller, Newton IV, 421
Miller, Newton IV, 1069
Miller, Newton V, 99
Miller, Newton V, 956
Miller, Olcha III, 230
Miller, Olicer H. IV, 49
Miller, Olive III, 230
Miller, Olive T. III, 427
Miller, Oliver IV, 101
Miller, Oliver IV, 911
Miller, Ollie V, 1010
Miller, Osa B. V, 1010
Miller, Oscar V, 697
Miller, Oscar V, 1010
Miller, Otho V, 1010
Miller, Parry E. V, 817
Miller, Perry V, 1010
Miller, Peter II, 396
Miller, Peter II, 713
Miller, Peter IV, 49
Miller, Peter IV, 93
Miller, Peter IV, 130
Miller, Peter IV, 132
Miller, Phebe II, 35
Miller, Phebe II, 62
Miller, Phebe II, 87
Miller, Phebe III, 109
Miller, Phebe III, 228
Miller, Phebe III, 230
Miller, Phebe IV, 101
Miller, Phebe IV, 106
Miller, Phebe IV, 253
Miller, Phebe IV, 541
Miller, Phebe IV, 548
Miller, Phebe IV, 634
Miller, Phebe IV, 646
Miller, Phebe V, 810
Miller, Phebe V, 921
Miller, Phebe V, 969
Miller, Phebe V, 972
Miller, Phebe V, 973
Miller, Phebe VI, 423
Miller, Phebe Ann V, 99
Miller, Phebe Ann VI, 535
Miller, Phebe Ann VI, 663
Miller, Phebe Ann VI, 757
Miller, Phebe Ann VI, 766
Miller, Phebe C. III, 27
Miller, Phebe C. III, 122
Miller, Phebe C. III, 229
Miller, Phebe C. III, 230
Miller, Phebe C. III, 293
Miller, Phebe C. III, 326
Miller, Phebe C. III, 330
Miller, Phebe H. III, 229
Miller, Phebe Jane III, 128
Miller, Phebe Jane III, 230
Miller, Phebe W. III, 229
Miller, Phebe W. III, 230
Miller, Phebe, Jr. II, 35
Miller, Phebe, Jr. III, 229
Miller, Phebe, Sr. II, 35
Miller, Philip III, 230
Miller, Phineas VI, 663
Miller, Phinneas Janney VI, 766
Miller, Polly VI, 962
Miller, Polly VI, 998
Miller, Priscilla II, 48
Miller, Priscilla II, 87
Miller, Priscilla II, 113
Miller, Pyle Smith II, 34
Miller, Rachel II, 34
Miller, Rachel II, 54
Miller, Rachel II, 87
Miller, Rachel II, 88
Miller, Rachel II, 396
Miller, Rachel II, 465
Miller, Rachel II, 499
Miller, Rachel II, 597
Miller, Rachel II, 598
Miller, Rachel II, 607
Miller, Rachel II, 728
Miller, Rachel II, 756
Miller, Rachel II, 783
Miller, Rachel II, 838
Miller, Rachel II, 899
Miller, Rachel II, 986
Miller, Rachel II, 1015
Miller, Rachel II, 1056
Miller, Rachel II, 1076
Miller, Rachel II, 1081
Miller, Rachel II, 1086
Miller, Rachel II, 1088
Miller, Rachel IV, 252
Miller, Rachel IV, 253
Miller, Rachel IV, 329
Miller, Rachel IV, 343
Miller, Rachel IV, 421
Miller, Rachel IV, 541
Miller, Rachel IV, 741
Miller, Rachel IV, 1069
Miller, Rachel IV, 1070
Miller, Rachel IV, 1082
Miller, Rachel IV, 1217
Miller, Rachel IV, 1220
Miller, Rachel V, 99
Miller, Rachel V, 956
Miller, Rachel VI, 322
Miller, Rachel VI, 332
Miller, Rachel VI, 423
Miller, Rachel VI, 513
Miller, Rachel VI, 535
Miller, Rachel VI, 587
Miller, Rachel VI, 840
Miller, Rachel Biddle II, 810
Miller, Rachel Biddle II, 899
Miller, Rachel J. IV, 49
Miller, Rachel Jane IV, 101
Miller, Rachel Jane V, 973
Miller, Ralph V, 349
Miller, Reatha VI, 766
Miller, Rebecca II, 34
Miller, Rebecca II, 35
Miller, Rebecca II, 48
Miller, Rebecca II, 87
Miller, Rebecca II, 88
Miller, Rebecca II, 121
Miller, Rebecca II, 598
Miller, Rebecca II, 713
Miller, Rebecca II, 756
Miller, Rebecca II, 1002
Miller, Rebecca II, 1015
Miller, Rebecca II, 1076
Miller, Rebecca III, 95
Miller, Rebecca III, 230
Miller, Rebecca III, 346
Miller, Rebecca IV, 33
Miller, Rebecca IV, 49
Miller, Rebecca IV, 51
Miller, Rebecca IV, 87
Miller, Rebecca IV, 95
Miller, Rebecca IV, 96
Miller, Rebecca IV, 101
Miller, Rebecca IV, 182
Miller, Rebecca IV, 740
Miller, Rebecca IV, 909
Miller, Rebecca IV, 911
Miller, Rebecca IV, 971
Miller, Rebecca IV, 980
Miller, Rebecca V, 172
Miller, Rebecca V, 190
Miller, Rebecca V, 557
Miller, Rebecca V, 586
Miller, Rebecca V, 969
Miller, Rebecca V, 973
Miller, Rebecca V, 979
Miller, Rebecca VI, 517
Miller, Rebecca VI, 543
Miller, Rebecca VI, 663
Miller, Rebecca VI, 746
Miller, Rebecca VI, 766
Miller, Rebecca VI, 767
Miller, Rebecca A. V, 1010
Miller, Rebecca G. IV, 49
Miller, Rebecca G. IV, 101
Miller, Rebecca G. IV, 1258
Miller, Rebecca G. V, 973
Miller, Rebecca H. II, 747
Miller, Rebecca H. II, 756
Miller, Rebecca L. IV, 588
Miller, Rebecca Lillian IV, 588
Miller, Rebecca Lillian IV, 593
Miller, Rebecca S. II, 713
Miller, Rebecca S. II, 811
Miller, Rebecca S. II, 899
Miller, Rebecca S. II, 902
Miller, Rebecka II, 446
Miller, Rebeckah II, 34
Miller, Rebeckah II, 77
Miller, Rebeckah IV, 101
Miller, Rebeckah V, 264
Miller, Rebeckah VI, 746
Miller, Rebekah II, 78
Miller, Rebekah II, 87
Miller, Rees IV, 1287
Miller, Reuben IV, 101
Miller, Reuben IV, 343
Miller, Reuben IV, 1069
Miller, Reuben V, 99
Miller, Reuben B. III, 230
Miller, Rhoda V, 697
Miller, Rhoda V, 970
Miller, Rhoda V, 973
Miller, Rhoda V, 979
Miller, Richard II, 19
Miller, Richard II, 35
Miller, Richard II, 48
Miller, Richard II, 49
Miller, Richard II, 87
Miller, Richard II, 88
Miller, Richard II, 96
Miller, Richard III, 229
Miller, Richard III, 230
Miller, Richard III, 427
Miller, Richard IV, 343
Miller, Richard IV, 488
Miller, Richard IV, 541
Miller, Richard, Jr. III, 230
Miller, Richardson III, 125
Miller, Robert III, 95
Miller, Robert III, 230
Miller, Robert IV, 49
Miller, Robert IV, 88
Miller, Robert IV, 96
Miller, Robert IV, 100
Miller, Robert IV, 101
Miller, Robert IV, 343
Miller, Robert IV, 390
Miller, Robert IV, 421
Miller, Robert IV, 588
Miller, Robert IV, 715
Miller, Robert IV, 740
Miller, Robert IV, 741
Miller, Robert IV, 834
Miller, Robert IV, 873
Miller, Robert IV, 878
Miller, Robert IV, 906
Miller, Robert IV, 910
Miller, Robert IV, 911
Miller, Robert IV, 918
Miller, Robert IV, 1069
Miller, Robert IV, 1174
Miller, Robert V, 99
Miller, Robert V, 789
Miller, Robert V, 973
Miller, Robert VI, 423
Miller, Robert VI, 535
Miller, Robert VI, 597
Miller, Robert VI, 601
Miller, Robert VI, 639
Miller, Robert VI, 676
Miller, Robert VI, 765
Miller, Robert VI, 879
Miller, Robert VI, 962
Miller, Robert H. II, 899
Miller, Robert H. II, 942
Miller, Robert H. VI, 518
Miller, Robert H. VI, 740
Miller, Robert H. VI, 745
Miller, Robert H. VI, 765
Miller, Robert H. VI, 766
Miller, Robert H. VI, 772
Miller, Robert Hartshorne VI, 517
Miller, Robert Hartshorne VI, 535
Miller, Robert Hartshorne VI, 753
Miller, Robert Hartshorne VI, 766
Miller, Robt. H. VI, 754
Miller, Rosa V, 634
Miller, Ross, Elizabeth IV, 548
Miller, Rueben V, 956
Miller, Ruth I, 921
Miller, Ruth II, 48
Miller, Ruth II, 87
Miller, Ruth II, 112
Miller, Ruth III, 169
Miller, Ruth IV, 49
Miller, Ruth IV, 100
Miller, Ruth IV, 101
Miller, Ruth IV, 103
Miller, Ruth IV, 343
Miller, Ruth IV, 488
Miller, Ruth IV, 541
Miller, Ruth V, 99
Miller, Ruth V, 972
Miller, Ruth V, 979
Miller, Ruth VI, 423
Miller, Ruth VI, 487
Miller, Ruth VI, 513
Miller, Ruth VI, 535
Miller, Ruth VI, 597
Miller, Ruth VI, 601
Miller, Ruth VI, 738
Miller, Ruth VI, 766
Miller, Ruth A. V, 349
Miller, Ruth A. V, 413
Miller, Ruth A. V, 973
Miller, Ruth A. V, 975
Miller, Ruth Ana IV, 741
Miller, Ruth Ann IV, 49
Miller, Ruth Anna IV, 684
Miller, Ruth Ellen IV, 1174
Miller, Ruth H. IV, 101
Miller, Ruth H. IV, 107
Miller, Ruth N. V, 586
Miller, Ruth N. V, 973
Miller, Ruth Rogers III, 427
Miller, Ruth Rogers III, 449
Miller, Ruth, Jr. II, 55
Miller, Ruth, Jr. II, 87
Miller, Ruthanna IV, 101
Miller, Sabina IV, 49
Miller, Sabina IV, 101
Miller, Sabina IV, 741
Miller, Sabina V, 973
Miller, Sallie V, 755
Miller, Sally VI, 840
Miller, Sally VI, 864
Miller, Sally VI, 942
Miller, Samantha V, 1010
Miller, Samantha Jane I, 115
Miller, Samuel II, 34
Miller, Samuel II, 88
Miller, Samuel II, 135
Miller, Samuel II, 242
Miller, Samuel II, 598
Miller, Samuel III, 210
Miller, Samuel III, 230
Miller, Samuel IV, 834
Miller, Samuel IV, 837
Miller, Samuel IV, 911
Miller, Samuel IV, 980
Miller, Samuel V, 349
Miller, Samuel V, 413
Miller, Samuel V, 979
Miller, Samuel V, 1010
Miller, Samuel VI, 423
Miller, Samuel VI, 462
Miller, Samuel VI, 535
Miller, Samuel VI, 766
Miller, Samuel VI, 767
Miller, Samuel C. V, 99
Miller, Samuel H. IV, 792
Miller, Samuel H. VI, 535
Miller, Samuel J. III, 329
Miller, Samuel M. V, 817
Miller, Samuel M., Jr. III, 18
Miller, Samuel S. II, 153
Miller, Samuel T. VI, 832
Miller, Samuel T. VI, 863
Miller, Samuel W. II, 135
Miller, Samuel W. III, 207
Miller, Samuel W. III, 230
Miller, Sarah II, 24
Miller, Sarah II, 34
Miller, Sarah II, 35
Miller, Sarah II, 48
Miller, Sarah II, 65
Miller, Sarah II, 66
Miller, Sarah II, 87
Miller, Sarah II, 88
Miller, Sarah II, 135
Miller, Sarah II, 226
Miller, Sarah II, 242
Miller, Sarah II, 483
Miller, Sarah II, 597
Miller, Sarah II, 756
Miller, Sarah II, 801
Miller, Sarah II, 899
Miller, Sarah II, 925
Miller, Sarah II, 928
Miller, Sarah II, 953
Miller, Sarah II, 960
Miller, Sarah II, 961
Miller, Sarah II, 965
Miller, Sarah II, 986
Miller, Sarah II, 996
Miller, Sarah II, 1001
Miller, Sarah II, 1015
Miller, Sarah II, 1038
Miller, Sarah II, 1076
Miller, Sarah III, 229
Miller, Sarah III, 329
Miller, Sarah IV, 67
Miller, Sarah IV, 95
Miller, Sarah IV, 98
Miller, Sarah IV, 101
Miller, Sarah IV, 253
Miller, Sarah IV, 343
Miller, Sarah IV, 421
Miller, Sarah IV, 488
Miller, Sarah IV, 537
Miller, Sarah IV, 541
Miller, Sarah IV, 834
Miller, Sarah IV, 905
Miller, Sarah IV, 911
Miller, Sarah IV, 1258
Miller, Sarah IV, 1287
Miller, Sarah V, 190
Miller, Sarah V, 264
Miller, Sarah V, 789
Miller, Sarah V, 921
Miller, Sarah V, 973
Miller, Sarah V, 975
Miller, Sarah V, 1010
Miller, Sarah VI, 423
Miller, Sarah VI, 424

er, Sarah VI, 485
er, Sarah VI, 507
er, Sarah VI, 535
er, Sarah VI, 578
er, Sarah VI, 601
er, Sarah VI, 663
er, Sarah VI, 745
er, Sarah VI, 766
er, Sarah VI, 772
er, Sarah VI, 840
er, Sarah VI, 962
er, Sarah A. II, 810
er, Sarah A. III, 427
er, Sarah Ann III, 210
er, Sarah Ann III, 229
er, Sarah Ann III, 230
er, Sarah Ann IV, 421
er, Sarah Ann IV, 426
er, Sarah Ann IV, 911
er, Sarah C. IV, 980
er, Sarah Charity IV, 980
er, Sarah Charity V, 413
er, Sarah E. III, 229
er, Sarah Elisabeth I, 627
er, Sarah H. III, 230
er, Sarah Jane III, 228
er, Sarah Jane VI, 962
er, Sarah M. V, 1010
er, Sarah N. III, 96
er, Sarah O. IV, 911
er, Sarah P. VI, 767
er, Sarah R. II, 810
er, Sarah R. IV, 588
er, Sarah S. III, 229
er, Sarah S. III, 230
er, Sarah W. III, 441
er, Sarah Wyatt II, 19
er, Sarah Wyatt II, 35
er, Sarah Wyatt II, 49
er, Sarah Wyatt II, 88
er, Sarah, Jr. II, 1001
er, Sarah, Jr. II, 1015
er, Sarah, Jr. II, 1056
er, Sarles III, 229
er, Sarles III, 230
er, Sarles III, 329
er, Scytha V, 884
er, Simon VI, 888
er, Simon VI, 900
er, Simon VI, 1009
er, Simon, Jr. VI, 906
er, Simon, Jr. VI, 962
er, Sina IV, 343
er, Sina IV, 360
er, Sindella V, 1010
er, Sindula V, 1010
er, Solomon IV, 49
er, Solomon IV, 100
er, Solomon IV, 101
er, Solomon IV, 103
er, Solomon V, 99
er, Solomon V, 972
er, Solomon V, 979
er, Solomon VI, 423
er, Solomon VI, 507
er, Solomon VI, 535
er, Solomon VI, 601
er, Solomon W. V, 99
er, Solomon W. V, 973
er, Solomon, Jr. VI, 601
er, Sophia IV, 907
er, Sophia IV, 908
er, Sophia IV, 911
er, Sophia A. IV, 965
er, Stella May V, 697
er, Stephen II, 48
er, Stephen II, 597
er, Stephen III, 128
er, Stephen III, 129
er, Stephen III, 174
er, Stephen III, 229
er, Stephen III, 230
er, Stephen IV, 343
er, Stephen IV, 488
er, Stephen IV, 541
er, Stephen IV, 548
er, Susan II, 810
er, Susan V, 634
er, Susan V, 640
er, Susan V, 973
er, Susan V, 974
er, Susan C. II, 121
er, Susan Cadwaller II, 783
er, Susan E. II, 153
er, Susan E. II, 154
er, Susan G. II, 88
er, Susan R. II, 899
er, Susan Ridgway II, 810
er, Susanna II, 87
er, Susanna II, 455
er, Susanna II, 598
Miller, Susanna IV, 49
Miller, Susanna IV, 834
Miller, Susanna V, 264
Miller, Susanna V, 307
Miller, Susanna V, 979
Miller, Susanna VI, 888
Miller, Susanna VI, 916
Miller, Susanna VI, 962
Miller, Susanna K. IV, 911
Miller, Susannah II, 72
Miller, Susannah II, 87
Miller, Susannah II, 153
Miller, Susannah II, 154
Miller, Susannah IV, 343
Miller, Susannah IV, 646
Miller, Susannah IV, 653
Miller, Susannah IV, 665
Miller, Susannah IV, 741
Miller, Susannah IV, 787
Miller, Susannah IV, 834
Miller, Susannah IV, 911
Miller, Susannah V, 264
Miller, Susannah VI, 477
Miller, Susannah VI, 535
Miller, Susannah VI, 767
Miller, Susannah VI, 797
Miller, Susannah VI, 962
Miller, Susannah H. IV, 792
Miller, Susannah K. IV, 918
Miller, Tacy IV, 49
Miller, Tacy IV, 130
Miller, Tacy IV, 132
Miller, Theodocia II, 598
Miller, Thomas II, 48
Miller, Thomas II, 396
Miller, Thomas II, 508
Miller, Thomas II, 515
Miller, Thomas II, 597
Miller, Thomas II, 598
Miller, Thomas II, 976
Miller, Thomas II, 1015
Miller, Thomas II, 1056
Miller, Thomas II, 1076
Miller, Thomas II, 1086
Miller, Thomas III, 230
Miller, Thomas IV, 101
Miller, Thomas IV, 541
Miller, Thomas V, 99
Miller, Thomas V, 190
Miller, Thomas V, 264
Miller, Thomas V, 484
Miller, Thomas V, 517
Miller, Thomas V, 586
Miller, Thomas V, 817
Miller, Thomas V, 970
Miller, Thomas V, 973
Miller, Thomas V, 974
Miller, Thomas V, 975
Miller, Thomas V, 979
Miller, Thomas VI, 535
Miller, Thomas VI, 767
Miller, Thomas VI, 999
Miller, Thomas N. IV, 100
Miller, Thomas N. V, 99
Miller, Thomas P. VI, 535
Miller, Thomas P. VI, 767
Miller, Thomas Phillip VI, 767
Miller, Thos. II, 801
Miller, Thos. V, 969
Miller, Thos. V, 973
Miller, Thos. V, 1010
Miller, Thurman V, 697
Miller, Timothy IV, 1374
Miller, Vesla Eleanor V, 697
Miller, Vesta Eleanor V, 686
Miller, Vesta Eleanor V, 697
Miller, Viola V, 99
Miller, Viola V, 697
Miller, Viola V, 973
Miller, Virgil IV, 1174
Miller, Virgil V, 413
Miller, Walter V, 1010
Miller, Walton V, 1010
Miller, Warrick II, 597
Miller, Warrick IV, 101
Miller, Warrick IV, 343
Miller, Warrick IV, 421
Miller, Warrick VI, 746
Miller, Warrick P., Jr. VI, 766
Miller, Warwick IV, 101
Miller, Warwick VI, 487
Miller, Warwick VI, 513
Miller, Warwick VI, 535
Miller, Warwick VI, 738
Miller, Warwick VI, 766
Miller, Warwick Guyon VI, 765
Miller, Warwick Guyon VI, 766
Miller, Warwick Price II, 598
Miller, Warwick Price VI, 765
Miller, Warwick Price VI, 766
Miller, Warwrick Price VI, 782
Miller, Wd. Elijah V, 851
Miller, Wd. Juliann II, 801
Miller, Wd. Laura F. III, 26
Miller, Wd. Margaret II, 810
Miller, Wd. Mary VI, 962
Miller, Wd. Mary Johnson VI, 332
Miller, Wd. Mary White II, 810
Miller, Wd. Miriam II, 396
Miller, Wd. Phebe C. III, 26
Miller, Wd. Sallie Levis II, 820
Miller, Wilhelm III, 427
Miller, Wilhelm III, 440
Miller, Wilhelm III, 449
Miller, William II, 34
Miller, William II, 35
Miller, William II, 226
Miller, William II, 242
Miller, William II, 396
Miller, William III, 228
Miller, William IV, 49
Miller, William IV, 95
Miller, William IV, 101
Miller, William IV, 253
Miller, William IV, 343
Miller, William IV, 488
Miller, William IV, 541
Miller, William IV, 1069
Miller, William V, 99
Miller, William V, 697
Miller, William V, 851
Miller, William VI, 423
Miller, William VI, 535
Miller, William VI, 601
Miller, William VI, 911
Miller, William VI, 942
Miller, William VI, 944
Miller, William VI, 962
Miller, William VI, 981
Miller, William B. IV, 49
Miller, William B. IV, 911
Miller, William C. II, 783
Miller, William F. II, 34
Miller, William F. II, 35
Miller, William Foster II, 35
Miller, William H. II, 396
Miller, William H. IV, 101
Miller, William H. VI, 535
Miller, William H. VI, 766
Miller, William H. VI, 770
Miller, William Hartshorne VI, 535
Miller, William Henry IV, 49
Miller, William J. IV, 488
Miller, William R. V, 755
Miller, William S. VI, 962
Miller, William Thomas I, 1159
Miller, William Tyler III, 427
Miller, William, Jr. VI, 765
Miller, William, Jr. VI, 971
Miller, Willie IV, 1258
Miller, Willie V, 413
Miller, Wilmer IV, 911
Miller, Wilmer V, 413
Miller, Winfield II, 899
Miller, Wm. II, 66
Miller, Wm. II, 72
Miller, Wm. II, 87
Miller, Wm. II, 121
Miller, Wm. II, 153
Miller, Wm. II, 154
Miller, Wm. II, 502
Miller, Wm. II, 516
Miller, Wm. II, 597
Miller, Wm. II, 598
Miller, Wm. II, 810
Miller, Wm. IV, 87
Miller, Wm. IV, 96
Miller, Wm. IV, 252
Miller, Wm. IV, 1287
Miller, Wm. V, 461
Miller, Wm. V, 921
Miller, Wm. V, 956
Miller, Wm. V, 973
Miller, Wm. C. V, 190
Miller, Wm. Canby II, 783
Miller, Wm. D. III, 229
Miller, Wm. D. III, 326
Miller, Wm. F. II, 87
Miller, Wm. F. II, 88
Miller, Wm. F. II, 100
Miller, Wm. F. II, 114
Miller, Wm. F. II, 121
Miller, Wm. F. II, 135
Miller, Wm. Franklin V, 921
Miller, Wm. H. II, 756
Miller, Wm. H. V, 697
Miller, Wm. H. V, 1010
Miller, Wm. H. VI, 767
Miller, Wm. H. P. IV, 1287
Miller, Wm. Henry IV, 101
Miller, Wm. J. IV, 980
Miller, Wm. R. V, 973
Miller, Wm. Walton II, 783
Miller, Wyatt Acton II, 135
Miller, Wyatt Acton II, 153
Miller, Wyatt W. II, 127
Miller, Wyatt W. II, 135
Miller, Wyatt W. III, 140
Miller, Wyatt W. III, 230
Miller, Zadoc V, 246
Miller, Zadoc V, 399
Miller, Zadoc V, 413
Miller, Zadock IV, 911
Miller, Zadock V, 349
Miller, Zadock V, 413
Miller, Zadok V, 349
Miller, Zador V, 264
Miller, Zoe V, 190
Miller, Zoe L. V, 190
Miller, Zoe T. V, 190
Milleson, Abigail IV, 49
Milleson, Ann IV, 43
Milleson, Ann IV, 49
Milleson, Caleb IV, 101
Milleson, Dorothy IV, 49
Milleson, Elisha IV, 25
Milleson, Elisha IV, 49
Milleson, Elizabeth IV, 49
Milleson, Hannah IV, 25
Milleson, Hannah IV, 49
Milleson, James IV, 49
Milleson, James, Jr. IV, 49
Milleson, John IV, 49
Milleson, Jonathan IV, 49
Milleson, Lydia IV, 30
Milleson, Lydia IV, 49
Milleson, Mary IV, 43
Milleson, Mary IV, 49
Milleson, Rachel IV, 49
Milleson, Rachel IV, 57
Milleson, Sarah IV, 23
Milleson, Sarah IV, 49
Milleson, William IV, 49
Millet, Hannah IV, 1369
Millet, Hannah IV, 1374
Milley, ??? VI, 903
Millhoan, Elizabeth IV, 253
Millhoan, William IV, 253
Millhorn, John IV, 253
Millhorn, Josephine IV, 253
Millhous, Elizabeth P. IV, 49
Millhous, Sarah I, 1062
Millhous, Sarah I, 1063
Millhous, Sarah II, 705
Millhous, Sarah IV, 280
Millhouse, ??? IV, 1047
Millhouse, Ann I, 1057
Millhouse, Ann I, 1058
Millhouse, Ann V, 99
Millhouse, Anna IV, 1069
Millhouse, Anna IV, 1077
Millhouse, Anna V, 99
Millhouse, Charity IV, 1068
Millhouse, Charity IV, 1069
Millhouse, Charles I, 1034
Millhouse, Daniel IV, 154
Millhouse, Daniel IV, 421
Millhouse, Daniel Henry I, 1034
Millhouse, Dinah I, 1056
Millhouse, Dinah I, 1057
Millhouse, Dinah I, 1058
Millhouse, Elizabeth I, 1034
Millhouse, Elizabeth IV, 371
Millhouse, Elizabeth IV, 421
Millhouse, Elizabeth IV, 1060
Millhouse, Elizabeth IV, 1069
Millhouse, Elizabeth V, 99
Millhouse, Elizabeth P. IV, 35
Millhouse, Elizabeth P. IV, 49
Millhouse, Elizabeth P. IV, 70
Millhouse, Elizabeth P. IV, 208
Millhouse, Elizabeth P. IV, 209
Millhouse, Elizabeth P. IV, 252
Millhouse, Esther IV, 379
Millhouse, Esther IV, 421
Millhouse, Esther IV, 1068
Millhouse, Esther IV, 1069
Millhouse, Hannah IV, 154
Millhouse, Hannah IV, 160
Millhouse, Hannah IV, 644
Millhouse, Hannah IV, 646
Millhouse, Hannah IV, 1069
Millhouse, Henry I, 1015
Millhouse, Henry I, 1034
Millhouse, Henry I, 1055
Millhouse, Henry I, 1056
Millhouse, Henry I, 1057
Millhouse, Henry I, 1058
Millhouse, Henry I, 1059
Millhouse, Henry V, 99
Millhouse, Henry V, 469
Millhouse, Isaac IV, 1069
Millhouse, Jane IV, 154
Millhouse, Jane IV, 252
Millhouse, Jane IV, 269
Millhouse, Jane IV, 1069
Millhouse, Jean I, 1056
Millhouse, John I, 1034
Millhouse, John V, 99
Millhouse, John, Sr. I, 1034
Millhouse, Joshua IV, 35
Millhouse, Joshua V. IV, 70
Millhouse, Joshua V. IV, 208
Millhouse, Joshua V. IV, 209
Millhouse, Lavina I, 562
Millhouse, Martha IV, 70
Millhouse, Martha IV, 142
Millhouse, Martha IV, 416
Millhouse, Martha IV, 421
Millhouse, Martha IV, 422
Millhouse, Martha IV, 435
Millhouse, Martha IV, 468
Millhouse, Martha IV, 1069
Millhouse, Martha IV, 1076
Millhouse, Martha IV, 1077
Millhouse, Martha M. IV, 1118
Millhouse, Mary I, 1058
Millhouse, Mary I, 1059
Millhouse, Mary IV, 411
Millhouse, Mary IV, 421
Millhouse, Mary Elizabeth IV, 1068
Millhouse, Phebe IV, 154
Millhouse, Phebe IV, 160
Millhouse, Rachel IV, 1069
Millhouse, Rachel IV, 1078
Millhouse, Rachel IV, 1118
Millhouse, Rebecca I, 1034
Millhouse, Rebecca I, 1055
Millhouse, Rebecca I, 1056
Millhouse, Rebecca I, 1058
Millhouse, Rebecca IV, 142
Millhouse, Rebecca IV, 154
Millhouse, Rebecca IV, 468
Millhouse, Rebecca V, 99
Millhouse, Rebeckah I, 1058
Millhouse, Rebeckah I, 1059
Millhouse, Rebekah I, 1057
Millhouse, Rebekah I, 1058
Millhouse, Robart V, 99
Millhouse, Robert I, 1034
Millhouse, Robert I, 1056
Millhouse, Robert I, 1057
Millhouse, Robert I, 1058
Millhouse, Robert IV, 154
Millhouse, Robert IV, 371
Millhouse, Robert IV, 411
Millhouse, Robert IV, 416
Millhouse, Robert IV, 421
Millhouse, Robert IV, 422
Millhouse, Robert IV, 435
Millhouse, Robert IV, 1069
Millhouse, Robert IV, 1076
Millhouse, Robert IV, 1077
Millhouse, Robert IV, 1078
Millhouse, Robert IV, 1118
Millhouse, Robert V, 99
Millhouse, Robert V, 469
Millhouse, Ruth IV, 416
Millhouse, Ruth IV, 421
Millhouse, Ruth IV, 422
Millhouse, Ruth IV, 1069
Millhouse, Sally I, 1034
Millhouse, Sally V, 99
Millhouse, Samuel I, 60
Millhouse, Samuel I, 1034
Millhouse, Samuel IV, 421
Millhouse, Samuel V, 99
Millhouse, Sarah I, 1056
Millhouse, Sarah I, 1058
Millhouse, Sarah IV, 154
Millhouse, Sarah IV, 365
Millhouse, Sarah IV, 371
Millhouse, Sarah IV, 409
Millhouse, Sarah IV, 411
Millhouse, Sarah IV, 421
Millhouse, Sarah IV, 422
Millhouse, Sarah IV, 1069
Millhouse, Sarah V, 99
Millhouse, Stephen IV, 514
Millhouse, Stephen IV, 541
Millhouse, Thomas IV, 1069
Millhouse, Vickers IV, 252
Millhouse, Widow Jane I, 1034
Millhouse, William IV, 70
Millhouse, William IV, 154
Millhouse, William IV, 421
Millhouse, William IV, 1068
Millhouse, William, Jr. IV, 154
Millhouse, William, Jr. IV, 252
Millhouse, Wm. IV, 142
Millhouse, Wm. IV, 154

Millhouse, Wm. IV, 160
Millhouse, Wm. IV, 468
Millican, Abigail I, 540
Millican, Abigail I, 562
Millican, Ann V, 99
Millican, Baptist V, 99
Millican, Betsy V, 99
Millican, Eli V, 517
Millican, Eliza Ann I, 766
Millican, Eliza Ann I, 770
Millican, Hannah I, 767
Millican, Hannah I, 1116
Millican, Hannah I, 1126
Millican, Hannah V, 99
Millican, Jacob V, 99
Millican, John I, 894
Millican, John V, 99
Millican, John V, 517
Millican, Mary I, 1126
Millican, Mary V, 517
Millican, Polly V, 99
Millican, Rebecca I, 766
Millican, Rebecca I, 770
Millican, Sally V, 99
Millican, Samuel I, 894
Millican, Samuel V, 99
Millican, Sarah I, 767
Millican, William I, 1126
Millican, William V, 99
Millican, William Thomas V, 517
Millican, William, Sr. I, 1126
Millickan, Charles II, 396
Millickan, Charles P. II, 396
Milligan, Abigail IV, 50
Milligan, Abigail IV, 56
Milligan, Abigail IV, 646
Milligan, Abigail IV, 741
Milligan, Abigail IV, 1217
Milligan, Alice IV, 1217
Milligan, Ann IV, 50
Milligan, Ann IV, 741
Milligan, Ann IV, 972
Milligan, Ann IV, 979
Milligan, Clement IV, 50
Milligan, Clement IV, 741
Milligan, Earl IV, 741
Milligan, Elizabeth IV, 606
Milligan, Elizabeth IV, 646
Milligan, Elizabeth IV, 1217
Milligan, Elizabeth IV, 1287
Milligan, Elmira IV, 253
Milligan, Elmira E. IV, 253
Milligan, Elnora V, 461
Milligan, Elvira IV, 1217
Milligan, Elvira IV, 1228
Milligan, Emma V, 461
Milligan, Esther IV, 646
Milligan, Esther IV, 1217
Milligan, George V, 461
Milligan, Hannah II, 396
Milligan, Hannah IV, 1217
Milligan, Hannah Ruth IV, 646
Milligan, James IV, 50
Milligan, James IV, 741
Milligan, Jesse IV, 646
Milligan, Jesse IV, 980
Milligan, Jesse IV, 1217
Milligan, Jesse IV, 1228
Milligan, Jessie IV, 1217
Milligan, John IV, 50
Milligan, John IV, 56
Milligan, John IV, 646
Milligan, John IV, 741
Milligan, Joseph IV, 50
Milligan, Joseph IV, 488
Milligan, Joseph IV, 741
Milligan, Lindley H. IV, 646
Milligan, M??? IV, 741
Milligan, Maggie IV, 253
Milligan, Maggie B. IV, 253
Milligan, Mary Ann IV, 1217
Milligan, Rebecca Ann IV, 646
Milligan, Rebecca Ann IV, 1217
Milligan, Rebecca Ann IV, 1287
Milligan, Ruth IV, 646
Milligan, Ruth IV, 1217
Milligan, Ruth IV, 1228
Milligan, Samuel IV, 1217
Milligan, Samuel L. IV, 646
Milligan, Sarah Ann IV, 1287
Milligan, Sarah Ellen IV, 1217
Milligan, Tryphenia IV, 1217
Milligan, William II, 396
Milligan, William IV, 50
Milligan, William IV, 606
Milligan, William IV, 646
Milligan, William IV, 741
Milligan, Wm. IV, 1287
Millikan, Abigail I, 562
Millikan, Absalom Griffin I, 894
Millikan, Allen I, 750
Millikan, Allen I, 751
Millikan, Allen I, 767
Millikan, Almeda R. V, 586
Millikan, Almedia R. V, 586
Millikan, Almedia R. V, 697
Millikan, Almedie V, 586
Millikan, Alpheus Lundy I, 863
Millikan, Amanda M. I, 751
Millikan, Ann I, 510
Millikan, Ann I, 523
Millikan, Ann I, 562
Millikan, Ann I, 661
Millikan, Ann I, 662
Millikan, Ann I, 684
Millikan, Ann I, 685
Millikan, Ann I, 766
Millikan, Ann I, 847
Millikan, Ann I, 862
Millikan, Ann I, 870
Millikan, Ann I, 894
Millikan, Ann I, 927
Millikan, Anna Matilda I, 767
Millikan, Annie I, 614
Millikan, Archie C. I, 751
Millikan, Azel I, 750
Millikan, Azel I, 766
Millikan, Azel I, 767
Millikan, Bell V, 697
Millikan, Benjamin I, 338
Millikan, Benjamin I, 510
Millikan, Benjamin I, 625
Millikan, Benjamin I, 657
Millikan, Benjamin I, 661
Millikan, Benjamin I, 751
Millikan, Benjamin I, 862
Millikan, Benjamin I, 894
Millikan, Benjamin E. I, 751
Millikan, Binjamin G. I, 863
Millikan, Caroline I, 863
Millikan, Caroline I, 894
Millikan, Charity V, 553
Millikan, Charity V, 586
Millikan, Charley V, 586
Millikan, Clark I, 767
Millikan, D. W. I, 614
Millikan, Daniel W. I, 767
Millikan, Daniel Washington I, 751
Millikan, Dorcas I, 751
Millikan, Dorcas I, 767
Millikan, Eleazar I, 862
Millikan, Eleazar I, 881
Millikan, Eleazar I, 894
Millikan, Eleazar I, 930
Millikan, Eleazar I, 935
Millikan, Eleazar B., Jr. I, 862
Millikan, Eleazer B. I, 862
Millikan, Eli I, 894
Millikan, Eli V, 586
Millikan, Eli W. V, 586
Millikan, Eli W. V, 697
Millikan, Eliza I, 767
Millikan, Eliza Ann I, 750
Millikan, Eliza Ann I, 766
Millikan, Eliza Ann I, 767
Millikan, Eliza V. N. I, 751
Millikan, Elizabeth I, 510
Millikan, Elizabeth I, 685
Millikan, Elizabeth I, 692
Millikan, Elizabeth I, 862
Millikan, Elizabeth I, 874
Millikan, Elizabeth I, 894
Millikan, Elizabeth V, 697
Millikan, Emery C. I, 862
Millikan, Emily I, 921
Millikan, Emily V, 586
Millikan, Emily A. I, 872
Millikan, Emily A. I, 894
Millikan, Emma Jane I, 863
Millikan, Eunice P. I, 751
Millikan, Eunice Priscilla I, 767
Millikan, Flora Ellen I, 625
Millikan, Flora Ellen I, 767
Millikan, Grace I, 862
Millikan, Grace D. I, 881
Millikan, Grace D. I, 894
Millikan, Gurney Wilson I, 751
Millikan, Hannah I, 684
Millikan, Hannah I, 766
Millikan, Hannah I, 767
Millikan, Hannah I, 770
Millikan, Hannah I, 862
Millikan, Hannah I, 894
Millikan, Hannah I, 901
Millikan, Hannah V, 586
Millikan, Hannah C. V, 586
Millikan, Hannah C. V, 697
Millikan, Hannah T. I, 751
Millikan, Isaac S. I, 862
Millikan, Isabel V, 697
Millikan, Jacob I, 863
Millikan, Jacob I, 894
Millikan, James I, 684
Millikan, Jane I, 510
Millikan, Jane I, 657
Millikan, Jane I, 680
Millikan, Jane I, 684
Millikan, Jane I, 767
Millikan, Jane I, 862
Millikan, Jane I, 863
Millikan, Jane I, 884
Millikan, Jane I, 894
Millikan, Jess I, 894
Millikan, Jesse I, 510
Millikan, Jesse I, 662
Millikan, Jesse I, 862
Millikan, Jesse I, 863
Millikan, Jesse I, 894
Millikan, Jesse D. V, 586
Millikan, Jesse D. F. V, 586
Millikan, Jesse H. I, 946
Millikan, Jesse L. I, 862
Millikan, Jessie D. F. V, 697
Millikan, Joakim I, 862
Millikan, John I, 510
Millikan, John I, 661
Millikan, John I, 862
Millikan, John I, 863
Millikan, John I, 894
Millikan, John V, 586
Millikan, John V, 697
Millikan, John D. I, 862
Millikan, John Frazer I, 562
Millikan, John H. V, 586
Millikan, John H. V, 606
Millikan, John K. I, 751
Millikan, John K. I, 767
Millikan, Joseph T. I, 767
Millikan, Joseph Thomas I, 751
Millikan, Lindsey Henderson I, 750
Millikan, Londa Martitia I, 767
Millikan, Lydia I, 766
Millikan, Lydia I, 767
Millikan, Lydia V, 307
Millikan, Lydia Parthena I, 750
Millikan, Maggie I, 946
Millikan, Mahlon I, 862
Millikan, Mahlon I, 863
Millikan, Mahlon I, 894
Millikan, Margaret I, 526
Millikan, Margaret I, 562
Millikan, Margaret I, 657
Millikan, Margaret I, 862
Millikan, Margaret I, 894
Millikan, Margaret I, 905
Millikan, Margaret V, 586
Millikan, Margaret C. V, 697
Millikan, Margaret E. V, 586
Millikan, Margaret E. V, 697
Millikan, Margaret Eleanor V, 586
Millikan, Martha I, 562
Millikan, Martha I, 757
Millikan, Martha I, 766
Millikan, Martha I, 862
Millikan, Martha I, 863
Millikan, Martha I, 894
Millikan, Martha A. I, 894
Millikan, Martha Allice I, 767
Millikan, Martha C. I, 862
Millikan, Martha C. I, 894
Millikan, Martha J. V, 586
Millikan, Martha J. V, 697
Millikan, Mary I, 528
Millikan, Mary I, 562
Millikan, Mary I, 662
Millikan, Mary I, 750
Millikan, Mary I, 767
Millikan, Mary I, 862
Millikan, Mary I, 863
Millikan, Mary I, 871
Millikan, Mary I, 874
Millikan, Mary I, 894
Millikan, Mary I, 903
Millikan, Mary I, 1126
Millikan, Mary V, 586
Millikan, Mary Ann I, 863
Millikan, Mary Ann I, 901
Millikan, Mary E. V, 586
Millikan, Mary E. V, 697
Millikan, Mary I. I, 894
Millikan, Mary J. I, 751
Millikan, Mary J. I, 934
Millikan, Mary Jane I, 933
Millikan, Mattie J. I, 894
Millikan, Mattie J. I, 897
Millikan, Nancy I, 862
Millikan, Nancy I, 894
Millikan, Nancy Angeline I, 750
Millikan, Nathan V, 586
Millikan, Pamelia V, 586
Millikan, Pamelia A. V, 697
Millikan, Pearl I, 338
Millikan, Permela V, 558
Millikan, Priscilla V, 697
Millikan, Priscilla E. V, 586
Millikan, Priscilla E. V, 697
Millikan, Quincy I, 766
Millikan, Quincy M. I, 751
Millikan, Rachel I, 863
Millikan, Rachel I, 894
Millikan, Rachel A. I, 863
Millikan, Rachel A. I, 894
Millikan, Rachel C. V, 586
Millikan, Rachel C. V, 697
Millikan, Rachel Callista I, 751
Millikan, Rachel R. I, 751
Millikan, Rachel Roseline I, 767
Millikan, Rachel V. I, 751
Millikan, Rebecca I, 766
Millikan, Rebecca V, 586
Millikan, Rebecca A. I, 862
Millikan, Rebecca A. I, 894
Millikan, Rebecca L. I, 751
Millikan, Rhoda J. I, 862
Millikan, Ruth I, 888
Millikan, Ruth I, 894
Millikan, Ruth I, 930
Millikan, Ruth I, 935
Millikan, Ruth C. I, 862
Millikan, Ruth C. I, 894
Millikan, Sabina V, 697
Millikan, Sallie I, 625
Millikan, Sally I, 894
Millikan, Sally I, 901
Millikan, Sally M. I, 751
Millikan, Samuel I, 510
Millikan, Samuel I, 523
Millikan, Samuel I, 562
Millikan, Samuel I, 661
Millikan, Samuel I, 662
Millikan, Samuel I, 684
Millikan, Samuel I, 685
Millikan, Samuel I, 751
Millikan, Samuel I, 757
Millikan, Samuel I, 766
Millikan, Samuel I, 862
Millikan, Samuel I, 863
Millikan, Samuel I, 894
Millikan, Samuel C. I, 894
Millikan, Sarah I, 510
Millikan, Sarah I, 562
Millikan, Sarah I, 661
Millikan, Sarah I, 751
Millikan, Sarah I, 766
Millikan, Sarah I, 767
Millikan, Sarah I, 862
Millikan, Sarah I, 885
Millikan, Sarah I, 894
Millikan, Sarah I, 930
Millikan, Sarah I, 935
Millikan, Sarah I, 946
Millikan, Sarah I, 950
Millikan, Sarah I, 1108
Millikan, Sarah V, 697
Millikan, Sarah E. I, 751
Millikan, Sarah Elizabeth I, 750
Millikan, Sarah Ellen V, 586
Millikan, Sarah J. V, 586
Millikan, Sarah J. V, 697
Millikan, Sarah L. I, 751
Millikan, Susanna I, 862
Millikan, Susanna I, 877
Millikan, Susanna I, 894
Millikan, Susannah I, 862
Millikan, Susannah S. I, 894
Millikan, T. C. I, 894
Millikan, Tamer Delilah I, 750
Millikan, Thamer I, 863
Millikan, Thomas V, 586
Millikan, Thomas V, 697
Millikan, Thomas C. I, 863
Millikan, Thomas C. I, 894
Millikan, Thomas F. I, 751
Millikan, Thomas F. I, 767
Millikan, Thomas N. V, 586
Millikan, Thomas N. V, 697
Millikan, Thomas W. I, 862
Millikan, Thos. C. I, 894
Millikan, Troy Watson I, 751
Millikan, Vida I, 614
Millikan, Widow Mary I, 862
Millikan, William I, 510
Millikan, William I, 562
Millikan, William I, 661
Millikan, William I, 684
Millikan, William I, 862
Millikan, William I, 894
Millikan, William I, 1108
Millikan, William V, 99
Millikan, William V, 553
Millikan, William V, 586
Millikan, William P. I, 751
Millikan, William P. I, 766
Millikan, William P. I, 767
Millikan, William R. I, 862
Millikan, Winborn B. I, 751
Millikan, Wm. V, 586
Millikan, Zachariah V, 586
Milliken, Caroline I, 877
Milliken, Earl IV, 741
Milliken, Emily A. I, 850
Milliken, Martha IV, 741
Milliken, Martha M. II, 899
Milliken, William I, 1126
Millikens, Agnes IV, 1330
Millikin, Abigail IV, 741
Millikin, Ann IV, 741
Millikin, Benjamin I, 920
Millikin, Clement IV, 741
Millikin, Earl IV, 741
Millikin, Eleazar I, 874
Millikin, Hannah I, 674
Millikin, James IV, 741
Millikin, John IV, 741
Millikin, Joseph IV, 741
Millikin, M??? IV, 741
Millikin, Margaret I, 562
Millikin, Martha I, 540
Millikin, Martha I, 562
Millikin, Martha IV, 741
Millikin, Mary IV, 716
Millikin, Mary IV, 741
Millikin, Mattie J. I, 920
Millikin, Rebecca V, 561
Millikin, Rebecca V, 586
Millikin, Ruth C. I, 874
Millikin, Samuel I, 562
Millikin, Sarah I, 920
Millikin, William IV, 741
Milliman, Alice II, 736
Milliman, Alice II, 756
Milliner, Amos V, 264
Milliner, Beverly V, 264
Milliner, Elizabeth VI, 840
Milliner, John V, 264
Milliner, Joseph V, 264
Milliner, Luke V, 264
Milliner, Oliver V, 264
Milliner, R. Dudley V, 264
Milliner, Ruht VI, 300
Milliner, Ruth VI, 332
Milliner, William VI, 840
Millines, Betsy VI, 964
Millington, Alice III, 231
Millington, Frederick III, 231
Millington, John II, 1033
Millington, Wm. Henry III, 2
Million, John VI, 840
Million, Marietta V, 789
Million, Marietta V, 792
Million, Mary VI, 840
Millirons, Catharener VI, 903
Millirons, Elizabeth VI, 903
Millirons, Henry VI, 903
Millirons, Rosanna VI, 964
Millis, Elizabeth I, 829
Millis, Hiram I, 829
Millison, Abel IV, 541
Millison, Abigail IV, 24
Millison, Abigail IV, 49
Millison, Abigail IV, 101
Millison, Abigail IV, 323
Millison, Abigail IV, 343
Millison, Abigail IV, 509
Millison, Abigail IV, 541
Millison, Ann IV, 101
Millison, Ann IV, 343
Millison, Ann IV, 526
Millison, Ann IV, 541
Millison, Anne IV, 541
Millison, Caleb IV, 101
Millison, Dorothy IV, 44
Millison, Dorothy IV, 49
Millison, Dorothy IV, 343
Millison, Dorothy IV, 541
Millison, Elisha IV, 79
Millison, Elisha IV, 101
Millison, Elisha IV, 343
Millison, Elizabeth IV, 101
Millison, Elizabeth IV, 343
Millison, Elizabeth IV, 422
Millison, Elizabeth IV, 437
Millison, Hannah IV, 79
Millison, Hannah IV, 101
Millison, Hannah IV, 343
Millison, Hannah IV, 529
Millison, Hannah IV, 541
Millison, James IV, 24
Millison, James IV, 44
Millison, James IV, 49
Millison, James IV, 101
Millison, James IV, 541

ison, James, Jr. IV, 49
ison, James, Jr. IV, 343
ison, John IV, 44
ison, John IV, 101
ison, Jonathan IV, 343
ison, Jonathan IV, 541
ison, Leah IV, 541
ison, Lydia IV, 101
ison, Mary IV, 101
ison, Noah IV, 541
ison, Rachel IV, 541
ison, Rebecca IV, 541
lison, Sarah IV, 44
lison, Sarah IV, 101
lison, William IV, 343
lison, Wm. IV, 101
lmyer, Lucy Ann IV, 1217
lner, Albert G. VI, 962
lner, Albert G. VI, 970
lner, Albert G. VI, 983
lner, Albert G. VI, 1018
lner, Amey VI, 962
lner, Ann P. VI, 962
lner, Beverly VI, 332
lner, Beverly, Jr. V, 264
llner, Cassandra D. VI, 1005
llner, Catharine VI, 962
llner, Clarisa VI, 962
llner, Elizabeth V, 264
llner, Elizabeth VI, 962
llner, Jeremiah D. VI, 962
llner, Jeremiah D. VI, 964
llner, John VI, 332
llner, John VI, 962
llner, Joseph II, 998
llner, Joseph V, 350
llner, Joseph VI, 332
llner, Madison F. VI, 962
llner, Margaret V, 264
llner, Margaret VI, 919
llner, Marilla VI, 970
llner, Mary VI, 983
illner, Mildred H. VI, 962
illner, Nancy VI, 969
illner, Nancy VI, 970
illner, Owen VI, 962
illner, Patsy VI, 962
illner, Pleasant II, 998
illner, Polly VI, 962
illner, Polly VI, 970
illner, Prudence VI, 1018
illner, Robert VI, 962
illner, Robert D. V, 264
illner, Sally VI, 962
illner, Sarah II, 965
illner, Thomas VI, 962
illner, Wd. Pleasant II, 1015
illner, William III, 231
illner, William VI, 919
illner, William VI, 962
illner, William VI, 970
illner, William VI, 983
illner, William VI, 1005
illner, William VI, 1018
illner, Williamson VI, 962
illner, Wmson VI, 970
illnor, Ann II, 396
illnor, Elizabeth II, 396
illnor, Isaac II, 396
illnor, John II, 1015
illnor, John II, 1031
Millnor, Martha II, 1015
Millnor, Martha II, 1031
Millnor, Rachel II, 1015
Millnor, Rachel II, 1027
Milloum, Ann II, 1015
Milloum, Ann II, 1040
Milloum, Jane II, 1015
Milloum, Jane II, 1040
Mills, ??? III, 203
Mills, ??? IV, 1047
Mills, ??? V, 147
Mills, ??? V, 315
Mills, Aaron I, 510
Mills, Aaron I, 561
Mills, Aaron I, 562
Mills, Aaron I, 773
Mills, Aaron I, 789
Mills, Aaron I, 830
Mills, Aaron I, 967
Mills, Aaron I, 1101
Mills, Aaron I, 1105
Mills, Aaron I, 1126
Mills, Aaron I, 1127
Mills, Aaron V, 755
Mills, Abel III, 231
Mills, Abel IV, 50
Mills, Abigail I, 510
Mills, Abigail I, 978
Mills, Abigail I, 992
Mills, Abigail I, 993
Mills, Abijah IV, 50
Mills, Abner I, 1057
Mills, Abner IV, 1374
Mills, Abner V, 171
Mills, Abner V, 190
Mills, Abner V, 191
Mills, Abner V, 192
Mills, Abraham VI, 840
Mills, Achsa I, 510
Mills, Achsa I, 993
Mills, Ada V, 190
Mills, Ada V, 458
Mills, Adelaide III, 231
Mills, Adeline III, 231
Mills, Agnes V, 396
Mills, Agnes V, 412
Mills, Agnes V, 413
Mills, Agnes V, 414
Mills, Agness V, 425
Mills, Albert V, 413
Mills, Albert V, 414
Mills, Albert H. V, 634
Mills, Albert H. V, 697
Mills, Albert T. III, 191
Mills, Albert T. III, 231
Mills, Albert T. III, 271
Mills, Alexander I, 1034
Mills, Alexander I, 1036
Mills, Alexander IV, 50
Mills, Alexander V, 17
Mills, Alexander V, 192
Mills, Alexander V, 755
Mills, Alfred V, 634
Mills, Alias I, 510
Mills, Alice I, 511
Mills, Alice I, 562
Mills, Alice I, 662
Mills, Alice I, 967
Mills, Alice I, 1108
Mills, Alice I, 1109
Mills, Alice I, 1124
Mills, Alice I, 1125
Mills, Alice I, 1126
Mills, Alice I, 1127
Mills, Alice V, 192
Mills, Alice M. V, 697
Mills, Alice Rebecca V, 191
Mills, Allen V, 192
Mills, Amasa I, 1096
Mills, Ames V, 190
Mills, Ames V, 264
Mills, Amos I, 510
Mills, Amos I, 548
Mills, Amos I, 562
Mills, Amos I, 773
Mills, Amos I, 789
Mills, Amos I, 830
Mills, Amos V, 163
Mills, Amos V, 191
Mills, Amos V, 192
Mills, Amos Charles V, 191
Mills, Amy V, 191
Mills, Amy V, 192
Mills, Anabel M. V, 31
Mills, Anable V, 100
Mills, Ann I, 510
Mills, Ann I, 527
Mills, Ann I, 562
Mills, Ann I, 721
Mills, Ann I, 726
Mills, Ann I, 993
Mills, Ann I, 997
Mills, Ann I, 1109
Mills, Ann I, 1127
Mills, Ann V, 17
Mills, Ann V, 100
Mills, Ann V, 101
Mills, Ann V, 176
Mills, Ann V, 191
Mills, Ann V, 192
Mills, Ann V, 413
Mills, Ann V, 573
Mills, Ann V, 586
Mills, Ann V, 697
Mills, Ann V, 789
Mills, Ann P. V, 163
Mills, Ann P. V, 191
Mills, Ann P. V, 192
Mills, Anna I, 789
Mills, Anna I, 830
Mills, Anna I, 1109
Mills, Anna V, 100
Mills, Anna V, 101
Mills, Anna V, 349
Mills, Anna V, 738
Mills, Anna V, 755
Mills, Anna V, 817
Mills, Anna V, 818
Mills, Anna E. V, 101
Mills, Anna Maria I, 1127
Mills, Anna O. V, 414
Mills, Anna P. V, 956
Mills, Anne V, 414
Mills, Annie II, 851
Mills, Annie II, 899
Mills, Annie V, 402
Mills, Annie V, 414
Mills, Annis Levenia IV, 253
Mills, Arlie V, 192
Mills, Aron I, 1126
Mills, Arthur V, 192
Mills, Asa I, 789
Mills, Asa I, 830
Mills, Asa I, 1086
Mills, Asa I, 1101
Mills, Asa I, 1108
Mills, Asa I, 1126
Mills, Asa I, 1127
Mills, Austin V, 414
Mills, Axey I, 978
Mills, Benj. I, 510
Mills, Benjamin I, 409
Mills, Benjamin I, 1109
Mills, Benjamin I, 1127
Mills, Benjamin I, 1145
Mills, Benjamin I, 1159
Mills, Benjamin V, 101
Mills, Benjamin F. V, 100
Mills, Benjamin H. V, 101
Mills, Benjamin H. V, 191
Mills, Benjamin Jonathan I, 1108
Mills, Benjamin N. V, 192
Mills, Benona I, 563
Mills, Benoni I, 510
Mills, Benoni I, 562
Mills, Benoni I, 789
Mills, Benoni I, 829
Mills, Benoni I, 830
Mills, Benoni I, 841
Mills, Benoni I, 993
Mills, Benony I, 562
Mills, Bethia I, 1096
Mills, Bethiah I, 1096
Mills, Bethiah I, 1126
Mills, Bethiah I, 1127
Mills, Betsey I, 1109
Mills, Betsy Ann I, 1127
Mills, Betty I, 1055
Mills, Betty V, 159
Mills, Betty V, 191
Mills, Betty V, 192
Mills, Branson I, 1108
Mills, Branson I, 1109
Mills, Branson I, 1128
Mills, Caleb V, 190
Mills, Caleb V, 192
Mills, Calvin W. V, 634
Mills, Carrie V, 100
Mills, Carrie V, 101
Mills, Carroll H. IV, 253
Mills, Carry V, 101
Mills, Catharine I, 789
Mills, Catharine III, 228
Mills, Catharine V, 921
Mills, Catharine B. V, 414
Mills, Catharine B. V, 921
Mills, Catherine I, 1117
Mills, Catherine I, 1126
Mills, Catherine V, 100
Mills, Catherine V, 115
Mills, Catherine V, 414
Mills, Catherine V, 973
Mills, Catherine B. V, 414
Mills, Catherine B. V, 441
Mills, Charity I, 510
Mills, Charity I, 537
Mills, Charity I, 561
Mills, Charity I, 562
Mills, Charity I, 789
Mills, Charity I, 817
Mills, Charity I, 829
Mills, Charity I, 830
Mills, Charity I, 993
Mills, Charity I, 1101
Mills, Charity I, 1105
Mills, Charity I, 1108
Mills, Charity I, 1109
Mills, Charity I, 1119
Mills, Charity I, 1126
Mills, Charity I, 1127
Mills, Charity I, 1133
Mills, Charity V, 163
Mills, Charity V, 176
Mills, Charity V, 191
Mills, Charity V, 192
Mills, Charity V, 200
Mills, Charles I, 1057
Mills, Charles V, 17
Mills, Charles V, 101
Mills, Charles V, 175
Mills, Charles V, 191
Mills, Charles V, 586
Mills, Charles V, 789
Mills, Chas. V, 192
Mills, Chas. V, 573
Mills, Chas. V, 789
Mills, Christina V, 264
Mills, Ciceley I, 789
Mills, Cicila V, 230
Mills, Cicilia I, 511
Mills, Cicilia I, 554
Mills, Cicilia I, 562
Mills, Clara IV, 253
Mills, Clara J. V, 414
Mills, Clarissa I, 563
Mills, Clarissa I, 574
Mills, Clarissa I, 830
Mills, Clarissa I, 839
Mills, Clarissa IV, 154
Mills, Clarkson V, 413
Mills, Clarkson W. V, 413
Mills, Claude J. V, 634
Mills, Corah B. V, 414
Mills, Corah E. I, 1109
Mills, Coral V, 581
Mills, Cornelius IV, 1174
Mills, Cromwell III, 231
Mills, Curtis IV, 50
Mills, Curtis V, 100
Mills, Cynthia I, 1145
Mills, Cyrus V, 190
Mills, Cyrus V, 192
Mills, Daniel I, 830
Mills, Daniel I, 1057
Mills, Daniel V, 35
Mills, Daniel V, 100
Mills, Daniel V, 170
Mills, Daniel V, 191
Mills, Daniel V, 192
Mills, Daniel V, 264
Mills, David I, 562
Mills, David I, 789
Mills, David I, 1035
Mills, David I, 1109
Mills, David I, 1114
Mills, David I, 1127
Mills, David I, 1145
Mills, David I, 1159
Mills, David IV, 50
Mills, David V, 100
Mills, David V, 155
Mills, David V, 191
Mills, David V, 192
Mills, David V, 413
Mills, David V, 414
Mills, David V, 755
Mills, David C. V, 414
Mills, Deborah I, 830
Mills, Deborah V, 82
Mills, Deborah V, 100
Mills, Deborah V, 101
Mills, Deborah V, 818
Mills, Delila V, 328
Mills, Delila V, 349
Mills, Delila V, 414
Mills, Delilah I, 1145
Mills, Della V, 414
Mills, Dempsey V, 192
Mills, Demsy V, 190
Mills, Dena V, 192
Mills, Dinah I, 1057
Mills, Dinah V, 175
Mills, Dinah V, 190
Mills, Dinah V, 191
Mills, Dorcas V, 413
Mills, Dorcas V, 417
Mills, Dorcas A. V, 414
Mills, Dorcas A. V, 425
Mills, Dorothy G. III, 231
Mills, E. P. V, 634
Mills, Ede V, 100
Mills, Edgar V, 414
Mills, Edith IV, 422
Mills, Edith IV, 1069
Mills, Edith IV, 1107
Mills, Edith V, 81
Mills, Edith V, 100
Mills, Edith V, 817
Mills, Edmond J. VI, 962
Mills, Effia Anna V, 101
Mills, Effie Anna V, 100
Mills, Eldon H. III, 231
Mills, Eldon H., Jr. III, 231
Mills, Eleazibeth I, 789
Mills, Eli I, 562
Mills, Eli I, 789
Mills, Eli I, 978
Mills, Eli I, 985
Mills, Eli I, 993
Mills, Eli IV, 50
Mills, Eli IV, 102
Mills, Eli IV, 422
Mills, Eli IV, 1069
Mills, Eli V, 973
Mills, Eli R. IV, 50
Mills, Elias V, 697
Mills, Elias P. V, 634
Mills, Elias P. V, 697
Mills, Elihu I, 1109
Mills, Elihu V, 191
Mills, Elijah I, 1057
Mills, Elijah I, 1127
Mills, Elijah I, 1128
Mills, Elijah V, 100
Mills, Elijah V, 175
Mills, Elijah V, 176
Mills, Elijah V, 191
Mills, Elijah V, 192
Mills, Elijah Isaac V, 192
Mills, Elisabeth I, 832
Mills, Elisabeth I, 1108
Mills, Elisha IV, 50
Mills, Elisha IV, 422
Mills, Elisha IV, 1069
Mills, Elisha V, 100
Mills, Eliz. III, 96
Mills, Eliz. III, 219
Mills, Eliza V, 100
Mills, Elizabeth I, 510
Mills, Elizabeth I, 511
Mills, Elizabeth I, 544
Mills, Elizabeth I, 547
Mills, Elizabeth I, 548
Mills, Elizabeth I, 562
Mills, Elizabeth I, 563
Mills, Elizabeth I, 789
Mills, Elizabeth I, 806
Mills, Elizabeth I, 829
Mills, Elizabeth I, 830
Mills, Elizabeth I, 841
Mills, Elizabeth I, 1032
Mills, Elizabeth I, 1034
Mills, Elizabeth I, 1035
Mills, Elizabeth I, 1058
Mills, Elizabeth I, 1108
Mills, Elizabeth I, 1109
Mills, Elizabeth I, 1121
Mills, Elizabeth I, 1126
Mills, Elizabeth I, 1127
Mills, Elizabeth I, 1128
Mills, Elizabeth I, 1133
Mills, Elizabeth III, 231
Mills, Elizabeth IV, 34
Mills, Elizabeth IV, 44
Mills, Elizabeth IV, 50
Mills, Elizabeth IV, 54
Mills, Elizabeth IV, 69
Mills, Elizabeth IV, 102
Mills, Elizabeth IV, 154
Mills, Elizabeth IV, 253
Mills, Elizabeth IV, 332
Mills, Elizabeth IV, 343
Mills, Elizabeth IV, 422
Mills, Elizabeth V, 17
Mills, Elizabeth V, 28
Mills, Elizabeth V, 35
Mills, Elizabeth V, 100
Mills, Elizabeth V, 101
Mills, Elizabeth V, 118
Mills, Elizabeth V, 187
Mills, Elizabeth V, 190
Mills, Elizabeth V, 191
Mills, Elizabeth V, 192
Mills, Elizabeth V, 204
Mills, Elizabeth V, 214
Mills, Elizabeth V, 230
Mills, Elizabeth V, 264
Mills, Elizabeth VI, 424
Mills, Elizabeth VI, 887
Mills, Elizabeth VI, 962
Mills, Elizabeth Ann V, 634
Mills, Elizabeth H. III, 203
Mills, Elizabeth John VI, 424
Mills, Ellis Pugh V, 17
Mills, Elmer V, 192
Mills, Elvin I, 1145
Mills, Emily I, 1108
Mills, Emily I, 1123
Mills, Emily I, 1127
Mills, Emily I, 1128
Mills, Emily IV, 1374
Mills, Emily IV, 1383
Mills, Emma I, 622
Mills, Emma V, 517
Mills, Emma V, 634
Mills, Emma Bell V, 414
Mills, Emma J. V, 634
Mills, Enice IV, 50
Mills, Enoch V, 100
Mills, Enoch V, 190
Mills, Enoch V, 192
Mills, Enoch V, 200
Mills, Enoch V, 201
Mills, Enos I, 1109

Mills, Esther I, 1057
Mills, Esther IV, 50
Mills, Esther IV, 343
Mills, Esther IV, 349
Mills, Esther IV, 422
Mills, Esther IV, 1069
Mills, Esther V, 162
Mills, Esther V, 170
Mills, Esther V, 191
Mills, Esther V, 192
Mills, Etta V, 199
Mills, Eunice I, 1034
Mills, Eunice I, 1036
Mills, Eunice V, 17
Mills, Eunice V, 187
Mills, Eunice V, 191
Mills, Eunice V, 755
Mills, Eunice Anna V, 192
Mills, Eunice Annie V, 191
Mills, Ezra IV, 1069
Mills, Ezra IV, 1107
Mills, F. P. IV, 253
Mills, Fannie E. V, 634
Mills, Flora B. V, 414
Mills, Flora Etta V, 191
Mills, Florence III, 231
Mills, Florence Clayton II, 810
Mills, Frances V, 414
Mills, Francis I, 1128
Mills, Frank V, 192
Mills, Frank B. V, 697
Mills, Frankie V, 697
Mills, Frankie S. V, 697
Mills, Franklin V, 100
Mills, Franklin V, 192
Mills, Fred P. IV, 253
Mills, George I, 510
Mills, George I, 562
Mills, George V, 163
Mills, George V, 192
Mills, George D. V, 101
Mills, George D. V, 191
Mills, George D. V, 192
Mills, George M. II, 851
Mills, George M. II, 899
Mills, Georgia IV, 253
Mills, Georgia A. IV, 253
Mills, Gideon I, 789
Mills, Gideon IV, 154
Mills, Gideon IV, 422
Mills, Gideon IV, 1069
Mills, Gideon IV, 1107
Mills, Gulia Ann I, 1145
Mills, Hannah I, 451
Mills, Hannah I, 510
Mills, Hannah I, 560
Mills, Hannah I, 562
Mills, Hannah I, 571
Mills, Hannah I, 580
Mills, Hannah I, 785
Mills, Hannah I, 789
Mills, Hannah I, 794
Mills, Hannah I, 829
Mills, Hannah I, 830
Mills, Hannah I, 957
Mills, Hannah I, 967
Mills, Hannah I, 1057
Mills, Hannah I, 1086
Mills, Hannah I, 1105
Mills, Hannah I, 1108
Mills, Hannah I, 1109
Mills, Hannah I, 1119
Mills, Hannah I, 1120
Mills, Hannah I, 1126
Mills, Hannah I, 1127
Mills, Hannah I, 1130
Mills, Hannah I, 1135
Mills, Hannah III, 149
Mills, Hannah III, 231
Mills, Hannah III, 349
Mills, Hannah IV, 422
Mills, Hannah IV, 588
Mills, Hannah IV, 1374
Mills, Hannah V, 25
Mills, Hannah V, 100
Mills, Hannah V, 101
Mills, Hannah V, 162
Mills, Hannah V, 171
Mills, Hannah V, 191
Mills, Hannah V, 349
Mills, Hannah V, 369
Mills, Hannah V, 412
Mills, Hannah V, 413
Mills, Hannah V, 414
Mills, Hannah Isabel V, 192
Mills, Hanour I, 988
Mills, Harriet C. V, 517
Mills, Harriet C. V, 697
Mills, Harry V, 192
Mills, Harvey P. V, 192
Mills, Helen G. IV, 1174
Mills, Henry I, 409
Mills, Henry I, 487
Mills, Henry I, 510
Mills, Henry I, 562
Mills, Henry I, 773
Mills, Henry I, 785
Mills, Henry I, 789
Mills, Henry I, 794
Mills, Henry I, 829
Mills, Henry I, 967
Mills, Henry I, 1109
Mills, Henry I, 1126
Mills, Henry I, 1127
Mills, Henry I, 1135
Mills, Henry IV, 34
Mills, Henry IV, 44
Mills, Henry IV, 50
Mills, Henry IV, 54
Mills, Henry IV, 343
Mills, Henry IV, 349
Mills, Henry V, 191
Mills, Henry V, 414
Mills, Henry V, 461
Mills, Henry VI, 424
Mills, Henry C. V, 100
Mills, Henry F. V, 176
Mills, Henry F. V, 177
Mills, Henry F. V, 191
Mills, Henry M. IV, 50
Mills, Hepsibah V, 817
Mills, Hepzibah IV, 50
Mills, Hezekiah I, 789
Mills, Hezekiah I, 830
Mills, Hezekiah V, 264
Mills, Hezekiah V, 349
Mills, Hezekiah V, 417
Mills, High IV, 1107
Mills, Howard B. II, 810
Mills, Hugh I, 510
Mills, Hugh V, 69
Mills, Hugh V, 100
Mills, Hugh J. IV, 422
Mills, Hugh J. IV, 1069
Mills, Hulda Jane I, 1145
Mills, Huldah IV, 1278
Mills, Hur I, 343
Mills, Hur I, 487
Mills, Hur I, 510
Mills, Hur I, 789
Mills, Hur I, 830
Mills, Hur I, 957
Mills, Hur I, 965
Mills, Hur I, 1086
Mills, Hur I, 1096
Mills, Hurr I, 409
Mills, Ira I, 1109
Mills, Isaac I, 789
Mills, Isaac I, 830
Mills, Isaac I, 967
Mills, Isaac I, 1035
Mills, Isaac I, 1126
Mills, Isaac IV, 50
Mills, Isaac IV, 154
Mills, Isaac IV, 422
Mills, Isaac IV, 1069
Mills, Isaac V, 100
Mills, Isaac V, 115
Mills, Isaac V, 973
Mills, Isaac L. V, 31
Mills, Isaac L. V, 100
Mills, Issachar IV, 1069
Mills, J. B. IV, 253
Mills, J. Bertram IV, 253
Mills, J. Oscar Hill V, 264
Mills, Jabas V, 414
Mills, Jabez V, 413
Mills, Jabez H. V, 414
Mills, Jacob I, 789
Mills, Jacob I, 829
Mills, Jacob I, 830
Mills, Jacob I, 1086
Mills, Jacob I, 1096
Mills, Jacob I, 1127
Mills, James I, 510
Mills, James I, 978
Mills, James I, 993
Mills, James I, 1035
Mills, James I, 1108
Mills, James I, 1128
Mills, James III, 231
Mills, James IV, 50
Mills, James V, 17
Mills, James V, 28
Mills, James V, 65
Mills, James V, 100
Mills, James V, 101
Mills, James V, 190
Mills, James V, 209
Mills, James V, 264
Mills, James V, 414
Mills, James V, 634
Mills, James V, 817
Mills, James VI, 962
Mills, James VI, 999
Mills, James J. V, 101
Mills, Jane I, 510
Mills, Jane I, 677
Mills, Jane I, 685
Mills, Jane I, 789
Mills, Jane I, 796
Mills, Jane I, 830
Mills, Jane I, 1035
Mills, Jane I, 1109
Mills, Jane I, 1123
Mills, Jane I, 1126
Mills, Jane I, 1127
Mills, Jane I, 1128
Mills, Jane IV, 1217
Mills, Jane V, 177
Mills, Jane V, 192
Mills, Jane V, 204
Mills, Jane V, 547
Mills, Jane Jones I, 1127
Mills, Jane M. L. VI, 840
Mills, Jehu V, 191
Mills, Jehu V, 192
Mills, Jemima I, 562
Mills, Jemima I, 571
Mills, Jemima I, 822
Mills, Jemima I, 829
Mills, Jemima I, 830
Mills, Jemima I, 838
Mills, Jemima I, 1032
Mills, Jemima I, 1034
Mills, Jemima I, 1035
Mills, Jemima I, 1062
Mills, Jemima V, 100
Mills, Jemima V, 264
Mills, Jemimah I, 510
Mills, Jemimah V, 246
Mills, Jeremiah I, 789
Mills, Jeremiah I, 830
Mills, Jeremiah J. V, 634
Mills, Jesse I, 1108
Mills, Jesse I, 1109
Mills, Jesse V, 181
Mills, Jesse V, 191
Mills, Jesse Connor V, 192
Mills, Joanna II, 396
Mills, Job I, 1056
Mills, Job V, 159
Mills, Job V, 190
Mills, Job V, 191
Mills, Joel V, 100
Mills, Joel V, 146
Mills, Joel T. V, 973
Mills, John I, 343
Mills, John I, 409
Mills, John I, 487
Mills, John I, 510
Mills, John I, 511
Mills, John I, 562
Mills, John I, 662
Mills, John I, 685
Mills, John I, 789
Mills, John I, 829
Mills, John I, 967
Mills, John I, 1034
Mills, John I, 1035
Mills, John I, 1038
Mills, John I, 1055
Mills, John I, 1096
Mills, John I, 1101
Mills, John I, 1102
Mills, John I, 1108
Mills, John I, 1109
Mills, John I, 1118
Mills, John I, 1126
Mills, John I, 1145
Mills, John I, 1159
Mills, John II, 396
Mills, John IV, 50
Mills, John IV, 253
Mills, John V, 100
Mills, John V, 131
Mills, John V, 159
Mills, John V, 190
Mills, John V, 191
Mills, John V, 192
Mills, John V, 200
Mills, John V, 349
Mills, John V, 396
Mills, John V, 412
Mills, John V, 413
Mills, John V, 414
Mills, John V, 425
Mills, John V, 755
Mills, John V, 818
Mills, John VI, 357
Mills, John H. I, 1159
Mills, John Henry I, 1145
Mills, John J. IV, 253
Mills, John Lindley V, 191
Mills, John M. V, 413
Mills, John Marshill I, 1109
Mills, John Martin I, 1108
Mills, John Milton V, 414
Mills, John P. I, 1109
Mills, John, III I, 1126
Mills, John, Jr. I, 645
Mills, John, Jr. I, 1096
Mills, John, Jr. I, 1126
Mills, John, Jr. I, 1127
Mills, John, Jr. V, 100
Mills, John, Jr. VI, 357
Mills, John, Senr. I, 511
Mills, John, Sr. I, 1108
Mills, Jonathan I, 451
Mills, Jonathan I, 510
Mills, Jonathan I, 789
Mills, Jonathan I, 830
Mills, Jonathan I, 957
Mills, Jonathan I, 967
Mills, Jonathan I, 1086
Mills, Jonathan I, 1096
Mills, Jonathan I, 1109
Mills, Jonathan I, 1127
Mills, Jonathan V, 163
Mills, Jonathan V, 176
Mills, Jonathan V, 191
Mills, Jonathan V, 349
Mills, Jonathan V, 799
Mills, Jonathan C. V, 634
Mills, Jonathan Jessop V, 100
Mills, Joseph I, 451
Mills, Joseph I, 560
Mills, Joseph I, 562
Mills, Joseph I, 789
Mills, Joseph I, 829
Mills, Joseph I, 830
Mills, Joseph I, 967
Mills, Joseph I, 1126
Mills, Joseph IV, 50
Mills, Joseph IV, 55
Mills, Joseph IV, 343
Mills, Joseph V, 100
Mills, Joseph V, 191
Mills, Joseph V, 192
Mills, Joseph V, 349
Mills, Joseph V, 369
Mills, Joseph V, 396
Mills, Joseph V, 413
Mills, Joseph V, 414
Mills, Joseph V, 634
Mills, Joseph H. V, 413
Mills, Joseph H. V, 414
Mills, Joseph J. IV, 1374
Mills, Joseph J. IV, 1383
Mills, Joseph M. V, 412
Mills, Joseph M. V, 413
Mills, Joseph M. V, 414
Mills, Joseph Maris V, 413
Mills, Joseph O. V, 192
Mills, Joseph R. I, 1159
Mills, Joseph, Jr. IV, 102
Mills, Joseph, Jr. V, 414
Mills, Joshua I, 510
Mills, Joshua I, 554
Mills, Joshua L. IV, 50
Mills, Josiah V, 100
Mills, Josiah B. V, 101
Mills, Julia IV, 488
Mills, Kezia I, 815
Mills, Kezia I, 829
Mills, Keziah V, 264
Mills, Lanty I, 1109
Mills, Laura V, 192
Mills, Lavena V, 264
Mills, Layton V, 192
Mills, Layton Jay V, 17
Mills, Lelia V, 461
Mills, Levi I, 1108
Mills, Levi V, 187
Mills, Levi V, 191
Mills, Levi V, 192
Mills, Levi V, 414
Mills, Levi V, 515
Mills, Levi V, 517
Mills, Levi V, 697
Mills, Lewis I, 1145
Mills, Lewis IV, 422
Mills, Lewis IV, 1069
Mills, Lewis V, 413
Mills, Lewis V, 414
Mills, Lewis V, 441
Mills, Lewis V, 921
Mills, Lewis B. V, 634
Mills, Lewis G. V, 264
Mills, Lewis M. V, 414
Mills, Lewis M. V, 921
Mills, Lewis V. V, 264
Mills, Lindley V, 101
Mills, Lindley E. V, 192
Mills, Linley E. V, 192
Mills, Lisse I, 1128
Mills, Lois V, 396
Mills, Lois V, 412
Mills, Lois V, 413
Mills, Lois V, 414
Mills, Louella B. V, 192
Mills, Louisa A. I, 797
Mills, Louisa A. I, 830
Mills, Lucille Ella V, 414
Mills, Luella V, 101
Mills, Luella B. V, 192
Mills, Luke Jones I, 1128
Mills, Luzena I, 830
Mills, Lydda I, 967
Mills, Lydia I, 511
Mills, Lydia I, 562
Mills, Lydia I, 662
Mills, Lydia I, 1034
Mills, Lydia I, 1035
Mills, Lydia I, 1036
Mills, Lydia I, 1109
Mills, Lydia I, 1126
Mills, Lydia I, 1127
Mills, Lydia I, 1128
Mills, Lydia I, 1132
Mills, Lydia IV, 37
Mills, Lydia IV, 50
Mills, Lydia V, 21
Mills, Lydia V, 65
Mills, Lydia V, 69
Mills, Lydia V, 100
Mills, Lydia V, 101
Mills, Lydia V, 160
Mills, Lydia V, 182
Mills, Lydia V, 185
Mills, Lydia V, 190
Mills, Lydia V, 191
Mills, Lydia V, 414
Mills, Lydia V, 755
Mills, Lydia Ann V, 191
Mills, Lydia Ann V, 192
Mills, Lydia J. V, 101
Mills, Lydia J. V, 192
Mills, Lydia M. V, 414
Mills, Macy I, 1096
Mills, Madeleine III, 231
Mills, Mahlon I, 1108
Mills, Malona V, 155
Mills, Malona V, 191
Mills, Malona V, 192
Mills, Margaret I, 510
Mills, Margaret V, 402
Mills, Margaret V, 414
Mills, Margaret V, 581
Mills, Margaret Ann I, 1127
Mills, Maria V, 414
Mills, Marietta IV, 741
Mills, Marilyn III, 231
Mills, Maris I, 789
Mills, Maris I, 830
Mills, Maris I, 967
Mills, Maris I, 1124
Mills, Maris I, 1126
Mills, Maris V, 264
Mills, Mark V, 100
Mills, Mark V, 190
Mills, Mark V, 191
Mills, Mark V, 192
Mills, Mark V, 200
Mills, Marmaduke I, 1034
Mills, Marmaduke I, 1035
Mills, Marmaduke V, 57
Mills, Marmaduke V, 99
Mills, Marmaduke V, 100
Mills, Marmaduke V, 113
Mills, Marrietta I, 1128
Mills, Martha I, 562
Mills, Martha I, 565
Mills, Martha I, 789
Mills, Martha I, 1086
Mills, Martha I, 1119
Mills, Martha I, 1127
Mills, Martha III, 191
Mills, Martha IV, 50
Mills, Martha IV, 54
Mills, Martha IV, 404
Mills, Martha IV, 422
Mills, Martha V, 176
Mills, Martha V, 191
Mills, Martha V, 192
Mills, Martha V, 755
Mills, Martha Catharine III, 231
Mills, Martha Elizabeth V, 191
Mills, Martha P. III, 270
Mills, Martha R. III, 231
Mills, Mary I, 510
Mills, Mary I, 511
Mills, Mary I, 534
Mills, Mary I, 544
Mills, Mary I, 546

s, Mary I, 554
s, Mary I, 562
s, Mary I, 563
s, Mary I, 662
s, Mary I, 685
s, Mary I, 695
s, Mary I, 789
s, Mary I, 829
s, Mary I, 830
s, Mary I, 841
s, Mary I, 993
s, Mary I, 997
s, Mary I, 1034
s, Mary I, 1035
s, Mary I, 1057
s, Mary I, 1058
s, Mary I, 1086
s, Mary I, 1089
s, Mary I, 1096
s, Mary I, 1108
s, Mary I, 1109
s, Mary I, 1114
s, Mary I, 1118
s, Mary I, 1126
s, Mary I, 1127
s, Mary I, 1135
s, Mary I, 1145
s, Mary II, 598
s, Mary IV, 50
ls, Mary IV, 56
ls, Mary IV, 154
ls, Mary IV, 253
ls, Mary IV, 422
ls, Mary IV, 432
ls, Mary V, 100
ls, Mary V, 101
lls, Mary V, 113
lls, Mary V, 175
lls, Mary V, 176
lls, Mary V, 181
lls, Mary V, 190
lls, Mary V, 191
lls, Mary V, 192
lls, Mary V, 200
lls, Mary V, 204
lls, Mary V, 517
lls, Mary V, 697
lls, Mary V, 755
lls, Mary V, 789
lls, Mary V, 792
lls, Mary V, 799
lls, Mary VI, 424
lls, Mary VI, 962
ills, Mary Alma V, 414
ills, Mary Alma V, 921
ills, Mary Ann I, 1127
ills, Mary Ann IV, 50
ills, Mary Ann V, 973
ills, Mary Anna V, 414
ills, Mary B. V, 100
ills, Mary Beals I, 1145
ills, Mary Belle V, 100
ills, Mary E. V, 191
ills, Mary Elizabeth V, 163
ills, Mary Elizabeth V, 192
ills, Mary H. II, 851
ills, Mary H. II, 899
ills, Mary H. V, 697
ills, Mary H. VI, 957
Iills, Mary I. V, 755
Iills, Mary Jane I, 1109
Iills, Mary Jane V, 381
Iills, Mary Jane V, 413
Iills, Mary Jane V, 414
Iills, Mary M. V, 101
Iills, Mary Paty V, 17
Iills, Mary, Jr. V, 176
Iills, Mary, Jr. V, 192
Iills, Maryann I, 978
Iills, Matulda IV, 1174
Iills, May V, 101
Iills, Maynard V, 697
Iills, Melona V, 192
Iills, Micajah I, 510
Iills, Micajah I, 511
Iills, Micajah I, 544
Iills, Micajah I, 562
Mills, Micajah I, 726
Mills, Micajah I, 830
Mills, Michael I, 510
Mills, Millikan I, 1109
Mills, Milton I, 1127
Mills, Milton IV, 1217
Mills, Milton V, 101
Mills, Milton V, 192
Mills, Milton W. V, 100
Mills, Milton W. V, 101
Mills, Minnie V, 101
Mills, Minnie Elva V, 414
Mills, Minnie May V, 100
Mills, Miriam I, 1109
Mills, Molly VI, 838
Mills, Mordecai I, 789
Mills, Mordecai V, 101
Mills, Mordica V, 100
Mills, Mordicai V, 100
Mills, Moses I, 510
Mills, Moses I, 789
Mills, Moses I, 967
Mills, Moses I, 1109
Mills, Moses I, 1126
Mills, Moses I, 1127
Mills, Moses V, 740
Mills, Mrs. Christina V, 264
Mills, Mrs. Emma C. I, 638
Mills, Murray D. V, 414
Mills, Murry D. V, 414
Mills, Myrtle R. V, 697
Mills, Myrtle Rayburn V, 349
Mills, Nacy I, 1109
Mills, Nancy I, 1108
Mills, Nancy V, 264
Mills, Nancy V, 414
Mills, Nancy V, 517
Mills, Nancy V, 634
Mills, Nancy D. V, 192
Mills, Nancy J. I, 1128
Mills, Nancy J. I, 1135
Mills, Naomi I, 1145
Mills, Nathan I, 789
Mills, Nathan I, 830
Mills, Nathan I, 1108
Mills, Nathan I, 1109
Mills, Nathan I, 1127
Mills, Nathan I, 1128
Mills, Nathan IV, 154
Mills, Nathan IV, 422
Mills, Nathan V, 100
Mills, Nellie M. V, 697
Mills, Noah V, 973
Mills, Nora Grice V, 697
Mills, Oliver V, 755
Mills, Orleanna I, 1128
Mills, Orlistus V, 100
Mills, Orlistus R. V, 101
Mills, Orpha V, 264
Mills, Orval P. V, 192
Mills, Oscar V, 264
Mills, Parry I, 1109
Mills, Patience I, 957
Mills, Patience I, 965
Mills, Patience I, 967
Mills, Patience I, 1035
Mills, Patience I, 1086
Mills, Patience I, 1096
Mills, Patience I, 1127
Mills, Patience V, 57
Mills, Patience V, 82
Mills, Patience V, 99
Mills, Patience V, 100
Mills, Patience V, 113
Mills, Patience V, 182
Mills, Patience V, 191
Mills, Patience V, 740
Mills, Patience V, 808
Mills, Patience V, 816
Mills, Patience V, 817
Mills, Patience V, 818
Mills, Patience V, 819
Mills, Patince Susanna I, 1109
Mills, Patsy V, 190
Mills, Patsy V, 191
Mills, Patsy V, 201
Mills, Pearly V, 697
Mills, Perry I, 1127
Mills, Peter I, 510
Mills, Peter I, 993
Mills, Phebe I, 534
Mills, Phebe I, 562
Mills, Phebe I, 789
Mills, Phebe I, 1034
Mills, Phebe I, 1035
Mills, Phebe I, 1128
Mills, Phebe III, 231
Mills, Phebe V, 100
Mills, Phebe V, 177
Mills, Phebe V, 190
Mills, Phebe V, 191
Mills, Phebe V, 192
Mills, Phebe V, 200
Mills, Phebe V, 799
Mills, Phebe A. I, 1109
Mills, Phebe A. V, 191
Mills, Phebe Ann V, 177
Mills, Phebe G. V, 192
Mills, Phebe Jane III, 231
Mills, Philip V, 192
Mills, Phillip V, 191
Mills, Providence IV, 253
Mills, Prudence V, 100
Mills, Prudence V, 131
Mills, Pusey IV, 50
Mills, Rachel I, 510
Mills, Rachel I, 511
Mills, Rachel I, 547
Mills, Rachel I, 562
Mills, Rachel I, 662
Mills, Rachel I, 789
Mills, Rachel I, 805
Mills, Rachel I, 826
Mills, Rachel I, 829
Mills, Rachel I, 830
Mills, Rachel I, 843
Mills, Rachel I, 967
Mills, Rachel I, 1109
Mills, Rachel I, 1114
Mills, Rachel I, 1121
Mills, Rachel I, 1126
Mills, Rachel I, 1127
Mills, Rachel I, 1134
Mills, Rachel I, 1145
Mills, Rachel IV, 44
Mills, Rachel IV, 50
Mills, Rachel V, 17
Mills, Rachel V, 81
Mills, Rachel V, 99
Mills, Rachel V, 100
Mills, Rachel V, 104
Mills, Rachel V, 190
Mills, Rachel V, 191
Mills, Rachel V, 200
Mills, Rachel V, 264
Mills, Rachel Alice IV, 741
Mills, Rachel Alice IV, 745
Mills, Rachel Alice V, 100
Mills, Rachel Jane I, 1109
Mills, Rachel Jane I, 1128
Mills, Ray P. V, 192
Mills, Rebecah I, 789
Mills, Rebecca I, 1056
Mills, Rebecca I, 1109
Mills, Rebecca V, 50
Mills, Rebecca V, 101
Mills, Rebecca V, 158
Mills, Rebecca V, 159
Mills, Rebecca V, 191
Mills, Rebecca V, 192
Mills, Rebecca V, 204
Mills, Rebecca V, 413
Mills, Rebecca V, 414
Mills, Rebecca V, 417
Mills, Rebeckah I, 510
Mills, Rebeckah I, 562
Mills, Rebeckah I, 563
Mills, Rebeckah I, 978
Mills, Rebeckah I, 985
Mills, Rebeckah II, 64
Mills, Rebeckah II, 88
Mills, Rebekah I, 830
Mills, Rebekah I, 839
Mills, Regina V, 414
Mills, Reuben I, 562
Mills, Reuben I, 563
Mills, Reuben I, 565
Mills, Reuben I, 574
Mills, Reuben I, 773
Mills, Reuben I, 789
Mills, Reuben I, 967
Mills, Reuben I, 1126
Mills, Reuben IV, 154
Mills, Reuben IV, 253
Mills, Reuben IV, 422
Mills, Reuben IV, 432
Mills, Reuben IV, 1069
Mills, Reuben IV, 1107
Mills, Reuben V, 230
Mills, Reuben V, 414
Mills, Reuben, Jr. I, 830
Mills, Reuben, Jr. IV, 154
Mills, Rhoda I, 1109
Mills, Rhoda I, 1127
Mills, Rhoda V, 634
Mills, Rhoda V, 640
Mills, Richard I, 562
Mills, Richard I, 789
Mills, Richard I, 830
Mills, Richard I, 957
Mills, Richard I, 967
Mills, Richard I, 993
Mills, Richard I, 1086
Mills, Richard I, 1101
Mills, Richard I, 1108
Mills, Richard I, 1109
Mills, Richard I, 1126
Mills, Richard I, 1127
Mills, Richard V, 100
Mills, Richard V, 264
Mills, Richard V, 517
Mills, Richard V, 521
Mills, Richard L. I, 1109
Mills, Richard, Sr. I, 1109
Mills, Rigena V, 414
Mills, Robert V, 162
Mills, Robert V, 697
Mills, Robert VI, 952
Mills, Robert Franklin I, 1109
Mills, Robert J. V, 697
Mills, Robert Kelly V, 17
Mills, Robert S. VI, 962
Mills, Roscoe V, 264
Mills, Rowland R. V, 100
Mills, Rowland R. V, 973
Mills, Roy J. V, 101
Mills, Ruben I, 511
Mills, Ruben I, 554
Mills, Ruben I, 562
Mills, Ruben I, 789
Mills, Ruben I, 830
Mills, Ruth I, 510
Mills, Ruth I, 511
Mills, Ruth I, 662
Mills, Ruth I, 785
Mills, Ruth I, 821
Mills, Ruth I, 829
Mills, Ruth I, 830
Mills, Ruth I, 978
Mills, Ruth I, 987
Mills, Ruth I, 993
Mills, Ruth I, 1108
Mills, Ruth I, 1123
Mills, Ruth I, 1127
Mills, Ruth V, 100
Mills, Ruth V, 187
Mills, Ruth V, 190
Mills, Ruth V, 191
Mills, Ruth V, 192
Mills, Ruth V, 209
Mills, Ruth V, 397
Mills, Ruth V, 413
Mills, Ruth V, 414
Mills, Ruth V, 517
Mills, Ruth Ann V, 101
Mills, Ruth Ann V, 102
Mills, Ruth Hannah V, 100
Mills, Ruth W. V, 515
Mills, Ruth W. V, 517
Mills, Ruth W. V, 697
Mills, Ruthanna V, 100
Mills, Ruthanna V, 101
Mills, Ruthanna V, 102
Mills, Sally I, 789
Mills, Sally IV, 50
Mills, Sally IV, 154
Mills, Sally IV, 422
Mills, Sally IV, 457
Mills, Samuel I, 510
Mills, Samuel I, 789
Mills, Samuel I, 966
Mills, Samuel I, 1089
Mills, Samuel I, 1096
Mills, Samuel I, 1101
Mills, Samuel I, 1109
Mills, Samuel I, 1126
Mills, Samuel I, 1127
Mills, Samuel IV, 253
Mills, Samuel V, 349
Mills, Samuel V, 755
Mills, Samuel V, 973
Mills, Samuel H. I, 1109
Mills, Samuel L. IV, 253
Mills, Samuel W. V, 191
Mills, Sarah I, 400
Mills, Sarah I, 409
Mills, Sarah I, 451
Mills, Sarah I, 510
Mills, Sarah I, 511
Mills, Sarah I, 554
Mills, Sarah I, 562
Mills, Sarah I, 563
Mills, Sarah I, 565
Mills, Sarah I, 572
Mills, Sarah I, 662
Mills, Sarah I, 685
Mills, Sarah I, 690
Mills, Sarah I, 789
Mills, Sarah I, 829
Mills, Sarah I, 830
Mills, Sarah I, 967
Mills, Sarah I, 978
Mills, Sarah I, 1035
Mills, Sarah I, 1086
Mills, Sarah I, 1101
Mills, Sarah I, 1108
Mills, Sarah I, 1109
Mills, Sarah I, 1111
Mills, Sarah I, 1117
Mills, Sarah I, 1123
Mills, Sarah I, 1125
Mills, Sarah I, 1126
Mills, Sarah I, 1127
Mills, Sarah I, 1128
Mills, Sarah I, 1130
Mills, Sarah I, 1135
Mills, Sarah I, 1145
Mills, Sarah II, 242
Mills, Sarah II, 396
Mills, Sarah III, 149
Mills, Sarah III, 231
Mills, Sarah IV, 50
Mills, Sarah IV, 55
Mills, Sarah IV, 154
Mills, Sarah IV, 343
Mills, Sarah IV, 422
Mills, Sarah V, 17
Mills, Sarah V, 65
Mills, Sarah V, 100
Mills, Sarah V, 101
Mills, Sarah V, 172
Mills, Sarah V, 191
Mills, Sarah V, 192
Mills, Sarah V, 246
Mills, Sarah V, 264
Mills, Sarah V, 349
Mills, Sarah V, 350
Mills, Sarah V, 413
Mills, Sarah V, 755
Mills, Sarah V, 973
Mills, Sarah A. II, 848
Mills, Sarah A. II, 899
Mills, Sarah A. V, 100
Mills, Sarah A. V, 101
Mills, Sarah A. V, 192
Mills, Sarah Ann I, 1127
Mills, Sarah Anna II, 810
Mills, Sarah Arminda I, 1109
Mills, Sarah C. III, 231
Mills, Sarah Elizabeth IV, 50
Mills, Sarah H. V, 100
Mills, Sarah H. V, 101
Mills, Sarah Jane V, 413
Mills, Sarah W. V, 176
Mills, Sarah W. V, 191
Mills, Sarah, Jr. I, 1127
Mills, Sarah, Jr. I, 1128
Mills, Sarah, Sr. I, 1128
Mills, Selma P. IV, 253
Mills, Selma P. IV, 286
Mills, Seth I, 789
Mills, Seth I, 967
Mills, Seth I, 1126
Mills, Seth I, 1127
Mills, Seth V, 100
Mills, Seth V, 190
Mills, Seth V, 192
Mills, Sherelda I, 1127
Mills, Sidney IV, 50
Mills, Sidney V, 817
Mills, Sidney A. III, 231
Mills, Solomon I, 830
Mills, Solomon I, 1096
Mills, Solomon I, 1127
Mills, Solomon Hiatt I, 511
Mills, Sophia I, 1108
Mills, Sophia I, 1109
Mills, Sophia I, 1127
Mills, Stacy III, 149
Mills, Stacy III, 231
Mills, Stephen V, 160
Mills, Stephen V, 191
Mills, Strangeman V, 100
Mills, Strangman Stanley V, 100
Mills, Susan V, 818
Mills, Susan K. IV, 102
Mills, Susan R. VI, 952
Mills, Susanna I, 562
Mills, Susanna I, 830
Mills, Susanna I, 1127
Mills, Susanna V, 29
Mills, Susanna V, 100
Mills, Tabitha I, 510
Mills, Teressa I, 1159
Mills, Thomas I, 343
Mills, Thomas I, 409
Mills, Thomas I, 487
Mills, Thomas I, 562
Mills, Thomas I, 789
Mills, Thomas I, 822
Mills, Thomas I, 829
Mills, Thomas I, 830
Mills, Thomas I, 1086
Mills, Thomas IV, 422
Mills, Thomas IV, 1069
Mills, Thomas V, 17
Mills, Thomas V, 100
Mills, Thomas V, 192
Mills, Thomas V, 204
Mills, Thomas V, 246
Mills, Thomas V, 264
Mills, Thomas VI, 199
Mills, Thomas H. V, 100
Mills, Thomas K. IV, 102
Mills, Thomas W. IV, 1069
Mills, Thos. I, 562
Mills, Walter V, 414
Mills, Walter V, 921

Mills, Walter T. V, 414
Mills, Walter T. V, 921
Mills, Walter W. I, 622
Mills, Walter W., Jr. I, 622
Mills, Walter, Jr. I, 638
Mills, Walter, Jr. III, 231
Mills, Warren V, 581
Mills, Warren Elmer V, 192
Mills, Widow Bethiah I, 1086
Mills, Widow Elizabeth I, 789
Mills, Widow Jemima I, 830
Mills, Widow Mary I, 1038
Mills, Wilbur H. V, 101
Mills, Wilbur Henry V, 100
Mills, William I, 510
Mills, William I, 562
Mills, William I, 789
Mills, William I, 967
Mills, William I, 988
Mills, William I, 1034
Mills, William I, 1035
Mills, William I, 1036
Mills, William I, 1108
Mills, William I, 1109
Mills, William I, 1126
Mills, William I, 1127
Mills, William I, 1145
Mills, William I, 1159
Mills, William II, 396
Mills, William IV, 50
Mills, William IV, 253
Mills, William V, 100
Mills, William V, 175
Mills, William V, 182
Mills, William V, 187
Mills, William V, 190
Mills, William V, 191
Mills, William V, 192
Mills, William V, 204
Mills, William V, 634
Mills, William Andrew I, 1109
Mills, William F. III, 231
Mills, William H. V, 100
Mills, William H. V, 101
Mills, William N. I, 1109
Mills, William Riley I, 1128
Mills, William, Jr. IV, 253
Mills, William, Sr. IV, 253
Mills, Wm. I, 1057
Mills, Wm. I, 1058
Mills, Wm. I, 1109
Mills, Wm. V, 190
Mills, Wm. V, 191
Mills, Wm. V, 192
Mills, Wm. V, 214
Mills, Wm. V, 634
Mills, Wm. F. III, 231
Mills, Zachariah I, 562
Mills, Zachariah I, 967
Mills, Zachariah I, 1109
Mills, Zachariah I, 1126
Mills, Zachariah I, 1127
Mills, Zacharias I, 511
Mills, Zacharias I, 662
Mills, Zillah V, 100
Mills, Zilpha V, 817
Mills, Zimry I, 1108
Millsap, J. Robert I, 1159
Millsap, Sally I, 980
Millsap, Sally I, 993
Millsaps, Sally I, 993
Millstead, Alexander B. VI, 813
Milner, Alfred V, 264
Milner, Alfred W. V, 264
Milner, Amos V, 264
Milner, Amos VI, 332
Milner, Ann V, 265
Milner, Ann VI, 332
Milner, Anna II, 598
Milner, Anna V, 264
Milner, Anna VI, 332
Milner, Anna Katherine Ruth Rachel V, 264
Milner, Anne VI, 332
Milner, Anne Kathy V, 264
Milner, Armistead VI, 896
Milner, Arthur III, 231
Milner, Arthur Hackney V, 264
Milner, Athanissa IV, 343
Milner, Beverly V, 264
Milner, Beverly VI, 332
Milner, Beverly, Jr. V, 264
Milner, Bulah II, 598
Milner, Caty VI, 332
Milner, Chas. Fremont V, 264
Milner, Clary E. V, 264
Milner, Clyde V, 264
Milner, Clyde Alonzo V, 264
Milner, Daniel VI, 300
Milner, David II, 1007
Milner, Dudley IV, 343
Milner, Dudley VI, 295
Milner, Dudley VI, 332
Milner, Elizabeth II, 396
Milner, Elizabeth II, 629
Milner, Elizabeth II, 1007
Milner, Elizabeth V, 264
Milner, Ella V, 264
Milner, Ella W. V, 264
Milner, Frank V, 264
Milner, Frank P. V, 265
Milner, Fremont B. V, 264
Milner, Fremont Beverly V, 264
Milner, Grace V, 461
Milner, Hannah II, 396
Milner, Hannah II, 1000
Milner, Hannah V, 264
Milner, Hannah V, 292
Milner, Hariet II, 598
Milner, Harry V, 265
Milner, Henry V, 264
Milner, Howard Edwin V, 264
Milner, Isaac II, 396
Milner, Isaac II, 598
Milner, Isaac II, 1039
Milner, James II, 396
Milner, James II, 629
Milner, Jesse V, 349
Milner, Jesse J. V, 350
Milner, John II, 396
Milner, John II, 598
Milner, John II, 1000
Milner, John V, 264
Milner, John A. V, 264
Milner, Joseph III, 231
Milner, Joseph V, 264
Milner, Joseph V, 349
Milner, Joseph V, 350
Milner, Joseph VI, 499
Milner, Josiah V, 264
Milner, Louisa F. V, 264
Milner, Luke V, 264
Milner, Lydia II, 598
Milner, Lydia B. IV, 741
Milner, Lydia B. IV, 753
Milner, Margaret V, 264
Milner, Mary IV, 343
Milner, Mary V, 264
Milner, Mary VI, 295
Milner, Mary VI, 332
Milner, Mary VI, 896
Milner, Mary Ann V, 264
Milner, Mary E. V, 264
Milner, Maud V, 249
Milner, Maud V, 264
Milner, Mellie IV, 1308
Milner, Michal J. V, 264
Milner, Moses VI, 332
Milner, Moses S. V, 264
Milner, Nancy E. V, 264
Milner, Nettie C. V, 461
Milner, Nina V, 458
Milner, Nina V, 461
Milner, Oliver V, 264
Milner, Phebe II, 598
Milner, Pleasant VI, 499
Milner, Pleasant VI, 586
Milner, Priscilla A. V, 350
Milner, Priscilla Ann V, 349
Milner, Priscilla Ann V, 350
Milner, R. Dudley V, 264
Milner, Rachel E. V, 265
Milner, Rachel E. V, 458
Milner, Rachel E. V, 461
Milner, Rebecca Denny V, 264
Milner, Rebecca S. V, 264
Milner, Robert V, 264
Milner, Robert D. V, 264
Milner, Ruth V, 264
Milner, Ruth V, 349
Milner, Ruth VI, 300
Milner, Ruth VI, 332
Milner, Ruth A. V, 264
Milner, Sallie V, 264
Milner, Sally V, 264
Milner, Samuel II, 396
Milner, Sarah II, 598
Milner, Sarah II, 629
Milner, Sarah II, 1013
Milner, Sarah V, 218
Milner, Sarah V, 264
Milner, Sarah VI, 332
Milner, Sidney II, 598
Milner, Stanley V, 461
Milner, Susanna V, 349
Milner, Susanna V, 350
Milner, Susanna VI, 535
Milner, Susannah IV, 741
Milner, Susannah V, 349
Milner, Susannah V, 350
Milner, Susannah V, 397
Milner, Susannah V, 414
Milner, Thomas V, 264
Milner, Wd. Martha II, 598
Milner, Wd. Martha II, 621
Milner, Wd. Sarah II, 1039
Milner, William II, 396
Milner, William III, 231
Milner, Willis V, 265
Milner, Winnifred V, 461
Milner, Wm. II, 1007
Milner, Wm. II, 1013
Milner, Wm. V, 349
Milner, Wm. G. V, 350
Milner, Wm. T. V, 350
Milnor, Ann II, 396
Milnor, Anna II, 396
Milnor, Anna II, 472
Milnor, Anna II, 574
Milnor, Anna II, 598
Milnor, Anna II, 756
Milnor, Anna IV, 154
Milnor, Armin II, 1056
Milnor, Beulah II, 598
Milnor, Beulah II, 756
Milnor, Bulah II, 598
Milnor, Caty IV, 154
Milnor, Charles II, 396
Milnor, Charles II, 598
Milnor, Daniel II, 1015
Milnor, David II, 1015
Milnor, David II, 1016
Milnor, Dudley IV, 154
Milnor, Elizabeth II, 396
Milnor, Elizabeth II, 598
Milnor, Elizabeth II, 1015
Milnor, Elizabeth II, 1016
Milnor, Elvira II, 998
Milnor, Elvira II, 1016
Milnor, Frances II, 519
Milnor, Frances II, 598
Milnor, George II, 396
Milnor, George Ashton II, 396
Milnor, George Aston II, 598
Milnor, Hannah II, 396
Milnor, Hannah II, 598
Milnor, Hannah II, 614
Milnor, Hannah II, 982
Milnor, Hannah II, 1015
Milnor, Hannah II, 1016
Milnor, Hariet II, 598
Milnor, Harriet II, 598
Milnor, Harriet II, 668
Milnor, Harriet II, 1016
Milnor, Harriett II, 598
Milnor, Harriot II, 598
Milnor, Isaac II, 396
Milnor, Isaac II, 598
Milnor, Isaac II, 965
Milnor, Isaac II, 1015
Milnor, Isaac II, 1016
Milnor, James II, 396
Milnor, James II, 598
Milnor, Jane M. II, 296
Milnor, Jane M. II, 297
Milnor, John II, 396
Milnor, John II, 472
Milnor, John II, 598
Milnor, John II, 1015
Milnor, John II, 1016
Milnor, John M. II, 1016
Milnor, John, Jr. II, 598
Milnor, Jonathan II, 982
Milnor, Jonathan II, 1015
Milnor, Jonathan II, 1016
Milnor, Joseph II, 993
Milnor, Joseph II, 1004
Milnor, Joseph II, 1015
Milnor, Joseph II, 1016
Milnor, Joseph II, 1023
Milnor, Katherine II, 1004
Milnor, Katherine II, 1015
Milnor, Letitia II, 1011
Milnor, Letitia II, 1016
Milnor, Lydia II, 598
Milnor, Mahlon II, 965
Milnor, Mahlon II, 998
Milnor, Mahlon II, 1014
Milnor, Mahlon II, 1015
Milnor, Mahlon II, 1016
Milnor, Mahlon II, 1041
Milnor, Mahlon II, 1076
Milnor, Maria S. II, 1016
Milnor, Maria S. II, 1041
Milnor, Martha II, 396
Milnor, Martha II, 598
Milnor, Martha II, 641
Milnor, Martha II, 993
Milnor, Martha II, 1015
Milnor, Mary II, 396
Milnor, Mary II, 577
Milnor, Mary II, 598
Milnor, Mary II, 1015
Milnor, Mary II, 1016
Milnor, Mary IV, 154
Milnor, Mary Ann II, 396
Milnor, Mary Ann II, 598
Milnor, Mercy Coates II, 396
Milnor, Mercy Coates II, 598
Milnor, Nathan II, 1016
Milnor, Nathaniel VI, 594
Milnor, Phebe II, 598
Milnor, Phebe II, 713
Milnor, Phebe II, 965
Milnor, Phebe II, 992
Milnor, Phebe II, 998
Milnor, Phebe II, 1015
Milnor, Phebe II, 1016
Milnor, Phebe II, 1041
Milnor, Phebe II, 1056
Milnor, Phebe II, 1062
Milnor, Pheby II, 1014
Milnor, Pheby II, 1016
Milnor, Priscilla II, 1014
Milnor, Priscilla II, 1015
Milnor, Rachel II, 1015
Milnor, Rachel II, 1016
Milnor, Rebecca II, 396
Milnor, Rebeckah II, 1003
Milnor, Rebeckah II, 1015
Milnor, Robert II, 396
Milnor, Robert II, 598
Milnor, Robert VI, 594
Milnor, Samuel II, 396
Milnor, Samuel II, 1016
Milnor, Samuel II, 1056
Milnor, Sarah II, 396
Milnor, Sarah II, 598
Milnor, Sarah II, 965
Milnor, Sarah II, 1008
Milnor, Sarah II, 1015
Milnor, Sarah II, 1016
Milnor, Sarah II, 1023
Milnor, Sidney II, 598
Milnor, Sidney II, 713
Milnor, Sidney II, 756
Milnor, Stephen II, 1015
Milnor, Theodosia II, 598
Milnor, Theodosia II, 612
Milnor, Thomas II, 396
Milnor, Thomas II, 598
Milnor, Thomas II, 1016
Milnor, Virena II, 965
Milnor, Wd. Martha II, 598
Milnor, Wd. Pleasant II, 1015
Milnor, Wd. Sarah II, 1015
Milnor, William II, 396
Milnor, Wm. II, 472
Milnor, Wm. II, 598
Milnor, Wm. II, 982
Milnor, Wm. II, 1015
Milnor, Wm., Jr. II, 598
Miltenberger, Emma V, 101
Milton, Absalom VI, 886
Milton, Absolem VI, 886
Milton, Alfred Day III, 231
Milton, Alfreda Amelia III, 231
Milton, Alice Florence III, 231
Milton, Amos IV, 154
Milton, Anderson VI, 885
Milton, Anderson VI, 984
Milton, Ann II, 713
Milton, Ann VI, 886
Milton, Anna IV, 541
Milton, Anna R. II, 899
Milton, Annie R. II, 899
Milton, Armella IV, 253
Milton, Elizabeth II, 706
Milton, Elizabeth VI, 886
Milton, Ellen III, 231
Milton, Fanny IV, 343
Milton, Henry IV, 154
Milton, James V, 439
Milton, John IV, 253
Milton, John V, 406
Milton, Jos. III, 231
Milton, Joseph Nathaniel III, 231
Milton, Joseph Nathaniel III, 285
Milton, Lucy VI, 942
Milton, Mary III, 231
Milton, Mary IV, 154
Milton, Mary IV, 253
Milton, Mary IV, 541
Milton, Mary VI, 422
Milton, Mary VI, 424
Milton, Mary VI, 676
Milton, Mary E. III, 231
Milton, Mary Ellen III, 231
Milton, Mary Ellen III, 285
Milton, Mary, Jr. III, 231
Milton, Mary, Jr. IV, 253
Milton, Mary, Jr. IV, 541
Milton, Moses IV, 154
Milton, Moses IV, 343
Milton, Nathaniel III, 231
Milton, Patience IV, 253
Milton, Patience IV, 541
Milton, Rebecca IV, 1069
Milton, Rebecca IV, 1135
Milton, Rebecca V, 406
Milton, Rebeckah VI, 886
Milton, Robert Heaton III, 23
Milton, Ruth Elizabeth III, 23
Milton, Sarah IV, 343
Milton, Thomas IV, 154
Milton, Thomas V, 695
Milton, Thomas, Jr. IV, 154
Milton, William IV, 343
Minard, ??? III, 231
Minard, Caroline III, 231
Minard, Caroline E. III, 231
Minard, Caroline E. III, 326
Minard, Carrie III, 231
Minard, David III, 231
Minard, Jane III, 117
Minard, Jane III, 137
Minard, Jane III, 371
Minard, John III, 64
Minard, John III, 231
Minard, John III, 319
Minard, Margaret III, 231
Minard, Mary F. III, 319
Minard, Mary Frances III, 231
Minard, Sarah IV, 646
Minard, Serena III, 231
Minard, Serena A. III, 64
Minard, Serena A. III, 231
Minard, Serena A. III, 319
Minard, Stephen III, 231
Minard, Walter W. III, 231
Minard, Walter W. III, 326
Minch, Edmund D. II, 135
Minch, Jennie H. II, 135
Minch, Margaret Ridgway II, 1
Minch, Martha II, 135
Minch, R. Leslie II, 135
Minchener, Lydia IV, 1286
Mincher, Rachel II, 598
Mincher, Rachel II, 664
Minchins, Rebekah I, 408
Minden, Elisha I, 152
Minden, Milisant, Jr. I, 152
Minden, Robert I, 152
Minden, Sarah I, 152
Minehart, Effie IV, 1258
Minehart, Jose V, 414
Minehart, Josie V, 414
Minehart, Mabel IV, 1258
Miner, Armstead VI, 880
Miner, Caroline IV, 646
Miner, Caroline IV, 652
Miner, Caroline P. IV, 646
Miner, Caroline P. IV, 652
Miner, Ellis IV, 741
Miner, Frances S. A. VI, 962
Miner, John VI, 962
Miner, Mildred VI, 902
Miner, Nancy VI, 880
Miner, Nancy E. VI, 919
Miner, Nellie C. IV, 1330
Miner, Robert VI, 999
Miner, Robert C. VI, 919
Miner, Sterling C. IV, 1330
Miner, William A. VI, 919
Minerva, Elizabeth V, 217
Ming, Dorothy VI, 840
Ming, Sarah I, 188
Ming, Sarah I, 196
Ming, Wm. II, 598
Ming, Wollery VI, 839
Ming, Wollery VI, 840
Minge, Anna Maria IV, 483
Minge, Anna Maria IV, 488
Minge, Anna Maria VI, 195
Minge, Anna Maria VI, 199
Minge, Cap VI, 199
Minge, Captain ??? VI, 171
Mingen, Sarah II, 235
Mingen, Sarah II, 242
Mingester, Amanda V, 1010
Miniard, Artie I, 1159
Miniard, James I, 1159
Minican, Gulielma IV, 422
Minican, Gulielma Maria IV, 50
Minican, Margaret IV, 422
Minican, Sarah IV, 422
Minikan, Ann IV, 102
Minikan, Hannah IV, 102
Minikan, John IV, 102
Minikan, Margaret IV, 102
Minikan, Mary IV, 102
Minikan, Sarah Simpson IV, 102
Minikan, William IV, 102
Miniken, Ann IV, 50
Miniken, Gulielma Maria IV, 50

en, Hannah IV, 50
en, John IV, 50
en, John IV, 102
en, Julia Elna Maria
V, 335
en, Margaret IV, 50
en, Margaret IV, 335
en, Margaret IV, 341
en, Margaret IV, 343
en, Mary IV, 50
en, Mary IV, 102
en, Sarah IV, 50
en, Sarah IV, 343
en, William IV, 50
kin, Ann IV, 102
kin, Gulielma IV, 102
kin, Gulielma Maria
enn IV, 102
kin, Gulielma Maria
enn IV, 343
kin, Hannah IV, 102
kin, John IV, 102
kin, Margaret IV, 102
kin, Margaret IV, 335
kin, Margaret IV, 343
kin, Maria Penn IV, 102
kin, Mary IV, 102
kin, Mary IV, 343
kin, Sarah IV, 102
kin, Sarah IV, 343
kin, Sarah Samson IV, 343
kin, Sarah Simpson IV, 102
kin, Sarah Simson IV, 102
kin, Simpson IV, 102
kin, William IV, 102
on, Margaret II, 598
ster, M. E. III, 78
ster, M. E. III, 325
near, George IV, 1174
near, Lydia IV, 1174
never, A. D. IV, 1258
never, George IV, 1258
never, Lucius IV, 1258
nick, Beulah II, 598
nick, Beulah II, 674
nick, Catharine VI, 962
nick, George W. VI, 962
nick, John VI, 962
nick, Louise Cox V, 350
nick, Mary Ann VI, 962
nikan, Margaret IV, 330
nikan, Mary IV, 330
nikan, Mary IV, 343
nikan, William IV, 330
nis, A. VI, 941
nis, Callohill VI, 907
nis, Callohill VI, 994
nis, Issac Calohill VI, 885
nis, Martha VI, 951
or, ??? III, 231
or, Ann Eliza VI, 908
or, Aristead VI, 962
or, Armistead VI, 962
or, Armistead VI, 982
or, Betsy VI, 962
or, Cath. III, 231
or, Catharine VI, 998
or, Edith W. VI, 884
or, Edith White VI, 962
or, Eliza VI, 962
or, Elizabeth VI, 908
or, Ephraim VI, 962
or, Fanny VI, 918
or, Frances S. A. VI, 962
or, Gabriel VI, 962
or, George III, 231
nor, John VI, 962
nor, Leroy VI, 962
nor, Letitia Marsh III, 231
nor, Martha VI, 883
nor, Mary M. III, 123
nor, Mary M. III, 231
nor, Milley VI, 962
nor, Nancy VI, 982
nor, Polly VI, 918
nor, Robert C. VI, 902
nor, Robert C. VI, 908
nor, Robert C. VI, 962
nor, Sarah V, 586
nor, Sarah V, 592
nor, Sarah V, 922
nor, Sarah V, 925
nor, Susan Jane VI, 962
nor, Thomas VI, 962
inor, Threeivellus VI, 918
inor, W. VI, 884
inor, W. VI, 918
inor, W. VI, 962
inor, William VI, 883
inor, William VI, 884
inor, Wm. VI, 998
Minroe, Quincy I, 766
Minsan, Benjamin II, 242
Minsan, Sarah II, 242
Minshall, Bertha V, 634
Minshall, Edward II, 599
Minshall, Evan II, 599
Minshall, Isaac II, 599
Minshall, Isaac II, 611
Minshall, Jacob II, 598
Minshall, Jacob II, 611
Minshall, Margaret II, 599
Minshall, Margaret II, 611
Minshall, R. M. IV, 1330
Minshall, Rachel II, 598
Minshall, Rachel II, 664
Minshall, Rebecca II, 599
Minshall, Rebecka II, 599
Minshall, Rebeckah II, 466
Minshall, Rebeckah II, 599
Minshall, Rebeckah II, 611
Minshall, Rebekah II, 599
Minshall, Reese IV, 1330
Minshall, Samuel II, 599
Minshall, Sarah II, 598
Minshall, Sarah II, 599
Minshall, Sarah II, 611
Minshall, Thomas II, 598
Minshall, Thomas II, 599
Minshall, Thomas II, 611
Minshall, Thos. II, 598
Minshall, Thos. II, 599
Minster, Mary II, 888
Minster, Mary II, 899
Minter, A. L. VI, 927
Minter, Agness VI, 996
Minter, Anne VI, 962
Minter, Anthony VI, 990
Minter, Augustus L. VI, 962
Minter, Betsy Ann VI, 927
Minter, Billey VI, 875
Minter, Billey VI, 960
Minter, Billey VI, 962
Minter, Billy VI, 936
Minter, Billy VI, 980
Minter, Billy VI, 996
Minter, Dolly G. VI, 962
Minter, Elizabeth VI, 960
Minter, Elvira VI, 962
Minter, Florentine J. VI, 962
Minter, James VI, 875
Minter, James VI, 936
Minter, James VI, 960
Minter, James VI, 962
Minter, Jane VI, 875
Minter, Jesse VI, 962
Minter, John VI, 990
Minter, Mary I, 386
Minter, Mary I, 409
Minter, Merit VI, 962
Minter, Polly VI, 990
Minter, Sally VI, 980
Minter, Sarah VI, 960
Minter, Susannah VI, 936
Minthorn, Ellan I, 891
Minthorn, Ellen I, 611
Minthorn, Ellen I, 894
Minthorn, Mary I, 895
Minthorn, Murtin L. I, 895
Minthorn, Theodore I, 895
Minton, Betty I, 1022
Minton, Celia C. VI, 841
Minton, Elizabeth I, 1062
Minton, Hannah I, 1022
Minton, John VI, 806
Minton, John VI, 841
Minton, Joseph I, 1022
Minton, Lydia I, 1022
Minton, Marget I, 1022
Minton, Mary I, 1022
Minton, Parthenay I, 1062
Minton, Parthenia I, 1022
Minton, Rachel I, 1022
Minton, Rachel I, 1060
Minton, Rachel I, 1062
Minton, Rebeckah I, 1022
Minton, Rebekah I, 1062
Minton, Richard I, 1022
Minton, Richard I, 1035
Minton, Sarah VI, 840
Minton, Simon VI, 840
Minton, Susan G. VI, 841
Minton, Thomas I, 1022
Minton, Thomas I, 1035
Minton, W. William VI, 841
Minton, William Y. VI, 801
Minton, William Y. VI, 841
Minton, William Y. VI, 860
Minturn, ??? III, 231
Minturn, ??? III, 271
Minturn, Benjamin G., Jr.
III, 231
Minturn, Eliza Ann III, 231
Minturn, Esther III, 271
Minturn, Hannah III, 231
Minturn, John III, 231
Minturn, Jonas III, 231
Minturn, Mary III, 41
Minturn, Mary III, 231
Minturn, Penelope III, 231
Minturn, Sarah II, 698
Minturn, Sarah III, 43
Minturn, Sarah III, 231
Minturn, William III, 231
Minus, Samuel I, 1091
Minus, Samuel I, 1092
Minus, Samuel I, 1095
Minus, Samuel I, 1096
Minyard, Artie I, 1159
Minyard, James I, 1159
Mipis, Phebe VI, 424
Mire, Nancy V, 423
Mirech, Howe VI, 138
Mirech, Howe VI, 143
Mires, Ann Eliza IV, 1152
Mires, Ann Eliza IV, 1174
Mires, Anna V, 517
Mires, Anna V, 586
Mires, Anna P. V, 956
Mires, Benjamin VI, 537
Mires, Bessie V, 517
Mires, Elijah VI, 537
Mires, Eliza V, 956
Mires, Elizabeth VI, 537
Mires, Esther VI, 537
Mires, Francis VI, 537
Mires, Hannah VI, 537
Mires, Harry IV, 1174
Mires, Isaac V, 586
Mires, Isaac VI, 537
Mires, John VI, 537
Mires, Jonathan VI, 537
Mires, Lydia I, 994
Mires, Mary IV, 1287
Mires, Mary VI, 537
Mires, Mary C. V, 956
Mires, Mary C. V, 959
Mires, Orpha IV, 34
Mires, Orpha IV, 51
Mires, Permelia V, 423
Mires, Rebecca IV, 1029
Mires, Rebecca IV, 1030
Mires, Samuel V, 423
Mires, Sarah VI, 537
Mires, Susannah VI, 537
Mires, Thirza IV, 909
Mires, Thirza IV, 911
Mires, Thomas VI, 537
Miris, David I, 409
Mirza, Youel V, 697
Misky, Clara II, 853
Misky, Clara II, 899
Misner, Mary IV, 128
Misner, Mary IV, 130
Misner, Mary V, 697
Misner, Wm. V, 697
Misseldine, Jemima V, 31
Misseldine, Jemima V, 101
Misseldine, John V, 101
Misseldine, John F. V, 101
Missouri, Lydia I, 46
Mitch, Alfred V, 1010
Mitch, Mrs. Bertha V, 1010
Mitchall, James VI, 991
Mitcham, Catharine VI, 840
Mitcham, Hargrove VI, 840
Mitchaner, Mary IV, 1029
Mitchcalf, Catharine VI, 944
Mitchel, Abraham II, 599
Mitchel, Abraham II, 614
Mitchel, Abraham II, 625
Mitchel, Abraham II, 638
Mitchel, Amelia II, 713
Mitchel, Ann II, 599
Mitchel, Ann II, 625
Mitchel, Ann IV, 50
Mitchel, David IV, 343
Mitchel, Edith IV, 741
Mitchel, Edith L. IV, 741
Mitchel, Edith L. IV, 769
Mitchel, Elisabeth I, 146
Mitchel, Elisabeth I, 151
Mitchel, Elizabeth IV, 78
Mitchel, Elizabeth IV, 102
Mitchel, Elizabeth VI, 767
Mitchel, Estella S. V, 517
Mitchel, Frances II, 1056
Mitchel, Frances VI, 950
Mitchel, George II, 1016
Mitchel, Grace V, 634
Mitchel, Hannah II, 599
Mitchel, Hannah II, 976
Mitchel, Hannah II, 1016
Mitchel, Hannah VI, 767
Mitchel, Hannah D. V, 517
Mitchel, Hannah D. V, 518
Mitchel, Hannah D. V, 587
Mitchel, Harriet II, 1051
Mitchel, Harriet II, 1056
Mitchel, Harriet II, 1073
Mitchel, Harriet II, 1076
Mitchel, Isabel IV, 741
Mitchel, James II, 396
Mitchel, John II, 976
Mitchel, John II, 1016
Mitchel, Joseph II, 976
Mitchel, Joshua II, 599
Mitchel, Joshua II, 1016
Mitchel, Joshua II, 1056
Mitchel, Lydia S. II, 959
Mitchel, Lydia S. IV, 576
Mitchel, Lydia S. IV, 588
Mitchel, M. IV, 1287
Mitchel, Mahlon Milnor II, 1056
Mitchel, Marietta B. V, 517
Mitchel, Mary II, 976
Mitchel, Mary IV, 50
Mitchel, Mary IV, 488
Mitchel, Mary V, 101
Mitchel, Mary V, 140
Mitchel, Mary VI, 424
Mitchel, Mathew VI, 767
Mitchel, Nelson IV, 488
Mitchel, Oliver V, 414
Mitchel, Oliver A. V, 414
Mitchel, Pearson II, 1016
Mitchel, Pleasant VI, 767
Mitchel, Rachel IV, 1287
Mitchel, Reading II, 1056
Mitchel, Rebecca II, 242
Mitchel, Rebecca II, 1016
Mitchel, Robert R. V, 517
Mitchel, Ruth I, 400
Mitchel, Ruth I, 409
Mitchel, Samuel IV, 50
Mitchel, Samuel VI, 424
Mitchel, Sarah II, 599
Mitchel, Sarah II, 614
Mitchel, Sarah II, 625
Mitchel, Sarah II, 638
Mitchel, Sarah IV, 50
Mitchel, Sarah V, 517
Mitchel, Sarah V, 541
Mitchel, Selah I, 1008
Mitchel, Selah I, 1011
Mitchel, Stephen VI, 950
Mitchel, Susanna IV, 50
Mitchel, Susannah VI, 424
Mitchel, Thomas II, 638
Mitchel, Thomas II, 1016
Mitchel, Thomas IV, 50
Mitchel, Thomas VI, 424
Mitchel, Wm. IV, 488
Mitchel-Ellicott, Mary VI, 782
Mitchell Ellicott, Mary VI, 654
Mitchell, ??? III, 49
Mitchell, ??? III, 203
Mitchell, ??? III, 232
Mitchell, ??? III, 427
Mitchell, ??? III, 472
Mitchell, A. C. IV, 253
Mitchell, Abel IV, 741
Mitchell, Abner III, 232
Mitchell, Abraham II, 396
Mitchell, Abraham II, 527
Mitchell, Abraham II, 529
Mitchell, Abraham II, 599
Mitchell, Abraham III, 126
Mitchell, Abraham III, 232
Mitchell, Abram II, 396
Mitchell, Acquilla VI, 963
Mitchell, Ada II, 810
Mitchell, Ada II, 836
Mitchell, Ada II, 900
Mitchell, Ada B. II, 887
Mitchell, Ada B. II, 900
Mitchell, Ada Begley II, 810
Mitchell, Adam VI, 808
Mitchell, Adam VI, 840
Mitchell, Addie IV, 253
Mitchell, Albert III, 305
Mitchell, Albert G. VI, 983
Mitchell, Alice Cummins IV, 1330
Mitchell, Alice J. III, 490
Mitchell, Alice J. III, 501
Mitchell, Allen II, 1043
Mitchell, Allen R. II, 836
Mitchell, Allen R. II, 885
Mitchell, Allen R. II, 887
Mitchell, Allen R. II, 900
Mitchell, Allen R., Jr. II, 810
Mitchell, Allen Robert II, 810
Mitchell, Amelia II, 713
Mitchell, Amelia II, 756
Mitchell, Amelia III, 232
Mitchell, Amelia Frances VI, 976
Mitchell, Amos II, 599
Mitchell, Andrew III, 232
Mitchell, Ann II, 599
Mitchell, Ann II, 1016
Mitchell, Ann III, 77
Mitchell, Ann IV, 42
Mitchell, Ann VI, 871
Mitchell, Ann VI, 963
Mitchell, Ann D. VI, 963
Mitchell, Ann E. VI, 964
Mitchell, Ann Eliza II, 810
Mitchell, Ann Eliza II, 1056
Mitchell, Ann Elizabeth III, 232
Mitchell, Ann H. VI, 932
Mitchell, Ann Lucy VI, 963
Mitchell, Anna II, 810
Mitchell, Anna II, 854
Mitchell, Anna II, 900
Mitchell, Anna J. II, 900
Mitchell, Anna M. II, 900
Mitchell, Anna Martha II, 810
Mitchell, Appic I, 311
Mitchell, Arch VI, 840
Mitchell, Becca I, 311
Mitchell, Benjamin II, 396
Mitchell, Benjamin II, 810
Mitchell, Benjamin VI, 881
Mitchell, Benjamin VI, 962
Mitchell, Benjamin VI, 963
Mitchell, Benjamin N. VI, 963
Mitchell, Benjamin N. VI, 964
Mitchell, Benjn. VI, 964
Mitchell, Betsey VI, 840
Mitchell, Betsey VI, 895
Mitchell, Betsey VI, 963
Mitchell, Beulah II, 810
Mitchell, Beulah L. II, 885
Mitchell, Beulah L. II, 900
Mitchell, C. VI, 960
Mitchell, Caroline II, 1070
Mitchell, Caroline II, 1076
Mitchell, Caroline H. III, 203
Mitchell, Caroline L. III, 232
Mitchell, Catharine VI, 964
Mitchell, Catharine M. II, 836
Mitchell, Catharine M. II, 900
Mitchell, Catherine III, 232
Mitchell, Catherine M. II, 810
Mitchell, Catherine S. VI, 845
Mitchell, Charity I, 311
Mitchell, Charles III, 427
Mitchell, Charles VI, 964
Mitchell, Charles L. VI, 963
Mitchell, Charles L. VI, 974
Mitchell, Charles M. II, 900
Mitchell, Charles S. VI, 943
Mitchell, Charles W. II, 900
Mitchell, Charles W. II, 1056
Mitchell, Charlotte V, 379
Mitchell, Charlotte Barnard
II, 810
Mitchell, Charlotte C. VI, 925
Mitchell, Chas. W. II, 810
Mitchell, Chas. W. II, 835
Mitchell, Chas. W. II, 900
Mitchell, Cora IV, 253
Mitchell, Daisy IV, 1217
Mitchell, Daniel VI, 871
Mitchell, Daniel VI, 874
Mitchell, Daniel VI, 933
Mitchell, Daniel VI, 963
Mitchell, Daniel Thornton
III, 232
Mitchell, Daniel, Jr. VI, 998
Mitchell, David III, 232
Mitchell, David IV, 343
Mitchell, David VI, 871
Mitchell, David VI, 897
Mitchell, David VI, 963
Mitchell, David T. II, 900
Mitchell, Deborah II, 396
Mitchell, Delia III, 232
Mitchell, Delia III, 326
Mitchell, Dorcas V, 193
Mitchell, Dr. Thomas P. VI, 963
Mitchell, Drewellen VI, 964
Mitchell, Edith II, 790
Mitchell, Edith III, 261
Mitchell, Edith IV, 741
Mitchell, Edith L. IV, 741
Mitchell, Edith M. II, 887
Mitchell, Edith M. II, 900
Mitchell, Edith Maud II, 810
Mitchell, Edward VI, 936
Mitchell, Edward VI, 965
Mitchell, Edward O. P. VI, 963
Mitchell, Edwin II, 810
Mitchell, Edwin II, 900
Mitchell, Edwin III, 232

Mitchell, Edy VI, 837
Mitchell, Eleanor VI, 901
Mitchell, Elenor VI, 987
Mitchell, Elijah VI, 963
Mitchell, Elijah VI, 980
Mitchell, Elijah VI, 1000
Mitchell, Eliz. III, 427
Mitchell, Eliza II, 900
Mitchell, Eliza V, 922
Mitchell, Eliza VI, 981
Mitchell, Eliza VI, 1019
Mitchell, Eliza A. VI, 963
Mitchell, Eliza Ann II, 1056
Mitchell, Eliza V. VI, 1002
Mitchell, Eliza. III, 232
Mitchell, Elizabeth II, 957
Mitchell, Elizabeth II, 958
Mitchell, Elizabeth II, 1016
Mitchell, Elizabeth III, 232
Mitchell, Elizabeth III, 322
Mitchell, Elizabeth III, 427
Mitchell, Elizabeth III, 439
Mitchell, Elizabeth IV, 741
Mitchell, Elizabeth VI, 535
Mitchell, Elizabeth VI, 555
Mitchell, Elizabeth VI, 767
Mitchell, Elizabeth VI, 808
Mitchell, Elizabeth VI, 840
Mitchell, Elizabeth VI, 894
Mitchell, Elizabeth VI, 900
Mitchell, Elizabeth VI, 902
Mitchell, Elizabeth VI, 909
Mitchell, Elizabeth VI, 963
Mitchell, Elizabeth VI, 976
Mitchell, Elizabeth A. VI, 874
Mitchell, Elizabeth T. III, 382
Mitchell, Ellwood II, 900
Mitchell, Elwood II, 873
Mitchell, Elwood II, 900
Mitchell, Emily II, 847
Mitchell, Emily II, 900
Mitchell, Emily VI, 881
Mitchell, Emily VI, 963
Mitchell, Enos VI, 903
Mitchell, Enos VI, 933
Mitchell, Ephraim J. VI, 963
Mitchell, Estella S. V, 517
Mitchell, Esther II, 396
Mitchell, Esther II, 527
Mitchell, Esther II, 599
Mitchell, Esther II, 645
Mitchell, Esther III, 126
Mitchell, Esther III, 232
Mitchell, Fanny H. II, 900
Mitchell, Ferris A. III, 232
Mitchell, Ferris A. III, 305
Mitchell, Flora IV, 1330
Mitchell, Frances II, 810
Mitchell, Frances II, 835
Mitchell, Frances II, 900
Mitchell, Frances II, 1016
Mitchell, Frances II, 1056
Mitchell, Frances VI, 850
Mitchell, Frances VI, 894
Mitchell, Frances VI, 933
Mitchell, Frances VI, 958
Mitchell, Frances VI, 962
Mitchell, Frances G. VI, 963
Mitchell, Frances R. VI, 893
Mitchell, Francis II, 864
Mitchell, Francis II, 900
Mitchell, Francis III, 232
Mitchell, Frank III, 232
Mitchell, Frank III, 233
Mitchell, Franklin III, 232
Mitchell, Franklin V, 922
Mitchell, Franklin V, 928
Mitchell, Geo. W. V, 193
Mitchell, George II, 1016
Mitchell, George V, 193
Mitchell, George Justice, Jr. II, 810
Mitchell, George L. II, 885
Mitchell, George L. II, 900
Mitchell, George Lippincott II, 810
Mitchell, George R. II, 810
Mitchell, Goode B. VI, 883
Mitchell, Gordon III, 427
Mitchell, Gove II, 810
Mitchell, Gove II, 814
Mitchell, Gove II, 836
Mitchell, Gove II, 854
Mitchell, Gove II, 873
Mitchell, Gove II, 900
Mitchell, Gove II, 965
Mitchell, Gove II, 1043
Mitchell, Greer VI, 874
Mitchell, Hannah II, 396
Mitchell, Hannah II, 599
Mitchell, Hannah II, 790
Mitchell, Hannah II, 965
Mitchell, Hannah II, 1016
Mitchell, Hannah III, 427
Mitchell, Hannah V, 922
Mitchell, Hannah VI, 535
Mitchell, Hannah VI, 767
Mitchell, Hannah VI, 883
Mitchell, Hannah VI, 963
Mitchell, Hannah D. III, 232
Mitchell, Hannah D. III, 233
Mitchell, Hannah D. III, 293
Mitchell, Hannah D. V, 586
Mitchell, Hannah D. V, 922
Mitchell, Hannah S. III, 233
Mitchell, Hannah W. III, 305
Mitchell, Hans II, 864
Mitchell, Hans II, 900
Mitchell, Harriet II, 1016
Mitchell, Harriet S. VI, 933
Mitchell, Helen II, 138
Mitchell, Henrietta II, 713
Mitchell, Henrietta II, 756
Mitchell, Henrietta III, 232
Mitchell, Henry III, 232
Mitchell, Henry III, 305
Mitchell, Henry III, 382
Mitchell, Henry III, 389
Mitchell, Henry V, 922
Mitchell, Henry VI, 874
Mitchell, Henry VI, 958
Mitchell, Henry VI, 963
Mitchell, Horace G. II, 810
Mitchell, Horace G. II, 900
Mitchell, Howard E. II, 810
Mitchell, I. Allen II, 854
Mitchell, I. Allen II, 900
Mitchell, Ignatious VI, 963
Mitchell, Ignatius VI, 963
Mitchell, Ignatius VI, 987
Mitchell, Isaac IV, 522
Mitchell, Isaac IV, 541
Mitchell, Isaac VI, 883
Mitchell, Isaac VI, 963
Mitchell, Isabel IV, 741
Mitchell, J. D. VI, 966
Mitchell, J. D. VI, 976
Mitchell, J. Howard II, 810
Mitchell, J. Howard II, 885
Mitchell, J. Howard II, 900
Mitchell, Jabez VI, 932
Mitchell, Jabez VI, 963
Mitchell, Jacob D. VI, 872
Mitchell, Jacob D. VI, 878
Mitchell, Jacob D. VI, 890
Mitchell, Jacob D. VI, 893
Mitchell, Jacob D. VI, 896
Mitchell, Jacob D. VI, 912
Mitchell, Jacob D. VI, 913
Mitchell, Jacob D. VI, 914
Mitchell, Jacob D. VI, 915
Mitchell, Jacob D. VI, 916
Mitchell, Jacob D. VI, 919
Mitchell, Jacob D. VI, 920
Mitchell, Jacob D. VI, 923
Mitchell, Jacob D. VI, 924
Mitchell, Jacob D. VI, 934
Mitchell, Jacob D. VI, 935
Mitchell, Jacob D. VI, 943
Mitchell, Jacob D. VI, 949
Mitchell, Jacob D. VI, 957
Mitchell, Jacob D. VI, 958
Mitchell, Jacob D. VI, 966
Mitchell, Jacob D. VI, 967
Mitchell, Jacob D. VI, 972
Mitchell, Jacob D. VI, 974
Mitchell, Jacob D. VI, 976
Mitchell, Jacob D. VI, 984
Mitchell, Jacob D. VI, 985
Mitchell, Jacob D. VI, 986
Mitchell, Jacob D. VI, 987
Mitchell, Jacob D. VI, 989
Mitchell, Jacob D. VI, 1000
Mitchell, Jacob D. VI, 1003
Mitchell, Jacob D. VI, 1004
Mitchell, Jacob D. VI, 1011
Mitchell, Jacob D. VI, 1012
Mitchell, Jacob D. VI, 1018
Mitchell, James II, 396
Mitchell, James III, 232
Mitchell, James III, 412
Mitchell, James III, 427
Mitchell, James VI, 840
Mitchell, James VI, 869
Mitchell, James VI, 870
Mitchell, James VI, 872
Mitchell, James VI, 873
Mitchell, James VI, 876
Mitchell, James VI, 877
Mitchell, James VI, 882
Mitchell, James VI, 884
Mitchell, James VI, 885
Mitchell, James VI, 889
Mitchell, James VI, 890
Mitchell, James VI, 891
Mitchell, James VI, 892
Mitchell, James VI, 893
Mitchell, James VI, 895
Mitchell, James VI, 896
Mitchell, James VI, 897
Mitchell, James VI, 898
Mitchell, James VI, 899
Mitchell, James VI, 900
Mitchell, James VI, 901
Mitchell, James VI, 902
Mitchell, James VI, 903
Mitchell, James VI, 906
Mitchell, James VI, 907
Mitchell, James VI, 908
Mitchell, James VI, 909
Mitchell, James VI, 910
Mitchell, James VI, 911
Mitchell, James VI, 912
Mitchell, James VI, 913
Mitchell, James VI, 916
Mitchell, James VI, 917
Mitchell, James VI, 919
Mitchell, James VI, 922
Mitchell, James VI, 923
Mitchell, James VI, 925
Mitchell, James VI, 926
Mitchell, James VI, 929
Mitchell, James VI, 931
Mitchell, James VI, 932
Mitchell, James VI, 933
Mitchell, James VI, 935
Mitchell, James VI, 936
Mitchell, James VI, 937
Mitchell, James VI, 939
Mitchell, James VI, 941
Mitchell, James VI, 942
Mitchell, James VI, 943
Mitchell, James VI, 946
Mitchell, James VI, 947
Mitchell, James VI, 949
Mitchell, James VI, 950
Mitchell, James VI, 951
Mitchell, James VI, 954
Mitchell, James VI, 957
Mitchell, James VI, 958
Mitchell, James VI, 961
Mitchell, James VI, 962
Mitchell, James VI, 963
Mitchell, James VI, 966
Mitchell, James VI, 967
Mitchell, James VI, 968
Mitchell, James VI, 970
Mitchell, James VI, 971
Mitchell, James VI, 972
Mitchell, James VI, 974
Mitchell, James VI, 976
Mitchell, James VI, 978
Mitchell, James VI, 979
Mitchell, James VI, 980
Mitchell, James VI, 981
Mitchell, James VI, 982
Mitchell, James VI, 983
Mitchell, James VI, 984
Mitchell, James VI, 986
Mitchell, James VI, 987
Mitchell, James VI, 988
Mitchell, James VI, 989
Mitchell, James VI, 990
Mitchell, James VI, 991
Mitchell, James VI, 992
Mitchell, James VI, 996
Mitchell, James VI, 997
Mitchell, James VI, 998
Mitchell, James VI, 999
Mitchell, James VI, 1000
Mitchell, James VI, 1001
Mitchell, James VI, 1003
Mitchell, James VI, 1004
Mitchell, James VI, 1006
Mitchell, James VI, 1007
Mitchell, James VI, 1008
Mitchell, James VI, 1009
Mitchell, James VI, 1010
Mitchell, James VI, 1011
Mitchell, James VI, 1012
Mitchell, James VI, 1014
Mitchell, James VI, 1016
Mitchell, James VI, 1017
Mitchell, James VI, 1018
Mitchell, James VI, 1019
Mitchell, James VI, 1021
Mitchell, James VI, 1022
Mitchell, James H. VI, 963
Mitchell, James Harvey VI, 963
Mitchell, James R. VI, 893
Mitchell, James R. VI, 943
Mitchell, James, Sr. VI, 1002
Mitchell, Jane III, 405
Mitchell, Jane III, 427
Mitchell, Jane VI, 795
Mitchell, Jane VI, 963
Mitchell, Jane E. VI, 983
Mitchell, Jane T. III, 232
Mitchell, Jeannette III, 232
Mitchell, Jeannette III, 305
Mitchell, Jesse V, 265
Mitchell, Jesse VI, 873
Mitchell, Jesse VI, 934
Mitchell, Jesse VI, 961
Mitchell, Jesse VI, 962
Mitchell, Jesse VI, 963
Mitchell, Jesse VI, 1014
Mitchell, Jethro III, 232
Mitchell, Jethro V, 922
Mitchell, Jethro, Jr. III, 232
Mitchell, Jethro, Jr. V, 922
Mitchell, Joann VI, 976
Mitchell, John II, 191
Mitchell, John II, 242
Mitchell, John II, 396
Mitchell, John II, 1016
Mitchell, John III, 305
Mitchell, John IV, 1258
Mitchell, John VI, 662
Mitchell, John VI, 739
Mitchell, John VI, 752
Mitchell, John VI, 767
Mitchell, John VI, 855
Mitchell, John VI, 876
Mitchell, John VI, 883
Mitchell, John VI, 897
Mitchell, John VI, 911
Mitchell, John VI, 923
Mitchell, John VI, 962
Mitchell, John VI, 963
Mitchell, John VI, 964
Mitchell, John A. VI, 964
Mitchell, John Allen II, 965
Mitchell, John Allen II, 1070
Mitchell, John Allen II, 1076
Mitchell, John C. III, 232
Mitchell, John H. VI, 964
Mitchell, John Howard, Jr. II, 810
Mitchell, John Joseph III, 305
Mitchell, John P. VI, 899
Mitchell, John P. VI, 943
Mitchell, John, Jr. VI, 886
Mitchell, John, Jr. VI, 894
Mitchell, John, Jr. VI, 963
Mitchell, John, Sr. VI, 963
Mitchell, Jonathan II, 1016
Mitchell, Jonathan B. II, 900
Mitchell, Jonathan B. II, 1056
Mitchell, Jonathan Buckman II, 810
Mitchell, Jonathan W. II, 1016
Mitchell, Joseph II, 396
Mitchell, Joseph II, 958
Mitchell, Joseph II, 965
Mitchell, Joseph II, 1016
Mitchell, Joseph Barnard II, 810
Mitchell, Joseph D. VI, 880
Mitchell, Joseph D. VI, 891
Mitchell, Joseph R. IV, 741
Mitchell, Joseph R. IV, 779
Mitchell, Josephine B. II, 846
Mitchell, Josephine B. II, 900
Mitchell, Joshua II, 396
Mitchell, Joshua II, 599
Mitchell, Joshua II, 810
Mitchell, Joshua II, 835
Mitchell, Joshua II, 900
Mitchell, Joshua II, 1016
Mitchell, Joshua II, 1043
Mitchell, Joshua II, 1056
Mitchell, Joshua III, 305
Mitchell, Joshua B. III, 305
Mitchell, Joshua W. III, 305
Mitchell, Jubal VI, 963
Mitchell, Jubal VI, 1000
Mitchell, Judith VI, 822
Mitchell, Judith VI, 823
Mitchell, Judith VI, 958
Mitchell, Judith VI, 963
Mitchell, Julia Ann VI, 893
Mitchell, Kitty VI, 962
Mitchell, Laban IV, 541
Mitchell, Latham III, 427
Mitchell, Lavina E. VI, 964
Mitchell, Lewis C. VI, 880
Mitchell, Lewis C. VI, 891
Mitchell, Lewis C. VI, 958
Mitchell, Lewis C. VI, 964
Mitchell, Lida IV, 1258
Mitchell, Lillie Estella I, 617
Mitchell, Lizzie V, 698
Mitchell, Lockey J. VI, 963
Mitchell, Louisa II, 900
Mitchell, Louisa VI, 840
Mitchell, Louise II, 810
Mitchell, Lucia II, 1016
Mitchell, Lucie M. VI, 964
Mitchell, Lucretia VI, 845
Mitchell, Lucretia M. II, 810
Mitchell, Lucretia M. II, 835
Mitchell, Lucretia M. II, 900
Mitchell, Lucy II, 965
Mitchell, Lucy II, 1001
Mitchell, Lucy II, 1016
Mitchell, Lucy VI, 963
Mitchell, Lucy VI, 997
Mitchell, Lucy M. VI, 963
Mitchell, Lydia II, 396
Mitchell, Lydia II, 946
Mitchell, Lydia IV, 522
Mitchell, Lydia IV, 1258
Mitchell, Lydia VI, 963
Mitchell, Lydia E. IV, 343
Mitchell, Lydia P. IV, 522
Mitchell, Lydia P. IV, 541
Mitchell, M. D. II, 873
Mitchell, M. Emily II, 900
Mitchell, Mahlon M. II, 1076
Mitchell, Mahlon Milnor II, 1
Mitchell, Mahlon Milnor II, 1
Mitchell, Maine III, 275
Mitchell, Margaret VI, 877
Mitchell, Margaret VI, 933
Mitchell, Margaret C. VI, 893
Mitchell, Margaret H. VI, 893
Mitchell, Margaret M. VI, 871
Mitchell, Marget VI, 897
Mitchell, Maria II, 900
Mitchell, Maria Louisa II, 900
Mitchell, Maria Louisa III, 30
Mitchell, Maria W. VI, 964
Mitchell, Marjory VI, 962
Mitchell, Martha VI, 840
Mitchell, Martha VI, 889
Mitchell, Martha VI, 893
Mitchell, Martha VI, 900
Mitchell, Martha VI, 963
Mitchell, Martha VI, 964
Mitchell, Martha A. VI, 963
Mitchell, Martha Ann II, 599
Mitchell, Martha Ann II, 637
Mitchell, Martha Ann VI, 891
Mitchell, Martha D. VI, 992
Mitchell, Martha M. VI, 952
Mitchell, Mary I, 311
Mitchell, Mary II, 396
Mitchell, Mary II, 529
Mitchell, Mary II, 599
Mitchell, Mary II, 819
Mitchell, Mary II, 965
Mitchell, Mary II, 1015
Mitchell, Mary II, 1016
Mitchell, Mary III, 232
Mitchell, Mary III, 305
Mitchell, Mary III, 405
Mitchell, Mary III, 412
Mitchell, Mary III, 424
Mitchell, Mary III, 427
Mitchell, Mary IV, 253
Mitchell, Mary VI, 739
Mitchell, Mary VI, 845
Mitchell, Mary VI, 877
Mitchell, Mary VI, 880
Mitchell, Mary VI, 903
Mitchell, Mary VI, 936
Mitchell, Mary VI, 958
Mitchell, Mary VI, 963
Mitchell, Mary VI, 969
Mitchell, Mary VI, 1014
Mitchell, Mary A. II, 810
Mitchell, Mary A. IV, 253
Mitchell, Mary Ann II, 810
Mitchell, Mary Ann II, 1087
Mitchell, Mary Ann II, 1088
Mitchell, Mary B. VI, 913
Mitchell, Mary C. VI, 929
Mitchell, Mary E. II, 885
Mitchell, Mary E. II, 900
Mitchell, Mary Ella II, 810
Mitchell, Mary Emily II, 810
Mitchell, Mary Jane VI, 964
Mitchell, Mary L. III, 490
Mitchell, Mary M. VI, 916
Mitchell, Mary S. II, 949
Mitchell, Mary S. II, 1087
Mitchell, Mary S. II, 1088
Mitchell, Mary V. II, 900
Mitchell, Mary V. VI, 964
Mitchell, Maryann II, 900
Mitchell, Mathew VI, 535
Mitchell, Mathew VI, 767
Mitchell, Matilda III, 305
Mitchell, Matilda VI, 998
Mitchell, Matthew III, 232

nell, Matthew VI, 767
hell, Melcena V, 379
hell, Mercides V, 307
hell, Mercy III, 232
hell, Mercy V, 922
nell, Mercy Ann II, 1056
hell, Mercy Ann II, 1059
hell, Meriot III, 232
hell, Mildred VI, 945
hell, Milley VI, 963
hell, Milley VI, 980
hell, Millicent VI, 964
hell, Minnie III, 232
hell, Minot III, 326
hell, Miriam III, 427
hell, Moses II, 756
hell, Mrs. Flora IV, 1330
hell, Myra V, 922
hell, Myra VI, 840
hell, Myron Colyer III, 490
hell, Myron Colyer III, 501
hell, Nancy VI, 808
hell, Nancy VI, 840
hell, Nancy VI, 874
hell, Nancy VI, 936
hell, Nancy VI, 963
hell, Nancy VI, 1017
hell, Nancy D. VI, 891
hell, Nancy H. VI, 963
hell, Nantucket Mary III, 331
chell, Nelly VI, 963
chell, Obed II, 713
chell, Obed II, 756
chell, Obed III, 232
chell, P. VI, 893
chell, Parthena Jane VI, 963
chell, Patience II, 810
chell, Patience J. II, 900
chell, Patton VI, 840
chell, Paulina Ann VI, 964
chell, Pearson II, 191
chell, Pearson II, 242
chell, Pearson II, 599
chell, Pearson II, 965
chell, Pearson II, 1016
chell, Peggy VI, 963
chell, Peirson II, 1043
chell, Peleg II, 1087
chell, Peleg II, 1088
chell, Pernicy I, 311
chell, Pheba I, 311
chell, Phebe III, 382
chell, Phebe B. III, 305
chell, Phebe H. II, 756
chell, Phebe H. III, 232
tchell, Philip J. II, 900
tchell, Pierson II, 810
tchell, Pierson II, 900
tchell, Pierson II, 1070
tchell, Pierson II, 1076
tchell, Pleasant VI, 535
tchell, Pleasant VI, 731
tchell, Pleasant VI, 767
tchell, Polly VI, 840
tchell, Polly VI, 897
tchell, Polly VI, 963
tchell, Polly E. VI, 1009
tchell, Poly Enos VI, 970
itchell, Prethia VI, 963
itchell, Priscilla III, 405
itchell, Priscilla III, 427
itchell, Rachel III, 232
itchell, Rachel V, 922
itchell, Reading II, 1056
itchell, Reading B. II, 1076
itchell, Rebecca II, 242
itchell, Rebecca II, 396
itchell, Rebecca II, 810
itchell, Rebecca II, 814
itchell, Rebecca II, 873
itchell, Rebecca II, 900
itchell, Rebecca II, 1016
itchell, Rebecca II, 1043
itchell, Rebecca V, 1010
itchell, Rebecca Allen II, 814
itchell, Rebeccah II, 191
itchell, Rebeccah II, 242
itchell, Rebeccah V, 1010
itchell, Rebeckah II, 396
itchell, Rebeckah II, 599
itchell, Rebeckah II, 965
itchell, Rebeckah VI, 840
itchell, Reese D. VI, 933
itchell, Rev. James VI, 943
itchell, Richard II, 599
itchell, Richard II, 1015
itchell, Richard II, 1016
itchell, Richard II, 1026
itchell, Richard H. III, 232
itchell, Richard, Jr. II, 1016
Mitchell, Ro. C. VI, 878
Mitchell, Ro. C. VI, 892
Mitchell, Ro. C. VI, 898
Mitchell, Ro. C. VI, 917
Mitchell, Ro. C. VI, 919
Mitchell, Ro. C. VI, 943
Mitchell, Ro. C. VI, 949
Mitchell, Ro. C. VI, 951
Mitchell, Ro. C. VI, 952
Mitchell, Ro. C. VI, 970
Mitchell, Ro. C. VI, 972
Mitchell, Ro. C. VI, 975
Mitchell, Ro. C. VI, 987
Mitchell, Ro. C. VI, 1004
Mitchell, Ro. C. VI, 1018
Mitchell, Robert III, 405
Mitchell, Robert III, 424
Mitchell, Robert III, 427
Mitchell, Robert VI, 877
Mitchell, Robert VI, 895
Mitchell, Robert VI, 921
Mitchell, Robert VI, 963
Mitchell, Robert VI, 964
Mitchell, Robert VI, 970
Mitchell, Robert VI, 996
Mitchell, Robert VI, 1018
Mitchell, Robert C. VI, 890
Mitchell, Robert C. VI, 902
Mitchell, Robert C. VI, 908
Mitchell, Robert C. VI, 919
Mitchell, Robert C. VI, 943
Mitchell, Robert C. VI, 949
Mitchell, Robert C. VI, 963
Mitchell, Robert C. VI, 1005
Mitchell, Robert M. VI, 840
Mitchell, Robert R. V, 922
Mitchell, Robert W. VI, 964
Mitchell, Robt. C. VI, 903
Mitchell, Robt. C. VI, 935
Mitchell, Robt. O. VI, 921
Mitchell, Rowland G. III, 232
Mitchell, Rowland G. V, 922
Mitchell, Sally VI, 855
Mitchell, Sally VI, 963
Mitchell, Sally VI, 1000
Mitchell, Sally Ann VI, 964
Mitchell, Sally P. VI, 934
Mitchell, Saml. VI, 968
Mitchell, Saml. P. VI, 963
Mitchell, Saml. P. VI, 968
Mitchell, Samuel II, 1016
Mitchell, Samuel VI, 840
Mitchell, Samuel VI, 893
Mitchell, Samuel VI, 911
Mitchell, Samuel VI, 917
Mitchell, Samuel VI, 943
Mitchell, Samuel VI, 961
Mitchell, Samuel VI, 963
Mitchell, Samuel VI, 966
Mitchell, Samuel VI, 989
Mitchell, Samuel VI, 1005
Mitchell, Samuel VI, 1009
Mitchell, Samuel VI, 1019
Mitchell, Samuel A. III, 305
Mitchell, Samuel K. V, 379
Mitchell, Samuel M. VI, 880
Mitchell, Samuel M. VI, 963
Mitchell, Samuel S. III, 232
Mitchell, Sarah II, 396
Mitchell, Sarah II, 504
Mitchell, Sarah II, 529
Mitchell, Sarah II, 599
Mitchell, Sarah II, 796
Mitchell, Sarah II, 813
Mitchell, Sarah II, 873
Mitchell, Sarah II, 900
Mitchell, Sarah II, 965
Mitchell, Sarah III, 49
Mitchell, Sarah III, 126
Mitchell, Sarah III, 232
Mitchell, Sarah III, 424
Mitchell, Sarah III, 427
Mitchell, Sarah V, 922
Mitchell, Sarah VI, 871
Mitchell, Sarah VI, 909
Mitchell, Sarah VI, 963
Mitchell, Sarah VI, 964
Mitchell, Sarah Ann II, 900
Mitchell, Sarah Ann VI, 943
Mitchell, Sarah Ann VI, 964
Mitchell, Sarah Ann VI, 983
Mitchell, Sarah B. II, 138
Mitchell, Sarah B. VI, 963
Mitchell, Sarah C. VI, 968
Mitchell, Sarah D. VI, 984
Mitchell, Sarah E. IV, 741
Mitchell, Sarah E. IV, 779
Mitchell, Sarah F. V, 922
Mitchell, Sarah J. L. II, 153
Mitchell, Sarah Jane VI, 964
Mitchell, Sarah M. VI, 881
Mitchell, Sarah S. V, 922
Mitchell, Sarah T. III, 427
Mitchell, Sarah, Jr. V, 922
Mitchell, Sarah, Jr. V, 928
Mitchell, Silas H. III, 305
Mitchell, Simon I, 311
Mitchell, Sinah VI, 963
Mitchell, Siner VI, 963
Mitchell, Sinor P. VI, 968
Mitchell, Sophia VI, 837
Mitchell, Spicey VI, 840
Mitchell, Stephen VI, 898
Mitchell, Stephen VI, 962
Mitchell, Stephen VI, 963
Mitchell, Stephen VI, 1017
Mitchell, Stephen A. VI, 964
Mitchell, Stephen E. VI, 916
Mitchell, Stephen E. VI, 952
Mitchell, Susan II, 900
Mitchell, Susan III, 232
Mitchell, Susan A. II, 900
Mitchell, Susan Matilda III, 305
Mitchell, Susanna II, 396
Mitchell, Susanna II, 599
Mitchell, Susanna II, 689
Mitchell, Susanna VI, 839
Mitchell, Susannah II, 891
Mitchell, Susannah II, 900
Mitchell, Susannah VI, 963
Mitchell, Susannah Wilson II, 900
Mitchell, Tacey II, 1070
Mitchell, Tacey II, 1076
Mitchell, Tacy II, 854
Mitchell, Tacy II, 900
Mitchell, Tacy VI, 662
Mitchell, Tacy VI, 739
Mitchell, Tacy VI, 752
Mitchell, Tacy VI, 758
Mitchell, Tacy VI, 767
Mitchell, Tarplin R. VI, 964
Mitchell, Tarpley VI, 981
Mitchell, Tarply VI, 983
Mitchell, Tellitha VI, 911
Mitchell, Thomas II, 396
Mitchell, Thomas II, 504
Mitchell, Thomas II, 599
Mitchell, Thomas II, 965
Mitchell, Thomas II, 1001
Mitchell, Thomas II, 1016
Mitchell, Thomas V, 922
Mitchell, Thomas VI, 934
Mitchell, Thomas VI, 998
Mitchell, Thomas A. VI, 964
Mitchell, Thomas D. VI, 958
Mitchell, Thomas D. VI, 1008
Mitchell, Thomas G. III, 232
Mitchell, Thomas P. VI, 984
Mitchell, Thos. V, 922
Mitchell, Tzzwell VI, 1015
Mitchell, W. J. IV, 1330
Mitchell, Walter III, 232
Mitchell, Walter V, 922
Mitchell, Wd. Eunice III, 232
Mitchell, Wd. Mary VI, 519
Mitchell, Wd. Mary VI, 767
Mitchell, Wd. Phebe II, 713
Mitchell, Wd. Susannah II, 810
Mitchell, William II, 965
Mitchell, William II, 1043
Mitchell, William III, 424
Mitchell, William III, 427
Mitchell, William VI, 802
Mitchell, William VI, 840
Mitchell, William VI, 901
Mitchell, William VI, 913
Mitchell, William VI, 958
Mitchell, William VI, 963
Mitchell, William VI, 964
Mitchell, William VI, 976
Mitchell, William C. VI, 963
Mitchell, William C. VI, 964
Mitchell, William C. VI, 1009
Mitchell, William H. VI, 964
Mitchell, Willie IV, 253
Mitchell, Wm. IV, 1330
Mitchell, Wm. F. III, 232
Mitchell, Wm. H. II, 138
Mitchell, Wm. H. III, 490
Mitchell, Wm. Reynolds Keeney II, 810
Mitchell-Ellicott, Mary VI, 668
Mitchell-Ellicott, Mary VI, 714
Mitchell-Ellicott, Mary VI, 749
Mitchell-Ellicott, Mary VI, 756
Mitchell-Ellicott, Mary VI, 758
Mitchell-Ellicott, Mary VI, 759
Mitchell-Ellivott, Mary VI, 664
Mitchem, Presilla VI, 840
Mitchem, William VI, 840
Mitchen, Dosha VI, 964
Mitchen, Lucy VI, 964
Mitchen, Micajah VI, 964
Mitchen, Samuel VI, 964
Mitchen, Thomas VI, 872
Mitchener, Alice V, 193
Mitchener, Alice V, 517
Mitchener, Barak IV, 421
Mitchener, Benjamin II, 599
Mitchener, Betsy V, 761
Mitchener, Chas. H. II, 898
Mitchener, David H. IV, 541
Mitchener, Elmor IV, 541
Mitchener, Esther IV, 102
Mitchener, Esther, Jr. IV, 102
Mitchener, Ethel V, 192
Mitchener, Ethel V, 193
Mitchener, Ezra II, 599
Mitchener, Florence V, 193
Mitchener, Hannah II, 599
Mitchener, Hannah IV, 102
Mitchener, Henrietta R. II, 809
Mitchener, Henrietta R. II, 898
Mitchener, Horace V, 193
Mitchener, Isaac IV, 541
Mitchener, Jacob L. V, 922
Mitchener, Jacob Lukens IV, 1173
Mitchener, John II, 599
Mitchener, John IV, 102
Mitchener, John IV, 541
Mitchener, John A. I, 214
Mitchener, John Waterman IV, 541
Mitchener, Jonathan IV, 102
Mitchener, Kinsey IV, 541
Mitchener, Lawrence V, 192
Mitchener, Lawrence V, 193
Mitchener, Louisa S. II, 898
Mitchener, Lydia IV, 102
Mitchener, Lydia IV, 109
Mitchener, Lydia IV, 1173
Mitchener, Lydia V, 922
Mitchener, Lydia Ann IV, 541
Mitchener, Lydia B. IV, 421
Mitchener, Lydia S. II, 809
Mitchener, Lydia S. II, 898
Mitchener, Mahlon II, 599
Mitchener, Margaret V, 192
Mitchener, Margaret V, 193
Mitchener, Martha V, 99
Mitchener, Mary Ann IV, 541
Mitchener, Mary C. IV, 541
Mitchener, Mary Evaline IV, 541
Mitchener, Mary P. V, 761
Mitchener, Mordecai IV, 102
Mitchener, Naomi IV, 102
Mitchener, Nathan S. IV, 541
Mitchener, Neomi IV, 102
Mitchener, Ollie P. I, 214
Mitchener, Rachel IV, 102
Mitchener, Rachel IV, 541
Mitchener, Rachel IV, 1173
Mitchener, Rebecca II, 599
Mitchener, Rebekah IV, 541
Mitchener, Reyner II, 809
Mitchener, Samuel V, 192
Mitchener, Samuel C. V, 192
Mitchener, Sarah II, 599
Mitchener, Sarah II, 612
Mitchener, Sarah Alice IV, 541
Mitchener, Thomas IV, 102
Mitchener, Thos. V, 761
Mitchener, Thurman V, 193
Mitchener, Virgo V, 193
Mitchener, Walter V, 193
Mitchener, William IV, 102
Mitchener, Wm. IV, 1173
Mitchener, Wm. Arthur IV, 541
Mitchenor, Esther, Jr. VI, 534
Mitchenor, John IV, 252
Mitchenor, Wm. VI, 534
Mitches, George II, 1016
Mitchiner, Daniel IV, 1217
Mitchiner, Samuel C. V, 192
Mitchiner, Wm. VI, 534
Mitchinor, Mahlon II, 599
Mitchner, Ethel V, 193
Mitchner, Jacob L. IV, 1153
Mitchner, Jacob L. IV, 1174
Mitchner, Jacob L. V, 922
Mitchner, Jacob Lukens IV, 1174
Mitchner, Jane IV, 488
Mitchner, John IV, 541
Mitchner, Lawrence V, 193
Mitchner, Luceta IV, 541
Mitchner, Lydia V, 922
Mitchner, Lydian IV, 1174
Mitchner, Lydien IV, 1153
Mitchner, Mary II, 395
Mitchner, Rebeckah IV, 541
Mitchner, Sarah IV, 541
Mitchoner, Benjamin II, 599
Mitchoner, Ezra II, 599
Mitchum, Elizabeth VI, 877
Mitchum, Elizabeth VI, 891
Mitchum, Macajar VI, 877
Mitfhell, Joel D. VI, 1018
Mitler, ??? V, 965
Mitten, Geo. V, 1011
Mitten, Lydia II, 242
Mitten, Margaret II, 599
Mitten, Sarah V, 1011
Mitzger, Margery VI, 426
Mitzger, Mary Jane I, 1128
Mixon, L. Simeon I, 412
Mizer, Esther I, 1159
Mizer, George M. Dallas I, 1159
MMoore, John VI, 931
Moar, Anthony II, 397
Moar, Mordecai I, 410
Moare, Elizabeth II, 397
Moare, John II, 397
Moats, Dorothy I, 411
Mobberly, Rebecca V, 365
Mobberly, Roy V, 365
Moberly, Catharine V, 698
Moberly, J. F. V, 698
Moberly, John F. V, 698
Moberly, Lydia V, 341
Moberly, Lydia V, 350
Moberly, Rebecca V, 350
Moberly, Roy V, 350
Mobley, Grace V, 193
Mobley, Jeannette V, 193
Mobly, Elizabeth VI, 965
Mobly, John VI, 965
Mochlen, Anna V, 354
Mochlenpage, Anna V, 350
Mock, Addison T. IV, 1040
Mock, Almeda V, 634
Mock, Almedia V, 634
Mock, C. S. V, 193
Mock, Cassius V, 634
Mock, Charles E. IV, 1258
Mock, Earl Frank IV, 1258
Mock, Marguerite Baird IV, 1330
Mocklenpage, Anna V, 350
Mocklenpage, August W. V, 350
Mocomb, Meribah II, 588
Mode, Hannah II, 396
Mode, Mary II, 396
Mode, Mary II, 599
Mode, Mary II, 635
Mode, Priscilla P. V, 922
Mode, Sarah II, 1016
Mode, Sarah II, 1034
Mode, William II, 396
Modlen, Bertha Ballard V, 698
Modlen, Pleasant I, 725
Modlen, Pleasant I, 731
Modlin, Ann I, 59
Modlin, Ann I, 62
Modlin, Ann I, 146
Modlin, Ann I, 725
Modlin, Ann I, 993
Modlin, Anna I, 993
Modlin, Anne I, 993
Modlin, Benjamin V, 755
Modlin, Charles I, 993
Modlin, Edmund I, 895
Modlin, George I, 993
Modlin, Hannah I, 993
Modlin, Ida I, 876
Modlin, Ida I, 895
Modlin, Jacob I, 895
Modlin, Jacob E. I, 863
Modlin, James I, 725
Modlin, Jesse I, 993
Modlin, John I, 59
Modlin, John I, 62
Modlin, John I, 725
Modlin, John I, 993
Modlin, John V, 755
Modlin, Joseph I, 726
Modlin, Leah I, 725
Modlin, Mark I, 725
Modlin, Martha I, 921
Modlin, Mary I, 863
Modlin, Mary I, 895
Modlin, Mourning I, 59
Modlin, Nathan I, 725
Modlin, Nathan I, 726
Modlin, Noah I, 863
Modlin, Noah I, 895
Modlin, Noah R. I, 895
Modlin, Peninah I, 136
Modlin, Peninah I, 146
Modlin, Samuel V, 755
Modlin, Sarah I, 408
Modlin, Sarah I, 726
Modlin, Sarah I, 993
Modlin, Shubal C. I, 863
Modlin, Shubal C. I, 895

Modlin, Thomas V, 755
Modlin, William I, 726
Modlin, William I, 993
Modling, Jesse I, 993
Modling, John I, 993
Moelling, ??? III, 82
Moelling, Sarah M. III, 82
Moelling, Sarah M. III, 232
Moelling, Theodore III, 232
Moetet, Rhoda C. IV, 1239
Moffatt, ??? III, 232
Moffatt, Abigail I, 863
Moffatt, Anthony G. III, 232
Moffatt, David L. I, 863
Moffatt, David V. I, 863
Moffatt, Dougan C. I, 863
Moffatt, Elizabeth I, 863
Moffatt, Elizabeth III, 232
Moffatt, Eugene III, 232
Moffatt, Howard A. III, 232
Moffatt, Isabella F. III, 232
Moffatt, John IV, 253
Moffatt, John L. III, 232
Moffatt, Lydia I, 863
Moffatt, Margaret IV, 253
Moffatt, Martha I, 863
Moffatt, Moses A. I, 863
Moffatt, Robert I, 863
Moffatt, Tabitha I, 863
Moffatt, Thomas I, 483
Moffatt, Wm. H. I, 863
Moffett, Amanda L. V, 193
Moffett, Anna IV, 1287
Moffett, Clara IV, 1287
Moffett, F. W. V, 193
Moffett, Francis W. V, 193
Moffett, James IV, 1287
Moffett, Mary I, 895
Moffett, Mary I, 896
Moffett, Sarah I, 895
Moffett, Sarah I, 901
Moffett, Solomon V, 265
Moffit, David I, 409
Moffit, Hannah V, 101
Moffit, Hugh I, 409
Moffit, Jeremiah V, 265
Moffit, John I, 409
Moffit, John IV, 253
Moffit, Joseph I, 409
Moffit, Libni I, 409
Moffit, Mary I, 381
Moffit, Mary V, 101
Moffit, Nathan I, 409
Moffit, Robert I, 409
Moffit, Ruth V, 265
Moffit, Sallie I, 614
Moffit, Susanna I, 402
Moffit, Susanna I, 409
Moffit, William I, 409
Moffitt, ??? I, 946
Moffitt, ??? III, 130
Moffitt, ??? III, 232
Moffitt, ??? V, 32
Moffitt, Aaron I, 483
Moffitt, Abbie T. I, 612
Moffitt, Abijah V, 853
Moffitt, Abijah V, 872
Moffitt, Achsah I, 901
Moffitt, Agnes II, 296
Moffitt, Agnes II, 297
Moffitt, Allen I, 920
Moffitt, Amey I, 470
Moffitt, Anna IV, 1287
Moffitt, Anna F. V, 853
Moffitt, Anna F. V, 866
Moffitt, Anthony G. III, 232
Moffitt, Catharine I, 382
Moffitt, Catharine I, 409
Moffitt, Charles I, 382
Moffitt, Charles I, 409
Moffitt, Charles I, 483
Moffitt, Charles V, 101
Moffitt, Charles S. I, 470
Moffitt, Charly C. I, 409
Moffitt, Colvin L. I, 863
Moffitt, Cynthia E. I, 484
Moffitt, David I, 409
Moffitt, David I, 483
Moffitt, David I, 895
Moffitt, David I, 903
Moffitt, David V. I, 895
Moffitt, David V. I, 1096
Moffitt, David Vestal I, 622
Moffitt, David, Jr. I, 483
Moffitt, Davidson I, 895
Moffitt, Dorcas III, 130
Moffitt, Dorcas III, 232
Moffitt, Eli I, 895
Moffitt, Elihu I, 895
Moffitt, Elisabeth I, 622
Moffitt, Elizabeth I, 382
Moffitt, Elizabeth I, 409
Moffitt, Elizabeth I, 895
Moffitt, Elizabeth I, 903
Moffitt, Elizabeth I, 1096
Moffitt, Elizabeth III, 232
Moffitt, Elizabeth V, 32
Moffitt, Elizabeth V, 101
Moffitt, Emma I, 920
Moffitt, Eugene III, 232
Moffitt, Faustine I, 895
Moffitt, Faustine I, 901
Moffitt, Frederic III, 232
Moffitt, Hannah I, 382
Moffitt, Hannah I, 409
Moffitt, Hannah I, 470
Moffitt, Hannah I, 483
Moffitt, Hannah I, 485
Moffitt, Hannah I, 895
Moffitt, Hannah V, 101
Moffitt, Hannah V, 250
Moffitt, Hannah V, 265
Moffitt, Hannah V, 307
Moffitt, Hannah J. I, 470
Moffitt, Hannah Jane I, 470
Moffitt, Harmon I, 459
Moffitt, Harmon I, 470
Moffitt, Harmon I, 483
Moffitt, Harmon I, 484
Moffitt, Harmon I, 485
Moffitt, Harmon L. I, 470
Moffitt, Harmon L. I, 483
Moffitt, Harmon Levi I, 470
Moffitt, Harriet I, 895
Moffitt, Harriet I, 1090
Moffitt, Harriet I, 1096
Moffitt, Harriett I, 920
Moffitt, Howard A. III, 232
Moffitt, Hugh I, 382
Moffitt, Hugh I, 409
Moffitt, Hugh I, 470
Moffitt, Hugh I, 483
Moffitt, Hugh V, 250
Moffitt, Hugh V, 265
Moffitt, Isabella F. III, 232
Moffitt, James IV, 1287
Moffitt, James V, 32
Moffitt, James A. I, 409
Moffitt, James M. I, 409
Moffitt, Jeremiah I, 409
Moffitt, Jeremiah V, 265
Moffitt, Jeremiah V, 307
Moffitt, Jesse III, 232
Moffitt, John I, 409
Moffitt, John I, 1096
Moffitt, John I, 1101
Moffitt, John I, 1128
Moffitt, John III, 232
Moffitt, John IV, 253
Moffitt, John L. III, 232
Moffitt, Joseph I, 409
Moffitt, Joseph V, 307
Moffitt, Joseph T. I, 470
Moffitt, Joshua I, 409
Moffitt, L. Elizabeth I, 922
Moffitt, Lela IV, 1330
Moffitt, Libni I, 409
Moffitt, Libni I, 423
Moffitt, Libni I, 895
Moffitt, Lizzie A. I, 409
Moffitt, Louiza I, 888
Moffitt, Louiza I, 895
Moffitt, Lydia I, 409
Moffitt, Lydia I, 426
Moffitt, Lydia I, 483
Moffitt, Lydia I, 876
Moffitt, Lydia I, 895
Moffitt, Lydia V, 853
Moffitt, Lydia V, 872
Moffitt, Lydia Elizabeth I, 874
Moffitt, Lydia Elizabeth I, 895
Moffitt, Lydia T. V, 853
Moffitt, Malinda I, 873
Moffitt, Malinda I, 895
Moffitt, Margaret I, 409
Moffitt, Margaret I, 423
Moffitt, Margaret I, 483
Moffitt, Mariam L. I, 893
Moffitt, Mariam L. I, 895
Moffitt, Martha I, 409
Moffitt, Martha I, 457
Moffitt, Martha I, 470
Moffitt, Martha I, 675
Moffitt, Martha I, 685
Moffitt, Martha I, 880
Moffitt, Martha I, 895
Moffitt, Martha I, 925
Moffitt, Martha I, 930
Moffitt, Martha E. I, 863
Moffitt, Mary I, 382
Moffitt, Mary I, 384
Moffitt, Mary I, 409
Moffitt, Mary I, 470
Moffitt, Mary I, 483
Moffitt, Mary I, 685
Moffitt, Mary I, 895
Moffitt, Mary V, 101
Moffitt, Mary L. I, 863
Moffitt, Minna B. I, 863
Moffitt, Miriam I, 409
Moffitt, Miriam I, 619
Moffitt, Miriam Launa I, 622
Moffitt, Moses A. I, 1090
Moffitt, Moses A. I, 1096
Moffitt, Mrs. Lela IV, 1330
Moffitt, Nathan I, 409
Moffitt, Nathan I, 895
Moffitt, Nathan V, 83
Moffitt, Nathan V, 101
Moffitt, Phebe I, 409
Moffitt, Presilla I, 409
Moffitt, Rachel I, 459
Moffitt, Rachel I, 760
Moffitt, Rachel I, 767
Moffitt, Rachel M. I, 470
Moffitt, Rebecca I, 409
Moffitt, Rebecca I, 470
Moffitt, Rhoda A. V, 968
Moffitt, Rhoda A. V, 973
Moffitt, Rhoda Ann V, 31
Moffitt, Rhoda Ann V, 83
Moffitt, Rhoda Ann V, 101
Moffitt, Robert I, 409
Moffitt, Robert I, 426
Moffitt, Robert I, 457
Moffitt, Robert I, 470
Moffitt, Robert I, 483
Moffitt, Robert I, 675
Moffitt, Robert I, 685
Moffitt, Robert I, 895
Moffitt, Rosannah I, 469
Moffitt, Ruth I, 409
Moffitt, Ruth V, 265
Moffitt, Samuel I, 409
Moffitt, Sarah I, 895
Moffitt, Solomon V, 265
Moffitt, Stephen I, 470
Moffitt, Stephen I, 483
Moffitt, Susanna I, 409
Moffitt, Thomas I, 470
Moffitt, Thomas I, 483
Moffitt, William I, 409
Moffitt, William I, 457
Moffitt, William I, 470
Moffitt, William I, 483
Moffitt, William I, 685
Moffitt, William A. I, 483
Moffitt, William D. I, 470
Moffitt, William Davis I, 470
Moffitt, William Tell I, 930
Moffitt, William, Sr. I, 470
Moffitt, Wilson Lee I, 930
Moffitt, Wm. I, 382
Moffitt, Wm. I, 409
Moffitt, Zeruah I, 884
Moffitt, Zeruah I, 895
Moffitt, Zimri S. I, 470
Moger, Abraham E. III, 234
Moger, Ann C. III, 232
Moger, Avis L. III, 234
Moger, Edwin III, 235
Moger, Eliza III, 234
Moger, Ezra C. III, 232
Moger, Hannah III, 232
Moger, Henry H. III, 235
Moger, John I. III, 232
Moger, Joseph III, 235
Moger, Julia Ann III, 235
Moger, Maria Ann III, 232
Moger, Nelson III, 235
Moger, Olive III, 235
Moger, Olive Ann III, 235
Moger, Seth III, 235
Moger, Simeon G. III, 232
Moger, Simmons III, 232
Moger, Simmons III, 328
Moger, Simmons G. III, 232
Moger, Simmons, Jr. III, 232
Moger, Smith III, 235
Moger, Wd. Hannah III, 328
Moher, Christian VI, 841
Moher, Frances VI, 841
Mohler, Joseph B. V, 698
Mohr, Christian VI, 830
Mohr, Mariah L. VI, 830
Mohrmyer, John V, 586
Moise, Abigail V, 463
Moise, Elizabeth V, 463
Moise, Ephraim V, 463
Moist, Emma V, 818
Moist, Laura V, 818
Molan, Daniel II, 397
Molan, James II, 397
Moland, Daniel II, 397
Moland, Elizabeth II, 599
Moland, James II, 397
Moland, Mary A. VI, 809
Moland, William N. II, 397
Moland, Wm. II, 599
Mole, Elonor II, 397
Mole, Roger II, 397
Moleneux, Ann III, 382
Moleneux, Anne III, 382
Moleneux, Benjamin III, 382
Moleneux, Henry III, 382
Moleneux, Jesse III, 382
Moleneux, Martha III, 382
Moleneux, Mary III, 382
Moleneux, Phebe III, 382
Moleneux, Royal III, 382
Moleneux, Samuel III, 382
Moleneux, Sarah III, 382
Moler, Albert V, 152
Moler, Emma L. V, 152
Moler, Etta V, 152
Moler, Ruth VI, 424
Molineaux, ??? III, 232
Molineaux, Elizabeth III, 237
Molineaux, Hannah III, 115
Molineaux, Hannah III, 237
Molineaux, Horsman III, 237
Molineaux, John III, 237
Molineaux, Joseph III, 237
Molineaux, Mary III, 237
Molineaux, Moses III, 115
Molineaux, Moses III, 237
Molineaux, Susanna III, 237
Moll, Jacob II, 446
Moll, John II, 446
Moll, John, Jr. II, 446
Mollayan, Alice III, 232
Mollayan, Alice Elizabeth III, 232
Mollayan, Krekor III, 232
Mollayan, Nazena III, 232
Mollayan, Virginia III, 232
Mollayan, Zaker III, 232
Molle, Arthur IV, 1330
Molle, Chas. IV, 1330
Molle, Elsie IV, 1330
Molle, Louisa IV, 1330
Moller, Caroline III, 427
Moller, Olaf III, 427
Moller, Sidney R. III, 427
Mollineux, ??? III, 434
Mollineux, Albert III, 427
Mollineux, Benjamin H. III, 427
Mollineux, Edgar III, 427
Mollineux, Henry III, 427
Mollineux, Henry III, 490
Mollineux, Horsman III, 427
Mollineux, Horsman III, 490
Mollineux, Irwin W. III, 427
Mollineux, J. III, 427
Mollineux, Jesse III, 427
Mollineux, Jesse III, 479
Mollineux, Jesse III, 490
Mollineux, John J. III, 427
Mollineux, Johnnie III, 427
Mollineux, Libbie III, 427
Mollineux, Lydia L. III, 427
Mollineux, Martha III, 427
Mollineux, Martha III, 434
Mollineux, Martin III, 427
Mollineux, Mary III, 427
Mollineux, Phebe III, 427
Mollineux, Phebe III, 479
Mollineux, Phebe III, 490
Mollineux, R. III, 427
Mollineux, Sarah III, 427
Mollineux, Sarah III, 490
Mollinex, Hannah III, 237
Mollinex, Henry III, 237
Mollinex, Horseman III, 237
Mollinex, Jesse III, 237
Mollinex, Moses III, 237
Mollinex, Phebe III, 237
Mollinex, Sarah III, 237
Molock, Ella IV, 1239
Molock, Phebe Jane IV, 1239
Molony, Sarah Briban VI, 770
Molony-P, Sarah Briban VI, 731
Molsby, Susannah VI, 362
Molten, Phebe II, 599
Molten, Samuel II, 599
Moltey, Susan IV, 1258
Molty, William F. VI, 894
Molyneaux, Ruth C. V, 656
Molyneaux, Ruth C. V, 698
Molyneaux, Scott V, 656
Molyneaux, Scott V, 698
Mombelly, ??? III, 229
Mombelly, ??? III, 232
Mombelly, Ethel III, 232
Mombelly, Ethel A. III, 229
Mombelly, Ethel A. III, 232
Monce, Clara V, 414
Monce, Edwin S. V, 414
Monce, Howard V, 414
Monce, Ulysses V, 414
Monce, Ulysses L. V, 414
Monce, Vivian V, 414
Monday, Barclay IV, 343
Monday, Esther V, 923
Monday, Susan IV, 343
Monday, Susanna IV, 343
Monden, Joseph I, 708
Monden, Joseph I, 727
Monden, Milisent I, 708
Mondy, Amanda V, 193
Money, Caroline IV, 1308
Money, Grace E. IV, 1308
Money, James I Sup 1, 11
Money, James IV, 1308
Money, John I Sup 1, 11
Money, Joseph I Sup 1, 11
Monger, Alice M. V, 101
Monghiman, Elizabeth May IV, 1330
Monghiman, May IV, 1330
Monington, Susanah II, 599
Monington, Susanah II, 680
Monington, William II, 397
Monington, Wm. II, 599
Monington, Wm. II, 680
Monro, Alex. A. III, 238
Monro, Mary E. III, 238
Monro, Rebecca II, 242
Monro, Rebeckah II, 242
Monro, Rebeckah II, 259
Monro, Thomas III, 238
Monrod, Andrew VI, 32
Monrod, Priest Andrew VI, 35
Monroe, Berlie IV, 1330
Monroe, Catharine VI, 841
Monroe, Charlotte VI, 852
Monroe, Cora Georgia IV, 133
Monroe, Cynthia VI, 841
Monroe, David III, 490
Monroe, Deborah IV, 1135
Monroe, Deborah IV, 1139
Monroe, Deborah IV, 1284
Monroe, Deborah IV, 1287
Monroe, Dorcas V, 414
Monroe, Dorothy II, 699
Monroe, Elisha VI, 841
Monroe, Elizabeth IV, 1291
Monroe, Elizabeth VI, 839
Monroe, Elizabeth B. I, 1159
Monroe, Elizabeth Rea IV, 128
Monroe, Frances VI, 841
Monroe, Frances VI, 866
Monroe, Frank II, 699
Monroe, Geo W. IV, 1330
Monroe, Georgia IV, 1330
Monroe, Gertrude V, 663
Monroe, Gertrude V, 698
Monroe, Gladys IV, 1330
Monroe, Hannah IV, 980
Monroe, Hannah IV, 995
Monroe, Hannah IV, 1002
Monroe, Hazel IV, 1330
Monroe, Henry IV, 1330
Monroe, Henry J. IV, 1330
Monroe, James V, 663
Monroe, James V, 698
Monroe, James VI, 841
Monroe, John IV, 1287
Monroe, John VI, 815
Monroe, John VI, 841
Monroe, John VI, 852
Monroe, John VI, 866
Monroe, John B. V, 414
Monroe, Jonathan VI, 841
Monroe, Jonathan VI, 853
Monroe, Lizzie I, 1159
Monroe, Margaret E. IV, 1330
Monroe, Martha II, 699
Monroe, Martha VI, 852
Monroe, Mary A. V, 414
Monroe, Mary Jane VI, 914
Monroe, Mary Jane VI, 916
Monroe, Maud IV, 1330
Monroe, Moses IV, 1287
Monroe, Moses IV, 1291
Monroe, Mrs. Cora IV, 1330
Monroe, Nancy VI, 832
Monroe, Nancy VI, 965
Monroe, Nancy J. VI, 852
Monroe, Orrin IV, 1330
Monroe, Rachel VI, 841
Monroe, Robert VI, 832
Monroe, Robert VI, 841
Monroe, Robert VI, 852
Monroe, Sally VI, 852
Monroe, Samuel John II, 699

oe, Sarah III, 232
oe, Susan VI, 866
oe, William VI, 965
oe, Wm. VI, 839
ose, Elizabeth II, 756
ose, Elizabeth II, 767
en, Courtney III, 134
en, Courtney III, 232
en, Sarah III, 134
en, Sarah III, 232
ague, Elizabeth I, 146
ague, George H. IV, 741
ague, Mary A. IV, 741
ague, Mary Ann IV, 741
ague, Thomas IV, 253
alzo, Maggie III, 84
alzo, Maggie III, 233
alzo, Mary III, 84
alzo, Mary III, 233
alzo, Ramon III, 84
alzo, Ramon III, 233
crief, Jennie IV, 834
crief, Mary IV, 834
crief, Thomas IV, 834
crief, Tom IV, 834
eague, Elizabeth I, 146
ez, Lola V, 713
ford, Filner W. VI, 59
gomery, A. Harvey V, 461
gomery, A. Newton V, 461
gomery, Amanda I, 934
gomery, Amanda I, 946
gomery, Amanda C. I, 930
gomery, Amanda C. I, 946
gomery, Amy IV, 1107
gomery, Anna V, 23
gomery, Anna V, 101
gomery, Bertha I, 946
gomery, Bertha V, 461
gomery, Bertha Louise
, 934
gomery, Bessie V, 461
gomery, Carrie V, 461
gomery, Clara Louise II, 897
gomery, Clarence IV, 741
tgomery, Cora V, 461
tgomery, David V, 101
tgomery, Dora V, 461
tgomery, Edwin H. III, 233
tgomery, Elizabeth II, 545
tgomery, Elizabeth II, 599
tgomery, Elizabeth V, 101
tgomery, Elva V, 461
tgomery, George I, 934
tgomery, George B. I, 930
tgomery, George M. I, 946
tgomery, George W. I, 930
tgomery, George W. I, 946
tgomery, Hannah V, 461
tgomery, Henry C. IV, 422
tgomery, Henry C. IV, 1107
tgomery, Huldah V, 461
tgomery, J. J. IV, 741
tgomery, J. L. V, 307
tgomery, James V, 462
tgomery, Jane IV, 422
tgomery, Jane IV, 1107
tgomery, Joel IV, 422
tgomery, Joel IV, 1107
tgomery, John L. V, 461
tgomery, Joseph IV, 1258
tgomery, Kezia I, 993
tgomery, Keziah I, 986
tgomery, Keziah I, 994
tgomery, Lena V, 414
tgomery, Leslie V, 461
tgomery, Lewis II, 897
tgomery, Lillie I, 930
tgomery, Lillie V, 101
tgomery, Lulua V, 461
tgomery, Lydia IV, 675
tgomery, Lydia IV, 741
tgomery, Margaret II, 397
tgomery, Martha I, 993
tgomery, Martha I, 1009
tgomery, Martha I, 1011
tgomery, Mary I, 930
tgomery, Mary II, 514
tgomery, Mary II, 599
tgomery, Mary IV, 422
tgomery, Mary IV, 1107
tgomery, Mary V, 307
tgomery, Mary V, 461
tgomery, Mary V, 462
ntgomery, Mildred IV, 871
ntgomery, Mildred IV, 878
ntgomery, Milton V, 461
ntgomery, Newton V, 461
ntgomery, Nina V, 461
ntgomery, Owen V, 101
ntgomery, Owen V, 193
Montgomery, Pearl V, 101
Montgomery, R. Marshall V, 461
Montgomery, Rachel I, 895
Montgomery, Rachel V, 461
Montgomery, Rebecca V, 101
Montgomery, Rebecca V, 137
Montgomery, Robert V, 461
Montgomery, Ruth Ann IV, 422
Montgomery, Ruthanna IV, 422
Montgomery, Sarah I, 1009
Montgomery, Sarah I, 1011
Montgomery, Sarah IV, 422
Montgomery, Sarah Ann IV, 422
Montgomery, Sarah E. V, 101
Montgomery, Sarahann IV, 1107
Montgomery, Sidney V, 101
Montgomery, Sidney V, 193
Montgomery, Theodore Leslie V, 307
Montgomery, Thomas IV, 422
Montgomery, Thomas IV, 1107
Montgomery, Thomas V, 461
Montgomery, W. H. V, 461
Montgomery, Wd. Margaret II, 599
Montgomery, Wilbur V, 461
Montgomery, William II, 397
Montgomery, William V, 461
Montgomery, William H. IV, 422
Montgomery, Wm. II, 514
Montgomery, Wm. II, 599
Montgomery, Wm. H. IV, 1107
Montgummery, Hugh VI, 76
Montgummery, Martha I, 993
Montjoy, Bathsheba V, 265
Montjoy, Bathsheba V, 272
Mood, Sarah II, 1016
Moode, Alexander II, 490
Moode, Alexander II, 599
Moode, Andrew II, 1016
Moode, Eleanor II, 599
Moode, Eleanor II, 1016
Moode, Eleanor II, 1034
Moode, Elizabeth II, 516
Moode, Elizabeth II, 599
Moode, Elizabeth III, 28
Moode, Hannah II, 490
Moode, Hannah II, 546
Moode, Hannah II, 599
Moode, Hannah II, 998
Moode, Hannah II, 1016
Moode, Joseph II, 1016
Moode, Lydia II, 1016
Moode, Lydia II, 1034
Moode, Mary II, 599
Moode, Sarah II, 1016
Moode, William II, 396
Moode, Wm. II, 490
Moode, Wm. II, 516
Moode, Wm. II, 599
Moode, Wm. II, 1016
Moodey, Jenny VI, 925
Moodey, Lucy VI, 991
Moodey, Susanah VI, 991
Moody, ??? III, 242
Moody, Abigail V, 157
Moody, Abigail V, 193
Moody, Abigail Jane I, 607
Moody, Catherine IV, 1239
Moody, Clara V, 698
Moody, Davis IV, 1287
Moody, Edith Emily V, 499
Moody, Edith Emily V, 517
Moody, Edith Emma V, 698
Moody, Eleanor III, 233
Moody, Eliza IV, 1287
Moody, Elizabeth VI, 903
Moody, George VI, 965
Moody, Jane IV, 1287
Moody, Jessie IV, 741
Moody, John I, 1145
Moody, John VI, 926
Moody, John VI, 965
Moody, John J. I, 1159
Moody, L. R. V, 698
Moody, Lora IV, 1287
Moody, Lucella Wilson IV, 1169
Moody, Lucella Wilson IV, 1174
Moody, Martha VI, 965
Moody, Mary V, 149
Moody, Mary V, 177
Moody, Mary V, 193
Moody, Mary V, 956
Moody, Mary VI, 965
Moody, Rebeckah VI, 73
Moody, Rebeckah VI, 76
Moody, Ruth V, 193
Moody, Ruth VI, 350
Moody, Ruth VI, 353
Moody, Ruth VI, 965
Moody, Salley VI, 965
Moody, Samuel V, 193
Moody, Samuel VI, 353
Moody, Samuel VI, 925
Moody, Samuel VI, 965
Moody, Sarah VI, 941
Moody, Susanna VI, 882
Moody, Thomas VI, 903
Moody, William VI, 965
Mooma, Latha S. V, 586
Mooma, Lewis V, 586
Mooma, Susan V, 586
Moomaw, Latha S. V, 586
Moomaw, Lewis V, 586
Moomaw, Susan V, 586
Moon, ??? V, 315
Moon, A. VI, 855
Moon, Aaron I, 511
Moon, Aaron V, 193
Moon, Aaron V, 265
Moon, Aaron V, 415
Moon, Aaron V, 417
Moon, Aaron V, 419
Moon, Aaron V, 420
Moon, Aaron V, 421
Moon, Aaron V, 517
Moon, Aaron V, 587
Moon, Aaron V, 756
Moon, Abbie V, 418
Moon, Abby S. V, 421
Moon, Abby S. V, 422
Moon, Abie V, 422
Moon, Abigail I, 361
Moon, Abigail I, 396
Moon, Abigail I, 409
Moon, Abigail V, 416
Moon, Abigail V, 419
Moon, Achsa Ann V, 419
Moon, Ada Bell V, 698
Moon, Adalask V, 422
Moon, Adalask W. V, 422
Moon, Agnes II, 965
Moon, Agnes II, 1016
Moon, Agnes II, 1022
Moon, Albert V, 417
Moon, Albert D. V, 193
Moon, Aletha B. II, 965
Moon, Aletha B. II, 1057
Moon, Alfred V, 416
Moon, Alfred V, 418
Moon, Alfred V, 420
Moon, Alfred Alonzo V, 193
Moon, Alfred H. I, 247
Moon, Alfred H. I, 258
Moon, Alfred H. II, 965
Moon, Alfred H. II, 1056
Moon, Alfred H. V, 421
Moon, Alfred H. V, 422
Moon, Alice II, 949
Moon, Alice II, 972
Moon, Alice II, 1016
Moon, Alice V, 418
Moon, Alice V, 421
Moon, Alice H. II, 982
Moon, Alice H. II, 1017
Moon, Alice L. V, 418
Moon, Alice L. V, 421
Moon, Alice L. V, 422
Moon, Allen V, 415
Moon, Allen V, 416
Moon, Allen V, 419
Moon, Allen V, 420
Moon, Allen Lewis V, 698
Moon, Allie V, 419
Moon, Alma V, 422
Moon, Almira V, 403
Moon, Almira V, 418
Moon, Almira V, 421
Moon, Alpheus V, 193
Moon, Alvin V, 416
Moon, Alvin V, 420
Moon, Amanda V, 417
Moon, Amanda V, 421
Moon, Amanda E. V, 418
Moon, Amaziah V, 422
Moon, Amos V, 350
Moon, Amos V, 415
Moon, Amos V, 416
Moon, Amos V, 421
Moon, Amos G. V, 418
Moon, Amos R. V, 417
Moon, Amos R. V, 420
Moon, Amos S. V, 418
Moon, Amy V, 437
Moon, Ana C. V, 698
Moon, Andrew V, 416
Moon, Andrew V, 418
Moon, Andrew V, 422
Moon, Andrew H. V, 417
Moon, Andrew H. V, 420
Moon, Ange Netta V, 418
Moon, Angenetta V, 422
Moon, Angenetta V, 587
Moon, Ann I, 346
Moon, Ann I, 361
Moon, Ann I, 396
Moon, Ann I, 409
Moon, Ann I, 410
Moon, Ann I, 420
Moon, Ann I, 550
Moon, Ann I, 563
Moon, Ann II, 965
Moon, Ann II, 966
Moon, Ann II, 984
Moon, Ann II, 985
Moon, Ann II, 1016
Moon, Ann II, 1017
Moon, Ann II, 1018
Moon, Ann II, 1022
Moon, Ann II, 1035
Moon, Ann V, 350
Moon, Ann V, 356
Moon, Ann V, 385
Moon, Ann V, 414
Moon, Ann V, 415
Moon, Ann V, 416
Moon, Ann V, 417
Moon, Ann V, 418
Moon, Ann V, 419
Moon, Ann V, 420
Moon, Ann V, 423
Moon, Ann V, 433
Moon, Ann VI, 424
Moon, Ann VI, 461
Moon, Ann VI, 965
Moon, Ann B. V, 418
Moon, Anna II, 1057
Moon, Anna II, 1061
Moon, Anna II, 1086
Moon, Anna V, 236
Moon, Anna V, 265
Moon, Anna V, 383
Moon, Anna V, 384
Moon, Anna V, 397
Moon, Anna V, 403
Moon, Anna V, 404
Moon, Anna V, 411
Moon, Anna V, 414
Moon, Anna V, 415
Moon, Anna V, 416
Moon, Anna V, 419
Moon, Anna V, 420
Moon, Anna V, 421
Moon, Anna V, 586
Moon, Anna V, 587
Moon, Anna Isabel V, 421
Moon, Anna Isabel V, 432
Moon, Anna Isabelle V, 416
Moon, Anna J. II, 716
Moon, Anna J. II, 721
Moon, Anna J. II, 965
Moon, Anna J. II, 1056
Moon, Anna J. II, 1058
Moon, Anna J. II, 1089
Moon, Anna Jennie II, 1086
Moon, Anna M. V, 437
Moon, Anne I, 361
Moon, Anne V, 419
Moon, Annie V, 417
Moon, Annie V, 418
Moon, Annie V, 421
Moon, Annie L. V, 418
Moon, Ansie V, 422
Moon, Arched. VI, 998
Moon, Archelaus VI, 950
Moon, Archelaus VI, 965
Moon, Archelous VI, 939
Moon, Archibald VI, 841
Moon, Archs. VI, 927
Moon, Archs. VI, 1001
Moon, Arksy Ann V, 415
Moon, Armandus V, 418
Moon, Arminda V, 418
Moon, Arminda V, 419
Moon, Arminda V, 421
Moon, Arsky Ann V, 421
Moon, Arthur V, 193
Moon, Arthur V, 417
Moon, Arthur V, 418
Moon, Arthur V, 421
Moon, Arthur V, 422
Moon, Arthur V, 437
Moon, Arthur H. V, 418
Moon, Asaph V, 416
Moon, Asaph V, 421
Moon, Ascenith V, 101
Moon, Asenath V, 61
Moon, Asenath V, 101
Moon, Asenath V, 102
Moon, Asenath V, 415
Moon, Asenath V, 517
Moon, Asenath V, 518
Moon, Aseneth I, 511
Moon, Asenith V, 102
Moon, Asenith V, 420
Moon, Austin VI, 841
Moon, Australia V, 698
Moon, Australia J. V, 419
Moon, Barclay II, 1057
Moon, Barclay V, 416
Moon, Barclay V, 420
Moon, Beatrice B. V, 698
Moon, Benjamin II, 446
Moon, Benjamin V, 414
Moon, Benjamin V, 415
Moon, Benjamin V, 416
Moon, Benjamin V, 419
Moon, Benjamin V, 420
Moon, Benjamin VI, 841
Moon, Benjamin H. V, 416
Moon, Bert G. V, 698
Moon, Bertha V, 422
Moon, Bertha V, 587
Moon, Bertha Cox V, 422
Moon, Betsy V, 422
Moon, Betsy H. V, 698
Moon, Betty V, 400
Moon, Betty H. V, 421
Moon, Beulah II, 1056
Moon, Beulah T. II, 965
Moon, Birtsel V, 419
Moon, Bridget II, 796
Moon, Bridget II, 965
Moon, Bridget II, 997
Moon, Bridget II, 1017
Moon, C. C. V, 437
Moon, Caleb V, 416
Moon, Caleb T. V, 420
Moon, Calvin V, 416
Moon, Calvin V, 417
Moon, Calvin P. V, 419
Moon, Carey V, 417
Moon, Carey E. V, 419
Moon, Carl V, 422
Moon, Carl A. V, 422
Moon, Caroline V, 386
Moon, Caroline V, 417
Moon, Caroline V, 420
Moon, Caroline V, 421
Moon, Caroline V, 422
Moon, Caroline VI, 729
Moon, Caroline VI, 730
Moon, Caroline VI, 767
Moon, Caroline VI, 793
Moon, Caroline B. VI, 793
Moon, Cassandra VI, 965
Moon, Catharine VI, 741
Moon, Catharine VI, 767
Moon, Catharine E. VI, 1013
Moon, Charity I, 361
Moon, Charity I, 378
Moon, Charity I, 409
Moon, Charity I, 410
Moon, Charity I, 413
Moon, Charity V, 415
Moon, Charity V, 420
Moon, Charity V, 956
Moon, Charles II, 965
Moon, Charles II, 1056
Moon, Charles II, 1086
Moon, Charles II, 1087
Moon, Charles II, 1089
Moon, Charles V, 193
Moon, Charles A. V, 421
Moon, Charles Allen V, 418
Moon, Charles H. V, 193
Moon, Charles H. V, 418
Moon, Charles H. V, 422
Moon, Charles Henry II, 330
Moon, Charles Henry II, 949
Moon, Charles Henry II, 952
Moon, Charles Henry II, 1086
Moon, Charles Henry II, 1089
Moon, Charles T. II, 965
Moon, Charles Thompson II, 1057
Moon, Charles W. V, 418
Moon, Charles William V, 421
Moon, Charlotta D. V, 518
Moon, Charlotte V, 417
Moon, Charlotte D. V, 389
Moon, Charlotte D. V, 420
Moon, Charlotte D. V, 421
Moon, Charlotte D. V, 493
Moon, Charlotte D. V, 518
Moon, Christopher V, 416
Moon, Christopher V, 420
Moon, Christopher VI, 906
Moon, Christopher VI, 942
Moon, Christopher VI, 949
Moon, Christopher VI, 1014
Moon, Clara V, 193
Moon, Clara L. V, 419
Moon, Clarence V, 418

Moon, Clarence V, 422
Moon, Clarkson V, 417
Moon, Clarkson V, 586
Moon, Clyde M. V, 193
Moon, Cora V, 418
Moon, Cora V, 422
Moon, Cora V, 698
Moon, Cora A. V, 418
Moon, Cora A. V, 670
Moon, Cora A. V, 698
Moon, Cyrus V, 389
Moon, Cyrus V, 415
Moon, Cyrus V, 417
Moon, Cyrus V, 419
Moon, Cyrus V, 420
Moon, Cyrus V, 421
Moon, Cyrus V, 563
Moon, Cyrus V, 586
Moon, Cyrus V, 587
Moon, Dallas N. V, 422
Moon, Dallis N. V, 418
Moon, Dallos N. V, 587
Moon, Daniel I, 1109
Moon, Daniel I, 1128
Moon, Daniel V, 101
Moon, Daniel V, 265
Moon, Daniel V, 350
Moon, Daniel V, 384
Moon, Daniel V, 395
Moon, Daniel V, 414
Moon, Daniel V, 415
Moon, Daniel V, 416
Moon, Daniel V, 417
Moon, Daniel V, 419
Moon, Daniel V, 422
Moon, Daniel V, 426
Moon, Daniel V, 436
Moon, Daniel C. V, 417
Moon, Daniel C. V, 418
Moon, Daniel C. V, 419
Moon, Daniel C. V, 421
Moon, Daniel C. V, 698
Moon, Daniel Edward V, 421
Moon, Daniel H. V, 375
Moon, Daniel H. V, 420
Moon, Daniel H. V, 421
Moon, Daniel H. V, 828
Moon, Daniel H. V, 853
Moon, Daniel H. V, 875
Moon, Daniel R. V, 415
Moon, Daniel R. V, 417
Moon, Daniel R. V, 419
Moon, Daniel R. V, 420
Moon, Daniel W. V, 421
Moon, David II, 397
Moon, David II, 600
Moon, David II, 1017
Moon, David V, 369
Moon, David I. V, 416
Moon, David I. V, 420
Moon, Delila V, 220
Moon, Delila V, 265
Moon, Delilah V, 373
Moon, Delilah V, 414
Moon, Delilah V, 417
Moon, Delilah V, 419
Moon, Della V, 698
Moon, Diantha V, 408
Moon, Diantha V, 416
Moon, Diantha V, 420
Moon, Dinah I, 358
Moon, Dinah I, 361
Moon, Dinah I, 402
Moon, Dinah I, 410
Moon, Dinah I, 511
Moon, Dinah I, 561
Moon, Dinah I, 563
Moon, Dinah V, 24
Moon, Dinah V, 101
Moon, Dinah V, 373
Moon, Dinah V, 416
Moon, Dinah V, 419
Moon, Dinah V, 517
Moon, Dinah V, 518
Moon, Dinah V, 956
Moon, Dinnah V, 101
Moon, Dora V, 417
Moon, Dorcas Ann V, 417
Moon, Dorcas Ann V, 420
Moon, Dorothy B. V, 418
Moon, Dorothy B. V, 421
Moon, Dorothy B. V, 422
Moon, Edgar II, 1056
Moon, Edgar V, 193
Moon, Edgar V, 417
Moon, Edgar V, 418
Moon, Edith C. II, 966
Moon, Edmund II, 1016
Moon, Edmund II, 1018
Moon, Edna V, 397
Moon, Edom V, 416
Moon, Edom V, 420
Moon, Edward II, 965
Moon, Edward V, 265
Moon, Edward P. II, 965
Moon, Edward P. II, 1057
Moon, Edwin J. V, 418
Moon, Edwin J. V, 422
Moon, Elbridge V, 418
Moon, Elbridge V, 421
Moon, Eleanor V, 415
Moon, Eleanor V, 417
Moon, Eleanor V, 419
Moon, Eleanor V, 421
Moon, Eleanor V, 426
Moon, Eleanor V, 433
Moon, Eli V, 415
Moon, Eli V, 419
Moon, Eli V, 420
Moon, Elias I, 410
Moon, Elias V, 415
Moon, Elias V, 420
Moon, Elida J. V, 193
Moon, Elisabeth II, 1005
Moon, Elisabeth B. I, 247
Moon, Eliza I, 1119
Moon, Eliza I, 1128
Moon, Eliza II, 965
Moon, Eliza V, 322
Moon, Eliza V, 350
Moon, Eliza V, 376
Moon, Eliza V, 414
Moon, Eliza V, 415
Moon, Eliza V, 416
Moon, Eliza V, 419
Moon, Eliza V, 421
Moon, Eliza V, 422
Moon, Eliza V, 436
Moon, Eliza V, 587
Moon, Eliza V, 597
Moon, Eliza E. V, 422
Moon, Eliza H. II, 1056
Moon, Eliza H. II, 1062
Moon, Eliza Jane V, 417
Moon, Eliza Jane V, 420
Moon, Eliza Jane V, 421
Moon, Eliza M. V, 418
Moon, Elizabeth I, 361
Moon, Elizabeth I, 410
Moon, Elizabeth I, 420
Moon, Elizabeth II, 242
Moon, Elizabeth II, 446
Moon, Elizabeth II, 965
Moon, Elizabeth II, 966
Moon, Elizabeth II, 985
Moon, Elizabeth II, 1012
Moon, Elizabeth II, 1016
Moon, Elizabeth II, 1017
Moon, Elizabeth II, 1022
Moon, Elizabeth II, 1044
Moon, Elizabeth II, 1056
Moon, Elizabeth III, 233
Moon, Elizabeth V, 193
Moon, Elizabeth V, 322
Moon, Elizabeth V, 350
Moon, Elizabeth V, 375
Moon, Elizabeth V, 392
Moon, Elizabeth V, 397
Moon, Elizabeth V, 414
Moon, Elizabeth V, 415
Moon, Elizabeth V, 416
Moon, Elizabeth V, 417
Moon, Elizabeth V, 418
Moon, Elizabeth V, 419
Moon, Elizabeth V, 420
Moon, Elizabeth V, 421
Moon, Elizabeth V, 422
Moon, Elizabeth V, 432
Moon, Elizabeth V, 437
Moon, Elizabeth V, 440
Moon, Elizabeth V, 955
Moon, Elizabeth V, 956
Moon, Elizabeth VI, 475
Moon, Elizabeth VI, 520
Moon, Elizabeth VI, 522
Moon, Elizabeth VI, 855
Moon, Elizabeth B. II, 1049
Moon, Elizabeth H. V, 416
Moon, Elizabeth Hadley V, 698
Moon, Elizabeth J. I, 410
Moon, Elizabeth Letitia II, 965
Moon, Elizabeth Letitia II, 1049
Moon, Elizabeth Letitia II, 1056
Moon, Elkanah V, 415
Moon, Elkanah V, 421
Moon, Ella V, 265
Moon, Ella V, 417
Moon, Ella V, 418
Moon, Ella V, 419
Moon, Ella Glenn V, 698
Moon, Ella May V, 418
Moon, Ella S. II, 1076
Moon, Ellen II, 965
Moon, Ellen V, 421
Moon, Ellen M. II, 966
Moon, Ellwood V, 419
Moon, Ellwood V, 420
Moon, Elmer V, 422
Moon, Elmina V, 422
Moon, Elmira M. V, 422
Moon, Elsie V, 634
Moon, Elsie V, 698
Moon, Elwood V, 416
Moon, Elwood V, 417
Moon, Elwood V, 421
Moon, Elwood V, 586
Moon, Elwood V, 587
Moon, Emerson V, 418
Moon, Emily V, 422
Moon, Emma V, 422
Moon, Emma Bell V, 418
Moon, Emma Jerusha V, 418
Moon, Emma W. II, 1086
Moon, Emy I, 361
Moon, Enoch V, 517
Moon, Enoch V, 518
Moon, Enoch V, 955
Moon, Enoch V, 956
Moon, Enoch L. V, 421
Moon, Enos V, 416
Moon, Enos V, 417
Moon, Enos V, 420
Moon, Enos Finley V, 419
Moon, Erlestus V, 421
Moon, Erlistus J. V, 418
Moon, Erlistus J. V, 419
Moon, Esther IV, 1069
Moon, Esther V, 415
Moon, Esther V, 416
Moon, Esther V, 417
Moon, Esther V, 419
Moon, Esther V, 420
Moon, Esther A. II, 949
Moon, Esther M. II, 949
Moon, Ethel V, 419
Moon, Ethel V, 422
Moon, Eunice V, 193
Moon, Eunice V, 417
Moon, Eunice V, 587
Moon, Eunice V, 756
Moon, Eunice E. V, 193
Moon, Eunice E. V, 420
Moon, Eunice Ellen V, 193
Moon, Eunice Ellen V, 421
Moon, Eunice Jane V, 417
Moon, Eva V, 193
Moon, Eva V, 418
Moon, Eva V, 421
Moon, Eva L. V, 193
Moon, Eva Mae V, 422
Moon, Eva May V, 419
Moon, Everett II, 965
Moon, Ezra V, 413
Moon, Ezra V, 415
Moon, Ezra V, 417
Moon, Ezra V, 420
Moon, Ezraetta II, 965
Moon, Ezraetta II, 1053
Moon, Ezraetta II, 1056
Moon, Florence Eva V, 418
Moon, Frances Marion V, 418
Moon, Francis V, 422
Moon, Francis M. V, 422
Moon, Francis M. V, 587
Moon, Francis Orville V, 421
Moon, Fred V, 437
Moon, Galen V, 422
Moon, Genette V, 421
Moon, Geo. V, 437
Moon, Geo. H. V, 350
Moon, Geo. Hodgson V, 350
Moon, George I, 361
Moon, George I, 409
Moon, George V, 415
Moon, George V, 416
Moon, George V, 418
Moon, George V, 586
Moon, George V, 590
Moon, George H. V, 419
Moon, Gertrude V, 419
Moon, Gertrude V, 422
Moon, Gertrude V, 922
Moon, Golden B. V, 698
Moon, Goodrich VI, 965
Moon, Grace V, 387
Moon, Grace V, 414
Moon, Grace V, 417
Moon, Haley V, 419
Moon, Hannah I, 361
Moon, Hannah I, 373
Moon, Hannah I, 409
Moon, Hannah I, 410
Moon, Hannah I, 417
Moon, Hannah I, 420
Moon, Hannah I, 667
Moon, Hannah II, 242
Moon, Hannah II, 600
Moon, Hannah II, 650
Moon, Hannah II, 965
Moon, Hannah II, 966
Moon, Hannah II, 1000
Moon, Hannah II, 1016
Moon, Hannah II, 1017
Moon, Hannah II, 1022
Moon, Hannah II, 1056
Moon, Hannah II, 1076
Moon, Hannah V, 176
Moon, Hannah V, 403
Moon, Hannah V, 415
Moon, Hannah V, 416
Moon, Hannah V, 419
Moon, Hannah V, 420
Moon, Hannah V, 421
Moon, Hannah V, 430
Moon, Hannah V, 698
Moon, Hannah V, 709
Moon, Hannah Bass I, 409
Moon, Hannah S. V, 416
Moon, Hannah S. V, 421
Moon, Hannah S. V, 422
Moon, Hannah S. V, 698
Moon, Harley V, 422
Moon, Harriet O. I, 247
Moon, Harriet O. I, 258
Moon, Harriett V, 193
Moon, Harry V, 419
Moon, Harry V, 422
Moon, Harry C. V, 698
Moon, Harvey II, 1056
Moon, Harvey V, 417
Moon, Harvey V, 419
Moon, Harvey V, 698
Moon, Hattie Delilah V, 418
Moon, Havilah V, 415
Moon, Havilah V, 419
Moon, Henrietta O. VI, 767
Moon, Henry V, 350
Moon, Henry V, 377
Moon, Henry V, 403
Moon, Henry V, 414
Moon, Henry V, 415
Moon, Henry V, 417
Moon, Henry V, 418
Moon, Henry V, 419
Moon, Henry V, 422
Moon, Henry V, 439
Moon, Henry B. II, 965
Moon, Henry B. II, 1056
Moon, Henry B. VI, 730
Moon, Henry B. VI, 737
Moon, Henry B. VI, 767
Moon, Henry B. VI, 788
Moon, Henry Bond VI, 767
Moon, Henry H. V, 420
Moon, Henry J. II, 1051
Moon, Henry J. II, 1056
Moon, Henry J., Jr. II, 965
Moon, Henry P. V, 416
Moon, Henry T. II, 965
Moon, Henry T. II, 966
Moon, Henry, Jr. V, 420
Moon, Hiram V, 415
Moon, Hiram V, 420
Moon, Hiram E. V, 403
Moon, Hiram E. V, 418
Moon, Hiram E. V, 421
Moon, Hiram E. V, 422
Moon, Hiram E. V, 587
Moon, Hiram Edwin V, 418
Moon, Hiram H. V, 417
Moon, Howard Haines II, 965
Moon, Huldah V, 350
Moon, Huldah V, 355
Moon, Huldah V, 411
Moon, Huldah V, 415
Moon, Huldah V, 417
Moon, Huldah V, 420
Moon, Huldah V, 421
Moon, Huldah V, 440
Moon, Huldah VI, 114
Moon, Huldah VI, 116
Moon, Ida V, 193
Moon, Ida May V, 418
Moon, Ida May V, 422
Moon, Ira V, 417
Moon, Ira V, 420
Moon, Irena V, 392
Moon, Irena V, 417
Moon, Irena V, 421
Moon, Irena V, 589
Moon, Isaac II, 966
Moon, Isaac V, 420
Moon, Isaac G. V, 417
Moon, Isaac G. V, 421
Moon, Isaac G. V, 518
Moon, Isabella I, 410
Moon, Isadora II, 965
Moon, Isaiah V, 415
Moon, Isaiah V, 419
Moon, Isaiah V, 421
Moon, J. Edward II, 1056
Moon, J. Morton II, 965
Moon, Jabez V, 415
Moon, Jabez V, 417
Moon, Jacob I, 358
Moon, Jacob I, 361
Moon, Jacob I, 368
Moon, Jacob I, 395
Moon, Jacob I, 409
Moon, Jacob I, 410
Moon, Jacob I, 428
Moon, Jacob V, 265
Moon, Jacob V, 415
Moon, Jacob V, 416
Moon, Jacob V, 420
Moon, Jacob V, 422
Moon, Jacob VI, 965
Moon, Jacob K. V, 421
Moon, Jacob, Jr. VI, 920
Moon, Jacob, Jr. VI, 980
Moon, James I, 346
Moon, James I, 361
Moon, James I, 409
Moon, James I, 410
Moon, James I, 511
Moon, James I, 563
Moon, James I, 683
Moon, James I, 685
Moon, James II, 965
Moon, James II, 966
Moon, James II, 985
Moon, James II, 993
Moon, James II, 997
Moon, James II, 998
Moon, James II, 1012
Moon, James II, 1016
Moon, James II, 1017
Moon, James II, 1022
Moon, James II, 1035
Moon, James II, 1044
Moon, James II, 1048
Moon, James II, 1056
Moon, James II, 1061
Moon, James II, 1062
Moon, James II, 1076
Moon, James V, 101
Moon, James V, 391
Moon, James V, 414
Moon, James V, 417
Moon, James V, 418
Moon, James V, 419
Moon, James V, 420
Moon, James V, 421
Moon, James V, 431
Moon, James V, 517
Moon, James V, 518
Moon, James V, 698
Moon, James VI, 424
Moon, James VI, 767
Moon, James VI, 820
Moon, James Arthur V, 417
Moon, James Arthur V, 441
Moon, James B. II, 965
Moon, James B. II, 1056
Moon, James C. V, 416
Moon, James C. V, 418
Moon, James C. V, 419
Moon, James C. V, 422
Moon, James C., Jr. V, 420
Moon, James C., Jr. V, 422
Moon, James Edward II, 966
Moon, James H. I, 247
Moon, James H. II, 965
Moon, James H. II, 1044
Moon, James H. V, 421
Moon, James H. V, 422
Moon, James K. II, 1049
Moon, James K. II, 1056
Moon, James M. II, 965
Moon, James M. II, 1053
Moon, James O. V, 698
Moon, James S. V, 420
Moon, James, Jr. II, 965
Moon, James, Jr. II, 1016
Moon, James, Jr. II, 1039
Moon, Jamima V, 422
Moon, Jane II, 397
Moon, Jane II, 957
Moon, Jane II, 965
Moon, Jane II, 966
Moon, Jane II, 970
Moon, Jane II, 1017
Moon, Jane II, 1044
Moon, Jane II, 1048
Moon, Jane II, 1049

, Jane II, 1056
, Jane II, 1058
, Jane II, 1061
, Jane II, 1062
, Jane II, 1076
, Jane V, 65
, Jane V, 101
n, Jane V, 104
, Jane V, 375
n, Jane V, 377
n, Jane V, 389
n, Jane V, 414
n, Jane V, 415
n, Jane V, 416
n, Jane V, 419
n, Jane V, 420
n, Jane V, 421
n, Jane V, 422
n, Jane V, 426
n, Jane V, 436
n, Jane V, 469
n, Jane V, 517
n, Jane V, 518
n, Jane V, 563
n, Jane V, 586
n, Jane V, 587
n, Jane V, 853
n, Jane VI, 1014
n, Jane C. I, 247
n, Jane C. I, 258
n, Jane C. II, 965
n, Jane C. II, 1048
n, Jane C. II, 1056
on, Jane Chace II, 1057
n, Jane Chace II, 1061
n, Jane G. V, 417
on, Jane G. V, 420
on, Jason V, 415
on, Jason V, 421
on, Jasper II, 966
on, Jean V, 350
on, Jehu V, 415
on, Jehu V, 420
on, Jenetie V, 418
on, Jenny VI, 841
on, Jephtha D. V, 698
on, Jeremiah V, 265
on, Jeremiah V, 350
on, Jeremiah V, 352
on, Jeremiah V, 415
on, Jeremiah V, 416
on, Jeremiah V, 419
on, Jeremiah V, 420
on, Jermiah I, 1109
on, Joseph V, 415
on, Jesse I, 361
on, Jesse I, 410
on, Jesse V, 373
on, Jesse V, 395
on, Jesse V, 414
on, Jesse V, 416
on, Jesse V, 417
on, Jesse V, 419
on, Jesse V, 420
on, Jesse V, 422
on, Jesse F. V, 421
on, Jesse H. V, 418
on, Jesse H. V, 422
on, Jessie F. VI, 730
oon, Jessie Freemont VI, 730
oon, Jessie Freemont VI, 767
on, Joab V, 416
on, Joab V, 420
oon, Job V, 417
oon, Joel V, 415
oon, Joel V, 420
oon, John I, 361
oon, John I, 367
oon, John I, 410
oon, John I, 511
oon, John I, 561
oon, John I, 563
oon, John I, 667
oon, John I, 1109
oon, John II, 446
oon, John II, 599
oon, John II, 949
oon, John II, 966
oon, John II, 982
oon, John II, 984
oon, John II, 1016
oon, John II, 1056
oon, John II, 1076
oon, John IV, 1287
oon, John V, 101
oon, John V, 193
oon, John V, 265
oon, John V, 350
oon, John V, 355
oon, John V, 415
oon, John V, 419
Moon, John V, 421
Moon, John V, 422
Moon, John V, 425
Moon, John V, 517
Moon, John V, 518
Moon, John V, 698
Moon, John V, 956
Moon, John VI, 729
Moon, John VI, 730
Moon, John VI, 767
Moon, John VI, 793
Moon, John B. II, 965
Moon, John C. V, 415
Moon, John C. V, 417
Moon, John C. V, 420
Moon, John C. V, 422
Moon, John Carter V, 419
Moon, John Carter V, 420
Moon, John D. V, 421
Moon, John Dalton V, 418
Moon, John Demrus V, 193
Moon, John Demrus V, 587
Moon, John Dewrus V, 421
Moon, John E. V, 698
Moon, John Eldridge V, 420
Moon, John H. V, 418
Moon, John Milton V, 415
Moon, John Milton V, 417
Moon, John P. V, 416
Moon, John P. V, 420
Moon, John R. V, 415
Moon, John R. V, 416
Moon, John R. V, 418
Moon, John R. V, 419
Moon, John R. V, 420
Moon, John T. V, 418
Moon, John T. V, 422
Moon, John T. V, 922
Moon, John Thos. V, 422
Moon, John W. V, 418
Moon, John Wesley V, 422
Moon, John Wilmer II, 949
Moon, John, Jr. II, 1017
Moon, John, Jr. V, 422
Moon, Jonas II, 965
Moon, Jonas II, 972
Moon, Jonas II, 1016
Moon, Jonathan I, 361
Moon, Jonathan I, 410
Moon, Jonathan V, 384
Moon, Jonathan V, 417
Moon, Jonathan V, 420
Moon, Jonathan V, 517
Moon, Jonathan R. II, 900
Moon, Joseph I, 196
Moon, Joseph I, 409
Moon, Joseph I, 1101
Moon, Joseph I, 1109
Moon, Joseph I, 1128
Moon, Joseph II, 1017
Moon, Joseph II, 1056
Moon, Joseph V, 265
Moon, Joseph V, 373
Moon, Joseph V, 376
Moon, Joseph V, 393
Moon, Joseph V, 414
Moon, Joseph V, 415
Moon, Joseph V, 416
Moon, Joseph V, 417
Moon, Joseph V, 418
Moon, Joseph V, 419
Moon, Joseph B. V, 416
Moon, Joseph B. V, 420
Moon, Joseph D. V, 417
Moon, Joseph D. V, 419
Moon, Joseph D. V, 436
Moon, Joseph E. V, 418
Moon, Joseph H. V, 324
Moon, Joseph H. V, 350
Moon, Joseph H. V, 380
Moon, Joseph H. V, 414
Moon, Joseph H. V, 415
Moon, Joseph H. V, 418
Moon, Joseph H. V, 419
Moon, Joseph H. V, 420
Moon, Joseph H. V, 421
Moon, Joseph H. V, 422
Moon, Joseph Harley V, 418
Moon, Joseph Harley V, 422
Moon, Joseph, Jr. V, 419
Moon, Joseph, Sr. V, 416
Moon, Josiah P. VI, 795
Moon, Josiah P. VI, 855
Moon, Judith I, 511
Moon, Judith I, 563
Moon, Judith I, 685
Moon, Judith V, 65
Moon, Judith V, 101
Moon, Judith V, 102
Moon, Judith V, 416
Moon, Judith V, 419
Moon, Judith V, 517
Moon, Judith V, 518
Moon, Judith VI, 260
Moon, Julia II, 1056
Moon, Julia Ann V, 422
Moon, Julia French II, 1051
Moon, Julia French II, 1056
Moon, Julia H. II, 965
Moon, Julian II, 1056
Moon, Julian II, 1076
Moon, Juliann II, 965
Moon, Juliann II, 984
Moon, Juliann II, 1017
Moon, L. VI, 819
Moon, L. R. V, 698
Moon, Larkin I, 410
Moon, Latitia II, 1049
Moon, Lavinah V, 416
Moon, Lavinah V, 431
Moon, Leah V, 393
Moon, Leah V, 415
Moon, Leah V, 417
Moon, Leah V, 419
Moon, Leah V, 420
Moon, Leah VI, 424
Moon, Leah VI, 436
Moon, Leander V, 416
Moon, Leander V, 420
Moon, Leander V, 421
Moon, Lee V, 422
Moon, Leighton V, 422
Moon, Leonidas V, 421
Moon, Levi V, 416
Moon, Levi V, 418
Moon, Levi V, 419
Moon, Levi V, 421
Moon, Levina V, 391
Moon, Levina V, 417
Moon, Levina V, 418
Moon, Levina V, 419
Moon, Levina V, 420
Moon, Lewis V, 415
Moon, Lewis V, 418
Moon, Lewis V, 419
Moon, Lewis V, 421
Moon, Lewis V, 698
Moon, Lewis C. V, 666
Moon, Lewis C. V, 698
Moon, Lida V, 182
Moon, Lida E. V, 418
Moon, Lida E. V, 698
Moon, Lilley V, 418
Moon, Lilly V, 422
Moon, Lindley II, 965
Moon, Lindley V, 417
Moon, Lindley V, 420
Moon, Lindley V, 422
Moon, Lindley M. V, 416
Moon, Lindley Murry V, 417
Moon, Linley V, 441
Moon, Linton V, 417
Moon, Lisbon V, 417
Moon, Lizzie V, 440
Moon, Loena V, 417
Moon, Loena V, 420
Moon, Lois R. V, 698
Moon, Loranna V, 422
Moon, Loreena V, 422
Moon, Lottie V, 422
Moon, Louella V, 417
Moon, Louisa II, 1089
Moon, Louisa V, 384
Moon, Louisa V, 416
Moon, Louisa V, 417
Moon, Louisa V, 421
Moon, Louisa P. V, 634
Moon, Louisa P. V, 698
Moon, Louisa S. VI, 767
Moon, Louisa S. VI, 788
Moon, Louisa S. VI, 789
Moon, Louise S. VI, 767
Moon, Lowranna I, 346
Moon, Lowry I, 347
Moon, Lucetta V, 193
Moon, Lucetta E. V, 193
Moon, Lucinda V, 413
Moon, Lucinda V, 415
Moon, Lucinda V, 419
Moon, Lucinda V, 421
Moon, Lucinda B. V, 418
Moon, Lucretia II, 949
Moon, Lucy V, 417
Moon, Lucy V, 421
Moon, Lucy V, 422
Moon, Lucy VI, 884
Moon, Lucy Ann VI, 884
Moon, Lucy Belle V, 193
Moon, Luella V, 422
Moon, Lulu V, 698
Moon, Lurany I, 361
Moon, Lurany I, 410
Moon, Lydia V, 101
Moon, Lydia V, 102
Moon, Lydia V, 265
Moon, Lydia V, 293
Moon, Lydia V, 373
Moon, Lydia V, 377
Moon, Lydia V, 415
Moon, Lydia V, 416
Moon, Lydia V, 417
Moon, Lydia V, 419
Moon, Lydia V, 420
Moon, Lydia V, 421
Moon, Lydia V, 422
Moon, Lydia V, 425
Moon, Lydia V, 518
Moon, Lydia V, 586
Moon, Lydia V, 698
Moon, Lydia VI, 841
Moon, Lydia C. V, 422
Moon, Lydia E. V, 265
Moon, Lydia J. V, 421
Moon, Lydia Jane V, 375
Moon, Lydia Jane V, 416
Moon, Lydia Jane V, 418
Moon, Lydia Jane V, 421
Moon, Lydia M. V, 414
Moon, Lydia M. V, 418
Moon, Lydia Margaret V, 416
Moon, Lydia Margaret V, 422
Moon, Madge Brown V, 422
Moon, Mae V, 698
Moon, Maggie G. V, 422
Moon, Mahala V, 373
Moon, Mahala V, 416
Moon, Mahala V, 417
Moon, Mahlon II, 965
Moon, Mahlon II, 966
Moon, Mahlon II, 1017
Moon, Mahlon II, 1049
Moon, Mahlon II, 1056
Moon, Mahlon II, 1058
Moon, Malachi I, 563
Moon, Malachia I, 563
Moon, Malakiah I, 563
Moon, Maliciah I, 511
Moon, Malinda I, 410
Moon, Malinda V, 415
Moon, Malinda V, 421
Moon, Manary B. V, 417
Moon, Margaret I, 361
Moon, Margaret I, 410
Moon, Margaret I, 528
Moon, Margaret I, 563
Moon, Margaret II, 965
Moon, Margaret V, 377
Moon, Margaret V, 415
Moon, Margaret V, 417
Moon, Margaret V, 420
Moon, Margaret V, 421
Moon, Margaret V, 422
Moon, Margaret V, 437
Moon, Margaret VI, 371
Moon, Margaret E. V, 418
Moon, Margaret Ellen V, 265
Moon, Margaret Ellin V, 265
Moon, Margaret Emily V, 421
Moon, Margaret Lydia V, 418
Moon, Maria V, 418
Moon, Maria V, 421
Moon, Maria B. II, 966
Moon, Maria Balderston II, 1044
Moon, Maria Balderston II, 1056
Moon, Maria L. V, 419
Moon, Maria O. VI, 819
Moon, Mariah VI, 841
Moon, Marian I, 511
Moon, Marietta II, 949
Moon, Marion C. I, 410
Moon, Marion Jane II, 1086
Moon, Martha II, 599
Moon, Martha II, 646
Moon, Martha II, 965
Moon, Martha II, 982
Moon, Martha II, 984
Moon, Martha II, 985
Moon, Martha II, 990
Moon, Martha II, 1017
Moon, Martha II, 1063
Moon, Martha V, 392
Moon, Martha V, 418
Moon, Martha V, 421
Moon, Martha V, 422
Moon, Martha VI, 730
Moon, Martha VI, 737
Moon, Martha VI, 767
Moon, Martha VI, 788
Moon, Martha VI, 795
Moon, Martha VI, 965
Moon, Martha D. VI, 767
Moon, Martha Emily V, 417
Moon, Martha R. II, 1056
Moon, Marthena Davis VI, 767
Moon, Mary I, 361
Moon, Mary I, 368
Moon, Mary I, 410
Moon, Mary I, 428
Moon, Mary I, 429
Moon, Mary I, 563
Moon, Mary I, 577
Moon, Mary I, 734
Moon, Mary I, 1109
Moon, Mary I, 1128
Moon, Mary II, 600
Moon, Mary II, 659
Moon, Mary II, 965
Moon, Mary II, 966
Moon, Mary II, 1010
Moon, Mary II, 1017
Moon, Mary II, 1027
Moon, Mary II, 1033
Moon, Mary II, 1039
Moon, Mary II, 1049
Moon, Mary II, 1056
Moon, Mary II, 1072
Moon, Mary II, 1076
Moon, Mary II, 1086
Moon, Mary V, 102
Moon, Mary V, 193
Moon, Mary V, 236
Moon, Mary V, 265
Moon, Mary V, 350
Moon, Mary V, 375
Moon, Mary V, 384
Moon, Mary V, 395
Moon, Mary V, 405
Moon, Mary V, 410
Moon, Mary V, 413
Moon, Mary V, 414
Moon, Mary V, 415
Moon, Mary V, 416
Moon, Mary V, 417
Moon, Mary V, 418
Moon, Mary V, 419
Moon, Mary V, 420
Moon, Mary V, 421
Moon, Mary V, 426
Moon, Mary V, 427
Moon, Mary V, 429
Moon, Mary V, 431
Moon, Mary V, 432
Moon, Mary V, 439
Moon, Mary V, 441
Moon, Mary V, 461
Moon, Mary V, 498
Moon, Mary V, 517
Moon, Mary V, 518
Moon, Mary V, 698
Moon, Mary V, 828
Moon, Mary V, 853
Moon, Mary V, 875
Moon, Mary VI, 424
Moon, Mary VI, 673
Moon, Mary A. V, 182
Moon, Mary A. V, 421
Moon, Mary A. V, 436
Moon, Mary Ann V, 99
Moon, Mary Ann V, 101
Moon, Mary Ann V, 102
Moon, Mary Ann V, 417
Moon, Mary Anna II, 949
Moon, Mary B. II, 1056
Moon, Mary Brown II, 965
Moon, Mary C. II, 965
Moon, Mary C. II, 1050
Moon, Mary C. II, 1087
Moon, Mary C. II, 1089
Moon, Mary C. V, 698
Moon, Mary E. I, 410
Moon, Mary E. V, 145
Moon, Mary E. V, 389
Moon, Mary E. V, 418
Moon, Mary E. V, 421
Moon, Mary E. V, 461
Moon, Mary E. VI, 942
Moon, Mary Edith V, 418
Moon, Mary Elizabeth V, 417
Moon, Mary Elizabeth V, 420
Moon, Mary Ellen V, 375
Moon, Mary Ellen V, 416
Moon, Mary Ellen V, 421
Moon, Mary Emily V, 421
Moon, Mary Emma V, 193
Moon, Mary Etta V, 418
Moon, Mary Eva V, 193
Moon, Mary Eva V, 421
Moon, Mary Eva V, 587
Moon, Mary Halcie V, 422
Moon, Mary J. V, 418
Moon, Mary Jane V, 373
Moon, Mary Jane V, 403
Moon, Mary Jane V, 416
Moon, Mary Jane V, 420

Moon, Mary Jane V, 422
Moon, Mary Louesa V, 418
Moon, Mary Louisa II, 949
Moon, Mary Louisa II, 1089
Moon, Mary Louise II, 1086
Moon, Mary Louise V, 419
Moon, Mary Lydia II, 965
Moon, Mary Lydia V, 417
Moon, Mary Platt II, 1056
Moon, Mary Stricklen I, 726
Moon, Mary, Jr. II, 1076
Moon, Mary-ann Elizabeth V, 193
Moon, Maryann V, 518
Moon, Massy Jemima V, 193
Moon, Mathew V, 415
Moon, Mathew V, 420
Moon, Matthew VI, 866
Moon, May E. V, 698
Moon, Melinda V, 410
Moon, Melinda V, 419
Moon, Melissa V, 416
Moon, Melissa V, 420
Moon, Melissa V, 437
Moon, Mellie V, 193
Moon, Miles V, 415
Moon, Miles V, 417
Moon, Miles V, 421
Moon, Miles C. V, 518
Moon, Miles H. V, 389
Moon, Miles H. V, 420
Moon, Miles H. V, 493
Moon, Miles H. V, 518
Moon, Milla I, 563
Moon, Milley I, 511
Moon, Milton V, 193
Moon, Milton W. V, 698
Moon, Minerva L. VI, 949
Moon, Minnie V, 422
Moon, Minnie A. V, 698
Moon, Minnie D. V, 422
Moon, Minnie D. V, 587
Moon, Minnie Dolphenia V, 418
Moon, Minnie O. V, 422
Moon, Minnie Olive V, 418
Moon, Minnie Ollie V, 422
Moon, Miriam V, 517
Moon, Morton V, 421
Moon, Moses II, 965
Moon, Moses II, 985
Moon, Moses II, 1017
Moon, Moses V, 392
Moon, Moses V, 415
Moon, Moses V, 417
Moon, Moses V, 419
Moon, Moses V, 440
Moon, Myra V, 422
Moon, Myrta V, 421
Moon, Nancy V, 419
Moon, Nancy V, 420
Moon, Nancy V, 424
Moon, Nancy VI, 841
Moon, Nancy VI, 927
Moon, Naomi V, 422
Moon, Narcess V, 420
Moon, Narcissa V, 416
Moon, Nathan V, 415
Moon, Nathan V, 419
Moon, Nathan V, 420
Moon, Nathan V, 421
Moon, Nathan V, 422
Moon, Nathan B. V, 417
Moon, Nathan W. V, 417
Moon, Nelson V, 417
Moon, Nelson V, 421
Moon, Nelson V, 586
Moon, Nelson Lydia V, 587
Moon, Neri V, 182
Moon, Neri V, 193
Moon, Neri V, 415
Moon, Neri V, 421
Moon, Nina V, 419
Moon, Nixon V, 415
Moon, Nixon V, 419
Moon, Nora E. V, 193
Moon, Obadiah V, 417
Moon, Obadiah V, 420
Moon, Oland J. V, 634
Moon, Oland J. V, 698
Moon, Olin V, 698
Moon, Olive V, 421
Moon, Olive R. V, 698
Moon, Oliver V, 193
Moon, Oliver V, 417
Moon, Oliver V, 420
Moon, Oliver V, 421
Moon, Oliver V, 756
Moon, Oliver Arthur V, 587
Moon, Ora V, 422
Moon, Orland V, 698
Moon, Orlando V, 634
Moon, Orpha V, 421
Moon, Oscar V, 698
Moon, Ossian V, 418
Moon, Ossian V, 421
Moon, Othello V, 419
Moon, Otto V, 422
Moon, Otto V, 698
Moon, Otto J. V, 418
Moon, Parham VI, 841
Moon, Parker V, 417
Moon, Parker V, 421
Moon, Patrick VI, 841
Moon, Percy S. VI, 767
Moon, Peter I, 370
Moon, Peter I, 409
Moon, Phebe V, 193
Moon, Phebe V, 355
Moon, Phebe V, 373
Moon, Phebe V, 385
Moon, Phebe V, 395
Moon, Phebe V, 414
Moon, Phebe V, 415
Moon, Phebe V, 416
Moon, Phebe V, 417
Moon, Phebe V, 419
Moon, Phebe V, 420
Moon, Phebe V, 421
Moon, Phebe V, 422
Moon, Phebe V, 432
Moon, Phebe VI, 767
Moon, Pleasant V, 411
Moon, Pleasant V, 415
Moon, Pleasant V, 417
Moon, Pleasant V, 419
Moon, Pleasant V, 421
Moon, Pleasant V, 440
Moon, Pleasant V, 441
Moon, Polly V, 167
Moon, Polly V, 193
Moon, Polly V, 415
Moon, Polly V, 421
Moon, Priscilla V, 324
Moon, Priscilla V, 350
Moon, Priscilla V, 377
Moon, Priscilla V, 380
Moon, Priscilla V, 416
Moon, Priscilla V, 419
Moon, Priscilla V, 420
Moon, Priscilla V, 421
Moon, Priscilla S. V, 421
Moon, Quintillius V. V, 421
Moon, R. Barclay II, 965
Moon, Rachel I, 361
Moon, Rachel I, 367
Moon, Rachel I, 370
Moon, Rachel I, 409
Moon, Rachel I, 410
Moon, Rachel I, 420
Moon, Rachel I, 427
Moon, Rachel I, 563
Moon, Rachel I, 577
Moon, Rachel I, 667
Moon, Rachel I, 1111
Moon, Rachel II, 965
Moon, Rachel II, 985
Moon, Rachel II, 1017
Moon, Rachel II, 1056
Moon, Rachel II, 1061
Moon, Rachel V, 350
Moon, Rachel V, 352
Moon, Rachel V, 384
Moon, Rachel V, 393
Moon, Rachel V, 395
Moon, Rachel V, 397
Moon, Rachel V, 402
Moon, Rachel V, 411
Moon, Rachel V, 415
Moon, Rachel V, 416
Moon, Rachel V, 417
Moon, Rachel V, 418
Moon, Rachel V, 419
Moon, Rachel V, 420
Moon, Rachel V, 421
Moon, Rachel V, 422
Moon, Rachel V, 425
Moon, Rachel V, 436
Moon, Rachel Ann II, 965
Moon, Rachel Anna II, 965
Moon, Rachel Anna II, 970
Moon, Rachel Anna II, 1058
Moon, Rachel Jane V, 416
Moon, Rachel Jane V, 421
Moon, Rachel Jane V, 853
Moon, Rachel T. II, 965
Moon, Rachel T. II, 1056
Moon, Ralph V, 698
Moon, Ralph L. V, 698
Moon, Raymond V, 422
Moon, Rebecca II, 1066
Moon, Rebecca II, 1076
Moon, Rebecca V, 176
Moon, Rebecca V, 413
Moon, Rebecca V, 414
Moon, Rebecca V, 417
Moon, Rebecca V, 418
Moon, Rebecca V, 420
Moon, Rebecca V, 421
Moon, Rebecca V, 422
Moon, Rebecca VI, 767
Moon, Rebecca VI, 793
Moon, Rebecca W. II, 1056
Moon, Rebeckah II, 990
Moon, Rebeckah II, 1017
Moon, Reece II, 966
Moon, Reuben C. V, 416
Moon, Rhoda V, 73
Moon, Richard I, 511
Moon, Richard I, 563
Moon, Richard I, 1107
Moon, Richard I, 1109
Moon, Richard V, 24
Moon, Richard V, 82
Moon, Richard V, 101
Moon, Richard V, 265
Moon, Richard V, 395
Moon, Richard V, 415
Moon, Richard V, 417
Moon, Richard V, 419
Moon, Richard V, 420
Moon, Richard V, 421
Moon, Richard V, 429
Moon, Richard V, 517
Moon, Richard V, 518
Moon, Richard VI, 424
Moon, Richard E. V, 418
Moon, Richard, Jr. I, 563
Moon, Robert V, 415
Moon, Robert V, 417
Moon, Robert V, 418
Moon, Robert V, 420
Moon, Robert V, 421
Moon, Robert Barclay II, 965
Moon, Robert E. V, 418
Moon, Robert E. V, 422
Moon, Robert E. V, 587
Moon, Robert Ellwood V, 422
Moon, Rodger II, 1016
Moon, Rodger II, 1018
Moon, Roger II, 965
Moon, Roger II, 966
Moon, Roger II, 985
Moon, Roger II, 1010
Moon, Roger II, 1012
Moon, Roger II, 1016
Moon, Roger II, 1017
Moon, Roger II, 1022
Moon, Ruby V, 422
Moon, Russell V, 193
Moon, Russell W. V, 193
Moon, Ruth I, 358
Moon, Ruth I, 361
Moon, Ruth I, 368
Moon, Ruth I, 395
Moon, Ruth I, 409
Moon, Ruth I, 410
Moon, Ruth I, 1109
Moon, Ruth I, 1128
Moon, Ruth V, 101
Moon, Ruth V, 265
Moon, Ruth V, 350
Moon, Ruth V, 395
Moon, Ruth V, 407
Moon, Ruth V, 415
Moon, Ruth V, 416
Moon, Ruth V, 417
Moon, Ruth V, 419
Moon, Ruth V, 420
Moon, Ruth V, 426
Moon, Ruth V, 436
Moon, Ruth V, 698
Moon, Ruth Anna V, 698
Moon, Ruthanna V, 666
Moon, Ruthanna V, 698
Moon, Salina V, 469
Moon, Saline V, 517
Moon, Sally VI, 841
Moon, Samantha B. V, 421
Moon, Samantha B. V, 422
Moon, Samantha B. V, 586
Moon, Samantha B. V, 587
Moon, Samantha B. V, 591
Moon, Samantha Louella V, 416
Moon, Samantha Luella V, 420
Moon, Samira V, 418
Moon, Samuel I, 1109
Moon, Samuel II, 599
Moon, Samuel II, 600
Moon, Samuel II, 965
Moon, Samuel II, 966
Moon, Samuel II, 982
Moon, Samuel II, 984
Moon, Samuel II, 985
Moon, Samuel II, 990
Moon, Samuel II, 1016
Moon, Samuel II, 1017
Moon, Samuel II, 1056
Moon, Samuel II, 1057
Moon, Samuel II, 1061
Moon, Samuel V, 193
Moon, Samuel V, 265
Moon, Samuel V, 415
Moon, Samuel V, 416
Moon, Samuel V, 417
Moon, Samuel V, 419
Moon, Samuel V, 420
Moon, Samuel V, 422
Moon, Samuel V, 426
Moon, Samuel V, 441
Moon, Samuel A. VI, 942
Moon, Samuel B. II, 970
Moon, Samuel C. II, 965
Moon, Samuel C. II, 1058
Moon, Sanford V, 422
Moon, Sanford A. V, 417
Moon, Sarah I, 361
Moon, Sarah I, 397
Moon, Sarah I, 409
Moon, Sarah I, 410
Moon, Sarah I, 420
Moon, Sarah I, 1128
Moon, Sarah II, 242
Moon, Sarah II, 446
Moon, Sarah II, 600
Moon, Sarah II, 966
Moon, Sarah II, 974
Moon, Sarah II, 985
Moon, Sarah II, 993
Moon, Sarah II, 998
Moon, Sarah II, 1016
Moon, Sarah II, 1017
Moon, Sarah V, 349
Moon, Sarah V, 350
Moon, Sarah V, 373
Moon, Sarah V, 377
Moon, Sarah V, 391
Moon, Sarah V, 393
Moon, Sarah V, 395
Moon, Sarah V, 402
Moon, Sarah V, 403
Moon, Sarah V, 414
Moon, Sarah V, 415
Moon, Sarah V, 416
Moon, Sarah V, 417
Moon, Sarah V, 419
Moon, Sarah V, 420
Moon, Sarah V, 422
Moon, Sarah V, 426
Moon, Sarah V, 439
Moon, Sarah V, 517
Moon, Sarah VI, 260
Moon, Sarah VI, 767
Moon, Sarah Ann I, 410
Moon, Sarah Ann II, 965
Moon, Sarah Ann II, 1056
Moon, Sarah Ann V, 379
Moon, Sarah Ann V, 392
Moon, Sarah Ann V, 416
Moon, Sarah Ann V, 417
Moon, Sarah Ann V, 420
Moon, Sarah Ann V, 421
Moon, Sarah Ann V, 422
Moon, Sarah C. II, 1086
Moon, Sarah E. V, 392
Moon, Sarah E. V, 415
Moon, Sarah E. V, 421
Moon, Sarah Elizabeth V, 388
Moon, Sarah Elizabeth V, 415
Moon, Sarah Elizabeth V, 416
Moon, Sarah Elizabeth V, 417
Moon, Sarah Elizabeth V, 421
Moon, Sarah H. V, 420
Moon, Sarah Jane V, 420
Moon, Sarah M. V, 421
Moon, Sary I, 1109
Moon, Selima I, 563
Moon, Selina I, 563
Moon, Selina V, 518
Moon, Seth V, 414
Moon, Seth V, 415
Moon, Seth V, 416
Moon, Seth V, 417
Moon, Seth V, 421
Moon, Silas V, 415
Moon, Silas V, 416
Moon, Silas V, 420
Moon, Simeon VI, 424
Moon, Simon I, 347
Moon, Simon I, 361
Moon, Simon I, 409
Moon, Simon I, 410
Moon, Simon I, 420
Moon, Simon I, 511
Moon, Simon I, 563
Moon, Simon I, 685
Moon, Simon II, 966
Moon, Simon V, 65
Moon, Simon V, 101
Moon, Simon V, 102
Moon, Simon V, 517
Moon, Simon V, 518
Moon, Simon VI, 371
Moon, Simon P. V, 418
Moon, Simon P. V, 421
Moon, Simon Peter V, 416
Moon, Simon, Jr. I, 563
Moon, Simon, Jr. V, 517
Moon, Simon, Jr. V, 518
Moon, Solina I, 683
Moon, Solina I, 685
Moon, Solomon V, 415
Moon, Solomon V, 417
Moon, Solomon V, 418
Moon, Solomon V, 419
Moon, Solomon L. V, 421
Moon, Solomon, Jr. V, 419
Moon, Stephen V, 415
Moon, Stephen V, 420
Moon, Stephen VI, 841
Moon, Stephen O. V, 417
Moon, Susan V, 422
Moon, Susana V, 956
Moon, Susanna I, 511
Moon, Susanna I, 539
Moon, Susanna I, 557
Moon, Susanna I, 563
Moon, Susanna I, 1107
Moon, Susanna V, 376
Moon, Susanna V, 416
Moon, Susanna V, 420
Moon, Susanna V, 436
Moon, Susanna V, 586
Moon, Susanna V, 590
Moon, Susanna A. V, 418
Moon, Susanna W. VI, 855
Moon, Susannah I, 361
Moon, Susannah V, 322
Moon, Susannah V, 350
Moon, Susannah V, 375
Moon, Susannah V, 415
Moon, Susannah V, 416
Moon, Susannah V, 417
Moon, Susannah V, 418
Moon, Susannah V, 419
Moon, Susannah V, 421
Moon, Susannah V, 422
Moon, Susannah V, 436
Moon, Susannah V, 441
Moon, Susannah Beeson VI, 42
Moon, Susannah Brown VI, 42
Moon, Susannah C. VI, 841
Moon, Sylvanus V, 416
Moon, T. E. V, 698
Moon, T. Elwood V, 634
Moon, Talbert V, 417
Moon, Tamar V, 379
Moon, Tamar V, 414
Moon, Tamar V, 420
Moon, Thomas I, 361
Moon, Thomas II, 446
Moon, Thomas II, 1056
Moon, Thomas V, 414
Moon, Thomas V, 415
Moon, Thomas V, 416
Moon, Thomas V, 417
Moon, Thomas V, 418
Moon, Thomas V, 419
Moon, Thomas V, 420
Moon, Thomas V, 421
Moon, Thomas V, 422
Moon, Thomas V, 426
Moon, Thomas V, 430
Moon, Thomas V, 431
Moon, Thomas V, 698
Moon, Thomas V, 853
Moon, Thomas VI, 424
Moon, Thomas Branson V, 420
Moon, Thomas E. V, 634
Moon, Thomas H. III, 233
Moon, Thomas J. V, 418
Moon, Thomas J. V, 421
Moon, Thomas J. V, 422
Moon, Thomas J. V, 698
Moon, Thomas W. V, 416
Moon, Thomas W. V, 418
Moon, Thomas W. V, 420
Moon, Thomas W. V, 421
Moon, Thomas W. V, 422
Moon, Thomas, Jr. V, 419
Moon, Thomas, Jr. V, 420
Moon, Thomas, Sr. V, 421
Moon, Thos. V, 709
Moon, Timothy II, 966
Moon, Timothy II, 1016
Moon, Ursola V, 419
Moon, Ursola V, 425

on, Ursula V, 350
on, Ursula V, 355
on, Ursula V, 416
on, Vashti I, 511
on, Vashti I, 563
on, Vashti V, 24
on, Vashti V, 82
on, Vashti V, 101
on, Vashti V, 416
on, Vashti V, 419
on, Vashti V, 517
on, Vashti V, 518
on, Vashti, Jr. V, 101
on, Vesta I, 563
on, W. T. V, 419
on, Walter V, 418
on, Walter V, 422
on, Walter Clarence V, 422
on, Walter E. V, 418
on, Walter E. V, 421
on, Walter West V, 422
on, Wanda V, 690
on, Wanda V, 698
on, Wd. Elizabeth II, 1016
on, Wd. Elizabeth II, 1018
on, Wd. Joan II, 965
on, Wd. Mary II, 446
on, Wilkerson T. V, 102
on, Wilkerson T. V, 417
oon, Wilkerson T. V, 421
on, William I, 361
on, William I, 409
oon, William I, 563
oon, William I, 1109
oon, William II, 966
oon, William V, 176
on, William V, 265
oon, William V, 350
oon, William V, 414
oon, William V, 415
oon, William V, 417
oon, William V, 418
oon, William V, 419
oon, William V, 420
oon, William V, 421
oon, William V, 853
oon, William VI, 841
oon, William VI, 844
oon, William VI, 849
oon, William VI, 855
oon, William VI, 927
oon, William A. V, 587
oon, William Bazzle V, 193
oon, William C. V, 421
oon, William D. V, 417
oon, William Ellis V, 418
oon, William F. V, 419
oon, William H. II, 965
oon, William H. II, 966
oon, William H. V, 418
oon, William H. V, 422
oon, William H. V, 587
oon, William J. V, 417
oon, William K. V, 416
oon, William K. V, 853
oon, William R. V, 421
oon, William R. Hockett V, 420
oon, William Riley V, 415
oon, William Riley V, 420
oon, William T. V, 415
oon, William T. V, 416
oon, William T. V, 421
oon, William T. V, 422
oon, William W. V, 437
oon, William Willet II, 965
Moon, Willis D. V, 419
Moon, Wilson T. V, 422
Moon, Wm. II, 600
Moon, Wm. II, 1016
Moon, Wm. II, 1017
Moon, Wm. II, 1018
Moon, Wm. II, 1076
Moon, Wm. V, 356
Moon, Wm. V, 416
Moon, Wm. V, 419
Moon, Wm. V, 433
Moon, Wm. VI, 980
Moon, Wm. B. V, 193
Moon, Wm. Hockett V, 419
Moon, Wm. P. V, 634
Moon, Wm. P. V, 698
Moon, Zimri V, 350
Moon, Zimri V, 416
Moon, Zimri V, 419
Moon, Zimri V, 420
Moone, Mary II, 600
Mooney, Ann I, 410
Mooney, Anne I, 1044
Mooney, Catherine V, 234
Mooney, Catherine V, 265
Mooney, Deborah I, 1044
Mooney, Edward IV, 488
Mooney, Elizabeth IV, 253
Mooney, Elizabeth VI, 423
Mooney, Elizabeth VI, 424
Mooney, Esther VI, 404
Mooney, Esther VI, 424
Mooney, Eva P. IV, 488
Mooney, F. H. IV, 488
Mooney, H. E. IV, 488
Mooney, Hattie IV, 1174
Mooney, J. H. IV, 488
Mooney, James V, 265
Mooney, James, Sr. V, 265
Mooney, John I, 1044
Mooney, John I, 1049
Mooney, Joseph I, 410
Mooney, Joseph I, 1041
Mooney, Joseph I, 1044
Mooney, Joseph I, 1049
Mooney, Lelia A. C. VI, 841
Mooney, Malcolm IV, 488
Mooney, Marie IV, 488
Mooney, Martha I, 410
Mooney, Martha I, 1044
Mooney, Martha II, 600
Mooney, Martha Neal I, 410
Mooney, Mary I, 393
Mooney, Mary I, 410
Mooney, Mary I, 1044
Mooney, Mary V, 234
Mooney, Mary V, 265
Mooney, Mary E. IV, 488
Mooney, Michael VI, 841
Mooney, N. O. IV, 488
Mooney, Patience V, 301
Mooney, Patience V, 307
Mooney, Phebe V, 230
Mooney, Phebe V, 265
Mooney, Phebe VI, 362
Mooney, Phebe VI, 424
Mooney, Polly V, 265
Mooney, Prudence I, 1044
Mooney, Rachel I, 410
Mooney, Samuel I, 410
Mooney, Sarah I, 1044
Mooney, Wm. IV, 488
Moony, Ann I, 380
Moony, Ann I, 409
Moony, Ann I, 410
Moony, Ann Miller I, 422
Moony, Elizabeth VI, 424
Moony, Esther VI, 424
Moony, John I, 1049
Moony, Joseph I, 1049
Moony, Joseph VI, 424
Moony, Martha I, 411
Moony, Martha Neal I, 410
Moony, Mary I, 410
Moony, Phebe VI, 424
Moony, Rachel I, 410
Moony, Sidney V, 422
Moony, Sidney C. V, 422
Moor, Abigail I, 37
Moor, Abigail I, 60
Moor, Abigail I, 423
Moor, Abigail Thomas I, 410
Moor, Alexander I, 1049
Moor, Ann V, 265
Moor, Ann VI, 593
Moor, Ann VI, 601
Moor, Anne VI, 260
Moor, Anthony I, 1096
Moor, Anthony II, 446
Moor, Anthony VI, 601
Moor, Benjamin, Jr. II, 191
Moor, Benjamin, Jr. II, 242
Moor, Camm I, 526
Moor, Camm I, 563
Moor, Charles Harrison III, 233
Moor, David VI, 601
Moor, David R. V, 518
Moor, E. Katy I, 1159
Moor, Edward T. V, 518
Moor, Eliza Ann I, 196
Moor, Elizabeth I Sup 1, 4
Moor, Elizabeth II, 397
Moor, Elmira V, 102
Moor, Elmira V, 518
Moor, Francis I, 185
Moor, Gilpah VI, 601
Moor, Hannah I, 185
Moor, Hannah IV, 28
Moor, Hannah IV, 50
Moor, Hannah VI, 380
Moor, Isabel I, 60
Moor, James I, 1035
Moor, James I, 1049
Moor, John I, 60
Moor, John I, 196
Moor, John I, 410
Moor, John I, 563
Moor, John II, 397
Moor, Joseph I, 185
Moor, Joseph V, 265
Moor, Lancaster John I, 338
Moor, Leah Jane I, 60
Moor, Lydia Ann V, 518
Moor, Margaret I, 60
Moor, Mary I, 146
Moor, Mary I, 153
Moor, Mary I, 185
Moor, Mary II, 191
Moor, Mary II, 242
Moor, Mary II, 446
Moor, Mary II, 600
Moor, Mary VI, 601
Moor, Mary Peele I, 196
Moor, Milton Y. V, 518
Moor, Mirriam I, 60
Moor, Mordecai I, 1035
Moor, Nancy I, 196
Moor, Patience II, 242
Moor, Peninah I, 60
Moor, Peninah I, 196
Moor, Phebe V, 265
Moor, Prudence I, 410
Moor, Rachel V, 265
Moor, Rachel V, 884
Moor, Rachel VI, 601
Moor, Rebecca II, 446
Moor, Richard I, 1041
Moor, Robert I, 1096
Moor, Robert VI, 601
Moor, Ruth VI, 601
Moor, Samuel S. V, 518
Moor, Sarah II, 397
Moor, Sarah V, 265
Moor, Sarah V, 518
Moor, Sarah VI, 601
Moor, Sarah Elizabeth V, 518
Moor, Seaborn V, 884
Moor, Sophia I, 526
Moor, Sophia I, 563
Moor, Thomas II, 397
Moor, William I Sup 1, 4
Moor, William VI, 260
Moor, Wm., Sr. I Sup 1, 3
Moor, Wm., Sr. I Sup 1, 6
Moore, ??? III, 96
Moore, ??? III, 220
Moore, ??? III, 233
Moore, ??? III, 329
Moore, ??? V, 587
Moore, ??? V, 823
Moore, ??? VI, 283
Moore, A. K. I, 638
Moore, Aaron I, 34
Moore, Aaron I, 60
Moore, Abigail I, 60
Moore, Abigail I, 423
Moore, Abigail I, 789
Moore, Abigail I, 801
Moore, Abigail I, 830
Moore, Abigail III, 233
Moore, Abigail V, 307
Moore, Abigail V, 518
Moore, Abigail VI, 424
Moore, Abigail VI, 601
Moore, Abigail C. I, 831
Moore, Abigail L. III, 383
Moore, Abigail S. II, 756
Moore, Abigail S. II, 761
Moore, Abigail Thomas I, 410
Moore, Abner II, 600
Moore, Abner II, 601
Moore, Abner IV, 102
Moore, Abner VI, 535
Moore, Abner VI, 536
Moore, Abner VI, 601
Moore, Abner VI, 676
Moore, Abraham II, 397
Moore, Abraham V, 508
Moore, Abraham V, 518
Moore, Ada VI, 424
Moore, Ada VI, 439
Moore, Adaline E. V, 587
Moore, Addison I, 589
Moore, Adelbert V, 699
Moore, Aggy VI, 965
Moore, Agnes II, 601
Moore, Agnes T. II, 713
Moore, Albert A. V, 885
Moore, Albert K. V, 518
Moore, Albert R. III, 233
Moore, Albert R. V, 588
Moore, Alexander I, 1049
Moore, Alexander V, 102
Moore, Alexander V, 832
Moore, Alexander V, 854
Moore, Alexander VI, 965
Moore, Alfred II, 900
Moore, Alfred III, 490
Moore, Alfred III, 491
Moore, Alfred III, 505
Moore, Alfred B. V, 588
Moore, Alfred B. V, 698
Moore, Alfred H. III, 490
Moore, Alfred H. III, 506
Moore, Alice I, 638
Moore, Alice I, 895
Moore, Alice I, 903
Moore, Alice I, 1044
Moore, Alice I, 1128
Moore, Alice II, 397
Moore, Alice II, 947
Moore, Alice V, 102
Moore, Alice V, 699
Moore, Alice V, 854
Moore, Alice V, 861
Moore, Alice L. D. III, 233
Moore, Alice T. I, 622
Moore, Allen II, 810
Moore, Allen II, 863
Moore, Allen II, 900
Moore, Allen V, 580
Moore, Allie V, 588
Moore, Alphonzo Ralph I, 338
Moore, Amanda IV, 253
Moore, Amanda IV, 1174
Moore, Amanda IV, 1181
Moore, Amanda M. V, 1011
Moore, Amelia I, 270
Moore, Amelia I, 274
Moore, America V, 699
Moore, Amy VI, 571
Moore, Amy L. III, 149
Moore, Amy L. III, 233
Moore, Andrew V, 518
Moore, Andrew Robeson II, 810
Moore, Ann I, 34
Moore, Ann I, 60
Moore, Ann I, 68
Moore, Ann I, 511
Moore, Ann I, 563
Moore, Ann I, 595
Moore, Ann II, 242
Moore, Ann II, 397
Moore, Ann II, 511
Moore, Ann II, 520
Moore, Ann II, 600
Moore, Ann II, 810
Moore, Ann II, 863
Moore, Ann III, 233
Moore, Ann V, 26
Moore, Ann V, 102
Moore, Ann V, 265
Moore, Ann V, 587
Moore, Ann VI, 260
Moore, Ann VI, 421
Moore, Ann VI, 424
Moore, Ann VI, 429
Moore, Ann VI, 501
Moore, Ann VI, 527
Moore, Ann VI, 530
Moore, Ann VI, 535
Moore, Ann VI, 536
Moore, Ann VI, 564
Moore, Ann VI, 575
Moore, Ann VI, 586
Moore, Ann VI, 601
Moore, Ann VI, 677
Moore, Ann VI, 708
Moore, Ann VI, 711
Moore, Ann VI, 783
Moore, Ann Eliza II, 1088
Moore, Ann Eliza II, 1089
Moore, Ann Gane I, 563
Moore, Ann Gane I, 569
Moore, Ann T. II, 810
Moore, Ann T. II, 900
Moore, Ann W. II, 809
Moore, Ann W. II, 897
Moore, Ann W. II, 900
Moore, Ann Williams II, 806
Moore, Anna I, 563
Moore, Anna I, 586
Moore, Anna I, 589
Moore, Anna I, 963
Moore, Anna I, 967
Moore, Anna II, 788
Moore, Anna II, 843
Moore, Anna II, 887
Moore, Anna III, 383
Moore, Anna IV, 253
Moore, Anna IV, 343
Moore, Anna IV, 1258
Moore, Anna V, 265
Moore, Anna V, 350
Moore, Anna V, 854
Moore, Anna F. III, 316
Moore, Anna F. III, 382
Moore, Anna Mary I, 563
Moore, Anna Mott III, 233
Moore, Anne I, 511
Moore, Anne I, 549
Moore, Anne I, 563
Moore, Anne II, 197
Moore, Anne II, 600
Moore, Anne V, 587
Moore, Anne VI, 260
Moore, Anne VI, 286
Moore, Anne Grace I, 563
Moore, Anney VI, 841
Moore, Annie I, 326
Moore, Annie I, 338
Moore, Anthony I, 1128
Moore, Anthony II, 397
Moore, Anthony II, 480
Moore, Anthony II, 600
Moore, Anthony VI, 424
Moore, Anthony VI, 601
Moore, Ariadna I, 546
Moore, Ariadna I, 563
Moore, Ariedny I, 563
Moore, Armelle I, 274
Moore, Arthur I, 338
Moore, Arthur V, 699
Moore, Arthur K. I, 638
Moore, Arthur K. V, 699
Moore, Arthur K., Jr. I, 622
Moore, Arthur Kirby I, 622
Moore, Asa II, 600
Moore, Asa VI, 366
Moore, Asa VI, 424
Moore, Asa VI, 472
Moore, Asa VI, 501
Moore, Asa VI, 527
Moore, Asa VI, 536
Moore, Asa VI, 575
Moore, Asa VI, 586
Moore, Asa VI, 587
Moore, Asa VI, 664
Moore, Asa L. V, 307
Moore, Asahel II, 1088
Moore, Asahel II, 1089
Moore, Asenath C. II, 810
Moore, Aseneth C. II, 900
Moore, Auerila I, 1044
Moore, Austin V, 350
Moore, Austin VI, 841
Moore, Barbary VI, 800
Moore, Barclay V, 854
Moore, Bathsheba IV, 50
Moore, Bathsheba IV, 102
Moore, Bathsheba V, 828
Moore, Bathsheba V, 854
Moore, Bell V, 518
Moore, Ben VI, 822
Moore, Benajah V, 102
Moore, Benajah V, 854
Moore, Benjamin II, 35
Moore, Benjamin II, 73
Moore, Benjamin II, 88
Moore, Benjamin II, 242
Moore, Benjamin II, 1017
Moore, Benjamin II, 1057
Moore, Benjamin V, 587
Moore, Benjamin V, 698
Moore, Benjamin VI, 424
Moore, Benjamin VI, 601
Moore, Benjamin VI, 841
Moore, Benjamin VI, 905
Moore, Benjamin VI, 974
Moore, Benjamin, Jr. II, 88
Moore, Benjamin, Jr. II, 242
Moore, Bertha V, 1011
Moore, Betsey V, 307
Moore, Betsey VI, 841
Moore, Betsey Ann I, 311
Moore, Betsy VI, 935
Moore, Betsy VI, 974
Moore, Betty I, 46
Moore, Betty I, 60
Moore, Blanch I, 638
Moore, Blanch Ida V, 350
Moore, Blanche I, 638
Moore, C. A. IV, 1287
Moore, C. H. VI, 835
Moore, C. R. VI, 640
Moore, Caleb V, 698
Moore, Calvin IV, 253
Moore, Calvin IV, 299
Moore, Calvin C. IV, 741
Moore, Camm I, 511
Moore, Camm I, 563
Moore, Camm I, 586
Moore, Camm I, 589
Moore, Camm I, 967
Moore, Camm VI, 260
Moore, Campbell G. VI, 841
Moore, Caroline I, 589
Moore, Caroline V, 350
Moore, Carrie Elma V, 587
Moore, Carrie Willets III, 233

Moore, Carrie Wilson I, 338
Moore, Catharine II, 601
Moore, Catharine II, 806
Moore, Catharine II, 810
Moore, Catharine II, 887
Moore, Catharine II, 892
Moore, Catharine II, 900
Moore, Catharine III, 316
Moore, Catharine VI, 965
Moore, Catharine D. I, 329
Moore, Catharine D. I, 330
Moore, Catharine Randolph II, 805
Moore, Cecelia III, 233
Moore, Cecelie III, 196
Moore, Celia I, 338
Moore, Celia C. VI, 841
Moore, Celie I, 336
Moore, Chalkley II, 35
Moore, Charles I, 563
Moore, Charles I, 586
Moore, Charles I, 589
Moore, Charles I, 595
Moore, Charles I, 963
Moore, Charles I, 967
Moore, Charles II, 600
Moore, Charles IV, 253
Moore, Charles V, 350
Moore, Charles VI, 841
Moore, Charles Cameron I, 622
Moore, Charles Cameron I, 638
Moore, Charles Edward II, 901
Moore, Charles F. III, 293
Moore, Charles F. R. III, 233
Moore, Charles H. I, 563
Moore, Charles H. VI, 639
Moore, Charles Harrison III, 233
Moore, Charles Hubbard I, 511
Moore, Charles O. I, 622
Moore, Charles Oscar V, 699
Moore, Charles S. I, 933
Moore, Charlie V, 588
Moore, Charlie R. V, 698
Moore, Charlotte III, 490
Moore, Charlotte III, 491
Moore, Charlotte III, 505
Moore, Chas. V, 1011
Moore, Chas. J. V, 1011
Moore, Chester M. IV, 1330
Moore, Choicey IV, 253
Moore, Christian VI, 841
Moore, Christiana VI, 748
Moore, Christopher VI, 804
Moore, Christopher VI, 835
Moore, Christopher VI, 841
Moore, Clara V, 588
Moore, Clara M. V, 587
Moore, Clara Marcilla V, 350
Moore, Clara May V, 699
Moore, Clark V, 588
Moore, Clark V, 698
Moore, Clark V, 699
Moore, Clarke I, 830
Moore, Clarkson I, 511
Moore, Clarkson I, 563
Moore, Clarkson IV, 741
Moore, Clarky I, 789
Moore, Clementine III, 233
Moore, Clifton V, 587
Moore, Clifton V, 699
Moore, Clive VI, 799
Moore, Colvin C. IV, 741
Moore, Cornelia III, 233
Moore, Cornelius I, 60
Moore, Cornelius I, 68
Moore, Curtis I, 311
Moore, Curtis P. I, 287
Moore, Curtis P. I, 326
Moore, Curtis P. I, 330
Moore, Cyrus II, 323
Moore, Cyrus IV, 50
Moore, Cyrus IV, 102
Moore, D. F. McKiney I, 326
Moore, Dally VI, 841
Moore, Daniel VI, 841
Moore, Daniel Williams I, 326
Moore, Dasey Sanders I, 326
Moore, David I, 1128
Moore, David I, 1145
Moore, David I, 1159
Moore, David IV, 50
Moore, David IV, 102
Moore, David V, 102
Moore, David V, 854
Moore, David V, 884
Moore, David V, 885
Moore, David VI, 424
Moore, David VI, 601
Moore, David VI, 854
Moore, David VI, 965
Moore, David C. V, 102
Moore, David C. V, 885
Moore, David M. V, 854
Moore, David Nathaniel V, 884
Moore, David P. III, 293
Moore, David R. V, 102
Moore, David R. V, 518
Moore, David Richard IV, 894
Moore, David S. I, 326
Moore, David S. I, 330
Moore, David S. V, 587
Moore, David Sanders I, 326
Moore, David Sanders I, 330
Moore, David, Jr. V, 854
Moore, David, Jr. V, 884
Moore, Davis S. I, 329
Moore, Deborah II, 583
Moore, Deborah II, 600
Moore, Deborah III, 293
Moore, Deborah III, 427
Moore, Deborah A. V, 973
Moore, Deborah A. V, 976
Moore, Deborah White I, 616
Moore, Demey V, 854
Moore, Dempsey I, 563
Moore, Dempsey I, 1016
Moore, Dempsey V, 102
Moore, Demsy V, 854
Moore, Dinah Ann II, 751
Moore, Dinah Ann II, 756
Moore, Dinah Creek V, 854
Moore, Dinah Creek V, 872
Moore, Dinah G. I, 338
Moore, Dora I, 338
Moore, Dosha V, 698
Moore, Douglas V, 350
Moore, Dr. John II, 810
Moore, Dr. John Wilson II, 823
Moore, Drucilla V, 1011
Moore, Drusilla II, 179
Moore, Drusilla II, 296
Moore, E. B. I, 338
Moore, E. B., Jr. I, 338
Moore, E. Katy I, 1159
Moore, Earl III, 233
Moore, Earl F. V, 350
Moore, Eastburn Richey III, 293
Moore, Edith I, 830
Moore, Edith I, 931
Moore, Edith II, 900
Moore, Edith Ann V, 102
Moore, Edith Elisabeth I, 622
Moore, Edith Elizabeth I, 638
Moore, Edith R. IV, 1258
Moore, Editha VI, 965
Moore, Edna I, 511
Moore, Edna V, 518
Moore, Eduth I, 622
Moore, Edward III, 146
Moore, Edward III, 233
Moore, Edward IV, 104
Moore, Edward IV, 154
Moore, Edward IV, 1069
Moore, Edward V, 588
Moore, Edward A. V, 885
Moore, Edward Andrew V, 885
Moore, Edward B. I, 326
Moore, Edward B. I, 338
Moore, Edward G. V, 102
Moore, Edward M. III, 383
Moore, Edward T. IV, 154
Moore, Edward T. V, 518
Moore, Edward Thomas IV, 894
Moore, Edwin II, 901
Moore, Edwin III, 233
Moore, Edwin Bunting III, 53
Moore, Edwin Bunting III, 70
Moore, Edwin Bunting III, 233
Moore, Edwin D. VI, 966
Moore, Edwin P. II, 713
Moore, Edwin P. II, 756
Moore, Egtna IV, 1330
Moore, Elam I, 831
Moore, Elam B. I, 790
Moore, Eleanor IV, 1107
Moore, Eleanor IV, 1122
Moore, Eleanor V, 193
Moore, Elecsander I, 563
Moore, Elisabeth I, 60
Moore, Elisabeth I, 61
Moore, Elisabeth I, 86
Moore, Elisha V, 854
Moore, Eliz. III, 233
Moore, Eliza V, 698
Moore, Eliza V, 884
Moore, Eliza V, 885
Moore, Eliza A. V, 350
Moore, Eliza Ann I, 196
Moore, Eliza Ann V, 701
Moore, Eliza Henderson VI, 1010
Moore, Eliza K. V, 885
Moore, Elizabeth I, 326
Moore, Elizabeth I, 330
Moore, Elizabeth I, 338
Moore, Elizabeth I, 563
Moore, Elizabeth I, 567
Moore, Elizabeth I, 831
Moore, Elizabeth I Sup 1, 4
Moore, Elizabeth I Sup 1, 5
Moore, Elizabeth I Sup 1, 8
Moore, Elizabeth II, 88
Moore, Elizabeth II, 323
Moore, Elizabeth II, 397
Moore, Elizabeth II, 485
Moore, Elizabeth II, 600
Moore, Elizabeth II, 601
Moore, Elizabeth II, 676
Moore, Elizabeth II, 713
Moore, Elizabeth II, 727
Moore, Elizabeth II, 756
Moore, Elizabeth II, 810
Moore, Elizabeth II, 871
Moore, Elizabeth II, 900
Moore, Elizabeth III, 293
Moore, Elizabeth IV, 50
Moore, Elizabeth IV, 80
Moore, Elizabeth IV, 102
Moore, Elizabeth V, 82
Moore, Elizabeth V, 102
Moore, Elizabeth V, 132
Moore, Elizabeth V, 307
Moore, Elizabeth V, 518
Moore, Elizabeth V, 587
Moore, Elizabeth V, 588
Moore, Elizabeth V, 698
Moore, Elizabeth V, 699
Moore, Elizabeth V, 832
Moore, Elizabeth V, 854
Moore, Elizabeth V, 884
Moore, Elizabeth V, 888
Moore, Elizabeth VI, 259
Moore, Elizabeth VI, 260
Moore, Elizabeth VI, 265
Moore, Elizabeth VI, 266
Moore, Elizabeth VI, 267
Moore, Elizabeth VI, 367
Moore, Elizabeth VI, 424
Moore, Elizabeth VI, 472
Moore, Elizabeth VI, 474
Moore, Elizabeth VI, 505
Moore, Elizabeth VI, 509
Moore, Elizabeth VI, 518
Moore, Elizabeth VI, 519
Moore, Elizabeth VI, 520
Moore, Elizabeth VI, 527
Moore, Elizabeth VI, 535
Moore, Elizabeth VI, 536
Moore, Elizabeth VI, 538
Moore, Elizabeth VI, 564
Moore, Elizabeth VI, 570
Moore, Elizabeth VI, 572
Moore, Elizabeth VI, 575
Moore, Elizabeth VI, 586
Moore, Elizabeth VI, 619
Moore, Elizabeth VI, 620
Moore, Elizabeth VI, 663
Moore, Elizabeth VI, 676
Moore, Elizabeth VI, 713
Moore, Elizabeth VI, 756
Moore, Elizabeth VI, 757
Moore, Elizabeth VI, 766
Moore, Elizabeth VI, 772
Moore, Elizabeth VI, 841
Moore, Elizabeth VI, 849
Moore, Elizabeth VI, 854
Moore, Elizabeth VI, 867
Moore, Elizabeth VI, 965
Moore, Elizabeth A. II, 179
Moore, Elizabeth A. II, 280
Moore, Elizabeth A. II, 296
Moore, Elizabeth A. M. II, 280
Moore, Elizabeth A. M. II, 296
Moore, Elizabeth B. V, 102
Moore, Elizabeth B. VI, 784
Moore, Elizabeth C. II, 296
Moore, Elizabeth Kay II, 810
Moore, Elizabeth R. II, 323
Moore, Elizabeth R. II, 712
Moore, Elizabeth R. II, 713
Moore, Elizabeth Walker I, 511
Moore, Elizabeth, Jr. VI, 472
Moore, Elizabeth, Jr. VI, 536
Moore, Ella L. II, 713
Moore, Ellen V, 350
Moore, Ellen VI, 259
Moore, Ellen VI, 260
Moore, Ellen D. II, 179
Moore, Ellen D. II, 280
Moore, Ellen D. II, 296
Moore, Ellwood Burdsall III, 233
Moore, Elma IV, 1330
Moore, Elmira V, 102
Moore, Elmira V, 518
Moore, Eloise V, 193
Moore, Elva I, 338
Moore, Elva Jewell I, 338
Moore, Elvira IV, 894
Moore, Elwood Burdsall III, 53
Moore, Ema V, 518
Moore, Emily VI, 841
Moore, Emily Frances VI, 965
Moore, Emma V, 265
Moore, Emma V, 350
Moore, Emma V, 580
Moore, Emma V, 699
Moore, Emma V, 922
Moore, Emma J. V, 587
Moore, Emma J. V, 698
Moore, Emma S. II, 901
Moore, Emmaline L. II, 863
Moore, Emmaline L. II, 900
Moore, Emmaline Louisa II, 810
Moore, Estella V, 699
Moore, Estella V, 721
Moore, Esther II, 88
Moore, Esther II, 100
Moore, Esther II, 713
Moore, Esther II, 798
Moore, Esther II, 900
Moore, Esther V, 854
Moore, Esther VI, 767
Moore, Esther VI, 778
Moore, Esther A. II, 947
Moore, Eunice Fitz II, 805
Moore, Eva I, 622
Moore, Eva V, 587
Moore, Eva V, 698
Moore, Eva Bilbro I, 638
Moore, Evaline V, 587
Moore, Evaline V, 588
Moore, Evaline V, 698
Moore, Evangeline II, 849
Moore, Evangeline II, 901
Moore, Evans V, 854
Moore, Eveline V, 588
Moore, Ewel I, 589
Moore, Fam V, 588
Moore, Fannie H. II, 901
Moore, Fannie H. II, 921
Moore, Flavius J. V, 350
Moore, Flavus J. V, 350
Moore, Flora II, 788
Moore, Florence V, 587
Moore, Floyd William I, 326
Moore, France I, 511
Moore, Frances I, 548
Moore, Frances I, 563
Moore, Frances IV, 628
Moore, Frances IV, 763
Moore, Frances IV, 981
Moore, Frances VI, 844
Moore, Frances VI, 864
Moore, Frances A. VI, 835
Moore, Frances C. IV, 741
Moore, Francis I, 13
Moore, Francis V, 587
Moore, Francis VI, 841
Moore, Francis I. V, 698
Moore, Frankey VI, 833
Moore, Franklin V, 518
Moore, Franklin V, 535
Moore, Franklin J. III, 233
Moore, Franklin J. V, 518
Moore, Frederick III, 233
Moore, Frederick III, 383
Moore, Frederick V, 518
Moore, Frederick L. V, 588
Moore, Freeman VI, 800
Moore, Freeman VI, 804
Moore, Freeman VI, 821
Moore, Freeman VI, 841
Moore, G. W. IV, 253
Moore, Gainer II, 713
Moore, Gainer II, 734
Moore, Gainer II, 751
Moore, Gainer II, 756
Moore, Gainer II, 760
Moore, Gainer IV, 253
Moore, Geo. V, 350
Moore, George I, 338
Moore, George II, 397
Moore, George IV, 253
Moore, George VI, 841
Moore, George C. I, 338
Moore, George C. I, 829
Moore, George C. I, 831
Moore, George Curtis I, 326
Moore, George Curtis I, 338
Moore, George Ernest I, 338
Moore, George H. III, 383
Moore, George Smedley II, 397
Moore, George Smedley II, 600
Moore, George W. V, 350
Moore, George W. VI, 842
Moore, Gerressa E. V, 956
Moore, Gertrude Elizabeth I,
Moore, Gideon I, 274
Moore, Gideon II, 600
Moore, Gilbert III, 383
Moore, Gilbert A. III, 383
Moore, Gilbert H. III, 233
Moore, Gilpah VI, 601
Moore, Gladys V, 350
Moore, Goodrich VI, 814
Moore, Goodrich VI, 841
Moore, Goodrich VI, 965
Moore, Goodrich VI, 987
Moore, Grace IV, 102
Moore, Grace IV, 253
Moore, Grace Ella I, 563
Moore, Graftian A. V, 350
Moore, Grafton V, 350
Moore, Gulielma V, 587
Moore, Gulielma V, 698
Moore, H. Allen II, 810
Moore, Hadassah III, 382
Moore, Haines V, 587
Moore, Hannah I, 60
Moore, Hannah I, 196
Moore, Hannah I, 589
Moore, Hannah I, 595
Moore, Hannah II, 35
Moore, Hannah II, 73
Moore, Hannah II, 88
Moore, Hannah II, 508
Moore, Hannah II, 600
Moore, Hannah II, 601
Moore, Hannah II, 699
Moore, Hannah II, 713
Moore, Hannah II, 818
Moore, Hannah III, 44
Moore, Hannah III, 139
Moore, Hannah III, 233
Moore, Hannah III, 293
Moore, Hannah IV, 50
Moore, Hannah IV, 253
Moore, Hannah IV, 272
Moore, Hannah IV, 1174
Moore, Hannah V, 102
Moore, Hannah V, 508
Moore, Hannah V, 518
Moore, Hannah V, 905
Moore, Hannah V, 922
Moore, Hannah VI, 116
Moore, Hannah VI, 601
Moore, Hannah D. III, 232
Moore, Hannah D. III, 233
Moore, Hannah D. III, 293
Moore, Hannah D. V, 518
Moore, Hannah D. V, 586
Moore, Hannah D. V, 587
Moore, Hannah D. V, 588
Moore, Hannah L. II, 882
Moore, Hannah L. II, 900
Moore, Hannah Lewis II, 900
Moore, Hannah S. III, 233
Moore, Hannah W. II, 756
Moore, Hannah W., Jr. II, 713
Moore, Hannah W., Jr. II, 756
Moore, Hannah West II, 600
Moore, Hannah West II, 637
Moore, Hannah, Jr. I, 196
Moore, Harley M. IV, 981
Moore, Harley M. IV, 1258
Moore, Harriet V, 265
Moore, Harriett V, 587
Moore, Harriett M. V, 587
Moore, Harris V, 587
Moore, Harris C. V, 587
Moore, Harris C. V, 588
Moore, Harris C. V, 698
Moore, Harry IV, 628
Moore, Harry IV, 981
Moore, Harry E. IV, 741
Moore, Harry E. IV, 763
Moore, Hattie V, 698
Moore, Hattie E. V, 588
Moore, Hazel V, 669
Moore, Hazel V, 699
Moore, Hazel Everett V, 699
Moore, Helen IV, 1330
Moore, Helen VI, 259
Moore, Helen VI, 260
Moore, Helen C. IV, 1330
Moore, Henry I, 196
Moore, Henry II, 446
Moore, Henry II, 805
Moore, Henry M. II, 887
Moore, Hezekiah I, 60
Moore, Hibberd D. II, 713
Moore, Hiram VI, 841
Moore, Horace E. II, 713
Moore, Howard B. III, 196
Moore, Howard B. III, 233
Moore, Howard L. III, 233

re, Hubbard I, 563
re, Hugh W. I, 338
re, Hugh Watson I, 338
re, Ida IV, 210
re, Ida Eliza I, 326
re, Idella H. V, 102
re, Irene Hatch I, 326
re, Isaac II, 88
re, Isaac III, 293
re, Isaac V, 350
re, Isaac V, 518
re, Isaac V, 587
re, Isaac W. II, 901
re, Isaac W. II, 921
re, Isaac W. V, 885
re, Isabel I, 60
re, Isabel V, 307
re, Isabel V, 587
re, Isabel V, 677
re, Isabel V, 699
re, Isabel Ann V, 587
re, Isabel Ann V, 595
re, Isabel Reeder III, 70
re, Isabel Reeder III, 233
re, Isabella IV, 154
re, Isabella IV, 1069
re, Isabella IV, 1071
re, Isabella V, 551
re, Isabella V, 699
re, Isabella A. V, 566
re, Isabelle I, 60
re, Isabelle I, 62
re, Isabelle V, 699
re, J. Clarence III, 293
re, J. Frank I, 338
re, J. L. I, 326
re, J. Wilson II, 882
re, J. Wilson II, 900
re, Jacob III, 293
re, Jacob V, 518
re, Jacob Hubbard I, 511
re, James I, 410
re, James I, 1044
re, James I, 1049
re, James II, 197
re, James II, 242
re, James II, 397
re, James II, 492
re, James II, 713
re, James II, 798
re, James III, 233
re, James III, 293
re, James V, 102
re, James V, 518
re, James V, 536
re, James V, 885
re, James V, 888
re, James V, 907
re, James VI, 424
re, James VI, 505
re, James VI, 518
re, James VI, 519
re, James VI, 535
re, James VI, 536
re, James VI, 538
re, James VI, 566
re, James VI, 569
re, James VI, 570
re, James VI, 601
re, James VI, 651
re, James VI, 663
re, James VI, 676
re, James VI, 709
re, James VI, 801
re, James VI, 815
re, James VI, 836
re, James VI, 841
re, James VI, 849
re, James B. III, 293
re, James D. VI, 842
re, James Douglass II, 713
re, James G. III, 293
re, James L. I, 410
re, James L. VI, 800
re, James L. VI, 841
re, James R. VI, 834
re, James R. VI, 841
re, James Robert IV, 981
re, James Trayern VI, 677
re, James W. I, 1145
re, James, Jr. VI, 767
re, James, Jr. VI, 778
re, Jane I, 146
re, Jane I, 330
re, Jane I, 410
re, Jane I, 424
re, Jane I, 923
re, Jane II, 397
re, Jane II, 589
re, Jane II, 600
re, Jane II, 1017
Moore, Jane IV, 343
Moore, Jane IV, 422
Moore, Jane V, 307
Moore, Jane V, 350
Moore, Jane V, 698
Moore, Jane V, 907
Moore, Jane V, 1011
Moore, Jane VI, 821
Moore, Jane VI, 841
Moore, Jane VI, 850
Moore, Jane VI, 864
Moore, Jane R. III, 53
Moore, Jane R. III, 233
Moore, Jasper III, 293
Moore, Jeany VI, 850
Moore, Jehu III, 233
Moore, Jehu V, 518
Moore, Jehu V, 586
Moore, Jehu V, 587
Moore, Jehu C. III, 232
Moore, Jehu C. III, 233
Moore, Jehu C. III, 293
Moore, Jehu C. V, 587
Moore, Jehu C. V, 588
Moore, Jemima III, 293
Moore, Jemimah I, 196
Moore, Jenie V, 1011
Moore, Jennetta V, 587
Moore, Jennetta Belle V, 699
Moore, Jennie IV, 253
Moore, Jennie Arnold III, 233
Moore, Jennie E. I, 336
Moore, Jennie E. I, 338
Moore, Jennie H. I, 338
Moore, Jennie R. III, 233
Moore, Jenny VI, 841
Moore, Jenny VI, 965
Moore, Jeremiah S. II, 901
Moore, Jesse I, 60
Moore, Jesse I, 128
Moore, Jesse I, 146
Moore, Jesse I, 185
Moore, Jesse I, 189
Moore, Jesse I, 196
Moore, Jesse I, 787
Moore, Jesse I, 789
Moore, Jesse I, 790
Moore, Jesse I, 798
Moore, Jesse I, 830
Moore, Jesse I, 895
Moore, Jesse V, 350
Moore, Jesse VI, 841
Moore, Jesse H. I, 311
Moore, Jesse H. I, 326
Moore, Jesse Hollowell I, 330
Moore, Jesse R. VI, 820
Moore, Jesse, Sr. I, 789
Moore, Jessie V, 350
Moore, Jewell I, 338
Moore, Jno. P. VI, 853
Moore, Job II, 601
Moore, Job VI, 259
Moore, Job VI, 260
Moore, Job R. VI, 260
Moore, Job, Jr. III, 233
Moore, John I, 60
Moore, John I, 67
Moore, John I, 192
Moore, John I, 196
Moore, John I, 274
Moore, John I, 321
Moore, John I, 330
Moore, John I, 410
Moore, John I, 511
Moore, John I, 563
Moore, John I, 1049
Moore, John I, 1128
Moore, John I Sup 1, 5
Moore, John II, 397
Moore, John II, 485
Moore, John II, 600
Moore, John II, 756
Moore, John II, 806
Moore, John II, 810
Moore, John II, 900
Moore, John II, 947
Moore, John II, 1088
Moore, John II, 1089
Moore, John III, 149
Moore, John III, 233
Moore, John III, 293
Moore, John IV, 50
Moore, John IV, 71
Moore, John IV, 102
Moore, John IV, 154
Moore, John IV, 1069
Moore, John V, 350
Moore, John V, 518
Moore, John V, 587
Moore, John V, 1011
Moore, John VI, 260
Moore, John VI, 267
Moore, John VI, 286
Moore, John VI, 424
Moore, John VI, 809
Moore, John VI, 819
Moore, John VI, 841
Moore, John VI, 965
Moore, John VI, 977
Moore, John VI, 980
Moore, John A. IV, 253
Moore, John B. I, 831
Moore, John B. V, 350
Moore, John Benjamin V, 350
Moore, John Enoch IV, 253
Moore, John Franklin I, 338
Moore, John G. VI, 944
Moore, John H. V, 566
Moore, John H. V, 588
Moore, John H. V, 699
Moore, John Haines V, 587
Moore, John Haines V, 698
Moore, John Haines V, 699
Moore, John Henry I, 326
Moore, John M. II, 751
Moore, John M. II, 756
Moore, John P. V, 956
Moore, John P. V, 973
Moore, John Parker I, 196
Moore, John R. I, 326
Moore, John R. I, 329
Moore, John R. I, 330
Moore, John R. I, 1159
Moore, John Riley I, 1145
Moore, John Robert I, 326
Moore, John Robert I, 330
Moore, John S. I, 326
Moore, John Sanders I, 330
Moore, John Thomas I, 511
Moore, John W. V, 350
Moore, John W. V, 588
Moore, John W. V, 698
Moore, John Wilmer II, 947
Moore, John Wilson II, 900
Moore, John, Jr. IV, 102
Moore, John, Jr. VI, 259
Moore, John, Jr. VI, 260
Moore, John, Jr. VI, 265
Moore, John, Jr. VI, 266
Moore, John, Jr. VI, 286
Moore, John, Sr. VI, 260
Moore, Jonah I, 1128
Moore, Jonathan I, 60
Moore, Jonathan I, 146
Moore, Jonathan V, 307
Moore, Jonathan R. II, 810
Moore, Jonathan R. II, 900
Moore, Jonathan R. II, 901
Moore, Jonathan R. II, 922
Moore, Jonathan R. III, 233
Moore, Jonathan Robeson II, 810
Moore, Jonathan Robeson II, 818
Moore, Jos. T. III, 382
Moore, Josehine L. II, 901
Moore, Joseph I, 13
Moore, Joseph I, 60
Moore, Joseph I, 63
Moore, Joseph I, 66
Moore, Joseph I, 196
Moore, Joseph I, 202
Moore, Joseph I, 563
Moore, Joseph II, 242
Moore, Joseph II, 397
Moore, Joseph II, 541
Moore, Joseph II, 589
Moore, Joseph II, 600
Moore, Joseph II, 671
Moore, Joseph II, 1057
Moore, Joseph III, 233
Moore, Joseph III, 427
Moore, Joseph IV, 50
Moore, Joseph IV, 102
Moore, Joseph V, 265
Moore, Joseph V, 422
Moore, Joseph V, 441
Moore, Joseph V, 518
Moore, Joseph V, 587
Moore, Joseph V, 698
Moore, Joseph V, 699
Moore, Joseph V, 701
Moore, Joseph V, 854
Moore, Joseph V, 956
Moore, Joseph V, 960
Moore, Joseph V, 973
Moore, Joseph V, 976
Moore, Joseph V, 1011
Moore, Joseph VI, 116
Moore, Joseph VI, 396
Moore, Joseph VI, 424
Moore, Joseph VI, 536
Moore, Joseph VI, 601
Moore, Joseph VI, 676
Moore, Joseph VI, 965
Moore, Joseph C. III, 233
Moore, Joseph F. III, 53
Moore, Joseph F. III, 233
Moore, Joseph H. III, 293
Moore, Joseph Harry IV, 981
Moore, Joseph J. V, 1011
Moore, Joseph S. I, 338
Moore, Joseph Samuel I, 326
Moore, Joseph T. II, 900
Moore, Joseph T. III, 316
Moore, Joseph T. III, 382
Moore, Joseph T. III, 383
Moore, Josephine D. II, 296
Moore, Josephine L. II, 922
Moore, Josephine Lea II, 810
Moore, Josephine Lea II, 818
Moore, Joshua I, 60
Moore, Joshua I, 196
Moore, Joshua I, 586
Moore, Joshua I, 589
Moore, Joshua I, 895
Moore, Joshua I, 907
Moore, Joshua I Sup 1, 8
Moore, Joshua III, 233
Moore, Joshua IV, 50
Moore, Joshua IV, 102
Moore, Joshua V, 518
Moore, Joshua V, 533
Moore, Joshua V, 587
Moore, Joshua V, 698
Moore, Joshua VI, 108
Moore, Joshua VI, 116
Moore, Joshua VI, 841
Moore, Joshua Anderson I, 196
Moore, Joshua Anderson I, 830
Moore, Joshua M. V, 518
Moore, Joshua M. V, 699
Moore, Joshua R. II, 179
Moore, Joshua R. II, 280
Moore, Joshua R. II, 296
Moore, Joshua, Jr. V, 587
Moore, Josiah I, 60
Moore, Josiah I, 86
Moore, Josiah II, 35
Moore, Josiah V, 307
Moore, Josiah M. VI, 965
Moore, Judith I, 274
Moore, Judith III, 293
Moore, Judith VI, 804
Moore, Judith VI, 838
Moore, Judith W. VI, 808
Moore, Judy B. VI, 841
Moore, Juilianna V, 518
Moore, Julia I, 338
Moore, Julia F. I, 338
Moore, Julia F. M. I, 338
Moore, Julia Fisk I, 829
Moore, Julia Fisk I, 831
Moore, Julianna V, 471
Moore, Junietta V, 193
Moore, Katharine II, 897
Moore, Katherine II, 397
Moore, Katie D. I, 326
Moore, Katie D. I, 338
Moore, Kearnhappuck I, 185
Moore, Keranhappuck I, 60
Moore, Keranhappuck I, 68
Moore, Kesiah V, 848
Moore, Kesiah V, 854
Moore, Keturah IV, 905
Moore, Keturah IV, 911
Moore, Keturah IV, 981
Moore, Keziah V, 854
Moore, Kirkwood II, 713
Moore, Kirkwood II, 756
Moore, Kissiah VI, 841
Moore, Kittie V, 265
Moore, L. D. VI, 841
Moore, L. J. I, 330
Moore, L. J. I, 331
Moore, L. J. I, 338
Moore, Lambert I, 511
Moore, Lambert I, 563
Moore, Lancaster I, 330
Moore, Lancaster I, 831
Moore, Lancaster J. I, 326
Moore, Lancaster J. I, 330
Moore, Lancaster John I, 338
Moore, Laura I, 633
Moore, Laura I, 638
Moore, Laura II, 856
Moore, Laura A. I, 633
Moore, Laura A. I, 638
Moore, Laura De II, 901
Moore, Laura E. VI, 639
Moore, Laura E. VI, 640
Moore, Laura E. VI, 676
Moore, Laura E. B. I, 338
Moore, Laura Elizabeth I, 326
Moore, Laura J. I, 1159
Moore, Laura M. I, 336
Moore, Laura M. I, 338
Moore, Leah I, 53
Moore, Leah I, 60
Moore, Leah V, 307
Moore, Leah Ann II, 901
Moore, Leah Jane I, 60
Moore, Leah Moor V, 307
Moore, Leander V, 1011
Moore, Lemuel Peele I, 196
Moore, Levi I, 1128
Moore, Levi VI, 601
Moore, Libbie III, 233
Moore, Libbie III, 330
Moore, Lindley III, 383
Moore, Lindley V, 265
Moore, Lindley M. III, 383
Moore, Lindley M. V, 587
Moore, Lindley M. V, 588
Moore, Lindley Murray III, 233
Moore, Lindley Murray III, 383
Moore, Lizzie V, 461
Moore, Lizzie Smith I, 338
Moore, Lloyd W. I, 338
Moore, Lola B. I, 338
Moore, Lola Bell I, 326
Moore, Lola S. I, 338
Moore, Louelma I, 338
Moore, Louisa J. V, 1011
Moore, Louisa Nye V, 698
Moore, Louise V, 1011
Moore, Louiza V, 265
Moore, Lucinda J. I, 1145
Moore, Lucretia II, 947
Moore, Lucy I, 563
Moore, Lucy IV, 734
Moore, Lucy IV, 741
Moore, Lucy IV, 763
Moore, Lucy E. VI, 965
Moore, Lucy H. I, 563
Moore, Lucy J. VI, 841
Moore, Ludie I, 624
Moore, Luelma I, 335
Moore, Luelma I, 338
Moore, Lula I, 338
Moore, Lula I, 340
Moore, Lula S. I, 338
Moore, Luna I, 1159
Moore, Luna Adkin I, 1145
Moore, Luona May I, 326
Moore, Luther H. V, 699
Moore, Luzena I, 831
Moore, Lydia I, 13
Moore, Lydia I, 60
Moore, Lydia I, 189
Moore, Lydia I, 196
Moore, Lydia III, 491
Moore, Lydia III, 505
Moore, Lydia IV, 154
Moore, Lydia IV, 253
Moore, Lydia IV, 1069
Moore, Lydia V, 307
Moore, Lydia V, 350
Moore, Lydia Ann IV, 894
Moore, Lydia Ann V, 102
Moore, Lydia Ann V, 518
Moore, Lydia B. III, 233
Moore, Lydia B. V, 973
Moore, Lydia B. V, 976
Moore, Lydia R. III, 207
Moore, Lyman H. I, 338
Moore, Lymon Lyndon I, 338
Moore, Mahlon I, 1128
Moore, Mahlon VI, 601
Moore, Malachi I, 274
Moore, Manline I, 622
Moore, Maple V, 756
Moore, Margaret I, 60
Moore, Margaret I, 61
Moore, Margaret I, 78
Moore, Margaret I, 185
Moore, Margaret I, 192
Moore, Margaret I, 196
Moore, Margaret I, 787
Moore, Margaret I, 789
Moore, Margaret I, 828
Moore, Margaret I, 830
Moore, Margaret I, 895
Moore, Margaret II, 516
Moore, Margaret II, 600
Moore, Margaret II, 626
Moore, Margaret II, 901
Moore, Margaret II, 921
Moore, Margaret III, 233
Moore, Margaret V, 265
Moore, Margaret V, 272
Moore, Margaret V, 634
Moore, Margaret V, 650
Moore, Margaret VI, 800
Moore, Margaret Ann IV, 981
Moore, Margaret C. VI, 835

Moore, Margaret E. V, 587
Moore, Margaret E. V, 634
Moore, Margaret Ellen V, 587
Moore, Margaret Ellen V, 698
Moore, Margaret Virginia IV, 253
Moore, Margery III, 293
Moore, Margrett II, 397
Moore, Marietta II, 947
Moore, Marion IV, 104
Moore, Mark VI, 841
Moore, Martha I, 51
Moore, Martha I, 57
Moore, Martha I, 60
Moore, Martha I, 61
Moore, Martha I, 589
Moore, Martha I, 831
Moore, Martha I, 844
Moore, Martha I, 933
Moore, Martha II, 397
Moore, Martha II, 577
Moore, Martha II, 600
Moore, Martha II, 713
Moore, Martha II, 756
Moore, Martha II, 900
Moore, Martha IV, 154
Moore, Martha IV, 1069
Moore, Martha V, 570
Moore, Martha V, 587
Moore, Martha V, 698
Moore, Martha V, 956
Moore, Martha V, 973
Moore, Martha VI, 107
Moore, Martha VI, 817
Moore, Martha VI, 824
Moore, Martha VI, 841
Moore, Martha VI, 842
Moore, Martha VI, 859
Moore, Martha VI, 963
Moore, Martha A. II, 794
Moore, Martha A. II, 810
Moore, Martha A. IV, 646
Moore, Martha Ann V, 587
Moore, Martha F. IV, 629
Moore, Martha F. IV, 646
Moore, Martha F. IV, 715
Moore, Martha Frances IV, 628
Moore, Martha Frances IV, 715
Moore, Martha Frances IV, 741
Moore, Martha H. V, 699
Moore, Martha M. II, 863
Moore, Martha M. II, 900
Moore, Martha M. II, 901
Moore, Martha M. II, 916
Moore, Martha R. II, 810
Moore, Martha T. I, 790
Moore, Mary I, 13
Moore, Mary I, 60
Moore, Mary I, 61
Moore, Mary I, 62
Moore, Mary I, 63
Moore, Mary I, 67
Moore, Mary I, 85
Moore, Mary I, 128
Moore, Mary I, 146
Moore, Mary I, 185
Moore, Mary I, 196
Moore, Mary I, 274
Moore, Mary I, 276
Moore, Mary I, 300
Moore, Mary I, 311
Moore, Mary I, 511
Moore, Mary I, 563
Moore, Mary I, 565
Moore, Mary I, 787
Moore, Mary I, 789
Moore, Mary I, 790
Moore, Mary I, 798
Moore, Mary I, 830
Moore, Mary I, 831
Moore, Mary I, 873
Moore, Mary I, 895
Moore, Mary I, 1128
Moore, Mary I Sup 1, 5
Moore, Mary II, 35
Moore, Mary II, 88
Moore, Mary II, 242
Moore, Mary II, 397
Moore, Mary II, 574
Moore, Mary II, 581
Moore, Mary II, 600
Moore, Mary II, 601
Moore, Mary II, 637
Moore, Mary II, 653
Moore, Mary II, 685
Moore, Mary II, 689
Moore, Mary II, 712
Moore, Mary II, 713
Moore, Mary II, 818
Moore, Mary II, 900
Moore, Mary II, 1057
Moore, Mary II, 1076
Moore, Mary III, 220
Moore, Mary III, 233
Moore, Mary III, 316
Moore, Mary III, 383
Moore, Mary IV, 50
Moore, Mary IV, 102
Moore, Mary IV, 104
Moore, Mary IV, 518
Moore, Mary IV, 741
Moore, Mary IV, 872
Moore, Mary IV, 878
Moore, Mary V, 102
Moore, Mary V, 350
Moore, Mary V, 854
Moore, Mary V, 884
Moore, Mary V, 885
Moore, Mary V, 960
Moore, Mary V, 1011
Moore, Mary VI, 233
Moore, Mary VI, 396
Moore, Mary VI, 424
Moore, Mary VI, 429
Moore, Mary VI, 474
Moore, Mary VI, 498
Moore, Mary VI, 536
Moore, Mary VI, 552
Moore, Mary VI, 567
Moore, Mary VI, 601
Moore, Mary VI, 620
Moore, Mary VI, 663
Moore, Mary VI, 676
Moore, Mary VI, 677
Moore, Mary VI, 841
Moore, Mary VI, 850
Moore, Mary VI, 853
Moore, Mary VI, 965
Moore, Mary A. I, 326
Moore, Mary A. I, 328
Moore, Mary A. I, 329
Moore, Mary A. I, 330
Moore, Mary A. I, 338
Moore, Mary A. I, 622
Moore, Mary A. I, 638
Moore, Mary A. V, 102
Moore, Mary A. V, 699
Moore, Mary A. VI, 846
Moore, Mary A. Blanche I, 622
Moore, Mary Alice V, 588
Moore, Mary Ann I, 43
Moore, Mary Ann I, 61
Moore, Mary Ann I, 287
Moore, Mary Ann V, 102
Moore, Mary Ann V, 582
Moore, Mary Ann V, 587
Moore, Mary Ann VI, 851
Moore, Mary Anna II, 947
Moore, Mary Anna II, 948
Moore, Mary Anna II, 1088
Moore, Mary Anna II, 1089
Moore, Mary B. III, 233
Moore, Mary B. III, 329
Moore, Mary B. V, 102
Moore, Mary B. V, 518
Moore, Mary B. V, 535
Moore, Mary B. V, 885
Moore, Mary Brown II, 600
Moore, Mary Brown V, 885
Moore, Mary Brown V, 886
Moore, Mary C. II, 713
Moore, Mary C. II, 734
Moore, Mary C. II, 751
Moore, Mary C. II, 756
Moore, Mary C. II, 760
Moore, Mary C. IV, 253
Moore, Mary C. V, 102
Moore, Mary Catharine V, 699
Moore, Mary Christiana VI, 737
Moore, Mary E. I, 326
Moore, Mary E. I, 328
Moore, Mary E. I, 330
Moore, Mary E. I, 1145
Moore, Mary E. II, 713
Moore, Mary E. II, 756
Moore, Mary E. IV, 741
Moore, Mary E. V, 698
Moore, Mary E. V, 885
Moore, Mary E. VI, 871
Moore, Mary E. VI, 872
Moore, Mary Elizabeth V, 885
Moore, Mary Ellen V, 587
Moore, Mary Frances I, 622
Moore, Mary Frances I, 638
Moore, Mary H. IV, 741
Moore, Mary H. IV, 763
Moore, Mary H. V, 518
Moore, Mary Hicks III, 383
Moore, Mary J. I, 563
Moore, Mary J. VI, 804
Moore, Mary J. VI, 841
Moore, Mary L. I, 330
Moore, Mary L. I, 331
Moore, Mary L. II, 882
Moore, Mary L. II, 900
Moore, Mary L. III, 383
Moore, Mary Louisa I, 326
Moore, Mary M. VI, 836
Moore, Mary P. I, 507
Moore, Mary P. I, 558
Moore, Mary P. I, 563
Moore, Mary Peele I, 196
Moore, Mary Preyer I, 563
Moore, Mary Puryear I, 511
Moore, Mary T. I, 563
Moore, Mary U. V, 518
Moore, Mary W. VI, 965
Moore, Mary Wilson II, 790
Moore, Mary, Jr. VI, 474
Moore, Maryan I, 309
Moore, Maryan I, 311
Moore, Mathew VI, 834
Moore, Mathew VI, 841
Moore, Mathilde III, 196
Moore, Mathilde III, 233
Moore, Matilda III, 233
Moore, Matilda Ann V, 385
Moore, Matilda Ann V, 422
Moore, Mattie IV, 1287
Moore, Mattie V, 518
Moore, Mattie M. I, 933
Moore, Maud I, 338
Moore, Maurine I, 638
Moore, May III, 233
Moore, May III, 293
Moore, May IV, 1287
Moore, Melinday I, 589
Moore, Mellis S. III, 316
Moore, Mentra V, 1011
Moore, Meret Elmore V, 350
Moore, Meriam II, 600
Moore, Meriam II, 644
Moore, Merian II, 242
Moore, Mescanorid V, 854
Moore, Mescanorid??? V, 854
Moore, Micajah V, 587
Moore, Micajah V, 698
Moore, Micajah C. V, 588
Moore, Michael I, 274
Moore, Michal I, 274
Moore, Mifflin Young IV, 894
Moore, Milcah II, 600
Moore, Milcah M. II, 179
Moore, Milcah Martha II, 215
Moore, Milcah Martha II, 243
Moore, Milcah Martha II, 601
Moore, Mildred VI, 812
Moore, Milisent I, 60
Moore, Milisent I, 75
Moore, Millie Frederick I, 326
Moore, Milly VI, 841
Moore, Milton VI, 676
Moore, Milton J. V, 102
Moore, Milton Y. V, 518
Moore, Minnie I, 1159
Moore, Minnie I, 1160
Moore, Minnie III, 233
Moore, Minnie Elzena I, 330
Moore, Miriam I, 189
Moore, Miriam I, 196
Moore, Miriam II, 253
Moore, Miriam Moor V, 307
Moore, Mirriam I, 60
Moore, Mordecai I, 410
Moore, Mordecai II, 583
Moore, Mordecai II, 600
Moore, Mordecai II, 810
Moore, Mordecai IV, 50
Moore, Mordecai IV, 102
Moore, Mordecai V, 422
Moore, Mordecai V, 854
Moore, Mordecai V, 863
Moore, Mordecai VI, 424
Moore, Mordecai C. V, 587
Moore, Morris I, 831
Moore, Moses II, 712
Moore, Moses II, 713
Moore, Moses IV, 741
Moore, Mourning VI, 950
Moore, Nancy I, 196
Moore, Nancy III, 233
Moore, Nancy V, 265
Moore, Nancy V, 350
Moore, Nancy V, 461
Moore, Nancy V, 518
Moore, Nancy V, 533
Moore, Nancy V, 587
Moore, Nancy V, 680
Moore, Nancy V, 698
Moore, Nancy VI, 805
Moore, Nancy VI, 841
Moore, Nancy VI, 849
Moore, Nancy VI, 965
Moore, Nancy VI, 1020
Moore, Nancy Ann Cely I, 326
Moore, Nannie Virginia I, 926
Moore, Nannie Virginia I, 946
Moore, Naomi III, 233
Moore, Nathan I, 13
Moore, Nathan I, 189
Moore, Nathan I, 196
Moore, Nathan I, 1128
Moore, Nathan V, 854
Moore, Nathaniel V, 828
Moore, Nathaniel V, 854
Moore, Nathaniel V, 884
Moore, Nereus Mendenhall I, 338
Moore, Nusetta V, 518
Moore, Obediah VI, 841
Moore, Obediah VI, 965
Moore, Obedience VI, 841
Moore, Oceanus C. V, 350
Moore, Olive VI, 853
Moore, Oliver V, 587
Moore, Oliver V, 588
Moore, Oliver VI, 841
Moore, Oliver C. V, 698
Moore, Oliver C. V, 699
Moore, Ophelia V, 518
Moore, Ophelia V, 588
Moore, Ophelia V, 698
Moore, Ophelia V, 699
Moore, Ophelia A. V, 518
Moore, Ora I, 622
Moore, Ora I, 638
Moore, Oscar V, 699
Moore, Oscar V, 721
Moore, Oscar A. V, 699
Moore, Ottie V, 699
Moore, Patience II, 242
Moore, Patience VI, 950
Moore, Patrick VI, 841
Moore, Patsey VI, 841
Moore, Patsy VI, 841
Moore, Paul I, 338
Moore, Paulina V, 518
Moore, Pearl IV, 1217
Moore, Pearl V, 518
Moore, Pemberton IV, 741
Moore, Penina V, 701
Moore, Peninah I, 60
Moore, Peninah I, 66
Moore, Peninah I, 196
Moore, Pennianah I, 196
Moore, Penninah I, 196
Moore, Permelia A. VI, 834
Moore, Peter VI, 965
Moore, Phebe II, 600
Moore, Phebe II, 601
Moore, Phebe II, 671
Moore, Phebe II, 756
Moore, Phebe II, 760
Moore, Phebe II, 781
Moore, Phebe II, 824
Moore, Phebe III, 146
Moore, Phebe III, 233
Moore, Phebe V, 102
Moore, Phebe V, 265
Moore, Phebe V, 587
Moore, Phebe V, 832
Moore, Phebe V, 854
Moore, Phebe V, 885
Moore, Phebe V, 888
Moore, Phebe VI, 518
Moore, Phebe VI, 519
Moore, Phebe VI, 535
Moore, Phebe VI, 536
Moore, Phebe VI, 566
Moore, Phebe VI, 601
Moore, Phebe VI, 663
Moore, Phebe VI, 676
Moore, Phebe Ann II, 1057
Moore, Phebe Ann II, 1088
Moore, Phebe Ann II, 1089
Moore, Phebe D. V, 587
Moore, Phebe E. II, 900
Moore, Phebe Elizabeth II, 900
Moore, Phebe Elizabeth II, 936
Moore, Phebe Jane V, 922
Moore, Phebe M. III, 233
Moore, Phebe P. III, 491
Moore, Phebe P. III, 506
Moore, Phebe R. II, 901
Moore, Phebe W. V, 885
Moore, Phyllis Gaye IV, 981
Moore, Polinia I, 926
Moore, Polly VI, 965
Moore, Polly A. VI, 841
Moore, Predem VI, 841
Moore, Predham VI, 846
Moore, Priscilla Jane V, 518
Moore, Priscilla Jane V, 536
Moore, Prisscilla VI, 841
Moore, Prudence I, 410
Moore, Rachel I, 1113
Moore, Rachel I, 1128
Moore, Rachel I, 1145
Moore, Rachel I, 1159
Moore, Rachel II, 184
Moore, Rachel II, 397
Moore, Rachel II, 600
Moore, Rachel II, 1057
Moore, Rachel IV, 226
Moore, Rachel IV, 253
Moore, Rachel IV, 517
Moore, Rachel IV, 541
Moore, Rachel IV, 1068
Moore, Rachel IV, 1069
Moore, Rachel V, 265
Moore, Rachel V, 422
Moore, Rachel V, 441
Moore, Rachel V, 587
Moore, Rachel V, 698
Moore, Rachel V, 854
Moore, Rachel V, 863
Moore, Rachel V, 884
Moore, Rachel VI, 424
Moore, Rachel VI, 536
Moore, Rachel VI, 549
Moore, Rachel VI, 571
Moore, Rachel VI, 601
Moore, Rachel VI, 768
Moore, Rachel VI, 771
Moore, Rachel G. V, 422
Moore, Rachel W. V, 518
Moore, Rachel W. V, 588
Moore, Rachel Wilson II, 823
Moore, Ralph Richard IV, 741
Moore, Ransom S. I, 326
Moore, Reba V, 699
Moore, Rebecca I, 196
Moore, Rebecca I, 789
Moore, Rebecca I, 830
Moore, Rebecca I, 831
Moore, Rebecca I, 1128
Moore, Rebecca I Sup 1, 5
Moore, Rebecca II, 88
Moore, Rebecca II, 239
Moore, Rebecca II, 242
Moore, Rebecca II, 397
Moore, Rebecca II, 480
Moore, Rebecca II, 600
Moore, Rebecca II, 901
Moore, Rebecca V, 51
Moore, Rebecca V, 102
Moore, Rebecca V, 854
Moore, Rebecca V, 907
Moore, Rebecca VI, 708
Moore, Rebecca VI, 830
Moore, Rebecca B. III, 233
Moore, Rebecca T. VI, 544
Moore, Rebecca T. VI, 688
Moore, Rebecca W. II, 781
Moore, Rebeccah I, 830
Moore, Rebeckah I, 60
Moore, Rebeckah I, 73
Moore, Rebeckah II, 35
Moore, Rebeckah II, 73
Moore, Rebeckah II, 88
Moore, Rebeckah II, 480
Moore, Rebeckah II, 600
Moore, Rebekah I, 185
Moore, Rebekah VI, 651
Moore, Reuben Green V, 587
Moore, Rhoda VI, 866
Moore, Rhoda G. V, 587
Moore, Richard I, 410
Moore, Richard I, 563
Moore, Richard I, 1016
Moore, Richard II, 397
Moore, Richard II, 516
Moore, Richard II, 600
Moore, Richard II, 626
Moore, Richard II, 637
Moore, Richard II, 900
Moore, Richard V, 102
Moore, Richard V, 854
Moore, Richard VI, 11
Moore, Richard VI, 841
Moore, Richard M. II, 900
Moore, Richard M. II, 901
Moore, Richard W. I, 563
Moore, Richard Wells II, 600
Moore, Richard Woodson I, 511
Moore, Ridgeway II, 863
Moore, Ridgeway II, 900
Moore, Ridgeway Kay II, 810
Moore, Ridgway II, 756
Moore, Ridgway II, 900
Moore, Robert I, 196
Moore, Robert I, 338
Moore, Robert I, 1128
Moore, Robert II, 88
Moore, Robert II, 100
Moore, Robert II, 600
Moore, Robert II, 900

ore, Robert VI, 424
ore, Robert VI, 601
ore, Robert VI, 841
ore, Robert VI, 963
ore, Robert B. IV, 741
ore, Robert B. IV, 981
ore, Robert Barclay IV, 981
ore, Robert C. V, 698
ore, Robert Griffen III, 233
ore, Robert H. V, 587
ore, Robert M. VI, 965
ore, Robert R. III, 382
ore, Robert Wain V, 350
ore, Roberta I, 338
ore, Roberta May I, 326
ore, Robeson II, 900
ore, Robt. VI, 935
ore, Roose II, 446
ore, Rosa Alice V, 885
ore, Roy V, 588
ore, Ruben VI, 424
ore, Ruth I, 1128
ore, Ruth I, 1134
ore, Ruth IV, 170
ore, Ruth IV, 253
ore, Ruth V, 193
ore, Ruth V, 566
ore, Ruth V, 587
ore, Ruth V, 698
ore, Ruth VI, 601
ore, Ruth A. V, 699
ore, Ruth Bernice IV, 763
ore, Ruthanna II, 699
ore, Ruthanna II, 713
ore, Ruthanna V, 518
ore, Ruthanna W. II, 727
ore, Salem IV, 741
ore, Salina V, 350
ore, Sallie VI, 815
ore, Sallie E. I, 326
ore, Sallie E. VI, 841
ore, Sally I, 302
ore, Sally I, 311
ore, Sally VI, 795
ore, Sally VI, 841
ore, Sally VI, 965
ore, Sam'l III, 233
ore, Sampson VI, 833
ore, Sampson VI, 841
ore, Samson, Jr. VI, 809
ore, Samuel I, 13
ore, Samuel I, 60
ore, Samuel I, 62
ore, Samuel I, 78
ore, Samuel I, 146
ore, Samuel I, 148
ore, Samuel I, 196
ore, Samuel I, 789
ore, Samuel I, 830
ore, Samuel I, 831
ore, Samuel I, 873
ore, Samuel I, 895
ore, Samuel I, 1128
ore, Samuel IV, 154
ore, Samuel IV, 1069
ore, Samuel V, 265
ore, Samuel V, 350
ore, Samuel V, 587
ore, Samuel V, 588
ore, Samuel V, 698
ore, Samuel V, 884
ore, Samuel V, 888
ore, Samuel VI, 841
ore, Samuel Ayers V, 350
ore, Samuel B. V, 28
oore, Samuel B. V, 102
oore, Samuel B. V, 884
oore, Samuel B. V, 885
oore, Samuel Brown V, 854
oore, Samuel J. V, 350
oore, Samuel L. II, 727
oore, Samuel Lewis II, 699
oore, Samuel Lewis II, 713
oore, Samuel M. III, 427
oore, Samuel Preston II, 397
oore, Samuel S. V, 102
oore, Samuel S. V, 518
oore, Samuel Spencer IV, 894
oore, Sanders I, 330
oore, Sarah I, 38
oore, Sarah I, 57
oore, Sarah I, 60
oore, Sarah I, 146
oore, Sarah I, 148
oore, Sarah I, 273
oore, Sarah I, 274
oore, Sarah I, 410
oore, Sarah I, 589
oore, Sarah I, 789
oore, Sarah I, 831
oore, Sarah I, 1128
Moore, Sarah II, 242
Moore, Sarah II, 397
Moore, Sarah II, 516
Moore, Sarah II, 541
Moore, Sarah II, 583
Moore, Sarah II, 589
Moore, Sarah II, 600
Moore, Sarah II, 671
Moore, Sarah II, 723
Moore, Sarah II, 756
Moore, Sarah II, 802
Moore, Sarah II, 810
Moore, Sarah II, 818
Moore, Sarah III, 233
Moore, Sarah IV, 88
Moore, Sarah IV, 102
Moore, Sarah IV, 253
Moore, Sarah IV, 299
Moore, Sarah IV, 343
Moore, Sarah IV, 422
Moore, Sarah IV, 741
Moore, Sarah IV, 894
Moore, Sarah IV, 1065
Moore, Sarah IV, 1069
Moore, Sarah V, 28
Moore, Sarah V, 102
Moore, Sarah V, 265
Moore, Sarah V, 518
Moore, Sarah V, 580
Moore, Sarah V, 587
Moore, Sarah V, 588
Moore, Sarah V, 698
Moore, Sarah V, 699
Moore, Sarah V, 828
Moore, Sarah V, 839
Moore, Sarah V, 854
Moore, Sarah V, 884
Moore, Sarah VI, 366
Moore, Sarah VI, 424
Moore, Sarah VI, 472
Moore, Sarah VI, 490
Moore, Sarah VI, 492
Moore, Sarah VI, 529
Moore, Sarah VI, 536
Moore, Sarah VI, 541
Moore, Sarah VI, 553
Moore, Sarah VI, 557
Moore, Sarah VI, 565
Moore, Sarah VI, 566
Moore, Sarah VI, 567
Moore, Sarah VI, 601
Moore, Sarah VI, 676
Moore, Sarah VI, 801
Moore, Sarah VI, 809
Moore, Sarah VI, 812
Moore, Sarah VI, 815
Moore, Sarah VI, 841
Moore, Sarah A. V, 587
Moore, Sarah A. V, 698
Moore, Sarah A. VI, 842
Moore, Sarah Allennetta II, 795
Moore, Sarah Ann V, 511
Moore, Sarah Ann V, 518
Moore, Sarah Ann V, 587
Moore, Sarah Ann VI, 536
Moore, Sarah Bond V, 307
Moore, Sarah E. I, 328
Moore, Sarah E. I, 330
Moore, Sarah E. I, 615
Moore, Sarah E. III, 293
Moore, Sarah E. V, 102
Moore, Sarah E. VI, 970
Moore, Sarah Elizabeth I, 326
Moore, Sarah Elizabeth IV, 894
Moore, Sarah Elizabeth V, 518
Moore, Sarah Emily V, 350
Moore, Sarah Emily V, 554
Moore, Sarah Emily V, 587
Moore, Sarah H. III, 233
Moore, Sarah Jane V, 587
Moore, Sarah Jane V, 588
Moore, Sarah L. II, 888
Moore, Sarah L. II, 901
Moore, Sarah L. II, 922
Moore, Sarah M. V, 879
Moore, Sarah M. V, 885
Moore, Sarah P. II, 734
Moore, Sarah P. II, 756
Moore, Sarah W. IV, 253
Moore, Sarah W. IV, 741
Moore, Sarah W. V, 102
Moore, Sarah W. V, 885
Moore, Sarah W. VI, 804
Moore, Seaborn V, 854
Moore, Seaborn V, 863
Moore, Seaborn V, 884
Moore, Seborn V, 102
Moore, Seth V, 587
Moore, Smith V, 461
Moore, Smitha I, 287
Moore, Smithey I, 326
Moore, Smithson I, 330
Moore, Smithson C. I, 326
Moore, Smithson C. I, 330
Moore, Smithson D. I, 330
Moore, Smithy I, 330
Moore, Smithy J. I, 326
Moore, Smitson I, 311
Moore, Smyth I, 511
Moore, Smyth I, 563
Moore, Smythen I, 311
Moore, Sophia I, 511
Moore, Sophia I, 563
Moore, Sophia I, 586
Moore, Sophia I, 589
Moore, Sophia I, 967
Moore, Sophia VI, 836
Moore, Stacy II, 179
Moore, Stacy II, 296
Moore, Stanley I, 338
Moore, Stanley V, 350
Moore, Sudie I, 620
Moore, Susan IV, 343
Moore, Susan V, 265
Moore, Susan G. VI, 841
Moore, Susanna I, 563
Moore, Susanna I, 573
Moore, Susanna II, 397
Moore, Susanna IV, 322
Moore, Susanna V, 587
Moore, Susannah I, 511
Moore, Susannah I, 563
Moore, Susannah III, 233
Moore, Susannah III, 259
Moore, Susannah IV, 1107
Moore, Susannah IV, 1122
Moore, Susannah V, 518
Moore, Susannah V, 563
Moore, Susannah V, 587
Moore, T. Clarkson I, 563
Moore, Tabitha B. II, 790
Moore, Tabitha E. I, 329
Moore, Tabitha E. I, 330
Moore, Taylor V, 265
Moore, Taylor V, 587
Moore, Thomas I, 37
Moore, Thomas I, 60
Moore, Thomas I, 62
Moore, Thomas I, 274
Moore, Thomas I, 563
Moore, Thomas I, 589
Moore, Thomas I, 600
Moore, Thomas I, 1044
Moore, Thomas II, 242
Moore, Thomas II, 253
Moore, Thomas II, 397
Moore, Thomas II, 516
Moore, Thomas II, 541
Moore, Thomas II, 600
Moore, Thomas II, 601
Moore, Thomas III, 233
Moore, Thomas V, 518
Moore, Thomas V, 588
Moore, Thomas VI, 259
Moore, Thomas VI, 260
Moore, Thomas VI, 424
Moore, Thomas VI, 472
Moore, Thomas VI, 474
Moore, Thomas VI, 505
Moore, Thomas VI, 527
Moore, Thomas VI, 536
Moore, Thomas VI, 538
Moore, Thomas VI, 570
Moore, Thomas VI, 571
Moore, Thomas VI, 575
Moore, Thomas VI, 586
Moore, Thomas VI, 601
Moore, Thomas VI, 620
Moore, Thomas VI, 676
Moore, Thomas VI, 804
Moore, Thomas VI, 805
Moore, Thomas VI, 810
Moore, Thomas VI, 841
Moore, Thomas VI, 850
Moore, Thomas VI, 965
Moore, Thomas E. V, 699
Moore, Thomas E. V, 854
Moore, Thomas Elwood V, 854
Moore, Thomas F. VI, 804
Moore, Thomas F. VI, 841
Moore, Thomas Haynes III, 233
Moore, Thomas Seth V, 587
Moore, Thomas Seth V, 698
Moore, Thomas W. II, 900
Moore, Thomas W. VI, 965
Moore, Thomas, Jr. VI, 474
Moore, Thomas, Jr. VI, 536
Moore, Thomas, Jr. VI, 620
Moore, Thomas, Jr. VI, 676
Moore, Thomas, Jr. VI, 677
Moore, Thos. I, 507
Moore, Thos. I, 511
Moore, Thos. II, 788
Moore, Thos. II, 818
Moore, Thos. V, 307
Moore, Thos. V, 922
Moore, Thos. VI, 1010
Moore, Thos. Camm I, 511
Moore, Thos. R. III, 233
Moore, Thos. W. II, 900
Moore, Tiny I, 1159
Moore, Truman I, 53
Moore, Truman I, 60
Moore, Tucker W. VI, 841
Moore, U. G. I, 338
Moore, Uriah G. I, 338
Moore, Uriah Grantham I, 326
Moore, Ursley V, 1011
Moore, Valda IV, 734
Moore, Veda V, 587
Moore, Veda Hadley V, 588
Moore, Verba V, 699
Moore, Verletta Elizabeth V, 1011
Moore, Veva V, 699
Moore, Viola IV, 253
Moore, Viola V, 699
Moore, Virginia IV, 1258
Moore, Virginia A. IV, 1258
Moore, W. F. I, 338
Moore, W. M. I, 638
Moore, W. M. I, 946
Moore, W. R. VI, 841
Moore, Walter V, 973
Moore, Walter V, 976
Moore, Walter VI, 535
Moore, Walter Hadley V, 698
Moore, Walter T. IV, 741
Moore, Warren W. VI, 841
Moore, Washington VI, 841
Moore, Wd. ??? Moore II, 397
Moore, Wd. Dorothy II, 446
Moore, Wd. Jane II, 397
Moore, Wd. Rebeckah Talbott VI, 505
Moore, Wd. Rebekah VI, 570
Moore, Wd. Sarah II, 600
Moore, Wendall Richardson I, 622
Moore, Wendall Richardson I, 638
Moore, Widow Abigail I, 37
Moore, Widow Abigail I, 60
Moore, Widow Rebecca VI, 536
Moore, Widower Edward II, 600
Moore, Widower James II, 600
Moore, Wilfred IV, 734
Moore, Wilfred IV, 741
Moore, Wilfred IV, 763
Moore, Willard I, 563
Moore, Willard E. I, 563
Moore, William I, 60
Moore, William I, 61
Moore, William I, 326
Moore, William I, 330
Moore, William I, 338
Moore, William I, 622
Moore, William I, 926
Moore, William I, 931
Moore, William I, 1160
Moore, William I Sup 1, 4
Moore, William I Sup 1, 5
Moore, William II, 397
Moore, William II, 810
Moore, William III, 139
Moore, William III, 233
Moore, William III, 293
Moore, William IV, 154
Moore, William IV, 741
Moore, William V, 587
Moore, William VI, 260
Moore, William VI, 286
Moore, William VI, 424
Moore, William VI, 727
Moore, William VI, 796
Moore, William VI, 804
Moore, William VI, 808
Moore, William VI, 809
Moore, William VI, 820
Moore, William VI, 824
Moore, William VI, 830
Moore, William VI, 841
Moore, William VI, 846
Moore, William VI, 850
Moore, William VI, 872
Moore, William VI, 965
Moore, William A. VI, 859
Moore, William B. I, 326
Moore, William E. I, 338
Moore, William Ernest I, 338
Moore, William Jaron I, 326
Moore, William Lea III, 233
Moore, William M. I, 326
Moore, William M. I, 338
Moore, William M. I, 638
Moore, William M. VI, 835
Moore, William Madison I, 931
Moore, William Mathew I, 330
Moore, William P. I, 589
Moore, William R. I, 326
Moore, William R. I, 329
Moore, William R. I, 330
Moore, William R. VI, 807
Moore, William R. VI, 836
Moore, William Rufus I, 326
Moore, William Rufus I, 330
Moore, William T. I, 1159
Moore, Wilmouth VI, 852
Moore, Wilson V, 518
Moore, Winefred VI, 841
Moore, Wm. I, 622
Moore, Wm. II, 88
Moore, Wm. II, 574
Moore, Wm. II, 600
Moore, Wm. II, 900
Moore, Wm. II, 901
Moore, Wm. IV, 1069
Moore, Wm. V, 307
Moore, Wm. V, 1011
Moore, Wm. VI, 849
Moore, Wm. H. I, 946
Moore, Wm. H. V, 1011
Moore, Wm. Henry I, 511
Moore, Wm. J. II, 849
Moore, Wm. J. II, 856
Moore, Wm. J. II, 901
Moore, Wm. Rufus I, 338
Moore, Wm. Rufus I, 622
Moore, Wm. S. V, 1011
Moore, Wm. W. II, 790
Moore, Woodson I, 563
Moore, Zilpah I, 330
Moore, Zilpah I, 1128
Moore, Zilpha I, 311
Moore, Zilpha I, 326
Moore, Zilpha I, 330
Moore, Zilpha I, 338
Moore, Zilpha C. I, 326
Moore, Zilphia VI, 424
Moorehead, Adelaide V, 461
Moorehead, Bernice V, 461
Moorehead, Geo. V, 461
Moorehead, Jessie May V, 461
Moorelan, Elizabeth IV, 742
Moorelan, Hiram IV, 742
Moorelan, Huldah IV, 742
Moorelan, Jonah IV, 742
Moorelan, Joseph IV, 742
Moorelan, Mary IV, 742
Moorelan, Rhoda IV, 742
Moorelan, Stephen IV, 742
Mooreland, Barzillai IV, 742
Mooreland, Mary II, 722
Moorem, L. J. I, 330
Mooreman, Agatha VI, 253
Mooreman, Agatha VI, 260
Mooreman, Agatha VI, 332
Mooreman, Andrew VI, 261
Mooreman, Anna VI, 332
Mooreman, Betsy VI, 322
Mooreman, Betsy VI, 941
Mooreman, Betty VI, 332
Mooreman, Cety VI, 260
Mooreman, Cety VI, 275
Mooreman, Charles VI, 261
Mooreman, Charles VI, 931
Mooreman, Charles VI, 964
Mooreman, Clark T. VI, 261
Mooreman, Henry VI, 332
Mooreman, Jesse VI, 931
Mooreman, Judith VI, 260
Mooreman, Louisa VI, 252
Mooreman, Lucy C. VI, 801
Mooreman, Martha VI, 931
Mooreman, Mary VI, 964
Mooreman, Micajah VI, 233
Mooreman, Micajah VI, 260
Mooreman, Micajah VI, 941
Mooreman, Mildred VI, 260
Mooreman, Milley VI, 332
Mooreman, Milly VI, 941
Mooreman, Molley VI, 332
Mooreman, Permelia VI, 964
Mooreman, Pleasant T. VI, 842
Mooreman, Rachel VI, 332
Mooreman, Rachel VI, 802
Mooreman, Robert VI, 261
Mooreman, Sally VI, 920
Mooreman, Samuel VI, 332
Mooreman, Samuel VI, 964
Mooreman, Susannah VI, 233
Mooreman, Susannah VI, 260
Mooreman, Thomas VI, 252
Mooreman, Thomas VI, 260
Mooreman, Thomas VI, 291

Mooreman, Thomas VI, 332
Mooreman, Thomas VI, 801
Mooreman, Zaachas VI, 302
Mooreman, Zaachas VI, 802
Mooreman, Zachariah VI, 253
Mooreman, Zachariah VI, 332
Mooreman, Zachariah VI, 941
Mooreman, Zacheriah VI, 253
Mooreman, Zacheriah VI, 260
Mooreman, Zacheriah VI, 275
Moores, Rebecca B. III, 233
Moorlan, Jonah IV, 742
Moorlan, Sarah VI, 334
Moorlan, Sarah VI, 343
Moorlan, Stephen VI, 334
Moorland, Joseph VI, 334
Moorland, Rebecca VI, 329
Moorland, Rebecca VI, 345
Moorman, ??? VI, 293
Moorman, A VI, 334
Moorman, Abraham VI, 842
Moorman, Acchilles VI, 261
Moorman, Acchillis VI, 261
Moorman, Acculus VI, 260
Moorman, Achiles VI, 842
Moorman, Achilles VI, 261
Moorman, Achilles VI, 333
Moorman, Achilles VI, 797
Moorman, Achilles VI, 806
Moorman, Achilles VI, 822
Moorman, Achilles VI, 824
Moorman, Achilles VI, 831
Moorman, Achilles VI, 842
Moorman, Achilles L. VI, 824
Moorman, Achilles L. VI, 842
Moorman, Achilles V. VI, 806
Moorman, Achilles, Jr. VI, 863
Moorman, Achillias VI, 286
Moorman, Achsah I, 411
Moorman, Achsah I, 831
Moorman, Achsah I, 1071
Moorman, Achsah I, 1072
Moorman, Affrica V, 265
Moorman, Affrica VI, 332
Moorman, Africa V, 102
Moorman, Africa V, 265
Moorman, Africa VI, 333
Moorman, Africa VI, 334
Moorman, Africai V, 265
Moorman, Agatha V, 102
Moorman, Agatha V, 254
Moorman, Agatha V, 266
Moorman, Agatha VI, 252
Moorman, Agatha VI, 260
Moorman, Agatha VI, 317
Moorman, Agatha VI, 318
Moorman, Agatha VI, 322
Moorman, Agatha VI, 332
Moorman, Agatha VI, 333
Moorman, Agatha VI, 334
Moorman, Agathy V, 265
Moorman, Agg???torn I, 1067
Moorman, Agge VI, 286
Moorman, Agnes I, 831
Moorman, Agnes VI, 261
Moorman, Agness I, 410
Moorman, Agness I, 411
Moorman, Agness I, 1071
Moorman, Agness I, 1072
Moorman, Agness VI, 854
Moorman, Agnis I, 1067
Moorman, Alfred V, 350
Moorman, Alfred J. V, 350
Moorman, Algerney V, 635
Moorman, Alice Matilda V, 635
Moorman, Allice V, 636
Moorman, Alpheus V, 635
Moorman, Alpheus Aljourney V, 635
Moorman, Alrica V, 518
Moorman, Alva Augburn V, 635
Moorman, Alvah V, 636
Moorman, Amealy VI, 333
Moorman, Americus V, 635
Moorman, Americus V, 636
Moorman, Andrew I, 410
Moorman, Andrew VI, 234
Moorman, Andrew VI, 261
Moorman, Andrew VI, 325
Moorman, Andrew VI, 333
Moorman, Andrew VI, 805
Moorman, Andrew VI, 829
Moorman, Ann I, 410
Moorman, Ann I, 411
Moorman, Ann I, 1071
Moorman, Ann V, 635
Moorman, Ann V, 646
Moorman, Ann R. VI, 835
Moorman, Ann S. VI, 842
Moorman, Anna I, 411
Moorman, Anna I, 831
Moorman, Anna I, 1068
Moorman, Anna I, 1071
Moorman, Anna V, 102
Moorman, Anna VI, 260
Moorman, Anna VI, 304
Moorman, Anna VI, 332
Moorman, Anna VI, 333
Moorman, Anna M. V, 636
Moorman, Apharacia V, 506
Moorman, Apharacia V, 519
Moorman, Apharacia V, 623
Moorman, Apharacia V, 634
Moorman, Apharacia V, 635
Moorman, Apharacia VI, 332
Moorman, Aphraca V, 518
Moorman, Aphracia V, 194
Moorman, Archelaus I, 1066
Moorman, Archilles VI, 261
Moorman, Archilus I, 726
Moorman, Archilus V, 350
Moorman, Ariann V, 350
Moorman, Arianna V, 350
Moorman, Ashley VI, 251
Moorman, Austin VI, 842
Moorman, Barckley V, 635
Moorman, Barrett G. V, 194
Moorman, Benjamin I, 343
Moorman, Benjamin I, 392
Moorman, Benjamin I, 410
Moorman, Benjamin I, 790
Moorman, Benjamin I, 1049
Moorman, Benjamin I, 1067
Moorman, Benjamin I, 1068
Moorman, Benjamin V, 636
Moorman, Benjamin B. V, 519
Moorman, Benjamin B. V, 635
Moorman, Benjamin B. V, 636
Moorman, Betsy V, 102
Moorman, Betsy V, 265
Moorman, Betsy VI, 319
Moorman, Betsy VI, 322
Moorman, Betsy VI, 325
Moorman, Betsy VI, 333
Moorman, Betsy VI, 334
Moorman, Betsy VI, 842
Moorman, Betsy Ann V, 519
Moorman, Betsy Ann V, 634
Moorman, Betsy Ann VI, 334
Moorman, Betsy Ann VI, 338
Moorman, Betsy H. VI, 842
Moorman, Betty VI, 260
Moorman, Betty VI, 286
Moorman, Betty VI, 287
Moorman, Betty VI, 320
Moorman, Betty VI, 332
Moorman, Betty VI, 333
Moorman, Bety VI, 260
Moorman, Bety VI, 274
Moorman, Caroline V, 636
Moorman, Caroline VI, 333
Moorman, Catharine V, 636
Moorman, Catherine V, 636
Moorman, Catherine VI, 842
Moorman, Cety VI, 260
Moorman, Charity I, 790
Moorman, Charity I, 1067
Moorman, Charles I, 410
Moorman, Charles I, 1049
Moorman, Charles V, 102
Moorman, Charles V, 253
Moorman, Charles V, 265
Moorman, Charles V, 268
Moorman, Charles V, 518
Moorman, Charles V, 634
Moorman, Charles V, 635
Moorman, Charles VI, 240
Moorman, Charles VI, 258
Moorman, Charles VI, 260
Moorman, Charles VI, 261
Moorman, Charles VI, 275
Moorman, Charles VI, 286
Moorman, Charles VI, 317
Moorman, Charles VI, 332
Moorman, Charles VI, 333
Moorman, Charles VI, 334
Moorman, Charles VI, 799
Moorman, Charles VI, 964
Moorman, Charles VI, 1005
Moorman, Charles VI, 1011
Moorman, Charles Clinton V, 635
Moorman, Charles H. VI, 842
Moorman, Charles P. VI, 964
Moorman, Charles T. V, 610
Moorman, Charles Terrell VI, 332
Moorman, Charles Thos. V, 635
Moorman, Charles William V, 635
Moorman, Charles, Sr. VI, 286
Moorman, Charlotte E. V, 518
Moorman, Charlotte E. V, 524
Moorman, Charlotte E. VI, 334
Moorman, Chas. VI, 797
Moorman, Chas. VI, 854
Moorman, Chas. VI, 904
Moorman, Chas. R. V, 636
Moorman, Chas. T. V, 636
Moorman, Chas. Thos. V, 634
Moorman, Chas., Jr. V, 636
Moorman, Childas V, 265
Moorman, Childers E. V, 266
Moorman, Childress E. V, 266
Moorman, Childs V, 518
Moorman, Chiles V, 265
Moorman, Chiles V, 266
Moorman, Chiles VI, 332
Moorman, Chiles VI, 334
Moorman, Chloe Alice V, 635
Moorman, Christopher V, 518
Moorman, Christopher V, 634
Moorman, Christopher Elsworth V, 635
Moorman, Chuza I, 1068
Moorman, Clark VI, 261
Moorman, Clark T. VI, 261
Moorman, Clark T. VI, 274
Moorman, Clark T. VI, 276
Moorman, Clark T. VI, 333
Moorman, Clark Terrell VI, 247
Moorman, Clark Terrell VI, 333
Moorman, Clark Terrill VI, 261
Moorman, Clarke VI, 856
Moorman, Collins V, 265
Moorman, David V, 102
Moorman, David V, 636
Moorman, David H. VI, 831
Moorman, David H. VI, 842
Moorman, Delilah I, 410
Moorman, Dewannah VI, 854
Moorman, Diggs I, 411
Moorman, Dorcas VI, 334
Moorman, Dorcus VI, 842
Moorman, Dorothy V, 102
Moorman, Dosha V, 492
Moorman, Dosha V, 518
Moorman, Dosha V, 519
Moorman, Dosha V, 620
Moorman, Dosha V, 623
Moorman, Dosha V, 634
Moorman, Dosha V, 635
Moorman, Dosha V, 638
Moorman, Dosha V, 647
Moorman, Dosha VI, 332
Moorman, Dosha VI, 333
Moorman, Dosha VI, 334
Moorman, Dosha VI, 340
Moorman, Dosha VI, 341
Moorman, Dosha Paxton V, 518
Moorman, Doshy VI, 340
Moorman, Drury C. VI, 802
Moorman, Drury C. VI, 830
Moorman, Drury C. VI, 964
Moorman, E. Granville VI, 835
Moorman, Ed. P. VI, 797
Moorman, Ed. P. VI, 858
Moorman, Edmund V, 102
Moorman, Edmund P. VI, 803
Moorman, Edmund P. VI, 851
Moorman, Edward I, 790
Moorman, Edward I, 831
Moorman, Edward I, 841
Moorman, Edward I, 1066
Moorman, Edward I, 1067
Moorman, Edward I, 1071
Moorman, Edward G. VI, 842
Moorman, Edwin V, 265
Moorman, Eli I, 790
Moorman, Eli I, 1067
Moorman, Eli V, 266
Moorman, Eli V, 636
Moorman, Eli Watson V, 634
Moorman, Elizabeth I, 410
Moorman, Elizabeth I, 1049
Moorman, Elizabeth V, 102
Moorman, Elizabeth V, 253
Moorman, Elizabeth V, 265
Moorman, Elizabeth V, 266
Moorman, Elizabeth V, 268
Moorman, Elizabeth V, 518
Moorman, Elizabeth V, 519
Moorman, Elizabeth V, 609
Moorman, Elizabeth V, 610
Moorman, Elizabeth V, 630
Moorman, Elizabeth V, 634
Moorman, Elizabeth V, 635
Moorman, Elizabeth V, 636
Moorman, Elizabeth V, 651
Moorman, Elizabeth VI, 255
Moorman, Elizabeth VI, 260
Moorman, Elizabeth VI, 261
Moorman, Elizabeth VI, 286
Moorman, Elizabeth VI, 321
Moorman, Elizabeth VI, 322
Moorman, Elizabeth VI, 332
Moorman, Elizabeth VI, 333
Moorman, Elizabeth VI, 805
Moorman, Elizabeth VI, 806
Moorman, Elizabeth VI, 811
Moorman, Elizabeth VI, 842
Moorman, Elizabeth VI, 856
Moorman, Elizabeth VI, 964
Moorman, Elizabeth A. VI, 964
Moorman, Elizabeth A. C. VI, 986
Moorman, Elizabeth B. VI, 334
Moorman, Elizabeth B. VI, 842
Moorman, Elizabeth Betty VI, 316
Moorman, Elizabeth C. C. VI, 842
Moorman, Elizabeth M. VI, 842
Moorman, Elnora V, 636
Moorman, Emily V, 253
Moorman, Emily V, 265
Moorman, Emily V, 305
Moorman, Emily V, 307
Moorman, Emily V, 519
Moorman, Emily V, 618
Moorman, Emily V, 634
Moorman, Emily V, 635
Moorman, Emmily V, 265
Moorman, Esther VI, 842
Moorman, Fanny I, 410
Moorman, Fanny V, 102
Moorman, Fanny V, 265
Moorman, Fanny VI, 334
Moorman, Fanny Herndon VI, 332
Moorman, Fenton Thomas V, 635
Moorman, Frances E. VI, 964
Moorman, Frank V, 194
Moorman, Frank V, 636
Moorman, Frank Hope V, 635
Moorman, Genevra V, 636
Moorman, Gilbert V, 350
Moorman, Granville A. VI, 851
Moorman, Hannah I, 1068
Moorman, Hannah I, 1071
Moorman, Hannah I, 1072
Moorman, Hannah V, 102
Moorman, Hannah V, 266
Moorman, Hannah V, 351
Moorman, Hannah V, 636
Moorman, Hannah E. V, 350
Moorman, Hannah Sexton V, 194
Moorman, Harriet VI, 327
Moorman, Harriet VI, 334
Moorman, Harriet E. VI, 942
Moorman, Harriett I, 1068
Moorman, Harry Leroy V, 635
Moorman, Harry T. V, 636
Moorman, Henry I, 1068
Moorman, Henry VI, 260
Moorman, Henry VI, 332
Moorman, Henry VI, 333
Moorman, Henry VI, 805
Moorman, Henry VI, 811
Moorman, Henry VI, 830
Moorman, Henry F. VI, 842
Moorman, Henry T. V, 194
Moorman, Henry T. V, 519
Moorman, Henry T. V, 634
Moorman, Henry T. V, 635
Moorman, Henry T. V, 636
Moorman, Henry T. VI, 334
Moorman, Henry T. VI, 842
Moorman, Hope Chiles VI, 333
Moorman, Howard V, 636
Moorman, Ida V, 1011
Moorman, Iola V, 1011
Moorman, J. M. VI, 920
Moorman, J. M. VI, 942
Moorman, Jacob VI, 964
Moorman, James I, 1055
Moorman, James I, 1067
Moorman, James V, 102
Moorman, James V, 194
Moorman, James V, 201
Moorman, James V, 265
Moorman, James V, 518
Moorman, James V, 519
Moorman, James V, 634
Moorman, James VI, 251
Moorman, James VI, 261
Moorman, James VI, 332
Moorman, James VI, 334
Moorman, James VI, 842
Moorman, James VI, 851
Moorman, James VI, 895
Moorman, James VI, 911
Moorman, James VI, 918
Moorman, James VI, 964
Moorman, James VI, 980
Moorman, James VI, 981
Moorman, James VI, 999
Moorman, James C. V, 636
Moorman, James C. VI, 796
Moorman, James C. VI, 806
Moorman, James C. VI, 835
Moorman, James Christopher V, 634
Moorman, James Christopher V, 635
Moorman, James Ellis V, 634
Moorman, James G. VI, 864
Moorman, James H. VI, 334
Moorman, James H. VI, 842
Moorman, James H. L. VI, 869
Moorman, James H. L. VI, 881
Moorman, James H. L. VI, 889
Moorman, James H. L. VI, 909
Moorman, James H. L. VI, 914
Moorman, James H. L. VI, 918
Moorman, James H. L. VI, 922
Moorman, James H. L. VI, 932
Moorman, James H. L. VI, 941
Moorman, James H. L. VI, 949
Moorman, James H. L. VI, 954
Moorman, James H. L. VI, 987
Moorman, James H. L. VI, 997
Moorman, James H. L. VI, 101
Moorman, James Leander V, 63
Moorman, James M. VI, 334
Moorman, James M. VI, 942
Moorman, James M. VI, 964
Moorman, James P. V, 519
Moorman, James S. V, 636
Moorman, James Sheridan V, 6
Moorman, James W. VI, 795
Moorman, James W. VI, 798
Moorman, James W. VI, 842
Moorman, James, Jr. V, 636
Moorman, James, Jr. VI, 848
Moorman, James, Sr. VI, 813
Moorman, Jane V, 350
Moorman, Jane VI, 842
Moorman, Jane R. VI, 796
Moorman, Jesse I, 1067
Moorman, Jesse V, 266
Moorman, Jesse V, 634
Moorman, Jesse V, 636
Moorman, Jesse VI, 805
Moorman, Jesse VI, 806
Moorman, Jesse VI, 842
Moorman, Jesse VI, 851
Moorman, Jesse VI, 870
Moorman, Jesse Crew VI, 261
Moorman, John I, 410
Moorman, John I, 411
Moorman, John I, 831
Moorman, John I, 1066
Moorman, John I, 1067
Moorman, John I, 1068
Moorman, John I, 1071
Moorman, John V, 634
Moorman, John V, 635
Moorman, John VI, 285
Moorman, John VI, 286
Moorman, John VI, 287
Moorman, John VI, 842
Moorman, John Allen V, 635
Moorman, John C. V, 634
Moorman, John C. VI, 332
Moorman, John C. VI, 842
Moorman, John H. V, 519
Moorman, John H. V, 636
Moorman, John H. VI, 319
Moorman, John H. VI, 325
Moorman, John H. VI, 333
Moorman, John H. VI, 334
Moorman, John H. VI, 986
Moorman, John Hampton V, 519
Moorman, John Hampton V, 635
Moorman, John Hampton V, 636
Moorman, John Hope VI, 332
Moorman, John J. VI, 842
Moorman, John T. V, 266
Moorman, John T. V, 307
Moorman, John Thomas VI, 334
Moorman, John Winston V, 265
Moorman, Joseph V, 266
Moorman, Joseph Watkins V, 26
Moorman, Joshua V, 102
Moorman, Juda VI, 842
Moorman, Jude VI, 286
Moorman, Judith I, 411
Moorman, Judith I, 831
Moorman, Judith VI, 234
Moorman, Judith VI, 251
Moorman, Judith VI, 260
Moorman, Judith VI, 795
Moorman, Judith VI, 806
Moorman, Judith VI, 811
Moorman, Judith VI, 824

orman, Judith VI, 825
orman, Judith VI, 833
orman, Judith VI, 842
orman, Julia A. V, 629
orman, Julia A. V, 635
orman, Katy VI, 964
orman, Kitty V, 253
orman, Kitty Winstone V, 265
orman, Laura Elizabeth V, 635
oorman, Lehiles V, 102
oorman, Lemuel VI, 964
oorman, Letitia M. VI, 797
oorman, Lettice V, 102
oorman, Levi Stratton V, 635
oorman, Lewis I, 1067
oorman, Lidia VI, 333
oorman, Lillie V, 636
oorman, Lishee I, 410
oorman, Lishy I, 1049
oorman, Liza I, 1068
oorman, Lodouk VI, 334
oorman, Lodowick VI, 334
oorman, Lodowick VI, 842
oorman, Lodowick A. VI, 986
oorman, Louisa V, 636
oorman, Louisa G. VI, 921
oorman, Lucy I, 392
oorman, Lucy I, 410
oorman, Lucy VI, 253
oorman, Lucy VI, 260
oorman, Lucy VI, 286
oorman, Lucy VI, 797
oorman, Lucy VI, 798
oorman, Lucy VI, 811
oorman, Lucy VI, 824
oorman, Lucy VI, 851
oorman, Lucy Ann V, 519
oorman, Lucy Ann V, 522
oorman, Lucy Ann V, 635
oorman, Lucy F. VI, 833
oorman, Lucy J. VI, 920
oorman, Lucy Jane VI, 312
oorman, Lucy Jane VI, 334
Moorman, Lydia V, 102
Moorman, Lydia V, 140
Moorman, Lydia V, 266
Moorman, Lydia V, 307
Moorman, Lydia V, 518
Moorman, Lydia V, 634
Moorman, Lydia V, 635
Moorman, Lydia VI, 324
Moorman, Lydia VI, 333
Moorman, Lydia VI, 334
Moorman, Lydia VI, 797
Moorman, Lydia Ann V, 265
Moorman, Malinda V, 266
Moorman, Malinda V, 636
Moorman, Malinda V, 638
Moorman, Mallisa V, 634
Moorman, Manerva V, 636
Moorman, Manson V, 588
Moorman, Manson V, 600
Moorman, Manson V, 634
Moorman, Manson H. V, 519
Moorman, Manson H. V, 635
Moorman, Marcella Jane V, 635
Moorman, Marcella Jane V, 636
Moorman, Margaret V, 102
Moorman, Margaret V, 299
Moorman, Margaret V, 307
Moorman, Margaret Matilda V, 634
Moorman, Margaret Matilda V, 635
Moorman, Maria V, 634
Moorman, Mariah V, 519
Moorman, Mariah W. V, 614
Moorman, Mariah W. V, 635
Moorman, Maris I, 1068
Moorman, Marshall V, 635
Moorman, Martha V, 102
Moorman, Martha V, 611
Moorman, Martha V, 634
Moorman, Martha V, 635
Moorman, Martha Ann V, 635
Moorman, Martha C. V, 620
Moorman, Martha E. V, 635
Moorman, Martha J. C. VI, 842
Moorman, Martha M. V, 635
Moorman, Martin V, 102
Moorman, Mary I, 410
Moorman, Mary I, 831
Moorman, Mary I, 841
Moorman, Mary I, 1055
Moorman, Mary I, 1067
Moorman, Mary I, 1068
Moorman, Mary I, 1070
Moorman, Mary I, 1071
Moorman, Mary V, 102
Moorman, Mary V, 194
Moorman, Mary V, 201
Moorman, Mary V, 266
Moorman, Mary V, 519
Moorman, Mary V, 623
Moorman, Mary V, 625
Moorman, Mary V, 634
Moorman, Mary V, 635
Moorman, Mary V, 636
Moorman, Mary V, 651
Moorman, Mary VI, 254
Moorman, Mary VI, 260
Moorman, Mary VI, 261
Moorman, Mary VI, 286
Moorman, Mary VI, 315
Moorman, Mary VI, 316
Moorman, Mary VI, 321
Moorman, Mary VI, 322
Moorman, Mary VI, 333
Moorman, Mary VI, 842
Moorman, Mary VI, 854
Moorman, Mary VI, 856
Moorman, Mary VI, 858
Moorman, Mary VI, 861
Moorman, Mary VI, 864
Moorman, Mary VI, 904
Moorman, Mary VI, 964
Moorman, Mary Agnesso V, 265
Moorman, Mary Alice V, 350
Moorman, Mary Alice V, 519
Moorman, Mary Alzina V, 635
Moorman, Mary Ann V, 588
Moorman, Mary Ann V, 591
Moorman, Mary E. VI, 825
Moorman, Mary G. VI, 964
Moorman, Mary Hope V, 635
Moorman, Mary M. VI, 798
Moorman, Mary Molly VI, 317
Moorman, Mary R. V, 350
Moorman, Mary Rebecca V, 350
Moorman, Mary S. VI, 842
Moorman, Matilda V, 102
Moorman, Matilda V, 519
Moorman, Matilda V, 610
Moorman, Matilda V, 634
Moorman, Matilda A. V, 635
Moorman, Matilda Ann V, 634
Moorman, Matthew V, 634
Moorman, Matthew V, 635
Moorman, Melissa V, 492
Moorman, Melissa V, 620
Moorman, Melissa V, 635
Moorman, Micajah V, 102
Moorman, Micajah V, 265
Moorman, Micajah V, 518
Moorman, Micajah V, 519
Moorman, Micajah V, 630
Moorman, Micajah V, 634
Moorman, Micajah V, 635
Moorman, Micajah V, 646
Moorman, Micajah VI, 233
Moorman, Micajah VI, 260
Moorman, Micajah VI, 261
Moorman, Micajah VI, 286
Moorman, Micajah VI, 317
Moorman, Micajah VI, 321
Moorman, Micajah VI, 322
Moorman, Micajah VI, 325
Moorman, Micajah VI, 332
Moorman, Micajah VI, 333
Moorman, Micajah VI, 334
Moorman, Micajah VI, 340
Moorman, Micajah VI, 830
Moorman, Micajah VI, 842
Moorman, Micajah C. V, 519
Moorman, Micajah C. V, 610
Moorman, Micajah C. V, 635
Moorman, Micajah Clark V, 518
Moorman, Micajah F. V, 629
Moorman, Micajah F. V, 634
Moorman, Micajah F. V, 635
Moorman, Micajah John VI, 333
Moorman, Micajah, Jr. VI, 325
Moorman, Micajah, Jr. VI, 334
Moorman, Micajah, Sr. V, 635
Moorman, Micijah VI, 829
Moorman, Mildred V, 518
Moorman, Mildred V, 630
Moorman, Mildred V, 634
Moorman, Mildred V, 635
Moorman, Mildred VI, 252
Moorman, Mildred VI, 253
Moorman, Mildred VI, 260
Moorman, Mildred VI, 286
Moorman, Mildred VI, 318
Moorman, Mildred VI, 848
Moorman, Milley I, 410
Moorman, Milley I, 418
Moorman, Milley VI, 260
Moorman, Milley VI, 322
Moorman, Milley VI, 332
Moorman, Milly I, 1049
Moorman, Milly VI, 318
Moorman, Milly VI, 322
Moorman, Milly VI, 324
Moorman, Milly VI, 333
Moorman, Milly VI, 805
Moorman, Milly VI, 829
Moorman, Molley VI, 286
Moorman, Molley VI, 332
Moorman, Molly V, 518
Moorman, Molly VI, 260
Moorman, Molly VI, 332
Moorman, Molly VI, 334
Moorman, Mycajah VI, 332
Moorman, Nancy I, 1068
Moorman, Nancy V, 102
Moorman, Nancy V, 255
Moorman, Nancy V, 265
Moorman, Nancy V, 266
Moorman, Nancy V, 268
Moorman, Nancy V, 307
Moorman, Nancy V, 308
Moorman, Nancy V, 351
Moorman, Nancy V, 518
Moorman, Nancy V, 519
Moorman, Nancy V, 535
Moorman, Nancy V, 634
Moorman, Nancy V, 635
Moorman, Nancy V, 647
Moorman, Nancy VI, 319
Moorman, Nancy VI, 332
Moorman, Nancy VI, 333
Moorman, Nancy VI, 334
Moorman, Nancy VI, 335
Moorman, Nancy VI, 805
Moorman, Nancy VI, 842
Moorman, Nancy VI, 901
Moorman, Nancy VI, 948
Moorman, Nancy C. VI, 842
Moorman, Nancy Elizabeth V, 635
Moorman, Nancy H. VI, 842
Moorman, Nancy J. V, 350
Moorman, Nancy J. V, 351
Moorman, Nancy John Thomas V, 518
Moorman, Nancy W. V, 609
Moorman, Nancy W. V, 634
Moorman, Nancy W. V, 635
Moorman, Naomi VI, 332
Moorman, Nettie E. V, 636
Moorman, Obediance V, 102
Moorman, Obedience V, 102
Moorman, Palinah VI, 334
Moorman, Paschal Lewis V, 634
Moorman, Patsey VI, 831
Moorman, Patsy V, 102
Moorman, Patsy VI, 842
Moorman, Paulina VI, 333
Moorman, Pauline VI, 296
Moorman, Pauline VI, 796
Moorman, Paxon Hope V, 634
Moorman, Paxton Hope V, 635
Moorman, Peggy V, 102
Moorman, Permelia VI, 964
Moorman, Peter V, 102
Moorman, Pleasant VI, 260
Moorman, Pleasant VI, 286
Moorman, Pleasant VI, 334
Moorman, Pleasant VI, 842
Moorman, Polley V, 634
Moorman, Polley V, 635
Moorman, Polly V, 518
Moorman, Polly VI, 318
Moorman, Polly VI, 334
Moorman, Polly VI, 824
Moorman, Polly VI, 842
Moorman, Polly VI, 921
Moorman, Pricilla V, 102
Moorman, Rachel I, 410
Moorman, Rachel IV, 253
Moorman, Rachel V, 32
Moorman, Rachel V, 102
Moorman, Rachel V, 252
Moorman, Rachel V, 422
Moorman, Rachel V, 623
Moorman, Rachel V, 634
Moorman, Rachel V, 635
Moorman, Rachel VI, 247
Moorman, Rachel VI, 260
Moorman, Rachel VI, 261
Moorman, Rachel VI, 286
Moorman, Rachel VI, 296
Moorman, Rachel VI, 297
Moorman, Rachel VI, 302
Moorman, Rachel VI, 315
Moorman, Rachel VI, 322
Moorman, Rachel VI, 332
Moorman, Rachel VI, 333
Moorman, Rachel VI, 842
Moorman, Rachel VI, 922
Moorman, Rachel Ann V, 588
Moorman, Rachel Ann V, 600
Moorman, Rachel Ann V, 635
Moorman, Rachel Fisher V, 351
Moorman, Rachel Susanna VI, 260
Moorman, Raindy V, 102
Moorman, Reames V, 102
Moorman, Rebecah I, 1067
Moorman, Rebecca I, 790
Moorman, Rebecca I, 831
Moorman, Rebecca V, 102
Moorman, Rebecca V, 351
Moorman, Rebecca VI, 1011
Moorman, Rebeckah I, 1071
Moorman, Rebekah I, 410
Moorman, Rebekah I, 411
Moorman, Reuben V, 634
Moorman, Reuben VI, 324
Moorman, Reuben VI, 333
Moorman, Reuben VI, 334
Moorman, Reuben Albert V, 635
Moorman, Reuben Chiles V, 634
Moorman, Reubin VI, 333
Moorman, Reubin VI, 334
Moorman, Rhoda VI, 227
Moorman, Rhoda VI, 282
Moorman, Rhoda VI, 318
Moorman, Rhoda VI, 323
Moorman, Rhoda VI, 332
Moorman, Rhoda VI, 333
Moorman, Richard F. V, 350
Moorman, Rickman V, 102
Moorman, Robert V, 102
Moorman, Robert V, 265
Moorman, Robert V, 266
Moorman, Robert VI, 260
Moorman, Robert VI, 261
Moorman, Robert VI, 286
Moorman, Robert VI, 334
Moorman, Robert Alexander VI, 332
Moorman, Rosetta Harriet V, 635
Moorman, Rozetta Harriet V, 635
Moorman, Ruben VI, 332
Moorman, Ruben VI, 333
Moorman, Ruebin V, 518
Moorman, Rufus V, 635
Moorman, Ruth I, 1068
Moorman, Ruth I, 1070
Moorman, Ruth I, 1071
Moorman, S. T. VI, 938
Moorman, S. T. VI, 941
Moorman, Salley VI, 261
Moorman, Salley VI, 274
Moorman, Salley VI, 276
Moorman, Sally VI, 333
Moorman, Sally VI, 341
Moorman, Sally VI, 797
Moorman, Sally VI, 839
Moorman, Sally VI, 948
Moorman, Sally Ann VI, 334
Moorman, Sally Ann VI, 842
Moorman, Sally Ann VI, 964
Moorman, Sally Mary V, 635
Moorman, Saml. VI, 901
Moorman, Saml. P. R. VI, 894
Moorman, Saml. P. R. VI, 944
Moorman, Samuel V, 102
Moorman, Samuel VI, 332
Moorman, Samuel VI, 842
Moorman, Samuel VI, 964
Moorman, Samuel P. R. VI, 985
Moorman, Samuel T. VI, 964
Moorman, Sarah I, 410
Moorman, Sarah I, 821
Moorman, Sarah I, 831
Moorman, Sarah I, 1067
Moorman, Sarah I, 1068
Moorman, Sarah V, 102
Moorman, Sarah V, 194
Moorman, Sarah V, 266
Moorman, Sarah V, 636
Moorman, Sarah VI, 251
Moorman, Sarah VI, 260
Moorman, Sarah VI, 332
Moorman, Sarah A. VI, 795
Moorman, Sarah A. VI, 830
Moorman, Sarah Eveline V, 635
Moorman, Sarah Eveline V, 636
Moorman, Sarah J. VI, 985
Moorman, Sarah Jane V, 635
Moorman, Sarah Jane V, 636
Moorman, Selia I, 1068
Moorman, Sophia VI, 964
Moorman, Stella V, 636
Moorman, Stephen V, 102
Moorman, Sucky VI, 964
Moorman, Susana VI, 261
Moorman, Susanah I, 1071
Moorman, Susanna I, 383
Moorman, Susanna I, 410
Moorman, Susanna I, 411
Moorman, Susanna I, 831
Moorman, Susanna V, 219
Moorman, Susanna V, 265
Moorman, Susanna V, 518
Moorman, Susanna VI, 318
Moorman, Susanna VI, 322
Moorman, Susanna VI, 325
Moorman, Susanna VI, 332
Moorman, Susanna VI, 333
Moorman, Susanna VI, 334
Moorman, Susanna VI, 340
Moorman, Susanna VI, 829
Moorman, Susanna VI, 842
Moorman, Susanna W. VI, 842
Moorman, Susannah I, 1067
Moorman, Susannah I, 1071
Moorman, Susannah V, 102
Moorman, Susannah V, 266
Moorman, Susannah V, 518
Moorman, Susannah V, 519
Moorman, Susannah V, 522
Moorman, Susannah V, 610
Moorman, Susannah V, 630
Moorman, Susannah V, 634
Moorman, Susannah V, 635
Moorman, Susannah V, 636
Moorman, Susannah V, 638
Moorman, Susannah VI, 233
Moorman, Susannah VI, 260
Moorman, Susannah VI, 261
Moorman, Susannah VI, 333
Moorman, Susannah VI, 911
Moorman, Susannah H. V, 635
Moorman, Susannah Ruth V, 636
Moorman, Sussanna VI, 335
Moorman, Tabitha VI, 285
Moorman, Tabitha VI, 286
Moorman, Tabitha VI, 287
Moorman, Tarlton I, 1067
Moorman, Tarlton I, 1068
Moorman, Tarlton I, 1071
Moorman, Tarlton I, 1072
Moorman, Thomas I, 383
Moorman, Thomas I, 410
Moorman, Thomas I, 831
Moorman, Thomas I, 1067
Moorman, Thomas I, 1068
Moorman, Thomas I, 1071
Moorman, Thomas V, 102
Moorman, Thomas V, 265
Moorman, Thomas V, 266
Moorman, Thomas V, 307
Moorman, Thomas V, 492
Moorman, Thomas V, 518
Moorman, Thomas V, 519
Moorman, Thomas V, 635
Moorman, Thomas V, 699
Moorman, Thomas VI, 17
Moorman, Thomas VI, 147
Moorman, Thomas VI, 260
Moorman, Thomas VI, 261
Moorman, Thomas VI, 286
Moorman, Thomas VI, 315
Moorman, Thomas VI, 332
Moorman, Thomas VI, 333
Moorman, Thomas VI, 334
Moorman, Thomas VI, 797
Moorman, Thomas VI, 805
Moorman, Thomas VI, 811
Moorman, Thomas VI, 828
Moorman, Thomas VI, 829
Moorman, Thomas VI, 835
Moorman, Thomas VI, 842
Moorman, Thomas B. VI, 964
Moorman, Thomas C. V, 519
Moorman, Thomas C. V, 611
Moorman, Thomas C. V, 634
Moorman, Thomas C. V, 635
Moorman, Thomas C., Jr. V, 102
Moorman, Thomas E. V, 635
Moorman, Thomas Harris, Jr. VI, 261
Moorman, Thomas P. V, 620
Moorman, Thomas P. V, 623
Moorman, Thomas P. V, 634
Moorman, Thomas P. V, 635
Moorman, Thomas P. V, 638
Moorman, Thomas P. V, 647
Moorman, Thomas T. VI, 825
Moorman, Thomas, Sr. V, 194
Moorman, Thos. VI, 830
Moorman, Thos. C. V, 636
Moorman, Thos. Clark V, 634
Moorman, Thos., Sr. V, 635
Moorman, Trenton Thos. V, 636
Moorman, Uriah I, 1068
Moorman, Uriah I, 1071
Moorman, Uriah V, 265
Moorman, Ursala V, 227
Moorman, Ursala V, 266

Moorman, Virginia J. VI, 830
Moorman, Watson V, 636
Moorman, Wd. Apharacia V, 635
Moorman, William I, 410
Moorman, William V, 102
Moorman, William V, 253
Moorman, William V, 265
Moorman, William V, 266
Moorman, William VI, 332
Moorman, William VI, 334
Moorman, William VI, 814
Moorman, William VI, 842
Moorman, William VI, 847
Moorman, William F. V, 635
Moorman, William H. V, 266
Moorman, William H. VI, 853
Moorman, William Thomas V, 265
Moorman, Wm. C. V, 636
Moorman, Wm. D. V, 636
Moorman, Wm. M. VI, 848
Moorman, Wm. Newton V, 634
Moorman, Wm. Newton V, 635
Moorman, Z. VI, 1007
Moorman, Zacaheriah VI, 260
Moorman, Zacariah VI, 286
Moorman, Zacharia I, 831
Moorman, Zachariah I, 1067
Moorman, Zachariah I, 1071
Moorman, Zachariah V, 266
Moorman, Zachariah VI, 260
Moorman, Zachariah VI, 309
Moorman, Zachariah VI, 318
Moorman, Zachariah VI, 320
Moorman, Zachariah VI, 322
Moorman, Zachariah VI, 323
Moorman, Zachariah VI, 332
Moorman, Zachariah VI, 333
Moorman, Zachariah VI, 813
Moorman, Zachariah VI, 842
Moorman, Zachariah G. VI, 833
Moorman, Zachariah W. VI, 801
Moorman, Zachariah William VI, 334
Moorman, Zachariah William VI, 842
Moorman, Zacheriah VI, 260
Moorman, Zacheriah VI, 274
Moormans, ??? VI, 283
Moormon, Apharacia V, 496
Moorton, John II, 595
Moorton, Mary II, 595
Moorton, Randol II, 446
Moory, Benjamin F. V, 351
Moory, George A. V, 351
Moos, Ann II, 88
Moose, Hannah III, 44
Moose, Jane VI, 842
Moose, John VI, 842
Moots, Charles A. V, 699
Moots, Chas. A. V, 678
Moots, Minnie V, 678
Moots, Minnie V, 699
Moppin, Elizabeth I, 1096
Moppin, Elizabeth, Jr. I, 1086
Moppin, George I, 1159
Moppin, George W. I, 1086
Moppin, George W. I, 1092
Moppin, George W. I, 1096
Moppin, Jacob I, 1086
Moppin, Louiza Ann I, 1086
Moppin, Lydia I, 1086
Moppin, Martha I, 1086
Moppin, Martha I, 1092
Moppin, Martha I, 1096
Moppin, Mary I, 1086
Moppin, Morgan G. I, 1096
Moppin, Sarah I, 1086
Moramoon, Benjamin I, 246
Moran, Susanna III, 281
Moran, Susanna III, 300
Morann, Mary Ann I, 991
Morann, Mary Ann I, 994
Morany, Rachel I, 826
Morason, Stephen I, 451
Mordecai, Ann IV, 911
Mordecai, Deborah IV, 911
Mordecai, Elizabeth IV, 911
Mordecai, Emily IV, 911
Mordecai, James IV, 911
Mordecai, Jonah IV, 911
Mordecai, Lydia IV, 911
Mordecai, Nathan IV, 911
Mordecai, Phebe IV, 911
Mordock, Priscilla VI, 101
Mordock, Priscilla VI, 116
Mordock, Sally VI, 956
Mordock, William VI, 956
More, ??? V, 877
More, Aaron I, 60
More, Abigail I, 790
More, Abigail III, 233
More, Abraham VI, 201
More, Albert IV, 1287
More, Albert R. III, 233
More, Alice L. D. III, 233
More, Amy L. III, 233
More, An I, 451
More, Ann I, 451
More, Ann III, 233
More, Ann VI, 424
More, Ann R. IV, 817
More, Ann R. IV, 834
More, Anthony I, 1128
More, Anthony II, 397
More, Anthony II, 446
More, Bell V, 518
More, Benjamin II, 242
More, Benjamin II, 265
More, Benjamin II, 275
More, Benjamin II, 1076
More, Benjamin F. II, 1076
More, C. A. IV, 1287
More, Calvin C. IV, 741
More, Calvin C. IV, 783
More, Carrie Willets III, 233
More, David I, 1128
More, David V, 102
More, Deborah IV, 1197
More, Deborah IV, 1198
More, Drusilla II, 179
More, Edith I, 815
More, Edith I, 830
More, Edna V, 518
More, Effie I, 761
More, Effie I, 767
More, Eli J. I, 790
More, Elizabeth I, 109
More, Elizabeth II, 88
More, Elizabeth II, 601
More, Elizabeth II, 603
More, Elizabeth V, 548
More, Elizabeth V, 587
More, Elizabeth VI, 565
More, Elizabeth B. V, 102
More, Ema V, 518
More, Gainer II, 756
More, Gerressa E. V, 956
More, Grace II, 446
More, Gulielma V, 563
More, Gulielma V, 587
More, Hannah II, 601
More, Hannah D. III, 233
More, Hannah D. V, 517
More, Hannah D. V, 518
More, Harriet V, 265
More, Harriett V, 587
More, Harriett M. V, 579
More, Harriett M. V, 587
More, Henry II, 446
More, Hulda Atwater I, 790
More, Isaac II, 88
More, Isaac V, 518
More, James V, 518
More, Jane I, 131
More, Jane I, 410
More, Jane II, 397
More, Jehu III, 233
More, Jehu V, 517
More, Jehu V, 518
More, Jemimah I, 193
More, Jemimah I, 196
More, Jenie V, 1011
More, Jennie IV, 1287
More, Jesse I, 907
More, Jesse L. I, 761
More, Jesse L. I, 767
More, John I, 563
More, John II, 1076
More, John III, 233
More, John VI, 270
More, John VI, 424
More, John B. I, 790
More, Joseph II, 242
More, Joseph II, 275
More, Joseph II, 1076
More, Joseph B. I, 790
More, Joshua M. V, 518
More, Katherine II, 397
More, Katherine II, 446
More, Keturah IV, 911
More, Laura J. I, 1159
More, Louisa J. V, 1011
More, Luzena I, 800
More, Luzena I, 831
More, Lydia IV, 253
More, Lydia B. III, 233
More, Malachi I, 272
More, Malachi I, 274
More, Martha VI, 199
More, Martha VI, 200
More, Martha VI, 201
More, Martha A. IV, 608
More, Martha A. IV, 646
More, Mary I, 146
More, Mary I, 299
More, Mary I, 311
More, Mary I, 790
More, Mary I, 802
More, Mary I, 830
More, Mary II, 88
More, Mary II, 446
More, Mary II, 600
More, Mary II, 601
More, Mary II, 900
More, Mary II, 1076
More, Mary IV, 701
More, Mary IV, 1287
More, Mary V, 102
More, Mary Ann V, 102
More, Mary B. V, 518
More, Mary Brown II, 600
More, Mary C. II, 756
More, Mary C. V, 102
More, Mary U. V, 518
More, Mattie IV, 1287
More, Mattie V, 518
More, May IV, 1287
More, Michal I, 272
More, Michal I, 274
More, Milcah II, 600
More, Minnie III, 233
More, Morries I, 790
More, Nicholas II, 446
More, Nickolas II, 446
More, Nusetta V, 518
More, Ophelia V, 518
More, Ophelia A. V, 518
More, Patience II, 242
More, Patience II, 275
More, Paulina V, 518
More, Pearl V, 518
More, Phebe II, 756
More, Phebe V, 587
More, Phebe D. V, 567
More, Phebe D. V, 587
More, Rachel II, 1076
More, Rachel V, 257
More, Rachel V, 265
More, Rachel W. V, 518
More, Rebecah I, 790
More, Rebecca I, 830
More, Rebecca I, 834
More, Rebecca I, 1128
More, Rebecca I Sup 1, 5
More, Rebecca I Sup 1, 6
More, Rebecca W. II, 1076
More, Rebecka II, 446
More, Reuben Green V, 587
More, Rhoda G. V, 587
More, Richard I, 410
More, Richard W. I, 563
More, Robert I, 1128
More, Robert II, 1076
More, Ruthanna V, 518
More, Samuel I, 790
More, Samuel II, 446
More, Samuel B. V, 102
More, Sarah I, 35
More, Sarah I, 60
More, Sarah II, 242
More, Sarah II, 265
More, Sarah II, 756
More, Sarah IV, 741
More, Sarah IV, 783
More, Sarah V, 102
More, Sarah Emily V, 587
More, Sarah Jane V, 567
More, Sarah Jane V, 587
More, Smitson I, 311
More, Smythen I, 311
More, Stacy II, 179
More, Susanna II, 446
More, Susannah V, 587
More, Taylor V, 265
More, Thomas I, 274
More, Thomas II, 242
More, Thomas II, 1076
More, Thomas V, 518
More, Thomas VI, 565
More, Thos. R. III, 233
More, William I, 109
More, William I Sup 1, 5
More, William I Sup 1, 6
More, William VI, 199
More, William VI, 200
More, William VI, 201
More, Wilson V, 518
More, Zilpha I, 303
More, Zilpha I, 311
Moreal, Violet B. II, 901
Moreal, Violet B. II, 907
Moreau, Mr. Nicholas VI, 147
Moree, Abigail III, 427
Morehead, Hannah IV, 385
Morehead, Hannah IV, 422
Morehead, John II, 446
Morehouse, Albert R. III, 234
Morehouse, Charles V, 1011
Morehouse, Elizabeth III, 218
Morehouse, Elizabeth III, 234
Morehouse, Minnie III, 233
Morehouse, Noly IV, 1239
Morehouse, Wd. Elizabeth III, 234
Morehouse, Wd. Elizabeth III, 334
Morehouse, William IV, 1174
Morehouse, William H. III, 234
Morehouse, Wm. H. III, 218
Morehouse, Wm. H. III, 234
Morehouse, Wm. H. III, 334
Morelan, Abigal VI, 334
Morelan, Aden IV, 639
Morelan, Aden IV, 647
Morelan, Aden VI, 334
Morelan, Albert IV, 1135
Morelan, Albert M. IV, 742
Morelan, Amelia IV, 742
Morelan, Amy IV, 639
Morelan, Amy IV, 647
Morelan, Ann IV, 742
Morelan, Ann VI, 537
Morelan, Ann VI, 551
Morelan, Barzilla IV, 647
Morelan, Caroline IV, 742
Morelan, Caroline IV, 1135
Morelan, Edwin IV, 742
Morelan, Eliza IV, 742
Morelan, Eliza Ann ??? IV, 742
Morelan, Elizabeth IV, 50
Morelan, Elizabeth IV, 727
Morelan, Elizabeth IV, 742
Morelan, Elmira IV, 742
Morelan, Emela IV, 647
Morelan, Huldah VI, 334
Morelan, Isaac VI, 334
Morelan, Jason IV, 50
Morelan, Jason IV, 1135
Morelan, Jason VI, 537
Morelan, Jason VI, 551
Morelan, Joel IV, 1135
Morelan, Jonah IV, 647
Morelan, Jonah VI, 334
Morelan, Jonas IV, 51
Morelan, Lanora IV, 742
Morelan, Lydia F ??? IV, 742
Morelan, Martha IV, 742
Morelan, Martha Elizabeth IV, 1135
Morelan, Mary IV, 50
Morelan, Mary IV, 647
Morelan, Mary IV, 648
Morelan, Mary IV, 1135
Morelan, Mary VI, 334
Morelan, Mary M. IV, 742
Morelan, Micajah IV, 742
Morelan, Mordecai IV, 742
Morelan, Mordica VI, 334
Morelan, Newberry IV, 742
Morelan, Rebecca IV, 1135
Morelan, Richard VI, 334
Morelan, Robert IV, 1135
Morelan, Roxan IV, 742
Morelan, Roxany IV, 742
Morelan, Ruth Anna IV, 647
Morelan, Sarah IV, 911
Morelan, Sarah VI, 334
Morelan, Sarah VI, 343
Morelan, Sarah P. IV, 742
Morelan, Stephen IV, 742
Morelan, Stephen IV, 878
Morelan, Stephen VI, 334
Morelan, Theophilus IV, 742
Morelan, William VI, 334
Moreland, ??? III, 352
Moreland, Abigal VI, 334
Moreland, Aden IV, 913
Moreland, Aden VI, 334
Moreland, Albert IV, 1135
Moreland, Amy IV, 647
Moreland, Amy IV, 834
Moreland, Ann IV, 1106
Moreland, Ann VI, 334
Moreland, Ann VI, 354
Moreland, Huldah IV, 742
Moreland, Huldah IV, 834
Moreland, Huldah VI, 334
Moreland, Isaac VI, 334
Moreland, Jane III, 234
Moreland, Jane III, 352
Moreland, Jane VI, 344
Moreland, Jane VI, 894
Moreland, Jason IV, 1106
Moreland, Jason IV, 1135
Moreland, Jason VI, 328
Moreland, Jason VI, 334
Moreland, Jason VI, 343
Moreland, Jason VI, 354
Moreland, Jennet III, 234
Moreland, Jennet III, 352
Moreland, John VI, 344
Moreland, John VI, 894
Moreland, Jonah IV, 647
Moreland, Jonah VI, 334
Moreland, Joseph IV, 834
Moreland, Joseph VI, 296
Moreland, Joseph VI, 334
Moreland, Lydia IV, 742
Moreland, Martha VI, 334
Moreland, Martha VI, 343
Moreland, Marthew VI, 334
Moreland, Marthew VI, 343
Moreland, Mary IV, 647
Moreland, Mary IV, 655
Moreland, Mary IV, 1106
Moreland, Mary IV, 1135
Moreland, Mary VI, 334
Moreland, Mary VI, 344
Moreland, Mary F. IV, 834
Moreland, Mordecai IV, 834
Moreland, Mordica VI, 334
Moreland, Mourning VI, 296
Moreland, Mourning VI, 334
Moreland, Nancy VI, 328
Moreland, Nancy VI, 334
Moreland, Nathan Kirk IV, 834
Moreland, Rebecca IV, 1107
Moreland, Rebecca IV, 1135
Moreland, Rebecca VI, 345
Moreland, Rebeckah VI, 328
Moreland, Rebeckah VI, 334
Moreland, Rebeckah VI, 344
Moreland, Rhoda IV, 742
Moreland, Richard VI, 334
Moreland, Richard VI, 344
Moreland, Robert IV, 1135
Moreland, Sarah IV, 742
Moreland, Sarah IV, 913
Moreland, Sarah VI, 334
Moreland, Sarah VI, 344
Moreland, Sarah VI, 424
Moreland, Stephen IV, 834
Moreland, Stephen VI, 334
Moreland, William VI, 334
Morell, Mary IV, 619
Morell, Mary IV, 646
Moreman, Achsah I, 831
Moreman, Affrica VI, 332
Moreman, Agnes I, 831
Moreman, Agness I, 410
Moreman, Agness I, 426
Moreman, Alrica V, 518
Moreman, Ann I, 379
Moreman, Ann I, 410
Moreman, Anna I, 726
Moreman, Anna I, 831
Moreman, Aphraca V, 518
Moreman, Archaleaus I, 831
Moreman, Archilus I, 726
Moreman, Arihelus I, 726
Moreman, Arihelus I, 1066
Moreman, Benjamin I, 726
Moreman, Benjamin I, 831
Moreman, Celia I, 726
Moreman, Charles I, 410
Moreman, Charles V, 518
Moreman, Charles Terrell VI, 332
Moreman, Childs V, 518
Moreman, Chiles VI, 332
Moreman, Christopher V, 518
Moreman, Cuza I, 831
Moreman, Delilah I, 370
Moreman, Delilah I, 410
Moreman, Dosha V, 518
Moreman, Dosha V, 523
Moreman, Edward I, 831
Moreman, Eli I, 831
Moreman, Eliza I, 726
Moreman, Elizabeth I, 410
Moreman, Elizabeth I, 831
Moreman, Elizabeth V, 505
Moreman, Elizabeth V, 518
Moreman, Fanny I, 381
Moreman, Fanny I, 410
Moreman, Hannah I, 703
Moreman, Hannah I, 726
Moreman, Hannah I, 831
Moreman, Henry I, 703
Moreman, Henry I, 726
Moreman, James I, 726
Moreman, James I, 831
Moreman, James V, 518
Moreman, James VI, 332

oreman, Jesse I, 726
oreman, Jesse I, 831
oreman, John I, 726
oreman, John I, 727
oreman, John I, 831
oreman, John Hope VI, 332
oreman, Joseph I, 831
oreman, Judith I, 411
oreman, Judith I, 726
oreman, Judith I, 831
oreman, Julia I, 726
oreman, Lidia VI, 319
oreman, Lidia VI, 333
oreman, Lishee I, 410
oreman, Lucy I, 383
oreman, Lucy I, 410
oreman, Lydia VI, 333
oreman, Mary I, 408
oreman, Mary I, 410
oreman, Mary I, 726
oreman, Mary I, 831
oreman, Micajah V, 518
oreman, Micajah VI, 333
oreman, Mildred V, 518
oreman, Mycajah VI, 332
oreman, Nancy I, 726
oreman, Nancy V, 494
oreman, Nancy V, 518
oreman, Nancy VI, 332
oreman, Paulina VI, 333
oreman, Polly V, 518
oreman, Rachel I, 370
oreman, Rachel I, 410
oreman, Rebecah I, 726
oreman, Rebecca I, 831
oreman, Rebekah I, 385
oreman, Rebekah I, 410
oreman, Reuben VI, 319
oreman, Reuben VI, 333
oreman, Richard I, 703
oreman, Ruben VI, 332
oreman, Ruben VI, 333
oreman, Ruth I, 726
oreman, Ruth I, 831
Moreman, Sampey I, 726
Moreman, Sarah I, 410
Moreman, Sarah I, 726
Moreman, Sarah I, 831
Moreman, Sarah VI, 332
Moreman, Sarah VI, 341
Moreman, Susanna I, 726
Moreman, Susanna I, 831
Moreman, Susannah V, 518
Moreman, Tarlton I, 703
Moreman, Tarlton I, 726
Moreman, Tarlton I, 831
Moreman, Thomas I, 703
Moreman, Thomas I, 726
Moreman, Thomas I, 831
Moreman, Thomas V, 518
Moreman, Thomas VI, 332
Moreman, Uriah I, 831
Moreman, Widow Susanna I, 726
Moreman, Wilson I, 726
Moreman, Zacharia I, 831
Moreman, Zachariah I, 831
Moren, Elizabeth V, 885
Moreton, Ann IV, 51
Moreton, Edith IV, 51
Moreton, Elizabeth IV, 51
Moreton, Hannah IV, 51
Moreton, John II, 397
Moreton, Mary II, 397
Moreton, Mary IV, 51
Moreton, Phebe IV, 51
Moreton, Rebecca IV, 51
Moreton, Samuel IV, 51
Moreton, Sarah IV, 51
Moreton, Susanna IV, 51
Moreton, Thomas IV, 51
Moreton, William IV, 51
Morey, Amos III, 234
Morey, Benjamin V, 351
Morey, Benjamin F. V, 351
Morey, Daniel B. V, 351
Morey, Daniel B. V, 699
Morey, Fannie III, 44
Morey, Fannie III, 234
Morey, Frederick R. III, 234
Morey, Gardner P. III, 44
Morey, Gardner P. III, 234
Morey, George A. V, 351
Morey, Hannah B. III, 234
Morey, James S. III, 234
Morey, Jemima III, 234
Morey, John II, 446
Morey, Levi III, 234
Morey, Lydia III, 44
Morey, Lydia III, 234
Morey, Margaret V, 351
Morey, Margaret V, 353
Morey, Nettie Estelle III, 234
Morey, Sarah J. V, 351
Morey, Sarah Jane V, 351
Morford, Eliza T. VI, 1004
Morford, Esther II, 200
Morford, Esther II, 243
Morford, Hern Brian II, 243
Morford, Ruth Ann V, 101
Morford, Ruth Ann V, 102
Morford, Ruthanna V, 101
Morford, Ruthanna V, 102
Morford, Thomas V, 102
Morgan, ??? V, 194
Morgan, Abbie VI, 651
Morgan, Abigail I, 790
Morgan, Abigail I, 1110
Morgan, Abigail I, 1114
Morgan, Abigail I, 1115
Morgan, Abigail I, 1128
Morgan, Abigail I, 1129
Morgan, Abigail C. I, 831
Morgan, Abigail C. I, 1110
Morgan, Abigail C. I, 1129
Morgan, Abigal I, 1129
Morgan, Abraham VI, 904
Morgan, Abraham VI, 964
Morgan, Abraham VI, 996
Morgan, Adaline VI, 965
Morgan, Agness VI, 900
Morgan, Albina IV, 1174
Morgan, Albina IV, 1217
Morgan, Alexander V, 285
Morgan, Alexander VI, 965
Morgan, Allen I, 1145
Morgan, Allexander II, 601
Morgan, Allexander II, 636
Morgan, Amanda IV, 1287
Morgan, Amy VI, 840
Morgan, Ann I, 61
Morgan, Ann I, 67
Morgan, Ann I, 102
Morgan, Ann I, 147
Morgan, Ann I, 171
Morgan, Ann I, 175
Morgan, Ann I, 375
Morgan, Ann I, 492
Morgan, Ann I, 511
Morgan, Ann I, 1145
Morgan, Ann I, 1155
Morgan, Ann I, 1160
Morgan, Ann II, 397
Morgan, Ann II, 509
Morgan, Ann II, 537
Morgan, Ann II, 601
Morgan, Ann II, 639
Morgan, Ann II, 641
Morgan, Ann III, 234
Morgan, Ann IV, 50
Morgan, Ann IV, 53
Morgan, Ann IV, 54
Morgan, Ann IV, 102
Morgan, Ann IV, 488
Morgan, Ann IV, 834
Morgan, Ann V, 153
Morgan, Ann V, 160
Morgan, Ann V, 176
Morgan, Ann V, 181
Morgan, Ann V, 194
Morgan, Ann V, 956
Morgan, Ann Eliza IV, 27
Morgan, Ann Eliza IV, 48
Morgan, Ann Eliza IV, 50
Morgan, Ann Eliza IV, 102
Morgan, Ann Eliza IV, 834
Morgan, Ann Maria III, 234
Morgan, Ann Waln II, 601
Morgan, Ann Waln II, 641
Morgan, Anna I, 103
Morgan, Anna V, 194
Morgan, Anna L. V, 103
Morgan, Anna Maria III, 362
Morgan, Anne I, 411
Morgan, Annie L. V, 194
Morgan, Archelaus I, 218
Morgan, Arthur I, 247
Morgan, Asa IV, 154
Morgan, Asa IV, 344
Morgan, Asa V, 194
Morgan, Asa V, 266
Morgan, Asseneth I, 1062
Morgan, Asseneth I, 1063
Morgan, B. T. IV, 253
Morgan, Benj. VI, 768
Morgan, Benjamin I, 102
Morgan, Benjamin I, 140
Morgan, Benjamin I, 147
Morgan, Benjamin I, 148
Morgan, Benjamin I, 563
Morgan, Benjamin I, 581
Morgan, Benjamin I, 726
Morgan, Benjamin II, 397
Morgan, Benjamin II, 601
Morgan, Benjamin II, 636
Morgan, Benjamin V, 756
Morgan, Benjamin H. VI, 957
Morgan, Benjamin R. II, 601
Morgan, Benjamin Townsend IV, 742
Morgan, Benjamin Townsend IV, 834
Morgan, Benjamin, Jr. I, 147
Morgan, Benjamin, Jr. II, 601
Morgan, Benjamin, Sr. I, 102
Morgan, Betsey VI, 952
Morgan, Betsy VI, 888
Morgan, Camilla F. I, 922
Morgan, Carl S. V, 194
Morgan, Carl Sherwood V, 103
Morgan, Caroline I, 1145
Morgan, Catharine I, 511
Morgan, Catharine I, 563
Morgan, Catharine I, 582
Morgan, Catharine I, 831
Morgan, Catharine I, 1128
Morgan, Catharine I, 1129
Morgan, Catharine I, 1130
Morgan, Catharine II, 397
Morgan, Catharine IV, 338
Morgan, Catharine IV, 339
Morgan, Catharine IV, 344
Morgan, Catharine V, 194
Morgan, Catharine Elizabeth I, 1110
Morgan, Catherine I, 1110
Morgan, Catherine I, 1129
Morgan, Catherine V, 159
Morgan, Catherine V, 194
Morgan, Catherine, Jr. I, 1129
Morgan, Cathrine VI, 897
Morgan, Cecil IV, 1258
Morgan, Charles I, 61
Morgan, Charles I, 96
Morgan, Charles I, 102
Morgan, Charles I, 103
Morgan, Charles I, 132
Morgan, Charles I, 147
Morgan, Charles I, 155
Morgan, Charles I, 563
Morgan, Charles I, 726
Morgan, Charles IV, 102
Morgan, Charles IV, 253
Morgan, Charles IV, 254
Morgan, Charles IV, 834
Morgan, Charles V, 756
Morgan, Charles W. II, 397
Morgan, Charles W. II, 601
Morgan, Charles Waln II, 601
Morgan, Charlotte V, 20
Morgan, Charlotte V, 103
Morgan, Charlotte V, 922
Morgan, Charlotte VI, 964
Morgan, Charlotte A. V, 922
Morgan, Charlotte C. VI, 958
Morgan, Chas. E. II, 853
Morgan, Chas. E. II, 901
Morgan, Chester O. III, 234
Morgan, Chris. VI, 887
Morgan, Christopher V, 922
Morgan, Christopher VI, 887
Morgan, Christopher VI, 964
Morgan, Christopher VI, 965
Morgan, Christopher A. V, 922
Morgan, Clarence V, 699
Morgan, Cornelia V, 922
Morgan, Cornelia V, 926
Morgan, Daniel VI, 425
Morgan, David I, 102
Morgan, David I, 148
Morgan, David I, 1110
Morgan, David I, 1145
Morgan, David I, 1157
Morgan, David I, 1160
Morgan, David II, 462
Morgan, David IV, 154
Morgan, David IV, 344
Morgan, David V, 28
Morgan, David V, 102
Morgan, David V, 103
Morgan, David V, 266
Morgan, David B. V, 266
Morgan, David B. V, 289
Morgan, David Bruce V, 266
Morgan, David Bruce VI, 334
Morgan, David C. VI, 830
Morgan, David C. VI, 840
Morgan, David, Jr. V, 103
Morgan, Debborah VI, 425
Morgan, Deborah I, 1049
Morgan, Deborah II, 397
Morgan, Deborah IV, 102
Morgan, Deborah IV, 834
Morgan, Deborah VI, 395
Morgan, Deborah VI, 418
Morgan, Deborah VI, 425
Morgan, Deborah VI, 767
Morgan, Deborah L. VI, 425
Morgan, Dolly VI, 830
Morgan, Dolly VI, 840
Morgan, Edith IV, 102
Morgan, Edith IV, 742
Morgan, Edith IV, 834
Morgan, Edward II, 397
Morgan, Edward IV, 102
Morgan, Edward IV, 834
Morgan, Edward VI, 425
Morgan, Edward J. V, 922
Morgan, Edward, Jr. V, 285
Morgan, Edwin V, 701
Morgan, Edwin Tasco V, 699
Morgan, Edwin Tasso V, 699
Morgan, Eleanor III, 427
Morgan, Eleanor III, 450
Morgan, Elijah IV, 50
Morgan, Elisa S. III, 234
Morgan, Elisabeth I, 37
Morgan, Elisabeth I, 46
Morgan, Elisabeth I, 61
Morgan, Elisabeth I, 130
Morgan, Elisabeth I, 132
Morgan, Elisabeth I, 142
Morgan, Elisabeth I, 147
Morgan, Elisabeth I, 158
Morgan, Elisabeth I, 196
Morgan, Elisabeth I, 198
Morgan, Elisabeth I, 247
Morgan, Elisabeth I, 1110
Morgan, Elisabeth I, 1113
Morgan, Elisabeth I, 1129
Morgan, Elisha I, 1110
Morgan, Elisha Hall I, 147
Morgan, Eliza II, 509
Morgan, Eliza II, 601
Morgan, Eliza IV, 646
Morgan, Eliza IV, 665
Morgan, Eliza IV, 742
Morgan, Eliza IV, 834
Morgan, Eliza IV, 851
Morgan, Eliza VI, 530
Morgan, Eliza VI, 536
Morgan, Eliza VI, 744
Morgan, Eliza VI, 763
Morgan, Eliza VI, 767
Morgan, Eliza VI, 768
Morgan, Eliza A. VI, 840
Morgan, Eliza A. VI, 965
Morgan, Eliza Ann VI, 882
Morgan, Eliza N. IV, 834
Morgan, Eliza Nailor IV, 834
Morgan, Eliza Nailor IV, 857
Morgan, Elizabeth I, 96
Morgan, Elizabeth I, 102
Morgan, Elizabeth I, 247
Morgan, Elizabeth I, 252
Morgan, Elizabeth I, 511
Morgan, Elizabeth II, 397
Morgan, Elizabeth II, 601
Morgan, Elizabeth II, 674
Morgan, Elizabeth IV, 50
Morgan, Elizabeth IV, 102
Morgan, Elizabeth IV, 154
Morgan, Elizabeth IV, 344
Morgan, Elizabeth IV, 646
Morgan, Elizabeth IV, 665
Morgan, Elizabeth IV, 894
Morgan, Elizabeth V, 102
Morgan, Elizabeth V, 194
Morgan, Elizabeth V, 266
Morgan, Elizabeth V, 284
Morgan, Elizabeth VI, 199
Morgan, Elizabeth VI, 216
Morgan, Elizabeth VI, 536
Morgan, Elizabeth VI, 767
Morgan, Elizabeth VI, 840
Morgan, Elizabeth VI, 860
Morgan, Elizabeth VI, 878
Morgan, Elizabeth VI, 964
Morgan, Elizabeth Ann VI, 1018
Morgan, Elizabeth D. VI, 897
Morgan, Elizabeth D. VI, 995
Morgan, Elizabeth F. VI, 897
Morgan, Elizabeth J. VI, 958
Morgan, Elizabeth O. V, 922
Morgan, Elizabeth S. IV, 1040
Morgan, Ellen M. VI, 765
Morgan, Ellen M. VI, 767
Morgan, Ellen M. VI, 768
Morgan, Elme J. VI, 874
Morgan, Elmira C. VI, 965
Morgan, Emily I, 1145
Morgan, Ephraim V, 922
Morgan, Esther IV, 50
Morgan, Esther IV, 63
Morgan, Esther IV, 498
Morgan, Esther IV, 741
Morgan, Esther IV, 834
Morgan, Evan II, 397
Morgan, Evan II, 446
Morgan, Fennette Jane VI, 965
Morgan, Florentine W. VI, 1012
Morgan, Flossie Stuart I, 946
Morgan, Floyd S. III, 427
Morgan, Floyd S. N. III, 450
Morgan, Frances E. III, 49
Morgan, Francis III, 234
Morgan, Francis III, 362
Morgan, Francis VI, 840
Morgan, Frank IV, 254
Morgan, Frederick Y. IV, 253
Morgan, Garland VI, 901
Morgan, Garland VI, 947
Morgan, Garland VI, 955
Morgan, Garland VI, 985
Morgan, Garland VI, 995
Morgan, Garland VI, 1016
Morgan, George IV, 50
Morgan, George IV, 834
Morgan, Gerrard J. V, 266
Morgan, Gerrard Johnson V, 266
Morgan, Grace V, 266
Morgan, Grace V, 289
Morgan, Grady Lee I, 946
Morgan, Hannah I, 50
Morgan, Hannah I, 61
Morgan, Hannah I, 102
Morgan, Hannah I, 103
Morgan, Hannah I, 140
Morgan, Hannah I, 142
Morgan, Hannah I, 147
Morgan, Hannah I, 158
Morgan, Hannah I, 1110
Morgan, Hannah II, 115
Morgan, Hannah II, 121
Morgan, Hannah II, 397
Morgan, Hannah II, 537
Morgan, Hannah II, 601
Morgan, Hannah II, 722
Morgan, Hannah II, 1017
Morgan, Hannah III, 234
Morgan, Hannah IV, 50
Morgan, Hannah IV, 102
Morgan, Hannah IV, 154
Morgan, Hannah IV, 344
Morgan, Hannah IV, 742
Morgan, Hannah IV, 834
Morgan, Hannah V, 266
Morgan, Hannah V, 942
Morgan, Hannah VI, 917
Morgan, Hannah H. VI, 767
Morgan, Hannah Hallowy II, 828
Morgan, Hannah I. II, 862
Morgan, Hannah I. II, 901
Morgan, Hannah Irwin II, 901
Morgan, Hannah P. II, 722
Morgan, Helen II, 601
Morgan, Helen W. II, 397
Morgan, Henrietta V, 699
Morgan, Henry I, 492
Morgan, Henry I, 511
Morgan, Henry I, 563
Morgan, Henry I, 1110
Morgan, Henry VI, 425
Morgan, Henry VI, 840
Morgan, Henry B. V, 699
Morgan, Hezekiah I, 790
Morgan, Hezekiah I, 1110
Morgan, Hezekiah I, 1128
Morgan, Hezikiah I, 1145
Morgan, Hugh V, 266
Morgan, Hugh VI, 319
Morgan, Hugh VI, 325
Morgan, Hugh VI, 334
Morgan, Huldah I, 147
Morgan, Huldah I, 1110
Morgan, Huldah I, 1115
Morgan, Huldah I, 1129
Morgan, Ila I, 922
Morgan, Ila I, 931
Morgan, Isaac I, 102
Morgan, Isaac I, 147
Morgan, Isaac I, 175
Morgan, Isaac I, 1110
Morgan, Isaac II, 115
Morgan, Isaac II, 121
Morgan, Isaac II, 713
Morgan, Isaac II, 722
Morgan, Isaac IV, 154
Morgan, Isaac IV, 344
Morgan, Isaac V, 194
Morgan, Isaac V, 266
Morgan, Isaac V, 285
Morgan, Isaac V, 756
Morgan, Isaac VI, 425
Morgan, Isaac VI, 536
Morgan, Isaac, Jr. II, 115

Morgan, Isaac, Jr. II, 121
Morgan, Isabella III, 234
Morgan, Israel II, 601
Morgan, J. Wesley VI, 942
Morgan, Jacob V, 922
Morgan, James I, 50
Morgan, James I, 61
Morgan, James I, 102
Morgan, James I, 103
Morgan, James I, 140
Morgan, James I, 141
Morgan, James I, 147
Morgan, James I, 167
Morgan, James I, 1110
Morgan, James IV, 646
Morgan, James IV, 894
Morgan, James V, 922
Morgan, James VI, 1018
Morgan, James H. IV, 742
Morgan, James H. V, 103
Morgan, James H. V, 194
Morgan, James T. V, 922
Morgan, James W. V, 194
Morgan, James, Jr. I, 146
Morgan, James, Jr. I, 147
Morgan, James, Sr. I, 103
Morgan, Jane I, 895
Morgan, Jane I, 905
Morgan, Jane II, 397
Morgan, Jane II, 601
Morgan, Jane II, 636
Morgan, Jane VI, 768
Morgan, Jane VI, 830
Morgan, Jane VI, 840
Morgan, Jane B. II, 853
Morgan, Jane B. II, 901
Morgan, Jemima III, 234
Morgan, Jennie V, 699
Morgan, Jephthah I, 1110
Morgan, Jesse VI, 944
Morgan, Jesse VI, 964
Morgan, Jesse VI, 965
Morgan, Jesse VI, 1012
Morgan, Jesse VI, 1017
Morgan, Jesse VI, 1018
Morgan, Jessee I, 147
Morgan, Jessee I, 156
Morgan, Joanna II, 397
Morgan, Joanna II, 465
Morgan, Joanna II, 601
Morgan, Joel IV, 646
Morgan, John I, 61
Morgan, John I, 196
Morgan, John I, 218
Morgan, John I, 247
Morgan, John I, 511
Morgan, John I, 563
Morgan, John I, 726
Morgan, John I, 1110
Morgan, John III, 362
Morgan, John IV, 50
Morgan, John IV, 102
Morgan, John IV, 834
Morgan, John IV, 1287
Morgan, John V, 102
Morgan, John V, 194
Morgan, John VI, 190
Morgan, John VI, 193
Morgan, John VI, 199
Morgan, John VI, 216
Morgan, John VI, 424
Morgan, John VI, 425
Morgan, John VI, 530
Morgan, John VI, 536
Morgan, John VI, 763
Morgan, John VI, 765
Morgan, John VI, 767
Morgan, John VI, 768
Morgan, John VI, 860
Morgan, John VI, 897
Morgan, John A. I, 922
Morgan, John B. I, 831
Morgan, John B. I, 1110
Morgan, John B. I, 1129
Morgan, John B. II, 853
Morgan, John B. II, 901
Morgan, John C. IV, 646
Morgan, John D. IV, 1287
Morgan, John H. VI, 887
Morgan, John W. V, 266
Morgan, John W. VI, 965
Morgan, John Watkins V, 266
Morgan, Jonathan I, 102
Morgan, Jonathan I, 103
Morgan, Jonathan I, 148
Morgan, Jonathan I, 1110
Morgan, Jonathan IV, 154
Morgan, Jonathan IV, 344
Morgan, Jonathan V, 102
Morgan, Jonathan V, 194
Morgan, Jonathan V, 266
Morgan, Josep. I, 102
Morgan, Joseph I, 218
Morgan, Joseph I, 247
Morgan, Joseph I, 1145
Morgan, Joseph II, 179
Morgan, Joseph II, 901
Morgan, Joseph II, 910
Morgan, Joseph IV, 834
Morgan, Joseph V, 102
Morgan, Joseph V, 103
Morgan, Joseph V, 285
Morgan, Joseph VI, 393
Morgan, Joseph VI, 424
Morgan, Joseph VI, 425
Morgan, Joseph VI, 530
Morgan, Joseph VI, 536
Morgan, Joseph VI, 601
Morgan, Joseph VI, 763
Morgan, Joseph VI, 768
Morgan, Joseph VI, 840
Morgan, Joseph Wright IV, 834
Morgan, Joseph, Jr. II, 785
Morgan, Josephine V, 422
Morgan, Josephine E. V, 422
Morgan, Josephine E. V, 439
Morgan, Joshua I, 147
Morgan, Joshua IV, 646
Morgan, Joshua IV, 894
Morgan, Joshua W. IV, 646
Morgan, Josiah I, 132
Morgan, Josiah IV, 1287
Morgan, Judith V, 266
Morgan, Judith VI, 319
Morgan, Judith VI, 325
Morgan, Judith VI, 334
Morgan, Juliana Jane VI, 965
Morgan, Katherine I, 1160
Morgan, Katherine III, 249
Morgan, Katherine, Jr. I, 1129
Morgan, Lee I, 946
Morgan, Lemmuel I, 182
Morgan, Lemmuel I, 196
Morgan, Lemuel I, 50
Morgan, Lemuel I, 61
Morgan, Lemuel I, 103
Morgan, Lemuel I, 147
Morgan, Lemuel I, 196
Morgan, Lemuel I, 726
Morgan, Levi I, 1110
Morgan, Levi I, 1128
Morgan, Lewis IV, 646
Morgan, Lewis IV, 894
Morgan, Lewis VI, 888
Morgan, Lewis VI, 1014
Morgan, Lina I, 946
Morgan, Lizzie V, 194
Morgan, Louisa VI, 850
Morgan, Lovey VI, 964
Morgan, Loving VI, 963
Morgan, Lucinda I, 1145
Morgan, Lucinda I, 1157
Morgan, Lucinda I, 1160
Morgan, Lucy II, 798
Morgan, Lucy VI, 903
Morgan, Lurany VI, 1020
Morgan, Lyda I, 102
Morgan, Lydda I, 196
Morgan, Lyddia I, 132
Morgan, Lyddia I, 147
Morgan, Lydia I, 103
Morgan, Lydia I, 140
Morgan, Lydia I, 147
Morgan, Lydia I, 196
Morgan, Lydia I, 1110
Morgan, Lydia I, 1120
Morgan, Lydia I, 1126
Morgan, Lydia I, 1128
Morgan, Lydia I, 1129
Morgan, Lydia IV, 834
Morgan, Lydia V, 285
Morgan, Lydia VI, 425
Morgan, Lydia VI, 441
Morgan, Mahala VI, 980
Morgan, Mahlon VI, 965
Morgan, Mahlon VI, 1020
Morgan, Margaret I, 103
Morgan, Margaret I, 141
Morgan, Margaret I, 147
Morgan, Margaret I, 148
Morgan, Margaret VI, 651
Morgan, Margaret D. I, 1110
Morgan, Margret Jane I, 1145
Morgan, Maria IV, 741
Morgan, Maria IV, 834
Morgan, Maria IV, 837
Morgan, Mariah IV, 834
Morgan, Martha I, 145
Morgan, Martha I, 147
Morgan, Martha I, 156
Morgan, Martha IV, 1275
Morgan, Martha IV, 1287
Morgan, Martha V, 103
Morgan, Martha V, 518
Morgan, Martha V, 524
Morgan, Martha VI, 393
Morgan, Martha VI, 424
Morgan, Martha VI, 425
Morgan, Martha VI, 530
Morgan, Martha VI, 536
Morgan, Martha VI, 763
Morgan, Martha VI, 768
Morgan, Martha A. V, 103
Morgan, Martha A. V, 194
Morgan, Martha A. VI, 963
Morgan, Martha Ann V, 194
Morgan, Martha L. VI, 982
Morgan, Mary I, 61
Morgan, Mary I, 102
Morgan, Mary I, 103
Morgan, Mary I, 132
Morgan, Mary I, 146
Morgan, Mary I, 147
Morgan, Mary I, 150
Morgan, Mary I, 159
Morgan, Mary I, 175
Morgan, Mary I, 182
Morgan, Mary I, 191
Morgan, Mary I, 196
Morgan, Mary I, 218
Morgan, Mary I, 247
Morgan, Mary I, 831
Morgan, Mary I, 1129
Morgan, Mary II, 115
Morgan, Mary II, 121
Morgan, Mary II, 179
Morgan, Mary II, 296
Morgan, Mary II, 446
Morgan, Mary II, 478
Morgan, Mary II, 555
Morgan, Mary II, 601
Morgan, Mary II, 713
Morgan, Mary II, 785
Morgan, Mary IV, 50
Morgan, Mary IV, 89
Morgan, Mary IV, 102
Morgan, Mary IV, 834
Morgan, Mary V, 194
Morgan, Mary V, 922
Morgan, Mary V, 942
Morgan, Mary VI, 190
Morgan, Mary VI, 193
Morgan, Mary VI, 199
Morgan, Mary VI, 379
Morgan, Mary VI, 424
Morgan, Mary VI, 425
Morgan, Mary VI, 429
Morgan, Mary VI, 900
Morgan, Mary VI, 927
Morgan, Mary Ann II, 719
Morgan, Mary Ann II, 756
Morgan, Mary Ann VI, 767
Morgan, Mary Ann VI, 768
Morgan, Mary Ann VI, 964
Morgan, Mary Anna II, 713
Morgan, Mary B. I, 1110
Morgan, Mary C. VI, 965
Morgan, Mary Cooper II, 804
Morgan, Mary E. IV, 243
Morgan, Mary E. IV, 253
Morgan, Mary Frances VI, 944
Morgan, Mary G. II, 397
Morgan, Mary Genevieve V, 699
Morgan, Mary Genevive V, 701
Morgan, Mary H. II, 901
Morgan, Mary Lincoln II, 901
Morgan, Mary N. VI, 798
Morgan, Mary Payton VI, 425
Morgan, Mary V. V, 922
Morgan, Mary W. VI, 944
Morgan, Mathew I, 146
Morgan, Mathew I, 164
Morgan, Mathews IV, 102
Morgan, Matilda I, 1110
Morgan, Matilda I, 1113
Morgan, Matilda I, 1129
Morgan, Matilda IV, 498
Morgan, Matilda IV, 742
Morgan, Matilda IV, 834
Morgan, Matilda IV, 846
Morgan, Matilda V, 103
Morgan, Matilda V, 171
Morgan, Matilda V, 194
Morgan, Matthew I, 61
Morgan, Mattie V, 103
Morgan, McGilbert VI, 840
Morgan, Meriam I, 196
Morgan, Meriam I, 726
Morgan, Merimon A. VI, 980
Morgan, Mertie V, 699
Morgan, Micajah I, 102
Morgan, Micajah V, 756
Morgan, Michal I, 726
Morgan, Milisant, Jr. I, 147
Morgan, Milisant, Jr. I, 152
Morgan, Miliscent I, 147
Morgan, Miliscent I, 150
Morgan, Milisent I, 147
Morgan, Milisent I, 167
Morgan, Millisant I, 103
Morgan, Millisent I, 103
Morgan, Mills Lee I, 946
Morgan, Miranda VI, 768
Morgan, Miriam I, 50
Morgan, Miriam I, 61
Morgan, Miriam I, 103
Morgan, Miriam I, 146
Morgan, Miriam I, 147
Morgan, Miriam I, 180
Morgan, Miriam I, 790
Morgan, Miriam I, 1110
Morgan, Miriam I, 1128
Morgan, Miriam IV, 50
Morgan, Mordecai I, 150
Morgan, Mordecai II, 397
Morgan, Mordecai VI, 903
Morgan, Mordecai VI, 964
Morgan, Mordica VI, 964
Morgan, Mordicai VI, 948
Morgan, Moreman VI, 840
Morgan, Morgan IV, 742
Morgan, Morgan VI, 357
Morgan, Morgan VI, 874
Morgan, Morgan VI, 952
Morgan, Morgan VI, 964
Morgan, Morgan VI, 969
Morgan, Morgan, Jr. VI, 944
Morgan, Morgin VI, 958
Morgan, Morgin VI, 964
Morgan, Morris II, 397
Morgan, Nancy V, 922
Morgan, Nancy VI, 965
Morgan, Nancy E. VI, 811
Morgan, Naomi I, 563
Morgan, Naomi I, 581
Morgan, Naomi I, 622
Morgan, Naomi I, 726
Morgan, Naomy I, 726
Morgan, Nathan I, 103
Morgan, Nathan I, 147
Morgan, Nathan VI, 651
Morgan, Nathan W. I, 102
Morgan, Nathaniel VI, 965
Morgan, Obadiah I, 1110
Morgan, Obadiah I, 1128
Morgan, Obadiah I, 1145
Morgan, Obadiah I, 1155
Morgan, Obadiah I, 1160
Morgan, Obediah I, 790
Morgan, Obediah I, 1128
Morgan, Obediah I, 1160
Morgan, Ola V, 636
Morgan, Oliver IV, 50
Morgan, Oliver IV, 102
Morgan, Olover IV, 102
Morgan, Orpha IV, 254
Morgan, Orpha V, 461
Morgan, Orpha V, 699
Morgan, Patience VI, 1020
Morgan, Patsy I, 148
Morgan, Patsy VI, 964
Morgan, Patty VI, 964
Morgan, Peninah I, 147
Morgan, Peninnah I, 102
Morgan, Penninah I, 137
Morgan, Penninah I, 147
Morgan, Penninah I, 718
Morgan, Penninah I, 726
Morgan, Permelia VI, 948
Morgan, Phamay I, 1057
Morgan, Phamy V, 176
Morgan, Phamy V, 194
Morgan, Phebe VI, 425
Morgan, Phebe VI, 436
Morgan, Phebe VI, 904
Morgan, Plato V, 266
Morgan, Plato V, 922
Morgan, Polly VI, 964
Morgan, Price M. VI, 917
Morgan, Rachel I, 147
Morgan, Rachel I, 193
Morgan, Rachel I, 196
Morgan, Rachel I, 726
Morgan, Rachel I, 1115
Morgan, Rachel I, 1129
Morgan, Rachel IV, 50
Morgan, Rachel IV, 62
Morgan, Rachel VI, 425
Morgan, Randolph I, 563
Morgan, Reace VI, 964
Morgan, Rebecah I, 1128
Morgan, Rebecca I, 1110
Morgan, Rebecca I, 1123
Morgan, Rebecca I, 1128
Morgan, Rebecca I, 1129
Morgan, Rebecca IV, 102
Morgan, Rebecca IV, 103
Morgan, Rebecca IV, 834
Morgan, Rebecca V, 28
Morgan, Rebecca V, 102
Morgan, Rebecca V, 103
Morgan, Rebecca VI, 878
Morgan, Rebecca VI, 995
Morgan, Rebecca Mathews IV, 102
Morgan, Rebecca Mathews IV, 834
Morgan, Rebecca Waln II, 601
Morgan, Rebecca Waln II, 639
Morgan, Rebeccah I, 790
Morgan, Rebeccah I, 831
Morgan, Rebeccah I, 1110
Morgan, Rebeckah I, 511
Morgan, Rebeckah I, 562
Morgan, Rebeckah I, 563
Morgan, Rebeckah I, 578
Morgan, Rebekah I, 1128
Morgan, Rebekah M. IV, 102
Morgan, Rece VI, 934
Morgan, Reece VI, 963
Morgan, Reese VI, 904
Morgan, Reese VI, 1020
Morgan, Reuben I, 831
Morgan, Reuben I, 1128
Morgan, Rex IV, 254
Morgan, Rhoda I, 1110
Morgan, Rhoda I, 1129
Morgan, Rhoda I, 1135
Morgan, Rhoda VI, 887
Morgan, Rhoda VI, 952
Morgan, Rhodah I, 1110
Morgan, Richard VI, 803
Morgan, Richard VI, 811
Morgan, Richard VI, 840
Morgan, Richard VI, 843
Morgan, Rosanna VI, 964
Morgan, Roxana C. I, 1110
Morgan, Ruben I, 511
Morgan, Ruben I, 1128
Morgan, Rueben I, 1102
Morgan, Russell V, 103
Morgan, Ruth I, 36
Morgan, Ruth I, 61
Morgan, Ruth I, 790
Morgan, Ruth I, 831
Morgan, Ruth I, 843
Morgan, Ruth I, 1110
Morgan, Ruth I, 1115
Morgan, Ruth I, 1128
Morgan, Ruth I, 1129
Morgan, Ruth I, 1160
Morgan, Ruth IV, 50
Morgan, Ruth V, 181
Morgan, Ruth V, 194
Morgan, Ruth Edna V, 194
Morgan, Salem IV, 50
Morgan, Sally VI, 874
Morgan, Sally VI, 879
Morgan, Sally VI, 928
Morgan, Sally VI, 964
Morgan, Sally VI, 1002
Morgan, Samuel I, 103
Morgan, Samuel I, 145
Morgan, Samuel I, 147
Morgan, Samuel V, 285
Morgan, Samuel VI, 952
Morgan, Samuel B. V, 102
Morgan, Samuel B. V, 103
Morgan, Samuel B. VI, 958
Morgan, Samuel B. VI, 965
Morgan, Samuel G. II, 601
Morgan, Samuel Griffith II, 397
Morgan, Samuel J. V, 922
Morgan, Samuel M. I, 1110
Morgan, Samuel P. V, 922
Morgan, Sarah I, 102
Morgan, Sarah I, 103
Morgan, Sarah I, 136
Morgan, Sarah I, 137
Morgan, Sarah I, 138
Morgan, Sarah I, 140
Morgan, Sarah I, 146
Morgan, Sarah I, 147
Morgan, Sarah I, 164
Morgan, Sarah I, 196
Morgan, Sarah I, 719
Morgan, Sarah I, 726
Morgan, Sarah I, 1110
Morgan, Sarah II, 397
Morgan, Sarah II, 601
Morgan, Sarah II, 756
Morgan, Sarah II, 760
Morgan, Sarah II, 901
Morgan, Sarah II, 910
Morgan, Sarah IV, 646

rgan, Sarah IV, 818
rgan, Sarah IV, 834
rgan, Sarah V, 922
rgan, Sarah VI, 359
rgan, Sarah VI, 424
rgan, Sarah VI, 536
rgan, Sarah VI, 537
rgan, Sarah VI, 549
rgan, Sarah VI, 663
rgan, Sarah VI, 756
rgan, Sarah VI, 768
rgan, Sarah VI, 771
rgan, Sarah VI, 964
rgan, Sarah VI, 965
rgan, Sarah A. VI, 887
rgan, Sarah Ann I, 1110
rgan, Sarah Ann V, 922
rgan, Sarah Elizabeth I, 1110
rgan, Sarah F. II, 853
rgan, Sarah F. II, 901
rgan, Sarah H. I, 726
rgan, Sarah P. II, 901
rgan, Seth I, 102
rgan, Seth I, 147
rgan, Seth I, 158
rgan, Seth I, 196
rgan, Seth I, 198
rgan, Seth I, 1110
rgan, Seth I, 1129
rgan, Sisley II, 85
rgan, Sisley II, 88
rgan, Slater B. II, 901
rgan, Slater Brown II, 901
rgan, Sophia I, 1145
rgan, Sophia IV, 275
rgan, Sophia R. VI, 970
rgan, Sophia W. VI, 840
rgan, Stephen VI, 900
rgan, Stephen VI, 964
rgan, Susan IV, 646
rgan, Susan IV, 894
rgan, Susan VI, 840
rgan, Susan A. VI, 840
rgan, Susan W. II, 601
rgan, Susan W. II, 639
rgan, Susan Waln II, 601
rgan, Susanah I, 1129
rgan, Susanna I, 563
rgan, Susanna I, 726
rgan, Susanna IV, 646
rgan, Susanna VI, 904
rgan, Susanna VI, 917
rgan, Susannah I, 102
rgan, Susannah I, 147
rgan, Susannah I, 155
rgan, Susannah I, 196
rgan, Susannah I, 726
rgan, Susannah I, 1110
rgan, Susannah I, 1115
rgan, Susannah II, 465
rgan, Susannah II, 601
rgan, Swan H. VI, 840
rgan, Terrell VI, 811
rgan, Terrell VI, 840
rgan, Thomas I, 511
rgan, Thomas I, 790
rgan, Thomas I, 831
rgan, Thomas I, 843
rgan, Thomas I, 1110
rgan, Thomas I, 1128
rgan, Thomas I, 1145
rgan, Thomas I, 1160
rgan, Thomas II, 397
rgan, Thomas II, 509
rgan, Thomas II, 537
rgan, Thomas II, 601
rgan, Thomas II, 639
rgan, Thomas II, 641
rgan, Thomas IV, 498
rgan, Thomas IV, 646
rgan, Thomas V, 160
rgan, Thomas V, 176
rgan, Thomas V, 194
rgan, Thomas VI, 768
rgan, Thomas VI, 840
rgan, Thomas VI, 917
rgan, Thomas VI, 964
rgan, Thomas VI, 1002
rgan, Thomas A. VI, 964
rgan, Thomas D. VI, 840
rgan, Thomas J. VI, 964
rgan, Thomas M. III, 234
rgan, Thomas P. VI, 767
rgan, Thomas W. II, 397
rgan, Thomas W. II, 537
rgan, Thomas W. II, 601
rgan, Thompson I, 1145
rgan, Thos. VI, 904
rgan, Tymanda I, 1145
rgan, Waln II, 601
rgan, Wd. Esther IV, 857
Morgan, Wd. Mary II, 179
Morgan, Widow Miliscent I, 147
Morgan, Widow Rebeckah I, 563
Morgan, William I, 147
Morgan, William I, 218
Morgan, William I, 247
Morgan, William I, 511
Morgan, William I, 562
Morgan, William I, 563
Morgan, William I, 790
Morgan, William I, 831
Morgan, William I, 1101
Morgan, William I, 1110
Morgan, William I, 1126
Morgan, William I, 1128
Morgan, William I, 1129
Morgan, William II, 397
Morgan, William IV, 50
Morgan, William IV, 665
Morgan, William IV, 742
Morgan, William IV, 834
Morgan, William V, 103
Morgan, William V, 181
Morgan, William V, 194
Morgan, William VI, 291
Morgan, William VI, 536
Morgan, William VI, 537
Morgan, William VI, 549
Morgan, William VI, 726
Morgan, William VI, 768
Morgan, William VI, 771
Morgan, William VI, 882
Morgan, William VI, 964
Morgan, William B. I, 719
Morgan, William B. I, 726
Morgan, William B. I, 1110
Morgan, William B. III, 234
Morgan, William B. VI, 878
Morgan, William B. VI, 965
Morgan, William H. I, 1129
Morgan, William H. I, 1160
Morgan, William H. V, 194
Morgan, William H. V, 699
Morgan, William J. I, 1145
Morgan, William M. IV, 50
Morgan, William P. II, 713
Morgan, William, Jr. I, 1128
Morgan, William, Jr. I, 1129
Morgan, William, Jr. VI, 768
Morgan, Winifred V, 194
Morgan, Winney I, 236
Morgan, Winney I, 247
Morgan, Wm. I, 1110
Morgan, Wm. II, 601
Morgan, Wm. V, 171
Morgan, Wm. V, 194
Morgan, Wm. VI, 663
Morgan, Wm. VI, 768
Morgan, Wm. H. V, 194
Morgan, Wm. Henry V, 103
Morgan, Wm. P. II, 756
Morgan, Wm., Jr. I, 1110
Morgan, Wm., Jr. I, 1130
Morgan, Zilla II, 901
Morgan, Zillah II, 810
Morgen, Josiah IV, 1287
Morgen, Sarah IV, 646
Morgin, ??? VI, 879
Morgin, Elizabeth V, 266
Morgin, Hannah V, 266
Morgin, Morgin VI, 874
Morgin, Morgin VI, 964
Morgin, Morgin VI, 969
Morgin, Morgin VI, 989
Morgin, Morgin, Sr. VI, 964
Morgin, Sally VI, 964
Morgin, Susanna I, 719
Morgin, Susanna I, 726
Morgin, Susannah VI, 1020
Morgin, Thomas VI, 1020
Morgin, William I, 967
Morice, George I, 563
Morice, Lawrence II, 212
Morice, Virgin II, 212
Moris, Ann IV, 351
Moris, Anthony, Jr. II, 626
Moris, Damaris I, 91
Moris, Edith V, 51
Moris, Edith V, 103
Moris, Elizabeth I, 91
Moris, Mary II, 626
Moris, Sarah II, 626
Morison, Damaris I, 1
Morison, Damaris I, 61
Morison, Damaris I, 70
Morison, Damaris I, 78
Morison, Edith I, 451
Morison, Elizabeth I, 451
Morison, Elizabeth I, 454
Morison, James I, 451
Morison, Mary I, 451
Morison, Nathaniel I, 1145
Morison, Stephen I, 451
Morison, Stephen I, 454
Morison, William I, 451
Morlan, ??? VI, 348
Morlan, Abigail VI, 351
Morlan, Abigail VI, 354
Morlan, Abigail VI, 537
Morlan, Abner IV, 646
Morlan, Abner IV, 647
Morlan, Achsah IV, 878
Morlan, Achsah IV, 879
Morlan, Achsah IV, 882
Morlan, Adem IV, 856
Morlan, Aden IV, 632
Morlan, Aden IV, 647
Morlan, Aden IV, 728
Morlan, Aden IV, 742
Morlan, Aden IV, 878
Morlan, Aden VI, 354
Morlan, Albert IV, 646
Morlan, Albert IV, 647
Morlan, Albert IV, 648
Morlan, Albert IV, 742
Morlan, Albert IV, 1107
Morlan, Albert IV, 1135
Morlan, Albert M. IV, 742
Morlan, Albert M. IV, 743
Morlan, Alma Jane IV, 742
Morlan, Amanda IV, 627
Morlan, Amanda IV, 648
Morlan, Amanda IV, 878
Morlan, Amelia IV, 647
Morlan, Amelia IV, 648
Morlan, Amelia IV, 742
Morlan, Amelia E. IV, 742
Morlan, Amos IV, 646
Morlan, Amos IV, 647
Morlan, Amos IV, 894
Morlan, Amy IV, 647
Morlan, Amy IV, 728
Morlan, Amy IV, 742
Morlan, Amy IV, 878
Morlan, Amy J. IV, 856
Morlan, Amy Jane IV, 648
Morlan, Amy Jane IV, 743
Morlan, Amy Jane IV, 878
Morlan, Angeline IV, 879
Morlan, Angeline IV, 886
Morlan, Anjelina IV, 878
Morlan, Ann IV, 638
Morlan, Ann IV, 646
Morlan, Ann IV, 647
Morlan, Ann IV, 742
Morlan, Ann IV, 878
Morlan, Ann IV, 879
Morlan, Ann IV, 894
Morlan, Ann IV, 1174
Morlan, Ann VI, 353
Morlan, Ann VI, 354
Morlan, Ann VI, 355
Morlan, Ann VI, 537
Morlan, Anna IV, 401
Morlan, Anna IV, 407
Morlan, Anna IV, 628
Morlan, Anna IV, 647
Morlan, Anna IV, 648
Morlan, Anna IV, 743
Morlan, Anna IV, 878
Morlan, Anna IV, 1012
Morlan, Anna ??? IV, 742
Morlan, Anna M. IV, 628
Morlan, Anna M. IV, 743
Morlan, Anna Mary IV, 647
Morlan, Anna Mary IV, 648
Morlan, Anna Mary IV, 743
Morlan, Anna Mary IV, 981
Morlan, Armella IV, 878
Morlan, Barsilla IV, 647
Morlan, Barzilla IV, 640
Morlan, Barzilla IV, 646
Morlan, Barzilla IV, 647
Morlan, Barzillai IV, 742
Morlan, Barzillan IV, 647
Morlan, Barzillia VI, 354
Morlan, Caroline IV, 647
Morlan, Caroline IV, 648
Morlan, Caroline IV, 742
Morlan, Caroline IV, 911
Morlan, Caroline O. IV, 648
Morlan, Charity IV, 643
Morlan, Charity IV, 646
Morlan, Charity IV, 647
Morlan, Charles IV, 864
Morlan, Charles IV, 878
Morlan, Charles L. IV, 646
Morlan, Charles L. IV, 648
Morlan, Charles P. IV, 621
Morlan, Charles P. IV, 647
Morlan, Charles P. IV, 648
Morlan, Charles P. IV, 742
Morlan, Charles P. IV, 743
Morlan, Charles P. IV, 981
Morlan, Chas. IV, 646
Morlan, Chas. P. IV, 647
Morlan, Chas. P. IV, 981
Morlan, Christopher Anthony VI, 354
Morlan, David IV, 742
Morlan, David F. IV, 608
Morlan, David H. IV, 647
Morlan, David H. IV, 648
Morlan, David H. IV, 743
Morlan, David H. IV, 878
Morlan, Deborah IV, 878
Morlan, DeLorma IV, 878
Morlan, Eden VI, 537
Morlan, Edward IV, 743
Morlan, Edwin IV, 742
Morlan, Edwin IV, 911
Morlan, Edwin C. IV, 648
Morlan, Edwin D. IV, 647
Morlan, Elisabeth IV, 646
Morlan, Eliza IV, 742
Morlan, Eliza A. IV, 647
Morlan, Eliza Ann IV, 647
Morlan, Eliza Ann IV, 648
Morlan, Eliza Ann IV, 742
Morlan, Eliza Ann IV, 911
Morlan, Eliza Ann IV, 981
Morlan, Eliza Ann ??? IV, 742
Morlan, Eliza M. IV, 608
Morlan, Elizaann IV, 903
Morlan, Elizabeth IV, 643
Morlan, Elizabeth IV, 647
Morlan, Elizabeth IV, 742
Morlan, Elizabeth IV, 743
Morlan, Elizabeth IV, 878
Morlan, Elizabeth IV, 981
Morlan, Elizabeth VI, 354
Morlan, Elizabeth VI, 914
Morlan, Elizabeth Amanda IV, 878
Morlan, Elizabeth Ann IV, 865
Morlan, Elizabeth Ann IV, 878
Morlan, Elizabeth Ann IV, 879
Morlan, Elizann IV, 911
Morlan, Ellen IV, 648
Morlan, Ellen IV, 742
Morlan, Elmira IV, 647
Morlan, Elmira IV, 648
Morlan, Elmira IV, 742
Morlan, Elmira IV, 911
Morlan, Emela IV, 647
Morlan, Emily IV, 647
Morlan, Emily IV, 878
Morlan, Erwin C. IV, 646
Morlan, Eva D. IV, 618
Morlan, Eva D. IV, 647
Morlan, Eva D. IV, 648
Morlan, Eva D. IV, 742
Morlan, Eva D. IV, 743
Morlan, Frances IV, 627
Morlan, Frances IV, 648
Morlan, Frances IV, 864
Morlan, Frances IV, 878
Morlan, Hannah VI, 537
Morlan, Harriet IV, 646
Morlan, Harriet IV, 647
Morlan, Harriet IV, 656
Morlan, Harvey IV, 648
Morlan, Hiram IV, 742
Morlan, Hosea IV, 638
Morlan, Hosea IV, 647
Morlan, Hosea VI, 354
Morlan, Hulda IV, 1217
Morlan, Huldah IV, 647
Morlan, Huldah IV, 657
Morlan, Huldah IV, 742
Morlan, Huldah IV, 1217
Morlan, Huldah VI, 351
Morlan, Huldah VI, 354
Morlan, Huldah A. IV, 894
Morlan, Ida E. IV, 742
Morlan, Irene R. IV, 742
Morlan, Irene R. IV, 743
Morlan, Isaac IV, 646
Morlan, Isaac IV, 647
Morlan, Isaac IV, 648
Morlan, Isaac IV, 667
Morlan, Isaac IV, 742
Morlan, Isaac IV, 790
Morlan, Isaac VI, 354
Morlan, James IV, 878
Morlan, James H. IV, 646
Morlan, James H. IV, 648
Morlan, James Hervy IV, 878
Morlan, Jason IV, 646
Morlan, Jason IV, 647
Morlan, Jason IV, 878
Morlan, Jason IV, 879
Morlan, Jason IV, 1107
Morlan, Jason VI, 352
Morlan, Jason VI, 353
Morlan, Jason VI, 354
Morlan, Jason VI, 355
Morlan, Jason VI, 537
Morlan, Jason VI, 552
Morlan, Jesse Lewis IV, 647
Morlan, Joel IV, 646
Morlan, John IV, 648
Morlan, John IV, 742
Morlan, John IV, 878
Morlan, John IV, 955
Morlan, Jonah IV, 647
Morlan, Jonah IV, 742
Morlan, Jonah IV, 878
Morlan, Jonah IV, 1174
Morlan, Jonah VI, 354
Morlan, Jonah VI, 356
Morlan, Jonah VI, 537
Morlan, Joseph IV, 646
Morlan, Joseph IV, 647
Morlan, Joseph IV, 742
Morlan, Joseph IV, 1167
Morlan, Joseph IV, 1174
Morlan, Joseph IV, 1217
Morlan, Joseph VI, 353
Morlan, Joseph VI, 537
Morlan, Joseph VI, 964
Morlan, Katy VI, 354
Morlan, Katy VI, 964
Morlan, Lanora IV, 647
Morlan, Lanora IV, 742
Morlan, Laurence L. IV, 647
Morlan, Laurence Louis IV, 981
Morlan, Lawrence L. IV, 648
Morlan, Lawrence L. IV, 743
Morlan, Lawrence L. IV, 981
Morlan, Lemuel IV, 878
Morlan, Lenora IV, 647
Morlan, Lenora M. IV, 648
Morlan, Leonora M. IV, 640
Morlan, Lewis T. IV, 618
Morlan, Lewis T. IV, 647
Morlan, Lewis T. IV, 648
Morlan, Louis T. IV, 647
Morlan, Louis T. IV, 742
Morlan, Louis T. IV, 743
Morlan, Louisa IV, 870
Morlan, Louisa IV, 878
Morlan, Louisa IV, 879
Morlan, Louisa IV, 911
Morlan, Lucy IV, 894
Morlan, Lucy IV, 895
Morlan, Lucy Ann IV, 894
Morlan, Lydia IV, 647
Morlan, Lydia IV, 709
Morlan, Lydia IV, 742
Morlan, Lydia IV, 829
Morlan, Lydia IV, 856
Morlan, Lydia IV, 878
Morlan, Lydia IV, 911
Morlan, Lydia IV, 918
Morlan, Lydia IV, 955
Morlan, Lydia IV, 981
Morlan, Lydia IV, 1016
Morlan, Lydia Ann IV, 647
Morlan, Lydia Ann IV, 648
Morlan, Lydia Ann IV, 661
Morlan, Lydia F ??? IV, 742
Morlan, Lydia F. IV, 639
Morlan, Lydia F. IV, 981
Morlan, Martha IV, 646
Morlan, Martha IV, 647
Morlan, Martha IV, 648
Morlan, Martha IV, 665
Morlan, Martha IV, 667
Morlan, Martha IV, 742
Morlan, Martha IV, 790
Morlan, Martha IV, 863
Morlan, Martha IV, 878
Morlan, Martha IV, 1217
Morlan, Martha VI, 354
Morlan, Martha B. IV, 878
Morlan, Mary IV, 417
Morlan, Mary IV, 623
Morlan, Mary IV, 639
Morlan, Mary IV, 646
Morlan, Mary IV, 647
Morlan, Mary IV, 648
Morlan, Mary IV, 742
Morlan, Mary IV, 743
Morlan, Mary IV, 824
Morlan, Mary IV, 878
Morlan, Mary IV, 879
Morlan, Mary IV, 1107
Morlan, Mary IV, 1167
Morlan, Mary IV, 1174
Morlan, Mary IV, 1217
Morlan, Mary VI, 351
Morlan, Mary VI, 352
Morlan, Mary VI, 354

Morlan, Mary VI, 356
Morlan, Mary VI, 537
Morlan, Mary VI, 551
Morlan, Mary Elizabeth IV, 1217
Morlan, Mary F. IV, 647
Morlan, Mary F. IV, 648
Morlan, Mary F. IV, 743
Morlan, Mary I. IV, 743
Morlan, Mary I. IV, 784
Morlan, Mary M. IV, 641
Morlan, Mary M. IV, 647
Morlan, Mary M. IV, 648
Morlan, Mary M. IV, 742
Morlan, Mary M. IV, 743
Morlan, Mary M. IV, 878
Morlan, Matilda IV, 647
Morlan, Melva S. IV, 647
Morlan, Micajah IV, 647
Morlan, Micajah IV, 648
Morlan, Micajah IV, 742
Morlan, Micajah IV, 911
Morlan, Micajah M. IV, 742
Morlan, Micajah M. IV, 743
Morlan, Mordecai IV, 647
Morlan, Mordecai IV, 742
Morlan, Mordecai IV, 834
Morlan, Mordecai IV, 878
Morlan, Mordecai IV, 903
Morlan, Mordecai IV, 911
Morlan, Mordecai IV, 981
Morlan, Mordecia IV, 742
Morlan, Mordecia VI, 354
Morlan, Mordicai IV, 648
Morlan, Mordicai IV, 897
Morlan, Morning VI, 353
Morlan, Nathan IV, 878
Morlan, Newberry IV, 647
Morlan, Newberry IV, 648
Morlan, Newberry IV, 742
Morlan, Newberry IV, 911
Morlan, Phebe IV, 878
Morlan, Phebe IV, 917
Morlan, Rachel IV, 646
Morlan, Rachel IV, 647
Morlan, Rachel IV, 894
Morlan, Rebecca IV, 632
Morlan, Rebecca IV, 640
Morlan, Rebecca IV, 646
Morlan, Rebecca IV, 647
Morlan, Rebecca IV, 878
Morlan, Rebecca VI, 537
Morlan, Rezin IV, 878
Morlan, Rhoda IV, 742
Morlan, Richard IV, 623
Morlan, Richard IV, 646
Morlan, Richard IV, 647
Morlan, Richard IV, 648
Morlan, Richard VI, 354
Morlan, Rosea IV, 646
Morlan, Rosina IV, 647
Morlan, Roxan IV, 742
Morlan, Roxana IV, 647
Morlan, Roxana IV, 648
Morlan, Roxana IV, 666
Morlan, Roxana IV, 911
Morlan, Roxany IV, 742
Morlan, Ruth IV, 878
Morlan, Ruth IV, 1174
Morlan, Ruth IV, 1217
Morlan, Ruth Anna IV, 647
Morlan, S. Ellen IV, 743
Morlan, S. Ellen IV, 981
Morlan, Sally Ann IV, 646
Morlan, Sally Ann IV, 647
Morlan, Sally Ann IV, 894
Morlan, Samuel E. IV, 646
Morlan, Samuel E. IV, 648
Morlan, Sarah IV, 742
Morlan, Sarah IV, 743
Morlan, Sarah IV, 878
Morlan, Sarah IV, 911
Morlan, Sarah IV, 914
Morlan, Sarah IV, 923
Morlan, Sarah IV, 981
Morlan, Sarah VI, 354
Morlan, Sarah VI, 537
Morlan, Sarah P. IV, 628
Morlan, Sarah P. IV, 647
Morlan, Sarah P. IV, 648
Morlan, Sarah P. IV, 723
Morlan, Sarah P. IV, 742
Morlan, Sarah P. IV, 743
Morlan, Sarah P. IV, 878
Morlan, Sarah P. IV, 981
Morlan, Semira Ellen IV, 621
Morlan, Semira Ellen IV, 647
Morlan, Smith IV, 1217
Morlan, Stephen IV, 646
Morlan, Stephen IV, 647
Morlan, Stephen IV, 742
Morlan, Stephen IV, 834
Morlan, Stephen IV, 878
Morlan, Stephen VI, 351
Morlan, Stephen VI, 354
Morlan, Stephen VI, 537
Morlan, Stephen VI, 551
Morlan, Stephen R. IV, 646
Morlan, Stephen R. IV, 648
Morlan, Stephen R. IV, 878
Morlan, Theophelus IV, 647
Morlan, Theophilis IV, 648
Morlan, Theophilos IV, 743
Morlan, Theophilus IV, 628
Morlan, Theophilus IV, 639
Morlan, Theophilus IV, 647
Morlan, Theophilus IV, 648
Morlan, Theophilus IV, 709
Morlan, Theophilus IV, 723
Morlan, Theophilus IV, 742
Morlan, Theophilus IV, 743
Morlan, Theophilus IV, 829
Morlan, Theophilus IV, 911
Morlan, Theophilus IV, 923
Morlan, Theophilus IV, 981
Morlan, Theopholus IV, 878
Morlan, Theophulus IV, 955
Morlan, Theophulus IV, 981
Morlan, Wd. Lydia T. IV, 802
Morlan, William VI, 354
Morlan, William VI, 537
Morlan, William VI, 551
Morlan, William VI, 914
Morlan, William H. IV, 878
Morlan, William H. IV, 879
Morlan, William S. IV, 648
Morlan, William, Jr. VI, 537
Morlan, Wilson C. IV, 647
Morlan, Wilson J. IV, 743
Morlan, Wilson J. IV, 981
Morlan, Wilson Jesse IV, 981
Morlan, Wm. IV, 646
Morlan, Wm. IV, 647
Morlan, Wm. S. IV, 646
Morlan, Wm., Jr. VI, 504
Morland, ??? IV, 861
Morland, ??? IV, 1125
Morland, Albert IV, 742
Morland, Albert IV, 1107
Morland, Albert M. IV, 743
Morland, Alma Jane IV, 742
Morland, Amy Jane IV, 743
Morland, Ann IV, 1107
Morland, Anna M. IV, 743
Morland, Benjamin VI, 964
Morland, Caroline IV, 1135
Morland, Charles P. IV, 743
Morland, David IV, 742
Morland, David H. IV, 743
Morland, Eliza Ann IV, 742
Morland, Elizabeth IV, 50
Morland, Elizabeth IV, 647
Morland, Emily IV, 254
Morland, Isaac VI, 354
Morland, Jason IV, 50
Morland, Jason IV, 1107
Morland, John IV, 742
Morland, Jonas IV, 51
Morland, Joseph IV, 1217
Morland, Joseph VI, 964
Morland, Joshua IV, 1107
Morland, Katy VI, 964
Morland, Keziah VI, 964
Morland, Lulu IV, 254
Morland, Lydia Ann IV, 647
Morland, Martha IV, 648
Morland, Martha IV, 653
Morland, Martha VI, 354
Morland, Martha Elizabeth IV, 1135
Morland, Martha Elizabeth IV, 1137
Morland, Mary IV, 50
Morland, Mary IV, 647
Morland, Mary IV, 742
Morland, Mary IV, 743
Morland, Mary IV, 1107
Morland, Mary F. IV, 830
Morland, Mary M. IV, 743
Morland, Micajah M. IV, 743
Morland, Mordecia IV, 742
Morland, Phebe IV, 879
Morland, Rebecca IV, 1107
Morland, Robert IV, 1135
Morland, Sarah IV, 742
Morland, Sarah IV, 743
Morland, Sarah P. IV, 743
Morland, Stephen I, 1096
Morland, Stephen R. IV, 879
Morland, Theophilos IV, 743
Morland, Theophilus IV, 743
Morlick, James B. VI, 842
Morlick, Mary J. VI, 842
Morlin, Emily IV, 608
Morlin, Emily IV, 647
Morlin, Rebecca IV, 647
Morline, Clia V, 1011
Morline, Elice V, 1011
Morline, Millie V, 1011
Morline, Solomon V, 1011
Morman, Anna I, 1066
Morman, Arthur V, 699
Morman, Benjamin I, 1066
Morman, Benjamin B. V, 519
Morman, Bety VI, 260
Morman, Celia I, 1066
Morman, Charles V, 265
Morman, Charles V, 518
Morman, Childas V, 265
Morman, Dosha V, 518
Morman, Dosha V, 519
Morman, Edward I, 1071
Morman, Eli V, 266
Morman, Elisa I, 1066
Morman, Elizabeth V, 519
Morman, Elizabeth VI, 261
Morman, Emily V, 519
Morman, Hannah I, 1066
Morman, Hannah V, 48
Morman, Hannah V, 102
Morman, Henry I, 1066
Morman, Henry T. V, 194
Morman, James I, 1066
Morman, James V, 519
Morman, James P. V, 519
Morman, Jesse I, 1066
Morman, John I, 726
Morman, John I, 1066
Morman, John H. V, 519
Morman, John, II I, 1066
Morman, Judith I, 1066
Morman, Julia I, 1066
Morman, Kitty Winstone V, 253
Morman, Lucy Ann V, 519
Morman, Manson H. V, 519
Morman, Mary I, 1066
Morman, Mary I, 1071
Morman, Mary V, 519
Morman, Mary Alice V, 519
Morman, Micajah V, 265
Morman, Micajah C. V, 519
Morman, Nancy I, 1066
Morman, Nancy V, 351
Morman, Nancy V, 519
Morman, Rachel V, 389
Morman, Rachel V, 422
Morman, Raindy V, 102
Morman, Rebecah I, 1066
Morman, Rebecca V, 351
Morman, Ruth I, 1066
Morman, Sampey I, 1066
Morman, Sarah I, 1066
Morman, Tarlton I, 1066
Morman, Thomas I, 1066
Morman, Thomas V, 265
Morman, Thomas V, 518
Morman, Thomas V, 519
Morman, Thomas VI, 260
Morman, Thomas C. V, 519
Morman, Thomas C., Jr. V, 102
Morman, Uriah V, 265
Morman, Widow Susanna I, 726
Morman, Widow Susanna I, 1066
Morman, William V, 253
Morman, Wilson I, 1066
Morman, Zacaheriah VI, 260
Morman, Zachariah I, 1071
Morman, Zachariah V, 266
Mormon, Charles V, 265
Mormon, John I, 727
Mormon, Micajah VI, 260
Mormon, Rachel Ann V, 588
Mormon, Robert V, 265
Mormon, William V, 265
Mornington, Susannah II, 397
Mornington, Thomas II, 397
Mornington, William II, 397
Morre, Thomas VI, 805
Morrell, Anna III, 257
Morrell, Daniel J. II, 756
Morrell, Daniel J. II, 768
Morrell, Elizabeth III, 427
Morrell, Elizabeth W. III, 417
Morrell, George VI, 93
Morrell, John A. II, 756
Morrell, John A. L. II, 756
Morrell, John A. L. V, 922
Morrell, Jonathan III, 234
Morrell, Judith III, 41
Morrell, Judith III, 234
Morrell, Phebe III, 427
Morrell, Philip III, 427
Morrell, Philip III, 433
Morrell, Rebecca III, 124
Morrell, Rebecca III, 234
Morrell, Rebecca III, 427
Morrell, Rebecca III, 433
Morrell, Sarah Ann II, 889
Morrell, Sarah Ann II, 901
Morrell, Sarah Ann III, 234
Morrell, Susan II, 756
Morrell, Susan II, 768
Morrell, Susanna L. II, 756
Morrell, Susanna L. II, 768
Morrell, Thaddeus II, 756
Morrell, Thaddeus II, 768
Morrell, Thaddeus C. V, 922
Morrey, Mary Jenkinson IV, 1123
Morrice, James VI, 965
Morrice, Jemima I, 197
Morrice, John VI, 965
Morrice, Polly VI, 965
Morrice, William VI, 939
Morrice, William VI, 965
Morril, Philip III, 433
Morril, Rebecca III, 433
Morriott, Peter II, 440
Morris, ??? I, 279
Morris, ??? II, 597
Morris, ??? II, 815
Morris, ??? IV, 1059
Morris, ??? IV, 1085
Morris, ??? IV, 1125
Morris, ??? V, 422
Morris, Aaron I, 103
Morris, Aaron I, 104
Morris, Aaron I, 105
Morris, Aaron I, 106
Morris, Aaron I, 113
Morris, Aaron I, 114
Morris, Aaron I, 137
Morris, Aaron I, 138
Morris, Aaron I, 148
Morris, Aaron I, 149
Morris, Aaron I, 150
Morris, Aaron I, 151
Morris, Aaron I, 154
Morris, Aaron I, 162
Morris, Aaron I, 164
Morris, Aaron I, 291
Morris, Aaron I, 967
Morris, Aaron I, 1068
Morris, Aaron IV, 154
Morris, Aaron IV, 422
Morris, Aaron IV, 423
Morris, Aaron IV, 429
Morris, Aaron IV, 541
Morris, Aaron IV, 543
Morris, Aaron IV, 1070
Morris, Aaron IV, 1100
Morris, Aaron IV, 1107
Morris, Aaron IV, 1108
Morris, Aaron IV, 1123
Morris, Aaron Morris, Sr. I, 148
Morris, Aaron, Jr. I, 103
Morris, Aaron, Jr. I, 148
Morris, Aaron, Jr. I, 149
Morris, Aaron, Sr. I, 137
Morris, Aaron, Sr. I, 148
Morris, Aaron, Sr. I, 149
Morris, Aaron, Sr. I, 169
Morris, Abel I, 291
Morris, Abel Horn I, 312
Morris, Abel Trueblood I, 148
Morris, Abigael I, 106
Morris, Abigail I, 105
Morris, Abigail I, 106
Morris, Abigail I, 148
Morris, Abigail I, 149
Morris, Abigail I, 150
Morris, Abigail I, 157
Morris, Abigail I, 163
Morris, Abigail II, 209
Morris, Abigail II, 237
Morris, Abigail II, 243
Morris, Abigail II, 397
Morris, Abigail II, 398
Morris, Abigail II, 508
Morris, Abigail II, 591
Morris, Abigail II, 603
Morris, Abigail III, 70
Morris, Abigail III, 201
Morris, Abigail III, 234
Morris, Abigail IV, 154
Morris, Abraham I, 197
Morris, Abraham II, 243
Morris, Abraham IV, 344
Morris, Abraham IV, 694
Morris, Abraham IV, 743
Morris, Abraham IV, 792
Morris, Abraham IV, 938
Morris, Abraham IV, 981
Morris, Abraham IV, 1205
Morris, Abraham IV, 1210
Morris, Abraham IV, 1217
Morris, Abraham IV, 1227
Morris, Abraham D. V, 756
Morris, Abraham W. IV, 981
Morris, Abraham W. IV, 1174
Morris, Abraham W. IV, 1217
Morris, Abram IV, 743
Morris, Abram IV, 744
Morris, Achilles VI, 834
Morris, Achilles G. VI, 834
Morris, Adoni IV, 45
Morris, Agnes II, 397
Morris, Agnes II, 601
Morris, Agnes VI, 965
Morris, Albert I, 1160
Morris, Albert IV, 1218
Morris, Albert V, 266
Morris, Albert V, 267
Morris, Albert V, 519
Morris, Albert V, 699
Morris, Albina IV, 743
Morris, Alice II, 243
Morris, Alice IV, 422
Morris, Alice IV, 588
Morris, Alice IV, 589
Morris, Alice IV, 599
Morris, Alice IV, 1070
Morris, Alice IV, 1107
Morris, Alice IV, 1111
Morris, Alice IV, 1130
Morris, Alice IV, 1135
Morris, Alice IV, 1136
Morris, Alice M. III, 234
Morris, Alice Unice IV, 1136
Morris, Alonzo V, 266
Morris, Alonzo V, 267
Morris, Alvaretta V, 267
Morris, Alvaretta V, 699
Morris, Amanda IV, 51
Morris, Amasa IV, 648
Morris, Amasa IV, 879
Morris, Ambrose VI, 864
Morris, Ambrose VI, 879
Morris, Ambrose VI, 966
Morris, Amos W. IV, 1107
Morris, Amos W. IV, 1108
Morris, Amy IV, 648
Morris, Amy VI, 965
Morris, Anderson I, 25
Morris, Anderson I, 103
Morris, Anderson I, 106
Morris, Anderson I, 150
Morris, Anderson I, 151
Morris, Anderson VI, 965
Morris, Ann I, 103
Morris, Ann I, 104
Morris, Ann I, 105
Morris, Ann I, 106
Morris, Ann I, 118
Morris, Ann I, 142
Morris, Ann I, 148
Morris, Ann I, 149
Morris, Ann I, 150
Morris, Ann I, 151
Morris, Ann I, 156
Morris, Ann I, 167
Morris, Ann I, 168
Morris, Ann I, 311
Morris, Ann I, 1068
Morris, Ann II, 243
Morris, Ann II, 397
Morris, Ann II, 559
Morris, Ann II, 602
Morris, Ann II, 603
Morris, Ann II, 612
Morris, Ann II, 655
Morris, Ann II, 798
Morris, Ann IV, 45
Morris, Ann IV, 254
Morris, Ann IV, 588
Morris, Ann IV, 1111
Morris, Ann VI, 965
Morris, Ann H. II, 901
Morris, Ann Jess II, 243
Morris, Anna I, 105
Morris, Anna I, 291
Morris, Anna I, 831
Morris, Anna I, 1071
Morris, Anna I, 1072
Morris, Anna II, 243
Morris, Anna II, 398
Morris, Anna II, 602
Morris, Anna II, 603
Morris, Anna II, 650
Morris, Anna II, 756
Morris, Anna II, 810
Morris, Anna II, 901
Morris, Anna IV, 45
Morris, Anna IV, 254
Morris, Anna IV, 344
Morris, Anna IV, 358
Morris, Anna IV, 743

Morris, Anna H. I, 563
Morris, Anna H. I, 568
Morris, Anna H. III, 155
Morris, Anna Margaretta II, 296
Morris, Anne I, 61
Morris, Anne I, 85
Morris, Anne I, 311
Morris, Anne IV, 254
Morris, Anthony II, 179
Morris, Anthony II, 243
Morris, Anthony II, 397
Morris, Anthony II, 398
Morris, Anthony II, 469
Morris, Anthony II, 476
Morris, Anthony II, 480
Morris, Anthony II, 524
Morris, Anthony II, 538
Morris, Anthony II, 558
Morris, Anthony II, 579
Morris, Anthony II, 596
Morris, Anthony II, 601
Morris, Anthony II, 602
Morris, Anthony II, 603
Morris, Anthony II, 620
Morris, Anthony II, 626
Morris, Anthony II, 643
Morris, Anthony II, 649
Morris, Anthony II, 662
Morris, Anthony II, 677
Morris, Anthony II, 679
Morris, Anthony IV, 103
Morris, Anthony IV, 685
Morris, Anthony IV, 743
Morris, Anthony IV, 744
Morris, Anthony IV, 919
Morris, Anthony IV, 928
Morris, Anthony IV, 935
Morris, Anthony IV, 981
Morris, Anthony Cadwallader II, 569
Morris, Anthony Cadwallader II, 602
Morris, Anthony Cadwallader II, 603
Morris, Anthony P. II, 398
Morris, Anthony P. II, 603
Morris, Anthony P. II, 756
Morris, Anthony P. II, 901
Morris, Anthony P. III, 155
Morris, Anthony Paschall II, 810
Morris, Anthony Paschall II, 901
Morris, Anthony Paschall, Jr. II, 810
Morris, Anthony, Jr. II, 179
Morris, Anthony, Jr. II, 243
Morris, Anthony, Jr. II, 397
Morris, Anthony, Jr. II, 527
Morris, Anthony, Jr. II, 601
Morris, Anthony, Jr. II, 602
Morris, Ara I, 291
Morris, Aron I, 103
Morris, Aron I, 104
Morris, Arthur IV, 1135
Morris, Arthur IV, 1136
Morris, Ava IV, 422
Morris, Ava IV, 577
Morris, Ava IV, 588
Morris, Ava IV, 743
Morris, Ava IV, 1056
Morris, Ava IV, 1069
Morris, Ava IV, 1070
Morris, Avice IV, 154
Morris, Avis I, 320
Morris, Barkley IV, 879
Morris, Barzilla II, 243
Morris, Barzilla IV, 103
Morris, Barzilla IV, 648
Morris, Barzillai II, 179
Morris, Barzillai II, 243
Morris, Barzillai IV, 696
Morris, Barzillai IV, 743
Morris, Barzillai IV, 981
Morris, Barzillar IV, 981
Morris, Bathsheba II, 179
Morris, Bathsheba II, 243
Morris, Ben VI, 879
Morris, Benajah IV, 1107
Morris, Benajah IV, 1136
Morris, Benedict II, 398
Morris, Benedict Dorsey II, 397
Morris, Beniamin I, 103
Morris, Benj. II, 184
Morris, Benj. H. IV, 981
Morris, Benjamin I, 45
Morris, Benjamin I, 61
Morris, Benjamin I, 74
Morris, Benjamin I, 103
Morris, Benjamin I, 104
Morris, Benjamin I, 105
Morris, Benjamin I, 132
Morris, Benjamin I, 138
Morris, Benjamin I, 148
Morris, Benjamin I, 149
Morris, Benjamin I, 151
Morris, Benjamin I, 157
Morris, Benjamin I, 196
Morris, Benjamin I, 197
Morris, Benjamin I, 291
Morris, Benjamin I, 311
Morris, Benjamin I, 703
Morris, Benjamin II, 397
Morris, Benjamin II, 398
Morris, Benjamin II, 602
Morris, Benjamin IV, 154
Morris, Benjamin IV, 422
Morris, Benjamin IV, 585
Morris, Benjamin IV, 588
Morris, Benjamin IV, 589
Morris, Benjamin IV, 743
Morris, Benjamin V, 267
Morris, Benjamin VI, 879
Morris, Benjamin F. IV, 1136
Morris, Benjamin F. V, 267
Morris, Benjamin F. V, 423
Morris, Benjamin F. V, 699
Morris, Benjamin Wistar II, 603
Morris, Benjamin Wistar II, 681
Morris, Benjamin, Jr. I, 149
Morris, Bennajah R. V, 267
Morris, Benoni I, 103
Morris, Benoni I, 104
Morris, Benoni I, 106
Morris, Benoni I, 150
Morris, Benoni I, 171
Morris, Benoni I, 895
Morris, Benoni IV, 254
Morris, Betsey I, 291
Morris, Betsey VI, 879
Morris, Betsy I, 312
Morris, Betsy VI, 1015
Morris, Betsy Ann VI, 966
Morris, Bette I, 104
Morris, Betty I, 148
Morris, Betty I, 167
Morris, Beulah II, 243
Morris, Beulah II, 706
Morris, Beulah IV, 45
Morris, Beulah IV, 344
Morris, Beulah W. IV, 743
Morris, Beulah W. IV, 981
Morris, Branch H. VI, 842
Morris, Bryan IV, 1217
Morris, Byron IV, 1217
Morris, Cadwalader II, 602
Morris, Cadwallader II, 602
Morris, Cadwallader II, 654
Morris, Caleb I, 104
Morris, Caleb I, 106
Morris, Caleb I, 150
Morris, Caleb I, 151
Morris, Caleb I, 1068
Morris, Caleb II, 243
Morris, Caleb IV, 344
Morris, Caleb IV, 982
Morris, Caleb Shinn IV, 743
Morris, Caleb Shinn IV, 981
Morris, Caleb Trueblood I, 148
Morris, Calmer IV, 1217
Morris, Calmer J. IV, 1218
Morris, Calmers J. IV, 1217
Morris, Carl IV, 1218
Morris, Caroline V, 267
Morris, Caroline VI, 1006
Morris, Carrie IV, 488
Morris, Caspar W. II, 603
Morris, Casper II, 602
Morris, Catharine I, 104
Morris, Catharine I, 150
Morris, Catharine I, 895
Morris, Catharine II, 603
Morris, Catharine II, 885
Morris, Catharine II, 901
Morris, Catherine IV, 45
Morris, Catherine V, 267
Morris, Catherine J. V, 194
Morris, Catherine W. II, 713
Morris, Celia I, 291
Morris, Celia I, 303
Morris, Celia I, 311
Morris, Celia I, 312
Morris, Celina IV, 1210
Morris, Celina IV, 1217
Morris, Charity I, 291
Morris, Charity I, 311
Morris, Charity I, 313
Morris, Charles I, 105
Morris, Charles II, 713
Morris, Charles V, 699
Morris, Charles VI, 768
Morris, Charles K. IV, 1135
Morris, Charles K. IV, 1136
Morris, Charles Wistar II, 398
Morris, Charles Wistar II, 756
Morris, Charley V, 266
Morris, Charlott I, 150
Morris, Charlotte I, 197
Morris, Chas. Wistar II, 901
Morris, Christian II, 398
Morris, Christian IV, 1218
Morris, Christina IV, 1218
Morris, Christopher I, 103
Morris, Christopher I, 104
Morris, Christopher I, 116
Morris, Christopher I, 133
Morris, Christopher I, 149
Morris, Christopher I, 150
Morris, Clara V, 636
Morris, Clarence I. IV, 1136
Morris, Clarke I, 105
Morris, Clarkey I, 105
Morris, Clarkey I, 148
Morris, Clarkey I, 149
Morris, Clarkey I, 162
Morris, Col. Lewis III, 234
Morris, Col. Thomas VI, 865
Morris, Cora IV, 254
Morris, Cynthia IV, 45
Morris, Cynthia IV, 911
Morris, Daniel II, 398
Morris, Daniel II, 559
Morris, Daniel II, 602
Morris, Daniel II, 611
Morris, Daniel VI, 966
Morris, Daniel E. IV, 1135
Morris, Daniel M. IV, 1136
Morris, David I, 61
Morris, David I, 104
Morris, David I, 106
Morris, David I, 151
Morris, David I, 163
Morris, David I, 291
Morris, David II, 35
Morris, David II, 81
Morris, David II, 88
Morris, David II, 243
Morris, David II, 601
Morris, David II, 602
Morris, David II, 603
Morris, David II, 622
Morris, David II, 655
Morris, David IV, 45
Morris, David IV, 102
Morris, David IV, 103
Morris, David IV, 588
Morris, David IV, 589
Morris, David IV, 879
Morris, David IV, 1070
Morris, David IV, 1107
Morris, David IV, 1108
Morris, David IV, 1111
Morris, David IV, 1123
Morris, David V, 266
Morris, David V, 307
Morris, David V, 447
Morris, David VI, 425
Morris, David E. IV, 254
Morris, David Linneaus IV, 1107
Morris, David Linneaus IV, 1135
Morris, David Linneaus IV, 1136
Morris, David P. IV, 1108
Morris, Deborah II, 184
Morris, Deborah II, 243
Morris, Deborah II, 398
Morris, Deborah II, 527
Morris, Deborah II, 602
Morris, Deborah II, 603
Morris, Deborah IV, 910
Morris, Deborah D. IV, 911
Morris, Delphi IV, 254
Morris, Delphia IV, 254
Morris, Demcey I, 104
Morris, Demcy I, 189
Morris, Demcy I, 197
Morris, Demsey I, 61
Morris, Demsey I, 149
Morris, Demsey I, 150
Morris, Demsey I, 197
Morris, Demsey I, 291
Morris, Demsy I, 150
Morris, Demsy I, 197
Morris, Dennie V, 267
Morris, Dr. John II, 209
Morris, Dr. John II, 243
Morris, Dr. John II, 397
Morris, Dr. John II, 398
Morris, Dr. M. R. III, 234
Morris, Dr. M. R. III, 274
Morris, Draper I, 151
Morris, E. Ann IV, 981
Morris, Earnestine P. V, 699
Morris, Easter VI, 895
Morris, Edith II, 243
Morris, Edith IV, 1136
Morris, Edith V, 103
Morris, Edith A. V, 103
Morris, Edith L. IV, 254
Morris, Edith L. IV, 937
Morris, Edith Thornburg V, 267
Morris, Edmund II, 179
Morris, Edmund II, 296
Morris, Edna V. IV, 1136
Morris, Edward II, 243
Morris, Edward II, 398
Morris, Edward II, 446
Morris, Edward II, 580
Morris, Edward II, 602
Morris, Edward II, 603
Morris, Edward II, 654
Morris, Edward III, 234
Morris, Edward IV, 102
Morris, Edward IV, 103
Morris, Edward IV, 107
Morris, Edward IV, 238
Morris, Edward IV, 254
Morris, Edward IV, 310
Morris, Edward VI, 425
Morris, Edward S. II, 810
Morris, Edward Stabler II, 901
Morris, Edwin IV, 403
Morris, Edwin IV, 422
Morris, Edwin IV, 588
Morris, Edwin IV, 589
Morris, Edwin IV, 1070
Morris, Edwin IV, 1107
Morris, Edwin IV, 1135
Morris, Edwin H. IV, 1135
Morris, Effa J. V, 267
Morris, Effa J. V, 423
Morris, Effie J. V, 267
Morris, Eldo V, 267
Morris, Eleanor IV, 589
Morris, Eleanor IV, 1070
Morris, Eleanor V, 266
Morris, Eley VI, 963
Morris, Eli I, 104
Morris, Eli I, 150
Morris, Eli I, 193
Morris, Eli I, 197
Morris, Eli IV, 1107
Morris, Eli IV, 1108
Morris, Elias IV, 254
Morris, Elias Albertson I, 149
Morris, Elisabeth I, 61
Morris, Elisabeth I, 103
Morris, Elisabeth I, 104
Morris, Elisabeth I, 106
Morris, Elisabeth I, 113
Morris, Elisabeth I, 131
Morris, Elisabeth I, 146
Morris, Elisabeth I, 148
Morris, Elisabeth I, 149
Morris, Elisabeth I, 150
Morris, Elisabeth I, 151
Morris, Elisabeth I, 157
Morris, Elisabeth I, 160
Morris, Elisabeth I, 163
Morris, Elisabeth I, 165
Morris, Elisabeth I, 168
Morris, Elisabeth I, 197
Morris, Elisabeth II, 558
Morris, Elisabeth VI, 989
Morris, Eliza IV, 51
Morris, Eliza IV, 62
Morris, Eliza IV, 254
Morris, Eliza IV, 313
Morris, Eliza IV, 315
Morris, Eliza Ann IV, 879
Morris, Eliza Ann IV, 884
Morris, Eliza Ann IV, 973
Morris, Eliza Ann IV, 982
Morris, Eliza Ann IV, 1108
Morris, Eliza Ann IV, 1118
Morris, Eliza Ann IV, 1134
Morris, Eliza Ann IV, 1135
Morris, Eliza M. IV, 1108
Morris, Elizabeth I, 99
Morris, Elizabeth I, 103
Morris, Elizabeth I, 104
Morris, Elizabeth I, 105
Morris, Elizabeth I, 139
Morris, Elizabeth I, 150
Morris, Elizabeth I, 162
Morris, Elizabeth I, 191
Morris, Elizabeth I, 196
Morris, Elizabeth I, 291
Morris, Elizabeth I, 311
Morris, Elizabeth I, 831
Morris, Elizabeth I, 863
Morris, Elizabeth I, 895
Morris, Elizabeth I, 1068
Morris, Elizabeth II, 397
Morris, Elizabeth II, 398
Morris, Elizabeth II, 532
Morris, Elizabeth II, 572
Morris, Elizabeth II, 579
Morris, Elizabeth II, 601
Morris, Elizabeth II, 602
Morris, Elizabeth II, 603
Morris, Elizabeth II, 649
Morris, Elizabeth II, 677
Morris, Elizabeth II, 679
Morris, Elizabeth II, 713
Morris, Elizabeth II, 756
Morris, Elizabeth II, 877
Morris, Elizabeth II, 901
Morris, Elizabeth II, 1017
Morris, Elizabeth II, 1037
Morris, Elizabeth III, 234
Morris, Elizabeth IV, 37
Morris, Elizabeth IV, 45
Morris, Elizabeth IV, 51
Morris, Elizabeth IV, 102
Morris, Elizabeth IV, 107
Morris, Elizabeth IV, 254
Morris, Elizabeth IV, 344
Morris, Elizabeth IV, 488
Morris, Elizabeth IV, 585
Morris, Elizabeth IV, 588
Morris, Elizabeth IV, 743
Morris, Elizabeth IV, 879
Morris, Elizabeth IV, 881
Morris, Elizabeth IV, 935
Morris, Elizabeth IV, 974
Morris, Elizabeth IV, 981
Morris, Elizabeth IV, 982
Morris, Elizabeth IV, 1028
Morris, Elizabeth IV, 1029
Morris, Elizabeth IV, 1090
Morris, Elizabeth IV, 1103
Morris, Elizabeth IV, 1107
Morris, Elizabeth IV, 1128
Morris, Elizabeth IV, 1129
Morris, Elizabeth IV, 1135
Morris, Elizabeth V, 243
Morris, Elizabeth V, 266
Morris, Elizabeth V, 267
Morris, Elizabeth V, 278
Morris, Elizabeth V, 699
Morris, Elizabeth VI, 425
Morris, Elizabeth VI, 677
Morris, Elizabeth VI, 696
Morris, Elizabeth VI, 904
Morris, Elizabeth VI, 984
Morris, Elizabeth VI, 1017
Morris, Elizabeth Ann IV, 1109
Morris, Elizabeth B. II, 603
Morris, Elizabeth B. II, 621
Morris, Elizabeth E. V, 885
Morris, Elizabeth H. III, 184
Morris, Elizabeth H. III, 234
Morris, Elizabeth H. VI, 865
Morris, Elizabeth I. IV, 743
Morris, Elizabeth J. II, 243
Morris, Elizabeth J. II, 244
Morris, Elizabeth J. II, 603
Morris, Elizabeth J. II, 757
Morris, Elizabeth J. II, 769
Morris, Elizabeth J. IV, 744
Morris, Elizabeth M. II, 296
Morris, Elizabeth M. II, 301
Morris, Elizabeth Marshall II, 814
Morris, Elizabeth Maud V, 699
Morris, Elizabeth R. II, 603
Morris, Elizabeth, Jr. II, 655
Morris, Ellen II, 296
Morris, Ellen II, 297
Morris, Ellen IV, 422
Morris, Ellen IV, 588
Morris, Ellen IV, 743
Morris, Ellen IV, 1029
Morris, Ellen IV, 1136
Morris, Ellen V, 1011
Morris, Ellis II, 398
Morris, Ellwood II, 603
Morris, Emeline IV, 870
Morris, Emily IV, 45
Morris, Emlen IV, 1136
Morris, Emlen I. IV, 1135
Morris, Emma V, 266
Morris, Emma V, 267
Morris, Emma E. IV, 815
Morris, Emma Lizzie IV, 1136
Morris, Emma R. V, 267
Morris, Emmet V, 266
Morris, Emmit V, 266
Morris, Enos V, 266
Morris, Enos V, 267
Morris, Err T. IV, 1135
Morris, Ester II, 243
Morris, Esther I, 150
Morris, Esther I, 193
Morris, Esther I, 197
Morris, Esther II, 179
Morris, Esther II, 243

Morris, Esther II, 603
Morris, Esther II, 613
Morris, Esther IV, 45
Morris, Esther IV, 103
Morris, Esther IV, 344
Morris, Esther IV, 612
Morris, Esther IV, 648
Morris, Esther IV, 702
Morris, Esther IV, 743
Morris, Esther IV, 744
Morris, Esther IV, 928
Morris, Esther IV, 952
Morris, Esther IV, 981
Morris, Esther VI, 895
Morris, Esther Pugh V, 699
Morris, Ethel J. IV, 1135
Morris, Eunice V, 194
Morris, Evaline B. VI, 842
Morris, Evan II, 601
Morris, Everet IV, 254
Morris, Everett IV, 254
Morris, Everett IV, 1136
Morris, Everett C. IV, 1136
Morris, Exum I, 291
Morris, Exum I, 312
Morris, Ezekiel VI, 965
Morris, Fannie V, 636
Morris, Fannie V, 699
Morris, Fannie C. V, 699
Morris, Fern IV, 744
Morris, Feroby I, 895
Morris, Flora Jane V, 267
Morris, Frances II, 451
Morris, Frances II, 452
Morris, Frances II, 603
Morris, Frances VI, 757
Morris, Franklin IV, 1135
Morris, Frederick IV, 488
Morris, Gainer II, 601
Morris, George I, 104
Morris, George I, 150
Morris, George I, 563
Morris, George I, 863
Morris, George I, 895
Morris, George II, 243
Morris, George IV, 744
Morris, Goshen IV, 981
Morris, Grace II, 88
Morris, Grace II, 112
Morris, Grace IV, 744
Morris, Griffith IV, 45
Morris, Gulielma I, 104
Morris, Gulielma I, 133
Morris, Gulielma I, 149
Morris, Gulielma I, 863
Morris, Gulielma I, 895
Morris, Gulielma II, 398
Morris, Gulielma Maria II, 243
Morris, Gulielma Maria II, 262
Morris, Gulielma Marie II, 602
Morris, Haner VI, 904
Morris, Hannah I, 35
Morris, Hannah I, 61
Morris, Hannah I, 104
Morris, Hannah I, 105
Morris, Hannah I, 106
Morris, Hannah I, 132
Morris, Hannah I, 138
Morris, Hannah I, 148
Morris, Hannah I, 149
Morris, Hannah I, 150
Morris, Hannah I, 151
Morris, Hannah I, 157
Morris, Hannah I, 291
Morris, Hannah I, 311
Morris, Hannah I, 831
Morris, Hannah I, 1068
Morris, Hannah II, 179
Morris, Hannah II, 243
Morris, Hannah II, 364
Morris, Hannah II, 397
Morris, Hannah II, 398
Morris, Hannah II, 480
Morris, Hannah II, 596
Morris, Hannah II, 602
Morris, Hannah II, 603
Morris, Hannah II, 621
Morris, Hannah IV, 45
Morris, Hannah IV, 102
Morris, Hannah IV, 103
Morris, Hannah IV, 107
Morris, Hannah IV, 185
Morris, Hannah IV, 238
Morris, Hannah IV, 254
Morris, Hannah IV, 310
Morris, Hannah IV, 648
Morris, Hannah IV, 685
Morris, Hannah IV, 743
Morris, Hannah IV, 910
Morris, Hannah IV, 928
Morris, Hannah IV, 935
Morris, Hannah IV, 971
Morris, Hannah IV, 981
Morris, Hannah IV, 982
Morris, Hannah IV, 1016
Morris, Hannah IV, 1135
Morris, Hannah V, 266
Morris, Hannah V, 267
Morris, Hannah V, 423
Morris, Hannah V, 519
Morris, Hannah V, 541
Morris, Hannah V, 1011
Morris, Hannah VI, 425
Morris, Hannah VI, 842
Morris, Hannah VI, 966
Morris, Hannah Alice IV, 1135
Morris, Hannah G. V, 258
Morris, Hannah G. V, 266
Morris, Hannah J. IV, 254
Morris, Hannah Jane IV, 254
Morris, Hannah Jane IV, 1136
Morris, Hannah Jane IV, 1217
Morris, Hannah P. II, 603
Morris, Harmon IV, 743
Morris, Harriett IV, 1217
Morris, Harriett Lucretia IV, 1217
Morris, Harry VI, 965
Morris, Harry B. IV, 744
Morris, Helen E. II, 877
Morris, Helen E. II, 901
Morris, Henry C. IV, 51
Morris, Henry G. V, 885
Morris, Henry J. V, 267
Morris, Henry P. IV, 254
Morris, Henryetta IV, 1217
Morris, Herbert L. III, 184
Morris, Herbert L. III, 234
Morris, Hester II, 243
Morris, Hetty II, 798
Morris, Homer V, 636
Morris, Howard IV, 254
Morris, Hudson VI, 831
Morris, Huldah I, 105
Morris, Huldah I, 148
Morris, Huldah I, 153
Morris, Ida IV, 676
Morris, Ida Margaret III, 234
Morris, Irael II, 398
Morris, Isaac I, 103
Morris, Isaac I, 104
Morris, Isaac I, 133
Morris, Isaac I, 150
Morris, Isaac I, 291
Morris, Isaac I, 300
Morris, Isaac I, 311
Morris, Isaac I, 863
Morris, Isaac I, 895
Morris, Isaac I, 967
Morris, Isaac II, 397
Morris, Isaac II, 602
Morris, Isaac II, 603
Morris, Isaac IV, 45
Morris, Isaac IV, 910
Morris, Isaac V, 266
Morris, Isaac V, 588
Morris, Isaac P. II, 713
Morris, Isaac T. IV, 254
Morris, Isaac Thomas IV, 254
Morris, Isaac W. II, 700
Morris, Isaac W. II, 713
Morris, Isaac Wistar II, 603
Morris, Isaac Wistar II, 616
Morris, Isaack I, 104
Morris, Isaiah IV, 648
Morris, Isaiah IV, 743
Morris, Isaiah IV, 879
Morris, Isaiah IV, 981
Morris, Isaiah IV, 1217
Morris, Isaiah IV, 1225
Morris, Isaiah V, 266
Morris, Isaiah V, 267
Morris, Isaiah V, 699
Morris, Israel II, 397
Morris, Israel II, 398
Morris, Israel II, 474
Morris, Israel II, 602
Morris, Israel VI, 898
Morris, Israel W. II, 603
Morris, Israel W. II, 734
Morris, Israel W. II, 756
Morris, Israel, Jr. II, 398
Morris, Israel, Jr. II, 603
Morris, Isrel VI, 904
Morris, J. Sam Armistead VI, 827
Morris, Jacob I, 61
Morris, Jacob I, 104
Morris, Jacob I, 149
Morris, Jacob I, 150
Morris, Jacob I, 170
Morris, Jacob I, 191
Morris, Jacob I, 196
Morris, Jacob III, 427
Morris, Jacob IV, 45
Morris, Jacob VI, 895
Morris, Jacob VI, 963
Morris, Jacob VI, 965
Morris, Jacob VI, 984
Morris, Jacob VI, 986
Morris, Jael II, 35
Morris, Jael II, 88
Morris, Jael II, 602
Morris, Jael II, 649
Morris, Jale II, 83
Morris, Jale II, 88
Morris, James I, 105
Morris, James I, 106
Morris, James II, 397
Morris, James II, 398
Morris, James II, 572
Morris, James II, 601
Morris, James II, 603
Morris, James II, 986
Morris, James II, 1017
Morris, James III, 234
Morris, James V, 243
Morris, James V, 258
Morris, James V, 266
Morris, James V, 267
Morris, James V, 278
Morris, James V, 519
Morris, James V, 541
Morris, James V, 544
Morris, James VI, 939
Morris, James VI, 965
Morris, James B. IV, 981
Morris, James D. II, 877
Morris, James D. II, 901
Morris, James H. VI, 842
Morris, James P. II, 398
Morris, James T. II, 713
Morris, James T. II, 757
Morris, James W. I, 151
Morris, Jane II, 35
Morris, Jane II, 398
Morris, Jane II, 567
Morris, Jane II, 601
Morris, Jane IV, 45
Morris, Jane IV, 102
Morris, Jane IV, 103
Morris, Jane IV, 254
Morris, Jane IV, 981
Morris, Jane IV, 1012
Morris, Jane IV, 1174
Morris, Jane IV, 1209
Morris, Jane IV, 1217
Morris, Jane V, 266
Morris, Jane VI, 425
Morris, Jane VI, 966
Morris, Jane F. VI, 966
Morris, Jane M. II, 296
Morris, Jane M. II, 297
Morris, Jason IV, 45
Morris, Jean II, 81
Morris, Jean II, 88
Morris, Jehoshaphat I, 104
Morris, Jehoshaphat I, 150
Morris, Jehoshaphat I, 171
Morris, Jehoshaphat I, 175
Morris, Jehosphaphat I, 103
Morris, Jehosphaphat I, 105
Morris, Jehu IV, 45
Morris, Jehu H. IV, 1107
Morris, Jemima I, 150
Morris, Jemima I, 189
Morris, Jemima I, 197
Morris, Jennie IV, 1330
Morris, Jennie V, 267
Morris, Jennie V, 636
Morris, Jennie B. V, 267
Morris, Jennie B. V, 351
Morris, Jeremiah I, 291
Morris, Jeremiah I, 301
Morris, Jeremiah I, 311
Morris, Jeremiah I, 312
Morris, Jeremiah I, 320
Morris, Jeremiah II, 398
Morris, Jeremiah V, 194
Morris, Jeremiah V, 266
Morris, Jeremiah V, 267
Morris, Jerry V, 194
Morris, Jerry V, 519
Morris, Jesse I, 60
Morris, Jesse I, 104
Morris, Jesse I, 105
Morris, Jesse I, 106
Morris, Jesse I, 150
Morris, Jesse I, 197
Morris, Jesse I, 831
Morris, Jesse II, 243
Morris, Jesse IV, 45
Morris, Jesse IV, 422
Morris, Jesse IV, 588
Morris, Jesse IV, 743
Morris, Jesse IV, 1135
Morris, Jesse IV, 1136
Morris, Jesse IV, 1137
Morris, Jesse VI, 842
Morris, Jesse Brown I, 247
Morris, Jesse J. IV, 1136
Morris, Jessee I, 150
Morris, Jethro I, 103
Morris, Jhon I, 114
Morris, Jno. II, 179
Morris, Joanna II, 580
Morris, Joanna II, 602
Morris, Joanna II, 603
Morris, Joanna II, 654
Morris, Job I, 197
Morris, Joel II, 602
Morris, Joel IV, 1107
Morris, Joel IV, 1123
Morris, Johanna II, 398
Morris, Johanna II, 602
Morris, Johanna II, 654
Morris, John I, 61
Morris, John I, 68
Morris, John I, 101
Morris, John I, 103
Morris, John I, 104
Morris, John I, 105
Morris, John I, 116
Morris, John I, 148
Morris, John I, 149
Morris, John I, 150
Morris, John I, 154
Morris, John I, 166
Morris, John I, 167
Morris, John I, 291
Morris, John I, 831
Morris, John I, 1068
Morris, John I, 1160
Morris, John II, 179
Morris, John II, 237
Morris, John II, 243
Morris, John II, 397
Morris, John II, 398
Morris, John II, 508
Morris, John II, 549
Morris, John II, 601
Morris, John II, 602
Morris, John II, 603
Morris, John II, 662
Morris, John II, 757
Morris, John II, 769
Morris, John III, 234
Morris, John IV, 45
Morris, John IV, 344
Morris, John IV, 648
Morris, John IV, 743
Morris, John IV, 744
Morris, John IV, 879
Morris, John IV, 981
Morris, John IV, 1174
Morris, John IV, 1207
Morris, John IV, 1217
Morris, John IV, 1218
Morris, John V, 103
Morris, John V, 266
Morris, John V, 519
Morris, John V, 557
Morris, John VI, 842
Morris, John VI, 852
Morris, John VI, 865
Morris, John VI, 896
Morris, John VI, 963
Morris, John VI, 965
Morris, John VI, 966
Morris, John VI, 998
Morris, John VI, 1015
Morris, John A. I, 151
Morris, John Anderson I, 103
Morris, John C. V, 636
Morris, John Griffith I, 106
Morris, John H. II, 135
Morris, John H. IV, 1108
Morris, John H. V, 194
Morris, John H. VI, 1018
Morris, John P. I, 1160
Morris, John P. IV, 1218
Morris, John Price I, 149
Morris, John S. V, 423
Morris, John Symons, Sr. I, 148
Morris, John T. II, 757
Morris, John Thompson II, 713
Morris, John Toms I, 106
Morris, John W. IV, 815
Morris, John W. IV, 981
Morris, John W. IV, 982
Morris, John W. IV, 1131
Morris, John W. IV, 1135
Morris, John Webster IV, 1135
Morris, John Wesley IV, 254
Morris, John Winslow I, 106
Morris, John Y. IV, 254
Morris, John, Jr. I, 148
Morris, John, Jr. I, 177
Morris, John, Jr. VI, 852
Morris, John, Sr. I, 148
Morris, Jonathan I, 105
Morris, Jonathan I, 149
Morris, Jonathan I, 150
Morris, Jonathan I, 156
Morris, Jonathan I, 168
Morris, Jonathan I, 291
Morris, Jonathan I, 312
Morris, Jonathan I, 1068
Morris, Jonathan II, 35
Morris, Jonathan II, 398
Morris, Jonathan II, 602
Morris, Jonathan IV, 51
Morris, Jonathan IV, 62
Morris, Jonathan IV, 254
Morris, Jonathan IV, 422
Morris, Jonathan IV, 588
Morris, Jonathan IV, 589
Morris, Jonathan IV, 743
Morris, Jonathan IV, 879
Morris, Jonathan IV, 1069
Morris, Jonathan IV, 1070
Morris, Jonathan IV, 1080
Morris, Jonathan IV, 1104
Morris, Jonathan IV, 1107
Morris, Jonathan IV, 1108
Morris, Jonathan V, 266
Morris, Jonathan V, 267
Morris, Jonathan Price I, 149
Morris, Jonathan Smith II, 602
Morris, Josep I, 105
Morris, Joseph I, 61
Morris, Joseph I, 72
Morris, Joseph I, 97
Morris, Joseph I, 103
Morris, Joseph I, 104
Morris, Joseph I, 105
Morris, Joseph I, 112
Morris, Joseph I, 118
Morris, Joseph I, 141
Morris, Joseph I, 143
Morris, Joseph I, 148
Morris, Joseph I, 149
Morris, Joseph I, 150
Morris, Joseph I, 151
Morris, Joseph I, 153
Morris, Joseph I, 162
Morris, Joseph I, 197
Morris, Joseph I, 200
Morris, Joseph I, 201
Morris, Joseph I, 247
Morris, Joseph I, 563
Morris, Joseph I, 568
Morris, Joseph II, 30
Morris, Joseph II, 35
Morris, Joseph II, 58
Morris, Joseph II, 88
Morris, Joseph II, 243
Morris, Joseph II, 397
Morris, Joseph II, 398
Morris, Joseph II, 524
Morris, Joseph II, 591
Morris, Joseph II, 596
Morris, Joseph II, 597
Morris, Joseph II, 602
Morris, Joseph II, 603
Morris, Joseph II, 655
Morris, Joseph II, 798
Morris, Joseph IV, 154
Morris, Joseph IV, 344
Morris, Joseph IV, 589
Morris, Joseph IV, 648
Morris, Joseph IV, 738
Morris, Joseph IV, 743
Morris, Joseph IV, 744
Morris, Joseph IV, 772
Morris, Joseph IV, 879
Morris, Joseph IV, 930
Morris, Joseph IV, 952
Morris, Joseph IV, 981
Morris, Joseph IV, 1107
Morris, Joseph IV, 1174
Morris, Joseph IV, 1209
Morris, Joseph IV, 1217
Morris, Joseph IV, 1218
Morris, Joseph IV, 1227
Morris, Joseph C. IV, 981
Morris, Joseph C. IV, 982
Morris, Joseph C. IV, 1012
Morris, Joseph C. IV, 1217
Morris, Joseph C. IV, 1218
Morris, Joseph Draper I, 103
Morris, Joseph Earl IV, 1136
Morris, Joseph H. I, 151
Morris, Joseph H. I, 197
Morris, Joseph H. VI, 848

rris, Joseph Henley I, 105
rris, Joseph Henley I, 106
rris, Joseph Henley I, 148
rris, Joseph Henley I, 149
rris, Joseph John I, 1160
rris, Joseph Jones IV, 422
rris, Joseph K. IV, 1108
rris, Joseph M. I, 151
rris, Joseph Rhodes IV, 254
rris, Joseph Rhodes IV, 743
rris, Joseph S. II, 603
rris, Joseph, Jr. I, 148
rris, Joseph, Jr. I, 150
rris, Joseph, Jr. I, 157
rris, Joseph, Jr. IV, 743
rris, Joseph, Sr. I, 148
rris, Joshua I, 35
rris, Joshua I, 61
rris, Joshua I, 103
rris, Joshua I, 105
rris, Joshua I, 106
rris, Joshua I, 142
rris, Joshua I, 147
rris, Joshua I, 148
rris, Joshua I, 149
rris, Joshua I, 150
rris, Joshua I, 151
rris, Joshua I, 153
rris, Joshua I, 167
rris, Joshua I, 177
rris, Joshua I, 197
rris, Joshua I, 291
rris, Joshua II, 35
rris, Joshua II, 398
rris, Joshua II, 446
rris, Joshua II, 756
rris, Joshua II, 901
rris, Joshua IV, 154
rris, Joshua IV, 422
rris, Joshua IV, 588
rris, Joshua IV, 589
rris, Joshua IV, 694
rris, Joshua IV, 743
rris, Joshua IV, 879
rris, Joshua IV, 1070
rris, Joshua IV, 1089
rris, Joshua IV, 1135
rris, Joshua IV, 1217
rris, Joshua IV, 1218
rris, Joshua C. V, 699
rris, Joshua, Jr. IV, 879
rris, Joshua, Jr. IV, 884
rris, Joshua, Jr. IV, 1108
rris, Joshua, Jr. IV, 1118
rris, Joshua, Jr. IV, 1136
rris, Joshua, Sr. I, 150
rris, Josiah I, 104
rris, Josiah I, 895
rris, Josiah Bundy I, 148
rris, Josiah Bundy I, 895
rris, Josiah C. V, 699
rris, Julia III, 234
rris, Julian VI, 926
rris, Keziah I, 149
rris, Keziah IV, 1217
rris, Keziah IV, 1218
rris, Larrence II, 243
rris, Lavina V, 267
rris, Lavisa IV, 1136
rris, Leaah I, 311
rris, Leah I, 105
rris, Leah I, 291
rris, Leah IV, 154
rris, Leah IV, 743
rris, Leah IV, 785
rris, LeeRoy V, 194
rris, Lemuel I, 105
rris, Lemuel I, 151
rris, Leola Usher I, 564
rris, Leota IV, 254
rris, Leroy V, 194
rris, LeRoy V, 194
rris, Levina VI, 879
rris, Lew III, 13
rris, Lewis II, 35
rris, Lewis II, 88
rris, Lewis II, 112
rris, Lewis II, 602
rris, Lewis II, 649
rris, Lewis IV, 45
rris, Lewis IV, 1135
rris, Lewis IV, 1136
rris, Lidia I, 280
rris, Lindley IV, 1135
rris, Lindley IV, 1136
rris, Lizzie IV, 1135
rris, Louisa II, 603
rris, Louisa IV, 1127
rris, Louisa IV, 1136
rris, Louisa V, 194
rris, Louisa VI, 842
Morris, Louisa P. II, 398
Morris, Lucinda V, 267
Morris, Lucinda VI, 842
Morris, Lucretia I, 106
Morris, Lucretia I, 142
Morris, Lucretia I, 149
Morris, Lucretia I, 150
Morris, Lucretia IV, 1217
Morris, Lucretia VI, 842
Morris, Lucy VI, 966
Morris, Luke I, 320
Morris, Luke II, 397
Morris, Luke II, 602
Morris, Luke II, 633
Morris, Luke W. II, 603
Morris, Luke W. II, 621
Morris, Luretta V, 267
Morris, Lyda I, 149
Morris, Lyda I, 150
Morris, Lydda I, 103
Morris, Lyddia I, 61
Morris, Lyddia I, 74
Morris, Lyddia I, 105
Morris, Lyddia I, 106
Morris, Lyddia I, 149
Morris, Lydia I, 103
Morris, Lydia I, 105
Morris, Lydia I, 149
Morris, Lydia I, 150
Morris, Lydia I, 156
Morris, Lydia I, 291
Morris, Lydia I, 311
Morris, Lydia II, 151
Morris, Lydia II, 153
Morris, Lydia II, 795
Morris, Lydia IV, 51
Morris, Lydia IV, 102
Morris, Lydia IV, 103
Morris, Lydia IV, 154
Morris, Lydia IV, 238
Morris, Lydia IV, 254
Morris, Lydia IV, 422
Morris, Lydia IV, 423
Morris, Lydia IV, 542
Morris, Lydia IV, 557
Morris, Lydia IV, 589
Morris, Lydia IV, 648
Morris, Lydia IV, 727
Morris, Lydia IV, 743
Morris, Lydia IV, 787
Morris, Lydia IV, 879
Morris, Lydia IV, 1069
Morris, Lydia IV, 1070
Morris, Lydia IV, 1094
Morris, Lydia IV, 1107
Morris, Lydia IV, 1108
Morris, Lydia IV, 1136
Morris, Lydia V, 103
Morris, Lydia V, 266
Morris, Lydia V, 267
Morris, Lydia V, 298
Morris, Lydia V, 307
Morris, Lydia V, 447
Morris, Lydia V, 557
Morris, Lydia V, 583
Morris, Lydia V, 667
Morris, Lydia VI, 425
Morris, Lydia VI, 980
Morris, Lydia Frances IV, 254
Morris, Lydia K. II, 153
Morris, Lydia Keasby II, 135
Morris, Lydia M. V, 267
Morris, Lydia Maria V, 267
Morris, Lydia Maria V, 699
Morris, Lydia P. IV, 1136
Morris, Lydia S. IV, 1135
Morris, Lydia T. II, 757
Morris, Lydia Thompson II, 713
Morris, Lydia, Jr. I, 137
Morris, Lydia, Jr. I, 149
Morris, Lyle C. V, 194
Morris, Magdalen II, 601
Morris, Magdalen II, 674
Morris, Maggie V, 249
Morris, Mahala I, 291
Morris, Mahala I, 312
Morris, Mahalia I, 309
Morris, Mahalia I, 312
Morris, Mahitable J. IV, 744
Morris, Mahlon V, 266
Morris, Mahlon V, 267
Morris, Margaret I, 101
Morris, Margaret I, 103
Morris, Margaret I, 104
Morris, Margaret I, 105
Morris, Margaret I, 106
Morris, Margaret I, 142
Morris, Margaret I, 144
Morris, Margaret I, 145
Morris, Margaret I, 148
Morris, Margaret I, 149
Morris, Margaret I, 150
Morris, Margaret I, 151
Morris, Margaret I, 154
Morris, Margaret I, 171
Morris, Margaret I, 197
Morris, Margaret I, 209
Morris, Margaret I, 291
Morris, Margaret I, 301
Morris, Margaret I, 311
Morris, Margaret I, 312
Morris, Margaret I, 320
Morris, Margaret I, 831
Morris, Margaret I, 863
Morris, Margaret I, 895
Morris, Margaret II, 179
Morris, Margaret II, 184
Morris, Margaret II, 209
Morris, Margaret II, 243
Morris, Margaret II, 262
Morris, Margaret II, 289
Morris, Margaret II, 398
Morris, Margaret II, 508
Morris, Margaret II, 549
Morris, Margaret II, 601
Morris, Margaret II, 603
Morris, Margaret IV, 254
Morris, Margaret IV, 1258
Morris, Margaret VI, 827
Morris, Margaret VI, 965
Morris, Margaret E. II, 296
Morris, Margaret E. II, 297
Morris, Margaret E. II, 301
Morris, Margaret J. IV, 241
Morris, Margaret J. IV, 254
Morris, Margaret Jane V, 699
Morris, Margaret, Jr. I, 151
Morris, Margarett II, 691
Morris, Margret II, 602
Morris, Maria II, 603
Morris, Maria II, 697
Morris, Maria IV, 311
Morris, Maria IV, 313
Morris, Maria IV, 1135
Morris, Maria V, 194
Morris, Maria V, 423
Morris, Marium I, 150
Morris, Mark I, 103
Morris, Mark I, 149
Morris, Martha I, 106
Morris, Martha I, 150
Morris, Martha I, 151
Morris, Martha I, 176
Morris, Martha I, 197
Morris, Martha I, 200
Morris, Martha I, 203
Morris, Martha I, 312
Morris, Martha I, 957
Morris, Martha I, 1068
Morris, Martha II, 289
Morris, Martha II, 398
Morris, Martha II, 524
Morris, Martha II, 580
Morris, Martha II, 597
Morris, Martha II, 602
Morris, Martha II, 603
Morris, Martha II, 613
Morris, Martha II, 713
Morris, Martha III, 234
Morris, Martha IV, 743
Morris, Martha IV, 879
Morris, Martha IV, 981
Morris, Martha V, 266
Morris, Martha V, 461
Morris, Martha V, 756
Morris, Martha VI, 820
Morris, Martha VI, 998
Morris, Martha A. IV, 648
Morris, Martha A. IV, 662
Morris, Martha A. V, 699
Morris, Martha Ann VI, 966
Morris, Martha E. V, 194
Morris, Martha M. II, 237
Morris, Martha M. II, 243
Morris, Martin IV, 588
Morris, Martin IV, 589
Morris, Martin IV, 1070
Morris, Martin IV, 1090
Morris, Martin IV, 1103
Morris, Martin IV, 1107
Morris, Martin IV, 1128
Morris, Martin IV, 1135
Morris, Mary I, 25
Morris, Mary I, 60
Morris, Mary I, 61
Morris, Mary I, 101
Morris, Mary I, 103
Morris, Mary I, 104
Morris, Mary I, 105
Morris, Mary I, 106
Morris, Mary I, 112
Morris, Mary I, 114
Morris, Mary I, 116
Morris, Mary I, 121
Morris, Mary I, 128
Morris, Mary I, 129
Morris, Mary I, 132
Morris, Mary I, 133
Morris, Mary I, 138
Morris, Mary I, 147
Morris, Mary I, 148
Morris, Mary I, 149
Morris, Mary I, 150
Morris, Mary I, 151
Morris, Mary I, 153
Morris, Mary I, 154
Morris, Mary I, 158
Morris, Mary I, 160
Morris, Mary I, 162
Morris, Mary I, 163
Morris, Mary I, 164
Morris, Mary I, 165
Morris, Mary I, 166
Morris, Mary I, 169
Morris, Mary I, 170
Morris, Mary I, 173
Morris, Mary I, 177
Morris, Mary I, 291
Morris, Mary I, 304
Morris, Mary I, 311
Morris, Mary I, 319
Morris, Mary I, 320
Morris, Mary I, 831
Morris, Mary I, 1068
Morris, Mary II, 134
Morris, Mary II, 151
Morris, Mary II, 179
Morris, Mary II, 239
Morris, Mary II, 243
Morris, Mary II, 251
Morris, Mary II, 262
Morris, Mary II, 296
Morris, Mary II, 397
Morris, Mary II, 398
Morris, Mary II, 519
Morris, Mary II, 567
Morris, Mary II, 568
Morris, Mary II, 569
Morris, Mary II, 591
Morris, Mary II, 601
Morris, Mary II, 602
Morris, Mary II, 603
Morris, Mary II, 620
Morris, Mary II, 622
Morris, Mary II, 626
Morris, Mary II, 633
Morris, Mary II, 643
Morris, Mary II, 662
Morris, Mary II, 681
Morris, Mary II, 734
Morris, Mary II, 756
Morris, Mary II, 810
Morris, Mary III, 252
Morris, Mary IV, 45
Morris, Mary IV, 51
Morris, Mary IV, 62
Morris, Mary IV, 76
Morris, Mary IV, 102
Morris, Mary IV, 154
Morris, Mary IV, 415
Morris, Mary IV, 422
Morris, Mary IV, 588
Morris, Mary IV, 648
Morris, Mary IV, 682
Morris, Mary IV, 743
Morris, Mary IV, 744
Morris, Mary IV, 747
Morris, Mary IV, 879
Morris, Mary IV, 911
Morris, Mary IV, 928
Morris, Mary IV, 938
Morris, Mary IV, 981
Morris, Mary IV, 1028
Morris, Mary IV, 1029
Morris, Mary IV, 1108
Morris, Mary IV, 1112
Morris, Mary IV, 1123
Morris, Mary IV, 1210
Morris, Mary IV, 1212
Morris, Mary IV, 1217
Morris, Mary IV, 1227
Morris, Mary IV, 1239
Morris, Mary V, 103
Morris, Mary V, 266
Morris, Mary V, 267
Morris, Mary V, 269
Morris, Mary V, 519
Morris, Mary VI, 842
Morris, Mary VI, 879
Morris, Mary VI, 965
Morris, Mary ??? III, 234
Morris, Mary A. I, 151
Morris, Mary A. I, 176
Morris, Mary A. I, 593
Morris, Mary A. I, 595
Morris, Mary Abigail I, 25
Morris, Mary Abigail I, 103
Morris, Mary Ann II, 602
Morris, Mary Ann II, 603
Morris, Mary Ann II, 713
Morris, Mary Ann II, 734
Morris, Mary Ann II, 756
Morris, Mary Ann IV, 154
Morris, Mary Ann IV, 161
Morris, Mary Ann IV, 1217
Morris, Mary Anne IV, 1217
Morris, Mary Anne IV, 1225
Morris, Mary C. V, 956
Morris, Mary E. IV, 422
Morris, Mary E. IV, 423
Morris, Mary E. IV, 1107
Morris, Mary E. IV, 1108
Morris, Mary E. IV, 1117
Morris, Mary E. V, 956
Morris, Mary Elizabeth II, 756
Morris, Mary Ella IV, 1136
Morris, Mary Ellen IV, 1135
Morris, Mary Ellen IV, 1136
Morris, Mary Ellen IV, 1137
Morris, Mary H. II, 135
Morris, Mary H. II, 153
Morris, Mary H. IV, 911
Morris, Mary Hildreth II, 135
Morris, Mary Hildreth II, 151
Morris, Mary Hildreth II, 153
Morris, Mary P. II, 296
Morris, Mary P. IV, 981
Morris, Mary P. IV, 982
Morris, Mary P. IV, 1009
Morris, Mary R. II, 603
Morris, Mary S. II, 243
Morris, Mary S. II, 296
Morris, Mary S. II, 713
Morris, Mary S. IV, 51
Morris, Mary S. IV, 744
Morris, Mary S. IV, 1131
Morris, Mary S. IV, 1135
Morris, Mary Sanders I, 105
Morris, Mary Susanna IV, 1136
Morris, Mary T. IV, 1107
Morris, Mary T. IV, 1108
Morris, Mary T. IV, 1112
Morris, Mary, Jr. I, 138
Morris, Mary, Jr. I, 148
Morris, Mary, Jr. I, 157
Morris, Mary, Jr. I, 164
Morris, Mary, Sr. I, 148
Morris, Matil IV, 45
Morris, Matilda I, 150
Morris, Matilda IV, 45
Morris, Matilda IV, 422
Morris, Matilda IV, 1136
Morris, Matilda P. IV, 1135
Morris, Matilda P. IV, 1136
Morris, Maud IV, 254
Morris, Maurice II, 398
Morris, Mauris II, 398
Morris, Mehetable IV, 1217
Morris, Mehetable J. IV, 694
Morris, Mehetable J. IV, 743
Morris, Mehitable J. IV, 1205
Morris, Mehitable J. IV, 1217
Morris, Melicent I, 148
Morris, Melvina VI, 842
Morris, Meribah IV, 981
Morris, Merihab IV, 924
Morris, Miaram I, 103
Morris, Michael IV, 254
Morris, Mifflin II, 603
Morris, Mifflin II, 756
Morris, Mifflin II, 901
Morris, Milicent I, 104
Morris, Milicent I, 138
Morris, Milicent I, 148
Morris, Milicent I, 311
Morris, Milisant I, 149
Morris, Milisant I, 168
Morris, Miliscent I, 45
Morris, Miliscent I, 61
Morris, Miliscent I, 104
Morris, Miliscent I, 105
Morris, Miliscent I, 106
Morris, Miliscent I, 150
Morris, Milley VI, 963
Morris, Milley VI, 965
Morris, Millicent I, 291
Morris, Millicent I, 300
Morris, Millicent I, 311
Morris, Millicent I, 1011
Morris, Millicent V, 266
Morris, Millisent I, 150
Morris, Milly I, 1001
Morris, Milly V, 307
Morris, Minnie IV, 254

Morris, Minta V, 266
Morris, Miriam I, 97
Morris, Miriam I, 103
Morris, Miriam I, 105
Morris, Miriam I, 106
Morris, Miriam I, 113
Morris, Miriam I, 129
Morris, Miriam I, 137
Morris, Miriam I, 148
Morris, Miriam I, 149
Morris, Miriam I, 150
Morris, Miriam I, 151
Morris, Miriam I, 164
Morris, Miriam I, 169
Morris, Miriam I, 230
Morris, Miriam I, 247
Morris, Miriam I, 712
Morris, Miriam I, 727
Morris, Miriam IV, 879
Morris, Miriam, Jr. I, 148
Morris, Mordeca I, 106
Morris, Mordecai I, 103
Morris, Mordecai I, 105
Morris, Mordecai I, 106
Morris, Mordecai I, 125
Morris, Mordecai I, 147
Morris, Mordecai I, 148
Morris, Mordecai I, 149
Morris, Mordecai I, 150
Morris, Mordecai I, 151
Morris, Mordecai I, 157
Morris, Mordecai I, 165
Morris, Mordecai I, 169
Morris, Mordecai I, 197
Morris, Mordecai I, 291
Morris, Mordecai IV, 422
Morris, Mordecai IV, 588
Morris, Mordecai IV, 589
Morris, Mordecai IV, 599
Morris, Mordecai IV, 743
Morris, Mordecai IV, 1070
Morris, Mordecai IV, 1107
Morris, Mordecai IV, 1136
Morris, Mordecai, Jr. I, 106
Morris, Mordecai, Jr. I, 150
Morris, Mordecai, Sr. I, 106
Morris, Mordecai, Sr. I, 151
Morris, Mordica I, 197
Morris, Mordica I, 203
Morris, Morgan VI, 966
Morris, Morris II, 602
Morris, Morris II, 611
Morris, Morris, Jr. II, 398
Morris, N. J. II, 480
Morris, Nancy IV, 1028
Morris, Nancy IV, 1029
Morris, Nancy VI, 852
Morris, Nancy VI, 939
Morris, Nancy VI, 986
Morris, Nancy Ann IV, 872
Morris, Nancy Ann IV, 879
Morris, Naomi Jordan I, 151
Morris, Nathan I, 104
Morris, Nathan I, 105
Morris, Nathan I, 106
Morris, Nathan I, 129
Morris, Nathan I, 149
Morris, Nathan I, 150
Morris, Nathan I, 151
Morris, Nathan I, 291
Morris, Nathan I, 1068
Morris, Nathan IV, 422
Morris, Nathan IV, 423
Morris, Nathan IV, 429
Morris, Nathan IV, 541
Morris, Nathan IV, 543
Morris, Nathan IV, 588
Morris, Nathan IV, 589
Morris, Nathan IV, 743
Morris, Nathan IV, 1069
Morris, Nathan IV, 1070
Morris, Nathan IV, 1107
Morris, Nathan O. I, 105
Morris, Nathan O. I, 151
Morris, Nathan Overman I, 150
Morris, Nathan P. I, 151
Morris, Nathan Thomas I, 312
Morris, Nathan, Jr. I, 149
Morris, Nathan, Sr. I, 106
Morris, Nathan, Sr. I, 151
Morris, Nathaniel VI, 965
Morris, Nettie B. IV, 254
Morris, Nixon IV, 241
Morris, Nixon IV, 254
Morris, Oliver T. IV, 1107
Morris, Ona IV, 1258
Morris, Ora IV, 1258
Morris, Owen II, 398
Morris, Owen II, 567
Morris, Owen II, 601
Morris, Owen II, 602
Morris, Peggy I, 150
Morris, Peggy I, 171
Morris, Peggy VI, 966
Morris, Penelope I, 105
Morris, Penelope I, 149
Morris, Penelope I, 168
Morris, Peninah I, 133
Morris, Peninah I, 150
Morris, Peninah I, 291
Morris, Penninah I, 150
Morris, Penninah I, 163
Morris, Peter I, 104
Morris, Pharabe I, 895
Morris, Pharaby I, 133
Morris, Pharaby I, 150
Morris, Pharaby I, 863
Morris, Phebe II, 397
Morris, Phebe II, 398
Morris, Phebe II, 474
Morris, Phebe II, 538
Morris, Phebe II, 601
Morris, Phebe II, 602
Morris, Phebe II, 603
Morris, Phebe III, 227
Morris, Phebe III, 234
Morris, Phebe IV, 422
Morris, Phebe IV, 423
Morris, Phebe IV, 429
Morris, Phebe IV, 541
Morris, Phebe IV, 542
Morris, Phebe IV, 543
Morris, Phebe IV, 879
Morris, Phebe IV, 885
Morris, Phebe IV, 1064
Morris, Phebe IV, 1070
Morris, Phebe IV, 1107
Morris, Phebe IV, 1108
Morris, Phebe IV, 1123
Morris, Phebe Ann IV, 1107
Morris, Phebe Ann IV, 1108
Morris, Phebe R. II, 398
Morris, Phebe, Jr. II, 398
Morris, Pheraby I, 104
Morris, Phinehas I, 895
Morris, Phinehas Nixon I, 150
Morris, Pierce IV, 879
Morris, Polly VI, 898
Morris, Polly VI, 965
Morris, Polly VI, 966
Morris, Polly Ann VI, 966
Morris, Polly T. VI, 842
Morris, Powel II, 901
Morris, Powell II, 901
Morris, Precilla Jane IV, 1217
Morris, Prichard I, 150
Morris, Priscilla I, 105
Morris, Priscilla Ann IV, 1217
Morris, Priscilla Jane IV, 1217
Morris, Priscillaann IV, 1207
Morris, Priscillaann IV, 1217
Morris, Pritchard I, 103
Morris, Pritchard I, 104
Morris, Pritchard I, 150
Morris, Prudance II, 88
Morris, Prudence II, 30
Morris, Prudence II, 58
Morris, Prudence II, 243
Morris, Prudence II, 244
Morris, Prudence II, 603
Morris, Prudence II, 757
Morris, Prudence II, 769
Morris, Prudence IV, 488
Morris, Pryor V, 636
Morris, Rachel I, 104
Morris, Rachel II, 603
Morris, Rachel II, 713
Morris, Rachel IV, 45
Morris, Rachel IV, 254
Morris, Rachel IV, 344
Morris, Rachel IV, 403
Morris, Rachel IV, 422
Morris, Rachel IV, 423
Morris, Rachel IV, 588
Morris, Rachel IV, 589
Morris, Rachel IV, 694
Morris, Rachel IV, 738
Morris, Rachel IV, 743
Morris, Rachel IV, 744
Morris, Rachel IV, 879
Morris, Rachel IV, 919
Morris, Rachel IV, 930
Morris, Rachel IV, 952
Morris, Rachel IV, 981
Morris, Rachel IV, 983
Morris, Rachel IV, 1069
Morris, Rachel IV, 1070
Morris, Rachel IV, 1089
Morris, Rachel IV, 1107
Morris, Rachel IV, 1108
Morris, Rachel IV, 1135
Morris, Rachel IV, 1210
Morris, Rachel IV, 1217
Morris, Rachel A. I, 1160
Morris, Rachel A. IV, 1128
Morris, Rachel A. IV, 1136
Morris, Rachel Ann I, 1160
Morris, Rachel Ann IV, 1090
Morris, Rachel Ann IV, 1135
Morris, Rachel Ann IV, 1217
Morris, Rachel B. IV, 1129
Morris, Rachel H. IV, 1107
Morris, Rachel K. IV, 254
Morris, Rachel M. IV, 1136
Morris, Rebecah I, 105
Morris, Rebecca I, 99
Morris, Rebecca I, 104
Morris, Rebecca I, 131
Morris, Rebecca I, 151
Morris, Rebecca I, 247
Morris, Rebecca I, 291
Morris, Rebecca I, 309
Morris, Rebecca I, 311
Morris, Rebecca II, 243
Morris, Rebecca II, 398
Morris, Rebecca II, 480
Morris, Rebecca II, 602
Morris, Rebecca II, 603
Morris, Rebecca II, 609
Morris, Rebecca II, 616
Morris, Rebecca II, 620
Morris, Rebecca II, 663
Morris, Rebecca II, 681
Morris, Rebecca II, 702
Morris, Rebecca II, 713
Morris, Rebecca IV, 102
Morris, Rebecca IV, 103
Morris, Rebecca IV, 254
Morris, Rebecca IV, 344
Morris, Rebecca IV, 422
Morris, Rebecca IV, 588
Morris, Rebecca IV, 743
Morris, Rebecca IV, 772
Morris, Rebecca IV, 981
Morris, Rebecca IV, 1070
Morris, Rebecca IV, 1107
Morris, Rebecca IV, 1135
Morris, Rebecca IV, 1217
Morris, Rebecca V, 103
Morris, Rebecca W. II, 398
Morris, Rebeccah I, 104
Morris, Rebeccah I, 151
Morris, Rebeccah I, 163
Morris, Rebecka II, 398
Morris, Rebeckah I, 150
Morris, Rebeckah I, 171
Morris, Rebeckah I, 174
Morris, Rebeckah I, 895
Morris, Rebekah I, 140
Morris, Rebekah I, 148
Morris, Rebekah I, 149
Morris, Rebekah I, 167
Morris, Rebekah I, 895
Morris, Rebekah II, 602
Morris, Rebekas I, 106
Morris, Rhoda C. V, 699
Morris, Richard II, 179
Morris, Richard II, 243
Morris, Richard II, 398
Morris, Richard IV, 51
Morris, Richard IV, 103
Morris, Richard VI, 842
Morris, Richard Hill II, 243
Morris, Richard Hill II, 262
Morris, Richard Wistar II, 603
Morris, Robert I, 291
Morris, Robert I, 311
Morris, Robert II, 602
Morris, Robert IV, 588
Morris, Robert IV, 879
Morris, Robert IV, 911
Morris, Robert IV, 1107
Morris, Robert VI, 842
Morris, Robert VI, 863
Morris, Robert VI, 965
Morris, Robert L. IV, 589
Morris, Robert M. IV, 1258
Morris, Robert N. IV, 1107
Morris, Ruben I, 727
Morris, Rudderah II, 55
Morris, Rudderah II, 88
Morris, Rudra II, 35
Morris, Ruth I, 103
Morris, Ruth I, 104
Morris, Ruth I, 105
Morris, Ruth I, 132
Morris, Ruth I, 148
Morris, Ruth I, 149
Morris, Ruth I, 150
Morris, Ruth I, 162
Morris, Ruth I, 177
Morris, Ruth I, 863
Morris, Ruth I, 895
Morris, Ruth II, 179
Morris, Ruth II, 243
Morris, Ruth II, 296
Morris, Ruth II, 297
Morris, Ruth IV, 175
Morris, Ruth IV, 254
Morris, Ruth IV, 422
Morris, Ruth IV, 589
Morris, Ruth IV, 879
Morris, Ruth IV, 1069
Morris, Ruth IV, 1070
Morris, Ruth IV, 1136
Morris, Ruth V, 267
Morris, Ruth V, 412
Morris, Ruth V, 423
Morris, Ruth V, 519
Morris, Ruth V, 531
Morris, Ruth V, 699
Morris, Ruth Anna IV, 1070
Morris, Ruth Anna IV, 1135
Morris, Ruth M. V, 267
Morris, Ruth P. IV, 1101
Morris, Ruthann IV, 1099
Morris, Ruthann IV, 1107
Morris, Ruthanna IV, 51
Morris, Ruthanna V. IV, 1069
Morris, Ruty IV, 1107
Morris, Salley IV, 358
Morris, Sally I, 291
Morris, Sally I, 311
Morris, Sally IV, 154
Morris, Sally IV, 415
Morris, Sally IV, 422
Morris, Sally IV, 427
Morris, Sally IV, 648
Morris, Sally IV, 743
Morris, Sally IV, 787
Morris, Sally IV, 1107
Morris, Sally IV, 1123
Morris, Sally VI, 963
Morris, Sally VI, 965
Morris, Saml. VI, 871
Morris, Samson II, 446
Morris, Samuel I, 103
Morris, Samuel I, 105
Morris, Samuel I, 148
Morris, Samuel I, 150
Morris, Samuel I, 291
Morris, Samuel I, 303
Morris, Samuel I, 311
Morris, Samuel II, 397
Morris, Samuel II, 398
Morris, Samuel II, 480
Morris, Samuel II, 569
Morris, Samuel II, 602
Morris, Samuel II, 603
Morris, Samuel II, 616
Morris, Samuel II, 620
Morris, Samuel II, 681
Morris, Samuel II, 691
Morris, Samuel II, 1017
Morris, Samuel II, 1057
Morris, Samuel II, 1076
Morris, Samuel IV, 45
Morris, Samuel IV, 154
Morris, Samuel IV, 358
Morris, Samuel IV, 415
Morris, Samuel IV, 422
Morris, Samuel IV, 423
Morris, Samuel IV, 588
Morris, Samuel IV, 589
Morris, Samuel IV, 743
Morris, Samuel IV, 787
Morris, Samuel IV, 1069
Morris, Samuel IV, 1070
Morris, Samuel IV, 1107
Morris, Samuel IV, 1117
Morris, Samuel IV, 1123
Morris, Samuel V, 885
Morris, Samuel V, 1011
Morris, Samuel VI, 965
Morris, Samuel VI, 998
Morris, Samuel A. I, 1160
Morris, Samuel A. IV, 1217
Morris, Samuel B. II, 603
Morris, Samuel B. II, 621
Morris, Samuel, Jr. II, 398
Morris, Samuel, Jr. II, 602
Morris, Sarah I, 37
Morris, Sarah I, 61
Morris, Sarah I, 68
Morris, Sarah I, 72
Morris, Sarah I, 101
Morris, Sarah I, 103
Morris, Sarah I, 104
Morris, Sarah I, 105
Morris, Sarah I, 106
Morris, Sarah I, 126
Morris, Sarah I, 128
Morris, Sarah I, 138
Morris, Sarah I, 141
Morris, Sarah I, 144
Morris, Sarah I, 146
Morris, Sarah I, 148
Morris, Sarah I, 149
Morris, Sarah I, 150
Morris, Sarah I, 151
Morris, Sarah I, 158
Morris, Sarah I, 159
Morris, Sarah I, 163
Morris, Sarah I, 177
Morris, Sarah I, 291
Morris, Sarah I, 311
Morris, Sarah I, 312
Morris, Sarah I, 320
Morris, Sarah I, 831
Morris, Sarah I, 957
Morris, Sarah I, 1068
Morris, Sarah I, 1071
Morris, Sarah I, 1160
Morris, Sarah II, 35
Morris, Sarah II, 64
Morris, Sarah II, 88
Morris, Sarah II, 179
Morris, Sarah II, 186
Morris, Sarah II, 243
Morris, Sarah II, 248
Morris, Sarah II, 397
Morris, Sarah II, 398
Morris, Sarah II, 446
Morris, Sarah II, 474
Morris, Sarah II, 591
Morris, Sarah II, 597
Morris, Sarah II, 601
Morris, Sarah II, 602
Morris, Sarah II, 603
Morris, Sarah II, 616
Morris, Sarah II, 677
Morris, Sarah II, 691
Morris, Sarah II, 700
Morris, Sarah II, 713
Morris, Sarah II, 756
Morris, Sarah II, 810
Morris, Sarah II, 814
Morris, Sarah II, 838
Morris, Sarah II, 901
Morris, Sarah III, 155
Morris, Sarah III, 234
Morris, Sarah III, 274
Morris, Sarah IV, 45
Morris, Sarah IV, 103
Morris, Sarah IV, 142
Morris, Sarah IV, 154
Morris, Sarah IV, 254
Morris, Sarah IV, 344
Morris, Sarah IV, 422
Morris, Sarah IV, 443
Morris, Sarah IV, 588
Morris, Sarah IV, 648
Morris, Sarah IV, 685
Morris, Sarah IV, 696
Morris, Sarah IV, 743
Morris, Sarah IV, 744
Morris, Sarah IV, 763
Morris, Sarah IV, 879
Morris, Sarah IV, 974
Morris, Sarah IV, 977
Morris, Sarah IV, 981
Morris, Sarah IV, 982
Morris, Sarah IV, 1070
Morris, Sarah IV, 1107
Morris, Sarah V, 267
Morris, Sarah V, 699
Morris, Sarah VI, 537
Morris, Sarah VI, 574
Morris, Sarah Ann I, 106
Morris, Sarah Ann I, 135
Morris, Sarah Ann I, 151
Morris, Sarah Ann IV, 743
Morris, Sarah Ann IV, 744
Morris, Sarah Ann IV, 911
Morris, Sarah Ann IV, 938
Morris, Sarah Ann IV, 981
Morris, Sarah Ann V, 266
Morris, Sarah C. IV, 974
Morris, Sarah C. IV, 981
Morris, Sarah E. I, 564
Morris, Sarah F. V, 922
Morris, Sarah G. I, 1160
Morris, Sarah G. IV, 1217
Morris, Sarah J. IV, 1135
Morris, Sarah Jane IV, 51
Morris, Sarah P. II, 713
Morris, Sarah R. IV, 911
Morris, Sarah S. II, 825
Morris, Sarah S. IV, 1217
Morris, Sarah S. IV, 1227
Morris, Sarah Sanders I, 105
Morris, Sarah Saunders II, 782
Morris, Sarah T. IV, 1108
Morris, Sarah Whinery V, 266
Morris, Sarah Whinery V, 519

ris, Sarah, Jr. II, 476
ris, Selah I, 312
ris, Selea I, 311
ris, Selea I, 315
ris, Selia I, 291
ris, Selia I, 1068
ris, Serepta V, 266
ris, Silas IV, 1136
ris, Silas S. IV, 1135
ris, Stephen I, 104
ris, Stephen II, 179
ris, Stephen II, 243
ris, Stephen IV, 743
ris, Stephen IV, 744
ris, Stephen IV, 981
ris, Stephen IV, 982
ris, Stephen IV, 1217
ris, Stephen VI, 969
ris, Stephen VI, 1006
ris, Stephen P. II, 713
ris, Stephen P. II, 734
ris, Stephen P. II, 756
ris, Susan II, 772
ris, Susan II, 798
ris, Susan IV, 51
ris, Susan C. VI, 896
ris, Susan H. IV, 1104
ris, Susan H. IV, 1107
rris, Susan Jane IV, 589
ris, Susan Jane IV, 596
ris, Susana I, 103
ris, Susanah I, 104
ris, Susanah VI, 966
ris, Susann IV, 1107
rris, Susanna I, 105
rris, Susanna I, 149
rris, Susanna I, 162
ris, Susanna I, 291
rris, Susanna I, 302
rris, Susanna I, 311
rris, Susanna II, 370
rris, Susanna II, 398
rris, Susanna III, 234
rris, Susanna IV, 45
rris, Susanna IV, 96
rris, Susanna IV, 103
rris, Susanna IV, 588
rris, Susanna IV, 589
rris, Susanna IV, 815
rris, Susanna IV, 1069
rris, Susanna IV, 1070
rris, Susanna IV, 1100
rris, Susanna IV, 1107
rris, Susanna IV, 1108
rris, Susanna IV, 1113
rris, Susanna V, 885
rris, Susanna VI, 871
rris, Susanna VI, 965
rris, Susannah I, 105
rris, Susannah I, 106
rris, Susannah I, 125
rris, Susannah I, 148
rris, Susannah I, 149
rris, Susannah I, 151
rris, Susannah I, 154
rris, Susannah I, 175
rris, Susannah II, 398
rris, Susannah II, 797
orris, Susannah IV, 45
orris, Susannah IV, 154
orris, Susannah IV, 422
orris, Susannah IV, 428
orris, Susannah IV, 577
orris, Susannah IV, 588
orris, Susannah IV, 648
orris, Susannah IV, 743
orris, Susannah IV, 1059
orris, Susannah IV, 1070
orris, Susie IV, 1330
orris, Tabitha IV, 981
orris, Tabitha IV, 1174
orris, Tabitha IV, 1209
orris, Tabitha IV, 1217
orris, Tabitha VI, 989
orris, Tacie IV, 541
orris, Tacie IV, 543
orris, Tacy II, 398
orris, Tacy II, 525
orris, Tacy II, 559
orris, Tacy II, 602
orris, Tacy II, 611
orris, Tacy IV, 422
orris, Tacy IV, 423
orris, Tacy IV, 429
orris, Tacy IV, 541
orris, Tacy IV, 588
orris, Tacy IV, 589
orris, Tacy IV, 1069
orris, Tacy IV, 1070
orris, Tacy IV, 1107
orris, Tamson IV, 588
Morris, Theodate IV, 1069
Morris, Theodate IV, 1070
Morris, Theodate IV, 1080
Morris, Theodate IV, 1107
Morris, Thomas I, 103
Morris, Thomas I, 104
Morris, Thomas I, 105
Morris, Thomas I, 106
Morris, Thomas I, 142
Morris, Thomas I, 144
Morris, Thomas I, 149
Morris, Thomas I, 150
Morris, Thomas I, 151
Morris, Thomas I, 174
Morris, Thomas I, 291
Morris, Thomas I, 303
Morris, Thomas I, 311
Morris, Thomas I, 312
Morris, Thomas I, 957
Morris, Thomas I, 967
Morris, Thomas I, 1066
Morris, Thomas I, 1068
Morris, Thomas I, 1071
Morris, Thomas II, 398
Morris, Thomas II, 567
Morris, Thomas II, 591
Morris, Thomas II, 601
Morris, Thomas II, 602
Morris, Thomas II, 643
Morris, Thomas II, 691
Morris, Thomas IV, 103
Morris, Thomas IV, 154
Morris, Thomas IV, 161
Morris, Thomas IV, 254
Morris, Thomas IV, 648
Morris, Thomas IV, 743
Morris, Thomas IV, 981
Morris, Thomas IV, 982
Morris, Thomas IV, 1107
Morris, Thomas C. V, 699
Morris, Thomas E. IV, 254
Morris, Thomas Elwood IV, 1108
Morris, Thomas F. IV, 981
Morris, Thomas Henley I, 106
Morris, Thomas Husband II, 810
Morris, Thomas Jordan I, 149
Morris, Thomas, Jr. I, 151
Morris, Thomas, Jr. II, 591
Morris, Thomas, Jr. II, 603
Morris, Thomas, Jr. IV, 254
Morris, Thomas, Sr. I, 151
Morris, Thomason II, 88
Morris, Thomason IV, 738
Morris, Thomason IV, 743
Morris, Thomesson IV, 981
Morris, Thos. II, 810
Morris, Thos. II, 814
Morris, Thos. II, 901
Morris, Thos. E. IV, 254
Morris, Thos. Gurley III, 234
Morris, Tomas A. I, 151
Morris, Trenton II, 480
Morris, Trifena IV, 1217
Morris, Tryphena IV, 1218
Morris, Vincent VI, 879
Morris, Vincent VI, 965
Morris, Vinson VI, 938
Morris, Viola Chlotilda IV, 981
Morris, Virgin II, 243
Morris, Walter E. V, 266
Morris, Warder II, 398
Morris, Warner V, 194
Morris, Wd. Elizabeth II, 398
Morris, Wd. Joanna II, 602
Morris, Wd. Mary II, 612
Morris, Wd. Mary P. II, 179
Morris, Wd. Mary S. II, 179
Morris, Wd. Sarah II, 179
Morris, Wd. Sarah II, 243
Morris, Widow Charlotte I, 201
Morris, Widow Elizabeth I, 151
Morris, Widow Lyddia I, 137
Morris, Widow Mary I, 104
Morris, Widow Mary I, 151
Morris, Widow Miliscent I, 147
Morris, Widow Miriam I, 143
Morris, Widow Miriam I, 148
Morris, Widow Sally I, 303
Morris, Widow Sally I, 311
Morris, Willard V, 267
Morris, William I, 92
Morris, William I, 105
Morris, William I, 106
Morris, William I, 291
Morris, William I, 302
Morris, William I, 311
Morris, William I, 312
Morris, William II, 243
Morris, William II, 262
Morris, William II, 397
Morris, William II, 398
Morris, William IV, 45
Morris, William IV, 154
Morris, William IV, 422
Morris, William IV, 588
Morris, William IV, 589
Morris, William IV, 743
Morris, William IV, 919
Morris, William IV, 1069
Morris, William VI, 842
Morris, William VI, 966
Morris, William VI, 989
Morris, William B. VI, 966
Morris, William E. I, 291
Morris, William E. V, 267
Morris, William Exum I, 312
Morris, William H. II, 296
Morris, William H. VI, 966
Morris, William Muse I, 103
Morris, William P. IV, 1070
Morris, William P. IV, 1107
Morris, William P. V, 267
Morris, William R. V, 267
Morris, William, Jr. II, 398
Morris, Wilson V, 266
Morris, Wilson V, 267
Morris, Winnie IV, 254
Morris, Wm. II, 135
Morris, Wm. II, 151
Morris, Wm. II, 153
Morris, Wm. II, 262
Morris, Wm. II, 474
Morris, Wm. II, 480
Morris, Wm. II, 508
Morris, Wm. II, 549
Morris, Wm. II, 602
Morris, Wm. II, 603
Morris, Wm. II, 612
Morris, Wm. II, 1017
Morris, Wm. IV, 577
Morris, Wm. IV, 588
Morris, Wm. IV, 743
Morris, Wm. IV, 974
Morris, Wm. IV, 1059
Morris, Wm. IV, 1070
Morris, Wm. IV, 1108
Morris, Wm. C. IV, 974
Morris, Wm. H. II, 301
Morris, Wm. W. IV, 1107
Morris, Wm. Wharton II, 1017
Morris, Wm. Wright IV, 1136
Morris, Wm., Jr. II, 602
Morris, Wm., Jr. II, 677
Morris, Wm., Jr. IV, 588
Morris, Zachariah I, 61
Morris, Zachariah I, 85
Morris, Zachariah I, 104
Morris, Zachariah I, 105
Morris, Zachariah I, 106
Morris, Zachariah I, 149
Morris, Zachariah I, 158
Morris, Zachariah I, 291
Morris, Zachariah I, 309
Morris, Zachariah I, 311
Morris, Zachariah I, 312
Morris, Zachariah I, 315
Morris, Zachariah V, 267
Morris, Zadoc V, 267
Morrish, William II, 446
Morrison, Alexander C. III, 234
Morrison, Alson W. V, 267
Morrison, Alson W. V, 351
Morrison, Ann II, 35
Morrison, Ann IV, 1108
Morrison, Ann IV, 1110
Morrison, Anna II, 88
Morrison, Anna II, 90
Morrison, Anna E. II, 179
Morrison, Anne E. II, 244
Morrison, Annie C. L. III, 234
Morrison, Barbara II, 398
Morrison, Catharine I, 445
Morrison, Catharine I, 451
Morrison, Catharine I, 454
Morrison, Daniel IV, 1174
Morrison, Deborah I, 361
Morrison, Deborah I, 448
Morrison, Deborah I, 451
Morrison, Dinah I, 451
Morrison, Edith I, 451
Morrison, Eli I, 439
Morrison, Elisabeath I, 135
Morrison, Elisabeath I, 151
Morrison, Elizabeth I, 451
Morrison, Elizabeth II, 713
Morrison, Elizabeth IV, 834
Morrison, Elizabeth IV, 1174
Morrison, Elizabeth V, 266
Morrison, Ellen V, 922
Morrison, Ellen T. V, 922
Morrison, Enoch I, 439
Morrison, Enoch I, 451
Morrison, Enoch I, 452
Morrison, Evan II, 603
Morrison, Evan II, 604
Morrison, George II, 398
Morrison, George II, 489
Morrison, George II, 603
Morrison, George, Jr. II, 398
Morrison, Gilbert V, 351
Morrison, Gilbert G. V, 351
Morrison, Gilbert Gurey V, 267
Morrison, Hannah I, 361
Morrison, Hannah I, 411
Morrison, Hannah I, 428
Morrison, Hannah I, 431
Morrison, Hannah I, 451
Morrison, Hannah IV, 83
Morrison, Hannah V, 66
Morrison, Hannah V, 103
Morrison, Hannah V, 497
Morrison, Hannah V, 519
Morrison, Harlan I, 439
Morrison, Harlon I, 439
Morrison, James I, 361
Morrison, James I, 411
Morrison, James I, 451
Morrison, James I, 454
Morrison, James I, 727
Morrison, James I, 1160
Morrison, Jane I, 361
Morrison, Jane I, 408
Morrison, Jane I, 411
Morrison, Jane IV, 83
Morrison, Jane IV, 103
Morrison, Jane V, 266
Morrison, Jane Isabella II, 703
Morrison, Jennie V, 267
Morrison, Jennie L. V, 351
Morrison, John I, 151
Morrison, John II, 398
Morrison, John III, 234
Morrison, John V, 266
Morrison, John V, 351
Morrison, John VI, 796
Morrison, John VI, 808
Morrison, John VI, 1016
Morrison, John I. V, 351
Morrison, John Q. V, 267
Morrison, John W. V, 267
Morrison, Jonas IV, 834
Morrison, Josiah L. II, 604
Morrison, Katharine I, 361
Morrison, Lindley M. V, 351
Morrison, Louis A. III, 234
Morrison, Lucy VI, 410
Morrison, Lucy VI, 425
Morrison, Maggie IV, 1174
Morrison, Mamie V, 461
Morrison, Margaret III, 234
Morrison, Mary I, 361
Morrison, Mary I, 439
Morrison, Mary I, 447
Morrison, Mary I, 451
Morrison, Mary II, 398
Morrison, Mary II, 489
Morrison, Mary II, 603
Morrison, Mary II, 604
Morrison, Mary V, 461
Morrison, Mary A. V, 351
Morrison, Mary Atlantic V, 267
Morrison, Mary Atlantic V, 279
Morrison, Mary M. III, 234
Morrison, Matilda IV, 911
Morrison, Matthew II, 35
Morrison, Nathaniel I, 1129
Morrison, Phebe III, 234
Morrison, Priscilla V, 240
Morrison, Priscilla V, 267
Morrison, Robert I, 361
Morrison, Robert I, 411
Morrison, Robert I, 428
Morrison, Robert I, 451
Morrison, Robert I, 695
Morrison, Robert V, 461
Morrison, Robert, Sr. I, 439
Morrison, Ruth I, 361
Morrison, Ruth I, 451
Morrison, Ruth I, 454
Morrison, Sabra A. VI, 774
Morrison, Sarah I, 411
Morrison, Sidney II, 398
Morrison, Sidney II, 603
Morrison, Simon I, 361
Morrison, Stephen I, 451
Morrison, Thomas W. V, 267
Morrison, Thomas W. V, 351
Morrison, William I, 361
Morrison, William I, 451
Morrison, William I, 457
Morrison, William II, 398
Morrison, William V, 351
Morrison, William VI, 842
Morrison, William John III, 234
Morrison, Wm. II, 603
Morrison, Wm. II, 604
Morrison, Wm. IV, 83
Morrison, Wm. IV, 1174
Morriss, Agnes II, 397
Morriss, Anna II, 398
Morriss, Anthony II, 397
Morriss, Anthony II, 398
Morriss, Anthony P. II, 398
Morriss, Anthony, Jr. II, 397
Morriss, Benjamin II, 398
Morriss, Charles Wistar II, 398
Morriss, Christian II, 398
Morriss, Deborah II, 243
Morriss, Elizabeth II, 398
Morriss, Elizabeth IV, 1029
Morriss, Ellis II, 398
Morriss, Grissell II, 446
Morriss, Gulielma Maria II, 243
Morriss, Hannah II, 243
Morriss, Hannah II, 397
Morriss, Israel II, 398
Morriss, James II, 398
Morriss, James P. II, 398
Morriss, John II, 398
Morriss, John VI, 816
Morriss, Joseph I, 247
Morriss, Joshua II, 398
Morriss, Larrence II, 212
Morriss, Larrence II, 243
Morriss, Louisa P. II, 398
Morriss, Mahaley VI, 816
Morriss, Margaret II, 243
Morriss, Margaret II, 398
Morriss, Mary II, 398
Morriss, Mary VI, 1001
Morriss, Owen II, 398
Morriss, Phebe II, 398
Morriss, Phebe R. II, 398
Morriss, Rachel II, 713
Morriss, Rebecca W. II, 398
Morriss, Rebecka II, 398
Morriss, Richard II, 243
Morriss, Samuel II, 397
Morriss, Sarah II, 243
Morriss, Sarah II, 398
Morriss, Sarah VI, 850
Morriss, Stephen II, 243
Morriss, Susan VI, 933
Morriss, Thomas II, 398
Morriss, Virgin II, 212
Morriss, Virgin II, 243
Morrisson, Catharine I, 451
Morrisson, Enoch I, 451
Morrisson, Hannah I, 451
Morrisson, John II, 398
Morrisson, Mary I, 451
Morrisson, Mary I, 452
Morrisson, Robert I, 451
Morrisson, Ruth I, 451
Morrland, Joseph VI, 297
Morrland, Mouring VI, 297
Morror, Phebe I, 564
Morrough, Rebecca IV, 982
Morrough, Rebecca IV, 1001
Morrow, A. C. I, 662
Morrow, Adelia V, 461
Morrow, Albert V, 461
Morrow, Alice V, 307
Morrow, Andrew I, 361
Morrow, Andrew V, 103
Morrow, Andrew V, 756
Morrow, Bessie M. I, 338
Morrow, Celia V, 636
Morrow, Celia V, 699
Morrow, Charles W. V, 423
Morrow, Charlie W. V, 423
Morrow, Clarence O. V, 307
Morrow, Delia V, 461
Morrow, Elizabeth I, 411
Morrow, Fannie V, 636
Morrow, Florence V, 423
Morrow, Hannah I, 362
Morrow, Hannah I, 407
Morrow, Hannah I, 411
Morrow, Hannah V, 103
Morrow, Hannah V, 756
Morrow, Harry Franklin V, 519
Morrow, Helen V, 423
Morrow, Inas V, 461
Morrow, Inez V, 423
Morrow, J. D. V, 307
Morrow, John I, 361
Morrow, John I, 411
Morrow, John I, 420
Morrow, John I, 595
Morrow, John V, 103
Morrow, John V, 756
Morrow, Joseph I, 361
Morrow, Joseph V, 103

Morrow, Joseph V, 756
Morrow, Lavina K. V, 519
Morrow, Lee V, 461
Morrow, Letta V, 423
Morrow, Letta Lee V, 307
Morrow, Lettie S. V, 423
Morrow, Lois Marie V, 461
Morrow, Lucile V, 519
Morrow, Lucinda I, 595
Morrow, Lucinda I, 597
Morrow, Lucinda IV, 473
Morrow, Margaret I, 685
Morrow, Martha L. V, 588
Morrow, Mary I, 361
Morrow, Mary I, 362
Morrow, Mary I, 411
Morrow, Mary I, 420
Morrow, Mary V, 103
Morrow, Mary V, 756
Morrow, Mary E. V, 423
Morrow, Mary Elizabeth V, 423
Morrow, Meriam M. I, 685
Morrow, Miriam I, 662
Morrow, Miriam M. I, 685
Morrow, Rachel I, 361
Morrow, Rachel I, 411
Morrow, Rhoda B. I, 593
Morrow, Rhoda B. I, 595
Morrow, Rose V, 699
Morrow, Ruth I, 362
Morrow, Ruth V, 103
Morrow, Ruth V, 756
Morrow, Samuel C. V, 588
Morrow, Sarah I, 402
Morrow, Sarah I, 411
Morrow, Susan B. V, 423
Morrow, Susan L. V, 87
Morrow, Susan L. V, 103
Morrow, Susan L. V, 588
Morrow, Susanna I, 595
Morrow, Vernon V, 461
Morrow, Warren V, 423
Morrow, Wm. I, 411
Morrs, Helena E. II, 901
Morrs, Julia II, 901
Morrs, Thos. L. II, 901
Morse, Abigail II, 604
Morse, Abigail V, 267
Morse, Arthur H. III, 148
Morse, Arthur H. III, 234
Morse, Augusta III, 234
Morse, Charles F. III, 234
Morse, Elizabeth II, 244
Morse, Ellen III, 234
Morse, Emma IV, 648
Morse, Emma Jane IV, 744
Morse, Ephraim II, 244
Morse, Esther II, 244
Morse, Esther F. III, 148
Morse, Esther F. III, 234
Morse, Fred Callender III, 254
Morse, Gershom Perdue V, 267
Morse, Glennie Lucile IV, 1330
Morse, H. Kate III, 234
Morse, Hannah II, 244
Morse, Harold Edwin IV, 1330
Morse, Helena Emma II, 809
Morse, Irene III, 254
Morse, Jacob Wilcot II, 244
Morse, James Herbert III, 133
Morse, James Herbert III, 234
Morse, Jane IV, 648
Morse, Kenneth IV, 648
Morse, Kenneth IV, 744
Morse, Lucinda III, 234
Morse, Lucy III, 133
Morse, Lucy III, 234
Morse, Milly VI, 975
Morse, Perry IV, 648
Morse, Raymond III, 234
Morse, Rilla IV, 1174
Morse, Robert Wayne IV, 1330
Morse, Sarah W. III, 234
Morse, Waldo J. III, 234
Morse, Wm. VI, 984
Morse, Wm. H. IV, 648
Morse, Wm. H. Perry IV, 744
Morsell, Rachel VI, 546
Morss, Helena E. II, 897
Morss, Julia II, 897
Morss, Thos. L. II, 897
Morten, Albert F. IV, 1287
Morten, Ann IV, 76
Morten, Samuel IV, 71
Morten, Susanna IV, 103
Mortimer, Robert V, 1011
Morton, Abigail II, 398
Morton, Abigail II, 604
Morton, Abigail II, 679
Morton, Agnes E. V, 922
Morton, Albert F. IV, 1287
Morton, Alexander V, 956
Morton, Allie Arnett I, 622
Morton, Alvada V, 684
Morton, Alvada V, 699
Morton, Ann II, 604
Morton, Ann IV, 51
Morton, Ann IV, 103
Morton, Ann IV, 154
Morton, Ann IV, 254
Morton, Anna II, 289
Morton, Anna II, 604
Morton, Anna II, 640
Morton, Anna VI, 842
Morton, Anna M. IV, 834
Morton, Anna M. IV, 842
Morton, Annie I, 946
Morton, Arthur Winston I, 622
Morton, Benjamin IV, 51
Morton, Benjamin IV, 154
Morton, Calvin Wister V, 699
Morton, Cassander IV, 471
Morton, Cassander IV, 488
Morton, Cassandra IV, 488
Morton, Cassandra IV, 542
Morton, Clarence IV, 1218
Morton, Clorinda Bell V, 699
Morton, Edith IV, 51
Morton, Edith IV, 103
Morton, Elenora V, 922
Morton, Elisabeth I, 622
Morton, Elizabeth I, 359
Morton, Elizabeth IV, 51
Morton, Ella M. V, 699
Morton, Emma W. II, 901
Morton, Esther II, 505
Morton, Esther II, 604
Morton, Esther II, 638
Morton, Everett Perry V, 699
Morton, Florence IV, 1218
Morton, Frank I, 946
Morton, Hannah II, 604
Morton, Hannah II, 619
Morton, Hannah IV, 32
Morton, Hannah IV, 51
Morton, Hannah IV, 103
Morton, Hannah IV, 117
Morton, Hannah IV, 154
Morton, Hannah IV, 488
Morton, Hannah IV, 542
Morton, Hannah J. V, 885
Morton, Hannah J. V, 887
Morton, Hannah, Sr. IV, 103
Morton, Hannah, Sr. IV, 110
Morton, Ishmael Earl V, 699
Morton, James II, 398
Morton, James II, 505
Morton, James II, 580
Morton, James II, 604
Morton, James M. V, 699
Morton, James Pemberton II, 604
Morton, Jane M. II, 604
Morton, Jane M. II, 640
Morton, Jemima II, 676
Morton, Joanna V, 956
Morton, John II, 398
Morton, John II, 505
Morton, John II, 604
Morton, John II, 679
Morton, John IV, 51
Morton, John IV, 154
Morton, John IV, 488
Morton, John V, 956
Morton, John R. IV, 254
Morton, Josiah VI, 842
Morton, Josiah VI, 903
Morton, Josiah VI, 907
Morton, Josiah VI, 919
Morton, Josiah VI, 1009
Morton, Josiah VI, 1011
Morton, Josiah VI, 1016
Morton, Josiah VI, 1019
Morton, Josiah VI, 1021
Morton, Lida IV, 254
Morton, Lola B. I, 338
Morton, Lucinda IV, 1218
Morton, M V, 956
Morton, M??? V, 956
Morton, Manervy Jane V, 956
Morton, Maria V, 699
Morton, Martha V, 956
Morton, Mary I, 359
Morton, Mary I, 595
Morton, Mary II, 179
Morton, Mary II, 604
Morton, Mary IV, 51
Morton, Mary IV, 103
Morton, Mary IV, 117
Morton, Mary IV, 154
Morton, Mary IV, 488
Morton, Myrtle IV, 1041
Morton, Nancy VI, 842
Morton, Nancy VI, 937
Morton, Phebe I, 946
Morton, Phebe II, 398
Morton, Phebe II, 580
Morton, Phebe II, 604
Morton, Phebe II, 619
Morton, Phebe IV, 51
Morton, Phebe IV, 103
Morton, Phebe Pemberton II, 604
Morton, R. R. IV, 1218
Morton, Rachel W. II, 179
Morton, Rebecca IV, 51
Morton, Rebecca IV, 103
Morton, Rebecca IV, 254
Morton, Rebecca IV, 1155
Morton, Rebecca IV, 1174
Morton, Richard VI, 842
Morton, Robert II, 604
Morton, Robert II, 619
Morton, Rufus I, 622
Morton, Sally VI, 842
Morton, Samuel I, 359
Morton, Samuel II, 398
Morton, Samuel II, 580
Morton, Samuel II, 604
Morton, Samuel II, 619
Morton, Samuel IV, 32
Morton, Samuel IV, 51
Morton, Samuel IV, 117
Morton, Samuel G. II, 604
Morton, Samuel G. II, 640
Morton, Samuel, Jr. II, 604
Morton, Sarah I, 595
Morton, Sarah II, 398
Morton, Sarah IV, 32
Morton, Sarah IV, 51
Morton, Sarah A. I, 946
Morton, Sarah Ann I, 895
Morton, Sarah Jane IV, 411
Morton, Sarah Jane IV, 423
Morton, Susanna IV, 51
Morton, Susanna IV, 103
Morton, Thomas II, 604
Morton, Thomas IV, 51
Morton, Thomas IV, 103
Morton, Thomas D. I, 895
Morton, Uriah II, 179
Morton, William II, 398
Morton, William IV, 51
Morton, William IV, 103
Morton, William VI, 842
Mory, Daniel B. V, 351
Mory, Daniel B. V, 699
Mory, Lucy Ann IV, 1239
Mory, Mary V, 699
Mory, Sarah Jane V, 699
Mory, Verna V, 699
Mosby, Agnes VI, 158
Mosby, Agnes VI, 159
Mosby, Agnes VI, 199
Mosby, Agness VI, 159
Mosby, Benjamin VI, 842
Mosby, Catharine E. VI, 970
Mosby, Curles VI, 200
Mosby, Edward VI, 149
Mosby, Edward VI, 158
Mosby, Edward VI, 199
Mosby, Edward VI, 209
Mosby, Edward VI, 216
Mosby, Edward VI, 217
Mosby, Edwd VI, 148
Mosby, Edwd VI, 199
Mosby, Elizabeth VI, 966
Mosby, Henry VI, 199
Mosby, John VI, 205
Mosby, John G. VI, 199
Mosby, Jos VI, 199
Mosby, Margaret Emily VI, 966
Mosby, Mary II, 604
Mosby, Mary II, 623
Mosby, Mary VI, 199
Mosby, Mary VI, 208
Mosby, Mary VI, 216
Mosby, Mary VI, 217
Mosby, Mildred A. VI, 1007
Mosby, Mildred G. VI, 842
Mosby, Nancy VI, 966
Mosby, P. W. VI, 971
Mosby, P. W. VI, 1007
Mosby, Poindexter W. VI, 966
Mosby, Powhatan VI, 966
Mosby, Salley VI, 1009
Mosby, Sally VI, 1009
Mosby, Sarah VI, 148
Mosby, Sarah VI, 199
Mosby, Susanna VI, 947
Mosby, Ursley VI, 282
Mose, Isaac II, 88
Moseby, Elizabeth H. VI, 825
Moseby, Elizabeth Jane VI, 988
Moseby, Poindexter W. VI, 988
Moseby, Salley VI, 1009
Moseby, Sally VI, 1009
Moseley, Arthur VI, 874
Moseley, Arthur VI, 882
Moseley, Arthur VI, 966
Moseley, Belinda R. VI, 842
Moseley, Catharine III, 234
Moseley, Catharine VI, 966
Moseley, Daniel VI, 966
Moseley, Daniel N. VI, 1010
Moseley, Edward VI, 862
Moseley, Edward Mozley VI, 979
Moseley, Eleanor J. VI, 950
Moseley, Elizabeth VI, 889
Moseley, Elizabeth VI, 966
Moseley, Elizabeth W. VI, 950
Moseley, Geo. C. VI, 889
Moseley, Geo. C. VI, 950
Moseley, Geo. C. VI, 974
Moseley, George C. VI, 966
Moseley, James VI, 425
Moseley, James VI, 842
Moseley, John VI, 842
Moseley, John VI, 966
Moseley, Joseph VI, 842
Moseley, Keziah VI, 842
Moseley, Martha VI, 889
Moseley, Mary A. VI, 842
Moseley, Mary Ann VI, 797
Moseley, Mary D. VI, 966
Moseley, Mary M. VI, 889
Moseley, Nancy VI, 966
Moseley, Pamelia VI, 935
Moseley, Pamelia VI, 966
Moseley, Patty VI, 842
Moseley, Sarah VI, 979
Moseley, William VI, 966
Mosely, Arthur VI, 975
Moser, Caleb VI, 425
Moses, Eliza S. W. VI, 807
Moses, Joseph M. VI, 846
Moses, Mary E. VI, 842
Moses, Nathan U. IV, 1174
Moses, Richard P. III, 234
Moses, William H. VI, 842
Mosgrove, Margaretta V, 588
Mosgrove, Watson R. V, 588
Mosher, ??? IV, 1141
Mosher, Abbie III, 480
Mosher, Abbie III, 491
Mosher, Abial T. IV, 1374
Mosher, Abial T., Jr. IV, 1374
Mosher, Abial, Jr. IV, 1374
Mosher, Abraham E. III, 234
Mosher, Adaline IV, 1218
Mosher, Adelaide III, 235
Mosher, Albert V, 103
Mosher, Alice V, 103
Mosher, Allen IV, 254
Mosher, Allen IV, 1175
Mosher, Allen IV, 1176
Mosher, Alvate III, 480
Mosher, Alvate III, 491
Mosher, Alvate??? III, 480
Mosher, Alvate??? III, 491
Mosher, Andrew C. II, 885
Mosher, Andrew C. II, 901
Mosher, Ann C. III, 232
Mosher, Asa IV, 1174
Mosher, Asa IV, 1175
Mosher, Asa IV, 1176
Mosher, Asa IV, 1195
Mosher, Asa V, 103
Mosher, Asa V, 956
Mosher, Asa Obediah IV, 1175
Mosher, Asa Obediah V, 956
Mosher, Asa W. IV, 1175
Mosher, Asa, Jr. IV, 1150
Mosher, Asa, Jr. IV, 1175
Mosher, Avis L. III, 234
Mosher, Bethia IV, 1174
Mosher, Bethiah IV, 1159
Mosher, Bethiah IV, 1175
Mosher, Bethiah IV, 1195
Mosher, Bethiah V, 57
Mosher, Beulah IV, 1175
Mosher, Beulah IV, 1176
Mosher, Beulah IV, 1179
Mosher, Beulah V, 103
Mosher, Calista IV, 1175
Mosher, Calista V, 58
Mosher, Calista V, 103
Mosher, Cassander IV, 1175
Mosher, Cassander IV, 1176
Mosher, Charity II, 808
Mosher, Chas. F. IV, 1258
Mosher, Chester IV, 1218
Mosher, Claude Nathan IV, 879
Mosher, Comport IV, 1175
Mosher, Cynthia IV, 1374
Mosher, Cynthia W. IV, 1175
Mosher, Daniel IV, 254
Mosher, Daniel IV, 1149
Mosher, Daniel IV, 1175
Mosher, Daniel IV, 1176
Mosher, David IV, 254
Mosher, David IV, 1176
Mosher, David W. IV, 1175
Mosher, Deborah IV, 1201
Mosher, Deborah IV, 1218
Mosher, Dennis IV, 1175
Mosher, Edgar II, 885
Mosher, Edgar II, 901
Mosher, Edgar C. II, 901
Mosher, Edith IV, 1159
Mosher, Edith IV, 1175
Mosher, Edith IV, 1186
Mosher, Edith IV, 1218
Mosher, Edith Ann IV, 1175
Mosher, Edwin III, 235
Mosher, Elias H. IV, 1374
Mosher, Elijah IV, 1175
Mosher, Eliza III, 234
Mosher, Eliza Ann IV, 1374
Mosher, Elizabeth IV, 1175
Mosher, Elizabeth IV, 1176
Mosher, Elizabeth IV, 1368
Mosher, Elizabeth IV, 1374
Mosher, Elizabeth N. II, 885
Mosher, Elizabeth N. II, 901
Mosher, Elma IV, 1175
Mosher, Elsie IV, 879
Mosher, Elsie Roane IV, 879
Mosher, Elsy Bethiah IV, 1175
Mosher, Elsy Bethiah IV, 1176
Mosher, Emma II, 901
Mosher, Emma C. II, 885
Mosher, Emma C. II, 901
Mosher, Esther IV, 1175
Mosher, Esther IV, 1195
Mosher, Esther Ann IV, 1175
Mosher, Esther Ann IV, 1176
Mosher, Eunice IV, 1175
Mosher, Eunice V, 30
Mosher, Eunice V, 103
Mosher, Eunice V, 956
Mosher, Ezra C. III, 232
Mosher, Flora IV, 1218
Mosher, Frances Cornelia II, 88
Mosher, Frances Cornelia II, 90
Mosher, Gershom IV, 254
Mosher, Gershon IV, 1175
Mosher, Gideon IV, 1175
Mosher, Gideon IV, 1176
Mosher, Gideon IV, 1218
Mosher, Guli Elma IV, 1175
Mosher, Guli Elma IV, 1176
Mosher, Gulielma IV, 254
Mosher, H. H. IV, 1218
Mosher, Hannah III, 232
Mosher, Hannah IV, 1144
Mosher, Hannah IV, 1175
Mosher, Hannah B. IV, 1176
Mosher, Hannah B. IV, 1202
Mosher, Hannah B. IV, 1218
Mosher, Harriet IV, 1175
Mosher, Harriet IV, 1176
Mosher, Henry IV, 1175
Mosher, Henry IV, 1176
Mosher, Henry H. III, 235
Mosher, Henry H. IV, 1218
Mosher, Isaac IV, 1374
Mosher, Isaac H. IV, 1368
Mosher, Isaac H. IV, 1374
Mosher, Israel IV, 1175
Mosher, J. Raymond IV, 1218
Mosher, James IV, 1218
Mosher, John IV, 1175
Mosher, John IV, 1176
Mosher, John V, 956
Mosher, John I. III, 232
Mosher, Jonathan IV, 1175
Mosher, Jonathan IV, 1218
Mosher, Jonathan B. IV, 1176
Mosher, Jonathan B. V, 103
Mosher, Jonathan R. IV, 1374
Mosher, Joseph III, 235
Mosher, Joseph IV, 254
Mosher, Joseph IV, 1175
Mosher, Joseph IV, 1176
Mosher, Joseph IV, 1179
Mosher, Julia Ann III, 235
Mosher, Lemuel IV, 1175
Mosher, Lemuel Obedia IV, 1176
Mosher, Lemuel Obediah IV, 1175
Mosher, Loretta M. IV, 1374
Mosher, Lucy IV, 1357
Mosher, Lucy IV, 1374
Mosher, Lucy Ellen IV, 1374
Mosher, Lulu IV, 1218
Mosher, Mable A. IV, 1206

her, Mable A. IV, 1218
her, Mae Casey IV, 1218
her, Manford IV, 1175
her, Manford IV, 1176
her, Maria Ann III, 232
her, Marie IV, 1218
her, Mary IV, 1155
her, Mary IV, 1158
her, Mary IV, 1175
her, Mary IV, 1176
her, Mary IV, 1207
her, Mary IV, 1218
her, Mary IV, 1258
her, Mary V, 103
her, Mary Ann IV, 1175
her, Mary Ann V, 956
her, Mary Evelyn IV, 1218
her, Mary F. IV, 1175
her, Mary M. IV, 1218
her, Mary S. IV, 1175
her, Mary S. IV, 1176
her, Mary, Jr. IV, 1175
her, Minnie IV, 1218
her, Minnie D. IV, 1218
her, Minnie Ong IV, 1258
her, Moses IV, 1374
her, Nancy IV, 1149
her, Nancy IV, 1175
her, Nathan IV, 1176
her, Nathan N. IV, 1175
her, Nathan N. IV, 1218
her, Nelson III, 235
her, Obediah IV, 1175
her, Olive III, 235
her, Olive Ann III, 235
her, Olive J. IV, 1218
her, Oscar III, 235
her, Paulina IV, 1176
her, Pauline IV, 1175
her, Peace IV, 1174
her, Peace IV, 1175
her, Peace IV, 1176
her, Peace IV, 1197
her, Pearl IV, 1175
her, Peleg IV, 1150
her, Peleg IV, 1175
her, Peleg, Jr. IV, 1175
her, Perlina IV, 1175
her, Phebe IV, 1175
her, Phebe IV, 1186
her, Phebe A. IV, 1218
her, Rachel IV, 1173
her, Rachel IV, 1175
her, Rachel IV, 1176
sher, Ralph Harlan IV, 1218
sher, Ralph N. IV, 1218
sher, Robert IV, 879
sher, Robert IV, 1159
sher, Robert IV, 1175
sher, Robert IV, 1186
sher, Robert Allen IV, 1218
sher, Robert E. IV, 1218
sher, Robert F. IV, 1218
sher, Rosellen IV, 1218
sher, Ruth IV, 254
sher, Ruth IV, 1175
sher, Ruth IV, 1176
sher, Ruth IV, 1186
sher, Ruth IV, 1189
sher, Ruth IV, 1194
sher, Ruth IV, 1374
sher, Ruth Ann IV, 1374
sher, Samuel IV, 254
sher, Samuel J. IV, 1218
sher, Sarah IV, 1175
sher, Sarah IV, 1357
sher, Sarah IV, 1374
sher, Sarah V, 103
sher, Sarah V, 956
sher, Sarah A. V, 956
sher, Sarah Angelina IV, 1175
sher, Sarah P. IV, 1150
osher, Sarah P. IV, 1175
sher, Sarah T. IV, 1175
osher, Scolista V, 956
sher, Seneca IV, 1175
osher, Seneca IV, 1176
osher, Seth III, 235
osher, Shirley IV, 1218
osher, Simeon G. III, 232
osher, Simmons III, 232
osher, Simmons G. III, 232
osher, Simmons, Jr. III, 232
osher, Smith III, 235
osher, Smith Ruth IV, 1175
osher, Stephen IV, 1158
osher, Stephen IV, 1175
osher, Stephen IV, 1176
osher, Stephen IV, 1186
osher, Stephen IV, 1218
osher, Stephen V, 956
Mosher, Stephen, Jr. IV, 1175
Mosher, Susan C. IV, 1175
Mosher, Susanna B. V, 956
Mosher, Susanna C. IV, 1150
Mosher, Susanna C. IV, 1175
Mosher, Susannah B. IV, 1175
Mosher, Susannah C. IV, 1175
Mosher, Susannah C. V, 956
Mosher, Thomas IV, 1357
Mosher, Thomas IV, 1374
Mosher, Thomas R. IV, 1374
Mosher, Virgil IV, 1218
Moshier, Isaac IV, 1374
Moshier, Lucy IV, 1374
Moshier, Sarah IV, 1374
Moshier, Thomas IV, 1374
Moshure, ??? V, 1011
Mosier, ??? V, 1011
Mosier, Albert V, 1011
Mosier, Daisy V, 699
Mosier, Daisy T. V, 699
Mosier, Ellen V, 1011
Mosier, Emily V, 1011
Mosier, Etta V, 1011
Mosier, Freddie V, 1011
Mosier, Frederick V, 1011
Mosier, George W. V, 1011
Mosier, Granville V, 699
Mosier, Harriet V, 699
Mosier, Henry V, 1011
Mosier, James V, 588
Mosier, Jonathan V, 57
Mosier, Laura E. V, 1011
Mosier, Louisa V, 1011
Mosier, Mary IV, 1258
Mosier, Mary V, 57
Mosier, Rachel V, 1011
Mosier, Samuel V, 1011
Mosier, Sarah V, 1011
Mosier, Sarah A. V, 954
Mosier, Sarah A. V, 956
Mosier, Susanna B. V, 950
Mosier, Susanna B. V, 956
Mosier, Viola V, 1011
Mosley, Arther, Jr. VI, 200
Mosley, Arther, Jr. VI, 204
Mosley, Joseph VI, 842
Mosley, Judith A. J. VI, 862
Mosley, Patty VI, 842
Mosley, Robert B. VI, 862
Mosley, Thomas VI, 862
Mosley, Virginia Ann VI, 493
Mosman, Frances Doan V, 700
Moss, Abigail II, 604
Moss, Abraham II, 35
Moss, Abraham II, 86
Moss, Abraham II, 88
Moss, Abraham II, 98
Moss, Abraham II, 398
Moss, Abraham II, 604
Moss, Alexander VI, 842
Moss, Andrew V, 194
Moss, Ann II, 88
Moss, Ann II, 98
Moss, Ann VI, 961
Moss, Celia VI, 966
Moss, Charity III, 235
Moss, Daniel VI, 843
Moss, Dell I, 853
Moss, Della E. I, 616
Moss, Dolly VI, 992
Moss, Drury VI, 842
Moss, Drury VI, 966
Moss, Edw. VI, 998
Moss, Edward VI, 966
Moss, Eliza III, 57
Moss, Eliza III, 235
Moss, Eliza VI, 808
Moss, Elizabeth II, 244
Moss, Elizabeth V, 194
Moss, Elizabeth VI, 815
Moss, Elizabeth VI, 842
Moss, Ephraim II, 244
Moss, Esther II, 244
Moss, Fanny VI, 842
Moss, Florence Rush I, 946
Moss, Frances V, 922
Moss, Frances Matilda V, 103
Moss, Francis VI, 843
Moss, Hannah II, 35
Moss, Hannah II, 244
Moss, Hannah II, 398
Moss, Hannah VI, 998
Moss, Harrison V, 194
Moss, Harry VI, 842
Moss, Henry II, 398
Moss, Henry VI, 901
Moss, Henry VI, 948
Moss, Hope II, 88
Moss, Hope II, 98
Moss, Isaac II, 35
Moss, Isaac II, 88
Moss, Isaac II, 398
Moss, Isaac II, 604
Moss, Isaac III, 235
Moss, Israel III, 235
Moss, Jacob L. III, 235
Moss, Jacob Wilcot II, 244
Moss, James III, 235
Moss, Jane III, 235
Moss, John III, 57
Moss, John III, 235
Moss, Jonathan VI, 815
Moss, Jonathan VI, 820
Moss, Joseph II, 604
Moss, Julia V, 194
Moss, Keziah VI, 843
Moss, Lewis V, 194
Moss, Littleberry VI, 816
Moss, Littleberry VI, 842
Moss, Littleberry VI, 843
Moss, Mamaroneck III, 235
Moss, Manerva VI, 820
Moss, Margaret IV, 648
Moss, Martha VI, 966
Moss, Martha A. VI, 853
Moss, Mary II, 604
Moss, Mary VI, 200
Moss, Mary Ann Amanda VI, 901
Moss, Mary J. V, 267
Moss, Memmry VI, 821
Moss, Milly VI, 842
Moss, Ned VI, 966
Moss, Nelley VI, 843
Moss, Peter VI, 842
Moss, Polly VI, 843
Moss, Rachel VI, 966
Moss, Rachel VI, 998
Moss, Rebecca II, 244
Moss, Rebecca II, 604
Moss, Rebecca VI, 843
Moss, Rebeckah II, 35
Moss, Rebeckah II, 56
Moss, Rebeckah II, 88
Moss, Rebeckah II, 90
Moss, Rebeckah II, 244
Moss, Rebekah II, 86
Moss, Rebekah II, 88
Moss, Rebekah II, 98
Moss, Rebekah II, 604
Moss, Richard II, 35
Moss, Richard II, 88
Moss, Richard II, 98
Moss, Richard VI, 842
Moss, Richard VI, 922
Moss, Richard VI, 998
Moss, Sally VI, 966
Moss, Samuel VI, 843
Moss, Sarah II, 1017
Moss, Sarah V, 899
Moss, Sarah V, 922
Moss, Sarah VI, 842
Moss, Sarah Eliza III, 57
Moss, Sarah Eliza III, 235
Moss, Solomon III, 235
Moss, Thomas II, 35
Moss, Thomas VI, 808
Moss, Thomas VI, 815
Moss, Thomas VI, 816
Moss, Thomas VI, 992
Moss, Thomas Daniel VI, 853
Moss, William VI, 843
Moss, William VI, 966
Moss, William C. III, 235
Moss, Winney VI, 842
Mossbarger, Nellie V, 700
Mossbarger, Nettie V, 700
Mossbarger, Nettie V, 713
Mossbarger, Thomas M. V, 700
Mossbarger, Thos. M. V, 713
Mossberger, Nellie V, 700
Mossburgh, Susanna IV, 488
Mossburgh, Susannah IV, 423
Mossin, Peter IV, 1330
Mostez, Mary F. IV, 254
Mosure, Albert V, 1011
Mosure, Frederick V, 1011
Mosure, George W. V, 1011
Mosure, Henry V, 1011
Mosure, Rachel V, 1011
Mosure, Samuel V, 1011
Mote, Aann M. V, 758
Mote, Aaron V, 103
Mote, Aaron V, 756
Mote, Aaron V, 757
Mote, Aaron V, 758
Mote, Albert Louis V, 757
Mote, Alice Harvey V, 758
Mote, Alvah E. V, 758
Mote, Alvale Eugene V, 757
Mote, Ann I, 1049
Mote, Ann V, 103
Mote, Ann V, 756
Mote, Anna V, 750
Mote, Anna V, 756
Mote, Anna V, 758
Mote, Anna E. V, 758
Mote, Anna E. V, 772
Mote, Anna Maria V, 757
Mote, Anna S. V, 104
Mote, Anna S. V, 756
Mote, Annie M. V, 758
Mote, Anson V, 757
Mote, Anson V, 758
Mote, Arena V, 89
Mote, Arena E. V, 89
Mote, Arena E. V, 103
Mote, Arena E. V, 757
Mote, Arena E. V, 774
Mote, Arriadne V, 757
Mote, Arrie L. V, 741
Mote, Asa V, 744
Mote, Asa V, 756
Mote, Asa V, 758
Mote, Barbara V, 726
Mote, Barbara V, 756
Mote, Barbara V, 758
Mote, Bertie E. V, 104
Mote, C. V, 741
Mote, Carrie Albertine V, 758
Mote, Celeste Susan V, 74
Mote, Celestia Susan V, 757
Mote, Charity V, 748
Mote, Charity V, 756
Mote, Charity V, 774
Mote, Charity J. V, 757
Mote, Clara E. V, 104
Mote, Clarence Leslie V, 104
Mote, Cordelia Bayes V, 757
Mote, Daniel V, 756
Mote, Daniel V, 758
Mote, Daniel H. V, 757
Mote, David I, 411
Mote, David I, 1015
Mote, David I, 1035
Mote, David I, 1041
Mote, David I, 1049
Mote, David V, 103
Mote, David V, 726
Mote, David V, 747
Mote, David V, 754
Mote, David V, 756
Mote, David V, 757
Mote, David Noah V, 818
Mote, David, Jr. I, 1015
Mote, David, Jr. V, 756
Mote, David, Jr. V, 757
Mote, David, Jr. V, 758
Mote, Deborah V, 748
Mote, Deborah V, 757
Mote, Dora V, 588
Mote, Dorcas I, 411
Mote, Dorcas V, 103
Mote, Dorcas V, 747
Mote, Dorcas V, 756
Mote, Dorcas V, 757
Mote, Dorkis V, 103
Mote, Dorothy I, 411
Mote, Dr. John V, 757
Mote, Edwin E. V, 758
Mote, Edwin Enos V, 757
Mote, Edwin L. V, 103
Mote, Edwin M. V, 103
Mote, Elijah V, 756
Mote, Elijah V, 758
Mote, Elisha J. V, 757
Mote, Elisha J. V, 758
Mote, Elizabeth V, 103
Mote, Elizabeth V, 732
Mote, Elizabeth V, 756
Mote, Elizabeth V, 757
Mote, Elizabeth V, 758
Mote, Elizabeth C. V, 729
Mote, Elizabeth C. V, 757
Mote, Emily V, 758
Mote, Emma V, 104
Mote, Emma V. V, 104
Mote, Enoch V, 756
Mote, Enos V, 756
Mote, Enos V, 757
Mote, Enos V, 758
Mote, Enos V, 763
Mote, Ethan A. V, 757
Mote, Ethan A. V, 758
Mote, Ezekel V, 818
Mote, Ezekiel V, 818
Mote, George H. V, 104
Mote, Grace V, 758
Mote, Grace V, 818
Mote, Hannah V, 756
Mote, Hannah V, 757
Mote, Hannah L. V, 740
Mote, Hannah L. V, 758
Mote, Harvey V, 758
Mote, Henry D. V, 103
Mote, Henry Davis V, 103
Mote, Isaiah V, 103
Mote, Isaiah V, 756
Mote, Jane V, 757
Mote, Jeremiah I, 1049
Mote, Jeremiah V, 103
Mote, Jeremiah V, 723
Mote, Jeremiah V, 756
Mote, Jeremiah V, 757
Mote, Jesse V, 758
Mote, Jesse J. V, 758
Mote, Jesse Jordan V, 756
Mote, Jessie E. V, 104
Mote, Jodie E. V, 104
Mote, John I, 1049
Mote, John V, 103
Mote, John V, 729
Mote, John V, 732
Mote, John V, 746
Mote, John V, 756
Mote, John V, 757
Mote, John V, 818
Mote, John Franklin V, 757
Mote, John Franklin V, 758
Mote, John J. V, 757
Mote, John W. V, 756
Mote, John W. V, 758
Mote, John Webster V, 756
Mote, John, Jr. V, 757
Mote, John, Jr. V, 766
Mote, Jonathan I, 1049
Mote, Jonathan V, 74
Mote, Jonathan V, 103
Mote, Jonathan V, 723
Mote, Jonathan V, 756
Mote, Jonathan, Jr. V, 757
Mote, Jonathan, Sr. V, 757
Mote, Jonithan V, 757
Mote, Jonothan V, 103
Mote, Joseph V, 519
Mote, Joseph V, 522
Mote, Joseph V, 756
Mote, Joseph V, 757
Mote, Joseph V, 758
Mote, Joseph V, 759
Mote, Kezia V, 744
Mote, Keziah V, 756
Mote, Keziah V, 758
Mote, Kirk V, 104
Mote, Kirk V, 758
Mote, Kirk L. V, 103
Mote, Kirk L. V, 104
Mote, Kirk Linus V, 67
Mote, Kirk Linus V, 103
Mote, Kirk Linus V, 757
Mote, Kirke V, 758
Mote, L. S. V, 741
Mote, L. Smith V, 774
Mote, Ledru Rollin V, 757
Mote, Linas V, 740
Mote, Linas V, 758
Mote, Linnaeus V, 758
Mote, Linneous V, 758
Mote, Linnias V, 757
Mote, Linus V, 756
Mote, Linus V, 757
Mote, Lottie V, 757
Mote, Lottie V, 758
Mote, Lottie B. V, 104
Mote, Lottie B. V, 758
Mote, Louis Albert V, 758
Mote, Louis Albert V, 772
Mote, Louis K. V, 758
Mote, Louis Kossuth V, 757
Mote, Louis Kossuth V, 758
Mote, Luke V, 757
Mote, Luke S. V, 748
Mote, Luke Smith V, 756
Mote, Luke Smith V, 757
Mote, Lydia V, 757
Mote, Lydia Ann V, 67
Mote, Lydia Chloria V, 757
Mote, Lydia Chloris V, 758
Mote, M. B. V, 758
Mote, Marcus V, 103
Mote, Marcus V, 756
Mote, Marcus V, 757
Mote, Marcus V, 758
Mote, Marcus Benson V, 757
Mote, Margaret V, 758
Mote, Margaret V, 818
Mote, Margaret L. V, 756
Mote, Margaret S. V, 744
Mote, Margaret S. V, 757
Mote, Martha V, 519
Mote, Martha V, 522
Mote, Martha Ann V, 757
Mote, Martha Ann V, 758
Mote, Martha Ann V, 763

Mote, Martha J. V, 758
Mote, Martha J. V, 771
Mote, Martha P. V, 519
Mote, Martha P. V, 757
Mote, Martha P. V, 758
Mote, Mary I, 1049
Mote, Mary V, 103
Mote, Mary V, 519
Mote, Mary V, 723
Mote, Mary V, 726
Mote, Mary V, 733
Mote, Mary V, 747
Mote, Mary V, 756
Mote, Mary V, 757
Mote, Mary V, 758
Mote, Mary V, 813
Mote, Mary Ann V, 756
Mote, Mary Ann V, 757
Mote, Mary E. V, 758
Mote, Mary Elizabeth V, 757
Mote, Mary Elizabeth V, 758
Mote, Mary Ellen V, 757
Mote, Mary J. V, 758
Mote, Mary Melona V, 757
Mote, Mary Olivia V, 757
Mote, Matilda V, 756
Mote, Minnie V, 104
Mote, Miriam V, 754
Mote, Miriam V, 756
Mote, Miriam V, 757
Mote, Miriam V, 758
Mote, Nancy V, 756
Mote, Nancy V, 758
Mote, Nancy V, 771
Mote, Nancy V. V, 756
Mote, Nathan V, 756
Mote, Neva V, 758
Mote, Omar V, 758
Mote, Orrin L. V, 757
Mote, Orrin S. V, 758
Mote, Orrin S. V, 771
Mote, Orris S. V, 758
Mote, Phebe L. V, 756
Mote, Phebe S. V, 758
Mote, Rachel I, 1049
Mote, Rachel V, 103
Mote, Rachel V, 732
Mote, Rachel V, 737
Mote, Rachel V, 746
Mote, Rachel V, 749
Mote, Rachel V, 756
Mote, Rachel V, 757
Mote, Rachel V, 758
Mote, Rachel V, 818
Mote, Rachel Caroline V, 756
Mote, Rachel, Jr. V, 758
Mote, Raymond V, 758
Mote, Rebecca V, 746
Mote, Rebecca V, 756
Mote, Rebecca V, 758
Mote, Rebecca H. V, 741
Mote, Rebecca H. V, 758
Mote, Rhoda V, 103
Mote, Rhoda V, 126
Mote, Rhoda V, 729
Mote, Rhoda V, 756
Mote, Rhoda V, 757
Mote, Rhoda V, 758
Mote, Rhoda V, 766
Mote, Rhoda V, 818
Mote, Rhoda L. V, 103
Mote, Rhoda M. V, 758
Mote, Rhoda Matilda V, 757
Mote, Rhoda Matlda V, 758
Mote, Rhoda T. V, 757
Mote, Roy Dale V, 758
Mote, Sally C. V, 818
Mote, Samuel V, 104
Mote, Samuel Kersey V, 103
Mote, Samuel S. V, 103
Mote, Samuel S. V, 104
Mote, Samuel Steddom V, 103
Mote, Samuel Steddom V, 104
Mote, Samuel Steddom V, 757
Mote, Samuel T. V, 757
Mote, Samuel T. V, 758
Mote, Samuel Teague V, 756
Mote, Sarah V, 103
Mote, Sarah V, 756
Mote, Sarah V, 758
Mote, Sarah Elizabeth V, 758
Mote, Sarah P. V, 756
Mote, Spencer Joyce V, 758
Mote, Susan Margaret V, 756
Mote, Susanna V, 74
Mote, Susanna V, 103
Mote, Susanna Jane V, 103
Mote, Susannah V, 756
Mote, Susannah V, 758
Mote, Susannah J. V, 103
Mote, Thos. Clarkson V, 757
Mote, Thos. Elwood V, 756
Mote, Timothy I, 1049
Mote, Timothy V, 103
Mote, Timothy V, 723
Mote, Timothy V, 756
Mote, Timothy V, 757
Mote, Wd. Rebecca V, 757
Mote, William I, 1035
Mote, William V, 103
Mote, William R. V, 758
Mote, William, Jr. V, 757
Mote, William, Sr. V, 757
Mote, Wm. V, 756
Mote, Wm. Aldin V, 757
Mote, Wm. Oscar V, 757
Mote, Zeno V, 748
Mote, Zeno V, 756
Mote, Zeno V, 757
Motes, Dorcas I, 411
Motesham, Carrie Barley IV, 744
Motley, David VI, 966
Motley, Elizabeth A. VI, 843
Motley, Jno. VI, 966
Motley, Joel VI, 843
Motley, John VI, 966
Motley, John VI, 1020
Motley, Martha VI, 966
Motley, Mary VI, 966
Motley, Susie IV, 1258
Motley, Tacey II, 398
Mott, ??? III, 236
Mott, ??? III, 428
Mott, ??? III, 433
Mott, ??? III, 457
Mott, ??? III, 462
Mott, ??? III, 488
Mott, ??? III, 491
Mott, ??? IV, 1125
Mott, Abigail II, 244
Mott, Abigail II, 263
Mott, Abigail II, 604
Mott, Abigail II, 689
Mott, Abigail III, 235
Mott, Abigail III, 236
Mott, Abigail III, 237
Mott, Abigail III, 321
Mott, Abigail III, 395
Mott, Abigail III, 407
Mott, Abigail III, 427
Mott, Abigail III, 428
Mott, Abigail III, 429
Mott, Abigail III, 487
Mott, Abigail IV, 1049
Mott, Abigail IV, 1070
Mott, Abigail IV, 1127
Mott, Abigail IV, 1136
Mott, Abigail B. IV, 1070
Mott, Abigail B. IV, 1136
Mott, Achsah IV, 1108
Mott, Achsah IV, 1132
Mott, Achsah IV, 1136
Mott, Ada IV, 1330
Mott, Ada M. IV, 1330
Mott, Adam II, 811
Mott, Adam III, 88
Mott, Adam III, 235
Mott, Adam III, 236
Mott, Adam III, 237
Mott, Adam III, 282
Mott, Adam III, 395
Mott, Adam III, 397
Mott, Adam III, 419
Mott, Adam III, 427
Mott, Adam III, 428
Mott, Adam III, 429
Mott, Adam III, 430
Mott, Adam III, 436
Mott, Adam III, 444
Mott, Adam III, 460
Mott, Adam III, 470
Mott, Adam III, 473
Mott, Adam III, 476
Mott, Albert E. III, 235
Mott, Albert Edwin III, 235
Mott, Alfred III, 236
Mott, Alfred A. III, 235
Mott, Alma IV, 254
Mott, Alma S. IV, 254
Mott, Amelia Smith II, 179
Mott, Amelia Smith II, 289
Mott, Amelia Smith II, 297
Mott, Amy III, 428
Mott, Amy III, 429
Mott, Amy III, 430
Mott, Amy III, 446
Mott, Amy III, 466
Mott, Amy III, 472
Mott, Amy IV, 1108
Mott, Amy IV, 1136
Mott, Amy Ann III, 428
Mott, Andrew III, 236
Mott, Andrew V, 922
Mott, Andrew U. III, 235
Mott, Andrew V. III, 491
Mott, Ann II, 244
Mott, Ann II, 256
Mott, Ann II, 979
Mott, Ann II, 988
Mott, Ann II, 1017
Mott, Ann III, 38
Mott, Ann III, 203
Mott, Ann III, 236
Mott, Ann III, 237
Mott, Ann III, 269
Mott, Ann III, 423
Mott, Ann III, 427
Mott, Ann III, 428
Mott, Ann III, 429
Mott, Ann IV, 215
Mott, Ann Eliz. III, 265
Mott, Ann Eliza III, 237
Mott, Ann Elizabeth III, 236
Mott, Ann M. III, 127
Mott, Ann M. III, 235
Mott, Ann M. III, 237
Mott, Ann Maria III, 491
Mott, Anna II, 604
Mott, Anna II, 801
Mott, Anna II, 878
Mott, Anna II, 901
Mott, Anna III, 414
Mott, Anna III, 429
Mott, Anna IV, 254
Mott, Anna B. II, 179
Mott, Anna M. III, 491
Mott, Anna M. IV, 214
Mott, Anna M. IV, 254
Mott, Anna W. III, 417
Mott, Anna W. III, 420
Mott, Anne II, 811
Mott, Anne III, 88
Mott, Anne III, 236
Mott, Anne III, 419
Mott, Anne N. III, 237
Mott, Annetta III, 235
Mott, Annetta H. III, 235
Mott, Annetta H. ??? III, 236
Mott, Arthur III, 236
Mott, Arthur H. IV, 678
Mott, Asher II, 398
Mott, Asher II, 516
Mott, Asher II, 556
Mott, Asher II, 604
Mott, Asher II, 689
Mott, Asher II, 988
Mott, Asher II, 1017
Mott, Asher IV, 374
Mott, Asher IV, 423
Mott, Asher IV, 589
Mott, Asher IV, 1070
Mott, Asher IV, 1108
Mott, Asher IV, 1128
Mott, Asher IV, 1136
Mott, Asher IV, 1137
Mott, Avis III, 236
Mott, Avis B. III, 113
Mott, Avis B. III, 235
Mott, Benj. III, 479
Mott, Benjamin III, 235
Mott, Benjamin III, 428
Mott, Benjamin III, 430
Mott, Benjamin III, 446
Mott, Benjamin III, 491
Mott, Benjamin III, 504
Mott, Bennie H. III, 430
Mott, Berger IV, 1239
Mott, Bernard IV, 1330
Mott, Bernard E. IV, 254
Mott, Bernard E. IV, 1330
Mott, Burger IV, 1176
Mott, Burger IV, 1239
Mott, Caroline III, 236
Mott, Caroline III, 269
Mott, Caroline III, 428
Mott, Caroline III, 449
Mott, Caroline D. III, 237
Mott, Caroline S. III, 236
Mott, Catharine III, 394
Mott, Catharine III, 428
Mott, Catharine III, 429
Mott, Catharine III, 430
Mott, Catharine III, 472
Mott, Catharine A. III, 429
Mott, Catharine T. IV, 1374
Mott, Catherine III, 428
Mott, Charity III, 491
Mott, Charity Ann III, 491
Mott, Charles II, 757
Mott, Charles III, 236
Mott, Charles III, 491
Mott, Charles E. III, 235
Mott, Charles F. III, 103
Mott, Charles F. III, 168
Mott, Charlotte F. III, 236
Mott, Chas. II, 810
Mott, Chas. II, 901
Mott, Chas. A. IV, 1330
Mott, Chas. R. IV, 1330
Mott, Clendenon IV, 1108
Mott, Daniel III, 236
Mott, Daniel III, 428
Mott, Daniel III, 446
Mott, Daniel IV, 423
Mott, Daniel M. IV, 589
Mott, Daniel M. IV, 1105
Mott, Daniel M. IV, 1108
Mott, Daniel M. IV, 1136
Mott, Daniel Millhouse IV, 589
Mott, Daniel W. III, 237
Mott, Daniel W. III, 383
Mott, David C. IV, 1136
Mott, Deborah II, 398
Mott, Deborah II, 556
Mott, Deborah II, 604
Mott, Deborah III, 235
Mott, Dorothy A. IV, 254
Mott, Dorothy A. IV, 282
Mott, Dr. Henry III, 235
Mott, Dr. Valentine III, 237
Mott, Ebenezer II, 244
Mott, Ebenezer, Jr. II, 244
Mott, Edith IV, 1330
Mott, Edith M. IV, 834
Mott, Edith May IV, 816
Mott, Edith May IV, 834
Mott, Edmond III, 442
Mott, Edmund III, 428
Mott, Edward III, 237
Mott, Edward III, 429
Mott, Edward IV, 1330
Mott, Edward K. III, 428
Mott, Edward K. III, 431
Mott, Edward Thomas II, 811
Mott, Eleanor IV, 423
Mott, Eleanor IV, 589
Mott, Eleanor IV, 1108
Mott, Eleanor IV, 1136
Mott, Elenor IV, 1136
Mott, Eli P. IV, 1136
Mott, Eliz. III, 46
Mott, Eliz. III, 236
Mott, Eliz. III, 428
Mott, Eliz. III, 508
Mott, Eliz. M. III, 236
Mott, Eliza III, 235
Mott, Eliza III, 383
Mott, Eliza A. III, 236
Mott, Eliza A. III, 428
Mott, Eliza Ann III, 446
Mott, Elizabeth II, 813
Mott, Elizabeth II, 846
Mott, Elizabeth II, 901
Mott, Elizabeth III, 113
Mott, Elizabeth III, 159
Mott, Elizabeth III, 235
Mott, Elizabeth III, 236
Mott, Elizabeth III, 237
Mott, Elizabeth III, 383
Mott, Elizabeth III, 393
Mott, Elizabeth III, 417
Mott, Elizabeth III, 423
Mott, Elizabeth III, 427
Mott, Elizabeth III, 428
Mott, Elizabeth III, 429
Mott, Elizabeth III, 430
Mott, Elizabeth III, 459
Mott, Elizabeth III, 473
Mott, Elizabeth III, 476
Mott, Elizabeth III, 488
Mott, Elizabeth III, 489
Mott, Elizabeth III, 491
Mott, Elizabeth IV, 744
Mott, Elizabeth IV, 1108
Mott, Elizabeth IV, 1136
Mott, Elizabeth IV, 1330
Mott, Elizabeth IV, 1374
Mott, Elizabeth A. III, 235
Mott, Elizabeth B. III, 428
Mott, Elizabeth H. IV, 1258
Mott, Elizabeth H. IV, 1330
Mott, Elizabeth K. III, 430
Mott, Elizabeth M. III, 292
Mott, Ellen I, 210
Mott, Ellen I, 235
Mott, Ellen I, 247
Mott, Ellison III, 428
Mott, Elma IV, 678
Mott, Elmira IV, 1130
Mott, Elmira IV, 1136
Mott, Elvira IV, 1136
Mott, Emily III, 491
Mott, Emma F. IV, 744
Mott, Ernest H. Copeland I, 247
Mott, Esther III, 383
Mott, Esther IV, 961
Mott, Esther IV, 1136
Mott, Esther W. III, 235
Mott, Florence III, 130
Mott, Frances B. IV, 744
Mott, Frances S. IV, 678
Mott, Frances S. IV, 744
Mott, Francis E. IV, 678
Mott, Francis E. IV, 744
Mott, Francis S. IV, 678
Mott, Franklin III, 237
Mott, Frederick IV, 1108
Mott, G. W. IV, 1136
Mott, Geo. W. IV, 1136
Mott, George III, 428
Mott, George Harvey IV, 1136
Mott, George Hervey IV, 1136
Mott, George W. IV, 589
Mott, George W. IV, 1049
Mott, George W. IV, 1070
Mott, George W. IV, 1108
Mott, George W. IV, 1127
Mott, George W. IV, 1136
Mott, George Wm. IV, 589
Mott, Gersham IV, 374
Mott, Gersham IV, 423
Mott, Gershom IV, 1108
Mott, Gershom IV, 1128
Mott, Gershom IV, 1130
Mott, Gershom IV, 1136
Mott, Gershon IV, 589
Mott, Grace III, 491
Mott, Gulielma III, 235
Mott, Gulielma VI, 501
Mott, Gulielma VI, 537
Mott, Gulielma M. III, 428
Mott, Hannah III, 235
Mott, Hannah III, 397
Mott, Hannah III, 410
Mott, Hannah III, 417
Mott, Hannah III, 428
Mott, Hannah III, 429
Mott, Hannah III, 430
Mott, Hannah III, 433
Mott, Hannah III, 475
Mott, Hannah III, 491
Mott, Hannah Ann IV, 1105
Mott, Hannah Ann IV, 1108
Mott, Hannah Ann IV, 1136
Mott, Hannah B. II, 244
Mott, Hannah B. II, 263
Mott, Hannah B. II, 297
Mott, Hannah B. II, 304
Mott, Hannah B. III, 235
Mott, Hannah B. III, 236
Mott, Hannah C. III, 473
Mott, Hannah D. III, 235
Mott, Hannah H. IV, 1330
Mott, Henrietta R. II, 901
Mott, Henrietta Roh II, 811
Mott, Henry III, 235
Mott, Henry III, 236
Mott, Henry III, 237
Mott, Henry III, 383
Mott, Henry III, 417
Mott, Henry III, 419
Mott, Henry III, 428
Mott, Henry III, 429
Mott, Henry III, 430
Mott, Henry III, 464
Mott, Henry B. III, 428
Mott, Henry Franklin III, 235
Mott, Henry Franklin III, 237
Mott, Hulda II, 224
Mott, Hulda II, 244
Mott, Huldah II, 398
Mott, Huldah II, 604
Mott, Isaac III, 428
Mott, Isabel Pelham II, 812
Mott, J. Cromwell III, 428
Mott, Jackson III, 491
Mott, Jacob III, 235
Mott, Jacob III, 420
Mott, Jacob III, 428
Mott, Jacob III, 463
Mott, Jacob III, 466
Mott, Jacob III, 491
Mott, Jacob T. III, 428
Mott, James II, 398
Mott, James II, 604
Mott, James II, 801
Mott, James II, 811
Mott, James II, 846
Mott, James II, 855
Mott, James II, 856
Mott, James II, 871
Mott, James II, 878
Mott, James II, 901
Mott, James III, 55
Mott, James III, 423

, James III, 427
, James III, 428
, James III, 430
, James III, 441
, James III, 459
, James III, 489
, James IV, 744
, James IV, 1108
, James E. IV, 243
, James E. IV, 254
, James E. IV, 589
, James E. IV, 1108
, James E. IV, 1132
, James E. IV, 1134
, James E. IV, 1136
, James, Jr. II, 604
, James, Jr. III, 428
, Jane III, 41
, Jane III, 55
, Jane III, 235
, Jane III, 236
, Jane III, 237
, Jane III, 253
, Jane III, 282
, Jane III, 383
, Jane III, 428
, Jane III, 429
, Jane III, 430
, Jane III, 443
, Jane III, 444
, Jane III, 464
, Jane IV, 1133
, Jane ??? III, 235
, Jarvis III, 491
, Jas. Frederick IV, 1136
, Jehu III, 428
, Jehu III, 437
, Jemima III, 405
, Jennette III, 236
, Jerusha III, 428
, Jerusha III, 430
, Jesse D. IV, 982
, John II, 244
, John III, 235
, John III, 236
, John III, 417
, John III, 428
, John III, 430
, John III, 453
, John III, 480
, John III, 487
, John III, 491
, John IV, 423
, John IV, 589
, John B. III, 235
, John Bowne III, 236
, John Bowne III, 237
, John C. III, 236
, John Dewees IV, 945
, John Dewees IV, 982
, John W. III, 235
, John W. III, 236
, John W. III, 383
, John W. IV, 400
, John W. IV, 423
, John W. IV, 589
, John W. IV, 617
, John W. IV, 693
, John W. IV, 1136
, Jos. III, 428
, Jos. III, 443
, Joseph III, 236
, Joseph III, 428
, Joseph III, 430
, Joseph K. III, 429
, Joseph L. III, 236
, Joseph S. III, 236
, Katharine III, 428
, Katharine III, 442
, Kezia III, 420
, Kezia III, 428
, Kezia III, 429
, Kezia III, 444
, Kezia III, 463
, Kezia III, 466
, Leonard III, 417
, Leonard III, 473
, Letitia III, 426
, Letitia III, 430
, Lillian U. III, 236
, Louisa III, 236
, Louise III, 236
, Louise III, 269
, Lucretia II, 398
, Lucretia II, 604
, Lucretia II, 801
, Lucretia II, 811
, Lucretia II, 846
, Lucretia II, 855
, Lucretia II, 878
, Lucretia II, 901
Mott, Lucretia II, 906
Mott, Lucretia III, 397
Mott, Lucretia III, 428
Mott, Lucretia III, 429
Mott, Lucretia V, 751
Mott, Lydia III, 57
Mott, Lydia III, 103
Mott, Lydia III, 168
Mott, Lydia III, 236
Mott, Lydia III, 427
Mott, Lydia III, 429
Mott, Lydia III, 430
Mott, Lydia III, 443
Mott, Lydia III, 457
Mott, Lydia III, 460
Mott, Lydia P. II, 323
Mott, Lydia P. III, 236
Mott, Lydia P. III, 491
Mott, Lydia P. V, 104
Mott, Lydia P. V, 922
Mott, Margaret III, 428
Mott, Margaret IV, 945
Mott, Margaret IV, 982
Mott, Maria II, 604
Mott, Maria II, 790
Mott, Maria II, 855
Mott, Maria II, 901
Mott, Maria III, 96
Mott, Maria III, 235
Mott, Maria III, 236
Mott, Maria III, 237
Mott, Maria III, 383
Mott, Mariah II, 811
Mott, Marie ??? III, 235
Mott, Marjarie A. IV, 1136
Mott, Marjorie A. IV, 1108
Mott, Martha II, 901
Mott, Martha III, 159
Mott, Martha III, 411
Mott, Martha III, 429
Mott, Martha III, 430
Mott, Martha III, 470
Mott, Martha III, 479
Mott, Martha III, 491
Mott, Martha IV, 514
Mott, Martha IV, 542
Mott, Martha IV, 678
Mott, Martha B. III, 159
Mott, Martha B. III, 236
Mott, Martha B. IV, 542
Mott, Martha H. III, 467
Mott, Martha Jane IV, 1136
Mott, Martha W. III, 411
Mott, Martha W. III, 428
Mott, Martha W. III, 449
Mott, Martha, Jr. II, 811
Mott, Mary II, 377
Mott, Mary II, 556
Mott, Mary II, 604
Mott, Mary II, 701
Mott, Mary II, 988
Mott, Mary II, 1017
Mott, Mary III, 282
Mott, Mary III, 408
Mott, Mary III, 417
Mott, Mary III, 427
Mott, Mary III, 428
Mott, Mary III, 429
Mott, Mary III, 430
Mott, Mary III, 431
Mott, Mary III, 441
Mott, Mary III, 444
Mott, Mary III, 453
Mott, Mary III, 459
Mott, Mary III, 480
Mott, Mary III, 491
Mott, Mary IV, 589
Mott, Mary IV, 1070
Mott, Mary IV, 1108
Mott, Mary IV, 1131
Mott, Mary IV, 1136
Mott, Mary Ann III, 491
Mott, Mary E. IV, 678
Mott, Mary Elizabeth III, 429
Mott, Mary Elvira IV, 1136
Mott, Mary Elvira IV, 1137
Mott, Mary F. III, 236
Mott, Mary F. III, 237
Mott, Mary F. III, 358
Mott, Mary F. III, 388
Mott, Mary F. III, 491
Mott, Mary J. III, 397
Mott, Mary J. III, 428
Mott, Mary J. III, 429
Mott, Mary Jane III, 491
Mott, Mary P. IV, 243
Mott, Mary P. IV, 254
Mott, Mary P. IV, 1108
Mott, Mary P. IV, 1134
Mott, Mary P. IV, 1136
Mott, Mary S. IV, 1136
Mott, Mary T. IV, 1374
Mott, Mary U. III, 419
Mott, Mary U. III, 428
Mott, Mary W. III, 429
Mott, Mary W. III, 430
Mott, Mary, Jr. III, 436
Mott, Matilda III, 236
Mott, Matilda Jane IV, 1108
Mott, Matilda Jane IV, 1129
Mott, Matilda Jane IV, 1136
Mott, Matthew Bernard III, 236
Mott, Merribeth III, 429
Mott, Micajah III, 394
Mott, Micajah III, 417
Mott, Micajah III, 429
Mott, Michajah III, 444
Mott, Mildred IV, 744
Mott, Mildred C. IV, 1108
Mott, Mildred Carroll IV, 1108
Mott, Mildred Elizabeth IV, 744
Mott, Milford IV, 816
Mott, Milford IV, 834
Mott, Milhouse IV, 423
Mott, Miriam III, 428
Mott, Miriam III, 443
Mott, Oliver III, 429
Mott, Phebe III, 127
Mott, Phebe III, 227
Mott, Phebe III, 235
Mott, Phebe III, 236
Mott, Phebe III, 237
Mott, Phebe III, 358
Mott, Phebe III, 427
Mott, Phebe III, 428
Mott, Phebe III, 429
Mott, Phebe III, 436
Mott, Phebe III, 447
Mott, Phebe III, 463
Mott, Phebe III, 470
Mott, Phebe III, 476
Mott, Phebe III, 480
Mott, Phebe III, 491
Mott, Phebe A. III, 406
Mott, Phebe A. III, 429
Mott, Phebe E. III, 236
Mott, Phebe S. III, 235
Mott, Rachel III, 394
Mott, Rachel III, 413
Mott, Rachel III, 420
Mott, Rachel III, 428
Mott, Rachel III, 429
Mott, Rachel III, 444
Mott, Rachel III, 479
Mott, Rachel III, 491
Mott, Rachel III, 494
Mott, Rachel III, 504
Mott, Rachel Tacy IV, 617
Mott, Rachel Tacy IV, 693
Mott, Rachel Tacy IV, 694
Mott, Rachel Tacy IV, 744
Mott, Rebecca III, 399
Mott, Rebecca III, 428
Mott, Rebecca III, 429
Mott, Rhoda C. IV, 1239
Mott, Richard II, 179
Mott, Richard II, 244
Mott, Richard II, 263
Mott, Richard III, 235
Mott, Richard III, 236
Mott, Richard III, 407
Mott, Richard III, 428
Mott, Richard III, 429
Mott, Richard III, 430
Mott, Richard III, 432
Mott, Richard III, 447
Mott, Richard IV, 214
Mott, Richard IV, 423
Mott, Richard IV, 542
Mott, Richard IV, 582
Mott, Richard IV, 589
Mott, Richard IV, 1108
Mott, Richard F. II, 179
Mott, Richard F. II, 289
Mott, Richard F. II, 297
Mott, Richard F. II, 304
Mott, Richard F. III, 236
Mott, Richard, Jr. III, 236
Mott, Richard, Jr. III, 292
Mott, Richard, Jr. IV, 1374
Mott, Richbell III, 428
Mott, Richbell III, 429
Mott, Richbell III, 444
Mott, Robert III, 235
Mott, Robert III, 423
Mott, Robert III, 429
Mott, Robert F. II, 179
Mott, Robert F. II, 244
Mott, Robert F. II, 263
Mott, Robert F. II, 297
Mott, Robert F. II, 304
Mott, Robert F. III, 236
Mott, Robert S. III, 236
Mott, Robert T. II, 179
Mott, Ruth II, 196
Mott, Ruth II, 244
Mott, Ruth III, 417
Mott, Ruth III, 428
Mott, Ruth III, 437
Mott, Ruth III, 487
Mott, Ruth III, 491
Mott, Ruth ??? III, 236
Mott, Ruth Anna IV, 423
Mott, Ruthanna IV, 374
Mott, Ruthanna IV, 423
Mott, Ruthanna IV, 1128
Mott, Ruthanna IV, 1136
Mott, S. Louisa III, 393
Mott, S. Louisa III, 430
Mott, Samuel III, 108
Mott, Samuel III, 113
Mott, Samuel III, 126
Mott, Samuel III, 159
Mott, Samuel III, 235
Mott, Samuel III, 236
Mott, Samuel III, 237
Mott, Samuel III, 365
Mott, Samuel III, 394
Mott, Samuel III, 427
Mott, Samuel III, 430
Mott, Samuel III, 472
Mott, Samuel III, 475
Mott, Samuel III, 491
Mott, Samuel C. III, 429
Mott, Samuel Cornell III, 429
Mott, Samuel F. III, 203
Mott, Samuel F. III, 236
Mott, Samuel F. III, 269
Mott, Samuel F., Jr. III, 236
Mott, Samuel G. III, 236
Mott, Samuel N. III, 236
Mott, Samuel N. III, 237
Mott, Samuel W. III, 429
Mott, Samuel, Jr. III, 236
Mott, Sana A. IV, 693
Mott, Sara IV, 214
Mott, Sarah II, 226
Mott, Sarah II, 244
Mott, Sarah II, 516
Mott, Sarah II, 604
Mott, Sarah III, 88
Mott, Sarah III, 108
Mott, Sarah III, 126
Mott, Sarah III, 235
Mott, Sarah III, 236
Mott, Sarah III, 237
Mott, Sarah III, 272
Mott, Sarah III, 365
Mott, Sarah III, 388
Mott, Sarah III, 393
Mott, Sarah III, 394
Mott, Sarah III, 412
Mott, Sarah III, 421
Mott, Sarah III, 427
Mott, Sarah III, 428
Mott, Sarah III, 429
Mott, Sarah III, 430
Mott, Sarah III, 432
Mott, Sarah III, 455
Mott, Sarah III, 460
Mott, Sarah III, 491
Mott, Sarah IV, 254
Mott, Sarah IV, 374
Mott, Sarah IV, 423
Mott, Sarah IV, 542
Mott, Sarah IV, 589
Mott, Sarah IV, 1070
Mott, Sarah IV, 1108
Mott, Sarah IV, 1128
Mott, Sarah IV, 1131
Mott, Sarah IV, 1136
Mott, Sarah A. III, 394
Mott, Sarah A. III, 419
Mott, Sarah A. III, 420
Mott, Sarah A. III, 429
Mott, Sarah A. III, 472
Mott, Sarah J. IV, 1108
Mott, Sarah J. IV, 1136
Mott, Sarah W. III, 393
Mott, Sarah W. IV, 423
Mott, Sarah W. IV, 582
Mott, Sarah W. IV, 589
Mott, Silas III, 429
Mott, Silas III, 430
Mott, Sina IV, 617
Mott, Sina A. IV, 400
Mott, Sina A. IV, 423
Mott, Smith III, 430
Mott, Smith IV, 1136
Mott, Smith H. IV, 1108
Mott, Smith H. IV, 1129
Mott, Smith H. IV, 1136
Mott, Stephen III, 237
Mott, Stephen III, 388
Mott, Stephen III, 412
Mott, Stephen III, 428
Mott, Stephen III, 429
Mott, Stephen III, 430
Mott, Stephen III, 472
Mott, Stephen III, 476
Mott, Stephen III, 491
Mott, Susan II, 179
Mott, Susan II, 297
Mott, Susan II, 304
Mott, Susan III, 237
Mott, Susan III, 491
Mott, Susan M. III, 237
Mott, Susan T. II, 179
Mott, Susan T. II, 289
Mott, Susan T. II, 297
Mott, Susannah III, 487
Mott, Susannah III, 491
Mott, Susie M. III, 235
Mott, Tacie M. IV, 678
Mott, Temperance III, 419
Mott, Temperance III, 428
Mott, Thomas II, 398
Mott, Thomas II, 604
Mott, Thomas II, 901
Mott, Thomas III, 428
Mott, Thomas III, 430
Mott, Thomas III, 449
Mott, Thomas III, 470
Mott, Thomas C. II, 398
Mott, Thomas C. II, 604
Mott, Thomas E. IV, 514
Mott, Thomas E. IV, 542
Mott, Thomas U. III, 428
Mott, Thos. III, 411
Mott, Thos. III, 449
Mott, Thos. III, 467
Mott, Valentine III, 235
Mott, Valentine III, 237
Mott, Valentine III, 265
Mott, Valentine III, 383
Mott, Valentine III, 430
Mott, Valentine III, 491
Mott, Walter III, 235
Mott, Walter III, 237
Mott, Way III, 235
Mott, Wd. Hannah B. II, 179
Mott, Wd. Phebe III, 407
Mott, Wd. Sarah III, 429
Mott, Willard IV, 1330
Mott, William III, 38
Mott, William III, 236
Mott, William III, 237
Mott, William III, 393
Mott, William III, 410
Mott, William III, 428
Mott, William III, 430
Mott, William III, 433
Mott, William III, 444
Mott, William III, 459
Mott, William IV, 154
Mott, William IV, 254
Mott, William IV, 344
Mott, William IV, 423
Mott, William IV, 589
Mott, William IV, 678
Mott, William IV, 1136
Mott, William B. III, 430
Mott, William C. IV, 1136
Mott, William Elton II, 179
Mott, William F. II, 179
Mott, William F. III, 127
Mott, William F. III, 237
Mott, William F., Jr. III, 237
Mott, William K. III, 393
Mott, William K. III, 428
Mott, William W. III, 237
Mott, William, Jr. IV, 1136
Mott, William, Sr. III, 430
Mott, Witson III, 491
Mott, Wm. III, 408
Mott, Wm. IV, 254
Mott, Wm. IV, 423
Mott, Wm. IV, 589
Mott, Wm. IV, 1070
Mott, Wm. IV, 1108
Mott, Wm. IV, 1131
Mott, Wm. IV, 1136
Mott, Wm. A. IV, 254
Mott, Wm. A. IV, 282
Mott, Wm. B III, 430
Mott, Wm. B. III, 426
Mott, Wm. C. IV, 254
Mott, Wm. F. III, 227
Mott, Wm. F. III, 235
Mott, Wm. F. III, 237
Mott, Wm. F. III, 358
Mott, Wm. F. J., Jr. III, 237
Mott, Wm. F., Jr. III, 41
Mott, Wm. F., Jr. III, 235

Mott, Wm. F., Jr. III, 236
Mott, Wm. F., Jr. III, 237
Mott, Wm. K. III, 393
Mott, Wm. Kirby III, 430
Motte, Anson V, 758
Motte, Arena E. V, 757
Motte, Arriadne V, 757
Motte, Celestia Susan V, 757
Motte, Charity J. V, 757
Motte, Cordelia Bayes V, 757
Motte, David V, 756
Motte, David V, 757
Motte, Elisha J. V, 757
Motte, Jeremiah V, 756
Motte, John V, 757
Motte, John, Jr. V, 739
Motte, John, Jr. V, 757
Motte, Luke Smith V, 757
Motte, Lydia V, 757
Motte, Lydia Hasket V, 739
Motte, Marcus Benson V, 757
Motte, Mary Melona V, 757
Motte, Miriam V, 757
Motte, Rachel V, 757
Motte, Rhoda T. V, 735
Motte, Sarah Elizabeth V, 758
Motte, Spencer Joyce V, 758
Motte, Wm. Aldin V, 757
Mottishaw, Carrie IV, 1041
Mottishaw, Elizabeth IV, 1041
Mottishaw, Mildred IV, 1041
Mottishaw, Opal IV, 1041
Mouce, Clara V, 104
Mouce, Clara V, 923
Mouce, Edward K. V, 923
Mouce, Edwin V, 923
Mouce, Edwin W. V, 104
Mouce, Howard V, 104
Mouce, Howard V, 923
Mouce, Howard J. V, 104
Mouce, Howard J. V, 923
Mouce, Irvin V, 923
Mouce, Ulysses L. V, 104
Mouce, Ulysses L. V, 923
Mouce, Vivian V, 104
Mouce, Vivian V, 923
Mouce, Vivien V, 104
Mouch, Blanch Brown IV, 1218
Moudling, Jesse I, 725
Moughiman, May IV, 1330
Moulden, Aquilla VI, 966
Moulden, Dosha VI, 966
Moulder, Sarah II, 481
Moulder, Sarah II, 604
Moulson, Deborah II, 604
Moulson, Deborah II, 757
Moulson, Deborah II, 811
Moulson, Deborah II, 901
Moulson, Deborah III, 237
Moulson, John II, 604
Moulson, John II, 811
Moulson, Sarah II, 604
Moulson, Sarah II, 757
Moulson, Sarah II, 811
Moulson, Sarah II, 901
Moulton, Benjamin H. VI, 966
Moulton, Mary S. VI, 966
Mounford, Mody A. VI, 77
Mount, Abigail II, 88
Mount, Elizabeth I, 1129
Mount, Mary II, 604
Mount, Mary II, 610
Mount, Mary Jane I, 1129
Mount, Samuel I, 1129
Mount, Sarah II, 902
Mount, Sarah II, 941
Mount, Victory Elizabeth I, 1129
Mountain, Charles III, 119
Mountain, Charles H. III, 237
Mountain, Hannah III, 119
Mountain, Hannah III, 237
Mountain, Hannah B. III, 237
Mountaine, Edward II, 966
Mountaine, Mary II, 966
Mountaine, Richard II, 966
Mountaine, Richard II, 1017
Mountaine, Richard II, 1020
Mounteague, Widow Elizabeth I, 106
Mountford, Susan VI, 77
Mounticue, Elizabeth I, 146
Mounts, Belle V, 588
Mounts, Beulah Haviland IV, 744
Mounts, Edith V, 663
Mounts, Edith V, 700
Mounts, Ida Jane IV, 978
Mounts, Neil V, 663
Mounts, Neil V, 700
Mountz, Grace IV, 975
Mountz, Grace Linton IV, 982
Mourfin, Mary II, 244
Mourfin, Mary II, 261
Mourland, Elmira IV, 742
Mourland, Elmira IV, 752
Mourland, Lydia IV, 742
Mourman, Elizabeth V, 102
Mourman, Obediance V, 102
Mourning, Agness V, 285
Mouton, Samuel II, 398
Mouton, Sarah II, 398
Mowell, Elizabeth III, 74
Mowen, Lydia V, 493
Mowen, Lydia V, 519
Mower, Ann IV, 1374
Mower, Ann IV, 1381
Mower, Ellen IV, 1374
Mower, George IV, 1374
Mower, John IV, 1374
Mower, Rebecca IV, 1374
Mowray, Lucy Ann IV, 1235
Mowray, Lucy Ann IV, 1239
Mowry, Mary V, 699
Mowry, Verna V, 699
Moxham, John, Jr. III, 237
Moyce, Clara V, 923
Moyce, Jane IV, 1287
Moyce, Lucy IV, 1287
Moyce, Lucy V, 923
Moyce, Lucy Ann V, 923
Moye, Bettie I, 312
Moye, Penny I, 338
Moye, Stanley I, 312
Moyer, Elmer V, 1011
Moyer, Lucy II, 733
Moyer, Lucy II, 757
Moyer, Mary V, 1011
Moyer, Wm. V, 1011
Moyers, Ann II, 398
Moyers, Benjamin II, 398
Moyers, Catherine V, 700
Moyers, Samuel V, 700
Mozeley, Susannah VI, 953
Mozeley, Walter VI, 953
Mozier, Adelaide III, 235
Mozier, Oscar III, 235
Mozley, James VI, 979
Mtchell, James VI, 1004
Mucdaneld, John VI, 287
Muchlenthal, Clara III, 32
Muckans, Hannah II, 399
Muckelseed, Elinor II, 446
Muckey, Oliver M. IV, 1176
Mudge, Alice III, 430
Mudge, Alice G. III, 430
Mudge, Amy III, 430
Mudge, Ann III, 430
Mudge, Anna III, 420
Mudge, Anne III, 454
Mudge, Coles III, 404
Mudge, Coles III, 430
Mudge, Coles III, 465
Mudge, Daniel III, 420
Mudge, Daniel III, 430
Mudge, Dorothy III, 404
Mudge, Dorothy III, 430
Mudge, Dorothy III, 465
Mudge, Eliz. III, 462
Mudge, Elizabeth III, 419
Mudge, ELizabeth III, 430
Mudge, Elizabeth III, 430
Mudge, ELizabeth III, 430
Mudge, Elizabeth III, 430
Mudge, Elizabeth III, 451
Mudge, Elizabeth III, 454
Mudge, Elizabeth III, 461
Mudge, Hannah III, 430
Mudge, Hannah III, 452
Mudge, Henry W. III, 430
Mudge, Irene III, 430
Mudge, Irene III, 448
Mudge, Irene S. III, 430
Mudge, Jacob III, 430
Mudge, Jacob III, 452
Mudge, James III, 437
Mudge, Jane III, 404
Mudge, Jane III, 430
Mudge, Jane III, 437
Mudge, Martha III, 420
Mudge, Martha III, 430
Mudge, Martha III, 470
Mudge, Martha T. III, 430
Mudge, Mary III, 437
Mudge, Melisande III, 430
Mudge, Mesalinda III, 407
Mudge, Michael III, 420
Mudge, Michael III, 430
Mudge, Michael III, 454
Mudge, Sarah III, 420
Mudge, Sarah III, 430
Mudge, Sarah III, 454
Mudge, Sterling W. III, 430
Mudge, Todd Wm. III, 430
Mudge, William III, 430
Mudge, William III, 470
Mudge, William J. III, 430
Mudge, William S. III, 430
Mudge, Wm. III, 470
Mudge, Wm. J. III, 430
Mudge, Wm. J. III, 448
Mudge, Wm. S. III, 407
Mudge, Wm. S. III, 430
Mueller, Elsa II, 720
Muetzel, Alma C. IV, 1330
Muggleston, Edward II, 399
Muglestone, Margaret II, 244
Muglestone, Margaret II, 268
Muglestone, Rebecca II, 268
Muglestone, William II, 268
Mugrage, Girden H. IV, 1258
Muhlenberg, Rev. Wm. III, 380
Muirhead, Clara W. III, 237
Muirhead, William III, 237
Mulane, Martha E. V, 345
Mulane, Martha E. V, 351
Mulenix, Gideon IV, 1218
Mulford, Anna VI, 768
Mulford, Charles V, 588
Mulford, Edith VI, 740
Mulford, Edith VI, 768
Mulford, Emma VI, 737
Mulford, Emma VI, 768
Mulford, Furman Lawrence VI, 768
Mulford, Furman Lloyd VI, 737
Mulford, Furman Lloyd VI, 740
Mulford, Furman Lloyd VI, 768
Mulford, Isaac II, 135
Mulford, Julia V, 588
Mulford, Mable V, 588
Mulford, Mary II, 153
Mulford, Mary D. II, 139
Mulford, Mary M. II, 135
Mulford, Mary M. II, 153
Mulford, Ruth V, 588
Mulforf, Mary II, 160
Muliner, Elizabeth V, 758
Mull, ??? V, 194
Mull, Blanch May V, 461
Mull, Frances V, 104
Mull, Lydia II, 999
Mull, Lydia II, 1017
Mull, Margaret V, 194
Mull, Noah V, 194
Mullen, ??? II, 179
Mullen, A. R. V, 1011
Mullen, Aaron V, 104
Mullen, Aaron V, 957
Mullen, Aaron V, 974
Mullen, Alexander V, 1011
Mullen, Alpha V, 519
Mullen, Alpheus V, 519
Mullen, Ann II, 244
Mullen, Ann V, 104
Mullen, Ann V, 519
Mullen, Ann V, 533
Mullen, Ann V, 973
Mullen, Ann V, 974
Mullen, Bathsheba V, 957
Mullen, Bethuel V, 957
Mullen, Beulah V, 104
Mullen, Catherine V, 1011
Mullen, Charley V, 519
Mullen, Charlie V, 519
Mullen, Chas. W. V, 1011
Mullen, Christian V, 973
Mullen, Christiana V, 104
Mullen, Cleo V, 1011
Mullen, Clyde D. V, 519
Mullen, Daniel V, 1011
Mullen, David V, 104
Mullen, Dora V, 519
Mullen, Edward II, 244
Mullen, Eli V, 104
Mullen, Elizabeth V, 87
Mullen, Elizabeth V, 104
Mullen, Elizabeth V, 973
Mullen, Elizabeth K. II, 179
Mullen, Elizabeth K. II, 297
Mullen, Ella V, 1011
Mullen, Ellenor V, 519
Mullen, Elma R. V, 957
Mullen, Elvira V, 1011
Mullen, Emeline V, 677
Mullen, Emily B. V, 588
Mullen, Emma V, 566
Mullen, Esther II, 179
Mullen, Etta V, 1011
Mullen, Eunice D. V, 519
Mullen, Eunice Medora V, 519
Mullen, Flora V, 519
Mullen, Hallie O. V, 519
Mullen, Hannah II, 198
Mullen, Hannah II, 244
Mullen, Hannah IV, 51
Mullen, Hannah V, 104
Mullen, Harley V, 519
Mullen, Henry V, 519
Mullen, Henry L. V, 519
Mullen, Huldah V, 104
Mullen, Isaac V, 104
Mullen, Isaac V, 957
Mullen, Isaac V, 974
Mullen, Isaiah IV, 51
Mullen, Isaiah V, 104
Mullen, Isaiah V, 519
Mullen, Isaiah M. V, 519
Mullen, Jacob Taylor V, 519
Mullen, James V, 104
Mullen, James V, 519
Mullen, Jane IV, 51
Mullen, Jane V, 101
Mullen, Jane V, 104
Mullen, Jane V, 957
Mullen, Jane V, 968
Mullen, Jane V, 974
Mullen, Jehu V, 974
Mullen, Job V, 104
Mullen, Job V, 974
Mullen, John II, 244
Mullen, John IV, 51
Mullen, John V, 104
Mullen, John W. V, 1011
Mullen, John, Jr. II, 244
Mullen, John, Jr. V, 104
Mullen, Joseph II, 244
Mullen, Joseph V, 104
Mullen, Joseph H. V, 519
Mullen, Levina P. V, 519
Mullen, Lydia IV, 51
Mullen, Lydia V, 104
Mullen, Lydia V, 974
Mullen, Lydia Ann V, 104
Mullen, Maria V, 104
Mullen, Maria V, 974
Mullen, Marie V, 700
Mullen, Mary II, 244
Mullen, Mary V, 1011
Mullen, Mary VI, 966
Mullen, Mary Ann V, 104
Mullen, Mary Ann V, 974
Mullen, Mary Frances V, 1011
Mullen, Mattie V, 1011
Mullen, Meribah II, 239
Mullen, Meribah II, 244
Mullen, Nancy V, 1011
Mullen, Nancy Ann V, 1011
Mullen, Nathan V, 104
Mullen, Nathan V, 974
Mullen, Noah V, 104
Mullen, Noah V, 974
Mullen, Oella V, 104
Mullen, Oella V, 118
Mullen, Pollie V, 1011
Mullen, Polly V, 1011
Mullen, Rachel IV, 51
Mullen, Rachel V, 23
Mullen, Rachel V, 104
Mullen, Rebecca II, 244
Mullen, Rebecca V, 104
Mullen, Robert VI, 966
Mullen, Ruth V, 104
Mullen, Ruth V, 957
Mullen, Ruth V, 973
Mullen, Samuel IV, 51
Mullen, Samuel IV, 255
Mullen, Samuel V, 104
Mullen, Samuel A. II, 179
Mullen, Samuel A. II, 297
Mullen, Sarah II, 179
Mullen, Sarah II, 297
Mullen, Sarah IV, 51
Mullen, Sarah V, 90
Mullen, Sarah V, 104
Mullen, Seth V, 104
Mullen, Seth V, 974
Mullen, Stacy B. II, 297
Mullen, Thomas III, 237
Mullen, William V, 104
Mullen, William C. II, 297
Mullen, Wm. V, 973
Mullener, Elizabeth V, 758
Mullenex, ??? III, 232
Mullenex, Hannah III, 199
Mullenex, Moses III, 199
Mullenix, Aaron IV, 1176
Mullenix, Ann IV, 1148
Mullenix, Ann IV, 1176
Mullenix, Anna IV, 1176
Mullenix, Anna IV, 1190
Mullenix, Edna Sanders V, 351
Mullenix, Gideon IV, 1176
Mullenix, Gideon IV, 1218
Mullenix, Hannah IV, 1218
Mullenix, Joshua W. IV, 1218
Mullenix, Martha IV, 1176
Mullenix, Moses IV, 1176
Mullenix, Priscilla IV, 1176
Mullenix, Rhoda IV, 1176
Mullenix, Rhoda IV, 1188
Mullenix, Rhoda IV, 1195
Mullenix, Samuel IV, 1176
Mullenix, Thomas IV, 1176
Mullennix, George F. IV, 1176
Mullennix, Gideon IV, 1176
Mullennix, Gideon IV, 1192
Mullennix, Hannah IV, 1176
Mullennix, Hannah IV, 1192
Mullennix, Moses IV, 1176
Mullennix, Priscilla IV, 1176
Mullennix, Rhoda IV, 1176
Mullennix, William IV, 1176
Mullens, Mary VI, 872
Mullens, Thomas VI, 872
Muller, Agatha C. III, 237
Muller, Bertha Margaret III, 2
Muller, John B. III, 237
Mullett, Cora IV, 671
Mullett, Della IV, 671
Mullett, George IV, 671
Mullett, Mrs. ??? IV, 744
Mullican, Mille VI, 966
Mullican, Thomas VI, 966
Mullican, William VI, 966
Mullice, J. G. I, 638
Mullice, Kirby Errol I, 638
Mullice, Lelia B. I, 638
Mullice, Mrs. J. G I, 638
Mullice, Robie I, 638
Mullies, J. G. I, 638
Mullies, Kirby Errol I, 638
Mullies, Mrs. J. G I, 638
Mulligan, Charles P. II, 399
Mulligan, Maria III, 237
Mulligan, Maria Louisa III, 71
Mulligan, Maria Louisa III, 23
Mulligan, William III, 71
Mulligan, William III, 237
Mullin, Aaron V, 974
Mullin, Abigail V, 885
Mullin, Abigail V, 887
Mullin, Abraham V, 854
Mullin, Abraham V, 885
Mullin, Ann V, 970
Mullin, Ann V, 973
Mullin, Ann V, 974
Mullin, Ann V, 977
Mullin, Beulah V, 104
Mullin, Beulah V, 885
Mullin, Christian V, 973
Mullin, Clyde D. V, 519
Mullin, David V, 104
Mullin, David V, 885
Mullin, Edward II, 244
Mullin, Edward II, 265
Mullin, Eli V, 104
Mullin, Elizabeth V, 104
Mullin, Elizabeth V, 973
Mullin, Elizabeth M. VI, 882
Mullin, Hannah II, 244
Mullin, Hannah V, 49
Mullin, Hannah V, 104
Mullin, Hannah V, 854
Mullin, Hannah V, 879
Mullin, Hannah V, 885
Mullin, Hannah VI, 601
Mullin, Isaac V, 885
Mullin, Isaac V, 974
Mullin, Isaiah V, 104
Mullin, Isaiah VI, 601
Mullin, James V, 104
Mullin, James V, 977
Mullin, Jane V, 62
Mullin, Jane VI, 601
Mullin, Jehu V, 974
Mullin, Job V, 974
Mullin, John II, 244
Mullin, John V, 104
Mullin, John VI, 601
Mullin, John VI, 604
Mullin, John S. V, 854
Mullin, John, Jr. V, 104
Mullin, Joseph IV, 254
Mullin, Joseph V, 104
Mullin, Joshua V, 885
Mullin, Lydia V, 104
Mullin, Lydia V, 854
Mullin, Lydia V, 882
Mullin, Lydia V, 885
Mullin, Lydia V, 974
Mullin, Lydia VI, 601
Mullin, Lydia VI, 604
Mullin, Lydia Ann V, 37
Mullin, Lydia Ann V, 104
Mullin, Maria V, 967
Mullin, Maria V, 974

in, Mary II, 244
in, Mary II, 265
in, Mary III, 82
in, Mary Ann V, 104
in, Mary Ann V, 854
in, Mary Ann V, 885
in, Matthew M. VI, 882
in, Nathan V, 974
in, Noah V, 974
in, Phebe S. II, 807
in, Rachel V, 100
in, Rachel V, 104
in, Rachel VI, 601
in, Rebecca II, 218
in, Rebecca II, 244
in, Rebecca V, 104
in, Rebecca V, 885
in, Ruth V, 973
in, Samuel IV, 254
in, Samuel IV, 255
in, Samuel V, 104
in, Samuel V, 854
in, Samuel V, 885
in, Samuel VI, 601
in, Sarah V, 880
in, Sarah V, 885
in, Sarah V, 977
in, Sarah VI, 601
in, William V, 104
in, Wm. V, 973
in, Wm. V, 974
naux, Susanna III, 237
inex, Elizabeth III, 163
inex, Elizabeth III, 237
inex, Hannah III, 237
inex, Henry III, 237
inex, Horseman III, 237
inex, Horsman III, 163
inex, Horsman III, 237
inex, Jesse III, 237
inex, John III, 237
inex, Joseph III, 237
inex, Mary III, 237
inex, Moses III, 237
inex, Phebe III, 237
inex, Sarah III, 237
inex, Susanna III, 237
inix, Aaron IV, 1176
inix, Gideon IV, 1176
inix, Martha IV, 1176
inix, Moses IV, 1176
inix, Priscilla IV, 1176
inix, Rhoda IV, 1176
inix, Samuel IV, 1176
inix, Thomas IV, 1176
ins, Annie Roberts II, 805
ins, Betsy VI, 843
ins, James VI, 843
ins, Joannoh VI, 846
ins, John VI, 966
ins, Joshua VI, 843
ins, Lula I, 613
ins, Mary VI, 966
ins, Mary Ann V, 879
ins, Milly VI, 966
ins, Robert VI, 966
ins, William VI, 799
is, Bonnie Jean I, 622
is, Isabel I, 621
is, James I, 622
is, James Gurney I, 622
is, Kirby Earl I, 622
is, Lelia I, 622
is, Mary I, 614
is, Mary A. I, 622
is, Roxie V. I, 622
is, Ruby Lammie I, 622
iss, Lula I, 628
vaney, Phebe II, 902
vaney, Phebe P. II, 902
naugh, Alice V, 1011
nby, Joseph H. III, 237
nby, Joseph H. III, 308
nby, Rachel III, 237
nby, Robt. III, 237
nby, Tabitha III, 237
nby, Tabitha III, 308
nford, Ann II, 399
nford, Ann III, 237
nford, Ann III, 249
nford, Ann VI, 200
nford, Betsy VI, 61
nford, Cephas VI, 77
nford, James VI, 61
nford, James VI, 77
nford, Jeffrey VI, 200
nford, John S. II, 244
nford, Lucy VI, 61
nford, Lucy VI, 77
nford, Mary II, 399
nford, Thomas II, 399
Mumford, Thomasine II, 244
Mumma, E. R. V, 818
Mumma, Elizabeth V, 818
Munda, Rhoda I, 152
Munday, Esther V, 928
Munday, Esther F. V, 923
Munday, Fanny VI, 537
Munday, George W. VI, 537
Munday, George W. VI, 583
Munday, Mary VI, 537
Munday, Mary VI, 583
Munday, Robert VI, 537
Munday, Susanna IV, 343
Munday, Susanna IV, 347
Munden, Ann I, 197
Munden, Aseaneth I, 185
Munden, Aseanth I, 152
Munden, Benjamin I, 35
Munden, Benjamin I, 61
Munden, Benjamin I, 106
Munden, Betty I, 35
Munden, Betty I, 61
Munden, Betty I, 151
Munden, Betty I, 176
Munden, Calvin A. I, 152
Munden, Carolina I, 152
Munden, Caroline I, 107
Munden, Caroline I, 152
Munden, Caroline I, 157
Munden, Chalkley I, 61
Munden, Chalkley I, 185
Munden, Chalkley I, 197
Munden, Colvin Albertson I, 185
Munden, Darkas I, 152
Munden, Elisabeth I, 46
Munden, Elisabeth I, 61
Munden, Elisabeth I, 151
Munden, Elisha I, 152
Munden, Elizabeth I, 107
Munden, Hannah I, 61
Munden, Hannah I, 70
Munden, Hannah I, 107
Munden, Hannah I, 185
Munden, Henry Thornton I, 61
Munden, Jesse I, 61
Munden, Jesse I, 107
Munden, Jesse I, 152
Munden, Jesse I, 185
Munden, Jesse I, 197
Munden, Jesse I, 200
Munden, Jesse I, 727
Munden, Jesse I, 895
Munden, Jesse I, 896
Munden, John I, 152
Munden, Joseph I, 54
Munden, Joseph I, 61
Munden, Joseph I, 106
Munden, Joseph I, 107
Munden, Joseph I, 152
Munden, Joseph I, 185
Munden, Joseph I, 197
Munden, Joseph I, 727
Munden, Kezia I, 37
Munden, Kezia I, 61
Munden, Kezia I, 130
Munden, Keziah I, 106
Munden, Keziah I, 152
Munden, Levi I, 37
Munden, Levi I, 61
Munden, Levi I, 66
Munden, Levi I, 75
Munden, Levi I, 106
Munden, Levi I, 107
Munden, Levi I, 127
Munden, Levi I, 130
Munden, Levi I, 152
Munden, Levi I, 180
Munden, Levi I, 185
Munden, Levi I, 189
Munden, Levi I, 197
Munden, Levi, Jr. I, 197
Munden, Levi, Sr. I, 61
Munden, Levy I, 34
Munden, Levy I, 61
Munden, Levy I, 107
Munden, Lyda I, 152
Munden, Margaret I, 61
Munden, Margaret I, 107
Munden, Margaret I, 152
Munden, Margaret I, 185
Munden, Margaret I, 197
Munden, Mark I, 61
Munden, Mark I, 106
Munden, Mark I, 152
Munden, Mark I, 188
Munden, Mark I, 197
Munden, Mark I, 727
Munden, Mary I, 54
Munden, Mary I, 61
Munden, Mary I, 79
Munden, Mary I, 107
Munden, Mary I, 151
Munden, Mary I, 152
Munden, Mary I, 185
Munden, Mary I, 189
Munden, Mary I, 197
Munden, Mary I, 200
Munden, Mary I, 895
Munden, Mary I, 896
Munden, Miles I, 185
Munden, Miles I, 197
Munden, Milicent I, 727
Munden, Milisant, Jr. I, 147
Munden, Milisant, Jr. I, 152
Munden, Milisent I, 727
Munden, Miriam I, 61
Munden, Miriam I, 107
Munden, Miriam I, 152
Munden, Miriam I, 158
Munden, Miriam I, 185
Munden, Miriam I, 192
Munden, Miriam I, 197
Munden, Nathan I, 152
Munden, Nathan I, 197
Munden, Nathaniel I, 61
Munden, Nathaniel I, 107
Munden, Nathaniel I, 152
Munden, Penina I, 727
Munden, Peninah I, 188
Munden, Peninah I, 197
Munden, Peninah I, 727
Munden, Peter I, 151
Munden, Rachel I, 130
Munden, Rachel I, 151
Munden, Rachel I, 197
Munden, Rachel I, 199
Munden, Rhoda I, 34
Munden, Rhoda I, 61
Munden, Rhoda I, 107
Munden, Rhoda I, 127
Munden, Rhoda I, 152
Munden, Rhoda I, 180
Munden, Rhoda I, 185
Munden, Robert I, 152
Munden, Robert Evans I, 197
Munden, Ruth I, 107
Munden, Ruth I, 141
Munden, Ruth I, 152
Munden, Sarah I, 46
Munden, Sarah I, 61
Munden, Sarah I, 66
Munden, Sarah I, 152
Munden, Sarah I, 194
Munden, Sarah I, 197
Munden, Simon I, 152
Munden, Susanah I, 152
Munden, Susanah I, 185
Munden, Susannah I, 152
Munden, Susannah I, 160
Munden, Widow Hannah I, 185
Munden, Widow Mary I, 200
Munden, William I, 46
Munden, William I, 61
Munden, William I, 107
Munden, William I, 185
Munden, William I, 895
Munden, William, Jr. I, 152
Munden, Zilpha I, 152
Mundens, Benjamin I, 106
Mundens, Betty I, 106
Mundens, Elishai I, 106
Mundens, Hannah I, 106
Mundens, Zelpha I, 106
Mundin, John I, 152
Mundin, Levi I, 152
Mundy, Alexander VI, 966
Mundy, Catharine E. VI, 966
Mundy, Ester V, 923
Mundy, Esther V, 923
Mundy, Esther V, 974
Mundy, Esther F. V, 923
Mundy, Joseph I, 727
Munger, Avis B. V, 700
Munger, Helen A. III, 125
Munger, Helen Adeline III, 229
Munger, Walter IV, 1330
Mungo, Edward G. I, 622
Mungo, Lona I, 622
Mungo, Luciel E. I, 946
Mungo, Lucile I, 622
Mungo, Scott V, 636
Munier, Anna Josephine III, 73
Munier, Anna Josephine III, 238
Munier, Chas. III, 73
Munier, Chas. III, 238
Munier, Mary A. III, 73
Munier, Mary E. III, 238
Munnett, Abigail III, 238
Munroe, Alex. A. III, 238
Munroe, James III, 238
Munroe, Mary E. III, 238
Munroe, Thomas III, 238
Munsall, Nora Michel IV, 982
Munsay, Mary E. IV, 255
Munsell, Nora IV, 982
Munsell, Nora Michel IV, 982
Munsell, Stanton IV, 982
Munsey, Nathan IV, 1258
Munson, Catharine III, 430
Munson, Catharine M. III, 411
Munson, Frances H. III, 430
Munson, Francis S. III, 430
Munson, Kate III, 430
Munson, Levi III, 411
Munson, Levi III, 430
Munson, Lydia Jane IV, 1374
Munson, Lydia Jane IV, 1385
Munson, Mary III, 430
Munson, Rachel III, 430
Muntford, Aleck VI, 76
Muntford, Bell VI, 76
Muntford, Bessie VI, 76
Muntford, Bessie VI, 77
Muntford, Carr VI, 77
Muntford, Carr VI, 82
Muntford, Carrie VI, 76
Muntford, Cephas VI, 76
Muntford, Cephas VI, 77
Muntford, Charles L. VI, 77
Muntford, Eliza VI, 52
Muntford, Eliza VI, 76
Muntford, Eliza VI, 77
Muntford, Ellen VI, 76
Muntford, Ellen VI, 77
Muntford, Franklin VI, 77
Muntford, George D. VI, 76
Muntford, Harry VI, 76
Muntford, Harry VI, 77
Muntford, Henry VI, 77
Muntford, James VI, 76
Muntford, James VI, 77
Muntford, Joseph's VI, 77
Muntford, Lucy VI, 77
Muntford, Mary Jane VI, 53
Muntford, Mody VI, 76
Muntford, Mody A. VI, 77
Muntford, Moody VI, 77
Muntford, Moody A. VI, 77
Muntford, Moody A. VI, 81
Muntford, Moody A. VI, 82
Muntford, Richard VI, 77
Muntford, Ruby VI, 76
Muntford, Ruth VI, 76
Muntford, Sallie VI, 53
Muntford, Sallie VI, 76
Muntford, Sallie VI, 77
Muntford, Susan VI, 76
Muntford, Susan VI, 77
Muntford, Susan VI, 81
Muntford, Susan VI, 82
Muntford, Wade VI, 53
Muntford, Wade VI, 77
Muntford, William VI, 52
Muntford, William VI, 76
Muntford, William VI, 77
Muntford, Wilmoth VI, 82
Muntford, Wilmoth L. VI, 76
Muntford, Wm. VI, 77
Murchell, Rachel II, 604
Murcherson, John VI, 827
Murcheson, John VI, 840
Murcock, Ann I Sup 1, 9
Murcock, John I Sup 1, 9
Murdah, John VI, 23
Murdah, John VI, 33
Murdah, Lydda I, 61
Murdaugh, Ann VI, 73
Murdaugh, Ann VI, 77
Murdaugh, John I, 51
Murdaugh, John I, 61
Murdaugh, John VI, 8
Murdaugh, John VI, 23
Murdaugh, John VI, 27
Murdaugh, John VI, 33
Murdaugh, John VI, 116
Murdaugh, John VI, 121
Murdaugh, Josiah VI, 63
Murdaugh, Josiah VI, 73
Murdaugh, Josiah VI, 77
Murdaugh, Lemuel I Sup 1, 7
Murdaugh, Milicent VI, 77
Murdaugh, Milicent VI, 87
Murdaugh, Sarah Sebrel VI, 116
Murdaugh, Thomas Trotter VI, 77
Murdaugh, Widow Sarah I, 61
Murdin, Ethelbert H. V, 588
Murdin, Susan D. V, 588
Murdoch, Agnes B. II, 713
Murdoch, Charles II, 713
Murdoch, Guy Charles II, 713
Murdoch, Ian Lachlan II, 713
Murdoch, Kennearly Gavin II, 713
Murdoch, Mary L. II, 713
Murdoch, Mary Sylvia II, 713
Murdoch, William T. II, 713
Murdock, ??? III, 143
Murdock, ??? III, 238
Murdock, Alexander I, 767
Murdock, Ann I, 448
Murdock, Ann I, 450
Murdock, Betsey VI, 998
Murdock, Catharine II, 819
Murdock, Charlotte VI, 966
Murdock, David I, 767
Murdock, Elijah VI, 965
Murdock, Elijah VI, 966
Murdock, Elijah VI, 969
Murdock, Elijah VI, 998
Murdock, Gilbert VI, 966
Murdock, James V, 588
Murdock, James E. V, 588
Murdock, James E., Jr. II, 902
Murdock, James Edward, Jr. II, 811
Murdock, John I, 143
Murdock, John I, 152
Murdock, Jonathan H. IV, 1287
Murdock, Juliet V, 250
Murdock, Juliet V, 267
Murdock, Mary III, 143
Murdock, Mary III, 238
Murdock, Miriam I, 143
Murdock, Miriam I, 152
Murdock, Phebe II, 399
Murdock, Polly VI, 956
Murdock, Polly VI, 966
Murdock, Prudence I Sup 1, 9
Murdock, Rachel V, 818
Murdock, Rev. ??? III, 411
Murdock, Samuel II, 399
Murdock, Sarah I, 760
Murdock, Sarah I, 767
Murdock, Susan II, 811
Murdock, Susan V, 33
Murdock, Susan V, 104
Murdock, Susan V, 588
Murdock, Susan B. II, 902
Murdock, Susan B. V, 104
Murdock, Susan B. V, 588
Murdock, Thomas F. V, 588
Murdock, Thos. F. II, 902
Murdock, Wm. B. II, 902
Murdock, Wm. B. V, 588
Murdock, Wm. Butterworth, Jr. II, 811
Murdor, John VI, 8
Murdough, John I, 61
Murdough, Joseph I, 61
Murdough, Josiah I, 35
Murdough, Josiah I, 61
Murdough, Lemuel I, 61
Murdough, Lydda I, 61
Murdough, Lydia I, 35
Murdough, Lydia I, 61
Murdough, Mary I, 60
Murdough, Mary I, 61
Murdough, Mary I, 73
Murdough, Miriam I, 61
Murdough, Miriam I, 85
Murdough, Widow Sarah I, 61
Murell, Nancy VI, 814
Murell, Thos. VI, 814
Murfe, William II, 446
Murfee, Charles VI, 58
Murfee, Margret I, 378
Murfee, Margret I, 411
Murfey, Barnabey II, 399
Murfey, Jane II, 1017
Murfey, Wm. II, 604
Murfin, Katherine II, 197
Murfin, Katherine II, 244
Murfin, Mary II, 244
Murfin, Mary II, 260
Murfit, Eliz. III, 249
Murfit, Eliza. III, 83
Murgrage, Girden F. IV, 1331
Murgrage, Mildred P. IV, 1331
Murie, Ann IV, 255
Murie, Effie IV, 255
Murie, Jennie IV, 255
Murie, Jesse IV, 255
Murie, Jewsie IV, 255
Murie, John, Sr. IV, 255
Murie, Louis IV, 255
Murie, Mary IV, 255
Murie, Peter IV, 255
Murie, Thomas IV, 255
Murie, Vernon IV, 255
Murie, William IV, 255
Muriel, Mary Ward III, 274
Muriel, Mildred IV, 985
Muritt, Ann III, 82
Murphey, Aaron F. VI, 425

Murphey, Almira II, 811
Murphey, Almira II, 820
Murphey, Almira II, 902
Murphey, Almira R. II, 902
Murphey, Almira R. II, 922
Murphey, Anna V, 1011
Murphey, Blanch V, 1011
Murphey, Cynthia V, 351
Murphey, Cynthia V, 365
Murphey, Edward R. II, 902
Murphey, Elanor VI, 918
Murphey, Elma V, 351
Murphey, Elma V, 366
Murphey, Elva V, 351
Murphey, Elva V, 361
Murphey, Frank V, 1011
Murphey, Fred V, 1011
Murphey, Hannah II, 996
Murphey, Hattie V, 1011
Murphey, Henry V, 1011
Murphey, Huldah V, 1011
Murphey, Ira V, 1011
Murphey, Isabella VI, 967
Murphey, Jane II, 1017
Murphey, Jane V, 1011
Murphey, John VI, 978
Murphey, Joseph I, 99
Murphey, Joseph II, 902
Murphey, Leatitia II, 63
Murphey, Letitia II, 811
Murphey, Letitia II, 902
Murphey, Lillie V, 1011
Murphey, Lydia V, 473
Murphey, Lydia V, 519
Murphey, Mamie IV, 1330
Murphey, Margaret II, 814
Murphey, Martha I, 99
Murphey, Martha V, 519
Murphey, Martha E. V, 1011
Murphey, Martha I. V, 1011
Murphey, Mary II, 820
Murphey, Mary V, 1011
Murphey, Mary J. II, 811
Murphey, Mary J. II, 902
Murphey, Mary J. II, 922
Murphey, May V, 1011
Murphey, Nella V, 1011
Murphey, Neoma V, 1011
Murphey, Rachel F. II, 811
Murphey, Rachel F. II, 902
Murphey, Rachel T. II, 902
Murphey, Rolla V, 1011
Murphey, Rosa Ann V, 1011
Murphey, Sam V, 1011
Murphey, Samuel V, 1011
Murphey, Sarah II, 902
Murphey, Sarah C. II, 902
Murphey, Sarah E. II, 902
Murphey, Sarah E. II, 921
Murphey, Susan C. II, 811
Murphey, Susan C. II, 902
Murphey, Truman V, 351
Murphey, Walter V, 1011
Murphey, William VI, 967
Murphey, William Craig II, 811
Murphey, Wm. II, 63
Murphey, Wm. C. II, 902
Murphey, Wm. C. II, 922
Murphey, Wm. Craig II, 820
Murphey, Zola V, 351
Murphy, Aaron F. VI, 425
Murphy, Abigail I, 920
Murphy, Abigail Jane I, 923
Murphy, Albert V, 194
Murphy, Albert L. A. I, 662
Murphy, Almira II, 902
Murphy, Almira R. II, 902
Murphy, Ann II, 88
Murphy, Arbulissa B. I, 618
Murphy, Asenath IV, 1101
Murphy, Asenath IV, 1108
Murphy, Barnabey II, 399
Murphy, Bennett M. VI, 938
Murphy, C. S. I, 946
Murphy, Caleb IV, 1364
Murphy, Calvin Bond I, 618
Murphy, Catharine D. V, 424
Murphy, Catherine V, 580
Murphy, Charles VI, 768
Murphy, Charles F. I, 946
Murphy, Charles S. I, 931
Murphy, Clemment I, 727
Murphy, Daniel III, 238
Murphy, Dorothy I, 139
Murphy, Dorothy I, 152
Murphy, Edward R. II, 902
Murphy, Elijah T. VI, 877
Murphy, Elijah T. VI, 967
Murphy, Elisabeth I, 152
Murphy, Eliz'h T. VI, 425
Murphy, Elizabeth I, 152
Murphy, Elizabeth I, 156
Murphy, Elizabeth I, 165
Murphy, Elizabeth I, 727
Murphy, Elizabeth T. VI, 372
Murphy, Elizabeth T. VI, 624
Murphy, Elizabeth T. VI, 625
Murphy, Ella V, 380
Murphy, Emelia VI, 967
Murphy, Estella V, 519
Murphy, Flora E. IV, 1364
Murphy, Flora E. IV, 1374
Murphy, Florance Annie I, 931
Murphy, Frances VI, 967
Murphy, Franklin I, 923
Murphy, Georgie III, 491
Murphy, Greenberry V, 424
Murphy, Isaac Penrose IV, 1108
Murphy, Isabella VI, 967
Murphy, J. VI, 966
Murphy, James V, 519
Murphy, James VI, 966
Murphy, James VI, 983
Murphy, Jamie III, 491
Murphy, Jane V, 1011
Murphy, Jane VI, 885
Murphy, Jeremiah VI, 967
Murphy, Jerusha V, 424
Murphy, John IV, 744
Murphy, John VI, 335
Murphy, John VI, 954
Murphy, John VI, 966
Murphy, John L. I, 662
Murphy, John L. I, 685
Murphy, John, Jr. VI, 966
Murphy, John, Jr. VI, 1021
Murphy, Joseph I, 152
Murphy, Joseph II, 902
Murphy, Julius A. I, 662
Murphy, Katy VI, 966
Murphy, Laura V, 588
Murphy, Leatitia II, 88
Murphy, Letitia II, 902
Murphy, Lettitia II, 88
Murphy, Lucy VI, 967
Murphy, Lyddia I, 727
Murphy, Lydia I, 152
Murphy, Lydia I, 727
Murphy, Lydia V, 519
Murphy, Lydia Jane I, 923
Murphy, Mahlon II, 35
Murphy, Mahlon II, 88
Murphy, Margaret I, 411
Murphy, Margaret I, 618
Murphy, Margaret I, 927
Murphy, Margaret IV, 834
Murphy, Margaret IV, 894
Murphy, Margaret V, 104
Murphy, Margaret VI, 937
Murphy, Margaret Ann I, 936
Murphy, Margaret J. I, 662
Murphy, Margarett VI, 966
Murphy, Margret I, 411
Murphy, Martha I, 107
Murphy, Martha I, 140
Murphy, Martha I, 152
Murphy, Martha I, 156
Murphy, Martha II, 121
Murphy, Martha III, 491
Murphy, Martha V, 519
Murphy, Martha K. II, 121
Murphy, Mary I, 145
Murphy, Mary I, 152
Murphy, Mary II, 399
Murphy, Mary IV, 381
Murphy, Mary IV, 423
Murphy, Mary E. V, 423
Murphy, Mary G. I, 662
Murphy, Mary J. II, 902
Murphy, Mary Jane IV, 1108
Murphy, Michael I, 107
Murphy, Michael I, 152
Murphy, Michael I, 165
Murphy, Miles I, 107
Murphy, Miles I, 139
Murphy, Miles I, 152
Murphy, Miles I, 727
Murphy, Miranda IV, 1364
Murphy, Miriam I, 662
Murphy, Miriam E. I, 676
Murphy, Miriam E. I, 685
Murphy, Nancy VI, 814
Murphy, Nancy VI, 961
Murphy, Nancy VI, 967
Murphy, Nancy, Sr. VI, 961
Murphy, Naomi II, 35
Murphy, Naomia II, 88
Murphy, Neah II, 88
Murphy, Nixon VI, 967
Murphy, Noah II, 35
Murphy, Noah II, 88
Murphy, Noah II, 107
Murphy, Noah II, 244
Murphy, Noah S. II, 244
Murphy, Pamelia VI, 978
Murphy, Phebe V, 490
Murphy, Phebe V, 519
Murphy, Pleasant VI, 992
Murphy, Polley VI, 966
Murphy, Polly VI, 977
Murphy, Rachel F. II, 902
Murphy, Rachel T. II, 902
Murphy, Robert I, 107
Murphy, Robert I, 152
Murphy, Robert I, 727
Murphy, Rosa Holland V, 194
Murphy, Ruth V, 854
Murphy, Ruth V, 872
Murphy, Ruth VI, 814
Murphy, Ruth VI, 966
Murphy, Sam V, 1011
Murphy, Samuel VI, 966
Murphy, Sarah I, 564
Murphy, Sarah I, 936
Murphy, Sarah II, 902
Murphy, Sarah IV, 648
Murphy, Sarah IV, 652
Murphy, Sarah IV, 744
Murphy, Sarah V, 580
Murphy, Sarah C. II, 902
Murphy, Sarah C. III, 34
Murphy, Sarah C. III, 339
Murphy, Sarah E. I, 662
Murphy, Sarah E. II, 902
Murphy, Sarah Elizabeth II, 921
Murphy, Silas I, 831
Murphy, Smith II, 35
Murphy, Smith II, 88
Murphy, Stephen VI, 967
Murphy, Susan C. II, 902
Murphy, Susan Cox II, 820
Murphy, Theodosha VI, 966
Murphy, Thomas I, 107
Murphy, Timothy III, 238
Murphy, Truman V, 351
Murphy, Wd. Lettitia II, 35
Murphy, William I, 152
Murphy, William I, 156
Murphy, William I, 936
Murphy, William II, 35
Murphy, William III, 491
Murphy, William VI, 967
Murphy, William Henry III, 491
Murphy, Willie V, 194
Murphy, Wm. II, 88
Murphy, Wm. II, 604
Murphy, Wm. C. II, 902
Murphy, Zachary I, 152
Murray, ??? III, 43
Murray, ??? III, 238
Murray, ??? III, 253
Murray, Agnes Taber III, 239
Murray, Alfred IV, 1258
Murray, Ann Eliza III, 238
Murray, Anna V, 104
Murray, Anna T. III, 90
Murray, Anna T. III, 238
Murray, Anna T. III, 324
Murray, Anna T. III, 329
Murray, Anna T. III, 330
Murray, Anna Taber III, 239
Murray, Avis III, 253
Murray, Beulah III, 168
Murray, Beulah III, 238
Murray, Caroline III, 238
Murray, Caroline III, 253
Murray, Catharine III, 40
Murray, Catharine III, 183
Murray, Catharine III, 238
Murray, Catharine III, 239
Murray, Catharine III, 253
Murray, Catharine B. III, 238
Murray, Catherine II, 594
Murray, Catherine II, 605
Murray, Catherine VI, 92
Murray, Chap. III, 239
Murray, Charles Taber III, 239
Murray, Cora T. V, 104
Murray, D. Colden III, 239
Murray, David III, 253
Murray, David VI, 928
Murray, David Colden III, 238
Murray, David Colden III, 239
Murray, Donal Powell V, 104
Murray, Edward L. III, 238
Murray, Effie IV, 255
Murray, Effingham C. III, 99
Murray, Effingham C. III, 238
Murray, Effingham C. III, 239
Murray, Eliz. III, 238
Murray, Eliz. C. III, 117
Murray, Eliz. C. III, 179
Murray, Eliz. C. III, 238
Murray, Eliza III, 29
Murray, Eliza III, 81
Murray, Eliza III, 238
Murray, Elizabeth II, 605
Murray, Elizabeth II, 679
Murray, Elizabeth VI, 928
Murray, Elizabeth C. III, 238
Murray, Elizabeth C. III, 239
Murray, Elizabeth Colden III, 239
Murray, Elizabeth W. VI, 967
Murray, Ella IV, 1331
Murray, Elsie V, 104
Murray, Emely V, 104
Murray, Frances K. III, 239
Murray, Gertrude III, 239
Murray, Gertrude Colden III, 179
Murray, Gertrude Colden III, 238
Murray, Hannah II, 581
Murray, Hannah II, 604
Murray, Hannah III, 238
Murray, Hannah III, 239
Murray, Hannah W. III, 239
Murray, Hannah W. III, 288
Murray, Hannah, Jr. III, 238
Murray, Harriet III, 57
Murray, Harriet C. III, 57
Murray, Harriet C. III, 238
Murray, Harriet C. III, 239
Murray, James I, 247
Murray, James III, 238
Murray, James V, 1011
Murray, James V, 1012
Murray, James VI, 967
Murray, Jane M. III, 238
Murray, Janet Helen V, 104
Murray, John II, 476
Murray, John II, 581
Murray, John II, 604
Murray, John III, 253
Murray, John, Jr. III, 40
Murray, John, Jr. III, 238
Murray, John, Jr. III, 239
Murray, Joseph K. III, 238
Murray, Kate V, 104
Murray, Lindley III, 68
Murray, Lindley III, 81
Murray, Lindley III, 193
Murray, Lindley III, 238
Murray, Lindley III, 239
Murray, Lindley Murray III, 253
Murray, Lindley, Jr. III, 238
Murray, London III, 238
Murray, Louisa III, 238
Murray, Lowell Thomas V, 104
Murray, Margaret VI, 948
Murray, Margaret C. III, 238
Murray, Margaretta C. III, 81
Murray, Marie III, 99
Murray, Marie III, 238
Murray, Mary II, 581
Murray, Mary II, 604
Murray, Mary III, 26
Murray, Mary III, 117
Murray, Mary III, 238
Murray, Mary III, 239
Murray, Mary III, 253
Murray, Mary III, 360
Murray, Mary Ann III, 193
Murray, Mary Ann III, 238
Murray, Mary Ann III, 239
Murray, Mary Ellen V, 104
Murray, Mary K. III, 238
Murray, Natalie Eliza V, 104
Murray, Opal V, 349
Murray, Opal V, 351
Murray, Phebe Ann III, 57
Murray, Phebe Anna III, 57
Murray, Phebe Anna III, 238
Murray, Phebe Anna III, 239
Murray, Polly VI, 967
Murray, Rebecca H. V, 104
Murray, Robert III, 238
Murray, Robert III, 239
Murray, Robert III, 263
Murray, Robert I. III, 117
Murray, Robert I. III, 238
Murray, Robert I. III, 239
Murray, Robert I. III, 288
Murray, Robert I., Jr. III, 239
Murray, Robert Lindley III, 239
Murray, Roberta I. III, 239
Murray, Robt. I III, 179
Murray, Robt. I. III, 57
Murray, Robt. I. III, 238
Murray, Robt. I. III, 239
Murray, Robt. I., Jr. III, 238
Murray, Robt. I., Jr. III, 239
Murray, Robt. L. III, 238
Murray, Robt. Lindley III, 238
Murray, Robt. Lindley III, 239
Murray, Robt. Lindley III, 324
Murray, Russel J. V, 588
Murray, Ruth III, 239
Murray, Ruth V, 588
Murray, Ruth Barrett V, 588
Murray, Ruth S. III, 238
Murray, Ruth S. III, 239
Murray, Ruth S. III, 324
Murray, Sarah II, 604
Murray, Sarah S. III, 239
Murray, Susanah I, 451
Murray, Susanna VI, 967
Murray, Susannah II, 217
Murray, Susannah II, 244
Murray, Susannah III, 238
Murray, Susannah III, 239
Murray, Susannah III, 356
Murray, Thomas VI, 967
Murray, Walter V, 349
Murray, Walter V, 351
Murray, William III, 238
Murray, William III, 239
Murray, William VI, 948
Murray, William VI, 967
Murray, William T. III, 239
Murray, William Taber III, 23
Murrell, Alice VI, 843
Murrell, Armintha IV, 825
Murrell, Armintha IV, 834
Murrell, Caroline VI, 843
Murrell, Charles VI, 967
Murrell, Cordelia V, 194
Murrell, Cordelia V, 692
Murrell, Cordelia V, 700
Murrell, Cordelia M. V, 700
Murrell, David G. VI, 843
Murrell, Eliza Ann VI, 901
Murrell, Eliza Ann VI, 967
Murrell, Elizabeth VI, 843
Murrell, Elizabeth VI, 901
Murrell, Elizabeth VI, 974
Murrell, Evaline V, 636
Murrell, Eveline V, 636
Murrell, Frances VI, 843
Murrell, Frances C. VI, 843
Murrell, Fred A. VI, 853
Murrell, Frederick VI, 843
Murrell, George VI, 33
Murrell, George VI, 37
Murrell, Grant V, 636
Murrell, Grant V, 700
Murrell, James VI, 843
Murrell, Jane V, 636
Murrell, Jeffrey VI, 200
Murrell, Jeffrey VI, 807
Murrell, Jeffrey VI, 843
Murrell, Jennie V, 636
Murrell, John VI, 843
Murrell, John VI, 844
Murrell, John VI, 967
Murrell, John VI, 974
Murrell, John C. VI, 830
Murrell, John C. VI, 843
Murrell, Levina VI, 843
Murrell, Mabel V, 700
Murrell, Mabel A. V, 700
Murrell, Mable V, 194
Murrell, Mable V, 719
Murrell, Margaret F. VI, 830
Murrell, Mary V, 636
Murrell, Mary VI, 33
Murrell, Mary VI, 37
Murrell, Mary VI, 843
Murrell, Mary Ann VI, 967
Murrell, Mildred VI, 834
Murrell, Nancy VI, 843
Murrell, Ora V, 194
Murrell, Ora V, 700
Murrell, Ora H. V, 194
Murrell, Polly VI, 299
Murrell, Polly VI, 799
Murrell, Polly VI, 843
Murrell, Reuben T. VI, 910
Murrell, S. J. V, 636
Murrell, Sallie B. VI, 843
Murrell, Seley VI, 854
Murrell, Stella V, 636
Murrell, Susan E. VI, 830
Murrell, Thomas VI, 799
Murrell, Thomas VI, 832
Murrell, Thomas VI, 843
Murrell, Thomas VI, 854
Murrell, U. G. V, 194
Murrell, U. Grant V, 700
Murrell, Ulysses Grant V, 194
Murrell, William VI, 200
Murrell, William VI, 843
Murrell, William G. VI, 843
Murrell, Wm. VI, 834
Murrey, ??? VI, 39
Murrey, Ann II, 399

ey, Humphrey II, 399
ey, Humphrey II, 446
ey, John II, 446
ey, Lucinda I, 595
ey, Mary VI, 45
ey, Phebe Anna III, 75
ey, Rebeckah II, 446
ey, Rhoda I, 595
ey, Richardson II, 446
ey, Robert S. III, 75
ey, Ruth Barrett V, 461
ey, Sarah II, 446
ey, Susanna I, 564
ey, Thomas II, 446
ill, Jane VI, 940
ill, Sarah VI, 910
ill, Wm. VI, 940
tt, Mattie I, 311
ow, Dora I, 618
ow, John I, 831
ow, Margaret I, 685
ow, Martha I, 617
ow, Mary E. I, 662
ow, Phebe I, 564
ow, Sarah I, 831
ow, Sarah I, 841
ow, Sheubal I, 662
ow, Susan I, 564
ow, Susanna I, 831
y, Andrew II, 399
y, Ann II, 399
y, Ann IV, 255
y, Ann VI, 601
y, Anne T. IV, 834
y, Anne T. IV, 848
y, Donal Powell V, 104
y, Elizabeth II, 446
y, Elizabeth VI, 33
y, Elizabeth VI, 38
y, Elizabeth W. VI, 967
y, Emely V, 104
y, Hannah II, 399
y, Humphrey II, 399
y, James VI, 967
y, Janet Helen V, 104
y, John II, 446
y, John VI, 17
y, John VI, 33
y, John VI, 38
y, Kate V, 104
y, Lindley V, 267
y, Martha VI, 843
y, Mary Ellen V, 104
y, Mary R. IV, 542
y, Mary R. IV, 559
y, Natalie Eliza V, 104
y, Rebecca H. V, 36
y, Rebecca H. V, 104
y, Robert II, 399
y, Robert V, 194
y, Ruth Barrett V, 461
y, Sarah II, 446
y, Sarah IV, 21
y, Sarah IV, 51
y, Susannah II, 244
y, Thomas II, 446
y, Thomas Tuke VI, 17
y, William II, 399
y, William VI, 843
y, Wm. V, 461
on, C. E. IV, 1329
in, Sarah IV, 607
, Susanah I, 451
, Grace IV, 1331
, Nancy VI, 967
, William W. VI, 967
grave, Aaron II, 605
grave, Abigail I, 309
grave, Abigail I, 312
grave, Abigail II, 605
grave, Abraham I, 291
grave, Andrew I, 291
grave, Ann I, 291
grave, Ann I, 312
grave, Anna I, 291
grave, Anne I, 312
grave, Arcada I, 312
grave, Arcada I, 317
grave, Avey I, 312
grave, Avis I, 292
grave, Avis I, 312
grave, Avis I, 317
grave, Betty I, 312
grave, Caleb I, 312
grave, Caleb I, 1071
grave, Catharine I, 312
grave, Charity I, 292
grave, Charity I, 312
grave, Charity I, 1071
grave, Christian I, 280
grave, Christiana I, 312
Musgrave, Christiana I, 313
Musgrave, Edward I, 312
Musgrave, Elizabeth I, 291
Musgrave, Elizabeth I, 292
Musgrave, Elizabeth I, 303
Musgrave, Elizabeth I, 312
Musgrave, Elizabeth I, 1071
Musgrave, Emelia I, 300
Musgrave, Emelia I, 312
Musgrave, Esther II, 605
Musgrave, Furney I, 312
Musgrave, Hannah I, 291
Musgrave, Hannah I, 308
Musgrave, Hannah I, 312
Musgrave, Harret Telitha I, 312
Musgrave, Harriett Tabitha I, 291
Musgrave, Isabella I, 330
Musgrave, James I, 291
Musgrave, James I, 292
Musgrave, James I, 312
Musgrave, Joel I, 292
Musgrave, Joel I, 304
Musgrave, Joel I, 312
Musgrave, John I, 305
Musgrave, John I, 312
Musgrave, Jonathan I, 292
Musgrave, Jonathan I, 312
Musgrave, Josiah I, 312
Musgrave, Josiah I, 317
Musgrave, Lovicia I, 312
Musgrave, Mary I, 291
Musgrave, Mary I, 303
Musgrave, Mary I, 312
Musgrave, Micajah I, 312
Musgrave, Millia I, 312
Musgrave, Nathan I, 291
Musgrave, Nathan I, 292
Musgrave, Nathan I, 312
Musgrave, Rachel II, 588
Musgrave, Rebecca I, 292
Musgrave, Rebecca I, 312
Musgrave, Rebeckah I, 304
Musgrave, Rebeckah I, 312
Musgrave, Sallyann I, 312
Musgrave, Sarah I, 305
Musgrave, Sarah I, 311
Musgrave, Sarah I, 312
Musgrave, Sarah I, 1071
Musgrave, Thomas I, 292
Musgrave, William I, 292
Musgrave, William I, 312
Musgrave, William I, 317
Musgrave, Wm. IV, 154
Musgrove, Aaron II, 399
Musgrove, Aaron II, 593
Musgrove, Aaron II, 605
Musgrove, Aaron, Sr. II, 605
Musgrove, Abigail II, 605
Musgrove, Abraham II, 605
Musgrove, Agathy VI, 967
Musgrove, Ann II, 521
Musgrove, Ann II, 605
Musgrove, Ann Eliza VI, 989
Musgrove, Benj. VI, 1015
Musgrove, Benj. B. VI, 921
Musgrove, Benjamin VI, 967
Musgrove, Benjamin VI, 976
Musgrove, Benjamin B. VI, 875
Musgrove, Benjamin B. VI, 967
Musgrove, Caleb I, 312
Musgrove, Christopher VI, 926
Musgrove, Christopher VI, 958
Musgrove, Christopher VI, 967
Musgrove, Christopher VI, 976
Musgrove, Christopher VI, 989
Musgrove, Christopher VI, 1015
Musgrove, D. P. VI, 1015
Musgrove, Demetrius P. VI, 967
Musgrove, Elijah II, 605
Musgrove, Eliza E. VI, 967
Musgrove, Elizabeth II, 593
Musgrove, Elizabeth II, 605
Musgrove, Esther II, 605
Musgrove, Furney I, 312
Musgrove, Grace VI, 584
Musgrove, Hannah II, 605
Musgrove, Israel II, 605
Musgrove, Israel VI, 537
Musgrove, Israel VI, 584
Musgrove, James I, 312
Musgrove, James II, 399
Musgrove, James II, 605
Musgrove, Job II, 605
Musgrove, Joel II, 399
Musgrove, John II, 605
Musgrove, John VI, 1015
Musgrove, John H. VI, 921
Musgrove, John H. VI, 967
Musgrove, John H. VI, 1015
Musgrove, Jonathan I, 312
Musgrove, Josiah I, 312
Musgrove, Kesiah VI, 1015
Musgrove, Kezia VI, 967
Musgrove, Keziah VI, 1015
Musgrove, Keziah E. VI, 958
Musgrove, Lucy VI, 967
Musgrove, Magdaline S. VI, 1015
Musgrove, Martha A. VI, 967
Musgrove, Mary II, 605
Musgrove, Mary IV, 344
Musgrove, Mary VI, 634
Musgrove, Mary VI, 677
Musgrove, Millicent VI, 871
Musgrove, Minerva N. VI, 875
Musgrove, Moses II, 399
Musgrove, Moses II, 605
Musgrove, Nathan I, 312
Musgrove, Rachel II, 605
Musgrove, Rachel VI, 1015
Musgrove, Rebecca VI, 976
Musgrove, Rezia VI, 1015
Musgrove, Ruth II, 605
Musgrove, Sally Ann VI, 967
Musgrove, Sarah VI, 537
Musgrove, Sarah VI, 572
Musgrove, Sarah M. VI, 1015
Musgrove, Tabitha VI, 921
Musgrove, Thomas VI, 572
Musgrove, Thomas VI, 967
Musgrove, William I, 312
Musgrove, Wm. II, 605
Musser, ??? III, 69
Musser, Caroline III, 69
Mussetter, Alvin V, 519
Mussetter, Clarence W. V, 519
Mussetter, Maria V, 194
Mussetter, Minnie Carl V, 519
Mussetter, Sarah V, 519
Mustgrave, Charity I, 1071
Mutersbaugh, Dora IV, 1239
Mutersbaugh, J. A. IV, 1239
Muth, Henry IV, 1258
Muth, Winona L. IV, 1258
Muyskins, Rev. John III, 435
Myars, Catharine V, 517
Myars, John II, 605
Myars, Mary IV, 35
Myars, Mary IV, 51
Myars, Susanna II, 605
Myer, Job II, 755
Myers, A. C. VI, 495
Myers, Abigail IV, 1287
Myers, Aggy VI, 814
Myers, Albert V, 1012
Myers, Albert Cook VI, 490
Myers, Albert Cook VI, 491
Myers, Albert Cook VI, 495
Myers, Albert Cook VI, 567
Myers, Alice IV, 648
Myers, Alice VI, 537
Myers, Alice VI, 586
Myers, Alice G. VI, 677
Myers, Alice Graham VI, 677
Myers, Ambrose Worthington IV, 420
Myers, Amelia V, 423
Myers, Ann III, 134
Myers, Ann III, 239
Myers, Ann IV, 575
Myers, Ann IV, 589
Myers, Ann VI, 538
Myers, Anna IV, 1331
Myers, Annie V, 1012
Myers, Archie I, 930
Myers, Augusta IV, 1218
Myers, Augustus IV, 1218
Myers, Aurelia H. I, 922
Myers, Barbara E. IV, 720
Myers, Benjamin II, 399
Myers, Benjamin II, 605
Myers, Benjamin VI, 537
Myers, Benjamin VI, 677
Myers, Benjamin VI, 687
Myers, Bernice L. IV, 420
Myers, Biola Gertrude V, 267
Myers, C. Nolen V, 1012
Myers, Catherine VI, 475
Myers, Charles IV, 1258
Myers, Charles IV, 1259
Myers, Charles Lionel IV, 420
Myers, Charles W. IV, 662
Myers, Charles William Henry V, 267
Myers, Clara IV, 1258
Myers, Clara IV, 1259
Myers, Clark IV, 1041
Myers, Claus A. IV, 1331
Myers, Clifford D. V, 194
Myers, Cynthia IV, 911
Myers, Cynthia IV, 912
Myers, D. Loretta I, 611
Myers, David IV, 744
Myers, Diana Luatta I, 922
Myers, Dora V, 634
Myers, Dorothy IV, 1259
Myers, Dr. Albert Cook I, 487
Myers, Edith V, 517
Myers, Elaine IV, 1218
Myers, Elen V, 267
Myers, Eli IV, 720
Myers, Elijah VI, 468
Myers, Elijah VI, 475
Myers, Elijah VI, 537
Myers, Elijah VI, 538
Myers, Elijah VI, 542
Myers, Elijah VI, 555
Myers, Elijah VI, 623
Myers, Elijah VI, 677
Myers, Elisha VI, 556
Myers, Eliza Jane IV, 744
Myers, Elizabeth II, 605
Myers, Elizabeth IV, 648
Myers, Elizabeth IV, 686
Myers, Elizabeth IV, 744
Myers, Elizabeth IV, 835
Myers, Elizabeth IV, 911
Myers, Elizabeth IV, 917
Myers, Elizabeth VI, 475
Myers, Elizabeth VI, 512
Myers, Elizabeth VI, 537
Myers, Elizabeth VI, 601
Myers, Elizabeth VI, 677
Myers, Elizabeth VI, 687
Myers, Elizabeth A. V, 104
Myers, Elizabeth W. IV, 662
Myers, Ella VI, 633
Myers, Ella VI, 634
Myers, Ella VI, 677
Myers, Ella VI, 738
Myers, Ellen V, 267
Myers, Esther IV, 1259
Myers, Esther VI, 475
Myers, Esther VI, 476
Myers, Esther VI, 500
Myers, Esther VI, 505
Myers, Esther VI, 527
Myers, Esther VI, 537
Myers, Esther VI, 547
Myers, Esther VI, 548
Myers, Esther VI, 645
Myers, Esther VI, 651
Myers, Esther VI, 688
Myers, Esther, Jr. VI, 475
Myers, Ethel I, 937
Myers, Ethel I, 946
Myers, Ethel B. I, 946
Myers, Eva V, 423
Myers, Eva C. V, 423
Myers, Fannie VI, 677
Myers, Floyd VI, 677
Myers, Floyd VI, 711
Myers, Floyd VI, 713
Myers, Francis VI, 537
Myers, Frank IV, 1218
Myers, Frank J. Russell VI, 768
Myers, Frank M. VI, 677
Myers, Frank Richard IV, 1041
Myers, George V, 267
Myers, George V, 461
Myers, George VI, 475
Myers, George C. V, 267
Myers, George C. V, 461
Myers, George, Jr. V, 267
Myers, Gertrude Whitman IV, 1331
Myers, Grace Ann IV, 1239
Myers, H. M. IV, 1287
Myers, Hannah II, 294
Myers, Hannah II, 297
Myers, Hannah IV, 835
Myers, Hannah VI, 537
Myers, Hannah VI, 587
Myers, Hannah VI, 677
Myers, Hannah VI, 768
Myers, Hannah D. II, 297
Myers, Hannah E. II, 806
Myers, Hannah E. IV, 831
Myers, Hannah E. IV, 835
Myers, Hannah S. VI, 475
Myers, Hannah S. VI, 538
Myers, Hannah S. VI, 623
Myers, Hannah S. VI, 677
Myers, Hattie V, 1012
Myers, Henry V, 423
Myers, Henry VI, 475
Myers, Henry VI, 476
Myers, Henry, Jr. VI, 475
Myers, Herbert V, 1012
Myers, Hiram VI, 475
Myers, Ida IV, 982
Myers, Ida V, 1012
Myers, Iota V, 461
Myers, Isaac VI, 475
Myers, Isaac VI, 537
Myers, Isaac VI, 677
Myers, Isaac, Jr. VI, 475
Myers, Isaiah VI, 537
Myers, Isaiah VI, 586
Myers, Israel IV, 744
Myers, J. P. VI, 475
Myers, Jacob II, 179
Myers, Jacob VI, 475
Myers, Jacob VI, 677
Myers, Jacob VI, 687
Myers, Jane IV, 835
Myers, Jane VI, 768
Myers, Jane V. II, 902
Myers, Jane V. IV, 744
Myers, John II, 605
Myers, John V, 267
Myers, John V, 423
Myers, John V, 1012
Myers, John VI, 476
Myers, John VI, 537
Myers, John A. IV, 1239
Myers, John F. V, 423
Myers, John George VI, 677
Myers, John W. III, 239
Myers, John W. III, 276
Myers, John Wesley VI, 775
Myers, John Wesley Myers VI, 768
Myers, John, Jr. VI, 475
Myers, John, Sr. VI, 476
Myers, Jonathan IV, 835
Myers, Jonathan IV, 911
Myers, Jonathan VI, 468
Myers, Jonathan VI, 537
Myers, Jonathan VI, 547
Myers, Jonathan VI, 586
Myers, Joseph V, 1012
Myers, Joseph VI, 536
Myers, Joseph VI, 537
Myers, Joseph VI, 548
Myers, Joseph VI, 557
Myers, Joseph VI, 688
Myers, Joseph VI, 768
Myers, Joseph E. IV, 420
Myers, Josie III, 239
Myers, Josie B. VI, 768
Myers, Josie B. VI, 775
Myers, Josie M. III, 276
Myers, Julia A. II, 902
Myers, Julia A. IV, 744
Myers, Julia Ann VI, 768
Myers, Julianna IV, 835
Myers, Lemuel IV, 662
Myers, Lena IV, 879
Myers, Leona IV, 879
Myers, Lillian II, 128
Myers, Lillian IV, 835
Myers, Louisa II, 605
Myers, Luatta I, 920
Myers, Luetta I, 922
Myers, Lydia I, 994
Myers, Mahala IV, 835
Myers, Mahlon VI, 537
Myers, Margaret A. III, 276
Myers, Margaret A. IV, 1331
Myers, Margaret Alice III, 239
Myers, Margaret Alice VI, 768
Myers, Margaret Alice VI, 775
Myers, Martha VI, 476
Myers, Martha A. IV, 982
Myers, Martha E. VI, 548
Myers, Martha E. VI, 688
Myers, Martha J. IV, 720
Myers, Mary II, 244
Myers, Mary IV, 835
Myers, Mary IV, 1041
Myers, Mary IV, 1259
Myers, Mary IV, 1287
Myers, Mary V, 194
Myers, Mary V, 200
Myers, Mary VI, 425
Myers, Mary VI, 468
Myers, Mary VI, 475
Myers, Mary VI, 476
Myers, Mary VI, 537
Myers, Mary VI, 538
Myers, Mary VI, 542
Myers, Mary VI, 547
Myers, Mary VI, 555
Myers, Mary VI, 556
Myers, Mary VI, 586
Myers, Mary VI, 623
Myers, Mary VI, 768
Myers, Mary A. VI, 425
Myers, Mary Ellen VI, 538
Myers, Mary Ellen VI, 677
Myers, Mary Ellen VI, 711
Myers, Mary Ellen VI, 713
Myers, Mary Esther VI, 475

Myers, Mary F. IV, 835
Myers, Mary F. IV, 836
Myers, Mary J. V, 267
Myers, Mary T. IV, 648
Myers, Mary T. IV, 661
Myers, Mary W. IV, 420
Myers, Mattie I, 930
Myers, Minnie V, 194
Myers, Minnie V, 1012
Myers, Mrs. Jennie V, 1012
Myers, Myrtle May V, 1012
Myers, Nancy V, 267
Myers, Nancy V, 423
Myers, Nancy Hall IV, 835
Myers, Nettie V, 1012
Myers, Nimrod T. Bennett VI, 768
Myers, Olitha V, 586
Myers, Ollah V, 267
Myers, Pamelia VI, 537
Myers, Pamelia VI, 542
Myers, Paul IV, 1041
Myers, Paulina IV, 744
Myers, Paulina VI, 768
Myers, Pauline IV, 835
Myers, Permelia V, 423
Myers, Phebe VI, 518
Myers, Phebe VI, 519
Myers, Phebe VI, 535
Myers, Phebe VI, 536
Myers, Phebe VI, 537
Myers, Phebe VI, 566
Myers, Phebe VI, 663
Myers, Phebe VI, 676
Myers, Phebe VI, 767
Myers, Priscilla V, 267
Myers, Priscilla V, 423
Myers, Prudence V, 200
Myers, Rachel IV, 835
Myers, Rachel VI, 687
Myers, Rachel VI, 768
Myers, Ralph V, 200
Myers, Ralph J. V, 423
Myers, Rebecca IV, 744
Myers, Rebecca VI, 538
Myers, Richard, Jr. VI, 475
Myers, Russel Abram V, 1012
Myers, Ruth Hannah VI, 538
Myers, S. Ethel I, 931
Myers, Sadie V, 1012
Myers, Samuel IV, 744
Myers, Samuel IV, 835
Myers, Samuel V, 267
Myers, Samuel V, 423
Myers, Samuel V, 517
Myers, Samuel VI, 538
Myers, Samuel VI, 768
Myers, Sarah IV, 744
Myers, Sarah V, 461
Myers, Sarah V, 517
Myers, Sarah VI, 475
Myers, Sarah VI, 501
Myers, Sarah VI, 537
Myers, Sarah VI, 538
Myers, Sarah VI, 555
Myers, Sarah VI, 562
Myers, Sarah VI, 677
Myers, Sarah Ann IV, 744
Myers, Sarah E. VI, 731
Myers, Sarah E. VI, 768
Myers, Sarah Eliza VI, 538
Myers, Sarah H. IV, 710
Myers, Sarah H. IV, 744
Myers, Sarah H. IV, 835
Myers, Sarah H. VI, 768
Myers, Sarah J. V, 267
Myers, Sarah J. V, 461
Myers, Stacy Janney VI, 476
Myers, Susan IV, 1259
Myers, Susanna II, 605
Myers, Susanna IV, 1258
Myers, Susannah II, 399
Myers, Susannah VI, 475
Myers, Susannah VI, 537
Myers, Susannah VI, 538
Myers, Susannah VI, 549
Myers, Susannah VI, 677
Myers, Tacey VI, 538
Myers, Tacey VI, 555
Myers, Tacey VI, 557
Myers, Tacey VI, 567
Myers, Tacy VI, 476
Myers, Tacy VI, 556
Myers, Tacy VI, 624
Myers, Tacy VI, 697
Myers, Thirza IV, 911
Myers, Thomas VI, 537
Myers, Thomas VI, 677
Myers, Thyra Jane IV, 420
Myers, Verna IV, 1041
Myers, Violet Mae IV, 1041
Myers, Vivian I, 930
Myers, Wd. Mary II, 179
Myers, Wd. Phebe VI, 557
Myers, William I, 922
Myers, William IV, 648
Myers, William IV, 835
Myers, William V, 267
Myers, William VI, 538
Myers, William VI, 623
Myers, William VI, 677
Myers, William VI, 768
Myers, William H. V, 267
Myers, Wm VI, 633
Myers, Wm. IV, 835
Myers, Wm. V, 1012
Myers, Wm. VI, 475
Myers, Wm. VI, 623
Myers, Wm. VI, 677
Myers, Zeb V, 267
Myers, Zebedee V, 267
Myler, Betsey VI, 882
Myler, Elizabeth T. VI, 967
Myler, Henry VI, 961
Myler, Henry W. VI, 875
Myler, Henry W. VI, 877
Myler, Henry W. VI, 967
Myler, Mary A. VI, 875
Myler, Mat. VI, 877
Myler, Mat. VI, 882
Myler, Mat. VI, 961
Myler, Nelly VI, 961
Myler, Peachey VI, 843
Myler, Thomas VI, 843
Myles, Sarah I, 152
Mynotte, Edwin J. III, 239
Mynotte, Frances D. III, 239
Myres, Alice IV, 51
Myres, Alice, Jr. VI, 537
Myres, David IV, 51
Myres, David VI, 537
Myres, Elizabeth IV, 51
Myres, Elizabeth VI, 601
Myres, Elizabeth Ann V, 46
Myres, Elizabeth Ann V, 98
Myres, George C. V, 267
Myres, Harry V, 98
Myres, Isaiah IV, 51
Myres, Isaiah VI, 537
Myres, Israel VI, 537
Myres, Jacob VI, 537
Myres, Mary IV, 51
Myres, Mary V, 579
Myres, Mary A. I, 622
Myres, Ollah V, 267
Myres, Orpha IV, 51
Myres, Phebe IV, 51
Myres, Priscilla V, 228
Myres, Priscilla V, 267
Myres, Rachel VI, 537
Myres, Samuel IV, 835
Myres, Samuel V, 228
Myres, Samuel V, 267
Myres, Sarah VI, 537
Myres, Sarah H. IV, 817
Myres, Sarah H. IV, 835
Myres, Sarah J. V, 267
Myres, William IV, 51
Myres, William VI, 537
Myric, Mary IV, 1287
Myrick, Alabama I, 622
Myrick, David B. I, 622
Myrick, J. A. I, 638
Myrick, Miriam I, 622
Myrick, Miriam H. I, 638
Myrick, Naomi I, 622
Myrick, Reuben I, 622
Myrick, Stephen S. I, 638
Myrick, Stephen S., Jr. I, 638
Myrick, Stephen Stanton I, 622
Myrick, Stephen Stanton, Jr. I, 622
Myrick, Stephen Stanton, Jr. I, 638
Myrie, Howel VI, 72
Myrie, Howel VI, 77
Myrtle, Mrs. G. B. I, 640

Nabholz, Hedwig II, 713
Nabholz, Hedwig Mary III, 239
Nabholz, Mary III, 239
Nabholz, Mary H. III, 239
Nabholz, Paul II, 713
Nabholz, Paul III, 239
Nabholz, Paul V. III, 239
Nabholz, Roland Paul III, 239
Nabors, James VI, 968
Nabors, Nancy VI, 968
Nackbar, Amy D. V, 1012
Nadenbousch, Agness VI, 423
Nadenbousch, Agness VI, 425
Nading, Catharine P. I, 863
Nading, Catherine I, 882
Nading, Catherine I, 895
Nading, Granville A. I, 863
Nading, Granville Adolpheus I, 895
Nading, John H. S. I, 863
Nading, John Henry Shelton I, 895
Nading, William I, 863
Nading, William I, 895
Nading, William I, 946
Naftal, Nicholas II, 605
Naftel, Joseph III, 239
Naftel, Mary II, 605
Naftel, Mary III, 239
Naftel, Nicholas II, 605
Naftel, Nicholas III, 239
Nagel, Adeline IV, 1331
Naggle, Lena V, 519
Naggle, Lena L. V, 519
Nagle, Baltus II, 811
Nagle, Elizabeth II, 811
Nagle, Hannah II, 605
Nagle, Lena V, 519
Naglee, Hannah II, 795
Naglee, Rachel II, 795
Naglee, Rachel II, 820
Naglee, Thos. Clarkson II, 795
Nail, Carrie V, 1012
Nail, J. H. V, 1012
Nail, Lydia IV, 542
Nail, Lydia IV, 551
Nail, Martha I, 451
Naile, Baltus II, 811
Naile, Elizabeth II, 811
Nailer, Beulah IV, 744
Nailer, Eliza IV, 742
Nailer, Elizabeth II, 399
Nailer, John II, 399
Nailer, Joseph II, 399
Nailer, Lane II, 399
Nailer, Sarah II, 399
Nailor, Abigail IV, 1070
Nailor, Beulah IV, 744
Nailor, Beulah W. IV, 744
Nailor, Charles IV, 982
Nailor, John II, 446
Nailor, John II, 536
Nailor, John II, 605
Nailor, Mary II, 446
Nailor, Mary II, 536
Nailor, Mary IV, 473
Nailor, Mary IV, 489
Nailor, Rachel IV, 744
Nailor, Thomas II, 446
Nainby, John II, 605
Naiper, Charles VI, 822
Naiper, Lucy VI, 822
Naler, Wm. V, 461
Nally, Elizabeth VI, 967
Nally, Patsy VI, 967
Nally, Sarah VI, 677
Nally, Sarah VI, 695
Nally, William VI, 887
Nally, William VI, 967
Nameth, Helen IV, 255
Nameth, Pearl IV, 255
Nancarrow, Grace II, 569
Nancarrow, Grace II, 605
Nancarrow, John II, 569
Nancarrow, John II, 605
Nancarrow, John, Jr. II, 605
Nancarrow, Susanna II, 569
Nancarrow, Susanna II, 605
Nancarrow, Susannah II, 244
Nance, Albert G. VI, 967
Nance, Allen B. VI, 967
Nance, Allen B. VI, 998
Nance, Allen B. VI, 1009
Nance, Archd., Sr. VI, 967
Nance, Archibald VI, 937
Nance, Archibald VI, 967
Nance, Benjamin E. VI, 967
Nance, Campbel V, 461
Nance, Celia A. VI, 887
Nance, Chapple VI, 170
Nance, Delia VI, 849
Nance, Deliley VI, 815
Nance, Dillity I, 564
Nance, Edwin T. VI, 967
Nance, Edwin T. VI, 1022
Nance, Elizabeth V, 461
Nance, Elizabeth VI, 170
Nance, Elizabeth VI, 200
Nance, Elizabeth VI, 967
Nance, Elizabeth Ladd VI, 170
Nance, Elizabeth R. VI, 967
Nance, Elvira VI, 1001
Nance, France VI, 849
Nance, G. W. V, 1012
Nance, Henry VI, 170
Nance, Jane G. VI, 967
Nance, Jesse VI, 170
Nance, Joannah VI, 967
Nance, Joel VI, 967
Nance, John VI, 887
Nance, John VI, 967
Nance, John VI, 1009
Nance, John VI, 1022
Nance, John Q. A. VI, 1022
Nance, Joseph VI, 170
Nance, Joseph Crew VI, 200
Nance, Joshua VI, 170
Nance, Judith VI, 170
Nance, Lancelot VI, 170
Nance, Laura V, 267
Nance, Laura E. V, 462
Nance, Lucinda VI, 1009
Nance, Lucy A. VI, 849
Nance, Lydia V, 267
Nance, Margaret VI, 170
Nance, Martha VI, 967
Nance, Martha E. VI, 1022
Nance, Mary VI, 881
Nance, Mary VI, 967
Nance, Mary VI, 1009
Nance, Mary Ann VI, 849
Nance, Mary G. VI, 1022
Nance, Molley VI, 988
Nance, Mornig VI, 881
Nance, Mourin VI, 881
Nance, Nancy V, 1012
Nance, Nancy VI, 170
Nance, Nancy VI, 937
Nance, Nancy VI, 967
Nance, Nancy VI, 1009
Nance, Obadiah V, 1012
Nance, Obediah VI, 170
Nance, Owen Milton VI, 170
Nance, P. W. VI, 1009
Nance, Paschal VI, 904
Nance, Paschal VI, 920
Nance, Paschal W. VI, 967
Nance, Paschal W. VI, 1009
Nance, Paschall VI, 967
Nance, Patsy VI, 967
Nance, Peter VI, 980
Nance, Polly VI, 877
Nance, Polly VI, 904
Nance, Polly VI, 988
Nance, Polly A. VI, 967
Nance, Sally VI, 967
Nance, Sally VI, 980
Nance, Sarah V, 267
Nance, Sarah V, 461
Nance, Sarah VI, 170
Nance, Sarah C. VI, 967
Nance, Sarah Elizabeth VI, 967
Nance, Terrell VI, 170
Nance, Thaddeus VI, 967
Nance, Thaddeus C. VI, 948
Nance, Thomas VI, 967
Nance, Thomas VI, 980
Nance, Thorp H. VI, 967
Nance, Thorp. H. VI, 1022
Nance, William VI, 967
Nance, Wilmuth VI, 920
Nancy, Ann IV, 584
Nangle, Eliz. III, 73
Nangle, Eliza III, 193
Nants, Dillity I, 564
Nanzer, George Henry V, 519
Nanzer, John V, 519
Nanzer, Melinda V, 519
Nanzer, William Harland V, 519
Naphtal, Joseph III, 239
Naphtal, Mary III, 239
Naphtal, Nicholas III, 239
Napier, Ashford VI, 881
Napier, Elizabeth VI, 881
Napier, Mary VI, 818
Napper, Eunice II, 605
Napper, Eunice II, 678
Napper, George II, 605
Napper, George II, 678
Napper, Hannah VI, 850
Napper, Milley VI, 850
Naramore, Arna IV, 744
Naramore, David IV, 744
Naramore, David IV, 784
Naramore, John IV, 744
Naramore, Rebecca IV, 744
Naramore, Rebecca IV, 784
Naramore, Rebecca W. IV, 744
Narsau, Elizabeth II, 605
Narsau, Helen II, 605
Narsau, Sarah II, 605
Narsh, Elizabeth II, 399
Narsh, Hannah II, 399
Narsworthy, Christian VI, 45
Narsworthy, Christian VI, 46
Narsworthy, George VI, 33
Narsworthy, George VI, 38
Narward, Asenath I, 443
Narward, Asenath I, 451
Nase, Emeline III, 239
Nase, Lulu III, 111
Nase, Lulu III, 239
Nase, M. Helena III, 239
Nase, Mary III, 239
Nase, Mary G. III, 239
Nase, Mary G. III, 247
Nase, Mary H. III, 239
Nase, Mary Helen III, 239
Nase, William Augustus III,
Nase, Wm. III, 239
Nase, Wm. Augusta III, 247
Nase, Wm. Augustus III, 239
Nash, Abner VI, 843
Nash, Catherine VI, 843
Nash, Clara III, 102
Nash, Clara III, 239
Nash, Eliza VI, 843
Nash, Ellen IV, 1331
Nash, Frances W. VI, 843
Nash, Francis II, 605
Nash, Francis III, 239
Nash, Francis III, 426
Nash, Francis III, 431
Nash, George F. III, 239
Nash, Isaac III, 239
Nash, James VI, 823
Nash, James M. VI, 843
Nash, John II, 399
Nash, John VI, 158
Nash, John VI, 200
Nash, John A. III, 102
Nash, John A. III, 239
Nash, Juliette III, 239
Nash, Kate III, 218
Nash, Lucy VI, 260
Nash, Lucy A. VI, 843
Nash, Margaret III, 218
Nash, Margaret III, 239
Nash, Martha II, 399
Nash, Mary VI, 467
Nash, Mary VI, 491
Nash, Missouri VI, 843
Nash, Nancy VI, 823
Nash, Nellie III, 239
Nash, Polly VI, 843
Nash, Rebecca VI, 806
Nash, Rebecca VI, 843
Nash, Robert VI, 831
Nash, Robert D. VI, 843
Nash, Sally VI, 831
Nash, Sarah Abner VI, 795
Nash, Susanna III, 239
Nash, Susanna III, 426
Nash, Susanna III, 431
Nash, Theodore III, 239
Nash, Theron IV, 1331
Nash, William VI, 843
Nassau, Elizabeth II, 605
Nassau, Hannah II, 605
Nassau, Helen II, 605
Nassau, Sarah II, 605
Nassaw, Hannah II, 605
Nation, Alonzo O. IV, 255
Nation, Emma IV, 255
Nation, Maggie IV, 255
Nation, Mrs. Alonzo IV, 255
Nations, Marry I, 960
Nations, Marry I, 967
Natts, Sarah VI, 967
Natts, Zafanine VI, 967
Naudicks, Thomas II, 446
Naughan, Frances Ann VI, 2
Naughan, Hannah VI, 216
Naughan, Shields VI, 216
Naughan, William Shields VI, 216
Naughan, Wm. Shields VI, 2
Nayler, Mary II, 244
Naylor, ??? II, 811
Naylor, ??? IV, 423
Naylor, Abigail IV, 464
Naylor, Abigail IV, 489
Naylor, Abigail IV, 1070
Naylor, Abraham IV, 474
Naylor, Abraham IV, 488
Naylor, Abraham IV, 489
Naylor, Abraham IV, 505
Naylor, Abraham IV, 1070
Naylor, Abraham G. IV, 489
Naylor, Abraham P. IV, 488
Naylor, Abraham P. IV, 1070
Naylor, Abraham P. IV, 1072
Naylor, Abram IV, 489
Naylor, Absalom P. IV, 489
Naylor, Addison IV, 1070
Naylor, Addison Wood IV, 10

or, Albert IV, 489
or, Albert IV, 1070
or, Ann IV, 489
or, Ann IV, 940
or, Ann IV, 982
or, Ann Eliza IV, 255
or, Annie E. IV, 489
or, Bartley G. IV, 489
or, Benjamin II, 811
or, Benjamin IV, 255
or, Benjamin IV, 589
or, Beulah IV, 744
or, Beulah IV, 982
or, Beulah W. IV, 982
or, Caroline IV, 488
or, Caroline IV, 489
or, Catharine T. III, 240
or, Celia Marie IV, 982
or, Charles IV, 489
or, Charles IV, 982
or, Charles A. IV, 982
or, Charles B. IV, 423
or, Charles B. IV, 542
or, Charles P. IV, 488
or, Charles W. IV, 489
or, Chas. IV, 943
or, Chas. A. IV, 982
or, David IV, 488
or, David IV, 489
or, David IV, 589
or, David IV, 1137
or, David E. IV, 130
or, David E. IV, 589
or, David E. IV, 1137
or, Deborah IV, 488
or, Deborah IV, 493
or, Elisabeth II, 501
or, Elisabeth II, 605
or, Eliz. III, 240
or, Eliza Ann IV, 255
or, Eliza Ann IV, 488
or, Eliza J. IV, 489
or, Elizabeth II, 88
or, Elizabeth II, 399
or, Elizabeth II, 491
or, Elizabeth II, 605
or, Elizabeth IV, 255
or, Elizabeth IV, 294
or, Elizabeth IV, 473
or, Elizabeth IV, 488
or, Elizabeth IV, 489
or, Elizabeth IV, 1016
or, Elliott IV, 489
or, Ethel IV, 982
or, Etta Jane IV, 489
or, Ezra IV, 255
or, Ezra IV, 423
or, Ezra IV, 589
or, Ezra W. IV, 423
or, Ezra W. IV, 542
or, Ezra W. IV, 552
or, Ezra W. IV, 589
or, Farland IV, 489
or, Farlend IV, 589
or, Farlin IV, 488
or, Farlin IV, 589
or, Florence IV, 734
or, Florence Elizabeth
IV, 982
or, George IV, 488
or, George IV, 489
or, George G. IV, 130
or, George G. IV, 1137
or, George Gilbert IV, 1137
or, Gladys Cox V, 267
or, H. S. IV, 982
or, Hannah II, 399
or, Hannah IV, 982
lor, Hannah Lloyd IV, 982
or, Harry IV, 489
or, Harry IV, 734
or, Harry C. IV, 489
or, Harry S. IV, 982
lor, Howard IV, 489
or, Ida Lucille IV, 982
or, J. Oscar IV, 489
or, James IV, 255
lor, James IV, 423
lor, James IV, 474
lor, James IV, 489
lor, James IV, 542
lor, James IV, 589
lor, James N. IV, 589
lor, James, Sr. IV, 589
lor, Jane IV, 255
lor, Jane IV, 474
lor, Jane IV, 485
lor, Jane IV, 488
or, Jane IV, 589
lor, Jane IV, 600
lor, Jessie Belle IV, 489
Naylor, Job Rogers III, 240
Naylor, John II, 399
Naylor, John II, 605
Naylor, John IV, 130
Naylor, John IV, 255
Naylor, John IV, 463
Naylor, John IV, 485
Naylor, John IV, 488
Naylor, John IV, 489
Naylor, John IV, 571
Naylor, John IV, 589
Naylor, John IV, 1133
Naylor, John IV, 1136
Naylor, John IV, 1137
Naylor, John L. IV, 488
Naylor, John N. IV, 488
Naylor, John Oscar IV, 489
Naylor, John S. IV, 255
Naylor, John, Jr. IV, 124
Naylor, John, Jr. IV, 130
Naylor, John, Jr. IV, 489
Naylor, John, Sr. IV, 589
Naylor, Joseph II, 399
Naylor, Joseph IV, 488
Naylor, Joseph IV, 489
Naylor, Joseph C. IV, 982
Naylor, Joseph P. IV, 488
Naylor, Joseph Sylvester IV, 982
Naylor, Lane II, 399
Naylor, Levena IV, 982
Naylor, Lewis IV, 255
Naylor, Lewis IV, 423
Naylor, Lewis IV, 435
Naylor, Lewis IV, 489
Naylor, Lewis IV, 542
Naylor, Lewis IV, 566
Naylor, Lewis IV, 589
Naylor, Louis IV, 375
Naylor, Louis IV, 423
Naylor, Lulu IV, 489
Naylor, Madge N. III, 240
Naylor, Margaret IV, 255
Naylor, Margaret IV, 375
Naylor, Margaret IV, 376
Naylor, Margaret IV, 423
Naylor, Margaret IV, 474
Naylor, Margaret IV, 488
Naylor, Margaret IV, 489
Naylor, Margaret IV, 589
Naylor, Margaret H. IV, 375
Naylor, Margaret H. IV, 423
Naylor, Margaret H. IV, 589
Naylor, Margaret Jane IV, 489
Naylor, Maria IV, 423
Naylor, Maria IV, 489
Naylor, Maria Elizabeth IV, 130
Naylor, Maria W. IV, 423
Naylor, Maria W. IV, 589
Naylor, Mariah IV, 464
Naylor, Marietta IV, 734
Naylor, Marietta IV, 982
Naylor, Martha IV, 130
Naylor, Martha IV, 463
Naylor, Martha IV, 488
Naylor, Martha Elizabeth IV, 130
Naylor, Martha Elizabeth
IV, 1135
Naylor, Martha Elizabeth
IV, 1137
Naylor, Mary II, 244
Naylor, Mary II, 605
Naylor, Mary IV, 255
Naylor, Mary IV, 482
Naylor, Mary IV, 486
Naylor, Mary IV, 488
Naylor, Mary IV, 489
Naylor, Mary IV, 504
Naylor, Mary B. IV, 542
Naylor, Mary E. IV, 423
Naylor, Mary E. IV, 435
Naylor, Mary E. IV, 464
Naylor, Mary H. IV, 435
Naylor, Mary H. IV, 489
Naylor, Mary Jane IV, 489
Naylor, Mary Jane IV, 1070
Naylor, Mary Jane IV, 1072
Naylor, Mary Jane IV, 1108
Naylor, Mary Jane IV, 1111
Naylor, Mary K. IV, 423
Naylor, Mary K. IV, 589
Naylor, Mary, Sr. IV, 255
Naylor, Mary, Sr. IV, 488
Naylor, Matilda IV, 488
Naylor, Matilda IV, 489
Naylor, Myrtle IV, 376
Naylor, Myrtle IV, 423
Naylor, Naomi IV, 488
Naylor, Naomi IV, 489
Naylor, Narcissa IV, 489
Naylor, Narcissa IV, 589
Naylor, Narcissa IV, 1137
Naylor, Narsissa IV, 488
Naylor, Nathan IV, 589
Naylor, Nathan M. IV, 255
Naylor, Nathan M. IV, 488
Naylor, Nathan M. IV, 489
Naylor, Nathan O. IV, 489
Naylor, Oliver IV, 489
Naylor, Oliver G. IV, 489
Naylor, Oliver P. IV, 255
Naylor, Oliver P. IV, 489
Naylor, Oliver Price IV, 255
Naylor, Oliver Price IV, 488
Naylor, Oscar IV, 489
Naylor, Oscar I. IV, 489
Naylor, Presley I. IV, 488
Naylor, Rachel IV, 255
Naylor, Rachel IV, 369
Naylor, Rachel IV, 375
Naylor, Rachel IV, 423
Naylor, Rachel IV, 435
Naylor, Rachel IV, 472
Naylor, Rachel IV, 489
Naylor, Rachel IV, 542
Naylor, Rachel IV, 566
Naylor, Rachel IV, 589
Naylor, Rachel IV, 744
Naylor, Rachel IV, 1070
Naylor, Rachel IV, 1072
Naylor, Rachel Ann IV, 505
Naylor, Rachel Ann IV, 1070
Naylor, Rachel E. IV, 423
Naylor, Rachel E. IV, 542
Naylor, Rachel E. IV, 552
Naylor, Rachel F. IV, 423
Naylor, Rachel F. IV, 589
Naylor, Rachel N. IV, 589
Naylor, Rebecca IV, 255
Naylor, Rebecca IV, 476
Naylor, Rebecca IV, 488
Naylor, Rebecca IV, 489
Naylor, Rebecca IV, 1133
Naylor, Rebecca Ethel IV, 982
Naylor, Rebecca P. IV, 476
Naylor, Rebecca P. IV, 488
Naylor, Rebeckah IV, 489
Naylor, Roberta IV, 982
Naylor, Roberta Asenath IV, 982
Naylor, Ross IV, 423
Naylor, Ross D. IV, 423
Naylor, Ross D. IV, 542
Naylor, Ruth IV, 474
Naylor, Ruth IV, 488
Naylor, Ruth IV, 489
Naylor, Ruthanna IV, 1137
Naylor, Samuel IV, 255
Naylor, Samuel IV, 464
Naylor, Samuel IV, 476
Naylor, Samuel IV, 488
Naylor, Samuel IV, 489
Naylor, Samuel G. IV, 255
Naylor, Samuel G. IV, 488
Naylor, Samuel G. IV, 489
Naylor, Samuel, Jr. IV, 489
Naylor, Sarah II, 399
Naylor, Sarah IV, 130
Naylor, Sarah IV, 488
Naylor, Sarah IV, 489
Naylor, Sarah IV, 494
Naylor, Sarah IV, 1136
Naylor, Sarah IV, 1137
Naylor, Sarah Lorena IV, 982
Naylor, Sarah R. IV, 124
Naylor, Sarah R. IV, 130
Naylor, Sarah R. IV, 571
Naylor, Sarah R. IV, 589
Naylor, Stephen IV, 255
Naylor, Stephen B. IV, 589
Naylor, Tabitha IV, 255
Naylor, Tabitha Jane IV, 589
Naylor, Talitha IV, 589
Naylor, Talitha IV, 595
Naylor, Uriah C. IV, 130
Naylor, Uriah C. IV, 1137
Naylor, Virginia IV, 489
Naylor, William IV, 488
Naylor, William IV, 489
Naylor, William B. IV, 255
Naylor, William B. IV, 489
Naylor, William Bates IV, 488
Naylor, William Henry IV, 489
Naylor, William R. IV, 255
Nayloy, Deborah IV, 489
Neadham, Edmond II, 399
Neadly, Benjamin II, 1017
Neadly, Christiana II, 1017
Neadly, Ebenezer II, 1017
Neadly, Elizabeth II, 1017
Neadly, Hannah II, 1017
Neadly, Jonathan II, 1017
Neadly, Maria II, 1017
Neadly, Sarah II, 1017
Neal, ??? VI, 293
Neal, Abel VI, 538
Neal, Ann II, 1017
Neal, Ann IV, 745
Neal, Ann V, 104
Neal, Ann VI, 538
Neal, Ann VI, 902
Neal, Ann VI, 923
Neal, Ann VI, 967
Neal, Anna V, 758
Neal, Anna V, 789
Neal, Anna Mary IV, 835
Neal, Anne I, 564
Neal, Archibald IV, 489
Neal, Benjamin I, 1086
Neal, Benjamin I, 1096
Neal, Benjamin V, 104
Neal, Benjamin V, 818
Neal, Benjamin VI, 677
Neal, Binjamin I, 411
Neal, Charles VI, 335
Neal, Comfort IV, 648
Neal, Daniel VI, 907
Neal, Daniel VI, 961
Neal, Daniel VI, 967
Neal, David II, 1057
Neal, Edith IV, 745
Neal, Elam II, 1017
Neal, Eleanor IV, 648
Neal, Elenor IV, 615
Neal, Eli II, 1017
Neal, Eli II, 1018
Neal, Eli V, 818
Neal, Eli, Jr. II, 1018
Neal, Elijah IV, 648
Neal, Elinor II, 1017
Neal, Eliza IV, 835
Neal, Elizabeth II, 1017
Neal, Elizabeth V, 815
Neal, Elizabeth V, 816
Neal, Elizabeth V, 818
Neal, Elizabeth VI, 538
Neal, Elizabeth VI, 928
Neal, Elizabeth VI, 997
Neal, Elme IV, 835
Neal, Emilia VI, 967
Neal, Enos H. IV, 615
Neal, Enos H. IV, 648
Neal, Enos. IV, 648
Neal, Enos. H. IV, 648
Neal, Esther V, 818
Neal, Fanny VI, 873
Neal, Fanny VI, 928
Neal, George I, 411
Neal, George I, 1096
Neal, George VI, 538
Neal, George VI, 677
Neal, Guli Elma IV, 745
Neal, Hannah II, 605
Neal, Hannah II, 1017
Neal, Hannah II, 1057
Neal, Henry I, 411
Neal, Henry I, 1086
Neal, Henry I, 1094
Neal, Henry I, 1096
Neal, Henry I, 1097
Neal, Henry V, 104
Neal, Henry V, 723
Neal, Henry V, 816
Neal, Henry V, 818
Neal, Henry V, 821
Neal, Henry VI, 677
Neal, Isaac C. II, 902
Neal, Jacob VI, 967
Neal, Jacob VI, 981
Neal, James I, 375
Neal, James I, 411
Neal, James I, 1096
Neal, James II, 1017
Neal, James V, 758
Neal, James V, 789
Neal, James V, 818
Neal, James VI, 677
Neal, James B. V, 789
Neal, James E. IV, 835
Neal, James F. II, 757
Neal, Jane II, 1017
Neal, Jesse VI, 538
Neal, Joel VI, 1002
Neal, John II, 1017
Neal, John IV, 489
Neal, John IV, 648
Neal, John IV, 835
Neal, John V, 818
Neal, John VI, 538
Neal, John VI, 878
Neal, John VI, 920
Neal, John VI, 935
Neal, John VI, 967
Neal, John, Jr. II, 1017
Neal, John, Jr. IV, 814
Neal, John, Jr. IV, 835
Neal, Joseph II, 1017
Neal, Joseph VI, 538
Neal, Joseph Pemberton V, 807
Neal, Jusline Ann IV, 1218
Neal, Lewis VI, 538
Neal, Lydia V, 818
Neal, Lydia VI, 538
Neal, Mahlon I, 411
Neal, Mahlon I, 1096
Neal, Mahlon V, 104
Neal, Mahlon V, 789
Neal, Mahlon V, 818
Neal, Mahlon VI, 677
Neal, Malon V, 806
Neal, Malon V, 818
Neal, Margaret IV, 489
Neal, Margaret IV, 648
Neal, Margaret IV, 835
Neal, Margaret V, 818
Neal, Margaret Louise V, 104
Neal, Maria IV, 489
Neal, Martha I, 411
Neal, Martha I, 451
Neal, Martha II, 1017
Neal, Martha IV, 835
Neal, Mary I, 411
Neal, Mary I, 1093
Neal, Mary I, 1096
Neal, Mary II, 1018
Neal, Mary II, 1057
Neal, Mary IV, 73
Neal, Mary IV, 103
Neal, Mary IV, 835
Neal, Mary V, 104
Neal, Mary V, 789
Neal, Mary V, 794
Neal, Mary V, 818
Neal, Mary V, 821
Neal, Mary V, 974
Neal, Mary VI, 902
Neal, Mary VI, 967
Neal, Mary Ann IV, 835
Neal, Mary M. IV, 814
Neal, Mary M. IV, 835
Neal, Mary O. V, 758
Neal, Morton IV, 745
Neal, Nathan V, 1012
Neal, Patty VI, 967
Neal, Phebe I, 1086
Neal, Phebe V, 104
Neal, Polly VI, 967
Neal, Rachel I, 411
Neal, Rachel I, 1086
Neal, Rachel I, 1094
Neal, Rachel I, 1096
Neal, Rachel II, 1017
Neal, Rachel V, 104
Neal, Rachel V, 794
Neal, Rachel V, 806
Neal, Rachel V, 818
Neal, Rachel VI, 425
Neal, Rachel VI, 538
Neal, Rachel VI, 677
Neal, Rachel VI, 967
Neal, Rebecca I, 1096
Neal, Rebecca IV, 632
Neal, Rebecca IV, 648
Neal, Rebecca V, 104
Neal, Rebecca V, 723
Neal, Rebecca V, 816
Neal, Rebecca VI, 538
Neal, Rebecca B. II, 902
Neal, Rebeccah VI, 538
Neal, Rebeckah I, 1096
Neal, Rebeckah I, 1097
Neal, Ruth IV, 101
Neal, Ruth IV, 103
Neal, Ruth IV, 810
Neal, Ruth IV, 835
Neal, Ruth Ann IV, 835
Neal, Sally VI, 878
Neal, Sally VI, 967
Neal, Samuel IV, 835
Neal, Samuel V, 588
Neal, Sarah I, 406
Neal, Sarah I, 411
Neal, Sarah II, 757
Neal, Sarah II, 773
Neal, Sarah V, 789
Neal, Sarah VI, 538
Neal, Sarahetta IV, 982
Neal, Sarahetta IV, 1018
Neal, Susanna IV, 103
Neal, Susanna VI, 837
Neal, Susanna VI, 967
Neal, Susannah V, 807
Neal, Susannah V, 818
Neal, Tace V, 807
Neal, Thomas VI, 837
Neal, Thompson IV, 835

Neal, Widow Mary I, 375
Neal, Wilhelmina V, 104
Neal, William I, 411
Neal, William I, 1015
Neal, William I, 1077
Neal, William I, 1086
Neal, William I, 1096
Neal, William IV, 103
Neal, William IV, 835
Neal, William V, 104
Neal, William V, 723
Neal, William VI, 538
Neal, William VI, 677
Neal, William VI, 902
Neal, William VI, 928
Neal, William VI, 967
Neal, Wm. II, 1017
Neal, Wm. IV, 835
Neal, Wm. V, 789
Neal, Wm. V, 818
Neal, Zachariah VI, 873
Neal, Zephannah VI, 923
Neald, Ann II, 966
Neald, Ely II, 966
Neald, James II, 903
Neald, James II, 966
Neald, Joseph II, 1017
Neald, Martha II, 966
Neald, Mary II, 1018
Neald, Rachel II, 966
Neald, Rachel II, 1017
Neale, Alfred V, 923
Neale, Alfred Wm. V, 923
Neale, Anna Maria V, 923
Neale, Barak IV, 1176
Neale, Caroline III, 240
Neale, Daniel A. III, 107
Neale, Daniel A. III, 240
Neale, Edward V, 923
Neale, Edwin V, 923
Neale, Eliza T. II, 902
Neale, Elizabeth II, 757
Neale, Emily V, 923
Neale, James Henry V, 923
Neale, John III, 240
Neale, John, Jr. II, 1017
Neale, Joseph III, 491
Neale, Josiah IV, 1176
Neale, Justine A. IV, 1176
Neale, Louisa V, 923
Neale, Louise V, 923
Neale, Lydia M. III, 240
Neale, Margaret Louisa V, 923
Neale, Margarett VI, 961
Neale, Mary II, 1076
Neale, Mary III, 107
Neale, Mary III, 240
Neale, Mary V, 923
Neale, Maybelle II, 757
Neale, R. W. IV, 1331
Neale, Richard V, 923
Neale, Richard Webb V, 923
Neale, Ruth II, 857
Neale, Ruth II, 902
Neale, Sarah III, 240
Neale, Wilhelmina V, 923
Neale, Wilhelmina Louisa V, 923
Neale, William I, 1096
Nealins, Rachel IV, 51
Neall, ??? II, 811
Neall, Ann E. II, 811
Neall, Anna E. II, 902
Neall, Anna Vaughn II, 804
Neall, Anna Vaughn II, 811
Neall, Anna Vaughn II, 884
Neall, Anna Vaughn II, 902
Neall, Cecelia Helen II, 811
Neall, Cecilia II, 811
Neall, Cecilia II, 831
Neall, Cecilia II, 869
Neall, Cecilia II, 902
Neall, Cecilia H. II, 884
Neall, Cecilia Helen II, 902
Neall, Daniel II, 757
Neall, Daniel II, 811
Neall, Daniel II, 831
Neall, Daniel II, 869
Neall, Daniel II, 884
Neall, Daniel II, 902
Neall, Daniel, Jr. II, 757
Neall, Daniel, Jr. II, 811
Neall, Daniel, Jr. II, 831
Neall, Daniel, Jr. II, 902
Neall, Daniel, Sr. II, 811
Neall, Daniell II, 902
Neall, Eliza Ann II, 785
Neall, Eliza E. V, 423
Neall, Eliza Ellen V, 423
Neall, Eliza J. II, 902
Neall, Eliza T. II, 902
Neall, Eliza Townsend II, 811
Neall, Elizabeth II, 757
Neall, Elizabeth II, 902
Neall, Elizabeth J. II, 902
Neall, Frank L. II, 902
Neall, Frank Lesley II, 811
Neall, Frank Lesley II, 869
Neall, Frank Lesley II, 902
Neall, Frank Leslie II, 811
Neall, Hannah II, 399
Neall, Hannah II, 713
Neall, Hannah Woodnut II, 811
Neall, Hannah Woodnut II, 869
Neall, Hannah Woodnut II, 902
Neall, Isaac C. II, 713
Neall, Isaac C. II, 811
Neall, Isaac C. II, 899
Neall, Isaac C. II, 902
Neall, Isaac I. II, 902
Neall, Isaac J. II, 811
Neall, James II, 713
Neall, James II, 803
Neall, James II, 811
Neall, James II, 899
Neall, James II, 902
Neall, James B. II, 811
Neall, James F. II, 757
Neall, James Francisco II, 713
Neall, James, Jr. II, 713
Neall, James, Jr. II, 902
Neall, John II, 902
Neall, John M. II, 811
Neall, John M. II, 902
Neall, Jonathan II, 811
Neall, Margaret II, 902
Neall, Margaret A. II, 902
Neall, Margaret Acton II, 811
Neall, Margaret J. II, 902
Neall, Mary II, 902
Neall, Mary V, 104
Neall, Mary VI, 390
Neall, Mary VI, 425
Neall, Maybelle II, 713
Neall, Maybelle II, 757
Neall, Rachel II, 803
Neall, Rachel II, 899
Neall, Rachel II, 902
Neall, Rachel C. II, 902
Neall, Rachel E. II, 902
Neall, Rebecca B. II, 902
Neall, Rebecca J. II, 902
Neall, Rebecca S. II, 713
Neall, Rebecca S. II, 811
Neall, Rebecca S. II, 899
Neall, Rebecca S. II, 902
Neall, Rebecca T. II, 902
Neall, Ruth II, 902
Neall, Ruthanna II, 803
Neall, Sarah II, 757
Neall, Sarah II, 811
Neall, Sarah II, 831
Neall, Sarah II, 902
Neall, Susan M. II, 902
Neall, Wd. Eliza Ann II, 803
Neall, William VI, 390
Neall, William VI, 425
Neally, Nancy Jane V, 1012
Nealy, Annie V, 1012
Nealy, Hannah IV, 210
Nealy, Hannah IV, 255
Nealy, James V, 1012
Nealy, Nancy Jane V, 1012
Nealy, Orynthee V, 923
Nealy, Rachel Orynthia V, 923
Nealy, Stephen A. V, 1012
Nean, Alexander V, 105
Nean, Anna Elizabeth V, 105
Nean, Elizabeth V, 105
Nean, Martin V, 105
Nean, Thompson V, 105
Neane, Thompson V, 105
Near, Ada V, 1012
Near, Ada Barber V, 1012
Near, Ann IV, 891
Near, Ann IV, 894
Near, Cora D. V, 1012
Near, Edward V, 1012
Near, Emanuel V, 1012
Near, Etta V, 1012
Near, Flow V, 1012
Near, James V, 1012
Near, James C. V, 1012
Near, Mary A. V, 1012
Near, Mary Ann V, 1012
Near, Maud V, 1012
Near, Maude V, 1012
Near, Samuel V, 1012
Near, Samuel Peter V, 1012
Near, Wm. V, 1012
Nease, Elvira H. IV, 1029
Neave, Albert V, 924
Neave, Alexander II, 605
Neave, Alexander II, 606
Neave, Alexander V, 923
Neave, Ann Elizabeth V, 923
Neave, Anna V, 923
Neave, Anna P. V, 923
Neave, Charles II, 605
Neave, Charles II, 606
Neave, Charles IV, 154
Neave, Charles IV, 155
Neave, Charles V, 923
Neave, Chas. V, 923
Neave, Edward P. V, 923
Neave, Elizabeth II, 399
Neave, Elizabeth II, 605
Neave, Elizabeth II, 606
Neave, Elizabeth V, 923
Neave, Elizabeth V, 925
Neave, Elizabeth V, 944
Neave, Elizabeth J., Jr. V, 924
Neave, Elizabeth M. V, 923
Neave, Elizabeth Merrified II, 605
Neave, Emma V, 924
Neave, Emma V, 929
Neave, Frances V, 923
Neave, Frank M. V, 923
Neave, Hannah II, 605
Neave, Hannah II, 606
Neave, Hannah V, 923
Neave, Hannah V, 943
Neave, Hattie Lupton V, 923
Neave, Isaac P. V, 923
Neave, Jeremiah II, 399
Neave, Jeremiah II, 605
Neave, Jeremiah V, 923
Neave, Jeremiah V, 925
Neave, Joel II, 605
Neave, Joell II, 399
Neave, Martin V, 923
Neave, Mary Susannah V, 923
Neave, Oliver Martin V, 923
Neave, Sarah II, 399
Neave, Sarah V, 923
Neave, Sophia III, 117
Neave, Susannah Martin V, 923
Neave, Thompson II, 605
Neave, Thompson V, 923
Neave, Thompson V, 944
Neave, Thompson, Jr. V, 923
Neave, Thomson II, 605
Neave, Thos. Jefferson V, 923
Neave, William V, 923
Neave, Wm. V, 923
Neave, Wm. V, 924
Neavet, Ruth VI, 425
Neavitt, Elizabeth VI, 426
Necalls, Elezabeath I, 152
Necalls, Elezabeath I, 154
Necem, Elizabeth I, 720
Necem, Luke I, 720
Nedarman, John I, 1062
Nedarman, Sarah I, 1062
Nedarman, Widow Sarah I, 1060
Neddles, Cornelia VI, 577
Neddles, Edward M. VI, 577
Nederman, John I, 1060
Nedler, Alonzo V, 461
Nedler, Belle V, 461
Nedry, Eliza V, 105
Needdom, Elizabeth I, 727
Needdom, Elizabeth I, 737
Neederman, John I, 1035
Needham, Ann I, 727
Needham, Ann I, 732
Needham, Anna II, 606
Needham, Edmond II, 399
Needham, Elisabeth I, 139
Needham, Elisabeth I, 152
Needham, Elizabeth I, 99
Needham, Elizabeth I, 727
Needham, Elizabeth II, 399
Needham, Florence VI, 843
Needham, Frances VI, 978
Needham, Hannah II, 562
Needham, Hannah II, 606
Needham, Jane VI, 799
Needham, John II, 399
Needham, John II, 606
Needham, Joseph VI, 799
Needham, Joseph VI, 978
Needham, Lydia II, 781
Needham, Lydia II, 816
Needham, Mary I, 727
Needham, Mary II, 399
Needham, Mary II, 446
Needham, Mary II, 606
Needham, Mary Ann VI, 950
Needham, Mary Yates I, 727
Needham, William VI, 843
Needles, Alice M. II, 811
Needles, Alice Matthews II, 891
Needles, Alice Matthews II, 903
Needles, Anna V, 105
Needles, Anna Maria II, 811
Needles, Anne M. II, 902
Needles, Caleb H. II, 902
Needles, Caleb H. II, 903
Needles, Caleb Hathaway II, 811
Needles, Cornelia II, 811
Needles, Cornelia II, 903
Needles, Cornelia II, 943
Needles, Cornelia VI, 538
Needles, Cornelia VI, 677
Needles, Cornelia VI, 717
Needles, Cornelia J. II, 902
Needles, Cornelia J. II, 934
Needles, Cornelia Jenkins II, 811
Needles, Cornelia Jenkins II, 829
Needles, Cornelia Jenkins II, 943
Needles, Edith B. II, 811
Needles, Edith N. II, 842
Needles, Edith N. II, 903
Needles, Edward II, 606
Needles, Edward II, 811
Needles, Edward II, 902
Needles, Edward II, 903
Needles, Edward II, 934
Needles, Edward M. II, 891
Needles, Edward M. II, 902
Needles, Edward M. II, 903
Needles, Edward M. II, 934
Needles, Edward M. II, 943
Needles, Edward M. VI, 538
Needles, Edward M. VI, 677
Needles, Edward Man II, 811
Needles, Eliza II, 811
Needles, Eliza VI, 575
Needles, Eliza J. II, 903
Needles, Eliza J. II, 934
Needles, Eliza J. VI, 488
Needles, Eliza J. VI, 538
Needles, Eliza J. VI, 577
Needles, Eliza J. VI, 635
Needles, Eliza J. VI, 677
Needles, Eliza J. VI, 717
Needles, Eliza Jenkins II, 811
Needles, Eliza M. II, 902
Needles, Hannah Y. II, 902
Needles, Harry Norwood II, 811
Needles, Helen M. II, 811
Needles, Helen M. II, 903
Needles, James B. IV, 103
Needles, John II, 811
Needles, John II, 947
Needles, John II, 1086
Needles, John, Jr. II, 606
Needles, John, Jr. II, 757
Needles, Joseph II, 606
Needles, Joseph A. II, 606
Needles, Lydia Ann II, 757
Needles, Mary II, 606
Needles, Mary II, 811
Needles, Patience H. II, 811
Needles, Patience H. II, 882
Needles, Patience H. II, 903
Needles, Patience J. II, 891
Needles, Rachel H. II, 902
Needles, Sarah II, 949
Needles, Sarah II, 1089
Needles, Sarah T. II, 902
Needles, Sarah Y. II, 811
Needles, Wd. Sarah M. II, 947
Needles, Wm. Jenkins II, 811
Needles, Wm. N. II, 902
Needles, Wm. Norwood II, 811
Needom, Ann I, 727
Needom, Ezekiel II, 446
Needom, Mary I, 727
Needom, Mary I, 739
Needom, Mary Yates I, 727
Needom, Nicholas II, 446
Neel, Ann VI, 967
Neel, Elioner II, 1022
Neel, Emilia VI, 967
Neel, James II, 998
Neel, James II, 1017
Neel, Jane II, 1017
Neel, Jane II, 1032
Neel, John II, 1032
Neel, John, Jr. II, 1022
Neel, Martha II, 980
Neel, Martha II, 1017
Neel, Rachel II, 998
Neel, Walter VI, 967
Neel, William VI, 967
Neel, Zachariah VI, 967
Neelan, Rachel IV, 103
Neeld, Ann II, 1017
Neeld, Ann II, 1020
Neeld, Ann II, 1039
Neeld, Elam II, 1017
Neeld, Eli II, 998
Neeld, Eli II, 1017
Neeld, Eli II, 1039
Neeld, Eliza E. V, 423
Neeld, Eliza E. V, 438
Neeld, Elizabeth II, 1006
Neeld, Elizabeth II, 1017
Neeld, Hannah II, 998
Neeld, Hannah II, 1049
Neeld, Hannah II, 1057
Neeld, James II, 903
Neeld, James II, 1017
Neeld, James II, 1020
Neeld, Mary II, 1057
Neele, Eliza Ellen V, 437
Neele, Ellen V, 437
Neele, Joseph V, 437
Neely, Anna IV, 1287
Neely, Anna IV, 1291
Neely, Bettie F. I, 831
Neely, Cassius M. IV, 1287
Neely, Edith IV, 1287
Neely, Elizabeth VI, 328
Neely, Elizabeth VI, 335
Neely, Florence Christine IV,
Neely, Irena V, 105
Neely, Irena V, 118
Neely, James V, 1012
Neely, Leonora I, 831
Neely, Levi IV, 1287
Neely, Levi H. IV, 1287
Neely, Lowis IV, 1287
Neely, Mabel IV, 880
Neely, Mary Abigail IV, 1287
Neely, Orynthee V, 923
Neely, Rebecca IV, 1287
Neer, Edward V, 1012
Neer, Mary A. V, 1012
Neers, Susanna VI, 539
Neff, Benjamin V, 588
Neff, Bert H. IV, 1259
Neff, Ersie V, 854
Neff, Ersie V, 856
Neff, Ethel IV, 1259
Neff, Frances V, 588
Neff, Grace IV, 1331
Neff, Hannah May II, 877
Neff, Hannah May II, 903
Neff, Henry V, 461
Neff, Isabel Frances V, 588
Neff, James IV, 1331
Neff, Lillie May V, 461
Neff, Louise J. White V, 588
Neff, Lucile IV, 1259
Neff, Mabel V, 461
Neff, Marion V, 461
Neff, Mary IV, 1331
Neff, Narcissa V, 924
Neff, Narcissa V, 941
Neff, Paul Adam V, 588
Neff, Rebecca IV, 344
Neff, Thos. H. IV, 1331
Neff, William II, 399
Neffner, Anna V, 423
Neffner, Annie V, 423
Neffner, Artie V, 423
Neffner, Edward V, 423
Neffner, Henry V, 423
Neffner, Margaret V, 423
Neffner, R. T. V, 423
Nefner, Annie V, 423
Negas, Catharine VI, 840
Negle, Mary Jane IV, 1259
Neglee, Hannah II, 605
Neglee, Hannah II, 690
Negrin, Jesse IV, 119
Negus, Abel V, 951
Negus, Abraham II, 399
Negus, Albert IV, 983
Negus, Albert Burdg IV, 51
Negus, Albert Burge IV, 982
Negus, Albert C. IV, 131
Negus, Albert J. IV, 255
Negus, Albert Purdy IV, 983
Negus, Amacy IV, 745
Negus, Amasa IV, 225
Negus, Amasa IV, 255
Negus, Amasa L. IV, 255
Negus, Amasa L. IV, 745
Negus, Amasa Lipsey IV, 744
Negus, Amos L. IV, 255
Negus, Ann IV, 255
Negus, Anna IV, 255
Negus, Anna B. IV, 255
Negus, Benjamin Willard IV,
Negus, Bracken IV, 255
Negus, Bracken IV, 744
Negus, Brackin IV, 255
Negus, Caleb B. IV, 180
Negus, Caleb B. IV, 255
Negus, Caleb B. IV, 983
Negus, Caleb Bracken IV, 51

s, Caleb Bracken IV, 982
s, Caleb Bracken IV, 983
s, Caleb E. IV, 255
s, David IV, 835
s, Deborah IV, 255
s, Deborah IV, 282
s, Deborah IV, 286
s, Deborah S. IV, 200
s, Earl Curtis II, 399
s, Elisha IV, 51
s, Elisha IV, 704
s, Elisha IV, 744
s, Elisha IV, 982
s, Elisha IV, 983
s, Eliza IV, 103
s, Eliza IV, 130
s, Eliza IV, 131
s, Eliza IV, 255
s, Eliza IV, 489
s, Eliza IV, 502
s, Eliza IV, 835
s, Eliza IV, 852
s, Eliza A. V, 951
s, Eliza A. V, 957
s, Eliza Ann IV, 79
s, Eliza Ann IV, 103
s, Eliza Ann IV, 131
s, Eliza J. IV, 180
s, Eliza J. IV, 200
s, Eliza J. IV, 255
s, Ellis W. IV, 255
s, Ellwood IV, 982
s, Elma IV, 835
s, Elvira IV, 704
s, Elvira IV, 744
s, Elvira IV, 745
s, Elwood IV, 51
s, Elwood IV, 983
s, Emily IV, 983
s, Esther IV, 131
s, Esther IV, 704
s, Esther IV, 744
s, Esther IV, 835
s, Esther IV, 848
s, Esther IV, 982
s, Esther IV, 983
s, Esther Fawcett IV, 982
s, Esther T. IV, 983
s, Hannah V, 951
s, Hannah Lavinah IV, 131
s, Isaac IV, 131
s, Isaac IV, 982
s, Isaac IV, 983
s, Isabel IV, 131
s, Israel IV, 87
s, Israel IV, 103
s, Israel IV, 130
s, Israel IV, 131
s, Israel IV, 982
s, Israel IV, 1012
s, Jacob IV, 103
s, Jacob IV, 131
s, Jason IV, 983
s, Jesse IV, 983
s, Jesse Leah C. IV, 835
s, Jessie C. IV, 255
s, Jessie C. IV, 283
s, Jessie Leah C. IV, 255
s, Jessie Leah C. IV, 835
s, Jessie Leah C. IV, 844
s, John II, 244
s, John II, 399
s, John IV, 51
s, John IV, 77
s, John IV, 103
s, John IV, 130
s, John IV, 655
s, John IV, 704
s, John IV, 744
s, John IV, 745
s, John IV, 747
s, John IV, 835
s, John IV, 982
s, John IV, 983
s, John IV, 991
s, John IV, 1011
s, John Thompson IV, 835
s, John W. IV, 131
s, John W. IV, 744
s, John W. IV, 745
s, John W. IV, 983
s, John Watson IV, 489
s, John Wayts IV, 131
s, John Wayts IV, 982
s, Jonathan B. IV, 131
s, Joseph IV, 79
s, Joseph IV, 103
s, Joseph IV, 131
s, Joseph IV, 835
s, Joshua II, 244
s, Joshua IV, 51
Negus, Joshua IV, 103
Negus, Laura E. IV, 255
Negus, Lavina IV, 983
Negus, Levina II, 244
Negus, Levina IV, 51
Negus, Levinah IV, 103
Negus, Levinah IV, 130
Negus, Lovina IV, 982
Negus, Lydia IV, 87
Negus, Lydia IV, 103
Negus, Lydia IV, 131
Negus, Lydia IV, 225
Negus, Lydia IV, 255
Negus, Lydia IV, 835
Negus, Lydia IV, 850
Negus, Lydia IV, 982
Negus, Lydia IV, 983
Negus, Lydia IV, 1011
Negus, Lydia G. IV, 103
Negus, Lydia G. IV, 983
Negus, Lydia L. IV, 131
Negus, Lydia S. IV, 131
Negus, Margaret B. IV, 131
Negus, Maria IV, 51
Negus, Maria W. IV, 983
Negus, Mariam IV, 655
Negus, Mariam IV, 983
Negus, Martha IV, 835
Negus, Martha IV, 848
Negus, Mary II, 399
Negus, Mary IV, 131
Negus, Mary IV, 133
Negus, Mary IV, 835
Negus, Mary B. V, 957
Negus, Mary B. V, 960
Negus, Mary Eliza IV, 131
Negus, Mary M. IV, 131
Negus, Mary M. IV, 744
Negus, Mary M. IV, 745
Negus, Mary M. IV, 747
Negus, Mary M. IV, 983
Negus, Mary Martin IV, 131
Negus, Mary Martin IV, 982
Negus, Mary R. IV, 255
Negus, Mary Rebecca IV, 200
Negus, Mary Rebecca IV, 255
Negus, Mary Whitacre IV, 983
Negus, Meria Whitacre IV, 982
Negus, Miriam IV, 23
Negus, Miriam IV, 51
Negus, Miriam IV, 77
Negus, Miriam IV, 103
Negus, Miriam IV, 130
Negus, Miriam IV, 131
Negus, Miriam IV, 704
Negus, Miriam IV, 744
Negus, Miriam IV, 745
Negus, Miriam IV, 747
Negus, Miriam IV, 982
Negus, Miriam IV, 983
Negus, Miriam IV, 991
Negus, Miriam, Jr. IV, 744
Negus, Mirium IV, 1011
Negus, Oliver IV, 255
Negus, Oliver S. IV, 200
Negus, Oliver S. IV, 255
Negus, Oliver S. IV, 282
Negus, Oliver S. IV, 286
Negus, Plummer IV, 255
Negus, Rachel IV, 22
Negus, Rachel IV, 51
Negus, Rachel IV, 255
Negus, Rachel IV, 305
Negus, Rachel IV, 744
Negus, Rachel IV, 982
Negus, Rachel IV, 983
Negus, Rachel E. IV, 255
Negus, Rebecca IV, 51
Negus, Rebecca IV, 131
Negus, Rebecca IV, 983
Negus, Rebecca M. IV, 983
Negus, Rebecca Miller IV, 982
Negus, Rebecca Miller IV, 983
Negus, Rebeckah II, 244
Negus, Reese IV, 200
Negus, Ruth IV, 200
Negus, Ruth IV, 983
Negus, Ruth IV, 1012
Negus, Ruthana IV, 131
Negus, Sara D. IV, 255
Negus, Sara Debora IV, 286
Negus, Sarah II, 244
Negus, Sarah II, 262
Negus, Sarah IV, 51
Negus, Sarah IV, 103
Negus, Sarah IV, 113
Negus, Sarah IV, 130
Negus, Sarah IV, 131
Negus, Sarah IV, 133
Negus, Sarah IV, 255
Negus, Sarah IV, 446
Negus, Sarah IV, 655
Negus, Sarah IV, 744
Negus, Sarah IV, 760
Negus, Sarah IV, 814
Negus, Sarah IV, 835
Negus, Sarah IV, 982
Negus, Sarah IV, 983
Negus, Sarah IV, 991
Negus, Sarah D. IV, 423
Negus, Sarah D. IV, 446
Negus, Sarah S. IV, 255
Negus, Sarah S. IV, 305
Negus, Sarah S. IV, 983
Negus, Sarah Smith IV, 982
Negus, Sarah Smith IV, 983
Negus, Shaidlock IV, 22
Negus, Shaidlock IV, 51
Negus, Shaidlock IV, 67
Negus, Shaidlock IV, 103
Negus, Shaidlock IV, 131
Negus, Shaidlock IV, 744
Negus, Shaidlock IV, 982
Negus, Shaidlock IV, 983
Negus, Shedloc IV, 305
Negus, Shedlock II, 244
Negus, Shedlock II, 262
Negus, Shedlock IV, 51
Negus, Shedlock IV, 983
Negus, Thaidlock IV, 255
Negus, Wayte IV, 744
Negus, West IV, 131
Negus, West IV, 133
Negus, West IV, 835
Negus, William IV, 131
Negus, William IV, 835
Negus, Wilson IV, 255
Negus, Wilson A. IV, 255
Negus, Wilson A. IV, 283
Negus, Wilson A. IV, 835
Negus, Wilson A. IV, 844
Negus, Wilson N. IV, 255
Negus, Wm. IV, 131
Negus, Wm. IV, 835
Nehrenst, Katharine IV, 1306
Nehrenst, Katherine IV, 1331
Nehrnst, Catherine IV, 1331
Nehrnst, Katherine IV, 1331
Neidigh, Ella IV, 1176
Neighbors, Amanda VI, 839
Neighbors, Anne VI, 843
Neighbors, Benjamin VI, 968
Neighbors, Brences VI, 843
Neighbors, Ednery A. VI, 804
Neighbors, Elizabeth VI, 835
Neighbors, Elizabeth A. VI, 968
Neighbors, Fleming VI, 913
Neighbors, James VI, 843
Neighbors, Jane VI, 843
Neighbors, Jemima VI, 845
Neighbors, John VI, 817
Neighbors, Julian VI, 913
Neighbors, Lotsey VI, 795
Neighbors, Louisa VI, 798
Neighbors, Mary VI, 968
Neighbors, Nancy VI, 843
Neighbors, Nancy VI, 873
Neighbors, Polly VI, 843
Neighbors, Richard VI, 843
Neighbors, Richard VI, 968
Neighbors, Ro. VI, 845
Neighbors, Ro. R. VI, 843
Neighbors, Robert R. VI, 839
Neighbors, Robert R. VI, 843
Neighbors, Susanna VI, 817
Neighbors, Thomas E. VI, 843
Neighbors, William VI, 843
Neighbors, William R. VI, 798
Neighbors, William R. VI, 843
Neighbors, Wm. VI, 835
Neighbours, Anderson VI, 968
Neighbours, Benjamin VI, 968
Neighbours, Elizabeth A. VI, 968
Neighbours, Fleming VI, 968
Neighbours, Hannah VI, 968
Neighbours, Henry VI, 968
Neighbours, James VI, 968
Neighbours, Joel VI, 937
Neighbours, John VI, 998
Neighbours, Lucinda VI, 968
Neighbours, Mary VI, 937
Neighbours, Mary VI, 968
Neighbours, Nancy VI, 968
Neighbours, Rebeckah VI, 924
Neighbours, Richard VI, 968
Neighbours, Sally VI, 968
Neighbours, Susan VI, 968
Neil, Barack IV, 1176
Neil, Barak IV, 1176
Neil, Elma IV, 1176
Neil, Harriet IV, 1331
Neil, John IV, 835
Neil, John IV, 859
Neil, Jonathan IV, 1176
Neil, Josiah IV, 1176
Neil, Justin Ann IV, 1176
Neil, Justine IV, 1176
Neil, Justine A. IV, 1176
Neil, Lewis, Jr. VI, 425
Neil, Margaret IV, 489
Neil, Martha IV, 648
Neil, Martha IV, 664
Neil, Mary M. IV, 835
Neil, Mary W. IV, 1176
Neil, Omar IV, 1176
Neil, Omar O. IV, 1176
Neil, Phebe Elma IV, 1176
Neil, Rachel VI, 425
Neil, Richard T. IV, 1176
Neil, Richard Thomas IV, 1176
Neil, Ruth IV, 605
Neil, Ruth IV, 648
Neil, Ruth IV, 879
Neil, Ruth. VI, 425
Neil, Samuel IV, 835
Neil, Susanna IV, 103
Neil, Susanna IV, 879
Neil, William IV, 103
Neil, William IV, 879
Neil, William A. IV, 1176
Neil, Wm. IV, 879
Neil, Wm. IV, 1176
Neild, Eli II, 980
Neild, Eli II, 1017
Neild, Martha II, 980
Neile, Ann VI, 425
Neill, Abraham VI, 425
Neill, Ann IV, 648
Neill, Ann IV, 745
Neill, Ann IV, 866
Neill, Ann IV, 879
Neill, Ann IV, 880
Neill, Ann V, 104
Neill, Ann V, 140
Neill, Ann VI, 376
Neill, Ann VI, 425
Neill, Ann VI, 435
Neill, Ann VI, 441
Neill, Ann VI, 450
Neill, Ann VI, 462
Neill, Ann VI, 506
Neill, Ann VI, 555
Neill, Ann VI, 571
Neill, Ann VI, 601
Neill, Ann VI, 768
Neill, Ann VI, 776
Neill, Anna IV, 1331
Neill, Anna Mary IV, 1331
Neill, Comfort IV, 648
Neill, Daniel VI, 768
Neill, Dillwin B. IV, 615
Neill, Edith IV, 745
Neill, Edith C. IV, 648
Neill, Edith C. IV, 879
Neill, Edith E. IV, 648
Neill, Edith E. IV, 657
Neill, Eleanor IV, 648
Neill, Eleanor C. IV, 648
Neill, Elijah IV, 648
Neill, Eliza IV, 868
Neill, Eliza IV, 879
Neill, Eliza IV, 880
Neill, Elizabeth IV, 648
Neill, Elizabeth IV, 879
Neill, Elizabeth IV, 880
Neill, Elizabeth IV, 882
Neill, Elizabeth C. IV, 648
Neill, Ella C. IV, 615
Neill, Enos H. IV, 648
Neill, Enos. IV, 648
Neill, Enos. H. IV, 648
Neill, Eva M. IV, 615
Neill, Eva M. IV, 648
Neill, Eva M. IV, 691
Neill, Eva M. IV, 745
Neill, Frederick VI, 592
Neill, Gula Elma IV, 745
Neill, Gulaelma IV, 745
Neill, Guli Elma IV, 648
Neill, Guli Elma IV, 745
Neill, Guli Elma IV, 879
Neill, Guliema E. IV, 745
Neill, Hannah IV, 745
Neill, Hannah IV, 868
Neill, Hannah IV, 879
Neill, Hannah IV, 880
Neill, Hannah VI, 592
Neill, Hannah W. IV, 648
Neill, Harriet IV, 1331
Neill, Isaac VI, 425
Neill, James Cope IV, 879
Neill, John IV, 648
Neill, John IV, 835
Neill, John IV, 879
Neill, John IV, 880
Neill, John V, 140
Neill, John VI, 376
Neill, John VI, 450
Neill, John VI, 462
Neill, John VI, 506
Neill, John VI, 538
Neill, John VI, 571
Neill, John VI, 601
Neill, John Hadley IV, 879
Neill, John Jr. IV, 911
Neill, John, Jr. IV, 904
Neill, Jonathan VI, 592
Neill, Joseph IV, 865
Neill, Joseph IV, 879
Neill, Joseph IV, 880
Neill, Joseph IV, 911
Neill, Joseph VI, 421
Neill, Joseph VI, 462
Neill, Joseph VI, 592
Neill, Joseph VI, 601
Neill, Joseph VI, 751
Neill, Joseph VI, 768
Neill, Joseph VI, 769
Neill, Justin Ann IV, 1176
Neill, Justine Ann IV, 880
Neill, Justine Ann IV, 911
Neill, Lewis VI, 371
Neill, Lewis VI, 410
Neill, Lewis VI, 425
Neill, Lewis VI, 435
Neill, Lewis VI, 441
Neill, Lewis VI, 457
Neill, Lewis VI, 462
Neill, Lewis VI, 506
Neill, Lewis VI, 538
Neill, Lewis VI, 555
Neill, Lewis VI, 581
Neill, Lewis VI, 601
Neill, Lewis VI, 734
Neill, Lewis VI, 759
Neill, Lewis VI, 768
Neill, Lewis VI, 769
Neill, Lewis VI, 776
Neill, Lewis Neill VI, 768
Neill, Lewis, Jr. VI, 425
Neill, Lizzie E. IV, 1331
Neill, Lulu VI, 677
Neill, Lydia VI, 425
Neill, Lydia VI, 457
Neill, Lydia VI, 462
Neill, Lydia VI, 506
Neill, Lydia VI, 538
Neill, Lydia VI, 581
Neill, Lydia VI, 601
Neill, Lydia VI, 768
Neill, Mahlon Scholfield VI, 768
Neill, Malissa IV, 879
Neill, Malissa Ann IV, 880
Neill, Malissa Ann IV, 882
Neill, Margaret IV, 648
Neill, Margaret IV, 864
Neill, Margaret IV, 879
Neill, Margaret IV, 880
Neill, Martha IV, 648
Neill, Martha IV, 880
Neill, Mary IV, 835
Neill, Mary IV, 865
Neill, Mary IV, 866
Neill, Mary IV, 872
Neill, Mary IV, 879
Neill, Mary IV, 880
Neill, Mary IV, 911
Neill, Mary VI, 421
Neill, Mary VI, 425
Neill, Mary VI, 450
Neill, Mary VI, 462
Neill, Mary VI, 571
Neill, Mary VI, 601
Neill, Mary VI, 751
Neill, Mary VI, 768
Neill, Mary VI, 769
Neill, Mary Agnes IV, 648
Neill, Mary Ann IV, 879
Neill, Mary Ann IV, 880
Neill, Mary J. IV, 880
Neill, Mary M. IV, 904
Neill, Mary P. VI, 677
Neill, Merton IV, 745
Neill, Moreton IV, 745
Neill, Morton IV, 648
Neill, Morton IV, 745
Neill, Morton IV, 866
Neill, Morton IV, 879
Neill, Morton IV, 880
Neill, Phebe V, 140
Neill, Phebe VI, 376
Neill, Phebe VI, 425
Neill, Phebe VI, 462
Neill, R. W. IV, 1331

Neill, Rachel VI, 371
Neill, Rachel VI, 410
Neill, Rachel VI, 425
Neill, Rachel VI, 441
Neill, Rachel VI, 457
Neill, Rachel VI, 462
Neill, Rachel VI, 538
Neill, Rachel VI, 555
Neill, Rachel VI, 581
Neill, Rachel VI, 734
Neill, Rachel VI, 759
Neill, Rachel VI, 769
Neill, Rachel VI, 776
Neill, Rachel Neill VI, 768
Neill, Rebecca IV, 648
Neill, Rebecca IV, 872
Neill, Rebecca IV, 879
Neill, Rebecca VI, 405
Neill, Rebecca VI, 410
Neill, Rebecca VI, 462
Neill, Rebecca VI, 751
Neill, Rebecca VI, 755
Neill, Rebecca VI, 759
Neill, Rebecca VI, 769
Neill, Rebeccah VI, 425
Neill, Rebeckah VI, 601
Neill, Rebekah VI, 421
Neill, Rebekah VI, 425
Neill, Rebekah VI, 462
Neill, Rebekah VI, 768
Neill, Richard Webb IV, 1331
Neill, Ruth IV, 648
Neill, Ruth IV, 879
Neill, Ruth VI, 425
Neill, Ruth VI, 601
Neill, Ruth Ann IV, 880
Neill, Ruth. VI, 425
Neill, Samuel IV, 866
Neill, Samuel IV, 872
Neill, Samuel IV, 879
Neill, Samuel Morton IV, 879
Neill, Sara IV, 879
Neill, Sarah IV, 863
Neill, Sarah IV, 880
Neill, Sarah VI, 371
Neill, Sarah VI, 462
Neill, Sarah VI, 592
Neill, Sarah VI, 601
Neill, Sarah VI, 734
Neill, Sarah VI, 769
Neill, Susan IV, 879
Neill, Susanna IV, 879
Neill, Susannah IV, 879
Neill, Thomas VI, 421
Neill, Thomas VI, 425
Neill, Thomas VI, 462
Neill, Thomas VI, 769
Neill, Willets A. IV, 880
Neill, William IV, 103
Neill, William IV, 879
Neill, William IV, 880
Neill, William VI, 425
Neill, Willits Allison IV, 879
Neill, Wm. IV, 879
Neille, Dilwyn B. IV, 941
Neille, Ella IV, 941
Neille, Eva W. IV, 941
Neille, Joseph IV, 911
Neille, Justine Ann IV, 911
Neille, Lewis VI, 522
Neille, Lewis VI, 538
Neille, Lydia VI, 522
Neille, Lydia VI, 538
Neille, Mary IV, 911
Neille, Rachel VI, 522
Neille, Rachel VI, 538
Neilluck, Mary VI, 751
Neilor, Beulah W. IV, 982
Neilson, Agnes III, 206
Neilson, Agnes III, 240
Neilson, Archibald J. III, 206
Neilson, Archibald J. III, 240
Neilson, Catharine I, 1022
Neilson, Deborah III, 240
Neilson, Jesse I, 1022
Neilson, Mary I, 1022
Neilson, Samuel I, 1022
Neiswanger, Clarissa IV, 319
Neiswanger, Clarissa IV, 344
Neiswanger, Elizabeth IV, 319
Neiswanger, Elizabeth IV, 344
Neitert, Zella V, 679
Neitert, Zella V, 700
Neitzke, ??? III, 395
Neitzke, Jas. Harvey III, 431
Neitzke, Martha S. III, 395
Neitzke, Martha S. III, 431
Neitzke, Mary Emily III, 431
Nellson, Rob II, 446
Nelms, Charles VI, 952
Nelms, Charles, Jr. VI, 968
Nelms, Ebenezer VI, 968
Nelms, Elizabeth VI, 952
Nelms, Fanny VI, 980
Nelms, Hiram VI, 968
Nelms, Malinda VI, 968
Nelms, Malinda P. VI, 978
Nelms, Matilda VI, 980
Nelms, Mildred Jane VI, 968
Nelms, Moses VI, 980
Nelms, Nancy VI, 980
Nelms, Sarah VI, 968
Nelms, Sarah C. VI, 968
Nelms, Sinor P. VI, 968
Nelms, William VI, 968
Nelson, Agnes III, 240
Nelson, Alexander I, 61
Nelson, Alexander F. I, 411
Nelson, Alice V, 105
Nelson, Amy W. IV, 1331
Nelson, Amy Wilhelmina IV, 1331
Nelson, Andrew III, 240
Nelson, Ann III, 58
Nelson, Ann III, 397
Nelson, Ann III, 431
Nelson, Arbella V, 700
Nelson, Arbelle V, 700
Nelson, Archibald J. III, 240
Nelson, Augusta IV, 952
Nelson, Catharine I, 365
Nelson, Catharine I, 411
Nelson, Catharine III, 240
Nelson, Catharine III, 397
Nelson, Catharine A. III, 240
Nelson, Catherine III, 431
Nelson, Caty III, 58
Nelson, Caty III, 240
Nelson, Christian L. IV, 1331
Nelson, Christopher C. V, 700
Nelson, Cynthia VI, 981
Nelson, Deborah II, 606
Nelson, Deborah II, 757
Nelson, Deborah III, 115
Nelson, Deborah III, 240
Nelson, Deborah III, 383
Nelson, Dinah I, 411
Nelson, Dora I, 621
Nelson, Edna V, 700
Nelson, Edna E. V, 700
Nelson, Eli E. III, 90
Nelson, Eli E. III, 240
Nelson, Eliza III, 240
Nelson, Elizabeth II, 131
Nelson, Elizabeth V, 267
Nelson, Elizabeth V, 351
Nelson, Esther III, 240
Nelson, Eugene III, 240
Nelson, Ezra III, 431
Nelson, George V, 1012
Nelson, Harriett III, 90
Nelson, Harriett III, 240
Nelson, Henrietta V, 841
Nelson, Henrietta V, 854
Nelson, Henry III, 240
Nelson, Henry A. III, 216
Nelson, Henry A. III, 240
Nelson, Henry Augustus III, 240
Nelson, Henry E. III, 431
Nelson, Hester III, 240
Nelson, Hester III, 370
Nelson, Horatio III, 240
Nelson, James I, 627
Nelson, James II, 1002
Nelson, James II, 1003
Nelson, James II, 1018
Nelson, James III, 240
Nelson, Jesse I, 411
Nelson, Jesse I, 1035
Nelson, John I, 1015
Nelson, John II, 1018
Nelson, John VI, 886
Nelson, John VI, 893
Nelson, John VI, 940
Nelson, John VI, 968
Nelson, John VI, 981
Nelson, John C. III, 240
Nelson, John E. IV, 1331
Nelson, Lizzie V, 700
Nelson, Lucy III, 240
Nelson, Lucy III, 431
Nelson, Lucy VI, 886
Nelson, Lydia III, 431
Nelson, Margaret II, 1002
Nelson, Margaret II, 1003
Nelson, Margaret II, 1018
Nelson, Margaret III, 412
Nelson, Mary I, 365
Nelson, Mary I, 411
Nelson, Mary I, 421
Nelson, Mary I, 1035
Nelson, Mary II, 1018
Nelson, Mary II, 1057
Nelson, Mary II, 1077
Nelson, Mary III, 216
Nelson, Mary III, 240
Nelson, Mary III, 370
Nelson, Mary VI, 968
Nelson, Mary, Jr. II, 1018
Nelson, Nancy VI, 968
Nelson, Nannie I, 207
Nelson, Olive IV, 1331
Nelson, Paul Gordon IV, 1331
Nelson, Peter C. VI, 843
Nelson, Phebe III, 431
Nelson, Polly VI, 968
Nelson, Prudence I, 564
Nelson, Prudence I, 586
Nelson, Prudence I, 594
Nelson, Prudence I, 595
Nelson, Rebecca I, 924
Nelson, Rebekah I, 411
Nelson, Sallie I, 627
Nelson, Sally I, 1034
Nelson, Sally I, 1062
Nelson, Sally VI, 886
Nelson, Samuel I, 365
Nelson, Samuel I, 411
Nelson, Samuel I, 1015
Nelson, Samuel I, 1035
Nelson, Sarah VI, 843
Nelson, Sarah A. VI, 843
Nelson, Stephen III, 412
Nelson, Susanna II, 399
Nelson, Thomas III, 58
Nelson, Thomas III, 240
Nelson, Thomas III, 397
Nelson, Thomas III, 431
Nelson, Thomas H. VI, 843
Nelson, Thomas H. VI, 939
Nelson, Vinson VI, 968
Nelson, Vinson VI, 998
Nelson, Wayne I, 638
Nelson, William I, 411
Nelson, Wright III, 240
Nelson, Zilpha I, 627
Nenney, Lucy VI, 968
Nenney, Patrick VI, 968
Neptune, Jane VI, 538
Neptune, Jane VI, 587
Neptune, Ruth VI, 538
Neptune, Sarah IV, 585
Neptune, Sarah IV, 589
Neptune, Sarah IV, 599
Nerdeman, Peter VI, 910
Nerhooff, John III, 240
Nerwby, Elizabeth I, 198
Nerwby, Jesse I, 198
Nerwby, Margaret I, 198
Nerwby, Nancy I, 198
Nerwby, Thomas I, 198
Nesbit, Gertrude VI, 742
Nesbit, Gertrude VI, 784
Nesbit, John II, 606
Nesbit, Mary II, 244
Nesbit, Mary II, 606
Nesbit, Mary V, 924
Nesbitt, Mary III, 606
Nesby, Rachel I, 1056
Ness, Abbie VI, 261
Ness, Abbie A. VI, 261
Ness, Abigail VI, 261
Netro, Abraham V, 1012
Netro, J. V, 1012
Netro, Joseph C. V, 1012
Netro, Samuel V, 1012
Nettnay, Madeline IV, 1331
Nettron, Joseph C. V, 1012
Netzley, Alice V, 758
Netzley, Angie V, 758
Neuben, Nicholas IV, 489
Neuenschwander, Maud III, 240
Neuenschwander, Ramona T. III, 240
Neuenschwander, Ramona T. III, 279
Neuenschwander, W. J. III, 240
Neuenschwander, Wm. J. III, 279
Neuenschwander, Wm. J., Jr. III, 240
Neuenschwander, Wm. J., Jr. III, 279
Neugean, Azariah I, 564
Neule, Daniel VI, 952
Neuman, Elizabeth II, 83
Neve, Alexander V, 923
Neve, Anna V, 919
Neve, Anna V, 923
Nevel, Elizabeth II, 244
Nevet, Catharine IV, 256
Nevet, Catharine IV, 308
Nevet, Mary IV, 256
Nevett, Isaac VI, 425
Nevett, Thomas VI, 426
Nevil, Benjamin IV, 1218
Nevil, Benjamin G. IV, 1218
Nevil, Rhoda E. IV, 1218
Nevil, Thomas Hancock II, 606
Nevill, Agnes III, 240
Nevill, Agnes V, 924
Nevill, Alfred III, 240
Nevill, Alfred IV, 1176
Nevill, Alfred V, 924
Nevill, Alfred W. IV, 1239
Nevill, Benj. G. V, 924
Nevill, Benj. Greenwood V, 924
Nevill, Benjamin IV, 1176
Nevill, Benjamin IV, 1218
Nevill, Benjamin G. IV, 1176
Nevill, Benjamin G. IV, 1218
Nevill, Benjamin G. IV, 1227
Nevill, Benjamin G. IV, 1239
Nevill, Benjamin Greenwood III, 240
Nevill, Benjamin Greenwood V, 924
Nevill, Edward III, 240
Nevill, Edward V, 924
Nevill, Elizabeth III, 240
Nevill, Elizabeth V, 924
Nevill, Ernest G. IV, 1239
Nevill, G. B. IV, 1239
Nevill, Greenwood IV, 1176
Nevill, James III, 240
Nevill, James V, 924
Nevill, Joseph III, 240
Nevill, Joseph IV, 1218
Nevill, Joseph V, 924
Nevill, Joseph W. V, 924
Nevill, Joseph Wattis V, 924
Nevill, Joseph Watts III, 240
Nevill, Mary Agnes IV, 1176
Nevill, Mary Agnes IV, 1239
Nevill, Mary Agness IV, 1239
Nevill, Rhoda IV, 1176
Nevill, Rhoda IV, 1239
Nevill, Rhoda E. IV, 1176
Nevill, Rhoda E. IV, 1218
Nevill, Rhoda E. IV, 1227
Nevill, Sarah E. IV, 1239
Nevill, Sarah Elizabeth IV, 1176
Nevill, Sarah Elizabeth IV, 1239
Nevill, Susanna III, 240
Nevill, Susanna IV, 1210
Nevill, Susanna IV, 1218
Nevill, Susanna V, 924
Nevill, Susannah V, 924
Neville, Agnes V, 910
Neville, Benj. G. V, 924
Neville, Benjamin V, 910
Neville, James V, 924
Neville, Joseph W. V, 924
Neville, Susannah V, 910
Nevins, Achsa II, 606
Nevins, Achsa II, 688
Nevins, Achsah II, 866
Nevins, Achsah II, 914
Nevins, Adalaide II, 817
Nevins, Agnes VI, 843
Nevins, John VI, 843
Nevins, Jonathan Willis II, 817
Nevins, Pim II, 606
Nevins, Pim, Jr. II, 606
Nevins, Thomas III, 240
Nevins, Wd. Achsah II, 817
Nevis, Ann IV, 983
Nevis, Esther IV, 983
Nevit, Eliza IV, 255
Nevit, Eliza IV, 344
Nevit, Grace IV, 255
Nevit, Grace IV, 344
Nevit, Isaac IV, 255
Nevit, Isaac IV, 344
Nevit, Isaac IV, 349
Nevit, Isaac IV, 542
Nevit, John IV, 255
Nevit, John IV, 542
Nevit, Joseph IV, 542
Nevit, Keziah IV, 542
Nevit, Rachel IV, 255
Nevit, Rachel IV, 344
Nevit, Rachel IV, 349
Nevit, Rachel IV, 525
Nevit, Rachel IV, 542
Nevit, Rachel, Jr. IV, 542
Nevit, Ruth IV, 255
Nevit, Ruth IV, 344
Nevit, Ruth IV, 349
Nevit, Ruth VI, 425
Nevit, Ruth VI, 677
Nevit, Thomas IV, 542
Nevitt, ??? III, 240
Nevitt, Catharine IV, 255
Nevitt, Catharine IV, 256
Nevitt, Catharine IV, 535
Nevitt, Catharine IV, 542
Nevitt, Catharine VI, 426
Nevitt, Charles Henry III, 24
Nevitt, David IV, 542
Nevitt, Eliza IV, 255
Nevitt, Eliza IV, 344
Nevitt, Eliza IV, 523
Nevitt, Eliza IV, 542
Nevitt, Eliza VI, 426
Nevitt, Elizabeth VI, 426
Nevitt, Grace IV, 255
Nevitt, Grace IV, 344
Nevitt, Grace IV, 542
Nevitt, Grace IV, 546
Nevitt, Grace VI, 426
Nevitt, Hannah VI, 426
Nevitt, Hannah, Jr. VI, 426
Nevitt, Hopewell VI, 425
Nevitt, Isaac IV, 255
Nevitt, Isaac IV, 344
Nevitt, Isaac IV, 542
Nevitt, Isaac VI, 362
Nevitt, Isaac VI, 425
Nevitt, Isaac VI, 426
Nevitt, Isaac, Jr. IV, 542
Nevitt, Jemima III, 240
Nevitt, Jno. IV, 542
Nevitt, John II, 606
Nevitt, John IV, 255
Nevitt, John IV, 535
Nevitt, John IV, 542
Nevitt, John VI, 426
Nevitt, Joseph IV, 542
Nevitt, Joseph VI, 426
Nevitt, Katharine IV, 542
Nevitt, Katherine VI, 425
Nevitt, Keziah IV, 542
Nevitt, Keziah IV, 546
Nevitt, Luvina IV, 542
Nevitt, Mary IV, 255
Nevitt, Mary IV, 256
Nevitt, Mary VI, 426
Nevitt, Maryann IV, 542
Nevitt, Matilda III, 240
Nevitt, Rachel IV, 255
Nevitt, Rachel IV, 344
Nevitt, Rachel IV, 542
Nevitt, Rachel VI, 362
Nevitt, Rachel VI, 425
Nevitt, Rachel VI, 426
Nevitt, Rachel, Jr. IV, 256
Nevitt, Rachel, Jr. IV, 542
Nevitt, Ruth IV, 255
Nevitt, Ruth IV, 344
Nevitt, Ruth VI, 384
Nevitt, Ruth VI, 425
Nevitt, Ruth VI, 426
Nevitt, Sarah VI, 411
Nevitt, Sarah VI, 426
Nevitt, Thomas IV, 542
Nevitt, Thomas IV, 546
Nevitt, Thomas VI, 425
Nevitt, Thomas VI, 426
Nevitt, Thomas J. IV, 542
Nevitte, Ruth VI, 426
New, Mary VI, 167
New, Mary VI, 200
New, Phebe IV, 103
Newbe, James I, 108
Newbe, Jamima I, 108
Newbe, Naomi I, 108
Newbe, Nathan I, 108
Newbe, Sarah I, 108
Newbe, Thomas I, 108
Newbern, Amy V, 974
Newbern, Jacob IV, 51
Newbern, Jacob IV, 983
Newbern, Lydia IV, 983
Newbern, Mary IV, 983
Newberry, Ann III, 241
Newberry, Ann III, 273
Newberry, James M. VI, 843
Newberry, Jane VI, 843
Newberry, John I, 564
Newberry, Lucy VI, 843
Newberry, Margaret II, 507
Newberry, Margaret II, 606
Newberry, Margret II, 507
Newberry, Mary Ann V, 588
Newberry, Mary Ann V, 602
Newberry, Walter II, 606
Newberry, Walter III, 241
Newberry, Walter III, 273
Newberry, William VI, 843
Newbery, William II, 244
Newbey, Ann I, 107
Newbey, Benjamin I, 107
Newbey, Benjamin I, 153
Newbey, Dorcas I, 153
Newbey, Dorcas I, 164
Newbey, Elezabeath I, 152

bey, Elizabeth I, 152
bey, Elizabeth I, 155
bey, Elizabeth I, 172
bey, Gabriel, Sr. I, 107
bey, Hannah I, 107
bey, Isabelle I, 60
bey, Isabelle I, 62
bey, Jeams I, 107
bey, John I, 152
bey, Joseph I, 155
bey, Mary I, 107
bey, Mary I, 108
bey, Miriam I, 108
bey, Samuel I, 107
bey, Sarah I, 108
bey, Sarah I, 153
bey, Thomas I, 108
bey, William, Jr. I, 152
bie, Nathan VI, 33
bold, Abigail II, 399
bold, Abigail II, 606
bold, Agnes Webster II, 966
bold, Albert G. II, 966
bold, Albert G. II, 1057
bold, Alice H. II, 966
bold, Ann II, 179
bold, Ann II, 244
bold, Ann II, 245
bold, Anna II, 237
bold, Anna II, 244
bold, Anna M. II, 966
bold, Anna M. II, 1057
bold, Caleb II, 227
bold, Caleb II, 244
bold, Caleb III, 138
bold, Caleb III, 201
bold, Caleb III, 240
bold, Caroline II, 286
bold, Caroline A. II, 286
bold, Caroline A. II, 297
bold, Caroline Amelia II, 297
bold, Catharine II, 606
bold, Charles II, 399
bold, Charlotte II, 22
bold, Charlotte II, 46
bold, Charlotte II, 47
bold, Clara VI, 677
bold, Clara VI, 678
bold, Clayton II, 516
bold, Clayton II, 606
bold, Clayton III, 240
bold, Deborah II, 606
bold, Deborah II, 1018
bold, Edith II, 244
bold, Edith II, 1007
bold, Edith II, 1018
bold, Eleanor Parsons II, 966
bold, Elizabeth II, 179
bold, Elizabeth II, 297
bold, Elizabeth II, 903
bold, Elizabeth II, 1077
bold, Elizabeth II, 1081
bold, Elizabeth H. II, 903
bold, Elizabeth L. II, 702
bold, Elizabeth P. II, 179
bold, Elizabeth P. II, 286
bold, Elizabeth P. II, 297
bold, Emaline II, 1057
bold, Emaline Parsons II, 1045
bold, Emeline II, 966
bold, Emeline P. II, 966
bold, Emeline P. II, 1057
bold, Emily III, 25
bold, Emily III, 240
bold, Emma II, 903
bold, George II, 516
bold, George II, 606
bold, George III, 240
bold, George A. VI, 677
bold, George A. VI, 678
bold, Godfrey II, 399
bold, Hannah II, 179
bold, Hannah II, 208
bold, Hannah II, 245
bold, Hannah II, 606
bold, Hannah VI, 677
bold, Hannah C. VI, 677
bold, Hannah C. VI, 678
bold, Hannah R. II, 966
bold, Hannah R. II, 1052
bold, Hannah R. II, 1057
bold, Isaac II, 606
bold, James E. III, 240
bold, James Emlen III, 240
bold, James S. II, 757
bold, James S. II, 966
bold, James S. II, 1018
bold, James S. II, 1045
bold, James S. II, 1057
bold, James Simpson II, 606
Newbold, James W. II, 1077
Newbold, Jane K. II, 1077
Newbold, John II, 198
Newbold, John II, 233
Newbold, John II, 245
Newbold, John II, 606
Newbold, John III, 25
Newbold, John III, 240
Newbold, Joseph H. II, 903
Newbold, Joseph W. II, 208
Newbold, Joseph W. II, 245
Newbold, Joshua II, 179
Newbold, Joshua II, 244
Newbold, Joshua II, 245
Newbold, Joshua II, 903
Newbold, Josiah II, 966
Newbold, Josiah H. II, 757
Newbold, Josiah H. II, 1052
Newbold, Josiah H. II, 1057
Newbold, Josiah H., Jr. II, 966
Newbold, Lydia II, 903
Newbold, Margaret II, 606
Newbold, Margaret Hutton II, 966
Newbold, Martha II, 198
Newbold, Martha II, 245
Newbold, Martha II, 606
Newbold, Mary II, 198
Newbold, Mary II, 233
Newbold, Mary II, 245
Newbold, Mary II, 516
Newbold, Mary II, 606
Newbold, Mary II, 903
Newbold, Mary II, 1045
Newbold, Mary II, 1077
Newbold, Mary III, 240
Newbold, Mary A. II, 966
Newbold, Mary Anderson II, 1045
Newbold, Mary Anderson II, 1057
Newbold, Mary Ann III, 240
Newbold, Mary E. III, 240
Newbold, Mary H. II, 903
Newbold, Mary L. II, 297
Newbold, Michael II, 89
Newbold, Michael II, 606
Newbold, Michall II, 244
Newbold, Pose Anna P. II, 1057
Newbold, Rebecca II, 179
Newbold, Rebecca II, 244
Newbold, Rebecca II, 245
Newbold, Rebecca II, 966
Newbold, Rebecca II, 1052
Newbold, Rebecca II, 1057
Newbold, Rebecca H. II, 1057
Newbold, Rose Anna P. II, 966
Newbold, Samuel II, 179
Newbold, Samuel II, 233
Newbold, Samuel II, 244
Newbold, Samuel II, 245
Newbold, Samuel II, 399
Newbold, Samuel II, 606
Newbold, Samuel II, 903
Newbold, Samuel Hough II, 903
Newbold, Sarah II, 179
Newbold, Sarah II, 227
Newbold, Sarah II, 244
Newbold, Sarah II, 245
Newbold, Sarah II, 399
Newbold, Sarah II, 606
Newbold, Sarah III, 138
Newbold, Sarah III, 201
Newbold, Sarah III, 240
Newbold, Sarah S. II, 757
Newbold, Susan II, 757
Newbold, Susan III, 25
Newbold, Susan III, 240
Newbold, Susanna II, 179
Newbold, Susanna II, 244
Newbold, Susanna II, 297
Newbold, Susanna II, 606
Newbold, Susanna H. II, 399
Newbold, Susannah II, 244
Newbold, Susannah III, 240
Newbold, Thomas II, 179
Newbold, Thomas II, 237
Newbold, Thomas II, 244
Newbold, Thomas II, 606
Newbold, Thomas II, 966
Newbold, Thomas II, 1077
Newbold, Thomas H. II, 1057
Newbold, William II, 208
Newbold, William II, 245
Newbold, William F. II, 179
Newbold, William F. II, 286
Newbold, William F. II, 297
Newbold, William F. 'VI, 678
Newbold, William R. II, 966
Newbold, Wm. F. VI, 677
Newbold, Wm. L. II, 606
Newbold, Wm. R. II, 1052
Newbold, Wm. R. II, 1057
Newborn, Amy V, 885
Newborn, David V, 105
Newborn, David V, 885
Newborn, George V, 885
Newborn, Gulie Elma V, 885
Newborn, Jacob IV, 983
Newborn, John V, 105
Newborn, John B. V, 885
Newborn, Lydia IV, 983
Newborn, Lydia V, 885
Newborn, Mary IV, 983
Newborn, Virgin B. V, 885
Newborn, Warner L. V, 885
Newbould, Ann II, 244
Newbould, Ann II, 256
Newbould, Catharine II, 606
Newbould, Edith II, 208
Newbould, Edith II, 244
Newbould, Michall II, 244
Newbould, Michall II, 257
Newbould, Samuel II, 606
Newbould, Susanna II, 244
Newbould, Susannah II, 244
Newbould, Susannah II, 257
Newbould, Thomas II, 208
Newbould, Thomas II, 244
Newbourn, David IV, 51
Newbourn, David IV, 69
Newbourn, Dorothy IV, 51
Newbourn, George IV, 51
Newbourn, George IV, 64
Newbourn, Hannah IV, 51
Newbourn, Jacob IV, 51
Newbourn, Jacob IV, 64
Newbourn, Jacob IV, 69
Newbourn, John IV, 51
Newbourn, Lydia IV, 51
Newbourn, Lydia IV, 64
Newbourn, Mary IV, 64
Newbourn, Mary IV, 69
Newbourn, Rachel IV, 51
Newbourn, Sarah IV, 51
Newbourn, Tamer IV, 51
Newbourn, Thamer IV, 51
Newbourn, Thamer IV, 69
Newbry, Harrold V, 267
Newbry, Kenneth Lloyd V, 267
Newbry, Lee V, 267
Newbry, Stella V, 267
Newburn, Amy V, 885
Newburn, Amy V, 974
Newburn, Ann IV, 51
Newburn, Ann IV, 103
Newburn, Beulah V, 829
Newburn, Beulah V, 854
Newburn, David IV, 51
Newburn, David IV, 69
Newburn, David IV, 103
Newburn, David V, 105
Newburn, David V, 829
Newburn, David V, 854
Newburn, David V, 885
Newburn, David, Jr. IV, 103
Newburn, David, Jr. V, 885
Newburn, Dorothy IV, 51
Newburn, George IV, 51
Newburn, George IV, 103
Newburn, George V, 885
Newburn, Gulie Elma V, 885
Newburn, Hannah IV, 51
Newburn, Jacob IV, 51
Newburn, Jacob IV, 69
Newburn, Jacob IV, 103
Newburn, Jacob IV, 924
Newburn, John II, 89
Newburn, John IV, 51
Newburn, John IV, 103
Newburn, John V, 974
Newburn, John B. V, 854
Newburn, John B. V, 885
Newburn, Lydia IV, 51
Newburn, Lydia IV, 675
Newburn, Lydia IV, 745
Newburn, Lydia IV, 924
Newburn, Lydia IV, 983
Newburn, Lydia V, 885
Newburn, Mary IV, 51
Newburn, Mary IV, 69
Newburn, Mary IV, 103
Newburn, Mary IV, 113
Newburn, Mary IV, 924
Newburn, Rachel IV, 51
Newburn, Rachel IV, 103
Newburn, Rachel V, 854
Newburn, Sarah IV, 51
Newburn, Sarah IV, 103
Newburn, Sarah IV, 117
Newburn, Susanna II, 89
Newburn, Susannah II, 89
Newburn, Tamar V, 854
Newburn, Tamer IV, 51
Newburn, Tamer IV, 103
Newburn, Thamer IV, 51
Newburn, Thamer IV, 69
Newburn, Virgin B. V, 854
Newburn, Virgin B. V, 885
Newburn, Warner L. V, 885
Newburn, William IV, 103
Newburn, Wm. II, 89
Newbury, ??? III, 29
Newbury, Ann III, 241
Newbury, Anna III, 240
Newbury, Anna B. III, 241
Newbury, Anna K. III, 29
Newbury, Anna K. III, 240
Newbury, Charles E. III, 240
Newbury, Charles E. III, 241
Newbury, John III, 240
Newbury, Jonathan III, 240
Newbury, Nelson III, 241
Newbury, Phebe III, 240
Newbury, Walter III, 241
Newby, ??? VI, 95
Newby, Abigail I, 703
Newby, Abigail I, 728
Newby, Adaline V, 342
Newby, Adaline V, 351
Newby, Albert I, 64
Newby, Albert Edward V, 588
Newby, Amy I, 475
Newby, Amy I, 484
Newby, Amy Lane I, 484
Newby, Ann I, 13
Newby, Ann I, 59
Newby, Ann I, 62
Newby, Ann I, 107
Newby, Ann I, 152
Newby, Ann I, 153
Newby, Ann I, 167
Newby, Ann I, 228
Newby, Ann I, 550
Newby, Ann I, 564
Newby, Ann I, 662
Newby, Ann I, 682
Newby, Ann I, 685
Newby, Ann I, 703
Newby, Ann I, 704
Newby, Ann VI, 106
Newby, Ann VI, 116
Newby, Ann Davis VI, 116
Newby, Anna I, 703
Newby, Anna I, 727
Newby, Anna I, 729
Newby, Anna A. I, 64
Newby, Anna May V, 700
Newby, Anne I, 142
Newby, Anne I, 146
Newby, Anne I, 152
Newby, Annie E. I, 14
Newby, Asenath I, 728
Newby, Axey V, 171
Newby, Axey V, 194
Newby, Axum I, 728
Newby, Axum I, 738
Newby, Baker I, 64
Newby, Barnaba I, 728
Newby, Barnabas I, 728
Newby, Barnaby I, 63
Newby, Barnaby I, 703
Newby, Barnaby I, 716
Newby, Barnaby I, 727
Newby, Barnaby I, 728
Newby, Benjamin I, 59
Newby, Benjamin I, 62
Newby, Benjamin I, 63
Newby, Benjamin I, 85
Newby, Benjamin I, 107
Newby, Benjamin I, 127
Newby, Benjamin I, 152
Newby, Benjamin I, 153
Newby, Benjamin I, 197
Newby, Benoni I, 727
Newby, Benoni I, 728
Newby, Benoni I, 896
Newby, Caleb I, 197
Newby, Caroline I, 728
Newby, Caroline I, 738
Newby, Caroline V, 351
Newby, Catharine I, 64
Newby, Catharine I, 884
Newby, Catharine I, 895
Newby, Catharine I, 896
Newby, Catherine I, 154
Newby, Charity I, 728
Newby, Cudger I, 62
Newby, Cyrus I, 863
Newby, Cyrus V, 854
Newby, Darcas I, 108
Newby, Demcy I, 108
Newby, Demcy V, 307
Newby, Demcy V, 351
Newby, Dempsy V, 351
Newby, Demsey I, 153
Newby, Demsey I, 164
Newby, Demsey I, 180
Newby, Demsey V, 351
Newby, Dillen I, 198
Newby, Dilling I, 727
Newby, Dorcas I, 153
Newby, Dorothy I, 153
Newby, Dorothy I, 156
Newby, Dorothy I, 913
Newby, Dorrithy VI, 27
Newby, Dorrithy VI, 33
Newby, Edith I, 703
Newby, Edith I, 724
Newby, Edith I, 728
Newby, Edmund I, 153
Newby, Edmund I, 174
Newby, Edmund I, 198
Newby, Edward I, 197
Newby, Edward I Sup 1, 4
Newby, Edward I Sup 1, 5
Newby, Edwd. I, 13
Newby, Eleanor I, 767
Newby, Eleanor V, 307
Newby, Eleanor V, 340
Newby, Eleanor V, 351
Newby, Eleazar I, 728
Newby, Eleazar I, 738
Newby, Eleonar I, 728
Newby, Elezabeath I, 152
Newby, Elezabeath I, 154
Newby, Elezabeath Necalls I Sup 1, 8
Newby, Elias I, 703
Newby, Elias I, 728
Newby, Elias I, 731
Newby, Elisabeth I, 13
Newby, Elisabeth I, 14
Newby, Elisabeth I, 37
Newby, Elisabeth I, 43
Newby, Elisabeth I, 55
Newby, Elisabeth I, 56
Newby, Elisabeth I, 57
Newby, Elisabeth I, 59
Newby, Elisabeth I, 62
Newby, Elisabeth I, 63
Newby, Elisabeth I, 64
Newby, Elisabeth I, 70
Newby, Elisabeth I, 71
Newby, Elisabeth I, 76
Newby, Elisabeth I, 78
Newby, Elisabeth I, 86
Newby, Elisabeth I, 87
Newby, Elisabeth I, 88
Newby, Elisabeth I, 129
Newby, Elisabeth I, 130
Newby, Elisabeth I, 137
Newby, Elisabeth I, 152
Newby, Elisabeth I, 153
Newby, Elisabeth I, 154
Newby, Elisabeth I, 161
Newby, Elisabeth I, 170
Newby, Elisha I, 704
Newby, Elisha I, 727
Newby, Eliza I, 13
Newby, Eliza I, 64
Newby, Elizabeth I, 107
Newby, Elizabeth I, 108
Newby, Elizabeth I, 109
Newby, Elizabeth I, 127
Newby, Elizabeth I, 152
Newby, Elizabeth I, 153
Newby, Elizabeth I, 197
Newby, Elizabeth I, 200
Newby, Elizabeth I, 564
Newby, Elizabeth I, 662
Newby, Elizabeth I, 679
Newby, Elizabeth I, 685
Newby, Elizabeth I, 687
Newby, Elizabeth I, 695
Newby, Elizabeth I, 703
Newby, Elizabeth I, 704
Newby, Elizabeth I, 727
Newby, Elizabeth I, 728
Newby, Elizabeth I, 729
Newby, Elizabeth I, 731
Newby, Elizabeth I, 735
Newby, Elizabeth I, 863
Newby, Elizabeth I, 895
Newby, Elizabeth I Sup 1, 3
Newby, Elizabeth I Sup 1, 5
Newby, Elizabeth I Sup 1, 7
Newby, Elizabeth V, 238
Newby, Elizabeth V, 268
Newby, Elizabeth V, 307
Newby, Elizabeth V, 339
Newby, Elizabeth V, 351
Newby, Elizabeth V, 466
Newby, Elizabeth V, 854

Newby, Elizabeth VI, 30
Newby, Elizabeth VI, 33
Newby, Elizabeth C. I, 1160
Newby, Elkanah I, 703
Newby, Ellasent I, 703
Newby, Elleonor I, 728
Newby, Ellicent I, 153
Newby, Elva III, 241
Newby, Elva D. III, 241
Newby, Elvira I, 154
Newby, Elvira I, 169
Newby, Emily V, 588
Newby, Emily V, 594
Newby, Emily P. V, 588
Newby, Emma V, 700
Newby, Emma Caroline V, 351
Newby, Enoch I, 107
Newby, Enoch I, 153
Newby, Enoch I, 154
Newby, Esther I, 13
Newby, Esther I, 54
Newby, Esther I, 64
Newby, Esther I, 957
Newby, Esther I, 965
Newby, Esther I, 967
Newby, Esther I, 1001
Newby, Esther I, 1011
Newby, Esther V, 267
Newby, Esther V, 268
Newby, Ewing V, 461
Newby, Exum I, 13
Newby, Exum I, 63
Newby, Exum I, 64
Newby, Exum I, 153
Newby, Exum I, 154
Newby, Exum I, 197
Newby, Exum I, 727
Newby, Exum II, 245
Newby, Exum, Jr. I, 63
Newby, Exum, Jr. I, 197
Newby, Exum, Jr. III, 241
Newby, Exum, Sr. I, 63
Newby, Fanny I, 704
Newby, Fanny I, 727
Newby, Francis I, 13
Newby, Francis I, 55
Newby, Francis I, 62
Newby, Francis I, 153
Newby, Francis I, 197
Newby, Francis I, 727
Newby, Francis I Sup 1, 5
Newby, Francis I Sup 1, 6
Newby, Francis I Sup 1, 7
Newby, Francis VI, 183
Newby, Francis VI, 200
Newby, Francis White I, 197
Newby, Frederic I, 13
Newby, Frederic I, 64
Newby, Frederic I, 763
Newby, Frederic I, 767
Newby, Frederick I, 63
Newby, Frederick I, 64
Newby, Frederick I, 81
Newby, Frederick I, 662
Newby, Frederick I, 727
Newby, Frederick I, 728
Newby, Frederick I, 767
Newby, Fredrick I, 704
Newby, Gabrel I, 703
Newby, Gabrel I, 704
Newby, Gabriel I, 1
Newby, Gabriel I, 3
Newby, Gabriel I, 13
Newby, Gabriel I, 61
Newby, Gabriel I, 62
Newby, Gabriel I, 63
Newby, Gabriel I, 76
Newby, Gabriel I, 79
Newby, Gabriel I, 142
Newby, Gabriel I, 152
Newby, Gabriel I, 662
Newby, Gabriel I, 703
Newby, Gabriel I, 727
Newby, Gabriel I, 731
Newby, Gabriel I Sup 1, 5
Newby, Gabriel I Sup 1, 6
Newby, Gabriel I Sup 1, 7
Newby, Gabriel VI, 183
Newby, Gabriel VI, 200
Newby, Gabriel, Jr. I Sup 1, 6
Newby, Gabril I, 63
Newby, Gabril I, 197
Newby, Gediar I, 728
Newby, George I, 728
Newby, Gideon I, 35
Newby, Gideon I, 63
Newby, Gideon I, 484
Newby, Gideon I, 703
Newby, Gideon I, 727
Newby, Gideon I, 728
Newby, Glasgo I, 62
Newby, Gulyelma I, 228
Newby, Hagar I, 62
Newby, Hannah I, 133
Newby, Hannah I, 153
Newby, Hannah I, 185
Newby, Hannah I, 197
Newby, Hannah I, 728
Newby, Hannah I Sup 1, 7
Newby, Hannah II, 455
Newby, Hannah II, 606
Newby, Harry I, 62
Newby, Hennery I, 107
Newby, Henry I, 13
Newby, Henry I, 64
Newby, Henry I, 274
Newby, Henry I, 703
Newby, Henry I, 728
Newby, Henry I, 735
Newby, Henry IV, 51
Newby, Henry IV, 423
Newby, Henry V, 854
Newby, Hudah I, 63
Newby, Hugh I, 13
Newby, Huldah I, 13
Newby, Huldah I, 47
Newby, Huldah I, 58
Newby, Huldah I, 63
Newby, Huldah I, 64
Newby, Huldah I, 105
Newby, Huldah I, 148
Newby, Huldah I, 153
Newby, Huldah VI, 183
Newby, Huldah VI, 200
Newby, Hulde I, 108
Newby, Isaac I, 728
Newby, Isaac I, 1160
Newby, Isaac V, 267
Newby, Isaac V, 268
Newby, Isaac V, 307
Newby, Isaac V, 461
Newby, Isaac V, 466
Newby, Isaac K. V, 351
Newby, Isaac Wilson I, 63
Newby, Isabel I, 13
Newby, Isabel I, 153
Newby, Isabella IV, 256
Newby, Isabella IV, 288
Newby, Isabelle I, 62
Newby, Jabez I, 728
Newby, Jabez Hunt I, 895
Newby, Jack I, 62
Newby, Jacob I, 728
Newby, James I, 14
Newby, James I, 62
Newby, James I, 64
Newby, James I, 92
Newby, James I, 107
Newby, James I, 108
Newby, James I, 131
Newby, James I, 137
Newby, James I, 152
Newby, James I, 153
Newby, James I, 172
Newby, James I, 274
Newby, James I, 275
Newby, James I Sup 1, 5
Newby, James IV, 51
Newby, James IV, 256
Newby, James IV, 423
Newby, James IV, 489
Newby, James Atkinson II, 606
Newby, James M. V, 700
Newby, James, Jr. I, 153
Newby, Jamima I, 63
Newby, Jamima I, 704
Newby, Jamimah I, 704
Newby, Jane I, 14
Newby, Jane I, 39
Newby, Jane I, 61
Newby, Jane I, 64
Newby, Jane I, 564
Newby, Jane V, 351
Newby, Jane V, 353
Newby, Jeams I, 107
Newby, Jeams I, 108
Newby, Jemima I, 8
Newby, Jemima I, 13
Newby, Jemima I, 14
Newby, Jemima I, 19
Newby, Jemima I, 39
Newby, Jemima I, 47
Newby, Jemima I, 62
Newby, Jemima I, 63
Newby, Jemima I, 68
Newby, Jemima I, 153
Newby, Jemima I, 895
Newby, Jemima, Jr. I, 62
Newby, Jemima, Sr. I, 62
Newby, Jemimah I, 717
Newby, Jemimah I, 727
Newby, Jemimah I, 879
Newby, Jemimah I, 895
Newby, Jennie Brazil V, 700
Newby, Jesse I, 13
Newby, Jesse I, 14
Newby, Jesse I, 62
Newby, Jesse I, 63
Newby, Jesse I, 64
Newby, Jesse I, 76
Newby, Jesse I, 153
Newby, Jesse I, 154
Newby, Jesse I, 703
Newby, Jesse I, 704
Newby, Jesse I, 727
Newby, Jesse I, 728
Newby, Jesse IV, 423
Newby, Jesse VI, 183
Newby, Jesse VI, 200
Newby, Jesse Wilson I, 14
Newby, Job IV, 51
Newby, Job IV, 256
Newby, Job IV, 423
Newby, Job IV, 489
Newby, Joeh I, 62
Newby, John I, 62
Newby, John I, 64
Newby, John I, 107
Newby, John I, 152
Newby, John I, 153
Newby, John I, 154
Newby, John I, 172
Newby, John I, 185
Newby, John I, 190
Newby, John I, 197
Newby, John I, 198
Newby, John I, 200
Newby, John I, 703
Newby, John I, 727
Newby, John I, 896
Newby, John I Sup 1, 7
Newby, John I Sup 1, 8
Newby, John V, 351
Newby, John VI, 116
Newby, John VI, 968
Newby, John Henley I, 727
Newby, John Henley I, 728
Newby, John L. I, 63
Newby, John L. I, 896
Newby, John L. II, 606
Newby, John L. VI, 200
Newby, John Lawrence I, 13
Newby, John Lawrence I, 63
Newby, John Lawrence VI, 200
Newby, John M. V, 461
Newby, John M. V, 700
Newby, John Thomas I, 13
Newby, John W. V, 351
Newby, John Westly V, 351
Newby, Jonathan I, 55
Newby, Jonathan I, 63
Newby, Jonathan I, 197
Newby, Jonathan I, 703
Newby, Joseph I, 13
Newby, Joseph I, 62
Newby, Joseph I, 63
Newby, Joseph I, 64
Newby, Joseph I, 86
Newby, Joseph I, 87
Newby, Joseph I, 88
Newby, Joseph I, 107
Newby, Joseph I, 108
Newby, Joseph I, 132
Newby, Joseph I, 146
Newby, Joseph I, 152
Newby, Joseph I, 153
Newby, Joseph I, 154
Newby, Joseph I, 167
Newby, Joseph I, 197
Newby, Joseph I, 198
Newby, Joseph I, 201
Newby, Joseph I, 274
Newby, Joseph I, 275
Newby, Joseph I, 679
Newby, Joseph I, 685
Newby, Joseph I, 703
Newby, Joseph I, 727
Newby, Joseph I, 728
Newby, Joseph I, 913
Newby, Joseph I, 957
Newby, Joseph I, 967
Newby, Joseph IV, 256
Newby, Joseph IV, 423
Newby, Joseph V, 267
Newby, Joseph V, 268
Newby, Joseph VI, 45
Newby, Joseph VI, 116
Newby, Joseph VI, 261
Newby, Joseph VI, 283
Newby, Joseph P. I, 14
Newby, Joseph Wilson I, 14
Newby, Joseph Wilson I, 64
Newby, Joseph, Jr. I, 62
Newby, Joseph, Jr. I, 78
Newby, Joseph, Jr. I, 197
Newby, Joshua I, 198
Newby, Joshua I, 662
Newby, Joshua I, 685
Newby, Joshua I, 703
Newby, Joshua I, 704
Newby, Joshua I, 727
Newby, Joshua I, 728
Newby, Joshua Moore I, 197
Newby, Josiah I, 127
Newby, Josiah I, 704
Newby, Josiah I, 727
Newby, Josiah V, 267
Newby, Josiah V, 268
Newby, Josiah V, 307
Newby, Josiah V, 343
Newby, Josiah V, 351
Newby, Judah I, 62
Newby, Julia I, 933
Newby, Julia V, 351
Newby, Julia A. V, 351
Newby, Julia Ann I, 928
Newby, Keran I, 63
Newby, Keran I, 66
Newby, Keron I Sup 1, 8
Newby, Kezia I, 63
Newby, Kezia I, 131
Newby, Kezia I, 153
Newby, Keziah I, 62
Newby, Keziah I, 68
Newby, Keziah I, 107
Newby, Keziah I, 131
Newby, Keziah I, 153
Newby, Keziah I, 154
Newby, Keziah I, 197
Newby, Leah I, 13
Newby, Leah I, 63
Newby, Lenoer I, 728
Newby, Lewis I, 197
Newby, Lucinda V, 268
Newby, Lucinda V, 461
Newby, Lucinda V, 466
Newby, Luke I, 63
Newby, Lydia I, 64
Newby, Lydia I, 88
Newby, Lydia I, 728
Newby, Lydia I, 731
Newby, Malachi Jolly IV, 489
Newby, Margaret I, 3
Newby, Margaret I, 13
Newby, Margaret I, 14
Newby, Margaret I, 62
Newby, Margaret I, 64
Newby, Margaret I, 69
Newby, Margaret I, 81
Newby, Margaret I, 153
Newby, Margaret I, 154
Newby, Margaret I, 703
Newby, Margaret I, 931
Newby, Margaret IV, 256
Newby, Margaret A. I, 64
Newby, Margaret A. I, 67
Newby, Margaret Ann I, 14
Newby, Margaret Ann I, 15
Newby, Mark I, 13
Newby, Mark I, 62
Newby, Mark I, 63
Newby, Mark I, 65
Newby, Mark I, 69
Newby, Mark I, 108
Newby, Mark I, 153
Newby, Mark I, 154
Newby, Mark I, 197
Newby, Mark Bogue I, 198
Newby, Marry I, 896
Newby, Martha I, 13
Newby, Martha I, 14
Newby, Martha I, 63
Newby, Martha I, 64
Newby, Martha I, 88
Newby, Martha I, 128
Newby, Martha I, 154
Newby, Martha I, 197
Newby, Martha A. I, 64
Newby, Martha P. I, 14
Newby, Martha P. I, 64
Newby, Martha P. IV, 227
Newby, Martha P. IV, 256
Newby, Martha Rix I, 13
Newby, Martha Rix I, 63
Newby, Martha Rix I, 81
Newby, Mary I, 13
Newby, Mary I, 14
Newby, Mary I, 19
Newby, Mary I, 34
Newby, Mary I, 35
Newby, Mary I, 36
Newby, Mary I, 45
Newby, Mary I, 55
Newby, Mary I, 58
Newby, Mary I, 59
Newby, Mary I, 60
Newby, Mary I, 61
Newby, Mary I, 62
Newby, Mary I, 63
Newby, Mary I, 64
Newby, Mary I, 69
Newby, Mary I, 70
Newby, Mary I, 72
Newby, Mary I, 76
Newby, Mary I, 79
Newby, Mary I, 85
Newby, Mary I, 87
Newby, Mary I, 90
Newby, Mary I, 107
Newby, Mary I, 108
Newby, Mary I, 146
Newby, Mary I, 153
Newby, Mary I, 154
Newby, Mary I, 164
Newby, Mary I, 174
Newby, Mary I, 189
Newby, Mary I, 197
Newby, Mary I, 198
Newby, Mary I, 201
Newby, Mary I, 203
Newby, Mary I, 484
Newby, Mary I, 703
Newby, Mary I, 704
Newby, Mary I, 715
Newby, Mary I, 727
Newby, Mary I, 728
Newby, Mary I, 886
Newby, Mary I, 895
Newby, Mary I, 896
Newby, Mary I, 913
Newby, Mary I, 914
Newby, Mary I Sup 1, 3
Newby, Mary I Sup 1, 4
Newby, Mary I Sup 1, 5
Newby, Mary I Sup 1, 6
Newby, Mary I Sup 1, 8
Newby, Mary III, 241
Newby, Mary V, 343
Newby, Mary V, 351
Newby, Mary VI, 17
Newby, Mary VI, 45
Newby, Mary VI, 46
Newby, Mary VI, 183
Newby, Mary VI, 200
Newby, Mary Ann I, 716
Newby, Mary Ann I, 921
Newby, Mary Christine III, 2
Newby, Mary Isabella I, 64
Newby, Mary Lucas V, 461
Newby, Mary, Jr. VI, 116
Newby, Mary, Sr. VI, 116
Newby, Melinda I, 763
Newby, Melinda I, 767
Newby, Mellicent I, 198
Newby, Meriam I, 57
Newby, Meriam I, 62
Newby, Merrium I, 727
Newby, Merrium I, 729
Newby, Micah I, 153
Newby, Micah I, 197
Newby, Micah I, 198
Newby, Micah I, 201
Newby, Micajah I, 728
Newby, Milesant I, 197
Newby, Milesant I, 201
Newby, Milicent I, 63
Newby, Milicent I, 76
Newby, Milicent I, 703
Newby, Milicent I, 712
Newby, Milicent I, 727
Newby, Milicent I, 728
Newby, Miliscent I, 107
Newby, Miliscent I, 153
Newby, Milisent I, 197
Newby, Milisent I, 703
Newby, Milisent I, 728
Newby, Millisent I, 703
Newby, Milly I, 703
Newby, Miriam I, 13
Newby, Miriam I, 35
Newby, Miriam I, 45
Newby, Miriam I, 52
Newby, Miriam I, 62
Newby, Miriam I, 63
Newby, Miriam I, 75
Newby, Miriam I, 107
Newby, Miriam I, 108
Newby, Miriam I, 153
Newby, Miriam I, 155
Newby, Miriam I, 703
Newby, Miriam I, 704
Newby, Miriam I, 728
Newby, Miriam V, 346
Newby, Miriam V, 351
Newby, Miriam Elizabeth V, 3

Newby, Miryam I, 108
Newby, Molly I, 728
Newby, Moorning I, 153
Newby, Mordceas I, 62
Newby, Mordeca I, 59
Newby, Mordeca I, 62
Newby, Mordecai I, 108
Newby, Mordecai I, 153
Newby, Morgan I, 728
Newby, Mourning I, 62
Newby, Mourning I, 63
Newby, Mourning I, 69
Newby, Mourning I, 108
Newby, Nancy I, 14
Newby, Nancy I, 15
Newby, Nancy I, 64
Newby, Nancy I, 203
Newby, Nancy I, 728
Newby, Nancy V, 302
Newby, Nancy V, 307
Newby, Nancy VI, 968
Newby, Naomi I, 152
Newby, Naomi I, 172
Newby, Naomi I, 197
Newby, Naomi I, 264
Newby, Naomi I, 274
Newby, Naomiah I, 107
Newby, Naomy I, 144
Newby, Naomy I, 153
Newby, Naomy I, 154
Newby, Nathan I, 13
Newby, Nathan I, 43
Newby, Nathan I, 58
Newby, Nathan I, 62
Newby, Nathan I, 63
Newby, Nathan I, 64
Newby, Nathan I, 68
Newby, Nathan I, 90
Newby, Nathan I, 107
Newby, Nathan I, 153
Newby, Nathan I, 704
Newby, Nathan I, 727
Newby, Nathan I, 728
Newby, Nathan I, 863
Newby, Nathan I, 896
Newby, Nathan I, 957
Newby, Nathan I, 965
Newby, Nathan I, 967
Newby, Nathan I, 1011
Newby, Nathan I Sup 1, 5
Newby, Nathan I Sup 1, 6
Newby, Nathan V, 267
Newby, Nathan V, 268
Newby, Nathan V, 307
Newby, Nathan V, 351
Newby, Nathan V, 588
Newby, Nathan VI, 8
Newby, Nathan VI, 17
Newby, Nathan VI, 23
Newby, Nathan VI, 30
Newby, Nathan VI, 33
Newby, Nathan Johnson I, 727
Newby, Nathaniel I, 197
Newby, Nicholson I Sup 1, 8
Newby, Olive B. IV, 256
Newby, Olive B. IV, 288
Newby, Olive P. IV, 256
Newby, Oliver I, 64
Newby, Patience I, 62
Newby, Patience I, 154
Newby, Patience I, 171
Newby, Patience I, 197
Newby, Patience VI, 45
Newby, Patient I, 154
Newby, Penelope I, 679
Newby, Penelope I, 685
Newby, Penelope I, 695
Newby, Penelope I, 703
Newby, Penelope I, 728
Newby, Penina I, 721
Newby, Penina I, 727
Newby, Penlope I, 728
Newby, Pennelope I, 728
Newby, Penninah I, 63
Newby, Penninah I, 76
Newby, Penninah I, 703
Newby, Penninah I, 704
Newby, Phebe I, 727
Newby, Phebe I, 728
Newby, Phebe I, 885
Newby, Phebe I, 896
Newby, Phinehas I, 107
Newby, Phinehas I, 154
Newby, Pinninah I, 713
Newby, Pinninah I, 727
Newby, Pleasant I, 63
Newby, Pleasant I, 79
Newby, Pleasant I, 108
Newby, R. B. I, 14
Newby, Rachel I, 13
Newby, Rachel I, 62
Newby, Rachel I, 63
Newby, Rachel I, 64
Newby, Rachel I, 67
Newby, Rachel I, 87
Newby, Rachel I, 153
Newby, Rachel I, 685
Newby, Rachel I, 703
Newby, Rachel I, 716
Newby, Rachel I, 723
Newby, Rachel I, 727
Newby, Rachel I, 728
Newby, Rachel V, 267
Newby, Rachel V, 268
Newby, Rebecka I, 63
Newby, Rebeckah I, 152
Newby, Rebeckah I, 156
Newby, Rebeckah I, 727
Newby, Rebekah I, 703
Newby, Rebekah I, 728
Newby, Richard V, 461
Newby, Richard R. V, 700
Newby, Rix I, 197
Newby, Rix I, 727
Newby, Rix I, 728
Newby, Robert I, 8
Newby, Robert I, 13
Newby, Robert I, 14
Newby, Robert I, 19
Newby, Robert I, 60
Newby, Robert I, 62
Newby, Robert I, 63
Newby, Robert I, 68
Newby, Robert I, 72
Newby, Robert I, 107
Newby, Robert I, 153
Newby, Robert V, 267
Newby, Robert V, 268
Newby, Robert B. I, 14
Newby, Robert B. I, 63
Newby, Robert B. I, 64
Newby, Robert B. II, 606
Newby, Robert Betson I, 13
Newby, Ruth I, 62
Newby, Ruth I, 85
Newby, Ruth I, 107
Newby, Ruth I, 108
Newby, Ruth I, 153
Newby, Ruth I, 475
Newby, Ruth I, 484
Newby, Samantha Ellen V, 351
Newby, Samuel I, 13
Newby, Samuel I, 62
Newby, Samuel I, 63
Newby, Samuel I, 67
Newby, Samuel I, 71
Newby, Samuel I, 85
Newby, Samuel I, 86
Newby, Samuel I, 108
Newby, Samuel I, 153
Newby, Samuel I, 189
Newby, Samuel I, 197
Newby, Samuel I, 475
Newby, Samuel I, 484
Newby, Samuel I, 662
Newby, Samuel I, 685
Newby, Samuel I, 703
Newby, Samuel I, 704
Newby, Samuel I, 721
Newby, Samuel I, 727
Newby, Samuel I, 728
Newby, Samuel I, 885
Newby, Samuel I, 896
Newby, Samuel I Sup 1, 3
Newby, Samuel I Sup 1, 5
Newby, Samuel, Jr. I, 153
Newby, Samuel, Sr. I, 108
Newby, Sarah I, 8
Newby, Sarah I, 13
Newby, Sarah I, 14
Newby, Sarah I, 23
Newby, Sarah I, 34
Newby, Sarah I, 49
Newby, Sarah I, 59
Newby, Sarah I, 62
Newby, Sarah I, 63
Newby, Sarah I, 64
Newby, Sarah I, 66
Newby, Sarah I, 70
Newby, Sarah I, 78
Newby, Sarah I, 81
Newby, Sarah I, 88
Newby, Sarah I, 97
Newby, Sarah I, 107
Newby, Sarah I, 108
Newby, Sarah I, 127
Newby, Sarah I, 132
Newby, Sarah I, 136
Newby, Sarah I, 152
Newby, Sarah I, 153
Newby, Sarah I, 155
Newby, Sarah I, 168
Newby, Sarah I, 172
Newby, Sarah I, 188
Newby, Sarah I, 189
Newby, Sarah I, 197
Newby, Sarah I, 274
Newby, Sarah I, 275
Newby, Sarah I, 662
Newby, Sarah I, 703
Newby, Sarah I, 704
Newby, Sarah I, 715
Newby, Sarah I, 727
Newby, Sarah I, 728
Newby, Sarah I, 729
Newby, Sarah I, 735
Newby, Sarah I, 957
Newby, Sarah I, 967
Newby, Sarah I Sup 1, 5
Newby, Sarah V, 307
Newby, Sarah V, 337
Newby, Sarah V, 351
Newby, Sarah V, 396
Newby, Sarah A. I, 14
Newby, Sarah Ann I, 64
Newby, Sarah Eula I, 14
Newby, Sarah Eula I, 64
Newby, Sarah I. I, 64
Newby, Sarah Isabella I, 14
Newby, Sarah Jane V, 351
Newby, Sarah, Sr. I, 153
Newby, Seba I, 728
Newby, Selia I, 727
Newby, Selia I, 896
Newby, Seth I, 716
Newby, Sue I, 62
Newby, Susanna I, 152
Newby, Susanna I, 157
Newby, Susanna IV, 51
Newby, Susannah I, 154
Newby, Susannah I, 185
Newby, Susannah I, 197
Newby, Susannah I, 200
Newby, Susannah IV, 413
Newby, Susannah IV, 423
Newby, Susannah IV, 480
Newby, Susannah IV, 489
Newby, Thomas I, 13
Newby, Thomas I, 14
Newby, Thomas I, 15
Newby, Thomas I, 23
Newby, Thomas I, 62
Newby, Thomas I, 63
Newby, Thomas I, 64
Newby, Thomas I, 72
Newby, Thomas I, 78
Newby, Thomas I, 97
Newby, Thomas I, 107
Newby, Thomas I, 108
Newby, Thomas I, 144
Newby, Thomas I, 153
Newby, Thomas I, 154
Newby, Thomas I, 155
Newby, Thomas I, 157
Newby, Thomas I, 176
Newby, Thomas I, 189
Newby, Thomas I, 197
Newby, Thomas I, 203
Newby, Thomas I, 703
Newby, Thomas I, 727
Newby, Thomas I, 728
Newby, Thomas I, 863
Newby, Thomas I, 928
Newby, Thomas IV, 256
Newby, Thomas V, 267
Newby, Thomas V, 268
Newby, Thomas V, 854
Newby, Thomas VI, 17
Newby, Thomas VI, 45
Newby, Thomas VI, 77
Newby, Thomas VI, 116
Newby, Thomas VI, 118
Newby, Thomas Cox I, 484
Newby, Thomas Pretlow VI, 116
Newby, Thomas R. I, 14
Newby, Thomas R. I, 64
Newby, Thos. VI, 46
Newby, Tom I, 62
Newby, Violet I, 928
Newby, Widow Elisabehth I, 153
Newby, Widow Elisabeth I, 63
Newby, Widow Elisabeth I, 76
Newby, Widow Elizabeth I, 900
Newby, Widow Kezia I, 65
Newby, Widow Keziah I, 62
Newby, Widow Keziah I, 65
Newby, Widow Leah I, 57
Newby, Widow Leah I, 63
Newby, Widow Margaret I, 176
Newby, Widow Mary I, 197
Newby, Widow Mary I, 201
Newby, Widow Penninah I, 43
Newby, Widow Sarah I, 153
Newby, Widow Sarah I, 157
Newby, Widow Sarah Walton I, 64
Newby, Wike I, 13
Newby, William I, 13
Newby, William I, 14
Newby, William I, 61
Newby, William I, 62
Newby, William I, 63
Newby, William I, 64
Newby, William I, 70
Newby, William I, 108
Newby, William I, 133
Newby, William I, 153
Newby, William I, 174
Newby, William I, 185
Newby, William I, 197
Newby, William I, 228
Newby, William I, 475
Newby, William I, 484
Newby, William I, 564
Newby, William I, 662
Newby, William I, 685
Newby, William I, 687
Newby, William I, 695
Newby, William I, 703
Newby, William I, 704
Newby, William I, 727
Newby, William I, 728
Newby, William I, 729
Newby, William I, 863
Newby, William I, 895
Newby, William I, 896
Newby, William I, 900
Newby, William V, 267
Newby, William V, 268
Newby, William V, 351
Newby, William V, 854
Newby, William VI, 27
Newby, William VI, 33
Newby, William Albert V, 351
Newby, William C. I, 64
Newby, William Milton V, 351
Newby, William Nicholson I, 14
Newby, William, Jr. I, 62
Newby, William, Jr. I, 142
Newby, William, Jr. I, 152
Newby, William, Sr. I, 62
Newby, Willis I, 13
Newby, Wlliam I, 39
Newby, Wm. V, 307
Newby, Wm. V, 396
Newby, Wm. A. V, 461
Newby, Wm. C. IV, 256
Newby, Wm. C. IV, 288
Newby, Wyke I, 13
Newby, Wyke I, 14
Newby, Zachariah I, 62
Newby, Zachariah I, 153
Newby, Zachariah I, 198
Newby, Zimri I, 728
Newcom, Mary II, 245
Newcomb, John III, 241
Newcomb, Mary III, 241
Newcombe, Elizabeth II, 606
Newcombe, Elizabeth II, 632
Newcome, Elizabeth II, 606
Newcome, Mary II, 606
Newcomer, Edwin B. II, 903
Newcomer, Grace V, 195
Newcomer, Maria K. II, 903
Newel, Adam H. V, 700
Newel, Carrie V, 700
Newel, Emma V, 700
Newel, Grant V, 700
Newel, Jane V, 700
Newel, Jayne V, 700
Newel, John P. V, 700
Newel, Lewis V, 268
Newel, Lewis V, 700
Newel, Tabitha II, 798
Newell, Blanche E. I, 618
Newell, Carrie J. V, 268
Newell, Cary Jane V, 268
Newell, Dorothy Eula II, 713
Newell, Dwight Watson I, 618
Newell, Eliza I, 338
Newell, Elizabeth G. II, 138
Newell, Emma B. V, 268
Newell, Harold Arthur II, 713
Newell, James E. II, 138
Newell, Kate I, 618
Newell, Lewis V, 268
Newell, Mamie I, 338
Newell, Mammie I, 338
Newell, Margaret II, 136
Newell, Margaret Emeline V, 351
Newell, Margaret Emily V, 351
Newell, Martha II, 713
Newell, Mary Harris II, 136
Newell, Mattie I, 338
Newell, Robert II, 136
Newell, Samuel John II, 713
Newell, Sarah II, 89
Newell, Sarah E. II, 138
Newell, Simeon I, 338
Newell, Simson I, 338
Newell, Thomas VI, 879
Newell, Ulysses V, 268
Newett, Ruth IV, 155
Newgan, Poly Enos VI, 970
Newgan, Richard VI, 970
Newgen, Jacob I, 564
Newgent, Azariah I, 564
Newgent, Jacob I, 564
Newgent, Rhoda I, 1009
Newgent, Rhoda I, 1011
Newhall, Abby II, 713
Newhall, Annetta W. II, 903
Newhall, Annetta W. II, 943
Newhall, Annette W. II, 903
Newhall, Betsey III, 241
Newhall, Edwin R. III, 241
Newhall, Elizabeth III, 241
Newhall, Elizabeth H. III, 241
Newhall, George II, 713
Newhall, Hannah II, 713
Newhall, Hannah J. II, 713
Newhall, Joseph P. III, 241
Newhall, Lydia C. III, 147
Newhall, Lydia C. III, 241
Newhall, Mary II, 713
Newhall, Mary II, 757
Newhall, Paul II, 713
Newhall, Paul Wing II, 606
Newhall, Paul Wing II, 757
Newhall, Richard III, 241
Newhall, Richard M. III, 147
Newhall, Richard W. III, 241
Newhouse, Ethland III, 241
Newhouse, Florence Anna III, 241
Newhouse, Silas III, 241
Newhouse, Walter S. III, 241
Newhouse, Walter Scott, Jr. III, 241
Newkirk, Alice V, 924
Newkirk, C. Claudius V, 924
Newkirk, Charles W. V, 924
Newkirk, Chas. W. V, 924
Newkirk, Chas. Wesley V, 924
Newkirk, Elias Claudius V, 924
Newkirk, Jesse B. V, 924
Newkirk, Jesse Buchanan V, 924
Newkirk, Jessie B. V, 924
Newkirk, Lydia B. II, 135
Newkirk, Martha II, 146
Newkirk, Martha II, 154
Newkirk, Mary II, 154
Newkirk, Mary II, 155
Newkirk, Mary H. II, 135
Newkirk, Mary H. II, 154
Newkirk, Quinton K. II, 135
Newkirk, Wm. Buchanan V, 924
Newlan, Catherine VI, 426
Newlan, Harvey I. I, 247
Newland, Catherine VI, 426
Newland, David VI, 426
Newland, David VI, 678
Newland, Deborah VI, 426
Newland, Deborah VI, 630
Newland, Deborah VI, 678
Newland, Elijah VI, 426
Newland, Elijah VI, 678
Newland, Gainer VI, 426
Newland, Hannah VI, 426
Newland, Ira V, 588
Newland, Ira Earl V, 588
Newland, James VI, 426
Newland, James VI, 678
Newland, Jesse VI, 426
Newland, Jesse VI, 678
Newland, John VI, 426
Newland, John VI, 678
Newland, Margaret VI, 426
Newland, Margaret VI, 678
Newland, Margaret VI, 698
Newland, Mary VI, 386
Newland, Mary VI, 426
Newland, Rebekah I, 412
Newland, Sarah VI, 426
Newland, Sarah VI, 678
Newland, Tamar VI, 426
Newland, Tamer VI, 678
Newland, Thamer VI, 678
Newland, William VI, 426
Newland, William VI, 678
Newland, William, Sr. VI, 426
Newland, William, Sr. VI, 678
Newland, Wm. VI, 426
Newland, Wm., Jr. VI, 426
Newland, Wm., Sr. VI, 678

Newlet, Richard V, 105
Newlet, Sarah V, 105
Newlin, Aaron I, 767
Newlin, Aaron S. I, 751
Newlin, Aaron S. I, 767
Newlin, Abigail II, 982
Newlin, Abigail II, 1018
Newlin, Achsa I, 411
Newlin, Achsa I, 412
Newlin, Achsa I, 451
Newlin, Achsa I, 751
Newlin, Achsa I, 767
Newlin, Achsah I, 411
Newlin, Akcea I, 451
Newlin, Alice IV, 423
Newlin, Alice IV, 438
Newlin, Alice IV, 440
Newlin, Ann IV, 103
Newlin, Ann IV, 131
Newlin, Anna IV, 490
Newlin, Annesley II, 154
Newlin, Annesley II, 160
Newlin, Annie IV, 490
Newlin, Antinet I, 439
Newlin, Asie I, 451
Newlin, Benjamin II, 154
Newlin, Benjamin II, 160
Newlin, Candace I, 452
Newlin, Catharine I, 439
Newlin, Catharine I, 446
Newlin, Catharine I, 451
Newlin, Catharine I, 452
Newlin, Catharine I, 751
Newlin, Catharine I, 767
Newlin, Catharine Adela I, 767
Newlin, Charles I, 452
Newlin, Charles V, 351
Newlin, Charles V, 423
Newlin, Chas. G. IV, 489
Newlin, Clarice I, 931
Newlin, Clarice E. I, 946
Newlin, Cyrus I, 439
Newlin, Cyrus II, 982
Newlin, Cyrus II, 1018
Newlin, David I, 439
Newlin, David I, 452
Newlin, David V, 589
Newlin, David VI, 678
Newlin, Deborah I, 362
Newlin, Deborah I, 404
Newlin, Deborah I, 411
Newlin, Deborah I, 412
Newlin, Deborah I, 439
Newlin, Deborah I, 442
Newlin, Deborah I, 451
Newlin, Deborah I, 452
Newlin, Deborah I, 751
Newlin, Deborah I, 767
Newlin, Deborah VI, 630
Newlin, Deborah VI, 678
Newlin, Deborah Jane I, 439
Newlin, Della M. I, 527
Newlin, Della M. I, 564
Newlin, Della N. I, 850
Newlin, Delphina I, 247
Newlin, Delphina E. I, 564
Newlin, Delphina Jane I, 751
Newlin, Dicene S. I, 294
Newlin, Dicene S. I, 767
Newlin, Dicene S. I, 768
Newlin, Duncan I, 439
Newlin, Duncan I, 751
Newlin, Edith I, 377
Newlin, Edith I, 411
Newlin, Edith I, 412
Newlin, Edith I, 451
Newlin, Edith IV, 126
Newlin, Edith IV, 131
Newlin, Edith IV, 835
Newlin, Edith IV, 841
Newlin, Edith M. IV, 757
Newlin, Edna V, 700
Newlin, Edna B. V, 700
Newlin, Eleanor I, 439
Newlin, Eleanor I, 444
Newlin, Eleanor I, 452
Newlin, Eleanor V, 105
Newlin, Eleanor V, 589
Newlin, Eleanor C. V, 105
Newlin, Elener I, 446
Newlin, Elener I, 451
Newlin, Elenor I, 439
Newlin, Eli I, 247
Newlin, Eli I, 391
Newlin, Eli I, 411
Newlin, Eli I, 412
Newlin, Eli I, 439
Newlin, Eli I, 451
Newlin, Eli I, 751
Newlin, Eli IV, 438
Newlin, Eli V, 105
Newlin, Eli V, 268
Newlin, Eli V, 351
Newlin, Eli V, 373
Newlin, Eli V, 423
Newlin, Eli V, 519
Newlin, Eli V, 589
Newlin, Eli V, 591
Newlin, Elias I, 439
Newlin, Elias I, 452
Newlin, Elias V, 589
Newlin, Elihu I, 439
Newlin, Elihugh I, 452
Newlin, Elijah IV, 131
Newlin, Elijah VI, 678
Newlin, Elisabeth I, 622
Newlin, Eliza Jane I, 767
Newlin, Elizabeth I, 638
Newlin, Elizabeth I, 685
Newlin, Elizabeth I, 690
Newlin, Elizabeth I, 751
Newlin, Elizabeth I, 767
Newlin, Elizabeth I, 931
Newlin, Elizabeth II, 154
Newlin, Elizabeth II, 160
Newlin, Elizabeth II, 161
Newlin, Elizabeth II, 607
Newlin, Elizabeth IV, 100
Newlin, Elizabeth IV, 103
Newlin, Elizabeth IV, 131
Newlin, Elizabeth IV, 490
Newlin, Elizabeth A. IV, 466
Newlin, Elizabeth A. IV, 489
Newlin, Elizabeth G. II, 154
Newlin, Ellen IV, 835
Newlin, Ellen B. IV, 835
Newlin, Ellen B. IV, 841
Newlin, Ely V, 351
Newlin, Emiley I, 452
Newlin, Emily J. I, 760
Newlin, Emily J. I, 767
Newlin, Enoch I, 439
Newlin, Esther I, 1129
Newlin, Esther V, 105
Newlin, Esther V, 128
Newlin, Esther V, 268
Newlin, Esther V, 423
Newlin, Esther V, 519
Newlin, Esther V, 589
Newlin, Esther Irene IV, 813
Newlin, Esther Irene IV, 835
Newlin, Farnando I, 439
Newlin, Franklin VI, 77
Newlin, Gulielma I, 439
Newlin, Hannah I, 356
Newlin, Hannah I, 362
Newlin, Hannah I, 399
Newlin, Hannah I, 411
Newlin, Hannah I, 439
Newlin, Hannah I, 445
Newlin, Hannah I, 451
Newlin, Hannah I, 452
Newlin, Hannah I, 747
Newlin, Hannah I, 751
Newlin, Hannah I, 767
Newlin, Hannah Gilbert IV, 835
Newlin, Harvey I, 247
Newlin, Harvey I. I, 247
Newlin, Henry V, 105
Newlin, Hessie I, 247
Newlin, Hester V, 105
Newlin, Hettie I, 247
Newlin, Ida A. IV, 716
Newlin, Ida A. IV, 720
Newlin, Ida A. IV, 757
Newlin, Ida A. IV, 820
Newlin, Ida A. IV, 835
Newlin, Ida A. IV, 841
Newlin, Isaac I, 439
Newlin, Jabes I, 767
Newlin, Jabez I, 767
Newlin, Jabez F. I, 751
Newlin, Jacob I, 362
Newlin, Jacob I, 411
Newlin, Jacob I, 426
Newlin, Jacob I, 439
Newlin, Jacob I, 452
Newlin, Jacob I, 455
Newlin, Jacob VI, 77
Newlin, James I, 362
Newlin, James I, 404
Newlin, James I, 411
Newlin, James I, 412
Newlin, James I, 439
Newlin, James I, 442
Newlin, James I, 451
Newlin, James I, 452
Newlin, James I, 685
Newlin, James I, 690
Newlin, James I, 695
Newlin, James I, 747
Newlin, James I, 767
Newlin, James IV, 490
Newlin, James VI, 678
Newlin, James M. I, 247
Newlin, James N. I, 622
Newlin, James Newton I, 751
Newlin, Jane IV, 131
Newlin, Jane V, 589
Newlin, Jas. IV, 466
Newlin, Jehu I, 439
Newlin, Jehu I, 452
Newlin, Jehu VI, 64
Newlin, Jehu VI, 77
Newlin, Jehugh I, 452
Newlin, Jesse VI, 678
Newlin, Jno. V, 589
Newlin, Joel V, 589
Newlin, John I, 356
Newlin, John I, 362
Newlin, John I, 405
Newlin, John I, 411
Newlin, John I, 412
Newlin, John I, 439
Newlin, John I, 451
Newlin, John I, 452
Newlin, John I, 455
Newlin, John I, 685
Newlin, John I, 728
Newlin, John I, 741
Newlin, John I, 762
Newlin, John I, 767
Newlin, John I, 931
Newlin, John II, 606
Newlin, John V, 105
Newlin, John V, 128
Newlin, John V, 268
Newlin, John V, 519
Newlin, John VI, 678
Newlin, John D. V, 105
Newlin, John D. V, 589
Newlin, John N. I, 751
Newlin, John S. II, 607
Newlin, John Togan I, 751
Newlin, John, Jr. I, 399
Newlin, John, Jr. I, 411
Newlin, John, Jr. I, 452
Newlin, Jonathan I, 439
Newlin, Jonathan I, 451
Newlin, Jonathan I, 452
Newlin, Joseph I, 294
Newlin, Joseph I, 439
Newlin, Joseph I, 452
Newlin, Joseph I, 751
Newlin, Joseph I, 760
Newlin, Joseph I, 767
Newlin, Joseph Charles I, 751
Newlin, Joseph John I, 751
Newlin, Joseph O. I, 247
Newlin, Joseph Oliver I, 751
Newlin, Joshua I, 411
Newlin, Joshua I, 412
Newlin, Joshua I, 451
Newlin, Joshua I, 767
Newlin, Joshua V, 589
Newlin, Kathrine I, 362
Newlin, Lydia I, 439
Newlin, Lydia I, 447
Newlin, Lydia I, 452
Newlin, Lydia V, 268
Newlin, Lydia V, 351
Newlin, Lydia V, 373
Newlin, Lydia V, 423
Newlin, Lydia V, 591
Newlin, Lydia B. V, 268
Newlin, Lydia B. V, 423
Newlin, Lydia Osborn V, 589
Newlin, Mahlon I, 247
Newlin, Maine VI, 77
Newlin, Malen I, 439
Newlin, Margaret I, 685
Newlin, Margaret I, 690
Newlin, Margaret I, 767
Newlin, Margaret VI, 678
Newlin, Marion VI, 77
Newlin, Martha I, 946
Newlin, Martha Ann I, 751
Newlin, Martha E. I, 247
Newlin, Martha E. I, 931
Newlin, Martha E. I, 946
Newlin, Martha Elisabeth I, 622
Newlin, Martha Ellen I, 931
Newlin, Martha Jane I, 767
Newlin, Mary I, 356
Newlin, Mary I, 362
Newlin, Mary I, 386
Newlin, Mary I, 391
Newlin, Mary I, 411
Newlin, Mary I, 412
Newlin, Mary I, 414
Newlin, Mary I, 416
Newlin, Mary I, 439
Newlin, Mary I, 451
Newlin, Mary I, 452
Newlin, Mary I, 751
Newlin, Mary I, 767
Newlin, Mary I, 769
Newlin, Mary II, 154
Newlin, Mary II, 160
Newlin, Mary II, 982
Newlin, Mary II, 1018
Newlin, Mary IV, 438
Newlin, Mary V, 50
Newlin, Mary V, 105
Newlin, Mary V, 560
Newlin, Mary V, 568
Newlin, Mary V, 589
Newlin, Mary A. I, 445
Newlin, Mary A. I, 452
Newlin, Mary Alida I, 439
Newlin, Mary Ann I, 439
Newlin, Mary Edwards V, 589
Newlin, Mary Ellen I, 751
Newlin, Mary Heston I, 751
Newlin, Mary Margaret I, 751
Newlin, Mary Margaret I, 767
Newlin, Mary S. I, 751
Newlin, Mary W. II, 154
Newlin, Matilda IV, 466
Newlin, Matilda IV, 490
Newlin, Miranda I, 452
Newlin, Moranda I, 439
Newlin, Nancy I, 439
Newlin, Nancy H. I, 447
Newlin, Nancy H. I, 452
Newlin, Nannie G. I, 247
Newlin, Nathan I, 767
Newlin, Nathaniel I, 372
Newlin, Nathaniel I, 412
Newlin, Nathaniel I, 439
Newlin, Nathaniel I, 446
Newlin, Nathaniel I, 451
Newlin, Nathaniel I, 452
Newlin, Nathaniel I, 457
Newlin, Nathaniel I, 767
Newlin, Nathaniel N. I, 751
Newlin, Nathaniel, Jr. I, 451
Newlin, Newton I, 751
Newlin, Newton I, 767
Newlin, Olive I, 439
Newlin, Olive I, 447
Newlin, Olive I, 452
Newlin, Olive W. V, 700
Newlin, Oliver I, 247
Newlin, Oliver I, 439
Newlin, Oliver I, 452
Newlin, Phinehas V, 589
Newlin, Rebecca I, 439
Newlin, Rebecca I, 451
Newlin, Rebecca I, 452
Newlin, Rebekah I, 405
Newlin, Rebekah I, 412
Newlin, Robenia Ethel Hair I, 439
Newlin, Robert II, 982
Newlin, Robert II, 1018
Newlin, Robert, Jr. II, 903
Newlin, Roseland I, 247
Newlin, Ruth I, 294
Newlin, Ruth I, 362
Newlin, Ruth I, 398
Newlin, Ruth I, 411
Newlin, Ruth I, 412
Newlin, Ruth I, 426
Newlin, Ruth I, 439
Newlin, Ruth I, 444
Newlin, Ruth I, 451
Newlin, Ruth I, 452
Newlin, Ruth I, 454
Newlin, Ruth I, 455
Newlin, Ruth I, 751
Newlin, Ruth I, 760
Newlin, Ruth I, 762
Newlin, Ruth I, 767
Newlin, Ruth V, 589
Newlin, Ruth VI, 77
Newlin, Ruth Emily I, 751
Newlin, Ruth Isabelle I, 751
Newlin, Sally I, 412
Newlin, Sally I, 425
Newlin, Samuel G. I, 751
Newlin, Sarah I, 362
Newlin, Sarah I, 372
Newlin, Sarah I, 391
Newlin, Sarah I, 399
Newlin, Sarah I, 411
Newlin, Sarah I, 412
Newlin, Sarah I, 431
Newlin, Sarah I, 439
Newlin, Sarah I, 451
Newlin, Sarah I, 452
Newlin, Sarah I, 455
Newlin, Sarah I, 685
Newlin, Sarah I, 741
Newlin, Sarah I, 767
Newlin, Sarah II, 154
Newlin, Sarah II, 160
Newlin, Sarah IV, 177
Newlin, Sarah IV, 256
Newlin, Sarah V, 105
Newlin, Sarah V, 589
Newlin, Sarah VI, 678
Newlin, Sarah VI, 689
Newlin, Sarah Decena I, 751
Newlin, Sarah Dicena I, 751
Newlin, Sarah Frances I, 439
Newlin, Sarah L. IV, 256
Newlin, Sarah W. VI, 64
Newlin, Sarah W. VI, 77
Newlin, Sarah W. VI, 92
Newlin, Simon IV, 131
Newlin, Sylvester I, 931
Newlin, Sylvester I, 946
Newlin, Tamer VI, 678
Newlin, Telitha I, 439
Newlin, Temple V, 351
Newlin, Temple V, 423
Newlin, Thomas I, 362
Newlin, Thomas I, 412
Newlin, Thomas I, 439
Newlin, Thomas I, 452
Newlin, Thomas I, 685
Newlin, Thomas I, 690
Newlin, Thomas I, 767
Newlin, Thomas II, 154
Newlin, Thomas II, 160
Newlin, Thomas II, 607
Newlin, Thomas V, 700
Newlin, Thomas E. I, 439
Newlin, Thomas, Jr. II, 607
Newlin, Thomas, Jr. II, 757
Newlin, William I, 439
Newlin, William I, 451
Newlin, William I, 452
Newlin, William I, 751
Newlin, William I, 767
Newlin, William V, 50
Newlin, William V, 105
Newlin, William V, 351
Newlin, William V, 423
Newlin, William V, 589
Newlin, William VI, 426
Newlin, William VI, 678
Newlin, William B. I, 452
Newlin, William Benton I, 439
Newlin, William W. IV, 835
Newlin, William, Sr. VI, 678
Newlin, Wm. IV, 841
Newlin, Wm. V, 351
Newlin, Wm. V, 560
Newlin, Wm. W. IV, 757
Newlin, Wm. W. IV, 841
Newlin, Zilla I, 452
Newlin, Zimri I, 439
Newlon, Ann IV, 131
Newlon, Elijah IV, 131
Newlon, Hannah VI, 944
Newlon, James VI, 959
Newlon, John VI, 944
Newlon, Priscilla VI, 959
Newlon, Simon IV, 131
Newlyn, Eli V, 220
Newlyn, Lydia V, 220
Newman, ??? VI, 39
Newman, Adam VI, 906
Newman, Adam VI, 968
Newman, Alfred VI, 871
Newman, Alfred VI, 887
Newman, Alfred VI, 975
Newman, Alfred VI, 979
Newman, Alfred VI, 990
Newman, Alfred VI, 1000
Newman, Alfred VI, 1022
Newman, Ann I, 380
Newman, Ann I, 412
Newman, Ann I, 1102
Newman, Ann I, 1110
Newman, Ann I, 1129
Newman, Ann V, 105
Newman, Anna V, 105
Newman, Anna V, 137
Newman, Anna V, 423
Newman, Annie V, 423
Newman, Anny V, 50
Newman, Arthur VI, 898
Newman, Arthur VI, 919
Newman, Arthur VI, 968
Newman, Arthur, Jr. VI, 914
Newman, Arthur, Jr. VI, 920
Newman, Arthur, Jr. VI, 968
Newman, Arthur, Jr. VI, 972
Newman, Arthur, Sr. VI, 920
Newman, Asenath V, 589
Newman, Bailey VI, 968
Newman, Benjamin F. V, 589

man, Betsey VI, 898
man, Callohill VI, 968
man, Catherine VI, 1015
man, Cena VI, 942
man, Clark VI, 968
man, Conrad VI, 944
man, Conrad VI, 968
man, Conrad VI, 1015
man, Deborah VI, 968
man, Delilah VI, 999
man, Dorothy VI, 925
man, Edward I, 564
man, Edwin III, 241
man, Eleanor I, 685
man, Elias VI, 968
man, Elisabeth I, 1110
man, Elizabeth I, 412
man, Elizabeth I, 685
man, Elizabeth I, 1129
man, Elizabeth II, 83
man, Elizabeth II, 89
man, Elizabeth II, 607
man, Elizabeth V, 50
man, Elizabeth V, 105
man, Elizabeth VI, 939
man, Elizabeth VI, 968
man, Elizabeth VI, 998
man, Elizabeth H. VI, 968
man, Elizabeth King VI, 968
man, Elizabeth Knight II, 35
man, Elizabeth Knight II, 89
man, Ella V, 423
man, Elusty VI, 898
man, Emily VI, 1015
man, Frances VI, 1002
man, Franklin B. V, 589
man, G. A. V, 105
man, Garett VI, 972
man, Garrett VI, 872
man, Garrett VI, 898
man, Geo. V, 423
man, George V, 423
man, H. N. V, 700
man, Hannah II, 607
man, Hannah II, 621
man, Hannah VI, 968
man, Harriett J. VI, 968
man, Hattie V, 351
man, Hattie V, 423
man, Hattie E. V, 423
man, Henry V, 700
man, Henry VI, 872
man, Henry VI, 898
man, Henry VI, 940
man, Henry VI, 961
man, Henry VI, 968
man, Huldah I, 685
man, Huldah I, 689
man, James VI, 968
man, James M. C. V, 105
man, Jane VI, 900
man, Jesse VI, 968
man, Jesse M. VI, 968
man, Joel V, 105
man, John I, 685
man, John I, 689
man, John I, 767
man, John I, 896
man, John I, 1110
man, John V, 105
man, John VI, 968
man, John Knight II, 89
man, John L. VI, 947
man, Johnathan I, 1102
man, Johnathan I, 1129
man, Jonathan I, 380
man, Jonathan I, 412
man, Jonathan I, 831
man, Jonathan I, 1110
man, Jonathan I, 1129
man, Jonathan V, 50
man, Jonathan V, 105
man, Jonathan V, 137
man, Jonathan Thomas V, 105
man, Jonothan V, 105
man, Joseph I, 412
man, Joseph I, 685
man, Joseph V, 105
man, Julia Ann VI, 968
man, Laura V, 105
man, Levina VI, 898
man, Lillie C. V, 423
man, Lovely VI, 933
man, Lucinda VI, 898
man, Lucinda VI, 972
man, Lucy VI, 960
man, Lucy VI, 968
man, Lucy Ann VI, 1019
man, Margaret VI, 899
man, Martha VI, 968
Newman, Mary I, 564
Newman, Mary I, 721
Newman, Mary I, 728
Newman, Mary I, 819
Newman, Mary I, 831
Newman, Mary I, 1129
Newman, Mary V, 589
Newman, Mary V, 794
Newman, Mary VI, 33
Newman, Mary VI, 34
Newman, Mary VI, 877
Newman, Mary VI, 898
Newman, Mary VI, 944
Newman, Mary VI, 968
Newman, Mary VI, 972
Newman, Mary Earl I, 1110
Newman, Mary Earl V, 105
Newman, Mary Earl V, 137
Newman, Mary Jane VI, 968
Newman, Mary M. V, 589
Newman, Mildred VI, 968
Newman, Nancie A. V, 423
Newman, Nancy V, 423
Newman, Nancy VI, 888
Newman, Nancy VI, 920
Newman, Nancy VI, 968
Newman, Nancy A. V, 423
Newman, Nathan VI, 960
Newman, Nathan VI, 1002
Newman, Nathaniel VI, 968
Newman, Nimrod VI, 898
Newman, Nimrod VI, 936
Newman, Nimrod VI, 942
Newman, Nimrod VI, 968
Newman, Parthena VI, 998
Newman, Patsey VI, 936
Newman, Paul II, 399
Newman, Permelia VI, 968
Newman, Polly P. VI, 968
Newman, Rachel I, 674
Newman, Rachel I, 685
Newman, Rice VI, 815
Newman, Ruhamah I, 685
Newman, Sally VI, 872
Newman, Sally VI, 877
Newman, Sally VI, 1002
Newman, Sally VI, 1012
Newman, Sarah II, 89
Newman, Sarah VI, 968
Newman, Silas III, 491
Newman, Sindey VI, 898
Newman, Susan VI, 947
Newman, Susannah VI, 898
Newman, Thomas VI, 33
Newman, Thomas VI, 34
Newman, Thomas VI, 968
Newman, Tulitha I, 452
Newman, Walter III, 241
Newman, William V, 589
Newman, William VI, 933
Newman, William VI, 972
Newman, William Lambert I, 564
Newman, Zilopha VI, 968
Newmans, Jonathan I, 831
Newnon, Abigail I, 564
Newnon, Edward I, 564
Newnum, Abigail I, 530
Newnum, Abigail I, 564
Newport, Aaron IV, 17
Newport, Aaron IV, 23
Newport, Aaron IV, 51
Newport, Aaron IV, 52
Newport, Aaron IV, 103
Newport, Aaron IV, 150
Newport, Aaron IV, 157
Newport, Aaron IV, 745
Newport, Aaron VI, 426
Newport, Aaron VI, 561
Newport, Aaron VI, 678
Newport, Aaron VI, 705
Newport, Abigail IV, 52
Newport, Abigail IV, 155
Newport, Abigail IV, 157
Newport, Abigail IV, 545
Newport, Amanda V, 105
Newport, Amanda V, 144
Newport, Amanda Ann V, 105
Newport, Amanda Ann V, 144
Newport, Anna B. II, 903
Newport, Anna B. II, 912
Newport, Anna Maria IV, 344
Newport, Anna Mariah IV, 344
Newport, Bernard IV, 344
Newport, Caroline IV, 155
Newport, Caroline IV, 256
Newport, Clara May II, 903
Newport, Clara May II, 912
Newport, David II, 399
Newport, David Noble IV, 344
Newport, David, Jr. II, 607
Newport, Edith IV, 52
Newport, Edith IV, 150
Newport, Edith IV, 155
Newport, Edith IV, 159
Newport, Edith IV, 478
Newport, Edith IV, 490
Newport, Elizabeth II, 399
Newport, Elizabeth II, 607
Newport, Elizabeth IV, 51
Newport, Elizabeth IV, 52
Newport, Elizabeth IV, 103
Newport, Elizabeth IV, 107
Newport, Elizabeth IV, 145
Newport, Elizabeth IV, 155
Newport, Elizabeth IV, 256
Newport, Elizabeth IV, 703
Newport, Elizabeth IV, 745
Newport, Elvira IV, 344
Newport, Eunice Ann V, 968
Newport, Eunice Ann V, 974
Newport, Fawcett T. IV, 155
Newport, Hannah II, 446
Newport, James V, 589
Newport, James V, 758
Newport, Jane V, 758
Newport, Jason V, 758
Newport, Jesse II, 399
Newport, Jesse IV, 51
Newport, Jesse IV, 52
Newport, Jesse IV, 103
Newport, Jesse IV, 155
Newport, Jesse IV, 256
Newport, Jesse R. IV, 344
Newport, Jesse W. II, 607
Newport, John IV, 52
Newport, John William IV, 155
Newport, Jonah IV, 52
Newport, Jonah IV, 155
Newport, Jonah IV, 159
Newport, Jonah IV, 344
Newport, Jonah C. VI, 561
Newport, Jonah C. VI, 678
Newport, Jonah C. VI, 705
Newport, Jonathan V, 924
Newport, Joseph IV, 52
Newport, Joseph IV, 103
Newport, Joseph IV, 155
Newport, Joseph IV, 256
Newport, Joseph V, 924
Newport, Julia M. IV, 155
Newport, Julia M. IV, 158
Newport, Julia Maria IV, 256
Newport, Julia Maria IV, 269
Newport, Julia Meriah IV, 155
Newport, Lidia Ann IV, 155
Newport, Lydia IV, 52
Newport, Lydia IV, 54
Newport, Lydia Ann IV, 152
Newport, Lydia Ann IV, 155
Newport, Lydia Ann IV, 240
Newport, Lydia Ann IV, 256
Newport, Mary II, 399
Newport, Mary IV, 23
Newport, Mary IV, 51
Newport, Mary IV, 52
Newport, Mary IV, 85
Newport, Mary IV, 103
Newport, Mary IV, 150
Newport, Mary IV, 155
Newport, Mary IV, 256
Newport, Mary IV, 609
Newport, Mary IV, 648
Newport, Mary IV, 745
Newport, Mary VI, 561
Newport, Mary VI, 678
Newport, Mary VI, 705
Newport, Mary Ann IV, 155
Newport, Mary Ann IV, 157
Newport, Narcissa IV, 155
Newport, Nathan IV, 52
Newport, Nathan IV, 103
Newport, Nathan IV, 145
Newport, Nathan IV, 155
Newport, Nathan IV, 703
Newport, Nathan IV, 745
Newport, Noble IV, 52
Newport, Noble IV, 155
Newport, Noble IV, 256
Newport, Rachel IV, 155
Newport, Rachel IV, 159
Newport, Rachel IV, 344
Newport, Rachel VI, 678
Newport, Rachel VI, 705
Newport, Rachel S. VI, 678
Newport, Rebecca IV, 51
Newport, Reece IV, 52
Newport, Reece IV, 103
Newport, Rees IV, 52
Newport, Rees IV, 256
Newport, Reese IV, 155
Newport, Reese IV, 256
Newport, Richard IV, 52
Newport, Rodman B. II, 903
Newport, Rodman B. II, 912
Newport, Ruth IV, 52
Newport, Ruth IV, 103
Newport, Ruth IV, 150
Newport, Ruth IV, 155
Newport, Ruthanna IV, 344
Newport, Sarah IV, 313
Newport, Sarah IV, 314
Newport, Taylor IV, 344
Newport, Thomas II, 446
Newport, Thomas IV, 51
Newport, Thomas IV, 71
Newport, Thomas IV, 85
Newport, Thomas IV, 103
Newport, William V, 758
Newport, William Hoyle IV, 490
Newport, Wm. C. II, 903
Newport, Wm. C. II, 912
News, Sarah I, 308
Newsom, Bell IV, 1218
Newsom, Braxton VI, 969
Newsom, Charity I, 292
Newsom, Charity I, 312
Newsom, Charity IV, 424
Newsom, Charles IV, 424
Newsom, Charlotty I, 312
Newsom, Clarkey I, 302
Newsom, Clarkey I, 312
Newsom, Clarky I, 313
Newsom, Daniel I, 292
Newsom, Daniel I, 302
Newsom, Daniel I, 312
Newsom, David I, 247
Newsom, David I, 292
Newsom, David I, 312
Newsom, David I, 320
Newsom, David M. VI, 968
Newsom, Davis I, 292
Newsom, Edith III, 241
Newsom, Edith A. III, 241
Newsom, Edith Armstrong III, 241
Newsom, Edwin IV, 423
Newsom, Edwin IV, 424
Newsom, Elisabeth I, 292
Newsom, Elizabeth I, 312
Newsom, Elizabeth I, 319
Newsom, Elizabeth I, 728
Newsom, Elizabeth III, 241
Newsom, Elizabeth IV, 423
Newsom, Elizabeth VI, 979
Newsom, Elizabeth R. III, 241
Newsom, Esther W. IV, 1218
Newsom, Esther W. IV, 1228
Newsom, Everett III, 241
Newsom, Everett H. III, 241
Newsom, Exum I, 312
Newsom, Isaac I, 312
Newsom, James I, 339
Newsom, Jesse I, 312
Newsom, Joab I, 292
Newsom, Joel I, 292
Newsom, Joel I, 312
Newsom, Joel I, 320
Newsom, John I, 292
Newsom, John I, 312
Newsom, John L. V, 636
Newsom, John W. VI, 968
Newsom, Jordan IV, 423
Newsom, Jordan IV, 424
Newsom, Jordon I, 292
Newsom, Jordon I, 312
Newsom, Jordon IV, 424
Newsom, Jose I, 292
Newsom, Joseph I, 292
Newsom, Joseph IV, 423
Newsom, Joseph IV, 424
Newsom, Joseph Jourdan IV, 424
Newsom, Josie I, 312
Newsom, L. Octavia VI, 968
Newsom, Lany I, 312
Newsom, Luke I, 312
Newsom, Lydia I, 292
Newsom, Lydia I, 303
Newsom, Lydia I, 312
Newsom, Martha IV, 423
Newsom, Mary I, 243
Newsom, Mary I, 247
Newsom, Mary I, 280
Newsom, Mary I, 292
Newsom, Mary I, 312
Newsom, Mary IV, 423
Newsom, Mary A. VI, 969
Newsom, Mary F. VI, 968
Newsom, Mary, Jr. I, 312
Newsom, Micajah I, 312
Newsom, Mildraid I, 312
Newsom, Milicent I, 300
Newsom, Milicent I, 312
Newsom, Millicent I, 292
Newsom, Nathan I, 292
Newsom, Nathan I, 312
Newsom, Nathaniel VI, 969
Newsom, Nathaniel VI, 1022
Newsom, Patty I, 312
Newsom, Peninah I, 292
Newsom, Peninah I, 312
Newsom, Peninah I, 320
Newsom, Pheriba I, 312
Newsom, Pheriby I, 292
Newsom, Pininah I, 312
Newsom, Rachel IV, 423
Newsom, Rachel IV, 424
Newsom, Rachel IV, 1070
Newsom, Rebekah I, 312
Newsom, Robert I, 292
Newsom, Rosabel IV, 1218
Newsom, Sarah I, 247
Newsom, Sarah I, 253
Newsom, Sarah I, 292
Newsom, Sarah I, 302
Newsom, Sarah I, 307
Newsom, Sarah I, 312
Newsom, Sarah I, 313
Newsom, Sophia Ann VI, 968
Newsom, Susan IV, 424
Newsom, Susanna IV, 1070
Newsom, Susannah IV, 423
Newsom, Thomas I, 312
Newsom, William I, 243
Newsom, William I, 247
Newsom, William I, 292
Newsom, William I, 312
Newsom, William IV, 423
Newsom, William IV, 424
Newsom, William VI, 968
Newsom, William VI, 979
Newsom, William VI, 983
Newsom, Willis I, 292
Newsom, Willis I, 302
Newsom, Willis I, 303
Newsom, Willis I, 312
Newsom, Wm. IV, 1070
Newsom, Zilpha I, 302
Newsom, Zilpha I, 312
Newsom, Zilpha I, 318
Newsom, Zilphia I, 292
Newsome, Abigail I, 728
Newsome, Bertie I, 339
Newsome, Charity IV, 419
Newsome, Charity IV, 424
Newsome, Ebbie I, 339
Newsome, Edwin IV, 424
Newsome, Elizabeth I, 304
Newsome, Elizabeth I, 720
Newsome, Elizabeth I, 728
Newsome, James I, 339
Newsome, John Obed I, 339
Newsome, Luke I, 720
Newsome, Luke I, 728
Newsome, Martha I, 728
Newsome, Ramsom I, 728
Newsome, Sarah I, 728
Newsome, William IV, 424
Newsome, William VI, 832
Newsome, William F. I, 728
Newson, Abigail I, 728
Newson, Abigail I, 734
Newson, Charlotty I, 308
Newson, Charlotty I, 312
Newson, Clarkey I, 312
Newson, Daniel I, 312
Newson, David I, 312
Newson, Isaac I, 312
Newson, Jesse I, 312
Newson, Joel I, 312
Newson, John I, 312
Newson, Josie I, 312
Newson, Luke I, 312
Newson, Micajah I, 312
Newson, Mildraid I, 312
Newson, Rachel IV, 1070
Newson, Thomas I, 312
Newson, William I, 312
Newson, William F. I, 728
Newson, Willis I, 312
Newsum, David VI, 77
Newsum, David VI, 83
Newsum, John L. V, 636
Newsum, Margaret VI, 843
Newsum, William VI, 843
Newton, ??? III, 431
Newton, Ann I, 445
Newton, Basil II, 399
Newton, Charles V, 423
Newton, Daniel II, 245
Newton, Elisabeth II, 607
Newton, Elizabeth II, 399
Newton, Elizabeth II, 510
Newton, Elizabeth II, 607
Newton, Elizabeth B. II, 286

Newton, Elizabeth B. II, 297
Newton, Esther III, 387
Newton, Hannah II, 180
Newton, Hannah II, 214
Newton, Hannah II, 238
Newton, Hannah II, 245
Newton, Ida May V, 423
Newton, Isaac I, 530
Newton, Isaac II, 245
Newton, Jane V, 885
Newton, Jesse I, 946
Newton, John V, 351
Newton, John C. V, 351
Newton, Lula I, 946
Newton, Lula A. I, 946
Newton, Lula Angeline I, 931
Newton, Mary I, 895
Newton, Mary I, 896
Newton, Mary II, 180
Newton, Mary II, 235
Newton, Mary II, 245
Newton, Mary II, 269
Newton, Matilda II, 789
Newton, Richard III, 33
Newton, Robert II, 180
Newton, Samuel II, 180
Newton, Samuel II, 238
Newton, Samuel II, 245
Newton, Samuel VI, 8
Newton, Samuel VI, 17
Newton, Samuel, Jr. II, 180
Newton, Samuel, Jr. II, 245
Newton, Samuel, Sr. II, 180
Newton, Sarah I, 444
Newton, Sarah I, 452
Newton, Sarah Ann II, 238
Newton, Sarah Ann II, 245
Newton, Susanna II, 399
Newton, Theodore VI, 651
Newton, Wd. Hannah II, 180
Newton, William II, 399
Newton, William V, 423
Newville, Lorie IV, 1176
Newville, Myrtle IV, 1176
Newzum, Hannah IV, 104
Newzum, Richard IV, 104
Niblack, Sarah IV, 527
Niblack, Sarah IV, 542
Niblock, Mary IV, 424
Niblock, Mary IV, 436
Nicar, Eliza Henry VI, 968
Nicar, Hugh M. VI, 875
Nicar, Hugh M. VI, 968
Nicas, Hugh M. VI, 843
Nicas, Sarah L. VI, 843
Niccols, Catherin I, 245
Niccols, Catherin I, 247
Nice, Mary II, 607
Nice, William II, 399
Nicelson, Mary IV, 419
Nicelson, Mary IV, 424
Nicely, Minnie V, 636
Nichalls, Elias II, 1018
Nichalls, John II, 1018
Nichison, Mrs. ??? IV, 490
Nichol, E. Marion III, 94
Nichol, Samuel II, 399
Nichol, Thomason II, 399
Nicholas, Anna B. III, 241
Nicholas, Anna B. III, 305
Nicholas, Anthony II, 494
Nicholas, Anthony II, 496
Nicholas, Anthony II, 607
Nicholas, Anthony II, 651
Nicholas, Elmer IV, 1239
Nicholas, Emily IV, 740
Nicholas, Emily IV, 759
Nicholas, Evaline IV, 1239
Nicholas, Flora M. IV, 358
Nicholas, James I, 1035
Nicholas, Jno VI, 291
Nicholas, John II, 399
Nicholas, John II, 607
Nicholas, John IV, 1287
Nicholas, Jonathan II, 607
Nicholas, Lydia IV, 542
Nicholas, Mamie IV, 1259
Nicholas, Martha II, 496
Nicholas, Martha II, 607
Nicholas, Mary II, 494
Nicholas, Mary II, 496
Nicholas, Mary II, 518
Nicholas, Mary II, 607
Nicholas, Mary VI, 373
Nicholas, Mary Jane III, 241
Nicholas, Mary Jane III, 305
Nicholas, Rebecca II, 607
Nicholas, Rebecca II, 651
Nicholas, Robert B. III, 305
Nicholas, Robt. B. III, 241
Nicholas, Samuel II, 399
Nicholas, Samuel II, 518
Nicholas, Samuel II, 607
Nicholas, Samuel II, 651
Nicholas, Stephen III, 241
Nicholas, Stephen III, 305
Nicholas, Thomas VI, 886
Nicholas, Tryphena IV, 835
Nicholas, Wd. Mary II, 632
Nicholds, Sarah I, 445
Nicholds, Sarah I, 452
Nicholes, Elizabeth II, 229
Nicholes, Elizabeth II, 245
Nicholes, Mamie IV, 1259
Nicholes, Tacy N. IV, 1259
Nicholl, Avis M. III, 241
Nicholl, Avis M. III, 263
Nicholl, Marion III, 241
Nicholl, Marion III, 263
Nicholl, Thomas J. III, 263
Nicholl, Thos. J. III, 241
Nicholls, Anthony II, 399
Nicholls, Catharine VI, 978
Nicholls, Frederick I, 767
Nicholls, John VI, 978
Nicholls, Martha II, 607
Nicholls, Mary II, 494
Nicholls, Mary II, 607
Nicholls, Mrs. Mary VI, 11
Nicholls, Solomon IV, 155
Nicholls, Wm. II, 607
Nichols, ??? VI, 681
Nichols, Abdon VI, 634
Nichols, Absalom VI, 634
Nichols, Adline VI, 969
Nichols, Agnes V, 700
Nichols, Albert IV, 344
Nichols, Albert VI, 678
Nichols, Alpheus IV, 649
Nichols, Amon VI, 969
Nichols, Amor IV, 344
Nichols, Amor VI, 624
Nichols, Amor VI, 654
Nichols, Amor VI, 678
Nichols, Amor VI, 682
Nichols, Amor VI, 683
Nichols, Amos VI, 678
Nichols, Amos VI, 681
Nichols, Amos VI, 683
Nichols, Amy IV, 155
Nichols, Amy IV, 321
Nichols, Amy IV, 344
Nichols, Amy VI, 684
Nichols, Andrew J. VI, 904
Nichols, Ann I, 1032
Nichols, Ann I, 1035
Nichols, Ann IV, 344
Nichols, Ann V, 105
Nichols, Ann V, 195
Nichols, Ann VI, 426
Nichols, Ann VI, 505
Nichols, Ann VI, 539
Nichols, Ann VI, 634
Nichols, Ann VI, 678
Nichols, Ann VI, 680
Nichols, Ann VI, 696
Nichols, Ann VI, 969
Nichols, Ann Eliza III, 462
Nichols, Ann Elizabeth VI, 685
Nichols, Anna V, 195
Nichols, Anna Branch VI, 669
Nichols, Anna Branch VI, 678
Nichols, Anna Branch VI, 685
Nichols, Anna E. VI, 662
Nichols, Anna E. VI, 678
Nichols, Annie Elizabeth VI, 662
Nichols, Anson V, 195
Nichols, Anson L. V, 195
Nichols, Anson S. V, 195
Nichols, Anthony II, 399
Nichols, Arch VI, 969
Nichols, Archibald VI, 927
Nichols, Archibald VI, 944
Nichols, Archibald VI, 966
Nichols, Archibald VI, 969
Nichols, Archilis VI, 969
Nichols, Arthur VI, 683
Nichols, Athanissa IV, 1198
Nichols, Athenessa IV, 1218
Nichols, Athenissa IV, 1177
Nichols, Athenissa IV, 1218
Nichols, Avis M. III, 241
Nichols, Badel VI, 1000
Nichols, Bartlett VI, 969
Nichols, Basdale VI, 969
Nichols, Bazdell VI, 984
Nichols, Bazdell, Jr. VI, 969
Nichols, Benj. F. III, 90
Nichols, Benj. F. III, 241
Nichols, Benjamin IV, 649
Nichols, Benjamin IV, 745
Nichols, Benjamin VI, 683
Nichols, Calvin V, 700
Nichols, Caroline VI, 681
Nichols, Cassandra IV, 649
Nichols, Cassandra VI, 426
Nichols, Cassandra VI, 621
Nichols, Cassandra VI, 678
Nichols, Cassandra VI, 681
Nichols, Cassandra VI, 685
Nichols, Cassandria VI, 426
Nichols, Catharine VI, 647
Nichols, Catharine VI, 648
Nichols, Catharine VI, 684
Nichols, Catharine VI, 693
Nichols, Catharine VI, 698
Nichols, Catharine VI, 969
Nichols, Catharine VI, 988
Nichols, Catherin I, 247
Nichols, Catherine VI, 503
Nichols, Catherine VI, 538
Nichols, Catherine VI, 642
Nichols, Catherine VI, 678
Nichols, Catherine VI, 936
Nichols, Charity VI, 335
Nichols, Charity VI, 679
Nichols, Charles IV, 344
Nichols, Charles IV, 424
Nichols, Charles IV, 745
Nichols, Charles VI, 637
Nichols, Charles VI, 670
Nichols, Charles VI, 673
Nichols, Charles VI, 679
Nichols, Charles VI, 680
Nichols, Charles VI, 681
Nichols, Charles VI, 682
Nichols, Charles VI, 718
Nichols, Charles Leach VI, 679
Nichols, Charlotte VI, 938
Nichols, Clarissa VI, 969
Nichols, Clayton Amor IV, 344
Nichols, Clayton Amor VI, 682
Nichols, Cornelia VI, 681
Nichols, Cornelia G. VI, 662
Nichols, Cornelia G. VI, 663
Nichols, Cornelia G. VI, 683
Nichols, D. F. VI, 683
Nichols, Daniel IV, 155
Nichols, Daniel VI, 625
Nichols, Daniel VI, 627
Nichols, Daniel VI, 684
Nichols, Daniel VI, 869
Nichols, Daniel VI, 952
Nichols, Daniel VI, 969
Nichols, Daniel McPherson VI, 681
Nichols, Daniel W. VI, 879
Nichols, Danile VI, 679
Nichols, David IV, 344
Nichols, David Alpheus IV, 649
Nichols, Donald VI, 679
Nichols, Dr. Charles H. III, 241
Nichols, E. Norman III, 144
Nichols, Edgar IV, 344
Nichols, Edgar VI, 682
Nichols, Edith III, 241
Nichols, Edith V, 195
Nichols, Edith VI, 638
Nichols, Edith VI, 644
Nichols, Edith VI, 679
Nichols, Edith VI, 700
Nichols, Edith VI, 709
Nichols, Edith C. III, 144
Nichols, Edith H. VI, 679
Nichols, Edith H. VI, 684
Nichols, Edward II, 399
Nichols, Edward IV, 745
Nichols, Edward IV, 880
Nichols, Edward VI, 679
Nichols, Edward VI, 680
Nichols, Edward Enoch VI, 670
Nichols, Edward Enoch VI, 679
Nichols, Edwin Wilson VI, 681
Nichols, Eli IV, 155
Nichols, Eli IV, 256
Nichols, Eli IV, 341
Nichols, Eli IV, 344
Nichols, Eli IV, 424
Nichols, Eli IV, 1176
Nichols, Eli VI, 426
Nichols, Eli VI, 538
Nichols, Eli VI, 678
Nichols, Eli VI, 679
Nichols, Eli VI, 683
Nichols, Eli Janney VI, 649
Nichols, Eli Janney VI, 679
Nichols, Eli Janney VI, 681
Nichols, Elijah V, 195
Nichols, Elisha VI, 912
Nichols, Elisha VI, 969
Nichols, Eliza IV, 344
Nichols, Eliza IV, 424
Nichols, Eliza IV, 1176
Nichols, Eliza Ann VI, 681
Nichols, Eliza E. III, 241
Nichols, Elizabeth III, 431
Nichols, Elizabeth IV, 52
Nichols, Elizabeth IV, 82
Nichols, Elizabeth IV, 155
Nichols, Elizabeth IV, 344
Nichols, Elizabeth IV, 354
Nichols, Elizabeth IV, 531
Nichols, Elizabeth V, 195
Nichols, Elizabeth VI, 506
Nichols, Elizabeth VI, 620
Nichols, Elizabeth VI, 625
Nichols, Elizabeth VI, 630
Nichols, Elizabeth VI, 637
Nichols, Elizabeth VI, 642
Nichols, Elizabeth VI, 643
Nichols, Elizabeth VI, 645
Nichols, Elizabeth VI, 653
Nichols, Elizabeth VI, 654
Nichols, Elizabeth VI, 659
Nichols, Elizabeth VI, 665
Nichols, Elizabeth VI, 679
Nichols, Elizabeth VI, 680
Nichols, Elizabeth VI, 684
Nichols, Elizabeth VI, 685
Nichols, Elizabeth VI, 691
Nichols, Elizabeth VI, 704
Nichols, Elizabeth VI, 707
Nichols, Elizabeth VI, 708
Nichols, Elizabeth VI, 714
Nichols, Elizabeth VI, 718
Nichols, Elizabeth VI, 721
Nichols, Elizabeth VI, 722
Nichols, Elizabeth VI, 843
Nichols, Elizabeth J. V, 195
Nichols, Elizabeth P. III, 241
Nichols, Ella V, 1012
Nichols, Ellen F. VI, 679
Nichols, Ellen F. VI, 682
Nichols, Ellen F. VI, 700
Nichols, Ellis IV, 104
Nichols, Elmer IV, 1239
Nichols, Elsie VI, 679
Nichols, Elsie VI, 682
Nichols, Elsie VI, 723
Nichols, Elvira VI, 835
Nichols, Elwood K. IV, 649
Nichols, Elwood K. IV, 650
Nichols, Elwood K. IV, 835
Nichols, Elwood K. IV, 837
Nichols, Elwood Keagy IV, 649
Nichols, Emily VI, 426
Nichols, Emily VI, 656
Nichols, Emily VI, 662
Nichols, Emily VI, 679
Nichols, Emily VI, 680
Nichols, Emily VI, 681
Nichols, Emily VI, 685
Nichols, Emily VI, 707
Nichols, Emily Engle II, 903
Nichols, Emmor IV, 344
Nichols, Enoch V, 105
Nichols, Enoch V, 181
Nichols, Enoch V, 195
Nichols, Erickson Norman III, 241
Nichols, Ernest III, 241
Nichols, Ernest Lee III, 241
Nichols, Ernest Lee III, 268
Nichols, Ernestine Agnes III, 241
Nichols, Estelle VI, 679
Nichols, Estelle VI, 686
Nichols, Esther VI, 984
Nichols, Esther Jean III, 241
Nichols, Etta V, 1012
Nichols, Eugene IV, 344
Nichols, Eugene IV, 1176
Nichols, Faithful IV, 645
Nichols, Faithful IV, 649
Nichols, Flail VI, 969
Nichols, Flavius J. VI, 683
Nichols, Flora M. IV, 344
Nichols, Flora Mariah IV, 344
Nichols, Flora Mariah VI, 682
Nichols, Frail VI, 912
Nichols, Francis Annie VI, 679
Nichols, Francis E. VI, 683
Nichols, Geo. IV, 332
Nichols, Geo. W. VI, 700
Nichols, George VI, 538
Nichols, George VI, 936
Nichols, George H. IV, 256
Nichols, George S. VI, 681
Nichols, George W. VI, 679
Nichols, George W. VI, 682
Nichols, George W. VI, 700
Nichols, Georgie M. VI, 681
Nichols, Grace VI, 669
Nichols, Grace VI, 678
Nichols, Grace VI, 682
Nichols, Gracetta VI, 653
Nichols, Griffin VI, 938
Nichols, Griffin VI, 953
Nichols, Griffin VI, 969
Nichols, Hannah II, 806
Nichols, Hannah IV, 155
Nichols, Hannah IV, 321
Nichols, Hannah IV, 344
Nichols, Hannah IV, 424
Nichols, Hannah VI, 496
Nichols, Hannah VI, 539
Nichols, Hannah VI, 621
Nichols, Hannah VI, 626
Nichols, Hannah VI, 647
Nichols, Hannah VI, 656
Nichols, Hannah VI, 679
Nichols, Hannah VI, 684
Nichols, Hannah VI, 685
Nichols, Hannah VI, 688
Nichols, Hannah VI, 689
Nichols, Hannah VI, 690
Nichols, Hannah VI, 696
Nichols, Hannah VI, 713
Nichols, Hannah VI, 714
Nichols, Hannah Mary VI, 68
Nichols, Harold V, 1012
Nichols, Harriet VI, 681
Nichols, Hattie V, 1012
Nichols, Hattie E. VI, 680
Nichols, Helen IV, 155
Nichols, Helen VI, 684
Nichols, Hendrick VI, 969
Nichols, Henry VI, 679
Nichols, Henry VI, 700
Nichols, Henry J. VI, 683
Nichols, Herbert Lee III, 241
Nichols, Horace Mann VI, 684
Nichols, Hortentia IV, 344
Nichols, Hortentia IV, 1176
Nichols, I. M. V, 1012
Nichols, Isaac VI, 426
Nichols, Isaac VI, 493
Nichols, Isaac VI, 539
Nichols, Isaac VI, 609
Nichols, Isaac VI, 624
Nichols, Isaac VI, 625
Nichols, Isaac VI, 634
Nichols, Isaac VI, 644
Nichols, Isaac VI, 648
Nichols, Isaac VI, 656
Nichols, Isaac VI, 660
Nichols, Isaac VI, 663
Nichols, Isaac VI, 674
Nichols, Isaac VI, 679
Nichols, Isaac VI, 680
Nichols, Isaac VI, 681
Nichols, Isaac VI, 682
Nichols, Isaac VI, 685
Nichols, Isaac VI, 692
Nichols, Isaac VI, 722
Nichols, Isaac VI, 969
Nichols, Isaac VI, 980
Nichols, Isaac H. VI, 684
Nichols, Isaac H. VI, 685
Nichols, Isaac H. VI, 969
Nichols, Isaac, Jr. VI, 539
Nichols, Isaac, Jr. VI, 640
Nichols, Isaac, Jr. VI, 672
Nichols, Isaac, Jr. VI, 676
Nichols, Isaac, Jr. VI, 680
Nichols, Isaac, Jr. VI, 684
Nichols, Isaac, Jr. VI, 718
Nichols, Isaiah VI, 539
Nichols, Jacob IV, 1177
Nichols, Jacob VI, 426
Nichols, Jacob VI, 539
Nichols, Jacob VI, 578
Nichols, Jacob VI, 648
Nichols, Jacob VI, 680
Nichols, Jacob VI, 684
Nichols, James I, 1032
Nichols, James I, 1035
Nichols, James III, 241
Nichols, James IV, 155
Nichols, James IV, 256
Nichols, James V, 105
Nichols, James V, 195
Nichols, James VI, 654
Nichols, James VI, 683
Nichols, James VI, 684
Nichols, James Benton VI, 66
Nichols, James Benton VI, 68
Nichols, James H. IV, 745
Nichols, James W. VI, 680
Nichols, James William VI, 68
Nichols, Jane II, 607
Nichols, Jane II, 636
Nichols, Jane III, 172
Nichols, Jane III, 241
Nichols, Jane IV, 256
Nichols, Jane IV, 332

chols, Jane IV, 341
chols, Jane IV, 344
chols, Jane IV, 424
chols, Jane VI, 426
chols, Jane VI, 904
chols, Jane VI, 969
chols, Jas. VI, 684
chols, Jean IV, 155
chols, Jefferson VI, 904
chols, Jemima VI, 969
chols, Jenny VI, 869
chols, Jenny VI, 969
chols, Jeremiah I, 94
chols, Jeremiah I, 131
chols, Jeremiah I, 154
chols, Jesse IV, 344
chols, Jesse IV, 424
chols, Jesse IV, 613
chols, Jesse IV, 649
chols, Jesse IV, 745
chols, Jesse VI, 426
chols, Jesse VI, 624
chols, Jesse VI, 625
chols, Jesse VI, 637
chols, Jesse VI, 642
chols, Jesse VI, 679
chols, Jesse VI, 680
chols, Jesse VI, 682
ichols, Jesse VI, 685
ichols, Jesse VI, 904
ichols, Jesse VI, 930
ichols, Jesse VI, 969
ichols, Jesse M. VI, 681
ichols, John II, 607
ichols, John II, 636
ichols, John IV, 155
ichols, John IV, 256
ichols, John IV, 542
ichols, John IV, 1287
ichols, John V, 1012
ichols, John VI, 505
ichols, John VI, 506
ichols, John VI, 539
ichols, John VI, 563
ichols, John VI, 624
ichols, John VI, 625
ichols, John VI, 626
ichols, John VI, 628
ichols, John VI, 649
ichols, John VI, 655
ichols, John VI, 679
ichols, John VI, 680
ichols, John VI, 681
ichols, John VI, 682
ichols, John VI, 683
ichols, John VI, 684
ichols, John VI, 843
ichols, John VI, 869
ichols, John VI, 936
ichols, John VI, 952
Nichols, John VI, 969
Nichols, John VI, 1000
Nichols, John VI, 1013
Nichols, John B. VI, 683
Nichols, John F. VI, 944
Nichols, John F. VI, 969
Nichols, John J. VI, 969
Nichols, John M. III, 149
Nichols, John M. III, 241
Nichols, John M. VI, 969
Nichols, John P. VI, 681
Nichols, John P. VI, 962
Nichols, John Wilbur IV, 344
Nichols, John Wilbur VI, 682
Nichols, John, Jr. VI, 1001
Nichols, John, Sr. VI, 952
Nichols, Jonah T. VI, 681
Nichols, Jonathan III, 431
Nichols, Joseph V, 195
Nichols, Joseph VI, 626
Nichols, Joseph VI, 659
Nichols, Joseph VI, 666
Nichols, Joseph VI, 674
Nichols, Joseph VI, 681
Nichols, Joseph VI, 682
Nichols, Joseph VI, 683
Nichols, Joseph VI, 685
Nichols, Joseph VI, 686
Nichols, Joseph VI, 708
Nichols, Joseph VI, 837
Nichols, Joseph VI, 856
Nichols, Joseph H. VI, 685
Nichols, Joshua II, 399
Nichols, Joshua VI, 426
Nichols, Joshua VI, 458
Nichols, Joshua VI, 539
Nichols, Joshua VI, 626
Nichols, Joshua VI, 680
Nichols, Joshua VI, 681
Nichols, Joshua VI, 682
Nichols, Joshua VI, 720
Nichols, Joshua VI, 723
Nichols, Joshua Pancoast VI, 681
Nichols, Judith VI, 969
Nichols, Julia IV, 649
Nichols, Julia IV, 650
Nichols, Julia B. VI, 681
Nichols, Julia Eliza VI, 685
Nichols, Julia R. IV, 835
Nichols, Julia R. IV, 837
Nichols, Julia Rachel IV, 835
Nichols, Julian VI, 969
Nichols, Kenneth Evans VI, 679
Nichols, Keziah I, 94
Nichols, Keziah I, 131
Nichols, Keziah I, 154
Nichols, Keziah I, 157
Nichols, Kitturah VI, 879
Nichols, Laura VI, 684
Nichols, Laura V. VI, 679
Nichols, Laura V. VI, 681
Nichols, Lauretta H III, 90
Nichols, Lauretta H. III, 241
Nichols, Lauretta Hessin III, 90
Nichols, Lavanny VI, 969
Nichols, Leatitia VI, 667
Nichols, Leatitia VI, 681
Nichols, Lena VI, 658
Nichols, Lena VI, 681
Nichols, Letitia VI, 522
Nichols, Letitia VI, 681
Nichols, Letitia VI, 953
Nichols, Levica VI, 843
Nichols, Lewis VI, 835
Nichols, Lewis VI, 840
Nichols, Lindley Kendall III, 241
Nichols, Linhoss IV, 649
Nichols, Lizzie V, 195
Nichols, Lloyd IV, 344
Nichols, Lloyd IV, 424
Nichols, Lloyd IV, 1176
Nichols, Locky VI, 962
Nichols, Lot VI, 426
Nichols, Louis VI, 843
Nichols, Louisa VI, 976
Nichols, Louisa J. VI, 612
Nichols, Louisa J. VI, 637
Nichols, Louisa J. VI, 680
Nichols, Louisa Jane VI, 670
Nichols, Louisa Jane VI, 673
Nichols, Louisa Jane VI, 679
Nichols, Louisa Jane VI, 681
Nichols, Louisa Jane VI, 682
Nichols, Louisa Jane VI, 718
Nichols, Lucretia VI, 681
Nichols, Lucy VI, 937
Nichols, Lucy VI, 966
Nichols, Lucy A. II, 802
Nichols, Lucy A. VI, 666
Nichols, Lucy A. VI, 667
Nichols, Lucy A. VI, 681
Nichols, Lula VI, 630
Nichols, Lydia IV, 344
Nichols, Lydia IV, 424
Nichols, Lydia IV, 542
Nichols, Lydia VI, 518
Nichols, Lydia VI, 539
Nichols, Lydia VI, 648
Nichols, Lydia VI, 656
Nichols, Lydia VI, 661
Nichols, Lydia VI, 679
Nichols, Lydia VI, 680
Nichols, Lydia VI, 681
Nichols, Lydia VI, 685
Nichols, Lydia VI, 689
Nichols, Lydia VI, 718
Nichols, Lydia VI, 722
Nichols, Lydia Ann IV, 344
Nichols, Lydia Ann IV, 353
Nichols, Lydia Ann VI, 662
Nichols, Lydia Ann VI, 678
Nichols, Lydia Ann VI, 685
Nichols, Lydia C. VI, 681
Nichols, Lydia E. VI, 649
Nichols, Lydia E. VI, 679
Nichols, Lydia E. VI, 681
Nichols, Lydia J. IV, 424
Nichols, Lydia J. IV, 745
Nichols, Lydia Jane VI, 685
Nichols, Lydia Janney VI, 683
Nichols, Mabel Alice VI, 673
Nichols, Mabel Alice VI, 679
Nichols, Mabel Alice VI, 681
Nichols, Mahlon IV, 649
Nichols, Mahlon IV, 650
Nichols, Mahlon VI, 681
Nichols, Mahlon VI, 685
Nichols, Mahlon VI, 686
Nichols, Mahlon Janney VI, 681
Nichols, Mamie IV, 1259
Nichols, Margaret II, 399
Nichols, Margaret VI, 539
Nichols, Margaret VI, 563
Nichols, Margaret VI, 682
Nichols, Margery IV, 645
Nichols, Margery IV, 649
Nichols, Margery VI, 423
Nichols, Margery VI, 426
Nichols, Margery VI, 648
Nichols, Margery VI, 682
Nichols, Margery VI, 685
Nichols, Margrett II, 399
Nichols, Maria IV, 344
Nichols, Maria VI, 624
Nichols, Maria VI, 654
Nichols, Maria VI, 678
Nichols, Maria VI, 682
Nichols, Maria VI, 683
Nichols, Maria P. IV, 344
Nichols, Maria Priscilla VI, 625
Nichols, Maria Priscilla VI, 628
Nichols, Maria Priscilla VI, 681
Nichols, Maria Priscilla VI, 682
Nichols, Mariah VI, 679
Nichols, Mariah VI, 700
Nichols, Marion III, 241
Nichols, Mark V, 195
Nichols, Martha IV, 344
Nichols, Martha IV, 1331
Nichols, Martha VI, 681
Nichols, Martha VI, 952
Nichols, Martha Ann IV, 649
Nichols, Martha Ann VI, 624
Nichols, Martha Ann VI, 625
Nichols, Martha Ann VI, 681
Nichols, Martha Ann VI, 684
Nichols, Martha Ann VI, 685
Nichols, Martha B. IV, 344
Nichols, Martha B. VI, 678
Nichols, Martha Elizabeth VI, 685
Nichols, Martha Jane VI, 683
Nichols, Mary I, 154
Nichols, Mary II, 399
Nichols, Mary II, 446
Nichols, Mary II, 489
Nichols, Mary II, 564
Nichols, Mary II, 607
Nichols, Mary III, 241
Nichols, Mary IV, 155
Nichols, Mary IV, 256
Nichols, Mary IV, 332
Nichols, Mary IV, 341
Nichols, Mary IV, 344
Nichols, Mary IV, 424
Nichols, Mary IV, 605
Nichols, Mary IV, 649
Nichols, Mary VI, 426
Nichols, Mary VI, 477
Nichols, Mary VI, 518
Nichols, Mary VI, 519
Nichols, Mary VI, 522
Nichols, Mary VI, 539
Nichols, Mary VI, 544
Nichols, Mary VI, 587
Nichols, Mary VI, 621
Nichols, Mary VI, 624
Nichols, Mary VI, 625
Nichols, Mary VI, 626
Nichols, Mary VI, 627
Nichols, Mary VI, 634
Nichols, Mary VI, 636
Nichols, Mary VI, 640
Nichols, Mary VI, 642
Nichols, Mary VI, 643
Nichols, Mary VI, 644
Nichols, Mary VI, 646
Nichols, Mary VI, 648
Nichols, Mary VI, 653
Nichols, Mary VI, 654
Nichols, Mary VI, 657
Nichols, Mary VI, 661
Nichols, Mary VI, 664
Nichols, Mary VI, 665
Nichols, Mary VI, 667
Nichols, Mary VI, 669
Nichols, Mary VI, 672
Nichols, Mary VI, 674
Nichols, Mary VI, 676
Nichols, Mary VI, 678
Nichols, Mary VI, 679
Nichols, Mary VI, 680
Nichols, Mary VI, 681
Nichols, Mary VI, 682
Nichols, Mary VI, 684
Nichols, Mary VI, 685
Nichols, Mary VI, 688
Nichols, Mary VI, 689
Nichols, Mary VI, 690
Nichols, Mary VI, 692
Nichols, Mary VI, 708
Nichols, Mary VI, 712
Nichols, Mary VI, 713
Nichols, Mary VI, 942
Nichols, Mary VI, 969
Nichols, Mary A. III, 241
Nichols, Mary A. K. VI, 685
Nichols, Mary Alice III, 90
Nichols, Mary Allen VI, 426
Nichols, Mary Ann VI, 624
Nichols, Mary Ann VI, 625
Nichols, Mary Ann VI, 626
Nichols, Mary Ann VI, 659
Nichols, Mary Ann VI, 666
Nichols, Mary Ann VI, 674
Nichols, Mary Ann VI, 681
Nichols, Mary Ann VI, 682
Nichols, Mary Ann VI, 683
Nichols, Mary Ann VI, 685
Nichols, Mary Ann VI, 708
Nichols, Mary Ann VI, 980
Nichols, Mary C. IV, 745
Nichols, Mary C. VI, 631
Nichols, Mary C. VI, 642
Nichols, Mary C. VI, 643
Nichols, Mary C. VI, 656
Nichols, Mary C. VI, 680
Nichols, Mary C. VI, 692
Nichols, Mary C. G. VI, 684
Nichols, Mary Cassandra VI, 680
Nichols, Mary Cornelia VI, 681
Nichols, Mary Cornelia VI, 682
Nichols, Mary Cornelia VI, 708
Nichols, Mary E. IV, 613
Nichols, Mary E. IV, 649
Nichols, Mary E. VI, 682
Nichols, Mary E. VI, 692
Nichols, Mary E. VI, 699
Nichols, Mary Elizabeth VI, 624
Nichols, Mary Elizabeth VI, 625
Nichols, Mary Elizabeth VI, 627
Nichols, Mary Elizabeth VI, 679
Nichols, Mary Elizabeth VI, 680
Nichols, Mary Emma IV, 344
Nichols, Mary Emma VI, 682
Nichols, Mary Esther VI, 679
Nichols, Mary G. VI, 637
Nichols, Mary Jane VI, 644
Nichols, Mary Jane VI, 685
Nichols, Mary Janney VI, 680
Nichols, Mary Janney VI, 681
Nichols, Mary Lydia Ann VI, 678
Nichols, Mary Virginia IV, 649
Nichols, Mary, Jr. VI, 667
Nichols, Matthewson V, 1012
Nichols, Mattie E. VI, 684
Nichols, Melinda VI, 1000
Nichols, Mercy Ann IV, 344
Nichols, Mercy Ann IV, 424
Nichols, Milton Alpheus VI, 679
Nichols, Milton Stanley VI, 679
Nichols, Milton Stanley VI, 682
Nichols, Milton Stanley VI, 723
Nichols, Minnie IV, 649
Nichols, Minnie L. IV, 649
Nichols, Miram G. VI, 681
Nichols, Miriam VI, 680
Nichols, Miriam VI, 692
Nichols, Miriam G. VI, 385
Nichols, Miriam G. VI, 426
Nichols, Miriam G. VI, 458
Nichols, Miriam G. VI, 681
Nichols, Miriam G. VI, 682
Nichols, Miriam G. VI, 723
Nichols, Morgan VI, 679
Nichols, Morgan J. VI, 679
Nichols, Mr. ??? IV, 1331
Nichols, Mrs. ??? IV, 1331
Nichols, Mrs. Ella IV, 1331
Nichols, Myrtle L. VI, 681
Nichols, N. B. IV, 358
Nichols, Nancey VI, 969
Nichols, Nancy VI, 634
Nichols, Nancy VI, 662
Nichols, Nancy VI, 678
Nichols, Nancy VI, 680
Nichols, Nancy VI, 685
Nichols, Nancy VI, 837
Nichols, Nancy VI, 912
Nichols, Nancy VI, 969
Nichols, Naomi VI, 426
Nichols, Naomi VI, 458
Nichols, Naomi VI, 626
Nichols, Naomi VI, 680
Nichols, Naomi VI, 681
Nichols, Naomi VI, 682
Nichols, Naomi VI, 720
Nichols, Naomi VI, 723
Nichols, Nathan VI, 653
Nichols, Nathan VI, 680
Nichols, Nathan VI, 682
Nichols, Nathan B. IV, 344
Nichols, Nathan B. IV, 358
Nichols, Nathan B. VI, 632
Nichols, Nathan B. VI, 652
Nichols, Nathan B. VI, 654
Nichols, Nathan B. VI, 678
Nichols, Nathan B. VI, 682
Nichols, Nathan B. VI, 685
Nichols, Nathan B. VI, 699
Nichols, Nathan Clifford IV, 344
Nichols, Nathan Clifford VI, 682
Nichols, Nathan Clifford VI, 699
Nichols, Nehemiah VI, 969
Nichols, Nellie VI, 718
Nichols, Nellie Grace VI, 679
Nichols, Nellie Grace VI, 682
Nichols, Nellie Grace VI, 683
Nichols, Netta Hannah VI, 683
Nichols, Netta Hannah VI, 684
Nichols, Nettie IV, 256
Nichols, Noami VI, 682
Nichols, Olivia VI, 634
Nichols, Olivia VI, 663
Nichols, Olivia VI, 680
Nichols, Olivia VI, 684
Nichols, Olivia M. VI, 660
Nichols, Pamelia VI, 952
Nichols, Patsy VI, 912
Nichols, Patty VI, 856
Nichols, Paul Adam IV, 649
Nichols, Paxton IV, 424
Nichols, Peggy VI, 937
Nichols, Peggy VI, 969
Nichols, Phebe VI, 426
Nichols, Phebe VI, 625
Nichols, Phebe VI, 626
Nichols, Phebe VI, 627
Nichols, Phebe VI, 682
Nichols, Phebe VI, 683
Nichols, Phebe VI, 969
Nichols, Phebe Alice VI, 680
Nichols, Phebe Ann VI, 681
Nichols, Phebe G. VI, 676
Nichols, Phebe G. VI, 680
Nichols, Philpot VI, 969
Nichols, Phineas VI, 624
Nichols, Phineas J. VI, 625
Nichols, Phineas Janney VI, 681
Nichols, Polly VI, 969
Nichols, Polly VI, 1000
Nichols, Polly VI, 1001
Nichols, Rachel IV, 256
Nichols, Rachel IV, 344
Nichols, Rachel IV, 424
Nichols, Rachel IV, 1176
Nichols, Rachel IV, 1218
Nichols, Ralph Eugene VI, 679
Nichols, Rebecca IV, 351
Nichols, Rebecca IV, 424
Nichols, Rebecca VI, 426
Nichols, Rebecca VI, 503
Nichols, Rebecca VI, 660
Nichols, Rebecca VI, 679
Nichols, Rebecca VI, 680
Nichols, Rebecca VI, 682
Nichols, Rebecca VI, 684
Nichols, Rebecca VI, 685
Nichols, Rebecca VI, 693
Nichols, Rebecca H. VI, 681
Nichols, Rebecca J. VI, 626
Nichols, Rebecca J. VI, 681
Nichols, Rebecca J. VI, 683
Nichols, Rebecca K. VI, 624
Nichols, Rebecca K. VI, 625
Nichols, Rebecca K. VI, 679
Nichols, Rebecca M. VI, 683
Nichols, Rebecca M. VI, 709
Nichols, Rebeccah VI, 683
Nichols, Rebecka II, 399
Nichols, Rebeckah VI, 539
Nichols, Rebeckah VI, 648
Nichols, Rebekah VI, 493
Nichols, Rebekah VI, 539
Nichols, Rebekah VI, 625
Nichols, Rebekah VI, 679
Nichols, Rebekah VI, 680
Nichols, Rebekah VI, 684
Nichols, Rhoda V, 181
Nichols, Rhoda V, 195
Nichols, Rhoda VI, 969
Nichols, Richard Elwood IV, 649
Nichols, Robert II, 446
Nichols, Robert H. VI, 681
Nichols, Robt II, 446
Nichols, Ruth III, 241
Nichols, Ruth VI, 539
Nichols, Ruth VI, 541
Nichols, Ruth VI, 634
Nichols, Ruth VI, 686
Nichols, Ruth VI, 722
Nichols, Ruth Ann VI, 942
Nichols, Ruth Esther VI, 637
Nichols, Ruth Esther VI, 679
Nichols, Ruth Esther VI, 683

Nichols, Ruth Esther VI, 693
Nichols, Ruth Hannah IV, 649
Nichols, Ruth Hannah IV, 650
Nichols, Ruth Hannah VI, 681
Nichols, Ruth Hannah VI, 683
Nichols, Ruth Hannah VI, 685
Nichols, Ruth Hannah VI, 686
Nichols, S. Thornton VI, 662
Nichols, S. Thornton VI, 713
Nichols, Sallie VI, 681
Nichols, Sallie VI, 683
Nichols, Sallie VI, 684
Nichols, Sally VI, 944
Nichols, Sally VI, 952
Nichols, Sally VI, 969
Nichols, Samuel II, 399
Nichols, Samuel II, 489
Nichols, Samuel II, 607
Nichols, Samuel IV, 82
Nichols, Samuel IV, 649
Nichols, Samuel IV, 820
Nichols, Samuel IV, 835
Nichols, Samuel VI, 426
Nichols, Samuel VI, 624
Nichols, Samuel VI, 626
Nichols, Samuel VI, 634
Nichols, Samuel VI, 646
Nichols, Samuel VI, 678
Nichols, Samuel VI, 680
Nichols, Samuel VI, 681
Nichols, Samuel VI, 683
Nichols, Samuel VI, 685
Nichols, Samuel VI, 942
Nichols, Samuel VI, 969
Nichols, Samuel E. VI, 685
Nichols, Samuel Thornton VI, 660
Nichols, Samuel Thornton VI, 663
Nichols, Samuel Thornton VI, 683
Nichols, Samuel, Jr. VI, 518
Nichols, Samuel, Jr. VI, 667
Nichols, Sarah II, 607
Nichols, Sarah II, 651
Nichols, Sarah IV, 344
Nichols, Sarah IV, 424
Nichols, Sarah VI, 426
Nichols, Sarah VI, 522
Nichols, Sarah VI, 539
Nichols, Sarah VI, 563
Nichols, Sarah VI, 621
Nichols, Sarah VI, 624
Nichols, Sarah VI, 625
Nichols, Sarah VI, 626
Nichols, Sarah VI, 628
Nichols, Sarah VI, 640
Nichols, Sarah VI, 649
Nichols, Sarah VI, 655
Nichols, Sarah VI, 656
Nichols, Sarah VI, 657
Nichols, Sarah VI, 667
Nichols, Sarah VI, 670
Nichols, Sarah VI, 672
Nichols, Sarah VI, 679
Nichols, Sarah VI, 680
Nichols, Sarah VI, 682
Nichols, Sarah VI, 683
Nichols, Sarah VI, 684
Nichols, Sarah VI, 685
Nichols, Sarah VI, 690
Nichols, Sarah VI, 904
Nichols, Sarah VI, 952
Nichols, Sarah VI, 962
Nichols, Sarah VI, 969
Nichols, Sarah VI, 996
Nichols, Sarah Alice VI, 684
Nichols, Sarah Ann III, 149
Nichols, Sarah Ann III, 241
Nichols, Sarah Ann VI, 936
Nichols, Sarah E. IV, 358
Nichols, Sarah E. VI, 632
Nichols, Sarah E. VI, 652
Nichols, Sarah E. VI, 683
Nichols, Sarah E. VI, 685
Nichols, Sarah E. VI, 699
Nichols, Sarah Eleanor VI, 654
Nichols, Sarah Eleanor VI, 682
Nichols, Sarah Elenor IV, 344
Nichols, Sarah Paxson II, 1057
Nichols, Solomon IV, 155
Nichols, Solomon IV, 321
Nichols, Solomon VI, 496
Nichols, Solomon VI, 539
Nichols, Solomon VI, 684
Nichols, Sophia VI, 660
Nichols, Sophia Susanna VI, 634
Nichols, Sophia Susanna VI, 684
Nichols, Spencer I. IV, 745
Nichols, Stacy IV, 645
Nichols, Stacy IV, 649
Nichols, Stacy VI, 426
Nichols, Stacy VI, 624
Nichols, Stacy VI, 625
Nichols, Stacy VI, 684
Nichols, Stacy VI, 685
Nichols, Stephen II, 48
Nichols, Susan IV, 344
Nichols, Susan IV, 1176
Nichols, Susan VI, 960
Nichols, Susanna IV, 27
Nichols, Susanna IV, 52
Nichols, Susanna IV, 82
Nichols, Susanna IV, 104
Nichols, Susanna VI, 684
Nichols, Susanna VI, 969
Nichols, Susannah IV, 1287
Nichols, Susannah VI, 539
Nichols, Susannah VI, 660
Nichols, Swithen VI, 426
Nichols, Swithen VI, 679
Nichols, Swithin VI, 625
Nichols, Swithin VI, 648
Nichols, Swithin VI, 660
Nichols, Swithin VI, 679
Nichols, Swithin VI, 680
Nichols, Swithin VI, 682
Nichols, Swithin VI, 684
Nichols, Swithin VI, 685
Nichols, T. J. VI, 683
Nichols, T. J. VI, 684
Nichols, Tacey VI, 335
Nichols, Tacey VI, 684
Nichols, Tacy IV, 1176
Nichols, Tacy VI, 335
Nichols, Tacy VI, 539
Nichols, Tacy VI, 578
Nichols, Tacy VI, 648
Nichols, Tacy VI, 685
Nichols, Tamson Ann VI, 680
Nichols, Thamasin C. VI, 683
Nichols, Thomas II, 607
Nichols, Thomas III, 172
Nichols, Thomas III, 431
Nichols, Thomas IV, 344
Nichols, Thomas IV, 649
Nichols, Thomas VI, 13
Nichols, Thomas VI, 426
Nichols, Thomas VI, 513
Nichols, Thomas VI, 518
Nichols, Thomas VI, 522
Nichols, Thomas VI, 538
Nichols, Thomas VI, 539
Nichols, Thomas VI, 634
Nichols, Thomas VI, 661
Nichols, Thomas VI, 662
Nichols, Thomas VI, 678
Nichols, Thomas VI, 679
Nichols, Thomas VI, 680
Nichols, Thomas VI, 681
Nichols, Thomas VI, 684
Nichols, Thomas VI, 685
Nichols, Thomas VI, 707
Nichols, Thomas VI, 958
Nichols, Thomas VI, 969
Nichols, Thomas Fuller III, 241
Nichols, Thomas J. VI, 683
Nichols, Thomas T. IV, 344
Nichols, Thomas W. VI, 969
Nichols, Thomason II, 399
Nichols, Thos VI, 656
Nichols, Thos Janney VI, 683
Nichols, Thos. IV, 155
Nichols, Thos. VI, 684
Nichols, Thos. J. III, 241
Nichols, Tirza VI, 1020
Nichols, Triphena IV, 649
Nichols, Triphena IV, 745
Nichols, Triphena IV, 820
Nichols, Triphena IV, 835
Nichols, Tryphena IV, 649
Nichols, Tryphena IV, 820
Nichols, Tryphena IV, 835
Nichols, Tryphena VI, 646
Nichols, Tryphena VI, 683
Nichols, Tryphena VI, 685
Nichols, Tryphena Hannah IV, 835
Nichols, Virginia IV, 745
Nichols, Virginia VI, 680
Nichols, Virginia J. VI, 621
Nichols, Virginia J. VI, 651
Nichols, Virginia J. VI, 658
Nichols, Virginia J. VI, 659
Nichols, Virginia J. VI, 681
Nichols, Virginia J. VI, 685
Nichols, Warren VI, 684
Nichols, Wd. Elizabeth VI, 513
Nichols, Widow Elizabeth VI, 538
Nichols, Widow Emily VI, 685
Nichols, Widow Grace VI, 685
Nichols, Widow Margaret VI, 655
Nichols, Willard Alvin IV, 256
Nichols, William II, 399
Nichols, William II, 446
Nichols, William III, 431
Nichols, William IV, 256
Nichols, William IV, 344
Nichols, William IV, 649
Nichols, William V, 195
Nichols, William VI, 426
Nichols, William VI, 539
Nichols, William VI, 621
Nichols, William VI, 624
Nichols, William VI, 657
Nichols, William VI, 667
Nichols, William VI, 680
Nichols, William VI, 681
Nichols, William VI, 683
Nichols, William VI, 684
Nichols, William VI, 685
Nichols, William VI, 690
Nichols, William VI, 969
Nichols, William VI, 984
Nichols, William VI, 1000
Nichols, William Albert VI, 678
Nichols, William Edgar VI, 632
Nichols, William Edgar VI, 685
Nichols, William F. VI, 843
Nichols, William H. VI, 681
Nichols, William J. IV, 745
Nichols, William S. VI, 685
Nichols, William W. VI, 681
Nichols, William, Jr. VI, 621
Nichols, William, Jr. VI, 685
Nichols, Willis IV, 880
Nichols, Winifred III, 241
Nichols, Winifred III, 268
Nichols, Wm. II, 607
Nichols, Wm. II, 903
Nichols, Wm. IV, 605
Nichols, Wm. IV, 649
Nichols, Wm. V, 195
Nichols, Wm. VI, 522
Nichols, Wm. VI, 563
Nichols, Wm. VI, 640
Nichols, Wm. VI, 644
Nichols, Wm. VI, 646
Nichols, Wm. VI, 667
Nichols, Wm. VI, 678
Nichols, Wm. VI, 680
Nichols, Wm. VI, 682
Nichols, Wm. VI, 685
Nichols, Wm. VI, 988
Nichols, Wm. VI, 995
Nichols, Wm. Alpheus VI, 680
Nichols, Wm. D. VI, 969
Nichols, Wm. E. VI, 652
Nichols, Wm. E. VI, 653
Nichols, Wm. Edgar VI, 669
Nichols, Wm. Harvey VI, 679
Nichols, Wm. I. III, 241
Nichols, Wm. J. VI, 685
Nichols, Wm. W. VI, 681
Nichols, Wm., Jr. VI, 685
Nichols, Zilpha IV, 649
Nicholson, ??? I, 22
Nicholson, ??? I, 23
Nicholson, ??? II, 811
Nicholson, ??? III, 241
Nicholson, Abel II, 35
Nicholson, Abel II, 36
Nicholson, Abel II, 70
Nicholson, Abel II, 89
Nicholson, Abel II, 598
Nicholson, Abel II, 607
Nicholson, Abel II, 810
Nicholson, Abel, Sr. II, 64
Nicholson, Abel, Sr. II, 89
Nicholson, Abell II, 35
Nicholson, Abell II, 89
Nicholson, Abell II, 107
Nicholson, Abigail I Sup 1, 3
Nicholson, Abigail I Sup 1, 5
Nicholson, Abigail II, 713
Nicholson, Abigail III, 30
Nicholson, Abigail III, 241
Nicholson, Abigail V, 589
Nicholson, Abigail P. III, 241
Nicholson, Agnes II, 719
Nicholson, Agnes II, 757
Nicholson, Agnes II, 769
Nicholson, Aletta IV, 490
Nicholson, Aletta IV, 501
Nicholson, Alice I, 25
Nicholson, Alice I, 613
Nicholson, Alice I, 930
Nicholson, Alice IV, 490
Nicholson, Alice IV, 589
Nicholson, Alice L. I, 24
Nicholson, Alice L. N. I, 936
Nicholson, Alice Lanton I, 14
Nicholson, Alice Lauton I, 64
Nicholson, Alice Lauton I, 84
Nicholson, Alice W. II, 135
Nicholson, Alice W. II, 154
Nicholson, Allice IV, 589
Nicholson, Ann I, 1
Nicholson, Ann I, 35
Nicholson, Ann I, 61
Nicholson, Ann I, 64
Nicholson, Ann I, 76
Nicholson, Ann II, 18
Nicholson, Ann II, 35
Nicholson, Ann II, 36
Nicholson, Ann II, 58
Nicholson, Ann II, 89
Nicholson, Ann II, 99
Nicholson, Ann II, 121
Nicholson, Ann II, 135
Nicholson, Ann II, 154
Nicholson, Ann II, 160
Nicholson, Ann II, 399
Nicholson, Ann II, 607
Nicholson, Ann II, 657
Nicholson, Ann II, 811
Nicholson, Ann II, 903
Nicholson, Ann Jane IV, 542
Nicholson, Ann N. II, 139
Nicholson, Anna I, 14
Nicholson, Anna I, 23
Nicholson, Anna I, 64
Nicholson, Anna I, 70
Nicholson, Anna I, 612
Nicholson, Anna I, 923
Nicholson, Anna I, 932
Nicholson, Anna III, 241
Nicholson, Anna Almy I, 14
Nicholson, Anna H. II, 704
Nicholson, Anna N. I, 16
Nicholson, Anne I, 64
Nicholson, Bathsheba V, 175
Nicholson, Bathsheba V, 195
Nicholson, Bathsheba V, 573
Nicholson, Bathsheba V, 589
Nicholson, Bathshebe V, 572
Nicholson, Benjamin I, 14
Nicholson, Benjamin I, 109
Nicholson, Benjamin II, 36
Nicholson, Benjamin II, 89
Nicholson, Benjamin II, 135
Nicholson, Benjamin C. IV, 256
Nicholson, Benjamin C. IV, 490
Nicholson, Benjamin C. IV, 542
Nicholson, Beulah II, 36
Nicholson, Beulah II, 89
Nicholson, Beulah II, 239
Nicholson, Beulah II, 399
Nicholson, Beulah II, 607
Nicholson, Caleb Harvey, Jr. V, 589
Nicholson, Carolina I, 108
Nicholson, Caroline I, 109
Nicholson, Caroline I, 154
Nicholson, Caroline I, 176
Nicholson, Caroline I, 685
Nicholson, Caroline I, 692
Nicholson, Caroline M. V, 105
Nicholson, Catharine I, 909
Nicholson, Catharine C. II, 714
Nicholson, Charles II, 35
Nicholson, Charles II, 135
Nicholson, Charles IV, 256
Nicholson, Charles IV, 490
Nicholson, Charles IV, 542
Nicholson, Charles Herbert I, 623
Nicholson, Charles Herbert I, 638
Nicholson, Charles L. IV, 490
Nicholson, Charles White I, 14
Nicholson, Charlotte III, 241
Nicholson, Chas. IV, 469
Nicholson, Christo. I, 1
Nicholson, Christopher I, 1
Nicholson, Christopher I, 14
Nicholson, Christopher I, 35
Nicholson, Christopher I, 64
Nicholson, Christopher I, 108
Nicholson, Christopher I, 109
Nicholson, Christopher I, 142
Nicholson, Christopher I, 148
Nicholson, Christopher I, 154
Nicholson, Christopher I, 155
Nicholson, Christopher I, 161
Nicholson, Christopher I Sup 1, 5
Nicholson, Christopher I Sup 1, 8
Nicholson, Cleo I Sup 1, 7
Nicholson, Content II, 607
Nicholson, Daniel II, 36
Nicholson, Daniel IV, 424
Nicholson, Daniel V, 105
Nicholson, Daniel V, 175
Nicholson, Daniel V, 195
Nicholson, Daniel S. IV, 424
Nicholson, Darkin II, 35
Nicholson, Darkin II, 55
Nicholson, Darkin II, 58
Nicholson, Darkin II, 89
Nicholson, David White I, 623
Nicholson, Eden Finley V, 105
Nicholson, Edith J. II, 903
Nicholson, Edith J. II, 941
Nicholson, Edwin II, 135
Nicholson, Edwin II, 154
Nicholson, Elezabeath I, 152
Nicholson, Elezabeath I, 154
Nicholson, Elisabeth I, 14
Nicholson, Elisabeth I, 42
Nicholson, Elisabeth I, 62
Nicholson, Elisabeth I, 64
Nicholson, Elisabeth I, 108
Nicholson, Elisabeth I, 137
Nicholson, Elisabeth I, 154
Nicholson, Elisabeth I, 155
Nicholson, Elisabeth I, 162
Nicholson, Elisabeth I, 166
Nicholson, Elisabeth I, 177
Nicholson, Elisabeth II, 36
Nicholson, Elisabeth A. I, 84
Nicholson, Elisabeth W. I, 64
Nicholson, Elisabeth W. I, 65
Nicholson, Elisha II, 36
Nicholson, Elisha II, 89
Nicholson, Elisha II, 607
Nicholson, Elisha V, 924
Nicholson, Eliza IV, 490
Nicholson, Eliza IV, 496
Nicholson, Eliza IV, 542
Nicholson, Eliza Jane IV, 536
Nicholson, Eliza Jane Crew IV, 256
Nicholson, Eliza Jane Crew IV, 542
Nicholson, Elizabeth I, 108
Nicholson, Elizabeth I, 109
Nicholson, Elizabeth I, 135
Nicholson, Elizabeth I, 154
Nicholson, Elizabeth I, 685
Nicholson, Elizabeth I, 687
Nicholson, Elizabeth I Sup 1, 3
Nicholson, Elizabeth I Sup 1, 5
Nicholson, Elizabeth I Sup 1, 7
Nicholson, Elizabeth II, 35
Nicholson, Elizabeth II, 36
Nicholson, Elizabeth II, 55
Nicholson, Elizabeth II, 58
Nicholson, Elizabeth II, 70
Nicholson, Elizabeth II, 74
Nicholson, Elizabeth II, 89
Nicholson, Elizabeth II, 153
Nicholson, Elizabeth II, 154
Nicholson, Elizabeth II, 239
Nicholson, Elizabeth II, 245
Nicholson, Elizabeth II, 399
Nicholson, Elizabeth II, 598
Nicholson, Elizabeth II, 607
Nicholson, Elizabeth II, 624
Nicholson, Elizabeth II, 713
Nicholson, Elizabeth III, 241
Nicholson, Elizabeth III, 242
Nicholson, Elizabeth III, 335
Nicholson, Elizabeth IV, 52
Nicholson, Elizabeth IV, 104
Nicholson, Elizabeth IV, 155
Nicholson, Elizabeth IV, 344
Nicholson, Elizabeth IV, 424
Nicholson, Elizabeth IV, 458
Nicholson, Elizabeth IV, 542
Nicholson, Elizabeth V, 105
Nicholson, Elizabeth V, 175
Nicholson, Elizabeth V, 195
Nicholson, Elizabeth V, 957
Nicholson, Elizabeth Ann IV, 256
Nicholson, Elizabeth Ann IV, 490
Nicholson, Elizabeth Ann IV, 517
Nicholson, Elizabeth Ann IV, 542
Nicholson, Elizabeth D. II, 135
Nicholson, Elizabeth D. T. II, 154
Nicholson, Elizabeth Gertrude I, 623
Nicholson, Elizabeth Haines II, 810
Nicholson, Elizabeth R. III, 241
Nicholson, Elizabeth R. III, 365
Nicholson, Elizabeth V. H. II, 720
Nicholson, Elizabeth V. H. II, 757
Nicholson, Elizabeth V. H. II, 770
Nicholson, Ellen I, 623
Nicholson, Ellen I, 936
Nicholson, Ellen M. I, 14
Nicholson, Ellen M. I, 16
Nicholson, Ellen M. I, 25
Nicholson, Ellen M. I, 64
Nicholson, Ellen M. B. I, 64

cholson, Esther I, 155
cholson, Esther I, 174
cholson, Esther I, 185
cholson, Esther I, 198
cholson, Esther I, 200
cholson, Esther II, 35
cholson, Esther II, 43
cholson, Esther II, 89
cholson, Esther II, 106
cholson, Ezra I, 109
cholson, F. H. I, 65
cholson, F. H. I, 638
cholson, F. Herbert I, 638
cholson, Frances Herbert I, 14
cholson, Francis Herbert I, 14
cholson, Francis Herbert I, 623
cholson, Frank Cob I, 638
cholson, Frank Cole I, 623
cholson, Gabriel I, 108
cholson, Gabriel I, 109
cholson, Gabril I, 155
cholson, Gabril I, 169
cholson, George I, 186
cholson, George I, 198
cholson, George II, 35
cholson, George II, 135
cholson, George II, 154
cholson, George II, 204
cholson, George II, 214
cholson, George II, 245
cholson, George IV, 104
cholson, George IV, 155
cholson, George IV, 344
cholson, George IV, 424
cholson, George IV, 745
cholson, George V, 195
cholson, George Edwin IV, 256
cholson, George Edwin IV, 490
cholson, George Edwin IV, 542
cholson, George K. II, 135
cholson, George T. I, 64
cholson, George Thos. I, 14
cholson, George White I, 14
cholson, Gertrude I, 14
cholson, Grace II, 36
cholson, Grace II, 89
cholson, Grace II, 105
cholson, Grace II, 607
cholson, Hannah I, 14
cholson, Hannah I, 109
cholson, Hannah I, 267
cholson, Hannah I Sup 1, 4
cholson, Hannah I Sup 1, 5
cholson, Hannah I Sup 1, 6
cholson, Hannah I Sup 1, 8
cholson, Hannah II, 35
cholson, Hannah II, 49
cholson, Hannah II, 64
cholson, Hannah II, 75
cholson, Hannah II, 89
cholson, Hannah II, 120
cholson, Hannah II, 121
cholson, Hannah II, 135
cholson, Hannah II, 152
cholson, Hannah II, 154
cholson, Hannah II, 214
cholson, Hannah II, 245
cholson, Hannah II, 598
cholson, Hannah II, 607
cholson, Hannah II, 783
cholson, Hannah II, 791
cholson, Hannah II, 810
cholson, Hannah II, 813
cholson, Hannah IV, 104
cholson, Hannah IV, 155
cholson, Hannah IV, 344
cholson, Hannah IV, 424
cholson, Hannah IV, 429
cholson, Hannah IV, 745
cholson, Hannah A. II, 154
cholson, Hannah, Jr. II, 87
cholson, Hannah, Jr. II, 89
cholson, Harrie L. II, 135
cholson, Harrold Linneus I, 623
cholson, Hattie IV, 1176
cholson, Henley I, 108
cholson, Henly I, 108
cholson, Henry I, 155
cholson, Henry I, 158
cholson, Huldah I, 109
cholson, Huldah III, 241
cholson, Isaac II, 35
cholson, Isaac II, 70
cholson, Isaac II, 135
cholson, Isaac II, 152
cholson, Isaac II, 154
cholson, Isaac II, 399
cholson, Isaac II, 607
cholson, Isaac IV, 104
cholson, Isaac, Jr. II, 135
Nicholson, Isabel, Sr. II, 64
Nicholson, Isabel, Sr. II, 89
Nicholson, Isabella II, 293
Nicholson, Isabella II, 297
Nicholson, Isabella III, 241
Nicholson, Jacob I, 109
Nicholson, Jacob IV, 424
Nicholson, Jael II, 89
Nicholson, Jael II, 100
Nicholson, James II, 35
Nicholson, James II, 89
Nicholson, James IV, 52
Nicholson, James IV, 104
Nicholson, James IV, 155
Nicholson, James IV, 900
Nicholson, James Carey Thomas II, 757
Nicholson, Jane I Sup 1, 7
Nicholson, Jane III, 241
Nicholson, Jane IV, 900
Nicholson, Jane V, 105
Nicholson, Jane V, 136
Nicholson, Jane V, 957
Nicholson, Jane S. V, 105
Nicholson, Jean II, 89
Nicholson, Jean II, 103
Nicholson, Jesse IV, 1176
Nicholson, Jesse V, 195
Nicholson, Jesse B. F. IV, 1176
Nicholson, Jno. I, 1
Nicholson, Job S. IV, 424
Nicholson, Job Scott IV, 424
Nicholson, John I, 14
Nicholson, John I, 64
Nicholson, John I, 76
Nicholson, John I, 108
Nicholson, John I, 109
Nicholson, John I, 154
Nicholson, John I, 185
Nicholson, John I, 196
Nicholson, John I, 198
Nicholson, John I, 909
Nicholson, John II, 35
Nicholson, John II, 64
Nicholson, John II, 89
Nicholson, John II, 93
Nicholson, John II, 121
Nicholson, John II, 607
Nicholson, John II, 757
Nicholson, John III, 241
Nicholson, John IV, 256
Nicholson, John IV, 344
Nicholson, John IV, 490
Nicholson, John IV, 542
Nicholson, John H. II, 121
Nicholson, John H. II, 135
Nicholson, John H. II, 154
Nicholson, John Haines II, 35
Nicholson, John W. I, 64
Nicholson, John White I, 14
Nicholson, Jonathan IV, 835
Nicholson, Joseph I, 14
Nicholson, Joseph I, 64
Nicholson, Joseph I, 65
Nicholson, Joseph I, 108
Nicholson, Joseph I, 109
Nicholson, Joseph I, 113
Nicholson, Joseph I, 145
Nicholson, Joseph I, 154
Nicholson, Joseph I, 155
Nicholson, Joseph I, 162
Nicholson, Joseph I, 685
Nicholson, Joseph I Sup 1, 3
Nicholson, Joseph I Sup 1, 5
Nicholson, Joseph II, 35
Nicholson, Joseph II, 36
Nicholson, Joseph II, 89
Nicholson, Joseph II, 121
Nicholson, Joseph II, 135
Nicholson, Joseph II, 154
Nicholson, Joseph II, 204
Nicholson, Joseph II, 245
Nicholson, Joseph II, 607
Nicholson, Joseph II, 903
Nicholson, Joseph III, 30
Nicholson, Joseph III, 241
Nicholson, Joseph IV, 52
Nicholson, Joseph IV, 102
Nicholson, Joseph IV, 104
Nicholson, Joseph IV, 155
Nicholson, Joseph IV, 344
Nicholson, Joseph IV, 424
Nicholson, Joseph IV, 458
Nicholson, Joshua I, 198
Nicholson, Joshua II, 399
Nicholson, Joshua II, 607
Nicholson, Joshua T. II, 399
Nicholson, Joshua T. II, 607
Nicholson, Josiah I, 14
Nicholson, Josiah I, 16
Nicholson, Josiah I, 25
Nicholson, Josiah I, 64
Nicholson, Josiah I, 65
Nicholson, Josiah I, 71
Nicholson, Josiah I, 84
Nicholson, Josiah I, 154
Nicholson, Josiah I, 623
Nicholson, Josiah I, 936
Nicholson, Josiah Winslow I, 14
Nicholson, Juliet VI, 782
Nicholson, Katharine II, 204
Nicholson, Katharine II, 245
Nicholson, Katherine C. II, 757
Nicholson, Keziah I, 40
Nicholson, Keziah I, 64
Nicholson, Lafayette IV, 1259
Nicholson, Leonard III, 242
Nicholson, Lindsay II, 607
Nicholson, Lindsey II, 399
Nicholson, Lindsey II, 607
Nicholson, Lindsey III, 241
Nicholson, Lindzey II, 239
Nicholson, Lindzey II, 245
Nicholson, Lindzey II, 607
Nicholson, Lindzey II, 713
Nicholson, Louisa V, 105
Nicholson, Lydia I, 84
Nicholson, Lydia I, 109
Nicholson, Lydia III, 241
Nicholson, Lydia V, 195
Nicholson, Lydia A. II, 721
Nicholson, Lydia T. IV, 1176
Nicholson, M. C. IV, 745
Nicholson, Malissa V, 105
Nicholson, Margaret I, 103
Nicholson, Margaret I, 148
Nicholson, Margaret I, 154
Nicholson, Margrate I, 109
Nicholson, Mariam I, 198
Nicholson, Marian Frances I, 623
Nicholson, Marian L. V, 105
Nicholson, Marianna I, 14
Nicholson, Marion L. V, 105
Nicholson, Mark II, 89
Nicholson, Martha II, 89
Nicholson, Martha IV, 567
Nicholson, Martha IV, 589
Nicholson, Martha Jane V, 105
Nicholson, Mary I, 51
Nicholson, Mary I, 64
Nicholson, Mary I, 101
Nicholson, Mary I, 104
Nicholson, Mary I, 108
Nicholson, Mary I, 109
Nicholson, Mary I, 135
Nicholson, Mary I, 142
Nicholson, Mary I, 148
Nicholson, Mary I, 153
Nicholson, Mary I, 154
Nicholson, Mary I, 155
Nicholson, Mary I, 161
Nicholson, Mary I, 169
Nicholson, Mary I, 173
Nicholson, Mary I, 186
Nicholson, Mary I, 198
Nicholson, Mary I Sup 1, 7
Nicholson, Mary I Sup 1, 8
Nicholson, Mary II, 35
Nicholson, Mary II, 55
Nicholson, Mary II, 89
Nicholson, Mary II, 107
Nicholson, Mary II, 131
Nicholson, Mary II, 297
Nicholson, Mary III, 30
Nicholson, Mary III, 241
Nicholson, Mary III, 242
Nicholson, Mary IV, 102
Nicholson, Mary IV, 104
Nicholson, Mary IV, 155
Nicholson, Mary IV, 424
Nicholson, Mary IV, 587
Nicholson, Mary IV, 589
Nicholson, Mary IV, 900
Nicholson, Mary A. K. IV, 1176
Nicholson, Mary Anne I, 64
Nicholson, Mary Clark II, 713
Nicholson, Mary Clark II, 757
Nicholson, Mary Clark II, 770
Nicholson, Mary Ellen V, 105
Nicholson, Mary Ellen V, 957
Nicholson, Mary Emily V, 105
Nicholson, Mary Hunter, Jr. II, 297
Nicholson, Mary Lippincott II, 399
Nicholson, Mary N. V, 565
Nicholson, Mary Symons I, 22
Nicholson, Mary W. II, 757
Nicholson, Mary Webb I, 623
Nicholson, Mary Webb I, 638
Nicholson, Mary Webb I, 639
Nicholson, Matthew I, 40
Nicholson, Matthew I, 64
Nicholson, Matthew I, 109
Nicholson, Matthew I, 154
Nicholson, Mehetabel I, 64
Nicholson, Mehetabel I, 65
Nicholson, Mehitabel I, 154
Nicholson, Mehitabel I, 155
Nicholson, Mehittabel I, 108
Nicholson, Meriam I, 728
Nicholson, Michael II, 607
Nicholson, Milicent I, 108
Nicholson, Miliscent I, 154
Nicholson, Miliscent I, 173
Nicholson, Millicent I, 108
Nicholson, Millicent II, 36
Nicholson, Milton II, 36
Nicholson, Milton II, 89
Nicholson, Miriam I, 94
Nicholson, Miriam I, 108
Nicholson, Miriam I, 109
Nicholson, Miriam I, 129
Nicholson, Miriam I, 130
Nicholson, Miriam I, 154
Nicholson, Miriam I, 155
Nicholson, Mirum I, 198
Nicholson, Mrs. ??? IV, 490
Nicholson, Mrs. Mary IV, 745
Nicholson, Narcissa IV, 256
Nicholson, Narcissa IV, 469
Nicholson, Narcissa IV, 490
Nicholson, Narcissa IV, 542
Nicholson, Nathan I, 109
Nicholson, Nathan I, 154
Nicholson, Nathan I, 155
Nicholson, Nathan I, 185
Nicholson, Nathan I, 198
Nicholson, Nathan I, 199
Nicholson, Nathan P. I, 186
Nicholson, Nathaniel I, 14
Nicholson, Nathaniel I Sup 1, 4
Nicholson, Nathaniel I Sup 1, 5
Nicholson, Nicholas I, 64
Nicholson, Nicholas I, 78
Nicholson, Nicholas I, 95
Nicholson, Nicholas I, 109
Nicholson, Nicholas I, 154
Nicholson, Nicholas I, 155
Nicholson, Nicholas I, 198
Nicholson, Nicolas I, 109
Nicholson, Noah II, 36
Nicholson, Parker I, 198
Nicholson, Peninah I, 198
Nicholson, Peninah I, 199
Nicholson, Peninnah I, 185
Nicholson, Penninah I, 198
Nicholson, Pharaby I, 185
Nicholson, Phebe II, 721
Nicholson, Phebe Ann Greenfield IV, 542
Nicholson, Phebe Ann Greenfield IV, 558
Nicholson, Pheraby I, 188
Nicholson, Pheraby I, 198
Nicholson, Polly IV, 835
Nicholson, Priscila I, 64
Nicholson, Priscila I, 76
Nicholson, Priscilla I Sup 1, 4
Nicholson, Priscilla I Sup 1, 5
Nicholson, Rachel I, 95
Nicholson, Rachel I, 109
Nicholson, Rachel I, 132
Nicholson, Rachel I, 154
Nicholson, Rachel II, 17
Nicholson, Rachel II, 35
Nicholson, Rachel II, 36
Nicholson, Rachel II, 72
Nicholson, Rachel II, 80
Nicholson, Rachel II, 89
Nicholson, Rachel II, 99
Nicholson, Rachel II, 101
Nicholson, Rachel II, 607
Nicholson, Rebecca II, 35
Nicholson, Rebecca II, 70
Nicholson, Rebecca II, 89
Nicholson, Rebecca II, 121
Nicholson, Rebecca II, 135
Nicholson, Rebecca II, 150
Nicholson, Rebecca II, 152
Nicholson, Rebecca II, 154
Nicholson, Rebecca II, 607
Nicholson, Rebecca IV, 424
Nicholson, Rebeckah I, 108
Nicholson, Rebeckah II, 492
Nicholson, Rebeckah II, 607
Nicholson, Rebekah I, 145
Nicholson, Rebekah I, 154
Nicholson, Rebekah I, 160
Nicholson, Rex I, 154
Nicholson, Rhoda Elma III, 242
Nicholson, Richard II, 607
Nicholson, Richard IV, 835
Nicholson, Richard L. II, 713
Nicholson, Richard L. II, 757
Nicholson, Richard L. II, 770
Nicholson, Richard L. III, 241
Nicholson, Richard L. III, 242
Nicholson, Richard L. III, 335
Nicholson, Ricks I, 109
Nicholson, Ruth II, 35
Nicholson, Ruth II, 36
Nicholson, Ruth II, 50
Nicholson, Ruth II, 68
Nicholson, Ruth II, 89
Nicholson, Ruth II, 111
Nicholson, Ruth II, 607
Nicholson, Ruth III, 242
Nicholson, Ruth IV, 1273
Nicholson, Ruth IV, 1287
Nicholson, Ruth V, 105
Nicholson, Ruth V, 957
Nicholson, Ruth W. V, 105
Nicholson, S. Edgar III, 242
Nicholson, Saml. I, 42
Nicholson, Saml. I, 64
Nicholson, Samuel I, 14
Nicholson, Samuel I, 154
Nicholson, Samuel I Sup 1, 5
Nicholson, Samuel I Sup 1, 7
Nicholson, Samuel I Sup 1, 8
Nicholson, Samuel II, 17
Nicholson, Samuel II, 18
Nicholson, Samuel II, 35
Nicholson, Samuel II, 36
Nicholson, Samuel II, 49
Nicholson, Samuel II, 66
Nicholson, Samuel II, 89
Nicholson, Samuel II, 121
Nicholson, Samuel II, 135
Nicholson, Samuel II, 154
Nicholson, Samuel II, 239
Nicholson, Samuel II, 245
Nicholson, Samuel II, 607
Nicholson, Samuel F. II, 135
Nicholson, Samuel Greer III, 242
Nicholson, Samuel, Jr. II, 89
Nicholson, Samuel, Jr. II, 121
Nicholson, Samuell I Sup 1, 7
Nicholson, Samuell II, 17
Nicholson, Sanuell I Sup 1, 5
Nicholson, Sarah I, 14
Nicholson, Sarah I, 55
Nicholson, Sarah I, 64
Nicholson, Sarah I, 78
Nicholson, Sarah I, 80
Nicholson, Sarah I, 108
Nicholson, Sarah I, 109
Nicholson, Sarah I, 154
Nicholson, Sarah I, 155
Nicholson, Sarah I, 158
Nicholson, Sarah I, 168
Nicholson, Sarah I, 185
Nicholson, Sarah I, 190
Nicholson, Sarah I, 196
Nicholson, Sarah I, 198
Nicholson, Sarah I Sup 1, 4
Nicholson, Sarah I Sup 1, 5
Nicholson, Sarah II, 20
Nicholson, Sarah II, 35
Nicholson, Sarah II, 36
Nicholson, Sarah II, 50
Nicholson, Sarah II, 66
Nicholson, Sarah II, 89
Nicholson, Sarah II, 93
Nicholson, Sarah II, 99
Nicholson, Sarah II, 107
Nicholson, Sarah II, 121
Nicholson, Sarah II, 135
Nicholson, Sarah II, 139
Nicholson, Sarah II, 154
Nicholson, Sarah II, 160
Nicholson, Sarah II, 399
Nicholson, Sarah II, 496
Nicholson, Sarah II, 607
Nicholson, Sarah III, 241
Nicholson, Sarah IV, 104
Nicholson, Sarah IV, 155
Nicholson, Sarah IV, 458
Nicholson, Sarah A. I, 14
Nicholson, Sarah A. I, 64
Nicholson, Sarah Alice IV, 542
Nicholson, Sarah Allas IV, 256
Nicholson, Sarah Allen II, 135
Nicholson, Sarah Ann II, 607
Nicholson, Sarah Ann II, 903
Nicholson, Sarah N. I, 64
Nicholson, Sarah Newby I, 22
Nicholson, Sarah T. II, 89
Nicholson, Sarah W. I, 14
Nicholson, Sarah W. I, 64
Nicholson, Sarah W. I, 82
Nicholson, Sarah, Jr. II, 36
Nicholson, Sary I, 155

Nicholson, Sibyl I, 14
Nicholson, Sibyl I, 65
Nicholson, Susan I, 155
Nicholson, Susan II, 297
Nicholson, Susan E. II, 153
Nicholson, Susan E. II, 154
Nicholson, Susan G. II, 154
Nicholson, Susan G. II, 903
Nicholson, Susanah I, 108
Nicholson, Susanna II, 446
Nicholson, Susannah I, 108
Nicholson, Susannah I, 148
Nicholson, Susannah I, 154
Nicholson, Susannah I, 155
Nicholson, Susannah I, 162
Nicholson, Susannah I, 169
Nicholson, T. H. I, 65
Nicholson, Tempa I, 185
Nicholson, Tempy I, 198
Nicholson, Thomas I, 14
Nicholson, Thomas I, 51
Nicholson, Thomas I, 64
Nicholson, Thomas I, 80
Nicholson, Thomas I, 94
Nicholson, Thomas I, 101
Nicholson, Thomas I, 103
Nicholson, Thomas I, 104
Nicholson, Thomas I, 108
Nicholson, Thomas I, 109
Nicholson, Thomas I, 154
Nicholson, Thomas I, 155
Nicholson, Thomas I, 164
Nicholson, Thomas I, 168
Nicholson, Thomas I, 174
Nicholson, Thomas I, 177
Nicholson, Thomas I, 412
Nicholson, Thomas I, 728
Nicholson, Thomas II, 36
Nicholson, Thomas II, 607
Nicholson, Thomas II, 757
Nicholson, Thomas III, 242
Nicholson, Thomas William I, 198
Nicholson, Thos. I, 267
Nicholson, Thos. II, 811
Nicholson, Timothy I, 14
Nicholson, Timothy I, 64
Nicholson, Timothy I, 82
Nicholson, Valentine V, 105
Nicholson, Valentine V, 136
Nicholson, Valentine V, 195
Nicholson, Valentine V, 957
Nicholson, Wd. Ann II, 607
Nicholson, Widow Anne I, 71
Nicholson, Widow Rebeckah I, 108
Nicholson, Widow Sarah Walton I, 64
Nicholson, William I, 14
Nicholson, William I, 64
Nicholson, William I, 108
Nicholson, William I, 155
Nicholson, William II, 35
Nicholson, William II, 36
Nicholson, William II, 135
Nicholson, William II, 154
Nicholson, William II, 399
Nicholson, William IV, 104
Nicholson, William IV, 256
Nicholson, William IV, 344
Nicholson, William IV, 424
Nicholson, William IV, 490
Nicholson, William IV, 542
Nicholson, William IV, 1176
Nicholson, William L. IV, 490
Nicholson, William, Jr. II, 36
Nicholson, William, Sr. II, 36
Nicholson, Wm. II, 50
Nicholson, Wm. II, 89
Nicholson, Wm. II, 99
Nicholson, Wm. II, 103
Nicholson, Wm. II, 107
Nicholson, Wm. II, 135
Nicholson, Wm. II, 139
Nicholson, Wm. II, 153
Nicholson, Wm. II, 154
Nicholson, Wm. II, 160
Nicholson, Wm. II, 607
Nicholson, Wm. II, 903
Nicholson, Wm. IV, 155
Nicholson, Wm., Jr. II, 89
Nicholson, Wm., Jr. II, 607
Nicholson, Zachariah I, 108
Nicholson, Zachariah I, 154
Nicholson, Zachariah I, 685
Nicholson, Zachariah I, 687
Nicholson, Zacharias I, 154
Nicholson, Zacharias I, 166
Nicholson, Zebedee II, 721
Nichos, John II, 399
Nichos, Samuel II, 399
Nichual, Wm. II, 903
Nick, Charles V, 631
Nickels, Ann K. IV, 745
Nickels, Lydia I, 1083
Nickels, Lydia I, 1086
Nickels, Mary IV, 745
Nickels, Mary Anna K. IV, 739
Nickels, Wm. IV, 739
Nickels, Wm. IV, 745
Nickelson, George II, 245
Nickelson, George II, 276
Nickelson, Hannah II, 245
Nickelson, Hannah II, 276
Nickerson, Abbie P. V, 953
Nickerson, Abbie P. V, 957
Nickerson, Adelaide III, 17
Nickerson, Adelaide III, 242
Nickerson, Clark V, 957
Nickerson, David A. V, 953
Nickerson, David A. V, 957
Nickerson, Elizabeth A. II, 903
Nickerson, Jonathan IV, 344
Nickerson, Joshua V, 519
Nickerson, Martha V, 957
Nickerson, Polly IV, 344
Nickerson, Polly IV, 354
Nickerson, Sarah III, 17
Nickerson, Sarah III, 242
Nickerson, Stephen III, 17
Nickerson, Stephen III, 242
Nickerson, Susie V, 676
Nickilson, Benjamin C. IV, 256
Nickilson, Elizabeth Ann IV, 256
Nickilson, George Edwin IV, 256
Nickilson, John IV, 256
Nickilson, Narcissa IV, 256
Nickilson, William IV, 256
Nickison, Alice IV, 1239
Nickison, William IV, 1239
Nickkols, Locky VI, 962
Nicklen, Dr. John VI, 510
Nicklen, Elizabeth VI, 510
Nicklers, Martha M. IV, 155
Nickles, Athenissa IV, 1177
Nickles, Jane VI, 602
Nickles, Lydia VI, 602
Nickles, Rachel IV, 256
Nickleson, Jonathan IV, 835
Nickleson, Joshua V, 519
Nickleson, Mary V, 485
Nickleson, Mary V, 519
Nicklin, Dr. John VI, 539
Nicklin, Elizabeth VI, 539
Nickola, Lewis IV, 745
Nickold, Margaret VI, 656
Nickols, Amos VI, 678
Nickols, Amy VI, 684
Nickols, Ann VI, 426
Nickols, Ann K. IV, 745
Nickols, Bazdel VI, 964
Nickols, Benjamin IV, 745
Nickols, Cassandra VI, 371
Nickols, Charles IV, 745
Nickols, Daniel VI, 684
Nickols, David VI, 372
Nickols, Edward IV, 745
Nickols, Eli IV, 341
Nickols, Eli IV, 344
Nickols, Eli VI, 678
Nickols, Elizabeth VI, 518
Nickols, Elizabeth VI, 684
Nickols, Elizabeth VI, 964
Nickols, George VI, 538
Nickols, George S. IV, 745
Nickols, Hannah VI, 684
Nickols, Helen VI, 684
Nickols, Isaac VI, 539
Nickols, Isaac VI, 602
Nickols, Isaac VI, 607
Nickols, Isaac VI, 608
Nickols, Isaac VI, 610
Nickols, Isaac VI, 681
Nickols, Isaac, Jr. VI, 539
Nickols, Isaiah VI, 539
Nickols, Isaiah VI, 587
Nickols, Jacob IV, 1177
Nickols, James VI, 684
Nickols, James H. IV, 745
Nickols, Jane VI, 602
Nickols, Jesse IV, 745
Nickols, Jesse M. IV, 745
Nickols, John VI, 682
Nickols, John VI, 684
Nickols, John VI, 707
Nickols, John O. IV, 745
Nickols, Joseph VI, 681
Nickols, Joshua VI, 539
Nickols, Lydia IV, 745
Nickols, Lydia VI, 602
Nickols, Lydia VI, 607
Nickols, Lydia VI, 608
Nickols, Lydia Ann VI, 663
Nickols, Lydia J. IV, 745
Nickols, Mahlon IV, 745
Nickols, Margaret VI, 682
Nickols, Maria VI, 678
Nickols, Mariam G. VI, 692
Nickols, Mary IV, 745
Nickols, Mary VI, 506
Nickols, Mary VI, 539
Nickols, Mary VI, 587
Nickols, Mary VI, 681
Nickols, Mary Ann VI, 681
Nickols, Mary C. IV, 745
Nickols, Mary Lydia Ann VI, 678
Nickols, Miriam G. VI, 458
Nickols, Nathan B. VI, 678
Nickols, Rachel IV, 341
Nickols, Rachel IV, 344
Nickols, Rachel Alice IV, 741
Nickols, Rachel Alice IV, 745
Nickols, Rebecca VI, 684
Nickols, Rebecca J. VI, 681
Nickols, Rebeckah VI, 539
Nickols, Robert H. IV, 745
Nickols, Ruth IV, 745
Nickols, Ruth Hannah IV, 745
Nickols, Sarah VI, 602
Nickols, Solomon VI, 684
Nickols, Spencer I. IV, 745
Nickols, Susannah VI, 486
Nickols, Susannah VI, 539
Nickols, Tacy IV, 1176
Nickols, Tacy VI, 685
Nickols, Thomas VI, 538
Nickols, Thos. VI, 684
Nickols, Triphena IV, 745
Nickols, Virginia IV, 745
Nickols, Virginia J. VI, 681
Nickols, Walter IV, 745
Nickols, Widow Elizabeth VI, 538
Nickols, Wilbur IV, 745
Nickols, William VI, 371
Nickols, William VI, 602
Nickols, William Albert VI, 678
Nickols, William J. IV, 745
Nickols, Wm. IV, 745
Nickolson, Elizabeth I, 109
Nickolson, Joseph I, 109
Nickolson, Presala I, 109
Nickolson, Sammuell, Jr. I, 109
Nickolson, Samuel I, 1
Nickolson, Samuel I, 90
Nickolson, Samuel I, 109
Nickson, Jane II, 89
Nickson, Jane II, 104
Nickson, Jane II, 608
Nickson, Jane II, 674
Nickson, Joseph I, 896
Nickson, Rachel II, 400
Nickson, Rachel II, 466
Nickson, Thomas II, 466
Nickson, Thomas II, 608
Nickson, Wd. Rachel II, 608
Nickum, Ann Eliza P. IV, 745
Nickum, Eliza T. IV, 685
Nickum, Eliza T. IV, 745
Nicodemus, Elizabeth IV, 971
Nicolas, Barbara Ann V, 768
Nicoll, Gloriana M. III, 383
Nicoll, Gloriana M. III, 387
Nicoll, Sam'l Benj. III, 387
Nicoll, Samuel Benj. III, 383
Nicoll, Sarah III, 383
Nicoll, Sarah III, 387
Nicolot, Agnes V, 700
Nicols, Athenessa IV, 1218
Nicols, Benjamin III, 483
Nicols, Benjamin III, 491
Nicols, Eli IV, 241
Nicols, Eli IV, 256
Nicols, Jane IV, 256
Nicols, Mary III, 483
Nicols, Mary III, 491
Nicols, Rachel IV, 241
Nicols, Rachel IV, 256
Nidy, Margaret E. V, 636
Niell, Omar O. IV, 1176
Nielson, Deborah II, 89
Nieman, Carl IV, 1331
Nieman, Harry IV, 1331
Nieman, Harry H. IV, 1331
Niers, Ann VI, 484
Niers, Ann VI, 539
Niers, Susanna VI, 539
Niers, Susanna VI, 547
Nieweg, Anna III, 358
Nigby, Elizabeth VI, 805
Nigh, Mary IV, 626
Nigh, Mary IV, 649
Night, Abel I, 824
Night, Abram I, 824
Night, Anna I, 824
Night, Ruth I, 824
Night, Samuel IV, 911
Night, Samuel V, 184
Night, Sarah IV, 911
Night, Susannah IV, 911
Nightengale, Florence I, 666
Nigley, Sarah VI, 817
Nigue, Fred IV, 1331
Niles, Amanda V, 758
Niles, Emma V, 758
Niles, Hezekiah II, 607
Niles, Hezekiah II, 608
Niles, John W. II, 608
Niles, Mrs. William V, 758
Niles, Sadie V, 758
Nilson, Eliz. Paxson III, 242
Nilson, Ellen Y. III, 242
Nilson, Harold L. III, 242
Nilson, Richard S. III, 242
Nimits, Chester W. VI, 757
Nimmo, Anny VI, 1013
Nimmo, David VI, 969
Nimmo, Elizabeth VI, 885
Nimmo, Frances VI, 969
Nimmo, Harriet H. VI, 969
Nimmo, James VI, 969
Nimmo, Jenny VI, 969
Nimmo, John VI, 965
Nimmo, John M. VI, 956
Nimmo, John M. VI, 969
Nimmo, Martha VI, 969
Nimmo, Mary VI, 969
Nimmo, Mary A. VI, 969
Nimmo, Mary M. VI, 956
Nimmo, Milly VI, 928
Nimmo, Olive W. IV, 403
Nimmo, Olive W. IV, 424
Nimmo, Robert VI, 885
Nimmo, Robert VI, 956
Nimmo, Robert VI, 969
Nimmo, Robert VI, 1013
Nimmo, Sarah VI, 1013
Nimmo, Susan VI, 965
Nimmo, Thomas VI, 964
Nimmo, Thomas J. VI, 969
Ninde, Benjamin V, 105
Ninde, Benjamin V, 140
Ninde, Frederick V, 106
Ninde, Henry P. V, 106
Ninde, James V, 105
Ninde, James William V, 106
Ninde, Jane V, 105
Ninde, Jane V, 140
Ninde, Lindley V, 106
Ninde, Margaret V, 106
Ninde, Martha V, 106
Ninde, Miliorah V, 105
Ninde, Priscilla V, 105
Ninde, Rebecka V, 106
Ninde, Rhoda V, 106
Nipper, Ann I, 1049
Nippes, Mary II, 757
Nippes, Mary II, 762
Nisbet, Mary V, 900
Nisbet, Mary V, 924
Nisbit, Mary II, 606
Nisbitt, Mary II, 606
Nishwitz, J. E. V, 758
Nishwitz, Jacob E. V, 758
Niss, Johannis II, 446
Niss, Susanna II, 446
Nite, Jonathan I, 556
Nitobe, Inazo II, 714
Nitobe, Inazo II, 738
Nitobe, Inazo II, 757
Nitobe, Juijero II, 738
Nitobe, Juijero II, 757
Nitobe, Mary P. II, 714
Nitobe, Mary P. II, 738
Nitobe, Mary P. II, 757
Nitobe, Mary P. E. II, 757
Nitobe, Seki II, 738
Nitobe, Seki II, 757
Nitobe, Thomasu II, 714
Nitobe, Yoshio II, 714
Nitobe, Yoshio II, 757
Nitrow, Abraham V, 1012
Niven, ??? III, 242
Niven, George III, 242
Niven, Jeannette III, 242
Niven, Mary III, 242
Niven, Robert III, 242
Niver, Lavina H. IV, 1239
Nix, Edward VI, 969
Nix, Elizabeth VI, 969
Nixom, Elizabeth I, 704
Nixom, Luke I, 704
Nixom, Martha I, 704
Nixon, Abigail I, 109
Nixon, Abigail I, 156
Nixon, Abigail I, 729
Nixon, Abigail I, 863
Nixon, Abigail I, 896
Nixon, Achsah I, 65
Nixon, Achsah I, 81
Nixon, Achsah I, 156
Nixon, Achsah I, 198
Nixon, Alonzo I, 339
Nixon, Alonzo I, 412
Nixon, Alonzo I, 638
Nixon, Alonzo I, 946
Nixon, Amy I, 412
Nixon, Ann I, 110
Nixon, Ann I, 149
Nixon, Ann I, 156
Nixon, Ann V, 106
Nixon, Ann V, 307
Nixon, Ann V, 855
Nixon, Ann VI, 685
Nixon, Ann VI, 717
Nixon, Ann P. V, 352
Nixon, Ann P. V, 854
Nixon, Ann P. V, 855
Nixon, Ann Skinner I, 111
Nixon, Anna I, 194
Nixon, Anna I, 198
Nixon, Anna I, 704
Nixon, Anna I, 729
Nixon, Anna I, 738
Nixon, Anna V, 589
Nixon, Anna V, 854
Nixon, Anna V, 855
Nixon, Anne V, 974
Nixon, Annie J. I, 11
Nixon, Barnabas I, 729
Nixon, Barnabe I, 110
Nixon, Barnabe I, 155
Nixon, Barnaby I, 110
Nixon, Barnaby I, 153
Nixon, Barnaby I, 155
Nixon, Barnaby I, 704
Nixon, Barnaby VI, 17
Nixon, Barnaby VI, 116
Nixon, Barnaby VI, 133
Nixon, Barnaby VI, 138
Nixon, Barnaby VI, 194
Nixon, Barnebe I, 102
Nixon, Barnebe I, 110
Nixon, Barneby I, 110
Nixon, Barneby I, 155
Nixon, Barralias I, 704
Nixon, Benjamin I, 111
Nixon, Benjamin I, 156
Nixon, Beulah VI, 769
Nixon, Beulah VI, 770
Nixon, Caleb I, 110
Nixon, Caleb I, 156
Nixon, Caleb I, 729
Nixon, Caleb I, 896
Nixon, Damaris I, 110
Nixon, Damaris I, 155
Nixon, Damaris I, 161
Nixon, David VI, 116
Nixon, David A. I, 623
Nixon, Delphina E. I, 412
Nixon, Delphinia Matilda I, 70
Nixon, Dorathy I, 140
Nixon, Dorathy I, 156
Nixon, Dorethe I, 109
Nixon, Dorithy I, 111
Nixon, Dorithy I, 155
Nixon, Dority I, 110
Nixon, Dorothy I, 109
Nixon, Dorothy I, 153
Nixon, Dorothy I, 156
Nixon, Elenor I, 729
Nixon, Elezabeath I, 155
Nixon, Elezabeath I, 159
Nixon, Elisabeth I, 14
Nixon, Elisabeth I, 35
Nixon, Elisabeth I, 57
Nixon, Elisabeth I, 65
Nixon, Elisabeth I, 110
Nixon, Elisabeth I, 152
Nixon, Elisabeth I, 155
Nixon, Elisabeth I, 156
Nixon, Elisabeth I, 191
Nixon, Elisabeth I, 198
Nixon, Elizabeth I, 110
Nixon, Elizabeth I, 130
Nixon, Elizabeth I, 152
Nixon, Elizabeth I, 155
Nixon, Elizabeth I, 156
Nixon, Elizabeth I, 161
Nixon, Elizabeth I, 186
Nixon, Elizabeth I, 704
Nixon, Elizabeth I, 729
Nixon, Elizabeth I, 767
Nixon, Elizabeth I, 990
Nixon, Elizabeth I, 994
Nixon, Elizabeth I Sup 1, 5

Nixon, Elizabeth V, 268
Nixon, Elizabeth V, 423
Nixon, Elizabeth, Sr. I, 110
Nixon, Ella Maria I, 729
Nixon, Ella Mariah I, 832
Nixon, Esther I, 555
Nixon, Esther I, 564
Nixon, Esther V, 854
Nixon, Esther Jane I, 729
Nixon, Evaline I, 412
Nixon, Evaline I, 638
Nixon, Eveline I, 313
Nixon, Eveline I, 339
Nixon, Eveline I, 638
Nixon, Eveline I, 946
Nixon, Everette V, 589
Nixon, Flora I, 389
Nixon, Flora I, 412
Nixon, Flora I, 729
Nixon, Flora M. I, 412
Nixon, Flora M. I, 704
Nixon, Flora M. I, 729
Nixon, Flora M. I, 832
Nixon, Foster I, 186
Nixon, Foster I, 198
Nixon, Frances I, 65
Nixon, Francis I, 14
Nixon, Francis I, 62
Nixon, Francis I, 65
Nixon, Francis I, 110
Nixon, Francis I, 156
Nixon, Frederick I, 65
Nixon, Frederick I, 109
Nixon, Frederick I, 111
Nixon, Frederick I, 155
Nixon, Fredric I, 65
Nixon, Gabrel I, 704
Nixon, Gabriel I, 729
Nixon, Gabriel I, 828
Nixon, Gabriel I, 832
Nixon, George IV, 256
Nixon, George V, 350
Nixon, George F. I, 832
Nixon, George Fox I, 729
Nixon, George Fox I, 832
Nixon, Hannah I, 34
Nixon, Hannah I, 65
Nixon, Hannah I, 109
Nixon, Hannah I, 110
Nixon, Hannah I, 155
Nixon, Hannah I, 274
Nixon, Hannah I, 275
Nixon, Hannah II, 77
Nixon, Hannah II, 90
Nixon, Hannah V, 307
Nixon, Hannah V, 973
Nixon, Hannah V, 974
Nixon, Hannah VI, 539
Nixon, Hannah VI, 587
Nixon, Hannah, Jr. I, 136
Nixon, Hannah, Jr. I, 155
Nixon, Hanner I, 155
Nixon, Harry V, 1012
Nixon, Henley I, 704
Nixon, Henley I, 729
Nixon, Henrietta V, 352
Nixon, Henrietta V, 854
Nixon, Henrietta V, 855
Nixon, Isaac II, 90
Nixon, Jacob I, 110
Nixon, Jacob I, 155
Nixon, Jacob I, 729
Nixon, Jacob I, 994
Nixon, James I, 65
Nixon, James I, 135
Nixon, James I, 156
Nixon, James I, 164
Nixon, James I, 704
Nixon, James I, 893
Nixon, James I, 896
Nixon, Jane I, 155
Nixon, Jane I, 156
Nixon, Jane I, 896
Nixon, Jane II, 89
Nixon, Jane II, 608
Nixon, Jean I, 110
Nixon, Jean I, 729
Nixon, Jemima I, 110
Nixon, Jemima I, 121
Nixon, Jemima I, 155
Nixon, Jemima I, 170
Nixon, Jemima I, 994
Nixon, Jennie V, 1012
Nixon, Jesse I, 662
Nixon, Jesse I, 704
Nixon, Jesse I, 729
Nixon, John I, 34
Nixon, John I, 65
Nixon, John I, 108
Nixon, John I, 110
Nixon, John I, 111
Nixon, John I, 139
Nixon, John I, 149
Nixon, John I, 152
Nixon, John I, 155
Nixon, John I, 156
Nixon, John I, 167
Nixon, John I, 172
Nixon, John I, 186
Nixon, John I, 194
Nixon, John I, 198
Nixon, John I, 704
Nixon, John I, 729
Nixon, John I, 896
Nixon, John I Sup 1, 5
Nixon, John V, 854
Nixon, John V, 1012
Nixon, John Anderson I, 198
Nixon, John C. I, 11
Nixon, Joseph I, 65
Nixon, Joseph I, 110
Nixon, Joseph I, 152
Nixon, Joseph I, 156
Nixon, Joseph I, 161
Nixon, Joseph I, 186
Nixon, Joseph I, 198
Nixon, Joseph I, 704
Nixon, Joseph I, 729
Nixon, Joseph I, 831
Nixon, Joseph I, 896
Nixon, Joseph I, 994
Nixon, Joseph II, 89
Nixon, Joseph Butler I, 831
Nixon, Joseph Harrison II, 90
Nixon, Josiah I, 110
Nixon, Josiah I, 155
Nixon, Josiah I, 156
Nixon, Josiah I, 729
Nixon, Josiah I, 895
Nixon, Josiah I, 896
Nixon, Julia V, 1012
Nixon, Kezia I, 63
Nixon, Kezia I, 65
Nixon, Keziah I, 62
Nixon, Keziah I, 71
Nixon, Keziah I, 110
Nixon, Keziah I, 142
Nixon, Keziah I, 155
Nixon, L. S. I, 947
Nixon, L. Simeon I, 339
Nixon, L. Simeon I, 412
Nixon, L. Simeon I, 638
Nixon, L. Simeon I, 946
Nixon, Laura Emma I, 704
Nixon, Laura Emma I, 729
Nixon, Laura Emma I, 832
Nixon, Liddia I, 109
Nixon, Lorenzo I, 339
Nixon, Lorenzo I, 412
Nixon, Lorenzo I, 638
Nixon, Lorenzo I, 946
Nixon, Lyda I, 156
Nixon, Lydda I, 35
Nixon, Lydda I, 65
Nixon, Lydda I, 186
Nixon, Lyddea I, 110
Nixon, Lyddia I, 155
Nixon, Lydia I, 65
Nixon, Lydia I, 149
Nixon, Lydia I, 156
Nixon, Lydia I, 186
Nixon, Lydia I, 704
Nixon, Lydia I, 709
Nixon, Lydia I, 722
Nixon, Lydia I, 729
Nixon, Lydia I, 896
Nixon, Margaret I, 65
Nixon, Margaret I, 110
Nixon, Margaret I, 111
Nixon, Margaret I, 123
Nixon, Margaret I, 134
Nixon, Margaret I, 145
Nixon, Margaret I, 156
Nixon, Margaret I, 172
Nixon, Margaret I, 186
Nixon, Margaret I, 187
Nixon, Margaret I, 188
Nixon, Margaret I, 189
Nixon, Margaret I, 198
Nixon, Margaret I, 202
Nixon, Margaret I, 704
Nixon, Martha I, 65
Nixon, Martha I, 76
Nixon, Martha I, 110
Nixon, Martha I, 147
Nixon, Martha I, 156
Nixon, Martha I, 186
Nixon, Martha I, 198
Nixon, Martha I, 704
Nixon, Martha I, 729
Nixon, Martha IV, 256
Nixon, Martha V, 63
Nixon, Martha V, 106
Nixon, Martha V, 307
Nixon, Martha V, 842
Nixon, Martha V, 854
Nixon, Martha V, 855
Nixon, Martha V, 974
Nixon, Martha VI, 75
Nixon, Martha VI, 77
Nixon, Martha Ann V, 106
Nixon, Martha Ann V, 307
Nixon, Martha Ann V, 854
Nixon, Martha Ann V, 855
Nixon, Martha Ann V, 974
Nixon, Martha L. I, 156
Nixon, Martha L. IV, 256
Nixon, Martha L. IV, 285
Nixon, Martha L. IV, 745
Nixon, Martha L. IV, 772
Nixon, Mary I, 55
Nixon, Mary I, 65
Nixon, Mary I, 68
Nixon, Mary I, 78
Nixon, Mary I, 93
Nixon, Mary I, 109
Nixon, Mary I, 110
Nixon, Mary I, 111
Nixon, Mary I, 135
Nixon, Mary I, 139
Nixon, Mary I, 155
Nixon, Mary I, 156
Nixon, Mary I, 164
Nixon, Mary I, 173
Nixon, Mary I, 181
Nixon, Mary I, 186
Nixon, Mary I, 198
Nixon, Mary I, 662
Nixon, Mary I, 685
Nixon, Mary I, 704
Nixon, Mary I, 712
Nixon, Mary I, 729
Nixon, Mary I, 734
Nixon, Mary I, 828
Nixon, Mary I, 832
Nixon, Mary I, 895
Nixon, Mary I, 896
Nixon, Mary I, 994
Nixon, Mary I Sup 1, 5
Nixon, Mary I Sup 1, 6
Nixon, Mary II, 90
Nixon, Mary II, 297
Nixon, Mary II, 301
Nixon, Mary II, 608
Nixon, Mary IV, 155
Nixon, Mary V, 106
Nixon, Mary V, 246
Nixon, Mary V, 268
Nixon, Mary V, 307
Nixon, Mary V, 350
Nixon, Mary V, 352
Nixon, Mary V, 519
Nixon, Mary V, 522
Nixon, Mary V, 842
Nixon, Mary V, 854
Nixon, Mary V, 974
Nixon, Mary VI, 77
Nixon, Mary VI, 130
Nixon, Mary VI, 133
Nixon, Mary VI, 138
Nixon, Mary VI, 497
Nixon, Mary VI, 539
Nixon, Mary Ada I, 704
Nixon, Mary Ann V, 48
Nixon, Mary Ann V, 106
Nixon, Mary Everigin I, 109
Nixon, Mary F. I, 65
Nixon, Mary Roberts II, 800
Nixon, Mary, Jr. I, 65
Nixon, Maudlin II, 399
Nixon, Mehatabell I, 14
Nixon, Mehetabel I, 64
Nixon, Mehetabel I, 65
Nixon, Mehitabel I, 154
Nixon, Mehitabel I, 155
Nixon, Milicen I, 679
Nixon, Milicent I, 695
Nixon, Milicent I, 704
Nixon, Milicent I, 723
Nixon, Milicent I, 729
Nixon, Milicent I, 832
Nixon, Milicent IV, 285
Nixon, Milicent Adelaid I, 704
Nixon, Milicent J. I, 729
Nixon, Milicent J. I, 737
Nixon, Millicent I, 662
Nixon, Millicent I, 704
Nixon, Millicent I, 729
Nixon, Millison I, 564
Nixon, Miriam I, 108
Nixon, Miriam I, 110
Nixon, Miriam I, 153
Nixon, Miriam I, 155
Nixon, Miriam I, 156
Nixon, Miriam I, 195
Nixon, Miriam I, 198
Nixon, Miriam I, 729
Nixon, Miriam I, 896
Nixon, Morris I, 110
Nixon, Morris I, 156
Nixon, Morriss VI, 75
Nixon, Morriss VI, 77
Nixon, Mrs. Nancy I, 638
Nixon, Nancy I, 729
Nixon, Nancy A. I, 623
Nixon, Nancy A. I, 638
Nixon, Nancy J. I, 719
Nixon, Nancy J. I, 729
Nixon, Narcissa I, 704
Nixon, Narcissa I, 729
Nixon, Narcissa I, 893
Nixon, Narcissa I, 896
Nixon, Nathan I, 35
Nixon, Nathan I, 65
Nixon, Nathan I, 110
Nixon, Nathan I, 155
Nixon, Nathan I, 156
Nixon, Nathan I, 186
Nixon, Nathan I, 189
Nixon, Nathan I, 198
Nixon, Nettie V, 1012
Nixon, Nobert V, 1012
Nixon, Oliver W. V, 106
Nixon, Oreana W. I, 832
Nixon, Orianna Wilson I, 729
Nixon, Orianna Wilson I, 832
Nixon, Orlando I, 339
Nixon, Orlando I, 412
Nixon, Orlando I, 638
Nixon, Orlando I, 946
Nixon, Pearce I, 65
Nixon, Pearce I, 74
Nixon, Pearce I, 704
Nixon, Pegga I, 729
Nixon, Peggy VI, 59
Nixon, Peirce I, 65
Nixon, Peirce I, 110
Nixon, Peirce I, 155
Nixon, Peirce I, 166
Nixon, Peirce V, 246
Nixon, Penina I, 65
Nixon, Penina I, 74
Nixon, Penina V, 106
Nixon, Peninah I, 65
Nixon, Peninah I, 110
Nixon, Peninah I, 155
Nixon, Peninah I, 685
Nixon, Peninah I, 704
Nixon, Peninah I, 729
Nixon, Peninah I, 994
Nixon, Peninah V, 246
Nixon, Peninah V, 307
Nixon, Peninah V, 854
Nixon, Peninah V, 855
Nixon, Peninah V, 974
Nixon, Penninah I, 156
Nixon, Perice I, 65
Nixon, Pheriba I, 186
Nixon, Pheriba I, 190
Nixon, Pheriba I, 198
Nixon, Phinas I, 729
Nixon, Phineas I, 65
Nixon, Phineas I, 93
Nixon, Phineas I, 110
Nixon, Phineas I, 181
Nixon, Phineas I, 555
Nixon, Phineas I, 564
Nixon, Phineas I, 832
Nixon, Phinehas I, 65
Nixon, Phinehas I, 110
Nixon, Phinehas I, 121
Nixon, Phinehas I, 155
Nixon, Phinehas I, 156
Nixon, Phinehas I, 186
Nixon, Phinehas I, 195
Nixon, Phinehas I, 198
Nixon, Phinehas I, 662
Nixon, Phinehas I, 679
Nixon, Phinehas I, 685
Nixon, Phinehas I, 695
Nixon, Phinehas I, 704
Nixon, Phinehas I, 729
Nixon, Phinehas, Jr. I, 704
Nixon, Phinenas, Sr. I, 704
Nixon, Phineus I, 65
Nixon, Phineus I, 68
Nixon, Phinis I, 729
Nixon, Phinnehas I Sup 1, 5
Nixon, Phinnehas I Sup 1, 6
Nixon, Piearce I, 685
Nixon, Pierce I, 155
Nixon, Pierce I, 156
Nixon, Pierce I, 729
Nixon, Pierce I, 994
Nixon, Pirce I, 156
Nixon, Rachel I, 43
Nixon, Rachel I, 65
Nixon, Rachel I, 110
Nixon, Rachel I, 155
Nixon, Rachel I, 187
Nixon, Rachel I, 198
Nixon, Rachel I, 685
Nixon, Rachel II, 400
Nixon, Rachel V, 268
Nixon, Rachel V, 350
Nixon, Rachel V, 352
Nixon, Ratchel I, 994
Nixon, Rebeca VI, 59
Nixon, Rebecca I, 128
Nixon, Rebecca I, 155
Nixon, Rhoda I, 529
Nixon, Rhoda I, 530
Nixon, Rhoda I, 564
Nixon, Rhoda I, 832
Nixon, Rhoda V, 855
Nixon, Robert IV, 285
Nixon, Robert V, 1012
Nixon, Robert Butler I, 831
Nixon, Rodah I, 832
Nixon, Sadie F. V, 1012
Nixon, Samuel I, 43
Nixon, Samuel I, 65
Nixon, Samuel I, 110
Nixon, Samuel I, 123
Nixon, Samuel I, 187
Nixon, Samuel I, 198
Nixon, Samuel I, 529
Nixon, Samuel I, 530
Nixon, Samuel I, 564
Nixon, Samuel I, 831
Nixon, Samuel I, 832
Nixon, Samuel V, 307
Nixon, Samuel V, 352
Nixon, Samuel V, 854
Nixon, Samuel V, 855
Nixon, Samuel V, 974
Nixon, Samuel VI, 116
Nixon, Samuel VI, 138
Nixon, Samuel VI, 769
Nixon, Samuel VI, 770
Nixon, Samuel R. I, 156
Nixon, Samuel R. V, 974
Nixon, Samuel, Jr. V, 106
Nixon, Sarah I, 65
Nixon, Sarah I, 74
Nixon, Sarah I, 93
Nixon, Sarah I, 109
Nixon, Sarah I, 110
Nixon, Sarah I, 111
Nixon, Sarah I, 127
Nixon, Sarah I, 153
Nixon, Sarah I, 154
Nixon, Sarah I, 155
Nixon, Sarah I, 156
Nixon, Sarah I, 159
Nixon, Sarah I, 161
Nixon, Sarah I, 164
Nixon, Sarah I, 166
Nixon, Sarah I, 181
Nixon, Sarah I, 186
Nixon, Sarah I, 193
Nixon, Sarah I, 196
Nixon, Sarah I, 198
Nixon, Sarah V, 106
Nixon, Sarah V, 307
Nixon, Sarah V, 519
Nixon, Sarah V, 829
Nixon, Sarah V, 854
Nixon, Sarah V, 855
Nixon, Sarah V, 880
Nixon, Sarah V, 885
Nixon, Sarah V, 974
Nixon, Sarah V, 1012
Nixon, Sarah VI, 17
Nixon, Sarah VI, 116
Nixon, Sarah A. V, 1012
Nixon, Sarah Ann V, 519
Nixon, Sarah May V, 854
Nixon, Simeon I, 313
Nixon, Simeon I, 339
Nixon, Simmons Creek VI, 116
Nixon, Stephen I, 704
Nixon, Susan I, 832
Nixon, Susanna I, 110
Nixon, Susanna I, 704
Nixon, Susanna V, 106
Nixon, Susannah I, 102
Nixon, Susannah I, 142
Nixon, Susannah I, 147
Nixon, Susannah I, 155
Nixon, Susannah I, 156
Nixon, Susannah I, 729
Nixon, Susannah V, 307
Nixon, Susannah V, 854
Nixon, Susannah V, 855

Nixon, Susannah V, 974
Nixon, Susannah VI, 769
Nixon, Susannah VI, 770
Nixon, Thomas I, 65
Nixon, Thomas I, 74
Nixon, Thomas I, 109
Nixon, Thomas I, 110
Nixon, Thomas I, 155
Nixon, Thomas I, 156
Nixon, Thomas I, 166
Nixon, Thomas I, 186
Nixon, Thomas I, 198
Nixon, Thomas I, 704
Nixon, Thomas I, 709
Nixon, Thomas I, 728
Nixon, Thomas I, 729
Nixon, Thomas I, 734
Nixon, Thomas I, 896
Nixon, Thomas I, 994
Nixon, Thomas II, 399
Nixon, Thomas II, 400
Nixon, Thomas II, 608
Nixon, Thomas IV, 52
Nixon, Thomas V, 106
Nixon, Thomas VI, 59
Nixon, Thomas VI, 77
Nixon, Thomas VI, 116
Nixon, Thomas VI, 138
Nixon, Thomas Jefferson I, 704
Nixon, Tomes I, 198
Nixon, Toms I, 186
Nixon, Wd. Anna V, 63
Nixon, Wd. Magdalen II, 608
Nixon, Wd. Rachel II, 608
Nixon, Widow Jane I, 110
Nixon, Widow Jane I, 167
Nixon, Widow Kezia I, 65
Nixon, Widow Kezia I, 69
Nixon, Widow Keziah I, 62
Nixon, Widow Keziah I, 65
Nixon, Widow Margaret I, 198
Nixon, William I, 110
Nixon, William I, 111
Nixon, William I, 155
Nixon, William I, 156
Nixon, William I, 729
Nixon, William I, 990
Nixon, William I, 994
Nixon, William V, 63
Nixon, William V, 106
Nixon, William V, 268
Nixon, William V, 423
Nixon, William V, 842
Nixon, William V, 854
Nixon, William V, 855
Nixon, William V, 974
Nixon, William E. J. I, 719
Nixon, William E. J. I, 729
Nixon, William E. T. I, 729
Nixon, William M. I, 65
Nixon, William M. I, 156
Nixon, William M. I, 198
Nixon, William Muse I, 110
Nixon, William Muse I, 156
Nixon, William N. I, 81
Nixon, William P. I, 832
Nixon, William Penn I, 729
Nixon, William Penn I, 832
Nixon, Wm. V, 307
Nixon, Wm. V, 924
Nixon, Wm. V, 974
Nixon, Wm. V, 1012
Nixon, Zac. I, 198
Nixon, Zacaria I, 110
Nixon, Zacarias I, 110
Nixon, Zach. I, 65
Nixon, Zach. I, 69
Nixon, Zachariah I, 14
Nixon, Zachariah I, 35
Nixon, Zachariah I, 65
Nixon, Zachariah I, 76
Nixon, Zachariah I, 78
Nixon, Zachariah I, 92
Nixon, Zachariah I, 109
Nixon, Zachariah I, 110
Nixon, Zachariah I, 111
Nixon, Zachariah I, 155
Nixon, Zachariah I, 156
Nixon, Zachariah I, 173
Nixon, Zachariah I, 186
Nixon, Zachariah I, 189
Nixon, Zachariah I, 198
Nixon, Zachariah I, 704
Nixon, Zachariah I, 729
Nixon, Zachariah I Sup 1, 4
Nixon, Zachariah I Sup 1, 5
Nixon, Zachariah, Jr. I, 155
Nixon, Zachariah, Jr. I, 156
Nixon, Zachariah, Sr. I, 54
Nixon, Zachariah, Sr. I, 65
Nixon, Zachariah, Sr. I, 68
Nixon, Zacharias I, 110
Nixon, Zacharias I, 155
Nixon, Zacharias I, 159
Nixon, Zachary I, 14
Nixson, Elizabeth I, 110
Nixson, Elizabeth I, 767
Nixson, Elizabeth I, 994
Nixson, Jemima I, 994
Nixson, Magdalen II, 462
Nixson, Mary I, 110
Nixson, Phineas I, 110
Nixson, Rebeckah I, 110
Nixson, Sarah I, 110
Nixson, Thomas I, 110
Nixson, Thomas II, 400
Nixson, Thomas II, 462
Nixson, Thomas II, 608
Nixson, Wd. Magdalen II, 608
Noah, Dorothy I, 638
Noah, Dorothy I, 642
Noah, Eva V, 195
Noah, J. I. V, 195
Noah, John O. V, 195
Noah, Max I, 638
Nobblitt, Mary I, 994
Noble, Abel II, 400
Noble, Abel II, 446
Noble, Abel II, 608
Noble, Amanda IV, 256
Noble, Ann III, 242
Noble, Anthony II, 400
Noble, Arthur IV, 1177
Noble, Benjamin VI, 969
Noble, Catherine VI, 969
Noble, Eliz. H. III, 242
Noble, Eliza Jane IV, 490
Noble, Elizabeth II, 400
Noble, Elizabeth III, 242
Noble, Elizabeth Hallock III, 242
Noble, Emily Lucile III, 242
Noble, Evelyn III, 431
Noble, Evelyn III, 448
Noble, Frank IV, 1177
Noble, Franklin II, 903
Noble, Franklin III, 147
Noble, Franklin III, 242
Noble, George L. IV, 256
Noble, Grace III, 147
Noble, Grace III, 242
Noble, Irene IV, 1177
Noble, Irene Elizabeth IV, 1177
Noble, Isaac II, 400
Noble, James A. IV, 1177
Noble, James Arthur IV, 1177
Noble, Jennie V, 1012
Noble, Joseph II, 245
Noble, Joseph II, 252
Noble, Joseph II, 261
Noble, Joseph II, 400
Noble, Joseph II, 608
Noble, Joseph II, 682
Noble, Joseph IV, 256
Noble, Joseph VI, 969
Noble, Joshua VI, 888
Noble, Joshua VI, 909
Noble, Joshua VI, 969
Noble, Leroy Eugene III, 242
Noble, Lindsley Hallock III, 242
Noble, Lucy VI, 969
Noble, Lydia II, 608
Noble, Lyman A. IV, 490
Noble, Marianna III, 147
Noble, Marianna III, 242
Noble, Marinda E. VI, 890
Noble, Martha II, 180
Noble, Martha II, 400
Noble, Mary II, 245
Noble, Mary II, 252
Noble, Mary II, 261
Noble, Mary II, 400
Noble, Mary II, 446
Noble, Mary II, 608
Noble, Mary II, 682
Noble, Mary Blanch IV, 1177
Noble, Mary Blanche IV, 1177
Noble, Mary M. IV, 1177
Noble, Nancy VI, 969
Noble, Polly VI, 888
Noble, Ralph IV, 1177
Noble, Richard II, 17
Noble, Richard II, 400
Noble, Rose IV, 490
Noble, Ross IV, 490
Noble, Samuel II, 400
Noble, Samuel II, 608
Noble, Samuel W. III, 242
Noble, Sarah II, 608
Noble, Sarah VI, 969
Noble, Stuart L. IV, 1287
Noble, Thomas Burling III, 242
Noble, Thomas L. III, 147
Noble, Thomas L. III, 242
Noble, Will IV, 256
Noble, William II, 400
Noble, William III, 242
Noble, William IV, 256
Noble, William VI, 888
Noble, William VI, 969
Noble, William H. IV, 256
Noble, Wily VI, 880
Noblet, Abraham I, 412
Noblet, Ann I, 412
Noblet, Anna II, 90
Noblet, John I, 412
Noblet, Jos. I, 971
Noblet, Joseph I, 412
Noblet, Joseph I, 994
Noblet, Joseph II, 90
Noblet, Laetitia II, 63
Noblet, Leatitia II, 79
Noblet, Leatitia II, 90
Noblet, Lettitia II, 90
Noblet, Margaret II, 90
Noblet, Mary I, 376
Noblet, Mary I, 412
Noblet, Mary I, 420
Noblet, Mary II, 90
Noblet, Mary II, 98
Noblet, Rebecca I, 412
Noblet, Rebekah I, 412
Noblet, Thomas I, 1160
Noblet, William I, 412
Noblet, Wm. II, 90
Noblett, Abraham I, 362
Noblett, Abraham I, 832
Noblett, Ann I, 362
Noblett, Anne I, 364
Noblett, John I, 362
Noblett, John I, 364
Noblett, Joseph I, 362
Noblett, Joseph I, 832
Noblett, Mary I, 362
Noblett, Mary I, 364
Noblett, Rebecah I, 832
Noblett, Rebecca I, 362
Noblett, Thomas I, 362
Noblett, William I, 362
Noblett, William I, 832
Noblit, Abraham I, 994
Noblit, Anna II, 88
Noblit, Anna II, 90
Noblit, Joseph I, 994
Noblit, Margaret II, 90
Noblit, Margaret II, 107
Noblit, Mary I, 994
Noblit, Mary II, 70
Noblit, Mary II, 90
Noblit, Rebekah I, 412
Noblit, Rebekah I, 993
Noblit, Rebekah I, 994
Noblit, William I, 994
Noblitt, Abraham I, 832
Noblitt, Joseph II, 90
Noblitt, Lettitia II, 90
Nobrage, Elizabeth IV, 256
Nobrage, John G. IV, 256
Nock, Daniel IV, 542
Nock, Daniel C. IV, 542
Nock, Ezekiel IV, 542
Nock, Jane IV, 542
Nock, Phebe IV, 542
Nock, Rachel IV, 542
Nock, Sarah IV, 542
Nock, William IV, 542
Nock, William VI, 11
Noe, A. L. III, 174
Noe, A. L. III, 242
Noe, Clarence III, 242
Noe, Dinah I, 408
Noe, Dinah I, 412
Noe, James H. III, 174
Noe, James H. III, 242
Noe, Josephine H. III, 174
Noe, Josephine H. III, 242
Noel, Aldrovantus VI, 843
Noel, Ann VI, 843
Noel, Edward VI, 843
Noel, Elizabeth VI, 986
Noel, Fanny VI, 969
Noel, German C. VI, 843
Noel, Jane VI, 843
Noel, John A. VI, 417
Noel, John A. VI, 426
Noel, Lida IV, 1331
Noel, Louisa VI, 426
Noel, Louisa Marie VI, 417
Noel, Lurany VI, 843
Noel, Martha VI, 860
Noel, Mary VI, 843
Noel, Matthew VI, 843
Noel, Polly VI, 843
Noel, Roderick VI, 843
Noel, Simon VI, 969
Noel, Victoria VI, 417
Noel, Victoria VI, 426
Noel, Victoria V. VI, 417
Noell, Addison A. VI, 970
Noell, Alexander J. VI, 970
Noell, Almagro VI, 919
Noell, Almegro VI, 930
Noell, Alonzo VI, 876
Noell, America H. VI, 1015
Noell, Ann VI, 894
Noell, Ann Eliza VI, 970
Noell, Ann Miller VI, 890
Noell, Anne VI, 970
Noell, Caleb VI, 918
Noell, Caleb VI, 970
Noell, Caleb R. VI, 890
Noell, Caleb R. VI, 943
Noell, Candall VI, 860
Noell, Caroline VI, 929
Noell, Catharine VI, 970
Noell, Catharine B. VI, 970
Noell, Catharine N. VI, 917
Noell, Charles VI, 917
Noell, Charles VI, 919
Noell, Charles VI, 1012
Noell, Charles P. VI, 878
Noell, Cornelius VI, 929
Noell, Cornelius VI, 938
Noell, Cornelius VI, 969
Noell, Cornelius, Jr. VI, 951
Noell, Cornelius, Jr. VI, 967
Noell, Cornelius, Jr. VI, 970
Noell, Cornelius, Jr. VI, 1015
Noell, Cornelius, Jr. VI, 1016
Noell, Cornelius, Senr. VI, 912
Noell, Cornelius, Sr. VI, 890
Noell, Cornelius, Sr. VI, 941
Noell, Cornelius, Sr. VI, 943
Noell, Cornelius, Sr. VI, 961
Noell, Cornelius, Sr. VI, 962
Noell, Corns VI, 894
Noell, Corns., Sr. VI, 986
Noell, Dematris A. VI, 876
Noell, Dosha VI, 877
Noell, Doshea VI, 885
Noell, Eleanor VI, 970
Noell, Eliza J. VI, 940
Noell, Elizabeth VI, 919
Noell, Elizabeth T. VI, 970
Noell, Erasmus VI, 970
Noell, Ethelinda L. VI, 970
Noell, Fanny VI, 969
Noell, Frances J. VI, 970
Noell, Frances S. A. VI, 962
Noell, German C. VI, 860
Noell, James VI, 940
Noell, James VI, 962
Noell, James VI, 970
Noell, James VI, 1015
Noell, Jane VI, 849
Noell, Jesse VI, 969
Noell, Jesse VI, 970
Noell, Jesse VI, 986
Noell, Jesse A. VI, 970
Noell, Jesse M. VI, 1000
Noell, John VI, 912
Noell, John VI, 970
Noell, John VI, 1013
Noell, John C. VI, 876
Noell, John C. VI, 1010
Noell, John G. VI, 970
Noell, Joice VI, 860
Noell, Joyce VI, 849
Noell, Judith C. VI, 1000
Noell, Judith M. VI, 970
Noell, Judith S. VI, 894
Noell, Judith Shelton VI, 970
Noell, Kitty VI, 913
Noell, Lafayette VI, 970
Noell, Livingston P. VI, 894
Noell, Maria Elizabeth VI, 943
Noell, Martha H. VI, 985
Noell, Mathew VI, 865
Noell, Miss ??? VI, 938
Noell, Nancy VI, 929
Noell, Nancy VI, 969
Noell, Nancy VI, 970
Noell, Palestine VI, 970
Noell, Pamelia VI, 908
Noell, Peggy VI, 912
Noell, Polly VI, 962
Noell, Polly VI, 970
Noell, Polly B. VI, 1015
Noell, Salley VI, 894
Noell, Sally VI, 962
Noell, Sally M. VI, 918
Noell, Sarah Ann VI, 970
Noell, Sarah C. VI, 951
Noell, Sarah E. VI, 970
Noell, Simon VI, 969
Noell, Simon M. VI, 895
Noell, Simon M. VI, 901
Noell, Susan VI, 961
Noell, Susan VI, 985
Noell, Susan Ann VI, 970
Noell, Thomas VI, 877
Noell, Thomas VI, 908
Noell, Thomas VI, 929
Noell, Thomas VI, 970
Noell, Thomas VI, 971
Noell, Thos. VI, 913
Noell, William VI, 962
Noell, William E. VI, 919
Noell, William E. VI, 985
Noell, William E. VI, 1012
Noftsinger, Abraham VI, 970
Noftsinger, Eliza VI, 970
Noggle, Bell V, 195
Noggle, David V, 195
Noggle, David J. V, 195
Noggle, Ella L. V, 195
Noggle, Ella L. C. V, 195
Noggle, Henry V, 1012
Noggle, Henry O. V, 195
Noggle, Henry S. V, 195
Noggle, Jesse F. V, 195
Noggle, Mary Jane V, 195
Noggle, Myrtle C. V, 195
Noggle, Nannie G. V, 195
Noggle, Pearl C. V, 195
Noggle, Wm. C. V, 195
Nogle, Betsy V, 1012
Nogle, Henry V, 1012
Nogle, Hiram V, 1012
Noice, Elizabeth IV, 1350
Noice, Elizabeth IV, 1374
Nolan, Abram I, 247
Nolan, Belinda I, 14
Nolan, Belinda Maria I, 14
Nolan, Belinda Maria I, 65
Nolan, Bellinda I, 65
Nolan, Evelyn I, 247
Nolan, Evelyn Frances I, 14
Nolan, Evelyn Frances I, 65
Nolan, Evelyn Frances I, 236
Nolan, Evelyn Frances I, 247
Nolan, Henry P. I, 14
Nolan, Henry P. I, 65
Nolan, Henry Peile I, 49
Nolan, Henry Peile I, 65
Nolan, John I, 14
Nolan, John I, 65
Nolan, John Villiers I, 14
Nolan, John Villiers I, 65
Nolan, Josephine I, 65
Nolan, Josephine I, 210
Nolan, Josephine Constance I,
Nolan, Maria I, 14
Nolan, Maria I, 65
Nolan, Mariah I, 247
Nolan, Mariah F. I, 236
Nolan, Mariah F. I, 247
Nolan, Mary I, 49
Nolan, Sarah I, 247
Nolan, Walter E. I, 247
Nolan, Walter Ernest I, 14
Nolan, Walter Ernest I, 65
Nolan, Walter Ernest I, 247
Noland, Belinda Maria I, 65
Noland, Henry P. I, 65
Noland, Mary Ann IV, 1127
Noland, Mary Ann IV, 1137
Noland, Sarah Maria IV, 1127
Noland, Sarah Maria IV, 1137
Nolder, Samuel A. V, 423
Nolder, Samuel M. V, 423
Nolder, Samuel N. V, 423
Nole, Dr. ??? III, 294
Nole, Phebe III, 294
Nole, Rachel III, 294
Nolen, Josephine III, 97
Nolen, Josephine III, 242
Nolton, Jane V, 1012
Nolton, Joseph VI, 200
Nolton, Robt. Pleasants VI, 20
Nolton, Sarah VI, 200
Nolton, Theodore V, 1012
Noltz, Charles V, 700
Noltz, David C. V, 700
Noltz, Dennis D. V, 700
Noltz, Elizabeth V, 700
Noltz, Florence V, 700
Nolwin, Ann T. VI, 843
Nolwin, Thomas VI, 843
Nolye, Charles V, 700
Nolye, Charles H. V, 700
Nolye, David C. V, 700
Nolye, Dennis D. V, 700
Nolye, Dlorence V. V, 700
Nolye, Elizabeth V, 700
Nolye, Florence V, 700

lye, Lewis D. V, 700
ode, ??? III, 242
oks, Susanna II, 608
oks, Susanna II, 641
radyke, Elizabeth I, 564
radyke, Sugar I, 564
rberry, Jane II, 90
rberry, Rebekah II, 53
rberry, Rebekah II, 90
rbury, Nathan II, 400
rbury, Sarah III, 134
rcross, Eliz. III, 240
rcross, Elizabeth II, 258
rcross, Frances VI, 970
rcross, Hannah II, 180
rcross, Hannah II, 245
rcross, Jane II, 245
rcross, John II, 192
rcross, John II, 245
rcross, Joseph II, 245
rcross, Joshua II, 245
rcross, Lucy II, 220
rcross, Lucy II, 245
rcross, Mary II, 192
rcross, Mary II, 245
rcross, Rachel II, 189
rcross, Rachel II, 245
rcross, Rachel II, 275
rcross, Rachel II, 991
rcross, Rachel II, 1018
rcross, Rebecca II, 245
rcross, Rebecca II, 249
rcross, Samuel II, 180
rcross, Samuel II, 245
rcross, Samuel VI, 970
rcross, Sarah II, 245
rcross, Simeon II, 245
rcross, Susannah II, 214
rcross, Susannah II, 245
rcross, William II, 245
rcross, William II, 249
rcross, William II, 258
rd, Paul H. IV, 1331
rdby, Hilma Kindlund III, 213
rder, Hannah IV, 1331
rder, Miss Hanna A. IV, 1331
rdike, Abraham I, 913
rdike, Abraham II, 245
rdike, Charity V, 315
rdike, Henrietta P. V, 106
rdike, Judith I, 832
rdike, Judith I, 835
rdike, Phebe I, 832
rdike, Phebe I, 837
rdike, Sally B. I, 994
rdy, Hilma Kindlund III, 242
rdyke, Aaron B. V, 268
rdyke, Aaron B. V, 325
rdyke, Aaron B. V, 352
rdyke, Aaron B. V, 353
rdyke, Abraham I, 832
rdyke, Abraham I, 909
rdyke, Abraham I, 913
rdyke, Abraham I, 967
rdyke, Abraham I, 994
rdyke, Abraham I, 1044
rdyke, Abraham I, 1050
rdyke, Abraham I, 1129
rdyke, Abraham II, 245
rdyke, Abraham II, 255
rdyke, Abraham V, 106
rdyke, Abraham V, 145
rdyke, Abraham V, 352
rdyke, Abraham, Jr. V, 317
rdyke, Abraham, Jr. V, 352
rdyke, Abram Andrews V, 352
rdyke, Adan I, 1050
rdyke, Aden I, 909
rdyke, Adin I, 821
rdyke, Adin I, 832
rdyke, Adin II, 245
rdyke, Albert V, 424
rdyke, Albert H. V, 268
rdyke, Albert H. V, 423
rdyke, Alice V, 679
rdyke, Alice V, 700
rdyke, Almeda H. V, 700
rdyke, Almedia V, 318
rdyke, Almedia V, 352
rdyke, Almedia V, 353
rdyke, Almedia V, 610
rdyke, Almedia V, 636
rdyke, Almedia V, 700
rdyke, Alpheus V, 352
rdyke, Alpheus V, 353
rdyke, Angeline V, 352
rdyke, Ann V, 260
rdyke, Ann V, 352
rdyke, Ann V, 353
rdyke, Ann V, 419
rdyke, Ann V, 423
Nordyke, Ann V, 424
Nordyke, Ann V, 505
Nordyke, Ann V, 520
Nordyke, Ann Elizabeth V, 700
Nordyke, Ann Elizabeth Henry V, 701
Nordyke, Anna V, 346
Nordyke, Anna V, 347
Nordyke, Anna V, 352
Nordyke, Anna V, 378
Nordyke, Anna V, 424
Nordyke, Anna E. V, 589
Nordyke, Anna J. V, 589
Nordyke, Asa V, 318
Nordyke, Asa V, 342
Nordyke, Asa V, 352
Nordyke, Asa V, 353
Nordyke, Asa V, 610
Nordyke, Asa V, 636
Nordyke, Asa V, 700
Nordyke, Benajah I, 832
Nordyke, Benajah I, 967
Nordyke, Benajah I, 1050
Nordyke, Benajah I, 1129
Nordyke, Benajah II, 245
Nordyke, Benajah V, 352
Nordyke, Benajah V, 353
Nordyke, Benajah V, 505
Nordyke, Benajah V, 520
Nordyke, Benjamin V, 353
Nordyke, Beulah I, 832
Nordyke, Beverley I, 1050
Nordyke, Bulah I, 967
Nordyke, Callie V, 700
Nordyke, Calvin J. V, 268
Nordyke, Caroline V, 353
Nordyke, Caroline V, 700
Nordyke, Caroline E. V, 352
Nordyke, Charity I, 909
Nordyke, Charity I, 1129
Nordyke, Charity V, 268
Nordyke, Charity V, 337
Nordyke, Charity V, 345
Nordyke, Charity V, 352
Nordyke, Charity V, 354
Nordyke, Charity V, 362
Nordyke, Charity V, 636
Nordyke, Charles A. V, 352
Nordyke, Charles M. V, 589
Nordyke, Charley V, 424
Nordyke, Charty I, 1118
Nordyke, Ciciley I, 832
Nordyke, Ciciley I, 837
Nordyke, Clayton B. V, 353
Nordyke, Cyrus V, 352
Nordyke, Daniel I, 832
Nordyke, Daniel I, 967
Nordyke, Daniel I, 1050
Nordyke, David V, 352
Nordyke, David V, 362
Nordyke, Edgar M. V, 352
Nordyke, Edgar M. V, 353
Nordyke, Edgar M. V, 700
Nordyke, Edith I, 927
Nordyke, Edith H. V, 352
Nordyke, Edith H. V, 361
Nordyke, Edmund V, 352
Nordyke, Edmund V, 353
Nordyke, Edward L. V, 352
Nordyke, Edward S. V, 353
Nordyke, Eli M. V, 353
Nordyke, Elias V, 347
Nordyke, Elijah V, 353
Nordyke, Elijah V, 700
Nordyke, Eliza V, 349
Nordyke, Eliza V, 352
Nordyke, Elizabeth I, 832
Nordyke, Elizabeth I, 1129
Nordyke, Elizabeth V, 347
Nordyke, Elizabeth A. V, 332
Nordyke, Elizabeth A. V, 353
Nordyke, Ella V, 353
Nordyke, Ella V, 424
Nordyke, Ella M. V, 700
Nordyke, Ella S. V, 353
Nordyke, Ella S. V, 424
Nordyke, Ellen C. V, 352
Nordyke, Ellis V, 352
Nordyke, Ellwood V, 268
Nordyke, Elmore V, 347
Nordyke, Elmore V, 352
Nordyke, Elwood V, 268
Nordyke, Eunice V, 352
Nordyke, Eunice V, 353
Nordyke, Eunice V, 520
Nordyke, Florence Rosetta V, 589
Nordyke, Frank V, 353
Nordyke, Frank V, 520
Nordyke, Frank V, 700
Nordyke, Frank H. V, 589
Nordyke, Hannah V, 352
Nordyke, Hannah V, 354
Nordyke, Hannah V, 974
Nordyke, Hannah V, 975
Nordyke, Hannah Ellen V, 268
Nordyke, Harriet A. V, 353
Nordyke, Harriet A. V, 700
Nordyke, Harriett V, 700
Nordyke, Harvey D. V, 268
Nordyke, Hattie V, 700
Nordyke, Hattie A. V, 353
Nordyke, Henrietta P. V, 145
Nordyke, Henrietta P. V, 352
Nordyke, Henry V, 352
Nordyke, Henry V, 361
Nordyke, Henry V, 589
Nordyke, Henry V, 595
Nordyke, Herbert V, 353
Nordyke, Hezekiah V, 347
Nordyke, Hezekiah V, 352
Nordyke, Hiram I, 832
Nordyke, Hiram I, 967
Nordyke, Hiram I, 1050
Nordyke, Hiram I, 1129
Nordyke, Hiram V, 106
Nordyke, Hiram V, 268
Nordyke, Hiram V, 352
Nordyke, Ida V, 700
Nordyke, Ida M. V, 589
Nordyke, Inez V, 353
Nordyke, Irene V, 353
Nordyke, Isaac V, 352
Nordyke, Isaac E. V, 352
Nordyke, Isaac E. V, 353
Nordyke, Isabella A. V, 352
Nordyke, Israel I, 832
Nordyke, Israel I, 1050
Nordyke, Israel I, 1129
Nordyke, Israel II, 245
Nordyke, Israel V, 346
Nordyke, Israel V, 347
Nordyke, Israel V, 352
Nordyke, Israel Nordyke V, 347
Nordyke, Isrel I, 832
Nordyke, James V, 352
Nordyke, Jane V, 351
Nordyke, Jane V, 353
Nordyke, Jesse V, 251
Nordyke, Jesse V, 268
Nordyke, Jesse V, 340
Nordyke, Jesse V, 352
Nordyke, John V, 423
Nordyke, John V, 424
Nordyke, John Archer Elmore I, 909
Nordyke, John M. V, 423
Nordyke, John Milton V, 424
Nordyke, Joseph T. V, 353
Nordyke, Joseph Thornburg V, 352
Nordyke, Judith I, 832
Nordyke, Judith I, 909
Nordyke, Judith V, 372
Nordyke, Judith V, 424
Nordyke, Lavina V, 251
Nordyke, Lavina V, 268
Nordyke, Levina V, 268
Nordyke, Levina V, 340
Nordyke, Levina V, 352
Nordyke, Lewis V, 320
Nordyke, Lewis V, 352
Nordyke, Lewis V, 353
Nordyke, Lewis V, 613
Nordyke, Lewis V, 636
Nordyke, Linley M. V, 268
Nordyke, Loran V, 353
Nordyke, Loren V, 353
Nordyke, Luther V, 423
Nordyke, Luther V, 424
Nordyke, Lydia Ann V, 347
Nordyke, Lydia J. V, 352
Nordyke, Lydia J. V, 362
Nordyke, Margaret V, 351
Nordyke, Margaret V, 353
Nordyke, Maria V, 347
Nordyke, Martha I, 821
Nordyke, Martha I, 832
Nordyke, Martha I, 907
Nordyke, Martha I, 909
Nordyke, Martha I, 913
Nordyke, Martha Helen V, 352
Nordyke, Mary I, 832
Nordyke, Mary I, 909
Nordyke, Mary I, 967
Nordyke, Mary I, 1050
Nordyke, Mary I, 1129
Nordyke, Mary II, 245
Nordyke, Mary II, 255
Nordyke, Mary V, 106
Nordyke, Mary V, 327
Nordyke, Mary V, 337
Nordyke, Mary V, 346
Nordyke, Mary V, 352
Nordyke, Mary V, 397
Nordyke, Mary V, 423
Nordyke, Mary V, 700
Nordyke, Mary A. V, 353
Nordyke, Mary Angelina V, 352
Nordyke, Mary Ann V, 324
Nordyke, Mary Ann V, 352
Nordyke, Mary Anna V, 424
Nordyke, Mary B. V, 353
Nordyke, Mary Bell V, 352
Nordyke, Mary E. V, 268
Nordyke, Mary Elizabeth V, 268
Nordyke, Mary Emeline V, 347
Nordyke, Mary F. V, 700
Nordyke, Mary Frances V, 352
Nordyke, Mary Frances V, 353
Nordyke, Mary H. V, 342
Nordyke, Mary H. V, 352
Nordyke, Mary Isabel V, 353
Nordyke, Micaijah I, 967
Nordyke, Micajah I, 832
Nordyke, Micajah I, 1050
Nordyke, Micajah I, 1118
Nordyke, Micajah I, 1129
Nordyke, Micajah V, 268
Nordyke, Micajah V, 337
Nordyke, Micajah V, 345
Nordyke, Micajah V, 352
Nordyke, Micajah V, 354
Nordyke, Micajah V, 362
Nordyke, Micajah V, 589
Nordyke, Micajah V, 636
Nordyke, Micajah V, 700
Nordyke, Michael V, 352
Nordyke, Milton V, 353
Nordyke, Milton H. V, 700
Nordyke, Milton Henry V, 700
Nordyke, Morgan V, 347
Nordyke, Morgan E. V, 352
Nordyke, Morgan Elmore V, 352
Nordyke, Mycajah I, 1129
Nordyke, Nancy V, 424
Nordyke, Nellie V, 520
Nordyke, Nora E. V, 589
Nordyke, Phebe I, 832
Nordyke, Phebe I, 909
Nordyke, Phebe I, 967
Nordyke, Phebe I, 1050
Nordyke, Phebe I, 1118
Nordyke, Phebe I, 1129
Nordyke, Phebe V, 345
Nordyke, Phebe V, 352
Nordyke, Phebe V, 361
Nordyke, Phebe V, 589
Nordyke, Phebe V, 595
Nordyke, Rachel V, 320
Nordyke, Rachel V, 353
Nordyke, Rachel A. V, 353
Nordyke, Rachel A. V, 613
Nordyke, Rachel A. V, 636
Nordyke, Rachel Ann V, 353
Nordyke, Rachel M. V, 636
Nordyke, Rebecca V, 347
Nordyke, Rebecca V, 353
Nordyke, Rhoda V, 352
Nordyke, Rhoda Ann V, 352
Nordyke, Robert I, 832
Nordyke, Robert I, 909
Nordyke, Sally B. I, 913
Nordyke, Sally B. I, 994
Nordyke, Sally B. I, 1000
Nordyke, Samuel V, 352
Nordyke, Sarah I, 1129
Nordyke, Sarah V, 325
Nordyke, Sarah V, 352
Nordyke, Sarah V, 362
Nordyke, Sarah V, 372
Nordyke, Sarah V, 424
Nordyke, Sarah Bell I, 909
Nordyke, Sarah Emily V, 268
Nordyke, Sarah J. V, 353
Nordyke, Sary Emly V, 268
Nordyke, Sicily I, 909
Nordyke, Solomon V, 423
Nordyke, Solomon V, 424
Nordyke, Susanna B. V, 353
Nordyke, Susannah B. V, 352
Nordyke, Sylvanus V, 353
Nordyke, Sylvester V, 423
Nordyke, Sylvester V, 424
Nordyke, Sylvester B. V, 424
Nordyke, Thomas Johnson I, 909
Nordyke, Thomas K. V, 353
Nordyke, Thomas R. V, 352
Nordyke, Thomas R. V, 353
Nordyke, Thos. R. V, 332
Nordyke, Thos. R. V, 353
Nordyke, Unice V, 353
Nordyke, William V, 347
Nordyke, William Lewis V, 347
Nordyke, Wm. V, 347
Nordyke, Wm. M. V, 353
Norgrave, Gertrude C. II, 811
Norgrave, Malinda Phebe II, 811
Norgrave, Malinda Phebe II, 841
Norgrave, Malinda Phebe II, 903
Norgrave, Mary Jane II, 841
Norgrave, Mary Jane II, 903
Norgrave, Thos. A. II, 841
Norgrave, Thos. A. II, 903
Norgrave, Woodward Thomas II, 811
Norgrave, Woodward Thomas II, 841
Norgrave, Woodward Thomas II, 903
Noridike, Elizabeth I, 832
Noridyke, Hiram V, 268
Noriss, Hannah II, 400
Noriss, Isaac II, 400
Noriss, Mary II, 400
Noriss, Rachel II, 400
Noriss, Thomas II, 400
Norling, Coyt IV, 911
Norling, Lewis IV, 912
Norling, Mary A. IV, 912
Norman, Alfred VI, 970
Norman, Ann VI, 216
Norman, Ann VI, 261
Norman, Charles IV, 1331
Norman, Charles VI, 200
Norman, Charles VI, 216
Norman, Charles VI, 261
Norman, Charles Lightfoot VI, 261
Norman, Chas. A. IV, 1331
Norman, Cora Lee IV, 1331
Norman, Daniel V, 1012
Norman, Deborah Ann VI, 261
Norman, Eliza VI, 261
Norman, Eliza Pleasants VI, 261
Norman, Elizabeth II, 787
Norman, Estelle VI, 679
Norman, Estelle VI, 686
Norman, Florence IV, 1287
Norman, George W. IV, 256
Norman, Hannah VI, 216
Norman, Henry H. VI, 686
Norman, Henry H. VI, 689
Norman, Jean Gore VI, 539
Norman, Lydia I, 685
Norman, Margaret I, 1062
Norman, Margaret VI, 487
Norman, Margaret VI, 539
Norman, Mary II, 811
Norman, Mary G. II, 903
Norman, Mary Hannah VI, 686
Norman, Mary Hannah VI, 689
Norman, Mary Leake VI, 970
Norman, Mary S. II, 903
Norman, Mildred VI, 200
Norman, Rena I, 924
Norman, Samuel VI, 200
Norman, Samuel VI, 261
Normand, Cora Lee IV, 1331
Normand, Jean Gore VI, 539
Normandy, Herndon M. VI, 762
Normandy, Herndon Myers VI, 762
Normandy, Herndon Myers VI, 769
Normandy, Ruth Anna VI, 762
Normandy, Ruth Anna VI, 769
Normant, Ann VI, 200
Normant, Charles VI, 200
Normant, Deborah Ann VI, 200
Normant, Elizabeth VI, 200
Normant, Lightfoot VI, 200
Normart, Anna R. II, 714
Normart, Anna R. II, 718
Normart, Frank M. II, 714
Normart, Frank M. II, 718
Normart, Joseph John II, 714
Normart, Lydia B. II, 714
Normart, Mary II, 714
Normart, Mary II, 718
Normart, Mary T. II, 714
Norment, Ann VI, 200
Norment, Betsy G. VI, 200
Norment, Charles VI, 200
Norment, Charles Lightfoot VI, 200
Norment, Charles Lightfoot VI, 261
Norment, Deborah Ann VI, 200
Norment, Eliza VI, 200
Norment, Elizabeth VI, 200
Norment, Elizabeth VI, 209
Norment, John VI, 200
Norment, Lightfoot VI, 200
Norment, Mildred VI, 200

Norment, Nancy VI, 200
Norment, Samuel VI, 200
Norment, Samuel VI, 261
Norodyke, Abraham V, 106
Norodyke, Benejah V, 106
Norodyke, Charity V, 106
Norodyke, Elijah V, 106
Norodyke, Henrietta P. V, 106
Norodyke, Hezekiah V, 106
Norodyke, Hiram V, 106
Norodyke, Isaac V, 106
Norodyke, Israel V, 106
Norodyke, Mary V, 106
Norodyke, Micajah V, 106
Norodyke, Phebe V, 106
Norodyke, Sarah V, 106
Norres, Isaac II, 584
Norres, Isaac II, 608
Norres, Sarah II, 584
Norres, Sarah II, 608
Norrigan, Elizabeth V, 195
Norris, Ann IV, 345
Norris, Ann Caroline II, 400
Norris, Augustus C. II, 148
Norris, Augustus C. II, 154
Norris, Benjamin II, 400
Norris, Benjamin VI, 568
Norris, Benjamin F. VI, 539
Norris, Bert V, 1012
Norris, Burgoine V, 1012
Norris, Calista V, 1012
Norris, Charles II, 245
Norris, Charles II, 252
Norris, Charles II, 400
Norris, Charles II, 527
Norris, Charles II, 584
Norris, Charles II, 608
Norris, Cordelia D. VI, 539
Norris, Cordelia D. VI, 568
Norris, Cornelia L. VI, 762
Norris, Daniel VI, 540
Norris, Debby II, 584
Norris, Debby II, 608
Norris, Deborah II, 400
Norris, Edgar J. II, 903
Norris, Elizabeth II, 245
Norris, Elizabeth II, 400
Norris, Elizabeth II, 516
Norris, Elizabeth II, 608
Norris, Elizabeth IV, 256
Norris, Elizabeth IV, 373
Norris, Elizabeth IV, 424
Norris, Elizabeth F. II, 154
Norris, Elizabeth Fox II, 400
Norris, Elizabeth G. IV, 256
Norris, Elizabeth Hill II, 527
Norris, Elizabeth Hill II, 608
Norris, Elizabeth Lippincott II, 148
Norris, Elizabeth Lippincott II, 154
Norris, Ellen II, 400
Norris, Ellen II, 608
Norris, Ellis V, 1012
Norris, Emily II, 400
Norris, Emily II, 608
Norris, Emma V, 1012
Norris, Eugene Wesley III, 242
Norris, Floyd IV, 256
Norris, Frances III, 242
Norris, Frances VI, 844
Norris, Geo. V, 1012
Norris, George II, 608
Norris, George V, 1012
Norris, George W. II, 400
Norris, Hannah II, 400
Norris, Hannah II, 543
Norris, Hannah II, 608
Norris, Hannah II, 691
Norris, Hannah II, 714
Norris, Hannah V, 1012
Norris, Hannah Fox II, 400
Norris, Hannah Wood II, 714
Norris, Harold IV, 256
Norris, Harriet S. V, 1012
Norris, Harriett V, 1012
Norris, Helen II, 798
Norris, Henry II, 608
Norris, Hershel Augustus II, 148
Norris, Hershel Augustus II, 154
Norris, Humphrey II, 400
Norris, Humphrey II, 608
Norris, Humphrey II, 686
Norris, Isaac II, 245
Norris, Isaac II, 252
Norris, Isaac II, 400
Norris, Isaac II, 543
Norris, Isaac II, 583
Norris, Isaac II, 608
Norris, Isaac II, 714
Norris, Isaac, Jr. II, 608
Norris, James II, 400
Norris, Jane IV, 542
Norris, Jane R. IV, 542
Norris, Jesse V, 1012
Norris, Joel VI, 539
Norris, Joel VI, 568
Norris, John II, 400
Norris, John II, 446
Norris, John V, 1012
Norris, John VI, 844
Norris, John W. V, 1012
Norris, Joseph I, 313
Norris, Joseph II, 400
Norris, Joseph P. II, 400
Norris, Joseph P., Jr. II, 608
Norris, Joseph Parker II, 400
Norris, Joseph Parker II, 516
Norris, Joseph Parker II, 527
Norris, Joseph Parker II, 608
Norris, Libie V, 1012
Norris, Lillie V, 1012
Norris, Lloyd II, 608
Norris, Lula M. IV, 1259
Norris, Lulu M. IV, 1259
Norris, Lydia H. II, 148
Norris, Lydia H. II, 154
Norris, Maggie V, 1012
Norris, Margaret II, 245
Norris, Margaret II, 252
Norris, Margaret II, 400
Norris, Margaret II, 608
Norris, Margrett II, 400
Norris, Mary II, 90
Norris, Mary II, 245
Norris, Mary II, 400
Norris, Mary II, 446
Norris, Mary II, 505
Norris, Mary II, 527
Norris, Mary II, 583
Norris, Mary II, 584
Norris, Mary II, 608
Norris, Mary V, 1012
Norris, Mary Ann II, 714
Norris, Mary P. II, 516
Norris, Mary P. II, 608
Norris, Mary Parker II, 400
Norris, Mary, Jr. II, 536
Norris, Miriam II, 57
Norris, Miriam II, 90
Norris, Moses II, 400
Norris, Nancy II, 400
Norris, Pleasant IV, 336
Norris, Pleasant IV, 344
Norris, Prudence II, 400
Norris, Rachel II, 400
Norris, Rachel II, 608
Norris, Rachel II, 686
Norris, Rachel VI, 539
Norris, Rachel VI, 568
Norris, Rebecca II, 811
Norris, Rebeka II, 400
Norris, Rose IV, 256
Norris, Ruby IV, 256
Norris, Ruth II, 245
Norris, Sally II, 506
Norris, Samuel II, 400
Norris, Samuel II, 608
Norris, Sarah II, 400
Norris, Sarah II, 481
Norris, Sarah II, 608
Norris, Sarah VI, 540
Norris, Sarah Ann VI, 539
Norris, Sarah Ann VI, 568
Norris, Sylvanus V, 1012
Norris, Sytanis Calista J. V, 1012
Norris, Tabitha IV, 80
Norris, Tabitha IV, 104
Norris, Tallie V, 1012
Norris, Thomas II, 90
Norris, Thomas II, 400
Norris, Thomas II, 608
Norris, Thomas Lloyd II, 400
Norris, Thos. II, 57
Norris, Thos. II, 90
Norris, William II, 714
Norriss, Hannah II, 400
Norriss, Humphrey II, 400
Norriss, Isaac II, 400
Norriss, James II, 446
Norriss, John II, 446
Norriss, Joseph II, 400
Norriss, Margaret II, 400
Norriss, Mary II, 400
Norriss, Rachel II, 400
Norriss, Rachel II, 446
Norriss, Rebecka II, 446
Norriss, Sarah II, 446
Norriss, Thomas II, 400
Norros, Mary II, 90
Norsworthy, George VI, 32
Nort, John VI, 994
North, Abel II, 903
North, Abel IV, 649
North, Abraham VI, 942
North, Abraham VI, 962
North, Abraham VI, 970
North, Abraham VI, 987
North, Abraham R. VI, 844
North, Abram VI, 985
North, Abram. VI, 873
North, Ada V, 1013
North, Ann I, 987
North, Ann I, 994
North, Ann VI, 844
North, Ann Smith VI, 758
North, Ann Smith VI, 764
North, Annie V, 1013
North, Anthony VI, 853
North, Anthony A. VI, 846
North, Anthony W. VI, 861
North, Arthur C. VI, 801
North, Bessie V, 1013
North, Betsey VI, 962
North, Catherine VI, 844
North, Charity V, 756
North, Daniel I, 994
North, David VI, 919
North, David VI, 970
North, David VI, 978
North, David VI, 986
North, Dolly VI, 844
North, Dorothy VI, 840
North, Edney Elizabeth VI, 915
North, Elizabeth IV, 649
North, Elizabeth IV, 652
North, Elizabeth IV, 745
North, Elizabeth IV, 835
North, Elizabeth IV, 983
North, Elizabeth VI, 818
North, Elizabeth VI, 844
North, Elizabeth VI, 970
North, Ellie V, 1013
North, Emily II, 715
North, Esther V, 1013
North, Fenton VI, 841
North, Gustavious IV, 835
North, Gustavis IV, 745
North, Gustavus IV, 745
North, Gustavus IV, 983
North, Ira V, 1012
North, Ira V, 1013
North, Irena V, 1013
North, Isaac V, 1013
North, James VI, 844
North, James O. VI, 844
North, Jesse IV, 649
North, Jesse IV, 652
North, Jesse IV, 745
North, Jesse IV, 835
North, Jesse IV, 983
North, John IV, 649
North, John IV, 745
North, John IV, 835
North, John IV, 983
North, John VI, 873
North, John VI, 910
North, John VI, 919
North, John VI, 937
North, John VI, 942
North, John VI, 949
North, John R. VI, 978
North, John R. VI, 986
North, John, Jr. VI, 970
North, Kezia I, 994
North, Keziah I, 800
North, Keziah I, 832
North, Loretta V, 1013
North, Lydia II, 608
North, Lydia II, 627
North, Margaret IV, 649
North, Maria Ann B. VI, 970
North, Martha VI, 861
North, Martha J. V, 1013
North, Martha Jane V, 1012
North, Mary VI, 844
North, Mary VI, 915
North, Mary E. V, 1013
North, Mary E. VI, 853
North, Mary Jane IV, 649
North, Mary Jane IV, 745
North, Mary Jane IV, 829
North, Mary Jane IV, 835
North, Mary Jane IV, 983
North, Mary L. IV, 745
North, May V, 1013
North, Minnie V, 1013
North, Nancy VI, 840
North, Nancy VI, 844
North, Nancy VI, 873
North, Nancy VI, 978
North, Owen L. VI, 844
North, Patsey VI, 942
North, Pearl V, 1013
North, Permelia M. VI, 910
North, Peter VI, 844
North, Polly VI, 818
North, Polly VI, 970
North, Poly VI, 937
North, Rachel I, 994
North, Rachel I, 999
North, Rachel II, 903
North, Richard II, 608
North, Richard VI, 844
North, Ruth II, 400
North, Ruth II, 478
North, Ruth II, 608
North, Sally VI, 919
North, Sally VI, 987
North, Sarah I, 274
North, Sarah II, 608
North, Sarah II, 624
North, Sarah IV, 649
North, Sarah IV, 745
North, Sarah IV, 804
North, Sarah IV, 835
North, Sarah IV, 983
North, Sarah VI, 844
North, Sarah L. VI, 844
North, Sarah L. VI, 937
North, Sarah Povall VI, 949
North, Sarah S. II, 460
North, Sarah S. II, 608
North, Susanna V, 1012
North, Susanna V, 1013
North, Susanna VI, 985
North, Susanna VI, 986
North, Susannah C. VI, 841
North, Thomas V, 1013
North, Thomas VI, 807
North, Thomas VI, 844
North, Thomas VI, 853
North, Thomas VI, 861
North, Thomas VI, 950
North, Thomas A. VI, 861
North, Thos., Jr. VI, 1013
North, William VI, 844
North, William VI, 901
North, William VI, 970
Northall, Rebecca M. III, 102
Northam, Emily Ann I, 682
Northam, Emily Ann I, 685
Northam, Matilda I, 685
Northam, Matilda I, 690
Northcote, Mrs. Wm. IV, 1331
Northcott, Anna W. IV, 1331
Northcott, Annie IV, 1320
Northcott, Mrs. Wm. IV, 1331
Northdike, Abraham I, 1044
Northdike, Aden I, 1044
Northdike, Benajah I, 1044
Northdike, Beulah I, 1044
Northdike, Daniel I, 1044
Northdike, Hiram I, 1044
Northdike, Israel I, 1044
Northdike, Mary I, 1044
Northdike, Micajah I, 1044
Northdike, Phebe I, 1044
Northrop, Anna III, 78
Northrop, Anna III, 242
Northrop, Annie III, 78
Northrop, Annie Claire III, 242
Northrop, Eaton B. III, 78
Northrop, Eaton B. III, 242
Northrop, Eleanor III, 242
Northrop, John III, 242
Northrop, Sarah Ann III, 2÷2
Northrup, ??? III, 352
Northrup, Eleanor III, 242
Northrup, John III, 242
Northrup, Sarah Ann III, 242
Northrup, Sarah Ann III, 352
Northstein, Clara IV, 1259
Northstein, Edith IV, 1259
Northstein, Elizabeth Miller IV, 1259
Northstein, Mable IV, 1259
Norton, Almena III, 404
Norton, Almena III, 431
Norton, Amelia III, 166
Norton, Amelia III, 242
Norton, Ann I, 662
Norton, Ann I, 767
Norton, Ann I, 1129
Norton, Anna I, 913
Norton, Anna I, 914
Norton, Anna Jane I, 910
Norton, Anson III, 404
Norton, Anson III, 431
Norton, Charles E. III, 166
Norton, Charles E. III, 242
Norton, Chas. E. III, 166
Norton, Denis I, 595
Norton, Dennis I, 662
Norton, Dennis I, 910
Norton, Dennis I, 911
Norton, Dennis I, 913
Norton, Edward I, 412
Norton, Edward I, 564
Norton, Edward I, 662
Norton, Edward I, 685
Norton, Edward I, 913
Norton, Edward VI, 524
Norton, Edward VI, 540
Norton, Elizabeth I, 412
Norton, Elizabeth I, 526
Norton, Elizabeth I, 564
Norton, Elizabeth I, 662
Norton, Elizabeth I, 674
Norton, Elizabeth I, 685
Norton, Elizabeth I, 741
Norton, Elizabeth I, 767
Norton, Elizabeth I, 913
Norton, Elizabeth VI, 464
Norton, Elizabeth VI, 540
Norton, Elizabeth Caroline I, 9
Norton, Gains III, 242
Norton, George III, 428
Norton, George III, 431
Norton, Grace II, 608
Norton, Hannah III, 242
Norton, Jacob Janney VI, 540
Norton, Jesse I, 662
Norton, John V, 700
Norton, John H. V, 700
Norton, Jonathan II, 608
Norton, Lidia II, 90
Norton, Lidia II, 245
Norton, Margaret I, 378
Norton, Margaret I, 412
Norton, Margaret V, 395
Norton, Margaret V, 424
Norton, Margaret VI, 540
Norton, Margery II, 608
Norton, Maria A. III, 404
Norton, Maria A. III, 431
Norton, Mary I, 685
Norton, Mary I, 690
Norton, Mary II, 545
Norton, Mary II, 608
Norton, Mary II, 609
Norton, Mary III, 242
Norton, Mary III, 428
Norton, Mary III, 431
Norton, Mary VI, 477
Norton, Mary VI, 540
Norton, Rachel IV, 1056
Norton, Rachel IV, 1070
Norton, Richard I, 564
Norton, Richard I, 645
Norton, Richard I, 662
Norton, Richard I, 767
Norton, Richard I, 913
Norton, Robert III, 242
Norton, Samuel II, 609
Norton, Sarah I, 910
Norton, Sarah I, 911
Norton, Sarah I, 913
Norton, Sarah II, 400
Norton, Wd. Mary VI, 476
Norton, Wd. Mary VI, 524
Norton, William I, 412
Norton, William I, 564
Norton, William I, 662
Norton, Wm. II, 545
Norton, Wm. II, 608
Norton, Wm. II, 609
Norton, Wm. VI, 540
Norton, Wm., Jr. II, 608
Norus, Elizabeth II, 203
Norvald, Grace Kersey V, 700
Norvald, Gretchen V, 700
Norvald, Harriet B. V, 700
Norvald, Harriett V, 700
Norvald, John V, 700
Norvald, John R. V, 700
Norvald, John, Jr. V, 700
Norvall, Elizabeth VI, 802
Norvall, Will. VI, 802
Norvell, E. B. VI, 805
Norvell, George, Jr. VI, 970
Norvell, John VI, 970
Norvell, Lorenzo VI, 995
Norvell, Mary VI, 805
Norvell, Nancy VI, 970
Norvell, Polly VI, 844
Norvell, Reuben VI, 844
Norvell, Sophia R. VI, 970
Norvell, Will VI, 867
Norvell, William VI, 865
Norville, Jessie IV, 1287
Norwood, Annah II, 798
Norwood, Cornelia Frances I, 61
Norwood, Elizabeth I, 264
Norwood, Lucy I, 615

rwood, Nettie I, 247
rwood, Susann I, 247
rwood, Theaophilas I, 264
rwood, Theaophilas I, 274
rwood, W. J. I, 247
rwood, William I, 615
rwood, William G. I, 247
strand, ??? III, 479
strand, Ann III, 491
strand, Daniel III, 493
strand, Fannie III, 491
strand, Hewlett III, 491
strand, Jacob T. III, 431
strand, Jemima III, 491
strand, John R. III, 491
strand, Rachel III, 479
strand, Rachel III, 491
strand, Sarah Ann III, 431
strand, Sarah P. III, 491
strand, Susannah III, 491
strand, Susannah III, 493
thstine, Henry IV, 1259
tman, Henry T. III, 242
tman, Henry T. III, 282
tman, Josephine R. III, 242
tman, Josephine R. III, 282
tshire, Claude IV, 1259
tshire, Della IV, 1259
tshire, Hevy IV, 1259
tshire, Mary E. IV, 1259
tshire, Noble IV, 1259
ttingham, Joseph III, 242
ttingham, Mary II, 609
ttingham, Mary III, 242
ttingham, Samuel II, 609
ttingham, Samuel III, 242
urse, Rebecca II, 603
urse, Rebecca II, 609
wrold, Harriett V, 661
wrold, John V, 661
well, Fanny VI, 971
wland, Mary VI, 839
wlin, Bryan W. VI, 863
wlin, Elizabeth H. VI, 970
wlin, Elizabeth S. VI, 844
wlin, Fanny VI, 844
wlin, James H. VI, 844
wlin, James H. VI, 970
wlin, Jane VI, 970
wlin, Jemima Claywell VI, 827
wlin, Malinda B. VI, 844
wlin, Matthew B. VI, 970
wlin, Robert W. VI, 844
wlin, Samuel VI, 844
wlin, Samuel John Nelson VI, 1019
wlin, Sarah VI, 827
wlin, Sarah VI, 1019
x, Elizabeth I, 349
x, Mary I, 349
x, Thomas I, 349
yes, ??? III, 242
yes, ??? III, 243
yes, Bessie V, 424
yes, Caroline III, 242
yes, Caroline III, 361
yes, Caroline J. III, 222
yes, Catharine III, 159
yes, Clara G. III, 222
yes, Clara G. III, 242
yes, Estella V, 424
yes, George V, 424
yes, Georgia V, 424
yes, Glen H. III, 222
yes, Glen H. III, 242
yes, Glen H. III, 361
yes, Henry T. III, 242
yes, Henry T. III, 357
yes, Kate J. III, 159
yes, Kate J. III, 242
yes, Lucinda III, 242
yes, Lucinda III, 357
yes, Mary V, 424
yes, Sybil J. III, 147
yes, Sybil J. III, 243
yes, T. Wilson III, 222
yes, T. Wilson III, 242
yes, William V, 424
by, Ruth I, 153
cem, Luke I, 728
cum, Nancy VI, 810
dd, Ella Abby VI, 749
gan, Poly Enos VI, 970
gan, Richard VI, 970
gent, Eunice V, 320
ll, Amy IV, 1259
ll, Clara IV, 1259
ll, Emma IV, 1259
ll, George IV, 1259
ll, Joseph F. V, 1013
ll, William IV, 1259
Nullinger, Eva S. IV, 1331
Nullinger, Fred E. IV, 1331
Numan, Barberry VI, 1015
Numan, Geret VI, 898
Numan, Marget VI, 917
Numan, Nimrod VI, 810
Numan, Rebecca VI, 810
Numan, Rosenah VI, 917
Nume, John V, 353
Nume, John W. V, 353
Nume, Ora V, 353
Numo, Thomas J. VI, 908
Nunn, Catharine V, 636
Nunn, Marion V, 636
Nunn, Martha V, 636
Nunn, Mary V, 636
Nunn, Milton O. V, 636
Nunnally, Elizabeth VI, 970
Nunnally, Joshua D. VI, 844
Nunnally, June VI, 844
Nunnally, Richard VI, 970
Nunnally, Sophia A. VI, 844
Nunnally, William B. VI, 844
Nunnally, Wishington VI, 970
Nunnery, Ch VI, 970
Nunnery, Polly VI, 970
Nuse, Charles III, 243
Nuse, George III, 103
Nuse, George III, 243
Nuse, Harriett Alida III, 103
Nuse, Harriett Alida III, 243
Nuse, Mary III, 243
Nuson, Nathaniel VI, 933
Nut, Elizabeth IV, 649
Nut, Hannah IV, 649
Nut, Jonathan IV, 649
Nut, Rebekah VI, 467
Nutler, Carl IV, 1331
Nutler, Henry V, 924
Nutt, Aaron V, 106
Nutt, Ann II, 245
Nutt, Ann II, 966
Nutt, Ann II, 997
Nutt, Ann II, 1016
Nutt, Ann II, 1018
Nutt, Ann II, 1040
Nutt, Ann C. V, 53
Nutt, Ann C. V, 106
Nutt, E. N. IV, 1177
Nutt, Edmond II, 995
Nutt, Edmond II, 1018
Nutt, Edmund II, 1018
Nutt, Edmund II, 1040
Nutt, Elizabeth II, 989
Nutt, Elizabeth II, 995
Nutt, Elizabeth II, 1018
Nutt, Elizabeth IV, 649
Nutt, Elizabeth VI, 474
Nutt, Elizabeth VI, 540
Nutt, Elizabeth VI, 574
Nutt, George V, 1013
Nutt, Hannah IV, 52
Nutt, Hannah IV, 60
Nutt, Hannah IV, 104
Nutt, Hannah V, 1013
Nutt, Hannah VI, 540
Nutt, John II, 966
Nutt, John II, 989
Nutt, John II, 1018
Nutt, John, Jr. II, 1018
Nutt, Jonathan II, 966
Nutt, Jonathan II, 995
Nutt, Jonathan II, 997
Nutt, Jonathan II, 1011
Nutt, Jonathan II, 1018
Nutt, Jonathan II, 1040
Nutt, Jonathan IV, 649
Nutt, Jonathan VI, 540
Nutt, Jonathan VI, 574
Nutt, Joseph II, 1018
Nutt, Joseph II, 1040
Nutt, Joseph VI, 540
Nutt, Joseph, Jr. VI, 540
Nutt, Martha II, 966
Nutt, Martha V, 44
Nutt, Martha V, 106
Nutt, Mary II, 704
Nutt, Mary II, 719
Nutt, Mary II, 966
Nutt, Mary II, 982
Nutt, Mary II, 1018
Nutt, Mary V, 106
Nutt, Rebecca II, 723
Nutt, Rebecca II, 1018
Nutt, Rebecca VI, 540
Nutt, Rebecca VI, 544
Nutt, Rebeckah II, 1018
Nutt, Rebeckah II, 1040
Nutt, Rebekah VI, 540
Nutt, Sarah III, 243
Nutt, Sarah III, 431
Nutt, Susannah II, 966
Nutt, Susannah II, 975
Nutt, Susannah II, 1011
Nutt, Susannah II, 1018
Nutt, Susannah VI, 503
Nutt, Susannah VI, 540
Nutt, Thomas II, 1018
Nutt, Thomas VI, 540
Nutt, Wd. Ann II, 245
Nutt, Wd. Elizabeth II, 1016
Nutt, Wd. Elizabeth II, 1018
Nuzum, George IV, 104
Nuzum, Hannah IV, 104
Nuzum, Richard IV, 104
Nuzum, William IV, 104
Nye, Achsah III, 498
Nye, Eunice V, 898
Nye, Eunice V, 924
Nyhart, Hattie IV, 256
Nyholm, ??? III, 243
Nyholm, Fred H. III, 87
Nyholm, Fred H. III, 243
Nyholm, Frederick Howard, Jr. III, 243
Nyholm, Hannah Maria III, 46
Nyholm, Hannah Marie III, 243
Nyholm, Lillian Florence III, 243
Nyholm, Marion H. III, 87
Nyholm, Marion H. III, 243
Nyholm, Sarah R. III, 87

O'Brian, Betsey VI, 869
O'Brian, David V, 106
O'Brian, Elizabeth II, 195
O'Brian, Elizabeth II, 246
O'Brian, Elizabeth V, 106
O'Brian, Esther V, 106
O'Brian, Jonothan V, 106
O'Brian, Lucy I, 642
O'Brian, Mary V, 106
O'Brian, Mary VI, 985
O'Brian, Mathew VI, 985
O'Brian, Nancy V, 106
O'Brian, Rebecca V, 106
O'Brian, Susanna VI, 869
O'Brian, Thomas V, 106
O'Brian, Thomas V, 520
O'Brian, Thos. V, 924
O'Brian, William VI, 869
O'Brien, Ignatius Jerome III, 243
O'Brien, John IV, 959
O'Brien, Mary E. IV, 981
O'Brien, Mary Ellen IV, 959
O'Brien, Mary J. III, 243
O'Brien, Rhoda VI, 970
O'Brien, Sarah III, 243
O'Brien, Thomas V, 106
O'Brien, William VI, 970
O'Connel, Thelma IV, 746
O'Connell, Blanch Fay IV, 745
O'Connell, Charles IV, 745
O'Connell, Grace IV, 700
O'Connell, Grace IV, 745
O'Connell, Kenneth IV, 745
O'Connell, Kenneth IV, 746
O'Connell, Lois IV, 745
O'Connell, Lois IV, 746
O'Connell, Nancy Jane IV, 745
O'Connell, Thelma IV, 745
O'Connell, Thelma IV, 746
O'Connell, William V, 424
O'Conner, Ann II, 609
O'Conner, Ann II, 628
O'Conner, Gertrude L. V, 700
O'Conner, John V, 353
O'Conner, Uritta V, 915
O'Conner, Uritta V, 924
O'Connor, Maria III, 213
O'Daniel, Martha I, 933
O'Day, John C. IV, 1218
O'Dell, ??? III, 308
O'Dell, Florence R. III, 308
O'Dell, Mariah G. IV, 1369
O'Deniel, John VI, 870
O'Deniel, Winney VI, 870
O'Doherty, Daniel VI, 844
O'Doherty, Lively Susan VI, 844
O'Donals, Sarah V, 424
O'Hara, Chas. VI, 663
O'Hara, Emma Linton V, 589
O'Hara, J. H. O. VI, 261
O'Hara, Mary Jane VI, 663
O'Hara, Mary Jane VI, 756
O'Hara, Priscilla VI, 663
O'Hara, Sara I, 617
O'Hare, ??? III, 243
O'Hare, James III, 243
O'Kane, Henry VI, 844
O'Kane, Sarah VI, 844
O'Keefe, Jesse V, 107
O'Mahondra, Mary V. VI, 844
O'Mahondra, Robt. M. VI, 844
O'Neal, ??? V, 965
O'Neal, Abigail I, 564
O'Neal, Abigail I, 1016
O'Neal, Abigail IV, 52
O'Neal, Abijah I, 1035
O'Neal, Abijah IV, 52
O'Neal, Abijah V, 83
O'Neal, Achsah I, 564
O'Neal, Achsah I, 1016
O'Neal, Ann I, 564
O'Neal, Ann I, 1016
O'Neal, Ann I, 1035
O'Neal, Ann IV, 257
O'Neal, Anna IV, 52
O'Neal, Anna V, 17
O'Neal, Anna V, 83
O'Neal, Anna V, 129
O'Neal, Anna V, 974
O'Neal, Anna Swain V, 107
O'Neal, Bartley VI, 844
O'Neal, Cary I, 564
O'Neal, Cary I, 1016
O'Neal, Clara I, 617
O'Neal, Daniel VI, 1008
O'Neal, Elizabeth V, 759
O'Neal, Elizabeth VI, 971
O'Neal, Hannah I, 564
O'Neal, Hannah I, 1016
O'Neal, Hannah IV, 345
O'Neal, Hannaueel I, 564
O'Neal, Hannaueel I, 1016
O'Neal, Henry I, 564
O'Neal, Henry I, 1016
O'Neal, Henry I, 1035
O'Neal, Hephziba I, 564
O'Neal, Hephziba I, 1016
O'Neal, Hepsibah I, 1035
O'Neal, Hiram I, 564
O'Neal, Hiram I, 1016
O'Neal, Hugh I, 564
O'Neal, Hugh I, 896
O'Neal, Hugh I, 1016
O'Neal, Hugh I, 1035
O'Neal, Jacob VI, 971
O'Neal, James VI, 602
O'Neal, James Mills V, 17
O'Neal, John I, 564
O'Neal, John I, 617
O'Neal, John I, 896
O'Neal, John I, 1015
O'Neal, John I, 1016
O'Neal, John I, 1035
O'Neal, John IV, 52
O'Neal, John VI, 602
O'Neal, John VI, 604
O'Neal, John VI, 971
O'Neal, John Belton I, 564
O'Neal, John Belton I, 1016
O'Neal, John Foster I, 564
O'Neal, John Kelly V, 79
O'Neal, John Kelly V, 107
O'Neal, John Kelly V, 971
O'Neal, John Kelly V, 974
O'Neal, Jonathan V, 970
O'Neal, Kelly IV, 52
O'Neal, Lizzie V, 636
O'Neal, Lydia V, 17
O'Neal, Mark I, 564
O'Neal, Mark I, 1016
O'Neal, Mary I, 564
O'Neal, Mary I, 617
O'Neal, Mary I, 1016
O'Neal, Mary I, 1035
O'Neal, Mary V, 80
O'Neal, Mary V, 107
O'Neal, Mary V, 129
O'Neal, Mary V, 970
O'Neal, Mary V, 971
O'Neal, Mary V, 974
O'Neal, Mary V, 977
O'Neal, Mary VI, 971
O'Neal, Mary VI, 1008
O'Neal, Mary J. V, 567
O'Neal, Mary J. V, 589
O'Neal, Maryann IV, 52
O'Neal, Mathias V, 589
O'Neal, Matthias V, 107
O'Neal, Matthias V, 974
O'Neal, Nansey I, 564
O'Neal, Patience I, 1035
O'Neal, Polly VI, 971
O'Neal, Priscilla I, 564
O'Neal, Priscilla I, 1016
O'Neal, Rebecca II, 1018
O'Neal, Rebecca IV, 52
O'Neal, Rebecca V, 83
O'Neal, Rebeckah VI, 602
O'Neal, Rebeckah VI, 604
O'Neal, Rebekah I, 564
O'Neal, Rebekah I, 1016
O'Neal, Rhoda I, 564
O'Neal, Rhoda I, 1016
O'Neal, Rhoda IV, 52
O'Neal, Robert I, 564
O'Neal, Robert I, 1016
O'Neal, Robert VI, 602
O'Neal, Sarah I, 564
O'Neal, Sarah I, 896
O'Neal, Sarah I, 1016
O'Neal, Sarah I, 1035
O'Neal, Sarah IV, 52
O'Neal, Susannah VI, 844
O'Neal, Thomas I, 564
O'Neal, Thomas I, 1016
O'Neal, Thomas I, 1035
O'Neal, Thornton VI, 916
O'Neal, Thornton VI, 971
O'Neal, Walter VI, 967
O'Neal, Walter VI, 971
O'Neal, William I, 564
O'Neal, William I, 896
O'Neal, William I, 1016
O'Neal, William I, 1035
O'Neal, William IV, 52
O'Neall, Abijah I, 1022
O'Neall, Abijah I, 1033
O'Neall, Abijah I, 1035
O'Neall, Abijah V, 107
O'Neall, Abijah P. V, 55
O'Neall, Abijah P. V, 107
O'Neall, Albert E. V, 107
O'Neall, Ann I, 1022
O'Neall, Ann I, 1033
O'Neall, Ann I, 1035
O'Neall, Anna V, 107
O'Neall, Anna C. V, 55
O'Neall, Anna M. V, 107
O'Neall, Anna Swain V, 107
O'Neall, Charles F. V, 107
O'Neall, Elisha I, 1022
O'Neall, Elisha V, 107
O'Neall, Henry I, 1022
O'Neall, Henry I, 1034
O'Neall, Henry I, 1035
O'Neall, Hepsibah I, 1035
O'Neall, Hepzibah I, 1030
O'Neall, Hugh I, 1022
O'Neall, Hugh I, 1033
O'Neall, Hugh I, 1035
O'Neall, Hugh T. V, 107
O'Neall, Irama V, 107
O'Neall, J. Kelly V, 107
O'Neall, John I, 1022
O'Neall, John I, 1030
O'Neall, John I, 1035
O'Neall, John Kelly V, 107
O'Neall, Margaret H. V, 107
O'Neall, Martha V, 107
O'Neall, Martha L. V, 107
O'Neall, Mary I, 1022
O'Neall, Mary I, 1034
O'Neall, Mary I, 1035
O'Neall, Mary V, 107
O'Neall, Mary Ann I, 1022
O'Neall, Mary Ann V, 107
O'Neall, Maryann I, 1022
O'Neall, Maryann V, 107
O'Neall, Matthias V, 107
O'Neall, Rebecah I, 1022
O'Neall, Rebecca V, 107
O'Neall, Rhoda V, 107
O'Neall, Sarah I, 1022
O'Neall, Sarah I, 1029
O'Neall, Sarah I, 1035
O'Neall, Sarah V, 107
O'Neall, Thomas I, 1022
O'Neall, Thomas I, 1029
O'Neall, Thomas I, 1035
O'Neall, William I, 1022
O'Neall, William I, 1035
O'Neall, William V, 107
O'Neall, William E. V, 107
O'Neall, Wm. VI, 427
O'Neil, Rebecca II, 1042
O'Neill, Abijah VI, 427
O'Neill, Agnes III, 244
O'Neill, Agnes III, 317
O'Neill, Agnes III, 319
O'Neill, Ann VI, 427
O'Neill, Gregory III, 244
O'Neill, Gregory III, 319
O'Neill, Hannah VI, 427
O'Neill, James II, 446
O'Neill, John VI, 427
O'Neill, Margaret VI, 427
O'Neill, Margrett II, 446
O'Neill, Mary VI, 427
O'Neill, Owen II, 446
O'Neill, Rebekah VI, 427
O'Neill, Sarah VI, 427

O'Neill, William VI, 427
O'Neill, Wm. VI, 427
O'Rourke, Thomas IV, 836
O'Rowrk, Edna Cohen IV, 1332
O'Sayle, Prudence I, 1029
O'Sayle, Prudence I, 1035
O'Shuff, Aaron III, 244
O'Sullivan, Elizabeth II, 246
Oaborn, Kazia II, 699
Oackes, C. V, 759
Oacks, Emily V, 759
Oads, Thos. II, 34
Oads???, Thos. II, 34
Oak, Ann VI, 90
Oak, Richmond VI, 157
Oak, Wayn VI, 157
Oak, Wayne VI, 90
Oakes, Stella H. III, 491
Oakfor, John II, 246
Oakford, Aaron II, 90
Oakford, Aaron II, 400
Oakford, Aaron II, 609
Oakford, Amos II, 36
Oakford, Ann II, 90
Oakford, Ann II, 99
Oakford, Ann II, 400
Oakford, Ann II, 609
Oakford, Benjamin II, 609
Oakford, Benjamin W. II, 90
Oakford, Benjamin Webber II, 90
Oakford, Benjamin Webber II, 400
Oakford, Charles II, 36
Oakford, Charles II, 76
Oakford, Charles II, 90
Oakford, Charles II, 113
Oakford, Chas. II, 36
Oakford, Deborah II, 90
Oakford, Deborah II, 105
Oakford, Easter II, 36
Oakford, Elizabeth II, 36
Oakford, Elizabeth II, 61
Oakford, Elizabeth II, 82
Oakford, Elizabeth II, 90
Oakford, Elizabeth II, 91
Oakford, Elizabeth II, 400
Oakford, Elizabeth II, 609
Oakford, Ester II, 90
Oakford, Esther II, 36
Oakford, Esther II, 76
Oakford, Esther II, 90
Oakford, Esther II, 106
Oakford, Franklin II, 400
Oakford, George II, 90
Oakford, Grace II, 85
Oakford, Grace II, 90
Oakford, Hannah II, 36
Oakford, Hannah II, 62
Oakford, Hannah II, 90
Oakford, Hannah II, 811
Oakford, Hannah Ann II, 811
Oakford, Hannah Ann II, 903
Oakford, Hannah Ann VI, 769
Oakford, Hannah L. II, 903
Oakford, Hannah Lloyd II, 811
Oakford, Hannah Shallcross II, 811
Oakford, Isaac II, 90
Oakford, Isaac II, 400
Oakford, Isaac II, 609
Oakford, Isaac II, 811
Oakford, Jacob II, 66
Oakford, Jacob II, 90
Oakford, James II, 36
Oakford, John II, 36
Oakford, John II, 62
Oakford, John II, 90
Oakford, John II, 91
Oakford, John II, 246
Oakford, John, Jr. II, 90
Oakford, Joseph II, 36
Oakford, Joseph II, 400
Oakford, Joseph Lloyd II, 609
Oakford, Leah II, 66
Oakford, Leah II, 90
Oakford, Lettitia II, 90
Oakford, Loyd II, 609
Oakford, Mabel II, 36
Oakford, Mabel II, 60
Oakford, Mabel II, 90
Oakford, Margaret II, 36
Oakford, Margaret II, 90
Oakford, Margaret II, 108
Oakford, Margret II, 36
Oakford, Margret II, 90
Oakford, Margret II, 113
Oakford, Mary II, 36
Oakford, Mary II, 90
Oakford, Mary II, 609
Oakford, Rebecca II, 36
Oakford, Rebecca S. II, 903
Oakford, Rebecca Serrill II, 811
Oakford, Rebeck II, 90
Oakford, Rebeckah II, 36
Oakford, Rebeckah II, 88
Oakford, Rebeckah II, 90
Oakford, Richard II, 609
Oakford, Richard II, 811
Oakford, Samuel II, 36
Oakford, Sarah II, 36
Oakford, Sarah II, 62
Oakford, Sarah II, 78
Oakford, Sarah II, 90
Oakford, Susanna II, 57
Oakford, Susanna II, 90
Oakford, Susannah II, 36
Oakford, Susannah II, 90
Oakford, Wade Samuel II, 60
Oakford, Wade Samuel II, 90
Oakford, Waid Samuel II, 246
Oakford, William II, 36
Oakford, Wm. II, 62
Oakford, Wm. II, 88
Oakford, Wm. II, 90
Oakforde, Susannah II, 61
Oakforde, Susannah II, 90
Oakham, Jacob II, 529
Oakham, Jacob II, 609
Oakham, Rebecca II, 550
Oakham, Rebecca II, 609
Oakham, Rebeckah II, 529
Oakley, Alice Ann IV, 649
Oakley, Alicean IV, 649
Oakley, Alisana IV, 649
Oakley, Baltimore IV, 649
Oakley, Berneice C. IV, 1041
Oakley, Bernice IV, 1041
Oakley, Elisana IV, 649
Oakley, Elizabeth III, 483
Oakley, Elizabeth III, 491
Oakley, Frances V, 268
Oakley, George V, 106
Oakley, George V, 146
Oakley, George V, 223
Oakley, George V, 268
Oakley, George V, 353
Oakley, Hannah III, 431
Oakley, Hannah III, 443
Oakley, Hannah III, 491
Oakley, Hannah III, 497
Oakley, Henry III, 431
Oakley, Henry III, 443
Oakley, Henry III, 491
Oakley, Henry III, 497
Oakley, Katherine V, 223
Oakley, Katherine V, 268
Oakley, Latitia III, 488
Oakley, Latitia III, 491
Oakley, Mary III, 491
Oakley, Mary III, 499
Oakley, Nathaniel III, 491
Oakley, Sarah III, 243
Oakley, William IV, 256
Oakley, William V, 268
Oaks, C. V, 759
Oaks, Emily V, 759
Oaks, Fanney VI, 935
Oaks, Frances VI, 974
Oaks, Franke Dixon VI, 935
Oaks, Laviney VI, 935
Oaks, Susanna V, 737
Oaks, Susannah V, 758
Oale, Maria IV, 1331
Oasburn, Hannah II, 246
Oatley, Lloyd IV, 1331
Oatley, Ola IV, 1331
Oatley, Olga Smithson IV, 1331
Oatley, Vincent IV, 1331
Oats, Rachel VI, 418
Oats, Rachel VI, 426
Obenshain, Ann E. VI, 970
Obenshain, Samuel VI, 970
Oberthier, Fam IV, 1331
Oberthier, John IV, 1331
Oberthier, Magdalena IV, 1331
Oberthier, Mrs. Lena IV, 1331
Oblinger, Hannah IV, 1070
Oblinger, Hannah G. IV, 589
Oblinger, Hannah Townsend IV, 1070
Oblinger, Sarah IV, 578
Oblinger, Sarah IV, 589
Oblinger, Sarah T. IV, 589
Oblinger, Sarah T. IV, 1070
Oblinger, Stephen IV, 1070
Obrion, Anna IV, 1331
Obrion, Ava IV, 1331
Obrion, Jay IV, 1331
Obrion, William IV, 1331
Ocher, Ella IV, 1218
Ockford, Elizabeth II, 90
Odam, Sarah VI, 201
Odan, Sarah VI, 155
Oday, Maggie V, 1013
Oddie, Robert III, 243
Oddie, William III, 243
Ode, Rachel VI, 426
Odear, Mary I, 896
Odell, Almira IV, 1239
Odell, Ann II, 214
Odell, Ann II, 246
Odell, Anson IV, 1353
Odell, Benjamin III, 243
Odell, Charlotte IV, 1353
Odell, Daisy V, 1013
Odell, Daniel III, 243
Odell, Fanny III, 243
Odell, Florence III, 243
Odell, Gabriel III, 243
Odell, Hannah III, 243
Odell, Hannah D. III, 243
Odell, Jacob III, 243
Odell, John I, 623
Odell, John J. P. III, 48
Odell, Lettie IV, 1239
Odell, Maria IV, 1353
Odell, Maria IV, 1374
Odell, Mary Jane I, 623
Odell, Mary Jane I, 638
Odell, Mary L. III, 48
Odell, Nancy I, 623
Odell, Rebecca I, 623
Odell, Sarah III, 243
Odell, Wesley IV, 1239
Oden, Catharine VI, 970
Oden, Elisha VI, 970
Oden, William VI, 970
Oden, Winney VI, 970
Oden, Winney VI, 977
Odenmald, Albert IV, 1259
Odenmald, Louisa IV, 1259
Odenmald, Louisa C. IV, 1259
Oders, Mary I, 896
Odey, Florence IV, 746
Odey, Irma B. IV, 746
Odey, Irma Belle IV, 746
Odey, Janice IV, 746
Odey, Maggie V, 1013
Odey, Mrs. E. C. IV, 746
Odey, Ralph E. IV, 746
Odey, Ralph, Jr. IV, 746
Odey, Robert IV, 746
Odiam, John VI, 201
Odineal, Eliza P. VI, 970
Odineal, Elizabeth VI, 970
Odineal, George D. VI, 970
Odineal, Tarleton J. VI, 970
Odle, Betty I, 767
Odle, Daniel I, 767
Odle, Daniel I, 768
Odle, Mary I, 767
Odle, Mary I, 768
Odle, Patience I, 767
Odom, Bettie I, 339
Odom, Bud I, 220
Odom, Genettae I, 339
Odom, Jennie I, 220
Odom, Josiah I, 218
Odom, Josiah I, 339
Odom, Josiah S. I, 339
Odom, Martha I, 218
Odom, Martha A. I, 247
Odom, Martha A. I, 249
Odom, Sallie I, 339
Odom, Sarah I, 215
Odom, Sarah I, 339
Odom, Sylvester I, 339
Odom, W. B. I, 339
Odom, William B. I, 339
Odoms, Charles V, 589
Odon, Sallie I, 339
Odon, Sylvester I, 339
Odum, Abraham VI, 199
Odum, Abraham VI, 200
Odum, John VI, 201
Odum, Martha VI, 199
Odum, Martha VI, 200
Odum, Martha VI, 201
Odum, Martha Ann I, 218
Odum, Sarah VI, 201
Oesch, Opal L. IV, 782
Oesch, Walter IV, 782
Offley, Caleb II, 501
Offley, Caleb II, 609
Offley, Caleb II, 990
Offley, Caleb II, 1018
Offley, Daniel I, 1016
Offley, Daniel II, 400
Offley, Daniel II, 501
Offley, Daniel II, 609
Offley, Daniel III, 243
Offley, David II, 518
Offley, David II, 609
Offley, Eliza Ann II, 609
Offley, Elizabeth II, 990
Offley, Elizabeth II, 1018
Offley, Harriet II, 757
Offley, Martha I, 1016
Offley, Mary II, 518
Offley, Mary II, 609
Offley, Mary Anna II, 903
Offley, Rachel II, 609
Offley, Rebecca II, 903
Offley, Thomas II, 400
Offley, Wd. Rachel II, 501
Offley, Wm. II, 903
Offly, Daniel II, 400
Offly, Thomas II, 400
Ogan, Catharine V, 622
Ogan, Catharine V, 636
Ogan, Catherine V, 818
Ogborn, Allen V, 106
Ogborn, Amelia V, 462
Ogborn, Amelia F. V, 462
Ogborn, Ann II, 180
Ogborn, Ann II, 246
Ogborn, Ann V, 106
Ogborn, Anna L. II, 715
Ogborn, Anna L. II, 716
Ogborn, Caleb II, 246
Ogborn, Caleb II, 811
Ogborn, Caleb, Jr. II, 246
Ogborn, Caleb, Jr. V, 106
Ogborn, David H. V, 589
Ogborn, Dicy Ella V, 268
Ogborn, Earnest V, 462
Ogborn, Earnest Francis V, 462
Ogborn, Edwin V, 106
Ogborn, Eliza V, 268
Ogborn, Eliza V, 462
Ogborn, Eliza V, 560
Ogborn, Eliza V, 589
Ogborn, Eliza Jane V, 462
Ogborn, Elizabeth II, 246
Ogborn, Elizabeth II, 247
Ogborn, Elizabeth V, 106
Ogborn, Ellwood V, 924
Ogborn, Elwood II, 246
Ogborn, Elwood V, 924
Ogborn, Esther V, 106
Ogborn, Evan V, 106
Ogborn, Ezra V, 106
Ogborn, Fathergill II, 717
Ogborn, Flora C. V, 462
Ogborn, Florence C. V, 268
Ogborn, Fothergill II, 246
Ogborn, Grace V, 462
Ogborn, Hannah II, 904
Ogborn, Hannah V, 106
Ogborn, Harriett M. V, 589
Ogborn, Henry V, 268
Ogborn, Henry M. V, 268
Ogborn, Henry M. V, 462
Ogborn, Henry M. V, 589
Ogborn, Isaac A. V, 106
Ogborn, Isaac F. V, 589
Ogborn, Jesse T. Butterworth V, 106
Ogborn, John II, 246
Ogborn, John II, 273
Ogborn, John V, 106
Ogborn, Joseph II, 246
Ogborn, Joseph V, 106
Ogborn, Joseph P. V, 106
Ogborn, Joseph Parker V, 106
Ogborn, Lydia V, 106
Ogborn, Maria VI, 491
Ogborn, Maria VI, 512
Ogborn, Martha V, 924
Ogborn, Martha C. V, 924
Ogborn, Mary II, 246
Ogborn, Mary II, 273
Ogborn, Mary V, 106
Ogborn, Matilda V, 462
Ogborn, Matilda A. V, 268
Ogborn, Morris II, 714
Ogborn, Pamelia F. V, 268
Ogborn, Rachel P. II, 717
Ogborn, Rebecca V, 106
Ogborn, Rebeccah V, 106
Ogborn, Ruth E. V, 32
Ogborn, Ruth E. V, 106
Ogborn, Samuel V, 106
Ogborn, Samuel V, 462
Ogborn, Samuel F. V, 106
Ogborn, Samuel F. V, 353
Ogborn, Sarah II, 246
Ogborn, Sarah B. V, 106
Ogborn, Sarah E. V, 589
Ogborn, Sarah W. II, 717
Ogborn, Susan G. II, 714
Ogborn, Susan S. II, 757
Ogborn, Susannah F. II, 246
Ogborn, Wd. Hannah II, 811
Ogborn, William II, 246
Ogborn, William II, 247
Ogborn, William V, 462
Ogborn, Wm. Elwood V, 924
Ogborn, Wm. Layton V, 462
Ogbourn, Joseph II, 246
Ogburn, Adaline V, 714
Ogburn, Allen I, 550
Ogburn, Allen V, 106
Ogburn, Ann II, 246
Ogburn, Ansalom I, 550
Ogburn, Asa I, 550
Ogburn, Buly I, 550
Ogburn, Buly I, 564
Ogburn, Caleb, Jr. V, 106
Ogburn, David H. V, 589
Ogburn, David H. V, 701
Ogburn, Edward H. II, 904
Ogburn, Edwin V, 106
Ogburn, Elihu I, 550
Ogburn, Elwood V, 924
Ogburn, Esther V, 106
Ogburn, Evan V, 106
Ogburn, Fothergill II, 246
Ogburn, Hannah II, 903
Ogburn, Hannah II, 904
Ogburn, Harriet B. V, 701
Ogburn, Harriett M. V, 589
Ogburn, Henry V, 268
Ogburn, Huldah I, 550
Ogburn, Ithamar I, 550
Ogburn, John V, 106
Ogburn, Joseph V, 106
Ogburn, Juliatha I, 550
Ogburn, Louisa I, 928
Ogburn, Lydia V, 106
Ogburn, Mahlon F. V, 701
Ogburn, Margaret I, 550
Ogburn, Martha C. V, 924
Ogburn, Mary V, 106
Ogburn, Miriam I, 550
Ogburn, Pheaby VI, 116
Ogburn, Phenias I, 550
Ogburn, Ruth E. V, 33
Ogburn, Ruth E. V, 106
Ogburn, Samuel V, 106
Ogburn, Sarah E. V, 589
Ogburn, Sarah E. V, 701
Ogburn, Sarah M. II, 904
Ogburn, Solomon I, 550
Ogburn, Thomas, II I, 550
Ogburn, Zodac I, 550
Ogden, ??? III, 480
Ogden, Abigail II, 135
Ogden, Alberta Sherron II, 135
Ogden, Alberta Sherron II, 153
Ogden, Alberta Sherron II, 154
Ogden, Alis II, 475
Ogden, Alis II, 609
Ogden, Ann II, 609
Ogden, Ann II, 612
Ogden, Ann IV, 686
Ogden, Ann Maria III, 204
Ogden, Ann Maria III, 243
Ogden, Anna II, 120
Ogden, Anna II, 121
Ogden, Anna F. III, 243
Ogden, Anna M. II, 297
Ogden, Anna M. II, 304
Ogden, Anna M. IV, 686
Ogden, Anna M. IV, 746
Ogden, Anna M. IV, 983
Ogden, Anna Margaret II, 297
Ogden, Anna Maria IV, 746
Ogden, Anna Mariah II, 121
Ogden, Armistead H. VI, 970
Ogden, Benjamin IV, 836
Ogden, Benjamin Barton IV, 83
Ogden, Beulah P. II, 121
Ogden, Beulah P. II, 125
Ogden, Beulah Pancoast II, 82
Ogden, Catharine VI, 970
Ogden, Catharine E. VI, 970
Ogden, Catherine II, 400
Ogden, Champness VI, 971
Ogden, Charles II, 121
Ogden, Charles III, 243
Ogden, Charles G. II, 297
Ogden, Charles G. II, 304
Ogden, Charles S. II, 297
Ogden, Charles S. II, 904
Ogden, Charles Smith II, 811
Ogden, Chas. S. II, 904
Ogden, Clarkson II, 121
Ogden, David II, 90
Ogden, David II, 475
Ogden, David II, 609
Ogden, Deborah II, 714
Ogden, Dorothea II, 811
Ogden, Edward H. II, 811
Ogden, Edward H. II, 909

den, Elijah VI, 964
den, Elijah VI, 970
den, Elijah VI, 974
den, Eliz. III, 110
den, Eliz. III, 243
den, Eliz. T. III, 173
den, Elizabeth II, 121
den, Elizabeth II, 476
den, Elizabeth III, 243
den, Elizabeth VI, 971
den, Elizabeth H. VI, 977
den, Elizabeth L. II, 904
den, Elizabeth M. II, 859
den, Elizabeth M. II, 904
den, Elizabeth M. VI, 974
den, Elizabeth Morris II, 811
den, Ellen C. IV, 614
den, Ellen C. IV, 636
den, Ellen C. IV, 649
den, Ellen C. H. IV, 649
den, Emily VI, 983
den, Emma II, 811
den, Emma II, 853
den, Emma II, 904
den, Esther II, 36
den, Esther II, 609
den, Esther II, 791
den, Francis J. III, 243
den, Francis Perot II, 811
den, George II, 400
den, George II, 609
den, George P. II, 135
den, Gilbert III, 243
den, Gilbert III, 491
den, Hannah II, 121
den, Hannah II, 400
den, Hannah II, 401
den, Hannah II, 501
den, Hannah II, 578
den, Hannah II, 609
den, Hannah II, 611
den, Hannah II, 683
den, Hannah II, 823
den, Hannah II, 829
den, Hannah IV, 649
den, Hannah IV, 836
den, Hannah IV, 880
den, Hannah W. II, 297
den, Hannah W. II, 304
den, Hannah W. II, 904
den, Hannah W. II, 914
den, Hannah W. IV, 649
den, Harriet II, 853
den, Harriet II, 904
den, Harriet II, 909
den, Harriet VI, 958
den, Harriet M. II, 811
den, Harriett II, 904
den, Henry III, 243
den, Henry VI, 1013
den, Henry Corbit II, 811
den, Henry Corbit II, 904
den, Henry Corbit III, 110
den, Henry Corbit III, 243
den, Henry M. VI, 908
den, Henry M. VI, 956
den, Henry M. VI, 970
den, Henry M. VI, 977
gden, Henry T. VI, 860
gden, Henry T. VI, 902
den, Hester II, 542
den, Hester II, 609
gden, Hugh II, 609
gden, Hugh II, 811
gden, Jamima II, 609
gden, Jemima II, 400
gden, Jemima II, 609
gden, Jemimah II, 558
gden, Jemimah II, 609
gden, Jesse II, 400
gden, Jesse II, 811
gden, Jesse II, 904
gden, John II, 135
gden, John II, 297
gden, John II, 304
gden, John II, 400
gden, John II, 401
gden, John II, 501
gden, John II, 609
gden, John II, 611
gden, John II, 904
gden, John II, 914
gden, John IV, 649
gden, John IV, 686
gden, John VI, 958
gden, John VI, 983
gden, John James VI, 974
gden, John L. VI, 997
gden, John M. II, 853
gden, John M. II, 904
gden, John M. II, 909
Ogden, John W. II, 757
Ogden, John W. II, 904
Ogden, John W. II, 914
Ogden, Jonathan II, 558
Ogden, Jonathan II, 609
Ogden, Joseph II, 36
Ogden, Joseph II, 121
Ogden, Joseph II, 149
Ogden, Joseph II, 154
Ogden, Joseph II, 400
Ogden, Joseph II, 401
Ogden, Joseph II, 558
Ogden, Joseph II, 609
Ogden, Joseph, Jr. II, 609
Ogden, Lavina E. VI, 964
Ogden, Lydia II, 570
Ogden, Lydia II, 609
Ogden, Lydia VI, 659
Ogden, Lydia VI, 686
Ogden, Marie III, 110
Ogden, Marie III, 243
Ogden, Marilla VI, 970
Ogden, Martha II, 19
Ogden, Martha II, 401
Ogden, Martha IV, 558
Ogden, Martha A. II, 121
Ogden, Martha Ann VI, 970
Ogden, Martha H. IV, 746
Ogden, Martha H. IV, 768
Ogden, Martha H. IV, 788
Ogden, Mary II, 36
Ogden, Mary II, 475
Ogden, Mary II, 476
Ogden, Mary II, 500
Ogden, Mary II, 609
Ogden, Mary II, 684
Ogden, Mary II, 801
Ogden, Mary III, 480
Ogden, Mary III, 491
Ogden, Mary VI, 1013
Ogden, Mary Ann II, 36
Ogden, Mary Ann II, 79
Ogden, Mary Ann II, 90
Ogden, Mary Ann II, 119
Ogden, Mary Ann II, 121
Ogden, Mary Ann II, 149
Ogden, Mary Ann II, 154
Ogden, Mary G. III, 204
Ogden, Mary J. VI, 908
Ogden, Middleton II, 811
Ogden, Mildred VI, 956
Ogden, Nancy VI, 970
Ogden, Prudence II, 149
Ogden, Prudence II, 154
Ogden, Richard T. IV, 636
Ogden, Richard T. IV, 649
Ogden, Robert II, 609
Ogden, Samuel II, 36
Ogden, Samuel II, 79
Ogden, Samuel II, 90
Ogden, Samuel II, 149
Ogden, Samuel II, 154
Ogden, Samuel II, 246
Ogden, Samuel II, 609
Ogden, Samuel II, 684
Ogden, Samuel VI, 540
Ogden, Sarah II, 401
Ogden, Sarah VI, 964
Ogden, Sarah Ann VI, 983
Ogden, Sarah L. II, 135
Ogden, Sarah M. II, 909
Ogden, Sarah Morris II, 811
Ogden, Stephen IV, 649
Ogden, Stephen IV, 836
Ogden, Stephen IV, 880
Ogden, Susan VI, 971
Ogden, Susannah H. II, 904
Ogden, Susannah H. II, 914
Ogden, Sybil II, 793
Ogden, Thomas II, 476
Ogden, Walker R. VI, 970
Ogden, Wd. Eliz. B. III, 125
Ogden, Wd. Hannah II, 609
Ogden, Wd. Mary II, 609
Ogden, Wharton II, 121
Ogden, William VI, 958
Ogden, William VI, 971
Ogden, Wm. II, 609
Ogdon, Anna Mariah II, 121
Ogdon, Champness VI, 977
Ogdon, Elijah VI, 964
Ogdon, Elizabeth VI, 971
Ogdon, Hannah II, 400
Ogdon, Hannah II, 401
Ogdon, Henry T. VI, 971
Ogdon, John II, 400
Ogdon, John II, 401
Ogdon, John VI, 971
Ogdon, John VI, 982
Ogdon, John VI, 997
Ogdon, Louisey L. VI, 997
Ogdon, Lucy Jane VI, 982
Ogdon, Margaret E. VI, 971
Ogdon, Martha II, 401
Ogdon, Sarah II, 401
Ogelby, Rebecca II, 401
Ogelsby, John II, 401
Ogen, Jane VI, 409
Ogen, Jane VI, 426
Oggborne, Mary II, 246
Oggborne, Mary II, 247
Oggborne, William II, 246
Ogilby, Everad II, 401
Ogilby, James II, 401
Ogilby, John II, 401
Ogilby, Joseph II, 609
Ogilby, Joseph II, 792
Ogilby, Justinian II, 401
Ogilby, Margaret II, 401
Ogilby, Margaret II, 792
Ogilby, Martha II, 401
Ogilby, Mary II, 401
Ogilby, Patrick II, 401
Ogilby, Patrick II, 609
Ogilby, Patrick, Jr. II, 609
Ogilby, Rachel II, 609
Ogilby, Rebecca II, 401
Ogilby, Rebecca II, 609
Ogilby, Rebekah II, 609
Ogilby, Wd. Mary Austin II, 792
Ogilby, Wd. Rebecca II, 401
Ogilby, Wd. Rebecca II, 609
Ogilsby, Patrick III, 431
Ogilsby, Rebecca III, 431
Ogin, Jane VI, 426
Ogin, Phame VI, 365
Ogin, Phame VI, 426
Ogleby, Alexander VI, 426
Ogleby, Catharine V, 974
Ogleby, Elizabeth VI, 808
Ogleby, Joseph II, 609
Ogleby, Justinian II, 401
Ogleby, Mary VI, 808
Ogleby, Patrick II, 401
Ogleby, Patrick III, 475
Ogleby, Phebe VI, 426
Ogleby, Wd. Rebecca II, 401
Oglesbe, Anna V, 1013
Oglesbe, Ida V, 1013
Oglesbe, Ida Y. V, 1013
Oglesbee, ??? V, 589
Oglesbee, Alice M. V, 107
Oglesbee, Alice Mae V, 106
Oglesbee, Alice Mae V, 195
Oglesbee, Alonzo V, 520
Oglesbee, Anna V, 520
Oglesbee, Anna V, 701
Oglesbee, Anna T. V, 589
Oglesbee, Christopher R. V, 520
Oglesbee, Edward V, 520
Oglesbee, Edward V, 701
Oglesbee, Edward D. V, 520
Oglesbee, Eric V, 520
Oglesbee, Errick J. V, 520
Oglesbee, Eva V, 520
Oglesbee, Eva V, 701
Oglesbee, Eva Foland V, 195
Oglesbee, Eva Foland V, 520
Oglesbee, Floid V, 520
Oglesbee, Floyd V, 701
Oglesbee, Floyd H. V, 520
Oglesbee, Francis V, 520
Oglesbee, Franklin V, 701
Oglesbee, George V, 106
Oglesbee, George D. V, 107
Oglesbee, Lenna V, 520
Oglesbee, Leontine V, 520
Oglesbee, Lucinda V, 491
Oglesbee, Lucinda V, 520
Oglesbee, Martha A. V, 106
Oglesbee, Martha A. M. V, 195
Oglesbee, Martha M. V, 107
Oglesbee, Martha Morgan V, 195
Oglesbee, Mary Bell V, 520
Oglesbee, Mary Emily V, 520
Oglesbee, Mary Emily V, 701
Oglesbee, Mary Esther V, 520
Oglesbee, Miranda V, 701
Oglesbee, Oscar Leroy V, 520
Oglesbee, Phaniah V, 520
Oglesbee, Phebe V, 520
Oglesbee, Pheniah V, 501
Oglesbee, Pheniah V, 520
Oglesbee, Priscilla Gladys V, 520
Oglesbee, Rebecca V, 520
Oglesbee, Rebecca V, 701
Oglesbee, Rebecca A. V, 520
Oglesbee, Reece V, 520
Oglesbee, Reece V, 701
Oglesbee, Robert V, 520
Oglesbee, Robert V, 701
Oglesbee, Roy V, 520
Oglesbee, Ruth V, 520
Oglesbee, Ruth V, 589
Oglesbee, Ruth V, 701
Oglesbee, Sarah Margaret V, 520
Oglesbee, Winnifred V, 520
Oglesby, Alonzo V, 520
Oglesby, Anna V, 520
Oglesby, Anne VI, 844
Oglesby, Catharine V, 969
Oglesby, Catharine S. VI, 954
Oglesby, Christian VI, 934
Oglesby, Constance VI, 900
Oglesby, Conway VI, 817
Oglesby, Daniel VI, 844
Oglesby, Daniel VI, 864
Oglesby, Daniel VI, 971
Oglesby, David VI, 817
Oglesby, David VI, 844
Oglesby, David VI, 917
Oglesby, David, Jr. VI, 971
Oglesby, Edward D. V, 520
Oglesby, Elizabeth VI, 844
Oglesby, Errick J. V, 520
Oglesby, Eva V, 520
Oglesby, Eva Foland V, 520
Oglesby, Fanny VI, 971
Oglesby, Floyd H. V, 520
Oglesby, Frances VI, 810
Oglesby, Frances VI, 829
Oglesby, Frances W. VI, 1018
Oglesby, Francis V, 520
Oglesby, Jacob VI, 844
Oglesby, Jacob VI, 917
Oglesby, Jinny VI, 917
Oglesby, Judith E. VI, 900
Oglesby, Keziah VI, 800
Oglesby, Lenna V, 520
Oglesby, Leontine V, 520
Oglesby, Lucinda V, 491
Oglesby, Lucinda V, 520
Oglesby, Margaret IV, 649
Oglesby, Margaret IV, 658
Oglesby, Margaret W. VI, 956
Oglesby, Margaret W. VI, 971
Oglesby, Martha VI, 971
Oglesby, Mary I, 1022
Oglesby, Mary VI, 800
Oglesby, Mary VI, 844
Oglesby, Mary VI, 858
Oglesby, Mary VI, 971
Oglesby, Mary Bell V, 520
Oglesby, Mary Emily V, 520
Oglesby, Mary Esther V, 520
Oglesby, Mary S. VI, 900
Oglesby, Nancy VI, 844
Oglesby, Nancy VI, 1013
Oglesby, Oscar Leroy V, 520
Oglesby, Phaniah V, 501
Oglesby, Phaniah V, 520
Oglesby, Phebe V, 520
Oglesby, Phebe VI, 426
Oglesby, Phebe VI, 602
Oglesby, Polly VI, 858
Oglesby, Priscilla Gladys V, 520
Oglesby, Rebecca V, 520
Oglesby, Reece V, 520
Oglesby, Rhoda Ann VI, 971
Oglesby, Richard VI, 971
Oglesby, Robert V, 520
Oglesby, Ruth V, 520
Oglesby, Sally VI, 845
Oglesby, Sarah VI, 856
Oglesby, Sarah A. VI, 923
Oglesby, Sarah Margaret V, 520
Oglesby, Susanna VI, 817
Oglesby, Thomas VI, 850
Oglesby, Thomas VI, 858
Oglesby, Thomas VI, 971
Oglesby, William VI, 844
Oglesby, William VI, 864
Oglesby, William VI, 954
Oglesby, William VI, 971
Oglesby, William VI, 1005
Oglesby, William VI, 1010
Oglesby, William H. VI, 831
Oglesby, William, Jr. VI, 844
Oglesby, William, Jr. VI, 1018
Oglesby, Winnifred V, 520
Oglesby, Wm. VI, 928
Oglisby, William VI, 1005
Oher, Boyer II, 446
Ohlhausen, Cassandra VI, 971
Ohlhausen, Henry V. VI, 971
Ohlhausen, John V. VI, 971
Ohlhausen, Mary H. VI, 971
Ohmstead, Mary Jane III, 169
Ohmstead, Mary Jane III, 243
Ohnemus, Frank H. III, 243
Oiler, Hannah V, 589
Oiler, Hannah Maria V, 589
Oiler, Margaret A. V, 589
Oiler, Margaret Ann V, 571
Oiler, Margaret Ann V, 589
Okeford, Charles II, 65
Okeford, Charles II, 90
Okeford, Mary II, 65
Okeford, Mary II, 90
Okeley, Alicean IV, 649
Okeley, Alicean IV, 666
Okie, Gertrude II, 795
Olaphant, William H. IV, 746
Olcott, ??? III, 329
Olcott, Eliz. M. III, 20
Olcott, Eliz. M. III, 66
Olcott, Maria C. III, 243
Olcott, Maria C. III, 329
Olcott, Phebe C. III, 243
Olcott, Stephen III, 243
Old, Eliza W. VI, 844
Old, Martha J. VI, 858
Old, Thomas J. VI, 844
Oldacre, Elizabeth VI, 335
Oldacre, Elizabeth VI, 343
Oldacre, Martha VI, 426
Oldacre, Marthe VI, 426
Oldacre, Polley VI, 928
Oldaker, Hannah VI, 1010
Oldaker, John VI, 941
Oldaker, John VI, 1010
Oldaker, Rebecca VI, 941
Oldakers, Elizabeth VI, 335
Oldakers, Elizabeth VI, 971
Oldakers, Hannah VI, 971
Oldakers, Henry VI, 335
Oldakers, Henry VI, 971
Oldakers, Henry VI, 1015
Oldakers, Isaac VI, 971
Oldakers, John VI, 335
Oldakers, John VI, 971
Oldakers, John VI, 1015
Oldakers, Rebecca VI, 1015
Oldane, Martha VI, 540
Oldden, Benjamin II, 610
Oldden, David II, 610
Oldden, Elizabeth II, 401
Oldden, Elizabeth II, 610
Oldden, Esther II, 610
Oldden, James II, 610
Oldden, James, Jr. II, 610
Oldden, John II, 401
Oldden, Mary II, 604
Oldden, Mary II, 610
Oldden, Mary II, 635
Oldden, Rachel II, 515
Oldden, Rachel II, 610
Oldden, Rebecca B. II, 610
Oldden, Rebecca B. II, 635
Oldden, Thomas H. II, 610
Oldden, William II, 401
Olden, Ann II, 401
Olden, Ann II, 610
Olden, Benjamin II, 401
Olden, Benjamin II, 610
Olden, Burling II, 401
Olden, Burling II, 610
Olden, Catharine II, 610
Olden, Catherine II, 225
Olden, David II, 610
Olden, Eliza II, 401
Olden, Elizabeth II, 401
Olden, Elizabeth II, 610
Olden, Emma II, 401
Olden, Emma II, 610
Olden, Ephraim II, 246
Olden, Esther II, 401
Olden, Esther II, 610
Olden, James II, 401
Olden, James II, 610
Olden, James, Jr. II, 610
Olden, John II, 401
Olden, John II, 610
Olden, Martha VI, 540
Olden, Mary II, 210
Olden, Mary II, 246
Olden, Mary II, 401
Olden, Mary II, 610
Olden, Mary Hough II, 401
Olden, Mary W. III, 448
Olden, Phebe Ann II, 1057
Olden, Phebe Ann II, 1060
Olden, Rachel II, 610
Olden, Robert II, 401
Olden, Robert II, 610
Olden, Thomas H. II, 610
Olden, Thomas Hough II, 401
Olden, William II, 401
Oldfather, Dolly V, 818
Oldfield, Hannah I, 832
Oldham, Abner W. V, 957
Oldham, Ann V, 957
Oldham, Anna V, 957
Oldham, Anne V, 268

Oldham, Anne V, 288
Oldham, Blanch IV, 1332
Oldham, Blanche IV, 1332
Oldham, James G. V, 957
Oldham, Jane G. V, 950
Oldham, Jane G. V, 957
Oldham, John II, 446
Oldham, John V, 957
Oldham, John VI, 427
Oldham, Joseph V, 957
Oldham, Levi W. V, 957
Oldham, Lydia Ellen V, 957
Oldham, Margaret W. V, 957
Oldham, Martha VI, 540
Oldham, Mary II, 610
Oldham, Mary II, 688
Oldham, Mary A. V, 954
Oldham, Mary A. V, 957
Oldham, Massie W. V, 957
Oldham, Rachel I, 546
Oldham, Rachel I, 564
Oldham, Rachel VI, 359
Oldham, William IV, 69
Oldham, William VI, 427
Oldhausen, Henry V. VI, 971
Oldhausen, Mary H. VI, 971
Oldman, Ann II, 574
Oldman, Ann II, 610
Oldman, Elizabeth II, 401
Oldman, Elizabeth II, 531
Oldman, Elizabeth II, 610
Oldman, Esther II, 552
Oldman, Esther II, 610
Oldman, James II, 401
Oldman, Jane II, 610
Oldman, Jane II, 686
Oldman, Jane II, 811
Oldman, Jane Garret II, 827
Oldman, Joseph II, 401
Oldman, Joseph II, 592
Oldman, Joseph II, 610
Oldman, Mary II, 401
Oldman, Mary II, 610
Oldman, Samuel II, 610
Oldman, Sarah II, 513
Oldman, Sarah II, 592
Oldman, Sarah II, 610
Oldman, Thomas II, 401
Oldman, Thomas II, 513
Oldman, Thomas II, 531
Oldman, Thomas II, 610
Oldman, Thomas II, 686
Oldman, Wd. Elizabeth II, 401
Oldman, Wd. Mary II, 513
Oldman, Wd. Mary II, 610
Oldreg, Liddia II, 90
Oldreg, Rebeca II, 90
Olds, Alice IV, 1332
Olds, Alice M. IV, 256
Olds, Ella IV, 1259
Olds, George IV, 1259
Olds, Maggie IV, 1239
Olds, O. L. IV, 1332
Olds, Orcelius L. IV, 256
Olds, Orcetues IV, 1332
Olen, Alce II, 446
Olen, John II, 446
Olephant, Elizabeth IV, 1208
Olephant, Ephraim IV, 1208
Olephant, Ruth IV, 1208
Olephant, Ruth IV, 1218
Olephant, Seth S. IV, 1218
Oler, George III, 243
Oler, Hazel III, 243
Oler, Hazel III, 364
Olind, Joyce II, 241
Olind, Joyce II, 246
Olinger, Jane V, 462
Oliphant, ??? IV, 983
Oliphant, Abner IV, 650
Oliphant, Abner IV, 746
Oliphant, Abner IV, 880
Oliphant, Abner IV, 1218
Oliphant, Alice M. IV, 787
Oliphant, Alice M. IV, 836
Oliphant, Alice Marie IV, 679
Oliphant, Alice Marie IV, 746
Oliphant, Alice Marie IV, 800
Oliphant, Alice Marie IV, 836
Oliphant, Ann IV, 52
Oliphant, Ann IV, 610
Oliphant, Ann IV, 649
Oliphant, Ann IV, 650
Oliphant, Ann IV, 746
Oliphant, Ann IV, 903
Oliphant, Ann IV, 912
Oliphant, Ann VI, 354
Oliphant, Anna B. IV, 836
Oliphant, Anna B. H. IV, 836
Oliphant, Anna M. B. IV, 836
Oliphant, Anna Sina IV, 746
Oliphant, Anna Sina IV, 747
Oliphant, Anne Mary IV, 513
Oliphant, Arthur IV, 836
Oliphant, Arthur B. IV, 846
Oliphant, Arthur G. IV, 542
Oliphant, Arthur G. IV, 836
Oliphant, Barton Dean IV, 912
Oliphant, Beulah H. IV, 542
Oliphant, Beulah H. IV, 836
Oliphant, Beulah Ruth IV, 836
Oliphant, Charlotte Eleanor VI, 971
Oliphant, David S. VI, 971
Oliphant, Eliza IV, 180
Oliphant, Eliza IV, 256
Oliphant, Eliza IV, 683
Oliphant, Eliza IV, 746
Oliphant, Eliza Ann IV, 650
Oliphant, Elizabeth IV, 52
Oliphant, Elizabeth IV, 606
Oliphant, Elizabeth IV, 610
Oliphant, Elizabeth IV, 619
Oliphant, Elizabeth IV, 624
Oliphant, Elizabeth IV, 631
Oliphant, Elizabeth IV, 649
Oliphant, Elizabeth IV, 650
Oliphant, Elizabeth IV, 704
Oliphant, Elizabeth IV, 727
Oliphant, Elizabeth IV, 746
Oliphant, Elizabeth IV, 880
Oliphant, Elizabeth IV, 983
Oliphant, Elizabeth VI, 313
Oliphant, Elizabeth VI, 354
Oliphant, Elizabeth VI, 646
Oliphant, Elizabeth VI, 647
Oliphant, Elizabeth M. IV, 746
Oliphant, Elizabeth M. IV, 836
Oliphant, Elizabeth M. IV, 851
Oliphant, Elizabeth M. IV, 1013
Oliphant, Elizabeth W. IV, 746
Oliphant, Ellazan IV, 542
Oliphant, Ellazan IV, 836
Oliphant, Ellazan H. IV, 746
Oliphant, Ellazan R. IV, 534
Oliphant, Ellazan R. IV, 542
Oliphant, Ephraim IV, 610
Oliphant, Ephraim IV, 624
Oliphant, Ephraim IV, 631
Oliphant, Ephraim IV, 649
Oliphant, Ephraim IV, 650
Oliphant, Ephraim IV, 704
Oliphant, Ephraim IV, 746
Oliphant, Ephraim IV, 880
Oliphant, Ephraim IV, 983
Oliphant, Ephraim IV, 994
Oliphant, Ephraim IV, 1218
Oliphant, Ephraim VI, 354
Oliphant, Eprhaim IV, 52
Oliphant, George Barclay IV, 836
Oliphant, Hannah IV, 746
Oliphant, Hannah IV, 836
Oliphant, Hannah IV, 851
Oliphant, Hannah P. IV, 542
Oliphant, Hannah P. IV, 746
Oliphant, Hannah P. IV, 787
Oliphant, Hannah P. IV, 819
Oliphant, Hannah P. IV, 836
Oliphant, Harriet V, 107
Oliphant, Henry M. IV, 610
Oliphant, Howard John IV, 542
Oliphant, Howard John IV, 800
Oliphant, Howard John IV, 836
Oliphant, Israel IV, 650
Oliphant, Israel IV, 746
Oliphant, Israel IV, 747
Oliphant, Israel IV, 983
Oliphant, Israel IV, 1218
Oliphant, Israel IV, 1219
Oliphant, Jacob IV, 610
Oliphant, John IV, 542
Oliphant, John IV, 632
Oliphant, John IV, 650
Oliphant, John IV, 746
Oliphant, John IV, 787
Oliphant, John IV, 819
Oliphant, John IV, 836
Oliphant, John IV, 851
Oliphant, John Howard IV, 679
Oliphant, John Howard IV, 746
Oliphant, John Oliphant IV, 610
Oliphant, John Wilton IV, 1218
Oliphant, Jonathan IV, 650
Oliphant, Jonathan IV, 746
Oliphant, Jonathan IV, 983
Oliphant, Laura M. IV, 836
Oliphant, Laura M. IV, 846
Oliphant, Lucretia IV, 1218
Oliphant, Lucretia IV, 1219
Oliphant, Lulu Bell IV, 1218
Oliphant, Lydia IV, 650
Oliphant, Lydia IV, 746
Oliphant, Lydia IV, 931
Oliphant, Lydia IV, 983
Oliphant, Lydia B. IV, 686
Oliphant, Lydia B. IV, 746
Oliphant, Lydia B. IV, 747
Oliphant, Lydia B. IV, 983
Oliphant, Mahlon IV, 610
Oliphant, Mahlon IV, 620
Oliphant, Mahlon IV, 650
Oliphant, Mahlon IV, 746
Oliphant, Maria IV, 632
Oliphant, Maria IV, 650
Oliphant, Maria IV, 746
Oliphant, Maria H. IV, 746
Oliphant, Maria K. IV, 746
Oliphant, Mary I, 1096
Oliphant, Mary Ann IV, 650
Oliphant, Mary Ann IV, 746
Oliphant, Mary Ann IV, 1212
Oliphant, Mary Letta IV, 1218
Oliphant, Nathan H., Jr. IV, 863
Oliphant, Olive IV, 843
Oliphant, Olive H. IV, 215
Oliphant, Olive H. IV, 256
Oliphant, Olive H. IV, 819
Oliphant, Olive H. IV, 836
Oliphant, Phebe L. IV, 792
Oliphant, Phebe S. IV, 746
Oliphant, Rachel IV, 52
Oliphant, Rachel IV, 607
Oliphant, Rachel IV, 608
Oliphant, Rachel IV, 610
Oliphant, Rachel IV, 619
Oliphant, Rachel IV, 631
Oliphant, Rachel IV, 649
Oliphant, Rachel IV, 650
Oliphant, Rachel IV, 683
Oliphant, Rachel IV, 746
Oliphant, Rachel IV, 836
Oliphant, Rachel IV, 983
Oliphant, Rachel VI, 354
Oliphant, Rebecca IV, 52
Oliphant, Rebecca IV, 610
Oliphant, Rebecca IV, 649
Oliphant, Rebeccah IV, 606
Oliphant, Rebeckah VI, 354
Oliphant, Richard IV, 610
Oliphant, Richard W. IV, 836
Oliphant, Ruth IV, 650
Oliphant, Ruth IV, 746
Oliphant, Ruth IV, 983
Oliphant, Ruth IV, 1218
Oliphant, Samuel IV, 52
Oliphant, Samuel IV, 606
Oliphant, Samuel IV, 607
Oliphant, Samuel IV, 608
Oliphant, Samuel IV, 610
Oliphant, Samuel IV, 619
Oliphant, Samuel IV, 631
Oliphant, Samuel IV, 649
Oliphant, Samuel IV, 650
Oliphant, Samuel IV, 683
Oliphant, Samuel IV, 746
Oliphant, Samuel IV, 836
Oliphant, Samuel IV, 983
Oliphant, Samuel VI, 313
Oliphant, Samuel VI, 354
Oliphant, Samuel VI, 501
Oliphant, Samuel VI, 502
Oliphant, Samuel VI, 540
Oliphant, Samuel H. IV, 746
Oliphant, Samuel, Jr. IV, 650
Oliphant, Samuel, Jr. IV, 746
Oliphant, Sarah IV, 607
Oliphant, Sarah IV, 624
Oliphant, Sarah IV, 650
Oliphant, Sarah IV, 704
Oliphant, Sarah IV, 705
Oliphant, Sarah IV, 746
Oliphant, Sarah IV, 863
Oliphant, Sarah IV, 880
Oliphant, Sarah IV, 983
Oliphant, Sarah IV, 994
Oliphant, Sarah Ann IV, 620
Oliphant, Sarah Ann IV, 650
Oliphant, Sarah H. IV, 650
Oliphant, Sarah H. IV, 746
Oliphant, Sarah H. IV, 880
Oliphant, Seth S. IV, 1218
Oliphant, Sina IV, 608
Oliphant, Sina IV, 650
Oliphant, Sina IV, 746
Oliphant, Sina W. IV, 650
Oliphant, Sina W. IV, 657
Oliphant, Sina W. IV, 746
Oliphant, Sina W. IV, 792
Oliphant, Sinah IV, 746
Oliphant, Virginia E. IV, 836
Oliphant, Wd. Elizabeth VI, 501
Oliphant, Widow Elizabeth VI, 540
Oliphant, William B. IV, 746
Oliphant, William D. IV, 836
Oliphant, William H. IV, 650
Oliphant, William H. IV, 657
Oliphant, William H. IV, 686
Oliphant, William H. IV, 746
Oliphant, William H. IV, 747
Oliphant, William W. IV, 746
Oliphant, Wm. IV, 649
Oliphant, Wm. IV, 650
Oliphant, Wm. IV, 836
Oliphant, Wm. IV, 1219
Oliphant, Wm. D. IV, 513
Oliphant, Wm. D. IV, 534
Oliphant, Wm. D. IV, 542
Oliphant, Wm. D. IV, 746
Oliphant, Wm. D. IV, 836
Oliphant, Wm. H. IV, 746
Oliphant, Wm. H. IV, 792
Oliphant, Wm. H. IV, 931
Oliphant, Wm. H. IV, 983
Olive, Isaac Marriott II, 246
Olive, Joyce II, 246
Olive, Mary II, 219
Olive, Mary II, 246
Olive, Richard II, 246
Olive, Thomas II, 163
Olive, Thomas II, 246
Oliver, Agness VI, 971
Oliver, Amanda VI, 844
Oliver, Amos V, 636
Oliver, Anise IV, 1177
Oliver, Ann A. VI, 802
Oliver, Ann M. VI, 844
Oliver, Anna II, 958
Oliver, Annis IV, 1177
Oliver, Asa V, 701
Oliver, Asa V, 720
Oliver, Asa Lee V, 701
Oliver, Benjamin VI, 827
Oliver, Benjamin VI, 828
Oliver, Benjamin VI, 845
Oliver, Benjamin VI, 860
Oliver, Berdyrine VI, 844
Oliver, Charles VI, 844
Oliver, Charles I. VI, 844
Oliver, Charles W. VI, 971
Oliver, Daniel II, 401
Oliver, Daniel IV, 257
Oliver, Daniel IV, 424
Oliver, Daniel IV, 543
Oliver, Daniel VI, 971
Oliver, Delilah H. IV, 747
Oliver, Elizabeth II, 534
Oliver, Elizabeth II, 610
Oliver, Elizabeth II, 814
Oliver, Elizabeth II, 958
Oliver, Elizabeth VI, 828
Oliver, Elizabeth VI, 966
Oliver, Elizabeth VI, 971
Oliver, Elizabeth Breed II, 966
Oliver, Elma II, 948
Oliver, Elma II, 949
Oliver, Elma II, 1057
Oliver, Elma II, 1087
Oliver, Elma II, 1089
Oliver, Elma F. II, 949
Oliver, Elma F. IV, 747
Oliver, Elma French II, 966
Oliver, Elma French II, 1060
Oliver, Emma Ellison V, 636
Oliver, Emma Talbott II, 966
Oliver, Esther IV, 257
Oliver, Esther IV, 424
Oliver, Esther IV, 543
Oliver, Esther IV, 1177
Oliver, Esther V. IV, 1177
Oliver, Evan II, 401
Oliver, Evan II, 610
Oliver, George IV, 1177
Oliver, George V, 701
Oliver, George V, 715
Oliver, George C. IV, 1177
Oliver, Hazel V, 701
Oliver, Hazel V, 720
Oliver, James VI, 844
Oliver, James VI, 946
Oliver, James VI, 971
Oliver, James C. VI, 946
Oliver, Jane II, 401
Oliver, Jane V, 1013
Oliver, John IV, 257
Oliver, Joseph VI, 822
Oliver, Judith A. VI, 844
Oliver, Lucille Sharpless II, 966
Oliver, Lynn II, 1060
Oliver, Margaret Emily VI, 966
Oliver, Marguerite V, 701
Oliver, Marguerite V, 715
Oliver, Mary II, 610
Oliver, Mary II, 966
Oliver, Mary VI, 887
Oliver, Mary VI, 946
Oliver, Mary Genevieve V, 699
Oliver, Mary Genevive V, 701
Oliver, Mary Sydney II, 1057
Oliver, Mary Sydney II, 1060
Oliver, Mary T. VI, 822
Oliver, Mildred VI, 860
Oliver, Minerva Ann VI, 946
Oliver, Oliver T. II, 966
Oliver, Rachel IV, 983
Oliver, Randal VI, 844
Oliver, Reuben II, 610
Oliver, Sally VI, 971
Oliver, Sarah IV, 543
Oliver, Sarah J. II, 1087
Oliver, Sarah J. II, 1089
Oliver, Sarah M. V, 636
Oliver, Susan II, 966
Oliver, Theresa II, 401
Oliver, Thomas II, 401
Oliver, Thomas II, 610
Oliver, Thomas VI, 887
Oliver, Thos. VI, 971
Oliver, Wd. Jane II, 401
Oliver, Wendall French II, 1060
Oliver, Wendell F. II, 1057
Oliver, Wendell French II, 966
Oliver, Wendell French II, 1057
Oliver, William VI, 815
Oliver, William VI, 844
Oliver, William VI, 971
Oliver, William B. II, 966
Oliver, William B. II, 1087
Oliver, William B. II, 1089
Oliver, William T. II, 948
Oliver, William T. II, 949
Oliver, William T. II, 958
Oliver, William T. II, 1087
Oliver, William T. II, 1089
Oliver, William Theodore II, 966
Oliver, William W. VI, 946
Oliver, William Wendell II, 966
Oliver, Wm. Theodore II, 1057
Oliver, Wm. Theodore II, 1060
Ollden, Catharine II, 457
Ollden, Catharine II, 610
Ollden, James II, 457
Ollden, James II, 610
Ollden, John II, 610
Ollden, Mary II, 457
Ollden, Mary II, 610
Ollifant, Samuel VI, 335
Olliphant, Ann IV, 746
Olliphant, Eliza IV, 746
Olliphant, Elizabeth VI, 335
Olliphant, Ellazan IV, 542
Olliphant, Hannah VI, 335
Olliphant, Harris VI, 335
Olliphant, Israel IV, 746
Olliphant, John IV, 746
Olliphant, Jonas VI, 335
Olliphant, Levi VI, 335
Olliphant, Mary VI, 335
Olliphant, Rachel IV, 746
Olliphant, Samuel VI, 335
Olliphant, Samuel, Jr. IV, 746
Olliphant, Sarah IV, 746
Olliphant, William H. IV, 746
Olliphant, William, Jr. VI, 335
Olliphent, Abner IV, 650
Olliphent, Sarah IV, 650
Ollive, Joyce II, 235
Ollive, Joyce II, 241
Ollive, Joyce II, 246
Ollive, Mary II, 246
Ollive, Mary II, 273
Ollive, Richard II, 235
Ollive, Richard II, 241
Ollive, Richard II, 246
Ollive, Thomas II, 246
Ollive, Thomas II, 273
Olmstead, Anna IV, 747
Olmstead, Anne IV, 747
Olmstead, Elmer IV, 1177
Olmstead, Elmer C. IV, 1177
Olmstead, Louisa III, 243
Olmstead, Mary Jane III, 243
Olmstead, William IV, 747
Olmstead, William B. III, 243
Olney, Edwin III, 410
Olney, Elizabeth III, 410
Olney, Elizabeth III, 431
Olney, Lafayette III, 420
Olney, Lafayette III, 431
Olney, Mary III, 410
Olney, Wd. Lafayette III, 410
Olophant, Elizabeth IV, 633
Olophant, Ephraim IV, 633
Olophant, Mary Ann IV, 633
Olophant, Mary Ann IV, 650

er, Elma F. IV, 709
er, Elma F. IV, 747
n, Caroline L. III, 83
n, Caroline III, 51
n, Caroline III, 83
n, John A. IV, 1332
n, Mrs. Mariah IV, 1332
n, Oscar V, 1013
s, Charles M. V, 589
s, Clay V, 589
s, Edna V, 107
s, Edna V, 589
s, Edna V, 701
s, Edna R. V, 701
s, Ella V, 701
s, Elmira V, 701
s, Eva V, 589
s, Frank V, 589
s, Laverne V, 107
s, Laverne V, 589
s, Lovina C. V, 589
s, Rebecca V, 589
s, Samuel William V, 107
s, Sherman V, 589
s, William V, 107
s, William P. V, 107
s, Willie V, 589
s, Wm. V, 589
s, Wm. V, 701
s, Wm. H. V, 589
s, Wm. P. V, 589
n, Eli IV, 52
n, Eli IV, 131
n, Judah IV, 747
n, Susan Chase IV, 747
n, Susan E. IV, 747
erdenk, Dr. Francis S. Jr III, 173
erdenk, Franziska III, 173
erdonk, Adrian C. III, 243
erdonk, Bertha III, 243
erdonk, Elizabeth III, 243
erdonk, Elizabeth III, 302
erdonk, Elizabeth S. III, 243
erdonk, Fanny III, 243
erdonk, Francis III, 243
erdonk, Francis S. III, 243
erdonk, Francis S., Jr. III, 243
erdonk, Franziska III, 243
erdonk, Henry III, 443
erdonk, J. W. III, 83
erdonk, John III, 243
erdonk, John W. III, 83
erdonk, John W. III, 243
erdonk, John W. III, 302
erdonk, John Wm. III, 81
erdonk, John Wm. III, 243
erdonk, Latitia III, 443
erdonk, Lydia III, 443
erdonk, Margaret III, 81
erdonk, Margaret III, 83
erdonk, Margaret III, 243
erdonk, Margaret III, 302
erdonk, Margaret, Jr. III, 243
erdonk, Mary F. III, 243
erduck, Elizabeth III, 149
Elizabeth II, 90
al, Ann IV, 268
all, Abijah V, 83
all, Abijah V, 110
all, Abijah P. V, 107
all, Anna V, 83
all, Anna V, 110
all, Martha V, 107
all, Mary Ann V, 43
all, Mary Ann V, 107
all, Rebecca V, 107
all, Rhoda V, 83
all, Rhoda V, 107
all, Sarah V, 107
all, Sarah V, 110
all, William V, 107
all, William VI, 427
y, Ann Elizabeth VI, 971
y, Charles B. VI, 971
y, Demarius VI, 945
y, Eliza VI, 1009
y, James VI, 882
y, James VI, 934
y, James VI, 971
y, James L. VI, 934
y, James W. VI, 971
y, Mary VI, 891
y, Mary C. VI, 971
y, Mary F. VI, 971
y, Nancy VI, 944
y, Polly VI, 971
y, Susannah M. VI, 77
y, Susannah M. VI, 89
Oney, Thomas VI, 891
Oney, Thomas VI, 925
Oney, Thomas VI, 935
Oney, Thomas VI, 944
Oney, Thomas VI, 945
Oney, Thomas VI, 947
Oney, Thomas VI, 971
Oney, Thomas VI, 1009
Ong, A. R. IV, 490
Ong, A. R. IV, 491
Ong, Albert R. IV, 491
Ong, Amanda IV, 257
Ong, Amanda IV, 490
Ong, Amanda IV, 491
Ong, Amanda IV, 926
Ong, Amanda IV, 984
Ong, Anderson C. IV, 257
Ong, Anderson C. IV, 490
Ong, Anderson C. IV, 491
Ong, Anderson C. IV, 984
Ong, Anderson C. IV, 1259
Ong, Ann IV, 75
Ong, Ann IV, 104
Ong, Ann IV, 490
Ong, Ann Eliza IV, 257
Ong, Ann Eliza IV, 490
Ong, Anna IV, 257
Ong, Anna IV, 466
Ong, Anna IV, 480
Ong, Anna IV, 481
Ong, Anna IV, 490
Ong, Anna IV, 491
Ong, Anna IV, 497
Ong, Anne IV, 104
Ong, Annie E. IV, 984
Ong, Annie L. IV, 491
Ong, C. A. IV, 474
Ong, Catharine IV, 257
Ong, Catharine IV, 490
Ong, Celia IV, 487
Ong, Celia IV, 491
Ong, Celia A. IV, 490
Ong, Chas. IV, 257
Ong, Clarence IV, 490
Ong, Clarence IV, 491
Ong, Clarence W. IV, 491
Ong, Delbert IV, 491
Ong, Delbert B. IV, 490
Ong, Delbert L. IV, 491
Ong, Delbert T. IV, 491
Ong, Delbert T. IV, 984
Ong, Delbert T. IV, 1259
Ong, Dinah IV, 104
Ong, Dinah IV, 155
Ong, Effa Lorena IV, 984
Ong, Effie IV, 1219
Ong, Effie IV, 1259
Ong, Effie Lorena IV, 1041
Ong, Effie Lourena IV, 1259
Ong, Eilene IV, 257
Ong, Eliza IV, 257
Ong, Eliza IV, 483
Ong, Elizabeth IV, 99
Ong, Elizabeth IV, 104
Ong, Elizabeth IV, 131
Ong, Elizabeth IV, 482
Ong, Elizabeth IV, 490
Ong, Elizana IV, 483
Ong, Elizana IV, 491
Ong, Elizanna IV, 490
Ong, Ella P. IV, 491
Ong, Elmira IV, 257
Ong, Elmira IV, 490
Ong, Elmira IV, 491
Ong, Elmira IV, 494
Ong, Elmira IV, 983
Ong, Elmira IV, 984
Ong, Elmira IV, 1259
Ong, Elmyra IV, 984
Ong, Elva L. IV, 491
Ong, Emily IV, 467
Ong, Emily IV, 491
Ong, Emma IV, 257
Ong, Emma IV, 491
Ong, Emma L. IV, 491
Ong, Emma L. IV, 497
Ong, Enly IV, 490
Ong, Ethel IV, 1259
Ong, Findley IV, 257
Ong, Finley IV, 52
Ong, Finley IV, 104
Ong, Finley IV, 155
Ong, Finley IV, 466
Ong, Finley IV, 480
Ong, Finley IV, 483
Ong, Finley IV, 490
Ong, Finley IV, 491
Ong, Finley VI, 427
Ong, Finley K. IV, 257
Ong, Finley K. IV, 490
Ong, Florence IV, 1259
Ong, Fred IV, 490
Ong, George IV, 1259
Ong, George Lewis IV, 1041
Ong, George Lewis IV, 1259
Ong, Gertrude IV, 1259
Ong, Gideon Swain IV, 257
Ong, Hannah IV, 257
Ong, Hannah IV, 490
Ong, Harlem IV, 490
Ong, Harlen IV, 490
Ong, Harlin IV, 491
Ong, Howard IV, 490
Ong, Howard IV, 491
Ong, Ida E. IV, 474
Ong, Iola IV, 257
Ong, Iola IV, 491
Ong, Iola C. IV, 257
Ong, Iola C. IV, 491
Ong, Isaac IV, 104
Ong, Isaac IV, 155
Ong, Isaac IV, 257
Ong, Isaac IV, 490
Ong, Isabel IV, 131
Ong, Isabel IV, 132
Ong, Isabella IV, 104
Ong, Isabella IV, 131
Ong, J. IV, 490
Ong, J. B. IV, 245
Ong, J. F. IV, 490
Ong, Jacob IV, 52
Ong, Jacob IV, 71
Ong, Jacob IV, 104
Ong, Jacob IV, 137
Ong, Jacob IV, 155
Ong, Jacob IV, 167
Ong, Jacob IV, 257
Ong, Jacob IV, 481
Ong, Jacob IV, 485
Ong, Jacob IV, 490
Ong, Jacob VI, 427
Ong, Jacob, Jr. IV, 490
Ong, James IV, 104
Ong, James IV, 131
Ong, Jane IV, 104
Ong, Jane IV, 131
Ong, Jesse IV, 104
Ong, Jesse IV, 131
Ong, Jessie L. IV, 490
Ong, John IV, 104
Ong, John IV, 155
Ong, Joseph II, 401
Ong, Joseph IV, 491
Ong, Joseph IV, 1259
Ong, Joseph P. IV, 257
Ong, Joseph P. IV, 490
Ong, Joseph P. IV, 491
Ong, Joseph P. IV, 498
Ong, Joseph P. IV, 984
Ong, Joseph P. IV, 1005
Ong, Joseph P. IV, 1041
Ong, L. B. IV, 1259
Ong, Lemuel IV, 257
Ong, Lemuel IV, 490
Ong, Lemuel M. IV, 491
Ong, Lewis IV, 257
Ong, Lewis IV, 490
Ong, Lewis IV, 491
Ong, Lewis IV, 494
Ong, Lewis IV, 983
Ong, Lewis IV, 984
Ong, Lewis IV, 1259
Ong, Lewis B. IV, 491
Ong, Lewis B. IV, 984
Ong, Lewis B. IV, 1259
Ong, Lewis H. IV, 491
Ong, Lida D. IV, 1259
Ong, Lindley IV, 1259
Ong, Lindley H. IV, 257
Ong, Lindley H. IV, 490
Ong, Lizzie IV, 474
Ong, Lizzie IV, 491
Ong, Lonore IV, 1259
Ong, Louis B. IV, 1259
Ong, M. IV, 474
Ong, M. IV, 490
Ong, M. J. IV, 490
Ong, Mabel C. IV, 490
Ong, Martha IV, 491
Ong, Martha A. IV, 257
Ong, Martha Ann IV, 490
Ong, Mary IV, 52
Ong, Mary IV, 71
Ong, Mary IV, 104
Ong, Mary IV, 131
Ong, Mary IV, 134
Ong, Mary IV, 155
Ong, Mary IV, 245
Ong, Mary IV, 257
Ong, Mary IV, 481
Ong, Mary IV, 485
Ong, Mary IV, 490
Ong, Mary IV, 491
Ong, Mary VI, 427
Ong, Mary B. IV, 466
Ong, Mary B. IV, 490
Ong, Mary C. IV, 490
Ong, Mary Eliza IV, 257
Ong, Mary Elizabeth IV, 257
Ong, Mary Elizabeth IV, 491
Ong, Mary H. IV, 491
Ong, Mary R. IV, 465
Ong, Mary R. IV, 491
Ong, Mary S. T. IV, 257
Ong, Mary T. IV, 257
Ong, Matilda IV, 490
Ong, Matthias F. IV, 490
Ong, Mattie IV, 491
Ong, Miffen IV, 490
Ong, Miffin IV, 482
Ong, Mifflin IV, 257
Ong, Mifflin IV, 465
Ong, Mifflin IV, 490
Ong, Mifflin IV, 491
Ong, Mifflin J. IV, 490
Ong, Miflin IV, 257
Ong, Minnie IV, 1259
Ong, Minnie R. IV, 1259
Ong, Moses IV, 490
Ong, Moses H. IV, 257
Ong, Moses H. IV, 490
Ong, Moses H. IV, 491
Ong, Naomi IV, 491
Ong, Nathan IV, 104
Ong, Nathan IV, 155
Ong, Nathan IV, 257
Ong, Nathan IV, 490
Ong, O. B. IV, 257
Ong, Oliver IV, 257
Ong, Oliver IV, 490
Ong, Oliver IV, 491
Ong, Osborn IV, 257
Ong, Osborn IV, 491
Ong, Osborn B. IV, 257
Ong, Plummer IV, 257
Ong, Plummer IV, 490
Ong, Rachel Ann IV, 216
Ong, Rachel Ann IV, 257
Ong, Rachel Ann IV, 474
Ong, Rachel Ann IV, 490
Ong, Rachel Ann IV, 491
Ong, Rachel E. IV, 490
Ong, Ralph IV, 257
Ong, Ralph O. IV, 257
Ong, Rebecca IV, 52
Ong, Rebecca IV, 99
Ong, Rebecca IV, 104
Ong, Rebecca IV, 480
Ong, Rebecca IV, 490
Ong, Rebecca IV, 491
Ong, Rebecca VI, 427
Ong, Rebecca D. IV, 579
Ong, Rebeccah II, 401
Ong, Rebeckah IV, 104
Ong, Rhoda IV, 491
Ong, Rhoda IV, 498
Ong, Rhoda IV, 1259
Ong, Rhoda S. IV, 984
Ong, Rhoda S. IV, 1005
Ong, Rhoda S. IV, 1041
Ong, Rosa IV, 491
Ong, Ross IV, 491
Ong, Sarah IV, 218
Ong, Sarah IV, 257
Ong, Sarah J. IV, 257
Ong, Sarah J. IV, 490
Ong, Sarah J. IV, 491
Ong, Sarah Jane IV, 257
Ong, Shepherd IV, 491
Ong, W. P. IV, 1259
Ong, William IV, 257
Ong, William IV, 490
Ong, William IV, 491
Ong, William P. IV, 257
Ong, William P. IV, 490
Ong, William P. IV, 491
Ong, William P. IV, 984
Ong, Wm. IV, 490
Ong, Zola IV, 490
Ongin, Charles II, 401
Oosley, Betty V, 954
Oosley, Betty V, 957
Oosley, Keturah V, 953
Oosley, Keturah V, 957
Opal, Pearl IV, 985
Opey, Mary G. III, 450
Opey, Mary Garetta III, 450
Oplinger, Hannah G. IV, 589
Oplinger, Sarah T. IV, 589
Oram, Hester II, 446
Oram, Mira II, 757
Oram, Rachel W. II, 714
Oram, Rebecca VI, 490
Oram, Rebecca VI, 540
Oram, Wm. II, 446
Oran, Alfred V, 637
Oran, Esther V, 172
Oran, Esther V, 195
Oran, Esther V, 622
Oran, Esther V, 637
Oran, James V, 637
Oran, Joannah V, 610
Oran, Joannah V, 637
Oran, John V, 622
Oran, John A. V, 610
Oran, John A. V, 637
Oran, Lydia V, 622
Oran, Margaret V, 637
Oran, Margaret Ellen V, 637
Oran, Mary V, 637
Oran, Sarah Ann V, 637
Oran, Thomas Chalkley V, 637
Orange, Catharine J. VI, 918
Orange, Wm. S. VI, 918
Orbaugh, Ruth Anna IV, 747
Orbin, Anna Lou V, 701
Orbin, Anna Lou V, 708
Orbin, Sleva Wm. V, 708
Orbin, Sleve William V, 701
Ordway, Joshua III, 244
Ore, America VI, 971
Ore, Caroline I, 1160
Ore, Edward VI, 947
Ore, Edward VI, 964
Ore, Edward VI, 971
Ore, Edward VI, 1020
Ore, Elizabeth VI, 901
Ore, Evelina VI, 971
Ore, George L. I, 1160
Ore, James A. VI, 881
Ore, James A. VI, 971
Ore, Jas. A. VI, 1020
Ore, Jenny VI, 901
Ore, Judy F. VI, 971
Ore, Mary Ann VI, 1020
Ore, Matthew J. VI, 936
Ore, Matthew J. VI, 950
Ore, Matthew J. VI, 971
Ore, Ramsom I, 1160
Ore, Rebecca VI, 971
Ore, Ruthanna IV, 543
Ore, Ruthanna IV, 546
Ore, Sarah VI, 971
Ore, Sarah Jane VI, 901
Ore, Sarah Jane VI, 964
Ore, William VI, 901
Ore, William VI, 964
Ore, William VI, 971
Ore, William H. VI, 963
Ore, William H. VI, 971
Ore, Wm. H. VI, 964
Oreiley, Clara B. IV, 1259
Oren, Abigail V, 268
Oren, Abigail V, 472
Oren, Abigail V, 520
Oren, Abigail V, 637
Oren, Absalom V, 636
Oren, Absalom V, 637
Oren, Alex V, 353
Oren, Alexander V, 353
Oren, Alexander V, 362
Oren, Alexander V, 491
Oren, Alexander V, 520
Oren, Alexander V, 637
Oren, Alexandria V, 520
Oren, Alexandria V, 544
Oren, Alfeus V, 520
Oren, Alfred V, 462
Oren, Alfred V, 520
Oren, Alfred V, 521
Oren, Alfred V, 637
Oren, Allis V, 637
Oren, Alva W. V, 195
Oren, Alvan V, 701
Oren, Alvin V, 520
Oren, Alvin V, 521
Oren, Alvin V, 637
Oren, Angeline V, 637
Oren, Anna V, 701
Oren, Arthur E. V, 521
Oren, Asa V, 637
Oren, Asaneth V, 195
Oren, Asenath V, 512
Oren, Asenath V, 520
Oren, Asenath V, 521
Oren, Asenath V, 637
Oren, Aseneth V, 828
Oren, Asenith V, 512
Oren, Asenith V, 520
Oren, Chalkley V, 353
Oren, Chalkley V, 520
Oren, Chalkley V, 521
Oren, Charles V, 462
Oren, Charles B. V, 462

Oren, Charles H. V, 521
Oren, Clara J. V, 521
Oren, Daniel V, 353
Oren, Daniel B. V, 520
Oren, Daniel B. V, 637
Oren, David V, 520
Oren, David V, 636
Oren, David V, 701
Oren, Elie V, 637
Oren, Elihu V, 520
Oren, Elijah V, 195
Oren, Elijah V, 637
Oren, Elijah V, 957
Oren, Eliza V, 637
Oren, Eliza V, 644
Oren, Elizabeth V, 161
Oren, Elizabeth V, 195
Oren, Elizabeth V, 462
Oren, Elizabeth V, 621
Oren, Elizabeth V, 637
Oren, Elizabeth V, 650
Oren, Elizabeth L. V, 462
Oren, Elizabeth Lydia Abigail V, 637
Oren, Ephraim V, 636
Oren, Ephraim V, 637
Oren, Ephrim V, 621
Oren, Esther V, 195
Oren, Esther V, 353
Oren, Esther V, 636
Oren, Esther V, 637
Oren, Esther B. V, 353
Oren, Ezekiel V, 353
Oren, Ezekiel V, 520
Oren, Ezekiel V, 637
Oren, Frank V, 658
Oren, Frank V, 701
Oren, Hannah V, 195
Oren, Hannah V, 353
Oren, Hannah V, 520
Oren, Hannah V, 542
Oren, Hannah V, 544
Oren, Hannah V, 636
Oren, Hannah V, 637
Oren, Hannah Jane V, 637
Oren, Henry V, 637
Oren, Henry G. V, 353
Oren, Henry G. V, 637
Oren, Henry Gilpin V, 195
Oren, Ira V, 195
Oren, Isabella V, 637
Oren, Isaiah V, 637
Oren, J. A. V, 462
Oren, Jacob V, 636
Oren, Jacob L. V, 621
Oren, Jacob L. V, 637
Oren, James V, 195
Oren, James V, 353
Oren, James V, 520
Oren, James V, 521
Oren, James V, 637
Oren, James V, 701
Oren, James V, 957
Oren, James E. V, 520
Oren, James E. V, 521
Oren, James E. V, 701
Oren, James Ezekiel V, 637
Oren, Jane V, 195
Oren, Jane V, 520
Oren, Jane V, 536
Oren, Jane V, 637
Oren, Jesse V, 520
Oren, Jesse N. V, 521
Oren, Joanna V, 520
Oren, Joanna V, 637
Oren, Joanna A. V, 462
Oren, Joannah V, 637
Oren, Joel Starbeck V, 637
Oren, John I, 1096
Oren, John V, 195
Oren, John V, 257
Oren, John V, 268
Oren, John V, 353
Oren, John V, 462
Oren, John V, 520
Oren, John V, 609
Oren, John V, 628
Oren, John V, 636
Oren, John V, 637
Oren, John V, 639
Oren, John V, 957
Oren, John A. V, 353
Oren, John A. V, 462
Oren, John A. V, 520
Oren, John A. V, 521
Oren, John A. V, 637
Oren, John F. V, 353
Oren, John F. V, 520
Oren, John F. V, 637
Oren, John, Jr. V, 610
Oren, John, Jr. V, 637
Oren, Joseph V, 176
Oren, Joseph V, 195
Oren, Joseph V, 268
Oren, Joseph V, 512
Oren, Joseph V, 520
Oren, Joseph V, 636
Oren, Joseph V, 637
Oren, Joseph V, 701
Oren, Joseph V, 828
Oren, Joseph V, 957
Oren, Laura E. V, 268
Oren, Laura E. V, 462
Oren, Leslie V, 521
Oren, Levi V, 462
Oren, Levi V, 637
Oren, Levi B. V, 462
Oren, Lewis V, 637
Oren, Lizzie V, 462
Oren, Lydia V, 257
Oren, Lydia V, 268
Oren, Lydia V, 353
Oren, Lydia V, 362
Oren, Lydia V, 472
Oren, Lydia V, 491
Oren, Lydia V, 520
Oren, Lydia V, 544
Oren, Lydia V, 609
Oren, Lydia V, 636
Oren, Lydia V, 637
Oren, Lydia Ann V, 353
Oren, Lydia Ann V, 520
Oren, Lydia, Jr. V, 353
Oren, Lydia, Sr. V, 637
Oren, Margaret V, 195
Oren, Margaret V, 472
Oren, Margaret V, 520
Oren, Margaret V, 637
Oren, Margaret V, 701
Oren, Margaret V, 828
Oren, Margaret V, 957
Oren, Margaret E. V, 520
Oren, Margaret E. V, 637
Oren, Margaret Ellen V, 637
Oren, Martha V, 610
Oren, Martha V, 637
Oren, Martha V, 644
Oren, Martha J. V, 628
Oren, Martha J. V, 637
Oren, Mary V, 268
Oren, Mary V, 520
Oren, Mary V, 521
Oren, Mary V, 621
Oren, Mary V, 637
Oren, Mary V, 701
Oren, Mary Ann V, 177
Oren, Mary Ann V, 195
Oren, Mary Ann V, 637
Oren, Mary B. V, 520
Oren, Mary B. V, 521
Oren, Mary B. V, 701
Oren, Moses V, 637
Oren, Moses F. V, 353
Oren, Moses F. V, 520
Oren, Phebe V, 172
Oren, Phebe V, 195
Oren, Phebe V, 353
Oren, Phebe V, 520
Oren, Phebe V, 636
Oren, Phebe V, 637
Oren, Phebe Hannah Jane V, 637
Oren, Phebee V, 506
Oren, Philip M. V, 521
Oren, Rachel V, 520
Oren, Rachel V, 701
Oren, Rachel L. V, 520
Oren, Rachel L. V, 701
Oren, Rebecca V, 331
Oren, Rebecca V, 353
Oren, Rebecca V, 637
Oren, Rebecca F. V, 353
Oren, Ruth V, 176
Oren, Ruth V, 195
Oren, Ruth V, 353
Oren, Ruth V, 362
Oren, Ruth V, 462
Oren, Ruth V, 520
Oren, Ruth V, 609
Oren, Ruth V, 636
Oren, Ruth V, 637
Oren, Ruth V, 639
Oren, Ruth V, 655
Oren, Ruth V, 701
Oren, Sarah V, 160
Oren, Sarah V, 176
Oren, Sarah V, 520
Oren, Sarah V, 636
Oren, Sarah V, 637
Oren, Sarah V, 701
Oren, Sarah A. V, 520
Oren, Sarah Ann V, 268
Oren, Sarah Ann V, 520
Oren, Sarah Ann V, 521
Oren, Sarah Ann V, 637
Oren, Sarah H. V, 520
Oren, Sarah H. V, 701
Oren, Susan V, 268
Oren, Susan V, 520
Oren, Susan V, 521
Oren, Susanna V, 195
Oren, Susannah V, 637
Oren, Susannah V, 645
Oren, Susannah V, 957
Oren, Tessie C. V, 658
Oren, Tessie C. V, 701
Oren, Thomas V, 520
Oren, Thomas V, 701
Oren, Thomas C. V, 520
Oren, Thomas C. V, 637
Oren, Thomas Chalkley V, 637
Oren, Thomas H. V, 520
Oren, Thomas H. V, 701
Oren, William V, 195
Oren, William A. V, 195
Oren, Wm. V, 637
Oren, Wm. V, 957
Orenduff, Jesse VI, 953
Organ, Anne VI, 844
Organ, Behethaland VI, 971
Organ, Betsey VI, 844
Organ, Elcy VI, 844
Organ, Elizabeth VI, 812
Organ, Elizabeth VI, 844
Organ, Elizabeth A. VI, 844
Organ, Erness VI, 952
Organ, Henry A. VI, 844
Organ, Holcombe VI, 844
Organ, James VI, 844
Organ, John VI, 844
Organ, John J. VI, 917
Organ, John J. VI, 971
Organ, Mary VI, 832
Organ, Mary Ann P. VI, 971
Organ, Mary P. VI, 844
Organ, Milly VI, 819
Organ, Samuel VI, 814
Organ, Samuel VI, 971
Organ, Sarah VI, 812
Organ, Susan W. VI, 844
Organ, William VI, 832
Organ, William VI, 835
Organ, William VI, 844
Orin, Abigail V, 947
Orin, John I, 1096
Orin, John V, 947
Orison, Helen IV, 345
Orist, Erastus I, 7
Orist, Ida Leanora I, 7
Orm, Deborah B. VI, 427
Orm, Harriet P. VI, 427
Orm, Phebe R. VI, 427
Ormdorf, Sarah Ann IV, 1259
Orme, Harriet P. VI, 427
Orme, Mary II, 610
Orme, Mary II, 665
Orme, Richard II, 610
Orme, Richard II, 665
Ormerod, Daisy Eliz III, 158
Ormerod, Daisy Elizabeth III, 244
Ormerod, Eliz. III, 244
Ormerod, Elizabeth III, 158
Ormerod, John III, 158
Ormerod, John III, 244
Orms, Richard II, 401
Ormsby, ??? II, 811
Ormsby, Anna M. II, 811
Ormsby, Anna M. II, 904
Ormsby, Anna Maria II, 714
Ormsby, Blanch IV, 747
Ormsby, Caroline A. II, 714
Ormsby, Carolyn S. II, 757
Ormsby, Catharine IV, 747
Ormsby, Catherine II, 811
Ormsby, Elizabeth IV, 1041
Ormsby, Harry IV, 747
Ormsby, Henry II, 812
Ormsby, Henry II, 904
Ormsby, Henry G., Jr. II, 757
Ormsby, Henry George II, 714
Ormsby, Henry George II, 757
Ormsby, Henry George II, 811
Ormsby, Henry George II, 904
Ormsby, Henry George, Jr. II, 714
Ormsby, Henry George, Jr. II, 812
Ormsby, Henry S. II, 714
Ormsby, Iva IV, 747
Ormsby, Ivy IV, 747
Ormsby, James IV, 747
Ormsby, Jane II, 904
Ormsby, Lizzie IV, 1041
Ormsby, Malisa IV, 747
Ormsby, Malisa IV, 763
Ormsby, Mary II, 904
Ormsby, Mary IV, 747
Ormsby, Mary K. II, 904
Ormsby, Robert S. II, 714
Ormsby, Wd. Jane II, 812
Ormsby, Wm. IV, 747
Orn, Ann IV, 424
Orn, Ann IV, 434
Ornstein, Bertha III, 243
Oron, Alexander V, 353
Oron, Ezekiel V, 353
Oron, Hannah V, 353
Oron, James V, 353
Oron, John F. V, 353
Oron, Lydia V, 353
Oron, Lydia Ann V, 353
Oron, Moses F. V, 353
Oron, Phebe V, 353
Orr, Ann IV, 543
Orr, Ann VI, 540
Orr, Anna IV, 543
Orr, Anna IV, 548
Orr, Asa V, 590
Orr, Elizabeth V, 589
Orr, Elizabeth VI, 844
Orr, George V, 589
Orr, George V, 590
Orr, Gertrude V, 589
Orr, Gertrude V, 590
Orr, Harold V, 590
Orr, Harold N. V, 590
Orr, Harriet M. IV, 912
Orr, Harry V, 589
Orr, Hershel B. V, 590
Orr, Howard V, 589
Orr, Howard W. V, 590
Orr, Jeanette IV, 900
Orr, Jeannett IV, 984
Orr, Jesse Kirk V, 590
Orr, John VI, 844
Orr, Lalia Lucile V, 590
Orr, Mary IV, 487
Orr, Mary IV, 491
Orr, Mary IV, 900
Orr, Mary E. IV, 912
Orr, Mary M. III, 108
Orr, Odis V, 590
Orr, Osee V, 590
Orr, Parker IV, 900
Orr, Parker IV, 912
Orr, Ruthanna IV, 543
Orr, S. B. V, 589
Orr, W. V, 590
Orr, Zion M. E. IV, 912
Orrison, Amos IV, 447
Orrison, Helen IV, 447
Orrison, Rebecca IV, 424
Orrison, Rebecca IV, 447
Orsband, Selah I, 565
Orsborn, G. W. I, 1160
Orsborn, George E. I, 1160
Orsborn, George W. I, 1160
Orsborn, Sarah I, 1160
Orsborn, Wm. R. I, 1160
Orsen, Mary Moon V, 701
Ort, Evalena III, 244
Ort, Evalena III, 323
Orten, Hannah II, 149
Orten, Hannah II, 154
Ortloff, Frank III, 244
Ortloff, Thomas P. E. III, 244
Orton, Hannah II, 119
Orton, Hannah II, 121
Orton, Hannah II, 149
Orton, Hannah II, 154
Orton, Helen C. V, 701
Orton, Luella Cook V, 701
Orum, Benjamin II, 401
Orum, Elizabeth II, 401
Orum, Mary II, 401
Orum, Mira II, 757
Orum, Mira O. II, 757
Orum, Mira O. II, 762
Orum, Rachel W. II, 757
Orville, Emma M. V, 590
Orvis, Edward Ernest III, 244
Orvis, Emma II, 732
Orvis, Emma II, 757
Orvis, Emma III, 244
Orvis, Emma G. III, 130
Orvis, Emma G. III, 161
Orvis, Emma G. III, 244
Orvis, Eugene Luvois III, 244
Orvis, Francis W. III, 130
Orvis, Francis W. III, 161
Orvis, Francis W. III, 244
Orvis, Francis Wayland II, 732
Orvis, Francis Wayland II, 757
Orvis, Harold H. II, 757
Orvis, Harold Heacock II, 714
Orvis, Harold Heacock II, 732
Orvis, Harold Heacock II, 757
Orvis, Harold Heacock III, 24
Orvis, Leora A. C. II, 714
Orvis, Leora Alice II, 732
Orvis, Leora Alice II, 757
Orvis, Ora Lucile III, 244
Orvis, Ora Lucille III, 130
Orvis, Ora Lucille III, 244
Orwig, A. W. IV, 1332
Orwig, Kate IV, 1332
Orwig, Mrs. A. W. IV, 1332
Osbern, Beulah I, 896
Osbern, Charlotte V, 850
Osbern, Charlotte V, 855
Osbern, William H. V, 521
Osbin, Ann I, 994
Osboarn, Anne I, 994
Osborn, ??? IV, 1141
Osborn, ??? V, 590
Osborn, ??? V, 591
Osborn, A. W. IV, 1259
Osborn, Abigail I, 412
Osborn, Abigail V, 591
Osborn, Abigail Esther I, 595
Osborn, Abner III, 361
Osborn, Abraham I, 412
Osborn, Abraham I, 729
Osborn, Abraham I, 832
Osborn, Abraham I, 994
Osborn, Abram I, 729
Osborn, Adaline V, 701
Osborn, Adam V, 590
Osborn, Adam V, 591
Osborn, Adam V, 701
Osborn, Addie King I, 1160
Osborn, Adelbert D. IV, 1178
Osborn, Adeline V, 590
Osborn, Albert W. V, 591
Osborn, Albert W. V, 701
Osborn, Alexander I, 729
Osborn, Alfred V, 424
Osborn, Alfred V, 590
Osborn, Alfred V, 591
Osborn, Alfred V, 592
Osborn, Alfred V, 599
Osborn, Alfred V, 701
Osborn, Alice IV, 1177
Osborn, Alice IV, 1178
Osborn, Alice V, 195
Osborn, Alice A. V, 590
Osborn, Alice C. V, 590
Osborn, Alice C. V, 701
Osborn, Alicutt P. IV, 1177
Osborn, Allen I, 512
Osborn, Allen I, 565
Osborn, Allen I, 1130
Osborn, Alletta V, 590
Osborn, Alletta V, 592
Osborn, Allettia V, 701
Osborn, Alpheus I, 662
Osborn, Amanda M. V, 591
Osborn, Amanda Madora I, 5
Osborn, Amanda May V, 701
Osborn, Amy I, 1130
Osborn, Angeline V, 521
Osborn, Angeline V, 590
Osborn, Angeline V, 591
Osborn, Angeline V, 701
Osborn, Angelkne V, 591
Osborn, Ann I, 565
Osborn, Ann I, 729
Osborn, Ann I, 994
Osborn, Ann II, 246
Osborn, Ann V, 548
Osborn, Ann V, 592
Osborn, Ann V, 637
Osborn, Ann B. IV, 1239
Osborn, Ann B. IV, 1242
Osborn, Ann E. V, 590
Osborn, Ann E. V, 591
Osborn, Ann Eliza V, 591
Osborn, Ann Eliza V, 701
Osborn, Ann Elizabeth Henry V, 701
Osborn, Anna I, 565
Osborn, Anna I, 573
Osborn, Anna I, 729
Osborn, Anna IV, 257
Osborn, Anna IV, 1177
Osborn, Anna V, 590
Osborn, Anna V, 591
Osborn, Anna V, 702
Osborn, Anna C. V, 424
Osborn, Anna C. V, 591
Osborn, Anna Gertrude IV, 11
Osborn, Anna H. V, 462
Osborn, Anna Mancher V, 42
Osborn, Anne I, 896
Osborn, Anne I, 994

orn, Anne IV, 1177
orn, Annie V, 702
orn, Annie J. V, 601
orn, Argus V, 195
orn, Arthur E. IV, 1194
orn, Asenath I, 729
orn, Asenath I, 832
orn, Asenath H. I, 662
orn, Azur IV, 1177
orn, Benjamin V, 107
orn, Benjamin V, 591
orn, Benjamin A. I, 1160
orn, Bertha V, 195
orn, Beulah I, 896
orn, Blanche L. V, 702
orn, Branson I, 595
orn, C. N. V, 701
orn, Calvin V, 590
orn, Calvin J. V, 702
orn, Carolin V, 590
orn, Caroline IV, 1177
orn, Caroline V, 521
orn, Caroline V, 701
orn, Catherine V, 562
orn, Catherine V, 590
orn, Catherine V, 591
orn, Catherine M. V, 701
orn, Cecil O. IV, 1178
orn, Cecil V. IV, 1178
orn, Celea I, 565
orn, Celia I, 512
orn, Celia I, 565
orn, Celia I, 832
orn, Charity IV, 1149
orn, Charity IV, 1177
orn, Charles I, 662
orn, Charles I, 832
orn, Charles I, 1086
orn, Charles I, 1096
orn, Charles I, 1102
orn, Charles I, 1110
orn, Charles I, 1111
orn, Charles I, 1129
orn, Charles I, 1130
orn, Charles I, 1132
orn, Charles I, 1137
orn, Charles IV, 257
orn, Charles IV, 1177
orn, Charles V, 107
orn, Charles V, 562
orn, Charles V, 590
orn, Charles V, 591
orn, Charles V, 701
orn, Charles H. I, 1160
orn, Charles J. V, 521
orn, Charles N. V, 107
orn, Charles N. V, 591
orn, Charles W. V, 590
orn, Charles, Jr. V, 590
orn, Charles, Jr. V, 591
orn, Charlotte A. IV, 1177
orn, Chas. IV, 257
orn, Chas. V, 555
orn, Clara J. IV, 836
orn, Clara J. IV, 857
orn, Clarabelle IV, 1177
orn, Clark V, 521
orn, Clark V, 590
orn, Clark V, 591
orn, Clark V, 701
orn, Clinton V, 702
orn, Clinton L. V, 590
orn, Cora J. IV, 1177
orn, Courtis V, 424
orn, Cuthbert H. I, 662
orn, Cynthia IV, 257
orn, Cynthia V, 107
orn, Cynthia V, 195
orn, Cynthia V, 591
orn, Daniel I, 412
orn, Daniel I, 565
orn, Daniel I, 1096
orn, Daniel I, 1101
orn, Daniel I, 1110
orn, Daniel I, 1130
orn, Daniel IV, 1149
orn, Daniel IV, 1153
orn, Daniel IV, 1177
orn, Daniel IV, 1194
orn, Daniel IV, 1195
orn, Daniel IV, 1198
orn, Daniel V, 701
orn, Daniel Azur IV, 257
orn, Daniel Henman V, 521
orn, Daniel, Jr. I, 1129
orn, Daniel, Senr. I, 662
orn, David I, 565
orn, David I, 567
orn, David I, 573
orn, David I, 967
orn, David I, 994
Osborn, David IV, 257
Osborn, David IV, 1177
Osborn, David IV, 1193
Osborn, David IV, 1198
Osborn, David V, 521
Osborn, David V, 590
Osborn, David M. I, 565
Osborn, David Madason I, 512
Osborn, David S. V, 590
Osborn, David S. V, 591
Osborn, David, Jr. I, 565
Osborn, David, Jr. IV, 1177
Osborn, David, Jr. IV, 1194
Osborn, Deborah II, 246
Osborn, Deborah IV, 1177
Osborn, Deborah IV, 1194
Osborn, Deborah Dunn II, 90
Osborn, Dell D. IV, 1178
Osborn, Della H. IV, 1178
Osborn, Delphina V, 590
Osborn, Desire IV, 1177
Osborn, Desire IV, 1195
Osborn, Dorcas IV, 257
Osborn, Dorcas IV, 1177
Osborn, Dorcas IV, 1197
Osborn, Dorcas IV, 1198
Osborn, Edgar IV, 1178
Osborn, Edith I, 687
Osborn, Edith IV, 1194
Osborn, Edward V, 521
Osborn, Edward V, 701
Osborn, Edward V, 702
Osborn, Edward M. V, 195
Osborn, Edward W. IV, 1177
Osborn, Edwin IV, 1177
Osborn, Edwin V, 592
Osborn, Edwin M. V, 195
Osborn, Effa A. V, 592
Osborn, Effie V, 702
Osborn, Effie E. V, 592
Osborn, Elard Lindsey I, 664
Osborn, Elenora V, 424
Osborn, Eli I, 686
Osborn, Eli I, 687
Osborn, Eli V, 590
Osborn, Eli M. V, 590
Osborn, Elihu I, 1086
Osborn, Elihu I, 1096
Osborn, Elihu I, 1099
Osborn, Elihu I, 1110
Osborn, Elihu I, 1130
Osborn, Elijah I, 1110
Osborn, Elijah IV, 257
Osborn, Elisha V, 591
Osborn, Elisha B. V, 590
Osborn, Elisha B. V, 591
Osborn, Elisha B. V, 701
Osborn, Eliza V, 397
Osborn, Eliza V, 424
Osborn, Eliza V, 462
Osborn, Eliza V, 591
Osborn, Eliza V, 592
Osborn, Eliza V, 702
Osborn, Eliza V, 924
Osborn, Eliza Ann V, 590
Osborn, Eliza Ann V, 591
Osborn, Eliza Ann V, 602
Osborn, Eliza Ann V, 701
Osborn, Eliza D. V, 591
Osborn, Eliza D. V, 701
Osborn, Elizabeth I, 412
Osborn, Elizabeth I, 565
Osborn, Elizabeth I, 662
Osborn, Elizabeth I, 729
Osborn, Elizabeth I, 832
Osborn, Elizabeth I, 994
Osborn, Elizabeth I, 1129
Osborn, Elizabeth I, 1130
Osborn, Elizabeth I, 1132
Osborn, Elizabeth II, 246
Osborn, Elizabeth V, 107
Osborn, Elizabeth V, 424
Osborn, Elizabeth V, 512
Osborn, Elizabeth V, 521
Osborn, Elizabeth V, 584
Osborn, Elizabeth V, 590
Osborn, Elizabeth V, 591
Osborn, Elizabeth V, 701
Osborn, Elizabeth VI, 540
Osborn, Elizabeth Angeline V, 521
Osborn, Elizabeth D. V, 590
Osborn, Elizabeth D. V, 702
Osborn, Elizabeth W. IV, 1177
Osborn, Elizabeth, Sr. V, 591
Osborn, Ella III, 361
Osborn, Ellwood V, 590
Osborn, Ellwood V, 701
Osborn, Elmore IV, 1177
Osborn, Elnor V, 591
Osborn, Elnora V, 424
Osborn, Elnora V, 591
Osborn, Elwin I, 638
Osborn, Elwood V, 592
Osborn, Elwood V, 702
Osborn, Emily V, 521
Osborn, Emma V, 606
Osborn, Emma N. V, 702
Osborn, Emma U. V, 702
Osborn, Enoch I, 994
Osborn, Ernest IV, 1178
Osborn, Ernest Franklin IV, 1178
Osborn, Esther I, 565
Osborn, Esther IV, 1160
Osborn, Esther IV, 1177
Osborn, Esther IV, 1184
Osborn, Esther IV, 1194
Osborn, Esther IV, 1219
Osborn, Esther IV, 1222
Osborn, Ethel IV, 1177
Osborn, Ethel V, 924
Osborn, Ethel K. IV, 1183
Osborn, Ethel M. V, 924
Osborn, Ethel W. V, 924
Osborn, Eva M. V, 592
Osborn, Eva R. V, 702
Osborn, Eva Rosa V, 591
Osborn, Fay V, 592
Osborn, Fay V, 702
Osborn, Fay H. V, 592
Osborn, Floyd V, 592
Osborn, Floyd I. V, 592
Osborn, Francene L. IV, 1178
Osborn, Francine L. IV, 1177
Osborn, Francis V, 521
Osborn, Frank V, 590
Osborn, Frank V, 592
Osborn, Frank L. V, 590
Osborn, Frank T. V, 424
Osborn, Frank T. V, 701
Osborn, Franklin W. I, 595
Osborn, Freda V, 606
Osborn, Frederick V, 701
Osborn, Frederick D. V, 590
Osborn, Frieda E. IV, 1259
Osborn, G. W. I, 1160
Osborn, Geo. IV, 1147
Osborn, George I, 1160
Osborn, George A. IV, 1178
Osborn, George Craft II, 246
Osborn, George E. I, 1160
Osborn, George E. V, 521
Osborn, George Eddie V, 701
Osborn, George Eddie V, 702
Osborn, George Eddy V, 590
Osborn, George Edwin V, 521
Osborn, George W. I, 1160
Osborn, Gideon S. V, 107
Osborn, Gideon S. V, 591
Osborn, Gideon Swayne IV, 257
Osborn, Gilbert I, 1160
Osborn, Gilbert V, 592
Osborn, Gilbert S. V, 591
Osborn, Gilbert S. V, 701
Osborn, Gilbert, Jr. IV, 1259
Osborn, Glenn V, 702
Osborn, Glenn V, 709
Osborn, Grace IV, 1178
Osborn, Grace IV, 1259
Osborn, Grace Gertrude IV, 1178
Osborn, Hannah I, 832
Osborn, Hannah I, 994
Osborn, Hannah I, 1130
Osborn, Hannah I, 1132
Osborn, Hannah II, 246
Osborn, Hannah II, 611
Osborn, Hannah III, 172
Osborn, Hannah IV, 257
Osborn, Hannah V, 107
Osborn, Hannah V, 424
Osborn, Hannah V, 521
Osborn, Hannah V, 567
Osborn, Hannah V, 590
Osborn, Hannah V, 591
Osborn, Hannah V, 656
Osborn, Hannah V, 659
Osborn, Hannah V, 701
Osborn, Hannah V, 702
Osborn, Hannah H. I, 662
Osborn, Harry V, 521
Osborn, Hattie IV, 1178
Osborn, Helen V, 702
Osborn, Helen A. IV, 1259
Osborn, Henry I, 546
Osborn, Henry I, 565
Osborn, Henry IV, 257
Osborn, Henry IV, 1160
Osborn, Henry IV, 1177
Osborn, Henry Edwin IV, 1177
Osborn, Henry Edwin IV, 1178
Osborn, Hessy V, 521
Osborn, Hettie V, 590
Osborn, Hubert H. IV, 1178
Osborn, I. H. V, 592
Osborn, Idena V, 195
Osborn, Isaac I, 1096
Osborn, Isaac I, 1129
Osborn, Isaac III, 172
Osborn, Isabel I, 889
Osborn, Isabel I, 896
Osborn, Isabel V, 107
Osborn, Isaiah I, 1110
Osborn, Isaiah I, 1129
Osborn, Isaiah IV, 257
Osborn, Isaiah V, 590
Osborn, Isaiah V, 591
Osborn, Isaiah V, 701
Osborn, Isaiah H. V, 590
Osborn, Isaiah H. V, 592
Osborn, Izabel I, 412
Osborn, J. T. V, 592
Osborn, James I, 1110
Osborn, James I, 1129
Osborn, James I, 1160
Osborn, James IV, 257
Osborn, James R. I, 595
Osborn, Jane I, 565
Osborn, Jane I, 994
Osborn, Jane I, 1096
Osborn, Jane I, 1099
Osborn, Jane III, 33
Osborn, Jean I, 994
Osborn, Jemima V, 555
Osborn, Jemima V, 590
Osborn, Jennie IV, 1259
Osborn, Jeremiah I, 412
Osborn, Jeremiah I, 452
Osborn, Jeremiah I, 470
Osborn, Jeremiah I, 484
Osborn, Jeremiah I, 729
Osborn, Jeremiah I, 896
Osborn, Jeremiah I, 1130
Osborn, Jeremiah T. I, 484
Osborn, Jesse I, 832
Osborn, Jesse I, 994
Osborn, Jesse B. I, 1160
Osborn, Jesse W. V, 702
Osborn, Jesse W. V, 924
Osborn, Jesse Wm. V, 424
Osborn, Jesse Wm. V, 462
Osborn, Jesse Wm. V, 591
Osborn, Jesse Wm. V, 702
Osborn, Jessee I, 470
Osborn, Job I, 565
Osborn, John I, 564
Osborn, John I, 832
Osborn, John I, 893
Osborn, John I, 896
Osborn, John I, 1110
Osborn, John I, 1129
Osborn, John IV, 257
Osborn, John IV, 424
Osborn, John IV, 1177
Osborn, John IV, 1178
Osborn, John V, 590
Osborn, John D. IV, 1177
Osborn, John D. IV, 1178
Osborn, John T. V, 591
Osborn, John Thomas V, 590
Osborn, John Thomas V, 701
Osborn, Jonathan I, 565
Osborn, Jonathan I, 889
Osborn, Jonathan I, 896
Osborn, Jonathan I, 967
Osborn, Jonathan I, 994
Osborn, Jonathan V, 521
Osborn, Jonothan V, 107
Osborn, Jordan V, 107
Osborn, Joseph I, 565
Osborn, Joseph V, 107
Osborn, Joseph V, 521
Osborn, Joseph V, 592
Osborn, Joseph B. V, 521
Osborn, Joseph Osborn II, 246
Osborn, Joseph P. V, 590
Osborn, Joseph Peter V, 701
Osborn, Josephine IV, 1177
Osborn, Josephus IV, 1177
Osborn, Josephus IV, 1178
Osborn, Josephus F. IV, 1177
Osborn, Josiah I, 1110
Osborn, Josiah I, 1129
Osborn, Josiah II, 67
Osborn, Josiah II, 90
Osborn, Josiah IV, 257
Osborn, Josie V, 211
Osborn, Josie Bell V, 195
Osborn, Judith II, 544
Osborn, Judith II, 610
Osborn, Julia A. III, 362
Osborn, Julia C. III, 53
Osborn, Kate IV, 1163
Osborn, Kate IV, 1182
Osborn, Katherine V, 591
Osborn, Katie O. IV, 1147
Osborn, Laura IV, 1177
Osborn, Laura IV, 1183
Osborn, Laura B. IV, 1194
Osborn, Laura M. V, 701
Osborn, Lemuel I, 1130
Osborn, Lenora W. IV, 1178
Osborn, Lenore W. IV, 1177
Osborn, Leona L. V, 590
Osborn, Leona S. V, 701
Osborn, Letitia I, 484
Osborn, Lida T. V, 592
Osborn, Lizzie IV, 1178
Osborn, Lottie IV, 1178
Osborn, Lucy E. V, 590
Osborn, Lucy E. V, 701
Osborn, Lutitia I, 484
Osborn, Lutitia A. I, 470
Osborn, Luzena I, 832
Osborn, Lydia I, 565
Osborn, Lydia I, 686
Osborn, Lydia I, 994
Osborn, Lydia I, 1110
Osborn, Lydia I, 1129
Osborn, Lydia II, 512
Osborn, Lydia II, 610
Osborn, Lydia II, 611
Osborn, Lydia IV, 257
Osborn, Lydia IV, 1177
Osborn, Lydia IV, 1182
Osborn, Lydia IV, 1195
Osborn, Lydia V, 521
Osborn, Lydia V, 590
Osborn, Lydia V, 591
Osborn, Lydia V, 705
Osborn, Lydia A. V, 591
Osborn, Lydia Ann IV, 1177
Osborn, Lydia Ann IV, 1178
Osborn, Mae V, 702
Osborn, Maranda V, 591
Osborn, Maranda V, 592
Osborn, Margaret I, 412
Osborn, Margaret I, 1101
Osborn, Margaret I, 1110
Osborn, Margaret I, 1130
Osborn, Margaret V, 424
Osborn, Margaret V, 521
Osborn, Margaret V, 525
Osborn, Margaret V, 584
Osborn, Margaret V, 585
Osborn, Margaret V, 590
Osborn, Margaret V, 591
Osborn, Margaret V, 606
Osborn, Margaret V, 695
Osborn, Margaret Francis I, 664
Osborn, Margaret J. V, 521
Osborn, Margaret J. V, 590
Osborn, Margaret Jane V, 521
Osborn, Margaret Jane V, 591
Osborn, Margaret Jane V, 701
Osborn, Margaret Marsh V, 591
Osborn, Margrett VI, 540
Osborn, Maria I, 832
Osborn, Mariah I, 565
Osborn, Mariah I, 832
Osborn, Marjorie S. IV, 1194
Osborn, Martha IV, 424
Osborn, Martha IV, 1070
Osborn, Martha IV, 1075
Osborn, Martha IV, 1177
Osborn, Martha V, 521
Osborn, Martha V, 556
Osborn, Martha V, 591
Osborn, Martha V, 701
Osborn, Martha V, 702
Osborn, Martha C. V, 590
Osborn, Martha E. V, 590
Osborn, Martha E. V, 592
Osborn, Martha Emily V, 591
Osborn, Martha Emily V, 599
Osborn, Martha Emly V, 701
Osborn, Martha J. V, 424
Osborn, Martha J. V, 577
Osborn, Martha J. V, 591
Osborn, Martha J. V, 592
Osborn, Martha J. V, 662
Osborn, Martha J. V, 701
Osborn, Martha Jane V, 424
Osborn, Martha Jane V, 591
Osborn, Martha P. V, 591
Osborn, Martha P. V, 701
Osborn, Martha Sibbil I, 662
Osborn, Mary I, 412
Osborn, Mary I, 452
Osborn, Mary I, 460
Osborn, Mary I, 470
Osborn, Mary I, 484
Osborn, Mary I, 564
Osborn, Mary I, 565
Osborn, Mary I, 994

Osborn, Mary II, 90
Osborn, Mary IV, 424
Osborn, Mary IV, 1177
Osborn, Mary V, 521
Osborn, Mary V, 590
Osborn, Mary V, 591
Osborn, Mary V, 603
Osborn, Mary VI, 540
Osborn, Mary A. IV, 1178
Osborn, Mary A. V, 521
Osborn, Mary A. V, 604
Osborn, Mary Ann I, 512
Osborn, Mary Ann I, 565
Osborn, Mary Ann I, 832
Osborn, Mary Ann V, 424
Osborn, Mary Ann V, 588
Osborn, Mary Ann V, 591
Osborn, Mary Cory V, 521
Osborn, Mary E. V, 584
Osborn, Mary E. V, 590
Osborn, Mary E. V, 710
Osborn, Mary Emily V, 582
Osborn, Mary Emily V, 591
Osborn, Mary Jane V, 547
Osborn, Mary Jane V, 590
Osborn, Mary Jane V, 591
Osborn, Mary Netta IV, 1219
Osborn, Mary R. V, 591
Osborn, Mary R. V, 701
Osborn, Mary W. IV, 1177
Osborn, Mary W. IV, 1193
Osborn, Mary W. IV, 1288
Osborn, Mary W. IV, 1299
Osborn, Mathew I, 470
Osborn, Mathew I, 512
Osborn, Mathew I, 565
Osborn, Matthew I, 412
Osborn, Matthew I, 452
Osborn, Matthew I, 470
Osborn, Matthew I, 484
Osborn, Matthew I, 564
Osborn, Matthew I, 565
Osborn, Matthew I, 967
Osborn, Matthew I, 994
Osborn, Maud H. V, 592
Osborn, May IV, 1178
Osborn, May V, 689
Osborn, May V, 702
Osborn, Melissa V, 702
Osborn, Melville S. V, 702
Osborn, Merritt IV, 1177
Osborn, Merritt J. IV, 1178
Osborn, Mikle W. V, 590
Osborn, Millie R. IV, 1178
Osborn, Minerva IV, 1177
Osborn, Minerva IV, 1178
Osborn, Minnie V, 702
Osborn, Minnie V, 709
Osborn, Minnie Loyd V, 702
Osborn, Miranda V, 701
Osborn, Miriam V, 521
Osborn, Morrow IV, 1193
Osborn, Myrtle A. IV, 1177
Osborn, Nancy I, 565
Osborn, Nancy Ellen V, 590
Osborn, Nancy Ellen V, 591
Osborn, Narcissa IV, 257
Osborn, Narcissa V, 107
Osborn, Narcissa V, 591
Osborn, Nathan II, 90
Osborn, Nellie IV, 424
Osborn, Nellie A. V, 701
Osborn, Nettie J. V, 591
Osborn, Obadiah H. IV, 1194
Osborn, Oliett P. IV, 1178
Osborn, Olive A. V, 590
Osborn, Olive Ann V, 701
Osborn, Ollie V, 592
Osborn, Omer V, 424
Osborn, Owen I, 994
Osborn, Owen IV, 424
Osborn, Parker V, 107
Osborn, Parker Jordan V, 591
Osborn, Paul II, 610
Osborn, Paulina J. V, 590
Osborn, Paulina J. V, 701
Osborn, Pauline V, 592
Osborn, Peter II, 812
Osborn, Peter V, 521
Osborn, Peter V, 567
Osborn, Peter V, 590
Osborn, Peter V, 591
Osborn, Peter V, 602
Osborn, Peter V, 606
Osborn, Peter V, 701
Osborn, Peter V, 702
Osborn, Peter A. V, 591
Osborn, Peter A. V, 592
Osborn, Peter Alfred V, 701
Osborn, Peter, Jr. V, 521
Osborn, Peter, Jr. V, 590
Osborn, Peter, Jr. V, 591
Osborn, Phebe II, 180
Osborn, Phebe II, 297
Osborn, Phebe IV, 1184
Osborn, Priscilla IV, 1162
Osborn, Priscilla IV, 1177
Osborn, Rachel I, 565
Osborn, Rachel Catharine I, 595
Osborn, Ralph H. IV, 1178
Osborn, Randall V, 592
Osborn, Rebecah I, 994
Osborn, Rebecca I, 686
Osborn, Rebecca I, 994
Osborn, Rebecca IV, 424
Osborn, Rebecca IV, 1288
Osborn, Rebecca V, 521
Osborn, Rebeccah I, 994
Osborn, Rebeckah I, 412
Osborn, Rebeckah I, 985
Osborn, Rebeckah I, 994
Osborn, Rebeckah IV, 424
Osborn, Rhoda II, 67
Osborn, Rhoda II, 90
Osborn, Richard I, 967
Osborn, Richard I, 994
Osborn, Richard III, 33
Osborn, Robert I, 1160
Osborn, Robert C. IV, 1194
Osborn, Ruth I, 612
Osborn, Ruth IV, 678
Osborn, Ruth IV, 1153
Osborn, Ruth IV, 1177
Osborn, Ruth IV, 1246
Osborn, Ruth A. V, 597
Osborn, Ruth Ann V, 590
Osborn, Ruth Ann V, 591
Osborn, Ruth Ann V, 598
Osborn, Ruth Ann V, 710
Osborn, Ruth E. V, 590
Osborn, Ruth Ellen V, 521
Osborn, Ruth Ellen V, 591
Osborn, Ruth Ellen V, 701
Osborn, Ruth Irena V, 701
Osborn, Ruth J. V, 590
Osborn, Sallie I, 1160
Osborn, Sallie V, 592
Osborn, Sally III, 120
Osborn, Sally T. V, 590
Osborn, Samantha V, 424
Osborn, Samantha V, 591
Osborn, Samantha B. V, 586
Osborn, Samantha B. V, 591
Osborn, Samuel I, 565
Osborn, Sarah I, 412
Osborn, Sarah I, 452
Osborn, Sarah I, 470
Osborn, Sarah I, 546
Osborn, Sarah I, 564
Osborn, Sarah I, 565
Osborn, Sarah I, 595
Osborn, Sarah I, 729
Osborn, Sarah I, 832
Osborn, Sarah I, 893
Osborn, Sarah I, 896
Osborn, Sarah I, 994
Osborn, Sarah I, 1096
Osborn, Sarah I, 1110
Osborn, Sarah I, 1129
Osborn, Sarah I, 1130
Osborn, Sarah I, 1160
Osborn, Sarah II, 246
Osborn, Sarah II, 611
Osborn, Sarah III, 361
Osborn, Sarah IV, 1147
Osborn, Sarah IV, 1177
Osborn, Sarah V, 107
Osborn, Sarah V, 195
Osborn, Sarah V, 567
Osborn, Sarah V, 590
Osborn, Sarah V, 591
Osborn, Sarah V, 701
Osborn, Sarah Benedict IV, 1198
Osborn, Sarah Ellen V, 577
Osborn, Sarah Ellen V, 591
Osborn, Sarah J. V, 195
Osborn, Sarah Jane I, 512
Osborn, Sarah Jane I, 565
Osborn, Sarah Jane V, 590
Osborn, Sarah Jane V, 591
Osborn, Sarah Jane V, 604
Osborn, Sarah P. IV, 1194
Osborn, Sarah Saunders II, 812
Osborn, Sarah Theodocia V, 701
Osborn, Scott V, 521
Osborn, Selah I, 565
Osborn, Seth IV, 1178
Osborn, Seth IV, 1259
Osborn, Seth V, 590
Osborn, Seth V, 591
Osborn, Seth V, 701
Osborn, Seth C. IV, 1178
Osborn, Seth W. V, 590
Osborn, Seth W. V, 591
Osborn, Seth W. V, 592
Osborn, Simon I, 484
Osborn, Solomon V, 590
Osborn, Solomon V, 591
Osborn, Sophia I, 452
Osborn, Sophia I, 453
Osborn, Sophia I, 470
Osborn, Stephen V, 591
Osborn, Susan IV, 1177
Osborn, Susan IV, 1193
Osborn, Susan IV, 1194
Osborn, Susan G. II, 812
Osborn, Susan George II, 812
Osborn, Susanna II, 644
Osborn, Susanna V, 586
Osborn, Susanna V, 590
Osborn, Susannah V, 591
Osborn, Syrena V, 424
Osborn, Tamer I, 832
Osborn, Thomas I, 412
Osborn, Thomas I, 512
Osborn, Thomas I, 565
Osborn, Thomas I, 768
Osborn, Thomas I, 832
Osborn, Thomas I, 967
Osborn, Thomas I, 985
Osborn, Thomas I, 994
Osborn, Thomas IV, 424
Osborn, Thomas V, 590
Osborn, Thomas V, 591
Osborn, Thomas Clarkson IV, 1194
Osborn, Thos. II, 67
Osborn, Thos. II, 90
Osborn, Unice M. V, 591
Osborn, Vanette V, 592
Osborn, Vannette J. V, 592
Osborn, Vionette J. V, 701
Osborn, W. Herbert IV, 1178
Osborn, Walter Albert V, 592
Osborn, Walter D. V, 590
Osborn, Walter D. V, 701
Osborn, Walter S. V, 590
Osborn, Walter Stanton V, 701
Osborn, Wd. Ada III, 120
Osborn, Wesley V, 195
Osborn, Wilfing I, 1130
Osborn, William I, 412
Osborn, William I, 512
Osborn, William I, 565
Osborn, William I, 686
Osborn, William I, 729
Osborn, William I, 832
Osborn, William I, 967
Osborn, William I, 994
Osborn, William I, 1096
Osborn, William I, 1129
Osborn, William I, 1130
Osborn, William I, 1160
Osborn, William III, 244
Osborn, William V, 107
Osborn, William V, 424
Osborn, William V, 521
Osborn, William V, 590
Osborn, William V, 591
Osborn, William V, 702
Osborn, William Abraham I, 832
Osborn, William C. V, 590
Osborn, William Elmore IV, 1177
Osborn, William H. V, 521
Osborn, William H. V, 590
Osborn, William Jesse I, 664
Osborn, William N. V, 591
Osborn, William Pembroke I, 751
Osborn, William, Jr. V, 590
Osborn, William, Jr. V, 591
Osborn, Wilson J. V, 195
Osborn, Wm. IV, 1184
Osborn, Wm. V, 424
Osborn, Wm. V, 462
Osborn, Wm. V, 591
Osborn, Wm. V, 702
Osborn, Wm. Elmore IV, 1178
Osborn, Wm. Elmore IV, 1183
Osborn, Wm. H. V, 701
Osborn, Wm. N. V, 556
Osborn, Wm. R. I, 1160
Osborn, Wm., Jr. V, 567
Osborn, Wm., Jr. V, 591
Osborne, ??? III, 244
Osborne, Abigail I, 685
Osborne, Abigail III, 244
Osborne, Abner III, 244
Osborne, Abraham I, 685
Osborne, Achsah I, 686
Osborne, Ada I, 638
Osborne, Ada S. I, 623
Osborne, Adella Eunice I, 768
Osborne, Alexander I, 662
Osborne, Alexander I, 686
Osborne, Alta Mae I, 947
Osborne, Ann I, 685
Osborne, Ann I, 686
Osborne, Ann II, 610
Osborne, Anna I, 664
Osborne, Anna I, 686
Osborne, Anna I, 767
Osborne, Arilla I, 638
Osborne, Asenath I, 686
Osborne, Asenath I, 815
Osborne, Aurilla I, 623
Osborne, Aurilla I, 638
Osborne, Barsina I, 663
Osborne, Benjamin Franklin I, 664
Osborne, Benjamin Lundy I, 663
Osborne, Beulah I, 890
Osborne, Beulah I, 896
Osborne, Beulah L. I, 790
Osborne, Beulah Luzena I, 686
Osborne, Branch VI, 948
Osborne, Byran L. I, 638
Osborne, Byrom L. I, 623
Osborne, Byron IV, 1332
Osborne, Byron L. IV, 1332
Osborne, C. F. I, 638
Osborne, Caroline E. I, 751
Osborne, Celia I, 768
Osborne, Celia III, 244
Osborne, Center I, 685
Osborne, Charles I, 686
Osborne, Charles I, 815
Osborne, Charles I, 832
Osborne, Charles IV, 1288
Osborne, Charles V, 843
Osborne, Charles V, 855
Osborne, Charles VI, 180
Osborne, Charles VI, 427
Osborne, Charles F. I, 638
Osborne, Charles Franklin I, 623
Osborne, Charles Wyrick I, 623
Osborne, Charlotte IV, 1288
Osborne, Cyrena I, 677
Osborne, Cyrena I, 686
Osborne, Daniel I, 623
Osborne, Daniel I, 685
Osborne, Daniel I, 686
Osborne, Daniel II, 610
Osborne, Daniel E. I, 663
Osborne, David I, 686
Osborne, David S. I, 751
Osborne, Delphina C. I, 686
Osborne, Delphina Cornelia I, 662
Osborne, Diana I, 686
Osborne, Diana I, 689
Osborne, Donald Jay I, 623
Osborne, Doris I, 623
Osborne, Dorland I, 638
Osborne, Dwight I, 638
Osborne, Dwight H. I, 623
Osborne, Edith I, 686
Osborne, Eli I, 686
Osborne, Elihu I, 1096
Osborne, Elisabeth I, 685
Osborne, Eliza I, 686
Osborne, Eliza I, 767
Osborne, Eliza V, 353
Osborne, Elizabeth I, 664
Osborne, Elizabeth I, 685
Osborne, Elizabeth I, 686
Osborne, Elizabeth I, 751
Osborne, Elizabeth I, 758
Osborne, Elizabeth I, 768
Osborne, Elizabeth II, 401
Osborne, Elizabeth II, 547
Osborne, Elizabeth II, 610
Osborne, Elizabeth II, 660
Osborne, Elizabeth II, 789
Osborne, Elizabeth II, 812
Osborne, Elizabeth VI, 948
Osborne, Elizabeth Ann II, 610
Osborne, Elizabeth Atkinson II, 610
Osborne, Ella III, 122
Osborne, Ella III, 244
Osborne, Ella III, 360
Osborne, Elsie I, 638
Osborne, Elsie I, 643
Osborne, Elsie L. I, 623
Osborne, Elwin I, 623
Osborne, Elwin I, 638
Osborne, Elwin I, 662
Osborne, Elwin I, 663
Osborne, Ephraim I, 663
Osborne, Esther I, 686
Osborne, Esther IV, 1288
Osborne, Eunice I, 768
Osborne, Eunice Lowder I, 664
Osborne, Frances VI, 948
Osborne, George I, 1160
Osborne, Grace IV, 1178
Osborne, Grace Lee III, 244
Osborne, Gretchin I, 623
Osborne, Hannah I, 623
Osborne, Hannah I, 663
Osborne, Hannah I, 685
Osborne, Hannah I, 686
Osborne, Hannah I, 691
Osborne, Hannah II, 610
Osborne, Hannah II, 611
Osborne, Hannah II, 714
Osborne, Hannah III, 244
Osborne, Hannah V, 656
Osborne, Hannah V, 702
Osborne, Hannah H. I, 686
Osborne, Harry Dorland I, 62
Osborne, Helen E. I, 947
Osborne, Huldah I, 685
Osborne, Ila Spencer I, 947
Osborne, Isaac III, 244
Osborne, J. Norman I, 638
Osborne, Jabes I, 767
Osborne, Jabez I, 744
Osborne, Jabez I, 751
Osborne, Jabez I, 758
Osborne, Jabez I, 767
Osborne, Jane I, 565
Osborne, Jane I, 638
Osborne, Jane I, 1096
Osborne, Jane III, 244
Osborne, Jane III, 395
Osborne, Jane III, 431
Osborne, Jeramiah I, 439
Osborne, Jeremiah I, 452
Osborne, Jeremiah I, 662
Osborne, Jeremiah I, 663
Osborne, Jeremiah I, 686
Osborne, Jeremiah I, 765
Osborne, Jeremiah I, 768
Osborne, Jeremiah I, 896
Osborne, Jeremiah T. I, 484
Osborne, Jesse I, 439
Osborne, Jesse I, 685
Osborne, Jesse I, 686
Osborne, Jesse I, 767
Osborne, Jesse I, 768
Osborne, Jesse I, 770
Osborne, Jesse R. I, 623
Osborne, Jobe I, 663
Osborne, John I, 662
Osborne, John I, 685
Osborne, John I, 686
Osborne, John I, 790
Osborne, John I, 890
Osborne, John I, 896
Osborne, John III, 244
Osborne, Joseph I, 685
Osborne, Joseph III, 244
Osborne, Judith II, 610
Osborne, Lena L. I, 623
Osborne, Letitia I, 484
Osborne, Lindley C. I, 686
Osborne, Lindley E. I, 623
Osborne, Lindley E. I, 638
Osborne, Lorenzo I, 663
Osborne, Lorenzo I, 686
Osborne, Louesa E. I, 686
Osborne, Louesa E. I, 691
Osborne, Lutitia I, 484
Osborne, Lydia I, 623
Osborne, Lydia I, 685
Osborne, Lydia I, 686
Osborne, Lydia II, 610
Osborne, Lydia II, 611
Osborne, Maron I, 663
Osborne, Martha I, 685
Osborne, Martha I, 686
Osborne, Martha I, 768
Osborne, Mary I, 439
Osborne, Mary I, 445
Osborne, Mary I, 452
Osborne, Mary I, 685
Osborne, Mary I, 686
Osborne, Mary V, 480
Osborne, Mary Ann I, 663
Osborne, Mary Ann I, 768
Osborne, Mary Cory V, 521
Osborne, Mary E. I, 624
Osborne, Mary M. I, 768
Osborne, Mary Margaret I, 7
Osborne, Mary Mastin I, 623
Osborne, Mary N. I, 623
Osborne, Mary W. IV, 1288
Osborne, Matthew I, 439
Osborne, Matthew I, 445
Osborne, Matthew I, 452
Osborne, Matthew I, 484
Osborne, Matthew I, 662
Osborne, Matthew I, 685
Osborne, Matthew I, 686

rne, Mattie IV, 1157
rne, Minnie M. I, 623
rne, Mourning I, 685
rne, Mrs. ??? IV, 1332
rne, Mrs. Lenora IV, 1332
rne, Nathaniel Pearsall's
II, 244
rne, Norman J. I, 623
rne, Obed I, 623
rne, Obed I, 663
rne, Obed I, 686
rne, Obed I, 691
rne, Owen I, 623
rne, Owen IV, 1332
rne, Paul II, 610
rne, Peeter II, 401
rne, Peter II, 610
rne, Peter II, 812
rne, Phebe I, 685
rne, Phebe I, 686
rne, Rachel I, 686
rne, Rachel I, 765
rne, Rachel I, 768
rne, Rachel Eliza I, 686
rne, Rachel Mary Ann I, 676
rne, Rachel Mary Ann I, 686
rne, Rebecca I, 658
rne, Rebecca I, 685
rne, Rebecca I, 686
rne, Rebecca I, 758
rne, Rebecca I, 767
rne, Rebecca I, 770
rne, Rebecca IV, 424
rne, Rebecca IV, 1288
rne, Rebecka I, 767
rne, Rebeckah I, 767
rne, Rhoda II, 90
rne, Richard I, 686
rne, Richard III, 244
rne, Richard III, 395
rne, Richard III, 431
rne, Robert II, 627
rne, Robt. C. III, 244
rne, Ruth I, 686
rne, Ruth IV, 1332
rne, Ruth M. IV, 1332
rne, Samuel I, 685
rne, Samuel I, 686
rne, Sarah I, 452
rne, Sarah I, 662
rne, Sarah I, 663
rne, Sarah I, 685
rne, Sarah I, 686
rne, Sarah I, 768
rne, Sarah I, 896
rne, Sarah II, 610
rne, Sarah II, 611
rne, Sarah II, 627
rne, Sarah II, 812
rne, Sarah III, 244
rne, Sarah V, 759
rne, Sarah B. III, 97
rne, Sarah B. III, 244
orne, Sarah J. III, 244
rne, Sarah L. I, 790
rne, Sealey III, 244
orne, Seth G. IV, 1332
orne, Simon I, 662
orne, Simon I, 663
orne, Sophia I, 439
orne, Sophronia II, 611
orne, Sophronia L. II, 757
orne, Spencer I, 947
orne, Susan III, 244
orne, Susanna I, 663
orne, Susanna II, 610
orne, Susanna II, 611
orne, Tamer I, 685
orne, Thomas I, 565
orne, Thomas I, 658
orne, Thomas I, 768
orne, Thomas IV, 424
orne, Thomas Henry IV, 1288
orne, Widow Elizabeth I, 744
orne, William I, 664
orne, William I, 685
orne, William I, 686
orne, William I, 767
orne, William III, 244
orne, William G. III, 244
orne, William H. III, 97
orne, William H. III, 244
orne, William P. I, 686
oroune, Byron L. IV, 1328
oroune, Ruth IV, 1328
ourn, Alexander I, 728
ourn, Alexander I, 729
ourn, Ann II, 610
ourn, Charles I, 1129
ourn, David V, 521
ourn, Elizabeth I, 728
Osbourn, Elizabeth II, 246
Osbourne, Elizabeth II, 456
Osbourne, Elizabeth II, 610
Osbourne, Elizabeth Ann II, 610
Osbourne, Elizabeth Atkinson
II, 610
Osbourne, Enoch I, 994
Osbourne, Hannah II, 610
Osbourne, John VI, 1004
Osbourne, Lydia II, 610
Osbourne, Margaret VI, 1004
Osbourne, Sarah II, 610
Osbourne, Sarah II, 904
Osbourne, Susanna II, 610
Osbourne, Susanna II, 611
Osbun, Charles V, 855
Osbun, Charlotty V, 855
Osbun, Daniel I, 412
Osbun, Daniel I, 420
Osbun, David I, 664
Osbun, Elwood V, 855
Osbun, Hannah I, 664
Osbun, Huldah I, 669
Osbun, Jesse I, 767
Osbun, John I, 663
Osbun, John I, 669
Osbun, Jonathan I, 664
Osbun, Jonathan V, 855
Osbun, Margaret I, 420
Osbun, Mary I, 663
Osbun, Mary I, 664
Osbun, Mary V, 855
Osbun, Matthew I, 664
Osbun, Polly V, 855
Osbun, Rebecah I, 664
Osbun, Richard I, 664
Osbun, Sarah I, 663
Osbun, Sarah I, 669
Osbun, Susanna V, 844
Osbun, Susanna V, 855
Osbun, Thomas I, 664
Osbun, William I, 663
Osbun, William I, 664
Osburn, Addie King I, 1160
Osburn, Ann I, 729
Osburn, Asenath I, 832
Osburn, Betsey VI, 841
Osburn, Daniel V, 268
Osburn, David I, 967
Osburn, Elizabeth I, 412
Osburn, Elizabeth I, 994
Osburn, Elizabeth II, 610
Osburn, Elizabeth V, 107
Osburn, Elizabeth V, 268
Osburn, Elizabeth VI, 540
Osburn, George VI, 841
Osburn, Isaac I, 1129
Osburn, James I, 1160
Osburn, Jane III, 244
Osburn, Jesse I, 767
Osburn, John IV, 345
Osburn, John V, 268
Osburn, John VI, 971
Osburn, Jonathan I, 967
Osburn, Margaret I, 412
Osburn, Margrett VI, 540
Osburn, Mariah I, 832
Osburn, Mary I, 994
Osburn, Mary V, 268
Osburn, Mary V, 603
Osburn, Mary VI, 540
Osburn, Mary VI, 569
Osburn, Mary VI, 971
Osburn, Mary Albina VI, 569
Osburn, Matthew I, 967
Osburn, Mortimer VI, 569
Osburn, Nathaniel Pearsall's
III, 244
Osburn, Nicholas VI, 965
Osburn, Nicholas VI, 971
Osburn, Rachel VI, 971
Osburn, Rebecca IV, 131
Osburn, Rebecca IV, 133
Osburn, Richard I, 967
Osburn, Richard III, 244
Osburn, Samuel VI, 971
Osburn, Sarah I, 832
Osburn, Sarah V, 268
Osburn, Susanna II, 610
Osburn, Susanna V, 268
Osburn, Thomas I, 565
Osburn, Thomas I, 967
Osburn, William I, 967
Osburn, William I, 1160
Osburn, William V, 521
Osburne, Elizabeth II, 610
Osburne, Susanna II, 610
Osgood, Mary III, 126
Osgood, Mary III, 244
Osiola, Elmira IV, 1355
Osiola, Elmira IV, 1375
Osler, Harmon II, 904
Osler, Harmon II, 925
Osler, Leah W. VI, 567
Osler, Leah Walker II, 904
Osler, Leah Walker II, 925
Osler, Leonora A. II, 904
Osler, Leonora A. II, 925
Osler, Wilbur Fiske II, 904
Osler, Wilbur Fiske II, 925
Osler, Wm. F. VI, 567
Osmassen, Annie II, 968
Osment, Mary I, 896
Osmint, Martha E. I, 565
Osmond, Amelia II, 200
Osmond, Amelia II, 246
Osmond, Amelia VI, 412
Osmond, Amelia VI, 427
Osmond, Eunice II, 200
Osmond, Eunice II, 246
Osmond, Eunice VI, 427
Osmond, Eunice VI, 462
Osmond, John II, 192
Osmond, John II, 246
Osmond, John VI, 427
Osmond, John VI, 462
Osmond, Martha II, 192
Osmond, Martha II, 200
Osmond, Martha II, 246
Osmond, Martha VI, 369
Osmond, Martha VI, 462
Osmond, Sarah IV, 1178
Osmond, Sarah IV, 1259
Osmond, Unus II, 246
Osmund, Amelia II, 246
Osmund, Eunice II, 246
Osmund, Sarah II, 195
Ost, Mae IV, 1332
Ostrander, ??? III, 368
Ostrander, Hetty III, 244
Ostrander, Mary III, 244
Ostrander, Maurice III, 244
Ostrander, Sarah III, 244
Ostrander, Sarah III, 368
Ostrone, Catharine V, 957
Ostrone, Sarah V, 957
Ostrosci, Agnes IV, 257
Ostroski, Agnes IV, 257
Ostroski, Mamie IV, 257
Ostroski, Mary IV, 257
Ostroski, Moxie IV, 257
Ostroski, Stana IV, 257
Ostrosky, Moxie IV, 257
Oten, James V, 874
Oten, Joel V, 874
Oten, Lewis V, 874
Oten, Martha V, 874
Oten, Thomas V, 874
Otey, Armistead VI, 935
Otey, Armistead VI, 949
Otey, Armistead VI, 971
Otey, Armistead VI, 989
Otey, Armistead VI, 1016
Otey, Betsey VI, 971
Otey, Colo. Armistead VI, 989
Otey, Dr. John A. VI, 972
Otey, Edwin W. VI, 945
Otey, Eliza J. VI, 943
Otey, Frances VI, 885
Otey, Frances VI, 933
Otey, Frances VI, 949
Otey, Frances VI, 989
Otey, Frances M. C. VI, 972
Otey, Frances O. VI, 972
Otey, Frazier VI, 887
Otey, Frazier VI, 935
Otey, Frazier VI, 962
Otey, Frazier VI, 971
Otey, Frazier VI, 990
Otey, Harriet P. VI, 992
Otey, Isaac VI, 949
Otey, Isaac VI, 971
Otey, Isaac VI, 972
Otey, Isaac VI, 978
Otey, Isaac N. VI, 977
Otey, James VI, 885
Otey, James VI, 890
Otey, John VI, 926
Otey, John B. VI, 945
Otey, John H. VI, 943
Otey, John H. VI, 971
Otey, John H. VI, 972
Otey, John H. VI, 992
Otey, John H., Jr. VI, 972
Otey, John H., Jr. VI, 990
Otey, John W. VI, 972
Otey, Julian K. VI, 977
Otey, Martha VI, 978
Otey, Mary VI, 971
Otey, Mary C. VI, 972
Otey, Mary G. VI, 972
Otey, Mildred VI, 971
Otey, Mildred VI, 972
Otey, Mildred L. VI, 990
Otey, Nelson VI, 972
Otey, Permelia C. VI, 925
Otey, Polly VI, 925
Otey, Polly B. VI, 933
Otey, Prudence B. VI, 971
Otey, Robt. B. VI, 943
Otey, Sally VI, 896
Otey, Sally VI, 971
Otey, Sarah VI, 972
Otey, Sarah A. R. VI, 981
Otey, Sarah Ann E. VI, 945
Otey, Thomas J. VI, 905
Otey, Thomas J. VI, 990
Otey, William VI, 887
Otey, William L. VI, 972
Otey, Wm. L. VI, 1004
Otis, ??? III, 111
Otis, Adelbert IV, 1239
Otis, Bethiah B. III, 244
Otis, Carlton IV, 836
Otis, Charles II, 949
Otis, Charles II, 1088
Otis, Charles II, 1089
Otis, Charlotte E. II, 297
Otis, Charlotte Ellen II, 290
Otis, Charlotte Ellen II, 297
Otis, Deborah IV, 836
Otis, Dillwyn IV, 836
Otis, Eliza G. III, 111
Otis, Eliza G. III, 244
Otis, Elizabeth IV, 836
Otis, Elizabeth IV, 1239
Otis, Ella H. IV, 535
Otis, Ella H. IV, 543
Otis, Ella H. IV, 554
Otis, Ellen E. II, 290
Otis, Ellen E. II, 297
Otis, James D. II, 1088
Otis, James D. II, 1089
Otis, James J. II, 290
Otis, James J. II, 297
Otis, Joshua D. III, 244
Otis, Loretta IV, 1239
Otis, Louis II, 949
Otis, Marianna II, 1089
Otis, Marianna W. II, 1057
Otis, Marianna W. II, 1063
Otis, Martha II, 949
Otis, Martha II, 1088
Otis, Martha II, 1089
Otis, Martha K. II, 949
Otis, Martha K. II, 1087
Otis, Martha K. II, 1089
Otis, Martha K. IV, 731
Otis, Martha K. IV, 747
Otis, Mary Amy II, 949
Otis, Mary M. II, 1088
Otis, Mary M. II, 1089
Otis, Rebecca G. III, 244
Otis, Stephen G. II, 1089
Otis, Theodore IV, 1239
Otlip, Catherine IV, 747
Otlip, Felix IV, 701
Otlip, John IV, 747
Otlip, Mary IV, 676
Otlip, Mary IV, 701
Otlip, Rose M. IV, 701
Otlip, Viola IV, 747
Otlip, Viola Mary IV, 747
Ott, Hannah V, 901
Ott, Hannah V, 924
Ott, Ira IV, 1332
Ott, Ira W. IV, 1332
Ott, Irene IV, 1332
Ott, Irene Z. IV, 1332
Ott, John IV, 702
Ott, Loma Pauline IV, 952
Ott, Lorna Pauline IV, 702
Ott, Martha G. VI, 427
Ott, Mary IV, 702
Ott, Matha G. VI, 394
Otter, John II, 401
Otter, John II, 467
Otter, John II, 611
Otter, L. VI, 973
Otter, Mary II, 611
Ottey, Lucy Price II, 715
Otto, Rebecca M. II, 904
Otto, Sarah II, 1018
Otto, Sarah II, 1021
Otwell, Addison Grant I, 262
Otwell, Adison G. I, 664
Otwell, Anna M. I, 664
Otwell, Archie W. I, 623
Otwell, Archie W. I, 631
Otwell, Archie W. I, 638
Otwell, Archie W. I, 664
Otwell, Archie W., Jr. I, 623
Otwell, Bascomb Lee I, 623
Otwell, Bessie I, 623
Otwell, Bessie I, 631
Otwell, Bessie I, 638
Otwell, Elizabeth I, 262
Otwell, Eunice I, 262
Otwell, Eunice I, 623
Otwell, Eunice I, 664
Otwell, J. H. I, 623
Otwell, Mary N. I, 623
Otwell, Myrtle I, 638
Otwell, Ronald Coble I, 623
Otwell, S. G. I, 623
Otwell, S. G. I, 638
Otwell, S. Garnett I, 623
Otwell, Sheubal G. I, 664
Otwell, William I, 262
Oudeland, Christian VI, 31
Oudeland, Christian VI, 33
Oudeland, Tho. Taberer VI, 31
Oudelant, Christian VI, 37
Oudelant, Wm. VI, 29
Oudelants, William VI, 35
Oudlant, Christian VI, 37
Oudlant, Elizabeth VI, 33
Oudlant, Elizabeth Oudelants
VI, 33
Oudlant, William VI, 33
Oudlant, William VI, 37
Ouldfeild, Christopher VI, 33
Oulldford, Crestofer I, 91
Ousbun, Ann II, 210
Ousbun, Ann II, 246
Ousler, Elener II, 223
Ousler, Elener II, 246
Ousley, Anna L. V, 424
Ousley, Anna Louisa V, 424
Ousley, Annie L. V, 424
Ousley, Carrie V, 424
Ousley, Cassius Carl V, 424
Ousley, Catharine D. V, 424
Ousley, Catherine V, 424
Ousley, Catherine D. V, 424
Ousley, Clarence V, 424
Ousley, Elizabeth V, 424
Ousley, Ethel V, 424
Ousley, Ethel H. V, 424
Ousley, Harvey V, 424
Ousley, John V, 424
Ousley, John D. V, 424
Ousley, Lille V, 424
Ousley, Mary V, 424
Ousley, Maud E. V, 424
Ousley, Moses V, 424
Ousley, Nancy V, 420
Ousley, Nancy V, 424
Ousley, Nellie V, 424
Ousley, Nettie V, 424
Ousley, Ollie V, 424
Ousley, Ollie M. V, 424
Ousley, Richard V, 424
Ousley, William H. V, 424
Ousley, William Henry V, 424
Ousley, Wm. Henry V, 424
Outeland, William VI, 33
Outelants, William VI, 33
Outhouse, Marie III, 46
Outland, ??? I, 279
Outland, ??? IV, 1269
Outland, ??? VI, 48
Outland, A. F. I, 250
Outland, A. J. I, 208
Outland, Abbigail P. I, 250
Outland, Abigail I, 220
Outland, Abigail I, 228
Outland, Abigail I, 237
Outland, Abigail I, 248
Outland, Abigail I, 330
Outland, Abigail C. I, 221
Outland, Abigail C. I, 249
Outland, Abigail C. I, 259
Outland, Abigail P. I, 219
Outland, Abigail P. I, 249
Outland, Abigail P. I, 250
Outland, Abigail P. I, 329
Outland, Abigail P. I, 330
Outland, Ada Belle I, 219
Outland, Addison J. I, 221
Outland, Addison J. I, 262
Outland, Agatha I, 292
Outland, Agatha I, 308
Outland, Agatha I, 313
Outland, Alfred J. I, 211
Outland, Alfred J. I, 218
Outland, Alfred J. I, 232
Outland, Alfred J. I, 235
Outland, Alfred J. I, 249
Outland, Alfred J. I, 250
Outland, Alfred Jordan I, 219
Outland, Alice Judith I, 219
Outland, Aline I, 262
Outland, Amazetta IV, 1288

Outland, Ann I, 218
Outland, Ann I, 220
Outland, Ann I, 221
Outland, Ann I, 234
Outland, Ann I, 245
Outland, Ann I, 247
Outland, Ann I, 248
Outland, Ann I, 292
Outland, Ann I, 313
Outland, Ann IV, 590
Outland, Ann V, 957
Outland, Ann B. IV, 1288
Outland, Ann C. I, 219
Outland, Ann P. IV, 424
Outland, Ann P. IV, 453
Outland, Anna Brown I, 221
Outland, Anna C. I, 262
Outland, Anna Cora I, 221
Outland, Anna E. I, 219
Outland, Anna Mary I, 232
Outland, Anna Mary I, 250
Outland, Anna Mary K. I, 219
Outland, Anna May I, 208
Outland, Anne I, 248
Outland, Anne I, 254
Outland, Annie E. I, 221
Outland, Arabella I, 219
Outland, Arthur F. I, 219
Outland, Asenath I, 66
Outland, Asenath I, 248
Outland, Asenith I, 221
Outland, Assenath I, 66
Outland, Assenath I, 70
Outland, Benjamin Porter I, 221
Outland, Benjamin T. I, 220
Outland, Benjamin T. I, 249
Outland, Bennett IV, 1288
Outland, Betcy I, 233
Outland, Betcy I, 248
Outland, Betsy I, 220
Outland, Betty I, 220
Outland, Betty I, 292
Outland, Betty I, 313
Outland, Beulah Elma I, 218
Outland, Bewel IV, 1288
Outland, Boddie VI, 39
Outland, Boddy VI, 39
Outland, Catharin E. I, 219
Outland, Cecil Pascns I, 220
Outland, Charity I, 292
Outland, Charity I, 304
Outland, Charity I, 311
Outland, Charity I, 313
Outland, Charles IV, 1288
Outland, Charles Henry I, 220
Outland, Charles Lyndon I, 219
Outland, Charles T. I, 214
Outland, Charles T. I, 239
Outland, Charles T. I, 249
Outland, Charles T. I, 250
Outland, Charles Thomas I, 219
Outland, Christian I, 219
Outland, Christian I, 220
Outland, Christian VI, 33
Outland, Christian VI, 45
Outland, Cinthyann IV, 1288
Outland, Cora IV, 1288
Outland, Cornelius I, 219
Outland, Cornelius I, 220
Outland, Cornelius I, 221
Outland, Cornelius I, 248
Outland, Cornelius I, 249
Outland, Cornelius I, 254
Outland, Cornelius I, 292
Outland, Cornelius I, 311
Outland, Cornelius I, 313
Outland, Cornelius I, 317
Outland, Cornelius VI, 7
Outland, Cornelius VI, 33
Outland, Courtney I, 221
Outland, David I, 219
Outland, David I, 220
Outland, David I, 234
Outland, David I, 248
Outland, David I, 249
Outland, David A. I, 219
Outland, Deborah I, 219
Outland, Deborah I, 295
Outland, Deborah D. I, 244
Outland, Deborah D. I, 248
Outland, Della D. I, 250
Outland, Dorothy Delphina I, 220
Outland, Dorothy J. I, 235
Outland, Dorothy J. I, 249
Outland, Dorothy Jane I, 221
Outland, E. Meredith I, 221
Outland, Earl I, 262
Outland, Earl P. I, 262
Outland, Edgar Francis I, 220
Outland, Edith C. I, 219
Outland, Edith Gertrude I, 219
Outland, Edmon IV, 1288
Outland, Edmond IV, 1288
Outland, Edmund VI, 77
Outland, Edward Borough I, 219
Outland, Edward Burrough I, 220
Outland, Edward E. I, 219
Outland, Effie G. I, 221
Outland, Elfred R. I, 219
Outland, Eli I, 220
Outland, Elijah I, 207
Outland, Elijah I, 209
Outland, Elijah I, 218
Outland, Elijah I, 219
Outland, Elijah I, 221
Outland, Elijah I, 223
Outland, Elijah I, 239
Outland, Elijah I, 249
Outland, Elijah I, 250
Outland, Elijah P. I, 219
Outland, Elijah P. I, 249
Outland, Elijah P. I, 619
Outland, Elijah Peele I, 221
Outland, Elinda I, 249
Outland, Elisabeth I, 236
Outland, Elisabeth I, 248
Outland, Elisabeth I, 249
Outland, Elisabeth I, 257
Outland, Elisabeth I, 325
Outland, Elisabeth H. I, 232
Outland, Elisabeth H. I, 249
Outland, Elisha I, 623
Outland, Elisha IV, 1288
Outland, Elizabeth I, 220
Outland, Elizabeth I, 221
Outland, Elizabeth I, 292
Outland, Elizabeth I, 309
Outland, Elizabeth I, 310
Outland, Elizabeth I, 313
Outland, Elizabeth IV, 378
Outland, Elizabeth IV, 424
Outland, Elizabeth IV, 437
Outland, Elizabeth VI, 21
Outland, Elizabeth VI, 33
Outland, Elizabeth VI, 41
Outland, Elizabeth VI, 45
Outland, Elizabeth VI, 46
Outland, Elizabeth Ann I, 221
Outland, Elizabeth H. I, 208
Outland, Elizabeth H. I, 221
Outland, Elizabeth Helena I, 232
Outland, Elizabeth Helena I, 249
Outland, Elizabeth Oudelants VI, 33
Outland, Elizabeth, Jr. I, 313
Outland, Elizabeth, Sr. I, 313
Outland, Ella G. I, 219
Outland, Ellen IV, 1288
Outland, Ellena R. I, 221
Outland, Elsie I, 262
Outland, Elsie J. I, 623
Outland, Elsie S. I, 638
Outland, Elton G. I, 219
Outland, Emma E. IV, 1288
Outland, Ernest F. I, 262
Outland, Essie M. I, 249
Outland, Exum I, 156
Outland, Exum I, 159
Outland, Exum I, 219
Outland, Exum I, 220
Outland, Exum I, 248
Outland, Exum I, 292
Outland, Exum I, 295
Outland, Exum I, 308
Outland, Exum I, 313
Outland, Ezra IV, 1288
Outland, Felix I, 221
Outland, Felix G. I, 262
Outland, Fernando Claud I, 220
Outland, Fleetwood F. I, 220
Outland, Fleetwood Farmer I, 249
Outland, Florence II, 711
Outland, Florence IV, 393
Outland, Floyd I, 262
Outland, Francis Nicholson I, 221
Outland, Fred I, 250
Outland, Fred Lewter I, 220
Outland, G. T. I, 330
Outland, George E. I, 219
Outland, George Everett I, 219
Outland, Grace M. I, 220
Outland, Gulielma I, 228
Outland, Gulielma P. I, 219
Outland, H. T. I, 330
Outland, Hannah VI, 33
Outland, Harold S. I, 220
Outland, Harriet A. I, 221
Outland, Harriet A. I, 227
Outland, Harriet Ann I, 221
Outland, Harris Ellis I, 220
Outland, Hattie A. I, 249
Outland, Hattie A. I, 257
Outland, Helen I, 219
Outland, Henrietta T. I, 220
Outland, Henry I, 249
Outland, Henry IV, 1288
Outland, Henry Edmon I, 220
Outland, Henry Edwin I, 219
Outland, Henry T. I, 219
Outland, Henry T. I, 220
Outland, Henry T. I, 228
Outland, Henry T. I, 249
Outland, Henry T. I, 250
Outland, Henry T. I, 329
Outland, Henry T. I, 330
Outland, Henry T., Jr. I, 220
Outland, Henry Thomas I, 219
Outland, Henry Thomas I, 221
Outland, Hettie IV, 1288
Outland, Homer Bryon I, 220
Outland, Howard E. I, 221
Outland, Iola T. I, 262
Outland, Iolah I, 221
Outland, Ira DeCane I, 220
Outland, Isaac Felton I, 220
Outland, Isaac Overman I, 219
Outland, Isaac Overman I, 248
Outland, Isaac P. I, 220
Outland, Isaac P. I, 249
Outland, Isaac P. I, 250
Outland, Isaac Parker I, 220
Outland, Isabella I, 219
Outland, Isabella I, 249
Outland, Isabella I, 262
Outland, Isabella Dora I, 252
Outland, Isabella O. I, 223
Outland, Isaiah IV, 1288
Outland, Izabella E. I, 221
Outland, J. F. VI, 77
Outland, J. Wesley IV, 1288
Outland, James IV, 1288
Outland, James A. I, 220
Outland, James A. I, 250
Outland, James Albert I, 221
Outland, James Archie I, 218
Outland, James C. I, 220
Outland, James Henry I, 219
Outland, James Percy I, 219
Outland, Jane I, 211
Outland, Jane I, 220
Outland, Jane I, 221
Outland, Jane I, 233
Outland, Jane I, 248
Outland, Jane I, 249
Outland, Jane IV, 1288
Outland, Janie I, 221
Outland, Janie I, 262
Outland, Jehu J. I, 249
Outland, Jehu J. II, 757
Outland, Jehu Jackson I, 219
Outland, Jehu T. I, 250
Outland, Jennie I, 220
Outland, Jephtha Edwin I, 219
Outland, Jeremiah I, 220
Outland, Jeremiah I, 248
Outland, Jeremiah IV, 1288
Outland, Jeremiah V, 107
Outland, Jesse I, 221
Outland, Jesse I, 249
Outland, Jesse I, 292
Outland, Jesse I, 313
Outland, Jesse H. I, 220
Outland, Jesse Harvey I, 249
Outland, Jesse Herman I, 220
Outland, Joel I, 250
Outland, Joel Bean I, 219
Outland, John I, 156
Outland, John I, 160
Outland, John I, 220
Outland, John I, 221
Outland, John I, 233
Outland, John I, 248
Outland, John I, 249
Outland, John I, 251
Outland, John I, 292
Outland, John VI, 45
Outland, John VI, 46
Outland, John VI, 77
Outland, John Edwin I, 219
Outland, John Henry I, 220
Outland, John L. I, 250
Outland, John Lewter I, 219
Outland, John Lewter I, 220
Outland, John Peele I, 219
Outland, John T. I, 250
Outland, John Thomas I, 221
Outland, John Thomas I, 292
Outland, Jona I, 249
Outland, Jonah M. I, 220
Outland, Jonah M. I, 250
Outland, Jonah Morris I, 219
Outland, Jonathan I, 221
Outland, Jonathan I, 248
Outland, Jonathan I, 292
Outland, Jonathan I, 313
Outland, Jonathan Eli I, 219
Outland, Joseph I, 35
Outland, Joseph I, 53
Outland, Joseph I, 65
Outland, Joseph I, 66
Outland, Joseph I, 69
Outland, Joseph I, 87
Outland, Joseph I, 99
Outland, Joseph I, 156
Outland, Joseph I, 220
Outland, Joseph I, 249
Outland, Joseph I, 262
Outland, Joseph I, 292
Outland, Joseph I, 313
Outland, Joseph IV, 393
Outland, Joseph VI, 77
Outland, Joseph E. I, 249
Outland, Joseph Exum I, 220
Outland, Joseph John I, 220
Outland, Joseph John I, 249
Outland, Joseph Richard I, 221
Outland, Josephine I, 220
Outland, Josephine I, 249
Outland, Josiah I, 219
Outland, Josiah I, 220
Outland, Josiah I, 221
Outland, Josiah I, 227
Outland, Josiah I, 246
Outland, Josiah I, 247
Outland, Josiah I, 248
Outland, Josiah I, 249
Outland, Josiah IV, 424
Outland, Josiah IV, 590
Outland, Josiah IV, 1288
Outland, Josiah V, 107
Outland, Josiah B. I, 221
Outland, Josiah P. I, 221
Outland, Josiah Peele I, 221
Outland, Josiah, Jr. I, 248
Outland, Josie Estella I, 220
Outland, Judith I, 248
Outland, Judith I, 251
Outland, Judith I, 313
Outland, Judith Ann I, 221
Outland, Julia E. I, 220
Outland, Julia Elisabeth I, 249
Outland, Julia Eller I, 219
Outland, Julia M. I, 220
Outland, Julia U. I, 249
Outland, Julia W. I, 221
Outland, Kate I, 227
Outland, Kexia I, 248
Outland, Kezia I, 246
Outland, Kezia I, 248
Outland, Keziah IV, 1288
Outland, Keziah V, 107
Outland, Laura IV, 393
Outland, Le Anna I, 262
Outland, Levi A. I, 249
Outland, Levi Anderson I, 219
Outland, Levi Anderson I, 220
Outland, Lidia Jane I, 221
Outland, Lillian I, 619
Outland, Lola M. I, 219
Outland, Louise I, 219
Outland, Lucinda IV, 1288
Outland, Lula V. I, 250
Outland, Lydia I, 241
Outland, Lydia I, 248
Outland, Lydia Peele I, 219
Outland, Mabel I, 219
Outland, Maggie Mae I, 219
Outland, Mahlon Hockett I, 219
Outland, Margaret I, 65
Outland, Margaret I, 69
Outland, Margaret I, 207
Outland, Margaret I, 209
Outland, Margaret I, 218
Outland, Margaret I, 219
Outland, Margaret I, 221
Outland, Margaret I, 223
Outland, Margaret I, 249
Outland, Margaret I, 250
Outland, Margaret I, 313
Outland, Margaret IV, 155
Outland, Margaret IV, 424
Outland, Margaret IV, 437
Outland, Margaret IV, 447
Outland, Margaret IV, 590
Outland, Margaret IV, 1288
Outland, Margaret A. I, 219
Outland, Margaret A. I, 232
Outland, Margaret A. I, 234
Outland, Margaret A. I, 239
Outland, Margaret A. I, 249
Outland, Margaret A. I, 250
Outland, Margaret Abigail I,
Outland, Margaret Ann I, 21
Outland, Margaret Ann I, 22
Outland, Margaret Edna I, 2
Outland, Margaret Gertrude I, 219
Outland, Margaret Helen I,
Outland, Margaret Lola I, 21
Outland, Margaretta I, 219
Outland, Margret I, 313
Outland, Marhta J. I, 251
Outland, Maria J. I, 234
Outland, Maria J. I, 249
Outland, Maria Jane I, 221
Outland, Mariah J. I, 211
Outland, Mariam I, 219
Outland, Mark B. I, 219
Outland, Marth I, 313
Outland, Martha I, 66
Outland, Martha I, 152
Outland, Martha I, 156
Outland, Martha I, 220
Outland, Martha I, 221
Outland, Martha I, 233
Outland, Martha I, 234
Outland, Martha I, 248
Outland, Martha I, 249
Outland, Martha I, 292
Outland, Martha I, 313
Outland, Martha IV, 424
Outland, Martha IV, 443
Outland, Martha IV, 1288
Outland, Martha IV, 1292
Outland, Martha A. I, 247
Outland, Martha A. I, 249
Outland, Martha Ann I, 220
Outland, Martha J. I, 216
Outland, Martha J. I, 221
Outland, Martha J. I, 249
Outland, Martha J. I, 257
Outland, Martha Jane I, 220
Outland, Martha Jane I, 249
Outland, Martha R. I, 219
Outland, Martha R. I, 221
Outland, Martha R. I, 234
Outland, Martha R. I, 248
Outland, Martha R. I, 249
Outland, Martha R. I, 330
Outland, Martitia I. I, 219
Outland, Mary I, 35
Outland, Mary I, 37
Outland, Mary I, 65
Outland, Mary I, 66
Outland, Mary I, 156
Outland, Mary I, 160
Outland, Mary I, 208
Outland, Mary I, 219
Outland, Mary I, 220
Outland, Mary I, 227
Outland, Mary I, 248
Outland, Mary I, 249
Outland, Mary I, 258
Outland, Mary I, 292
Outland, Mary I, 313
Outland, Mary I, 623
Outland, Mary IV, 1288
Outland, Mary VI, 45
Outland, Mary VI, 46
Outland, Mary Ann I, 221
Outland, Mary Annis I, 221
Outland, Mary Annis I, 249
Outland, Mary C. I, 220
Outland, Mary E. I, 219
Outland, Mary E. I, 619
Outland, Mary Eleanor I, 219
Outland, Mary Eliza I, 219
Outland, Mary Eliza I, 220
Outland, Mary Elizabeth IV, 1288
Outland, Mary F. I, 208
Outland, Mary F. I, 218
Outland, Mary F. I, 235
Outland, Mary F. I, 249
Outland, Mary F. I, 250
Outland, Mary Florence I, 211
Outland, Mary J. I, 220
Outland, Mary J. I, 245
Outland, Mary J. I, 249
Outland, Mary Jane I, 220
Outland, Mary Jane I, 249
Outland, Mary W. I, 220
Outland, Matilda IV, 1288
Outland, Melinda I, 249
Outland, Melissa IV, 1288
Outland, Mildred I, 262
Outland, Mildred E. I, 623
Outland, Mildred E. I, 638
Outland, Milecent I, 248
Outland, Milercent I, 220
Outland, Milercent I, 221

nd, Milicent I, 248
nd, Milisent I, 156
nd, Milisent I, 233
nd, Milisent I, 247
nd, Milisent I, 248
nd, Milisent I, 254
nd, Milisint I, 247
nd, Milisint I, 253
nd, Miriam I, 156
and, Miriam I, 248
and, Miriam I, 295
and, Miriam I, 329
and, Miriam E. I, 249
and, Miriam E. I, 259
and, Miriam Elisabeth I, 249
and, Mirium I, 248
and, Nanney I, 292
and, Nannie Ellen I, 262
and, Naomi IV, 1288
and, Nora IV, 1288
and, Nora V, 569
and, Nora V, 592
and, Oliver IV, 1288
land, Oliver Winfield I, 221
land, Ora B. I, 249
land, Oren IV, 1288
land, Ozella C. I, 209
land, Ozella C. I, 232
land, Ozella C. I, 250
land, Ozella Cora I, 219
land, Patsy V, 107
land, Pattie IV, 1288
land, Pegga I, 219
land, Peter IV, 1288
land, Phebe IV, 424
land, Phebe IV, 448
land, Phebe D. IV, 393
land, Rachel I, 219
land, Rachel I, 220
land, Rachel I, 221
land, Rachel I, 248
land, Rachel I, 249
tland, Rachel I, 254
tland, Rachel I, 261
tland, Rachel IV, 1288
tland, Rachel VI, 46
tland, Rachel Abigail I, 220
tland, Rachel Elma I, 221
tland, Rebecca I, 221
tland, Rebecca IV, 424
tland, Rebecca IV, 447
tland, Rever M. I, 249
tland, Richard Exum VI, 77
tland, Robert I, 216
tland, Robert I, 220
tland, Robert I, 221
tland, Robert I, 248
tland, Robert I, 249
tland, Robert I, 251
tland, Robert I, 257
tland, Robert I, 313
tland, Robert Barcley C. I, 292
tland, Robert Marmon V, 107
tland, Russell D. I, 220
tland, Ruth Anna I, 249
tland, Ruth E. I, 221
tland, Sallie I, 239
tland, Sallie I, 248
utland, Sallie F. I, 239
utland, Sallie F. I, 249
utland, Sallie Lee Olia I, 220
utland, Sally I, 219
utland, Samuel IV, 1288
utland, Sarah I, 65
utland, Sarah I, 66
utland, Sarah I, 87
utland, Sarah I, 99
utland, Sarah I, 140
utland, Sarah I, 156
utland, Sarah I, 219
utland, Sarah I, 220
utland, Sarah I, 221
utland, Sarah I, 234
utland, Sarah I, 241
utland, Sarah I, 248
utland, Sarah I, 249
utland, Sarah I, 250
utland, Sarah I, 251
utland, Sarah I, 292
utland, Sarah I, 313
utland, Sarah I, 317
Outland, Sarah IV, 1288
Outland, Sarah Ann IV, 1288
Outland, Sarah Elizabeth I, 220
Outland, Sarah F. I, 250
Outland, Sarah Florence I, 214
Outland, Sarah Florence I, 219
Outland, Sarah J. I, 207
Outland, Sarah Jane I, 219
Outland, Sophronia I, 262
Outland, Sophronia I, 623
Outland, Sophronia A. I, 638
Outland, Stanley Ellis I, 220
Outland, Susan IV, 1288
Outland, Susanah I, 221
Outland, Susanna IV, 1288
Outland, Tho VI, 33
Outland, Thomas I, 211
Outland, Thomas I, 220
Outland, Thomas I, 221
Outland, Thomas I, 233
Outland, Thomas I, 237
Outland, Thomas I, 241
Outland, Thomas I, 247
Outland, Thomas I, 248
Outland, Thomas I, 249
Outland, Thomas I, 292
Outland, Thomas I, 313
Outland, Thomas I, 325
Outland, Thomas VI, 33
Outland, Thomas VI, 45
Outland, Thomas VI, 77
Outland, Thomas Earl I, 221
Outland, Thomas Elwood I, 219
Outland, Thomas J. I, 66
Outland, Thomas J. I, 70
Outland, Thomas J. I, 248
Outland, Thomas J. I, 249
Outland, Thomas Jordon I, 221
Outland, Thomas P. I, 221
Outland, Thomas P. I, 250
Outland, Thomas P. I, 262
Outland, Thomas Peele I, 220
Outland, Thomas Pemberton I, 221
Outland, Thomas, Jr. I, 248
Outland, Thomas, Sr. I, 249
Outland, Thos. I, 218
Outland, Thos. VI, 46
Outland, Vashti R. I, 221
Outland, Vincent I, 262
Outland, Walter I, 638
Outland, Walter C. I, 262
Outland, Walter C. I, 623
Outland, Walter C. I, 638
Outland, Walter C., Jr. I, 262
Outland, Walter C., Jr. I, 623
Outland, Walter C., Jr. I, 638
Outland, Walter Carlton I, 219
Outland, Warrick P. I, 262
Outland, Warrick Penn I, 221
Outland, Wilfred F. I, 221
Outland, William I, 220
Outland, William I, 221
Outland, William I, 234
Outland, William I, 247
Outland, William I, 248
Outland, William I, 249
Outland, William I, 292
Outland, William I, 313
Outland, William IV, 155
Outland, William IV, 590
Outland, William IV, 1288
Outland, William VI, 33
Outland, William VI, 45
Outland, William VI, 46
Outland, William VI, 116
Outland, William VI, 120
Outland, William Albert I, 220
Outland, William C. I, 219
Outland, William C. I, 221
Outland, William C. I, 227
Outland, William C. I, 234
Outland, William C. I, 248
Outland, William C. I, 249
Outland, William C. I, 330
Outland, William Copeland I, 221
Outland, William Eoodrow I, 220
Outland, William F. I, 208
Outland, William F. I, 221
Outland, William Franklin I, 219
Outland, William Franklin I, 232
Outland, William Franklin I, 249
Outland, William Fredrick I, 219
Outland, William H. I, 249
Outland, William Henry I, 221
Outland, William M. I, 221
Outland, William M. I, 249
Outland, William Micajah I, 220
Outland, William O. I, 232
Outland, William O. I, 249
Outland, William P. I, 249
Outland, William Thomas I, 221
Outland, Wm. IV, 437
Outland, Wm. IV, 447
Outland, Wm. VI, 46
Outlaw, Margaret II, 700
Outline, Cornelius I, 249
Overacre, Emily M. VI, 972
Overacre, George W. VI, 972
Overacre, Sally VI, 972
Overacre, Thomas VI, 972
Overba, Mary VI, 810
Overcash, Mattie B. V, 759
Overdell, Albert Eugene III, 244
Overdell, Elizabeth III, 244
Overdell, Martha III, 244
Overdell, Martha E. III, 244
Overdell, Martha E. III, 322
Overdell, Otto III, 244
Overdell, Otto III, 322
Overend, Margaret II, 72
Overend, Margaret II, 90
Overfelt, Alithea VI, 986
Overfelt, Ann VI, 527
Overfelt, Ann VI, 540
Overfelt, Charles VI, 972
Overfelt, Michael VI, 972
Overfelt, Michael VI, 986
Overfelt, Polly VI, 972
Overfield, Ann VI, 540
Overfield, Jonathan IV, 1288
Overfield, Martha IV, 1288
Overfield, Samuel IV, 1288
Overfield, Sarah VI, 540
Overholser, Harry V, 759
Overholt, Florence IV, 1332
Overholts, Benjamin Bruce V, 855
Overholts, L. O. V, 855
Overholts, Lee V, 855
Overholts, Lee O. V, 855
Overholts, Mae V, 855
Overholts, Martha Elizabeth V, 855
Overholts, Ruby Mae V, 855
Overholtz, Benjamin Bruce V, 855
Overholtz, Lee O. V, 855
Overholtz, Mae V, 855
Overholtzer, Julia A. II, 874
Overholtzer, Julia A. II, 904
Overholtzer, Julia Ann II, 799
Overleace, Susannah V, 759
Overleace, Susannah V, 765
Overleece, Susannah V, 759
Overleece, Susannah V, 765
Overly, Clara B. IV, 1259
Overman, ??? I, 279
Overman, Aaron I, 292
Overman, Aaron I, 293
Overman, Aaron I, 312
Overman, Aaron I, 313
Overman, Aaron I, 320
Overman, Aaron, Jr. I, 313
Overman, Abagail I, 111
Overman, Abba I, 293
Overman, Abigail I, 106
Overman, Abigail I, 111
Overman, Abigail I, 112
Overman, Abigail I, 148
Overman, Abigail I, 157
Overman, Abigail I, 158
Overman, Abigail I, 159
Overman, Abigail I, 161
Overman, Abigail I, 170
Overman, Abigail I, 293
Overman, Abigail I, 363
Overman, Abigail I, 680
Overman, Abigail I, 686
Overman, Abigail I, 729
Overman, Abigial V, 107
Overman, Abner I, 159
Overman, Achilles V, 308
Overman, Achsah I, 293
Overman, Adelia V, 462
Overman, Agatha C. I, 293
Overman, Agatha Caroline I, 313
Overman, Alexander I, 313
Overman, Alva V, 269
Overman, Alva V, 462
Overman, Amanda V, 462
Overman, Amee I, 135
Overman, Amee I, 157
Overman, Ann I, 111
Overman, Ann I, 112
Overman, Ann I, 113
Overman, Ann I, 131
Overman, Ann I, 156
Overman, Ann I, 157
Overman, Ann I, 158
Overman, Ann I, 159
Overman, Ann I, 166
Overman, Ann I, 167
Overman, Ann V, 107
Overman, Ann V, 298
Overman, Ann V, 308
Overman, Anna I, 293
Overman, Anna I, 313
Overman, Anna I, 320
Overman, Anna I, 730
Overman, Anna V, 107
Overman, Anna V, 268
Overman, Anna V, 447
Overman, Anna M. I, 293
Overman, Anne I, 111
Overman, Anne I, 303
Overman, Anne I, 313
Overman, Anne V, 298
Overman, Anne V, 308
Overman, Anne V, 309
Overman, Benjamin I, 66
Overman, Benjamin I, 85
Overman, Benjamin I, 96
Overman, Benjamin I, 111
Overman, Benjamin I, 112
Overman, Benjamin I, 158
Overman, Benjamin I, 159
Overman, Benjamin I, 730
Overman, Benjamin I, 896
Overman, Benjamin S. I, 159
Overman, Benjm. I, 157
Overman, Bennoni I, 111
Overman, Benoni I, 157
Overman, Betty I, 112
Overman, Betty I, 158
Overman, Betty I, 292
Overman, Betty I, 313
Overman, Binjamin I, 896
Overman, Caleb I, 292
Overman, Caleb I, 313
Overman, Carline I, 186
Overman, Caroline I, 152
Overman, Caroline I, 157
Overman, Caroline I, 198
Overman, Catharine I, 292
Overman, Chalkey I, 309
Overman, Chalkley I, 292
Overman, Chalkley I, 313
Overman, Charity I, 293
Overman, Charity Frances I, 313
Overman, Charles I, 34
Overman, Charles I, 52
Overman, Charles I, 66
Overman, Charles I, 111
Overman, Charles I, 127
Overman, Charles I, 145
Overman, Charles I, 156
Overman, Charles I, 157
Overman, Charles I, 158
Overman, Charles I, 159
Overman, Charles I, 166
Overman, Charles I, 293
Overman, Charles I, 313
Overman, Charles V, 447
Overman, Chelley E. I, 327
Overman, Christian I, 313
Overman, Christiana I, 292
Overman, Christiana I, 312
Overman, Christiana I, 313
Overman, Christopher I, 111
Overman, Christopher I, 112
Overman, Christopher I, 157
Overman, Christopher I, 165
Overman, Clarkey I, 52
Overman, Clarkey I, 186
Overman, Clarkey I, 704
Overman, Clarky I, 66
Overman, Cornelas I, 327
Overman, Cornelia V, 462
Overman, Cornelius I, 293
Overman, Cornelius I, 313
Overman, Cornelius I, 330
Overman, Daniel I, 111
Overman, David V, 107
Overman, David V, 139
Overman, David E. I, 327
Overman, David H. I, 327
Overman, David H. I, 339
Overman, Deborah I, 159
Overman, Deborah I, 174
Overman, Demcey V, 308
Overman, Dempsey I, 727
Overman, Dempsey I, 729
Overman, Dempsey V, 107
Overman, Dempsey V, 268
Overman, Dempsey V, 308
Overman, Dempsey V, 462
Overman, Dempsy V, 301
Overman, Demsey I, 730
Overman, Demsey C. V, 308
Overman, Domsy I, 729
Overman, Eleanor V, 307
Overman, Eleanor V, 308
Overman, Eli I, 111
Overman, Eli I, 896
Overman, Eli I, 967
Overman, Eli IV, 1178
Overman, Eli V, 308
Overman, Eli V, 390
Overman, Eli V, 759
Overman, Eli V, 855
Overman, Elias I, 729
Overman, Elias V, 107
Overman, Elias V, 268
Overman, Elias V, 301
Overman, Elias V, 308
Overman, Elias V, 462
Overman, Elijah I, 330
Overman, Elijah V, 308
Overman, Elijah J. I, 293
Overman, Elisabeth I, 111
Overman, Elisabeth I, 129
Overman, Elisabeth I, 147
Overman, Elisabeth I, 148
Overman, Elisabeth I, 157
Overman, Elisabeth I, 158
Overman, Elisabeth I, 159
Overman, Elisabeth I, 176
Overman, Elisabeth I, 196
Overman, Elisabeth I, 198
Overman, Elisabeth I, 832
Overman, Elisha I, 729
Overman, Elisha I, 967
Overman, Elisha V, 107
Overman, Elisha V, 308
Overman, Eliza I, 159
Overman, Eliza I, 313
Overman, Elizabeth I, 93
Overman, Elizabeth I, 104
Overman, Elizabeth I, 111
Overman, Elizabeth I, 112
Overman, Elizabeth I, 134
Overman, Elizabeth I, 138
Overman, Elizabeth I, 145
Overman, Elizabeth I, 150
Overman, Elizabeth I, 157
Overman, Elizabeth I, 159
Overman, Elizabeth I, 186
Overman, Elizabeth I, 292
Overman, Elizabeth I, 293
Overman, Elizabeth I, 313
Overman, Elizabeth I, 330
Overman, Elizabeth I, 664
Overman, Elizabeth I, 719
Overman, Elizabeth I, 729
Overman, Elizabeth I, 730
Overman, Elizabeth I, 732
Overman, Elizabeth I, 830
Overman, Elizabeth I, 832
Overman, Elizabeth IV, 1178
Overman, Elizabeth V, 298
Overman, Elizabeth V, 308
Overman, Elizabeth V, 311
Overman, Elizabeth C. V, 108
Overman, Elizabeth Cooper V, 107
Overman, Elizabeth Cooper V, 139
Overman, Ellen V, 307
Overman, Elva H. I, 339
Overman, Ely I, 664
Overman, Enoch I, 729
Overman, Enoch V, 107
Overman, Enoch V, 268
Overman, Enoch V, 308
Overman, Enos V, 308
Overman, Epherim, Sr. I, 111
Overman, Ephraigm I, 159
Overman, Ephraim I, 111
Overman, Ephraim I, 129
Overman, Ephraim I, 156
Overman, Ephraim I, 157
Overman, Ephraim I, 158
Overman, Ephraim I, 161
Overman, Ephraim I, 165
Overman, Ephraim I, 170
Overman, Ephraim I, 293
Overman, Ephraim I, 313
Overman, Ephraim I, 664
Overman, Ephraim I, 695
Overman, Ephraim I, 729
Overman, Ephraim I, 832
Overman, Ephraim I, 967
Overman, Ephraim I, 1011
Overman, Ephraim V, 759
Overman, Ephraim V, 855
Overman, Ephram I, 363
Overman, Ephram I, 704
Overman, Ephriam I, 111
Overman, Exum I, 159
Overman, Exum I, 293
Overman, Exum I, 313
Overman, Exum I, 326
Overman, Exum I, 330
Overman, Ezekiel D. I, 293
Overman, Fanny I, 721
Overman, Frank W. V, 353
Overman, Frank W. V, 924
Overman, George F. I, 159
Overman, Gideon I, 111
Overman, Gideon I, 157
Overman, Hannah I, 111
Overman, Hannah I, 112
Overman, Hannah I, 147

Overman, Hannah I, 148
Overman, Hannah I, 157
Overman, Hannah I, 158
Overman, Hannah I, 163
Overman, Hannah I, 165
Overman, Hannah I, 198
Overman, Hannah I, 280
Overman, Hannah I, 292
Overman, Hannah I, 293
Overman, Hannah I, 313
Overman, Hannah V, 305
Overman, Hannah V, 308
Overman, Hannah, Sr. I, 158
Overman, Harrett E. I, 327
Overman, Helen V, 462
Overman, Henry I, 159
Overman, Henry I, 313
Overman, Henry V, 855
Overman, Hettie I, 337
Overman, Hettie I, 339
Overman, Hettie O. I, 619
Overman, Huldah I, 111
Overman, Huldah I, 293
Overman, Isaac I, 111
Overman, Isaac I, 137
Overman, Isaac I, 139
Overman, Isaac I, 157
Overman, Isaac I, 158
Overman, Isaac I, 159
Overman, Isaac I, 162
Overman, Isaac I, 170
Overman, Isaac I, 412
Overman, Isaac I, 664
Overman, Isaac I, 686
Overman, Isaac I, 729
Overman, Isaac I, 967
Overman, Isaac V, 107
Overman, Isaac V, 308
Overman, Isabel I, 111
Overman, Isabel I, 159
Overman, Isac I, 159
Overman, Isbel I, 158
Overman, Isbel I, 170
Overman, Isbell I, 111
Overman, Jacob I, 92
Overman, Jacob I, 111
Overman, Jacob I, 152
Overman, Jacob I, 156
Overman, Jacob I, 157
Overman, Jacob I, 186
Overman, Jacob I, 198
Overman, Jacob, Jr. I, 112
Overman, James I, 111
Overman, James I, 112
Overman, James I, 152
Overman, James I, 157
Overman, James I, 158
Overman, James I, 159
Overman, James I, 170
Overman, James I, 174
Overman, James I, 412
Overman, James I, 768
Overman, James, Sr. I, 112
Overman, James, Sr. I, 159
Overman, Jeams I, 111
Overman, Jeams I, 112
Overman, Jesse I, 293
Overman, Jesse I, 308
Overman, Jesse I, 313
Overman, Jesse I, 321
Overman, Jesse I, 664
Overman, Jesse I, 967
Overman, Jesse V, 759
Overman, Jesse V, 855
Overman, Jesse V, 863
Overman, Jesse B. V, 308
Overman, Jesse T. I, 330
Overman, Jesse Thomas I, 293
Overman, Jesse Thomas I, 326
Overman, Joh I, 159
Overman, John I, 66
Overman, John I, 106
Overman, John I, 111
Overman, John I, 112
Overman, John I, 152
Overman, John I, 157
Overman, John I, 158
Overman, John I, 159
Overman, John I, 163
Overman, John I, 165
Overman, John I, 180
Overman, John I, 186
Overman, John I, 197
Overman, John I, 198
Overman, John I, 292
Overman, John I, 293
Overman, John I, 303
Overman, John I, 305
Overman, John I, 313
Overman, John I, 315
Overman, John I, 721
Overman, John I, 729
Overman, John I, 730
Overman, John V, 107
Overman, John V, 265
Overman, John V, 268
Overman, John V, 307
Overman, John V, 308
Overman, John M. V, 301
Overman, John M. V, 308
Overman, John Milton V, 308
Overman, John R. I, 327
Overman, John R. I, 330
Overman, John R. I, 339
Overman, John Thomas I, 330
Overman, John, Jr. I, 313
Overman, John, Sr. I, 112
Overman, John, Sr. I, 293
Overman, John, Sr. I, 313
Overman, Jonas I, 159
Overman, Joseph I, 50
Overman, Joseph I, 66
Overman, Joseph I, 111
Overman, Joseph I, 112
Overman, Joseph I, 114
Overman, Joseph I, 125
Overman, Joseph I, 157
Overman, Joseph I, 158
Overman, Joseph I, 172
Overman, Joseph I, 313
Overman, Joseph I, 729
Overman, Joseph I, 730
Overman, Joshua I, 112
Overman, Joshua I, 138
Overman, Joshua I, 157
Overman, Joshua I, 293
Overman, Joshua I, 313
Overman, Josiah I, 159
Overman, Judith I, 293
Overman, Judith I, 309
Overman, Judith I, 313
Overman, Judith Ann I, 327
Overman, Julia I, 615
Overman, Kezia I, 664
Overman, Kezia V, 855
Overman, Kezia V, 863
Overman, Kezia K. V, 243
Overman, Kezia K. V, 268
Overman, Keziah I, 154
Overman, Keziah I, 157
Overman, Keziah I, 704
Overman, Keziah K. V, 390
Overman, Leah V, 301
Overman, Leah V, 308
Overman, Libbie V, 462
Overman, Lydda I, 186
Overman, Lydda V, 759
Overman, Lydia I, 190
Overman, Lydia I, 198
Overman, Lydia I, 664
Overman, Lydia V, 308
Overman, Margaret I, 112
Overman, Margaret I, 158
Overman, Margaret I, 159
Overman, Margaret I, 327
Overman, Margaret I, 339
Overman, Margaret I, 619
Overman, Margaret I, 730
Overman, Mariam I, 158
Overman, Mariam I, 170
Overman, Mariam I, 730
Overman, Mariam I, 737
Overman, Marth I, 313
Overman, Martha I, 112
Overman, Martha I, 114
Overman, Martha I, 125
Overman, Martha I, 135
Overman, Martha I, 144
Overman, Martha I, 157
Overman, Martha I, 159
Overman, Martha I, 172
Overman, Martha I, 293
Overman, Martha I, 308
Overman, Martha I, 313
Overman, Martha I, 562
Overman, Martha I, 565
Overman, Martha I, 664
Overman, Martha I, 832
Overman, Martha V, 308
Overman, Martha Clark I, 158
Overman, Mary I, 34
Overman, Mary I, 66
Overman, Mary I, 106
Overman, Mary I, 111
Overman, Mary I, 112
Overman, Mary I, 122
Overman, Mary I, 127
Overman, Mary I, 137
Overman, Mary I, 139
Overman, Mary I, 143
Overman, Mary I, 147
Overman, Mary I, 149
Overman, Mary I, 157
Overman, Mary I, 158
Overman, Mary I, 159
Overman, Mary I, 167
Overman, Mary I, 170
Overman, Mary I, 171
Overman, Mary I, 174
Overman, Mary I, 186
Overman, Mary I, 193
Overman, Mary I, 197
Overman, Mary I, 198
Overman, Mary I, 292
Overman, Mary I, 293
Overman, Mary I, 301
Overman, Mary I, 306
Overman, Mary I, 309
Overman, Mary I, 311
Overman, Mary I, 313
Overman, Mary I, 320
Overman, Mary I, 729
Overman, Mary I, 730
Overman, Mary I, 896
Overman, Mary IV, 1178
Overman, Mary IV, 1193
Overman, Mary V, 107
Overman, Mary V, 215
Overman, Mary V, 268
Overman, Mary V, 306
Overman, Mary V, 308
Overman, Mary Ann I, 327
Overman, Mary Ann V, 308
Overman, Mary G. I, 327
Overman, Mary W. IV, 1178
Overman, Mary, Jr. I, 148
Overman, Mary, Jr. I, 157
Overman, Mary, Jr. V, 308
Overman, Matthew I, 147
Overman, Matthew I, 159
Overman, Mehetable I, 339
Overman, Merrium I, 727
Overman, Merrium I, 729
Overman, Miliscent I, 112
Overman, Millescent I, 158
Overman, Millia I, 326
Overman, Millie I, 293
Overman, Milton V, 107
Overman, Miriam I, 99
Overman, Miriam I, 111
Overman, Miriam I, 112
Overman, Miriam I, 139
Overman, Miriam I, 142
Overman, Miriam I, 152
Overman, Miriam I, 156
Overman, Miriam I, 157
Overman, Miriam I, 158
Overman, Miriam I, 159
Overman, Miriam I, 163
Overman, Miriam I, 171
Overman, Miriam I, 292
Overman, Miriam I, 308
Overman, Miriam I, 313
Overman, Miriam I, 730
Overman, Miriam V, 107
Overman, Mourning I, 66
Overman, Mourning I, 85
Overman, Mourning I, 96
Overman, Mourning I, 132
Overman, Myriam I, 140
Overman, Myriam I, 159
Overman, Nancy V, 265
Overman, Nancy V, 268
Overman, Nancy V, 307
Overman, Nancy V, 308
Overman, Nancy V, 309
Overman, Nanny I, 293
Overman, Nathan I, 106
Overman, Nathan I, 111
Overman, Nathan I, 112
Overman, Nathan I, 113
Overman, Nathan I, 136
Overman, Nathan I, 140
Overman, Nathan I, 157
Overman, Nathan I, 158
Overman, Nathan I, 159
Overman, Nathan I, 167
Overman, Nathan I, 293
Overman, Nathan I, 729
Overman, Nathan I, 730
Overman, Nathan I, 732
Overman, Nathan V, 107
Overman, Nathan V, 268
Overman, Nathan V, 308
Overman, Needham I, 313
Overman, Nehemiah I, 157
Overman, Nehemiah I, 172
Overman, Nixon IV, 1178
Overman, Nixon IV, 1193
Overman, Norman V, 462
Overman, Norman M. V, 308
Overman, Obadiah I, 412
Overman, Obadiah I, 565
Overman, Obadiah I, 664
Overman, Obadiah I, 729
Overman, Obadiah I, 967
Overman, Obadiah V, 107
Overman, Obadiah V, 268
Overman, Obediah I, 111
Overman, Obediah I, 157
Overman, Obediah I, 412
Overman, Obediah I, 562
Overman, Obediah I, 565
Overman, Obediah I, 680
Overman, Obediah I, 686
Overman, Obediah I, 832
Overman, Onias I, 112
Overman, Onias I, 158
Overman, Onious I, 159
Overman, Peggy Mariah I, 293
Overman, Peninah I, 163
Overman, Phebe Jane V, 301
Overman, Phebe Jane V, 308
Overman, Phinehas I, 704
Overman, Phinehas I, 967
Overman, Piety V, 390
Overman, Pininah I, 293
Overman, Polly Ann I, 293
Overman, Polly Ann M. I, 327
Overman, Rachel I, 111
Overman, Rachel I, 157
Overman, Rachel I, 158
Overman, Rachel I, 165
Overman, Rachel I, 293
Overman, Rachel I, 304
Overman, Rachel I, 313
Overman, Rachel I, 327
Overman, Rachel I, 664
Overman, Rachel I, 695
Overman, Rachel I, 704
Overman, Rachel I, 729
Overman, Rachel I, 832
Overman, Rachel I, 1001
Overman, Rachel I, 1011
Overman, Rachel V, 304
Overman, Rachel V, 308
Overman, Rachel V, 759
Overman, Rachel V, 855
Overman, Rebecca I, 111
Overman, Rebecca I, 112
Overman, Rebecca I, 127
Overman, Rebecca I, 156
Overman, Rebecca I, 157
Overman, Rebecca I, 172
Overman, Rebecca V, 308
Overman, Rebecca V, 309
Overman, Rebeckah I, 152
Overman, Rebeckah I, 156
Overman, Rebekah I, 156
Overman, Rebekah I, 158
Overman, Rebekah I, 172
Overman, Rebekah I, 186
Overman, Reuben I, 147
Overman, Reuben I, 158
Overman, Reuben I, 159
Overman, Reuben I, 186
Overman, Reuben I, 198
Overman, Reuben V, 759
Overman, Rhoda V, 308
Overman, Richard I, 313
Overman, Richard I, 330
Overman, Robert I, 293
Overman, Robert V, 462
Overman, Robert Morris I, 313
Overman, Ruebin I, 158
Overman, Ruth I, 111
Overman, Ruth I, 157
Overman, Ruth I, 158
Overman, Ruth I, 165
Overman, Ruth I, 170
Overman, Ruth V, 462
Overman, Sally H. V, 254
Overman, Sally H. V, 268
Overman, Samuel I, 157
Overman, Sarah I, 50
Overman, Sarah I, 66
Overman, Sarah I, 73
Overman, Sarah I, 108
Overman, Sarah I, 111
Overman, Sarah I, 112
Overman, Sarah I, 129
Overman, Sarah I, 131
Overman, Sarah I, 136
Overman, Sarah I, 141
Overman, Sarah I, 146
Overman, Sarah I, 149
Overman, Sarah I, 155
Overman, Sarah I, 156
Overman, Sarah I, 157
Overman, Sarah I, 158
Overman, Sarah I, 159
Overman, Sarah I, 161
Overman, Sarah I, 162
Overman, Sarah I, 163
Overman, Sarah I, 165
Overman, Sarah I, 186
Overman, Sarah I, 292
Overman, Sarah I, 293
Overman, Sarah I, 301
Overman, Sarah I, 305
Overman, Sarah I, 313
Overman, Sarah I, 315
Overman, Sarah I, 412
Overman, Sarah I, 562
Overman, Sarah I, 565
Overman, Sarah I, 727
Overman, Sarah I, 729
Overman, Sarah I, 730
Overman, Sarah V, 25
Overman, Sarah V, 107
Overman, Sarah V, 301
Overman, Sarah V, 308
Overman, Sarah V, 353
Overman, Silas V, 759
Overman, Simeon I, 158
Overman, Smithy J. I, 339
Overman, Sophia V, 302
Overman, Sophia V, 308
Overman, Susan I, 832
Overman, Susanna I, 152
Overman, Susanna I, 157
Overman, Susanna I, 730
Overman, Susanna I, 832
Overman, Susannah I, 111
Overman, Susannah I, 130
Overman, Susannah I, 157
Overman, Tamer I, 135
Overman, Tamer I, 158
Overman, Thaddeus I, 158
Overman, Thamer I, 111
Overman, Thamer I, 157
Overman, Thamer I, 158
Overman, Thamer I, 172
Overman, Thomas I, 111
Overman, Thomas I, 112
Overman, Thomas I, 131
Overman, Thomas I, 141
Overman, Thomas I, 157
Overman, Thomas I, 158
Overman, Thomas I, 159
Overman, Thomas I, 171
Overman, Thomas I, 186
Overman, Thomas I, 198
Overman, Thomas I, 293
Overman, Thomas I, 304
Overman, Thomas I, 313
Overman, Thomas I, 330
Overman, Thomas C. I, 327
Overman, Thomas C. I, 330
Overman, Thomas, Sr. I, 157
Overman, Vernon V, 269
Overman, Vernon V, 462
Overman, W. H. I, 339
Overman, W. O. V, 308
Overman, Widow Elizabeth I, 730
Overman, Widow Mary I, 313
Overman, Widow Mourning I, 157
Overman, Widow Sarah I, 153
Overman, Widow Sarah I, 157
Overman, William I, 108
Overman, William I, 111
Overman, William I, 112
Overman, William I, 122
Overman, William I, 148
Overman, William I, 157
Overman, William I, 158
Overman, William I, 159
Overman, William I, 171
Overman, William I, 293
Overman, William I, 301
Overman, William I, 330
Overman, William V, 269
Overman, William V, 308
Overman, William V, 462
Overman, William Exum I, 293
Overman, William Exum I, 326
Overman, William F. I, 339
Overman, William Frankling I, 330
Overman, William H. I, 327
Overman, William H. I, 330
Overman, William H. I, 339
Overman, William Henry I, 330
Overman, William P. V, 308
Overman, William T. I, 293
Overman, William T. I, 327
Overman, William Thomas I, 313
Overman, Willis I, 158
Overman, Wm. II, 611
Overman, Wm. V, 462
Overman, Wm. H. I, 619
Overman, Wm. O. V, 462
Overman, Zabulon I, 729

man, Zadoc V, 107
man, Zadock I, 111
man, Zadok I, 157
man, Zebelon I, 967
man, Zebulon I, 111
man, Zebulon I, 152
man, Zebulon I, 158
man, Zebulon I, 729
man, Zebulon I, 730
man, Zebulon V, 215
man, Zebulon V, 268
man, Zebulon V, 308
man, Zebulon V, 311
man, Zebulum V, 107
man, Zodac I, 729
man, Zodock I, 967
man???, Elizabeth I, 159
mon, Frances I, 704
mon, John I, 704
mon, Margaret I, 704
mon, Mary I, 704
mon, Mordicah I, 704
mon, Sarah I, 704
stree, Archibald VI, 873
street, Adline B. VI, 1018
street, Alexander S. VI, 973
street, Alfred N. VI, 972
street, Alfred N. VI, 973
street, Amanda VI, 972
street, Ann E. VI, 973
street, Ann L. VI, 908
street, Archibald VI, 933
street, Archibald VI, 972
street, Armistead VI, 972
street, Barsheba VI, 899
street, Benjamin T. VI, 973
street, Benoney VI, 898
street, Benoney VI, 972
street, Benoney VI, 973
street, C. VI, 972
street, Caleb F. VI, 973
street, Catharine VI, 972
street, Catharine P. VI, 972
street, Charles VI, 973
street, Charles H. VI, 972
street, David VI, 909
street, Dolly VI, 844
street, Eady VI, 972
street, Ebe VI, 972
street, Elizabeth VI, 955
street, Elizabeth VI, 972
street, Elizabeth VI, 984
street, Elizabeth VI, 1001
street, Elizabeth H. VI, 943
street, Elizabeth R. VI, 984
street, Emily J. VI, 873
street, Emily Jame VI, 891
street, Eunice VI, 972
street, Frances VI, 972
street, Frances VI, 1012
street, Frances VI, 1014
street, Frances Elizabeth
VI, 933
street, George VI, 955
street, George W. VI, 972
street, Granville VI, 973
street, Harriet A. R. VI, 972
street, Harrison VI, 946
street, Henrietta VI, 972
street, Henry J. VI, 971
street, Henry J. VI, 972
street, Henry J. VI, 984
street, Hiram VI, 973
street, Jack VI, 972
street, James VI, 844
street, James VI, 943
street, James VI, 955
street, James VI, 972
street, James VI, 992
street, James VI, 1012
street, James P. VI, 844
street, Jane VI, 972
street, Jane VI, 992
street, Jeremiah VI, 972
street, Jeremiah VI, 973
street, Jeremiah VI, 999
street, Jesse VI, 972
street, Jesse VI, 973
street, John VI, 882
street, John VI, 902
street, John VI, 919
street, John VI, 922
street, John VI, 926
street, John VI, 946
street, John VI, 972
street, John VI, 973
street, John VI, 979
street, John VI, 984
rstreet, John VI, 990
rstreet, John VI, 1012
rstreet, John VI, 1013
Overstreet, John E. VI, 972
Overstreet, John, Jr. VI, 972
Overstreet, John, Jr. VI, 1002
Overstreet, Joicy VI, 900
Overstreet, Joshua VI, 973
Overstreet, Jubal VI, 972
Overstreet, Judith VI, 909
Overstreet, Lewis VI, 899
Overstreet, Littleberry VI, 972
Overstreet, Lockey VI, 882
Overstreet, Lucinda VI, 909
Overstreet, Lucinda VI, 972
Overstreet, Lucy VI, 972
Overstreet, Lucy VI, 1001
Overstreet, Malinda VI, 999
Overstreet, Marinda VI, 973
Overstreet, Martha VI, 972
Overstreet, Martha VI, 973
Overstreet, Martha A. VI, 917
Overstreet, Martha Ann VI, 973
Overstreet, Mary VI, 908
Overstreet, Mary VI, 955
Overstreet, Mary VI, 972
Overstreet, Mary VI, 973
Overstreet, Mary A. VI, 973
Overstreet, Mary J. VI, 973
Overstreet, Mary Jane Rebecca
VI, 973
Overstreet, Mary Sophia VI, 972
Overstreet, Mildred VI, 933
Overstreet, Milley VI, 972
Overstreet, Minerva A. VI, 926
Overstreet, Minerva A. VI, 973
Overstreet, Nancy VI, 835
Overstreet, Nancy VI, 844
Overstreet, Nancy VI, 909
Overstreet, Nancy VI, 926
Overstreet, Nancy VI, 938
Overstreet, Nancy VI, 940
Overstreet, Nancy VI, 972
Overstreet, Nancy VI, 973
Overstreet, Nancy A. VI, 1017
Overstreet, Parkey VI, 1013
Overstreet, Peggy VI, 972
Overstreet, Pelina VI, 946
Overstreet, Permelia VI, 973
Overstreet, Permelia L. VI, 972
Overstreet, Polly VI, 919
Overstreet, Polly VI, 938
Overstreet, Polly VI, 972
Overstreet, Polly Ann VI, 972
Overstreet, Polly P. VI, 972
Overstreet, Polly P. VI, 973
Overstreet, Ruth VI, 972
Overstreet, Sally VI, 1002
Overstreet, Sarah VI, 901
Overstreet, Sarah VI, 956
Overstreet, Seaney VI, 972
Overstreet, Stephen VI, 972
Overstreet, Stephen VI, 973
Overstreet, Susannah VI, 972
Overstreet, Tabithy VI, 973
Overstreet, Thomas VI, 901
Overstreet, Thomas VI, 938
Overstreet, Thomas VI, 955
Overstreet, Thomas VI, 956
Overstreet, Thomas VI, 972
Overstreet, Thomas VI, 1014
Overstreet, Thomas, Jr. VI, 938
Overstreet, Thomas, Sr. VI, 1002
Overstreet, Tilghman J. VI, 972
Overstreet, Tilmon VI, 972
Overstreet, Uney VI, 955
Overstreet, Unice VI, 1018
Overstreet, William VI, 972
Overstreet, William VI, 1017
Overstreet, William B. VI, 973
Overstreet, William H. VI, 908
Overstreet, William H. VI, 973
Overstrett, Archibald VI, 900
Overtake, Henry C. V, 353
Overtake, John F. V, 353
Overtake, Lucinda V, 353
Overtake, Lucinda E. V, 353
Overtake, Margaret V, 353
Overtake, Margaret J. V, 353
Overtakes, Henry C. V, 353
Overtakes, John F. V, 353
Overtakes, Lucinda E. V, 353
Overtakes, Margaret V, 353
Overton, David II, 180
Overton, David II, 246
Overton, Samuel II, 611
Overtsreet, Suckey VI, 882
Ovington, Adele III, 226
Ovington, Adele III, 244
Ovington, Clara G. IV, 747
Ovington, Louise III, 226
Ovington, Louise III, 244
Ovington, Theodore T. III, 226
Ovington, Theodore T. III, 244
Owell, Elizabeth VI, 988
Owell, Eunice I, 623
Owell, Mary VI, 978
Owell, Myrtle I, 623
Owen, ??? II, 643
Owen, Abigail H. V, 885
Owen, Agness Harriet VI, 973
Owen, Alexander VI, 973
Owen, Alice II, 946
Owen, Amos V, 759
Owen, Ann II, 154
Owen, Ann II, 156
Owen, Ann II, 401
Owen, Ann II, 779
Owen, Ann IV, 700
Owen, Ann VI, 33
Owen, Ann VI, 36
Owen, Ann VI, 938
Owen, Anna V, 190
Owen, Arelius II, 401
Owen, Aurelius II, 401
Owen, Barnett VI, 973
Owen, Bartholomew II, 611
Owen, Benjamin I, 1044
Owen, Benjamin II, 36
Owen, Benjamin II, 91
Owen, Benjamin V, 108
Owen, Benjamin V, 172
Owen, Benjamin V, 759
Owen, Benjamin V, 957
Owen, Benjamin F. S. II, 297
Owen, Benjamin Franklin II, 297
Owen, Benjamin P. VI, 890
Owen, Bernard VI, 973
Owen, Bernard L. VI, 920
Owen, Bessie V, 855
Owen, Bessie V, 860
Owen, Betsey VI, 942
Owen, Byron IV, 700
Owen, Cassius E. V, 354
Owen, Catharine II, 401
Owen, Charleen V, 354
Owen, Charles II, 611
Owen, David II, 36
Owen, David II, 91
Owen, David VI, 895
Owen, David VI, 967
Owen, David VI, 973
Owen, David VI, 989
Owen, David VI, 1010
Owen, Deborah V, 108
Owen, Delih VI, 973
Owen, Delpha VI, 973
Owen, Dinah V, 209
Owen, Edward II, 401
Owen, Edward II, 572
Owen, Edward II, 611
Owen, Effa A. IV, 1041
Owen, Elazan IV, 1041
Owen, Eleanor II, 805
Owen, Elisan IV, 984
Owen, Elisan IV, 1011
Owen, Elizabeth I, 1045
Owen, Elizabeth II, 90
Owen, Elizabeth II, 401
Owen, Elizabeth II, 452
Owen, Elizabeth II, 611
Owen, Elizabeth II, 715
Owen, Elizabeth IV, 747
Owen, Elizabeth V, 108
Owen, Elizabeth VI, 931
Owen, Elizabeth VI, 973
Owen, Elizabeth A. V, 382
Owen, Emeline M. VI, 973
Owen, Ephraim I, 1044
Owen, Ephraim I, 1045
Owen, Ephraim V, 108
Owen, Ephraim V, 723
Owen, Ephraim V, 759
Owen, Esther II, 401
Owen, Esther II, 501
Owen, Esther II, 611
Owen, Esther V, 172
Owen, Esther V, 957
Owen, Evan II, 401
Owen, Evan II, 554
Owen, Evan II, 611
Owen, Frances II, 446
Owen, Frances IV, 747
Owen, Gainor II, 611
Owen, George II, 611
Owen, Gilbert VI, 33
Owen, Gilbert VI, 36
Owen, Griffith II, 91
Owen, Griffith II, 401
Owen, Griffith II, 542
Owen, Griffith II, 572
Owen, Griffith II, 598
Owen, Griffith II, 599
Owen, Griffith II, 611
Owen, Griffith II, 643
Owen, Hannah II, 247
Owen, Hannah II, 401
Owen, Hannah II, 609
Owen, Hannah II, 611
Owen, Hannah V, 108
Owen, Harrison VI, 844
Owen, Harvey A. IV, 1041
Owen, Henry M. V, 354
Owen, Humphrey II, 247
Owen, Isaac E. V, 354
Owen, Israel IV, 744
Owen, Israel IV, 747
Owen, James VI, 829
Owen, James VI, 876
Owen, James VI, 929
Owen, James VI, 931
Owen, James VI, 942
Owen, James F. N. VI, 973
Owen, Jane II, 401
Owen, Jane II, 494
Owen, Jane II, 518
Owen, Jane II, 542
Owen, Jane II, 544
Owen, Jane II, 611
Owen, Jemima VI, 844
Owen, Jesse IV, 984
Owen, Jesse VI, 973
Owen, John I, 1044
Owen, John I, 1045
Owen, John II, 401
Owen, John II, 542
Owen, John II, 544
Owen, John II, 611
Owen, John V, 108
Owen, John V, 159
Owen, John V, 759
Owen, John VI, 881
Owen, John VI, 937
Owen, John VI, 944
Owen, John VI, 973
Owen, John VI, 995
Owen, John VI, 1019
Owen, John A. I, 947
Owen, John W. II, 715
Owen, John, Jr. VI, 973
Owen, Joice VI, 1011
Owen, Jonathan Coppock II, 611
Owen, Jordan VI, 973
Owen, Joseph II, 36
Owen, Joseph II, 91
Owen, Joseph II, 154
Owen, Joseph II, 156
Owen, Joseph Hall II, 805
Owen, Joshua II, 154
Owen, Joshua II, 156
Owen, Joshua II, 200
Owen, Joshua II, 204
Owen, Joshua II, 218
Owen, Joshua II, 246
Owen, Joshua II, 250
Owen, Joshua II, 258
Owen, Joshua II, 779
Owen, Joshua IV, 747
Owen, Jourdan VI, 872
Owen, Judith VI, 973
Owen, Judith Ann Elizabeth
VI, 988
Owen, Julia IV, 700
Owen, Julia A. IV, 700
Owen, Katharine II, 401
Owen, Lewis II, 82
Owen, Lewis II, 90
Owen, Lewis II, 91
Owen, Lewis II, 111
Owen, Lillie M. IV, 1041
Owen, Louisa VI, 937
Owen, Louise C. VI, 899
Owen, Lynch VI, 844
Owen, Maggie B. II, 715
Owen, Maggie May I, 947
Owen, Margaret II, 212
Owen, Margaret II, 246
Owen, Margaret II, 247
Owen, Margaret V, 188
Owen, Margaret VI, 937
Owen, Margery I, 1045
Owen, Margery V, 108
Owen, Marget VI, 973
Owen, Maria Louisa VI, 920
Owen, Martha II, 156
Owen, Martha II, 238
Owen, Martha II, 246
Owen, Martha II, 258
Owen, Martha II, 401
Owen, Martha II, 611
Owen, Martha II, 814
Owen, Martha A. V, 382
Owen, Mary I, 1044
Owen, Mary I, 1045
Owen, Mary II, 204
Owen, Mary II, 246
Owen, Mary II, 247
Owen, Mary II, 250
Owen, Mary II, 401
Owen, Mary II, 554
Owen, Mary II, 611
Owen, Mary IV, 410
Owen, Mary IV, 747
Owen, Mary V, 108
Owen, Mary VI, 920
Owen, Mary VI, 938
Owen, Mary VI, 1000
Owen, Mary F. IV, 835
Owen, Mary F. IV, 836
Owen, Mary J. VI, 890
Owen, Mary L. VI, 973
Owen, Mary M. IV, 744
Owen, Mary M. IV, 745
Owen, Mary M. IV, 747
Owen, Mary V. VI, 964
Owen, Matthew II, 246
Owen, Mercy II, 36
Owen, Mercy II, 91
Owen, Michael IV, 700
Owen, Milicent II, 154
Owen, Milicent II, 155
Owen, Millicent II, 154
Owen, Mourning I, 992
Owen, Mourning I, 994
Owen, N. W. VI, 920
Owen, Nancy VI, 931
Owen, Naomi II, 247
Owen, Nathaniel IV, 747
Owen, Nicholas W. VI, 964
Owen, Nicholas W. VI, 973
Owen, Nicholas W. VI, 988
Owen, Owen II, 611
Owen, Owen VI, 938
Owen, Owen VI, 973
Owen, Owen VI, 1000
Owen, Pamelia A. VI, 973
Owen, Parker II, 611
Owen, Parmelia VI, 832
Owen, Parthena VI, 973
Owen, Parvis M. IV, 1178
Owen, Patsy VI, 844
Owen, Pattsey VI, 1010
Owen, Phebe IV, 747
Owen, Phebe IV, 1178
Owen, Philip VI, 828
Owen, Philip VI, 973
Owen, Prudence II, 90
Owen, Prudence II, 111
Owen, Prudence II, 250
Owen, Prudence II, 779
Owen, Rachel II, 91
Owen, Rachel II, 103
Owen, Rachel II, 401
Owen, Rachel II, 904
Owen, Rachel V, 159
Owen, Rachel VI, 1000
Owen, Rebecca II, 218
Owen, Rebecca II, 246
Owen, Rebecca II, 401
Owen, Rebecca II, 599
Owen, Rebecca II, 752
Owen, Rebecca V, 606
Owen, Rebecca G. IV, 700
Owen, Rebecka II, 401
Owen, Rebeckah II, 599
Owen, Rebeckah II, 611
Owen, Rebeckah V, 159
Owen, Rebekah II, 611
Owen, Robert II, 401
Owen, Robert II, 554
Owen, Robert II, 558
Owen, Robert II, 611
Owen, Robert VI, 832
Owen, Robert VI, 844
Owen, Robert VI, 939
Owen, Robert C. V, 354
Owen, Rosa A. IV, 1041
Owen, Rowland II, 250
Owen, Ruth I, 1045
Owen, Ruth I, 1057
Owen, Ruth II, 247
Owen, Ruth V, 108
Owen, Ruth VI, 973
Owen, Salley VI, 931
Owen, Sally VI, 828
Owen, Samuel I, 1045
Owen, Samuel II, 401
Owen, Samuel II, 611
Owen, Samuel V, 108
Owen, Samuel V, 159
Owen, Samuel V, 188
Owen, Samuel V, 190
Owen, Samuel V, 209
Owen, Samuel V, 759
Owen, Samuel VI, 973
Owen, Samuel S. II, 297
Owen, Samuel S. II, 757

Owen, Samuel S. II, 758
Owen, Samuel S. II, 1057
Owen, Samuel Stocton II, 297
Owen, Sarah I, 1044
Owen, Sarah I, 1045
Owen, Sarah II, 200
Owen, Sarah II, 247
Owen, Sarah II, 259
Owen, Sarah II, 401
Owen, Sarah II, 464
Owen, Sarah II, 494
Owen, Sarah II, 598
Owen, Sarah II, 599
Owen, Sarah II, 611
Owen, Sarah II, 643
Owen, Sarah IV, 699
Owen, Sarah IV, 747
Owen, Sarah V, 108
Owen, Sarah V, 188
Owen, Sarah V, 190
Owen, Sarah V, 759
Owen, Sarah VI, 973
Owen, Sarah Owen V, 759
Owen, Sarah S. V, 354
Owen, Stacy IV, 1041
Owen, Susanna II, 401
Owen, Susanna II, 558
Owen, Susanna II, 572
Owen, Susanna II, 611
Owen, Susanna VI, 828
Owen, Susanna VI, 844
Owen, Susannah II, 82
Owen, Susannah II, 90
Owen, Susannah II, 583
Owen, Susannah II, 611
Owen, Tacy II, 602
Owen, Tacy II, 611
Owen, Taliaferro VI, 973
Owen, Taliaffero VI, 899
Owen, Thomas II, 297
Owen, Thomas II, 443
Owen, Thomas II, 611
Owen, Thomas IV, 835
Owen, Thomas IV, 836
Owen, Thomas M. II, 297
Owen, Thomas Matthews II, 297
Owen, Thomas Matthews II, 758
Owen, Thomas, Jr. II, 401
Owen, Thomas, Jr. II, 611
Owen, Ursley VI, 828
Owen, Ursly VI, 973
Owen, Wd. Ann II, 401
Owen, Wd. Jane II, 401
Owen, Wd. Martha II, 246
Owen, Wd. Mary II, 401
Owen, Wd. Sarah II, 611
Owen, Wd. Susanna II, 478
Owen, William VI, 1011
Owen, William B. VI, 973
Owen, William C. V, 354
Owen, William Waring II, 401
Owen, Winfield IV, 747
Owen, Wm. II, 91
Owen, Wm. II, 103
Owen, Wm. VI, 815
Owen, Wm. G. V, 382
Owen, Wm. T. VI, 899
Owen, Wm. Waring II, 611
Owenby, Nancy VI, 946
Owens, Alexander VI, 973
Owens, Amos V, 196
Owens, Ann V, 196
Owens, Anna V, 196
Owens, Anne V, 196
Owens, Belle IV, 1259
Owens, Benjamin I, 274
Owens, Benjamin V, 195
Owens, Benjamin V, 196
Owens, Bethia I, 274
Owens, Bethiah I, 268
Owens, Bethiah I, 274
Owens, Cashius E. V, 354
Owens, Cassius E. V, 354
Owens, Charity V, 195
Owens, Charity V, 196
Owens, Charleen V, 354
Owens, Chasteen V, 354
Owens, Dinah V, 196
Owens, Edgar V, 702
Owens, Edgar T. V, 702
Owens, Eleanor I, 565
Owens, Eliza I, 565
Owens, Eliza Ann IV, 1332
Owens, Ella V, 702
Owens, Emeline M. VI, 973
Owens, Emily I, 896
Owens, Ephraim V, 195
Owens, Ephraim V, 196
Owens, Esther C. V, 196
Owens, Frances IV, 747
Owens, Henry IV, 1219
Owens, Henry M. V, 354
Owens, Isaac A. V, 354
Owens, Isaac E. V, 354
Owens, James V, 196
Owens, John V, 195
Owens, John V, 196
Owens, Jonathan V, 196
Owens, Lizzie V, 667
Owens, Lizzie V, 702
Owens, M. Anna I, 1160
Owens, Margaret V, 196
Owens, Margery V, 195
Owens, Margery V, 196
Owens, Martha V, 354
Owens, Mary I, 274
Owens, Mary I, 412
Owens, Mary II, 401
Owens, Mary V, 195
Owens, Mary V, 196
Owens, Mary VI, 901
Owens, Mary Annie V, 196
Owens, Maud V, 269
Owens, Mrs. Ford V, 1013
Owens, Myrtle IV, 1259
Owens, Owen VI, 901
Owens, Pamelia A. VI, 917
Owens, Phebe IV, 1178
Owens, Philip VI, 886
Owens, Polly VI, 901
Owens, Rachel V, 196
Owens, Rebecca V, 196
Owens, Rebeckah V, 196
Owens, Richard V, 353
Owens, Richard V, 354
Owens, Robert C. V, 353
Owens, Robert C. V, 354
Owens, Samuel V, 195
Owens, Samuel V, 196
Owens, Samuel V, 469
Owens, Samuel Griffin V, 196
Owens, Sarah V, 195
Owens, Sarah V, 196
Owens, Sarah Maria V, 196
Owens, Sarah S. V, 354
Owens, Sarah W. II, 717
Owens, Taliaferro VI, 917
Owens, Tamar V, 196
Owens, Thomas VI, 11
Owens, Wd. Hannah II, 811
Owens, William V, 354
Owens, William C. V, 354
Owerton, Constantine II, 1033
Owin, Mary VI, 201
Owin, Marye VI, 261
Owl, John Thomas VI, 802
Ownbey, Nancy VI, 973
Ownbey, Powell VI, 986
Ownbey, William VI, 973
Ownby, Ann VI, 973
Ownby, Catharine VI, 911
Ownby, Catharine J. VI, 973
Ownby, Charles VI, 973
Ownby, Edward VI, 973
Ownby, Eliza VI, 943
Ownby, Elizabeth VI, 973
Ownby, Elizabeth VI, 1000
Ownby, Jane VI, 1009
Ownby, Matilda VI, 973
Ownby, Nancy VI, 911
Ownby, Nancy VI, 973
Ownby, Nancy VI, 1000
Ownby, Powell VI, 957
Ownby, Powell, Jr. VI, 957
Ownby, Powell, Jr. VI, 973
Ownby, Powell, Sr. VI, 973
Ownby, William VI, 973
Ownes, Mary V, 521
Ownesby, Matilda VI, 1011
Ownesby, Powell VI, 1011
Ownesby, Powell Ownbey VI, 1004
Ownesby, Powell, Jr. VI, 1011
Ownesby, Susanna VI, 1004
Ownly, Joel I, 66
Ownly, Sarah I, 66
Ownsbey, Nancy VI, 973
Ownsbey, Powell, Sr. VI, 973
Ownsby, Elizabeth VI, 957
Ownsby, Nancy VI, 946
Ownsby, Sally VI, 986
Owsley, Wm. Henry V, 424
Oxley, Ada IV, 257
Oxley, Ann II, 446
Oxley, Charles IV, 257
Oxley, Elizabeth May IV, 257
Oxley, George IV, 257
Oxley, Grace IV, 1064
Oxley, Grace IV, 1070
Oxley, Hannah Jane IV, 104
Oxley, Henry VI, 502
Oxley, Henry VI, 540
Oxley, Henry Troth IV, 104
Oxley, Honnor II, 371
Oxley, Honour II, 542
Oxley, Honour II, 611
Oxley, James E. IV, 257
Oxley, Joel IV, 104
Oxley, Joel IV, 112
Oxley, Joel IV, 257
Oxley, Joel VI, 427
Oxley, John II, 401
Oxley, John II, 611
Oxley, John VI, 940
Oxley, John VI, 961
Oxley, John VI, 973
Oxley, John W. IV, 257
Oxley, Joseph II, 446
Oxley, Joseph II, 611
Oxley, Margaret Truman IV, 104
Oxley, Mary II, 611
Oxley, Mary IV, 104
Oxley, Mary IV, 112
Oxley, Mary IV, 257
Oxley, Nancy VI, 938
Oxley, Nathaniel VI, 973
Oxley, Polly VI, 973
Oxley, Rachel IV, 170
Oxley, Rachel IV, 257
Oxley, Rebecca VI, 973
Oxley, Sally VI, 973
Oxley, Saml. VI, 938
Oxley, Samuel VI, 894
Oxley, Samuel VI, 973
Oxley, Sarah IV, 104
Oxley, Walter II, 758
Oxley, Wd. Ann II, 401
Oxley, William II, 401
Oxley, William IV, 491
Oxley, Wm. II, 446
Oxtoby, Mary Ann III, 244
Oxtoby, William III, 244
Oyler, Hannah Maria V, 589
Oyler, Hannah Maria V, 924
Oyler, John VI, 940
Oyler, Nancy J. VI, 973
Oyler, Valentine W. VI, 973
Oyster, Amy IV, 984
Oyster, Amy IV, 1001
Oyster, Carrie IV, 671
Oyster, Carrie IV, 792
Oyster, Mary Ann IV, 940
Oyster, Mary Ann IV, 984
Oyster, Samuel IV, 671
Oyster, Samuel IV, 792
Oyster, Sarah J. IV, 671
Oyster, Sarah J. IV, 792
Oyster, Sarah J. IV, 836
Ozan, Mrs. ??? IV, 1332
Ozanne, Mrs. ??? IV, 1332
Ozanne, Mrs. Julian L. IV, 1332
Ozbern, Sarah I, 994
Ozbon, Sarah I, 565
Ozbon, William Abraham I, 832
Ozborn, Abigail I, 511
Ozborn, Abner H. I, 511
Ozborn, Abraham I, 729
Ozborn, Abram I, 729
Ozborn, Anna I, 727
Ozborn, Daniel I, 565
Ozborn, Daniel I, 645
Ozborn, David I, 511
Ozborn, David I, 535
Ozborn, Elijah I, 512
Ozborn, Eliza I, 751
Ozborn, Elizabeth I, 512
Ozborn, Hannah I, 511
Ozborn, Ira I, 512
Ozborn, Iva I, 512
Ozborn, Jane I, 511
Ozborn, Jean I, 994
Ozborn, Jesse I, 512
Ozborn, Jesse I, 751
Ozborn, Job I, 511
Ozborn, Joel I, 512
Ozborn, Joseph I, 511
Ozborn, Lydia I, 511
Ozborn, Lydia I, 535
Ozborn, Lydia J. I, 512
Ozborn, Margaret I, 412
Ozborn, Mary I, 511
Ozborn, Mary V, 517
Ozborn, Mary V, 521
Ozborn, Matthew I, 511
Ozborn, Matthew I, 645
Ozborn, Matthew I, 994
Ozborn, Meria I, 511
Ozborn, Rachel I, 512
Ozborn, Rachel I, 679
Ozborn, Rebecca I, 751
Ozborn, Samuel I, 512
Ozborn, Thomas I, 994
Ozborn, William I, 511
Ozborn, William I, 727
Ozborn, William I, 729
Ozborn, William I, 994
Ozbourn, Rebecca I, 994
Ozbourn, William I, 412
Ozbourne, David I, 994
Ozbum, Sarah I, 412
Ozbun, Abigail I, 384
Ozbun, Abigail I, 662
Ozbun, Abigail I, 663
Ozbun, Abigail I, 685
Ozbun, Abigail I, 691
Ozbun, Abner I, 663
Ozbun, Abraham I, 384
Ozbun, Abraham I, 412
Ozbun, Abraham I, 662
Ozbun, Abraham I, 663
Ozbun, Abraham I, 682
Ozbun, Abraham I, 685
Ozbun, Abraham I, 978
Ozbun, Abraham I, 994
Ozbun, Ann I, 663
Ozbun, Ann I, 682
Ozbun, Ann I, 684
Ozbun, Ann I, 685
Ozbun, Ann I, 686
Ozbun, Anna I, 558
Ozbun, Anna I, 565
Ozbun, Anna I, 664
Ozbun, Anne I, 896
Ozbun, Anne I, 900
Ozbun, Charles I, 662
Ozbun, Charles I, 663
Ozbun, Charles I, 1129
Ozbun, Charles V, 855
Ozbun, Charlotte V, 855
Ozbun, Charlotty V, 855
Ozbun, Daniel I, 662
Ozbun, Daniel I, 663
Ozbun, Daniel I, 675
Ozbun, Daniel I, 685
Ozbun, Daniel V, 268
Ozbun, Daniel, Jr. I, 1129
Ozbun, David I, 511
Ozbun, David I, 663
Ozbun, David I, 994
Ozbun, Eli I, 664
Ozbun, Elisabeth I, 685
Ozbun, Elisha V, 855
Ozbun, Elisha G. V, 855
Ozbun, Elizabeth I, 420
Ozbun, Elizabeth I, 662
Ozbun, Elizabeth I, 663
Ozbun, Elizabeth I, 681
Ozbun, Elvira V, 855
Ozbun, Elwood V, 838
Ozbun, Elwood V, 855
Ozbun, Enoch I, 664
Ozbun, Esther III, 244
Ozbun, Hannah I, 364
Ozbun, Hannah I, 662
Ozbun, Hannah I, 663
Ozbun, Hannah I, 664
Ozbun, Hannah I, 685
Ozbun, Hannah I, 690
Ozbun, Henry I, 664
Ozbun, Hulda V, 855
Ozbun, Huldah I, 685
Ozbun, Huldah I, 691
Ozbun, Isaac I, 662
Ozbun, Isabel I, 662
Ozbun, Isabel I, 663
Ozbun, Isabell I, 663
Ozbun, Isabella V, 855
Ozbun, James III, 244
Ozbun, James H. V, 855
Ozbun, James K. V, 855
Ozbun, Jane I, 982
Ozbun, Jane I, 994
Ozbun, Jeremiah I, 385
Ozbun, Jeremiah I, 412
Ozbun, Jeremiah I, 663
Ozbun, Jesse I, 663
Ozbun, Jesse I, 664
Ozbun, Jesse I, 681
Ozbun, Jesse I, 685
Ozbun, Job I, 511
Ozbun, John I, 524
Ozbun, John I, 564
Ozbun, John I, 686
Ozbun, John V, 268
Ozbun, John V, 318
Ozbun, John V, 844
Ozbun, Jonathan I, 663
Ozbun, Jonathan I, 994
Ozbun, Jonathan V, 855
Ozbun, Joseph I, 663
Ozbun, Joseph V, 855
Ozbun, Lydia I, 511
Ozbun, Lydia I, 663
Ozbun, Lydia I, 673
Ozbun, Lydia I, 685
Ozbun, Lydia I, 994
Ozbun, Lydia I, 1129
Ozbun, Lydia V, 838
Ozbun, Lydia V, 855
Ozbun, Margaret I, 662
Ozbun, Martha I, 682
Ozbun, Martha I, 685
Ozbun, Mary I, 364
Ozbun, Mary I, 511
Ozbun, Mary I, 663
Ozbun, Mary I, 673
Ozbun, Mary I, 684
Ozbun, Mary I, 685
Ozbun, Mary I, 978
Ozbun, Mary V, 318
Ozbun, Mary V, 354
Ozbun, Mary V, 855
Ozbun, Matthew I, 343
Ozbun, Matthew I, 364
Ozbun, Matthew I, 412
Ozbun, Matthew I, 511
Ozbun, Matthew I, 662
Ozbun, Matthew I, 663
Ozbun, Matthew I, 664
Ozbun, Matthew I, 978
Ozbun, Matthew I, 982
Ozbun, Matthew I, 994
Ozbun, Matthew, Sr. I, 663
Ozbun, Melinda I, 663
Ozbun, Mourning I, 675
Ozbun, Mourning I, 685
Ozbun, Nathan I, 663
Ozbun, Obed I, 664
Ozbun, Peter I, 662
Ozbun, Phebe I, 663
Ozbun, Phebe I, 681
Ozbun, Polly V, 855
Ozbun, Rachel I, 511
Ozbun, Rachel I, 662
Ozbun, Rachel I, 663
Ozbun, Rachel I, 686
Ozbun, Rebecca I, 362
Ozbun, Rebecca I, 663
Ozbun, Richard I, 663
Ozbun, Ruth I, 663
Ozbun, Ruth I, 679
Ozbun, Ruth I, 686
Ozbun, Samuel I, 662
Ozbun, Samuel I, 663
Ozbun, Samuel I, 681
Ozbun, Samuel I, 685
Ozbun, Sarah I, 385
Ozbun, Sarah I, 524
Ozbun, Sarah I, 664
Ozbun, Sarah I, 685
Ozbun, Sarah I, 686
Ozbun, Sarah I, 687
Ozbun, Sarah I, 691
Ozbun, Sarah V, 318
Ozbun, Sarah V, 844
Ozbun, Sarah V, 855
Ozbun, Seth I, 663
Ozbun, Susanna V, 843
Ozbun, Susanna V, 844
Ozbun, Susanna V, 855
Ozbun, Susannah I, 664
Ozbun, Susannah V, 855
Ozbun, Tamar I, 662
Ozbun, Tamer I, 685
Ozbun, Tamer I, 687
Ozbun, Thomas I, 362
Ozbun, Thomas I, 412
Ozbun, Thomas I, 420
Ozbun, Thomas I, 511
Ozbun, Thomas I, 994
Ozbun, William I, 412
Ozbun, William I, 558
Ozbun, William I, 565
Ozbun, William I, 662
Ozbun, William I, 663
Ozbun, William I, 664
Ozbun, William I, 684
Ozbun, William I, 685
Ozbun, William I, 729
Ozbun, William I, 978
Ozbun, William I, 994
Ozbun, William I, 1129
Ozbun, Wm. I, 362
Ozburn, Abigail I, 412
Ozburn, Abraham I, 512
Ozburn, Ann I, 565
Ozburn, Daniel V, 354
Ozburn, David I, 512
Ozburn, David I, 565
Ozburn, Eliza B. V, 354
Ozburn, Elizabeth I, 362
Ozburn, Elizabeth I, 512
Ozburn, Elizabeth I, 556
Ozburn, Elizabeth I, 565
Ozburn, Elizabeth V, 354

rn, Elvira V, 855
rn, Elwood V, 354
rn, Enoch I, 982
rn, Enoch I, 994
rn, Exum V, 354
rn, Hannah I, 412
rn, Hannah I, 420
rn, Henry V, 354
rn, Henry M. V, 354
rn, Isaac Samuel V, 354
rn, Isabel V, 354
rn, Isabella V, 354
rn, Isabella V, 855
rn, Isable I, 512
rn, Jesse I, 768
rn, John I, 564
rn, John V, 354
rn, Jonathan I, 512
rn, Jonathan V, 354
rn, Joseph I, 523
rn, Joseph I, 565
rn, Lydia I, 565
rn, Margaret I, 362
rn, Margaret I, 412
rn, Margaret I, 418
rn, Marshall V, 354
rn, Mary I, 523
rn, Mary I, 564
rn, Mary I, 565
rn, Mary I, 568
rn, Mary V, 354
rn, Mary V, 834
rn, Mary V, 855
rn, Matthew I, 512
rn, Matthew I, 564
rn, Matthew I, 565
rn, Matthew I, 568
rn, Mourning V, 354
rn, Peeter II, 401
rn, Rebecca I, 362
rn, Rebecka I, 767
rn, Rebeckah I, 512
rn, Rebeckah I, 767
rn, Richard I, 512
rn, Richard I, 994
rn, Samuel I, 556
rn, Samuel I, 565
rn, Samuel V, 354
rn, Sarah I, 540
rn, Sarah I, 564
rn, Sarah I, 565
rn, Sarah I, 982
rn, Sarah I, 994
rn, Sarah I, 1129
rn, Sarah V, 354
rn, Susanna V, 354
rn, Thomas I, 362
rn, Thomas I, 512
rn, William I, 362
rn, William I, 412
rn, William I, 512
rn, William I, 729
rn, William I, 967
rn, William I, 994
rn, Wm. I, 362
ent, Velna I, 623
ent, Walter R. I, 623
ond, Amelia VI, 427
orn, Matthew I, 565

Elizabeth III, 125
Sarah Ellen I, 615
Sarah Jane I, 615
William I, 615
, Esther I, 919
, Hardy I, 452
, John VI, 844
, Margaret VI, 844
, Mary II, 523
, Mary II, 611
, Nancy I, 445
, Nancy I, 452
, Susanna I, 452
, George V, 668
, George V, 702
, Marianne V, 668
, Marianne V, 702
, Samuel IV, 1259
ard, Clara Bell IV, 1332
ard, Cora IV, 1345
ard, Cora Bell IV, 1332
ard, Curtis H. IV, 1332
ard, Duty IV, 1332
ard, Jennie IV, 1332
ard, Jenny Duty IV, 1332
ard, John IV, 1332
ard, Mrs. John IV, 1332
ard, Ruth IV, 1332
ard, Winnie III, 244
er, ??? IV, 310

Packer, Aaron IV, 257
Packer, Aaron IV, 258
Packer, Aaron IV, 310
Packer, Aaron IV, 424
Packer, Aaron IV, 891
Packer, Aaron IV, 894
Packer, Abigail IV, 258
Packer, Abijah IV, 424
Packer, Abijah IV, 543
Packer, Abijah IV, 590
Packer, Abraham IV, 257
Packer, Abraham IV, 345
Packer, Abraham IV, 424
Packer, Abraham IV, 526
Packer, Abraham IV, 543
Packer, Abraham IV, 590
Packer, Abram IV, 517
Packer, Alice M. IV, 258
Packer, Allen IV, 257
Packer, Amos A. IV, 257
Packer, Ann II, 144
Packer, Ann II, 154
Packer, Ann IV, 258
Packer, Ann IV, 313
Packer, Ann IV, 562
Packer, Ann IV, 891
Packer, Ann IV, 894
Packer, Ann V, 108
Packer, Ann V, 957
Packer, Ann C. II, 904
Packer, Asenath IV, 257
Packer, Asenath IV, 258
Packer, Asenath V, 108
Packer, Benjamin IV, 257
Packer, Benjamin IV, 310
Packer, Calvin H. IV, 313
Packer, Cassandra IV, 864
Packer, Cassandra IV, 880
Packer, Catharine IV, 171
Packer, Catharine V, 108
Packer, Cathärineb IV, 258
Packer, Catherine V, 108
Packer, Christiana II, 737
Packer, Christiana II, 758
Packer, Christianna D. II, 758
Packer, Christianna L. II, 758
Packer, David IV, 543
Packer, Edith IV, 170
Packer, Edith IV, 258
Packer, Edith J. IV, 258
Packer, Eli IV, 257
Packer, Eli IV, 258
Packer, Eli IV, 894
Packer, Elisha IV, 257
Packer, Elisha IV, 258
Packer, Elisha IV, 310
Packer, Elisha IV, 313
Packer, Elisha V, 108
Packer, Eliza V, 957
Packer, Eliza V, 962
Packer, Elizabeth IV, 257
Packer, Elizabeth IV, 258
Packer, Elizabeth IV, 836
Packer, Elizabeth IV, 848
Packer, Elizabeth IV, 894
Packer, Ella IV, 921
Packer, Ella IV, 984
Packer, Ella C. IV, 984
Packer, Elva J. IV, 258
Packer, Ephraim J. IV, 257
Packer, Esther C. II, 737
Packer, Esther C. II, 758
Packer, Ethel M. IV, 258
Packer, Eve IV, 257
Packer, Eve IV, 258
Packer, Eve IV, 543
Packer, Franklin IV, 257
Packer, Franklin IV, 258
Packer, Franklin V, 59
Packer, Franklin V, 108
Packer, Fredrick E. IV, 258
Packer, George IV, 104
Packer, George IV, 258
Packer, George IV, 313
Packer, George IV, 562
Packer, George IV, 650
Packer, George IV, 836
Packer, George IV, 880
Packer, Grace IV, 245
Packer, Grace IV, 257
Packer, Grace IV, 258
Packer, Grace A. IV, 258
Packer, Hannah L. IV, 258
Packer, Hannah L. IV, 313
Packer, Hannah L. IV, 562
Packer, Isaac IV, 257
Packer, Isaac IV, 258
Packer, Isaac IV, 310
Packer, Isaac IV, 543
Packer, Israel IV, 257
Packer, James II, 904

Packer, Jesse IV, 258
Packer, Joel V, 108
Packer, John II, 737
Packer, John II, 758
Packer, John IV, 239
Packer, John IV, 258
Packer, John V, 108
Packer, John Thomas IV, 257
Packer, John Thomas IV, 258
Packer, Jordan IV, 543
Packer, Lambern IV, 258
Packer, Lamborn IV, 562
Packer, Levi IV, 257
Packer, Levi IV, 258
Packer, Levi IV, 543
Packer, Lewess IV, 313
Packer, Lewessa IV, 562
Packer, Lillian IV, 258
Packer, Louesa IV, 258
Packer, Lydia C. IV, 258
Packer, Lydia C. IV, 313
Packer, Lydia C. IV, 562
Packer, Margaret IV, 46
Packer, Margaret IV, 52
Packer, Margaret IV, 313
Packer, Margaretta V, 108
Packer, Marianna V, 108
Packer, Mary IV, 258
Packer, Mary IV, 424
Packer, Mary IV, 543
Packer, Mary IV, 590
Packer, Mary E. V, 59
Packer, Mary E. V, 108
Packer, Mary Elizabeth G. V, 108
Packer, Mary P. IV, 517
Packer, Milton W. IV, 257
Packer, Moses IV, 52
Packer, Moses IV, 104
Packer, Moses IV, 155
Packer, Moses IV, 258
Packer, Moses IV, 491
Packer, Moses IV, 1178
Packer, Oren V, 957
Packer, Phebe Ann IV, 258
Packer, Phebe Ann IV, 313
Packer, Phebe Ann IV, 562
Packer, Philena IV, 258
Packer, Philena IV, 313
Packer, Philena IV, 562
Packer, Rachel M. IV, 171
Packer, Rebecca IV, 169
Packer, Rebecca IV, 171
Packer, Rebecca IV, 239
Packer, Rebecca IV, 257
Packer, Rebecca IV, 258
Packer, Rebecca IV, 310
Packer, Rebecca IV, 311
Packer, Rebecca IV, 313
Packer, Rebecca V. IV, 258
Packer, Ruth IV, 170
Packer, Ruth IV, 258
Packer, S. M. IV, 258
Packer, Samuel II, 904
Packer, Samuel V, 108
Packer, Sarah II, 401
Packer, Sarah IV, 257
Packer, Sarah IV, 258
Packer, Sarah IV, 310
Packer, Sarah IV, 336
Packer, Sarah IV, 345
Packer, Sarah IV, 424
Packer, Sarah IV, 517
Packer, Sarah IV, 526
Packer, Sarah IV, 543
Packer, Sarah IV, 590
Packer, Sarah IV, 901
Packer, Sarah IV, 912
Packer, Sarah V, 108
Packer, Sarah Ann II, 904
Packer, Sarah P. IV, 313
Packer, Sarah P. IV, 314
Packer, Seth F. IV, 257
Packer, Seth T. IV, 258
Packer, Sophia IV, 1029
Packer, Susanna II, 457
Packer, Susanna II, 611
Packer, Susanna IV, 205
Packer, Susanna IV, 258
Packer, Susanna IV, 590
Packer, Susannah IV, 526
Packer, Thomas IV, 258
Packer, Thomas IV, 310
Packer, Thomas E. IV, 171
Packer, William V, 108
Packer, William Paul V, 108
Packer, Wilson IV, 313
Packer, Wm. II, 904
Packer, Wm. IV, 171
Packer, Wm. Atkinson IV, 258
Packer, Wm. F. IV, 170
Packer, Wm. F. IV, 258

Packer, Wm. L. IV, 313
Packhard, Winnie III, 333
Packingham, Rachel IV, 1070
Paddock, ??? III, 154
Paddock, ??? III, 155
Paddock, Alice V, 108
Paddock, Alice V, 925
Paddock, Alice V, 934
Paddock, Amy V, 925
Paddock, Ann I, 565
Paddock, Ann V, 108
Paddock, Ann V, 925
Paddock, Anna V, 924
Paddock, Avis V, 924
Paddock, Avis V, 925
Paddock, Barclay V, 924
Paddock, Benj. F. V, 925
Paddock, Benj. S. III, 244
Paddock, Benjamin V, 108
Paddock, Benjamin V, 924
Paddock, Benjamin V, 925
Paddock, Charles V, 108
Paddock, Chas. V, 925
Paddock, Cornelia III, 154
Paddock, Cornelia III, 244
Paddock, Deborah V, 108
Paddock, Deborah V, 924
Paddock, Deborah V, 925
Paddock, Elizabeth V, 899
Paddock, Elizabeth V, 925
Paddock, Elizabeth S. V, 925
Paddock, Elizabeth Stanton V, 898
Paddock, Emma III, 244
Paddock, Gertrude III, 155
Paddock, Gertrude III, 244
Paddock, Jemima V, 108
Paddock, Jemimah V, 924
Paddock, Jemimah V, 925
Paddock, Joseph V, 108
Paddock, Joseph V, 925
Paddock, Joseph, Jr. V, 925
Paddock, Lucretia V, 108
Paddock, Lucretia V, 924
Paddock, Lucretia P. V, 925
Paddock, Lydia V, 108
Paddock, Lydia V, 925
Paddock, Lydia V, 926
Paddock, Lydia V, 942
Paddock, Lydia F. V, 925
Paddock, Lydia Folger V, 941
Paddock, Mary V, 925
Paddock, Mary C. V, 924
Paddock, Nantucket I, 565
Paddock, Nathaniel I, 565
Paddock, Phebe V, 108
Paddock, Phebe V, 898
Paddock, Phebe V, 925
Paddock, Priscilla I, 532
Paddock, Priscilla I, 565
Paddock, Rebecca V, 910
Paddock, Rebecca H. V, 909
Paddock, Rebecca H. V, 925
Paddock, Reuben V, 108
Paddock, Reuben V, 925
Paddock, Samuel V, 108
Paddock, Samuel V, 924
Paddock, Samuel V, 925
Paddock, Sarah S. V, 925
Paddock, Sherborn I, 565
Paddock, Susannah V, 924
Paddock, Susannah M. V, 925
Paddock, Tristram V, 108
Paddock, Tristram V, 925
Paddock, William V, 108
Paddock, William V, 925
Paddock, William C. V, 925
Paddock, Wm. V, 898
Paddock, Wm. V, 925
Paden, Celia IV, 624
Paden, Celia IV, 650
Paden, Hannah VI, 427
Paden, Isaac IV, 624
Paden, Isaac IV, 650
Paden, Isaac VI, 427
Paden, Jacob VI, 427
Paden, Lydia IV, 258
Paden, Margaret IV, 258
Paden, Rachel IV, 258
Paden, Rebecca IV, 650
Paden, Rebecca VI, 427
Padg, John II, 91
Padg, Rebeck II, 91
Padget, Alexander V, 702
Padget, Alice V, 702
Padget, Alice Ann V, 702
Padget, Charles V, 702
Padget, Elizabeth VI, 973
Padget, Farrell Benjamin V, 702
Padget, Lillie May V, 702
Padget, Lilly May V, 702

Padget, Phaso V, 702
Padget, Sarah Elizabeth Ann V, 702
Padget, William VI, 973
Padgett, Alice V, 521
Padgett, Ann VI, 973
Padgett, Ann VI, 974
Padgett, Beverly VI, 871
Padgett, Beverly VI, 974
Padgett, Beverly H. VI, 974
Padgett, Clarisa VI, 962
Padgett, Elizabeth VI, 973
Padgett, Elizabeth M. VI, 974
Padgett, Fredck. VI, 923
Padgett, Frederick VI, 973
Padgett, Frederick VI, 974
Padgett, Fredrick VI, 973
Padgett, Gideon VI, 876
Padgett, Gideon VI, 974
Padgett, James A. VI, 890
Padgett, James A. VI, 974
Padgett, John R. VI, 974
Padgett, Kitturah VI, 974
Padgett, Lucy VI, 923
Padgett, Lucy VI, 974
Padgett, Mary A. C. VI, 803
Padgett, Mary Ann VI, 974
Padgett, Matilda VI, 973
Padgett, Nancy VI, 923
Padgett, Permelia VI, 974
Padgett, Pleasant VI, 973
Padgett, Polly VI, 973
Padgett, Sarah F. VI, 974
Padgett, Seaton VI, 803
Padgett, Thomas VI, 974
Padgett, Waller VI, 973
Padgett, Walter VI, 973
Padgett, William VI, 962
Padgett, William VI, 973
Padgett, Winney VI, 970
Padgett, Wm. VI, 1003
Padgitt, Frederick VI, 894
Padgitt, James A. VI, 974
Padgitt, John R. VI, 974
Paff, Phebe II, 1018
Pagan, Carter VI, 974
Pagan, David VI, 874
Pagan, David VI, 974
Pagan, Elizabeth VI, 335
Pagan, Joseph VI, 974
Pagan, Mary VI, 974
Pagan, Nancy L. VI, 974
Pagan, Peggy VI, 890
Pagan, Suana VI, 974
Pagans, Carter VI, 974
Pagans, Nancy L. VI, 974
Page, Abigail II, 91
Page, Abigail II, 105
Page, Abigail H. II, 297
Page, Agnes II, 296
Page, Agnes II, 297
Page, Alce VI, 33
Page, Alice V, 424
Page, Alse VI, 33
Page, Alta V, 424
Page, Amelia III, 244
Page, Amelia III, 245
Page, Amelia III, 319
Page, Amelia III, 431
Page, Amelia C. III, 245
Page, Amelia E. III, 225
Page, Amy II, 401
Page, Ann II, 586
Page, Ann II, 612
Page, Ann VI, 974
Page, Anna V, 354
Page, Anna VI, 162
Page, Anna VI, 201
Page, Annie L. III, 319
Page, Annie S. III, 244
Page, Archibald, Jr. VI, 949
Page, Bennett VI, 974
Page, Bennett VI, 1014
Page, Bennett VI, 1015
Page, Betsey Ann VI, 974
Page, Betsey Ann VI, 1003
Page, Bettie I, 621
Page, Charles V, 424
Page, David G. III, 244
Page, Deborah II, 462
Page, Deborah II, 612
Page, Dora IV, 1288
Page, E. III, 245
Page, Edmd. VI, 910
Page, Edmund G. VI, 974
Page, Edward T. III, 244
Page, Elezabeath I, 155
Page, Elezabeath I, 159
Page, Eliza I, 565
Page, Eliza Ann VI, 974
Page, Elizabeth I, 91

Page, Elizabeth I, 110
Page, Elizabeth VI, 33
Page, Elizabeth VI, 844
Page, Elizabeth VI, 910
Page, Elizabeth VI, 974
Page, Elizabeth VI, 1003
Page, Elizabeth F. II, 297
Page, Elizabeth H. II, 297
Page, Emeline Smith III, 244
Page, Emily VI, 974
Page, Enoch III, 245
Page, Fanny VI, 1003
Page, Felicia VI, 29
Page, Frances VI, 974
Page, Franklin III, 245
Page, George II, 586
Page, George II, 612
Page, George III, 244
Page, Grant V, 424
Page, Hannah II, 32
Page, Hannah II, 78
Page, Hannah II, 91
Page, Hannah II, 247
Page, Hannah II, 259
Page, Hannah III, 244
Page, Hannah III, 245
Page, Henry II, 247
Page, Henry IV, 1288
Page, Henry VI, 33
Page, Isaac I, 92
Page, Isaac I, 112
Page, Isabell VI, 32
Page, Isabell VI, 33
Page, Isack I, 91
Page, Isacke I, 110
Page, Isacke I, 159
Page, James II, 36
Page, James VI, 937
Page, James VI, 974
Page, James VI, 1003
Page, James H. VI, 974
Page, Jane VI, 729
Page, John I, 250
Page, John II, 32
Page, John II, 36
Page, John II, 54
Page, John II, 91
Page, John II, 247
Page, John II, 402
Page, John II, 586
Page, John II, 612
Page, John III, 244
Page, John III, 245
Page, John VI, 30
Page, John VI, 33
Page, John VI, 844
Page, John VI, 974
Page, John G. VI, 974
Page, Joseph II, 402
Page, Joseph II, 612
Page, L. O. V, 683
Page, L. O. V, 702
Page, Louisa III, 244
Page, Louisa III, 245
Page, Louisa IV, 258
Page, Lucinda VI, 974
Page, Lucy III, 134
Page, Lucy III, 245
Page, Lucy VI, 974
Page, Lydia Ann III, 245
Page, Martha VI, 1014
Page, Martha B. VI, 974
Page, Mary I, 313
Page, Mary I, 715
Page, Mary I, 730
Page, Mary II, 36
Page, Mary II, 91
Page, Mary II, 109
Page, Mary II, 402
Page, Mary II, 612
Page, Mary II, 670
Page, Mary VI, 33
Page, Mary VI, 34
Page, Mary Frances III, 254
Page, Mary Mann VI, 760
Page, Mary Mann VI, 785
Page, Mary R. VI, 974
Page, Mattie E. VI, 684
Page, Nancy VI, 874
Page, Nancy VI, 937
Page, Nancy VI, 974
Page, Nathaniel I, 565
Page, Nellie V, 683
Page, Nellie V, 702
Page, Peace III, 245
Page, Pelatiah III, 245
Page, Pelatiah P. III, 245
Page, Pelatiah P. III, 319
Page, Pelatiah P. III, 431
Page, Pelatian P. III, 225
Page, Pilatiah P. III, 244
Page, Polly VI, 974
Page, Polly VI, 1003
Page, Rachel II, 36
Page, Rachel W. III, 431
Page, Rachel W. III, 441
Page, Rebecca II, 32
Page, Rebecca III, 245
Page, Rebecca VI, 29
Page, Rebecca VI, 33
Page, Rebecca, Jr. II, 91
Page, Rebeccah II, 402
Page, Rebeck II, 91
Page, Rebeckah II, 36
Page, Rebeckah II, 91
Page, Rebeckah VI, 33
Page, Rebekah II, 54
Page, Rebekah II, 91
Page, Robert II, 247
Page, Sarah I, 307
Page, Sarah I, 313
Page, Sarah I, 717
Page, Sarah I, 730
Page, Sarah II, 36
Page, Sarah II, 78
Page, Sarah II, 297
Page, Sarah II, 402
Page, Sarah V, 925
Page, Sarah V, 929
Page, Sophronia I, 681
Page, Susanna VI, 802
Page, Susannah II, 247
Page, Thomas VI, 8
Page, Thomas VI, 17
Page, Thomas VI, 29
Page, Thomas VI, 32
Page, Thomas VI, 33
Page, Thomas VI, 34
Page, Thomas VI, 36
Page, Thomas VI, 974
Page, Thomas VI, 983
Page, Thomas VI, 1020
Page, Wessley VI, 974
Page, William IV, 1178
Page, William VI, 33
Page, William VI, 974
Page, William H. VI, 974
Page, Wilson M. III, 245
Page, Wilson M. III, 431
Page, Wilson M. III, 441
Page, Wm. R. IV, 1178
Pagen, David VI, 996
Pagen, Sarah VI, 996
Pagett, Alice V, 637
Pagett, Edward V, 638
Pagett, Harry L. V, 638
Pagett, Myra E. V, 638
Pagin, Joseph VI, 974
Pagin, Suana VI, 974
Pagitt, Ann VI, 974
Pagitt, Beverly VI, 974
Pagitt, Beverly VI, 1022
Pagitt, Elisabetha VI, 970
Pagitt, Elizabeth VI, 973
Pagitt, Frederick VI, 923
Pagitt, Frederick VI, 973
Pagitt, Frederick VI, 974
Pagitt, Frederick VI, 977
Pagitt, Jack R. VI, 974
Pagitt, John R. VI, 1001
Pagitt, John R. VI, 1018
Pagitt, Matilda VI, 973
Pagitt, Pleasant VI, 973
Pagitt, Pleasant M. VI, 973
Pagitt, Thomas VI, 970
Pagon, Elizabeth VI, 310
Paige, ??? III, 348
Paige, Alice B. III, 348
Paige, Alice Browning I, 947
Paige, Alice Browning III, 245
Paige, Alice P. I, 936
Paige, Anna I, 936
Paige, Elwood J. I, 936
Pailen, Ann I, 113
Pailen, Elizabeth I, 113
Pailen, Henry I, 113
Pailen, Henry, Jr. I, 159
Pailen, Mary I, 113
Pailen, Miriam I, 113
Pailen, Thomas I, 113
Pailin, Henry I, 730
Pailin, Mary I, 159
Pailin, Nixon I, 730
Pailin, Sarah I, 159
Pailon, Henry I, 730
Pailon, Henry I, 896
Pain, Charles Lynch VI, 262
Pain, Ellinor II, 617
Pain, Ellinor II, 663
Pain, George VI, 201
Pain, George VI, 206
Pain, John II, 402
Pain, John VI, 262
Pain, Libbie V, 462
Pain, Lydia V, 759
Pain, Lydia V, 769
Pain, Margaret II, 617
Pain, Mary II, 402
Pain, Mary II, 446
Pain, Rachel I, 1086
Pain, Samuel II, 446
Pain, Sarah I, 897
Paine, ??? III, 245
Paine, Bryant I, 967
Paine, Charlotte I, 925
Paine, Daniel I, 967
Paine, Dolly II, 617
Paine, Dolly II, 668
Paine, Elizabeth II, 234
Paine, Elizabeth II, 247
Paine, Elizabeth II, 258
Paine, Elizabeth II, 275
Paine, Frail VI, 954
Paine, Frank V, 269
Paine, Joanna VI, 954
Paine, John VI, 335
Paine, Letitia V, 269
Paine, Lettie V, 269
Paine, Mabel Jane V, 702
Paine, Mary II, 617
Paine, Mary VI, 335
Paine, Matthew II, 37
Paine, Nancy Bryant I, 967
Paine, Nathaniel II, 247
Paine, Nathaniel II, 275
Paine, Patsy VI, 1013
Paine, Polley VI, 886
Paine, Ruth VI, 335
Paine, Sarah II, 227
Paine, Sarah II, 247
Paine, Thomas I, 967
Paine, William VI, 335
Paine, William VI, 886
Pains, John VI, 291
Painter, ??? II, 446
Painter, ??? IV, 984
Painter, Abigail IV, 52
Painter, Abigail IV, 650
Painter, Abigail IV, 703
Painter, Abigail IV, 747
Painter, Abigail IV, 748
Painter, Abigail VI, 427
Painter, Abigail VI, 449
Painter, Abigail VI, 602
Painter, Abraham IV, 747
Painter, Abraham IV, 748
Painter, Abraham VI, 602
Painter, Adna Griffith IV, 984
Painter, Agnes IV, 748
Painter, Agnes E. IV, 747
Painter, Aletha L. V, 522
Painter, Almira V, 508
Painter, Amanda Jane V, 522
Painter, Amos IV, 713
Painter, Anderson V, 521
Painter, Ann II, 402
Painter, Ann IV, 698
Painter, Ann IV, 747
Painter, Ann IV, 748
Painter, Ann IV, 768
Painter, Ann IV, 770
Painter, Ann IV, 785
Painter, Ann IV, 916
Painter, Ann V, 521
Painter, Ann Pusey II, 612
Painter, Anna B. IV, 984
Painter, Anna Maria V, 508
Painter, Annie V, 1013
Painter, Asenath V, 522
Painter, Asenith V, 521
Painter, Bertha V, 522
Painter, Berthina V, 521
Painter, Beulah VI, 602
Painter, Bulah VI, 415
Painter, Bulah VI, 428
Painter, Bulah VI, 592
Painter, Bulay VI, 592
Painter, Burthenia O. V, 485
Painter, Calvin C. V, 508
Painter, Charley IV, 1288
Painter, Chester V, 522
Painter, David IV, 52
Painter, David IV, 650
Painter, David IV, 698
Painter, David IV, 747
Painter, David IV, 748
Painter, David IV, 770
Painter, David IV, 785
Painter, David IV, 916
Painter, David V, 354
Painter, David V, 469
Painter, David V, 491
Painter, David V, 521
Painter, David V, 522
Painter, David V, 621
Painter, David V, 638
Painter, David V, 702
Painter, David VI, 387
Painter, David VI, 427
Painter, David VI, 602
Painter, David A. V, 519
Painter, David A. V, 521
Painter, David A. V, 522
Painter, David Faulkner VI, 427
Painter, David Pidgeon V, 702
Painter, David S. V, 269
Painter, David S. V, 522
Painter, David S. V, 638
Painter, Davis S. V, 241
Painter, Dayton V, 521
Painter, Dayton V, 522
Painter, Deborah II, 612
Painter, Deborah II, 649
Painter, Deborah V, 521
Painter, Deborah L. V, 522
Painter, Deborah S. V, 538
Painter, Deborah T. V, 505
Painter, Demo V, 522
Painter, Docia V, 521
Painter, Donald H. V, 196
Painter, Donald Hinshaw V, 702
Painter, Dora F. V, 522
Painter, Edith IV, 698
Painter, Edith IV, 748
Painter, Edmund Franklin V, 521
Painter, Edmund Franklin V, 522
Painter, Edward V, 508
Painter, Eliza V, 521
Painter, Elizabeth IV, 747
Painter, Elizabeth IV, 748
Painter, Elizabeth IV, 770
Painter, Elizabeth IV, 836
Painter, Elizabeth IV, 916
Painter, Elizabeth V, 521
Painter, Elizabeth V, 522
Painter, Elizabeth V, 529
Painter, Elizabeth V, 638
Painter, Elizabeth VI, 387
Painter, Elizabeth VI, 427
Painter, Elizabeth VI, 594
Painter, Elizabeth VI, 602
Painter, Elizabeth Ann V, 491
Painter, Elizabeth Ann Fawcett V, 522
Painter, Elva V, 196
Painter, Elva V, 702
Painter, Elva H. V, 702
Painter, Elva Hinshaw V, 196
Painter, Elva Hinshaw V, 702
Painter, Elwood IV, 747
Painter, Elwood IV, 748
Painter, Elwood G. IV, 748
Painter, Ethel L. V, 521
Painter, Eunice IV, 345
Painter, Eunice VI, 427
Painter, Eunice VI, 462
Painter, Florence V, 1013
Painter, George II, 402
Painter, George II, 506
Painter, George II, 612
Painter, George II, 649
Painter, George Edward V, 702
Painter, Hampton W. V, 269
Painter, Hannah IV, 52
Painter, Hannah IV, 650
Painter, Hannah IV, 653
Painter, Hannah IV, 748
Painter, Hannah IV, 763
Painter, Hannah V, 19
Painter, Hannah V, 108
Painter, Hannah V, 196
Painter, Hannah V, 510
Painter, Hannah V, 521
Painter, Hannah V, 522
Painter, Hannah V, 528
Painter, Hannah V, 630
Painter, Hannah V, 638
Painter, Hannah V, 644
Painter, Hannah VI, 427
Painter, Hannah VI, 602
Painter, Hannah A. V, 522
Painter, Hannah E. IV, 747
Painter, Hannah E. IV, 748
Painter, Hannah E. IV, 763
Painter, Hannah F. IV, 713
Painter, Hannah L. V, 521
Painter, Hannah L. V, 522
Painter, Hannah L. V, 638
Painter, Hannah Lewis V, 522
Painter, Hannah S. V, 196
Painter, Hannah S. V, 207
Painter, Hannah S. V, 522
Painter, Hannah S. V, 638
Painter, Harriet M. V, 196
Painter, Harriet M. V, 207
Painter, Harriet M. V, 269
Painter, Harriet M. V, 283
Painter, Harriet M. V, 521
Painter, Harriet M. V, 638
Painter, Harriett M. V, 522
Painter, Hazel V, 702
Painter, Hazel V, 722
Painter, Hazel T. V, 702
Painter, Helen M. V, 196
Painter, Helen Maria V, 702
Painter, Helena V, 521
Painter, Helena V, 522
Painter, Henry V, 702
Painter, Henry F. V, 508
Painter, Herbert J. V, 196
Painter, Herbert J. V, 702
Painter, Herbert Joseph V, 7
Painter, Irene V, 522
Painter, Irene J. V, 522
Painter, Isaac V, 506
Painter, Isaac V, 521
Painter, Isaac V, 522
Painter, Isaac VI, 427
Painter, Isaac VI, 602
Painter, Isaac G. IV, 748
Painter, Isaac G. IV, 836
Painter, Isaac, Sr. VI, 602
Painter, J. Henry V, 196
Painter, J. Henry V, 702
Painter, Jacob IV, 52
Painter, Jacob IV, 650
Painter, Jacob IV, 747
Painter, Jacob IV, 748
Painter, Jacob IV, 749
Painter, Jacob IV, 836
Painter, Jacob IV, 859
Painter, Jacob V, 269
Painter, Jacob V, 521
Painter, Jacob V, 522
Painter, Jacob V, 638
Painter, Jacob VI, 427
Painter, Jacob VI, 598
Painter, Jacob VI, 602
Painter, Jesse IV, 52
Painter, Jesse V, 519
Painter, Jesse V, 521
Painter, Jesse V, 522
Painter, Jesse V, 529
Painter, Jesse V, 635
Painter, Jesse V, 638
Painter, Jesse VI, 602
Painter, Jesse Moses V, 522
Painter, Jesse S. V, 522
Painter, Joanna V, 522
Painter, Joanna T. V, 506
Painter, Joanna T. V, 522
Painter, John II, 446
Painter, John IV, 748
Painter, John V, 521
Painter, John V, 522
Painter, John VI, 387
Painter, John VI, 403
Painter, John VI, 427
Painter, John VI, 594
Painter, John VI, 595
Painter, John VI, 602
Painter, John H. IV, 698
Painter, John H. IV, 747
Painter, John H. IV, 748
Painter, John Henry V, 196
Painter, John, Jr. VI, 427
Painter, Joseph IV, 52
Painter, Joseph IV, 650
Painter, Joseph IV, 747
Painter, Joseph IV, 748
Painter, Joseph IV, 984
Painter, Joseph V, 196
Painter, Joseph V, 521
Painter, Joseph C. V, 196
Painter, Joseph C. V, 207
Painter, Joseph C. V, 521
Painter, Joseph C. V, 522
Painter, Joseph C. V, 528
Painter, Joseph C. V, 630
Painter, Joseph C. V, 638
Painter, Joseph C. V, 644
Painter, Joseph G. V, 522
Painter, Joseph H. V, 638
Painter, Joseph Henry V, 638
Painter, Joseph S. V, 522
Painter, Joseph Willets IV, 98
Painter, Joseph Willis IV, 984
Painter, Joshua IV, 747
Painter, Julian V, 521
Painter, Julian V, 522
Painter, Lawrence IV, 1259
Painter, Lewis IV, 748
Painter, Lidia V, 521
Painter, Lillian V, 702
Painter, Lillian V, 712

er, Lillian P. V, 638
er, Lillian Pidgeon V, 702
er, Livinus V, 508
er, Lorenso IV, 748
er, Lorenzo IV, 747
er, Lorenzo IV, 836
er, Lorenzo D. V, 521
er, Louisa I, 896
er, Louisa IV, 747
er, Louisa IV, 748
er, Louisa IV, 836
er, Louisa V, 508
er, Louisa V, 521
er, Louisa V, 522
er, Louiza IV, 748
ter, Louiza IV, 777
ter, Lucinda IV, 714
ter, Lucinda IV, 747
er, Lucinda IV, 748
er, Lucinda IV, 836
er, Lucy Ann V, 519
ter, Lucy Ann V, 522
ter, Lucy J. V, 1013
ter, Lydia II, 402
ter, Lydia II, 612
ter, Lydia A. V, 462
ter, Lydia Ann IV, 747
ter, Lydia E. IV, 748
ter, Lydia E. V, 521
ter, Lydia Fraizer V, 521
ter, Lydia S. V, 522
ter, Lydia S. V, 535
ter, Mahlon VI, 602
ter, Margaret VI, 597
ter, Margaret Ann V, 522
ter, Margaret Ann V, 630
ter, Margaret Ann V, 638
ter, Margaret F. V, 241
ter, Margaret F. V, 269
ter, Margery VI, 602
ter, Martha IV, 52
ter, Martha IV, 748
ter, Martha V, 17
ter, Martha V, 354
ter, Martha V, 482
ter, Martha V, 519
ter, Martha V, 521
ter, Martha V, 522
ter, Martha V, 759
ter, Martha VI, 387
ter, Martha VI, 427
ter, Martha VI, 602
ter, Martha C. V, 521
ter, Martha Coate V, 522
ter, Martha L. V, 521
ter, Martha P. V, 757
ter, Martha S. V, 522
ter, Martha W. IV, 747
ter, Martha W. IV, 776
ter, Mary II, 402
ter, Mary IV, 52
ter, Mary IV, 443
ter, Mary IV, 445
ter, Mary IV, 650
ter, Mary IV, 720
ter, Mary IV, 747
ter, Mary IV, 748
ter, Mary IV, 770
ter, Mary IV, 836
ter, Mary IV, 916
ter, Mary IV, 951
ter, Mary IV, 984
ter, Mary V, 269
ter, Mary V, 354
ter, Mary V, 365
nter, Mary V, 462
nter, Mary V, 491
nter, Mary V, 519
nter, Mary V, 521
nter, Mary V, 522
nter, Mary V, 621
nter, Mary V, 638
nter, Mary V, 757
nter, Mary V, 1013
nter, Mary VI, 595
nter, Mary VI, 597
nter, Mary VI, 598
nter, Mary VI, 602
nter, Mary Ann IV, 747
nter, Mary Ann IV, 748
nter, Mary Ann IV, 749
nter, Mary Ann IV, 984
nter, Mary Anna IV, 984
nter, Mary Emma V, 196
nter, Mary Emma V, 638
nter, Mary Emy V, 638
nter, Mary Frances V, 522
nter, Mary H. V, 522
nter, Maurice V, 522
nter, Maurice V, 702
nter, Mercy Ann V, 507
Painter, Mercy Ann V, 522
Painter, Miriam IV, 747
Painter, Miriam IV, 748
Painter, Miriam IV, 749
Painter, Miriam IV, 836
Painter, Miriam IV, 840
Painter, Miriam G. IV, 740
Painter, Miriam G. IV, 748
Painter, Mordacai W. V, 522
Painter, Mordecai V, 521
Painter, Mordecai W. V, 521
Painter, Mordicai W. V, 519
Painter, Mordicai W. V, 522
Painter, Morris E. V, 522
Painter, Moses V, 521
Painter, Naomi V, 196
Painter, Naomi V, 269
Painter, Naomi V, 521
Painter, Naomi V, 522
Painter, Naomi V, 638
Painter, Naomi Hannah V, 638
Painter, Nathan IV, 747
Painter, Orville E. V, 522
Painter, Phebe IV, 704
Painter, Phebe IV, 748
Painter, Phebe IV, 953
Painter, Phebe IV, 984
Painter, Phebe V, 491
Painter, Phebe V, 522
Painter, Phebe VI, 602
Painter, Phebe E. IV, 698
Painter, Phebe E. IV, 747
Painter, Phebe E. IV, 748
Painter, Phebe F. IV, 713
Painter, Phebe F. IV, 748
Painter, Phebe W. V, 521
Painter, Rachel V, 555
Painter, Rachel VI, 427
Painter, Rachel VI, 435
Painter, Rachel VI, 602
Painter, Rachel VI, 769
Painter, Rachel Ann IV, 747
Painter, Rachel Ann IV, 748
Painter, Rachel Ann IV, 965
Painter, Rachel Ann IV, 984
Painter, Rachel W. V, 521
Painter, Rachel W. V, 522
Painter, Rachel W. V, 665
Painter, Ray V, 722
Painter, Rebecca IV, 714
Painter, Rebecca IV, 747
Painter, Rebecca IV, 748
Painter, Rebecca IV, 950
Painter, Rebecca IV, 984
Painter, Rebecca V, 521
Painter, Rebecca V, 522
Painter, Rebecca Ann IV, 1070
Painter, Rebecca F. V, 522
Painter, Rebecca F. V, 527
Painter, Rebeckah VI, 602
Painter, Reuben IV, 704
Painter, Reuben IV, 748
Painter, Reuben G. IV, 747
Painter, Reuben G. IV, 748
Painter, Reuben G. IV, 953
Painter, Reuben G. IV, 984
Painter, Rhoda V, 521
Painter, Rhoda V, 522
Painter, Richard II, 612
Painter, Robert IV, 52
Painter, Robert IV, 258
Painter, Robert IV, 650
Painter, Robert IV, 747
Painter, Robert IV, 748
Painter, Robert VI, 427
Painter, Robert VI, 462
Painter, Robert VI, 597
Painter, Robert VI, 602
Painter, Rosanna IV, 99
Painter, Rosanna IV, 104
Painter, Roy V, 522
Painter, Roy V, 702
Painter, Roy D. V, 521
Painter, Samuel IV, 52
Painter, Samuel IV, 650
Painter, Samuel IV, 720
Painter, Samuel IV, 747
Painter, Samuel IV, 748
Painter, Samuel IV, 836
Painter, Samuel V, 522
Painter, Samuel VI, 602
Painter, Samuel H. IV, 747
Painter, Samuel S. V, 521
Painter, Sarah IV, 715
Painter, Sarah IV, 747
Painter, Sarah IV, 748
Painter, Sarah IV, 836
Painter, Sarah IV, 855
Painter, Sarah V, 521
Painter, Sarah V, 522
Painter, Sarah V, 535
Painter, Sarah VI, 403
Painter, Sarah VI, 427
Painter, Sarah VI, 602
Painter, Sarah A. V, 269
Painter, Sarah Alice V, 462
Painter, Sarah Alice V, 638
Painter, Sarah Clarissa V, 508
Painter, Seth IV, 747
Painter, Seth IV, 748
Painter, Seth IV, 836
Painter, Seth V, 1013
Painter, Stephen IV, 747
Painter, Stephen IV, 748
Painter, Stephen IV, 836
Painter, Susan IV, 724
Painter, Susan IV, 748
Painter, Susan VI, 428
Painter, Susan VI, 437
Painter, Susanna I, 191
Painter, Susanna I, 198
Painter, Susanna II, 506
Painter, Susanna II, 612
Painter, Susannah I, 198
Painter, Susannah I, 202
Painter, Susannah IV, 747
Painter, Susannah V, 519
Painter, Susannah V, 521
Painter, Susannah V, 522
Painter, Susannah V, 635
Painter, Susannah V, 638
Painter, Susannah VI, 387
Painter, Susannah VI, 403
Painter, Susannah VI, 427
Painter, Susannah VI, 594
Painter, Susannah VI, 595
Painter, Susannah VI, 598
Painter, Susannah VI, 602
Painter, Theodocia V, 522
Painter, Thomas IV, 52
Painter, Thomas IV, 748
Painter, Thomas V, 354
Painter, Thomas V, 365
Painter, Thomas V, 521
Painter, Thomas V, 522
Painter, Thomas V, 592
Painter, Thomas V, 638
Painter, Thomas VI, 427
Painter, Thomas VI, 602
Painter, Thomas Ashley V, 522
Painter, Thos. V, 638
Painter, Thos. V, 757
Painter, Thos. Price IV, 747
Painter, Virginia V, 521
Painter, Virginia V, 522
Painter, Wd. Miriam IV, 836
Painter, William IV, 258
Painter, William IV, 747
Painter, William V, 521
Painter, William V, 522
Painter, Willis IV, 984
Painter, Wm. M. IV, 747
Painter, Wm. M. IV, 748
Painther, John, Jr. VI, 427
Painton, Alfred IV, 1332
Painton, Alfred T. IV, 1332
Pairent, Elizabeth V, 1013
Pairpoint, John VI, 432
Pairpoint, Jonathan IV, 836
Pairson, Elizabeth I, 357
Pairson, Jacob I, 357
Pairson, Mary I, 357
Paish, Charles V, 945
Paist, Abigail V, 196
Paist, Abigail V, 522
Paist, Abigail V, 523
Paist, Abigail V, 957
Paist, Ann II, 1017
Paist, Ann II, 1020
Paist, B. Franklin II, 904
Paist, Benjamin Franklin II, 904
Paist, Benjamin Franklin II, 925
Paist, Charles V, 196
Paist, Charles V, 522
Paist, Charles V, 523
Paist, Charles V, 957
Paist, Elizabeth V, 957
Paist, Elizabeth K. II, 323
Paist, Isaac V, 957
Paist, James V, 196
Paist, James V, 522
Paist, James V, 957
Paist, Lydia V, 957
Paist, Mary V, 953
Paist, Mary V, 957
Paist, Nettie II, 904
Paist, Nettie II, 925
Paist, Rachel II, 715
Paist, Susan V, 955
Paist, Susan V, 957
Paist, William V, 957
Paist, Wm. II, 1017
Paist, Wm. II, 1020
Paiste, Alcestack II, 904
Paiste, Anna II, 821
Paiste, Anna II, 904
Paiste, B. Franklin II, 904
Paiste, Benjamin Franklin II, 904
Paiste, Henry Thomas II, 904
Paiste, John II, 904
Paiste, Marion II, 904
Paiste, Nettie II, 904
Palamountain, Bennet III, 245
Palamountain, Bennett III, 245
Palamountain, David III, 245
Palamountain, Isaac Thorn III, 245
Palen, Henry I, 730
Palen, Henry I, 896
Palen, Mary I, 896
Palen, Nixon I, 896
Palen, Sarah I, 896
Pales, Harry IV, 1259
Paleske, Louisa II, 402
Palham, Margaret I, 896
Palimountain, Bennett III, 245
Palin, Ann I, 112
Palin, Ann I, 113
Palin, Ann I, 157
Palin, Ann I, 159
Palin, Elisabeth I, 135
Palin, Elisabeth I, 159
Palin, Elisabeth I, 162
Palin, Elizabeth I, 113
Palin, Elizabeth I, 159
Palin, Elizabeth I, 166
Palin, Exum I, 863
Palin, Henry I, 113
Palin, Henry I, 156
Palin, Henry I, 157
Palin, Henry I, 159
Palin, Henry I, 730
Palin, Henry I, 863
Palin, Henry, Jr. I, 143
Palin, Henry, Jr. I, 159
Palin, John I, 730
Palin, Mary I, 143
Palin, Mary I, 159
Palin, Mary I, 863
Palin, Miriam I, 141
Palin, Miriam I, 159
Palin, Nixon I, 113
Palin, Nixon I, 159
Palin, Nixon I, 730
Palin, Nixon I, 863
Palin, Penninah I, 113
Palin, Sarah I, 113
Palin, Sarah I, 156
Palin, Sarah I, 159
Palin, Sarah I, 730
Palin, Sarah I, 863
Palin, Susannah I, 159
Palin, Susannah I, 174
Palin, Thomas I, 113
Palin, Thomas I, 159
Palin, Thomas I, 166
Paling, Plesent II, 1015
Paling, Plesent II, 1018
Pallard, Dinah I, 967
Pallard, John I, 967
Pallmer, Amos II, 966
Pallmer, Rachel II, 1018
Palm, Ella E. II, 793
Palmbla, Mrs. ??? IV, 1332
Palmer, ??? II, 1018
Palmer, ??? III, 17
Palmer, ??? III, 245
Palmer, ??? III, 246
Palmer, Aaron II, 612
Palmer, Aaron III, 246
Palmer, Abigail IV, 258
Palmer, Abigail IV, 345
Palmer, Abner II, 1019
Palmer, Agnes II, 1077
Palmer, Agnes L. II, 1077
Palmer, Agnes S. II, 1066
Palmer, Alfred II, 1019
Palmer, Alice II, 1000
Palmer, Alice II, 1019
Palmer, Alice C. II, 1066
Palmer, Alice Smedly III, 245
Palmer, Aliph G. III, 292
Palmer, Aliph Gertrude III, 245
Palmer, Amos II, 966
Palmer, Amos II, 981
Palmer, Amos II, 1018
Palmer, Amy II, 1019
Palmer, Ann II, 323
Palmer, Ann II, 609
Palmer, Ann II, 612
Palmer, Ann II, 966
Palmer, Ann II, 967
Palmer, Ann II, 977
Palmer, Ann II, 986
Palmer, Ann II, 1019
Palmer, Ann II, 1030
Palmer, Ann II, 1037
Palmer, Ann IV, 1157
Palmer, Ann IV, 1178
Palmer, Ann Mariah VI, 974
Palmer, Ann, Jr. II, 1004
Palmer, Ann, Jr. II, 1019
Palmer, Ann, Jr. II, 1035
Palmer, Ann, Jr. II, 1057
Palmer, Ann, Jr. Watson II, 1018
Palmer, Anna II, 1066
Palmer, Anna II, 1072
Palmer, Anna II, 1077
Palmer, Anna C. IV, 425
Palmer, Anna C. IV, 442
Palmer, Anna D. II, 904
Palmer, Anna Dora II, 812
Palmer, Anna Dora II, 864
Palmer, Anna Dora II, 904
Palmer, Anna M. III, 120
Palmer, Anna M. III, 245
Palmer, Anna R. II, 1077
Palmer, Anna Stanton IV, 425
Palmer, Anne II, 966
Palmer, Anne, Jr. II, 1009
Palmer, Anne, Jr. II, 1019
Palmer, Arthur C. II, 1066
Palmer, Asa VI, 797
Palmer, Asa W. VI, 837
Palmer, Asenath II, 967
Palmer, Ben. VI, 973
Palmer, Benjamin II, 955
Palmer, Benjamin II, 966
Palmer, Benjamin II, 979
Palmer, Benjamin II, 982
Palmer, Benjamin II, 1000
Palmer, Benjamin II, 1019
Palmer, Benjamin II, 1033
Palmer, Benjamin III, 246
Palmer, Benjamin VI, 983
Palmer, Benjamin P. II, 1019
Palmer, Benjamin, Jr. II, 1019
Palmer, Blanche V, 638
Palmer, Blanchie V, 638
Palmer, Blandina II, 402
Palmer, Blandine II, 612
Palmer, Bricket III, 104
Palmer, Caleb II, 966
Palmer, Caleb II, 1019
Palmer, Caroline III, 245
Palmer, Caroline III, 246
Palmer, Caroline E. III, 245
Palmer, Caroline French II, 812
Palmer, Carrie V, 638
Palmer, Carrie B. V, 638
Palmer, Catharine IV, 1375
Palmer, Catherine IV, 1375
Palmer, Charles II, 402
Palmer, Charles II, 904
Palmer, Charles III, 182
Palmer, Charles III, 245
Palmer, Charles F. II, 904
Palmer, Charles Follen II, 812
Palmer, Charles Lewis II, 812
Palmer, Charles W. IV, 424
Palmer, Charles W. IV, 442
Palmer, Charlotte II, 955
Palmer, Charlotte II, 982
Palmer, Charlotte II, 1019
Palmer, Chas. II, 904
Palmer, Chas. K. II, 812
Palmer, Christian II, 989
Palmer, Christian II, 1018
Palmer, Clarence V, 638
Palmer, Clarissa III, 245
Palmer, Clarissa III, 246
Palmer, Daniel II, 966
Palmer, Daniel II, 992
Palmer, Daniel II, 1004
Palmer, Daniel II, 1018
Palmer, Daniel II, 1019
Palmer, Daniel III, 245
Palmer, Daniel III, 246
Palmer, Daniel IV, 345
Palmer, Daniel IV, 543
Palmer, Daniel Hunt II, 1019
Palmer, Daniel, Jr. II, 1019
Palmer, David II, 612
Palmer, David II, 646
Palmer, David II, 966
Palmer, David II, 967
Palmer, David II, 1018
Palmer, David II, 1019
Palmer, David II, 1037
Palmer, David II, 1057
Palmer, David II, 1066
Palmer, David II, 1077
Palmer, David II, 1078

Palmer, David II, 1080
Palmer, David, Jr. II, 1057
Palmer, David, Jr. II, 1077
Palmer, David, Jr. II, 1080
Palmer, Deborah III, 246
Palmer, Delbert IV, 1332
Palmer, Delbert E. IV, 1332
Palmer, Dorinda Bouten III, 246
Palmer, Drake III, 246
Palmer, Ebenezer C. III, 246
Palmer, Edith II, 967
Palmer, Edith II, 1057
Palmer, Edith A. III, 245
Palmer, Edith N. III, 245
Palmer, Edmund III, 245
Palmer, Edw. III, 245
Palmer, Edward II, 904
Palmer, Edward II, 1077
Palmer, Edward III, 245
Palmer, Edward III, 246
Palmer, Edward VI, 627
Palmer, Edward VI, 686
Palmer, Edward VI, 769
Palmer, Edward A. III, 245
Palmer, Edward Maria Theresa III, 245
Palmer, Edward Pennock III, 245
Palmer, Edward Pennock, Jr. III, 245
Palmer, Edwin II, 904
Palmer, Edwin L. II, 812
Palmer, Edwin L. II, 864
Palmer, Edwin L. II, 904
Palmer, Eleanor II, 940
Palmer, Eli III, 245
Palmer, Eli III, 299
Palmer, Elihu III, 246
Palmer, Eliza III, 246
Palmer, Eliza W. II, 755
Palmer, Eliza W. II, 758
Palmer, Elizabeth II, 402
Palmer, Elizabeth II, 524
Palmer, Elizabeth II, 612
Palmer, Elizabeth II, 624
Palmer, Elizabeth II, 634
Palmer, Elizabeth II, 804
Palmer, Elizabeth II, 812
Palmer, Elizabeth II, 966
Palmer, Elizabeth II, 1018
Palmer, Elizabeth II, 1019
Palmer, Elizabeth II, 1040
Palmer, Elizabeth II, 1066
Palmer, Elizabeth II, 1077
Palmer, Elizabeth III, 245
Palmer, Elizabeth III, 246
Palmer, Elizabeth III, 431
Palmer, Elizabeth III, 454
Palmer, Elizabeth IV, 345
Palmer, Elizabeth IV, 543
Palmer, Elizabeth IV, 1178
Palmer, Elizabeth V, 957
Palmer, Elizabeth VI, 974
Palmer, Elizabeth R. II, 1075
Palmer, Elizabeth R. II, 1077
Palmer, Elizabeth Smith III, 245
Palmer, Ellen H. II, 904
Palmer, Ellen P. III, 245
Palmer, Ellis II, 466
Palmer, Ellis II, 612
Palmer, Elsie VI, 627
Palmer, Elsie VI, 686
Palmer, Elsie VI, 733
Palmer, Elsie VI, 769
Palmer, Elsie VI, 773
Palmer, Emeline IV, 1375
Palmer, Emeline IV, 1379
Palmer, Emily III, 245
Palmer, Emily III, 246
Palmer, Emma II, 812
Palmer, Ephraim IV, 1375
Palmer, Esther II, 955
Palmer, Esther II, 979
Palmer, Esther II, 982
Palmer, Esther II, 1000
Palmer, Esther II, 1019
Palmer, Esther II, 1033
Palmer, Esther III, 245
Palmer, Esther III, 246
Palmer, Eugene V, 1013
Palmer, Eva M. II, 898
Palmer, Eva M. II, 904
Palmer, Fern V, 1013
Palmer, Fern P. V, 1013
Palmer, Florence III, 245
Palmer, Florence III, 299
Palmer, Florence G. IV, 258
Palmer, Frances II, 812
Palmer, Frances II, 829
Palmer, Frances II, 837
Palmer, Frances II, 904
Palmer, Frances II, 943
Palmer, Frances II, 966
Palmer, Frances II, 967
Palmer, Frances II, 1012
Palmer, Frances II, 1018
Palmer, Francis II, 994
Palmer, Francis II, 1018
Palmer, Francis H. II, 904
Palmer, Francis Henry II, 812
Palmer, Francis J. III, 245
Palmer, Frank V, 1013
Palmer, Franklin II, 1077
Palmer, George II, 402
Palmer, George II, 1075
Palmer, George II, 1077
Palmer, George IV, 345
Palmer, George A. IV, 1178
Palmer, Hannah I, 896
Palmer, Hannah I, 1016
Palmer, Hannah II, 966
Palmer, Hannah II, 1001
Palmer, Hannah II, 1018
Palmer, Hannah II, 1019
Palmer, Hannah II, 1030
Palmer, Hannah II, 1033
Palmer, Hannah II, 1040
Palmer, Hannah III, 50
Palmer, Hannah III, 245
Palmer, Hannah III, 246
Palmer, Hannah IV, 543
Palmer, Hannah V, 925
Palmer, Hannah VI, 262
Palmer, Hannah VI, 769
Palmer, Hannah F. III, 245
Palmer, Hannah Fisher IV, 345
Palmer, Hannah H. II, 864
Palmer, Hannah H. II, 904
Palmer, Hannah, Jr. II, 981
Palmer, Harriet III, 245
Palmer, Harriet M. III, 182
Palmer, Harriet M. III, 245
Palmer, Harriet W. II, 812
Palmer, Harriette M. III, 245
Palmer, Harrison III, 50
Palmer, Harrison III, 245
Palmer, Harvey IV, 1375
Palmer, Henry II, 904
Palmer, Henry III, 245
Palmer, Henry IV, 1375
Palmer, Henry F. IV, 1375
Palmer, Henry Freleigh IV, 1375
Palmer, Ida III, 297
Palmer, Ida V, 1013
Palmer, Ida VI, 782
Palmer, Isaac Allen III, 246
Palmer, Isabel II, 1012
Palmer, Isabel II, 1018
Palmer, Israel D. III, 245
Palmer, Jael II, 1018
Palmer, James II, 1077
Palmer, James III, 185
Palmer, James III, 246
Palmer, Jane II, 466
Palmer, Jane II, 612
Palmer, Jane II, 966
Palmer, Jane III, 246
Palmer, Jane K. II, 1077
Palmer, Japheth III, 245
Palmer, Jeal II, 1019
Palmer, Jesse II, 402
Palmer, Jesse II, 967
Palmer, Joel VI, 974
Palmer, John I, 412
Palmer, John II, 241
Palmer, John II, 247
Palmer, John II, 402
Palmer, John II, 612
Palmer, John II, 812
Palmer, John II, 904
Palmer, John II, 966
Palmer, John II, 967
Palmer, John II, 1001
Palmer, John II, 1003
Palmer, John II, 1018
Palmer, John II, 1032
Palmer, John II, 1057
Palmer, John II, 1077
Palmer, John II, 1080
Palmer, John III, 104
Palmer, John III, 245
Palmer, John IV, 345
Palmer, John IV, 543
Palmer, John V, 638
Palmer, John V, 1013
Palmer, John VI, 77
Palmer, John B. III, 245
Palmer, John, Jr. II, 1019
Palmer, Jonathan II, 812
Palmer, Jonathan II, 943
Palmer, Jonathan II, 966
Palmer, Jonathan II, 967
Palmer, Jonathan II, 977
Palmer, Jonathan II, 980
Palmer, Jonathan II, 994
Palmer, Jonathan II, 995
Palmer, Jonathan II, 1018
Palmer, Jonathan II, 1019
Palmer, Jonathan II, 1026
Palmer, Jonathan II, 1030
Palmer, Jonathan II, 1035
Palmer, Jonathan II, 1037
Palmer, Jonathan II, 1057
Palmer, Jonathan II, 1073
Palmer, Jonathan II, 1077
Palmer, Jonathan III, 245
Palmer, Jonathan, Jr. II, 812
Palmer, Jonathan, Jr. II, 829
Palmer, Jonathan, Jr. II, 904
Palmer, Jonathan, Jr. II, 1018
Palmer, Jonathan, Jr. II, 1035
Palmer, Joseph I, 412
Palmer, Joseph II, 402
Palmer, Joseph II, 966
Palmer, Joseph II, 967
Palmer, Joseph II, 1019
Palmer, Joseph II, 1057
Palmer, Joseph II, 1077
Palmer, Joseph III, 245
Palmer, Joseph VI, 428
Palmer, Joseph VI, 541
Palmer, Joseph M. II, 904
Palmer, Joseph Monroe II, 831
Palmer, Joseph Monroe II, 904
Palmer, Josephine Mable V, 1013
Palmer, Joshua II, 966
Palmer, Joshua II, 1019
Palmer, Joshua K. II, 1071
Palmer, Joshua K. II, 1077
Palmer, Judith VI, 973
Palmer, Julietta V, 925
Palmer, Latitia II, 988
Palmer, Latitia II, 1019
Palmer, Levick II, 804
Palmer, Levick II, 812
Palmer, Levick II, 904
Palmer, Levick IV, 345
Palmer, Levick IV, 543
Palmer, Levick VI, 769
Palmer, Lewis II, 864
Palmer, Lewis II, 904
Palmer, Lewis II, 1057
Palmer, Lewis II, 1063
Palmer, Lewis IV, 424
Palmer, Lizzie V, 638
Palmer, Lizzie E. V, 638
Palmer, Louisa IV, 1375
Palmer, Lucy IV, 590
Palmer, Lucy M. V, 638
Palmer, Lydia II, 984
Palmer, Lydia II, 1019
Palmer, Lydia II, 1057
Palmer, Lydia IV, 1375
Palmer, Lydia VI, 262
Palmer, Lydia L. V, 925
Palmer, Lydia S. V, 925
Palmer, Mareb VI, 686
Palmer, Mareb VI, 698
Palmer, Margaret I, 159
Palmer, Margaret I, 168
Palmer, Margaret II, 402
Palmer, Margaret II, 612
Palmer, Margaret II, 629
Palmer, Margaret II, 966
Palmer, Margery II, 1004
Palmer, Margery II, 1019
Palmer, Maria II, 1077
Palmer, Maria II, 1080
Palmer, Maria III, 246
Palmer, Mariah II, 1077
Palmer, Marianna III, 245
Palmer, Marianna III, 299
Palmer, Marjorie II, 966
Palmer, Mark II, 966
Palmer, Mark II, 1057
Palmer, Mark II, 1066
Palmer, Mark II, 1071
Palmer, Mark II, 1072
Palmer, Mark II, 1077
Palmer, Mark, Jr. II, 1057
Palmer, Mark, Jr. II, 1077
Palmer, Martha II, 967
Palmer, Martha II, 1057
Palmer, Martha II, 1073
Palmer, Martha II, 1077
Palmer, Martha III, 245
Palmer, Martha III, 246
Palmer, Martha III, 263
Palmer, Martha S. II, 1077
Palmer, Martin VI, 153
Palmer, Martin VI, 201
Palmer, Mary II, 402
Palmer, Mary II, 831
Palmer, Mary II, 904
Palmer, Mary II, 966
Palmer, Mary II, 967
Palmer, Mary II, 992
Palmer, Mary II, 1004
Palmer, Mary II, 1018
Palmer, Mary II, 1019
Palmer, Mary II, 1037
Palmer, Mary II, 1057
Palmer, Mary III, 104
Palmer, Mary III, 120
Palmer, Mary III, 245
Palmer, Mary III, 246
Palmer, Mary IV, 336
Palmer, Mary IV, 345
Palmer, Mary IV, 543
Palmer, Mary IV, 568
Palmer, Mary IV, 590
Palmer, Mary V, 1013
Palmer, Mary Adaline V, 702
Palmer, Mary Adeline V, 702
Palmer, Mary Ann III, 246
Palmer, Mary Ann IV, 1172
Palmer, Mary Ann IV, 1178
Palmer, Mary Anna II, 1077
Palmer, Mary C. II, 1057
Palmer, Mary C. II, 1063
Palmer, Mary C. III, 246
Palmer, Mary C. IV, 424
Palmer, Mary C. V, 1013
Palmer, Mary R. II, 755
Palmer, Mary R. II, 758
Palmer, Mary R. II, 1066
Palmer, Mary, Jr. II, 1013
Palmer, Mary, Jr. II, 1019
Palmer, Mary, Jr. II, 1057
Palmer, Mary, Jr. II, 1077
Palmer, Mary, Jr. II, 1078
Palmer, Matilda II, 812
Palmer, Matilda II, 904
Palmer, Matilda IV, 345
Palmer, Matilda IV, 357
Palmer, Merab VI, 541
Palmer, Merab VI, 686
Palmer, Minnie IV, 1332
Palmer, Minnie V, 1013
Palmer, Miss Florence IV, 258
Palmer, Moses II, 967
Palmer, Moses VI, 769
Palmer, Moses D. V, 925
Palmer, Moses D. VI, 262
Palmer, Myra IV, 1332
Palmer, Myra Litty IV, 748
Palmer, Myra Litty IV, 1332
Palmer, Nancey VI, 983
Palmer, Nancy II, 1057
Palmer, Nancy II, 1073
Palmer, Nancy II, 1077
Palmer, Naomi II, 1003
Palmer, Naomi II, 1018
Palmer, Nathan III, 245
Palmer, Nathan III, 246
Palmer, Nehemiah III, 246
Palmer, Obadiah III, 245
Palmer, Obadiah III, 246
Palmer, Olinda IV, 322
Palmer, Olinda IV, 345
Palmer, P. Edward III, 292
Palmer, Pamela II, 1019
Palmer, Pamela II, 1033
Palmer, Paul I Sup 1, 5
Palmer, Pennell VI, 763
Palmer, Pennell VI, 764
Palmer, Pennell VI, 769
Palmer, Peter D. III, 246
Palmer, Phebe II, 1079
Palmer, Phebe III, 15
Palmer, Phebe III, 50
Palmer, Phebe III, 245
Palmer, Philip I, 412
Palmer, Priscilla II, 1019
Palmer, Prudence IV, 1178
Palmer, Prudence V, 957
Palmer, R. D. VI, 828
Palmer, R. D. VI, 844
Palmer, R. D. VI, 867
Palmer, Rachel II, 241
Palmer, Rachel II, 247
Palmer, Rachel II, 402
Palmer, Rachel II, 983
Palmer, Rachel II, 1018
Palmer, Rachel II, 1019
Palmer, Rachel II, 1032
Palmer, Rachel II, 1071
Palmer, Rachel II, 1072
Palmer, Rachel II, 1077
Palmer, Randall IV, 1375
Palmer, Randell IV, 1375
Palmer, Rebecca II, 402
Palmer, Rebecca II, 612
Palmer, Rebecca II, 1071
Palmer, Rebecca II, 1077
Palmer, Rebecca N. VI, 763
Palmer, Rebecca N. VI, 764
Palmer, Rebecca N. VI, 769
Palmer, Rebeckah II, 612
Palmer, Rebeckah II, 696
Palmer, Richard II, 1019
Palmer, Richard III, 245
Palmer, Richard III, 246
Palmer, Robert II, 1019
Palmer, Robert T. VI, 826
Palmer, Rosaline III, 246
Palmer, Ruth II, 1003
Palmer, Ruth II, 1018
Palmer, Ruth IV, 336
Palmer, Ruth IV, 345
Palmer, Samuel II, 966
Palmer, Samuel II, 967
Palmer, Samuel II, 1009
Palmer, Samuel II, 1013
Palmer, Samuel II, 1018
Palmer, Samuel II, 1019
Palmer, Samuel II, 1079
Palmer, Samuel III, 245
Palmer, Samuel III, 246
Palmer, Samuel IV, 543
Palmer, Samuel A. III, 246
Palmer, Samuel F. II, 812
Palmer, Samuel Fisher IV, 34
Palmer, Samuel L. III, 120
Palmer, Samuel L. III, 245
Palmer, Sarah I, 151
Palmer, Sarah I, 159
Palmer, Sarah I, 413
Palmer, Sarah II, 402
Palmer, Sarah II, 812
Palmer, Sarah II, 829
Palmer, Sarah II, 966
Palmer, Sarah II, 967
Palmer, Sarah II, 977
Palmer, Sarah II, 995
Palmer, Sarah II, 1004
Palmer, Sarah II, 1018
Palmer, Sarah II, 1019
Palmer, Sarah II, 1026
Palmer, Sarah II, 1057
Palmer, Sarah II, 1063
Palmer, Sarah II, 1073
Palmer, Sarah II, 1077
Palmer, Sarah III, 98
Palmer, Sarah III, 151
Palmer, Sarah III, 245
Palmer, Sarah III, 246
Palmer, Sarah III, 314
Palmer, Sarah III, 431
Palmer, Sarah III, 454
Palmer, Sarah IV, 984
Palmer, Sarah IV, 1015
Palmer, Sarah V, 1013
Palmer, Sarah Ann II, 831
Palmer, Sarah Ann II, 904
Palmer, Sarah Ann IV, 345
Palmer, Sarah B. III, 245
Palmer, Sarah Cowgill II, 804
Palmer, Sarah Cowgill IV, 345
Palmer, Sarah E. II, 1077
Palmer, Sarah E. III, 120
Palmer, Sarah H. II, 904
Palmer, Sarah H. II, 943
Palmer, Sarah H. III, 245
Palmer, Sarah T. II, 1066
Palmer, Sarah T. II, 1072
Palmer, Sarah T. II, 1077
Palmer, Sarah T. III, 185
Palmer, Sarah T. III, 246
Palmer, Sarah Tatum II, 812
Palmer, Silvanus III, 246
Palmer, Solomon II, 1019
Palmer, Solomon III, 151
Palmer, Solomon III, 246
Palmer, Solomon III, 431
Palmer, Solomon III, 454
Palmer, Sophia V, 1013
Palmer, Sophia J. V, 1013
Palmer, Stephen IV, 1375
Palmer, Stephen H. IV, 1375
Palmer, Susan II, 1077
Palmer, Susan II, 1080
Palmer, Susan VI, 627
Palmer, Susan VI, 686
Palmer, Susan VI, 769
Palmer, Susan Boyd VI, 733
Palmer, Susanna I, 413
Palmer, Susanna II, 1057
Palmer, Susanna II, 1077
Palmer, Susanna II, 1080
Palmer, Susannah II, 1019
Palmer, Susannah III, 246
Palmer, Sylvester V, 1013
Palmer, Tace II, 967
Palmer, Tacey II, 402
Palmer, Tacy II, 402

er, Tacy II, 1057
er, Tacy, Jr. II, 1077
er, Tacy, Jr. II, 1078
er, Tamar II, 1019
er, Tamar II, 1077
er, Tamar II, 1078
er, Tamar II, 1080
er, Tamer II, 1019
er, Tamer II, 1077
er, Tamer II, 1078
er, Theodocia II, 1019
er, Theodosia II, 598
er, Theodosia II, 612
er, Thomas I, 412
er, Thomas II, 402
er, Thomas II, 599
er, Thomas II, 612
er, Thomas VI, 541
er, Thomas VI, 903
er, Thomas VI, 974
er, Thomas Chalkley
I, 1057
er, Thomas Chalkley
I, 1063
er, Thos. II, 1033
er, Virginia L. II, 857
er, Virginia L. II, 904
er, Wd. Ann II, 966
er, Wd. Christian II, 966
er, Wd. Hannah F. III, 50
er, Wd. Margaret II, 466
er, Wd. Margaret II, 612
er, Wd. Sarah Cowgill
I, 804
er, William II, 402
er, William II, 966
er, William III, 120
er, William III, 246
er, William IV, 748
er, William Henry IV, 748
er, Willis I, 159
er, Wj. H. V, 638
er, Wm. II, 1019
er, Wm. II, 1079
er, Wm. III, 246
er, Wm. H. V, 638
er, Wm. J. II, 904
er, Wm. M. II, 831
er, Wm. M. II, 904
green, ??? III, 246
green, Antoinette III, 246
green, Margaret III, 246
green, Oluff III, 246
or, John VI, 970
ore, Benj. VI, 920
ore, Benjamin VI, 899
ore, Benjamin VI, 907
ore, Benjamin VI, 912
ore, Benjamin VI, 950
ore, Benjamin VI, 991
ore, Benjamin VI, 1011
ore, Betsy VI, 974
ore, Charles R. VI, 974
ore, John II, 446
ore, John VI, 973
ore, John VI, 974
ore, John VI, 991
ore, Joseph VI, 428
ore, Lauraina VI, 899
ore, Mary VI, 950
ore, Mary VI, 974
ore, Mildred M. VI, 974
ore, Rhoda VI, 1011
ore, Sarah VI, 912
ore, William VI, 974
mar, Asa VI, 844
mar, Eliza VI, 844
plin, Armistead VI, 824
plin, Elizabeth VI, 798
plin, Elizabeth VI, 824
plin, William VI, 798
ast, Sarah VI, 428
khurst, John II, 248
o, Sarah II, 936
oas, Martha Jane VI, 719
oast, ??? III, 247
coast, Aaron II, 136
coast, Aaron II, 247
coast, Aaron II, 248
coast, Aaron II, 815
coast, Aaron II, 905
coast, Aaron, Jr. II, 122
coast, Aaron, Jr. II, 905
coast, Abdon VI, 537
coast, Abdon VI, 677
coast, Abdon VI, 686
coast, Abdon VI, 687
coast, Abigail II, 247
coast, Abigail II, 248
coast, Abigail II, 455
coast, Abigail II, 603
Pancoast, Abigail II, 612
Pancoast, Abigail II, 1004
Pancoast, Abigail II, 1019
Pancoast, Abigail VI, 489
Pancoast, Abigail VI, 537
Pancoast, Abigail VI, 541
Pancoast, Abigail VI, 677
Pancoast, Abigail VI, 686
Pancoast, Abigail VI, 687
Pancoast, Ada III, 246
Pancoast, Ada B. II, 862
Pancoast, Ada B. II, 905
Pancoast, Aden VI, 489
Pancoast, Aden VI, 541
Pancoast, Adin II, 247
Pancoast, Adin II, 248
Pancoast, Adin VI, 541
Pancoast, Albert E. Fletcher
VI, 628
Pancoast, Albertson H. II, 905
Pancoast, Alfred IV, 425
Pancoast, Anita Mary II, 135
Pancoast, Ann II, 122
Pancoast, Ann II, 136
Pancoast, Ann II, 180
Pancoast, Ann II, 185
Pancoast, Ann II, 247
Pancoast, Ann II, 248
Pancoast, Ann II, 263
Pancoast, Ann II, 282
Pancoast, Ann II, 297
Pancoast, Ann II, 612
Pancoast, Ann II, 725
Pancoast, Ann II, 758
Pancoast, Ann II, 812
Pancoast, Ann II, 815
Pancoast, Ann II, 817
Pancoast, Ann IV, 345
Pancoast, Ann VI, 383
Pancoast, Ann VI, 630
Pancoast, Ann VI, 634
Pancoast, Ann VI, 686
Pancoast, Ann Arundel VI, 541
Pancoast, Ann M. II, 91
Pancoast, Anna VI, 685
Pancoast, Anna D. II, 905
Pancoast, Anna H. II, 135
Pancoast, Anna Hilliard II, 36
Pancoast, Anna Hilliard II, 122
Pancoast, Anna M. II, 136
Pancoast, Anna M. II, 154
Pancoast, Anne II, 133
Pancoast, Annie P. II, 136
Pancoast, Arthalinda P. II, 136
Pancoast, Arthanissa IV, 345
Pancoast, Arthur Ballanger II, 36
Pancoast, Arthur Ballinger
II, 122
Pancoast, Asa I, 1075
Pancoast, Asa III, 247
Pancoast, Athanissa IV, 343
Pancoast, Athanissa IV, 345
Pancoast, Benjamin II, 234
Pancoast, Benjamin II, 247
Pancoast, Bennett Smedley II, 36
Pancoast, Bennett Smedley
II, 122
Pancoast, Bertha VI, 616
Pancoast, Bertha VI, 702
Pancoast, Bertha E. VI, 686
Pancoast, Bertha E. VI, 702
Pancoast, Bertha E. VI, 707
Pancoast, Caleb II, 248
Pancoast, Caleb II, 612
Pancoast, Caleb II, 968
Pancoast, Caleb II, 1059
Pancoast, Caleb Copeland II, 248
Pancoast, Carolina T. VI, 686
Pancoast, Caroline II, 122
Pancoast, Caroline II, 136
Pancoast, Caroline II, 815
Pancoast, Caroline VI, 686
Pancoast, Caroline T. VI, 686
Pancoast, Carrie Almenia II, 812
Pancoast, Catharine II, 180
Pancoast, Charles E. II, 91
Pancoast, Charles E. II, 154
Pancoast, Charles F. II, 154
Pancoast, Charles F. II, 905
Pancoast, Charles Fithian II, 135
Pancoast, Chas. Edward II, 136
Pancoast, Chas. F. II, 905
Pancoast, Chas. Fithian II, 154
Pancoast, Curtis II, 180
Pancoast, David II, 180
Pancoast, David II, 590
Pancoast, David II, 612
Pancoast, David II, 812
Pancoast, David II, 893
Pancoast, David II, 905
Pancoast, David VI, 541
Pancoast, David VI, 554
Pancoast, David VI, 577
Pancoast, David VI, 602
Pancoast, David VI, 605
Pancoast, David VI, 769
Pancoast, David VI, 775
Pancoast, David VI, 789
Pancoast, David C. II, 135
Pancoast, David, Jr. II, 905
Pancoast, Davis II, 154
Pancoast, Deborah II, 968
Pancoast, Deborah Duer II, 1019
Pancoast, Diadamy VI, 541
Pancoast, Diadema II, 247
Pancoast, Diedamia VI, 489
Pancoast, Diedamia VI, 541
Pancoast, Dorcas II, 91
Pancoast, Dorcas II, 122
Pancoast, Dorcas II, 135
Pancoast, Dorcas II, 151
Pancoast, Dorcas II, 154
Pancoast, Dorcas S. II, 91
Pancoast, Dorcas S. II, 136
Pancoast, Dorothy Virginia II, 36
Pancoast, Dorothy Virginia
II, 122
Pancoast, Edward VI, 686
Pancoast, Edward VI, 701
Pancoast, Edwin II, 905
Pancoast, Edwin A. II, 905
Pancoast, Eleanor VI, 707
Pancoast, Eliakim II, 91
Pancoast, Elisabeth II, 247
Pancoast, Elisabeth II, 270
Pancoast, Elizabeth II, 122
Pancoast, Elizabeth II, 246
Pancoast, Elizabeth II, 247
Pancoast, Elizabeth II, 812
Pancoast, Elizabeth II, 905
Pancoast, Elizabeth II, 1019
Pancoast, Elizabeth IV, 345
Pancoast, Elizabeth IV, 348
Pancoast, Elizabeth VI, 428
Pancoast, Elizabeth VI, 488
Pancoast, Elizabeth VI, 509
Pancoast, Elizabeth VI, 541
Pancoast, Elizabeth VI, 565
Pancoast, Elizabeth VI, 566
Pancoast, Elizabeth VI, 567
Pancoast, Elizabeth VI, 602
Pancoast, Elizabeth VI, 627
Pancoast, Elizabeth A. II, 91
Pancoast, Elizabeth A. II, 135
Pancoast, Elizabeth A. II, 154
Pancoast, Elizabeth A. II, 857
Pancoast, Elizabeth A. II, 905
Pancoast, Elizabeth Atkinson
II, 36
Pancoast, Elizabeth Atkinson
II, 122
Pancoast, Elizabeth B. II, 812
Pancoast, Elizabeth Duer
II, 1019
Pancoast, Elizabeth E. II, 905
Pancoast, Elizabeth S. II, 905
Pancoast, Ephraim J. IV, 345
Pancoast, Esther II, 247
Pancoast, Esther II, 250
Pancoast, Franklin II, 122
Pancoast, George II, 180
Pancoast, George II, 248
Pancoast, George II, 297
Pancoast, George II, 812
Pancoast, George Elwood II, 248
Pancoast, George Elwood II, 297
Pancoast, Hannah II, 91
Pancoast, Hannah II, 122
Pancoast, Hannah II, 180
Pancoast, Hannah II, 247
Pancoast, Hannah II, 248
Pancoast, Hannah II, 253
Pancoast, Hannah II, 257
Pancoast, Hannah II, 270
Pancoast, Hannah II, 297
Pancoast, Hannah II, 298
Pancoast, Hannah II, 586
Pancoast, Hannah II, 612
Pancoast, Hannah III, 113
Pancoast, Hannah III, 246
Pancoast, Hannah III, 247
Pancoast, Hannah VI, 473
Pancoast, Hannah VI, 506
Pancoast, Hannah VI, 541
Pancoast, Hannah VI, 619
Pancoast, Hannah VI, 700
Pancoast, Hannah VI, 777
Pancoast, Hannah K. II, 91
Pancoast, Hannah K. II, 135
Pancoast, Hannah K. II, 151
Pancoast, Hannah K. II, 154
Pancoast, Hannah K. II, 820
Pancoast, Harriet II, 133
Pancoast, Harriet II, 135
Pancoast, Harriet II, 136
Pancoast, Henry II, 180
Pancoast, Henry Runrath II, 812
Pancoast, Henry T. VI, 686
Pancoast, Isaiah II, 91
Pancoast, Isaiah II, 248
Pancoast, Israel II, 247
Pancoast, Israel VI, 541
Pancoast, James II, 248
Pancoast, James II, 612
Pancoast, James C. II, 122
Pancoast, Jane VI, 686
Pancoast, Jane Stribling VI, 686
Pancoast, John II, 74
Pancoast, John II, 91
Pancoast, John II, 139
Pancoast, John II, 213
Pancoast, John II, 246
Pancoast, John II, 247
Pancoast, John II, 248
Pancoast, John II, 263
Pancoast, John II, 725
Pancoast, John II, 758
Pancoast, John II, 817
Pancoast, John IV, 345
Pancoast, John VI, 539
Pancoast, John VI, 541
Pancoast, John VI, 569
Pancoast, John VI, 570
Pancoast, John VI, 634
Pancoast, John VI, 686
Pancoast, John VI, 722
Pancoast, John Beaumont
II, 1019
Pancoast, John M. II, 136
Pancoast, John, Jr. VI, 686
Pancoast, Jonathan II, 91
Pancoast, Jonathan II, 248
Pancoast, Jonathan VI, 541
Pancoast, Joseph II, 133
Pancoast, Joseph II, 135
Pancoast, Joseph II, 136
Pancoast, Joseph II, 180
Pancoast, Joseph II, 234
Pancoast, Joseph II, 246
Pancoast, Joseph II, 247
Pancoast, Joseph II, 248
Pancoast, Joseph II, 253
Pancoast, Joseph II, 257
Pancoast, Joseph II, 277
Pancoast, Joseph II, 402
Pancoast, Joseph II, 725
Pancoast, Joseph II, 758
Pancoast, Joseph IV, 345
Pancoast, Joseph IV, 355
Pancoast, Joseph D. II, 135
Pancoast, Joseph D. II, 154
Pancoast, Joseph Duer II, 1019
Pancoast, Joseph Duer, Jr.
II, 1019
Pancoast, Joseph H. VI, 637
Pancoast, Joseph H. VI, 638
Pancoast, Joseph H. VI, 686
Pancoast, Joseph H. VI, 707
Pancoast, Joseph H. VI, 711
Pancoast, Joseph, Jr. III, 246
Pancoast, Joshua II, 402
Pancoast, Joshua II, 586
Pancoast, Joshua II, 612
Pancoast, Joshua VI, 624
Pancoast, Joshua VI, 627
Pancoast, Joshua VI, 681
Pancoast, Joshua VI, 686
Pancoast, Joshua VI, 722
Pancoast, Josiah II, 91
Pancoast, Josiah II, 122
Pancoast, Josiah II, 136
Pancoast, Josiah II, 154
Pancoast, Laura G. II, 877
Pancoast, Laura G. II, 905
Pancoast, Laura P. II, 905
Pancoast, Leonidas H., Jr. II, 36
Pancoast, Leonidas Horner II, 36
Pancoast, Leonidias II, 122
Pancoast, Lillian Sharpless II, 36
Pancoast, Lillian Sharpless
II, 122
Pancoast, Louisa VI, 686
Pancoast, Louisa C. VI, 711
Pancoast, Louisa C. VI, 716
Pancoast, Louisa E. VI, 708
Pancoast, Louisa E. VI, 711
Pancoast, Louisa E. VI, 713
Pancoast, Louise E. VI, 686
Pancoast, Lydia IV, 345
Pancoast, Lydia IV, 355
Pancoast, Lydia Alice VI, 686
Pancoast, Lydia Alice VI, 712
Pancoast, Mabel Couch II, 36
Pancoast, Mable Couch II, 122
Pancoast, Marian Ballanger
II, 36
Pancoast, Marion Ballinger
II, 122
Pancoast, Marmaduk S. II, 297
Pancoast, Marmaduke S. II, 298
Pancoast, Martha VI, 625
Pancoast, Martha Jane VI, 621
Pancoast, Martha Jane VI, 622
Pancoast, Martha Jane VI, 623
Pancoast, Martha Jane VI, 624
Pancoast, Martha Jane VI, 625
Pancoast, Martha Jane VI, 626
Pancoast, Martha Jane VI, 627
Pancoast, Martha Jane VI, 635
Pancoast, Martha Jane VI, 638
Pancoast, Martha Jane VI, 648
Pancoast, Martha Jane VI, 652
Pancoast, Martha Jane VI, 686
Pancoast, Martha Jane VI, 689
Pancoast, Martha Jane VI, 721
Pancoast, Mary II, 36
Pancoast, Mary II, 91
Pancoast, Mary II, 122
Pancoast, Mary II, 151
Pancoast, Mary II, 154
Pancoast, Mary II, 200
Pancoast, Mary II, 213
Pancoast, Mary II, 246
Pancoast, Mary II, 247
Pancoast, Mary II, 248
Pancoast, Mary II, 270
Pancoast, Mary II, 297
Pancoast, Mary II, 603
Pancoast, Mary II, 612
Pancoast, Mary II, 674
Pancoast, Mary II, 804
Pancoast, Mary II, 809
Pancoast, Mary II, 825
Pancoast, Mary II, 826
Pancoast, Mary II, 1019
Pancoast, Mary III, 156
Pancoast, Mary III, 246
Pancoast, Mary III, 356
Pancoast, Mary IV, 334
Pancoast, Mary IV, 345
Pancoast, Mary IV, 425
Pancoast, Mary IV, 491
Pancoast, Mary IV, 748
Pancoast, Mary VI, 428
Pancoast, Mary VI, 506
Pancoast, Mary VI, 541
Pancoast, Mary VI, 554
Pancoast, Mary VI, 569
Pancoast, Mary VI, 570
Pancoast, Mary VI, 602
Pancoast, Mary VI, 605
Pancoast, Mary VI, 775
Pancoast, Mary A. II, 905
Pancoast, Mary Ann IV, 345
Pancoast, Mary Davis II, 135
Pancoast, Mary H. II, 905
Pancoast, Mary Hurley II, 893
Pancoast, Mary Hurley II, 905
Pancoast, Mary Jane II, 135
Pancoast, Mary Jane II, 139
Pancoast, Mary Jane II, 154
Pancoast, Mary S. II, 905
Pancoast, Mary S., Jr. II, 905
Pancoast, Mary W. II, 117
Pancoast, Mary W. II, 122
Pancoast, Mercy IV, 345
Pancoast, Morris H. II, 154
Pancoast, Morris Hall II, 135
Pancoast, Morris Hall II, 154
Pancoast, Nathan Townsend
VI, 627
Pancoast, Omar B. II, 905
Pancoast, Phebe Gumery IV, 345
Pancoast, Priscilla Ballanger
II, 36
Pancoast, Priscilla Ballinger
II, 122
Pancoast, Rachel Duer II, 1019
Pancoast, Ralph Cowgill II, 1019
Pancoast, Raymond G. II, 136
Pancoast, Rebecca II, 36
Pancoast, Rebecca II, 122
Pancoast, Rebecca II, 725
Pancoast, Rebecca II, 758
Pancoast, Rhoda II, 968
Pancoast, Ruth VI, 539
Pancoast, Ruth VI, 541
Pancoast, Ruth VI, 634
Pancoast, Ruth VI, 686
Pancoast, Ruth VI, 722
Pancoast, Ruth Esther VI, 637
Pancoast, Ruth Esther VI, 638
Pancoast, Ruth Esther VI, 686
Pancoast, Ruth Esther VI, 707

Pancoast, Ruth Esther VI, 711
Pancoast, Ruth Hannah IV, 649
Pancoast, Ruth Hannah IV, 650
Pancoast, Ruth Hannah VI, 681
Pancoast, Ruth Hannah VI, 685
Pancoast, Ruth Hannah VI, 686
Pancoast, S. Thompson VI, 686
Pancoast, S. Thompson VI, 712
Pancoast, Sallie III, 431
Pancoast, Sallie E. II, 849
Pancoast, Sallie E. II, 905
Pancoast, Sallie P. III, 404
Pancoast, Sallie S. II, 862
Pancoast, Sallie S. II, 905
Pancoast, Sally III, 58
Pancoast, Sally III, 120
Pancoast, Sally III, 246
Pancoast, Sally VI, 686
Pancoast, Sally VI, 701
Pancoast, Samuel II, 91
Pancoast, Samuel II, 121
Pancoast, Samuel II, 135
Pancoast, Samuel II, 136
Pancoast, Samuel II, 151
Pancoast, Samuel II, 154
Pancoast, Samuel II, 247
Pancoast, Samuel II, 455
Pancoast, Samuel II, 586
Pancoast, Samuel II, 603
Pancoast, Samuel II, 612
Pancoast, Samuel II, 660
Pancoast, Samuel II, 674
Pancoast, Samuel II, 812
Pancoast, Samuel II, 825
Pancoast, Samuel II, 905
Pancoast, Samuel II, 1004
Pancoast, Samuel II, 1019
Pancoast, Samuel IV, 345
Pancoast, Samuel IV, 425
Pancoast, Samuel S. II, 91
Pancoast, Sarah II, 74
Pancoast, Sarah II, 91
Pancoast, Sarah II, 139
Pancoast, Sarah II, 198
Pancoast, Sarah II, 234
Pancoast, Sarah II, 243
Pancoast, Sarah II, 247
Pancoast, Sarah II, 248
Pancoast, Sarah II, 253
Pancoast, Sarah II, 297
Pancoast, Sarah II, 408
Pancoast, Sarah II, 455
Pancoast, Sarah II, 587
Pancoast, Sarah II, 590
Pancoast, Sarah II, 612
Pancoast, Sarah II, 660
Pancoast, Sarah II, 674
Pancoast, Sarah II, 812
Pancoast, Sarah II, 817
Pancoast, Sarah II, 867
Pancoast, Sarah II, 905
Pancoast, Sarah II, 911
Pancoast, Sarah II, 934
Pancoast, Sarah II, 978
Pancoast, Sarah II, 1019
Pancoast, Sarah III, 22
Pancoast, Sarah III, 246
Pancoast, Sarah IV, 155
Pancoast, Sarah IV, 355
Pancoast, Sarah IV, 425
Pancoast, Sarah VI, 428
Pancoast, Sarah VI, 529
Pancoast, Sarah VI, 537
Pancoast, Sarah VI, 541
Pancoast, Sarah VI, 554
Pancoast, Sarah VI, 555
Pancoast, Sarah VI, 570
Pancoast, Sarah VI, 577
Pancoast, Sarah VI, 602
Pancoast, Sarah VI, 605
Pancoast, Sarah VI, 627
Pancoast, Sarah VI, 677
Pancoast, Sarah VI, 681
Pancoast, Sarah VI, 686
Pancoast, Sarah VI, 687
Pancoast, Sarah VI, 688
Pancoast, Sarah VI, 722
Pancoast, Sarah VI, 769
Pancoast, Sarah VI, 775
Pancoast, Sarah VI, 789
Pancoast, Sarah A. VI, 541
Pancoast, Sarah A., Jr. VI, 495
Pancoast, Sarah A., Jr. VI, 541
Pancoast, Sarah Ann VI, 627
Pancoast, Sarah F. II, 905
Pancoast, Sarah G. II, 91
Pancoast, Sarah S. II, 849
Pancoast, Sarah S. II, 905
Pancoast, Sarah Saunders II, 812
Pancoast, Sarah Stephens II, 825
Pancoast, Seth II, 812
Pancoast, Seth II, 849
Pancoast, Seth II, 862
Pancoast, Seth II, 905
Pancoast, Seth III, 120
Pancoast, Seth III, 246
Pancoast, Seth S. II, 849
Pancoast, Seth S. II, 905
Pancoast, Shadlock II, 91
Pancoast, Shadlock II, 248
Pancoast, Shadrach II, 247
Pancoast, Solomon II, 248
Pancoast, Solomon III, 156
Pancoast, Solomon III, 246
Pancoast, Stacy L. II, 905
Pancoast, Stephen II, 812
Pancoast, Stephen IV, 334
Pancoast, Stephen IV, 345
Pancoast, Stephen IV, 425
Pancoast, Susan VI, 541
Pancoast, Susan G. II, 905
Pancoast, Susan George II, 812
Pancoast, Susannah II, 210
Pancoast, Susannah II, 247
Pancoast, Susannah II, 991
Pancoast, Susannah II, 1019
Pancoast, T. B. Reed II, 136
Pancoast, Tacie II, 794
Pancoast, Tacy II, 248
Pancoast, Tacy II, 828
Pancoast, Tacy II, 977
Pancoast, Tacy II, 1019
Pancoast, Thomas II, 180
Pancoast, Thomas II, 247
Pancoast, Thomas II, 248
Pancoast, Thomas II, 253
Pancoast, Thomasin II, 247
Pancoast, Thomasin II, 257
Pancoast, Thomasin II, 277
Pancoast, Thomasin III, 247
Pancoast, Unity II, 248
Pancoast, Unity III, 113
Pancoast, Unity III, 247
Pancoast, Unity III, 355
Pancoast, Walter III, 246
Pancoast, Wd. Mary II, 180
Pancoast, Wd. Mary II, 612
Pancoast, Wd. Mary VI, 769
Pancoast, Wd. Sarah II, 180
Pancoast, Widow Mary VI, 541
Pancoast, Widow Mary VI, 577
Pancoast, William II, 154
Pancoast, William II, 180
Pancoast, William II, 213
Pancoast, William II, 247
Pancoast, William II, 248
Pancoast, William II, 257
Pancoast, William II, 270
Pancoast, William VI, 495
Pancoast, William VI, 541
Pancoast, William VI, 570
Pancoast, William H. II, 297
Pancoast, William H. VI, 628
Pancoast, William Hoge II, 247
Pancoast, William S. II, 812
Pancoast, William Stacy II, 36
Pancoast, William, Jr. II, 247
Pancoast, Wm. II, 91
Pancoast, Wm. II, 122
Pancoast, Wm. II, 135
Pancoast, Wm. II, 590
Pancoast, Wm. II, 612
Pancoast, Wm. IV, 345
Pancoast, Wm. VI, 541
Pancoast, Wm. S. II, 905
Pancoast, Wm. Stacy II, 122
Pancoast-Saunders, Wd. Mary VI, 789
Pancoss, Elizabeth II, 1019
Pancoss, Mary II, 1019
Pancoss, Samuel II, 1019
Pancoss, Tacy II, 1019
Pancost, Ann II, 135
Pancost, Ann M. II, 91
Pancost, Charles E. II, 91
Pancost, David II, 135
Pancost, Diadema II, 247
Pancost, Dorcas II, 91
Pancost, Dorcas II, 122
Pancost, Dorcas S. II, 91
Pancost, Elizabeth II, 122
Pancost, Elizabeth II, 247
Pancost, Hannah II, 91
Pancost, Hannah II, 122
Pancost, Hannah II, 194
Pancost, Hannah II, 247
Pancost, Hannah II, 1055
Pancost, Isaiah II, 91
Pancost, James C. II, 122
Pancost, John II, 138
Pancost, Jonathan II, 91
Pancost, Josiah II, 91
Pancost, Martha II, 135
Pancost, Mary II, 91
Pancost, Mary II, 114
Pancost, Mary II, 232
Pancost, Mary Jane II, 138
Pancost, Samuel II, 91
Pancost, Samuel S. II, 91
Pancost, Sarah II, 138
Pancost, Sarah II, 612
Pancost, Shadlock II, 91
Pancost, Shadrach II, 194
Pancost, Shadrach II, 247
Pancost, Thomas II, 248
Pancost, Wm. II, 91
Pandrich, Ann II, 708
Pandrich, Ann II, 714
Pandrich, Ann S. II, 748
Pandrich, Ann S. II, 758
Pandrich, Ellen S. II, 708
Pandrich, George II, 708
Pandrich, George II, 714
Pandrich, George II, 748
Pandrich, George II, 758
Pandrich, Margaret II, 708
Pandrich, Margaret II, 714
Pandrich, Margaret II, 748
Pandrich, Margaret II, 758
Pandrich, Rebecca C. II, 714
Pandrich, Rebecca C. II, 758
Pandrick, Ellen S. II, 966
Pandrick, Margaret II, 758
Panecast, Mary IV, 425
Pangle, Abraham V. V, 1013
Pangle, Jennie V, 1013
Pangle, Louisa V, 1013
Pangle, Mary M. V, 1013
Pangle, Wm. V, 1013
Pankett, Lucretia Bell V, 638
Pankey, Ann VI, 974
Pankey, Elizabeth VI, 201
Pankey, James VI, 795
Pankey, Philip VI, 974
Pankhurst, Jane II, 248
Pankhurst, John II, 248
Pankhurst, John II, 260
Pankhurst, Mary II, 248
Pankhurst, Mary II, 260
Pannil, Morton VI, 845
Pannil, Polly B. VI, 845
Pannill, Ann M. VI, 821
Pannill, Ann T. VI, 845
Pannill, Catherine VI, 845
Pannill, David VI, 821
Pannill, Elizabeth VI, 850
Pannill, Fanny VI, 844
Pannill, J. VI, 824
Pannill, Jane VI, 850
Pannill, Jeremiah VI, 845
Pannill, John VI, 850
Pannill, Judith VI, 844
Pannill, Judith VI, 865
Pannill, Mary VI, 795
Pannill, Mary VI, 824
Pannill, Mildred Ann VI, 974
Pannill, Morton VI, 865
Pannill, Morton, Jr. VI, 845
Pannill, S. VI, 795
Pannill, Sam VI, 824
Pannill, Sam VI, 845
Pannill, Samuel VI, 821
Pannill, Samuel VI, 844
Pannill, Samuel VI, 865
Pannill, Sarah B. M. VI, 845
Pannill, William VI, 974
Paray, Frances I, 826
Paray, Frances I, 832
Parce, Ezekiel III, 383
Parce, Mary III, 383
Pardy, Ann V, 108
Pardy, Martha V, 108
Pardy, Martha V, 139
Parent, Edith V, 1013
Parent, Elizabeth V, 1013
Parent, Ella V, 1013
Parent, Franklin V, 1013
Parent, John V, 1013
Parent, Samuel V, 1013
Parham, Benajah V, 108
Parham, Benejah V, 855
Parham, Delila V, 108
Parham, Elizabeth V, 108
Parham, James L. VI, 77
Parham, James L. VI, 89
Parham, Margaret I, 877
Parham, Mary V, 818
Parham, Mary V, 855
Parham, Peter V, 108
Parham, Rachel V, 108
Parham, Rachel V, 855
Parham, William VI, 138
Parham, William VI, 139
Parham, Zachaus V, 855
Parham, Zacheus V, 855
Parham, Zaheus V, 108
Parime, Sarah IV, 36
Parime, Sarah IV, 52
Paris, Elijah VI, 974
Paris, Gabriel II, 614
Paris, Gabriel II, 758
Paris, Lida V, 354
Paris, Mary S. VI, 974
Paris, Polly Ann VI, 966
Paris, Sarah V, 354
Paris, Susan VI, 944
Paris, Zebediah VI, 944
Paris, Zedekiah VI, 966
Parish, Avery I, 565
Parish, Eleanor D. VI, 769
Parish, James E. I, 832
Parish, John II, 403
Parish, John B. I, 897
Parish, John W. I, 314
Parish, Joseph II, 248
Parish, Joseph VI, 915
Parish, Littleberry VI, 974
Parish, Marcellus A. I, 314
Parish, Margaret V, 638
Parish, Mary VI, 945
Parish, Mary VI, 974
Parish, Michaels II, 574
Parish, Patty VI, 974
Parish, Pearcy I, 314
Parish, Peggy VI, 845
Parish, Polly I, 314
Parish, Rachel IV, 425
Parish, Rachel IV, 491
Parish, Robert II, 403
Parish, Susannah II, 248
Parish, Thos. H. V, 638
Parish, William II, 403
Parish, William VI, 845
Parish, William VI, 974
Parish, William J. I, 832
Parish, William W. I, 314
Parishaw, Ruth I, 1001
Parisher, Samuel I, 274
Parisho, Abilisant I, 274
Parisho, Camewell I, 274
Parisho, Cammel I, 274
Parisho, Cammell I, 274
Parisho, Campbell I, 274
Parisho, Catharine I, 274
Parisho, Cornwill I, 274
Parisho, Eleanor I, 96
Parisho, James I, 967
Parisho, James V, 269
Parisho, Jeams I, 965
Parisho, Jeams I, 967
Parisho, Jean I, 967
Parisho, John I, 967
Parisho, Joseph I, 274
Parisho, Martha I, 274
Parisho, Mary I, 274
Parisho, Mary IV, 104
Parisho, Ruth I, 965
Parisho, Ruth I, 967
Parisho, Ruth I, 1011
Parisho, Samuel I, 274
Parisho, Sarah I, 274
Parishoe, James I, 68
Pariss, John VI, 858
Park, ??? VI, 283
Park, Almira B. IV, 947
Park, Asenath IV, 933
Park, Asenath IV, 984
Park, Asenath L. IV, 985
Park, Asenath L. IV, 986
Park, Asenath Lorena IV, 984
Park, Asenith IV, 947
Park, Asenith IV, 985
Park, Benoni I, 66
Park, Bertha Elizabeth IV, 984
Park, David IV, 947
Park, David IV, 984
Park, David IV, 985
Park, David James IV, 984
Park, Duncan IV, 984
Park, Elisabeth I, 66
Park, Elisabeth I, 85
Park, Elizabeth IV, 982
Park, Elizabeth IV, 984
Park, Elizabeth IV, 999
Park, Ethel V, 759
Park, Ethel S. V, 759
Park, Florence IV, 984
Park, Hannah II, 613
Park, Henry E. IV, 1288
Park, Humphrey I, 66
Park, Humphrey I, 74
Park, Humphry I, 66
Park, Humphry I, 85
Park, Ingram II, 180
Park, Ingram II, 298
Park, James IV, 1288
Park, Jane II, 613
Park, Joseph I, 198
Park, Joseph I, 250
Park, Joseph III, 247
Park, Lewis Lincoln IV, 984
Park, Lida IV, 984
Park, Lida Ridgway IV, 984
Park, Margaret II, 298
Park, Marietta IV, 982
Park, Marietta IV, 984
Park, Martha IV, 748
Park, Mary I, 48
Park, Mary I, 66
Park, Mary II, 758
Park, Mary IV, 984
Park, Mary T. III, 247
Park, Nathan I, 66
Park, Peninah I, 60
Park, Peninah I, 66
Park, Roberts IV, 984
Park, Ruthanna IV, 965
Park, Ruthanna IV, 984
Park, Samuel I, 66
Park, Sarah I, 36
Park, Sarah I, 61
Park, Sarah I, 63
Park, Sarah I, 66
Park, Sarah I, 250
Park, Sarah Emily IV, 984
Park, Sarah W. IV, 984
Park, Silvester IV, 982
Park, Sylvester IV, 984
Park, Sylvester G. IV, 984
Park, Sylvester G. IV, 999
Park, Thomas II, 613
Park, Widow Sarah I, 47
Park, Widow Sarah I, 66
Park, Widow Sarah I, 74
Parke, Benoni I, 66
Parke, Dr. Thomas II, 402
Parke, Hannah II, 613
Parke, Jacob II, 613
Parke, James P. II, 758
Parke, James P. II, 905
Parke, James Pemberton II, 9
Parke, Jane II, 576
Parke, Jane II, 613
Parke, Jane II, 619
Parke, Joseph II, 613
Parke, Joshua II, 812
Parke, Joshua C. II, 613
Parke, Joshua C. II, 714
Parke, Margaret II, 501
Parke, Margaret II, 613
Parke, Mary II, 758
Parke, Nathan I, 66
Parke, Peninah I, 66
Parke, Rachel II, 402
Parke, Rachel II, 613
Parke, Rachel II, 619
Parke, Richard II, 613
Parke, Sarah I, 66
Parke, Sarah II, 782
Parke, Sarah II, 905
Parke, Susanna II, 612
Parke, Susanna II, 613
Parke, Thomas II, 613
Parke, Thomas II, 619
Parke, Thomas, Jr. II, 613
Parke, Wd. Sarah II, 812
Parke, Widower Richard II, 6
Parkeley, Timonson III, 247
Parker, ??? III, 247
Parker, ??? IV, 1125
Parker, Aaron I, 113
Parker, Aaron I, 221
Parker, Aaron I, 223
Parker, Aaron I, 248
Parker, Aaron I, 251
Parker, Aaron I, 252
Parker, Aaron IV, 259
Parker, Aaron Ausborn I, 222
Parker, Aaron B. VI, 975
Parker, Abigail I, 222
Parker, Abigail I, 223
Parker, Abigail I, 244
Parker, Abigail I, 250
Parker, Abigail I, 251
Parker, Abigail III, 247
Parker, Abigail IV, 155
Parker, Abigail IV, 223
Parker, Abigail IV, 258
Parker, Abigail IV, 259
Parker, Abigail IV, 281
Parker, Abigail IV, 535
Parker, Abigail IV, 543
Parker, Abraham I, 274
Parker, Abraham II, 402
Parker, Abraham IV, 259

er, Ada I, 17
er, Ada B. V, 855
er, Adah R. I, 67
er, Adah R. I, 72
er, Adam V, 269
er, Adam V, 462
er, Alethia I, 20
er, Alexander I, 222
er, Alexander I, 223
er, Alexander I, 250
er, Alexander II, 402
er, Alexander II, 613
er, Alexander II, 667
er, Alexander VI, 845
er, Alexandria I, 251
er, Alice II, 701
er, Alice II, 732
er, Alice II, 757
er, Allen Julian I, 931
er, Alvanus V, 855
er, Alvin I, 947
er, Alvin Scott I, 15
er, Alvin Scott I, 896
er, Alvin Scott I, 931
er, Alvin Scott I, 947
er, Alvin Scott I, 950
er, Ammon H. VI, 975
er, Amos I, 222
er, Amos I, 250
er, Anderson IV, 1108
er, Anderson J. IV, 259
er, Anderson J. IV, 1108
er, Ann I, 309
er, Ann I, 314
er, Ann II, 402
er, Ann II, 492
er, Ann II, 613
er, Ann II, 614
er, Ann II, 617
er, Ann II, 758
er, Ann IV, 210
er, Ann IV, 259
er, Ann IV, 313
er, Ann IV, 339
er, Ann IV, 345
er, Ann IV, 391
er, Ann IV, 425
er, Ann IV, 650
er, Ann IV, 905
er, Ann IV, 912
er, Ann VI, 66
er, Ann VI, 78
er, Ann VI, 542
er, Ann VI, 633
er, Ann VI, 687
er, Ann VI, 736
er, Ann VI, 769
er, Ann C. II, 905
er, Ann Cash VI, 974
er, Ann Catharine III, 344
er, Ann F. IV, 650
er, Ann F. IV, 748
er, Ann R. I, 139
er, Ann R. I, 160
er, Ann Robinson I, 98
er, Ann Robinson I, 113
er, Anna I, 314
er, Anna IV, 202
er, Anna IV, 249
er, Anna IV, 258
er, Anna IV, 259
er, Anna IV, 425
er, Anna B. IV, 425
er, Anna Isabel V, 702
er, Anna Isabella V, 702
er, Anna Isabelle V, 702
er, Anne I, 293
er, Anne I, 1068
er, Anne I, 1071
er, Anne VI, 78
er, Annie I, 223
er, Aron I, 251
er, Asa I, 222
er, Asa I, 252
ker, Asenath I, 251
ker, Asenath I, 304
ker, Asenath I, 314
ker, Aseneth I, 223
ker, Asher III, 247
ker, Barbara I, 222
ker, Barbara I, 252
ker, Barbary I, 252
ker, Behala VI, 979
ker, Benaiah I, 251
ker, Benajah IV, 259
ker, Benajah IV, 262
ker, Benajah IV, 425
ker, Benajah IV, 427
ker, Benajah V, 413
ker, Benajah V, 424
ker, Benj. IV, 259
Parker, Benj. A. III, 20
Parker, Benjamin I, 222
Parker, Benjamin I, 293
Parker, Benjamin I, 304
Parker, Benjamin I, 314
Parker, Benjamin II, 180
Parker, Benjamin II, 279
Parker, Benjamin II, 298
Parker, Benjamin II, 812
Parker, Benjamin II, 905
Parker, Benjamin III, 247
Parker, Benjamin VI, 937
Parker, Benjamin J. I, 222
Parker, Benjamin J. I, 252
Parker, Betsey I, 293
Parker, Betsey VI, 937
Parker, Bettee V, 925
Parker, Betty M. V, 925
Parker, Beulah II, 402
Parker, Beulah II, 613
Parker, Beulah II, 614
Parker, Beulah II, 647
Parker, Beulah II, 714
Parker, Beulah II, 812
Parker, Beulah C. II, 714
Parker, Beulah P. II, 735
Parker, Beulah P. II, 758
Parker, Beulah R. IV, 425
Parker, Beulah Roads IV, 425
Parker, Beverly B. V, 462
Parker, Britton I, 251
Parker, Caleb I, 222
Parker, Caleb IV, 258
Parker, Caleb IV, 259
Parker, Caleb D. VI, 917
Parker, Caleb D. VI, 975
Parker, Caleb D. VI, 979
Parker, Camilla A. VI, 975
Parker, Caroline II, 402
Parker, Caroline II, 758
Parker, Carrie Ellen V, 462
Parker, Catharine I, 223
Parker, Catharine I, 251
Parker, Catharine II, 402
Parker, Catharine II, 613
Parker, Catharine II, 617
Parker, Catharine II, 622
Parker, Catherine II, 613
Parker, Cathrine II, 664
Parker, Cedren I, 252
Parker, Cedron Gerow I, 223
Parker, Cedron Jero I, 252
Parker, Charity IV, 259
Parker, Charity IV, 425
Parker, Charles II, 402
Parker, Charles II, 613
Parker, Charles IV, 1239
Parker, Charles V, 462
Parker, Charles Harold I, 931
Parker, Charles Harrold I, 623
Parker, Charles Tomlinson I, 931
Parker, Charles Townsend II, 613
Parker, Charlotte I, 67
Parker, Charlotte I, 931
Parker, Charlotte III, 247
Parker, Charlotte McA. I, 15
Parker, Charlotte McAdams I, 22
Parker, Charlotte McAdams I, 67
Parker, Charlotte McAdams I, 83
Parker, Charlotte White I, 931
Parker, Chas. IV, 1332
Parker, Chas. H. VI, 979
Parker, Chas. J. IV, 1332
Parker, Chas. M. II, 905
Parker, Chauncy B. I, 222
Parker, Clarke I, 113
Parker, Clarkey I, 53
Parker, Clarkey I, 66
Parker, Claude W. II, 714
Parker, Claude W. II, 758
Parker, Claudius IV, 912
Parker, Claudius Galin IV, 259
Parker, Claudius Galin IV, 650
Parker, Cola Godden III, 411
Parker, Cola Godden III, 431
Parker, Cora White I, 931
Parker, Cornelius II, 402
Parker, Cynthia VI, 630
Parker, Cynthia VI, 687
Parker, Cyrus Bay I, 252
Parker, Cyrus Ray I, 222
Parker, D. Anna II, 864
Parker, D. Anna II, 905
Parker, D. Howard IV, 425
Parker, D. Ralph, Jr. I, 931
Parker, Damaris II, 248
Parker, Daniel II, 402
Parker, Daniel III, 247
Parker, David I, 15
Parker, David VI, 918
Parker, David Howard IV, 425
Parker, David Ralph I, 897
Parker, David Ralph I, 931
Parker, Deborah I, 67
Parker, Deborah I, 565
Parker, Deborah I, 931
Parker, Deborah I, 947
Parker, Deborah I, 950
Parker, Deborah II, 402
Parker, Deborah II, 613
Parker, Deborah A. I, 15
Parker, Deborah A. I, 67
Parker, Deborah A. I, 252
Parker, Deborah A. V, 424
Parker, Deborah Ann I, 252
Parker, Deborah Ann I, 255
Parker, Deborah Ann V, 413
Parker, Deborah Ann V, 424
Parker, Deborah Annie II, 905
Parker, Deborah H. IV, 1288
Parker, Diana I, 274
Parker, Dianah I, 274
Parker, Dianna I, 274
Parker, Dora V, 1013
Parker, Dorothy IV, 1332
Parker, Doshia VI, 1008
Parker, Douglas V, 702
Parker, Douglas L. V, 702
Parker, Douglas L. V, 707
Parker, Douglas Ross V, 702
Parker, Dr. Isaac IV, 259
Parker, E. Thomas I, 252
Parker, Ed. Augustus II, 402
Parker, Edith I, 293
Parker, Edith I, 304
Parker, Edith I, 314
Parker, Edith II, 714
Parker, Edward II, 402
Parker, Edward II, 613
Parker, Edward II, 714
Parker, Edward II, 758
Parker, Edward IV, 425
Parker, Edward Augustus II, 758
Parker, Edward P. I, 67
Parker, Edward P. I, 565
Parker, Edward Peele I, 15
Parker, Edward Thornburgh IV, 425
Parker, Edward W. VI, 891
Parker, Edward W. VI, 946
Parker, Edward W. VI, 975
Parker, Edward W. VI, 988
Parker, Edwin IV, 258
Parker, Efhraim V, 957
Parker, Elaner I, 1007
Parker, Elaner I, 1011
Parker, Eleanor I, 947
Parker, Eleanor II, 527
Parker, Eleanor II, 613
Parker, Eleanor V, 424
Parker, Eleanor V, 433
Parker, Eleanor VI, 974
Parker, Eleanor Gertrude I, 623
Parker, Eleanor Gertrude I, 931
Parker, Elexander I, 241
Parker, Elexander I, 250
Parker, Eli I, 222
Parker, Eli I, 252
Parker, Elias T. I, 66
Parker, Eliazer Thomas I, 222
Parker, Elijah Alpheus I, 222
Parker, Elina VI, 917
Parker, Elisabeth I, 34
Parker, Elisabeth I, 66
Parker, Elisabeth I, 87
Parker, Elisabeth I, 113
Parker, Elisabeth I, 149
Parker, Elisabeth I, 159
Parker, Elisabeth I, 160
Parker, Elisabeth I, 176
Parker, Elisabeth I, 199
Parker, Elisabeth I, 251
Parker, Elisabeth I, 254
Parker, Elisabeth I, 280
Parker, Elisabeth I, 623
Parker, Elisha I, 66
Parker, Elisha I, 113
Parker, Elisha I, 159
Parker, Elisha I, 293
Parker, Elisha I, 314
Parker, Elisha I, 832
Parker, Elisha I, 1066
Parker, Elisha I, 1071
Parker, Elisha IV, 425
Parker, Elisha IV, 543
Parker, Elisha IV, 1108
Parker, Eliza I, 222
Parker, Eliza II, 402
Parker, Eliza II, 614
Parker, Eliza II, 647
Parker, Eliza II, 714
Parker, Eliza II, 812
Parker, Eliza II, 905
Parker, Eliza II, 913
Parker, Eliza III, 247
Parker, Eliza IV, 258
Parker, Eliza IV, 259
Parker, Eliza VI, 687
Parker, Eliza VI, 891
Parker, Eliza A. III, 20
Parker, Eliza Parker VI, 687
Parker, Elizabeth I, 98
Parker, Elizabeth I, 113
Parker, Elizabeth I, 125
Parker, Elizabeth I, 199
Parker, Elizabeth I, 222
Parker, Elizabeth I, 223
Parker, Elizabeth I, 251
Parker, Elizabeth I, 252
Parker, Elizabeth I, 274
Parker, Elizabeth I, 293
Parker, Elizabeth I, 302
Parker, Elizabeth I, 314
Parker, Elizabeth I, 315
Parker, Elizabeth I, 667
Parker, Elizabeth I, 832
Parker, Elizabeth I, 991
Parker, Elizabeth I, 994
Parker, Elizabeth I, 1068
Parker, Elizabeth I, 1071
Parker, Elizabeth II, 248
Parker, Elizabeth II, 250
Parker, Elizabeth II, 402
Parker, Elizabeth II, 531
Parker, Elizabeth II, 540
Parker, Elizabeth II, 613
Parker, Elizabeth II, 664
Parker, Elizabeth II, 670
Parker, Elizabeth II, 812
Parker, Elizabeth II, 905
Parker, Elizabeth III, 247
Parker, Elizabeth IV, 122
Parker, Elizabeth IV, 131
Parker, Elizabeth IV, 259
Parker, Elizabeth IV, 260
Parker, Elizabeth VI, 542
Parker, Elizabeth VI, 677
Parker, Elizabeth VI, 687
Parker, Elizabeth VI, 873
Parker, Elizabeth A. VI, 968
Parker, Elizabeth Ann I, 222
Parker, Elizabeth Ann IV, 369
Parker, Elizabeth Ann IV, 425
Parker, Elizabeth Anna IV, 369
Parker, Elizabeth Anna IV, 425
Parker, Elizabeth D. VI, 947
Parker, Elizabeth H. III, 241
Parker, Elizabeth J. I, 223
Parker, Elizabeth Louise V, 702
Parker, Elizabeth P. I, 223
Parker, Elizabeth Slatie III, 247
Parker, Elizabeth V. IV, 259
Parker, Elizabeth, Jr. I, 314
Parker, Elizah VI, 542
Parker, Ella V, 855
Parker, Ella M. III, 431
Parker, Ellen V, 301
Parker, Ellen V, 454
Parker, Ellen B. IV, 388
Parker, Ellen B. IV, 425
Parker, Ellen E. IV, 425
Parker, Ellen M. W. I, 931
Parker, Elmer E. III, 247
Parker, Elwood W. I, 222
Parker, Elwood Whittier I, 252
Parker, Emlen IV, 258
Parker, Emma II, 402
Parker, Emma II, 758
Parker, Emma II, 905
Parker, Emma IV, 259
Parker, Emma IV, 262
Parker, Emma IV, 425
Parker, Emmet N. V, 108
Parker, Emmet N. V, 925
Parker, Enoch I, 66
Parker, Enoch I, 86
Parker, Enoch I, 160
Parker, Enoch I, 199
Parker, Ephraim IV, 259
Parker, Ephraim V, 952
Parker, Ephraim I. IV, 313
Parker, Esther I, 314
Parker, Esther II, 402
Parker, Esther II, 471
Parker, Esther II, 613
Parker, Esther IV, 1375
Parker, Esther IV, 1376
Parker, Esther VI, 975
Parker, Esther M. II, 834
Parker, Esther M. II, 905
Parker, Ethel Louise V, 1013
Parker, Eulalia IV, 1219
Parker, Eunice I, 931
Parker, Eunice IV, 1332
Parker, Eunice Anderson I, 931
Parker, Eunice Anderson I, 947
Parker, Eva IV, 543
Parker, Eva IV, 1239
Parker, Eva IV, 1288
Parker, Eve IV, 525
Parker, Eveline I, 730
Parker, Ezra IV, 425
Parker, Ezra IV, 543
Parker, Ezra IV, 1108
Parker, Ezra VI, 922
Parker, Ezra VI, 950
Parker, Ezra VI, 974
Parker, Ezra VI, 999
Parker, Ezra VI, 1006
Parker, Ezra M. II, 714
Parker, Faith I, 244
Parker, Faith I, 250
Parker, Faith I, 251
Parker, Faith IV, 258
Parker, Faith IV, 259
Parker, Faitha I, 222
Parker, Fidelia IV, 1178
Parker, Fidella I, 896
Parker, Frances I, 235
Parker, Frances I, 252
Parker, Frances IV, 1102
Parker, Frances IV, 1108
Parker, Frances VI, 900
Parker, Frances VI, 974
Parker, Frances C. IV, 260
Parker, Frances H. VI, 975
Parker, Frances S. I, 947
Parker, Francis I, 252
Parker, Francis V, 269
Parker, Frank B. IV, 1332
Parker, Frank English I, 931
Parker, Frank English I, 947
Parker, Fred B. IV, 1332
Parker, Galen IV, 912
Parker, Garnetta I, 222
Parker, Garnetta I, 252
Parker, Garnetta D. I, 222
Parker, Geo. I, 222
Parker, Geo. IV, 425
Parker, Geo. IV, 1117
Parker, Geo. H. I, 223
Parker, Geo. S. III, 431
Parker, Geo. W. III, 247
Parker, George I, 222
Parker, George I, 223
Parker, George I, 251
Parker, George II, 248
Parker, George II, 402
Parker, George II, 613
Parker, George III, 247
Parker, George III, 373
Parker, George IV, 259
Parker, George IV, 425
Parker, George IV, 543
Parker, George IV, 828
Parker, George IV, 836
Parker, George IV, 859
Parker, George IV, 1108
Parker, George VI, 906
Parker, George VI, 974
Parker, George E. I, 222
Parker, George H. I, 222
Parker, George H. I, 225
Parker, George H. I, 232
Parker, George H. I, 252
Parker, George H. I, 255
Parker, George H. I, 257
Parker, George Hanson I, 222
Parker, George Howard III, 247
Parker, George Howard III, 298
Parker, Gilbert III, 247
Parker, Glenn Falls V, 702
Parker, Grace II, 471
Parker, Grace II, 613
Parker, Grace III, 247
Parker, Grace IV, 259
Parker, Grace IV, 262
Parker, Grace IV, 425
Parker, Grace IV, 427
Parker, Grace V, 424
Parker, Grace S. III, 239
Parker, Grace S. III, 247
Parker, Grezilla May I, 252
Parker, Grizilda May I, 223
Parker, Gulielma M. II, 402
Parker, Gulielma Maria II, 758
Parker, Gulielma Maria II, 773
Parker, Hannah II, 248
Parker, Hannah II, 402
Parker, Hannah II, 613
Parker, Hannah II, 614
Parker, Hannah II, 714
Parker, Hannah II, 1057
Parker, Hannah III, 247

Parker, Hannah IV, 224
Parker, Hannah IV, 259
Parker, Hannah IV, 296
Parker, Hannah V, 196
Parker, Hannah VI, 975
Parker, Hannah Ann IV, 259
Parker, Hannah Ann IV, 425
Parker, Hannah L. IV, 259
Parker, Hannah M. II, 860
Parker, Hannah M. II, 905
Parker, Harriett V, 462
Parker, Harrold I, 947
Parker, Henderson I, 250
Parker, Henderson I, 251
Parker, Henrietta VI, 979
Parker, Henry I, 15
Parker, Henry I, 32
Parker, Henry II, 402
Parker, Henry II, 758
Parker, Henry Edmon I, 222
Parker, Henry Edmund I, 251
Parker, Herbert I, 931
Parker, Herbert I, 947
Parker, Herbert Winston I, 931
Parker, Hetty II, 798
Parker, Humphrey I, 66
Parker, Humphrey II, 1019
Parker, Humphrey II, 1020
Parker, Humphrey, Jr. II, 1019
Parker, I. T. I, 252
Parker, Iael I, 160
Parker, Ida V, 855
Parker, Ida T. V, 855
Parker, Ida T. V, 860
Parker, Ida T. V, 1013
Parker, Ira VI, 974
Parker, Isaa I, 294
Parker, Isaa??? I, 294
Parker, Isaac I, 34
Parker, Isaac I, 66
Parker, Isaac I, 222
Parker, Isaac I, 223
Parker, Isaac I, 250
Parker, Isaac I, 251
Parker, Isaac I, 252
Parker, Isaac I, 254
Parker, Isaac I, 293
Parker, Isaac I, 314
Parker, Isaac II, 402
Parker, Isaac II, 613
Parker, Isaac II, 614
Parker, Isaac II, 714
Parker, Isaac II, 758
Parker, Isaac II, 812
Parker, Isaac II, 905
Parker, Isaac IV, 155
Parker, Isaac IV, 200
Parker, Isaac IV, 223
Parker, Isaac IV, 224
Parker, Isaac IV, 258
Parker, Isaac IV, 259
Parker, Isaac IV, 260
Parker, Isaac IV, 425
Parker, Isaac IV, 590
Parker, Isaac IV, 904
Parker, Isaac IV, 1108
Parker, Isaac V, 269
Parker, Isaac T. IV, 425
Parker, Isaac Thomas Elwood I, 222
Parker, Isaac, Jr. IV, 259
Parker, Isaac, Jr. IV, 590
Parker, Isaac, Jr. IV, 1108
Parker, Isaac, Sr. I, 314
Parker, Isabel I, 66
Parker, Isabel I, 76
Parker, Isabel I, 250
Parker, Isabel I, 254
Parker, Isabela I, 113
Parker, Isabella I, 66
Parker, Isabella I, 98
Parker, Isabella I, 113
Parker, Isabella I, 139
Parker, Isabella I, 160
Parker, Isabella I, 219
Parker, Isabella I, 223
Parker, Isabella I, 249
Parker, Isabella I, 251
Parker, Isabella Dora I, 252
Parker, Isabella O. I, 223
Parker, Isabelle I, 66
Parker, Isiac I, 251
Parker, J. Gurney I, 252
Parker, J. Robert I, 67
Parker, J. Robert I, 931
Parker, J. Robert I, 947
Parker, J. W. I, 339
Parker, Jacob I, 66
Parker, Jacob I, 222
Parker, Jacob I, 237
Parker, Jacob I, 244
Parker, Jacob I, 250
Parker, Jacob I, 251
Parker, Jacob IV, 155
Parker, Jacob IV, 258
Parker, Jacob IV, 259
Parker, Jacob IV, 425
Parker, Jacob IV, 1108
Parker, Jacob B. IV, 425
Parker, Jacob B. IV, 543
Parker, Jacob Belman IV, 543
Parker, Jacob Bolman IV, 425
Parker, Jacob H. IV, 259
Parker, Jacob Hervey IV, 258
Parker, Jacob, Jr. I, 251
Parker, Jacob, Sr. I, 251
Parker, Jael I, 186
Parker, Jail I, 199
Parker, James I, 222
Parker, James I, 251
Parker, James II, 402
Parker, James II, 446
Parker, James II, 905
Parker, James IV, 155
Parker, James IV, 259
Parker, James VI, 900
Parker, James VI, 974
Parker, James VI, 975
Parker, James H. I, 222
Parker, James H. VI, 975
Parker, James Henry I, 222
Parker, James Lawrence II, 714
Parker, James Loid I, 222
Parker, James M. VI, 916
Parker, James M. VI, 975
Parker, James M. VI, 979
Parker, James P. I, 565
Parker, James Peele I, 15
Parker, James R. I, 67
Parker, James Robert I, 15
Parker, James Robert I, 67
Parker, James Robert I, 83
Parker, James Robert I, 222
Parker, James Robert I, 896
Parker, James S. VI, 975
Parker, James S. VI, 997
Parker, James Walton I, 223
Parker, Jamima V, 424
Parker, Jamima V, 433
Parker, Jane I, 113
Parker, Jane I, 223
Parker, Jane I, 251
Parker, Jane I, 252
Parker, Jane II, 402
Parker, Jane II, 532
Parker, Jane II, 613
Parker, Jane IV, 258
Parker, Jane IV, 259
Parker, Jane IV, 1178
Parker, Jane VI, 957
Parker, Jane Gilpin II, 613
Parker, Jane H. I, 222
Parker, Jane H. I, 251
Parker, Jane H. IV, 425
Parker, Jane J. I, 252
Parker, Jane T. VI, 975
Parker, Jas. VI, 1008
Parker, Jay Russel V, 855
Parker, Jemima I, 223
Parker, Jemima I, 251
Parker, Jencey VI, 974
Parker, Jeptha I, 947
Parker, Jeptha M. I, 947
Parker, Jeptha McAdams I, 15
Parker, Jeptha McAdams I, 896
Parker, Jeremiah I, 63
Parker, Jeremiah I, 66
Parker, Jeremiah I, 222
Parker, Jeremiah I, 223
Parker, Jeremiah I, 250
Parker, Jeremiah I, 251
Parker, Jeremiah I Sup 1, 8
Parker, Jeremiah II, 714
Parker, Jerome I, 896
Parker, Jesse I, 222
Parker, Jesse I, 251
Parker, Jesse I, 293
Parker, Jesse I, 309
Parker, Jesse I, 314
Parker, Jesse I, 1068
Parker, Jesse IV, 202
Parker, Jesse IV, 210
Parker, Jesse IV, 249
Parker, Jesse IV, 258
Parker, Jesse IV, 259
Parker, Jesse IV, 296
Parker, Jesse IV, 425
Parker, Jesse Peele I, 222
Parker, Jessie Gertrude I, 623
Parker, Jessie Gertrude I, 931
Parker, Jessie Gertrude I, 947
Parker, Jno. W. IV, 260
Parker, Joanna II, 402
Parker, Joanna II, 446
Parker, Joanna II, 816
Parker, Joanna II, 905
Parker, Joanna II, 913
Parker, Joanna P. II, 758
Parker, Joanna P. II, 761
Parker, Job I, 66
Parker, Job I, 113
Parker, Job I, 160
Parker, Job I, 250
Parker, Job I, 254
Parker, Jobe I, 113
Parker, Joel I, 160
Parker, Joel I, 293
Parker, Joel I, 314
Parker, Joel IV, 258
Parker, Joel IV, 425
Parker, Joel Judkins IV, 425
Parker, John I, 113
Parker, John I, 159
Parker, John I, 160
Parker, John I, 186
Parker, John I, 199
Parker, John I, 222
Parker, John I, 251
Parker, John I, 832
Parker, John II, 248
Parker, John II, 402
Parker, John II, 446
Parker, John II, 507
Parker, John II, 613
Parker, John II, 664
Parker, John III, 239
Parker, John III, 247
Parker, John IV, 258
Parker, John IV, 259
Parker, John IV, 425
Parker, John VI, 687
Parker, John VI, 918
Parker, John VI, 937
Parker, John VI, 975
Parker, John Cherington IV, 258
Parker, John D. VI, 975
Parker, John G. I, 219
Parker, John Gurney I, 222
Parker, John Gurney I, 223
Parker, John Gurney I, 249
Parker, John Gurney I, 252
Parker, John H. I, 623
Parker, John H. I, 896
Parker, John K. II, 714
Parker, John N. I, 67
Parker, John Newby I, 15
Parker, John Peele I, 113
Parker, John Peelle I, 250
Parker, John S. III, 247
Parker, John W. I, 339
Parker, John Warder II, 402
Parker, Jonathan I, 160
Parker, Jonathan I, 223
Parker, Jonathan I, 250
Parker, Jonathan I, 257
Parker, Jonathan I, 565
Parker, Jonathan V, 855
Parker, Jonathan J. I, 223
Parker, Jonathan W. V, 855
Parker, Jordan I, 15
Parker, Jordan I, 21
Parker, Jordan I, 67
Parker, Jordan IV, 258
Parker, Jordan VI, 89
Parker, Jordon I, 222
Parker, Jordon IV, 259
Parker, Jos. VI, 542
Parker, Joseph I, 14
Parker, Joseph I, 15
Parker, Joseph I, 66
Parker, Joseph I, 67
Parker, Joseph I, 70
Parker, Joseph I, 82
Parker, Joseph I, 98
Parker, Joseph I, 113
Parker, Joseph I, 125
Parker, Joseph I, 149
Parker, Joseph I, 160
Parker, Joseph I, 222
Parker, Joseph I, 223
Parker, Joseph I, 244
Parker, Joseph I, 250
Parker, Joseph I, 251
Parker, Joseph I, 252
Parker, Joseph I, 254
Parker, Joseph II, 248
Parker, Joseph II, 277
Parker, Joseph II, 402
Parker, Joseph II, 403
Parker, Joseph II, 531
Parker, Joseph II, 613
Parker, Joseph II, 617
Parker, Joseph II, 664
Parker, Joseph II, 812
Parker, Joseph IV, 155
Parker, Joseph IV, 259
Parker, Joseph IV, 425
Parker, Joseph IV, 650
Parker, Joseph IV, 1108
Parker, Joseph IV, 1137
Parker, Joseph VI, 78
Parker, Joseph VI, 542
Parker, Joseph VI, 687
Parker, Joseph VI, 942
Parker, Joseph VI, 975
Parker, Joseph Elcanatts I, 222
Parker, Joseph J. I, 209
Parker, Joseph J. I, 232
Parker, Joseph J. I, 252
Parker, Joseph J. IV, 425
Parker, Joseph J. IV, 543
Parker, Joseph John I, 222
Parker, Joseph John I, 223
Parker, Joseph John IV, 259
Parker, Joseph John IV, 650
Parker, Joseph John IV, 912
Parker, Joseph Jones IV, 425
Parker, Joseph Jones IV, 543
Parker, Joseph Pennington I, 223
Parker, Joseph R. I, 15
Parker, Joseph R. I, 64
Parker, Joseph R. I, 67
Parker, Joseph R. I, 160
Parker, Joseph R. I, 252
Parker, Joseph R. I, 565
Parker, Joseph R. I, 931
Parker, Joseph Robinson I, 113
Parker, Joseph Robinson I, 252
Parker, Joseph Robinson I, 255
Parker, Joseph W. I, 67
Parker, Joseph W. I, 565
Parker, Joseph Wilson I, 15
Parker, Joseph, Jr. IV, 259
Parker, Josephine I, 896
Parker, Joshua II, 613
Parker, Joshua Davis I, 314
Parker, Josiah I, 33
Parker, Josiah I, 223
Parker, Josiah I, 250
Parker, Josiah I, 251
Parker, Josiah I, 254
Parker, Josiah I, 260
Parker, Josiah I, 293
Parker, Josiah Outland I, 314
Parker, Josiah Thomas I, 251
Parker, Judith I, 222
Parker, Judith I, 223
Parker, Judith I, 233
Parker, Judith I, 234
Parker, Judith I, 248
Parker, Judith I, 250
Parker, Judith I, 251
Parker, Judith A. I, 213
Parker, Judith A. I, 223
Parker, Judith A. I, 252
Parker, Judith Ann I, 221
Parker, Judith Ann I, 252
Parker, Julia I, 17
Parker, Julia I, 223
Parker, Julia I, 251
Parker, Julia I, 252
Parker, Julia I, 254
Parker, Julia I, 257
Parker, Julia IV, 258
Parker, Julia IV, 259
Parker, Julia J. I, 222
Parker, Julia W. I, 896
Parker, Julia White I, 15
Parker, Julian I, 33
Parker, Julian Floyd I, 223
Parker, Julian Floyd I, 252
Parker, Juliana I, 251
Parker, Juliana I, 261
Parker, July I, 251
Parker, Keran I, 63
Parker, Keran I, 66
Parker, Keran I, 251
Parker, Keran I Sup 1, 8
Parker, Keren I, 251
Parker, Keron I Sup 1, 8
Parker, Kezia I, 66
Parker, Kezia I, 86
Parker, Laura J. II, 714
Parker, Laura J. II, 758
Parker, Lawrence II, 446
Parker, Leah I, 223
Parker, Leah I, 250
Parker, Leah I, 300
Parker, Leah I, 314
Parker, Leroy V, 855
Parker, Leroy Alvanus V, 855
Parker, Leslie M. I, 222
Parker, Lidya II, 613
Parker, Lidya II, 677
Parker, Lillian Frances V, 855
Parker, Lindley IV, 425
Parker, Lindley IV, 543
Parker, Lindley IV, 1108
Parker, Linfoot F. III, 247
Parker, Lotta IV, 1259
Parker, Lotta B. IV, 1332
Parker, Lottie IV, 1259
Parker, Lottie IV, 1332
Parker, Louelma I, 896
Parker, Louisa I, 67
Parker, Louisa I, 896
Parker, Louisa IV, 985
Parker, Louise M. III, 247
Parker, Louise M. III, 298
Parker, Lucinda VI, 950
Parker, Lucy A. III, 247
Parker, Lyddia I, 66
Parker, Lydia I, 10
Parker, Lydia I, 47
Parker, Lydia I, 66
Parker, Lydia I, 160
Parker, Lydia I, 223
Parker, Lydia I, 236
Parker, Lydia I, 250
Parker, Lydia I, 251
Parker, Lydia I, 929
Parker, Lydia II, 279
Parker, Lydia II, 298
Parker, Lydia II, 402
Parker, Lydia II, 527
Parker, Lydia II, 540
Parker, Lydia II, 613
Parker, Lydia II, 715
Parker, Lydia IV, 258
Parker, Lydia IV, 259
Parker, Lydia IV, 425
Parker, Lydia IV, 543
Parker, Lydia V, 462
Parker, Lydia A. II, 721
Parker, Lydia Ann V, 226
Parker, Lydia Ann V, 269
Parker, Lydia Ann V, 462
Parker, Lydia C. IV, 259
Parker, Lydia J. I, 231
Parker, Lydia J. I, 252
Parker, Lydia Jane I, 222
Parker, Lydia Jane IV, 259
Parker, Lydia Jane IV, 293
Parker, Lydia Jane IV, 425
Parker, Lydia Jane IV, 448
Parker, Lydia M. IV, 1108
Parker, Lydia M. IV, 1121
Parker, M. Elisabeth I, 222
Parker, Mabel J. I, 223
Parker, Macajah I, 251
Parker, Marcilla I, 222
Parker, Margaret I, 14
Parker, Margaret I, 113
Parker, Margaret I, 160
Parker, Margaret I, 175
Parker, Margaret I, 244
Parker, Margaret I, 250
Parker, Margaret I, 251
Parker, Margaret I, 931
Parker, Margaret II, 279
Parker, Margaret II, 298
Parker, Margaret II, 402
Parker, Margaret III, 247
Parker, Margaret V, 855
Parker, Margaret A. I, 64
Parker, Margaret A. I, 67
Parker, Margaret A. I, 160
Parker, Margaret Ann I, 15
Parker, Margaret F. I, 222
Parker, Margaret F. I, 252
Parker, Margaret F. I, 255
Parker, Margaret Morris I, 15
Parker, Margaret Ruth V, 855
Parker, Marhta J. I, 251
Parker, Marjory III, 247
Parker, Martha I, 33
Parker, Martha I, 66
Parker, Martha I, 222
Parker, Martha I, 223
Parker, Martha I, 250
Parker, Martha I, 251
Parker, Martha I, 254
Parker, Martha II, 402
Parker, Martha II, 603
Parker, Martha II, 613
Parker, Martha II, 758
Parker, Martha II, 769
Parker, Martha II, 1019
Parker, Martha III, 247
Parker, Martha III, 411
Parker, Martha III, 431
Parker, Martha IV, 258
Parker, Martha IV, 259
Parker, Martha IV, 383
Parker, Martha IV, 425

er, Martha IV, 1108
er, Martha IV, 1137
er, Martha VI, 542
er, Martha VI, 559
er, Martha VI, 687
er, Martha D. VI, 845
er, Martha D. VI, 942
er, Martha J. I, 249
er, Martha J. I, 251
er, Martha Jane I, 249
er, Martha Jane I, 251
er, Martha R. I, 67
er, Martha R. I, 160
er, Mary I, 15
er, Mary I, 39
er, Mary I, 66
er, Mary I, 87
er, Mary I, 113
er, Mary I, 125
er, Mary I, 160
er, Mary I, 177
er, Mary I, 219
er, Mary I, 222
er, Mary I, 223
er, Mary I, 241
er, Mary I, 250
er, Mary I, 251
er, Mary I, 301
er, Mary I, 314
er, Mary I, 947
er, Mary II, 400
er, Mary II, 402
er, Mary II, 507
er, Mary II, 532
er, Mary II, 613
er, Mary II, 679
er, Mary II, 714
er, Mary III, 239
er, Mary III, 247
er, Mary IV, 155
er, Mary IV, 200
er, Mary IV, 258
er, Mary IV, 259
er, Mary IV, 425
er, Mary IV, 517
er, Mary IV, 543
er, Mary IV, 904
er, Mary IV, 1332
er, Mary V, 301
er, Mary V, 385
er, Mary V, 424
er, Mary V, 454
er, Mary V, 462
er, Mary VI, 492
er, Mary VI, 542
er, Mary VI, 687
er, Mary VI, 720
er, Mary VI, 845
er, Mary VI, 975
er, Mary VI, 999
er, Mary VI, 1012
er, Mary VI, 1018
er, Mary A. I, 252
er, Mary A. III, 20
er, Mary Ann I, 234
er, Mary Ann I, 252
er, Mary Ann IV, 206
er, Mary Ann IV, 259
er, Mary Ann IV, 724
er, Mary Bell IV, 260
er, Mary Bell IV, 1260
er, Mary E. I, 223
er, Mary Elisabeth I, 15
er, Mary Elizabeth I, 947
er, Mary Ella I, 222
er, Mary Ellen I, 210
er, Mary Endom I, 223
er, Mary G. III, 239
er, Mary G. III, 247
er, Mary G. IV, 425
er, Mary G. IV, 543
er, Mary G. IV, 1108
er, Mary G. IV, 1117
er, Mary Grace III, 247
er, Mary I. IV, 425
er, Mary Iddings II, 905
er, Mary J. I, 222
er, Mary J. I, 223
er, Mary J. I, 225
er, Mary J. I, 252
er, Mary J. I, 255
er, Mary Jane I, 222
er, Mary Jones II, 714
er, Mary K. II, 905
er, Mary Margaret II, 812
er, Mary Margaret II, 905
er, Mary R. II, 905
er, Mary R. VI, 979
er, Mary, Jr. I, 231
er, Mary, Jr. I, 250
er, Mary, Jr. I, 251
Parker, Maryann IV, 258
Parker, Maryann IV, 337
Parker, Maryann IV, 345
Parker, Massey II, 402
Parker, Massey II, 613
Parker, Massey II, 714
Parker, Matilda IV, 249
Parker, Matilda IV, 258
Parker, Matilda IV, 259
Parker, Mattie J. I, 222
Parker, Mattie J. I, 894
Parker, Mattie J. I, 897
Parker, Maude I, 223
Parker, Melancthan IV, 650
Parker, Melanethon IV, 650
Parker, Meribah II, 248
Parker, Micajah I, 222
Parker, Micajah I, 223
Parker, Micajah I, 251
Parker, Micajah I, 254
Parker, Micajah IV, 258
Parker, Micajah IV, 259
Parker, Mildred I, 222
Parker, Mildred I, 239
Parker, Mildred I, 251
Parker, Mildred W. VI, 942
Parker, Milicent I, 66
Parker, Miliscent I, 160
Parker, Milla A. V, 855
Parker, Millicent I, 293
Parker, Millicent I, 303
Parker, Millicent I, 314
Parker, Milly VI, 975
Parker, Milly Anna V, 855
Parker, Minerva Lewis VI, 922
Parker, Miriam I, 241
Parker, Miriam I, 251
Parker, Miriam I, 299
Parker, Miriam I, 314
Parker, Miriam I, 931
Parker, Miriam I, 947
Parker, Miriam C. I, 947
Parker, Moses VI, 891
Parker, Moses VI, 945
Parker, Moses VI, 957
Parker, Moses VI, 974
Parker, Moses VI, 1002
Parker, Nan Francis I, 947
Parker, Nancy I, 160
Parker, Nancy IV, 259
Parker, Nancy Ann VI, 1002
Parker, Nancy Ray I, 222
Parker, Nancy T. IV, 192
Parker, Nancy T. IV, 259
Parker, Nannie E. I, 223
Parker, Nannie E. I, 252
Parker, Nathan I, 15
Parker, Nathan I, 49
Parker, Nathan I, 66
Parker, Nathan I, 160
Parker, Nathan I, 221
Parker, Nathan I, 222
Parker, Nathan I, 223
Parker, Nathan I, 248
Parker, Nathan I, 250
Parker, Nathan I, 251
Parker, Nathan I, 293
Parker, Nathan I, 314
Parker, Nathan I, 1071
Parker, Nathan IV, 52
Parker, Nathan IV, 192
Parker, Nathan IV, 258
Parker, Nathan IV, 259
Parker, Nathan IV, 425
Parker, Nathan IV, 1288
Parker, Nathaniel VI, 968
Parker, Nathaniel VI, 974
Parker, Nicholas VI, 542
Parker, Noah IV, 1288
Parker, Nora I, 252
Parker, Nora Ann I, 223
Parker, Nora Ann I, 252
Parker, Norman I, 223
Parker, Norman I, 252
Parker, Oliver IV, 259
Parker, Orpah P. II, 905
Parker, Orpha Pratt II, 812
Parker, Osborn I, 222
Parker, Patience I, 242
Parker, Patience I, 250
Parker, Patience I, 314
Parker, Patience I, 613
Parker, Patience VI, 922
Parker, Patsey I, 293
Parker, Paul E. IV, 1219
Parker, Paul, Jr. IV, 1219
Parker, Pearl V, 522
Parker, Penelope I, 15
Parker, Penelope I, 21
Parker, Penelope I, 67
Parker, Penelope VI, 89
Parker, Penina I, 186
Parker, Peninah I, 66
Parker, Peninah I, 113
Parker, Peninah I, 198
Parker, Peninah I, 199
Parker, Peninah I, 222
Parker, Peninah I, 230
Parker, Peninah I, 250
Parker, Peninah I, 307
Parker, Peninah I, 314
Parker, Peninah IV, 258
Parker, Penninah I, 1068
Parker, Peter I, 66
Parker, Peter II, 279
Parker, Peter II, 298
Parker, Peter II, 402
Parker, Peter III, 247
Parker, Phebe II, 714
Parker, Phebe IV, 259
Parker, Phebe IV, 339
Parker, Phebe IV, 1375
Parker, Phebe V, 424
Parker, Phebe V, 952
Parker, Phebe V, 957
Parker, Phebe Ann III, 247
Parker, Phebe May I, 223
Parker, Pheraby I, 66
Parker, Philena IV, 259
Parker, Philip IV, 1332
Parker, Philip B. IV, 1332
Parker, Philip Draper IV, 259
Parker, Philip Draper IV, 425
Parker, Philip W. IV, 1332
Parker, Phinehas I, 293
Parker, Phinehas I, 301
Parker, Phinehas I, 314
Parker, Piety I, 293
Parker, Piety I, 294
Parker, Piety I, 306
Parker, Piety I, 314
Parker, Polley VI, 937
Parker, Polly VI, 974
Parker, Priscilla I, 251
Parker, Priscilla I, 257
Parker, Priscilla II, 471
Parker, Priscilla II, 613
Parker, Rachel I, 197
Parker, Rachel I, 199
Parker, Rachel I, 223
Parker, Rachel I, 250
Parker, Rachel I, 261
Parker, Rachel IV, 259
Parker, Rachel IV, 337
Parker, Rachel IV, 425
Parker, Rachel IV, 543
Parker, Rachel IV, 724
Parker, Rachel IV, 828
Parker, Rachel IV, 836
Parker, Rachel IV, 1108
Parker, Rachel IV, 1117
Parker, Rachel V, 855
Parker, Rachel VI, 481
Parker, Rachel A. IV, 425
Parker, Rachel Ann IV, 425
Parker, Rachel Ann IV, 1108
Parker, Rachel Ann IV, 1130
Parker, Rachel Ann IV, 1137
Parker, Ralph I, 15
Parker, Rebecah I, 251
Parker, Rebecca I, 222
Parker, Rebecca I, 223
Parker, Rebecca I, 233
Parker, Rebecca I, 251
Parker, Rebecca II, 540
Parker, Rebecca II, 613
Parker, Rebecca IV, 258
Parker, Rebecca IV, 259
Parker, Rebecca IV, 1108
Parker, Rebecca IV, 1288
Parker, Rebecca V, 702
Parker, Rebecca V, 707
Parker, Rebecca V, 855
Parker, Rebecca Andleton I, 222
Parker, Rebecca J. V, 702
Parker, Rebecca Jane V, 702
Parker, Rebecca V. V, 957
Parker, Rebeccah I, 314
Parker, Rebeckah I, 149
Parker, Rebekah I, 230
Parker, Rebekah I, 251
Parker, Rebekah VI, 635
Parker, Rebekah VI, 649
Parker, Rebekah VI, 658
Parker, Rebekah VI, 660
Parker, Rebekah VI, 687
Parker, Rebekah VI, 690
Parker, Reuben VI, 974
Parker, Reuben VI, 975
Parker, Reuben VI, 1018
Parker, Rhoda I, 222
Parker, Rhoda I, 237
Parker, Rhoda I, 250
Parker, Rhoda I, 251
Parker, Rhoda IV, 186
Parker, Rhoda IV, 258
Parker, Rhoda IV, 259
Parker, Rhoda IV, 425
Parker, Rhoda IV, 1108
Parker, Rhoda VI, 975
Parker, Rhoda D. IV, 425
Parker, Rhoda D. IV, 543
Parker, Rhoda D. IV, 1108
Parker, Richard I, 223
Parker, Richard I, 251
Parker, Richard II, 402
Parker, Richard II, 527
Parker, Richard II, 540
Parker, Richard II, 586
Parker, Richard II, 613
Parker, Richard II, 664
Parker, Richard II, 677
Parker, Richard II, 714
Parker, Robert I, 22
Parker, Robert I, 223
Parker, Robert I, 931
Parker, Robert Blair I, 947
Parker, Rosabel I, 252
Parker, Rosabell I, 223
Parker, Ruth I, 49
Parker, Ruth I, 66
Parker, Ruth I, 186
Parker, Ruth I, 190
Parker, Ruth I, 199
Parker, Ruth I, 223
Parker, Ruth E. IV, 1332
Parker, Ruth Edna IV, 1332
Parker, Ruth Eva I, 223
Parker, Ruth Eva I, 225
Parker, Ruth Eva I, 255
Parker, Ruth Louise III, 247
Parker, Sally I, 293
Parker, Sally VI, 918
Parker, Sally VI, 974
Parker, Sally VI, 975
Parker, Sally Ann VI, 975
Parker, Samuel I, 222
Parker, Samuel I, 223
Parker, Samuel I, 230
Parker, Samuel I, 250
Parker, Samuel I, 251
Parker, Samuel II, 154
Parker, Samuel II, 402
Parker, Samuel II, 613
Parker, Samuel II, 714
Parker, Samuel II, 905
Parker, Samuel V, 301
Parker, Samuel V, 454
Parker, Samuel V, 462
Parker, Samuel VI, 542
Parker, Samuel VI, 687
Parker, Samuel O. V, 462
Parker, Sarah I, 49
Parker, Sarah I, 66
Parker, Sarah I, 113
Parker, Sarah I, 160
Parker, Sarah I, 186
Parker, Sarah I, 195
Parker, Sarah I, 199
Parker, Sarah I, 222
Parker, Sarah I, 223
Parker, Sarah I, 240
Parker, Sarah I, 248
Parker, Sarah I, 250
Parker, Sarah I, 251
Parker, Sarah I, 254
Parker, Sarah I, 314
Parker, Sarah I, 319
Parker, Sarah I, 1068
Parker, Sarah II, 223
Parker, Sarah II, 248
Parker, Sarah II, 257
Parker, Sarah II, 402
Parker, Sarah II, 589
Parker, Sarah II, 613
Parker, Sarah II, 667
Parker, Sarah III, 247
Parker, Sarah IV, 200
Parker, Sarah IV, 223
Parker, Sarah IV, 258
Parker, Sarah IV, 259
Parker, Sarah IV, 396
Parker, Sarah IV, 425
Parker, Sarah IV, 904
Parker, Sarah IV, 1108
Parker, Sarah IV, 1112
Parker, Sarah VI, 78
Parker, Sarah VI, 891
Parker, Sarah VI, 975
Parker, Sarah VI, 979
Parker, Sarah A. VI, 975
Parker, Sarah Ann I, 223
Parker, Sarah Ann I, 251
Parker, Sarah Ann II, 905
Parker, Sarah Ann VI, 1006
Parker, Sarah E. I, 623
Parker, Sarah G. VI, 975
Parker, Sarah I. VI, 78
Parker, Sarah I. VI, 89
Parker, Sarah Isabella I, 15
Parker, Sarah Isabella I, 21
Parker, Sarah Isabella I, 223
Parker, Sarah Isabella I, 251
Parker, Sarah J. I, 15
Parker, Sarah J. I, 32
Parker, Sarah J. I, 67
Parker, Sarah J. I, 89
Parker, Sarah J. I, 232
Parker, Sarah J. I, 252
Parker, Sarah J. I, 896
Parker, Sarah Jane I, 209
Parker, Sarah Jane I, 223
Parker, Sarah M. I, 252
Parker, Sarah Maria I, 221
Parker, Sarah Maria I, 223
Parker, Sarah Rebecca V, 855
Parker, Sarah T. II, 714
Parker, Sarrah IV, 258
Parker, Schooley IV, 1178
Parker, Selah I, 1068
Parker, Seth I, 186
Parker, Seth I, 199
Parker, Seth W. I, 72
Parker, Sidney III, 247
Parker, Silas I, 251
Parker, Silas VI, 542
Parker, Silas VI, 687
Parker, Sophronia I, 237
Parker, Sophronia I, 252
Parker, Sophronia Jane I, 221
Parker, Stanton I, 223
Parker, Stanton J. IV, 259
Parker, Sumner III, 431
Parker, Susan Devilla I, 222
Parker, Susan E. II, 714
Parker, Susan Julia II, 714
Parker, Susanna IV, 543
Parker, Susannah II, 402
Parker, Susannah IV, 259
Parker, Sylvanua T. II, 714
Parker, Sylvanus T. II, 714
Parker, Sylvanus T. II, 758
Parker, Tabitha E. VI, 924
Parker, Tamer II, 1019
Parker, Tamer II, 1020
Parker, Tamur Burges I, 222
Parker, Therin I, 250
Parker, Thomas I, 160
Parker, Thomas I, 223
Parker, Thomas I, 233
Parker, Thomas I, 251
Parker, Thomas I, 293
Parker, Thomas I, 832
Parker, Thomas I, 1068
Parker, Thomas I, 1071
Parker, Thomas II, 402
Parker, Thomas II, 540
Parker, Thomas II, 613
Parker, Thomas II, 647
Parker, Thomas II, 714
Parker, Thomas II, 758
Parker, Thomas IV, 724
Parker, Thomas VI, 930
Parker, Thomas VI, 975
Parker, Thomas C. IV, 258
Parker, Thomas C. IV, 259
Parker, Thomas C. IV, 293
Parker, Thomas C. IV, 425
Parker, Thomas E. I, 252
Parker, Thomas E. IV, 388
Parker, Thomas E. IV, 425
Parker, Thomas L. IV, 259
Parker, Thomas Smith II, 402
Parker, Thomas Smith II, 613
Parker, Thomas W. II, 402
Parker, Thomas, Jr. II, 402
Parker, Thomas, Jr. II, 613
Parker, Thomas, Jr. II, 647
Parker, Thomas, Jr. II, 758
Parker, Thomas, Jr. II, 812
Parker, Thompson II, 402
Parker, Thompson II, 613
Parker, Thos. II, 392
Parker, Thos. II, 714
Parker, Thos. II, 812
Parker, Thos. II, 905
Parker, Thos. II, 913
Parker, Thos. IV, 337
Parker, Thos. C. IV, 448
Parker, Thos., Jr. II, 905
Parker, Thos., Sr. II, 812
Parker, Timothy IV, 425
Parker, Tyler William III, 247
Parker, Valentine III, 431

Parker, Viney VI, 974
Parker, Vivean I, 618
Parker, Vivian I, 623
Parker, Vivian I, 638
Parker, Vivian I, 639
Parker, Vivian Herbert I, 623
Parker, Vivian Herbert I, 931
Parker, Vivian J. I, 634
Parker, Vivian J. I, 638
Parker, Vivian J. I, 947
Parker, Vivian Jordan I, 15
Parker, Vivian Jordan I, 896
Parker, Vivian Jordan I, 931
Parker, W. Raleigh I, 210
Parker, Walter F. V, 462
Parker, Walter J. I, 223
Parker, Walter Jay I, 222
Parker, Wd. Margaret II, 180
Parker, Wd. Priscilla II, 586
Parker, Wd. Rachel VI, 542
Parker, Wiatt I, 730
Parker, Widow Dianna I, 270
Parker, Widow Martha R. I, 82
Parker, Widow Mary I, 70
Parker, William I, 223
Parker, William I, 251
Parker, William I, 293
Parker, William I, 314
Parker, William I, 315
Parker, William I, 730
Parker, William II, 208
Parker, William II, 248
Parker, William II, 402
Parker, William II, 403
Parker, William IV, 155
Parker, William IV, 259
Parker, William IV, 425
Parker, William IV, 650
Parker, William V, 269
Parker, William V, 522
Parker, William VI, 845
Parker, William E. I, 225
Parker, William Edgar I, 222
Parker, William Edgar I, 223
Parker, William Edgar I, 252
Parker, William Edgar I, 255
Parker, William J. I, 252
Parker, William J. IV, 259
Parker, William J. IV, 391
Parker, William J. IV, 425
Parker, William J. IV, 650
Parker, William J. IV, 905
Parker, William J. IV, 912
Parker, William Joseph I, 221
Parker, William L. VI, 975
Parker, William L. VI, 979
Parker, William L. VI, 1008
Parker, William T. I, 67
Parker, William T. I, 565
Parker, William T. I, 947
Parker, William T. IV, 260
Parker, William Thomas I, 15
Parker, William Thomas I, 931
Parker, William W. II, 402
Parker, Willis R. V, 855
Parker, Willits II, 714
Parker, Wilson I, 66
Parker, Wilson I, 160
Parker, Wm. II, 531
Parker, Wm. II, 613
Parker, Wm. II, 614
Parker, Wm. II, 758
Parker, Wm. IV, 339
Parker, Wm. IV, 650
Parker, Wm. V, 462
Parker, Wm. V, 952
Parker, Wm. V, 957
Parker, Wm. Darwin IV, 258
Parker, Wm. Henry II, 812
Parker, Wm. W. II, 714
Parker, Wm. W. II, 758
Parker, Wyatt I, 686
Parker, Wyatt A. I, 730
Parker, Zachariah I, 149
Parker, Zachariah VI, 975
Parker, Zerusah I, 241
Parker, Zerusah I, 250
Parker, Zilpha I, 314
Parker, Zilpha, Sr. I, 314
Parkerson, Phebe IV, 1359
Parkerson, Phebe IV, 1375
Parkerson, Sarah IV, 1359
Parkerson, Sarah IV, 1375
Parkings, Hannah VI, 605
Parkins, Abigail VI, 402
Parkins, Abigail VI, 428
Parkins, Abigail VI, 506
Parkins, Abigail VI, 507
Parkins, Abigail VI, 542
Parkins, Abigail VI, 568
Parkins, Abigail VI, 578
Parkins, Abigail VI, 654
Parkins, Abigail VI, 719
Parkins, Alfred VI, 468
Parkins, Alfred VI, 542
Parkins, Alfred VI, 591
Parkins, Alfred VI, 729
Parkins, Amy VI, 428
Parkins, Ann IV, 543
Parkins, Anne IV, 155
Parkins, Charles I, 1036
Parkins, Charles VI, 423
Parkins, Charles VI, 428
Parkins, David IV, 155
Parkins, David IV, 543
Parkins, David IV, 1108
Parkins, David VI, 428
Parkins, David VI, 602
Parkins, David, Jr. IV, 1108
Parkins, Ebenezer VI, 428
Parkins, Eliza IV, 543
Parkins, Elizabeth I, 1034
Parkins, Elizabeth I, 1036
Parkins, Elizabeth I, 1145
Parkins, Elizabeth IV, 155
Parkins, Elizabeth VI, 428
Parkins, Elizabeth VI, 443
Parkins, Elizabeth VI, 459
Parkins, Elizabeth VI, 601
Parkins, Elizabeth VI, 602
Parkins, Hannah IV, 155
Parkins, Hannah IV, 562
Parkins, Hannah IV, 1178
Parkins, Hannah VI, 419
Parkins, Hannah VI, 428
Parkins, Hannah VI, 469
Parkins, Hannah VI, 529
Parkins, Hannah VI, 602
Parkins, Hannah VI, 674
Parkins, Henry VI, 428
Parkins, Henry VI, 542
Parkins, Isaac IV, 155
Parkins, Isaac IV, 543
Parkins, Isaac IV, 548
Parkins, Isaac IV, 562
Parkins, Isaac IV, 1178
Parkins, Isaac VI, 402
Parkins, Isaac VI, 414
Parkins, Isaac VI, 419
Parkins, Isaac VI, 428
Parkins, Isaac VI, 480
Parkins, Isaac VI, 507
Parkins, Isaac VI, 527
Parkins, Isaac VI, 542
Parkins, Isaac VI, 592
Parkins, Isaac VI, 595
Parkins, Isaac VI, 602
Parkins, Isaac VI, 729
Parkins, Isaac VI, 761
Parkins, Isaac VI, 769
Parkins, Isaac J. VI, 428
Parkins, Isaac, Jr. VI, 428
Parkins, Jacob IV, 543
Parkins, Jacob IV, 1108
Parkins, James IV, 543
Parkins, Jane IV, 155
Parkins, Jane IV, 522
Parkins, Jane IV, 543
Parkins, Jane IV, 562
Parkins, Jane IV, 1178
Parkins, Jane VI, 370
Parkins, Jane VI, 428
Parkins, Jane VI, 602
Parkins, Jemima I, 1034
Parkins, Jemima I, 1036
Parkins, Jesse IV, 543
Parkins, Jesse IV, 562
Parkins, Jesse IV, 1178
Parkins, Jesse IV, 1219
Parkins, John IV, 543
Parkins, John IV, 1108
Parkins, John VI, 428
Parkins, John VI, 602
Parkins, Jonathan IV, 155
Parkins, Jonathan IV, 543
Parkins, Jonathan IV, 1108
Parkins, Jonathan VI, 370
Parkins, Jonathan VI, 427
Parkins, Jonathan VI, 428
Parkins, Jonathan VI, 443
Parkins, Jonathan VI, 459
Parkins, Jonathan VI, 602
Parkins, Jonathan, Jr. VI, 428
Parkins, Jonathan, Jr. VI, 602
Parkins, Joseph IV, 260
Parkins, Joseph VI, 467
Parkins, Joseph VI, 468
Parkins, Joseph VI, 569
Parkins, Joseph VI, 592
Parkins, Joseph VI, 602
Parkins, Joseph VI, 729
Parkins, Joseph VI, 769
Parkins, Joseph VI, 771
Parkins, Levi IV, 543
Parkins, Levi IV, 1108
Parkins, Louisa IV, 543
Parkins, Louisa IV, 1178
Parkins, Lucinda IV, 543
Parkins, Lucinda IV, 1108
Parkins, Luis IV, 562
Parkins, Lydia IV, 155
Parkins, Lydia IV, 526
Parkins, Lydia IV, 543
Parkins, Lydia IV, 1108
Parkins, Lydia IV, 1178
Parkins, Lydia VI, 414
Parkins, Lydia VI, 428
Parkins, Lydia VI, 761
Parkins, Lydia VI, 769
Parkins, Margaret A. VI, 392
Parkins, Margaret A. VI, 428
Parkins, Margaret A. VI, 495
Parkins, Margaret A. VI, 542
Parkins, Maria VI, 542
Parkins, Maria VI, 729
Parkins, Maria VI, 769
Parkins, Maria VI, 771
Parkins, Mariah VI, 468
Parkins, Martha VI, 592
Parkins, Mary IV, 543
Parkins, Mary IV, 1103
Parkins, Mary IV, 1108
Parkins, Mary IV, 1178
Parkins, Mary VI, 402
Parkins, Mary VI, 414
Parkins, Mary VI, 419
Parkins, Mary VI, 428
Parkins, Mary VI, 443
Parkins, Mary VI, 480
Parkins, Mary VI, 507
Parkins, Mary VI, 527
Parkins, Mary VI, 542
Parkins, Mary VI, 602
Parkins, Mary VI, 729
Parkins, Mary VI, 761
Parkins, Mary VI, 769
Parkins, Mary, Jr. VI, 428
Parkins, Miriam VI, 392
Parkins, Mishael IV, 543
Parkins, Nancy IV, 543
Parkins, Nancy IV, 548
Parkins, Nancy IV, 562
Parkins, Nancy IV, 1178
Parkins, Nathan IV, 155
Parkins, Nathan VI, 392
Parkins, Nathan VI, 428
Parkins, Nathan VI, 495
Parkins, Nathan VI, 542
Parkins, Nathan VI, 602
Parkins, Patience I, 1036
Parkins, Patience VI, 423
Parkins, Patience VI, 428
Parkins, Phebe IV, 541
Parkins, Phebe IV, 543
Parkins, Phebe VI, 428
Parkins, Phebe VI, 459
Parkins, Phebe VI, 561
Parkins, Phebe VI, 586
Parkins, Phebe VI, 702
Parkins, Rachel IV, 543
Parkins, Rachel IV, 1108
Parkins, Rachel VI, 428
Parkins, Rachel VI, 601
Parkins, Rachel VI, 602
Parkins, Rebecca IV, 514
Parkins, Rebecca IV, 543
Parkins, Ruth VI, 375
Parkins, Ruth VI, 428
Parkins, Ruth VI, 480
Parkins, Ruth VI, 542
Parkins, Samuel VI, 428
Parkins, Sarah IV, 543
Parkins, Sarah IV, 562
Parkins, Sarah IV, 1178
Parkins, Sarah IV, 1183
Parkins, Sarah IV, 1219
Parkins, Sarah VI, 468
Parkins, Sarah VI, 729
Parkins, Sarah Elizabeth VI, 392
Parkins, Sarah Elizabeth VI, 428
Parkins, Sarah H. VI, 542
Parkins, Sarah H. VI, 569
Parkins, Sarah J. IV, 543
Parkins, Sarah J. IV, 1108
Parkins, Sarah Jane IV, 1108
Parkins, Schooley IV, 1178
Parkins, Sidney VI, 428
Parkins, Stephen IV, 155
Parkins, Stephen IV, 543
Parkins, Stephen VI, 428
Parkins, Stephen VI, 602
Parkins, Susannah VI, 542
Parkins, Susannah VI, 569
Parkins, Susannah VI, 592
Parkins, Susannah VI, 602
Parkins, Susannah VI, 769
Parkins, Susannah VI, 771
Parkins, Sydney VI, 392
Parkins, Sydney VI, 495
Parkins, Sydney VI, 542
Parkins, Tacie IV, 541
Parkins, Tacie IV, 543
Parkins, Tacy IV, 543
Parkins, Thomas VI, 428
Parkins, Wd. Susannah VI, 467
Parkins, Widow Lydia VI, 527
Parkins, William IV, 260
Parkinson, Eugenia III, 256
Parkinson, Fanny V, 1013
Parkinson, Joseph V, 638
Parkinson, Joseph V, 1013
Parkinson, Sarah II, 494
Parkinson, Sarah II, 614
Parks, Aaron I, 314
Parks, Addie I, 314
Parks, Altheann IV, 1369
Parks, Altheann IV, 1375
Parks, Arzilla I, 314
Parks, Asenath IV, 748
Parks, Benjamin VI, 975
Parks, Berry I, 314
Parks, Berry Ann I, 314
Parks, Bertha Elizabeth IV, 984
Parks, Bessie L. IV, 748
Parks, Bettie I, 314
Parks, Clem IV, 748
Parks, David IV, 748
Parks, Duncan IV, 984
Parks, Earl VI, 372
Parks, Edwin I, 314
Parks, Elisabeth I, 54
Parks, Elisabeth I, 66
Parks, Elizabeth I, 314
Parks, Elizabeth IV, 1219
Parks, Emma III, 499
Parks, Ethel V, 759
Parks, Fannie A. I, 314
Parks, Foster II, 403
Parks, Henry Isaac IV, 491
Parks, Hepsee I, 314
Parks, J. B. I, 314
Parks, James I, 314
Parks, John L. IV, 748
Parks, John W. IV, 491
Parks, John Wm. IV, 491
Parks, Joseph B. I, 314
Parks, Lincoln S. IV, 748
Parks, Lizzie I, 314
Parks, Lucy IV, 748
Parks, Margaret II, 480
Parks, Margaret II, 613
Parks, Marguerite Ford IV, 491
Parks, Mariah A. IV, 491
Parks, Marietta IV, 1219
Parks, Martha IV, 748
Parks, Martha E. IV, 748
Parks, Mary II, 403
Parks, Mary IV, 748
Parks, Mary IV, 984
Parks, Mary E. I, 314
Parks, Mary Emaline I, 1160
Parks, Mary Etta IV, 1219
Parks, Mary Ida IV, 748
Parks, Mary Margaret IV, 491
Parks, Mary Williaman IV, 748
Parks, Pamelia VI, 975
Parks, Pauline May IV, 491
Parks, Phillis Jane IV, 491
Parks, Rachel Ann IV, 1130
Parks, Rachel Ann IV, 1137
Parks, Ray I, 639
Parks, Richard II, 481
Parks, Richard II, 613
Parks, Ruth E. VI, 372
Parks, Sallie I, 314
Parks, Samuel I, 54
Parks, Samuel I, 66
Parks, Sarah I, 484
Parks, Susanna II, 612
Parks, Susanna II, 613
Parks, Susannah II, 481
Parks, Sylvester IV, 1219
Parks, Sylvester G. IV, 1219
Parks, Virlinche VI, 975
Parks, Widower Richard II, 612
Parks, William G. IV, 491
Parks, William H. VI, 975
Parks, William W. IV, 491
Parks, Wm. IV, 491
Parks, Wm. K. IV, 748
Parlet, Emma IV, 260
Parlet, William II, 967
Parlett, David V, 108
Parlett, Harry IV, 260
Parlett, Jesse V, 108
Parlett, Mary V, 108
Parlett, Rusell V, 108
Parlett, Samuel S. IV, 260
Parlette, David V, 108
Parlette, David E. V, 522
Parlette, Jesse V, 108
Parlette, Mary V, 108
Parlette, Rusell V, 108
Parlot, Elizabeth II, 967
Parlot, William II, 967
Parlot, William C. V, 522
Parlott, David E. V, 522
Parlott, Elizabeth V, 522
Parlott, Emma IV, 260
Parlott, Frances C. V, 522
Parlott, Harry IV, 260
Parlott, Jemima V, 638
Parlott, Margaret Jane V, 638
Parlott, Samuel S. IV, 260
Parlott, Sarah E. V, 522
Parlott, William C. V, 522
Parmenter, Albert IV, 1288
Parmenter, Albert O. IV, 1288
Parmenter, Bessie V. IV, 1288
Parmenter, Carrie IV, 1288
Parmenter, Mary V, 1013
Parmenter, Wat IV, 1332
Parmenter, Watt IV, 1332
Parmer, Mareb VI, 686
Parmer, Mareb VI, 698
Parmer, Randal IV, 1375
Parmer, Sarah II, 1020
Parmer, Sarah II, 1033
Parmore, Pledge VI, 975
Parmore, Sally VI, 975
Parnel, Elizabeth I, 1022
Parnel, Elizabeth I, 1060
Parnel, Elizabeth I, 1062
Parnel, Esther I, 1022
Parnel, Esther I, 1035
Parnel, Esther I, 1038
Parnel, Esther I Sup 1, 11
Parnel, Esther IV, 52
Parnel, George I, 1022
Parnel, George IV, 52
Parnel, Hester V, 112
Parnel, James I, 1022
Parnel, James I, 1035
Parnel, James I, 1038
Parnel, James I Sup 1, 11
Parnel, James IV, 52
Parnel, James V, 196
Parnel, John I, 1022
Parnel, Ruth IV, 52
Parnell, Amos V, 196
Parnell, Benjamin V, 176
Parnell, Esther I, 1053
Parnell, Esther V, 77
Parnell, Esther V, 196
Parnell, George V, 196
Parnell, Hannah V, 175
Parnell, Hannah V, 196
Parnell, Hester V, 108
Parnell, James I, 1057
Parnell, James V, 77
Parnell, James V, 175
Parnell, James V, 176
Parnell, James V, 196
Parnell, John V, 196
Parnell, Jonathan V, 196
Parnell, Margaret V, 175
Parnell, Margaret V, 196
Parnell, Margret I, 1057
Parnell, Mary II, 248
Parnell, Mary II, 275
Parnell, Mary V, 196
Parnell, Phamy V, 176
Parnell, Phebe V, 196
Parnell, Ruth V, 196
Parnell, Sarah V, 77
Parnell, Sarah V, 108
Parnell, Sarah V, 176
Parnerl, George V, 108
Parnerl, James V, 108
Parpham, Ida V, 1013
Parphan, Ida V, 1013
Parr, ??? VI, 78
Parr, Alfred V, 269
Parr, Andrew F. V, 269
Parr, Ann II, 403
Parr, Ann II, 614
Parr, Anna II, 403
Parr, Anthony VI, 57
Parr, Elizabeth II, 403
Parr, Elizabeth II, 540
Parr, Elizabeth II, 614
Parr, Elizabeth II, 696
Parr, Elizabeth VI, 201
Parr, James II, 403
Parr, Joseph II, 614

-rr, Joshua II, 403
-rr, Liddia II, 403
-rr, Lucinda A. V, 269
-rr, Lydia II, 446
-rr, Mary V, 269
-rr, Nancy V, 1013
-rr, Nathaniel II, 403
-rr, Nathaniel II, 614
-rr, Nathaniel II, 696
-rr, Richard VI, 57
-rr, Samuel II, 403
-rr, Samuel II, 446
-rr, Spencer V, 269
-rr, Susanna VI, 542
-rr, Thomas VI, 201
-rr, William II, 403
-rr, William VI, 57
-rr, William VI, 201
-rr, Wm. II, 614
-rr, Wm. II, 696
-rr, Wm. V, 1013
-arrall, Hugh VI, 357
-arram, Benajah V, 108
-arram, Delila V, 108
-arram, Elizabeth V, 108
-arram, Peter V, 108
-arram, Zaheus V, 108
-arren, Bertha V, 425
-arren, Elias V, 425
-arren, George V, 424
-arren, George V, 425
-arren, John H. V, 425
-arren, Melvin V, 425
-arren, Sarah V, 425
-arrett, Cora Bell V, 269
-arrett, Elmer V, 269
-arrett, George V, 269
-arrett, Huldah V, 269
-arrett, Mary Ann I, 413
-arrett, Silas V, 269
-arrin, Adelbert IV, 1219
-arris, Betsy A. VI, 943
-arris, Frances VI, 919
-arris, Gabriel II, 614
-arris, Jemima VI, 845
-arris, John VI, 845
-arris, Zedekiah VI, 919
Parrish, Abigail II, 466
Parrish, Abigail II, 614
Parrish, Abraham II, 403
Parrish, Abraham Mitchell II, 403
Parrish, Aletha I, 627
Parrish, Alexander VI, 993
Parrish, Alfred II, 813
Parrish, Alfred II, 906
Parrish, Alice I, 614
Parrish, Alice I, 931
Parrish, Alice M. II, 812
Parrish, Alice M. II, 906
Parrish, Ann II, 180
Parrish, Ann II, 403
Parrish, Ann II, 614
Parrish, Ann II, 689
Parrish, Ann Cox II, 298
Parrish, Ann Cox II, 312
Parrish, Ann Cox II, 323
Parrish, Ann Cox II, 758
Parrish, Ann Cox II, 813
Parrish, Ann Cox II, 905
Parrish, Ann Richardson II, 812
Parrish, Anna I, 897
Parrish, Anna II, 403
Parrish, Anna II, 813
Parrish, Anna II, 879
Parrish, Anna II, 906
Parrish, Anna M. II, 813
Parrish, Anna M. II, 906
Parrish, Avery I, 565
Parrish, Avery I, 931
Parrish, C. G. I, 947
Parrish, Caleb Gaskill II, 312
Parrish, Caleb Gaskill II, 323
Parrish, Carolina G. I, 947
Parrish, Caroline II, 323
Parrish, Caroline G. I, 947
Parrish, Caroline L. II, 312
Parrish, Caroline L. III, 247
Parrish, Charles II, 312
Parrish, Charles II, 323
Parrish, Charles II, 614
Parrish, Charles II, 906
Parrish, Charles VI, 769
Parrish, Chas. II, 812
Parrish, Clemens II, 906
Parrish, Clemmons II, 812
Parrish, Clemmons II, 906
Parrish, Clemmons III, 247
Parrish, Clemmons III, 257
Parrish, Deborah II, 403
Parrish, Deborah II, 614
Parrish, Deborah II, 694
Parrish, Dillwyn II, 403
Parrish, Dillwyn II, 758
Parrish, Dillwyn II, 812
Parrish, Dillwyn II, 813
Parrish, Dillwyn II, 905
Parrish, Dillwyn II, 926
Parrish, Dillwyn II, 929
Parrish, Dillwyn, Jr. II, 813
Parrish, Dillwynn, Jr. II, 906
Parrish, Dr. ??? II, 174
Parrish, Dr. Edward III, 123
Parrish, Dr. Joseph II, 812
Parrish, Dr. Matthew III, 457
Parrish, Edward II, 403
Parrish, Edward II, 758
Parrish, Edward II, 812
Parrish, Edward II, 813
Parrish, Edward II, 846
Parrish, Edward II, 861
Parrish, Edward II, 879
Parrish, Edward II, 905
Parrish, Edward II, 906
Parrish, Edward III, 112
Parrish, Edward III, 247
Parrish, Edward, Jr. II, 812
Parrish, Edward, Jr. III, 247
Parrish, Eleanor Douglas VI, 734
Parrish, Eleanor Douglas VI, 769
Parrish, Elizabeth II, 312
Parrish, Elizabeth II, 403
Parrish, Elizabeth II, 522
Parrish, Elizabeth II, 614
Parrish, Elizabeth II, 621
Parrish, Elizabeth II, 794
Parrish, Elizabeth II, 812
Parrish, Elizabeth II, 905
Parrish, Elizabeth A. II, 905
Parrish, Elizabeth A. II, 929
Parrish, Elizabeth Archer II, 812
Parrish, Elizabeth B. II, 906
Parrish, Elizabeth H. II, 906
Parrish, Elizabeth Hunt II, 812
Parrish, Elizabeth Longstreth II, 812
Parrish, Elizabeth M. II, 756
Parrish, Elizabeth M. II, 758
Parrish, Elizabeth W. II, 174
Parrish, Elizabeth W. II, 288
Parrish, Elizabeth W. II, 298
Parrish, Elizabeth W. II, 312
Parrish, Elizabeth W. II, 323
Parrish, Elizabeth W. II, 758
Parrish, Elizabeth W. II, 761
Parrish, Elizabeth W. II, 866
Parrish, Elizabeth W. II, 899
Parrish, Elizabeth W. II, 905
Parrish, Elizabeth W. II, 906
Parrish, Elizabeth W. II, 912
Parrish, Elizabeth Williams II, 812
Parrish, Elizabeth Wright II, 813
Parrish, Emma III, 247
Parrish, Emma III, 257
Parrish, Eugene S. I, 947
Parrish, Fanny II, 813
Parrish, Fanny II, 846
Parrish, Fanny II, 906
Parrish, Frederick II, 812
Parrish, Frederick Maxfield II, 906
Parrish, George II, 403
Parrish, George D. II, 758
Parrish, George D. II, 905
Parrish, George D. II, 906
Parrish, George D. II, 912
Parrish, George Dillwyn II, 812
Parrish, George Dillwyn II, 813
Parrish, George Dillwyn II, 905
Parrish, George Dillwyn, Jr. II, 812
Parrish, Grace Louise III, 123
Parrish, Grizzie Ann I, 639
Parrish, Gussey Ann I, 897
Parrish, Hannah II, 598
Parrish, Hannah II, 614
Parrish, Hannah VI, 769
Parrish, Hannah M. II, 906
Parrish, Hannah M. II, 907
Parrish, Hannah Miller II, 813
Parrish, Helen II, 812
Parrish, Helen II, 906
Parrish, Helen Longstreth II, 812
Parrish, Henry M. V, 1013
Parrish, Herbert I, 931
Parrish, Hetty L. II, 906
Parrish, Hetty Longstreth II, 812
Parrish, Howard II, 813
Parrish, Hugh Roberts II, 812
Parrish, Hugh Roberts II, 906
Parrish, Isaac II, 211
Parrish, Isaac II, 248
Parrish, Isaac II, 403
Parrish, Isaac II, 498
Parrish, Isaac II, 599
Parrish, Isaac II, 614
Parrish, Isaac II, 694
Parrish, Isaac II, 758
Parrish, Isaac II, 812
Parrish, Isaac II, 813
Parrish, Isaac II, 892
Parrish, Isaac II, 905
Parrish, Isaac, Jr. II, 403
Parrish, Isaac, Jr. II, 812
Parrish, Isabel Pelham II, 812
Parrish, J. L. I, 947
Parrish, James II, 614
Parrish, James C. II, 906
Parrish, James Cresson II, 812
Parrish, James L. I, 947
Parrish, James Loten I, 947
Parrish, John I, 639
Parrish, John II, 174
Parrish, John II, 298
Parrish, John II, 312
Parrish, John II, 323
Parrish, John II, 403
Parrish, John II, 466
Parrish, John II, 491
Parrish, John II, 591
Parrish, John II, 599
Parrish, John II, 614
Parrish, John II, 689
Parrish, John II, 758
Parrish, John II, 812
Parrish, John II, 861
Parrish, John II, 866
Parrish, John II, 905
Parrish, John II, 906
Parrish, John B. I, 897
Parrish, John C. II, 323
Parrish, John C. III, 247
Parrish, John Cox II, 312
Parrish, John Cox II, 323
Parrish, John S. I, 897
Parrish, John S. II, 906
Parrish, John W. I, 314
Parrish, John, Jr. II, 323
Parrish, John, Jr. II, 327
Parrish, Joseph II, 180
Parrish, Joseph II, 211
Parrish, Joseph II, 248
Parrish, Joseph II, 288
Parrish, Joseph II, 298
Parrish, Joseph II, 312
Parrish, Joseph II, 323
Parrish, Joseph II, 403
Parrish, Joseph II, 614
Parrish, Joseph II, 714
Parrish, Joseph II, 758
Parrish, Joseph II, 812
Parrish, Joseph II, 813
Parrish, Joseph II, 866
Parrish, Joseph II, 879
Parrish, Joseph II, 892
Parrish, Joseph II, 899
Parrish, Joseph II, 905
Parrish, Joseph II, 906
Parrish, Joseph II, 912
Parrish, Joseph II, 929
Parrish, Joseph II, 938
Parrish, Joseph George II, 812
Parrish, Joseph W. II, 813
Parrish, Joseph, Jr. II, 288
Parrish, Joseph, Jr. II, 298
Parrish, Joseph, Jr. II, 758
Parrish, Joseph, Sr. II, 813
Parrish, Joshua Longstreth II, 812
Parrish, Lawrence Thompson VI, 734
Parrish, Lawrence Thompson VI, 769
Parrish, Lellia J. I, 947
Parrish, Lillie Roberta I, 947
Parrish, Louise III, 247
Parrish, Louzeba I, 565
Parrish, Lucy I, 897
Parrish, Lydia II, 174
Parrish, Lydia II, 180
Parrish, Lydia II, 288
Parrish, Lydia II, 298
Parrish, Lydia II, 312
Parrish, Lydia II, 318
Parrish, Lydia II, 323
Parrish, Lydia G. II, 323
Parrish, Lydia W. II, 906
Parrish, Lydia Williams II, 812
Parrish, Margaret II, 861
Parrish, Margaret II, 906
Parrish, Margaret Callender II, 812
Parrish, Margaret S. II, 846
Parrish, Margaret S. II, 879
Parrish, Margaret S. II, 906
Parrish, Margaret S. III, 247
Parrish, Margaret Shreve II, 812
Parrish, Margaret Shreve II, 813
Parrish, Margaret W. II, 312
Parrish, Margaret W. II, 323
Parrish, Margarett W. II, 324
Parrish, Martha VI, 950
Parrish, Mary II, 180
Parrish, Mary II, 403
Parrish, Mary II, 491
Parrish, Mary II, 614
Parrish, Mary II, 689
Parrish, Mary II, 813
Parrish, Mary II, 906
Parrish, Mary II, 925
Parrish, Mary K. II, 861
Parrish, Mary K. II, 906
Parrish, Mary K. III, 112
Parrish, Mary K. III, 247
Parrish, Matthew III, 457
Parrish, Max Algy I, 931
Parrish, Miers Fisher II, 812
Parrish, Minnie Evans I, 947
Parrish, Minnie Melissa I, 947
Parrish, Morris Longstreth II, 812
Parrish, Myrtle I, 947
Parrish, Nance E. I, 947
Parrish, Onslow I, 947
Parrish, Onslow Cassidy I, 931
Parrish, Patience II, 591
Parrish, Patience II, 614
Parrish, Patience II, 808
Parrish, Pearl I, 931
Parrish, Priscilla II, 906
Parrish, Rachel IV, 260
Parrish, Rachel IV, 334
Parrish, Rachel IV, 345
Parrish, Rachel P. II, 906
Parrish, Rachel S. II, 906
Parrish, Richard P. II, 906
Parrish, Richard Price II, 812
Parrish, Roanna I, 927
Parrish, Robert II, 403
Parrish, Robert II, 614
Parrish, Robert II, 689
Parrish, Rosa Myrth I, 947
Parrish, Sallie H. II, 323
Parrish, Sallie H. II, 327
Parrish, Samuel II, 403
Parrish, Samuel II, 813
Parrish, Samuel II, 879
Parrish, Samuel II, 906
Parrish, Samuel Franklin II, 812
Parrish, Samuel Longstreth II, 812
Parrish, Sarah II, 211
Parrish, Sarah II, 248
Parrish, Sarah II, 403
Parrish, Sarah II, 498
Parrish, Sarah II, 599
Parrish, Sarah II, 614
Parrish, Sarah II, 694
Parrish, Sarah II, 758
Parrish, Sarah II, 813
Parrish, Sarah II, 905
Parrish, Sarah II, 906
Parrish, Sarah III, 247
Parrish, Sarah VI, 993
Parrish, Sarah H. II, 312
Parrish, Sarah H. II, 323
Parrish, Sarah H. III, 247
Parrish, Sarah Jane II, 813
Parrish, Sarah L. II, 906
Parrish, Sarah L. II, 912
Parrish, Sarah Longstreth II, 812
Parrish, Sarah R. II, 892
Parrish, Sarah R. II, 905
Parrish, Sarah R., Jr. II, 906
Parrish, Sarah Redwood II, 753
Parrish, Sarah Redwood II, 812
Parrish, Sarah, Jr. II, 498
Parrish, Stephen II, 812
Parrish, Stephen II, 906
Parrish, Sula I, 639
Parrish, Susan II, 298
Parrish, Susan II, 714
Parrish, Susan II, 758
Parrish, Susan D. II, 298
Parrish, Susanna II, 312
Parrish, Susanna II, 403
Parrish, Susanna II, 614
Parrish, Susanna II, 714
Parrish, Susanna II, 758
Parrish, Susannah II, 211
Parrish, Susannah II, 248
Parrish, Susannah II, 288
Parrish, Susannah II, 298
Parrish, Susannah II, 812
Parrish, Susannah II, 813
Parrish, Susannah II, 866
Parrish, Susannah II, 879
Parrish, Susannah II, 892
Parrish, Susannah II, 899
Parrish, Susannah II, 905
Parrish, Susannah II, 906
Parrish, Susannah II, 912
Parrish, Susannah II, 929
Parrish, Susannah II, 938
Parrish, Susannah Dillwyn II, 826
Parrish, Susannah Dillwyn II, 906
Parrish, Susannah Dillwyn II, 938
Parrish, Susannah M. II, 905
Parrish, Thos. C. II, 906
Parrish, Thos. Clarkson II, 812
Parrish, Thos. Clarkson II, 813
Parrish, Thos. Clarkson II, 846
Parrish, Thos. Clarkson II, 906
Parrish, Thos. F. VI, 950
Parrish, Wd. Abigail II, 614
Parrish, William II, 403
Parrish, William Dillwyn II, 403
Parrish, William G. III, 247
Parrish, William Gaskill II, 312
Parrish, William Gaskill II, 323
Parrish, Wm. II, 614
Parrish, Wm. II, 905
Parrish, Wm. D. II, 899
Parrish, Wm. D. II, 905
Parrish, Wm. D. II, 906
Parrish, Wm. D. II, 907
Parrish, Wm. Dillwyn II, 758
Parrish, Wm. Dillwyn II, 813
Parrish, Wm. G. II, 906
Parrish, Wm. Gaskill II, 906
Parrish, Wm. W. II, 906
Parrish, Wm. Wright II, 813
Parrish, Zerviah III, 457
Parrishaw, Ruth I, 1011
Parrock, Elizabeth II, 403
Parrock, Hannah II, 403
Parrock, Ja. II, 403
Parrock, James II, 403
Parrock, James II, 489
Parrock, James II, 517
Parrock, James II, 545
Parrock, James II, 565
Parrock, James II, 614
Parrock, James, Jr. II, 403
Parrock, John II, 403
Parrock, John II, 462
Parrock, John II, 614
Parrock, Liddia II, 403
Parrock, Martha II, 545
Parrock, Martha II, 614
Parrock, Mary II, 462
Parrock, Mary II, 614
Parrock, Priscilla II, 489
Parrock, Priscilla II, 614
Parrock, Sarah II, 403
Parrock, Sarah II, 565
Parrock, Sarah II, 614
Parrock, Wd. Hannah II, 517
Parrot, Elizabeth II, 212
Parrot, Elizabeth II, 248
Parrot, Mary II, 403
Parrott, Agness VI, 801
Parrott, Ann VI, 845
Parrott, Avey VI, 845
Parrott, Elizabeth II, 403
Parrott, Hannah VI, 845
Parrott, James II, 403
Parrott, Jane VI, 845
Parrott, Jesse Smith II, 813
Parrott, John II, 614
Parrott, John VI, 28
Parrott, John VI, 32
Parrott, John VI, 34
Parrott, John VI, 845
Parrott, Julia Ann II, 814
Parrott, Martha II, 403
Parrott, Mary II, 403
Parrott, Mary Smith II, 813
Parrott, Sarah II, 403
Parrott, William J. VI, 845
Parrum, Marry VI, 829
Parrut, Edith V, 1013
Parry, Alice II, 298
Parry, Alice II, 302
Parry, Alice II, 312
Parry, Alice II, 323
Parry, Alice II, 325
Parry, Alice IV, 426
Parry, Alice IV, 590
Parry, Amelia W. III, 247
Parry, Ann II, 614

Parry, Ann II, 615
Parry, Ann II, 616
Parry, Ann Shoemaker II, 248
Parry, Ann Wilson II, 615
Parry, Anna II, 248
Parry, Anna II, 615
Parry, Anna II, 758
Parry, Anna Lutitia IV, 590
Parry, Anne II, 248
Parry, Anne II, 614
Parry, Anne II, 650
Parry, Anne II, 758
Parry, Anne Shoemaker II, 614
Parry, Annie II, 947
Parry, Asa IV, 367
Parry, Asa IV, 426
Parry, Asa IV, 566
Parry, Asa IV, 590
Parry, Asenath IV, 372
Parry, Asenath IV, 399
Parry, Asenath IV, 426
Parry, Asenath IV, 453
Parry, Asenath IV, 590
Parry, Benjamin II, 614
Parry, Benjamin II, 714
Parry, Benjamin II, 758
Parry, Benjamin IV, 590
Parry, Benjamin F. IV, 590
Parry, Catharine II, 615
Parry, Catharine II, 690
Parry, Charles II, 298
Parry, Charles C. III, 69
Parry, Charles C. III, 247
Parry, Clara L. IV, 590
Parry, David IV, 426
Parry, David IV, 525
Parry, David IV, 544
Parry, Deborah IV, 260
Parry, Deborah IV, 313
Parry, Deborah IV, 399
Parry, Deborah IV, 426
Parry, Deborah IV, 453
Parry, Deborah IV, 544
Parry, Deborah B. IV, 260
Parry, Edwin S. II, 312
Parry, Edwin S. II, 323
Parry, Eli IV, 426
Parry, Eli IV, 590
Parry, Elijah II, 248
Parry, Elijah III, 247
Parry, Eliza Jane IV, 426
Parry, Eliza Jane IV, 453
Parry, Elizabeth II, 248
Parry, Elizabeth II, 323
Parry, Elizabeth II, 614
Parry, Elizabeth II, 615
Parry, Elizabeth II, 758
Parry, Elizabeth II, 813
Parry, Elizabeth II, 906
Parry, Elizabeth IV, 367
Parry, Elizabeth IV, 397
Parry, Elizabeth IV, 426
Parry, Elizabeth IV, 429
Parry, Elizabeth IV, 566
Parry, Elizabeth IV, 590
Parry, Elizabeth V, 925
Parry, Elizabeth V, 928
Parry, Elizabeth Shoemaker II, 614
Parry, Ella IV, 570
Parry, Ella IV, 590
Parry, Ella Viola IV, 590
Parry, Ephraim IV, 367
Parry, Ephraim IV, 426
Parry, Ephraim IV, 566
Parry, Ephraim IV, 590
Parry, Geo. V, 925
Parry, Gibbons IV, 260
Parry, Gibbons IV, 313
Parry, Hannah II, 298
Parry, Hannah III, 247
Parry, Hannah IV, 425
Parry, Hannah IV, 426
Parry, Hannah IV, 525
Parry, Hannah IV, 544
Parry, Hannah H. IV, 395
Parry, Harrison III, 247
Parry, Isaac II, 142
Parry, Isaac II, 154
Parry, Isaac II, 553
Parry, Isaac II, 614
Parry, Isaac II, 615
Parry, Isaac II, 758
Parry, Isaac II, 906
Parry, Isaac C. III, 355
Parry, Israel Hallowell II, 813
Parry, Jacob II, 553
Parry, Jacob II, 614
Parry, Jacob II, 615
Parry, Jacob II, 1057
Parry, James C. IV, 260
Parry, Jane II, 614
Parry, Job IV, 372
Parry, Job IV, 399
Parry, Job IV, 426
Parry, Job IV, 453
Parry, Job IV, 544
Parry, Job IV, 590
Parry, Job G. IV, 544
Parry, Job, Jr. IV, 426
Parry, John II, 614
Parry, John II, 813
Parry, John IV, 425
Parry, John IV, 426
Parry, John IV, 543
Parry, John IV, 544
Parry, John IV, 1178
Parry, John S. II, 920
Parry, John Stubbs II, 813
Parry, Johnathan II, 614
Parry, Jonathan II, 614
Parry, Jos. S. III, 356
Parry, Joseph II, 614
Parry, Joseph III, 247
Parry, Joseph S. III, 247
Parry, Joseph S., Jr. III, 247
Parry, Joshua L. II, 813
Parry, Lucy IV, 590
Parry, Lucy B. IV, 590
Parry, Lydia III, 247
Parry, Lydia C. III, 247
Parry, Lydia S. II, 312
Parry, Lydia S. II, 323
Parry, Margaret II, 614
Parry, Margaret II, 813
Parry, Margaret P. II, 1054
Parry, Margaret P. II, 1057
Parry, Maria Willetts III, 247
Parry, Mariam IV, 1121
Parry, Martha II, 614
Parry, Martha II, 615
Parry, Martha II, 806
Parry, Martha II, 813
Parry, Martha H. II, 890
Parry, Martha H. II, 906
Parry, Mary II, 248
Parry, Mary II, 614
Parry, Mary II, 615
Parry, Mary II, 650
Parry, Mary II, 758
Parry, Mary II, 818
Parry, Mary V, 132
Parry, Mary A. II, 312
Parry, Mary A. II, 323
Parry, Mary E. II, 890
Parry, Mary E. II, 906
Parry, Mary Elizabeth II, 806
Parry, Mary Elizabeth II, 813
Parry, Mary Esther IV, 590
Parry, Mary J. IV, 525
Parry, Mary J. IV, 748
Parry, Mary Thompson II, 142
Parry, Mary Thompson II, 154
Parry, Mary, Jr. V, 108
Parry, Mary, Jr. V, 132
Parry, Minnie H. III, 69
Parry, Minnie H. III, 247
Parry, Miriam IV, 1108
Parry, Oliver II, 142
Parry, Oliver II, 154
Parry, Oliver II, 312
Parry, Oliver II, 323
Parry, Oliver II, 615
Parry, Oliver II, 758
Parry, Oliver II, 906
Parry, Parry IV, 260
Parry, Phebe II, 403
Parry, Phebe IV, 367
Parry, Phebe IV, 426
Parry, Philena M. II, 154
Parry, Priscilla II, 615
Parry, Priscilla II, 758
Parry, Priscilla II, 806
Parry, Priscilla II, 813
Parry, Priscilla II, 890
Parry, Priscilla II, 906
Parry, Priscilla II, 920
Parry, Rachel IV, 372
Parry, Rachel IV, 425
Parry, Rachel IV, 426
Parry, Rachel IV, 543
Parry, Rachel IV, 544
Parry, Rachel VI, 470
Parry, Rachel P. II, 920
Parry, Rhevanna IV, 543
Parry, Rhoda V, 925
Parry, Robert II, 91
Parry, Robert II, 122
Parry, Robert II, 248
Parry, Robert II, 1057
Parry, Robert R. III, 356
Parry, Rosella IV, 426
Parry, Rosella IV, 590
Parry, Ruannah IV, 425
Parry, Ruth III, 69
Parry, Ruth III, 247
Parry, Ruth IV, 367
Parry, Ruth IV, 426
Parry, Samuel II, 615
Parry, Samuel II, 758
Parry, Samuel II, 806
Parry, Samuel II, 813
Parry, Samuel II, 890
Parry, Samuel II, 906
Parry, Samuel V, 925
Parry, Samuel, Jr. II, 813
Parry, Sarah II, 403
Parry, Sarah II, 553
Parry, Sarah II, 614
Parry, Sarah II, 615
Parry, Sarah II, 650
Parry, Sarah II, 758
Parry, Sarah II, 782
Parry, Sarah II, 818
Parry, Sarah II, 906
Parry, Sarah III, 355
Parry, Sarah IV, 383
Parry, Sarah IV, 426
Parry, Sarah IV, 544
Parry, Sarah Ann IV, 367
Parry, Sarah Ann IV, 421
Parry, Sarah Ann IV, 426
Parry, Sarah Ann IV, 544
Parry, Sarah Ann IV, 566
Parry, Sarah Ann IV, 590
Parry, Sarah P. III, 356
Parry, Sarah S. II, 615
Parry, Sarah S. II, 758
Parry, Sarah Shoemaker II, 248
Parry, Sarah Shoemaker II, 615
Parry, Sarah Shoemaker II, 758
Parry, Sarahann IV, 426
Parry, Seneca II, 813
Parry, Seneca II, 920
Parry, Tacey III, 247
Parry, Tacey III, 356
Parry, Tacie III, 15
Parry, Tacie III, 431
Parry, Tacie P. III, 355
Parry, Tacie P. III, 471
Parry, Tacy W. III, 247
Parry, Thomas II, 614
Parry, Thomas II, 615
Parry, Thomas II, 758
Parry, Thomas III, 247
Parry, Thomas IV, 426
Parry, Thomas IV, 544
Parry, Thomas Gibbons IV, 260
Parry, Thos. II, 813
Parry, Thos. II, 906
Parry, William II, 312
Parry, William II, 323
Parry, William II, 325
Parry, Wm. P. II, 920
Parshal, Allie V, 462
Parshal, Austie V, 462
Parshal, Ida V, 108
Parshal, Tina V, 462
Parshall, Alphaus IV, 491
Parshall, Alpheus IV, 491
Parshall, Helen V, 108
Parshall, Ida V, 108
Parshall, M. L. V, 108
Parshall, Olive V, 108
Parsins, Hannah V, 957
Parson, Abner IV, 24
Parson, Abner IV, 52
Parson, Abraham IV, 52
Parson, Adeline I, 930
Parson, Agnes IV, 24
Parson, Agness IV, 52
Parson, Alice IV, 491
Parson, Ann II, 615
Parson, Ann IV, 52
Parson, Ann IV, 59
Parson, Ann V, 269
Parson, Chas. IV, 491
Parson, Elizabeth II, 615
Parson, Gainor IV, 491
Parson, Ganah IV, 491
Parson, Ganor IV, 491
Parson, George IV, 260
Parson, Hannah IV, 260
Parson, Isabel I, 526
Parson, Isabel I, 565
Parson, Israel IV, 260
Parson, Jacob V, 269
Parson, Joel IV, 52
Parson, John II, 562
Parson, John II, 634
Parson, Joseph VI, 211
Parson, Joshua IV, 52
Parson, Joshua V, 269
Parson, Juliann IV, 491
Parson, Margaret V, 269
Parson, Mary IV, 260
Parson, Mary IV, 491
Parson, Mary V, 269
Parson, Miriam IV, 52
Parson, Nathan I, 995
Parson, Polly I, 314
Parson, Rachel I, 730
Parson, Rachel IV, 201
Parson, Rachel IV, 260
Parson, Ruth II, 615
Parson, Samuel I, 995
Parson, Samuel Jairus V, 269
Parson, Samuel James V, 269
Parson, Sarah V, 297
Parson, Sarah V, 308
Parson, Susanna IV, 491
Parson, Vincent IV, 52
Parson, William I, 995
Parson, William IV, 491
Parson, William V, 269
Parson, Wm. II, 615
Parsons, Agnes I, 931
Parsons, Agnes I, 945
Parsons, Agnes I, 947
Parsons, Alice IV, 492
Parsons, Amos IV, 463
Parsons, Amos IV, 492
Parsons, Ann II, 615
Parsons, Ann II, 625
Parsons, Anna III, 248
Parsons, Anna III, 383
Parsons, Anne II, 180
Parsons, Asenath I, 565
Parsons, Asenath I, 575
Parsons, Augustus Taber III, 248
Parsons, Benjamin IV, 426
Parsons, Benjamin Johnson Crew VI, 262
Parsons, Benjamin L. IV, 426
Parsons, Bennett VI, 913
Parsons, Bennett VI, 975
Parsons, Bennett VI, 984
Parsons, Betsey VI, 975
Parsons, Catharine B. III, 248
Parsons, Daniel VI, 923
Parsons, David H. I, 947
Parsons, David H., Jr. I, 947
Parsons, David Henry I, 931
Parsons, David Henry, Jr. I, 931
Parsons, Doris Novene IV, 748
Parsons, Edith Augusta III, 248
Parsons, Edw. W. III, 248
Parsons, Edward H. III, 308
Parsons, Edward W. III, 248
Parsons, Edward Willis III, 248
Parsons, Eliza III, 74
Parsons, Eliza III, 248
Parsons, Eliza F. III, 248
Parsons, Eliza T. III, 248
Parsons, Elizabeth II, 446
Parsons, Elizabeth II, 615
Parsons, Elizabeth II, 1056
Parsons, Elizabeth II, 1057
Parsons, Elizabeth III, 59
Parsons, Elizabeth III, 248
Parsons, Elizabeth IV, 567
Parsons, Elizabeth IV, 572
Parsons, Elizabeth IV, 590
Parsons, Elizabeth VI, 191
Parsons, Elizabeth VI, 201
Parsons, Elizabeth VI, 202
Parsons, Elizabeth F. III, 248
Parsons, Elizabeth M. VI, 166
Parsons, Elizabeth M. VI, 201
Parsons, Elizabeth M. VI, 262
Parsons, Elizabeth T. VI, 202
Parsons, Elizabeth Tucker VI, 262
Parsons, Ellwood II, 958
Parsons, Elvira I, 686
Parsons, Elvira I, 690
Parsons, Emaline II, 1057
Parsons, Emeline II, 966
Parsons, Emeline P. II, 966
Parsons, Emily III, 167
Parsons, Emily III, 248
Parsons, Emily L. III, 248
Parsons, Fanny VI, 975
Parsons, Florence II, 615
Parsons, Floyd IV, 748
Parsons, Floyd Wesley IV, 748
Parsons, Gayner IV, 1070
Parsons, Gaynor IV, 463
Parsons, Gaynor IV, 492
Parsons, Gaynor IV, 1070
Parsons, George III, 248
Parsons, George IV, 519
Parsons, George IV, 544
Parsons, George IV, 562
Parsons, George H. III, 248
Parsons, Hannah II, 977
Parsons, Hannah II, 1020
Parsons, Hannah IV, 519
Parsons, Hannah IV, 544
Parsons, Hannah IV, 560
Parsons, Hannah IV, 562
Parsons, Harry IV, 748
Parsons, Helen Mary III, 248
Parsons, Hugh II, 403
Parsons, Hugh II, 615
Parsons, Isaac II, 966
Parsons, Isaac IV, 544
Parsons, Isabel I, 565
Parsons, Israel IV, 519
Parsons, Israel IV, 544
Parsons, Israel IV, 562
Parsons, Jabez IV, 748
Parsons, Jacob IV, 562
Parsons, Jacob Louis Crew VI, 262
Parsons, James I, 931
Parsons, James III, 55
Parsons, James III, 248
Parsons, James III, 372
Parsons, James III, 383
Parsons, James III, 431
Parsons, James III, 473
Parsons, James III, 480
Parsons, James III, 491
Parsons, James III, 507
Parsons, James B. III, 74
Parsons, James B. III, 248
Parsons, James, Jr. III, 248
Parsons, Jane I, 67
Parsons, Jane I, 71
Parsons, Jane II, 615
Parsons, Jane III, 248
Parsons, Jane III, 372
Parsons, Jane III, 431
Parsons, Jane III, 473
Parsons, Jane III, 491
Parsons, Jane III, 507
Parsons, Jane Ann III, 248
Parsons, Jas. B. III, 248
Parsons, Joel IV, 52
Parsons, John II, 180
Parsons, John II, 403
Parsons, John II, 446
Parsons, John II, 615
Parsons, John II, 625
Parsons, John III, 248
Parsons, John III, 491
Parsons, John VI, 11
Parsons, John VI, 34
Parsons, John VI, 975
Parsons, John B. III, 248
Parsons, John Bowne III, 248
Parsons, John Bowne III, 383
Parsons, Joseph VI, 201
Parsons, Joseph VI, 220
Parsons, Joseph Anthony VI, 202
Parsons, Joseph H. IV, 562
Parsons, Joseph, Jr. VI, 201
Parsons, Joseph, Jr. VI, 219
Parsons, Joshua II, 180
Parsons, Josiah VI, 201
Parsons, Josiah VI, 202
Parsons, Judith VI, 201
Parsons, Judy VI, 913
Parsons, Julia III, 248
Parsons, Julia III, 264
Parsons, Julia Frances III, 248
Parsons, Julia Frances III, 264
Parsons, Julia Frances III, 276
Parsons, Juliann IV, 463
Parsons, Katharine III, 248
Parsons, Katharine III, 324
Parsons, Katharine Pansy III, 248
Parsons, Kenyon III, 248
Parsons, Lydia Ann II, 966
Parsons, Lydia P. II, 958
Parsons, M. Herschel III, 248
Parsons, Mahlon H. IV, 562
Parsons, Margaret V, 734
Parsons, Margaret VI, 202
Parsons, Margaret VI, 262
Parsons, Margaret P. VI, 202
Parsons, Margaret Pleasants VI, 262
Parsons, Martha IV, 562
Parsons, Martha Turner III, 248
Parsons, Mary I, 686
Parsons, Mary III, 55
Parsons, Mary III, 248
Parsons, Mary III, 377
Parsons, Mary III, 383
Parsons, Mary III, 480
Parsons, Mary III, 491
Parsons, Mary IV, 492

sons, Mary IV, 499
sons, Mary IV, 544
sons, Mary VI, 34
sons, Mary VI, 201
sons, Mary VI, 219
sons, Mary B. III, 248
sons, Mary B. III, 383
sons, Mary F. III, 248
sons, Mary F. III, 308
sons, Mary J. III, 248
sons, Melvin Herschel III, 248
sons, Mercy A. II, 958
sons, Nellie IV, 748
sons, Patsy VI, 919
sons, Phebe Ellen IV, 748
sons, Polley VI, 975
rsons, Rachael I, 730
rsons, Rachel I, 730
rsons, Rachel IV, 408
rsons, Rachel IV, 426
rsons, Rachel IV, 519
rsons, Rachel IV, 544
rsons, Rachel L. I, 686
rsons, Rachel L. I, 690
rsons, Rebecca IV, 572
rsons, Rebecca IV, 590
rsons, Robert B. III, 383
rsons, Robert W. III, 248
rsons, Robert W. III, 276
rsons, Robert William III, 248
rsons, Robt. Wm. III, 248
rsons, Robt. Wm. III, 264
rsons, Rosana III, 59
rsons, Rosanna III, 248
rsons, Ruth II, 615
rsons, Sally VI, 975
rsons, Sam'l B. III, 248
rsons, Saml. VI, 984
rsons, Samuel I, 931
rsons, Samuel III, 248
rsons, Samuel III, 377
rsons, Samuel III, 383
rsons, Samuel III, 491
rsons, Samuel VI, 17
rsons, Samuel VI, 161
rsons, Samuel VI, 198
rsons, Samuel VI, 201
rsons, Samuel VI, 202
rsons, Samuel VI, 203
rsons, Samuel VI, 207
rsons, Samuel VI, 262
rsons, Samuel VI, 276
rsons, Samuel VI, 279
rsons, Samuel VI, 975
rsons, Samuel B. III, 248
rsons, Samuel P. VI, 191
rsons, Samuel P. VI, 201
rsons, Samuel P. VI, 202
rsons, Samuel Pleasants VI, 201
rsons, Samuel Pleasants VI, 262
rsons, Sarah I, 37
rsons, Sarah I, 67
rsons, Sarah I, 931
rsons, Sarah I, 1075
arsons, Sarah VI, 201
arsons, Sarah VI, 202
arsons, Sarah VI, 203
arsons, Sarah VI, 207
arsons, Sarah VI, 208
arsons, Sarah VI, 262
arsons, Sarah VI, 984
arsons, Sarah Pleasants VI, 262
arsons, Sophia IV, 519
arsons, Sophia IV, 544
arsons, Sophia IV, 562
arsons, Stephen III, 59
arsons, Stephen III, 248
arsons, Susan IV, 748
arsons, Susan H. III, 248
arsons, Susanna VI, 201
arsons, Susanna VI, 202
arsons, Susanna VI, 220
arsons, Susannah VI, 201
arsons, Thomas II, 615
arsons, Thomas III, 248
arsons, Ursula VI, 202
arsons, Ursulah VI, 201
arsons, Wd. Ann II, 403
arsons, William II, 180
arsons, William VI, 161
arsons, William VI, 201
arsons, William B. III, 248
arsons, William B. III, 383
arsons, Wm. II, 615
arsons, Wm. B. III, 204
arsons, Wm. H. III, 167
arsons, Woodson VI, 202
artall, Elizabeth II, 1020
Partall, Wm. II, 1020
Partall, Wm. Lacy II, 1020
Parten, John IV, 427
Parten, Rachel IV, 427
Parthemore, Sarah IV, 1178
Parthmore, Fred IV, 1178
Parthmore, Frederick IV, 1178
Parthmore, Rose IV, 1178
Parthmore, Sarah IV, 1178
Partington, ??? IV, 985
Partington, Edna May IV, 260
Partington, Eliezer IV, 260
Partington, Eliezur IV, 260
Partington, Flora IV, 985
Partington, Flora H. IV, 985
Partington, Gerard Joseph II, 813
Partington, Jennie IV, 260
Partington, John Edwin IV, 985
Partington, Lee Paul IV, 985
Partington, Margaret IV, 260
Partington, Mary Alice II, 813
Partlow, Alta IV, 1259
Partlow, Alta M. IV, 1260
Partlow, John IV, 1260
Partlow, John W. IV, 1260
Parton, Ann III, 119
Parton, Eliz. III, 248
Parton, Elizabeth III, 119
Parton, F. III, 248
Parton, Geo. III, 248
Parton, George B. III, 119
Parton, Lemuel E. III, 119
Parton, Lemuel E. III, 248
Parton, Mary III, 119
Parton, Mary III, 248
Partridge, Edward S. II, 813
Partridge, Ella III, 338
Partridge, Ella May III, 30
Partridge, Ella May III, 248
Partridge, Harry M. III, 30
Partridge, Harry W. III, 248
Partridge, Johnetta B. VI, 262
Partridge, Margaret H. III, 338
Partridge, Mason H. III, 338
Partridge, Sarah B. II, 813
Partridge, Susannah II, 813
Partridge, Tho. VI, 93
Parviance, ??? IV, 104
Parviance, David IV, 52
Parviance, David IV, 106
Parviance, David VI, 428
Parviance, Deborah IV, 260
Parviance, Deborah IV, 274
Parviance, Elizabeth IV, 52
Parviance, Elizabeth IV, 155
Parviance, Elizabeth IV, 260
Parviance, Elizabeth IV, 497
Parviance, Elizabeth VI, 428
Parviance, Esther IV, 143
Parviance, Esther IV, 155
Parviance, George IV, 52
Parviance, George IV, 106
Parviance, George IV, 143
Parviance, George IV, 155
Parviance, George VI, 428
Parviance, James IV, 52
Parviance, James IV, 106
Parviance, James IV, 155
Parviance, James IV, 260
Parviance, James IV, 497
Parviance, James VI, 428
Parviance, James, Jr. IV, 106
Parviance, John IV, 52
Parviance, John VI, 428
Parviance, Joseph IV, 52
Parviance, Joseph IV, 260
Parviance, Joseph IV, 274
Parviance, Joseph VI, 428
Parviance, Mary IV, 106
Parviance, Nathaniel IV, 52
Parviance, Nathaniel VI, 428
Parviance, Richard IV, 52
Parviance, Richard IV, 106
Parviance, Richard VI, 428
Parviance, Sarah IV, 106
Parviance, Sarah IV, 491
Parviance, Sarah IV, 497
Parviance, Thomas IV, 52
Parviance, Thomas IV, 106
Parviance, Thomas VI, 428
Parviance, William IV, 52
Parviance, William IV, 106
Parviance, William VI, 428
Parvin, Ann II, 479
Parvin, Ann II, 615
Parvin, Benjamin C. II, 615
Parvin, Benjamin C. III, 249
Parvin, Benjamin Care II, 615
Parvin, Carrie II, 714
Parvin, Carrie J. H. II, 758
Parvin, Charlotte II, 723
Parvin, Deborah II, 714
Parvin, Deborah II, 715
Parvin, Deborah Starr II, 714
Parvin, Deborah Starr II, 758
Parvin, Eleanor II, 615
Parvin, Elizabeth II, 615
Parvin, Elizabeth II, 758
Parvin, Elizabeth II, 813
Parvin, Elizabeth II, 906
Parvin, Francis II, 403
Parvin, Francis II, 813
Parvin, Francis II, 816
Parvin, Hannah II, 481
Parvin, Hannah II, 615
Parvin, Hannah II, 906
Parvin, Hannah III, 249
Parvin, Jacob II, 714
Parvin, Jeremiah II, 615
Parvin, Jeremiah Paul II, 615
Parvin, John II, 615
Parvin, John III, 249
Parvin, Margaret II, 131
Parvin, Mary II, 481
Parvin, Mary II, 615
Parvin, Mary II, 679
Parvin, Mordecai S. II, 714
Parvin, Mordecai S. II, 758
Parvin, Pearson II, 481
Parvin, Pearson II, 615
Parvin, Pearson II, 813
Parvin, Phebe II, 615
Parvin, Phebe II, 679
Parvin, Pheby II, 615
Parvin, Rebecca Hartman II, 714
Parvin, Rebecca Hartman II, 758
Parvin, Sarah Paul II, 615
Parvin, Susanna II, 816
Parvin, Susannah II, 813
Parvin, Susannah II, 816
Parvin, Wd. Hannah II, 813
Parvin, Winifred II, 131
Parvin, Wm. II, 615
Parvin, Wm. II, 679
Pary, Elizabeth II, 906
Pary, Isaac II, 906
Pary, Oliver II, 906
Pary, Priscilla II, 906
Pary, Samuel II, 906
Pary, Sarah II, 906
Pary, Thos. II, 906
Pascall, Joanna II, 446
Pascall, Stephen II, 403
Pascall, Thomas, Sr. II, 446
Pascall, William II, 446
Paschal, Cyrus I, 565
Paschal, Elizabeth II, 489
Paschal, Elizabeth II, 615
Paschal, Elzira I, 565
Paschal, Esperan A. I, 413
Paschal, Hannah II, 551
Paschal, Hannah II, 615
Paschal, Joseph II, 489
Paschal, Joseph II, 615
Paschal, Julius I, 565
Paschal, Robert I, 413
Paschal, Sarah Elisabeth I, 627
Paschal, Vera M. I, 931
Paschal, Vera Magdaline I, 947
Paschall, Abraham II, 616
Paschall, Abraham Johnson II, 616
Paschall, Ann II, 403
Paschall, Ann II, 484
Paschall, Ann II, 615
Paschall, Ann II, 616
Paschall, Ann D. II, 906
Paschall, Benj. II, 567
Paschall, Benj. II, 616
Paschall, Benjamin II, 403
Paschall, Benjamin II, 554
Paschall, Benjamin II, 567
Paschall, Benjamin II, 615
Paschall, Benjamin II, 616
Paschall, Beulah II, 403
Paschall, Edward II, 616
Paschall, Edward Johnson II, 616
Paschall, Elizabeth II, 403
Paschall, Elizabeth II, 554
Paschall, Elizabeth II, 567
Paschall, Elizabeth II, 615
Paschall, Elizabeth II, 616
Paschall, Elizabeth Coates II, 536
Paschall, Elizabeth Coates II, 616
Paschall, Frances II, 615
Paschall, Hannah II, 403
Paschall, Hannah II, 615
Paschall, Hannah II, 636
Paschall, Isaac II, 403
Paschall, Isaac II, 536
Paschall, Isaac II, 597
Paschall, Isaac II, 603
Paschall, Isaac II, 615
Paschall, Isaac II, 616
Paschall, Jane II, 403
Paschall, Jesse Zane II, 616
Paschall, John II, 615
Paschall, Jonathan II, 403
Paschall, Joseph II, 403
Paschall, Joseph II, 404
Paschall, Joseph II, 597
Paschall, Joseph II, 615
Paschall, Margaret II, 558
Paschall, Margaret II, 615
Paschall, Margaret Worth II, 791
Paschall, Martha II, 403
Paschall, Martha II, 567
Paschall, Martha II, 615
Paschall, Martha II, 616
Paschall, Mary II, 403
Paschall, Mary II, 615
Paschall, Mary II, 644
Paschall, Patience II, 403
Paschall, Patience II, 536
Paschall, Patience II, 597
Paschall, Patience II, 603
Paschall, Patience II, 615
Paschall, Patience II, 616
Paschall, Rebecca II, 403
Paschall, Rebecca II, 615
Paschall, Rebecca II, 626
Paschall, Samuel II, 403
Paschall, Sarah II, 403
Paschall, Sarah II, 404
Paschall, Sarah II, 603
Paschall, Sarah II, 615
Paschall, Sarah II, 616
Paschall, Sarah II, 681
Paschall, Sarah II, 700
Paschall, Sarah II, 713
Paschall, Stephen II, 403
Paschall, Stephen II, 615
Paschall, Stephen, Jr. II, 616
Paschall, Thomas II, 403
Paschall, Thomas II, 404
Paschall, Thomas II, 446
Paschall, Thomas II, 484
Paschall, Thomas II, 550
Paschall, Thomas II, 615
Paschall, Thomas G. II, 616
Paschall, Thomas Garrett II, 616
Paschall, Thos. G. II, 906
Paschall, Wd. Margaret II, 599
Paschall, William II, 403
Paschall, William II, 404
Paschall, Wm. II, 615
Pasco, Mary II, 404
Pases???, Electa A. I, 625
Pasmore, Augustine VI, 428
Pason, Hannah IV, 261
Passan, Ann II, 446
Passan, Francis II, 446
Passmore, Abigail II, 713
Passmore, Abijah II, 906
Passmore, Alice M. IV, 749
Passmore, Alice, Jr. IV, 749
Passmore, Ann II, 616
Passmore, Ann II, 653
Passmore, Ann IV, 1027
Passmore, Anna II, 906
Passmore, Anna M. II, 906
Passmore, Anna M. II, 938
Passmore, Benj. W. II, 704
Passmore, Deborah Ann II, 906
Passmore, Deby Ann II, 906
Passmore, Edward S. IV, 749
Passmore, Elizabeth VI, 770
Passmore, Elizabeth VI, 772
Passmore, Elizabeth T. L. II, 906
Passmore, Ellen VI, 770
Passmore, Ellen VI, 772
Passmore, Ellen C. II, 906
Passmore, Ellen C. II, 938
Passmore, Ellis P. IV, 749
Passmore, Elma IV, 749
Passmore, Frederick Lawrence VI, 772
Passmore, Geo. IV, 1029
Passmore, George IV, 748
Passmore, George IV, 749
Passmore, George IV, 1021
Passmore, George IV, 1027
Passmore, George VI, 770
Passmore, George VI, 772
Passmore, Hannah Ann IV, 749
Passmore, Hannah Ann IV, 1029
Passmore, Hannah Mary II, 798
Passmore, Hannah W. II, 906
Passmore, John W. IV, 749
Passmore, Joseph Harlan IV, 749
Passmore, Joseph Harlin IV, 749
Passmore, Lewis II, 906
Passmore, Lewis II, 938
Passmore, Lincoln K. IV, 749
Passmore, Lindley IV, 749
Passmore, Manrel IV, 1029
Passmore, Mansel IV, 749
Passmore, Mary II, 704
Passmore, Mary II, 906
Passmore, Naomi II, 843
Passmore, Naomi II, 906
Passmore, Pamela IV, 749
Passmore, Pamela IV, 1025
Passmore, Pamela IV, 1029
Passmore, Pamelia IV, 749
Passmore, Pennock VI, 542
Passmore, Phebe IV, 749
Passmore, Phebe IV, 1027
Passmore, Phebe IV, 1029
Passmore, Phebe H. IV, 748
Passmore, Phebe H. IV, 749
Passmore, Phebe H. IV, 1021
Passmore, Samuel W. II, 906
Passmore, Sarah II, 704
Passmore, Sarah W. II, 703
Passmore, Sarah W. II, 704
Passmore, Sarah W. II, 719
Passmore, Wm. II, 616
Passmore, Wm. II, 653
Passmore, Wm. C. II, 906
Passmore, Wm. C. II, 938
Past, Alcesta II, 1007
Past, Alcesta II, 1020
Past, Alcesta II, 1077
Past, Alcestack II, 904
Past, Alcestack II, 926
Past, Ann II, 1020
Past, Anna II, 904
Past, Anna II, 926
Past, Elizabeth II, 1020
Past, John II, 904
Past, John II, 926
Past, John II, 1007
Past, John II, 1020
Past, John II, 1077
Past, John C. II, 1077
Past, Lavina IV, 1178
Past, Rachel H. II, 1077
Past, Samuel IV, 1178
Past, William II, 1020
Paste, Abi II, 1020
Paste, Aby II, 1020
Paste, Achsah S. II, 1057
Paste, Albert II, 1057
Paste, Alcesta II, 1020
Paste, Alcester II, 1020
Paste, Alcester II, 1077
Paste, Alice II, 1009
Paste, Alice II, 1020
Paste, Alice, Jr. II, 1020
Paste, Ann II, 1020
Paste, Anna II, 904
Paste, Anna II, 1020
Paste, Benjamin II, 1020
Paste, Beulah II, 1057
Paste, Elizabeth II, 967
Paste, Elizabeth II, 1020
Paste, Elizabeth II, 1057
Paste, Euclaides II, 1020
Paste, Euclidus II, 1020
Paste, George II, 1020
Paste, John II, 1020
Paste, John II, 1057
Paste, Jolly II, 967
Paste, Jolly II, 1020
Paste, Jolly II, 1057
Paste, Jonathan II, 1020
Paste, Martha II, 1020
Paste, Martha K. II, 1020
Paste, Mary C. II, 1057
Paste, Mary C. II, 1058
Paste, Mercy II, 1020
Paste, Mercy II, 1021
Paste, Rachel II, 967
Paste, Rachel II, 1020
Paste, Rachel II, 1057
Paste, Rachel II, 1077
Paste, Rachel II, 1078
Paste, Rachel H. II, 1020
Paste, Robert II, 1020
Paste, Robert II, 1021
Paste, Sarah II, 967
Paste, Sarah II, 1020
Paste, Sarah II, 1057
Paste, Sarah K. II, 1020
Paste, Thomas S. II, 1057
Paste, William II, 1020
Paste, Wm. II, 1020
Paston, A. E. I, 932
Paston, Aubrey I, 932
Paston, Aubrey E. I, 947

Paston, Scovia I, 932
Paston, Scovia I, 947
Pastor, Isaac IV, 845
Pastores, Hannah II, 616
Pastorius, Hannah II, 616
Pastorius, Sarah II, 581
Pastorius, Sarah II, 616
Pastrous, Hannah II, 595
Patch, Francis V, 702
Patchel, Susannah V, 393
Patchel, Susannah V, 425
Patchin, Albert M. IV, 1041
Patchin, Lawson K. IV, 1041
Patching, Ann III, 96
Patching, Ann III, 304
Patching, John F. III, 249
Pate, Agnes VI, 930
Pate, Alice I, 339
Pate, Alma I, 639
Pate, Alma Lorena I, 623
Pate, Ann I, 314
Pate, Anne VI, 885
Pate, Avis L. J. I, 314
Pate, Avis Levana Jenety I, 294
Pate, Benjamin Allen VI, 975
Pate, Betty VI, 975
Pate, Charlotte IV, 52
Pate, Charlotte IV, 60
Pate, Charlotte IV, 95
Pate, Charlotte IV, 104
Pate, Cornelius VI, 885
Pate, Cornelius VI, 920
Pate, Cornelius VI, 975
Pate, Cornelius VI, 1022
Pate, Debah Ann Sophronia I, 294
Pate, E. F. I, 639
Pate, Edmd. VI, 993
Pate, Edmund VI, 845
Pate, Edwin James Gilbert I, 294
Pate, Eli F. I, 623
Pate, Eli Fernando Cartland I, 294
Pate, Elisabeth I, 623
Pate, Elizabeth I, 294
Pate, Elizabeth I, 314
Pate, Harriet Elizabeth VI, 975
Pate, Henry IV, 1375
Pate, Jane VI, 970
Pate, Jane VI, 975
Pate, Jeremiah VI, 975
Pate, John VI, 869
Pate, John VI, 873
Pate, John VI, 896
Pate, John VI, 930
Pate, John VI, 939
Pate, John VI, 943
Pate, John VI, 949
Pate, John VI, 959
Pate, John VI, 975
Pate, John VI, 980
Pate, John VI, 985
Pate, John VI, 993
Pate, John B. VI, 975
Pate, John D. VI, 940
Pate, John D. VI, 975
Pate, John D. VI, 982
Pate, John W. B. I, 314
Pate, John William Bryan I, 294
Pate, Joseph I, 294
Pate, Joseph I, 314
Pate, Joseph W. I, 294
Pate, Joseph W. I, 623
Pate, Judith VI, 888
Pate, Judith VI, 975
Pate, Margaret VI, 845
Pate, Mary IV, 1375
Pate, Mary VI, 955
Pate, Mary VI, 975
Pate, Mary A. M. VI, 975
Pate, Mary Ann VI, 920
Pate, Mary E. J. I, 314
Pate, Mary Elva Juleta I, 294
Pate, Mary L. E. VI, 975
Pate, Mathew VI, 955
Pate, Matthew VI, 885
Pate, Matthew VI, 888
Pate, Matthew VI, 920
Pate, Matthew VI, 930
Pate, Nancy VI, 930
Pate, Osmond C. I, 623
Pate, Osmond C. I, 639
Pate, Rhoda VI, 993
Pate, Sallie Ann I, 314
Pate, Sallie Ann I, 316
Pate, Samuel Jethro Stanton I, 294
Pate, Sarah E. I, 623
Pate, William H. VI, 927
Pate, William H. VI, 975
Patee, Mary IV, 1178
Paterson, Faith I, 252
Paterson, Frances IV, 1332
Paterson, Jane I, 833
Paterson, John I, 595
Paterson, John II, 616
Paterson, Margaret I, 833
Paterson, Margaret I, 834
Paterson, Mary I, 595
Paterson, Mary I, 994
Paterson, Mary I, 995
Paterson, Patience I, 252
Paterson, Priscilla I, 253
Paterson, Sarah I, 594
Paterson, Sarah I, 595
Paterson, Sarah I, 994
Paterson, Tempey I, 253
Patey, Lacy VI, 803
Patey, Nancy VI, 803
Pathemore, Fred IV, 1178
Pathemore, Rose IV, 1178
Patience, Thomas IV, 779
Patin, William III, 249
Patison, Amelia VI, 202
Patison, Anselm I, 253
Patison, Benjamin VI, 188
Patison, Benjamin VI, 202
Patison, Benjamin VI, 203
Patison, Benjamin VI, 211
Patison, Betsy I, 913
Patison, Burle VI, 202
Patison, Burleigh VI, 202
Patison, Elizabeth VI, 188
Patison, Elizabeth VI, 202
Patison, Elizabeth VI, 211
Patison, Elizabeth VI, 212
Patison, Hannah VI, 198
Patison, Hannah VI, 199
Patison, Hannah VI, 202
Patison, Hannah VI, 203
Patison, John VI, 199
Patison, John VI, 202
Patison, John VI, 203
Patison, Joseph VI, 177
Patison, Joseph VI, 198
Patison, Joseph VI, 202
Patison, Joseph VI, 203
Patison, Joseph VI, 212
Patison, Joseph, Jr. VI, 211
Patison, Martha VI, 202
Patison, Martha VI, 203
Patison, Mary VI, 202
Patison, Mary VI, 211
Patison, Mathew VI, 855
Patison, Obedience VI, 199
Patison, Peter VI, 199
Patison, Sarah VI, 202
Patison, William VI, 198
Patison, William VI, 202
Patison, Wm. VI, 203
Paton, Ann VI, 752
Paton, Joseph B. VI, 752
Paton, Mary VI, 425
Paton, Mary VI, 429
Paton, Rebecca VI, 735
Paton, Rebecca VI, 770
Patredge, Mary VI, 34
Patredge, Thomas VI, 34
Patric, Francis V, 1013
Patric, Margaret V, 1013
Patrick, Abner S. II, 136
Patrick, Abner S. II, 154
Patrick, Abner S. II, 156
Patrick, Alice Reeves II, 136
Patrick, Anna L. II, 140
Patrick, B. Jennie II, 154
Patrick, B. Jennie II, 156
Patrick, Beulah Jane II, 136
Patrick, Catherine VI, 797
Patrick, David F. VI, 845
Patrick, Edmond VI, 797
Patrick, Elizabeth VI, 975
Patrick, Elmer IV, 1288
Patrick, Ettie IV, 1288
Patrick, Frances Curn V, 108
Patrick, Francis V, 1013
Patrick, George G. II, 140
Patrick, Helena G. II, 140
Patrick, Isaac VI, 845
Patrick, Jane Robinson II, 136
Patrick, John II, 136
Patrick, John II, 404
Patrick, John V, 1013
Patrick, John VI, 797
Patrick, John VI, 830
Patrick, John VI, 845
Patrick, John VI, 884
Patrick, John VI, 954
Patrick, John VI, 975
Patrick, John F. VI, 819
Patrick, John R. II, 154
Patrick, John R. II, 156
Patrick, Lillian II, 136
Patrick, Lillian II, 156
Patrick, Lillian Acton II, 154
Patrick, Margaret V, 1013
Patrick, Mary II, 142
Patrick, Mary II, 154
Patrick, Mary VI, 428
Patrick, Matilda VI, 845
Patrick, Minnie IV, 837
Patrick, Minnie IV, 1288
Patrick, Mrs. Judith VI, 6
Patrick, Mrs. Judith VI, 11
Patrick, Nancy VI, 845
Patrick, Sarah VI, 830
Patrick, Sarah B. M. VI, 845
Patrick, Sarah E. V, 1013
Patrick, Sarah F. VI, 854
Patrick, William VI, 827
Patrick, William VI, 836
Patrick, William VI, 845
Patrick, William VI, 851
Patrick, William VI, 856
Patridge, Ella III, 248
Patridge, Margaret H. III, 248
Patridge, Mason H. III, 248
Patsey, Martha I, 30
Pattan, Ann I, 1050
Pattan, Grace I, 1050
Pattan, Hannah IV, 1071
Pattan, Hannah IV, 1078
Pattan, Isaac I, 1050
Pattan, Mahlon I, 1050
Pattan, Mary I, 1050
Pattan, Phebe IV, 1078
Pattan, Rachel I, 1050
Pattan, William I, 1050
Pattan, Wm. IV, 1078
Patten, Abraham IV, 1062
Patten, Abraham IV, 1070
Patten, Abraham IV, 1071
Patten, Adaline V, 618
Patten, Adaline V, 638
Patten, Alfred IV, 801
Patten, Alfred IV, 836
Patten, Alfred A. IV, 805
Patten, Alfred W. IV, 835
Patten, Anna IV, 366
Patten, Anna IV, 428
Patten, Anna B. IV, 428
Patten, Bertha E. IV, 428
Patten, Bertha Elizabeth IV, 428
Patten, Beulah IV, 428
Patten, Beulah Lydia IV, 428
Patten, Caleb S. IV, 1071
Patten, Caroline V, 831
Patten, Caroline V, 856
Patten, Charity IV, 373
Patten, Clara Elizabeth IV, 805
Patten, Clara Elizabeth IV, 837
Patten, Clarence Edgar IV, 837
Patten, Clarence R. IV, 366
Patten, Clarence R. IV, 428
Patten, Cyrus V, 638
Patten, Edwin IV, 805
Patten, Elihu H. IV, 428
Patten, Elihu H. IV, 1070
Patten, Elihu H. IV, 1071
Patten, Eliza Jane IV, 1070
Patten, Eliza Jane IV, 1071
Patten, Elizabeth IV, 801
Patten, Elizabeth IV, 805
Patten, Elizabeth IV, 835
Patten, Elizabeth IV, 836
Patten, Elizabeth IV, 837
Patten, Elizabeth VI, 845
Patten, Elizabeth C. IV, 836
Patten, Elizabeth C. IV, 837
Patten, Ephraim IV, 373
Patten, Ephraim IV, 428
Patten, Esther IV, 1070
Patten, Esther IV, 1071
Patten, Euphamy IV, 428
Patten, Euphemia IV, 428
Patten, Evaline V, 638
Patten, Ezekiel IV, 428
Patten, George IV, 1071
Patten, George D. IV, 1071
Patten, Grace IV, 425
Patten, Grace IV, 427
Patten, Hannah IV, 805
Patten, Hannah IV, 1070
Patten, Hannah IV, 1071
Patten, Hannah Ann IV, 428
Patten, Helen V, 702
Patten, Helen V, 704
Patten, Isaac IV, 1070
Patten, Isaac IV, 1071
Patten, James VI, 845
Patten, James Wm. IV, 837
Patten, Jane IV, 1071
Patten, Jared IV, 1070
Patten, Jared IV, 1071
Patten, Jeanie Maury VI, 770
Patten, Jennie V, 696
Patten, Jennie V, 702
Patten, Jesse IV, 1071
Patten, Jesse E. IV, 373
Patten, John IV, 427
Patten, John IV, 428
Patten, John IV, 1049
Patten, John IV, 1050
Patten, John IV, 1070
Patten, John IV, 1071
Patten, John IV, 1076
Patten, John Dewhurst VI, 770
Patten, John Quincy IV, 1070
Patten, Joseph IV, 428
Patten, Joseph IV, 1070
Patten, Joseph IV, 1071
Patten, Julia IV, 649
Patten, Julia IV, 650
Patten, Julia R. IV, 835
Patten, Julia R. IV, 837
Patten, Julia Rachel IV, 837
Patten, Juliett Craik VI, 770
Patten, Lydia IV, 428
Patten, Lydia IV, 1070
Patten, Lydia IV, 1071
Patten, Lydia IV, 1074
Patten, Mahlon IV, 428
Patten, Mahlon IV, 1070
Patten, Mahlon IV, 1071
Patten, Mahlon IV, 1108
Patten, Mary IV, 428
Patten, Mary IV, 1050
Patten, Mary IV, 1070
Patten, Mary IV, 1071
Patten, Mary Ellen IV, 1071
Patten, Mary Ellen IV, 1136
Patten, Mary Ellen IV, 1137
Patten, Mary H. IV, 428
Patten, Mary H. IV, 433
Patten, Mary P. IV, 373
Patten, Merrick IV, 1070
Patten, Merrick IV, 1071
Patten, Oscar Marion IV, 428
Patten, Phebe IV, 428
Patten, Phebe IV, 1070
Patten, Phebe IV, 1071
Patten, Phebe Ann IV, 1071
Patten, Polly VI, 845
Patten, Rachel IV, 292
Patten, Rachel IV, 425
Patten, Rachel IV, 427
Patten, Rachel IV, 428
Patten, Rachel IV, 445
Patten, Rachel IV, 1070
Patten, Rachel IV, 1071
Patten, Rachel B. IV, 428
Patten, Rachel B. IV, 1071
Patten, Rachel B. IV, 1076
Patten, Rebecca IV, 373
Patten, Rebecca IV, 428
Patten, Rebecca IV, 1049
Patten, Rebecca IV, 1070
Patten, Rebecca IV, 1071
Patten, Rebecca IV, 1076
Patten, Rebecca VI, 770
Patten, Rhoda IV, 428
Patten, Rhoda IV, 1049
Patten, Rhoda IV, 1070
Patten, Rhoda IV, 1071
Patten, Richard IV, 428
Patten, Richard IV, 1070
Patten, Richard IV, 1071
Patten, Richard IV, 1074
Patten, Roanice IV, 406
Patten, Roanice IV, 428
Patten, Ruth IV, 373
Patten, Ruth IV, 428
Patten, Ruth IV, 1062
Patten, Ruth IV, 1071
Patten, Sally IV, 373
Patten, Sally IV, 427
Patten, Sarah IV, 260
Patten, Sarah IV, 292
Patten, Sarah IV, 427
Patten, Sarah IV, 428
Patten, Sarah IV, 1070
Patten, Sarah IV, 1071
Patten, Sarah S. IV, 1071
Patten, Smith IV, 428
Patten, Susanna VI, 955
Patten, Vincent VI, 845
Patten, Welmet I, 1130
Patten, William IV, 406
Patten, William IV, 427
Patten, William IV, 428
Patten, William IV, 1070
Patten, William IV, 1071
Patten, William, Jr. IV, 427
Patten, Wilson H. IV, 373
Patten, Wm. IV, 292
Patten, Wm. IV, 373
Patten, Wm. IV, 425
Patten, Wm. IV, 428
Patten, Wm. IV, 836
Patten, Wm. IV, 1071
Patten, Wm. Bailey IV, 1071
Patten, Wm., Jr. IV, 1071
Pattern, Elizabeth VI, 845
Pattern, William VI, 845
Patters, James VI, 845
Patters, Sophia VI, 845
Patterson, ??? IV, 1085
Patterson, Abigail P. IV, 1109
Patterson, Achsa IV, 243
Patterson, Achsa IV, 260
Patterson, Achsa IV, 261
Patterson, Achsah I, 238
Patterson, Achsah I, 253
Patterson, Achsah IV, 426
Patterson, Achsah IV, 427
Patterson, Achsah IV, 1109
Patterson, Acsah IV, 592
Patterson, Agnes VI, 817
Patterson, Albert IV, 261
Patterson, Albert IV, 427
Patterson, Alfred F. IV, 260
Patterson, Alice IV, 208
Patterson, Alice IV, 407
Patterson, Amacy IV, 427
Patterson, Amasa I, 253
Patterson, Amasa IV, 261
Patterson, Amasa IV, 427
Patterson, Amasa IV, 443
Patterson, Amasa IV, 591
Patterson, Amasa IV, 1109
Patterson, Amasa L. IV, 260
Patterson, Amos IV, 260
Patterson, Amos IV, 261
Patterson, Amos IV, 426
Patterson, Amos IV, 427
Patterson, Amos IV, 1071
Patterson, Amos IV, 1109
Patterson, Amy IV, 261
Patterson, Amy IV, 569
Patterson, Amy IV, 570
Patterson, Amy IV, 590
Patterson, Amy IV, 592
Patterson, Andrew VI, 901
Patterson, Andrew VI, 975
Patterson, Angelina I, 230
Patterson, Angelina I, 253
Patterson, Angelina IV, 426
Patterson, Angelina IV, 427
Patterson, Angelina IV, 591
Patterson, Angelina P. IV, 447
Patterson, Angeline IV, 426
Patterson, Ann I, 253
Patterson, Ann I, 259
Patterson, Ann I, 994
Patterson, Ann II, 404
Patterson, Ann II, 614
Patterson, Ann II, 616
Patterson, Ann II, 631
Patterson, Ann IV, 427
Patterson, Ann IV, 458
Patterson, Ann IV, 591
Patterson, Ann IV, 1071
Patterson, Ann IV, 1108
Patterson, Ann IV, 1110
Patterson, Ann VI, 542
Patterson, Ann VI, 845
Patterson, Ann B. VI, 976
Patterson, Anna I, 224
Patterson, Anna I, 253
Patterson, Anna I, 259
Patterson, Anna IV, 427
Patterson, Anna IV, 585
Patterson, Anna IV, 586
Patterson, Anna IV, 591
Patterson, Anna IV, 592
Patterson, Anna VI, 335
Patterson, Anna VI, 945
Patterson, Anne IV, 385
Patterson, Anne IV, 590
Patterson, Anne IV, 600
Patterson, Anne IV, 1064
Patterson, Anne IV, 1071
Patterson, Anne Doudna IV, 426
Patterson, Anne W. IV, 591
Patterson, Anne Williams IV, 57
Patterson, Anselem IV, 224
Patterson, Anselem IV, 260
Patterson, Anselm I, 253
Patterson, Anselum I, 224
Patterson, Anslem I, 244
Patterson, Armistead VI, 976
Patterson, Arnal IV, 261
Patterson, Arnald IV, 261
Patterson, Arnold IV, 260
Patterson, Arnold IV, 287

terson, Arnold IV, 427
terson, Arnold IV, 590
terson, Arnold IV, 592
terson, Arnold IV, 1071
terson, Arnold IV, 1091
terson, Arnold IV, 1109
terson, Arnold IV, 1118
terson, Artemisa IV, 427
terson, Asa IV, 261
terson, Asa IV, 590
terson, Asa IV, 592
terson, Asael IV, 260
terson, Asahel IV, 261
terson, Asahel H. IV, 89
terson, Asahel H. IV, 104
terson, Asahel H. IV, 209
terson, Asahel H. IV, 260
terson, Asahel H. IV, 261
terson, Asenath I, 253
terson, Asenath IV, 365
terson, Asenath IV, 366
terson, Asenath IV, 426
terson, Asenath IV, 427
terson, Asenath IV, 591
terson, Ashley VI, 324
terson, Ashley VI, 335
terson, Axem IV, 261
terson, Axim IV, 155
terson, Axum IV, 427
terson, Bailey IV, 261
terson, Bailey IV, 590
terson, Bailey IV, 592
terson, Benja. I, 224
terson, Benja. I, 252
terson, Benjamin I, 224
terson, Benjamin I, 241
terson, Benjamin I, 252
terson, Benjamin I, 253
terson, Benjamin I, 994
terson, Benjamin I, 995
terson, Benjamin IV, 155
terson, Benjamin IV, 260
terson, Benjamin IV, 261
terson, Benjamin IV, 426
terson, Benjamin IV, 450
terson, Benjamin IV, 458
terson, Benjamin IV, 591
terson, Benjamin IV, 592
terson, Benjamin VI, 99
terson, Benjamin VI, 117
terson, Benjamin B. III, 230
terson, Benjamin B. III, 249
terson, Benjamin, Jr. IV, 427
terson, Benje. I, 224
terson, Bessie V, 522
terson, Betsey VI, 975
terson, Betsey VI, 993
terson, Beulah V, 108
terson, Beulah V, 856
terson, Beulah V, 925
terson, Beulah VI, 769
terson, Beulah VI, 770
terson, Bicks IV, 590
tterson, Blanche A. VI, 1014
tterson, Blancum A. VI, 975
tterson, Caleb IV, 590
tterson, Caleb IV, 1071
terson, Caleb IV, 1109
terson, Capt. Alfred III, 431
tterson, Carl IV, 1109
tterson, Carl IV, 1110
terson, Casandra VI, 845
terson, Catharine I, 224
tterson, Catharine IV, 155
tterson, Catharine IV, 260
tterson, Catharine IV, 261
tterson, Catharine IV, 426
tterson, Catharine IV, 450
tterson, Catharine J. IV, 1109
tterson, Charles IV, 261
terson, Charles IV, 407
terson, Charles IV, 427
tterson, Charles IV, 1109
tterson, Charles IV, 1219
tterson, Charles VI, 845
tterson, Charles C. VI, 881
tterson, Charles C. VI, 941
tterson, Charles Carter
IV, 1109
tterson, Chas. A. IV, 1219
tterson, Chas. C. VI, 882
tterson, Chas. C. VI, 965
tterson, Chas. C. VI, 992
tterson, Cindarilla VI, 975
tterson, Clara I, 639
tterson, Clara S. V, 522
tterson, Clarey IV, 261
tterson, Clarimon I, 224
tterson, Clark IV, 590
tterson, Clark IV, 1071
tterson, Clark IV, 1109
Patterson, Clary IV, 260
Patterson, Clary IV, 279
Patterson, Claudia IV, 592
Patterson, D. P. VI, 805
Patterson, Daniel V, 638
Patterson, David I, 224
Patterson, David I, 246
Patterson, David I, 252
Patterson, David I, 253
Patterson, David IV, 261
Patterson, David IV, 366
Patterson, David IV, 427
Patterson, David IV, 443
Patterson, David IV, 590
Patterson, David IV, 591
Patterson, David IV, 592
Patterson, David IV, 595
Patterson, David IV, 1288
Patterson, David VI, 811
Patterson, David VI, 817
Patterson, David VI, 833
Patterson, David VI, 845
Patterson, David VI, 851
Patterson, David VI, 854
Patterson, David VI, 855
Patterson, David B. VI, 811
Patterson, Dawcella VI, 306
Patterson, Dawcella VI, 808
Patterson, Deborah II, 705
Patterson, Deborah IV, 155
Patterson, Deborah IV, 221
Patterson, Deborah IV, 260
Patterson, Deborah IV, 427
Patterson, Deborah IV, 592
Patterson, Deborah H. II, 711
Patterson, Deborah H. II, 753
Patterson, Deborah H. II, 759
Patterson, Deborah H. IV, 591
Patterson, Deborh IV, 749
Patterson, Delia IV, 407
Patterson, Devereaux VI, 832
Patterson, Devereaux VI, 845
Patterson, Dorothy IV, 749
Patterson, Dorothy Kuhns
IV, 749
Patterson, Dortha B. IV, 1091
Patterson, Dortha B. IV, 1110
Patterson, Dortha Beulah
IV, 1109
Patterson, Edith IV, 1109
Patterson, Edith IV, 1110
Patterson, Edith IV, 1114
Patterson, Edith L. IV, 937
Patterson, Edna IV, 1109
Patterson, Edna T. IV, 590
Patterson, Edna T. IV, 592
Patterson, Edward VI, 993
Patterson, Edwin IV, 261
Patterson, Edwin IV, 328
Patterson, Edwin IV, 345
Patterson, Edwin IV, 426
Patterson, Edwin IV, 427
Patterson, Edwin IV, 590
Patterson, Edwin IV, 591
Patterson, Edwin IV, 600
Patterson, Elam IV, 155
Patterson, Elam IV, 261
Patterson, Elam IV, 426
Patterson, Elam IV, 458
Patterson, Elbina Smith IV, 447
Patterson, Eli IV, 261
Patterson, Eli IV, 319
Patterson, Eli IV, 345
Patterson, Eli IV, 386
Patterson, Eli IV, 566
Patterson, Eli IV, 567
Patterson, Eli IV, 574
Patterson, Eli IV, 576
Patterson, Eli IV, 579
Patterson, Eli IV, 590
Patterson, Eli IV, 591
Patterson, Eli IV, 592
Patterson, Eli IV, 593
Patterson, Eli Henry I, 1160
Patterson, Elihu I, 253
Patterson, Elihu IV, 427
Patterson, Elihu IV, 591
Patterson, Elijah IV, 155
Patterson, Elijah IV, 260
Patterson, Elijah IV, 261
Patterson, Elijah IV, 427
Patterson, Elim IV, 591
Patterson, Elisabeth I, 244
Patterson, Elisabeth I, 253
Patterson, Elisha IV, 590
Patterson, Elisha IV, 592
Patterson, Elisha V, 638
Patterson, Eliza I, 253
Patterson, Eliza IV, 427
Patterson, Eliza IV, 568
Patterson, Eliza IV, 591
Patterson, Eliza Ann IV, 426
Patterson, Eliza F. VI, 913
Patterson, Eliza Jane IV, 426
Patterson, Elizabeth I, 224
Patterson, Elizabeth I, 247
Patterson, Elizabeth I, 252
Patterson, Elizabeth I, 258
Patterson, Elizabeth I, 994
Patterson, Elizabeth I, 995
Patterson, Elizabeth I, 998
Patterson, Elizabeth I, 1130
Patterson, Elizabeth IV, 155
Patterson, Elizabeth IV, 261
Patterson, Elizabeth IV, 364
Patterson, Elizabeth IV, 398
Patterson, Elizabeth IV, 417
Patterson, Elizabeth IV, 426
Patterson, Elizabeth IV, 427
Patterson, Elizabeth IV, 428
Patterson, Elizabeth IV, 430
Patterson, Elizabeth IV, 443
Patterson, Elizabeth IV, 447
Patterson, Elizabeth IV, 568
Patterson, Elizabeth IV, 581
Patterson, Elizabeth IV, 586
Patterson, Elizabeth IV, 590
Patterson, Elizabeth IV, 591
Patterson, Elizabeth IV, 592
Patterson, Elizabeth IV, 1071
Patterson, Elizabeth IV, 1088
Patterson, Elizabeth IV, 1105
Patterson, Elizabeth IV, 1109
Patterson, Elizabeth V, 638
Patterson, Elizabeth V, 642
Patterson, Elizabeth VI, 123
Patterson, Elizabeth VI, 137
Patterson, Elizabeth VI, 845
Patterson, Elizabeth VI, 975
Patterson, Elizabeth Ann
IV, 1109
Patterson, Elizabeth H. VI, 968
Patterson, Elizabeth Jane
VI, 881
Patterson, Elizabeth K. VI, 975
Patterson, Ellen IV, 427
Patterson, Ellen IV, 436
Patterson, Ellen IV, 591
Patterson, Ellen IV, 593
Patterson, Ellen M. III, 249
Patterson, Elum IV, 260
Patterson, Elvy IV, 592
Patterson, Elwood IV, 261
Patterson, Elwood IV, 590
Patterson, Elwood IV, 592
Patterson, Elwood IV, 1109
Patterson, Elwood V, 108
Patterson, Elwood V, 925
Patterson, Emily III, 417
Patterson, Emily III, 431
Patterson, Emily IV, 590
Patterson, Emily IV, 592
Patterson, Emily IV, 1106
Patterson, Emily IV, 1109
Patterson, Emily IV, 1110
Patterson, Emily A. IV, 1095
Patterson, Emily A. IV, 1110
Patterson, Emly IV, 1109
Patterson, Enselem IV, 260
Patterson, Ephamy IV, 1109
Patterson, Epsey VI, 993
Patterson, Esther I, 224
Patterson, Esther I, 241
Patterson, Esther I, 252
Patterson, Esther IV, 35
Patterson, Esther IV, 53
Patterson, Esther IV, 155
Patterson, Esther IV, 208
Patterson, Esther IV, 209
Patterson, Esther IV, 260
Patterson, Esther IV, 392
Patterson, Esther IV, 403
Patterson, Esther IV, 427
Patterson, Esther IV, 450
Patterson, Esther IV, 458
Patterson, Esther IV, 591
Patterson, Esther IV, 1060
Patterson, Esther IV, 1071
Patterson, Esther VI, 997
Patterson, Esther G. IV, 104
Patterson, Esther J. IV, 261
Patterson, Esther P. IV, 89
Patterson, Esther P. IV, 104
Patterson, Esther P. IV, 261
Patterson, Eunice IV, 366
Patterson, Eunice IV, 427
Patterson, Eunice IV, 443
Patterson, Eunice IV, 591
Patterson, Eunice IV, 592
Patterson, Eunice IV, 595
Patterson, Eunice IV, 1109
Patterson, Eva L. IV, 366
Patterson, Eva L. IV, 375
Patterson, Eva L. IV, 427
Patterson, Eva L. IV, 442
Patterson, Eva L. IV, 592
Patterson, Eva Luzena IV, 591
Patterson, Eva Luzene IV, 261
Patterson, Exum IV, 261
Patterson, Exum IV, 385
Patterson, Exum IV, 585
Patterson, Exum IV, 586
Patterson, Exum IV, 590
Patterson, Exum IV, 591
Patterson, Faith I, 252
Patterson, Faith I, 253
Patterson, Faith IV, 260
Patterson, Faith IV, 261
Patterson, Faith IV, 345
Patterson, Faith IV, 591
Patterson, Faith IV, 1109
Patterson, Faith VI, 99
Patterson, Faith Bailey VI, 117
Patterson, Fanny VI, 826
Patterson, Fanny VI, 839
Patterson, Finetta J. VI, 1014
Patterson, Frances IV, 1332
Patterson, Frances VI, 969
Patterson, Frances E. IV, 592
Patterson, Francis IV, 1332
Patterson, Francis E. IV, 1109
Patterson, Garrad I, 224
Patterson, Garred I, 253
Patterson, Geo. IV, 428
Patterson, Geo. A. IV, 1091
Patterson, Geo. Wilson IV, 261
Patterson, George IV, 427
Patterson, George IV, 1109
Patterson, George IV, 1110
Patterson, George Arnold
IV, 1109
Patterson, George D. VI, 975
Patterson, George D. VI, 981
Patterson, George N. IV, 1260
Patterson, George S. IV, 426
Patterson, George W. IV, 592
Patterson, George Wilson IV, 427
Patterson, Gerrad VI, 138
Patterson, Gerred I, 230
Patterson, Gerred I, 253
Patterson, Gladney IV, 590
Patterson, Gladys IV, 261
Patterson, Gorden I, 995
Patterson, Grace IV, 1088
Patterson, Grace IV, 1109
Patterson, Guli Elma IV, 591
Patterson, Gulielma IV, 261
Patterson, Gulielma IV, 328
Patterson, Gulielma IV, 345
Patterson, Guly Elma IV, 590
Patterson, H. P. I, 639
Patterson, H??? IV, 260
Patterson, Hannah I, 224
Patterson, Hannah I, 246
Patterson, Hannah I, 252
Patterson, Hannah II, 404
Patterson, Hannah II, 616
Patterson, Hannah II, 759
Patterson, Hannah IV, 261
Patterson, Hannah IV, 398
Patterson, Hannah IV, 407
Patterson, Hannah IV, 426
Patterson, Hannah IV, 427
Patterson, Hannah IV, 446
Patterson, Hannah IV, 455
Patterson, Hannah IV, 565
Patterson, Hannah IV, 583
Patterson, Hannah IV, 590
Patterson, Hannah IV, 591
Patterson, Hannah IV, 592
Patterson, Harold Truesdell
III, 417
Patterson, Harold Truesdell
III, 431
Patterson, Harriet W. VI, 833
Patterson, Harriot IV, 590
Patterson, Hezekiah I, 1130
Patterson, Howard IV, 1178
Patterson, Ida I, 921
Patterson, Ida I, 925
Patterson, Ira IV, 260
Patterson, Ira IV, 261
Patterson, Ira IV, 287
Patterson, Ira IV, 427
Patterson, Ira IV, 590
Patterson, Ira IV, 591
Patterson, Ira IV, 592
Patterson, Ira IV, 650
Patterson, Ira IV, 1109
Patterson, Ira IV, 1120
Patterson, Isaac IV, 261
Patterson, Isaac IV, 345
Patterson, Isaac IV, 381
Patterson, Isaac IV, 426
Patterson, Isaac IV, 427
Patterson, Isaac IV, 590
Patterson, Isaac IV, 720
Patterson, Isaac B. IV, 592
Patterson, Isaac B. IV, 1071
Patterson, Isabella IV, 1069
Patterson, Isabella IV, 1071
Patterson, Isom V, 638
Patterson, J. W. IV, 1260
Patterson, Jacob I, 224
Patterson, Jacob I, 253
Patterson, Jacob IV, 261
Patterson, Jacob IV, 427
Patterson, Jacob V, 108
Patterson, Jacob VI, 324
Patterson, Jacob VI, 845
Patterson, James I, 253
Patterson, James II, 404
Patterson, James IV, 260
Patterson, James IV, 261
Patterson, James IV, 427
Patterson, James IV, 591
Patterson, James IV, 592
Patterson, James IV, 1071
Patterson, James IV, 1109
Patterson, James VI, 769
Patterson, James VI, 906
Patterson, James VI, 975
Patterson, James B. IV, 426
Patterson, James B. IV, 427
Patterson, James B. IV, 443
Patterson, James B. IV, 592
Patterson, James E. VI, 965
Patterson, James E. VI, 975
Patterson, James E. VI, 994
Patterson, James Edward
VI, 976
Patterson, James F. VI, 936
Patterson, James F. VI, 951
Patterson, James F. VI, 973
Patterson, James F. VI, 1014
Patterson, James G. VI, 845
Patterson, James G. VI, 851
Patterson, Jane IV, 590
Patterson, Jane IV, 1099
Patterson, Jane IV, 1109
Patterson, Jane IV, 1361
Patterson, Jane IV, 1375
Patterson, Jane VI, 769
Patterson, Jane VI, 845
Patterson, Jane VI, 975
Patterson, Jane VI, 1003
Patterson, Jane H. IV, 79
Patterson, Jane H. IV, 104
Patterson, Jane H. IV, 187
Patterson, Jane H. IV, 260
Patterson, Jane Knight II, 804
Patterson, Jared I, 253
Patterson, Jared IV, 426
Patterson, Jared IV, 427
Patterson, Jared IV, 590
Patterson, Jared IV, 591
Patterson, Jared IV, 592
Patterson, Jared IV, 1071
Patterson, Jared IV, 1109
Patterson, Jared VI, 429
Patterson, Jarret VI, 975
Patterson, Jemima I, 224
Patterson, Jemima I, 990
Patterson, Jemima I, 995
Patterson, Jemima IV, 261
Patterson, Jemima IV, 287
Patterson, Jemima IV, 426
Patterson, Jemima IV, 427
Patterson, Jemima IV, 446
Patterson, Jenny I, 565
Patterson, Jenny VI, 856
Patterson, Jeremiah I, 224
Patterson, Jeremiah I, 252
Patterson, Jeremiah I, 253
Patterson, Jeremiah IV, 155
Patterson, Jeremiah IV, 260
Patterson, Jeremiah IV, 261
Patterson, Jeremiah IV, 345
Patterson, Jeremiah IV, 426
Patterson, Jeremiah IV, 427
Patterson, Jeremiah IV, 430
Patterson, Jeremiah IV, 568
Patterson, Jeremiah IV, 590
Patterson, Jeremiah IV, 591
Patterson, Jeremiah IV, 592
Patterson, Jeremiah IV, 1071
Patterson, Jeremiah IV, 1088
Patterson, Jeremiah IV, 1109
Patterson, Jeremiah VI, 99
Patterson, Jeremiah VI, 117
Patterson, Jesse I, 224
Patterson, Jesse I, 994
Patterson, Jesse IV, 591
Patterson, Jesse IV, 592

Patterson, Jesse K. IV, 1109
Patterson, Jno. I, 252
Patterson, Joanna IV, 590
Patterson, Joannah VI, 827
Patterson, Joel I, 224
Patterson, Joel IV, 261
Patterson, Joel IV, 363
Patterson, Joel IV, 426
Patterson, Joel IV, 427
Patterson, Joel IV, 591
Patterson, Joel IV, 592
Patterson, John I, 224
Patterson, John I, 252
Patterson, John I, 253
Patterson, John I, 563
Patterson, John I, 565
Patterson, John I, 595
Patterson, John I, 833
Patterson, John II, 404
Patterson, John II, 616
Patterson, John IV, 260
Patterson, John IV, 261
Patterson, John IV, 365
Patterson, John IV, 426
Patterson, John IV, 427
Patterson, John IV, 585
Patterson, John IV, 590
Patterson, John IV, 591
Patterson, John V, 522
Patterson, John V, 638
Patterson, John VI, 845
Patterson, John VI, 975
Patterson, John VI, 981
Patterson, John D. VI, 924
Patterson, John D. VI, 1010
Patterson, John G. IV, 592
Patterson, John G. IV, 1109
Patterson, John Mosby IV, 447
Patterson, John S. IV, 1110
Patterson, John S. IV, 1118
Patterson, John Schofield IV, 1109
Patterson, John W. IV, 1110
Patterson, John William IV, 1109
Patterson, Jonathan I, 224
Patterson, Jonathan I, 229
Patterson, Jonathan I, 252
Patterson, Jonathan I, 253
Patterson, Jonathan I, 254
Patterson, Jonathan IV, 155
Patterson, Jonathan IV, 260
Patterson, Jonathan IV, 261
Patterson, Jonathan IV, 426
Patterson, Jonathan IV, 429
Patterson, Jonathan IV, 591
Patterson, Jordan I, 833
Patterson, Jordan I, 978
Patterson, Jordan I, 995
Patterson, Jordan IV, 240
Patterson, Jordan IV, 260
Patterson, Jordan IV, 261
Patterson, Jordan IV, 1071
Patterson, Jordan IV, 1109
Patterson, Jordden I, 994
Patterson, Jordon I, 224
Patterson, Jordon IV, 261
Patterson, Joseph I, 224
Patterson, Joseph I, 236
Patterson, Joseph I, 245
Patterson, Joseph I, 246
Patterson, Joseph I, 252
Patterson, Joseph I, 253
Patterson, Joseph I, 565
Patterson, Joseph I, 833
Patterson, Joseph I, 978
Patterson, Joseph I, 984
Patterson, Joseph I, 994
Patterson, Joseph I, 995
Patterson, Joseph IV, 155
Patterson, Joseph IV, 212
Patterson, Joseph IV, 243
Patterson, Joseph IV, 260
Patterson, Joseph IV, 261
Patterson, Joseph IV, 279
Patterson, Joseph IV, 396
Patterson, Joseph IV, 398
Patterson, Joseph IV, 426
Patterson, Joseph IV, 427
Patterson, Joseph IV, 446
Patterson, Joseph IV, 455
Patterson, Joseph IV, 590
Patterson, Joseph IV, 591
Patterson, Joseph IV, 1060
Patterson, Joseph IV, 1071
Patterson, Joseph IV, 1088
Patterson, Joseph IV, 1109
Patterson, Joseph IV, 1178
Patterson, Joseph VI, 17
Patterson, Joseph VI, 99
Patterson, Joseph VI, 117
Patterson, Joseph VI, 896
Patterson, Joseph VI, 901
Patterson, Joseph VI, 997
Patterson, Joseph B. IV, 1109
Patterson, Joseph S. I, 991
Patterson, Joseph S. I, 995
Patterson, Joseph W. I, 995
Patterson, Joseph, Jr. I, 253
Patterson, Joseph, Jr. IV, 261
Patterson, Joseph, Sr. I, 253
Patterson, Joseph, Sr. IV, 427
Patterson, Joshua I, 224
Patterson, Joshua I, 994
Patterson, Joshua I, 995
Patterson, Joshua IV, 590
Patterson, Joshua IV, 592
Patterson, Julia E. IV, 1219
Patterson, Keziah I, 224
Patterson, Keziah I, 252
Patterson, Keziah I, 253
Patterson, Keziah IV, 181
Patterson, Keziah IV, 260
Patterson, L. W. IV, 1260
Patterson, Laban IV, 260
Patterson, Laban IV, 426
Patterson, Laban IV, 591
Patterson, Laban B. IV, 407
Patterson, Laban B. IV, 427
Patterson, Laban B. IV, 583
Patterson, Laban B. IV, 591
Patterson, Laban B. IV, 1071
Patterson, Laband IV, 155
Patterson, Laben B. IV, 582
Patterson, Landis VI, 799
Patterson, Laura IV, 1332
Patterson, Lemuel IV, 260
Patterson, Lemuel IV, 261
Patterson, Lemuel IV, 565
Patterson, Lemuel IV, 583
Patterson, Lemuel IV, 590
Patterson, Lester John IV, 749
Patterson, Lettice I, 984
Patterson, Lettice I, 995
Patterson, Lettis P. I, 978
Patterson, Lewis IV, 427
Patterson, Lewis IV, 591
Patterson, Lindley IV, 261
Patterson, Lindley IV, 591
Patterson, Lindley IV, 592
Patterson, Lindley IV, 1109
Patterson, Littleberry VI, 800
Patterson, Littleberry VI, 811
Patterson, Loisa IV, 261
Patterson, Loretta IV, 261
Patterson, Loretta IV, 591
Patterson, Loretta F. IV, 576
Patterson, Loretta F. IV, 591
Patterson, Louis IV, 427
Patterson, Louisa IV, 386
Patterson, Louisa IV, 459
Patterson, Louisa IV, 574
Patterson, Louisa IV, 591
Patterson, Louisa IV, 642
Patterson, Louisa IV, 650
Patterson, Louisa IV, 1109
Patterson, Louiza IV, 591
Patterson, Lucetta C. IV, 591
Patterson, Lucinda IV, 261
Patterson, Lucinda IV, 1109
Patterson, Lucinda V, 269
Patterson, Lucinda VI, 854
Patterson, Lucy IV, 365
Patterson, Lucy IV, 426
Patterson, Lucy IV, 591
Patterson, Lucy VI, 805
Patterson, Lucy VI, 811
Patterson, Lucy VI, 975
Patterson, Lucy VI, 993
Patterson, Lucy Mason IV, 447
Patterson, Luvena VI, 1003
Patterson, Lydia I, 224
Patterson, Lydia I, 230
Patterson, Lydia I, 253
Patterson, Lydia IV, 396
Patterson, Lydia IV, 407
Patterson, Lydia IV, 426
Patterson, Lydia IV, 427
Patterson, Lydia IV, 443
Patterson, Lydia IV, 590
Patterson, Lydia V, 638
Patterson, Lydia VI, 380
Patterson, Lydia VI, 429
Patterson, Lydia VI, 913
Patterson, Lydia Ann IV, 582
Patterson, Lydia Ann IV, 591
Patterson, Lydia Ann IV, 592
Patterson, Lydia Ann IV, 1071
Patterson, Lydia H. IV, 260
Patterson, Lydia H. IV, 304
Patterson, Maggie IV, 1210
Patterson, Maggie Hays IV, 1219
Patterson, Mahala IV, 260
Patterson, Mahala IV, 261
Patterson, Mahala IV, 427
Patterson, Mahala IV, 590
Patterson, Mahala IV, 592
Patterson, Mahala IV, 650
Patterson, Mahala IV, 1109
Patterson, Mahlon IV, 104
Patterson, Mahlon IV, 187
Patterson, Mahlon IV, 221
Patterson, Mahlon IV, 226
Patterson, Mahlon IV, 260
Patterson, Mahlon IV, 261
Patterson, Mahlon IV, 304
Patterson, Malinda II, 704
Patterson, Malinda II, 714
Patterson, Malinda IV, 332
Patterson, Malinda IV, 345
Patterson, Malinda IV, 389
Patterson, Malinda IV, 577
Patterson, Malinda IV, 591
Patterson, Malinda VI, 851
Patterson, Margaret I, 224
Patterson, Margaret IV, 155
Patterson, Margaret IV, 260
Patterson, Margaret IV, 261
Patterson, Margaret IV, 426
Patterson, Margaret IV, 458
Patterson, Margaret IV, 937
Patterson, Maria IV, 1089
Patterson, Maria IV, 1109
Patterson, Mariam IV, 260
Patterson, Marmaduke IV, 592
Patterson, Marmaduke IV, 1109
Patterson, Martha I, 224
Patterson, Martha I, 230
Patterson, Martha I, 252
Patterson, Martha I, 253
Patterson, Martha I, 994
Patterson, Martha IV, 260
Patterson, Martha IV, 261
Patterson, Martha IV, 590
Patterson, Martha IV, 1109
Patterson, Martha VI, 975
Patterson, Martha B. VI, 811
Patterson, Mary I, 224
Patterson, Mary I, 236
Patterson, Mary I, 252
Patterson, Mary I, 253
Patterson, Mary I, 563
Patterson, Mary I, 565
Patterson, Mary I, 595
Patterson, Mary I, 833
Patterson, Mary I, 907
Patterson, Mary I, 978
Patterson, Mary I, 994
Patterson, Mary I, 995
Patterson, Mary III, 230
Patterson, Mary III, 249
Patterson, Mary IV, 155
Patterson, Mary IV, 181
Patterson, Mary IV, 212
Patterson, Mary IV, 240
Patterson, Mary IV, 243
Patterson, Mary IV, 260
Patterson, Mary IV, 261
Patterson, Mary IV, 279
Patterson, Mary IV, 426
Patterson, Mary IV, 427
Patterson, Mary IV, 429
Patterson, Mary IV, 447
Patterson, Mary IV, 457
Patterson, Mary IV, 583
Patterson, Mary IV, 590
Patterson, Mary IV, 591
Patterson, Mary IV, 592
Patterson, Mary IV, 1060
Patterson, Mary IV, 1071
Patterson, Mary IV, 1109
Patterson, Mary IV, 1116
Patterson, Mary V, 522
Patterson, Mary V, 638
Patterson, Mary VI, 99
Patterson, Mary VI, 826
Patterson, Mary VI, 845
Patterson, Mary VI, 975
Patterson, Mary A. IV, 720
Patterson, Mary A. VI, 845
Patterson, Mary Ann I, 887
Patterson, Mary Ann I, 897
Patterson, Mary Ann IV, 104
Patterson, Mary Ann IV, 187
Patterson, Mary Ann IV, 221
Patterson, Mary Ann IV, 226
Patterson, Mary Ann IV, 260
Patterson, Mary Ann IV, 304
Patterson, Mary Bailey VI, 117
Patterson, Mary E. IV, 427
Patterson, Mary E. VI, 936
Patterson, Mary Elizabeth IV, 427
Patterson, Mary G. IV, 1109
Patterson, Mary G. IV, 1114
Patterson, Mary R. VI, 802
Patterson, Mary Rachel I, 253
Patterson, Mary W. VI, 965
Patterson, Maryann IV, 187
Patterson, Mathew IV, 1105
Patterson, Mathew IV, 1109
Patterson, Mathew T. IV, 590
Patterson, Mathew T. IV, 592
Patterson, Mathew T. IV, 1109
Patterson, Matthew IV, 426
Patterson, Matthew IV, 642
Patterson, Matthew IV, 650
Patterson, Meriam I, 244
Patterson, Meriam I, 253
Patterson, Meriam I, 994
Patterson, Merriam IV, 260
Patterson, Michael IV, 155
Patterson, Michal IV, 260
Patterson, Michal IV, 261
Patterson, Milicent Jones IV, 427
Patterson, Milton IV, 261
Patterson, Milton IV, 590
Patterson, Milton IV, 591
Patterson, Miriam I, 224
Patterson, Miriam I, 253
Patterson, Miriam IV, 224
Patterson, Miriam IV, 260
Patterson, Miriam IV, 585
Patterson, Moal II, 616
Patterson, Moles II, 404
Patterson, Moles II, 616
Patterson, Moles II, 631
Patterson, Moses II, 404
Patterson, Moultrie VI, 976
Patterson, Mrs. ??? VI, 890
Patterson, Nancy VI, 826
Patterson, Nancy VI, 882
Patterson, Nancy VI, 975
Patterson, Nathan IV, 426
Patterson, Nathan IV, 427
Patterson, Nathan IV, 457
Patterson, Nathan IV, 591
Patterson, Nathan IV, 592
Patterson, Nelson A. VI, 972
Patterson, Nelson A. VI, 976
Patterson, Nicholas Crews VI, 814
Patterson, Obediah VI, 799
Patterson, Obedience IV, 427
Patterson, Ohio R. IV, 591
Patterson, Olive R. IV, 579
Patterson, Olive R. IV, 591
Patterson, Oney VI, 993
Patterson, Oscar IV, 260
Patterson, Oscar W. IV, 261
Patterson, Oscar W. IV, 937
Patterson, Pamelia VI, 814
Patterson, Patience I, 252
Patterson, Patience IV, 426
Patterson, Patience VI, 99
Patterson, Patience VI, 117
Patterson, Patience Bailey VI, 117
Patterson, Penina IV, 591
Patterson, Peninah IV, 592
Patterson, Penninah IV, 363
Patterson, Penninah IV, 426
Patterson, Peter I, 224
Patterson, Peter I, 253
Patterson, Peter VI, 993
Patterson, Pharaba IV, 566
Patterson, Pharabi IV, 386
Patterson, Pharaby IV, 260
Patterson, Pharaby IV, 261
Patterson, Pharaby IV, 590
Patterson, Pharaby IV, 591
Patterson, Pharaby IV, 592
Patterson, Pharaby IV, 1109
Patterson, Pharaby IV, 1166
Patterson, Pharaby IV, 1179
Patterson, Pharaby J. IV, 224
Patterson, Pharaby J. IV, 260
Patterson, Phariba IV, 261
Patterson, Phariba IV, 377
Patterson, Phariba IV, 427
Patterson, Phariba IV, 591
Patterson, Phebe IV, 590
Patterson, Pherby I, 224
Patterson, Phereby IV, 1109
Patterson, Pheriba IV, 574
Patterson, Pheriba IV, 1071
Patterson, Phreeby IV, 1087
Patterson, Phreeby IV, 1109
Patterson, Polly V, 638
Patterson, Polly VI, 975
Patterson, Polly VI, 976
Patterson, Priscilla I, 253
Patterson, Priscilla IV, 592
Patterson, Priscilla IV, 1109
Patterson, Prysilla I, 253
Patterson, Rachel I, 253
Patterson, Rachel II, 91
Patterson, Rachel II, 108
Patterson, Rachel II, 699
Patterson, Rachel II, 704
Patterson, Rachel II, 711
Patterson, Rachel IV, 155
Patterson, Rachel IV, 260
Patterson, Rachel IV, 261
Patterson, Rachel IV, 287
Patterson, Rachel IV, 365
Patterson, Rachel IV, 426
Patterson, Rachel IV, 427
Patterson, Rachel IV, 428
Patterson, Rachel IV, 430
Patterson, Rachel IV, 443
Patterson, Rachel IV, 576
Patterson, Rachel IV, 577
Patterson, Rachel IV, 590
Patterson, Rachel IV, 591
Patterson, Rachel IV, 592
Patterson, Rachel IV, 1071
Patterson, Rachel IV, 1088
Patterson, Rachel IV, 1091
Patterson, Rachel IV, 1109
Patterson, Rachel IV, 1118
Patterson, Rachel VI, 981
Patterson, Rachel B. IV, 1109
Patterson, Rachel E. II, 714
Patterson, Rachel E. II, 744
Patterson, Rachel E. II, 753
Patterson, Rachel E. II, 759
Patterson, Rachel E. IV, 261
Patterson, Rachel E. IV, 427
Patterson, Rachel F. IV, 1109
Patterson, Rachel F. IV, 1118
Patterson, Rachel P. IV, 426
Patterson, Randall IV, 749
Patterson, Randall James IV, 74
Patterson, Rebecca I, 224
Patterson, Rebecca I, 799
Patterson, Rebecca I, 833
Patterson, Rebecca I, 995
Patterson, Rebecca II, 744
Patterson, Rebecca II, 759
Patterson, Rebecca IV, 53
Patterson, Rebecca IV, 64
Patterson, Rebecca IV, 261
Patterson, Rebecca IV, 345
Patterson, Rebecca IV, 381
Patterson, Rebecca IV, 426
Patterson, Rebecca IV, 427
Patterson, Rebecca IV, 590
Patterson, Rebecca IV, 591
Patterson, Rebecca IV, 592
Patterson, Rebecca IV, 1071
Patterson, Rebecca IV, 1109
Patterson, Rebecca IV, 1120
Patterson, Rebecca V, 638
Patterson, Rebecca Jane V, 638
Patterson, Rebecca W. IV, 1110
Patterson, Rebeckah VI, 896
Patterson, Rhoda I, 224
Patterson, Rhoda I, 246
Patterson, Rhoda I, 252
Patterson, Rhoda IV, 427
Patterson, Rhoda IV, 1288
Patterson, Ricks IV, 260
Patterson, Ricks IV, 261
Patterson, Rix IV, 261
Patterson, Rix IV, 592
Patterson, Rix IV, 1109
Patterson, Robert I, 67
Patterson, Robert I, 160
Patterson, Robert I, 224
Patterson, Robert II, 616
Patterson, Robert II, 631
Patterson, Robert IV, 590
Patterson, Robert IV, 591
Patterson, Robert IV, 1071
Patterson, Robert IV, 1109
Patterson, Robert VI, 879
Patterson, Robt. L. III, 249
Patterson, Ruth I, 229
Patterson, Ruth I, 253
Patterson, Ruth IV, 155
Patterson, Ruth IV, 260
Patterson, Ruth IV, 261
Patterson, Ruth IV, 426
Patterson, Ruth IV, 591
Patterson, Ruth IV, 1109
Patterson, Ruth IV, 1122
Patterson, Ruth Anna IV, 445
Patterson, Ruth Anna IV, 566
Patterson, Ruthanna IV, 79
Patterson, Ruthanna IV, 104
Patterson, Ruthanna IV, 187
Patterson, Ruthanna IV, 260
Patterson, Ruthanna IV, 590
Patterson, Ruthanna IV, 591
Patterson, Ruthanna IV, 936

terson, Sally V, 638
terson, Sally VI, 799
terson, Sally VI, 845
terson, Saml. D. VI, 960
terson, Samuel I, 224
terson, Samuel I, 253
terson, Samuel II, 404
terson, Samuel IV, 155
terson, Samuel IV, 574
terson, Samuel IV, 590
terson, Samuel IV, 592
terson, Samuel V, 108
terson, Samuel VI, 802
terson, Samuel VI, 845
terson, Samuel A. VI, 827
terson, Samuel D. VI, 936
terson, Samuel D. VI, 950
terson, Samuel D. VI, 968
terson, Samuel L. VI, 1001
terson, Samuel N. V, 108
terson, Samuel N. V, 925
terson, Sarah I, 224
terson, Sarah I, 230
terson, Sarah I, 245
terson, Sarah I, 253
terson, Sarah I, 565
terson, Sarah I, 595
terson, Sarah I, 833
terson, Sarah I, 994
terson, Sarah IV, 156
terson, Sarah IV, 164
terson, Sarah IV, 260
terson, Sarah IV, 261
terson, Sarah IV, 407
terson, Sarah IV, 426
terson, Sarah IV, 427
terson, Sarah IV, 455
terson, Sarah IV, 574
terson, Sarah IV, 582
terson, Sarah IV, 583
terson, Sarah IV, 586
terson, Sarah IV, 590
terson, Sarah IV, 591
terson, Sarah IV, 592
terson, Sarah IV, 1071
terson, Sarah IV, 1083
terson, Sarah IV, 1100
terson, Sarah IV, 1109
terson, Sarah IV, 1110
terson, Sarah IV, 1112
terson, Sarah IV, 1118
terson, Sarah V, 522
terson, Sarah V, 586
terson, Sarah V, 592
terson, Sarah V, 638
terson, Sarah V, 922
terson, Sarah V, 925
terson, Sarah VI, 901
terson, Sarah VI, 976
terson, Sarah A. IV, 591
terson, Sarah Ann IV, 427
terson, Sarah Ann IV, 946
terson, Sarah Ann IV, 985
terson, Sarah Ann IV, 1091
terson, Sarah Ann IV, 1109
terson, Sarah Ann VI, 941
terson, Sarah B. IV, 426
terson, Sarah E. IV, 369
terson, Sarah E. IV, 427
terson, Sarah F. III, 431
terson, Sarah J. II, 699
terson, Sarah J. IV, 427
terson, Sarah J. IV, 591
terson, Sarah J. VI, 855
terson, Sarah M. IV, 585
terson, Sarah W. VI, 975
terson, Sarahann IV, 591
terson, Sidna IV, 590
terson, Silas I, 224
terson, Silas IV, 155
terson, Silas IV, 261
terson, Silas IV, 365
terson, Silas IV, 426
terson, Silas IV, 427
terson, Silas IV, 443
terson, Silas IV, 590
terson, Silas IV, 592
terson, Silas IV, 1071
terson, Silva I, 240
terson, Silva I, 253
terson, Silva IV, 363
terson, Simeon IV, 447
terson, Simmons I, 833
terson, Stewart VI, 913
terson, Susan IV, 1109
terson, Susan IV, 1121
terson, Susan VI, 976
terson, Susan Benson VI, 890
terson, Susan L. II, 180
terson, Susannah II, 294
terson, Susannah II, 298
Patterson, Susannah VI, 800
Patterson, Susannah VI, 879
Patterson, Sylva I, 224
Patterson, Sylvia IV, 398
Patterson, Sylvia IV, 399
Patterson, Tabitha IV, 261
Patterson, Tabitha IV, 319
Patterson, Tabitha IV, 345
Patterson, Tabitha IV, 423
Patterson, Tabitha IV, 565
Patterson, Tabitha IV, 567
Patterson, Tabitha IV, 591
Patterson, Tabitha IV, 592
Patterson, Tabitha IV, 593
Patterson, Tace IV, 261
Patterson, Tacey IV, 212
Patterson, Tacey IV, 260
Patterson, Tacy IV, 400
Patterson, Tacyendon I, 224
Patterson, Talitha I, 224
Patterson, Talitha IV, 155
Patterson, Talitha IV, 261
Patterson, Talitha IV, 427
Patterson, Talitha IV, 576
Patterson, Talitha IV, 579
Patterson, Talitha IV, 589
Patterson, Tamer IV, 427
Patterson, Tarleton VI, 845
Patterson, Tarlton VI, 856
Patterson, Tempe I, 253
Patterson, Temperance I, 253
Patterson, Temperance IV, 429
Patterson, Temperance VI, 975
Patterson, Tempey I, 253
Patterson, Tempy I, 252
Patterson, Tempy I, 254
Patterson, Thomas I, 238
Patterson, Thomas I, 253
Patterson, Thomas II, 404
Patterson, Thomas IV, 407
Patterson, Thomas IV, 426
Patterson, Thomas IV, 427
Patterson, Thomas IV, 591
Patterson, Thomas VI, 975
Patterson, Thomas B. VI, 845
Patterson, Thomas J. IV, 590
Patterson, Thomas P. IV, 592
Patterson, Thomas P. IV, 1109
Patterson, Thomas T. IV, 592
Patterson, Thomas T. IV, 1109
Patterson, Thomas W. VI, 968
Patterson, Tilitha IV, 364
Patterson, Tilitha IV, 426
Patterson, Tillman IV, 427
Patterson, Tilman II, 699
Patterson, Tilman II, 704
Patterson, Tilman II, 711
Patterson, Tilman II, 714
Patterson, Tilman II, 753
Patterson, Tilman II, 759
Patterson, Tilman IV, 261
Patterson, Tilman IV, 332
Patterson, Tilman IV, 345
Patterson, Tilman IV, 427
Patterson, Tilman IV, 576
Patterson, Tilman IV, 577
Patterson, Tilman IV, 591
Patterson, Tilman IV, 592
Patterson, Tilman, Jr. IV, 261
Patterson, Tilman, Jr. IV, 369
Patterson, Tilman, Jr. IV, 427
Patterson, Tilmon II, 744
Patterson, Tilmon II, 759
Patterson, Tilmon IV, 261
Patterson, Tilmon IV, 591
Patterson, Tremon IV, 261
Patterson, Unice IV, 427
Patterson, Uriah I, 224
Patterson, Uriah I, 994
Patterson, Wayne Franklin IV, 749
Patterson, William I, 224
Patterson, William I, 244
Patterson, William I, 247
Patterson, William I, 252
Patterson, William I, 253
Patterson, William I, 833
Patterson, William I, 994
Patterson, William II, 404
Patterson, William II, 714
Patterson, William IV, 260
Patterson, William IV, 261
Patterson, William IV, 427
Patterson, William IV, 590
Patterson, William IV, 591
Patterson, William IV, 1109
Patterson, William V, 269
Patterson, William V, 522
Patterson, William V, 638
Patterson, William VI, 769
Patterson, William VI, 770
Patterson, William VI, 826
Patterson, William VI, 855
Patterson, William VI, 882
Patterson, William VI, 889
Patterson, William VI, 945
Patterson, William VI, 975
Patterson, William VI, 979
Patterson, William VI, 993
Patterson, William VI, 1003
Patterson, William A. IV, 261
Patterson, William A. VI, 845
Patterson, William A. VI, 975
Patterson, William C. VI, 969
Patterson, William C. VI, 1003
Patterson, William L. IV, 426
Patterson, William P. IV, 407
Patterson, William, Jr. I, 224
Patterson, William, Jr. I, 252
Patterson, William, Jr. I, 253
Patterson, William, Jr. I, 994
Patterson, William, Jr. IV, 261
Patterson, William, Sr. I, 253
Patterson, Willis IV, 260
Patterson, Wilson IV, 261
Patterson, Wilson IV, 427
Patterson, Winney I, 994
Patterson, Winny I, 991
Patterson, Winny I, 994
Patterson, Wm. II, 616
Patterson, Wm. II, 759
Patterson, Wm. IV, 181
Patterson, Wm. IV, 364
Patterson, Wm. IV, 426
Patterson, Wm. IV, 430
Patterson, Wm. IV, 569
Patterson, Wm. IV, 591
Patterson, Wm. IV, 1071
Patterson, Wm., Jr. IV, 155
Patteson, Ann I, 512
Patteson, Ann B. VI, 976
Patteson, Cornelis III, 311
Patteson, Deborah IV, 155
Patteson, Elizabeth I, 512
Patteson, Elizabeth VI, 975
Patteson, Esther IV, 155
Patteson, Godfrey III, 311
Patteson, Hannah II, 230
Patteson, Hannah II, 248
Patteson, Hannah VI, 503
Patteson, Hannah VI, 555
Patteson, Hannah VI, 746
Patteson, James VI, 975
Patteson, Jemime I, 512
Patteson, Jenne I, 512
Patteson, Jenny I, 526
Patteson, Jenny I, 565
Patteson, John I, 512
Patteson, John, II I, 512
Patteson, Jordan I, 512
Patteson, Joseph I, 512
Patteson, Joseph IV, 155
Patteson, Laband IV, 155
Patteson, Martha VI, 975
Patteson, Mary IV, 155
Patteson, Nelson A. VI, 976
Patteson, Samuel IV, 155
Patteson, Sarah I, 512
Patteson, Simmeon I, 512
Patteson, Thos. I, 512
Patteson, William I, 512
Patteson, William II, 230
Patteson, William II, 248
Patteson, Wm. VI, 503
Pattin, Hannah II, 616
Pattin, Hannah II, 639
Pattirson, Anna I, 621
Pattison, Ann VI, 533
Pattison, Ann VI, 542
Pattison, Ann VI, 657
Pattison, Ann VI, 675
Pattison, Anna I, 790
Pattison, Benj. VI, 101
Pattison, Benj. VI, 215
Pattison, Benjamin I, 252
Pattison, Benjamin VI, 115
Pattison, Benjamin VI, 116
Pattison, Benjamin VI, 117
Pattison, Betsy I, 913
Pattison, Charles I, 790
Pattison, Cornelia III, 249
Pattison, Elizabeth I, 833
Pattison, Elizabeth I, 834
Pattison, Elizabeth I, 913
Pattison, Elizabeth I, 914
Pattison, Elizabeth VI, 115
Pattison, Elizabeth VI, 116
Pattison, Elizabeth VI, 117
Pattison, Faith Bailey VI, 117
Pattison, Godfrey III, 249
Pattison, Hannah VI, 117
Pattison, Hezekiah I, 913
Pattison, Hugh I, 833
Pattison, James I, 833
Pattison, James III, 249
Pattison, James III, 312
Pattison, Jane I, 833
Pattison, Jane I, 910
Pattison, Jane I, 914
Pattison, Jane III, 249
Pattison, Jane III, 312
Pattison, Jemima I, 821
Pattison, Jemima I, 833
Pattison, Jeremiah VI, 117
Pattison, John I, 586
Pattison, John I, 833
Pattison, John I, 907
Pattison, John I, 913
Pattison, John, Jr. I, 833
Pattison, John, Jr. I, 913
Pattison, Jordan I, 790
Pattison, Jordan I, 804
Pattison, Jordan I, 833
Pattison, Joseph I, 565
Pattison, Joseph I, 773
Pattison, Joseph I, 790
Pattison, Joseph I, 833
Pattison, Joseph I, 913
Pattison, Joseph I, 914
Pattison, Joseph VI, 117
Pattison, Joseph VI, 215
Pattison, Joseph, Jr. I, 833
Pattison, Kesiah VI, 117
Pattison, Luzena I, 913
Pattison, Magdelane I, 913
Pattison, Margaret I, 833
Pattison, Margaret I, 913
Pattison, Margaret VI, 117
Pattison, Mary I, 790
Pattison, Mary I, 804
Pattison, Mary I, 833
Pattison, Mary Bailey VI, 117
Pattison, Moal II, 616
Pattison, Patience VI, 117
Pattison, Patience Bailey VI, 117
Pattison, Rebecca I, 833
Pattison, Sarah I, 790
Pattison, Sarah I, 819
Pattison, Sarah I, 823
Pattison, Sarah I, 833
Pattison, Simmons I, 833
Pattison, Simmons I, 907
Pattison, Simmons I, 913
Pattison, William I, 252
Pattison, William I, 790
Pattison, William I, 833
Pattison, William I, 913
Pattison, William VI, 117
Patton, ??? IV, 1047
Patton, Albert IV, 1288
Patton, Alice V, 702
Patton, Allie V, 196
Patton, Ann I, 1045
Patton, Anna V, 462
Patton, Anna V, 702
Patton, Anna V, 722
Patton, Annes V, 662
Patton, Annes V, 722
Patton, Annis V, 702
Patton, Blanch V, 702
Patton, Caleb S. IV, 1071
Patton, Catharine III, 128
Patton, Catharine III, 249
Patton, D. Hubert V, 703
Patton, Drusilla V, 269
Patton, Eliza I, 985
Patton, Eliza I, 995
Patton, Eliza Jane IV, 1071
Patton, Eliza Jane IV, 1110
Patton, Elizabeth V, 269
Patton, Ephraim IV, 428
Patton, Esta V, 269
Patton, Euphamy IV, 1110
Patton, Euphema Alice V, 269
Patton, Euphemia IV, 428
Patton, Ezekiel IV, 428
Patton, Geo V, 269
Patton, George D. IV, 1071
Patton, Gladys V, 269
Patton, Gladys V, 703
Patton, Grace I, 1045
Patton, Grace IV, 165
Patton, Hannah I, 1127
Patton, Hannah I, 1130
Patton, Hannah II, 616
Patton, Hardenia Ellen V, 269
Patton, Helen V, 702
Patton, Isaac I, 1045
Patton, Isaac V, 702
Patton, James V, 269
Patton, James M. V, 269
Patton, Jane IV, 1110
Patton, Jayn II, 64
Patton, Jayn II, 91
Patton, Jennie V, 702
Patton, John I, 1045
Patton, John IV, 165
Patton, John IV, 428
Patton, John IV, 446
Patton, John IV, 1110
Patton, John V, 269
Patton, John V, 592
Patton, Joseph IV, 428
Patton, Lena V, 269
Patton, Lilly IV, 1288
Patton, Lydia IV, 1071
Patton, Lydia IV, 1110
Patton, Mahlon I, 1045
Patton, Mahlon IV, 165
Patton, Mahlon IV, 428
Patton, Mahlon IV, 1052
Patton, Mahlon IV, 1071
Patton, Mahlon IV, 1110
Patton, Mary I, 1045
Patton, Mary IV, 420
Patton, Mary IV, 428
Patton, Mary IV, 1071
Patton, Mary V, 269
Patton, Mary Ellen IV, 1071
Patton, Mary Ellen IV, 1110
Patton, Mary Ellin IV, 1110
Patton, Phebe IV, 390
Patton, Phebe IV, 1052
Patton, Phebe IV, 1071
Patton, Rachel I, 1045
Patton, Rachel IV, 165
Patton, Rachel IV, 397
Patton, Rachel IV, 427
Patton, Rachel IV, 428
Patton, Rachel IV, 1052
Patton, Rachel IV, 1071
Patton, Rachel B. IV, 428
Patton, Rachel B. IV, 436
Patton, Rebecca IV, 428
Patton, Rebecca IV, 446
Patton, Rhoda IV, 428
Patton, Rhoda IV, 567
Patton, Richard IV, 1071
Patton, Richard IV, 1110
Patton, Ruth IV, 428
Patton, Ruth V, 269
Patton, Sally IV, 422
Patton, Sally IV, 427
Patton, Sally IV, 1260
Patton, Sarah I, 1045
Patton, Sarah IV, 165
Patton, Sarah IV, 260
Patton, Sarah IV, 1071
Patton, Sarah IV, 1079
Patton, Sarah Arbelle V, 269
Patton, Sarah E. V, 308
Patton, Sarah S. IV, 1052
Patton, Sarah S. IV, 1071
Patton, Scott V, 638
Patton, Sherman V, 269
Patton, Silas B. III, 128
Patton, Silas B. III, 249
Patton, Smith IV, 428
Patton, Susan V, 53
Patton, Susan V, 108
Patton, Susan V, 269
Patton, Vincent VI, 836
Patton, Violet Lenore V, 703
Patton, Warren J. V, 269
Patton, Welmet I, 1130
Patton, Wilbur V, 269
Patton, William I, 1045
Patton, William IV, 422
Patton, William IV, 427
Patton, William IV, 428
Patton, William T. V, 269
Patton, Wm. IV, 165
Patton, Wm. IV, 390
Patton, Wm. IV, 397
Patton, Wm. IV, 428
Patton, Wm. IV, 1052
Patton, Wm. IV, 1071
Patton, Wm. IV, 1110
Patton, Wm. V, 269
Patton, Wm. Bailey IV, 1071
Pattrage, Bell V, 462
Pattrage, Cora V, 462
Patty, ??? I, 1160
Patty, Ann I, 1035
Patty, Ann V, 108
Patty, Anna V, 108
Patty, Anna V, 759
Patty, Anna V, 789
Patty, Anna V, 790
Patty, Anna V, 818
Patty, Anne V, 730
Patty, Avey VI, 845
Patty, Charles I, 1022
Patty, Charles I, 1032

Patty, Charles I, 1035
Patty, Charles IV, 53
Patty, Charles V, 196
Patty, Charles V, 522
Patty, Charles V, 759
Patty, Charles V, 818
Patty, Chas. V, 196
Patty, Chas. V, 759
Patty, Chas. V, 781
Patty, Chas. V, 790
Patty, Elijah VI, 845
Patty, Elizabeth V, 790
Patty, Enoch V, 759
Patty, Enoch V, 790
Patty, George I, 1160
Patty, Hannah V, 844
Patty, Hannah V, 856
Patty, Hugh V, 759
Patty, James I, 1035
Patty, James V, 108
Patty, James V, 723
Patty, James V, 759
Patty, James V, 789
Patty, James V, 818
Patty, James V, 856
Patty, James, Jr. V, 790
Patty, Jesse I, 1160
Patty, John V, 759
Patty, John V, 790
Patty, Josiah I, 1160
Patty, Lot V, 759
Patty, Maggie V, 818
Patty, Margaret V, 108
Patty, Margaret V, 818
Patty, Margery V, 108
Patty, Margery V, 126
Patty, Margery V, 818
Patty, Mark V, 108
Patty, Mark V, 749
Patty, Mark V, 759
Patty, Mark V, 787
Patty, Mark V, 789
Patty, Mark V, 818
Patty, Martha VI, 737
Patty, Mary I, 1022
Patty, Mary I, 1032
Patty, Mary I, 1035
Patty, Mary IV, 53
Patty, Mary V, 749
Patty, Mary V, 759
Patty, Mary V, 781
Patty, Mary V, 787
Patty, Mary V, 789
Patty, Mary V, 790
Patty, Mary V, 808
Patty, Mary V, 818
Patty, Mary V, 856
Patty, Nancy V, 108
Patty, Nancy V, 759
Patty, Nancy V, 783
Patty, Nancy V, 790
Patty, Pheba V, 781
Patty, Phebe V, 108
Patty, Phebe V, 759
Patty, Phebe V, 790
Patty, Phebe V, 818
Patty, Rachel I, 1035
Patty, Rebecca V, 108
Patty, Rebecca V, 126
Patty, Rebecca V, 759
Patty, Rebecca V, 789
Patty, Rebecca V, 818
Patty, Samuel V, 108
Patty, Samuel V, 759
Patty, Sarah I, 1022
Patty, Sarah I, 1035
Patty, Sarah V, 108
Patty, Sarah V, 730
Patty, Sarah V, 759
Patty, Sarah VI, 798
Patty, Susanna V, 760
Patty, Wm. V, 759
Patty, Wm. V, 818
Patty, Zorobabel I, 1160
Pattyson, Benj. VI, 160
Pattyson, Benjamin VI, 202
Pattyson, Benjamin VI, 203
Pattyson, Benjamin VI, 213
Pattyson, Elizabeth VI, 177
Pattyson, John VI, 202
Pattyson, John VI, 203
Pattyson, Joseph VI, 202
Pattyson, Joseph VI, 203
Pattyson, Joseph VI, 211
Pattyson, Joseph VI, 212
Pattyson, Martha VI, 202
Pattyson, Martha VI, 203
Pattyson, Martha VI, 210
Pattyson, Mary VI, 210
Pattyson, Sarah VI, 202
Pattyson, Sarah VI, 211
Pattyson, Sarah VI, 212
Pattyson, William VI, 202
Paty, Anna V, 108
Paty, Charles I, 1035
Paty, Charles V, 196
Paty, Ester I, 1062
Paty, James V, 108
Paty, James V, 856
Paty, Mark V, 108
Paty, Mary I, 1035
Paty, Mary I, 1060
Paty, Mary I, 1062
Paty, Mary V, 794
Paty, Nancy V, 108
Paty, Phebe V, 108
Paty, Phebe V, 794
Paty, Rachel I, 1033
Paty, Rachel I, 1035
Paty, Rebecca V, 794
Paty, Samuel V, 108
Paty, Sarah I, 1033
Paty, Sarah I, 1035
Paty, Sarah V, 108
Pauckett, Clarence V, 703
Pauckett, Dora V, 703
Pauckett, Frank V, 703
Pauken, Astrid E. III, 128
Paukett, Clarence V, 703
Paukett, Dora V, 703
Paukett, Frank V, 703
Paukett, R. Franklin V, 703
Paul, Abigail II, 155
Paul, Abigail K. IV, 651
Paul, Abigail R. II, 136
Paul, Abigail R. II, 155
Paul, Abigail R. II, 906
Paul, Abigail Reeves II, 813
Paul, Abigail W. IV, 651
Paul, Ann II, 404
Paul, Ann II, 495
Paul, Ann II, 616
Paul, Ann II, 974
Paul, Ann II, 1020
Paul, Ann II, 1042
Paul, Anna II, 813
Paul, Bettle II, 404
Paul, Bettle II, 616
Paul, Bettle II, 813
Paul, Bettle II, 906
Paul, Clara Alice II, 813
Paul, Clara E. II, 813
Paul, Clara E. II, 898
Paul, Clara E. II, 906
Paul, Eleanor II, 616
Paul, Elizabeth II, 59
Paul, Elizabeth II, 91
Paul, Elizabeth II, 248
Paul, Elizabeth II, 255
Paul, Elizabeth II, 404
Paul, Elizabeth II, 507
Paul, Elizabeth II, 616
Paul, Elizabeth II, 630
Paul, Florence M. II, 813
Paul, Hannah II, 59
Paul, Hannah II, 91
Paul, Hannah II, 616
Paul, Hannah II, 679
Paul, Hannah II, 1058
Paul, Hannah II, 1077
Paul, Hannah T. II, 906
Paul, Hannah T. II, 907
Paul, Hannah T. IV, 651
Paul, Hattie IV, 1344
Paul, Henry II, 404
Paul, Herbert G. II, 813
Paul, Herbert Mickle II, 813
Paul, Howard M. II, 907
Paul, Howard Mickle II, 813
Paul, Isaac II, 404
Paul, Jacob II, 759
Paul, James II, 404
Paul, James II, 616
Paul, Jane II, 404
Paul, Jennie IV, 1332
Paul, Jennie IV, 1344
Paul, Jennie Viola IV, 1332
Paul, Jeremiah II, 404
Paul, Jeremiah II, 616
Paul, Jeremiah II, 813
Paul, Jno. S. II, 906
Paul, John II, 404
Paul, John II, 456
Paul, John II, 616
Paul, John II, 974
Paul, John II, 1020
Paul, John Stackhouse II, 813
Paul, Jonathan II, 813
Paul, Joseph II, 404
Paul, Joseph II, 616
Paul, Joseph II, 759
Paul, Joseph II, 974
Paul, Joseph II, 1020
Paul, Joseph II, 1042
Paul, Joseph II, 1058
Paul, Joseph II, 1077
Paul, Joseph M. II, 616
Paul, Joseph W. II, 759
Paul, Josiah II, 404
Paul, Josiah II, 616
Paul, Lydia II, 404
Paul, Lydia II, 456
Paul, Lydia II, 616
Paul, Lydia II, 906
Paul, Lydia S. II, 813
Paul, Martha II, 616
Paul, Mary II, 404
Paul, Mary II, 616
Paul, Mary Ann II, 813
Paul, Mary Ann IV, 651
Paul, Michal IV, 651
Paul, Mickle C. II, 813
Paul, Mickle C. II, 898
Paul, Mickle C. II, 906
Paul, Nathan II, 404
Paul, Pamelia A. VI, 976
Paul, Pheby Parvin II, 616
Paul, Phoebe K. II, 821
Paul, Rebecca II, 404
Paul, Rebecca II, 616
Paul, Rebecca II, 813
Paul, Rebecca, Jr. II, 616
Paul, Richard II, 59
Paul, Richard Butler II, 91
Paul, Samuel II, 59
Paul, Samuel II, 91
Paul, Samuel W. II, 759
Paul, Sarah II, 404
Paul, Sarah II, 616
Paul, Sarah II, 906
Paul, Sarah II, 1042
Paul, Sarah II, 1058
Paul, Sarah IV, 651
Paul, Sarah Ann II, 616
Paul, Sarah Ann II, 813
Paul, Sidney II, 404
Paul, Sidney II, 456
Paul, Sidney II, 616
Paul, Sidney II, 630
Paul, Susanna II, 404
Paul, Thomas II, 616
Paul, Wd. Mary II, 616
Paul, Wd. Sidney II, 616
Paul, William IV, 651
Paul, William H. VI, 976
Paul, William M. IV, 651
Paul, Wm. II, 616
Paul, Wm. M. II, 813
Paul, Wm. P. IV, 1344
Paul, Wm. W. II, 759
Paul, Yeamans II, 616
Paul, Yeamons II, 616
Paul, Yen III, 206
Paul, Yhamans II, 616
Paule, Jane II, 404
Paule, John II, 496
Paule, John II, 616
Paule, Sarah II, 496
Paule, Sarah II, 497
Paule, Sarah II, 616
Paule, Sidney II, 404
Paule, Sidney II, 496
Paule, Sidney II, 616
Paulet, Nelson VI, 845
Paulet, William VI, 845
Paulett, Amanda VI, 845
Paulett, Anderson VI, 845
Paulett, Elizabeth VI, 845
Paulett, Elizabeth VI, 867
Paulett, Holcombe VI, 845
Paulett, Mary VI, 845
Paulett, Nancy VI, 845
Paulett, Nelson VI, 845
Paulett, Sally A. VI, 845
Paulett, William VI, 845
Paulett, William R. VI, 845
Pauley, Angeline V, 462
Pauley, Chance V, 462
Pauley, Chas. V, 462
Pauley, James V, 462
Pauley, Louella V, 462
Pauley, Mary V, 462
Pauley, Mary G. V, 462
Pauley, Rebecca V, 894
Pauley, Rebecca V, 925
Pauley, Rebecca V, 929
Pauley, Rufus F. V, 462
Pauley, Rufus T. V, 462
Pauley, Samantha V, 462
Paulin, Charles A. V, 638
Paulin, David V, 638
Paulin, Enos V, 638
Paulin, Lelia V, 638
Paulin, Malinda V, 636
Paulin, Malinda V, 638
Paulin, Martha II, 616
Paulin, Mary II, 1017
Paulin, Mary II, 1020
Paulin, Mary IV, 749
Paulin, Stephen II, 446
Pauling, Hannah II, 616
Pauling, Martha II, 616
Paull, Elizabeth II, 616
Paull, Gideon III, 249
Paull, Joseph II, 616
Paullin, Lelia V, 638
Paulsgrove, Anna V, 759
Paunoff, Viola IV, 244
Paunoff, Viola IV, 261
Pavey, Frederic V, 703
Pavey, Louis V, 703
Pavey, Margaret E. V, 269
Pavey, Mary V, 269
Pavey, Mary V, 703
Pavey, Minnie V, 703
Pavey, Wm. V, 703
Pavy, Mary V, 266
Pawlen, Ruth V, 957
Pawlen, Ruth V, 961
Pawley, George II, 446
Pawley, Sarah II, 455
Pawley, Sarah II, 616
Pawlin, Pleasant II, 1015
Pawling, Hannah II, 616
Paxon, Aaron IV, 345
Paxon, Achsah I, 957
Paxon, Achsah I, 967
Paxon, Ailee I, 967
Paxon, Alice V, 241
Paxon, Amos VI, 542
Paxon, Ann I, 967
Paxon, Ann Deroza VI, 512
Paxon, Ann Derozzo VI, 543
Paxon, Ann Derroza VI, 512
Paxon, Ann Derrozo VI, 509
Paxon, Ann Derrozo VI, 542
Paxon, Anna B. II, 907
Paxon, Anthony B. II, 907
Paxon, Asaph V, 523
Paxon, Benjamin II, 617
Paxon, Benjamin IV, 345
Paxon, Benjamin VI, 542
Paxon, Betsy II, 1020
Paxon, Betsy II, 1058
Paxon, Burr VI, 509
Paxon, Burr VI, 512
Paxon, Burr VI, 542
Paxon, Cathrine I, 957
Paxon, Charles IV, 345
Paxon, Charles V, 703
Paxon, Effie J. IV, 749
Paxon, Elizabeth II, 907
Paxon, Elizabeth II, 1021
Paxon, Elizabeth II, 1058
Paxon, Elizabeth IV, 1289
Paxon, Elizabeth VI, 577
Paxon, Esther II, 1058
Paxon, Fenton D. VI, 543
Paxon, Frances E. II, 759
Paxon, Glenn V, 703
Paxon, Hannah IV, 301
Paxon, Henrietta VI, 512
Paxon, Henrietta Chalmers VI, 543
Paxon, Henry II, 617
Paxon, Isaac IV, 345
Paxon, Jacob I, 967
Paxon, Jacob II, 617
Paxon, Jacob IV, 749
Paxon, James VI, 543
Paxon, James, Jr. VI, 543
Paxon, Jesse IV, 749
Paxon, John I, 957
Paxon, John I, 967
Paxon, John IV, 345
Paxon, John VI, 332
Paxon, John VI, 429
Paxon, John VI, 543
Paxon, John W. II, 907
Paxon, Joseph II, 617
Paxon, Joseph VI, 543
Paxon, Joseph J. IV, 837
Paxon, Latitia II, 1058
Paxon, Leona V, 703
Paxon, Lydia IV, 345
Paxon, Maria IV, 749
Paxon, Martha VI, 746
Paxon, Martha VI, 777
Paxon, Mary I, 957
Paxon, Mary I, 967
Paxon, Mary IV, 345
Paxon, Mary VI, 429
Paxon, Mary VI, 471
Paxon, Mary VI, 543
Paxon, Mary Ann V, 523
Paxon, Mary Ann V, 535
Paxon, Mary Ann VI, 543
Paxon, Mary Jane VI, 512
Paxon, Mary Jane VI, 543
Paxon, Nancy VI, 332
Paxon, Nellie VI, 687
Paxon, Nellie VI, 719
Paxon, Nora V, 703
Paxon, Phineas II, 1058
Paxon, Rachel IV, 345
Paxon, Rebecca IV, 464
Paxon, Rebecca IV, 491
Paxon, Reuben I, 967
Paxon, Reuben VI, 543
Paxon, Robert V, 109
Paxon, Ruth IV, 345
Paxon, Sally IV, 328
Paxon, Sally IV, 345
Paxon, Samuel II, 617
Paxon, Samuel IV, 345
Paxon, Sarah IV, 651
Paxon, Sarah VI, 543
Paxon, Sarah W. II, 907
Paxon, Sidney H. IV, 1289
Paxon, Thomas II, 1058
Paxon, Webster IV, 345
Paxon, William VI, 770
Paxon, Wm. H. VI, 543
Paxson, ??? II, 813
Paxson, ??? III, 249
Paxson, ??? IV, 861
Paxson, ??? IV, 1269
Paxson, Aaron II, 1008
Paxson, Aaron II, 1020
Paxson, Aaron IV, 345
Paxson, Abigail II, 1020
Paxson, Abigail IV, 837
Paxson, Achsah IV, 1288
Paxson, Achsah V, 269
Paxson, Ada II, 813
Paxson, Ada II, 907
Paxson, Alfred II, 404
Paxson, Alfred II, 617
Paxson, Alice I, 1009
Paxson, Alice I, 1011
Paxson, Alice II, 617
Paxson, Alice II, 813
Paxson, Alice II, 814
Paxson, Alice II, 907
Paxson, Alice IV, 1289
Paxson, Alice V, 269
Paxson, Alice VI, 602
Paxson, Alice C. II, 813
Paxson, Alice C. II, 870
Paxson, Alma E. III, 83
Paxson, Alma E. III, 249
Paxson, Amos IV, 837
Paxson, Amos VI, 542
Paxson, Amos Cooper II, 828
Paxson, Amy Eleanor V, 269
Paxson, Amy Eleanor V, 278
Paxson, Amy Ellen IV, 1289
Paxson, Ann II, 248
Paxson, Ann II, 404
Paxson, Ann II, 509
Paxson, Ann II, 613
Paxson, Ann II, 617
Paxson, Ann II, 967
Paxson, Ann II, 1020
Paxson, Ann II, 1021
Paxson, Ann III, 249
Paxson, Ann III, 432
Paxson, Ann IV, 837
Paxson, Ann VI, 602
Paxson, Ann B. IV, 797
Paxson, Ann B. IV, 837
Paxson, Ann Derozo VI, 543
Paxson, Ann Derozzo VI, 543
Paxson, Ann Derrozo VI, 542
Paxson, Anna II, 404
Paxson, Anna II, 613
Paxson, Anna II, 617
Paxson, Anna II, 759
Paxson, Anna II, 813
Paxson, Anna II, 1013
Paxson, Anna II, 1020
Paxson, Anna II, 1070
Paxson, Anna II, 1077
Paxson, Anna III, 431
Paxson, Anna IV, 1288
Paxson, Anna IV, 1289
Paxson, Anna V, 269
Paxson, Anna B. II, 907
Paxson, Anna Elizabeth IV, 12
Paxson, Anna Maria II, 617
Paxson, Anna P. II, 813
Paxson, Anna P. II, 907
Paxson, Anna P. II, 927
Paxson, Anna Pickering II, 82
Paxson, Anna R. II, 907

son, Anna R. II, 1077
son, Anna W. II, 813
son, Anna W. II, 907
son, Anne II, 617
son, Anne II, 759
son, Anne Elizabeth IV, 1289
son, Anthony II, 1077
son, Anthony B. II, 907
son, Anthony Burton II, 813
son, Anthony Burton II, 907
son, Anthony Burton II, 922
son, Anthony Burton II, 1077
son, Arthur VI, 542
son, Asaph IV, 1288
son, Asaph IV, 1289
son, Asaph V, 512
son, Asaph V, 522
son, Asaph V, 523
son, Asaph Elwood IV, 1289
son, Asaph H. V, 512
son, Asaph H. V, 523
son, Aseph V, 522
son, Aseph V, 523
son, Aseph Elwood IV, 1289
son, Banjamin II, 1031
son, Benjamin II, 404
son, Benjamin II, 617
son, Benjamin II, 813
son, Benjamin II, 1020
son, Benjamin IV, 53
son, Benjamin IV, 335
son, Benjamin IV, 345
son, Benjamin IV, 651
son, Benjamin IV, 663
son, Benjamin IV, 837
son, Benjamin VI, 335
son, Benjamin VI, 336
son, Benjamin VI, 354
son, Benjamin VI, 542
xson, Benjamin T. II, 617
xson, Benjamin Taylor II, 404
xson, Benjamin W. IV, 837
xson, Bessie IV, 749
xson, Betsey II, 1020
xson, Betsy II, 1020
xson, Betsy II, 1058
xson, Burr VI, 542
xson, Burr VI, 543
xson, Camila IV, 1288
xson, Caroline II, 1060
xson, Caroline II, 1061
xson, Caroline Ely II, 967
xson, Catharine II, 404
xson, Catharine II, 617
xson, Catherine K. II, 1021
xson, Charles II, 617
xson, Charles II, 813
xson, Charles IV, 651
xson, Charles IV, 749
xson, Charles IV, 1289
xson, Charles Henry II, 759
xson, Charles Robert V, 523
xson, Chas. II, 813
xson, Chas. II, 907
xson, Dale IV, 749
xson, Dallas IV, 749
xson, David IV, 1289
xson, Deborah II, 813
xson, Deborah II, 907
xson, Deborah II, 967
xson, Deborah II, 1020
xson, Deborah II, 1031
xson, Dhosha VI, 335
xson, Dilce IV, 1288
xson, Dosha V, 523
xson, Dosha VI, 334
xson, Eddy IV, 1289
xson, Edith K. III, 57
xson, Edmund II, 404
xson, Edmund II, 617
xson, Edward IV, 837
xson, Edward Ely II, 813
xson, Edward S. II, 404
xson, Edward S. II, 617
xson, Effie J. IV, 749
xson, Effie J. IV, 837
xson, Eldora A. V, 522
xson, Eldora Elizabeth V, 523
xson, Eleanor Mary II, 813
xson, Eleanor Mary II, 907
xson, Elias II, 967
xson, Elias V, 269
xson, Elias G. IV, 1288
xson, Elias G. IV, 1289
xson, Elias G. V, 269
xson, Elias G. V, 522
xson, Elias G. V, 523
xson, Elijah VI, 543
xson, Elisas G. IV, 1289
xson, Eliz. III, 249
xson, Eliz. D. III, 85
Paxson, Eliz. D. III, 249
Paxson, Eliza Ann IV, 1289
Paxson, Eliza. III, 83
Paxson, Elizabeth II, 248
Paxson, Elizabeth II, 259
Paxson, Elizabeth II, 298
Paxson, Elizabeth II, 404
Paxson, Elizabeth II, 509
Paxson, Elizabeth II, 617
Paxson, Elizabeth II, 708
Paxson, Elizabeth II, 794
Paxson, Elizabeth II, 814
Paxson, Elizabeth II, 907
Paxson, Elizabeth II, 967
Paxson, Elizabeth II, 1021
Paxson, Elizabeth II, 1058
Paxson, Elizabeth II, 1077
Paxson, Elizabeth III, 79
Paxson, Elizabeth III, 249
Paxson, Elizabeth IV, 837
Paxson, Elizabeth IV, 1289
Paxson, Elizabeth D. III, 249
Paxson, Elizabeth L. II, 864
Paxson, Elizabeth L. II, 907
Paxson, Elizabeth S. II, 404
Paxson, Elizabeth S. II, 617
Paxson, Elizann IV, 1289
Paxson, Ella W. II, 813
Paxson, Ella W. II, 907
Paxson, Ella W. II, 922
Paxson, Elliott D. II, 907
Paxson, Elliott D. III, 249
Paxson, Elroy IV, 1289
Paxson, Emma F. II, 907
Paxson, Enos Eddy IV, 1289
Paxson, Enos L. IV, 1289
Paxson, Ester II, 617
Paxson, Esther II, 1058
Paxson, Esther IV, 837
Paxson, Esther Ann IV, 1289
Paxson, Ethel II, 814
Paxson, Ethel II, 850
Paxson, Ethel II, 907
Paxson, Ethel III, 79
Paxson, Ethel III, 361
Paxson, Fanny II, 404
Paxson, Florence II, 814
Paxson, Florence N. IV, 1289
Paxson, Frances III, 249
Paxson, Frances C. II, 714
Paxson, Frances E. II, 759
Paxson, Frank W. II, 907
Paxson, Frank Wilson II, 813
Paxson, Franklin IV, 1289
Paxson, Frederick II, 813
Paxson, Frederick II, 863
Paxson, Frederick II, 864
Paxson, Frederick II, 870
Paxson, Frederick II, 907
Paxson, Frederick II, 921
Paxson, Frederick II, 927
Paxson, Frederick L. II, 907
Paxson, Frederick, Jr. II, 814
Paxson, George Walker II, 1020
Paxson, Glen Dawson V, 523
Paxson, Grace II, 813
Paxson, Hannah II, 967
Paxson, Hannah II, 1046
Paxson, Hannah II, 1058
Paxson, Hannah IV, 261
Paxson, Hannah IV, 1289
Paxson, Hannah A. II, 907
Paxson, Hannah Drinker III, 249
Paxson, Hannah Elizabeth IV, 1289
Paxson, Hannameel II, 1058
Paxson, Harriet II, 792
Paxson, Harvey S. III, 83
Paxson, Harvey S. III, 249
Paxson, Helen II, 814
Paxson, Henrietta VI, 543
Paxson, Henrietta Chalmers VI, 543
Paxson, Henry II, 248
Paxson, Henry II, 258
Paxson, Henry II, 617
Paxson, Henry II, 967
Paxson, Henry II, 1020
Paxson, Henry II, 1021
Paxson, Henry Drinker III, 249
Paxson, Henry M. II, 813
Paxson, Heston IV, 837
Paxson, Heston C. IV, 837
Paxson, Hetty D. III, 249
Paxson, Howard II, 813
Paxson, Howard III, 249
Paxson, Irena V, 269
Paxson, Isaac II, 404
Paxson, Isaac II, 617
Paxson, Isaac II, 1020
Paxson, Isaac IV, 651
Paxson, Isabelle IV, 749
Paxson, Isaiah II, 794
Paxson, Isaiah II, 864
Paxson, Isaiah II, 907
Paxson, Isaiah II, 1008
Paxson, Isaiah II, 1020
Paxson, Isaiah IV, 859
Paxson, Israel II, 404
Paxson, Israel II, 613
Paxson, Israel II, 617
Paxson, Israel III, 432
Paxson, Israel IV, 1289
Paxson, J. Edward Moon II, 1046
Paxson, Jacob II, 617
Paxson, Jacob IV, 651
Paxson, Jacob IV, 749
Paxson, Jacob IV, 837
Paxson, Jacob IV, 1288
Paxson, Jacob V, 115
Paxson, Jacob VI, 335
Paxson, Jacob VI, 542
Paxson, Jacob VI, 602
Paxson, Jacob C. IV, 837
Paxson, James II, 1002
Paxson, James II, 1020
Paxson, James IV, 1288
Paxson, James IV, 1289
Paxson, James VI, 543
Paxson, James H. IV, 1289
Paxson, James H. V, 522
Paxson, James Hamilton IV, 1289
Paxson, James, Jr. VI, 543
Paxson, Jane II, 967
Paxson, Jane II, 1020
Paxson, Jane IV, 837
Paxson, Jane E. IV, 837
Paxson, Jane P. II, 907
Paxson, Jane Pyle II, 813
Paxson, Janney II, 907
Paxson, Jesse IV, 749
Paxson, Jesse IV, 837
Paxson, Jesse IV, 1289
Paxson, Jesse E. IV, 837
Paxson, Jesse G. IV, 1289
Paxson, Jessie IV, 749
Paxson, Jessie D. IV, 749
Paxson, Jessie D. IV, 837
Paxson, Joel C. IV, 1288
Paxson, John I, 1011
Paxson, John II, 1021
Paxson, John IV, 53
Paxson, John IV, 651
Paxson, John IV, 1288
Paxson, John IV, 1289
Paxson, John V, 269
Paxson, John V, 278
Paxson, John VI, 335
Paxson, John VI, 354
Paxson, John VI, 543
Paxson, John VI, 602
Paxson, John Henry IV, 1289
Paxson, John Townsend IV, 1288
Paxson, John W. II, 813
Paxson, John W. II, 907
Paxson, John W. II, 1070
Paxson, John W. II, 1077
Paxson, Jonathan II, 984
Paxson, Jonathan II, 1020
Paxson, Jonathan II, 1058
Paxson, Jonathan G. IV, 1289
Paxson, Joseph II, 248
Paxson, Joseph II, 259
Paxson, Joseph II, 617
Paxson, Joseph II, 792
Paxson, Joseph IV, 837
Paxson, Joseph VI, 543
Paxson, Joseph A. II, 907
Paxson, Joseph Armitage II, 813
Paxson, Joseph Coates II, 814
Paxson, Joseph Dure II, 1020
Paxson, Joseph J. IV, 837
Paxson, Joseph Palmer II, 1077
Paxson, Joseph R. II, 617
Paxson, Joseph S. II, 404
Paxson, Joseph S. II, 759
Paxson, Joseph Shoemaker II, 617
Paxson, Joseph Shoemaker II, 759
Paxson, Joseph T. II, 907
Paxson, Joshua II, 813
Paxson, Joshua II, 1077
Paxson, Joshua III, 431
Paxson, Latitia II, 1008
Paxson, Latitia II, 1020
Paxson, Latitia II, 1058
Paxson, Leona Margaret V, 523
Paxson, Leonides IV, 1289
Paxson, Letitia II, 1020
Paxson, Louis Cooper II, 813
Paxson, Lydia II, 813
Paxson, Lydia III, 79
Paxson, Lydia IV, 345
Paxson, Lydia IV, 837
Paxson, Lydia Ann II, 1077
Paxson, Lydia B. II, 863
Paxson, Lydia B. II, 864
Paxson, Lydia B. II, 870
Paxson, Lydia B. II, 907
Paxson, Lydia B. II, 921
Paxson, Lydia B. II, 927
Paxson, Lydia M. II, 708
Paxson, Lydia M. II, 814
Paxson, Lydia M. II, 907
Paxson, Lydia M. II, 921
Paxson, Lydia S. II, 850
Paxson, Lydia S. II, 907
Paxson, Mahlon IV, 1288
Paxson, Mahlon B. II, 864
Paxson, Mahlon B. II, 907
Paxson, Mahlon Betts II, 813
Paxson, Margaret II, 967
Paxson, Margaret II, 1002
Paxson, Margaret II, 1020
Paxson, Margaret IV, 1289
Paxson, Margaret V, 512
Paxson, Margaret V, 523
Paxson, Margaret Ann IV, 1289
Paxson, Margaret Chandlee III, 432
Paxson, Margaret L. IV, 1289
Paxson, Margaret L. V, 523
Paxson, Margery II, 967
Paxson, Maria IV, 749
Paxson, Maria IV, 837
Paxson, Martha II, 248
Paxson, Martha M. IV, 837
Paxson, Mary I, 1011
Paxson, Mary II, 198
Paxson, Mary II, 248
Paxson, Mary II, 258
Paxson, Mary II, 617
Paxson, Mary II, 716
Paxson, Mary II, 794
Paxson, Mary II, 813
Paxson, Mary II, 864
Paxson, Mary II, 907
Paxson, Mary II, 967
Paxson, Mary II, 984
Paxson, Mary II, 1008
Paxson, Mary II, 1020
Paxson, Mary II, 1035
Paxson, Mary III, 249
Paxson, Mary IV, 53
Paxson, Mary IV, 345
Paxson, Mary IV, 651
Paxson, Mary IV, 663
Paxson, Mary VI, 335
Paxson, Mary VI, 354
Paxson, Mary VI, 542
Paxson, Mary VI, 543
Paxson, Mary VI, 602
Paxson, Mary Ann II, 792
Paxson, Mary Ann V, 523
Paxson, Mary Ann VI, 543
Paxson, Mary Betts II, 813
Paxson, Mary Betts II, 863
Paxson, Mary Betts II, 907
Paxson, Mary D. III, 249
Paxson, Mary Drinker III, 249
Paxson, Mary E. IV, 1289
Paxson, Mary E. V, 269
Paxson, Mary Ellen IV, 1289
Paxson, Mary Jane IV, 1289
Paxson, Mary Jane VI, 543
Paxson, Mary Jennie II, 907
Paxson, Mary N. IV, 837
Paxson, Mary P. IV, 825
Paxson, Mary P. IV, 837
Paxson, Mary Platt II, 1046
Paxson, Mary Shoemaker II, 814
Paxson, Mary W. II, 907
Paxson, Mary W. II, 967
Paxson, Mary W. II, 1058
Paxson, Mary W. II, 1077
Paxson, Matilda IV, 837
Paxson, Mercy II, 813
Paxson, Michael II, 617
Paxson, Milton IV, 1288
Paxson, Milton IV, 1289
Paxson, Miriam Louise III, 432
Paxson, Moses II, 907
Paxson, Nancy VI, 332
Paxson, Nelson W. IV, 1289
Paxson, Newton W. V, 522
Paxson, Nora I. V, 523
Paxson, Nora T. V, 523
Paxson, Olie J. V, 269
Paxson, Oliver II, 967
Paxson, Oliver II, 1046
Paxson, Oliver II, 1058
Paxson, Owen Shoemaker II, 814
Paxson, Pamelia VI, 542
Paxson, Phebe IV, 1289
Paxson, Phebe Ann II, 617
Paxson, Phebe B. IV, 1289
Paxson, Phineas II, 1058
Paxson, Phineas II, 1077
Paxson, Phinehas II, 1058
Paxson, Phinias II, 1077
Paxson, Portius IV, 1289
Paxson, Princes IV, 1289
Paxson, Rachel II, 298
Paxson, Rachel II, 828
Paxson, Rachel II, 967
Paxson, Rachel II, 984
Paxson, Rachel II, 1020
Paxson, Rachel II, 1058
Paxson, Rachel II, 1077
Paxson, Rachel III, 432
Paxson, Rachel IV, 53
Paxson, Rachel IV, 335
Paxson, Rachel IV, 345
Paxson, Rachel IV, 651
Paxson, Rachel IV, 826
Paxson, Rachel IV, 837
Paxson, Rachel IV, 1288
Paxson, Rachel VI, 354
Paxson, Rachel VI, 543
Paxson, Rachel G. IV, 1289
Paxson, Rebecca II, 813
Paxson, Rebecca W. II, 813
Paxson, Rebecca W. II, 864
Paxson, Rebecca W. II, 907
Paxson, Rebeckah II, 1013
Paxson, Rebeckah II, 1020
Paxson, Reuben II, 617
Paxson, Reuben IV, 1288
Paxson, Reuben IV, 1289
Paxson, Reuben V, 269
Paxson, Reuben VI, 543
Paxson, Richard II, 248
Paxson, Richard II, 259
Paxson, Richard II, 404
Paxson, Richard II, 617
Paxson, Richard II, 759
Paxson, Richard Chandlee III, 432
Paxson, Richard, Jr. II, 759
Paxson, Richards S. II, 404
Paxson, Rolin IV, 1289
Paxson, Rowland IV, 1288
Paxson, Ruben VI, 602
Paxson, Ruth II, 404
Paxson, Ruth II, 617
Paxson, Ruth III, 399
Paxson, Ruth III, 432
Paxson, Ruth IV, 53
Paxson, Ruth IV, 335
Paxson, Ruth IV, 345
Paxson, Ruth IV, 651
Paxson, Ruth IV, 1289
Paxson, Ruth V, 523
Paxson, Ruth VI, 335
Paxson, Ruth VI, 336
Paxson, Ruth VI, 354
Paxson, Ruth Alice IV, 1289
Paxson, Ruth Anna II, 967
Paxson, Sally IV, 651
Paxson, Samuel II, 617
Paxson, Samuel III, 249
Paxson, Samuel IV, 651
Paxson, Samuel IV, 749
Paxson, Samuel C. II, 404
Paxson, Samuel C. II, 509
Paxson, Samuel C. II, 617
Paxson, Samuel C. III, 249
Paxson, Sarah II, 248
Paxson, Sarah II, 259
Paxson, Sarah II, 404
Paxson, Sarah II, 617
Paxson, Sarah II, 907
Paxson, Sarah II, 967
Paxson, Sarah II, 999
Paxson, Sarah II, 1000
Paxson, Sarah II, 1018
Paxson, Sarah II, 1020
Paxson, Sarah II, 1021
Paxson, Sarah II, 1034
Paxson, Sarah II, 1070
Paxson, Sarah II, 1077
Paxson, Sarah III, 432
Paxson, Sarah IV, 651
Paxson, Sarah IV, 837
Paxson, Sarah IV, 847
Paxson, Sarah IV, 1288
Paxson, Sarah IV, 1289
Paxson, Sarah V, 242
Paxson, Sarah VI, 543
Paxson, Sarah B. II, 1077
Paxson, Sarah Ely II, 967
Paxson, Sarah J. II, 907

Paxson, Sarah Jane IV, 749
Paxson, Sarah P. II, 836
Paxson, Sarah P. II, 907
Paxson, Sarah R. II, 759
Paxson, Sarah Rodman II, 617
Paxson, Sarah Rodman II, 759
Paxson, Sarah W. II, 878
Paxson, Sarah W. II, 907
Paxson, Sarah W. II, 967
Paxson, Sarah W. II, 1058
Paxson, Sidney IV, 1288
Paxson, Sidney H. IV, 1289
Paxson, Sitnah V, 115
Paxson, Stephen Smith II, 617
Paxson, Susan II, 404
Paxson, Susan II, 617
Paxson, Susan II, 907
Paxson, Susan J. II, 967
Paxson, Susan J. II, 1046
Paxson, Susan J. II, 1058
Paxson, Susan Shoemaker II, 759
Paxson, Susanna Moorman V, 523
Paxson, Susannah IV, 1288
Paxson, Taylor, Sarah IV, 837
Paxson, Thomas II, 248
Paxson, Thomas II, 994
Paxson, Thomas II, 999
Paxson, Thomas II, 1000
Paxson, Thomas II, 1008
Paxson, Thomas II, 1020
Paxson, Thomas II, 1046
Paxson, Thomas II, 1058
Paxson, Thomas II, 1077
Paxson, Thomas T. IV, 1289
Paxson, Thomas, Sr. II, 1008
Paxson, Thomas, Sr. II, 1020
Paxson, Thos. W. IV, 1289
Paxson, Timothy II, 617
Paxson, Timothy II, 1020
Paxson, Walter P. III, 399
Paxson, Walter P. III, 431
Paxson, Walter P. III, 432
Paxson, Wd. Hannah Johnson II, 828
Paxson, Webster IV, 345
Paxson, Willett II, 813
Paxson, Willett II, 907
Paxson, Willett II, 1070
Paxson, Willett II, 1077
Paxson, William II, 404
Paxson, William II, 714
Paxson, William II, 967
Paxson, William II, 1020
Paxson, William III, 249
Paxson, William IV, 53
Paxson, William IV, 651
Paxson, William IV, 837
Paxson, William IV, 1288
Paxson, William IV, 1289
Paxson, William V, 494
Paxson, William V, 523
Paxson, William VI, 354
Paxson, William B. II, 813
Paxson, William Betts II, 708
Paxson, William Betts II, 814
Paxson, William P. II, 404
Paxson, William Parker II, 404
Paxson, William, Jr. III, 249
Paxson, Wm. II, 509
Paxson, Wm. II, 613
Paxson, Wm. II, 617
Paxson, Wm. II, 759
Paxson, Wm. II, 1002
Paxson, Wm. II, 1013
Paxson, Wm. II, 1020
Paxson, Wm. II, 1022
Paxson, Wm. II, 1035
Paxson, Wm. IV, 837
Paxson, Wm. IV, 1289
Paxson, Wm. B. II, 850
Paxson, Wm. B. II, 907
Paxson, Wm. B. II, 921
Paxson, Wm. Betts III, 79
Paxson, Wm. H. VI, 543
Paxson, Wm. L. II, 759
Paxson, Wm. L. II, 907
Paxson, Wm., Jr. II, 1020
Paxton, Aaron IV, 428
Paxton, Abigail II, 1020
Paxton, Abigail IV, 910
Paxton, Abigail IV, 912
Paxton, Adella IV, 1016
Paxton, Alice II, 617
Paxton, Ann II, 404
Paxton, Anna Elizabeth IV, 1289
Paxton, Anna Elizabeth V, 957
Paxton, Arthur VI, 537
Paxton, Arthur VI, 542
Paxton, Asaph IV, 1289
Paxton, Aseph V, 523
Paxton, Benjamin IV, 345
Paxton, Benjamin IV, 428
Paxton, Benjamin VI, 335
Paxton, Benjamin VI, 336
Paxton, Charles IV, 345
Paxton, Charles IV, 428
Paxton, Charles Robert V, 523
Paxton, Cynthia IV, 1287
Paxton, Cynthia IV, 1289
Paxton, Dhosha VI, 335
Paxton, Dosha V, 518
Paxton, Dosha V, 523
Paxton, Dosha VI, 335
Paxton, Edward IV, 261
Paxton, Edward W. IV, 261
Paxton, Eldora Elizabeth V, 523
Paxton, Elias V, 196
Paxton, Elias G. IV, 1289
Paxton, Elias G. V, 425
Paxton, Elizabeth II, 248
Paxton, Elizabeth II, 298
Paxton, Elizabeth IV, 1016
Paxton, Elizabeth IV, 1279
Paxton, Elizabeth VI, 718
Paxton, Esther IV, 837
Paxton, Esther A. IV, 1289
Paxton, Esther A. IV, 1293
Paxton, Florence V, 957
Paxton, Florence N. IV, 1289
Paxton, Francis Marion V, 425
Paxton, Hannah IV, 156
Paxton, Hannah IV, 164
Paxton, Hannah IV, 261
Paxton, Hannah L. W. IV, 156
Paxton, Hannah L. W. IV, 163
Paxton, Henrietta VI, 510
Paxton, Henrietta C. VI, 512
Paxton, Henrietta Chalmers VI, 510
Paxton, Henry II, 248
Paxton, Isaac IV, 345
Paxton, Isaac IV, 428
Paxton, Israel II, 404
Paxton, Israel II, 617
Paxton, Jacob IV, 1219
Paxton, Jacob V, 108
Paxton, Jacob V, 109
Paxton, Jacob VI, 335
Paxton, Jacob VI, 537
Paxton, Jacob VI, 542
Paxton, James IV, 1289
Paxton, James V, 425
Paxton, James VI, 561
Paxton, James Hamilton IV, 1289
Paxton, John II, 298
Paxton, John IV, 345
Paxton, John IV, 1289
Paxton, John V, 108
Paxton, John V, 109
Paxton, John V, 425
Paxton, John VI, 333
Paxton, John VI, 335
Paxton, John VI, 429
Paxton, Jonathan G. IV, 1289
Paxton, Jonathan G. V, 425
Paxton, Joseph T. II, 907
Paxton, Lydia IV, 428
Paxton, Lydia IV, 837
Paxton, Margaret IV, 1289
Paxton, Margaret V, 523
Paxton, Margaret A. V, 425
Paxton, Margaret Ann IV, 1289
Paxton, Margaret Ann V, 425
Paxton, Margaret L. V, 523
Paxton, Maria IV, 834
Paxton, Maria IV, 837
Paxton, Mary I, 1011
Paxton, Mary II, 248
Paxton, Mary II, 617
Paxton, Mary IV, 156
Paxton, Mary IV, 164
Paxton, Mary IV, 345
Paxton, Mary IV, 428
Paxton, Mary IV, 651
Paxton, Mary IV, 657
Paxton, Mary V, 108
Paxton, Mary V, 109
Paxton, Mary VI, 335
Paxton, Mary VI, 429
Paxton, Mary VI, 537
Paxton, Mary VI, 542
Paxton, Mary VI, 602
Paxton, Mary VI, 668
Paxton, Mary Ann V, 523
Paxton, Mary Betts VI, 335
Paxton, Mary Ellen IV, 1289
Paxton, Mary Ellen V, 957
Paxton, Mary J. V, 425
Paxton, Mary Jane IV, 1289
Paxton, Mary Jane V, 425
Paxton, Mary Jane VI, 510
Paxton, Michael II, 617
Paxton, Nancy VI, 333
Paxton, Nancy VI, 335
Paxton, Nancy Susannah V, 109
Paxton, Nelson W. IV, 1289
Paxton, Nora T. V, 523
Paxton, Pamelia VI, 537
Paxton, Pamelia VI, 542
Paxton, Phebe IV, 1227
Paxton, Phebe Ann V, 957
Paxton, Phebe B. IV, 1219
Paxton, Phebe B. IV, 1289
Paxton, Rachel II, 298
Paxton, Rachel IV, 345
Paxton, Rachel IV, 631
Paxton, Rachel IV, 651
Paxton, Rachel VI, 298
Paxton, Rachel VI, 335
Paxton, Rachel VI, 345
Paxton, Rachel VI, 867
Paxton, Rachel G. IV, 1289
Paxton, Rachel G. V, 425
Paxton, Rachel J. V, 425
Paxton, Reuben I, 967
Paxton, Reuben II, 617
Paxton, Reuben IV, 1289
Paxton, Reuben V, 425
Paxton, Richard II, 248
Paxton, Robert V, 109
Paxton, Rowland R. IV, 1219
Paxton, Rowland R. IV, 1227
Paxton, Ruth IV, 345
Paxton, Ruth IV, 428
Paxton, Ruth IV, 1289
Paxton, Ruth V, 494
Paxton, Ruth V, 523
Paxton, Ruth V, 957
Paxton, Ruth VI, 335
Paxton, Ruth VI, 336
Paxton, Ruth A. V, 425
Paxton, Ruth Alice IV, 1289
Paxton, Ruth Alice V, 425
Paxton, Sally IV, 345
Paxton, Sally IV, 428
Paxton, Samuel IV, 345
Paxton, Sarah II, 298
Paxton, Sarah IV, 816
Paxton, Sarah IV, 837
Paxton, Sarah IV, 1289
Paxton, Sarah V, 425
Paxton, Sarah VI, 561
Paxton, Sarah, Jr. VI, 561
Paxton, Sitnah IV, 1219
Paxton, Sitnah V, 108
Paxton, Susan II, 907
Paxton, Sussanna VI, 335
Paxton, Thos. W. IV, 1289
Paxton, Webster IV, 428
Paxton, William II, 1020
Paxton, William IV, 651
Paxton, William V, 109
Paxton, Wm. II, 617
Paxton, Wm. IV, 834
Paxton, Wm. IV, 837
Paxton, Wm. IV, 1016
Paxton, Wm. IV, 1289
Paxton, Wm. VI, 510
Paxton, Wm. VI, 512
Payn, Anica VI, 335
Payn, Henry VI, 1020
Payn, John VI, 262
Payn, John VI, 335
Payn, John VI, 429
Payn, Mary VI, 335
Payn, Pollard VI, 1004
Payn, Rachel VI, 429
Payn, Ruth VI, 335
Payn, Sarah VI, 429
Payn, Sarah VI, 447
Payn, William VI, 335
Payne, ??? VI, 293
Payne, Ada IV, 492
Payne, Adda IV, 492
Payne, Alce VI, 429
Payne, Alex. VI, 854
Payne, Alice VI, 429
Payne, Alice VI, 444
Payne, Amanda VI, 868
Payne, Amy VI, 969
Payne, Ann M. VI, 814
Payne, Ann T. VI, 845
Payne, Anna I, 897
Payne, Baldwin VI, 845
Payne, Barnett VI, 909
Payne, Barnett VI, 976
Payne, Benjamin VI, 865
Payne, Betsey VI, 976
Payne, Braddock H. VI, 976
Payne, Catherine W. VI, 845
Payne, Charles Lynch VI, 262
Payne, Charles Wesley IV, 261
Payne, Charlotte E. VI, 866
Payne, Chas. Wesley IV, 261
Payne, Clarissa A. VI, 864
Payne, Comilla VI, 852
Payne, Dinah VI, 976
Payne, Dolly I, 512
Payne, Dolly II, 617
Payne, Dolly VI, 262
Payne, E. J. I, 897
Payne, Elizabeth VI, 262
Payne, Elizabeth VI, 884
Payne, Elizabeth VI, 909
Payne, Elizabeth VI, 964
Payne, Elizabeth VI, 965
Payne, Elizabeth VI, 976
Payne, Elizabeth A. VI, 976
Payne, Elizabeth Ann VI, 960
Payne, Elizabeth L. VI, 802
Payne, Elizabeth S. VI, 844
Payne, Ellinor II, 617
Payne, Elvira W. VI, 866
Payne, Emeline VI, 976
Payne, Emiline I, 926
Payne, Emily I, 639
Payne, Emily Florence IV, 261
Payne, Eva V, 852
Payne, Flail P. VI, 989
Payne, Frances VI, 687
Payne, Frances VI, 712
Payne, Frances VI, 870
Payne, Garland VI, 852
Payne, George VI, 429
Payne, George VI, 444
Payne, George VI, 976
Payne, Hannah V, 853
Payne, Hannah V, 856
Payne, Hannah VI, 870
Payne, Harriet H. III, 216
Payne, Harriet H. III, 249
Payne, Helen IV, 1260
Payne, Horace III, 216
Payne, Horace III, 249
Payne, James VI, 876
Payne, James VI, 914
Payne, James VI, 965
Payne, James VI, 976
Payne, James VI, 984
Payne, James VI, 1010
Payne, James F. VI, 866
Payne, James H. VI, 976
Payne, Jammy VI, 845
Payne, Jane VI, 810
Payne, Jane VI, 976
Payne, Jane VI, 984
Payne, Jno. VI, 904
Payne, Jno. S. VI, 844
Payne, Joanna VI, 954
Payne, Joel VI, 976
Payne, John I, 512
Payne, John I, 565
Payne, John II, 404
Payne, John II, 617
Payne, John VI, 242
Payne, John VI, 262
Payne, John VI, 429
Payne, John VI, 868
Payne, John VI, 870
Payne, John VI, 883
Payne, John VI, 960
Payne, John VI, 964
Payne, John VI, 969
Payne, John VI, 976
Payne, John VI, 984
Payne, John F. I, 897
Payne, John F. I, 947
Payne, John L. VI, 845
Payne, John S. VI, 814
Payne, John S. VI, 852
Payne, John Todd, Jr. II, 617
Payne, John W. VI, 845
Payne, John W. VI, 852
Payne, Jonathan V, 853
Payne, Jonathan V, 856
Payne, Joseph VI, 871
Payne, Joseph VI, 872
Payne, Joseph VI, 876
Payne, Joseph VI, 891
Payne, Joseph VI, 896
Payne, Joseph VI, 943
Payne, Joseph VI, 954
Payne, Joseph VI, 976
Payne, Joseph VI, 984
Payne, Joseph H. VI, 984
Payne, Jubal VI, 1019
Payne, Leonard IV, 261
Payne, Louisa VI, 954
Payne, Louisa VI, 976
Payne, Louisa W. VI, 807
Payne, Lucinda VI, 876
Payne, Lucretia VI, 845
Payne, Lucy VI, 1011
Payne, Lutitia IV, 261
Payne, Margaret II, 617
Payne, Margory VI, 928
Payne, Mariah VI, 976
Payne, Martha VI, 429
Payne, Martha VI, 444
Payne, Martha VI, 927
Payne, Martha Ann VI, 976
Payne, Mary I, 512
Payne, Mary II, 404
Payne, Mary II, 617
Payne, Mary VI, 262
Payne, Mary VI, 335
Payne, Mary VI, 845
Payne, Mary VI, 883
Payne, Mary Ann VI, 976
Payne, Mary C. VI, 852
Payne, Mary Jane VI, 874
Payne, Mary L. IV, 261
Payne, Mildred Jane VI, 976
Payne, Nancy VI, 969
Payne, Nancy VI, 976
Payne, Nanie B. VI, 854
Payne, Nathaniel VI, 845
Payne, Paulina H. VI, 976
Payne, Peggy VI, 976
Payne, Philip VI, 802
Payne, Philip VI, 810
Payne, Philip VI, 852
Payne, Philip A. VI, 845
Payne, Philip, Jr. VI, 976
Payne, Phillip VI, 807
Payne, Phillip VI, 845
Payne, Phillip VI, 864
Payne, Phillip W. VI, 866
Payne, Phoebe VI, 914
Payne, Pollard VI, 976
Payne, Rachel VI, 429
Payne, Rachel VI, 444
Payne, Rhoda VI, 976
Payne, Rodah VI, 1020
Payne, Rodney VI, 976
Payne, Sally VI, 954
Payne, Sally VI, 976
Payne, Sara VI, 964
Payne, Sarah I, 897
Payne, Sarah II, 828
Payne, Sarah III, 383
Payne, Sarah III, 387
Payne, Sarah VI, 429
Payne, Sarah VI, 845
Payne, Sarah VI, 870
Payne, Sarah VI, 883
Payne, Sarah VI, 969
Payne, Sarah VI, 976
Payne, Sarah Braddock VI, 1011
Payne, Sarah Eva V, 853
Payne, Susan R. VI, 865
Payne, Susanna M. II, 716
Payne, Susannah E. VI, 845
Payne, Tabitha VI, 845
Payne, Thomas VI, 884
Payne, Thomas VI, 969
Payne, Thomas VI, 976
Payne, Thomas VI, 1020
Payne, Thomas Q. VI, 976
Payne, Thomas Q. VI, 980
Payne, Thos. VI, 976
Payne, Walter I, 512
Payne, Walter II, 617
Payne, Walter VI, 262
Payne, Walter T. VI, 896
Payne, William VI, 874
Payne, William VI, 883
Payne, William VI, 928
Payne, William VI, 969
Payne, William VI, 976
Payne, William A. VI, 872
Payne, William A. VI, 976
Payne, William E. IV, 261
Payne, William Irvin IV, 261
Payne, William Temple VI, 262
Payne, Wm. VI, 826
Payne, Wm. Temple I, 512
Paynter, James II, 404
Paynter, John II, 404
Paynter, Richard II, 404
Paynter, Richard II, 612
Paynter, Richard III, 249
Payter, Jane III, 56
Payton, Anna V, 462
Payton, Archie V, 462
Payton, Cathrine II, 617
Payton, Clyde V, 462
Payton, Joseph E. V, 462
Payton, Mary VI, 429
Payton, Richard Allen V, 462
Payton, Stephen II, 617
Payton, Thomas IV, 53
Payty, Charles I, 1035
Peables, William VI, 203

body, Alma IV, 1239
body, Anna G. III, 249
body, Anna G. May III, 172
body, Frederick W. III, 172
body, Frederick W. III, 249
body, Mary May III, 172
body, Mary May III, 249
ce, Bertha E. I, 947
ce, Bertha Elsie I, 932
ce, Bertha P. I, 932
ce, Charlotte A. III, 249
ce, Clarence N. I, 932
ce, Corella Beatrice I, 932
ce, Delilah I, 932
ce, Dora I, 947
ce, Elizabeth I, 566
ce, Elizabeth I, 833
ce, Elizabeth I, 897
ce, Emma I, 932
ce, George III, 249
ce, James I, 947
ce, James Reid I, 932
ce, John I, 932
ce, John I, 935
ce, John I, 947
ce, Lucy G. I, 947
ce, Mary III, 251
ce, Mary III, 358
ce, Mary III, 473
ce, Nellie I, 935
ce, Nellie I, 947
ce, Nettie F. I, 932
ce, Rella I, 935
ce, Rella I, 947
ce, Sarah I, 932
ce, Sarah C. I, 932
ce, Sarah C. I, 947
ce, Silas I, 932
ce, Silas H. I, 947
cemaker, Foster V, 196
cemaker, Foster V, 523
cemaker, Myrtle V, 196
cemaker, Myrtle V, 523
cemaker, Thelma V, 196
cemaker, Thelma V, 523
ch, Elizabeth VI, 770
ch, Mary VI, 770
ch, Samuel VI, 770
ch, Samuel, Sr. VI, 770
ch, Sarah VI, 770
che, Phebe II, 249
che, Thomas II, 249
che, William II, 249
chee, Ann II, 163
chee, William II, 249
chey, Ann II, 180
chey, Joseph II, 180
chey, Mary II, 154
chey, Mary II, 155
chey, Rebecah II, 180
chey, Sarah II, 180
chey, Thomas II, 180
chey, William II, 180
co, Mary Louise III, 249
cock, ??? IV, 861
cock, Abraham I, 306
cock, Abraham I, 314
cock, Abraham I, 552
cock, Abraham I, 566
cock, Abraham I, 704
cock, Abraham I, 730
cock, Abram I, 294
cock, Abram I, 730
cock, Abram IV, 261
cock, Achsah I, 294
cock, Achsah I, 704
cock, Achsah I, 720
cock, Achsah I, 730
cock, Albert V, 818
cock, Amanda Jane V, 818
cock, Amos I, 294
cock, Amos I, 704
cock, Amos I, 720
cock, Amos I, 730
cock, Ann II, 779
cock, Anna I, 552
cock, Anna I, 566
cock, Anna I, 704
cock, Anna I, 730
cock, Anna I, 741
cock, Arlistes V, 818
cock, Arsinoe IV, 621
cock, Charles V, 818
cock, Daniel III, 249
cock, David II, 814
cock, Elizabeth I, 304
cock, Elizabeth I, 314
cock, Elizabeth VI, 976
cock, Ella C. III, 249
cock, Elsa Margaret III, 249
cock, Elve I, 730
Peacock, Elvy I, 294
Peacock, Elvy I, 704
Peacock, Elvy I, 711
Peacock, Elvy I, 730
Peacock, Elwood IV, 170
Peacock, Elwood IV, 261
Peacock, Elwood IV, 428
Peacock, Elwood V, 818
Peacock, Francis G. III, 249
Peacock, Hampton I, 294
Peacock, Hampton I, 704
Peacock, Hannah I, 566
Peacock, Hannah I, 704
Peacock, Hannah I, 720
Peacock, Hannah I, 730
Peacock, Hans G. III, 249
Peacock, Harley Loyde V, 818
Peacock, Harry W. IV, 401
Peacock, Harry Wetherill IV, 428
Peacock, Howard IV, 575
Peacock, Jemimah I, 314
Peacock, Jesse V, 818
Peacock, Jesse A. V, 818
Peacock, Jesse C. V, 818
Peacock, John I, 566
Peacock, John VI, 976
Peacock, John Jay I, 704
Peacock, John Jones V, 818
Peacock, Jonas I, 704
Peacock, Jonathan IV, 1375
Peacock, Josephine IV, 401
Peacock, Leona Belle V, 818
Peacock, Levy L. III, 249
Peacock, Lois J. IV, 428
Peacock, Lois Josephine IV, 428
Peacock, Lydia H. IV, 261
Peacock, Lydia H. IV, 592
Peacock, Lydia M. IV, 214
Peacock, Lydia M. IV, 261
Peacock, Margaret I, 294
Peacock, Margaret I, 314
Peacock, Margaret I, 704
Peacock, Margaret I, 730
Peacock, Margery H. IV, 574
Peacock, Margery H. IV, 575
Peacock, Margery H. IV, 592
Peacock, Margret I, 306
Peacock, Marjarie H. IV, 592
Peacock, Mary III, 460
Peacock, Mary Eadith V, 818
Peacock, Mary Jane IV, 261
Peacock, Miriam I, 704
Peacock, Morris IV, 214
Peacock, Morris IV, 261
Peacock, Morris IV, 592
Peacock, Naomi V, 703
Peacock, Naomi V, 818
Peacock, Osrow Elwood V, 818
Peacock, Patience I, 566
Peacock, Patsey I, 925
Peacock, Pheraby I, 294
Peacock, Pheraby I, 704
Peacock, Pheriby I, 730
Peacock, Rena IV, 428
Peacock, Rena J. IV, 261
Peacock, Rena Jane IV, 170
Peacock, Rena Jane IV, 261
Peacock, Rosetta V, 818
Peacock, Sarah II, 298
Peacock, Sarah II, 907
Peacock, Sarah P. III, 460
Peacock, Silas I, 294
Peacock, Silas I, 704
Peacock, Silas I, 730
Peacock, Susanna I, 413
Peacock, Susanna I, 429
Peacock, Tacy V, 974
Peacock, Tacy V, 978
Peacock, Thomas V, 703
Peacock, Wd. Sarah H. II, 814
Peacock, Wilie I, 314
Peacock, William I, 314
Peacock, Wm. III, 460
Peacock, Wm. IV, 574
Peacock, Wm. Howard IV, 592
Peaden, Alexander IV, 262
Peaden, Joseph IV, 262
Peaden, Thomas IV, 105
Peadon, Alexander IV, 262
Peake, Elizabeth II, 249
Peake, Hannah II, 617
Peake, Hannah II, 654
Peake, Wm. II, 617
Peake, Wm. II, 654
Peal, Ann IV, 429
Peal, Anna IV, 428
Peal, Christian I, 315
Peal, Cloe I, 1011
Peal, Cloe I, 1012
Peal, James VI, 66
Peal, James VI, 78
Peal, Phillis VI, 953
Peal, Reuben I, 995
Peal, Rhoda I, 995
Peal, Rhoda I, 1001
Peal, Robert VI, 59
Peal, Ruth VI, 66
Peal, Ruth VI, 78
Peal, Sarah I, 993
Peal, Sarah I, 995
Peal, Sarah I, 1011
Peal, Zilpha I, 995
Peale, Albert VI, 78
Peale, Charles W. II, 618
Peale, Hannah II, 618
Peale, Lydia V, 297
Peale, Lydia V, 308
Peale, Mark I, 995
Peale, Pharaby VI, 71
Peale, Pharaby Johnson VI, 78
Peale, Robert IV, 262
Peale, Robert VI, 71
Peale, Robert VI, 78
Peale, Ruth VI, 78
Pealen, Henry I, 896
Pealen, Mary I, 896
Pealen, Sarah I, 896
Peanock, William VI, 335
Pearce, Amanda Catharine VI, 976
Pearce, Ann II, 405
Pearce, Anna I, 314
Pearce, Archelaus IV, 985
Pearce, Archiles IV, 985
Pearce, Asenath L. IV, 985
Pearce, Benjamin V, 309
Pearce, Catharine V, 309
Pearce, Charles V, 270
Pearce, Charles V, 309
Pearce, Charles Brooke II, 405
Pearce, Clarence E. I, 947
Pearce, Clarkson V, 821
Pearce, Daniel II, 405
Pearce, David I, 68
Pearce, Deborah Ann II, 405
Pearce, Edward II, 405
Pearce, Edward II, 908
Pearce, Elizabeth II, 405
Pearce, Elizabeth III, 75
Pearce, Elizabeth III, 400
Pearce, Elizabeth III, 432
Pearce, Elizabeth VI, 976
Pearce, Ganer I, 967
Pearce, George I, 967
Pearce, George Chandler II, 405
Pearce, Gideon II, 908
Pearce, Hannah II, 215
Pearce, Hannah II, 249
Pearce, Hannah C. II, 405
Pearce, Isaac II, 405
Pearce, Jacob V, 309
Pearce, James I, 314
Pearce, James I, 567
Pearce, James I, 967
Pearce, James III, 400
Pearce, James III, 432
Pearce, James IV, 87
Pearce, Jesse I, 833
Pearce, John I, 36
Pearce, John I, 68
Pearce, John I, 967
Pearce, John II, 405
Pearce, John II, 446
Pearce, Joseph I, 68
Pearce, Joseph II, 405
Pearce, Joshua II, 405
Pearce, Josiah VI, 976
Pearce, Lacy Ann V, 821
Pearce, Leonard W. IV, 985
Pearce, Lowrethe I, 1132
Pearce, Lydia I, 36
Pearce, Lydia V, 303
Pearce, Lydia V, 309
Pearce, Marcey II, 506
Pearce, Marcey II, 618
Pearce, Mariam IV, 87
Pearce, Martha IV, 87
Pearce, Martha IV, 104
Pearce, Martha IV, 985
Pearce, Mary II, 206
Pearce, Mary II, 249
Pearce, Mary II, 298
Pearce, Mary II, 405
Pearce, Mary II, 703
Pearce, Mary IV, 87
Pearce, Mary IV, 104
Pearce, Mary IV, 105
Pearce, Mercy II, 618
Pearce, Meriba V, 309
Pearce, Miriam I, 36
Pearce, Miriam I, 68
Pearce, Moses V, 355
Pearce, Nathan V, 309
Pearce, Nicholas II, 405
Pearce, Polly VI, 307
Pearce, Polly VI, 335
Pearce, Rachel II, 219
Pearce, Rachel II, 225
Pearce, Rachel II, 249
Pearce, Ray IV, 985
Pearce, Rebecca III, 94
Pearce, Rebecca III, 182
Pearce, Richard II, 225
Pearce, Richard II, 249
Pearce, Richard II, 405
Pearce, Richard II, 618
Pearce, Richard VI, 976
Pearce, Robert I, 413
Pearce, Robert, Sr. I, 1130
Pearce, Robert, Sr. I, 1132
Pearce, Ruth II, 249
Pearce, Ruth V, 309
Pearce, Samuel I, 967
Pearce, Sarah I, 897
Pearce, Susanna II, 298
Pearce, Susanna VI, 432
Pearce, Susannah VI, 432
Pearce, Tempa I, 314
Pearce, Thomas I, 1
Pearce, Thomas I, 967
Pearce, Thomas I, 1130
Pearce, Thomas II, 405
Pearce, Thomas H. IV, 985
Pearce, William I, 833
Pearce, Willis Ray IV, 985
Pearcey, Isham VI, 976
Pearcey, Jenny VI, 976
Pearcey, Nancy VI, 1010
Pearcy, Abner VI, 976
Pearcy, Catharine VI, 994
Pearcy, Charles VI, 884
Pearcy, Charles VI, 895
Pearcy, Charles VI, 976
Pearcy, Clarey VI, 976
Pearcy, Edmund VI, 986
Pearcy, Eliza VI, 976
Pearcy, Henry VI, 917
Pearcy, Henry VI, 924
Pearcy, Henry VI, 976
Pearcy, Henry VI, 994
Pearcy, Henry VI, 995
Pearcy, Henry VI, 1010
Pearcy, Isham VI, 976
Pearcy, Jacob VI, 976
Pearcy, James VI, 986
Pearcy, Jenny VI, 976
Pearcy, Joaner VI, 993
Pearcy, Joannah VI, 976
Pearcy, John VI, 962
Pearcy, John VI, 970
Pearcy, John VI, 976
Pearcy, John VI, 1010
Pearcy, Kitty VI, 976
Pearcy, Marg. VI, 962
Pearcy, Martha Ann VI, 993
Pearcy, Mary VI, 917
Pearcy, Nancy VI, 884
Pearcy, Nancy VI, 976
Pearcy, Nancy VI, 1010
Pearcy, Necy VI, 924
Pearcy, Nicholas VI, 995
Pearcy, Patty VI, 986
Pearcy, Polly VI, 976
Pearcy, Rachel VI, 924
Pearcy, Sally VI, 1010
Pearcy, Sarah VI, 962
Pearcy, Thomas VI, 994
Pearcy, Ursula VI, 995
Pearl, Ada VI, 668
Pearl, Edward V, 354
Pearl, Edwin V, 354
Pearl, Isabella I, 16
Pearl, Martha IV, 1256
Pearl, Martha E. IV, 1256
Pearl, Salina IV, 926
Pearle, Lettie III, 464
Pearle, Lettie III, 475
Pearman, Grieg VI, 845
Pearman, James III, 249
Pearman, James C. VI, 825
Pearman, Polly VI, 845
Pears, Aaron I, 512
Pears, Charles II, 405
Pears, George I, 512
Pears, George I, 567
Pears, Hannah I, 512
Pears, Hepzibeth I, 512
Pears, Hepzibeth I, 558
Pears, Hepzibeth I, 567
Pears, Isaac I, 512
Pears, Mary I, 512
Pears, Mattie A. V, 111
Pears, Moses I, 512
Pears, Thomas I, 512
Pears, Thomas I, 558
Pears, Thomas I, 567
Pears, Wm. V, 1013
Pearsal, Amy III, 491
Pearsal, Ann III, 491
Pearsal, Edmund III, 355
Pearsal, Thomas III, 491
Pearsall, ??? III, 251
Pearsall, ??? III, 433
Pearsall, ??? III, 438
Pearsall, Abigail III, 432
Pearsall, Abigail III, 433
Pearsall, Alfred E. III, 249
Pearsall, Amy III, 46
Pearsall, Amy III, 249
Pearsall, Amy III, 251
Pearsall, Amy III, 282
Pearsall, Amy III, 300
Pearsall, Amy III, 381
Pearsall, Amy III, 383
Pearsall, Amy III, 432
Pearsall, Amy III, 492
Pearsall, Andries III, 492
Pearsall, Ann II, 404
Pearsall, Ann III, 59
Pearsall, Ann III, 237
Pearsall, Ann III, 249
Pearsall, Ann III, 250
Pearsall, Ann III, 251
Pearsall, Ann III, 319
Pearsall, Ann III, 381
Pearsall, Ann III, 383
Pearsall, Ann III, 387
Pearsall, Ann III, 432
Pearsall, Ann III, 472
Pearsall, Ann III, 473
Pearsall, Ann III, 474
Pearsall, Ann III, 479
Pearsall, Ann III, 491
Pearsall, Ann III, 492
Pearsall, Ann III, 508
Pearsall, Ann L. II, 714
Pearsall, Ann P. III, 387
Pearsall, Ann S. II, 906
Pearsall, Ann S. II, 907
Pearsall, Anna III, 432
Pearsall, Anna Arabella III, 250
Pearsall, Anna Arabella III, 275
Pearsall, Anna M. III, 251
Pearsall, Anna S. II, 759
Pearsall, Anne III, 249
Pearsall, Anne III, 383
Pearsall, Anne III, 432
Pearsall, Anne III, 435
Pearsall, Anne III, 492
Pearsall, Antoinette Graham III, 249
Pearsall, Antoinette Graham III, 383
Pearsall, Arthur Wood III, 433
Pearsall, Beth III, 432
Pearsall, Caroline III, 251
Pearsall, Catharine III, 383
Pearsall, Charles III, 383
Pearsall, Charles W. III, 249
Pearsall, Charles W. III, 250
Pearsall, Charles W. III, 492
Pearsall, Charlotte III, 251
Pearsall, Charlotte T. III, 249
Pearsall, Charlotte T. III, 313
Pearsall, Clara W. III, 237
Pearsall, Daniel III, 249
Pearsall, Daniel III, 251
Pearsall, Daniel III, 432
Pearsall, Edmund III, 250
Pearsall, Edmund III, 251
Pearsall, Edmund III, 383
Pearsall, Edward III, 251
Pearsall, Elijah III, 492
Pearsall, Eliz. III, 43
Pearsall, Eliz. III, 250
Pearsall, Eliz. III, 293
Pearsall, Eliza III, 23
Pearsall, Eliza III, 249
Pearsall, Eliza III, 250
Pearsall, Eliza III, 380
Pearsall, Eliza III, 383
Pearsall, Eliza A. III, 432
Pearsall, Eliza Ann III, 250
Pearsall, Elizabeth III, 23
Pearsall, Elizabeth III, 24
Pearsall, Elizabeth III, 58
Pearsall, Elizabeth III, 80
Pearsall, Elizabeth III, 102
Pearsall, Elizabeth III, 250
Pearsall, Elizabeth III, 251
Pearsall, Elizabeth III, 383
Pearsall, Elizabeth III, 400
Pearsall, Elizabeth III, 432
Pearsall, Elizabeth III, 492

Pearsall, Elizabeth P. II, 907
Pearsall, Elizabeth Parrish II, 907
Pearsall, Elizabeth S. II, 404
Pearsall, Elizabeth S. II, 617
Pearsall, Elizabeth W. III, 254
Pearsall, Emeline D. III, 250
Pearsall, Esther III, 251
Pearsall, Esther III, 381
Pearsall, Esther III, 383
Pearsall, Francis II, 759
Pearsall, Freelove III, 250
Pearsall, Freelove III, 251
Pearsall, Freelove III, 433
Pearsall, George III, 250
Pearsall, George III, 251
Pearsall, George H. III, 251
Pearsall, Gilbert III, 383
Pearsall, Gilbert H. III, 249
Pearsall, Gilbert H. III, 250
Pearsall, Gilbert H. III, 380
Pearsall, Gilbert H. III, 383
Pearsall, Hannah III, 43
Pearsall, Hannah III, 159
Pearsall, Hannah III, 250
Pearsall, Hannah III, 272
Pearsall, Hannah III, 414
Pearsall, Hannah III, 432
Pearsall, Hannah III, 492
Pearsall, Hannah III, 493
Pearsall, Hannah III, 494
Pearsall, Hannah M. II, 906
Pearsall, Hannah M. II, 907
Pearsall, Henry III, 249
Pearsall, Henry III, 260
Pearsall, Henry III, 432
Pearsall, Henry III, 433
Pearsall, Henry III, 452
Pearsall, Henry III, 453
Pearsall, Henry III, 474
Pearsall, Henry III, 492
Pearsall, Israel III, 250
Pearsall, Jacob III, 251
Pearsall, Jacob III, 383
Pearsall, Jacob III, 389
Pearsall, Jane III, 52
Pearsall, Jane III, 251
Pearsall, Jane III, 346
Pearsall, Jane III, 432
Pearsall, Jane III, 492
Pearsall, Jane Stratton III, 250
Pearsall, Jean III, 250
Pearsall, John II, 249
Pearsall, John III, 492
Pearsall, John III, 493
Pearsall, John III, 494
Pearsall, John G. III, 251
Pearsall, John W. III, 433
Pearsall, Joseph II, 617
Pearsall, Joseph III, 159
Pearsall, Joseph III, 250
Pearsall, Joseph III, 272
Pearsall, Joseph III, 432
Pearsall, Julia L. III, 250
Pearsall, Katharine F. III, 250
Pearsall, Katherine III, 249
Pearsall, Kezia III, 492
Pearsall, Margaret III, 164
Pearsall, Margaret III, 250
Pearsall, Margaret III, 251
Pearsall, Margaret III, 383
Pearsall, Margaret III, 387
Pearsall, Margaret B. III, 159
Pearsall, Margaret B. III, 250
Pearsall, Margaret H. III, 250
Pearsall, Martha III, 74
Pearsall, Martha III, 250
Pearsall, Martha III, 251
Pearsall, Martha III, 400
Pearsall, Martha III, 432
Pearsall, Martha III, 457
Pearsall, Martha C. III, 250
Pearsall, Mary II, 249
Pearsall, Mary II, 907
Pearsall, Mary III, 24
Pearsall, Mary III, 126
Pearsall, Mary III, 237
Pearsall, Mary III, 249
Pearsall, Mary III, 250
Pearsall, Mary III, 251
Pearsall, Mary III, 260
Pearsall, Mary III, 272
Pearsall, Mary III, 313
Pearsall, Mary III, 319
Pearsall, Mary III, 383
Pearsall, Mary III, 388
Pearsall, Mary III, 405
Pearsall, Mary III, 424
Pearsall, Mary III, 432
Pearsall, Mary III, 433
Pearsall, Mary III, 444
Pearsall, Mary III, 452
Pearsall, Mary III, 453
Pearsall, Mary III, 492
Pearsall, Mary III, 494
Pearsall, Mary A. III, 250
Pearsall, Mary Ann III, 250
Pearsall, Mary H. III, 251
Pearsall, Mary H. III, 383
Pearsall, Mary L. III, 249
Pearsall, Mary L. III, 250
Pearsall, Mary L. III, 251
Pearsall, Mary L. III, 313
Pearsall, Mary W. III, 250
Pearsall, Nath. III, 432
Pearsall, Nathaniel III, 74
Pearsall, Nathaniel III, 126
Pearsall, Nathaniel III, 250
Pearsall, Nathaniel III, 251
Pearsall, Nathaniel III, 424
Pearsall, Nathaniel III, 432
Pearsall, Nathaniel III, 457
Pearsall, Nicholas III, 250
Pearsall, Nicholas III, 313
Pearsall, Phebe III, 87
Pearsall, Phebe III, 250
Pearsall, Phebe III, 251
Pearsall, Phebe III, 417
Pearsall, Phebe III, 432
Pearsall, Phebe III, 492
Pearsall, Phebe III, 500
Pearsall, Phebe H. III, 433
Pearsall, Phineas C. III, 249
Pearsall, Rachel III, 250
Pearsall, Rachel III, 355
Pearsall, Rachel III, 383
Pearsall, Rachel III, 432
Pearsall, Rachel III, 474
Pearsall, Rachel III, 492
Pearsall, Rachel III, 508
Pearsall, Rachel C. III, 250
Pearsall, Rachel C. III, 293
Pearsall, Rebecca G. III, 250
Pearsall, Richard III, 250
Pearsall, Richard III, 251
Pearsall, Richard III, 383
Pearsall, Richard III, 492
Pearsall, Richard F. III, 275
Pearsall, Richard Franklin III, 250
Pearsall, Richard O. III, 250
Pearsall, Richard O. III, 251
Pearsall, Robert II, 404
Pearsall, Robert II, 617
Pearsall, Robert II, 714
Pearsall, Robert II, 759
Pearsall, Robert II, 906
Pearsall, Robert II, 907
Pearsall, Robert III, 80
Pearsall, Robert III, 250
Pearsall, Robert III, 251
Pearsall, Robert III, 293
Pearsall, Robert III, 383
Pearsall, Robert III, 432
Pearsall, Robert III, 492
Pearsall, Robert W. III, 250
Pearsall, Robert W. III, 254
Pearsall, Robert W. III, 383
Pearsall, Robert, Jr. II, 617
Pearsall, Robert, Jr. III, 250
Pearsall, Rowland III, 250
Pearsall, Rowland III, 432
Pearsall, Rowland III, 435
Pearsall, Rowland III, 492
Pearsall, Rowland III, 500
Pearsall, Samuel III, 164
Pearsall, Samuel III, 251
Pearsall, Samuel III, 383
Pearsall, Samuel III, 387
Pearsall, Samuel III, 432
Pearsall, Samuel III, 492
Pearsall, Samuel C. III, 432
Pearsall, Samuel G. III, 251
Pearsall, Sarah II, 714
Pearsall, Sarah III, 59
Pearsall, Sarah III, 110
Pearsall, Sarah III, 250
Pearsall, Sarah III, 251
Pearsall, Sarah III, 313
Pearsall, Sarah III, 331
Pearsall, Sarah III, 383
Pearsall, Sarah III, 398
Pearsall, Sarah III, 414
Pearsall, Sarah III, 429
Pearsall, Sarah III, 432
Pearsall, Sarah III, 444
Pearsall, Sarah III, 452
Pearsall, Sarah III, 453
Pearsall, Sarah III, 457
Pearsall, Sarah III, 460
Pearsall, Sarah B. III, 250
Pearsall, Sarah L. II, 714
Pearsall, Silas III, 251
Pearsall, Silas III, 432
Pearsall, T. W. III, 313
Pearsall, Thomas III, 58
Pearsall, Thomas III, 59
Pearsall, Thomas III, 102
Pearsall, Thomas III, 249
Pearsall, Thomas III, 250
Pearsall, Thomas III, 319
Pearsall, Thomas III, 331
Pearsall, Thomas III, 358
Pearsall, Thomas III, 381
Pearsall, Thomas III, 383
Pearsall, Thomas III, 394
Pearsall, Thomas III, 400
Pearsall, Thomas III, 414
Pearsall, Thomas III, 429
Pearsall, Thomas III, 432
Pearsall, Thomas III, 444
Pearsall, Thomas III, 460
Pearsall, Thomas III, 472
Pearsall, Thomas III, 474
Pearsall, Thomas III, 492
Pearsall, Thomas III, 508
Pearsall, Thomas W. III, 250
Pearsall, Thomas W. III, 251
Pearsall, Thomas W. III, 383
Pearsall, Thomas W., Jr. III, 251
Pearsall, Thomas, Jr. III, 87
Pearsall, Thomas, Jr. III, 251
Pearsall, Thos. III, 43
Pearsall, Thos. III, 250
Pearsall, Thos. III, 251
Pearsall, Thos. W. III, 249
Pearsall, Thos. W. III, 250
Pearsall, Thos. W. III, 313
Pearsall, Violet B. II, 901
Pearsall, Violet B. II, 907
Pearsall, Wait III, 432
Pearsall, Wait III, 492
Pearsall, Wd. Beth. Ann III, 438
Pearsall, Wd. Sarah Mott III, 394
Pearsall, William II, 714
Pearsall, William III, 24
Pearsall, William III, 250
Pearsall, William III, 251
Pearsall, William III, 432
Pearsall, William III, 492
Pearsall, Wm. II, 759
Pearsall, Wm. II, 906
Pearsall, Wm. II, 907
Pearsall, Wm. III, 23
Pearsall, Wm. III, 237
Pearsall, Wm. III, 250
Pearsall, Wm. Parrish II, 901
Pearsall, Wm. Parrish II, 907
Pearse, Hannah I, 567
Pearse, Polly I, 199
Pearses, Irons II, 405
Pearshall, Elizabeth III, 58
Pearsoll, Anna S. II, 759
Pearsoll, Francis II, 759
Pearsoll, Robert II, 759
Pearsoll, Wm. II, 759
Pearson, ??? I, 279
Pearson, ??? III, 174
Pearson, ??? V, 109
Pearson, Abigail V, 779
Pearson, Abigail V, 792
Pearson, Abigail V, 797
Pearson, Abigail V, 819
Pearson, Abigail V, 820
Pearson, Abner V, 638
Pearson, Abner V, 639
Pearson, Abraham I, 294
Pearson, Abraham IV, 105
Pearson, Abram V, 819
Pearson, Abram V, 820
Pearson, Achsa V, 639
Pearson, Achsa A. I, 768
Pearson, Achsah IV, 1289
Pearson, Achsah V, 638
Pearson, Achsah A. I, 751
Pearson, Achsah Ann I, 751
Pearson, Ada J. V, 761
Pearson, Ada J. V, 768
Pearson, Adah Jeanette V, 760
Pearson, Adah Jeanette V, 775
Pearson, Adelbert V, 760
Pearson, Albert V, 639
Pearson, Albert M. VI, 687
Pearson, Albert Millhollen VI, 687
Pearson, Alice IV, 105
Pearson, Alice IV, 339
Pearson, Alice IV, 345
Pearson, Alice V, 639
Pearson, Alice V, 760
Pearson, Alice J. V, 761
Pearson, Alicia III, 251
Pearson, Alpha V, 760
Pearson, Amanda J. II, 896
Pearson, Amanda J. II, 907
Pearson, Amanda Rachel V, 819
Pearson, Amanuel Jesse V, 819
Pearson, Amos IV, 1110
Pearson, Amos V, 790
Pearson, Amos V, 791
Pearson, Amos J. V, 819
Pearson, Amy V, 794
Pearson, Angeline V, 703
Pearson, Ann I, 61
Pearson, Ann I, 160
Pearson, Ann I, 294
Pearson, Ann I, 307
Pearson, Ann I, 314
Pearson, Ann I, 705
Pearson, Ann I, 730
Pearson, Ann I, 995
Pearson, Ann I, 1022
Pearson, Ann I, 1023
Pearson, Ann I, 1029
Pearson, Ann I, 1032
Pearson, Ann I, 1035
Pearson, Ann I, 1036
Pearson, Ann I, 1038
Pearson, Ann II, 451
Pearson, Ann II, 527
Pearson, Ann II, 618
Pearson, Ann II, 872
Pearson, Ann II, 907
Pearson, Ann II, 984
Pearson, Ann II, 1021
Pearson, Ann IV, 105
Pearson, Ann IV, 262
Pearson, Ann IV, 313
Pearson, Ann IV, 428
Pearson, Ann IV, 749
Pearson, Ann V, 100
Pearson, Ann V, 109
Pearson, Ann V, 747
Pearson, Ann V, 760
Pearson, Ann V, 786
Pearson, Ann V, 787
Pearson, Ann V, 789
Pearson, Ann V, 790
Pearson, Ann V, 791
Pearson, Ann V, 794
Pearson, Ann V, 819
Pearson, Ann, Jr. IV, 345
Pearson, Anna I, 113
Pearson, Anna I, 160
Pearson, Anna I, 704
Pearson, Anna I, 714
Pearson, Anna I, 718
Pearson, Anna I, 730
Pearson, Anna I, 1057
Pearson, Anna I, 1121
Pearson, Anna I, 1130
Pearson, Anna II, 404
Pearson, Anna II, 714
Pearson, Anna II, 759
Pearson, Anna II, 907
Pearson, Anna IV, 345
Pearson, Anna IV, 1286
Pearson, Anna IV, 1289
Pearson, Anna V, 109
Pearson, Anna V, 175
Pearson, Anna V, 196
Pearson, Anna V, 753
Pearson, Anna V, 760
Pearson, Anna V, 761
Pearson, Anna V, 791
Pearson, Anna V, 819
Pearson, Anna V, 820
Pearson, Anna Beatrice I, 315
Pearson, Anna J. V, 760
Pearson, Anna Jane V, 791
Pearson, Anna Macy V, 760
Pearson, Anna Marie IV, 1110
Pearson, Anna Mary V, 760
Pearson, Anne I, 995
Pearson, Anne I, 1023
Pearson, Anne I, 1036
Pearson, Anne IV, 156
Pearson, Anne V, 638
Pearson, Annie IV, 1289
Pearson, Annie V, 820
Pearson, Arlyn V, 761
Pearson, Arthur V, 761
Pearson, Asenath V, 270
Pearson, Asenath V, 523
Pearson, Asenath V, 638
Pearson, Aseneth V, 639
Pearson, Aseneth V, 646
Pearson, Avis C. I, 339
Pearson, Axum V, 639
Pearson, B. H. V, 760
Pearson, Barney I, 294
Pearson, Benj. IV, 345
Pearson, Benj. V, 759
Pearson, Benj. V, 761
Pearson, Benj. V, 762
Pearson, Benj. V, 791
Pearson, Benj. V, 797
Pearson, Benj. V, 815
Pearson, Benj. V, 819
Pearson, Benj. H. V, 760
Pearson, Benjamin I, 1015
Pearson, Benjamin I, 1022
Pearson, Benjamin I, 1023
Pearson, Benjamin I, 1029
Pearson, Benjamin I, 1035
Pearson, Benjamin I, 1036
Pearson, Benjamin I, 1056
Pearson, Benjamin II, 404
Pearson, Benjamin IV, 156
Pearson, Benjamin IV, 262
Pearson, Benjamin IV, 544
Pearson, Benjamin IV, 1071
Pearson, Benjamin IV, 1110
Pearson, Benjamin V, 109
Pearson, Benjamin V, 703
Pearson, Benjamin V, 748
Pearson, Benjamin V, 755
Pearson, Benjamin V, 759
Pearson, Benjamin V, 760
Pearson, Benjamin V, 761
Pearson, Benjamin V, 790
Pearson, Benjamin V, 791
Pearson, Benjamin V, 795
Pearson, Benjamin V, 818
Pearson, Benjamin V, 819
Pearson, Benjamin VI, 429
Pearson, Benjamin H. V, 753
Pearson, Benjamin J. V, 792
Pearson, Benjamin, Jr. V, 820
Pearson, Benson V, 790
Pearson, Bertie I, 339
Pearson, Betty I, 35
Pearson, Betty I, 67
Pearson, Betty I, 294
Pearson, Betty I, 314
Pearson, Betty I, 317
Pearson, Betty I Sup 1, 5
Pearson, Buma V, 639
Pearson, Calvin W. IV, 1375
Pearson, Calvin W. IV, 1381
Pearson, Catharine I, 705
Pearson, Catharine I, 730
Pearson, Catharine IV, 544
Pearson, Catharine IV, 1071
Pearson, Catharine IV, 1110
Pearson, Catharine IV, 1289
Pearson, Catharine V, 772
Pearson, Catharine V, 780
Pearson, Catharine V, 790
Pearson, Catharine V, 794
Pearson, Catharine R. V, 760
Pearson, Catherine IV, 322
Pearson, Catherine IV, 345
Pearson, Charity I, 1030
Pearson, Charity I, 1036
Pearson, Charity IV, 1179
Pearson, Charity IV, 1193
Pearson, Charity V, 109
Pearson, Charity V, 760
Pearson, Charity V, 772
Pearson, Charity V, 786
Pearson, Charity V, 790
Pearson, Charity V, 791
Pearson, Charity V, 819
Pearson, Charles E. V, 761
Pearson, Charles Edgar II, 907
Pearson, Charles Edgar II, 924
Pearson, Charley E. V, 761
Pearson, Chas. V, 639
Pearson, Chas. E. V, 760
Pearson, Chas. Edgar II, 907
Pearson, Chas. G. V, 639
Pearson, Christian VI, 543
Pearson, Christian VI, 546
Pearson, Christopher I, 67
Pearson, Clark V, 761
Pearson, Cynthia IV, 345
Pearson, Cynthia IV, 351
Pearson, Cynthia IV, 544
Pearson, Cynthia IV, 1071
Pearson, Cynthia IV, 1110
Pearson, Cynthia V, 856
Pearson, Daniel V, 760
Pearson, David I, 897
Pearson, David I, 1130
Pearson, David IV, 544
Pearson, David IV, 1071
Pearson, David IV, 1110
Pearson, David V, 790
Pearson, David V, 791
Pearson, David V, 819
Pearson, David V, 820
Pearson, David S. V, 760
Pearson, Deborah II, 527
Pearson, Deborah II, 618

son, Deborah II, 715
son, Deborah II, 997
son, Deborah II, 1021
son, Decena S. I, 768
son, Delbert V, 761
son, Delpha V, 794
son, Delphina V, 759
son, Delphina V, 761
son, Dicena I, 315
son, Dicene S. I, 294
son, Dicene S. I, 767
son, Dicene S. I, 768
son, Donna V, 761
son, Dorcas I, 294
son, Dorcas II, 868
son, Dorcas II, 907
son, Dorcas V, 748
son, Dorcas V, 753
son, Dorcas V, 760
rson, Dorcas V, 761
rson, Dorcas V, 762
rson, Dorcas P. V, 760
rson, Dr. H. R. V, 761
rson, E. L. I, 294
rson, E. Louvenia I, 315
rson, Eber V, 760
rson, Edith V, 760
rson, Edna I, 1023
rson, Edna I, 1036
rson, Edward Wilson II, 618
son, Eldred J. I, 315
rson, Eli V, 639
rson, Eli V, 703
rson, Eli V, 790
rson, Eli V, 791
rson, Eli V, 792
rson, Elihu V, 760
rson, Elihu V, 761
rson, Elihu V, 790
son, Elijah V, 109
rson, Elijah V, 790
rson, Elijah V, 791
rson, Elisabeth I, 37
son, Elisabeth I, 45
rson, Elisabeth I, 57
rson, Elisabeth I, 67
rson, Elisabeth II, 249
son, Elisabeth II, 466
rson, Elisabeth II, 618
rson, Elisha V, 109
rson, Elisha V, 790
rson, Elisha V, 791
rson, Elizabeth I, 294
son, Elizabeth I, 314
son, Elizabeth I, 315
rson, Elizabeth I, 400
rson, Elizabeth I, 413
rson, Elizabeth I, 512
rson, Elizabeth I, 566
rson, Elizabeth I, 897
rson, Elizabeth I, 995
rson, Elizabeth I, 1022
rson, Elizabeth I, 1035
rson, Elizabeth I, 1036
rson, Elizabeth I, 1062
rson, Elizabeth I, 1130
rson, Elizabeth II, 249
rson, Elizabeth II, 254
rson, Elizabeth II, 404
rson, Elizabeth II, 463
rson, Elizabeth II, 572
rson, Elizabeth II, 584
rson, Elizabeth II, 617
rson, Elizabeth II, 618
rson, Elizabeth II, 701
rson, Elizabeth II, 715
rson, Elizabeth II, 994
rson, Elizabeth II, 1000
rson, Elizabeth II, 1021
rson, Elizabeth IV, 156
rson, Elizabeth IV, 544
rson, Elizabeth IV, 550
rson, Elizabeth IV, 880
rson, Elizabeth V, 308
rson, Elizabeth V, 747
rson, Elizabeth V, 759
rson, Elizabeth V, 760
rson, Elizabeth V, 786
rson, Elizabeth V, 790
rson, Elizabeth V, 791
rson, Elizabeth V, 819
rson, Elizabeth V, 820
rson, Elizabeth VI, 976
rson, Elizabeth G. II, 731
rson, Elizabeth G. II, 759
rson, Elizabeth S. IV, 1110
rson, Elliott V, 856
rson, Ellwood IV, 1110
rson, Elma V, 761
rson, Elmer V, 761
rson, Elmira V, 791
Pearson, Elmira V, 792
Pearson, Elmira V, 820
Pearson, Elsie Weatherly I, 623
Pearson, Embree IV, 1071
Pearson, Emily V, 760
Pearson, Emily R. I, 294
Pearson, Enoch I, 1015
Pearson, Enoch I, 1022
Pearson, Enoch I, 1023
Pearson, Enoch I, 1028
Pearson, Enoch I, 1029
Pearson, Enoch I, 1035
Pearson, Enoch I, 1036
Pearson, Enoch I Sup 1, 11
Pearson, Enoch II, 967
Pearson, Enoch II, 994
Pearson, Enoch II, 1021
Pearson, Enoch II, 1027
Pearson, Enoch IV, 544
Pearson, Enoch IV, 1071
Pearson, Enoch IV, 1110
Pearson, Enoch V, 109
Pearson, Enoch V, 723
Pearson, Enoch V, 760
Pearson, Enoch V, 762
Pearson, Enoch V, 780
Pearson, Enoch V, 787
Pearson, Enoch V, 790
Pearson, Enoch V, 791
Pearson, Enoch V, 792
Pearson, Enoch V, 799
Pearson, Enoch V, 815
Pearson, Enoch V, 818
Pearson, Enoch V, 819
Pearson, Enoch V, 820
Pearson, Enoch VI, 429
Pearson, Enoch J. V, 820
Pearson, Enoch K. V, 761
Pearson, Enoch Keifer V, 792
Pearson, Enoch S. V, 791
Pearson, Enoch, Jr. V, 779
Pearson, Enoch, Jr. V, 791
Pearson, Enoch, Jr. V, 819
Pearson, Ernest V, 761
Pearson, Ester I, 1060
Pearson, Esther I, 1029
Pearson, Esther I, 1036
Pearson, Esther I, 1056
Pearson, Esther V, 109
Pearson, Esther V, 125
Pearson, Esther V, 126
Pearson, Esther V, 639
Pearson, Esther V, 755
Pearson, Esther V, 760
Pearson, Esther V, 790
Pearson, Esther V, 791
Pearson, Esther V, 795
Pearson, Esther V, 797
Pearson, Esther V, 815
Pearson, Esther V, 818
Pearson, Esther V, 819
Pearson, Esther V, 820
Pearson, Etta Hall V, 761
Pearson, Eunice I, 1022
Pearson, Eunice I, 1034
Pearson, Eunice I, 1036
Pearson, Eunice V, 761
Pearson, Eunice V, 789
Pearson, Eunice V, 791
Pearson, Eunice V, 815
Pearson, Eunice V, 818
Pearson, Eunice V, 819
Pearson, Eunice V, 820
Pearson, Eunice Anna V, 196
Pearson, Eva V, 760
Pearson, Eva Brumbaugh V, 760
Pearson, Eva May V, 639
Pearson, Evelyn V, 761
Pearson, Everett V, 760
Pearson, Everett V, 761
Pearson, Exile I, 566
Pearson, Exile I, 1016
Pearson, Exile V, 109
Pearson, Exile William I, 1023
Pearson, Exum I, 995
Pearson, Ezra II, 618
Pearson, Ezra V, 791
Pearson, Ezra V, 792
Pearson, Ezra V, 819
Pearson, Fannie C. VI, 687
Pearson, Fannie C. VI, 710
Pearson, Franklin V, 639
Pearson, Geo. V, 925
Pearson, George I, 512
Pearson, George I, 566
Pearson, George I, 1130
Pearson, George II, 780
Pearson, George III, 251
Pearson, George IV, 544
Pearson, George IV, 1071
Pearson, George IV, 1110
Pearson, George V, 354
Pearson, George V, 638
Pearson, George V, 639
Pearson, George V, 703
Pearson, George V, 925
Pearson, George VI, 976
Pearson, Georgia III, 174
Pearson, Georgia III, 251
Pearson, Georgiana III, 251
Pearson, Georgina III, 174
Pearson, Grace II, 547
Pearson, Grace II, 617
Pearson, Hal VI, 982
Pearson, Hal L. VI, 976
Pearson, Hannah I, 566
Pearson, Hannah I, 897
Pearson, Hannah I, 1011
Pearson, Hannah I, 1012
Pearson, Hannah I, 1016
Pearson, Hannah I, 1022
Pearson, Hannah I, 1033
Pearson, Hannah I, 1036
Pearson, Hannah II, 222
Pearson, Hannah II, 249
Pearson, Hannah II, 404
Pearson, Hannah II, 618
Pearson, Hannah II, 715
Pearson, Hannah II, 759
Pearson, Hannah V, 270
Pearson, Hannah V, 523
Pearson, Hannah V, 638
Pearson, Hannah V, 639
Pearson, Hannah V, 760
Pearson, Hannah V, 780
Pearson, Hannah V, 790
Pearson, Hannah V, 791
Pearson, Hannah V, 794
Pearson, Hannah V, 819
Pearson, Hannah VI, 429
Pearson, Hannah Ann IV, 1110
Pearson, Hariet V, 819
Pearson, Harris Preston I, 623
Pearson, Harry W. V, 639
Pearson, Harry W. V, 703
Pearson, Henry I, 1023
Pearson, Henry I, 1036
Pearson, Henry II, 404
Pearson, Henry IV, 1289
Pearson, Henry V, 109
Pearson, Henry V, 639
Pearson, Henry V, 791
Pearson, Henry A. V, 760
Pearson, Henry C. V, 792
Pearson, Henry J. V, 761
Pearson, Henry Jones V, 760
Pearson, Henry S. V, 792
Pearson, Herbert R. V, 760
Pearson, Herbert R. V, 775
Pearson, Hezekiah V, 270
Pearson, Hiram V, 109
Pearson, Hiram V, 759
Pearson, Hiram V, 761
Pearson, Hiram V, 786
Pearson, Hiram V, 790
Pearson, Hiram V, 791
Pearson, Hiram V, 819
Pearson, Hiram V, 820
Pearson, Homer V, 761
Pearson, Homer V, 820
Pearson, Horace M. V, 761
Pearson, Horace Melvin V, 760
Pearson, Horace Melvin V, 775
Pearson, Hosea V, 819
Pearson, Hulda I, 730
Pearson, Hulda I, 995
Pearson, Huldah I, 113
Pearson, Huldah I, 294
Pearson, Huldah I, 730
Pearson, Huldah I, 995
Pearson, Hyram V, 791
Pearson, Ichabod I, 57
Pearson, Ichabod I, 67
Pearson, Ichabod I, 160
Pearson, Ichabod I, 294
Pearson, Ichabod I, 315
Pearson, Ichabod IV, 1289
Pearson, Ichabod E. I, 294
Pearson, Ichabod E. I, 315
Pearson, Idella V, 760
Pearson, Irene Louella V, 703
Pearson, Isaac I, 294
Pearson, Isaac I, 512
Pearson, Isaac I, 897
Pearson, Isaac I, 967
Pearson, Isaac I, 1022
Pearson, Isaac I, 1096
Pearson, Isaac I, 1130
Pearson, Isaac II, 222
Pearson, Isaac II, 232
Pearson, Isaac II, 249
Pearson, Isaac II, 404
Pearson, Isaac II, 539
Pearson, Isaac II, 617
Pearson, Isaac II, 618
Pearson, Isaac IV, 345
Pearson, Isaac IV, 1375
Pearson, Isaac V, 109
Pearson, Isaac V, 639
Pearson, Isaac V, 748
Pearson, Isaac V, 759
Pearson, Isaac V, 790
Pearson, Isaac V, 791
Pearson, Isaac V, 792
Pearson, Isaac V, 804
Pearson, Isaac V, 819
Pearson, Isaac V, 820
Pearson, Isaac C. V, 780
Pearson, Isaac C. V, 792
Pearson, Isaac C. V, 820
Pearson, Isaac L. II, 618
Pearson, Isaac Lobdell II, 404
Pearson, Isaac R. V, 791
Pearson, Isaac, Jr. II, 618
Pearson, Isaac, Jr. V, 792
Pearson, Isabel I, 897
Pearson, Jacob I, 413
Pearson, Jacob J. III, 251
Pearson, James I, 1022
Pearson, James II, 404
Pearson, James II, 543
Pearson, James II, 618
Pearson, James II, 814
Pearson, James IV, 1110
Pearson, James V, 639
Pearson, James V, 760
Pearson, James V, 790
Pearson, James B. I, 339
Pearson, James Hart II, 618
Pearson, James R. I, 294
Pearson, Jane II, 404
Pearson, Jane II, 547
Pearson, Jane II, 618
Pearson, Jane II, 646
Pearson, Jane II, 656
Pearson, Jane IV, 345
Pearson, Jane IV, 544
Pearson, Jane IV, 1110
Pearson, Jane V, 621
Pearson, Jane V, 638
Pearson, Jane V, 639
Pearson, Jane V, 759
Pearson, Jane V, 791
Pearson, Jane V, 792
Pearson, Jane V, 819
Pearson, Jane V, 820
Pearson, Jane V, 925
Pearson, Jane Ann III, 251
Pearson, Jane Ann V, 925
Pearson, Jasper N. V, 761
Pearson, Jasper Newton V, 760
Pearson, Jasper Newton V, 775
Pearson, Jean V, 761
Pearson, Jeffery Hawkins II, 1021
Pearson, Jehu I. V, 197
Pearson, Jehu S. V, 196
Pearson, Jehu S. V, 197
Pearson, Jemimah I, 314
Pearson, Jeremiah V, 761
Pearson, Jeremiah V, 791
Pearson, Jeremiah V, 792
Pearson, Jeremiah V, 820
Pearson, Jesse I, 299
Pearson, Jesse I, 314
Pearson, Jesse I, 730
Pearson, Jesse I, 1023
Pearson, Jesse I, 1036
Pearson, Jesse IV, 156
Pearson, Jesse IV, 345
Pearson, Jesse IV, 351
Pearson, Jesse IV, 544
Pearson, Jesse IV, 1071
Pearson, Jesse IV, 1110
Pearson, Jesse V, 109
Pearson, Jesse V, 270
Pearson, Jesse V, 523
Pearson, Jesse V, 638
Pearson, Jesse V, 639
Pearson, Jesse V, 790
Pearson, Jesse V, 791
Pearson, Jesse V, 792
Pearson, Jesse V, 808
Pearson, Jesse V, 819
Pearson, Jesse V, 820
Pearson, Jesse William V, 196
Pearson, Joanna I, 1022
Pearson, Joanna I, 1036
Pearson, Joanna I, 1037
Pearson, Job I, 294
Pearson, Job II, 618
Pearson, Job V, 791
Pearson, John I, 45
Pearson, John I, 67
Pearson, John I, 294
Pearson, John I, 705
Pearson, John I, 897
Pearson, John I, 967
Pearson, John I, 1011
Pearson, John I, 1012
Pearson, John I, 1035
Pearson, John I, 1036
Pearson, John I Sup 1, 5
Pearson, John I Sup 1, 11
Pearson, John II, 618
Pearson, John IV, 544
Pearson, John IV, 1110
Pearson, John IV, 1289
Pearson, John V, 270
Pearson, John V, 523
Pearson, John V, 638
Pearson, John V, 748
Pearson, John V, 759
Pearson, John V, 790
Pearson, John V, 791
Pearson, John V, 792
Pearson, John V, 819
Pearson, John V, 820
Pearson, John V, 925
Pearson, John F. V, 638
Pearson, John F. V, 639
Pearson, John F. V, 818
Pearson, John F. V, 819
Pearson, John Furnas V, 109
Pearson, John H. V, 639
Pearson, John Mills V, 109
Pearson, John N. I, 294
Pearson, John N. I, 315
Pearson, John N. I, 339
Pearson, John Newlin I, 339
Pearson, John P. V, 759
Pearson, John Paschall II, 404
Pearson, John R. V, 760
Pearson, John R. V, 761
Pearson, John R. V, 762
Pearson, John S. II, 701
Pearson, John S. II, 715
Pearson, John S. II, 731
Pearson, John S. II, 759
Pearson, John T. I, 294
Pearson, John T. I, 315
Pearson, John T. I, 767
Pearson, John T. I, 768
Pearson, John Thomas I, 315
Pearson, John W. I, 339
Pearson, Jonas I, 1023
Pearson, Jonas I, 1035
Pearson, Jonas I, 1036
Pearson, Jonathan I, 46
Pearson, Jonathan I, 67
Pearson, Jonathan I, 132
Pearson, Jonathan I, 160
Pearson, Jonathan I, 294
Pearson, Jonathan I, 310
Pearson, Jonathan I, 314
Pearson, Jonathan I, 315
Pearson, Jonathan I, 730
Pearson, Jonathan I, 995
Pearson, Jonathan I Sup 1, 5
Pearson, Jonathan V, 354
Pearson, Jonathan V, 791
Pearson, Joseph I, 897
Pearson, Joseph I, 1022
Pearson, Joseph I, 1023
Pearson, Joseph I, 1035
Pearson, Joseph I, 1036
Pearson, Joseph II, 618
Pearson, Joseph II, 715
Pearson, Joseph V, 109
Pearson, Joseph V, 270
Pearson, Joseph V, 523
Pearson, Joseph V, 621
Pearson, Joseph V, 637
Pearson, Joseph V, 638
Pearson, Joseph V, 639
Pearson, Joseph V, 759
Pearson, Joseph V, 790
Pearson, Joseph V, 818
Pearson, Joseph V, 819
Pearson, Joseph V, 925
Pearson, Joseph A. V, 819
Pearson, Joseph D. I, 294
Pearson, Joseph F. V, 639
Pearson, Joseph Hibberd II, 618
Pearson, Joseph Hiram V, 819
Pearson, Joseph John V, 925
Pearson, Joseph L. I, 294
Pearson, Joseph L. I, 315
Pearson, Joseph, Jr. V, 791
Pearson, Joshua II, 404
Pearson, Joshua II, 466
Pearson, Joshua II, 618
Pearson, Joshua V, 791
Pearson, Joshua V, 819

Pearson, Joshua V, 820
Pearson, Josiah V, 790
Pearson, Judah II, 618
Pearson, Judah II, 672
Pearson, Juliann V, 819
Pearson, Katharine V, 791
Pearson, Katherine V, 793
Pearson, Kesiah V, 523
Pearson, Kezia, Jr. V, 761
Pearson, Keziah V, 109
Pearson, Keziah V, 638
Pearson, Keziah V, 639
Pearson, Keziah V, 756
Pearson, Keziah V, 759
Pearson, Keziah V, 819
Pearson, Keziah H. V, 760
Pearson, L. A. V, 761
Pearson, L. A., Jr. V, 761
Pearson, Laura E. V, 761
Pearson, Laura Ellayne V, 760
Pearson, Laura Ellayne V, 775
Pearson, Laura M. V, 639
Pearson, Laura M. V, 703
Pearson, Lawrence I, 1035
Pearson, Lawrence I, 1036
Pearson, Lawrence I Sup 1, 11
Pearson, Lawrence II, 991
Pearson, Lawrence II, 1021
Pearson, Lazaris I, 768
Pearson, Lazarus I, 283
Pearson, Lazarus I, 294
Pearson, Lazarus I, 315
Pearson, Lazarus I, 768
Pearson, Lazerous I, 294
Pearson, Lazerus I, 315
Pearson, Lellis I, 730
Pearson, Lemuel F. V, 787
Pearson, Leonidas V, 760
Pearson, Leslie I, 315
Pearson, Leslie I, 339
Pearson, Letitia II, 1014
Pearson, Letitia II, 1021
Pearson, Levi I, 37
Pearson, Levi I, 67
Pearson, Levi I, 705
Pearson, Levi V, 196
Pearson, Levi V, 197
Pearson, Levi V, 204
Pearson, Levi V, 791
Pearson, Levi V, 792
Pearson, Levi V, 820
Pearson, Levi H. I, 339
Pearson, Lillis I, 730
Pearson, Lindley V, 819
Pearson, Lizzie V, 760
Pearson, Lizzie V, 761
Pearson, Lon A. V, 639
Pearson, Louisa V, 780
Pearson, Louisa V, 792
Pearson, Louisa V, 804
Pearson, Louisa V, 819
Pearson, Louisa V, 820
Pearson, Lova V, 735
Pearson, Lova V, 761
Pearson, Lova L. V, 760
Pearson, Luvenia V, 760
Pearson, Lydia IV, 528
Pearson, Lydia IV, 544
Pearson, Lydia IV, 1289
Pearson, Lydia V, 638
Pearson, Lydia V, 791
Pearson, Lydia V, 819
Pearson, Lydia V, 820
Pearson, Maelea V, 760
Pearson, Mahala V, 760
Pearson, Mahala V, 761
Pearson, Mahala V, 768
Pearson, Mahala V, 775
Pearson, Mahala V, 790
Pearson, Mahala V, 792
Pearson, Mahala V, 811
Pearson, Mahala V, 819
Pearson, Mahalah V, 785
Pearson, Marcus J. V, 197
Pearson, Marcus John V, 196
Pearson, Marcus John V, 197
Pearson, Margaret I, 294
Pearson, Margaret I, 301
Pearson, Margaret I, 315
Pearson, Margaret II, 249
Pearson, Margaret II, 967
Pearson, Margaret II, 1021
Pearson, Margaret II, 1027
Pearson, Margaret V, 759
Pearson, Margaret V, 760
Pearson, Margaret V, 761
Pearson, Margaret V, 819
Pearson, Margaret Susan V, 639
Pearson, Margaret Z. I, 752
Pearson, Margery V, 786
Pearson, Margery V, 790
Pearson, Margery O. V, 196
Pearson, Maria II, 868
Pearson, Maria II, 907
Pearson, Marietta V, 789
Pearson, Marietta V, 792
Pearson, Mark I, 57
Pearson, Mark I, 67
Pearson, Mark I, 160
Pearson, Mark I, 294
Pearson, Mark I, 967
Pearson, Mark V, 308
Pearson, Martaret S. II, 759
Pearson, Martha I, 834
Pearson, Martha I, 897
Pearson, Martha I, 1022
Pearson, Martha I, 1023
Pearson, Martha I, 1035
Pearson, Martha I, 1036
Pearson, Martha I, 1038
Pearson, Martha II, 404
Pearson, Martha II, 618
Pearson, Martha II, 715
Pearson, Martha II, 759
Pearson, Martha II, 986
Pearson, Martha II, 1021
Pearson, Martha V, 125
Pearson, Martha V, 638
Pearson, Martha V, 639
Pearson, Martha VI, 429
Pearson, Martha Ann V, 819
Pearson, Martha B. II, 907
Pearson, Martha Bazilian II, 814
Pearson, Martha G. III, 83
Pearson, Marthanna IV, 1375
Pearson, Marthanna IV, 1381
Pearson, Mary I, 54
Pearson, Mary I, 60
Pearson, Mary I, 67
Pearson, Mary I, 87
Pearson, Mary I, 315
Pearson, Mary I, 339
Pearson, Mary I, 400
Pearson, Mary I, 413
Pearson, Mary I, 512
Pearson, Mary I, 623
Pearson, Mary I, 705
Pearson, Mary I, 708
Pearson, Mary I, 730
Pearson, Mary I, 761
Pearson, Mary I, 897
Pearson, Mary I, 1022
Pearson, Mary I, 1023
Pearson, Mary I, 1027
Pearson, Mary I, 1029
Pearson, Mary I, 1032
Pearson, Mary I, 1034
Pearson, Mary I, 1035
Pearson, Mary I, 1036
Pearson, Mary I, 1038
Pearson, Mary I Sup 1, 5
Pearson, Mary II, 122
Pearson, Mary II, 124
Pearson, Mary II, 404
Pearson, Mary II, 547
Pearson, Mary II, 618
Pearson, Mary II, 672
Pearson, Mary II, 701
Pearson, Mary II, 759
Pearson, Mary II, 780
Pearson, Mary II, 814
Pearson, Mary II, 907
Pearson, Mary II, 967
Pearson, Mary II, 1021
Pearson, Mary II, 1033
Pearson, Mary III, 251
Pearson, Mary IV, 518
Pearson, Mary IV, 544
Pearson, Mary IV, 953
Pearson, Mary IV, 985
Pearson, Mary IV, 1071
Pearson, Mary IV, 1110
Pearson, Mary IV, 1289
Pearson, Mary V, 109
Pearson, Mary V, 196
Pearson, Mary V, 197
Pearson, Mary V, 204
Pearson, Mary V, 425
Pearson, Mary V, 633
Pearson, Mary V, 638
Pearson, Mary V, 639
Pearson, Mary V, 640
Pearson, Mary V, 723
Pearson, Mary V, 755
Pearson, Mary V, 759
Pearson, Mary V, 760
Pearson, Mary V, 761
Pearson, Mary V, 779
Pearson, Mary V, 786
Pearson, Mary V, 789
Pearson, Mary V, 790
Pearson, Mary V, 791
Pearson, Mary V, 792
Pearson, Mary V, 794
Pearson, Mary V, 799
Pearson, Mary V, 800
Pearson, Mary V, 804
Pearson, Mary V, 808
Pearson, Mary V, 811
Pearson, Mary V, 815
Pearson, Mary V, 816
Pearson, Mary V, 818
Pearson, Mary V, 819
Pearson, Mary V, 820
Pearson, Mary V, 856
Pearson, Mary V, 925
Pearson, Mary VI, 429
Pearson, Mary VI, 602
Pearson, Mary A. II, 731
Pearson, Mary Achsah I, 294
Pearson, Mary Ann II, 715
Pearson, Mary Ann IV, 1088
Pearson, Mary Ann IV, 1110
Pearson, Mary Ann V, 629
Pearson, Mary Ann V, 639
Pearson, Mary C. M. I, 339
Pearson, Mary D. I, 751
Pearson, Mary E. I, 315
Pearson, Mary E. V, 639
Pearson, Mary E. V, 820
Pearson, Mary Eveline V, 760
Pearson, Mary Eveline V, 775
Pearson, Mary Foulke II, 618
Pearson, Mary Jane I, 751
Pearson, Mary Jane IV, 544
Pearson, Mary Jane IV, 1071
Pearson, Mary Jane IV, 1096
Pearson, Mary Jane IV, 1110
Pearson, Mary Jane V, 760
Pearson, Mary Jane V, 791
Pearson, Mary M. I, 294
Pearson, Mary M. I, 339
Pearson, Mary P. V, 820
Pearson, Mary R. V, 820
Pearson, Mary S. V, 197
Pearson, Mary S. V, 820
Pearson, Mary Webb I, 623
Pearson, Mary Webb I, 638
Pearson, Mary Webb I, 639
Pearson, Mary Wilson II, 618
Pearson, Mary, Jr. V, 819
Pearson, Mary, Sr. I, 1036
Pearson, Maryan V, 790
Pearson, Maryann IV, 544
Pearson, Massey Emma V, 196
Pearson, Mastin VI, 845
Pearson, Mathias V, 792
Pearson, Mathias V, 820
Pearson, May V, 761
Pearson, Mealin I, 1036
Pearson, Melia I, 1022
Pearson, Meolia V, 790
Pearson, Milly V, 730
Pearson, Milly V, 794
Pearson, Mina V, 761
Pearson, Minnie Whitaker I, 294
Pearson, Miriam I, 48
Pearson, Miriam I, 57
Pearson, Miriam I, 67
Pearson, Miriam I, 294
Pearson, Miriam I, 304
Pearson, Miriam I, 314
Pearson, Miriam I, 315
Pearson, Mordecai W. II, 715
Pearson, Moses V, 109
Pearson, Moses V, 760
Pearson, Moses V, 761
Pearson, Moses V, 789
Pearson, Moses V, 791
Pearson, Moses V, 811
Pearson, Moses V, 815
Pearson, Moses V, 818
Pearson, Moses V, 819
Pearson, Moses V, 820
Pearson, Moses W. V, 792
Pearson, Myron V, 761
Pearson, Mzry A. II, 759
Pearson, Nancy V, 759
Pearson, Nancy V, 790
Pearson, Nancy V, 791
Pearson, Nancy C. V, 792
Pearson, Nancy C. V, 793
Pearson, Nathan I, 67
Pearson, Nathan I, 113
Pearson, Nathan I, 154
Pearson, Nathan I, 160
Pearson, Nathan I, 315
Pearson, Nathan I, 512
Pearson, Nathan I, 704
Pearson, Nathan I, 705
Pearson, Nathan I, 708
Pearson, Nathan I, 730
Pearson, Nathan I, 751
Pearson, Nathan I, 995
Pearson, Nathan I, 1096
Pearson, Nathan I Sup 1, 5
Pearson, Nathan V, 760
Pearson, Nathan V, 819
Pearson, Nathan T. I, 294
Pearson, Nathan T. I, 315
Pearson, Nathan T. I, 761
Pearson, Nathan T. I, 768
Pearson, Nathaniel V, 792
Pearson, Nathaniel V, 820
Pearson, Noah V, 790
Pearson, Noah V, 791
Pearson, Obed V, 760
Pearson, Obed V, 761
Pearson, Obed A. V, 819
Pearson, Olive I, 1036
Pearson, Olive I, 1037
Pearson, Olive V, 109
Pearson, Olive V, 790
Pearson, Olive V, 794
Pearson, Omar V, 760
Pearson, Omar V, 761
Pearson, Orlando V, 819
Pearson, Paul V, 760
Pearson, Paul V, 761
Pearson, Paul V, 791
Pearson, Paul M. V, 792
Pearson, Pearson II, 249
Pearson, Peninah I, 192
Pearson, Peninah I, 199
Pearson, Peter I, 61
Pearson, Peter I, 67
Pearson, Peter I, 160
Pearson, Peter I, 294
Pearson, Peter I, 314
Pearson, Peter I, 705
Pearson, Peter I, 730
Pearson, Peter I Sup 1, 5
Pearson, Peter VI, 34
Pearson, Peter VI, 41
Pearson, Peter, Jr. I, 67
Pearson, Pheba V, 760
Pearson, Phebe I, 413
Pearson, Phebe I, 565
Pearson, Phebe I, 897
Pearson, Phebe I, 995
Pearson, Phebe I, 1022
Pearson, Phebe I, 1028
Pearson, Phebe I, 1035
Pearson, Phebe I, 1130
Pearson, Phebe II, 618
Pearson, Phebe IV, 105
Pearson, Phebe IV, 109
Pearson, Phebe IV, 262
Pearson, Phebe V, 794
Pearson, Phebe V, 815
Pearson, Phebe V, 818
Pearson, Phebe V, 819
Pearson, Phebe V, 820
Pearson, Phebe Smith IV, 1110
Pearson, Phebe W. II, 896
Pearson, Phebe W. II, 907
Pearson, Phebe Willits II, 809
Pearson, Phelig V, 820
Pearson, Polly I, 299
Pearson, Polly I, 314
Pearson, Polly I, 730
Pearson, Polly VI, 976
Pearson, Polly Ann V, 760
Pearson, Powel I, 566
Pearson, Powel I, 1016
Pearson, Powel V, 786
Pearson, Powel V, 790
Pearson, Powell V, 791
Pearson, Powell V, 792
Pearson, Prudence V, 760
Pearson, Prudence V, 761
Pearson, Prudence V, 762
Pearson, Prudence V, 791
Pearson, Rachel I, 36
Pearson, Rachel I, 62
Pearson, Rachel I, 67
Pearson, Rachel I, 301
Pearson, Rachel I, 314
Pearson, Rachel I, 897
Pearson, Rachel I Sup 1, 5
Pearson, Rachel II, 547
Pearson, Rachel IV, 1375
Pearson, Rachel V, 109
Pearson, Rachel V, 638
Pearson, Rachel V, 760
Pearson, Rachel V, 761
Pearson, Rachel V, 790
Pearson, Rachel V, 791
Pearson, Rachel V, 792
Pearson, Rachel V, 794
Pearson, Rachel V, 808
Pearson, Rachel V, 819
Pearson, Rachel V, 820
Pearson, Rachel VI, 845
Pearson, Rachel P. I, 751
Pearson, Rebeca I, 1028
Pearson, Rebecah I, 1022
Pearson, Rebecakah I, 1023
Pearson, Rebecca I, 160
Pearson, Rebecca I, 294
Pearson, Rebecca I, 299
Pearson, Rebecca I, 315
Pearson, Rebecca I, 1036
Pearson, Rebecca II, 195
Pearson, Rebecca II, 206
Pearson, Rebecca II, 249
Pearson, Rebecca II, 404
Pearson, Rebecca II, 547
Pearson, Rebecca IV, 1110
Pearson, Rebecca IV, 1115
Pearson, Rebecca IV, 1289
Pearson, Rebecca V, 109
Pearson, Rebecca V, 270
Pearson, Rebecca V, 523
Pearson, Rebecca V, 638
Pearson, Rebecca V, 639
Pearson, Rebecca V, 780
Pearson, Rebecca V, 786
Pearson, Rebecca V, 787
Pearson, Rebecca V, 790
Pearson, Rebecca V, 791
Pearson, Rebecca V, 797
Pearson, Rebecca V, 819
Pearson, Rebecca V, 856
Pearson, Rebecca VI, 976
Pearson, Rebecca C. V, 791
Pearson, Rebecca H. IV, 1110
Pearson, Rebeckah I, 46
Pearson, Rebeckah I, 67
Pearson, Rebeckah I, 113
Pearson, Rebeckah I, 160
Pearson, Rebeckah V, 790
Pearson, Rebekah I, 154
Pearson, Rebekah I, 160
Pearson, Rebekah I, 704
Pearson, Rebekah I, 1022
Pearson, Rhoda I, 294
Pearson, Rhoda I, 301
Pearson, Rhoda I, 314
Pearson, Rhoda I, 315
Pearson, Rhoda V, 760
Pearson, Rhoda V, 819
Pearson, Rice V, 790
Pearson, Richmond M. I, 294
Pearson, Robdfg II, 896
Pearson, Robert I, 566
Pearson, Robert I, 1016
Pearson, Robert I, 1022
Pearson, Robert I, 1030
Pearson, Robert I, 1036
Pearson, Robert II, 907
Pearson, Robert V, 109
Pearson, Robert V, 759
Pearson, Robert V, 761
Pearson, Robert V, 772
Pearson, Robert V, 780
Pearson, Robert V, 786
Pearson, Robert V, 790
Pearson, Robert V, 791
Pearson, Robert V, 793
Pearson, Robert V, 794
Pearson, Robert V, 819
Pearson, Robert Heaton II, 61
Pearson, Robert L. II, 907
Pearson, Robert Lee V, 760
Pearson, Robert V. V, 761
Pearson, Robert W. V, 792
Pearson, Robert, Jr. V, 791
Pearson, Rodah I, 314
Pearson, Rosanna V, 760
Pearson, Rosanna V, 762
Pearson, Rosanna V, 791
Pearson, Rosanna V, 794
Pearson, Rosannah V, 779
Pearson, Rosannah V, 790
Pearson, Rosannah V, 792
Pearson, Rose A. II, 907
Pearson, Rose A. II, 924
Pearson, Ruanna IV, 1289
Pearson, Ruth I, 67
Pearson, Ruth I, 86
Pearson, Ruth I, 1036
Pearson, Ruth V, 109
Pearson, Ruth V, 637
Pearson, Ruth V, 639
Pearson, Ruth V, 748
Pearson, Ruth V, 759
Pearson, Ruth V, 760
Pearson, Ruth V, 790
Pearson, Ruth V, 792
Pearson, Ruth V, 794
Pearson, Ruth E. I, 315
Pearson, Ruth Ellen I, 751
Pearson, Rutha VI, 877
Pearson, Sallie I, 294

son, Sallie I, 315
son, Sallie A. I, 283
son, Sallie A. I, 294
son, Sallie J. I, 339
son, Sally I, 315
son, Sally I, 1036
son, Sally V, 790
son, Sally V, 808
son, Sampson V, 790
son, Sampson V, 791
son, Samuel I, 413
son, Samuel I, 487
son, Samuel I, 512
son, Samuel I, 566
son, Samuel I, 897
son, Samuel I, 971
son, Samuel I, 995
son, Samuel I, 1015
son, Samuel I, 1022
son, Samuel I, 1023
son, Samuel I, 1027
son, Samuel I, 1032
son, Samuel I, 1035
son, Samuel I, 1036
son, Samuel I, 1038
son, Samuel I, 1096
son, Samuel I, 1130
son, Samuel V, 109
son, Samuel V, 760
son, Samuel V, 786
son, Samuel V, 789
son, Samuel V, 790
son, Samuel V, 791
son, Samuel V, 792
son, Samuel V, 794
son, Samuel V, 808
son, Samuel V, 818
son, Samuel V, 819
son, Samuel V, 820
son, Samuel VI, 429
son, Samuel VI, 543
son, Samuel VI, 546
son, Samuel P. VI, 166
son, Samuel Y. V, 791
son, Samuel, Jr. V, 791
on, Sarah I, 46
on, Sarah I, 56
on, Sarah I, 67
on, Sarah I, 113
on, Sarah I, 160
on, Sarah I, 283
son, Sarah I, 294
son, Sarah I, 299
on, Sarah I, 314
on, Sarah I, 315
on, Sarah I, 339
son, Sarah I, 400
on, Sarah I, 413
son, Sarah I, 512
son, Sarah I, 678
son, Sarah I, 686
son, Sarah I, 704
son, Sarah I, 730
on, Sarah I, 768
on, Sarah I, 897
son, Sarah I, 995
son, Sarah I, 1023
son, Sarah I, 1029
son, Sarah I, 1036
son, Sarah II, 232
son, Sarah II, 249
son, Sarah II, 618
son, Sarah II, 814
son, Sarah II, 907
son, Sarah II, 986
son, Sarah II, 1021
on, Sarah II, 1038
on, Sarah IV, 105
son, Sarah IV, 345
son, Sarah IV, 420
son, Sarah IV, 428
on, Sarah IV, 651
son, Sarah IV, 653
son, Sarah IV, 880
son, Sarah V, 109
on, Sarah V, 760
on, Sarah V, 786
son, Sarah V, 790
on, Sarah V, 791
on, Sarah V, 792
son, Sarah V, 794
son, Sarah V, 811
son, Sarah V, 819
son, Sarah V, 820
son, Sarah V, 1014
son, Sarah A. I, 302
son, Sarah A. I, 315
on, Sarah A. V, 760
on, Sarah Ann IV, 880
on, Sarah Ann V, 791
son, Sarah E. I, 751
Pearson, Sarah Elizabeth V, 819
Pearson, Sarah Ellen V, 820
Pearson, Sarah Hill I, 704
Pearson, Sarah J. I, 315
Pearson, Sarah Jane V, 196
Pearson, Sarah Jane V, 197
Pearson, Sarah Jane V, 820
Pearson, Sarah S. I, 339
Pearson, Sarah S. V, 761
Pearson, Sarah Starr II, 759
Pearson, Sarah T. C. V, 354
Pearson, Sarah T. H. V, 354
Pearson, Sarepta V, 819
Pearson, Seth W. V, 791
Pearson, Seth W. V, 792
Pearson, Sewell I, 751
Pearson, Sidney I, 1023
Pearson, Sidney V, 820
Pearson, Sidney A. IV, 1289
Pearson, Silas I, 199
Pearson, Smith IV, 1110
Pearson, Solebury II, 1021
Pearson, Stephen IV, 1110
Pearson, Stephen V, 761
Pearson, Stephen A. V, 761
Pearson, Stephen B. IV, 1110
Pearson, Susan II, 715
Pearson, Susan V, 820
Pearson, Susan Carter V, 639
Pearson, Susanna I, 512
Pearson, Susanna I, 566
Pearson, Susanna I, 1016
Pearson, Susanna II, 404
Pearson, Susanna II, 618
Pearson, Susanna IV, 105
Pearson, Susanna IV, 345
Pearson, Susanna IV, 1289
Pearson, Susanna V, 748
Pearson, Susanna V, 812
Pearson, Susanna P. IV, 1174
Pearson, Susanna P. IV, 1179
Pearson, Susannah II, 543
Pearson, Susannah II, 618
Pearson, Susannah II, 626
Pearson, Susannah II, 814
Pearson, Susannah IV, 428
Pearson, Susannah IV, 880
Pearson, Susannah V, 625
Pearson, Susannah V, 638
Pearson, Susannah V, 639
Pearson, Susannah V, 786
Pearson, Susannah V, 790
Pearson, Susannah V, 791
Pearson, Susannah V, 794
Pearson, Susannah V, 819
Pearson, Susie V, 703
Pearson, Sydney V, 760
Pearson, Sydney V, 762
Pearson, Sydnie V, 760
Pearson, T. Gilbert I, 639
Pearson, Tamer IV, 1101
Pearson, Tamer IV, 1110
Pearson, Theresa V, 761
Pearson, Theresa V, 774
Pearson, Thomas I, 413
Pearson, Thomas I, 512
Pearson, Thomas I, 897
Pearson, Thomas I, 1022
Pearson, Thomas I, 1023
Pearson, Thomas I, 1027
Pearson, Thomas I, 1035
Pearson, Thomas I, 1036
Pearson, Thomas I, 1037
Pearson, Thomas II, 404
Pearson, Thomas II, 543
Pearson, Thomas II, 617
Pearson, Thomas II, 618
Pearson, Thomas II, 967
Pearson, Thomas IV, 544
Pearson, Thomas IV, 1071
Pearson, Thomas IV, 1110
Pearson, Thomas IV, 1289
Pearson, Thomas V, 109
Pearson, Thomas V, 196
Pearson, Thomas V, 638
Pearson, Thomas V, 761
Pearson, Thomas V, 779
Pearson, Thomas V, 790
Pearson, Thomas V, 791
Pearson, Thomas V, 792
Pearson, Thomas V, 797
Pearson, Thomas V, 799
Pearson, Thomas V, 819
Pearson, Thomas VI, 976
Pearson, Thomas Barnest I, 623
Pearson, Thomas C. V, 639
Pearson, Thomas Elwood V, 196
Pearson, Thomas Elwood V, 197
Pearson, Thomas Gilbert I, 623
Pearson, Thomas O. I, 294
Pearson, Thomas, Jr. I, 897
Pearson, Thomas, Jr. I, 1036
Pearson, Thomas, Jr. V, 791
Pearson, Thomas, Jr. V, 792
Pearson, Thos. I, 512
Pearson, Thos. IV, 544
Pearson, Thos. V, 639
Pearson, Thos. V, 760
Pearson, Thos. V, 791
Pearson, Thos. B. V, 639
Pearson, Thursey V, 761
Pearson, Thursey V, 762
Pearson, Thurza V, 790
Pearson, Timothy V, 791
Pearson, Timothy V, 819
Pearson, Timothy V, 820
Pearson, Unice VI, 429
Pearson, Valentine V, 790
Pearson, Valentine V, 792
Pearson, Valeria V, 761
Pearson, Virginia V, 761
Pearson, Walter V, 639
Pearson, Walter J. II, 907
Pearson, Walter Jones II, 907
Pearson, Warren V, 760
Pearson, Wd. Deborah II, 618
Pearson, Wd. Deborah II, 672
Pearson, Wd. Grace II, 404
Pearson, Wd. Mary II, 824
Pearson, Wd. Phebe Harper II, 780
Pearson, West A. VI, 687
Pearson, West A. VI, 710
Pearson, Widow Mary I, 1027
Pearson, Widow Mary I, 1038
Pearson, Widow Phebe I, 566
Pearson, Widow Phebe I, 1016
Pearson, Widow Sarah I, 132
Pearson, Widow Sarah I, 160
Pearson, Widow Sarah I, 310
Pearson, Widow Sarah I, 314
Pearson, Wilkinson V, 109
Pearson, Wilkinson V, 819
Pearson, William I, 48
Pearson, William I, 67
Pearson, William I, 199
Pearson, William I, 294
Pearson, William I, 512
Pearson, William I, 897
Pearson, William I, 995
Pearson, William I, 1015
Pearson, William I, 1022
Pearson, William I, 1023
Pearson, William I, 1036
Pearson, William I, 1038
Pearson, William I, 1096
Pearson, William I, 1130
Pearson, William I Sup 1, 11
Pearson, William II, 404
Pearson, William II, 715
Pearson, William II, 967
Pearson, William II, 1021
Pearson, William IV, 156
Pearson, William IV, 544
Pearson, William IV, 1071
Pearson, William IV, 1110
Pearson, William IV, 1289
Pearson, William V, 109
Pearson, William V, 175
Pearson, William V, 197
Pearson, William V, 270
Pearson, William V, 354
Pearson, William V, 760
Pearson, William V, 790
Pearson, William V, 791
Pearson, William V, 792
Pearson, William V, 819
Pearson, William VI, 429
Pearson, William E. I, 294
Pearson, William E. I, 315
Pearson, William L. I, 294
Pearson, William L. I, 315
Pearson, William L. V, 760
Pearson, William S. I, 751
Pearson, William S. IV, 345
Pearson, William S. V, 760
Pearson, William Spencer V, 760
Pearson, William, Jr. I, 897
Pearson, Wm. II, 527
Pearson, Wm. II, 618
Pearson, Wm. II, 759
Pearson, Wm. II, 868
Pearson, Wm. II, 907
Pearson, Wm. II, 994
Pearson, Wm. IV, 322
Pearson, Wm. IV, 1071
Pearson, Wm. IV, 1115
Pearson, Wm. V, 197
Pearson, Wm. V, 760
Pearson, Wm. V, 768
Pearson, Wm. V, 786
Pearson, Wm. V, 790
Pearson, Wm. V, 791
Pearson, Wm. V, 812
Pearson, Wm. V, 820
Pearson, Wm. A. V, 760
Pearson, Wm. A. V, 775
Pearson, Wm. Savery II, 618
Pearson, Wm. T. V, 639
Pearson, Zeno I, 995
Pearson, Zilpah V, 768
Pearson, Zilpah V, 790
Pearson, Zilpah V, 791
Pearson, Zilpah V, 793
Pearson, Zilpha V, 760
Pearson, Zilpha V, 769
Pearson, Zimri V, 819
Pearsons, Ann I, 67
Pearsons, Mary V, 109
Pearsons, Thomas V, 109
Peart, Elizabeth II, 898
Peart, Elizabeth II, 908
Peart, Hannah II, 446
Peart, Joshua II, 715
Peart, Mary II, 618
Peart, Mary II, 898
Peart, Mary II, 907
Peart, Mary Ann II, 789
Peart, Thomas II, 446
Peart, Thomas II, 618
Peart, Thos. II, 898
Peart, Thos. II, 907
Pease, ??? III, 26
Pease, Fanny II, 146
Pease, Mary III, 145
Pease, Mary III, 171
Pease, Mary III, 251
Pease, Mary III, 358
Pease, Mary III, 473
Pease, Nancy II, 133
Pease, Nancy A. II, 146
Pease, Phebe III, 251
Pease, Wm. II, 146
Peaseley, Edgar III, 251
Peaseley, Edgar Everet III, 251
Peaseley, Florence III, 251
Peaseley, George III, 251
Peaseley, George E. III, 251
Peaseley, Jonathan III, 433
Peaseley, Rachel III, 251
Peaseley, Rachel III, 433
Peaseley, Wd. Rachel III, 433
Peaser, William R. III, 433
Peaslee, Amos II, 142
Peaslee, Amos II, 155
Peaslee, Amos J. II, 155
Peaslee, Amos J. II, 159
Peaslee, Elijah II, 142
Peaslee, Elijah II, 155
Peaslee, Emma S. II, 155
Peaslee, Emma S. II, 159
Peaslee, Emma W. II, 155
Peaslee, Esther II, 142
Peaslee, Esther II, 155
Peaslee, Gideon II, 155
Peaslee, Gideon II, 159
Peaslee, Hanna Lippincott VI, 429
Peaslee, Hannah II, 155
Peaslee, Hannah II, 159
Peaslee, Hannah L. VI, 368
Peaslee, Hannah Lippincott VI, 367
Peaslee, Jonathan III, 433
Peaslee, Rachel III, 433
Peaslee, Sarah Allen II, 155
Peaslee, Sarah N. II, 142
Peaslee, Sarah N. II, 155
Peaslee, Wd. Rachel III, 433
Peasley, Abraham IV, 1375
Peasley, Amy IV, 880
Peasley, Amy IV, 1179
Peasley, Amy IV, 1219
Peasley, Amy Ann IV, 1179
Peasley, Ann IV, 1219
Peasley, Ann IV, 1220
Peasley, Ann Eliza IV, 1219
Peasley, Betsy IV, 1179
Peasley, Betsy IV, 1219
Peasley, Chalkey IV, 880
Peasley, Chalkley IV, 863
Peasley, Chalkley IV, 1143
Peasley, Chalkley IV, 1179
Peasley, Chalkley IV, 1219
Peasley, Charles IV, 1179
Peasley, Charles IV, 1219
Peasley, Charles Enoch IV, 1219
Peasley, Charles L. IV, 1179
Peasley, Charles L. IV, 1219
Peasley, Chocley IV, 1219
Peasley, Cynthia IV, 1219
Peasley, David IV, 1179
Peasley, Eliza L. IV, 1219
Peasley, Eliza S. IV, 1219
Peasley, Enoch IV, 1179
Peasley, Enoch IV, 1219
Peasley, Florence III, 205
Peasley, George E. III, 205
Peasley, Henry G. IV, 1179
Peasley, Henry G. IV, 1219
Peasley, Henry G. IV, 1220
Peasley, Irie IV, 1219
Peasley, Jacob A. IV, 1179
Peasley, Jacob A. IV, 1219
Peasley, Jane IV, 1179
Peasley, Jane IV, 1219
Peasley, Jane A. IV, 1219
Peasley, John IV, 1219
Peasley, Jonathan II, 404
Peasley, Jonathan IV, 1219
Peasley, Jonathan W. IV, 1179
Peasley, Joseph IV, 880
Peasley, Joseph IV, 1179
Peasley, Joseph IV, 1219
Peasley, Joseph John IV, 1179
Peasley, Joseph, Jr. IV, 1179
Peasley, Lydia IV, 1179
Peasley, Margaret IV, 863
Peasley, Margaret IV, 880
Peasley, Margaret IV, 1143
Peasley, Margaret IV, 1179
Peasley, Margaret IV, 1219
Peasley, Marion IV, 880
Peasley, Martha IV, 1219
Peasley, Martha IV, 1228
Peasley, Martha P. IV, 1219
Peasley, Mary IV, 1179
Peasley, Mary IV, 1219
Peasley, Mary Jane IV, 1179
Peasley, Mary Jane IV, 1219
Peasley, Mary Jane IV, 1224
Peasley, Micajah IV, 1179
Peasley, Micajah IV, 1219
Peasley, Minerva IV, 1219
Peasley, Narcissa IV, 1219
Peasley, Narcissa IV, 1221
Peasley, Narsissa IV, 1219
Peasley, Phebe Ann IV, 1179
Peasley, Phebe Ann IV, 1219
Peasley, Pheby Jane IV, 1219
Peasley, Rachel II, 404
Peasley, Rachel III, 251
Peasley, Rhoda Ann IV, 1219
Peasley, Samuel IV, 1179
Peasley, Samuel IV, 1219
Peasley, Samuel IV, 1224
Peasley, Samuel Wm. IV, 1179
Peasley, Samuel Wm. IV, 1219
Peasley, Sarah IV, 1219
Peasley, Sarah J. IV, 1219
Peasley, Sarah Jane IV, 1219
Peasley, Susanna IV, 1224
Peasley, Watson H. IV, 1219
Peasley, William IV, 1179
Peasley, Wm. IV, 1179
Peasley, Wm. IV, 1219
Peasly, Mary II, 618
Peasly, Rachel II, 404
Peasly, Rachel II, 618
Peatman, ??? III, 56
Peatman, Lillie B. III, 56
Peatross, Amey VI, 262
Peatross, Amey VI, 280
Peatross, Amey VI, 962
Peatross, Amy VI, 280
Peatross, Ann VI, 262
Peatross, Anna VI, 262
Peatross, Caroline VI, 280
Peatross, Eliza VI, 203
Peatross, Eliza VI, 262
Peatross, Elizabeth VI, 262
Peatross, James VI, 962
Peatross, James VI, 983
Peatross, John VI, 203
Peatross, John VI, 238
Peatross, John VI, 262
Peatross, John VI, 280
Peatross, Mahala Terrell VI, 262
Peatross, Mary VI, 238
Peatross, Mary VI, 239
Peatross, Mary VI, 262
Peatross, Matthew VI, 262
Peatross, Nelson VI, 262
Peatross, Polley VI, 983
Peatross, Rhoda VI, 262
Peatross, Sally VI, 262
Peatross, Sarah VI, 238
Peatross, Sarah VI, 262
Peatross, Wd. Sarah VI, 203
Peatross, Wd. Sarah VI, 262
Peaty, Ann V, 108
Peaty, Charles I, 1035
Peaty, James I, 1035
Peaty, James V, 108

Peaty, Mark V, 108
Peaty, Mary I, 1035
Peaty, Samuel V, 108
Pebbles, Charity V, 110
Pebbles, Jessie V, 110
Pebbles, Nelson III, 251
Pebles, Elizabeth VI, 203
Pebles, Mary L. V, 703
Pebles, Peter VI, 203
Peck, Ann IV, 651
Peck, Ann IV, 652
Peck, Caroline III, 187
Peck, Caroline III, 251
Peck, Catharine I, 1128
Peck, Catharine I, 1130
Peck, Catherine I, 1130
Peck, Charlotte E. IV, 749
Peck, Ethel IV, 1332
Peck, Geo. III, 275
Peck, George III, 187
Peck, George III, 251
Peck, Hannah IV, 53
Peck, Harriet I, 566
Peck, Harriett I, 566
Peck, John IV, 53
Peck, John IV, 105
Peck, Mina VI, 845
Peck, Sarah II, 404
Peck, Sarah III, 187
Peck, Sarah III, 251
Peck, Sarah III, 275
Peck, W. Prentice IV, 1332
Peck, William III, 251
Peck, William VI, 820
Peck, William VI, 845
Peckham, Avis II, 823
Peckham, Daniel J. IV, 428
Peckham, Errol D. III, 252
Peckham, Errol D. IV, 1332
Peckham, Errol Devere IV, 1332
Peckham, Errol Kellogg III, 252
Peckham, James D. III, 252
Peckham, James S. IV, 1179
Peckham, Marian E. IV, 428
Peckham, Mary III, 252
Peckham, Mary III, 323
Peckham, Mary A. III, 252
Peckham, Nancy J. IV, 428
Peckham, Richard IV, 1375
Peckham, Seneca James IV, 1179
Peckham, William G. III, 252
Peckingham, Rachel IV, 1069
Peckover, Edmund V, 109
Peckover, Octavius III, 252
Peckum, Seneca James IV, 1179
Peckwith, Ann Eliza II, 823
Pedan, Alexander IV, 53
Pedan, Isaac IV, 17
Pedan, Joseph IV, 53
Pedan, Lydia IV, 53
Pedan, Margaret IV, 53
Pedan, Rachel IV, 53
Pedan, Thomas IV, 105
Peddicord, Oscar, Jr. V, 703
Peddicow, Elizabeth C. II, 973
Peddicow, James M. II, 973
Peddicow, Mary Rebecca II, 973
Peddrick, Ann V, 40
Peddrick, Catharine IV, 749
Peddrick, Elizabeth IV, 749
Peddrick, Elizabeth Pedrick IV, 749
Peddrick, Hugh IV, 749
Peddrick, Isaac V, 40
Peddrick, Jesse Townsend IV, 749
Peddrick, Judith IV, 749
Peddrick, Judith IV, 778
Peddrick, Keturah IV, 749
Peddrick, Philip IV, 749
Peddrick, Philip IV, 778
Peden, Abigail IV, 53
Peden, Abigail IV, 65
Peden, Alexander IV, 53
Peden, Alexander IV, 62
Peden, Alexander IV, 65
Peden, Ann IV, 50
Peden, Ann IV, 53
Peden, Darius IV, 53
Peden, Hannah IV, 77
Peden, Hannah IV, 105
Peden, Isaac IV, 105
Peden, Jacob IV, 105
Peden, Jesse IV, 53
Peden, Joseph IV, 53
Peden, Lydia IV, 53
Peden, Lydia IV, 62
Peden, Lydia, Jr. IV, 53
Peden, Lydia, Sr. IV, 53
Peden, Margaret IV, 53
Peden, Obadiah IV, 53
Peden, Rachel IV, 53
Peden, Rachel IV, 91
Peden, Rachel IV, 105
Peden, Rebecca IV, 78
Peden, Rebecca IV, 105
Peden, Ruth IV, 92
Peden, Ruth IV, 105
Peden, Samuel IV, 53
Peden, Susannah IV, 88
Peden, Susannah IV, 105
Peden, Thomas IV, 53
Peden, Thomas IV, 105
Peden, William I, 566
Pederick, Joseph II, 404
Pederick, Mary II, 100
Pederick, Philyp II, 91
Pederick, Tybithia II, 91
Pederick, Wm. II, 92
Pederson, Florence IV, 1332
Pedley, Sarah III, 67
Pedley, Sarah III, 252
Pedlow, James Green III, 252
Pedlow, Sinton III, 252
Pednick, Catherine V, 109
Pednick, Elizabeth V, 109
Pednick, Jesse Townsend V, 109
Pednick, Judith V, 109
Pednick, Keturah V, 109
Pednick, Mary V, 109
Pednick, Phillip V, 109
Pednick, Rcchard V, 109
Pednick, Richard V, 109
Pedon, Henry I, 566
Pedon, William I, 566
Pedric, Richard V, 883
Pedric, Richard V, 885
Pedric, Susanna V, 883
Pedric, Susanna V, 885
Pedrick, ??? II, 91
Pedrick, Adam II, 404
Pedrick, Ann V, 109
Pedrick, Ann V, 568
Pedrick, Ann V, 592
Pedrick, Ann Somers II, 92
Pedrick, Anna II, 65
Pedrick, Anna II, 91
Pedrick, Benjamin V, 109
Pedrick, Caleb II, 91
Pedrick, Carolyn II, 136
Pedrick, Catharine IV, 749
Pedrick, Catherine V, 109
Pedrick, Charles II, 37
Pedrick, Charles II, 92
Pedrick, Chester V, 109
Pedrick, Clayton V, 109
Pedrick, Daniel II, 36
Pedrick, Daniel II, 79
Pedrick, Daniel II, 91
Pedrick, Daniel II, 92
Pedrick, Elihu II, 53
Pedrick, Elihu II, 91
Pedrick, Elihu II, 122
Pedrick, Elihu II, 759
Pedrick, Elihu II, 814
Pedrick, Elihu II, 908
Pedrick, Elihu III, 252
Pedrick, Elihu V, 109
Pedrick, Elizabeth II, 36
Pedrick, Elizabeth II, 37
Pedrick, Elizabeth II, 56
Pedrick, Elizabeth II, 90
Pedrick, Elizabeth II, 91
Pedrick, Elizabeth II, 92
Pedrick, Elizabeth IV, 779
Pedrick, Elizabeth V, 109
Pedrick, Elizabeth A. II, 135
Pedrick, Elizabeth Pedrick IV, 749
Pedrick, Emma II, 814
Pedrick, Emma II, 908
Pedrick, Emma T. II, 134
Pedrick, Estor II, 91
Pedrick, George II, 122
Pedrick, Hannah II, 25
Pedrick, Hannah II, 36
Pedrick, Hannah II, 37
Pedrick, Hannah II, 41
Pedrick, Hannah II, 91
Pedrick, Hannah II, 92
Pedrick, Hannah II, 103
Pedrick, Hannah II, 122
Pedrick, Hannah V, 35
Pedrick, Hannah V, 52
Pedrick, Hannah V, 109
Pedrick, Hannah V, 197
Pedrick, Helen A. II, 136
Pedrick, Hester II, 37
Pedrick, Hester II, 92
Pedrick, Hezekiah II, 91
Pedrick, Hugh II, 36
Pedrick, Hugh II, 37
Pedrick, Hugh II, 56
Pedrick, Hugh II, 91
Pedrick, Isaac II, 25
Pedrick, Isaac II, 37
Pedrick, Isaac II, 41
Pedrick, Isaac II, 91
Pedrick, Isaac II, 122
Pedrick, Isaac II, 814
Pedrick, Isaac V, 35
Pedrick, Isaac V, 52
Pedrick, Isaac V, 109
Pedrick, Jacob II, 92
Pedrick, Jacob II, 135
Pedrick, James II, 36
Pedrick, James II, 91
Pedrick, Jane II, 122
Pedrick, Jesse Townsend IV, 749
Pedrick, Jesse Townsend V, 109
Pedrick, Jessee II, 92
Pedrick, John II, 36
Pedrick, John II, 91
Pedrick, John II, 122
Pedrick, Joseph II, 122
Pedrick, Joseph II, 134
Pedrick, Joseph II, 404
Pedrick, Joseph II, 908
Pedrick, Joseph D. II, 814
Pedrick, Joseph D. II, 908
Pedrick, Joseph Thorne II, 814
Pedrick, Judith IV, 749
Pedrick, Judith V, 109
Pedrick, Judith V, 974
Pedrick, Julia V, 109
Pedrick, Kesiah II, 91
Pedrick, Kesiah II, 817
Pedrick, Kesiah VI, 772
Pedrick, Keturah IV, 749
Pedrick, Keturah V, 109
Pedrick, Keziah II, 36
Pedrick, Keziah VI, 747
Pedrick, Lidya II, 69
Pedrick, Lidya II, 91
Pedrick, Lydia V, 35
Pedrick, Lydia V, 109
Pedrick, Margaret V, 109
Pedrick, Martha II, 25
Pedrick, Martha II, 37
Pedrick, Mary II, 36
Pedrick, Mary II, 37
Pedrick, Mary II, 41
Pedrick, Mary II, 76
Pedrick, Mary II, 91
Pedrick, Mary II, 92
Pedrick, Mary II, 97
Pedrick, Mary V, 52
Pedrick, Mary V, 109
Pedrick, Mary Ann II, 53
Pedrick, Mary Ann II, 91
Pedrick, Mary Ann II, 122
Pedrick, Mary Ann II, 126
Pedrick, Mary P. V, 109
Pedrick, Michael II, 37
Pedrick, Michael II, 91
Pedrick, Mirabe II, 92
Pedrick, Naomi II, 36
Pedrick, Naomi II, 79
Pedrick, Naomi II, 91
Pedrick, Naomi II, 92
Pedrick, Neomy II, 91
Pedrick, Phebe II, 37
Pedrick, Philip II, 36
Pedrick, Philip IV, 749
Pedrick, Philip V, 974
Pedrick, Phillip V, 109
Pedrick, Philyp II, 91
Pedrick, Rcchard V, 109
Pedrick, Rebeck II, 91
Pedrick, Rebeck II, 104
Pedrick, Rebeckah II, 37
Pedrick, Rebeckah II, 81
Pedrick, Rebeckah II, 91
Pedrick, Rebeckah II, 98
Pedrick, Richard II, 36
Pedrick, Richard V, 52
Pedrick, Richard V, 109
Pedrick, Samuel II, 37
Pedrick, Samuel II, 78
Pedrick, Samuel II, 91
Pedrick, Sarah II, 37
Pedrick, Sarah II, 91
Pedrick, Sarah II, 92
Pedrick, Sarah II, 134
Pedrick, Sarah II, 136
Pedrick, Sarah B. II, 155
Pedrick, Sarah B. II, 814
Pedrick, Sarah B. II, 908
Pedrick, Susannah II, 37
Pedrick, Tabitha II, 78
Pedrick, Tabitha II, 91
Pedrick, Thomas II, 91
Pedrick, Thomas II, 618
Pedrick, Tybithia II, 91
Pedrick, William II, 37
Pedrick, William V, 109
Pedrick, Wm. II, 69
Pedrick, Wm. II, 91
Pedrick, Wm. II, 92
Pedrick, Wm. II, 97
Pedrick, Wm. M. II, 136
Peeble, Charity V, 110
Peeble, Isaac V, 973
Peeble, Susan V, 973
Peebles, ??? VI, 95
Peebles, Abigail IV, 373
Peebles, Abigail IV, 428
Peebles, Abigail IV, 1071
Peebles, Abigail VI, 102
Peebles, Abigail VI, 117
Peebles, Abigail VI, 138
Peebles, Abigail Brock VI, 118
Peebles, Adaline V, 979
Peebles, Agness VI, 117
Peebles, Almeda V, 639
Peebles, Almedia V, 353
Peebles, Almedia V, 354
Peebles, Almedia V, 639
Peebles, Amanda V, 979
Peebles, Amelia IV, 1110
Peebles, Anderson IV, 392
Peebles, Ann V, 628
Peebles, Ann V, 973
Peebles, Ann V, 974
Peebles, Ann VI, 117
Peebles, Ann VI, 120
Peebles, Ann VI, 139
Peebles, Anna VI, 117
Peebles, Asenath IV, 428
Peebles, Asenath IV, 449
Peebles, Asenath IV, 1071
Peebles, Asenath IV, 1092
Peebles, Asenath IV, 1100
Peebles, Asenath IV, 1110
Peebles, Benjamin VI, 139
Peebles, Benjamin Franklin V, 639
Peebles, Burwell IV, 428
Peebles, Burwell IV, 449
Peebles, Burwell IV, 1071
Peebles, Burwell IV, 1092
Peebles, Burwell IV, 1100
Peebles, Burwell IV, 1110
Peebles, Burwell VI, 139
Peebles, Butler VI, 117
Peebles, Caroline V, 639
Peebles, Caroline V, 974
Peebles, Caroline VI, 139
Peebles, Catharina V, 639
Peebles, Catharine V, 639
Peebles, Catharine V, 642
Peebles, Catherine V, 109
Peebles, Catherine VI, 139
Peebles, Catherine VI, 976
Peebles, Chalkley IV, 428
Peebles, Chalkley IV, 1071
Peebles, Chalkley IV, 1110
Peebles, Charity H. V, 979
Peebles, Christian V, 639
Peebles, Christiana V, 109
Peebles, Christianna V, 639
Peebles, Christianna VI, 138
Peebles, Christianna VI, 139
Peebles, Clarissa V, 974
Peebles, Daniel IV, 428
Peebles, Daniel IV, 1071
Peebles, Daniel IV, 1110
Peebles, David V, 639
Peebles, Deborah IV, 386
Peebles, Deborah IV, 392
Peebles, Deborah IV, 428
Peebles, Deborah IV, 568
Peebles, Deborah V, 109
Peebles, Deborah V, 110
Peebles, Deborah V, 639
Peebles, Deborah V, 974
Peebles, Deborah V, 975
Peebles, Deborah V, 979
Peebles, Deborah VI, 117
Peebles, Deborah VI, 138
Peebles, Deborah VI, 139
Peebles, Deborah VI, 141
Peebles, Deborah Jane IV, 1110
Peebles, Deborah Jane IV, 1111
Peebles, Deborah Simmons IV, 428
Peebles, Deborah, Sr. VI, 139
Peebles, Drury VI, 117
Peebles, Edna IV, 1092
Peebles, Edna IV, 1110
Peebles, Edna VI, 136
Peebles, Edna VI, 139
Peebles, Edwin Auber V, 703
Peebles, Eli IV, 1110
Peebles, Eli IV, 1111
Peebles, Elihu V, 592
Peebles, Elihu V, 595
Peebles, Elihu V, 974
Peebles, Elihu V, 975
Peebles, Elihu V, 979
Peebles, Elihu VI, 117
Peebles, Elihu VI, 139
Peebles, Elijah V, 109
Peebles, Elijah V, 110
Peebles, Elijah V, 425
Peebles, Elijah V, 523
Peebles, Elijah V, 639
Peebles, Elijah VI, 17
Peebles, Elijah VI, 100
Peebles, Elijah VI, 102
Peebles, Elijah VI, 117
Peebles, Elijah VI, 118
Peebles, Elijah VI, 135
Peebles, Elijah VI, 138
Peebles, Elijah VI, 139
Peebles, Elizabeth IV, 1071
Peebles, Elizabeth IV, 1110
Peebles, Elizabeth IV, 1111
Peebles, Elizabeth IV, 1113
Peebles, Elizabeth V, 639
Peebles, Elizabeth VI, 104
Peebles, Elizabeth VI, 111
Peebles, Elizabeth VI, 113
Peebles, Elizabeth VI, 117
Peebles, Elizabeth VI, 118
Peebles, Elizabeth VI, 120
Peebles, Elizabeth VI, 136
Peebles, Elizabeth VI, 138
Peebles, Elizabeth VI, 139
Peebles, Elizabeth A. V, 979
Peebles, Elizabeth Ann V, 97
Peebles, Elizabeth Ann V, 97
Peebles, Elizabeth H. IV, 111
Peebles, Elizabeth H. IV, 111
Peebles, Elizabeth H. IV, 111
Peebles, Elizabeth Hollowell V, 639
Peebles, Emaline V, 979
Peebles, Emily V, 618
Peebles, Emily V, 639
Peebles, Emlen V, 639
Peebles, Emlin VI, 139
Peebles, Hannah V, 352
Peebles, Hannah V, 354
Peebles, Hannah V, 974
Peebles, Hannah V, 975
Peebles, Hannah V, 979
Peebles, Henrietta V, 612
Peebles, Henrietta V, 639
Peebles, Henrietta V, 974
Peebles, Henry V, 639
Peebles, Huldah IV, 392
Peebles, Huldah VI, 114
Peebles, Huldah VI, 117
Peebles, Huldah VI, 118
Peebles, Huldah VI, 120
Peebles, Huldah Ladd VI, 11
Peebles, Isaac V, 974
Peebles, Isabel V, 703
Peebles, James V, 639
Peebles, James VI, 98
Peebles, James VI, 117
Peebles, James VI, 118
Peebles, James VI, 138
Peebles, James VI, 139
Peebles, James VI, 976
Peebles, James Brock VI, 118
Peebles, James H. V, 975
Peebles, James S. V, 523
Peebles, James, Jr. VI, 103
Peebles, John IV, 1111
Peebles, John V, 523
Peebles, John V, 618
Peebles, John V, 628
Peebles, John V, 639
Peebles, John V, 971
Peebles, John V, 974
Peebles, John VI, 103
Peebles, John VI, 117
Peebles, John VI, 118
Peebles, John VI, 130
Peebles, John VI, 139
Peebles, John E. V, 639
Peebles, John Sears VI, 117
Peebles, John W. IV, 1110
Peebles, John, Jr. V, 974
Peebles, John, Jr. VI, 120
Peebles, Joseph VI, 103
Peebles, Joseph VI, 154
Peebles, Joshua V, 639
Peebles, Josiah IV, 1110
Peebles, Josiah IV, 1111
Peebles, Josiah VI, 117
Peebles, Josiah VI, 134
Peebles, Josiah VI, 136
Peebles, Josiah VI, 138

les, Julia E. V, 979
les, Julietta V, 639
les, July Etta V, 639
les, July Etta V, 649
les, Ladd VI, 117
les, Louisa Ann V, 979
les, Lucy V, 974
les, Lucy VI, 117
les, Lucy VI, 139
les, Lucy Ann V, 618
les, Lucy Ann V, 639
les, Lucy Ann VI, 139
les, Marcia L. V, 979
les, Margaret VI, 117
les, Margaret VI, 135
les, Margaret VI, 138
les, Martha IV, 386
les, Martha IV, 428
les, Martha IV, 575
les, Martha IV, 592
les, Martha IV, 1110
les, Martha IV, 1111
les, Martha V, 974
les, Martha VI, 120
les, Martha VI, 139
les, Mary IV, 373
les, Mary IV, 428
les, Mary IV, 569
les, Mary IV, 592
les, Mary V, 703
les, Mary V, 974
les, Mary V, 975
les, Mary VI, 100
les, Mary VI, 117
les, Mary VI, 131
les, Mary VI, 138
les, Mary VI, 139
les, Mary VI, 154
les, Mary Ann IV, 1111
les, Mary Ann IV, 1121
les, Mary Ann V, 523
les, Mary Ann V, 592
les, Mary Ann V, 595
les, Mary Ann V, 639
les, Mary Ann V, 971
les, Mary Ann V, 974
les, Mary Ann V, 975
les, Mary Ann V, 976
les, Mary Ann V, 979
les, Mary Jane V, 639
les, Mary L. V, 703
les, Mary, Jr. IV, 428
les, Mary, Jr. VI, 139
les, Micajah V, 979
les, Micajah VI, 117
les, Micajah VI, 131
les, Micajah VI, 133
les, Micajah VI, 138
les, Micajah VI, 139
les, Micajah VI, 140
les, Micajah Hunnicutt
V, 639
les, Micajah William V, 639
les, Michael V, 618
les, Michal V, 639
les, Michal V, 974
les, Michal VI, 130
les, Michal VI, 139
les, Miriam VI, 103
les, Mordecai IV, 373
les, Mordecai IV, 386
les, Mordecai IV, 428
les, Mordecai IV, 568
les, Mordecai IV, 1110
les, Mordecai IV, 1111
les, Mordecai VI, 138
les, Mordecai VI, 139
les, Mordecay VI, 139
les, Mordecia VI, 102
les, Mordecia VI, 117
les, Mordica VI, 118
les, Mordica VI, 138
les, Mordicai VI, 139
les, Mordicia VI, 138
les, Mordicia VI, 141
les, Mourning VI, 117
les, Mourning VI, 118
les, Mourning VI, 138
les, Mourning III VI, 108
les, Nathaniel V, 979
les, Oliver V, 639
les, Oliver VI, 139
les, Oliver Emlen V, 109
les, Penninah VI, 117
les, Penninah VI, 131
les, Penninah VI, 138
les, Peter VI, 17
les, Peter VI, 108
les, Peter VI, 117
les, Peter VI, 120
les, Peter VI, 138
Peebles, Peter VI, 139
Peebles, Peter, Jr. VI, 117
Peebles, Peter, Jr. VI, 118
Peebles, Peter, Sr. VI, 114
Peebles, Peter, Sr. VI, 117
Peebles, Peter, Sr. VI, 118
Peebles, Pleasant Dilworth
V, 109
Peebles, Pleasant Dilworth
V, 639
Peebles, Pleasant Dilworth
VI, 139
Peebles, Pleasant Dilworth
Catharine V, 639
Peebles, Polly VI, 134
Peebles, Polly VI, 138
Peebles, Rachel IV, 428
Peebles, Rachel IV, 431
Peebles, Rachel IV, 1071
Peebles, Rachel IV, 1110
Peebles, Rachel IV, 1111
Peebles, Rachel E. IV, 1071
Peebles, Rachel E. IV, 1110
Peebles, Rachel T. IV, 428
Peebles, Rachel T. IV, 1071
Peebles, Reuben V, 639
Peebles, Rhoda V, 639
Peebles, Richard V, 979
Peebles, Richard S. V, 979
Peebles, Robert IV, 1110
Peebles, Robert IV, 1112
Peebles, Robert IV, 1113
Peebles, Robert IV, 1117
Peebles, Ruanna IV, 1110
Peebles, Ruanna IV, 1111
Peebles, Ruanna IV, 1113
Peebles, Ruanna IV, 1114
Peebles, Samuel V, 109
Peebles, Samuel V, 639
Peebles, Samuel V, 925
Peebles, Samuel V, 974
Peebles, Samuel VI, 117
Peebles, Samuel VI, 120
Peebles, Samuel VI, 139
Peebles, Sarah V, 354
Peebles, Sarah V, 973
Peebles, Sarah V, 974
Peebles, Sarah V, 975
Peebles, Sarah VI, 98
Peebles, Sarah VI, 110
Peebles, Sarah VI, 117
Peebles, Sarah VI, 118
Peebles, Sarah VI, 120
Peebles, Sarah VI, 138
Peebles, Sarah VI, 139
Peebles, Sarah Ann V, 592
Peebles, Sarah Ann V, 975
Peebles, Sarah Ann V, 979
Peebles, Sarah H. V, 974
Peebles, Sarah Hunnicutt VI, 118
Peebles, Sarah L. IV, 1111
Peebles, Sarah L. IV, 1113
Peebles, Sarah Louisa IV, 1103
Peebles, Sarah Louisa IV, 1112
Peebles, Sarah Louiza IV, 1110
Peebles, Sarah, Jr. V, 974
Peebles, Sarah, Sr. V, 974
Peebles, Scott VI, 117
Peebles, Sibbilla IV, 1100
Peebles, Sibbilla IV, 1110
Peebles, Silviah VI, 117
Peebles, Silviah VI, 129
Peebles, Silviah VI, 138
Peebles, Simmons V, 974
Peebles, Stephen IV, 1110
Peebles, Stephen IV, 1111
Peebles, Stephen V, 352
Peebles, Stephen V, 354
Peebles, Stephen V, 639
Peebles, Stephen V, 974
Peebles, Stephen V, 975
Peebles, Stephen V, 979
Peebles, Stephen VI, 104
Peebles, Stephen VI, 110
Peebles, Stephen VI, 117
Peebles, Stephen VI, 118
Peebles, Stephen VI, 138
Peebles, Stephen Bailey VI, 118
Peebles, Stephen Thomas V, 639
Peebles, Stephen Thos. V, 639
Peebles, Steven V, 979
Peebles, Steven VI, 138
Peebles, Steven VI, 139
Peebles, Susan IV, 428
Peebles, Susan V, 974
Peebles, Susan M. V, 975
Peebles, Susanna IV, 592
Peebles, Susanna IV, 1071
Peebles, Susanna VI, 102
Peebles, Susanna VI, 110
Peebles, Susanna VI, 117
Peebles, Susanna VI, 118
Peebles, Susanna VI, 123
Peebles, Susanna L. IV, 1071
Peebles, Susanna Ladd VI, 139
Peebles, Susannah V, 974
Peebles, Susannah VI, 117
Peebles, Susannah VI, 118
Peebles, Susannah VI, 123
Peebles, Susannah VI, 139
Peebles, Susannah L. IV, 568
Peebles, Susannah L. IV, 592
Peebles, Susannah Ladd IV, 428
Peebles, Thomas VI, 113
Peebles, Wallace VI, 103
Peebles, Wallis VI, 103
Peebles, Wd. Sarah V, 639
Peebles, Wd. Sarah VI, 138
Peebles, William IV, 428
Peebles, William IV, 431
Peebles, William IV, 1110
Peebles, William V, 639
Peebles, William V, 979
Peebles, William VI, 102
Peebles, William VI, 117
Peebles, William VI, 118
Peebles, William S. VI, 139
Peebles, William Simmons
IV, 428
Peebles, William Simmons
VI, 139
Peebles, William T. V, 979
Peebles, Wm. IV, 1071
Peebles, Wm. IV, 1111
Peebles, Wm. V, 974
Peebles, Wm. A. IV, 1111
Peebles, Wm. H. V, 639
Peebles, Wm. S. IV, 1071
Peebles, Wm. S. IV, 1110
Peebles, Wm. S. V, 974
Peebles, Wm. S. V, 976
Peebles, Wm. S. V, 979
Peebles, Zalinda V, 975
Peebles, Zalinda V, 976
Peebles, Zalinda V, 979
Peel, Amy I, 336
Peel, Amy I, 339
Peel, Ann II, 405
Peel, Ann II, 618
Peel, Anna IV, 428
Peel, Anna IV, 455
Peel, Anthony II, 405
Peel, Charity I, 45
Peel, Charity I, 67
Peel, Charles W. II, 618
Peel, Cloe I, 1011
Peel, Elijah I, 67
Peel, Elisha I, 67
Peel, Ellen I, 336
Peel, Ellen I, 339
Peel, Emily I, 897
Peel, Esther Ann I, 897
Peel, Excum I, 897
Peel, Exum I, 897
Peel, Grant I, 897
Peel, Hannah II, 405
Peel, Hannah II, 618
Peel, Henry Jay I, 897
Peel, Hester Ann I, 897
Peel, Hester Ann Frances I, 897
Peel, Hunter VI, 977
Peel, James I, 67
Peel, James I, 897
Peel, Jane VI, 953
Peel, Jennie IV, 1274
Peel, John II, 405
Peel, John II, 618
Peel, John IV, 455
Peel, John V, 308
Peel, Jonathan I, 897
Peel, Joseph IV, 1333
Peel, Joseph H. IV, 1332
Peel, Joseph J. I, 897
Peel, Josiah IV, 262
Peel, Laura E. I, 897
Peel, Lucy I, 897
Peel, Ludia II, 618
Peel, Luke II, 618
Peel, Lydia II, 405
Peel, Lydia V, 308
Peel, Mable IV, 1289
Peel, Margaret A. I, 240
Peel, Martha I, 315
Peel, Mary I, 995
Peel, Mary I, 1011
Peel, Mary J. I, 897
Peel, Mary Jane I, 897
Peel, Mary Olve I, 897
Peel, Molly I, 315
Peel, Oswald II, 405
Peel, Oswell II, 405
Peel, Peggy I, 1011
Peel, Peggy VI, 977
Peel, Rachel II, 405
Peel, Rachel II, 618
Peel, Rachel VI, 65
Peel, Reuben I, 1011
Peel, Rhoda I, 1011
Peel, Robert I, 45
Peel, Robert I, 67
Peel, Ruth I, 67
Peel, Sarah I, 1011
Peel, Sarah V, 794
Peel, Sarah Letitia I, 897
Peel, Sarah W. I, 67
Peel, Tabitha I, 1071
Peel, Thomas VI, 65
Peel, William Franklin I, 339
Peele, Abba I, 225
Peele, Abbie I, 242
Peele, Abbie I, 254
Peele, Abner I, 225
Peele, Abner I, 294
Peele, Albert I, 226
Peele, Albert I, 255
Peele, Albert I, 512
Peele, Albert I, 535
Peele, Albert I, 566
Peele, Albert I, 920
Peele, Albert IV, 1000
Peele, Albert VI, 78
Peele, Albert VI, 92
Peele, Amanda I, 339
Peele, Amanda C. I, 339
Peele, Amy I, 339
Peele, Ann I, 15
Peele, Ann I, 224
Peele, Ann I, 306
Peele, Ann I, 315
Peele, Ann II, 618
Peele, Ann E. I, 68
Peele, Ann E. I, 225
Peele, Ann E. W. I, 255
Peele, Ann Elesabeth I, 84
Peele, Ann Elisabeth I, 24
Peele, Ann Elisabeth I, 68
Peele, Ann Elizabeth I, 224
Peele, Ann Elizabeth I, 947
Peele, Ann Elizabeth W. I, 932
Peele, Anna I, 225
Peele, Anna I, 315
Peele, Anna IV, 592
Peele, Anna F. I, 255
Peele, Anne I, 254
Peele, Anne I, 294
Peele, Anne I, 303
Peele, Anne I, 315
Peele, Anne I, 1071
Peele, Bertha A. I, 232
Peele, Bertha A. I, 255
Peele, Bertha Ann I, 225
Peele, Bertha Ann I, 339
Peele, Betsey I, 225
Peele, Betsey I, 295
Peele, Betsey I, 306
Peele, Betsey I, 315
Peele, Caleb III, 197
Peele, Caleb III, 252
Peele, Caleb III, 255
Peele, Carrie O. I, 339
Peele, Catharine I, 254
Peele, Charity I, 67
Peele, Charity I, 206
Peele, Charity I, 225
Peele, Charity I, 253
Peele, Charity I, 254
Peele, Charity I, 555
Peele, Charity I, 566
Peele, Christian I, 225
Peele, Christian I, 240
Peele, Christian I, 253
Peele, Christian I, 295
Peele, Christian I, 315
Peele, Christian I, 316
Peele, Christiana I, 295
Peele, Clinton III, 255
Peele, Cloe I, 315
Peele, David I, 225
Peele, David I, 253
Peele, David I, 294
Peele, David I, 306
Peele, David I, 315
Peele, Deborah A. I, 15
Peele, Deborah A. I, 252
Peele, Deborah Ann I, 225
Peele, Deborah Ann I, 252
Peele, Deborah Ann I, 255
Peele, Delphin E. I, 339
Peele, Delphin Elizabeth I, 339
Peele, Edmon I, 226
Peele, Edmond I, 225
Peele, Edmond I, 254
Peele, Edmund I, 224
Peele, Edmund I, 254
Peele, Edmund I, 1092
Peele, Edmund I, 1096
Peele, Edna I, 294
Peele, Edna I, 305
Peele, Edna I, 315
Peele, Edwin I, 226
Peele, Eleanor V, 687
Peele, Elijah I, 15
Peele, Elijah I, 19
Peele, Elijah I, 54
Peele, Elijah I, 67
Peele, Elijah I, 68
Peele, Elijah I, 224
Peele, Elijah I, 225
Peele, Elijah I, 255
Peele, Elijah I, 935
Peele, Elisabeth I, 67
Peele, Elisabeth I, 68
Peele, Elisabeth I, 240
Peele, Elisabeth I, 254
Peele, Elisabeth I. I, 255
Peele, Elisabeth P. I, 255
Peele, Elisha I, 67
Peele, Eliza Jane I, 226
Peele, Eliza Jane I, 255
Peele, Elizabeth I, 222
Peele, Elizabeth I, 224
Peele, Elizabeth I, 225
Peele, Elizabeth I, 226
Peele, Elizabeth I, 237
Peele, Elizabeth I, 251
Peele, Elizabeth I, 253
Peele, Elizabeth I, 254
Peele, Elizabeth I, 255
Peele, Elizabeth I, 257
Peele, Elizabeth I, 295
Peele, Elizabeth I, 314
Peele, Elizabeth I, 315
Peele, Elizabeth I, 934
Peele, Elizabeth J. I, 226
Peele, Elizabeth P. I, 225
Peele, Elizabeth R. I, 255
Peele, Elma Iola I, 225
Peele, Elsie I, 225
Peele, Elujah I, 255
Peele, Emily V, 630
Peele, Esther I, 225
Peele, Esther V, 523
Peele, Esther E. I, 19
Peele, Esther E. I, 67
Peele, Esther E. I, 68
Peele, Esther E. I, 84
Peele, Esther Mae I, 223
Peele, Exum I, 254
Peele, Exum I, 897
Peele, Farriba I, 1096
Peele, Fletcher I, 294
Peele, Fletcher I, 315
Peele, Franklin I, 339
Peele, George Conrad I, 223
Peele, Grace I, 226
Peele, Harriet M. V, 523
Peele, Henry I, 224
Peele, Henry I, 226
Peele, Henry I, 248
Peele, Henry I, 254
Peele, Henry E. I, 254
Peele, Henry E. III, 252
Peele, Henry Edmon I, 225
Peele, Henry Exum I, 226
Peele, Henry W. I, 255
Peele, Henry Whittier I, 225
Peele, Ichabod I, 339
Peele, Inez III, 252
Peele, Inez B. III, 16
Peele, Inez B. III, 252
Peele, Iona May I, 637
Peele, Ionia May I, 639
Peele, Irma M. I, 639
Peele, Irma Maie I, 622
Peele, Isaac I, 225
Peele, Isaac I, 255
Peele, Isabel I, 250
Peele, Isabel I, 254
Peele, Isabell I, 225
Peele, J. Willis I, 339
Peele, Jaehovah I, 253
Peele, James I, 15
Peele, James I, 32
Peele, James I, 67
Peele, James I, 224
Peele, James I, 254
Peele, James I, 255
Peele, James I, 260
Peele, James I, 294
Peele, James I, 315
Peele, James I, 339
Peele, James VI, 78
Peele, James Bryan I, 295
Peele, James D. I, 315

Peele, James Edgar I, 223
Peele, James Hare I, 225
Peele, James Henry I, 226
Peele, James Johnson I, 225
Peele, James L. I, 214
Peele, James L. I, 223
Peele, James L. I, 225
Peele, James L. I, 239
Peele, James L. I, 255
Peele, James Lloyd I, 225
Peele, James Lloyd I, 226
Peele, James Loyd I, 255
Peele, James N. I, 255
Peele, Jane I, 225
Peele, Jane I, 231
Peele, Jane I, 254
Peele, Jane I, 255
Peele, Jeremiah I, 225
Peele, Jeremiah I, 237
Peele, Jeremiah I, 254
Peele, Jeremiah I, 295
Peele, Jeremiah I, 566
Peele, Jesse I, 24
Peele, Jesse I, 67
Peele, Jesse I, 68
Peele, Jesse I, 222
Peele, Jesse I, 223
Peele, Jesse I, 224
Peele, Jesse I, 225
Peele, Jesse I, 226
Peele, Jesse I, 240
Peele, Jesse I, 254
Peele, Jesse I, 255
Peele, Jesse I, 295
Peele, Jesse I, 315
Peele, Jesse I, 319
Peele, Jesse V, 633
Peele, Jesse U. I, 255
Peele, Jesse W. I, 19
Peele, Jesse W. I, 67
Peele, Jesse W. I, 68
Peele, Jesse W. I, 84
Peele, Jesse W. I, 225
Peele, Jesse W. I, 255
Peele, Jesse William I, 226
Peele, Jesse, II I, 226
Peele, Joel I, 225
Peele, Joel I, 254
Peele, John I, 67
Peele, John I, 216
Peele, John I, 225
Peele, John I, 226
Peele, John I, 251
Peele, John I, 253
Peele, John I, 254
Peele, John I, 294
Peele, John I, 295
Peele, John I, 303
Peele, John I, 315
Peele, John I, 967
Peele, John I, 1071
Peele, John Bryan I, 226
Peele, John G. I, 225
Peele, John G. I, 255
Peele, John Grellet I, 226
Peele, John Grellet I, 255
Peele, John Grellet I, 257
Peele, John H. I, 255
Peele, John H. VI, 78
Peele, John H. VI, 79
Peele, John Hall I, 225
Peele, John Hare I, 225
Peele, John Thomas I, 15
Peele, John Thomas I, 67
Peele, John Thomas I, 224
Peele, John, Jr. I, 254
Peele, Jonathan E. I, 226
Peele, Jonathan E. I, 255
Peele, Jose I, 315
Peele, Joseph IV, 1333
Peele, Joseph H. I, 622
Peele, Joseph H. I, 637
Peele, Joseph H. I, 639
Peele, Joseph John I, 225
Peele, Joseph W. I, 255
Peele, Joseph Wheeler I, 226
Peele, Joseph Winbourn I, 226
Peele, Josey I, 225
Peele, Josey I, 286
Peele, Josiah I, 226
Peele, Josiah I, 253
Peele, Josiah I, 254
Peele, Josiah I, 314
Peele, Josiah I, 315
Peele, Josiah IV, 262
Peele, Josse I, 295
Peele, Judith I, 225
Peele, Judith I, 254
Peele, Judith I, 302
Peele, Judith I, 315
Peele, Judith A. I, 255
Peele, Julia I, 224
Peele, Julia I, 251
Peele, Julia I, 254
Peele, Julian A. I, 225
Peele, Juliana I, 225
Peele, Julianna I, 216
Peele, Julianna I, 225
Peele, Julianna I, 240
Peele, Julianna I, 255
Peele, Kathryn V, 659
Peele, Lee F. I, 339
Peele, Lee Franklin I, 339
Peele, Lillie I, 339
Peele, Lizzie I, 920
Peele, Louisa VI, 78
Peele, Louisa VI, 79
Peele, Louisa Porter VI, 78
Peele, Louise III, 197
Peele, Louise III, 252
Peele, Lucinda I, 339
Peele, Ludia II, 618
Peele, Lula I, 335
Peele, Lula I, 339
Peele, Lydia I, 226
Peele, Lydia I, 254
Peele, Lydia II, 638
Peele, Lydia V, 623
Peele, Lydia Ann I, 224
Peele, Lydia P. I, 255
Peele, Lydia Winborn I, 224
Peele, Lydia, Sr. I, 254
Peele, Margaret I, 208
Peele, Margaret I, 223
Peele, Margaret I, 226
Peele, Margaret I, 253
Peele, Margaret I, 295
Peele, Margaret I, 512
Peele, Margaret I, 920
Peele, Margaret VI, 65
Peele, Margaret A. I, 223
Peele, Margaret A. I, 225
Peele, Margaret A. I, 226
Peele, Margaret A. I, 231
Peele, Margaret A. I, 239
Peele, Margaret A. I, 240
Peele, Margaret A. I, 255
Peele, Margaret A. VI, 65
Peele, Margaret A. VI, 78
Peele, Margaret Ann I, 214
Peele, Margaret B. I, 225
Peele, Margaret E. I, 255
Peele, Margaret E. I, 535
Peele, Margaret E. I, 566
Peele, Margaret E. VI, 78
Peele, Margaret Edna VI, 92
Peele, Margaret F. I, 252
Peele, Margaret F. I, 255
Peele, Maria W. III, 197
Peele, Maria W. III, 252
Peele, Maria W. III, 255
Peele, Mark I, 967
Peele, Mark I, 985
Peele, Mark I, 995
Peele, Martha I, 225
Peele, Martha I, 250
Peele, Martha I, 254
Peele, Martha I, 255
Peele, Martha I, 315
Peele, Martha Jane I, 224
Peele, Mary I, 68
Peele, Mary I, 206
Peele, Mary I, 224
Peele, Mary I, 225
Peele, Mary I, 226
Peele, Mary I, 241
Peele, Mary I, 243
Peele, Mary I, 253
Peele, Mary I, 254
Peele, Mary I, 295
Peele, Mary I, 310
Peele, Mary I, 315
Peele, Mary I, 985
Peele, Mary I, 995
Peele, Mary A. I, 225
Peele, Mary A. I, 255
Peele, Mary A. I, 261
Peele, Mary Ann I, 32
Peele, Mary Ann I, 225
Peele, Mary Ann I, 226
Peele, Mary Ann I, 254
Peele, Mary Ann I, 261
Peele, Mary Ann IV, 1000
Peele, Mary Anna I, 566
Peele, Mary E. I, 24
Peele, Mary E. I, 67
Peele, Mary E. I, 226
Peele, Mary E. I, 236
Peele, Mary E. I, 255
Peele, Mary E. I, 932
Peele, Mary Eliza I, 15
Peele, Mary Eliza I, 19
Peele, Mary Eliza I, 67
Peele, Mary Eliza I, 224
Peele, Mary Eliza I, 935
Peele, Mary Elizabeth I, 226
Peele, Mary Geneva I, 223
Peele, Mary J. I, 222
Peele, Mary J. I, 225
Peele, Mary J. I, 252
Peele, Mary J. I, 255
Peele, Mary Jane I, 1092
Peele, Mary Jane I, 1096
Peele, Mary Julia I, 255
Peele, Mary Julia I, 257
Peele, Mary W. I, 226
Peele, Matthew I, 295
Peele, Mildred I, 295
Peele, Milercent I, 224
Peele, Milercent I, 225
Peele, Miles L. V, 687
Peele, Milisent I, 248
Peele, Milisent I, 254
Peele, Milisint I, 247
Peele, Milisint I, 253
Peele, Molley I, 295
Peele, Molly I, 315
Peele, Mylercent I, 255
Peele, Nanny I, 295
Peele, Nathan I, 295
Peele, Oswald II, 405
Peele, Owen I, 295
Peele, Pasco I, 1071
Peele, Passco I, 225
Peele, Passco I, 1071
Peele, Patience I, 286
Peele, Patience I, 295
Peele, Patience I, 315
Peele, Patience I, 319
Peele, Pegga I, 315
Peele, Peggy I, 295
Peele, Peninah I, 295
Peele, Peninah I, 315
Peele, Peninnah I, 316
Peele, Pharaby I, 225
Peele, Pharaby Johnson VI, 78
Peele, Phebe A. V, 633
Peele, Pherby I, 226
Peele, Phereba I, 254
Peele, Pheriba I, 295
Peele, Pheriba I, 301
Peele, Pheriba I, 309
Peele, Pheriba I, 315
Peele, Pollie I, 286
Peele, Polly I, 294
Peele, Priscilla I, 294
Peele, Priscilla I, 306
Peele, Priscilla I, 315
Peele, Rache I, 254
Peele, Rachel I, 211
Peele, Rachel I, 216
Peele, Rachel I, 225
Peele, Rachel I, 226
Peele, Rachel I, 254
Peele, Rachel I, 255
Peele, Rachel I, 315
Peele, Rachel I, 316
Peele, Rachel I, 566
Peele, Rachel Outland I, 224
Peele, Rebeckah I, 995
Peele, Reuben I, 314
Peele, Reuben I, 315
Peele, Reuben I, 967
Peele, Reuben I, 995
Peele, Rhoda I, 314
Peele, Rhoda I, 315
Peele, Rhoda I, 995
Peele, Robert I, 67
Peele, Robert I, 206
Peele, Robert I, 224
Peele, Robert I, 225
Peele, Robert I, 226
Peele, Robert I, 253
Peele, Robert I, 254
Peele, Robert I, 294
Peele, Robert I, 295
Peele, Robert I, 315
Peele, Robert I, 1096
Peele, Robert VI, 78
Peele, Robert B. I, 315
Peele, Robert, Jr. I, 225
Peele, Robert, Jr. I, 253
Peele, Robert, Sr. I, 254
Peele, Ruth I, 15
Peele, Ruth I, 32
Peele, Ruth I, 67
Peele, Ruth I, 224
Peele, Ruth I, 226
Peele, Ruth I, 254
Peele, Ruth I, 255
Peele, Ruth VI, 78
Peele, Ruth Anna I, 15
Peele, Ruth Anna I, 67
Peele, Ruth Eleonor I, 223
Peele, Ruth Eva I, 223
Peele, Ruth Eva I, 225
Peele, Ruth Eva I, 255
Peele, Ruthannah I, 224
Peele, Salley I, 295
Peele, Sallie I, 339
Peele, Sally I, 301
Peele, Sally I, 315
Peele, Sarah I, 67
Peele, Sarah I, 68
Peele, Sarah I, 225
Peele, Sarah I, 226
Peele, Sarah I, 250
Peele, Sarah I, 253
Peele, Sarah I, 254
Peele, Sarah I, 255
Peele, Sarah I, 313
Peele, Sarah I, 314
Peele, Sarah I, 315
Peele, Sarah I, 935
Peele, Sarah I, 995
Peele, Sarah III, 255
Peele, Sarah J. I, 235
Peele, Sarah J. I, 255
Peele, Sarah Jane I, 211
Peele, Sarah Jane I, 226
Peele, Sarah S. III, 255
Peele, Sarah W. I, 15
Peele, Sarah W. I, 19
Peele, Sarah W. I, 54
Peele, Sarah W. I, 67
Peele, Sarah W. I, 68
Peele, Sarah W. I, 255
Peele, Seddie I, 339
Peele, Selah I, 225
Peele, Selea I, 315
Peele, Selia I, 315
Peele, Tabbitha I, 1071
Peele, Tabitha I, 315
Peele, Tabitha I, 833
Peele, Tabitha I, 1071
Peele, Tempe I, 225
Peele, Tempy I, 252
Peele, Tempy I, 254
Peele, Thomas I, 68
Peele, Thomas I, 211
Peele, Thomas I, 216
Peele, Thomas I, 224
Peele, Thomas I, 225
Peele, Thomas I, 226
Peele, Thomas I, 254
Peele, Thomas I, 255
Peele, Thomas I, 566
Peele, Thomas C. I, 208
Peele, Thomas C. I, 225
Peele, Thomas C. I, 226
Peele, Thomas C. I, 231
Peele, Thomas C. I, 240
Peele, Thomas C. I, 255
Peele, Thomas Clarkson I, 225
Peele, Thomas Clarkston I, 225
Peele, Thomas Herbert I, 226
Peele, Vida M. I, 339
Peele, Vida May I, 339
Peele, W. F. I, 339
Peele, Webster W. I, 339
Peele, Webster Woodard I, 339
Peele, William I, 225
Peele, William I, 226
Peele, William I, 254
Peele, William I, 255
Peele, William I, 257
Peele, William I, 1071
Peele, William Franklin I, 339
Peele, William H. I, 255
Peele, William Herschal I, 255
Peele, William Hershal I, 512
Peele, William T. I, 226
Peele, William Thomas I, 226
Peele, William W. I, 566
Peele, Willis I, 295
Peele, Willis I, 306
Peele, Willis I, 315
Peele, Willis I, 339
Peele, Willis K. I, 339
Peele, Winnie I, 339
Peele, Zilpha I, 985
Peele, Zilpha I, 995
Peelee, Rachel I, 315
Peeler, D. H. I, 614
Peeler, Henrietta I, 614
Peeler, Mary Anna I, 614
Peeles, ??? IV, 1269
Peell, John II, 618
Peell, Luke II, 618
Peelle, Aaron V, 640
Peelle, Abigail V, 640
Peelle, Albert IV, 985
Peelle, Alfred V, 703
Peelle, Alfred Earl V, 640
Peelle, Alfred Earl V, 703
Peelle, Alice Arline V, 703
Peelle, Alice H. V, 703
Peelle, Alice Jane V, 640
Peelle, Alonzo V, 197
Peelle, Alonzo V, 640
Peelle, Alvan A. V, 703
Peelle, Ann IV, 428
Peelle, Ann IV, 429
Peelle, Ann V, 566
Peelle, Anna I, 315
Peelle, Anna IV, 428
Peelle, Anna V, 703
Peelle, Anna Belle V, 703
Peelle, Annabelle V, 640
Peelle, Anne I, 248
Peelle, Anne I, 254
Peelle, Annetta V, 640
Peelle, Anzonetta IV, 1289
Peelle, Aromethea V, 640
Peelle, Asa V, 640
Peelle, Benjamin W. IV, 1289
Peelle, Bertha V, 354
Peelle, Bertha V, 640
Peelle, Bertha V, 658
Peelle, Bertha V, 703
Peelle, Bertha Barbara V, 70
Peelle, Caleb III, 252
Peelle, Caleb Morris III, 252
Peelle, Calvin W. V, 703
Peelle, Caroline IV, 1289
Peelle, Carrie V, 523
Peelle, Cary V, 640
Peelle, Charity I, 244
Peelle, Charity I, 254
Peelle, Charles V, 523
Peelle, Charles Edward V, 70
Peelle, Chas. Edward V, 640
Peelle, Chas. Edward V, 703
Peelle, Clara S. V, 354
Peelle, Clara S. V, 703
Peelle, Clarissa V, 425
Peelle, Clarissa V, 615
Peelle, Clarissa V, 640
Peelle, Clarissa V, 645
Peelle, Clarissa A. V, 703
Peelle, Clarkson V, 640
Peelle, David I, 253
Peelle, Delpha O. IV, 1289
Peelle, Dorcas V, 425
Peelle, Dorcas V, 666
Peelle, Dorcas V, 703
Peelle, Dorcas A. V, 414
Peelle, Dorcas A. V, 425
Peelle, Dorcas A. V, 640
Peelle, Dorcas A. V, 703
Peelle, Dorothy V, 704
Peelle, Edmund I, 254
Peelle, Edna V, 640
Peelle, Edna C. V, 703
Peelle, Edna Street V, 703
Peelle, Eleanor V, 703
Peelle, Elias V, 640
Peelle, Elias H. V, 640
Peelle, Elihu C. V, 640
Peelle, Elijah I, 67
Peelle, Elijah I, 84
Peelle, Elijah I, 255
Peelle, Elijah J. V, 640
Peelle, Elisabeth I, 67
Peelle, Elizabeth IV, 1289
Peelle, Elizabeth V, 640
Peelle, Elizabeth V, 641
Peelle, Elizabeth V, 703
Peelle, Ella V, 640
Peelle, Ellen V, 703
Peelle, Ellen V, 707
Peelle, Elmer V, 703
Peelle, Elton V, 703
Peelle, Emery S. V, 703
Peelle, Emily V, 640
Peelle, Emma V, 425
Peelle, Emma V, 612
Peelle, Emma V, 640
Peelle, Emma E. V, 640
Peelle, Emma Lucile V, 703
Peelle, Emory V, 640
Peelle, Emory V, 703
Peelle, Enos V, 640
Peelle, Enos P. V, 703
Peelle, Esther V, 523
Peelle, Esther V, 640
Peelle, Esther B. V, 703
Peelle, Exum I, 254
Peelle, Fletcher I, 315
Peelle, Frances Charlotte III,
Peelle, Frank III, 252
Peelle, Frank A. V, 640
Peelle, Frank Alton V, 703
Peelle, Gertrude V, 703
Peelle, Gladys V, 703

, Gladys Marie V, 703
, Harley V, 703
, Harley H. V, 703
, Harriet M. V, 523
, Harriet M. V, 640
, Harriett Florence V, 640
, Hattie M. V, 703
, Hazel Ellen V, 703
, Henry III, 252
, Henry IV, 1289
, Henry V, 640
, Henry B. III, 252
, Henry E. III, 252
, Henry E. V, 640
, Henry Edmund III, 252
, Hubert Wayne V, 425
, Inez III, 252
, Inez B. III, 252
, Inez Marilyn III, 252
, Isaiah V, 634
, Isaiah V, 640
, Isaiah V, 703
, Isaiah Morris V, 703
, J. Irving V, 703
, J. Will V, 641
, James I, 254
, James I, 315
, James Walter III, 252
, Jesse I, 315
, Jesse V, 262
, Jesse V, 354
, Jesse V, 640
, Jesse V, 703
, Jesse W. I, 255
, Joel I, 254
, John I, 253
, John I, 254
, John I, 315
, John I, 967
, John IV, 141
, John IV, 156
, John IV, 1289
, John V, 270
, John V, 615
, John V, 640
, John V, 703
, John P. V, 640
, John Thomas I, 67
, John W. V, 640
, John, Jr. I, 254
, John, Jr. V, 414
, John, Jr. V, 425
, Jonathan R. V, 640
, Jose I, 315
, Joshua M. IV, 1289
, Josiah I, 253
, Josiah I, 315
, Josiah IV, 262
, Josiah IV, 1289
, Josiah V, 640
, Josie V, 640
, Judith I, 236
, Judith I, 254
, Judith I, 315
, Judith I, 318
, Kathryn V, 703
, Kathryn Marie V, 703
, Lawrence V, 640
, Lawrence D. V, 703
, Leroy V, 640
, Leroy V, 703
, Lillian V, 703
, Lina M. V, 523
, Louisa V, 245
, Louisa V, 270
, Louisa V, 625
, Louisa V, 640
, Louise III, 252
, Louise W. III, 252
, Luther Allen V, 640
, Lydia IV, 141
, Lydia IV, 156
, Lydia V, 270
, Lydia V, 640
, Lydia V, 703
, Lydia Arametha V, 640
, Lydia B. V, 615
, Lydia B. V, 640
, Lydia B. V, 703
, Lydia C. V, 640
, Lydia D. V, 703
, Lydia Deborah V, 523
, Lydia Deborah V, 703
, Lydia, Sr. I, 254
, Mable IV, 1289
, Mae V, 425
, Margaret E. V, 640
, Margaret Emily V, 640
, Margaretta V, 354
, Margaretta C. V, 703
, Maria W. III, 252
Peelle, Mark I, 967
Peelle, Mark V, 640
Peelle, Mark Clinton V, 658
Peelle, Mary I, 254
Peelle, Mary I, 300
Peelle, Mary I, 304
Peelle, Mary I, 315
Peelle, Mary III, 252
Peelle, Mary V, 639
Peelle, Mary V, 640
Peelle, Mary Ann IV, 985
Peelle, Mary Arlene V, 703
Peelle, Mary E. I, 67
Peelle, Mary E. I, 84
Peelle, Mary E. I, 236
Peelle, Mary E. V, 640
Peelle, Mary Eleanor V, 640
Peelle, Mary Eliza I, 67
Peelle, Mary Emma V, 197
Peelle, Mary Esther V, 197
Peelle, Mary Esther V, 703
Peelle, Mary J. I, 255
Peelle, Mary Vantress V, 523
Peelle, Maude V, 703
Peelle, May V, 704
Peelle, Melisa IV, 1289
Peelle, Miles L. V, 703
Peelle, Minna R. V, 640
Peelle, Minnie R. V, 640
Peelle, Moses V, 640
Peelle, Mylercent I, 255
Peelle, Nora V, 523
Peelle, Oliver V, 703
Peelle, Orrin V, 703
Peelle, Orrin G. V, 640
Peelle, Orrin G. V, 703
Peelle, Oscar V, 703
Peelle, Oscar D. V, 703
Peelle, Oscar V. V, 703
Peelle, Parker V, 523
Peelle, Parker S. V, 523
Peelle, Paul V, 523
Peelle, Pearl V, 682
Peelle, Pearl V, 703
Peelle, Phebe V, 640
Peelle, Phebe A. V, 262
Peelle, Phebe A. V, 640
Peelle, Phebe N. V, 640
Peelle, Phereba I, 254
Peelle, Rache I, 254
Peelle, Rachel I, 248
Peelle, Rachel I, 306
Peelle, Rachel I, 315
Peelle, Rachel IV, 985
Peelle, Reuben I, 967
Peelle, Reuben I, 995
Peelle, Reuben IV, 156
Peelle, Reuben V, 640
Peelle, Rhoda IV, 156
Peelle, Rhoda V, 634
Peelle, Rhoda V, 640
Peelle, Robert I, 67
Peelle, Robert I, 247
Peelle, Robert I, 254
Peelle, Robert III, 252
Peelle, Robert IV, 262
Peelle, Robert IV, 1289
Peelle, Robert B. I, 315
Peelle, Robert B. III, 252
Peelle, Robert, Jr. I, 253
Peelle, Roscoe V, 703
Peelle, Roscoe E. V, 703
Peelle, Russell G. V, 703
Peelle, Ruth Anna I, 67
Peelle, Ruth Anna V, 640
Peelle, Ruth Annie V, 703
Peelle, Sarah I, 247
Peelle, Sarah I, 253
Peelle, Sarah I, 315
Peelle, Sarah V, 640
Peelle, Sarah V, 703
Peelle, Sarah V, 794
Peelle, Sarah Ann V, 622
Peelle, Sarah Ann V, 640
Peelle, Sarah E. V, 523
Peelle, Sarah E. V, 640
Peelle, Sarah S. III, 252
Peelle, Sarah W. I, 67
Peelle, Selea I, 311
Peelle, Selea I, 315
Peelle, Selma V. V, 703
Peelle, Seth V, 640
Peelle, Seth V, 703
Peelle, Susan V, 634
Peelle, Susan V, 640
Peelle, Susan V, 703
Peelle, Susan M. V, 640
Peelle, Susan M. V, 703
Peelle, Susannah V, 615
Peelle, Susannah V, 640
Peelle, Thelma V. V, 704
Peelle, Thomas I, 248
Peelle, Thomas I, 254
Peelle, Thomas IV, 985
Peelle, Virgil Leroy V, 640
Peelle, Virgil Leroy V, 703
Peelle, Virginia B. R. V, 640
Peelle, Virginia Rhonemus Bosworth V, 703
Peelle, Waldo V, 703
Peelle, Walter V, 425
Peelle, Walter D. V, 640
Peelle, Weldon V, 640
Peelle, Weldon V, 641
Peelle, William I, 255
Peelle, William V, 245
Peelle, William V, 270
Peelle, William V, 425
Peelle, William V, 640
Peelle, William Ruskin V, 354
Peelle, Willis I, 304
Peelle, Willis I, 315
Peelle, Wilson V, 640
Peelle, Wilson C. V, 523
Peelle, Wm. V, 615
Peelle, Wm. V, 625
Peelle, Wm. V, 640
Peelle, Wm. V, 645
Peelle, Wm. C. V, 640
Peelle, Wm. C. V, 703
Peelle, Wm. R. V, 703
Peelle, Wm. Ruskin V, 354
Peene, Caroline III, 151
Peene, Caroline III, 252
Peene, George III, 151
Peene, George III, 252
Peene, Jennie E. III, 151
Peene, Jinnie E. III, 252
Peeper, Rachel IV, 429
Peeples, Dinah IV, 985
Peeples, Harry L. IV, 937
Peeples, James IV, 985
Peeples, James R. IV, 985
Peeples, Lucinda IV, 985
Peeples, Margaret A. IV, 937
Peeples, Nora IV, 937
Peer, Frances V, 1014
Peer, Frankie V, 197
Peer, Frankie V, 1014
Peer, George Francis V, 197
Peer, George Francis V, 1014
Peerman, Benjamin F. VI, 797
Peerman, Benjamin F. VI, 845
Peerman, Caroline C. VI, 845
Peerman, Catherine S. VI, 845
Peerman, Dancy VI, 796
Peerman, Dancy VI, 820
Peerman, Dancy VI, 825
Peerman, Mary J. VI, 845
Peerman, Sarah M. VI, 820
Peerman, William H. VI, 845
Peers, Elizabeth II, 814
Peers, George II, 814
Peerson, Jonathan I, 995
Peerson, Samuel I, 897
Peery, John V, 462
Peery, Mary V, 462
Peet, Anna Grace V, 250
Peet, George II, 405
Peg, Achsa I, 566
Peg, Barbara II, 405
Peg, Daniel II, 405
Peg, Mary II, 405
Peg, Nathan II, 405
Peg, Rebecah II, 405
Pegg, Achsa I, 566
Pegg, Anna Corina I, 919
Pegg, Barbara II, 405
Pegg, Barbara II, 567
Pegg, Barbara II, 618
Pegg, Daniel II, 405
Pegg, Daniel II, 567
Pegg, Daniel II, 618
Pegg, David I, 833
Pegg, David Valentine I, 833
Pegg, Davis I, 833
Pegg, Davis I, 836
Pegg, Elias II, 446
Pegg, Elizabeth I, 566
Pegg, Elizabeth I, 833
Pegg, Ellen I, 641
Pegg, Hiram IV, 311
Pegg, Hiram IV, 313
Pegg, James I, 833
Pegg, Jane I, 833
Pegg, Jane I, 836
Pegg, Jane I, 919
Pegg, John I, 833
Pegg, John V, 197
Pegg, Lydia I, 833
Pegg, Margaret I, 833
Pegg, Marget I, 833
Pegg, Mary I, 828
Pegg, Mary I, 833
Pegg, Mary I Sup 1, 10
Pegg, Mary II, 405
Pegg, Mary V, 819
Pegg, Mary Ann V, 820
Pegg, Mary, Jr. I, 833
Pegg, Maryann V, 820
Pegg, Nathan II, 405
Pegg, Rebecah II, 405
Pegg, Ruth I, 833
Pegg, Sarah I, 833
Pegg, Sarah IV, 311
Pegg, Sarah IV, 313
Pegg, Valentine I, 806
Pegg, Valentine I, 833
Pegg, Widow Mary I, 806
Peggans, Lucinda VI, 876
Peggot, Benjamin V, 761
Peggot, Joshua V, 761
Peglow, Elfriede III, 252
Peglow, Walter III, 252
Pegram, Anna I, 611
Pegram, Anna I, 639
Pegram, Annie I, 566
Pegram, Annie I, 616
Pegram, Annie C. I, 566
Pegram, Annie C. I, 624
Pegram, Annie C. I, 639
Pegram, Daniel VI, 942
Pegram, E. T. W. VI, 996
Pegram, Edward VI, 202
Pegram, Edward VI, 203
Pegram, Elizabeth Ann I, 947
Pegram, Ella I, 639
Pegram, Ella I, 640
Pegram, Ella V. I, 624
Pegram, Ella Virginia I, 566
Pegram, Elle E. I, 639
Pegram, Ina I, 633
Pegram, Ina I, 639
Pegram, Ina E. I, 616
Pegram, Ina W. I, 639
Pegram, J. H. I, 566
Pegram, James L. VI, 977
Pegram, James L. VI, 1001
Pegram, John VI, 132
Pegram, John VI, 139
Pegram, John VI, 144
Pegram, Josephine I, 931
Pegram, Julian K. VI, 977
Pegram, Julius H. I, 566
Pegram, Julius M. I, 611
Pegram, Julius M. I, 616
Pegram, Julius M. I, 624
Pegram, Julius M. I, 639
Pegram, Lula Smitherman I, 947
Pegram, Mary VI, 964
Pegram, Nancy E. I, 624
Pegram, Nathaniel VI, 135
Pegram, Nathaniel VI, 142
Pegram, Nathaniel J. VI, 135
Pegram, Nathaniel J. VI, 139
Pegram, R. B. I, 947
Pegram, Vivian I, 629
Pegram, Vivian I, 639
Pegram, Vivian A. I, 624
Pegram, Vivian A. I, 639
Pegram, William VI, 202
Pegram, William VI, 203
Pegram, William VI, 210
Peirc, Ann I, 15
Peirc, Deborah I, 15
Peirc, Jemima I, 15
Peirc, John I, 15
Peirc, Joseph I, 15
Peirc, Kerenhapprick I, 15
Peirc, Keziah I, 15
Peirc, Mary I, 15
Peirc, Rebekah I, 15
Peirc, Sarrah I, 15
Peirc, Thomas I, 15
Peirce, ??? V, 795
Peirce, Abigail II, 405
Peirce, Abigail II, 513
Peirce, Abigail II, 619
Peirce, Abner I, 68
Peirce, Abram L. V, 821
Peirce, Albert V, 820
Peirce, Albert Loving II, 814
Peirce, Alexander V, 925
Peirce, Alexander V, 926
Peirce, Alfred II, 619
Peirce, Alic I, 15
Peirce, Alice Marion II, 908
Peirce, Alvin V, 820
Peirce, Alvine V, 761
Peirce, Amanda Alice V, 821
Peirce, Amanda J. V, 821
Peirce, Amelia V, 811
Peirce, Ann I, 60
Peirce, Ann I, 68
Peirce, Ann II, 405
Peirce, Ann II, 618
Peirce, Ann V, 821
Peirce, Ann B. II, 814
Peirce, Ann B. II, 908
Peirce, Anna I, 995
Peirce, Anna I, 1131
Peirce, Anna II, 405
Peirce, Anna V, 821
Peirce, Anna B. II, 908
Peirce, Anne I, 68
Peirce, Anne II, 759
Peirce, Anne B. II, 844
Peirce, Anne B. II, 855
Peirce, Anne B. II, 908
Peirce, Anne B. Davis II, 818
Peirce, Benj. D. V, 821
Peirce, Benjamin V, 309
Peirce, Benjamin V, 761
Peirce, Benjamin D. V, 821
Peirce, Bertha V, 761
Peirce, Caleb I, 1130
Peirce, Caleb II, 405
Peirce, Caleb II, 618
Peirce, Caleb II, 619
Peirce, Caleb II, 715
Peirce, Caleb II, 743
Peirce, Caleb II, 759
Peirce, Caleb II, 814
Peirce, Caleb V, 925
Peirce, Caleb D. II, 759
Peirce, Caleb D. II, 908
Peirce, Calvin H. V, 821
Peirce, Carolin V, 821
Peirce, Catharine V, 309
Peirce, Catharine A. II, 908
Peirce, Catharine A. II, 927
Peirce, Chandlee II, 814
Peirce, Charity I, 1130
Peirce, Charles II, 405
Peirce, Charles V, 761
Peirce, Charles V, 925
Peirce, Charles Brooke II, 405
Peirce, Charles Brooke II, 619
Peirce, Charles Brooks II, 619
Peirce, Charles Hamlin V, 821
Peirce, Charritty I, 1132
Peirce, Chas. II, 814
Peirce, Chas. V, 926
Peirce, Chas. W. II, 908
Peirce, Chas. W. II, 927
Peirce, Clarkson V, 820
Peirce, Clarkson V, 821
Peirce, Clarkson T. V, 821
Peirce, Copeland I, 15
Peirce, Cornelia V, 953
Peirce, Cornelia V, 958
Peirce, Cyrus II, 619
Peirce, Cyrus II, 788
Peirce, Cyrus II, 814
Peirce, Cyrus II, 827
Peirce, Daniel II, 405
Peirce, David I, 68
Peirce, David V, 925
Peirce, Deborah Ann II, 405
Peirce, Deborah Ann II, 619
Peirce, Delilah V, 821
Peirce, Edward II, 405
Peirce, Edward II, 619
Peirce, Edward II, 908
Peirce, Edward W. II, 908
Peirce, Edwin L. II, 908
Peirce, Edwin Leedom II, 908
Peirce, Elisabeth I, 15
Peirce, Eliza Ann V, 821
Peirce, Elizabeth II, 405
Peirce, Elizabeth II, 619
Peirce, Elizabeth II, 814
Peirce, Elizabeth IV, 740
Peirce, Elizabeth V, 807
Peirce, Elizabeth V, 820
Peirce, Elizabeth V, 923
Peirce, Elizabeth V, 925
Peirce, Elizabeth L. II, 908
Peirce, Elizabeth Oliver II, 788
Peirce, Ellwood Chandlee II, 814
Peirce, Elmira V, 820
Peirce, Elmira F. V, 797
Peirce, Elmira F. V, 820
Peirce, Elwood II, 908
Peirce, Elwood C. II, 908
Peirce, Emma J. V, 820
Peirce, Emma W. V, 958
Peirce, Emma W. V, 962
Peirce, Enos E. V, 820
Peirce, Erie Dudley V, 761
Peirce, Ermina V, 761
Peirce, Ermina V, 820
Peirce, Esta V, 761
Peirce, Esther V, 34

Peirce, Esther V, 820
Peirce, Ethel V, 761
Peirce, Eunice V, 820
Peirce, Ezra L. V, 820
Peirce, Fidella V, 820
Peirce, Flora Malinda V, 821
Peirce, Frances B. II, 908
Peirce, Gainer V, 761
Peirce, Gainer V, 792
Peirce, Gainer V, 820
Peirce, Gainor V, 820
Peirce, Gainor A. V, 820
Peirce, Ganer IV, 781
Peirce, George I, 1130
Peirce, George II, 618
Peirce, George V, 761
Peirce, George V, 821
Peirce, George Chandler II, 405
Peirce, George Chandler II, 619
Peirce, George W. V, 820
Peirce, George, Jr. I, 1130
Peirce, Gideon II, 814
Peirce, Gideon II, 908
Peirce, Gideon V, 925
Peirce, Hannah I, 1124
Peirce, Hannah I, 1130
Peirce, Hannah II, 249
Peirce, Hannah II, 619
Peirce, Hannah II, 759
Peirce, Hannah II, 787
Peirce, Hannah II, 814
Peirce, Hannah II, 827
Peirce, Hannah II, 855
Peirce, Hannah II, 908
Peirce, Hannah V, 800
Peirce, Hannah V, 820
Peirce, Hannah V, 821
Peirce, Hannah VI, 482
Peirce, Hannah C. II, 405
Peirce, Hannah C. II, 619
Peirce, Hannah C. V, 801
Peirce, Hannah C. V, 820
Peirce, Hannah D. V, 958
Peirce, Hannah M. V, 821
Peirce, Henry I, 1131
Peirce, Henry D. V, 820
Peirce, Hephsabah I, 1130
Peirce, Hepzebah I, 1124
Peirce, Hepzebah I, 1130
Peirce, Howard V, 761
Peirce, Ida II, 814
Peirce, Ida II, 844
Peirce, Ida II, 908
Peirce, Irons II, 405
Peirce, Isaac II, 405
Peirce, Isaac II, 619
Peirce, Isaac IV, 740
Peirce, Isaac IV, 750
Peirce, Isaac M. I, 1131
Peirce, Isaac Newton IV, 710
Peirce, Isaac Newton IV, 750
Peirce, Jacob II, 619
Peirce, Jacob II, 759
Peirce, James I, 68
Peirce, James II, 908
Peirce, James V, 524
Peirce, James V, 592
Peirce, James V, 761
Peirce, James V, 821
Peirce, James V, 925
Peirce, James V, 926
Peirce, James E. II, 844
Peirce, James E. II, 908
Peirce, James Emlen II, 814
Peirce, James Emlen II, 855
Peirce, James Loring II, 814
Peirce, James Loving II, 814
Peirce, James M. V, 821
Peirce, Jane I, 1119
Peirce, Jane I, 1130
Peirce, Jane II, 405
Peirce, Jane II, 619
Peirce, Jane II, 715
Peirce, Jane II, 743
Peirce, Jane II, 759
Peirce, Jane II, 814
Peirce, Jane V, 792
Peirce, Jane V, 820
Peirce, Jane V, 821
Peirce, Jemima I, 62
Peirce, Jemima I, 68
Peirce, Jemima V, 821
Peirce, John I, 15
Peirce, John I, 17
Peirce, John I, 180
Peirce, John I, 199
Peirce, John I Sup 1, 5
Peirce, John II, 405
Peirce, John II, 814
Peirce, John V, 309
Peirce, John V, 592
Peirce, John V, 761
Peirce, John V, 807
Peirce, John V, 820
Peirce, John V, 821
Peirce, John D. II, 908
Peirce, John F. V, 524
Peirce, John T. V, 821
Peirce, Jonathan V, 958
Peirce, Joseph I, 15
Peirce, Joseph I, 49
Peirce, Joseph I, 90
Peirce, Joseph I Sup 1, 5
Peirce, Joseph II, 234
Peirce, Joseph II, 249
Peirce, Joseph II, 405
Peirce, Joseph II, 618
Peirce, Joshua II, 405
Peirce, Joshua II, 618
Peirce, Joshua II, 619
Peirce, Joshua II, 855
Peirce, Joshua II, 908
Peirce, Joshua VI, 482
Peirce, Keranhappuck I, 60
Peirce, Keranhappuck I, 68
Peirce, Kersey V, 925
Peirce, Keziah I, 62
Peirce, Keziah I, 68
Peirce, Lacy Ann V, 821
Peirce, Lavina E. V, 821
Peirce, Lida V, 925
Peirce, Liddia I, 56
Peirce, Liddia I, 68
Peirce, Lois T. V, 821
Peirce, Loren II, 827
Peirce, Lucy Ann V, 821
Peirce, Lydia V, 911
Peirce, Lydia V, 925
Peirce, Lydia B. II, 619
Peirce, Lydia B. II, 759
Peirce, Lydia C. V, 820
Peirce, Lydia J. II, 759
Peirce, M. F. V, 761
Peirce, Maggie V, 761
Peirce, Malinda V, 820
Peirce, Manerva V, 820
Peirce, Marcey II, 618
Peirce, Margaret V, 807
Peirce, Margaret V, 811
Peirce, Margaret V, 820
Peirce, Margaret Ann V, 821
Peirce, Maria II, 806
Peirce, Maria IV, 710
Peirce, Mariam V, 592
Peirce, Martha IV, 104
Peirce, Martha IV, 781
Peirce, Martha V, 518
Peirce, Martha V, 524
Peirce, Martin Elleman V, 820
Peirce, Mary I, 1
Peirce, Mary I, 15
Peirce, Mary I, 17
Peirce, Mary I, 38
Peirce, Mary I, 68
Peirce, Mary I, 1121
Peirce, Mary I, 1130
Peirce, Mary I Sup 1, 4
Peirce, Mary I Sup 1, 5
Peirce, Mary I Sup 1, 8
Peirce, Mary II, 234
Peirce, Mary II, 249
Peirce, Mary II, 405
Peirce, Mary V, 59
Peirce, Mary V, 111
Peirce, Mary V, 524
Peirce, Mary V, 560
Peirce, Mary V, 592
Peirce, Mary V, 761
Peirce, Mary V, 807
Peirce, Mary V, 820
Peirce, Mary V, 821
Peirce, Mary V, 926
Peirce, Mary V, 931
Peirce, Mary B. V, 797
Peirce, Mary B. V, 821
Peirce, Mary Elizabeth V, 821
Peirce, Mary S. II, 908
Peirce, Mary S. II, 927
Peirce, Matilda I, 1130
Peirce, Matilda V, 821
Peirce, Maurice V, 761
Peirce, Maurice Kensel II, 814
Peirce, Melicia V, 820
Peirce, Melinda V, 761
Peirce, Melinda V, 797
Peirce, Melinda V, 820
Peirce, Mercy II, 618
Peirce, Mercy IV, 750
Peirce, Meriam I, 50
Peirce, Meriam I, 68
Peirce, Merium I, 15
Peirce, Milly V, 745
Peirce, Milly V, 792
Peirce, Milly V, 797
Peirce, Milly V, 800
Peirce, Milly V, 801
Peirce, Milly V, 811
Peirce, Milly V, 820
Peirce, Milly V, 821
Peirce, Minnie V, 761
Peirce, Miriam I, 40
Peirce, Miriam I, 49
Peirce, Miriam I, 51
Peirce, Miriam I, 68
Peirce, Miriam I, 180
Peirce, Miriam V, 524
Peirce, Moses V, 820
Peirce, Moses C. V, 820
Peirce, Moses C. V, 821
Peirce, Nathan I, 68
Peirce, Nicholas II, 405
Peirce, Noah V, 820
Peirce, Oliver II, 908
Peirce, Orean II, 814
Peirce, Oren V, 820
Peirce, Oreon II, 908
Peirce, Patrick I, 1131
Peirce, Penelope I, 90
Peirce, Phebe II, 405
Peirce, Phebe II, 619
Peirce, Phebe II, 703
Peirce, Phebe II, 743
Peirce, Phebe II, 759
Peirce, Pheriba I, 37
Peirce, Pheriba I, 68
Peirce, Priscilla II, 814
Peirce, Priscilla V, 925
Peirce, Prudence V, 820
Peirce, Rachel I, 1116
Peirce, Rachel I, 1131
Peirce, Rachel II, 619
Peirce, Rachel II, 759
Peirce, Rachel V, 761
Peirce, Rachel V, 821
Peirce, Rachel Moon II, 814
Peirce, Rebecca II, 814
Peirce, Rebecca IV, 750
Peirce, Rebecca IV, 781
Peirce, Rebecca VI, 631
Peirce, Rebecca B. II, 405
Peirce, Rebecca B. II, 715
Peirce, Rebeckah I, 68
Peirce, Rebeckah I, 85
Peirce, Rebeckah I Sup 1, 5
Peirce, Rebeckah I Sup 1, 6
Peirce, Rebekah I, 15
Peirce, Richard II, 405
Peirce, Richard II, 618
Peirce, Richard V, 111
Peirce, Richard V, 524
Peirce, Richard V, 560
Peirce, Richard V, 592
Peirce, Robert I, 1132
Peirce, Robert V, 820
Peirce, Robert, Jr. I, 1130
Peirce, Rolen Nelson V, 821
Peirce, Rosella T. V, 821
Peirce, Ruth II, 788
Peirce, Ruth II, 814
Peirce, Ruth V, 761
Peirce, Ruth V, 810
Peirce, Ruth V, 820
Peirce, Ruth V, 821
Peirce, Ruth A. II, 908
Peirce, Ruth Anna II, 856
Peirce, Ruth Anna II, 908
Peirce, Ruth S. II, 619
Peirce, Ruth S. II, 827
Peirce, Sam'l V, 800
Peirce, Samuel V, 745
Peirce, Samuel V, 761
Peirce, Samuel V, 792
Peirce, Samuel V, 797
Peirce, Samuel V, 801
Peirce, Samuel V, 811
Peirce, Samuel V, 820
Peirce, Samuel V, 821
Peirce, Samuel V, 911
Peirce, Samuel V, 925
Peirce, Samuel V, 926
Peirce, Samuel Harrison V, 820
Peirce, Samuel N. V, 925
Peirce, Samuel, Jr. V, 807
Peirce, Samuel, Jr. V, 820
Peirce, Samuel, Jr. V, 821
Peirce, Sarah I, 15
Peirce, Sarah I, 61
Peirce, Sarah I, 68
Peirce, Sarah I Sup 1, 5
Peirce, Sarah I Sup 1, 6
Peirce, Sarah Ann II, 814
Peirce, Sarah D. II, 908
Peirce, Sarah Dicks II, 814
Peirce, Sarah E. IV, 740
Peirce, Sarah H. II, 856
Peirce, Sarah H. II, 908
Peirce, Sarah Harriet II, 814
Peirce, Sarah I. II, 619
Peirce, Sarah J. II, 619
Peirce, Sarah W. II, 234
Peirce, Sarah W. II, 249
Peirce, Susan V, 761
Peirce, Sydney V, 925
Peirce, Thomas I, 15
Peirce, Thomas I, 37
Peirce, Thomas I, 50
Peirce, Thomas I, 62
Peirce, Thomas I, 68
Peirce, Thomas I, 199
Peirce, Thomas I Sup 1, 5
Peirce, Thomas II, 405
Peirce, Thomas V, 925
Peirce, Thomas, Jr. I, 68
Peirce, Thomas, Sr. I, 68
Peirce, Thos. I, 90
Peirce, Thos. I Sup 1, 6
Peirce, Thos. V, 923
Peirce, Thos. V, 925
Peirce, Walter Clarence V, 821
Peirce, Wd. Ann V, 820
Peirce, Widow Isabel I, 68
Peirce, Widow Miriam I, 49
Peirce, Widow Miriam I, 68
Peirce, William I, 199
Peirce, William E. V, 821
Peirce, William R. V, 761
Peirce, William R. V, 820
Peirce, Wm. V, 821
Peirce, Wm. C. II, 908
Peirce, Wm. C. II, 927
Peirce, Wm. D. V, 953
Peirce, Wm. D. V, 958
Peirce, Wm. R. V, 820
Peirce, Zenas V, 820
Peirce, Zenas V, 821
Peirce, Zenas Cary V, 821
Peirces, John I, 1
Peirpoint, Ann IV, 749
Peirpoint, Ann IV, 859
Peirpoint, Benjamin IV, 749
Peirpoint, Jonathan IV, 749
Peirpoint, William Obed IV, 749
Peirpoint, Wm. IV, 859
Peirpont, Sarah II, 52
Peirpont, Sarah II, 92
Peirport, Mary H. VI, 789
Peirson, David I, 864
Peirson, Elizabeth I, 834
Peirson, Elizabeth I, 864
Peirson, Elizabeth I, 1087
Peirson, George I, 566
Peirson, Hannah I, 889
Peirson, Hannah I, 897
Peirson, Hannah II, 404
Peirson, Isaac I, 864
Peirson, Isaac I, 889
Peirson, Isaac I, 897
Peirson, Isaac I, 1087
Peirson, Nathan I, 864
Peirson, Nathan I, 1087
Peirson, Phebe I, 389
Peirson, Phebe I, 863
Peirson, Phebe I, 1087
Peirson, Rebecca I, 864
Peirson, Samuel I, 389
Peirson, Samuel I, 413
Peirson, Samuel I, 863
Peirson, Samuel I, 1087
Peirson, Sarah I, 897
Peirson, Solomon I, 864
Peirson, Thomas I, 897
Peirson, William I, 864
Peirson, William I, 1087
Peitsel, George VI, 977
Peitsel, Polly VI, 977
Peitsmeyer, Abigail V, 270
Peitsmeyer, Albertine IV, 1111
Peitsmeyer, Albertine V, 463
Peitsmeyer, Anna V, 270
Peitsmeyer, Anna J. V, 463
Peitsmeyer, Anna Jane V, 270
Peitsmeyer, Anne V, 463
Peitsmeyer, Carrie S. V, 110
Peitsmeyer, Charles V, 110
Peitsmeyer, Charles V, 270
Peitsmeyer, Charles G. V, 463
Peitsmeyer, Chas. V, 463
Peitsmeyer, Chas. Eugene V, 463
Peitsmeyer, Christian V, 270
Peitsmeyer, Christian V, 463
Peitsmeyer, Edward V, 270
Peitsmeyer, Eliza V, 463
Peitsmeyer, Eliza L. V, 270
Peitsmeyer, Eliza Louisa V, 110
Peitsmeyer, Eliza O. V, 463
Peitsmeyer, Eliza Olivia V, 2
Peitsmeyer, Elizabeth H. V, 4
Peitsmeyer, Elizabeth Hannah V, 270
Peitsmeyer, Elma L. V, 110
Peitsmeyer, Emma V, 463
Peitsmeyer, Ernest V, 463
Peitsmeyer, Gilbert C. V, 463
Peitsmeyer, Grace A. V, 463
Peitsmeyer, Grace Amy V, 27
Peitsmeyer, Gulielma V, 110
Peitsmeyer, Gulielma M. V, 2
Peitsmeyer, Hattie E. V, 463
Peitsmeyer, Isaac V, 270
Peitsmeyer, Isaac C. V, 463
Peitsmeyer, Joseph V, 270
Peitsmeyer, Joseph V, 463
Peitsmeyer, Joseph M. V, 463
Peitsmeyer, Joseph Morse V,
Peitsmeyer, Louisa V, 463
Peitsmeyer, Louisa A. V, 463
Peitsmeyer, Louiza V, 270
Peitsmeyer, Martha V, 270
Peitsmeyer, Mary V, 463
Peitsmeyer, Mary E. V, 463
Peitsmeyer, Mary Esther V, 2
Peitsmeyer, Mattie V, 463
Peitsmeyer, Nancy Dunhue V, 463
Peitsmeyer, Otto V, 270
Peitsmeyer, Otto V, 463
Peitsmeyer, Sallie M. V, 110
Peitsmire, Albertine IV, 1111
Peitsmyer, Charles V, 354
Peitsmyer, Chas. V, 358
Peitsmyer, Christian V, 354
Peitsmyer, Edith V, 271
Peitsmyer, Eliza L. V, 271
Peitsmyer, Gulielma V, 271
Peitsmyer, Gulielma V, 358
Peitsmyer, Gulielma M. V, 35
Peitsmyer, Jane V, 271
Peitsmyer, Joseph V, 271
Peitsmyer, Kite V, 271
Peitsmyer, Louisa V, 354
Peitsmyer, Miriam V, 271
Peitsmyer, Rebekah V, 271
Peitsmyer, Stephen V, 271
Peitsmyer, Thomas V, 271
Peitsmyer, Whittier V, 271
Peitzmeyer, Gulielma V, 110
Pelham, Martha II, 490
Pelham, Martha II, 619
Pell, ??? III, 88
Pell, ??? III, 173
Pell, ??? III, 252
Pell, Aaron III, 252
Pell, Abraham III, 252
Pell, Ann III, 433
Pell, Barney III, 252
Pell, Benjamin III, 252
Pell, Benjamin III, 433
Pell, Benjamin III, 453
Pell, Caleb III, 252
Pell, Cornelia III, 88
Pell, Cornelia III, 252
Pell, Edward H. III, 252
Pell, Edward Howland III, 25
Pell, Elijah III, 87
Pell, Elijah III, 252
Pell, Elizabeth III, 252
Pell, Ferris III, 252
Pell, Gilbert III, 252
Pell, Gilbert Titus III, 252
Pell, Hannah III, 428
Pell, Hannah III, 430
Pell, Hannah III, 433
Pell, Henry I, 932
Pell, Henry J. I, 932
Pell, Henry J. I, 947
Pell, Isaiah III, 252
Pell, John H. III, 252
Pell, Joshua III, 433
Pell, Josiah III, 252
Pell, Lettie I, 932
Pell, Mary III, 87
Pell, Mary III, 252
Pell, Mary III, 383
Pell, Mary III, 433
Pell, Mary III, 453
Pell, Mary C. III, 252
Pell, Mary E. III, 252
Pell, Mary R. III, 173
Pell, Mary R. III, 252
Pell, Phebe III, 252
Pell, Phebe III, 433
Pell, Philip III, 428
Pell, Philip III, 430
Pell, Philip III, 433
Pell, Rebecca III, 252

ands III, 252
arah III, 252
usan III, 252
usan F. III, 252
usan Rebecca III, 252
usannah III, 252
homas III, 433
Vm. Henry I, 897
, James II, 622
James II, 691
, Mary II, 622
Mary II, 691
, ??? IV, 861
Abel IV, 53
Abel John IV, 880
Albert IV, 1179
Albert IV, 1289
, Allen IV, 1179
Ann IV, 880
Catherine IV, 1289
Eleanor IV, 53
, Eleanor IV, 875
Eleanor IV, 880
Elisha IV, 1179
Elizabeth IV, 53
, Elizabeth IV, 880
, Emmett IV, 1289
Evaline IV, 1289
Frances IV, 1289
, Francis IV, 53
, Francis IV, 880
Francis IV, 894
George IV, 1179
George IV, 1289
, Harrison IV, 1179
, John IV, 53
Joseph IV, 880
Joseph IV, 894
, Katherine IV, 1289
, Laura IV, 1289
Lorenzo IV, 880
Mary IV, 53
, Mary IV, 875
, Mary IV, 880
, Mary IV, 894
Mary Elanor IV, 1179
Mary Ellen IV, 1179
, Matilda IV, 880
, Rachel IV, 880
Salathiel IV, 1179
Sarah IV, 894
, Sarah IV, 1179
, Sarah IV, 1289
Seth IV, 1179
Uniay IV, 1179
, Unity IV, 262
Unity IV, 1179
Vincent IV, 880
er, Abbey S. III, 252
er, Carrie Louise III, 175
er, Carrie Louise III, 253
er, Eugene A. III, 252
er, Hartley G. III, 175
er, Hartley G. III, 252
er, Hartley G. III, 253
, Abel IV, 651
, Abel J. IV, 871
, Abel J. IV, 880
, Abel John IV, 219
, Abel John IV, 262
, Abel John IV, 880
, Albert IV, 1179
, Allen IV, 880
, Allen IV, 1179
, Ann IV, 880
, Anne IV, 880
, Anne IV, 881
, Eleanor IV, 651
, Eleanor IV, 880
, Elisha IV, 880
, Elisha IV, 1179
, Elizabeth IV, 651
, Elizabeth IV, 873
, Elizabeth IV, 880
, Francis IV, 262
, Francis IV, 651
, Francis IV, 873
, Francis IV, 880
, George IV, 880
, George IV, 1179
, Harrison IV, 880
, Harrison IV, 1179
, John IV, 651
, Joseph IV, 880
, Joseph IV, 893
, Katharine IV, 1280
, Lorenzo IV, 880
, Mary IV, 262
, Mary IV, 651
, Mary IV, 873
, Mary IV, 880
Pellett, Mary Elanor IV, 1179
Pellett, Mary Eleanor IV, 880
Pellett, Mary Ellen IV, 880
Pellett, Mary Ellen IV, 1179
Pellett, Matilda IV, 880
Pellett, Rachel IV, 878
Pellett, Rachel IV, 880
Pellett, Salathiel IV, 880
Pellett, Salathiel IV, 1179
Pellett, Sarah IV, 872
Pellett, Sarah IV, 880
Pellett, Sarah IV, 893
Pellett, Sarah IV, 894
Pellett, Sarah IV, 1179
Pellett, Seth IV, 880
Pellett, Seth IV, 1179
Pellett, Uniay IV, 1179
Pellett, Unity IV, 219
Pellett, Unity IV, 262
Pellett, Unity IV, 871
Pellett, Unity IV, 880
Pellett, Unity IV, 1179
Pellett, Vincent IV, 880
Pellette, Francis IV, 880
Pellette, Lorenzo IV, 880
Pellette, Mary IV, 880
Pellette, Matilda IV, 880
Pellit, Albert IV, 1289
Pellott, Joseph IV, 837
Pellott, Mary IV, 837
Pellott, Sarah IV, 837
Pellowe, Helen III, 151
Pellowe, Helen III, 253
Pellowe, William III, 151
Pellowe, William III, 253
Pellowe, William H. III, 151
Pellowe, William H. III, 253
Pelmer, Abigail IV, 258
Pelmer, Abigail IV, 306
Pelo, Dorothy E. IV, 749
Pelo, Dorothy Elizabeth IV, 749
Pelo, Essie IV, 749
Pelo, Hervey IV, 749
Pelo, James IV, 749
Pelo, Mrs. ??? IV, 749
Pelo, Mrs. Elsie IV, 749
Pelo, Richard N. IV, 749
Pelo, Richard Nelson IV, 749
Pelo, Ruth Janet IV, 749
Pelo, Sarah IV, 749
Pelt, Anna IV, 1260
Pelt, Anna W. IV, 492
Pelt, Anna W. IV, 1260
Pelt, Annie M. IV, 1260
Pelt, C. R. I, 315
Pelt, Elma IV, 1260
Pelt, Henry I, 315
Pelt, Mary Elma IV, 1260
Pelt, Polly I, 315
Pelt, R. A. I, 315
Pelt, Robert IV, 1260
Pelt, Robert A. IV, 262
Pelt, S. H. I, 315
Pelt, William T. I, 315
Pelter, Kate VI, 429
Pelter, Kate VI, 439
Pelter, Kater VI, 422
Pelter, Kater VI, 439
Pelter, Nancy VI, 977
Pelter, Peter VI, 977
Pelter, Phineas S. VI, 429
Pemb, Elizabeth Mary II, 364
Pemberton, ??? V, 795
Pemberton, ??? V, 800
Pemberton, Abigail II, 1006
Pemberton, Abigail II, 1021
Pemberton, Albert V, 762
Pemberton, Albert L. IV, 985
Pemberton, Albert Lindley IV, 985
Pemberton, Albert Lindley IV, 1013
Pemberton, Alders V, 762
Pemberton, Alice II, 249
Pemberton, Alice II, 1002
Pemberton, Alice II, 1021
Pemberton, Alta V, 762
Pemberton, Amy E. V, 762
Pemberton, Ann I, 1023
Pemberton, Ann I, 1036
Pemberton, Ann I, 1038
Pemberton, Ann II, 405
Pemberton, Ann II, 528
Pemberton, Ann II, 619
Pemberton, Ann II, 620
Pemberton, Ann V, 804
Pemberton, Ann V, 821
Pemberton, Ann, Jr. II, 620
Pemberton, Anna V, 821
Pemberton, Anna B. V, 762
Pemberton, Anna Mary V, 762
Pemberton, Anne I, 1036
Pemberton, Anne V, 810
Pemberton, Benj. Aldus V, 762
Pemberton, Benj. Y. V, 762
Pemberton, Bertha H. IV, 985
Pemberton, Caroline T. II, 893
Pemberton, Caroline T. II, 908
Pemberton, Charles II, 405
Pemberton, Charles II, 527
Pemberton, Charles II, 555
Pemberton, Charles II, 619
Pemberton, Charles II, 620
Pemberton, Charles V, 762
Pemberton, Clara V, 354
Pemberton, Clara V, 425
Pemberton, Clarence V, 762
Pemberton, Clarence Leland IV, 985
Pemberton, Cyrus L. IV, 985
Pemberton, David V, 761
Pemberton, David V, 762
Pemberton, David V, 821
Pemberton, Dorcas M. Arvilla V, 761
Pemberton, Dorcas P. V, 762
Pemberton, Dorothy Mabel IV, 985
Pemberton, Dorsey E. V, 762
Pemberton, Drucilla V, 800
Pemberton, Drucilla V, 812
Pemberton, Drusilla V, 736
Pemberton, Drusilla V, 761
Pemberton, Drusilla V, 762
Pemberton, Drusilla V, 806
Pemberton, Drusilla V, 821
Pemberton, Ealse II, 1021
Pemberton, Earl Othel IV, 985
Pemberton, Elijah V, 801
Pemberton, Elijah V, 821
Pemberton, Elizabeth I, 1023
Pemberton, Elizabeth I, 1036
Pemberton, Elizabeth II, 405
Pemberton, Elizabeth II, 619
Pemberton, Elizabeth II, 620
Pemberton, Elizabeth V, 110
Pemberton, Elizabeth V, 736
Pemberton, Elizabeth V, 739
Pemberton, Elizabeth V, 761
Pemberton, Elizabeth V, 762
Pemberton, Elizabeth V, 767
Pemberton, Elizabeth V, 768
Pemberton, Elizabeth V, 769
Pemberton, Elizabeth V, 813
Pemberton, Elizabeth V, 821
Pemberton, Elizabeth VI, 845
Pemberton, Elma J. V, 762
Pemberton, Elma S. IV, 985
Pemberton, Elmer Lemuel IV, 985
Pemberton, Elmer Lloyd IV, 985
Pemberton, Enos V, 761
Pemberton, Enos V, 762
Pemberton, Enos V, 821
Pemberton, Esther II, 405
Pemberton, Esther II, 527
Pemberton, Esther II, 555
Pemberton, Esther II, 619
Pemberton, Esther II, 620
Pemberton, Esther V, 110
Pemberton, Esther V, 761
Pemberton, Esther V, 762
Pemberton, Esther V, 767
Pemberton, Esther V, 769
Pemberton, Esther V, 821
Pemberton, Esther, Jr. II, 619
Pemberton, Eunice V, 733
Pemberton, Eunice V, 761
Pemberton, Eunice V, 810
Pemberton, Eunice V, 820
Pemberton, Eunice V, 821
Pemberton, Eunice Anna V, 821
Pemberton, Fannie J. V, 801
Pemberton, George I, 1023
Pemberton, George I, 1036
Pemberton, Ginsey V, 761
Pemberton, H. Elmer V, 704
Pemberton, Hannah I, 1023
Pemberton, Hannah I, 1036
Pemberton, Hannah II, 405
Pemberton, Hannah II, 583
Pemberton, Hannah II, 604
Pemberton, Hannah II, 613
Pemberton, Hannah II, 619
Pemberton, Hannah II, 697
Pemberton, Hannah V, 821
Pemberton, Hannah VI, 845
Pemberton, Harry IV, 1289
Pemberton, Helen V, 762
Pemberton, Helen Mae IV, 985
Pemberton, Henry II, 893
Pemberton, Henry II, 908
Pemberton, Henry III, 253
Pemberton, Henry V, 761
Pemberton, Henry, Jr. II, 893
Pemberton, Henry, Jr. II, 908
Pemberton, Hester II, 405
Pemberton, Irena M. IV, 985
Pemberton, Isa V, 767
Pemberton, Isaac V, 761
Pemberton, Isaac V, 762
Pemberton, Isaac V, 807
Pemberton, Isaac V, 821
Pemberton, Isaiah I, 1023
Pemberton, Isaiah I, 1036
Pemberton, Isaiah V, 110
Pemberton, Isaiah V, 760
Pemberton, Isaiah V, 761
Pemberton, Isaiah V, 762
Pemberton, Isaiah V, 811
Pemberton, Isaiah V, 813
Pemberton, Isaiah V, 821
Pemberton, Isaiah, Jr. I, 1036
Pemberton, Isaiah, Jr. V, 762
Pemberton, Isiah I, 1023
Pemberton, Isiah I, 1036
Pemberton, Israel II, 249
Pemberton, Israel II, 262
Pemberton, Israel II, 405
Pemberton, Israel II, 528
Pemberton, Israel II, 571
Pemberton, Israel II, 583
Pemberton, Israel II, 619
Pemberton, Israel II, 630
Pemberton, Israel II, 633
Pemberton, Israel II, 697
Pemberton, Israel II, 1007
Pemberton, Israel II, 1021
Pemberton, Israel, Jr. II, 405
Pemberton, Israel, Jr. II, 619
Pemberton, James II, 249
Pemberton, James II, 262
Pemberton, James II, 405
Pemberton, James II, 583
Pemberton, James II, 603
Pemberton, James II, 604
Pemberton, James II, 613
Pemberton, James II, 619
Pemberton, James II, 620
Pemberton, James VI, 845
Pemberton, James VI, 851
Pemberton, Jane II, 405
Pemberton, Jesse V, 820
Pemberton, Jesse V, 821
Pemberton, John I, 1023
Pemberton, John I, 1036
Pemberton, John II, 405
Pemberton, John II, 619
Pemberton, John II, 620
Pemberton, John II, 697
Pemberton, John V, 110
Pemberton, John V, 736
Pemberton, John V, 743
Pemberton, John V, 800
Pemberton, John V, 806
Pemberton, John V, 810
Pemberton, John V, 821
Pemberton, John E. V, 725
Pemberton, John E. V, 761
Pemberton, John E. V, 768
Pemberton, John E. V, 797
Pemberton, John E. V, 803
Pemberton, John E. V, 804
Pemberton, John E. V, 816
Pemberton, John E. V, 821
Pemberton, Joseph II, 405
Pemberton, Joseph II, 528
Pemberton, Joseph II, 577
Pemberton, Joseph II, 619
Pemberton, Joseph II, 620
Pemberton, Joseph V, 760
Pemberton, Joseph V, 761
Pemberton, Joseph V, 762
Pemberton, Joseph V, 820
Pemberton, Joseph V, 821
Pemberton, Joseph VI, 862
Pemberton, Joseph, Jr. II, 619
Pemberton, Joshua II, 405
Pemberton, Jude I, 1036
Pemberton, Judeth I, 1023
Pemberton, Julia Etta IV, 928
Pemberton, Julia Etta IV, 985
Pemberton, Julietta IV, 612
Pemberton, Julietta IV, 651
Pemberton, Kate V, 704
Pemberton, Katherine V, 679
Pemberton, Katherine V, 704
Pemberton, Kathryn V, 704
Pemberton, Lawrence II, 619
Pemberton, Lawrence Lindley IV, 985
Pemberton, Lemuel IV, 985
Pemberton, Lemuel V, 807
Pemberton, Lemuel V, 821
Pemberton, Levina VI, 862
Pemberton, Lidde I, 1036
Pemberton, Louie V, 762
Pemberton, Louisa II, 603
Pemberton, Louisa IV, 985
Pemberton, Louisa M. IV, 985
Pemberton, Luie V, 762
Pemberton, Luranah V, 821
Pemberton, Lydia V, 736
Pemberton, Lydia V, 800
Pemberton, Mahala V, 762
Pemberton, Margaret V, 821
Pemberton, Margaret F. V, 761
Pemberton, Margareta J. IV, 985
Pemberton, Mary II, 527
Pemberton, Mary II, 571
Pemberton, Mary II, 603
Pemberton, Mary II, 619
Pemberton, Mary II, 620
Pemberton, Mary II, 623
Pemberton, Mary IV, 985
Pemberton, Mary V, 110
Pemberton, Mary V, 762
Pemberton, Mary V, 807
Pemberton, Mary V, 818
Pemberton, Mary V, 821
Pemberton, Mary Ann V, 762
Pemberton, Mary E. IV, 985
Pemberton, Mary Elizabeth IV, 985
Pemberton, Mary Elizabeth IV, 1013
Pemberton, Mary M. V, 762
Pemberton, Mary P. V, 761
Pemberton, Maryan V, 761
Pemberton, Max V, 704
Pemberton, May V, 762
Pemberton, Mildred IV, 985
Pemberton, Mildred Muriel IV, 985
Pemberton, Nancy V, 812
Pemberton, Nancy V, 821
Pemberton, Nannie I, 616
Pemberton, Nannie Frazier I, 639
Pemberton, Pearl IV, 985
Pemberton, Pearl Opal IV, 985
Pemberton, Phebe II, 405
Pemberton, Phebe II, 603
Pemberton, Phebe II, 619
Pemberton, Philadelphia II, 577
Pemberton, Phineas II, 232
Pemberton, Phineas II, 249
Pemberton, Phineas II, 405
Pemberton, Phineas II, 619
Pemberton, Phineas II, 630
Pemberton, Phineas II, 952
Pemberton, Phinehas II, 1002
Pemberton, Phinehas II, 1021
Pemberton, Prudence V, 760
Pemberton, Prudence V, 761
Pemberton, Prudence V, 762
Pemberton, Prudence V, 801
Pemberton, Prudence V, 811
Pemberton, Prudence V, 820
Pemberton, Prudence V, 821
Pemberton, Rachel I, 1036
Pemberton, Rachel II, 249
Pemberton, Rachel II, 262
Pemberton, Rachel II, 405
Pemberton, Rachel II, 613
Pemberton, Rachel II, 619
Pemberton, Rachel II, 630
Pemberton, Rachel V, 760
Pemberton, Rachel V, 761
Pemberton, Rachel V, 762
Pemberton, Rachell II, 405
Pemberton, Rebecca II, 405
Pemberton, Rebecca II, 488
Pemberton, Rebecca II, 620
Pemberton, Rebecca V, 812
Pemberton, Rebecca V, 816
Pemberton, Rhoda V, 762
Pemberton, Rhoda V, 769
Pemberton, Rhoda V, 821
Pemberton, Richard I, 1023
Pemberton, Richard I, 1036
Pemberton, Richard V, 736
Pemberton, Robert V, 110
Pemberton, Robert V, 733
Pemberton, Robert V, 761
Pemberton, Robert V, 810
Pemberton, Robert V, 820
Pemberton, Robert V, 821
Pemberton, Rosa V, 762
Pemberton, Ruth I, 1023
Pemberton, Ruth I, 1036
Pemberton, Ruth I, 1038
Pemberton, Ruth V, 820
Pemberton, Ruth V, 821

Pemberton, Samuel II, 619
Pemberton, Samuel V, 818
Pemberton, Sarah I, 1023
Pemberton, Sarah I, 1036
Pemberton, Sarah I, 1038
Pemberton, Sarah II, 249
Pemberton, Sarah II, 262
Pemberton, Sarah II, 364
Pemberton, Sarah II, 405
Pemberton, Sarah II, 619
Pemberton, Sarah II, 620
Pemberton, Sarah II, 633
Pemberton, Sarah II, 1007
Pemberton, Sarah II, 1021
Pemberton, Sarah IV, 985
Pemberton, Sarah V, 725
Pemberton, Sarah V, 761
Pemberton, Sarah V, 797
Pemberton, Sarah V, 801
Pemberton, Sarah M. IV, 927
Pemberton, Sarah M. IV, 985
Pemberton, Sidney V, 820
Pemberton, Sophia V, 808
Pemberton, Susan II, 908
Pemberton, Susanna II, 405
Pemberton, Susanna V, 768
Pemberton, Susanna V, 810
Pemberton, Susannah II, 405
Pemberton, Susannah V, 743
Pemberton, Susannah V, 761
Pemberton, Susannah V, 762
Pemberton, Susannah V, 803
Pemberton, Susannah V, 804
Pemberton, Susannah V, 816
Pemberton, Susannah V, 821
Pemberton, Susannah E. V, 813
Pemberton, Susannah E. V, 821
Pemberton, Sydney V, 762
Pemberton, Sydnie V, 760
Pemberton, Tace V, 807
Pemberton, Tace V, 821
Pemberton, Temperance V, 821
Pemberton, Theoline Vera IV, 985
Pemberton, Theresa V, 762
Pemberton, Thomas I, 1023
Pemberton, Thomas I, 1036
Pemberton, Thomas II, 405
Pemberton, Thursey V, 762
Pemberton, Unice V, 821
Pemberton, Walter V, 354
Pemberton, Walter S. I, 616
Pemberton, Wd. Hannah II, 405
Pemberton, Wd. Mary II, 619
Pemberton, Weltha IV, 1289
Pemberton, William I, 1015
Pemberton, William I, 1023
Pemberton, William I, 1036
Pemberton, William V, 762
Pemberton, Wm. II, 619
Pemberton, Wm. V, 801
Pemberton, Wm. A. V, 762
Pemberton, Wm. H. V, 762
Pembleton, Harriet M. II, 707
Pembleton, Harriet M. II, 715
Pembleton, Levi II, 707
Pembleton, Levi II, 715
Pembleton, Louise II, 707
Pembleton, Louise II, 715
Pembleton, Sally IV, 1352
Pembleton, Sally IV, 1375
Pemty, Maria II, 822
Pen, Margaret I, 1113
Pen, Margaret I, 1130
Pen, Martha VI, 846
Pen, Nancy P. VI, 918
Pen, William VI, 846
Penberton, Susannah E. V, 750
Pence, Allie V, 1014
Pence, Anna V, 1014
Pence, Bertha V, 1014
Pence, Clifford V, 1014
Pence, Clifford B. V, 1014
Pence, Daniel V, 1014
Pence, Glenn V, 354
Pence, Glenn V, 366
Pence, Jocie V, 1014
Pence, Mildred V, 354
Pence, Mildred V, 366
Pence, Mildred Wright V, 354
Pence, Morgan V, 1014
Pence, Oscar V, 1014
Pencer Lawrence, Judith VI, 528
Pendarvis, John I, 1076
Pendarvis???, John I, 1076
Pendelton, Rachel VI, 846
Pendelton, Wiatt W. VI, 846
Pender, Margaret I, 413
Pender, Minnie I, 413
Pendergrass, Margaret I, 921
Pendleton, Ann E. VI, 846
Pendleton, Aunalutitia I, 101
Pendleton, Cornelia V, 922
Pendleton, Cornelia V, 926
Pendleton, David B. VI, 846
Pendleton, David V. VI, 798
Pendleton, Elisabeth I, 143
Pendleton, Elisabeth I, 160
Pendleton, Estelle III, 253
Pendleton, Estelle III, 349
Pendleton, Henry VI, 977
Pendleton, James VI, 846
Pendleton, James G. VI, 846
Pendleton, James W. VI, 846
Pendleton, Judith VI, 855
Pendleton, Lydia G. III, 349
Pendleton, Martha I, 142
Pendleton, Martha I, 160
Pendleton, Martha VI, 837
Pendleton, Mary I, 101
Pendleton, Mary I, 136
Pendleton, Mary I, 151
Pendleton, Mary I, 160
Pendleton, Mary G. VI, 846
Pendleton, Mildred Ann VI, 977
Pendleton, Nancy VI, 846
Pendleton, Nancy VI, 977
Pendleton, Nathan III, 253
Pendleton, Nathan III, 349
Pendleton, Patsey VI, 977
Pendleton, Penelope I, 143
Pendleton, Penelope I, 160
Pendleton, Philip VI, 977
Pendleton, Sarah I, 160
Pendleton, Sarah I, 164
Pendleton, Sarah I Sup 1, 8
Pendleton, Thomas I, 101
Pendleton, Thomas VI, 977
Pendleton, William VI, 846
Pendley, Ann II, 620
Pendley, Ann II, 651
Pendley, John II, 620
Pendley, Mary II, 620
Pendry, ??? I, 932
Pendry, Bertha Elsie I, 932
Pendry, Bertha P. I, 932
Pendry, Dinah I, 897
Pendry, Dinah I, 1130
Pendry, Dinah I, 1133
Pendry, Eli I, 566
Pendry, Eli I, 790
Pendry, Eli I, 897
Pendry, Elizabeth I, 833
Pendry, James I, 566
Pendry, James I, 790
Pendry, James I, 833
Pendry, Jamima I, 877
Pendry, Jamima I, 897
Pendry, Jemima I, 566
Pendry, Jemima I, 790
Pendry, Jemima I, 833
Pendry, Martha I, 897
Pendry, Ruth I, 897
Pendry, Sarah I, 566
Pendry, Sarah I, 790
Pendry, Sarah I, 833
Pendry, Sarah I, 879
Pendry, Sarah I, 897
Pendry, Sinah I, 833
Penel, Mary III, 253
Penfield, Edmund III, 383
Pengelly, Catherine Sophia Louisa Hicks II, 715
Pengelly, Catherine Sophia Louisa Hicks II, 759
Pengelly, J. L. II, 715
Penick, Catharine VI, 835
Penick, Charles VI, 818
Penick, Charles VI, 835
Penick, Charles VI, 855
Penick, Edwin VI, 818
Penick, Edwin A. VI, 855
Penick, Frances VI, 855
Penick, Rebecca VI, 818
Penick, Robert VI, 835
Penington, Abigail IV, 1375
Penington, Ann II, 967
Penington, Ann II, 979
Penington, Ann II, 1021
Penington, Daniel II, 249
Penington, Daniel II, 1021
Penington, Edward II, 235
Penington, Edward II, 249
Penington, Edward II, 405
Penington, Edward II, 967
Penington, Francis B. V, 926
Penington, Hannah II, 405
Penington, Hannah IV, 1375
Penington, Isaac II, 405
Penington, Isaac II, 967
Penington, Isaac II, 979
Penington, Isaac II, 1021
Penington, Israel IV, 1375
Penington, Jane IV, 902
Penington, Jane IV, 912
Penington, John IV, 1375
Penington, Joseph IV, 1375
Penington, Levi IV, 902
Penington, Levi IV, 912
Penington, Levi V, 926
Penington, Lydia IV, 909
Penington, Margaret II, 985
Penington, Margaret II, 1021
Penington, Martha II, 620
Penington, Martha II, 659
Penington, Mary II, 405
Penington, Mary II, 967
Penington, Mary II, 1021
Penington, Mary IV, 1375
Penington, Mary V, 926
Penington, Mary Ann IV, 910
Penington, Sarah II, 235
Penington, Sarah II, 249
Penington, Sarah II, 264
Penington, Sarah II, 967
Penington, Sarah II, 1021
Penington, Sarah Ann IV, 1211
Penington, Thomas II, 620
Penington, Thomas II, 659
Penington, Thomas II, 967
Penland, Stella V, 641
Penley, Ann II, 620
Penley, John II, 620
Penley, Mary II, 620
Penman, Thomas H. IV, 262
Penn, Abraham VI, 977
Penn, Abram VI, 977
Penn, Catharine VI, 977
Penn, Christina VI, 846
Penn, Clark VI, 977
Penn, Daniel B. VI, 846
Penn, David VI, 846
Penn, Edney VI, 977
Penn, Elisabeth J. VI, 943
Penn, Eliza E. H. VI, 846
Penn, Elizabeth II, 620
Penn, Elizabeth VI, 823
Penn, Fanny VI, 986
Penn, Frances R. VI, 977
Penn, Gabriel VI, 977
Penn, Golda IV, 492
Penn, Governor ??? II, 620
Penn, Governor William II, 405
Penn, Greenville VI, 977
Penn, Gulielma Maria II, 620
Penn, Gulielma Maria II, 652
Penn, Hannah II, 405
Penn, Hannah II, 620
Penn, James VI, 823
Penn, James VI, 977
Penn, James, Jr. VI, 845
Penn, John II, 405
Penn, Joseph VI, 977
Penn, Louie R. V, 354
Penn, Lucinda DeWitt VI, 846
Penn, Lucy VI, 846
Penn, Lucy VI, 977
Penn, Mary M. VI, 977
Penn, Matilda VI, 845
Penn, Moses VI, 977
Penn, Patsy VI, 977
Penn, Peggy VI, 977
Penn, Peter P. VI, 977
Penn, Polly VI, 977
Penn, Rebecca IV, 1131
Penn, Rebecca IV, 1137
Penn, Richard VI, 846
Penn, Richeson M. VI, 921
Penn, Richeson M. VI, 961
Penn, Robert VI, 977
Penn, Robert C. VI, 846
Penn, Robert C. VI, 986
Penn, Robert C. VI, 998
Penn, Sally VI, 977
Penn, Sarah VI, 977
Penn, Thomas II, 620
Penn, William II, 15
Penn, William II, 18
Penn, William II, 163
Penn, William II, 329
Penn, William VI, 977
Penn, Wm. II, 620
Penn, Wm. II, 652
Penncock, Sina F. IV, 705
Pennel, Abraham IV, 53
Pennel, Amos IV, 53
Pennel, Amos Cook IV, 53
Pennel, Dinah IV, 53
Pennel, Elizabeth IV, 53
Pennel, George IV, 262
Pennel, Hannah IV, 105
Pennel, Hannah VI, 603
Pennel, James M. V, 926
Pennel, James M. V, 975
Pennel, Jane IV, 40
Pennel, Jane IV, 53
Pennel, Jesse IV, 105
Pennel, Jesse VI, 429
Pennel, Jesse VI, 603
Pennel, John IV, 53
Pennel, Jonathan IV, 262
Pennel, Jonathan V, 926
Pennel, Jonathan V, 975
Pennel, Joshua IV, 40
Pennel, Joshua IV, 56
Pennel, Lewis M. V, 926
Pennel, Lewis M. V, 975
Pennel, Louis M. V, 926
Pennel, Mary IV, 105
Pennel, Mary VI, 603
Pennel, Mary Ann V, 926
Pennel, Mary Ann V, 975
Pennel, Nathan II, 797
Pennel, Rhoda IV, 356
Pennel, Rosanna IV, 262
Pennel, Rosanna V, 926
Pennel, Rosanna V, 975
Pennel, Ruth IV, 53
Pennel, Sarah IV, 53
Pennel, Sarah IV, 56
Pennel, Stephen IV, 53
Pennel, Susanna IV, 40
Pennel, Susanna IV, 588
Pennel, Susanna IV, 592
Pennel, Susannah II, 797
Pennel, Susannah IV, 56
Pennel, William IV, 429
Pennel, Wm. H. IV, 1072
Pennell, Alice III, 47
Pennell, Ann II, 620
Pennell, Anne G. II, 819
Pennell, Beulah IV, 105
Pennell, Charles Leslie II, 715
Pennell, Charles Leslie II, 759
Pennell, Clarence Edward II, 715
Pennell, Clarence Edward II, 759
Pennell, Cydney II, 908
Pennell, Cydney II, 927
Pennell, Dell II, 749
Pennell, Dell II, 759
Pennell, Eli IV, 262
Pennell, Eli V, 975
Pennell, Eliza IV, 75
Pennell, Eliza IV, 105
Pennell, Elizabeth Owens II, 715
Pennell, Elizabeth Owens II, 759
Pennell, Elizabeth P. II, 908
Pennell, Elizabeth P. II, 927
Pennell, Ely Y. IV, 262
Pennell, Esther IV, 105
Pennell, Francis W. III, 253
Pennell, G. Howard II, 715
Pennell, George IV, 105
Pennell, George IV, 262
Pennell, George W. IV, 105
Pennell, Hannah II, 722
Pennell, Hannah II, 749
Pennell, Hannah II, 759
Pennell, Hannah IV, 93
Pennell, Hannah IV, 105
Pennell, Hannah VI, 395
Pennell, Hannah VI, 429
Pennell, Hill II, 749
Pennell, Hill II, 759
Pennell, Howard L. IV, 1260
Pennell, Howard Lewis IV, 1260
Pennell, James IV, 262
Pennell, James M. IV, 262
Pennell, James M. V, 926
Pennell, James M. V, 975
Pennell, Jesse IV, 93
Pennell, Jesse IV, 105
Pennell, Jesse VI, 395
Pennell, Jesse VI, 429
Pennell, John II, 620
Pennell, Jonathan IV, 262
Pennell, Jonathan V, 975
Pennell, Joseph II, 405
Pennell, Joseph II, 620
Pennell, Joseph II, 759
Pennell, Larkin II, 759
Pennell, Lewis IV, 262
Pennell, Lewis M. V, 975
Pennell, Louise Mabel IV, 1260
Pennell, Mabel Marie IV, 1260
Pennell, Maggie B. II, 715
Pennell, Maggie B. II, 759
Pennell, Malcolm Harold IV, 1260
Pennell, Maria IV, 105
Pennell, Maria G. IV, 93
Pennell, Maria G. IV, 105
Pennell, Martha II, 620
Pennell, Mary II, 715
Pennell, Mary II, 837
Pennell, Mary II, 908
Pennell, Mary III, 253
Pennell, Mary III, 270
Pennell, Mary IV, 105
Pennell, Mary Ann IV, 262
Pennell, Mary Ann V, 975
Pennell, Mary E. II, 706
Pennell, Mary G. II, 706
Pennell, Mary L. II, 908
Pennell, Nathan II, 706
Pennell, Nathan II, 715
Pennell, Rachel II, 749
Pennell, Rachel II, 759
Pennell, Rebecca A. II, 759
Pennell, Rhoda IV, 346
Pennell, Robert II, 405
Pennell, Robert II, 908
Pennell, Robert II, 927
Pennell, Robert D. IV, 105
Pennell, Robert Dell IV, 105
Pennell, Rosanna IV, 262
Pennell, Rosanna V, 975
Pennell, Samuel F. II, 715
Pennell, Samuel F. II, 759
Pennell, Samuel Howard II,
Pennell, Sarah IV, 97
Pennell, Sarah IV, 105
Pennell, Susanna IV, 105
Pennell, Susannah IV, 105
Pennell, William IV, 105
Pennell, Wm. Dell IV, 105
Pennell, Wm. Grubb IV, 105
Pennell, Wm. H. IV, 1072
Penner, Clarence V, 692
Penner, Elizabeth V, 692
Pennett, Mable V, 1014
Pennewit, Ann VI, 429
Pennewitt, Ann VI, 424
Pennewitt, Melissa E. V, 197
Pennill, Hannah VI, 603
Pennill, Jesse VI, 603
Pennill, Joseph II, 405
Pennill, Mary VI, 603
Pennill, Robert II, 405
Penniman, A. Warren II, 869
Penniman, A. Warren II, 908
Penniman, Anson II, 869
Penniman, Anson II, 908
Penniman, Anson W. II, 869
Penniman, Anson W. II, 908
Penniman, Anson Warren II,
Penniman, Anson Warren II,
Penniman, Caroline C. II, 869
Penniman, Caroline C. II, 908
Penniman, Caroline P. II, 869
Penniman, Caroline P. II, 908
Penniman, Ellen II, 814
Penniman, Ellen M. II, 869
Penniman, Ellen M. II, 908
Penniman, Jane Whitelock, Jr. II, 908
Penniman, Jane Whitlock, Jr. II, 869
Penniman, Russell S. II, 869
Penniman, Russell S. II, 908
Penniman, Russell Sylvanus II, 814
Penningtom, Margaret IV, 358
Pennington, Abigail IV, 1375
Pennington, Alice IV, 175
Pennington, Alice IV, 262
Pennington, Alice L. IV, 262
Pennington, Ann IV, 1028
Pennington, Ann V, 97
Pennington, Ann V, 110
Pennington, Ann V, 425
Pennington, Ann V, 641
Pennington, Ann V, 975
Pennington, Anna V, 425
Pennington, Anna V, 641
Pennington, Anna M. IV, 985
Pennington, Anne II, 405
Pennington, Anne V, 397
Pennington, Anne V, 425
Pennington, Barclay IV, 1179
Pennington, Barclay IV, 1219
Pennington, Benjamin IV, 102
Pennington, Benjamin A. IV, 1289
Pennington, Benjamin F. V, 64
Pennington, Caroline IV, 1179
Pennington, Caroline V, 425
Pennington, Caroline V, 641
Pennington, Charity IV, 429
Pennington, Charity IV, 456
Pennington, Charity IV, 834
Pennington, Charity IV, 837
Pennington, Charity P. IV, 837
Pennington, Charles IV, 1289
Pennington, Chas. V, 641
Pennington, Daniel II, 1021

ngton, Deborah IV, 262
ngton, Deborah IV, 429
ngton, Deborah IV, 985
ngton, Deborah IV, 1260
ngton, Deborah V, 110
ngton, Edward II, 405
ngton, Edward II, 565
ngton, Edward II, 620
ngton, Edward II, 649
ngton, Edward II, 967
ngton, Edward V, 425
ngton, Edwin IV, 1179
ngton, Edwin IV, 1219
ngton, Edwin V, 425
ngton, Eliza IV, 429
ngton, Eliza V, 110
ngton, Eliza V, 145
ngton, Eliza V, 926
ngton, Eliza V, 975
ngton, Elizabeth I, 413
ngton, Elizabeth II, 822
ngton, Elizabeth IV, 429
ngton, Elizabeth IV, 448
ngton, Elizabeth V, 926
ngton, Ella V, 425
ngton, Emma IV, 259
ngton, Emma IV, 262
ngton, Eva IV, 262
ngton, Frances IV, 912
ngton, Frances B. IV, 837
ngton, Frances B. IV, 912
ngton, Frances B. V, 900
ngton, Frances B. V, 926
ngton, Francis B. V, 926
ngton, Frank V, 425
ngton, Fred IV, 262
ngton, Fred W. IV, 262
ngton, Hannah II, 405
ngton, Hannah IV, 1375
ngton, Hannah I. V, 388
ngton, Hannah Isabel
, 388
ngton, Hannah Isabel
425
ngton, Hannah Jane II, 833
ngton, Hannah Jane II, 908
ngton, Hazel V, 691
ngton, Hazel V, 704
ngton, Hazel L. V, 704
ngton, Helen V, 702
ngton, Helen V, 704
ngton, Helen M. VI, 731
ngton, Helen M. VI, 739
ngton, Helen M. VI, 770
ngton, Henry VI, 731
ngton, Henry VI, 770
ngton, Henry C. V, 917
ngton, Hezekiah B. IV, 837
ngton, Hezekiah B. V, 926
ngton, Hezekiah Bye
', 837
ngton, Isaac I, 413
ngton, Isaac I, 566
ngton, Isaac II, 405
ngton, Isaac II, 620
ngton, Isaac II, 649
ngton, Isaac II, 967
ngton, Isaac IV, 1179
ngton, Isaac IV, 1219
ngton, Isaac IV, 1375
ngton, Isaac VI, 34
ngton, Isaac V. V, 704
ngton, Israel II, 620
ngton, Israel IV, 1375
ngton, Jane V, 425
ngton, Jane Wilson P.
', 320
ngton, John IV, 262
ngton, John IV, 429
ngton, John IV, 985
ngton, John IV, 1260
ngton, John IV, 1375
ngton, John V, 110
ngton, John V, 425
ngton, John V, 856
ngton, John V, 926
ngton, John V, 975
ngton, John Edwin V, 641
ngton, John Henry V, 704
ngton, John, Jr. IV, 1375
ngton, Joseph IV, 262
ngton, Joseph IV, 1179
ngton, Joseph IV, 1219
ngton, Joseph IV, 1375
ngton, Josiah IV, 429
ngton, Josiah V, 110
ngton, Josiah V, 425
ngton, Laura Ann V, 704
ngton, Lee V, 641
ngton, Leroy Talbott
', 429
Pennington, Levi I, 413
Pennington, Levi I, 566
Pennington, Levi I, 833
Pennington, Levi IV, 429
Pennington, Levi IV, 837
Pennington, Levi IV, 859
Pennington, Levi IV, 911
Pennington, Levi IV, 912
Pennington, Levi V, 425
Pennington, Levi V, 917
Pennington, Levi V, 926
Pennington, Levi Miller, Jr.
IV, 749
Pennington, Levi T. IV, 259
Pennington, Levi T. IV, 262
Pennington, Levi T. IV, 985
Pennington, Levi Talbot V, 110
Pennington, Levi, Jr. I, 413
Pennington, Lewis IV, 1179
Pennington, Lewis IV, 1219
Pennington, Lucretia M. IV, 1289
Pennington, Lydia IV, 837
Pennington, Lydia IV, 912
Pennington, Lydia IV, 1028
Pennington, Lydia IV, 1029
Pennington, Lydia IV, 1289
Pennington, Lydia V, 420
Pennington, Lydia V, 425
Pennington, Lydia Jane V, 425
Pennington, Margaret IV, 346
Pennington, Margaret IV, 352
Pennington, Margaret Ann V, 704
Pennington, Margaret W. V, 957
Pennington, Maria IV, 837
Pennington, Maria IV, 1179
Pennington, Maria IV, 1215
Pennington, Maria IV, 1219
Pennington, Maria IV, 1239
Pennington, Maria IV, 1289
Pennington, Maria IV, 1300
Pennington, Mariah IV, 741
Pennington, Mariah IV, 749
Pennington, Mariah IV, 834
Pennington, Mariah IV, 837
Pennington, Martha I, 413
Pennington, Martha I, 566
Pennington, Martha I, 664
Pennington, Martha II, 620
Pennington, Martha IV, 834
Pennington, Martha IV, 837
Pennington, Martha IV, 911
Pennington, Martha E. V, 641
Pennington, Martha Elma V, 425
Pennington, Mary I, 390
Pennington, Mary I, 413
Pennington, Mary II, 405
Pennington, Mary II, 620
Pennington, Mary II, 654
Pennington, Mary IV, 429
Pennington, Mary IV, 837
Pennington, Mary IV, 911
Pennington, Mary IV, 912
Pennington, Mary IV, 1375
Pennington, Mary IV, 1379
Pennington, Mary V, 110
Pennington, Mary V, 425
Pennington, Mary V, 704
Pennington, Mary V, 926
Pennington, Mary Ann IV, 837
Pennington, Mary Ann IV, 912
Pennington, Mary Anna IV, 1289
Pennington, Mary C. V, 641
Pennington, Mary E. V, 425
Pennington, Mary Elizabeth
IV, 1289
Pennington, Mary Elizabeth
V, 425
Pennington, Mary Engle VI, 770
Pennington, Mary Graham
V, 425
Pennington, Mary Grave I, 413
Pennington, Nancy V, 425
Pennington, Nancy E. V, 641
Pennington, Nancy Emma V, 425
Pennington, Nora V, 592
Pennington, Parker V, 197
Pennington, Paul V, 110
Pennington, Paul V, 957
Pennington, Rachel I, 566
Pennington, Rachel IV, 429
Pennington, Rachel V, 110
Pennington, Rebecca IV, 985
Pennington, Rebecca IV, 1260
Pennington, Rebecca W. IV, 262
Pennington, Reverence V, 197
Pennington, Robert IV, 1179
Pennington, Robert IV, 1219
Pennington, Robert V, 975
Pennington, Robert M. V, 926
Pennington, Robert Morris V, 110
Pennington, Roscor V, 704
Pennington, Rowena B. V, 197
Pennington, Ruth Ann V, 704
Pennington, Ruth Anna V, 704
Pennington, S. E. IV, 1239
Pennington, Samuel IV, 1289
Pennington, Samuel C. IV, 1289
Pennington, Samuel C. IV, 1300
Pennington, Samuel Edwin
IV, 1239
Pennington, Samuel Edwin
IV, 1289
Pennington, Sarah I, 373
Pennington, Sarah I, 413
Pennington, Sarah II, 405
Pennington, Sarah II, 565
Pennington, Sarah II, 620
Pennington, Sarah II, 649
Pennington, Sarah II, 967
Pennington, Sarah IV, 837
Pennington, Sarah IV, 1179
Pennington, Sarah IV, 1219
Pennington, Sarah V, 917
Pennington, Sarah V, 926
Pennington, Sarah Ann IV, 1179
Pennington, Sarah B. IV, 837
Pennington, Sarah Briban
VI, 731
Pennington, Sarah Briban
VI, 770
Pennington, Sarah M. V, 704
Pennington, Sina V, 532
Pennington, Sina Stoops V, 704
Pennington, Stanley V, 691
Pennington, Stanley V, 704
Pennington, Stephen P. V, 592
Pennington, Susanna V, 110
Pennington, Susannah IV, 429
Pennington, Talbert IV, 429
Pennington, Thomas II, 620
Pennington, William IV, 837
Pennington, William V, 425
Pennington, William K. IV, 1179
Pennington, William R. V, 425
Pennington, Wm. II, 620
Pennington, Wm. IV, 1219
Pennington, Wm. V, 641
Pennington, Wm. R. V, 425
Pennington, Wm. R. V, 641
Pennock, ??? VI, 348
Pennock, Abraham II, 620
Pennock, Abraham L. II, 715
Pennock, Abraham Liddon
II, 405
Pennock, Abraham Liddon
II, 620
Pennock, Alice IV, 749
Pennock, Alice VI, 352
Pennock, Alice VI, 354
Pennock, Ann IV, 750
Pennock, Ann E. IV, 750
Pennock, Annie H. II, 890
Pennock, Annie H. II, 909
Pennock, Caleb IV, 692
Pennock, Caspar Wistar II, 405
Pennock, Cynthia IV, 911
Pennock, Cynthia IV, 912
Pennock, Cynthia IV, 1111
Pennock, David IV, 912
Pennock, David IV, 1111
Pennock, David IV, 1140
Pennock, Deborah II, 620
Pennock, Dinah IV, 912
Pennock, E. Eldridge II, 715
Pennock, Elin IV, 912
Pennock, Elisabeth II, 620
Pennock, Elisabeth II, 685
Pennock, Elizabeth II, 405
Pennock, Elizabeth II, 406
Pennock, Elizabeth II, 620
Pennock, Elizabeth II, 685
Pennock, Elizabeth IV, 711
Pennock, Elizabeth IV, 749
Pennock, Elizabeth IV, 750
Pennock, Elizabeth IV, 837
Pennock, Elizabeth IV, 838
Pennock, Elizabeth IV, 912
Pennock, Elizabeth IV, 1290
Pennock, Elizabeth Ellen IV, 749
Pennock, Elizabeth H. IV, 750
Pennock, Elizabeth T. II, 890
Pennock, Elizabeth T. II, 909
Pennock, Elon IV, 1111
Pennock, Emeline IV, 1025
Pennock, Emeline IV, 1029
Pennock, Esther II, 816
Pennock, Eunice IV, 943
Pennock, George II, 405
Pennock, George II, 406
Pennock, George II, 620
Pennock, George W. II, 909
Pennock, Gilpin S. II, 909
Pennock, Gilpin Stubbs II, 814
Pennock, Grace IV, 912
Pennock, Hanna IV, 512
Pennock, Hannah II, 405
Pennock, Hannah II, 828
Pennock, Hannah IV, 29
Pennock, Hannah IV, 53
Pennock, Hannah IV, 651
Pennock, Hannah IV, 728
Pennock, Hannah IV, 749
Pennock, Hannah IV, 750
Pennock, Hannah IV, 837
Pennock, Hannah IV, 838
Pennock, Hannah IV, 909
Pennock, Hannah IV, 912
Pennock, Hannah VI, 335
Pennock, Hannah VI, 352
Pennock, Hannah VI, 354
Pennock, Hannah, Jr. IV, 912
Pennock, Isaac IV, 749
Pennock, Isaac IV, 750
Pennock, Isaac W. II, 620
Pennock, Isaac W. IV, 750
Pennock, Isabella II, 405
Pennock, Isabella L. II, 620
Pennock, J. Thompson II, 814
Pennock, J. Thompson II, 909
Pennock, Jacob IV, 1111
Pennock, James IV, 750
Pennock, James Stevens II, 620
Pennock, Jane IV, 749
Pennock, Jane IV, 832
Pennock, Jane IV, 837
Pennock, Jane IV, 909
Pennock, Jane VI, 354
Pennock, John II, 405
Pennock, John II, 406
Pennock, John IV, 651
Pennock, John IV, 663
Pennock, John IV, 748
Pennock, John IV, 749
Pennock, John IV, 750
Pennock, John IV, 837
Pennock, John IV, 838
Pennock, John VI, 335
Pennock, John VI, 352
Pennock, John VI, 354
Pennock, John Pim IV, 837
Pennock, John Pim IV, 838
Pennock, John Pim IV, 1290
Pennock, John Sellers II, 620
Pennock, John, Jr. IV, 750
Pennock, John, Jr. IV, 837
Pennock, Jonathan IV, 912
Pennock, Jonathan IV, 1111
Pennock, Joseph II, 406
Pennock, Joseph II, 620
Pennock, Joseph II, 715
Pennock, Joseph IV, 29
Pennock, Joseph IV, 53
Pennock, Joseph IV, 859
Pennock, Joseph IV, 909
Pennock, Joseph IV, 911
Pennock, Joseph IV, 912
Pennock, Joseph Liddon II, 620
Pennock, Joseph Siddon II, 405
Pennock, Joshua IV, 837
Pennock, Judith IV, 123
Pennock, Judith IV, 131
Pennock, Levis II, 890
Pennock, Levis II, 909
Pennock, Lewis T. II, 909
Pennock, Lydia II, 715
Pennock, Lydia IV, 749
Pennock, Lydia IV, 750
Pennock, Lydia IV, 837
Pennock, Lydia IV, 838
Pennock, Lydia Maria IV, 837
Pennock, Lydia Maria IV, 1290
Pennock, Mary II, 405
Pennock, Mary II, 406
Pennock, Mary II, 620
Pennock, Mary IV, 131
Pennock, Mary IV, 651
Pennock, Mary IV, 689
Pennock, Mary IV, 692
Pennock, Mary IV, 728
Pennock, Mary IV, 749
Pennock, Mary IV, 781
Pennock, Mary VI, 354
Pennock, Mary VI, 757
Pennock, Mary VI, 770
Pennock, Mary Ann IV, 748
Pennock, Mary Ann IV, 749
Pennock, Mary C. IV, 937
Pennock, Mary Coleman II, 620
Pennock, Mary H. II, 909
Pennock, Mary J. IV, 1041
Pennock, Mary Phebe Jane
VI, 335
Pennock, Mary W. II, 814
Pennock, Mary W. II, 908
Pennock, Mary W. II, 909
Pennock, Mary, Jr. IV, 749
Pennock, Mary, Jr. VI, 354
Pennock, Matilda IV, 1111
Pennock, Matilda IV, 1128
Pennock, Matilda IV, 1140
Pennock, Morris C. IV, 750
Pennock, Morris E. IV, 837
Pennock, Moses IV, 123
Pennock, Moses IV, 131
Pennock, Moses IV, 749
Pennock, Moses VI, 335
Pennock, Moses VI, 354
Pennock, Nathaniel VI, 757
Pennock, Nathaniel VI, 770
Pennock, Phebe II, 708
Pennock, Phebe IV, 174
Pennock, Phebe IV, 262
Pennock, Phebe IV, 749
Pennock, Phebe IV, 781
Pennock, Phebe IV, 798
Pennock, Phebe IV, 837
Pennock, Phebe VI, 354
Pennock, Philena II, 909
Pennock, Philena C. II, 909
Pennock, Priscilla IV, 53
Pennock, Priscilla IV, 56
Pennock, Rachel II, 822
Pennock, Rachel IV, 837
Pennock, Rachel IV, 838
Pennock, Rachel IV, 985
Pennock, Rachel IV, 1290
Pennock, Rachel Maston IV, 985
Pennock, Rachel P. IV, 750
Pennock, Rebecca IV, 837
Pennock, Rebecca IV, 912
Pennock, Rebecca IV, 1111
Pennock, Rebecca IV, 1140
Pennock, Robert L. II, 814
Pennock, Robert L. II, 909
Pennock, Ruth IV, 912
Pennock, Ruth IV, 915
Pennock, Samuel II, 405
Pennock, Samuel II, 406
Pennock, Samuel II, 620
Pennock, Samuel II, 685
Pennock, Samuel IV, 749
Pennock, Samuel IV, 750
Pennock, Samuel J. II, 890
Pennock, Samuel J. II, 909
Pennock, Sarah II, 405
Pennock, Sarah II, 620
Pennock, Sarah II, 642
Pennock, Sarah II, 715
Pennock, Sarah IV, 615
Pennock, Sarah IV, 651
Pennock, Sarah IV, 663
Pennock, Sarah IV, 692
Pennock, Sarah IV, 741
Pennock, Sarah IV, 749
Pennock, Sarah IV, 750
Pennock, Sarah IV, 785
Pennock, Sarah IV, 837
Pennock, Sarah IV, 838
Pennock, Sarah IV, 941
Pennock, Sarah IV, 1017
Pennock, Sarah VI, 757
Pennock, Sarah VI, 770
Pennock, Sarah S. IV, 837
Pennock, Sarah Savory IV, 1290
Pennock, Sarah W. II, 620
Pennock, Sidney IV, 750
Pennock, Sidney IV, 837
Pennock, Sidney IV, 838
Pennock, Sina F. IV, 750
Pennock, Susanna C. II, 909
Pennock, Susannah C. II, 814
Pennock, Susannah C. II, 909
Pennock, Sydney IV, 750
Pennock, Thamazin II, 794
Pennock, Thomas IV, 837
Pennock, Thomas IV, 1290
Pennock, Thomas Elwood
IV, 1290
Pennock, Thos. IV, 838
Pennock, Thosl IV, 838
Pennock, Tolman II, 620
Pennock, Walker C. II, 909
Pennock, Wd. Mary Emma
II, 814
Pennock, William IV, 651
Pennock, William IV, 749
Pennock, William VI, 335
Pennock, William VI, 352
Pennock, William VI, 354
Pennock, William E. II, 814
Pennock, William Elizabeth
VI, 354
Pennock, William, Jr. IV, 750
Pennock, William, Jr. VI, 354

Pennock, Wm. IV, 131
Pennock, Wm. IV, 728
Pennock, Wm. IV, 781
Pennock, Wm. E. II, 814
Pennock, Wm. E. II, 908
Pennock, Wm. Edward II, 909
Pennock, Wm. F. II, 909
Pennock, Wm. Sallway II, 620
Pennock, Wm. Salway II, 620
Pennocl, Alice VI, 335
Pennocl, Mary VI, 335
Pennran, Thomas H. IV, 262
Pennrose, ??? IV, 1125
Penny, Esther I, 1062
Penny, Esther I, 1063
Penny, Joseph I, 1063
Penny, Lydia I, 1063
Penny, Mary II, 298
Penny, Mary III, 253
Penny, Richard I, 1063
Pennywit, Ann VI, 429
Pennywit, Mary VI, 424
Pennywit, Mary VI, 429
Penock, Cynthia IV, 912
Penock, David IV, 912
Penock, Elin IV, 912
Penock, Elizabeth IV, 912
Penock, Grace IV, 912
Penock, Hannah IV, 912
Penock, Jonathan IV, 912
Penock, Joseph II, 620
Penock, Rebecca IV, 912
Penquite, Esther VI, 687
Penquite, Mary II, 249
Penquite, Mary II, 278
Penrod, Justin G. IV, 1333
Penrod, Justus G. IV, 1333
Penros, Benjamin IV, 912
Penros, John IV, 912
Penros, William IV, 912
Penrose, ??? III, 253
Penrose, ??? IV, 1085
Penrose, ???ildred IV, 1083
Penrose, A. Elizabeth IV, 1072
Penrose, Abraham IV, 105
Penrose, Abraham VI, 603
Penrose, Adaline IV, 1090
Penrose, Adaline M. IV, 1072
Penrose, Adaline W. IV, 1111
Penrose, Albert IV, 346
Penrose, Albert IV, 1072
Penrose, Alice W. II, 878
Penrose, Alice W. II, 909
Penrose, Alton W. IV, 1072
Penrose, Ann IV, 105
Penrose, Ann IV, 346
Penrose, Ann IV, 1072
Penrose, Ann IV, 1179
Penrose, Ann Elizabeth IV, 429
Penrose, Ann Elizabeth IV, 1072
Penrose, Ann Elizabeth IV, 1077
Penrose, Ann Elizabeth IV, 1111
Penrose, Ann Elizabeth IV, 1137
Penrose, Anna IV, 469
Penrose, Anna IV, 492
Penrose, Anna IV, 1067
Penrose, Anna IV, 1072
Penrose, Annah II, 798
Penrose, Barclay IV, 429
Penrose, Barclay IV, 592
Penrose, Barclay IV, 1072
Penrose, Barclay IV, 1073
Penrose, Barclay IV, 1131
Penrose, Barclay IV, 1137
Penrose, Benjamin IV, 105
Penrose, Benjamin IV, 912
Penrose, Benjamin VI, 603
Penrose, Charles IV, 1072
Penrose, Charles IV, 1073
Penrose, Christopher II, 620
Penrose, Clarkson T. IV, 1072
Penrose, Clarkson T. IV, 1106
Penrose, Clarkson T. IV, 1111
Penrose, Daniel Dalbey II, 814
Penrose, Deborah Jane IV, 1067
Penrose, Deborah Jane IV, 1073
Penrose, Edith IV, 985
Penrose, Edwin IV, 262
Penrose, Edwin IV, 346
Penrose, Edwin IV, 352
Penrose, Edwin IV, 429
Penrose, Edwin IV, 1179
Penrose, Eliza IV, 346
Penrose, Eliza IV, 1179
Penrose, Eliza Ann IV, 1179
Penrose, Eliza Jane IV, 1129
Penrose, Eliza Jane IV, 1137
Penrose, Elizabeth IV, 1072
Penrose, Elizabeth IV, 1073
Penrose, Elizabeth IV, 1090
Penrose, Elizabeth IV, 1128
Penrose, Elizabeth IV, 1137
Penrose, Elizabeth Corbit II, 798
Penrose, Elizabeth L. IV, 1051
Penrose, Elizabeth L. IV, 1073
Penrose, Elizabeth L. IV, 1137
Penrose, Elizabeth S. IV, 1072
Penrose, Elizabeth S. IV, 1073
Penrose, Elizabeth S. IV, 1084
Penrose, Ella II, 814
Penrose, Ellen S. II, 782
Penrose, Ellen W. II, 837
Penrose, Ellen W. II, 909
Penrose, Ellen Widdefield II, 782
Penrose, Elvira IV, 1072
Penrose, Emlen IV, 1111
Penrose, Esther IV, 750
Penrose, Esther IV, 838
Penrose, Esther IV, 912
Penrose, Geo. Pike III, 253
Penrose, Hanna S. IV, 181
Penrose, Hannah II, 814
Penrose, Hannah II, 871
Penrose, Hannah II, 909
Penrose, Hannah IV, 204
Penrose, Hannah IV, 205
Penrose, Hannah IV, 249
Penrose, Hannah IV, 262
Penrose, Hannah IV, 279
Penrose, Hannah IV, 1066
Penrose, Hannah IV, 1067
Penrose, Hannah IV, 1072
Penrose, Hannah C. IV, 1111
Penrose, Hannah G. IV, 262
Penrose, Hannah M. IV, 240
Penrose, Hannah M. IV, 262
Penrose, Hannah M. IV, 1072
Penrose, Hannah S. II, 871
Penrose, Hannah S. II, 909
Penrose, Hannah S. IV, 262
Penrose, Hannah S. IV, 283
Penrose, Hannah S. IV, 1072
Penrose, Hannah S. IV, 1073
Penrose, Hannah S. IV, 1077
Penrose, Hannah Smith II, 798
Penrose, Hervey IV, 1111
Penrose, Hughes IV, 262
Penrose, Isaac IV, 156
Penrose, Isaac IV, 262
Penrose, Isaac IV, 346
Penrose, Isaac IV, 429
Penrose, Isaac IV, 1070
Penrose, Isaac IV, 1072
Penrose, Isaac IV, 1073
Penrose, Isaac IV, 1111
Penrose, Isaac Roberts Davis
II, 798
Penrose, Jacob IV, 1072
Penrose, Jacob Hibbs IV, 262
Penrose, James II, 406
Penrose, James IV, 262
Penrose, James IV, 492
Penrose, James IV, 905
Penrose, James IV, 912
Penrose, James IV, 985
Penrose, James IV, 1072
Penrose, James IV, 1111
Penrose, James, Jr. IV, 985
Penrose, Jane IV, 1072
Penrose, Jane IV, 1073
Penrose, Jane IV, 1076
Penrose, Jason IV, 1061
Penrose, Jason IV, 1072
Penrose, Jason IV, 1111
Penrose, Jesse IV, 105
Penrose, Jesse IV, 117
Penrose, Jesse IV, 156
Penrose, Jesse IV, 262
Penrose, Jesse IV, 346
Penrose, Jesse IV, 429
Penrose, Jesse IV, 1073
Penrose, Jesse IV, 1179
Penrose, Jesse VI, 603
Penrose, John II, 406
Penrose, John IV, 105
Penrose, John IV, 240
Penrose, John IV, 469
Penrose, John IV, 492
Penrose, John IV, 838
Penrose, John IV, 912
Penrose, John IV, 985
Penrose, John IV, 1066
Penrose, John IV, 1067
Penrose, John IV, 1072
Penrose, John IV, 1137
Penrose, John A. IV, 1072
Penrose, John Adison IV, 1137
Penrose, John C. III, 253
Penrose, John D. IV, 1072
Penrose, John F. IV, 750
Penrose, Joseph IV, 103
Penrose, Joseph IV, 105
Penrose, Joseph IV, 117
Penrose, Joseph IV, 492
Penrose, Joseph IV, 1072
Penrose, Joseph IV, 1073
Penrose, Joseph IV, 1083
Penrose, Joseph IV, 1111
Penrose, Joseph IV, 1123
Penrose, Joseph IV, 1128
Penrose, Joseph IV, 1136
Penrose, Joseph IV, 1137
Penrose, Joseph V, 110
Penrose, Joseph V, 975
Penrose, Joseph VI, 603
Penrose, Lavina IV, 262
Penrose, Lavina IV, 346
Penrose, Lindley IV, 1137
Penrose, Louisa IV, 410
Penrose, Lovina IV, 1179
Penrose, M. Josephine IV, 985
Penrose, Mahlon IV, 262
Penrose, Mahlon IV, 1072
Penrose, Mahlon IV, 1073
Penrose, Margaret II, 620
Penrose, Margaret II, 653
Penrose, Margaret IV, 1072
Penrose, Margaret Ann IV, 1072
Penrose, Margaret Ann IV, 1073
Penrose, Margaret Ann IV, 1077
Penrose, Maria IV, 1052
Penrose, Maria IV, 1072
Penrose, Maria IV, 1111
Penrose, Maria Ada IV, 1111
Penrose, Mariah IV, 1111
Penrose, Mark IV, 262
Penrose, Mark IV, 346
Penrose, Martha IV, 1061
Penrose, Martha IV, 1072
Penrose, Martha IV, 1111
Penrose, Mary II, 620
Penrose, Mary IV, 103
Penrose, Mary IV, 105
Penrose, Mary IV, 117
Penrose, Mary IV, 346
Penrose, Mary IV, 352
Penrose, Mary IV, 429
Penrose, Mary IV, 838
Penrose, Mary IV, 1072
Penrose, Mary IV, 1111
Penrose, Mary IV, 1136
Penrose, Mary IV, 1179
Penrose, Mary V, 110
Penrose, Mary V, 975
Penrose, Mary VI, 603
Penrose, Mary Anna IV, 1106
Penrose, Mary Anna IV, 1111
Penrose, Mary B. IV, 429
Penrose, Mary Eliza IV, 1072
Penrose, Mary Elvira IV, 1136
Penrose, Mary Elvira IV, 1137
Penrose, Mary H. IV, 1073
Penrose, Mary J. II, 798
Penrose, Mary J. II, 871
Penrose, Mary J. II, 909
Penrose, Mary Jane II, 814
Penrose, Mary Jane IV, 1070
Penrose, Mary Jane IV, 1072
Penrose, Mary Jane IV, 1073
Penrose, Mary Jane IV, 1111
Penrose, Mary Needles II, 621
Penrose, Mary P. IV, 429
Penrose, Mary P. IV, 592
Penrose, Mary P. IV, 1072
Penrose, Mary P. IV, 1073
Penrose, Mary P. IV, 1075
Penrose, Mary P. IV, 1076
Penrose, Mary P. IV, 1131
Penrose, Mary P. IV, 1137
Penrose, Mary R. IV, 89
Penrose, Mary R. IV, 105
Penrose, Mary R. V, 270
Penrose, Mildred IV, 1072
Penrose, Mildred IV, 1111
Penrose, Mildred IV, 1123
Penrose, Mildred IV, 1128
Penrose, Mildred IV, 1137
Penrose, Morgan IV, 105
Penrose, Morris II, 814
Penrose, Morris II, 909
Penrose, Naomi IV, 1072
Penrose, Nathan II, 814
Penrose, Nathan II, 878
Penrose, Nathan II, 909
Penrose, Nathan L. IV, 1179
Penrose, Nathan Linville
IV, 1179
Penrose, Norwood II, 621
Penrose, Oliver J. IV, 429
Penrose, Oliver J. IV, 1072
Penrose, Oliver J. IV, 1073
Penrose, Osborn IV, 1072
Penrose, Osborn IV, 1082
Penrose, Osborn IV, 1111
Penrose, Osborn IV, 1121
Penrose, Pearson II, 909
Penrose, Phebe II, 827
Penrose, Phebe IV, 81
Penrose, Phebe IV, 105
Penrose, Phebe VI, 603
Penrose, Pierson M. II, 909
Penrose, R. W. II, 837
Penrose, Rachel IV, 156
Penrose, Rachel IV, 346
Penrose, Rachel IV, 429
Penrose, Rachel IV, 1062
Penrose, Rachel IV, 1072
Penrose, Rachel IV, 1073
Penrose, Rachel IV, 1179
Penrose, Rachel Ann IV, 1072
Penrose, Rachel Eva IV, 1111
Penrose, Rebecca II, 406
Penrose, Rebecca II, 620
Penrose, Rebecca II, 909
Penrose, Rebecca IV, 905
Penrose, Rebecca IV, 912
Penrose, Rebecca IV, 1072
Penrose, Rebecca IV, 1137
Penrose, Rebecca A. II, 909
Penrose, Rebecca Allen II, 814
Penrose, Rebecca W. II, 909
Penrose, Rebecca W. II, 939
Penrose, Richard IV, 262
Penrose, Richard IV, 429
Penrose, Richard IV, 1072
Penrose, Richard IV, 1077
Penrose, Richard IV, 1111
Penrose, Richard IV, 1137
Penrose, Richard H. IV, 985
Penrose, Richard Hawley IV, 985
Penrose, Robert II, 620
Penrose, Robert IV, 262
Penrose, Robert IV, 346
Penrose, Robert IV, 1179
Penrose, Ruth IV, 1073
Penrose, Samuel II, 814
Penrose, Samuel S. II, 909
Penrose, Samuel S. II, 939
Penrose, Sarah II, 464
Penrose, Sarah II, 620
Penrose, Sarah II, 647
Penrose, Sarah II, 814
Penrose, Sarah IV, 105
Penrose, Sarah IV, 116
Penrose, Sarah IV, 117
Penrose, Sarah IV, 156
Penrose, Sarah IV, 162
Penrose, Sarah IV, 262
Penrose, Sarah IV, 279
Penrose, Sarah IV, 346
Penrose, Sarah IV, 429
Penrose, Sarah IV, 492
Penrose, Sarah IV, 912
Penrose, Sarah IV, 1058
Penrose, Sarah IV, 1062
Penrose, Sarah IV, 1072
Penrose, Sarah IV, 1137
Penrose, Sarah VI, 603
Penrose, Sarah Ann IV, 492
Penrose, Sarah Ann IV, 1058
Penrose, Sarah Ann IV, 1072
Penrose, Sarah Ann IV, 1099
Penrose, Sarah Ann IV, 1111
Penrose, Sarah D. II, 878
Penrose, Sarah D. II, 909
Penrose, Sarah Elizabeth
IV, 1060
Penrose, Sarah Elizabeth
IV, 1072
Penrose, Susan IV, 1072
Penrose, Susan A. IV, 1072
Penrose, Susan A. IV, 1073
Penrose, Susan A. IV, 1082
Penrose, Susan A. IV, 1111
Penrose, Susan A. IV, 1121
Penrose, Susan G. IV, 726
Penrose, Susan G. IV, 750
Penrose, Susan H. IV, 750
Penrose, Susan H. IV, 1072
Penrose, Susan H. IV, 1111
Penrose, Tacy S. II, 791
Penrose, Thomas IV, 89
Penrose, Thomas IV, 105
Penrose, Thomas IV, 262
Penrose, Thomas IV, 279
Penrose, Thomas IV, 492
Penrose, Thomas IV, 838
Penrose, Thomas IV, 1052
Penrose, Thomas IV, 1058
Penrose, Thomas IV, 1072
Penrose, Thomas IV, 1073
Penrose, Thomas IV, 1111
Penrose, Thomas, Jr. IV, 262
Penrose, Thomas, Jr. IV, 492
Penrose, Thos IV, 912
Penrose, Thos. IV, 262
Penrose, Thos. IV, 492
Penrose, Washington H. II,
Penrose, Washington H. II,
Penrose, Washington Hicks
II, 814
Penrose, Wd. Rebecca II, 81
Penrose, William II, 798
Penrose, William III, 253
Penrose, William IV, 105
Penrose, William IV, 912
Penrose, William IV, 1072
Penrose, William VI, 603
Penrose, William H. IV, 107
Penrose, William W. IV, 111
Penrose, Wm. II, 620
Penrose, Wm. II, 798
Penrose, Wm. II, 871
Penrose, Wm. II, 909
Penrose, Wm. IV, 1072
Penrose, Wm. IV, 1073
Penrose, Wm. IV, 1137
Penry, James I, 566
Pense, Abbie IV, 1290
Pense, Bertha V, 1014
Pense, Daniel V, 1014
Pense, Oscar V, 1014
Pentan, Ida V, 1014
Pentecoast, David VI, 846
Pentecoast, Eliza VI, 846
Pentecoast, John G. VI, 846
Pentecoast, Sarah E. VI, 84
Pentecost, Mary Louisa IV,
Pentecost, Mary Louise IV,
Penticost, John G. VI, 846
Penticost, Mary Louisa IV,
Penticost, Mary Louisa IV,
Penton, Harriet II, 133
Penton, Harriet II, 135
Penton, Harriet II, 136
Penton, Rachel II, 122
Penton, Rachel II, 124
Penton, Sarah II, 92
Penton, Sarah II, 104
Peobells, Hannah VI, 202
Peobells, Hannah VI, 203
Peobells, William VI, 202
Peobells, William VI, 203
Peobles, Elizabeth VI, 203
Peobles, Hannah VI, 203
Peobles, Huldah VI, 192
Peobles, Huldah VI, 203
Peobles, Joseph VI, 154
Peobles, Joseph VI, 203
Peobles, Mary VI, 203
Peobles, Peter VI, 192
Peobles, Peter VI, 203
Peobles, William VI, 203
Peopells, William VI, 203
Peoples, Elijah VI, 78
Peoples, Harriet Stanley I, 6
Peoples, James R. IV, 985
Peoples, Josiah VI, 78
Peoples, Lucinda IV, 985
Peoples, Mary VI, 100
Peoples, Mary VI, 117
Peper, Frances II, 446
Peper, Germeins II, 446
Peper, Wm. II, 446
Pepper, Alexander II, 814
Pepper, Elijah S. V, 762
Pepper, Elizabeth II, 806
Pepper, Frances II, 446
Pepper, George II, 814
Pepper, Germine II, 446
Pepper, Irene Kinsey V, 197
Pepper, Julia Ann II, 814
Pepper, Margaret II, 814
Pepper, Wm. II, 446
Peppiott, Barbara II, 621
Peppiott, Barbara II, 694
Perbin, Edward VI, 34
Percell, Francis A. V, 425
Perceval, Geo. VI, 873
Percival, Benjamin II, 715
Percival, Benjamin II, 759
Percival, George Fox II, 759
Percival, Mary K. II, 719
Percival, Mary K. II, 759
Percival, Phebe II, 759
Percival, Sarah E. VI, 988
Percy, Abbey III, 253
Percy, Eliz. S. III, 274
Percy, Elizabeth III, 253
Percy, Elizabeth III, 305
Percy, Geo. R. III, 253
Percy, John III, 253
Percy, John C. III, 253
Percy, John C. III, 274
Percy, John C. III, 305

, Sarah III, 253
, Sarah E. III, 253
, Sarah Eliz. III, 253
, Sarah Eliz. III, 274
w, Charles IV, 346
w, Francis VI, 796
w, Jane VI, 796
w, Jennie VI, 796
ue, ??? VI, 348
ue, Abigail IV, 1290
ue, Abigail V, 270
ue, Abigail V, 463
ue, Alice V, 463
ue, Bennett VI, 336
ue, Bennett VI, 354
ue, Bennett VI, 977
ue, Charles IV, 346
ue, Charles IV, 429
ue, Charles A. IV, 156
ue, Charles A. IV, 346
ue, Charles Atkinson IV, 262
ue, David VI, 846
ue, David VI, 847
ue, David B. VI, 977
ue, Edith V, 463
ue, Elisha V, 270
ue, Eliza V, 463
ue, Eliza L. V, 270
ue, Eliza L. V, 271
ue, Elizabeth V, 49
ue, Elizabeth V, 110
ue, Elizabeth VI, 829
ue, Elizabeth VI, 846
ue, Elizabeth VI, 876
ue, Ezekiel VI, 847
ue, Frances VI, 841
ue, Gershom V, 49
ue, Gershom V, 110
ue, Gershom V, 270
ue, Gershom V, 463
ue, Gershom VI, 283
ue, Gershom VI, 336
ue, Gershom VI, 354
ue, Gershon IV, 1290
ue, Gladis V, 463
ue, Gulielma VI, 336
ue, Hannah VI, 977
ue, Hannah D. V, 110
ue, Helen V, 463
ue, Henry VI, 829
ue, Henry VI, 858
ue, Homer V, 463
ue, Isabella VI, 847
ue, Isham VI, 846
ue, Isham VI, 847
ue, Izak VI, 848
ue, Jacob V, 463
ue, Jacob VI, 336
ue, Jacob VI, 354
ue, Jane M. V, 463
ue, Jemima V, 110
ue, Jemima V, 231
ue, Jemima V, 463
ue, Jemima V, 523
ue, Jemima V, 592
ue, Jemima VI, 336
ue, Jemima VI, 354
ue, Jemima VI, 355
ue, Jennie V, 704
ue, Jesse VI, 846
ue, Jesse VI, 876
ue, Jesse Mable V, 704
ue, Joannoh VI, 846
ue, John VI, 977
ue, John R. VI, 846
ue, John W. VI, 876
ue, Lizzie V, 463
ue, Lucy Jane VI, 977
ue, Martin VI, 846
ue, Mary IV, 910
ue, Mary IV, 912
ue, Mary VI, 846
ue, Mary S. VI, 846
ue, Mentor P. V, 231
ue, Mentor P. V, 463
ue, Mentor Pim VI, 336
ue, Mentor Pim VI, 354
ue, Mentorpimm V, 110
ue, Minter VI, 354
ue, Minter Pim VI, 336
ue, Mintor Pim VI, 17
ue, Miriam VI, 680
ue, Miriam VI, 692
ue, Miriam G. VI, 682
ue, Morton V, 463
ue, Myra V, 463
ue, Pearl M. V, 704
ue, Pearl Marie V, 704
ue, Priscilla VI, 977
ue, Rebecca V, 231
ue, Rebecca V, 270
Perdue, Rebecca VI, 336
Perdue, Rebeckah VI, 355
Perdue, Rebeckah VI, 846
Perdue, Rhoda VI, 846
Perdue, Richard VI, 846
Perdue, Sally VI, 841
Perdue, Sarah IV, 346
Perdue, Sarah IV, 429
Perdue, Sarah VI, 682
Perdue, Sarah VI, 692
Perdue, Sarah S. IV, 156
Perdue, Stephen VI, 336
Perdue, Stephen VI, 354
Perdue, Susannah VI, 846
Perdue, Thomas V, 704
Perdue, Thomas VI, 680
Perdue, Thomas H. VI, 682
Perdue, Thomas H. VI, 692
Perdue, Thomas K. V, 463
Perdue, Whittier V, 463
Perdue, William VI, 336
Perdue, William VI, 682
Perdue, William VI, 687
Perdue, William VI, 692
Perdue???, Sarah VI, 692
Perdue???, William VI, 692
Perdy, Elizabeth VI, 846
Perdy, Henry VI, 846
Peregay, Marion IV, 1333
Peregay, Marion Frances IV, 1333
Peregoy, Marion Francis V, 856
Peregoy, Miriam Francis V, 856
Pereira, Lillie III, 56
Pereira, Lillie III, 253
Pereira, Lillie P. III, 56
Pereira, Lillie P. III, 253
Pereira, Russell III, 56
Pereira, Russell III, 253
Perera, Carolyn III, 253
Perera, Charles III, 253
Perera, Charles A. III, 46
Perera, Charles A. III, 253
Perera, John Brinton III, 253
Perera, Lionello III, 253
Perera, Ruth III, 253
Perera, Ruth Hoops III, 46
Perera, Ruth Hoops III, 253
Perera, Sylvia Brinton III, 253
Pereshew, Mary I, 255
Perfater, John VI, 977
Perfater, Sally VI, 977
Perie, John V, 462
Perie, Mary V, 462
Perie, Walter V, 308
Perie, Walter V, 462
Perigow, A. L. III, 174
Perigow, A. L. III, 242
Perisho, Ann I, 68
Perisho, Ann I, 140
Perisho, Anna I, 72
Perisho, Cammel I, 274
Perisho, Clerkey I, 160
Perisho, Clerkey I, 166
Perisho, Elenor I, 160
Perisho, Elinor I, 36
Perisho, Elinor I, 68
Perisho, Elinor I, 160
Perisho, Elinor I Sup 1, 7
Perisho, Elisabeth I, 68
Perisho, Elisabeth I, 71
Perisho, Elisabeth I, 113
Perisho, Elisabeth I, 140
Perisho, Elisabeth I, 160
Perisho, Elisabeth I, 199
Perisho, Elizabeth I, 113
Perisho, Elizabeth I, 188
Perisho, Elizabeth I, 199
Perisho, James I, 68
Perisho, James I, 113
Perisho, James I, 255
Perisho, James I, 967
Perisho, Jane I, 38
Perisho, Jane I, 68
Perisho, John I, 35
Perisho, John I, 68
Perisho, John I, 113
Perisho, John I, 199
Perisho, Joseph I, 68
Perisho, Joseph I, 71
Perisho, Joseph I, 160
Perisho, Joseph I, 188
Perisho, Joseph I, 199
Perisho, Joseph I, 274
Perisho, Joshoua I, 113
Perisho, Joshua I, 68
Perisho, Joshua I, 113
Perisho, Joshua I, 140
Perisho, Joshua I, 160
Perisho, Joshua I, 169
Perisho, Joshua Morris I, 113
Perisho, Joshua, Jr. I, 160
Perisho, Josiah I, 68
Perisho, Josiah I, 74
Perisho, Josiah I, 160
Perisho, Lydia C. I, 613
Perisho, Martha I, 113
Perisho, Martha Ann I, 160
Perisho, Mary I, 35
Perisho, Mary I, 68
Perisho, Mary I, 113
Perisho, Mary I, 144
Perisho, Mary I, 145
Perisho, Mary I, 156
Perisho, Mary I, 160
Perisho, Mary I, 315
Perisho, Mary Elma I, 113
Perisho, Mary Elma I, 160
Perisho, Miriam I, 132
Perisho, Miriam I, 160
Perisho, Miriam I, 169
Perisho, Nathan I, 113
Perisho, Nathan I, 145
Perisho, Nathan I, 160
Perisho, Penina I, 68
Perisho, Peninah I, 160
Perisho, Pennina I, 68
Perisho, Penninah I, 68
Perisho, Rachel I, 68
Perisho, Rachel I, 74
Perisho, Rachel I, 113
Perisho, Samuel I, 274
Perisho, Sarah I, 274
Perisho, Sarah I, 315
Perisho, Widow Miriam I, 113
Perishoe, Elenor I, 132
Perishoe, Elenor I, 160
Perishoe, James I, 255
Perishoe, James I, 256
Perishoe, Mary I, 255
Perkens, Isaac V, 469
Perkens, Phenia V, 469
Perkin, Edward VI, 7
Perkin, Elizabeth I, 1096
Perkin, Robert VI, 13
Perkins, ??? III, 492
Perkins, ??? VI, 39
Perkins, Aaron I, 295
Perkins, Aaron I, 316
Perkins, Abigail II, 180
Perkins, Abigail II, 249
Perkins, Abigail II, 251
Perkins, Abigail IV, 53
Perkins, Abigail V, 522
Perkins, Abigail V, 523
Perkins, Abigail V, 957
Perkins, Abijah V, 110
Perkins, Abijah V, 197
Perkins, Abijah V, 523
Perkins, Achsah I, 295
Perkins, Allen I, 295
Perkins, Ann I, 370
Perkins, Ann I, 413
Perkins, Ann I, 566
Perkins, Ann I, 686
Perkins, Ann IV, 53
Perkins, Ann IV, 59
Perkins, Ann IV, 151
Perkins, Ann IV, 165
Perkins, Ann IV, 750
Perkins, Ann V, 72
Perkins, Ann V, 110
Perkins, Ann V, 500
Perkins, Ann V, 523
Perkins, Anna I, 413
Perkins, Anna I, 589
Perkins, Anne V, 110
Perkins, Asenath C. I, 316
Perkins, Avis I, 296
Perkins, Axey I, 316
Perkins, Barna I, 316
Perkins, Barney E. I, 295
Perkins, Barney E. I, 296
Perkins, Barney E. I, 316
Perkins, Benj. D. II, 759
Perkins, Benjamin VI, 977
Perkins, Benjamin D. II, 759
Perkins, Benjamin D. III, 238
Perkins, Benjamin D. III, 253
Perkins, Benjamin D. III, 383
Perkins, Bertrion Eugene I, 339
Perkins, Betcy I, 589
Perkins, Beulah I, 566
Perkins, Caleb I, 566
Perkins, Caleb IV, 53
Perkins, Caleb V, 110
Perkins, Calvin G. I, 296
Perkins, Calvin G. I, 316
Perkins, Calvin G. I, 625
Perkins, Calvin G. W. I, 296
Perkins, Caroline III, 78
Perkins, Celia I, 595
Perkins, Charity E. I, 296
Perkins, Charity E. I, 316
Perkins, Charles I, 1036
Perkins, Charles F. I, 316
Perkins, Charlie F. I, 295
Perkins, Christian I, 295
Perkins, Clara W. II, 319
Perkins, Clara W. II, 323
Perkins, Clarissa IV, 1041
Perkins, Constantine VI, 846
Perkins, Cora I, 295
Perkins, Daniel I, 1036
Perkins, David I, 68
Perkins, David IV, 338
Perkins, David IV, 346
Perkins, David IV, 1041
Perkins, David Sanders I, 339
Perkins, Deborah I, 295
Perkins, Deborah D. I, 316
Perkins, Deborah D. I, 329
Perkins, Deborah D. I, 330
Perkins, Delano F. I, 316
Perkins, Delano S. S. I, 296
Perkins, Deler L. I, 295
Perkins, Demaris A. VI, 977
Perkins, Deverna IV, 1041
Perkins, Dinah I, 566
Perkins, Dinah I, 567
Perkins, Doctor Borden I, 296
Perkins, Dola I, 625
Perkins, Dora I, 316
Perkins, Dora I, 624
Perkins, Dr. Jared I, 589
Perkins, E. P. IV, 1290
Perkins, Edda I, 295
Perkins, Edward I, 339
Perkins, Edward VI, 22
Perkins, Edward VI, 33
Perkins, Edward VI, 34
Perkins, Edward VI, 40
Perkins, Elias I, 589
Perkins, Elias I, 595
Perkins, Elisabeth I, 623
Perkins, Elisha III, 253
Perkins, Elizabeth I, 294
Perkins, Elizabeth I, 295
Perkins, Elizabeth I, 539
Perkins, Elizabeth I, 566
Perkins, Elizabeth I, 1036
Perkins, Elizabeth I, 1130
Perkins, Elizabeth III, 492
Perkins, Elizabeth IV, 342
Perkins, Elizabeth IV, 346
Perkins, Elizabeth IV, 426
Perkins, Elizabeth IV, 429
Perkins, Elizabeth V, 354
Perkins, Elizabeth M. VI, 958
Perkins, Ella I, 295
Perkins, Elva T. I, 316
Perkins, Elvira I, 295
Perkins, Faithy I, 295
Perkins, Faithy I, 296
Perkins, Faithy I, 316
Perkins, Flocy I, 295
Perkins, Floid IV, 1041
Perkins, Florence Maud I, 327
Perkins, Florence Maude I, 339
Perkins, Frances E. I, 296
Perkins, Gladys H. I, 624
Perkins, Gladys H. I, 639
Perkins, Glenn IV, 1041
Perkins, Gulia E. I, 296
Perkins, Hannah I, 566
Perkins, Hannah I, 600
Perkins, Hannah I, 607
Perkins, Hannah IV, 342
Perkins, Hannah IV, 346
Perkins, Hannah IV, 424
Perkins, Hannah IV, 429
Perkins, Hannah IV, 1179
Perkins, Henry VI, 543
Perkins, Henry VI, 770
Perkins, Hillary W. I, 316
Perkins, Hillory W. I, 296
Perkins, Hillory W. I, 316
Perkins, I. III, 78
Perkins, Isaac I, 370
Perkins, Isaac I, 413
Perkins, Isaac I, 512
Perkins, Isaac I, 566
Perkins, Isaac I, 589
Perkins, Isaac I, 683
Perkins, Isaac I, 686
Perkins, Isaac I, 897
Perkins, Isaac IV, 53
Perkins, Isaac IV, 1179
Perkins, Isaac V, 17
Perkins, Isaac V, 110
Perkins, Isaac V, 197
Perkins, Isaac V, 523
Perkins, Isaac V, 957
Perkins, Isaac VI, 357
Perkins, Isaac VI, 447
Perkins, Isaac, Jr. VI, 428
Perkins, James I, 295
Perkins, James H. VI, 846
Perkins, Jane I, 595
Perkins, Jane IV, 1219
Perkins, Jane Louisa IV, 1179
Perkins, Jane W. VI, 846
Perkins, Jared I, 566
Perkins, Jared I, 586
Perkins, Jared I, 589
Perkins, Jared I, 595
Perkins, Jared, Jr. I, 595
Perkins, Jemima I, 1036
Perkins, Jered I, 566
Perkins, Jeremiah I, 256
Perkins, Jeremiah I, 295
Perkins, Jeremiah I, 296
Perkins, Jeremiah I, 316
Perkins, Jesse IV, 1179
Perkins, Jesse IV, 1219
Perkins, Joan I, 589
Perkins, John I, 284
Perkins, John I, 294
Perkins, John I, 295
Perkins, John I, 305
Perkins, John I, 316
Perkins, John I, 566
Perkins, John I, 567
Perkins, John I, 607
Perkins, John IV, 53
Perkins, John V, 110
Perkins, John V, 488
Perkins, John V, 523
Perkins, John B. I, 295
Perkins, John B. I, 296
Perkins, John B. I, 316
Perkins, John B. I, 329
Perkins, John B. I, 330
Perkins, John H. I, 316
Perkins, John Henry I, 295
Perkins, John K. V, 197
Perkins, John K. V, 523
Perkins, John Kelly V, 197
Perkins, John L. V, 523
Perkins, John M. VI, 977
Perkins, John Murray III, 383
Perkins, John Needham I, 339
Perkins, John William I, 295
Perkins, Jonathan IV, 346
Perkins, Jonathan IV, 543
Perkins, Jonathan IV, 750
Perkins, Jonathan IV, 838
Perkins, Joseph I, 413
Perkins, Joseph I, 560
Perkins, Joseph I, 566
Perkins, Joseph I, 603
Perkins, Joseph I, 607
Perkins, Joseph I, 686
Perkins, Joseph V, 110
Perkins, Joseph V, 197
Perkins, Joseph V, 523
Perkins, Joseph VI, 846
Perkins, Joseph, Jr. I, 607
Perkins, Joseph, Sr. I, 607
Perkins, Julia Ann V, 110
Perkins, Julia Ann V, 523
Perkins, Juliana V, 488
Perkins, Juliana V, 523
Perkins, Keziah I, 1145
Perkins, Kisiah VI, 977
Perkins, L. J. I, 331
Perkins, Laura E. I, 295
Perkins, Laura E. I, 316
Perkins, Lerry I, 339
Perkins, Levania T. I, 284
Perkins, Levina I, 295
Perkins, Lew Evey I, 295
Perkins, Lidda Roxanah I, 295
Perkins, Lillie Gertrude I, 339
Perkins, Lindley III, 383
Perkins, Lindley Murray II, 759
Perkins, Lois E. IV, 750
Perkins, Lola I, 625
Perkins, Lorany I, 607
Perkins, Louisa IV, 1219
Perkins, Louvena P. I, 316
Perkins, Lucetta I, 295
Perkins, Lucretia S. W. III, 253
Perkins, Ludie I, 624
Perkins, Lydia I, 1034
Perkins, Lydia I, 1036
Perkins, Lydia IV, 53
Perkins, Lydia IV, 338
Perkins, Lydia IV, 346
Perkins, Lydia V, 110
Perkins, Lydia V, 523
Perkins, Lydia V, 540
Perkins, Mahlon D. I, 296
Perkins, Mahlon D. I, 316
Perkins, Marenda I, 295

Perkins, Marenda I, 316
Perkins, Maria VI, 770
Perkins, Mariam Elizabeth I, 316
Perkins, Mark I, 295
Perkins, Martha I, 566
Perkins, Martha I, 920
Perkins, Martha V, 44
Perkins, Martha V, 110
Perkins, Martha V, 425
Perkins, Martha V, 428
Perkins, Martha A. VI, 819
Perkins, Mary I, 68
Perkins, Mary I, 229
Perkins, Mary I, 256
Perkins, Mary I, 295
Perkins, Mary I, 303
Perkins, Mary I, 316
Perkins, Mary I, 558
Perkins, Mary I, 566
Perkins, Mary I, 578
Perkins, Mary I, 589
Perkins, Mary I, 995
Perkins, Mary I, 1145
Perkins, Mary II, 226
Perkins, Mary II, 249
Perkins, Mary III, 238
Perkins, Mary III, 253
Perkins, Mary VI, 428
Perkins, Mary VI, 447
Perkins, Mary VI, 846
Perkins, Mary Ann V, 110
Perkins, Mary Ann V, 197
Perkins, Mary Ann V, 523
Perkins, Mary E. I, 296
Perkins, Mary E. I, 316
Perkins, Mary Ellen III, 187
Perkins, Mary Ellen III, 253
Perkins, Mary Frances Ann Maria VI, 977
Perkins, Mary G. VI, 806
Perkins, Mary Jane I, 295
Perkins, Mary L. I, 330
Perkins, Mary L. I, 331
Perkins, Mary Louise I, 339
Perkins, Mary S. I, 327
Perkins, Mary S. III, 228
Perkins, Mary S. III, 253
Perkins, Mary S. III, 383
Perkins, Maryann V, 189
Perkins, Maryann V, 197
Perkins, May VI, 655
Perkins, May E. VI, 508
Perkins, May E. VI, 543
Perkins, May Janee I, 316
Perkins, Miriam Elizabeth I, 295
Perkins, Moses I, 295
Perkins, Moses I, 316
Perkins, N. T. I, 316
Perkins, Nancy I, 284
Perkins, Nancy I, 566
Perkins, Nancy I, 586
Perkins, Nancy I, 589
Perkins, Nancy IV, 1179
Perkins, Nathan I, 284
Perkins, Nathan I, 295
Perkins, Nathan I, 296
Perkins, Nathan I, 316
Perkins, Nathan IV, 346
Perkins, Nathaniel I, 566
Perkins, Nathaniel I, 607
Perkins, Needham Eli I, 295
Perkins, Needham S. I, 295
Perkins, Needham S. I, 316
Perkins, Needham Samuel I, 295
Perkins, Needham T. I, 296
Perkins, Needham T. I, 297
Perkins, Needham T. I, 303
Perkins, Needham T. I, 304
Perkins, Needham T. I, 316
Perkins, Needham T. I, 328
Perkins, Needham T. I, 330
Perkins, Needham T. I, 331
Perkins, Needham T. I, 616
Perkins, Needham T. I, 624
Perkins, Newton I, 607
Perkins, Octavia I, 616
Perkins, Ordee Alphus I, 339
Perkins, P. G. I, 316
Perkins, Patience I, 295
Perkins, Patience I, 1036
Perkins, Patience A. I, 316
Perkins, Penelope I, 284
Perkins, Penelopy I, 316
Perkins, Peninah V, 110
Perkins, Pennelope I, 295
Perkins, Penninah IV, 53
Perkins, Penninah D. I, 316
Perkins, Pharabe I, 316
Perkins, Pharaby I, 256
Perkins, Pharaby I, 316
Perkins, Pharoah G. I, 295
Perkins, Pharoah G. I, 316
Perkins, Pharoh G. I, 624
Perkins, Phebe IV, 422
Perkins, Phebe IV, 429
Perkins, Phemia V, 957
Perkins, Phenia I, 566
Perkins, Phenia V, 523
Perkins, Pheniah I, 566
Perkins, Pheniah V, 110
Perkins, Pheniah V, 523
Perkins, Pheninah V, 197
Perkins, Pheriba I, 295
Perkins, Phineas V, 523
Perkins, Phiniah I, 683
Perkins, Phiniah I, 686
Perkins, Phiniah V, 17
Perkins, Pinninah D. I, 328
Perkins, Pinninah D. I, 330
Perkins, Pizarro IV, 1041
Perkins, Polly VI, 325
Perkins, Polly VI, 829
Perkins, Polly VI, 977
Perkins, Priscilla I, 560
Perkins, Priscilla I, 566
Perkins, Priscilla I, 607
Perkins, Priscilla V, 110
Perkins, Priscilla V, 523
Perkins, Priscilla V, 704
Perkins, Priscilla H. V, 523
Perkins, Prucey Ann I, 295
Perkins, Prucy A. I, 316
Perkins, Rachel I, 295
Perkins, Rachel I, 296
Perkins, Rachel I, 297
Perkins, Rachel I, 316
Perkins, Rachel I, 330
Perkins, Rachel I, 624
Perkins, Rachel IV, 346
Perkins, Rachel IV, 1111
Perkins, Rachel IV, 1114
Perkins, Rachel L. L. I, 296
Perkins, Rachel M. I, 296
Perkins, Rachel M. I, 316
Perkins, Rachel M. I, 624
Perkins, Rachel P. I, 295
Perkins, Rebecca I, 595
Perkins, Rebecca I, 620
Perkins, Rebeccah I, 566
Perkins, Rebeckah I, 589
Perkins, Reginald I, 624
Perkins, Reginald I, 639
Perkins, Richard VI, 806
Perkins, Richard VI, 819
Perkins, Richard VI, 846
Perkins, Robert IV, 53
Perkins, Robert V, 428
Perkins, Robert VI, 13
Perkins, Robert W. I, 296
Perkins, Robert W. I, 316
Perkins, Roxey Aner I, 295
Perkins, Ruth I, 295
Perkins, Ruth I, 605
Perkins, Ruth I, 607
Perkins, Sabinah IV, 53
Perkins, Salinah V, 110
Perkins, Salley W. I, 297
Perkins, Sallie I, 284
Perkins, Sallie I, 294
Perkins, Sallie I, 620
Perkins, Sallie I, 624
Perkins, Sallie I, 639
Perkins, Sallie Ann I, 314
Perkins, Sallie Ann I, 316
Perkins, Sallie E. I, 331
Perkins, Sallie Elisabeth I, 624
Perkins, Sallie W. I, 316
Perkins, Sallie W. I, 616
Perkins, Sallie Woodard I, 303
Perkins, Sallie Woodard I, 316
Perkins, Sallie, Sr. I, 316
Perkins, Sally I, 295
Perkins, Sally I, 305
Perkins, Sally I, 316
Perkins, Sally Ann I, 295
Perkins, Sally W. I, 296
Perkins, Sally W. I, 328
Perkins, Sally W. I, 330
Perkins, Saly M. I, 295
Perkins, Samuel I, 295
Perkins, Samuel I, 296
Perkins, Samuel I, 316
Perkins, Samuel I, 317
Perkins, Samuel I, 330
Perkins, Samuel R. I, 296
Perkins, Samuel T. I, 296
Perkins, Samuel T. I, 316
Perkins, Samuel, Sr. I, 296
Perkins, Sarah I, 295
Perkins, Sarah I, 296
Perkins, Sarah I, 316
Perkins, Sarah I, 318
Perkins, Sarah I, 566
Perkins, Sarah I, 607
Perkins, Sarah III, 253
Perkins, Sarah IV, 1179
Perkins, Sarah IV, 1219
Perkins, Sarah V, 107
Perkins, Sarah V, 110
Perkins, Sarah V, 189
Perkins, Sarah V, 197
Perkins, Sarah V, 523
Perkins, Sarah B. IV, 1211
Perkins, Sarah B. IV, 1219
Perkins, Sarah J. I, 308
Perkins, Sarah J. I, 316
Perkins, Sarah J. H. I, 296
Perkins, Sarah J. H. I, 316
Perkins, Sarah W. I, 304
Perkins, Sarah W. I, 316
Perkins, Savannah L. I, 920
Perkins, Selina V, 523
Perkins, Seth David I, 295
Perkins, Sidney I, 327
Perkins, Sidney I, 920
Perkins, Sidney E. I, 316
Perkins, Sidney E. I, 330
Perkins, Sidney E. I, 331
Perkins, Sidney E. I, 620
Perkins, Sidney E. I, 624
Perkins, Sidney Eugene I, 296
Perkins, Sophronia P. I, 677
Perkins, Sophronia P. I, 686
Perkins, Stephen IV, 346
Perkins, Sudie I, 620
Perkins, Susanna I, 512
Perkins, Susanna I, 566
Perkins, Susanna I, 995
Perkins, Susanna V, 42
Perkins, Susanna V, 110
Perkins, Susannah I, 995
Perkins, Susannah V, 483
Perkins, Susannah V, 523
Perkins, Susannah VI, 846
Perkins, Tacy IV, 422
Perkins, Tacy IV, 429
Perkins, Temple VI, 846
Perkins, Thomas I, 566
Perkins, Thomas I, 1036
Perkins, Thomas I Sup 1, 11
Perkins, Thomas II, 180
Perkins, Thomas IV, 53
Perkins, Thomas V, 17
Perkins, Thomas V, 107
Perkins, Thomas V, 110
Perkins, Thomas V, 189
Perkins, Thomas V, 197
Perkins, Thomas V, 523
Perkins, Thomas VI, 846
Perkins, Van Buren I, 624
Perkins, Van Buren I, 639
Perkins, Viola Falecia I, 296
Perkins, William I, 589
Perkins, William I, 595
Perkins, William VI, 977
Perkins, William Jones I, 295
Perkins, William Octavus A. O. I, 296
Perkins, William R. I, 296
Perkins, William R. I, 316
Perkins, William R. I, 328
Perkins, William R. I, 330
Perkins, William Samuel I, 295
Perkins, William T. I, 316
Perkins, William W. VI, 958
Perkins, William W. VI, 995
Perkins, Zeno E. I, 295
Perkinson, Ann II, 249
Perkinson, John S. Rogers II, 249
Perkinson, Mary II, 249
Perkinson, Mary II, 440
Perkinson, Thomas II, 440
Perkison, Ann II, 249
Perkison, Mary II, 249
Perkison, Mary II, 255
Perman, Paul P. IV, 1333
Permar, Edwin H. IV, 1260
Permat, Edwin H. IV, 1260
Perot, Ann II, 406
Perot, Ann S. II, 715
Perot, Ann S. II, 760
Perot, Annie Lovering II, 814
Perot, Caroline II, 853
Perot, Caroline R. II, 814
Perot, Caroline R. II, 909
Perot, Charles P. II, 759
Perot, Charles P. II, 760
Perot, Elizabeth II, 814
Perot, Elizabeth M. II, 853
Perot, Elizabeth M. II, 904
Perot, Elizabeth M. II, 909
Perot, Elizabeth M. II, 922
Perot, Elizabeth Marshall II, 814
Perot, Elizabeth Morris II, 814
Perot, Elizabeth W. II, 715
Perot, Elizabeth W. II, 759
Perot, Elizabeth W. II, 760
Perot, Elleston II, 909
Perot, Ellister II, 406
Perot, Elliston II, 406
Perot, Elliston II, 603
Perot, Elliston II, 621
Perot, Elliston II, 715
Perot, Elliston II, 759
Perot, Elliston II, 760
Perot, Elliston II, 814
Perot, Elliston II, 853
Perot, Elliston II, 909
Perot, Elliston, Jr. II, 814
Perot, Francis II, 406
Perot, Francis II, 621
Perot, Francis II, 760
Perot, Francis II, 814
Perot, Francis II, 838
Perot, Francis II, 853
Perot, Francis II, 904
Perot, Francis II, 909
Perot, Francis II, 922
Perot, Francis II, 933
Perot, Francis, Jr. II, 814
Perot, Francis, Jr. II, 909
Perot, Francis, Jr. III, 253
Perot, Hannah II, 406
Perot, Hannah II, 603
Perot, Hannah II, 621
Perot, Hannah II, 759
Perot, Hannah II, 760
Perot, Hannah II, 762
Perot, Henry Corbit II, 814
Perot, James P. II, 759
Perot, James P. II, 760
Perot, Joseph II, 406
Perot, Joseph II, 621
Perot, Laititia P. II, 760
Perot, Latitia P. II, 759
Perot, Mary W. II, 708
Perot, Mary W. II, 715
Perot, Mary W. II, 759
Perot, Mary W. II, 760
Perot, Mary W. II, 762
Perot, Mary Wm. II, 760
Perot, Morris II, 909
Perot, Rebecca C. II, 909
Perot, Rebecca C. II, 922
Perot, Sallie C. II, 909
Perot, Sallie Corbit II, 814
Perot, Sally S. II, 708
Perot, Sally S. II, 760
Perot, Samuel II, 406
Perot, Sansom II, 406
Perot, Sansom II, 759
Perot, Sansom II, 760
Perot, Sarah II, 406
Perot, Sarah II, 603
Perot, Sarah II, 621
Perot, Sarah II, 814
Perot, Sarah M. II, 759
Perot, Sarah M. II, 904
Perot, Sarah M. II, 909
Perot, Sarah Morris II, 760
Perot, Sarah Morris II, 811
Perot, Sarah Morris II, 909
Perot, Sarah S. II, 759
Perot, Thomas Morris II, 759
Perot, Thomas Morris II, 760
Perot, Thos. II, 909
Perot, Thos. Morris II, 814
Perot, Thos. Morris II, 922
Perot, William S. II, 715
Perot, William Sansom II, 406
Perot, Wm. L. II, 760
Perot, Wm. L. II, 762
Perot, Wm. S. II, 621
Perot, Wm. S. II, 708
Perot, Wm. S. II, 759
Perot, Wm. S. II, 760
Perot, Wm. Sansom II, 715
Perott, John VI, 29
Perott, Sarah Morris II, 760
Perren, Letty VI, 926
Perren, Patsy VI, 926
Perrey, Elisabeth I, 85
Perrey, Elizabeth I, 68
Perrey, Esther I, 68
Perrey, Reuben I, 68
Perrig, Susannah I, 152
Perrig, Susannah I, 160
Perrin, ??? III, 433
Perrin, Adelbert IV, 1219
Perrin, Ann VI, 933
Perrin, Bertha V, 441
Perrin, Bertha V, 704
Perrin, Charles VI, 933
Perrin, Charles VI, 955
Perrin, Charles VI, 978
Perrin, Charles VI, 991
Perrin, Charles E. IV, 1220
Perrin, Charles Earl IV, 122[illegible]
Perrin, Elias V, 271
Perrin, Elias V, 441
Perrin, Eliza V, 197
Perrin, Eliza VI, 892
Perrin, Elizabeth VI, 955
Perrin, Elizabeth A. VI, 977
Perrin, Elmer V, 354
Perrin, Estella V, 197
Perrin, Frank V, 354
Perrin, George V, 441
Perrin, George T. V, 197
Perrin, James IV, 1219
Perrin, James E. IV, 1220
Perrin, James Eber IV, 1220
Perrin, Jane VI, 977
Perrin, Jathniel III, 412
Perrin, Jathniel III, 433
Perrin, John VI, 933
Perrin, John VI, 977
Perrin, John VI, 991
Perrin, John H. V, 441
Perrin, John W. VI, 977
Perrin, Josephine L. III, 412
Perrin, Josephine L. III, 433
Perrin, Judah VI, 991
Perrin, Leta Lickliter V, 197
Perrin, Letty VI, 846
Perrin, Lucy W. III, 412
Perrin, Lucy W. III, 433
Perrin, Martha VI, 926
Perrin, Mary V, 354
Perrin, Mary VI, 991
Perrin, Melvin V, 425
Perrin, Melvin V, 441
Perrin, Nancey VI, 977
Perrin, Pearl V, 197
Perrin, Riece E. V, 271
Perrin, Sarah V, 425
Perrin, Sarah V, 441
Perrin, Sarah N. VI, 892
Perrin, Verna V, 354
Perrin, Walter V, 197
Perrin, William VI, 846
Perrin, William VI, 892
Perrin, William VI, 977
Perrine, Altha IV, 492
Perrine, Mrs. ??? IV, 1333
Perrine, Mrs. Nettie IV, 1333
Perrisho, Elisabeth I, 51
Perrisho, Elisabeth I, 68
Perrisho, Joseph I, 51
Perrisho, Joseph I, 68
Perrisho, Joshua I, 51
Perrisho, Joshua I, 68
Perrisho, Pennina I, 51
Perrisho, Penninah I, 68
Perrishoe, John I, 68
Perrishoe, Pennina I, 68
Perrot, Elliston II, 621
Perrot, John VI, 7
Perrot, Sarah II, 621
Perrott, ??? VI, 40
Perrott, Ann II, 406
Perrott, Elliston II, 621
Perrott, John VI, 40
Perrow, Amy A. VI, 846
Perrow, Andrew VI, 859
Perrow, Andrew J. VI, 820
Perrow, Caroline C. VI, 856
Perrow, Celia B. VI, 820
Perrow, Charles VI, 846
Perrow, Christiana VI, 846
Perrow, Daniel VI, 811
Perrow, Daniel VI, 817
Perrow, Daniel B. VI, 820
Perrow, Daniel B. VI, 846
Perrow, Dolly VI, 846
Perrow, Dolly VI, 852
Perrow, Elizabeth VI, 847
Perrow, Elizabeth VI, 862
Perrow, Elizabeth VI, 864
Perrow, Elizabeth VI, 977
Perrow, Elizabeth H. VI, 977
Perrow, Frances VI, 811
Perrow, James S. VI, 977
Perrow, John F. VI, 835
Perrow, John F. VI, 846
Perrow, John L. VI, 819
Perrow, Martha F. VI, 846
Perrow, Mary VI, 817
Perrow, Mary A. VI, 842
Perrow, Stephen VI, 846
Perrow, Stephen VI, 852
Perrow, Stephen VI, 856
Perrow, Stephen VI, 862
Perrow, Stephen VI, 977
Perrow, Stephen W. VI, 862

, ??? III, 429
, Amos V, 760
, Ann I, 23
, Ann I, 68
, Ann I, 87
, Anna E. V, 905
, Anna E. V, 926
, Anne II, 621
, Anne Shoemaker II, 621
, Arther IV, 750
, Arthur, Jr. IV, 726
, Arthur, Jr. IV, 750
, Asa IV, 262
, Asenath IV, 262
, Atlas J. I, 452
, Belle V, 1014
, Benjamin II, 621
, Beulah IV, 986
, Blanch V, 308
, Blanche V, 462
, Carpelona I, 413
, Cecil V, 308
, Charles V, 462
, Charles W. V, 462
, Cora V, 1014
, Daniel IV, 53
, David IV, 262
, David IV, 708
, Deborah IV, 346
, Deborah IV, 398
, Deborah IV, 429
, Dorcas I, 69
, Easter I, 186
, Edward V, 462
, Elisabeth I, 16
, Elisabeth I, 54
, Elisabeth I, 57
, Elisabeth I, 67
, Elisabeth I, 68
, Elisabeth I, 69
, Elisabeth I, 80
, Eliza Jane IV, 453
, Elizabeth I, 68
, Elizabeth I, 186
, Elizabeth I, 612
, Elizabeth IV, 262
, Elizabeth V, 926
, Elizabeth V, 941
, Elizabeth VI, 822
, Elizabeth VI, 878
, Elizabeth Shoemaker
I, 621
, Ella IV, 986
, Ella M. IV, 986
, Elmina I, 413
, Elmina I, 423
, Emma I, 16
, Emma IV, 750
, Emma R. I, 16
, Emma R. I, 33
, Emma R. I, 69
, Ephraim IV, 262
, Ernest V, 462
, Esek IV, 986
, Esek H. IV, 986
, Esther I, 16
, Esther I, 40
, Esther I, 69
, Esther I, 87
, Eva V, 1014
, Ezra A. V, 1014
, Fannie Reynolds IV, 1260
, Fred J. IV, 986
, Fredona F. V, 271
, Gail Duane IV, 1260
, Hannah I, 15
, Hannah I, 51
, Hannah I, 69
, Hannah I, 186
, Hannah I, 595
, Hannah IV, 346
, Hannah IV, 708
, Hardy I, 24
, Harold Kent, Jr. IV, 1260
, Hazel A. V, 1014
, Hazel Doyle IV, 1239
, Herman IV, 986
, Hermon L. IV, 986
, Homer V, 308
, Howard Dewitt V, 462
, Ibbie A. I, 69
, Isabella A. I, 69
, Isabella A. I, 89
, Isabelle I, 16
, Isabelle I, 33
, Jacob I, 16
, Jacob I, 69
, Jacob I, 186
, Jacob Rix I, 15
, James VI, 846
, James C. IV, 262
Perry, Jane II, 621
Perry, Jane III, 253
Perry, Jesse I, 15
Perry, Jesse I, 16
Perry, Jesse I, 57
Perry, Jesse I, 69
Perry, Jesse I, 186
Perry, Jessie IV, 1239
Perry, Job IV, 262
Perry, Job IV, 346
Perry, Job, Jr. IV, 262
Perry, John I, 15
Perry, John I, 16
Perry, John I, 51
Perry, John I, 69
Perry, John I, 186
Perry, John II, 440
Perry, John IV, 346
Perry, John IV, 398
Perry, John IV, 1179
Perry, John V, 462
Perry, John VI, 822
Perry, John Ellwood I, 15
Perry, John Elwood I, 69
Perry, John Elwood I, 186
Perry, John W. I, 16
Perry, Joseph L. I, 16
Perry, Joseph L. I, 69
Perry, Joshua V, 1014
Perry, Katie V, 1014
Perry, Lavina V, 1014
Perry, Letitia IV, 262
Perry, Lindley H. I, 39
Perry, Lucy B. I, 16
Perry, Lucy P. I, 69
Perry, Ludena I, 24
Perry, Ludona I, 69
Perry, Lydia III, 253
Perry, Lydia III, 433
Perry, Lydia IV, 53
Perry, Lydia IV, 149
Perry, Lydia IV, 156
Perry, Lydia IV, 346
Perry, Lydia IV, 348
Perry, Lydia V, 925
Perry, Lydia V, 926
Perry, Lydia P. III, 462
Perry, Lydia P. III, 492
Perry, M. William IV, 986
Perry, M. Wm. IV, 986
Perry, Maggie P. I, 16
Perry, Maggie P. I, 69
Perry, Mahlon IV, 986
Perry, Maria III, 236
Perry, Maria III, 253
Perry, Marian B. VI, 846
Perry, Martha V, 889
Perry, Mary I, 3
Perry, Mary I, 15
Perry, Mary I, 16
Perry, Mary I, 46
Perry, Mary I, 68
Perry, Mary I, 69
Perry, Mary I, 186
Perry, Mary I, 413
Perry, Mary IV, 262
Perry, Mary V, 462
Perry, Mary V, 760
Perry, Mary A. V, 1014
Perry, Mary E. I, 39
Perry, Mary J. IV, 708
Perry, Mary J. IV, 750
Perry, Mary Parry II, 621
Perry, Mary Penelope I, 15
Perry, Mary R. I, 10
Perry, Milea I, 69
Perry, Milicent I, 69
Perry, Milisent I, 69
Perry, Milisent I, 186
Perry, Millicent I, 16
Perry, Mylea I, 186
Perry, Nancy Jane I, 15
Perry, Nathan I, 16
Perry, Nathan I, 68
Perry, Nathan I, 186
Perry, Phebe IV, 262
Perry, Rachel I, 37
Perry, Rachel I, 69
Perry, Rachel I, 566
Perry, Rachel IV, 262
Perry, Rachel IV, 346
Perry, Rachel IV, 398
Perry, Rachel IV, 750
Perry, Rachel V, 760
Perry, Ralph E. D. I, 16
Perry, Ralph E. D. I, 69
Perry, Rebecca IV, 750
Perry, Rebecca Savry IV, 726
Perry, Rebecca Savry IV, 750
Perry, Restore I, 3
Perry, Restore I, 15
Perry, Restore I, 16
Perry, Restore I, 39
Perry, Restore I, 69
Perry, Restore I, 186
Perry, Reuben I, 11
Perry, Reuben I, 16
Perry, Reuben I, 57
Perry, Reuben I, 67
Perry, Reuben I, 69
Perry, Reuben I, 87
Perry, Reuben I, 186
Perry, Roy T. W. I, 16
Perry, Roy T. W. I, 69
Perry, Ruanna IV, 346
Perry, Rueben I, 68
Perry, Ruth I, 40
Perry, Ruth I, 69
Perry, Samuel IV, 262
Perry, Sarah I, 11
Perry, Sarah I, 15
Perry, Sarah I, 16
Perry, Sarah I, 41
Perry, Sarah I, 57
Perry, Sarah I, 69
Perry, Sarah I, 137
Perry, Sarah I, 161
Perry, Sarah I, 186
Perry, Sarah IV, 262
Perry, Sarah Ann I, 15
Perry, Sarah Parry II, 621
Perry, Susan Ellen I, 16
Perry, T. Eri I, 69
Perry, Thomas II, 621
Perry, Thomas IV, 346
Perry, Thomas E. I, 69
Perry, Thomas E. I, 89
Perry, Thomas Erie I, 16
Perry, Thomas Jay I, 16
Perry, Thos. Eri I, 33
Perry, Verley V, 462
Perry, W. Mahlon IV, 986
Perry, Walter V, 308
Perry, Walter V, 462
Perry, Widow Hannah I, 58
Perry, Widow Hannah I, 69
Perry, Wm. III, 253
Perry, Wm. IV, 986
Perry, Wm. V, 1014
Perry, Wm. Griffin I, 10
Perry, Wyatt M. IV, 986
Perryman, Cynthia I, 897
Perryman, Cynthia I, 906
Perryman, Mary I, 889
Perryman, Mary I, 897
Perse, An I, 199
Perse, Damaris I, 155
Perse, Joseph I, 155
Perse, Joseph I, 161
Persey, Charles VI, 931
Persey, Spicy VI, 931
Persinger, Minnie V, 704
Persinger, Rilla V, 704
Person, Aaron II, 440
Person, Benjamin VI, 429
Person, Clary VI, 870
Person, Elizabeth I, 524
Person, Elizabeth I, 566
Person, Elizabeth I, 897
Person, Elizabeth II, 249
Person, Elizabeth II, 263
Person, Elizabeth II, 572
Person, Elizabeth II, 617
Person, Enoch VI, 429
Person, George I, 567
Person, Huldah I, 995
Person, Isaac I, 897
Person, Margaret II, 234
Person, Margaret II, 249
Person, Mark I, 67
Person, Martin VI, 846
Person, Mary I, 67
Person, Mary I, 566
Person, Mary VI, 429
Person, Nathan I, 730
Person, Rachel VI, 846
Person, Samuel I, 566
Person, Samuel I, 567
Person, Samuel I, 1130
Person, Samuel VI, 429
Person, Sarah I, 567
Person, Sarah I, 719
Person, Sarah I, 730
Person, Sarah I, 884
Person, Sarah I, 897
Person, Sarah I, 995
Person, Thomas I, 524
Person, Thomas I, 566
Person, Thomas, Jr. I, 897
Person, William VI, 429
Persons, George I, 567
Persons, Mary I, 566
Persons, Ruth II, 615
Perts, Joshua V, 1014
Perviance, Amanda IV, 1181
Perviance, Cynthia IV, 1181
Perviance, Deborah IV, 494
Perviance, Eleanor IV, 265
Perviance, Elizabeth IV, 71
Perviance, Elizabeth IV, 106
Perviance, Evan IV, 265
Perviance, Henry IV, 1181
Perviance, James IV, 71
Perviance, Joseph IV, 106
Perviance, Joseph E. IV, 1181
Perviance, Martha M. IV, 1181
Perviance, Sarah IV, 106
Perviance, William H. IV, 1181
Pervies, John IV, 429
Pervis, Ann IV, 429
Pervis, Ann IV, 1074
Pervis, Edward IV, 1220
Pervis, Elijah IV, 1111
Pervis, John I, 296
Pervis, John IV, 429
Pervis, Jonathan IV, 429
Pervis, Jonn IV, 426
Pervis, Levi IV, 429
Pervis, Levi IV, 1074
Pervis, Mary IV, 426
Pervis, Mary IV, 429
Pervis, Mary IV, 1111
Pervis, Moses I, 296
Pervis, Moses I, 303
Pervis, Moses I, 316
Pervis, Moses IV, 1074
Pervis, Polly I, 316
Pervis, Stephen I, 316
Pervis, Susanna I, 296
Pervis, Susanna I, 302
Pervis, Susanna I, 316
Pervis, Susannah I, 303
Pervis, Susannah I, 316
Pervis, Winifred IV, 429
Pervis, Winneferd I, 316
Pervis, Winneford I, 296
Pervow, Jane I, 449
Pervow, Jane I, 452
Pery, Sarah I, 156
Pery, Sarah I, 161
Perygo, Sarah IV, 429
Peshine, Emma III, 99
Pete, Cornelius VI, 875
Peteate, John VI, 357
Petell, Martha II, 621
Peter, Lucy C. VI, 1007
Peter, Sovrin VI, 1007
Peter, Thomas, Sr. II, 446
Peter, William II, 446
Peterman, George VI, 977
Peterman, Joseph McKinney
V, 704
Peterman, Margaret VI, 977
Peters, ??? III, 501
Peters, Abigail II, 406
Peters, Addie VI, 770
Peters, Alma I, 1160
Peters, Amanda V, 573
Peters, Amy III, 253
Peters, An II, 406
Peters, Ann II, 406
Peters, Ann II, 473
Peters, Ann II, 621
Peters, Ann II, 641
Peters, Ann J. VI, 977
Peters, Ann Sophia III, 253
Peters, Anna M. II, 909
Peters, Anne III, 253
Peters, Aurelia C. VI, 1006
Peters, Benjamin II, 406
Peters, Bertha II, 909
Peters, Bertha Gilpin II, 814
Peters, Carl W. IV, 403
Peters, Catherine Dare VI, 770
Peters, Charles C. VI, 941
Peters, Charlotte II, 621
Peters, Chas. IV, 1333
Peters, Chas. P. II, 814
Peters, Chas. P. II, 909
Peters, Chas. P. II, 939
Peters, Chester B. IV, 403
Peters, Clarence C. II, 909
Peters, Clarence C. II, 939
Peters, Clayton III, 508
Peters, Clayton A. III, 492
Peters, Clayton Ames III, 492
Peters, Clifton C. VI, 977
Peters, Corydon Ovid I, 1146
Peters, David II, 406
Peters, David II, 621
Peters, David III, 253
Peters, Deborah III, 253
Peters, Dell D. II, 909
Peters, Dell P. II, 760
Peters, Dell P. II, 909
Peters, Dr. Charles III, 454
Peters, Dr. Chas. III, 433
Peters, Ed K. V, 704
Peters, Edith Mary V, 704
Peters, Edna Vickers VI, 770
Peters, Edna Vickers VI, 786
Peters, Edward IV, 403
Peters, Edward K. V, 704
Peters, Eleanor II, 406
Peters, Elisabeth II, 621
Peters, Elisabeth II, 660
Peters, Elisha VI, 927
Peters, Elisha VI, 995
Peters, Elisha VI, 1006
Peters, Eliza IV, 1239
Peters, Elizabeth II, 406
Peters, Elizabeth II, 486
Peters, Elizabeth II, 621
Peters, Elizabeth III, 492
Peters, Elizabeth III, 501
Peters, Elizabeth A. VI, 941
Peters, Elnora Elizabeth IV, 1333
Peters, Evan II, 406
Peters, Evan II, 621
Peters, Frank I, 1160
Peters, Frank IV, 1179
Peters, Frank IV, 1239
Peters, Frederick G. VI, 977
Peters, George II, 406
Peters, Hannah II, 406
Peters, Hannah II, 607
Peters, Hannah II, 621
Peters, Hannah Eliza I, 1146
Peters, Hannah P. II, 909
Peters, Hugh IV, 1239
Peters, Isaac II, 621
Peters, J. A. I, 1160
Peters, J. Frank I, 1160
Peters, Jacob I, 1145
Peters, Jacob I, 1160
Peters, James II, 621
Peters, James III, 433
Peters, James V, 573
Peters, James Arthur I, 1146
Peters, James S. II, 621
Peters, Jane II, 621
Peters, Jane II, 689
Peters, Jane IV, 1260
Peters, Jane VI, 989
Peters, Jane VI, 995
Peters, Jane Ann III, 253
Peters, Jas. A. I, 1160
Peters, Jennie V, 573
Peters, Jennie V, 680
Peters, John I, 69
Peters, John II, 406
Peters, John II, 516
Peters, John II, 621
Peters, John III, 253
Peters, John IV, 1260
Peters, John VI, 770
Peters, John L. I, 1160
Peters, Jonathan II, 406
Peters, Jonathan IV, 1260
Peters, Joseph I, 1160
Peters, Joseph II, 406
Peters, Joseph Alexander I, 1146
Peters, Julia D. B. VI, 926
Peters, Kate IV, 1239
Peters, Kearsey II, 621
Peters, Kersey II, 621
Peters, Kitty II, 621
Peters, Margaret II, 621
Peters, Margret Esther I, 1146
Peters, Margrett II, 406
Peters, Mari anna E. IV, 403
Peters, Maria Evaline V, 704
Peters, Marian H. IV, 403
Peters, Marion III, 492
Peters, Marion III, 508
Peters, Martha II, 597
Peters, Martha II, 621
Peters, Martha II, 1021
Peters, Martha VI, 977
Peters, Mary II, 406
Peters, Mary II, 516
Peters, Mary II, 574
Peters, Mary II, 621
Peters, Mary II, 630
Peters, Mary II, 643
Peters, Mary II, 909
Peters, Mary III, 433
Peters, Mary III, 454
Peters, Mary III, 492
Peters, Mary III, 508
Peters, Mary IV, 1260
Peters, Mary A. II, 814
Peters, Mary A. II, 909
Peters, Mary A. II, 939

Peters, Mary A. IV, 1333
Peters, Mary D. II, 909
Peters, Mary E. I, 1146
Peters, Mary Jane IV, 1260
Peters, Mary K. III, 492
Peters, Maude I, 1160
Peters, Meriam II, 621
Peters, Miriam II, 406
Peters, Miriam II, 493
Peters, Miriam Julia III, 253
Peters, Mordecai C. II, 621
Peters, Mordecai C. III, 253
Peters, Moza VI, 989
Peters, Mrs. Elnora E. IV, 1333
Peters, Mrs. Mary VI, 941
Peters, Myrtle D. IV, 402
Peters, Myrtle D. IV, 429
Peters, Nicholas II, 136
Peters, Orville Sherwin VI, 770
Peters, Orville Sherwin VI, 786
Peters, Rachel II, 406
Peters, Rebecca II, 500
Peters, Rebecca II, 621
Peters, Rebecca H. II, 406
Peters, Rebeckah II, 1021
Peters, Reece II, 406
Peters, Reece, Jr. II, 406
Peters, Rees II, 598
Peters, Rees II, 621
Peters, Reese II, 473
Peters, Reese II, 486
Peters, Reese II, 597
Peters, Reese II, 621
Peters, Reese, Jr. II, 621
Peters, Robert IV, 429
Peters, Ruth III, 253
Peters, Ruth E. I, 1160
Peters, Ruth Emeline I, 1145
Peters, Ruthemaline I, 1096
Peters, Samuel E. I, 1160
Peters, Samuel Everett I, 1146
Peters, Sarah II, 406
Peters, Sarah II, 460
Peters, Sarah II, 621
Peters, Sarah II, 674
Peters, Sarah T. III, 253
Peters, Sophia III, 148
Peters, Sophia III, 253
Peters, Stephen J. VI, 1006
Peters, Susan Ann VI, 977
Peters, Susanna II, 406
Peters, Susannah II, 406
Peters, Tho. II, 1033
Peters, Thomas II, 406
Peters, Thomas II, 516
Peters, Thomas II, 607
Peters, Thomas II, 621
Peters, Thomas II, 630
Peters, Thomas, Sr. II, 406
Peters, Valentine III, 253
Peters, Wd. Martha II, 598
Peters, Wd. Martha II, 621
Peters, Wesley VI, 989
Peters, Wharton Smith II, 406
Peters, William II, 406
Peters, William III, 253
Peters, William VI, 977
Peters, Wilson Mifflin IV, 403
Peters, Wm. J. VI, 770
Peters, Wm., Jr. II, 621
Peterson, Alice S. IV, 263
Peterson, Anna II, 406
Peterson, Anna II, 760
Peterson, Anna II, 909
Peterson, Archie V, 197
Peterson, Archie E. V, 197
Peterson, Bertha J. IV, 1220
Peterson, Bessie L. V, 197
Peterson, Carl V, 197
Peterson, Carl L. V, 197
Peterson, Clarence V, 523
Peterson, Cora V, 197
Peterson, Elizabeth IV, 263
Peterson, Elizabeth IV, 287
Peterson, Elizabeth V, 656
Peterson, Elizabeth V, 704
Peterson, Esther II, 406
Peterson, Esther II, 909
Peterson, Esther Evans II, 760
Peterson, Florence IV, 1333
Peterson, Frances M. II, 909
Peterson, Frances Maria II, 814
Peterson, Garfield V, 197
Peterson, George II, 406
Peterson, George II, 621
Peterson, George II, 760
Peterson, George II, 791
Peterson, George II, 814
Peterson, George II, 840
Peterson, George II, 909
Peterson, George, Jr. II, 406
Peterson, George, Jr. II, 621
Peterson, Halliel Holland V, 197
Peterson, Hannah M. II, 840
Peterson, Hannah M. II, 909
Peterson, Hattie E. V, 197
Peterson, Helen II, 909
Peterson, Helen Longstreth II, 814
Peterson, Henry II, 406
Peterson, Henry II, 909
Peterson, Isaac O. V, 197
Peterson, Israel II, 814
Peterson, Jane II, 37
Peterson, Jane II, 92
Peterson, Jane II, 406
Peterson, Jane II, 621
Peterson, Jane II, 760
Peterson, Jane II, 791
Peterson, Jane II, 814
Peterson, Jane II, 840
Peterson, Jane II, 909
Peterson, Jennie E. V, 197
Peterson, Lizzie K. I, 339
Peterson, Lula V, 704
Peterson, Mary IV, 1333
Peterson, Mary A. II, 810
Peterson, Minnie Kennedy I, 339
Peterson, Nicholas II, 122
Peterson, Nicholson II, 92
Peterson, Olive Wilson V, 197
Peterson, Pearson Serrill II, 814
Peterson, Pearson Serrill II, 909
Peterson, Philena II, 909
Peterson, Philena Marshall II, 814
Peterson, Rachel II, 92
Peterson, Rachel II, 406
Peterson, Rachel II, 909
Peterson, Rachel Evans II, 621
Peterson, Rachel Evans II, 760
Peterson, Rachel Evans II, 791
Peterson, Rebecca II, 805
Peterson, Richard II, 406
Peterson, Richard II, 760
Peterson, Richard II, 909
Peterson, Robert E. II, 840
Peterson, Robert E. II, 909
Peterson, Robert Evans II, 406
Peterson, Robert Evans II, 621
Peterson, Robert Evans II, 760
Peterson, Robert Evans II, 909
Peterson, Ruthanna V, 197
Peterson, Sarah II, 37
Peterson, Sarah II, 92
Peterson, Svend M. V, 656
Peterson, Svend M. V, 704
Peterson, William E. V, 197
Petet, Mary III, 165
Peticrew, James VI, 977
Peticrew, Winney VI, 977
Petiford, Chas. V, 1014
Petiford, Frederick V, 1014
Petiford, Mareanna V, 1014
Petiford, Margaret A. V, 1014
Petiford, Reuben M. V, 1014
Petiford, William V, 1014
Petit, Ann II, 122
Petit, Ann II, 123
Petit, Ann II, 155
Petit, Bula Ann IV, 750
Petit, Caroline II, 155
Petit, Caroline E. II, 910
Petit, Charles C. II, 155
Petit, Charles W. II, 155
Petit, Charlotte II, 155
Petit, David II, 155
Petit, David II, 160
Petit, Elihu II, 155
Petit, Elihu N. II, 155
Petit, Elihu R. II, 155
Petit, Elizabeth II, 137
Petit, Elizabeth V, 792
Petit, Elizabeth VI, 1011
Petit, Elizabeth P. II, 155
Petit, Eugene II, 910
Petit, Frankey VI, 987
Petit, Franklin II, 155
Petit, George W. II, 155
Petit, George W. II, 910
Petit, Hannah P. II, 143
Petit, Hannah P. II, 155
Petit, Huldah II, 155
Petit, Jas. J. II, 137
Petit, Jonathan II, 155
Petit, Joseph II, 155
Petit, Joseph Frederick II, 910
Petit, Lewis II, 155
Petit, Lewis VI, 1011
Petit, Margaret R. II, 155
Petit, Martha II, 155
Petit, Martha II, 160
Petit, Martha B. II, 155
Petit, Mary II, 136
Petit, Mary L. II, 910
Petit, Rachel II, 55
Petit, Rachel II, 92
Petit, Rachel II, 129
Petit, Sarah II, 55
Petit, Sarah II, 92
Petit, Sarah II, 123
Petit, Sarah II, 129
Petit, Sarah II, 130
Petit, Sarah II, 136
Petit, Sarah II, 155
Petit, Sarah B. II, 130
Petit, Sarah F. II, 155
Petit, Sarah F. II, 160
Petit, Sarah L. IV, 263
Petit, Sidney J. V, 37
Petit, Thomas VI, 1011
Petit, Wd. Sarah B. II, 136
Petit, Woodnutt II, 55
Petit, Woodnutt II, 92
Petit, Woodnutt II, 123
Petit, Woodnutt II, 129
Petit, Woodnutt II, 130
Petit, Woodnutt II, 136
Petit, Woodnutt II, 155
Petit, Woodnutt II, 160
Petitt, Beulah Ann IV, 873
Petitt, Beulah Ann IV, 881
Petitt, Charles IV, 873
Petitt, Permelia IV, 873
Petre, Mildred G. IV, 1333
Petros, John VI, 262
Petros, Rhoda VI, 262
Petross, Sarah VI, 262
Petsmyre, Carrie S. V, 110
Petsmyre, Charles V, 110
Petsmyre, Elma L. V, 110
Petsmyre, Gulielma V, 110
Petsmyre, Sallie M. V, 110
Pettet, Charles II, 323
Pettet, Charles IV, 651
Pettet, Daniel IV, 651
Pettet, Elizabeth II, 760
Pettet, Elizabeth K. II, 323
Pettet, Elnathan IV, 492
Pettet, Howard S. II, 323
Pettet, John G. IV, 263
Pettet, Joseph E. IV, 986
Pettet, Lucretia IV, 651
Pettet, Lydia S. IV, 986
Pettet, Margaret H. IV, 492
Pettet, Martha IV, 651
Pettet, Mary IV, 492
Pettet, Mary Jane IV, 190
Pettet, Mary Jane IV, 263
Pettet, Milton R. IV, 263
Pettet, Nathaniel II, 760
Pettet, Rebecca IV, 651
Pettet, Ruth V, 46
Pettet, Ruth V, 110
Pettet, Sarah I, 995
Pettet, Sarah I, 998
Pettet, Sarah C. IV, 978
Pettet, Sarah C. IV, 986
Pettet, Wm. IV, 986
Pettet, Wm. P. IV, 492
Pettet, Wm., Jr. IV, 978
Pettet, Wm., Jr. IV, 986
Pettett, Francis IV, 881
Pettett, Hannah IV, 1220
Pettett, Mary IV, 1213
Pettett, Mary IV, 1220
Petticrew, Ann VI, 819
Petticrew, Ann VI, 846
Petticrew, David VI, 846
Petticrew, Elizabeth VI, 819
Petticrew, Emeline VI, 846
Petticrew, James VI, 846
Petticrew, Jennet VI, 803
Petticrew, John VI, 819
Petticrew, John VI, 846
Petticrew, John VI, 856
Petticrew, Martha L. VI, 846
Petticrew, Mary A. VI, 846
Petticrew, Matthew VI, 846
Petticrew, Samuel VI, 846
Petticrew, Sarah A. VI, 846
Petticrew, Susan VI, 846
Petticrew, William VI, 846
Pettie, Mary V. I, 897
Pettie, William C. I, 897
Pettiford, Alexander V, 1014
Pettiford, Bessie V, 1014
Pettiford, Chas. V, 1014
Pettiford, Chas. B. V, 1014
Pettiford, Frederick V, 1014
Pettiford, Mareanna V, 1014
Pettiford, Margaret A. V, 1014
Pettiford, Margaret Ann V, 1014
Pettiford, Marianna V, 1014
Pettiford, Reuben M. V, 1014
Pettiford, William V, 1014
Pettiford, Wm. V, 1014
Pettis, Daniel IV, 750
Pettis, Lucinda IV, 750
Pettis, Lucy IV, 750
Pettis, Lucy J. IV, 750
Pettit, ??? IV, 603
Pettit, ??? IV, 795
Pettit, ??? IV, 912
Pettit, ??? IV, 1303
Pettit, A. J. Jeneura IV, 1239
Pettit, Abel J. IV, 881
Pettit, Abigail IV, 838
Pettit, Abigail IV, 853
Pettit, Abigail IV, 913
Pettit, Abigail VI, 543
Pettit, Abigail VI, 583
Pettit, Acsah II, 323
Pettit, Allie R. IV, 1239
Pettit, Andrew IV, 838
Pettit, Andrew IV, 1239
Pettit, Ann II, 92
Pettit, Ann II, 122
Pettit, Ann II, 136
Pettit, Ann II, 155
Pettit, Ann II, 804
Pettit, Ann II, 909
Pettit, Ann II, 910
Pettit, Ann IV, 881
Pettit, Ann VI, 950
Pettit, Anna IV, 750
Pettit, Anna Elizabeth IV, 263
Pettit, Annie E. IV, 973
Pettit, Asahel H. IV, 912
Pettit, Augusta IV, 912
Pettit, Augusta M. II, 18
Pettit, Benjamin IV, 263
Pettit, Benjamin IV, 750
Pettit, Benjamin IV, 912
Pettit, Beulah Ann IV, 750
Pettit, Beulah Ann IV, 881
Pettit, Beulah Ann IV, 913
Pettit, Blanch IV, 750
Pettit, Bula Ann IV, 750
Pettit, Buly Ann IV, 838
Pettit, Caroline II, 136
Pettit, Caroline II, 155
Pettit, Caroline II, 815
Pettit, Caroline II, 910
Pettit, Caroline E. II, 136
Pettit, Caroline E. II, 155
Pettit, Caroline E. II, 910
Pettit, Carolyn II, 136
Pettit, Charity IV, 912
Pettit, Charity D. IV, 913
Pettit, Charity D. IV, 915
Pettit, Charity D. IV, 986
Pettit, Charity D. IV, 989
Pettit, Charles II, 122
Pettit, Charles II, 323
Pettit, Charles IV, 651
Pettit, Charles IV, 838
Pettit, Charles C. II, 136
Pettit, Charles C. II, 155
Pettit, Charles W. II, 92
Pettit, Charles W. II, 136
Pettit, Charles W. II, 155
Pettit, Charlotte II, 92
Pettit, Charlotte II, 122
Pettit, Charlotte II, 136
Pettit, Charlotte II, 155
Pettit, Charlotte IV, 899
Pettit, Charlotte IV, 908
Pettit, Charlotte IV, 912
Pettit, Charlotte IV, 913
Pettit, Clarkson II, 136
Pettit, Clyde IV, 986
Pettit, Cora IV, 1239
Pettit, Cursey IV, 913
Pettit, Curtice G. IV, 263
Pettit, Curtis H. IV, 912
Pettit, Daniel IV, 651
Pettit, Daniel IV, 958
Pettit, Daniel IV, 986
Pettit, Daniel R. IV, 750
Pettit, Daniel R. IV, 986
Pettit, David II, 37
Pettit, David II, 92
Pettit, David II, 136
Pettit, David II, 155
Pettit, David II, 158
Pettit, David II, 910
Pettit, Deborah IV, 838
Pettit, Deborah IV, 853
Pettit, Elihu II, 155
Pettit, Elihu N. II, 155
Pettit, Elihu R. II, 136
Pettit, Elihu R. II, 155
Pettit, Elizabeth II, 165
Pettit, Elizabeth II, 312
Pettit, Elizabeth II, 760
Pettit, Elizabeth II, 910
Pettit, Elizabeth IV, 750
Pettit, Elizabeth IV, 759
Pettit, Elizabeth IV, 881
Pettit, Elizabeth IV, 912
Pettit, Elizabeth IV, 913
Pettit, Elizabeth IV, 914
Pettit, Elizabeth IV, 915
Pettit, Elizabeth IV, 986
Pettit, Elizabeth V, 794
Pettit, Elizabeth H. IV, 105
Pettit, Elizabeth H. IV, 986
Pettit, Elizabeth K. II, 323
Pettit, Elizabeth P. II, 155
Pettit, Elizabeth P. II, 804
Pettit, Elizabeth R. II, 155
Pettit, Ellen IV, 1239
Pettit, Elma IV, 209
Pettit, Elmyra IV, 912
Pettit, Elnathan IV, 200
Pettit, Elnathan IV, 263
Pettit, Elnathan IV, 307
Pettit, Elnathan IV, 492
Pettit, Elnathan IV, 505
Pettit, Elnathan IV, 750
Pettit, Elnathan IV, 912
Pettit, Elnathan IV, 1260
Pettit, Elnathan, Jr. IV, 263
Pettit, Elnathen IV, 913
Pettit, Emma IV, 263
Pettit, Emma IV, 273
Pettit, Emma C. IV, 263
Pettit, Emma S. IV, 958
Pettit, Eugene II, 136
Pettit, Eugene II, 155
Pettit, Eugene II, 910
Pettit, Ferdinand G. III, 433
Pettit, Francis IV, 881
Pettit, Frank R. IV, 263
Pettit, Franklin II, 136
Pettit, Franklin II, 155
Pettit, Franklin R. IV, 263
Pettit, Genevra IV, 1239
Pettit, George II, 136
Pettit, George II, 155
Pettit, George W. II, 136
Pettit, George W. II, 155
Pettit, George W. II, 910
Pettit, Hannah II, 92
Pettit, Hannah II, 122
Pettit, Hannah II, 136
Pettit, Hannah II, 155
Pettit, Hannah II, 158
Pettit, Hannah IV, 208
Pettit, Hannah IV, 227
Pettit, Hannah IV, 908
Pettit, Hannah IV, 913
Pettit, Hannah G. IV, 210
Pettit, Hannah G. IV, 226
Pettit, Hannah G. IV, 263
Pettit, Hannah G. IV, 913
Pettit, Hannah J. IV, 200
Pettit, Hannah J. IV, 263
Pettit, Hannah Streeter II, 1
Pettit, Hannah W. IV, 750
Pettit, Hannah Z. IV, 912
Pettit, Howard II, 312
Pettit, Howard S. II, 323
Pettit, Hulda II, 92
Pettit, Huldah II, 122
Pettit, Huldah II, 136
Pettit, Huldah II, 155
Pettit, J. Lawrence II, 155
Pettit, James II, 155
Pettit, James J. II, 136
Pettit, James J., Jr. II, 136
Pettit, Jane II, 165
Pettit, Jane II, 909
Pettit, Jane II, 910
Pettit, Jane IV, 986
Pettit, Jane P. IV, 263
Pettit, Jane R. II, 298
Pettit, Jane R. IV, 105
Pettit, Jane R. IV, 226
Pettit, Jane R. IV, 263
Pettit, Jane R. IV, 750
Pettit, Jane R. IV, 967
Pettit, Jane R. IV, 986
Pettit, Jane R. IV, 1333
Pettit, Jared H. IV, 912
Pettit, Jeannette III, 29
Pettit, Jeannette III, 254
Pettit, Jesse K. IV, 899
Pettit, Jesse K. IV, 908
Pettit, Jesse K. IV, 913
Pettit, Jesse Kersey IV, 912
Pettit, John III, 29
Pettit, John III, 254
Pettit, John IV, 1073

t, John G. IV, 263
t, John G. VI, 833
t, John Grubb IV, 263
, John Laurence II, 155
, John Lawrence II, 136
t, Jonathan II, 37
t, Jonathan II, 92
t, Jonathan II, 122
t, Jonathan II, 136
t, Jonathan II, 155
t, Jonathan II, 814
t, Jos. Frederick II, 136
t, Joseph II, 37
it, Joseph II, 54
t, Joseph II, 92
t, Joseph II, 136
t, Joseph II, 155
it, Joseph II, 814
it, Joseph II, 910
it, Joseph IV, 208
it, Joseph IV, 226
it, Joseph IV, 263
it, Joseph IV, 266
it, Joseph IV, 750
it, Joseph IV, 881
it, Joseph IV, 912
it, Joseph IV, 913
it, Joseph IV, 986
it, Joseph VI, 543
it, Joseph VI, 583
it, Joseph C. IV, 986
it, Joseph E. IV, 750
it, Joseph E. IV, 923
it, Joseph E. IV, 986
it, Joseph E. IV, 1000
it, Joseph Frederick II, 155
it, Joseph Frederick II, 910
it, Joseph, Jr. II, 136
it, Joseph, Jr. II, 910
tit, Judith VI, 977
tit, Laura IV, 986
tit, Laura IV, 1041
tit, Laura E. IV, 986
tit, Laura S. IV, 1041
tit, Lewis II, 92
tit, Lewis II, 122
tit, Lewis II, 136
tit, Lewis II, 155
tit, Lewis VI, 950
tit, Lewis VI, 977
tit, Lewis VI, 1011
tit, Lucinda VI, 846
tit, Lucretia IV, 620
tit, Lucretia IV, 651
tit, Lucretia M. IV, 912
tit, Lucretia P. IV, 798
tit, Lucretia P. IV, 838
tit, Lucretia P. IV, 899
tit, Lydia IV, 750
tit, Lydia IV, 923
tit, Lydia IV, 1000
tit, Lydia S. IV, 986
ttit, Lydia W. IV, 263
ttit, Lydia W. IV, 266
ttit, M. Elma IV, 208
ttit, M. Elma IV, 263
ttit, Mabel L. IV, 923
ttit, Margaret IV, 263
ttit, Margaret IV, 912
ttit, Margaret H. IV, 263
ttit, Margaret H. IV, 307
ttit, Margaret H. IV, 492
ttit, Margaret H. IV, 505
ttit, Margaret H. IV, 1260
ttit, Margaret R. II, 155
ttit, Margarett II, 136
ttit, Maria II, 312
ttit, Maria II, 323
ttit, Maria II, 327
ttit, Martha II, 136
ttit, Martha II, 155
ttit, Martha II, 910
ttit, Martha IV, 645
ttit, Martha IV, 651
ettit, Martha IV, 913
ettit, Martha B. II, 136
ettit, Martha B. II, 155
ettit, Martha B. II, 158
ettit, Martha E. II, 136
ettit, Martha J. VI, 806
ettit, Mary I Sup 1, 5
ettit, Mary II, 37
ettit, Mary II, 79
ettit, Mary II, 92
ettit, Mary II, 136
ettit, Mary II, 760
ettit, Mary II, 909
ettit, Mary II, 910
ettit, Mary III, 433
ettit, Mary IV, 263
ettit, Mary IV, 492
Pettit, Mary IV, 651
Pettit, Mary IV, 750
Pettit, Mary IV, 832
Pettit, Mary IV, 838
Pettit, Mary IV, 881
Pettit, Mary IV, 883
Pettit, Mary IV, 912
Pettit, Mary IV, 913
Pettit, Mary IV, 915
Pettit, Mary VI, 977
Pettit, Mary VI, 1011
Pettit, Mary A. IV, 986
Pettit, Mary Ann IV, 248
Pettit, Mary Ann IV, 263
Pettit, Mary Augusta II, 136
Pettit, Mary Augusta II, 155
Pettit, Mary C. IV, 227
Pettit, Mary C. IV, 263
Pettit, Mary Colson II, 155
Pettit, Mary Elma IV, 90
Pettit, Mary Elma IV, 105
Pettit, Mary Elma IV, 263
Pettit, Mary Frances III, 29
Pettit, Mary Frances III, 254
Pettit, Mary Jane IV, 190
Pettit, Mary Jane IV, 263
Pettit, Mary Jane IV, 492
Pettit, Mary Jane IV, 838
Pettit, Mary L. II, 910
Pettit, Mary P. IV, 912
Pettit, Mary, Jr. IV, 881
Pettit, Mary, Jr. IV, 913
Pettit, Milton IV, 912
Pettit, Milton E. IV, 263
Pettit, Milton E., Jr. IV, 263
Pettit, Milton R. IV, 210
Pettit, Milton R. IV, 227
Pettit, Milton R. IV, 236
Pettit, Milton R. IV, 263
Pettit, Mordecai L. IV, 1041
Pettit, Mott III, 433
Pettit, Myrtle II, 312
Pettit, Nancy IV, 1179
Pettit, Nathaniel II, 760
Pettit, Nathaniel II, 804
Pettit, Nathaniel II, 909
Pettit, Nathaniel II, 910
Pettit, Paris IV, 838
Pettit, Permela IV, 859
Pettit, Rachel II, 37
Pettit, Rachel II, 92
Pettit, Rachel Helen II, 136
Pettit, Rebecca IV, 651
Pettit, Rebecca IV, 750
Pettit, Rebecca IV, 958
Pettit, Rebecca IV, 986
Pettit, Rebecca W. IV, 711
Pettit, Rebecca W. IV, 750
Pettit, Rebecca W. IV, 986
Pettit, Russell II, 312
Pettit, Ruth II, 136
Pettit, Sam'l. VI, 806
Pettit, Samuel VI, 843
Pettit, Samuel VI, 846
Pettit, Sarah II, 37
Pettit, Sarah II, 54
Pettit, Sarah II, 92
Pettit, Sarah II, 122
Pettit, Sarah II, 136
Pettit, Sarah II, 155
Pettit, Sarah II, 789
Pettit, Sarah II, 814
Pettit, Sarah II, 910
Pettit, Sarah IV, 651
Pettit, Sarah IV, 912
Pettit, Sarah IV, 913
Pettit, Sarah IV, 936
Pettit, Sarah IV, 986
Pettit, Sarah Ann II, 136
Pettit, Sarah Bassett II, 789
Pettit, Sarah C. IV, 986
Pettit, Sarah F. II, 136
Pettit, Sarah F. II, 155
Pettit, Sarah L. IV, 236
Pettit, Sarah L. IV, 263
Pettit, Sarah, Jr. II, 122
Pettit, Susan B. II, 789
Pettit, Thomas II, 37
Pettit, Thomas II, 92
Pettit, Thomas VI, 977
Pettit, Thomas VI, 1011
Pettit, Thos. VI, 987
Pettit, Unity IV, 881
Pettit, Wd. Sarah B. II, 136
Pettit, Wesley IV, 1239
Pettit, William II, 165
Pettit, William IV, 105
Pettit, William IV, 263
Pettit, William IV, 750
Pettit, William IV, 912
Pettit, William IV, 915
Pettit, William IV, 967
Pettit, William IV, 986
Pettit, William IV, 1239
Pettit, William B. IV, 263
Pettit, William H. II, 312
Pettit, William P. IV, 263
Pettit, William, Jr. IV, 105
Pettit, William, Jr. VI, 687
Pettit, Wm. IV, 226
Pettit, Wm. IV, 263
Pettit, Wm. IV, 915
Pettit, Wm. IV, 986
Pettit, Wm. H. II, 136
Pettit, Wm. H. II, 155
Pettit, Wm. H. IV, 1239
Pettit, Wm. Henry II, 136
Pettit, Wm. P. IV, 492
Pettit, Wm., Jr. IV, 986
Pettit, Woodnut II, 92
Pettit, Woodnut II, 136
Pettit, Woodnutt II, 37
Pettit, Woodnutt II, 92
Pettit, Woodnutt II, 122
Pettit, Woodnutt II, 136
Pettit, Woodnutt II, 155
Pettit, Woodnutt II, 158
Pettit, Woodnutt II, 789
Pettit, Woodnutt II, 814
Pettitt, Caroline E. II, 873
Pettitt, Caroline E. II, 910
Pettitt, Elizabeth IV, 881
Pettitt, Elnathan IV, 750
Pettitt, James VI, 863
Pettitt, Margaret H. IV, 492
Pettitt, Sarah A. VI, 863
Pettitt, Unity IV, 881
Pettress, Eliza VI, 262
Pettress, John VI, 262
Pettress, Wd. Sarah VI, 262
Pettros, Ann VI, 262
Pettros, John VI, 262
Pettros, Sarah VI, 262
Petty, Annie F. I, 863
Petty, Catharine VI, 831
Petty, Charles M. I, 643
Petty, Charles W. I, 639
Petty, Charles Watson I, 624
Petty, Charles Watson I, 863
Petty, Charles Worth I, 624
Petty, D. M. I, 639
Petty, David M. I, 863
Petty, David M. I, 897
Petty, Eliza K. VI, 846
Petty, Elizabeth VI, 846
Petty, Emma L. I, 619
Petty, Emma L. I, 863
Petty, Frances I, 624
Petty, Frances I, 633
Petty, Frances I, 639
Petty, Freda I, 624
Petty, Frieda V. I, 639
Petty, Frieda V. I, 643
Petty, Frieda Victoria I, 639
Petty, G. Edgar I, 639
Petty, George Edgar I, 624
Petty, George Edgar I, 863
Petty, Herbert I, 639
Petty, Herbert C. I, 633
Petty, Herbert C. I, 639
Petty, Herbert C. I, 863
Petty, Herbert Clinton I, 624
Petty, James W. VI, 846
Petty, Jane II, 249
Petty, Jane II, 621
Petty, John W. I, 863
Petty, John W. I, 897
Petty, Julius V, 926
Petty, Laura I, 619
Petty, Laura I, 624
Petty, Laura I, 878
Petty, Laura I, 897
Petty, Laura I. I, 897
Petty, Laura J. I, 863
Petty, Louise I, 920
Petty, Luther W. I, 863
Petty, Lydia I, 686
Petty, Lydia I, 731
Petty, Lydia I, 863
Petty, Lydia I, 920
Petty, Lydia I, 992
Petty, Lydia I, 995
Petty, M. Victoria I, 626
Petty, M. Victoria I, 639
Petty, Mary I, 534
Petty, Mary I, 567
Petty, Mary I, 897
Petty, Mary I, 903
Petty, Mary C. I, 639
Petty, Mary E. I, 863
Petty, Mary Lizzie I, 863
Petty, Mary M. I, 639
Petty, Mary M. I, 897
Petty, Mary Macy I, 863
Petty, Mary Maria I, 624
Petty, Mary V. I, 897
Petty, Mary Victoria I, 619
Petty, Mary Victoria I, 624
Petty, Mary Victoria I, 863
Petty, Nancy I, 932
Petty, Rebecca II, 245
Petty, Rebecca II, 249
Petty, Richard W. VI, 861
Petty, Roela I. I, 897
Petty, Roella I, 626
Petty, Roella J. I, 639
Petty, Roella J. I, 863
Petty, Roella Jane I, 624
Petty, Ruth I, 624
Petty, Ruth I, 639
Petty, Ruth I, 643
Petty, Ruth W. I, 639
Petty, Sarah V, 1014
Petty, Sarah Elisabeth I, 624
Petty, Sarah Louisa I, 920
Petty, Sarah M. I, 639
Petty, Sarah M. I, 643
Petty, Thomas M. I, 639
Petty, Thomas M. I, 643
Petty, Thomas Macy I, 624
Petty, Thomas Worth I, 639
Petty, Victoria I, 639
Petty, W. C. I, 626
Petty, W. C. I, 863
Petty, Walter C. I, 863
Petty, Walter C. I, 897
Petty, Watson I, 863
Petty, Watson I, 920
Petty, William II, 245
Petty, William II, 249
Petty, William C. I, 897
Petty, William Clinton I, 624
Petty, William R. VI, 846
Petty, William, Sr. II, 249
Petty, Wm. II, 621
Petty, Wm. Clinton I, 619
Petty, Wm. Clinton I, 624
Pew, Achillas IV, 263
Pew, Ann II, 312
Pew, Ann II, 323
Pew, Ann II, 325
Pew, David I, 1062
Pew, David II, 406
Pew, Eli I, 416
Pew, Eli I, 828
Pew, Eli I, 835
Pew, Ellis II, 406
Pew, Esther I, 416
Pew, Hannah IV, 263
Pew, James Allen II, 312
Pew, Jane II, 612
Pew, Joseph H. II, 312
Pew, Joshua II, 312
Pew, Lydia II, 312
Pew, Lydia II, 317
Pew, Lydia II, 323
Pew, Martha V, 523
Pew, Mary I, 416
Pew, Miriam I, 828
Pew, Miriam L. I, 416
Pew, Miriam S. I, 416
Pew, Nancy P. VI, 918
Pew, Rachel I, 416
Pew, Rachel I, 1037
Pew, Rebecca II, 92
Pew, Thomas I, 568
Pew, Timothy I, 898
Pew, William N. II, 323
Pew, William N. II, 325
Pew, William N., Jr. II, 312
Pew, William, Jr. II, 323
Pewsey, Elizabeth II, 621
Pewsey, Joseph IV, 348
Pewsey, Martha IV, 348
Pewsey, Mary II, 621
Pewsey, Nathan IV, 348
Pewsey, Sarah II, 621
Peyton, Mary V, 592
Peyton, Polly VI, 978
Peyton, Pruey VI, 951
Peyton, William VI, 978
Pfaffle, Charles C. VI, 762
Pfaffle, Charles C. VI, 770
Pfaffle, Elsa Marvel VI, 762
Pfaffle, Elsa Marvel VI, 770
Pfaffle, Sophia VI, 762
Pfaffle, Sophia VI, 770
Pfister, Gertrude V, 425
Pfister, Lena M. V, 425
Pfister, Lenna Margaret V, 425
Pfister, Lewis V, 425
Pfister, Melcena V, 425
Pfister, Orlando V, 425
Pfister, Sarah V, 425
Pfister, Sarah A. V, 425
Pfister, Sarah Jane V, 425
Pflumer, Sadie V, 110
Phagen, Ephemia IV, 651
Phagin, Harmin IV, 651
Phagin, Lydia IV, 651
Phagon, Ephemia IV, 651
Phagon, Harmin IV, 651
Phagon, Harmon IV, 651
Phagon, Lydia IV, 651
Phagon, Uphemia IV, 651
Phalan, Affinity I, 1050
Phalan, Mary I, 1050
Phalen, Margaret V, 856
Phalin, Margaret V, 856
Phamy, Mary V, 177
Phamy, Mary V, 197
Phares, Bertha V, 865
Phares, Blanche V, 856
Phares, Clayton V, 856
Phares, Mary V, 856
Phares, Mary Hannah V, 856
Phares, Meribah V, 856
Phares, Thelma V, 856
Phares, William T. V, 856
Pharmer, William, Jr. I, 1048
Pharo, Allen II, 967
Pharo, Allen R. II, 283
Pharo, Allen R. II, 298
Pharo, Allen R. II, 715
Pharo, Allen R. II, 716
Pharo, Allen R. II, 760
Pharo, Allen R. II, 761
Pharo, Allen R. II, 1058
Pharo, Allen R. II, 1062
Pharo, Ann II, 249
Pharo, Ann II, 252
Pharo, Anna II, 283
Pharo, Anna II, 298
Pharo, Anna II, 720
Pharo, Anna L. II, 715
Pharo, Anna L. II, 716
Pharo, Anna L. II, 760
Pharo, Anna L. II, 761
Pharo, Edgar R. H. II, 298
Pharo, Edgar R. H. II, 967
Pharo, Edgar R. H. II, 1058
Pharo, Edward A. II, 715
Pharo, Elizabeth II, 249
Pharo, Elizabeth IV, 651
Pharo, Florence M. II, 715
Pharo, Florence M. II, 760
Pharo, Jarvis II, 249
Pharo, Joseph W. III, 254
Pharo, Marian II, 760
Pharo, Marian II, 761
Pharo, Marion II, 715
Pharo, Martha II, 180
Pharo, Martha W. II, 298
Pharo, Martha W. II, 967
Pharo, Martha W. II, 1058
Pharo, Mary Ann II, 283
Pharo, Mary Ann II, 298
Pharo, Mercianna Y. II, 1062
Pharo, Phebe II, 711
Pharo, Phebe B. II, 1058
Pharo, Phebe B. II, 1062
Pharo, Phoebe B. II, 715
Pharo, Rachel W. II, 711
Pharo, Robert II, 283
Pharo, Robert II, 298
Pharo, Robert II, 711
Pharo, Robert II, 1058
Pharo, Robert L. II, 967
Pharo, Robert S. II, 1058
Pharo, Robert S. II, 1062
Pharo, Robert T. II, 298
Pharo, Robert T. II, 1058
Pharo, Sophia II, 1058
Pharo, Sophia T. II, 298
Pharo, Sophia T. II, 967
Pharo, Sophia T. II, 1058
Pharo, Thomas Ridgway II, 249
Pharo, Walter T. II, 298
Pharo, Walter T. II, 967
Pharo, Walter T. II, 1058
Pharr, Dion C. VI, 846
Pharr, Mary J. VI, 846
Phearus, Blanche V, 856
Phearus, Thelma V, 856
Phearus, William T. V, 856
Phebus, Amy IV, 263
Phegan, Euphemy IV, 814
Pheimey, Earl G. IV, 1260
Pheimey, Eral G. IV, 1260
Pheimey, John A. IV, 1260
Pheimey, Lucian M. IV, 1260
Pheimey, Lucy M. IV, 1260
Pheimey, Mary E. IV, 1260
Pheimey, May E. IV, 1260

Phelan, Affinity I, 1050
Phelan, Ann I, 1045
Phelan, Elizabeth I, 1045
Phelan, Elizabeth I, 1050
Phelan, Evane I, 1045
Phelan, Evans I, 1050
Phelan, Jeremiah I, 1045
Phelan, Jeremiah I, 1050
Phelan, Mary I, 1045
Phelan, Mary I, 1050
Phelan, Thomas I, 1045
Phelan, Thomas I, 1050
Phelphot, Anna IV, 263
Phelphot, Harry IV, 263
Phelphot, Lewis IV, 263
Phelps, Alexander III, 292
Phelps, Ann I, 1160
Phelps, Bathsheba VI, 924
Phelps, Benjamin I, 69
Phelps, Benjamin I, 256
Phelps, Charlotte V, 271
Phelps, Christianna I, 731
Phelps, D. B. VI, 866
Phelps, Dorethy I, 55
Phelps, Dorethy I, 69
Phelps, Eli V, 271
Phelps, Eli V, 447
Phelps, Elisabeth I, 69
Phelps, Elisabeth I, 75
Phelps, Elisabeth I, 87
Phelps, Eliz. B. III, 250
Phelps, Eliza I, 69
Phelps, Elizabeth I, 90
Phelps, Elizabeth I, 126
Phelps, Elizabeth I, 727
Phelps, Elizabeth I, 731
Phelps, Elizabeth I Sup 1, 5
Phelps, Elizabeth I Sup 1, 6
Phelps, Elizabeth III, 250
Phelps, Elizabeth III, 271
Phelps, Elizabeth B. III, 254
Phelps, Elizabeth W. III, 254
Phelps, Frances E. VI, 978
Phelps, George VI, 846
Phelps, Hannah I, 1
Phelps, Hannah I, 69
Phelps, Hannah I, 72
Phelps, Henry I, 62
Phelps, Henry I, 69
Phelps, James VI, 846
Phelps, James VI, 978
Phelps, James M. VI, 892
Phelps, Jefferson W. VI, 978
Phelps, Jemima VI, 914
Phelps, Jessie S. III, 254
Phelps, Jessie S. III, 292
Phelps, Jnoa I, 42
Phelps, Jnoa. I, 64
Phelps, Jnoh I, 36
Phelps, Jnoh. I, 68
Phelps, Joel V, 447
Phelps, John V, 271
Phelps, John V, 447
Phelps, John VI, 886
Phelps, John VI, 914
Phelps, John VI, 924
Phelps, John VI, 930
Phelps, John VI, 978
Phelps, John A. VI, 846
Phelps, Jona I, 1
Phelps, Jona I, 36
Phelps, Jona. I, 85
Phelps, Jonathan I, 1
Phelps, Jonathan I, 55
Phelps, Jonathan I, 62
Phelps, Jonathan I, 69
Phelps, Jonathan I, 90
Phelps, Jonathan I, 731
Phelps, Jonathan I Sup 1, 3
Phelps, Jonathan I Sup 1, 5
Phelps, Jonathan I Sup 1, 6
Phelps, Joseph James III, 254
Phelps, Justice M. III, 292
Phelps, Justis III, 254
Phelps, Justise III, 254
Phelps, Justus III, 184
Phelps, Justus III, 254
Phelps, Lauretta III, 292
Phelps, Lucy VI, 930
Phelps, Malinda P. VI, 978
Phelps, Margaret I, 62
Phelps, Margaret I, 65
Phelps, Margaret I, 69
Phelps, Margret I, 69
Phelps, Mariam V, 271
Phelps, Martha V, 447
Phelps, Martha B. VI, 861
Phelps, Martin V, 447
Phelps, Mary I, 62
Phelps, Mary I, 69
Phelps, Mary V, 447
Phelps, Mary VI, 846
Phelps, Mary Ann VI, 846
Phelps, Mary L. III, 292
Phelps, Meriam V, 447
Phelps, Mourning I, 62
Phelps, Mourning I, 69
Phelps, Nancy VI, 846
Phelps, Nancy VI, 886
Phelps, Nancy VI, 914
Phelps, Nancy VI, 978
Phelps, Peter W. VI, 978
Phelps, Phebe III, 184
Phelps, Phebe III, 254
Phelps, Polly VI, 914
Phelps, Randolph VI, 923
Phelps, Richard VI, 978
Phelps, Robert VI, 914
Phelps, Roy D. IV, 1290
Phelps, Ruth VI, 978
Phelps, Samuel VI, 846
Phelps, Sarah IV, 651
Phelps, Sarah V, 447
Phelps, Sarah VI, 978
Phelps, Sarah B. VI, 846
Phelps, Susanna VI, 889
Phelps, Susanna VI, 978
Phelps, Susannah IV, 612
Phelps, Susannah IV, 651
Phelps, Thomas VI, 812
Phelps, Thomas VI, 859
Phelps, Thomas VI, 978
Phelps, Thomas VI, 998
Phelps, Thomas J. VI, 978
Phelps, Thos. W. III, 250
Phelps, Thos. W. III, 254
Phelps, Wilber J. IV, 1333
Phelps, Wilbur IV, 1333
Phelps, William VI, 850
Phelps, William VI, 875
Phenix, James II, 406
Phentress, Elisabeth I, 139
Pheobus, Anna Eliza III, 305
Pheonbus, Anna Eliza III, 305
Pheres, Meribah V, 825
Pheres, Meribah V, 856
Pherington, Theodore IV, 1278
Phifer, John VI, 707
Phifer, Rebecca Ruth VI, 707
Phihysie, ??? I, 4
Phihysie, Mary E. I, 4
Phihysie???, ??? I, 4
Phihysie???, Mary E. I, 4
Phila, Mary II, 505
Philbrook, Wm. C. IV, 1179
Phile, Elizabeth II, 614
Phile, Elizabeth II, 621
Philip, Clarence IV, 780
Philipps, Sarah II, 1058
Philips, ??? II, 815
Philips, Albina II, 815
Philips, Amy Ann VI, 770
Philips, Ann I, 816
Philips, Ann I, 833
Philips, Ann I, 971
Philips, Ann I, 995
Philips, Ann Hinshaw I, 995
Philips, Anna II, 622
Philips, Anna II, 655
Philips, Anna II, 796
Philips, Anne VI, 877
Philips, Asenath IV, 977
Philips, Benjamin II, 756
Philips, Benjamin II, 760
Philips, Burroughs II, 815
Philips, Calvin II, 815
Philips, Calvin II, 853
Philips, Calvin II, 910
Philips, Caroline V, 704
Philips, Caroline E. II, 849
Philips, Caroline E. II, 910
Philips, Catharine J. II, 815
Philips, Catharine M. II, 910
Philips, Charles II, 760
Philips, Cynthia V, 856
Philips, Dixon C. II, 815
Philips, Edith IV, 84
Philips, Edith IV, 105
Philips, Edward II, 760
Philips, Edward M. II, 910
Philips, Eli IV, 53
Philips, Eli VI, 543
Philips, Elizabeth IV, 53
Philips, Elizabeth VI, 543
Philips, Elizabeth Janney VI, 429
Philips, Elizabeth Sutton II, 815
Philips, Elizabeth Sutton II, 849
Philips, Elizabeth Sutton II, 910
Philips, Ellis IV, 53
Philips, Elma IV, 53
Philips, Elma IV, 61
Philips, Esther II, 815
Philips, George C. II, 910
Philips, George Chapman II, 815
Philips, Hannah II, 756
Philips, Hannah II, 760
Philips, Henry II, 760
Philips, Henry C. II, 815
Philips, Henry C. II, 910
Philips, Horace G. II, 849
Philips, Horace G. II, 910
Philips, Horace Greely II, 815
Philips, Howard J. II, 910
Philips, Isaac II, 756
Philips, Isaac II, 760
Philips, Isaac D. II, 849
Philips, Isaac D. II, 910
Philips, James IV, 53
Philips, James IV, 105
Philips, James V, 523
Philips, James VI, 543
Philips, Jane II, 815
Philips, Jane I. II, 853
Philips, Jane I. II, 910
Philips, John I, 833
Philips, John I, 995
Philips, John II, 622
Philips, John VI, 544
Philips, John C. II, 815
Philips, Jonathan IV, 53
Philips, Joseph I, 833
Philips, Joseph I, 995
Philips, Kate Bailey V, 592
Philips, Lena IV, 1041
Philips, Letitia VI, 717
Philips, Lucretia M. II, 790
Philips, Lucretia M. II, 853
Philips, Lucretia M. II, 910
Philips, Lucy Eveline V, 1014
Philips, Lucy Eveline V, 1022
Philips, Maria Louisa II, 815
Philips, Martha IV, 53
Philips, Martha Jane IV, 53
Philips, Mary I, 995
Philips, Mary II, 622
Philips, Mary IV, 53
Philips, Mary IV, 346
Philips, Mary VI, 875
Philips, Mary VI, 978
Philips, Mary Caroline II, 815
Philips, Mary Elizabeth IV, 618
Philips, Mary Elizabeth IV, 651
Philips, Mercy IV, 429
Philips, Mery IV, 346
Philips, Nancy VI, 972
Philips, Pearl V, 110
Philips, Phebe II, 756
Philips, Phebe II, 760
Philips, Phebe M. II, 760
Philips, Rachel VI, 429
Philips, Rayland W. II, 910
Philips, Rebecca II, 622
Philips, Richard V, 856
Philips, Robert R. II, 815
Philips, Ruth IV, 53
Philips, Ruth VI, 543
Philips, Ryland W. II, 910
Philips, Sally VI, 814
Philips, Samuel IV, 53
Philips, Samuel IV, 105
Philips, Samuel VI, 989
Philips, Samuel J. II, 910
Philips, Sarah II, 1061
Philips, Sarah IV, 79
Philips, Sarah VI, 989
Philips, Sidney G. II, 760
Philips, Solomon IV, 53
Philips, Solomon VI, 543
Philips, Solomon, Jr. IV, 105
Philips, Susannah I, 1036
Philips, Thomas IV, 53
Philips, Thomas VI, 429
Philips, Thomas VI, 978
Philips, Walter J. IV, 1041
Philips, Wd. Elizabeth Wilson II, 815
Philips, Widow Ann I, 833
Philips, William IV, 53
Philips, Wm. M. II, 760
Philips, Zachariah VI, 877
Phillen, Elizabeth II, 228
Philles, John II, 446
Philles, Margrett II, 446
Phillias, Joseph II, 446
Phillias, Mathew II, 446
Phillip, Anna Lucile IV, 1041
Phillip, Donald D. IV, 1041
Phillip, Effie M. I, 947
Phillip, Eppie I, 947
Phillip, Eppie I, 949
Phillip, Frances Zorada IV, 1041
Phillip, Henrietta I, 639
Phillip, James I, 639
Phillip, Jas. E. I, 639
Phillip, Margaret I, 639
Phillip, Mary U. I, 639
Phillip, Pearl L. I, 639
Phillip, Roxie I, 945
Phillip, Roxie I, 947
Phillip, Roxie I, 949
Phillip, Roxie L. I, 639
Phillip, Roxie L. I, 947
Phillip, Thomas M. I, 639
Phillip, Thos. M. I, 639
Phillip, William C. I, 484
Phillipa, Amy Ann VI, 535
Philliphs, Rachel VI, 429
Phillips, ??? II, 815
Phillips, ??? III, 416
Phillips, A. W. VI, 564
Phillips, Addie I, 413
Phillips, Albert IV, 429
Phillips, Albert IV, 986
Phillips, Albert C. II, 908
Phillips, Albert C. II, 910
Phillips, Albert S. IV, 429
Phillips, Alice L. III, 145
Phillips, Alice L. III, 254
Phillips, Alice Marion II, 908
Phillips, Alice Marion II, 910
Phillips, Alonzo C. IV, 263
Phillips, Alonzo C. IV, 986
Phillips, Alonzo E. IV, 986
Phillips, Amanda IV, 727
Phillips, Amelia IV, 1154
Phillips, Amy Ann VI, 535
Phillips, Amy Ann VI, 543
Phillips, Amy Ann VI, 544
Phillips, Amy Ann VI, 766
Phillips, Ann I, 993
Phillips, Ann II, 760
Phillips, Ann II, 792
Phillips, Ann IV, 875
Phillips, Ann IV, 881
Phillips, Ann VI, 544
Phillips, Ann Lucy VI, 963
Phillips, Anna III, 20
Phillips, Anna III, 93
Phillips, Anna V, 923
Phillips, Anna E. IV, 1041
Phillips, Anna Jane IV, 226
Phillips, Anna Jane IV, 263
Phillips, Anna Lucile IV, 1041
Phillips, Arthur W. VI, 494
Phillips, Arthur W. VI, 543
Phillips, Arthur W. VI, 544
Phillips, Arthur W. VI, 564
Phillips, Arthur W. VI, 641
Phillips, Arthur W. VI, 687
Phillips, Arthur W. VI, 688
Phillips, Asenath IV, 986
Phillips, Benjamin II, 715
Phillips, Benjamin II, 760
Phillips, Benjamin IV, 1179
Phillips, Benjamin IV, 1198
Phillips, Benjamina VI, 118
Phillips, Bertha IV, 750
Phillips, Betty VI, 543
Phillips, Brook IV, 750
Phillips, Brooke K. IV, 750
Phillips, Brooks IV, 750
Phillips, Burroughs II, 815
Phillips, Caleb VI, 978
Phillips, Calvin II, 910
Phillips, Caroline V, 704
Phillips, Caroline E. II, 910
Phillips, Carrie IV, 1041
Phillips, Catharin IV, 986
Phillips, Catharine II, 406
Phillips, Catharine III, 254
Phillips, Catharine J. II, 815
Phillips, Catharine M. II, 910
Phillips, Charles II, 760
Phillips, Charles C. III, 254
Phillips, Charles C. III, 357
Phillips, Charles Henry II, 715
Phillips, Charley G. V, 1014
Phillips, Chas. V, 1014
Phillips, Chas. C. III, 254
Phillips, Chloe V, 1014
Phillips, Chloe I. V, 1014
Phillips, Clara IV, 986
Phillips, Clara IV, 1041
Phillips, Clara H. IV, 960
Phillips, Clara H. IV, 1041
Phillips, Clara S. IV, 1041
Phillips, Clifford Towey V, 1014
Phillips, Cornelia I, 930
Phillips, Cornelia I, 932
Phillips, Cornelia I, 933
Phillips, Cornelius VI, 978
Phillips, Curtis IV, 750
Phillips, Cynthia V, 856
Phillips, Daniel III, 254
Phillips, Daniel III, 343
Phillips, Deborah IV, 881
Phillips, Deby II, 717
Phillips, Dinah VI, 543
Phillips, Dinah VI, 544
Phillips, Dinah VI, 587
Phillips, Donald D. IV, 1041
Phillips, Dorothy Mae IV, 104
Phillips, Dorothy Simons V, 7
Phillips, Dwight L. IV, 1041
Phillips, Edith IV, 105
Phillips, Edmond I, 1130
Phillips, Edmund I, 413
Phillips, Edmund VI, 544
Phillips, Edmund VI, 563
Phillips, Edmund VI, 687
Phillips, Edmund VI, 688
Phillips, Edmund, Jr. VI, 543
Phillips, Edmund, Jr. VI, 544
Phillips, Edmund, Jr. VI, 687
Phillips, Edna M. IV, 1041
Phillips, Edward II, 715
Phillips, Edward II, 760
Phillips, Edward IV, 1041
Phillips, Edward M. II, 910
Phillips, Effie I, 933
Phillips, Effie Marie IV, 1041
Phillips, Eleanor VI, 978
Phillips, Eli VI, 543
Phillips, Eli VI, 544
Phillips, Elizabeth II, 22
Phillips, Elizabeth II, 1058
Phillips, Elizabeth III, 254
Phillips, Elizabeth III, 258
Phillips, Elizabeth III, 261
Phillips, Elizabeth III, 344
Phillips, Elizabeth III, 456
Phillips, Elizabeth IV, 53
Phillips, Elizabeth IV, 98
Phillips, Elizabeth IV, 105
Phillips, Elizabeth IV, 116
Phillips, Elizabeth IV, 881
Phillips, Elizabeth IV, 986
Phillips, Elizabeth IV, 1333
Phillips, Elizabeth V, 1014
Phillips, Elizabeth VI, 497
Phillips, Elizabeth VI, 543
Phillips, Elizabeth VI, 544
Phillips, Elizabeth VI, 549
Phillips, Elizabeth VI, 635
Phillips, Elizabeth VI, 814
Phillips, Elizabeth VI, 863
Phillips, Elizabeth A. VI, 847
Phillips, Elizabeth J. VI, 429
Phillips, Elizabeth J. VI, 560
Phillips, Elizabeth Jane I, 413
Phillips, Elizabeth Janney VI, 444
Phillips, Elizabeth Janney VI, 494
Phillips, Elizabeth Janney VI, 543
Phillips, Elizabeth Janney VI, 544
Phillips, Elizabeth Janney VI, 560
Phillips, Elizabeth Janney VI, 641
Phillips, Elizabeth Janney VI, 687
Phillips, Elizabeth Johnson VI, 543
Phillips, Elizabeth Johnson VI, 687
Phillips, Elizabeth Sutton II, 9
Phillips, Ella I, 413
Phillips, Ella IV, 1260
Phillips, Ellen Rhoda IV, 1154
Phillips, Ellis IV, 53
Phillips, Ellis IV, 98
Phillips, Ellis IV, 105
Phillips, Ellis IV, 106
Phillips, Ellis IV, 1333
Phillips, Elmore IV, 263
Phillips, Elmore IV, 986
Phillips, Elsie IV, 1041
Phillips, Emily IV, 838
Phillips, Emily IV, 986
Phillips, Emily IV, 1041
Phillips, Emily Margaret IV, 98
Phillips, Eppie M. I, 932
Phillips, Evan VI, 543
Phillips, Evan VI, 544
Phillips, Evelyn IV, 1041
Phillips, Fanny V, 1014
Phillips, Florence V, 71
Phillips, Florence V, 110
Phillips, Frances III, 254
Phillips, Frances VI, 978
Phillips, Frances L. VI, 935
Phillips, Frances R. VI, 855

ips, Frances Zorada IV, 1041
ips, Frank V, 762
ips, Frank E. IV, 986
ips, Franklin III, 145
ips, Franklin III, 254
ips, Frederick III, 254
ips, Frederick Morris
III, 254
ips, Geo. W. IV, 923
ips, George V, 110
ips, George V, 1014
ips, George VI, 118
ips, George VI, 978
ips, George C. II, 910
ips, George Chapman II, 815
ips, Hannah I, 484
ips, Hannah II, 760
ips, Hannah II, 1021
ips, Hannah II, 1037
ips, Hannah III, 254
ips, Hannah III, 456
ips, Hannah IV, 986
ips, Hannah V, 762
ips, Hannah V, 923
ips, Hannah VI, 543
ips, Hannah VI, 544
ips, Hannah VI, 687
ips, Harry V, 1014
ips, Helen IV, 986
ips, Helen Mae IV, 1041
ips, Helen S. IV, 960
ips, Helen S. IV, 1041
ips, Henery VI, 262
ips, Henrietta I, 614
ips, Henrietta I, 624
ips, Henry II, 760
ips, Henry III, 254
ips, Henry VI, 118
ips, Henry VI, 543
ips, Henry C. II, 815
ips, Henry C. II, 910
ips, Herbert Elma I, 316
ips, Homer IV, 986
ips, Homer IV, 1041
ips, Homer C. IV, 960
ips, Homer C. IV, 986
ips, Homer C. IV, 1041
ips, Horace G. II, 910
ips, Howard J. II, 910
ips, Howard M. II, 910
ips, Icy V, 1014
ips, Ida IV, 263
ips, Ida IV, 304
ips, Ida Bell IV, 263
ips, Irene III, 234
ips, Irene III, 254
ips, Isaac II, 760
ips, Isaac V, 923
ips, Isaac D. II, 910
ips, Jacob R. III, 254
ips, James IV, 105
ips, James V, 523
ips, James VI, 118
ips, James VI, 543
ips, James VI, 570
ips, James A. I, 930
ips, James A. I, 932
ips, James A. I, 933
ips, James E. I, 413
ips, James E. I, 624
ips, James Evan IV, 263
ips, Jane III, 254
ips, Jane IV, 881
ips, Jane E. VI, 846
ips, Jane I. II, 910
ips, Jane J. II, 910
ips, Jane M. III, 254
ips, Jemima VI, 846
ips, Jenkins IV, 1179
ips, Jenkins IV, 1198
ips, Jeremiah I, 413
ips, Jericho III, 254
ips, Jesse IV, 1041
ips, Jesse C. II, 910
ips, Jesse E. IV, 263
ips, Jesse W. II, 910
ips, Jno. VI, 950
ips, John II, 406
ips, John IV, 1041
ips, John IV, 1154
ips, John VI, 544
ips, John VI, 688
ips, John VI, 814
ips, John VI, 821
ips, John VI, 846
ips, John VI, 863
ips, John VI, 978
ips, John B. VI, 803
ips, John B. VI, 846
ips, John B. VI, 847
ips, John E. IV, 986
Phillips, John G. VI, 846
Phillips, John H. I, 413
Phillips, John P. III, 254
Phillips, John Roberts VI, 262
Phillips, John T. VI, 855
Phillips, John W. I, 413
Phillips, Johnson Phillips VI, 543
Phillips, Jonathan IV, 53
Phillips, Jonathan IV, 105
Phillips, Joseph I, 833
Phillips, Joseph IV, 838
Phillips, Joseph IV, 986
Phillips, Joseph VI, 570
Phillips, Joseph VI, 839
Phillips, Joseph VI, 847
Phillips, Joseph E. IV, 986
Phillips, Josephine IV, 221
Phillips, Josephine IV, 263
Phillips, Josephine E. IV, 263
Phillips, Josiah V, 1014
Phillips, Julia IV, 1179
Phillips, Julia IV, 1198
Phillips, Julian III, 254
Phillips, Katharine M. II, 910
Phillips, Katherine IV, 986
Phillips, Kathleen IV, 1041
Phillips, Lena IV, 1041
Phillips, Leonard VI, 978
Phillips, Letitia VI, 494
Phillips, Letitia VI, 543
Phillips, Letitia VI, 544
Phillips, Letitia VI, 564
Phillips, Letitia VI, 641
Phillips, Letitia VI, 687
Phillips, Letitia VI, 688
Phillips, Letitia A. VI, 544
Phillips, Letta IV, 1179
Phillips, Letta IV, 1198
Phillips, Lillie I, 413
Phillips, Lizzie IV, 986
Phillips, Lou I, 624
Phillips, Louella IV, 1041
Phillips, Lowrana I, 413
Phillips, Lucinda VI, 978
Phillips, Lucretia M. II, 910
Phillips, Lucy Eveline V, 1014
Phillips, Lucy Mae IV, 1041
Phillips, Luella IV, 986
Phillips, Luella B. IV, 1041
Phillips, Luna I. V, 1014
Phillips, Lydia I, 413
Phillips, Lydia II, 715
Phillips, Lydia II, 760
Phillips, Lydia VI, 544
Phillips, Lydia VI, 563
Phillips, Lydia VI, 687
Phillips, Marcie III, 254
Phillips, Margaret I, 413
Phillips, Margaret I, 614
Phillips, Margaret I, 616
Phillips, Margaret I, 624
Phillips, Margaret II, 22
Phillips, Margaret IV, 838
Phillips, Margaret IV, 986
Phillips, Margaret VI, 543
Phillips, Margaret VI, 544
Phillips, Margaret VI, 563
Phillips, Margaret VI, 687
Phillips, Marguerite III, 254
Phillips, Marguerite IV, 1041
Phillips, Maria III, 254
Phillips, Maria L. II, 910
Phillips, Maria Louisa II, 815
Phillips, Maria Louisa III, 357
Phillips, Maria Louise III, 254
Phillips, Maria W. III, 160
Phillips, Maria W. III, 254
Phillips, Maris L. II, 848
Phillips, Maris L. II, 910
Phillips, Martha IV, 53
Phillips, Martha IV, 98
Phillips, Martha IV, 105
Phillips, Martha A. I, 413
Phillips, Mary I, 308
Phillips, Mary I, 316
Phillips, Mary I, 413
Phillips, Mary I, 418
Phillips, Mary II, 406
Phillips, Mary II, 586
Phillips, Mary II, 622
Phillips, Mary III, 115
Phillips, Mary III, 254
Phillips, Mary III, 343
Phillips, Mary III, 433
Phillips, Mary III, 456
Phillips, Mary IV, 332
Phillips, Mary IV, 346
Phillips, Mary IV, 986
Phillips, Mary V, 1014
Phillips, Mary VI, 846
Phillips, Mary VI, 978
Phillips, Mary Ann VI, 543
Phillips, Mary Ann VI, 978
Phillips, Mary C. II, 910
Phillips, Mary C. II, 926
Phillips, Mary C. M. VI, 919
Phillips, Mary Emily III, 234
Phillips, Mary Emily III, 254
Phillips, Mary Evelyn IV, 1041
Phillips, Mary Jane VI, 950
Phillips, Mary N. I, 413
Phillips, Mary Sidwell VI, 564
Phillips, Mary Sidwell VI, 687
Phillips, Mary Sidwell VI, 688
Phillips, Mary Sidwell VI, 708
Phillips, Mary Sidwell Phillips
VI, 543
Phillips, Mary U. I, 624
Phillips, Mathew II, 406
Phillips, Matilda C. VI, 846
Phillips, Matthew VI, 846
Phillips, Mercy IV, 429
Phillips, Mercy VI, 544
Phillips, Mercy VI, 687
Phillips, Mollie I, 413
Phillips, Mr. R. W. IV, 750
Phillips, Mrs. ??? IV, 750
Phillips, Nancy VI, 814
Phillips, Nancy VI, 961
Phillips, Nancy VI, 978
Phillips, Nancy Laura IV, 986
Phillips, Nannie J. I, 413
Phillips, Nellie V, 1014
Phillips, Nelson VI, 846
Phillips, Noah L. I, 413
Phillips, Nora Ethel I, 316
Phillips, Pamelia VI, 978
Phillips, Pardon III, 254
Phillips, Pearl V, 110
Phillips, Pearl L. I, 624
Phillips, Pearlie V, 110
Phillips, Pearly L. I, 413
Phillips, Peggy VI, 846
Phillips, Perley I, 413
Phillips, Phebe II, 715
Phillips, Phebe II, 760
Phillips, Phebe IV, 98
Phillips, Phebe IV, 105
Phillips, Phebe IV, 106
Phillips, Phebe M. II, 760
Phillips, Phiby VI, 803
Phillips, R. W. IV, 750
Phillips, Rachel I, 413
Phillips, Rachel I, 418
Phillips, Rachel VI, 429
Phillips, Rachel VI, 543
Phillips, Rachel VI, 544
Phillips, Rachel VI, 560
Phillips, Rachel VI, 572
Phillips, Rachel VI, 687
Phillips, Rachel VI, 766
Phillips, Rachel VI, 770
Phillips, Rachel VI, 824
Phillips, Rachel Robert VI, 535
Phillips, Rayland W. II, 910
Phillips, Rebecca IV, 881
Phillips, Rebecca IV, 923
Phillips, Rebecca IV, 986
Phillips, Rebecca VI, 540
Phillips, Rebecca VI, 544
Phillips, Rebecca A. III, 254
Phillips, Reuben Enos III, 254
Phillips, Reuben Eves III, 234
Phillips, Rhoda VI, 978
Phillips, Richard V, 856
Phillips, Robert H. III, 433
Phillips, Robert James IV, 1041
Phillips, Robert L. II, 910
Phillips, Robert R. II, 815
Phillips, Ronie Lovanna I, 624
Phillips, Rosamond VI, 846
Phillips, Roxie I, 930
Phillips, Roxie L. I, 932
Phillips, Roxie L. I, 947
Phillips, Rufus D. I, 316
Phillips, Ruth III, 254
Phillips, Ruth III, 309
Phillips, Ruth IV, 53
Phillips, Ruth IV, 105
Phillips, Ruth VI, 543
Phillips, Ruth VI, 544
Phillips, Ruth VI, 687
Phillips, Ruth VI, 688
Phillips, Ruth VI, 696
Phillips, Ryland W. II, 910
Phillips, S. VI, 915
Phillips, S. VI, 963
Phillips, S. VI, 992
Phillips, Sadie IV, 1041
Phillips, Sadie V, 1014
Phillips, Sallie IV, 986
Phillips, Sally Burlingham III, 254
Phillips, Sally W. VI, 846
Phillips, Saml. VI, 978
Phillips, Samuel II, 22
Phillips, Samuel III, 254
Phillips, Samuel IV, 105
Phillips, Samuel VI, 118
Phillips, Samuel VI, 978
Phillips, Samuel J. II, 910
Phillips, Samuel J. V, 1014
Phillips, Sara III, 254
Phillips, Sarah II, 760
Phillips, Sarah II, 1058
Phillips, Sarah III, 416
Phillips, Sarah IV, 105
Phillips, Sarah IV, 116
Phillips, Sarah V, 1014
Phillips, Sarah VI, 544
Phillips, Sarah VI, 687
Phillips, Sarah VI, 688
Phillips, Sarah VI, 846
Phillips, Sarah VI, 847
Phillips, Sarah VI, 978
Phillips, Sarah A. IV, 1179
Phillips, Sarah A. IV, 1198
Phillips, Sarah H. III, 433
Phillips, Sarah M. VI, 544
Phillips, Sarah M. VI, 582
Phillips, Sidney II, 760
Phillips, Sidney G. II, 760
Phillips, Simeon A. III, 254
Phillips, Smiley E. IV, 263
Phillips, Smylie S. IV, 263
Phillips, Solomon IV, 53
Phillips, Solomon IV, 98
Phillips, Solomon IV, 105
Phillips, Solomon IV, 106
Phillips, Solomon VI, 543
Phillips, Solomon VI, 544
Phillips, Solomon, Jr. IV, 105
Phillips, Sophia VI, 978
Phillips, Stephen VI, 978
Phillips, Susan III, 254
Phillips, Susan III, 343
Phillips, Susan C. II, 715
Phillips, Susan C. II, 760
Phillips, Susanna IV, 263
Phillips, Susanna IV, 268
Phillips, Susanna VI, 877
Phillips, Susannah I, 1026
Phillips, Susannah II, 822
Phillips, Theophilus III, 437
Phillips, Theophilus III, 456
Phillips, Thomas I, 614
Phillips, Thomas I, 616
Phillips, Thomas I, 624
Phillips, Thomas II, 406
Phillips, Thomas III, 254
Phillips, Thomas VI, 444
Phillips, Thomas VI, 494
Phillips, Thomas VI, 535
Phillips, Thomas VI, 543
Phillips, Thomas VI, 544
Phillips, Thomas VI, 560
Phillips, Thomas VI, 572
Phillips, Thomas VI, 641
Phillips, Thomas VI, 687
Phillips, Thomas VI, 766
Phillips, Thomas VI, 770
Phillips, Thomas VI, 923
Phillips, Thomas VI, 961
Phillips, Thomas VI, 978
Phillips, Thomas J. I, 413
Phillips, Thomas M. I, 413
Phillips, Thomas W. IV, 986
Phillips, Thos. IV, 1041
Phillips, Thos. M. I, 639
Phillips, W. Hayes IV, 1333
Phillips, Walter J. IV, 1041
Phillips, Wd. Elizabeth III, 437
Phillips, Wd. Elizabeth Wilson
II, 815
Phillips, Wendell IV, 1041
Phillips, Wesley VI, 950
Phillips, Wesley VI, 978
Phillips, Wesly VI, 978
Phillips, Widow Henrietta I, 616
Phillips, William III, 115
Phillips, William III, 254
Phillips, William III, 309
Phillips, William VI, 802
Phillips, William VI, 814
Phillips, William VI, 846
Phillips, William VI, 978
Phillips, William Augustus
III, 254
Phillips, William C. I, 484
Phillips, William Dixon II, 715
Phillips, William G. VI, 846
Phillips, William H. I, 413
Phillips, William I. III, 254
Phillips, Wilmer IV, 1041
Phillips, Witham M. II, 715
Phillips, Wm. IV, 1333
Phillips, Wm. Hays IV, 1333
Phillips, Wm. I. III, 160
Phillips, Wm. M. II, 760
Phillips, Zachariah VI, 801
Phillips, Zachariah VI, 846
Phillips, Zachariah VI, 858
Phillips, Zachariah VI, 978
Phillis, Catharin IV, 986
Phillis, Elizabeth IV, 986
Phillis, Helen Mae IV, 1041
Phillis, Lucy Mae IV, 1041
Phillis, Rebecca IV, 986
Phillis, Thomas W. IV, 986
Philpin, Mary II, 601
Philpin, Mary II, 622
Philpot, Anna IV, 263
Philpot, Harry IV, 263
Philpot, Lewis IV, 263
Philpot, Lewis J. IV, 263
Philpot, William IV, 263
Philpott, Anna IV, 263
Philpott, Lewis IV, 263
Philpott, Mary II, 68
Philpott, Mary II, 69
Philpott, Mary II, 92
Philpott, Susanna II, 69
Phinelias, Ann I, 402
Phinney, Barbary IV, 986
Phinney, Edward IV, 986
Phinney, Ella IV, 1307
Phinney, Fam IV, 1333
Phinney, Harold IV, 1333
Phinney, L. P. IV, 1307
Phinney, Lauren IV, 1041
Phinney, Loren A. IV, 1041
Phinney, Lucian IV, 1333
Phinney, Mae IV, 1307
Phinney, Roslie IV, 1333
Phinney, Steril IV, 1333
Phipp, Isaac II, 406
Phipp, Thomas II, 406
Phipps, Adriadna II, 786
Phipps, Amy II, 622
Phipps, Amy II, 760
Phipps, Amy II, 871
Phipps, Amy II, 910
Phipps, Artelia Jennie I, 621
Phipps, Benj IV, 912
Phipps, Bessie I, 612
Phipps, Bessie I, 613
Phipps, Charles II, 622
Phipps, Charles II, 760
Phipps, Charles IV, 492
Phipps, Chas. II, 910
Phipps, Chas. II, 921
Phipps, Daniel II, 406
Phipps, Deborah II, 406
Phipps, Deborah II, 497
Phipps, Deborah II, 574
Phipps, Deborah II, 622
Phipps, Deborah II, 647
Phipps, Deborah II, 760
Phipps, Deborah II, 815
Phipps, Deborah II, 910
Phipps, E. W. IV, 475
Phipps, E. W. IV, 492
Phipps, Earla IV, 492
Phipps, Earla E. IV, 492
Phipps, Edith S. II, 319
Phipps, Edith S. II, 323
Phipps, Elias H. II, 319
Phipps, Elias H. II, 323
Phipps, Elisha W. IV, 492
Phipps, Elizabeth II, 622
Phipps, Elizabeth II, 647
Phipps, Elizabeth II, 779
Phipps, Elizabeth II, 819
Phipps, Elizabeth II, 821
Phipps, Elizabeth K. II, 323
Phipps, Ellie II, 910
Phipps, Ellie II, 921
Phipps, Emma I, 621
Phipps, Emma I, 637
Phipps, Emma I, 639
Phipps, Emma IV, 492
Phipps, Emma W. IV, 492
Phipps, Eva IV, 492
Phipps, Frances II, 622
Phipps, Frances II, 815
Phipps, Francis II, 622
Phipps, Francis II, 910
Phipps, Geo. Washington I, 621
Phipps, George I, 639
Phipps, H. E. IV, 488
Phipps, Hannah II, 459
Phipps, Hannah II, 622
Phipps, Hannah II, 786
Phipps, Isaac II, 406
Phipps, Isaac II, 622

Phipps, Isaac II, 786
Phipps, Jemima II, 782
Phipps, Joel H. II, 323
Phipps, John II, 406
Phipps, John II, 622
Phipps, Jonathan II, 406
Phipps, Joseph II, 406
Phipps, Joseph II, 715
Phipps, Joseph II, 815
Phipps, Joseph II, 910
Phipps, Margaret IV, 912
Phipps, Marie IV, 492
Phipps, Mary II, 249
Phipps, Mary II, 406
Phipps, Mary II, 540
Phipps, Mary II, 622
Phipps, Mary II, 812
Phipps, Mary IV, 492
Phipps, Mary IV, 912
Phipps, Mary E. IV, 475
Phipps, Mary E. IV, 492
Phipps, Peter II, 406
Phipps, Rachel Emily IV, 1111
Phipps, Rachel Emily IV, 1122
Phipps, Rebecca II, 406
Phipps, Rebecca II, 540
Phipps, Rebecca II, 622
Phipps, Rebecca II, 760
Phipps, Rebecca II, 815
Phipps, Rebecca II, 901
Phipps, Rebecca II, 910
Phipps, Rebecca, Jr. II, 715
Phipps, Rebecca, Jr. II, 760
Phipps, Rebekah II, 406
Phipps, Rebekah II, 622
Phipps, Robinson II, 622
Phipps, Robinson II, 760
Phipps, Robinson II, 910
Phipps, Sarah II, 249
Phipps, Sarah II, 406
Phipps, Sarah II, 622
Phipps, Sarah II, 756
Phipps, Sarah II, 760
Phipps, Sarah II, 901
Phipps, Sarah II, 910
Phipps, Stephen II, 406
Phipps, Stephen II, 497
Phipps, Stephen II, 574
Phipps, Stephen II, 622
Phipps, Stephen II, 647
Phipps, Stephen II, 815
Phipps, Susanna II, 622
Phipps, Susanna II, 680
Phipps, Susanna IV, 492
Phipps, Tacy II, 406
Phipps, Thomas II, 406
Phipps, Thomas II, 540
Phipps, Thomas II, 574
Phipps, Thomas II, 622
Phipps, Thomas II, 760
Phipps, Thomas, Jr. II, 760
Phipps, Thomas, Jr. II, 815
Phipps, Thos. II, 815
Phipps, Thos. II, 901
Phipps, Thos. II, 910
Phipps, W. E. IV, 475
Phipps, W. E. IV, 492
Phipps, William II, 406
Phipps, William II, 815
Phipps, William IV, 492
Phipps, Wm. II, 910
Phipps, Wm. IV, 492
Phipps, Zephaniah II, 406
Phips, Edith IV, 106
Phips, Edith IV, 113
Phips, Isaac II, 622
Phoebus, Anna Eliza III, 266
Phound, Elizabeth L. IV, 810
Phound, Thomas C. IV, 810
Phouts, Peter V, 739
Phrasey, Joseph II, 249
Phukeway, A. VI, 985
Phukeway, A. VI, 1014
Physico, Peter I, 274
Physicoe, Abigail I, 274
Physioe, Abigail I, 274
Physioe, Dianna I, 274
Physioe, John I, 274
Physioe, Mary I, 274
Physioe, Peter I, 270
Physioe, Peter I, 274
Physioe, Susanna I, 274
Physioe, Widow Dianna I, 270
Physioe, Widow Dianna I, 274
Piat, Elizabeth IV, 429
Piat, Elizabeth IV, 439
Piat, Lucinda IV, 429
Piatt, Lillian IV, 1333
Piatt, Lillian E. IV, 1333
Piatt, Lorenzo J. IV, 1333
Piatt, Mary IV, 339
Piatt, Mary IV, 347
Piatti, Antonia III, 254
Piatti, Patrizio III, 254
Piatti, Selina A. III, 122
Piatti, Selina A. III, 254
Piatti, Virgil C. III, 122
Piatti, Virgil C. III, 254
Piborn, Jacob VI, 910
Piborn, Sarah VI, 910
Pickard, Catharine I, 452
Pickard, Elenor I, 452
Pickard, Elenor I, 455
Pickard, Rebecca II, 570
Pickard, Rebecca II, 622
Pickard, Sarah I, 452
Pickens, Keziah V, 704
Pickerd, Catharine I, 413
Pickerel, Achsah V, 110
Pickerel, Catharine I, 415
Pickerel, Catharine I, 429
Pickerel, Catherine V, 110
Pickerel, Henry V, 110
Pickerel, Jacob V, 975
Pickerel, John V, 110
Pickerell, Achsah I, 957
Pickerell, Achsah I, 967
Pickerell, Catharin I, 967
Pickerell, Catharine I, 967
Pickerell, Catherine I, 957
Pickerell, Dinah I, 967
Pickerell, Henry I, 957
Pickerell, Henry I, 967
Pickerell, John I, 957
Pickerell, John I, 967
Pickering, ??? IV, 137
Pickering, Abel IV, 156
Pickering, Abel IV, 264
Pickering, Abel IV, 346
Pickering, Abel IV, 544
Pickering, Abel VI, 430
Pickering, Abigail IV, 544
Pickering, Abijah I, 1087
Pickering, Abijah I, 1097
Pickering, Able IV, 562
Pickering, Abner IV, 544
Pickering, Alexander IV, 156
Pickering, Alice IV, 1107
Pickering, Alice IV, 1111
Pickering, Alice V, 762
Pickering, Amanda IV, 156
Pickering, Amanda IV, 264
Pickering, Amanda IV, 346
Pickering, Amanda M. IV, 162
Pickering, Amelia IV, 141
Pickering, Amelia IV, 156
Pickering, Amelia IV, 337
Pickering, Amelia IV, 347
Pickering, Ann II, 312
Pickering, Ann II, 323
Pickering, Ann II, 1021
Pickering, Ann II, 1036
Pickering, Ann IV, 156
Pickering, Ann IV, 165
Pickering, Ann IV, 346
Pickering, Ann IV, 359
Pickering, Ann V, 957
Pickering, Ann V, 961
Pickering, Ann Eliza II, 312
Pickering, Ann Eliza II, 323
Pickering, Ann F. IV, 347
Pickering, Ann F. V, 957
Pickering, Anna IV, 156
Pickering, Anna IV, 343
Pickering, Anna IV, 347
Pickering, Anna Miller IV, 347
Pickering, Anna V. IV, 264
Pickering, Annie Eliza II, 318
Pickering, Annie Eliza II, 323
Pickering, Aquilla IV, 264
Pickering, Armelia IV, 544
Pickering, Armelia IV, 1111
Pickering, Benj. V, 816
Pickering, Benjamin I, 967
Pickering, Benjamin I, 1077
Pickering, Benjamin I, 1086
Pickering, Benjamin I, 1097
Pickering, Benjamin I, 1127
Pickering, Benjamin I, 1130
Pickering, Benjamin V, 110
Pickering, Benjamin V, 309
Pickering, Benjamin VI, 384
Pickering, Benjamin VI, 429
Pickering, Benjamin VI, 430
Pickering, Benjamin VI, 431
Pickering, Benjamin VI, 603
Pickering, Benjamin Jonathan I, 1097
Pickering, Benjamin, Senior I, 1086
Pickering, Betty I, 1087
Pickering, Caroline IV, 156
Pickering, Channing R. II, 323
Pickering, Channing Ridgway II, 312
Pickering, Charity I, 1087
Pickering, Charles II, 446
Pickering, Charles IV, 156
Pickering, Charles Henry II, 815
Pickering, Charles W. II, 815
Pickering, Chas. L. IV, 347
Pickering, Chas. Lewis IV, 347
Pickering, Chas. W. II, 910
Pickering, Clyde Ward IV, 264
Pickering, David I, 1087
Pickering, David IV, 156
Pickering, David IV, 346
Pickering, David V, 271
Pickering, David V, 309
Pickering, David VI, 430
Pickering, David VI, 431
Pickering, Deborah I, 1086
Pickering, Deborah I, 1087
Pickering, Deborah I, 1097
Pickering, Dorothy V, 1014
Pickering, Ealeanor VI, 429
Pickering, Edmond IV, 150
Pickering, Eleanor IV, 347
Pickering, Eleanor IV, 429
Pickering, Eleanor V, 309
Pickering, Eleanor VI, 431
Pickering, Elenor IV, 347
Pickering, Elenor V, 271
Pickering, Elenor V, 274
Pickering, Elenor V, 447
Pickering, Elenor VI, 430
Pickering, Elias IV, 346
Pickering, Elias IV, 347
Pickering, Elias IV, 1107
Pickering, Elias IV, 1111
Pickering, Elias VI, 430
Pickering, Elias VI, 603
Pickering, Elihu IV, 264
Pickering, Elijah I, 1087
Pickering, Elijah IV, 146
Pickering, Elijah IV, 156
Pickering, Elijah IV, 347
Pickering, Elijah IV, 1029
Pickering, Elinor IV, 330
Pickering, Elinor IV, 347
Pickering, Elisabeth I, 1130
Pickering, Elisha I, 1087
Pickering, Elisha I, 1097
Pickering, Elisha IV, 140
Pickering, Elisha IV, 156
Pickering, Elisha IV, 157
Pickering, Elisha IV, 347
Pickering, Eliza II, 312
Pickering, Eliza II, 323
Pickering, Eliza C. IV, 264
Pickering, Elizabeth I, 1086
Pickering, Elizabeth I, 1087
Pickering, Elizabeth I, 1094
Pickering, Elizabeth I, 1097
Pickering, Elizabeth II, 249
Pickering, Elizabeth II, 298
Pickering, Elizabeth II, 312
Pickering, Elizabeth IV, 144
Pickering, Elizabeth IV, 156
Pickering, Elizabeth IV, 264
Pickering, Elizabeth IV, 322
Pickering, Elizabeth IV, 328
Pickering, Elizabeth IV, 346
Pickering, Elizabeth IV, 347
Pickering, Elizabeth IV, 392
Pickering, Elizabeth IV, 429
Pickering, Elizabeth IV, 544
Pickering, Elizabeth IV, 556
Pickering, Elizabeth IV, 562
Pickering, Elizabeth IV, 592
Pickering, Elizabeth IV, 1073
Pickering, Elizabeth VI, 382
Pickering, Elizabeth VI, 429
Pickering, Elizabeth VI, 430
Pickering, Elizabeth VI, 440
Pickering, Elizabeth Ellis VI, 603
Pickering, Elizabeth L. IV, 1111
Pickering, Elizabeth, Jr. I, 1087
Pickering, Ellen IV, 347
Pickering, Ellis I, 967
Pickering, Ellis I, 1086
Pickering, Ellis I, 1087
Pickering, Ellis I, 1096
Pickering, Ellis I, 1097
Pickering, Ellis VI, 430
Pickering, Ellis H. IV, 264
Pickering, Emmaline Moore II, 815
Pickering, Emmaline Moore II, 910
Pickering, Enos I, 967
Pickering, Enos I, 1086
Pickering, Enos I, 1087
Pickering, Enos I, 1097
Pickering, Enos I, 1130
Pickering, Enos IV, 156
Pickering, Enos IV, 346
Pickering, Enos VI, 429
Pickering, Enos VI, 430
Pickering, Enos VI, 603
Pickering, Enos, Jr. I, 1087
Pickering, Esther IV, 544
Pickering, Evan IV, 264
Pickering, Evan IV, 544
Pickering, Evan IV, 1111
Pickering, Evan VI, 430
Pickering, Evan VI, 603
Pickering, Francis Drake IV, 347
Pickering, George II, 863
Pickering, George II, 910
Pickering, Grace V, 299
Pickering, Grace V, 309
Pickering, Grace VI, 415
Pickering, Grace VI, 429
Pickering, Grace VI, 430
Pickering, Grace VI, 431
Pickering, Grace VI, 603
Pickering, Grace VI, 608
Pickering, Hannah I, 1086
Pickering, Hannah I, 1087
Pickering, Hannah II, 863
Pickering, Hannah II, 910
Pickering, Hannah IV, 156
Pickering, Hannah IV, 264
Pickering, Hannah IV, 331
Pickering, Hannah IV, 346
Pickering, Hannah IV, 544
Pickering, Hannah IV, 1024
Pickering, Hannah V, 271
Pickering, Hannah V, 309
Pickering, Hannah VI, 365
Pickering, Hannah VI, 383
Pickering, Hannah VI, 384
Pickering, Hannah VI, 429
Pickering, Hannah VI, 430
Pickering, Hannah VI, 431
Pickering, Hannah VI, 461
Pickering, Hannah VI, 603
Pickering, Hannah VI, 608
Pickering, Hannah F. IV, 325
Pickering, Hannah Hartley IV, 1029
Pickering, Hannah K. IV, 347
Pickering, Hannah K. IV, 1029
Pickering, Hannah Kemp IV, 1029
Pickering, Hannah S. C. II, 910
Pickering, Hannah, Jr. IV, 156
Pickering, Helena IV, 544
Pickering, Henry IV, 156
Pickering, Henry C. II, 910
Pickering, Henry F. IV, 325
Pickering, Henry F. IV, 347
Pickering, Henry Fox IV, 156
Pickering, Henry Fox IV, 347
Pickering, Henry Fox IV, 1024
Pickering, Henry Fox IV, 1029
Pickering, Henry T. V, 957
Pickering, Henry T. V, 961
Pickering, Hester V, 814
Pickering, Hester V, 820
Pickering, Hetty V, 816
Pickering, Hiram IV, 346
Pickering, Hiram IV, 544
Pickering, Isaac IV, 144
Pickering, Isaac IV, 264
Pickering, Isaac IV, 328
Pickering, Isaac IV, 346
Pickering, Isaac IV, 347
Pickering, Isaac IV, 1111
Pickering, Isaac V, 271
Pickering, Isaac VI, 429
Pickering, Isaac VI, 430
Pickering, Isaac VI, 431
Pickering, Isaac VI, 459
Pickering, Isaac VI, 603
Pickering, Jacob IV, 145
Pickering, Jacob IV, 163
Pickering, Jacob IV, 226
Pickering, Jacob IV, 264
Pickering, Jacob IV, 326
Pickering, Jacob IV, 331
Pickering, Jacob IV, 429
Pickering, Jacob IV, 540
Pickering, Jacob IV, 544
Pickering, Jacob IV, 562
Pickering, Jacob VI, 361
Pickering, Jacob VI, 383
Pickering, Jacob VI, 384
Pickering, Jacob VI, 429
Pickering, Jacob VI, 430
Pickering, Jacob, Jr. IV, 156
Pickering, Jacob, Jr. IV, 264
Pickering, Jacob, Jr. IV, 338
Pickering, Jacob, Jr. IV, 346
Pickering, Jacob, Jr. IV, 544
Pickering, Jacob, Jr. VI, 430
Pickering, James IV, 346
Pickering, James IV, 347
Pickering, James IV, 544
Pickering, James Rees V, 447
Pickering, Jane I, 1086
Pickering, Jane II, 312
Pickering, Jane IV, 328
Pickering, Jane IV, 329
Pickering, Jane IV, 337
Pickering, Jane IV, 346
Pickering, Jane VI, 384
Pickering, Jane VI, 430
Pickering, Jane W. IV, 347
Pickering, Jeremiah II, 622
Pickering, Jesse B. IV, 562
Pickering, Joanna IV, 156
Pickering, Joanna IV, 346
Pickering, John I, 1086
Pickering, John I, 1087
Pickering, John I, 1097
Pickering, John II, 978
Pickering, John II, 1021
Pickering, John II, 1036
Pickering, John IV, 156
Pickering, John IV, 158
Pickering, John IV, 159
Pickering, John IV, 165
Pickering, John IV, 328
Pickering, John IV, 337
Pickering, John IV, 346
Pickering, John IV, 347
Pickering, John IV, 430
Pickering, John V, 271
Pickering, John VI, 384
Pickering, John VI, 429
Pickering, John VI, 430
Pickering, John C. IV, 156
Pickering, John C. IV, 347
Pickering, John Charles IV, 3
Pickering, John Chas. IV, 347
Pickering, John E. IV, 347
Pickering, John Elliott IV, 34
Pickering, John H. IV, 264
Pickering, John Hurford IV, 2
Pickering, John L. IV, 347
Pickering, John R. II, 910
Pickering, John, Jr. II, 1021
Pickering, John, Sr. IV, 264
Pickering, Jonas IV, 147
Pickering, Jonas IV, 156
Pickering, Jonas IV, 544
Pickering, Jonas VI, 603
Pickering, Jonathan I, 1086
Pickering, Jonathan IV, 156
Pickering, Jonathan IV, 264
Pickering, Jonathan IV, 346
Pickering, Jonathan IV, 544
Pickering, Jonathan IV, 1111
Pickering, Jonathan V, 271
Pickering, Jonathan V, 274
Pickering, Jonathan V, 309
Pickering, Jonathan V, 447
Pickering, Jonathan VI, 362
Pickering, Jonathan VI, 389
Pickering, Jonathan VI, 429
Pickering, Jonathan VI, 430
Pickering, Jonathan VI, 431
Pickering, Jonathan VI, 440
Pickering, Jonathan VI, 603
Pickering, Jonathan E. IV, 26
Pickering, Jonathan, Jr. V, 30
Pickering, Jonathan, Jr. VI, 4
Pickering, Jonathan, Sr. V, 27
Pickering, Jonathan, Sr. V, 30
Pickering, Jordan IV, 544
Pickering, Joseph II, 323
Pickering, Joseph II, 1021
Pickering, Joseph II, 1036
Pickering, Joseph IV, 156
Pickering, Joseph IV, 346
Pickering, Joseph IV, 544
Pickering, Joseph VI, 430
Pickering, Joseph S. II, 622
Pickering, Joseph S. II, 815
Pickering, Joseph W. II, 323
Pickering, Joseph Watson II,
Pickering, Joshua IV, 544
Pickering, Joshua VI, 430
Pickering, Joshua VI, 431
Pickering, Joshua VI, 603
Pickering, Josiah F. IV, 264
Pickering, Josiah Fox IV, 347
Pickering, Keturah V, 816
Pickering, Lamira IV, 156
Pickering, Lamira IV, 347
Pickering, Leah IV, 156
Pickering, Leah IV, 159
Pickering, Leah IV, 346

ering, Leah IV, 352
ering, Lemira IV, 347
ering, Levi I, 1086
ering, Levi I, 1097
ering, Levi IV, 156
ering, Levi IV, 326
ering, Levi IV, 346
ering, Levi IV, 429
kering, Levi IV, 619
ering, Levi IV, 651
kering, Levi VI, 603
kering, Levi, Jr. IV, 347
kering, Lewis IV, 156
kering, Lewis IV, 162
kering, Lewis Henry Hoover IV, 347
kering, Lidia VI, 429
kering, Lydia IV, 156
kering, Lydia IV, 163
kering, Lydia IV, 326
kering, Lydia IV, 430
kering, Lydia IV, 540
kering, Lydia IV, 544
kering, Lydia V, 271
kering, Lydia V, 298
kering, Lydia V, 309
kering, Lydia V, 447
kering, Lydia VI, 361
kering, Lydia VI, 430
kering, Lydia VI, 431
ckering, Lydia Ann IV, 156
kering, Mahlon IV, 544
ckering, Margaret Ann I, 1087
ckering, Margaret Ann I, 1097
ckering, Margaret E. IV, 750
ckering, Margaret J. IV, 347
ckering, Mariam I, 1097
ckering, Martha VI, 593
ckering, Mary I, 1086
ckering, Mary I, 1095
ckering, Mary I, 1097
ckering, Mary II, 1021
ckering, Mary II, 1025
ckering, Mary IV, 106
ckering, Mary IV, 140
ckering, Mary IV, 145
ckering, Mary IV, 150
ckering, Mary IV, 156
ckering, Mary IV, 157
ckering, Mary IV, 159
ickering, Mary IV, 264
ickering, Mary IV, 321
ickering, Mary IV, 326
ickering, Mary IV, 328
ickering, Mary IV, 329
ickering, Mary IV, 346
ickering, Mary IV, 347
ickering, Mary IV, 429
ickering, Mary IV, 515
ickering, Mary IV, 544
ickering, Mary VI, 383
ickering, Mary VI, 384
ickering, Mary VI, 387
ickering, Mary VI, 429
ickering, Mary VI, 430
ickering, Mary VI, 431
ickering, Mary VI, 603
Pickering, Mary Ann IV, 145
Pickering, Mary Ann IV, 156
Pickering, Mary Ann IV, 199
Pickering, Mary Ann IV, 264
Pickering, Mary Ann IV, 346
Pickering, Mary C. P. IV, 320
Pickering, Mary C. P. IV, 347
Pickering, Mary Elizabeth IV, 347
Pickering, Mary Rebecca II, 312
Pickering, Mary S. IV, 157
Pickering, Mary S. IV, 347
Pickering, Mercy II, 813
Pickering, Mercy II, 1020
Pickering, Mercy II, 1021
Pickering, Mercy V, 309
Pickering, Mercy VI, 417
Pickering, Mercy VI, 429
Pickering, Mercy VI, 431
Pickering, Mery VI, 431
Pickering, Milla IV, 156
Pickering, Miller IV, 156
Pickering, Miriam I, 1087
Pickering, Mordecai IV, 1111
Pickering, Naomi IV, 264
Pickering, Nathaniel I, 1086
Pickering, Nathaniel I, 1097
Pickering, Phebe IV, 150
Pickering, Phebe IV, 156
Pickering, Phebe IV, 326
Pickering, Phebe IV, 340
Pickering, Phebe IV, 346
Pickering, Phebe IV, 359
Pickering, Phebe IV, 544
Pickering, Phebe IV, 651
Pickering, Phebe V, 271
Pickering, Phebe V, 274
Pickering, Phebe V, 309
Pickering, Phebe VI, 362
Pickering, Phebe VI, 413
Pickering, Phebe VI, 430
Pickering, Phebe VI, 431
Pickering, Phebe VI, 603
Pickering, Phebe Ann IV, 143
Pickering, Phebe Ann IV, 156
Pickering, Phebe Ann IV, 157
Pickering, Phenehas I, 1086
Pickering, Phineas I, 1097
Pickering, Phinehas I, 1097
Pickering, Phinehas I, 1099
Pickering, Phinneas I, 1097
Pickering, Rachel I, 1087
Pickering, Rachel I, 1097
Pickering, Rachel I, 1099
Pickering, Rachel II, 312
Pickering, Rachel II, 323
Pickering, Rachel II, 978
Pickering, Rachel II, 1021
Pickering, Rachel II, 1036
Pickering, Rachel IV, 226
Pickering, Rachel IV, 264
Pickering, Rachel IV, 338
Pickering, Rachel IV, 340
Pickering, Rachel IV, 346
Pickering, Rachel IV, 347
Pickering, Rachel IV, 429
Pickering, Rachel IV, 471
Pickering, Rachel IV, 492
Pickering, Rachel IV, 525
Pickering, Rachel IV, 544
Pickering, Rachel V, 271
Pickering, Rachel V, 309
Pickering, Rachel VI, 429
Pickering, Rachel VI, 431
Pickering, Rachel D. II, 318
Pickering, Rachel D. II, 323
Pickering, Rachel E. IV, 320
Pickering, Rachel E. IV, 347
Pickering, Rebecca I, 1096
Pickering, Rebecca IV, 150
Pickering, Rebecca IV, 156
Pickering, Rebecca IV, 158
Pickering, Rebecca IV, 228
Pickering, Rebecca IV, 264
Pickering, Rebecca IV, 337
Pickering, Rebecca IV, 346
Pickering, Rebecca IV, 347
Pickering, Rebecca IV, 429
Pickering, Rebecca IV, 544
Pickering, Rebecca IV, 1029
Pickering, Rebecca V, 302
Pickering, Rebecca V, 309
Pickering, Rebecca VI, 430
Pickering, Rebecca VI, 431
Pickering, Rebecca J. IV, 264
Pickering, Rebecca Jane I, 1087
Pickering, Rebecca Jane I, 1097
Pickering, Rebecca Stevens IV, 146
Pickering, Rebecca Stevens IV, 156
Pickering, Rebecca W. II, 910
Pickering, Rebeccah VI, 430
Pickering, Rebeckah I, 1086
Pickering, Rebeckah I, 1096
Pickering, Rebeckah I, 1097
Pickering, Rebeckah IV, 156
Pickering, Rebeckah VI, 430
Pickering, Rebeckah VI, 603
Pickering, Rebekah I, 1086
Pickering, Rebekah I, 1087
Pickering, Rebekah VI, 384
Pickering, Rebekah VI, 430
Pickering, Rees IV, 347
Pickering, Reese IV, 157
Pickering, Rhoda IV, 156
Pickering, Rhoda IV, 326
Pickering, Rhoda IV, 346
Pickering, Rhoda IV, 544
Pickering, Rhoda VI, 430
Pickering, Riley David I, 1087
Pickering, Riley David I, 1097
Pickering, Rosa May IV, 264
Pickering, Rose V, 425
Pickering, Ruth IV, 147
Pickering, Ruth IV, 156
Pickering, Ruth IV, 544
Pickering, Ruth V, 271
Pickering, Ruth V, 309
Pickering, Ruth VI, 431
Pickering, Ruthanna IV, 346
Pickering, Ruthanna IV, 347
Pickering, Ruthanna IV, 544
Pickering, Samira John Eliot IV, 347
Pickering, Samuel I, 967
Pickering, Samuel I, 1086
Pickering, Samuel I, 1087
Pickering, Samuel I, 1096
Pickering, Samuel I, 1097
Pickering, Samuel II, 1021
Pickering, Samuel II, 1025
Pickering, Samuel IV, 150
Pickering, Samuel IV, 156
Pickering, Samuel IV, 264
Pickering, Samuel IV, 320
Pickering, Samuel IV, 326
Pickering, Samuel IV, 328
Pickering, Samuel IV, 346
Pickering, Samuel IV, 347
Pickering, Samuel IV, 359
Pickering, Samuel IV, 429
Pickering, Samuel IV, 430
Pickering, Samuel IV, 544
Pickering, Samuel IV, 651
Pickering, Samuel VI, 387
Pickering, Samuel VI, 429
Pickering, Samuel VI, 603
Pickering, Samuel VI, 608
Pickering, Samuel Scarborough VI, 429
Pickering, Samuel, Jr. VI, 413
Pickering, Samuel, Jr. VI, 430
Pickering, Samuel, Jr. VI, 593
Pickering, Samuel, Jr. VI, 603
Pickering, Sarah I, 1127
Pickering, Sarah I, 1130
Pickering, Sarah II, 312
Pickering, Sarah IV, 141
Pickering, Sarah IV, 150
Pickering, Sarah IV, 156
Pickering, Sarah IV, 158
Pickering, Sarah IV, 163
Pickering, Sarah IV, 165
Pickering, Sarah IV, 264
Pickering, Sarah IV, 320
Pickering, Sarah IV, 346
Pickering, Sarah IV, 347
Pickering, Sarah IV, 429
Pickering, Sarah IV, 544
Pickering, Sarah IV, 1098
Pickering, Sarah IV, 1111
Pickering, Sarah V, 271
Pickering, Sarah V, 309
Pickering, Sarah VI, 365
Pickering, Sarah VI, 379
Pickering, Sarah VI, 384
Pickering, Sarah VI, 389
Pickering, Sarah VI, 429
Pickering, Sarah VI, 430
Pickering, Sarah VI, 431
Pickering, Sarah VI, 450
Pickering, Sarah Ann IV, 264
Pickering, Sarah Ann IV, 347
Pickering, Sarah Ann IV, 352
Pickering, Sarah E. IV, 347
Pickering, Sarah F. IV, 347
Pickering, Sarah F. IV, 350
Pickering, Sarah Fox IV, 156
Pickering, Sarah Fox IV, 347
Pickering, Sarah Jane II, 323
Pickering, Sarah Jane IV, 324
Pickering, Sarah Jane IV, 347
Pickering, Sarrah IV, 156
Pickering, Sidney V, 271
Pickering, Sidney VI, 430
Pickering, Sidney VI, 459
Pickering, Simeon IV, 347
Pickering, Stacy II, 622
Pickering, Susan L. II, 323
Pickering, Susan S. II, 321
Pickering, Susan S. II, 323
Pickering, Susan Savery II, 312
Pickering, Susanna I, 962
Pickering, Susanna I, 967
Pickering, Susanna IV, 343
Pickering, Susanna IV, 346
Pickering, Susanna IV, 347
Pickering, Susanna IV, 544
Pickering, Susanna, Jr. IV, 347
Pickering, Susannah I, 1087
Pickering, Susannah I, 1097
Pickering, Susannah IV, 326
Pickering, Susannah IV, 346
Pickering, Susannah IV, 429
Pickering, Susannah IV, 619
Pickering, Susannah IV, 651
Pickering, Susannah Elizabeth I, 1087
Pickering, Susannah Elizabeth I, 1097
Pickering, Tacy P. II, 863
Pickering, Tacy P. II, 910
Pickering, Tacy Pancoast II, 815
Pickering, Thomas I, 1086
Pickering, Thomas I, 1097
Pickering, Thomas IV, 346
Pickering, Thomas IV, 347
Pickering, Thomas VI, 430
Pickering, Thomas V. IV, 156
Pickering, Vada V, 1014
Pickering, Watson II, 312
Pickering, Watson II, 323
Pickering, Wd Phebe IV, 328
Pickering, Wd. Ann II, 446
Pickering, Wd. Mary VI, 429
Pickering, Wd. Rebecca II, 815
Pickering, William I, 1087
Pickering, William I, 1097
Pickering, William IV, 347
Pickering, William IV, 544
Pickering, William V, 271
Pickering, William VI, 365
Pickering, William VI, 384
Pickering, William VI, 430
Pickering, William VI, 431
Pickering, William Coates II, 815
Pickering, William Robert I, 1087
Pickering, William Robert I, 1097
Pickering, William T. IV, 347
Pickering, Wm. II, 1025
Pickering, Wm. V, 309
Pickering, Wm. V, 447
Pickering, Wm. C. II, 863
Pickering, Wm. C. II, 910
Pickering, Yeomans II, 978
Pickering, Yeomans II, 1021
Picket, Abigail V, 111
Picket, Anna V, 111
Picket, Anna V, 523
Picket, Anna V, 856
Picket, Anne V, 523
Picket, Annie R. IV, 1073
Picket, Benjamin V, 110
Picket, Catharine I, 406
Picket, Catharine I, 415
Picket, Charity I, 833
Picket, Edward IV, 1073
Picket, Eli IV, 347
Picket, Elisha IV, 592
Picket, Elizabeth IV, 430
Picket, Elizabeth IV, 1073
Picket, Elizabeth V, 111
Picket, Ellen V, 111
Picket, Ester V, 111
Picket, Hannah I, 686
Picket, Hannah IV, 430
Picket, Hannah IV, 750
Picket, Hannah IV, 1073
Picket, Hannah IV, 1111
Picket, Hannah, Jr. IV, 1073
Picket, Harriet I, 453
Picket, Henry IV, 1073
Picket, Isaac IV, 1073
Picket, James IV, 1073
Picket, Jemima I, 403
Picket, Jemima I, 415
Picket, Jeremiah I, 833
Picket, Jesse IV, 1073
Picket, John I, 686
Picket, John II, 622
Picket, John IV, 1073
Picket, Joseph I, 833
Picket, Joseph I, 844
Picket, Joseph IV, 1073
Picket, Joseph V, 111
Picket, Joseph V, 523
Picket, Joseph V, 856
Picket, Joshua V, 110
Picket, Louisa IV, 1073
Picket, Lydia V, 111
Picket, Lydia V, 523
Picket, Lydia V, 856
Picket, Marjary I, 898
Picket, Martha I, 686
Picket, Martha I, 687
Picket, Martha IV, 1073
Picket, Martha IV, 1111
Picket, Mary II, 622
Picket, Mary IV, 386
Picket, Mary IV, 430
Picket, Mary IV, 438
Picket, Mary IV, 575
Picket, Mary IV, 592
Picket, Mary IV, 1073
Picket, Mary IV, 1078
Picket, Mary IV, 1083
Picket, Mary IV, 1117
Picket, Mary V, 110
Picket, Mary V, 111
Picket, Mary V, 523
Picket, Mary V, 856
Picket, Mary Ann IV, 750
Picket, Mary H. IV, 264
Picket, Mary H. IV, 286
Picket, Matilda IV, 1073
Picket, Matilda IV, 1083
Picket, Moses IV, 430
Picket, Moses IV, 1073
Picket, Nathan IV, 1073
Picket, Perley IV, 430
Picket, Perley IV, 434
Picket, Perley IV, 1073
Picket, Phebe IV, 430
Picket, Phebe IV, 750
Picket, Pricilla V, 111
Picket, Priscilla I, 833
Picket, Priscilla I, 844
Picket, Priscilla V, 523
Picket, Rachel IV, 1073
Picket, Rachel IV, 1083
Picket, Rebecca IV, 430
Picket, Rebecca IV, 1073
Picket, Rebecca IV, 1078
Picket, Rebecca M. IV, 430
Picket, Rebecca M. IV, 434
Picket, Rebeckah V, 308
Picket, Reuben E. IV, 750
Picket, Rhoda IV, 1073
Picket, Ruth I, 415
Picket, Sarah I, 453
Picket, Sarah IV, 1073
Picket, Sarah IV, 1111
Picket, Sarah IV, 1117
Picket, Sarah V, 110
Picket, Sarah V, 111
Picket, Sarah V, 523
Picket, Sarah V, 856
Picket, Sarah M. IV, 1073
Picket, Simeon I, 686
Picket, Simeon I, 687
Picket, Tamar V, 111
Picket, Tamer V, 523
Picket, Tamer V, 856
Picket, Thamar V, 523
Picket, Thomas IV, 386
Picket, Thomas IV, 430
Picket, Thomas IV, 1073
Picket, Thomas IV, 1117
Picket, William I, 453
Picket, William IV, 430
Picket, William IV, 1073
Picket, Wm. IV, 1073
Picket, Wm. A. IV, 1078
Pickett, ??? IV, 1047
Pickett, ??? VI, 688
Pickett, Abigail I, 413
Pickett, Abigail I, 414
Pickett, Abigail I, 731
Pickett, Abigal I, 731
Pickett, Alfred M. I, 415
Pickett, Alice II, 622
Pickett, Alice II, 632
Pickett, Alice II, 665
Pickett, Alice L. II, 1058
Pickett, Alice Lydia II, 967
Pickett, Ann I, 484
Pickett, Ann IV, 848
Pickett, Anna IV, 215
Pickett, Anna IV, 264
Pickett, Anna IV, 289
Pickett, Anna IV, 819
Pickett, Annie R. IV, 1073
Pickett, Benj. I, 414
Pickett, Benjamin I, 413
Pickett, Benjamin I, 414
Pickett, Benjamin I, 415
Pickett, Benjamin I, 452
Pickett, Benjamin I, 453
Pickett, Benjamin, Jr. I, 414
Pickett, Catharine I, 414
Pickett, Catharine I, 415
Pickett, Catharine I, 452
Pickett, Charity I, 413
Pickett, Charity I, 414
Pickett, Charity I, 833
Pickett, Daniel VI, 431
Pickett, David I, 415
Pickett, Deborah B. II, 723
Pickett, Edith I, 414
Pickett, Edith I, 452
Pickett, Edith IV, 553
Pickett, Edith R. IV, 430
Pickett, Edith R. IV, 445
Pickett, Edith R. IV, 544
Pickett, Edith R. IV, 553
Pickett, Edward IV, 430
Pickett, Edward IV, 1073
Pickett, Elihu I, 386
Pickett, Elihu I, 415
Pickett, Eliza V, 425
Pickett, Eliza A. I, 708
Pickett, Eliza A. I, 731
Pickett, Eliza H. R. I, 731
Pickett, Elizabeth I, 414
Pickett, Elizabeth I, 731
Pickett, Elizabeth IV, 430
Pickett, Elizabeth IV, 1073

Pickett, Elizabeth D. I, 415
Pickett, Elizabeth Jane I, 415
Pickett, Elmer II, 967
Pickett, Elmer II, 1058
Pickett, Ethel IV, 401
Pickett, Ethel IV, 403
Pickett, Ethel IV, 961
Pickett, Ethel IV, 986
Pickett, Francis I, 415
Pickett, George III, 254
Pickett, Gertrude IV, 766
Pickett, Gertrude IV, 824
Pickett, Gertrude IV, 844
Pickett, Grace I, 616
Pickett, Hannah I, 363
Pickett, Hannah I, 413
Pickett, Hannah I, 414
Pickett, Hannah I, 415
Pickett, Hannah I, 452
Pickett, Hannah I, 453
Pickett, Hannah I, 484
Pickett, Hannah IV, 430
Pickett, Hannah IV, 448
Pickett, Hannah IV, 1062
Pickett, Hannah IV, 1115
Pickett, Hannah VI, 387
Pickett, Hannah VI, 431
Pickett, Hannah VI, 603
Pickett, Hannah P. I, 374
Pickett, Hannah P. I, 415
Pickett, Hannah R. I, 484
Pickett, Hannah, Jr. IV, 1073
Pickett, Hannah, Sr. VI, 603
Pickett, Hariet I, 453
Pickett, Harriet I, 453
Pickett, Harriett IV, 401
Pickett, Harriett IV, 819
Pickett, Harvey IV, 176
Pickett, Harvey IV, 264
Pickett, Henery I, 363
Pickett, Hiram T. I, 415
Pickett, Hiram Taylor I, 415
Pickett, Irene IV, 264
Pickett, Irene J. II, 967
Pickett, Irene J. IV, 820
Pickett, Isaac IV, 1073
Pickett, Isaiah I, 414
Pickett, Isaiah I, 415
Pickett, James I, 414
Pickett, James I, 415
Pickett, James V, 425
Pickett, James VI, 978
Pickett, James Barclay V, 425
Pickett, Jemima I, 415
Pickett, Jemima I, 833
Pickett, Jeremiah I, 413
Pickett, Jeremiah I, 414
Pickett, Jeremiah I, 415
Pickett, Jeremiah I, 452
Pickett, Jeremiah I, 484
Pickett, Jeremiah I, 833
Pickett, Jeremiah H. I, 484
Pickett, Jeremiah, Jr. I, 413
Pickett, Jesse I, 363
Pickett, Jesse I, 415
Pickett, Jesse IV, 1073
Pickett, John I, 363
Pickett, John I, 413
Pickett, John I, 414
Pickett, John I, 415
Pickett, John I, 452
Pickett, John I, 453
Pickett, John II, 622
Pickett, John II, 632
Pickett, John IV, 1073
Pickett, John Newlin I, 414
Pickett, Jonathan I, 415
Pickett, Joseph I, 414
Pickett, Joseph I, 415
Pickett, Joseph I, 833
Pickett, Joseph V, 111
Pickett, Joshua I, 414
Pickett, Joshua I, 415
Pickett, Louella I, 639
Pickett, Louisa IV, 430
Pickett, Louisa IV, 444
Pickett, Louisa IV, 1073
Pickett, Louisa D. IV, 444
Pickett, Louisa D. IV, 1077
Pickett, Lucinda C. I, 415
Pickett, Mahlon I, 383
Pickett, Mahlon I, 415
Pickett, Margaret IV, 1333
Pickett, Margery I, 413
Pickett, Margery I, 414
Pickett, Martha I, 414
Pickett, Mary I, 363
Pickett, Mary I, 386
Pickett, Mary I, 404
Pickett, Mary I, 413
Pickett, Mary I, 414
Pickett, Mary I, 415
Pickett, Mary I, 452
Pickett, Mary I, 453
Pickett, Mary II, 622
Pickett, Mary IV, 386
Pickett, Mary IV, 430
Pickett, Mary IV, 446
Pickett, Mary IV, 1055
Pickett, Mary IV, 1073
Pickett, Mary IV, 1115
Pickett, Mary Ann I, 484
Pickett, Mary E. V, 425
Pickett, Mary Emily I, 415
Pickett, Mary H. IV, 264
Pickett, Mary P. IV, 446
Pickett, Mary Williams II, 622
Pickett, Maryland I, 413
Pickett, Melva A. II, 1058
Pickett, Melva Alice II, 967
Pickett, Merle E. II, 1058
Pickett, Merle Elmer II, 967
Pickett, Milicent J. I, 415
Pickett, Moses IV, 430
Pickett, Nancy I, 415
Pickett, Nancy VI, 978
Pickett, Nathan I, 363
Pickett, Nathan I, 414
Pickett, Nathan I, 453
Pickett, Patience I, 386
Pickett, Patience I, 414
Pickett, Patience I, 415
Pickett, Patience I, 453
Pickett, Perley IV, 264
Pickett, Perley IV, 282
Pickett, Perley IV, 430
Pickett, Perley IV, 444
Pickett, Perley IV, 445
Pickett, Perley IV, 1073
Pickett, Phebe I, 402
Pickett, Phebe I, 414
Pickett, Phebe I, 415
Pickett, Phebe IV, 430
Pickett, Phineas IV, 401
Pickett, Phineas IV, 819
Pickett, Priscilla I, 414
Pickett, Priscilla I, 415
Pickett, Priscilla I, 833
Pickett, Priscilla I, 834
Pickett, Rachel I, 413
Pickett, Rachel I, 414
Pickett, Rachel I, 452
Pickett, Rachel IV, 1095
Pickett, Rachel IV, 1122
Pickett, Rachel VI, 370
Pickett, Rachel VI, 431
Pickett, Rebecca I, 363
Pickett, Rebecca I, 415
Pickett, Rebecca I, 452
Pickett, Rebecca II, 715
Pickett, Rebecca IV, 176
Pickett, Rebecca IV, 177
Pickett, Rebecca IV, 264
Pickett, Rebecca IV, 430
Pickett, Rebecca IV, 444
Pickett, Rebecca IV, 1073
Pickett, Rebecca IV, 1077
Pickett, Rebecca IV, 1083
Pickett, Rebecca V, 271
Pickett, Rebecca Binns IV, 264
Pickett, Rebecca C. I, 383
Pickett, Rebecca C. I, 415
Pickett, Rebecca M. IV, 430
Pickett, Rebeckah I, 414
Pickett, Rebekah I, 413
Pickett, Rebekah I, 414
Pickett, Rebekah I, 452
Pickett, Rhoda IV, 430
Pickett, Rhoda IV, 1055
Pickett, Rhoda IV, 1073
Pickett, Robert II, 967
Pickett, Robert IV, 264
Pickett, Robert B. IV, 820
Pickett, Ruth I, 414
Pickett, Ruth I, 415
Pickett, Ruth I, 453
Pickett, Ruth VI, 689
Pickett, Ruth Amy IV, 820
Pickett, Ruth Amy IV, 838
Pickett, Ruth K. II, 715
Pickett, Ruth Kennard II, 760
Pickett, Ruth S. I, 484
Pickett, Samuel I, 363
Pickett, Samuel I, 414
Pickett, Samuel R. I, 639
Pickett, Samuel Randolph I, 415
Pickett, Sara M. II, 715
Pickett, Sarah I, 363
Pickett, Sarah I, 413
Pickett, Sarah I, 414
Pickett, Sarah I, 415
Pickett, Sarah I, 452
Pickett, Sarah I, 453
Pickett, Sarah IV, 1073
Pickett, Sarah Ann Maria I, 415
Pickett, Sarah E. IV, 264
Pickett, Sarah E. IV, 282
Pickett, Sarah E. IV, 430
Pickett, Sarah E. IV, 444
Pickett, Sarah E. IV, 445
Pickett, Sarah E. S. IV, 264
Pickett, Sarah J. I, 462
Pickett, Sarah J. I, 478
Pickett, Sarah J. I, 484
Pickett, Sarah M. II, 760
Pickett, Sarah M. IV, 430
Pickett, Simeon I, 386
Pickett, Simeon I, 415
Pickett, Simon I, 414
Pickett, Simon I, 484
Pickett, Simon S. I, 484
Pickett, Solomon I, 414
Pickett, Taylor I, 415
Pickett, Thomas IV, 430
Pickett, Thomas IV, 1055
Pickett, Thomas IV, 1073
Pickett, Thomas IV, 1115
Pickett, Thos. IV, 430
Pickett, Warren E. II, 715
Pickett, Warren E. II, 760
Pickett, Widow Sarah I, 413
Pickett, Wiley I, 731
Pickett, William I, 363
Pickett, William I, 413
Pickett, William I, 414
Pickett, William I, 415
Pickett, William I, 452
Pickett, William I, 453
Pickett, William I, 484
Pickett, William I, 833
Pickett, William I, 834
Pickett, William IV, 430
Pickett, William IV, 1073
Pickett, William V, 271
Pickett, William A. I, 484
Pickett, Wm. I, 363
Pickett, Wm. I, 414
Pickett, Wm. II, 715
Pickett, Wm. IV, 264
Pickett, Wm. IV, 430
Pickett, Wm. IV, 444
Pickett, Wm. IV, 1073
Pickett, Wm. IV, 1077
Pickett, Wm. IV, 1083
Pickford, Sarah E. III, 254
Pickhard, Catharine I, 452
Pickhart, Sarah I, 452
Pickheart, Catharine I, 372
Pickheart, Catharine I, 413
Pickle, Mary IV, 838
Pickle, Sarah IV, 53
Pickle, Sarah IV, 55
Pickle, Sarah IV, 106
Pickle, Sarah IV, 107
Pickoring, Charles II, 446
Pickott, Hannah VI, 603
Pickott, John II, 622
Pickott, Moses VI, 603
Pickott, Rachel VI, 603
Pickrel, Catharine I, 415
Pickrell, ??? IV, 1269
Pickrell, Achsa I, 1011
Pickrell, Achsah I, 1001
Pickrell, Asa IV, 1290
Pickrell, Carrie IV, 1333
Pickrell, Catharin I, 967
Pickrell, Catharine I, 955
Pickrell, Catharine I, 1011
Pickrell, Catharine IV, 1290
Pickrell, Catherine I, 1001
Pickrell, Dina I, 959
Pickrell, Dinah I, 955
Pickrell, Dinah I, 967
Pickrell, Esther W. IV, 1290
Pickrell, Hannah W. IV, 1290
Pickrell, Harlen IV, 1290
Pickrell, Henry I, 1011
Pickrell, Henry IV, 1290
Pickrell, Henry Harvey IV, 1290
Pickrell, Isaiah IV, 1290
Pickrell, Jacob IV, 1290
Pickrell, John I, 955
Pickrell, John I, 967
Pickrell, Lindley H. IV, 1290
Pickrell, Mahlon IV, 1290
Pickrell, Martha IV, 1290
Pickrell, Mary I, 1011
Pickrell, Mary IV, 1290
Pickrell, Peter M. IV, 1290
Pickrell, Rachel IV, 1290
Pickrell, Ruth Ann IV, 1290
Pickrell, Sarah Jane IV, 1290
Pickrell, Susannah W. IV, 1290
Pickrell, William IV, 1290
Pickring, Benjamin VI, 603
Pickring, Elias VI, 603
Pickring, Elizabeth Ellis VI, 603
Pickring, Enos VI, 603
Pickring, Evan VI, 603
Pickring, Isaac VI, 603
Pickring, Jonas VI, 603
Pickring, Jonathan VI, 603
Pickring, Joshua VI, 603
Pickring, Levi VI, 603
Pickring, Mary VI, 603
Pickring, Rebeckah VI, 603
Pickring, Samuel VI, 603
Pickron, Elenor V, 447
Pickum, Seneca James IV, 1164
Picral, Mary I, 1011
Pidgen, Charles, Jr. I, 594
Pidgeon, ??? VI, 293
Pidgeon, ??? VI, 348
Pidgeon, Abel Lewis VI, 431
Pidgeon, Achsa I, 898
Pidgeon, Achsah I, 589
Pidgeon, Achsah I, 595
Pidgeon, Achsah I, 596
Pidgeon, Achsah I, 597
Pidgeon, Achsah I, 864
Pidgeon, Addison I, 589
Pidgeon, Addison V, 355
Pidgeon, Addison V, 641
Pidgeon, Alice IV, 54
Pidgeon, Alice VI, 349
Pidgeon, Alice VI, 355
Pidgeon, Amos IV, 474
Pidgeon, Amos IV, 492
Pidgeon, Amos IV, 1060
Pidgeon, Amos IV, 1073
Pidgeon, Amos IV, 1111
Pidgeon, Ann II, 180
Pidgeon, Ann II, 249
Pidgeon, Ann IV, 347
Pidgeon, Ann IV, 474
Pidgeon, Ann IV, 492
Pidgeon, Ann IV, 1060
Pidgeon, Ann IV, 1073
Pidgeon, Ann IV, 1074
Pidgeon, Ann IV, 1111
Pidgeon, Ann VI, 336
Pidgeon, Anne IV, 157
Pidgeon, Anne VI, 312
Pidgeon, Anzanetta IV, 986
Pidgeon, Benjamin IV, 54
Pidgeon, Benjamin VI, 355
Pidgeon, C. Chandlee VI, 770
Pidgeon, Carl J. V, 641
Pidgeon, Caroline C. V, 641
Pidgeon, Caroline P. V, 641
Pidgeon, Cassie VI, 431
Pidgeon, Catharine V, 354
Pidgeon, Catharine V, 355
Pidgeon, Catharine V, 641
Pidgeon, Charles I, 589
Pidgeon, Charles I, 595
Pidgeon, Charles I, 596
Pidgeon, Charles I, 686
Pidgeon, Charles I, 807
Pidgeon, Charles I, 818
Pidgeon, Charles I, 834
Pidgeon, Charles I, 864
Pidgeon, Charles I, 898
Pidgeon, Charles IV, 157
Pidgeon, Charles IV, 347
Pidgeon, Charles V, 354
Pidgeon, Charles V, 355
Pidgeon, Charles V, 641
Pidgeon, Charles VI, 312
Pidgeon, Charles VI, 336
Pidgeon, Charles VI, 355
Pidgeon, Charles VI, 490
Pidgeon, Charles VI, 544
Pidgeon, Charles M. VI, 384
Pidgeon, Charles M. VI, 431
Pidgeon, Charles M. VI, 739
Pidgeon, Charles M. VI, 770
Pidgeon, Charles, II I, 864
Pidgeon, Charles, Jr. I, 596
Pidgeon, Charles, Jr. I, 834
Pidgeon, Charles, Sr. I, 589
Pidgeon, Charles, Sr. I, 596
Pidgeon, Chas. V, 355
Pidgeon, Chas. V, 641
Pidgeon, Chas. A. V, 354
Pidgeon, Chas. A. V, 641
Pidgeon, Chas. B. V, 355
Pidgeon, Cornelia V, 355
Pidgeon, Cornelia C. I, 589
Pidgeon, Cornelia C. V, 354
Pidgeon, Daniel A. V, 641
Pidgeon, David I, 589
Pidgeon, David I, 595
Pidgeon, David I, 596
Pidgeon, David I, 686
Pidgeon, David I, 692
Pidgeon, David I, 864
Pidgeon, David A. V, 641
Pidgeon, Dorcas II, 65
Pidgeon, Dorcas II, 92
Pidgeon, Dorothy VI, 431
Pidgeon, Dorothy Everett VI, 3
Pidgeon, Dorothy Everett VI, 4
Pidgeon, Edward W. VI, 431
Pidgeon, Edward Walker VI, 4
Pidgeon, Eliza I, 589
Pidgeon, Eliza C. VI, 431
Pidgeon, Elizabeth I, 589
Pidgeon, Elizabeth I, 595
Pidgeon, Elizabeth I, 596
Pidgeon, Elizabeth I, 686
Pidgeon, Elizabeth I, 807
Pidgeon, Elizabeth I, 834
Pidgeon, Elizabeth I, 864
Pidgeon, Elizabeth I, 892
Pidgeon, Elizabeth I, 898
Pidgeon, Elizabeth IV, 54
Pidgeon, Elizabeth IV, 157
Pidgeon, Elizabeth IV, 621
Pidgeon, Elizabeth IV, 651
Pidgeon, Elizabeth IV, 1073
Pidgeon, Elizabeth IV, 1074
Pidgeon, Elizabeth IV, 1090
Pidgeon, Elizabeth IV, 1111
Pidgeon, Elizabeth V, 72
Pidgeon, Elizabeth V, 111
Pidgeon, Elizabeth V, 355
Pidgeon, Elizabeth V, 641
Pidgeon, Elizabeth VI, 301
Pidgeon, Elizabeth VI, 312
Pidgeon, Elizabeth VI, 336
Pidgeon, Elizabeth VI, 355
Pidgeon, Elizabeth VI, 378
Pidgeon, Elizabeth VI, 397
Pidgeon, Elizabeth VI, 431
Pidgeon, Elizabeth VI, 454
Pidgeon, Ella V, 641
Pidgeon, Ella V, 704
Pidgeon, Emilly I, 589
Pidgeon, Ethel May VI, 770
Pidgeon, Hannah I, 589
Pidgeon, Hannah I, 592
Pidgeon, Hannah V, 641
Pidgeon, Hannah VI, 311
Pidgeon, Hannah VI, 336
Pidgeon, Hannah VI, 352
Pidgeon, Hannah VI, 355
Pidgeon, Hannah Charles I, 596
Pidgeon, Harriet IV, 474
Pidgeon, Harriet IV, 492
Pidgeon, Harriet IV, 1060
Pidgeon, Harriet IV, 1073
Pidgeon, Henry V, 355
Pidgeon, Henry H. V, 354
Pidgeon, Henry H. V, 641
Pidgeon, Henry H. V, 704
Pidgeon, Henry P. I, 589
Pidgeon, Homer V, 641
Pidgeon, Ida May C. V, 641
Pidgeon, Isaac I, 487
Pidgeon, Isaac I, 790
Pidgeon, Isaac I, 834
Pidgeon, Isaac I, 864
Pidgeon, Isaac I, 890
Pidgeon, Isaac I, 898
Pidgeon, Isaac IV, 157
Pidgeon, Isaac V, 111
Pidgeon, Isaac V, 704
Pidgeon, Isaac VI, 312
Pidgeon, Isaac VI, 336
Pidgeon, Isaac VI, 351
Pidgeon, Isaac VI, 367
Pidgeon, Isaac VI, 378
Pidgeon, Isaac VI, 397
Pidgeon, Isaac VI, 402
Pidgeon, Isaac VI, 431
Pidgeon, Isaac VI, 454
Pidgeon, Isaac E. VI, 336
Pidgeon, Isaac H. V, 704
Pidgeon, Isaac, Jr. VI, 431
Pidgeon, Isaac, Jr. VI, 544
Pidgeon, Jane I, 596
Pidgeon, Jane I, 864
Pidgeon, Jane I, 898
Pidgeon, Jane Jackson VI, 770
Pidgeon, Jean I, 589
Pidgeon, Jean I, 595
Pidgeon, Jeffry I, 589
Pidgeon, Jesse I, 589
Pidgeon, John I, 589
Pidgeon, John IV, 492
Pidgeon, John IV, 1073
Pidgeon, John V, 641
Pidgeon, John VI, 336
Pidgeon, John VI, 544

geon, John B. IV, 986
geon, John Hammer VI, 431
dgeon, John M. I, 596
dgeon, John M. V, 641
dgeon, John S. IV, 1073
dgeon, Joseph IV, 492
dgeon, Joseph IV, 1073
dgeon, Joseph Fisher VI, 336
dgeon, Joseph W. IV, 492
dgeon, Joseph W. IV, 1073
dgeon, Joseph W. IV, 1090
dgeon, Joseph W. IV, 1111
dgeon, Julia I, 589
dgeon, Julia V, 355
dgeon, Julia V, 641
dgeon, Julia A. V, 354
dgeon, Julia A. V, 641
dgeon, Katharine I, 589
dgeon, Katharine I, 596
dgeon, Katharine I, 818
dgeon, Katharine I, 834
idgeon, Katie VI, 384
idgeon, Katie VI, 431
idgeon, Katie VI, 739
idgeon, Katie VI, 770
idgeon, Laura Bell V, 641
idgeon, Lewis VI, 365
idgeon, Lewis VI, 431
idgeon, Lewis VI, 457
idgeon, Lewis VI, 544
idgeon, Lewis VI, 582
idgeon, Lillian V, 712
idgeon, Louisa I, 589
idgeon, Louisa V, 355
idgeon, Louisa V, 360
idgeon, Louisa M. V, 641
idgeon, Louise M. V, 354
idgeon, Luther Duval VI, 770
idgeon, Lydia A. IV, 986
idgeon, Martha IV, 722
idgeon, Martha IV, 751
idgeon, Mary I, 589
idgeon, Mary I, 596
idgeon, Mary I, 597
idgeon, Mary I, 834
idgeon, Mary I, 864
idgeon, Mary I, 898
Pidgeon, Mary IV, 54
Pidgeon, Mary IV, 751
Pidgeon, Mary IV, 838
Pidgeon, Mary IV, 840
Pidgeon, Mary V, 111
Pidgeon, Mary V, 355
Pidgeon, Mary VI, 355
Pidgeon, Mary VI, 431
Pidgeon, Mary VI, 448
Pidgeon, Mary Elizabeth VI, 431
Pidgeon, Mary J. V, 641
Pidgeon, Mildred VI, 770
Pidgeon, Minnie Cornelia V, 641
Pidgeon, Orpah I, 864
Pidgeon, Oscar L. V, 641
Pidgeon, Oscar Leonard V, 641
Pidgeon, Pauline VI, 770
Pidgeon, Phebe I, 864
Pidgeon, Phebe I, 898
Pidgeon, Prudence I, 588
Pidgeon, Prudence I, 589
Pidgeon, Prudence I, 594
Pidgeon, Prudence I, 595
Pidgeon, Prudence I, 596
Pidgeon, Prudence I, 864
Pidgeon, Prudence I, 898
Pidgeon, Rachel I, 589
Pidgeon, Rachel I, 596
Pidgeon, Rachel I, 686
Pidgeon, Rachel I, 692
Pidgeon, Rachel IV, 54
Pidgeon, Rachel IV, 157
Pidgeon, Rachel IV, 359
Pidgeon, Rachel IV, 410
Pidgeon, Rachel IV, 927
Pidgeon, Rachel VI, 329
Pidgeon, Rachel VI, 335
Pidgeon, Rachel VI, 336
Pidgeon, Rachel VI, 355
Pidgeon, Rachel VI, 378
Pidgeon, Rachel VI, 431
Pidgeon, Rachel VI, 483
Pidgeon, Rachel VI, 490
Pidgeon, Rachel VI, 544
Pidgeon, Rachel, Jr. VI, 544
Pidgeon, Rebecca Jane VI, 431
Pidgeon, Rezin Edward VI, 770
Pidgeon, Robert II, 249
Pidgeon, Ruth I, 864
Pidgeon, Ruth VI, 335
Pidgeon, Ruth VI, 336
Pidgeon, Saml I, 864
Pidgeon, Samuel I, 589
Pidgeon, Samuel I, 834
Pidgeon, Samuel I, 898
Pidgeon, Samuel IV, 157
Pidgeon, Samuel V, 74
Pidgeon, Samuel V, 111
Pidgeon, Samuel VI, 431
Pidgeon, Samuel L. VI, 376
Pidgeon, Samuel L. VI, 431
Pidgeon, Samuel L. VI, 544
Pidgeon, Samuel L. VI, 582
Pidgeon, Samuel L. VI, 770
Pidgeon, Samuel Lukens VI, 431
Pidgeon, Samuel Luther VI, 770
Pidgeon, Samuel T. V, 641
Pidgeon, Sarah I, 834
Pidgeon, Sarah I, 847
Pidgeon, Sarah I, 864
Pidgeon, Sarah I, 898
Pidgeon, Sarah IV, 347
Pidgeon, Sarah IV, 359
Pidgeon, Sarah V, 74
Pidgeon, Sarah V, 111
Pidgeon, Sarah VI, 336
Pidgeon, Sarah VI, 355
Pidgeon, Sarah VI, 367
Pidgeon, Sarah VI, 402
Pidgeon, Sarah VI, 431
Pidgeon, Sarah VI, 770
Pidgeon, Sarah Chandlee VI, 431
Pidgeon, Sarah M. VI, 376
Pidgeon, Sarah M. VI, 431
Pidgeon, Sarah M. VI, 582
Pidgeon, Sarah Mildred VI, 770
Pidgeon, Susan VI, 365
Pidgeon, Susan T. VI, 431
Pidgeon, Susan T. VI, 457
Pidgeon, Susan T. VI, 582
Pidgeon, Susanna I, 589
Pidgeon, Susanna I, 595
Pidgeon, Susanna I, 864
Pidgeon, Susanna I, 898
Pidgeon, Susanna IV, 492
Pidgeon, Willard V, 641
Pidgeon, Willard V, 704
Pidgeon, Willard T. V, 641
Pidgeon, William I, 589
Pidgeon, William I, 864
Pidgeon, William IV, 838
Pidgeon, William IV, 859
Pidgeon, William IV, 881
Pidgeon, William VI, 335
Pidgeon, William VI, 336
Pidgeon, William VI, 340
Pidgeon, William VI, 349
Pidgeon, William VI, 352
Pidgeon, William VI, 355
Pidgeon, William VI, 365
Pidgeon, William VI, 431
Pidgeon, William VI, 483
Pidgeon, William VI, 490
Pidgeon, William VI, 544
Pidgeon, William, Jr. IV, 54
Pidgeon, William, Jr. VI, 355
Pidgeon, Wm. IV, 157
Pidgeon, Wm. IV, 359
Pidgeon, Wm. IV, 840
Pidgeon, Wm. VI, 336
Pidgeon, Wm. VI, 490
Pidgin, Elizabeth VI, 336
Pidgin, Isaac I, 567
Pidgion, Charles, Sr. I, 596
Pidgion, Elizabeth IV, 157
Pidgion, Isaac IV, 157
Pidgion, Oscar Leonard V, 641
Pidgion, Samuel IV, 157
Pidgon, Isaac I, 567
Pidgon, Mary V, 321
Pidgon, Mary V, 355
Piearce, Jane I, 978
Piefer, Pearl IV, 1220
Piepho, Sarah K. V, 111
Piepho, Sarah R. V, 111
Pier, Elizabeth III, 254
Pier, Flora V, 197
Pier, Frances V, 592
Pier, Frankie V, 197
Pier, Frankie V, 592
Pier, Geo. V, 592
Pier, Geo. Frank V, 197
Pier, George F. V, 197
Pier, George F. V, 592
Pier, Hannah III, 254
Pier, John III, 254
Pier, Joseph III, 254
Pier, Julia III, 234
Pier, Mary III, 254
Pier, Matthew III, 254
Pier, Samuel III, 254
Pier, Sarah III, 254
Pierc, Benjamin I, 161
Pierc, Isabel I, 161
Pierc, Isabell I, 162
Pierc, Thomas I, 161
Pierc, Thomas I, 162
Pierce, ??? III, 271
Pierce, Aaron I, 512
Pierce, Aaron I, 1097
Pierce, Aaron I, 1110
Pierce, Abigail I, 567
Pierce, Abigail III, 254
Pierce, Abigail III, 271
Pierce, Abigail A. I, 1087
Pierce, Abigail Amanda I, 1097
Pierce, Abigail R. I, 1087
Pierce, Abraham III, 254
Pierce, Albert L. II, 908
Pierce, Alexander R. I, 1087
Pierce, Alexander R. I, 1097
Pierce, Alfred II, 619
Pierce, Alfred III, 254
Pierce, Alfred III, 255
Pierce, Alice H. III, 254
Pierce, Alice Marion II, 910
Pierce, Amanda III, 128
Pierce, Amanda III, 255
Pierce, Amanda J. V, 821
Pierce, Amy I, 1110
Pierce, Amy B. IV, 376
Pierce, Amy B. IV, 430
Pierce, An I, 199
Pierce, Ann III, 312
Pierce, Ann III, 352
Pierce, Ann IV, 901
Pierce, Ann V, 306
Pierce, Ann V, 309
Pierce, Anna I, 186
Pierce, Anna I, 958
Pierce, Anna I, 1087
Pierce, Anna I, 1097
Pierce, Anna I, 1131
Pierce, Anna V, 794
Pierce, Anna V, 821
Pierce, Anna B. II, 908
Pierce, Anne V, 309
Pierce, Annie III, 95
Pierce, Annie III, 255
Pierce, Asenath L. IV, 986
Pierce, Benj. D. V, 821
Pierce, Benjamin I, 161
Pierce, Benjamin V, 111
Pierce, Benjamin V, 309
Pierce, Benjamin V, 761
Pierce, Caleb I, 1130
Pierce, Caleb II, 618
Pierce, Caleb D. III, 69
Pierce, Calvin H. V, 821
Pierce, Carolin V, 821
Pierce, Carrie III, 169
Pierce, Casper G. I, 1087
Pierce, Casper G. I, 1097
Pierce, Catharine V, 309
Pierce, Charity I, 1110
Pierce, Charity I, 1130
Pierce, Charity V, 355
Pierce, Charles V, 309
Pierce, Charles V, 761
Pierce, Charles E. I, 1097
Pierce, Charles E. I, 1131
Pierce, Charles Eddy I, 1087
Pierce, Charritty I, 1130
Pierce, Christopher I, 274
Pierce, Christopher I, 567
Pierce, Clarkson V, 820
Pierce, Clarkson V, 821
Pierce, Clementine V, 300
Pierce, Clementine V, 309
Pierce, Clemma V, 309
Pierce, Cornelia V, 958
Pierce, Cynthia II, 706
Pierce, Cyrus II, 619
Pierce, Daniel VI, 897
Pierce, Darwin IV, 838
Pierce, David I, 1110
Pierce, David V, 309
Pierce, Deborah III, 118
Pierce, Deborah III, 255
Pierce, Dick V, 704
Pierce, Dorothy III, 255
Pierce, Edward II, 908
Pierce, Edward W. II, 908
Pierce, Edwin IV, 838
Pierce, Edwin V, 958
Pierce, Eli I, 1130
Pierce, Eli III, 254
Pierce, Elias H. III, 254
Pierce, Eliza V, 704
Pierce, Eliza Ann I, 1087
Pierce, Eliza Ann V, 821
Pierce, Elizabeth II, 619
Pierce, Elizabeth III, 116
Pierce, Elizabeth III, 335
Pierce, Elizabeth III, 432
Pierce, Elizabeth V, 309
Pierce, Elizabeth V, 794
Pierce, Elizabeth E. I, 1087
Pierce, Elizabeth J. I, 1097
Pierce, Elizabeth J. I, 1100
Pierce, Elizabeth Jane I, 1097
Pierce, Elizabeth Ridgeway V, 463
Pierce, Ella P. IV, 1290
Pierce, Elmira F. V, 820
Pierce, Elwood C. IV, 1290
Pierce, Emeline III, 255
Pierce, Emma V, 111
Pierce, Emma W. V, 958
Pierce, Erasmus IV, 838
Pierce, Esther V, 111
Pierce, Esther V, 524
Pierce, Esther W. V, 34
Pierce, Esther W. V, 111
Pierce, Esther W. V, 524
Pierce, Ethel V, 761
Pierce, Ezekiel III, 255
Pierce, Ezekiel III, 383
Pierce, Ezra I, 1087
Pierce, Ezra I, 1097
Pierce, Ezra S. I, 1087
Pierce, Ezra Smith I, 1097
Pierce, Ezria I, 1097
Pierce, Flora IV, 1290
Pierce, Florence IV, 1290
Pierce, Frances I, 567
Pierce, Francis H. III, 255
Pierce, Gainer I, 1011
Pierce, Gainer IV, 901
Pierce, Gainer V, 761
Pierce, Gainer V, 780
Pierce, Gainer VI, 432
Pierce, Gainor V, 820
Pierce, Gainor A. V, 820
Pierce, George I, 512
Pierce, George I, 567
Pierce, George I, 1097
Pierce, George I, 1110
Pierce, George I, 1130
Pierce, George I, 1131
Pierce, George II, 618
Pierce, George V, 761
Pierce, George M. I, 1097
Pierce, George M. I, 1100
Pierce, George R. I, 1087
Pierce, George R. I, 1097
Pierce, George R. I, 1131
Pierce, George, Jr. I, 1130
Pierce, Gideon II, 908
Pierce, Hannah I, 512
Pierce, Hannah I, 567
Pierce, Hannah I, 1130
Pierce, Hannah II, 180
Pierce, Hannah II, 249
Pierce, Hannah II, 619
Pierce, Hannah III, 322
Pierce, Hannah IV, 838
Pierce, Hannah V, 111
Pierce, Hannah V, 820
Pierce, Hannah D. IV, 838
Pierce, Hannah D. V, 958
Pierce, Hannah E. I, 1087
Pierce, Hannah M. III, 83
Pierce, Hannah M. IV, 1290
Pierce, Hannah Verona IV, 1290
Pierce, Harry IV, 986
Pierce, Henry I, 1110
Pierce, Henry I, 1131
Pierce, Hephsabah I, 1130
Pierce, Hephzibah I, 567
Pierce, Hepzebah I, 1097
Pierce, Hepzebah I, 1130
Pierce, Hepzibeth I, 512
Pierce, Hepzibeth I, 567
Pierce, Hiram W. IV, 1290
Pierce, Howall V, 111
Pierce, Howard V, 761
Pierce, Isaac I, 512
Pierce, Isaac I, 1097
Pierce, Isaac II, 619
Pierce, Isaac III, 255
Pierce, Isaac IV, 750
Pierce, Isaac M. I, 1087
Pierce, Isaac M. I, 1097
Pierce, Isaac M. I, 1131
Pierce, Isaac Macy I, 1097
Pierce, Isaac Newton IV, 750
Pierce, Isaam M. I, 1110
Pierce, Isabel I, 161
Pierce, Jacob IV, 838
Pierce, Jacob V, 37
Pierce, Jacob V, 111
Pierce, Jacob V, 309
Pierce, James I, 274
Pierce, James I, 567
Pierce, James III, 255
Pierce, James III, 432
Pierce, James IV, 651
Pierce, James IV, 986
Pierce, James V, 111
Pierce, James V, 524
Pierce, James V, 592
Pierce, James V, 761
Pierce, James V, 838
Pierce, James E. II, 908
Pierce, James Pennington I, 274
Pierce, Jane I, 1130
Pierce, Jane III, 255
Pierce, Jane IV, 651
Pierce, Jane IV, 838
Pierce, Jane IV, 901
Pierce, Jane V, 780
Pierce, Jemima V, 821
Pierce, Jesse I, 567
Pierce, Joanna I, 1131
Pierce, John I, 54
Pierce, John I, 68
Pierce, John I, 70
Pierce, John I, 186
Pierce, John I, 199
Pierce, John III, 118
Pierce, John III, 255
Pierce, John V, 309
Pierce, John V, 524
Pierce, John V, 592
Pierce, John V, 761
Pierce, John V, 794
Pierce, John V, 820
Pierce, John V, 821
Pierce, John VI, 847
Pierce, John F. V, 111
Pierce, John F. V, 524
Pierce, John F. V, 704
Pierce, John L. V, 111
Pierce, Jonathan I, 1110
Pierce, Jonathan IV, 838
Pierce, Jonathan V, 111
Pierce, Jonathan V, 958
Pierce, Joseph I, 68
Pierce, Joseph I, 70
Pierce, Joseph I, 161
Pierce, Joseph I, 186
Pierce, Joseph II, 180
Pierce, Joseph II, 249
Pierce, Joseph II, 618
Pierce, Joseph II, 706
Pierce, Joseph G. I, 1097
Pierce, Joseph I. I, 1131
Pierce, Joseph J. I, 1087
Pierce, Joshua II, 619
Pierce, Josiah I, 186
Pierce, Josiah I, 199
Pierce, Lavina E. V, 821
Pierce, Leonard W. IV, 986
Pierce, Lilla J. III, 128
Pierce, Lilla J. III, 255
Pierce, Lillian I, 639
Pierce, Lois T. V, 821
Pierce, Lowrethe I, 1130
Pierce, Lucien B. III, 95
Pierce, Lucien B. III, 255
Pierce, Lucy Ann V, 821
Pierce, Luretta A. IV, 1290
Pierce, Lydia I, 1130
Pierce, Lydia V, 309
Pierce, Lydia V, 881
Pierce, Lydia V, 885
Pierce, Lydia B. II, 743
Pierce, Lydia J. II, 715
Pierce, Lydia J. II, 759
Pierce, Lyman IV, 1240
Pierce, M. F. V, 761
Pierce, Malinda V, 820
Pierce, Manuel V, 309
Pierce, Margaret II, 878
Pierce, Margaret V, 792
Pierce, Margaret V, 820
Pierce, Maria IV, 750
Pierce, Maria G. IV, 751
Pierce, Maria G. IV, 1029
Pierce, Mariam V, 592
Pierce, Marie IV, 751
Pierce, Marie IV, 1333
Pierce, Marion S. IV, 1290
Pierce, Martha III, 254
Pierce, Martha V, 111
Pierce, Martha V, 524
Pierce, Martha V, 838
Pierce, Martha A. I, 1087
Pierce, Martha A. I, 1097
Pierce, Martha E. III, 322
Pierce, Mary I, 65
Pierce, Mary I, 70
Pierce, Mary I, 512
Pierce, Mary I, 1084
Pierce, Mary I, 1097
Pierce, Mary I, 1130
Pierce, Mary II, 180

Pierce, Mary II, 249
Pierce, Mary II, 968
Pierce, Mary III, 255
Pierce, Mary III, 383
Pierce, Mary IV, 105
Pierce, Mary V, 111
Pierce, Mary V, 524
Pierce, Mary V, 592
Pierce, Mary V, 761
Pierce, Mary V, 820
Pierce, Mary VI, 847
Pierce, Mary VI, 984
Pierce, Mary A. IV, 1290
Pierce, Mary E. I, 1087
Pierce, Mary Maria I, 958
Pierce, Masie IV, 751
Pierce, Matilda I, 1130
Pierce, Matilda V, 355
Pierce, Matilda V, 821
Pierce, Mattie A. V, 111
Pierce, Melinda V, 779
Pierce, Melinda V, 792
Pierce, Mercy IV, 750
Pierce, Mercy L. III, 255
Pierce, Mercy L. IV, 751
Pierce, Meriba V, 309
Pierce, Meribah V, 309
Pierce, Merriam V, 838
Pierce, Merritt III, 128
Pierce, Merritt III, 255
Pierce, Milly V, 820
Pierce, Milly V, 821
Pierce, Minnie V, 761
Pierce, Minnie Lea I, 639
Pierce, Miriam I, 68
Pierce, Miriam I, 186
Pierce, Miriam I, 199
Pierce, Miriam V, 37
Pierce, Miriam V, 111
Pierce, Miriam V, 524
Pierce, Miriam V, 543
Pierce, Moses I, 512
Pierce, Moses I, 1097
Pierce, Moses I, 1130
Pierce, Moses V, 355
Pierce, Moses M. V, 355
Pierce, Myra III, 255
Pierce, Nancy II, 706
Pierce, Nathan V, 309
Pierce, Nathan R. I, 1087
Pierce, Nathan R. I, 1097
Pierce, Nathan R. I, 1131
Pierce, Orabell I, 639
Pierce, Oral J. I, 639
Pierce, Patrick I, 1130
Pierce, Patrick I, 1131
Pierce, Perry B. VI, 544
Pierce, Perry B. VI, 576
Pierce, Perry B. VI, 577
Pierce, Perry B. VI, 717
Pierce, Phariby I, 186
Pierce, Phebe II, 967
Pierce, Phebe III, 69
Pierce, Phebe III, 255
Pierce, Phebe IV, 1260
Pierce, Phebe Jane IV, 1132
Pierce, Phebe Jane IV, 1137
Pierce, Pheriba I, 199
Pierce, Polly I, 199
Pierce, Polly VI, 307
Pierce, Rachael I, 199
Pierce, Rachel I, 1087
Pierce, Rachel I, 1110
Pierce, Rachel I, 1131
Pierce, Rachel II, 180
Pierce, Rachel II, 249
Pierce, Rachel V, 761
Pierce, Rachel V, 821
Pierce, Rachel VI, 984
Pierce, Ray IV, 987
Pierce, Rebecca III, 254
Pierce, Rebecca IV, 750
Pierce, Rebecca VI, 706
Pierce, Retta III, 95
Pierce, Retta III, 255
Pierce, Reuben III, 255
Pierce, Richard II, 249
Pierce, Richard V, 111
Pierce, Richard V, 524
Pierce, Richard V, 592
Pierce, Richard V, 704
Pierce, Robert I, 413
Pierce, Robert I, 1110
Pierce, Robert I, 1130
Pierce, Robert, Jr. I, 1130
Pierce, Robert, Junr. I, 1130
Pierce, Robert, Sr. I, 1130
Pierce, Rosella T. V, 821
Pierce, Ruth I, 1001
Pierce, Ruth I, 1011
Pierce, Ruth II, 249
Pierce, Ruth V, 309
Pierce, Ruth V, 761
Pierce, Ruth V, 820
Pierce, Ruth V, 821
Pierce, Ruth L. IV, 1179
Pierce, Ruth L. IV, 1196
Pierce, Ruth T. V, 958
Pierce, Samuel V, 820
Pierce, Samuel V, 821
Pierce, Sarah I, 36
Pierce, Sarah I, 1131
Pierce, Sarah I Sup 1, 3
Pierce, Sarah II, 1021
Pierce, Sarah II, 1038
Pierce, Sarah III, 180
Pierce, Sarah D. II, 908
Pierce, Sarah E. I, 1087
Pierce, Sarah E. I, 1097
Pierce, Sarah E. I, 1131
Pierce, Sarah E. III, 255
Pierce, Sarah E. IV, 750
Pierce, Sarah E. IV, 751
Pierce, Sarah J. II, 619
Pierce, Sarah W. II, 249
Pierce, Sarah W. III, 255
Pierce, Sarah W. III, 314
Pierce, Sarah W. III, 326
Pierce, Sarah W. III, 329
Pierce, Sidney Maria IV, 1029
Pierce, Smith I, 1131
Pierce, Susan IV, 838
Pierce, Susan VI, 544
Pierce, Susan VI, 576
Pierce, Susan VI, 577
Pierce, Susan VI, 717
Pierce, Susan VI, 771
Pierce, Susan D. IV, 838
Pierce, Susan W. VI, 544
Pierce, Susan W. VI, 688
Pierce, Susanna I, 1084
Pierce, Susanna II, 249
Pierce, Susanna VI, 432
Pierce, Susannah II, 249
Pierce, Susannah VI, 432
Pierce, Thomas I, 54
Pierce, Thomas I, 65
Pierce, Thomas I, 68
Pierce, Thomas I, 70
Pierce, Thomas I, 161
Pierce, Thomas I, 186
Pierce, Thomas I, 199
Pierce, Thomas I, 512
Pierce, Thomas I, 565
Pierce, Thomas I, 567
Pierce, Thomas I, 1084
Pierce, Thomas I, 1087
Pierce, Thomas I, 1097
Pierce, Thomas I, 1130
Pierce, Thomas III, 255
Pierce, Thomas V, 111
Pierce, Thomas Elwood I, 186
Pierce, Thomas H. IV, 986
Pierce, Thomas L. III, 255
Pierce, Thomas L. III, 322
Pierce, Thos. I Sup 1, 4
Pierce, Wd. Mary II, 180
Pierce, William I, 199
Pierce, William III, 255
Pierce, William V, 355
Pierce, William E. I, 1097
Pierce, William E. I, 1131
Pierce, William Ezra I, 1087
Pierce, William R. V, 761
Pierce, William R. V, 820
Pierce, Willie V, 704
Pierce, Willis IV, 986
Pierce, Wm. I, 958
Pierce, Wm. III, 255
Pierce, Wm. V, 309
Pierce, Wm. V, 821
Pierce, Wm. A. V, 958
Pierce, Wm. C. II, 908
Pierce, Wm. D. IV, 838
Pierce, Wm. D. V, 958
Pierce, Zenas V, 820
Pierce, Zenas V, 821
Pierman, James III, 255
Pierpoint, Ann IV, 430
Pierpoint, Benjamin IV, 430
Pierpoint, Eli IV, 430
Pierpoint, Eli VI, 547
Pierpoint, Elizabeth IV, 430
Pierpoint, Elizabeth VI, 547
Pierpoint, Elizabeth VI, 548
Pierpoint, Emaline E. IV, 1095
Pierpoint, Emily II, 967
Pierpoint, Emily C. II, 1058
Pierpoint, Esther VI, 547
Pierpoint, Esther VI, 771
Pierpoint, Hannah VI, 547
Pierpoint, John IV, 430
Pierpoint, John Edwin VI, 771
Pierpoint, John R. VI, 771
Pierpoint, Jonathan IV, 430
Pierpoint, Jonathan VI, 565
Pierpoint, Jonathan W. VI, 771
Pierpoint, Lydia IV, 428
Pierpoint, Mary IV, 430
Pierpoint, Mary H. VI, 771
Pierpoint, Matilda IV, 365
Pierpoint, Matilda IV, 430
Pierpoint, Matilda IV, 1080
Pierpoint, Obed IV, 430
Pierpoint, Obed VI, 547
Pierpoint, Obed VI, 771
Pierpoint, Obed J. VI, 548
Pierpoint, Phebe IV, 1080
Pierpoint, Rebecca J. VI, 548
Pierpoint, Sarah Ann VI, 547
Pierpoint, Sarah R. VI, 513
Pierpoint, William IV, 430
Pierpoint, William W. VI, 771
Pierpoint, Wm. IV, 365
Pierpoint, Wm. IV, 1080
Pierpoint, Wm. Henry VI, 771
Pierponnt, Rebecca L. IV, 1115
Pierpont, ??? IV, 1047
Pierpont, ??? VI, 646
Pierpont, Albert B. VI, 547
Pierpont, Amos VI, 547
Pierpont, Ann IV, 838
Pierpont, Ann IV, 1060
Pierpont, Ann IV, 1074
Pierpont, Ann VI, 547
Pierpont, Ann VI, 548
Pierpont, Ann, Jr. VI, 547
Pierpont, Ann, Jr. VI, 548
Pierpont, Ann, Jr. VI, 565
Pierpont, Benjamin IV, 838
Pierpont, Benjamin IV, 1074
Pierpont, Betsy VI, 475
Pierpont, Calbe VI, 537
Pierpont, Caleb VI, 480
Pierpont, Caleb VI, 547
Pierpont, Caleb VI, 572
Pierpont, Caleb VI, 587
Pierpont, Charles VI, 547
Pierpont, Charles VI, 552
Pierpont, Charles VI, 572
Pierpont, Charles VI, 688
Pierpont, David VI, 548
Pierpont, Delitha IV, 1074
Pierpont, Edmund IV, 1074
Pierpont, Eli IV, 838
Pierpont, Eli IV, 1074
Pierpont, Eli VI, 500
Pierpont, Eli VI, 528
Pierpont, Eli VI, 547
Pierpont, Eli VI, 548
Pierpont, Eli VI, 672
Pierpont, Eli VI, 688
Pierpont, Elizabeth IV, 838
Pierpont, Elizabeth IV, 1060
Pierpont, Elizabeth IV, 1074
Pierpont, Elizabeth VI, 432
Pierpont, Elizabeth VI, 475
Pierpont, Elizabeth VI, 527
Pierpont, Elizabeth VI, 548
Pierpont, Elizabeth VI, 584
Pierpont, Elizabeth VI, 622
Pierpont, Elizabeth VI, 688
Pierpont, Elizabeth A. VI, 500
Pierpont, Elizabeth A. VI, 548
Pierpont, Elizabeth A. VI, 688
Pierpont, Emaline E. IV, 1112
Pierpont, Esther VI, 475
Pierpont, Esther VI, 500
Pierpont, Esther VI, 505
Pierpont, Esther VI, 527
Pierpont, Esther VI, 537
Pierpont, Esther VI, 547
Pierpont, Esther VI, 645
Pierpont, Esther VI, 651
Pierpont, Esther VI, 688
Pierpont, Esther Myers VI, 528
Pierpont, Frances, Jr. VI, 547
Pierpont, Francis VI, 547
Pierpont, Francis VI, 548
Pierpont, Francis VI, 552
Pierpont, Francis, Jr. VI, 547
Pierpont, Francis, Sr. VI, 547
Pierpont, Hannah IV, 1074
Pierpont, Hannah VI, 528
Pierpont, Hannah VI, 547
Pierpont, Hannah VI, 548
Pierpont, Hannah VI, 672
Pierpont, Hannah VI, 688
Pierpont, Henry VI, 547
Pierpont, Jabis VI, 547
Pierpont, James VI, 547
Pierpont, John IV, 838
Pierpont, John IV, 1074
Pierpont, John VI, 432
Pierpont, John VI, 547
Pierpont, John R. VI, 432
Pierpont, John R. VI, 548
Pierpont, John William VI, 547
Pierpont, Jonah IV, 1179
Pierpont, Jonathan IV, 838
Pierpont, Jonathan IV, 1060
Pierpont, Jonathan IV, 1074
Pierpont, Jonathan VI, 547
Pierpont, Jonathan VI, 688
Pierpont, Jonathan W. VI, 548
Pierpont, Joseph VI, 432
Pierpont, Joseph VI, 500
Pierpont, Joseph VI, 547
Pierpont, Joseph VI, 548
Pierpont, Joseph VI, 622
Pierpont, Joseph VI, 623
Pierpont, Joseph VI, 645
Pierpont, Joseph VI, 688
Pierpont, Leah IV, 1074
Pierpont, Lerura Ann VI, 645
Pierpont, Lerura Ann VI, 688
Pierpont, Lydia IV, 1071
Pierpont, Lydia IV, 1074
Pierpont, Margaret VI, 688
Pierpont, Martha E. VI, 548
Pierpont, Martha E. VI, 688
Pierpont, Mary IV, 838
Pierpont, Mary IV, 1074
Pierpont, Mary IV, 1082
Pierpont, Mary VI, 476
Pierpont, Mary VI, 505
Pierpont, Mary VI, 547
Pierpont, Mary VI, 548
Pierpont, Mary VI, 552
Pierpont, Mary VI, 650
Pierpont, Mary VI, 651
Pierpont, Mary VI, 665
Pierpont, Mary VI, 688
Pierpont, Mary VI, 704
Pierpont, Mary VI, 710
Pierpont, Mary Ann IV, 1051
Pierpont, Mary Ann IV, 1074
Pierpont, Mary E. VI, 658
Pierpont, Mary E. VI, 688
Pierpont, Mary Esther VI, 475
Pierpont, Mary Esther VI, 500
Pierpont, Mary Esther VI, 548
Pierpont, Mary Esther VI, 623
Pierpont, Mary Esther VI, 625
Pierpont, Mary Esther VI, 688
Pierpont, Mary H. VI, 548
Pierpont, Mary Jane VI, 688
Pierpont, Maryann Sarah Esther IV, 1074
Pierpont, Matilda IV, 1071
Pierpont, Matilda IV, 1074
Pierpont, Moses VI, 547
Pierpont, Obed IV, 838
Pierpont, Obed IV, 1074
Pierpont, Obed VI, 475
Pierpont, Obed VI, 500
Pierpont, Obed VI, 505
Pierpont, Obed VI, 527
Pierpont, Obed VI, 528
Pierpont, Obed VI, 537
Pierpont, Obed VI, 645
Pierpont, Obed VI, 651
Pierpont, Obed VI, 688
Pierpont, Obed J. VI, 547
Pierpont, Obed J. VI, 622
Pierpont, Obed J. VI, 688
Pierpont, Phebe IV, 1074
Pierpont, Pleasant VI, 645
Pierpont, Rachel IV, 1074
Pierpont, Rebecca IV, 1112
Pierpont, Rebecca VI, 548
Pierpont, Rebecca J. VI, 688
Pierpont, Rebecca L. IV, 1112
Pierpont, Rue Ann VI, 500
Pierpont, Rue Ann VI, 548
Pierpont, Rue Ann VI, 622
Pierpont, Rue Ann VI, 623
Pierpont, Rue Ann VI, 645
Pierpont, Rue Ann VI, 688
Pierpont, Samuel VI, 432
Pierpont, Samuel VI, 475
Pierpont, Samuel VI, 548
Pierpont, Samuel VI, 584
Pierpont, Sarah VI, 513
Pierpont, Sarah VI, 528
Pierpont, Sarah VI, 537
Pierpont, Sarah VI, 547
Pierpont, Sarah VI, 548
Pierpont, Sarah VI, 552
Pierpont, Sarah VI, 658
Pierpont, Sarah Ann VI, 688
Pierpont, Sarah C. IV, 1179
Pierpont, Sarah Catherine VI, 646
Pierpont, Sarah Catherine VI, 688
Pierpont, Sarah E. VI, 584
Pierpont, Sarah Esther VI, 548
Pierpont, Sarah R. VI, 548
Pierpont, Sarah R. VI, 688
Pierpont, Sidney VI, 547
Pierpont, Sidney VI, 552
Pierpont, Sidney VI, 572
Pierpont, Sydney VI, 547
Pierpont, William IV, 838
Pierpont, William IV, 1074
Pierpont, Wm. IV, 1071
Pierpont, Wm. IV, 1074
Pierport, John R. VI, 789
Piersol, Edith IV, 131
Piersol, Edith IV, 132
Piersol, Sarah IV, 131
Piersol, Sarah IV, 133
Pierson, Abraham IV, 105
Pierson, Alice IV, 838
Pierson, Amy III, 58
Pierson, Amy III, 334
Pierson, Ann II, 1021
Pierson, Ann IV, 838
Pierson, Ann, Jr. IV, 345
Pierson, Annie IV, 1289
Pierson, Arthur N. III, 255
Pierson, Arthur N. III, 323
Pierson, Betty I, 686
Pierson, Betty I, 689
Pierson, Catherine C. III, 255
Pierson, Catherine C. III, 323
Pierson, Cert I, 834
Pierson, Chas. W. IV, 1333
Pierson, Christopher I, 67
Pierson, David I, 897
Pierson, Elisabeth I, 67
Pierson, Elisabeth I, 68
Pierson, Elizabeth I, 664
Pierson, Elizabeth I, 675
Pierson, Elizabeth I, 682
Pierson, Elizabeth I, 686
Pierson, Elizabeth I, 834
Pierson, Elizabeth I, 863
Pierson, Elizabeth I, 864
Pierson, Elizabeth I, 897
Pierson, Elizabeth I, 1008
Pierson, Elizabeth I, 1011
Pierson, Elizabeth I, 1130
Pierson, Emma V, 606
Pierson, Fannie C. VI, 710
Pierson, Fannie C. VI, 711
Pierson, George I, 1130
Pierson, George I, 1131
Pierson, George IV, 1333
Pierson, Hannah I, 664
Pierson, Hannah I, 674
Pierson, Hannah I, 686
Pierson, Hannah I, 834
Pierson, Hannah I, 897
Pierson, Hannah I, 1011
Pierson, Henry V, 109
Pierson, Hulda I, 730
Pierson, Huldah I, 683
Pierson, Huldah I, 686
Pierson, Isaac I, 834
Pierson, Isaac I, 897
Pierson, Isaac I, 967
Pierson, Isaac IV, 345
Pierson, Isabel I, 664
Pierson, Isabel I, 674
Pierson, Isabel I, 686
Pierson, Isabel I, 897
Pierson, Isabela I, 834
Pierson, Jane IV, 345
Pierson, John I, 815
Pierson, John I, 834
Pierson, John I, 864
Pierson, John I, 897
Pierson, John I, 1011
Pierson, John II, 618
Pierson, John II, 644
Pierson, John IV, 1289
Pierson, Jonathan I, 686
Pierson, Jonathan V, 354
Pierson, Joseph I, 864
Pierson, Mark I, 967
Pierson, Mark I, 1011
Pierson, Mark V, 308
Pierson, Martha I, 815
Pierson, Martha I, 834
Pierson, Martha I, 897
Pierson, Martha L. IV, 749
Pierson, Martha L. IV, 774
Pierson, Mary I, 678
Pierson, Mary I, 686
Pierson, Mary I, 897
Pierson, Mary T. II, 37
Pierson, Nathan I, 683
Pierson, Nathan I, 686

erson, Orilla L. IV, 1333
erson, Orilla Lorain IV, 1333
erson, Phebe I, 686
erson, Phebe I, 897
erson, Phebe I, 1130
erson, Rachel I, 864
erson, Rachel I, 871
erson, Rachel I, 897
erson, Rebecca V, 631
erson, Rebecca V, 639
erson, Robert V, 606
erson, Roscoe IV, 1333
erson, Ruanna IV, 1289
erson, Ruth Irene IV, 1333
erson, Sadie F. III, 255
erson, Sadie F. III, 323
erson, Samuel I, 686
erson, Samuel I, 897
erson, Samuel V, 109
erson, Sarah I, 686
erson, Sarah I, 864
erson, Sarah I, 872
erson, Sarah II, 907
erson, Sarah IV, 838
erson, Smith I, 1131
erson, Susanna IV, 838
erson, Susannah IV, 422
erson, Susannah IV, 428
erson, Susie V, 703
erson, Thomas I, 664
erson, Thomas I, 686
erson, Thomas I, 834
erson, Thomas I, 864
erson, Thomas I, 897
erson, Thomas IV, 1289
erson, West A. VI, 710
erson, West A. VI, 711
erson, William I, 675
erson, William I, 686
erson, William I, 834
erson, William I, 864
erson, William I, 897
erson, William V, 109
erson, William V, 354
esley, Mary II, 618
et, Elizabeth IV, 429
et, Elizabeth IV, 439
etmier, Edward V, 355
etsmire, Edward V, 355
geon, ??? II, 446
geon, Addison V, 355
geon, Alice IV, 699
geon, Alice IV, 723
geon, Alice IV, 751
geon, Alice IV, 765
geon, Anne IV, 157
geon, Benj. IV, 751
geon, Benjamin IV, 751
geon, Catharine V, 354
geon, Charles I, 834
geon, Charles IV, 157
geon, Charles IV, 347
geon, Charles V, 354
geon, Charles V, 641
geon, Chas. A. V, 354
geon, Cornelia C. V, 354
geon, Elizabeth I, 898
geon, Elizabeth IV, 699
geon, Elizabeth IV, 751
geon, Harriet IV, 475
geon, Henry H. V, 354
geon, Isaac V, 111
geon, Isaac VI, 431
geon, Isabel II, 446
geon, Joseph II, 446
geon, Julia A. V, 354
geon, Katharine I, 834
geon, Louise M. V, 354
geon, Martha IV, 751
geon, Mary I, 809
geon, Mary IV, 751
geon, Mary IV, 765
geon, Mary V, 355
geon, Phebe I, 898
geon, Rachel I, 686
geon, Rachel IV, 723
geon, Rachel IV, 751
geon, Richard II, 446
geon, Samuel I, 809
geon, Samuel I, 834
geon, Sarah I, 883
geon, Sarah I, 898
geon, Susan T. VI, 580
geon, William, Jr. IV, 751
geon, Wm. IV, 699
geon, Wm. IV, 723
geon, Wm. IV, 751
geon, Wm. IV, 765
ggatt, Mary I, 691
ggot, ??? IV, 137
ggot, Albert V, 463
Piggot, Alice II, 622
Piggot, Alice II, 632
Piggot, Benjamin I, 452
Piggot, Burr VI, 688
Piggot, Elinor IV, 352
Piggot, Elizabeth D. VI, 688
Piggot, Hannah VI, 423
Piggot, Hannah VI, 432
Piggot, Hannah VI, 688
Piggot, Hannah, Sr. VI, 432
Piggot, John I, 452
Piggot, John I, 455
Piggot, John II, 622
Piggot, John II, 632
Piggot, John IV, 352
Piggot, John VI, 432
Piggot, John Newlin I, 414
Piggot, John, Jr. VI, 432
Piggot, Joseph I, 833
Piggot, Joshua I, 414
Piggot, Lyddia VI, 432
Piggot, Mary IV, 544
Piggot, Mary IV, 556
Piggot, Mary VI, 432
Piggot, Mary VI, 688
Piggot, Moses VI, 432
Piggot, Phebe E. IV, 347
Piggot, Phebe E. IV, 352
Piggot, Rachel VI, 432
Piggot, Rebecca I, 452
Piggot, Rebecca I, 455
Piggot, Samuel I, 567
Piggot, Sarah I, 414
Piggot, Thomas VI, 432
Piggot, William VI, 688
Piggoth, Abigail I, 712
Piggoth, Abigail I, 731
Piggott, ??? III, 82
Piggott, ??? VI, 688
Piggott, Aaron I, 363
Piggott, Abigail I, 359
Piggott, Abigail I, 362
Piggott, Abigail I, 363
Piggott, Abigail I, 406
Piggott, Abigail I, 413
Piggott, Abigail I, 414
Piggott, Abigal I, 731
Piggott, Adeline IV, 523
Piggott, Adeline IV, 545
Piggott, Albert B. VI, 689
Piggott, Alberta J. VI, 621
Piggott, Alberta J. VI, 688
Piggott, Amos IV, 347
Piggott, Ann IV, 347
Piggott, Anna I, 362
Piggott, Anna I, 790
Piggott, Anna IV, 157
Piggott, Anna V, 111
Piggott, Benj. I, 349
Piggott, Benj. I, 362
Piggott, Benj. I, 363
Piggott, Benj. I, 367
Piggott, Benj. I, 414
Piggott, Benjamin I, 354
Piggott, Benjamin I, 362
Piggott, Benjamin I, 363
Piggott, Benjamin I, 407
Piggott, Benjamin I, 413
Piggott, Benjamin I, 414
Piggott, Benjamin I, 446
Piggott, Benjamin I, 453
Piggott, Benjamin I, 984
Piggott, Benjamin I, 995
Piggott, Benjamin V, 110
Piggott, Benjamin, Jr. I, 414
Piggott, Betty VI, 688
Piggott, Burr VI, 621
Piggott, Burr VI, 656
Piggott, Burr VI, 679
Piggott, Burr VI, 689
Piggott, Burr VI, 690
Piggott, Burr VI, 713
Piggott, Burr VI, 714
Piggott, Bushrod VI, 621
Piggott, Bushrod VI, 688
Piggott, Bushrod VI, 689
Piggott, Caleb I, 362
Piggott, Catharine I, 414
Piggott, Catharine I, 450
Piggott, Catharine I, 452
Piggott, Charity I, 409
Piggott, Charity I, 414
Piggott, Charity I, 567
Piggott, Charles III, 255
Piggott, Clara VI, 432
Piggott, Clara VI, 438
Piggott, Clara VI, 439
Piggott, Clara Elma VI, 439
Piggott, Clara Elma VI, 689
Piggott, Clara Emma VI, 695
Piggott, David I, 362
Piggott, David IV, 544
Piggott, Dinah I, 362
Piggott, Ebenezer VI, 689
Piggott, Edith I, 414
Piggott, Eleanor IV, 430
Piggott, Eleazar I, 567
Piggott, Elenor I, 363
Piggott, Elenor IV, 347
Piggott, Elenor IV, 348
Piggott, Eli IV, 347
Piggott, Eli L. IV, 347
Piggott, Eliazar I, 363
Piggott, Elizabeth I, 346
Piggott, Elizabeth I, 362
Piggott, Elizabeth I, 363
Piggott, Elizabeth I, 367
Piggott, Elizabeth I, 375
Piggott, Elizabeth I, 414
Piggott, Elizabeth I, 428
Piggott, Elizabeth I, 550
Piggott, Elizabeth I, 567
Piggott, Elizabeth I, 864
Piggott, Elizabeth I, 885
Piggott, Elizabeth I, 898
Piggott, Elizabeth I, 1011
Piggott, Elizabeth IV, 347
Piggott, Elizabeth VI, 475
Piggott, Elizabeth VI, 477
Piggott, Elizabeth VI, 484
Piggott, Elizabeth VI, 544
Piggott, Elizabeth VI, 548
Piggott, Elizabeth VI, 623
Piggott, Elizabeth VI, 624
Piggott, Elizabeth VI, 625
Piggott, Elizabeth VI, 626
Piggott, Elizabeth VI, 628
Piggott, Elizabeth VI, 682
Piggott, Elizabeth VI, 683
Piggott, Elizabeth VI, 689
Piggott, Elizabeth VI, 690
Piggott, Elizabeth VI, 699
Piggott, Elizabeth A. III, 255
Piggott, Elizabeth D. I, 378
Piggott, Elizabeth D. I, 415
Piggott, Elizabeth Dinah VI, 656
Piggott, Elizabeth Dinah VI, 690
Piggott, Elizabeth Rogers VI, 690
Piggott, Emma VI, 690
Piggott, Eunice I, 363
Piggott, George I, 363
Piggott, George III, 255
Piggott, Grace I, 853
Piggott, Grace I, 898
Piggott, Gracett I, 864
Piggott, Gracset I, 878
Piggott, Gracset I, 898
Piggott, Hannah I, 346
Piggott, Hannah I, 349
Piggott, Hannah I, 354
Piggott, Hannah I, 362
Piggott, Hannah I, 363
Piggott, Hannah I, 384
Piggott, Hannah I, 391
Piggott, Hannah I, 396
Piggott, Hannah I, 413
Piggott, Hannah I, 414
Piggott, Hannah I, 415
Piggott, Hannah I, 422
Piggott, Hannah I, 425
Piggott, Hannah I, 452
Piggott, Hannah I, 470
Piggott, Hannah I, 864
Piggott, Hannah I, 882
Piggott, Hannah I, 898
Piggott, Hannah IV, 157
Piggott, Hannah IV, 347
Piggott, Hannah IV, 430
Piggott, Hannah VI, 432
Piggott, Hannah VI, 447
Piggott, Hannah VI, 462
Piggott, Hannah VI, 603
Piggott, Hannah VI, 621
Piggott, Hannah VI, 626
Piggott, Hannah VI, 656
Piggott, Hannah VI, 679
Piggott, Hannah VI, 689
Piggott, Hannah VI, 690
Piggott, Hannah VI, 713
Piggott, Hannah VI, 714
Piggott, Hannah N. I, 864
Piggott, Hannah, Jr. IV, 157
Piggott, Hannah, Jr. IV, 430
Piggott, Hannah, Sr. VI, 432
Piggott, Hannah, Sr. VI, 603
Piggott, Harriet IV, 347
Piggott, Henry IV, 347
Piggott, Henry VI, 422
Piggott, Henry VI, 462
Piggott, Henry VI, 676
Piggott, Henry Eugene VI, 689
Piggott, Henry Eugene VI, 701
Piggott, Hugh VI, 690
Piggott, Isaac IV, 544
Piggott, Isaac VI, 432
Piggott, Isaac VI, 648
Piggott, Isaac VI, 681
Piggott, Isaac VI, 686
Piggott, Isaac VI, 688
Piggott, Isaac VI, 689
Piggott, Isaac VI, 690
Piggott, Isaac VI, 705
Piggott, Isaac VI, 714
Piggott, Isabel I, 864
Piggott, Isaiah I, 363
Piggott, Isaiah I, 414
Piggott, Israel IV, 544
Piggott, Israel IV, 545
Piggott, James I, 363
Piggott, James IV, 157
Piggott, James VI, 432
Piggott, James VI, 603
Piggott, Jemima I, 833
Piggott, Jenney VI, 545
Piggott, Jeremiah I, 343
Piggott, Jeremiah I, 362
Piggott, Jeremiah I, 363
Piggott, Jeremiah I, 408
Piggott, Jeremiah I, 413
Piggott, Jeremiah I, 414
Piggott, Jeremiah I, 415
Piggott, Jeremiah I, 422
Piggott, Jeremiah I, 451
Piggott, Jeremiah I, 452
Piggott, Jeremiah I, 470
Piggott, Jeremiah I, 484
Piggott, Jeremiah I, 567
Piggott, Jeremiah I, 864
Piggott, Jeremiah I, 898
Piggott, Jeremiah, Jr. I, 409
Piggott, Jeremiah, Jr. I, 413
Piggott, Jesse VI, 689
Piggott, Jesse VI, 690
Piggott, John I, 346
Piggott, John I, 362
Piggott, John I, 363
Piggott, John I, 391
Piggott, John I, 413
Piggott, John I, 414
Piggott, John I, 415
Piggott, John I, 425
Piggott, John I, 452
Piggott, John II, 622
Piggott, John II, 686
Piggott, John IV, 157
Piggott, John IV, 324
Piggott, John IV, 326
Piggott, John IV, 347
Piggott, John IV, 348
Piggott, John IV, 430
Piggott, John IV, 544
Piggott, John VI, 432
Piggott, John VI, 484
Piggott, John VI, 544
Piggott, John VI, 545
Piggott, John VI, 595
Piggott, John VI, 603
Piggott, John VI, 682
Piggott, John VI, 688
Piggott, John VI, 689
Piggott, John VI, 690
Piggott, John Crosley IV, 544
Piggott, John W. VI, 681
Piggott, John W. VI, 689
Piggott, John, Jr. IV, 157
Piggott, John, Jr. VI, 432
Piggott, John, Jr. VI, 689
Piggott, Jonathan I, 362
Piggott, Jonathan I, 415
Piggott, Jordan IV, 544
Piggott, Jos. John Gurney I, 864
Piggott, Joseph I, 362
Piggott, Joseph I, 414
Piggott, Joseph I, 567
Piggott, Joseph I, 790
Piggott, Joseph I, 864
Piggott, Joseph I, 898
Piggott, Joseph V, 111
Piggott, Joshua I, 362
Piggott, Joshua I, 363
Piggott, Joshua I, 384
Piggott, Joshua I, 414
Piggott, Joshua IV, 544
Piggott, Joshua IV, 545
Piggott, Joshua V, 110
Piggott, Katharine I, 363
Piggott, Louisa M. III, 82
Piggott, Lucinda IV, 347
Piggott, Lyddia VI, 432
Piggott, Lydia I, 790
Piggott, Lydia IV, 142
Piggott, Lydia V, 111
Piggott, Lydia VI, 432
Piggott, Lydia VI, 681
Piggott, Lydia VI, 689
Piggott, Mahlon I, 362
Piggott, Margaret I, 362
Piggott, Margery I, 349
Piggott, Margery I, 362
Piggott, Margery I, 363
Piggott, Margery I, 376
Piggott, Margery I, 382
Piggott, Margery I, 413
Piggott, Margery I, 414
Piggott, Margery I, 567
Piggott, Margery I, 892
Piggott, Margery I, 898
Piggott, Margery VI, 484
Piggott, Maria III, 255
Piggott, Marjary I, 898
Piggott, Martha Jane VI, 689
Piggott, Mary I, 349
Piggott, Mary I, 362
Piggott, Mary I, 363
Piggott, Mary I, 367
Piggott, Mary I, 403
Piggott, Mary I, 413
Piggott, Mary I, 414
Piggott, Mary I, 415
Piggott, Mary I, 417
Piggott, Mary I, 425
Piggott, Mary I, 453
Piggott, Mary I, 454
Piggott, Mary I, 567
Piggott, Mary I, 790
Piggott, Mary I, 995
Piggott, Mary IV, 157
Piggott, Mary IV, 347
Piggott, Mary IV, 430
Piggott, Mary IV, 544
Piggott, Mary V, 110
Piggott, Mary V, 111
Piggott, Mary VI, 422
Piggott, Mary VI, 432
Piggott, Mary VI, 477
Piggott, Mary VI, 544
Piggott, Mary VI, 603
Piggott, Mary VI, 625
Piggott, Mary VI, 627
Piggott, Mary VI, 648
Piggott, Mary VI, 675
Piggott, Mary VI, 676
Piggott, Mary VI, 679
Piggott, Mary VI, 682
Piggott, Mary VI, 689
Piggott, Mary VI, 690
Piggott, Mary Elizabeth VI, 689
Piggott, Mary Hannah VI, 686
Piggott, Mary Hannah VI, 689
Piggott, Mary Jane VI, 686
Piggott, Mary Jane VI, 688
Piggott, Mary Jane VI, 689
Piggott, Mary Jane VI, 711
Piggott, Mary Jane VI, 713
Piggott, Mary Jane VI, 714
Piggott, Maryland I, 413
Piggott, Moses IV, 157
Piggott, Moses IV, 430
Piggott, Moses VI, 432
Piggott, Moses VI, 447
Piggott, Moses VI, 462
Piggott, Moses VI, 603
Piggott, Nancy I, 415
Piggott, Nathan I, 363
Piggott, Nathan I, 414
Piggott, Nathan I, 453
Piggott, Nathan I, 454
Piggott, Nathan IV, 142
Piggott, Nathan VI, 689
Piggott, Patience I, 349
Piggott, Patience I, 362
Piggott, Patience I, 381
Piggott, Patience I, 414
Piggott, Patience I, 446
Piggott, Patience I, 453
Piggott, Pearl VI, 689
Piggott, Pearl VI, 701
Piggott, Phebe I, 363
Piggott, Phebe I, 391
Piggott, Phebe I, 414
Piggott, Phebe IV, 142
Piggott, Phebe IV, 157
Piggott, Phebe IV, 347
Piggott, Phebe VI, 544
Piggott, Phebe VI, 545
Piggott, Phebe VI, 603
Piggott, Phebe VI, 682
Piggott, Phebe VI, 689
Piggott, Phebe VI, 690
Piggott, Phebe VI, 709
Piggott, Phebe Ann VI, 689
Piggott, Phebe Ann VI, 705
Piggott, Phebe E. IV, 347
Piggott, Pricilla V, 111

Piggott, Priscilla I, 790
Piggott, Priscilla I, 864
Piggott, Priscilla I, 877
Piggott, Priscilla I, 898
Piggott, Rachel I, 362
Piggott, Rachel I, 363
Piggott, Rachel I, 376
Piggott, Rachel I, 408
Piggott, Rachel I, 413
Piggott, Rachel I, 414
Piggott, Rachel I, 452
Piggott, Rachel I, 567
Piggott, Rachel I, 898
Piggott, Rachel IV, 157
Piggott, Rachel IV, 544
Piggott, Rachel VI, 432
Piggott, Rachel VI, 595
Piggott, Rachel VI, 603
Piggott, Rebecca I, 362
Piggott, Rebecca I, 363
Piggott, Rebecca I, 567
Piggott, Rebecca IV, 157
Piggott, Rebecca IV, 544
Piggott, Rebecca VI, 432
Piggott, Rebecca VI, 705
Piggott, Rebecca B. VI, 705
Piggott, Rebecca E. VI, 689
Piggott, Rebecca M. VI, 690
Piggott, Rebecca Mary VI, 648
Piggott, Rebecca Mary VI, 681
Piggott, Rebecca Mary VI, 689
Piggott, Rebeckah I, 549
Piggott, Rebeckah I, 567
Piggott, Rebekah I, 400
Piggott, Rebekah I, 413
Piggott, Rebekah I, 414
Piggott, Rebekah I, 452
Piggott, Rebekah I, 1011
Piggott, Rebekah VI, 544
Piggott, Rebekah VI, 603
Piggott, Rhoda IV, 157
Piggott, Ruth I, 354
Piggott, Ruth I, 362
Piggott, Ruth I, 363
Piggott, Ruth I, 399
Piggott, Ruth I, 414
Piggott, Ruth I, 415
Piggott, Ruth I, 448
Piggott, Ruth I, 453
Piggott, Ruth I, 470
Piggott, Ruth I, 984
Piggott, Ruth I, 995
Piggott, Ruth IV, 157
Piggott, Ruth VI, 432
Piggott, Ruth VI, 689
Piggott, Ruth Hannah VI, 689
Piggott, Samuel I, 363
Piggott, Samuel I, 414
Piggott, Samuel I, 549
Piggott, Samuel I, 567
Piggott, Samuel III, 255
Piggott, Samuel IV, 544
Piggott, Samuel IV, 545
Piggott, Samuel VI, 544
Piggott, Samuel VI, 689
Piggott, Samuel H. VI, 689
Piggott, Sarah I, 343
Piggott, Sarah I, 359
Piggott, Sarah I, 362
Piggott, Sarah I, 363
Piggott, Sarah I, 384
Piggott, Sarah I, 388
Piggott, Sarah I, 401
Piggott, Sarah I, 411
Piggott, Sarah I, 413
Piggott, Sarah I, 414
Piggott, Sarah I, 431
Piggott, Sarah I, 440
Piggott, Sarah I, 451
Piggott, Sarah I, 452
Piggott, Sarah I, 453
Piggott, Sarah I, 567
Piggott, Sarah I, 1011
Piggott, Sarah III, 177
Piggott, Sarah III, 255
Piggott, Sarah IV, 326
Piggott, Sarah IV, 347
Piggott, Sarah IV, 544
Piggott, Sarah V, 110
Piggott, Sarah VI, 621
Piggott, Sarah VI, 625
Piggott, Sarah VI, 626
Piggott, Sarah VI, 627
Piggott, Sarah VI, 678
Piggott, Sarah VI, 679
Piggott, Sarah VI, 682
Piggott, Sarah VI, 689
Piggott, Sarah VI, 690
Piggott, Sarah VI, 710
Piggott, Sarah VI, 711
Piggott, Sarah A. VI, 689
Piggott, Sarah Ann IV, 539
Piggott, Sarah Ann IV, 545
Piggott, Sarah Ann VI, 626
Piggott, Sarah Ann VI, 675
Piggott, Sarah Ann VI, 688
Piggott, Sarah Ann VI, 689
Piggott, Sarah Ann VI, 690
Piggott, Sarah Ann VI, 695
Piggott, Sarah Ann VI, 701
Piggott, Sarahann IV, 544
Piggott, Shirley Thomas VI, 689
Piggott, Simon I, 363
Piggott, Simon I, 414
Piggott, Simon S. I, 470
Piggott, Solomon I, 363
Piggott, Susahhan VI, 523
Piggott, Susannah IV, 347
Piggott, Susannah VI, 464
Piggott, Susannah VI, 545
Piggott, Tamar I, 790
Piggott, Tamar V, 111
Piggott, Thomas I, 363
Piggott, Thomas IV, 157
Piggott, Thomas IV, 430
Piggott, Thomas VI, 432
Piggott, Thomas VI, 603
Piggott, Thomas VI, 626
Piggott, Thomas VI, 675
Piggott, Thomas VI, 688
Piggott, Thomas VI, 689
Piggott, Thomas VI, 690
Piggott, Thomas VI, 695
Piggott, Thomas VI, 701
Piggott, Thomas Hatcher VI, 689
Piggott, Widow Sarah I, 413
Piggott, William I, 343
Piggott, William I, 344
Piggott, William I, 362
Piggott, William I, 363
Piggott, William I, 407
Piggott, William I, 413
Piggott, William I, 414
Piggott, William I, 415
Piggott, William I, 440
Piggott, William I, 450
Piggott, William I, 452
Piggott, William I, 453
Piggott, William I, 567
Piggott, William I, 833
Piggott, William I, 834
Piggott, William I, 864
Piggott, William I, 898
Piggott, William IV, 430
Piggott, William IV, 544
Piggott, William VI, 477
Piggott, William VI, 544
Piggott, William VI, 625
Piggott, William VI, 627
Piggott, William VI, 656
Piggott, William VI, 679
Piggott, William VI, 682
Piggott, William VI, 689
Piggott, William VI, 690
Piggott, William Burr VI, 689
Piggott, Wm Burr VI, 675
Piggott, Wm. I, 359
Piggott, Wm. I, 401
Piggott, Wm. I, 567
Piggott, Wm. VI, 648
Pigion, Alice IV, 751
Pigion, Joseph II, 446
Pigion, Mary II, 446
Pigion, Susanna II, 446
Pigion, Wm. IV, 751
Pigot, Anna V, 856
Pigot, Edith I, 452
Pigot, Joseph V, 856
Pigot, Lydia V, 856
Pigot, Mary I, 452
Pigot, Mary V, 856
Pigot, Sarah I, 451
Pigot, Sarah I, 452
Pigot, Sarah V, 856
Pigot, Tamer V, 856
Pigott, Anna IV, 165
Pigott, Hannah IV, 157
Pigott, James IV, 157
Pigott, Moses IV, 157
Pigott, Rachel IV, 157
Pigott, Thomas IV, 157
Pik, Hannah VI, 432
Pike, ??? I, 279
Pike, Abigail I, 146
Pike, Abigail I, 157
Pike, Abigail I, 161
Pike, Abigail I, 343
Pike, Abigail I, 351
Pike, Abigail I, 358
Pike, Abigail I, 363
Pike, Abigail I, 364
Pike, Abigail I, 365
Pike, Abigail I, 367
Pike, Abigail I, 368
Pike, Abigail I, 413
Pike, Abigail I, 415
Pike, Abigail I, 421
Pike, Abigail I, 425
Pike, Abigail I, 790
Pike, Abigail I, 806
Pike, Abigail I, 834
Pike, Abigail V, 271
Pike, Abigail V, 292
Pike, Abigail V, 309
Pike, Abigail V, 355
Pike, Absilla I, 297
Pike, Absilla I, 305
Pike, Absilla I, 316
Pike, Achsah I, 297
Pike, Achsah I, 310
Pike, Achsah I, 317
Pike, Achsah I, 624
Pike, Albert I, 297
Pike, Alfred Florence I, 686
Pike, Alpheus IV, 617
Pike, Alpheus IV, 819
Pike, Aner Jane V, 425
Pike, Ann I, 114
Pike, Ann I, 161
Pike, Ann I, 172
Pike, Ann I, 316
Pike, Ann I, 363
Pike, Ann I, 415
Pike, Ann I, 731
Pike, Ann V, 355
Pike, Anne I, 243
Pike, Anne I, 256
Pike, Annie I, 624
Pike, Annie Louise I, 624
Pike, Annie Tomlinson I, 639
Pike, Arcada I, 286
Pike, Arcada I, 296
Pike, Arcada I, 297
Pike, Arcada I, 305
Pike, Arcada I, 312
Pike, Arcada I, 317
Pike, Avis I, 297
Pike, Avis I, 312
Pike, Avis I, 317
Pike, Axey I, 297
Pike, Barnabas I, 297
Pike, Barney E. I, 317
Pike, Barny I, 317
Pike, Benj. I, 364
Pike, Benjamin I, 114
Pike, Benjamin I, 161
Pike, Benjamin I, 296
Pike, Benjamin I, 317
Pike, Benjamin I, 731
Pike, Benjamin I, 1066
Pike, Benjamin, Jr. I, 161
Pike, Benjn. I, 161
Pike, Betsy I, 296
Pike, Carel Alphonso I, 297
Pike, Carl I, 339
Pike, Carl I, 639
Pike, Carl A. I, 317
Pike, Carl A. I, 339
Pike, Carl A. I, 624
Pike, Carl Leon I, 624
Pike, Carl N. IV, 1333
Pike, Caroline I, 416
Pike, Caroline Stepney II, 910
Pike, Caroline Stepney II, 927
Pike, Carrie V, 355
Pike, Catharine II, 520
Pike, Catharine II, 613
Pike, Catharine II, 622
Pike, Catherine II, 406
Pike, Celia IV, 617
Pike, Celia IV, 618
Pike, Celia IV, 651
Pike, Charity I, 296
Pike, Charlotte I, 287
Pike, Charlotte I, 296
Pike, Charlotte I, 305
Pike, Charlotte I, 317
Pike, Charty I, 296
Pike, Christian I, 296
Pike, Christian I, 297
Pike, Christian I, 315
Pike, Christian I, 316
Pike, Christian I, 317
Pike, Christian P. I, 297
Pike, Christian, Jr. I, 317
Pike, Clarkey I, 296
Pike, Cornelius I, 416
Pike, Cynthia Luzenia I, 416
Pike, Daniel K. V, 425
Pike, Daniel Kester V, 426
Pike, David I, 296
Pike, David I, 297
Pike, David I, 315
Pike, David I, 316
Pike, Deborah I, 69
Pike, Deborah V, 592
Pike, Doctor Leonedas I, 686
Pike, Dora I, 416
Pike, Dorcas I, 398
Pike, Dorcas I, 416
Pike, Earl D. IV, 1333
Pike, Edna I, 297
Pike, Elam I, 910
Pike, Eli V, 355
Pike, Eli V, 426
Pike, Elisabeth I, 135
Pike, Elisabeth I, 161
Pike, Elizabeth I, 97
Pike, Elizabeth I, 114
Pike, Elizabeth I, 351
Pike, Elizabeth I, 363
Pike, Elizabeth I, 364
Pike, Elizabeth I, 365
Pike, Elizabeth I, 415
Pike, Elizabeth I, 416
Pike, Elizabeth I, 421
Pike, Elizabeth I, 429
Pike, Elizabeth I, 773
Pike, Elizabeth I, 790
Pike, Elizabeth I, 834
Pike, Elizabeth I, 843
Pike, Elizabeth I, 910
Pike, Elizabeth I, 914
Pike, Elizabeth IV, 879
Pike, Elizabeth IV, 881
Pike, Elizabeth V, 271
Pike, Elizabeth VI, 582
Pike, Elizabeth C. V, 271
Pike, Elizabeth J. II, 910
Pike, Elizabeth J. II, 927
Pike, Elizabeth L. V, 272
Pike, Emily Jane I, 416
Pike, Exum I, 296
Pike, Exum I, 303
Pike, Exum I, 317
Pike, Fannah I, 161
Pike, Fanny I, 114
Pike, George W. I, 364
Pike, George W. I, 416
Pike, George W. I, 686
Pike, George W. I, 687
Pike, Georgie M. VI, 681
Pike, Hannah V, 274
Pike, Hannah V, 355
Pike, Hannah V, 447
Pike, Hannah L. I, 416
Pike, Harriet Elen V, 426
Pike, Harriet Ellen V, 355
Pike, Henry II, 1077
Pike, Henry Allen I, 296
Pike, Himelius I, 910
Pike, Howard M. IV, 1333
Pike, Huldah I, 299
Pike, Huldah I, 316
Pike, Huldah V, 350
Pike, Huldah V, 355
Pike, Huldy V, 355
Pike, Ida May V, 355
Pike, James III, 255
Pike, James V, 355
Pike, James V, 425
Pike, James V, 426
Pike, James Berry I, 296
Pike, James E. I, 296
Pike, James E. I, 297
Pike, James E. I, 317
Pike, Jane I, 114
Pike, Jane I, 172
Pike, Jane IV, 617
Pike, Jane IV, 819
Pike, Jean I, 161
Pike, Jean I, 363
Pike, Jemima A. I, 416
Pike, Jesse I, 161
Pike, Jesse I, 364
Pike, Jesse I, 416
Pike, Jesse I, 731
Pike, Jesse I, 1066
Pike, Jessee I, 114
Pike, John I, 114
Pike, John I, 157
Pike, John I, 161
Pike, John I, 166
Pike, John I, 296
Pike, John I, 297
Pike, John I, 317
Pike, John I, 343
Pike, John I, 351
Pike, John I, 358
Pike, John I, 363
Pike, John I, 364
Pike, John I, 365
Pike, John I, 367
Pike, John I, 368
Pike, John I, 414
Pike, John I, 415
Pike, John I, 416
Pike, John I, 731
Pike, John I, 790
Pike, John I, 834
Pike, John I, 836
Pike, John I, 1066
Pike, John II, 622
Pike, John II, 662
Pike, John V, 271
Pike, John V, 274
Pike, John V, 280
Pike, John V, 292
Pike, John V, 309
Pike, John V, 355
Pike, John V, 425
Pike, John V, 426
Pike, John Elder I, 686
Pike, John William I, 296
Pike, John, II I, 364
Pike, John, Jr. I, 161
Pike, John, Jr. I, 415
Pike, Jonathan I, 114
Pike, Jonathan I, 161
Pike, Jonathan I, 286
Pike, Jonathan I, 287
Pike, Jonathan I, 296
Pike, Jonathan I, 297
Pike, Jonathan I, 307
Pike, Jonathan I, 316
Pike, Jonathan I, 317
Pike, Jonathan, Jr. I, 317
Pike, Jordan I, 114
Pike, Jordan I, 161
Pike, Joseph I, 114
Pike, Joseph I, 161
Pike, Julia I, 296
Pike, Julia Ann V, 426
Pike, Juliann V, 425
Pike, Kesiah I, 686
Pike, Kezia I, 460
Pike, Kezia I, 673
Pike, Keziah I, 686
Pike, Lavina Angilina I, 364
Pike, Lawson G. I, 416
Pike, Leah I, 834
Pike, Leah I, 836
Pike, Leah I, 967
Pike, Leah I, 1001
Pike, Leah V, 271
Pike, Leah V, 274
Pike, Leah V, 280
Pike, Leah V, 292
Pike, Leah V, 309
Pike, Levi V, 355
Pike, Lewis I, 295
Pike, Lewis I, 296
Pike, Lewis I, 317
Pike, Lindley W. IV, 820
Pike, Loren D. IV, 1333
Pike, Loucindie I, 317
Pike, Loueza I, 409
Pike, Loueza I, 416
Pike, Louisa J. I, 416
Pike, Lucinda I, 317
Pike, Lucinda E. I, 296
Pike, Lucinda E. I, 317
Pike, Lucy V, 226
Pike, Lucy V, 271
Pike, Lucy V, 337
Pike, Lucy V, 350
Pike, Lucy V, 355
Pike, Lucy M. IV, 1333
Pike, Luzena I, 910
Pike, Lydda I, 114
Pike, Lydia I, 161
Pike, Lydia V, 337
Pike, Lydia V, 355
Pike, Lydia V, 394
Pike, Lydia V, 397
Pike, Lydia V, 425
Pike, Lydia V, 426
Pike, Mable Ovela I, 624
Pike, Margaret I, 133
Pike, Margaret I, 161
Pike, Margaret I, 364
Pike, Margaret I, 385
Pike, Margaret I, 415
Pike, Margaret I, 790
Pike, Margaret I, 833
Pike, Margaret I, 834
Pike, Margaret V, 265
Pike, Margaret V, 272
Pike, Margaret V, 309
Pike, Mariam I, 161
Pike, Marietta V, 355
Pike, Mark I, 296
Pike, Mark I, 297
Pike, Mark I, 315
Pike, Mark I, 316

ke, Mark E. I, 297
ke, Mark E. I, 317
ke, Martha I, 161
ke, Martha I, 295
ke, Martha I, 301
ke, Martha I, 317
ke, Martha G. I, 947
ke, Martha H. V, 271
ke, Martha Isadore V, 426
ke, Martha Isodre V, 355
ke, Mary I, 114
ke, Mary I, 287
ke, Mary I, 296
ke, Mary I, 297
ke, Mary I, 299
ke, Mary I, 305
ke, Mary I, 311
ke, Mary I, 316
ke, Mary I, 317
ke, Mary I, 364
ke, Mary I, 385
ke, Mary I, 396
ke, Mary I, 414
ke, Mary I, 415
ke, Mary I, 423
ke, Mary I, 790
ke, Mary I, 834
ke, Mary I, 907
ke, Mary I, 910
ke, Mary I, 913
ke, Mary I, 914
ke, Mary I, 995
ke, Mary II, 298
ke, Mary II, 622
ke, Mary II, 662
ke, Mary II, 1077
ke, Mary V, 355
ke, Mary A. I, 416
ke, Mary Ann I, 161
ke, Mary Ann I, 364
ke, Mary Ann I, 398
ke, Mary Ann I, 416
ke, Mary Ann V, 355
ke, Mary Lizar I, 296
ke, Mary Lola I, 624
ke, Mathew I, 296
ke, Mathew I, 297
ke, Mathew I, 317
ke, Mathew I, 731
ke, Mathew I, 1066
ke, Mathew Simpson I, 296
ke, Matthew I, 114
ke, Matthew I, 296
ke, Matthew I, 297
ke, Micajah I, 296
ke, Micajah I, 297
ke, Micajah I, 317
ke, Michael T. I, 297
ke, Michael T. I, 317
ke, Milah I, 114
ke, Miley I, 161
ke, Milisent I, 114
ke, Miriam I, 114
ke, Miriam I, 123
ke, Miriam I, 161
ke, Miriam I, 173
ke, Miriam I, 303
ke, Miriam I, 317
ke, Mrs. Anna IV, 1333
ke, Myrtle IV, 1333
ke, Nancy I, 415
ke, Nathan I, 114
ke, Nathan I, 161
ke, Nathan I, 256
ke, Nathan I, 287
ke, Nathan I, 296
ke, Nathan I, 297
ke, Nathan I, 311
ke, Nathan I, 316
ke, Nathan I, 317
ke, Nathan I, 363
ke, Nathan I, 364
ke, Nathan I, 415
ke, Nathan I, 416
ke, Nathan I, 429
ke, Nathan I, 567
ke, Nathan I, 600
ke, Nathan I, 773
ke, Nathan I, 790
ke, Nathan I, 834
ke, Nathan I, 907
ke, Nathan I, 910
ke, Nathan I, 913
ke, Nathan I, 914
ke, Nathan I, 967
ke, Nathan I, 995
ke, Nathan V, 271
ke, Nathan VI, 582
ke, Nathan E. I, 416
ke, Nathan K. I, 317
ke, Nathan, Jr. I, 317
Pike, Newby I, 910
Pike, Novella I, 639
Pike, Orpha I, 296
Pike, Orpha I, 299
Pike, Orpha I, 317
Pike, Orpha IV, 820
Pike, Orpha IV, 838
Pike, Orpha J. IV, 819
Pike, Ovella I, 624
Pike, Ovilla I, 639
Pike, Patience I, 114
Pike, Patience I, 295
Pike, Peninah I, 161
Pike, Peninah I, 296
Pike, Peninah I, 315
Pike, Peninnah I, 316
Pike, Penniah I, 114
Pike, Penniah I, 317
Pike, Phebe I, 790
Pike, Phebe I, 825
Pike, Phebe I, 834
Pike, Phebe I, 910
Pike, Phebe V, 271
Pike, Phebe V, 324
Pike, Phebe V, 355
Pike, Philip I, 296
Pike, Philip Barnabas I, 296
Pike, Priscilla I, 364
Pike, Priscilla I, 414
Pike, Priscilla I, 415
Pike, Priscilla I, 790
Pike, Priscilla I, 834
Pike, Priscilla I, 845
Pike, Rachel I, 287
Pike, Rachel I, 296
Pike, Rachel I, 297
Pike, Rachel I, 311
Pike, Rachel I, 316
Pike, Rachel I, 317
Pike, Rachel I, 339
Pike, Rachel I, 363
Pike, Rachel I, 364
Pike, Rachel I, 368
Pike, Rachel I, 384
Pike, Rachel I, 415
Pike, Rachel I, 419
Pike, Rachel I, 429
Pike, Rachel I, 624
Pike, Rachel I, 639
Pike, Rachel I, 731
Pike, Rachel I, 1066
Pike, Rachel V, 271
Pike, Rachel V, 280
Pike, Rachel V, 309
Pike, Rachel V, 524
Pike, Rachel V, 530
Pike, Rachel V, 762
Pike, Rachel VI, 582
Pike, Rachel M. I, 624
Pike, Rachel R. I, 339
Pike, Rachel, Jr. I, 317
Pike, Ralph M. IV, 1333
Pike, Rebeca Ann Mariah I, 296
Pike, Rebecca I, 296
Pike, Rebecca I, 297
Pike, Rebecca I, 317
Pike, Rebecca II, 250
Pike, Rebecca II, 298
Pike, Rebecca V, 641
Pike, Rebeckah V, 111
Pike, Rhoda I, 114
Pike, Rhoda I, 256
Pike, Robert I, 317
Pike, Ruth I, 363
Pike, Ruth I, 367
Pike, Ruth I, 386
Pike, Ruth I, 416
Pike, Ruth V, 271
Pike, Ruth V, 274
Pike, Ruth V, 309
Pike, Ruth Jane Elizabeth I, 296
Pike, Sallie I, 286
Pike, Sallie I, 287
Pike, Sallie I, 317
Pike, Sallie A. I, 317
Pike, Sally I, 296
Pike, Sally A. I, 297
Pike, Samuel I, 114
Pike, Samuel I, 123
Pike, Samuel I, 157
Pike, Samuel I, 161
Pike, Samuel I, 165
Pike, Samuel I, 243
Pike, Samuel I, 256
Pike, Samuel I, 316
Pike, Samuel I, 363
Pike, Samuel I, 396
Pike, Samuel I, 415
Pike, Samuel I, 416
Pike, Samuel I, 686
Pike, Samuel V, 272
Pike, Samuel V, 309
Pike, Samuel V, 355
Pike, Samuel V, 426
Pike, Samuel Kirby I, 416
Pike, Samuel O. I, 416
Pike, Samuel O. I, 686
Pike, Samuel Taylor I, 364
Pike, Sarah I, 114
Pike, Sarah I, 157
Pike, Sarah I, 161
Pike, Sarah I, 166
Pike, Sarah I, 296
Pike, Sarah I, 297
Pike, Sarah I, 300
Pike, Sarah I, 303
Pike, Sarah I, 307
Pike, Sarah I, 316
Pike, Sarah I, 317
Pike, Sarah I, 363
Pike, Sarah I, 364
Pike, Sarah I, 415
Pike, Sarah I, 790
Pike, Sarah II, 250
Pike, Sarah II, 298
Pike, Sarah V, 425
Pike, Sarah V, 432
Pike, Sarah V, 723
Pike, Sarah V, 762
Pike, Sarah M. I, 416
Pike, Silas I, 317
Pike, Silas C. I, 297
Pike, Solomon F. I, 416
Pike, Sophia II, 406
Pike, Stephen II, 180
Pike, Stephen II, 250
Pike, Stephen II, 622
Pike, Susanna I, 97
Pike, Susanna I, 114
Pike, Susanna I, 358
Pike, Susanna I, 363
Pike, Susanna I, 385
Pike, Susanna I, 404
Pike, Susanna I, 415
Pike, Susanna I, 686
Pike, Susannah I, 136
Pike, Susannah I, 161
Pike, Tabitha I, 161
Pike, Tabitha I, 165
Pike, Talitha C. I, 686
Pike, Talitha C. I, 687
Pike, Taylor I, 416
Pike, Thomas II, 298
Pike, Thomas Ellwood V, 426
Pike, Thomas Elwood V, 425
Pike, Thornton II, 910
Pike, Thornton II, 927
Pike, Trecinda I, 297
Pike, Tristram I, 790
Pike, Tristram V, 355
Pike, Ursola V, 419
Pike, Ursola V, 425
Pike, Ursula V, 350
Pike, Ursula V, 355
Pike, Virgil I, 339
Pike, Widow Elizabeth I, 834
Pike, Widow Jane I, 161
Pike, Wilie I, 317
Pike, William I, 296
Pike, William I, 297
Pike, William I, 317
Pike, William I, 364
Pike, William I, 415
Pike, William I, 624
Pike, William I, 639
Pike, William I, 790
Pike, William I, 910
Pike, William V, 226
Pike, William V, 271
Pike, William V, 355
Pike, William V, 426
Pike, William B. I, 296
Pike, William C. I, 624
Pike, William E. I, 317
Pike, William E. I, 339
Pike, William E. I, 624
Pike, William E. G. I, 297
Pike, William F. I, 317
Pike, William Franklin I, 416
Pike, William G. I, 416
Pike, William Howard I, 624
Pike, William J. V, 425
Pike, William J. V, 426
Pike, William M. I, 416
Pike, William T. I, 339
Pike, William T. I, 624
Pike, William W. V, 271
Pike, Willie I, 296
Pike, Willie I, 339
Pike, Willis I, 297
Pike, Willson I, 114
Pike, Wilson I, 114
Pike, Wilson I, 161
Pike, Wm. I, 364
Pike, Wm. I, 415
Pike, Wm. V, 324
Pike, Wm. V, 337
Pike, Wm. V, 350
Pike, Wm. V, 355
Pike, Wm. G. I, 364
Pike, Wm. L. I, 624
Pike, Wm. T. I, 339
Pike, Wm. T. I, 624
Pike, Zoe E. IV, 1333
Pilcher, Orlando V, 641
Pilcher, Sattie V, 641
Pile, Ann II, 629
Pile, Ann II, 680
Pile, Jane II, 629
Pile, John VI, 432
Pile, John L. II, 715
Pile, John L. II, 760
Pile, Joseph VI, 432
Pile, Mary I, 453
Pile, Nicholas II, 629
Pile, Nicholas II, 680
Pile, Rachel II, 715
Pile, Rachel H. II, 910
Pile, Wm. Henry II, 715
Piles, Elizabeth II, 407
Piles, Joseph VI, 432
Piles, Zachariah IV, 1290
Pilings, Rosa IV, 264
Pilkington, Edward II, 622
Pilkington, Edward II, 680
Pilkington, Mary II, 622
Pilkington, Mary II, 680
Pilkington, Sarah III, 492
Pilkinton, Adam II, 407
Pilkinton, Thomas II, 407
Pillar, Alfred Ernest III, 255
Pillar, Elizabeth II, 446
Pillar, Francis III, 255
Pillar, Isaac II, 622
Pillar, Isaac II, 691
Pillar, James II, 407
Pillar, James II, 446
Pillar, James II, 622
Pillar, James II, 691
Pillar, Mary II, 622
Pillar, Mary II, 691
Pillar, Rebecka II, 407
Pillar, Sarah II, 622
Pillar, Sarah II, 691
Pillar, Tamar II, 407
Pillar, Tamer II, 446
Piller, ??? II, 446
Piller, Gainer II, 407
Piller, Isaac II, 622
Piller, James II, 407
Piller, James II, 446
Piller, Rebecka II, 407
Piller, Ruth II, 407
Piller, Sarah II, 622
Piller, Tamar II, 407
Piller, Tamer II, 446
Piller, Tamor II, 407
Pilling, Chas. B. III, 445
Pilling, Eliz. C. III, 445
Pilling, Elizabeth III, 424
Pilling, Elizabeth III, 433
Pilling, Katharine III, 424
Pilling, Katharine III, 433
Pilling, Katharine V. III, 433
Pilling, Katharine Valerie III, 445
Pilling, Katharine Valine III, 433
Pilling, Martha II, 1021
Pilling, Simeon III, 433
Pilling, Simeon O. III, 424
Pilling, Thomas II, 1021
Pillow, Edith VI, 839
Pillow, Elizabeth VI, 839
Pillow, Elizabeth VI, 847
Pillow, Franklin VI, 847
Pillow, Franklin VI, 857
Pillow, Jasper VI, 839
Pillow, Jasper VI, 847
Pillow, John VI, 847
Pillow, Patsy VI, 847
Pillow, Polly VI, 847
Pillow, Rebecca VI, 847
Pillow, Thomas J. VI, 847
Pillows, Agness VI, 867
Pillows, Freeman V, 1014
Pilot, Lucile IV, 1333
Pilot, Wm. ??? IV, 1333
Pilot, Wm. H. IV, 1333
Pim, Aaron IV, 913
Pim, Abigail IV, 833
Pim, Abigail IV, 838
Pim, Abigail IV, 913
Pim, Abigail IV, 914
Pim, Aden IV, 838
Pim, Aden IV, 913
Pim, Aden IV, 987
Pim, Alfred V, 926
Pim, Alice IV, 1220
Pim, Alice IV, 1228
Pim, Alice E. IV, 913
Pim, Alice E. IV, 914
Pim, Allen IV, 913
Pim, Amy IV, 913
Pim, Ann II, 801
Pim, Ann IV, 738
Pim, Ann IV, 751
Pim, Ann IV, 913
Pim, Anna IV, 987
Pim, Anna IV, 1007
Pim, Anna Arwilda IV, 913
Pim, Anne IV, 987
Pim, Anne IV, 1007
Pim, Asa IV, 838
Pim, Asa IV, 913
Pim, Asa IV, 987
Pim, Benjamin IV, 913
Pim, Benjamin IV, 987
Pim, Bertice IV, 987
Pim, Bertie IV, 987
Pim, Blanch IV, 838
Pim, Blanch IV, 846
Pim, Blanche IV, 751
Pim, C IV, 651
Pim, Caroline IV, 651
Pim, Caroline S. IV, 652
Pim, Caroline S. IV, 913
Pim, Caroline S. IV, 914
Pim, Charles IV, 913
Pim, Charles IV, 987
Pim, Chas. IV, 944
Pim, Curtis Binford IV, 913
Pim, Eliza IV, 651
Pim, Eliza IV, 652
Pim, Eliza IV, 913
Pim, Elizabeth IV, 913
Pim, Elizabeth IV, 972
Pim, Elizabeth IV, 987
Pim, Emily IV, 944
Pim, Eneas IV, 913
Pim, Enos IV, 838
Pim, Enos IV, 904
Pim, Enos IV, 913
Pim, Enos IV, 914
Pim, Enos IV, 987
Pim, Esther IV, 751
Pim, Eva E. IV, 1333
Pim, Franklin IV, 913
Pim, Frederick C. IV, 913
Pim, Garret IV, 652
Pim, Garret IV, 838
Pim, Garret IV, 914
Pim, Garrett IV, 652
Pim, Garrett IV, 904
Pim, Garrett IV, 913
Pim, Hannah II, 92
Pim, Hannah IV, 652
Pim, Hannah IV, 903
Pim, Hannah IV, 913
Pim, Hannah IV, 914
Pim, Harvey IV, 652
Pim, Harvy IV, 913
Pim, Henry III, 255
Pim, Isaac IV, 651
Pim, Isaac IV, 652
Pim, Isaac IV, 838
Pim, Isaac IV, 913
Pim, Isaac IV, 914
Pim, Israel IV, 913
Pim, Jabez IV, 913
Pim, Jarrett IV, 833
Pim, Jarrett IV, 838
Pim, John II, 622
Pim, John II, 760
Pim, John III, 255
Pim, John IV, 913
Pim, John IV, 987
Pim, Jonathan II, 622
Pim, Jonathan II, 760
Pim, Joseph II, 92
Pim, Joseph IV, 913
Pim, Joseph G. IV, 913
Pim, Joseph G. IV, 914
Pim, Joseph G. IV, 1041
Pim, Laura IV, 913
Pim, Laura IV, 1333
Pim, Lauretta IV, 913
Pim, Lauretta IV, 987
Pim, Lawretta IV, 1041
Pim, Lena IV, 751
Pim, Lewis IV, 911
Pim, Lewis IV, 913
Pim, Lewis IV, 914
Pim, Lewis IV, 987
Pim, Lewis G. IV, 751

Pim, Lewis G. IV, 838
Pim, Lewis G. IV, 913
Pim, Lewis G. IV, 1333
Pim, Lewis G. V, 197
Pim, Lidia II, 92
Pim, Loren IV, 751
Pim, Lydia IV, 652
Pim, Lydia IV, 838
Pim, Lydia IV, 913
Pim, Lydia IV, 914
Pim, Lydia G. IV, 987
Pim, Maggie IV, 944
Pim, Maggie IV, 987
Pim, Maggie Vietta IV, 944
Pim, Maggie Vietta IV, 987
Pim, Margaret II, 710
Pim, Mary II, 92
Pim, Mary II, 104
Pim, Mary IV, 652
Pim, Mary IV, 913
Pim, Mary V, 197
Pim, Mary Ann IV, 913
Pim, Mary Ann IV, 987
Pim, Mary Anna IV, 987
Pim, Mary B. IV, 751
Pim, Mary Barrett IV, 1333
Pim, Mary Vietta IV, 913
Pim, Mary Vietta IV, 914
Pim, Nathan IV, 838
Pim, Nathan IV, 859
Pim, Nathan IV, 903
Pim, Nathan IV, 913
Pim, Nathan IV, 914
Pim, Norman IV, 751
Pim, Phebe IV, 904
Pim, Phebe IV, 913
Pim, Phebe IV, 914
Pim, Phebe IV, 987
Pim, Rachel IV, 838
Pim, Rachel IV, 913
Pim, Rebecca IV, 904
Pim, Rebecca IV, 913
Pim, Rebecca IV, 914
Pim, Rhoda IV, 751
Pim, Rhoda IV, 966
Pim, Rhoda IV, 987
Pim, Sarah IV, 651
Pim, Sarah IV, 652
Pim, Sarah IV, 838
Pim, Sarah IV, 911
Pim, Sarah IV, 913
Pim, Sarah IV, 914
Pim, Sarah IV, 987
Pim, Sarah IV, 1179
Pim, Sarah IV, 1197
Pim, Sarah E. IV, 913
Pim, Sarah E. IV, 914
Pim, Sarah Emily IV, 987
Pim, Sarah Emma IV, 987
Pim, Sina Ann IV, 913
Pim, Thomas II, 710
Pim, Thomas IV, 913
Pim, Walter A. IV, 913
Pim, Warren Lewis IV, 913
Pim, Wd. Sarah IV, 809
Pim, Wd. Sarah IV, 838
Pim, Willard IV, 751
Pim, Willard IV, 987
Pim, Willard Lorain IV, 987
Pim, William IV, 751
Pim, William Lecky II, 715
Pim, Wm. Lecky II, 760
Pimm, Alfred V, 926
Pimm, Caroline S. IV, 652
Pimm, Elizabeth II, 62
Pimm, Elizabeth II, 92
Pimm, Enos IV, 987
Pimm, Garrett IV, 652
Pimm, Hannah II, 92
Pimm, Hannah II, 137
Pimm, Hannah IV, 652
Pimm, Harvey IV, 652
Pimm, Isaac IV, 652
Pimm, John II, 92
Pimm, John II, 105
Pimm, John II, 622
Pimm, John Joseph II, 92
Pimm, Joseph II, 92
Pimm, Joseph II, 137
Pimm, Joseph A. II, 910
Pimm, Joseph, Jr. II, 92
Pimm, Levi II, 92
Pimm, Levy II, 92
Pimm, Lewis G. V, 197
Pimm, Lidia II, 92
Pimm, Lydia II, 92
Pimm, Lydia IV, 903
Pimm, Lydia IV, 914
Pimm, Mary II, 92
Pimm, Mary V, 197
Pimm, Mary B. V, 197
Pimm, Sarah II, 92
Pimm, Sarah II, 105
Pimm, Sarah IV, 652
Pimm, Teresa II, 92
Pimm, Teresa II, 137
Pinchin, David II, 815
Pinchin, Elizabeth II, 815
Pinchin, Elizabeth A. II, 831
Pinchin, Elizabeth A. II, 910
Pindar, Antrim II, 967
Pindar, Mary Ann II, 967
Pindegar, Amos II, 407
Pindegar, Samuel II, 407
Pinder, George IV, 1179
Pinder, Ivah IV, 1179
Pinder, John IV, 1179
Pinder, Laura S. IV, 1179
Pinder, Mary IV, 1179
Pinder, Orley IV, 1179
Pinder, Samuel IV, 1179
Pindle, Nancy J. V, 463
Pine, Cath. Jane III, 67
Pine, Cath. Jane III, 255
Pine, Catharine III, 255
Pine, Chalkley II, 122
Pine, Chalkley II, 136
Pine, Chalkley II, 155
Pine, Chalkley II, 815
Pine, Chalkley II, 910
Pine, Edith III, 442
Pine, Edwin II, 910
Pine, Elizabeth I, 932
Pine, Elizabeth III, 433
Pine, Elizabeth III, 474
Pine, Elizabeth IV, 706
Pine, Elizabeth IV, 751
Pine, Elizabeth G. III, 255
Pine, Ellen A. II, 910
Pine, Ellen B. II, 910
Pine, Gilbert G. III, 255
Pine, Hannah II, 52
Pine, Hannah II, 92
Pine, Hannah II, 815
Pine, Hannah II, 910
Pine, Hannah III, 442
Pine, Hannah B. II, 37
Pine, Hannah B. II, 122
Pine, Hannah D. II, 136
Pine, Hannah D. II, 155
Pine, Hannah D. II, 815
Pine, Hannah D. II, 910
Pine, Isaac III, 255
Pine, James III, 433
Pine, James III, 442
Pine, James III, 474
Pine, James Arnold V, 111
Pine, Joseph II, 37
Pine, Joseph II, 52
Pine, Joseph II, 92
Pine, Joseph II, 122
Pine, Joseph II, 136
Pine, Joseph II, 155
Pine, Joseph II, 815
Pine, Joseph II, 820
Pine, Joseph II, 910
Pine, Joseph B. II, 910
Pine, Joshua II, 815
Pine, Joshua Brooks II, 815
Pine, Judith II, 52
Pine, Judith II, 92
Pine, Judith II, 136
Pine, Margaret Elizabeth II, 910
Pine, Martha II, 37
Pine, Martha II, 52
Pine, Martha II, 92
Pine, Martha II, 122
Pine, Martha II, 136
Pine, Martha II, 155
Pine, Martha II, 815
Pine, Martha II, 820
Pine, Martha II, 910
Pine, Martha, Jr. II, 815
Pine, Mary II, 37
Pine, Mary II, 122
Pine, Mary II, 136
Pine, Mary II, 815
Pine, Mary II, 910
Pine, Mary III, 67
Pine, Mary III, 255
Pine, Mary V, 926
Pine, Mary A. II, 155
Pine, Mary A. II, 910
Pine, Mary Allen II, 815
Pine, Mary Allen II, 910
Pine, Mary Ann II, 815
Pine, Mary Ann Wing II, 815
Pine, Mary H. II, 815
Pine, Mary H. V, 111
Pine, Mary Johnson V, 111
Pine, Priscilla II, 37
Pine, Priscilla II, 122
Pine, Priscilla II, 136
Pine, Priscilla II, 155
Pine, Priscilla II, 820
Pine, Priscilla II, 910
Pine, Priscilla II, 923
Pine, Rachel III, 255
Pine, Rachel III, 373
Pine, Rachel III, 433
Pine, Rachel III, 476
Pine, Ruth Eleanor V, 111
Pine, Ruth Hannah V, 111
Pine, Samuel II, 52
Pine, Samuel II, 92
Pine, Samuel II, 815
Pine, Samuel II, 910
Pine, Samuel III, 255
Pine, Samuel III, 373
Pine, Samuel III, 433
Pine, Samuel III, 476
Pine, Samuel T. II, 910
Pine, Samuel Thorne II, 815
Pine, Sarah II, 37
Pine, Sarah II, 122
Pine, Sarah V, 88
Pine, Sarah V, 111
Pine, Sarah Ann III, 255
Pine, Sarah B. II, 136
Pine, Sarah B. II, 155
Pine, Sarah B. II, 863
Pine, Sarah B. II, 910
Pine, Simeon V, 975
Pine, Simon V, 111
Pine, Smith III, 255
Pine, Wd. Rachel III, 433
Pine, William III, 255
Pine, William H. V, 111
Pine, Wm. II, 52
Pine, Wm. II, 92
Pine, Wm. II, 136
Pine, Wm. II, 815
Pine, Wm. III, 67
Pine, Wm. V, 926
Pinemore, Samuel II, 407
Pingard, John II, 407
Pingleton, Dorothy V, 856
Pingleton, Ersie V, 854
Pingleton, Ersie V, 856
Pinkam, Shubael I, 834
Pinkerton, Albert V, 355
Pinkerton, Anna M. II, 808
Pinkerton, Charlotte V, 355
Pinkerton, Helen IV, 264
Pinkerton, Lida B. IV, 264
Pinkerton, Michael L. IV, 264
Pinkerton, Mrs. Mike IV, 264
Pinkerton, Richard P. V, 355
Pinkerton, Ruth A. V, 355
Pinkham, Abigail III, 383
Pinkham, Abigail III, 389
Pinkham, Abigail IV, 751
Pinkham, Amy III, 433
Pinkham, Amy III, 467
Pinkham, Ann III, 384
Pinkham, Arthur Edward IV, 264
Pinkham, Arthur Edward IV, 751
Pinkham, Arthur Edwin IV, 264
Pinkham, Caroline H. IV, 106
Pinkham, Caroline H. IV, 131
Pinkham, Caroline H. IV, 751
Pinkham, Cornelia IV, 751
Pinkham, Daniel III, 384
Pinkham, Ebenezer III, 492
Pinkham, Elijah IV, 751
Pinkham, Eliz. III, 492
Pinkham, Elizabeth IV, 751
Pinkham, Emma IV, 751
Pinkham, Emma C. IV, 264
Pinkham, Emma C. IV, 697
Pinkham, Emma C. IV, 751
Pinkham, Emma C. IV, 1333
Pinkham, Fanny S. III, 255
Pinkham, Gilbert L. IV, 751
Pinkham, Gilbert Lately IV, 751
Pinkham, Gilbert Latey IV, 106
Pinkham, Gilbert Latey IV, 751
Pinkham, Gilbod IV, 106
Pinkham, Huldah Caroline IV, 751
Pinkham, James Parnel IV, 751
Pinkham, James Parnell IV, 106
Pinkham, James Parnell IV, 131
Pinkham, James Parnell IV, 751
Pinkham, John III, 384
Pinkham, Libni III, 383
Pinkham, Libni III, 492
Pinkham, Libni III, 494
Pinkham, Libny III, 255
Pinkham, Mary IV, 106
Pinkham, Mary IV, 709
Pinkham, Mary IV, 751
Pinkham, Mary IV, 955
Pinkham, Mary IV, 987
Pinkham, Mary B. IV, 106
Pinkham, Mary B. IV, 131
Pinkham, Mary B. IV, 751
Pinkham, Mary B. IV, 987
Pinkham, Mary Cornelia IV, 264
Pinkham, Mary Cornelia IV, 751
Pinkham, Mary Elizabeth IV, 106
Pinkham, Mary Elizabeth IV, 131
Pinkham, Mary Elizabeth IV, 737
Pinkham, Mary Elizabeth IV, 751
Pinkham, Mary F. IV, 264
Pinkham, Obed III, 384
Pinkham, Ruth III, 255
Pinkham, Sarah III, 255
Pinkham, Sarah III, 383
Pinkham, Sarah III, 492
Pinkham, Sarah III, 494
Pinkham, Thomas IV, 106
Pinkham, Thomas IV, 131
Pinkham, Thomas IV, 264
Pinkham, Thomas IV, 751
Pinkham, Thomas Edward IV, 106
Pinkham, Thomas Edward IV, 131
Pinkham, Thomas Edward IV, 709
Pinkham, Thomas Edward IV, 955
Pinkham, Thomas Edward IV, 987
Pinkham, Thos. IV, 987
Pinkham, Thos. Edward IV, 264
Pinkham, Thos. Edward IV, 751
Pinkham, Wendall IV, 1313
Pinkham, William P. IV, 264
Pinkham, William P. IV, 751
Pinkham, William Penn IV, 106
Pinkham, William Penn IV, 751
Pinkham, Wm. P. IV, 264
Pinkham, Wm. P. IV, 697
Pinkham, Wm. P. IV, 751
Pinkham, Wm. P. IV, 1333
Pinkham, Wm. Penn IV, 131
Pinkham, Wm. Penn IV, 751
Pinkham, Zebulun III, 384
Pinkham, Zebulun III, 433
Pinkham, Zebulun III, 467
Pinkhan, Gilbod IV, 106
Pinkhan, Mary IV, 106
Pinkhan, Thomas IV, 106
Pinkney, Clara Eleanor II, 815
Pinkney, George II, 815
Pinkney, William III, 255
Pinnear, John VI, 46
Pinnear, Sarah VI, 46
Pinner, Clark I, 256
Pinner, Clarke I, 256
Pinner, Clarkey I, 52
Pinner, Clarkey I, 69
Pinner, Clarkey I, 226
Pinner, John I, 52
Pinner, John I, 69
Pinner, John I, 226
Pinner, John I, 256
Pinner, John VI, 46
Pinner, John VI, 118
Pinner, John, Jr. I, 226
Pinner, Joseph I, 226
Pinner, Joseph I, 256
Pinner, Mrs. Richard VI, 11
Pinner, Rebeckah VI, 45
Pinner, Rebeckah VI, 46
Pinner, Sallie I, 929
Pinner, Sarah I, 226
Pinner, Sarah I, 256
Pinner, Sarah VI, 46
Pinner, Sarah VI, 118
Pinner, Sarah VI, 120
Pinney, Addie B. III, 83
Pinney, Addie B. III, 89
Pinnock, Joseph IV, 53
Pinock, Alice VI, 335
Pinock, Mary VI, 335
Pinson, Abijah I, 512
Pinson, Abijah I, 567
Pinson, Abijah I, 958
Pinson, Abijah I, 965
Pinson, Abijah I, 967
Pinson, Ann I, 958
Pinson, Ann I, 965
Pinson, Ann I, 967
Pinson, Bowater I, 512
Pinson, Eliza I, 958
Pinson, Jesse Franklin I, 958
Pinson, Joel I, 512
Pinson, John I, 958
Pinson, Maacah I, 512
Pinson, Maacah I, 957
Pinson, Maacah I, 967
Pinson, Maacha I, 957
Pinson, Maache I, 967
Pinson, Mary I, 512
Pinson, Mary I, 567
Pinson, Mary I, 957
Pinson, Mary I, 964
Pinson, Mary I, 967
Pinson, Mica I, 958
Pinson, Mica I, 967
Pinson, Nathan I, 512
Pinson, Nathan I, 567
Pinson, Nathan I, 967
Pinson, Obadiah I, 967
Pinson, Obediah I, 512
Pinson, Obediah I, 567
Pinson, Rebecca I, 1050
Pinson, Richard I, 512
Pinson, Richard I, 567
Pinson, Richard I, 953
Pinson, Richard I, 957
Pinson, Richard I, 958
Pinson, Richard I, 967
Pinson, Sarah I, 512
Pinson, Sarah I, 567
Pinson, Sarah I, 957
Pinson, Sarah I, 966
Pinson, Sarah I, 967
Pintard, Ann III, 255
Pintard, Mary III, 255
Pinter, Sarah IV, 855
Pinyard, Elinor II, 446
Pinyard, John II, 446
Pinyard, Joseph II, 407
Pinyard, Mary II, 622
Pinyard, Rebecca II, 407
Pinyard, Thomas II, 446
Piott, Mary IV, 347
Piott, Susanna IV, 347
Piper, Effie IV, 1290
Piper, Elisabeth I, 161
Piper, Elisabeth I, 170
Piper, Elizabeth I, 153
Piper, Elizabeth I, 161
Piper, Emma IV, 1290
Piper, George IV, 1290
Piper, Hal V, 853
Piper, Hal V, 856
Piper, Harry L. III, 255
Piper, James I, 161
Piper, James I, 834
Piper, James IV, 985
Piper, Joseph I, 161
Piper, Lucinda IV, 985
Piper, Margaret IV, 985
Piper, Mary I, 161
Piper, Mary Jane IV, 1290
Piper, Nathan I, 120
Piper, Nathan I, 161
Piper, Nathaniel I, 153
Piper, Nathaniel I, 161
Piper, Sarah IV, 330
Piper, Sarah IV, 347
Piper, Susan IV, 995
Piper, Thomas I, 161
Piper, Wd. Sarah Eva V, 853
Piper, Wd. Sarah Eva V, 856
Pipes, George D. IV, 751
Pipes, Lizzie IV, 1220
Pipkin, Marshal Howard I, 339
Pippet, Benjamin II, 180
Pippet, Wd. Ann II, 180
Pippett, Barbara II, 694
Pippett, Susan R. IV, 696
Pippett, Susan R. IV, 751
Pippie, Isaac II, 407
Pippie, Joseph II, 407
Pippin, Oney VI, 850
Pippitt, Benjamin II, 407
Pippitt, Charles II, 407
Pirals, Henry I, 968
Pirce, Ganer I, 967
Pirce, James I, 967
Pirce, John I, 967
Pirce, Samuel I, 967
Pirce, Thomas I, 967
Pirkins, Abijah V, 197
Pirkins, Ann I, 512
Pirkins, Anna I, 413
Pirkins, Asenath C. I, 311
Pirkins, Asenath C. I, 316
Pirkins, Bety I, 512
Pirkins, Caleb I, 512
Pirkins, Hannah I, 607
Pirkins, Hillary W. I, 311
Pirkins, Hillary W. I, 316
Pirkins, Isaac V, 197
Pirkins, Jared I, 512
Pirkins, John I, 316
Pirkins, John I, 512
Pirkins, John B. I, 330
Pirkins, John K. V, 197

kins, John Kelly V, 197
kins, Joseph I, 512
kins, Joseph II, 407
rkins, Joseph V, 197
rkins, Mary I, 512
rkins, Mary Ann V, 197
kins, Moses I, 316
rkins, Pheninah V, 197
rkins, Sarah I, 512
rkins, Sarah II, 407
rkins, Sarah V, 197
rkins, Thomas I, 512
rkins, Thomas V, 197
rstey, Solomon VI, 291
rvis, Moses I, 256
sley, Deborah Ann II, 828
storias, Sarah II, 581
tcairn, Emma C. III, 255
tcairn, Martha III, 255
tcairn, Mary III, 255
tcairn, Robert III, 255
tcairn, Robert Brower III, 255
itcher, Abigail V, 524
tcher, Abigail V, 535
itcher, Hugh B. III, 252
itcher, Hugh B. III, 255
itcher, Sarah S. III, 252
itcher, Sarah S. III, 255
itchford, Ann VI, 177
itchford, Ann VI, 203
itchford, Frances VI, 177
itchford, Frances VI, 203
itchford, Samuel VI, 177
itchford, Samuel VI, 203
itcock, Ellen II, 152
itcock, Ellen II, 155
ites, Thomas II, 407
itfield, Ann II, 1058
itfield, Ann B. II, 1058
itfield, Ann E. II, 250
itfield, Ann Eliza II, 953
itfield, Ann Eliza II, 954
itfield, Ann Eliza II, 955
Pitfield, Ann Eliza II, 1058
Pitfield, Ann Elizabeth II, 250
Pitfield, Benjamin II, 525
Pitfield, Benjamin II, 623
Pitfield, Elizabeth II, 180
Pitfield, Elizabeth II, 250
Pitfield, Elizabeth II, 525
Pitfield, Elizabeth II, 623
Pitfield, Elizabeth II, 715
Pitfield, Elizabeth II, 955
Pitfield, Elizabeth II, 1058
Pitfield, Grace II, 407
Pitfield, Grace II, 525
Pitfield, Grace II, 623
Pitfield, Grace II, 1012
Pitfield, Grace II, 1021
Pitfield, Rebecca II, 180
Pitfield, Rebecca II, 250
Pitfield, Robert II, 180
Pitfield, Robert II, 623
Pitfield, Robert II, 955
Pitfield, Robert L. II, 250
Pitfield, Robert L. II, 623
Pitfield, Robert L. II, 715
Pitfield, Robert L. II, 1058
Pitfield, Robert Lucas II, 250
Pitfield, Robert Lucas II, 525
Pitfield, Robert Lucas II, 623
Pitfield, William II, 250
Pitfield, Wm. F. II, 1058
Pitman, Aaron II, 1058
Pitman, Aaron IV, 348
Pitman, Aaron IV, 430
Pitman, Abel II, 180
Pitman, Abel II, 250
Pitman, Abia I, 226
Pitman, Abigail II, 180
Pitman, Abigail II, 250
Pitman, Abigail B. II, 250
Pitman, Amy I, 226
Pitman, Ann IV, 157
Pitman, Ann IV, 348
Pitman, Ann IV, 430
Pitman, Anthony IV, 157
Pitman, Anthony IV, 264
Pitman, Anthony IV, 348
Pitman, Anthony IV, 354
Pitman, Anthony IV, 430
Pitman, Anthony IV, 1179
Pitman, Anthony IV, 1180
Pitman, Anthony V, 111
Pitman, Beulah IV, 157
Pitman, Beulah IV, 1175
Pitman, Beulah IV, 1179
Pitman, Beulah IV, 1180
Pitman, Bula IV, 430
Pitman, Bulah IV, 348
Pitman, Caleb III, 207
Pitman, Caleb III, 255
Pitman, Catharine II, 250
Pitman, Catherine II, 180
Pitman, Catherine II, 250
Pitman, Daniel II, 180
Pitman, Daniel II, 250
Pitman, Daniel II, 623
Pitman, Delilah I, 513
Pitman, Delilah I, 567
Pitman, Delilah I, 834
Pitman, Elias IV, 157
Pitman, Elias IV, 264
Pitman, Elias IV, 348
Pitman, Elias IV, 430
Pitman, Elias IV, 1179
Pitman, Elias IV, 1180
Pitman, Elias V, 111
Pitman, Eliz III, 283
Pitman, Eliza IV, 157
Pitman, Eliza IV, 264
Pitman, Eliza IV, 348
Pitman, Eliza IV, 1179
Pitman, Eliza IV, 1180
Pitman, Eliza V, 111
Pitman, Elizabeth I, 69
Pitman, Elizabeth I, 226
Pitman, Elizabeth II, 250
Pitman, Elizabeth II, 1021
Pitman, Elizabeth II, 1058
Pitman, Elizabeth III, 207
Pitman, Elizabeth III, 255
Pitman, Elizabeth IV, 106
Pitman, Elizabeth IV, 157
Pitman, Elizabeth IV, 348
Pitman, Elizabeth IV, 351
Pitman, Elizabeth IV, 1175
Pitman, Elizabeth D. III, 207
Pitman, Ephraim II, 250
Pitman, Ephraim II, 623
Pitman, Esther IV, 264
Pitman, Esther IV, 348
Pitman, Esther IV, 430
Pitman, Esther IV, 1179
Pitman, Esther IV, 1180
Pitman, Esther V, 111
Pitman, Faith I, 226
Pitman, Frances II, 324
Pitman, Howard Franklin II, 715
Pitman, James I, 513
Pitman, James I, 567
Pitman, James I, 819
Pitman, James I, 834
Pitman, John IV, 157
Pitman, John IV, 348
Pitman, Joseph I, 69
Pitman, Joseph I, 206
Pitman, Joseph I, 226
Pitman, Joseph I, 256
Pitman, Judith I, 819
Pitman, Judith I, 834
Pitman, Levi II, 250
Pitman, Levi IV, 106
Pitman, Levi IV, 157
Pitman, Levi IV, 348
Pitman, Levi IV, 430
Pitman, Levi IV, 1175
Pitman, Lucy Price II, 715
Pitman, Margaret II, 250
Pitman, Margaret IV, 157
Pitman, Margaret IV, 264
Pitman, Margaret IV, 348
Pitman, Margaret IV, 354
Pitman, Margaret IV, 430
Pitman, Margaret IV, 1179
Pitman, Margaret IV, 1180
Pitman, Margaret V, 111
Pitman, Margaret V. IV, 1179
Pitman, Margaret V. IV, 1180
Pitman, Marion II, 715
Pitman, Mary I, 567
Pitman, Mary I, 806
Pitman, Mary I, 834
Pitman, Mary II, 180
Pitman, Mary II, 250
Pitman, Mary II, 407
Pitman, Mary II, 1021
Pitman, Mary II, 1058
Pitman, Mary II, 1077
Pitman, Mary VI, 978
Pitman, Moses I, 69
Pitman, Patience I, 226
Pitman, Peter B. II, 250
Pitman, Peter Barker II, 180
Pitman, Rebecca IV, 264
Pitman, Rebecca IV, 348
Pitman, Rebecca IV, 430
Pitman, Rebecca IV, 1179
Pitman, Rebecca IV, 1180
Pitman, Rebecca V, 111
Pitman, Reuben VI, 978
Pitman, Robert I, 567
Pitman, Robert I, 834
Pitman, Robert II, 180
Pitman, Robert II, 250
Pitman, Robert II, 623
Pitman, Robert Asher II, 715
Pitman, Ruth I, 513
Pitman, Ruth I, 567
Pitman, Samuel Emlen II, 180
Pitman, Sarah II, 180
Pitman, Sarah II, 250
Pitman, Thomas I, 226
Pitman, Uriah IV, 157
Pitman, Uriah IV, 348
Pitman, Wd. Catharine II, 180
Pitman, William I, 513
Pitmon, James I, 567
Pitmon, Robert I, 567
Pitner, Rachel I, 1116
Pitner, Rachel I, 1131
Pits, Elizabeth I, 556
Pits, Elizabeth I, 567
Pits, Mary I, 543
Pits, Mary I, 567
Pitser, William V, 355
Pitser, Wm. V, 355
Pitsmyer, Edward V, 355
Pitsmyer, Gulielma V, 355
Pitt, Anna III, 256
Pitt, Anna III, 304
Pitt, Anna III, 305
Pitt, Charlotte III, 256
Pitt, Dorsetshire II, 48
Pitt, Edith II, 48
Pitt, Henry VI, 34
Pitt, John B. III, 256
Pitt, Joseph II, 48
Pitt, Thomas VI, 32
Pitt, Thomas VI, 34
Pitt, Thomas VI, 35
Pitt, William R. III, 256
Pitt, William R. III, 304
Pitt, Wm. R. III, 305
Pittebone, DeForrest L. VI, 1013
Pittfield, Ann II, 1046
Pittfield, Ann Eliza II, 1046
Pittfield, Elizabeth II, 1046
Pittfield, Robert L. II, 623
Pittfield, Robert L. II, 1046
Pittfield, Wm. F. II, 1046
Pittfield, Wm. F. II, 1058
Pittis, Emma VI, 771
Pittis, William VI, 771
Pittman, Aaron IV, 430
Pittman, Abel II, 180
Pittman, Abel II, 234
Pittman, Abigail II, 234
Pittman, Abigail II, 250
Pittman, Abigail B. II, 250
Pittman, Ann IV, 335
Pittman, Ann IV, 348
Pittman, Ann IV, 430
Pittman, Anthony IV, 1179
Pittman, Beulah IV, 1180
Pittman, Bula IV, 430
Pittman, Catherine II, 180
Pittman, Catherine II, 234
Pittman, Daniel II, 623
Pittman, Delilah I, 567
Pittman, Elias IV, 1179
Pittman, Eliza IV, 1179
Pittman, Elizabeth IV, 345
Pittman, Elizabeth IV, 348
Pittman, Ephraim II, 250
Pittman, Esther IV, 1179
Pittman, Frances II, 298
Pittman, James I, 834
Pittman, Judith I, 834
Pittman, Levi IV, 348
Pittman, Margaret II, 250
Pittman, Margaret II, 255
Pittman, Margaret IV, 1179
Pittman, Martha M. II, 298
Pittman, Mary I, 567
Pittman, Mary II, 212
Pittman, Mary II, 250
Pittman, Peggy VI, 921
Pittman, Rebecca IV, 1179
Pittman, Robert I, 834
Pittman, Robert II, 623
Pittman, Samuel Emlen II, 180
Pittman, Sarah II, 250
Pittman, Susan II, 298
Pittman, Wd. Catharine II, 180
Pitts, Abigail I, 932
Pitts, Andrew I, 567
Pitts, Andrew I, 834
Pitts, Avis L. J. I, 317
Pitts, Cadwalader I, 910
Pitts, Cadwallader I, 834
Pitts, Cadwallader I, 907
Pitts, Cadwallader I, 914
Pitts, Charity I, 914
Pitts, Clarkey I, 790
Pitts, Cornelia I, 898
Pitts, Cornelia I, 948
Pitts, Daniel W. I, 790
Pitts, Elihu I, 790
Pitts, Elihu E. I, 834
Pitts, Elizabeth I, 317
Pitts, Elizabeth I, 567
Pitts, Elizabeth I, 572
Pitts, Elizabeth I, 600
Pitts, Elizabeth I, 790
Pitts, Elizabeth I, 833
Pitts, Elizabeth I, 834
Pitts, Elizabeth I, 898
Pitts, Elizabeth I, 907
Pitts, Elizabeth I, 910
Pitts, Elizabeth I, 914
Pitts, G. O. I, 624
Pitts, George I, 995
Pitts, Henry I, 790
Pitts, Isla I, 948
Pitts, Isla Luzena I, 898
Pitts, James I, 790
Pitts, James I, 830
Pitts, James I, 834
Pitts, Jemima I, 790
Pitts, Jesse I, 790
Pitts, John I, 833
Pitts, John I, 834
Pitts, John I, 907
Pitts, John B. I, 790
Pitts, John W. B. I, 317
Pitts, John Wesley I, 898
Pitts, John Wesley I, 932
Pitts, Jonathan I, 790
Pitts, Joseph W. I, 317
Pitts, Leuzena I, 983
Pitts, Louzena I, 995
Pitts, Lucy VI, 847
Pitts, Luzena I, 995
Pitts, Mamie I, 624
Pitts, Martha I, 834
Pitts, Martha IV, 1220
Pitts, Martha J. I, 790
Pitts, Martha J. I, 834
Pitts, Mary I, 567
Pitts, Mary I, 624
Pitts, Mary I, 790
Pitts, Mary E. I, 835
Pitts, Mary E. I, 898
Pitts, Mary E. J. I, 317
Pitts, Rebecca I, 830
Pitts, Rebecca I, 834
Pitts, Rebeka I, 790
Pitts, Ritchie VI, 847
Pitts, Samuel I, 790
Pitts, Samuel I, 932
Pitts, Sarah I, 790
Pitts, Sarah I, 796
Pitts, Sarah I, 814
Pitts, Sarah I, 834
Pitts, Sarah I, 910
Pitts, Sarah I, 914
Pitts, Temperance I, 596
Pitts, William I, 790
Pitts, William I, 834
Pitzer, Albert V, 272
Pitzer, Anna V, 272
Pitzer, Clara V, 272
Pitzer, Ella V, 272
Pitzer, Lizzie V, 272
Pitzer, Mary W. VI, 432
Pitzer, Wm. V, 355
Pixley, Ann III, 256
Pixley, John H. III, 256
Pixley, Thomas III, 256
Place, Aaron Lancaster I, 114
Place, Aaron Lancaster I, 161
Place, Benjamin IV, 1180
Place, Benjamin V, 958
Place, Benjamin E. V, 958
Place, Eliza IV, 1180
Place, Eliza V, 958
Place, Elizabeth V, 958
Place, Hannah E. IV, 1180
Place, Isaac I, 114
Place, Isaac I, 161
Place, Isaac IV, 1180
Place, Isaac V, 958
Place, Isaac I. III, 256
Place, Jain I, 161
Place, Jane I, 114
Place, Jane I, 161
Place, Jane IV, 1180
Place, Jane IV, 1185
Place, Jane V, 958
Place, Jeane I, 161
Place, Joan I, 114
Place, Joseph III, 256
Place, Martha I, 161
Place, Martha V, 958
Place, Martha N. IV, 1185
Place, Mary V, 958
Place, Mary V, 962
Place, Mary Ann III, 256
Place, Maurice I, 161
Place, Maurice IV, 1180
Place, Maurice V, 111
Place, Maurice V, 524
Place, Maurice V, 958
Place, Maurice V, 962
Place, Morris I, 161
Place, Morris IV, 1180
Place, Ruth I, 161
Place, William I, 161
Place, William V, 856
Place, Wm. IV, 1180
Plack, Mary Belle V, 856
Plackett, Mary Griscom II, 155
Pladwell, Sarah II, 623
Pladwell, Sarah II, 628
Plais, Aaron Lancaster V, 111
Plais, Jane V, 111
Plais, Jane C. V, 111
Plais, Morris V, 111
Plank, Mary V, 197
Plank, Mollie M. V, 197
Plank, Nancy V, 197
Plankenhorn, Thomas II, 407
Plankenhorne, John II, 623
Plankett, B. Franklin V, 641
Plankinghorn, Hannah II, 623
Plankinghorn, Hannah II, 677
Plankinghorn, Jane II, 623
Plankinghorn, John II, 623
Plankinghorn, Susanna II, 623
Plankinghorn, Thomas II, 623
Plankinghorn, Thomas H. II, 623
Plankinhorn, Jane II, 407
Plankinhorn, John II, 407
Plankinhorn, Susanna III, 256
Plankinhorn, Thomas II, 407
Plasket, Margaret II, 1013
Plasket, Margaret II, 1021
Plasket, Wm. II, 1021
Plasket, Wm. Plasket II, 1013
Plaskett, Phebe II, 465
Plaskett, Phebe II, 623
Plaster, Susanna VI, 479
Plaster, Susanna VI, 545
Plats, Sarah II, 92
Platt, Benjamin IV, 264
Platt, Benjamin IV, 1180
Platt, Charity III, 114
Platt, Charity III, 256
Platt, Charles S. II, 760
Platt, Charles S. II, 769
Platt, Charlotte III, 433
Platt, Edith II, 760
Platt, Edith II, 769
Platt, Edith S. II, 715
Platt, Eleanor III, 256
Platt, Elizabeth III, 256
Platt, Emma S. III, 256
Platt, Esther Ann III, 256
Platt, George II, 623
Platt, Hannah A. IV, 751
Platt, Hannah A. IV, 779
Platt, Hiram IV, 751
Platt, Hiram IV, 779
Platt, Isadora II, 965
Platt, Isadora Elizabeth II, 700
Platt, Isadora Elizabeth II, 720
Platt, J. Hull III, 256
Platt, Joseph E. II, 715
Platt, Joseph Eyre II, 760
Platt, Joseph Eyre II, 769
Platt, Kezia III, 433
Platt, Kezia III, 466
Platt, Maria Louisa III, 339
Platt, Martha E. II, 760
Platt, Martha E. II, 769
Platt, Mary III, 256
Platt, Richard III, 114
Platt, Richard III, 256
Platt, Sarah IV, 751
Platt, Simeon IV, 751
Platt, William III, 433
Platt, Zopha H. III, 433
Platts, Elizabeth II, 37
Platts, Jane II, 37
Platts, Jane II, 71
Platts, Jane II, 92
Platts, Jean II, 59
Platts, Jean II, 92
Platts, Jonah II, 92
Platts, Jonah II, 102
Platts, Jonathan II, 37
Platts, Jonathan II, 59
Platts, Jonathan II, 92
Platts, Sarah II, 92

Platts, Sarah II, 102
Platts, Thomas II, 37
Platwell, Ann II, 623
Player, Jacob II, 446
Pleadwell, Ann II, 623
Pleadwell, Edward II, 407
Pleadwell, Edward II, 503
Pleadwell, Edward II, 623
Pleadwell, Grace II, 407
Pleadwell, Grace II, 503
Pleadwell, Grace II, 623
Pleadwell, Hannah II, 407
Pleadwell, Sarah II, 407
Pleadwell, Sarah II, 623
Pleas, Aaron V, 111
Pleas, Aaron Lancaster V, 111
Pleas, Achsah I, 928
Pleas, Benjamin IV, 1180
Pleas, Eliza IV, 1180
Pleas, Elizabeth VI, 545
Pleas, Elizabeth VI, 579
Pleas, Hannah IV, 1157
Pleas, Hannah IV, 1180
Pleas, Hannah E. IV, 1180
Pleas, Isaac IV, 1180
Pleas, Isaac V, 111
Pleas, Jane IV, 1180
Pleas, Jane V, 111
Pleas, Jane C. V, 111
Pleas, Lancaster V, 111
Pleas, Mariba Newby V, 111
Pleas, Maurice IV, 1157
Pleas, Maurice IV, 1180
Pleas, Maurice V, 111
Pleas, Morris IV, 1180
Pleas, Morris V, 111
Pleas, William V, 111
Pleas, Wm. IV, 1180
Pleasant, Ann II, 578
Pleasant, Ann II, 623
Pleasant, Anne VI, 183
Pleasant, C. E. IV, 1260
Pleasant, Caleb E. II, 760
Pleasant, Charles II, 578
Pleasant, Charles II, 623
Pleasant, Deborah VI, 781
Pleasant, Elizabeth VI, 545
Pleasant, Elizabeth J. V, 926
Pleasant, Ezra VI, 545
Pleasant, Frances V. II, 578
Pleasant, Frances V. II, 623
Pleasant, Genito VI, 263
Pleasant, George VI, 545
Pleasant, Isabella VI, 847
Pleasant, Israel P. V, 926
Pleasant, Jacob VI, 545
Pleasant, James VI, 184
Pleasant, James VI, 545
Pleasant, Jeremiah VI, 545
Pleasant, John II, 584
Pleasant, John II, 623
Pleasant, John Scott VI, 545
Pleasant, Joseph VI, 545
Pleasant, Margaret VI, 183
Pleasant, Mary II, 527
Pleasant, Mary II, 584
Pleasant, Mary II, 623
Pleasant, Mary Ann VI, 184
Pleasant, Miriam VI, 183
Pleasant, Robert VI, 218
Pleasant, Robert VI, 243
Pleasant, Robert VI, 545
Pleasant, Samuel II, 527
Pleasant, Samuel II, 623
Pleasant, Samuel VI, 847
Pleasant, Sarah II, 527
Pleasant, Sarah II, 623
Pleasant, Sarah VI, 545
Pleasant, Thomas, Jr. VI, 85
Pleasant-Stabler, Mary VI, 472
Pleasants, ??? VI, 262
Pleasants, ??? VI, 263
Pleasants, A. Janney VI, 265
Pleasants, Agnes VI, 178
Pleasants, Agnes VI, 203
Pleasants, Aline VI, 764
Pleasants, Allan A. VI, 764
Pleasants, Ann II, 364
Pleasants, Ann II, 407
Pleasants, Ann II, 516
Pleasants, Ann II, 623
Pleasants, Ann VI, 205
Pleasants, Ann VI, 207
Pleasants, Ann VI, 545
Pleasants, Ann B. II, 623
Pleasants, Ann Hunnicutt VI, 206
Pleasants, Ann Josephine VI, 263
Pleasants, Ann Josephine VI, 265
Pleasants, Ann P. II, 623
Pleasants, Ann Thomas VI, 203
Pleasants, Anna VI, 203
Pleasants, Anna VI, 208
Pleasants, Anne VI, 205
Pleasants, Archabald VI, 263
Pleasants, Archable VI, 263
Pleasants, Arthanahious Barnett VI, 264
Pleasants, Asa Jenney VI, 265
Pleasants, Bazil VI, 432
Pleasants, Bazile VI, 432
Pleasants, Beaver VI, 264
Pleasants, Belle VI, 237
Pleasants, Benjamin VI, 263
Pleasants, Benjamin B. VI, 263
Pleasants, Caleb E. II, 407
Pleasants, Caleb E. II, 760
Pleasants, Caleb Emlen II, 623
Pleasants, Cary VI, 207
Pleasants, Cary VI, 264
Pleasants, Cassandra VI, 545
Pleasants, Catharine III, 159
Pleasants, Charles II, 407
Pleasants, Charles II, 516
Pleasants, Charles II, 623
Pleasants, Charles VI, 206
Pleasants, Charles VI, 207
Pleasants, Charles VI, 208
Pleasants, Charles Emlen II, 407
Pleasants, Charles Emlen II, 623
Pleasants, Charles P. VI, 208
Pleasants, Charles Pemberton II, 760
Pleasants, Charles Thomas VI, 264
Pleasants, Charley Forest VI, 263
Pleasants, Clementina VI, 207
Pleasants, Deborah VI, 196
Pleasants, Deborah VI, 208
Pleasants, Deborah VI, 264
Pleasants, Deborah VI, 267
Pleasants, Deborah VI, 545
Pleasants, Deborah VI, 564
Pleasants, Deborah VI, 771
Pleasants, Deborah VI, 780
Pleasants, Deborah VI, 783
Pleasants, Deborah Stabler VI, 18
Pleasants, Dillwyn VI, 263
Pleasants, Dorothea VI, 205
Pleasants, Dorothy VI, 148
Pleasants, Dorothy VI, 188
Pleasants, Dorothy VI, 203
Pleasants, Dorothy VI, 204
Pleasants, Dorothy VI, 206
Pleasants, Dorothy VI, 207
Pleasants, Dr. Samuel, Jr. II, 407
Pleasants, Edward VI, 229
Pleasants, Edward S. VI, 263
Pleasants, Eliza II, 623
Pleasants, Eliza VI, 200
Pleasants, Eliza VI, 203
Pleasants, Eliza VI, 207
Pleasants, Eliza VI, 208
Pleasants, Eliza VI, 237
Pleasants, Eliza VI, 263
Pleasants, Eliza VI, 265
Pleasants, Eliza VI, 662
Pleasants, Eliza VI, 753
Pleasants, Eliza A. VI, 208
Pleasants, Eliza J. VI, 265
Pleasants, Eliza J. VI, 266
Pleasants, Eliza R. II, 623
Pleasants, Eliza R. VI, 264
Pleasants, Elizabeth II, 407
Pleasants, Elizabeth VI, 18
Pleasants, Elizabeth VI, 46
Pleasants, Elizabeth VI, 194
Pleasants, Elizabeth VI, 196
Pleasants, Elizabeth VI, 203
Pleasants, Elizabeth VI, 204
Pleasants, Elizabeth VI, 205
Pleasants, Elizabeth VI, 206
Pleasants, Elizabeth VI, 207
Pleasants, Elizabeth VI, 219
Pleasants, Elizabeth VI, 231
Pleasants, Elizabeth VI, 262
Pleasants, Elizabeth VI, 263
Pleasants, Elizabeth VI, 264
Pleasants, Elizabeth VI, 267
Pleasants, Elizabeth VI, 545
Pleasants, Elizabeth VI, 564
Pleasants, Elizabeth VI, 587
Pleasants, Elizabeth VI, 771
Pleasants, Elizabeth VI, 781
Pleasants, Elizabeth VI, 783
Pleasants, Elizabeth Elmore VI, 264
Pleasants, Elizabeth R. II, 623
Pleasants, Elizabeth Snowden VI, 262
Pleasants, Elizabeth T. VI, 202
Pleasants, Elizabeth T. VI, 208
Pleasants, Elizabeth T. VI, 221
Pleasants, Elizabeth T. VI, 264
Pleasants, Elizabeth, Jr. VI, 207
Pleasants, Esther D. II, 737
Pleasants, Esther D. II, 760
Pleasants, Fitz Henry VI, 207
Pleasants, Fitz Henry VI, 208
Pleasants, Frances II, 407
Pleasants, Frances III, 204
Pleasants, Frances V. II, 623
Pleasants, Francis Vant III, 126
Pleasants, Genito VI, 263
Pleasants, Genito VI, 264
Pleasants, George II, 407
Pleasants, George VI, 203
Pleasants, George VI, 263
Pleasants, George VI, 545
Pleasants, George D. VI, 265
Pleasants, George E. II, 623
Pleasants, Hannah II, 623
Pleasants, Henrico VI, 203
Pleasants, Henrico VI, 204
Pleasants, Henrico VI, 207
Pleasants, Henrietta M. VI, 264
Pleasants, Henrietta Maria VI, 228
Pleasants, Henry VI, 18
Pleasants, Henry VI, 263
Pleasants, Henry A. VI, 265
Pleasants, Henry Abijah VI, 263
Pleasants, Isaac VI, 263
Pleasants, Israel II, 407
Pleasants, Israel II, 623
Pleasants, Israel P. II, 760
Pleasants, Israel Pemberton II, 623
Pleasants, Jacob VI, 203
Pleasants, Jacob VI, 262
Pleasants, Jacob VI, 529
Pleasants, James II, 407
Pleasants, James II, 623
Pleasants, James VI, 203
Pleasants, James VI, 207
Pleasants, James VI, 208
Pleasants, James VI, 263
Pleasants, James A. VI, 208
Pleasants, James B. VI, 264
Pleasants, James Brooks VI, 264
Pleasants, James G. Whitlock VI, 265
Pleasants, Jane VI, 18
Pleasants, Jane VI, 148
Pleasants, Jane VI, 149
Pleasants, Jane VI, 204
Pleasants, Jane VI, 207
Pleasants, Jane VI, 264
Pleasants, Jesse Stanley VI, 265
Pleasants, Jessie VI, 206
Pleasants, John II, 407
Pleasants, John II, 619
Pleasants, John II, 623
Pleasants, John VI, 8
Pleasants, John VI, 17
Pleasants, John VI, 18
Pleasants, John VI, 46
Pleasants, John VI, 111
Pleasants, John VI, 118
Pleasants, John VI, 145
Pleasants, John VI, 146
Pleasants, John VI, 147
Pleasants, John VI, 148
Pleasants, John VI, 149
Pleasants, John VI, 172
Pleasants, John VI, 178
Pleasants, John VI, 184
Pleasants, John VI, 188
Pleasants, John VI, 196
Pleasants, John VI, 203
Pleasants, John VI, 204
Pleasants, John VI, 205
Pleasants, John VI, 207
Pleasants, John VI, 208
Pleasants, John VI, 214
Pleasants, John VI, 219
Pleasants, John VI, 220
Pleasants, John VI, 263
Pleasants, John B. Crenshaw VI, 265
Pleasants, John Barnett VI, 263
Pleasants, John S. VI, 203
Pleasants, John S. VI, 208
Pleasants, John S. VI, 264
Pleasants, John Scott VI, 264
Pleasants, John Scott VI, 529
Pleasants, John Thomas VI, 263
Pleasants, John, Jr. VI, 164
Pleasants, John, Jr. VI, 203
Pleasants, John, Jr. VI, 205
Pleasants, John, Jr. VI, 206
Pleasants, John, Jr. VI, 207
Pleasants, John, Jr. VI, 263
Pleasants, John, Senior VI, 203
Pleasants, John, Senior VI, 205
Pleasants, John, Sr. VI, 161
Pleasants, John, Sr. VI, 206
Pleasants, Jordan VI, 207
Pleasants, Joseph II, 407
Pleasants, Joseph II, 623
Pleasants, Joseph VI, 8
Pleasants, Joseph VI, 18
Pleasants, Joseph VI, 148
Pleasants, Joseph VI, 154
Pleasants, Joseph VI, 185
Pleasants, Joseph VI, 188
Pleasants, Joseph VI, 203
Pleasants, Joseph VI, 204
Pleasants, Joseph VI, 207
Pleasants, Joseph VI, 211
Pleasants, Joseph VI, 212
Pleasants, Joseph VI, 218
Pleasants, Joseph VI, 219
Pleasants, Joseph VI, 229
Pleasants, Joseph VI, 265
Pleasants, Joseph J. VI, 208
Pleasants, Joseph J. VI, 229
Pleasants, Joseph Jordan VI, 263
Pleasants, Joseph, Jr. VI, 204
Pleasants, Josephine V. VI, 764
Pleasants, Josiah VI, 206
Pleasants, Julia M. VI, 265
Pleasants, Julia Maria VI, 263
Pleasants, Julia W. Winston VI, 265
Pleasants, Keziah VI, 545
Pleasants, Laura II, 760
Pleasants, Lydia VI, 188
Pleasants, Lydia VI, 203
Pleasants, Lydia VI, 205
Pleasants, Lydia Alice VI, 263
Pleasants, M. Belle VI, 265
Pleasants, Margaret VI, 17
Pleasants, Margaret VI, 18
Pleasants, Margaret VI, 184
Pleasants, Margaret VI, 203
Pleasants, Margaret VI, 204
Pleasants, Margaret VI, 206
Pleasants, Margaret VI, 208
Pleasants, Margaret VI, 263
Pleasants, Margaret VI, 516
Pleasants, Margaret VI, 735
Pleasants, Margaret Ann VI, 263
Pleasants, Margaret Iaabella VI, 263
Pleasants, Margret VI, 18
Pleasants, Martha VI, 148
Pleasants, Martha VI, 158
Pleasants, Martha VI, 203
Pleasants, Martha VI, 204
Pleasants, Martha VI, 215
Pleasants, Martha VI, 229
Pleasants, Martha VI, 263
Pleasants, Martha VI, 265
Pleasants, Martha Belle VI, 265
Pleasants, Martha Ellen VI, 263
Pleasants, Martha Isabella VI, 237
Pleasants, Martha Isabella VI, 263
Pleasants, Martha R. II, 760
Pleasants, Mary II, 364
Pleasants, Mary II, 407
Pleasants, Mary II, 516
Pleasants, Mary II, 588
Pleasants, Mary II, 604
Pleasants, Mary II, 619
Pleasants, Mary II, 623
Pleasants, Mary II, 760
Pleasants, Mary VI, 18
Pleasants, Mary VI, 178
Pleasants, Mary VI, 179
Pleasants, Mary VI, 190
Pleasants, Mary VI, 194
Pleasants, Mary VI, 199
Pleasants, Mary VI, 203
Pleasants, Mary VI, 204
Pleasants, Mary VI, 205
Pleasants, Mary VI, 207
Pleasants, Mary VI, 208
Pleasants, Mary VI, 218
Pleasants, Mary VI, 219
Pleasants, Mary VI, 244
Pleasants, Mary VI, 263
Pleasants, Mary VI, 264
Pleasants, Mary VI, 267
Pleasants, Mary VI, 268
Pleasants, Mary VI, 545
Pleasants, Mary VI, 564
Pleasants, Mary VI, 587
Pleasants, Mary VI, 731
Pleasants, Mary VI, 771
Pleasants, Mary VI, 780
Pleasants, Mary VI, 781
Pleasants, Mary VI, 782
Pleasants, Mary C. III, 159
Pleasants, Mary S. VI, 265
Pleasants, Mary Snowden VI, 263
Pleasants, Mary, Jr. VI, 207
Pleasants, Mary, Junior VI, 205
Pleasants, Mary, Senior VI, 205
Pleasants, Mary, Sr. VI, 206
Pleasants, Matthew VI, 207
Pleasants, Meriam VI, 206
Pleasants, Micajah VI, 263
Pleasants, Mildred VI, 189
Pleasants, Miriam VI, 111
Pleasants, Miriam VI, 118
Pleasants, Miriam VI, 206
Pleasants, Miriam VI, 263
Pleasants, Miriam VI, 264
Pleasants, Miriam VI, 545
Pleasants, Miriam Margaret VI, 206
Pleasants, Moses VI, 545
Pleasants, Mr. ??? VI, 145
Pleasants, Nathaniel B. Crenshaw VI, 265
Pleasants, Pemberton II, 623
Pleasants, Phebe R. VI, 432
Pleasants, Phillip VI, 207
Pleasants, Phoebe VI, 208
Pleasants, Richard VI, 204
Pleasants, Richmond VI, 263
Pleasants, Robert II, 407
Pleasants, Robert II, 623
Pleasants, Robert VI, 17
Pleasants, Robert VI, 18
Pleasants, Robert VI, 87
Pleasants, Robert VI, 150
Pleasants, Robert VI, 163
Pleasants, Robert VI, 184
Pleasants, Robert VI, 193
Pleasants, Robert VI, 199
Pleasants, Robert VI, 204
Pleasants, Robert VI, 205
Pleasants, Robert VI, 207
Pleasants, Robert VI, 208
Pleasants, Robert VI, 215
Pleasants, Robert VI, 220
Pleasants, Robert VI, 221
Pleasants, Robert VI, 264
Pleasants, Robert VI, 291
Pleasants, Robert VI, 516
Pleasants, Robert, Jr. VI, 203
Pleasants, Robert, Jr. VI, 205
Pleasants, Robert, Jr. VI, 206
Pleasants, Robert, Jr. VI, 207
Pleasants, Robert, Jr. VI, 263
Pleasants, Robert, Sr. VI, 205
Pleasants, Robert, Sr. VI, 206
Pleasants, Robt. VI, 193
Pleasants, Ruth VI, 545
Pleasants, Sally VI, 208
Pleasants, Samuel II, 407
Pleasants, Samuel II, 516
Pleasants, Samuel II, 619
Pleasants, Samuel II, 623
Pleasants, Samuel VI, 194
Pleasants, Samuel VI, 206
Pleasants, Samuel VI, 207
Pleasants, Samuel VI, 208
Pleasants, Samuel Parsons VI, 264
Pleasants, Samuel, Jr. II, 623
Pleasants, Samuel, Jr. VI, 263
Pleasants, Samuel, Jr. VI, 545
Pleasants, Sarah II, 407
Pleasants, Sarah II, 623
Pleasants, Sarah VI, 18
Pleasants, Sarah VI, 164
Pleasants, Sarah VI, 201
Pleasants, Sarah VI, 202
Pleasants, Sarah VI, 203
Pleasants, Sarah VI, 206
Pleasants, Sarah VI, 207
Pleasants, Sarah VI, 208
Pleasants, Sarah VI, 262
Pleasants, Sarah VI, 263
Pleasants, Sarah VI, 264
Pleasants, Sarah VI, 529
Pleasants, Sarah VI, 545
Pleasants, Sarah L. VI, 203
Pleasants, Sarah L. VI, 208
Pleasants, Sarah Lownes VI, 264
Pleasants, Sophia VI, 207
Pleasants, Susanna VI, 172
Pleasants, Susanna VI, 203
Pleasants, Susanna VI, 206
Pleasants, Susanna VI, 207
Pleasants, Susanna VI, 214
Pleasants, Susannah VI, 204

easants, Susannah VI, 219
easants, Susannah VI, 262
easants, Tabitha VI, 240
easants, Tace VI, 229
easants, Tace VI, 263
easants, Tacy E. VI, 229
easants, Tacy E. VI, 263
easants, Talitha VI, 263
easants, Tallitha VI, 238
easants, Talrton W. VI, 263
easants, Tarlton VI, 207
easants, Tarlton VI, 238
easants, Tarlton VI, 240
easants, Tarlton W. VI, 18
easants, Tarlton W. VI, 208
easants, Tarlton W. VI, 238
easants, Tarlton W. VI, 264
easants, Tarlton W., Jr. VI, 208
easants, Thomas II, 623
easants, Thomas VI, 17
easants, Thomas VI, 18
easants, Thomas VI, 149
easants, Thomas VI, 161
easants, Thomas VI, 177
easants, Thomas VI, 184
easants, Thomas VI, 188
easants, Thomas VI, 189
easants, Thomas VI, 203
easants, Thomas VI, 204
easants, Thomas VI, 205
easants, Thomas VI, 206
easants, Thomas VI, 207
easants, Thomas VI, 216
easants, Thomas VI, 228
easants, Thomas VI, 262
easants, Thomas VI, 263
easants, Thomas VI, 267
easants, Thomas VI, 276
easants, Thomas VI, 564
easants, Thomas VI, 587
easants, Thomas VI, 771
easants, Thomas VI, 781
easants, Thomas VI, 783
easants, Thomas E. VI, 264
leasants, Thomas Exum VI, 264
easants, Thomas F. II, 623
leasants, Thomas Franklin II, 623
leasants, Thomas S. VI, 264
leasants, Thomas Snowden VI, 262
leasants, Thomas Snowden VI, 263
leasants, Thomas Snowden VI, 276
leasants, Thomas, Jr. VI, 78
leasants, Thomas, Jr. VI, 87
leasants, Thomas, Jr. VI, 203
leasants, Thomas, Jr. VI, 206
leasants, Thomas, Sr. VI, 262
leasants, Thomas, Sr. VI, 263
leasants, Thomax VI, 771
leasants, Thos. VI, 209
leasants, Thos. VI, 263
leasants, Tomas VI, 545
leasants, Ursula VI, 172
leasants, Ursula VI, 203
leasants, Ursula VI, 206
leasants, Ursula VI, 207
leasants, Walter A. Ricks VI, 265
leasants, Walter F. II, 623
leasants, Walter F. VI, 265
leasants, Walter Frederick VI, 263
leasants, Wd. Dorothy VI, 204
leasants, Wd. Mrs. Jane VI, 146
leasants, Widow Jane VI, 147
leasants, Wiliam VI, 263
leasants, William H. VI, 18
leasants, William H. VI, 190
leasants, William H. VI, 194
leasants, William H. VI, 208
leasants, William H. VI, 237
leasants, William H. VI, 263
leasants, William H. VI, 264
leasants, William H. VI, 265
leasants, William H. VI, 432
leasants, William Henry VI, 203
leasants, William Henry VI, 263
leasants, William Henry VI, 264
leasants, William Henry VI, 265
leasants, William Henry VI, 272
leasants, William Henry VI, 432
leasants, William Henry VI, 662
leasants, Willing VI, 263
leasants, Wm. C. III, 159
leasants, Wm. H. VI, 263
leasants, Wm. Henry VI, 753
lease, Isaac I, 161
lease, Margret IV, 752
Pledger, Elizabeth II, 37
Pledger, Hannah II, 61
Pledger, Hannah II, 92
Pledger, Hannah II, 104
Pledger, John II, 37
Pledger, John II, 61
Pledger, John II, 92
Pledger, John, Jr. II, 82
Pledger, John, Jr. II, 92
Pledger, Joseph II, 37
Pledger, Joseph II, 81
Pledger, Joseph II, 92
Pledger, Mary II, 81
Pledger, Mary II, 82
Pledger, Mary II, 92
Pledgitt, Eliza Ann VI, 894
Pledwell, Ann II, 407
Pledwell, Edward II, 407
Pledwell, Grace II, 407
Pledwell, Hannah II, 407
Pledwell, Sarah II, 407
Ploger, Emma IV, 1180
Ploger, Emma J. IV, 1180
Ploger, Emma Ploger Sutmiller IV, 1180
Ploger, Jehu H. IV, 1180
Ploger, John Francis IV, 1180
Plott, Dr. J. Hull III, 154
Plott, Emma S. III, 154
Plotts, Anna M. II, 709
Plotts, Anna M. II, 715
Plotts, Anna M. II, 760
Plotts, Dwight II, 715
Plotts, Dwight II, 760
Plotts, Edith Augusta II, 715
Plotts, George F. II, 709
Plotts, George F. II, 715
Plotts, Grace II, 709
Plotts, Grace Greenwood II, 715
Plotts, Grace Greenwood II, 760
Plotts, Mildred Margaret II, 715
Plotts, Mildred Margaret II, 760
Plotts, Thelma Margaret II, 709
Plow, Charity IV, 1240
Plow, Samuel IV, 1240
Plowman, Magnes II, 561
Plowman, Magnes II, 624
Plowman, Margaret II, 624
Plowman, Margaret II, 760
Plowman, Sarah II, 561
Plowman, Sarah II, 624
Plowman, Thomas II, 624
Plowman, Thomas L. II, 760
Plumber, Eleanor VI, 546
Plumber, Richard VI, 546
Plumber, Samuel VI, 546
Plumber, Sarah VI, 546
Plumber, Thomas VI, 546
Plumbley, Charles IV, 1220
Plumer, Alice IV, 348
Plumer, Eli IV, 431
Plumer, Elizabeth II, 92
Plumer, Elizabeth IV, 426
Plumer, Ezra V, 111
Plumer, Greenberry G. IV, 157
Plumer, Joseph IV, 264
Plumer, Mahala V, 68
Plumer, Mahala V, 111
Plumer, Mary IV, 264
Plumer, Rachel IV, 426
Plumer, Robert IV, 426
Plumer, Tacy V, 111
Plumley, Ann II, 1020
Plumley, Ann II, 1021
Plumley, Anna IV, 430
Plumley, Anna IV, 454
Plumley, Anna IV, 1220
Plumley, B. Rush II, 911
Plumley, Charles IV, 1220
Plumley, Clarkson IV, 430
Plumley, Elizabeth IV, 1112
Plumley, Elizabeth IV, 1120
Plumley, Hannah IV, 577
Plumley, Hannah IV, 592
Plumley, Jacob N. IV, 430
Plumley, John L. II, 911
Plumley, Jonathan S. IV, 430
Plumley, M. W. IV, 1220
Plumley, M. Wilson II, 911
Plumley, Margaret C. II, 911
Plumley, Mary Ann IV, 430
Plumley, Peasley IV, 430
Plumley, Rebecca II, 911
Plumley, Rebecca IV, 430
Plumley, Rebecca IV, 1112
Plumley, Rebecca IV, 1117
Plumley, Ruthanna IV, 336
Plumley, Ruthanna IV, 348
Plumley, William D. IV, 430
Plumly, Anna IV, 1220
Plumly, B. Rush II, 815
Plumly, B. Rush II, 911
Plumly, Charles IV, 1220
Plumly, John L. II, 911
Plumly, John Longshore II, 815
Plumly, M. W. IV, 1220
Plumly, M. Wilson II, 911
Plumly, Margaret C. II, 911
Plumly, Margaret P. II, 831
Plumly, Margaret P. II, 911
Plumly, Rebecca II, 815
Plumly, Rebecca II, 911
Plummer, Aaron VI, 545
Plummer, Aaron VI, 690
Plummer, Abigail III, 433
Plummer, Abigail III, 492
Plummer, Abigail P. III, 351
Plummer, Abraham IV, 157
Plummer, Abraham IV, 431
Plummer, Abraham IV, 1074
Plummer, Abraham IV, 1112
Plummer, Abram IV, 264
Plummer, Abram IV, 375
Plummer, Abram IV, 381
Plummer, Abram IV, 430
Plummer, Abram IV, 431
Plummer, Abram IV, 445
Plummer, Abram IV, 1101
Plummer, Abram IV, 1112
Plummer, Abram IV, 1122
Plummer, Achsah VI, 505
Plummer, Albert III, 492
Plummer, Alfred A. IV, 431
Plummer, Alice IV, 157
Plummer, Alice IV, 264
Plummer, Alice IV, 348
Plummer, Alice IV, 360
Plummer, Alice IV, 491
Plummer, Alice IV, 492
Plummer, Amos IV, 1112
Plummer, Amos VI, 546
Plummer, Amos P. IV, 492
Plummer, Angelina IV, 431
Plummer, Angeline IV, 1102
Plummer, Angeline IV, 1112
Plummer, Anjaline IV, 430
Plummer, Ann IV, 106
Plummer, Ann IV, 157
Plummer, Ann IV, 159
Plummer, Ann IV, 431
Plummer, Ann IV, 492
Plummer, Ann IV, 1074
Plummer, Ann VI, 518
Plummer, Ann VI, 519
Plummer, Ann VI, 541
Plummer, Ann VI, 558
Plummer, Ann VI, 569
Plummer, Ann VI, 570
Plummer, Ann VI, 645
Plummer, Ann VI, 661
Plummer, Ann VI, 663
Plummer, Ann VI, 665
Plummer, Ann VI, 667
Plummer, Ann VI, 674
Plummer, Ann VI, 676
Plummer, Ann VI, 755
Plummer, Anna VI, 336
Plummer, Anna VI, 519
Plummer, Anna VI, 545
Plummer, Anna VI, 663
Plummer, Anna VI, 671
Plummer, Anna VI, 709
Plummer, Anna VI, 785
Plummer, Anna D. IV, 431
Plummer, Anne VI, 756
Plummer, Anthony VI, 546
Plummer, Asa V, 60
Plummer, Asa V, 200
Plummer, Asa V, 272
Plummer, Asa VI, 300
Plummer, Asa VI, 336
Plummer, Asa VI, 337
Plummer, Axum IV, 1112
Plummer, Benj. IV, 1333
Plummer, Benjamin IV, 1333
Plummer, Benjamin L. IV, 492
Plummer, Caleb IV, 264
Plummer, Caleb IV, 431
Plummer, Caleb IV, 492
Plummer, Caspar IV, 1074
Plummer, Caspar IV, 1112
Plummer, Caspar M. IV, 1112
Plummer, Casper IV, 431
Plummer, Cassandra VI, 468
Plummer, Cassandra VI, 562
Plummer, Chas. V, 641
Plummer, Clarence V, 1014
Plummer, Clarence O. IV, 431
Plummer, David V, 641
Plummer, David N. III, 492
Plummer, Deborah IV, 264
Plummer, Deborah IV, 431
Plummer, Deborah IV, 492
Plummer, Deborah IV, 592
Plummer, Deborah IV, 1112
Plummer, Deborah IV, 1122
Plummer, Deborah VI, 336
Plummer, Deborah Jane IV, 1059
Plummer, Deborah Jane IV, 1074
Plummer, Deborah Talitha IV, 430
Plummer, Dinah IV, 148
Plummer, Dinah IV, 157
Plummer, Edward D. IV, 431
Plummer, Elanor VI, 575
Plummer, Eleanor II, 160
Plummer, Eleanor IV, 157
Plummer, Eleanor VI, 548
Plummer, Elenor IV, 347
Plummer, Elenor IV, 348
Plummer, Eli IV, 360
Plummer, Eli IV, 431
Plummer, Eli V, 272
Plummer, Eli VI, 336
Plummer, Eli VI, 337
Plummer, Elinor VI, 548
Plummer, Elizabeth II, 92
Plummer, Elizabeth III, 433
Plummer, Elizabeth III, 481
Plummer, Elizabeth III, 492
Plummer, Elizabeth IV, 106
Plummer, Elizabeth IV, 157
Plummer, Elizabeth IV, 264
Plummer, Elizabeth IV, 430
Plummer, Elizabeth IV, 431
Plummer, Elizabeth IV, 441
Plummer, Elizabeth IV, 442
Plummer, Elizabeth IV, 445
Plummer, Elizabeth IV, 592
Plummer, Elizabeth IV, 715
Plummer, Elizabeth IV, 1074
Plummer, Elizabeth IV, 1101
Plummer, Elizabeth IV, 1112
Plummer, Elizabeth IV, 1122
Plummer, Elizabeth V, 22
Plummer, Elizabeth V, 111
Plummer, Elizabeth VI, 484
Plummer, Elizabeth VI, 494
Plummer, Elizabeth VI, 495
Plummer, Elizabeth VI, 502
Plummer, Elizabeth VI, 519
Plummer, Elizabeth VI, 520
Plummer, Elizabeth VI, 641
Plummer, Elizabeth VI, 661
Plummer, Elizabeth VI, 744
Plummer, Elizabeth P. IV, 430
Plummer, Ellen VI, 548
Plummer, Ellen VI, 575
Plummer, Emily V, 200
Plummer, Emily V, 272
Plummer, Emily N. V, 197
Plummer, Enoch III, 407
Plummer, Enoch III, 433
Plummer, Enoch III, 492
Plummer, Evaline C. IV, 431
Plummer, Evalyn C. IV, 375
Plummer, Evalyn C. IV, 431
Plummer, Exum IV, 430
Plummer, Exum IV, 431
Plummer, Exum IV, 592
Plummer, Exum IV, 1112
Plummer, Ezra V, 111
Plummer, Ezra V, 272
Plummer, Ezra VI, 336
Plummer, Ezra VI, 337
Plummer, Ezra VI, 690
Plummer, Flora A. I, 898
Plummer, Flossie V, 1014
Plummer, Gerard VI, 771
Plummer, Gerard, Jr. VI, 771
Plummer, Grace V, 60
Plummer, Grace V, 111
Plummer, Grace V, 200
Plummer, Grace V, 272
Plummer, Grace VI, 300
Plummer, Grace VI, 336
Plummer, Grace VI, 337
Plummer, Grace VI, 546
Plummer, Granville IV, 1074
Plummer, Granville W. IV, 1074
Plummer, Greenberry IV, 1112
Plummer, Greenberry G. IV, 157
Plummer, Greenberry G. IV, 264
Plummer, Hammah W. IV, 411
Plummer, Hannah II, 708
Plummer, Hannah IV, 264
Plummer, Hannah IV, 412
Plummer, Hannah IV, 431
Plummer, Hannah W. IV, 431
Plummer, Herbert IV, 431
Plummer, Herbert E. IV, 431
Plummer, Herbert W. IV, 431
Plummer, I. S. IV, 264
Plummer, Ida IV, 431
Plummer, Ira IV, 1074
Plummer, Isaac IV, 1112
Plummer, Isaac VI, 546
Plummer, Isaac VI, 548
Plummer, Israel Ann VI, 536
Plummer, J. L. IV, 492
Plummer, Jacob VI, 545
Plummer, James IV, 157
Plummer, James IV, 360
Plummer, Jane IV, 157
Plummer, Jane IV, 264
Plummer, Jane IV, 365
Plummer, Jane IV, 386
Plummer, Jane IV, 393
Plummer, Jane IV, 411
Plummer, Jane IV, 431
Plummer, Jane IV, 441
Plummer, Jane IV, 707
Plummer, Jane M. IV, 157
Plummer, Jane M. IV, 264
Plummer, Jane M. V, 111
Plummer, Janney VI, 545
Plummer, Jesse V, 272
Plummer, Jesse VI, 336
Plummer, Jesse VI, 337
Plummer, Jesse VI, 546
Plummer, Jesse VI, 548
Plummer, Joannah H. V, 926
Plummer, Joanora V, 926
Plummer, John III, 351
Plummer, John III, 481
Plummer, John III, 492
Plummer, John III, 494
Plummer, John III, 500
Plummer, John IV, 157
Plummer, John IV, 264
Plummer, John IV, 390
Plummer, John IV, 426
Plummer, John IV, 428
Plummer, John IV, 430
Plummer, John IV, 431
Plummer, John IV, 491
Plummer, John IV, 592
Plummer, John IV, 1074
Plummer, John IV, 1112
Plummer, John IV, 1122
Plummer, John D. IV, 431
Plummer, John F. V, 926
Plummer, John Franklin I, 898
Plummer, John J. III, 492
Plummer, John T. V, 926
Plummer, John, Jr. III, 492
Plummer, Jos. IV, 471
Plummer, Jos. IV, 476
Plummer, Jos. IV, 492
Plummer, Joseph IV, 264
Plummer, Joseph IV, 374
Plummer, Joseph IV, 431
Plummer, Joseph IV, 470
Plummer, Joseph IV, 474
Plummer, Joseph IV, 491
Plummer, Joseph IV, 492
Plummer, Joseph VI, 506
Plummer, Joseph VI, 519
Plummer, Joseph VI, 545
Plummer, Joseph VI, 572
Plummer, Joseph VI, 661
Plummer, Joseph P. V, 926
Plummer, Joseph W. IV, 431
Plummer, Joshua IV, 492
Plummer, Joshua IV, 1074
Plummer, Joshua T. IV, 1074
Plummer, Julia A. IV, 174
Plummer, Julia A. IV, 264
Plummer, Juliann IV, 492
Plummer, Kinsey IV, 1112
Plummer, Leroy IV, 1112
Plummer, Lewis W. IV, 384
Plummer, Lewis W. IV, 431
Plummer, Lidia V, 926
Plummer, Lot V, 272
Plummer, Lott VI, 337
Plummer, Louis W. IV, 431
Plummer, Lydia IV, 264
Plummer, Lydia IV, 431
Plummer, Lydia IV, 492
Plummer, Lydia V, 926
Plummer, Lydia Ann IV, 1062
Plummer, Lydia Ann IV, 1074
Plummer, Lydia W. IV, 492
Plummer, Mahala IV, 492
Plummer, Mahala V, 67
Plummer, Mahala V, 272
Plummer, Mahala V, 573
Plummer, Mahala V, 592
Plummer, Mahale IV, 476
Plummer, Mahale IV, 492
Plummer, Margaret IV, 465
Plummer, Margaret IV, 492
Plummer, Margaret IV, 1074

Plummer, Margaret IV, 1112
Plummer, Margaret B. IV, 1074
Plummer, Mariam IV, 381
Plummer, Mariam IV, 431
Plummer, Marry Susannah VI, 577
Plummer, Martha III, 492
Plummer, Martha III, 494
Plummer, Martha III, 500
Plummer, Martha Ann IV, 374
Plummer, Martha Ann IV, 431
Plummer, Mary III, 454
Plummer, Mary III, 492
Plummer, Mary IV, 264
Plummer, Mary IV, 386
Plummer, Mary IV, 390
Plummer, Mary IV, 431
Plummer, Mary IV, 443
Plummer, Mary IV, 470
Plummer, Mary IV, 474
Plummer, Mary IV, 476
Plummer, Mary IV, 491
Plummer, Mary IV, 492
Plummer, Mary IV, 500
Plummer, Mary IV, 1074
Plummer, Mary IV, 1112
Plummer, Mary V, 641
Plummer, Mary VI, 546
Plummer, Mary VI, 572
Plummer, Mary VI, 574
Plummer, Mary VI, 771
Plummer, Mary Ann IV, 1074
Plummer, Mary Ann IV, 1075
Plummer, Mary Ann IV, 1112
Plummer, Mary Ann VI, 771
Plummer, Mary B. IV, 430
Plummer, Mary B. IV, 592
Plummer, Mary B. IV, 1112
Plummer, Mary E. IV, 1112
Plummer, Mary L. V, 641
Plummer, Mary M. V, 926
Plummer, Mary P. III, 492
Plummer, Mary P. III, 500
Plummer, Mary R. IV, 431
Plummer, Mary S. IV, 471
Plummer, Mary S. IV, 492
Plummer, Mary T. IV, 430
Plummer, Md. John West VI, 572
Plummer, Micajah IV, 264
Plummer, Micajah IV, 431
Plummer, Micajah C. IV, 431
Plummer, Miriam IV, 375
Plummer, Miriam IV, 431
Plummer, Moses IV, 106
Plummer, Nellie IV, 1112
Plummer, Nellie J. IV, 1112
Plummer, Park V, 641
Plummer, Park S. V, 641
Plummer, Pearl V, 1014
Plummer, Phebe IV, 148
Plummer, Phebe IV, 157
Plummer, Phebe IV, 347
Plummer, Philip VI, 771
Plummer, Rachel IV, 157
Plummer, Rachel IV, 264
Plummer, Rachel IV, 328
Plummer, Rachel IV, 348
Plummer, Rachel IV, 390
Plummer, Rachel IV, 426
Plummer, Rachel IV, 428
Plummer, Rachel IV, 430
Plummer, Rachel IV, 431
Plummer, Rachel IV, 443
Plummer, Rachel IV, 592
Plummer, Rachel IV, 1074
Plummer, Rachel IV, 1101
Plummer, Rachel IV, 1112
Plummer, Rachel IV, 1122
Plummer, Rachel VI, 539
Plummer, Rachel VI, 546
Plummer, Rachel A. IV, 1112
Plummer, Rachel E. IV, 393
Plummer, Rachel E. IV, 431
Plummer, Rachel E. IV, 707
Plummer, Rachel E. IV, 771
Plummer, Rachel E. IV, 1071
Plummer, Rachel T. IV, 430
Plummer, Ralph H. IV, 431
Plummer, Ralph N. IV, 431
Plummer, Raymond IV, 431
Plummer, Raymond I. IV, 431
Plummer, Rebecca IV, 54
Plummer, Rebecca IV, 492
Plummer, Rebecca IV, 592
Plummer, Rebecca IV, 1074
Plummer, Rebecca IV, 1112
Plummer, Rebecca VI, 771
Plummer, Rebecca C. II, 136
Plummer, Richard IV, 492
Plummer, Richard IV, 1074
Plummer, Richard Hopkins VI, 771
Plummer, Robert IV, 157
Plummer, Robert IV, 264
Plummer, Robert IV, 365
Plummer, Robert IV, 386
Plummer, Robert IV, 393
Plummer, Robert IV, 411
Plummer, Robert IV, 430
Plummer, Robert IV, 431
Plummer, Robert IV, 441
Plummer, Robert IV, 443
Plummer, Robert IV, 592
Plummer, Robert IV, 707
Plummer, Robert IV, 1112
Plummer, Robert Allen IV, 431
Plummer, Robert S. IV, 1074
Plummer, Ruth IV, 106
Plummer, Ruth VI, 506
Plummer, Ruth VI, 546
Plummer, Ruth VI, 548
Plummer, Ruth Ann IV, 431
Plummer, Ruth Ann IV, 1112
Plummer, Ruth Ann IV, 1122
Plummer, Ruthann IV, 431
Plummer, Ruthanna IV, 1074
Plummer, S. IV, 492
Plummer, Saml VI, 517
Plummer, Samuel IV, 492
Plummer, Samuel IV, 1074
Plummer, Samuel VI, 506
Plummer, Samuel VI, 521
Plummer, Samuel VI, 545
Plummer, Samuel VI, 548
Plummer, Samuel VI, 574
Plummer, Sarah III, 492
Plummer, Sarah IV, 106
Plummer, Sarah IV, 431
Plummer, Sarah IV, 470
Plummer, Sarah IV, 492
Plummer, Sarah IV, 1074
Plummer, Sarah IV, 1109
Plummer, Sarah IV, 1112
Plummer, Sarah VI, 506
Plummer, Sarah VI, 517
Plummer, Sarah VI, 519
Plummer, Sarah VI, 521
Plummer, Sarah VI, 545
Plummer, Sarah VI, 546
Plummer, Sarah VI, 548
Plummer, Sarah VI, 572
Plummer, Sarah VI, 574
Plummer, Sarah VI, 661
Plummer, Sarah C. V, 926
Plummer, Sarah J. IV, 1106
Plummer, Sarah J. IV, 1112
Plummer, Sarah S. IV, 430
Plummer, Sina IV, 343
Plummer, Sina IV, 360
Plummer, Sinah IV, 157
Plummer, Susanna IV, 465
Plummer, Susanna IV, 492
Plummer, Susanna IV, 1074
Plummer, Susanna VI, 548
Plummer, Susanna W. IV, 1074
Plummer, Susannah IV, 431
Plummer, Susannah IV, 492
Plummer, Tabitha IV, 431
Plummer, Tabitha IV, 1104
Plummer, Tabitha IV, 1112
Plummer, Tacy V, 60
Plummer, Tacy V, 172
Plummer, Tacy V, 197
Plummer, Tacy V, 272
Plummer, Tacy VI, 337
Plummer, Talbert IV, 431
Plummer, Talbert IV, 1112
Plummer, Talbott IV, 1074
Plummer, Talbott IV, 1106
Plummer, Talbott IV, 1112
Plummer, Talitha IV, 430
Plummer, Talitha IV, 592
Plummer, Thomas IV, 148
Plummer, Thomas IV, 347
Plummer, Thomas IV, 431
Plummer, Thomas IV, 492
Plummer, Thomas IV, 1074
Plummer, Thomas IV, 1075
Plummer, Thomas IV, 1112
Plummer, Thomas VI, 548
Plummer, Thomas VI, 575
Plummer, Thomas VI, 771
Plummer, Thomas C. IV, 1112
Plummer, Thomas Gilpin V, 197
Plummer, Thos. IV, 465
Plummer, Thos. IV, 492
Plummer, Thos. IV, 1112
Plummer, Wd. Abigail III, 407
Plummer, William IV, 430
Plummer, William IV, 492
Plummer, William IV, 592
Plummer, William VI, 546
Plummer, William VI, 548
Plummer, William A. I, 624
Plummer, William A. I, 639
Plummer, William A. I, 898
Plummer, William T. III, 256
Plummer, Wm. II, 136
Plummer, Wm. IV, 1112
Plummer, Wm., Jr. II, 136
Plummer, Wm., Jr. II, 155
Plummer-Harris, Elizabeth VI, 522
Plummer-Harris, Moses VI, 522
Plummer-Harris, Widow Sarah VI, 522
Plumstead, Charles II, 407
Plumstead, Clement II, 407
Plumstead, Clement II, 624
Plumstead, Elizabeth II, 407
Plumstead, Elizabeth II, 624
Plumstead, Rebecca II, 407
Plumstead, Rebecca II, 624
Plumstead, Rebeccah II, 407
Plumstead, Sarah II, 407
Plumstead, Thomas II, 407
Plumstead, William II, 407
Plumstead, Wm. II, 624
Plumsted, Clement II, 572
Plumsted, Clement II, 612
Plumsted, Clement II, 624
Plumsted, Elizabeth II, 612
Plumsted, Elizabeth II, 624
Plumsted, Rebecca II, 572
Plumsted, Rebecca II, 624
Plumsted, Rebeccah II, 407
Plumsted, William II, 407
Plumsted, Wm. II, 572
Plumsted, Wm. II, 624
Plunket, Adeline VI, 861
Plunkett, A. VI, 847
Plunkett, A. VI, 853
Plunkett, A. VI, 864
Plunkett, Adeline VI, 978
Plunkett, Agness VI, 847
Plunkett, Alexander A. N. VI, 978
Plunkett, Ambrose VI, 799
Plunkett, Ambrose VI, 808
Plunkett, Ambrose VI, 817
Plunkett, Ambrose VI, 838
Plunkett, Benjamin VI, 836
Plunkett, Benjamin VI, 847
Plunkett, Elizabeth VI, 847
Plunkett, Elizabeth J. VI, 838
Plunkett, Frances VI, 853
Plunkett, Jane H. VI, 847
Plunkett, John H. VI, 799
Plunkett, John H. VI, 847
Plunkett, John L. I, 687
Plunkett, Mildred VI, 867
Plunkett, Polly VI, 836
Plunkett, Sarah T. VI, 847
Plunkett, Serena VI, 864
Plunkett, Tallifero VI, 838
Plunkett, Talliferro VI, 864
Plunkett, Winnefred VI, 799
Plunkett, Wm. H. VI, 847
Plunner, John IV, 592
Plymale, Amy VI, 934
Plymale, Ardenia VI, 898
Plymale, Catharine VI, 880
Plymale, Christena VI, 879
Plymale, Irenia VI, 884
Plymale, Martha VI, 978
Plymale, Mary C. VI, 978
Plymale, Patty VI, 934
Plymale, Samuel VI, 978
Plymale, Thomas VI, 879
Plymale, Thomas VI, 884
Plymale, Thomas VI, 978
Plymire, Grace V, 666
Plymire, Grace V, 704
Plymire, Grace C. V, 704
Plymire, Harley V, 666
Plymire, Harley V, 704
Pnuover, Henrietta II, 717
Poage, Robert VI, 978
Poage, Sally Lewis VI, 978
Pobst, Arminda V, 419
Pobst, Frederick D. V, 400
Pobst, James V, 426
Pobst, Laura V, 426
Pobst, Mary Ann V, 400
Pobst, Mathias V, 419
Pobst, Sarah V, 419
Pockett, Benjamin F. V, 641
Pocoson, ??? VI, 13
Poe, Fannie E. VI, 494
Poe, Melvina I, 835
Poe, Melvina I, 846
Poe, Samuel VI, 797
Poe, Sarah I, 835
Poff, James W. V, 272
Poff, Joseph D. V, 272
Poff, Luke V, 272
Poff, Rachel F. V, 272
Poff, Sarah W. V, 272
Poff, Stephen W. V, 272
Pogue, Martha III, 30
Pogue, Martha III, 182
Pogue, Martha III, 341
Pogue, Mary VI, 830
Pohl, Adelaide III, 256
Pohl, Francis III, 256
Pohl, Francis Julius III, 256
Pohl, Fred'k Joseph III, 256
Pohl, Josephine III, 256
Poigner, Hattie Hosier V, 704
Poillon, Margaret III, 256
Poince, Elisabeth II, 624
Poince, Elizabeth II, 607
Poince, Elizabeth II, 624
Poince, Michael II, 624
Poince, Michaell II, 607
Poince, Michaell II, 624
Poindexter, Anderson VI, 978
Poindexter, Ann VI, 978
Poindexter, Ann E. VI, 978
Poindexter, Anne VI, 992
Poindexter, Capt. Samuel VI, 1013
Poindexter, Caroline VI, 843
Poindexter, Caroline VI, 1013
Poindexter, Caroline E. VI, 921
Poindexter, Dabney VI, 921
Poindexter, Dabney VI, 978
Poindexter, Davis D. VI, 978
Poindexter, Dionitia VI, 978
Poindexter, Elisa M. VI, 978
Poindexter, Elisha M. VI, 978
Poindexter, Elizabeth VI, 892
Poindexter, Elizabeth A. VI, 827
Poindexter, Emily P. VI, 978
Poindexter, Frances VI, 847
Poindexter, Francis VI, 854
Poindexter, J. D. VI, 845
Poindexter, James VI, 941
Poindexter, James H. VI, 928
Poindexter, James L. VI, 847
Poindexter, Jane A. VI, 829
Poindexter, Jane M. L. VI, 840
Poindexter, Jno. W. VI, 975
Poindexter, John VI, 847
Poindexter, John VI, 978
Poindexter, John S. VI, 941
Poindexter, John S. VI, 978
Poindexter, Joseph VI, 847
Poindexter, Joseph VI, 892
Poindexter, Joseph VI, 978
Poindexter, Joseph VI, 992
Poindexter, Joseph, Jr. VI, 848
Poindexter, Judith VI, 847
Poindexter, Laura J. I, 995
Poindexter, Lewis D. VI, 829
Poindexter, Martha VI, 978
Poindexter, Mary A. VI, 847
Poindexter, Mary W. VI, 978
Poindexter, Nancy VI, 847
Poindexter, Nancy VI, 978
Poindexter, Pauline A. VI, 928
Poindexter, Plutina R. I, 995
Poindexter, Reuben VI, 847
Poindexter, Richard VI, 827
Poindexter, Richard VI, 863
Poindexter, Richard W. VI, 928
Poindexter, Richard W. VI, 978
Poindexter, Sally VI, 847
Poindexter, Samuel VI, 892
Poindexter, Samuel VI, 978
Poindexter, Samuel VI, 1013
Poindexter, Samuel B. VI, 941
Poindexter, Sarah VI, 845
Poindexter, Sarah T. VI, 847
Poindexter, Sarah W. VI, 921
Poindexter, Susan M. VI, 838
Poindexter, Susan M. VI, 941
Poindexter, Thomas F. VI, 845
Poindexter, Wady VI, 847
Poindexter, William VI, 838
Poindexter, Willis VI, 978
Poindexter, Willis VI, 994
Poindexter, Wm. VI, 840
Point, Isaac II, 407
Point, Joshua II, 407
Point, Michall II, 407
Pointer, John VI, 847
Pointer, Polly VI, 847
Points, Elisabeth II, 624
Points, Elizabeth II, 607
Points, Michael II, 607
Points, Michael II, 624
Pole, Ann II, 624
Pole, Anna II, 472
Pole, Anna II, 624
Pole, Edward II, 407
Pole, Edward II, 624
Pole, Edward II, 678
Pole, Edward, Jr. II, 624
Pole, Elizabeth II, 407
Pole, Grace II, 407
Pole, John II, 250
Pole, John II, 261
Pole, John II, 407
Pole, John II, 472
Pole, John II, 624
Pole, John II, 678
Pole, Joseph Warner II, 624
Pole, Mary II, 407
Pole, Mary II, 624
Pole, Mary II, 678
Pole, Rachel II, 180
Pole, Rachel II, 250
Pole, Rachel II, 261
Pole, Rachel II, 407
Pole, Rachel II, 624
Pole, Rachel II, 678
Pole, Rachel Smith II, 624
Pole, Simeon II, 678
Pole, Thomas II, 250
Pole, Thomas II, 624
Polegreen, Elizabeth II, 624
Polin, Hannah II, 624
Poling, Ellen V, 762
Poling, Ephraim V, 1014
Poling, Ethel V, 762
Poling, Geo. V, 762
Poling, George V, 762
Poling, Gladdie V, 1014
Poling, Nancy V, 1014
Polk, Addie V, 272
Polk, Eva V, 355
Polk, Hannah V, 501
Polk, Hannah V, 524
Polk, Julia V, 243
Polk, Julia V, 272
Polk, Julia V, 355
Polk, Rachel V, 112
Pollard, Alice Elizabeth IV, 987
Pollard, Amy IV, 264
Pollard, Andrew IV, 838
Pollard, Andrew IV, 856
Pollard, Anna Janet IV, 838
Pollard, Benjamin IV, 264
Pollard, Betsy VI, 941
Pollard, Callohill VI, 997
Pollard, Catharine VI, 884
Pollard, Catharine VI, 923
Pollard, Catharine VI, 978
Pollard, Chizia VI, 978
Pollard, Dorothy Sarah IV, 987
Pollard, Edith Caroline IV, 987
Pollard, Edward John IV, 838
Pollard, Elizabeth IV, 264
Pollard, Elizabeth VI, 878
Pollard, Elizabeth VI, 978
Pollard, Elizabeth VI, 979
Pollard, Ellen H. IV, 987
Pollard, Emily IV, 264
Pollard, Emily IV, 838
Pollard, Emily IV, 856
Pollard, Emma Leota IV, 987
Pollard, Francis VI, 874
Pollard, Francis VI, 878
Pollard, Francis VI, 954
Pollard, Francis VI, 979
Pollard, Francis J. IV, 838
Pollard, Francis Joseph IV, 838
Pollard, Francis Joseph IV, 845
Pollard, Frankey VI, 945
Pollard, Geo. IV, 964
Pollard, George IV, 987
Pollard, George VI, 957
Pollard, George VI, 978
Pollard, George VI, 997
Pollard, George VI, 999
Pollard, Hannah IV, 264
Pollard, Henrietta VI, 979
Pollard, Jane VI, 984
Pollard, Janet IV, 838
Pollard, Jesse N. VI, 884
Pollard, Jesse N. VI, 978
Pollard, John IV, 264
Pollard, John IV, 838
Pollard, John VI, 978
Pollard, John VI, 984
Pollard, John A. VI, 979
Pollard, John, Jr. VI, 911
Pollard, Joseph IV, 264
Pollard, Joseph VI, 896
Pollard, Joseph VI, 978
Pollard, Judith VI, 923
Pollard, Judith VI, 952
Pollard, Kesiah VI, 957

ard, Lucinda IV, 838
ard, Lucinda IV, 845
ard, Lucinda S. IV, 838
ard, Mariah IV, 264
ard, Martha VI, 182
ard, Martha VI, 208
ard, Martha Irena IV, 987
ard, Martha Irene IV, 987
ard, Mary E. VI, 979
ard, Mary J. IV, 964
ard, Mary J. IV, 987
ard, Mildred VI, 997
ard, Molly VI, 928
ard, Nancy VI, 911
ard, Nancy VI, 978
ard, Nancy VI, 979
ard, Naomi IV, 264
ard, Ohizia VI, 978
ard, Patsey VI, 954
ard, Penelope Ann VI, 978
ard, Rachel L. IV, 987
ard, Rachel S. IV, 987
ard, Rebecca VI, 999
ard, Robert A. IV, 838
ard, Ruth IV, 1180
ard, Salley VI, 957
ard, Samuel IV, 264
ard, Samuel IV, 1375
ard, Samuel C. VI, 979
ard, Sarah IV, 964
ard, Sarah VI, 979
ard, Shepperd VI, 979
ard, Sophia VI, 923
ard, Susan N. VI, 874
ard, Thomas VI, 928
ard, Thomas VI, 941
ard, Thomas VI, 952
ard, Thomas VI, 957
ard, Thomas VI, 978
ard, Thomas VI, 979
ard, Thomas VI, 984
ard, Thomas VI, 999
ard, Thomas VI, 1006
ard, Warren W. IV, 1180
ard, Warren W. IV, 1260
ard, Wm. Henry IV, 987
ett, Chas. F. III, 256
ett, Josephine III, 256
ett, Lulu III, 256
in, Thomas II, 407
in, Warner II, 407
ock, Eugenia III, 256
ock, Eugenia III, 424
ock, Eugenia III, 433
ock, Grace IV, 1317
ock, Grace IV, 1333
ock, Irene IV, 1333
ock, Irene Graham IV, 1317
ock, James R. III, 256
ock, Jas. R. III, 424
ock, Jas. R. III, 433
ock, Levina IV, 752
ock, Levina IV, 766
ock, Mabel I, 219
ock, Mary E. IV, 1317
ock, Mary E. IV, 1333
ock, Mary Elizabeth IV, 1333
ock, Ruth Isabella III, 256
ock, Ruth Isabella III, 433
ock, Ruth Isabelle III, 424
ock, Willis C. IV, 1333
y, Eva V, 463
y, Mary V, 849
on, Elizabeth I, 563
on, Elizabeth I, 567
eroy, Elizabeth J. II, 751
eroy, Elizabeth J. II, 760
d, ??? IV, 1334
d, Annie E. V, 592
d, David V, 426
d, David V, 592
d, Eleanor V, 426
d, Ellenor V, 592
d, Hattie V, 691
d, Hattie V, 704
d, Jennie V, 592
d, Levi V, 426
d, Levi V, 592
d, Levi W. V, 426
d, Mr. ??? IV, 1333
d, Mrs. E. IV, 1333
d, Nancy J. V, 592
d, Phebe A. V, 592
d, Ralph IV, 1333
d, Robert II, 196
d, Robert II, 250
d, Rosa Ellen V, 592
d, Sarah II, 196
d, Sarah II, 250
d, Sarah H. IV, 893
d, Sylvester V, 355
Pond, Sylvester V, 426
Pond, Wm. E. IV, 1333
Pond, Zenas I. V, 592
Pontius, Grace IV, 1334
Pool, Abigail I, 731
Pool, Albinah IV, 881
Pool, Albinah VI, 690
Pool, Ane I, 114
Pool, Ann IV, 652
Pool, Ann IV, 752
Pool, Ann IV, 839
Pool, Ann IV, 881
Pool, Ann IV, 884
Pool, Ann IV, 987
Pool, Ann VI, 546
Pool, Ann VI, 551
Pool, Asaneth IV, 839
Pool, Ascenath IV, 881
Pool, Asenath IV, 881
Pool, Asenath IV, 987
Pool, Asenath C. I, 626
Pool, Asenath H. IV, 652
Pool, Asenath H. IV, 881
Pool, Asenith IV, 752
Pool, Asenith IV, 839
Pool, Assenath IV, 626
Pool, Benjamin VI, 546
Pool, Benjamin VI, 603
Pool, Benjamin VI, 649
Pool, Benjamin VI, 655
Pool, Benjamin VI, 658
Pool, Benjamin VI, 660
Pool, Benjamin VI, 690
Pool, Caleb V, 38
Pool, Charles I, 705
Pool, Charles V, 762
Pool, Clarkey I, 148
Pool, Clarkey I, 162
Pool, Clarkey I, 705
Pool, Clarkey I, 731
Pool, Cornelia Martitia I, 930
Pool, Cynthia Ann I, 69
Pool, Cynthia Ann I, 75
Pool, Dudley VI, 979
Pool, Elisabeth I, 127
Pool, Elisabeth I, 162
Pool, Elisabeth I, 195
Pool, Elisabeth I, 199
Pool, Elizabeth I, 93
Pool, Elizabeth I, 705
Pool, Elizabeth I, 711
Pool, Elizabeth I, 731
Pool, Elizabeth I, 733
Pool, Elizabeth IV, 493
Pool, Elizabeth V, 112
Pool, Elizabeth VI, 546
Pool, Elizabeth VI, 598
Pool, Elizabeth VI, 655
Pool, Elizabeth VI, 656
Pool, Elizabeth VI, 690
Pool, Elizabeth Ann V, 112
Pool, Elizabeth W. I, 705
Pool, Emily IV, 493
Pool, Felix I, 731
Pool, Florence A. I, 705
Pool, Gulielma I, 705
Pool, Gulielma I, 731
Pool, Hannah IV, 493
Pool, Hannah VI, 546
Pool, Hannah VI, 599
Pool, Hannah VI, 603
Pool, Hannah VI, 660
Pool, Hannah VI, 690
Pool, Henry B. I, 705
Pool, Henry B. I, 731
Pool, Isaac VI, 658
Pool, Israel IV, 881
Pool, Israel IV, 934
Pool, Israel VI, 658
Pool, Israel VI, 690
Pool, James IV, 884
Pool, Jane IV, 881
Pool, Jane IV, 934
Pool, Jane IV, 977
Pool, Jane IV, 987
Pool, Jane VI, 658
Pool, Jane VI, 690
Pool, Jesse VI, 690
Pool, John I, 705
Pool, John I, 711
Pool, John I, 731
Pool, John II, 446
Pool, John V, 112
Pool, John V, 762
Pool, John VI, 882
Pool, Jonas IV, 652
Pool, Jonas IV, 752
Pool, Jonas IV, 839
Pool, Jonas IV, 881
Pool, Jonas IV, 987
Pool, Jonas VI, 690
Pool, Jonie H. I, 705
Pool, Joseph IV, 493
Pool, Joseph V, 112
Pool, Joseph VI, 597
Pool, Joseph VI, 599
Pool, Joseph VI, 603
Pool, Joseph VI, 660
Pool, Joseph VI, 690
Pool, Joseph E. I, 705
Pool, Joseph Elwood I, 731
Pool, Joshua V, 309
Pool, Kathrine VI, 979
Pool, Lydia IV, 346
Pool, Lydia IV, 348
Pool, Lydia IV, 431
Pool, Lydia IV, 467
Pool, Lydia IV, 493
Pool, Lydia IV, 881
Pool, Lydia IV, 934
Pool, Lydia IV, 987
Pool, Lydia VI, 690
Pool, Margaret I, 161
Pool, Margaret I, 162
Pool, Margaret I, 174
Pool, Margret I, 705
Pool, Maria IV, 476
Pool, Maria IV, 493
Pool, Maria L. III, 256
Pool, Martha VI, 546
Pool, Mary I, 108
Pool, Mary I, 114
Pool, Mary I, 154
Pool, Mary I, 161
Pool, Mary II, 624
Pool, Mary VI, 649
Pool, Mary VI, 690
Pool, Mary M. I, 705
Pool, Millicent M. I, 705
Pool, Mirtle E. I, 705
Pool, Nancy I, 722
Pool, Nancy I, 731
Pool, Naomiah VI, 690
Pool, Nathaniel II, 408
Pool, Nathaniel II, 1012
Pool, Noah I, 930
Pool, Otis IV, 752
Pool, Phelix I, 731
Pool, Phineas IV, 881
Pool, Phineas VI, 690
Pool, Priscilla IV, 652
Pool, Priscilla IV, 752
Pool, Priscilla IV, 839
Pool, Priscilla IV, 881
Pool, Priscilla IV, 987
Pool, Priscilla H. IV, 652
Pool, Rachel VI, 655
Pool, Rebecca II, 677
Pool, Rebecca V, 38
Pool, Rebecca V, 67
Pool, Rebecca V, 112
Pool, Rebecca H. V, 112
Pool, Rebeckah VI, 603
Pool, Rebekah VI, 649
Pool, Rebekah VI, 658
Pool, Rebekah VI, 660
Pool, Rebekah VI, 690
Pool, Richard I, 114
Pool, Richard I, 161
Pool, Romulus R. I, 731
Pool, Roxanna I, 930
Pool, Ruth Ann V, 97
Pool, Ruth Ann V, 112
Pool, Samuel III, 256
Pool, Samuel IV, 157
Pool, Samuel IV, 348
Pool, Samuel IV, 431
Pool, Samuel IV, 493
Pool, Samuel VI, 690
Pool, Samuel S. II, 122
Pool, Sarah I, 111
Pool, Sarah I, 157
Pool, Sarah I, 161
Pool, Sarah I, 162
Pool, Sarah IV, 881
Pool, Sarah IV, 987
Pool, Sarah V, 38
Pool, Sarah VI, 636
Pool, Sarah VI, 690
Pool, Sarah Jane IV, 652
Pool, Sarah Jane IV, 752
Pool, Sarah Jane IV, 881
Pool, Sarah M. I, 731
Pool, Sollomon I, 161
Pool, Soloeman I, 114
Pool, Soloman I, 114
Pool, Solomon I, 92
Pool, Solomon I, 93
Pool, Solomon I, 111
Pool, Solomon I, 161
Pool, Susanna IV, 348
Pool, Susannah IV, 348
Pool, Susannah IV, 431
Pool, Susannah VI, 690
Pool, Thomas I, 162
Pool, Thomas I, 731
Pool, Timothy IV, 348
Pool, Timothy IV, 431
Pool, William I, 148
Pool, William I, 161
Pool, William I, 162
Pool, William I, 731
Pool, William V, 67
Pool, William V, 112
Poole, Ann II, 407
Poole, Ann II, 668
Poole, Arthur III, 256
Poole, Asenath C. I, 612
Poole, Asenath H. IV, 652
Poole, Caroline III, 384
Poole, Charles D. III, 492
Poole, Clara IV, 1260
Poole, Clark S. III, 256
Poole, Dorothy I, 924
Poole, Eliza III, 256
Poole, Elizabeth II, 408
Poole, Elizabeth II, 624
Poole, Elizabeth II, 781
Poole, Elizabeth II, 1021
Poole, Elizabeth II, 1042
Poole, Eugene III, 256
Poole, Gilpin III, 384
Poole, Hannah II, 408
Poole, Hannah II, 624
Poole, Hannah II, 687
Poole, Hannah VI, 546
Poole, Hannah VI, 580
Poole, Hannah VI, 603
Poole, John II, 408
Poole, John III, 492
Poole, John P. V, 97
Poole, Louise III, 384
Poole, Louise Hemstreet III, 381
Poole, Margaret I, 91
Poole, Margaret I, 161
Poole, Margrete I, 172
Poole, Maria L. III, 256
Poole, Mary II, 533
Poole, Mary II, 624
Poole, Milo Randolph III, 256
Poole, Nathaniel II, 407
Poole, Nathaniel II, 408
Poole, Nathaniel II, 587
Poole, Nathaniel II, 624
Poole, Nathaniel II, 668
Poole, Nathaniel II, 1021
Poole, Phineas B. V, 97
Poole, Priscilla H. IV, 652
Poole, Rachel II, 545
Poole, Rachel II, 624
Poole, Rebecca II, 624
Poole, Richard I, 161
Poole, Ruth Ann V, 97
Poole, Samuel III, 256
Poole, Sarah II, 608
Poole, Sarah II, 624
Poole, Sarah IV, 914
Poole, Sollomon I, 91
Poole, Sollomon I, 161
Poole, Sollomon I, 172
Poole, Sophronia Ellen III, 256
Poole, Wd. Ann II, 624
Poole, William III, 381
Poole, William III, 384
Pooley, Catherine VI, 546
Pooley, Elizabeth VI, 471
Pooley, Elizabeth VI, 546
Pooley, Matthias VI, 546
Pooley, Rebecca II, 1021
Poor, Joel VI, 847
Poor, Martha A. VI, 832
Poor, Mary I, 898
Poor, Susanna VI, 847
Poorman, Ella V, 524
Poorman, George V, 524
Poorman, Rebecca A. IV, 987
Poorman, Rebecca A. IV, 1008
Poorman, Rebecca Ann IV, 1137
Poorman, Rebecca Ann IV, 1138
Pope, ??? IV, 1303
Pope, ??? VI, 39
Pope, Abigail IV, 1272
Pope, Abigail IV, 1290
Pope, Abner VI, 769
Pope, Abner VI, 771
Pope, Abner James VI, 771
Pope, Alfred IV, 752
Pope, Alfred V, 272
Pope, Alfred A. IV, 752
Pope, Alfred S. IV, 1334
Pope, Alge VI, 34
Pope, Alice VI, 771
Pope, Alson G. I, 898
Pope, Alton IV, 752
Pope, Alton IV, 1334
Pope, Amy II, 324
Pope, Ann II, 250
Pope, Ann VI, 46
Pope, Ann VI, 690
Pope, Ann VI, 691
Pope, Ann VI, 695
Pope, Ann VI, 721
Pope, Aquila V, 272
Pope, Arthur IV, 1334
Pope, Bathsheba V, 265
Pope, Bathsheba V, 272
Pope, Betsy V, 112
Pope, Betsy V, 116
Pope, Carl W. IV, 1334
Pope, Carlyle W. IV, 752
Pope, Charlotte II, 237
Pope, Charlotte II, 250
Pope, Clifford H. III, 97
Pope, Clifford Hillhouse III, 256
Pope, Cora V, 641
Pope, Daniel N. III, 256
Pope, Darwin J. VI, 732
Pope, Darwin J. VI, 771
Pope, Dinah I, 566
Pope, Dinah I, 567
Pope, Dinah I, 835
Pope, E. M. Mariah I, 687
Pope, Edward VI, 771
Pope, Edward C. IV, 752
Pope, Edward M. IV, 752
Pope, Eliphalet VI, 771
Pope, Elizabeth I, 560
Pope, Elizabeth I, 567
Pope, Elizabeth I, 835
Pope, Elizabeth I, 898
Pope, Elizabeth II, 237
Pope, Elizabeth II, 250
Pope, Elizabeth II, 271
Pope, Elizabeth V, 112
Pope, Elizabeth V, 272
Pope, Elizabeth V, 641
Pope, Elizabeth C. V, 271
Pope, Elizabeth L. V, 272
Pope, Ellen IV, 752
Pope, Ellen V, 1014
Pope, Ellen M. IV, 752
Pope, Ellen Maria IV, 752
Pope, Emma B. V, 641
Pope, Folger VI, 690
Pope, Folger VI, 695
Pope, Folger VI, 721
Pope, Folger VI, 722
Pope, Folger VI, 771
Pope, Folger VI, 792
Pope, Francis E. IV, 752
Pope, Francis E. IV, 1334
Pope, Frank V, 641
Pope, Grace V, 94
Pope, Grace V, 112
Pope, Grace V, 272
Pope, Hannah II, 197
Pope, Hannah II, 224
Pope, Hannah II, 250
Pope, Hannah VI, 583
Pope, Hannah VI, 722
Pope, Hannah VI, 771
Pope, Hannah VI, 792
Pope, Harriet H. III, 256
Pope, Henrietta V, 641
Pope, Henrietta E. V, 641
Pope, Henry VI, 34
Pope, Henry VI, 78
Pope, Henry F. IV, 1334
Pope, Henry J. IV, 752
Pope, Herbert A. IV, 752
Pope, Herbert A. IV, 1334
Pope, Ida Clair III, 292
Pope, Ira C. V, 641
Pope, Ira Clinton V, 641
Pope, James III, 256
Pope, James V, 981
Pope, James V, 1014
Pope, James VI, 847
Pope, James L. V, 641
Pope, Jane I, 567
Pope, John II, 250
Pope, John II, 312
Pope, John II, 324
Pope, John II, 624
Pope, John V, 355
Pope, John VI, 34
Pope, John L. IV, 752
Pope, John L. IV, 1334
Pope, John S. IV, 752
Pope, Joseph II, 237
Pope, Joseph II, 250
Pope, Joseph F. I, 898
Pope, Joseph P. VI, 771
Pope, Lewis J. V, 272

Pope, Lewis John V, 272
Pope, Lorenzo D. V, 641
Pope, Louisa J. V, 641
Pope, Louisa Jane V, 641
Pope, Maria VI, 769
Pope, Maria VI, 771
Pope, Mariah I, 680
Pope, Mariah IV, 1290
Pope, Marie VI, 34
Pope, Mark C. III, 256
Pope, Martha I, 1011
Pope, Martha II, 624
Pope, Martha V, 112
Pope, Martha V, 116
Pope, Martha V, 215
Pope, Martha V, 248
Pope, Martha V, 272
Pope, Martha VI, 847
Pope, Martha E. V, 641
Pope, Martha R. V, 641
Pope, Mary I, 526
Pope, Mary I, 549
Pope, Mary I, 567
Pope, Mary II, 298
Pope, Mary II, 300
Pope, Mary II, 324
Pope, Mary VI, 29
Pope, Mary VI, 34
Pope, Mary VI, 432
Pope, Mary VI, 732
Pope, Mary VI, 771
Pope, Mary A. V, 641
Pope, Mary Ann V, 641
Pope, Mary Ann VI, 771
Pope, Mary E. I, 835
Pope, Mary E. I, 898
Pope, Minnie V, 641
Pope, Mourning VI, 78
Pope, Nathan V, 112
Pope, Nathaniel I, 567
Pope, Nathaniel II, 197
Pope, Nathaniel II, 250
Pope, Nathaniel II, 259
Pope, Nathaniel II, 624
Pope, Nathaniel V, 112
Pope, Nathaniel V, 116
Pope, Nathaniel V, 272
Pope, Nathaniel V, 355
Pope, Natheniel V, 215
Pope, Priscilla I, 407
Pope, Priscilla I, 416
Pope, Priscilla I, 567
Pope, Richard VI, 46
Pope, Richard VI, 870
Pope, Richard VI, 875
Pope, Richard VI, 877
Pope, Richard VI, 879
Pope, Richard VI, 895
Pope, Richard VI, 930
Pope, Richard VI, 938
Pope, Richard VI, 940
Pope, Richard VI, 954
Pope, Richard VI, 962
Pope, Richard VI, 975
Pope, Richard VI, 976
Pope, Richard VI, 980
Pope, Richard VI, 987
Pope, Richard VI, 1006
Pope, Sallie I, 317
Pope, Samuel I, 567
Pope, Samuel I, 835
Pope, Samuel I, 968
Pope, Samuel V, 355
Pope, Sarah II, 250
Pope, Sarah II, 259
Pope, Sarah H. III, 97
Pope, Sarah H. III, 256
Pope, Sarah M. V, 641
Pope, Tacy VI, 432
Pope, Theodata VI, 625
Pope, Theodate IV, 1334
Pope, Theodate VI, 690
Pope, Theodate VI, 691
Pope, Theodate VI, 721
Pope, Theodate VI, 722
Pope, Theodate VI, 723
Pope, Theodate VI, 771
Pope, Theodate VI, 792
Pope, Theodate S. IV, 752
Pope, Theodore VI, 771
Pope, Thomas II, 624
Pope, Uriah II, 250
Pope, Walter S. IV, 1334
Pope, William I, 835
Pope, William I, 898
Pope, William II, 250
Pope, William V, 94
Pope, William V, 112
Pope, William V, 272
Pope, William VI, 29
Pope, William VI, 34
Pope, William, Jr. V, 272
Pope, Wm VI, 7
Pope, Wm. VI, 22
Popenoe, Cath. Jane III, 255
Popes, Ann II, 250
Popes, Charlotte II, 250
Popes, Uriah II, 250
Popes, William II, 250
Popkins, Catharine VI, 553
Poplin, Callie I, 1160
Poplin, James I, 1160
Poponoe, Cath. Jane III, 67
Popp, Evelyn Miller VI, 771
Popp, Evelyn Miller VI, 773
Popp, Frederick W. VI, 771
Popp, Frederick W. VI, 773
Popp, Richard VI, 771
Popp, Selma VI, 771
Poppelton, Mary II, 81
Poppelton, Mary II, 92
Pore, Margrett II, 446
Porter, ??? III, 269
Porter, ??? VI, 48
Porter, ??? VI, 78
Porter, Amelia III, 256
Porter, Amy Bell IV, 264
Porter, Ann VI, 78
Porter, Ann VI, 847
Porter, Ann VI, 979
Porter, Anna VI, 79
Porter, Annie IV, 265
Porter, Archie V, 926
Porter, Belfield VI, 979
Porter, Belfield J. VI, 986
Porter, Benjamin VI, 861
Porter, Benjamin W. VI, 805
Porter, Betsy VI, 847
Porter, Betty VI, 45
Porter, Betty VI, 46
Porter, Burwell C. VI, 979
Porter, Cecil V, 926
Porter, Charles E. IV, 265
Porter, Claiborne N. VI, 851
Porter, Claibourne VI, 847
Porter, Deborah IV, 489
Porter, Deborah IV, 493
Porter, Edna VI, 66
Porter, Elander VI, 875
Porter, Eleanor II, 250
Porter, Eleanor II, 624
Porter, Eleanor III, 256
Porter, Eleanor V, 419
Porter, Eleanor V, 426
Porter, Eleazer III, 440
Porter, Elijah Hare VI, 78
Porter, Eliz. Ann III, 269
Porter, Eliza IV, 1180
Porter, Eliza Ann III, 256
Porter, Elizabeth II, 408
Porter, Elizabeth II, 624
Porter, Elizabeth II, 715
Porter, Elizabeth IV, 265
Porter, Elizabeth VI, 826
Porter, Elizabeth Ann III, 440
Porter, Ezekiel VI, 812
Porter, Ezekiel VI, 814
Porter, Frances Walker I, 619
Porter, Francis VI, 847
Porter, George II, 250
Porter, George III, 256
Porter, Hannah II, 715
Porter, Hannah V, 426
Porter, Hannah V, 427
Porter, Hannah E. II, 831
Porter, Hannah E. II, 911
Porter, Harrison IV, 265
Porter, Hershal Donavon V, 926
Porter, Ida M. IV, 264
Porter, Ida May IV, 264
Porter, Ida May IV, 265
Porter, James W. VI, 849
Porter, Jane VI, 817
Porter, Jennie V, 926
Porter, Jesse Copeland VI, 78
Porter, John II, 446
Porter, John III, 256
Porter, John VI, 7
Porter, John VI, 8
Porter, John VI, 18
Porter, John VI, 22
Porter, John VI, 23
Porter, John VI, 34
Porter, John VI, 45
Porter, John VI, 46
Porter, John VI, 66
Porter, John VI, 71
Porter, John VI, 78
Porter, John VI, 817
Porter, John VI, 847
Porter, John VI, 979
Porter, John VI, 1004
Porter, John A. VI, 861
Porter, John B. VI, 979
Porter, John G. III, 256
Porter, John G. III, 300
Porter, John S. VI, 1011
Porter, John's VI, 78
Porter, John, Jr. VI, 11
Porter, John, Jr. VI, 12
Porter, John, Jr. VI, 59
Porter, John, Jr. VI, 78
Porter, Joseph VI, 18
Porter, Joseph C. VI, 995
Porter, Joseph F. III, 256
Porter, Lizzie IV, 265
Porter, Lizzie Rankin IV, 264
Porter, Lorene IV, 1334
Porter, Louisa VI, 56
Porter, Louisa VI, 72
Porter, Louisa VI, 78
Porter, Louisa VI, 79
Porter, Louisa Jones VI, 78
Porter, Louisa R. VI, 979
Porter, Maggie IV, 987
Porter, Margaret Ann VI, 92
Porter, Margaret E. IV, 1334
Porter, Margt VI, 148
Porter, Margt VI, 208
Porter, Martha E. IV, 1334
Porter, Martha Ellen IV, 1334
Porter, Mary II, 250
Porter, Mary III, 256
Porter, Mary IV, 41
Porter, Mary IV, 54
Porter, Mary IV, 493
Porter, Mary V, 926
Porter, Mary VI, 78
Porter, Mary VI, 79
Porter, Mary VI, 91
Porter, Mary A. G. VI, 979
Porter, Mary Ann VI, 847
Porter, Mary C. VI, 78
Porter, Mary J. VI, 56
Porter, Mary J. VI, 78
Porter, Mary T. III, 256
Porter, Mathew II, 446
Porter, Mr. ??? IV, 1334
Porter, Mr. ??? VI, 12
Porter, Mr. John W. H. VI, 11
Porter, Mr. John, Sr. VI, 12
Porter, Mrs. ??? VI, 11
Porter, Mrs. ??? VI, 12
Porter, Nancy VI, 828
Porter, Nancy VI, 861
Porter, Nellie I, 209
Porter, Parthena VI, 973
Porter, Paul V, 704
Porter, Paul V, 716
Porter, Peggy VI, 808
Porter, Peggy VI, 863
Porter, Penelope Ann VI, 978
Porter, Rachel VI, 59
Porter, Rachel Copeland VI, 78
Porter, Rebecca IV, 431
Porter, Rebecca IV, 457
Porter, Ruth VI, 78
Porter, Sally Ware VI, 979
Porter, Sarah III, 256
Porter, Sarah III, 300
Porter, Sarah VI, 59
Porter, Sarah VI, 78
Porter, Sarah VI, 208
Porter, Sarah VI, 219
Porter, Sarah VI, 828
Porter, Sarah VI, 847
Porter, Sarah L. IV, 1290
Porter, Susan M. IV, 987
Porter, Susanna IV, 264
Porter, Temperance K. VI, 979
Porter, Thomas III, 256
Porter, Thomas VI, 847
Porter, Thomas C. G. III, 256
Porter, Veda V, 704
Porter, Veda V, 716
Porter, Violetta II, 587
Porter, Violetta II, 624
Porter, Virgil Randolph V, 926
Porter, Walter V, 926
Porter, William III, 256
Porter, William VI, 78
Porter, William VI, 146
Porter, William VI, 148
Porter, William VI, 178
Porter, William VI, 208
Porter, William VI, 847
Porter, William VI, 850
Porter, William VI, 889
Porter, William VI, 943
Porter, William VI, 973
Porter, William VI, 978
Porter, William C. VI, 979
Porter, William, Jr. VI, 148
Porter, William, Jr. VI, 149
Porter, William, Jr. VI, 188
Porter, William, Jr. VI, 208
Porter, William, Sr. VI, 208
Porter, Wm. VI, 59
Porter, Wm. R. VI, 1016
Porter, Zachariah VI, 56
Porter, Zachariah VI, 72
Porter, Zachariah VI, 78
Portes, Elizabeth I, 567
Portes, Elizabeth I, 573
Portes, Jane I, 898
Portes, Sarah I, 567
Portice, Elizabeth I, 721
Portice, Elizabeth I, 731
Portis, Elbert IV, 1334
Portis, Jane I, 898
Portis, Mary V, 856
Portwood, Amy G. VI, 834
Portwood, Giles B. VI, 817
Portwood, Giles B. VI, 834
Portwood, Mary C. VI, 834
Portwood, Nancy C. VI, 817
Portwood, Rebecca VI, 817
Posegate, Anne V, 309
Posegate, Charles V, 447
Posegate, Isaac V, 309
Posegate, Martha V, 355
Posegate, Mary Ann V, 309
Posey, Mary Ann VI, 956
Possom, Thomas II, 446
Possons, Elizabeth III, 256
Possons, Elizabeth Mary III, 256
Possons, Emily III, 256
Possons, George III, 256
Possons, William H. III, 256
Possons, Wm. H. III, 256
Post, ??? III, 488
Post, ??? III, 493
Post, Abigail III, 432
Post, Abigail III, 433
Post, Agnes Morgan III, 257
Post, Alanson III, 492
Post, Albert S. III, 492
Post, Alcesta II, 979
Post, Amelia III, 257
Post, Amelia III, 433
Post, Amy III, 488
Post, Amy III, 489
Post, Amy III, 492
Post, Amy III, 493
Post, Ann B. III, 510
Post, Arthur III, 433
Post, Arthur W. III, 435
Post, Arthur Willis III, 433
Post, Arthur Wood III, 393
Post, Arthur Wood III, 434
Post, Asa III, 511
Post, Asa J. III, 511
Post, Benjamin II, 979
Post, Benjamin III, 427
Post, Benjamin III, 433
Post, Benjamin III, 492
Post, Bessie V, 463
Post, Caroline III, 51
Post, Caroline III, 257
Post, Caroline III, 433
Post, Caroline III, 434
Post, Caroline III, 459
Post, Caroline III, 492
Post, Caroline III, 502
Post, Caroline Bulkley III, 257
Post, Caroline P. III, 256
Post, Catharine III, 433
Post, Catharine III, 434
Post, Catharine III, 435
Post, Catharine III, 441
Post, Catharine III, 459
Post, Catharine III, 467
Post, Catharine III, 473
Post, Catharine III, 492
Post, Catharine III, 493
Post, Catharine III, 501
Post, Catharine III, 507
Post, Catharine A. III, 434
Post, Catharine M. III, 433
Post, Catharine M. III, 434
Post, Catharine M. III, 474
Post, Catharine M. III, 492
Post, Catharine M. III, 508
Post, Charles III, 433
Post, Charles III, 434
Post, Charles III, 457
Post, Charles V, 463
Post, Charles M. III, 434
Post, Charls P. III, 462
Post, Cora V, 463
Post, Daniel III, 384
Post, Daniel III, 386
Post, Daniel III, 454
Post, Daniel III, 461
Post, Edmund III, 257
Post, Edmund III, 434
Post, Edmund III, 441
Post, Edmund III, 453
Post, Edmund III, 467
Post, Edmund III, 492
Post, Edmund III, 493
Post, Edmund III, 507
Post, Edmund, Jr. III, 441
Post, Edward III, 384
Post, Edward III, 434
Post, Elisha III, 434
Post, Elisha III, 493
Post, Eliz. III, 493
Post, Eliz. III, 503
Post, Eliza Jane III, 447
Post, Elizabeth III, 416
Post, Elizabeth III, 434
Post, Elizabeth III, 435
Post, Elizabeth III, 474
Post, Elizabeth III, 493
Post, Elizabeth III, 498
Post, Elizabeth C. III, 257
Post, Elizabeth C. III, 364
Post, Elizabeth C. III, 434
Post, Elizabeth K. III, 384
Post, Elizabeth R. III, 434
Post, Emily III, 433
Post, Emily III, 462
Post, Esther III, 381
Post, Esther III, 434
Post, Esther L. III, 434
Post, Esther L. III, 486
Post, Esther L. III, 493
Post, Esther P. III, 381
Post, Esther P. III, 384
Post, Ethel III, 435
Post, Ethel Mary III, 393
Post, Evie III, 493
Post, George III, 493
Post, Hannah III, 434
Post, Hannah III, 488
Post, Hannah III, 493
Post, Helen III, 129
Post, Helen III, 256
Post, Helen B. III, 289
Post, Helen Buckley III, 256
Post, Helen Bulkley III, 257
Post, Helen M. III, 435
Post, Helen M. III, 446
Post, Henry III, 256
Post, Henry III, 277
Post, Henry III, 435
Post, Henry III, 451
Post, Henry III, 453
Post, Henry III, 493
Post, Henry R. III, 257
Post, Henry R. III, 364
Post, Henry R. III, 434
Post, Henry T. III, 434
Post, Isaac III, 434
Post, Isaac III, 435
Post, Isaac III, 488
Post, Isaac III, 489
Post, Isaac III, 493
Post, James III, 425
Post, James III, 433
Post, James III, 434
Post, James III, 459
Post, James III, 473
Post, James III, 492
Post, James III, 493
Post, James III, 501
Post, James III, 507
Post, Jane III, 435
Post, Jane III, 453
Post, Jane III, 493
Post, Jarvis III, 486
Post, Jericho III, 434
Post, John II, 979
Post, John III, 432
Post, John III, 433
Post, John III, 434
Post, John III, 435
Post, John III, 436
Post, John III, 471
Post, John III, 473
Post, John III, 476
Post, John III, 493
Post, John III, 506
Post, John B. III, 510
Post, John W. III, 419
Post, John W. III, 434
Post, Joseph III, 416
Post, Joseph III, 421
Post, Joseph III, 433
Post, Joseph III, 434
Post, Joseph III, 440
Post, Joseph III, 474
Post, Joseph III, 492
Post, Joseph III, 493

, Joseph III, 495
, Joseph III, 508
, Jotham III, 257
, Jotham III, 434
, Jotham III, 435
, Lizzie V, 197
, Lydia III, 434
, Lydia III, 441
, Lydia III, 453
, Lydia III, 492
, M. Amelia III, 457
, Margaret Morgan III, 257
, Martha III, 427
, Martha III, 434
, Martha III, 442
, Martha III, 492
, Martha W. III, 434
, Mary III, 384
, Mary III, 421
, Mary III, 433
, Mary III, 434
, Mary III, 435
, Mary III, 441
, Mary III, 442
, Mary III, 443
, Mary III, 451
, Mary III, 453
, Mary III, 471
, Mary III, 473
, Mary III, 474
, Mary III, 493
, Mary III, 495
, Mary III, 506
, Mary A. III, 511
, Mary C. I, 1131
, Mary E. III, 493
, Mary Ella III, 482
, Mary Ella III, 493
, Mary Ethel III, 433
, Mary J. III, 470
, Mary Jane III, 257
, Mary Jane III, 434
, Mary Jane III, 468
, Mary Louisa III, 511
, Mary M. III, 511
, Mary N. III, 257
, Mary R. III, 257
, Mary R. III, 416
, Mary R. III, 434
, Mary T. III, 384
, Mary T. III, 386
, Mary T. III, 434
, Mary T. III, 461
, Mary U. III, 257
, Mary U. III, 468
, Mary W. III, 425
, Mary W. III, 434
, Mary W. III, 440
, Mary W. III, 492
, Mary W. III, 493
, Mary W. III, 508
, Micah III, 434
, Micah III, 435
, Micah III, 493
, Micah III, 503
, Michael III, 433
, Michael III, 493
, Morgan B. III, 256
, Morgan B. III, 257
, Morgan B. Helen III, 289
, Phebe III, 257
, Phebe III, 419
, Phebe III, 432
, Phebe III, 433
, Phebe III, 434
, Phebe III, 435
, Phebe III, 436
, Phebe III, 437
, Phebe III, 471
, Phebe III, 473
, Phebe III, 474
, Phebe III, 476
, Phebe III, 492
, Phebe III, 493
, Phebe III, 501
, Phebe III, 506
, Phebe III, 507
, Phebe W. III, 425
, Phebe W. III, 433
, Phebe W. III, 434
, Phebe W. III, 435
, Phebe W. III, 459
, Phebe W. III, 486
, Phebe W. III, 493
, Rachel III, 434
, Rebecca III, 427
, Rebecca III, 433
, Rich. III, 474
, Richard III, 257
, Richard III, 433
, Richard III, 434
Post, Richard III, 435
Post, Richard III, 446
Post, Richard III, 473
Post, Richard III, 476
Post, Richard, Jr. III, 435
Post, Robert III, 434
Post, Robert F. III, 257
Post, Rosetta III, 384
Post, Rosetta III, 386
Post, Rosetta III, 434
Post, Rosetta III, 454
Post, Rosetta III, 461
Post, Ruth III, 493
Post, Ruth III, 494
Post, Sam'l III, 453
Post, Samuel III, 257
Post, Samuel III, 434
Post, Samuel III, 435
Post, Samuel III, 462
Post, Samuel III, 468
Post, Samuel III, 473
Post, Samuel C. III, 511
Post, Sarah III, 434
Post, Sarah III, 452
Post, Sarah III, 453
Post, Sarah III, 493
Post, Sarah H. III, 257
Post, Seaman III, 482
Post, Seaman III, 493
Post, Smith III, 257
Post, Smith III, 493
Post, Stephen III, 257
Post, Stephen III, 434
Post, Stephen III, 435
Post, Stephen R. III, 51
Post, Stephen R. III, 257
Post, Stephen R. III, 434
Post, Susannah III, 493
Post, Susannah III, 503
Post, Wd. Jane III, 462
Post, William III, 384
Post, William III, 434
Post, William F. III, 435
Post, William T. III, 381
Post, William T. III, 384
Post, Willis III, 257
Post, Wm. T. III, 381
Postgait, Charity V, 244
Postgait, Charity V, 272
Postgait, Charles V, 272
Postgait, Isaac V, 272
Postgait, John V, 272
Postgait, Mary V, 272
Postgait, Rachel V, 272
Postgait, Thomas V, 244
Postgait, Thomas V, 272
Postgate, Anna V, 355
Postgate, Anna V, 447
Postgate, Anne V, 308
Postgate, Anne V, 309
Postgate, Charles V, 272
Postgate, Charles V, 308
Postgate, Charles V, 309
Postgate, Charles V, 355
Postgate, Charles V, 447
Postgate, Isaac V, 272
Postgate, Isaac V, 309
Postgate, Isaac N. V, 355
Postgate, John V, 272
Postgate, Martha V, 355
Postgate, Mary V, 272
Postgate, Mary Ann V, 309
Postgate, Mary Ann V, 355
Postgate, Mary Ann V, 366
Postgate, Rachel V, 272
Postgate, Thomas V, 272
Postgate, Thomas V, 447
Postlethwaite, Althea III, 121
Postlethwaite, Althea III, 257
Postlethwaite, C. Gayton III, 121
Postlethwaite, C. Gayton III, 257
Postlethwaite, Charlotte III, 257
Postlethwaite, Charlotte L. III, 257
Postlethwaite, Charlotte L. III, 302
Postlethwaite, Clarence E. III, 257
Postlethwaite, Clarence E. III, 302
Postlethwaite, E. J. III, 257
Postlethwaite, Gayton III, 257
Postlethwaite, J. A. J. III, 257
Potee, Claudious IV, 1290
Potee, Claudius IV, 1290
Potee, Elben IV, 1290
Potee, Eliza Ann IV, 1290
Potee, Ella IV, 1290
Potee, Ema IV, 1290
Potee, Flora IV, 1290
Potee, Frank IV, 1290
Potee, Fred IV, 1290
Potee, Jeremiah IV, 1290
Potee, Jeremiah IV, 1292
Potee, Lewis IV, 1290
Potee, Lindley P. IV, 1290
Potee, Ruth IV, 1290
Potee, Sarah A. IV, 1290
Potee, Sarah A. IV, 1292
Potee, Sattie IV, 1290
Potee, Srefna IV, 1290
Potee, Susan IV, 1290
Pots, Margaretta II, 1021
Pots, Mary I, 1032
Pots, Mary I, 1036
Pots, Rachel II, 92
Pots, Stacy II, 1021
Potter, Abel III, 493
Potter, Abraham I, 567
Potter, Abraham VI, 432
Potter, Anna III, 493
Potter, Asa I, 1146
Potter, Asa I, 1160
Potter, Asa III, 493
Potter, Augustine VI, 799
Potter, Augustus C. III, 257
Potter, Augustus E. III, 138
Potter, Augustus E. III, 257
Potter, Chloe IV, 1180
Potter, Cordovia May V, 426
Potter, Edith Eloise III, 107
Potter, Edith Eloise III, 257
Potter, Eli Clarkson Jones I, 1160
Potter, Elisabeth II, 554
Potter, Elisha III, 257
Potter, Eliza I, 882
Potter, Eliza I, 898
Potter, Elizabeth III, 257
Potter, Ella III, 257
Potter, Frances III, 257
Potter, Frances R. III, 138
Potter, Frances R. III, 257
Potter, George VI, 979
Potter, Hannah V, 426
Potter, Hannah VI, 979
Potter, Henry I, 687
Potter, Isaac I, 1160
Potter, Isaac II, 554
Potter, Isaac II, 624
Potter, Jesse F. V, 426
Potter, Jesse James I, 1160
Potter, Jesse T. V, 426
Potter, Kezia I, 1008
Potter, Kezia I, 1011
Potter, Keziah I, 1011
Potter, Lois I, 890
Potter, Lois I, 898
Potter, Lois G. I, 687
Potter, Lonora H. I, 687
Potter, Lonora H. I, 688
Potter, Lowis I, 864
Potter, Lucinda IV, 1169
Potter, Lucinda IV, 1171
Potter, Lucinda IV, 1180
Potter, Mary II, 624
Potter, Mary II, 633
Potter, Mary IV, 752
Potter, Mary VI, 432
Potter, Mary E. I, 687
Potter, Nancy VI, 799
Potter, Rudolph I, 1160
Potter, Ruth III, 257
Potter, Ruth III, 493
Potter, T. R. I, 1160
Potter, William J. III, 107
Potter, William J. III, 257
Potter, William Johnson I, 1160
Potterf, Margaret V, 112
Pottinger, Almina V, 856
Pottinger, Lydia V, 856
Pottorf, Granville V, 112
Pottorf, Margaret V, 112
Pottorf, Simeon V, 112
Pottorf, Simeon L. V, 112
Potts, Abigail IV, 155
Potts, Abigail IV, 157
Potts, Abigail IV, 265
Potts, Abigail IV, 348
Potts, Abigail IV, 545
Potts, Alfred II, 408
Potts, Alfred IV, 157
Potts, Alfred IV, 348
Potts, Alfred IV, 545
Potts, Alice II, 498
Potts, Alice II, 624
Potts, Ann II, 408
Potts, Ann II, 446
Potts, Ann II, 599
Potts, Ann II, 811
Potts, Ann II, 911
Potts, Ann II, 944
Potts, Ann IV, 652
Potts, Ann VI, 716
Potts, Ann, Jr. VI, 546
Potts, Ann, Jr. VI, 716
Potts, Ann, Sr. VI, 546
Potts, Anna II, 625
Potts, Anna IV, 157
Potts, Anna IV, 348
Potts, Anna Frances II, 625
Potts, Anna Shipley II, 715
Potts, Benedict D. II, 408
Potts, Benjamin G. V, 1014
Potts, Betty I, 932
Potts, Caroline II, 408
Potts, Charles H. I, 948
Potts, Charles Hampton I, 932
Potts, Christian VI, 543
Potts, Christian VI, 547
Potts, David II, 408
Potts, David II, 498
Potts, David II, 624
Potts, David II, 625
Potts, David VI, 484
Potts, David VI, 546
Potts, David VI, 547
Potts, David, Jr. VI, 546
Potts, Deborah II, 408
Potts, Deborah II, 625
Potts, Deborah II, 688
Potts, Deborah IV, 157
Potts, Dorothy III, 257
Potts, Edward II, 408
Potts, Edward IV, 348
Potts, Edward IV, 545
Potts, Edward VI, 546
Potts, Edward G. IV, 155
Potts, Edward G. IV, 157
Potts, Edward G. IV, 348
Potts, Edward G. IV, 545
Potts, Edward Garrigus IV, 157
Potts, Elanor VI, 979
Potts, Elisabeth II, 624
Potts, Eliza II, 250
Potts, Elizabeth I, 932
Potts, Elizabeth I, 948
Potts, Elizabeth II, 37
Potts, Elizabeth II, 462
Potts, Elizabeth V, 1014
Potts, Elizabeth VI, 484
Potts, Elizabeth VI, 533
Potts, Elizabeth VI, 540
Potts, Elizabeth VI, 546
Potts, Elizabeth VI, 547
Potts, Elizabeth VI, 622
Potts, Elizabeth VI, 691
Potts, Elizabeth M. I, 932
Potts, Esther II, 247
Potts, Esther II, 250
Potts, Ezekiel VI, 546
Potts, Ezekiel VI, 979
Potts, Frances II, 625
Potts, George I, 932
Potts, Grace II, 446
Potts, Hannah II, 93
Potts, Hannah II, 108
Potts, Hannah II, 625
Potts, Hannah VI, 477
Potts, Hannah VI, 546
Potts, Hannah VI, 575
Potts, Harriet V, 1014
Potts, Hephzibah II, 625
Potts, Hepsebe II, 625
Potts, Humprey II, 462
Potts, Ida May V, 1014
Potts, Isaac II, 625
Potts, Isaac II, 688
Potts, Isaac W. II, 760
Potts, Isaac W. II, 911
Potts, Jacob II, 408
Potts, James II, 408
Potts, James R. I, 948
Potts, James Robert I, 932
Potts, Jane V, 1014
Potts, Jane VI, 484
Potts, Jane VI, 546
Potts, Jennie V, 1014
Potts, Jennings VI, 627
Potts, Jennings VI, 691
Potts, John II, 93
Potts, John II, 408
Potts, John II, 446
Potts, John II, 599
Potts, John II, 1008
Potts, John II, 1021
Potts, John IV, 348
Potts, John IV, 545
Potts, John V, 112
Potts, John V, 975
Potts, John VI, 547
Potts, John Morris II, 625
Potts, Jonas II, 408
Potts, Jonas VI, 465
Potts, Jonas VI, 477
Potts, Jonas VI, 484
Potts, Jonas VI, 540
Potts, Jonas VI, 546
Potts, Jonas VI, 547
Potts, Jonas VI, 568
Potts, Jonas VI, 592
Potts, Jonas VI, 603
Potts, Jonas, Jr. VI, 477
Potts, Jonas, Jr. VI, 546
Potts, Jonas, Sr. VI, 477
Potts, Jonas, Sr. VI, 568
Potts, Jonathan II, 30
Potts, Jonathan II, 37
Potts, Jonathan II, 61
Potts, Jonathan II, 93
Potts, Jonathan VI, 546
Potts, Jonathan VI, 547
Potts, Jonathan, Jr. II, 92
Potts, Jonathan, Jr. VI, 547
Potts, Joseph I, 639
Potts, Joseph I, 640
Potts, Joseph I, 948
Potts, Joseph II, 250
Potts, Joseph II, 298
Potts, Joseph II, 324
Potts, Joseph II, 408
Potts, Joseph II, 569
Potts, Joseph II, 599
Potts, Joseph II, 624
Potts, Joseph II, 1008
Potts, Joseph II, 1021
Potts, Joseph V, 704
Potts, Joseph K. II, 625
Potts, Judith I, 932
Potts, Judith I, 989
Potts, Judith I, 995
Potts, Judith III, 257
Potts, Judith III, 294
Potts, Lawrence M. II, 911
Potts, Lawrence M. II, 944
Potts, Lewis I, 948
Potts, Lindley IV, 157
Potts, Lindley IV, 348
Potts, Lindley IV, 545
Potts, Lindley V, 975
Potts, Lindly V, 112
Potts, Louis I. I, 932
Potts, Lydia II, 30
Potts, Lydia II, 75
Potts, Lydia II, 93
Potts, Lydia VI, 624
Potts, Lydia VI, 691
Potts, Margaret II, 911
Potts, Margaret II, 944
Potts, Margaret VI, 547
Potts, Margaret W. II, 911
Potts, Margaretta II, 1021
Potts, Margarette II, 1021
Potts, Margarette II, 1042
Potts, Martha II, 408
Potts, Martha II, 625
Potts, Martha II, 688
Potts, Mary II, 408
Potts, Mary II, 462
Potts, Mary II, 624
Potts, Mary II, 625
Potts, Mary II, 1008
Potts, Mary II, 1021
Potts, Mary III, 257
Potts, Mary III, 287
Potts, Mary IV, 157
Potts, Mary IV, 348
Potts, Mary IV, 360
Potts, Mary IV, 545
Potts, Mary V, 112
Potts, Mary V, 975
Potts, Mary VI, 467
Potts, Mary VI, 477
Potts, Mary VI, 484
Potts, Mary VI, 546
Potts, Mary VI, 547
Potts, Mary VI, 568
Potts, Mary VI, 603
Potts, Mary Ann IV, 155
Potts, Mary Ann IV, 157
Potts, Mary Ann IV, 158
Potts, Mary Letitia VI, 627
Potts, Mary Letitia VI, 691
Potts, Mary P. II, 715
Potts, Mary P. II, 760
Potts, Mary Powel II, 569
Potts, Mary Powel II, 625
Potts, Miriam II, 408
Potts, Nathan II, 625
Potts, Nathan VI, 504
Potts, Nathan VI, 547
Potts, Nathan R. II, 408
Potts, Nicholas I, 932
Potts, Nicholas I, 948
Potts, Nicholas H. I, 932

Potts, Nutt II, 408
Potts, Oliver IV, 157
Potts, Oliver Goldsmith IV, 157
Potts, Phebe VI, 477
Potts, Phebe VI, 546
Potts, Phebe VI, 592
Potts, Phebe VI, 603
Potts, Phineas II, 408
Potts, Rachel II, 78
Potts, Rachel II, 92
Potts, Rachel II, 93
Potts, Rachel II, 446
Potts, Rachel VI, 546
Potts, Rachel VI, 547
Potts, Rebecca II, 782
Potts, Rebecca II, 785
Potts, Rebecca II, 826
Potts, Rebecca IV, 157
Potts, Rebecca IV, 348
Potts, Rebecca IV, 360
Potts, Rebecca IV, 545
Potts, Rebecca Ann II, 809
Potts, Rebecca P. IV, 558
Potts, Rebecka II, 408
Potts, Rebecka II, 446
Potts, Rebeckah II, 446
Potts, Richard II, 250
Potts, Richard VI, 477
Potts, Rufina I, 948
Potts, Rufina R. I, 932
Potts, Ruth II, 599
Potts, Ruth IV, 157
Potts, Ruth IV, 348
Potts, Ruth VI, 482
Potts, Ruth VI, 547
Potts, Ruth Anna IV, 157
Potts, Ruth Elizabeth VI, 626
Potts, Ruth Elizabeth VI, 627
Potts, Ruth Elizabeth VI, 691
Potts, Ruthanna V, 112
Potts, Ruthanna V, 140
Potts, Ruthanna V, 141
Potts, Samuel II, 625
Potts, Samuel II, 911
Potts, Samuel II, 944
Potts, Samuel IV, 157
Potts, Samuel IV, 348
Potts, Samuel IV, 360
Potts, Samuel IV, 545
Potts, Samuel V, 112
Potts, Samuel V, 975
Potts, Samuel VI, 547
Potts, Sarah II, 30
Potts, Sarah II, 37
Potts, Sarah II, 61
Potts, Sarah II, 70
Potts, Sarah II, 93
Potts, Sarah II, 408
Potts, Sarah II, 508
Potts, Sarah II, 566
Potts, Sarah II, 569
Potts, Sarah II, 570
Potts, Sarah II, 624
Potts, Sarah II, 625
Potts, Sarah VI, 547
Potts, Sarah, Jr. II, 37
Potts, Sarah, Jr. II, 93
Potts, Sones I, 948
Potts, Stacey II, 247
Potts, Stacey II, 250
Potts, Stacey II, 625
Potts, Stacy II, 408
Potts, Stacy II, 625
Potts, Stacy II, 1021
Potts, Stacy II, 1042
Potts, Stephen VI, 933
Potts, Susanna VI, 539
Potts, Susanna VI, 547
Potts, Thomas II, 408
Potts, Thomas II, 446
Potts, Thomas III, 257
Potts, Thomas III, 294
Potts, Thurston VI, 626
Potts, Thurston VI, 627
Potts, Thurston VI, 691
Potts, William H. I, 948
Potts, William Henry I, 932
Potts, Wm. II, 462
Potts, Wm. II, 625
Potts, Y. H. V, 1014
Poulson, Albert IV, 1260
Poulson, Mary Bell IV, 1260
Poulter, James II, 446
Poulter, Margrett II, 446
Poultney Gover, Anthony VI, 522
Poultney Gover, Sarah VI, 522
Poultney, ??? III, 257
Poultney, Alice II, 625
Poultney, Alice II, 668
Poultney, Ann II, 408
Poultney, Ann II, 541
Poultney, Ann II, 625
Poultney, Ann II, 643
Poultney, Ann II, 911
Poultney, Ann VI, 548
Poultney, Ann VI, 571
Poultney, Ann Williams II, 625
Poultney, Anthony VI, 490
Poultney, Anthony VI, 548
Poultney, Benj. II, 625
Poultney, Benj. II, 655
Poultney, Benj. II, 667
Poultney, Benjamin II, 408
Poultney, Benjamin II, 625
Poultney, Benjamin II, 687
Poultney, Benjamin III, 257
Poultney, Charles Williams II, 408
Poultney, Charles Williams II, 625
Poultney, Chas. Williams II, 911
Poultney, Chas. Wm. II, 911
Poultney, Daniel Burns II, 911
Poultney, Daniel Byrnes II, 408
Poultney, Daniel Byrnes II, 625
Poultney, Daniel Byrnes II, 911
Poultney, Eleanor II, 625
Poultney, Eleanor VI, 548
Poultney, Eliza III, 257
Poultney, Elizabeth II, 408
Poultney, Elizabeth II, 625
Poultney, Elizabeth II, 643
Poultney, Elizabeth II, 668
Poultney, Elizabeth II, 687
Poultney, Elizabeth II, 823
Poultney, Elizabeth VI, 571
Poultney, Gulielma II, 408
Poultney, Gulielma Evans II, 625
Poultney, Hannah II, 408
Poultney, Hannah II, 625
Poultney, Hannah II, 655
Poultney, Hannah II, 687
Poultney, Hannah III, 257
Poultney, James II, 408
Poultney, James II, 625
Poultney, James II, 687
Poultney, James II, 715
Poultney, James II, 911
Poultney, Jane T. E. III, 257
Poultney, John II, 408
Poultney, John II, 541
Poultney, John II, 625
Poultney, John II, 643
Poultney, John VI, 546
Poultney, John VI, 548
Poultney, John VI, 575
Poultney, John, Jr. II, 625
Poultney, Joseph VI, 548
Poultney, Laetitia II, 911
Poultney, Latitia II, 625
Poultney, Latitia II, 687
Poultney, Letitia II, 408
Poultney, Letitia II, 625
Poultney, Letitia II, 715
Poultney, Letitia II, 736
Poultney, Letitia II, 911
Poultney, Lydia II, 408
Poultney, Lydia II, 625
Poultney, Lydia II, 667
Poultney, Lydia II, 720
Poultney, Lydia II, 911
Poultney, Lydia B. II, 625
Poultney, Lydia B. II, 911
Poultney, Maria III, 257
Poultney, Mary II, 408
Poultney, Mary II, 541
Poultney, Mary II, 625
Poultney, Mary VI, 490
Poultney, Mary VI, 548
Poultney, Mary VI, 575
Poultney, Mary W. II, 715
Poultney, Mary Williams II, 625
Poultney, Md. Thomas, Jr. VI, 571
Poultney, Phebe II, 408
Poultney, Phebe II, 625
Poultney, Phebe II, 667
Poultney, Rebecca II, 625
Poultney, Rebecca II, 655
Poultney, Richard VI, 548
Poultney, Richard VI, 575
Poultney, Samuel II, 408
Poultney, Samuel II, 625
Poultney, Sarah II, 408
Poultney, Sarah II, 625
Poultney, Sarah II, 687
Poultney, Sarah II, 723
Poultney, Sarah II, 867
Poultney, Sarah II, 911
Poultney, Sarah VI, 490
Poultney, Sarah VI, 491
Poultney, Sarah VI, 546
Poultney, Sarah VI, 548
Poultney, Sarah Pancoast II, 625
Poultney, Sarah Pancoast II, 911
Poultney, Susanna VI, 548
Poultney, Susannah VI, 490
Poultney, Thomas II, 408
Poultney, Thomas II, 625
Poultney, Thomas II, 643
Poultney, Thomas II, 668
Poultney, Thomas II, 687
Poultney, Thomas VI, 571
Poultney, Thomas, Jr. II, 625
Poultney, Thomas, Jr. VI, 548
Poultney, Thos. II, 823
Poultney, Wd. Alice II, 823
Poultney, William VI, 546
Poultney, Wm. II, 625
Poultney, Wm. Cook II, 625
Pound, Angelina E. IV, 839
Pound, Angeline E. IV, 894
Pound, Ann II, 408
Pound, Ann IV, 839
Pound, Ann IV, 893
Pound, Ann IV, 894
Pound, Ann IV, 1180
Pound, Ann H. IV, 839
Pound, Ann H. IV, 894
Pound, Ann H. IV, 1180
Pound, Asa IV, 894
Pound, Asa IV, 1180
Pound, Benj. H. IV, 1180
Pound, Benjamin H. IV, 839
Pound, Benjamin H. IV, 1180
Pound, Christopher II, 408
Pound, David IV, 839
Pound, David IV, 893
Pound, David IV, 894
Pound, David IV, 1180
Pound, Deborah II, 446
Pound, Elijah IV, 839
Pound, Elijah IV, 1180
Pound, Elizabeth L. IV, 810
Pound, Elizabeth L. IV, 839
Pound, Elizabeth L. IV, 894
Pound, Isabella IV, 839
Pound, Isabella IV, 894
Pound, Isabella IV, 1180
Pound, John II, 446
Pound, Margaret IV, 1180
Pound, Mary II, 408
Pound, Mary II, 625
Pound, Mary II, 691
Pound, Mary IV, 894
Pound, Mary IV, 1180
Pound, Mary H. IV, 839
Pound, Mary H. IV, 894
Pound, Mary H. IV, 1031
Pound, Mary H. IV, 1180
Pound, Robert II, 408
Pound, Robert II, 446
Pound, Samuel II, 446
Pound, Samuel S. III, 257
Pound, Sarah II, 446
Pound, Sarah H. IV, 839
Pound, Sarah H. IV, 894
Pound, Sarah H. IV, 1180
Pound, Susan IV, 752
Pound, Susan IV, 792
Pound, Susan IV, 826
Pound, Susan IV, 839
Pound, Susan I. IV, 752
Pound, Thomas IV, 826
Pound, Thomas C. IV, 752
Pound, Thomas C. IV, 792
Pound, Thomas C. IV, 810
Pound, Thomas C. IV, 839
Pound, Thomas C. IV, 1180
Pound, Thos. C. IV, 752
Pound, Thos. C. IV, 1180
Pound, Wm. I. IV, 752
Pounder, Appicarus II, 37
Pounder, Asher II, 93
Pounds, Ann VI, 451
Pounds, Samuel VI, 451
Pouts, ??? I, 715
Pouts, ??? I, 731
Pouts, Elizabeth I, 715
Pouts, Elizabeth IV, 54
Pouts, Jacob I, 695
Pouts, Jacob I, 715
Pouts, Jacob IV, 54
Pouts, Leanor IV, 54
Pouts, Levi IV, 54
Pouts, Linor I, 715
Pouts, Rebeckah I, 715
Pouts, William I, 715
Povall, Eliza T. VI, 937
Povall, Elizabeth VI, 937
Powar, Clementina VI, 847
Powar, Edward VI, 847
Powar, Helen VI, 847
Powar, Henry VI, 847
Powar, John F. VI, 823
Powar, Margaret VI, 864
Powar, Pamely VI, 864
Powar, Sina VI, 847
Powar, William VI, 847
Powar, William VI, 864
Powar, Wm. VI, 815
Poweel, Sarah II, 250
Powel, Aaron Draper VI, 79
Powel, Abraham I, 567
Powel, Abraham I, 645
Powel, Ann I, 416
Powel, Ann II, 686
Powel, Arlendo C. I, 752
Powel, Arlendo C. I, 768
Powel, Asenath I, 752
Powel, Asenath I, 768
Powel, Asenath I, 769
Powel, Benjamin II, 626
Powel, Benjamin V, 856
Powel, Charles VI, 62
Powel, Edmund F. I, 752
Powel, Edward F. I, 768
Powel, Eli I, 664
Powel, Eli I, 768
Powel, Elijah I, 664
Powel, Elijah I, 692
Powel, Elijah I, 768
Powel, Elizabeth I, 416
Powel, Elizabeth I, 567
Powel, Elizabeth I, 664
Powel, Elizabeth I, 768
Powel, Elizabeth II, 37
Powel, Elizabeth II, 163
Powel, Elizabeth II, 181
Powel, Elizabeth II, 201
Powel, Elizabeth II, 235
Powel, Elizabeth II, 250
Powel, Elizabeth II, 653
Powel, Elizabeth IV, 54
Powel, Elizabeth VI, 432
Powel, Esther I, 416
Powel, Evan II, 626
Powel, Gerald V, 272
Powel, Gwen II, 626
Powel, Hannah IV, 48
Powel, Hannah IV, 54
Powel, Hannah V, 852
Powel, Henry I, 567
Powel, Henry I, 664
Powel, Henry I, 688
Powel, Henry I, 690
Powel, Henry I, 741
Powel, Henry I, 1093
Powel, Henry I, 1097
Powel, Jabez I, 752
Powel, Jabez I, 768
Powel, Jabez M. I, 768
Powel, Jabez Marcelous I, 752
Powel, Jacob I, 69
Powel, Jacob I, 1131
Powel, Jane I, 835
Powel, Jane II, 37
Powel, Jane II, 56
Powel, Jane II, 93
Powel, Jeremiah II, 37
Powel, Jeremiah II, 56
Powel, Jeremiah II, 93
Powel, John I, 343
Powel, John I, 416
Powel, John II, 37
Powel, John II, 212
Powel, John II, 250
Powel, John II, 276
Powel, John VI, 432
Powel, Joseph I, 768
Powel, Judith I, 832
Powel, Judith I, 835
Powel, Julianna II, 760
Powel, Letitia IV, 38
Powel, Letitia IV, 54
Powel, Lindon I, 768
Powel, Lydia I, 768
Powel, Lydia IV, 52
Powel, Lydia IV, 54
Powel, Lydia Jane I, 752
Powel, Lyndon I, 768
Powel, Lyndon W. I, 752
Powel, Margaret I, 416
Powel, Martha I, 664
Powel, Martha IV, 54
Powel, Mary I, 194
Powel, Mary I, 199
Powel, Mary I, 752
Powel, Mary I, 768
Powel, Mary II, 37
Powel, Mary II, 86
Powel, Mary II, 93
Powel, Mary V, 273
Powel, Mary VI, 79
Powel, Miriam I, 556
Powel, Miriam I, 567
Powel, Miriam VI, 62
Powel, Morning I, 692
Powel, Mournen I, 741
Powel, Naomi I, 664
Powel, Orlando C. I, 768
Powel, Oswin John VI, 79
Powel, Prudence II, 181
Powel, Rachel I, 416
Powel, Rachel IV, 54
Powel, Rachel V, 856
Powel, Rebecca I, 1121
Powel, Rebecca I, 1131
Powel, Rebecca II, 716
Powel, Rebecca VI, 34
Powel, Rebecca VI, 37
Powel, Richard II, 250
Powel, Robert II, 181
Powel, Robert II, 250
Powel, Robert R. V, 272
Powel, Samuel II, 626
Powel, Sarah I, 664
Powel, Sarah I, 688
Powel, Sarah I, 731
Powel, Sarah II, 37
Powel, Sarah II, 89
Powel, Sarah II, 93
Powel, Sarah II, 155
Powel, Sarah II, 250
Powel, Sarah II, 276
Powel, Sarah II, 577
Powel, Sarah II, 625
Powel, Sarah II, 626
Powel, Stimnson VI, 433
Powel, Susanna I, 416
Powel, Susanna I, 690
Powel, Susanna I, 768
Powel, Susanna II, 626
Powel, Susanna Eugenie I, 75
Powel, Susannah I, 741
Powel, Thomas II, 626
Powel, Thomas V, 197
Powel, Thomas C. I, 752
Powel, Thomas C. I, 768
Powel, Thomas L. I, 752
Powel, Thomas L. I, 768
Powel, Ugenia I, 768
Powel, Virgin II, 212
Powel, Virgin II, 250
Powel, Walter W. I, 768
Powel, Walter Winborn I, 752
Powel, Wm. II, 155
Powel, Wm. VI, 37
Powel, Woodard M. I, 752
Powel, Woodward C. I, 768
Powell, ??? III, 258
Powell, ??? III, 259
Powell, ??? III, 405
Powell, ??? III, 479
Powell, A. III, 477
Powell, Aaron VI, 906
Powell, Aaron Draper VI, 79
Powell, Abigail II, 408
Powell, Abigail II, 537
Powell, Abigail II, 626
Powell, Abigail III, 257
Powell, Abigail III, 258
Powell, Abigail III, 360
Powell, Abigail III, 413
Powell, Abigail III, 414
Powell, Abigail III, 428
Powell, Abigail III, 434
Powell, Abigail III, 435
Powell, Abigail III, 436
Powell, Abigail III, 437
Powell, Abigail III, 455
Powell, Abigail III, 470
Powell, Abigail III, 493
Powell, Abigail III, 494
Powell, Abner VI, 847
Powell, Abraham II, 911
Powell, Abraham III, 257
Powell, Abraham III, 493
Powell, Abraham III, 497
Powell, Abraham VI, 973
Powell, Abraham VI, 979
Powell, Abraham VI, 1021
Powell, Abraham VI, 1022
Powell, Abram II, 884
Powell, Abram II, 911
Powell, Adaline III, 494
Powell, Addie L. III, 494
Powell, Addie L. III, 495
Powell, Albina II, 626
Powell, Albinah II, 626
Powell, Alexander III, 247
Powell, Alexander III, 257
Powell, Alfred F. VI, 979
Powell, Alice III, 493
Powell, Alice III, 494

ell, Amanda I, 929
ell, Amanda V, 197
ell, Amelia III, 494
ell, Amey III, 258
ell, Amos III, 436
ell, Amos III, 437
ell, Amos III, 467
ell, Amos III, 469
ell, Amy II, 136
ell, Amy III, 257
ell, Amy III, 258
ell, Amy III, 428
ell, Amy III, 435
ell, Amy III, 437
ell, Amy III, 467
ell, Amy III, 470
ell, Amy III, 493
ell, Amy III, 501
ell, Amy III, 505
ell, Andrew III, 482
ell, Andrew III, 493
ell, Ann I, 687
ell, Ann II, 250
ell, Ann II, 408
ell, Ann II, 503
ell, Ann II, 544
ell, Ann II, 615
ell, Ann II, 625
ell, Ann II, 626
ell, Ann III, 258
ell, Ann III, 435
ell, Ann III, 464
ell, Ann III, 494
ell, Ann III, 511
ell, Ann VI, 979
ell, Ann Eliza VI, 979
ell, Anna II, 137
ell, Anna II, 911
ell, Anna II, 923
ell, Anna III, 257
ell, Anna III, 258
ell, Anna III, 432
ell, Anna III, 437
ell, Anna III, 464
ell, Anna E. II, 911
ell, Anna E. III, 181
ell, Anna L. III, 257
ell, Anna M. II, 139
ell, Anne III, 405
ell, Anne III, 432
ell, Anne III, 435
ell, Anne III, 437
ell, Anne III, 492
ell, Annie I, 339
ell, Annie III, 435
ell, Ansel III, 493
ell, Antoinette III, 493
ell, Antoinette III, 494
vell, Artie III, 494
ell, Barbara I, 921
ell, Barbara Ethel I, 922
vell, Benajah B. II, 298
vell, Benj. III, 494
vell, Benjamin II, 626
vell, Benjamin III, 436
vell, Benjamin III, 493
vell, Benjamin V, 856
vell, Benjamin Rush II, 715
vell, Benjamin Rush II, 760
vell, Benjamin Rush II, 815
vell, Benjamin Rush II, 911
vell, Benjamin W. VI, 771
vell, Bertha Kate I, 921
vell, Bertha Kate I, 922
vell, Bessie IV, 1260
vell, Beth III, 435
vell, Bethany III, 257
vell, Betsy VI, 802
vell, Beulah II, 140
vell, Caleb III, 413
vell, Caleb III, 435
vell, Caleb III, 437
vell, Caleb T. VI, 891
vell, Caroline III, 493
vell, Caroline III, 495
vell, Cath. III, 257
vell, Cath. III, 437
well, Catharine III, 257
well, Catharine III, 258
well, Catharine III, 435
well, Catharine III, 437
well, Catharine III, 493
well, Catharine III, 494
well, Charity III, 435
well, Charles III, 493
well, Charles VI, 79
well, Charles VI, 847
well, Charles VI, 856
well, Charles H. III, 493
well, Charles L. III, 493
well, Charles S. III, 493
Powell, Charles S. III, 494
Powell, Charles U. III, 435
Powell, Charles W. III, 493
Powell, Chas. IV, 493
Powell, Chas. Hallowell II, 911
Powell, Chas. U. III, 378
Powell, Chas. U. III, 384
Powell, Chester IV, 1260
Powell, Chester A. IV, 1041
Powell, Christopher II, 223
Powell, Christopher II, 250
Powell, Christopher III, 257
Powell, Clement III, 413
Powell, Clement III, 435
Powell, Clement III, 465
Powell, Clement III, 466
Powell, Clements III, 258
Powell, Cleopatra VI, 935
Powell, Coles C. III, 511
Powell, Cornelius III, 257
Powell, Cornelius III, 416
Powell, Cornelius III, 435
Powell, Cornelius VI, 797
Powell, Cornelius VI, 847
Powell, Cyrus III, 258
Powell, D. A. I, 929
Powell, Daniel III, 258
Powell, Daniel III, 435
Powell, Daniel III, 436
Powell, Daniel III, 494
Powell, Daniel, Jr. III, 435
Powell, David II, 184
Powell, David II, 408
Powell, David II, 626
Powell, David II, 638
Powell, David II, 653
Powell, David III, 435
Powell, David VI, 846
Powell, David VI, 847
Powell, David VI, 850
Powell, Davis II, 626
Powell, Deborah II, 250
Powell, Deborah II, 408
Powell, Deborah II, 516
Powell, Deborah II, 626
Powell, Deborah III, 258
Powell, Deborah III, 435
Powell, Deborah III, 437
Powell, Deborah III, 458
Powell, Deborah III, 465
Powell, Deborah III, 469
Powell, Deborah III, 501
Powell, Deborah III, 504
Powell, Deborah Jane III, 493
Powell, E. Georgina III, 493
Powell, Edith III, 257
Powell, Edmund III, 436
Powell, Eleanor E. VI, 1021
Powell, Eleanor Frost III, 378
Powell, Eleanor Frost III, 384
Powell, Elijah I, 687
Powell, Elijah V, 856
Powell, Elijah VI, 802
Powell, Elisabeth I, 69
Powell, Elisabeth I, 70
Powell, Elisha III, 414
Powell, Elisha III, 435
Powell, Elisha H. III, 63
Powell, Elisha H. III, 179
Powell, Elisha H. III, 257
Powell, Eliz. III, 451
Powell, Eliza III, 257
Powell, Eliza III, 493
Powell, Eliza III, 497
Powell, Eliza A. VI, 847
Powell, Elizabeth I, 317
Powell, Elizabeth I, 687
Powell, Elizabeth I, 1131
Powell, Elizabeth II, 65
Powell, Elizabeth II, 93
Powell, Elizabeth II, 184
Powell, Elizabeth II, 248
Powell, Elizabeth II, 250
Powell, Elizabeth II, 408
Powell, Elizabeth II, 565
Powell, Elizabeth II, 572
Powell, Elizabeth II, 625
Powell, Elizabeth II, 626
Powell, Elizabeth II, 651
Powell, Elizabeth II, 653
Powell, Elizabeth III, 107
Powell, Elizabeth III, 178
Powell, Elizabeth III, 247
Powell, Elizabeth III, 254
Powell, Elizabeth III, 257
Powell, Elizabeth III, 258
Powell, Elizabeth III, 319
Powell, Elizabeth III, 384
Powell, Elizabeth III, 434
Powell, Elizabeth III, 435
Powell, Elizabeth III, 436
Powell, Elizabeth III, 437
Powell, Elizabeth III, 444
Powell, Elizabeth III, 455
Powell, Elizabeth III, 456
Powell, Elizabeth III, 459
Powell, Elizabeth III, 471
Powell, Elizabeth III, 474
Powell, Elizabeth III, 493
Powell, Elizabeth III, 511
Powell, Elizabeth IV, 40
Powell, Elizabeth VI, 34
Powell, Elizabeth VI, 338
Powell, Elizabeth VI, 847
Powell, Elizabeth VI, 850
Powell, Elizabeth H. II, 751
Powell, Elizabeth H. II, 760
Powell, Elizabeth H. II, 884
Powell, Elizabeth H. II, 911
Powell, Elizabeth M. III, 324
Powell, Elizabeth U. III, 414
Powell, Elizabeth U. III, 435
Powell, Elizabeth W. III, 257
Powell, Elsie III, 179
Powell, Elsie III, 181
Powell, Elsie III, 194
Powell, Elsie III, 257
Powell, Elsie III, 258
Powell, Elsie III, 259
Powell, Elsie III, 493
Powell, Elsie Knapp III, 259
Powell, Emeline M. VI, 973
Powell, Emily III, 258
Powell, Emily III, 493
Powell, Emma III, 247
Powell, Emma III, 257
Powell, Emma III, 494
Powell, Emma L. II, 877
Powell, Emma L. II, 911
Powell, Emmeline III, 493
Powell, Essie IV, 493
Powell, Essie IV, 1041
Powell, Essie IV, 1260
Powell, Esther III, 435
Powell, Esther III, 437
Powell, Esther III, 467
Powell, Esther III, 493
Powell, Esther III, 505
Powell, Esther VI, 628
Powell, Esther VI, 691
Powell, Ethalenda III, 258
Powell, Etta III, 435
Powell, Eugene I, 948
Powell, Evan II, 626
Powell, Evelyn Turner I, 922
Powell, Fannie III, 494
Powell, Felicia VI, 34
Powell, Frances IV, 1180
Powell, Frances VI, 979
Powell, Francis VI, 838
Powell, Francis VI, 850
Powell, Frank V, 641
Powell, Frederick III, 257
Powell, Fredrika III, 259
Powell, Fredrika III, 267
Powell, Fredrika T. III, 259
Powell, Fredrika T. III, 267
Powell, Freelove III, 435
Powell, Freelove III, 436
Powell, Freelove III, 437
Powell, Freelove III, 464
Powell, Freelove III, 494
Powell, G. Thomas III, 414
Powell, G. Thomas III, 435
Powell, Geo S. III, 435
Powell, Geo. III, 181
Powell, Geo. S. III, 435
Powell, George II, 815
Powell, George II, 911
Powell, George II, 923
Powell, George III, 488
Powell, George III, 493
Powell, George F. III, 493
Powell, George S. II, 911
Powell, George S. III, 421
Powell, George S. III, 435
Powell, George Sellers II, 911
Powell, George T. III, 66
Powell, George Townsend III, 257
Powell, Gerald V, 272
Powell, Grace II, 223
Powell, Grace II, 250
Powell, Grace III, 435
Powell, Grace A. III, 414
Powell, Grace A. III, 435
Powell, Grace T. III, 435
Powell, Green III, 493
Powell, Gwen II, 626
Powell, Hannah II, 93
Powell, Hannah II, 446
Powell, Hannah II, 626
Powell, Hannah II, 815
Powell, Hannah III, 258
Powell, Hannah III, 435
Powell, Hannah III, 436
Powell, Hannah III, 437
Powell, Hannah III, 459
Powell, Hannah III, 465
Powell, Hannah III, 466
Powell, Hannah III, 468
Powell, Hannah III, 474
Powell, Hannah III, 492
Powell, Hannah III, 493
Powell, Hannah III, 494
Powell, Hannah V, 856
Powell, Hannah VI, 691
Powell, Hannah VI, 702
Powell, Hannah VI, 854
Powell, Hannah Ann III, 488
Powell, Hannah Ann III, 494
Powell, Hannah J. III, 435
Powell, Hannah Poultney II, 815
Powell, Hannah Poultney II, 911
Powell, Hannah Poultney II, 923
Powell, Hannah W. III, 63
Powell, Hannah W. III, 480
Powell, Hannah W. III, 493
Powell, Hannah, Jr. III, 421
Powell, Harriet III, 384
Powell, Harriet III, 493
Powell, Harriet F. VI, 979
Powell, Harriet Van Nostrand III, 378
Powell, Harriett III, 384
Powell, Helen Elizabeth II, 911
Powell, Helen W. II, 877
Powell, Helen W. II, 911
Powell, Henrietta III, 502
Powell, Henry I, 69
Powell, Henry I, 70
Powell, Henry I, 567
Powell, Henry I, 687
Powell, Henry I, 1087
Powell, Henry I, 1089
Powell, Henry I, 1097
Powell, Henry II, 446
Powell, Henry III, 422
Powell, Henry III, 435
Powell, Henry III, 493
Powell, Henry III, 508
Powell, Henry A. VI, 979
Powell, Henry D. VI, 900
Powell, Henry D. VI, 979
Powell, Henry J. III, 258
Powell, Hezekiah VI, 79
Powell, Hopy Ann VI, 878
Powell, Ida Elizabeth II, 799
Powell, Isaac II, 250
Powell, Isaac II, 626
Powell, Isaac III, 435
Powell, Isaac III, 437
Powell, Isaac III, 456
Powell, Isaac III, 465
Powell, Isaac III, 493
Powell, Isaac R. V, 856
Powell, Isaac Randal V, 856
Powell, Isaac, Jr. III, 435
Powell, Isaac, Jr. III, 436
Powell, Isaac, Jr. III, 493
Powell, Israel III, 258
Powell, Israel III, 494
Powell, Jackson III, 436
Powell, Jacob I, 69
Powell, Jacob I, 1131
Powell, Jacob II, 194
Powell, Jacob II, 250
Powell, Jacob III, 258
Powell, Jacob III, 435
Powell, Jacob III, 492
Powell, Jacob III, 493
Powell, Jacob V, 356
Powell, Jacob VI, 45
Powell, Jacob VI, 46
Powell, Jacob VI, 79
Powell, Jacob S. III, 437
Powell, James III, 258
Powell, James III, 321
Powell, James III, 467
Powell, James III, 493
Powell, James G. IV, 1334
Powell, James P. I, 921
Powell, Jamie III, 494
Powell, Jane II, 93
Powell, Jane III, 436
Powell, Jane III, 437
Powell, Jane III, 466
Powell, Jane III, 471
Powell, Jane III, 482
Powell, Jane III, 493
Powell, Jane VI, 979
Powell, Jane Duryea III, 493
Powell, Jarvis III, 494
Powell, Jarvis W. III, 494
Powell, Jas. G. IV, 1334
Powell, Jathina VI, 847
Powell, Jemima III, 402
Powell, Jemima III, 436
Powell, Jemima III, 437
Powell, Jemima III, 438
Powell, Jemima III, 494
Powell, Jemima III, 495
Powell, Jemina III, 436
Powell, Jenetta V, 197
Powell, Jennie III, 493
Powell, Jere II, 136
Powell, Jeremiah II, 49
Powell, Jeremiah II, 65
Powell, Jeremiah II, 93
Powell, Jeremiah II, 136
Powell, Jerusha III, 425
Powell, Jerusha III, 428
Powell, Jerusha III, 436
Powell, Jerusha III, 437
Powell, Jerusha III, 464
Powell, Jesse VI, 908
Powell, Jesse VI, 916
Powell, Jesse VI, 979
Powell, Jno. II, 250
Powell, Johanna VI, 846
Powell, John I, 687
Powell, John I, 1097
Powell, John II, 136
Powell, John II, 247
Powell, John II, 248
Powell, John II, 250
Powell, John II, 255
Powell, John II, 408
Powell, John II, 544
Powell, John II, 626
Powell, John II, 911
Powell, John II, 923
Powell, John III, 147
Powell, John III, 258
Powell, John III, 384
Powell, John III, 414
Powell, John III, 435
Powell, John III, 436
Powell, John III, 437
Powell, John III, 464
Powell, John III, 465
Powell, John III, 467
Powell, John III, 468
Powell, John III, 470
Powell, John III, 493
Powell, John III, 505
Powell, John IV, 431
Powell, John VI, 432
Powell, John VI, 847
Powell, John VI, 979
Powell, John D. III, 258
Powell, John Lewis II, 136
Powell, John R. I, 922
Powell, John S. II, 911
Powell, John Smith II, 815
Powell, John T. III, 511
Powell, John W. III, 186
Powell, John W. III, 258
Powell, John W. III, 428
Powell, John W. III, 436
Powell, John W. III, 437
Powell, John W. III, 441
Powell, John W. III, 469
Powell, John, Jr. III, 436
Powell, John, Jr. III, 459
Powell, John, Jr. III, 494
Powell, Jonah III, 258
Powell, Jonah III, 436
Powell, Jonah III, 485
Powell, Jonah III, 489
Powell, Jonah III, 494
Powell, Jonah III, 499
Powell, Jonas III, 435
Powell, Jonas III, 436
Powell, Jonas III, 437
Powell, Jonas III, 492
Powell, Jonas III, 494
Powell, Jonathan III, 435
Powell, Jonathan P. III, 258
Powell, Jonathan R. III, 257
Powell, Jonathan R. III, 258
Powell, Jones III, 258
Powell, Joseph I, 1097
Powell, Joseph II, 250
Powell, Josephine III, 493
Powell, Joshua II, 626
Powell, Joshua III, 258
Powell, Joshua III, 435
Powell, Joshua III, 436
Powell, Joshua III, 437
Powell, Joshua III, 455
Powell, Joshua III, 466
Powell, Joshua III, 467
Powell, Joshua III, 468
Powell, Joshua III, 470

Powell, Joshua III, 473
Powell, Joshua III, 493
Powell, Josiah V, 856
Powell, Josiah VI, 942
Powell, Josiah VI, 979
Powell, Judeth III, 258
Powell, Judith III, 258
Powell, Judith VI, 850
Powell, Juliana N. II, 298
Powell, Julianna II, 760
Powell, Julianna N. II, 760
Powell, Kate I, 948
Powell, Katharine III, 414
Powell, Katharine III, 436
Powell, Kezia III, 481
Powell, Kezia III, 494
Powell, Lessie III, 494
Powell, Letty III, 436
Powell, Lewis III, 436
Powell, Libbie W. III, 494
Powell, Louisa III, 493
Powell, Louisa VI, 916
Powell, Louisa Ann VI, 1021
Powell, Lucas E. VI, 979
Powell, Lucas E. VI, 1022
Powell, Lucy III, 482
Powell, Lucy III, 483
Powell, Lucy VI, 847
Powell, Lucy G. III, 258
Powell, Lucy G. III, 349
Powell, Lucy G. III, 494
Powell, Lucy Gertrude III, 503
Powell, Lula V, 762
Powell, Lydia II, 502
Powell, Lydia II, 626
Powell, Lydia V, 856
Powell, Major ??? VI, 847
Powell, Malinda VI, 902
Powell, Manervy VI, 847
Powell, Marcia III, 257
Powell, Marcia R. III, 66
Powell, Margaret II, 626
Powell, Margaret III, 147
Powell, Margaret III, 258
Powell, Margaret III, 435
Powell, Margaret III, 436
Powell, Margaret III, 465
Powell, Margaret III, 467
Powell, Margaret III, 468
Powell, Margaret III, 493
Powell, Margaret III, 505
Powell, Margaret VI, 800
Powell, Margaret VI, 847
Powell, Margaret VI, 854
Powell, Margaret VI, 979
Powell, Margaret E. II, 871
Powell, Margaret E. II, 911
Powell, Margaret Elgar II, 911
Powell, Margaret H. II, 911
Powell, Margaretta II, 626
Powell, Margarette A. I, 339
Powell, Margrett II, 408
Powell, Margt III, 437
Powell, Maria III, 395
Powell, Maria III, 437
Powell, Maria III, 494
Powell, Martha II, 408
Powell, Martha II, 626
Powell, Martha II, 716
Powell, Martha III, 258
Powell, Martha III, 321
Powell, Martha III, 435
Powell, Martha III, 436
Powell, Martha III, 437
Powell, Martha III, 453
Powell, Martha III, 456
Powell, Martha III, 465
Powell, Martha III, 492
Powell, Martha III, 494
Powell, Martha III, 500
Powell, Martha A. V, 835
Powell, Martha A. V, 856
Powell, Martha A. VI, 854
Powell, Martha Ann V, 856
Powell, Martha E. VI, 979
Powell, Martin II, 716
Powell, Martin II, 760
Powell, Mary I, 1131
Powell, Mary II, 93
Powell, Mary II, 194
Powell, Mary II, 247
Powell, Mary II, 250
Powell, Mary II, 298
Powell, Mary II, 408
Powell, Mary II, 551
Powell, Mary II, 601
Powell, Mary II, 626
Powell, Mary II, 630
Powell, Mary II, 649
Powell, Mary II, 800
Powell, Mary II, 911
Powell, Mary II, 923
Powell, Mary III, 181
Powell, Mary III, 258
Powell, Mary III, 355
Powell, Mary III, 363
Powell, Mary III, 402
Powell, Mary III, 422
Powell, Mary III, 435
Powell, Mary III, 436
Powell, Mary III, 437
Powell, Mary III, 439
Powell, Mary III, 455
Powell, Mary III, 465
Powell, Mary III, 466
Powell, Mary III, 471
Powell, Mary III, 481
Powell, Mary III, 485
Powell, Mary III, 490
Powell, Mary III, 492
Powell, Mary III, 493
Powell, Mary III, 494
Powell, Mary III, 500
Powell, Mary III, 504
Powell, Mary IV, 265
Powell, Mary VI, 32
Powell, Mary VI, 33
Powell, Mary VI, 34
Powell, Mary VI, 79
Powell, Mary A. VI, 900
Powell, Mary Alice III, 494
Powell, Mary Ann IV, 839
Powell, Mary Ann IV, 901
Powell, Mary Ann IV, 914
Powell, Mary Ann VI, 900
Powell, Mary B. VI, 79
Powell, Mary B. VI, 81
Powell, Mary B. VI, 82
Powell, Mary C. III, 181
Powell, Mary Cathron VI, 877
Powell, Mary D. III, 437
Powell, Mary D. III, 466
Powell, Mary E. III, 493
Powell, Mary Elizabeth VI, 942
Powell, Mary Emma III, 493
Powell, Mary J. III, 258
Powell, Mary J. III, 428
Powell, Mary Jane II, 136
Powell, Mary Jane III, 494
Powell, Mary L. II, 884
Powell, Mary L. II, 911
Powell, Mary N. III, 258
Powell, Mary, Jr. III, 258
Powell, Mary, Jr. III, 436
Powell, Matilda III, 258
Powell, Matilda III, 436
Powell, Matilda III, 441
Powell, Matilda VI, 1022
Powell, Melville R. III, 259
Powell, Mercy III, 436
Powell, Mercy III, 437
Powell, Mercy III, 444
Powell, Milly VI, 979
Powell, Miriam Draper VI, 79
Powell, Mordicia VI, 79
Powell, Morgan VI, 847
Powell, Morning I, 687
Powell, Moses III, 258
Powell, Moses III, 414
Powell, Moses III, 436
Powell, Moses III, 437
Powell, Mourning I, 317
Powell, Nancy VI, 847
Powell, Nancy A. VI, 838
Powell, Obadiah III, 435
Powell, Obadiah III, 469
Powell, Oliver VI, 1022
Powell, Oliver N. VI, 994
Powell, Oswin John VI, 79
Powell, Pamelia C. III, 494
Powell, Peggy VI, 854
Powell, Phebe III, 258
Powell, Phebe III, 384
Powell, Phebe III, 418
Powell, Phebe III, 435
Powell, Phebe III, 436
Powell, Phebe III, 437
Powell, Phebe III, 455
Powell, Phebe III, 466
Powell, Phebe III, 467
Powell, Phebe III, 468
Powell, Phebe III, 470
Powell, Phebe III, 473
Powell, Phebe III, 474
Powell, Phebe III, 493
Powell, Phebe III, 494
Powell, Phebe III, 505
Powell, Phebe III, 509
Powell, Phebe A. III, 437
Powell, Phebe A. III, 494
Powell, Philenah III, 258
Powell, Phineas III, 494
Powell, Polly VI, 979
Powell, Prudence II, 163
Powell, Prudence II, 247
Powell, Prudence II, 250
Powell, Prudence III, 494
Powell, Rachel III, 257
Powell, Rachel III, 258
Powell, Rachel III, 414
Powell, Rachel III, 416
Powell, Rachel III, 435
Powell, Rachel III, 436
Powell, Rachel III, 437
Powell, Rachel III, 471
Powell, Rachel III, 494
Powell, Rachel III, 499
Powell, Rachel IV, 22
Powell, Rachel V, 856
Powell, Rachel A. III, 259
Powell, Rachel D. III, 63
Powell, Rachel D. III, 179
Powell, Rachel D. III, 257
Powell, Rachel H. III, 258
Powell, Ralph IV, 1041
Powell, Rebecca I, 1131
Powell, Rebecca II, 136
Powell, Rebecca II, 615
Powell, Rebecca II, 626
Powell, Rebecca II, 716
Powell, Rebecca III, 437
Powell, Rebecca III, 469
Powell, Rebecca VI, 34
Powell, Rebeckah VI, 846
Powell, Reuben III, 257
Powell, Reuben III, 435
Powell, Reuben III, 437
Powell, Rich'd S. III, 63
Powell, Richard II, 250
Powell, Richard III, 258
Powell, Richard III, 425
Powell, Richard III, 435
Powell, Richard III, 437
Powell, Richard III, 464
Powell, Richard III, 467
Powell, Richard III, 493
Powell, Richard III, 505
Powell, Richard VI, 847
Powell, Richard C. VI, 800
Powell, Richard P. III, 494
Powell, Richard Post III, 470
Powell, Richard S. III, 480
Powell, Richard S. III, 493
Powell, Richard S. III, 494
Powell, Richard S. III, 495
Powell, Richard S. III, 502
Powell, Richard S. III, 509
Powell, Richard, Jr. III, 436
Powell, Richard, Jr. III, 438
Powell, Richard, Jr. III, 466
Powell, Richard, Jr. III, 494
Powell, Robert II, 163
Powell, Robert II, 247
Powell, Robert II, 250
Powell, Robert III, 493
Powell, Robert R. V, 272
Powell, Roney IV, 265
Powell, Ruben III, 464
Powell, Rueben III, 464
Powell, Ruth III, 398
Powell, Ruth III, 428
Powell, Ruth III, 437
Powell, Ruth III, 493
Powell, Ruth III, 494
Powell, Ruth III, 508
Powell, Ruth Alice III, 258
Powell, Ruth Alice III, 349
Powell, Ruth Alice III, 494
Powell, Ruth Alice III, 503
Powell, Ruth H. III, 488
Powell, Salley VI, 79
Powell, Sally VI, 979
Powell, Sam'l I, 1097
Powell, Sam'l II, 408
Powell, Samuel I, 1097
Powell, Samuel II, 136
Powell, Samuel II, 155
Powell, Samuel II, 408
Powell, Samuel II, 601
Powell, Samuel II, 626
Powell, Samuel II, 630
Powell, Samuel II, 636
Powell, Samuel II, 686
Powell, Samuel III, 258
Powell, Samuel III, 437
Powell, Samuel III, 481
Powell, Samuel III, 492
Powell, Samuel III, 493
Powell, Samuel VI, 79
Powell, Samuel VI, 81
Powell, Samuel VI, 82
Powell, Samuel B. III, 258
Powell, Samuel S. II, 911
Powell, Samuel, Jr. II, 408
Powell, Samuel, Jr. II, 537
Powell, Samuel, Jr. II, 626
Powell, Samuel, Jr. III, 437
Powell, Samuel, Sr. II, 408
Powell, Sarah I, 687
Powell, Sarah I, 1131
Powell, Sarah II, 93
Powell, Sarah II, 136
Powell, Sarah II, 140
Powell, Sarah II, 155
Powell, Sarah II, 223
Powell, Sarah II, 250
Powell, Sarah II, 255
Powell, Sarah II, 408
Powell, Sarah II, 454
Powell, Sarah II, 508
Powell, Sarah II, 529
Powell, Sarah II, 577
Powell, Sarah II, 601
Powell, Sarah II, 626
Powell, Sarah II, 636
Powell, Sarah II, 638
Powell, Sarah II, 791
Powell, Sarah III, 258
Powell, Sarah III, 259
Powell, Sarah III, 428
Powell, Sarah III, 435
Powell, Sarah III, 436
Powell, Sarah III, 437
Powell, Sarah III, 444
Powell, Sarah III, 464
Powell, Sarah III, 467
Powell, Sarah III, 479
Powell, Sarah III, 488
Powell, Sarah III, 492
Powell, Sarah III, 493
Powell, Sarah III, 494
Powell, Sarah III, 509
Powell, Sarah VI, 45
Powell, Sarah VI, 46
Powell, Sarah VI, 847
Powell, Sarah VI, 918
Powell, Sarah A. III, 437
Powell, Sarah A. III, 469
Powell, Sarah Ann III, 258
Powell, Sarah H. III, 49
Powell, Sarah H. III, 179
Powell, Sarah H. III, 181
Powell, Sarah H. III, 257
Powell, Sarah H. III, 258
Powell, Sarah Hopper III, 259
Powell, Sarah J. II, 155
Powell, Sarah K. II, 298
Powell, Sarah M. II, 871
Powell, Sarah M. II, 911
Powell, Sarah M. III, 186
Powell, Sarah M. III, 258
Powell, Sarah M. III, 437
Powell, Sarah M. III, 441
Powell, Sarah M. III, 469
Powell, Sarah T. III, 63
Powell, Sarah T. III, 480
Powell, Sarah T. III, 482
Powell, Sarah T. III, 493
Powell, Sarah T. III, 494
Powell, Sarah T. III, 495
Powell, Sarah T. III, 502
Powell, Sarah W. II, 131
Powell, Sarah Woolston II, 250
Powell, Sibbel III, 494
Powell, Sibyl III, 437
Powell, Silas III, 437
Powell, Solomon III, 258
Powell, Solomon III, 398
Powell, Solomon III, 428
Powell, Solomon III, 437
Powell, Sophia VI, 847
Powell, Stephen III, 258
Powell, Stephen III, 437
Powell, Stephen B. III, 437
Powell, Stephen D. III, 437
Powell, Stimnson VI, 433
Powell, Stimonson III, 395
Powell, Stimonson III, 437
Powell, Stimusson III, 466
Powell, Susan III, 511
Powell, Susan E. V, 272
Powell, Susana M. VI, 891
Powell, Susanna I, 687
Powell, Susanna II, 446
Powell, Susanna II, 626
Powell, Susanna V, 856
Powell, Susanna A. VI, 338
Powell, Susanna A. VI, 850
Powell, Susannah II, 250
Powell, Sybil III, 489
Powell, Sybil III, 492
Powell, Sybil III, 494
Powell, Sybyl III, 436
Powell, Tabitha III, 258
Powell, Thomas II, 408
Powell, Thomas II, 626
Powell, Thomas III, 254
Powell, Thomas III, 257
Powell, Thomas III, 258
Powell, Thomas III, 319
Powell, Thomas III, 355
Powell, Thomas III, 360
Powell, Thomas III, 413
Powell, Thomas III, 428
Powell, Thomas III, 435
Powell, Thomas III, 436
Powell, Thomas III, 437
Powell, Thomas III, 439
Powell, Thomas III, 444
Powell, Thomas III, 453
Powell, Thomas III, 455
Powell, Thomas III, 456
Powell, Thomas III, 465
Powell, Thomas III, 470
Powell, Thomas III, 473
Powell, Thomas III, 474
Powell, Thomas III, 493
Powell, Thomas III, 500
Powell, Thomas III, 504
Powell, Thomas IV, 493
Powell, Thomas IV, 1041
Powell, Thomas IV, 1220
Powell, Thomas V, 197
Powell, Thomas V, 426
Powell, Thomas VI, 847
Powell, Thomas E. V, 197
Powell, Thomas E. V, 272
Powell, Thomas E. V, 426
Powell, Thomas T. III, 258
Powell, Thomas U. III, 488
Powell, Thomas U. III, 494
Powell, Thomas, Sr. III, 437
Powell, Thos. II, 871
Powell, Thos. II, 911
Powell, Thos. III, 257
Powell, Thos. III, 434
Powell, Thos. III, 435
Powell, Thos. III, 437
Powell, Thos. III, 471
Powell, Timothy III, 258
Powell, Timothy M. III, 181
Powell, Townsend III, 257
Powell, Ura V, 197
Powell, Ura V, 272
Powell, Ura V, 426
Powell, Usley VI, 979
Powell, Vashty II, 93
Powell, Virgin II, 250
Powell, Virgin II, 255
Powell, Virginia C. I, 929
Powell, Wait III, 258
Powell, Wait III, 402
Powell, Wait III, 436
Powell, Wait III, 437
Powell, Wait III, 466
Powell, Wait III, 468
Powell, Wait III, 471
Powell, Wait III, 493
Powell, Wait III, 494
Powell, Wait Elisha III, 437
Powell, Wait, Jr. III, 432
Powell, Wait, Jr. III, 435
Powell, Walter I, 339
Powell, Walter III, 258
Powell, Walter III, 349
Powell, Walter III, 482
Powell, Walter III, 483
Powell, Walter III, 494
Powell, Walter IV, 493
Powell, Walter IV, 1041
Powell, Walter C. II, 871
Powell, Walter C. II, 911
Powell, Walter E. II, 911
Powell, Walter F. I, 339
Powell, Washington II, 626
Powell, Wd Sarah II, 626
Powell, Wd. Abigail III, 257
Powell, Wd. Ann III, 464
Powell, Wd. Elizabeth III, 467
Powell, Wd. Elizabeth VI, 34
Powell, Wd. Katharine III, 469
Powell, Wd. Margaret III, 470
Powell, Wd. Sarah II, 597
Powell, Wellington III, 494
Powell, Wellington III, 495
Powell, Whitson III, 494
Powell, Willet III, 437
Powell, Willet III, 443
Powell, Willete III, 436
Powell, Willets III, 494
Powell, William II, 408
Powell, William III, 437
Powell, William III, 511
Powell, William VI, 34
Powell, William VI, 979

ll, William J. III, 258
ll, William K. III, 493
ll, William S. III, 258
ll, William, Jr. II, 408
ll, Willie III, 494
ll, Wilmena V, 197
ll, Wilson III, 181
ell, Wilson III, 259
ell, Wilson M. III, 49
ell, Wilson M. III, 179
ell, Wilson M. III, 194
ell, Wilson M. III, 257
ell, Wilson M. III, 258
ell, Wilson M. III, 259
ell, Wilson M., Jr. III, 258
ell, Wilson Marcy III, 259
ell, Wilson Marcy III, 267
ell, Wm. II, 136
ell, Wm. II, 140
ell, Wm. II, 155
ell, Wm. II, 529
ell, Wm. II, 544
ell, Wm. II, 572
ell, Wm. II, 625
ell, Wm. II, 626
ell, Wm. II, 630
ell, Wm. II, 651
ell, Wm. VI, 32
ell, Wm. VI, 33
vell, Wm. VI, 34
vell, Wm. G. II, 877
vell, Wm. G. II, 911
vell, Wm. N. III, 258
vell, Wm., Jr. II, 454
vell, Wm., Jr. II, 626
vell, Zebulon III, 492
vell, Zebulon III, 494
welson, Albert A. IV, 1260
welson, Mary Bell IV, 1260
wer, Abigail IV, 1366
wer, Abigail IV, 1372
wer, Abraham IV, 1376
wer, Abraham L. IV, 1376
wer, Amy IV, 1376
wer, Arthur IV, 1376
wer, Arthur P. IV, 1376
wer, Bulah E. IV, 1376
wer, Deborah IV, 1376
wer, Duana IV, 1376
wer, Elisabeth VI, 1021
wer, Elizabeth IV, 1366
wer, Elizabeth VI, 872
wer, Elizabeth VI, 874
wer, Elizabeth VI, 976
wer, Elizabeth VI, 989
ower, Elizabeth, Sr. VI, 989
ower, Emeline IV, 1376
ower, Emeline IV, 1384
ower, Esther IV, 1375
ower, Esther IV, 1376
ower, Ethen L. IV, 1376
ower, Francis IV, 1376
ower, George IV, 1376
ower, Gideon IV, 1376
ower, Huldah A. IV, 1376
ower, Ira IV, 1376
ower, Ira S. IV, 1376
ower, Janetta F. VI, 1021
ower, Jared IV, 1376
ower, John IV, 1376
ower, John VI, 966
ower, John W. IV, 1376
ower, John Webb IV, 1376
ower, Lorenzo IV, 1376
ower, Mary IV, 1376
ower, Mary VI, 874
Power, Mary Lavina IV, 1376
Power, Matilda IV, 1376
Power, Nancy VI, 872
Power, Nathan IV, 1358
Power, Nathan IV, 1376
Power, Otis C. IV, 1376
Power, Patience IV, 1358
Power, Patience IV, 1376
Power, Patience C. IV, 1376
Power, Phebe M. IV, 1376
Power, Salinda IV, 1376
Power, Samuel IV, 1376
Power, Sarah IV, 1376
Power, Sarah VI, 976
Power, Sarah L. IV, 1366
Power, Sarah L. IV, 1372
Power, Sarah L. IV, 1376
Power, Selinda IV, 1376
Power, Thomas Hawly IV, 1366
Power, Vicena IV, 1366
Power, Vicena IV, 1376
Power, William IV, 1376
Power, William Lawton IV, 1366
Power, William Lawton IV, 1372
Powers, Agnes R. V, 926
Powers, Angeline L. VI, 979
Powers, Ann VI, 812
Powers, Anna L. II, 140
Powers, Arthur IV, 1180
Powers, Delilah J. VI, 847
Powers, Edward II, 408
Powers, Elizabeth VI, 838
Powers, Fayette VI, 979
Powers, Hazel Stingley V, 197
Powers, Henry VI, 812
Powers, Henry VI, 835
Powers, Henry VI, 838
Powers, Henry VI, 840
Powers, James Pearson II, 408
Powers, Jane IV, 265
Powers, Jane IV, 301
Powers, Katie V, 356
Powers, Locky J. VI, 836
Powers, Louisa VI, 840
Powers, Lydia IV, 125
Powers, Lydia IV, 131
Powers, Margaret II, 136
Powers, Margaret Vanneman II, 155
Powers, Mary V, 272
Powers, Mary V, 273
Powers, Mary Jane VI, 1002
Powers, Missouri VI, 835
Powers, Paul H. II, 136
Powers, Ruhama VI, 956
Powers, Sarah II, 559
Powers, Sarah L. V, 112
Powers, Susanna II, 408
Powers, Susannah II, 618
Powers, Susannah II, 626
Powers, Thomas VI, 847
Powers, Thomas VI, 956
Powers, Thomas VI, 1002
Powers, Wm. McAllister VI, 836
Powers, Zeno IV, 1180
Powers, Zeno Alvin IV, 1180
Powil, Mary II, 93
Powil, Mary II, 108
Powill, Hannah II, 93
Powill, Hannah II, 110
Powly, George II, 408
Powly, Mary II, 408
Pownal, George II, 1022
Pownal, Mary II, 1022
Pownal, Mary II, 1029
Pownal, Reuben II, 1022
Pownal, Reuben II, 1029
Pownall, Abigail II, 1002
Pownall, Abigail II, 1020
Pownall, Catharine II, 626
Pownall, Catharine II, 688
Pownall, Eleanor II, 1002
Pownall, Eleanor II, 1022
Pownall, Elenor II, 1020
Pownall, Elinor II, 1017
Pownall, Elioner II, 1022
Pownall, Elizabeth II, 791
Pownall, Elizabeth II, 818
Pownall, Elizabeth II, 989
Pownall, Elizabeth II, 1022
Pownall, Elsie II, 931
Pownall, George II, 1022
Pownall, Hannah Ann II, 798
Pownall, Mary II, 1022
Pownall, Rachel II, 1005
Pownall, Rachel II, 1022
Pownall, Reuben II, 1022
Pownall, Sarah II, 626
Pownall, Sarah II, 688
Pownall, Simeon II, 626
Pownall, Simeon II, 688
Pownel, John I, 416
Powner, Appicares II, 93
Powner, Asher II, 93
Powner, George II, 1004
Poyl, Ruth I, 453
Poynt, Pine II, 56
Prachen, Barbara II, 626
Prackett, Margaretta V, 908
Prackett, Margaretta V, 926
Pramer, John V, 198
Pratchin, Barbara II, 408
Prater, Sillei VI, 847
Prater, Thomas VI, 847
Prathar, Archilbald VI, 1002
Prathar, Mary Jane VI, 1002
Prather, Archibald VI, 979
Prather, David M. VI, 847
Prather, Euphemia VI, 847
Prather, Jonathan VI, 979
Prather, Margaret Ann V, 326
Prather, Mary Jean V, 704
Prather, Rebecca V, 356
Prather, Rebecca V, 359
Prather, Sally VI, 979
Prather, Sarah VI, 918
Prather, Sarah VI, 979
Prather, Sidney V, 112
Prather, Sidney V, 141
Prather, Thomas VI, 918
Pratt, Abijah IV, 1376
Pratt, Ada Marian IV, 1334
Pratt, Ada Marion IV, 1334
Pratt, Anna L. II, 911
Pratt, Betsey IV, 1376
Pratt, Betsy IV, 1376
Pratt, Charles III, 259
Pratt, Charles IV, 1376
Pratt, Charles Barton III, 259
Pratt, Charles Walter III, 28
Pratt, David, Jr. II, 626
Pratt, Davis R. II, 911
Pratt, Davis Richards II, 815
Pratt, Dicey VI, 911
Pratt, Doris V, 704
Pratt, Edwin D. II, 815
Pratt, Edwin D. II, 911
Pratt, Elizabeth II, 911
Pratt, Elizabeth II, 927
Pratt, Elizabeth IV, 1376
Pratt, Elizzbeth VI, 939
Pratt, Ella IV, 1334
Pratt, Ellen J. II, 911
Pratt, Ellen J. II, 943
Pratt, Ellen Janney II, 815
Pratt, Elmina III, 438
Pratt, Emma II, 815
Pratt, Emma II, 911
Pratt, Emma G. II, 911
Pratt, Franklin II, 815
Pratt, Hannah I, 272
Pratt, Hannah I, 274
Pratt, Hannah I, 553
Pratt, Hannah I, 568
Pratt, Hannah II, 822
Pratt, Ivanette Hathaway V, 198
Pratt, J. F. IV, 1334
Pratt, Jacob Arnold IV, 1376
Pratt, Jemima III, 438
Pratt, Jemima III, 494
Pratt, Jemima III, 495
Pratt, Jemina III, 436
Pratt, Jeremiah D. II, 626
Pratt, Jessie III, 259
Pratt, Jessie Emma III, 259
Pratt, John III, 438
Pratt, John VI, 939
Pratt, John VI, 979
Pratt, John C. III, 438
Pratt, Jonathan III, 494
Pratt, Jonathan III, 495
Pratt, Joseph VI, 833
Pratt, Joseph VI, 847
Pratt, Lewis II, 626
Pratt, Lillian V, 704
Pratt, Loraine Ethel III, 259
Pratt, Mariah IV, 1334
Pratt, Martha II, 815
Pratt, Martha II, 822
Pratt, Martha II, 928
Pratt, Martha K. II, 911
Pratt, Martha R. II, 911
Pratt, Martha R. II, 928
Pratt, Martha Roberts II, 822
Pratt, Martha V. II, 815
Pratt, Martha V. II, 911
Pratt, Martha V. II, 928
Pratt, Mary I, 553
Pratt, Mary I, 568
Pratt, Mary III, 438
Pratt, Mary VI, 916
Pratt, Nancy VI, 847
Pratt, Nancy VI, 945
Pratt, Nathan II, 815
Pratt, Nathan II, 822
Pratt, Nathan II, 911
Pratt, Nathan II, 928
Pratt, Ossining III, 259
Pratt, Polly VI, 979
Pratt, Rachel II, 626
Pratt, Rachel II, 630
Pratt, Roy V, 704
Pratt, Salley VI, 979
Pratt, Sarah I, 274
Pratt, Sarah H. III, 438
Pratt, Stephen VI, 889
Pratt, Stephen VI, 902
Pratt, Stephen VI, 945
Pratt, Stephen VI, 979
Pratt, T. C. V, 704
Pratt, Walter III, 259
Pratt, Walter B. III, 259
Pratt, Wd. Martha V. II, 815
Prawl, Chas. W. V, 1014
Prawl, Mary E. V, 1014
Pray, Anna Jane V, 845
Pray, Anna Jane V, 857
Pray, Anna Maria V, 592
Pray, Anna Mariah V, 592
Pray, Elisa V, 857
Pray, Elizabeth V, 857
Pray, Elizabeth M. V, 592
Pray, Elvira V, 592
Pray, Elvira V, 762
Pray, Elvira V, 856
Pray, Elvira V, 857
Pray, Elvira V, 864
Pray, Enos IV, 106
Pray, Enos V, 592
Pray, Enos V, 762
Pray, Enos V, 792
Pray, Enos V, 856
Pray, Enos V, 857
Pray, Enos V, 864
Pray, Enos Edwin V, 592
Pray, Enos G. V, 592
Pray, Joseph IV, 106
Pray, Joseph V, 592
Pray, Joseph V, 845
Pray, Joseph V, 857
Pray, Joseph J. V, 592
Pray, Mark V, 592
Pray, Martha V, 592
Pray, Martha V, 857
Pray, Martha H. V, 592
Pray, Mary IV, 106
Pray, Mary V, 856
Pray, Mary V, 857
Pray, Mary V, 864
Pray, Mary V, 868
Pray, Mary H. V, 857
Pray, Mary H. V, 868
Pray, Mattie V, 592
Pray, Nida V, 592
Pray, Rachel IV, 106
Pray, Rachel V, 592
Pray, Rachel V, 856
Pray, Rachel V, 857
Pray, Rachel V, 864
Pray, Rhoda J. V, 592
Pray, Ruth J. V, 592
Pray, Samuel IV, 106
Pray, Samuel Dilwin V, 592
Pray, Samuel M. V, 857
Pray, Sibil V, 857
Pray, Sybil J. V, 592
Pray, Wd Mary IV, 73
Pray, Wd Mary IV, 106
Pray, William IV, 73
Pray, William IV, 106
Pray, William V, 857
Pray, William S. V, 592
Pray, Wm. IV, 106
Pray, Wm. V, 856
Pray, Wm. V, 864
Pray, Wm. V, 868
Pray, Wm. S. V, 592
Preas, Behala VI, 979
Preas, Delila VI, 979
Preas, Elizabeth VI, 875
Preas, Elizabeth VI, 884
Preas, Elizabeth VI, 979
Preas, Elizabeth VI, 1001
Preas, Henry VI, 940
Preas, Henry VI, 979
Preas, Jane VI, 1019
Preas, John VI, 979
Preas, Joseph VI, 979
Preas, Joseph, Jr. VI, 968
Preas, Joseph, Jr. VI, 979
Preas, Margaret VI, 977
Preas, Mary VI, 919
Preas, Mary VI, 979
Preas, Mary Jane VI, 979
Preas, Mary R. VI, 979
Preas, Polly VI, 884
Preas, Rachel VI, 979
Preas, Rebecca VI, 875
Preas, Ruth VI, 1019
Preas, Sarah VI, 979
Preas, Thomas VI, 875
Preas, Thomas VI, 919
Preas, Thomas VI, 977
Preas, Thomas VI, 979
Preas, Thomas VI, 993
Preas, William VI, 979
Preas., Betsy VI, 911
Preason, Salley VI, 943
Preast, Elizabeth VI, 979
Preast, Henry VI, 979
Preast, Joseph VI, 979
Preast, Patsey VI, 977
Preast, Rachel VI, 1006
Preast, Sarah VI, 979
Prebles, Sarah V, 977
Prechet, Mathew I, 162
Prechett, ??? V, 315
Prediger, Friedericke III, 33
Preeman, James C. VI, 796
Preese, Elizabeth II, 626
Preese, Reese II, 626
Preese, Reese II, 686
Prentiss, Martha Elizabeth II, 703
Prescott, Francis II, 408
Present, Joannah II, 409
Presey, ??? V, 315
Preshall, Mary V, 419
Presley, Callie I, 1160
Presley, Francis I, 1160
Presley, Francis I, 1161
Presley, Isaac I, 1160
Presley, John I, 1160
Presley, Lizzie I, 1160
Presley, Polly I, 1160
Presley, Rufus I, 1161
Presley, Ruthie I, 1160
Presley, Sarah J. I, 1160
Presnal, Benoni V, 416
Presnal, Benoni V, 426
Presnal, Daniel V, 426
Presnal, Elagah I, 731
Presnal, Hannah I, 416
Presnal, Hannah I, 731
Presnal, Hannah V, 429
Presnal, Henry V, 426
Presnal, Isaac I, 731
Presnal, Islah I, 731
Presnal, James V, 426
Presnal, Jane V, 416
Presnal, Jane V, 426
Presnal, Jeremiah V, 426
Presnal, Mariam I, 722
Presnal, Mariam I, 731
Presnal, Mary V, 426
Presnal, Nathan I, 731
Presnal, Pleasant V, 426
Presnal, Ruth I, 731
Presnal, Sarah V, 426
Presnal, William V, 426
Presnal, Wm. V, 426
Presnall, Absolum I, 731
Presnall, Callie Eugenia IV, 1334
Presnall, Christianna I, 731
Presnall, Christina I, 731
Presnall, Christinea I, 731
Presnall, Christinea I, 737
Presnall, Daniel I, 725
Presnall, Daniel I, 731
Presnall, Daniel, Jr. I, 731
Presnall, Elagah I, 731
Presnall, Elias I, 731
Presnall, Elihu I, 731
Presnall, Elijah I, 731
Presnall, Elijah I, 995
Presnall, Elisha I, 484
Presnall, Elisha I, 731
Presnall, Elisha I, 995
Presnall, Elizabeth I, 731
Presnall, Esau I, 731
Presnall, Grace IV, 1334
Presnall, H. F. IV, 1334
Presnall, Hannah I, 731
Presnall, Hannah I, 732
Presnall, Howard F. IV, 1334
Presnall, Isaac I, 731
Presnall, Isaac I, 995
Presnall, Islah I, 731
Presnall, Israel I, 731
Presnall, Israel I, 995
Presnall, James I, 731
Presnall, Jane I, 731
Presnall, Jane I, 995
Presnall, Jehu I, 731
Presnall, Jeremiah L. I, 731
Presnall, John I, 731
Presnall, John M. I, 731
Presnall, Josiah I, 731
Presnall, Josiah I, 995
Presnall, Julia I, 731
Presnall, Lydia I, 722
Presnall, Lydia I, 728
Presnall, Lydia I, 731
Presnall, Lydia V, 112
Presnall, Maram I, 995
Presnall, Mariam I, 731
Presnall, Martha I, 731
Presnall, Mary I, 731
Presnall, Mary V, 426
Presnall, Mashach I, 995
Presnall, Massah I, 725
Presnall, Massah I, 731
Presnall, Meriam I, 731
Presnall, Michael I, 731
Presnall, Nathan I, 475
Presnall, Nathan I, 484
Presnall, Nathan I, 731
Presnall, Pleasant I, 725
Presnall, Pleasant I, 731

Presnall, Rachel I, 731
Presnall, Rebeca I, 731
Presnall, Rebecah I, 484
Presnall, Rebecca I, 475
Presnall, Rebecca I, 484
Presnall, Rebecca I, 731
Presnall, Rebekah I, 731
Presnall, Ruth I, 731
Presnall, Ruth I, 995
Presnall, Sarah I, 731
Presnall, Shadrick I, 731
Presnall, Shadrock I, 995
Presnall, Stephen I, 484
Presnall, Stephen I, 731
Presnall, Stephen I, 732
Presnall, Stephen I, 995
Presnel, Daniel I, 731
Presnel, Hannah I, 405
Presnel, John I, 405
Presnell, Christian I, 687
Presnell, Christian Reece I, 687
Presnell, Daniel I, 416
Presnell, Daniel I, 687
Presnell, Hannah I, 416
Presnell, John I, 416
Presnell, Robert II, 446
Pressick, Christopher II, 446
Pressnell, Sarah V, 420
Pressnell, Sarah V, 426
Prestley, Callie I, 1160
Prestley, John I, 1160
Prestley, Rufus I, 1161
Prestly, Francis I, 1161
Prestly, Thomas II, 409
Prestly, Thomas, Jr. II, 409
Prestly, William II, 409
Preston, Abel II, 409
Preston, Abel II, 627
Preston, Abell II, 409
Preston, Abi VI, 980
Preston, Agathy VI, 980
Preston, Albert VI, 337
Preston, Albert M. II, 911
Preston, Albert W. II, 815
Preston, Albert W. II, 911
Preston, Alwilda V, 1014
Preston, Amelia T. VI, 941
Preston, Amos II, 815
Preston, Amos II, 1009
Preston, Amos II, 1022
Preston, Amos IV, 859
Preston, Amos VI, 337
Preston, Amos VI, 549
Preston, Amos VI, 691
Preston, Ann II, 409
Preston, Ann II, 815
Preston, Ann II, 911
Preston, Ann II, 1022
Preston, Ann V, 112
Preston, Ann VI, 337
Preston, Ann VI, 549
Preston, Ann VI, 691
Preston, Ann M. VI, 847
Preston, Annis E. VI, 980
Preston, Arabella Jane VI, 980
Preston, Benjamin II, 409
Preston, Blanche B. V, 426
Preston, Bowker VI, 903
Preston, Bowker VI, 970
Preston, Bowker VI, 988
Preston, Christopher VI, 980
Preston, Debora M. IV, 839
Preston, Deborah IV, 752
Preston, Docia VI, 946
Preston, Doshia VI, 934
Preston, Elam VI, 337
Preston, Elinor II, 93
Preston, Elinor II, 95
Preston, Elisha VI, 980
Preston, Elisha H. VI, 916
Preston, Eliza VI, 980
Preston, Eliza A. VI, 963
Preston, Eliza H. II, 911
Preston, Eliza Hunt II, 815
Preston, Elizabeth II, 409
Preston, Elizabeth II, 531
Preston, Elizabeth II, 627
Preston, Elizabeth II, 648
Preston, Elizabeth VI, 337
Preston, Elizabeth VI, 340
Preston, Elizabeth VI, 847
Preston, Elizabeth VI, 930
Preston, Elizabeth VI, 979
Preston, Elizabeth H. VI, 970
Preston, Elizabeth S. VI, 980
Preston, Ellen S. VI, 368
Preston, Enoch VI, 337
Preston, Erban VI, 337
Preston, Fanny VI, 980
Preston, Frances VI, 980
Preston, Francis VI, 880
Preston, Francis VI, 980
Preston, Francis VI, 982
Preston, Francis VI, 995
Preston, Francis VI, 1014
Preston, Frank V, 1014
Preston, Fred V, 1014
Preston, Hannah II, 409
Preston, Hannah II, 482
Preston, Hannah II, 600
Preston, Hannah II, 626
Preston, Henry II, 409
Preston, Henry II, 446
Preston, Hester II, 1009
Preston, Hester II, 1022
Preston, Isaac VI, 968
Preston, Isaac VI, 980
Preston, J. H. V, 1014
Preston, James II, 251
Preston, James II, 409
Preston, James VI, 892
Preston, James VI, 915
Preston, Jane Bedward II, 627
Preston, Jennie V, 356
Preston, Jesse VI, 980
Preston, Jesse B. VI, 973
Preston, Jesse B. VI, 980
Preston, Jesse B. VI, 985
Preston, Joel VI, 913
Preston, Joel VI, 938
Preston, Joel VI, 956
Preston, Joel VI, 979
Preston, Joel VI, 980
Preston, Joel VI, 985
Preston, Joel L. VI, 980
Preston, John VI, 337
Preston, John VI, 549
Preston, John VI, 691
Preston, John VI, 870
Preston, John VI, 949
Preston, John VI, 979
Preston, John VI, 980
Preston, John F. VI, 980
Preston, John S. VI, 980
Preston, John, Senior VI, 337
Preston, John, Sr. VI, 337
Preston, Jonas II, 627
Preston, Jonas II, 815
Preston, Jonas II, 911
Preston, Jonas VI, 337
Preston, Joseph II, 627
Preston, Joseph IV, 265
Preston, Judith VI, 749
Preston, Judith VI, 785
Preston, Kalita VI, 337
Preston, Litten O. V, 426
Preston, Lloyd II, 409
Preston, Lorenzo D. VI, 980
Preston, Lucinda VI, 956
Preston, Lucinda M. VI, 915
Preston, Lucy VI, 979
Preston, Lydda VI, 980
Preston, Lydia V, 896
Preston, Lydia V, 926
Preston, Lydia Ann VI, 634
Preston, Lydia Ann VI, 691
Preston, Mahala VI, 980
Preston, Margaret II, 409
Preston, Margaret II, 600
Preston, Margaret II, 626
Preston, Margaret II, 815
Preston, Margaret VI, 903
Preston, Margaret VI, 1000
Preston, Mariah VI, 880
Preston, Martha VI, 980
Preston, Martha M. VI, 980
Preston, Mary II, 409
Preston, Mary II, 543
Preston, Mary II, 582
Preston, Mary II, 627
Preston, Mary IV, 752
Preston, Mary VI, 985
Preston, Mary Ann VI, 980
Preston, Mary E. VI, 980
Preston, Matilda VI, 980
Preston, Melon VI, 980
Preston, Merabe II, 409
Preston, Mildred Jane VI, 968
Preston, Milley VI, 980
Preston, Minerva S. VI, 892
Preston, Moses VI, 337
Preston, Moses VI, 549
Preston, Moses VI, 691
Preston, Moses VI, 980
Preston, Nancy VI, 980
Preston, Naomi II, 119
Preston, Naomi II, 122
Preston, Orpah II, 627
Preston, Patsy VI, 980
Preston, Paul II, 409
Preston, Paul II, 531
Preston, Paul II, 582
Preston, Paul II, 627
Preston, Paul IV, 265
Preston, Peter VI, 337
Preston, Peter VI, 549
Preston, Peter VI, 691
Preston, Peter VI, 980
Preston, Pleasant VI, 882
Preston, Pleasant VI, 978
Preston, Pleasant VI, 980
Preston, Pleasant VI, 1017
Preston, Polly VI, 938
Preston, Polly P. VI, 972
Preston, Polly T. VI, 916
Preston, Rachel II, 409
Preston, Rachel II, 583
Preston, Rachel II, 626
Preston, Rachell II, 409
Preston, Ralph C. IV, 839
Preston, Rebecca VI, 337
Preston, Rebecca VI, 549
Preston, Rebeckah VI, 337
Preston, Rebekah VI, 691
Preston, Richard II, 409
Preston, Robert II, 627
Preston, Robert E. II, 627
Preston, Robert H. V, 762
Preston, Sally VI, 980
Preston, Samuel II, 409
Preston, Samuel II, 576
Preston, Samuel II, 583
Preston, Samuel II, 600
Preston, Samuel II, 626
Preston, Samuel II, 627
Preston, Sarah II, 409
Preston, Sarah II, 481
Preston, Sarah II, 627
Preston, Sarah II, 686
Preston, Sarah IV, 265
Preston, Sarah IV, 914
Preston, Sarah VI, 337
Preston, Sarah VI, 549
Preston, Sarah VI, 691
Preston, Sarah VI, 931
Preston, Stephen VI, 887
Preston, Stephen VI, 938
Preston, Stephen VI, 946
Preston, Stephen VI, 979
Preston, Stephen VI, 980
Preston, Stephen, Jr. VI, 1007
Preston, Stephen, Sr. VI, 980
Preston, Suckey VI, 980
Preston, Susanna II, 409
Preston, Susanna VI, 870
Preston, Susanna VI, 938
Preston, Susannah VI, 980
Preston, Tamer VI, 980
Preston, Thomas II, 409
Preston, Thomas II, 627
Preston, Thomas VI, 903
Preston, Thomas VI, 924
Preston, Thomas VI, 980
Preston, Thomas VI, 1016
Preston, Thomas L. VI, 847
Preston, Thos. VI, 938
Preston, Vickers VI, 337
Preston, Walter V, 426
Preston, Wd Elizabeth II, 627
Preston, Wd Margaret II, 627
Preston, Wd. Ann II, 409
Preston, Wd. Elizabeth II, 694
Preston, Wd. Margaret II, 576
Preston, William II, 409
Preston, William VI, 337
Preston, William VI, 549
Preston, William VI, 691
Preston, William VI, 892
Preston, William VI, 915
Preston, William VI, 941
Preston, William VI, 963
Preston, William VI, 972
Preston, William VI, 980
Preston, William B. VI, 980
Preston, Wilson J. IV, 839
Preston, Wm. II, 531
Preston, Wm. II, 627
Preston, Wm. II, 760
Preston, Wm. II, 1022
Preston, Wm. B. VI, 938
Preston, Wm. B. VI, 949
Preston, Wm., Jr. II, 627
Preston, Zeanas VI, 549
Preston, Zenas VI, 337
Preston, Zenas VI, 340
Preston, Zenas VI, 847
Preston, Zenes VI, 691
Pretlo, Ann VI, 167
Pretlo, Joshua VI, 167
Pretlo, Joshua VI, 209
Pretlow, ??? VI, 48
Pretlow, ??? VI, 95
Pretlow, Abbie III, 66
Pretlow, Abbie III, 259
Pretlow, Abbie V, 705
Pretlow, Abigail V, 705
Pretlow, Ann VI, 61
Pretlow, Ann VI, 79
Pretlow, Ann VI, 80
Pretlow, Ann VI, 98
Pretlow, Ann VI, 101
Pretlow, Ann VI, 109
Pretlow, Ann VI, 118
Pretlow, Ann VI, 119
Pretlow, Ann VI, 209
Pretlow, Ann Bailey VI, 79
Pretlow, Ann C. VI, 80
Pretlow, Ann C. VI, 237
Pretlow, Ann Denson VI, 79
Pretlow, Ann Eliz. VI, 92
Pretlow, Ann Mary P. VI, 79
Pretlow, Anne VI, 118
Pretlow, Anselm VI, 80
Pretlow, Anselm VI, 118
Pretlow, Austin C. VI, 92
Pretlow, Austin Crenshaw VI, 79
Pretlow, Benjamin VI, 79
Pretlow, Benjamin VI, 119
Pretlow, Betsy Ann V, 926
Pretlow, Caroline Jordan VI, 79
Pretlow, Deborah VI, 79
Pretlow, Deborah VI, 80
Pretlow, Deborah VI, 84
Pretlow, Deborah VI, 265
Pretlow, Deborah VI, 266
Pretlow, Deborah H. VI, 80
Pretlow, Deborah R. VI, 80
Pretlow, Deborah R. VI, 92
Pretlow, Deborah R. Pretlow VI, 80
Pretlow, Denson VI, 79
Pretlow, Edna VI, 80
Pretlow, Elizabeth Ann V, 926
Pretlow, Elizabeth Ann V, 975
Pretlow, Emma F. V, 704
Pretlow, Emma T. III, 259
Pretlow, Emma T. V, 705
Pretlow, Fannie M. VI, 80
Pretlow, Fanny Murry VI, 79
Pretlow, Franklin VI, 79
Pretlow, Franklin VI, 80
Pretlow, Gertrude E. VI, 69
Pretlow, Gertrude E. VI, 79
Pretlow, Gertrude E. VI, 80
Pretlow, H. Virginia VI, 265
Pretlow, H. Virginia VI, 279
Pretlow, Isabella VI, 79
Pretlow, Isabella Chlotilda Ladd VI, 80
Pretlow, Isabella H. VI, 80
Pretlow, J. D. VI, 236
Pretlow, J. Denson VI, 60
Pretlow, James VI, 83
Pretlow, James T. VI, 69
Pretlow, James T. VI, 79
Pretlow, James T. VI, 80
Pretlow, Jane VI, 79
Pretlow, Jane VI, 80
Pretlow, Jane VI, 104
Pretlow, Jane VI, 119
Pretlow, Jane Denson VI, 79
Pretlow, Jane Denson VI, 80
Pretlow, Jane Denson Pretlow VI, 79
Pretlow, Jane W. VI, 61
Pretlow, Jane W. VI, 80
Pretlow, Jane W. VI, 92
Pretlow, Jane Watson VI, 79
Pretlow, Joel C. VI, 80
Pretlow, Joel E. VI, 79
Pretlow, John VI, 18
Pretlow, John VI, 79
Pretlow, John VI, 80
Pretlow, John VI, 84
Pretlow, John VI, 118
Pretlow, John VI, 265
Pretlow, John VI, 266
Pretlow, John E. VI, 79
Pretlow, John E. VI, 80
Pretlow, John Jordan VI, 80
Pretlow, John S. Sadler VI, 80
Pretlow, John, Sr. VI, 80
Pretlow, John, Sr. VI, 90
Pretlow, Jordan VI, 79
Pretlow, Jordan Denson VI, 80
Pretlow, Jorden Denson VI, 79
Pretlow, Joseph VI, 18
Pretlow, Joseph VI, 46
Pretlow, Joseph VI, 59
Pretlow, Joseph VI, 66
Pretlow, Joseph VI, 79
Pretlow, Joseph VI, 80
Pretlow, Joseph VI, 118
Pretlow, Joseph VI, 265
Pretlow, Joseph John VI, 80
Pretlow, Joshua VI, 56
Pretlow, Joshua VI, 61
Pretlow, Joshua VI, 79
Pretlow, Joshua VI, 80
Pretlow, Joshua VI, 111
Pretlow, Joshua VI, 118
Pretlow, Joshua VI, 209
Pretlow, Julia C. VI, 80
Pretlow, Julieta V, 975
Pretlow, Maria VI, 80
Pretlow, Maria L. VI, 69
Pretlow, Maria L. VI, 79
Pretlow, Maria L. VI, 80
Pretlow, Maria L. VI, 83
Pretlow, Martha VI, 135
Pretlow, Martha VI, 139
Pretlow, Mary VI, 18
Pretlow, Mary VI, 45
Pretlow, Mary VI, 46
Pretlow, Mary VI, 66
Pretlow, Mary VI, 79
Pretlow, Mary VI, 80
Pretlow, Mary VI, 98
Pretlow, Mary VI, 109
Pretlow, Mary VI, 113
Pretlow, Mary VI, 118
Pretlow, Mary VI, 119
Pretlow, Mary VI, 265
Pretlow, Mary VI, 266
Pretlow, Mary A. T. VI, 80
Pretlow, Mary Ann VI, 118
Pretlow, Mary Ann Sarah VI, 8
Pretlow, Mary Ann Terrell VI, 7
Pretlow, Mary H. VI, 80
Pretlow, Mary Helen VI, 79
Pretlow, Mary J. VI, 80
Pretlow, Mary J. D. VI, 60
Pretlow, Mary J. D. VI, 79
Pretlow, Mary J. D. VI, 80
Pretlow, Mary Jane VI, 80
Pretlow, Mary Jane VI, 92
Pretlow, Mary Jane VI, 236
Pretlow, Mary Jane VI, 237
Pretlow, Mary Jane VI, 265
Pretlow, Mary W. VI, 80
Pretlow, Mary W. VI, 84
Pretlow, Mary W. VI, 92
Pretlow, Mary Winston VI, 79
Pretlow, Rebecca VI, 42
Pretlow, Rebecca VI, 113
Pretlow, Rebecca VI, 118
Pretlow, Rebeckah VI, 111
Pretlow, Rebeckah VI, 113
Pretlow, Rebeckah VI, 118
Pretlow, Richard P. Clements VI, 80
Pretlow, Robert VI, 80
Pretlow, Robert VI, 118
Pretlow, Robert Binford VI, 80
Pretlow, Robert E. III, 259
Pretlow, Robert E. V, 704
Pretlow, Robert E. V, 705
Pretlow, Robert F. V, 705
Pretlow, Robert S. VI, 79
Pretlow, Robert S. VI, 80
Pretlow, Robert T. III, 259
Pretlow, Robert T. V, 705
Pretlow, Robt. E. III, 259
Pretlow, Samuel VI, 18
Pretlow, Samuel VI, 80
Pretlow, Samuel VI, 98
Pretlow, Samuel VI, 113
Pretlow, Samuel VI, 118
Pretlow, Samuel B. VI, 79
Pretlow, Samuel B. VI, 80
Pretlow, Samuel B. VI, 84
Pretlow, Samuel B., Jr. VI, 79
Pretlow, Samuel Calvert VI, 80
Pretlow, Sarah VI, 45
Pretlow, Sarah VI, 46
Pretlow, Sarah VI, 79
Pretlow, Sarah VI, 118
Pretlow, Sarah VI, 119
Pretlow, Sarah D. VI, 80
Pretlow, Sarah D. Julia VI, 79
Pretlow, Sarah Jordan VI, 80
Pretlow, Sophia S. VI, 80
Pretlow, Thomas VI, 18
Pretlow, Thomas VI, 46
Pretlow, Thomas VI, 61
Pretlow, Thomas VI, 79
Pretlow, Thomas VI, 80
Pretlow, Thomas VI, 90
Pretlow, Thomas VI, 98
Pretlow, Thomas VI, 106
Pretlow, Thomas VI, 118
Pretlow, Thomas VI, 172
Pretlow, Thomas VI, 209
Pretlow, Thomas, Jr. VI, 80
Pretlow, Thomas, Jr. VI, 98

w, Thomas, Jr. VI, 118
w, Thomas, Sr. VI, 80
w, Thos. VI, 46
w, William Joyner VI, 80
we, Samuel I, 65
we, Samuel I, 69
we, Widow Kezia I, 65
we, Widow Kezia I, 69
t, James VI, 848
t, Sarah VI, 848
st, Octaire Emile II, 790
st, Sophia VI, 750
st, Sophia VI, 771
Mary I, 1131
t, Rebeckah VI, 197
t, Rebeckah VI, 209
tt, Michael VI, 811
r, Hannah III, 260
r, Matthew III, 260
r, Wd. Ann III, 260
Elizabeth III, 40
Elizabeth III, 116
Elizabeth III, 260
Elizabeth III, 319
Elizabeth III, 410
Elizabeth VI, 823
Hannah III, 260
Hannah III, 319
John III, 40
John III, 260
John III, 319
Martha III, 85
Martha III, 405
Mary III, 85
Mary III, 260
Mary III, 329
Mary III, 405
Mary III, 410
Matt III, 116
Matthew III, 85
Matthew III, 260
Matthew III, 329
Matthew III, 405
Matthew III, 410
r, Wd. Ann III, 260
bie, John VI, 854
bie, Mary VI, 854
ble, Elizabeth VI, 957
ble, Garnet D. VI, 848
ble, Henry VI, 805
ble, Henry VI, 848
ble, Jacob A. VI, 848
ble, James VI, 806
ble, James VI, 848
ble, Jane VI, 814
ble, Jane VI, 848
ble, Jemima VI, 855
ble, John VI, 814
ble, John R. VI, 839
ble, John R. VI, 857
ble, John, Jr. VI, 848
bble, Lavina VI, 848
bble, Levina VI, 857
bble, Lucinda VI, 796
bble, Martha VI, 848
bble, Martha VI, 857
bble, Martin VI, 848
bble, Mary VI, 814
bble, Mary VI, 848
bble, Nancy VI, 848
bble, Nancy VI, 980
bble, Patience VI, 848
bble, Rachel VI, 848
bble, William VI, 957
bble, William VI, 980
bble, Zachaus VI, 855
ice, ??? III, 259
ice, ??? IV, 752
ice, ??? IV, 839
ice, ??? IV, 1303
ice, A. P. VI, 976
ice, Aaron V, 857
ice, Aaron Morris, Jr. I, 162
ice, Alex P. VI, 895
ice, Alex. P. VI, 939
ice, Alexander VI, 980
ice, Alexander P. VI, 874
ice, Alexander P. VI, 943
rice, Alexander P. VI, 980
ice, Alexr. VI, 1000
rice, Alice III, 16
rice, Alice III, 259
rice, Alice Maulsby II, 830
rice, Alice Maulsby II, 912
rice, Amanda IV, 1290
rice, Amanda V, 1014
rice, Amos V, 1014
rice, Amos Griffith IV, 54
rice, Amy Ann IV, 135
rice, Amy Ann IV, 839
rice, Angeline VI, 980
Price, Ann II, 409
Price, Ann II, 585
Price, Ann II, 627
Price, Ann II, 628
Price, Ann II, 652
Price, Ann II, 761
Price, Ann II, 816
Price, Ann II, 956
Price, Ann II, 967
Price, Ann II, 977
Price, Ann II, 985
Price, Ann II, 1022
Price, Ann II, 1058
Price, Ann II, 1078
Price, Ann IV, 485
Price, Ann IV, 493
Price, Ann V, 919
Price, Ann Eliza IV, 382
Price, Ann Eliza IV, 432
Price, Ann W. III, 259
Price, Anna I, 297
Price, Anna I, 317
Price, Anna II, 409
Price, Anna II, 1057
Price, Anna II, 1061
Price, Anna Callender II, 761
Price, Anna Coffin II, 798
Price, Anna M. II, 716
Price, Anna M. II, 761
Price, Anna Margaret II, 761
Price, Anna P. II, 912
Price, Anna P. II, 914
Price, Anna Price II, 911
Price, Anne II, 798
Price, Anne II, 1073
Price, Anne II, 1078
Price, Anne Callendar II, 771
Price, Anne Callender II, 761
Price, Anne P. II, 761
Price, Anne P. II, 762
Price, Annie II, 784
Price, Benj. II, 446
Price, Benj. F. IV, 1334
Price, Benjamin I, 162
Price, Benjamin I, 732
Price, Benjamin II, 446
Price, Benjamin II, 816
Price, Benjamin III, 59
Price, Bertha V, 198
Price, Bertha G. V, 198
Price, Bethany Eliza I, 340
Price, Betty I, 35
Price, Betty I, 69
Price, Betty I, 114
Price, Betty I, 128
Price, Betty I, 162
Price, Beulah IV, 752
Price, Beulah F. IV, 752
Price, Beulah R. IV, 471
Price, Beulah R. IV, 493
Price, Beulah R. IV, 752
Price, Bourne VI, 848
Price, Bourne VI, 849
Price, Bourne VI, 928
Price, Bourne VI, 980
Price, Callender II, 409
Price, Callender II, 761
Price, Calvin V, 524
Price, Caroline II, 761
Price, Caroline C. II, 912
Price, Carrie IV, 1334
Price, Carroll B. II, 912
Price, Catharine I, 297
Price, Catharine I, 300
Price, Catharine I, 317
Price, Catharine II, 815
Price, Catharine VI, 811
Price, Catharine VI, 980
Price, Catherine V, 112
Price, Catherine Ann V, 112
Price, Cena VI, 980
Price, Charity D. IV, 265
Price, Charles II, 627
Price, Charles III, 259
Price, Charles V, 705
Price, Charles VI, 871
Price, Charles VI, 877
Price, Charles VI, 881
Price, Charles VI, 888
Price, Charles VI, 892
Price, Charles VI, 895
Price, Charles VI, 897
Price, Charles VI, 898
Price, Charles VI, 903
Price, Charles VI, 910
Price, Charles VI, 920
Price, Charles VI, 923
Price, Charles VI, 925
Price, Charles VI, 926
Price, Charles VI, 932
Price, Charles VI, 933
Price, Charles VI, 942
Price, Charles VI, 944
Price, Charles VI, 948
Price, Charles VI, 955
Price, Charles VI, 957
Price, Charles VI, 962
Price, Charles VI, 973
Price, Charles VI, 992
Price, Charles VI, 1000
Price, Charles VI, 1004
Price, Charles VI, 1016
Price, Charles C. II, 912
Price, Charles C. IV, 652
Price, Charles C. IV, 752
Price, Charles Coale II, 815
Price, Charles Coale III, 16
Price, Charles Coale III, 259
Price, Charles Evans II, 815
Price, Charles Evans II, 912
Price, Charles F. V, 705
Price, Charles H. IV, 265
Price, Charles J. II, 627
Price, Charles W. VI, 980
Price, Chas S. II, 912
Price, Chas. I, 628
Price, Chas. II, 830
Price, Chas. II, 912
Price, Chas. IV, 1334
Price, Chas. VI, 871
Price, Chas. VI, 970
Price, Chas. C. II, 912
Price, Chas. Coale II, 912
Price, Chas. Coale, Jr. II, 815
Price, Chas. S. II, 920
Price, Clara Jane V, 356
Price, Clara Johnson V, 705
Price, Clara M. II, 912
Price, Clara M. IV, 752
Price, Clara May II, 903
Price, Clara May II, 912
Price, Clarence V, 926
Price, Clarence V, 940
Price, Clark B. IV, 1290
Price, Clinton II, 967
Price, Cornelia VI, 433
Price, Curtis V, 857
Price, Cynthia M. IV, 894
Price, Cynthia M. IV, 895
Price, Daniel III, 259
Price, Daniel IV, 54
Price, Daniel VI, 848
Price, Daniel VI, 969
Price, Daniel VI, 980
Price, Daniel B. II, 965
Price, Daniel B. II, 967
Price, Daniel B. II, 970
Price, Daniel B. II, 1022
Price, Daniel B. II, 1048
Price, Daniel B. II, 1056
Price, Daniel B. II, 1058
Price, Daniel B. II, 1061
Price, Daniel L. VI, 980
Price, David II, 409
Price, David II, 496
Price, David II, 627
Price, David B. I, 340
Price, Debby II, 628
Price, Debby II, 815
Price, Debby II, 911
Price, Deborah II, 409
Price, Deborah II, 558
Price, Deborah II, 627
Price, Deborah II, 628
Price, Dorcas IV, 752
Price, Doshea VI, 848
Price, Dr. Wm. II, 912
Price, Dr. Wm. II, 943
Price, Edgar IV, 1290
Price, Edgar VI, 937
Price, Edith IV, 48
Price, Edith IV, 54
Price, Edith IV, 265
Price, Edith IV, 348
Price, Edith IV, 353
Price, Edith IV, 431
Price, Edith IV, 447
Price, Edith IV, 464
Price, Edith IV, 493
Price, Edith IV, 501
Price, Edith M. IV, 54
Price, Edith M. IV, 752
Price, Edith Mary IV, 54
Price, Edwin VI, 848
Price, Edwin G. IV, 135
Price, Edwin G. IV, 652
Price, Edwin G. IV, 816
Price, Edwin G. IV, 839
Price, Eleanor R. IV, 1334
Price, Eli K. II, 628
Price, Eli M. VI, 549
Price, Eli M. VI, 555
Price, Eli M. VI, 556
Price, Elias Albertson I, 162
Price, Elijah V, 198
Price, Elijah V, 356
Price, Elijah V, 592
Price, Elisabeth I, 159
Price, Elisabeth I, 162
Price, Elisabeth G. I, 624
Price, Elisha II, 409
Price, Elissif C. VI, 874
Price, Eliza I, 339
Price, Eliza II, 761
Price, Eliza II, 785
Price, Eliza II, 816
Price, Eliza II, 967
Price, Eliza II, 1022
Price, Eliza II, 1038
Price, Eliza II, 1058
Price, Eliza II, 1078
Price, Eliza IV, 265
Price, Eliza IV, 313
Price, Eliza IV, 314
Price, Eliza V, 524
Price, Eliza Ann IV, 265
Price, Eliza Ann IV, 314
Price, Eliza Ann VI, 549
Price, Eliza Ann VI, 555
Price, Eliza Ann VI, 556
Price, Eliza C. II, 911
Price, Eliza Jane V, 524
Price, Elizabeth I, 297
Price, Elizabeth I, 331
Price, Elizabeth II, 251
Price, Elizabeth II, 409
Price, Elizabeth II, 446
Price, Elizabeth II, 496
Price, Elizabeth II, 627
Price, Elizabeth II, 628
Price, Elizabeth II, 716
Price, Elizabeth II, 806
Price, Elizabeth II, 911
Price, Elizabeth II, 967
Price, Elizabeth II, 970
Price, Elizabeth II, 1016
Price, Elizabeth II, 1022
Price, Elizabeth II, 1058
Price, Elizabeth II, 1061
Price, Elizabeth IV, 54
Price, Elizabeth IV, 135
Price, Elizabeth IV, 265
Price, Elizabeth IV, 321
Price, Elizabeth IV, 348
Price, Elizabeth IV, 493
Price, Elizabeth IV, 504
Price, Elizabeth IV, 836
Price, Elizabeth IV, 839
Price, Elizabeth IV, 1334
Price, Elizabeth IV, 1344
Price, Elizabeth VI, 234
Price, Elizabeth VI, 265
Price, Elizabeth VI, 487
Price, Elizabeth VI, 500
Price, Elizabeth VI, 501
Price, Elizabeth VI, 513
Price, Elizabeth VI, 535
Price, Elizabeth VI, 549
Price, Elizabeth VI, 738
Price, Elizabeth VI, 746
Price, Elizabeth VI, 766
Price, Elizabeth VI, 901
Price, Elizabeth VI, 916
Price, Elizabeth VI, 935
Price, Elizabeth VI, 969
Price, Elizabeth C. II, 409
Price, Elizabeth C. II, 628
Price, Elizabeth C. IV, 836
Price, Elizabeth C. IV, 839
Price, Elizabeth D. IV, 894
Price, Elizabeth D. IV, 895
Price, Elizabeth Evans II, 815
Price, Elizabeth Evans II, 912
Price, Elizabeth Evans III, 259
Price, Elizabeth G. II, 716
Price, Elizabeth G. II, 761
Price, Elizabeth G. II, 912
Price, Elizabeth P. VI, 871
Price, Elizabeth P. VI, 934
Price, Elizabeth P. VI, 943
Price, Elizabeth S. II, 628
Price, Elizabeth W. II, 409
Price, Elizabeth W. II, 758
Price, Elizabeth W. II, 761
Price, Elizabeth W. II, 905
Price, Elizabeth W. II, 912
Price, Elizabeth W. VI, 848
Price, Elizabeth Williams II, 812
Price, Elizabeth Williams II, 911
Price, Ellen A. IV, 471
Price, Ellen A. IV, 493
Price, Ellen F. IV, 752
Price, Ellen H. II, 815
Price, Ellen H. II, 912
Price, Ellen H. Evans II, 912
Price, Ellis II, 409
Price, Ellis II, 627
Price, Ellwood IV, 314
Price, Elvira VI, 1004
Price, Elwood IV, 265
Price, Emilie II, 409
Price, Emilie R. II, 628
Price, Emily W. II, 912
Price, Emily W. VI, 433
Price, Emily Walton II, 815
Price, Emma II, 815
Price, Emma II, 912
Price, Emma II, 937
Price, Emma III, 259
Price, Emma III, 263
Price, Emma V, 198
Price, Emma S. V, 198
Price, Emory V, 857
Price, Enoch II, 627
Price, Evan V, 198
Price, Ezekiel IV, 106
Price, Farrington III, 259
Price, Feby Ann II, 815
Price, Ferris II, 627
Price, Ferris II, 815
Price, Ferris W. II, 912
Price, Ferris W. IV, 652
Price, Ferris W. IV, 752
Price, Ferris Walton II, 815
Price, Ferris Walton II, 912
Price, Ferriss II, 627
Price, Flora Bell V, 524
Price, Flora Burden V, 524
Price, Flora Elizabeth V, 198
Price, Florence III, 259
Price, Florence III, 343
Price, Florence V, 926
Price, Florence L. IV, 752
Price, Frances IV, 265
Price, Frances IV, 493
Price, Frances VI, 980
Price, Frances E. IV, 617
Price, Frances E. IV, 652
Price, Francis IV, 135
Price, Francis IV, 839
Price, Francis E. IV, 808
Price, Francis E. IV, 839
Price, Francis Edward IV, 839
Price, Francis Price IV, 135
Price, Francis Walten II, 798
Price, Frank O. III, 259
Price, Frank O. III, 343
Price, Geo. I, 339
Price, Geo. Wm. IV, 1290
Price, George I, 339
Price, George II, 409
Price, George IV, 348
Price, George IV, 1290
Price, George G. IV, 135
Price, George G. IV, 839
Price, George J. IV, 348
Price, George W. I, 331
Price, George W. I, 339
Price, George Ward II, 815
Price, George Willis I, 339
Price, Gertrude H. II, 912
Price, Gertrude H. II, 920
Price, Gertrude H. S. II, 912
Price, Gideon V, 356
Price, Grace II, 409
Price, Hannah II, 521
Price, Hannah II, 627
Price, Hannah II, 912
Price, Hannah II, 965
Price, Hannah II, 970
Price, Hannah II, 1016
Price, Hannah II, 1022
Price, Hannah III, 235
Price, Hannah IV, 106
Price, Hannah IV, 131
Price, Hannah IV, 133
Price, Hannah IV, 265
Price, Hannah IV, 298
Price, Hannah B. II, 912
Price, Hannah B. II, 967
Price, Hannah B. II, 1048
Price, Hannah B. II, 1056
Price, Hannah B. II, 1058
Price, Hannah B. II, 1061
Price, Hannah B. IV, 652
Price, Hannah B. IV, 752
Price, Hannah Brinton II, 794
Price, Hannah Brinton II, 862
Price, Hannah Brinton II, 912
Price, Hannah F. II, 943
Price, Hannah Fisher II, 628
Price, Hannah G. II, 628
Price, Hannah V. IV, 265
Price, Hannah W. IV, 265
Price, Hannah W. IV, 308

Price, Hannah W. IV, 493
Price, Hannah W. IV, 501
Price, Harmon IV, 132
Price, Hatten VI, 980
Price, Hatton VI, 901
Price, Helen II, 815
Price, Helen II, 912
Price, Helen C. IV, 652
Price, Helen C. IV, 839
Price, Helen F. II, 716
Price, Helen F. II, 761
Price, Helen P. II, 751
Price, Helen P. II, 761
Price, Helen P. IV, 617
Price, Helen P. IV, 652
Price, Helen P. IV, 808
Price, Helen P. IV, 839
Price, Henrietta H. II, 912
Price, Henrietta H. II, 943
Price, Henrietta Hoskins II, 829
Price, Henry II, 627
Price, Henry II, 628
Price, Henry V, 705
Price, Henry V, 1014
Price, Henry C. V, 705
Price, Henry Ferris II, 815
Price, Henry Ferris II, 912
Price, Hubbard II, 816
Price, Ichabod II, 855
Price, Ichabod II, 912
Price, Ichabod III, 259
Price, Irena H. IV, 816
Price, Irene IV, 652
Price, Irene H. IV, 839
Price, Isaac II, 409
Price, Isaac II, 521
Price, Isaac II, 627
Price, Isaac II, 716
Price, Isaac IV, 131
Price, Isaac IV, 135
Price, Isaac IV, 493
Price, Isaac IV, 752
Price, Isaac IV, 839
Price, Isaac IV, 1112
Price, Isaac C. II, 911
Price, Isaac Coale II, 409
Price, Isaac Cook II, 628
Price, Isaachar II, 627
Price, Isachar II, 409
Price, Isachar II, 627
Price, Isachar II, 1022
Price, Isacher II, 409
Price, Isaiah II, 798
Price, Isaiah II, 986
Price, Isaiah II, 1022
Price, Isaiah II, 1058
Price, Isaiah II, 1072
Price, Isaiah II, 1073
Price, Isaiah II, 1078
Price, Isaiah II, 1083
Price, Israel IV, 106
Price, Israel IV, 265
Price, Israel IV, 493
Price, Israel Burgess II, 1022
Price, Issachar II, 627
Price, Issachar II, 1022
Price, Ivarrick IV, 265
Price, J. Randolph II, 155
Price, J. Randolph II, 815
Price, J. Randolph II, 912
Price, J. W. IV, 1334
Price, James I, 297
Price, James I, 339
Price, James II, 409
Price, James V, 705
Price, James V, 762
Price, James VI, 980
Price, James B. II, 628
Price, James M. II, 716
Price, James M. II, 761
Price, James M. II, 912
Price, James M. II, 937
Price, James M. IV, 131
Price, James Mott II, 798
Price, James Rice V, 112
Price, Jane II, 1078
Price, Jane D. II, 1072
Price, Jane D. II, 1078
Price, Jasper IV, 106
Price, Jasper IV, 131
Price, Jasper Oliver IV, 135
Price, Jehu VI, 433
Price, Jehu VI, 549
Price, Jehu VI, 555
Price, Jehu VI, 556
Price, Jesse II, 409
Price, Jesse II, 627
Price, Jesse IV, 1112
Price, Jesse IV, 1290
Price, Jessie I, 339
Price, Jhon I, 114
Price, Jno. A. VI, 871
Price, Joel IV, 48
Price, Joel IV, 54
Price, Joh I, 162
Price, John I, 35
Price, John I, 69
Price, John I, 114
Price, John I, 127
Price, John I, 128
Price, John I, 149
Price, John I, 159
Price, John I, 162
Price, John II, 409
Price, John II, 627
Price, John II, 903
Price, John II, 912
Price, John II, 967
Price, John II, 985
Price, John II, 1022
Price, John II, 1058
Price, John II, 1077
Price, John II, 1086
Price, John III, 235
Price, John III, 259
Price, John IV, 348
Price, John IV, 396
Price, John IV, 1112
Price, John IV, 1334
Price, John V, 356
Price, John VI, 433
Price, John F. II, 830
Price, John F. II, 862
Price, John F. II, 912
Price, John F. III, 259
Price, John F. IV, 752
Price, John Ferris II, 815
Price, John H. IV, 348
Price, John H. IV, 431
Price, John H. IV, 432
Price, John H. IV, 447
Price, John M. II, 409
Price, John M. VI, 848
Price, John Morris II, 815
Price, John Morris II, 912
Price, John Morris III, 259
Price, John Price I, 162
Price, John Randolph II, 816
Price, John Randolph II, 912
Price, John T. II, 912
Price, John T. IV, 652
Price, John W. IV, 493
Price, John W. IV, 1290
Price, John W. IV, 1334
Price, John W. IV, 1344
Price, John Wm. V, 926
Price, Joice VI, 980
Price, Jonathan I, 114
Price, Jonathan I, 127
Price, Jonathan I, 149
Price, Jonathan I, 162
Price, Jonathan II, 409
Price, Jonathan II, 627
Price, Jonathan Price I, 162
Price, Joseph II, 409
Price, Joseph II, 585
Price, Joseph II, 627
Price, Joseph II, 628
Price, Joseph II, 652
Price, Joseph II, 716
Price, Joseph II, 729
Price, Joseph II, 761
Price, Joseph II, 816
Price, Joseph II, 911
Price, Joseph II, 912
Price, Joseph II, 931
Price, Joseph II, 967
Price, Joseph II, 1022
Price, Joseph II, 1038
Price, Joseph II, 1058
Price, Joseph II, 1078
Price, Joseph IV, 265
Price, Joseph IV, 313
Price, Joseph VI, 433
Price, Joseph VI, 848
Price, Joseph G. I, 340
Price, Joseph Henley I, 162
Price, Joseph J. VI, 265
Price, Joseph K. IV, 1290
Price, Joseph N. II, 761
Price, Joseph R. IV, 1290
Price, Joseph, Jr. II, 761
Price, Joshua II, 761
Price, Joshua II, 815
Price, Joshua II, 816
Price, Joshua C. VI, 433
Price, Joshua L. II, 912
Price, Joshua Longstreth II, 409
Price, Joshua Longstreth II, 816
Price, Joshua Longstreth II, 911
Price, Judith Shelton VI, 970
Price, Julia V, 356
Price, Julia V, 857
Price, Julia A. V, 857
Price, Katharine III, 259
Price, Katharine III, 263
Price, Katharine VI, 693
Price, Keziah III, 259
Price, Laura Elizabeth IV, 752
Price, Letitia II, 409
Price, Letitia II, 501
Price, Letitia II, 627
Price, Levina IV, 391
Price, Levina IV, 431
Price, Levinia VI, 848
Price, Lewis IV, 308
Price, Louisa II, 912
Price, Louisa II, 931
Price, Lucretia Mott II, 798
Price, Lucy VI, 848
Price, Lydia II, 409
Price, Lydia II, 608
Price, Lydia II, 627
Price, Lydia II, 816
Price, Lydia II, 906
Price, Lydia II, 912
Price, Lydia II, 1086
Price, Lydia IV, 493
Price, Lydia IV, 903
Price, Lydia IV, 914
Price, Lydia VI, 847
Price, Lydia VI, 980
Price, Lydia B. II, 967
Price, Lydia B. II, 1022
Price, Lydia B. II, 1058
Price, Lydia N. II, 761
Price, Lydia W. II, 585
Price, Lydia W. II, 628
Price, Lydia W. II, 761
Price, Lydia W. II, 879
Price, Lydia W. II, 905
Price, Lydia W. II, 911
Price, Lydia Williams II, 708
Price, Lydia Williams II, 812
Price, Lydia Williams II, 816
Price, Mae V, 1014
Price, Magdeline VI, 848
Price, Maggie V, 857
Price, Mamie Ann V, 198
Price, Margaret II, 155
Price, Margaret II, 158
Price, Margaret II, 409
Price, Margaret II, 477
Price, Margaret II, 529
Price, Margaret II, 627
Price, Margaret II, 798
Price, Margaret II, 816
Price, Margaret II, 986
Price, Margaret II, 1022
Price, Margaret II, 1058
Price, Margaret II, 1072
Price, Margaret II, 1073
Price, Margaret II, 1078
Price, Margaret II, 1083
Price, Margaret IV, 106
Price, Margaret IV, 130
Price, Margaret IV, 131
Price, Margaret IV, 135
Price, Margaret IV, 688
Price, Margaret IV, 839
Price, Margaret VI, 980
Price, Margaret C. II, 627
Price, Margaret C. II, 652
Price, Margaret C. III, 259
Price, Margaret Callender II, 409
Price, Margaret H. II, 912
Price, Margaret H. II, 920
Price, Margaret S. II, 912
Price, Margaret Simmons II, 816
Price, Margaretta S. II, 829
Price, Margery II, 729
Price, Margery II, 761
Price, Margery II, 816
Price, Maria II, 798
Price, Marsia Anne III, 259
Price, Marsia Anne III, 343
Price, Martha I, 339
Price, Martha II, 815
Price, Martha II, 819
Price, Martha II, 1070
Price, Martha II, 1078
Price, Martha IV, 752
Price, Martha V, 705
Price, Martha VI, 265
Price, Martha Case II, 1058
Price, Martha D. VI, 848
Price, Martha J. IV, 265
Price, Martha J. V, 705
Price, Martha Jane IV, 265
Price, Mary I, 114
Price, Mary I, 297
Price, Mary I, 317
Price, Mary I, 340
Price, Mary II, 409
Price, Mary II, 446
Price, Mary II, 521
Price, Mary II, 627
Price, Mary II, 628
Price, Mary II, 641
Price, Mary II, 669
Price, Mary II, 965
Price, Mary II, 967
Price, Mary II, 986
Price, Mary II, 1022
Price, Mary II, 1038
Price, Mary II, 1058
Price, Mary II, 1078
Price, Mary III, 259
Price, Mary IV, 54
Price, Mary IV, 78
Price, Mary IV, 106
Price, Mary IV, 132
Price, Mary IV, 252
Price, Mary IV, 265
Price, Mary IV, 313
Price, Mary IV, 314
Price, Mary IV, 486
Price, Mary IV, 493
Price, Mary IV, 545
Price, Mary IV, 894
Price, Mary IV, 1334
Price, Mary V, 112
Price, Mary V, 857
Price, Mary VI, 500
Price, Mary VI, 549
Price, Mary VI, 848
Price, Mary Ann IV, 333
Price, Mary Ann IV, 348
Price, Mary Ann IV, 396
Price, Mary Ann IV, 431
Price, Mary Ann VI, 1016
Price, Mary C. II, 911
Price, Mary C. II, 967
Price, Mary Catharine V, 705
Price, Mary Coale II, 628
Price, Mary E. II, 912
Price, Mary Elizabeth II, 912
Price, Mary G. II, 912
Price, Mary Gertrude II, 815
Price, Mary L. II, 716
Price, Mary L. II, 761
Price, Mary Louisa II, 761
Price, Mary Melissa IV, 106
Price, Mary Melissa IV, 131
Price, Mary Melissa IV, 752
Price, Mary N. II, 912
Price, Mary P. V, 963
Price, Mary S. VI, 265
Price, Mary Susan I, 628
Price, Mary W. II, 830
Price, Maryann IV, 348
Price, Matilda V, 1014
Price, Mattock IV, 1334
Price, Maud IV, 265
Price, Mauda V, 1014
Price, Melissa V, 356
Price, Mercy IV, 106
Price, Mildred Early V, 593
Price, Miles V, 857
Price, Milford Leroy I, 339
Price, Mina V, 846
Price, Mina V, 857
Price, Minerva IV, 372
Price, Minerva IV, 431
Price, Miriam I, 114
Price, Miriam I, 128
Price, Miriam I, 143
Price, Miriam I, 162
Price, Moody V, 705
Price, Mordecai VI, 500
Price, Mordecai VI, 501
Price, Mordecai VI, 536
Price, Mordecai VI, 549
Price, Mordecai VI, 768
Price, Mordecai VI, 771
Price, Mrs. E. IV, 1334
Price, Nancy I, 628
Price, Nancy VI, 847
Price, Nancy VI, 879
Price, Nancy VI, 980
Price, Nancy A. VI, 916
Price, Narcissa V, 112
Price, Narcissa V, 125
Price, Narcissa V, 126
Price, Nathan Raymond Franklin I, 339
Price, Nathaniel II, 967
Price, Nathaniel II, 977
Price, Nathaniel II, 985
Price, Nathaniel II, 986
Price, Nathaniel II, 1022
Price, Nathaniel II, 1038
Price, Nathaniel VI, 980
Price, Nathaniel, Jr. II, 977
Price, Nathaniel, Jr. II, 1022
Price, Nellie V, 1014
Price, Oliver IV, 265
Price, Oliver IV, 493
Price, Opal IV, 1290
Price, Parker V, 524
Price, Paul V, 198
Price, Paul Robert IV, 1290
Price, Paulina H. VI, 976
Price, Penrose II, 798
Price, Phebe VI, 433
Price, Phebe Ann VI, 433
Price, Phebe B. II, 967
Price, Phebe B. II, 1058
Price, Phebe B. II, 1086
Price, Phebe O. III, 259
Price, Pheeby VI, 1008
Price, Philip II, 409
Price, Philip II, 521
Price, Philip II, 627
Price, Philip II, 911
Price, Philip, Jr. II, 627
Price, Philip, Jr. II, 628
Price, Philip, Jr. II, 785
Price, Philip, Jr. II, 816
Price, Philip, Jr. II, 911
Price, Phillip II, 912
Price, Polly VI, 980
Price, Polly P. VI, 1013
Price, Rachael II, 1078
Price, Rachel I, 162
Price, Rachel II, 409
Price, Rachel II, 460
Price, Rachel II, 478
Price, Rachel II, 627
Price, Rachel II, 679
Price, Rachel II, 967
Price, Rachel II, 985
Price, Rachel II, 1022
Price, Rachel II, 1058
Price, Rachel II, 1078
Price, Rachel IV, 106
Price, Rachel IV, 109
Price, Rachel IV, 308
Price, Rachel IV, 348
Price, Rachel IV, 396
Price, Rachel IV, 431
Price, Rachel IV, 432
Price, Rachel IV, 447
Price, Rachel VI, 536
Price, Rachel VI, 549
Price, Rachel VI, 768
Price, Rachel VI, 771
Price, Rachel Ann II, 965
Price, Rachel Ann II, 1056
Price, Rachel Anna II, 967
Price, Rachel Anna II, 970
Price, Rachel Anna II, 1058
Price, Rachel B. II, 967
Price, Rachel B. II, 1058
Price, Rachel B. II, 1078
Price, Rachel B. II, 1083
Price, Rachel C. II, 911
Price, Rachel Coale II, 785
Price, Rachel, Jr. I, 162
Price, Rachel, Jr. I, 174
Price, Randolph II, 160
Price, Rebecca II, 627
Price, Rebecca II, 708
Price, Rebecca II, 729
Price, Rebecca II, 761
Price, Rebecca IV, 135
Price, Rebecca IV, 136
Price, Rebecca IV, 493
Price, Rebecca IV, 839
Price, Rebecca B. IV, 265
Price, Rebecca B. IV, 296
Price, Rebecca B. IV, 493
Price, Rebecca B. IV, 501
Price, Rebecca Lillian IV, 588
Price, Rebecca Lillian IV, 593
Price, Rebecca Marie IV, 839
Price, Rebecca S. II, 761
Price, Rebecca Simmons II, 761
Price, Rebecca T. II, 879
Price, Rebecca T. II, 912
Price, Rebecca Thompson II, 816
Price, Rebecca W. II, 862
Price, Rebecca W. II, 903
Price, Rebecca W. II, 912
Price, Rebecca W. III, 259
Price, Rebecca W. IV, 652
Price, Rebecca W. IV, 752
Price, Rebecca Walmsley II, 816
Price, Rebekah VI, 433
Price, Reece II, 965
Price, Reuben Moore II, 912
Price, Rice I, 297
Price, Rice I, 312
Price, Rice V, 112
Price, Rice V, 762

Richard II, 409
Richard II, 446
Richard II, 627
Richard II, 679
Richard II, 708
Richard II, 761
Richard II, 798
Richard II, 812
Richard II, 816
Richard II, 879
Richard II, 905
Richard II, 906
Richard II, 911
Richard II, 912
Richard IV, 1334
Richard VI, 980
Richard, Jr. II, 585
Richard, Jr. II, 628
Rise I, 300
Rise I, 317
Robert I, 297
Robert IV, 1290
Robert V, 112
Robert V, 762
Robert V, 857
Robert VI, 845
Robert VI, 961
Robert VI, 1004
Robert Osborne II, 555
Ruth I, 114
Ruth I, 162
Ruth II, 628
Ruth II, 816
Ruth Anna II, 409
Ruth Anna II, 628
Ruth Anna II, 911
Ruth Kirk II, 912
Ruthann IV, 348
Ruthanna IV, 348
Ruthanna Lucy II, 816
Sally VI, 1016
Sally S. VI, 871
Samuel I, 114
Samuel I, 162
Samuel I, 174
Samuel I, 732
Samuel II, 446
Samuel II, 912
Samuel II, 920
Samuel IV, 265
Samuel V, 112
Samuel V, 592
Samuel VI, 811
Samuel D. VI, 959
Samuel G. II, 155
Samuel G. II, 160
Sarah I, 114
Sarah I, 162
Sarah I, 169
Sarah I, 199
Sarah I, 280
Sarah I, 297
Sarah I, 313
Sarah I, 317
Sarah II, 409
Sarah II, 555
Sarah II, 627
Sarah II, 667
Sarah II, 716
Sarah II, 786
Sarah II, 795
Sarah II, 816
Sarah II, 912
Sarah II, 977
Sarah II, 1022
Sarah III, 60
Sarah IV, 1112
Sarah V, 112
Sarah V, 762
Sarah VI, 536
Sarah VI, 537
Sarah VI, 549
Sarah VI, 768
Sarah VI, 771
Sarah Ann II, 967
Sarah B. II, 155
Sarah B. II, 160
Sarah J. I, 339
Sarah J. I, 340
Sarah L. II, 761
Sarah L. II, 906
Sarah L. II, 912
Sarah L. II, 937
Sarah Longstreth II, 812
Sarah Longstreth II, 816
Sarah T. II, 155
Sarah T. II, 160
Sarah T. II, 815
Sarah T. II, 912
Sarah Wistar II, 409
Sary I, 199
Price, Sophia VI, 501
Price, Sophia VI, 549
Price, Stephen S. II, 761
Price, Stephen Simmons II, 716
Price, Stephen Simmons II, 761
Price, Susan II, 855
Price, Susan II, 907
Price, Susan II, 912
Price, Susan III, 259
Price, Susan V, 919
Price, Susan VI, 848
Price, Susan M. II, 855
Price, Susan M. II, 912
Price, Susan Morris V, 926
Price, Susan Morris V, 940
Price, Susanah I, 162
Price, Susanna I, 149
Price, Susanna I, 162
Price, Susanna I, 723
Price, Susanna I, 732
Price, Susanna II, 627
Price, Susanna II, 691
Price, Susanna IV, 265
Price, Susanna IV, 485
Price, Susanna IV, 493
Price, Susanna IV, 504
Price, Susanna IV, 505
Price, Susanna J. IV, 414
Price, Susanna J. IV, 432
Price, Susanna M. II, 716
Price, Susannah I, 114
Price, Susannah I, 144
Price, Susannah I, 155
Price, Susannah I, 162
Price, Susannah III, 259
Price, Susannah IV, 265
Price, Susannah IV, 493
Price, Susannah VI, 549
Price, Susannah VI, 555
Price, Susannah VI, 556
Price, Susannah VI, 857
Price, Susie M. III, 235
Price, Sylvia IV, 1290
Price, Tace II, 409
Price, Theodore IV, 839
Price, Thomas II, 409
Price, Thomas II, 446
Price, Thomas IV, 106
Price, Thomas IV, 894
Price, Thomas IV, 895
Price, Thomas IV, 1112
Price, Thomas VI, 11
Price, Thomas VI, 433
Price, Thomas VI, 901
Price, Thomas VI, 980
Price, Thomas C. II, 628
Price, Thomas C. II, 761
Price, Thomas Callender II, 409
Price, Thomas Callender II, 761
Price, Thomas Jordan I, 162
Price, Thomas, Jr. IV, 1112
Price, Thornton Walton II, 815
Price, Thornton Walton II, 912
Price, Thornton Walton III, 259
Price, Ureann IV, 688
Price, Uriah IV, 132
Price, Uriah IV, 135
Price, Uriah IV, 136
Price, Uriah IV, 348
Price, Uriah IV, 391
Price, Uriah IV, 431
Price, Uriah IV, 839
Price, Ursley Goode VI, 980
Price, Violet IV, 1290
Price, Virginia L. VI, 980
Price, Voylet IV, 1290
Price, Wallace V, 857
Price, Walter V, 198
Price, Walter F. II, 716
Price, Walter F. II, 761
Price, Warick IV, 493
Price, Warrick IV, 265
Price, Warrick IV, 471
Price, Warrick IV, 485
Price, Warrick IV, 493
Price, Warrick IV, 505
Price, Warrick IV, 752
Price, Warrick IV, 1180
Price, Warrick V, 919
Price, Warrick, Sr. IV, 265
Price, Warrick, Sr. IV, 493
Price, Warwick IV, 1334
Price, Wd. Ann VI, 532
Price, Wd. Rebecca IV, 839
Price, Widow Ruth I, 149
Price, William I, 162
Price, William II, 409
Price, William III, 259
Price, William IV, 106
Price, William IV, 265
Price, William IV, 493
Price, William IV, 501
Price, William V, 272
Price, William VI, 799
Price, William VI, 848
Price, William VI, 903
Price, William VI, 980
Price, William B. IV, 471
Price, William B. IV, 493
Price, William B. IV, 752
Price, William F. IV, 752
Price, William L. II, 716
Price, William M. VI, 848
Price, William S. VI, 931
Price, William S. VI, 980
Price, Winslow I, 199
Price, Winslow I, 732
Price, Wm. II, 446
Price, Wm. II, 628
Price, Wm. II, 912
Price, Wm. II, 943
Price, Wm. IV, 132
Price, Wm. IV, 265
Price, Wm. IV, 298
Price, Wm. IV, 464
Price, Wm. IV, 501
Price, Wm. V, 272
Price, Wm. V, 705
Price, Wm. Ballinger IV, 493
Price, Wm. G. IV, 1290
Price, Wm. L. II, 761
Price, Wm. L. II, 912
Price, Wm. L. II, 937
Price, Wm. Lightfoot II, 815
Price, Wm. Lightfoot III, 259
Price, Wm. Lightfoot III, 263
Price, Wm. S. VI, 874
Price, Wm. T. IV, 1334
Price, Wm. Webb II, 912
Price, Zerinda G. VI, 1004
Price, Zilpha I, 317
Price, Zilpha V, 112
Price, Zilphia I, 297
Prichard, Ann I, 163
Prichard, Ann I, 173
Prichard, Ann II, 567
Prichard, Ann II, 628
Prichard, Barbara II, 409
Prichard, Barberah II, 409
Prichard, Benjamin I, 114
Prichard, Benjamin I, 115
Prichard, Benjamin I, 125
Prichard, Benjamin I, 453
Prichard, Benjamin, Jr. I, 163
Prichard, Bennone I, 115
Prichard, Benoni I, 115
Prichard, Cassie V, 1014
Prichard, Edith II, 628
Prichard, Elisabeth I, 151
Prichard, Elisabeth I, 163
Prichard, Elizabeth I, 114
Prichard, Elizabeth I, 115
Prichard, Emma V, 198
Prichard, Finley V, 1014
Prichard, Hannah I, 115
Prichard, Hariet I, 453
Prichard, John I, 115
Prichard, John II, 409
Prichard, Joseph I, 114
Prichard, Joseph I, 115
Prichard, Joseph VI, 80
Prichard, Joseph VI, 81
Prichard, Martha I, 114
Prichard, Martha I, 125
Prichard, Martha I, 162
Prichard, Martha I, 166
Prichard, Mary I, 66
Prichard, Mary I, 114
Prichard, Mary I, 143
Prichard, Mary I, 148
Prichard, Mary I, 163
Prichard, Mary II, 409
Prichard, Mary II, 628
Prichard, Mathew II, 547
Prichard, Matthew I, 114
Prichard, Matthew I, 115
Prichard, Matthew II, 628
Prichard, Miriam I, 115
Prichard, Miriam I, 162
Prichard, Miriam I, 167
Prichard, Rebecca II, 409
Prichard, Samuel I, 453
Prichard, Sarah I, 114
Prichard, Sarah I, 115
Prichard, Sarah I, 158
Prichard, Sarah I, 163
Prichard, Sarah II, 547
Prichard, Sarah II, 628
Prichard, Sarah L. V, 1014
Prichard, Thomas I, 114
Prichard, Thomas I, 115
Prichard, Thomas I, 151
Prichard, Thomas I, 154
Prichard, Thomas I, 163
Prichard, Thomas II, 409
Prichard, Widow Mary I, 70
Prichard, William II, 409
Prichard, Wm. II, 628
Prichet, Barbara II, 409
Prichet, Elizabeth IV, 652
Prichet, Hannah IV, 652
Prichet, Isaac IV, 652
Prichet, Joab IV, 652
Prichet, John IV, 652
Prichet, Mary II, 409
Prichet, Rachel IV, 652
Prichet, Sarah IV, 652
Prichet, Thomas II, 409
Prichett, Ann IV, 652
Prichett, Edith II, 628
Prichett, Elizabeth IV, 649
Prichett, Elizabeth IV, 652
Prichett, Elizabeth H. II, 716
Prichett, Hannah IV, 652
Prichett, Isaac IV, 652
Prichett, J. IV, 652
Prichett, Joab IV, 649
Prichett, Joab IV, 652
Prichett, Joab IV, 667
Prichett, Joel IV, 652
Prichett, John IV, 652
Prichett, John S. IV, 652
Prichett, Joseph IV, 612
Prichett, Joseph IV, 652
Prichett, Joseph IV, 667
Prichett, Mary IV, 649
Prichett, Mary IV, 652
Prichett, Mary IV, 667
Prichett, Mary Ann IV, 652
Prichett, P. IV, 652
Prichett, Phebe IV, 612
Prichett, Phebe IV, 652
Prichett, Phebe IV, 667
Prichett, Rachel IV, 617
Prichett, Rachel IV, 652
Prichett, Rebecca II, 409
Prichett, Reuben IV, 652
Prichett, Rheuben Emmett IV, 652
Prichett, Sarah IV, 648
Prichett, Sarah IV, 652
Prichett, William II, 409
Prichett, Wm. IV, 652
Prichett, Wm. Henry IV, 652
Pricket, Elizabeth H. II, 296
Pricket, Elizabeth H. II, 298
Pricket, Ezra E. II, 298
Prickett, Elizabeth VI, 980
Prickett, Elizabeth E. II, 713
Prickett, Ezra E. II, 298
Prickett, Mary W. II, 722
Prickett, Reuben VI, 980
Prickit, Mary II, 222
Prickit, Mary II, 251
Priddy, Chas. V, 1014
Priddy, Chas. F. V, 1014
Priddy, Fannie V, 1014
Priddy, Fanny M. V, 1014
Priddy, John V, 1014
Priddy, John F. V, 1014
Priddy, Lucinda V, 1014
Priddy, Lucy A. V, 1014
Priddy, Milla J. V, 1014
Priddy, Millie V, 1014
Priddy, Thos. D. V, 1014
Pride, ??? II, 446
Pride, Abraham II, 409
Pride, Abraham II, 446
Pride, Elizabeth II, 409
Pride, Elizabeth II, 446
Pride, Susanna II, 446
Priece, Ezekiel IV, 106
Priece, Mary IV, 81
Priece, Mary IV, 106
Priece, Mercy IV, 106
Priece, Thomas IV, 81
Priece, Thomas IV, 106
Prier, Amelia III, 260
Prier, Ann II, 410
Prier, Deborah III, 260
Prier, Elizabeth III, 260
Prier, Elizabeth III, 399
Prier, Elizabeth III, 438
Prier, James III, 260
Prier, John III, 260
Prier, John III, 399
Prier, John III, 438
Prier, Joseph III, 260
Prier, Mary II, 410
Prier, Mary III, 260
Prier, Mary Ann III, 260
Prier, Mary Ann III, 290
Prier, Matthew III, 260
Prier, Norton II, 410
Prier, Richard II, 410
Prier, Samuel III, 260
Prier, Samuel III, 290
Prier, Silas II, 410
Prier, Theodosia III, 260
Priers, Mary II, 410
Priers, Silus II, 410
Priest, ??? II, 409
Priest, Alice V, 272
Priest, Amanda V, 273
Priest, Amanda J. V, 272
Priest, Amanda Jane V, 272
Priest, Andrew V, 272
Priest, Andrew V, 273
Priest, Anna V, 272
Priest, Anna A. V, 272
Priest, Cordelia V, 273
Priest, Cordella V, 272
Priest, Dean V, 273
Priest, Edith V, 356
Priest, Elias V, 273
Priest, Emma V, 272
Priest, Emma A. V, 272
Priest, Flora P. V, 273
Priest, George II, 409
Priest, George V, 273
Priest, Gertie IV, 1290
Priest, Hannah II, 409
Priest, Hannah II, 591
Priest, Hannah II, 628
Priest, Herbert V, 273
Priest, Jacob Leslie V, 272
Priest, James II, 409
Priest, Jennie Lewis IV, 1220
Priest, John II, 409
Priest, John V, 272
Priest, John V, 273
Priest, John D. V, 272
Priest, John, Jr. II, 409
Priest, Joseph II, 409
Priest, Joseph Marshal II, 628
Priest, Laura V, 272
Priest, Levi V, 1015
Priest, Maggie V, 1015
Priest, Mamie V, 273
Priest, Margarite V, 273
Priest, Mary Edith V, 272
Priest, Mildred V, 273
Priest, Noble L. V, 272
Priest, Raymond E. V, 272
Priest, Reece II, 447
Priest, Robert II, 409
Priest, Sadie V, 273
Priest, Sarah II, 409
Priest, Sarah II, 623
Priest, Sarah II, 628
Priest, Sarah II, 642
Priest, Susanna VI, 691
Priest, Susannah VI, 636
Priest, Thomas V, 272
Priest, Thos. V, 272
Priest, William II, 409
Priest, William V, 273
Priest, Wm. V, 1015
Priest, Wm. M. V, 273
Priestly, Agnes II, 1016
Priestly, Agnes II, 1022
Priestly, John II, 520
Priestly, John II, 628
Priestly, Mary II, 520
Priestly, Mary II, 628
Priestly, Thomas II, 409
Priestly, Thomas II, 520
Priestly, Thomas II, 628
Priestly, William II, 409
Prill, Elizabeth V, 753
Prill, Matilda V, 753
Prill, Michael V, 753
Prim, Mille I, 768
Prim, Milly I, 768
Prim, Sarah C. I, 995
Primer, Ellen IV, 1180
Primm, Mille I, 762
Primm, Mille I, 768
Primmer, Elizabeth II, 409
Primmer, Richard II, 409
Prin, Mary III, 259
Prince, Ann III, 259
Prince, Ann VI, 971
Prince, Ann Elizabeth VI, 971
Prince, Geo. M. III, 486
Prince, George M. III, 486
Prince, George M. III, 495
Prince, Josephine III, 486
Prince, Josephine III, 495
Prince, Maria III, 30
Prince, Nicholas II, 628
Prince, Rebecca III, 259
Prince, Rebecca III, 359
Prince, Wd. Ann III, 384

Prince, William III, 384
Prindle, Almira III, 138
Prindle, Almira III, 259
Prindle, Almira L. III, 259
Prindle, Anna Louisa III, 369
Prindle, Anna Louise III, 259
Prindle, Charlotte III, 259
Prindle, Clara R. III, 259
Prindle, Clara Remson III, 29
Prindle, Cyrus III, 138
Prindle, Cyrus III, 259
Prindle, Elmira IV, 1334
Prindle, Elmira L. III, 259
Prindle, George W. III, 236
Prindle, Henry W. III, 259
Prindle, Henry Walker III, 29
Prindle, Judson III, 259
Prindle, Louise III, 236
Prindle, Mary W. III, 29
Prindle, Mary W. III, 259
Prindle, Wm. P. III, 259
Prindle, Wm. Porter III, 29
Pringle, Susan J. V, 593
Prinit, John III, 259
Prints, Asenath V, 112
Prints, Asenath V, 138
Printz, Henry VI, 373
Printze, Cynthia W. V, 112
Printze, Cynthia W. V, 113
Prinz, Alex Henry III, 438
Prinz, Alex. Chas. III, 438
Prinz, Alexander H. III, 438
Prinz, Alexander H. III, 447
Prinz, Elizabeth III, 438
Prinz, Louise III, 438
Prinz, Mary E. III, 438
Prinz, Mary Elizabeth III, 438
Prinz, Ruth III, 438
Prinz, Ruth B. III, 438
Prinz, Ruth B. III, 447
Prior, ??? III, 260
Prior, Amelia III, 260
Prior, Ann II, 628
Prior, Ann III, 432
Prior, Ann III, 438
Prior, Ann III, 474
Prior, Anna III, 438
Prior, Anne III, 260
Prior, Deborah III, 260
Prior, Edmund III, 259
Prior, Edmund III, 260
Prior, Edmund III, 395
Prior, Edmund III, 416
Prior, Edmund III, 438
Prior, Edmund III, 440
Prior, Edmund H. III, 260
Prior, Edmund H. III, 438
Prior, Eleanor H. III, 260
Prior, Elizabeth II, 410
Prior, Elizabeth III, 260
Prior, Elizabeth III, 393
Prior, Elizabeth III, 396
Prior, Elizabeth III, 411
Prior, Elizabeth III, 412
Prior, Elizabeth III, 438
Prior, Elizabeth III, 439
Prior, Elizabeth III, 455
Prior, Elizabeth III, 459
Prior, Elizabeth III, 463
Prior, Elizabeth III, 495
Prior, Elizabeth H. III, 438
Prior, Elizabeth M. III, 260
Prior, Elizabeth Moode III, 395
Prior, Elizabeth Moode III, 438
Prior, Elizabeth R. III, 438
Prior, Esther III, 260
Prior, Esther III, 438
Prior, George II, 251
Prior, George II, 628
Prior, Georgianna III, 438
Prior, Hannah II, 251
Prior, Hannah III, 74
Prior, Hannah III, 259
Prior, Hannah III, 260
Prior, Hannah III, 400
Prior, Hannah III, 403
Prior, Hannah III, 412
Prior, Hannah III, 438
Prior, Hannah III, 439
Prior, Hannah H. III, 440
Prior, Henrietta M. III, 438
Prior, Henrietta W. III, 260
Prior, Henrietta W. III, 463
Prior, Henry III, 260
Prior, Henry III, 438
Prior, Horace III, 260
Prior, Horace III, 438
Prior, Horace III, 447
Prior, James III, 260
Prior, James III, 398
Prior, James III, 438
Prior, Jericho III, 495
Prior, John III, 260
Prior, John III, 393
Prior, John III, 396
Prior, John III, 411
Prior, John III, 412
Prior, John III, 438
Prior, John III, 455
Prior, John III, 463
Prior, John III, 495
Prior, John VI, 848
Prior, John Augustus III, 260
Prior, John Augustus III, 438
Prior, John Augustus III, 495
Prior, Jos. III, 451
Prior, Joseph II, 251
Prior, Joseph II, 628
Prior, Joseph III, 259
Prior, Joseph III, 260
Prior, Joseph III, 438
Prior, Joseph III, 439
Prior, Joseph III, 454
Prior, Joseph III, 473
Prior, Joseph Augustus III, 260
Prior, Julia A. III, 438
Prior, Julia A. III, 447
Prior, M III, 438
Prior, Margaret II, 251
Prior, Martha III, 74
Prior, Martha III, 260
Prior, Martha III, 400
Prior, Martha III, 403
Prior, Martha III, 404
Prior, Martha III, 438
Prior, Martha III, 439
Prior, Martha III, 459
Prior, Martha III, 466
Prior, Martha III, 470
Prior, Mary II, 251
Prior, Mary III, 160
Prior, Mary III, 259
Prior, Mary III, 260
Prior, Mary III, 395
Prior, Mary III, 416
Prior, Mary III, 436
Prior, Mary III, 437
Prior, Mary III, 438
Prior, Mary III, 439
Prior, Mary III, 440
Prior, Mary III, 446
Prior, Mary III, 460
Prior, Mary Ann III, 260
Prior, Massee VI, 848
Prior, Mathew II, 410
Prior, Matt III, 260
Prior, Matthew III, 74
Prior, Matthew III, 260
Prior, Matthew III, 403
Prior, Matthew III, 404
Prior, Matthew III, 405
Prior, Matthew III, 432
Prior, Matthew III, 438
Prior, Matthew III, 474
Prior, Norton II, 410
Prior, Olive Florence III, 438
Prior, Phebe III, 259
Prior, Phebe III, 260
Prior, Phebe III, 438
Prior, Phebe III, 439
Prior, Phebe III, 451
Prior, Phebe III, 454
Prior, Phebe III, 472
Prior, Phebe III, 473
Prior, Phebe III, 506
Prior, Phebe W. III, 260
Prior, Phebe W. III, 393
Prior, Phebe W. III, 438
Prior, Phebe W. III, 495
Prior, Philemon III, 465
Prior, Philemon F. III, 260
Prior, Philemon H. III, 438
Prior, Philenor F. III, 260
Prior, Philenor T. III, 260
Prior, Philomon F. III, 495
Prior, Rachel III, 398
Prior, Rachel III, 438
Prior, Sam. III, 437
Prior, Samuel III, 260
Prior, Samuel III, 436
Prior, Samuel III, 438
Prior, Samuel III, 439
Prior, Samuel III, 446
Prior, Samuel III, 460
Prior, Sarah III, 260
Prior, Sarah III, 439
Prior, Sarah Ann II, 280
Prior, Sarah Ann II, 298
Prior, Sarah F. III, 260
Prior, Sarah J. III, 465
Prior, Sarah, Jr. III, 438
Prior, Silas II, 410
Prior, Susanna II, 628
Prior, Tacy II, 628
Prior, Telitha III, 260
Prior, Theodosia III, 260
Prior, Theodosia III, 438
Prior, Thomas III, 74
Prior, Thomas III, 400
Prior, Thomas III, 438
Prior, Thomas III, 439
Prior, Thomas III, 459
Prior, Thomas III, 470
Prior, Thos. III, 466
Prior, Wd. Ann III, 260
Prior, Wd. Beth. Ann III, 438
Prior, Wd. Elizabeth III, 438
Prior, Wd. Hannah III, 438
Prior, William III, 260
Prior, William III, 438
Prior, William Henry III, 438
Prior, William, Jr. III, 260
Prise, Nancy VI, 879
Prisgar, John II, 409
Prisgar, Mary II, 409
Prisnal, Jacob VI, 337
Prit, Daniel II, 409
Pritchard, ??? I, 25
Pritchard, Aaron I, 115
Pritchard, Aaron I, 163
Pritchard, Abigail I, 114
Pritchard, Abigail I, 115
Pritchard, Abigail I, 123
Pritchard, Abigail I, 150
Pritchard, Abigail I, 163
Pritchard, Abigail I, 175
Pritchard, Alfred George III, 260
Pritchard, Alonzo B. V, 112
Pritchard, Ann I, 115
Pritchard, Ann I, 163
Pritchard, Anna V, 593
Pritchard, Anna V, 705
Pritchard, Anna M. V, 593
Pritchard, Anna M. V, 705
Pritchard, Asenath I, 70
Pritchard, Asenath I, 115
Pritchard, Asenith I, 163
Pritchard, Assenath I, 66
Pritchard, Assenath I, 70
Pritchard, Barberah II, 409
Pritchard, Benjamin I, 70
Pritchard, Benjamin I, 79
Pritchard, Benjamin I, 80
Pritchard, Benjamin I, 103
Pritchard, Benjamin I, 112
Pritchard, Benjamin I, 114
Pritchard, Benjamin I, 115
Pritchard, Benjamin I, 137
Pritchard, Benjamin I, 142
Pritchard, Benjamin I, 150
Pritchard, Benjamin I, 162
Pritchard, Benjamin I, 163
Pritchard, Benjamin I, 169
Pritchard, Benjamin I, 173
Pritchard, Benjamin I, 453
Pritchard, Benjamin C. I, 2
Pritchard, Benjamin C. I, 70
Pritchard, Benjamin C. I, 71
Pritchard, Benjamin Morris I, 115
Pritchard, Benjamin Morris I, 163
Pritchard, Benjamin, Jr. I, 115
Pritchard, Benjamin, Jr. I, 163
Pritchard, Benjamin, Sr. I, 115
Pritchard, Benoni I, 118
Pritchard, Benoni I, 162
Pritchard, Benoni I, 163
Pritchard, Benoni I, 177
Pritchard, Benoni I, 687
Pritchard, Betsy I, 115
Pritchard, Betsy I, 163
Pritchard, Caleb I, 70
Pritchard, Caleb I, 87
Pritchard, Caleb I, 115
Pritchard, Caleb I, 163
Pritchard, Caleb W. I, 70
Pritchard, Calvin D. V, 705
Pritchard, Calvin W. V, 593
Pritchard, Calvin W. V, 705
Pritchard, Carlton V, 112
Pritchard, Carlton C. V, 112
Pritchard, Carlton C. V, 705
Pritchard, Clara Emily III, 260
Pritchard, Clifford V, 112
Pritchard, Clifford M. V, 112
Pritchard, Clifford M. V, 705
Pritchard, Daniel V, 112
Pritchard, David Heston I, 208
Pritchard, David T. V, 65
Pritchard, David T. V, 112
Pritchard, Edith Hannah III, 260
Pritchard, Edwin D. V, 705
Pritchard, Elisabeth I, 62
Pritchard, Elisabeth I, 70
Pritchard, Elisabeth I, 78
Pritchard, Elisabeth I, 148
Pritchard, Elisabeth I, 154
Pritchard, Elisabeth I, 162
Pritchard, Elisabeth I, 163
Pritchard, Eliza I, 143
Pritchard, Eliza I, 162
Pritchard, Eliza I, 615
Pritchard, Elizabeth I, 97
Pritchard, Elizabeth I, 109
Pritchard, Elizabeth I, 115
Pritchard, Elizabeth I, 127
Pritchard, Elizabeth I, 135
Pritchard, Elizabeth I, 162
Pritchard, Elizabeth I, 685
Pritchard, Elizabeth I, 687
Pritchard, Emily III, 260
Pritchard, Emily C. III, 260
Pritchard, Emma V, 112
Pritchard, Finley V, 1014
Pritchard, Frances V, 112
Pritchard, Frances V, 677
Pritchard, Francis I, 115
Pritchard, Francis I, 163
Pritchard, Grace B. I, 211
Pritchard, Hannah I, 115
Pritchard, Hannah I, 149
Pritchard, Hariet I, 453
Pritchard, Hariot I, 453
Pritchard, Harriet V, 112
Pritchard, Harriett I, 440
Pritchard, Helen Rachel I, 208
Pritchard, Isabel I, 114
Pritchard, Isabel I, 115
Pritchard, Isabel I, 142
Pritchard, Isabel I, 161
Pritchard, Isabel I, 162
Pritchard, Isabell I, 162
Pritchard, Izbel I, 115
Pritchard, James VI, 980
Pritchard, James VI, 1012
Pritchard, James Michle I, 208
Pritchard, John I, 114
Pritchard, John I, 115
Pritchard, John I, 163
Pritchard, John II, 409
Pritchard, John C. III, 260
Pritchard, John Charles III, 260
Pritchard, Jordan I, 115
Pritchard, Jordan I, 163
Pritchard, Joseph I, 62
Pritchard, Joseph I, 70
Pritchard, Joseph I, 78
Pritchard, Joseph I, 114
Pritchard, Joseph I, 115
Pritchard, Joseph I, 123
Pritchard, Joseph I, 129
Pritchard, Joseph I, 144
Pritchard, Joseph I, 162
Pritchard, Joseph I, 163
Pritchard, Joseph Richard I, 208
Pritchard, Josephus I, 115
Pritchard, Louisa I, 115
Pritchard, Louisa I, 163
Pritchard, Luella Rebecca I, 208
Pritchard, Mamie Henley I, 732
Pritchard, Margaret I, 115
Pritchard, Margaret I, 116
Pritchard, Margaret I, 123
Pritchard, Margaret I, 144
Pritchard, Margaret I, 151
Pritchard, Margaret I, 163
Pritchard, Martha I, 112
Pritchard, Martha I, 115
Pritchard, Martha I, 162
Pritchard, Martha I, 172
Pritchard, Martha I, 440
Pritchard, Martha Ann I, 208
Pritchard, Mary I, 70
Pritchard, Mary I, 87
Pritchard, Mary I, 103
Pritchard, Mary I, 114
Pritchard, Mary I, 115
Pritchard, Mary I, 116
Pritchard, Mary I, 132
Pritchard, Mary I, 137
Pritchard, Mary I, 150
Pritchard, Mary I, 162
Pritchard, Mary I, 163
Pritchard, Mary II, 628
Pritchard, Mary VI, 980
Pritchard, Mary Ann I, 115
Pritchard, Mary Ann I, 139
Pritchard, Mary Ann I, 163
Pritchard, Mary Lizzie I, 208
Pritchard, Mary Toms I, 114
Pritchard, Mathew I, 92
Pritchard, Mathew I, 162
Pritchard, Matthew I, 114
Pritchard, Matthew I, 115
Pritchard, Matthew I, 129
Pritchard, Matthew I, 162
Pritchard, Matthew I, 163
Pritchard, Matthew I, 732
Pritchard, Matthua I, 145
Pritchard, Matthua I, 162
Pritchard, Melia I, 163
Pritchard, Mila I, 70
Pritchard, Milay I, 163
Pritchard, Milea I, 70
Pritchard, Milea I, 80
Pritchard, Milea I, 115
Pritchard, Miley I, 25
Pritchard, Miley I Sup 1, 7
Pritchard, Minnie Straughn I, 640
Pritchard, Miriam I, 70
Pritchard, Miriam I, 115
Pritchard, Miriam I, 158
Pritchard, Miriam I, 162
Pritchard, Miriam I, 163
Pritchard, Miriam I, 169
Pritchard, Miriam I, 177
Pritchard, Nellie M. V, 112
Pritchard, Osmund I, 115
Pritchard, Penina I, 70
Pritchard, Penina I, 79
Pritchard, Peninah I, 70
Pritchard, Peninah I, 85
Pritchard, Peninah I, 115
Pritchard, Peninnah I, 162
Pritchard, Peninnah I, 173
Pritchard, Penninah I, 114
Pritchard, Penninah I, 115
Pritchard, Penninah I, 136
Pritchard, Penninah I, 139
Pritchard, Penninah I, 150
Pritchard, Penninah I, 163
Pritchard, Penninah I, 177
Pritchard, Rachel W. I, 70
Pritchard, Rachel W. I, 71
Pritchard, Rebeccah I, 151
Pritchard, Rebeccah I, 163
Pritchard, Rebeckah I, 115
Pritchard, Ricks I, 115
Pritchard, Rosannah I, 115
Pritchard, Rosannah I, 129
Pritchard, Rosannah I, 162
Pritchard, Ruth I, 115
Pritchard, Ruth Elma I, 208
Pritchard, Samuel I, 114
Pritchard, Samuel I, 163
Pritchard, Samuel I, 440
Pritchard, Samuel I, 453
Pritchard, Samuel V, 112
Pritchard, Samuel White I, 115
Pritchard, Samuel White I, 163
Pritchard, Sarah I, 70
Pritchard, Sarah I, 92
Pritchard, Sarah I, 112
Pritchard, Sarah I, 114
Pritchard, Sarah I, 115
Pritchard, Sarah I, 116
Pritchard, Sarah I, 127
Pritchard, Sarah I, 129
Pritchard, Sarah I, 137
Pritchard, Sarah I, 145
Pritchard, Sarah I, 162
Pritchard, Sarah I, 163
Pritchard, Sarah I, 719
Pritchard, Sarah I, 732
Pritchard, Sarah A. V, 65
Pritchard, Sarah A. V, 112
Pritchard, Sarah H. V, 112
Pritchard, Sarah L. V, 1014
Pritchard, Susanna II, 628
Pritchard, Susannah I, 115
Pritchard, Susannah I, 139
Pritchard, Susannah I, 163
Pritchard, Susannah II, 547
Pritchard, Susannah II, 560
Pritchard, Thomas I, 97
Pritchard, Thomas I, 109
Pritchard, Thomas I, 114
Pritchard, Thomas I, 115
Pritchard, Thomas I, 116
Pritchard, Thomas I, 132
Pritchard, Thomas I, 135
Pritchard, Thomas I, 150
Pritchard, Thomas I, 162
Pritchard, Thomas I, 163
Pritchard, Thomas II, 409
Pritchard, Thomas Jordan I, 115
Pritchard, Thomas, Sr. I, 115
Pritchard, Widow Elisabeth I, 138
Pritchard, Widow Elisabeth I, 162
Pritchard, Widow Mary I, 70
Pritchard, William I, 114

ard, William I, 163
ard, William I, 440
ard, William H. V, 593
ard, William H. V, 705
ard, William Winslow
115
ard, Wm. H. V, 705
art, Abigail V, 198
art, Adda V, 198
art, Alonzo V, 198
art, Anna V, 198
art, Benjamin V, 198
art, Daniel V, 198
art, Daniel R. V, 198
art, Elizabeth V, 198
art, Emma V, 198
art, Lara A. V, 198
et, Edith II, 628
et, Elizabeth II, 199
et, Elizabeth II, 251
et, Mary II, 251
et, Sarah I, 55
et, Sarah I, 70
et, Wm. II, 628
e, Elizabeth I Sup 1, 8
e, John I Sup 1, 8
e, Judah I Sup 1, 8
e, Leah I Sup 1, 8
e, Rachel I, 90
e, Rachel I Sup 1, 8
w, Ann C. VI, 60
w, Ann C. VI, 80
w, Benjamin VI, 119
w, John VI, 79
w, Joseph VI, 18
w, Joseph VI, 80
w, Samuel VI, 118
w, Thomas, Jr. VI, 118
owe, Elisabeth I, 16
owe, John I, 16
owe, Judith I, 16
owe, Leah I, 16
owe, Miriam I, 16
owe, Priscilla I, 16
owe, Rachel I, 16
owe, Rachel I Sup 1, 7
owe, Rebecca I, 16
owe, Rebecca I Sup 1, 7
s, Catherine II, 447
s, Henry II, 447
e, John V, 1015
ot, Erastus I, 7
ot, Ida Leanora I, 7
er, Addy II, 784
er, Adeline L. II, 841
er, Adeline L. II, 912
er, Maria II, 841
er, Maria II, 912
er, Peter II, 841
er, Peter II, 912
basco, Abraham III, 485
basco, Abraham III, 495
basco, Ada V, 657
basco, Ada V, 705
basco, Anna V, 551
basco, Anna V, 593
basco, Anna V, 705
basco, Bertha V, 705
basco, Carol Lee V, 641
basco, Charity III, 485
basco, Charity III, 495
basco, Charles D. V, 593
basco, Charles Donald V, 593
basco, Charles Donald V, 641
basco, Chas. V, 705
basco, Don V, 593
basco, Edith V, 705
basco, Emily V, 705
basco, Ethel V, 705
obasco, Eva Lucile V, 641
obasco, George W. V, 705
obasco, Hannah V, 705
obasco, Hannah VI, 433
obasco, Hannah VI, 458
obasco, Hannah J. V, 705
obasco, Harold R. V, 593
obasco, Inez V, 705
obasco, James V, 705
obasco, James C. V, 705
obasco, Jane III, 485
obasco, Jane III, 495
obasco, John V, 705
obasco, Joseph III, 485
obasco, Lewis Donald V, 641
obasco, Louise V, 658
obasco, Louise V, 705
obasco, Lucile V, 550
robasco, Lulu B. V, 641
robasco, Lydia V, 705
robasco, Malidsa V, 705
robasco, Mary Ann V, 705
Probasco, Mary Anna V, 593
Probasco, Mary Anna V, 705
Probasco, Mary Catherine V, 593
Probasco, Mary H. V, 705
Probasco, Mary Lucile V, 593
Probasco, Myra V, 593
Probasco, Myra V, 687
Probasco, Myra V, 705
Probasco, Nina V, 551
Probasco, Nina V, 593
Probasco, Raymond H. V, 593
Probasco, Robert M. V, 593
Probasco, Russell V, 655
Probasco, Russell V, 705
Probasco, Ruth V, 705
Probasco, Ruth V, 709
Probasco, Ruth Anna V, 705
Probasco, Vesta V, 655
Probasco, W. H. V, 593
Probasco, William V, 593
Probasco, William V, 705
Probasco, William A. V, 593
Probasco, Wm. V, 551
Probasco, Wm. V, 705
Probasco, Wm. Arthur V, 593
Probasco, Wm. Emmitt V, 641
Probasco, Wm. Russell V, 705
Proctor, Eva III, 260
Proctor, Eva H. III, 111
Proctor, Eva H. III, 260
Proctor, Isaac III, 260
Proctor, Izak II, 995
Proctor, Izak II, 1022
Proctor, James I, 948
Proctor, James I, 950
Proctor, Jas. Edward I, 948
Proctor, Margaret II, 282
Proctor, Margaret II, 298
Proctor, Mary III, 260
Proctor, Minnie IV, 1334
Proctor, Minnie May IV, 1334
Proctor, Nellie I, 948
Proctor, Nellie I, 950
Proctor, Nellie V. I, 932
Proctor, Oliver III, 111
Proctor, Oliver III, 260
Proctor, Rebecca II, 995
Proctor, Rebecca II, 1022
Proctor, Rebeckah II, 995
Proctor, Rebeckah II, 1022
Proctor, Roy IV, 1334
Proctor, Sarah III, 260
Proctor, Stephen II, 912
Proctor, Stephen II, 995
Proctor, Stephen II, 1022
Proctor, Thomas II, 410
Proctor, William II, 410
Proctor, Wm. Jay IV, 1334
Prosser, Ann II, 93
Prosser, Ann II, 181
Prosser, Ann II, 251
Prosser, Benjamin II, 93
Prosser, Benjamin II, 181
Prosser, Benjamin II, 251
Prosser, Benjamin II, 280
Prosser, Benjamin II, 298
Prosser, Catharine VI, 806
Prosser, Deborah II, 181
Prosser, Deborah II, 251
Prosser, Deborah II, 280
Prosser, Deborah II, 298
Prosser, Eliza II, 251
Prosser, Elizabeth II, 93
Prosser, Elizabeth II, 181
Prosser, Elizabeth II, 251
Prosser, Jane VI, 834
Prosser, John II, 93
Prosser, John II, 181
Prosser, John II, 251
Prosser, Martha II, 93
Prosser, Martha II, 251
Prosser, Mary II, 93
Prosser, Mary II, 181
Prosser, Mary II, 251
Prosser, Mary II, 280
Prosser, Mary II, 298
Prosser, Rebecca VI, 834
Prosser, Uriah II, 93
Prosser, Uriah II, 181
Prosser, Uriah II, 251
Prosser, Wd. Deborah II, 181
Prosser, William II, 181
Prosser, William II, 251
Prosser, William Stevenson
II, 181
Prosser, William Stevenson
II, 251
Prosser, Wm. II, 93
Prosser, Wm. Stephenson II, 93
Prosser, Zeriah II, 251
Prossor, Mary II, 251
Prothero, Evan II, 410
Prothero, Wd. Elizabeth II, 410
Proud, Amy III, 260
Proud, Ann II, 628
Proud, John II, 628
Proud, Robert II, 410
Proud, Robert II, 628
Proud, Wm. II, 628
Proudfoot, Andrew III, 260
Proudfoot, Faith G. IV, 1260
Proudfoot, Faith J. G. IV, 1260
Proudfoot, Jeannette III, 260
Proudfoot, Margaret IV, 752
Proudfoot, Margaret IV, 1334
Prous, Charles I, 91
Prous, Charles I, 116
Prous, Dorathy I, 116
Prouse, Ann I, 116
Prouse, Charles I, 116
Prouse, Deleverance I, 116
Prouse, Dorothy I, 91
Prouse, Elis I, 116
Prouse, Henry I, 116
Prouse, Jeremiah I, 116
Prouse, Mary Melar I, 116
Prouse, Patients I, 116
Prout, Geo. IV, 1334
Prout, Henry IV, 1334
Prout, Nellie IV, 1334
Prout, Selina IV, 1334
Prout, Selina J. IV, 1334
Prout, Stephen IV, 1334
Prouty, Rachel IV, 367
Prouty, Rachel IV, 432
Provost, Martha III, 327
Prows, Anna I, 1
Prows, Charles I, 1
Prows, Charles I Sup 1, 5
Prows, Dorothy I, 1
Prows, Henry I, 1
Prows, Henry I, 61
Prows, Henry I, 70
Prows, Henry I, 78
Prudden, Isabella S. III, 177
Prudden, Isabella S. III, 260
Prudden, Louise III, 177
Prudden, Louise III, 260
Prudden, Sidney C. III, 177
Prudden, Sidney C. III, 260
Prudhoe, Margaret IV, 1041
Pruet, Hester V, 108
Pruet, Hester V, 112
Pruitt, Charles Wilson V, 198
Pruitt, David VI, 866
Pruitt, Elizabeth V, 198
Pruitt, Elizabeth V, 213
Pruitt, Elizabeth VI, 869
Pruitt, Joshua VI, 848
Pruitt, Robert VI, 869
Pruitt, Sally VI, 866
Pryer, Ann III, 249
Pryer, Mary II, 237
Pryer, Mary III, 137
Pryer, Mary III, 260
Pryer, Matthew III, 137
Pryer, Matthew III, 249
Pryer, Matthew III, 260
Pryer, Sarah III, 137
Pryer, Sarah III, 260
Pryer, Thomas II, 237
Pryol, Jeremiah V, 593
Pryor, Ann II, 410
Pryor, Ann II, 479
Pryor, Ann II, 609
Pryor, Ann II, 628
Pryor, Ann II, 816
Pryor, Ann II, 912
Pryor, Anna II, 816
Pryor, Anna II, 912
Pryor, Benjamin P. VI, 980
Pryor, Betsey VI, 917
Pryor, Clyde M. IV, 1220
Pryor, Daniel II, 628
Pryor, Daniel II, 761
Pryor, Eliza II, 808
Pryor, Elizabeth II, 410
Pryor, Elizabeth II, 628
Pryor, Elizabeth II, 895
Pryor, Elizabeth II, 912
Pryor, Elizabeth VI, 635
Pryor, Elizabeth VI, 848
Pryor, Fanny B. VI, 980
Pryor, George II, 181
Pryor, George II, 251
Pryor, George II, 274
Pryor, George II, 410
Pryor, George II, 628
Pryor, Hanes VI, 917
Pryor, Hannah II, 181
Pryor, Hannah II, 251
Pryor, Hannah II, 271
Pryor, Hannah II, 274
Pryor, Hannah II, 477
Pryor, Hannah II, 628
Pryor, Hannah III, 260
Pryor, Hannah VI, 549
Pryor, Hannah, Jr. II, 251
Pryor, Harris VI, 917
Pryor, Harris VI, 959
Pryor, James VI, 549
Pryor, James VI, 635
Pryor, Jane II, 251
Pryor, Jennie Pearl IV, 1220
Pryor, Joanna II, 410
Pryor, John II, 251
Pryor, John VI, 848
Pryor, John VI, 980
Pryor, Joseph II, 181
Pryor, Joseph II, 251
Pryor, Joseph II, 628
Pryor, Joseph II, 816
Pryor, Joseph II, 912
Pryor, Juggy VI, 959
Pryor, Lydia II, 410
Pryor, Lydia II, 628
Pryor, Lydia II, 653
Pryor, Margaret II, 251
Pryor, Margaret II, 274
Pryor, Mary II, 251
Pryor, Mary II, 271
Pryor, Mary II, 410
Pryor, Mary II, 531
Pryor, Mary II, 628
Pryor, Mary III, 260
Pryor, Massee VI, 848
Pryor, Mathew II, 410
Pryor, Nancy VI, 982
Pryor, Norton II, 410
Pryor, Patsey VI, 959
Pryor, Polley VI, 959
Pryor, Polly VI, 933
Pryor, Priscilla II, 628
Pryor, Rachel IV, 1220
Pryor, Richard II, 181
Pryor, Richard II, 251
Pryor, Richard II, 410
Pryor, Richard II, 477
Pryor, Richard II, 628
Pryor, Sally VI, 980
Pryor, Samuel II, 410
Pryor, Samuel II, 628
Pryor, Sarah II, 628
Pryor, Sarah VI, 635
Pryor, Silas II, 410
Pryor, Silas II, 539
Pryor, Silas II, 628
Pryor, Silus II, 410
Pryor, Smith IV, 1220
Pryor, Spicy VI, 848
Pryor, Susanah II, 539
Pryor, Susanna II, 628
Pryor, Susannah VI, 497
Pryor, Tacy II, 410
Pryor, Tacy II, 628
Pryor, Tedford P. IV, 1220
Pryor, Thomas II, 181
Pryor, Thomas II, 251
Pryor, Thomas II, 271
Pryor, Thomas II, 274
Pryor, Thomas II, 410
Pryor, Thomas II, 477
Pryor, Thomas II, 531
Pryor, Thomas II, 628
Pryor, Thomas II, 653
Pryor, Thomas VI, 848
Pryor, Thomas White II, 251
Pryor, Thomas, Jr. II, 251
Pryor, Thomas, Jr. II, 628
Pryor, Wd Priscilla II, 628
Pryor, Wd. Letitia II, 410
Pryor, Wd. Priscilla II, 477
Pryor, William II, 181
Pryor, William II, 251
Pryor, William III, 260
Pryor, William VI, 848
Pryor, William VI, 917
Pryor, William VI, 959
Pryor-Dixon, Elizabeth VI, 549
Pryor-Dixon, James VI, 549
Pryor-Dixon, Susannah VI, 497
Pryor-Dixon, Susannah VI, 549
Puble, Willis J. I, 317
Pucket, Angeline V, 74
Pucket, Beuly I, 568
Pucket, Daniel V, 857
Pucket, Eli V, 427
Pucket, Elizabeth V, 319
Pucket, Elizabeth V, 356
Pucket, Enos V, 857
Pucket, Henry W. V, 926
Pucket, Isom I, 968
Pucket, James, Jr. V, 427
Pucket, Jane V, 857
Pucket, Keziah V, 427
Pucket, Levina I, 968
Pucket, Mary I, 1012
Pucket, Mary V, 309
Pucket, Mary V, 427
Pucket, Mary V, 857
Pucket, Mary V, 858
Pucket, Nancy M. V, 273
Pucket, Nathan V, 273
Pucket, Rhoda V, 846
Pucket, Rhoda E. V, 847
Pucket, Richard I, 568
Pucket, Richard I, 968
Pucket, Richard V, 857
Pucket, Sarah IV, 1112
Pucket, Susanna V, 857
Pucket, Susannah V, 857
Pucket, Tamar V, 857
Pucket, Thomas I, 568
Pucket, Thomas I, 968
Pucket, Thomas I, 1012
Pucket, Thomas V, 857
Pucket, Thomas V, 858
Pucket, Thomas, Jr. I, 968
Pucket, Vianna C. V, 857
Pucket, Vienna V, 857
Puckett, Aaron V, 426
Puckett, Aaron V, 427
Puckett, Albert V, 427
Puckett, Alice I, 968
Puckett, Alice V, 427
Puckett, Amelia V, 427
Puckett, Arzilla V, 426
Puckett, Barclay V, 426
Puckett, Bell V, 427
Puckett, Belle V, 427
Puckett, Benjamin I, 968
Puckett, Benjamin V, 273
Puckett, Benjamin V, 356
Puckett, Benjamin V, 369
Puckett, Benjamin V, 426
Puckett, Benjamin V, 427
Puckett, Bertha V, 463
Puckett, Betsy A. VI, 848
Puckett, Beulah I, 533
Puckett, Beulah I, 568
Puckett, Beuly I, 568
Puckett, Binjamin I, 968
Puckett, Catharine I, 968
Puckett, Catharine V, 427
Puckett, Catherine V, 273
Puckett, Catherine V, 426
Puckett, Catherine V, 427
Puckett, Charles V, 427
Puckett, Charles VI, 848
Puckett, Clarence V, 705
Puckett, Clayburn VI, 861
Puckett, Clinton V, 463
Puckett, Cyrus I, 968
Puckett, Daniel I, 533
Puckett, Daniel I, 568
Puckett, Daniel I, 968
Puckett, Daniel V, 273
Puckett, Daniel V, 369
Puckett, Daniel V, 426
Puckett, Daniel V, 427
Puckett, Daniel Roberts V, 426
Puckett, Daniel Roberts V, 427
Puckett, Daniel, Jr. V, 427
Puckett, Deborah I, 968
Puckett, Delilah Ann V, 426
Puckett, Edith I, 1010
Puckett, Edith I, 1012
Puckett, Eli I, 968
Puckett, Eli V, 427
Puckett, Eliza V, 427
Puckett, Elizabeth I, 968
Puckett, Elizabeth V, 273
Puckett, Elizabeth V, 356
Puckett, Elizabeth V, 426
Puckett, Emma V, 463
Puckett, Enos V, 426
Puckett, Enos V, 427
Puckett, Feraby I, 968
Puckett, Fleming VI, 848
Puckett, Flo V, 705
Puckett, Frank V, 427
Puckett, Gertie V, 427
Puckett, Grace V, 372
Puckett, Grace V, 426
Puckett, Grace V, 427
Puckett, Greenlee I, 968
Puckett, Gulielma V, 426
Puckett, Gulielma V, 427
Puckett, Hannah I, 968
Puckett, Hannah V, 426
Puckett, Hannah V, 427
Puckett, Henry V, 426
Puckett, Henry V, 427
Puckett, Henry D. VI, 848

Puckett, Henry W. V, 926
Puckett, Isaac V, 426
Puckett, Isham VI, 848
Puckett, Isom I, 968
Puckett, Isom V, 427
Puckett, James I, 968
Puckett, James V, 273
Puckett, James V, 356
Puckett, James V, 426
Puckett, James V, 427
Puckett, James B. V, 427
Puckett, James R. V, 426
Puckett, James, Jr. V, 427
Puckett, Jane V, 273
Puckett, Jane V, 356
Puckett, Jeremiah V, 426
Puckett, Jincy V, 427
Puckett, Joel I, 968
Puckett, John I, 968
Puckett, John V, 426
Puckett, John V, 427
Puckett, John T. VI, 848
Puckett, Joseph I, 968
Puckett, Joseph V, 356
Puckett, Joseph V, 401
Puckett, Joseph V, 426
Puckett, Joseph V, 427
Puckett, Joseph M. V, 426
Puckett, Joseph M. V, 427
Puckett, Keziah I, 968
Puckett, Keziah V, 273
Puckett, Keziah V, 427
Puckett, Leah V, 427
Puckett, Levina I, 968
Puckett, Levina V, 426
Puckett, Lucinda V, 112
Puckett, Lucinda V, 126
Puckett, Lydia V, 426
Puckett, Lydia V, 427
Puckett, Malinda V, 427
Puckett, Margaret V, 426
Puckett, Margaret V, 427
Puckett, Margaret Ann V, 427
Puckett, Martha VI, 799
Puckett, Martha VI, 848
Puckett, Martha Ann V, 426
Puckett, Martha E. VI, 861
Puckett, Mary I, 968
Puckett, Mary I, 1012
Puckett, Mary V, 273
Puckett, Mary V, 356
Puckett, Mary V, 385
Puckett, Mary V, 401
Puckett, Mary V, 419
Puckett, Mary V, 426
Puckett, Mary V, 427
Puckett, Mary V, 463
Puckett, Mary VI, 848
Puckett, Mary Ann V, 427
Puckett, Mary J. VI, 838
Puckett, Mary Jane V, 426
Puckett, Mary Jane V, 427
Puckett, Mary S. VI, 856
Puckett, Matilda V, 383
Puckett, Matilda V, 427
Puckett, Micajah V, 356
Puckett, Micajah V, 427
Puckett, Moses I, 968
Puckett, Moses V, 273
Puckett, Moses V, 426
Puckett, Moses V, 427
Puckett, Moses V, 436
Puckett, Nan V, 463
Puckett, Nancy V, 426
Puckett, Nancy V, 427
Puckett, Nancy V, 436
Puckett, Nancy VI, 848
Puckett, Nancy M. V, 273
Puckett, Nathan V, 273
Puckett, Nathan V, 426
Puckett, Nathan V, 427
Puckett, Nathaniel VI, 834
Puckett, Nelson VI, 848
Puckett, Nelson H. VI, 807
Puckett, Nelson H. VI, 838
Puckett, Nelson H. VI, 861
Puckett, Nora V, 463
Puckett, Ocie V, 463
Puckett, Olive Ann V, 427
Puckett, Patsy VI, 834
Puckett, Patty I, 968
Puckett, Phebe V, 273
Puckett, Pheby V, 427
Puckett, Pheraby V, 427
Puckett, Pheriby V, 427
Puckett, Polly VI, 848
Puckett, Rachel V, 846
Puckett, Rachel V, 847
Puckett, Rebecca V, 427
Puckett, Rhida E. V, 857
Puckett, Richard I, 568
Puckett, Richard I, 968
Puckett, Richard V, 426
Puckett, Richard V, 427
Puckett, Richerson VI, 848
Puckett, Sally I, 968
Puckett, Sally V, 427
Puckett, Sally VI, 848
Puckett, Sarah VI, 856
Puckett, Sarah E. VI, 807
Puckett, Sarah Jane V, 392
Puckett, Sarah Jane V, 426
Puckett, Sarah Jane V, 427
Puckett, Serene VI, 848
Puckett, Susannah V, 426
Puckett, Susannah V, 427
Puckett, Talbot B. V, 426
Puckett, Talbot B. V, 427
Puckett, Tamar V, 427
Puckett, Tamer V, 426
Puckett, Taylor V, 273
Puckett, Taylor V, 356
Puckett, Thomas I, 568
Puckett, Thomas I, 953
Puckett, Thomas I, 968
Puckett, Thomas I, 1012
Puckett, Thomas V, 426
Puckett, Thomas V, 427
Puckett, Thomas VI, 848
Puckett, Thomas E. VI, 824
Puckett, Thomas E. VI, 828
Puckett, Thomas Elwood V, 426
Puckett, Thomas, Jr. I, 968
Puckett, Tira V, 426
Puckett, Tirey V, 356
Puckett, Vienna V, 845
Puckett, Welcome V, 356
Puckett, Welcome V, 426
Puckett, William VI, 799
Puckett, William VI, 848
Puckett, Zachariah I, 968
Puckett, Zachariah V, 427
Pue, Edward II, 447
Pue, Owen II, 447
Puff, Phebe II, 987
Puff, Phebe II, 1022
Puggot, Jeremiah I, 567
Pugh, A. Henry V, 927
Pugh, Abraham VI, 848
Pugh, Achillas V, 142
Pugh, Achilles IV, 265
Pugh, Achilles V, 112
Pugh, Achilles V, 113
Pugh, Achilles V, 902
Pugh, Achilles V, 927
Pugh, Achilles Henry V, 112
Pugh, Achillies V, 927
Pugh, Albert Eston V, 705
Pugh, Alce, Jr. VI, 433
Pugh, Alice I, 625
Pugh, Alice I, 1023
Pugh, Alice VI, 364
Pugh, Alice VI, 433
Pugh, Alice Elizabeth VI, 433
Pugh, Ann I, 1023
Pugh, Ann I, 1037
Pugh, Ann II, 298
Pugh, Ann II, 302
Pugh, Ann II, 1022
Pugh, Ann IV, 265
Pugh, Ann IV, 651
Pugh, Ann IV, 652
Pugh, Ann V, 783
Pugh, Ann V, 926
Pugh, Ann V, 927
Pugh, Ann VI, 383
Pugh, Ann VI, 408
Pugh, Ann VI, 433
Pugh, Anna IV, 265
Pugh, Anna V, 927
Pugh, Anna M. V, 927
Pugh, Anna Maria V, 112
Pugh, Anna Maria V, 113
Pugh, Anna Maria V, 142
Pugh, Anna Maria V, 902
Pugh, Anna Maria V, 927
Pugh, Annamaria V, 113
Pugh, Azariah I, 1023
Pugh, Azariah I, 1036
Pugh, Azariah I, 1037
Pugh, Azariah I, 1039
Pugh, Azariah V, 113
Pugh, Azariah VI, 363
Pugh, Azariah VI, 433
Pugh, Bathsheba V, 112
Pugh, Bathsheba V, 784
Pugh, Belinda V, 112
Pugh, Benjamin VI, 433
Pugh, Bersheba V, 81
Pugh, Bersheba V, 112
Pugh, Bette I, 1023
Pugh, Betty I, 1032
Pugh, Betty I, 1036
Pugh, Caleb V, 113
Pugh, Caleb V, 926
Pugh, Caleb V, 927
Pugh, Caroline IV, 646
Pugh, Caroline IV, 652
Pugh, Caroline P. IV, 646
Pugh, Caroline P. IV, 652
Pugh, Casandaz I, 568
Pugh, Casander I, 898
Pugh, Casander I, 1016
Pugh, Catharine I, 568
Pugh, Catharine I, 1016
Pugh, Catherine I, 898
Pugh, Catherine VI, 549
Pugh, Charles V, 852
Pugh, Charles E. II, 912
Pugh, Charlotte II, 299
Pugh, Christopher V, 926
Pugh, Clara Esther V, 705
Pugh, Clara Ethel V, 705
Pugh, Credylla VI, 848
Pugh, Cynthia W. V, 112
Pugh, Cynthia W. V, 113
Pugh, David I, 1023
Pugh, David I, 1036
Pugh, David I, 1039
Pugh, David I, 1062
Pugh, David IV, 265
Pugh, David V, 81
Pugh, David V, 112
Pugh, David V, 113
Pugh, David V, 784
Pugh, David V, 927
Pugh, David VI, 433
Pugh, David VI, 838
Pugh, David VI, 848
Pugh, David Thos. V, 927
Pugh, David, Jr. V, 927
Pugh, David, Sr. V, 927
Pugh, Deborah VI, 433
Pugh, E. Jane I, 919
Pugh, Eli I, 416
Pugh, Eli I, 835
Pugh, Elijah I, 1050
Pugh, Elijah II, 788
Pugh, Elijah II, 816
Pugh, Elijah, Jr. II, 816
Pugh, Elijah, Jr. II, 912
Pugh, Eliza II, 912
Pugh, Eliza Ann V, 857
Pugh, Eliza E. H. VI, 848
Pugh, Elizabeth I, 416
Pugh, Elizabeth I, 898
Pugh, Elizabeth I, 1016
Pugh, Elizabeth V, 705
Pugh, Elizabeth V, 783
Pugh, Elizabeth VI, 433
Pugh, Elizabeth VI, 848
Pugh, Ellis I, 1036
Pugh, Ellis I, 1037
Pugh, Ellis IV, 54
Pugh, Ellis V, 112
Pugh, Ellis VI, 433
Pugh, Emma Mary V, 705
Pugh, Enoch I, 416
Pugh, Enoch V, 113
Pugh, Enoch V, 857
Pugh, Enoch V, 926
Pugh, Enoch V, 927
Pugh, Enoch VI, 433
Pugh, Estelle I, 612
Pugh, Ester IV, 265
Pugh, Esther I, 403
Pugh, Esther I, 416
Pugh, Esther III, 261
Pugh, Esther V, 112
Pugh, Esther V, 113
Pugh, Esther V, 926
Pugh, Esther V, 927
Pugh, Esther Alma V, 852
Pugh, Etta V, 857
Pugh, Evan IV, 652
Pugh, Gabriel McCool I, 1037
Pugh, Gabriel McCooll VI, 433
Pugh, Geo. E. V, 927
Pugh, George V, 705
Pugh, George David V, 705
Pugh, Hanna VI, 863
Pugh, Hannah I, 568
Pugh, Hannah I, 898
Pugh, Hannah I, 1016
Pugh, Hannah I, 1023
Pugh, Hannah I, 1036
Pugh, Hannah I, 1050
Pugh, Hannah II, 810
Pugh, Hannah II, 816
Pugh, Hannah IV, 265
Pugh, Hannah IV, 1220
Pugh, Hannah V, 112
Pugh, Hannah V, 926
Pugh, Hannah V, 927
Pugh, Hannah V, 930
Pugh, Hannah VI, 363
Pugh, Hannah VI, 433
Pugh, Hannah VI, 838
Pugh, Harriet V, 86
Pugh, Harriet V, 113
Pugh, Henry II, 410
Pugh, Henry A. V, 927
Pugh, Henry E. V, 113
Pugh, Himelius I, 835
Pugh, Hiram V, 113
Pugh, Isaac VI, 549
Pugh, Isaac VI, 771
Pugh, Ishmael V, 113
Pugh, Ismael V, 113
Pugh, James VI, 848
Pugh, James W. I, 612
Pugh, Jane I, 1023
Pugh, Jane VI, 364
Pugh, Jane VI, 382
Pugh, Jane VI, 433
Pugh, Jane VI, 470
Pugh, Jane VI, 530
Pugh, Jane, Jr. VI, 433
Pugh, Jean VI, 433
Pugh, Jesse I, 416
Pugh, Jesse I, 1036
Pugh, Jesse I, 1050
Pugh, Jesse II, 816
Pugh, Jesse V, 113
Pugh, Jesse VI, 364
Pugh, Jesse VI, 433
Pugh, Jesse VI, 549
Pugh, Joanna I, 1036
Pugh, Joanna I, 1037
Pugh, Job I, 1023
Pugh, Job V, 112
Pugh, Job V, 926
Pugh, Job V, 927
Pugh, Job V, 944
Pugh, Job VI, 433
Pugh, John I, 416
Pugh, John IV, 493
Pugh, John IV, 593
Pugh, John IV, 651
Pugh, John IV, 652
Pugh, John V, 112
Pugh, John V, 113
Pugh, John V, 857
Pugh, John VI, 407
Pugh, John VI, 433
Pugh, John VI, 520
Pugh, John VI, 666
Pugh, John VI, 797
Pugh, John VI, 848
Pugh, John A. V, 927
Pugh, John D. V, 113
Pugh, John D. V, 927
Pugh, John Davis V, 112
Pugh, John R. V, 705
Pugh, Jonathan II, 851
Pugh, Jonathan II, 884
Pugh, Jonathan IV, 652
Pugh, Jonathan VI, 838
Pugh, Jordan A. V, 927
Pugh, Joseph II, 816
Pugh, Joseph II, 1022
Pugh, Joseph IV, 652
Pugh, Joseph V, 113
Pugh, Joseph T. IV, 652
Pugh, Joshua II, 816
Pugh, Joshua V, 926
Pugh, Katherine VI, 549
Pugh, Leah V, 112
Pugh, Leah V, 927
Pugh, Leah C. V, 920
Pugh, Leah C. V, 927
Pugh, Lettice II, 816
Pugh, Lettuce II, 788
Pugh, Lidia VI, 433
Pugh, Locy VI, 838
Pugh, Lot V, 112
Pugh, Lot V, 145
Pugh, Lot V, 926
Pugh, Lot VI, 848
Pugh, Lydia I, 408
Pugh, Lydia I, 416
Pugh, Lydia I, 1023
Pugh, Lydia IV, 652
Pugh, Lydia VI, 433
Pugh, Margaret II, 612
Pugh, Margaret II, 628
Pugh, Margaret II, 629
Pugh, Margaret IV, 228
Pugh, Margaret IV, 265
Pugh, Martha VI, 848
Pugh, Martha I. VI, 823
Pugh, Martha Jane VI, 980
Pugh, Mary I, 400
Pugh, Mary I, 416
Pugh, Mary I, 430
Pugh, Mary II, 410
Pugh, Mary II, 628
Pugh, Mary II, 660
Pugh, Mary II, 788
Pugh, Mary V, 50
Pugh, Mary V, 113
Pugh, Mary V, 198
Pugh, Mary V, 705
Pugh, Mary V, 909
Pugh, Mary V, 927
Pugh, Mary VI, 433
Pugh, Mary VI, 848
Pugh, Mary A. VI, 819
Pugh, Mary Ann IV, 652
Pugh, Mary Ann IV, 655
Pugh, Mary F. V, 927
Pugh, Mary Jane VI, 934
Pugh, Mary L. I, 612
Pugh, Mary T. V, 112
Pugh, Mary T. V, 142
Pugh, Mary Taylor V, 112
Pugh, Mary Taylor V, 927
Pugh, Michel VI, 848
Pugh, Miriam I, 768
Pugh, Miriam I, 835
Pugh, Miriam L. I, 416
Pugh, Miriam S. I, 416
Pugh, Mishal VI, 433
Pugh, Moses Marshall VI, 98
Pugh, Nancy I, 898
Pugh, Nancy I, 1016
Pugh, Nancy VI, 805
Pugh, Nancy VI, 918
Pugh, Naomi I, 395
Pugh, Naomi I, 416
Pugh, Naomi I, 768
Pugh, Naomi I, 835
Pugh, Patience VI, 433
Pugh, Phebe I, 1037
Pugh, Phebe IV, 54
Pugh, Phebe V, 112
Pugh, Priscilla VI, 848
Pugh, Rachel I, 416
Pugh, Rachel I, 1023
Pugh, Rachel I, 1036
Pugh, Rachel I, 1037
Pugh, Rachel I, 1039
Pugh, Rachel III, 343
Pugh, Rachel IV, 265
Pugh, Rachel IV, 303
Pugh, Rachel V, 81
Pugh, Rachel V, 112
Pugh, Rachel V, 113
Pugh, Rachel V, 145
Pugh, Rachel V, 784
Pugh, Rachel V, 926
Pugh, Rachel V, 927
Pugh, Rachel VI, 408
Pugh, Rachel VI, 433
Pugh, Rachel Ann III, 343
Pugh, Rachel M. I, 898
Pugh, Rachel, Sr. V, 927
Pugh, Rebecca I, 416
Pugh, Rebecca I, 768
Pugh, Rebecca I, 835
Pugh, Rebecca II, 816
Pugh, Rebecca Mariah I, 835
Pugh, Rebekah I, 374
Pugh, Rebekah I, 416
Pugh, Reu V, 112
Pugh, Robertson G. VI, 848
Pugh, Rue V, 927
Pugh, Rues V, 113
Pugh, Ruth I, 898
Pugh, Ruth I, 1016
Pugh, Ruth V, 112
Pugh, Ruth V, 113
Pugh, Ruth VI, 407
Pugh, Ruth VI, 433
Pugh, Ruth VI, 520
Pugh, Ruth VI, 666
Pugh, Sally VI, 1016
Pugh, Samuel V, 927
Pugh, Samuel J. V, 927
Pugh, Sarah I, 568
Pugh, Sarah I, 898
Pugh, Sarah I, 1016
Pugh, Sarah I, 1023
Pugh, Sarah II, 1005
Pugh, Sarah II, 1022
Pugh, Sarah IV, 218
Pugh, Sarah IV, 265
Pugh, Sarah IV, 652
Pugh, Sarah V, 112
Pugh, Sarah V, 113
Pugh, Sarah V, 927
Pugh, Sarah V, 944
Pugh, Sarah VI, 433
Pugh, Sarah VI, 440
Pugh, Sarah VI, 772

Sarah VI, 838
Sarah VI, 848
Sarah A. VI, 848
Sarah M. V, 927
Sophia I, 1036
Sophia I, 1039
Sophia V, 113
Susanna V, 43
Susanna V, 113
Susanna VI, 848
Tabitha VI, 823
Tabitha VI, 848
Thomas I, 416
Thomas I, 568
Thomas I, 1023
Thomas I, 1036
Thomas I, 1037
Thomas I Sup 1, 9
Thomas II, 1005
Thomas II, 1022
Thomas V, 113
Thomas V, 927
Thomas VI, 408
Thomas VI, 433
Thomas VI, 848
Thomas VI, 918
Thomas VI, 1016
Thomas Joseph V, 113
Thomas, Sr. VI, 433
Thos. V, 783
Thos. V, 926
Thos. V, 927
Timothy I, 898
Timothy I, 1016
Verhindo I, 1023
Verlinda V, 113
Verlinda V, 129
Wd. Catharine II, 816
Wd. Catherine VI, 771
Wd. Eliza Wickersham
I, 816
William I, 568
William I, 1036
William I, 1037
William V, 112
William V, 927
William VI, 848
William W. VI, 848
Wm. I, 1016
Wm. H. V, 927
Zilpha IV, 265
ley, Charlotte Marie V, 705
ley, Elizabeth III, 261
ley, Jeanne V, 705
ley, Laura Bell V, 705
ley, Perci V, 705
ley, Phyllis V, 705
ley, Ruth V, 705
ley, Sybil V, 705
m, Anna May IV, 987
m, Burley T. IV, 987
m, Edith IV, 987
m, Edith Marie IV, 987
m, William VI, 855
n, Abraham B. VI, 915
n, Ann M. VI, 887
n, Archibald VI, 981
n, Capt. Thomas VI, 981
n, Charlotte VI, 1008
n, Elizabeth VI, 914
n, Elizabeth VI, 979
n, Elizabeth VI, 981
n, George B. VI, 878
n, Granville VI, 972
n, Granville VI, 981
n, Granville R. VI, 972
n, Huldah VI, 1021
n, Jane VI, 981
n, Jesse VI, 1008
n, Louisa W. VI, 1008
n, Lucinda VI, 930
n, Lucinda E. VI, 878
en, Lydda VI, 980
en, Martha VI, 981
en, Moses VI, 918
en, Moses VI, 981
en, Nancy VI, 890
en, Polly VI, 894
en, Polly VI, 981
en, Polly M. VI, 981
en, Pulley VI, 890
en, Quintilly VI, 1003
en, Salley VI, 1021
en, Sarah VI, 968
en, Siner VI, 963
en, Thomas VI, 880
en, Thomas VI, 887
en, Thomas VI, 889
en, Thomas VI, 894
en, Thomas VI, 963
en, Thomas VI, 968

Pullen, Thomas VI, 979
Pullen, Thomas VI, 980
Pullen, Thomas VI, 981
Pullen, Thomas, Sr. VI, 878
Pullen, Thomas, Sr. VI, 1021
Pullen, Thos. VI, 1021
Pullen, Tilghman VI, 887
Pullen, Tilmon A. VI, 884
Pullen, Tilmon A. VI, 968
Pullen, William VI, 981
Pullen, William F. VI, 887
Pullen, Winney VI, 930
Pullen, Zachariah VI, 930
Pulliam, Delphia VI, 848
Pulliam, Frances M. VI, 803
Pulliam, Iseam VI, 797
Pulliam, Mary A. VI, 848
Pulliam, Penelope VI, 797
Pulliam, Rawlings VI, 803
Pulliam, Thomas A. VI, 848
Pulliam, William VI, 848
Pullin, Elizabeth VI, 981
Pullin, George B. VI, 893
Pullin, Moses VI, 981
Pullin, Philip II, 410
Pullin, William II, 410
Pullium, Isham VI, 864
Pullium, Mary VI, 864
Pullwitz, Edith III, 261
Pullwitz, Edward Mitchell III, 50
Pullwitz, Edward Mitchell
III, 261
Pullwitz, Eunice III, 50
Pullwitz, Eunice III, 261
Pullwitz, Henry III, 261
Puls, Faye IV, 1334
Pulse, Bell V, 356
Pulse, Belle V, 344
Pummel, Alexander H. V, 273
Pummel, Hamilton V, 273
Pummel, Mary V, 273
Pummel, Mary E. V, 273
Pummelle, Margaret V, 655
Pummelle, Margaret V, 705
Pummelle, William V, 705
Pummelle, Wm. V, 655
Pumphrey, Mettie V, 463
Puoltney, James II, 911
Purcel, Elias H. IV, 1180
Purcel, Elias Hix IV, 1180
Purcel, Hannah IV, 1180
Purcel, Hannah E. IV, 1180
Purcel, John IV, 1180
Purcel, John Beedle IV, 1180
Purcel, Joseph William IV, 1181
Purcel, Joseph Wm. IV, 1180
Purcel, Lucy IV, 1180
Purcel, Lydia Ann IV, 1180
Purcel, Mahlon W. IV, 1180
Purcel, Mahlon W. IV, 1181
Purcel, Mary IV, 1180
Purcel, Nancy H. IV, 1181
Purcel, Nancy N. IV, 1180
Purcel, Nancy N. IV, 1191
Purcel, Peleg IV, 1180
Purcel, Priscilla H. IV, 1180
Purcel, Priscilla Hunt IV, 1180
Purcel, Rebecca Anney IV, 1180
Purcel, Rebecca J. IV, 1180
Purcel, Rosanna IV, 1180
Purcel, Rosannah IV, 1180
Purcel, Thomas V. IV, 1180
Purcel, Thos. V. IV, 1180
Purcel, Thos. V. IV, 1181
Purcel, Thos. V. IV, 1191
Purcell, Adeliah VI, 691
Purcell, Catherine V, 762
Purcell, Elias H. VI, 433
Purcell, Elias H. VI, 434
Purcell, Elias Hicks VI, 691
Purcell, Elias Hicks Purcell
VI, 434
Purcell, Elias Hix IV, 1180
Purcell, Elizabeth VI, 848
Purcell, Elizabeth S. VI, 948
Purcell, Ella V, 641
Purcell, Emma VI, 691
Purcell, Emma Stone VI, 265
Purcell, Frances VI, 691
Purcell, Francis A. V, 427
Purcell, Hannah VI, 691
Purcell, Hannah VI, 692
Purcell, Hannah VI, 710
Purcell, Hanney VI, 668
Purcell, John IV, 1180
Purcell, John VI, 414
Purcell, John VI, 433
Purcell, John VI, 434
Purcell, John VI, 435
Purcell, John VI, 667
Purcell, John VI, 668

Purcell, John VI, 691
Purcell, John VI, 692
Purcell, John VI, 710
Purcell, John VI, 713
Purcell, John B. VI, 691
Purcell, John Beedle IV, 1180
Purcell, John Beedle VI, 691
Purcell, John, Jr. VI, 434
Purcell, Joseph VI, 434
Purcell, Joseph J. VI, 691
Purcell, Joseph William VI, 434
Purcell, Leana V, 641
Purcell, Lena V, 641
Purcell, Lot VI, 434
Purcell, Lot VI, 668
Purcell, Lot VI, 691
Purcell, Lot VI, 692
Purcell, Lot VI, 710
Purcell, Lott VI, 434
Purcell, Lucy VI, 848
Purcell, Lydia VI, 691
Purcell, Lydia Ann IV, 1180
Purcell, Lydia Ann VI, 433
Purcell, Lydia Ann VI, 434
Purcell, Lydia Ann VI, 435
Purcell, Lydia Ann VI, 691
Purcell, Lydia J. VI, 668
Purcell, Lydia Jane VI, 663
Purcell, Lydia Jane VI, 668
Purcell, Mahlon W. VI, 434
Purcell, Malinda J. V, 392
Purcell, Martha III, 439
Purcell, Mary IV, 1180
Purcell, Mary VI, 414
Purcell, Mary VI, 433
Purcell, Mary VI, 434
Purcell, Mary VI, 435
Purcell, Mary VI, 667
Purcell, Mary VI, 668
Purcell, Mary VI, 691
Purcell, Mary VI, 692
Purcell, Mary VI, 710
Purcell, Mary VI, 713
Purcell, Mary Janney VI, 691
Purcell, Mary Janney VI, 692
Purcell, Mary Janney VI, 713
Purcell, Mordecai VI, 691
Purcell, Mordeica VI, 433
Purcell, Mordica VI, 434
Purcell, Nancy V, 392
Purcell, Nancy N. IV, 1191
Purcell, Nancy N. VI, 434
Purcell, Nancy N. VI, 691
Purcell, Nancy N. VI, 718
Purcell, Nathan H. VI, 668
Purcell, Pleasant VI, 691
Purcell, Pleasant VI, 692
Purcell, Pleasant VI, 709
Purcell, Pricilla H. VI, 691
Purcell, Pricilla Hunt VI, 691
Purcell, Priscilla H. VI, 433
Purcell, Priscilla H. VI, 434
Purcell, Priscilla Hunt IV, 1180
Purcell, Priscilla Hunt VI, 434
Purcell, Rebecca VI, 414
Purcell, Rebecca VI, 433
Purcell, Rebecca VI, 434
Purcell, Rebecca Anney IV, 1180
Purcell, Rebecca J. VI, 434
Purcell, Rebecca Janney VI, 434
Purcell, Rebecca Janney VI, 691
Purcell, Rosanna VI, 433
Purcell, Rosanna VI, 434
Purcell, Rosanna VI, 691
Purcell, Rosannah IV, 1180
Purcell, Stacy Janney VI, 691
Purcell, Susannah VI, 538
Purcell, Susannah VI, 549
Purcell, Thomas II, 629
Purcell, Thomas III, 439
Purcell, Thomas VI, 434
Purcell, Thomas VI, 691
Purcell, Thomas VI, 848
Purcell, Thomas VI, 864
Purcell, Thomas H. VI, 718
Purcell, Thomas L. VI, 433
Purcell, Thomas Pursell VI, 948
Purcell, Thomas V. VI, 434
Purcell, Thomas V. VI, 691
Purcell, Thomas Vernon VI, 691
Purcell, Thos. N. IV, 1191
Purcell, Valentine VI, 668
Purcell, Wm. V, 392
Purdee, Samuel A. I, 732
Purdie, Gulielma M. I, 732
Purdie, Gulielma M. I, 932
Purdie, Gulielma Maria I, 722
Purdie, Gulielma Maria I, 732
Purdie, Hugh V, 356
Purdie, Samuel I, 732
Purdie, Samuel A. I, 687

Purdie, Samuel A. I, 732
Purdie, Samuel Alexander I, 722
Purdie, Samuel Alexander I, 732
Purdie, Waity H. I, 732
Purdom, Benj. VI, 502
Purdom, Benjamin VI, 499
Purdom, Benjamin VI, 580
Purdom, Elizabeth VI, 581
Purdom, Elizabeth VI, 583
Purdom, Mary VI, 580
Purdue, Isaac VI, 692
Purdue, Mariam G. VI, 692
Purdue, Mary Virginia VI, 692
Purdue, Miriam VI, 692
Purdue, Miriam G. VI, 682
Purdue, Richard VI, 848
Purdue, Sarah VI, 682
Purdue, Susannah VI, 848
Purdue, Thomas H. VI, 682
Purdue, Thomas H. VI, 692
Purdue, William VI, 682
Purdum, Benjamin VI, 490
Purdum, Benjamin VI, 526
Purdum, Benjamin VI, 549
Purdum, Benjamin VI, 582
Purdum, Elizabeth VI, 490
Purdum, Wd. Elizabeth VI, 549
Purdy, ??? III, 261
Purdy, Abegail I, 948
Purdy, Abigail Jane I, 932
Purdy, Abigal I, 948
Purdy, Adamile III, 261
Purdy, Addie L. III, 494
Purdy, Addie L. III, 495
Purdy, Alchie III, 60
Purdy, Alchie III, 261
Purdy, Alex III, 261
Purdy, Alex. III, 60
Purdy, Alexander C. V, 705
Purdy, Alice Roberta III, 261
Purdy, Amelia F. I, 898
Purdy, Anna V, 356
Purdy, Elias Dawson II, 629
Purdy, Ellison R. I, 898
Purdy, Ellison R. V, 705
Purdy, Foliard Ridge II, 629
Purdy, Folliard II, 629
Purdy, George H. III, 261
Purdy, Grace V, 356
Purdy, Gulielma I, 948
Purdy, Harriett W. V, 705
Purdy, Helen V, 356
Purdy, Hugh V, 356
Purdy, James III, 261
Purdy, James Garfield III, 261
Purdy, Jane II, 543
Purdy, Jane II, 629
Purdy, Jeanette H. V, 705
Purdy, Julia D. III, 261
Purdy, Julia S. III, 60
Purdy, Juliette III, 261
Purdy, Monmouth III, 261
Purdy, Monroe III, 261
Purdy, Rose V, 463
Purdy, Theodore III, 261
Purham, Sarah III, 261
Purham, Sarah III, 331
Purington, Pelatiah I, 256
Purinton, ??? III, 261
Purinton, Avis III, 261
Purinton, Caroline H. IV, 1181
Purinton, John IV, 1181
Purinton, John H. IV, 1181
Purinton, Lydia G. IV, 1181
Purinton, Palatiah V, 927
Purinton, Pelatiah I, 256
Purinton, Philena IV, 1181
Purinton, Sara. III, 261
Purinton, Sarah III, 261
Purk, Katie V, 1015
Purkey, Gay V, 427
Purkey, Neale V, 427
Purkins, David I, 59
Purkins, David I, 68
Purkins, Mary I, 59
Purnal, Elizabeth VI, 981
Purnal, Elizabeth R. VI, 981
Purnal, Fletcher VI, 981
Purnal, John VI, 981
Purnal, Mary VI, 981
Purnal, Peter VI, 981
Purnal, Phebe VI, 981
Purnell, David II, 136
Purnell, Elizabeth VI, 981
Purnell, John VI, 981
Purnell, John H. VI, 880
Purnell, Joseph VI, 889
Purnell, Lucy VI, 956
Purnell, Mildred A. II, 136
Purnell, Sara II, 136
Pursel, Jonathan II, 1022

Pursel, Lydia II, 1022
Pursell, Ann II, 1016
Pursell, Ann II, 1022
Pursell, John II, 1022
Pursell, Jonathan II, 1022
Pursell, Joseph William IV, 1181
Pursell, Lucy VI, 1008
Pursell, Lydia II, 1022
Pursell, Lydia II, 1039
Pursell, Lydia C. VI, 999
Pursell, Mahlon II, 1022
Pursell, Mahlon W. IV, 1181
Pursell, Mary II, 1022
Pursell, Mary Ann P. VI, 971
Pursell, Mildred Ann VI, 974
Pursell, Nancy H. IV, 1181
Pursell, Sarah J. VI, 935
Pursell, Thomas VI, 971
Pursell, Thomas VI, 974
Pursell, Thomas VI, 999
Pursell, Thos. VI, 1008
Pursell, Thos. V. IV, 1181
Pursler, Rebecca Mary V, 593
Pursley, Sarah VI, 921
Pursley, William VI, 921
Purtee, Hazel V, 705
Purviance, ??? IV, 104
Purviance, Alfred IV, 494
Purviance, Alfred G. IV, 494
Purviance, Alice M. IV, 494
Purviance, Alice M. IV, 495
Purviance, Amanda IV, 1174
Purviance, Amanda IV, 1181
Purviance, Amos IV, 493
Purviance, Amos IV, 494
Purviance, Ann IV, 557
Purviance, Anna H. IV, 495
Purviance, Annie Hurford IV, 495
Purviance, Annie W. IV, 494
Purviance, Bessie IV, 495
Purviance, Charles L. IV, 494
Purviance, Charles T. IV, 494
Purviance, Chas. A. IV, 494
Purviance, Clementine IV, 545
Purviance, Cynthia IV, 1181
Purviance, D. IV, 494
Purviance, David IV, 106
Purviance, David IV, 113
Purviance, David IV, 158
Purviance, David IV, 265
Purviance, David IV, 493
Purviance, David IV, 494
Purviance, David IV, 503
Purviance, David IV, 509
Purviance, David IV, 534
Purviance, David IV, 545
Purviance, David IV, 557
Purviance, David VI, 428
Purviance, David, Jr. IV, 494
Purviance, David, Jr. IV, 545
Purviance, Deborah IV, 265
Purviance, Deborah IV, 467
Purviance, Deborah IV, 490
Purviance, Deborah IV, 493
Purviance, Deborah IV, 494
Purviance, Deborah IV, 497
Purviance, Deborah, Sr. IV, 494
Purviance, Eleanor IV, 265
Purviance, Eleanor IV, 274
Purviance, Elenor IV, 494
Purviance, Elis IV, 494
Purviance, Elisha IV, 494
Purviance, Eliza IV, 545
Purviance, Elizabeth IV, 106
Purviance, Elizabeth IV, 115
Purviance, Elizabeth IV, 265
Purviance, Elizabeth IV, 493
Purviance, Elizabeth IV, 494
Purviance, Elizabeth IV, 503
Purviance, Elizabeth L. IV, 495
Purviance, Elizabeth L. IV, 971
Purviance, Elizabeth L. IV, 987
Purviance, Elizabeth L. IV, 988
Purviance, Elizabeth M. IV, 495
Purviance, Ellen IV, 494
Purviance, Ellis IV, 494
Purviance, Ellis IV, 545
Purviance, Elmira IV, 490
Purviance, Elmira IV, 493
Purviance, Elmira IV, 494
Purviance, Elvira IV, 509
Purviance, Elvira IV, 545
Purviance, Elvira IV, 566
Purviance, Elvira IV, 567
Purviance, Elvira IV, 593
Purviance, Elwood IV, 493
Purviance, Elwood IV, 494
Purviance, Esther IV, 493
Purviance, Esther IV, 494
Purviance, Esther IV, 501
Purviance, Ethel May IV, 495

Purviance, Evan IV, 265
Purviance, Evan IV, 494
Purviance, Evan H. IV, 265
Purviance, Evan H. IV, 494
Purviance, Evan H. IV, 505
Purviance, Evan Hurford IV, 495
Purviance, George IV, 106
Purviance, George IV, 493
Purviance, George IV, 494
Purviance, George, Jr. IV, 494
Purviance, Guli Ann IV, 545
Purviance, Guliann IV, 545
Purviance, Hannah M. IV, 495
Purviance, Hannah May IV, 494
Purviance, Henry IV, 493
Purviance, Henry IV, 1181
Purviance, Henry S. IV, 494
Purviance, Henry S. IV, 1181
Purviance, Isaac IV, 493
Purviance, Israel IV, 493
Purviance, James IV, 106
Purviance, James IV, 158
Purviance, James IV, 265
Purviance, James IV, 493
Purviance, James IV, 494
Purviance, James VI, 428
Purviance, James, Jr. IV, 106
Purviance, James, Jr. IV, 494
Purviance, Jas. IV, 494
Purviance, Jos. IV, 490
Purviance, Jos. IV, 494
Purviance, Joseph IV, 106
Purviance, Joseph IV, 265
Purviance, Joseph IV, 493
Purviance, Joseph IV, 494
Purviance, Joseph IV, 497
Purviance, Joseph E. IV, 1181
Purviance, Joseph Elwood IV, 1181
Purviance, Joseph R. IV, 494
Purviance, Ketura H. IV, 545
Purviance, Lydia IV, 265
Purviance, Lydia B. IV, 494
Purviance, Lydia B. IV, 495
Purviance, Lydia B. IV, 505
Purviance, M. Amanda IV, 1181
Purviance, Mark W. IV, 545
Purviance, Marten Ezra IV, 545
Purviance, Martha IV, 493
Purviance, Martha IV, 494
Purviance, Martha IV, 496
Purviance, Martha IV, 1149
Purviance, Martha IV, 1181
Purviance, Martha M. IV, 1181
Purviance, Martin Ezra IV, 494
Purviance, Martin Ezra IV, 545
Purviance, Mary IV, 106
Purviance, Mary IV, 113
Purviance, Mary IV, 158
Purviance, Mary IV, 265
Purviance, Mary IV, 473
Purviance, Mary IV, 486
Purviance, Mary IV, 493
Purviance, Mary IV, 494
Purviance, Mary IV, 503
Purviance, Mary IV, 545
Purviance, Mary S. IV, 494
Purviance, Nathan IV, 493
Purviance, Nathan IV, 494
Purviance, Nathaniel IV, 494
Purviance, Nellie IV, 494
Purviance, Nellie IV, 495
Purviance, Owen IV, 493
Purviance, Owen IV, 494
Purviance, Plummer IV, 494
Purviance, Plummer W. IV, 494
Purviance, Rebecca IV, 494
Purviance, Richard IV, 106
Purviance, Richard IV, 467
Purviance, Richard IV, 494
Purviance, Richard B. IV, 493
Purviance, S. IV, 494
Purviance, Samuel IV, 493
Purviance, Samuel IV, 494
Purviance, Samuel IV, 495
Purviance, Samuel T. IV, 495
Purviance, Samutl T. IV, 494
Purviance, Sarah IV, 106
Purviance, Sarah IV, 158
Purviance, Sarah IV, 226
Purviance, Sarah IV, 265
Purviance, Sarah IV, 275
Purviance, Sarah IV, 473
Purviance, Sarah IV, 478
Purviance, Sarah IV, 489
Purviance, Sarah IV, 494
Purviance, Sarah IV, 495
Purviance, Sarah IV, 503
Purviance, Sarah IV, 509
Purviance, Sarah IV, 534
Purviance, Sarah IV, 545
Purviance, Sarah IV, 987
Purviance, Sarah IV, 988
Purviance, Sarah H. IV, 494
Purviance, Sarah W. IV, 557
Purviance, Semira IV, 545
Purviance, Semira Clementine IV, 534
Purviance, Semira Clementine IV, 545
Purviance, Semira Clementine IV, 552
Purviance, Sina IV, 265
Purviance, Sinah IV, 493
Purviance, Thomas IV, 106
Purviance, Thomas IV, 265
Purviance, Thomas IV, 494
Purviance, Thomas W. IV, 494
Purviance, Thomas Wm. IV, 494
Purviance, William IV, 106
Purviance, William IV, 265
Purviance, William IV, 478
Purviance, William IV, 493
Purviance, William IV, 494
Purviance, William IV, 495
Purviance, William IV, 987
Purviance, William H. IV, 1181
Purviance, William I. IV, 494
Purviance, William J. IV, 265
Purviance, William S. IV, 494
Purviance, William S. IV, 495
Purviance, Willie IV, 494
Purviance, Wm. IV, 226
Purviance, Wm. IV, 274
Purviance, Wm. IV, 494
Purviance, Wm. IV, 987
Purviance, Wm. IV, 988
Purviance, Wm. S. IV, 987
Purviance, Wm. S. IV, 988
Purvies, Ann IV, 1074
Purvies, Elijah IV, 1074
Purvies, Isaac IV, 1074
Purvies, John IV, 1074
Purvies, Jonathan IV, 1074
Purvies, Levi IV, 1074
Purvies, Mary IV, 1074
Purvies, Moses IV, 1074
Purvies, Rachel IV, 1074
Purvies, Sarah IV, 1074
Purvis, Alcinda I, 256
Purvis, Ann IV, 1074
Purvis, Anna Elizabeth I, 256
Purvis, Anna Rebecca I, 226
Purvis, Annette C. IV, 1220
Purvis, Daliah I, 207
Purvis, Edward IV, 1220
Purvis, Elijah IV, 1074
Purvis, Elijah IV, 1137
Purvis, Emily Ann IV, 1074
Purvis, Emily Ann IV, 1075
Purvis, Eunice V, 958
Purvis, Eunice V, 960
Purvis, Georgiana B. II, 816
Purvis, Hannah E. IV, 1220
Purvis, Harriet D. II, 816
Purvis, Harvey J. I, 207
Purvis, Isaac IV, 1074
Purvis, J. J. I, 226
Purvis, James I, 256
Purvis, James J. I, 241
Purvis, James J. I, 256
Purvis, John I, 256
Purvis, John IV, 1074
Purvis, Jonathan IV, 1074
Purvis, Julia Lois I, 226
Purvis, Junius J. I, 226
Purvis, Levi IV, 1074
Purvis, Lucy IV, 1150
Purvis, Lucy IV, 1220
Purvis, Lydia IV, 1203
Purvis, Lydia IV, 1220
Purvis, Margaret I, 226
Purvis, Margaret B. I, 241
Purvis, Margaret B. I, 256
Purvis, Martha R. I, 226
Purvis, Mary IV, 1074
Purvis, Mattie R. I, 235
Purvis, Mattie R. I, 256
Purvis, Moses I, 256
Purvis, Moses IV, 1074
Purvis, Paul I, 226
Purvis, Paul I, 256
Purvis, Paul W. I, 235
Purvis, Paul W. I, 256
Purvis, Peleg IV, 1220
Purvis, Peleg B. IV, 1220
Purvis, Rachel IV, 1074
Purvis, Robert II, 816
Purvis, Ruth Evelyn I, 226
Purvis, Sarah IV, 1074
Purvis, Sarah J. V, 955
Purvis, Sarah J. V, 958
Purvis, Viola IV, 1220
Purvis, William I, 256
Purvis, William IV, 1220
Purvis, Willie IV, 1220
Purvis, Winnifred I, 233
Purviss, John I, 256
Pusey, Andrew VI, 603
Pusey, Ann II, 410
Pusey, Ann II, 629
Pusey, Ann II, 685
Pusey, Ann II, 816
Pusey, Ann H. IV, 730
Pusey, Ann H. IV, 752
Pusey, Anne II, 629
Pusey, Caleb II, 629
Pusey, Caleb II, 685
Pusey, Caleb II, 761
Pusey, Caleb II, 816
Pusey, Caleb II, 912
Pusey, Caleb III, 261
Pusey, Caleb VI, 357
Pusey, Caroline F. C. II, 816
Pusey, Caroline F. C. II, 913
Pusey, Caroline F. C. II, 922
Pusey, Clara G. II, 816
Pusey, Clarence Carleton II, 816
Pusey, Cora Elma V. VI, 642
Pusey, Cora Elma V. VI, 692
Pusey, David VI, 549
Pusey, David VI, 603
Pusey, Edith Lewis II, 844
Pusey, Edith Lewis II, 913
Pusey, Elbert N. VI, 642
Pusey, Elbert N. VI, 692
Pusey, Elizabeth II, 410
Pusey, Elizabeth II, 629
Pusey, Elizabeth II, 716
Pusey, Elizabeth III, 261
Pusey, Elizabeth III, 344
Pusey, Elizabeth I. II, 913
Pusey, Elizabeth I. II, 942
Pusey, Elizabeth M. IV, 54
Pusey, Elizabeth Q. II, 913
Pusey, Ellwood Thos. II, 816
Pusey, Elwood II, 913
Pusey, Elwood T. II, 761
Pusey, Elwood T. II, 913
Pusey, Esther II, 816
Pusey, Esther II, 913
Pusey, Esther II, 942
Pusey, Frederick Taylor II, 913
Pusey, George IV, 38
Pusey, George IV, 54
Pusey, George V, 113
Pusey, George V, 356
Pusey, George VI, 434
Pusey, George VI, 549
Pusey, George • VI, 603
Pusey, Grace Edna II, 895
Pusey, Grace Edna II, 913
Pusey, Hannah II, 828
Pusey, Hannah V, 113
Pusey, Hannah V, 490
Pusey, Hannah V, 524
Pusey, Hannah Y. VI, 642
Pusey, Howard II, 913
Pusey, Jacob II, 913
Pusey, Jacob II, 922
Pusey, James II, 716
Pusey, Jesse D. VI, 642
Pusey, Jesse D. VI, 692
Pusey, Jesse F. V, 524
Pusey, Joel V, 113
Pusey, Joel V, 356
Pusey, Joel V, 490
Pusey, Joel V, 524
Pusey, Joel VI, 603
Pusey, John VI, 603
Pusey, John Marsh IV, 54
Pusey, Joice V, 113
Pusey, Jonas II, 828
Pusey, Joseph IV, 54
Pusey, Joseph IV, 348
Pusey, Joseph M. III, 261
Pusey, Joseph M. III, 344
Pusey, Joseph M. IV, 54
Pusey, Josephine Gertrude II, 816
Pusey, Josephine Gertrude II, 913
Pusey, Joshua II, 629
Pusey, Joshua II, 685
Pusey, Joshua II, 816
Pusey, Joshua II, 913
Pusey, Joshua II, 922
Pusey, Joshua IV, 54
Pusey, Joshua VI, 483
Pusey, Joshua VI, 549
Pusey, Joshua VI, 603
Pusey, Joshua VI, 656
Pusey, Joshua VI, 657
Pusey, Joshua VI, 692
Pusey, Joshua W. II, 629
Pusey, Joshua W. II, 761
Pusey, Joshua W. II, 912
Pusey, Louisa W. II, 913
Pusey, Louisa W. II, 922
Pusey, Lydia II, 592
Pusey, Lydia II, 629
Pusey, Lydia II, 716
Pusey, Lydia II, 761
Pusey, Lydia II, 828
Pusey, Lydia II, 913
Pusey, Lydia II, 942
Pusey, Lydia V, 113
Pusey, Lydia V, 331
Pusey, Lydia V, 356
Pusey, Lydia V, 621
Pusey, Lydia VI, 482
Pusey, Lydia VI, 483
Pusey, Lydia VI, 509
Pusey, Lydia VI, 554
Pusey, Lydia VI, 567
Pusey, Lydia VI, 603
Pusey, M'Kay VI, 603
Pusey, Margaret V, 113
Pusey, Margaret V, 356
Pusey, Margaret V, 360
Pusey, Margaret VI, 603
Pusey, Martha IV, 50
Pusey, Martha IV, 54
Pusey, Martha IV, 348
Pusey, Martha V, 113
Pusey, Martha V, 524
Pusey, Mary II, 410
Pusey, Mary II, 629
Pusey, Mary II, 799
Pusey, Mary II, 816
Pusey, Mary IV, 54
Pusey, Mary V, 113
Pusey, Mary V, 331
Pusey, Mary V, 356
Pusey, Mary V, 360
Pusey, Mary V, 621
Pusey, Mary VI, 483
Pusey, Mary VI, 597
Pusey, Mary VI, 602
Pusey, Mary VI, 603
Pusey, Mary Albino III, 261
Pusey, Mary Albino III, 344
Pusey, Mary Ann IV, 22
Pusey, Mary Ann IV, 54
Pusey, Mary Ellen VI, 656
Pusey, Mary Ellen VI, 657
Pusey, Mary Ellen VI, 692
Pusey, Mary G. IV, 54
Pusey, Mary H. IV, 54
Pusey, Mary M. IV, 54
Pusey, Mary Mifflin II, 913
Pusey, Mary Painter II, 629
Pusey, Mary, Jr. II, 629
Pusey, Mary, Jr. V, 356
Pusey, Massey VI, 491
Pusey, Nathan IV, 50
Pusey, Nathan IV, 54
Pusey, Nathan IV, 348
Pusey, Nathan V, 113
Pusey, Nathan V, 331
Pusey, Nathan V, 356
Pusey, Nathan V, 360
Pusey, Nathan V, 621
Pusey, Nathan VI, 592
Pusey, Nathan VI, 603
Pusey, Rachel II, 410
Pusey, Rachel V, 524
Pusey, Rachel VI, 603
Pusey, Rebecca K. II, 913
Pusey, Rebecca Rakestraw II, 816
Pusey, Reuben II, 816
Pusey, Reuben II, 913
Pusey, Reuben II, 942
Pusey, Sarah II, 629
Pusey, Sarah IV, 38
Pusey, Sarah IV, 54
Pusey, Sarah Baker II, 716
Pusey, Susanna II, 562
Pusey, Susanna II, 629
Pusey, Susanna II, 761
Pusey, Susanna II, 816
Pusey, Susannah II, 912
Pusey, Susannah VI, 603
Pusey, Susannah Y. VI, 692
Pusey, Tacy II, 410
Pusey, Walter Carrol II, 913
Pusey, Walter Carroll II, 844
Pusey, Wd. Mary II, 629
Pusey, William II, 410
Pusey, William IV, 54
Pusey, William V, 113
Pusey, William VI, 603
Pusey, Wm. II, 629
Pusey, Wm. II, 716
Pusey, Wm. V, 356
Pusey, Wm. E. IV, 839
Pushee, Addary P. V, 243
Pushee, Martha A. V, 243
Pushee, Minnie V, 243
Pushee, Walter H. V, 273
Pushey, Martha Ann V, 258
Pushey, Martha Ann V, 273
Pushie, Addie V, 273
Pushie, Adney P. V, 273
Pushie, Arthur V, 273
Pushie, Harley V, 273
Pushie, Margaret V, 273
Pushie, Martha V, 273
Pushie, Martha Ann V, 273
Pushie, Mellie F. V, 273
Pushie, Minnie V, 273
Pushie, Minnie M. V, 273
Pushie, Nellie V, 273
Pushie, Walter H. V, 273
Pussell, Ann II, 364
Pussell, Ann II, 410
Pussle, Mary II, 1011
Pussle, Mary II, 1022
Pusy, David VI, 434
Pusy, George VI, 434
Pusy, Mary VI, 371
Pusy, Mary VI, 434
Pusy, Nathan VI, 371
Pusy, Nathan VI, 434
Puterbaugh, Alberta V, 762
Puterbaugh, Mildred V, 762
Puterbaugh, Roy V, 762
Puterbaugh, William V, 762
Putman, Ann I, 568
Putman, Eva Gibson V, 427
Putman, Josiah I, 898
Putnam, ??? III, 486
Putnam, Ann I, 568
Putnam, Anna H. I, 563
Putnam, Anna H. I, 568
Putnam, Bessie IV, 1260
Putnam, Chas. V, 1015
Putnam, Chas. D. V, 1015
Putnam, Clifford V, 1015
Putnam, Elizabeth V, 1015
Putnam, Hazel V, 1015
Putnam, Howard IV, 1260
Putnam, Julia III, 486
Putnam, Julia III, 495
Putnam, Marsella IV, 1240
Putnam, Olive V, 1015
Putnam, Tillie V, 1015
Putnum, Ann I, 568
Putt, John II, 447
Putt, Nicholas II, 447
Puttway, Edward II, 447
Pyatt, Deborah VI, 549
Pyatt, John VI, 549
Pyatt, Julia B. IV, 752
Pyatt, Leroy C. IV, 752
Pyatt, Mary VI, 489
Pyatt, Mary VI, 549
Pyerce, George II, 618
Pygeon, Joseph II, 446
Pygeon, Mary II, 446
Pygeon, Rebecca II, 446
Pyle, ??? V, 705
Pyle, A. C. V, 594
Pyle, Aaron IV, 652
Pyle, Aaron IV, 881
Pyle, Abigail II, 817
Pyle, Abigail IV, 652
Pyle, Abigail V, 593
Pyle, Abijah V, 113
Pyle, Abijah V, 594
Pyle, Abijah H. V, 113
Pyle, Abijah H. V, 593
Pyle, Abijah H. V, 594
Pyle, Abraham V, 594
Pyle, Ada Laura V, 593
Pyle, Albert V, 593
Pyle, Albert C. V, 594
Pyle, Alfred C. V, 594
Pyle, Alfred Clark V, 705
Pyle, Allen V, 524
Pyle, Allen H. V, 593
Pyle, Allen H. V, 594
Pyle, Allen H. V, 641
Pyle, Allen T. V, 641
Pyle, Amanda Maria V, 566
Pyle, Amanda Maria V, 676
Pyle, Amy Q. II, 1088
Pyle, Amy Q. II, 1089
Pyle, Ann II, 629
Pyle, Ann IV, 50
Pyle, Ann IV, 54
Pyle, Ann Maria V, 593
Pyle, Anna C. V, 594
Pyle, Anna Garner V, 593
Pyle, Anna M. V, 593

e, Benjamin IV, 652
e, Benjamin IV, 873
e, Benjamin IV, 881
e, Caleb IV, 265
e, Caleb V, 593
e, Carrie V, 705
e, Charles C. V, 594
e, Charley V, 593
e, Chas. C. V, 594
e, Chas. W. V, 594
e, Curtice IV, 54
e, Curtis IV, 35
e, Curtis IV, 54
e, Cyrus II, 846
e, Cyrus II, 913
e, David V, 113
le, David V, 125
le, David V, 593
le, David V, 594
le, David V, 599
le, David Henry V, 641
le, David Lindley V, 594
le, David Lindley V, 705
le, David S. V, 356
le, David S. V, 593
le, David S. V, 594
le, David S. V, 604
le, David S. V, 641
le, David S. V, 705
le, Davis S. V, 641
le, Deborah IV, 207
le, Deborah IV, 265
le, Edith II, 31
le, Edward II, 949
le, Edward II, 1088
le, Edward II, 1089
yle, Elizabeth II, 807
le, Elizabeth IV, 652
le, Elizabeth IV, 865
yle, Elizabeth IV, 873
yle, Elizabeth IV, 881
yle, Elizabeth V, 524
yle, Elizabeth D. VI, 772
yle, Elizabeth S. IV, 881
yle, Ellen VI, 770
yle, Ellen VI, 772
yle, Ellwood IV, 881
yle, Elmira IV, 742
yle, Elmira IV, 752
yle, Elwood IV, 881
yle, Emily V, 588
yle, Emily V, 593
yle, Emily V, 594
yle, Emma V, 594
yle, Emma V, 705
yle, Esther IV, 35
yle, Esther IV, 54
yle, Esther IV, 873
yle, Esther IV, 881
yle, Esther V, 113
yle, Esther V, 125
yle, Esther V, 356
yle, Esther V, 427
yle, Esther V, 593
yle, Esther V, 594
yle, Esther V, 598
yle, Esther V, 599
yle, Esther V, 600
Pyle, Esther V, 641
Pyle, Esther V, 705
Pyle, Esther Ann V, 427
Pyle, Esther Jane V, 593
Pyle, Esther M. IV, 881
Pyle, Esther S. V, 113
Pyle, Evan V, 594
Pyle, Frank C. II, 823
Pyle, Frank W. V, 706
Pyle, Frederick VI, 772
Pyle, Frederick B. VI, 770
Pyle, Gardner IV, 652
Pyle, Geo. Madden, Jr. V, 594
Pyle, George IV, 265
Pyle, George C. V, 594
Pyle, George Palmer IV, 54
Pyle, Graham V, 593
Pyle, Graham V, 594
Pyle, Hannah II, 788
Pyle, Hannah II, 949
Pyle, Hannah IV, 881
Pyle, Hannah IV, 882
Pyle, Harland IV, 265
Pyle, Henry IV, 652
Pyle, Henry IV, 659
Pyle, Henry IV, 881
Pyle, Henry V, 705
Pyle, Howard O. V, 593
Pyle, Irena V, 593
Pyle, Irene V, 594
Pyle, Isaac II, 31
Pyle, Isaac IV, 265
Pyle, Isabella V, 593
Pyle, J. E. V, 594
Pyle, James IV, 273
Pyle, Jane II, 31
Pyle, Jane II, 629
Pyle, Jane IV, 207
Pyle, Jane IV, 265
Pyle, Jehu V, 554
Pyle, Jehu V, 593
Pyle, Jehu V, 598
Pyle, Jehu Evan V, 428
Pyle, Jehu Evans V, 705
Pyle, Jehu H. V, 594
Pyle, Jesse IV, 54
Pyle, Jesse IV, 158
Pyle, John IV, 54
Pyle, John V, 31
Pyle, John V, 113
Pyle, John V, 427
Pyle, John V, 552
Pyle, John V, 593
Pyle, John V, 594
Pyle, John V, 641
Pyle, John VI, 432
Pyle, John Evan V, 594
Pyle, John W. V, 705
Pyle, John Wm. V, 594
Pyle, Joseph II, 629
Pyle, Joseph IV, 652
Pyle, Joseph V, 593
Pyle, Joseph V, 594
Pyle, Joseph L. V, 705
Pyle, Joseph Luther V, 594
Pyle, Joseph S. V, 113
Pyle, Joseph S. V, 593
Pyle, Lamborn II, 949
Pyle, Lindley V, 593
Pyle, Louella Marie V, 705
Pyle, Louisa IV, 881
Pyle, Louisa IV, 885
Pyle, Louisa V, 554
Pyle, Louisa V, 593
Pyle, Louisa V, 594
Pyle, Louise V, 593
Pyle, Louiza V, 594
Pyle, Lydia IV, 273
Pyle, Lydia V, 594
Pyle, Lydia V, 705
Pyle, Lydia Ann II, 788
Pyle, Malinda V, 356
Pyle, Malinda V, 593
Pyle, Malinda V, 598
Pyle, Malinda V, 710
Pyle, Margaret V, 706
Pyle, Maria IV, 54
Pyle, Maria IV, 62
Pyle, Marietta V, 594
Pyle, Martha IV, 54
Pyle, Martha IV, 652
Pyle, Martha V, 593
Pyle, Martha V, 594
Pyle, Mary I, 453
Pyle, Mary II, 563
Pyle, Mary II, 629
Pyle, Mary II, 823
Pyle, Mary IV, 881
Pyle, Mary V, 113
Pyle, Mary V, 548
Pyle, Mary V, 593
Pyle, Mary V, 594
Pyle, Mary V, 706
Pyle, Mary VI, 787
Pyle, Mary VI, 790
Pyle, Mary A. II, 846
Pyle, Mary A. II, 913
Pyle, Mary A. V, 705
Pyle, Mary Abigail V, 594
Pyle, Mary Ann V, 31
Pyle, Mary Ann V, 113
Pyle, Mary Ann V, 552
Pyle, Mary Ann V, 593
Pyle, Mary Ann V, 594
Pyle, Mary E. V, 593
Pyle, Mary Emily V, 593
Pyle, Mary Emily V, 607
Pyle, Mary Emily V, 641
Pyle, Mary M. II, 846
Pyle, Mary M. II, 913
Pyle, Mary P. V, 594
Pyle, Mary P. V, 705
Pyle, Mary T. V, 553
Pyle, Mary T. V, 594
Pyle, Melinda V, 594
Pyle, Melinda V, 598
Pyle, Meriam V, 593
Pyle, Mildred V, 705
Pyle, Mildred V, 708
Pyle, Minerva Sarah II, 823
Pyle, Minnie M. V, 593
Pyle, Miriam C. V, 594
Pyle, Nancy V, 593
Pyle, Nancy V, 705
Pyle, Nancy F. V, 356
Pyle, Nancy F. V, 594
Pyle, Nancy J. V, 273
Pyle, Nancy J. V, 594
Pyle, Nancy T. V, 239
Pyle, Nancy T. V, 273
Pyle, Nancy T. V, 594
Pyle, Naomi IV, 652
Pyle, Nathan IV, 54
Pyle, Nicholas II, 629
Pyle, Olive V, 593
Pyle, Olive V, 594
Pyle, Omar V, 594
Pyle, Palmer IV, 54
Pyle, Phebe Ann II, 949
Pyle, Priscilla IV, 132
Pyle, Priscilla IV, 134
Pyle, Rachel II, 629
Pyle, Rachel II, 1077
Pyle, Rachel II, 1078
Pyle, Rachel V, 356
Pyle, Rachel V, 593
Pyle, Rachel V, 705
Pyle, Rachel H. II, 1078
Pyle, Rachel J. V, 594
Pyle, Rebecca IV, 54
Pyle, Rebecca IV, 62
Pyle, Rebecca IV, 652
Pyle, Rebecca IV, 659
Pyle, Rebecca V, 386
Pyle, Rebecca V, 427
Pyle, Rebecca V, 428
Pyle, Rebecca V, 562
Pyle, Rebecca V, 593
Pyle, Rebecca V, 594
Pyle, Rebecca V, 705
Pyle, Robert II, 788
Pyle, Robert L. VI, 772
Pyle, Ruth I, 404
Pyle, Ruth I, 416
Pyle, Ruth I, 440
Pyle, Ruth I, 453
Pyle, Ruth IV, 54
Pyle, Ruth V, 70
Pyle, Ruth V, 113
Pyle, Ruth V, 574
Pyle, Ruth V, 593
Pyle, Ruth V, 594
Pyle, Sallie C. II, 948
Pyle, Sallie C. II, 949
Pyle, Samuel V, 593
Pyle, Samuel C. V, 705
Pyle, Samuel W. V, 594
Pyle, Sarah IV, 54
Pyle, Sarah IV, 172
Pyle, Sarah IV, 265
Pyle, Sarah IV, 273
Pyle, Sarah IV, 652
Pyle, Sarah IV, 752
Pyle, Sarah IV, 759
Pyle, Sarah V, 113
Pyle, Sarah V, 126
Pyle, Sarah V, 356
Pyle, Sarah V, 593
Pyle, Sarah V, 594
Pyle, Sarah V, 599
Pyle, Sarah V, 641
Pyle, Sarah Emily V, 548
Pyle, Sarah Emily V, 594
Pyle, Sarah Malinda V, 356
Pyle, Sarah Malinda V, 593
Pyle, Sarah Malinda V, 594
Pyle, Sarah Malinda V, 705
Pyle, Sarah T. V, 593
Pyle, Sarah T. V, 604
Pyle, Sarah T. V, 641
Pyle, Susanna IV, 54
Pyle, Tamar Ann V, 594
Pyle, Tamar Ann V, 641
Pyle, Tamar Anna V, 356
Pyle, Tamar Anna V, 641
Pyle, Tamer Anna V, 593
Pyle, Thamer Ann V, 594
Pyle, Thomas V, 593
Pyle, Thomas V, 594
Pyle, Thomas Henry V, 593
Pyle, Thomas Henry V, 594
Pyle, Thos. V, 593
Pyle, Thos. Henry V, 641
Pyle, Walter V, 594
Pyle, William IV, 54
Pyle, William IV, 265
Pyle, William IV, 652
Pyle, William V, 113
Pyle, William V, 427
Pyle, William V, 428
Pyle, William V, 562
Pyle, William V, 593
Pyle, William V, 705
Pyle, William Howard V, 705
Pyle, William L. V, 594
Pyle, Wm. IV, 207
Pyle, Wm. V, 386
Pyle, Wm. V, 593
Pyle, Wm. L. V, 594
Pyle, Wm. T. V, 553
Pyle, Woodrow V, 593
Pyle, Woodrow B. V, 594
Pyley, Mary I, 446
Pymm, Lydia II, 84
Pymm, Lydia II, 92
Pyott, Ann IV, 353
Pyott, Deborah VI, 549
Pyott, John VI, 549
Pyott, Mary VI, 549
Pyper, Elizabeth I, 116
Pyper, James I, 116
Pyper, James I, 161
Pyper, Macedams I, 116
Pyper, Nethaniel I, 116
Pyris, Nellie IV, 1290

Quackenbos, Herman Minor II, 816
Quackenbos, Louis Henry II, 816
Quackenbos, Mary II, 816
Quackenbos, Philip Price II, 816
Quackenbos, Ruthanna Lucy II, 816
Quackenboss, Ruth Anna L. II, 913
Quackenbush, Arminta V, 1015
Quackenbush, Armirtie V, 1015
Quackenbush, Chrisie V, 1015
Quackenbush, Chrissy V, 1015
Quail, Asenith IV, 83
Quail, Asenith IV, 106
Quaintance, Abraham Morris IV, 1220
Quaintance, Abraham Morris IV, 1221
Quaintance, Ann IV, 266
Quaintance, Ann IV, 470
Quaintance, Ann IV, 495
Quaintance, Ann IV, 1181
Quaintance, Ann IV, 1207
Quaintance, Ann IV, 1219
Quaintance, Ann IV, 1220
Quaintance, Ann VI, 530
Quaintance, Ann VI, 549
Quaintance, Arthalinda P. II, 136
Quaintance, Betsy IV, 495
Quaintance, Betta IV, 481
Quaintance, Betty IV, 265
Quaintance, Betty IV, 495
Quaintance, Betty IV, 839
Quaintance, Betty IV, 1181
Quaintance, Betty IV, 1220
Quaintance, C. L. IV, 1221
Quaintance, Caleb IV, 1181
Quaintance, Caleb IV, 1220
Quaintance, Charles IV, 1181
Quaintance, Charles IV, 1221
Quaintance, Charles L. IV, 1220
Quaintance, Charles R. IV, 1181
Quaintance, Charlotte IV, 495
Quaintance, Charlotte IV, 1181
Quaintance, Charlotte IV, 1201
Quaintance, Charlotte IV, 1220
Quaintance, Chas. R. IV, 1220
Quaintance, Cintha J. IV, 1221
Quaintance, Cintha Jane IV, 1220
Quaintance, Dawson IV, 495
Quaintance, Dawson IV, 1181
Quaintance, Dawson IV, 1220
Quaintance, Edward C. IV, 1220
Quaintance, Edward Courtney IV, 495
Quaintance, Edward Courtney IV, 1181
Quaintance, Elem S. IV, 1220
Quaintance, Eli IV, 265
Quaintance, Eli IV, 266
Quaintance, Eli IV, 481
Quaintance, Eli IV, 495
Quaintance, Eli IV, 839
Quaintance, Eli IV, 1181
Quaintance, Eli IV, 1214
Quaintance, Eli IV, 1220
Quaintance, Eli IV, 1229
Quaintance, Eli D. IV, 1220
Quaintance, Eli P. IV, 495
Quaintance, Eli P. IV, 1181
Quaintance, Ellen L. IV, 1220
Quaintance, Ephron O. IV, 1221
Quaintance, Ephron Osnam IV, 1220
Quaintance, Esther IV, 495
Quaintance, Esther IV, 1181
Quaintance, Fisher IV, 266
Quaintance, Fisher IV, 495
Quaintance, Fisher IV, 826
Quaintance, Fisher IV, 839
Quaintance, Fisher IV, 859
Quaintance, Fisher IV, 1181
Quaintance, Fisher IV, 1219
Quaintance, Fisher IV, 1220
Quaintance, Fisher IV, 1221
Quaintance, Fisher IV, 1229
Quaintance, G. L. IV, 1221
Quaintance, George E. IV, 1181
Quaintance, George E. IV, 1221
Quaintance, George L. IV, 1220
Quaintance, Greenbury P. IV, 1220
Quaintance, Grenbery P. IV, 1220
Quaintance, Hannah IV, 495
Quaintance, Hannah IV, 1229
Quaintance, Hannah A. IV, 1214
Quaintance, Hannah A. IV, 1220
Quaintance, Hannah L. IV, 1220
Quaintance, Hannah Louisa IV, 1221
Quaintance, Hester IV, 1229
Quaintance, Ira IV, 1220
Quaintance, Irey IV, 495
Quaintance, Irey IV, 1181
Quaintance, Israel W. IV, 1220
Quaintance, Jos. IV, 481
Quaintance, Jos. IV, 495
Quaintance, Joseph IV, 265
Quaintance, Joseph IV, 470
Quaintance, Joseph IV, 495
Quaintance, Joseph IV, 839
Quaintance, Joseph IV, 1181
Quaintance, Joseph IV, 1220
Quaintance, Joseph IV, 1221
Quaintance, Joseph IV, 1229
Quaintance, Joseph D. IV, 1220
Quaintance, Joseph K. IV, 180
Quaintance, Joseph K. IV, 265
Quaintance, Joseph K. IV, 1181
Quaintance, Joseph O. IV, 1221
Quaintance, Joseph Orlando IV, 1220
Quaintance, Joseph R. IV, 1202
Quaintance, Joseph R. IV, 1220
Quaintance, Joseph W. IV, 495
Quaintance, Joseph W. IV, 1181
Quaintance, Joseph W. IV, 1220
Quaintance, Lewis IV, 1172
Quaintance, Lewis IV, 1181
Quaintance, Lewis IV, 1221
Quaintance, Lewis C. IV, 495
Quaintance, Lewis C. IV, 1220
Quaintance, Lewis Carey IV, 495
Quaintance, Lewis Cary IV, 495
Quaintance, Lewis Cary IV, 839
Quaintance, Lewis Coy IV, 1181
Quaintance, Livonia T. IV, 1220
Quaintance, Lovina IV, 1211
Quaintance, Lovina IV, 1221
Quaintance, Lucy Ann IV, 1220
Quaintance, Lydia IV, 1220
Quaintance, Lydia R. IV, 1220
Quaintance, Maria IV, 1172
Quaintance, Maria IV, 1181
Quaintance, Maria IV, 1221
Quaintance, Mariah M. IV, 1220
Quaintance, Martha IV, 1181
Quaintance, Mary C. IV, 1229
Quaintance, Mary Cordelia IV, 1220
Quaintance, Melvin IV, 1220
Quaintance, Melvin IV, 1221
Quaintance, Phebe IV, 180
Quaintance, Phebe IV, 265
Quaintance, Phebe IV, 266
Quaintance, Phebe IV, 1202
Quaintance, Phebe IV, 1220
Quaintance, Rachel IV, 495
Quaintance, Rachel IV, 1181
Quaintance, Rachel IV, 1217
Quaintance, Rachel IV, 1220
Quaintance, Rachel Angeline IV, 1221
Quaintance, Rachel Emma IV, 1220
Quaintance, Rebecca IV, 495
Quaintance, Rebecca IV, 1181
Quaintance, Rebecca Ann IV, 1181
Quaintance, Rebecca Ann IV, 1220
Quaintance, Rebecca B. IV, 1220
Quaintance, Sarah IV, 495
Quaintance, Sarah IV, 826
Quaintance, Sarah IV, 839
Quaintance, Sarah IV, 1181
Quaintance, Sarah IV, 1219
Quaintance, Sarah IV, 1220

Quaintance, Sarah IV, 1229
Quaintance, Sarah Ann IV, 1220
Quaintance, Sarah Ann IV, 1221
Quaintance, Sarah Jane IV, 1181
Quaintance, Sarahann IV, 1220
Quaintance, Saryann IV, 1221
Quaintance, Silas Lewis IV, 1220
Quaintance, Silas Lewis IV, 1221
Quaintance, Susanna IV, 265
Quaintance, Susanna IV, 266
Quaintance, Susanna IV, 470
Quaintance, Susanna IV, 481
Quaintance, Susanna IV, 495
Quaintance, Susanna IV, 1181
Quaintance, Susanna IV, 1220
Quaintance, Susannah IV, 495
Quaintance, Susannah IV, 1181
Quaintance, William IV, 266
Quaintance, William IV, 495
Quaintance, William IV, 1181
Quaintance, Wm. IV, 495
Quaintance, Wm. IV, 1220
Quaintance, Wm. P. IV, 1220
Quakingbush, Mary I, 411
Quakingbush, Mary I, 416
Quanitance, Susanna IV, 1156
Quarles, Ann VI, 981
Quarles, Betsey VI, 981
Quarles, Blancum A. VI, 975
Quarles, Chesteen M. VI, 1010
Quarles, D. W. VI, 1018
Quarles, David W. VI, 948
Quarles, David W. VI, 981
Quarles, David W. VI, 1010
Quarles, Doshia VI, 1010
Quarles, Eliza A. VI, 981
Quarles, Elizabeth Frances VI, 981
Quarles, Elizabeth Jane VI, 887
Quarles, Elizabeth R. VI, 981
Quarles, Elizabeth T. VI, 1016
Quarles, George L. VI, 981
Quarles, Giles T. VI, 981
Quarles, Giles T. VI, 1003
Quarles, Ira H. VI, 936
Quarles, Ira H. VI, 981
Quarles, James VI, 899
Quarles, James VI, 910
Quarles, James VI, 986
Quarles, Jane VI, 857
Quarles, Jeremiah W. VI, 981
Quarles, Jesse L. VI, 981
Quarles, John VI, 920
Quarles, Lucy VI, 1006
Quarles, Mary W. VI, 1018
Quarles, Nancey VI, 869
Quarles, Nancy VI, 848
Quarles, Nancy VI, 887
Quarles, Nancy VI, 981
Quarles, Polley VI, 981
Quarles, Polly VI, 937
Quarles, Rachel VI, 981
Quarles, Roger VI, 981
Quarles, Saml. VI, 899
Quarles, Saml. VI, 1016
Quarles, Saml. H. VI, 986
Quarles, Samuel VI, 1003
Quarles, Samuel VI, 1016
Quarles, Samuel H. VI, 981
Quarles, Sarah VI, 822
Quarles, Sarah VI, 1006
Quarles, Sarah VI, 1016
Quarles, Sarah A. R. VI, 981
Quarles, Sarah W. VI, 899
Quarles, Susan Jane VI, 1003
Quarles, Tabitha VI, 930
Quarles, Thomas VI, 975
Quarles, William VI, 887
Quarles, William VI, 930
Quarles, William VI, 937
Quarles, William J. A. VI, 981
Quarles, Wilmouth VI, 869
Quarles, Wm. VI, 848
Quarles, Wm. VI, 944
Quarles, Wm. I. A. VI, 869
Quarles, Wm. J. A. VI, 1016
Queans, Jonathan II, 410
Queans, Mary II, 410
Queans, Nathaniel II, 410
Queen, Estella IV, 1221
Queen, Mary E. IV, 1221
Queen, W. C. IV, 1221
Queen, Webb IV, 1221
Queer, Lydia IV, 893
Queer, Lydia IV, 894
Queer, Mary IV, 1029
Querdon, Nathaniel II, 410
Quest, ??? III, 261
Quest, ??? III, 368
Quest, Harriet R. III, 261
Quest, Harriet R. III, 368
Quest, Mary II, 251
Quick, David R. III, 120
Quick, David R. III, 261
Quick, Ellen V, 927
Quick, Ellen V, 928
Quick, Emma R. III, 120
Quick, Emma R. III, 261
Quick, Gordon P. IV, 1334
Quick, Jennie III, 120
Quick, Jennie III, 261
Quick, Maud IV, 1334
Quicksal, Daniel II, 629
Quicksal, John II, 181
Quicksal, Mary II, 629
Quicksall, Aaron II, 181
Quicksall, Aaron II, 251
Quicksall, Daniel II, 410
Quicksall, Daniel II, 629
Quicksall, John II, 181
Quicksall, John II, 251
Quicksall, John II, 410
Quicksall, Jonathan II, 251
Quicksall, Mary II, 629
Quicksall, Sarah L. II, 629
Quicksall, Sarah L. II, 741
Quicksall, Sarah L. II, 761
Quicksall, Wm. II, 629
Quig, Henry VI, 807
Quiggins, Edna IV, 1334
Quiggins, Edna H. IV, 1334
Quiggins, Robert IV, 1334
Quiggins, Robert K. IV, 1334
Quiggins, Robt. N. IV, 1334
Quigley, Caroline E. IV, 1041
Quigley, Michael V, 356
Quigley, Rhoda V. IV, 1041
Quigley, Wm. R. IV, 1041
Quilling, William V, 762
Quilling, William Henry V, 762
Quimby, Charles IV, 266
Quimby, George A. IV, 1260
Quimby, Jennie IV, 1260
Quinby, ??? III, 261
Quinby, Aaron II, 629
Quinby, Aaron II, 657
Quinby, Aaron V, 594
Quinby, Aaron VI, 473
Quinby, Aaron VI, 550
Quinby, Aaron B. V, 524
Quinby, Aaron B. V, 594
Quinby, Aaron J. III, 261
Quinby, Aaron J. III, 262
Quinby, Amy III, 261
Quinby, Amy III, 262
Quinby, Azariah III, 261
Quinby, Benjamin H. VI, 195
Quinby, Caleb III, 261
Quinby, Caroline III, 261
Quinby, Caroline A. III, 144
Quinby, Caroline A. III, 212
Quinby, Charles III, 261
Quinby, Daniel III, 261
Quinby, Daniel III, 314
Quinby, Daniel VI, 195
Quinby, Deborah III, 261
Quinby, Edward III, 261
Quinby, Edward S. III, 128
Quinby, Edward S. III, 262
Quinby, Eleanor II, 1022
Quinby, Elijah P. III, 261
Quinby, Eliz. C. III, 329
Quinby, Eliza III, 128
Quinby, Eliza III, 261
Quinby, Eliza III, 262
Quinby, Eliza F. III, 262
Quinby, Elizabeth V, 524
Quinby, Elizabeth V, 594
Quinby, Elizabeth VI, 195
Quinby, Elizabeth VI, 473
Quinby, Elizabeth VI, 476
Quinby, Elizabeth VI, 550
Quinby, Elizabeth Stackhouse II, 629
Quinby, Ellen II, 913
Quinby, Ellinor II, 1022
Quinby, Esther III, 261
Quinby, Esther III, 276
Quinby, Esther F. III, 261
Quinby, Esther F. III, 262
Quinby, Ezra A. V, 524
Quinby, Ezra A. V, 594
Quinby, Frances Eugene III, 261
Quinby, George W. III, 261
Quinby, George W. III, 262
Quinby, George W. III, 384
Quinby, Hannah II, 1022
Quinby, Hannah III, 153
Quinby, Hannah III, 154
Quinby, Hannah III, 261
Quinby, Hannah III, 405
Quinby, Hannah III, 439
Quinby, Isaiah III, 261
Quinby, Isaiah III, 262
Quinby, Jane II, 1022
Quinby, Jesaphine E. V, 594
Quinby, John III, 261
Quinby, John Jagger III, 261
Quinby, John, Jr. III, 261
Quinby, John, Jr. III, 262
Quinby, Jonathan II, 1022
Quinby, Josaphine E. V, 524
Quinby, Josephine E. V, 524
Quinby, Josephine E. V, 594
Quinby, Josephine E. V, 604
Quinby, Joshua III, 261
Quinby, Joshua S. III, 261
Quinby, Josiah II, 1022
Quinby, Josiah III, 261
Quinby, Josiah III, 262
Quinby, Josiah III, 405
Quinby, Josiah III, 439
Quinby, Josiah H. III, 261
Quinby, Latitia II, 1022
Quinby, Margaret L. III, 261
Quinby, Mary III, 177
Quinby, Mary III, 261
Quinby, Mary III, 262
Quinby, Mary III, 314
Quinby, Mary Ann V, 524
Quinby, Mary E. III, 127
Quinby, Mary Eliz. III, 128
Quinby, Mary Elizabeth III, 261
Quinby, Mary Elizabeth III, 262
Quinby, Mary Jane III, 261
Quinby, Mary Jane III, 262
Quinby, Mellicent III, 261
Quinby, Mercy Ann V, 524
Quinby, Mercy Ann V, 594
Quinby, Miriam V, 550
Quinby, Miriam V, 594
Quinby, Miriam E. V, 524
Quinby, Miriam E. V, 594
Quinby, Moses II, 629
Quinby, Moses II, 1022
Quinby, Moses I. III, 261
Quinby, Moses I. III, 262
Quinby, Moses I. III, 276
Quinby, Phebe II, 761
Quinby, Phebe III, 261
Quinby, Phebe Jane III, 261
Quinby, Sarah III, 262
Quinby, Sarah VI, 195
Quinby, Susannah II, 629
Quinby, Thomas M. V, 524
Quinby, Thomas M. V, 594
Quinby, Thos. M. V, 594
Quinby, Valentine III, 261
Quinby, Valentine H. III, 262
Quinby, Walter U. III, 262
Quinby, William III, 261
Quinby, William III, 262
Quinlan, Ellen III, 490
Quinlan, Ellen III, 495
Quinn, Ada G. IV, 266
Quinn, Ally Compton V, 679
Quinn, Ally Compton V, 706
Quinn, Bernard VI, 952
Quinn, Bernard VI, 953
Quinn, Catharine III, 156
Quinn, Charles C. IV, 266
Quinn, Dr. A. T. V, 706
Quinn, Elias V, 198
Quinn, George W. V, 198
Quinn, John VI, 981
Quinn, Lydda VI, 981
Quinn, Lydia VI, 1004
Quinn, Mabel M. V, 198
Quinn, Mary VI, 952
Quinn, Mary M. V, 198
Quinn, Mildred V, 198
Quinn, Ralph V, 198
Quinn, Robert V, 198
Quinstall, Thomas VI, 881
Quinton, Mary II, 93
Quinton, Mary II, 99
Quirk, Annie Eyre II, 816
Quirk, George Thos. II, 816
Quirk, Mathew John II, 816
Quisenberry, James VI, 848
Quisenberry, Mildred VI, 848

R. H., James VI, 994
R???, Anna III, 357
Raa, Rebeckah VI, 434
Raan, John VI, 1012
Rabb, Jennie IV, 495
Rabberman, Amos IV, 1103
Rabberman, Amos IV, 1112
Rabberman, Amos IV, 1113
Rabberman, Caroline IV, 1104
Rabberman, Caroline IV, 1112
Rabberman, Charlotte IV, 1099
Rabberman, Charlotte IV, 1112
Rabberman, Helena IV, 1104
Rabberman, Helena IV, 1112
Rabberman, Hellen IV, 1112
Rabberman, Henry IV, 1104
Rabberman, Henry IV, 1112
Rabberman, Henry D. IV, 1113
Rabberman, Henry, Jr. IV, 1112
Rabberman, Henry, Sr. IV, 1112
Rabberman, John IV, 1112
Rabberman, John E. IV, 1112
Rabberman, Jonathan IV, 1112
Rabberman, Jonathan H. IV, 1112
Rabberman, Lewis W. IV, 1112
Rabberman, Lydia IV, 1112
Rabberman, Lydia IV, 1113
Rabberman, Mary IV, 1108
Rabberman, Mary IV, 1112
Rabberman, Mary T. IV, 1108
Rabberman, Mary T. IV, 1112
Rabberman, Sarah IV, 1108
Rabberman, Sarah IV, 1112
Rabberman, Sarah L. IV, 1111
Rabberman, Sarah L. IV, 1113
Rabberman, Sarah Louisa IV, 1103
Rabberman, Sarah Louisa IV, 1112
Rabberman, Thelma Elizabeth IV, 1103
Rabberman, Thelma S. IV, 1112
Raber, Gotleib IV, 1041
Raber, Maggie IV, 1041
Raberman, Caroline IV, 654
Raberman, Hellena IV, 654
Raberman, Henry, Jr. IV, 654
Raberman, Lewis W. IV, 654
Raberman, Mary IV, 654
Rabern, Jane I, 1161
Rabey, Andrew Jackson VI, 81
Rabey, Emeline E. VI, 81
Rabey, Joseph W. VI, 65
Rabey, Joseph W. VI, 81
Rabey, Lois M. VI, 81
Rabey, Mary V. VI, 65
Rabey, Mary V. VI, 81
Rable, John IV, 1041
Raburn, Jane I, 1161
Raburn, Jennie I, 1161
Raburn, Susanna V, 594
Raburn, Susannah V, 594
Raby, Della M. I, 16
Raby, James IV, 137
Raby, James M. I, 16
Raby, James Oliver I, 16
Rach, Louise III, 196
Rachford, Alice II, 563
Rachford, Alice II, 639
Rachford, Dennis II, 563
Rachford, Dennis II, 639
Rachford, Joseph V, 356
Rachford, Solomon II, 563
Rachford, Solomon II, 639
Radcliff, Ann VI, 550
Radcliff, Edward II, 975
Radcliff, Harriet VI, 550
Radcliff, Harriet VI, 645
Radcliff, Harriett VI, 500
Radcliff, Joshua VI, 500
Radcliff, Joshua VI, 550
Radcliff, Mary E. VI, 550
Radcliff, Nancy VI, 500
Radcliff, Nancy VI, 550
Radcliff, Phebe II, 975
Radcliff, Sallie A. VI, 550
Radcliff, Sally VI, 550
Radcliff, Thomas VI, 550
Radcliffe, Edward II, 967
Radcliffe, Edward II, 1022
Radcliffe, Harriet VI, 500
Radcliffe, Harriett VI, 645
Radcliffe, Harriett VI, 692
Radcliffe, Henry Baker II, 1022
Radcliffe, Joshua VI, 572
Radcliffe, Joshua VI, 645
Radcliffe, Joshua VI, 692
Radcliffe, Martha II, 967
Radcliffe, Martha II, 1022
Radcliffe, Martha II, 1029
Radcliffe, Mary II, 975
Radcliffe, Mary II, 1022
Radcliffe, Nancy VI, 572
Radcliffe, Nancy VI, 645
Radcliffe, Nancy VI, 692
Radcliffe, Phebe II, 1022
Radcliffe, Phebe II, 1029
Radcliffe, Rebecca II, 999
Radcliffe, Rebecca II, 1022
Radcliffe, Richard II, 1022
Radcliffe, Richard II, 1029
Rader, Charles IV, 1260
Rader, Clara IV, 1260
Rader, Clara E. IV, 1260
Rader, Elizabeth VI, 795
Rader, James M. VI, 981
Rader, Malinda M. VI, 981
Radford, Ann R. VI, 877
Radford, Clara I, 317
Radford, Elizabeth VI, 926
Radford, John VI, 1020
Radford, Lulu I, 317
Radford, Mary VI, 915
Radford, Miles I, 317
Radford, Munford W. VI, 981
Radford, Sarah Elizabeth VI,
Radford, Starling B. I, 317
Radford, Starting I, 256
Radford, William VI, 877
Radford, Wm. VI, 986
Radigon, Frank IV, 1260
Radike, Gustave IV, 1334
Radike, Minnie IV, 1334
Radike, Robert A. IV, 1334
Radike, Walter O. IV, 1334
Radley, Cornelius V, 273
Radley, Daniel II, 410
Radley, Daniel II, 447
Radley, Daniel II, 470
Radley, Daniel II, 629
Radley, Daniell II, 410
Radley, James II, 410
Radley, Margrett II, 410
Radley, Mary II, 410
Radley, Mary II, 470
Radley, Mary II, 629
Radley, Miriam II, 410
Radley, Sarah II, 629
Radley, Sarah II, 686
Radley, Thomas II, 447
Radliffe, Rebecca II, 1022
Radwell, Kate II, 698
Radwell, Kate II, 718
Raeburn, Ethel V, 706
Raegan, Mary V, 113
Raegan, Reason V, 113
Rafell, Rene III, 133
Rafell, Rene III, 136
Rafford, Charlotte III, 256
Raford, Edwin VI, 82
Ragan, Amos I, 925
Ragan, Amos I, 929
Ragan, Beulah V, 59
Ragan, Beulah V, 114
Ragan, Elihu V, 198
Ragan, Eliza V, 730
Ragan, Eliza V, 800
Ragan, Huston V, 198
Ragan, James I, 948
Ragan, James L. I, 948
Ragan, Katharine I, 929
Ragan, Leah V, 114
Ragan, Lydia V, 198
Ragan, Martha I, 898
Ragan, Martha I, 925
Ragan, Martha I, 929
Ragan, Mary I, 1037
Ragan, Mary V, 114
Ragan, Mary V, 198
Ragan, Minnie E. I, 898
Ragan, Patience V, 198
Ragan, Rachel V, 198
Ragan, Robert R. I, 948
Ragan, Ruel V, 198
Ragan, Samuel V, 198
Ragan, Sarah V, 800
Ragan, Susan I, 881
Ragan, Susan I, 898
Ragan, Susan I, 921
Ragan, Susan I, 922
Ragan, Susan I, 936
Ragan, Susan B. I, 898
Ragan, Susan B. I, 942
Ragan, Susan B. I, 948
Ragan, Susan Belle I, 925
Ragan, Thos. V, 198
Ragan, William I, 898
Ragan, William P. I, 948
Ragan, Zadock V, 800
Ragen, Amos I, 932
Ragen, James L. I, 932
Ragen, Martha I, 932
Ragin, Mary V, 100
Ragin, Ruel V, 100
Ragin, Ruel V, 113
Ragland, Ann VI, 337
Ragland, Elizabeth VI, 981
Ragland, Elizabeth K. VI, 848
Ragland, James VI, 981
Ragland, Nancy VI, 981
Ragland, Reuben VI, 337

and, Reuben VI, 981
and, Reubin VI, 337
and, Samuel E. VI, 848
and, William VI, 869
sdale, Ruby V, 857
n, Louis IV, 1221
way, Elizabeth V, 927
way, Elizabeth M. V, 927
abaugh, Jacob R. V, 1015
abaugh, Peter IV, 1334
abough, Eva V, 1015
abough, Wm. V, 1015
er, Catharine V, 1015
nsly, Sarah I, 453
ord, Ada VI, 68
ord, Ada J. VI, 68
ord, Ada J. VI, 82
ord, Ada J. VI, 83
ord, Albert VI, 83
ord, Alemdie VI, 83
ord, Algie VI, 82
ord, Alice VI, 60
ord, Alice VI, 82
ord, Alice VI, 83
ord, Alice VI, 92
ord, Allan VI, 81
ord, Allen VI, 81
ord, Allen VI, 83
ord, Almeda VI, 92
ord, Almeda B. VI, 51
ord, Almedia VI, 82
ord, Almedia VI, 83
ord, Almedie VI, 51
ord, Almedie VI, 54
ord, Almedie VI, 81
ord, Almedie VI, 82
ord, Ammedia VI, 83
ord, Anise VI, 83
ord, Anise H. Raiford VI, 81
ord, Anise H. Raiford VI, 82
ord, Anna VI, 51
ord, Anna VI, 81
ord, Anna VI, 82
ord, Anna B. VI, 82
ord, Anna H. VI, 92
ord, Annie Hedgepeth VI, 81
ord, Annie M. W. VI, 81
ord, Annie M. W. VI, 83
ord, Annie May VI, 82
ord, Annie S. VI, 68
ord, Annie S. VI, 82
ord, Aquilla VI, 81
ord, Aquilla VI, 83
ord, Berlin VI, 82
ord, Berlin VI, 83
ord, Bettie F. VI, 82
ord, Bettie F. VI, 83
ord, Bettie F. VI, 90
ord, Caroline VI, 83
ord, Carrie VI, 82
ord, Charles E. VI, 81
ord, Charles E. VI, 83
ord, Cleora Delcine VI, 82
ord, Cloyd O. VI, 82
ord, Conley VI, 83
ord, Delia I, 31
ord, Diana VI, 54
ord, Diana VI, 82
ord, Diza VI, 81
ord, Diza VI, 83
ord, Eddie E. VI, 82
ord, Edith S. VI, 57
ord, Edith S. VI, 82
ord, Edith S. VI, 83
ord, Edward VI, 51
ord, Edward VI, 81
ord, Edward Francis VI, 81
ord, Edward J. VI, 51
ord, Edward J. VI, 81
ord, Edward J. VI, 82
ord, Edward J. VI, 83
ord, Edward J. VI, 90
ord, Edwin VI, 67
ord, Edwin VI, 82
ord, Edwin VI, 83
ord, Edwin VI, 92
ord, Edwin W. VI, 51
ord, Edwin W. VI, 83
ord, Edwin Walter VI, 81
ord, Edwin Walter VI, 90
ord, Effie T. VI, 81
ord, Eleanor VI, 82
ord, Elizabeth VI, 79
ord, Elizabeth VI, 81
ord, Elizabeth VI, 82
ord, Elizabeth VI, 83
ord, Elizabeth F. VI, 51
ord, Elizabeth F. VI, 81
ord, Elizabeth F. VI, 83
ord, Ella D. VI, 68
ord, Ella D. VI, 82
Raiford, Ellen VI, 82
Raiford, Ellen VI, 85
Raiford, Ellen Tabitha VI, 82
Raiford, Ellen Tabitha VI, 83
Raiford, Enrly Jarhone VI, 81
Raiford, Esther G. VI, 81
Raiford, Ethel T. VI, 81
Raiford, Eugene Roberts VI, 82
Raiford, Eula V. VI, 82
Raiford, Everitte VI, 69
Raiford, Everitte VI, 81
Raiford, Everitte VI, 82
Raiford, Everitte VI, 83
Raiford, Fabius VI, 81
Raiford, Fabius VI, 82
Raiford, Fannie VI, 83
Raiford, Fannie Henry Branche VI, 82
Raiford, Frederick VI, 82
Raiford, George VI, 82
Raiford, George VI, 83
Raiford, George F. VI, 83
Raiford, George Fox VI, 81
Raiford, George W. VI, 51
Raiford, George W. VI, 54
Raiford, George W. VI, 81
Raiford, George W. VI, 82
Raiford, George W. VI, 83
Raiford, Harris VI, 92
Raiford, Hattie M. VI, 83
Raiford, Hattie M. Branche VI, 82
Raiford, Henry VI, 76
Raiford, Henry VI, 79
Raiford, Henry VI, 81
Raiford, Henry VI, 82
Raiford, Henry VI, 83
Raiford, Hubert E. VI, 81
Raiford, Hubert E. VI, 83
Raiford, Hunter D. VI, 57
Raiford, Hunter D. VI, 81
Raiford, Hunter D. VI, 82
Raiford, Hunter D. VI, 83
Raiford, Jabez VI, 82
Raiford, James B. Hedgepeth VI, 83
Raiford, James E. VI, 81
Raiford, James E. VI, 83
Raiford, Jeremiah J. VI, 81
Raiford, Jesse Thomas VI, 82
Raiford, John VI, 92
Raiford, John Cary VI, 81
Raiford, John T. VI, 52
Raiford, John T. VI, 81
Raiford, John T. VI, 82
Raiford, John T. VI, 83
Raiford, Julia A. VI, 81
Raiford, Junietta VI, 83
Raiford, Junietta F. Raiford VI, 81
Raiford, Kenneth VI, 91
Raiford, Kenneth H. VI, 68
Raiford, Kenneth H. VI, 82
Raiford, Kinneth VI, 68
Raiford, Kinneth H. VI, 81
Raiford, Kinneth H. VI, 83
Raiford, Lee VI, 82
Raiford, Lee VI, 83
Raiford, Lelia F. VI, 51
Raiford, Lelia F. VI, 81
Raiford, Lelia F. VI, 82
Raiford, Lelia F. VI, 83
Raiford, Lelia T. VI, 92
Raiford, Lemuel VI, 54
Raiford, Levi P. VI, 60
Raiford, Levi P. VI, 82
Raiford, Levi P. VI, 83
Raiford, Lillie Maie I, 21
Raiford, Lilly May VI, 81
Raiford, Lizzie VI, 82
Raiford, Lizzie VI, 83
Raiford, Lizzie R. VI, 83
Raiford, Lorena VI, 82
Raiford, Lorena P. VI, 81
Raiford, Lorena P. VI, 83
Raiford, Lorena Pearl VI, 51
Raiford, Louisa VI, 52
Raiford, Louisa VI, 81
Raiford, Louisa VI, 83
Raiford, Louisa VI, 92
Raiford, Loula M. VI, 83
Raiford, Louna P. VI, 92
Raiford, Lula VI, 92
Raiford, Lula May VI, 81
Raiford, Lula May VI, 83
Raiford, Lulu VI, 83
Raiford, Lulu Jackson VI, 82
Raiford, Lulu M. VI, 51
Raiford, Lulu Mason VI, 76
Raiford, Lulu Mason VI, 81
Raiford, Lulu Mason VI, 82
Raiford, Lulu May VI, 51
Raiford, Lulu May VI, 82
Raiford, Mabel V. VI, 81
Raiford, Mable V. VI, 82
Raiford, Mable V. VI, 90
Raiford, Maggie A. VI, 82
Raiford, Maggie A. VI, 91
Raiford, Margaret Edna VI, 82
Raiford, Martha VI, 81
Raiford, Martha VI, 82
Raiford, Martha VI, 83
Raiford, Martha Ann VI, 81
Raiford, Martha Ann VI, 83
Raiford, Martha C. VI, 69
Raiford, Martha C. VI, 81
Raiford, Martha C. VI, 83
Raiford, Martha C. VI, 92
Raiford, Martha E. VI, 76
Raiford, Martha E. VI, 81
Raiford, Martha E. VI, 82
Raiford, Martha E. VI, 83
Raiford, Martha Elizabeth VI, 92
Raiford, Martha J. VI, 81
Raiford, Martha J. VI, 92
Raiford, Martha M. J. VI, 67
Raiford, Martha M. J. VI, 81
Raiford, Martha S. VI, 75
Raiford, Mary VI, 92
Raiford, Mary A. VI, 51
Raiford, Mary A. VI, 83
Raiford, Mary Agnes VI, 81
Raiford, Mary B. VI, 79
Raiford, Mary B. VI, 81
Raiford, Mary B. VI, 82
Raiford, Mary B. VI, 83
Raiford, Mary L. VI, 54
Raiford, Mary L. VI, 81
Raiford, Mary L. VI, 82
Raiford, Mary Lou VI, 82
Raiford, Mary Louisa VI, 81
Raiford, Mattie VI, 83
Raiford, Mattie J. VI, 83
Raiford, Mattie J. VI, 92
Raiford, Maude VI, 82
Raiford, Mills VI, 51
Raiford, Mills VI, 83
Raiford, Mills E. VI, 81
Raiford, Mills E. VI, 82
Raiford, Mills E. VI, 83
Raiford, Paul VI, 81
Raiford, Philip VI, 81
Raiford, Philip VI, 82
Raiford, Philip VI, 92
Raiford, Philip M. VI, 82
Raiford, Philiph VI, 81
Raiford, Philiph VI, 82
Raiford, Philiph VI, 83
Raiford, Raynor VI, 83
Raiford, Robert B. VI, 82
Raiford, Rosa D. VI, 81
Raiford, Rosa D. VI, 83
Raiford, Rufus L. VI, 81
Raiford, Rufus L. VI, 83
Raiford, Sallie VI, 54
Raiford, Sallie T. VI, 82
Raiford, Sallie T. VI, 83
Raiford, Sarah E. VI, 83
Raiford, Sarah Elizabeth VI, 81
Raiford, Sarah Elizabeth VI, 90
Raiford, Septimus VI, 82
Raiford, Seu J. Raiford VI, 82
Raiford, Sue VI, 81
Raiford, Sue J. VI, 63
Raiford, Sue J. VI, 82
Raiford, Sue J. VI, 83
Raiford, Susan VI, 76
Raiford, Susan VI, 81
Raiford, Susan VI, 82
Raiford, Susan VI, 83
Raiford, Susan VI, 92
Raiford, Susannah Jane VI, 82
Raiford, T. Philip VI, 54
Raiford, T. Philip Raiford VI, 82
Raiford, Tabitha VI, 81
Raiford, Tabitha VI, 82
Raiford, Tabitha VI, 83
Raiford, Tabitha VI, 92
Raiford, Theodore VI, 83
Raiford, Theodore Earnest VI, 82
Raiford, Theodore Earnest VI, 83
Raiford, Theodore P. VI, 63
Raiford, Theodore P. VI, 81
Raiford, Theodore P. VI, 83
Raiford, Theodore Philip VI, 82
Raiford, Theodore Sidney VI, 82
Raiford, Unity VI, 83
Raiford, Viola M. VI, 82
Raiford, Virlinda T. VI, 83
Raiford, Virny VI, 83
Raiford, W. G. VI, 83
Raiford, Waldo Emerson VI, 82
Raiford, William VI, 81
Raiford, William B. VI, 68
Raiford, William B. VI, 81
Raiford, William B. VI, 82
Raiford, William B. VI, 83
Raiford, William G. VI, 82
Raiford, William G. VI, 83
Raiford, William G. VI, 85
Raiford, William H. VI, 68
Raiford, William H. VI, 82
Raiford, William H. VI, 83
Raiford, Wilmoth VI, 82
Raiford, Wilmoth L. VI, 76
Raiford, Wistar VI, 81
Raiford, Wm. VI, 68
Raiford, Wm. VI, 81
Raiford, Wm. VI, 82
Raiford, Wm. H. VI, 83
Rail, Anna I, 596
Rail, Charles I, 513
Rail, David IV, 266
Rail, George I, 513
Rail, Hannah I, 513
Rail, James IV, 266
Rail, Margaret I, 568
Rail, Mary I, 513
Rail, Rachel I, 568
Rail, Thomas I, 568
Raile, Elizabeth I, 555
Raile, Elizabeth I, 568
Railey, Abigail VI, 434
Railey, Ann IV, 55
Railey, Ann IV, 266
Railey, Ann IV, 545
Railey, Ann IV, 988
Railey, Ann VI, 434
Railey, Asa IV, 266
Railey, Asa VI, 434
Railey, Asenath IV, 266
Railey, David IV, 266
Railey, David VI, 434
Railey, Edwin V, 642
Railey, Eli IV, 55
Railey, Eli VI, 434
Railey, Eli, Jr. IV, 266
Railey, Elizabeth IV, 266
Railey, Elizabeth V, 642
Railey, Hannah IV, 224
Railey, Hannah IV, 266
Railey, Hannah VI, 434
Railey, James IV, 266
Railey, James VI, 434
Railey, Jehu IV, 55
Railey, John IV, 55
Railey, John IV, 653
Railey, John VI, 434
Railey, Joseph VI, 434
Railey, Joshua VI, 434
Railey, Kersey IV, 55
Railey, Martha IV, 266
Railey, Martha V, 642
Railey, Mary IV, 55
Railey, Mary IV, 266
Railey, Mary VI, 434
Railey, Mary, Sr. IV, 266
Railey, Melissa IV, 266
Railey, Melissa Ann IV, 266
Railey, Newton IV, 266
Railey, Phebe IV, 55
Railey, Rachel IV, 266
Railey, Rachel VI, 434
Railey, Robert IV, 545
Railey, Sarah VI, 434
Railey, Thomas IV, 55
Railey, Thomas IV, 545
Railey, Unity C. IV, 988
Raily, Ann IV, 881
Raily, Eli VI, 434
Raily, Elma Iola I, 225
Raily, Frank R. I, 225
Raily, Jehu Dexon IV, 881
Raily, Kersey IV, 881
Raily, Mary IV, 881
Raily, Phebe IV, 881
Raily, Thomas IV, 881
Rainbow, Eugene IV, 270
Rainbow, Jefferson IV, 270
Rainbow, Mary IV, 256
Rainbow, Nettie May IV, 270
Rainbow, Rosa IV, 270
Rainbow, William IV, 270
Raine, Ann VI, 848
Raine, Caroline VI, 849
Raine, Geo. W. VI, 849
Raine, I. VI, 849
Raine, Jane I, 416
Raine, John VI, 848
Raine, Joseph S. VI, 849
Raine, Mary VI, 849
Raine, Ready VI, 849
Raine, William VI, 849
Raines, Armistead VI, 981
Raines, Eliza VI, 981
Raines, George V, 308
Raines, George V, 309
Raines, John VI, 963
Raines, Nancy V, 308
Raines, Nancy V, 309
Raines, Rebecca V, 309
Rainey, Eliza W. VI, 849
Rainey, Ella Louisa IV, 1074
Rainey, Ella Louisa IV, 1075
Rainey, James VI, 849
Rainey, Robert VI, 943
Rainey, Wm. VI, 849
Rains, Armistead VI, 981
Rains, Armistead H. VI, 981
Rains, Braxton VI, 981
Rains, Catherine V, 273
Rains, Cynthia VI, 981
Rains, David V, 273
Rains, Eliza VI, 981
Rains, Elizabeth VI, 981
Rains, John VI, 981
Rains, Lydia I, 484
Rains, Mary V, 272
Rains, Mary V, 273
Rains, Nancy V, 309
Rains, Nancy V, 313
Rains, William I, 470
Rains, William I, 484
Rainstein, Mae III, 64
Rainstein, Mae III, 262
Raisin, Joanna II, 816
Raisin, Mifflin II, 816
Raisin, Warner Mifflin II, 816
Raisin, Wm. Jenkins II, 816
Raison, Warner M. II, 913
Rake, Alice III, 43
Rake, Alice III, 262
Rake, Ann III, 262
Rake, John III, 262
Rake, John D. III, 43
Rake, John Dyke III, 262
Rake, Mary III, 262
Rake, Samuel III, 262
Rake-straw, Grace II, 537
Rake???, Mary II, 688
Rakes, Elizabeth VI, 926
Rakes, Henry VI, 926
Rakes, Henry VI, 1002
Rakes, Stashy VI, 1002
Rakestraw, ??? II, 410
Rakestraw, Abraham II, 181
Rakestraw, Abraham II, 243
Rakestraw, Abraham II, 251
Rakestraw, Abraham II, 274
Rakestraw, Amy IV, 940
Rakestraw, Amy IV, 988
Rakestraw, Ann II, 251
Rakestraw, Ann II, 410
Rakestraw, Ann II, 629
Rakestraw, Anthony II, 251
Rakestraw, Baven II, 629
Rakestraw, Benjamin IV, 988
Rakestraw, Benjamin H. M. IV, 752
Rakestraw, Bevan II, 410
Rakestraw, Elisabeth II, 572
Rakestraw, Elisabeth II, 629
Rakestraw, Elisha IV, 988
Rakestraw, Eliza II, 251
Rakestraw, Eliza IV, 752
Rakestraw, Elizabeth II, 410
Rakestraw, Elizabeth II, 454
Rakestraw, Elizabeth II, 598
Rakestraw, Elizabeth II, 629
Rakestraw, Elizabeth VI, 434
Rakestraw, Elizabeth VI, 603
Rakestraw, Ellen IV, 988
Rakestraw, Ellen IV, 999
Rakestraw, Esther II, 181
Rakestraw, Esther II, 251
Rakestraw, Grace II, 410
Rakestraw, Grace II, 629
Rakestraw, Grace II, 696
Rakestraw, Hannah II, 251
Rakestraw, Hannah II, 629
Rakestraw, Hannah IV, 752
Rakestraw, Hannah IV, 988
Rakestraw, Hannah VI, 434
Rakestraw, Hannah VI, 603
Rakestraw, Hannah Baldwin II, 913
Rakestraw, Haram B. IV, 988
Rakestraw, Haran B. IV, 988
Rakestraw, Haron B. IV, 752
Rakestraw, Henrietta IV, 1029
Rakestraw, Isaac IV, 752
Rakestraw, Isaac IV, 976
Rakestraw, Isaac IV, 988
Rakestraw, James IV, 752

Rakestraw, Jane II, 410
Rakestraw, Jane II, 629
Rakestraw, Jane IV, 988
Rakestraw, Jane IV, 1019
Rakestraw, Jane M. IV, 988
Rakestraw, John II, 410
Rakestraw, John II, 598
Rakestraw, John II, 629
Rakestraw, John II, 630
Rakestraw, John II, 913
Rakestraw, Joseph II, 410
Rakestraw, Joseph II, 629
Rakestraw, Joseph VI, 434
Rakestraw, Joseph VI, 603
Rakestraw, Joseph, Jr. II, 598
Rakestraw, Joseph, Jr. II, 629
Rakestraw, Joshua L. IV, 988
Rakestraw, Joshua L. IV, 999
Rakestraw, Justiana II, 629
Rakestraw, Justinian II, 410
Rakestraw, Justinian II, 629
Rakestraw, Justinian VI, 434
Rakestraw, Justinian VI, 603
Rakestraw, Levi IV, 752
Rakestraw, Levi IV, 976
Rakestraw, Levi IV, 988
Rakestraw, Lewis M. IV, 1041
Rakestraw, Lloyd M. IV, 1041
Rakestraw, Lydia IV, 988
Rakestraw, Lydia R. IV, 976
Rakestraw, Lydia R. IV, 988
Rakestraw, Margaret IV, 839
Rakestraw, Martha II, 410
Rakestraw, Martha II, 629
Rakestraw, Martha II, 630
Rakestraw, Mary II, 181
Rakestraw, Mary II, 243
Rakestraw, Mary II, 251
Rakestraw, Mary II, 274
Rakestraw, Mary II, 410
Rakestraw, Mary II, 629
Rakestraw, Mary IV, 988
Rakestraw, Mary Ann II, 913
Rakestraw, Mary Ann IV, 752
Rakestraw, Mary E. IV, 1041
Rakestraw, Nathan IV, 988
Rakestraw, Nathan IV, 999
Rakestraw, Olive IV, 988
Rakestraw, Orlin IV, 988
Rakestraw, Phebe IV, 1029
Rakestraw, Rachel II, 490
Rakestraw, Rachel II, 629
Rakestraw, Rebecca II, 447
Rakestraw, Rebecca II, 629
Rakestraw, Rebecca II, 630
Rakestraw, Rebecca IV, 752
Rakestraw, Rebecca IV, 839
Rakestraw, Rebecca IV, 976
Rakestraw, Rebecca IV, 988
Rakestraw, Rebecca B. IV, 976
Rakestraw, Rebecca B. IV, 988
Rakestraw, Ruth II, 410
Rakestraw, Ruthanna IV, 988
Rakestraw, Ruthanna IV, 999
Rakestraw, Sarah II, 251
Rakestraw, Sarah II, 274
Rakestraw, Sarah II, 410
Rakestraw, Sarah II, 598
Rakestraw, Sarah II, 629
Rakestraw, Sarah IV, 752
Rakestraw, Sarah IV, 924
Rakestraw, Sarah IV, 988
Rakestraw, Sarah VI, 434
Rakestraw, Sarah VI, 603
Rakestraw, Sidney II, 526
Rakestraw, Sidney II, 528
Rakestraw, Sidney II, 629
Rakestraw, Sidney II, 630
Rakestraw, Susan IV, 752
Rakestraw, Susan IV, 1021
Rakestraw, Susan IV, 1029
Rakestraw, Susanna II, 410
Rakestraw, Susanna II, 629
Rakestraw, Susanna Atkinson II, 630
Rakestraw, Susannah II, 456
Rakestraw, Susannah II, 629
Rakestraw, Susannah II, 630
Rakestraw, Thomas II, 181
Rakestraw, Thomas II, 251
Rakestraw, Thomas II, 410
Rakestraw, Thomas II, 447
Rakestraw, Thomas II, 629
Rakestraw, Thomas IV, 752
Rakestraw, Thomas IV, 1021
Rakestraw, Thomas IV, 1029
Rakestraw, Thomas, Jr. IV, 752
Rakestraw, Thos. Pennock II, 913
Rakestraw, Wd. Susanna II, 456
Rakestraw, Wd. Susanna II, 630
Rakestraw, William II, 410
Rakestraw, Wm. II, 454
Rakestraw, Wm. II, 490
Rakestraw, Wm. II, 629
Rakestraw, Wm. IV, 752
Rakestraw, Wm., Jr. II, 447
Rale, John III, 262
Raleigh, Amos IV, 988
Raleigh, Ann II, 761
Raleigh, Ann Jackson II, 630
Raleigh, Ann Jackson II, 761
Raleigh, Cora V, 706
Raleigh, Cora V, 710
Raleigh, Elazan IV, 681
Raleigh, Elazan IV, 752
Raleigh, Eliza IV, 988
Raleigh, Hannah II, 563
Raleigh, Hannah II, 630
Raleigh, Hannah II, 761
Raleigh, Hannah II, 769
Raleigh, James IV, 266
Raleigh, Joseph IV, 266
Raleigh, Samuel II, 410
Raleigh, Samuel II, 630
Raleigh, Tabitha IV, 545
Raleigh, Thomas IV, 545
Raleigh, Thomas IV, 653
Raleigh, Unity C. IV, 988
Raley, Abigail IV, 55
Raley, Abigail IV, 914
Raley, Abigail VI, 434
Raley, Abner IV, 545
Raley, Abraham Lincoln IV, 753
Raley, Alice II, 299
Raley, Amos IV, 988
Raley, Ann IV, 29
Raley, Ann IV, 54
Raley, Ann IV, 55
Raley, Ann IV, 61
Raley, Ann IV, 67
Raley, Ann IV, 132
Raley, Ann IV, 221
Raley, Ann IV, 266
Raley, Ann IV, 517
Raley, Ann IV, 530
Raley, Ann IV, 545
Raley, Ann IV, 546
Raley, Ann IV, 752
Raley, Ann IV, 839
Raley, Ann IV, 881
Raley, Ann IV, 988
Raley, Ann VI, 434
Raley, Ann VI, 551
Raley, Ann VI, 603
Raley, Asa IV, 55
Raley, Asa IV, 158
Raley, Asa IV, 249
Raley, Asa IV, 266
Raley, Asa IV, 271
Raley, Asa IV, 285
Raley, Asa IV, 432
Raley, Asa IV, 530
Raley, Asa IV, 545
Raley, Asa IV, 658
Raley, Asa IV, 770
Raley, Asa VI, 434
Raley, Asenath IV, 158
Raley, Asenath IV, 176
Raley, Asenath IV, 249
Raley, Asenath IV, 266
Raley, Asenath IV, 271
Raley, Asenath IV, 285
Raley, Asenath IV, 432
Raley, Asenath IV, 530
Raley, Asenath IV, 545
Raley, Asenath IV, 658
Raley, Asenath IV, 752
Raley, Asenath IV, 770
Raley, Clara M. IV, 801
Raley, Clara M. IV, 839
Raley, Clara Malinda IV, 753
Raley, David IV, 55
Raley, David IV, 266
Raley, David VI, 434
Raley, Eli IV, 50
Raley, Eli IV, 55
Raley, Eli VI, 434
Raley, Eli VI, 600
Raley, Eli VI, 603
Raley, Eli VI, 604
Raley, Eli, Jr. IV, 55
Raley, Eli, Jr. IV, 266
Raley, Elijah IV, 914
Raley, Eliza IV, 753
Raley, Eliza IV, 914
Raley, Eliza IV, 988
Raley, Eliza IV, 990
Raley, Elizabeth II, 299
Raley, Elizabeth IV, 55
Raley, Elizabeth IV, 266
Raley, Elizabeth IV, 432
Raley, Elizabeth IV, 913
Raley, Elizabeth IV, 914
Raley, Elizabeth VI, 209
Raley, Elizabeth T. IV, 266
Raley, Elizabeth T. IV, 432
Raley, Ellis VI, 434
Raley, Emmor IV, 752
Raley, Esther IV, 725
Raley, Esther IV, 753
Raley, Esther IV, 874
Raley, Esther IV, 881
Raley, Esther D. IV, 752
Raley, Flora B. IV, 839
Raley, Flora B. IV, 851
Raley, Flora Bell IV, 753
Raley, Frances IV, 17
Raley, Frances IV, 55
Raley, Frances VI, 434
Raley, Frances VI, 604
Raley, Hannah IV, 55
Raley, Hannah IV, 69
Raley, Hannah IV, 150
Raley, Hannah IV, 158
Raley, Hannah IV, 266
Raley, Hannah VI, 434
Raley, Isaac VI, 849
Raley, James II, 299
Raley, James IV, 55
Raley, James IV, 150
Raley, James IV, 221
Raley, James IV, 266
Raley, James IV, 839
Raley, James IV, 913
Raley, James IV, 914
Raley, James IV, 965
Raley, James IV, 988
Raley, James VI, 209
Raley, James VI, 434
Raley, James VI, 551
Raley, James VI, 603
Raley, James VI, 604
Raley, James VI, 606
Raley, Jane IV, 54
Raley, Jane IV, 67
Raley, Jane VI, 434
Raley, Jane P. II, 299
Raley, Jehu IV, 55
Raley, Jehu IV, 881
Raley, Jehu D. IV, 725
Raley, Jehu D. IV, 752
Raley, Jehu D. IV, 874
Raley, Jehu D. IV, 881
Raley, Jehu Dexon IV, 881
Raley, Jesse Cope IV, 55
Raley, Jesse Cope IV, 132
Raley, John IV, 17
Raley, John IV, 55
Raley, John IV, 123
Raley, John IV, 132
Raley, John IV, 653
Raley, John IV, 881
Raley, John IV, 914
Raley, John VI, 147
Raley, John VI, 209
Raley, John VI, 434
Raley, John VI, 551
Raley, John Raley IV, 55
Raley, John, Jr. IV, 55
Raley, Joseph IV, 32
Raley, Joseph IV, 55
Raley, Joseph IV, 176
Raley, Joseph IV, 202
Raley, Joseph IV, 266
Raley, Joseph IV, 807
Raley, Joseph IV, 839
Raley, Joseph IV, 897
Raley, Joseph IV, 914
Raley, Joseph VI, 434
Raley, Joshua IV, 55
Raley, Joshua VI, 434
Raley, Judith VI, 849
Raley, Kersey IV, 55
Raley, Kersey IV, 752
Raley, Kersey IV, 881
Raley, Laura IV, 752
Raley, Lidia VI, 209
Raley, Malinda IV, 914
Raley, Martha IV, 266
Raley, Martha IV, 271
Raley, Martha R. IV, 176
Raley, Mary IV, 17
Raley, Mary IV, 50
Raley, Mary IV, 55
Raley, Mary IV, 266
Raley, Mary IV, 641
Raley, Mary IV, 653
Raley, Mary IV, 722
Raley, Mary IV, 752
Raley, Mary IV, 753
Raley, Mary IV, 876
Raley, Mary IV, 881
Raley, Mary IV, 914
Raley, Mary VI, 434
Raley, Mary VI, 551
Raley, Mary VI, 600
Raley, Mary VI, 603
Raley, Mary VI, 604
Raley, Mary Ann IV, 752
Raley, Mary Ann IV, 813
Raley, Mary Ann IV, 839
Raley, Mary Frances II, 299
Raley, Mary H. IV, 266
Raley, Mary H. IV, 285
Raley, Mary H. IV, 653
Raley, Mary H. IV, 658
Raley, Mary H. IV, 659
Raley, Mary H. IV, 770
Raley, Mary H. IV, 771
Raley, Mary, Sr. IV, 266
Raley, Melissa IV, 266
Raley, Melissa Ann IV, 266
Raley, Michael IV, 55
Raley, Michael VI, 434
Raley, Milton IV, 752
Raley, Milton IV, 753
Raley, Milton IV, 839
Raley, Milton IV, 899
Raley, Milton IV, 914
Raley, Newton IV, 266
Raley, Phebe IV, 55
Raley, Phebe IV, 545
Raley, Phebe IV, 881
Raley, Phebe IV, 887
Raley, Rachel IV, 55
Raley, Rachel IV, 150
Raley, Rachel IV, 221
Raley, Rachel IV, 249
Raley, Rachel IV, 266
Raley, Rachel VI, 434
Raley, Rachel VI, 551
Raley, Rachel VI, 603
Raley, Rachel VI, 604
Raley, Rachel VI, 606
Raley, Rhoda IV, 881
Raley, Robert IV, 54
Raley, Robert IV, 55
Raley, Robert IV, 67
Raley, Robert IV, 132
Raley, Robert IV, 266
Raley, Robert IV, 545
Raley, Robert IV, 653
Raley, Robert IV, 914
Raley, Robert IV, 988
Raley, Robert VI, 434
Raley, Robert VI, 551
Raley, Robert VI, 603
Raley, Robert F. II, 299
Raley, Robert, Jr. VI, 434
Raley, Robert, Sr. IV, 55
Raley, Ruth IV, 55
Raley, Ruth IV, 132
Raley, Ruth IV, 266
Raley, Ruth A. IV, 752
Raley, Sally IV, 32
Raley, Sally IV, 55
Raley, Sally IV, 202
Raley, Sally IV, 266
Raley, Sarah IV, 27
Raley, Sarah IV, 50
Raley, Sarah IV, 54
Raley, Sarah IV, 55
Raley, Sarah IV, 123
Raley, Sarah IV, 132
Raley, Sarah IV, 752
Raley, Sarah IV, 753
Raley, Sarah IV, 899
Raley, Sarah IV, 914
Raley, Sarah IV, 988
Raley, Sarah VI, 434
Raley, Sarah Elizabeth IV, 752
Raley, Sarah Elizabeth IV, 839
Raley, Sarah Elizabeth IV, 841
Raley, Sarah Jane IV, 266
Raley, Sarah Jane IV, 545
Raley, Short IV, 55
Raley, Susanna IV, 839
Raley, Susannah IV, 807
Raley, Tabitha IV, 545
Raley, Talitha IV, 545
Raley, Talitha Ann IV, 266
Raley, Talitha Ann IV, 545
Raley, Talitha Ann IV, 546
Raley, Thirza IV, 914
Raley, Thomas IV, 29
Raley, Thomas IV, 55
Raley, Thomas IV, 266
Raley, Thomas IV, 517
Raley, Thomas IV, 545
Raley, Thomas IV, 546
Raley, Thomas IV, 752
Raley, Thomas IV, 881
Raley, Thomas VI, 209
Raley, Unity IV, 965
Raley, Unity IV, 988
Raley, Unity C. IV, 965
Raley, Unity C. IV, 988
Raley, William II, 299
Raley, Wm. IV, 752
Ralf, Sarah II, 93
Rallings, Mary VI, 910
Ralls, Elizabeth VI, 84
Ralls, John VI, 84
Ralls, Tabitha VI, 84
Ralph, Edward Garrigue II, 63
Ralph, Hannah II, 630
Ralph, Margaret II, 630
Ralph, Mary II, 552
Ralph, Mary Ralph II, 630
Ralph, Sarah II, 57
Ralph, Sarah II, 93
Ralston, Callie May V, 1015
Ralston, Elizabeth Marshall V, 198
Ralston, John W. V, 428
Ralston, John W. V, 846
Ralston, John W. V, 857
Ralston, John W. V, 1015
Ralston, Mary V, 428
Ralston, Mary H. V, 428
Ralston, Mary H. V, 846
Ralston, Mary H. V, 857
Rambo, Ada V, 356
Rambo, Benjamin V, 356
Rambo, Deborah VI, 434
Rambo, Deborah Rachel V, 35
Rambo, Edward B. V, 927
Rambo, Edward Burroughs V, 927
Rambo, Effie V, 428
Rambo, Elijah Coffin V, 927
Rambo, Elizabeth V, 927
Rambo, Francis A. V, 927
Rambo, Francis Howgill V, 92
Rambo, Herman V, 356
Rambo, Isaac V, 356
Rambo, Isaac VI, 434
Rambo, Isaac VI, 604
Rambo, Jackson VI, 434
Rambo, Jacob I, 568
Rambo, Jacob VI, 434
Rambo, Jacob VI, 602
Rambo, Jacob VI, 604
Rambo, Jacob, Jr. VI, 604
Rambo, James Parnell V, 927
Rambo, Jane V, 356
Rambo, Jane V, 357
Rambo, Jane M. V, 356
Rambo, John I, 1077
Rambo, Joseph VI, 604
Rambo, Joseph Allen VI, 604
Rambo, Lidia VI, 434
Rambo, Louis V, 356
Rambo, Mariam V, 927
Rambo, Martha II, 630
Rambo, Martha II, 660
Rambo, Miriam Allinson V, 92
Rambo, Monte V, 356
Rambo, Naomi C. V, 927
Rambo, Naomi Coffin V, 927
Rambo, Nathan V, 927
Rambo, Rebeccah VI, 434
Rambo, Rebeckah VI, 600
Rambo, Rebeckah VI, 602
Rambo, Rebeckah VI, 604
Rambo, Robert V, 356
Rambo, Ruth V, 356
Rambo, Sarah VI, 604
Rambo, Sarah S. V, 927
Rambo, Sarah Sylvania V, 92
Rambo, Sarah Sylvanus V, 92
Rambo, Tillie V, 356
Rambo, William V, 356
Rambo, William V, 428
Rambo, William A. V, 927
Rambo, Wm. V, 356
Rambo, Wm. A. V, 927
Ramey, George IV, 1260
Ramey, Hester IV, 1260
Ramie, George IV, 1260
Ramie, Hester IV, 1260
Rampson, Maria II, 1078
Ramsay, Barthl. VI, 981
Ramsay, Benjamin VI, 981
Ramsay, Betty VI, 981
Ramsay, William J. III, 262
Ramsdell, Eliza Ann IV, 1376
Ramsdell, Elizabeth IV, 1376
Ramsdell, Lydia Jane IV, 137
Ramsdell, Margaret IV, 1376
Ramsdell, Martha IV, 1376
Ramsdell, Thomas D. IV, 137
Ramsdell, William D. IV, 137
Ramsey, Albert V, 1015
Ramsey, Albert VI, 1019

nsey, Alice V, 1015
nsey, Ann E. VI, 824
nsey, Annis W. IV, 495
nsey, Annis W. IV, 503
nsey, Barbara VI, 984
nsey, Barthl. VI, 981
nsey, Ben VI, 981
nsey, Benja. VI, 889
nsey, Benjamin II, 630
nsey, Benjamin VI, 875
msey, Benjamin VI, 981
msey, Betty VI, 981
nsey, Caroline B. VI, 825
msey, Catherine Ryan V, 198
msey, Daniel VI, 981
msey, Dorcas VI, 981
msey, Eliza VI, 981
nsey, Elizabeth VI, 849
nsey, Elizabeth VI, 981
nsey, Elizabeth VI, 982
msey, Elizabeth A. D. VI, 832
msey, Elizabeth C. H. VI, 849
msey, Emily VI, 895
msey, Emily VI, 897
msey, Emily VI, 900
msey, Harriet V, 1015
msey, Harrison VI, 981
msey, Henry VI, 981
msey, James V, 1015
msey, James VI, 895
msey, James VI, 965
msey, James VI, 981
msey, James B. VI, 981
msey, James M. VI, 981
msey, John VI, 981
msey, John C. V, 1015
msey, Joseph T. VI, 849
msey, Lucy VI, 825
msey, Lydia IV, 42
msey, Lydia IV, 55
msey, Madison VI, 978
msey, Marget VI, 902
msey, Marlin V, 1015
msey, Martha IV, 511
msey, Martha IV, 545
msey, Martha VI, 828
msey, Martha VI, 981
msey, Martin VI, 981
msey, Mary VI, 981
msey, Mary E. VI, 682
msey, Mary E. VI, 692
msey, Matilda IV, 240
msey, Mattie V, 1015
msey, Murlin V, 1015
msey, Nancy V, 1015
msey, Nancy VI, 965
msey, Nancy VI, 981
msey, Nansy V, 1015
msey, Phebe VI, 849
msey, Polly VI, 981
msey, Rebecca II, 816
msey, Roaka V, 1015
msey, Robert C. VI, 965
msey, Robert C. VI, 982
msey, Sally VI, 981
msey, Sarah I, 1161
msey, Sarah V, 740
msey, Sarah VI, 981
msey, Sarah E. I, 1161
msey, Simon VI, 981
msey, Susanna IV, 106
msey, Susanna VI, 942
msey, Susannah IV, 114
msey, Susannah VI, 889
msey, Thomas VI, 828
msey, Thomas VI, 849
msey, Thomas T. VI, 849
msey, Walter V, 1015
msey, William III, 262
msey, William VI, 912
msey, William J. III, 262
mson, Henry III, 262
mson, Louisa III, 262
mson, Maria II, 1078
msy, Sarah E. I, 1161
my, Mary V, 198
nall, Jonas V, 858
anbury, Margrett II, 410
anbury, Mary II, 410
anbury, William II, 410
anch, Barbara IV, 676
anch, Catherine IV, 676
anch, Jacob IV, 676
andal, Abraham VI, 692
andal, Alfred V, 857
andal, Alfred V, 858
andal, Amy V, 857
andal, Amy V, 858
andal, Ann I, 1037
andal, Ann V, 857
andal, Ann V, 858
Randal, Ann V, 862
Randal, Ann VI, 692
Randal, Charity VI, 692
Randal, Charles E. V, 858
Randal, David V, 857
Randal, Delilah V, 858
Randal, Delilah V, 871
Randal, Elizabeth V, 857
Randal, Elizabeth V, 858
Randal, Elizabeth VI, 692
Randal, Emely V, 858
Randal, Emily V, 857
Randal, Emma V, 198
Randal, Hannah I, 1037
Randal, Hannah V, 857
Randal, Hannah VI, 692
Randal, Isaac I, 1037
Randal, Isaac V, 843
Randal, Isaac V, 857
Randal, Isaac V, 858
Randal, Isaac VI, 692
Randal, James I, 1037
Randal, Jane VI, 692
Randal, John V, 857
Randal, John V, 858
Randal, John VI, 692
Randal, John D. V, 706
Randal, Jonas I, 1037
Randal, Jonas V, 857
Randal, Jonas V, 858
Randal, Jonas P. V, 858
Randal, Jonas, Jr. V, 858
Randal, Jonathan V, 857
Randal, Jonathan V, 858
Randal, Joseph I, 1037
Randal, Joseph V, 845
Randal, Joseph V, 857
Randal, Joseph V, 858
Randal, Joseph VI, 692
Randal, Joseph, Jr. I, 1037
Randal, Joseph, Jr. V, 858
Randal, Joseph, Jr. VI, 692
Randal, Kesiah V, 845
Randal, Keziah V, 857
Randal, Keziah V, 858
Randal, Louisa V, 858
Randal, Lydia V, 857
Randal, Lydia V, 858
Randal, Margaret V, 858
Randal, Martha V, 857
Randal, Martha V, 858
Randal, Mary V, 706
Randal, Mary V, 857
Randal, Mary V, 858
Randal, Mary VI, 337
Randal, Mary VI, 338
Randal, Mary VI, 692
Randal, Mary Jane V, 858
Randal, Nancy V, 858
Randal, Naomi V, 858
Randal, Nathan V, 857
Randal, Phebe V, 843
Randal, Phebe V, 857
Randal, Rachel V, 857
Randal, Rachel V, 858
Randal, Rachel VI, 337
Randal, Rachel VI, 692
Randal, Rebecca II, 630
Randal, Rebecca V, 857
Randal, Rebeckah VI, 692
Randal, Richard V, 858
Randal, Ruth VI, 692
Randal, Sarah I, 1037
Randal, Sarah II, 1006
Randal, Sarah II, 1022
Randal, Sarah V, 843
Randal, Sarah V, 857
Randal, Sarah V, 858
Randal, Sarah VI, 692
Randal, Sarah, Jr. V, 858
Randal, Susanna V, 857
Randal, Susannah V, 858
Randal, Thomas I, 1037
Randal, William V, 858
Randal, Zimri V, 857
Randal, Zimri V, 858
Randale, Ann V, 857
Randale, Elizabeth V, 857
Randale, Hannah V, 857
Randale, Isaac V, 857
Randale, John V, 857
Randale, Jonas V, 857
Randale, Lydia V, 857
Randale, Martha V, 857
Randale, Phebe V, 857
Randale, Rachel V, 857
Randale, Sarah V, 857
Randall, ??? II, 826
Randall, Abraham VI, 550
Randall, Abraham VI, 693
Randall, Alverdie V, 594
Randall, Ann V, 851
Randall, Ann VI, 550
Randall, C. E. IV, 1290
Randall, Charity VI, 550
Randall, Charity VI, 693
Randall, Charles V, 594
Randall, Charles E. IV, 1290
Randall, Charles E. V, 858
Randall, Deborah II, 1073
Randall, Deborah II, 1078
Randall, Deborah F. II, 1078
Randall, Effie IV, 1261
Randall, Effie T. IV, 1261
Randall, Eliza V, 762
Randall, Eliza Ann V, 762
Randall, Elizabeth IV, 839
Randall, Elizabeth V, 849
Randall, Elizabeth V, 857
Randall, Elizabeth V, 858
Randall, Elizabeth VI, 501
Randall, Elizabeth VI, 550
Randall, Elizabeth VI, 645
Randall, Elizabeth VI, 696
Randall, Emma J. V, 762
Randall, George II, 447
Randall, Grace H. V, 706
Randall, Hannah VI, 550
Randall, Harry V, 762
Randall, Harry V, 763
Randall, Henrietta Wooley IV, 1290
Randall, I. A. V, 763
Randall, Isaac IV, 839
Randall, Isaac V, 849
Randall, Isaac V, 858
Randall, J. H. V, 762
Randall, James IV, 839
Randall, Jane VI, 550
Randall, Jane VI, 669
Randall, Jane VI, 693
Randall, John IV, 839
Randall, John V, 428
Randall, John V, 594
Randall, John V, 706
Randall, John V, 849
Randall, John VI, 550
Randall, John VI, 693
Randall, John D. V, 594
Randall, John D. V, 706
Randall, Jonathan H., Jr. V, 762
Randall, Joseph VI, 485
Randall, Joseph VI, 550
Randall, Joseph VI, 558
Randall, Joseph VI, 632
Randall, Joseph VI, 693
Randall, Joseph, Jr. VI, 693
Randall, Louisa V, 858
Randall, Lydia V, 849
Randall, Lydia V, 851
Randall, Lydia Ann V, 851
Randall, Martha V, 858
Randall, Martha V, 862
Randall, Mary IV, 432
Randall, Mary IV, 535
Randall, Mary IV, 545
Randall, Mary IV, 839
Randall, Mary V, 428
Randall, Mary V, 594
Randall, Mary V, 706
Randall, Mary VI, 550
Randall, Mary VI, 693
Randall, Mary VI, 715
Randall, Mary Jane V, 858
Randall, Mary M. T. II, 913
Randall, Melissa IV, 1290
Randall, Melissa V, 1015
Randall, Melissa A. V, 1015
Randall, Moses Dillon VI, 550
Randall, Naomi V, 858
Randall, Nettie IV, 1290
Randall, Oscar V, 763
Randall, Rachel II, 630
Randall, Rachel II, 716
Randall, Rachel VI, 485
Randall, Rachel VI, 503
Randall, Rachel VI, 550
Randall, Rachel VI, 558
Randall, Rachel VI, 632
Randall, Rachel VI, 647
Randall, Rachel VI, 693
Randall, Rachel VI, 698
Randall, Rebecca II, 535
Randall, Rebecca II, 630
Randall, Rebecca VI, 486
Randall, Rebekah VI, 550
Randall, Ruth VI, 485
Randall, Ruth VI, 550
Randall, Ruth VI, 632
Randall, Ruth VI, 693
Randall, Sarah II, 410
Randall, Sarah II, 630
Randall, Sarah V, 594
Randall, Sarah V, 849
Randall, Sarah V, 858
Randall, Sarah VI, 550
Randall, Sarah VI, 555
Randall, Sarah VI, 558
Randall, Sarah VI, 698
Randall, Susan II, 838
Randall, Susan II, 940
Randall, Warwick II, 410
Randall, Wm. IV, 839
Randall, Wm. S. B. V, 594
Randals, Ann IV, 821
Randals, Ann IV, 840
Randals, Isaac IV, 840
Randals, James IV, 821
Randals, James IV, 840
Randel, ??? V, 198
Randel, Ann I, 1023
Randel, Ann I, 1062
Randel, Ann I, 1063
Randel, Ann V, 857
Randel, Ann Roberts I, 1062
Randel, David V, 857
Randel, Elizabeth I, 1058
Randel, Elizabeth V, 198
Randel, Emma V, 198
Randel, Hannah I, 1023
Randel, Hannah I, 1062
Randel, Hannah I, 1063
Randel, Hannah V, 857
Randel, Hannah V, 958
Randel, Isaac I, 1023
Randel, Jehu I, 1058
Randel, Jehu V, 198
Randel, John I, 1023
Randel, John I, 1058
Randel, John V, 198
Randel, Jonas I, 1023
Randel, Jonas I, 1058
Randel, Jonas V, 198
Randel, Jonas V, 829
Randel, Jonathan I, 1058
Randel, Jonathan V, 198
Randel, Jonathan V, 857
Randel, Joseph I, 1023
Randel, Joseph V, 857
Randel, Lydia I, 1023
Randel, Lydia I, 1063
Randel, Margaret V, 858
Randel, Mary IV, 1074
Randel, Mary V, 829
Randel, Moses I, 1023
Randel, Nathan V, 857
Randel, Rachel I, 1023
Randel, Rachel I, 1060
Randel, Rachel I, 1062
Randel, Rebecca V, 198
Randel, Rebecca V, 857
Randel, Rebekah I, 1058
Randel, Robert I, 1058
Randel, Sarah I, 1023
Randel, Sarah IV, 825
Randel, Sarah IV, 840
Randel, Thomas I, 1023
Randel, Walter I, 1058
Randel, Walter V, 198
Randell, Ann II, 447
Randell, George II, 447
Randels, Ann IV, 840
Randels, Anna IV, 839
Randels, Elizabeth IV, 799
Randels, Elizabeth IV, 839
Randels, Elizabeth IV, 840
Randels, Isaac IV, 839
Randels, Isaac IV, 840
Randels, James IV, 839
Randels, James IV, 840
Randels, John IV, 839
Randels, John IV, 840
Randels, Maria IV, 839
Randels, Maria IV, 848
Randels, Mary IV, 838
Randels, Mary IV, 839
Randels, Mary IV, 840
Randels, Sarah IV, 798
Randels, Sarah IV, 839
Randels, Sarah IV, 840
Randels, William IV, 881
Randels, Wm. IV, 839
Randle, Ann V, 113
Randle, Ann V, 858
Randle, Ann Roberts I, 1062
Randle, Deborah F. II, 1078
Randle, Elizabeth I, 1060
Randle, Elizabeth I, 1062
Randle, Esther VI, 653
Randle, Hannah I, 1062
Randle, Isaac V, 858
Randle, Jehu V, 113
Randle, John V, 113
Randle, John V, 829
Randle, John V, 858
Randle, Jonas I, 1062
Randle, Jonas V, 113
Randle, Jonathan V, 113
Randle, Joseph V, 113
Randle, Joseph VI, 693
Randle, Joseph, Jr. VI, 693
Randle, Lydia I, 1062
Randle, Lydia V, 829
Randle, Lydia V, 858
Randle, Martha V, 858
Randle, Mary V, 113
Randle, Mary V, 857
Randle, Mary Jane V, 858
Randle, Rachel VI, 693
Randle, Rebekah I, 1061
Randle, Rebekah I, 1062
Randle, Sarah II, 630
Randle, Sarah V, 113
Randle, Sarah V, 858
Randle, William, Jr. IV, 653
Randles, Anna IV, 881
Randles, Anne IV, 880
Randles, Anne IV, 881
Randles, Elizabeth IV, 863
Randles, Elizabeth IV, 881
Randles, Esther IV, 753
Randles, Esther IV, 881
Randles, Isaac IV, 753
Randles, Isaac IV, 840
Randles, Isaac IV, 881
Randles, John IV, 881
Randles, Mary IV, 876
Randles, Mary IV, 881
Randles, William IV, 881
Randobaugh, John V, 1015
Randobaugh, Levi V, 1015
Randobaugh, Mariah V, 1015
Randobaugh, Mary V, 1015
Randobaugh, Tissie V, 1015
Randol, Jaeil II, 93
Randol, Lydia I, 1062
Randol, Mary VI, 338
Randol, Mary VI, 854
Randolf, Deborah IV, 806
Randolf, Deborah IV, 840
Randolf, Sarah II, 93
Randolf, Warrick II, 93
Randolph, ??? III, 121
Randolph, ??? V, 942
Randolph, ??? VI, 48
Randolph, Albert IV, 1221
Randolph, Ann II, 208
Randolph, Anna II, 761
Randolph, Anna II, 1086
Randolph, Anna J. II, 716
Randolph, Anna J. II, 721
Randolph, Anna J. II, 1056
Randolph, Anna J. II, 1058
Randolph, Anna J. II, 1089
Randolph, Anne II, 716
Randolph, Beverly VI, 849
Randolph, Caroline Eliza III, 262
Randolph, Chattie IV, 1181
Randolph, Col. William VI, 149
Randolph, Col. William VI, 209
Randolph, Dr. John Lindley III, 121
Randolph, Dr. John Lindley Fitz III, 358
Randolph, Edmund III, 121
Randolph, Edmund F. III, 262
Randolph, Edward II, 208
Randolph, Edward II, 251
Randolph, Edward II, 716
Randolph, Edward II, 721
Randolph, Edward II, 761
Randolph, Edward II, 949
Randolph, Edward II, 1086
Randolph, Edward II, 1089
Randolph, Edward III, 121
Randolph, Edward F. II, 630
Randolph, Edward F. II, 761
Randolph, Edward F. IV, 653
Randolph, Edward F. IV, 988
Randolph, Edward Fitts IV, 882
Randolph, Edward Fitz IV, 988
Randolph, Edward Taylor II, 716
Randolph, Edwin F. IV, 882
Randolph, Eliza III, 121
Randolph, Eliza III, 262
Randolph, Eliza III, 358
Randolph, Eliza F. III, 262
Randolph, Elizabeth II, 410
Randolph, Elizabeth VI, 200
Randolph, Elizabeth VI, 209
Randolph, Emma G. IV, 1334
Randolph, Eunice Fitz II, 805
Randolph, George II, 630
Randolph, George II, 716

Randolph, George II, 761
Randolph, George F. II, 208
Randolph, George F. II, 251
Randolph, George F. II, 410
Randolph, George F. II, 411
Randolph, George F. II, 630
Randolph, George F. II, 716
Randolph, George F. II, 761
Randolph, George F. II, 777
Randolph, George F., Jr. II, 411
Randolph, George W. II, 760
Randolph, George W. II, 761
Randolph, Grendon VI, 146
Randolph, Guliana II, 208
Randolph, Guliana II, 251
Randolph, Guy D. IV, 1181
Randolph, Hannah II, 208
Randolph, Hannah II, 251
Randolph, Hannah II, 410
Randolph, Hannah II, 630
Randolph, Hannah II, 716
Randolph, Hannah II, 761
Randolph, Hannah II, 777
Randolph, Hannah F. II, 630
Randolph, Hannah F. II, 761
Randolph, Hannah S. F. III, 262
Randolph, Hannah Skinner III, 262
Randolph, Harriet II, 716
Randolph, Harriet Ann F. III, 262
Randolph, Harriet S. F. III, 262
Randolph, Ira F. II, 410
Randolph, Ira F. II, 630
Randolph, J. Farland IV, 1334
Randolph, Jacob VI, 18
Randolph, Jacob F. VI, 209
Randolph, Jame F. II, 761
Randolph, James III, 262
Randolph, James C. F. III, 262
Randolph, James Cornwall III, 121
Randolph, James F. III, 262
Randolph, Jane II, 721
Randolph, Jane IV, 106
Randolph, Jane Chace II, 716
Randolph, Jane Chace II, 761
Randolph, Jane Chase II, 1086
Randolph, Jane F. II, 411
Randolph, Jas. F. III, 397
Randolph, Jennie II, 761
Randolph, Jennie C. II, 760
Randolph, John III, 262
Randolph, John F. III, 262
Randolph, John L. III, 121
Randolph, John L. III, 262
Randolph, John L. F. III, 262
Randolph, John R. F. III, 262
Randolph, John T. III, 262
Randolph, Joseph III, 262
Randolph, Joseph VI, 83
Randolph, Joseph K. F. III, 262
Randolph, Juliana F. II, 761
Randolph, Juliana F. II, 777
Randolph, Julianna F. II, 630
Randolph, Julianne II, 410
Randolph, King III, 262
Randolph, Margaret F. II, 716
Randolph, Margaret F. II, 761
Randolph, Margaret F. VI, 83
Randolph, Margaret F. VI, 90
Randolph, Marian II, 760
Randolph, Marian II, 761
Randolph, Marion II, 716
Randolph, Mary I, 565
Randolph, Mary II, 220
Randolph, Mary II, 251
Randolph, Mary II, 716
Randolph, Mary III, 262
Randolph, Mary Ann Tucker II, 784
Randolph, Mary B. III, 397
Randolph, Mary F. III, 262
Randolph, Mrs. Margaret Monroe IV, 1334
Randolph, Nancy VI, 849
Randolph, Nellie IV, 1181
Randolph, Percy Lloyd II, 716
Randolph, Percy Lloyd II, 760
Randolph, Percy Lloyd II, 761
Randolph, Phebe III, 121
Randolph, Randal II, 635
Randolph, Robert III, 121
Randolph, S. F. III, 262
Randolph, Samuel F. III, 262
Randolph, Sarah K. III, 262
Randolph, Sarah K. F. III, 262
Randolph, Sidney III, 262
Randolph, Susan F. VI, 800
Randolph, Susanna IV, 1108
Randolph, Susanna IV, 1113
Randolph, Thomas VI, 209
Randolph, William VI, 146
Randolph, William W. F. III, 262
Ranes, B. VI, 843
Ranes, Elizabeth VI, 843
Ranes, Nancy VI, 843
Raney, Robert VI, 882
Raney, Robert VI, 942
Raney, Robert VI, 982
Raney, Sally VI, 982
Ranger, Caroline Agnes III, 82
Ranier, Hannah II, 218
Ranier, Hannah II, 252
Rank, Edward V, 763
Rank, Henry V, 763
Rank, Lewis W. V, 763
Rank, Morris V, 763
Rank, Susan V, 763
Ranke, Ethel May VI, 770
Rankeen, Elizabeth VI, 849
Rankeen, Robert VI, 849
Rankin, Abigail III, 262
Rankin, Abigail IV, 266
Rankin, Abigail R. IV, 311
Rankin, Abigail R. IV, 314
Rankin, Ann VI, 434
Rankin, Elizabeth IV, 263
Rankin, Elizabeth IV, 266
Rankin, Isaac Walker VI, 434
Rankin, Jane I, 416
Rankin, John IV, 266
Rankin, John W. IV, 263
Rankin, Lydia IV, 266
Rankin, Lydia IV, 300
Rankin, Lydia W. IV, 263
Rankin, Lydia W. IV, 266
Rankin, Martha IV, 266
Rankin, Martha IV, 311
Rankin, Martha IV, 314
Rankin, Martha IV, 348
Rankin, Mary VI, 434
Rankin, Mary VI, 454
Rankin, Mary Branson IV, 314
Rankin, William IV, 266
Rankin, William J. W. IV, 266
Rankins, Martha IV, 348
Rankins, Martha IV, 545
Rannells, Clara Kirk V, 706
Rannells, Daisy Wright V, 706
Ransbarger, Elizabeth VI, 841
Ransbarger, Elizabeth VI, 849
Ransbarger, Philip VI, 841
Ransbarger, Philip VI, 849
Ranserry, Benjamin II, 411
Ransley, Catharine I, 453
Ransley, James I, 453
Ransley, John I, 417
Ransley, John I, 453
Ransley, Joseph I, 453
Ransley, Sarah I, 453
Ransom, ??? III, 262
Ransom, Benj. III, 262
Ransom, Blanch G. III, 262
Ransom, Catharine H. III, 262
Ransom, Egbert III, 262
Ransom, Eleanor Priscilla III, 262
Ransom, Eleanor Priscilla III, 263
Ransom, Eliza Elizabeth III, 262
Ransom, Elizabeth E. III, 262
Ransom, Frank III, 263
Ransom, Frank Edwin III, 262
Ransom, Frank Edwin III, 263
Ransom, Frank Fellows III, 262
Ransom, Henry III, 263
Ransom, John Fry III, 262
Ransom, Louisa III, 263
Ransom, Mary III, 438
Ransome, ??? III, 262
Ransome, Blanch G. III, 262
Ransome, Egbert III, 72
Ransome, Egbert III, 262
Ransome, Eleanor Priscilla III, 129
Ransome, Eleanor Priscilla III, 262
Ransome, Eliza Elizabeth III, 262
Ransome, Elizabeth E. III, 72
Ransome, Elizabeth E. III, 262
Ransome, Frank Edwin III, 129
Ransome, Frank Edwin III, 262
Ransome, Grace III, 365
Ransome, Henry III, 204
Ransome, Henry III, 263
Ransome, Louisa III, 204
Ransome, Louisa III, 263
Ranson, Price VI, 913
Ranstead, Caleb II, 411
Ranstead, Elizabeth II, 411
Ranstead, Elizabeth II, 580
Ranstead, Elizabeth II, 630
Ranstead, Hannah II, 411
Ranstead, Joseph II, 411
Ranstead, Joshua II, 411
Ranstead, Lydia II, 411
Ranstead, Mary II, 411
Ranstead, Mary II, 630
Ranstead, Mary II, 684
Ranstead, Sarah II, 411
Ranstead, Susanna II, 630
Ranstead, Thomas II, 411
Ranstead, William II, 411
Ranstead, Wm. II, 630
Ransted, Caleb II, 621
Ransted, Caleb II, 626
Ransted, Caleb II, 630
Ransted, Caleb II, 677
Ransted, Elizabeth II, 630
Ransted, Joseph II, 630
Ransted, Mary II, 621
Ransted, Mary II, 630
Ransted, Mary II, 677
Ransted, Rachel II, 626
Ransted, Rachel II, 630
Ransted, Susanna II, 630
Ransted, Wm. II, 621
Ransted, Wm. II, 630
Ranton, Elizabeth II, 616
Ranton, Elizabeth II, 630
Ranton, Mary, Jr. II, 411
Ranton, Sidney Paul II, 411
Raoch, Sarah VI, 582
Rapelye, Caroline III, 245
Rapelye, Caroline III, 263
Rapelye, Martha III, 263
Raper, Abigail II, 180
Raper, Abigail II, 181
Raper, Abigail II, 184
Raper, Abigail II, 251
Raper, Abigail II, 252
Raper, Abigail II, 261
Raper, Ann II, 411
Raper, Anne I, 948
Raper, Bonnie I, 948
Raper, Caleb II, 181
Raper, Caleb II, 208
Raper, Caleb II, 251
Raper, Daniel, Jr. II, 181
Raper, Hannah II, 181
Raper, Helen I, 948
Raper, Henry II, 626
Raper, Henry II, 630
Raper, Joshua II, 177
Raper, Joshua II, 181
Raper, Joshua II, 252
Raper, Lydia II, 181
Raper, Mariam I, 163
Raper, Martha II, 166
Raper, Martha II, 181
Raper, Martha II, 252
Raper, Mary II, 177
Raper, Mary II, 181
Raper, Mary II, 208
Raper, Mary II, 251
Raper, Mary II, 252
Raper, Mary II, 261
Raper, Mary II, 626
Raper, Mary II, 630
Raper, Miriam I, 163
Raper, Miriam I, 199
Raper, Miriam E. I, 817
Raper, Miriam E. I, 835
Raper, Rebecca II, 181
Raper, Sarah I, 159
Raper, Sarah I, 163
Raper, Sarah II, 181
Raper, Sarah II, 183
Raper, Sarah II, 252
Raper, Thomas II, 166
Raper, Thomas II, 181
Raper, Thomas II, 184
Raper, Thomas II, 208
Raper, Thomas II, 251
Raper, Thomas II, 252
Rapine, Sarah B. II, 1055
Rapine, Sarah B. II, 1058
Rapior, Abigail II, 249
Rapior, Abigail II, 251
Rapior, Thomas II, 249
Rapior, Thomas II, 251
Rapley, Eliza Maria VI, 749
Rapp, Emeline III, 305
Rapp, John V, 706
Rasche, Albert T. IV, 753
Rasche, Charles IV, 753
Rasche, Deborah IV, 753
Rasche, Elizabeth G. IV, 705
Rasche, Elizabeth G. IV, 753
Rasche, Elizabeth G. IV, 952
Rasche, Elizabeth G. IV, 988
Rasche, Florence I, 640
Rasche, Helena IV, 738
Rasche, Hellena Luella IV, 753
Rasche, Jacob IV, 738
Rasche, Julius IV, 705
Rasche, Julius IV, 753
Rasche, Julius IV, 952
Rasche, Julius IV, 988
Rasche, Matilda IV, 738
Rasche, Matilda IV, 753
Rascue, Elizabeth G. IV, 753
Rascue, Eoizabeth G. IV, 753
Rascue, Julius IV, 753
Rasec, Lucile IV, 1334
Rasey, Harrison IV, 1181
Rash, Matilda IV, 753
Rasin, Abraham II, 905
Rasin, Abraham II, 913
Rasin, Joanna II, 905
Rasin, Joanna II, 913
Rasin, Joanna P. II, 758
Rasin, Joanna P. II, 761
Rasin, Patience M. II, 905
Rasin, Patience M. II, 913
Rasin, Warner M. II, 905
Rasin, Warner M. II, 913
Rasmussen, Bertha III, 263
Rasmussen, Bertha C. III, 263
Rasmussen, Bertha C. III, 334
Rasmussen, Christian W. III, 263
Rasmussen, Christian W. III, 334
Rasor, Lucy M. IV, 1334
Rasor, Lucy Marie IV, 1334
Ratchford, Joseph V, 356
Ratclif, Abner I, 417
Ratclif, Edom I, 417
Ratclif, Harrison V, 273
Ratclif, Mary I, 417
Ratclif, Mildred V, 273
Ratclif, Richard VI, 34
Ratclif, Richard VI, 35
Ratclif, Sarah I, 417
Ratclif, Tamer I, 417
Ratcliff, ??? V, 315
Ratcliff, Abner I, 377
Ratcliff, Abner I, 416
Ratcliff, Abner I, 417
Ratcliff, Abner V, 113
Ratcliff, Abner V, 273
Ratcliff, Abner V, 356
Ratcliff, Abner V, 425
Ratcliff, Abner V, 428
Ratcliff, Abner V, 429
Ratcliff, Abner V, 431
Ratcliff, Abner, Jr. V, 428
Ratcliff, Abner, Sr. V, 428
Ratcliff, Alice Ann IV, 988
Ratcliff, Amos I, 377
Ratcliff, Amos I, 416
Ratcliff, Amos I, 417
Ratcliff, Amos V, 113
Ratcliff, Amos V, 273
Ratcliff, Amos V, 350
Ratcliff, Amos V, 356
Ratcliff, Amos V, 428
Ratcliff, Amos V, 429
Ratcliff, Amos Hibbs IV, 545
Ratcliff, Amos, Jr. V, 428
Ratcliff, Ann I, 377
Ratcliff, Ann I, 416
Ratcliff, Ann I, 417
Ratcliff, Ann I, 705
Ratcliff, Ann II, 411
Ratcliff, Ann II, 630
Ratcliff, Ann V, 113
Ratcliff, Ann V, 350
Ratcliff, Ann V, 356
Ratcliff, Ann V, 408
Ratcliff, Ann V, 428
Ratcliff, Ann Margaret V, 273
Ratcliff, Anna I, 996
Ratcliff, Anna V, 356
Ratcliff, Anna V, 428
Ratcliff, Anna Lydia IV, 267
Ratcliff, Anne V, 273
Ratcliff, Benj. B. IV, 251
Ratcliff, Benj. B. IV, 266
Ratcliff, Benjamin I, 163
Ratcliff, Benjamin I, 996
Ratcliff, Benjamin IV, 267
Ratcliff, Benjamin IV, 546
Ratcliff, Benjamin IV, 1075
Ratcliff, Benjamin B. IV, 545
Ratcliff, Benjamin B. IV, 1075
Ratcliff, Benjamin B. VI, 209
Ratcliff, Benjamin R. IV, 546
Ratcliff, Benjamin S. IV, 545
Ratcliff, Betty I, 314
Ratcliff, Betty I, 317
Ratcliff, Betty I, 996
Ratcliff, Blanche N. IV, 267
Ratcliff, Carl M. I, 1161
Ratcliff, Catharine I, 163
Ratcliff, Charles IV, 545
Ratcliff, Charles IV, 1075
Ratcliff, Charles Augustus IV, 267
Ratcliff, Chas. IV, 546
Ratcliff, Chas. Arthur IV, 267
Ratcliff, Cornelious VI, 34
Ratcliff, Cornelius V, 113
Ratcliff, Cornelius VI, 31
Ratcliff, Cornelius VI, 34
Ratcliff, Cyrus V, 429
Ratcliff, Damaris I Sup 1, 5
Ratcliff, Dorcas V, 273
Ratcliff, Dorcas V, 356
Ratcliff, Dorcas V, 428
Ratcliff, Dorcas V, 431
Ratcliff, E. Wood IV, 267
Ratcliff, Edom I, 377
Ratcliff, Edom I, 416
Ratcliff, Edom I, 417
Ratcliff, Edom V, 273
Ratcliff, Edom V, 428
Ratcliff, Edom V, 642
Ratcliff, Edom, Jr. V, 356
Ratcliff, Edward IV, 545
Ratcliff, Edward IV, 546
Ratcliff, Eleanor I, 377
Ratcliff, Eleanor I, 416
Ratcliff, Eleanor V, 113
Ratcliff, Eleanor V, 273
Ratcliff, Eleanor V, 350
Ratcliff, Eleanor V, 356
Ratcliff, Eleanor V, 428
Ratcliff, Elender I, 417
Ratcliff, Elenor V, 356
Ratcliff, Elenor V, 428
Ratcliff, Elias V, 273
Ratcliff, Elijah I, 835
Ratcliff, Elisha IV, 546
Ratcliff, Elisha B. IV, 545
Ratcliff, Eliza IV, 546
Ratcliff, Eliza W. IV, 545
Ratcliff, Elizabeth I, 405
Ratcliff, Elizabeth I, 416
Ratcliff, Elizabeth I, 685
Ratcliff, Elizabeth I, 687
Ratcliff, Elizabeth I, 705
Ratcliff, Elizabeth IV, 221
Ratcliff, Elizabeth IV, 238
Ratcliff, Elizabeth IV, 266
Ratcliff, Elizabeth IV, 267
Ratcliff, Elizabeth IV, 530
Ratcliff, Elizabeth IV, 546
Ratcliff, Elizabeth IV, 955
Ratcliff, Elizabeth IV, 988
Ratcliff, Elizabeth IV, 1075
Ratcliff, Elizabeth V, 113
Ratcliff, Elizabeth V, 273
Ratcliff, Elizabeth V, 332
Ratcliff, Elizabeth V, 356
Ratcliff, Elizabeth V, 428
Ratcliff, Elizabeth V, 429
Ratcliff, Elizabeth V, 434
Ratcliff, Elizabeth VI, 30
Ratcliff, Elizabeth VI, 31
Ratcliff, Elizabeth VI, 34
Ratcliff, Elizabeth VI, 209
Ratcliff, Elizabeth VI, 210
Ratcliff, Elizabeth VI, 265
Ratcliff, Elizabeth Ann V, 428
Ratcliff, Elizabeth Ann V, 429
Ratcliff, Ellenor V, 428
Ratcliff, Ellwood IV, 266
Ratcliff, Elwood IV, 198
Ratcliff, Elwood IV, 267
Ratcliff, Elwood IV, 288
Ratcliff, Elwood IV, 523
Ratcliff, Elwood IV, 545
Ratcliff, Elwood V, 975
Ratcliff, Elwood VI, 210
Ratcliff, Emmor IV, 988
Ratcliff, Ephraim I, 163
Ratcliff, Esther W. IV, 267
Ratcliff, Ettie V, 642
Ratcliff, Ezekiel V, 273
Ratcliff, Fleming IV, 267
Ratcliff, Fleming IV, 545
Ratcliff, Frederick W. IV, 267
Ratcliff, Gabriel I, 996
Ratcliff, George M. IV, 267
Ratcliff, Gideon VI, 18
Ratcliff, Gideon VI, 209
Ratcliff, Gideon VI, 265
Ratcliff, H. H. IV, 267
Ratcliff, Hannah I, 163
Ratcliff, Hannah I, 416
Ratcliff, Hannah I, 996
Ratcliff, Hannah IV, 226
Ratcliff, Hannah IV, 267
Ratcliff, Hannah IV, 545

tcliff, Hannah IV, 546
tcliff, Hannah IV, 1290
tcliff, Hannah VI, 209
tcliff, Hannah VI, 210
tcliff, Hannah A. I, 1161
tcliff, Hannah B. IV, 266
tcliff, Hannah B. IV, 267
tcliff, Hannah B. VI, 209
tcliff, Hannah B. VI, 210
tcliff, Hannah J. IV, 267
tcliff, Hannah Jane IV, 267
tcliff, Harrison IV, 55
tcliff, Harrison IV, 267
tcliff, Harrison V, 273
tcliff, Harrison VI, 209
tcliff, Harrison VI, 210
tcliff, Harrison VI, 265
tcliff, Horace H. IV, 267
tcliff, Horace Hussey, Jr. IV, 267
atcliff, Huldah V, 273
atcliff, Hurford IV, 988
atcliff, Isaac IV, 169
atcliff, Isaac IV, 227
atcliff, Isaac IV, 266
atcliff, Isaac IV, 267
atcliff, Isaac IV, 307
atcliff, Isaac IV, 546
atcliff, Isaac V, 273
atcliff, Isaac V, 356
atcliff, Isaac V, 428
atcliff, Isaac V, 975
atcliff, Isaac VI, 209
atcliff, Isaac VI, 210
atcliff, Isaac VI, 238
atcliff, Isaac VI, 265
atcliff, Isaac C. IV, 266
atcliff, Isaac C. IV, 267
atcliff, Isabel IV, 1290
atcliff, Jacob V, 273
atcliff, Jacob V, 356
atcliff, Jacob V, 428
atcliff, Jacob V, 429
atcliff, Jacob V, 628
atcliff, Jacob V, 642
atcliff, Jacob VI, 209
Ratcliff, Jacob F. IV, 545
Ratcliff, Jane IV, 545
Ratcliff, Jane V, 273
Ratcliff, Jaon IV, 389
Ratcliff, Jehu V, 273
Ratcliff, Jesse IV, 545
Ratcliff, Jesse IV, 546
Ratcliff, Jesse V, 273
Ratcliff, Jesse V, 356
Ratcliff, Jesse V, 428
Ratcliff, Jesse V, 429
Ratcliff, Jesse V, 434
Ratcliff, Jesse C. I, 1161
Ratcliff, Job I, 384
Ratcliff, Job I, 416
Ratcliff, Job I, 417
Ratcliff, Joel V, 273
Ratcliff, Joel V, 428
Ratcliff, John I, 317
Ratcliff, John I, 416
Ratcliff, John II, 630
Ratcliff, John IV, 226
Ratcliff, John IV, 266
Ratcliff, John IV, 267
Ratcliff, John IV, 545
Ratcliff, John IV, 546
Ratcliff, John IV, 1075
Ratcliff, John V, 113
Ratcliff, John V, 273
Ratcliff, John V, 356
Ratcliff, John V, 383
Ratcliff, John V, 428
Ratcliff, John V, 792
Ratcliff, John VI, 34
Ratcliff, John VI, 35
Ratcliff, John VI, 155
Ratcliff, John VI, 156
Ratcliff, John VI, 184
Ratcliff, John VI, 209
Ratcliff, John VI, 265
Ratcliff, John A. VI, 210
Ratcliff, John C. IV, 267
Ratcliff, John Milton V, 429
Ratcliff, John T. V, 428
Ratcliff, John T. V, 429
Ratcliff, Jonathan I, 705
Ratcliff, Jonathan I, 996
Ratcliff, Jonathan V, 273
Ratcliff, Jordan VI, 8
Ratcliff, Joseph I, 163
Ratcliff, Joseph I, 687
Ratcliff, Joseph I, 705
Ratcliff, Joseph I, 995
Ratcliff, Joseph IV, 1290
Ratcliff, Joseph V, 273
Ratcliff, Joshua I, 163
Ratcliff, Joshua IV, 545
Ratcliff, Josiah IV, 212
Ratcliff, Josiah IV, 266
Ratcliff, Josiah IV, 267
Ratcliff, Josiah IV, 432
Ratcliff, Josiah IV, 529
Ratcliff, Josiah IV, 988
Ratcliff, Josiah VI, 166
Ratcliff, Josiah VI, 170
Ratcliff, Josiah VI, 209
Ratcliff, Josiah VI, 210
Ratcliff, Josiah C. IV, 267
Ratcliff, Josiah C. IV, 432
Ratcliff, Josiah C. IV, 955
Ratcliff, Josiah C. IV, 988
Ratcliff, Josiah E. IV, 988
Ratcliff, Judith V, 428
Ratcliff, Julia A. IV, 267
Ratcliff, Lemuel IV, 545
Ratcliff, Lemuel IV, 546
Ratcliff, Lemuel IV, 1075
Ratcliff, Lewis IV, 545
Ratcliff, M. I, 1161
Ratcliff, Marcus I, 1161
Ratcliff, Margaret I, 163
Ratcliff, Margaret IV, 169
Ratcliff, Margaret IV, 267
Ratcliff, Margaret IV, 307
Ratcliff, Margaret V, 113
Ratcliff, Margaret V, 273
Ratcliff, Margaret V, 405
Ratcliff, Margaret V, 408
Ratcliff, Margaret V, 428
Ratcliff, Margaret V, 975
Ratcliff, Margaret VI, 209
Ratcliff, Margaret VI, 210
Ratcliff, Margaret VI, 238
Ratcliff, Margaret VI, 265
Ratcliff, Margaret Ann V, 273
Ratcliff, Margaret H. IV, 267
Ratcliff, Margaret H. V, 429
Ratcliff, Margaret W. IV, 227
Ratcliff, Margaret W. IV, 267
Ratcliff, Maria IV, 1075
Ratcliff, Martha IV, 251
Ratcliff, Martha IV, 266
Ratcliff, Martha IV, 267
Ratcliff, Martha IV, 307
Ratcliff, Martha IV, 515
Ratcliff, Martha IV, 529
Ratcliff, Martha IV, 545
Ratcliff, Martha IV, 546
Ratcliff, Martha IV, 1070
Ratcliff, Martha IV, 1075
Ratcliff, Martha V, 425
Ratcliff, Martha V, 428
Ratcliff, Martha VI, 210
Ratcliff, Martha VI, 265
Ratcliff, Martha J. IV, 266
Ratcliff, Martha J. IV, 267
Ratcliff, Martha J. V, 975
Ratcliff, Martha M. IV, 545
Ratcliff, Mary I, 377
Ratcliff, Mary I, 417
Ratcliff, Mary I, 697
Ratcliff, Mary I, 705
Ratcliff, Mary I, 996
Ratcliff, Mary I Sup 1, 5
Ratcliff, Mary IV, 106
Ratcliff, Mary IV, 109
Ratcliff, Mary IV, 169
Ratcliff, Mary IV, 198
Ratcliff, Mary IV, 212
Ratcliff, Mary IV, 238
Ratcliff, Mary IV, 266
Ratcliff, Mary IV, 267
Ratcliff, Mary IV, 389
Ratcliff, Mary IV, 432
Ratcliff, Mary IV, 523
Ratcliff, Mary IV, 545
Ratcliff, Mary IV, 546
Ratcliff, Mary IV, 950
Ratcliff, Mary IV, 988
Ratcliff, Mary V, 113
Ratcliff, Mary V, 428
Ratcliff, Mary VI, 33
Ratcliff, Mary VI, 34
Ratcliff, Mary VI, 155
Ratcliff, Mary VI, 156
Ratcliff, Mary VI, 209
Ratcliff, Mary VI, 210
Ratcliff, Mary VI, 265
Ratcliff, Mary VI, 810
Ratcliff, Mary B. IV, 187
Ratcliff, Mary B. IV, 266
Ratcliff, Mary B. IV, 267
Ratcliff, Mary E. V, 628
Ratcliff, Mary E. V, 642
Ratcliff, Mary Elizabeth IV, 267
Ratcliff, Mary Ellyson IV, 432
Ratcliff, Mary Judith IV, 988
Ratcliff, Mildred IV, 55
Ratcliff, Mildred IV, 267
Ratcliff, Mildred V, 273
Ratcliff, Mildred VI, 209
Ratcliff, Mildred VI, 337
Ratcliff, Mildred VI, 434
Ratcliff, Moses V, 113
Ratcliff, Moses V, 273
Ratcliff, Moses V, 356
Ratcliff, Moses V, 428
Ratcliff, Moses V, 429
Ratcliff, Nancy VI, 434
Ratcliff, Nathan I, 705
Ratcliff, Nathan I, 996
Ratcliff, Nathan V, 429
Ratcliff, Phinehas I, 996
Ratcliff, Rachel I, 377
Ratcliff, Rachel I, 416
Ratcliff, Rachel I, 417
Ratcliff, Rachel IV, 529
Ratcliff, Rachel V, 273
Ratcliff, Rachel V, 332
Ratcliff, Rachel V, 356
Ratcliff, Rachel V, 428
Ratcliff, Rachel V, 642
Ratcliff, Rachel VI, 166
Ratcliff, Rachel VI, 170
Ratcliff, Rachel VI, 209
Ratcliff, Rachel VI, 210
Ratcliff, Rachel M. IV, 1075
Ratcliff, Rebecca IV, 267
Ratcliff, Rebecca IV, 546
Ratcliff, Rebecca IV, 1075
Ratcliff, Rebecca IV, 1078
Ratcliff, Rebecca V, 273
Ratcliff, Rebecca V, 428
Ratcliff, Rebecca V, 429
Ratcliff, Rebecca V, 434
Ratcliff, Rebecca VI, 34
Ratcliff, Rebecca B. IV, 267
Ratcliff, Rebecca B. IV, 288
Ratcliff, Rich, Senior VI, 35
Ratcliff, Richard I, 314
Ratcliff, Richard I, 317
Ratcliff, Richard I, 705
Ratcliff, Richard I, 995
Ratcliff, Richard I, 996
Ratcliff, Richard I Sup 1, 3
Ratcliff, Richard VI, 8
Ratcliff, Richard VI, 18
Ratcliff, Richard VI, 30
Ratcliff, Richard VI, 31
Ratcliff, Richard VI, 32
Ratcliff, Richard VI, 34
Ratcliff, Richard VI, 35
Ratcliff, Richard VI, 37
Ratcliff, Richard VI, 41
Ratcliff, Richard VI, 42
Ratcliff, Richard Updegraff IV, 267
Ratcliff, Richard, Senior VI, 35
Ratcliff, Richard, Senior VI, 36
Ratcliff, Richard, Sr. VI, 34
Ratcliff, Robert IV, 267
Ratcliff, Robert IV, 546
Ratcliff, Robert F. IV, 432
Ratcliff, Robert F. IV, 546
Ratcliff, Robert Fleming VI, 210
Ratcliff, Ruby E. I, 1161
Ratcliff, Sally Ann IV, 266
Ratcliff, Sally Ann VI, 209
Ratcliff, Sara VI, 32
Ratcliff, Sara VI, 34
Ratcliff, Sarah I, 163
Ratcliff, Sarah I, 377
Ratcliff, Sarah I, 416
Ratcliff, Sarah I, 417
Ratcliff, Sarah IV, 185
Ratcliff, Sarah IV, 221
Ratcliff, Sarah IV, 226
Ratcliff, Sarah IV, 266
Ratcliff, Sarah IV, 267
Ratcliff, Sarah IV, 306
Ratcliff, Sarah IV, 545
Ratcliff, Sarah IV, 546
Ratcliff, Sarah IV, 559
Ratcliff, Sarah V, 113
Ratcliff, Sarah V, 273
Ratcliff, Sarah V, 356
Ratcliff, Sarah V, 359
Ratcliff, Sarah V, 383
Ratcliff, Sarah V, 428
Ratcliff, Sarah V, 429
Ratcliff, Sarah V, 431
Ratcliff, Sarah V, 434
Ratcliff, Sarah VI, 8
Ratcliff, Sarah VI, 34
Ratcliff, Sarah Ann IV, 545
Ratcliff, Sarah Ann IV, 546
Ratcliff, Sarah Ann IV, 1075
Ratcliff, Sarah Ann VI, 210
Ratcliff, Sarah E. IV, 267
Ratcliff, Sarah Eleanor V, 273
Ratcliff, Sarah Elizabeth V, 273
Ratcliff, Sarah Esther IV, 267
Ratcliff, Sarah Esther IV, 304
Ratcliff, Sarah Esther IV, 1290
Ratcliff, Sarah Esther IV, 1299
Ratcliff, Sarah J. IV, 267
Ratcliff, Sarah J. VI, 209
Ratcliff, Sarah J. VI, 210
Ratcliff, Sarah Jane V, 428
Ratcliff, Sarah Jane V, 429
Ratcliff, Sarah Jordan VI, 155
Ratcliff, Sarah Jordan VI, 156
Ratcliff, Sarah Jordan VI, 209
Ratcliff, Sary I, 417
Ratcliff, Silas V, 429
Ratcliff, Susan V, 428
Ratcliff, Susan V, 429
Ratcliff, Tacy IV, 389
Ratcliff, Tamer I, 384
Ratcliff, Tamer I, 416
Ratcliff, Tamer I, 417
Ratcliff, Thomas I, 163
Ratcliff, Thomas I, 835
Ratcliff, Thomas I, 996
Ratcliff, Thomas V, 273
Ratcliff, Thomas V, 356
Ratcliff, Thomas V, 428
Ratcliff, Thomas V, 429
Ratcliff, Wd. Elizabeth VI, 31
Ratcliff, Widow Mary I, 163
Ratcliff, William IV, 266
Ratcliff, William IV, 267
Ratcliff, William IV, 306
Ratcliff, William IV, 545
Ratcliff, William IV, 546
Ratcliff, William VI, 18
Ratcliff, William VI, 155
Ratcliff, William VI, 156
Ratcliff, William VI, 209
Ratcliff, William VI, 210
Ratcliff, William VI, 265
Ratcliff, William F. IV, 267
Ratcliff, William F. IV, 545
Ratcliff, William N. IV, 545
Ratcliff, William R. IV, 267
Ratcliff, William R. IV, 988
Ratcliff, Wm F. IV, 185
Ratcliff, Wm. IV, 238
Ratcliff, Wm. IV, 266
Ratcliff, Wm. IV, 267
Ratcliff, Wm. IV, 559
Ratcliff, Wm. F. IV, 266
Ratcliff, Wm. F. IV, 267
Ratcliff, Wm. F. IV, 546
Ratcliff, Wm. N. IV, 267
Ratcliff, Wm. R. IV, 267
Ratcliff, Wm. R. IV, 304
Ratcliff, Wm. R. IV, 1290
Ratcliff, Wm. R. IV, 1299
Ratcliffe, Ann VI, 550
Ratcliffe, Harriet VI, 550
Ratcliffe, Joshua VI, 550
Ratcliffe, Mary E. VI, 550
Ratcliffe, Nancy VI, 434
Ratcliffe, Nancy VI, 550
Ratcliffe, Sally VI, 550
Ratcliffe, Thomas VI, 550
Rate, John III, 263
Ratekin, John VI, 849
Ratekin, John, Jr. VI, 849
Ratekin, Lawrence VI, 819
Ratekin, Lawrence VI, 849
Ratekin, Martha VI, 815
Ratekin, Nancy VI, 849
Ratekin, Polly VI, 849
Ratekin, Rachel VI, 819
Ratekin, Rebekah VI, 819
Ratekin, Susan VI, 849
Rath, Alice III, 398
Rath, Alice III, 439
Rathbone, Anna D. III, 263
Rathbone, Francis III, 263
Rathbone, Francis H. III, 263
Rathbone, Hiram G. VI, 982
Rathbone, Susan III, 263
Rathbone, Susan III, 348
Rathbone, Tirzah VI, 982
Rathborne, Ann Maria III, 263
Rathborne, Charles Lambert III, 263
Rathborne, Chas. Lambert III, 143
Rathborne, Eliz. Leedom III, 143
Rathborne, Eliz. Leedom III, 263
Rathborne, Rich. III, 263
Rathburn, Hiram G. VI, 933
Rathburn, Pearl IV, 1181
Rather, Daniel B. VI, 911
Rather, Daniel B. VI, 982
Rather, Elizabeth VI, 964
Rather, James VI, 947
Rather, Martha L. VI, 982
Rather, Mary Ann VI, 930
Rather, Mary Ann, Sr. VI, 930
Rather, Nancy VI, 982
Rather, Rawley VI, 982
Rather, Sally VI, 979
Rather, Samuel VI, 964
Rather, Samuel VI, 979
Rather, Samuel VI, 999
Rathmel, John II, 1022
Rathmell, John II, 252
Rathmell, Mary II, 252
Rathmier, Ella IV, 267
Ratiken, James VI, 467
Ratiken, Jane VI, 467
Ratiken, Susannah VI, 467
Ratleiff, Lydia I, 996
Ratlife, Richard VI, 35
Ratliff, Abigail I, 705
Ratliff, Abigail I, 732
Ratliff, Abner I, 416
Ratliff, Abner V, 428
Ratliff, Abner V, 429
Ratliff, Amos V, 273
Ratliff, Amos V, 428
Ratliff, Ann I, 664
Ratliff, Ann I, 732
Ratliff, Ann V, 113
Ratliff, Ann V, 428
Ratliff, Ann V, 429
Ratliff, Anna I, 993
Ratliff, Anna I, 996
Ratliff, Axa I, 996
Ratliff, Benjamin I, 70
Ratliff, Benjamin I, 732
Ratliff, Benjamin I, 996
Ratliff, Benjamin B. IV, 1075
Ratliff, Bettie I, 664
Ratliff, Betty I, 317
Ratliff, Betty I, 732
Ratliff, Betty I, 996
Ratliff, Carl M. I, 1161
Ratliff, Catharine I, 163
Ratliff, Catharine I, 191
Ratliff, Catharine I, 199
Ratliff, Cathrine I, 199
Ratliff, Charles IV, 1075
Ratliff, Cornelis I, 42
Ratliff, Cornelis I, 70
Ratliff, Cornelius I, 70
Ratliff, Cornelius I, 695
Ratliff, Cornelius I, 705
Ratliff, Cornelius I, 732
Ratliff, Cornelius I, 733
Ratliff, Cornelius V, 89
Ratliff, Cornelius V, 113
Ratliff, Dorcas V, 428
Ratliff, Edom V, 428
Ratliff, Edward IV, 546
Ratliff, Eleanor V, 273
Ratliff, Eleanor V, 428
Ratliff, Elias I, 996
Ratliff, Elias V, 273
Ratliff, Elijah I, 1071
Ratliff, Elisabeth I, 42
Ratliff, Elisabeth I, 62
Ratliff, Elisabeth I, 70
Ratliff, Elisabeth I, 73
Ratliff, Elisabeth I, 199
Ratliff, Elisha IV, 546
Ratliff, Eliza I, 70
Ratliff, Elizabeth I, 70
Ratliff, Elizabeth I, 695
Ratliff, Elizabeth I, 705
Ratliff, Elizabeth I, 729
Ratliff, Elizabeth I, 732
Ratliff, Elizabeth I, 733
Ratliff, Elizabeth IV, 1075
Ratliff, Elizabeth V, 113
Ratliff, Elizabeth V, 273
Ratliff, Elizabeth V, 382
Ratliff, Elizabeth V, 428
Ratliff, Elizabeth VI, 34
Ratliff, Ellenor V, 428
Ratliff, Ephraim I, 70
Ratliff, Ephraim I, 732
Ratliff, Ephraim I, 996
Ratliff, Gabriel I, 996
Ratliff, Gulielma I, 705
Ratliff, Gulielma I, 732
Ratliff, Hannah I, 61
Ratliff, Hannah I, 70
Ratliff, Hannah I, 199
Ratliff, Hannah I, 732
Ratliff, Hannah I, 996
Ratliff, Hannah A. I, 1161
Ratliff, Isaac V, 428
Ratliff, Jacob V, 402

Ratliff, Jacob V, 428
Ratliff, Jas. VI, 962
Ratliff, Jehu V, 273
Ratliff, Jesse V, 428
Ratliff, Jesse C. I, 1161
Ratliff, Joel V, 428
Ratliff, John IV, 1075
Ratliff, John V, 428
Ratliff, Johnnathan I, 996
Ratliff, Jonathan I, 664
Ratliff, Jonathan I, 996
Ratliff, Jonathan V, 273
Ratliff, Joseph I, 49
Ratliff, Joseph I, 62
Ratliff, Joseph I, 70
Ratliff, Joseph I, 199
Ratliff, Joseph I, 487
Ratliff, Joseph I, 664
Ratliff, Joseph I, 705
Ratliff, Joseph I, 732
Ratliff, Joseph I, 991
Ratliff, Joseph I, 995
Ratliff, Joseph I, 996
Ratliff, Joseph V, 273
Ratliff, Joshua I, 70
Ratliff, Joshua I, 256
Ratliff, Joshua I, 732
Ratliff, Joshua I, 996
Ratliff, Juliemma I, 732
Ratliff, Juliemma I, 1066
Ratliff, Lemuel IV, 1075
Ratliff, Leticia I, 996
Ratliff, Lydia I, 996
Ratliff, M. I, 1161
Ratliff, Margaret I, 732
Ratliff, Margaret V, 428
Ratliff, Margaret Ann V, 273
Ratliff, Margret I, 70
Ratliff, Margret I, 996
Ratliff, Marjory VI, 962
Ratliff, Martha IV, 1075
Ratliff, Martha V, 428
Ratliff, Mary I, 49
Ratliff, Mary I, 70
Ratliff, Mary I, 705
Ratliff, Mary I, 732
Ratliff, Mary I, 734
Ratliff, Mary I, 898
Ratliff, Mary I, 985
Ratliff, Mary I, 996
Ratliff, Mary IV, 922
Ratliff, Mary IV, 988
Ratliff, Mary V, 89
Ratliff, Mary V, 113
Ratliff, Mary V, 402
Ratliff, Milicent I, 732
Ratliff, Milisant I, 705
Ratliff, Moses V, 273
Ratliff, Moses V, 428
Ratliff, Nathan I, 996
Ratliff, Phinehas I, 732
Ratliff, Phinehas I, 996
Ratliff, Phonhas I, 996
Ratliff, Polly I, 732
Ratliff, Polly I, 1066
Ratliff, Rachel V, 428
Ratliff, Rebecah I, 996
Ratliff, Rebecca V, 273
Ratliff, Rebekah I, 991
Ratliff, Rebekah I, 996
Ratliff, Richard I, 664
Ratliff, Richard I, 732
Ratliff, Richard I, 995
Ratliff, Richard I, 996
Ratliff, Ruby E. I, 1161
Ratliff, Ruth I, 705
Ratliff, Ruth Anne V, 927
Ratliff, Samuel I, 996
Ratliff, Sarah I, 62
Ratliff, Sarah I, 70
Ratliff, Sarah I, 90
Ratliff, Sarah I, 416
Ratliff, Sarah I, 705
Ratliff, Sarah I, 732
Ratliff, Sarah I, 991
Ratliff, Sarah I, 996
Ratliff, Sarah I, 1066
Ratliff, Sarah V, 113
Ratliff, Sarah V, 273
Ratliff, Sarah V, 428
Ratliff, Sarah V, 429
Ratliff, Sarah Ann IV, 1075
Ratliff, Sarah Eleanor V, 273
Ratliff, Sisley V, 794
Ratliff, Thomas I, 61
Ratliff, Thomas I, 70
Ratliff, Thomas I, 732
Ratliff, Thomas I, 996
Ratliff, Thomas I, 1066
Ratliff, Thomas V, 428
Ratliff, Thomas V, 429
Ratliff, Widow Sarah I, 45
Ratliff, Widow Sarah I, 70
Ratliff, Zachariah Nixon, Sr. I, 70
Ratliffe, Mary VI, 982
Ratliffe, Thomas VI, 982
Ratlifft, Dammaras I, 54
Ratlifft, Dammaras I, 65
Ratlifft, Dammaras I, 68
Ratlifft, Joseph I, 54
Ratlifft, Joseph I, 65
Ratlifft, Joseph I, 68
Ratlifft, Joseph I, 70
Ratlyff, Mary VI, 45
Ratlyff, Mary VI, 46
Rattakin, Catharine VI, 838
Rattcliff, Amos I, 417
Rattcliff, Ann I, 417
Rattcliff, Elender I, 417
Rattcliff, Elizabeth I, 416
Rattcliff, Elizabeth I, 419
Rattcliff, Hannah I, 416
Rattcliff, Jesse I, 416
Rattcliff, Job I, 416
Rattcliff, Job I, 417
Rattcliff, John I, 279
Rattcliff, Rachel I, 417
Rattcliff, Rebecca VI, 31
Rattcliff, Richard VI, 31
Rattcliff, Richard VI, 35
Rattcliff, Sarah I, 385
Rattcliff, Sarah I, 416
Rattcliff, Sary I, 417
Rattcliff, Tamer I, 416
Rattcliff, Thomas I, 416
Rattclift, Richard VI, 35
Rattekin, James VI, 500
Rattekin, James VI, 550
Rattekin, Ruth VI, 500
Rattekin, Ruth VI, 550
Rattekin, Sarah VI, 550
Rattekin, Susannah VI, 550
Rattikan, Ruth VI, 550
Rattikin, James VI, 499
Rattikin, Jas. VI, 502
Rattikin, Ruth VI, 499
Rattikin, Sarah VI, 587
Rattikin, Susannah VI, 499
Rattiskane, James IV, 267
Rattiskane, James Hague IV, 267
Rattiskane, Susanna IV, 267
Rattliff, Joseph I, 142
Rattliff, Mary I, 142
Rattliff, Richard VI, 35
Rattliff, Widow Mary I, 142
Rattliff, Widow Mary I, 163
Raub, Henry III, 263
Raub, Henry III, 372
Raub, Margaret III, 263
Raub, Margaret III, 372
Raudabaugh, Clara E. V, 1015
Raudabaugh, Eva V, 1015
Raudabaugh, Jacob R. V, 1015
Raudabaugh, Jessie V, 1015
Raudabaugh, Phoeba R. V, 1015
Raudabaugh, Wm. V, 1015
Raulings, Ann II, 244
Raulings, Ann II, 256
Raulings, Thomas II, 256
Raulings, Thos. II, 244
Raurton, Rebekah II, 411
Rausbarger, Phillip VI, 804
Rausbarger, Polly VI, 804
Rausin, Edward A. I, 1161
Ravenaugh, John I, 926
Ravenaugh, Katharine I, 926
Ravenaugh, Mary Ellen I, 926
Ravincraft, William I, 1037
Ravis, Nathaniel III, 263
Ravis, Peter III, 263
Ravis, Thomas III, 263
Rawle, Benjamin II, 630
Rawle, Beulah II, 411
Rawle, Beulah II, 630
Rawle, Beulah Howell II, 630
Rawle, Burge II, 630
Rawle, Caleb II, 557
Rawle, Edward II, 411
Rawle, Edward II, 630
Rawle, Edward Warner II, 630
Rawle, Edward Warner II, 650
Rawle, Elizabeth II, 411
Rawle, Elizabeth Margaret II, 411
Rawle, Francis II, 411
Rawle, Francis II, 478
Rawle, Francis II, 493
Rawle, Francis II, 550
Rawle, Francis II, 630
Rawle, Francis II, 672
Rawle, Francis II, 678
Rawle, Francis William II, 411
Rawle, Francis, Sr. II, 411
Rawle, Francis-Wm. II, 630
Rawle, George II, 557
Rawle, Hannah II, 558
Rawle, Hannah II, 630
Rawle, Henry II, 411
Rawle, Henry II, 630
Rawle, Horatio II, 411
Rawle, Horatio II, 630
Rawle, Jane II, 411
Rawle, Jane II, 630
Rawle, John II, 411
Rawle, Juliet II, 411
Rawle, Juliet II, 630
Rawle, Margaret II, 411
Rawle, Margaret II, 550
Rawle, Margaret Hodge II, 630
Rawle, Martha II, 411
Rawle, Martha II, 630
Rawle, Mary II, 411
Rawle, Mary II, 493
Rawle, Mary II, 630
Rawle, Mary II, 678
Rawle, Rebecca II, 411
Rawle, Rebecca II, 478
Rawle, Rebecca II, 630
Rawle, Rebecca II, 650
Rawle, Rebecca II, 678
Rawle, Rebecca Shoemaker II, 411
Rawle, Rebecca Shoemaker II, 630
Rawle, Rebeckah II, 678
Rawle, Robert II, 411
Rawle, Sarah II, 411
Rawle, Sarah II, 557
Rawle, Sarah II, 630
Rawle, Sarah Burge II, 411
Rawle, Sarah Coates II, 478
Rawle, Sarah Coates II, 630
Rawle, William II, 411
Rawle, Wm. II, 478
Rawle, Wm. II, 550
Rawle, Wm. II, 630
Rawles, Burwell V, 595
Rawles, Burwell VI, 138
Rawles, Burwell VI, 139
Rawles, David VI, 139
Rawles, Elizabeth V, 595
Rawles, Esther V, 595
Rawles, Francis II, 447
Rawles, Jane II, 517
Rawles, Jane II, 630
Rawles, Jesse V, 595
Rawles, John II, 411
Rawles, John V, 595
Rawles, Jonathan V, 595
Rawles, Martha II, 411
Rawles, Martha II, 447
Rawles, Mary Ann V, 595
Rawles, Mary Ann VI, 139
Rawles, Micajah V, 595
Rawles, Micajah VI, 139
Rawles, Michael V, 595
Rawles, Michel V, 595
Rawles, Robert II, 411
Rawles, Sarah II, 411
Rawles, Sarah V, 595
Rawles, Sarah VI, 138
Rawles, Sarah VI, 139
Rawles, Sarah Jane V, 595
Rawles, William V, 595
Rawlings, ??? VI, 637
Rawlings, ??? VI, 693
Rawlings, Abbie T. IV, 653
Rawlings, Abbie T. IV, 665
Rawlings, Alfred III, 263
Rawlings, Alvin VI, 812
Rawlings, Ann II, 256
Rawlings, Ann IV, 706
Rawlings, Annie Virginia VI, 637
Rawlings, Annie Virginia VI, 638
Rawlings, Annie Virginia VI, 640
Rawlings, Annie Virginia VI, 645
Rawlings, Annie Virginia VI, 693
Rawlings, James VI, 772
Rawlings, John VI, 772
Rawlings, John Edward III, 263
Rawlings, Joseph IV, 706
Rawlings, Margaret IV, 706
Rawlings, Margaret IV, 753
Rawlings, Margaret IV, 882
Rawlings, Marshall VI, 637
Rawlings, Marshall VI, 693
Rawlings, Mary VI, 736
Rawlings, Mary VI, 772
Rawlings, Robert VI, 772
Rawlings, Samuel VI, 772
Rawlings, W. Annie Virginia VI, 686
Rawlins, Lucy VI, 856
Rawlins, Mary VI, 834
Rawlins, Polly VI, 834
Rawlinson, Ann V, 273
Rawlinson, Elizabeth II, 630
Rawlinson, Maymie V, 273
Rawlinson, Thomas V, 273
Rawls, Berwell IV, 753
Rawls, Burnwell V, 642
Rawls, Burrel VI, 84
Rawls, Burrell VI, 84
Rawls, Burwell IV, 753
Rawls, Burwell IV, 914
Rawls, Burwell V, 524
Rawls, Burwell V, 595
Rawls, Burwell VI, 84
Rawls, Burwell VI, 139
Rawls, Catharine V, 639
Rawls, Catharine V, 642
Rawls, David IV, 753
Rawls, David IV, 914
Rawls, David VI, 84
Rawls, David VI, 139
Rawls, Elizabeth IV, 753
Rawls, Elizabeth IV, 914
Rawls, Elizabeth V, 524
Rawls, Elizabeth V, 595
Rawls, Elizabeth V, 642
Rawls, Elizabeth VI, 84
Rawls, Esther IV, 753
Rawls, Esther IV, 914
Rawls, Esther V, 524
Rawls, Esther V, 595
Rawls, Esther V, 609
Rawls, Esther V, 642
Rawls, Esther V, 975
Rawls, Esther F. V, 642
Rawls, Esther T. V, 975
Rawls, Jackson VI, 79
Rawls, Jackson VI, 83
Rawls, Jehu V, 975
Rawls, Jesse V, 524
Rawls, Jesse V, 595
Rawls, Jesse V, 642
Rawls, Jesse V, 975
Rawls, Jesse John V, 524
Rawls, John V, 524
Rawls, John V, 595
Rawls, John V, 642
Rawls, John V, 975
Rawls, John VI, 83
Rawls, John VI, 84
Rawls, Jonathan IV, 753
Rawls, Jonathan IV, 914
Rawls, Jonathan V, 524
Rawls, Jonathan V, 595
Rawls, Jonathan V, 642
Rawls, Margaret Ann VI, 92
Rawls, Maria VI, 79
Rawls, Maria VI, 83
Rawls, Maria L. VI, 79
Rawls, Maria L. VI, 83
Rawls, Mary VI, 84
Rawls, Mary Ann IV, 753
Rawls, Mary Ann IV, 914
Rawls, Mary Ann V, 592
Rawls, Mary Ann V, 642
Rawls, Mary Ann V, 975
Rawls, Mary Ann VI, 84
Rawls, Mary Ann VI, 139
Rawls, Micajah IV, 753
Rawls, Micajah IV, 914
Rawls, Micajah V, 642
Rawls, Micajah VI, 84
Rawls, Micajah VI, 139
Rawls, Michael IV, 753
Rawls, Michael IV, 914
Rawls, Michael V, 524
Rawls, Michal IV, 753
Rawls, Michal V, 642
Rawls, Michel V, 595
Rawls, Sarah IV, 753
Rawls, Sarah IV, 914
Rawls, Sarah V, 524
Rawls, Sarah V, 595
Rawls, Sarah V, 642
Rawls, Sarah V, 975
Rawls, Sarah V, 979
Rawls, Sarah VI, 84
Rawls, Sarah VI, 139
Rawls, Sarah Jane V, 524
Rawls, Sarah Jane V, 595
Rawls, Sarah Jane V, 616
Rawls, Sarah Jane V, 642
Rawls, Sarah Jane V, 975
Rawls, Tabitha VI, 84
Rawls, William IV, 753
Rawls, William IV, 914
Rawls, William V, 524
Rawls, William V, 642
Rawly, Francis, Sr. II, 411
Rawnsley, John I, 417
Rawnsley, John I, 447
Rawnsley, John I, 453
Rawnsley, Sarah I, 417
Rawnsley, Sarah I, 447
Rawnsly, Sarah I, 417
Rawson, Alice Leota IV, 267
Rawson, Arthur Joy III, 58
Rawson, Arthur Joy III, 263
Rawson, Arthur Joy VI, 693
Rawson, Charlotte III, 263
Rawson, Chas. E. IV, 267
Rawson, E. Marion III, 94
Rawson, Edward B. III, 263
Rawson, Edward B. III, 294
Rawson, Edward B. VI, 693
Rawson, Edward B. VI, 704
Rawson, Edward Briggs VI, 70
Rawson, Edward J. VI, 704
Rawson, Edward Joy VI, 664
Rawson, Edward Joy VI, 666
Rawson, Edward Joy VI, 693
Rawson, Edward Sidney III, 25
Rawson, Edward Sidney III, 26
Rawson, Edward Sidney VI, 69
Rawson, Eleanor III, 19
Rawson, Eliz. A. III, 263
Rawson, Eliza F. III, 263
Rawson, Eliza F. VI, 666
Rawson, Eliza F. VI, 693
Rawson, Eliza F. Coffin VI, 664
Rawson, Elizabeth VI, 693
Rawson, Elizabeth A. VI, 666
Rawson, Elizabeth A. VI, 693
Rawson, Elizabeth A. VI, 704
Rawson, Gertrude III, 195
Rawson, Gertrude III, 263
Rawson, Gertrude VI, 693
Rawson, Helen H. VI, 693
Rawson, Jane IV, 267
Rawson, Jonathan III, 263
Rawson, Jonathan A. III, 94
Rawson, Jonathan A. III, 263
Rawson, Jonathan A., Jr. III, 241
Rawson, Jonathan A., Jr. III, 26
Rawson, Katharine III, 259
Rawson, Katharine III, 263
Rawson, Katharine VI, 693
Rawson, Margaret III, 58
Rawson, Margaret III, 263
Rawson, Margaret VI, 693
Rawson, Marian N. III, 263
Rawson, Marianna III, 263
Rawson, Marianna III, 294
Rawson, Marianna VI, 693
Rawson, Marianna VI, 704
Rawson, Marianna S. III, 263
Rawson, Marianna S. VI, 693
Rawson, Marion III, 241
Rawson, Marion III, 263
Rawson, Mary VI, 693
Rawson, Mary Anna VI, 702
Rawson, Philip Nichols III, 195
Rawson, Philip Nichols III, 263
Rawson, Philip Nichols VI, 693
Rawson, Priscilla III, 94
Rawson, Priscilla III, 263
Rawson, Priscilla A. III, 263
Rawson, Priscilla Alden III, 263
Rawson, Samuel IV, 267
Rawson, Tabitha IV, 267
Rawson, Valentine Kirk III, 19
Ray, ??? III, 263
Ray, Albert V, 1015
Ray, Alce I, 1062
Ray, Alec I, 898
Ray, Allen VI, 434
Ray, Ann VI, 434
Ray, Anna C. III, 263
Ray, Benjamin VI, 982
Ray, Bessie I, 898
Ray, Christopher III, 263
Ray, Christopher III, 275
Ray, Christopher III, 279
Ray, Christopher III, 368
Ray, Clarissa VI, 982
Ray, Deborah VI, 434
Ray, Elizabeth II, 37
Ray, Elizabeth II, 56
Ray, Elizabeth II, 93
Ray, Elizabeth III, 263
Ray, Elizabeth III, 275
Ray, Elizabeth III, 368
Ray, Elizabeth IV, 83
Ray, Elizabeth IV, 101
Ray, Elizabeth IV, 107
Ray, Elizabeth V, 113
Ray, Emeline I, 882
Ray, Emeline I, 898
Ray, Fanny VI, 982
Ray, Fanny VI, 1002
Ray, Francis H. III, 263

ay, Francis H. VI, 693
ay, Frank A. III, 198
ay, Frank A. III, 263
ay, George VI, 982
ay, Hannah I, 408
ay, Hannah I, 417
ay, Hannah I, 453
ay, Hannah W. III, 275
ay, Hope VI, 982
ay, Hugh I, 70
ay, Hugh VI, 179
ay, Hugh VI, 210
ay, James I, 898
ay, James VI, 982
ay, John II, 411
ay, John III, 264
ay, John V, 463
ay, John VI, 434
ay, John VI, 604
ay, John VI, 970
ay, John VI, 982
ay, Jonathan I, 568
ay, Jonathan I Sup 1, 9
ay, Jonathan VI, 337
ay, Joseph I, 70
ay, Joseph VI, 265
ay, Joseph VI, 434
ay, Joseph Iddings I, 568
ay, Joseph S. II, 411
ay, Judith VI, 210
ay, Kate III, 198
ay, Kate III, 263
ay, Louisa IV, 805
ay, Louisa IV, 840
ay, Lucy VI, 818
ay, Lucy Jane VI, 982
ay, Lucy W. III, 263
ay, Luke VI, 982
ay, Luke John VI, 1002
ay, Luke, Jr. VI, 994
ay, Luke, Sr. VI, 970
ay, Luke, Sr. VI, 982
ay, Mae V, 463
ay, Marah IV, 840
ay, Margaret III, 263
ay, Margaret VI, 434
ay, Martha III, 263
ay, Mary II, 411
ay, Mary IV, 840
ay, Mary VI, 982
ay, Mary A. V, 273
ay, Pamela VI, 982
ay, Phebe IV, 101
ay, Phebe IV, 106
ay, Phebe IV, 107
ay, Polly VI, 970
ay, Polly VI, 982
ay, Rachel I, 453
ay, Rachel VI, 426
ay, Rachel J. V, 273
ay, Rebecca V, 113
ay, Rebecca VI, 434
ay, Rebeckah VI, 434
ay, Rebeckah, Jr. V, 113
ay, Rebekah V, 113
ay, Rebekah VI, 434
ay, Robert V, 113
ay, Robert VI, 434
ay, Ruth I, 932
ay, Sally VI, 982
ay, Sarah I, 256
ay, Sarah II, 93
ay, Sarah III, 279
ay, Sarah VI, 434
ay, Sarah VI, 982
ay, Sarah Sloan I, 948
ay, Schuyler G. VI, 982
ay, Simeon VI, 982
ay, Susanna VI, 434
ay, Thomas IV, 840
ay, Thomas VI, 434
ay, Thomas VI, 982
ay, Vena IV, 267
ay, William VI, 982
ay, Wm. IV, 101
ay, Wm. Anthony III, 263
ayborn, Ann E. V, 590
ayborn, James V, 594
ayborn, James W. IV, 1261
ayborn, Laura B. V, 594
ayborn, Samuel IV, 1261
ayborn, Samuel V, 594
ayborn, Susanna IV, 1261
ayborn, Susannah V, 594
ayburn, Ann Eliza V, 701
ayburn, Emeline V, 357
ayburn, Ethel V, 692
ayburn, Ethel V, 706
ayburn, James V, 594
ayburn, James V, 706
ayburn, James N. V, 113
Rayburn, James W. IV, 1261
Rayburn, James W. V, 594
Rayburn, Laura V, 706
Rayburn, Laura B. V, 594
Rayburn, Lydia V, 357
Rayburn, Margaret V, 113
Rayburn, Marley V, 357
Rayburn, May V, 357
Rayburn, Myrtie V, 357
Rayburn, Nellie V, 357
Rayburn, Samuel V, 594
Rayburn, Samuel V, 706
Rayburn, Susanna V, 594
Rayburn, Susannah V, 594
Rayburn, Susannah V, 706
Rayburn, Thomas W. V, 357
Rayburn, William V, 357
Rayburn, Wm. C. V, 357
Rayburne, James W. IV, 1261
Raydon, William II, 447
Rayer, Ida V, 1015
Rayer, Ida F. V, 1015
Rayer, Mamie IV, 1290
Rayfield, Angeline B. IV, 267
Rayford, Bertha Gertrude I, 212
Rayford, Edward I, 212
Rayl, Abigail Jane I, 603
Rayl, Adison I, 603
Rayl, Adison I, 607
Rayl, Adna I, 603
Rayl, Adna I, 607
Rayl, Adna Collins I, 513
Rayl, Ahiomelus I, 513
Rayl, Ahiomelus I, 603
Rayl, Alpeus P. I, 603
Rayl, Alphius I, 607
Rayl, Alphus I, 603
Rayl, Ann I, 513
Rayl, Ann I, 568
Rayl, Ann I, 600
Rayl, Ann I, 603
Rayl, Ann I, 607
Rayl, Asa I, 513
Rayl, Asa I, 603
Rayl, Asa P. I, 513
Rayl, Asia I, 607
Rayl, Athelbert IV, 267
Rayl, Betsy I, 603
Rayl, Caleb I, 513
Rayl, Caleb I, 568
Rayl, Caleb I, 603
Rayl, Caleb I, 607
Rayl, Charles I, 603
Rayl, Charles I, 607
Rayl, David P. IV, 267
Rayl, David S. IV, 267
Rayl, Delilah I, 607
Rayl, Delinda I, 603
Rayl, Docter F. I, 603
Rayl, Doctor ??? I, 607
Rayl, Doctor Franklin I, 568
Rayl, Eliza I, 603
Rayl, Eliza I, 606
Rayl, Eliza I, 607
Rayl, Elizabeth I, 513
Rayl, Elizabeth I, 568
Rayl, Elizabeth I, 600
Rayl, Elizabeth I, 603
Rayl, Elizabeth I, 607
Rayl, Elizabeth Ann I, 603
Rayl, Elizabeth W. I, 513
Rayl, Elizabeth W. I, 607
Rayl, Elmina I, 568
Rayl, Emily Jane I, 603
Rayl, Enoch Macy I, 568
Rayl, George I, 513
Rayl, George I, 568
Rayl, George I, 581
Rayl, George I, 603
Rayl, George I, 607
Rayl, George, Jr. I, 568
Rayl, George, Jr. I, 607
Rayl, Hannah I, 568
Rayl, Hannah I, 600
Rayl, Hannah IV, 267
Rayl, Hannah Jane IV, 267
Rayl, Harmon I, 603
Rayl, Harmon I, 607
Rayl, Harper I, 568
Rayl, Hymelus I, 568
Rayl, Isaac B. I, 603
Rayl, Isaac W. I, 513
Rayl, Isaac W. I, 568
Rayl, Isaac W. I, 603
Rayl, Jabas I, 603
Rayl, Jabez I, 568
Rayl, Jacob B. I, 603
Rayl, James I, 513
Rayl, James I, 603
Rayl, James H. I, 513
Rayl, James H. I, 568
Rayl, James H. I, 603
Rayl, James H. I, 607
Rayl, Jane I, 513
Rayl, Jane I, 568
Rayl, Jane I, 603
Rayl, John W. I, 603
Rayl, Judith I, 568
Rayl, Julia Emlin I, 603
Rayl, Julian I, 607
Rayl, Julyan I, 603
Rayl, Lewis I, 603
Rayl, Lewis I, 607
Rayl, Lindsey I, 568
Rayl, Lindsey I, 603
Rayl, Luas I, 607
Rayl, Lucy IV, 267
Rayl, Lucy Elizabeth IV, 267
Rayl, Lues I, 603
Rayl, Lynch I, 513
Rayl, Lynch I, 568
Rayl, Lynch I, 603
Rayl, Lynch I, 607
Rayl, Mahala I, 603
Rayl, Mahala I, 607
Rayl, Margaret I, 568
Rayl, Margaret I, 607
Rayl, Margret I, 603
Rayl, Martha I, 603
Rayl, Martha I, 607
Rayl, Mary I, 550
Rayl, Mary I, 568
Rayl, Mary I, 603
Rayl, Mary Elizabeth I, 603
Rayl, Matthew I, 568
Rayl, Matthew I, 603
Rayl, Nancy I, 513
Rayl, Nancy I, 559
Rayl, Nancy I, 568
Rayl, Nancy I, 603
Rayl, Nancy I, 607
Rayl, Nathan I, 513
Rayl, Nathan I, 568
Rayl, Nathan I, 578
Rayl, Nathan I, 600
Rayl, Nathan I, 603
Rayl, Nathan I, 607
Rayl, Perlina I, 603
Rayl, Perlina I, 607
Rayl, Pleasant I, 513
Rayl, Pleasant I, 603
Rayl, Pleasant I, 607
Rayl, Rachel I, 513
Rayl, Rachel I, 568
Rayl, Rachel I, 572
Rayl, Rachel I, 603
Rayl, Rebecca Jane I, 568
Rayl, Rebeckah I, 513
Rayl, Richard I, 513
Rayl, Robert T. I, 568
Rayl, Samuel IV, 267
Rayl, Samuel A. IV, 267
Rayl, Susanna I, 513
Rayl, Susanna I, 568
Rayl, Susanna I, 578
Rayl, Susannah I, 603
Rayl, Thomas I, 513
Rayl, Thomas I, 568
Rayl, Thomas I, 600
Rayl, Thomas I, 603
Rayl, Thomas I, 607
Rayl, Thomas C. I, 513
Rayl, Thomas C. I, 603
Rayl, Thomas E. I, 603
Rayl, Thomas, Jr. I, 607
Rayl, Thornburgh I, 568
Rayl, Thornburgh I, 603
Rayl, Vesti I, 607
Rayl, William I, 513
Rayl, William I, 568
Rayl, William I, 600
Rayl, William I, 607
Rayl, William E. I, 513
Rayl, William R. I, 603
Rayl, William, Jr. I, 607
Rayl, William, Sr. I, 603
Rayl, Zadock I, 603
Rayl, Zodoc I, 607
Rayl, Zodock I, 603
Rayl, Zodock I, 607
Rayle, Ann I, 513
Rayle, Ann I, 550
Rayle, Ann I, 568
Rayle, Elizabeth I, 513
Rayle, Eunice Ella V, 198
Rayle, George I, 513
Rayle, George I, 568
Rayle, Harper I, 568
Rayle, James H. I, 568
Rayle, Jeane I, 513
Rayle, Mary I, 513
Rayle, Matthew I, 513
Rayle, Nathan I, 513
Rayle, Rachel I, 513
Rayle, Susanna I, 568
Rayle, Thomas I, 513
Rayle, William I, 513
Raymond, ??? III, 30
Raymond, Abbie III, 221
Raymond, Abbie III, 263
Raymond, Abby B. III, 264
Raymond, Albern H. IV, 1376
Raymond, Alburn H. IV, 1376
Raymond, Caroline V, 1015
Raymond, Caroline E. III, 263
Raymond, Carrie E. III, 264
Raymond, Catharine IV, 1376
Raymond, Charles H. III, 221
Raymond, Charles H. III, 263
Raymond, Chas. V, 1015
Raymond, Chas. H. III, 264
Raymond, Clarence V, 555
Raymond, Ebenezer III, 119
Raymond, Ebenezer III, 263
Raymond, Eleanor B. III, 264
Raymond, Ellwood H. III, 263
Raymond, Elwood H. III, 264
Raymond, Esther IV, 1261
Raymond, Florence III, 263
Raymond, Florence III, 274
Raymond, Florence IV, 1334
Raymond, George III, 263
Raymond, Hannah III, 119
Raymond, Hannah III, 263
Raymond, Hannah III, 264
Raymond, Hannah T. III, 264
Raymond, Hannah T. III, 333
Raymond, Hariet V, 1015
Raymond, Harriett V, 1015
Raymond, Jacqueline III, 264
Raymond, Jno. Wm. III, 264
Raymond, John Wm. III, 264
Raymond, John Wm. III, 333
Raymond, John Wm., Jr. III, 264
Raymond, John Wm., Jr. III, 265
Raymond, Judith III, 264
Raymond, Lewis III, 264
Raymond, Lillie T. III, 56
Raymond, Lillie T. III, 264
Raymond, Louisa J. III, 271
Raymond, Lucretia IV, 1376
Raymond, Marguerite III, 264
Raymond, Marguerite III, 265
Raymond, Maria III, 264
Raymond, Maria L. III, 263
Raymond, Maria L. III, 264
Raymond, Olney Martin III, 264
Raymond, Richard Valentine III, 264
Raymond, Thomas II, 447
Raymond, Valentine Kirk III, 264
Raynard, Charles IV, 267
Raynolds, Lydia I, 996
Raynor, ??? III, 351
Raynor, Geo. III, 264
Raynor, Geo. III, 284
Raynor, George III, 264
Raynor, Joseph III, 439
Raynor, Martha III, 439
Raynor, Martha III, 447
Raynor, Mary III, 284
Raynor, Mary R. III, 264
Raynor, Mary R. III, 284
Raynor, Mary Rebecca III, 264
Raynor, Phebe III, 439
Raynor, Sarah Eliz. III, 264
Raynor, Sarah Elizabeth III, 152
Raynor, Sarah Elizabeth III, 264
Raynor, Susan III, 264
Raynor, Susan III, 351
Raynor, Susan W. III, 152
Raynor, Susan W. III, 264
Raynor, Susan W. III, 284
Razor, Aaron V, 763
Rea, Ann VI, 592
Rea, Carrie IV, 267
Rea, Deborah IV, 1271
Rea, Deborah IV, 1291
Rea, Elisabeth, Jr. I, 189
Rea, Elisabeth, Jr. I, 199
Rea, Elizabeth IV, 1291
Rea, Gains IV, 1291
Rea, Hannah VI, 390
Rea, Hannah VI, 596
Rea, Hannah VI, 604
Rea, Hiram IV, 267
Rea, Hugh VI, 179
Rea, Hugh VI, 210
Rea, Hugh VI, 265
Rea, Ida IV, 267
Rea, Isaac IV, 1269
Rea, Isaac IV, 1291
Rea, Isaiah IV, 1291
Rea, John II, 411
Rea, Joseph VI, 265
Rea, Joseph VI, 390
Rea, Joseph VI, 596
Rea, Joseph VI, 604
Rea, Judith VI, 179
Rea, Judith VI, 210
Rea, Judith VI, 265
Rea, Levi IV, 1291
Rea, Lot IV, 1291
Rea, Mary II, 411
Rea, Mary II, 663
Rea, Nancy IV, 267
Rea, Rebecca IV, 1273
Rea, Rebecca IV, 1291
Rea, Rebeckah VI, 596
Rea, Rebeckah VI, 604
Rea, Rebekah V, 113
Rea, Rebekah V, 128
Rea, Robert V, 128
Rea, Robert VI, 596
Rea, Robert VI, 604
Rea, Susannah VI, 390
Rea, Susannah VI, 596
Rea, Susannah VI, 604
Rea, Thomas IV, 1269
Rea, Thomas IV, 1291
Rea, Vena IV, 267
Reace, Ann V, 274
Reace, Elizabeth I, 847
Reace, Elizabeth Ann Sarah V, 274
Reace, Jane V, 274
Reace, Levi I, 996
Reace, Maryann I, 996
Reace, Ruth I, 996
Reace, Sarah I, 996
Reace, Sarah V, 274
Reace, Sylvira I, 996
Reace, William I, 996
Reache, Phebe II, 269
Reache, Thomas II, 269
Read, ??? III, 264
Read, A. Manson VI, 815
Read, A. S. VI, 806
Read, A. S. VI, 865
Read, Aaron M. VI, 849
Read, Alexander III, 264
Read, Anderson VI, 957
Read, Andrew B. VI, 982
Read, Ann J. VI, 977
Read, Betty IV, 840
Read, Blanche L. III, 191
Read, Caroline H. III, 281
Read, Caroline Seaman III, 264
Read, Charles II, 252
Read, Charles II, 584
Read, Charles II, 619
Read, Charles II, 630
Read, Charles IV, 840
Read, Charles IV, 859
Read, Daniel II, 1022
Read, Edward T. VI, 983
Read, Eliza A. VI, 983
Read, Eliza Jane IV, 55
Read, Elizabeth II, 631
Read, Elizabeth VI, 817
Read, Elizabeth VI, 849
Read, Elizabeth VI, 850
Read, Elizabeth VI, 905
Read, Elizabeth VI, 962
Read, Elizabeth VI, 981
Read, Elizabeth VI, 983
Read, Elvira VI, 983
Read, Emily Hussey II, 761
Read, Florence VI, 982
Read, Francis VI, 879
Read, Francis VI, 882
Read, Francis VI, 982
Read, Frank II, 816
Read, Frank II, 913
Read, George IV, 840
Read, Hannah III, 264
Read, Henry K. II, 913
Read, Isaac IV, 840
Read, Isabella G. VI, 895
Read, Isaiah IV, 348
Read, James III, 264
Read, James VI, 878
Read, James VI, 905
Read, James VI, 957
Read, Jenny VI, 879
Read, Jno. B. W. W. VI, 804
Read, Joel IV, 840
Read, Johanna VI, 987
Read, John IV, 55
Read, John VI, 336
Read, John VI, 849
Read, John VI, 858
Read, John VI, 919
Read, John T. W. VI, 849

Read, John T. W. VI, 977
Read, Joseph IV, 840
Read, Joseph VI, 1016
Read, Joseph Durose IV, 55
Read, Josiah VI, 849
Read, Joycy VI, 987
Read, Keziah VI, 829
Read, Luther III, 264
Read, Margaret VI, 982
Read, Martha III, 264
Read, Mary IV, 1113
Read, Mary VI, 849
Read, Mary VI, 870
Read, Mary E. VI, 815
Read, Mary E. VI, 849
Read, Mary Louisa II, 816
Read, Nancy VI, 882
Read, Nancy VI, 957
Read, Nancy VI, 982
Read, Nancy VI, 987
Read, Nelly VI, 799
Read, Nelly VI, 852
Read, Obediah VI, 829
Read, Obediah VI, 849
Read, Obediah VI, 850
Read, Obediah VI, 866
Read, Pamela III, 264
Read, Peggy VI, 849
Read, Polly VI, 827
Read, Priscilla C. IV, 55
Read, Prisscilla VI, 841
Read, R. D. P. VI, 958
Read, R. D. P. VI, 967
Read, Rachel II, 619
Read, Rachel II, 630
Read, Rachel V, 480
Read, Rachel V, 524
Read, Raldolph D. P. VI, 945
Read, Randolp D. P. VI, 927
Read, Randolph D. P. VI, 919
Read, Rebecca IV, 55
Read, Robert II, 252
Read, Robert II, 630
Read, Robert II, 631
Read, Robert II, 816
Read, Ruth I, 382
Read, Ruth I, 417
Read, Sally VI, 858
Read, Sally VI, 987
Read, Sam VI, 987
Read, Sam'l H. III, 264
Read, Samuel IV, 840
Read, Samuel IV, 882
Read, Samuel VI, 983
Read, Sarah II, 252
Read, Sarah II, 584
Read, Sarah II, 630
Read, Sarah II, 631
Read, Sarah II, 649
Read, Sarah VI, 848
Read, Sarah VI, 866
Read, Sarah E. VI, 919
Read, Sarah Elizabeth VI, 981
Read, Stella III, 157
Read, Stella III, 364
Read, Susanna VI, 878
Read, Thomas IV, 840
Read, W. VI, 962
Read, William III, 264
Read, William IV, 840
Read, William VI, 815
Read, William VI, 827
Read, William VI, 841
Read, William VI, 848
Read, William VI, 858
Read, William VI, 870
Read, William VI, 983
Read, William VI, 987
Read, William A. III, 281
Reade, Charles II, 181
Reade, Charles II, 1029
Reade, Luther VI, 73
Reade, Luther VI, 84
Reade, Mary II, 181
Readen, Rebecca VI, 849
Readen, Robert VI, 849
Readen, Wm. VI, 849
Reader, Achsah II, 1058
Reader, Achsah IV, 653
Reader, Alice IV, 840
Reader, Ann II, 1069
Reader, Ann II, 1078
Reader, Ann IV, 645
Reader, Ann IV, 653
Reader, Ann IV, 908
Reader, Ann VI, 550
Reader, Deborah IV, 840
Reader, Deborah IV, 843
Reader, Elizabeth VI, 337
Reader, Elizabeth VI, 935
Reader, Emma V, 274
Reader, Ethel V, 274
Reader, Hannah IV, 908
Reader, Hannah VI, 299
Reader, Hannah VI, 550
Reader, Hannah VI, 551
Reader, Hannah VI, 800
Reader, Hannah Elizabeth V, 219
Reader, Hannah Elizabeth V, 274
Reader, Isaac VI, 550
Reader, Jacob VI, 550
Reader, Jacob VI, 551
Reader, Jane II, 1078
Reader, John IV, 55
Reader, Joseph IV, 914
Reader, Joseph IV, 918
Reader, Joseph VI, 337
Reader, Julia I, 484
Reader, Lydia B. IV, 1029
Reader, Martha VI, 849
Reader, Mary IV, 914
Reader, Mary IV, 918
Reader, Mary VI, 550
Reader, Mary VI, 551
Reader, Mary VI, 693
Reader, Mary C. II, 1057
Reader, Priscilla II, 1006
Reader, Priscilla II, 1023
Reader, Priscilla IV, 653
Reader, Priscilla VI, 337
Reader, Samuel IV, 753
Reader, Samuel IV, 908
Reader, Samuel VI, 550
Reader, Samuel VI, 551
Reader, Sarah VI, 550
Reader, Sarah VI, 551
Reader, Sarah VI, 693
Reader, Sherman V, 274
Reader, Thomas IV, 653
Reader, Thomas IV, 753
Reader, Thomas VI, 337
Reader, Thomas VI, 550
Reader, Thomas VI, 849
Reader, William VI, 337
Reader, William VI, 550
Reader, William VI, 551
Reader, William VI, 693
Reader, William, Jr. VI, 550
Reader, William, Jr. VI, 551
Reader, Wm. VI, 551
Reader, Zilphia V, 274
Reading, Charles II, 411
Reading, Mary II, 411
Reading, Susanna II, 411
Reading, Susanna II, 562
Reading, Susanna II, 631
Reading, Wm. II, 631
Ready, Charles VI, 982
Ready, Charles VI, 1006
Ready, Jenny VI, 839
Ready, Katy VI, 1001
Ready, Kitty VI, 993
Ready, Mary VI, 982
Ready, Nancey VI, 1006
Ready, Nathan VI, 839
Reaford, Lewis II, 93
Reagan, ??? V, 147
Reagan, Beulah V, 114
Reagan, Charity V, 176
Reagan, Charity V, 198
Reagan, Dinah V, 114
Reagan, Dinah V, 182
Reagan, Dinah V, 198
Reagan, Dinah V, 213
Reagan, Eli H. V, 198
Reagan, Eli H. V, 199
Reagan, Elihu V, 198
Reagan, Hanah V, 154
Reagan, Hanah V, 198
Reagan, Hannah V, 198
Reagan, Huston V, 198
Reagan, Ina A. IV, 957
Reagan, Jehu S. V, 198
Reagan, Jehu S. V, 199
Reagan, Jesse V, 198
Reagan, Jesse V, 524
Reagan, John V, 114
Reagan, John V, 176
Reagan, John V, 198
Reagan, John V, 199
Reagan, Leah V, 114
Reagan, Lydia V, 198
Reagan, Mary V, 114
Reagan, Mary V, 163
Reagan, Mary V, 183
Reagan, Mary V, 198
Reagan, Mary V, 204
Reagan, Mary V, 209
Reagan, Mary S. V, 163
Reagan, Mary S. V, 198
Reagan, Patience V, 198
Reagan, Rachel V, 114
Reagan, Rachel V, 198
Reagan, Rachel V, 209
Reagan, Reasin V, 524
Reagan, Reasin Reuel V, 524
Reagan, Reason V, 114
Reagan, Reason V, 163
Reagan, Reason V, 198
Reagan, Reason V, 199
Reagan, Reason V, 204
Reagan, Reason V, 209
Reagan, Ruel V, 113
Reagan, Ruel V, 198
Reagan, Samuel V, 198
Reagan, Sarah Ann V, 198
Reagan, Sarah Ann V, 199
Reagan, Susannah V, 198
Reagan, Susannah V, 200
Reagan, Thomas V, 198
Reagan, Thos. V, 198
Reagan, Wiley V, 198
Reagan, William V, 198
Reagan, Wm. V, 198
Reagan, Wm. J. V, 199
Reagin, Mary V, 114
Reakes, Mary I, 256
Realey, Gem. VI, 870
Realey, Isaac VI, 870
Realey, Philip VI, 870
Realey, Sarah VI, 870
Reall, Wm. II, 631
Realow, John II, 631
Realow, John II, 632
Realow, Mary II, 631
Realow, Mary II, 632
Realy, John VI, 147
Ream, ??? IV, 1269
Ream, John V, 274
Reames, Abel F. IV, 1291
Reames, Abigail I, 226
Reames, Abigail I, 231
Reames, Abigail I, 256
Reames, Able Thomas IV, 1291
Reames, Ada IV, 1291
Reames, Anna IV, 1291
Reames, Arthur IV, 1291
Reames, Caleb I, 256
Reames, Caleb IV, 1291
Reames, Calib I, 226
Reames, Charles IV, 1291
Reames, Chas. H. IV, 1291
Reames, Chas. W. IV, 1291
Reames, Clara IV, 1291
Reames, Cora IV, 1291
Reames, Corena IV, 1291
Reames, David IV, 1291
Reames, Deborah Ann IV, 1291
Reames, Effie IV, 1291
Reames, Elias IV, 1291
Reames, Elijah I, 226
Reames, Elijah I, 256
Reames, Elijah IV, 1291
Reames, Elijah V, 274
Reames, Elisabeth I, 244
Reames, Eliza IV, 1291
Reames, Elizabeth I, 226
Reames, Elizabeth IV, 1291
Reames, Esther IV, 1291
Reames, Evangelina IV, 1291
Reames, Ezra IV, 1291
Reames, Florence Maud IV, 1291
Reames, Francis L. IV, 1291
Reames, Franklin IV, 1291
Reames, George IV, 1291
Reames, George C. IV, 1291
Reames, Glenn IV, 1291
Reames, Hannah I, 226
Reames, Hannah IV, 1291
Reames, Harlie M. IV, 1291
Reames, Harlyn IV, 1291
Reames, Harriet N. IV, 1291
Reames, Hezekiah IV, 1291
Reames, Hezekiah J. IV, 1291
Reames, Jennie IV, 1291
Reames, Jennie IV, 1294
Reames, Jeremiah I, 226
Reames, Jeremiah I, 256
Reames, Jesse IV, 1291
Reames, Joel V, 463
Reames, John I, 226
Reames, John I, 256
Reames, John IV, 1291
Reames, Jordan IV, 1291
Reames, Joseph Elwood IV, 1291
Reames, Josiah IV, 1291
Reames, Josiah F. IV, 1291
Reames, Juliana M. IV, 1291
Reames, Lettice V, 463
Reames, Levi IV, 1291
Reames, Lucretia IV, 1291
Reames, Luther IV, 1291
Reames, Lutheria IV, 1291
Reames, Lydia M. IV, 1291
Reames, Margaret I, 226
Reames, Margaret IV, 1291
Reames, Martha IV, 1291
Reames, Mary I, 226
Reames, Mary IV, 1291
Reames, Mary C. IV, 1291
Reames, Mary J. IV, 1291
Reames, Mary Jane IV, 1291
Reames, Matilda IV, 1291
Reames, Matilda V, 463
Reames, Melissa IV, 1291
Reames, Nancy Jane IV, 1291
Reames, Naomi I, 256
Reames, Naomi I, 259
Reames, Nelson IV, 1291
Reames, Obedience I, 226
Reames, Obedience I, 256
Reames, Olive IV, 1291
Reames, Olive M. IV, 1291
Reames, Orlando IV, 1291
Reames, Oswell IV, 1291
Reames, Pearlie IV, 1291
Reames, Perly A. IV, 1291
Reames, Peter I, 226
Reames, Peter I, 256
Reames, Rachel IV, 1291
Reames, Rebecca IV, 1291
Reames, Retta IV, 1291
Reames, Robert IV, 1291
Reames, Robert L. IV, 1291
Reames, Robert M. IV, 1291
Reames, Roswell K. IV, 1291
Reames, Samuel IV, 1291
Reames, Sarah IV, 1291
Reames, Sollomon P. IV, 1291
Reames, Tamer I, 256
Reames, Thomas IV, 1291
Reames, Unity IV, 1291
Reames, Virgil IV, 1291
Reames, Virgil F. IV, 1291
Reames, Wesley IV, 1291
Reames, William I, 226
Reames, William I, 256
Reames, William I, 259
Reames, William IV, 1291
Reames, Willie IV, 1291
Reames, Wm. M. IV, 1291
Reams, Anna IV, 1287
Reams, Anna IV, 1291
Reams, Benjamin Pattison VI, 119
Reams, Caleb IV, 1291
Reams, Catherine IV, 1261
Reams, Charles IV, 1261
Reams, Chas. IV, 1261
Reams, Chas. H. IV, 1291
Reams, Chas. W. IV, 1291
Reams, Clara IV, 1291
Reams, Cora IV, 1291
Reams, Corena IV, 1291
Reams, Cyrus IV, 1261
Reams, David IV, 1286
Reams, David IV, 1291
Reams, David V, 274
Reams, Deborah Ann IV, 1291
Reams, Deborah Ann IV, 1292
Reams, Earl V, 595
Reams, Effie IV, 1291
Reams, Elijah I, 256
Reams, Elijah V, 273
Reams, Elijah V, 274
Reams, Elisabeth I, 256
Reams, Elizabeth IV, 1291
Reams, Evangeline IV, 1261
Reams, Franklin IV, 1291
Reams, Gertrude Sise V, 595
Reams, Glenn IV, 1291
Reams, Glenn M. V, 595
Reams, Hannah V, 272
Reams, Hannah V, 273
Reams, Hannah V, 274
Reams, Harlie M. IV, 1291
Reams, Harriet N. IV, 1291
Reams, Hezekiah IV, 1291
Reams, Hezekiah VI, 119
Reams, Hezekiah J. IV, 1291
Reams, Jennie IV, 1291
Reams, Jeremiah I, 256
Reams, Jeremiah V, 273
Reams, Jeremiah V, 274
Reams, Jeremiah VI, 115
Reams, Jeremiah VI, 119
Reams, John I, 256
Reams, John V, 273
Reams, John V, 274
Reams, John VI, 210
Reams, Jonathan V, 273
Reams, Jonathan V, 274
Reams, Jordan IV, 1291
Reams, Jose V, 273
Reams, Joseph V, 274
Reams, Josiah IV, 1291
Reams, Letia V, 274
Reams, Lettice V, 357
Reams, Lettice V, 463
Reams, Lettis V, 274
Reams, Luther IV, 1291
Reams, Lutheria IV, 1291
Reams, Lydia M. IV, 1291
Reams, Malissa IV, 1281
Reams, Malissa IV, 1291
Reams, Margaret IV, 1286
Reams, Margaret IV, 1291
Reams, Margaret VI, 119
Reams, Martha VI, 210
Reams, Mary IV, 753
Reams, Mary IV, 1291
Reams, Mary V, 273
Reams, Mary V, 274
Reams, Mary VI, 202
Reams, Mary VI, 210
Reams, Mary I. IV, 1334
Reams, Mary J. IV, 1291
Reams, Mary Jane IV, 1291
Reams, Mary Louise V, 595
Reams, Matilda IV, 1291
Reams, Nancy Jane IV, 1291
Reams, Nettie IV, 1261
Reams, Obedience VI, 199
Reams, Obedience VI, 210
Reams, Olive M. IV, 1291
Reams, Orlando IV, 1291
Reams, Perly A. IV, 1291
Reams, Peter V, 274
Reams, Peter R. V, 274
Reams, Rachel IV, 1291
Reams, Rankin IV, 1261
Reams, Rankin Carl IV, 1261
Reams, Rebecca V, 273
Reams, Rebecca V, 274
Reams, Retta IV, 1291
Reams, Robert IV, 1291
Reams, Roswell K. IV, 1291
Reams, Samuel IV, 1291
Reams, Sarah IV, 1291
Reams, Sarah V, 273
Reams, Sarah V, 274
Reams, Sollomon P. IV, 1291
Reams, Virgil F. IV, 1291
Reams, W. J. IV, 1261
Reams, Walter IV, 1261
Reams, Walter Oren IV, 1261
Reams, Wesley IV, 1291
Reams, William I, 256
Reams, William IV, 1291
Reams, William V, 274
Reams, William VI, 95
Reams, William VI, 119
Reams, William VI, 199
Reams, William VI, 202
Reams, William VI, 210
Reams, William W. V, 273
Reams, William W. V, 274
Reams, Willie IV, 1291
Reams, Wm. IV, 1261
Reamsnyder, John V, 1015
Reanolds, Cyrus IV, 268
Reaps, Ann IV, 818
Reaps, Ann IV, 840
Reardon, Ella III, 264
Reardon, Ella III, 369
Reardon, Mary J. III, 264
Reardon, Mary J. III, 369
Reardon, Ralph III, 264
Reardon, Ralph III, 369
Reas, Isaiah IV, 1291
Rease, Ann I, 727
Rease, Ann I, 732
Rease, Arminta I, 568
Rease, Dempsey I, 732
Rease, Hannah I, 731
Rease, Hannah I, 732
Rease, John I, 727
Rease, John I, 732
Rease, Julia VI, 919
Rease, Tamer IV, 348
Rease, Tamor IV, 348
Reason, Edward V, 114
Reason, Edward V, 706
Reason, Elsie V, 114
Reason, Elsie M. V, 706
Reason, Hannah E. V, 114
Reason, Margaret R. V, 114
Reason, Paul V, 114
Reason, Paul V, 706
Reason, Percy V, 114
Reason, Percy V, 706
Reason, Sadie V, 114
Reason, Sadie V, 706
Reason, William H. V, 114
Reasor, Cecil V, 1015
Reave, Alexander V, 114

ave, Charles V, 114
ave, Elizabeth V, 114
ave, Hannah V, 114
ave, Jeremiah V, 114
ave, Sarah V, 114
ave, Thompson V, 114
aver, Adam Alfred IV, 1261
aver, Charles Russell IV, 1261
aver, Dorothy Rose IV, 1261
aver, John Pennington IV, 1261
aver, Ruth Silvia IV, 1261
aver, Stanley Hershel IV, 1261
aves, Ann IV, 653
aves, Bathsheba IV, 348
aves, Benjamin IV, 653
aves, Benjamin IV, 1291
aves, Charlotte E. V, 518
aves, Charlotte E. V, 524
aves, Esther V, 858
aves, Frances B. V, 199
aves, Harriett IV, 653
aves, John IV, 348
aves, John VI, 944
aves, Mary II, 93
aves, Mary VI, 944
aves, Mathew IV, 348
aves, Matilda IV, 653
aves, Ora Francis V, 199
aves, Robert V, 199
aves, Samuel IV, 348
aves, Susannah IV, 653
aves, Sybil I, 768
aves, Wm. Abraham V, 199
ay, ??? III, 263
ay, Allen Dale III, 264
ay, Anna C. III, 263
ay, Christopher III, 263
ay, Elizabeth III, 263
ay, Francis H. III, 263
ay, Frank A. III, 263
ay, John III, 264
ay, Kate III, 263
ay, Lucy W. III, 263
ay, Margaret III, 263
ay, Martha III, 263
ay, Wm. Anthony III, 263
ecca, Bracken IV, 683
ecca, Brackin IV, 683
er, Edith Alina II, 816
e, Sarah V, 429
kefuse, Mary II, 631
kett, Joseph II, 634
kett, William, Jr. II, 252
kett, Wm. II, 634
kitt, Joseph II, 634
kitt, Thomas IV, 158
kless, Joseph II, 252
kless, Joseph II, 256
kless, Margaret II, 252
kless, Margaret II, 256
kman, Samuel IV, 268
tor, ??? VI, 637
tor, ??? VI, 693
tor, Addie V, 463
tor, Anna VI, 647
tor, Anna VI, 693
tor, Betsey VI, 849
tor, Cora V, 463
tor, Eliza V, 463
tor, Elizabeth VI, 812
tor, Elizabeth VI, 849
tor, Eveline I, 985
tor, Eveline I, 996
tor, Fam V, 463
tor, Gan VI, 798
tor, Henry V, 463
tor, Jane VI, 799
tor, Jennie V, 706
tor, John V, 463
tor, John VI, 849
tor, John VI, 867
tor, Lewis VI, 849
tor, Martin VI, 849
tor, Mary VI, 648
tor, Mary VI, 694
tor, Mary VI, 849
tor, Myrtle V, 463
tor, Rebecca VI, 799
tor, Rosa V, 463
tor, Sally VI, 798
tor, Sarah VI, 849
l, George VI, 387
l, George VI, 435
l, Isaiah IV, 348
l, Mary IV, 546
l, Rachel VI, 387
ld, Adam VI, 434
ld, Ann IV, 432
ld, Ann IV, 444
ld, Ann IV, 495
Redd, Ann IV, 496
Redd, Catharine IV, 432
Redd, Charity IV, 268
Redd, Charity IV, 306
Redd, Charity IV, 348
Redd, Charity IV, 531
Redd, Charity VI, 435
Redd, Geo. IV, 306
Redd, Geo. IV, 422
Redd, George IV, 432
Redd, George IV, 504
Redd, George VI, 434
Redd, George VI, 435
Redd, George VI, 591
Redd, George VI, 604
Redd, Ichsah VI, 849
Redd, Isaac IV, 753
Redd, Isaiah IV, 348
Redd, Isaiah IV, 432
Redd, Isaiah IV, 444
Redd, Isaiah IV, 495
Redd, Isaiah IV, 496
Redd, Isaiah VI, 435
Redd, Israel IV, 432
Redd, Israel IV, 495
Redd, Israel VI, 435
Redd, John Paul VI, 849
Redd, Lydia IV, 495
Redd, Lydia IV, 504
Redd, Marget VI, 591
Redd, Mary IV, 348
Redd, Mary IV, 422
Redd, Mary IV, 432
Redd, Mary IV, 495
Redd, Mary IV, 1113
Redd, Meriam VI, 434
Redd, Miriam VI, 382
Redd, Miriam VI, 435
Redd, Rachel IV, 306
Redd, Rachel IV, 422
Redd, Rachel IV, 432
Redd, Rachel IV, 504
Redd, Rachel VI, 427
Redd, Rachel VI, 434
Redd, Rachel VI, 435
Redd, Rachel VI, 604
Redd, Robert VI, 434
Reddick, Frank V, 199
Reddick, George R. I, 30
Reddick, Margaret E. I, 30
Reddick, Martha A. I, 70
Reddick, Mary I, 939
Reddick, Mary I, 948
Reddick, Phebe V, 595
Reddick, Phebe V, 598
Reddick, Robert George I, 70
Redding, Elizabeth VI, 849
Redding, Eugenia I, 768
Redding, J. C. IV, 1335
Redding, James C. IV, 1335
Redding, Joseph VI, 849
Redding, Martha I, 628
Redding, Mary I, 484
Redding, Mary VI, 849
Redding, Mary Harmon I, 948
Redding, Robert VI, 849
Redding, Sallie I, 948
Redding, Sarah C. I, 948
Redding, Sarah Charlotte I, 932
Redding, Thomas VI, 849
Reddix, Alice I, 418
Reddix, John I, 418
Reddix, William I, 418
Reddock, Ann I, 418
Reddy, Mascilda VI, 808
Reden, Mary I, 484
Redenbaugh, John V, 1015
Redfern, Bessie V, 550
Redfern, Emma H. V, 595
Redfern, Lydia V, 301
Redfern, Rachel IV, 1162
Redfern, Rachel IV, 1181
Redfern, Rachel V, 62
Redfern, Rachel V, 114
Redford, Jane V, 301
Redford, Jane V, 309
Redford, Lydia V, 309
Redick, John V, 526
Redin, Charles II, 411
Redin, Mary II, 411
Redin, Susanna II, 411
Redknap, Joseph II, 565
Redknap, Joseph II, 631
Redknap, Rebecka II, 87
Redknap, Rebecka II, 93
Redknap, Wd. Elizabeth II, 565
Redknap, Wd. Elizabeth II, 631
Redman, ??? II, 447
Redman, Alexander II, 411
Redman, Allen V, 1015
Redman, Ann II, 616
Redman, Ann II, 631
Redman, Benjamin II, 411
Redman, Catherine II, 447
Redman, Edith V, 1015
Redman, Edith M. III, 264
Redman, Elizabeth II, 411
Redman, Elizabeth II, 447
Redman, Elizabeth VI, 982
Redman, Hannah II, 252
Redman, Hannah II, 271
Redman, Hannah II, 411
Redman, Hannah II, 631
Redman, Henry IV, 988
Redman, Holly III, 264
Redman, James II, 447
Redman, James A. II, 411
Redman, Jane II, 447
Redman, John II, 37
Redman, John II, 60
Redman, John II, 61
Redman, John II, 93
Redman, John II, 245
Redman, John II, 252
Redman, John II, 411
Redman, John II, 447
Redman, John II, 542
Redman, John II, 631
Redman, John II, 641
Redman, John E. II, 411
Redman, John E. II, 631
Redman, John E., Jr. II, 411
Redman, John, Jr. II, 447
Redman, Joseph II, 411
Redman, Joseph II, 447
Redman, Joseph II, 631
Redman, Lydia II, 411
Redman, Lydia II, 631
Redman, Lydia II, 649
Redman, Marcey II, 93
Redman, Margaret II, 245
Redman, Margaret II, 252
Redman, Maria IV, 988
Redman, Martha II, 411
Redman, Martha II, 631
Redman, Martha II, 693
Redman, Mary II, 24
Redman, Mary II, 37
Redman, Mary II, 60
Redman, Mary II, 93
Redman, Mary II, 245
Redman, Mary II, 252
Redman, Mary II, 411
Redman, Mary II, 631
Redman, Mary II, 641
Redman, Mercy II, 37
Redman, Mercy II, 65
Redman, Mercy II, 93
Redman, Narcissa IV, 1221
Redman, Narsissa IV, 1219
Redman, Neighbor Geo. III, 264
Redman, Penelope II, 411
Redman, Philip II, 411
Redman, Provided II, 411
Redman, Rachel II, 37
Redman, Rachel II, 60
Redman, Rachel II, 61
Redman, Rachel II, 93
Redman, Rebecca II, 252
Redman, Rebecca II, 271
Redman, Rebecca II, 411
Redman, Richard II, 411
Redman, Richard II, 631
Redman, Robert VI, 982
Redman, Samuel II, 411
Redman, Samuel II, 631
Redman, Samuel II, 693
Redman, Sarah II, 404
Redman, Sarah II, 542
Redman, Sarah II, 631
Redman, Sidney II, 411
Redman, Thomas II, 65
Redman, Thomas II, 93
Redman, Thomas II, 252
Redman, Thomas II, 271
Redman, Thomas II, 411
Redman, Thomas II, 542
Redman, Thomas II, 544
Redman, Thomas II, 616
Redman, Thomas II, 631
Redman, Wd. Sarah II, 411
Redman, Wd. Susanna II, 411
Redmon, Thomas II, 447
Redmond, ??? III, 264
Redmond, Abigail B. III, 264
Redmond, Ann III, 40
Redmond, Ann III, 264
Redmond, Anna G. II, 299
Redmond, Anna G. III, 264
Redmond, Caroline III, 264
Redmond, Charles P. III, 264
Redmond, Charles Philip III, 264
Redmond, Cornelia III, 264
Redmond, Esther VI, 975
Redmond, Frank IV, 729
Redmond, Hannah II, 499
Redmond, Hannah II, 631
Redmond, Hannah III, 264
Redmond, Hannah C. III, 127
Redmond, Hannah T. III, 264
Redmond, Henry S. III, 248
Redmond, Henry S. III, 264
Redmond, Herbert IV, 1261
Redmond, Irena VI, 975
Redmond, James M. III, 264
Redmond, Jas. Morton III, 40
Redmond, Jas. Norton III, 264
Redmond, John III, 265
Redmond, John C. III, 127
Redmond, John C. III, 264
Redmond, John C., Jr. III, 264
Redmond, John D. IV, 1261
Redmond, Julia III, 264
Redmond, Julia Frances III, 248
Redmond, Julia Frances III, 264
Redmond, Letitia III, 127
Redmond, Letitia III, 264
Redmond, Margaret IV, 1261
Redmond, Maria III, 264
Redmond, Mary Eliza III, 264
Redmond, Mary Katherine IV, 729
Redmond, Morton III, 264
Redmond, Myrtle IV, 729
Redmond, Philip III, 264
Redmond, Samuel G. III, 264
Redmond, William E. III, 264
Redmond, William F. III, 264
Rednap, ??? II, 411
Rednap, Elizabeth II, 411
Rednap, Joseph II, 411
Redrup, Thomas V, 1015
Redstreak, Frances II, 93
Redwood, Abraham II, 631
Redwood, Hannah II, 524
Redwood, Hannah II, 631
Redwood, John II, 447
Redwood, Jonas Langford II, 631
Redwood, Margaret IV, 1261
Redwood, Mehatible II, 631
Redwood, Rebecka II, 447
Redwood, Samuel II, 631
Redwood, Sarah II, 447
Redwood, Sarah II, 524
Redwood, Sarah II, 585
Redwood, Sarah II, 631
Redwood, Sarah II, 643
Redwood, Sarah II, 758
Redwood, William II, 411
Redwood, Wm. II, 524
Redwood, Wm. II, 631
Redwood, Wm. II, 643
Reece, Abiher I, 1131
Reece, Abraham I, 996
Reece, Ann I, 705
Reece, Ann I, 956
Reece, Ann I, 963
Reece, Ann I, 968
Reece, Ann V, 310
Reece, Ann V, 428
Reece, Ann V, 429
Reece, Anne I, 978
Reece, Asenath H. I, 720
Reece, Caleb I, 685
Reece, Caleb I, 687
Reece, Caleb I, 790
Reece, Caleb I, 898
Reece, Caleb I, 899
Reece, Caleb I, 968
Reece, Caleb I, 1131
Reece, Caleb V, 274
Reece, Caleb V, 309
Reece, Carey I, 215
Reece, Catharine I, 664
Reece, Catherine I, 1131
Reece, Christian I, 664
Reece, Christian I, 687
Reece, Christian I, 689
Reece, Christian I, 705
Reece, Christian I, 1131
Reece, Christianna I, 1131
Reece, Clement I, 640
Reece, Daniel I, 705
Reece, Daniel I, 790
Reece, Daniel V, 763
Reece, David I, 953
Reece, David I, 956
Reece, David I, 968
Reece, David I, 1012
Reece, David I, 1131
Reece, Davis I, 720
Reece, Davis I, 732
Reece, Dempsey V, 428
Reece, Dempsey V, 429
Reece, Edward II, 411
Reece, Edward VI, 551
Reece, Edward VI, 563
Reece, Elenor I, 616
Reece, Eli I, 624
Reece, Eli I, 640
Reece, Eli I, 932
Reece, Eli I, 948
Reece, Eli II, 913
Reece, Eli F. II, 816
Reece, Elias I, 705
Reece, Elizabeth I, 640
Reece, Elizabeth I, 932
Reece, Elizabeth I, 948
Reece, Elizabeth I, 956
Reece, Elizabeth I, 968
Reece, Elizabeth I, 1012
Reece, Elizabeth IV, 1181
Reece, Elizabeth IV, 1186
Reece, Ellwood I, 978
Reece, Evanna II, 913
Reece, Fran S. II, 913
Reece, France V, 274
Reece, Francis I, 664
Reece, Francis I, 968
Reece, Gideon VI, 604
Reece, Gurnay Birdsall I, 948
Reece, Gurney I, 932
Reece, Hannah I, 664
Reece, Hannah I, 687
Reece, Hannah I, 790
Reece, Hannah I, 963
Reece, Hannah I, 968
Reece, Hannah I, 978
Reece, Hannah I, 1131
Reece, Hannah V, 429
Reece, Hannah Jane I, 215
Reece, Hannah Rachel I, 1131
Reece, Hiram I, 978
Reece, Hiram I, 996
Reece, Huldah I, 664
Reece, Isaiah I, 1131
Reece, James I, 1131
Reece, James V, 114
Reece, Jane I, 705
Reece, Jane I, 1131
Reece, Jane V, 114
Reece, Jane V, 429
Reece, Jesse V, 310
Reece, John I, 664
Reece, John I, 705
Reece, Joseph Gordan I, 948
Reece, Joseph Gordon I, 624
Reece, Joseph Gordon I, 932
Reece, Joseph Gurney I, 640
Reece, Levi I, 996
Reece, Levi, Jr. I, 996
Reece, Lewis V, 114
Reece, Lewis VI, 604
Reece, Lucinda I, 996
Reece, Lucy T. II, 816
Reece, Lydia P. II, 913
Reece, M. Elma I, 948
Reece, Margaret V, 304
Reece, Margaret V, 310
Reece, Margaret VI, 600
Reece, Martha J. I, 988
Reece, Martha J. I, 996
Reece, Mary I, 790
Reece, Mary I, 899
Reece, Mary I, 906
Reece, Mary I, 978
Reece, Mary I, 984
Reece, Mary I, 987
Reece, Mary I, 996
Reece, Mary Alma I, 640
Reece, Mary Ann I, 624
Reece, Mary Ann I, 932
Reece, Mary Ann I, 985
Reece, Mary Ann I, 996
Reece, Mary Ellen I, 932
Reece, Mary Elma I, 624
Reece, Maryann I, 996
Reece, Michael I, 899
Reece, Millicent I, 705
Reece, Nancy VI, 1018
Reece, Nathan I, 705
Reece, Needham I, 705
Reece, Phebe V, 309
Reece, Phebe V, 311
Reece, Philip Eli I, 932
Reece, Philip Eli I, 948
Reece, Phillip I, 640
Reece, Rachel I, 664
Reece, Rachel I, 1009
Reece, Rachel I, 1012
Reece, Rachel I, 1131
Reece, Rachel VI, 694
Reece, Rachel VI, 709
Reece, Rebeckah I, 790

Reece, Rebeckah V, 309
Reece, Rebekah V, 304
Reece, Ruth I, 978
Reece, Ruth I, 985
Reece, Ruth I, 996
Reece, Ruth IV, 268
Reece, Ruth IV, 1335
Reece, Sarah I, 685
Reece, Sarah I, 687
Reece, Sarah I, 898
Reece, Sarah I, 899
Reece, Sarah I, 906
Reece, Sarah I, 971
Reece, Sarah I, 978
Reece, Sarah I, 996
Reece, Sarah V, 429
Reece, Sarah V, 499
Reece, Sarah V, 524
Reece, Sarah VI, 551
Reece, Sarah VI, 563
Reece, Sylvira I, 996
Reece, Thomas I, 1131
Reece, Thomas II, 411
Reece, Thomas V, 114
Reece, Thomas V, 429
Reece, Thomas, Jr. I, 1131
Reece, Thomas, Sr. I, 1131
Reece, Thos. Ellwood Lewis II, 816
Reece, William I, 624
Reece, William I, 932
Reece, William I, 968
Reece, William I, 996
Reece, William V, 114
Reece, William V, 274
Reece, William Clement I, 932
Reece, Willie V, 763
Reece, Yarnal I, 1131
Reece, Yarnel I, 1131
Reece, Zachariah I, 996
Reece, Zekeriah I, 978
Reed, Abigail S. II, 756
Reed, Abigail S. II, 761
Reed, Abraham II, 447
Reed, Alice IV, 1092
Reed, Alice IV, 1113
Reed, Amasa V, 199
Reed, Amesa V, 199
Reed, Angelina IV, 715
Reed, Angelina IV, 753
Reed, Ann I, 163
Reed, Ann I, 176
Reed, Anna II, 447
Reed, Anna V, 593
Reed, Avaline IV, 712
Reed, Avaline IV, 753
Reed, Avelina IV, 753
Reed, Belle V, 357
Reed, Bernice Virginia V, 524
Reed, Bertha L. II, 299
Reed, Caroline III, 493
Reed, Caroline III, 495
Reed, Caroline Sarah III, 403
Reed, Caroline Sarah III, 439
Reed, Catharine IV, 764
Reed, Catherine V, 706
Reed, Charles II, 411
Reed, Charles II, 447
Reed, Charles II, 1022
Reed, Charles IV, 882
Reed, Clara L. IV, 375
Reed, Daniel II, 1022
Reed, Daniel IV, 1240
Reed, Delilah Jane V, 706
Reed, Edward IV, 1291
Reed, Edward V, 524
Reed, Elijah VI, 798
Reed, Eliza Jane IV, 158
Reed, Elizabeth II, 631
Reed, Elizabeth II, 692
Reed, Elizabeth II, 808
Reed, Elizabeth II, 1006
Reed, Elizabeth II, 1023
Reed, Elizabeth IV, 495
Reed, Elizabeth IV, 502
Reed, Elizabeth IV, 1291
Reed, Elizabeth V, 706
Reed, Elizabeth VI, 993
Reed, Elizabeth A. V, 706
Reed, Elizabeth Ann V, 706
Reed, Ella V, 706
Reed, Ella M. V, 706
Reed, Elmer E. V, 706
Reed, Emily V, 114
Reed, Emily V, 118
Reed, Emily Fuller IV, 1335
Reed, Emily Hussey II, 761
Reed, Emma V, 595
Reed, Eva V, 199
Reed, Floramond V, 114
Reed, George I, 264
Reed, George IV, 882
Reed, Golda IV, 1261
Reed, Goldie IV, 1261
Reed, Harry IV, 375
Reed, Harry V, 763
Reed, Harvey O. V, 763
Reed, Henderson H. V, 706
Reed, Howard V, 763
Reed, Ida IV, 1261
Reed, Iota V, 463
Reed, Iota V, 524
Reed, Isabel IV, 131
Reed, Isabel IV, 132
Reed, J. F. IV, 1335
Reed, J. Harris II, 299
Reed, J. T. IV, 1335
Reed, Jacob VI, 982
Reed, James Edward V, 524
Reed, James H. III, 493
Reed, James H. III, 495
Reed, James L. V, 975
Reed, Jane II, 411
Reed, Jane II, 1023
Reed, Jane II, 1035
Reed, Jane VI, 849
Reed, Jas. H. III, 439
Reed, Jas. Harvey III, 403
Reed, Job IV, 764
Reed, John II, 411
Reed, John IV, 158
Reed, John V, 524
Reed, John V, 975
Reed, John VI, 814
Reed, John VI, 849
Reed, John B. T. VI, 849
Reed, John G. V, 757
Reed, John W. V, 706
Reed, Joseph IV, 882
Reed, Joseph IV, 1113
Reed, Joseph Durese IV, 158
Reed, Lavinia II, 913
Reed, Lavinia II, 930
Reed, Leah VI, 624
Reed, Leah VI, 694
Reed, Louella V, 706
Reed, Louisa A. VI, 849
Reed, Lucinda V, 706
Reed, Luther III, 265
Reed, Maggie B. V, 595
Reed, Margaret V, 763
Reed, Margery V, 199
Reed, Martha II, 761
Reed, Martha IV, 1291
Reed, Martha A. V, 706
Reed, Martha Ann V, 757
Reed, Martha Ann V, 758
Reed, Martha Ann V, 763
Reed, Martha Emily V, 706
Reed, Mary IV, 1113
Reed, Mary IV, 1261
Reed, Mary V, 199
Reed, Mary V, 706
Reed, Mary V, 974
Reed, Mary V, 975
Reed, Mary A. V, 595
Reed, Mary Ann V, 757
Reed, Mary Ann V, 975
Reed, Mary B. IV, 653
Reed, Mary C. IV, 1291
Reed, Mary E. IV, 1261
Reed, Miliscent IV, 753
Reed, Miliscent IV, 764
Reed, Minnie V, 763
Reed, Myrtle B. V, 357
Reed, Nancey VI, 982
Reed, Naomi Almira V, 114
Reed, Nettie IV, 1261
Reed, Pamela III, 265
Reed, Pamelia III, 137
Reed, Priscilla V, 706
Reed, Priscilla C. IV, 158
Reed, Rachel V, 524
Reed, Raymond V, 114
Reed, Rebecca IV, 158
Reed, Rebecca IV, 711
Reed, Rebecca IV, 753
Reed, Rebeckah II, 447
Reed, Robert II, 93
Reed, Robert II, 411
Reed, Ruth A. V, 706
Reed, Samuel IV, 882
Reed, Samuel J. V, 706
Reed, Samuel P. V, 706
Reed, Sarah II, 93
Reed, Sarah II, 252
Reed, Sarah III, 403
Reed, Sarah V, 199
Reed, Sarah V, 757
Reed, Sarah Ann V, 199
Reed, Sarah Ann V, 200
Reed, Sarah F. III, 439
Reed, Sarah Lavena Naylor IV, 988
Reed, Sidney L. II, 299
Reed, Susanna IV, 1240
Reed, Symon II, 447
Reed, T. Chandler II, 299
Reed, Theophilus Chandler II, 299
Reed, Valeria Maud II, 801
Reed, Virginia II, 825
Reed, Virginia P. II, 913
Reed, Virginia P. II, 933
Reed, Wd. Anne II, 411
Reed, William V, 706
Reed, Wm. V, 199
Reed, Wm. H. V, 706
Reeder, ??? IV, 753
Reeder, ??? IV, 795
Reeder, Abigail IV, 900
Reeder, Abigail IV, 914
Reeder, Abigail IV, 916
Reeder, Achsah II, 1058
Reeder, Achsah II, 1070
Reeder, Achsah II, 1076
Reeder, Achsah II, 1078
Reeder, Achsah IV, 653
Reeder, Achsah IV, 879
Reeder, Achsah IV, 882
Reeder, Achsah IV, 989
Reeder, Acsah II, 1023
Reeder, Acsah II, 1029
Reeder, Alice IV, 840
Reeder, Alice IV, 914
Reeder, Alice IV, 1029
Reeder, Alva IV, 915
Reeder, Amanda V, 274
Reeder, Amy Eleanor Smith V, 274
Reeder, Ann II, 1023
Reeder, Ann II, 1046
Reeder, Ann II, 1058
Reeder, Ann IV, 653
Reeder, Ann IV, 753
Reeder, Ann IV, 907
Reeder, Ann IV, 908
Reeder, Ann IV, 914
Reeder, Ann IV, 915
Reeder, Ann VI, 550
Reeder, Ann VI, 694
Reeder, Ann VI, 716
Reeder, Ann Eliza IV, 840
Reeder, Ann Eliza IV, 914
Reeder, Ann Sarah VI, 694
Reeder, Anna Eliza IV, 753
Reeder, Anne II, 967
Reeder, Benjamin IV, 753
Reeder, Benjamin IV, 914
Reeder, Benjamin N. IV, 753
Reeder, Calvin IV, 914
Reeder, Caroline IV, 753
Reeder, Carroll V, 274
Reeder, Charles II, 1023
Reeder, Charles II, 1029
Reeder, Charles II, 1058
Reeder, Charles II, 1076
Reeder, Charles II, 1078
Reeder, Charles M. II, 1070
Reeder, Charles M. II, 1078
Reeder, Charles, Jr. II, 1058
Reeder, Christiana II, 1023
Reeder, Christianna II, 1047
Reeder, Christianna II, 1058
Reeder, Christianna II, 1070
Reeder, Christianna II, 1078
Reeder, David II, 1023
Reeder, David II, 1029
Reeder, David IV, 753
Reeder, David IV, 1029
Reeder, David V, 199
Reeder, David B. III, 439
Reeder, David Battin IV, 914
Reeder, David W. IV, 753
Reeder, Deborah IV, 753
Reeder, Deborah IV, 787
Reeder, Deborah IV, 840
Reeder, Deborah V, 274
Reeder, Della May V, 763
Reeder, Eden IV, 914
Reeder, Eden IV, 915
Reeder, Eli IV, 915
Reeder, Eli D. IV, 753
Reeder, Eli D. IV, 914
Reeder, Eliza IV, 909
Reeder, Eliza IV, 914
Reeder, Elizabeth II, 1023
Reeder, Elizabeth II, 1029
Reeder, Elizabeth IV, 753
Reeder, Elizabeth IV, 840
Reeder, Elizabeth IV, 902
Reeder, Elizabeth IV, 914
Reeder, Elizabeth VI, 337
Reeder, Elizabeth VI, 694
Reeder, Elizabeth Cooper IV, 914
Reeder, Emma V, 274
Reeder, Eneas G. IV, 753
Reeder, Eneas G. IV, 914
Reeder, Enos V, 274
Reeder, Enos V, 278
Reeder, Esther F. IV, 753
Reeder, Esther F. IV, 763
Reeder, Esther F. IV, 914
Reeder, Esther T. IV, 914
Reeder, Esther T. IV, 916
Reeder, Ethel V, 274
Reeder, Ethel Grim V, 595
Reeder, Eunice V, 274
Reeder, Eva Cooper IV, 914
Reeder, Evan IV, 914
Reeder, Evan C. IV, 753
Reeder, Frank V, 763
Reeder, Franklin IV, 914
Reeder, G. W. IV, 268
Reeder, Gourly VI, 694
Reeder, Hannah IV, 228
Reeder, Hannah IV, 268
Reeder, Hannah IV, 627
Reeder, Hannah IV, 653
Reeder, Hannah IV, 753
Reeder, Hannah IV, 827
Reeder, Hannah IV, 840
Reeder, Hannah IV, 903
Reeder, Hannah IV, 909
Reeder, Hannah IV, 911
Reeder, Hannah IV, 914
Reeder, Hannah IV, 989
Reeder, Hannah V, 274
Reeder, Hannah VI, 648
Reeder, Hannah VI, 694
Reeder, Hannah C. IV, 914
Reeder, Hannah D. IV, 753
Reeder, Hannah D. IV, 914
Reeder, Hannah D. IV, 916
Reeder, Hannah E. V, 274
Reeder, Hannah Elizabeth IV, 915
Reeder, Hannah Elizabeth V, 274
Reeder, Harley Leroy V, 763
Reeder, Harvey W. V, 595
Reeder, Henry IV, 989
Reeder, Howard II, 1058
Reeder, Howard II, 1078
Reeder, Howell V, 763
Reeder, Jacob IV, 911
Reeder, Jacob IV, 914
Reeder, James IV, 753
Reeder, James IV, 810
Reeder, James IV, 840
Reeder, James IV, 858
Reeder, James IV, 914
Reeder, James IV, 916
Reeder, Jane II, 1078
Reeder, Jane V, 199
Reeder, Jesse IV, 914
Reeder, Jesse IV, 915
Reeder, Joanna IV, 753
Reeder, Joanna IV, 989
Reeder, Joanna IV, 1007
Reeder, Joanna IV, 1029
Reeder, John IV, 753
Reeder, John Sherman V, 274
Reeder, Joseph IV, 627
Reeder, Joseph IV, 653
Reeder, Joseph IV, 753
Reeder, Joseph IV, 908
Reeder, Joseph IV, 914
Reeder, Joseph IV, 989
Reeder, Joseph V, 274
Reeder, Joseph VI, 337
Reeder, Joseph VI, 694
Reeder, Josephine IV, 915
Reeder, Juliana IV, 915
Reeder, Latitia II, 1055
Reeder, Latitia II, 1058
Reeder, Letitia II, 1023
Reeder, Letitia W. II, 1076
Reeder, Letitia W. II, 1078
Reeder, Levi IV, 753
Reeder, Levi IV, 902
Reeder, Levi IV, 914
Reeder, Levi IV, 989
Reeder, Levi IV, 999
Reeder, Levi IV, 1007
Reeder, Levi V, 274
Reeder, Lewis IV, 753
Reeder, Louisa V, 269
Reeder, Louisa V, 274
Reeder, Louisa V, 278
Reeder, Louiza V, 274
Reeder, Lydia IV, 798
Reeder, Lydia IV, 840
Reeder, Lydia IV, 914
Reeder, Lydia IV, 1029
Reeder, Lydia IV, 1030
Reeder, Lydia Ann IV, 753
Reeder, Lydia Ann IV, 914
Reeder, Lydia B. IV, 741
Reeder, Lydia B. IV, 753
Reeder, Lydia B. IV, 1029
Reeder, Lydia, Jr. IV, 1029
Reeder, Malone IV, 914
Reeder, Margaret VI, 575
Reeder, Margaret C. II, 1049
Reeder, Margaret C. II, 1058
Reeder, Maria IV, 914
Reeder, Maria IV, 917
Reeder, Maria IV, 1029
Reeder, Maria IV, 1030
Reeder, Martha IV, 268
Reeder, Martha V, 595
Reeder, Martha C. IV, 268
Reeder, Martha J. V, 595
Reeder, Mary IV, 753
Reeder, Mary IV, 810
Reeder, Mary IV, 840
Reeder, Mary IV, 855
Reeder, Mary IV, 858
Reeder, Mary IV, 914
Reeder, Mary IV, 916
Reeder, Mary V, 1015
Reeder, Mary VI, 648
Reeder, Mary VI, 694
Reeder, Mary Buckingham VI, 694
Reeder, Mary C. II, 1058
Reeder, Mary T. IV, 1007
Reeder, Mary W. IV, 753
Reeder, Mellora Augusta III, 43
Reeder, Merihab IV, 909
Reeder, Parsilla VI, 337
Reeder, Pearl H. IV, 268
Reeder, Persilla VI, 337
Reeder, Philena D. IV, 753
Reeder, Philena Deborah IV, 91
Reeder, Pricilla VI, 694
Reeder, Priscilla II, 1023
Reeder, Priscilla IV, 653
Reeder, Priscilla IV, 753
Reeder, Priscilla IV, 798
Reeder, Priscilla IV, 840
Reeder, Priscilla IV, 902
Reeder, Priscilla VI, 337
Reeder, Priscilla VI, 694
Reeder, Rachel P. IV, 989
Reeder, Rachel P. IV, 999
Reeder, Rebecca IV, 907
Reeder, Rebecca IV, 914
Reeder, Rebecca IV, 1029
Reeder, Rebecca V, 763
Reeder, Rhoda M. III, 439
Reeder, Ruth IV, 127
Reeder, Ruth IV, 132
Reeder, Ruth IV, 914
Reeder, Ruth IV, 915
Reeder, Ruth E. IV, 914
Reeder, Samuel IV, 753
Reeder, Samuel IV, 840
Reeder, Samuel IV, 859
Reeder, Samuel IV, 914
Reeder, Sarah IV, 914
Reeder, Sarah VI, 644
Reeder, Sarah VI, 648
Reeder, Sarah VI, 649
Reeder, Sarah VI, 689
Reeder, Sarah VI, 694
Reeder, Sarah Ann IV, 899
Reeder, Sarah Ann IV, 915
Reeder, Sherman V, 274
Reeder, Stafford Joshua IV, 914
Reeder, Thomas IV, 228
Reeder, Thomas IV, 268
Reeder, Thomas IV, 653
Reeder, Thomas IV, 753
Reeder, Thomas IV, 827
Reeder, Thomas IV, 840
Reeder, Thomas VI, 337
Reeder, Thomas VI, 694
Reeder, Thomas Elwood V, 274
Reeder, Thomas, Jr. VI, 337
Reeder, Thos. IV, 902
Reeder, Washington IV, 268
Reeder, Wd. Rebecca V, 757
Reeder, Webster V, 274
Reeder, William IV, 753
Reeder, William IV, 914
Reeder, William IV, 1029
Reeder, William VI, 337
Reeder, William VI, 694
Reeder, Wm. IV, 753
Reeder, Wm. IV, 787
Reeder, Wm. IV, 798
Reeder, Wm. IV, 840
Reeder, Wm. IV, 915
Reeder, Wm. IV, 1030

eder, Wm. VI, 648
eder, Wm. VI, 694
eder, Yardley II, 1023
eder, Zilpah V, 274
eder, Zilphia V, 274
edy, Charles VI, 955
edy, Mary VI, 902
edy, Polly VI, 955
edy, Sarah E. IV, 1261
eks, Isaac VI, 8
eks, Isaac VI, 35
eks, Isack VI, 41
ems, Jeremiah I, 256
ems, John V, 273
es, Abraham V, 274
es, Alfred V, 309
es, Alfred VI, 436
es, Ann I, 1087
es, Ann I, 1093
es, Ann I, 1097
es, Ann V, 274
es, Ann V, 309
es, Ann V, 310
es, Ann V, 429
es, Ann V, 524
es, Ann VI, 415
es, Ann VI, 435
es, Ann VI, 436
es, Ann VI, 462
es, Ann VI, 600
es, Ann VI, 604
es, Ann VI, 694
es, Anna VI, 783
es, Anna J. III, 265
es, Anna J. V, 927
es, Anna Jackson V, 928
es, Anna T. III, 299
es, Annie VI, 435
es, Annie VI, 772
es, Annie J. III, 265
es, Annie J. V, 927
es, Annie J. VI, 436
es, Annie J., Jr. VI, 435
es, Annie J., Jr. VI, 436
es, Annie Jackson V, 927
ees, Annie Jackson VI, 436
ees, Annie R. VI, 436
ees, Annie, Jr. VI, 436
ees, Caleb V, 274
ees, Caleb V, 309
ees, Caroline V, 357
ees, Catherine I, 1097
ees, Catherine I, 1099
ees, Catherine I, 1131
ees, Catherine I, 1135
ees, Catherine VI, 435
ees, Charity I, 1097
ees, Charity I, 1098
ees, Charity I, 1099
ees, Charity V, 274
ees, Charity V, 309
ees, Charity VI, 383
ees, Charity VI, 409
ees, Charity VI, 435
ees, Christian I, 1131
ees, Clinton V, 357
ees, Cordelia IV, 1240
Rees, Dan VI, 436
Rees, David I, 1087
Rees, David I, 1098
Rees, David I, 1131
Rees, David VI, 435
Rees, David VI, 436
Rees, David VI, 440
Rees, David VI, 445
Rees, David VI, 457
Rees, David VI, 875
Rees, David B. VI, 843
Rees, David N. VI, 694
Rees, David Newcomer VI, 436
Rees, David Newcomer VI, 506
Rees, David, Jr. VI, 436
Rees, Deborah I, 1087
Rees, Delia IV, 1240
Rees, Edward VI, 694
Rees, Edward VI, 705
Rees, Eleanor V, 274
Rees, Eleanor V, 301
Rees, Eleanor V, 309
Rees, Eleanor V, 447
Rees, Eleanor VI, 436
Rees, Elenor V, 271
Rees, Elenor V, 274
Rees, Elenor V, 447
Rees, Elisha V, 309
Rees, Eliza Henry VI, 968
Rees, Eliza Ogborn V, 463
Rees, Elizabeth I, 1037
Rees, Elizabeth I, 1087
Rees, Elizabeth I, 1098
Rees, Elizabeth I, 1099
Rees, Elizabeth VI, 435
Rees, Elizabeth Ann Sarah V, 274
Rees, Ella V, 463
Rees, Ella VI, 645
Rees, Ella VI, 694
Rees, Ellen VI, 383
Rees, Ellen VI, 435
Rees, Ellis VI, 436
Rees, Elmore V, 357
Rees, Enoch VI, 435
Rees, Enoch VI, 436
Rees, Esther V, 357
Rees, Esther V, 360
Rees, Evan V, 309
Rees, Evan VI, 436
Rees, Evanna II, 854
Rees, Evans VI, 325
Rees, France V, 274
Rees, Frances VI, 849
Rees, Frank S. II, 854
Rees, Gideon VI, 435
Rees, Gideon VI, 604
Rees, H. M. V, 463
Rees, Hannah I, 732
Rees, Hannah I, 1117
Rees, Hannah I, 1131
Rees, Hannah II, 411
Rees, Hannah IV, 28
Rees, Hannah IV, 40
Rees, Hannah IV, 55
Rees, Hannah VI, 367
Rees, Hannah VI, 411
Rees, Hannah VI, 435
Rees, Hannah VI, 436
Rees, Hannah VI, 452
Rees, Henry VI, 415
Rees, Henry VI, 435
Rees, Henry VI, 451
Rees, Henry VI, 462
Rees, Henry VI, 600
Rees, Henry VI, 604
Rees, Herod VI, 849
Rees, Hester V, 357
Rees, Hester VI, 551
Rees, Jacob IV, 55
Rees, Jacob VI, 411
Rees, Jacob VI, 416
Rees, Jacob VI, 435
Rees, Jacob VI, 436
Rees, Jacob VI, 447
Rees, Jacob VI, 454
Rees, Jacob VI, 551
Rees, Jacob W. VI, 645
Rees, Jacob W. VI, 694
Rees, Jacob Walker VI, 436
Rees, Jacob Ward VI, 506
Rees, Jacob Ward VI, 694
Rees, James I, 1087
Rees, James I, 1097
Rees, James I, 1098
Rees, James V, 271
Rees, James V, 274
Rees, James V, 309
Rees, James V, 310
Rees, James V, 357
Rees, James V, 447
Rees, James, Jr. II, 716
Rees, Jane I, 1087
Rees, Jane I, 1131
Rees, Jane V, 274
Rees, Jane V, 357
Rees, Jane V, 927
Rees, Jane VI, 435
Rees, Jane VI, 436
Rees, Jane VI, 446
Rees, Jane VI, 454
Rees, Jane VI, 457
Rees, Jane VI, 752
Rees, Jane VI, 791
Rees, Jane Sidwell VI, 436
Rees, Jemima I, 1087
Rees, Jennie V, 463
Rees, Jesse V, 310
Rees, Joel IV, 55
Rees, Joel V, 274
Rees, Joel V, 310
Rees, John I, 1037
Rees, John I, 1087
Rees, John I, 1091
Rees, John I, 1097
Rees, John I, 1098
Rees, John V, 274
Rees, John V, 309
Rees, John VI, 435
Rees, John N. VI, 435
Rees, John, Jr. VI, 436
Rees, John, Sr. VI, 436
Rees, Jonah L. III, 265
Rees, Jonah L. III, 299
Rees, Jonah L. V, 927
Rees, Jonah L. VI, 406
Rees, Jonah L. VI, 435
Rees, Jonah L. VI, 772
Rees, Jonah L. VI, 783
Rees, Jonathan I, 1097
Rees, Jonathan V, 447
Rees, Joseph I, 1097
Rees, Joseph VI, 694
Rees, Josiah V, 309
Rees, Katherine VI, 435
Rees, Leah VI, 424
Rees, Leah VI, 436
Rees, Lewis VI, 435
Rees, Lewis VI, 604
Rees, Lucinda V, 274
Rees, Lucinda V, 289
Rees, Lydia V, 235
Rees, Lydia V, 274
Rees, Lydia V, 309
Rees, Lydia VI, 435
Rees, Lydia VI, 440
Rees, Lydia VI, 600
Rees, Lydia VI, 604
Rees, Lydia VI, 665
Rees, Lydia VI, 673
Rees, Lydia VI, 694
Rees, Lydia Ann VI, 435
Rees, Lydia Ann VI, 436
Rees, Lydia Ann VI, 506
Rees, Margaret I, 1091
Rees, Margaret I, 1097
Rees, Margaret I, 1099
Rees, Margaret V, 309
Rees, Margaret V, 310
Rees, Margaret V, 357
Rees, Margaret VI, 384
Rees, Margaret VI, 435
Rees, Margaret VI, 600
Rees, Margaret VI, 604
Rees, Margaret VI, 653
Rees, Margaret VI, 685
Rees, Margaret VI, 694
Rees, Margaret VI, 718
Rees, Martha VI, 422
Rees, Martha VI, 435
Rees, Martha VI, 436
Rees, Martha VI, 440
Rees, Martha VI, 445
Rees, Martha VI, 451
Rees, Martha VI, 457
Rees, Martha A. VI, 423
Rees, Martha A. VI, 436
Rees, Martha Jane VI, 875
Rees, Mary I, 1087
Rees, Mary V, 896
Rees, Mary V, 927
Rees, Mary VI, 381
Rees, Mary VI, 435
Rees, Mary VI, 436
Rees, Mary VI, 443
Rees, Mary VI, 445
Rees, Mary VI, 694
Rees, Mary VI, 714
Rees, Mary A. III, 299
Rees, Mary A. VI, 565
Rees, Mary Alcie VI, 783
Rees, Mary Alice III, 265
Rees, Mary Alice V, 927
Rees, Mary Alice V, 928
Rees, Mary Alice VI, 436
Rees, Mary Alice VI, 772
Rees, Mary Alice VI, 783
Rees, Mary Eleanor V, 309
Rees, Mary Ellen VI, 436
Rees, Matilda V, 297
Rees, Matilda V, 310
Rees, Matilda Jane V, 309
Rees, Matilda Jane VI, 436
Rees, Michael V, 274
Rees, Michael V, 309
Rees, Morris IV, 55
Rees, Morris VI, 384
Rees, Morris VI, 414
Rees, Morris VI, 435
Rees, Morris, Jr. VI, 435
Rees, Moses I, 1097
Rees, Moses I, 1098
Rees, Moses VI, 436
Rees, Moses, Jr. I, 1087
Rees, Moses, Sen. I, 1087
Rees, Mrs. Frida M. IV, 495
Rees, Nancy V, 274
Rees, Nathan IV, 55
Rees, Peter I, 1087
Rees, Peter I, 1098
Rees, Phebe I, 1087
Rees, Phebe I, 1091
Rees, Phebe I, 1097
Rees, Phebe I, 1098
Rees, Phebe V, 309
Rees, Phebe VI, 414
Rees, Phebe VI, 425
Rees, Phebe VI, 435
Rees, Phebe VI, 436
Rees, Phebe Elmore V, 274
Rees, Rachel I, 1087
Rees, Rachel I, 1131
Rees, Rachel IV, 268
Rees, Rachel V, 357
Rees, Rachel VI, 384
Rees, Rachel VI, 435
Rees, Rachel VI, 436
Rees, Rachel VI, 694
Rees, Rachel Annie VI, 406
Rees, Rachel Annie, Sr. VI, 435
Rees, Rebecca VI, 376
Rees, Rebecca VI, 436
Rees, Rebecca VI, 447
Rees, Rebecca Evaline I, 1098
Rees, Rebeckah V, 309
Rees, Robert VI, 413
Rees, Ruth I, 1098
Rees, Ruth I, 1099
Rees, Ruth IV, 268
Rees, Ruth VI, 435
Rees, Ruth VI, 447
Rees, Ruth VI, 454
Rees, Samuel V, 927
Rees, Samuel VI, 506
Rees, Samuel VI, 653
Rees, Samuel VI, 694
Rees, Samuel D. V, 927
Rees, Samuel D. VI, 435
Rees, Samuel D. VI, 436
Rees, Samuel David V, 927
Rees, Samuel David VI, 436
Rees, Sarah I, 611
Rees, Sarah I, 1087
Rees, Sarah I, 1097
Rees, Sarah I, 1098
Rees, Sarah IV, 53
Rees, Sarah IV, 55
Rees, Sarah IV, 106
Rees, Sarah IV, 107
Rees, Sarah V, 274
Rees, Sarah V, 309
Rees, Sarah V, 509
Rees, Sarah V, 524
Rees, Sarah VI, 414
Rees, Sarah VI, 420
Rees, Sarah VI, 435
Rees, Sarah VI, 436
Rees, Sarah VI, 694
Rees, Sarah VI, 705
Rees, Sarah L. VI, 843
Rees, Sarah, Sen. I, 1087
Rees, Sidney VI, 413
Rees, Sidney VI, 435
Rees, Silas IV, 268
Rees, Solomon I, 1037
Rees, Solomon I, 1097
Rees, Solomon I, 1098
Rees, Solomon I, 1099
Rees, Solomon VI, 436
Rees, Stephen IV, 268
Rees, Susannah I, 1087
Rees, Thamasin VI, 435
Rees, Thamasin M. VI, 416
Rees, Thamasin M. VI, 435
Rees, Thamsin VI, 416
Rees, Thomas I, 1097
Rees, Thomas V, 274
Rees, Thomas V, 357
Rees, Thomas VI, 383
Rees, Thomas VI, 435
Rees, Thomas VI, 436
Rees, Thomas, Jr. V, 309
Rees, Thomas, Jr. VI, 435
Rees, Thomas, Jur. VI, 436
Rees, Thomasin M. V, 927
Rees, Thomasine M. V, 927
Rees, Thos. V, 301
Rees, Thos. V, 309
Rees, Thos. V, 360
Rees, W. O. V, 463
Rees, Wd. Margaret VI, 551
Rees, Wd. Margaret Ward VI, 506
Rees, Widow Charity I, 1087
Rees, Widow Margaret VI, 653
Rees, Widow Margaret VI, 654
Rees, William I, 1077
Rees, William I, 1087
Rees, William I, 1097
Rees, William V, 274
Rees, William VI, 383
Rees, William VI, 436
Rees, William, Jr. I, 1087
Rees, William, Jr. I, 1097
Rees, William, Sen. I, 1087
Rees, Wm. I, 1087
Rees, Wm. V, 309
Rees, Zeno V, 357
Reese, ??? V, 114
Reese, Abraham I, 996
Reese, Abraham V, 274
Reese, Ann I, 513
Reese, Ann I, 732
Reese, Ann V, 484
Reese, Ann V, 524
Reese, Ann VI, 436
Reese, Ann VI, 551
Reese, Ann VI, 745
Reese, Ann VI, 772
Reese, Ann VI, 982
Reese, Anna II, 797
Reese, Anna VI, 982
Reese, Anna J. III, 265
Reese, Anna R. VI, 745
Reese, Annie VI, 772
Reese, Annie J. III, 265
Reese, Annie J. VI, 436
Reese, Annie Jackson III, 265
Reese, Annie Jackson VI, 436
Reese, Annie R. VI, 436
Reese, Arminta I, 568
Reese, Asa VI, 677
Reese, Asenath H. I, 732
Reese, Benj. F. VI, 965
Reese, Benjamin II, 411
Reese, Beulah VI, 772
Reese, Byron J. IV, 495
Reese, Byrum G. IV, 495
Reese, Caleb I, 835
Reese, Caleb I, 898
Reese, Caleb I, 899
Reese, Caleb I, 1012
Reese, Catharine I, 724
Reese, Catharine I, 732
Reese, Catharine VI, 982
Reese, Catherine VI, 435
Reese, Cathrine VI, 369
Reese, Charity I, 513
Reese, Charles V, 199
Reese, Christen I, 732
Reese, Christian I, 568
Reese, Christian I, 575
Reese, Christian I, 732
Reese, Daniel I, 835
Reese, David I, 568
Reese, David I, 1012
Reese, David II, 631
Reese, David VI, 436
Reese, David Newcomer VI, 436
Reese, David Newcomer VI, 551
Reese, David, Jr. VI, 982
Reese, Davis I, 732
Reese, Deborah VI, 772
Reese, Delia III, 265
Reese, Dempsey I, 732
Reese, Edith C. IV, 495
Reese, Edward II, 411
Reese, Edward II, 631
Reese, Edward VI, 494
Reese, Edward VI, 551
Reese, Eleanor VI, 436
Reese, Eli I, 948
Reese, Eliza M. VI, 982
Reese, Elizabeth I, 1012
Reese, Elizabeth V, 958
Reese, Elizabeth VI, 808
Reese, Ellen V, 114
Reese, Ellis VI, 436
Reese, Emily III, 85
Reese, Emily III, 265
Reese, Emily A. VI, 930
Reese, Emma IV, 1261
Reese, Enoch VI, 436
Reese, Featherston VI, 982
Reese, Frances VI, 849
Reese, Francis I, 732
Reese, Gerard H. VI, 756
Reese, Gerard H. VI, 758
Reese, Gerard H. VI, 772
Reese, Gerard Hopkins VI, 663
Reese, Hannah I, 732
Reese, Hannah I, 835
Reese, Hannah II, 411
Reese, Hannah II, 463
Reese, Hannah II, 481
Reese, Hannah II, 631
Reese, Hannah V, 958
Reese, Hannah VI, 436
Reese, Hannah VI, 440
Reese, Hannah VI, 551
Reese, Hannah R. V, 958
Reese, Henry VI, 369
Reese, Henry VI, 435
Reese, Henry VI, 766
Reese, Henry VI, 772
Reese, Herod VI, 808
Reese, Herod VI, 834
Reese, Herod VI, 849
Reese, Herod VI, 856

Reese, Hester VI, 551
Reese, Hulda Ann IV, 495
Reese, Huldah I, 732
Reese, Huldah I, 734
Reese, Huldah IV, 495
Reese, Huldah A. IV, 495
Reese, Isaiah I, 1131
Reese, Isaiah V, 1015
Reese, Jacob VI, 436
Reese, Jacob VI, 551
Reese, Jacob VI, 576
Reese, Jacob VI, 691
Reese, Jacob Walker VI, 436
Reese, Jacob Walker VI, 551
Reese, James I, 513
Reese, James V, 114
Reese, James VI, 982
Reese, James A. IV, 1261
Reese, Jane I, 1131
Reese, Jane V, 114
Reese, Jane V, 429
Reese, Jane VI, 436
Reese, Jane VI, 493
Reese, Jane VI, 551
Reese, Jane VI, 576
Reese, Jane VI, 582
Reese, Jason V, 958
Reese, Jennie V, 463
Reese, Jesse I, 732
Reese, Jno. M. VI, 944
Reese, Jno. M. VI, 968
Reese, Jno. M. VI, 975
Reese, Jno. M. VI, 981
Reese, Jno. M. VI, 1015
Reese, John I, 513
Reese, John I, 732
Reese, John VI, 884
Reese, John VI, 926
Reese, John VI, 982
Reese, John E. VI, 772
Reese, John M. VI, 887
Reese, John M. VI, 891
Reese, John M. VI, 954
Reese, John M. VI, 958
Reese, John W. VI, 982
Reese, John, Jr. VI, 436
Reese, Jonah L. III, 265
Reese, Jonah L. VI, 772
Reese, Jonathan V, 958
Reese, Jonathan G. V, 958
Reese, Joseph T. VI, 930
Reese, Joseph T. VI, 951
Reese, Joseph T. VI, 982
Reese, Joseph T. VI, 1014
Reese, Juday VI, 849
Reese, Kezia II, 631
Reese, Keziah II, 450
Reese, Lenius IV, 753
Reese, Lewis V, 114
Reese, Loring IV, 495
Reese, Loring W. IV, 495
Reese, Lucy McD. VI, 1014
Reese, Lydia VI, 551
Reese, Lydia Ann VI, 436
Reese, Lydia Ann VI, 691
Reese, Lydia P. II, 913
Reese, M. M. III, 85
Reese, M. M. III, 265
Reese, Margaret I, 513
Reese, Margaret VI, 405
Reese, Martha VI, 369
Reese, Martha VI, 435
Reese, Martha VI, 436
Reese, Martha VI, 940
Reese, Martha A. V, 114
Reese, Mary I, 513
Reese, Mary I, 568
Reese, Mary I, 835
Reese, Mary VI, 365
Reese, Mary VI, 436
Reese, Mary VI, 676
Reese, Mary VI, 763
Reese, Mary VI, 772
Reese, Mary VI, 982
Reese, Mary A. VI, 982
Reese, Mary Albina VI, 494
Reese, Mary Alice III, 265
Reese, Mary Alice VI, 436
Reese, Mary Alice VI, 772
Reese, Mary Anna VI, 766
Reese, Mary Anna VI, 772
Reese, Mary Elizabeth VI, 582
Reese, Mary Ellen VI, 436
Reese, Mary Jane VI, 756
Reese, Milly VI, 982
Reese, Morris VI, 551
Reese, Moses I, 513
Reese, Moses I, 568
Reese, Mrs. Frida M. IV, 495
Reese, Nancy VI, 877
Reese, Nancy VI, 982
Reese, Pamela VI, 982
Reese, Patsy VI, 982
Reese, Paul Dervit IV, 1261
Reese, Phebe V, 304
Reese, Phebe V, 309
Reese, Polly VI, 901
Reese, Polly VI, 982
Reese, Rachel I, 1012
Reese, Rachel II, 631
Reese, Rachel IV, 268
Reese, Rachel V, 323
Reese, Rachel V, 357
Reese, Rachel VI, 629
Reese, Rebecca I, 1007
Reese, Rebecca I, 1012
Reese, Rebekah I, 835
Reese, Rhoda VI, 884
Reese, Robert VI, 982
Reese, Robert W. VI, 877
Reese, Robert W. VI, 982
Reese, Robert W. VI, 999
Reese, Robt. VI, 940
Reese, Rosa V, 199
Reese, Ruth VI, 551
Reese, Ruth VI, 576
Reese, Ruth VI, 691
Reese, Sally V, 114
Reese, Sally VI, 982
Reese, Samuel VI, 551
Reese, Samuel VI, 577
Reese, Samuel D. V, 114
Reese, Samuel D. VI, 436
Reese, Samuel D. VI, 691
Reese, Samuel David VI, 436
Reese, Sarah I, 996
Reese, Sarah I, 1001
Reese, Sarah I, 1012
Reese, Sarah IV, 107
Reese, Sarah V, 429
Reese, Sarah V, 434
Reese, Sarah V, 699
Reese, Sarah V, 958
Reese, Sarah VI, 477
Reese, Sarah VI, 551
Reese, Sarah VI, 756
Reese, Sarah Jane VI, 663
Reese, Sarah Jane VI, 758
Reese, Sarah Jane VI, 772
Reese, Seth IV, 495
Reese, Seth C. IV, 495
Reese, Seth S. IV, 495
Reese, Silas G. VI, 982
Reese, Sloman VI, 884
Reese, Solomon VI, 436
Reese, Sophia VI, 926
Reese, Sophia S. VI, 1004
Reese, Stephen V, 958
Reese, Stephen VI, 982
Reese, Stephen D. V, 114
Reese, Stephen P. V, 958
Reese, Stephen R. V, 958
Reese, Tamar VI, 694
Reese, Tamer IV, 107
Reese, Thamizin M. V, 114
Reese, Thomas I, 513
Reese, Thomas I, 1131
Reese, Thomas II, 411
Reese, Thomas II, 412
Reese, Thomas II, 631
Reese, Thomas V, 114
Reese, Thomas VI, 436
Reese, Thomas VI, 551
Reese, Thomas VI, 676
Reese, Thomas VI, 772
Reese, Thomas L. VI, 763
Reese, Thomas L. VI, 772
Reese, Thomas, Jur. VI, 436
Reese, Wd. Margaret VI, 551
Reese, William I, 513
Reese, William I, 568
Reese, William II, 411
Reese, William V, 114
Reese, William V, 274
Reese, William V, 958
Reese, William VI, 982
Reese, William B. VI, 982
Reese, William W. III, 265
Reese, William W. VI, 981
Reese, William W. VI, 982
Reese, Wm. I, 513
Reese, Wm. Gould V, 958
Reese, Yarnal I, 1131
Reese, Zachery IV, 495
Reeser, A. V, 763
Reeser, Clarence A. V, 763
Reeser, Sarah V, 763
Reeseville, M. R. V, 706
Reeve, Abigail W. II, 816
Reeve, Abraham II, 181
Reeve, Abraham II, 762
Reeve, Abraham IV, 593
Reeve, Achsah II, 37
Reeve, Achsah S. II, 122
Reeve, Adelaide II, 283
Reeve, Adelaide II, 299
Reeve, Adelaide B. II, 299
Reeve, Alice B. II, 156
Reeve, Amanda IV, 989
Reeve, Amiliscent IV, 158
Reeve, Amos Preston IV, 859
Reeve, Ann II, 38
Reeve, Ann II, 299
Reeve, Ann II, 632
Reeve, Ann IV, 882
Reeve, Ann IV, 989
Reeve, Anna II, 761
Reeve, Anna II, 762
Reeve, Anna IV, 593
Reeve, Anna IV, 950
Reeve, Anna IV, 989
Reeve, Anna S. II, 283
Reeve, Anna S. II, 299
Reeve, Augustus H. II, 123
Reeve, Augustus Henry II, 38
Reeve, Belle S. III, 69
Reeve, Benjamin II, 37
Reeve, Benjamin II, 38
Reeve, Benjamin II, 58
Reeve, Benjamin II, 93
Reeve, Benjamin II, 107
Reeve, Benjamin II, 412
Reeve, Benjamin II, 471
Reeve, Benjamin II, 631
Reeve, Benjamin IV, 593
Reeve, Benjamin IV, 882
Reeve, Benjamin IV, 989
Reeve, Benjamin IV, 1291
Reeve, Benjamin IV, 1292
Reeve, Benjamin C. II, 37
Reeve, Benjamin C. II, 116
Reeve, Benjamin C. II, 123
Reeve, Benjamin Cooper II, 37
Reeve, Benjamin L. IV, 593
Reeve, Beulah II, 70
Reeve, Beulah II, 94
Reeve, Biddle II, 122
Reeve, Biddle II, 632
Reeve, C. Hildreth II, 156
Reeve, Caspar W. I, 1098
Reeve, Casper W. I, 1098
Reeve, Catharine II, 631
Reeve, Catharine IV, 974
Reeve, Catharine IV, 989
Reeve, Catharine V, 917
Reeve, Catherine II, 631
Reeve, Catherine IV, 989
Reeve, Charles II, 761
Reeve, Charles B. II, 156
Reeve, Chas. II, 632
Reeve, Clayton I, 1098
Reeve, Clement II, 632
Reeve, Dallas II, 38
Reeve, Dallas II, 122
Reeve, Dallas II, 123
Reeve, Daniel IV, 989
Reeve, David II, 252
Reeve, Dorcas IV, 989
Reeve, Dorcas Ann IV, 989
Reeve, Dorcas Ann IV, 1008
Reeve, Drusila IV, 859
Reeve, Edward II, 716
Reeve, Edward II, 762
Reeve, Eliza W. II, 716
Reeve, Elizabeth II, 37
Reeve, Elizabeth II, 58
Reeve, Elizabeth II, 93
Reeve, Elizabeth II, 122
Reeve, Elizabeth II, 299
Reeve, Elizabeth II, 301
Reeve, Elizabeth II, 631
Reeve, Elizabeth II, 632
Reeve, Elizabeth IV, 754
Reeve, Elizabeth IV, 874
Reeve, Elizabeth IV, 882
Reeve, Elizabeth IV, 967
Reeve, Elizabeth IV, 989
Reeve, Elizabeth IV, 1075
Reeve, Elizabeth IV, 1113
Reeve, Elizabeth Ann II, 913
Reeve, Elizabeth M. II, 122
Reeve, Elizabeth M. II, 124
Reeve, Ellen IV, 961
Reeve, Ellen IV, 989
Reeve, Ellen J. IV, 1042
Reeve, Ellen P. II, 123
Reeve, Ellin II, 52
Reeve, Ellin II, 93
Reeve, Elma Ann IV, 593
Reeve, Elonar II, 37
Reeve, Elonar II, 38
Reeve, Elwood II, 716
Reeve, Emma II, 38
Reeve, Emma II, 122
Reeve, Emma L. II, 156
Reeve, Emmer II, 114
Reeve, Emmer II, 116
Reeve, Emmer II, 122
Reeve, Emmer II, 123
Reeve, Emmor II, 37
Reeve, Emmor II, 122
Reeve, Esther IV, 1113
Reeve, George II, 37
Reeve, George II, 38
Reeve, Hannah II, 37
Reeve, Hannah II, 38
Reeve, Hannah II, 93
Reeve, Hannah II, 94
Reeve, Hannah II, 109
Reeve, Hannah II, 122
Reeve, Hannah II, 631
Reeve, Hannah II, 643
Reeve, Hannah IV, 754
Reeve, Hannah IV, 759
Reeve, Hannah IV, 989
Reeve, Hannah VI, 775
Reeve, Hannah Buzby II, 156
Reeve, Hannah C. II, 123
Reeve, Hannah Carpenter II, 38
Reeve, Hannah G. II, 38
Reeve, Hannah G. II, 122
Reeve, Hannah G. II, 124
Reeve, Henry II, 299
Reeve, Herbert E. II, 37
Reeve, Herbert E. II, 123
Reeve, Hildreth S. II, 156
Reeve, Isaac II, 1058
Reeve, Israel II, 632
Reeve, J. Morris II, 156
Reeve, J. Newbold II, 283
Reeve, J. Newbold II, 299
Reeve, James II, 37
Reeve, Joanna II, 156
Reeve, Joanna F. II, 156
Reeve, Joanna M. II, 156
Reeve, Job IV, 989
Reeve, Joel II, 632
Reeve, John II, 37
Reeve, John II, 58
Reeve, John II, 70
Reeve, John II, 93
Reeve, John II, 94
Reeve, John II, 252
Reeve, John II, 256
Reeve, John II, 412
Reeve, John II, 631
Reeve, John II, 639
Reeve, John II, 643
Reeve, John II, 716
Reeve, John IV, 989
Reeve, John Morris II, 156
Reeve, John N. II, 716
Reeve, John N. II, 762
Reeve, John, Jr. II, 94
Reeve, Joseph II, 37
Reeve, Joseph II, 38
Reeve, Joseph II, 52
Reeve, Joseph II, 60
Reeve, Joseph II, 93
Reeve, Joseph II, 94
Reeve, Joseph II, 122
Reeve, Joseph II, 154
Reeve, Joseph II, 155
Reeve, Joseph II, 156
Reeve, Joseph II, 632
Reeve, Joseph IV, 432
Reeve, Joseph IV, 593
Reeve, Joshua II, 37
Reeve, Joshua II, 94
Reeve, Joshua II, 109
Reeve, Joshua II, 122
Reeve, Joshua IV, 158
Reeve, Joshua IV, 754
Reeve, Joshua IV, 759
Reeve, Joshua IV, 874
Reeve, Joshua IV, 882
Reeve, Joshua IV, 967
Reeve, Joshua IV, 974
Reeve, Joshua IV, 989
Reeve, Joshua IV, 1041
Reeve, Joshua IV, 1075
Reeve, Joshua IV, 1113
Reeve, Joshua V, 917
Reeve, Josiah II, 38
Reeve, Josiah II, 94
Reeve, Josiah II, 180
Reeve, Josiah II, 299
Reeve, Josiah II, 301
Reeve, Josiah M. II, 38
Reeve, Josiah M. II, 94
Reeve, Josiah M. II, 122
Reeve, Josiah R. II, 299
Reeve, Josiah R. II, 301
Reeve, Latitia IV, 1113
Reeve, Leatitia II, 37
Reeve, Leatitia II, 38
Reeve, Leatitia II, 94
Reeve, Leatitia II, 114
Reeve, Leatitia II, 122
Reeve, Leatitia Ann II, 38
Reeve, Letitia II, 122
Reeve, Letitia II, 123
Reeve, Letitia II, 124
Reeve, Lettitia II, 87
Reeve, Lettitia II, 94
Reeve, Lettitia II, 122
Reeve, Lewis IV, 989
Reeve, Lillian II, 156
Reeve, Lillian A. II, 156
Reeve, Louisa II, 632
Reeve, Louisa II, 684
Reeve, Louiza M. II, 632
Reeve, Lydia IV, 1292
Reeve, Lydia Ann IV, 593
Reeve, Lydia B. IV, 1291
Reeve, Lydia F. II, 632
Reeve, Lydia F. II, 761
Reeve, Mahlon II, 94
Reeve, Margaret II, 137
Reeve, Margaret C. II, 156
Reeve, Margarett C. II, 156
Reeve, Maria II, 299
Reeve, Maria II, 301
Reeve, Maria S. II, 299
Reeve, Mark II, 37
Reeve, Mark II, 38
Reeve, Mark II, 93
Reeve, Mark II, 122
Reeve, Mark II, 181
Reeve, Mark II, 631
Reeve, Mark II, 761
Reeve, Mark M. II, 37
Reeve, Mark M. II, 761
Reeve, Martha II, 23
Reeve, Martha II, 38
Reeve, Martha II, 47
Reeve, Martha II, 58
Reeve, Martha II, 60
Reeve, Martha II, 94
Reeve, Martha II, 122
Reeve, Martha II, 154
Reeve, Martha II, 156
Reeve, Martha II, 161
Reeve, Martha Grier II, 156
Reeve, Martha W. II, 156
Reeve, Mary II, 37
Reeve, Mary II, 38
Reeve, Mary II, 93
Reeve, Mary II, 122
Reeve, Mary II, 252
Reeve, Mary II, 412
Reeve, Mary II, 631
Reeve, Mary II, 632
Reeve, Mary II, 634
Reeve, Mary II, 639
Reeve, Mary II, 761
Reeve, Mary II, 762
Reeve, Mary IV, 989
Reeve, Mary Ann II, 762
Reeve, Mary B. II, 38
Reeve, Mary B. II, 122
Reeve, Mary B. II, 716
Reeve, Mary B. II, 762
Reeve, Mary R. II, 37
Reeve, Mary R. II, 116
Reeve, Mary R. II, 123
Reeve, Mary R. C. II, 123
Reeve, Mary W. II, 38
Reeve, Mary W. II, 116
Reeve, Mary W. II, 122
Reeve, Mary W. II, 123
Reeve, Matilda Ann IV, 593
Reeve, Melescent IV, 882
Reeve, Melescent IV, 989
Reeve, Milicent II, 154
Reeve, Milicent II, 155
Reeve, Milicent IV, 989
Reeve, Miliscent IV, 974
Reeve, Milisent II, 122
Reeve, Millicent II, 38
Reeve, Millicent IV, 989
Reeve, Millicent V, 917
Reeve, Millisent II, 38
Reeve, Morris A. II, 156
Reeve, Mylicent II, 93
Reeve, Peter II, 37
Reeve, Peter II, 631
Reeve, Phebe IV, 989
Reeve, Priscilla II, 122
Reeve, Priscilla II, 123
Reeve, Priscilla M. II, 123
Reeve, Priscilla S. II, 122
Reeve, Priscilla W. II, 716
Reeve, Priscilla W., Jr. II, 122
Reeve, Prudence II, 37

ve, Prudence II, 122
ve, Prudence B. II, 116
ve, Prudence B. II, 123
ve, Rachel II, 37
ve, Rachel II, 93
ve, Rachel II, 107
ve, Rachel II, 412
ve, Rachel II, 761
ve, Rachel II, 762
ve, Rachel IV, 1376
ve, Rachel C. II, 37
ve, Rachel C. II, 123
ve, Rebecca II, 252
ve, Rebecca II, 256
ve, Rebecca C. II, 38
ve, Rebecca C. II, 123
ve, Rebecca F. I, 1098
ve, Richard II, 37
ve, Richard II, 94
ve, Richard II, 122
ve, Richard II, 123
ve, Richard II, 716
ve, Richard H. II, 38
ve, Richard Henry II, 38
ve, Richard Henry II, 116
ve, Richard Henry II, 122
ve, Richard M. II, 761
ve, Richard M. II, 762
ve, Robert I, 1098
ve, Robert I, 1099
ve, Ruth II, 37
ve, Ruth II, 38
ve, Ruth II, 58
ve, Ruth II, 93
ve, Ruth II, 471
ve, Ruth II, 631
ve, Samuel II, 38
ve, Samuel II, 94
ve, Samuel II, 122
ve, Samuel II, 632
ve, Samuel II, 761
ve, Samuel IV, 348
ve, Samuel IV, 432
ve, Samuel C. IV, 754
ve, Samuel C. IV, 950
ve, Samuel C. IV, 989
ve, Sarah II, 38
ve, Sarah II, 70
ve, Sarah II, 94
ve, Sarah II, 122
ve, Sarah II, 181
ve, Sarah II, 412
ve, Sarah II, 632
ve, Sarah A. II, 123
ve, Sarah B. II, 632
ve, Sarah C. II, 123
ve, Sarah Catherine II, 123
ve, Sarah Cooper II, 37
ve, Sarah W. II, 123
ve, Sarah Wyatt II, 37
ve, Sarah Wyatt II, 114
ve, Sarah Wyatt II, 116
ve, Sarah Wyatt II, 122
ve, Susan II, 38
ve, Susan II, 632
ve, Susan H. II, 94
ve, Susanna H. II, 94
ve, T. Whitle I, 1161
ve, T. Whittle I, 1161
ve, Tabitha II, 180
ve, Thomas II, 412
ve, Thomas IV, 754
ve, Thomas IV, 989
ve, Thomas C. II, 38
ve, Walter S. II, 283
ve, Walter S. II, 299
ve, Wd. Catharine II, 180
ve, Wd. Elizabeth Ann II, 816
ve, Wd. Mary II, 181
ve, Wd. Priscilla II, 38
ve, William II, 37
ve, William II, 38
ve, William IV, 989
ve, William F. II, 38
ve, Wm. II, 87
ve, Wm. II, 94
ve, Wm. II, 114
ve, Wm. II, 122
ve, Wm. II, 123
ve, Wm. II, 124
ve, Wm. II, 816
ve, Wm. F. II, 116
ve, Wm. F. II, 122
ve, Zechariah II, 181
ves, ??? V, 199
ves, Abigail II, 252
ves, Abigail II, 913
ves, Abigail W. II, 816
ves, Abraham II, 753
ves, Abraham II, 762
ves, Abraham II, 831
Reeves, Abraham II, 913
Reeves, Abraham IV, 593
Reeves, Abraham IV, 754
Reeves, Abraham IV, 1029
Reeves, Abram II, 797
Reeves, Adaline II, 913
Reeves, Adelaide II, 299
Reeves, Adelaide B. II, 299
Reeves, Alice B. II, 136
Reeves, Alice B. II, 147
Reeves, Alice B. II, 156
Reeves, Allen V, 858
Reeves, Amanda IV, 989
Reeves, Andrew C. III, 264
Reeves, Andrew C. III, 265
Reeves, Ann II, 252
Reeves, Ann II, 299
Reeves, Ann II, 632
Reeves, Ann IV, 653
Reeves, Ann IV, 654
Reeves, Ann IV, 676
Reeves, Ann IV, 754
Reeves, Ann IV, 882
Reeves, Ann IV, 1029
Reeves, Ann IV, 1031
Reeves, Ann B. IV, 1021
Reeves, Ann C. II, 913
Reeves, Ann C. II, 917
Reeves, Ann Catherine II, 816
Reeves, Ann H. V, 858
Reeves, Anna II, 753
Reeves, Anna II, 761
Reeves, Anna II, 762
Reeves, Anna II, 913
Reeves, Anna Naomi II, 719
Reeves, Anna Rachel II, 299
Reeves, Anna S. II, 299
Reeves, Anne IV, 432
Reeves, Annie I, 317
Reeves, Arthur M. V, 928
Reeves, Arthur Middleton V, 928
Reeves, Batavia IV, 1376
Reeves, Bell V, 199
Reeves, Belle V, 199
Reeves, Benjamin II, 412
Reeves, Benjamin II, 631
Reeves, Benjamin IV, 593
Reeves, Benjamin IV, 653
Reeves, Benjamin IV, 754
Reeves, Benjamin IV, 882
Reeves, Benjamin IV, 1292
Reeves, Beulah II, 299
Reeves, Biddle II, 122
Reeves, Biddle II, 123
Reeves, Biddle II, 252
Reeves, Biddle II, 632
Reeves, C. Hildreth II, 136
Reeves, C. Hildreth II, 147
Reeves, C. Hildreth II, 154
Reeves, C. Hildreth II, 156
Reeves, Caroline V, 928
Reeves, Caroline M. V, 928
Reeves, Catharine IV, 754
Reeves, Catherine V, 199
Reeves, Charles II, 136
Reeves, Charles II, 761
Reeves, Charles B. II, 156
Reeves, Charles B. II, 159
Reeves, Charles Hildreth II, 136
Reeves, Charlotte II, 299
Reeves, Chas. II, 632
Reeves, Chas. II, 816
Reeves, Chas. II, 913
Reeves, Claire V, 199
Reeves, Clayton I, 1087
Reeves, Clement II, 632
Reeves, Coats IV, 1376
Reeves, D. B. IV, 1029
Reeves, Daniel II, 299
Reeves, Daniel II, 913
Reeves, Daniel IV, 754
Reeves, Daniel IV, 1031
Reeves, Daniel B. IV, 1021
Reeves, David II, 252
Reeves, David IV, 754
Reeves, David IV, 840
Reeves, David Jesse II, 252
Reeves, Dorcas IV, 989
Reeves, Eli II, 252
Reeves, Eliza A. III, 476
Reeves, Eliza W. II, 716
Reeves, Elizabeth II, 123
Reeves, Elizabeth II, 252
Reeves, Elizabeth II, 299
Reeves, Elizabeth IV, 754
Reeves, Elizabeth IV, 1137
Reeves, Elizabeth V, 852
Reeves, Elizabeth V, 858
Reeves, Elizabeth Ann II, 913
Reeves, Elizabeth C. II, 299
Reeves, Elizabeth M. V, 858
Reeves, Elizabeth W. II, 324
Reeves, Elizabeth W. II, 327
Reeves, Ellen IV, 653
Reeves, Ellen IV, 754
Reeves, Elma Anna IV, 432
Reeves, Elmer D. V, 199
Reeves, Elmy Ann IV, 383
Reeves, Elmy Ann IV, 432
Reeves, Elwood II, 299
Reeves, Elwood II, 716
Reeves, Emma L. II, 136
Reeves, Emma L. II, 147
Reeves, Emma L. II, 154
Reeves, Emma L. II, 156
Reeves, Emma S. II, 154
Reeves, Emma S. II, 156
Reeves, Esther V, 858
Reeves, Ethel V, 199
Reeves, Etta V, 199
Reeves, Etta Mills V, 199
Reeves, Eva V, 199
Reeves, Frances B. V, 199
Reeves, Frank P. V, 199
Reeves, Frankie R. V, 199
Reeves, Freddie G. V, 199
Reeves, George IV, 754
Reeves, George M. IV, 754
Reeves, George S. V, 199
Reeves, George Sullivan V, 199
Reeves, Gilbert V, 199
Reeves, Grace Anna IV, 1029
Reeves, Grace Anna IV, 1030
Reeves, H. II, 893
Reeves, Hannah II, 299
Reeves, Hannah II, 816
Reeves, Hannah II, 831
Reeves, Hannah II, 913
Reeves, Hannah IV, 653
Reeves, Hannah IV, 754
Reeves, Hannah A. II, 913
Reeves, Hannah Ann II, 299
Reeves, Hannah Ann II, 913
Reeves, Hannah Ann II, 942
Reeves, Hannah Buzby II, 156
Reeves, Hannah Buzby II, 159
Reeves, Harriet IV, 613
Reeves, Harriet IV, 653
Reeves, Harriett IV, 653
Reeves, Harry V, 199
Reeves, Harry B. V, 199
Reeves, Henry II, 252
Reeves, Henry II, 299
Reeves, Henry II, 807
Reeves, Henry II, 816
Reeves, Henry IV, 732
Reeves, Henry, Jr. II, 831
Reeves, Henry, Jr. II, 913
Reeves, Hildreth S. II, 156
Reeves, Hildreth Stretch II, 136
Reeves, Hope II, 831
Reeves, Hope II, 913
Reeves, Isaac II, 299
Reeves, Isaac II, 967
Reeves, Isaac II, 1058
Reeves, Isaiah II, 299
Reeves, Israel II, 632
Reeves, J. Morris II, 134
Reeves, J. Morris II, 136
Reeves, J. Morris II, 137
Reeves, J. Morris II, 151
Reeves, J. Newbold II, 299
Reeves, J. Raymond V, 199
Reeves, James II, 138
Reeves, Jane II, 138
Reeves, Jessie I, 622
Reeves, Joanna II, 136
Reeves, Joanna II, 151
Reeves, Joanna II, 156
Reeves, Joanna F. II, 134
Reeves, Joanna F. II, 137
Reeves, Joanna F. II, 149
Reeves, Joanna F. II, 156
Reeves, Joanna M. II, 156
Reeves, Joanna M. II, 159
Reeves, Joanna Stretch II, 137
Reeves, Job IV, 754
Reeves, Job IV, 1137
Reeves, Joel II, 299
Reeves, Joel II, 632
Reeves, Joel II, 816
Reeves, John II, 252
Reeves, John II, 299
Reeves, John II, 412
Reeves, John II, 631
Reeves, John IV, 546
Reeves, John IV, 989
Reeves, John V, 199
Reeves, John J. V, 199
Reeves, John M. II, 913
Reeves, John Morris II, 156
Reeves, John Morris II, 159
Reeves, John W. V, 199
Reeves, Joseph II, 93
Reeves, Joseph II, 108
Reeves, Joseph II, 137
Reeves, Joseph II, 299
Reeves, Joseph II, 632
Reeves, Joseph IV, 432
Reeves, Joseph W. II, 913
Reeves, Josephine V, 199
Reeves, Josephine J. V, 199
Reeves, Joshua II, 137
Reeves, Joshua IV, 653
Reeves, Joshua IV, 754
Reeves, Joshua IV, 1137
Reeves, Josiah II, 94
Reeves, Josiah II, 299
Reeves, Josiah R. II, 299
Reeves, Katie V, 199
Reeves, Laura V, 199
Reeves, Lemuel H. I, 340
Reeves, Lewis IV, 754
Reeves, Lewis IV, 989
Reeves, Lillian II, 136
Reeves, Lillian II, 156
Reeves, Lillian A. II, 136
Reeves, Lillian Acton II, 154
Reeves, Louisa II, 299
Reeves, Louisa A. II, 893
Reeves, Louiza M. II, 632
Reeves, Lovisa II, 302
Reeves, Lydia IV, 579
Reeves, Lydia IV, 593
Reeves, Lydia IV, 1292
Reeves, Mansel P. IV, 754
Reeves, Margaret II, 137
Reeves, Margaret C. II, 156
Reeves, Marguerite III, 264
Reeves, Marguerite III, 265
Reeves, Maria II, 299
Reeves, Maria S. II, 299
Reeves, Mark II, 181
Reeves, Mark II, 299
Reeves, Mark E. V, 928
Reeves, Martha II, 137
Reeves, Martha II, 151
Reeves, Martha II, 156
Reeves, Martha Grier II, 134
Reeves, Martha Grier II, 151
Reeves, Martha Grier II, 156
Reeves, Martha W. II, 156
Reeves, Mary II, 58
Reeves, Mary II, 93
Reeves, Mary II, 252
Reeves, Mary II, 299
Reeves, Mary II, 412
Reeves, Mary II, 631
Reeves, Mary II, 632
Reeves, Mary II, 753
Reeves, Mary II, 761
Reeves, Mary II, 762
Reeves, Mary II, 797
Reeves, Mary IV, 268
Reeves, Mary IV, 653
Reeves, Mary IV, 732
Reeves, Mary IV, 754
Reeves, Mary IV, 1376
Reeves, Mary Ann II, 751
Reeves, Mary Ann II, 762
Reeves, Mary Anna IV, 1031
Reeves, Mary Ellen IV, 754
Reeves, Mary Jane II, 138
Reeves, Mary P. IV, 754
Reeves, Mary T. V, 928
Reeves, Mary Taylor V, 928
Reeves, Matilda IV, 653
Reeves, Matilda Ann IV, 383
Reeves, Matilda Ann IV, 432
Reeves, Matthew IV, 546
Reeves, Melicent II, 137
Reeves, Mellicent IV, 653
Reeves, Mercy II, 252
Reeves, Millisent IV, 754
Reeves, Miriam VI, 982
Reeves, Morris V, 199
Reeves, Morris A. II, 156
Reeves, Morris Acton II, 136
Reeves, Morris J. V, 199
Reeves, Mylicent II, 93
Reeves, Mylicent II, 108
Reeves, Nathan I, 622
Reeves, Nathan IV, 754
Reeves, Nathaniel VI, 982
Reeves, Ora F. V, 199
Reeves, Ora Francis V, 199
Reeves, Patience II, 221
Reeves, Patience II, 252
Reeves, Phebe II, 299
Reeves, Phebe IV, 732
Reeves, Phebe IV, 754
Reeves, Phebe Ann IV, 754
Reeves, Rachel II, 235
Reeves, Rachel II, 252
Reeves, Rachel II, 299
Reeves, Rachel II, 412
Reeves, Rachel II, 761
Reeves, Rachel II, 762
Reeves, Rachel IV, 1376
Reeves, Raymond V, 199
Reeves, Rebecca II, 252
Reeves, Rebecca II, 299
Reeves, Rebecca II, 793
Reeves, Rebecca II, 1023
Reeves, Robert V, 199
Reeves, Robert D. II, 299
Reeves, Robert D. II, 913
Reeves, Robert D. II, 917
Reeves, Robert Drake II, 816
Reeves, Samuel IV, 432
Reeves, Samuel C. IV, 432
Reeves, Samuel C. IV, 754
Reeves, Samuel C. IV, 989
Reeves, Samuel Carr IV, 653
Reeves, Sara G. C. III, 265
Reeves, Sarah II, 122
Reeves, Sarah II, 123
Reeves, Sarah II, 181
Reeves, Sarah II, 299
Reeves, Sarah II, 412
Reeves, Sarah II, 632
Reeves, Sarah A. C. III, 264
Reeves, Sarah B. II, 632
Reeves, Stacey II, 299
Reeves, Susan II, 632
Reeves, Susan H. II, 94
Reeves, Susanna H. II, 94
Reeves, Susannah IV, 646
Reeves, Susannah IV, 653
Reeves, Thomas II, 412
Reeves, Thomas IV, 754
Reeves, Thomas IV, 840
Reeves, Thomas IV, 989
Reeves, Viola IV, 1261
Reeves, Walter S. II, 299
Reeves, Wd. Elizabeth Ann II, 816
Reeves, William IV, 754
Reeves, William IV, 1376
Reeves, William A. V, 199
Reeves, William E. VI, 139
Reeves, Wm. II, 816
Reeves, Wm. Abraham V, 199
Reeves, Wm. E. VI, 139
Reeves, Wm. H. V, 199
Reeves, Zachariah II, 299
Reeves, Zechariah II, 181
Refford, John T. III, 265
Refford, Rachel II, 412
Refford, Rachel II, 635
Refford, William II, 412
Regaen, Mary I, 1058
Regaen, Reason I, 1058
Regal, Donna Jean IV, 754
Regal, Isabel IV, 754
Regal, Robert Lee IV, 754
Regal, Walter IV, 754
Regal, Walter Dean IV, 754
Regenhard, Olga III, 316
Regenhard, Olga M. III, 265
Regester, Aaron IV, 915
Regester, Abigail IV, 902
Regester, Abigail IV, 915
Regester, Ann IV, 915
Regester, Daniel IV, 915
Regester, David IV, 915
Regester, Hazel V, 1015
Regester, James Robetson IV, 915
Regester, Jane II, 632
Regester, Robert IV, 902
Regester, Robert IV, 915
Regester, Thomas IV, 915
Regester, William IV, 915
Regester, Wm. IV, 915
Register, Abigail IV, 55
Register, Evelyn I, 640
Register, Jane II, 632
Register, Malvina II, 809
Register, Robert IV, 55
Register, Thomas IV, 55
Register, William IV, 55
Regnier, Agnes III, 265
Regnier, Agnes III, 276
Regnier, Agnes III, 277
Regnier, Charles F. III, 265
Regnier, Charles F. III, 277
Regnier, M. Abby III, 265
Regnier, M. Abby III, 277
Regon, Martha I, 878
Regon, Martha I, 898
Reich, Adolphus II, 967
Reich, Alice M. II, 1045
Reich, Alice M. II, 1059
Reich, Alice Margaret II, 968

Reich, Alice Margaret II, 1058
Reich, Emma II, 967
Reich, Esther Mary II, 1045
Reich, Esther Mary II, 1058
Reich, Esther Mary II, 1059
Reich, Esther Mary C. II, 1058
Reich, Esther Mary Christine II, 968
Reich, Esther Mary, Jr. II, 968
Reich, Fanny I, 924
Reich, Fanny I, 940
Reich, Fanny I, 948
Reich, Florence II, 960
Reich, John F. II, 1059
Reich, John Frederic II, 968
Reich, Jos. Benjamin II, 968
Reich, Joseph Benjamin II, 1059
Reich, Laurence Max II, 968
Reich, Lawrence Max II, 1059
Reich, Mary I, 924
Reich, Mary II, 960
Reich, Mary II, 1059
Reich, Max II, 960
Reich, Max I. II, 1045
Reich, Max I. II, 1058
Reich, Max I. II, 1059
Reich, Max Isaac II, 967
Reich, Rufus I, 924
Reich, William George II, 968
Reich, Wm. G. II, 1059
Reichard, Lida McLaughlin IV, 268
Reichenbaugh, Clarence IV, 840
Reichenbaugh, Clarence E. IV, 840
Reichenbaugh, Frank IV, 840
Reichenbaugh, Glenn IV, 840
Reichenbaugh, Myrtle IV, 840
Reichenbaugh, Ray IV, 840
Reichenbaugh, Ray L. IV, 840
Reichenbaugh, Vera Pearl IV, 840
Reid, ??? III, 265
Reid, ??? III, 357
Reid, A. S. VI, 815
Reid, Albina House II, 913
Reid, Alex. VI, 991
Reid, Alexander III, 264
Reid, Alexander III, 265
Reid, Alfred L. VI, 849
Reid, Alice III, 265
Reid, Alice M. III, 191
Reid, Alice M. III, 265
Reid, Andrew B. VI, 982
Reid, Anna III, 265
Reid, Anna VI, 954
Reid, Anna Burling III, 271
Reid, Anna G. II, 712
Reid, Anne VI, 991
Reid, Arnold IV, 1181
Reid, Arnold S. IV, 1181
Reid, Betsey VI, 888
Reid, Beulah VI, 772
Reid, Catharine VI, 977
Reid, Cecelia VI, 838
Reid, Charles V, 1015
Reid, Clarissa VI, 823
Reid, Daniel III, 265
Reid, David C. III, 191
Reid, Dolly VI, 849
Reid, Edith Alina II, 816
Reid, Edward IV, 1291
Reid, Edward T. VI, 983
Reid, Effie IV, 1181
Reid, Eliza VI, 849
Reid, Eliza VI, 983
Reid, Eliza A. VI, 983
Reid, Eliza Jane IV, 37
Reid, Eliza Jane IV, 55
Reid, Elizabeth VI, 982
Reid, Elizabeth VI, 983
Reid, Ella Leslie II, 785
Reid, Ella Leslie II, 844
Reid, Ella Leslie II, 913
Reid, Elvira VI, 983
Reid, Emma IV, 1181
Reid, Esther VI, 982
Reid, Eugene A. IV, 1181
Reid, Fanny VI, 982
Reid, Florence VI, 982
Reid, France VI, 849
Reid, Francis VI, 977
Reid, Francis VI, 982
Reid, Francis VI, 988
Reid, Frank II, 816
Reid, Frank II, 913
Reid, George IV, 55
Reid, George IV, 882
Reid, George VI, 982
Reid, George Washington IV, 55
Reid, Harmon VI, 694
Reid, Harmon VI, 695
Reid, Helen VI, 694
Reid, Helen VI, 695
Reid, Henry K. II, 913
Reid, Herbert Wesley III, 265
Reid, Herbert Wesley III, 271
Reid, Ida III, 265
Reid, Jacob VI, 982
Reid, James III, 265
Reid, James VI, 849
Reid, James VI, 982
Reid, James VI, 991
Reid, Jane VI, 848
Reid, Jehu IV, 1181
Reid, Jene VI, 991
Reid, John IV, 55
Reid, John IV, 1181
Reid, John VI, 823
Reid, John VI, 849
Reid, John VI, 865
Reid, John C. VI, 982
Reid, John D. II, 716
Reid, John Hall IV, 55
Reid, John Miner II, 816
Reid, John Miner II, 913
Reid, John O. VI, 843
Reid, John T. W. VI, 983
Reid, Joseph VI, 982
Reid, Joseph D. II, 913
Reid, Joseph D. IV, 55
Reid, Joseph DuRose II, 785
Reid, Joseph Durose II, 813
Reid, Joseph Durose II, 816
Reid, Joseph Durose IV, 55
Reid, Josiah VI, 849
Reid, Kissiah VI, 841
Reid, Lavinia II, 913
Reid, Lucy A. VI, 849
Reid, Lula IV, 1181
Reid, Margaret VI, 982
Reid, Margaret Leslie II, 785
Reid, Margaret Leslie II, 813
Reid, Margaret Leslie II, 816
Reid, Margaretta Leslie II, 913
Reid, Margott VI, 988
Reid, Marjorie III, 265
Reid, Marjorie III, 357
Reid, Martha III, 264
Reid, Martha III, 265
Reid, Martha IV, 1291
Reid, Martha VI, 849
Reid, Martha VI, 865
Reid, Martha A. VI, 834
Reid, Martha B. IV, 1181
Reid, Martha F. VI, 853
Reid, Martha S. II, 716
Reid, Mary III, 265
Reid, Mary VI, 849
Reid, Mary VI, 991
Reid, Mary Alice II, 813
Reid, Mary Alice II, 913
Reid, Mary Ann VI, 849
Reid, Mary Ellen IV, 55
Reid, Mary Jane IV, 1181
Reid, Mary Louisa II, 816
Reid, Mary Louisa II, 913
Reid, Mary Rebecca II, 816
Reid, Milly VI, 982
Reid, Nancey VI, 982
Reid, Nancy VI, 820
Reid, Nancy VI, 849
Reid, Nancy VI, 982
Reid, Nathan VI, 849
Reid, Nathan VI, 888
Reid, Nathan VI, 925
Reid, Nathan VI, 934
Reid, Nathan VI, 935
Reid, Nathan VI, 977
Reid, Nathan VI, 983
Reid, Nathan, Jr. VI, 977
Reid, Nathaniel VI, 983
Reid, Obediah VI, 834
Reid, Obediah VI, 849
Reid, Pamela III, 264
Reid, Pamela Rebecca III, 265
Reid, Patsy VI, 977
Reid, Philip Sharpless II, 816
Reid, Priscilla C. IV, 55
Reid, Rachel VI, 982
Reid, Rebecca IV, 55
Reid, Rebecca VI, 831
Reid, Rebecca C. IV, 55
Reid, Rev. Wm. S. VI, 884
Reid, Robert II, 816
Reid, Robert II, 913
Reid, Ruth VI, 983
Reid, Samuel VI, 983
Reid, Samuel VI, 991
Reid, Sarah S. II, 913
Reid, Sophia VI, 849
Reid, Stella Imo IV, 1181
Reid, Theodore VI, 823
Reid, Thomas VI, 831
Reid, Thomas VI, 849
Reid, Thomas VI, 1013
Reid, Truax II, 913
Reid, Virginia P. II, 913
Reid, W. S. VI, 919
Reid, W. S. VI, 1009
Reid, William III, 264
Reid, William III, 265
Reid, William VI, 983
Reid, William Penn IV, 55
Reid, William S. VI, 893
Reid, William S. VI, 929
Reid, William S. VI, 1020
Reid, Wm. VI, 841
Reid, Wm. Henry III, 265
Reid, Wm. S. VI, 881
Reid, Wm. S. VI, 888
Reid, Wm. S. VI, 893
Reid, Wm. S. VI, 894
Reid, Wm. S. VI, 903
Reid, Wm. S. VI, 916
Reid, Wm. S. VI, 919
Reid, Wm. S. VI, 939
Reid, Wm. S. VI, 943
Reid, Wm. S. VI, 949
Reid, Wm. S. VI, 963
Reid, Wm. S. VI, 977
Reid, Wm. S. VI, 982
Reid, Wm. S. VI, 1010
Reiffsnyder, Ellen II, 913
Reiffsnyder, Howard II, 913
Reifsnyder, Agnes V. II, 834
Reifsnyder, Agnes V. II, 913
Reifsnyder, Ellen II, 816
Reifsnyder, Ellen II, 913
Reifsnyder, Gen. Washington II, 834
Reifsnyder, Gen. Washington II, 913
Reifsnyder, Hannah II, 816
Reifsnyder, Hannah II, 867
Reifsnyder, Hannah II, 914
Reifsnyder, Henry Gillam II, 816
Reifsnyder, Howard II, 816
Reifsnyder, Howard II, 867
Reifsnyder, Howard II, 913
Reifsnyder, Howard II, 914
Reifsnyder, Howard, Jr. II, 816
Reifsnyder, Isaac II, 816
Reifsnyder, Israel II, 816
Reigel, Martha IV, 268
Reighley, Ann IV, 266
Reiley, Ann VI, 551
Reiley, James VI, 604
Reiley, John VI, 551
Reiley, Mary VI, 551
Reiley, Rachel VI, 604
Reiley, Robert VI, 551
Reilly, Elizabeth V, 928
Reily, Eli VI, 604
Reily, Frances VI, 604
Reily, James VI, 604
Reily, Mary VI, 604
Reily, Rachel VI, 604
Reimer, Ann III, 61
Reimer, Anna III, 265
Reimer, Anna T. III, 211
Reimer, Anna Therese III, 61
Reimer, Anna Therese III, 265
Reimer, Carl H. G. III, 61
Reimer, Carl H. G. III, 265
Reine, Esther III, 32
Reinhardt, Elizabeth II, 156
Reinhardt, Elizabeth C. II, 137
Reinhardt, Elizabeth C. II, 156
Reinhardt, Elizabeth C. II, 914
Reinhardt, Ella III, 137
Reinhardt, Ester M. II, 156
Reinhardt, Esther M. II, 137
Reinhardt, Esther M. II, 914
Reinhardt, Lillian L. II, 156
Reinhardt, Lillian L. II, 914
Reinhardt, Lily L. II, 137
Reinhardt, Mary B. II, 137
Reinhardt, Mary B. II, 156
Reinhardt, Mary B. II, 914
Reinhardt, Rebecca II, 137
Reinhardt, Rebecca H. II, 156
Reinhardt, Rebecca H. II, 914
Reinhardt, Wm. D. II, 137
Reinhart, Chauncey III, 265
Reinhart, Chauncey O. III, 133
Reinhart, Chauncey R. III, 265
Reinhart, Chauncy III, 265
Reinhart, Loraine III, 265
Reinhart, Mabel III, 265
Reinhart, Mabel Elizabeth III, 133
Reinhart, Mabel Elizabeth III, 265
Reinhart, Mary M. III, 265
Reinhart, Rolfe Ormond III, 265
Reininger, Nevada IV, 1335
Reininger, Wm. N. IV, 1335
Reinington, John II, 632
Reinington, Sarah II, 632
Reins, George V, 309
Reinstein, Ada A. II, 914
Reinstein, Annabella T. II, 914
Reinstein, Chas. F. II, 914
Reinstein, Daniel K. II, 914
Reinstine, Ada A. II, 914
Reinstine, Annabella T. II, 914
Reinstine, Chas. F. II, 914
Reinstine, Daniel K. II, 914
Reis, Patience VI, 84
Reis, Patience VI, 88
Reise, Francis IV, 1335
Reiser, Ethel Anna II, 1072
Reiser, Ethel Anna II, 1078
Reiss, Francis IV, 1335
Reister, Lizzie III, 304
Reitzel, Jane II, 851
Reitzel, Jane II, 914
Reitzel, Wm. Wagner II, 816
Reitzel, Wm. Wagner II, 851
Reitzel, Wm. Wagner II, 914
Rejester, Jane II, 589
Reley, Absalom IV, 915
Reley, Albert IV, 29
Reley, Amos IV, 915
Reley, Ann IV, 28
Reley, Ann IV, 54
Reley, Ann IV, 988
Reley, Ann IV, 989
Reley, Ann IV, 1011
Reley, Ann VI, 551
Reley, Aseneth IV, 915
Reley, Elazan IV, 915
Reley, Elijah IV, 915
Reley, Eliza IV, 915
Reley, Elizabeth IV, 915
Reley, Esther IV, 915
Reley, Hannah IV, 69
Reley, Harrison IV, 29
Reley, James IV, 915
Reley, James VI, 551
Reley, James, Jr. IV, 915
Reley, John IV, 28
Reley, John IV, 69
Reley, John IV, 899
Reley, John IV, 914
Reley, John IV, 915
Reley, John IV, 989
Reley, John IV, 1011
Reley, John VI, 405
Reley, John VI, 551
Reley, John R. IV, 29
Reley, Jordan IV, 915
Reley, Joseph IV, 915
Reley, Levi IV, 915
Reley, Malinda IV, 899
Reley, Malinda IV, 914
Reley, Malinda IV, 915
Reley, Mary IV, 28
Reley, Mary IV, 69
Reley, Mary IV, 914
Reley, Mary IV, 915
Reley, Mary IV, 917
Reley, Mary VI, 405
Reley, Milton IV, 915
Reley, Peter IV, 29
Reley, Rachel VI, 551
Reley, Rebecca IV, 915
Reley, Robert IV, 62
Reley, Robert IV, 914
Reley, Robert IV, 915
Reley, Robert IV, 917
Reley, Robert IV, 989
Reley, Robert VI, 551
Reley, Robert Franklin IV, 915
Reley, Ruth IV, 915
Reley, Sarah IV, 62
Reley, Sarah IV, 915
Reley, Sarah IV, 989
Reley, Susannah IV, 915
Reley, Thomas IV, 915
Reley, William Pettit IV, 915
Relf, Sarah I, 151
Relf, Sarah I, 163
Rely, Ann IV, 20
Rely, Ann IV, 54
Rely, Jane IV, 54
Rely, Robert IV, 20
Remine, Hannah VI, 604
Remine, Hannah VI, 605
Remington, Alcy A. III, 265
Remington, Annabella L. II, 914
Remington, Annabella Laing II, 816
Remington, Annabella T. II, 914
Remington, Clement II, 745
Remington, Clement II, 762
Remington, Clement II, 914
Remington, Edward II, 914
Remington, Edward N. II, 914
Remington, Elizabeth C. II, 91
Remington, Isaac II, 745
Remington, Isaac II, 762
Remington, Isaac II, 914
Remington, Isaac II, 931
Remington, Isaac, Jr. II, 816
Remington, Isaac, Jr. II, 914
Remington, Jacobs II, 914
Remington, Jane W. IV, 348
Remington, Job B. II, 181
Remington, Job B. II, 299
Remington, John C. II, 914
Remington, John C. II, 942
Remington, John Clement II, 8
Remington, John Clement II, 9
Remington, John Clement II, 9
Remington, Joseph P. III, 265
Remington, Katharine Magill II, 914
Remington, Katherine Magill II, 848
Remington, Lydia II, 745
Remington, Lydia II, 762
Remington, Lydia II, 914
Remington, Lydia II, 942
Remington, Lydia H. II, 762
Remington, Lydia H. II, 914
Remington, Lydia H. II, 931
Remington, Margaret S. II, 914
Remington, Margaret S. II, 931
Remington, Margaret S. II, 942
Remington, Margaret Shoemaker II, 816
Remington, Mary IV, 1335
Remington, Needles II, 914
Remington, Samuel II, 914
Remington, Samuel J. II, 848
Remington, Samuel J. II, 914
Remington, Sarah II, 632
Remington, Sarah II, 745
Remington, Sarah II, 762
Remington, Sarah, Jr. II, 632
Remington, Stephen R. II, 914
Remley, Martha V, 274
Remley, William V, 274
Remmington, John II, 94
Remmington, Sarah II, 94
Remmington, Sarah, Jr. II, 632
Remmington, Susannah II, 94
Remond, Mary J. III, 205
Remond, Mary, Jr. III, 265
Remond, Narciss III, 265
Remos, Mary I, 233
Remos, Mary I, 256
Remsen, ??? III, 405
Remsen, Aris III, 439
Remsen, Daniel H. III, 439
Remsen, Henrietta III, 405
Remsen, Marian W. II, 914
Remsen, Martha III, 439
Remsen, Martha III, 495
Remsen, Rhyneer III, 481
Remsen, Rhyneer III, 495
Remsen, Sarah III, 439
Remsen, Wd. Martha III, 481
Remson, Celia M. III, 29
Renager, Hannah II, 472
Renager, Hannah II, 632
Rencho, Mary II, 631
Rencho, Mary II, 632
Rendles, Jane V, 595
Renear, Elizabeth II, 221
Renear, Elizabeth II, 252
Renear, Hannah II, 252
Renehall, Sarah VI, 210
Renfro, Widow Elizabeth VI, 35
Renn, Charles V, 357
Renn, Charles A. V, 357
Rennard, Jacob IV, 158
Rennard, John IV, 142
Rennard, John IV, 158
Rennard, Julia IV, 142
Rennard, Julia IV, 158
Rennard, Vilinda IV, 158
Rennell, Hannah M. VI, 210
Rennels, Clara V, 525
Rennels, Clyde V, 524
Rennels, Sarah Goldie V, 524
Rennels, Stephen Hire V, 524
Renner, Alice V, 595
Renner, Alice V, 706
Renner, Alice H. V, 595
Renner, Allie V, 595
Renner, Charles Marshall V, 70
Renner, Chas. Marshall V, 706
Renner, Clarence V, 595

er, Clarence V, 706
er, Clarence H. V, 595
er, E. Marshall V, 595
er, Elizabeth V, 706
er, Elizabeth M. V, 706
er, Gilman V, 595
er, Mahala G. V, 595
er, Marshall V, 595
er, Marshall V, 706
er, Mollie V, 706
er, Robert V, 595
er, Robert V, 706
ie, Mollie V, 690
ie, Mollie V, 706
ie, Robert V, 690
ie, Robert V, 706
olds, Elizabeth II, 49
olds, Elizabeth II, 94
olds, Francis II, 49
olds, Francis II, 94
olds, Rhoda I, 899
olds, Rutth VI, 1004
ols, Charles VI, 1004
Ella V, 1015
Etta V, 1015
Maggie V, 1015
S. W. I, 948
Wm. V, 1015
ds, Joseph IV, 349
nds, Eliz. III, 499
nds, Gilbert III, 499
nds, Hannah III, 499
nds, Hannah K. III, 499
nds, Justus III, 499
nds, Obadiah III, 499
nds, Sarah Ann III, 499
af, Hannah III, 23
af, Hannah III, 37
af, Hannah III, 265
af, Martha III, 265
af, Mary R. III, 265
af, Phebe III, 176
af, Phebe III, 265
af, Thomas III, 265
af, William III, 23
af, William III, 176
af, William III, 265
af, Wm. III, 265
aw, Alberta IV, 268
aw, Ann II, 412
aw, Ann II, 632
aw, Ann II, 659
aw, Elisabeth II, 632
aw, Elizabeth II, 412
aw, Elizabeth II, 632
aw, Elizabeth IV, 268
aw, Frank IV, 268
aw, Hannah II, 632
aw, Hannah II, 675
aw, James II, 632
aw, John II, 412
aw, John II, 632
aw, John II, 651
aw, Martha II, 252
aw, Martha II, 260
aw, Martha II, 632
aw, Martha II, 651
aw, Mary II, 412
aw, Mary II, 632
aw, Mary II, 659
aw, Mira O. II, 757
aw, Mira O. II, 762
aw, Rebeccah II, 412
aw, Richard II, 412
aw, Richard II, 632
aw, Samuel IV, 1335
aw, Sarah II, 632
aw, Thomas II, 412
aw, Thomas II, 632
er, Elizabeth II, 632
er, John II, 606
er, John II, 632
o, Mary II, 491
o, Elizabeth VI, 983
o, Moses VI, 983
ck, Margaret VI, 667
Frederick IV, 1181
Mary A. IV, 1181
olds, Joseph II, 632
olds, Sarah II, 632
rt, Clarence IV, 1335
rt, Ellsworth IV, 268
rt, Julia IV, 284
rt, Julia Stephens IV, 268
rt, Ruth IV, 268
e, Mary III, 265
, John W. V, 1015
Ceicil V, 1015
et, Clark IV, 780
et, Isaac IV, 780
et, Jane IV, 780
Ressket, Mary IV, 780
Ressket, Samuel IV, 780
Ressket, Sophia IV, 780
Ressler, Carrie IV, 754
Ressler, Druzilla IV, 754
Ressler, Elizabeth IV, 620
Ressler, Jacob IV, 754
Ressler, Magdaline IV, 620
Ressler, Martin IV, 620
Retallic, Edmund V, 114
Retallic, Emma V, 31
Retallic, Emma V, 114
Rethmell, John II, 252
Retman, Melissa V, 1015
Retter, Martha IV, 1181
Retter, Martha L. IV, 1221
Retter, Martha S. IV, 1221
Reubell, Rachel I, 835
Reubell, Rachel I, 841
Reuben, Annie M. II, 914
Reuben, Frederick II, 914
Reuben, Gertrude II, 914
Reuber, Annie M. II, 844
Reuber, Frederick II, 844
Reuber, Gertrude II, 844
Reuber, Mary Anna II, 785
Reush???, Elizabeth I, 731
Reush???, Elizabeth I, 733
Rev. Reid, Wm. S. VI, 907
Reve, Hannah II, 93
Reve, Joshua IV, 989
Reve, Mary II, 631
Reve, Mary II, 639
Reve, Milicent IV, 989
Reve, Rachel II, 93
Reve, Ruth II, 93
Revel, Ocena IV, 268
Revel, Rosa IV, 268
Reveley, Eliza VI, 849
Reveley, Isaac VI, 849
Reveley, John VI, 849
Reveley, John VI, 852
Reveley, Judith VI, 849
Reveley, Martha VI, 849
Reveley, Robert VI, 849
Revelle, Nellie V, 510
Revely, Eliza VI, 849
Revely, Elizabeth VI, 845
Revely, George F. VI, 849
Revely, Jane VI, 827
Revely, John VI, 827
Revely, John VI, 845
Revely, John VI, 859
Revely, Judy VI, 859
Revely, Margaret VI, 849
Revely, Robert VI, 802
Revely, Robert VI, 849
Reves, Eli II, 252
Reves, Elizabeth II, 252
Revve, Matthew IV, 546
Rexford, Abigail IV, 1181
Rexford, Abigail IV, 1191
Rexford, Hannah IV, 1240
Rexford, Hannah M. IV, 1237
Rexroat, John VI, 983
Rexroat, Katy VI, 983
Rextraw, Susannah II, 632
Reybold, Alice V, 854
Reyburn, Lida V, 359
Reyley, Ann VI, 551
Reyley, James VI, 551
Reyley, John VI, 551
Reyley, Mary VI, 551
Reyley, Rachel VI, 551
Reyley, Robert VI, 551
Reyly, Eli VI, 604
Reymer, James IV, 1292
Reymer, Lydia IV, 1292
Reynard, Adam V, 595
Reynard, Adam, Jr. V, 595
Reynard, Asa V, 595
Reynard, Catherine V, 597
Reynard, Elizabeth V, 595
Reynard, Elizabeth V, 597
Reynard, Jacob V, 595
Reynard, Jacob V, 597
Reynard, Joel V, 595
Reynard, Lydia V, 564
Reynard, Lydia V, 595
Reynard, Martha V, 714
Reynault, Mary Isabel III, 440
Reynear, Hannah II, 412
Reynear, Hannah II, 488
Reynear, Hannah II, 632
Reynear, Isaac II, 412
Reynear, Joseph II, 412
Reynear, Joseph II, 488
Reynear, Joseph II, 508
Reynear, Joseph II, 632
Reynear, Mary II, 412
Reynear, Rachel II, 412
Reynear, Rachel II, 508
Reynear, Rachel II, 632
Reynear, Stephen II, 412
Reynell, John II, 412
Reynell, John II, 607
Reynell, John II, 632
Reynell, Mary II, 607
Reynell, Sarah II, 412
Reynell, Wd. Mary II, 632
Reyner, Isaac II, 412
Reynier, Alice II, 632
Reyniers, Alice II, 622
Reyniers, Alice II, 632
Reynold, Alpheus Allen I, 688
Reynold, Dinah D. I, 688
Reynold, Joseph I, 688
Reynold, Mary V, 895
Reynold, Mary Ellen I, 688
Reynold, Milton E. I, 688
Reynold, William I, 688
Reynolds, ??? III, 41
Reynolds, ??? III, 265
Reynolds, ??? III, 327
Reynolds, Aaron I, 414
Reynolds, Aaron I, 417
Reynolds, Aaron I, 665
Reynolds, Aaron I, 687
Reynolds, Abel I, 666
Reynolds, Abia IV, 268
Reynolds, Abigail I, 666
Reynolds, Abigail I, 667
Reynolds, Abigail I, 688
Reynolds, Abigail I, 883
Reynolds, Abigail I, 899
Reynolds, Abigail III, 265
Reynolds, Abigail H. I, 687
Reynolds, Abigail H. I, 899
Reynolds, Abner VI, 960
Reynolds, Abner VI, 982
Reynolds, Abner VI, 983
Reynolds, Abner B. VI, 983
Reynolds, Abraham III, 265
Reynolds, Abraham III, 266
Reynolds, Abraham VI, 946
Reynolds, Achsa I, 768
Reynolds, Achsah I, 666
Reynolds, Addison I, 640
Reynolds, Adelia I, 864
Reynolds, Adella I, 666
Reynolds, Agnes VI, 231
Reynolds, Agnes VI, 265
Reynolds, Albert IV, 989
Reynolds, Alexander VI, 887
Reynolds, Alexander VI, 893
Reynolds, Alexander VI, 965
Reynolds, Alexander VI, 983
Reynolds, Alexander VI, 1011
Reynolds, Alexander VI, 1020
Reynolds, Alice Lucile IV, 1182
Reynolds, Allen IV, 817
Reynolds, Allen IV, 840
Reynolds, Allen IV, 989
Reynolds, Almyra I, 666
Reynolds, Alpheus Allen I, 688
Reynolds, Amelia I, 981
Reynolds, Amelia I, 996
Reynolds, Amelia O. VI, 832
Reynolds, Amey VI, 850
Reynolds, Amos B. V, 928
Reynolds, Amy I, 666
Reynolds, Amy I, 667
Reynolds, Amy I, 675
Reynolds, Amy I, 676
Reynolds, Amy I, 682
Reynolds, Amy I, 687
Reynolds, Amy I, 688
Reynolds, Amy B. II, 914
Reynolds, Amy B. II, 922
Reynolds, Amy J. I, 664
Reynolds, Amy Josephine I, 664
Reynolds, Anestasia II, 801
Reynolds, Angelia E. III, 447
Reynolds, Angeline E. VI, 933
Reynolds, Angeline E. VI, 983
Reynolds, Ann I, 626
Reynolds, Ann I, 665
Reynolds, Ann I, 666
Reynolds, Ann I, 667
Reynolds, Ann I, 676
Reynolds, Ann I, 683
Reynolds, Ann I, 687
Reynolds, Ann I, 689
Reynolds, Ann I, 899
Reynolds, Ann II, 252
Reynolds, Ann III, 265
Reynolds, Ann III, 405
Reynolds, Ann III, 406
Reynolds, Ann III, 439
Reynolds, Ann IV, 55
Reynolds, Ann IV, 257
Reynolds, Ann IV, 268
Reynolds, Ann IV, 653
Reynolds, Ann C. III, 237
Reynolds, Ann C. III, 265
Reynolds, Ann C. III, 266
Reynolds, Ann E. I, 688
Reynolds, Ann E. VI, 983
Reynolds, Ann Eliz. III, 265
Reynolds, Ann Eliza III, 237
Reynolds, Ann Elizabeth III, 266
Reynolds, Ann M. IV, 268
Reynolds, Ann Maria III, 265
Reynolds, Anna I, 569
Reynolds, Anna I, 620
Reynolds, Anna I, 625
Reynolds, Anna I, 640
Reynolds, Anna I, 641
Reynolds, Anna I, 688
Reynolds, Anna I, 932
Reynolds, Anna III, 172
Reynolds, Anna V, 463
Reynolds, Anna V, 928
Reynolds, Anna E. I, 666
Reynolds, Anna E. I, 871
Reynolds, Anna E. I, 899
Reynolds, Anna M. II, 816
Reynolds, Anna M. II, 914
Reynolds, Anne V, 928
Reynolds, Anne E. I, 899
Reynolds, Annie I, 624
Reynolds, Annie E. I, 624
Reynolds, Annie E. I, 864
Reynolds, Annie L. II, 717
Reynolds, Anthony I, 448
Reynolds, Anthony I, 453
Reynolds, Anthony I, 664
Reynolds, Anthony I, 665
Reynolds, Anthony I, 687
Reynolds, Archibald VI, 921
Reynolds, Aron I, 447
Reynolds, Aron I, 453
Reynolds, Aron I, 665
Reynolds, Asenath I, 665
Reynolds, Asenath I, 666
Reynolds, Asenath I, 688
Reynolds, Augustus V, 1015
Reynolds, B. Ventura I, 899
Reynolds, Benj. V, 928
Reynolds, Benj. C. V, 928
Reynolds, Benjamin II, 412
Reynolds, Benjamin V, 928
Reynolds, Benjamin VI, 970
Reynolds, Benjamin P. VI, 921
Reynolds, Benjamin P. VI, 983
Reynolds, Beulah II, 412
Reynolds, Byron I, 666
Reynolds, C. A. I, 640
Reynolds, Caleb VI, 983
Reynolds, Catharine I, 625
Reynolds, Catharine VI, 983
Reynolds, Catharine P. I, 688
Reynolds, Catharine P. I, 689
Reynolds, Catharine Payton I, 666
Reynolds, Celia VI, 983
Reynolds, Celinda VI, 1007
Reynolds, Cerceelia I, 864
Reynolds, Charity I, 417
Reynolds, Charity I, 427
Reynolds, Charity I, 667
Reynolds, Charity I, 687
Reynolds, Charles III, 265
Reynolds, Charles VI, 974
Reynolds, Charles VI, 983
Reynolds, Charles VI, 1009
Reynolds, Charles B. VI, 903
Reynolds, Charles B. VI, 951
Reynolds, Charles D., Jr. VI, 899
Reynolds, Charles D., Jr. VI, 983
Reynolds, Charles D., Sr. VI, 933
Reynolds, Charles Ernest V, 928
Reynolds, Charles P. VI, 983
Reynolds, Charles W. I, 624
Reynolds, Charlette V, 463
Reynolds, Charlie V, 429
Reynolds, Chas. VI, 983
Reynolds, Chas. B. VI, 912
Reynolds, Chas. D., Jr. VI, 933
Reynolds, Chas. Ernst V, 928
Reynolds, Christian I, 665
Reynolds, Christian I, 687
Reynolds, Christian I, 692
Reynolds, Christopher VI, 850
Reynolds, Clarissa V, 274
Reynolds, Clarkson I, 665
Reynolds, Clinton IV, 1182
Reynolds, Clinton O. IV, 1182
Reynolds, Clinton O. IV, 1335
Reynolds, Constance V, 1015
Reynolds, Cophire VI, 983
Reynolds, Cordelia I, 613
Reynolds, Cordelia I, 891
Reynolds, Cordelia I, 899
Reynolds, Cordelia B. I, 615
Reynolds, Cordelia B. I, 620
Reynolds, Cordelia B. I, 666
Reynolds, Cornelia V, 928
Reynolds, Cyntha E. I, 899
Reynolds, Cynthia E. I, 666
Reynolds, Cynthia E. I, 688
Reynolds, Cynthia E. I, 899
Reynolds, Cyrus I, 626
Reynolds, Cyrus I, 666
Reynolds, Cyrus I, 864
Reynolds, Cyrus I, 899
Reynolds, Cyrus IV, 268
Reynolds, Cyrus IV, 546
Reynolds, Cyrus A. I, 640
Reynolds, Cyrus Augustus I, 624
Reynolds, Daniel IV, 1182
Reynolds, Daniel IV, 1188
Reynolds, Daniel IV, 1221
Reynolds, Daniel IV, 1229
Reynolds, Daniel IV, 1240
Reynolds, Daniel V, 928
Reynolds, David I, 343
Reynolds, David I, 417
Reynolds, David I, 443
Reynolds, David I, 453
Reynolds, David I, 513
Reynolds, David I, 568
Reynolds, David I, 665
Reynolds, David I, 666
Reynolds, David I, 683
Reynolds, David I, 687
Reynolds, David I, 688
Reynolds, David V, 928
Reynolds, David VI, 850
Reynolds, David Calvin I, 667
Reynolds, Deborah I, 625
Reynolds, Deborah I, 640
Reynolds, Deborah I, 687
Reynolds, Delilah I, 665
Reynolds, Delilah I, 666
Reynolds, Dina I, 667
Reynolds, Dinah I, 484
Reynolds, Dinah I, 667
Reynolds, Dinah D. I, 688
Reynolds, Ditsey VI, 961
Reynolds, Dr. Charles H. III, 29
Reynolds, Dr. Charles H. III, 265
Reynolds, Ebanezar I, 665
Reynolds, Ebanezar I, 679
Reynolds, Ebanezar I, 687
Reynolds, Ebenezer I, 665
Reynolds, Ebenezar I, 687
Reynolds, Ebenezer L. II, 632
Reynolds, Edgar I, 640
Reynolds, Edgar Lee I, 625
Reynolds, Edgar Lee I, 640
Reynolds, Edith I, 625
Reynolds, Edith I, 640
Reynolds, Edith I, 665
Reynolds, Edith I, 686
Reynolds, Edith I, 687
Reynolds, Editha VI, 965
Reynolds, Edward VI, 911
Reynolds, Edward VI, 918
Reynolds, Edward VI, 951
Reynolds, Edward VI, 983
Reynolds, Edward J. VI, 983
Reynolds, Edwin J. VI, 912
Reynolds, Edwin J. VI, 943
Reynolds, Edwin J. VI, 984
Reynolds, Edwin J. VI, 989
Reynolds, Egbert I, 625
Reynolds, Eleanor I, 667
Reynolds, Eleanor I, 683
Reynolds, Eleanor I, 688
Reynolds, Eli II, 412
Reynolds, Elias III, 266
Reynolds, Elihu I, 665
Reynolds, Elihu I, 667
Reynolds, Elihu I, 683
Reynolds, Elihu I, 687
Reynolds, Elijah I, 665
Reynolds, Elisabeth I, 457
Reynolds, Elisabeth IV, 653
Reynolds, Elisha I, 667
Reynolds, Eliz. III, 266
Reynolds, Eliza IV, 268
Reynolds, Eliza IV, 754
Reynolds, Eliza IV, 840
Reynolds, Eliza VI, 946
Reynolds, Eliza Jane I, 768
Reynolds, Elizabeth I, 447
Reynolds, Elizabeth I, 448
Reynolds, Elizabeth I, 453
Reynolds, Elizabeth I, 664
Reynolds, Elizabeth I, 665
Reynolds, Elizabeth I, 667
Reynolds, Elizabeth I, 677
Reynolds, Elizabeth I, 683

Reynolds, Elizabeth I, 687
Reynolds, Elizabeth I, 813
Reynolds, Elizabeth I, 835
Reynolds, Elizabeth I, 978
Reynolds, Elizabeth II, 94
Reynolds, Elizabeth III, 266
Reynolds, Elizabeth III, 439
Reynolds, Elizabeth IV, 55
Reynolds, Elizabeth IV, 653
Reynolds, Elizabeth IV, 1221
Reynolds, Elizabeth V, 925
Reynolds, Elizabeth V, 928
Reynolds, Elizabeth VI, 265
Reynolds, Elizabeth VI, 838
Reynolds, Elizabeth VI, 850
Reynolds, Elizabeth VI, 983
Reynolds, Elizabeth VI, 1011
Reynolds, Elizabeth Ann VI, 983
Reynolds, Elizabeth Emily IV, 754
Reynolds, Elizabeth Emily IV, 840
Reynolds, Elizabeth J. D. VI, 921
Reynolds, Elizabeth Marie IV, 1182
Reynolds, Elma I, 666
Reynolds, Elma I, 688
Reynolds, Elvira VI, 937
Reynolds, Elwood I, 666
Reynolds, Emily VI, 731
Reynolds, Emily VI, 744
Reynolds, Emily VI, 772
Reynolds, Emily VI, 983
Reynolds, Emily Ann I, 667
Reynolds, Emily Ann I, 688
Reynolds, Enos I, 625
Reynolds, Enos I, 899
Reynolds, Enos Addeson I, 624
Reynolds, Enos Addison I, 666
Reynolds, Enos Addison I, 864
Reynolds, Esther III, 90
Reynolds, Esther III, 266
Reynolds, Esther IV, 268
Reynolds, Esther IV, 546
Reynolds, Esther Ann IV, 546
Reynolds, Esther R. III, 327
Reynolds, Eunice I, 666
Reynolds, Eunice I, 688
Reynolds, Evaline VI, 850
Reynolds, Ezra I, 665
Reynolds, Ezra IV, 840
Reynolds, Fannie V, 114
Reynolds, Frances I, 457
Reynolds, Frances I, 665
Reynolds, Frances I, 675
Reynolds, Frances I, 687
Reynolds, Frances VI, 974
Reynolds, Frances Jane VI, 983
Reynolds, Francis I, 417
Reynolds, Francis I, 453
Reynolds, Francis I, 665
Reynolds, Francis I, 666
Reynolds, Francis I, 677
Reynolds, Francis I, 687
Reynolds, Francis I, 768
Reynolds, Francis II, 94
Reynolds, Francis Henry III, 266
Reynolds, Frank V, 429
Reynolds, Franklin I, 640
Reynolds, Franklin IV, 754
Reynolds, Franklin V, 928
Reynolds, Franklin B. I, 625
Reynolds, Franklin C. I, 625
Reynolds, Franklin E. I, 864
Reynolds, Franklin Emlen I, 666
Reynolds, Franklin Emlon I, 899
Reynolds, George I, 978
Reynolds, George V, 642
Reynolds, George T. VI, 965
Reynolds, George T. VI, 983
Reynolds, George W. VI, 983
Reynolds, Gideon I, 667
Reynolds, Greenville B. W. VI, 983
Reynolds, Hannah I, 407
Reynolds, Hannah I, 409
Reynolds, Hannah I, 417
Reynolds, Hannah I, 513
Reynolds, Hannah I, 623
Reynolds, Hannah I, 656
Reynolds, Hannah I, 665
Reynolds, Hannah I, 666
Reynolds, Hannah I, 667
Reynolds, Hannah I, 680
Reynolds, Hannah I, 687
Reynolds, Hannah I, 688
Reynolds, Hannah I, 691
Reynolds, Hannah I, 794
Reynolds, Hannah IV, 55
Reynolds, Hannah IV, 268
Reynolds, Hannah IV, 650
Reynolds, Hannah IV, 653
Reynolds, Hannah IV, 754
Reynolds, Hannah IV, 818
Reynolds, Hannah IV, 840
Reynolds, Hannah V, 928
Reynolds, Hannah VI, 477
Reynolds, Hannah VI, 797
Reynolds, Hannah R. III, 284
Reynolds, Hannah R. IV, 570
Reynolds, Hannah R. IV, 614
Reynolds, Hannah R. V, 928
Reynolds, Harrison III, 90
Reynolds, Harrison B. VI, 983
Reynolds, Hattie I, 640
Reynolds, Hattie May I, 625
Reynolds, Helen V, 706
Reynolds, Henry I, 513
Reynolds, Henry II, 207
Reynolds, Henry II, 252
Reynolds, Henry III, 266
Reynolds, Henry IV, 55
Reynolds, Henry IV, 653
Reynolds, Henry V, 274
Reynolds, Henry VI, 477
Reynolds, Herbert I, 624
Reynolds, Herbert I, 640
Reynolds, Hiram L. II, 816
Reynolds, Hiram L. II, 914
Reynolds, Hiram L. II, 922
Reynolds, Irene IV, 1042
Reynolds, Isaac I, 664
Reynolds, Isaac I, 665
Reynolds, Isaac I, 762
Reynolds, Isaac I, 768
Reynolds, Isaac IV, 653
Reynolds, Isaac IV, 1182
Reynolds, Isaac VI, 822
Reynolds, Isaac VI, 832
Reynolds, Isaac VI, 858
Reynolds, Isaac VI, 983
Reynolds, Isaac P. V, 706
Reynolds, Isaac T. IV, 1182
Reynolds, Isaac Wells I, 667
Reynolds, Isabella I, 640
Reynolds, Isabella W. I, 625
Reynolds, J. W. IV, 1335
Reynolds, Jabez V, 928
Reynolds, Jacob VI, 850
Reynolds, James I, 996
Reynolds, James IV, 55
Reynolds, James IV, 653
Reynolds, James VI, 797
Reynolds, James VI, 834
Reynolds, James VI, 850
Reynolds, James VI, 860
Reynolds, James VI, 861
Reynolds, James VI, 946
Reynolds, James C. III, 266
Reynolds, James L. VI, 983
Reynolds, James S. VI, 850
Reynolds, Jamiah I, 443
Reynolds, Jamiah I, 453
Reynolds, Jane I, 835
Reynolds, Jane I, 978
Reynolds, Jane I, 996
Reynolds, Jane II, 82
Reynolds, Jane II, 94
Reynolds, Jane II, 484
Reynolds, Jane II, 632
Reynolds, Jane IV, 1169
Reynolds, Jane IV, 1182
Reynolds, Jane VI, 850
Reynolds, Jane E. VI, 983
Reynolds, Jane M. VI, 983
Reynolds, Jehu I, 665
Reynolds, Jemima I, 453
Reynolds, Jemima I, 687
Reynolds, Jemima VI, 983
Reynolds, Jemima VI, 1009
Reynolds, Jeremiah I, 378
Reynolds, Jeremiah I, 417
Reynolds, Jeremiah I, 446
Reynolds, Jeremiah I, 453
Reynolds, Jeremiah I, 484
Reynolds, Jeremiah I, 513
Reynolds, Jeremiah I, 568
Reynolds, Jeremiah I, 645
Reynolds, Jeremiah I, 656
Reynolds, Jeremiah I, 665
Reynolds, Jeremiah I, 666
Reynolds, Jeremiah I, 667
Reynolds, Jeremiah I, 675
Reynolds, Jeremiah I, 685
Reynolds, Jeremiah I, 687
Reynolds, Jeremiah I, 688
Reynolds, Jeremiah I, 695
Reynolds, Jeremiah I, 768
Reynolds, Jeremiah I, 794
Reynolds, Jeremiah I, 864
Reynolds, Jeremiah I, 899
Reynolds, Jeremiah IV, 268
Reynolds, Jeremiah IV, 546
Reynolds, Jeremieh I, 688
Reynolds, Jesse I, 665
Reynolds, Jesse I, 666
Reynolds, Jesse I, 667
Reynolds, Jesse VI, 887
Reynolds, Jesse VI, 918
Reynolds, Jesse VI, 928
Reynolds, Jesse VI, 950
Reynolds, Jesse VI, 956
Reynolds, Jesse White I, 625
Reynolds, Jesse White I, 640
Reynolds, Jessee VI, 1009
Reynolds, Jessie I, 640
Reynolds, Joash I, 620
Reynolds, Joash I, 624
Reynolds, Joash I, 625
Reynolds, Joash I, 666
Reynolds, Joash I, 688
Reynolds, Joash I, 864
Reynolds, Joash I, 871
Reynolds, Joash I, 899
Reynolds, Joash I, 932
Reynolds, Job I, 657
Reynolds, Job I, 666
Reynolds, Job I, 680
Reynolds, Job I, 687
Reynolds, Job I, 688
Reynolds, Job I, 768
Reynolds, Joel IV, 754
Reynolds, Joel IV, 840
Reynolds, Joel P. VI, 983
Reynolds, John I, 513
Reynolds, John I, 640
Reynolds, John I, 665
Reynolds, John I, 687
Reynolds, John II, 412
Reynolds, John II, 632
Reynolds, John IV, 55
Reynolds, John IV, 653
Reynolds, John VI, 801
Reynolds, John VI, 809
Reynolds, John VI, 822
Reynolds, John VI, 850
Reynolds, John VI, 921
Reynolds, John VI, 937
Reynolds, John VI, 946
Reynolds, John VI, 961
Reynolds, John VI, 983
Reynolds, John A. VI, 893
Reynolds, John A. VI, 983
Reynolds, John Addison I, 625
Reynolds, John Addison I, 640
Reynolds, John M. V, 463
Reynolds, John T. VI, 850
Reynolds, John W. III, 132
Reynolds, John W. III, 217
Reynolds, John W. III, 266
Reynolds, Johnson I, 667
Reynolds, Jonas I, 835
Reynolds, Jonas I, 978
Reynolds, Jonas I, 996
Reynolds, Jonas VI, 878
Reynolds, Jonas VI, 983
Reynolds, Jonas VI, 1007
Reynolds, Jonathan I, 417
Reynolds, Jonathan I, 513
Reynolds, Joseph I, 666
Reynolds, Joseph I, 667
Reynolds, Joseph I, 688
Reynolds, Joseph II, 412
Reynolds, Joseph II, 632
Reynolds, Joseph IV, 268
Reynolds, Joseph IV, 349
Reynolds, Joseph IV, 562
Reynolds, Joseph VI, 850
Reynolds, Joseph Harper I, 667
Reynolds, Joseph, Jr. IV, 268
Reynolds, Joseph, Jr. IV, 546
Reynolds, Josephine I, 666
Reynolds, Joshua I, 666
Reynolds, Joshua I, 688
Reynolds, Joshua I, 899
Reynolds, Joshua II, 412
Reynolds, Joshua V, 928
Reynolds, Josinah V, 847
Reynolds, Josinah V, 858
Reynolds, Judah VI, 983
Reynolds, Justice III, 266
Reynolds, Justin III, 266
Reynolds, Justus III, 266
Reynolds, Justus III, 439
Reynolds, Katherine VI, 747
Reynolds, Katherine VI, 763
Reynolds, Katherine VI, 791
Reynolds, L. Herbert IV, 1335
Reynolds, L. M. H. I, 640
Reynolds, Leanna VI, 801
Reynolds, Lettice IV, 268
Reynolds, Lettis IV, 218
Reynolds, Lettis IV, 268
Reynolds, Levany VI, 912
Reynolds, Levi I, 665
Reynolds, Levi IV, 268
Reynolds, Levi IV, 754
Reynolds, Levi IV, 840
Reynolds, Levi, Jr. IV, 840
Reynolds, Lewellen J. VI, 983
Reynolds, Lewice I, 899
Reynolds, Lewis I, 666
Reynolds, Lewis I, 667
Reynolds, Lewis I, 687
Reynolds, Lewis I, 688
Reynolds, Lewis I, 689
Reynolds, Lewis I, 835
Reynolds, Lewis I, 882
Reynolds, Lewis I, 899
Reynolds, Lewis V, 642
Reynolds, Lewis A. VI, 983
Reynolds, Lewis C. V, 642
Reynolds, Lindley H. I, 666
Reynolds, Lindley H. I, 864
Reynolds, Lindley H. I, 899
Reynolds, Lindley M. H. I, 932
Reynolds, Lindly Murray Hoag I, 948
Reynolds, Lois Esther IV, 1182
Reynolds, Lonora I, 666
Reynolds, Lonora H. I, 687
Reynolds, Lonora H. I, 688
Reynolds, Lorena I, 640
Reynolds, Lorena I, 666
Reynolds, Lorena I, 864
Reynolds, Louisa VI, 850
Reynolds, Lovena I, 640
Reynolds, Lucetta I, 666
Reynolds, Lucetta I, 682
Reynolds, Lucetta I, 688
Reynolds, Lucetta I, 922
Reynolds, Lucetta I, 934
Reynolds, Lucy VI, 887
Reynolds, Lucy VI, 983
Reynolds, Lurena I, 899
Reynolds, Lydia I, 665
Reynolds, Lydia I, 667
Reynolds, Lydia I, 674
Reynolds, Lydia I, 687
Reynolds, Lydia I, 996
Reynolds, Lydia IV, 268
Reynolds, Lydia IV, 309
Reynolds, Lydia C. V, 858
Reynolds, Lydia C. V, 859
Reynolds, Lydia K. III, 29
Reynolds, Lydia K. III, 265
Reynolds, Lydia K. III, 266
Reynolds, Lydia L. V, 858
Reynolds, Magdalen VI, 983
Reynolds, Mahala IV, 268
Reynolds, Mahala VI, 921
Reynolds, Mahaley VI, 983
Reynolds, Mahlon I, 665
Reynolds, Margaret I, 417
Reynolds, Margaret I, 453
Reynolds, Margaret I, 665
Reynolds, Margaret I, 666
Reynolds, Margaret I, 675
Reynolds, Margaret I, 687
Reynolds, Margaret I, 688
Reynolds, Margaret I, 768
Reynolds, Margaret III, 266
Reynolds, Margaretta IV, 754
Reynolds, Margaretta V, 928
Reynolds, Maria IV, 55
Reynolds, Maria IV, 653
Reynolds, Mariah IV, 639
Reynolds, Mariah IV, 653
Reynolds, Martha I, 665
Reynolds, Martha I, 666
Reynolds, Martha I, 677
Reynolds, Martha I, 680
Reynolds, Martha I, 686
Reynolds, Martha I, 687
Reynolds, Martha I, 688
Reynolds, Martha IV, 754
Reynolds, Martha IV, 989
Reynolds, Martha V, 928
Reynolds, Martha VI, 850
Reynolds, Martha VI, 861
Reynolds, Martha VI, 918
Reynolds, Martha VI, 983
Reynolds, Martha A. VI, 850
Reynolds, Martha Ann V, 858
Reynolds, Martha Ann V, 875
Reynolds, Martha Ann VI, 850
Reynolds, Martha Ann VI, 983
Reynolds, Martha Anna I, 624
Reynolds, Martha G. VI, 983
Reynolds, Martha H. IV, 840
Reynolds, Martha H. IV, 989
Reynolds, Martha Jane VI, 921
Reynolds, Martha K. IV, 840
Reynolds, Martha K. IV, 989
Reynolds, Martha S. I, 640
Reynolds, Martha S. I, 864
Reynolds, Mary I, 414
Reynolds, Mary I, 417
Reynolds, Mary I, 446
Reynolds, Mary I, 453
Reynolds, Mary I, 513
Reynolds, Mary I, 564
Reynolds, Mary I, 568
Reynolds, Mary I, 616
Reynolds, Mary I, 663
Reynolds, Mary I, 665
Reynolds, Mary I, 666
Reynolds, Mary I, 667
Reynolds, Mary I, 674
Reynolds, Mary I, 682
Reynolds, Mary I, 684
Reynolds, Mary I, 687
Reynolds, Mary I, 835
Reynolds, Mary I, 882
Reynolds, Mary I, 899
Reynolds, Mary I, 978
Reynolds, Mary I, 992
Reynolds, Mary I, 996
Reynolds, Mary II, 412
Reynolds, Mary III, 90
Reynolds, Mary III, 266
Reynolds, Mary III, 406
Reynolds, Mary IV, 754
Reynolds, Mary IV, 817
Reynolds, Mary IV, 840
Reynolds, Mary IV, 989
Reynolds, Mary IV, 1377
Reynolds, Mary V, 928
Reynolds, Mary VI, 265
Reynolds, Mary VI, 477
Reynolds, Mary VI, 834
Reynolds, Mary VI, 983
Reynolds, Mary A. I, 640
Reynolds, Mary A. I, 899
Reynolds, Mary A. III, 41
Reynolds, Mary A. III, 266
Reynolds, Mary Ann I, 624
Reynolds, Mary Ann I, 626
Reynolds, Mary Ann I, 666
Reynolds, Mary Ann I, 688
Reynolds, Mary Ann Eliza VI, 983
Reynolds, Mary B. VI, 934
Reynolds, Mary Caroline IV, 75
Reynolds, Mary Cornelia IV, 75
Reynolds, Mary Cornelia V, 928
Reynolds, Mary E. I, 677
Reynolds, Mary E. I, 688
Reynolds, Mary E. I, 864
Reynolds, Mary Ellen I, 688
Reynolds, Mary H. I, 666
Reynolds, Mary H. I, 688
Reynolds, Mary J. I, 624
Reynolds, Mary J. I, 625
Reynolds, Mary J. I, 640
Reynolds, Mary J. I, 899
Reynolds, Mary J. I, 905
Reynolds, Mary Jane IV, 268
Reynolds, Mary Jane IV, 546
Reynolds, Mary Jane IV, 1075
Reynolds, Mary Rachel I, 687
Reynolds, Mary V. IV, 1182
Reynolds, Matilda I, 996
Reynolds, Matilda I, 1000
Reynolds, Matilda IV, 268
Reynolds, Matilda IV, 546
Reynolds, Matilda IV, 549
Reynolds, Matthias VI, 983
Reynolds, Melinda I, 665
Reynolds, Merab I, 665
Reynolds, Mercy V, 928
Reynolds, Micajah VI, 983
Reynolds, Michael IV, 840
Reynolds, Michael IV, 859
Reynolds, Micheal IV, 268
Reynolds, Mille I, 978
Reynolds, Milo I, 665
Reynolds, Milo I, 667
Reynolds, Milo I, 688
Reynolds, Milton I, 665
Reynolds, Milton I, 666
Reynolds, Milton E. I, 688
Reynolds, Minnie R. V, 706
Reynolds, Miriam I, 666
Reynolds, Miriam I, 688
Reynolds, Miriam IV, 233
Reynolds, Miriam IV, 268
Reynolds, Miriam IV, 1182
Reynolds, Miriam IV, 1188
Reynolds, Miriam IV, 1221
Reynolds, Miriam IV, 1229
Reynolds, Miriam IV, 1240
Reynolds, Moriah IV, 653
Reynolds, Nancey VI, 983
Reynolds, Nancy I, 532

olds, Nancy I, 569
olds, Nancy III, 266
olds, Nancy IV, 653
olds, Nancy VI, 858
olds, Nancy VI, 860
olds, Nany VI, 912
olds, Naomi H. III, 266
olds, Nathaniel VI, 983
olds, Obadiah VI, 983
olds, Obediah VI, 983
olds, Oliver IV, 268
olds, Oliver IV, 349
olds, Oliver IV, 546
olds, Oliver P. V, 706
olds, Osborn II, 632
olds, Osborne II, 632
olds, Oscar L. I, 768
olds, Paran I, 808
olds, Paran I, 835
olds, Patria VI, 983
olds, Patsy VI, 912
olds, Patty I, 667
olds, Pauline I, 625
olds, Penelope III, 266
olds, Perin I, 688
olds, Perlina VI, 983
olds, Perrin I, 666
olds, Perrin I, 835
olds, Perthena VI, 983
olds, Peter III, 319
olds, Phebe I, 657
olds, Phebe I, 666
olds, Phebe I, 680
olds, Phebe I, 687
olds, Phebe I, 688
olds, Phebe I, 768
olds, Phebe III, 266
olds, Phebe IV, 1181
olds, Phebe IV, 1182
olds, Phebe IV, 1240
olds, Phebe V, 928
olds, Pheribah I, 667
olds, Philip VI, 983
olds, Pininnah I, 667
olds, Polley VI, 983
olds, Polly I, 666
olds, Polly IV, 1182
olds, Polly IV, 1192
olds, Polly VI, 974
olds, Polly VI, 983
olds, Polly VI, 1020
olds, Prudence I, 513
olds, Prudence I, 542
olds, Prudence I, 569
lds, Prudence II, 207
lds, Prudence II, 252
lds, Prudence VI, 477
lds, Rachel I, 513
lds, Rachel I, 664
lds, Rachel I, 665
lds, Rachel I, 666
lds, Rachel I, 667
lds, Rachel I, 676
lds, Rachel I, 677
lds, Rachel I, 679
lds, Rachel I, 687
lds, Rachel II, 412
lds, Rachel IV, 268
lds, Rachel IV, 546
lds, Rachel V, 274
lds, Rachel V, 279
lds, Rachel VI, 822
lds, Rebecca II, 632
lds, Rebecca II, 816
lds, Rebecca II, 914
lds, Rebecca IV, 55
lds, Rebecca IV, 268
lds, Rebecca IV, 301
lds, Rebecca IV, 615
lds, Rebecca IV, 653
lds, Rebecca V, 858
lds, Rebecca J. V, 846
lds, Rebecca Susanna
dia IV, 268
lds, Rebeckah VI, 850
lds, Rebekah IV, 653
lds, Reuben I, 666
lds, Reuben IV, 268
lds, Reuben IV, 546
lds, Rezin I, 667
lds, Rhoda I, 417
lds, Rhoda I, 667
lds, Rhoda I, 678
lds, Rhoda I, 687
lds, Rhoda I, 899
lds, Rhoda III, 266
lds, Rich. III, 237
lds, Rich. III, 266
lds, Rich. M. III, 266
lds, Richard III, 265
lds, Richard IV, 268
Reynolds, Richard IV, 546
Reynolds, Richard B. IV, 268
Reynolds, Richard B. IV, 546
Reynolds, Richard C. III, 266
Reynolds, Richard M. III, 90
Reynolds, Richard M. III, 266
Reynolds, Richard M. III, 405
Reynolds, Richard M. III, 439
Reynolds, Richardson III, 406
Reynolds, Roswell Lewis I, 667
Reynolds, Roy V, 706
Reynolds, Rueben V, 928
Reynolds, Rufus III, 90
Reynolds, Rufus III, 266
Reynolds, Rufus III, 406
Reynolds, Ruth I, 665
Reynolds, Ruth I, 687
Reynolds, Ruth Gladys IV, 1182
Reynolds, Ruthanna IV, 268
Reynolds, Ruthanna IV, 543
Reynolds, Ruthanna IV, 546
Reynolds, Sabrina VI, 956
Reynolds, Sally I, 657
Reynolds, Sally I, 666
Reynolds, Sally I, 768
Reynolds, Sally III, 266
Reynolds, Sally VI, 850
Reynolds, Samuel II, 82
Reynolds, Samuel II, 94
Reynolds, Samuel II, 412
Reynolds, Samuel III, 266
Reynolds, Samuel IV, 754
Reynolds, Samuel IV, 818
Reynolds, Samuel IV, 840
Reynolds, Samuel IV, 989
Reynolds, Samuel V, 928
Reynolds, Samuel Clarkson V, 928
Reynolds, Sanford VI, 744
Reynolds, Sarah I, 513
Reynolds, Sarah I, 665
Reynolds, Sarah I, 666
Reynolds, Sarah I, 667
Reynolds, Sarah I, 687
Reynolds, Sarah I, 688
Reynolds, Sarah I, 689
Reynolds, Sarah I, 762
Reynolds, Sarah I, 768
Reynolds, Sarah I, 899
Reynolds, Sarah II, 632
Reynolds, Sarah III, 266
Reynolds, Sarah IV, 55
Reynolds, Sarah IV, 651
Reynolds, Sarah IV, 653
Reynolds, Sarah IV, 989
Reynolds, Sarah IV, 1335
Reynolds, Sarah V, 928
Reynolds, Sarah VI, 731
Reynolds, Sarah VI, 744
Reynolds, Sarah VI, 809
Reynolds, Sarah Ann VI, 921
Reynolds, Sarah Ann VI, 983
Reynolds, Sarah B. VI, 912
Reynolds, Sarah E. III, 266
Reynolds, Sarah Ellen V, 846
Reynolds, Sarah Ellen V, 847
Reynolds, Sarah Ellen V, 858
Reynolds, Sarah Jane I, 667
Reynolds, Sarah Jane I, 688
Reynolds, Sarah P. VI, 893
Reynolds, Sarah Rodema I, 768
Reynolds, Siras IV, 546
Reynolds, Sisley VI, 1014
Reynolds, Smith I, 666
Reynolds, Smith I, 688
Reynolds, Solomon I, 513
Reynolds, Sophronia I, 808
Reynolds, Sophronia I, 835
Reynolds, Stephen IV, 268
Reynolds, Stephen V, 928
Reynolds, Stephen K. IV, 233
Reynolds, Stephen K. IV, 268
Reynolds, Susan I, 666
Reynolds, Susan I, 688
Reynolds, Susanna I, 378
Reynolds, Susanna I, 417
Reynolds, Susanna I, 453
Reynolds, Susanna I, 513
Reynolds, Susanna I, 665
Reynolds, Susanna I, 666
Reynolds, Susanna I, 667
Reynolds, Susanna I, 675
Reynolds, Susanna I, 687
Reynolds, Susanna I, 688
Reynolds, Susanna I, 691
Reynolds, Susanna I, 765
Reynolds, Susanna I, 768
Reynolds, Susanna I, 794
Reynolds, Susanna I, 864
Reynolds, Susanna I, 899
Reynolds, Susanna IV, 263
Reynolds, Susanna IV, 268
Reynolds, Susanna IV, 546
Reynolds, Susannah I, 484
Reynolds, Susannah I, 656
Reynolds, Susannah I, 665
Reynolds, Susannah I, 667
Reynolds, Tabitha IV, 840
Reynolds, Tabitha IV, 855
Reynolds, Tamer I, 685
Reynolds, Tamer I, 687
Reynolds, Tamer IV, 840
Reynolds, Tamer IV, 854
Reynolds, Theodore E. VI, 983
Reynolds, Theodoshey VI, 903
Reynolds, Thomas I, 417
Reynolds, Thomas I, 427
Reynolds, Thomas I, 513
Reynolds, Thomas I, 568
Reynolds, Thomas I, 569
Reynolds, Thomas I, 667
Reynolds, Thomas I, 687
Reynolds, Thomas I, 978
Reynolds, Thomas IV, 158
Reynolds, Thomas IV, 268
Reynolds, Thomas IV, 840
Reynolds, Valina I, 688
Reynolds, Valina I, 692
Reynolds, Velnia I, 666
Reynolds, Verus I, 666
Reynolds, Verus I, 688
Reynolds, Veturia I, 666
Reynolds, Veturia I, 864
Reynolds, Walter I, 625
Reynolds, Wd. Emily VI, 731
Reynolds, Wd. Mary II, 632
Reynolds, Wenlock I, 407
Reynolds, Wenlock I, 409
Reynolds, Wenlock I, 417
Reynolds, Wenlock I, 484
Reynolds, Wenlock I, 665
Reynolds, Wenlock I, 667
Reynolds, Wenlock I, 687
Reynolds, Wenlock I, 688
Reynolds, Wenlock I, 768
Reynolds, Wenlock, Jr. I, 688
Reynolds, Widow Susanna I, 666
Reynolds, William I, 343
Reynolds, William I, 417
Reynolds, William I, 513
Reynolds, William I, 532
Reynolds, William I, 568
Reynolds, William I, 569
Reynolds, William I, 663
Reynolds, William I, 665
Reynolds, William I, 666
Reynolds, William I, 667
Reynolds, William I, 687
Reynolds, William I, 688
Reynolds, William I, 883
Reynolds, William I, 899
Reynolds, William I, 978
Reynolds, William I, 996
Reynolds, William IV, 268
Reynolds, William IV, 754
Reynolds, William V, 847
Reynolds, William V, 858
Reynolds, William V, 928
Reynolds, William VI, 850
Reynolds, William VI, 983
Reynolds, William H. VI, 983
Reynolds, Williamd I, 678
Reynolds, Willis VI, 850
Reynolds, Wilmet I, 666
Reynolds, Winlock I, 765
Reynolds, Winlock I, 768
Reynolds, Wm. I, 417
Reynolds, Wm. I, 513
Reynolds, Wm. V, 928
Reynolds, Wm. G. IV, 989
Reynolds, Wm. K. V, 928
Reynolds, Wm. M. VI, 850
Reynolds, Zeno I, 665
Reynolds, Zeno I, 667
Reynolds, Zimri I, 665
Rhamstine, Henrietta III, 189
Rhea, Allen VI, 434
Rhea, Deborah VI, 434
Rhea, Hannah VI, 604
Rhea, Ida IV, 267
Rhea, John VI, 604
Rhea, Joseph VI, 434
Rhea, Joseph VI, 604
Rhea, Margaret VI, 434
Rhea, Rebecca V, 113
Rhea, Rebeckah VI, 604
Rhea, Rebeckah, Jr. VI, 604
Rhea, Rebekah VI, 434
Rhea, Robert V, 113
Rhea, Robert VI, 434
Rhea, Robert VI, 595
Rhea, Robert VI, 604
Rhea, Robert Hains VI, 604
Rhea, Sarah VI, 434
Rhea, Susanna VI, 434
Rhea, Susannah VI, 604
Rhea, Thomas VI, 434
Rheubel, Meriam IV, 465
Rheubel, Meriam IV, 495
Rhine, Elinor VI, 961
Rhinehart, Adam I, 364
Rhinehart, Adam V, 525
Rhinehart, Ann I, 364
Rhinehart, Ann V, 525
Rhinehart, Ann V, 529
Rhinehart, Asa V, 525
Rhinehart, Barbara V, 474
Rhinehart, Barbara V, 525
Rhinehart, Barbary I, 364
Rhinehart, Catharine V, 525
Rhinehart, Catrine I, 364
Rhinehart, Cherry Grove V, 525
Rhinehart, Elizabeth V, 638
Rhinehart, Elizabeth V, 642
Rhinehart, George I, 364
Rhinehart, George V, 525
Rhinehart, Isaac V, 525
Rhinehart, Jacob I, 364
Rhinehart, Jacob V, 525
Rhinehart, Jeremiah I, 364
Rhinehart, Jeremiah V, 525
Rhinehart, Joel V, 525
Rhinehart, Lydia V, 525
Rhinehart, Margaret I, 364
Rhinehart, Margaret V, 521
Rhinehart, Margaret V, 525
Rhinehart, Martha V, 525
Rhinehart, Rachel I, 364
Rhinehart, Rachel V, 525
Rhinehart, Solomon I, 364
Rhinehart, Solomon V, 525
Rhineheart, Jeremiah V, 525
Rhineholt, Lida V, 1015
Rhiner, Millie IV, 1335
Rhiner, Nellie IV, 1335
Rhinesmith, Wm. V, 1016
Rhoad, Mary V, 199
Rhoad, Phebe I, 978
Rhoades, ??? IV, 1125
Rhoades, Adam II, 412
Rhoades, Anna S. II, 914
Rhoades, Catherine II, 412
Rhoades, Dora V, 463
Rhoades, Edna V, 706
Rhoades, Elizabeth II, 633
Rhoades, Elizabeth IV, 840
Rhoades, Enos V, 463
Rhoades, Evan II, 412
Rhoades, Frances V, 463
Rhoades, Frank V, 706
Rhoades, Frank B. V, 706
Rhoades, George V, 679
Rhoades, George V, 706
Rhoades, Grace V, 679
Rhoades, Grace V, 706
Rhoades, Hannah II, 412
Rhoades, Hannah II, 904
Rhoades, Joseph IV, 1261
Rhoades, Lewis V, 463
Rhoades, Marilyn V, 706
Rhoades, Martha V, 463
Rhoades, Mary II, 290
Rhoades, Mary II, 299
Rhoades, Mary II, 633
Rhoades, Myra V, 706
Rhoades, Myra A. V, 706
Rhoades, Samuel II, 412
Rhoades, Samuel II, 904
Rhoades, Sarah II, 633
Rhoades, Susannah H. II, 904
Rhoades, Susannah H. II, 914
Rhoades, William V, 463
Rhoads, Abby II, 290
Rhoads, Abby II, 299
Rhoads, Abigail IV, 1377
Rhoads, Abigail VI, 436
Rhoads, Abigail VI, 437
Rhoads, Adam II, 412
Rhoads, Adam II, 632
Rhoads, Adam VI, 436
Rhoads, Alice S. II, 914
Rhoads, Alice Sellers II, 817
Rhoads, Alva V, 274
Rhoads, Alvah V, 274
Rhoads, Ann I, 417
Rhoads, Ann II, 412
Rhoads, Ann II, 632
Rhoads, Anna II, 704
Rhoads, Anna H. II, 704
Rhoads, Anna Ivins II, 816
Rhoads, Anna S. II, 914
Rhoads, Catherine II, 412
Rhoads, Charles II, 412
Rhoads, Charles II, 704
Rhoads, Charles II, 762
Rhoads, Cornell III, 365
Rhoads, Daniel J. II, 633
Rhoads, Daniel Jean II, 633
Rhoads, Edward II, 412
Rhoads, Edward II, 633
Rhoads, Eleanor II, 704
Rhoads, Eleanor II, 738
Rhoads, Elizabeth II, 412
Rhoads, Elizabeth II, 484
Rhoads, Elizabeth II, 524
Rhoads, Elizabeth II, 632
Rhoads, Elizabeth II, 633
Rhoads, Elizabeth II, 762
Rhoads, Enos V, 274
Rhoads, Evan II, 412
Rhoads, George II, 290
Rhoads, George II, 299
Rhoads, George II, 762
Rhoads, George, Jr. II, 762
Rhoads, Hannah II, 412
Rhoads, Hannah II, 632
Rhoads, Hannah II, 914
Rhoads, Israel II, 412
Rhoads, Jacob II, 412
Rhoads, Jacob II, 632
Rhoads, James II, 412
Rhoads, James E. II, 762
Rhoads, John II, 412
Rhoads, John II, 632
Rhoads, John II, 686
Rhoads, John III, 266
Rhoads, John P. II, 762
Rhoads, Joseph II, 412
Rhoads, Joseph II, 632
Rhoads, Joseph II, 633
Rhoads, Joseph II, 816
Rhoads, Joseph II, 825
Rhoads, Joseph II, 1074
Rhoads, Joseph II, 1078
Rhoads, Joshua II, 633
Rhoads, Joshua II, 816
Rhoads, Joshua II, 914
Rhoads, Joshua II, 1074
Rhoads, Joshua II, 1078
Rhoads, Julias Friedlander II, 816
Rhoads, Levi P. II, 762
Rhoads, Margaret II, 412
Rhoads, Margaret II, 632
Rhoads, Martha C. II, 817
Rhoads, Martha J. II, 762
Rhoads, Mary II, 299
Rhoads, Mary II, 412
Rhoads, Mary II, 527
Rhoads, Mary II, 632
Rhoads, Mary II, 633
Rhoads, Mary Ann II, 412
Rhoads, Mary Homer II, 290
Rhoads, Mary Homer II, 299
Rhoads, Mary Ivins II, 817
Rhoads, Naomi II, 412
Rhoads, Naomi II, 816
Rhoads, Naomi II, 817
Rhoads, Naomi II, 825
Rhoads, Naomi II, 1074
Rhoads, Naomi II, 1078
Rhoads, Naomi R. II, 836
Rhoads, Naomi R. II, 914
Rhoads, Naomy II, 633
Rhoads, Phianah III, 365
Rhoads, Rachel II, 557
Rhoads, Rachel II, 633
Rhoads, Rosanna II, 816
Rhoads, Rosanna II, 914
Rhoads, Rosanna II, 1053
Rhoads, Rosanna II, 1074
Rhoads, Rosanna II, 1078
Rhoads, Samuel II, 412
Rhoads, Samuel II, 484
Rhoads, Samuel II, 524
Rhoads, Samuel II, 527
Rhoads, Samuel II, 632
Rhoads, Samuel II, 914
Rhoads, Samuel, Jr. II, 412
Rhoads, Samuel, Jr. II, 619
Rhoads, Sarah II, 524
Rhoads, Sarah II, 619
Rhoads, Sarah II, 633
Rhoads, Sarah II, 825
Rhoads, Sarah V, 274
Rhoads, Susannah H. II, 914
Rhoads, Thomas Walter II, 817
Rhoads, William Braddock II, 290
Rhoads, William Braddock II, 299
Rhoda, Zimrada IV, 1380
Rhodabeck, Daniel O. IV, 1221
Rhode, Caleb V, 199

Rhode, Elizabeth V, 199
Rhode, Esther V, 199
Rhode, John V, 199
Rhode, Joseph V, 199
Rhode, Mary V, 199
Rhode, Mary V, 525
Rhode, Sarah V, 199
Rhode, Semour V, 199
Rhode, Thomas V, 199
Rhodes, ??? III, 266
Rhodes, ??? VI, 348
Rhodes, Aaron VI, 968
Rhodes, Abigail II, 252
Rhodes, Abigail VI, 475
Rhodes, Abigail VI, 551
Rhodes, Adam II, 412
Rhodes, Adam II, 632
Rhodes, Amanda V, 1016
Rhodes, Amy IV, 754
Rhodes, Amy IV, 778
Rhodes, Amy VI, 338
Rhodes, Amy VI, 355
Rhodes, Ann II, 632
Rhodes, Ann V, 114
Rhodes, Ann VI, 551
Rhodes, Ann VI, 986
Rhodes, Anna Eliza III, 266
Rhodes, Anna Eliza III, 305
Rhodes, Anna Morris IV, 269
Rhodes, Anna Morris IV, 754
Rhodes, Bertha V, 1016
Rhodes, Caroline IV, 653
Rhodes, Caroline IV, 661
Rhodes, Clarence V, 357
Rhodes, Cornelia III, 266
Rhodes, Cornelia III, 367
Rhodes, Cornelius H. III, 413
Rhodes, Cornelius H. III, 439
Rhodes, Cornell III, 266
Rhodes, David V, 1016
Rhodes, Dorothy V, 357
Rhodes, Drucilla I, 340
Rhodes, Drusilla I, 340
Rhodes, Edith Lee III, 266
Rhodes, Eliza III, 266
Rhodes, Elizabeth IV, 181
Rhodes, Elizabeth IV, 269
Rhodes, Elizabeth IV, 840
Rhodes, Elizabeth IV, 1075
Rhodes, Elizabeth IV, 1113
Rhodes, Elizabeth IV, 1117
Rhodes, Elizabeth IV, 1137
Rhodes, Elizabeth VI, 210
Rhodes, Elizabeth VI, 551
Rhodes, Elizabeth VI, 983
Rhodes, Elizabeth T. IV, 1113
Rhodes, Elizabeth Test IV, 1138
Rhodes, Elmer V, 1016
Rhodes, Estella V, 1016
Rhodes, Esther III, 22
Rhodes, Esther III, 34
Rhodes, Esther III, 145
Rhodes, Esther III, 266
Rhodes, Esther IV, 50
Rhodes, Esther IV, 55
Rhodes, Esther IV, 343
Rhodes, Esther IV, 349
Rhodes, Esther V, 525
Rhodes, Faye V, 357
Rhodes, Geo. E. III, 305
Rhodes, George V, 1016
Rhodes, George H. III, 266
Rhodes, George H. III, 367
Rhodes, Georgia III, 22
Rhodes, Georgia III, 266
Rhodes, Grace D. III, 266
Rhodes, Hannah II, 632
Rhodes, Hannah II, 651
Rhodes, Hannah VI, 533
Rhodes, Hannah VI, 551
Rhodes, Harman VI, 355
Rhodes, Harmon IV, 181
Rhodes, Harmon IV, 269
Rhodes, Harmon IV, 754
Rhodes, Harmon IV, 840
Rhodes, Harmon IV, 1075
Rhodes, Harmon IV, 1113
Rhodes, Harmon IV, 1117
Rhodes, Harmon IV, 1137
Rhodes, Harnan IV, 269
Rhodes, Harry III, 266
Rhodes, Henry III, 266
Rhodes, Henry VI, 986
Rhodes, Henry Mills IV, 55
Rhodes, Hiram III, 22
Rhodes, Hiram III, 34
Rhodes, Hiram III, 145
Rhodes, Hiram III, 266
Rhodes, Ira III, 266
Rhodes, Ira III, 305
Rhodes, Isaac IV, 269
Rhodes, Isaac IV, 1075
Rhodes, Isaac IV, 1113
Rhodes, Isaac IV, 1137
Rhodes, John III, 266
Rhodes, Jos. IV, 269
Rhodes, Joseph IV, 229
Rhodes, Joseph IV, 268
Rhodes, Joseph IV, 269
Rhodes, Joseph IV, 287
Rhodes, Joseph IV, 332
Rhodes, Joseph IV, 349
Rhodes, Joseph IV, 754
Rhodes, Joseph IV, 778
Rhodes, Joseph IV, 1137
Rhodes, Joseph V, 114
Rhodes, Joseph VI, 337
Rhodes, Joseph VI, 338
Rhodes, Joseph VI, 340
Rhodes, Joseph VI, 355
Rhodes, Joseph VI, 633
Rhodes, Joseph VI, 695
Rhodes, Joshua II, 1078
Rhodes, Josiah III, 266
Rhodes, Lidia IV, 269
Rhodes, Lindley V, 464
Rhodes, Louisa III, 266
Rhodes, Lydia IV, 229
Rhodes, Lydia IV, 269
Rhodes, Lydia IV, 754
Rhodes, Lydia V, 357
Rhodes, Margaret II, 412
Rhodes, Martha IV, 229
Rhodes, Martha IV, 269
Rhodes, Martha IV, 648
Rhodes, Martha IV, 653
Rhodes, Martha IV, 754
Rhodes, Martha IV, 778
Rhodes, Martha IV, 1075
Rhodes, Martha IV, 1102
Rhodes, Martha IV, 1113
Rhodes, Martha IV, 1137
Rhodes, Martha V, 114
Rhodes, Martha VI, 337
Rhodes, Martha VI, 338
Rhodes, Martha VI, 355
Rhodes, Martha VI, 633
Rhodes, Martha VI, 695
Rhodes, Martha Ann III, 266
Rhodes, Martha Rankin IV, 314
Rhodes, Mary II, 412
Rhodes, Mary IV, 269
Rhodes, Mary IV, 314
Rhodes, Mary IV, 332
Rhodes, Mary IV, 349
Rhodes, Mary IV, 696
Rhodes, Mary IV, 754
Rhodes, Mary V, 114
Rhodes, Mary V, 474
Rhodes, Mary V, 525
Rhodes, Mary VI, 476
Rhodes, Mary VI, 533
Rhodes, Mary VI, 537
Rhodes, Mary VI, 551
Rhodes, Mary VI, 632
Rhodes, Mary VI, 695
Rhodes, Mary VI, 935
Rhodes, Mary A. V, 1016
Rhodes, Mary Jr. IV, 696
Rhodes, Mary O. V, 1016
Rhodes, Mary, Jr. IV, 754
Rhodes, Mary, Jr. VI, 632
Rhodes, Moses IV, 343
Rhodes, Moses IV, 349
Rhodes, Moses IV, 721
Rhodes, Moses IV, 754
Rhodes, Moses V, 114
Rhodes, Moses VI, 338
Rhodes, Moses VI, 355
Rhodes, Moses VI, 695
Rhodes, Mrs. George IV, 754
Rhodes, Nancy VI, 968
Rhodes, Nettie V, 1016
Rhodes, Phebe I, 996
Rhodes, Phebe E. III, 413
Rhodes, Phebe E. III, 439
Rhodes, Phiannah III, 266
Rhodes, Polly VI, 986
Rhodes, Rebecca IV, 269
Rhodes, Rebecca IV, 295
Rhodes, Rebecca IV, 1075
Rhodes, Rebecca IV, 1113
Rhodes, Rebecca IV, 1117
Rhodes, Rebecca IV, 1137
Rhodes, Rendell V, 357
Rhodes, Richard Utter III, 266
Rhodes, Robert VI, 975
Rhodes, Rosanna II, 1059
Rhodes, Sally IV, 269
Rhodes, Sally IV, 287
Rhodes, Samuel II, 412
Rhodes, Sarah I, 303
Rhodes, Sarah I, 317
Rhodes, Sarah V, 274
Rhodes, Sarah VI, 215
Rhodes, Selina III, 266
Rhodes, Selina R. III, 305
Rhodes, Stanley Pumphrey III, 266
Rhodes, Susanna V, 114
Rhodes, Susannah IV, 343
Rhodes, Susannah IV, 721
Rhodes, Susannah IV, 754
Rhodes, Thomas III, 266
Rhodes, Thomas V, 474
Rhodes, Thomas V, 525
Rhodes, Wd. Georgia III, 22
Rhodes, Widow Mary VI, 551
Rhodes, William I, 996
Rhodes, William IV, 269
Rhodes, William IV, 1137
Rhodes, William VI, 355
Rhodes, William VI, 935
Rhodes, William VI, 983
Rhodes, William VI, 986
Rhodes, William VI, 1004
Rhodes, Wm. IV, 696
Rhodes, Wm. IV, 1075
Rhodes, Wm. VI, 632
Rhody, Mary VI, 84
Rhoetter, Tressie V, 763
Rhonimus, Jane V, 356
Rhonimus, Jane V, 357
Rhonimus, Martha V, 274
Rhoten, Maud Edwards V, 357
Rhubottom, Hannah I, 383
Rhubottom, Hannah I, 417
Rhubottom, Jane I, 383
Rhubottom, Jane I, 417
Rhubottom, Mary I, 386
Rhubottom, Mary I, 417
Rhude, Cora V, 706
Rhude, Howard Leonidas V, 706
Rhude, Mary V, 691
Rhude, Mary V, 706
Rhude, Mattie V, 706
Rhude, May V, 706
Rhude, Nancy V, 706
Rhuebottom, Elizabeth I, 417
Rhuebottom, Mary I, 417
Rhuebottom, Simon I, 417
Rhuebotton, Elizabeth I, 387
Rhuebotton, Elizabeth I, 417
Rhul, Eliza Jane IV, 989
Rhul, Eliza Jane IV, 1008
Riall, Mary II, 416
Riall, William II, 416
Riall, Wm. II, 631
Rian, Jeremiah II, 447
Rian, Martha II, 447
Rian, Samuel II, 447
Riblet, Clyde IV, 1335
Riblet, Cynthia V, 1016
Riblet, Hattie V, 1016
Riblet, Isaac R. V, 1016
Riblet, James James E., Jr. V, 1016
Riblet, Jennie V, 1016
Riblet, Oscar V, 1016
Riblet, Rebecca V, 1016
Riblet, Sylvanis V, 1016
Rice, ??? IV, 912
Rice, Alfred IV, 1292
Rice, Alley VI, 983
Rice, Alliance IV, 907
Rice, Amanda V. VI, 984
Rice, Angeline E. VI, 983
Rice, Ann II, 505
Rice, Ann II, 633
Rice, Ann VI, 984
Rice, Anna VI, 851
Rice, Augusta I, 569
Rice, Bailey VI, 983
Rice, Bailey VI, 984
Rice, Baley VI, 961
Rice, Ben VI, 962
Rice, Ben VI, 1010
Rice, Benj. F. IV, 1335
Rice, Benjamin VI, 923
Rice, Benjamin VI, 934
Rice, Benjamin VI, 983
Rice, Blanch V, 763
Rice, Blanche Mae IV, 1019
Rice, Catharine V, 790
Rice, Catherine IV, 1261
Rice, Charity IV, 269
Rice, Charity D. IV, 269
Rice, Charity D. IV, 915
Rice, Charity D. IV, 986
Rice, Charity D. IV, 989
Rice, Charles IV, 915
Rice, Charles VI, 850
Rice, Charles VI, 967
Rice, Charles H. IV, 269
Rice, Charles H. IV, 915
Rice, Charles H. IV, 986
Rice, Charles H. IV, 989
Rice, Charles, Sr. VI, 983
Rice, Charley D. IV, 989
Rice, Chas. H. IV, 269
Rice, Chas. R. VI, 850
Rice, David VI, 962
Rice, David VI, 967
Rice, David VI, 983
Rice, Deborah B. IV, 755
Rice, Deborah B. IV, 780
Rice, Deborah B. IV, 1042
Rice, Devolzo E. V, 642
Rice, Edith Louise IV, 756
Rice, Edith White VI, 962
Rice, Edward III, 266
Rice, Edwin IV, 754
Rice, Effie IV, 754
Rice, Eleanor Jane III, 266
Rice, Eliz. III, 68
Rice, Elizabeth IV, 915
Rice, Elizabeth VI, 813
Rice, Elizabeth VI, 1010
Rice, Elizabeth R. VI, 984
Rice, Ella IV, 755
Rice, Ellen IV, 1261
Rice, Elsie IV, 756
Rice, Fanny IV, 754
Rice, Fanny VI, 983
Rice, Frances III, 266
Rice, Frances VI, 962
Rice, Francis IV, 755
Rice, Francis C. IV, 754
Rice, Geo. W. VI, 850
Rice, George II, 633
Rice, George VI, 813
Rice, George VI, 831
Rice, Griffith II, 38
Rice, Hannah II, 38
Rice, Hannah VI, 551
Rice, Hannah VI, 552
Rice, Hattie III, 132
Rice, Hattie III, 188
Rice, Henry VI, 812
Rice, Hilda IV, 754
Rice, Hilda IV, 755
Rice, Jame M. IV, 299
Rice, Jane IV, 252
Rice, Jane IV, 269
Rice, Jane VI, 983
Rice, Jane M. IV, 269
Rice, Jesse D. V, 642
Rice, John II, 38
Rice, John VI, 851
Rice, John VI, 855
Rice, John VI, 983
Rice, Jonathan VI, 850
Rice, Jonathan Alexis VI, 984
Rice, Joseph II, 633
Rice, Joseph Robbins II, 633
Rice, Judith S. VI, 855
Rice, Judy VI, 850
Rice, Julia M. IV, 155
Rice, Julia M. IV, 158
Rice, Julia Maria IV, 256
Rice, Julia Maria IV, 269
Rice, Lawrence II, 505
Rice, Lawrence II, 633
Rice, Lester Allen IV, 754
Rice, Lilly Jessie V, 642
Rice, Liza VI, 961
Rice, Louis IV, 756
Rice, Lucinda W. VI, 984
Rice, Margaret V, 464
Rice, Margaretta V, 274
Rice, Martha IV, 754
Rice, Martha IV, 755
Rice, Martha VI, 30
Rice, Martha VI, 35
Rice, Martha Jane IV, 269
Rice, Martha Jane IV, 275
Rice, Mary IV, 1261
Rice, Mary VI, 240
Rice, Mary VI, 831
Rice, Mary VI, 850
Rice, Mary VI, 983
Rice, Mary Elizabeth IV, 882
Rice, Mary K. VI, 984
Rice, Mrs. Verna IV, 755
Rice, Nancy VI, 984
Rice, Paulina D. VI, 984
Rice, Phebe VI, 888
Rice, Philip II, 94
Rice, Phillip II, 38
Rice, Polley VI, 983
Rice, Priscilla I, 569
Rice, Rachel IV, 915
Rice, Rebecca I, 569
Rice, Rebecca II, 412
Rice, Rebecca VI, 850
Rice, Rebeckah VI, 983
Rice, Reuben VI, 984
Rice, Ruth VI, 437
Rice, Sally VI, 797
Rice, Sally VI, 983
Rice, Samuel VI, 850
Rice, Samuel VI, 983
Rice, Samuel VI, 984
Rice, Samuel B. VI, 984
Rice, Samuel D. VI, 905
Rice, Samuel D. VI, 992
Rice, Samuel D. D. VI, 984
Rice, Sarah II, 38
Rice, Sarah II, 79
Rice, Sarah II, 82
Rice, Sarah II, 94
Rice, Sarah II, 633
Rice, Sarah II, 638
Rice, Sarah IV, 942
Rice, Sarah IV, 989
Rice, Sarah IV, 1292
Rice, Sarah V, 469
Rice, Sarah VI, 943
Rice, Sarah VI, 984
Rice, Sarah D. VI, 984
Rice, Sarah J. VI, 850
Rice, Sarah L. V, 642
Rice, Susan V, 921
Rice, Susan V, 928
Rice, Susan VI, 850
Rice, Susan VI, 984
Rice, Susanna VI, 927
Rice, Thomas II, 38
Rice, Thomas II, 82
Rice, Thomas II, 94
Rice, Thomas VI, 984
Rice, Thomas J. VI, 984
Rice, W. P. IV, 907
Rice, Walter IV, 1261
Rice, Wd. Sarah II, 633
Rice, William I, 569
Rice, William IV, 915
Rice, William IV, 989
Rice, William VI, 797
Rice, William VI, 831
Rice, William VI, 961
Rice, William VI, 983
Rice, William VI, 984
Rice, William C. VI, 984
Rice, William H. VI, 932
Rice, William H. VI, 984
Rice, William H. VI, 997
Rice, William P. IV, 915
Rice, Wm. IV, 915
Rich, Aaron I, 667
Rich, Aaron I, 835
Rich, Aaron I, 899
Rich, Abigail I, 678
Rich, Abigail I, 688
Rich, Abigail I, 749
Rich, Abigail I, 752
Rich, Abigail I, 762
Rich, Abigail I, 768
Rich, Abigail I, 769
Rich, Ahineam I, 769
Rich, Ahinoam I, 768
Rich, Alfred I, 569
Rich, Allen VI, 850
Rich, Amy I, 688
Rich, Amy I, 768
Rich, Amy I, 769
Rich, Amy Jane I, 752
Rich, Amy Mariah I, 752
Rich, Anderson IV, 755
Rich, Ann II, 817
Rich, Ann II, 914
Rich, Ann V, 474
Rich, Ann V, 525
Rich, Ann V, 595
Rich, Ann VI, 551
Rich, Ann Gane I, 563
Rich, Ann Gane I, 569
Rich, Ann Jean I, 589
Rich, Anna I, 732
Rich, Anna I, 738
Rich, Anna I, 752
Rich, Anna I, 769
Rich, Anna Jane I, 596
Rich, Anna Jane I, 835
Rich, Anna Jean I, 596
Rich, Anna Jean I, 835
Rich, Anthony I, 470
Rich, Anthony T. I, 484
Rich, Aron I, 768
Rich, Asenath I, 769
Rich, Bartley V, 595
Rich, Benjamin II, 817
Rich, Betty I, 768
Rich, Clara B. IV, 755
Rich, Daniel C. II, 968

, David I, 768
, David I, 769
, David IV, 755
, David VI, 800
David VI, 850
, Deborah I, 762
, Deborah I, 768
, Deborah I, 769
, Deborah II, 968
Della Jane IV, 1030
, Dinah I, 569
, Dinah I, 667
, Dinah I, 676
Dinah I, 688
, Dinah I, 835
, Edith V, 66
, Edith V, 114
Edith V, 595
, Edward IV, 755
, Edwin G. II, 914
, Eliza I, 569
Elizabeth I, 561
Elizabeth I, 569
, Elizabeth I, 596
, Elizabeth I, 607
, Elizabeth I, 752
, Elizabeth I, 769
, Elizabeth II, 968
, Elizabeth II, 1023
, Elizabeth II, 1077
, Elizabeth II, 1078
, Elizabeth VI, 850
, Elizabeth C. II, 914
, Elizabeth C. V, 595
, Ellen D. IV, 1029
, Enion I, 732
, Enos I, 752
, Everett IV, 755
, Ezekel I, 752
, Ezekiel I, 768
, Ezekiel I, 769
, Francis B. IV, 681
, Francis B. IV, 755
, Frederick IV, 755
, Frederick C. IV, 755
, George I, 768
, Gertrude IV, 755
, Gertrude IV, 761
, Gladys IV, 755
, Gladys J. IV, 755
, Gordon IV, 755
, Grace IV, 755
, Hannah I, 596
, Hannah I, 762
, Hannah I, 768
, Hannah I, 769
, Hannah II, 968
, Helena I, 769
, Henry I, 667
, Henry I, 688
, Howard II, 968
, Isaac I, 513
, Isaac I, 762
, Isaac I, 768
, Isaac I, 769
, Isaac V, 114
, Isabel Ann V, 587
, Isabel Ann V, 595
, Isabela V, 595
, Isabella V, 471
, Isabella V, 525
, Isabella V, 547
, Isabella V, 595
, Isabella Ann V, 595
, Isabella Rich V, 525
, Isaiah I, 752
, Isaiah I, 769
, Isaiah II, 412
, J. Clifford II, 914
, J. Evert IV, 755
, Jacob I, 513
, Jacob V, 114
, James B. III, 266
, Jemima R. V, 595
, Jesse I, 752
, Jesse I, 769
, Joel VI, 850
, John I, 513
, John I, 569
, John I, 667
, John I, 688
, John I, 752
, John I, 768
, John I, 769
, John II, 968
, John II, 1023
, John V, 114
, John, Jr. I, 667
, John, Jr. I, 769
, Joseph I, 513
, Joseph I, 563

Rich, Joseph I, 569
Rich, Joseph I, 586
Rich, Joseph I, 589
Rich, Joseph I, 596
Rich, Joseph I, 667
Rich, Joseph I, 732
Rich, Joseph I, 768
Rich, Joseph I, 769
Rich, Joseph I, 835
Rich, Joseph II, 968
Rich, Joseph II, 1023
Rich, Joseph II, 1077
Rich, Joseph II, 1078
Rich, Joseph IV, 755
Rich, Joseph A. IV, 755
Rich, Joseph, Jr. II, 1077
Rich, Joseph, Jr. II, 1078
Rich, Judith I, 569
Rich, Judith I, 600
Rich, Judith V, 114
Rich, Levi M. V, 114
Rich, Lydia V, 114
Rich, Lydia V, 131
Rich, Lydia V, 525
Rich, Lydia V, 534
Rich, Maggie IV, 755
Rich, Maggie IV, 761
Rich, Mariam I, 569
Rich, Martha I, 569
Rich, Martha I, 589
Rich, Martha I, 596
Rich, Martha I, 667
Rich, Martha I, 688
Rich, Martha I, 692
Rich, Martha I, 752
Rich, Martha I, 768
Rich, Martha I, 835
Rich, Mary I, 542
Rich, Mary I, 569
Rich, Mary I, 688
Rich, Mary I, 752
Rich, Mary I, 767
Rich, Mary I, 768
Rich, Mary I, 769
Rich, Mary II, 968
Rich, Mary II, 1023
Rich, Mary II, 1078
Rich, Mary VI, 850
Rich, Mary Ann I, 752
Rich, Mary Ann V, 549
Rich, Mary Ann V, 595
Rich, Mary Ann Adsit V, 525
Rich, Mary Emily V, 595
Rich, Mary, Jr. II, 1077
Rich, Mary, Jr. II, 1078
Rich, Merrick V, 114
Rich, Millicent II, 968
Rich, Miriam I, 569
Rich, Miriam I, 684
Rich, Miriam I, 688
Rich, Moses I, 513
Rich, Moses I, 688
Rich, Moses I, 752
Rich, Moses I, 768
Rich, Moses I, 769
Rich, Moses, Jr. I, 769
Rich, Mrs. Marie IV, 755
Rich, Nancy V, 45
Rich, Nancy V, 114
Rich, Nancy VI, 800
Rich, Nancy Ann V, 45
Rich, Nancy Ann V, 114
Rich, Nathan I, 513
Rich, Nathan I, 569
Rich, Nathan V, 114
Rich, Nimrod VI, 800
Rich, Peter I, 569
Rich, Peter I, 667
Rich, Peter I, 688
Rich, Peter I, 732
Rich, Peter I, 768
Rich, Peter I, 769
Rich, Peter W. I, 769
Rich, Peter, Jr. I, 769
Rich, Petter I, 768
Rich, Phebe I, 667
Rich, Phebe I, 835
Rich, Phebe I, 838
Rich, Phebe V, 352
Rich, Phebe V, 589
Rich, Phebe V, 595
Rich, Preston I, 589
Rich, Rachel I, 596
Rich, Rachel II, 968
Rich, Rachel IV, 755
Rich, Rachel V, 114
Rich, Rebecca I, 752
Rich, Rebecca I, 762
Rich, Rebecca I, 768
Rich, Rebecca I, 769
Rich, Rebecca I, 914

Rich, Richard I, 762
Rich, Richard I, 768
Rich, Richard I, 769
Rich, Ritchard I, 768
Rich, Robert B. V, 595
Rich, Samuel I, 569
Rich, Samuel I, 678
Rich, Samuel I, 688
Rich, Samuel I, 768
Rich, Samuel I, 769
Rich, Samuel I, 835
Rich, Samuel V, 114
Rich, Samuel V, 131
Rich, Samuel V, 525
Rich, Samuel V, 534
Rich, Sarah I, 513
Rich, Sarah I, 569
Rich, Sarah I, 667
Rich, Sarah I, 678
Rich, Sarah I, 679
Rich, Sarah I, 687
Rich, Sarah I, 688
Rich, Sarah I, 752
Rich, Sarah I, 760
Rich, Sarah I, 768
Rich, Sarah I, 769
Rich, Sarah II, 633
Rich, Sarah II, 643
Rich, Sarah II, 817
Rich, Sarah II, 968
Rich, Sarah II, 1023
Rich, Sarah Carlile II, 803
Rich, Sarah Emeline I, 769
Rich, Sarah P. II, 914
Rich, Simeon I, 513
Rich, Simon V, 114
Rich, Sophia IV, 755
Rich, Sophiah I, 596
Rich, Susanna I, 513
Rich, Susannah V, 114
Rich, Thomas I, 513
Rich, Thomas I, 762
Rich, Thomas II, 412
Rich, Thomas II, 633
Rich, Thomas II, 643
Rich, Thomas V, 114
Rich, Thomas V, 357
Rich, Thomas V, 471
Rich, Thomas V, 525
Rich, Thomas V, 547
Rich, Thomas V, 595
Rich, Thomas VI, 546
Rich, Thomas VI, 551
Rich, Thomas P. V, 595
Rich, Thos. V, 595
Rich, Will IV, 755
Rich, William I, 596
Rich, William I, 678
Rich, William I, 688
Rich, William I, 732
Rich, William I, 752
Rich, William I, 768
Rich, William I, 769
Rich, William W. IV, 1029
Rich, Wm. IV, 755
Rich, Wm. IV, 761
Rich, Wm. C. II, 914
Richall, John II, 1023
Richard, Abigail VI, 437
Richard, Abijah II, 633
Richard, Abijah VI, 437
Richard, Aurelia H. I, 922
Richard, Ebenezer II, 633
Richard, Elisabeth I, 70
Richard, Ely VI, 437
Richard, Esther VI, 437
Richard, Hannah VI, 437
Richard, Isaac H. VI, 437
Richard, John II, 633
Richard, Lewis Walker VI, 437
Richard, Lydia II, 633
Richard, Lydia II, 669
Richard, Lydia V, 928
Richard, Lydia VI, 437
Richard, Lydia VI, 595
Richard, Richard II, 412
Richard, Roland VI, 437
Richard, Rowland II, 633
Richard, Rowland II, 669
Richard, Rowland V, 928
Richard, Rowland VI, 437
Richard, Samuel II, 669
Richard, Samuel VI, 437
Richard, Sarah II, 633
Richard, Townsend VI, 437
Richard, William I, 70
Richard, William II, 412
Richards, ??? IV, 755
Richards, ??? IV, 861
Richards, ??? VI, 348
Richards, Abigail II, 815

Richards, Abigail V, 506
Richards, Abigail V, 525
Richards, Abigail VI, 593
Richards, Abigail VI, 604
Richards, Abijah II, 633
Richards, Abijah IV, 55
Richards, Abijah IV, 56
Richards, Abijah IV, 638
Richards, Abijah IV, 653
Richards, Abijah IV, 869
Richards, Abijah IV, 882
Richards, Abijah IV, 905
Richards, Abijah VI, 337
Richards, Abijah VI, 355
Richards, Abijah VI, 437
Richards, Abijah VI, 604
Richards, Abijah VI, 633
Richards, Abijah VI, 695
Richards, Abijah, Jr. IV, 653
Richards, Andrew M'Kay VI, 604
Richards, Ann II, 412
Richards, Ann II, 447
Richards, Ann III, 266
Richards, Ann IV, 269
Richards, Ann IV, 311
Richards, Ann IV, 314
Richards, Ann F. VI, 984
Richards, Ann, Jr. IV, 269
Richards, Aquilla II, 412
Richards, Barbara VI, 984
Richards, Bartley V, 1016
Richards, Benjamin VI, 984
Richards, Benjamin VI, 995
Richards, Benjamin VI, 996
Richards, Beulah W. IV, 269
Richards, Bowland VI, 633
Richards, Catharine II, 819
Richards, Catharine IV, 55
Richards, Catherine V, 100
Richards, Catherine V, 115
Richards, Catherine VI, 604
Richards, Charles II, 123
Richards, Charles D. I, 1161
Richards, Charles Edward IV, 755
Richards, Chas. II, 817
Richards, Chas. W. II, 817
Richards, Cora V, 1016
Richards, Daniel II, 412
Richards, Daniel II, 782
Richards, Daniel IV, 755
Richards, David II, 412
Richards, Davis II, 815
Richards, Deborah V, 581
Richards, Ebenezer II, 633
Richards, Ebenezer VI, 604
Richards, Edith IV, 56
Richards, Edith IV, 620
Richards, Edith IV, 653
Richards, Edith VI, 355
Richards, Eleanor A. II, 914
Richards, Eleanor A. II, 933
Richards, Eleanor Ann II, 817
Richards, Eleanor Ann III, 190
Richards, Eleanor Ann III, 266
Richards, Eleanor Kenny II, 817
Richards, Elenor A. II, 914
Richards, Eli IV, 653
Richards, Eli IV, 882
Richards, Eli VI, 604
Richards, Elijah C. V, 1016
Richards, Elisabeth I, 70
Richards, Eliza II, 787
Richards, Elizabeth I, 317
Richards, Elizabeth II, 412
Richards, Elizabeth IV, 653
Richards, Elizabeth IV, 667
Richards, Elizabeth IV, 880
Richards, Elizabeth IV, 882
Richards, Elizabeth VI, 604
Richards, Elizabeth VI, 984
Richards, Elizabeth D. IV, 882
Richards, Elizabeth W. IV, 755
Richards, Ella V, 1016
Richards, Ellen V, 706
Richards, Ellen V, 1016
Richards, Emma III, 266
Richards, Emma III, 272
Richards, Emma IV, 269
Richards, Emma B. III, 266
Richards, Emma J. IV, 954
Richards, Esther IV, 55
Richards, Esther IV, 56
Richards, Esther IV, 638
Richards, Esther IV, 653
Richards, Esther IV, 882
Richards, Esther IV, 905
Richards, Esther VI, 337
Richards, Esther VI, 355
Richards, Esther VI, 695
Richards, Esther, Jr. IV, 882

Richards, Esther, Jr. VI, 633
Richards, Esther, Jr. VI, 695
Richards, Frederick III, 266
Richards, Frederick B. II, 762
Richards, Frederick Burge III, 266
Richards, Frederick D. B. II, 762
Richards, George IV, 1292
Richards, George W. II, 817
Richards, Gertrude E. IV, 717
Richards, Hannah II, 412
Richards, Hannah II, 633
Richards, Hannah II, 669
Richards, Hannah II, 793
Richards, Hannah II, 817
Richards, Hannah II, 846
Richards, Hannah II, 914
Richards, Hannah IV, 882
Richards, Hannah V, 76
Richards, Hannah VI, 598
Richards, Hannah VI, 604
Richards, Hannah Burge III, 266
Richards, Hannah R. IV, 755
Richards, Hannah R. IV, 763
Richards, Hannah Townsend II, 787
Richards, Hannah Townsend II, 818
Richards, Hannah Townsend II, 914
Richards, Harriet VI, 895
Richards, Helen V, 706
Richards, Henry B. VI, 984
Richards, Hester IV, 869
Richards, Huldah I, 70
Richards, Isaac W. III, 266
Richards, Isaac W. IV, 269
Richards, Jacob W. IV, 269
Richards, James V, 1016
Richards, Jane II, 817
Richards, Jesse P. II, 633
Richards, Jessie IV, 717
Richards, Jessie IV, 755
Richards, Joel VI, 984
Richards, John II, 412
Richards, John II, 447
Richards, John II, 633
Richards, John II, 817
Richards, John VI, 357
Richards, John VI, 882
Richards, John Hains VI, 604
Richards, Joseph II, 412
Richards, Joseph II, 451
Richards, Joseph II, 633
Richards, Joseph IV, 496
Richards, Joseph IV, 882
Richards, Joseph T. II, 914
Richards, Josiah C. V, 1016
Richards, Latham IV, 882
Richards, Lucy II, 745
Richards, Lucy II, 762
Richards, Lydia II, 633
Richards, Lydia II, 718
Richards, Lydia IV, 55
Richards, Lydia IV, 755
Richards, Lydia V, 17
Richards, Lydia V, 100
Richards, Lydia V, 104
Richards, Lydia V, 108
Richards, Lydia V, 928
Richards, Lydia VI, 593
Richards, Lydia VI, 598
Richards, Lydia VI, 601
Richards, Lydia VI, 603
Richards, Lydia VI, 604
Richards, Lydia B. IV, 755
Richards, Lydia II VI, 604
Richards, Malissa Ann IV, 882
Richards, Margaret II, 412
Richards, Margaret II, 633
Richards, Margaret II, 869
Richards, Martha II, 822
Richards, Martha IV, 269
Richards, Martha IV, 882
Richards, Martha VI, 882
Richards, Martha V. II, 815
Richards, Mary I, 70
Richards, Mary I, 317
Richards, Mary II, 412
Richards, Mary II, 451
Richards, Mary II, 514
Richards, Mary II, 602
Richards, Mary II, 624
Richards, Mary II, 633
Richards, Mary II, 718
Richards, Mary II, 787
Richards, Mary II, 796
Richards, Mary II, 817
Richards, Mary II, 846
Richards, Mary II, 914
Richards, Mary III, 266

Richards, Mary IV, 50
Richards, Mary IV, 55
Richards, Mary IV, 56
Richards, Mary IV, 83
Richards, Mary IV, 107
Richards, Mary IV, 194
Richards, Mary IV, 269
Richards, Mary IV, 653
Richards, Mary IV, 869
Richards, Mary IV, 882
Richards, Mary IV, 886
Richards, Mary IV, 905
Richards, Mary V, 100
Richards, Mary V, 706
Richards, Mary V, 1016
Richards, Mary VI, 355
Richards, Mary VI, 604
Richards, Mary VI, 633
Richards, Mary VI, 895
Richards, Mary Dix II, 817
Richards, Mary Dix II, 914
Richards, Mary P. IV, 312
Richards, Mary P. IV, 314
Richards, Mary, Jr. II, 914
Richards, Merrium IV, 882
Richards, Miriam V, 706
Richards, Mordecai Dawson II, 817
Richards, Mordecai Dawson II, 914
Richards, Mordecai Dawson II, 933
Richards, Nancy V, 525
Richards, Naomi V, 199
Richards, Naomi V, 525
Richards, Neomi V, 199
Richards, Penelope II, 447
Richards, Phebe II, 914
Richards, Phebe IV, 840
Richards, Phebe IV, 871
Richards, Phebe IV, 882
Richards, Philip II, 412
Richards, Philip II, 451
Richards, Philip II, 624
Richards, Philip II, 633
Richards, Philip III, 266
Richards, Phillip II, 412
Richards, Polly VI, 984
Richards, Rachel II, 412
Richards, Rachel II, 463
Richards, Rachel II, 633
Richards, Rachel II, 782
Richards, Rachel II, 827
Richards, Rachel IV, 882
Richards, Rachel IV, 885
Richards, Rachel Bettie II, 782
Richards, Rebecca II, 224
Richards, Rebecca II, 252
Richards, Rebecca II, 633
Richards, Rebecca B. II, 914
Richards, Rebecca H. II, 914
Richards, Rebecca Humphreys II, 817
Richards, Richard II, 412
Richards, Roland VI, 385
Richards, Roland VI, 598
Richards, Roland VI, 601
Richards, Roland VI, 604
Richards, Rolen V, 108
Richards, Rowland II, 543
Richards, Rowland II, 633
Richards, Rowland II, 669
Richards, Rowland IV, 55
Richards, Rowland IV, 653
Richards, Rowland IV, 882
Richards, Rowland V, 17
Richards, Rowland V, 100
Richards, Rowland VI, 593
Richards, Rowland VI, 599
Richards, Rowland VI, 604
Richards, Rowland VI, 695
Richards, Ruth Anna B. II, 914
Richards, Ruth Anna Brown II, 817
Richards, Ruth Anna S. II, 933
Richards, Sally VI, 882
Richards, Samuel II, 412
Richards, Samuel II, 633
Richards, Samuel II, 669
Richards, Samuel II, 718
Richards, Samuel II, 787
Richards, Samuel II, 796
Richards, Samuel II, 817
Richards, Samuel II, 846
Richards, Samuel II, 914
Richards, Samuel III, 266
Richards, Samuel IV, 55
Richards, Samuel IV, 269
Richards, Samuel IV, 653
Richards, Samuel IV, 755
Richards, Samuel IV, 882
Richards, Samuel IV, 885
Richards, Samuel V, 706
Richards, Samuel VI, 355
Richards, Samuel VI, 604
Richards, Samuel R. II, 914
Richards, Samuel Rowland II, 914
Richards, Samuel Rowland, Jr. II, 817
Richards, Samuel, Jr. II, 817
Richards, Sarah I, 70
Richards, Sarah I, 317
Richards, Sarah II, 412
Richards, Sarah II, 543
Richards, Sarah II, 633
Richards, Sarah IV, 55
Richards, Sarah IV, 269
Richards, Sarah IV, 832
Richards, Sarah IV, 840
Richards, Sarah V, 56
Richards, Sarah V, 115
Richards, Sarah VI, 604
Richards, Sarah H. V, 115
Richards, Sarah M. II, 786
Richards, Sidney IV, 55
Richards, Sidney VI, 604
Richards, Sitnah V, 108
Richards, Sitnah V, 115
Richards, Sitnah VI, 604
Richards, Stephen IV, 755
Richards, Stephen B. IV, 717
Richards, Susanna II, 412
Richards, Susannah II, 447
Richards, Susannah VI, 604
Richards, Tace IV, 882
Richards, Tace IV, 885
Richards, Thomas II, 224
Richards, Thomas II, 252
Richards, Thomas VI, 984
Richards, Townsend VI, 604
Richards, W. S. IV, 269
Richards, Warren V, 1016
Richards, Wd. Ann B. II, 817
Richards, Wd. Margaret Long II, 819
Richards, Wd. Martha V. II, 815
Richards, Wd. Phebe II, 817
Richards, Wd. Sarah Harrison II, 796
Richards, William I, 70
Richards, William I, 317
Richards, William II, 412
Richards, William II, 817
Richards, William III, 190
Richards, William III, 266
Richards, William VI, 984
Richards, Wm. II, 817
Richards, Wm. II, 819
Richards, Wm. II, 914
Richards, Wm. II, 933
Richards, Wm. V, 1016
Richards, Wm. P. II, 633
Richards, Wm. W. II, 817
Richardson, Abigail II, 533
Richardson, Abigail II, 633
Richardson, Abner B. II, 914
Richardson, Abraham VI, 552
Richardson, Abraham G. IV, 840
Richardson, Abram IV, 755
Richardson, Achsah II, 866
Richardson, Achsah II, 914
Richardson, Achsah N. II, 914
Richardson, Adline VI, 969
Richardson, Agness VI, 210
Richardson, Agness VI, 219
Richardson, Alexander IV, 207
Richardson, Alvin T. M. V, 595
Richardson, Amanda I, 899
Richardson, Amanda V, 595
Richardson, Amanda V, 707
Richardson, Amanda M. I, 864
Richardson, Amy III, 267
Richardson, Ann II, 220
Richardson, Ann II, 252
Richardson, Ann II, 412
Richardson, Ann II, 633
Richardson, Ann IV, 720
Richardson, Ann IV, 755
Richardson, Ann IV, 1075
Richardson, Ann V, 132
Richardson, Ann V, 958
Richardson, Ann VI, 487
Richardson, Ann VI, 537
Richardson, Ann VI, 551
Richardson, Ann VI, 552
Richardson, Ann VI, 559
Richardson, Ann VI, 573
Richardson, Anna P. II, 912
Richardson, Anna P. II, 914
Richardson, Anne III, 267
Richardson, Anne P. II, 761
Richardson, Anne P. II, 762
Richardson, Anne S. II, 781
Richardson, Anthony V, 595
Richardson, Anthony V, 707
Richardson, Aquilla VI, 552
Richardson, Archer VI, 984
Richardson, Ashton II, 723
Richardson, Ashton II, 762
Richardson, Ashton II, 774
Richardson, B. F. V, 707
Richardson, Barnett VI, 984
Richardson, Benjamin II, 412
Richardson, Benjamin Franklin V, 706
Richardson, Betsey VI, 874
Richardson, Buford Seigal IV, 269
Richardson, Caleb II, 413
Richardson, Caleb II, 634
Richardson, Caleb J. V, 958
Richardson, Catharine R. IV, 207
Richardson, Catherine VI, 551
Richardson, Caty VI, 958
Richardson, Celia I, 54
Richardson, Celia I, 70
Richardson, Charity B. V, 357
Richardson, Charles II, 760
Richardson, Charles II, 762
Richardson, Charles IV, 1261
Richardson, Charles Wharton II, 634
Richardson, Clara B. V, 706
Richardson, Clement II, 634
Richardson, Clinton VI, 928
Richardson, Clinton VI, 984
Richardson, David II, 412
Richardson, Deborah II, 412
Richardson, Deborah II, 634
Richardson, Deborah III, 266
Richardson, Deliverance III, 267
Richardson, Desmond IV, 269
Richardson, Dingee IV, 453
Richardson, Dolly VI, 851
Richardson, E. M. V, 357
Richardson, Eadith IV, 880
Richardson, Ede I, 257
Richardson, Edith V, 706
Richardson, Edward II, 412
Richardson, Elce I, 257
Richardson, Eleanor I, 921
Richardson, Eleanor IV, 269
Richardson, Eleanor IV, 297
Richardson, Eleanor IV, 1182
Richardson, Elinor II, 412
Richardson, Elisabeth II, 633
Richardson, Eliza II, 197
Richardson, Eliza II, 252
Richardson, Eliza IV, 1075
Richardson, Eliza Ann IV, 1292
Richardson, Elizabeth I, 417
Richardson, Elizabeth I, 769
Richardson, Elizabeth II, 412
Richardson, Elizabeth II, 413
Richardson, Elizabeth II, 633
Richardson, Elizabeth II, 634
Richardson, Elizabeth II, 680
Richardson, Elizabeth II, 683
Richardson, Elizabeth II, 781
Richardson, Elizabeth IV, 748
Richardson, Elizabeth IV, 755
Richardson, Elizabeth IV, 789
Richardson, Elizabeth IV, 836
Richardson, Elizabeth IV, 840
Richardson, Elizabeth VI, 372
Richardson, Elizabeth VI, 437
Richardson, Elizabeth VI, 441
Richardson, Elizabeth VI, 552
Richardson, Elizabeth VI, 851
Richardson, Elizabeth VI, 969
Richardson, Elizabeth VI, 984
Richardson, Ellen I, 625
Richardson, Elliot II, 866
Richardson, Elliott II, 817
Richardson, Elliott II, 914
Richardson, Emily VI, 963
Richardson, Emma V, 706
Richardson, Emma C. V, 707
Richardson, Emmit V, 357
Richardson, Enid M. III, 266
Richardson, Enid Mary III, 194
Richardson, Enid Mary III, 267
Richardson, Esther V, 595
Richardson, Esther Ann VI, 437
Richardson, Esther Ann VI, 615
Richardson, Esther Ann VI, 695
Richardson, Esther Sayers V, 707
Richardson, Eunice IV, 941
Richardson, Eunice IV, 989
Richardson, Eunice H. IV, 989
Richardson, Eva Leona IV, 207
Richardson, Eve VI, 984
Richardson, Faithful IV, 56
Richardson, Fielder IV, 755
Richardson, Fielder VI, 498
Richardson, Fielder VI, 552
Richardson, Flora Ellen I, 625
Richardson, Flora R. I, 640
Richardson, Frances II, 413
Richardson, Frances II, 914
Richardson, Frances A. V. VI, 850
Richardson, Francis II, 412
Richardson, Francis II, 413
Richardson, Francis II, 451
Richardson, Francis II, 464
Richardson, Francis II, 524
Richardson, Francis II, 533
Richardson, Francis II, 537
Richardson, Francis II, 555
Richardson, Francis II, 633
Richardson, Francis II, 634
Richardson, Francis II, 663
Richardson, Francis II, 762
Richardson, Francis VI, 85
Richardson, Francis VI, 548
Richardson, Francis, Jr. II, 634
Richardson, Frederick A. III, 259
Richardson, Frederick A. III, 267
Richardson, Fredrika T. III, 259
Richardson, Fredrika T. III, 267
Richardson, George II, 412
Richardson, George IV, 1292
Richardson, George IV, 1335
Richardson, George VI, 844
Richardson, George VI, 984
Richardson, Grace II, 412
Richardson, Granville M. IV, 1292
Richardson, Green VI, 982
Richardson, Gulielma IV, 880
Richardson, Hannah II, 412
Richardson, Hannah II, 413
Richardson, Hannah II, 486
Richardson, Hannah II, 633
Richardson, Hannah II, 634
Richardson, Hannah II, 693
Richardson, Hannah II, 760
Richardson, Hannah II, 762
Richardson, Hannah II, 774
Richardson, Hannah II, 870
Richardson, Hannah IV, 56
Richardson, Hannah IV, 132
Richardson, Hannah IV, 134
Richardson, Hannah IV, 645
Richardson, Hannah IV, 654
Richardson, Hannah IV, 755
Richardson, Hannah IV, 1075
Richardson, Hannah IV, 1081
Richardson, Hannah V, 59
Richardson, Hannah V, 60
Richardson, Hannah V, 958
Richardson, Hannah VI, 532
Richardson, Hannah VI, 552
Richardson, Hannah B. IV, 56
Richardson, Hannah D. IV, 132
Richardson, Hannah D. IV, 1075
Richardson, Hannah Dingy IV, 399
Richardson, Hannah Dingy IV, 432
Richardson, Hannah W. II, 716
Richardson, Hannah Y. II, 866
Richardson, Hannah Y. II, 914
Richardson, Harley V, 429
Richardson, Hattie IV, 1292
Richardson, Helen V, 429
Richardson, Henrietta III, 267
Richardson, Henrietta VI, 972
Richardson, Henrietta M. III, 194
Richardson, Henrietta M. V, 525
Richardson, Henrietta M. V, 595
Richardson, Henrietta Mary III, 267
Richardson, Henrietta P. III, 266
Richardson, Henriette V, 595
Richardson, Henry III, 194
Richardson, Henry III, 266
Richardson, Henry III, 267
Richardson, Henry V, 595
Richardson, Henry T. V, 525
Richardson, Henry T. V, 595
Richardson, Hubert Townsend III, 267
Richardson, Ida I, 948
Richardson, Ida May III, 363
Richardson, Ingram Henry III, 267
Richardson, Isaac IV, 755
Richardson, Isaac IV, 1075
Richardson, Isaac V, 958
Richardson, Isaac Decow II, 252
Richardson, Isaac G. IV, 755
Richardson, Isaac G. IV, 840
Richardson, J. C. IV, 269
Richardson, J. W. IV, 1240
Richardson, Jacob IV, 755
Richardson, Jacob IV, 840
Richardson, Jacob VI, 801
Richardson, Jacob VI, 850
Richardson, James VI, 984
Richardson, James N. II, 914
Richardson, Jane II, 412
Richardson, Jane IV, 1240
Richardson, Jane VI, 977
Richardson, Jane VI, 984
Richardson, Jemima I, 981
Richardson, Jemima I, 996
Richardson, Jesse V, 642
Richardson, Jesse VI, 913
Richardson, Jesse VI, 924
Richardson, Jesse VI, 982
Richardson, Jesse VI, 984
Richardson, Jno VI, 35
Richardson, Jno VI, 36
Richardson, Joel II, 634
Richardson, John I, 732
Richardson, John II, 252
Richardson, John II, 412
Richardson, John II, 413
Richardson, John II, 633
Richardson, John II, 634
Richardson, John II, 693
Richardson, John II, 716
Richardson, John II, 760
Richardson, John II, 762
Richardson, John III, 267
Richardson, John IV, 56
Richardson, John IV, 644
Richardson, John IV, 645
Richardson, John VI, 35
Richardson, John VI, 552
Richardson, John VI, 850
Richardson, John VI, 895
Richardson, John VI, 937
Richardson, John VI, 968
Richardson, John VI, 969
Richardson, John VI, 983
Richardson, John VI, 984
Richardson, John VI, 1001
Richardson, John C. V, 357
Richardson, John I. II, 914
Richardson, John I. II, 921
Richardson, John W. V, 357
Richardson, John W. V, 525
Richardson, John W. V, 595
Richardson, John, Jr. IV, 654
Richardson, Joseph II, 233
Richardson, Joseph II, 252
Richardson, Joseph II, 412
Richardson, Joseph II, 413
Richardson, Joseph II, 451
Richardson, Joseph II, 486
Richardson, Joseph II, 507
Richardson, Joseph II, 514
Richardson, Joseph II, 633
Richardson, Joseph II, 634
Richardson, Joseph II, 664
Richardson, Joseph II, 675
Richardson, Joseph IV, 56
Richardson, Joseph IV, 1075
Richardson, Joseph IV, 1221
Richardson, Joseph VI, 547
Richardson, Joseph VI, 552
Richardson, Joseph VI, 961
Richardson, Joseph VI, 968
Richardson, Joseph G. II, 76
Richardson, Joseph N. II, 41
Richardson, Joseph, Jr. II, 2
Richardson, Joseph, Jr. II, 2
Richardson, Joseph, Jr. II, 6
Richardson, Joshua II, 447
Richardson, Joshua II, 507
Richardson, Joshua II, 633
Richardson, Joshua II, 634
Richardson, Joshua VI, 984
Richardson, Joshuah II, 413
Richardson, Judith VI, 963
Richardson, Julia W. IV, 124
Richardson, Kate II, 914
Richardson, Kate II, 921
Richardson, Katherine N. II,
Richardson, Latitia II, 633
Richardson, Latitia II, 663
Richardson, Letitia II, 413
Richardson, Lewis VI, 984
Richardson, Libbie V, 357
Richardson, Lizzie V, 595
Richardson, Lizzie V, 707
Richardson, Lucretia VI, 552
Richardson, Lucy II, 970
Richardson, Lucy Jane VI, 9
Richardson, Lydia IV, 56
Richardson, Lydia IV, 453
Richardson, Lydia IV, 644

ardson, Lydia IV, 645
ardson, Lydia IV, 654
ardson, Lydia IV, 1075
ardson, Lydia P. IV, 432
ardson, Lydia P. IV, 453
ardson, Lydia P. IV, 1075
ardson, Lydia P. IV, 1081
ardson, Lydia, Jr. IV, 56
ardson, Malissa Ann IV, 880
ardson, Margaret IV, 1075
ardson, Margaret VI, 552
ardson, Margaret VI, 573
ardson, Margaret VI, 958
ardson, Margaret VI, 984
ardson, Margaret V. IV, 432
ardson, Margaret, Jr. VI, 552
ardson, Martha IV, 885
ardson, Martha IV, 1075
ardson, Martha V, 707
ardson, Martha G. II, 760
ardson, Martha G. II, 762
ardson, Martha L. V, 707
ardson, Martha V. IV, 1113
ardson, Mary I, 569
ardson, Mary I, 921
ardson, Mary II, 233
ardson, Mary II, 252
ardson, Mary II, 412
ardson, Mary II, 413
ardson, Mary II, 447
ardson, Mary II, 451
ardson, Mary II, 453
ardson, Mary II, 464
ardson, Mary II, 486
ardson, Mary II, 507
ardson, Mary II, 514
ardson, Mary II, 524
ardson, Mary II, 558
ardson, Mary II, 631
ardson, Mary II, 633
ardson, Mary II, 634
ardson, Mary II, 664
ardson, Mary II, 723
ardson, Mary II, 762
ardson, Mary II, 774
ardson, Mary II, 802
ardson, Mary II, 914
ardson, Mary II, 921
ardson, Mary III, 267
ardson, Mary IV, 50
ardson, Mary IV, 56
ardson, Mary IV, 654
ardson, Mary IV, 880
ardson, Mary IV, 1075
ardson, Mary VI, 476
ardson, Mary VI, 498
ardson, Mary VI, 517
ardson, Mary VI, 530
ardson, Mary VI, 547
ardson, Mary VI, 548
ardson, Mary VI, 552
ardson, Mary VI, 661
ardson, Mary VI, 753
ardson, Mary VI, 850
ardson, Mary VI, 961
ardson, Mary VI, 984
ardson, Mary C. V, 357
ardson, Mary C. V, 525
ardson, Mary C. V, 595
ardson, Mary Clarinda
', 525
ardson, Mary Clarinda
', 595
ardson, Mary Virginia
V, 269
ardson, Meriam VI, 552
ardson, Milcah VI, 552
ardson, Milcah VI, 573
ardson, Milly VI, 982
ardson, Milly VI, 984
ardson, Minnie V, 357
ardson, Miriam IV, 748
ardson, Miriam IV, 755
ardson, Miriam IV, 840
ardson, Molley VI, 984
ardson, Morgan VI, 850
ardson, N. Webster VI, 615
ardson, N. Webster VI, 695
ardson, Nancy VI, 937
ardson, Nancy VI, 961
ardson, Nancy VI, 984
ardson, Nathan IV, 1377
ardson, Nathaniel II, 413
ardson, Nathaniel II, 634
ardson, Nathaniel, Jr. II, 634
ardson, Nehemiah IV, 56
ardson, Olive V, 525
ardson, Olive V, 706
ardson, Olive V, 707
ardson, Oliver V, 595
ardson, Ollie V, 357
Richardson, Ollie P. V, 525
Richardson, Patience II, 633
Richardson, Penelope VI, 850
Richardson, Phebe M. I, 769
Richardson, Philip Burtt III, 267
Richardson, Polly VI, 969
Richardson, Polly VI, 984
Richardson, Priscilla VI, 984
Richardson, R. Edna V, 595
Richardson, Rachel II, 633
Richardson, Rachel II, 657
Richardson, Rachel IV, 1182
Richardson, Rachel VI, 984
Richardson, Rebecca II, 413
Richardson, Rebecca II, 555
Richardson, Rebecca II, 633
Richardson, Rebecca III, 267
Richardson, Rebecca IV, 1060
Richardson, Rebecca IV, 1075
Richardson, Rebecca VI, 984
Richardson, Rebecca W. IV, 399
Richardson, Rebecca W. IV, 1060
Richardson, Rebecca W. IV, 1075
Richardson, Rebecka II, 413
Richardson, Rebeckah II, 633
Richardson, Rebeckah II, 649
Richardson, Rebekah II, 633
Richardson, Rhoda VI, 961
Richardson, Rhue V, 429
Richardson, Richard II, 716
Richardson, Richard II, 762
Richardson, Richard II, 774
Richardson, Richard IV, 755
Richardson, Richard IV, 840
Richardson, Richard VI, 476
Richardson, Richard VI, 498
Richardson, Richard VI, 531
Richardson, Richard VI, 547
Richardson, Richard VI, 552
Richardson, Richard VI, 573
Richardson, Richard Pierpont
VI, 552
Richardson, Richard, Jr. VI, 548
Richardson, Richard, Jr. VI, 552
Richardson, Richd VI, 552
Richardson, Robert III, 267
Richardson, Robert W. II, 947
Richardson, Ruth II, 233
Richardson, Ruth II, 252
Richardson, Ruth II, 413
Richardson, Ruth II, 514
Richardson, Ruth II, 634
Richardson, Ruth IV, 1075
Richardson, Ruth V, 59
Richardson, Ruth V, 60
Richardson, Ruth V, 115
Richardson, Ruth V, 958
Richardson, Ruth C. IV, 1075
Richardson, Ruthanna II, 866
Richardson, Ruthanna II, 914
Richardson, Sally VI, 850
Richardson, Sally VI, 1001
Richardson, Saml. VI, 976
Richardson, Samuel II, 197
Richardson, Samuel II, 412
Richardson, Samuel II, 413
Richardson, Samuel II, 680
Richardson, Samuel II, 781
Richardson, Samuel IV, 56
Richardson, Samuel IV, 399
Richardson, Samuel IV, 453
Richardson, Samuel IV, 880
Richardson, Samuel IV, 1075
Richardson, Samuel VI, 532
Richardson, Samuel VI, 552
Richardson, Samuel VI, 984
Richardson, Samuel W. III, 267
Richardson, Samuel W. IV, 432
Richardson, Samuel W. IV, 1081
Richardson, Samuel, Jr. IV, 1075
Richardson, Sara I, 948
Richardson, Sarah II, 413
Richardson, Sarah II, 507
Richardson, Sarah II, 633
Richardson, Sarah II, 634
Richardson, Sarah II, 675
Richardson, Sarah IV, 620
Richardson, Sarah IV, 654
Richardson, Sarah V, 595
Richardson, Sarah V, 1016
Richardson, Sarah VI, 483
Richardson, Sarah VI, 547
Richardson, Sarah VI, 548
Richardson, Sarah VI, 552
Richardson, Sarah VI, 850
Richardson, Sarah VI, 968
Richardson, Sarah E. V, 595
Richardson, Sarah Esther V, 525
Richardson, Sarah Esther V, 595
Richardson, Sarah N. II, 634
Richardson, Sophia VI, 531
Richardson, Sophia VI, 552
Richardson, Sophia VI, 850
Richardson, Suckey VI, 984
Richardson, Susannah II, 781
Richardson, Susannah IV, 605
Richardson, Susannah IV, 654
Richardson, Teresa III, 187
Richardson, Thomas I, 257
Richardson, Thomas II, 412
Richardson, Thomas II, 413
Richardson, Thomas II, 555
Richardson, Thomas II, 633
Richardson, Thomas II, 634
Richardson, Thomas III, 267
Richardson, Thomas S. VI, 850
Richardson, Thos. VI, 479
Richardson, Thos. Taylor, Jr.
VI, 552
Richardson, Tully VI, 984
Richardson, Virginia IV, 269
Richardson, W. B. I, 921
Richardson, Walthall VI, 850
Richardson, Washington VI, 984
Richardson, Washington B. I, 625
Richardson, Wd. Achsah II, 817
Richardson, Wd. Leetitia II, 633
Richardson, Wd. Letitia II, 513
Richardson, Wd. Miriam IV, 836
Richardson, Wd. Sophia VI, 532
Richardson, Widow Sophia
VI, 543
Richardson, Wigton VI, 984
Richardson, William I, 899
Richardson, William III, 267
Richardson, William VI, 552
Richardson, William VI, 949
Richardson, William VI, 984
Richardson, William B. I, 625
Richardson, William B. I, 640
Richardson, William P. VI, 772
Richardson, William R. I, 864
Richardson, William R. I, 899
Richardson, William S. I, 864
Richardson, William S. I, 899
Richardson, Willie R. I, 899
Richardson, Wm. II, 587
Richardson, Wm. VI, 551
Richardson, Wm. VI, 850
Richardson, Wm. B I, 640
Richardson, Zachary II, 633
Riche, Ann II, 634
Riche, Ann II, 636
Riche, Mary II, 543
Riche, Mary II, 634
Richee, Ansley IV, 496
Richee, Edward IV, 496
Richee, Joseph Steer IV, 496
Richee, Mary IV, 496
Richee, Robert IV, 496
Richee, Samuel Steer IV, 496
Richee, Sarah IV, 496
Richerson, Agnes IV, 1068
Richerson, Hannah D. IV, 1075
Richerson, Hannah E. IV, 1068
Richerson, John VI, 841
Richerson, Samuel IV, 1068
Richeson, Elce I, 242
Richeson, Elce I, 257
Richey, Dora IV, 755
Richey, Elizabeth II, 634
Richey, Elizabeth II, 643
Richey, Isabella VI, 985
Richey, Mahlon II, 1078
Richey, Mary IV, 607
Richey, Mary IV, 654
Richey, Phebe Ann II, 1078
Richey, Robert VI, 985
Richey, Sara Ann II, 1078
Richey, Sarah IV, 840
Richie, Alta IV, 755
Richie, Ann II, 634
Richie, Anna Bailey II, 762
Richie, Anna Bailey II, 766
Richie, Ansley IV, 496
Richie, Aubery II, 634
Richie, Aubrey II, 453
Richie, Daniel W. IV, 755
Richie, David R. IV, 1335
Richie, David R. IV, 1336
Richie, Dora IV, 755
Richie, Earl IV, 755
Richie, Edith IV, 1336
Richie, Edith Russell IV, 1335
Richie, Edward II, 634
Richie, Edward II, 716
Richie, Edward IV, 269
Richie, Edward IV, 496
Richie, Edward Lawrence II, 762
Richie, Edward Lawrence II, 766
Richie, Edward Steer IV, 269
Richie, Elizabeth II, 634
Richie, Hannah II, 634
Richie, Hannah IV, 496
Richie, Hannah IV, 881
Richie, Hannah IV, 882
Richie, Hannah Harry II, 634
Richie, Isa Mary IV, 755
Richie, Joseph II, 634
Richie, Joseph Steer IV, 269
Richie, Joseph Steer IV, 496
Richie, Mary II, 634
Richie, Mary IV, 269
Richie, Mary IV, 496
Richie, Mary IV, 763
Richie, Mary Annesley IV, 496
Richie, Mary Ansley IV, 269
Richie, Mary B. II, 716
Richie, Mary E. IV, 755
Richie, Mrs. ??? IV, 755
Richie, Pearl E. A. IV, 763
Richie, Robert II, 634
Richie, Robert IV, 269
Richie, Robert IV, 281
Richie, Robert IV, 496
Richie, Samuel II, 634
Richie, Samuel Steer IV, 269
Richie, Samuel Steer IV, 496
Richie, Sarah II, 453
Richie, Sarah II, 634
Richie, Sarah II, 716
Richie, Sarah IV, 269
Richie, Sarah IV, 281
Richie, Sarah IV, 496
Richie, Sarah M. II, 299
Richie, Sarah M. III, 269
Richie, Sarah, Jr. V, 922
Richie, Sarah, Jr. V, 928
Richie, Vera IV, 755
Richie, Wd. Mary II, 453
Richie, Wd. Mary II, 634
Richie, William IV, 755
Richie, Wm. IV, 763
Richinson, Mary II, 68
Richinson, Mary II, 94
Richman, Sarah V, 320
Richmond, Bryan IV, 1182
Richmond, Chloe IV, 894
Richmond, Daniel IV, 894
Richmond, Dora IV, 1182
Richmond, Earnest IV, 1182
Richmond, Eliza IV, 894
Richmond, Ernest IV, 1182
Richmond, Esther R. IV, 891
Richmond, Esther R. IV, 894
Richmond, John II, 413
Richmond, John II, 634
Richmond, Lelia IV, 1182
Richmond, Lester IV, 1182
Richmond, Martin II, 447
Richmond, Mary IV, 892
Richmond, Mary IV, 894
Richmond, Mary S. II, 131
Richmond, Reba Milton II, 959
Richmond, Sarah V, 357
Richmond, Sarah A. V, 357
Richmond, William C. IV, 891
Richmond, William C. IV, 894
Richter, Margaret W. II, 156
Richter, Margaretta W. II, 156
Richwine, Clara L. IV, 1292
Richwine, James M. IV, 1292
Richy, Sara Ann II, 1073
Richy, Sara Ann II, 1078
Richy, Sarah IV, 805
Richy, Sarah IV, 840
Rick, Ann I, 304
Rick, Ann I, 317
Rickafuse, Mary II, 757
Rickafuse, Mary II, 762
Rickard, Isaac S. IV, 1240
Rickard, Jane IV, 1240
Rickard, Jennie T. IV, 1240
Rickard, Laura A. IV, 1156
Rickard, Laura A. IV, 1182
Rickard, Orange J. IV, 1240
Rickback, Mary A. III, 461
Rickers, William III, 267
Rickes, Abraham VI, 35
Rickes, Abrahm VI, 35
Rickes, Abralım VI, 48
Rickes, Benjamin VI, 35
Rickes, Catherin VI, 35
Rickes, Elizabeth VI, 35
Rickes, Isaac VI, 29
Rickes, Isaac VI, 35
Rickes, Isaac, Junior VI, 35
Rickes, Isaac, Senior VI, 35
Rickes, Isaac, Senior VI, 48
Rickes, J. Sarah VI, 35
Rickes, Jacob VI, 35
Rickes, Jeams VI, 35
Rickes, Jean VI, 35
Rickes, Jno VI, 48
Rickes, John VI, 35
Rickes, Kathren VI, 35
Rickes, Mary VI, 35
Rickes, Richard VI, 35
Rickes, Robart VI, 35
Rickes, Robert VI, 35
Rickes, Robt VI, 48
Rickes, Sarah VI, 35
Rickes, Wd. Mary VI, 29
Rickes, William VI, 35
Rickesis, Abraham VI, 27
Rickesis, Abraham VI, 35
Rickesis, Benjamin VI, 35
Rickesis, Elizabeth VI, 35
Rickesis, Isaac VI, 23
Rickesis, Isaac VI, 27
Rickesis, Isaac VI, 35
Rickesis, Isaac, Junior VI, 35
Rickesis, Isaace VI, 35
Rickesis, Jacob VI, 29
Rickesis, Jacob VI, 35
Rickesis, Jeams VI, 35
Rickesis, Jean VI, 35
Rickesis, John VI, 35
Rickesis, Kathren VI, 35
Rickesis, Mary VI, 27
Rickesis, Mary VI, 29
Rickesis, Mary VI, 35
Rickesis, Richard VI, 35
Rickesis, Robart VI, 35
Rickesis, Sarah VI, 35
Rickesis, William VI, 35
Rickeson, Prudence I, 1050
Ricket, Abigail V, 115
Ricket, Abigail V, 792
Ricket, Abigail V, 928
Ricket, Elizabeth V, 928
Ricket, Elizabeth V, 932
Ricket, Ellen V, 927
Ricket, Ellen V, 928
Ricket, Esther V, 928
Ricket, Esther Ellen V, 115
Ricket, Esther F. V, 923
Ricket, Esther G. V, 928
Ricket, Mary V, 115
Ricket, Mary V, 928
Ricket, Sarah V, 115
Ricket, Sarah V, 928
Ricket, Thomas IV, 349
Ricket, Thomas V, 115
Ricket, Thomas V, 792
Ricket, Thomas V, 928
Ricket, Thos. V, 928
Ricket, Thos. H. V, 928
Rickets, Abigail V, 115
Rickets, Eleanor V, 115
Rickets, Elizabeth II, 562
Rickets, Elizabeth II, 634
Rickets, Elizabeth V, 115
Rickets, Esther Fielding V, 115
Rickets, Harpalynce H. VI, 1012
Rickets, Isaac II, 413
Rickets, Lewis L. VI, 995
Rickets, Lewis L. VI, 1012
Rickets, Mary V, 115
Rickets, Wm., Jr. II, 634
Ricketson, Anna III, 267
Ricketson, Annie III, 25
Ricketson, Annie III, 267
Ricketson, Mary III, 19
Ricketson, Mary III, 25
Ricketson, Mary III, 267
Ricketson, Mary III, 309
Ricketson, May III, 25
Ricketson, Merribeth III, 429
Ricketson, Shadrach III, 19
Ricketson, Shadrach III, 25
Ricketson, Shadrach III, 267
Ricketson, Susan III, 267
Rickett, Abigail V, 97
Rickett, Abigail V, 115
Rickett, Abigail V, 928
Rickett, Eleanor V, 115
Rickett, Elizabeth V, 115
Rickett, Ellen V, 928
Rickett, Esther V, 928
Rickett, Esther Ellen V, 115
Rickett, Esther Fielding V, 115
Rickett, Frances VI, 850
Rickett, James VI, 850
Rickett, Mary V, 97
Rickett, Mary V, 115
Rickett, Mary V, 928
Rickett, Sarah V, 115
Rickett, Sarah V, 928
Rickett, Thomas V, 97
Rickett, Thomas V, 115
Rickett, Thomas V, 928
Rickett, Thos. V, 928
Ricketts, Elizabeth II, 413

Ricketts, Elizabeth II, 612
Ricketts, Elizabeth II, 634
Ricketts, Isaac II, 413
Ricketts, Isaac II, 612
Ricketts, Isaac II, 634
Ricketts, John II, 413
Ricketts, Joseph II, 634
Ricketts, Thomas II, 634
Ricketts, Warren V, 1016
Ricketts, Wm. II, 634
Ricketts, Wm., Jr. II, 634
Rickey, Alexander II, 968
Rickey, Alexander II, 978
Rickey, Alexander II, 1008
Rickey, Alexander II, 1015
Rickey, Alexander II, 1023
Rickey, Ann II, 413
Rickey, Ann II, 968
Rickey, Ann II, 1005
Rickey, Ann II, 1023
Rickey, Ann, Jr. II, 1008
Rickey, Ann, Jr. II, 1023
Rickey, Carol II, 497
Rickey, Carol II, 634
Rickey, Hannah II, 1023
Rickey, Hannah II, 1037
Rickey, James II, 413
Rickey, James II, 634
Rickey, James II, 968
Rickey, James II, 1005
Rickey, James II, 1023
Rickey, Jesse II, 1023
Rickey, Jesse II, 1059
Rickey, Jesse II, 1066
Rickey, John II, 968
Rickey, John II, 1003
Rickey, John II, 1004
Rickey, John II, 1023
Rickey, John M. II, 968
Rickey, John M. II, 1023
Rickey, John M. II, 1059
Rickey, Joseph II, 634
Rickey, Joseph II, 1023
Rickey, Joseph Kirkbride II, 1059
Rickey, Katharine II, 968
Rickey, Katherine II, 1004
Rickey, Katherine II, 1023
Rickey, Keirl II, 968
Rickey, Keirl II, 1003
Rickey, Keirl II, 1015
Rickey, Keirl II, 1023
Rickey, Keirll II, 1023
Rickey, Kirkbride II, 1078
Rickey, Kirkbride M. II, 1023
Rickey, Lambert II, 1023
Rickey, Lambert II, 1059
Rickey, Lambert II, 1066
Rickey, Mahlon II, 1023
Rickey, Mahlon II, 1059
Rickey, Mahlon II, 1078
Rickey, Martha II, 991
Rickey, Martha II, 1023
Rickey, Mary II, 413
Rickey, Mary II, 497
Rickey, Mary II, 634
Rickey, Mary II, 968
Rickey, Mary II, 1004
Rickey, Mary II, 1023
Rickey, Mary II, 1037
Rickey, Mary C. II, 716
Rickey, Mercy Ann II, 1056
Rickey, Mercy Ann II, 1059
Rickey, Phebe II, 968
Rickey, Phebe II, 1003
Rickey, Phebe II, 1013
Rickey, Phebe II, 1023
Rickey, Phebe II, 1059
Rickey, Phebe Ann II, 1066
Rickey, Rachel II, 968
Rickey, Rachel II, 978
Rickey, Rachel II, 1023
Rickey, Rachel II, 1030
Rickey, Samuel II, 413
Rickey, Samuel II, 497
Rickey, Samuel II, 634
Rickey, Samuel II, 1023
Rickey, Sarah II, 413
Rickey, Sarah II, 497
Rickey, Sarah II, 634
Rickey, Sarah II, 968
Rickey, Sarah II, 982
Rickey, Sarah II, 997
Rickey, Sarah II, 1003
Rickey, Sarah II, 1015
Rickey, Sarah II, 1023
Rickey, Sarah Ann II, 1023
Rickey, Sarah Ann II, 1051
Rickey, Sarah Ann II, 1059
Rickey, Thomas II, 968
Rickey, Thomas II, 1023
Rickey, Thomas II, 1037
Rickey, Thomas, Jr. II, 1023
Rickey, Violetta II, 982
Rickey, Violetta II, 1023
Rickles, Samuel II, 447
Rickman, William III, 267
Rickman, William III, 439
Ricks, ??? VI, 48
Ricks, ??? VI, 84
Ricks, Abraham VI, 48
Ricks, Alfred IV, 1292
Ricks, Alfred VI, 79
Ricks, Alfred VI, 84
Ricks, Alfred VI, 89
Ricks, Alfred VI, 265
Ricks, Alfred VI, 266
Ricks, Alfred VI, 274
Ricks, Alfred VI, 277
Ricks, Alfred VI, 279
Ricks, Alfred VI, 280
Ricks, Alfred W. VI, 265
Ricks, Alfred W. VI, 266
Ricks, Alpherd IV, 1292
Ricks, Angeline IV, 755
Ricks, Ann I, 257
Ricks, Ann I, 881
Ricks, Ann I, 899
Ricks, Ann IV, 174
Ricks, Ann VI, 45
Ricks, Ann VI, 46
Ricks, Ann VI, 84
Ricks, Ann VI, 90
Ricks, Ann VI, 119
Ricks, Ann VI, 218
Ricks, Ann Scott IV, 272
Ricks, Ann Scott Ricks IV, 272
Ricks, Anne VI, 266
Ricks, Anne Elizabeth VI, 266
Ricks, Anne R. VI, 266
Ricks, Anne R., Jr. VI, 266
Ricks, Arnold IV, 243
Ricks, Arnold VI, 79
Ricks, Arnold VI, 84
Ricks, Arnold VI, 218
Ricks, Arnold W. VI, 210
Ricks, Arnold W. VI, 217
Ricks, Arnold W. VI, 218
Ricks, Aseenoth I, 864
Ricks, Asenath I, 890
Ricks, Asenath I, 899
Ricks, Catherin VI, 35
Ricks, Charity Battle I, 257
Ricks, Christopher I, 864
Ricks, Christopher I, 899
Ricks, Deborah IV, 237
Ricks, Deborah VI, 79
Ricks, Deborah VI, 80
Ricks, Deborah VI, 84
Ricks, Deborah VI, 265
Ricks, Deborah VI, 266
Ricks, Deborah Ann IV, 243
Ricks, Deborah Ann IV, 272
Ricks, Deborah Ann IV, 1291
Ricks, Deborah Ann IV, 1292
Ricks, Deborah Ann VI, 210
Ricks, Edward I, 892
Ricks, Edward I, 899
Ricks, Edward IV, 272
Ricks, Edward Butts VI, 84
Ricks, Eliza VI, 84
Ricks, Eliza Ann V, 853
Ricks, Eliza Ann V, 858
Ricks, Eliza C. VI, 237
Ricks, Eliza C. VI, 265
Ricks, Eliza Catharine VI, 236
Ricks, Eliza J. VI, 266
Ricks, Eliza Kate VI, 237
Ricks, Eliza Kate VI, 266
Ricks, Elizabeth I, 899
Ricks, Elizabeth IV, 593
Ricks, Elizabeth VI, 46
Ricks, Elizabeth VI, 84
Ricks, Elizabeth VI, 89
Ricks, Elizabeth VI, 105
Ricks, Elizabeth VI, 119
Ricks, Elizabeth H. VI, 265
Ricks, Elizabeth H. VI, 266
Ricks, Elizabeth H. VI, 279
Ricks, Elizabeth P. VI, 266
Ricks, Emma I, 899
Ricks, Emma I, 900
Ricks, Geo. IV, 288
Ricks, Gwen I, 864
Ricks, Gwin I, 847
Ricks, Gwin I, 899
Ricks, Gwin, Jr. I, 899
Ricks, Hannah I, 870
Ricks, Hannah I, 899
Ricks, Henry Briggs VI, 84
Ricks, Henry Horn I, 257
Ricks, Isaac VI, 8
Ricks, Isaac VI, 18
Ricks, Isaac VI, 35
Ricks, Isaac VI, 48
Ricks, Isack VI, 41
Ricks, J. Hoge VI, 266
Ricks, J. Sarah VI, 35
Ricks, Jacob I, 257
Ricks, James I, 899
Ricks, James IV, 593
Ricks, James IV, 1292
Ricks, James A. I, 899
Ricks, James Hoge VI, 266
Ricks, James Hoge, Jr. VI, 266
Ricks, James Hoge, Sr. VI, 266
Ricks, James Jordan Scott VI, 84
Ricks, James M. IV, 1292
Ricks, James T. IV, 593
Ricks, James T. VI, 84
Ricks, Jane I, 864
Ricks, Jane I, 892
Ricks, Jane I, 899
Ricks, Joel Horn I, 257
Ricks, John I, 864
Ricks, John I, 899
Ricks, John IV, 593
Ricks, John IV, 1292
Ricks, John H. IV, 1292
Ricks, John M. IV, 1292
Ricks, John W. IV, 593
Ricks, John W. VI, 84
Ricks, Jonas I, 569
Ricks, Jonas I, 899
Ricks, Jonas, Jr. I, 899
Ricks, Joseph VI, 84
Ricks, Judith IV, 288
Ricks, Judith IV, 572
Ricks, Judith IV, 593
Ricks, Juleana VI, 84
Ricks, Julia IV, 272
Ricks, Julia VI, 265
Ricks, Julia Ann VI, 210
Ricks, Julia W. VI, 92
Ricks, Julia W. VI, 265
Ricks, Julia W. VI, 266
Ricks, Julia W. VI, 280
Ricks, Julia W. VI, 281
Ricks, Julian M. VI, 210
Ricks, Julian W. VI, 266
Ricks, Kate C. VI, 266
Ricks, Katherine C. VI, 266
Ricks, Lucy IV, 272
Ricks, Lucy K. IV, 272
Ricks, Lydia Maria IV, 1292
Ricks, Lynch IV, 272
Ricks, Marcia L. IV, 272
Ricks, Margaret IV, 272
Ricks, Margaret V, 975
Ricks, Margaret VI, 92
Ricks, Marha VI, 84
Ricks, Marsia VI, 75
Ricks, Martha I, 569
Ricks, Martha IV, 1292
Ricks, Martha VI, 45
Ricks, Martha VI, 46
Ricks, Martha VI, 265
Ricks, Martha S. VI, 266
Ricks, Martha S. VI, 279
Ricks, Mary I, 142
Ricks, Mary I, 163
Ricks, Mary VI, 46
Ricks, Mary VI, 84
Ricks, Mary VI, 266
Ricks, Mary A. VI, 79
Ricks, Mary A. VI, 84
Ricks, Mary A. VI, 89
Ricks, Mary A. VI, 266
Ricks, Mary A. VI, 279
Ricks, Mary Ann IV, 1292
Ricks, Mary Ann VI, 265
Ricks, Mary Ann VI, 266
Ricks, Mary Ann VI, 274
Ricks, Mary Ann VI, 277
Ricks, Mary Ann VI, 280
Ricks, Mary H. VI, 210
Ricks, Mary H. VI, 217
Ricks, Mary H. VI, 218
Ricks, Mary Jane IV, 1291
Ricks, Mary Jane IV, 1292
Ricks, Mary L. IV, 272
Ricks, Mary L. VI, 266
Ricks, Mary L. VI, 281
Ricks, Mary S. IV, 243
Ricks, Mary W. IV, 272
Ricks, Mary W. IV, 288
Ricks, Mary W. VI, 84
Ricks, Mary W. VI, 92
Ricks, Mary W. VI, 265
Ricks, Mary W. VI, 266
Ricks, Mary Winston VI, 79
Ricks, Maryann IV, 1292
Ricks, Milicent VI, 84
Ricks, Millicent IV, 272
Ricks, Morning VI, 45
Ricks, Morning VI, 46
Ricks, Nathaniel IV, 272
Ricks, Nathaniel VI, 84
Ricks, Nathaniel W. IV, 272
Ricks, Oswin IV, 272
Ricks, Oswin VI, 75
Ricks, Oswin VI, 84
Ricks, Phebe I, 899
Ricks, Phebe Ricks I, 257
Ricks, Pheriba Ellen IV, 1292
Ricks, Pheriba Green IV, 1292
Ricks, R. A. VI, 236
Ricks, R. A. VI, 237
Ricks, R. Arnold VI, 266
Ricks, Rachel I, 899
Ricks, Richard IV, 272
Ricks, Richard VI, 45
Ricks, Richard VI, 46
Ricks, Richard VI, 84
Ricks, Richard VI, 210
Ricks, Richard VI, 265
Ricks, Richard VI, 279
Ricks, Richard A. VI, 237
Ricks, Richard A. VI, 265
Ricks, Richard A. VI, 266
Ricks, Richard A. VI, 279
Ricks, Richard A. III VI, 266
Ricks, Richard Arnold VI, 266
Ricks, Richard J. IV, 1292
Ricks, Richard L. IV, 272
Ricks, Robert I, 142
Ricks, Robert I, 163
Ricks, Robert I, 835
Ricks, Robert I, 1037
Ricks, Robert IV, 272
Ricks, Robert IV, 572
Ricks, Robert IV, 593
Ricks, Robert IV, 1292
Ricks, Robert VI, 48
Ricks, Robert VI, 84
Ricks, Robert VI, 119
Ricks, Robert VI, 124
Ricks, Robert, Jr. VI, 119
Ricks, Robert, Sr. VI, 84
Ricks, Samuel VI, 119
Ricks, Samuel Jordan VI, 84
Ricks, Samuell T. VI, 265
Ricks, Samuella T. VI, 266
Ricks, Sarah I, 864
Ricks, Sarah I, 899
Ricks, Sarah I, 922
Ricks, Sarah VI, 79
Ricks, Seth I, 864
Ricks, Seth I, 899
Ricks, Thomas I, 257
Ricks, Thomas I, 899
Ricks, Thomas IV, 593
Ricks, Thomas VI, 84
Ricks, Thomas VI, 105
Ricks, Thomas VI, 119
Ricks, Thomas Draper VI, 84
Ricks, Walter A. VI, 266
Ricks, Wilkison VI, 84
Ricks, William I, 899
Ricks, William IV, 272
Ricks, William Jordan VI, 84
Ricks, William P. IV, 1292
Ricks, William R. VI, 84
Ricks, Winea VI, 84
Ricks, Winefred VI, 119
Ricks, Winifred VI, 124
Ricks, Winna VI, 119
Ricks, Winna VI, 124
Ricks, Winston IV, 272
Ricks, Zara I, 864
Ricks, Zaza I, 899
Ricksis, Isaac VI, 35
Ricky, Joseph II, 634
Ricky, Joseph Kirkbride II, 1059
Ricky, Mary C. II, 716
Ricky, Rachel II, 997
Ricky, Rachel II, 1023
Ricky, Thomas II, 997
Riddell, Lydia J. V, 199
Riddell, Robert V, 199
Ridder, Thomas II, 634
Ridder, Thos. II, 634
Riddick, A. F. I, 14
Riddick, A. F. I, 16
Riddick, A. F. I, 923
Riddick, A. F. I, 932
Riddick, Alice I, 70
Riddick, Alice Delphina I, 16
Riddick, Alice L. I, 948
Riddick, Alice Lawton I, 932
Riddick, Anna I, 64
Riddick, Anna I, 70
Riddick, Anna I, 612
Riddick, Anna I, 923
Riddick, Anna I, 932
Riddick, Anna Almy I, 14
Riddick, Anna M. I, 70
Riddick, Anna N. I, 16
Riddick, Anne I, 612
Riddick, Annie A. I, 933
Riddick, Archibald F. I, 612
Riddick, Archie Calvin I, 16
Riddick, Burrell I, 70
Riddick, Edgar B. I, 16
Riddick, Elisabeth I, 16
Riddick, George Robert I, 16
Riddick, Gustavus I, 16
Riddick, John Quincy I, 16
Riddick, Levert I, 16
Riddick, Margaret I, 16
Riddick, Margaret S. I, 16
Riddick, Martha VI, 74
Riddick, Martha VI, 85
Riddick, Martha A. I, 70
Riddick, Martha Levert Winslow) I, 31
Riddick, Mary I, 948
Riddick, Mary V, 882
Riddick, Mary V, 885
Riddick, Mary W. I, 923
Riddick, Mattie I, 70
Riddick, Mollie I, 16
Riddick, Robert I, 16
Riddick, Robert I, 70
Riddick, Robert George I, 70
Riddick, Samuel N. I, 70
Riddick, Samuel W. I, 16
Riddick, Samuel W. I, 31
Riddick, Sarah A. I, 70
Riddick, Sarah A. I, 83
Riddick, Sarah Abigail I, 70
Riddick, Theresa I, 948
Riddick, Theresa Alny I, 932
Riddle, Alexander IV, 269
Riddle, Bernice IV, 1041
Riddle, Bernice Oakley IV, 1(
Riddle, Eliza IV, 269
Riddle, Elizabeth V, 709
Riddle, Elizabeth V, 913
Riddle, Elizabeth V, 928
Riddle, James V, 357
Riddle, Jefferson I, 936
Riddle, Lura I, 923
Riddle, Lura Edna I, 936
Riddle, Mary I, 936
Riddle, Mary II, 221
Riddle, Mary II, 252
Riddle, Thomas VI, 266
Riddley, Dorothy IV, 1013
Riddley, Geo. IV, 1013
Riddley, Margaret IV, 1013
Ridegway, Charity VI, 364
Ridegway, Richard VI, 364
Ridell, Robert V, 199
Ridenhour, Julia Wollem IV,
Ridenhour, Margaret Ann I,
Ridenhour, Margaret Ann I,
Ridenour, Florence V, 1016
Ridenour, Florence VI, 749
Ridenour, Florence VI, 772
Ridenour, Florence VI, 792
Ridenour, Louis B. VI, 749
Ridenour, Louis B. VI, 772
Ridenour, Louis Beston VI, 7
Ridenour, Louis Beston VI, 7
Ridenour, Sylvia Belle VI, 77
Ridenour, Sylvia Belle VI, 79
Rideout, Nicholas II, 447
Rider, ??? III, 268
Rider, Ann V, 928
Rider, Ann V, 942
Rider, Anna III, 267
Rider, Arabella IV, 1240
Rider, Bridget III, 114
Rider, Bridget III, 268
Rider, Carrie III, 94
Rider, Carrie III, 267
Rider, Carrie III, 268
Rider, Carrie C. III, 94
Rider, Catharine III, 267
Rider, Catharine M. III, 267
Rider, Catharine W. III, 16
Rider, Catharine W. III, 267
Rider, Charles III, 267
Rider, Charles C. III, 267
Rider, Charles C. III, 268
Rider, Charles Henry III, 16
Rider, Charles Henry III, 26
Rider, Chas. C. III, 267
Rider, Chas. C. III, 268
Rider, Chas. Henry III, 267
Rider, Cora IV, 1240
Rider, Edna C. III, 267
Rider, Edwin III, 168
Rider, Edwin III, 267
Rider, Edwin Hanford III, 26

, Egbert S. III, 267
, Eliza IV, 1336
, Elizabeth VI, 984
, Ella III, 195
, Ella III, 267
, Ella III, 268
, Ella L. III, 66
, Ella L. III, 267
, Ella L. III, 268
, Emma IV, 1240
, Emma Louisa IV, 1240
, Florence Ruth III, 196
, Florence Ruth III, 267
r, Franklin III, 267
r, Franklin III, 268
r, Fred IV, 1240
r, Frederick IV, 1240
r, Frederick Aldrich III, 196
r, Frederick Aldrich III, 267
r, George III, 66
r, George III, 268
r, George F. IV, 1240
r, George W. III, 267
r, Grace IV, 1240
r, Henry III, 267
r, Isabella VI, 967
r, James VI, 984
r, James C. III, 267
r, James C. III, 268
r, James, Jr. III, 268
r, Jane VI, 984
er, Jarvis M. IV, 1377
er, Jas. L. IV, 1336
er, Jemimy VI, 1012
er, John III, 94
er, John III, 195
er, John IV, 1240
er, John VI, 898
er, John VI, 922
er, John VI, 939
er, John VI, 959
er, John VI, 967
er, John VI, 984
er, John VI, 1015
er, John R. III, 94
er, John R. III, 124
er, John R. III, 161
er, John R. III, 267
er, John R. III, 268
ler, John, Jr. III, 114
ler, John, Jr. III, 268
ler, John, Jr. VI, 922
ler, John, Sr. VI, 984
ler, Josiah C. III, 108
ler, Josiah C. III, 267
ler, Josiah C. III, 268
ler, Judeth III, 258
ler, Judith III, 258
ler, Julia Ann VI, 890
ler, Katharine III, 267
ler, Lydia A. III, 168
ler, Lydia A. III, 267
ler, Mary III, 268
ler, Mary VI, 898
der, Mary VI, 984
der, Mary Ann III, 267
der, Mary Ann III, 268
der, Mary Ann VI, 984
der, Mary E. VI, 922
der, Mary H. III, 267
der, Mary W. III, 94
der, Mary W. III, 124
der, Mary W. III, 161
der, Mary W. III, 195
der, Mary W. III, 267
der, Mary W. III, 268
ider, Matilda VI, 984
ider, Mehetable IV, 1377
ider, Mehettable T. IV, 1377
ider, Sarah H. III, 124
ider, Sarah H. III, 268
ider, Susanna VI, 1015
ider, Thomas VI, 898
ider, Thomas VI, 984
ider, Wilhelmina III, 108
ider, Wilhelmina III, 268
ider, William IV, 1240
ider, William VI, 984
Rider, Wm. IV, 1240
Riderpoke, Rosanna II, 804
Ridg, Sarah I, 732
Ridg, Sarah I, 734
Ridgaway, Daniel P. II, 156
Ridgaway, Jacob II, 156
Ridgaway, Kesiah P. II, 156
Ridgaway, Mercy II, 156
Ridge, Albert I, 948
Ridge, Albert Lee I, 933
Ridge, Albert Lee, Jr. I, 933
Ridge, Angelina I, 712
Ridge, Angelina I, 732
Ridge, Ann V, 115
Ridge, B. F. I, 948
Ridge, Clarice Virginia I, 933
Ridge, Claudia Abigail I, 933
Ridge, Daniel II, 447
Ridge, Eva Josephine I, 948
Ridge, Fanny I, 948
Ridge, Hannah V, 115
Ridge, Irene Marjory I, 933
Ridge, Jane V, 115
Ridge, Jaran B. I, 948
Ridge, John I, 417
Ridge, Kathleen I, 933
Ridge, Lee I, 948
Ridge, Lillian I, 948
Ridge, Luke I, 948
Ridge, Mahlon V, 115
Ridge, Margaret I, 417
Ridge, Margorie I, 948
Ridge, Martha II, 447
Ridge, Martha Fannie I, 933
Ridge, Mary I, 617
Ridge, Mary V, 115
Ridge, Noah I, 617
Ridge, Nona I, 948
Ridge, Nona Louise I, 933
Ridge, Sarah I, 732
Ridge, Sarah Addie Eliza I, 617
Ridge, Thomas A. I, 933
Ridgeaway, Rachel VI, 437
Ridgeley, Dan'l M. III, 268
Ridgeley, Daniel M. III, 21
Ridgeley, Ellen III, 21
Ridgeley, Ellen III, 268
Ridgeley, Eugenia III, 21
Ridgeley, Eugenia III, 268
Ridgely, Eugenia VI, 772
Ridgeon, Thomas H. I, 417
Ridges, R. Virginia III, 268
Ridgeway, Aaron IV, 546
Ridgeway, Aaron, Jr. IV, 547
Ridgeway, Abijah IV, 546
Ridgeway, Abijah J. IV, 546
Ridgeway, Allen II, 253
Ridgeway, Ann II, 253
Ridgeway, Ann IV, 546
Ridgeway, Anna IV, 546
Ridgeway, Anna P. II, 762
Ridgeway, Anne P. Miller II, 762
Ridgeway, Catharine II, 253
Ridgeway, Catharine II, 277
Ridgeway, Catharine IV, 546
Ridgeway, Charlotte II, 253
Ridgeway, Daniel II, 94
Ridgeway, Daniel IV, 546
Ridgeway, Daniel P. VI, 773
Ridgeway, Daniel Pedrick VI, 747
Ridgeway, Daniel Pedrick VI, 772
Ridgeway, Daniel Pedrick VI, 773
Ridgeway, David IV, 158
Ridgeway, David IV, 269
Ridgeway, David H. V, 357
Ridgeway, Edna V, 707
Ridgeway, Edward D. VI, 772
Ridgeway, Eliza IV, 546
Ridgeway, Elizabeth II, 252
Ridgeway, Elizabeth II, 253
Ridgeway, Elizabeth II, 272
Ridgeway, Elizabeth II, 762
Ridgeway, Elizabeth IV, 349
Ridgeway, Elizabeth IV, 546
Ridgeway, Elizabeth IV, 547
Ridgeway, Elizabeth IV, 1186
Ridgeway, Elizabeth V, 357
Ridgeway, Elizabeth V, 358
Ridgeway, Elizabeth Ann IV, 547
Ridgeway, Elizabeth, Jr. IV, 547
Ridgeway, Elizann IV, 546
Ridgeway, Elvira IV, 546
Ridgeway, Elvira R. IV, 538
Ridgeway, Elvira R. IV, 547
Ridgeway, Emma II, 762
Ridgeway, Emma R. Comley II, 762
Ridgeway, Esther II, 762
Ridgeway, Esther II, 915
Ridgeway, Esther IV, 547
Ridgeway, Esther VI, 984
Ridgeway, Francelia Williams VI, 772
Ridgeway, Francelia Williams VI, 773
Ridgeway, Frank V, 707
Ridgeway, Frederick VI, 437
Ridgeway, Frencelia Williams VI, 732
Ridgeway, Grace IV, 542
Ridgeway, Grace IV, 546
Ridgeway, Grace V, 357
Ridgeway, Hannah II, 203
Ridgeway, Hannah IV, 546
Ridgeway, Hannah VI, 437
Ridgeway, Hannah B. II, 915
Ridgeway, Hannah Burr II, 762
Ridgeway, Helen M. VI, 772
Ridgeway, Helen M. VI, 773
Ridgeway, Henrietta II, 762
Ridgeway, Henrietta II, 915
Ridgeway, Henry II, 203
Ridgeway, Henry VI, 815
Ridgeway, Henry W. II, 762
Ridgeway, Inez V, 707
Ridgeway, Inez V, 719
Ridgeway, Isaac II, 94
Ridgeway, Isaac IV, 546
Ridgeway, Isaac IV, 935
Ridgeway, Isabella IV, 935
Ridgeway, Jacob II, 94
Ridgeway, Jacob VI, 747
Ridgeway, Jacob VI, 772
Ridgeway, Jane IV, 546
Ridgeway, Jane IV, 547
Ridgeway, Jane VI, 420
Ridgeway, Jane VI, 437
Ridgeway, Jesse IV, 547
Ridgeway, Jesse C. II, 762
Ridgeway, Jesse C. II, 915
Ridgeway, Jesse Coates II, 762
Ridgeway, Job II, 94
Ridgeway, Job II, 253
Ridgeway, Job IV, 158
Ridgeway, Job Harvey VI, 732
Ridgeway, Job Harvey VI, 772
Ridgeway, Job Harvey VI, 773
Ridgeway, John IV, 158
Ridgeway, John IV, 349
Ridgeway, John IV, 546
Ridgeway, John VI, 420
Ridgeway, John VI, 437
Ridgeway, John J. IV, 546
Ridgeway, Jonathan IV, 546
Ridgeway, Joseph II, 208
Ridgeway, Joseph II, 253
Ridgeway, Joseph II, 762
Ridgeway, Joseph II, 915
Ridgeway, Joseph IV, 546
Ridgeway, Joseph IV, 547
Ridgeway, Joseph IV, 1182
Ridgeway, Joseph V, 357
Ridgeway, Joseph VI, 984
Ridgeway, Joseph P. II, 762
Ridgeway, Joseph P. II, 915
Ridgeway, Joseph, Jr. VI, 913
Ridgeway, Joseph, Jr. VI, 985
Ridgeway, Joseph, Sr. VI, 913
Ridgeway, Josiah II, 253
Ridgeway, Kesiah VI, 772
Ridgeway, Kezia IV, 546
Ridgeway, Keziah IV, 349
Ridgeway, Keziah IV, 542
Ridgeway, Keziah IV, 546
Ridgeway, Keziah VI, 747
Ridgeway, Lavina IV, 546
Ridgeway, Levina IV, 349
Ridgeway, Lydia IV, 546
Ridgeway, Lydia IV, 547
Ridgeway, Margaret VI, 420
Ridgeway, Margaret VI, 437
Ridgeway, Martha II, 94
Ridgeway, Martha II, 253
Ridgeway, Martha V, 300
Ridgeway, Martha V, 309
Ridgeway, Martha, Jr. V, 309
Ridgeway, Mary II, 208
Ridgeway, Mary II, 253
Ridgeway, Mary III, 470
Ridgeway, Mary IV, 546
Ridgeway, Mary IV, 547
Ridgeway, Mary IV, 1182
Ridgeway, Mary IV, 1186
Ridgeway, Mary V, 357
Ridgeway, Mary V, 707
Ridgeway, Mary V, 955
Ridgeway, Mary V, 958
Ridgeway, Mary VI, 530
Ridgeway, Mary VI, 552
Ridgeway, Mary Ann II, 762
Ridgeway, Mary Ann II, 915
Ridgeway, Mary Ann IV, 148
Ridgeway, Mary Ann IV, 158
Ridgeway, Mary Ann IV, 269
Ridgeway, Maryjane IV, 158
Ridgeway, Matilda IV, 547
Ridgeway, Michal IV, 158
Ridgeway, Michal IV, 349
Ridgeway, Michal IV, 546
Ridgeway, Michel IV, 349
Ridgeway, Miriam II, 253
Ridgeway, Moses C. II, 915
Ridgeway, Moses Coates II, 762
Ridgeway, Phebe II, 253
Ridgeway, Phebe IV, 546
Ridgeway, Polly VI, 913
Ridgeway, Polly VI, 960
Ridgeway, Posthema II, 253
Ridgeway, Posthema II, 259
Ridgeway, Rachel II, 94
Ridgeway, Rachel II, 253
Ridgeway, Rachel IV, 546
Ridgeway, Rachel VI, 420
Ridgeway, Rebecca II, 253
Ridgeway, Rebecca II, 762
Ridgeway, Rebecca II, 915
Ridgeway, Rebecca IV, 158
Ridgeway, Rebecca IV, 547
Ridgeway, Rebecca VI, 747
Ridgeway, Rebecca VI, 772
Ridgeway, Rebecca VI, 773
Ridgeway, Rebeckah II, 94
Ridgeway, Rees IV, 158
Ridgeway, Rees IV, 269
Ridgeway, Reese IV, 158
Ridgeway, Richard II, 253
Ridgeway, Richard III, 470
Ridgeway, Richard IV, 349
Ridgeway, Richard IV, 542
Ridgeway, Richard IV, 546
Ridgeway, Richard V, 357
Ridgeway, Richard VI, 420
Ridgeway, Richard VI, 437
Ridgeway, Richd VI, 552
Ridgeway, Robert V, 357
Ridgeway, Ruth IV, 349
Ridgeway, Ruth IV, 546
Ridgeway, Ruth Anna IV, 546
Ridgeway, Ruthanna IV, 546
Ridgeway, Sally VI, 985
Ridgeway, Sarah II, 94
Ridgeway, Sarah II, 253
Ridgeway, Sarah II, 762
Ridgeway, Sarah II, 915
Ridgeway, Sarah IV, 158
Ridgeway, Sarah Ridgway II, 762
Ridgeway, Solomon II, 253
Ridgeway, Susannah II, 253
Ridgeway, Tabitha Ann IV, 546
Ridgeway, Talitha Ann IV, 546
Ridgeway, Thomas II, 762
Ridgeway, Thomas IV, 349
Ridgeway, Thomas IV, 546
Ridgeway, Thomas IV, 547
Ridgeway, Thomas IV, 1186
Ridgeway, Thomas Elwood IV, 546
Ridgeway, Thos. IV, 546
Ridgeway, Timothy IV, 158
Ridgeway, Timothy IV, 349
Ridgeway, Timothy IV, 546
Ridgeway, Wilbur V, 357
Ridgeway, William II, 253
Ridgeway, William Penn VI, 773
Ridgeway, Wm. II, 762
Ridgeway, Wm. VI, 871
Ridgeway, Wm. P. II, 915
Ridgley, Ann IV, 478
Ridgley, Ann IV, 496
Ridgley, Francis II, 413
Ridgley, Wd. Harris II, 413
Ridglly, Francis II, 413
Ridglly, Wd. Harris II, 413
Ridgway, Abigail II, 181
Ridgway, Abigail II, 187
Ridgway, Abigail II, 253
Ridgway, Abigail II, 254
Ridgway, Abigail II, 260
Ridgway, Abigal II, 208
Ridgway, Abijah IV, 546
Ridgway, Abugal II, 253
Ridgway, Aden III, 268
Ridgway, Algernon S. VI, 437
Ridgway, Allen II, 253
Ridgway, Allen II, 413
Ridgway, Allen II, 807
Ridgway, Allen, Jr. II, 413
Ridgway, Andrews II, 253
Ridgway, Ann II, 38
Ridgway, Ann II, 94
Ridgway, Ann II, 95
Ridgway, Ann II, 113
Ridgway, Ann II, 123
Ridgway, Ann II, 137
Ridgway, Ann II, 156
Ridgway, Ann II, 249
Ridgway, Ann II, 252
Ridgway, Ann II, 253
Ridgway, Ann II, 254
Ridgway, Ann II, 265
Ridgway, Ann II, 413
Ridgway, Ann II, 915
Ridgway, Ann III, 439
Ridgway, Ann IV, 546
Ridgway, Anna II, 137
Ridgway, Anna II, 810
Ridgway, Anna IV, 551
Ridgway, Anna Bowen II, 137
Ridgway, Anna P. II, 899
Ridgway, Anna P. II, 915
Ridgway, Anne II, 137
Ridgway, Anne P. II, 756
Ridgway, Anne P. Miller II, 762
Ridgway, Aquila II, 634
Ridgway, Aquilla II, 635
Ridgway, Aquilla S. II, 299
Ridgway, Benjamin II, 181
Ridgway, Benjamin II, 254
Ridgway, Benjamin E. II, 254
Ridgway, Benjamin E. II, 299
Ridgway, Benjamin E. II, 312
Ridgway, Betty Jane II, 137
Ridgway, Beulah II, 181
Ridgway, Beulah II, 198
Ridgway, Beulah II, 208
Ridgway, Beulah II, 253
Ridgway, Beulah II, 254
Ridgway, Beulah II, 312
Ridgway, Bulah II, 94
Ridgway, Bulah VI, 437
Ridgway, Burr II, 254
Ridgway, Caleb II, 253
Ridgway, Caroline II, 413
Ridgway, Caroline II, 817
Ridgway, Caroline II, 895
Ridgway, Caroline II, 915
Ridgway, Caroline III, 45
Ridgway, Caroline III, 216
Ridgway, Caroline III, 217
Ridgway, Caroline III, 268
Ridgway, Caroline VI, 764
Ridgway, Caroline L. III, 217
Ridgway, Catharine II, 187
Ridgway, Catharine II, 253
Ridgway, Catherine II, 225
Ridgway, Charity II, 253
Ridgway, Charity VI, 437
Ridgway, Charity VI, 444
Ridgway, Charity VI, 452
Ridgway, Charity VI, 563
Ridgway, Charity VI, 695
Ridgway, Charity VI, 706
Ridgway, Charity, Jr. VI, 437
Ridgway, Charles II, 137
Ridgway, Charles II, 156
Ridgway, Charles II, 181
Ridgway, Charles II, 299
Ridgway, Charles II, 312
Ridgway, Charles II, 316
Ridgway, Charles II, 324
Ridgway, Charles S. II, 915
Ridgway, Charles Stowe II, 817
Ridgway, Charles Wood III, 217
Ridgway, Charlotte II, 253
Ridgway, Charlotte II, 818
Ridgway, Chas. S. II, 915
Ridgway, Chas. S. II, 922
Ridgway, Coates II, 635
Ridgway, Cornelia W. III, 217
Ridgway, Daniel II, 38
Ridgway, Daniel II, 63
Ridgway, Daniel II, 69
Ridgway, Daniel II, 94
Ridgway, Daniel II, 95
Ridgway, Daniel II, 137
Ridgway, Daniel II, 181
Ridgway, Daniel II, 253
Ridgway, Daniel II, 254
Ridgway, Daniel IV, 56
Ridgway, Daniel P. II, 95
Ridgway, Daniel P. II, 123
Ridgway, Daniel P. II, 137
Ridgway, Daniel P. II, 156
Ridgway, Daniel P. II, 915
Ridgway, Daniel Pedrick II, 817
Ridgway, David II, 181
Ridgway, David II, 203
Ridgway, David II, 253
Ridgway, David II, 254
Ridgway, David IV, 158
Ridgway, David IV, 269
Ridgway, David VI, 414
Ridgway, David VI, 421
Ridgway, David VI, 437
Ridgway, David H. V, 357
Ridgway, David H. V, 464
Ridgway, Delaplain II, 635
Ridgway, Delaplaine II, 413
Ridgway, Dillaplane II, 635
Ridgway, Dilliplain II, 634
Ridgway, Dinah IV, 107
Ridgway, Dorothy N. II, 137
Ridgway, Edith II, 299
Ridgway, Edith II, 312
Ridgway, Edith III, 217
Ridgway, Edmund II, 182
Ridgway, Edward II, 253

Ridgway, Edward VI, 421
Ridgway, Edward VI, 437
Ridgway, Edward Harvey II, 817
Ridgway, Edwin II, 135
Ridgway, Edwin L. II, 137
Ridgway, Elaine Agnes III, 268
Ridgway, Eleanor VI, 985
Ridgway, Eliz. III, 22
Ridgway, Eliz. III, 268
Ridgway, Eliza II, 281
Ridgway, Eliza II, 299
Ridgway, Eliza IV, 538
Ridgway, Eliza IV, 546
Ridgway, Eliza L. III, 217
Ridgway, Elizabeth II, 38
Ridgway, Elizabeth II, 94
Ridgway, Elizabeth II, 95
Ridgway, Elizabeth II, 137
Ridgway, Elizabeth II, 181
Ridgway, Elizabeth II, 201
Ridgway, Elizabeth II, 225
Ridgway, Elizabeth II, 252
Ridgway, Elizabeth II, 253
Ridgway, Elizabeth II, 254
Ridgway, Elizabeth II, 413
Ridgway, Elizabeth II, 634
Ridgway, Elizabeth II, 635
Ridgway, Elizabeth II, 788
Ridgway, Elizabeth II, 817
Ridgway, Elizabeth II, 850
Ridgway, Elizabeth II, 915
Ridgway, Elizabeth III, 22
Ridgway, Elizabeth III, 268
Ridgway, Elizabeth IV, 359
Ridgway, Elizabeth IV, 546
Ridgway, Elizabeth IV, 550
Ridgway, Elizabeth IV, 551
Ridgway, Elizabeth V, 357
Ridgway, Elizabeth V, 464
Ridgway, Elizabeth Anne II, 253
Ridgway, Elizabeth B. II, 915
Ridgway, Elizabeth C. II, 817
Ridgway, Elizabeth C. II, 853
Ridgway, Elizabeth C. II, 915
Ridgway, Elizabeth Coates II, 790
Ridgway, Ellis II, 635
Ridgway, Elsie II, 137
Ridgway, Emma II, 788
Ridgway, Emma II, 850
Ridgway, Emma II, 915
Ridgway, Emma R. II, 733
Ridgway, Emma R. Comley II, 762
Ridgway, Esther II, 413
Ridgway, Esther II, 635
Ridgway, Esther II, 790
Ridgway, Esther II, 794
Ridgway, Esther II, 808
Ridgway, Esther II, 817
Ridgway, Esther II, 866
Ridgway, Esther II, 915
Ridgway, Esther II, 922
Ridgway, Esther VI, 984
Ridgway, Esther C. II, 857
Ridgway, Esther C. II, 915
Ridgway, Eunice II, 94
Ridgway, Eunice II, 181
Ridgway, Eunice II, 635
Ridgway, Evelyn III, 268
Ridgway, Evelyn Ruth III, 268
Ridgway, Francelia II, 840
Ridgway, Francelia II, 915
Ridgway, Francelia Williams II, 817
Ridgway, Francis Townsend IV, 56
Ridgway, Franklin II, 137
Ridgway, Franklin II, 156
Ridgway, Franklin B. II, 817
Ridgway, Frederick VI, 437
Ridgway, Gabriel II, 181
Ridgway, George H. III, 217
Ridgway, Grace IV, 546
Ridgway, Grace V, 357
Ridgway, Hannah II, 38
Ridgway, Hannah II, 63
Ridgway, Hannah II, 94
Ridgway, Hannah II, 180
Ridgway, Hannah II, 181
Ridgway, Hannah II, 187
Ridgway, Hannah II, 191
Ridgway, Hannah II, 202
Ridgway, Hannah II, 203
Ridgway, Hannah II, 224
Ridgway, Hannah II, 247
Ridgway, Hannah II, 253
Ridgway, Hannah II, 254
Ridgway, Hannah II, 413
Ridgway, Hannah II, 635
Ridgway, Hannah II, 693
Ridgway, Hannah II, 817
Ridgway, Hannah VI, 437
Ridgway, Hannah VI, 459
Ridgway, Hannah B. II, 915
Ridgway, Hannah Burr II, 413
Ridgway, Hannah Burr II, 635
Ridgway, Hannah Burr II, 817
Ridgway, Hannah E. II, 181
Ridgway, Hannah E. II, 286
Ridgway, Hannah E. II, 299
Ridgway, Hannah Lydia II, 253
Ridgway, Harvey B. W. II, 915
Ridgway, Harvey Borton II, 817
Ridgway, Helen M. II, 915
Ridgway, Henrietta II, 94
Ridgway, Henrietta II, 635
Ridgway, Henrietta II, 692
Ridgway, Henrietta II, 693
Ridgway, Henrietta II, 720
Ridgway, Henrietta II, 723
Ridgway, Henrietta II, 915
Ridgway, Henrietta III, 268
Ridgway, Henrietta R. II, 862
Ridgway, Henrietta R. II, 915
Ridgway, Henry II, 94
Ridgway, Henry II, 156
Ridgway, Henry II, 181
Ridgway, Henry II, 253
Ridgway, Henry II, 635
Ridgway, Henry II, 692
Ridgway, Henry II, 817
Ridgway, Henry II, 915
Ridgway, Henry C. II, 156
Ridgway, Henry Clay II, 137
Ridgway, Henry Wright II, 635
Ridgway, Henry, Jr. III, 268
Ridgway, I. Harvey II, 840
Ridgway, I. Harvey II, 915
Ridgway, Isaac II, 94
Ridgway, Isaac II, 137
Ridgway, Isaac II, 156
Ridgway, Isaac II, 253
Ridgway, Isabel II, 253
Ridgway, Isabel II, 257
Ridgway, Isabella II, 226
Ridgway, Isabella II, 254
Ridgway, Isaiah II, 413
Ridgway, J. Harvey II, 915
Ridgway, Jacob II, 94
Ridgway, Jacob II, 112
Ridgway, Jacob II, 137
Ridgway, Jacob II, 140
Ridgway, Jacob II, 156
Ridgway, Jacob II, 226
Ridgway, Jacob II, 253
Ridgway, Jacob II, 254
Ridgway, Jacob II, 257
Ridgway, Jacob II, 413
Ridgway, Jacob II, 635
Ridgway, Jacob II, 817
Ridgway, Jacob, Jr. II, 253
Ridgway, James II, 225
Ridgway, James III, 268
Ridgway, James Bateman II, 809
Ridgway, James Smith II, 181
Ridgway, Jane II, 181
Ridgway, Jane II, 203
Ridgway, Jane II, 253
Ridgway, Jane II, 254
Ridgway, Jane II, 635
Ridgway, Jane IV, 546
Ridgway, Jane VI, 420
Ridgway, Jane VI, 437
Ridgway, Jeann Beeson VI, 421
Ridgway, Jennie Cecilia II, 891
Ridgway, Jennie Celia II, 915
Ridgway, Jennie H. II, 135
Ridgway, Jennie Lelia II, 915
Ridgway, Jeremiah II, 199
Ridgway, Jesse C. II, 915
Ridgway, Jesse Coates II, 413
Ridgway, Jesse Coates II, 817
Ridgway, Jno. II, 253
Ridgway, Job II, 38
Ridgway, Job II, 94
Ridgway, Job II, 123
Ridgway, Job II, 156
Ridgway, Job II, 202
Ridgway, Job II, 203
Ridgway, Job II, 204
Ridgway, Job II, 232
Ridgway, Job II, 253
Ridgway, Job II, 257
Ridgway, Job II, 268
Ridgway, Job II, 635
Ridgway, Job II, 817
Ridgway, Job IV, 56
Ridgway, Job IV, 63
Ridgway, Job IV, 107
Ridgway, Job IV, 156
Ridgway, Job IV, 158
Ridgway, Job IV, 269
Ridgway, Job Harvey II, 817
Ridgway, John II, 38
Ridgway, John II, 94
Ridgway, John II, 181
Ridgway, John II, 198
Ridgway, John II, 208
Ridgway, John II, 253
Ridgway, John II, 254
Ridgway, John II, 312
Ridgway, John II, 634
Ridgway, John II, 635
Ridgway, John II, 793
Ridgway, John II, 817
Ridgway, John III, 439
Ridgway, John III, 452
Ridgway, John III, 454
Ridgway, John IV, 56
Ridgway, John IV, 107
Ridgway, John IV, 158
Ridgway, John IV, 269
Ridgway, John IV, 344
Ridgway, John IV, 349
Ridgway, John IV, 546
Ridgway, John VI, 437
Ridgway, John J., Jr. II, 915
Ridgway, John Jacob II, 817
Ridgway, John W. B. II, 915
Ridgway, John, Jr. II, 635
Ridgway, Jonathan IV, 545
Ridgway, Jonathan IV, 546
Ridgway, Joseph II, 94
Ridgway, Joseph II, 180
Ridgway, Joseph II, 181
Ridgway, Joseph II, 186
Ridgway, Joseph II, 187
Ridgway, Joseph II, 191
Ridgway, Joseph II, 203
Ridgway, Joseph II, 204
Ridgway, Joseph II, 212
Ridgway, Joseph II, 253
Ridgway, Joseph II, 413
Ridgway, Joseph II, 634
Ridgway, Joseph II, 635
Ridgway, Joseph II, 790
Ridgway, Joseph II, 794
Ridgway, Joseph II, 808
Ridgway, Joseph II, 817
Ridgway, Joseph II, 866
Ridgway, Joseph II, 915
Ridgway, Joseph II, 922
Ridgway, Joseph III, 268
Ridgway, Joseph V, 357
Ridgway, Joseph V, 464
Ridgway, Joseph VI, 984
Ridgway, Joseph F. II, 254
Ridgway, Joseph F. II, 635
Ridgway, Joseph Fowler II, 181
Ridgway, Joseph P. II, 915
Ridgway, Joseph Parker II, 635
Ridgway, Joseph Parker II, 817
Ridgway, Joseph Parker II, 915
Ridgway, Joseph W. II, 137
Ridgway, Joseph, Jr. VI, 985
Ridgway, Josephine II, 817
Ridgway, Joshua II, 635
Ridgway, Josiah II, 253
Ridgway, Josiah VI, 437
Ridgway, Josiah, Jr. III, 217
Ridgway, Josias II, 201
Ridgway, Josias II, 253
Ridgway, Julian VI, 365
Ridgway, Julian VI, 437
Ridgway, Katherine II, 225
Ridgway, Katherine II, 253
Ridgway, Kesiah II, 817
Ridgway, Kesiah P. II, 156
Ridgway, Kezia II, 94
Ridgway, Kezia IV, 56
Ridgway, Kezia IV, 546
Ridgway, Kezia P. II, 915
Ridgway, Keziah II, 94
Ridgway, Keziah II, 112
Ridgway, Keziah II, 137
Ridgway, Keziah II, 140
Ridgway, Lavina IV, 56
Ridgway, Lavina IV, 107
Ridgway, Laviner IV, 56
Ridgway, Lee Henry II, 137
Ridgway, Levi II, 137
Ridgway, Levi II, 156
Ridgway, Lewis VI, 437
Ridgway, Lois D. II, 137
Ridgway, Lott II, 253
Ridgway, Lucy II, 253
Ridgway, Lydia II, 28
Ridgway, Lydia II, 69
Ridgway, Lydia II, 94
Ridgway, Lydia II, 137
Ridgway, Lydia II, 181
Ridgway, Lydia II, 240
Ridgway, Lydia II, 254
Ridgway, Lydia IV, 546
Ridgway, Lydia VI, 437
Ridgway, Lydia Ann II, 817
Ridgway, Lydia Bradway II, 817
Ridgway, Mamie V, 259
Ridgway, Marah IV, 56
Ridgway, Margaret II, 413
Ridgway, Margaret VI, 364
Ridgway, Margaret VI, 437
Ridgway, Margaret VI, 459
Ridgway, Margaret M. H. II, 135
Ridgway, Martha II, 94
Ridgway, Martha II, 120
Ridgway, Martha II, 123
Ridgway, Martha II, 181
Ridgway, Martha II, 232
Ridgway, Martha II, 253
Ridgway, Martha II, 254
Ridgway, Martha II, 783
Ridgway, Martha V, 115
Ridgway, Martha VI, 414
Ridgway, Martha VI, 421
Ridgway, Martha VI, 437
Ridgway, Martha VI, 444
Ridgway, Martha VI, 563
Ridgway, Martha VI, 695
Ridgway, Martha VI, 706
Ridgway, Martha, Jr. V, 115
Ridgway, Martha, Jr. VI, 437
Ridgway, Martha, Sr. VI, 437
Ridgway, Mary II, 94
Ridgway, Mary II, 137
Ridgway, Mary II, 156
Ridgway, Mary II, 181
Ridgway, Mary II, 182
Ridgway, Mary II, 186
Ridgway, Mary II, 187
Ridgway, Mary II, 195
Ridgway, Mary II, 203
Ridgway, Mary II, 212
Ridgway, Mary II, 216
Ridgway, Mary II, 224
Ridgway, Mary II, 226
Ridgway, Mary II, 252
Ridgway, Mary II, 253
Ridgway, Mary II, 254
Ridgway, Mary II, 257
Ridgway, Mary II, 267
Ridgway, Mary II, 268
Ridgway, Mary II, 272
Ridgway, Mary II, 273
Ridgway, Mary II, 281
Ridgway, Mary II, 285
Ridgway, Mary II, 286
Ridgway, Mary II, 299
Ridgway, Mary II, 312
Ridgway, Mary II, 413
Ridgway, Mary II, 599
Ridgway, Mary II, 635
Ridgway, Mary III, 268
Ridgway, Mary III, 360
Ridgway, Mary III, 439
Ridgway, Mary IV, 546
Ridgway, Mary V, 357
Ridgway, Mary V, 464
Ridgway, Mary VI, 412
Ridgway, Mary VI, 414
Ridgway, Mary VI, 437
Ridgway, Mary Ann II, 413
Ridgway, Mary Ann II, 635
Ridgway, Mary Ann II, 817
Ridgway, Mary Ann II, 915
Ridgway, Mary Ann IV, 269
Ridgway, Mary E. B. II, 156
Ridgway, Mary I. II, 922
Ridgway, Mary R. II, 316
Ridgway, Mary R. II, 324
Ridgway, Mary Rebecca II, 915
Ridgway, Mary Taylor II, 817
Ridgway, Maryjane IV, 158
Ridgway, Mercy II, 156
Ridgway, Mercy II, 254
Ridgway, Mercy II, 635
Ridgway, Mercy II, 817
Ridgway, Mercy II, 915
Ridgway, Merian II, 242
Ridgway, Michal IV, 56
Ridgway, Michal IV, 107
Ridgway, Michal IV, 158
Ridgway, Michal IV, 349
Ridgway, Michal IV, 546
Ridgway, Michel IV, 56
Ridgway, Michel IV, 349
Ridgway, Miriam II, 181
Ridgway, Miriam II, 253
Ridgway, Miriam II, 299
Ridgway, Miriam II, 312
Ridgway, Moses II, 635
Ridgway, Moses C. II, 915
Ridgway, Moses Coates II, 635
Ridgway, Naomi II, 94
Ridgway, Naomi II, 112
Ridgway, Naomi II, 140
Ridgway, Naomi II, 723
Ridgway, Patience VI, 364
Ridgway, Patience VI, 437
Ridgway, Paul IV, 56
Ridgway, Paul IV, 107
Ridgway, Peyton VI, 984
Ridgway, Phebe II, 80
Ridgway, Phebe II, 94
Ridgway, Phebe II, 95
Ridgway, Phebe II, 253
Ridgway, Phebe II, 787
Ridgway, Phebe II, 807
Ridgway, Phebe III, 439
Ridgway, Phebe III, 452
Ridgway, Phebe III, 454
Ridgway, Phebe IV, 546
Ridgway, Phebe IV, 550
Ridgway, Phebe VI, 362
Ridgway, Phebe VI, 437
Ridgway, Phebe Willits II, 809
Ridgway, Polley VI, 984
Ridgway, Posthema II, 253
Ridgway, Prudence II, 254
Ridgway, Prudence II, 299
Ridgway, Prudence II, 312
Ridgway, Rachel II, 38
Ridgway, Rachel II, 63
Ridgway, Rachel II, 69
Ridgway, Rachel II, 94
Ridgway, Rachel II, 95
Ridgway, Rachel II, 123
Ridgway, Rachel II, 137
Ridgway, Rachel II, 181
Ridgway, Rachel II, 201
Ridgway, Rachel II, 253
Ridgway, Rachel II, 254
Ridgway, Rachel VI, 437
Ridgway, Rachel VI, 452
Ridgway, Rebecca II, 94
Ridgway, Rebecca II, 198
Ridgway, Rebecca II, 204
Ridgway, Rebecca II, 253
Ridgway, Rebecca II, 254
Ridgway, Rebecca II, 291
Ridgway, Rebecca II, 299
Ridgway, Rebecca II, 413
Ridgway, Rebecca II, 635
Ridgway, Rebecca II, 716
Ridgway, Rebecca II, 793
Ridgway, Rebecca II, 817
Ridgway, Rebecca II, 896
Ridgway, Rebecca II, 915
Ridgway, Rebecca IV, 156
Ridgway, Rebecca IV, 158
Ridgway, Rebecca IV, 269
Ridgway, Rebecca B. II, 610
Ridgway, Rebecca B. II, 635
Ridgway, Rebecca R. II, 842
Ridgway, Rebecca R. II, 861
Ridgway, Rebeccah II, 94
Ridgway, Rebeckah II, 94
Ridgway, Rebeckah II, 199
Ridgway, Rebeckah II, 253
Ridgway, Rees IV, 269
Ridgway, Reese IV, 158
Ridgway, Reese IV, 269
Ridgway, Richard II, 181
Ridgway, Richard II, 191
Ridgway, Richard II, 212
Ridgway, Richard II, 252
Ridgway, Richard II, 253
Ridgway, Richard II, 254
Ridgway, Richard II, 272
Ridgway, Richard III, 268
Ridgway, Richard III, 360
Ridgway, Richard III, 439
Ridgway, Richard IV, 56
Ridgway, Richard IV, 546
Ridgway, Richard V, 357
Ridgway, Richard V, 464
Ridgway, Richard VI, 364
Ridgway, Richard VI, 437
Ridgway, Richard VI, 444
Ridgway, Richard VI, 452
Ridgway, Richard VI, 459
Ridgway, Richard VI, 563
Ridgway, Richard VI, 695
Ridgway, Richard VI, 706
Ridgway, Richard H. V, 464
Ridgway, Richard, Jr. II, 252
Ridgway, Richard, Jr. II, 273
Ridgway, Richard, Jr. VI, 448
Ridgway, Richard, Sr. VI, 460
Ridgway, Richd VI, 552
Ridgway, Ridgway II, 187
Ridgway, Robert II, 181
Ridgway, Robert II, 224
Ridgway, Robert II, 253

way, Robert II, 254
way, Robert II, 413
way, Robert III, 268
way, Robert V, 357
way, Robert V, 464
way, Robert Pearson II, 809
way, Rosanna VI, 850
way, Ruth IV, 344
way, Ruth IV, 349
way, Ruth IV, 546
way, Ruth Anna IV, 546
way, Sally VI, 985
way, Samuel II, 253
way, Samuel II, 254
way, Samuel II, 693
way, Samuel VI, 850
way, Sarah II, 79
way, Sarah II, 94
way, Sarah II, 181
way, Sarah II, 187
way, Sarah II, 204
way, Sarah II, 247
way, Sarah II, 253
way, Sarah II, 254
way, Sarah II, 413
way, Sarah II, 575
way, Sarah II, 635
way, Sarah II, 817
way, Sarah II, 915
way, Sarah III, 268
way, Sarah IV, 158
way, Sarah IV, 269
way, Sarah VI, 436
way, Sarah VI, 437
way, Sarah VI, 455
way, Sarah Ann II, 254
way, Sarah Ann II, 635
way, Sarah Ann III, 268
way, Sarah Barton II, 216
way, Sarah Barton II, 254
way, Sarah C. II, 866
way, Sarah C. II, 915
way, Sarah P. II, 835
way, Sarah P. II, 850
way, Sarah P. II, 895
way, Sarah P. II, 899
way, Sarah P. II, 915
way, Sarah Ridgway III, 217
way, Sarah W. II, 915
way, Sarah Willitts II, 817
way, Silas IV, 882
way, Silvanus J. III, 217
way, Silvanus J., Jr. III, 217
way, Solomon II, 181
way, Solomon II, 187
way, Solomon II, 203
way, Solomon II, 253
way, Solomon II, 254
way, Solomon II, 267
ay, Solomon, Jr. II, 253
ay, Solomon, Sr. II, 181
way, Sophia VI, 984
way, Susan R. II, 835
way, Susan R. II, 915
way, Susan Rotch II, 781
way, Susan Rotch II, 817
way, Susannah II, 201
way, Susannah II, 253
ay, T. Edwin II, 915
way, Tacy II, 137
way, Tacy VI, 432
way, Tacy Pope VI, 437
ay, Talitha IV, 545
way, Talitha Ann IV, 546
way, Teresa II, 137
way, Teresa II, 156
ay, Teressa II, 156
way, Thomas II, 202
way, Thomas II, 224
way, Thomas II, 249
way, Thomas II, 252
ay, Thomas II, 253
way, Thomas II, 268
way, Thomas II, 635
way, Thomas III, 216
ay, Thomas III, 268
way, Thomas IV, 56
way, Thomas IV, 107
way, Thomas IV, 349
way, Thomas IV, 359
way, Thomas IV, 550
way, Thomas IV, 551
way, Thomas H. III, 217
way, Thos. II, 817
way, Thos. II, 850
way, Thos. II, 895
way, Thos. II, 899
way, Thos. II, 915
way, Thos. III, 22
ay, Thos. III, 268
way, Thos. IV, 546
Ridgway, Thos. Edwin II, 817
Ridgway, Timothy II, 187
Ridgway, Timothy IV, 56
Ridgway, Timothy IV, 107
Ridgway, Timothy IV, 158
Ridgway, Timothy IV, 349
Ridgway, Timothy IV, 546
Ridgway, Tracy II, 156
Ridgway, Unice II, 254
Ridgway, Valentine Everit III, 217
Ridgway, W. P. II, 915
Ridgway, Waddington B. II, 137
Ridgway, Waddington B. II, 915
Ridgway, Wallace II, 809
Ridgway, Wd. Francelia W. II, 915
Ridgway, Wd. Henrietta II, 794
Ridgway, Wd. Mary II, 181
Ridgway, Wd. Rebecca II, 808
Ridgway, Wilbur V, 357
Ridgway, Wilbur V, 464
Ridgway, Willett Hicks II, 817
Ridgway, William II, 181
Ridgway, William II, 182
Ridgway, William II, 216
Ridgway, William II, 253
Ridgway, William II, 254
Ridgway, William II, 267
Ridgway, William II, 281
Ridgway, William II, 285
Ridgway, William II, 286
Ridgway, William II, 299
Ridgway, William II, 312
Ridgway, William VI, 984
Ridgway, William VI, 985
Ridgway, William Penn II, 413
Ridgway, William Penn II, 817
Ridgway, Wm. II, 137
Ridgway, Wm. P. II, 915
Ridgway, Wm. Penn II, 635
Ridgway, Wm. Penn II, 915
Ridick, Jean VI, 27
Ridick, Jean VI, 35
Ridick, Robert VI, 27
Ridick, Robert VI, 35
Riding, Susan VI, 428
Ridings, Susan VI, 437
Ridley, James II, 38
Ridley, James II, 95
Ridley, Mary II, 60
Ridley, Mary II, 95
Ridley, Miriam III, 254
Ridley, Rebecca II, 38
Ridley, Rebecka II, 95
Ridley, Rebecka II, 112
Ridley, Sarah II, 38
Ridley, Sarah II, 70
Ridley, Sarah II, 95
Ridley, Sarah II, 104
Ridley, Thomas VI, 85
Ridley, William II, 38
Ridley, Wm. II, 70
Ridley, Wm. II, 95
Ridly, Sarah II, 95
Ridshaw, Mary Ann I, 930
Ridugaway, Margaret VI, 437
Ridugaway, Margaret VI, 458
Ridway, John II, 783
Ridway, Kezia Reeves II, 784
Rieben, Eliza III, 164
Rieben, Eliza III, 268
Rieben, Pierce III, 164
Rieben, Pierre III, 268
Riece, Alfred V, 309
Riece, Caleb I, 968
Riece, Caleb I, 1012
Riece, Caleb V, 309
Riece, Eleanor V, 309
Riece, Elisha V, 309
Riece, Evan V, 309
Riece, Francis I, 968
Riece, Joel V, 310
Riece, John V, 309
Riece, Josiah V, 309
Riece, Margaret V, 309
Riece, Mary Eleanor V, 309
Riece, Matilda Jane V, 309
Riece, Michael V, 309
Riece, Sarah V, 309
Riece, Thomas, Jr. V, 309
Riece, Thos. V, 309
Riece, William I, 968
Riece, Wm. V, 309
Riehl, Anna III, 176
Riehl, Anna III, 268
Riehl, Anna M. F. III, 176
Riehl, Anna M. F. III, 268
Riehl, Ernst III, 268
Riehl, Ernst A. III, 176
Riehle, John V, 1016
Riehle, Maria Margaretta III, 75
Rieley, George VI, 879
Rieley, George VI, 901
Rieley, Mary VI, 901
Rieley, William G. VI, 901
Rieley, William G. VI, 925
Rielty, Margaret VI, 881
Rielty, Mary VI, 881
Riely, Eli VI, 604
Riely, Mary VI, 604
Riese, Tamer IV, 348
Rieser, Ethel Anna II, 1065
Rieser, Harry II, 1065
Rieson, Mary III, 268
Rieve, Ellen IV, 653
Rieve, Hannah IV, 653
Rieve, Joshua IV, 653
Rieve, Mellicent IV, 653
Rieve, Samuel Carr IV, 653
Rife, Abram IV, 1240
Rife, Abram, Sr. IV, 1240
Rife, Daisy M. IV, 1240
Rife, John IV, 1240
Rifes, Lizzie IV, 1221
Riffert, Edward II, 635
Riffert, Margaret II, 572
Riffert, Margaret II, 635
Riffert, Rachel II, 635
Riffert, Rachel II, 658
Riffets, Edward II, 635
Riffets, Rachel II, 635
Riffitts, Rachel II, 635
Rifford, John T. III, 268
Rig, Nathaniel IV, 269
Rig, Sarah IV, 269
Rigbie, Anna VI, 266
Rigbie, James VI, 266
Rigbie, Sarah VI, 266
Rigby, Abigail IV, 915
Rigby, Abigail IV, 916
Rigby, Daniel IV, 915
Rigby, Daniel IV, 916
Rigby, Mary IV, 916
Rigby, Tabitha VI, 883
Rigdon, David V, 1016
Rigdon, Jeptha V, 1016
Rigdon, Mary II, 254
Rigg, Abigail IV, 50
Rigg, Abigail IV, 56
Rigg, Anna IV, 269
Rigg, Clement IV, 50
Rigg, Clement IV, 56
Rigg, Clement IV, 65
Rigg, Clement, Jr. IV, 56
Rigg, David IV, 654
Rigg, David IV, 882
Rigg, David B. M. L. IV, 269
Rigg, David B. M. L. IV, 654
Rigg, David M. L. IV, 882
Rigg, Ephraim IV, 56
Rigg, Hannah IV, 654
Rigg, Hiram IV, 56
Rigg, Hiram IV, 269
Rigg, Hiram IV, 654
Rigg, Hiram IV, 882
Rigg, Jesse IV, 53
Rigg, Jesse IV, 56
Rigg, Jesse IV, 269
Rigg, Jesse IV, 370
Rigg, Jesse IV, 654
Rigg, Jesse IV, 882
Rigg, Joseph IV, 654
Rigg, Mary Ann IV, 269
Rigg, Mary Ann IV, 654
Rigg, Mary Ann IV, 882
Rigg, Matilda IV, 56
Rigg, Merium IV, 56
Rigg, Miriam IV, 56
Rigg, Miriam IV, 65
Rigg, Miriam IV, 269
Rigg, Nathaniel IV, 56
Rigg, Nathaniel IV, 269
Rigg, Priscilla IV, 53
Rigg, Priscilla IV, 56
Rigg, Sarah IV, 17
Rigg, Sarah IV, 50
Rigg, Sarah IV, 53
Rigg, Sarah IV, 56
Rigg, Sarah IV, 65
Rigg, Sarah IV, 269
Rigg, Sarah IV, 370
Rigg, Sarah IV, 432
Rigg, Sarah IV, 654
Rigg, Sarah IV, 882
Rigg, Sarah IV, 893
Rigg, Sarah IV, 894
Rigg, Sarah VI, 437
Rigg, Susanna IV, 269
Rigg, Thomas IV, 654
Rigg, Thomas W. IV, 654
Riggins, J. W. V, 1016
Riggins, Wm. V, 1016
Riggle, Lucy V, 707
Riggle, Lucy A. V, 707
Riggle, Sarah V, 707
Riggle, Sarah E. V, 707
Riggle, Sarah Leggit V, 707
Riggle, Susanna IV, 269
Riggle, Susanna IV, 290
Riggs, Daniel II, 490
Riggs, Daniel II, 635
Riggs, George VI, 850
Riggs, Helen C. II, 853
Riggs, Helen C. II, 915
Riggs, Martha II, 635
Riggs, Rhoda VI, 850
Riggs, William VI, 850
Riggs, Winifred III, 241
Riggs, Winifred III, 268
Right, Charles I, 583
Right, Cynthia I, 897
Right, Cynthia I, 906
Right, Dosia II, 113
Right, Dusia II, 113
Right, Elijah I, 583
Right, Elizabeth I, 535
Right, Elizabeth I, 583
Right, Emma V, 1016
Right, Esther I, 890
Right, Esther I, 906
Right, James I, 583
Right, James V, 1016
Right, Joshua I, 970
Right, Josia II, 113
Right, Keziah I, 584
Right, Nancy VI, 875
Right, Rachel VI, 345
Right, Rhoda IV, 559
Right, Robert II, 447
Right, Robert VI, 345
Righter, Elizabeth IV, 1261
Righter, Hannah G. IV, 270
Righter, Margaretta W. II, 137
Righter, Margaretta W. II, 150
Righter, Margaretta W. II, 156
Righter, Sarah II, 635
Righter, Sarah IV, 799
Righter, Sarah IV, 841
Righton, Agnes II, 635
Righton, Agnes II, 677
Righton, Frances II, 635
Righton, Francis II, 564
Righton, Mary II, 487
Righton, Mary II, 635
Righton, Sarah II, 222
Righton, Sarah II, 254
Righton, Sarah II, 413
Righton, William II, 222
Righton, William II, 254
Righton, Wm. II, 635
Righton, Wm. II, 677
Rightsel, Deborah I, 417
Rightsman, David I, 486
Rightsman, Leonard I, 486
Rightsman, Mary Ann I, 478
Rightsman, Mary Ann I, 486
Rightsman, Rachel I, 417
Rightsman, Rachel I, 430
Rightsmon, Katharine I, 453
Rigle, Sarah E. V, 707
Riker, Agnes S. III, 268
Riker, Alice III, 268
Riker, Delia III, 268
Riker, Elizabeth III, 268
Riker, Joseph III, 268
Riker, Lucy A. III, 268
Riker, Oliver Stokes III, 268
Riker, Rachel III, 268
Riker, Rachel S. III, 268
Riker, Ruth Anna III, 268
Riker, William A. III, 268
Riker, Wm. A. III, 268
Riks, Angeline IV, 755
Rileigh, Elias William V, 429
Riley, Andrew V, 1016
Riley, Ann VI, 690
Riley, Ann VI, 691
Riley, Ann VI, 695
Riley, Ann VI, 721
Riley, Carrie A. V, 1016
Riley, Charlene F. V, 707
Riley, Charles V, 595
Riley, Charley L. V, 707
Riley, Clara V, 1016
Riley, Clara S. III, 214
Riley, Clara S. III, 276
Riley, Clarence A. V, 199
Riley, Clarence H. V, 199
Riley, David F. V, 199
Riley, David T. V, 199
Riley, Dora J. V, 199
Riley, Elizabeth V, 928
Riley, Elizabeth VI, 762
Riley, Elizabeth VI, 773
Riley, Elizabeth VI, 985
Riley, Evolyn V, 1016
Riley, Florence V, 525
Riley, Florence V, 694
Riley, Florence V, 707
Riley, Flossie M. V, 199
Riley, Forest V, 1016
Riley, George William VI, 437
Riley, Harriet E. III, 439
Riley, Hazel R. V, 199
Riley, Helen V, 199
Riley, Helen D. III, 406
Riley, Helen D. III, 439
Riley, Helen R. V, 199
Riley, Henry D. III, 439
Riley, Henry M. III, 406
Riley, Henry M. III, 439
Riley, Hugh VI, 985
Riley, Isadora C. V, 464
Riley, Ivy V, 707
Riley, Jacob V, 1016
Riley, James V, 1016
Riley, James VI, 603
Riley, James VI, 985
Riley, Janette V, 1016
Riley, Jeremiah IV, 270
Riley, John IV, 1335
Riley, John V, 464
Riley, John V, 1016
Riley, John VI, 850
Riley, Joseph IV, 1292
Riley, Joseph VI, 985
Riley, Joshua VI, 762
Riley, Joshua VI, 773
Riley, Laurie V, 1016
Riley, Lauta V, 1016
Riley, Leah V, 1016
Riley, Leonard William VI, 417
Riley, Leonard William VI, 437
Riley, Levi V, 1016
Riley, Levi L. V, 1016
Riley, Levi S. V, 1016
Riley, Lucy VI, 985
Riley, Margaret I, 934
Riley, Margaret IV, 986
Riley, Martha Ann III, 439
Riley, Mary II, 95
Riley, Mary II, 413
Riley, Mary II, 635
Riley, Mary II, 762
Riley, Mary II, 773
Riley, Mary IV, 270
Riley, Mary IV, 1292
Riley, Mary VI, 850
Riley, Matilda IV, 1221
Riley, Matilda A. IV, 1221
Riley, Moses II, 413
Riley, Nancy VI, 985
Riley, Nettie IV, 1335
Riley, Nettie M. V, 1016
Riley, Nettie Smalley IV, 1335
Riley, Nevada V, 1016
Riley, Ray V, 1016
Riley, Raymond V, 1016
Riley, Robert T. III, 439
Riley, Rosella V, 199
Riley, Ruth IV, 859
Riley, Ruth IV, 860
Riley, Sarah I, 992
Riley, Sarah I, 996
Riley, Sarah J. V, 707
Riley, Sarah Jane V, 595
Riley, Shady II, 817
Riley, Shady II, 915
Riley, Silas M. V, 642
Riley, Silas W. V, 642
Riley, Sophia VI, 985
Riley, Susan V, 1016
Riley, Susie V, 1016
Riley, Thomas IV, 270
Riley, Thomas IV, 1292
Riley, Thomas VI, 551
Riley, Thomas Samuel IV, 270
Riley, Thos. Samuel IV, 270
Riley, Thos. W. III, 439
Riley, Victoria N. VI, 437
Riley, Virginia VI, 437
Riley, Virginia Noel VI, 417
Riley, Virginia Noel VI, 437
Riley, William VI, 985
Riley, William G. VI, 891
Riley, William S. V, 595
Riley, William S. V, 707
Riley, Wm. V, 199
Riley, Wm. V, 1016
Rimington, John II, 56
Rimington, John II, 94
Rimington, Sarah II, 94
Rimington, Susannah II, 56

Rimington, Susannah II, 94
Rinard, George V, 525
Rinard, Jeremiah V, 525
Rinard, Solomon V, 525
Rinchall, Sarah VI, 210
Rinchall, Sarah, Jr. VI, 210
Rinchall, Sarah, Sr. VI, 210
Rineard, Adom I, 417
Rinehart, Adam I, 417
Rinehart, Adam V, 115
Rinehart, Adom I, 417
Rinehart, Ann V, 115
Rinehart, Barbara V, 115
Rinehart, Barbary I, 417
Rinehart, Catharine I, 417
Rinehart, Catharine V, 525
Rinehart, Catherine V, 115
Rinehart, Ethel IV, 1221
Rinehart, Floyd E. IV, 1221
Rinehart, George I, 417
Rinehart, George V, 115
Rinehart, Grace W. IV, 1221
Rinehart, H. Stanley IV, 1335
Rinehart, Helen S. IV, 1335
Rinehart, Isaac V, 115
Rinehart, Jacob V, 115
Rinehart, James E. IV, 1221
Rinehart, Jeremiah I, 417
Rinehart, Jeremiah V, 115
Rinehart, Lydia V, 115
Rinehart, Margaret I, 417
Rinehart, Margaret V, 115
Rinehart, Marguerite IV, 1182
Rinehart, Margueritte IV, 1182
Rinehart, Mary B. IV, 1221
Rinehart, Rachel I, 417
Rinehart, Rachel I, 430
Rinehart, Solomon I, 417
Rinehart, Solomon V, 115
Rinehart, Thomas IV, 1221
Rineheart, Catharine I, 417
Rineheart, Margaret I, 417
Riner, Charles R. V, 858
Riner, George V, 858
Ring, ??? II, 826
Ring, ??? III, 236
Ring, Beatrice U. IV, 270
Ring, Catharine III, 269
Ring, Catharine III, 293
Ring, Charles Henry III, 269
Ring, Clementina III, 269
Ring, David Sands III, 269
Ring, Elias III, 269
Ring, Eliza III, 269
Ring, Eliza VI, 210
Ring, Elizabeth II, 413
Ring, Elizabeth II, 447
Ring, Enos IV, 1182
Ring, Eveline III, 269
Ring, Evelyn III, 269
Ring, Franklin Mott III, 269
Ring, Geo. W. III, 269
Ring, George Stewart III, 269
Ring, George W. III, 269
Ring, George Washington III, 269
Ring, Hannah II, 413
Ring, Hannah II, 447
Ring, Hannah B. II, 826
Ring, Harriet III, 269
Ring, Harriet III, 293
Ring, Henrietta III, 269
Ring, James III, 488
Ring, James III, 495
Ring, John III, 269
Ring, Joseph R. IV, 1377
Ring, Levinia V, 928
Ring, Louisa III, 236
Ring, Louisa III, 269
Ring, Louise III, 269
Ring, Marian IV, 1182
Ring, Martha IV, 567
Ring, Martha IV, 593
Ring, Martha G. III, 269
Ring, Mary Ann IV, 1182
Ring, Maude I, 223
Ring, Phebe III, 269
Ring, Phebe VI, 210
Ring, Rachel III, 269
Ring, Rachel IV, 432
Ring, Rachel W. III, 269
Ring, Raymond H. IV, 1335
Ring, Robert Elam III, 269
Ring, Sally Ann IV, 1182
Ring, Samuel II, 413
Ring, Samuel II, 447
Ring, Susannah II, 95
Ringer, Mary K. V, 805
Ringgold, Annie E. V, 937
Ringgold, Emma W. V, 928
Ringgold, Emma W. V, 937
Ringgold, Thomas V, 937
Ringley, Elpha IV, 989
Ringwald, Gertrude Ilane V, 1016
Rinker, Joseph VI, 773
Rino, Catharine III, 269
Rino, Elias III, 269
Rino, Mary III, 269
Rion, Priscilla V, 221
Rion, Priscilla V, 274
Ripits, ??? II, 413
Ripits, Paul II, 413
Ripley, Isabella VI, 985
Ripley, James VI, 985
Ripley, John IV, 270
Ripley, William I, 274
Riply, William I, 274
Ripton, Charles II, 413
Ripton, Josias II, 413
Risberger, Katherine II, 447
Risberger, Peter II, 447
Risdon, Ann II, 312
Risdon, Ann II, 324
Risdon, George II, 635
Rise, Nancy VI, 879
Riseley, Deborah Ann II, 324
Rish, Thomas V, 429
Risley, Deborah Ann II, 324
Risley, Deborah Ann II, 915
Risley, Deborah Ann II, 942
Risley, Enoch II, 95
Risley, Hannah C. II, 915
Risley, Hannah C. II, 942
Risley, Samuel L. II, 915
Risley, Samuel L. II, 942
Risley, Sarah II, 84
Risley, Sarah II, 95
Rislie, Enoch II, 95
Rison, Mary V, 525
Rison, Mary V, 531
Ritch, Ezekiel I, 768
Ritch, Isaac I, 768
Ritch, Isaiah I, 769
Ritch, Nancy VI, 843
Ritch, Phebe I, 835
Ritch, Ritchard I, 768
Ritch, William I, 768
Ritche, Mary II, 634
Ritchey, Charles J. VI, 1009
Ritchey, Earl IV, 755
Ritchey, Fanny VI, 985
Ritchey, Harvey F. VI, 985
Ritchey, Isabella VI, 985
Ritchey, Robert VI, 985
Ritchey, Saml. VI, 985
Ritchey, Samuel VI, 985
Ritchey, Sarah E. VI, 1009
Ritchey, Sarah J. VI, 985
Ritchie, Cornelius II, 156
Ritchie, Cornelius W. II, 137
Ritchie, Cornelius Wiltbank II, 146
Ritchie, Cornelius Wiltbank II, 156
Ritchie, Edith Russell IV, 1335
Ritchie, Elizabeth II, 413
Ritchie, Hannah II, 137
Ritchie, Hannah II, 146
Ritchie, Hannah II, 156
Ritchie, Hannah B. II, 152
Ritchie, Hannah B. II, 156
Ritchie, Hannah B. II, 158
Ritchie, Ida IV, 678
Ritchie, Isa Mary IV, 755
Ritchie, James II, 156
Ritchie, Mary E. II, 156
Ritchie, Mrs. ??? IV, 755
Ritchie, Robert V, 922
Ritchie, Sarah V, 922
Ritchie, Sarah F. V, 922
Ritchie, Sarah M. III, 269
Ritchison, Ann II, 252
Ritchison, Isaac Decow II, 252
Ritcliff, Julia A. IV, 244
Ritenour, Annie M. VI, 377
Ritenour, Annie M. VI, 437
Ritenour, Edith M. VI, 377
Ritenour, Edith M. VI, 437
Ritenour, Lettie V, 858
Ritenour, S. L. VI, 377
Ritenour, S. L. VI, 437
Ritson, Rebecca II, 635
Rittenauer, Joseph M. III, 439
Rittenhouse, ??? II, 413
Rittenhouse, David II, 413
Rittenhouse, Eleanor II, 413
Rittenhouse, Lola IV, 1261
Rittenhouse, Lula IV, 1261
Rittenhouse, Nora IV, 1261
Ritter, Hannah II, 485
Ritter, Hannah II, 635
Ritter, Jane S. II, 800
Ritter, Martha J. IV, 1182
Ritter, Rachel V, 305
Ritter, Rachel V, 310
Ritter, Sarah III, 187
Ritter, Sarah III, 251
Ritter, Sarah III, 275
Ritzie, Annie III, 212
Rively, Mary II, 779
River, Elizabeth VI, 27
River, Elizabeth VI, 32
River, Elizabeth VI, 34
River, Elizabeth VI, 36
River, Elizabeth VI, 38
River, George W. V, 870
River, Susan E. V, 870
Rivers, Isaac II, 447
Rivers, Mary II, 447
Rivers, Shallock II, 447
Rivers, Shatlock II, 447
Rives, Benjamin VI, 985
Rives, Benjamin VI, 1009
Rives, Elizabeth VI, 850
Rives, Landon C. VI, 850
Rives, Mariah VI, 850
Rives, Martha VI, 985
Rives, Rebecca VI, 985
Rives, Robert VI, 985
Rives, Robert, Jr. VI, 850
Rix, Abraham VI, 31
Rix, Abraham VI, 35
Rix, Ann I, 514
Rix, Ann I, 791
Rix, Arrena I, 892
Rix, Charity I, 892
Rix, Edward I, 513
Rix, Edward I, 791
Rix, Elizabeth I, 791
Rix, Elizabeth I, 863
Rix, Elizabeth I, 864
Rix, Elizabeth I, 892
Rix, Emma I, 864
Rix, Enoch I, 892
Rix, Gwen I, 791
Rix, Gwin I, 890
Rix, Gwin I, 899
Rix, Gwyn I, 513
Rix, Gwyn I, 791
Rix, Hanah I, 791
Rix, Hannah I, 513
Rix, James A. I, 864
Rix, Jane I, 899
Rix, John I, 514
Rix, John I, 791
Rix, John I, 863
Rix, John I, 864
Rix, John I, 899
Rix, John W. IV, 593
Rix, Jonas I, 791
Rix, Jones I, 513
Rix, Lydia I, 892
Rix, Margaret I, 892
Rix, Mary VI, 31
Rix, Mary VI, 35
Rix, Mary E. I, 863
Rix, Miles I, 892
Rix, Moses, Jr. I, 892
Rix, Phebe I, 892
Rix, Phebe I, 899
Rix, Rachel I, 899
Rix, Robert I, 835
Rix, Robert IV, 1292
Rix, Rosanna I, 892
Rix, Rudduck I, 892
Rix, Samuel I, 835
Rix, Sarah I, 835
Rix, Sarah I, 844
Rix, Sarah I, 899
Rix, Thomas I, 514
Rix, Thomas I, 791
Rix, Thomas I, 892
Rix, William I, 892
Rix, Zaza I, 899
Rix, Zodak I, 892
Ro???, John I, 1037
Ro???, Thomas I, 1037
Roach, ??? III, 301
Roach, Amy VI, 985
Roach, Amy Jane III, 269
Roach, Amy Jane III, 301
Roach, Basset VI, 985
Roach, Bassett VI, 985
Roach, Carrie IV, 1261
Roach, Chillion VI, 552
Roach, Cornelius VI, 985
Roach, Deborah VI, 501
Roach, Deborah VI, 552
Roach, Deborah VI, 553
Roach, Earl IV, 1261
Roach, Edmond VI, 552
Roach, Edmund VI, 553
Roach, Edna M. III, 212
Roach, Edna M. III, 269
Roach, Eliza A. VI, 847
Roach, Elizabeth VI, 496
Roach, Elizabeth VI, 552
Roach, Elizabeth VI, 553
Roach, Elizabeth VI, 795
Roach, Elizabeth VI, 846
Roach, Elizabeth VI, 850
Roach, Elizabeth VI, 985
Roach, Emma IV, 1261
Roach, Eunice I, 569
Roach, George V, 115
Roach, George VI, 552
Roach, Hannah V, 115
Roach, Hannah V, 141
Roach, Hannah VI, 496
Roach, Hannah VI, 551
Roach, Hannah VI, 552
Roach, Hannah VI, 553
Roach, Hannah VI, 554
Roach, Hannah VI, 579
Roach, Henry VI, 985
Roach, James I, 417
Roach, James VI, 496
Roach, James VI, 552
Roach, James VI, 553
Roach, James VI, 985
Roach, James H. I, 417
Roach, James, Jr. VI, 552
Roach, Jane VI, 985
Roach, John VI, 985
Roach, John A. VI, 985
Roach, John P. IV, 1261
Roach, Jonah VI, 552
Roach, Joshua VI, 850
Roach, Judith VI, 850
Roach, Julia Ann VI, 985
Roach, Lucy VI, 809
Roach, Lydia VI, 795
Roach, Mahlon VI, 552
Roach, Mahlon VI, 553
Roach, Martha D. VI, 985
Roach, Mary IV, 1261
Roach, Mary VI, 462
Roach, Mary VI, 553
Roach, Mary VI, 872
Roach, Mary E. III, 269
Roach, Mary Edna III, 212
Roach, Mary Elizabeth V, 115
Roach, Mary R. III, 347
Roach, Melvina IV, 1261
Roach, Micajah VI, 553
Roach, Mrs. Ursela VI, 872
Roach, Nancy Lydia I, 553
Roach, Nellie IV, 1261
Roach, Pearl S. IV, 1261
Roach, Phineas VI, 553
Roach, Phineas VI, 580
Roach, Polly VI, 985
Roach, Richard VI, 437
Roach, Richard VI, 496
Roach, Richard VI, 552
Roach, Richard VI, 553
Roach, Richard VI, 554
Roach, Richard VI, 579
Roach, Richard, Jr. VI, 437
Roach, Richard, Jr. VI, 553
Roach, Ruby S. III, 347
Roach, S. Ruby III, 269
Roach, Sarah VI, 553
Roach, Sarah VI, 579
Roach, Sarah VI, 720
Roach, Sarah VI, 840
Roach, Sarah VI, 850
Roach, Sarah Abner VI, 795
Roach, Tabitha VI, 553
Roach, Tabitha VI, 570
Roach, William VI, 800
Roach, William VI, 809
Roach, William VI, 840
Roach, William VI, 846
Roach, William VI, 850
Roades, Aaron D. VI, 986
Roades, Enos H. V, 464
Roades, Jane VI, 986
Roads, Alva V, 274
Roads, Ann I, 417
Roads, Ann II, 447
Roads, Ann V, 310
Roads, Ann VI, 551
Roads, Ann VI, 889
Roads, Caleb V, 199
Roads, Clarence V, 357
Roads, Dora V, 463
Roads, Dora E. V, 463
Roads, Dorothy V, 357
Roads, Edith V, 595
Roads, Edward II, 633
Roads, Edwin C. V, 310
Roads, Effie V, 310
Roads, Enos V, 463
Roads, Enos H. V, 464
Roads, Esther V, 469
Roads, Esther V, 510
Roads, Esther V, 525
Roads, Faye V, 357
Roads, Frances V, 463
Roads, Frank V, 463
Roads, Henry VI, 902
Roads, Jacob II, 632
Roads, Jacob II, 677
Roads, John II, 412
Roads, Joseph II, 633
Roads, Joseph VI, 338
Roads, Joshua II, 633
Roads, Judith VI, 902
Roads, Lewis V, 463
Roads, Lindley V, 464
Roads, Madge V, 464
Roads, Margaret II, 632
Roads, Margaret II, 677
Roads, Margrett II, 447
Roads, Martha V, 463
Roads, Mary V, 199
Roads, Naomy II, 633
Roads, Nellie V, 464
Roads, Phebe I, 417
Roads, Rendell V, 357
Roads, Semour V, 199
Roads, Thomas V, 199
Roads, William I, 996
Roads, William V, 463
Roads, Wm. VI, 902
Roads, Wm. L. V, 463
Roake, Mary, Jr. III, 269
Roan, Sarah II, 75
Roan, Sarah II, 95
Roark, Bernard VI, 850
Roark, Charles VI, 850
Roark, Elizabeth VI, 850
Roark, Littleberry E. VI, 850
Roark, Locky VI, 850
Roark, Owen VI, 850
Roark, Phebe VI, 850
Roas, Aquilla II, 415
Roatch, Lydia I, 553
Robards, Ann I, 1037
Robards, Ann I, 1039
Robards, Ann V, 115
Robards, Bethulah V, 858
Robards, David V, 115
Robards, Elizabeth VI, 338
Robards, Enoch VI, 329
Robards, Enoch VI, 338
Robards, John Lynch VI, 338
Robards, Jonathan I, 1059
Robards, Jonathan I, 1063
Robards, Mary I, 1059
Robards, Mary I, 1063
Robards, Maryann VI, 338
Robards, Matilda VI, 329
Robards, Matilda VI, 338
Robards, Phebe V, 115
Robards, Rebecah I, 1037
Robards, Rebecca V, 115
Robards, Samuel VI, 338
Robards, Sarah V, 115
Robards, Solomon V, 115
Robards, Thomas I, 1037
Robards, Thomas I, 1039
Robards, Thomas V, 115
Robards, Walter I, 1037
Robards, Walter V, 115
Robards, Whitson V, 115
Robards, William VI, 338
Robards, Zalinda VI, 338
Robarts, Ann V, 70
Robarts, Ann V, 275
Robarts, John V, 275
Robarts, Moses V, 275
Robarts, Rebecca V, 70
Robarts, Rebecca V, 115
Robarts, Thomas V, 70
Robb, Ann Eliza IV, 270
Robb, Ann Eliza IV, 290
Robb, Ann Eliza IV, 314
Robb, Jennie IV, 495
Robb, Theo IV, 1182
Robberman, Caroline IV, 654
Robberman, Charlotte IV, 654
Robberman, Hallena IV, 654
Robberman, Helena IV, 654
Robberman, Hellena IV, 654
Robberman, Henry IV, 654
Robberman, Henry D. IV, 654
Robberman, Henry, Jr. IV, 654
Robberman, Henry, Sr. IV, 654
Robberman, Lewis N. IV, 654
Robberman, Lewis W. IV, 654
Robberman, Mary IV, 654
Robberts, Abraham VI, 438
Robberts, Griffith VI, 438
Robberts, Lyddia VI, 438

rts, Lydia A. V, 275
rts, Rachel VI, 438
rts, Rebecca VI, 438
nett, Thos. V, 642
ns, ??? III, 498
ns, Abbie I, 948
ns, Abigail I, 948
ns, Abigail III, 385
ns, Abigail III, 439
ns, Abigail III, 470
ns, Abigail III, 495
ns, Abigail III, 506
ns, Abigail R. I, 934
ns, Albert A. I, 933
ns, Alexander I, 752
ns, Alexander I, 769
ns, Alexander I, 899
ns, Alexander S. I, 864
ns, Alexander S. I, 899
ins, Alice III, 270
ins, Almeda I, 732
ins, Almira I, 865
ins, Almy III, 439
ins, Amelia III, 471
ins, Angelina III, 270
ins, Ann II, 1023
ins, Ann Eliza III, 440
ins, Anna W. III, 495
ins, Anne III, 440
ins, Annette Rosalie VI, 757
ns, Annette Rosalie VI, 773
ins, Annie H. III, 495
ins, Annie H. III, 496
ins, Augustus W. III, 495
ns, Bathsheba V, 975
ins, Benjamin III, 495
ins, Caroline III, 486
ins, Caroline III, 495
ins, Carrie J. III, 495
ins, Carrie J. III, 496
ins, Carrie J. III, 502
ins, Charles Allen III, 269
ins, Charles W. III, 440
ins, Charles W. III, 495
ins, Clara III, 269
ins, Clara III, 270
ins, Claudia Abigail I, 933
ins, Cora III, 490
ins, Cora S. III, 495
ins, Cora S. III, 496
ins, Cornelia III, 482
ins, Cornelia III, 495
ins, Daniel III, 427
ins, Daniel III, 439
ins, Daniel III, 440
ins, Daniel C. III, 269
ins, Daniel, Jr. III, 439
ins, David S. I, 864
ins, David Yancey I, 899
ins, Deborah III, 269
ins, Derisa V, 1016
ins, Edith P. III, 269
ins, Edith P. III, 270
ins, Edward III, 270
ins, Edward III, 439
ins, Edward III, 440
ins, Edward III, 454
ins, Edward III, 482
ins, Edward III, 495
ins, Edward III, 496
ins, Edward III, 500
ins, Edward G. III, 495
ins, Edwin III, 270
ins, Edwin III, 495
ins, Elihu IV, 593
ins, Elihu IV, 1075
ins, Elisabeth II, 638
ins, Eliz. III, 43
ins, Eliz. III, 440
ins, Eliz. Ann III, 269
ins, Eliza I, 885
ins, Eliza I, 899
ins, Eliza Ann III, 256
ins, Eliza E. I, 865
ins, Eliza E. I, 899
ins, Elizabeth I, 899
ins, Elizabeth III, 74
ins, Elizabeth III, 110
ins, Elizabeth III, 269
ins, Elizabeth III, 270
ins, Elizabeth III, 397
ins, Elizabeth III, 400
ins, Elizabeth III, 401
ins, Elizabeth III, 421
ins, Elizabeth III, 427
ins, Elizabeth III, 439
ins, Elizabeth III, 440
ins, Elizabeth III, 441
ins, Elizabeth III, 460
ins, Elizabeth III, 468
ins, Elizabeth III, 472
Robbins, Elizabeth III, 485
Robbins, Elizabeth III, 495
Robbins, Elizabeth III, 496
Robbins, Elizabeth III, 504
Robbins, Elizabeth III, 505
Robbins, Elizabeth III, 506
Robbins, Elizabeth V, 763
Robbins, Elizabeth Ann III, 270
Robbins, Elizabeth Ann III, 440
Robbins, Ella III, 269
Robbins, Ella III, 270
Robbins, Ella III, 362
Robbins, Ella III, 486
Robbins, Ella III, 487
Robbins, Ella III, 495
Robbins, Ella A. III, 486
Robbins, Elliot III, 440
Robbins, Elliott III, 270
Robbins, Elliott Daniel VI, 757
Robbins, Elliott Daniel VI, 773
Robbins, Elmidia I, 732
Robbins, Elmira M. I, 899
Robbins, Emily III, 439
Robbins, Emily III, 440
Robbins, Emily W. III, 441
Robbins, Ernest III, 269
Robbins, Esther III, 270
Robbins, Esther III, 421
Robbins, Esther III, 434
Robbins, Esther III, 439
Robbins, Esther III, 440
Robbins, Esther III, 485
Robbins, Esther III, 493
Robbins, Esther III, 495
Robbins, Esther III, 496
Robbins, Esther III, 497
Robbins, Esther G. III, 480
Robbins, Esther G. III, 495
Robbins, Esther G. III, 496
Robbins, Esther G. III, 499
Robbins, Esther P. III, 485
Robbins, Esther P. III, 495
Robbins, Etta I, 948
Robbins, Eugene III, 495
Robbins, Eugene F. III, 479
Robbins, Eugene F. III, 495
Robbins, Eugene S. III, 486
Robbins, Flora I, 948
Robbins, Florry L. I, 933
Robbins, Forman III, 270
Robbins, Forman III, 440
Robbins, Forman C. III, 269
Robbins, Forman C. III, 440
Robbins, Franklin M. III, 495
Robbins, Furman C. II, 763
Robbins, George VI, 981
Robbins, Gulielma III, 440
Robbins, Hannah II, 447
Robbins, Hannah III, 74
Robbins, Hannah III, 110
Robbins, Hannah III, 269
Robbins, Hannah III, 270
Robbins, Hannah III, 354
Robbins, Hannah III, 399
Robbins, Hannah III, 400
Robbins, Hannah III, 402
Robbins, Hannah III, 439
Robbins, Hannah III, 440
Robbins, Hannah III, 448
Robbins, Hannah III, 453
Robbins, Hannah III, 495
Robbins, Hannah III, 496
Robbins, Hannah III, 497
Robbins, Hannah III, 505
Robbins, Hannah C. III, 421
Robbins, Hannah C. III, 439
Robbins, Hannah C. III, 485
Robbins, Hannah M. III, 269
Robbins, Hannah S. III, 486
Robbins, Hannah S. III, 495
Robbins, Hannah W. III, 270
Robbins, Harriet III, 256
Robbins, Harriet III, 269
Robbins, Harriet III, 270
Robbins, Harriet III, 409
Robbins, Harriet III, 440
Robbins, Herbert Daniel III, 269
Robbins, Huldah I, 769
Robbins, Iona Mae IV, 989
Robbins, Iredell I, 732
Robbins, Isaac III, 439
Robbins, J. T. I, 732
Robbins, J. W. III, 479
Robbins, J. W. III, 495
Robbins, J. Wesley I, 948
Robbins, Jacob III, 439
Robbins, Jacob III, 440
Robbins, Jacob III, 495
Robbins, Jacob III, 506
Robbins, James I, 865
Robbins, James I, 899
Robbins, James III, 439
Robbins, Jane II, 568
Robbins, Jane II, 638
Robbins, Jane III, 439
Robbins, Jane III, 440
Robbins, Jane III, 444
Robbins, Jennie T. II, 1078
Robbins, Jennie T. II, 1082
Robbins, Jere. III, 439
Robbins, Jere. III, 440
Robbins, Jeremiah III, 74
Robbins, Jeremiah III, 269
Robbins, Jeremiah III, 399
Robbins, Jeremiah III, 400
Robbins, Jeremiah III, 401
Robbins, Jeremiah III, 402
Robbins, Jeremiah III, 439
Robbins, Jeremiah III, 440
Robbins, Jeremiah III, 448
Robbins, Jeremiah III, 453
Robbins, Jeremiah III, 495
Robbins, Jessie Anna III, 269
Robbins, Job III, 439
Robbins, John II, 1023
Robbins, John III, 269
Robbins, John III, 398
Robbins, John III, 439
Robbins, John III, 440
Robbins, John III, 444
Robbins, John III, 495
Robbins, John Elliott III, 269
Robbins, John, Jr. III, 440
Robbins, Joseph I, 688
Robbins, Joseph I, 914
Robbins, Joseph II, 414
Robbins, Joseph II, 638
Robbins, Joseph II, 1078
Robbins, Joseph II, 1082
Robbins, Joshua D. I, 933
Robbins, Joshua D. I, 934
Robbins, Josiah III, 440
Robbins, Josie I, 899
Robbins, Julia III, 440
Robbins, Julia III, 495
Robbins, Julia III, 496
Robbins, Katherine III, 230
Robbins, Katherine III, 270
Robbins, Laura I, 899
Robbins, Laura A. I, 864
Robbins, Lavina I, 914
Robbins, Lettins II, 414
Robbins, Levina I, 914
Robbins, Louisa Matilda III, 269
Robbins, Mabel III, 269
Robbins, Margaret III, 423
Robbins, Margaret III, 440
Robbins, Margaret J. III, 440
Robbins, Margaret S. III, 269
Robbins, Maria III, 269
Robbins, Marian VI, 662
Robbins, Marion VI, 757
Robbins, Marion VI, 773
Robbins, Martha I, 613
Robbins, Martha III, 444
Robbins, Martha A. I, 899
Robbins, Martha C. III, 495
Robbins, Martha J. V, 357
Robbins, Martha M. I, 865
Robbins, Martha M. I, 899
Robbins, Martin I, 899
Robbins, Martin V. I, 864
Robbins, Martin V. I, 899
Robbins, Mary I, 899
Robbins, Mary I, 914
Robbins, Mary III, 43
Robbins, Mary III, 269
Robbins, Mary III, 270
Robbins, Mary III, 440
Robbins, Mary III, 448
Robbins, Mary III, 471
Robbins, Mary III, 495
Robbins, Mary III, 496
Robbins, Mary III, 499
Robbins, Mary III, 506
Robbins, Mary IV, 614
Robbins, Mary IV, 654
Robbins, Mary IV, 755
Robbins, Mary VI, 981
Robbins, Mary Ann IV, 593
Robbins, Mary Ann IV, 1075
Robbins, Mary E. III, 416
Robbins, Mary E. III, 440
Robbins, Mary G. I, 865
Robbins, Mary G. I, 899
Robbins, Mary H. III, 440
Robbins, Mary Isabel III, 440
Robbins, Mary J. I, 934
Robbins, Mary Jane I, 933
Robbins, Mary K. III, 440
Robbins, Mary K. III, 460
Robbins, Mary W. III, 434
Robbins, Mary W. III, 440
Robbins, Mary W. III, 493
Robbins, Matilda L. III, 269
Robbins, Matthew III, 486
Robbins, Matthew III, 497
Robbins, Matthew F. III, 486
Robbins, Matthew F. III, 495
Robbins, Matthew Franklin III, 270
Robbins, McKinley I, 948
Robbins, Milton III, 230
Robbins, Milton III, 270
Robbins, Miriam I, 899
Robbins, Miriam III, 440
Robbins, Miriam III, 444
Robbins, Miriam III, 495
Robbins, Miriam III, 496
Robbins, Miriam III, 498
Robbins, Miriam III, 506
Robbins, Miriam IV, 593
Robbins, Nancy I, 732
Robbins, Nathan I, 899
Robbins, Nellie O. IV, 1335
Robbins, Notra Gertrude I, 933
Robbins, Notra Gertrude I, 948
Robbins, Ollie C. I, 948
Robbins, Ona Mae IV, 989
Robbins, Phebe III, 486
Robbins, Phebe III, 495
Robbins, Phebe III, 504
Robbins, Phebe Ann III, 440
Robbins, Phebe T. III, 495
Robbins, Rachel III, 454
Robbins, Rachel W. III, 270
Robbins, Rachel W. III, 439
Robbins, Rachel W. III, 454
Robbins, Rachel W. III, 482
Robbins, Rachel W. III, 495
Robbins, Rachel W. III, 500
Robbins, Rebecca T. III, 440
Robbins, Rebecka II, 414
Robbins, Richard III, 486
Robbins, Richard H. III, 423
Robbins, Richard H. III, 440
Robbins, Rosanna M. I, 899
Robbins, Rosannia M. I, 865
Robbins, Rose I, 891
Robbins, Rose I, 899
Robbins, Roseannah III, 400
Robbins, Rowland III, 495
Robbins, Russell Frost III, 269
Robbins, Sallie III, 440
Robbins, Sally Ann III, 479
Robbins, Sally Ann III, 495
Robbins, Sam'l III, 256
Robbins, Samira E. I, 732
Robbins, Samuel II, 414
Robbins, Samuel III, 43
Robbins, Samuel III, 269
Robbins, Samuel III, 270
Robbins, Samuel III, 400
Robbins, Samuel III, 409
Robbins, Samuel III, 439
Robbins, Samuel III, 440
Robbins, Samuel III, 495
Robbins, Samuel III, 504
Robbins, Sarah I, 933
Robbins, Sarah II, 638
Robbins, Sarah III, 126
Robbins, Sarah III, 270
Robbins, Sarah III, 398
Robbins, Sarah III, 439
Robbins, Sarah III, 440
Robbins, Sarah III, 453
Robbins, Sarah III, 495
Robbins, Sarah A. II, 1078
Robbins, Sarah A. II, 1082
Robbins, Sarah E. III, 270
Robbins, Sarah E. III, 485
Robbins, Sarah E. III, 490
Robbins, Sarah E. III, 495
Robbins, Sarah E. III, 496
Robbins, Sarah E. III, 502
Robbins, Sarah Elizabeth III, 440
Robbins, Scudder III, 495
Robbins, Silas T. III, 269
Robbins, Silas T. III, 270
Robbins, Silas T. III, 282
Robbins, Silas T. III, 362
Robbins, Silas T. III, 495
Robbins, Silas T., Jr. III, 270
Robbins, Stephen III, 439
Robbins, Stephen III, 440
Robbins, Stephen III, 444
Robbins, Stephen III, 471
Robbins, Stephen III, 480
Robbins, Stephen III, 495
Robbins, Stephen III, 496
Robbins, Stephen III, 499
Robbins, Stephen III, 506
Robbins, Susan III, 270
Robbins, Susan H. III, 269
Robbins, Susan H. III, 270
Robbins, Susan H. III, 282
Robbins, Susan H. III, 362
Robbins, T. III, 495
Robbins, Thomas II, 414
Robbins, Thomas IV, 593
Robbins, Thos. Franklyn III, 440
Robbins, Valentine III, 270
Robbins, Valentine III, 440
Robbins, Violet I, 928
Robbins, Walter III, 440
Robbins, Walter III, 485
Robbins, Walter III, 490
Robbins, Walter III, 495
Robbins, Walter III, 496
Robbins, Walter III, 502
Robbins, Willet III, 270
Robbins, Willet III, 354
Robbins, Willet III, 434
Robbins, Willet III, 439
Robbins, Willet III, 440
Robbins, Willet III, 493
Robbins, Willet III, 495
Robbins, Willet III, 496
Robbins, Willet III, 497
Robbins, Willet S. III, 270
Robbins, Willet S. III, 495
Robbins, Willet S. III, 496
Robbins, Willett III, 270
Robbins, William I, 899
Robbins, William II, 414
Robbins, William III, 269
Robbins, William III, 439
Robbins, William III, 485
Robbins, William III, 495
Robbins, William III, 505
Robbins, William B. III, 440
Robbins, William C. III, 270
Robbins, William H. III, 495
Robbins, William M. III, 269
Robbins, William M. III, 270
Robbins, William M. III, 440
Robbins, William S. III, 270
Robbins, William S. III, 440
Robbins, William S. III, 496
Robbins, Willie E. III, 440
Robbins, Wm. B. III, 416
Robbins, Wm. B. III, 440
Robbins, Wm. J. III, 496
Robbins, Wm. M. III, 269
Robbins, Wm. M. III, 397
Robbins, Wm. S. III, 421
Robbins, Wm. S. III, 439
Robbins, Wm. S. III, 440
Robbins, Wm. S. III, 441
Robbins, Wm. S. III, 460
Robbins, Wm. S. III, 468
Robbins, Wm. S. III, 496
Robbins, Yancy I, 899
Robbins, Zacheriah IV, 1075
Robbins, Zacheriah H. IV, 593
Robbinson, John I, 70
Robens, John II, 414
Robenson, Abner I, 514
Robenson, Abner I, 569
Robenson, Ann I, 514
Robenson, Elizabeth I, 514
Robenson, Hannah I, 514
Robenson, Hannah I, 1012
Robenson, James I, 514
Robenson, James I, 1012
Robenson, Jehu I, 514
Robenson, Jehu I, 1012
Robenson, John I, 514
Robenson, John I, 569
Robenson, John I, 1012
Robenson, John, Sr. I, 1012
Robenson, Joshua I, 514
Robenson, Joshua I, 1012
Robenson, Levina I, 1012
Robenson, Lydia I, 514
Robenson, Lydia Ann VI, 439
Robenson, Mary I, 514
Robenson, Mary I, 549
Robenson, Mary I, 1012
Robenson, Nicholas I, 514
Robenson, Rachel I, 514
Robenson, Rebecca II, 638
Robenson, Richard II, 17
Robenson, Ruth I, 514
Robenson, Thomas I, 514
Robenson, William I, 514
Robenson, William I, 549
Robenson, William I, 569
Roberdes, John VI, 266
Roberds, Ann I, 1058
Roberds, Ann I, 1063
Roberds, Ann V, 199
Roberds, Ann V, 200
Roberds, Ann V, 858

Roberds, Asenath V, 200
Roberds, Asseneth I, 1062
Roberds, Asseneth I, 1063
Roberds, Bethula V, 873
Roberds, David I, 1058
Roberds, David V, 199
Roberds, Eleanor II, 637
Roberds, Esther I, 1063
Roberds, Hannah I, 1062
Roberds, Hannah I, 1063
Roberds, John I, 1063
Roberds, John V, 829
Roberds, Jonathan I, 1062
Roberds, Jonathan V, 873
Roberds, Mary I, 1060
Roberds, Mary I, 1063
Roberds, Mary IV, 1182
Roberds, Mary V, 194
Roberds, Mary V, 200
Roberds, Mary V, 842
Roberds, Mary V, 858
Roberds, Mary V, 873
Roberds, Rebecah I, 1058
Roberds, Rebecca V, 829
Roberds, Rebecca V, 849
Roberds, Rebecca V, 858
Roberds, Rebeckah V, 199
Roberds, Rebekah I, 1058
Roberds, Rebekah I, 1063
Roberds, Sarah I, 1063
Roberds, Thomas I, 1058
Roberds, Thomas I, 1062
Roberds, Thomas I, 1063
Roberds, Thomas V, 194
Roberds, Thomas V, 199
Roberds, Thomas V, 200
Roberds, Thomas V, 858
Roberds, Thomas V, 859
Roberds, Walter I, 1058
Roberds, Walter I, 1062
Roberds, Walter V, 199
Roberds, Walter V, 842
Roberds, Walter V, 858
Roberman, Caroline IV, 654
Roberman, Helena IV, 654
Roberman, Henry IV, 654
Roberman, Henry D. IV, 654
Roberman, Lewis N. IV, 654
Roberman, Mary IV, 654
Roberson, Abigale I, 274
Roberson, Ann VI, 139
Roberson, Ann VI, 141
Roberson, Anna Stanton I, 274
Roberson, Caroline I, 274
Roberson, Dolph A. I, 625
Roberson, Elizabeth I, 274
Roberson, Elizabeth VI, 910
Roberson, Fannie I, 625
Roberson, Gabriel I, 199
Roberson, George B. I, 625
Roberson, George B., Jr. I, 625
Roberson, Hannah I, 274
Roberson, Harry I, 640
Roberson, John I, 569
Roberson, John VI, 910
Roberson, M.D. George B. I, 640
Roberson, Mayson VI, 1021
Roberson, Mrs. G. B. I, 640
Roberson, Myrtle I, 625
Roberson, Orland W. IV, 1335
Roberson, Penina I, 274
Roberson, Ruth Harris I, 274
Roberson, Sophronia I, 209
Robert, ??? V, 823
Robert, Elizabeth II, 503
Robert, Gerard VI, 6
Robert, John V, 859
Robert, John VI, 266
Robert, Mary I, 569
Roberta, Robert III, 261
Roberta, Teressa III, 222
Roberts, ??? II, 447
Roberts, ??? IV, 547
Roberts, ??? VI, 293
Roberts, ??? VI, 447
Roberts, A. Alexander VI, 438
Roberts, Aaron IV, 200
Roberts, Aaron IV, 270
Roberts, Aaron IV, 325
Roberts, Aaron IV, 339
Roberts, Aaron IV, 349
Roberts, Aaron IV, 353
Roberts, Aaron IV, 432
Roberts, Aaron IV, 547
Roberts, Aaron IV, 1113
Roberts, Aaron IV, 1212
Roberts, Aaron IV, 1221
Roberts, Aaron Reuben IV, 1221
Roberts, Abel IV, 270
Roberts, Abel IV, 349
Roberts, Abel V, 310
Roberts, Abel V, 357
Roberts, Abel V, 429
Roberts, Abel V, 642
Roberts, Abel, Jr. V, 310
Roberts, Abigail III, 271
Roberts, Abigail IV, 915
Roberts, Abigail A. II, 763
Roberts, Abigail A. II, 769
Roberts, Abigail A. VI, 773
Roberts, Abigail A. VI, 786
Roberts, Abigail Ann II, 716
Roberts, Abigail Ann II, 749
Roberts, Abigail Ann II, 763
Roberts, Abigail Brick II, 817
Roberts, Able IV, 270
Roberts, Abraham II, 413
Roberts, Abraham II, 637
Roberts, Abraham IV, 102
Roberts, Abraham IV, 107
Roberts, Abraham IV, 270
Roberts, Abraham V, 275
Roberts, Abraham V, 310
Roberts, Abraham VI, 438
Roberts, Achsah A. VI, 773
Roberts, Agnes IV, 270
Roberts, Agnes IV, 349
Roberts, Agnes Haines II, 800
Roberts, Agness IV, 237
Roberts, Agness IV, 270
Roberts, Alban II, 636
Roberts, Albert IV, 1240
Roberts, Albert V, 859
Roberts, Albert C. II, 817
Roberts, Albert C. II, 861
Roberts, Albert C. II, 915
Roberts, Albert S. V, 859
Roberts, Albert S. V, 860
Roberts, Albina N. II, 1023
Roberts, Albina N. II, 1059
Roberts, Alena V. IV, 496
Roberts, Alfred III, 270
Roberts, Alfred C. III, 270
Roberts, Alfred H. VI, 417
Roberts, Alfred H. VI, 774
Roberts, Alfred Jas. III, 270
Roberts, Alice II, 137
Roberts, Alice II, 156
Roberts, Alice II, 940
Roberts, Alice IV, 1335
Roberts, Alice VI, 695
Roberts, Alice VI, 985
Roberts, Alice VI, 1019
Roberts, Alice A. VI, 773
Roberts, Alice M. II, 812
Roberts, Alice M. II, 906
Roberts, Allen I, 625
Roberts, Allen II, 413
Roberts, Allen II, 637
Roberts, Allen II, 638
Roberts, Almira II, 811
Roberts, Almira II, 820
Roberts, Almira II, 915
Roberts, Almira IV, 1171
Roberts, Almira IV, 1182
Roberts, Alonzo Frazee V, 859
Roberts, Alonzo J. V, 860
Roberts, Alpheus V, 859
Roberts, Alpheus V, 860
Roberts, Alta Bertha V, 859
Roberts, Alva III, 271
Roberts, Alvadare V, 860
Roberts, Alvadore V, 859
Roberts, Alvadore V, 860
Roberts, Alvadore Hornaday V, 859
Roberts, Amanda IV, 496
Roberts, Amos II, 636
Roberts, Amos II, 638
Roberts, Amos II, 716
Roberts, Amos IV, 547
Roberts, Amy IV, 349
Roberts, Ann I, 1037
Roberts, Ann I, 1062
Roberts, Ann I, 1063
Roberts, Ann II, 122
Roberts, Ann II, 123
Roberts, Ann II, 413
Roberts, Ann II, 414
Roberts, Ann II, 506
Roberts, Ann II, 634
Roberts, Ann II, 635
Roberts, Ann II, 636
Roberts, Ann II, 637
Roberts, Ann II, 640
Roberts, Ann II, 673
Roberts, Ann II, 763
Roberts, Ann IV, 158
Roberts, Ann IV, 270
Roberts, Ann IV, 333
Roberts, Ann IV, 349
Roberts, Ann IV, 562
Roberts, Ann IV, 1182
Roberts, Ann IV, 1221
Roberts, Ann V, 115
Roberts, Ann V, 275
Roberts, Ann V, 310
Roberts, Ann V, 312
Roberts, Ann V, 858
Roberts, Ann V, 859
Roberts, Ann VI, 478
Roberts, Ann VI, 553
Roberts, Ann VI, 773
Roberts, Ann VI, 985
Roberts, Ann J. II, 1055
Roberts, Ann Sophia II, 861
Roberts, Ann Sophia II, 915
Roberts, Anna II, 413
Roberts, Anna II, 716
Roberts, Anna II, 817
Roberts, Anna II, 870
Roberts, Anna II, 916
Roberts, Anna II, 968
Roberts, Anna II, 1023
Roberts, Anna III, 270
Roberts, Anna III, 361
Roberts, Anna IV, 237
Roberts, Anna IV, 349
Roberts, Anna IV, 353
Roberts, Anna IV, 547
Roberts, Anna IV, 1221
Roberts, Anna IV, 1224
Roberts, Anna B. III, 270
Roberts, Anna C. III, 49
Roberts, Anna C. III, 270
Roberts, Anna Eliza VI, 730
Roberts, Anna Eliza VI, 773
Roberts, Anna Eliza VI, 774
Roberts, Anna L. II, 968
Roberts, Anna Lovett II, 1061
Roberts, Anna M. II, 916
Roberts, Anna M. II, 920
Roberts, Anna Margaret, Jr. II, 817
Roberts, Anna Maria II, 716
Roberts, Anna Maria II, 762
Roberts, Anna Maria VI, 773
Roberts, Anna Miller VI, 774
Roberts, Anna Shaw II, 817
Roberts, Anne II, 636
Roberts, Anne II, 637
Roberts, Annie I, 621
Roberts, Annie II, 817
Roberts, Annoca VI, 850
Roberts, Aquila II, 414
Roberts, Aquila II, 636
Roberts, Aquilla II, 413
Roberts, Archibald VI, 136
Roberts, Archibald VI, 138
Roberts, Archibald VI, 139
Roberts, Archibald VI, 140
Roberts, Asa II, 817
Roberts, Asa II, 870
Roberts, Asa II, 916
Roberts, Asa IV, 1377
Roberts, Asenah VI, 438
Roberts, Asenath V, 642
Roberts, Asenath VI, 438
Roberts, Ashton II, 1023
Roberts, Asseneth I, 1063
Roberts, Aubrey II, 636
Roberts, Avis Jane IV, 1212
Roberts, Avis Jane IV, 1221
Roberts, Awbrey II, 601
Roberts, Awbrey II, 636
Roberts, Bathsheba II, 827
Roberts, Benjamin VI, 850
Roberts, Benjamin VI, 985
Roberts, Benjamin Hallowell VI, 773
Roberts, Benoni IV, 107
Roberts, Bertha V, 860
Roberts, Bertha Lee V, 860
Roberts, Bessie V, 855
Roberts, Bessie V, 859
Roberts, Bessie V, 860
Roberts, Bessie VI, 695
Roberts, Bethulah V, 115
Roberts, Bethulah V, 858
Roberts, Betsey VI, 850
Roberts, Betsey J. V, 429
Roberts, Betsy H. VI, 850
Roberts, Betty V, 226
Roberts, Betty J. V, 400
Roberts, Betty J. V, 429
Roberts, Beula IV, 432
Roberts, Beulah IV, 270
Roberts, Beulah IV, 349
Roberts, Beulah IV, 378
Roberts, Beulah IV, 547
Roberts, Beulah IV, 574
Roberts, Beulah IV, 1221
Roberts, Beulah R. IV, 378
Roberts, Blanch IV, 1221
Roberts, Bradford II, 636
Roberts, C. Dewitt V, 860
Roberts, Caleb II, 968
Roberts, Caleb C. II, 413
Roberts, Caleb C. II, 763
Roberts, Caleb H. VI, 774
Roberts, Caleb P. II, 968
Roberts, Caleb P. II, 1059
Roberts, Caleb Pancoast II, 1055
Roberts, Caroline I, 613
Roberts, Caroline II, 916
Roberts, Caroline III, 270
Roberts, Caroline V, 115
Roberts, Caroline French II, 827
Roberts, Caroline M. II, 850
Roberts, Caroline M. II, 916
Roberts, Carrie Annetta V, 115
Roberts, Catharine II, 413
Roberts, Catharine II, 414
Roberts, Catharine II, 481
Roberts, Catharine II, 505
Roberts, Catharine II, 533
Roberts, Catharine II, 636
Roberts, Catharine II, 637
Roberts, Catharine II, 638
Roberts, Catharine VI, 553
Roberts, Catherine II, 637
Roberts, Catherine VI, 546
Roberts, Catherine VI, 850
Roberts, Charles I, 625
Roberts, Charles I, 640
Roberts, Charles II, 156
Roberts, Charles II, 413
Roberts, Charles II, 414
Roberts, Charles II, 637
Roberts, Charles II, 638
Roberts, Charles II, 684
Roberts, Charles II, 716
Roberts, Charles II, 762
Roberts, Charles II, 763
Roberts, Charles II, 968
Roberts, Charles II, 1059
Roberts, Charles IV, 270
Roberts, Charles IV, 349
Roberts, Charles IV, 1182
Roberts, Charles IV, 1221
Roberts, Charles V, 274
Roberts, Charles V, 275
Roberts, Charles B. II, 1023
Roberts, Charles B. II, 1059
Roberts, Charles Dewitt V, 859
Roberts, Charles DeWitt V, 860
Roberts, Charles Elihu II, 716
Roberts, Charles F. V, 859
Roberts, Charles F. V, 860
Roberts, Charles H. II, 137
Roberts, Charles H. II, 156
Roberts, Charles H. II, 414
Roberts, Charles H. II, 638
Roberts, Charles H. II, 716
Roberts, Charles H. V, 115
Roberts, Charles H. VI, 773
Roberts, Charles R. VI, 771
Roberts, Charles R. VI, 773
Roberts, Charles Rubicam VI, 773
Roberts, Charles Rubicam VI, 777
Roberts, Charles Rubicam VI, 784
Roberts, Charles W. II, 1059
Roberts, Charles William II, 968
Roberts, Charley D. V, 275
Roberts, Charlotte VI, 900
Roberts, Chas. II, 122
Roberts, Chas. II, 123
Roberts, Chas. II, 638
Roberts, Chas. II, 808
Roberts, Chas. IV, 1214
Roberts, Chas. D. IV, 1335
Roberts, Chas. H. II, 915
Roberts, Chester II, 916
Roberts, Chester V, 860
Roberts, Chester E. V, 859
Roberts, Christan VI, 919
Roberts, Clara V, 859
Roberts, Clara B. V, 860
Roberts, Clarence M. IV, 496
Roberts, Clarissa IV, 915
Roberts, Clarissa IV, 1377
Roberts, Clauda V, 707
Roberts, Clayton II, 299
Roberts, Clayton II, 324
Roberts, Col. Winney VI, 822
Roberts, Curtis Boswell V, 859
Roberts, Curtis S. V, 859
Roberts, Cynthia IV, 1221
Roberts, Cynthia IV, 1377
Roberts, Daisy IV, 1182
Roberts, Daniel II, 414
Roberts, Daniel II, 637
Roberts, Daniel VI, 895
Roberts, David II, 413
Roberts, David II, 414
Roberts, David II, 1023
Roberts, David II, 1059
Roberts, David III, 270
Roberts, David V, 115
Roberts, David VI, 850
Roberts, David VI, 964
Roberts, David VI, 970
Roberts, David, Jr. II, 725
Roberts, David, Jr. II, 763
Roberts, Deborah II, 637
Roberts, Deborah II, 638
Roberts, Deborah II, 677
Roberts, Deborah II, 763
Roberts, Deborah II, 915
Roberts, Deborah II, 968
Roberts, Deborah D. II, 638
Roberts, Deborah H. II, 716
Roberts, Deborah H. II, 763
Roberts, Deborah W. II, 1059
Roberts, Delilah V, 852
Roberts, Delilah V, 853
Roberts, Delilah V, 858
Roberts, Delilah A. V, 853
Roberts, Delilah A. V, 859
Roberts, Donald A. III, 108
Roberts, Donald Alfred III, 2
Roberts, Edie II, 414
Roberts, Edith VI, 857
Roberts, Edith Adeline III, 2
Roberts, Edna V, 860
Roberts, Edw. C. III, 206
Roberts, Edward II, 413
Roberts, Edward II, 414
Roberts, Edward II, 468
Roberts, Edward II, 480
Roberts, Edward II, 496
Roberts, Edward II, 636
Roberts, Edward II, 637
Roberts, Edward II, 695
Roberts, Edward II, 762
Roberts, Edward III, 270
Roberts, Edward VI, 773
Roberts, Edward C. III, 225
Roberts, Edward C. III, 270
Roberts, Edward C. III, 271
Roberts, Edward H. II, 915
Roberts, Edwin II, 763
Roberts, Edwin II, 817
Roberts, Edwin II, 850
Roberts, Edwin II, 916
Roberts, Edwin V, 859
Roberts, Eleanor II, 637
Roberts, Eleanor II, 659
Roberts, Eleanor III, 225
Roberts, Eleanor III, 270
Roberts, Eleanor IV, 270
Roberts, Eleanor IV, 349
Roberts, Eleanor V, 310
Roberts, Eleanor V, 357
Roberts, Eleanor V, 429
Roberts, Eleanor VI, 553
Roberts, Eleanor L. II, 763
Roberts, Eleanor L. II, 772
Roberts, Eleanor M. III, 206
Roberts, Eleanor M. III, 271
Roberts, Elenor IV, 270
Roberts, Elenor V, 642
Roberts, Elias V, 274
Roberts, Elias V, 275
Roberts, Elihu II, 122
Roberts, Elihu II, 123
Roberts, Elihu II, 413
Roberts, Elihu II, 716
Roberts, Elihu II, 763
Roberts, Elihu V, 858
Roberts, Elihu V, 859
Roberts, Elihu H. V, 859
Roberts, Elisabeth I, 69
Roberts, Elisabeth I, 70
Roberts, Elisha II, 725
Roberts, Elisha II, 763
Roberts, Elisha IV, 1377
Roberts, Eliza II, 1023
Roberts, Eliza II, 1059
Roberts, Eliza Ann IV, 270
Roberts, Eliza Ann V, 859
Roberts, Eliza Jane V, 850
Roberts, Eliza Jane V, 858
Roberts, Eliza Jane V, 859
Roberts, Eliza Matilda II, 102
Roberts, Eliza Walker VI, 774
Roberts, Elizabeth I, 1075
Roberts, Elizabeth II, 309
Roberts, Elizabeth II, 324
Roberts, Elizabeth II, 414
Roberts, Elizabeth II, 458
Roberts, Elizabeth II, 478

rts, Elizabeth II, 481
rts, Elizabeth II, 485
rts, Elizabeth II, 502
rts, Elizabeth II, 505
rts, Elizabeth II, 539
rts, Elizabeth II, 600
rts, Elizabeth II, 616
rts, Elizabeth II, 635
rts, Elizabeth II, 636
rts, Elizabeth II, 637
rts, Elizabeth II, 649
rts, Elizabeth II, 738
rts, Elizabeth II, 820
rts, Elizabeth II, 870
rts, Elizabeth II, 915
rts, Elizabeth II, 916
rts, Elizabeth II, 1023
rts, Elizabeth II, 1059
rts, Elizabeth IV, 102
rts, Elizabeth IV, 107
rts, Elizabeth IV, 270
rts, Elizabeth IV, 276
rts, Elizabeth IV, 325
rts, Elizabeth IV, 339
rts, Elizabeth IV, 349
rts, Elizabeth IV, 353
rts, Elizabeth IV, 380
rts, Elizabeth IV, 432
rts, Elizabeth IV, 547
rts, Elizabeth IV, 1113
rts, Elizabeth IV, 1115
rts, Elizabeth IV, 1212
rts, Elizabeth IV, 1221
rts, Elizabeth V, 226
rts, Elizabeth V, 275
rts, Elizabeth V, 859
rts, Elizabeth VI, 329
rts, Elizabeth VI, 338
rts, Elizabeth VI, 530
rts, Elizabeth VI, 553
rts, Elizabeth VI, 764
rts, Elizabeth VI, 795
rts, Elizabeth VI, 850
rts, Elizabeth VI, 851
rts, Elizabeth VI, 970
erts, Elizabeth Ann IV, 312
erts, Elizabeth Ann IV, 314
erts, Elizabeth B. V, 859
erts, Elizabeth H. II, 861
erts, Elizabeth H. II, 915
erts, Elizabeth Hill II, 817
erts, Elizabeth Jr. IV, 1221
erts, Elizabeth K. II, 716
erts, Elizabeth K. II, 763
erts, Elizabeth K. II, 769
erts, Elizabeth L. II, 725
erts, Elizabeth L. II, 763
erts, Elizabeth M. II, 789
erts, Elizabeth M. III, 270
erts, Elizabeth P. V, 958
erts, Elizabeth S. II, 324
erts, Elizabeth W. II, 725
erts, Elizabeth W. II, 763
erts, Elizabeth W. III, 270
erts, Elizabeth W. III, 356
erts, Elizabeth Wolf V, 464
erts, Elizabeth, Jr. IV, 107
erts, Elizabeth, Jr. IV, 349
erts, Ella M. IV, 496
erts, Ellen II, 636
erts, Ellen II, 916
erts, Ellen VI, 85
erts, Ellen Gertrude II, 817
erts, Ellen T. II, 916
erts, Elliott VI, 985
erts, Ellis II, 636
erts, Ellwood III, 270
erts, Ellwood Walter III, 271
erts, Elonette V, 707
erts, Elsie V, 859
erts, Elsie V, 860
erts, Elsie Palmer VI, 627
erts, Elsie Palmer VI, 733
erts, Elsie Palmer VI, 734
erts, Elsie Palmer, Jr. VI, 773
erts, Elsie Palmer, Jr. VI, 774
erts, Elvira IV, 1182
erts, Elvira IV, 1221
erts, Elwood IV, 1182
erts, Emily V, 226
erts, Emily VI, 841
erts, Emily J. III, 114
erts, Emily J. III, 270
erts, Emma III, 290
erts, Emma A. II, 968
erts, Emma A. II, 1059
erts, Emma Elva V, 275
erts, Emma Florence V, 860
erts, Emma Ruth I, 625
erts, Emmett O. IV, 1335
erts, Emmor II, 916
Roberts, Emmor II, 940
Roberts, Enoch II, 414
Roberts, Enoch II, 637
Roberts, Enoch II, 638
Roberts, Enoch II, 801
Roberts, Enoch II, 811
Roberts, Enoch II, 823
Roberts, Enoch II, 915
Roberts, Enoch IV, 81
Roberts, Enoch VI, 311
Roberts, Enoch VI, 330
Roberts, Enoch VI, 331
Roberts, Enoch VI, 338
Roberts, Enoch VI, 839
Roberts, Enoch C. VI, 773
Roberts, Ephraim IV, 270
Roberts, Ephraim V, 310
Roberts, Ernest III, 358
Roberts, Esceneth V, 858
Roberts, Eseneth V, 859
Roberts, Esther I, 1063
Roberts, Esther II, 638
Roberts, Esther IV, 270
Roberts, Esther IV, 325
Roberts, Esther IV, 349
Roberts, Esther IV, 352
Roberts, Esther IV, 432
Roberts, Esther IV, 547
Roberts, Esther VI, 438
Roberts, Esther Anne IV, 1113
Roberts, Ethen IV, 1377
Roberts, Eugene IV, 1240
Roberts, Eugene Walton II, 817
Roberts, Eunice I, 625
Roberts, Eunice I, 640
Roberts, Eunice I, 643
Roberts, Eunice W. IV, 1335
Roberts, Eunice Worth IV, 1335
Roberts, Eunity II, 254
Roberts, Evan II, 968
Roberts, Evan II, 969
Roberts, Evan II, 977
Roberts, Evan II, 1023
Roberts, Evan II, 1055
Roberts, Evan II, 1059
Roberts, Evan II, 1061
Roberts, Evan L. II, 968
Roberts, Evelyn M. VI, 773
Roberts, Evelyn Miller VI, 771
Roberts, Evelyn Miller VI, 773
Roberts, Everet Olney IV, 1335
Roberts, Everett Arthur J. V, 860
Roberts, Ezekiel IV, 237
Roberts, Ezekiel IV, 270
Roberts, Ezekiel IV, 312
Roberts, Ezekiel IV, 314
Roberts, Ezekiel IV, 333
Roberts, Ezekiel IV, 349
Roberts, Ezekiel V, 310
Roberts, Flora R. II, 916
Roberts, Frances III, 270
Roberts, Frances VI, 850
Roberts, Frances VI, 964
Roberts, Frances VI, 972
Roberts, Frances VI, 1019
Roberts, Francis IV, 1221
Roberts, Frank IV, 270
Roberts, Franklin II, 716
Roberts, Franklin II, 763
Roberts, Franklin Ash VI, 773
Roberts, Fred C. V, 860
Roberts, Frederic C. Stubbs V, 859
Roberts, Frederic Coleman V, 859
Roberts, Fredric Lowell V, 859
Roberts, Frilla IV, 1292
Roberts, George II, 414
Roberts, George II, 527
Roberts, George II, 636
Roberts, George II, 637
Roberts, George II, 808
Roberts, George II, 915
Roberts, George IV, 270
Roberts, George IV, 349
Roberts, George VI, 677
Roberts, George VI, 694
Roberts, George VI, 695
Roberts, George VI, 712
Roberts, George S. VI, 438
Roberts, George, Jr. II, 637
Roberts, Gerard VI, 5
Roberts, Gerrard V, 274
Roberts, Gertrude Shaw II, 817
Roberts, Gertrude Stout I, 640
Roberts, Gervis S. II, 1023
Roberts, Grace I, 226
Roberts, Griffith IV, 87
Roberts, Griffith IV, 98
Roberts, Griffith IV, 107
Roberts, Griffith IV, 1182
Roberts, Griffith VI, 438
Roberts, Guy II, 817
Roberts, Guy II, 915
Roberts, Hannah I, 1063
Roberts, Hannah II, 95
Roberts, Hannah II, 122
Roberts, Hannah II, 123
Roberts, Hannah II, 182
Roberts, Hannah II, 413
Roberts, Hannah II, 414
Roberts, Hannah II, 527
Roberts, Hannah II, 589
Roberts, Hannah II, 615
Roberts, Hannah II, 636
Roberts, Hannah II, 637
Roberts, Hannah II, 638
Roberts, Hannah II, 649
Roberts, Hannah II, 687
Roberts, Hannah II, 716
Roberts, Hannah II, 763
Roberts, Hannah II, 821
Roberts, Hannah III, 270
Roberts, Hannah III, 498
Roberts, Hannah IV, 45
Roberts, Hannah IV, 56
Roberts, Hannah IV, 98
Roberts, Hannah IV, 107
Roberts, Hannah IV, 270
Roberts, Hannah IV, 1113
Roberts, Hannah IV, 1221
Roberts, Hannah IV, 1377
Roberts, Hannah V, 272
Roberts, Hannah V, 274
Roberts, Hannah V, 310
Roberts, Hannah V, 859
Roberts, Hannah V, 860
Roberts, Hannah V, 928
Roberts, Hannah VI, 438
Roberts, Hannah VI, 773
Roberts, Hannah VI, 850
Roberts, Hannah A. V, 859
Roberts, Hannah Ann V, 852
Roberts, Hannah Ann V, 853
Roberts, Hannah Ann V, 859
Roberts, Hannah F. II, 915
Roberts, Hannah Fell II, 817
Roberts, Hannah Kirk IV, 1221
Roberts, Hannah M. II, 414
Roberts, Hannah N. II, 817
Roberts, Hannah R. II, 749
Roberts, Hannah R. II, 763
Roberts, Hannah Rebecca II, 716
Roberts, Hannah Rebecca II, 763
Roberts, Hannah West II, 600
Roberts, Hannah West II, 637
Roberts, Hannah, Jr. II, 637
Roberts, Hannah, Jr. II, 684
Roberts, Harriett S. VI, 773
Roberts, Harriett Shepherd VI, 773
Roberts, Harriett Shepherd VI, 784
Roberts, Hattie V, 853
Roberts, Helen VI, 694
Roberts, Helen VI, 695
Roberts, Helen A. IV, 1214
Roberts, Helen A. IV, 1221
Roberts, Henery Philliphs VI, 266
Roberts, Henrietta II, 413
Roberts, Henrietta R. II, 752
Roberts, Henrietta R. II, 763
Roberts, Henry IV, 158
Roberts, Henry IV, 270
Roberts, Henry IV, 1182
Roberts, Henry VI, 553
Roberts, Henry VI, 850
Roberts, Henry C. II, 915
Roberts, Henry S. III, 270
Roberts, Henry W. II, 916
Roberts, Henry W. VI, 774
Roberts, Hester II, 414
Roberts, Homer C. V, 707
Roberts, Howard E. IV, 1335
Roberts, Hugh II, 137
Roberts, Hugh II, 156
Roberts, Hugh II, 413
Roberts, Hugh II, 414
Roberts, Hugh II, 480
Roberts, Hugh II, 527
Roberts, Hugh II, 600
Roberts, Hugh II, 636
Roberts, Hugh II, 637
Roberts, Hugh II, 673
Roberts, Hugh II, 677
Roberts, Hugh Walton VI, 774
Roberts, Hugh, Jr. II, 414
Roberts, Hugh, Sr. II, 414
Roberts, Ida VI, 771
Roberts, Ida VI, 773
Roberts, Ida VI, 777
Roberts, Ida VI, 784
Roberts, Irving V, 275
Roberts, Isaac II, 414
Roberts, Isaac II, 478
Roberts, Isaac II, 615
Roberts, Isaac II, 636
Roberts, Isaac II, 687
Roberts, Isaac V, 707
Roberts, Isaac VI, 760
Roberts, Isaac VI, 773
Roberts, Isaac Henry II, 716
Roberts, Isaac Henry II, 763
Roberts, Isaac Shoemaker II, 636
Roberts, Isaiah II, 637
Roberts, Isaiah IV, 158
Roberts, Isaiah IV, 270
Roberts, Isaiah IV, 1182
Roberts, Isham VI, 850
Roberts, Israel II, 414
Roberts, Israel IV, 270
Roberts, Jacob II, 478
Roberts, James II, 485
Roberts, James II, 636
Roberts, James V, 226
Roberts, James V, 464
Roberts, James W. V, 858
Roberts, James W. V, 859
Roberts, James W. VI, 627
Roberts, James W. VI, 734
Roberts, James Walker VI, 733
Roberts, James Walker VI, 773
Roberts, James Walker VI, 774
Roberts, Jane I, 899
Roberts, Jane II, 414
Roberts, Jane II, 523
Roberts, Jane II, 601
Roberts, Jane II, 607
Roberts, Jane II, 636
Roberts, Jane II, 637
Roberts, Jane II, 687
Roberts, Jane II, 696
Roberts, Jane II, 796
Roberts, Jane IV, 270
Roberts, Jane IV, 349
Roberts, Jane IV, 539
Roberts, Jane IV, 547
Roberts, Jane IV, 1171
Roberts, Jane IV, 1182
Roberts, Jane V, 274
Roberts, Jane VI, 810
Roberts, Jane H. III, 140
Roberts, Jean I, 164
Roberts, Jean H. VI, 417
Roberts, Jean Margaret III, 271
Roberts, Jean Margaret III, 358
Roberts, Jeannie III, 140
Roberts, Jeannie III, 271
Roberts, Jeannie H. III, 271
Roberts, Jennett II, 447
Roberts, Jennie V, 464
Roberts, Jennie V, 859
Roberts, Jennie T. V, 859
Roberts, Jervis S. II, 1023
Roberts, Jesse II, 637
Roberts, Jesse III, 271
Roberts, Jesse IV, 270
Roberts, Jesse IV, 349
Roberts, Jesse IV, 350
Roberts, Jesse IV, 432
Roberts, Jesse IV, 513
Roberts, Jesse IV, 547
Roberts, Jesse V, 226
Roberts, Jesse VI, 972
Roberts, Jesse VI, 985
Roberts, Jesse W. II, 637
Roberts, Jesse W. II, 638
Roberts, Jno. II, 637
Roberts, Job II, 672
Roberts, Joe VI, 850
Roberts, Joh VI, 266
Roberts, John I, 1063
Roberts, John II, 86
Roberts, John II, 95
Roberts, John II, 182
Roberts, John II, 216
Roberts, John II, 223
Roberts, John II, 254
Roberts, John II, 413
Roberts, John II, 414
Roberts, John II, 447
Roberts, John II, 573
Roberts, John II, 635
Roberts, John II, 636
Roberts, John II, 637
Roberts, John II, 696
Roberts, John II, 861
Roberts, John II, 915
Roberts, John II, 916
Roberts, John II, 968
Roberts, John II, 977
Roberts, John II, 1023
Roberts, John II, 1059
Roberts, John IV, 270
Roberts, John IV, 349
Roberts, John IV, 432
Roberts, John IV, 915
Roberts, John IV, 1221
Roberts, John IV, 1292
Roberts, John V, 115
Roberts, John V, 275
Roberts, John V, 310
Roberts, John V, 464
Roberts, John V, 642
Roberts, John V, 707
Roberts, John V, 826
Roberts, John V, 850
Roberts, John V, 858
Roberts, John V, 859
Roberts, John VI, 266
Roberts, John VI, 338
Roberts, John VI, 341
Roberts, John VI, 438
Roberts, John VI, 553
Roberts, John VI, 558
Roberts, John VI, 795
Roberts, John VI, 801
Roberts, John VI, 827
Roberts, John VI, 850
Roberts, John VI, 900
Roberts, John VI, 911
Roberts, John VI, 915
Roberts, John VI, 927
Roberts, John VI, 985
Roberts, John H. III, 191
Roberts, John H. III, 229
Roberts, John H. III, 270
Roberts, John H. III, 271
Roberts, John H. III, 356
Roberts, John H. III, 357
Roberts, John H. III, 361
Roberts, John H. VI, 773
Roberts, John I. III, 114
Roberts, John J. II, 637
Roberts, John J. Smith II, 637
Roberts, John L. IV, 1221
Roberts, John Lewis IV, 56
Roberts, John Lynch VI, 338
Roberts, John P. II, 324
Roberts, John S. III, 47
Roberts, John S. III, 49
Roberts, John S. III, 69
Roberts, John S. III, 270
Roberts, John S. III, 271
Roberts, John S. V, 257
Roberts, John S. V, 274
Roberts, John T. III, 271
Roberts, John Tompkins V, 226
Roberts, John, Jr. II, 637
Roberts, Jonathan I, 1062
Roberts, Jonathan II, 324
Roberts, Jonathan II, 637
Roberts, Jonathan IV, 1182
Roberts, Jonathan IV, 1186
Roberts, Jonathan V, 115
Roberts, Jonathan V, 226
Roberts, Jonathan V, 849
Roberts, Jonathan V, 858
Roberts, Jonathan V, 859
Roberts, Jonathan VI, 773
Roberts, Jonathan VI, 786
Roberts, Joseph I, 625
Roberts, Joseph II, 635
Roberts, Joseph II, 684
Roberts, Joseph II, 762
Roberts, Joseph II, 827
Roberts, Joseph IV, 158
Roberts, Joseph IV, 270
Roberts, Joseph IV, 349
Roberts, Joseph IV, 378
Roberts, Joseph IV, 547
Roberts, Joseph IV, 1214
Roberts, Joseph IV, 1221
Roberts, Joseph V, 226
Roberts, Joseph V, 274
Roberts, Joseph V, 275
Roberts, Joseph V, 310
Roberts, Joseph Fox II, 637
Roberts, Joseph H. II, 716
Roberts, Joseph H. V, 226
Roberts, Joseph L. VI, 773
Roberts, Joseph M. II, 817
Roberts, Joseph M. II, 916
Roberts, Joseph M. II, 920
Roberts, Joseph M. VI, 774
Roberts, Joseph M., Jr. II, 817
Roberts, Joseph Paull II, 635
Roberts, Joseph R. II, 916
Roberts, Joseph Rowland II, 817
Roberts, Joseph W. II, 915
Roberts, Joseph, Jr. II, 638
Roberts, Joseph, Jr. II, 716
Roberts, Joshua II, 299
Roberts, Josiah II, 817

Roberts, Josiah II, 916
Roberts, Josiah VI, 773
Roberts, Josiah F. II, 916
Roberts, Joyce V, 860
Roberts, Jr. Elizabeth IV, 1212
Roberts, Judah IV, 270
Roberts, Judah V, 271
Roberts, Judah V, 274
Roberts, Judah V, 275
Roberts, Judah V, 310
Roberts, Judith VI, 900
Roberts, Judith VI, 993
Roberts, Julia A. C. VI, 841
Roberts, Juliet V, 226
Roberts, Juliet V, 859
Roberts, Julietta V, 858
Roberts, Julietta V, 859
Roberts, Juliette V, 859
Roberts, Kalista VI, 985
Roberts, Katharine III, 271
Roberts, Katherine II, 447
Roberts, Kendall Cole VI, 773
Roberts, Keziah I, 145
Roberts, Keziah I, 164
Roberts, L. H. IV, 1335
Roberts, Latetia II, 968
Roberts, Latitia II, 968
Roberts, Latitia II, 977
Roberts, Latitia II, 1023
Roberts, Leander VI, 850
Roberts, Lelia A. C. VI, 841
Roberts, Leonard VI, 985
Roberts, Leticia V, 226
Roberts, Leverson IV, 1221
Roberts, Lewis IV, 270
Roberts, Lewis V, 310
Roberts, Lindley S. V, 860
Roberts, Lizzie VI, 82
Roberts, Lizzie VI, 85
Roberts, Lora M. V, 72
Roberts, Lora M. V, 115
Roberts, Lora M. V, 429
Roberts, Lorena V, 1016
Roberts, Louisa III, 270
Roberts, Louisa E. II, 156
Roberts, Louisa Elizabeth II, 137
Roberts, Louisa J. III, 271
Roberts, Louisa J. VI, 677
Roberts, Louisa J. VI, 694
Roberts, Louisa J. VI, 695
Roberts, Louisa J. VI, 712
Roberts, Louisa M. III, 206
Roberts, Louisa M. III, 270
Roberts, Lowell S. V, 860
Roberts, Luana V, 859
Roberts, Lucinda III, 270
Roberts, Lucretia V, 859
Roberts, Lucretia VI, 850
Roberts, Lucretia M. V, 859
Roberts, Lucy I, 625
Roberts, Lucy I, 640
Roberts, Lucy V, 272
Roberts, Luvina V, 860
Roberts, Lyddia VI, 438
Roberts, Lydia I, 130
Roberts, Lydia I, 164
Roberts, Lydia I, 1063
Roberts, Lydia II, 638
Roberts, Lydia II, 645
Roberts, Lydia II, 817
Roberts, Lydia II, 916
Roberts, Lydia IV, 87
Roberts, Lydia IV, 107
Roberts, Lydia IV, 349
Roberts, Lydia IV, 350
Roberts, Lydia IV, 354
Roberts, Lydia IV, 513
Roberts, Lydia IV, 547
Roberts, Lydia IV, 1113
Roberts, Lydia V, 50
Roberts, Lydia V, 115
Roberts, Lydia V, 858
Roberts, Lydia V, 859
Roberts, Lydia VI, 438
Roberts, Lydia VI, 583
Roberts, Lydia A. V, 275
Roberts, Lydia Ann V, 274
Roberts, Lydia C. V, 858
Roberts, Lydia C. V, 859
Roberts, Lydia L. II, 716
Roberts, Lydia L. II, 749
Roberts, Lydia L. II, 763
Roberts, Lydia Parry II, 916
Roberts, Lydia Parry II, 940
Roberts, Lyndley L. V, 859
Roberts, M. Franklin III, 498
Roberts, Mabel VI, 631
Roberts, Mabel A. VI, 621
Roberts, Mabel A. VI, 710
Roberts, Mabel A. VI, 711
Roberts, Mabel A. VI, 712
Roberts, Mabel Arbutus VI, 687
Roberts, Mabel Arbutus VI, 695
Roberts, Mabel Arbutus VI, 712
Roberts, Mack VI, 850
Roberts, Marcy II, 414
Roberts, Marcy II, 636
Roberts, Marcy II, 977
Roberts, Marcy II, 1023
Roberts, Margaret II, 254
Roberts, Margaret II, 414
Roberts, Margaret II, 637
Roberts, Margaret II, 638
Roberts, Margaret II, 703
Roberts, Margaret II, 817
Roberts, Margaret II, 1055
Roberts, Margaret III, 108
Roberts, Margaret III, 270
Roberts, Margaret IV, 270
Roberts, Margaret V, 310
Roberts, Margaret D. IV, 1261
Roberts, Margaret E. V, 707
Roberts, Margaret Harmon VI, 417
Roberts, Margaret Harmon VI, 438
Roberts, Margaret J. II, 1063
Roberts, Margaret L. V, 859
Roberts, Margaret M. II, 638
Roberts, Margarett II, 915
Roberts, Margaretta W. II, 716
Roberts, Margaretta W. II, 763
Roberts, Marguerite Shoemaker II, 968
Roberts, Marguerite Shoemaker II, 1059
Roberts, Marguerite Shoemaker II, 1061
Roberts, Maria II, 789
Roberts, Martha II, 414
Roberts, Martha II, 496
Roberts, Martha II, 534
Roberts, Martha II, 635
Roberts, Martha II, 636
Roberts, Martha II, 809
Roberts, Martha II, 916
Roberts, Martha II, 940
Roberts, Martha V, 226
Roberts, Martha VI, 856
Roberts, Martha Ann II, 599
Roberts, Martha Ann II, 637
Roberts, Martha Ann IV, 1221
Roberts, Martha C. IV, 1221
Roberts, Martha H. VI, 985
Roberts, Martha J. IV, 270
Roberts, Martha Jane V, 858
Roberts, Martha K. IV, 1221
Roberts, Martha P. III, 191
Roberts, Martha P. III, 270
Roberts, Martha P. III, 271
Roberts, Mary I, 127
Roberts, Mary I, 163
Roberts, Mary I, 732
Roberts, Mary I, 1063
Roberts, Mary I, 1066
Roberts, Mary II, 86
Roberts, Mary II, 95
Roberts, Mary II, 182
Roberts, Mary II, 216
Roberts, Mary II, 219
Roberts, Mary II, 223
Roberts, Mary II, 254
Roberts, Mary II, 413
Roberts, Mary II, 414
Roberts, Mary II, 480
Roberts, Mary II, 513
Roberts, Mary II, 527
Roberts, Mary II, 573
Roberts, Mary II, 590
Roberts, Mary II, 635
Roberts, Mary II, 636
Roberts, Mary II, 637
Roberts, Mary II, 638
Roberts, Mary II, 655
Roberts, Mary II, 673
Roberts, Mary II, 677
Roberts, Mary II, 695
Roberts, Mary II, 763
Roberts, Mary II, 779
Roberts, Mary II, 806
Roberts, Mary II, 915
Roberts, Mary II, 1059
Roberts, Mary III, 229
Roberts, Mary III, 270
Roberts, Mary III, 271
Roberts, Mary III, 342
Roberts, Mary III, 384
Roberts, Mary IV, 270
Roberts, Mary IV, 314
Roberts, Mary IV, 333
Roberts, Mary IV, 349
Roberts, Mary IV, 547
Roberts, Mary IV, 1113
Roberts, Mary IV, 1182
Roberts, Mary IV, 1186
Roberts, Mary IV, 1261
Roberts, Mary V, 115
Roberts, Mary V, 149
Roberts, Mary V, 226
Roberts, Mary V, 846
Roberts, Mary V, 849
Roberts, Mary V, 853
Roberts, Mary V, 857
Roberts, Mary V, 858
Roberts, Mary V, 859
Roberts, Mary VI, 438
Roberts, Mary VI, 454
Roberts, Mary VI, 553
Roberts, Mary VI, 558
Roberts, Mary VI, 760
Roberts, Mary VI, 773
Roberts, Mary VI, 850
Roberts, Mary VI, 978
Roberts, Mary VI, 985
Roberts, Mary A. VI, 331
Roberts, Mary A. VI, 839
Roberts, Mary Alma V, 859
Roberts, Mary Ann III, 134
Roberts, Mary Ann V, 859
Roberts, Mary Ann VI, 331
Roberts, Mary Ann VI, 338
Roberts, Mary Ann VI, 741
Roberts, Mary Ann VI, 742
Roberts, Mary Ann VI, 743
Roberts, Mary Ann VI, 762
Roberts, Mary Ann VI, 773
Roberts, Mary Ann VI, 774
Roberts, Mary Ashbridge II, 798
Roberts, Mary Ashbridge II, 820
Roberts, Mary B. III, 270
Roberts, Mary Ella VI, 773
Roberts, Mary Ella VI, 786
Roberts, Mary Emma VI, 774
Roberts, Mary F. II, 817
Roberts, Mary F. II, 916
Roberts, Mary H. II, 324
Roberts, Mary H. VI, 553
Roberts, Mary H. VI, 583
Roberts, Mary Hannah VI, 438
Roberts, Mary Henrietta VI, 584
Roberts, Mary J. II, 915
Roberts, Mary Jane IV, 925
Roberts, Mary Jane IV, 989
Roberts, Mary Jones II, 801
Roberts, Mary K. III, 270
Roberts, Mary K. III, 271
Roberts, Mary Luanna V, 865
Roberts, Mary M. V, 859
Roberts, Mary Margaret II, 915
Roberts, Mary Margarite V, 860
Roberts, Mary Oakford II, 808
Roberts, Mary P. III, 271
Roberts, Mary R. III, 47
Roberts, Mary W. II, 916
Roberts, Mary W. II, 920
Roberts, Mary W. III, 229
Roberts, Mary W. III, 270
Roberts, Mary W. III, 271
Roberts, Mary W. III, 297
Roberts, Mary W. VI, 730
Roberts, Mary W. VI, 773
Roberts, Mary W. VI, 774
Roberts, Maryann VI, 338
Roberts, Matilda IV, 200
Roberts, Matilda IV, 270
Roberts, Matilda IV, 1113
Roberts, Matilda VI, 299
Roberts, Matilda VI, 330
Roberts, Matilda VI, 338
Roberts, Matthew III, 271
Roberts, Melissa IV, 432
Roberts, Melissa IV, 440
Roberts, Mercy II, 505
Roberts, Mercy II, 636
Roberts, Mercy II, 637
Roberts, Mercy II, 684
Roberts, Mercy IV, 270
Roberts, Mercy VI, 553
Roberts, Meriam J. II, 324
Roberts, Michael L. V, 274
Roberts, Michael L. V, 275
Roberts, Michael Satterthwaite II, 1059
Roberts, Mildred Jackson VI, 850
Roberts, Mildred Louise III, 271
Roberts, Milten M. V, 1016
Roberts, Milton V, 859
Roberts, Milton V, 865
Roberts, Milton V, 1016
Roberts, Milton S. Stubbs V, 859
Roberts, Mira G. S. IV, 270
Roberts, Miriam II, 299
Roberts, Mordecai Yarnall II, 636
Roberts, Morris IV, 107
Roberts, Morris IV, 158
Roberts, Morris VI, 814
Roberts, Morris VI, 850
Roberts, Morton VI, 850
Roberts, Moses IV, 270
Roberts, Moses IV, 349
Roberts, Moses V, 275
Roberts, Moses V, 298
Roberts, Moses V, 310
Roberts, Moses V, 357
Roberts, Moses B. V, 429
Roberts, Moses B. Roberts V, 642
Roberts, Mrs. Eva A. V, 1016
Roberts, Nancy IV, 270
Roberts, Nancy IV, 349
Roberts, Nancy IV, 353
Roberts, Nancy V, 275
Roberts, Nancy V, 464
Roberts, Nancy VI, 985
Roberts, Nancy A. V, 464
Roberts, Nancy E. VI, 850
Roberts, Nathan II, 817
Roberts, Nathan II, 968
Roberts, Nathan IV, 496
Roberts, Nathan V, 272
Roberts, Nathan D. II, 968
Roberts, Nathan D. II, 1059
Roberts, Oliver V, 226
Roberts, Oney VI, 850
Roberts, Oressa May V, 859
Roberts, Orlando Stubbs V, 859
Roberts, Ottis V, 859
Roberts, Ottis V, 860
Roberts, Owen II, 414
Roberts, Owen II, 635
Roberts, Owen II, 636
Roberts, Owen II, 1033
Roberts, Paschall II, 414
Roberts, Patience II, 478
Roberts, Patience II, 535
Roberts, Patience II, 636
Roberts, Patsey VI, 865
Roberts, Paul E. V, 859
Roberts, Paul Ellis V, 860
Roberts, Penelope VI, 920
Roberts, Peter II, 414
Roberts, Peter II, 616
Roberts, Peter II, 635
Roberts, Phebe IV, 270
Roberts, Phebe IV, 300
Roberts, Phebe IV, 314
Roberts, Phebe IV, 315
Roberts, Phebe V, 115
Roberts, Phebe V, 226
Roberts, Phebe V, 858
Roberts, Phebe V, 859
Roberts, Philip VI, 972
Roberts, Philip VI, 985
Roberts, Phineas II, 414
Roberts, Phineas II, 636
Roberts, Phinehas II, 636
Roberts, Pleasant VI, 985
Roberts, Polly VI, 827
Roberts, Polly VI, 850
Roberts, Polly VI, 985
Roberts, Priscilla II, 414
Roberts, Priscilla II, 638
Roberts, Rachel II, 414
Roberts, Rachel II, 501
Roberts, Rachel II, 636
Roberts, Rachel II, 637
Roberts, Rachel II, 716
Roberts, Rachel II, 801
Roberts, Rachel II, 808
Roberts, Rachel II, 811
Roberts, Rachel II, 823
Roberts, Rachel II, 915
Roberts, Rachel III, 271
Roberts, Rachel IV, 81
Roberts, Rachel IV, 87
Roberts, Rachel IV, 93
Roberts, Rachel IV, 98
Roberts, Rachel IV, 107
Roberts, Rachel IV, 158
Roberts, Rachel IV, 270
Roberts, Rachel IV, 378
Roberts, Rachel IV, 1221
Roberts, Rachel V, 226
Roberts, Rachel VI, 338
Roberts, Rachel VI, 341
Roberts, Rachel VI, 438
Roberts, Rachel C. IV, 1214
Roberts, Rachel C. IV, 1221
Roberts, Rachel Elizabeth III, 271
Roberts, Rachel Elizabeth IV, 1221
Roberts, Rachel F. II, 414
Roberts, Rachel F. II, 638
Roberts, Rachel F. II, 915
Roberts, Rachel J. IV, 1113
Roberts, Rachel R. V, 115
Roberts, Rachel T. IV, 1113
Roberts, Raymond III, 140
Roberts, Raymond III, 271
Roberts, Raymond IV, 1335
Roberts, Raymond V, 707
Roberts, Rebecah I, 1037
Roberts, Rebecca II, 282
Roberts, Rebecca II, 299
Roberts, Rebecca II, 300
Roberts, Rebecca IV, 100
Roberts, Rebecca IV, 107
Roberts, Rebecca IV, 349
Roberts, Rebecca IV, 350
Roberts, Rebecca V, 115
Roberts, Rebecca V, 826
Roberts, Rebecca V, 850
Roberts, Rebecca V, 858
Roberts, Rebecca V, 859
Roberts, Rebecca V, 869
Roberts, Rebecca VI, 438
Roberts, Rebecca VI, 746
Roberts, Rebecca VI, 773
Roberts, Rebecca VI, 774
Roberts, Rebecca A. IV, 989
Roberts, Rebecca A. IV, 1012
Roberts, Rebecca W. II, 299
Roberts, Rebeccah VI, 438
Roberts, Rebecka II, 414
Roberts, Rebekah I, 1063
Roberts, Rebekah II, 451
Roberts, Rebekah II, 636
Roberts, Rebekah IV, 107
Roberts, Rebekah VI, 553
Roberts, Rebekah VI, 558
Roberts, Reese II, 637
Roberts, Retta V, 860
Roberts, Reuben II, 637
Roberts, Reuben III, 270
Roberts, Reuben IV, 547
Roberts, Reuben IV, 1221
Roberts, Reuben IV, 1377
Roberts, Reuben VI, 773
Roberts, Reuben L. IV, 1171
Roberts, Reuben L. IV, 1182
Roberts, Reuben L. IV, 1221
Roberts, Reuben M. VI, 773
Roberts, Reuben S. IV, 1182
Roberts, Reuben, Sr. VI, 773
Roberts, Rhoda II, 968
Roberts, Rhoda II, 969
Roberts, Rhoda VI, 919
Roberts, Rhoda S. II, 968
Roberts, Rhoda S. II, 1059
Roberts, Richard II, 414
Roberts, Richard II, 447
Roberts, Richard II, 505
Roberts, Richard II, 600
Roberts, Richard II, 636
Roberts, Richard II, 637
Roberts, Richard II, 808
Roberts, Richard IV, 158
Roberts, Richard IV, 270
Roberts, Richard VI, 553
Roberts, Richard VI, 558
Roberts, Richard VI, 583
Roberts, Richard VI, 730
Roberts, Richard VI, 773
Roberts, Richard VI, 774
Roberts, Richard VI, 850
Roberts, Richard VI, 919
Roberts, Richard VI, 937
Roberts, Richard VI, 985
Roberts, Richard Evan IV, 270
Roberts, Richard R. II, 916
Roberts, Richard R. II, 920
Roberts, Robert II, 414
Roberts, Robert II, 481
Roberts, Robert II, 505
Roberts, Robert II, 535
Roberts, Robert II, 636
Roberts, Robert II, 637
Roberts, Robert F. II, 916
Roberts, Robert F. VI, 751
Roberts, Robert F. VI, 774
Roberts, Robert P. II, 968
Roberts, Robert W. V, 860
Roberts, Robert Willis V, 859
Roberts, Robt. F. VI, 515
Roberts, Roland IV, 270
Roberts, Rosalie II, 916
Roberts, Roscoe V, 859
Roberts, Roscoe V, 860
Roberts, Rowland II, 817
Roberts, Rowland II, 916
Roberts, Rueben M. V, 956
Roberts, Rueben M. V, 958
Roberts, Ruth II, 636
Roberts, Ruth V, 271
Roberts, Ruth V, 274

rts, Ruth V, 275
rts, Ruth V, 859
rts, Ruth V, 860
rts, Ruth Ann VI, 751
rts, Ruth Ann VI, 774
rts, Ruth K. VI, 760
rts, Ruth K. VI, 773
rts, S. Raymond III, 271
rts, Sadie V, 859
rts, Sadie V, 860
rts, Sallie III, 361
rts, Sallie B. III, 229
rts, Sallie B. III, 270
rts, Sallie B. III, 271
rts, Sallie B. III, 357
rts, Sally Ann VI, 964
rts, Samuel II, 137
rts, Samuel II, 156
rts, Samuel II, 414
rts, Samuel II, 636
rts, Samuel II, 817
rts, Samuel V, 274
rts, Samuel V, 275
rts, Samuel V, 853
rts, Samuel V, 857
rts, Samuel V, 858
rts, Samuel V, 859
rts, Samuel VI, 338
rts, Samuel VI, 850
rts, Samuel A. II, 413
rts, Samuel H. II, 716
rts, Samuel H. II, 749
rts, Samuel H. II, 763
rts, Samuel H. II, 769
rts, Samuel Otis V, 859
rts, Samuel S. II, 915
rts, Sarah I, 1063
rts, Sarah II, 182
rts, Sarah II, 254
erts, Sarah II, 414
erts, Sarah II, 626
erts, Sarah II, 636
erts, Sarah II, 637
erts, Sarah II, 638
erts, Sarah II, 655
erts, Sarah II, 685
erts, Sarah II, 763
erts, Sarah II, 808
erts, Sarah II, 814
erts, Sarah II, 819
erts, Sarah II, 873
erts, Sarah II, 900
erts, Sarah II, 968
erts, Sarah II, 1012
erts, Sarah II, 1023
erts, Sarah III, 192
erts, Sarah III, 231
erts, Sarah III, 270
erts, Sarah III, 271
erts, Sarah III, 356
erts, Sarah IV, 128
erts, Sarah IV, 132
erts, Sarah IV, 339
erts, Sarah IV, 349
erts, Sarah IV, 547
erts, Sarah IV, 585
erts, Sarah IV, 593
erts, Sarah IV, 1113
erts, Sarah V, 88
erts, Sarah V, 115
erts, Sarah V, 225
erts, Sarah V, 226
erts, Sarah V, 275
erts, Sarah V, 464
erts, Sarah V, 725
erts, Sarah V, 775
erts, Sarah V, 858
erts, Sarah V, 859
erts, Sarah VI, 438
erts, Sarah VI, 471
erts, Sarah VI, 482
erts, Sarah VI, 554
erts, Sarah VI, 556
erts, Sarah VI, 675
erts, Sarah VI, 677
erts, Sarah VI, 695
erts, Sarah VI, 696
erts, Sarah VI, 704
erts, Sarah VI, 801
erts, Sarah A. II, 968
erts, Sarah A. II, 1055
erts, Sarah A. III, 271
erts, Sarah Ann II, 817
erts, Sarah Ann II, 916
erts, Sarah Ann III, 47
erts, Sarah Ann III, 69
erts, Sarah Ann III, 270
erts, Sarah Ann III, 271
erts, Sarah Anna III, 49
erts, Sarah B. III, 191
erts, Sarah C. II, 1059
Roberts, Sarah D. VI, 850
Roberts, Sarah Elizabeth II, 137
Roberts, Sarah Elizabeth II, 156
Roberts, Sarah Emily II, 794
Roberts, Sarah G. V, 257
Roberts, Sarah G. V, 274
Roberts, Sarah H. III, 270
Roberts, Sarah Josepha IV, 1221
Roberts, Sarah K. V, 115
Roberts, Sarah P. II, 316
Roberts, Sarah P. II, 324
Roberts, Sarah R. V, 826
Roberts, Sarah Roberts VI, 773
Roberts, Selma IV, 1261
Roberts, Septimus II, 637
Roberts, Septimus II, 638
Roberts, Septimus VI, 85
Roberts, Sidney V, 298
Roberts, Sidney V, 310
Roberts, Simeon II, 636
Roberts, Solomon V, 115
Roberts, Solomon W. II, 763
Roberts, Solomon White II, 413
Roberts, Spencer III, 271
Roberts, Spencer VI, 695
Roberts, Stephen V, 310
Roberts, Stokes L. II, 1023
Roberts, Stokes L. II, 1059
Roberts, Susan II, 299
Roberts, Susan II, 786
Roberts, Susan II, 817
Roberts, Susan II, 870
Roberts, Susan II, 915
Roberts, Susan II, 916
Roberts, Susan V, 844
Roberts, Susan V, 859
Roberts, Susan VI, 916
Roberts, Susan Ann VI, 985
Roberts, Susan F. II, 790
Roberts, Susan F. II, 915
Roberts, Susan H. II, 414
Roberts, Susan H. II, 638
Roberts, Susan H. II, 850
Roberts, Susan H. II, 916
Roberts, Susan M. V, 956
Roberts, Susan M. V, 958
Roberts, Susana II, 468
Roberts, Susana II, 636
Roberts, Susanah VI, 985
Roberts, Susanna II, 414
Roberts, Susanna S. II, 1059
Roberts, Susanna Wills II, 716
Roberts, Susannah VI, 437
Roberts, Susannah VI, 972
Roberts, Susannah S. II, 1051
Roberts, T. Ellwood II, 915
Roberts, Tacy II, 809
Roberts, Tacy II, 964
Roberts, Tacy II, 968
Roberts, Tacy II, 969
Roberts, Tacy II, 1059
Roberts, Tacy V, 226
Roberts, Thamzin II, 637
Roberts, Thamzin II, 696
Roberts, Thomas I, 164
Roberts, Thomas I, 1037
Roberts, Thomas I, 1063
Roberts, Thomas II, 254
Roberts, Thomas II, 414
Roberts, Thomas II, 451
Roberts, Thomas II, 501
Roberts, Thomas II, 534
Roberts, Thomas II, 635
Roberts, Thomas II, 636
Roberts, Thomas II, 637
Roberts, Thomas II, 1023
Roberts, Thomas IV, 270
Roberts, Thomas IV, 1335
Roberts, Thomas V, 115
Roberts, Thomas V, 226
Roberts, Thomas V, 274
Roberts, Thomas V, 275
Roberts, Thomas V, 310
Roberts, Thomas V, 858
Roberts, Thomas V, 859
Roberts, Thomas VI, 438
Roberts, Thomas VI, 916
Roberts, Thomas VI, 1019
Roberts, Thomas Ellwood II, 915
Roberts, Thomas Ellwood III, 271
Roberts, Thomas H. V, 226
Roberts, Thomas H. VI, 850
Roberts, Thomas M. II, 916
Roberts, Thomas W. Elkinton II, 763
Roberts, Thomasin II, 95
Roberts, Thomasine II, 527
Roberts, Thomasine II, 637
Roberts, Thos. Ellwood II, 817
Roberts, Thos. Ellwood III, 192
Roberts, Thos. Ellwood III, 270
Roberts, Thos. H. VI, 947
Roberts, Thos. M. II, 850
Roberts, Thos. M. II, 916
Roberts, Trilla IV, 1292
Roberts, Tristam V, 272
Roberts, Truman V, 1016
Roberts, Unity II, 254
Roberts, Usley VI, 856
Roberts, Ussley VI, 865
Roberts, Velma V, 707
Roberts, Verona V, 859
Roberts, Verona S. V, 860
Roberts, Viola V, 859
Roberts, Viola V, 1016
Roberts, Viretta Branson V, 859
Roberts, Virginia VI, 438
Roberts, W. Glenn III, 271
Roberts, Walter I, 1037
Roberts, Walter I, 1062
Roberts, Walter II, 916
Roberts, Walter II, 940
Roberts, Walter V, 115
Roberts, Walter V, 852
Roberts, Walter V, 858
Roberts, Walter V, 859
Roberts, Walter VI, 746
Roberts, Walter VI, 773
Roberts, Walter VI, 774
Roberts, Walter Ernest III, 271
Roberts, Walter Nelson V, 860
Roberts, Warren V, 464
Roberts, Wd Esther IV, 81
Roberts, Wd. Ann II, 786
Roberts, Wd. Margaret II, 968
Roberts, Wd. Martha II, 414
Roberts, Whitson V, 115
Roberts, Wilie VI, 985
Roberts, Willi J. V, 859
Roberts, William II, 414
Roberts, William IV, 270
Roberts, William IV, 1113
Roberts, William V, 274
Roberts, William V, 275
Roberts, William V, 859
Roberts, William V, 860
Roberts, William VI, 331
Roberts, William VI, 338
Roberts, William VI, 553
Roberts, William VI, 839
Roberts, William VI, 851
Roberts, William B. III, 270
Roberts, William Kennard IV, 593
Roberts, William L. II, 716
Roberts, William Pennell III, 270
Roberts, Wilson II, 1023
Roberts, Wilson V, 464
Roberts, Wilson P. V, 275
Roberts, Wm. II, 95
Roberts, Wm. II, 637
Roberts, Wm. II, 638
Roberts, Wm. II, 716
Roberts, Wm. II, 786
Roberts, Wm. IV, 158
Roberts, Wm. V, 464
Roberts, Wm. VI, 580
Roberts, Wm. Dawson II, 637
Roberts, Wm. J. II, 763
Roberts, Wm. L. II, 763
Roberts, Wm. Linneus IV, 1221
Roberts, Wm. P. II, 915
Roberts, Wm. Pennell III, 271
Roberts, Wm. R. II, 762
Roberts, Woodnut P. II, 716
Roberts, Zalinda VI, 338
Roberts, Zeno V, 859
Roberts, Zeno Addison V, 858
Robertson, ??? VI, 726
Robertson, Abram VI, 858
Robertson, Amanda A. VI, 896
Robertson, America VI, 934
Robertson, Andrew II, 414
Robertson, Archibald VI, 851
Robertson, Archibald W. VI, 985
Robertson, Arthur VI, 985
Robertson, Arthur H. VI, 897
Robertson, Benjamin V, 209
Robertson, Benjamin VI, 985
Robertson, Betsey VI, 985
Robertson, Betsy Ann VI, 334
Robertson, Betsy Ann VI, 338
Robertson, Biddy VI, 985
Robertson, Bird A. VI, 901
Robertson, Bridget E. VI, 851
Robertson, Byrd B. VI, 851
Robertson, Catharine VI, 851
Robertson, Catharine VI, 985
Robertson, Catherine VI, 210
Robertson, Charles IV, 270
Robertson, David VI, 830
Robertson, David VI, 849
Robertson, David VI, 851
Robertson, David VI, 866
Robertson, Edna IV, 1261
Robertson, Edward O. VI, 848
Robertson, Edwin VI, 985
Robertson, Elijah VI, 985
Robertson, Elijah VI, 994
Robertson, Eliza A. VI, 851
Robertson, Eliza H. VI, 815
Robertson, Eliza L. VI, 851
Robertson, Elizabeth VI, 851
Robertson, Elizabeth VI, 985
Robertson, Elizabeth S. VI, 985
Robertson, Elizabeth W. VI, 887
Robertson, Fleming W. VI, 985
Robertson, Frances VI, 851
Robertson, Frances VI, 985
Robertson, Frances A. VI, 851
Robertson, Francis W. VI, 985
Robertson, Gorrel VI, 985
Robertson, Hannah I, 968
Robertson, Hannah II, 414
Robertson, Henrietta VI, 897
Robertson, Henry VI, 821
Robertson, Henry VI, 845
Robertson, Henry VI, 851
Robertson, Holcomb VI, 850
Robertson, James I, 968
Robertson, James VI, 812
Robertson, James VI, 815
Robertson, James VI, 866
Robertson, James VI, 985
Robertson, James, Jr. VI, 846
Robertson, James, Jr. VI, 851
Robertson, Jane VI, 912
Robertson, Jeffrey VI, 985
Robertson, Jeffry VI, 939
Robertson, Jeffy VI, 922
Robertson, Jeffy VI, 972
Robertson, Jeffy VI, 981
Robertson, Jeffy VI, 985
Robertson, Jehu I, 968
Robertson, Jennett VI, 922
Robertson, Jesse VI, 985
Robertson, Jo. VI, 986
Robertson, John I, 569
Robertson, John I, 968
Robertson, John VI, 825
Robertson, John VI, 851
Robertson, John VI, 886
Robertson, John VI, 972
Robertson, John VI, 985
Robertson, John VI, 1006
Robertson, John J. VI, 919
Robertson, John, Jr. I, 968
Robertson, Johnson VI, 851
Robertson, Joseph A. VI, 851
Robertson, Joseph A. VI, 858
Robertson, Joshua I, 968
Robertson, Lucinda VI, 941
Robertson, Lucy VI, 1012
Robertson, Mahalah VI, 985
Robertson, Margaret V, 209
Robertson, Margaret VI, 849
Robertson, Mariah VI, 985
Robertson, Martha VI, 851
Robertson, Martha VI, 919
Robertson, Martha VI, 929
Robertson, Martha J. VI, 815
Robertson, Mary I, 968
Robertson, Mary V, 200
Robertson, Mary V, 208
Robertson, Mary VI, 774
Robertson, Mary VI, 851
Robertson, Mary VI, 985
Robertson, Mary Ann VI, 985
Robertson, Mary E. VI, 980
Robertson, Mary J. VI, 846
Robertson, Mary P. VI, 844
Robertson, Matilda VI, 994
Robertson, Milley VI, 895
Robertson, Mills VI, 919
Robertson, Mills VI, 985
Robertson, N. VI, 887
Robertson, N. VI, 929
Robertson, N. VI, 941
Robertson, N. VI, 975
Robertson, N. W. VI, 896
Robertson, Nancey VI, 985
Robertson, Nancy VI, 812
Robertson, Nancy VI, 851
Robertson, Nancy VI, 858
Robertson, Nancy VI, 886
Robertson, Nancy VI, 985
Robertson, Nancy A. VI, 985
Robertson, Nicholas I, 968
Robertson, Nicholas VI, 896
Robertson, Nicholas VI, 934
Robertson, Nicholas VI, 941
Robertson, Nicholas W. VI, 996
Robertson, Peasant I, 569
Robertson, Permelia VI, 985
Robertson, Polly M. VI, 981
Robertson, Rachel I, 968
Robertson, Rachel VI, 866
Robertson, Randolph VI, 985
Robertson, Rebecca II, 95
Robertson, Rebecca VI, 164
Robertson, Robert II, 638
Robertson, Robert VI, 851
Robertson, Sally VI, 851
Robertson, Sally VI, 963
Robertson, Sally Ann VI, 975
Robertson, Samuel II, 414
Robertson, Samuel II, 638
Robertson, Sarah VI, 985
Robertson, Sarah VI, 1001
Robertson, Sarah B. VI, 986
Robertson, Sophia VI, 985
Robertson, Sparger I, 948
Robertson, Susanna VI, 985
Robertson, T. W. VI, 892
Robertson, T. W. VI, 1012
Robertson, Teressa W. VI, 888
Robertson, Thomas I, 835
Robertson, Thomas II, 414
Robertson, Thomas VI, 300
Robertson, Thomas VI, 301
Robertson, Thomas VI, 302
Robertson, Thomas VI, 307
Robertson, Thomas VI, 329
Robertson, Thomas VI, 338
Robertson, Thomas VI, 886
Robertson, Thomas VI, 979
Robertson, Thomas VI, 985
Robertson, Thomas VI, 994
Robertson, Thomas VI, 1001
Robertson, Thomas VI, 1012
Robertson, Thomas John IV, 270
Robertson, Thomas W. VI, 980
Robertson, Thomas W. VI, 985
Robertson, Thos. VI, 340
Robertson, William I, 968
Robertson, William VI, 985
Robertson, William C. VI, 850
Robertson, Young W. VI, 851
Robertson, Zach. VI, 986
Robertson, Zachariah VI, 886
Robertson, Zachariah VI, 985
Robertson, Zechariah VI, 888
Robertson, Zechariah VI, 897
Robertson, Zedekiah VI, 931
Robeson, Catharine II, 806
Robeson, Catharine II, 810
Robeson, Ebenezer II, 414
Robeson, Edward II, 638
Robeson, George VI, 266
Robeson, Hannah V, 275
Robeson, Joseph I, 160
Robeson, Joseph I, 164
Robeson, Martha II, 414
Robeson, Martha II, 810
Robeson, Mary II, 414
Robeson, Morris II, 639
Robeson, Peter II, 810
Robeson, Samuel II, 447
Robeson, Sarah I, 160
Robeson, Sarah I, 164
Robeson, Sarah II, 254
Robeson, Tacy II, 639
Robeson, Thomas II, 414
Robeson, William II, 414
Robinet, Emma V, 642
Robinet, Thomas V, 707
Robinett, Anna V, 642
Robinett, Carl V, 642
Robinett, Eliza V, 642
Robinett, Elizabeth IV, 42
Robinett, Elizabeth IV, 56
Robinett, Elma V, 642
Robinett, Emma V, 642
Robinett, James IV, 42
Robinett, Leah Ellen V, 642
Robinett, Levica V, 642
Robinett, Levisa V, 200
Robinett, Mary V, 642
Robinett, Moses V, 707
Robinett, Priscilla IV, 42
Robinett, Priscilla IV, 56
Robinett, Sarah V, 642
Robinett, Thomas V, 707
Robinett, Thos. V, 642
Robinett, Zenas V, 642
Robinette, James IV, 69
Robinette, Priscilla IV, 56
Robinette, Priscilla IV, 69
Robingson, William I, 569
Robins, ??? III, 348
Robins, Aaron II, 254
Robins, Abel II, 817
Robins, Abner I, 514
Robins, Alexander I, 769

Robins, Alice V, 633
Robins, Ann I, 514
Robins, Ann II, 136
Robins, Ann II, 414
Robins, Arthur VI, 986
Robins, Asenath IV, 1075
Robins, Bathsheba V, 115
Robins, Deborah III, 194
Robins, Edith P. III, 53
Robins, Elihu IV, 582
Robins, Elihu IV, 593
Robins, Elihu IV, 1075
Robins, Elisabeth II, 638
Robins, Eliza I, 899
Robins, Elizabeth I, 514
Robins, Elizabeth I, 885
Robins, Elizabeth I, 899
Robins, Elizabeth II, 254
Robins, Elizabeth II, 517
Robins, Elizabeth IV, 103
Robins, Elizabeth IV, 107
Robins, Frances VI, 986
Robins, Frances G. VI, 922
Robins, Furman C. II, 763
Robins, George VI, 986
Robins, George W. II, 916
Robins, George Williams II, 817
Robins, Henry II, 414
Robins, James I, 899
Robins, Jane II, 638
Robins, Jaspar II, 414
Robins, Jennie T. II, 1078
Robins, Jinney VI, 986
Robins, John II, 414
Robins, John II, 447
Robins, John II, 638
Robins, John II, 652
Robins, John III, 194
Robins, Joseph I, 914
Robins, Joseph II, 414
Robins, Joseph II, 638
Robins, Joseph II, 1078
Robins, Josie I, 891
Robins, Josie I, 899
Robins, Laura I, 899
Robins, Lettins II, 414
Robins, Levina I, 914
Robins, Lydia II, 817
Robins, Lydia II, 916
Robins, Margarett II, 136
Robins, Margit William Mathews VI, 859
Robins, Maria III, 194
Robins, Maria III, 269
Robins, Mary I, 514
Robins, Mary I, 899
Robins, Mary II, 254
Robins, Mary II, 414
Robins, Mary II, 638
Robins, Mary II, 652
Robins, Mary II, 1053
Robins, Mary II, 1059
Robins, Mary Ann IV, 582
Robins, Mary Ann IV, 593
Robins, Mary Ann IV, 1075
Robins, Mary I. II, 1078
Robins, Miriam IV, 593
Robins, Moses V, 633
Robins, Nancy VI, 859
Robins, Nathan II, 136
Robins, Nicholas I, 514
Robins, Rebecca II, 1062
Robins, Rebecca II, 1078
Robins, Rebecka II, 414
Robins, Rebecka II, 447
Robins, Rhoda II, 817
Robins, Ruth I, 514
Robins, Ruth V, 633
Robins, Samuel II, 414
Robins, Samuel II, 447
Robins, Samuel II, 599
Robins, Samuel II, 638
Robins, Samuel III, 70
Robins, Sarah II, 599
Robins, Sarah II, 638
Robins, Sarah A. II, 1078
Robins, Silas T. III, 53
Robins, Susan H. III, 53
Robins, Thomas I, 514
Robins, Thomas II, 414
Robins, Thomas IV, 593
Robins, William I, 514
Robins, William II, 414
Robins, William D. IV, 1075
Robins, Wm. IV, 1075
Robins, Zachariah IV, 1075
Robins, Zachariah H. IV, 1075
Robins, Zacheriah IV, 1075
Robinson, ??? I, 27
Robinson, ??? III, 272
Robinson, A. Alexander VI, 438
Robinson, Aaron I, 116
Robinson, Abigail I, 1066
Robinson, Abigail II, 639
Robinson, Abigail III, 254
Robinson, Abigail III, 271
Robinson, Abner I, 569
Robinson, Abraham II, 639
Robinson, Abraham VI, 951
Robinson, Abraham VI, 986
Robinson, Ada VI, 424
Robinson, Ada VI, 439
Robinson, Albert G. VI, 439
Robinson, Alexander II, 414
Robinson, Alexander VI, 390
Robinson, Alice II, 456
Robinson, Alice II, 639
Robinson, Alice G. III, 54
Robinson, Alice G. III, 271
Robinson, Alice Gertrude III, 271
Robinson, Alida III, 271
Robinson, Alvin V, 763
Robinson, Amey II, 568
Robinson, Amey II, 638
Robinson, Amey II, 1023
Robinson, Amy II, 414
Robinson, Amy II, 638
Robinson, Amy II, 1023
Robinson, Amy III, 42
Robinson, Amy III, 272
Robinson, Amy J. III, 170
Robinson, Andrew II, 414
Robinson, Andrew II, 447
Robinson, Andrew VI, 438
Robinson, Andrew A. III, 272
Robinson, Andrew A. VI, 406
Robinson, Andrew A. VI, 438
Robinson, Andrew A. VI, 439
Robinson, Angelina H. VI, 986
Robinson, Anita Moon VI, 730
Robinson, Ann I, 3
Robinson, Ann I, 16
Robinson, Ann I, 26
Robinson, Ann I, 116
Robinson, Ann I, 164
Robinson, Ann I, 1012
Robinson, Ann II, 414
Robinson, Ann II, 587
Robinson, Ann II, 639
Robinson, Ann III, 271
Robinson, Ann III, 272
Robinson, Ann IV, 270
Robinson, Ann IV, 653
Robinson, Ann IV, 654
Robinson, Ann V, 275
Robinson, Ann V, 287
Robinson, Ann V, 969
Robinson, Ann V, 975
Robinson, Ann VI, 85
Robinson, Ann VI, 86
Robinson, Ann VI, 210
Robinson, Ann VI, 507
Robinson, Ann VI, 851
Robinson, Ann VI, 912
Robinson, Ann E. V, 642
Robinson, Ann W. VI, 869
Robinson, Anna I, 16
Robinson, Anna I, 71
Robinson, Anna I, 81
Robinson, Anna II, 415
Robinson, Anna II, 639
Robinson, Anna III, 271
Robinson, Anna IV, 271
Robinson, Anna IV, 314
Robinson, Anna IV, 1182
Robinson, Anna V, 275
Robinson, Anna VI, 851
Robinson, Anna Burling III, 271
Robinson, Anna Frances VI, 439
Robinson, Anna Frances VI, 695
Robinson, Anne I, 64
Robinson, Annie III, 131
Robinson, Annie III, 272
Robinson, Annie VI, 378
Robinson, Annie VI, 438
Robinson, Annie VI, 439
Robinson, Annie R. VI, 439
Robinson, Annie R. VI, 446
Robinson, Annie R. Sheridan VI, 438
Robinson, Annie Rebecca VI, 445
Robinson, Archibald VI, 368
Robinson, Archibald VI, 438
Robinson, Archibald VI, 439
Robinson, Archibald VI, 447
Robinson, Archibald VI, 553
Robinson, Archibald VI, 566
Robinson, Archibald VI, 567
Robinson, Archibald VI, 898
Robinson, Archibald VI, 1021
Robinson, Archibald S. VI, 438
Robinson, Archibald S. VI, 439
Robinson, Arthur VI, 410
Robinson, Arthur VI, 723
Robinson, Arthur VI, 851
Robinson, Arthur VI, 897
Robinson, Arthur VI, 912
Robinson, Austin VI, 438
Robinson, Austin F. VI, 439
Robinson, B. N. VI, 1005
Robinson, B. T. VI, 986
Robinson, Banner V, 275
Robinson, Barnabas IV, 1377
Robinson, Benj. N. VI, 978
Robinson, Benjamin VI, 940
Robinson, Benjamin VI, 962
Robinson, Benjamin VI, 978
Robinson, Benjamin VI, 986
Robinson, Benjamin VI, 1013
Robinson, Benjamin N. VI, 986
Robinson, Benjamin N. VI, 1005
Robinson, Benjamin T. VI, 986
Robinson, Bertha VI, 439
Robinson, Bertha M. III, 272
Robinson, Bertha Priscilla VI, 422
Robinson, Bertha Priscilla VI, 439
Robinson, Beulah Jane II, 136
Robinson, Burley VI, 870
Robinson, Burley VI, 986
Robinson, Caleb V, 275
Robinson, Capt. ??? III, 36
Robinson, Capt. ??? III, 272
Robinson, Caroline III, 97
Robinson, Caroline III, 271
Robinson, Catharine II, 639
Robinson, Catharine II, 916
Robinson, Catharine III, 271
Robinson, Catharine VI, 851
Robinson, Catherine III, 272
Robinson, Catherine V, 707
Robinson, Catherine VI, 210
Robinson, Chalkley IV, 314
Robinson, Charles III, 271
Robinson, Charles III, 272
Robinson, Charles IV, 107
Robinson, Charles IV, 496
Robinson, Charles IV, 1335
Robinson, Charles VI, 438
Robinson, Charles B. IV, 270
Robinson, Charles Branson IV, 314
Robinson, Charles G. VI, 438
Robinson, Charles Hunter VI, 438
Robinson, Charles Hunter VI, 439
Robinson, Charles W. VI, 398
Robinson, Charles W. VI, 439
Robinson, Chas. II, 815
Robinson, Chas. IV, 1335
Robinson, Chas. Alvin V, 642
Robinson, Chas. Branson IV, 271
Robinson, Christian II, 473
Robinson, Christian II, 638
Robinson, Christopher VI, 851
Robinson, Christopher L. VI, 829
Robinson, Clara VI, 432
Robinson, Clara VI, 438
Robinson, Clara VI, 439
Robinson, Clara Elma VI, 439
Robinson, Clara Elma VI, 689
Robinson, Clara Emma VI, 695
Robinson, Clarence V, 673
Robinson, Clarence V, 703
Robinson, Clarence V, 707
Robinson, Clarence V, 860
Robinson, Clarence VI, 439
Robinson, Clarence A. V, 860
Robinson, Clarence J. VI, 424
Robinson, Clarence J. VI, 438
Robinson, Clarence J. VI, 439
Robinson, Clemsey VI, 986
Robinson, Colin VI, 835
Robinson, Cora M. VI, 438
Robinson, Cyrus VI, 986
Robinson, Cyrus VI, 1014
Robinson, D. Arthur VI, 438
Robinson, D. Arthur VI, 439
Robinson, D. Arthur VI, 695
Robinson, David I, 116
Robinson, David II, 414
Robinson, David II, 415
Robinson, David VI, 375
Robinson, David VI, 438
Robinson, David Arthur VI, 438
Robinson, Davies VI, 851
Robinson, Dellie M. V, 642
Robinson, Doctor ??? II, 414
Robinson, Dorothy III, 394
Robinson, Dorothy III, 440
Robinson, Dorothy A. III, 425
Robinson, Dorothy A. III, 440
Robinson, Ebeneezer II, 558
Robinson, Ebenezer II, 254
Robinson, Ebenezer II, 414
Robinson, Ebenezer II, 415
Robinson, Ebenezer II, 568
Robinson, Ebenezer II, 581
Robinson, Ebenezer II, 638
Robinson, Ebenezer II, 639
Robinson, Ebenezer II, 1023
Robinson, Edith IV, 1261
Robinson, Edmond C. III, 271
Robinson, Edw. F. III, 271
Robinson, Edw. Fraser III, 271
Robinson, Edward II, 254
Robinson, Edward II, 415
Robinson, Edward II, 447
Robinson, Edward II, 473
Robinson, Edward II, 586
Robinson, Edward II, 638
Robinson, Edward II, 639
Robinson, Edward III, 271
Robinson, Edward III, 272
Robinson, Edward VI, 851
Robinson, Edward VI, 986
Robinson, Edward C. III, 271
Robinson, Edward F. III, 271
Robinson, Edward T. III, 54
Robinson, Edwin VI, 439
Robinson, Edwin VI, 986
Robinson, Edwin J. VI, 438
Robinson, Effa Steer VI, 418
Robinson, Effa Steer VI, 439
Robinson, Effie III, 170
Robinson, Effie III, 272
Robinson, Effie B. IV, 1335
Robinson, Eldred H. VI, 920
Robinson, Eldred H. VI, 986
Robinson, Eleanor III, 54
Robinson, Eleanor III, 271
Robinson, Eleanor VI, 851
Robinson, Eleanor M. III, 271
Robinson, Eleonor III, 170
Robinson, Eleonor Maxwell III, 169
Robinson, Eli V, 275
Robinson, Elihu D. VI, 732
Robinson, Elihu D. VI, 774
Robinson, Elinor II, 93
Robinson, Elinor II, 95
Robinson, Elinor II, 414
Robinson, Elisabeth I, 3
Robinson, Elisabeth I, 16
Robinson, Elisabeth I, 26
Robinson, Elisabeth I, 70
Robinson, Elisabeth I, 71
Robinson, Elisabeth I, 78
Robinson, Elisabeth I, 164
Robinson, Elisabeth I, 173
Robinson, Elisabeth Matilda I, 116
Robinson, Elisha V, 642
Robinson, Eliz. III, 272
Robinson, Eliza III, 271
Robinson, Eliza V, 275
Robinson, Eliza V, 283
Robinson, Elizabeth I, 101
Robinson, Elizabeth I, 116
Robinson, Elizabeth I, 164
Robinson, Elizabeth I, 532
Robinson, Elizabeth I, 561
Robinson, Elizabeth I, 569
Robinson, Elizabeth I, 968
Robinson, Elizabeth I, 1012
Robinson, Elizabeth II, 414
Robinson, Elizabeth II, 415
Robinson, Elizabeth II, 638
Robinson, Elizabeth II, 639
Robinson, Elizabeth II, 664
Robinson, Elizabeth III, 202
Robinson, Elizabeth III, 271
Robinson, Elizabeth III, 272
Robinson, Elizabeth IV, 48
Robinson, Elizabeth IV, 56
Robinson, Elizabeth IV, 270
Robinson, Elizabeth IV, 271
Robinson, Elizabeth IV, 314
Robinson, Elizabeth V, 52
Robinson, Elizabeth V, 53
Robinson, Elizabeth V, 115
Robinson, Elizabeth V, 275
Robinson, Elizabeth V, 525
Robinson, Elizabeth V, 538
Robinson, Elizabeth VI, 85
Robinson, Elizabeth VI, 947
Robinson, Elizabeth VI, 986
Robinson, Elizabeth VI, 1010
Robinson, Elizabeth VI, 1013
Robinson, Elizabeth A. C. VI, 986
Robinson, Elizabeth F. VI, 986
Robinson, Elizabeth Jordan I, 120
Robinson, Elizabeth L. III, 2
Robinson, Elizabeth M. V, 96
Robinson, Elizabeth M. V, 97
Robinson, Elizabeth M. VI, 8
Robinson, Elizabeth M. VI, 8
Robinson, Elizabeth P. V, 275
Robinson, Elizabeth P. V, 287
Robinson, Ella S. VI, 422
Robinson, Ella S. VI, 439
Robinson, Ellen III, 97
Robinson, Ellen III, 271
Robinson, Ellen V, 703
Robinson, Ellen V, 707
Robinson, Ellen M. VI, 732
Robinson, Ellen M. VI, 774
Robinson, Ellen M. VI, 791
Robinson, Elwood Ratcliff IV,
Robinson, Emily IV, 270
Robinson, Emily IV, 271
Robinson, Emily IV, 314
Robinson, Emily F. VI, 732
Robinson, Emily F. VI, 774
Robinson, Emily L. III, 272
Robinson, Emma III, 271
Robinson, Emma III, 272
Robinson, Emma IV, 1335
Robinson, Essie M. I, 933
Robinson, Essie Stuart I, 948
Robinson, Esther I, 16
Robinson, Esther I, 71
Robinson, Esther II, 414
Robinson, Esther III, 271
Robinson, Esther IV, 1292
Robinson, Esther S. VI, 438
Robinson, Eunice II, 973
Robinson, Fannie II, 973
Robinson, Femenine VI, 897
Robinson, Field VI, 986
Robinson, Florence J. VI, 412
Robinson, Florence J. VI, 438
Robinson, Florentine VI, 986
Robinson, Frances VI, 986
Robinson, Frances VI, 1021
Robinson, Frances G. VI, 851
Robinson, Frances R. VI, 893
Robinson, Frank Orlando V, 64
Robinson, Franklin III, 271
Robinson, Franklin III, 272
Robinson, Garrell VI, 985
Robinson, George I, 116
Robinson, George II, 414
Robinson, George II, 415
Robinson, George II, 639
Robinson, George II, 763
Robinson, George II, 916
Robinson, George III, 169
Robinson, George III, 271
Robinson, George III, 272
Robinson, George IV, 1292
Robinson, George V, 275
Robinson, George VI, 357
Robinson, George Brown III, 27
Robinson, George H. II, 414
Robinson, George H. II, 639
Robinson, George H. III, 271
Robinson, George N. VI, 438
Robinson, Gorrell VI, 892
Robinson, Gorrell VI, 897
Robinson, Gorrell VI, 919
Robinson, Hannah I, 958
Robinson, Hannah I, 968
Robinson, Hannah I, 970
Robinson, Hannah I, 1001
Robinson, Hannah I, 1012
Robinson, Hannah II, 254
Robinson, Hannah II, 414
Robinson, Hannah II, 415
Robinson, Hannah II, 586
Robinson, Hannah II, 616
Robinson, Hannah II, 638
Robinson, Hannah II, 639
Robinson, Hannah II, 652
Robinson, Hannah II, 716
Robinson, Hannah III, 271
Robinson, Hannah III, 272
Robinson, Hannah IV, 1292
Robinson, Hannah V, 275
Robinson, Hannah E. VI, 375
Robinson, Hannah Ellen VI, 438
Robinson, Hannah Ellen VI, 439
Robinson, Hannah Jacobs IV, 27
Robinson, Hannah Louisa III, 271
Robinson, Harriet VI, 986
Robinson, Henrietta E. VI, 1005
Robinson, Henry III, 271
Robinson, Henry III, 272
Robinson, Henry VI, 821
Robinson, Henry VI, 851

nson, Howard R. III, 202
nson, Howard Richards
II, 272
nson, Howell VI, 959
nson, Howell VI, 986
nson, Howell VI, 1008
nson, Huldah I, 142
nson, Huldah I, 164
nson, Ida Helen VI, 438
nson, Ida Helen VI, 439
nson, Idelia May V, 642
nson, Isaac N. I, 835
nson, Isabella VI, 819
nson, J. VI, 85
nson, J. VI, 87
nson, Jackson VI, 438
nson, Jackson VI, 445
nson, Jackson VI, 460
nson, Jacob IV, 56
nson, James I, 968
nson, James I, 970
nson, James I, 1012
nson, James II, 415
nson, James II, 639
nson, James III, 272
nson, James IV, 1292
nson, James V, 115
nson, James VI, 85
nson, James VI, 439
nson, James VI, 814
nson, James VI, 819
nson, James VI, 986
nson, James F. V, 642
nson, James H. VI, 986
nson, James J. II, 639
nson, James J. VI, 438
nson, James Kenneth
I, 364
nson, James Kenneth
I, 439
nson, James L. VI, 375
nson, James L. VI, 438
nson, James L. VI, 439
nson, James L. VI, 447
nson, James P. III, 272
nson, James W. VI, 689
nson, James W. VI, 851
nson, James William VI, 432
nson, James William VI, 438
nson, James William VI, 439
nson, James William VI, 689
nson, James Wm. VI, 695
nson, James, Jr. II, 456
nson, James, Jr. II, 639
nson, Jane I Sup 1, 4
nson, Jane I Sup 1, 5
nson, Jane II, 415
nson, Jane IV, 270
nson, Jane IV, 271
nson, Jane VI, 842
nson, Jane VI, 851
nson, Jane E. VI, 986
nson, Jane Estelle VI, 364
nson, Jane Estelle VI, 439
nson, Janne I Sup 1, 8
nson, Jeams I, 958
nson, Jehu I, 968
nson, Jehu I, 1012
nson, Jehu I, 1013
nson, Jemima I, 23
nson, Jemima I, 71
nson, Jemima I, 81
nson, Jemima I, 199
nson, Jemima III, 272
nson, Jenny VI, 851
nson, Jesse VI, 986
nson, Jessie B. V, 860
nson, John I, 16
nson, John I, 60
nson, John I, 62
nson, John I, 70
nson, John I, 78
nson, John I, 116
nson, John I, 148
nson, John I, 164
nson, John I, 569
nson, John I, 958
nson, John I, 968
nson, John I, 1012
nson, John II, 639
nson, John II, 1023
nson, John V, 275
nson, John V, 928
nson, John VI, 11
nson, John VI, 12
nson, John VI, 148
nson, John VI, 210
nson, John VI, 821
nson, John VI, 842
nson, John VI, 851
nson, John VI, 940
Robinson, John VI, 947
Robinson, John VI, 986
Robinson, John VI, 1010
Robinson, John VI, 1013
Robinson, John E. III, 272
Robinson, John F. VI, 438
Robinson, John F. VI, 439
Robinson, John Fenton VI, 695
Robinson, John H. VI, 986
Robinson, John Moor I, 70
Robinson, John S. III, 271
Robinson, John S. III, 272
Robinson, John, Jr. I, 968
Robinson, John, Sr. I, 1012
Robinson, Jonathan VI, 377
Robinson, Jonathan VI, 438
Robinson, Jonathan VI, 439
Robinson, Jonathan VI, 689
Robinson, Jonathan VI, 695
Robinson, Jos. III, 272
Robinson, Jos. VI, 372
Robinson, Jos. VI, 439
Robinson, Joseph I, 23
Robinson, Joseph I, 92
Robinson, Joseph I, 101
Robinson, Joseph I, 103
Robinson, Joseph I, 116
Robinson, Joseph I, 120
Robinson, Joseph I, 154
Robinson, Joseph I, 164
Robinson, Joseph I Sup 1, 5
Robinson, Joseph I Sup 1, 8
Robinson, Joseph II, 137
Robinson, Joseph II, 415
Robinson, Joseph III, 272
Robinson, Joseph VI, 36
Robinson, Joseph VI, 85
Robinson, Joseph VI, 388
Robinson, Joseph VI, 695
Robinson, Joseph Andrew VI, 438
Robinson, Joseph S. VI, 406
Robinson, Joseph S. VI, 422
Robinson, Joseph S. VI, 438
Robinson, Joseph S. VI, 439
Robinson, Joseph S. VI, 445
Robinson, Joseph W. IV, 270
Robinson, Joseph W. IV, 271
Robinson, Joseph Walker IV, 314
Robinson, Joseph, Sr. I, 164
Robinson, Joshua I, 958
Robinson, Joshua I, 968
Robinson, Joshua I, 1012
Robinson, Joshua IV, 1292
Robinson, Joshua V, 275
Robinson, Joshua V, 287
Robinson, Josiah I, 10
Robinson, Josiah I, 71
Robinson, Josiah I, 80
Robinson, Josiah I, 164
Robinson, Josiah VI, 438
Robinson, Josiah VI, 439
Robinson, Julia Florence VI, 439
Robinson, Julia M. VI, 986
Robinson, Kate VI, 439
Robinson, Kate Pelter VI, 418
Robinson, Kater VI, 422
Robinson, Kater VI, 439
Robinson, Katie Gould III, 299
Robinson, Katie Gould III, 351
Robinson, Kezia II, 254
Robinson, Keziah II, 415
Robinson, Laticia IV, 1292
Robinson, Laura A. VI, 410
Robinson, Laura Alice VI, 410
Robinson, Laura Alice VI, 438
Robinson, Laura Alice VI, 439
Robinson, Leona I. VI, 438
Robinson, Letha V, 673
Robinson, Letha V, 707
Robinson, Letha Gallimore V, 707
Robinson, Levina I, 968
Robinson, Levina I, 1012
Robinson, Lewis III, 272
Robinson, Lewis V, 200
Robinson, Lewis VI, 851
Robinson, Lewis A. III, 131
Robinson, Lewis A. III, 272
Robinson, Lewis A. VI, 438
Robinson, Lewis A. VI, 439
Robinson, Lidey I, 70
Robinson, Lidey I, 78
Robinson, Lillian IV, 1335
Robinson, Lucinda P. VI, 951
Robinson, Lucretia M. III, 128
Robinson, Lucretia M. III, 161
Robinson, Lucretia M. IV, 1027
Robinson, Lucretia M. IV, 1030
Robinson, Lucretia Macy II, 799
Robinson, Lucy VI, 851
Robinson, Lucy VI, 897
Robinson, Lucy Belle V, 200
Robinson, Ludia II, 618
Robinson, Luther H. VI, 438
Robinson, Luther H. VI, 439
Robinson, Lydia II, 415
Robinson, Lydia II, 638
Robinson, Lydia III, 44
Robinson, Lydia III, 234
Robinson, Lydia VI, 447
Robinson, Lydia Ann VI, 438
Robinson, Lydia Ann VI, 439
Robinson, Lydia Ann VI, 553
Robinson, Lydia Ann VI, 566
Robinson, Lydia Ann VI, 567
Robinson, Lydia J. VI, 438
Robinson, M. C. IV, 1292
Robinson, Mabel VI, 375
Robinson, Mabel VI, 376
Robinson, Mabel VI, 438
Robinson, Mabel VI, 439
Robinson, Mahala IV, 1292
Robinson, Mahala V, 275
Robinson, Margaret I, 116
Robinson, Margaret I, 139
Robinson, Margaret I, 164
Robinson, Margaret II, 415
Robinson, Margaret II, 504
Robinson, Margaret II, 639
Robinson, Margaret II, 763
Robinson, Margaret III, 272
Robinson, Margaret VI, 406
Robinson, Margaret VI, 438
Robinson, Margaret VI, 439
Robinson, Margaret Alice III, 170
Robinson, Margaret Ann I, 116
Robinson, Margaret Ann VI, 85
Robinson, Margaret C. VI, 438
Robinson, Margaret C. VI, 441
Robinson, Margaret Louise I, 27
Robinson, Margaret Robinson
VI, 438
Robinson, Margaret V. VI, 438
Robinson, Margaret, Jr. II, 763
Robinson, Margrett II, 415
Robinson, Maria IV, 1292
Robinson, Maria V, 717
Robinson, Martha IV, 1292
Robinson, Martha V, 275
Robinson, Martha VI, 85
Robinson, Martha Ann V, 707
Robinson, Martha I. VI, 85
Robinson, Martha I. VI, 87
Robinson, Martha J. IV, 267
Robinson, Martha J. IV, 271
Robinson, Martha J. V, 975
Robinson, Martha Jane VI, 986
Robinson, Martha Jones I, 116
Robinson, Martha M. VI, 851
Robinson, Martha N. VI, 893
Robinson, Martha W. VI, 897
Robinson, Mary I, 16
Robinson, Mary I, 62
Robinson, Mary I, 70
Robinson, Mary I, 71
Robinson, Mary I, 72
Robinson, Mary I, 78
Robinson, Mary I, 116
Robinson, Mary I, 155
Robinson, Mary I, 164
Robinson, Mary I, 166
Robinson, Mary I, 569
Robinson, Mary I, 968
Robinson, Mary I, 970
Robinson, Mary I, 1012
Robinson, Mary I, 1013
Robinson, Mary II, 137
Robinson, Mary II, 156
Robinson, Mary II, 254
Robinson, Mary II, 414
Robinson, Mary II, 415
Robinson, Mary II, 447
Robinson, Mary II, 456
Robinson, Mary II, 473
Robinson, Mary II, 558
Robinson, Mary II, 638
Robinson, Mary II, 639
Robinson, Mary II, 763
Robinson, Mary III, 106
Robinson, Mary III, 179
Robinson, Mary III, 250
Robinson, Mary III, 271
Robinson, Mary III, 272
Robinson, Mary IV, 1292
Robinson, Mary V, 200
Robinson, Mary V, 260
Robinson, Mary V, 275
Robinson, Mary VI, 398
Robinson, Mary VI, 438
Robinson, Mary VI, 439
Robinson, Mary VI, 511
Robinson, Mary VI, 512
Robinson, Mary VI, 563
Robinson, Mary VI, 564
Robinson, Mary VI, 774
Robinson, Mary VI, 780
Robinson, Mary VI, 781
Robinson, Mary VI, 783
Robinson, Mary VI, 819
Robinson, Mary VI, 948
Robinson, Mary VI, 982
Robinson, Mary VI, 986
Robinson, Mary A. V, 200
Robinson, Mary A. VI, 372
Robinson, Mary A. VI, 438
Robinson, Mary A. VI, 439
Robinson, Mary Ann V, 275
Robinson, Mary Anna I, 614
Robinson, Mary B. III, 272
Robinson, Mary E. I, 1161
Robinson, Mary E. V, 860
Robinson, Mary E. VI, 438
Robinson, Mary E. VI, 986
Robinson, Mary Elizabeth II, 763
Robinson, Mary Elizabeth
III, 272
Robinson, Mary Emily V, 860
Robinson, Mary F. VI, 377
Robinson, Mary Frances VI, 377
Robinson, Mary Frances VI, 438
Robinson, Mary Frances VI, 689
Robinson, Mary Frances VI, 695
Robinson, Mary Francis VI, 439
Robinson, Mary H. VI, 377
Robinson, Mary Hannah VI, 439
Robinson, Mary Jane VI, 378
Robinson, Mary Jane VI, 438
Robinson, Mary Jane VI, 439
Robinson, Mary O. VI, 438
Robinson, Mary Opal VI, 439
Robinson, Mary Opal VI, 447
Robinson, Mary P. III, 271
Robinson, Mary P. III, 272
Robinson, Mary P. III, 362
Robinson, Mary S. VI, 438
Robinson, Mary S. VI, 439
Robinson, Mary S. VI, 986
Robinson, Mary, Jr. I, 148
Robinson, Mary, Jr. I, 164
Robinson, Mary, Sr. I, 164
Robinson, Mason VI, 986
Robinson, Mathew II, 414
Robinson, Mathew II, 415
Robinson, Mathew II, 626
Robinson, Mathew II, 638
Robinson, Maude III, 426
Robinson, Mays VI, 893
Robinson, McClelan IV, 1292
Robinson, Meriam I, 71
Robinson, Meriam I, 78
Robinson, Miriam I, 103
Robinson, Miriam I, 116
Robinson, Miriam I, 148
Robinson, Miriam I, 164
Robinson, Morris II, 639
Robinson, Mrs. ??? VI, 11
Robinson, Mrs. Effie IV, 1335
Robinson, Mrs. John IV, 1335
Robinson, N. Robertson VI, 982
Robinson, Nancy III, 425
Robinson, Nancy III, 440
Robinson, Nancy VI, 821
Robinson, Nancy VI, 842
Robinson, Nancy VI, 851
Robinson, Nancy VI, 951
Robinson, Nancy VI, 978
Robinson, Nancy VI, 986
Robinson, Nancy VI, 996
Robinson, Nathaniel III, 272
Robinson, Nelson V, 200
Robinson, Nena VI, 422
Robinson, Nena VI, 438
Robinson, Nena VI, 439
Robinson, Neri V, 200
Robinson, Nicholas I, 569
Robinson, Nicholas I, 968
Robinson, Nicholas VI, 986
Robinson, Nichos VI, 897
Robinson, Norma Charlotte
V, 707
Robinson, Orpah I, 16
Robinson, Orpah I, 23
Robinson, Orpha I, 10
Robinson, Orpha I, 71
Robinson, Orpha I, 80
Robinson, Orpha I, 81
Robinson, Orpha I, 199
Robinson, Parmelia VI, 825
Robinson, Patrick II, 447
Robinson, Patty VI, 986
Robinson, Peter II, 415
Robinson, Phebe II, 509
Robinson, Phebe II, 638
Robinson, Phebe III, 272
Robinson, Philip III, 271
Robinson, Philip III, 272
Robinson, Phineas S. VI, 429
Robinson, Phineas S. VI, 438
Robinson, Phineas S. VI, 439
Robinson, Phinneas VI, 418
Robinson, Phinneas Steer VI, 422
Robinson, Phinneas Steer VI, 439
Robinson, Polly VI, 948
Robinson, Portia V, 678
Robinson, Portia V, 707
Robinson, Portia VI, 396
Robinson, Portia VI, 439
Robinson, Rachel I, 968
Robinson, Rachel II, 415
Robinson, Rachel III, 135
Robinson, Rachel III, 272
Robinson, Rachel VI, 851
Robinson, Rachel W. I, 16
Robinson, Rachel W. I, 70
Robinson, Rachel W. I, 71
Robinson, Rachel W. VI, 410
Robinson, Rachel W. VI, 438
Robinson, Rachel W. VI, 439
Robinson, Rachel W. VI, 695
Robinson, Rachel W. VI, 723
Robinson, Rachel W. Jollife
VI, 439
Robinson, Randolph VI, 963
Robinson, Ray VI, 438
Robinson, Ray VI, 439
Robinson, Ray, Jr. VI, 439
Robinson, Rebecca II, 123
Robinson, Rebecca II, 156
Robinson, Rebecca II, 415
Robinson, Rebecca II, 529
Robinson, Rebecca II, 638
Robinson, Rebecca II, 639
Robinson, Rebecca II, 815
Robinson, Rebecca IV, 270
Robinson, Rebecca IV, 271
Robinson, Rebecca IV, 314
Robinson, Rebecca VI, 164
Robinson, Rebecca VI, 210
Robinson, Rebecca VI, 372
Robinson, Rebecca VI, 406
Robinson, Rebecca VI, 422
Robinson, Rebecca VI, 438
Robinson, Rebecca VI, 439
Robinson, Rebecca VI, 445
Robinson, Rebecca C. II, 136
Robinson, Rebecca D. II, 137
Robinson, Rebecca D. II, 156
Robinson, Reuben B. III, 272
Robinson, Reuben Warren V, 642
Robinson, Rhoda I, 116
Robinson, Richard II, 93
Robinson, Richard II, 95
Robinson, Richard II, 254
Robinson, Richard II, 299
Robinson, Richard II, 415
Robinson, Richard II, 564
Robinson, Richard II, 638
Robinson, Richard VI, 35
Robinson, Robert Fennell III, 272
Robinson, Robt. John III, 109
Robinson, Roger Peelle V, 707
Robinson, Roland I, 116
Robinson, Rowland I, 116
Robinson, Rowland I, 155
Robinson, Rowland I, 164
Robinson, Rowland III, 272
Robinson, Rowland R. III, 272
Robinson, Rowland T. III, 135
Robinson, Rowland T. III, 272
Robinson, Rufus C. VI, 438
Robinson, Rufus C. VI, 439
Robinson, Ruth I, 569
Robinson, Ruth II, 415
Robinson, S. III, 272
Robinson, Sallie IV, 1292
Robinson, Sallie G. VI, 438
Robinson, Sallie G. VI, 439
Robinson, Sallie G. VI, 447
Robinson, Sally V, 275
Robinson, Sally VI, 986
Robinson, Samaria IV, 271
Robinson, Samaria I. IV, 311
Robinson, Samaria I. IV, 314
Robinson, Samaria J. IV, 270
Robinson, Samuel II, 414
Robinson, Samuel III, 271
Robinson, Samuel III, 272
Robinson, Samuel C. VI, 869
Robinson, Samuel C. VI, 897
Robinson, Samuel C. VI, 986
Robinson, Samuel Franklin
III, 272
Robinson, Samuel S. VI, 989
Robinson, Samuel T. III, 272
Robinson, Sarah I, 10

Robinson, Sarah I, 36
Robinson, Sarah I, 54
Robinson, Sarah I, 70
Robinson, Sarah I, 71
Robinson, Sarah I, 78
Robinson, Sarah I, 116
Robinson, Sarah I, 146
Robinson, Sarah I, 156
Robinson, Sarah I, 164
Robinson, Sarah I, 199
Robinson, Sarah I Sup 1, 8
Robinson, Sarah II, 254
Robinson, Sarah II, 299
Robinson, Sarah II, 395
Robinson, Sarah II, 414
Robinson, Sarah II, 415
Robinson, Sarah II, 564
Robinson, Sarah II, 596
Robinson, Sarah II, 626
Robinson, Sarah II, 638
Robinson, Sarah II, 639
Robinson, Sarah III, 42
Robinson, Sarah III, 73
Robinson, Sarah III, 126
Robinson, Sarah III, 271
Robinson, Sarah III, 272
Robinson, Sarah V, 642
Robinson, Sarah V, 860
Robinson, Sarah VI, 29
Robinson, Sarah VI, 36
Robinson, Sarah VI, 986
Robinson, Sarah Ann V, 199
Robinson, Sarah Ann V, 200
Robinson, Sarah Ann VI, 388
Robinson, Sarah Ann VI, 438
Robinson, Sarah Ann VI, 695
Robinson, Sarah B. VI, 986
Robinson, Sarah E. III, 68
Robinson, Sarah E. III, 272
Robinson, Sarah E. VI, 439
Robinson, Sarah Elizabeth J. VI, 438
Robinson, Sarah Emeline VI, 438
Robinson, Sarah Emeline VI, 445
Robinson, Sarah Emiline VI, 460
Robinson, Sarah G. VI, 375
Robinson, Sarah J. III, 271
Robinson, Sarah Jane III, 271
Robinson, Sarah Jane VI, 407
Robinson, Sarah Jane VI, 439
Robinson, Sarah Meriah V, 275
Robinson, Sarah R. III, 271
Robinson, Sarah White I, 116
Robinson, Seany VI, 851
Robinson, Silas D. VI, 439
Robinson, Silas Deane VI, 412
Robinson, Silas Deane VI, 438
Robinson, Silas Deane VI, 439
Robinson, Simeon VI, 986
Robinson, Smith II, 137
Robinson, Sophia VI, 439
Robinson, Sophia B. VI, 377
Robinson, Sophia B. VI, 410
Robinson, Sophia B. VI, 438
Robinson, Sophia B. VI, 439
Robinson, Sophie VI, 439
Robinson, Sophronia P. I, 835
Robinson, Susan III, 272
Robinson, Susan VI, 940
Robinson, Susanna II, 639
Robinson, Susanna VI, 986
Robinson, Susannah II, 781
Robinson, Sylvester II, 456
Robinson, Sylvester II, 639
Robinson, T. B. VI, 730
Robinson, T. K. IV, 1335
Robinson, Tabitha VI, 957
Robinson, Tacy II, 639
Robinson, Tacy IV, 271
Robinson, Tacy C. IV, 270
Robinson, Thomas I, 3
Robinson, Thomas I, 16
Robinson, Thomas I, 70
Robinson, Thomas I, 78
Robinson, Thomas I, 92
Robinson, Thomas I, 116
Robinson, Thomas I, 139
Robinson, Thomas I, 164
Robinson, Thomas I, 166
Robinson, Thomas I, 569
Robinson, Thomas I, 968
Robinson, Thomas I Sup 1, 8
Robinson, Thomas II, 414
Robinson, Thomas II, 415
Robinson, Thomas II, 473
Robinson, Thomas II, 638
Robinson, Thomas II, 639
Robinson, Thomas II, 973
Robinson, Thomas III, 42
Robinson, Thomas III, 272
Robinson, Thomas IV, 270
Robinson, Thomas IV, 271
Robinson, Thomas IV, 314
Robinson, Thomas IV, 1335
Robinson, Thomas VI, 35
Robinson, Thomas VI, 301
Robinson, Thomas VI, 302
Robinson, Thomas VI, 326
Robinson, Thomas VI, 329
Robinson, Thomas VI, 336
Robinson, Thomas VI, 337
Robinson, Thomas VI, 338
Robinson, Thomas VI, 340
Robinson, Thomas VI, 828
Robinson, Thomas VI, 851
Robinson, Thomas VI, 986
Robinson, Thomas Chalkley IV, 270
Robinson, Thomas Chalkley IV, 271
Robinson, Thomas Harold VI, 439
Robinson, Thomas Harold VI, 695
Robinson, Thomas Knox IV, 1335
Robinson, Thomas W. VI, 438
Robinson, Thomas W. VI, 439
Robinson, Thomas Wynne III, 170
Robinson, Thomas, Jr. I, 142
Robinson, Thomas, Jr. I, 164
Robinson, Thos. III, 272
Robinson, Thos. R. III, 272
Robinson, Virginia III, 272
Robinson, Virginia VI, 390
Robinson, Virginia VI, 439
Robinson, W. VI, 826
Robinson, W. R. III, 394
Robinson, W. R. III, 440
Robinson, Ward R. III, 440
Robinson, Ward Reid III, 425
Robinson, Wd. Elizabeth II, 447
Robinson, Wd. Mary II, 581
Robinson, Wd. Nena Mattison VI, 406
Robinson, Widow Anne I, 71
Robinson, Widow Elizabeth I, 164
Robinson, Willa VI, 439
Robinson, Willa VI, 457
Robinson, Willa VI, 695
Robinson, Willa VI, 723
Robinson, Willahmenia J. VI, 439
Robinson, William I, 16
Robinson, William I, 26
Robinson, William I, 70
Robinson, William I, 71
Robinson, William I, 78
Robinson, William I, 81
Robinson, William I, 116
Robinson, William I, 164
Robinson, William I, 525
Robinson, William I, 569
Robinson, William I, 847
Robinson, William I, 968
Robinson, William II, 414
Robinson, William II, 415
Robinson, William III, 272
Robinson, William IV, 270
Robinson, William IV, 271
Robinson, William V, 860
Robinson, William VI, 6
Robinson, William VI, 11
Robinson, William VI, 85
Robinson, William VI, 303
Robinson, William VI, 564
Robinson, William VI, 774
Robinson, William VI, 851
Robinson, William VI, 862
Robinson, William VI, 963
Robinson, William VI, 986
Robinson, William VI, 1003
Robinson, William B. VI, 986
Robinson, William Donald VI, 439
Robinson, William N. VI, 438
Robinson, William P. III, 272
Robinson, William Richardson III, 272
Robinson, William S. III, 272
Robinson, William T. III, 271
Robinson, William T. III, 272
Robinson, William T. VI, 377
Robinson, William T. VI, 410
Robinson, William T. VI, 438
Robinson, William T. VI, 439
Robinson, Wilson III, 170
Robinson, Wilson III, 272
Robinson, Winfield III, 97
Robinson, Winfield III, 271
Robinson, Wm Donald VI, 695
Robinson, Wm. II, 638
Robinson, Wm. II, 639
Robinson, Wm. II, 664
Robinson, Wm. V, 707
Robinson, Wm. V, 969
Robinson, Wm. V, 975
Robinson, Wm. VI, 12
Robinson, Wm. VI, 780
Robinson, Wm. A. II, 639
Robinson, Wm. Attmore II, 639
Robinson, Wm. P. III, 250
Robinson, Wm. P. III, 271
Robinson, Wm. P. III, 272
Robinson, Wm. R. V, 928
Robinson, Wm. T. III, 73
Robinson, Wm. T. III, 126
Robinson, Wm. T. III, 271
Robinson, Wm. T. III, 272
Robinson, Wm. T. VI, 439
Robinson, Wm. W. VI, 894
Robinson, Zachariah VI, 986
Robison, Edward II, 254
Robison, Elisha V, 642
Robison, Hannah I, 968
Robison, Hannah II, 254
Robison, Helen IV, 947
Robison, James F. V, 642
Robison, John I, 968
Robison, Laticia IV, 1292
Robison, Mary I, 958
Robison, Mary I, 968
Robison, Sarah V, 642
Robison, Sarrah II, 95
Robison, Sophronia P. I, 835
Robison, Thomas II, 414
Robson, Celia VI, 871
Robson, Leonard III, 272
Robson, Rebecca II, 67
Robson, Rebecca II, 95
Robson, Sampson IV, 158
Robson, Sampson, Jr. IV, 158
Robson, Sampson, Jr. IV, 271
Robson, Sampson, Jr. IV, 349
Robson, Sampson, Sr. IV, 158
Robson, Sampson, Sr. IV, 271
Robson, Sampson, Sr. IV, 349
Robson, Sarah II, 95
Robson, Sarrah II, 95
Robson, Wm. D. IV, 1335
Robuck, Gracie E. V, 429
Robuck, Pearl V, 688
Robuck, Pearl S. V, 429
Robuck, Ruth V, 688
Roby, Alexander V, 1016
Roby, Amanda F. V, 1016
Roby, Hannah IV, 1167
Roby, Hannah IV, 1182
Roby, Marjorie VI, 757
Roby, Maud IV, 1182
Roby, Mrs. Emily M. VI, 757
Roby, Stephen VI, 757
Roche, Deborah M. IV, 1201
Roche, Deborah M. IV, 1221
Rochel, Christianna I, 596
Rochel, Christianna I, 835
Rochel, Christiannah I, 589
Rochester, Addison G. III, 273
Rochester, Anna L. III, 273
Rochester, George A. III, 273
Rochester, Hannah VI, 211
Rochester, Julia III, 273
Rochester, Junius C. III, 149
Rochester, Junius C. III, 214
Rochester, Junius C. III, 273
Rochester, Lillian III, 149
Rochester, Lillian J. III, 214
Rochester, Wd. Lillian J. III, 273
Rochford, Alice II, 415
Rochford, Denness II, 415
Rochford, Dennia II, 415
Rochford, Dennis II, 415
Rochford, Denniss II, 415
Rochford, Elizabeth II, 415
Rochford, Hope III, 273
Rochford, Hope III, 338
Rochford, John III, 273
Rochford, Mary II, 415
Rochford, Mary Bell II, 415
Rochford, Patience II, 415
Rochford, Rebecca II, 415
Rochford, Rebecca II, 467
Rochford, Rebecca II, 639
Rochford, Rebekah II, 467
Rochford, Solomon II, 415
Rochford, Solomon II, 467
Rochford, Solomon II, 639
Rochford, Wd. Elizabeth II, 415
Rochford, Wd. Mary II, 415
Rochille, Christianna I, 835
Rock, Charles VI, 837
Rock, Mary VI, 837
Rockford, Alice II, 639
Rockford, Dennis II, 558
Rockford, Dennis II, 639
Rockford, Elizabeth II, 558
Rockford, Elizabeth II, 639
Rockford, Rebecca II, 639
Rockford, Solomon II, 639
Rockhil, Edward II, 182
Rockhil, Mary II, 182
Rockhil, Thomas II, 182
Rockhill, Agnes II, 828
Rockhill, Alice V, 707
Rockhill, Alice Caroline V, 696
Rockhill, Alice Caroline V, 707
Rockhill, Alice E. V, 707
Rockhill, Amelia V, 707
Rockhill, Amos II, 817
Rockhill, Amos II, 916
Rockhill, Anna IV, 894
Rockhill, Anna Cook II, 254
Rockhill, Benjamin V, 115
Rockhill, Calvin V, 525
Rockhill, Charles V, 525
Rockhill, Clement II, 38
Rockhill, Deborah II, 817
Rockhill, Deborah II, 916
Rockhill, Edward II, 182
Rockhill, Edward II, 254
Rockhill, Edward V, 707
Rockhill, Elizabeth II, 219
Rockhill, Elizabeth II, 254
Rockhill, Elizabeth II, 258
Rockhill, Elizabeth II, 1023
Rockhill, Elizabeth IV, 894
Rockhill, Elizabeth V, 525
Rockhill, Elizabeth V, 595
Rockhill, Ellis IV, 894
Rockhill, Grace II, 254
Rockhill, Hannah II, 38
Rockhill, Hannah II, 95
Rockhill, Hannah II, 182
Rockhill, Hannah II, 254
Rockhill, Hannah II, 639
Rockhill, J. H. V, 525
Rockhill, Jerusha II, 182
Rockhill, Jerusha II, 254
Rockhill, John II, 182
Rockhill, John II, 254
Rockhill, John II, 1023
Rockhill, Jonathan V, 525
Rockhill, Jonathan E. V, 525
Rockhill, Joseph II, 38
Rockhill, Joseph II, 95
Rockhill, Lidya II, 38
Rockhill, Lydia II, 639
Rockhill, Lydia II, 716
Rockhill, Lydia V, 525
Rockhill, Lydia H. V, 502
Rockhill, Lydia H. V, 525
Rockhill, Margaret IV, 894
Rockhill, Mary II, 38
Rockhill, Mary II, 95
Rockhill, Mary II, 182
Rockhill, Mary II, 254
Rockhill, Mary II, 299
Rockhill, Mary II, 1059
Rockhill, Mary V, 525
Rockhill, Millie V, 595
Rockhill, Nathan IV, 894
Rockhill, Robert II, 38
Rockhill, Robert II, 254
Rockhill, Robert II, 258
Rockhill, Ruth V, 115
Rockhill, Ruth V, 525
Rockhill, Salome W. II, 916
Rockhill, Salome Warner II, 817
Rockhill, Samuel II, 38
Rockhill, Samuel II, 182
Rockhill, Samuel II, 254
Rockhill, Samuel V, 860
Rockhill, Sarah II, 763
Rockhill, Sarah V, 525
Rockhill, Sarah V, 928
Rockhill, Serena Bell V, 525
Rockhill, Susan Mart V, 707
Rockhill, Susie M. V, 707
Rockhill, Thomas II, 182
Rockhills, Anna IV, 894
Rockhills, Ellis IV, 894
Rockhills, Margaret IV, 894
Rockhold, Ephraim V, 1016
Rockhold, Mary V, 1016
Rockolt, Mary V, 1016
Rockwell, ??? IV, 547
Rockwell, Alfred Edward IV, 547
Rockwell, Arthur R. IV, 432
Rockwell, Benjamin E. II, 716
Rockwell, Benjamin E. II, 763
Rockwell, Benjamin E. III, 273
Rockwell, Carl F. IV, 841
Rockwell, Carl Franklin IV, 432
Rockwell, Carl Franklin IV, 841
Rockwell, Cecil Floyd IV, 432
Rockwell, Chester Arthur IV,
Rockwell, Clara D. IV, 432
Rockwell, Donald West II, 13
Rockwell, Dorothy IV, 432
Rockwell, Edith M. IV, 547
Rockwell, Edward IV, 547
Rockwell, Edwin C. IV, 432
Rockwell, Edwin C. IV, 841
Rockwell, Eleanor M. IV, 432
Rockwell, Elizabeth IV, 389
Rockwell, Elizabeth IV, 432
Rockwell, Elizabeth IV, 547
Rockwell, Francis Hall IV, 43
Rockwell, Franklin II, 716
Rockwell, Franklin III, 273
Rockwell, Franklin IV, 432
Rockwell, Franklin IV, 841
Rockwell, Frederick Frye II,
Rockwell, Georgiana IV, 432
Rockwell, Gertrude Ellen IV,
Rockwell, Glenn R. IV, 389
Rockwell, Glenn R. IV, 432
Rockwell, Glenn R. IV, 841
Rockwell, Glenn Rudolph IV,
Rockwell, Glenn Rudolph IV,
Rockwell, Harvey IV, 547
Rockwell, Harvey Whiting IV, 432
Rockwell, Helen L. IV, 841
Rockwell, Helen Luella IV, 43
Rockwell, Helen Luella IV, 84
Rockwell, Heston Ellis IV, 432
Rockwell, Howard Francis IV, 432
Rockwell, Hubert Joshua IV,
Rockwell, Luella IV, 841
Rockwell, Luella W. IV, 432
Rockwell, Luella W. IV, 841
Rockwell, Margaret IV, 432
Rockwell, Margaret Evelyn II, 137
Rockwell, Margaret G. IV, 841
Rockwell, Margaret Georgianna IV, 841
Rockwell, Maria A. II, 716
Rockwell, Maria A. III, 273
Rockwell, Maria A. IV, 432
Rockwell, Mariah IV, 841
Rockwell, Marjorie H. II, 137
Rockwell, Martha II, 415
Rockwell, Martha IV, 547
Rockwell, Martha M. IV, 518
Rockwell, Martha M. IV, 547
Rockwell, Mary Moore IV, 547
Rockwell, Oletia A. IV, 432
Rockwell, Owen Lorenzo IV, 4
Rockwell, Reuben L. IV, 432
Rockwell, Rockwell IV, 547
Rockwell, Roy W. IV, 432
Rockwell, Ruth IV, 547
Rockwell, Wallace Henghan II, 137
Rockwood, Elizabeth II, 916
Rockwood, Elizabeth C. II, 916
Rockwood, Elizabeth C. II, 936
Rocky, Mary J. V, 763
Rocky, Thomas V, 763
Rodakiewicz, Erla III, 273
Roderick, Fannie VI, 510
Roderick, Fannie VI, 513
Roderick, Fannie VI, 553
Roderick, William VI, 510
Roderick, William VI, 513
Roderick, William VI, 553
Rodes, Aaron D. VI, 986
Rodes, Ann I, 417
Rodes, Ann VI, 986
Rodes, David VI, 986
Rodes, Fanny VI, 986
Rodes, Henry VI, 986
Rodes, Isaac VI, 986
Rodes, Jane VI, 986
Rodes, Martha Ann VI, 986
Rodes, Polly VI, 986
Rodes, Wd. Alender VI, 986
Rodes, William VI, 986
Rodes, Wm. Radford VI, 986
Rodgar, Susan I, 1161
Rodgers, ??? VI, 869
Rodgers, Alexander M. VI, 851
Rodgers, Allison IV, 496
Rodgers, Ann II, 250
Rodgers, Ann II, 255
Rodgers, Ann II, 817
Rodgers, Ann III, 273
Rodgers, Ann IV, 319
Rodgers, Ann IV, 349
Rodgers, Burton III, 273
Rodgers, Christianna I, 607
Rodgers, Clara A. V, 525
Rodgers, Cora E. IV, 1103

gers, Cora E. IV, 1113
gers, Elizabeth VI, 851
lgers, Esther IV, 186
lgers, Evan VI, 406
gers, Evan VI, 433
lgers, Evan, Jr. VI, 440
lgers, Farley I, 1161
lgers, Hannah IV, 331
lgers, Hannah IV, 349
lgers, Hannah VI, 436
lgers, Hannah VI, 440
lgers, Inez IV, 496
lgers, Jacob I, 569
lgers, James B. III, 273
lgers, Jane S. VI, 851
lgers, John II, 796
lgers, John V, 525
lgers, John VI, 869
dgers, John Edward V, 525
dgers, Lewis I, 1161
lgers, Lucy V, 275
lgers, Lydia IV, 1221
lgers, Lydia R. V, 525
lgers, Margaret II, 267
lgers, Margery IV, 186
lgers, Marie III, 273
lgers, Martha II, 255
lgers, Mary II, 245
dgers, Mary II, 255
dgers, Mary IV, 158
dgers, Mary Ann II, 156
dgers, Mary Ann II, 161
dgers, Moses II, 255
dgers, Priscilla IV, 56
dgers, Rebecca II, 200
dgers, Rebecca II, 255
dgers, Samuel VI, 851
dgers, Sarah II, 250
dgers, Sarah II, 255
dgers, Sarah VI, 433
dgers, Sarah VI, 440
dgers, Sarah Anna II, 316
dgers, Susanna IV, 1214
dgers, Susanna IV, 1221
dgers, Thernando I, 1161
dgers, Thomas II, 250
dgers, Thomas II, 255
dgers, Thomas VI, 821
dgers, Thos. II, 250
dgers, Wd. Deborah Hawley II, 796
dgers, Wm. IV, 1261
dgers, Wm. A. IV, 1261
dges, Jacob VI, 440
dgway, Elizabeth II, 95
dgway, Rachel II, 95
dman, ??? III, 273
dman, ??? III, 274
dman, Alfred II, 415
dman, Alfred II, 639
dman, Ann II, 255
dman, Ann II, 415
dman, Ann III, 118
dman, Ann III, 241
dman, Ann III, 273
dman, Anna II, 182
dman, Anna II, 255
dman, Anna II, 262
dman, Anna II, 273
dman, Anna C. III, 118
dman, Anna Marshall II, 182
dman, Anne III, 273
dman, Anne III, 274
dman, Benjamin II, 601
dman, Benjamin II, 639
dman, Caleb III, 118
dman, Caroline III, 40
dman, Caroline III, 273
dman, Caroline III, 274
dman, Catharine III, 273
dman, Catherine III, 118
dman, Charles III, 118
dman, Charles III, 273
dman, Charles M. III, 118
dman, Deborah III, 273
dman, Dr. John II, 254
dman, Dr. John III, 101
dman, Dr. John III, 241
dman, Dr. John III, 273
dman, Dr. John III, 375
dman, Edith T. IV, 1090
dman, Edith T. IV, 1113
dman, Eleanor III, 273
dman, Eliz. III, 159
dman, Eliz. III, 273
dman, Elizabeth II, 182
dman, Elizabeth II, 196
dman, Elizabeth II, 197
dman, Elizabeth II, 233
dman, Elizabeth II, 248
odman, Elizabeth II, 249
Rodman, Elizabeth II, 254
Rodman, Elizabeth II, 255
Rodman, Elizabeth II, 261
Rodman, Elizabeth II, 601
Rodman, Elizabeth II, 639
Rodman, Elizabeth III, 118
Rodman, Elizabeth III, 119
Rodman, Elizabeth III, 163
Rodman, Elizabeth III, 221
Rodman, Elizabeth III, 273
Rodman, Elizabeth III, 274
Rodman, Elizabeth III, 287
Rodman, Elizabeth III, 440
Rodman, Frampton II, 182
Rodman, George III, 273
Rodman, Hannah II, 790
Rodman, Hannah II, 794
Rodman, Hannah III, 101
Rodman, Hannah III, 273
Rodman, Hannah III, 274
Rodman, Hannah III, 438
Rodman, Hannah H. III, 440
Rodman, Harriet III, 273
Rodman, Helena III, 273
Rodman, Helena III, 354
Rodman, Henry A. II, 763
Rodman, Isaac Pearson II, 182
Rodman, Isaac Pearson II, 255
Rodman, Isaac Pearson II, 262
Rodman, Isaac Pearson II, 639
Rodman, Isaac Peason II, 639
Rodman, John II, 182
Rodman, John II, 255
Rodman, John II, 631
Rodman, John II, 763
Rodman, John III, 170
Rodman, John III, 221
Rodman, John III, 273
Rodman, John III, 274
Rodman, John III, 354
Rodman, John Barbados III, 273
Rodman, John, Jr. II, 254
Rodman, John, Jr. III, 360
Rodman, Joseph III, 41
Rodman, Joseph III, 201
Rodman, Joseph III, 273
Rodman, Joseph III, 354
Rodman, Judith III, 41
Rodman, Judith III, 234
Rodman, Judith III, 273
Rodman, Katharine III, 159
Rodman, Katharine III, 274
Rodman, Lawrence III, 273
Rodman, Lewis II, 916
Rodman, Margaret II, 182
Rodman, Margaret II, 233
Rodman, Margaret II, 250
Rodman, Margaret II, 255
Rodman, Margaret II, 270
Rodman, Margaret III, 273
Rodman, Marl. III, 118
Rodman, Martha III, 118
Rodman, Martha M. II, 900
Rodman, Martha M. II, 916
Rodman, Mary II, 182
Rodman, Mary II, 254
Rodman, Mary II, 255
Rodman, Mary II, 631
Rodman, Mary II, 639
Rodman, Mary II, 943
Rodman, Mary II, 974
Rodman, Mary II, 1023
Rodman, Mary III, 119
Rodman, Mary III, 164
Rodman, Mary III, 273
Rodman, Mary III, 274
Rodman, Mary III, 354
Rodman, Mary III, 355
Rodman, Mary III, 360
Rodman, Mary A. III, 411
Rodman, Mary A. III, 440
Rodman, Mary Anna II, 982
Rodman, Mary Anna II, 1023
Rodman, Mary W. III, 411
Rodman, Mary W. III, 440
Rodman, Pearson II, 255
Rodman, Penelope III, 273
Rodman, Penelope III, 274
Rodman, Penelope III, 287
Rodman, Phinehas Buckley II, 1023
Rodman, Rachel II, 182
Rodman, Rachel II, 255
Rodman, Rebecca II, 182
Rodman, Rebecca II, 255
Rodman, Rebecca II, 415
Rodman, Rebecca II, 572
Rodman, Rebecca II, 639
Rodman, Rebecca Waln II, 601
Rodman, Rebecca Waln II, 639
Rodman, Richards II, 763
Rodman, Samuel II, 255
Rodman, Samuel II, 415
Rodman, Samuel II, 601
Rodman, Samuel II, 639
Rodman, Samuel III, 164
Rodman, Samuel III, 273
Rodman, Samuel III, 355
Rodman, Samuel III, 440
Rodman, Samuel S. II, 182
Rodman, Samuel, Jr. III, 438
Rodman, Samuel, Jr. III, 440
Rodman, Sarah II, 182
Rodman, Sarah II, 255
Rodman, Sarah III, 201
Rodman, Sarah III, 273
Rodman, Sarah III, 274
Rodman, Scammon III, 273
Rodman, Susan II, 639
Rodman, Susan W. II, 601
Rodman, Susan W. II, 639
Rodman, Susanna II, 182
Rodman, Susanna II, 255
Rodman, Susanna II, 277
Rodman, Susannah II, 182
Rodman, Susannah II, 255
Rodman, Thomas II, 182
Rodman, Thomas II, 196
Rodman, Thomas II, 233
Rodman, Thomas II, 249
Rodman, Thomas II, 254
Rodman, Thomas II, 255
Rodman, Thomas II, 639
Rodman, Thomas III, 118
Rodman, Thomas III, 119
Rodman, Thomas III, 159
Rodman, Thomas III, 163
Rodman, Thomas III, 273
Rodman, Thomas III, 274
Rodman, Thomas, Jr. II, 182
Rodman, Thomas, Jr. II, 255
Rodman, Thomas, Jr. II, 639
Rodman, Thos. III, 40
Rodman, Thos. III, 273
Rodman, Thos. III, 287
Rodman, Thos. H. III, 411
Rodman, Thos. H. III, 440
Rodman, William II, 182
Rodman, William II, 254
Rodman, William II, 255
Rodman, William II, 415
Rodman, William III, 273
Rodman, Wm. II, 631
Rodman, Wm. II, 639
Rodman, Wm. R. II, 601
Rodman, Wm. R. II, 639
Rodney, Hannah II, 95
Rodney, Hannah II, 104
Rodney, Mary II, 639
Rodney, Thomas II, 447
Rodney, William II, 447
Rodney, Wm. II, 551
Rodney, Wm. II, 639
Roe, ??? III, 274
Roe, ??? III, 325
Roe, ??? III, 384
Roe, ??? III, 386
Roe, Ada III, 274
Roe, Ada III, 325
Roe, Ann II, 447
Roe, Ann III, 384
Roe, Ann III, 386
Roe, Clark IV, 1261
Roe, Claud IV, 1262
Roe, Claud H. IV, 1261
Roe, Claude IV, 1261
Roe, David II, 255
Roe, Ethel B. IV, 1261
Roe, Etta Luella IV, 1261
Roe, Grace IV, 1261
Roe, Grace IV, 1262
Roe, Helen V, 707
Roe, Hellen V, 707
Roe, Henry VI, 85
Roe, Lottie M. IV, 1261
Roe, Madeline IV, 1336
Roe, Madge IV, 1261
Roe, Magdeline Leigh IV, 1336
Roe, Margaret IV, 1261
Roe, Margaret IV, 1262
Roe, Margaret Logan IV, 1336
Roe, Mary II, 447
Roe, Ralph IV, 1261
Roe, Rebecca V, 626
Roe, Rebecca V, 643
Roe, Rebecca S. V, 275
Roe, Robert II, 447
Roebuck, Albert Warren V, 707
Roebuck, Pearl V, 707
Roebuck, Ruth V, 707
Roemmele, George J. II, 130
Roemmele, Mary II, 130
Roemmele, Vernon A. II, 130
Roepke, Ferdinand II, 713
Roepke, Friederike II, 713
Roepke, Hedwig II, 713
Roese, Grace IV, 1262
Roessler, Carrie IV, 755
Rofe, George VI, 6
Rogee, Ann II, 636
Rogee, Ann II, 640
Roger, Zettie V, 707
Rogers, ??? III, 274
Rogers, ??? III, 384
Rogers, ??? III, 388
Rogers, ??? III, 508
Rogers, ??? IV, 547
Rogers, Abaline IV, 1222
Rogers, Abigail II, 255
Rogers, Abigail II, 300
Rogers, Abigail V, 32
Rogers, Abigail V, 38
Rogers, Abigail V, 115
Rogers, Abigail V, 116
Rogers, Abigail C. II, 319
Rogers, Abigail C. II, 324
Rogers, Abilona B. IV, 1222
Rogers, Abner II, 255
Rogers, Abner II, 259
Rogers, Abner II, 300
Rogers, Abolone IV, 1221
Rogers, Aclice Ann IV, 624
Rogers, Addison IV, 271
Rogers, Agatha V, 763
Rogers, Agnes G. III, 274
Rogers, Alice IV, 56
Rogers, Alice IV, 158
Rogers, Alice IV, 349
Rogers, Alice IV, 433
Rogers, Alice VI, 370
Rogers, Alice VI, 440
Rogers, Alithea VI, 986
Rogers, Allen A. II, 916
Rogers, Allen D. V, 525
Rogers, Allen D. V, 707
Rogers, Alonzo IV, 1182
Rogers, Alonzo IV, 1221
Rogers, Alonzo IV, 1222
Rogers, Alonzo IV, 1377
Rogers, Amelia IV, 1377
Rogers, Amos II, 256
Rogers, Amos III, 417
Rogers, Amos V, 1016
Rogers, Amos Austin IV, 841
Rogers, Amos W. III, 440
Rogers, Amy II, 182
Rogers, Amy II, 255
Rogers, Amy II, 256
Rogers, Amy II, 258
Rogers, Ancel IV, 1182
Rogers, Ann I, 514
Rogers, Ann I, 550
Rogers, Ann I, 569
Rogers, Ann I, 899
Rogers, Ann II, 182
Rogers, Ann II, 231
Rogers, Ann II, 249
Rogers, Ann II, 255
Rogers, Ann II, 266
Rogers, Ann II, 300
Rogers, Ann II, 415
Rogers, Ann II, 604
Rogers, Ann II, 640
Rogers, Ann II, 717
Rogers, Ann II, 763
Rogers, Ann II, 817
Rogers, Ann II, 916
Rogers, Ann IV, 31
Rogers, Ann IV, 56
Rogers, Ann IV, 132
Rogers, Ann IV, 271
Rogers, Ann IV, 349
Rogers, Ann IV, 433
Rogers, Ann IV, 654
Rogers, Ann IV, 841
Rogers, Ann Lucretia II, 849
Rogers, Ann Lucretia II, 916
Rogers, Anna II, 255
Rogers, Anna II, 640
Rogers, Anna IV, 349
Rogers, Anna V, 1017
Rogers, Anna VI, 338
Rogers, Anna VI, 986
Rogers, Anna C. III, 150
Rogers, Anna C. III, 274
Rogers, Anna L. III, 274
Rogers, Anna L. VI, 742
Rogers, Anna L. VI, 743
Rogers, Anna L. VI, 774
Rogers, Anne II, 503
Rogers, Anne III, 461
Rogers, Ansel IV, 989
Rogers, Ansel IV, 1162
Rogers, Ansel IV, 1182
Rogers, Ansel IV, 1221
Rogers, Ansel IV, 1222
Rogers, Ansel IV, 1377
Rogers, Ansel V, 929
Rogers, Ansell IV, 1377
Rogers, Arthur IV, 1182
Rogers, Arthur IV, 1221
Rogers, Arthur VI, 685
Rogers, Arthur T. IV, 1222
Rogers, Asa II, 300
Rogers, Asa Wing IV, 1377
Rogers, Asa Wing IV, 1384
Rogers, Asa, Jr. II, 300
Rogers, Asberry V, 1016
Rogers, Asberry V, 1017
Rogers, Atlantic IV, 56
Rogers, Atlantic IV, 57
Rogers, Atlantic IV, 90
Rogers, Atlantic IV, 107
Rogers, Atlantic V, 975
Rogers, Benajah II, 300
Rogers, Beulah II, 224
Rogers, Beulah Ann II, 280
Rogers, Beulah Ann II, 300
Rogers, Bulah II, 255
Rogers, Callie I, 1161
Rogers, Caroline III, 440
Rogers, Caroline E. IV, 624
Rogers, Caroline H. III, 417
Rogers, Cassandra IV, 56
Rogers, Catharine III, 384
Rogers, Catharine III, 388
Rogers, Catharine IV, 271
Rogers, Catharine IV, 1182
Rogers, Catherine IV, 1182
Rogers, Celicia IV, 624
Rogers, Celora IV, 1222
Rogers, Charles V, 1016
Rogers, Charles B. VI, 986
Rogers, Charles R. III, 419
Rogers, Charles R. III, 440
Rogers, Charlotte III, 274
Rogers, Charlotte V, 979
Rogers, Charlotte A. IV, 755
Rogers, Charlotte A. V, 975
Rogers, Chas. V, 1017
Rogers, Christeana I, 569
Rogers, Christiana I, 569
Rogers, Christianna I, 607
Rogers, Clara V, 525
Rogers, Clara V, 1016
Rogers, Clara V, 1017
Rogers, Clara A. V, 525
Rogers, Clarkson III, 274
Rogers, Clarkson Van Duzen III, 274
Rogers, Clayton II, 256
Rogers, Clayton B. II, 858
Rogers, Clayton B. II, 916
Rogers, Clayton Taylor II, 818
Rogers, Cynthia IV, 1162
Rogers, Cynthia IV, 1182
Rogers, Cynthia IV, 1221
Rogers, Cynthia IV, 1377
Rogers, D. Davis II, 916
Rogers, Daniel III, 427
Rogers, Daniel III, 440
Rogers, Daniel T. IV, 939
Rogers, Daniel T. IV, 989
Rogers, Daniel T. IV, 990
Rogers, Daniel T. IV, 1204
Rogers, Daniel T. IV, 1222
Rogers, Daniel Y. IV, 990
Rogers, David II, 817
Rogers, David VI, 986
Rogers, David A. V, 763
Rogers, David Davis II, 817
Rogers, David G. IV, 57
Rogers, David Norman V, 763
Rogers, David, Jr. III, 274
Rogers, Dessie IV, 433
Rogers, Doratha I, 191
Rogers, Dorothy Lee V, 310
Rogers, Edith II, 182
Rogers, Edith II, 312
Rogers, Edith IV, 57
Rogers, Edith IV, 107
Rogers, Edith IV, 841
Rogers, Edith G. IV, 57
Rogers, Edith G. IV, 107
Rogers, Edith M. IV, 271
Rogers, Edith M. IV, 841
Rogers, Edith R. II, 316
Rogers, Edith R. II, 324
Rogers, Edward II, 182
Rogers, Edward II, 256
Rogers, Edward III, 274
Rogers, Edward VI, 376
Rogers, Edward VI, 440
Rogers, Edward VI, 742

Rogers, Edward VI, 743
Rogers, Edward VI, 774
Rogers, Edwin II, 415
Rogers, Edwin D. II, 916
Rogers, Edwin Davis II, 818
Rogers, Eleanor VI, 440
Rogers, Eli IV, 56
Rogers, Eli IV, 57
Rogers, Eli IV, 107
Rogers, Eli V, 979
Rogers, Eli H. IV, 755
Rogers, Eli H. V, 975
Rogers, Eli H. V, 979
Rogers, Elijah IV, 547
Rogers, Elijah IV, 562
Rogers, Elisabeth II, 256
Rogers, Elisabeth II, 258
Rogers, Elisha VI, 384
Rogers, Elisha T. III, 274
Rogers, Eliza I, 933
Rogers, Eliza V, 310
Rogers, Elizabeth I, 514
Rogers, Elizabeth I, 569
Rogers, Elizabeth I, 899
Rogers, Elizabeth II, 182
Rogers, Elizabeth II, 255
Rogers, Elizabeth II, 256
Rogers, Elizabeth II, 258
Rogers, Elizabeth II, 265
Rogers, Elizabeth II, 300
Rogers, Elizabeth II, 415
Rogers, Elizabeth II, 503
Rogers, Elizabeth II, 717
Rogers, Elizabeth II, 1024
Rogers, Elizabeth III, 274
Rogers, Elizabeth IV, 39
Rogers, Elizabeth IV, 42
Rogers, Elizabeth IV, 56
Rogers, Elizabeth IV, 57
Rogers, Elizabeth IV, 88
Rogers, Elizabeth IV, 107
Rogers, Elizabeth V, 25
Rogers, Elizabeth V, 115
Rogers, Elizabeth V, 1016
Rogers, Elizabeth V, 1017
Rogers, Elizabeth VI, 403
Rogers, Elizabeth VI, 430
Rogers, Elizabeth VI, 440
Rogers, Elizabeth VI, 620
Rogers, Elizabeth VI, 653
Rogers, Elizabeth VI, 656
Rogers, Elizabeth VI, 657
Rogers, Elizabeth VI, 690
Rogers, Elizabeth VI, 692
Rogers, Elizabeth VI, 695
Rogers, Elizabeth VI, 732
Rogers, Elizabeth VI, 749
Rogers, Elizabeth H. V, 116
Rogers, Elizabeth L. II, 860
Rogers, Elizabeth L. II, 916
Rogers, Elizabeth L. IV, 107
Rogers, Elizabeth, Jr. II, 640
Rogers, Ellen B. IV, 835
Rogers, Ellen B. IV, 841
Rogers, Elma IV, 624
Rogers, Elton II, 137
Rogers, Emma Delesta IV, 1222
Rogers, Emma Delista IV, 1222
Rogers, Empson V, 115
Rogers, Empson V, 116
Rogers, Esther V, 115
Rogers, Esther V, 763
Rogers, Eunice VI, 376
Rogers, Eunice VI, 440
Rogers, Eva M. V, 763
Rogers, Evan IV, 56
Rogers, Evan IV, 158
Rogers, Evan IV, 349
Rogers, Evan VI, 384
Rogers, Evan VI, 440
Rogers, Evan VI, 553
Rogers, Evan, Jr. VI, 440
Rogers, Evan, Jr. VI, 553
Rogers, Farley I, 1161
Rogers, Florence III, 263
Rogers, Florence III, 274
Rogers, Florence V, 1017
Rogers, Florence J. V, 1016
Rogers, Frank V, 707
Rogers, Frank Hellutt III, 274
Rogers, Furman Black III, 102
Rogers, Furman Black III, 274
Rogers, George F. III, 150
Rogers, George F. III, 274
Rogers, George T. III, 263
Rogers, George T. III, 274
Rogers, Grant V, 707
Rogers, Handy IV, 1222
Rogers, Hannah I, 607
Rogers, Hannah II, 197
Rogers, Hannah II, 255
Rogers, Hannah II, 312
Rogers, Hannah II, 324
Rogers, Hannah II, 447
Rogers, Hannah IV, 271
Rogers, Hannah IV, 349
Rogers, Hannah IV, 433
Rogers, Hannah IV, 1182
Rogers, Hannah V, 32
Rogers, Hannah V, 115
Rogers, Hannah VI, 376
Rogers, Hannah VI, 440
Rogers, Hannah VI, 679
Rogers, Hannah VI, 685
Rogers, Hannah VI, 696
Rogers, Hannah S. II, 324
Rogers, Harriet II, 300
Rogers, Harriet D. II, 916
Rogers, Harriet Disher II, 818
Rogers, Helen I, 625
Rogers, Henry II, 182
Rogers, Henry B. III, 274
Rogers, Henry, Jr. II, 300
Rogers, Hessie I, 1161
Rogers, Hope II, 255
Rogers, Hope II, 259
Rogers, Horace Kingsley III, 274
Rogers, Howard Taylor II, 818
Rogers, Howard Taylor II, 858
Rogers, Howard Taylor II, 916
Rogers, Ida V, 1016
Rogers, Ida V, 1017
Rogers, Isaac C. IV, 835
Rogers, Isaac C. IV, 841
Rogers, Isaaih V, 115
Rogers, Isaiah, Jr. V, 116
Rogers, J. Wesley V, 357
Rogers, Jacob I, 514
Rogers, Jacob I, 550
Rogers, Jacob I, 569
Rogers, Jacob I, 899
Rogers, Jacob VI, 440
Rogers, James III, 274
Rogers, James IV, 56
Rogers, James V, 1016
Rogers, James VI, 440
Rogers, James B. II, 818
Rogers, James C. III, 274
Rogers, James Clark III, 274
Rogers, James M. IV, 271
Rogers, James R. IV, 56
Rogers, James R. IV, 271
Rogers, James Swift III, 274
Rogers, Jane I, 607
Rogers, Jane II, 255
Rogers, Jane II, 415
Rogers, Jane II, 604
Rogers, Jane III, 274
Rogers, Jane IV, 56
Rogers, Jane IV, 158
Rogers, Jane IV, 342
Rogers, Jane IV, 349
Rogers, Jane M. II, 604
Rogers, Jane M. II, 640
Rogers, Jemima I, 514
Rogers, Jemima I, 569
Rogers, Jemima I, 899
Rogers, Jemima III, 482
Rogers, Jemima III, 496
Rogers, Jennie W. II, 916
Rogers, Jeremiah IV, 31
Rogers, Jeremiah IV, 56
Rogers, Jeremiah IV, 132
Rogers, Jesse I, 514
Rogers, Joan II, 447
Rogers, Job II, 300
Rogers, John II, 163
Rogers, John II, 182
Rogers, John II, 255
Rogers, John II, 257
Rogers, John II, 415
Rogers, John IV, 56
Rogers, John IV, 158
Rogers, John IV, 349
Rogers, John IV, 433
Rogers, John V, 525
Rogers, John VI, 440
Rogers, John VI, 553
Rogers, John Edward III, 274
Rogers, John Edward V, 525
Rogers, John F. V, 525
Rogers, John L. II, 256
Rogers, John S. II, 255
Rogers, John S. II, 256
Rogers, John Staples II, 255
Rogers, Johnathan I, 607
Rogers, Jonathan IV, 56
Rogers, Jonathan IV, 57
Rogers, Jonathan IV, 107
Rogers, Jonathan T. IV, 57
Rogers, Jonathan T. IV, 990
Rogers, Joseph II, 255
Rogers, Joseph II, 312
Rogers, Joseph II, 324
Rogers, Joseph II, 640
Rogers, Joseph IV, 107
Rogers, Joseph IV, 433
Rogers, Joseph IV, 547
Rogers, Joseph V, 115
Rogers, Joseph H. IV, 57
Rogers, Joseph P. II, 749
Rogers, Joseph P. II, 763
Rogers, Joseph Powel II, 255
Rogers, Joseph, Jr. IV, 547
Rogers, Joshua IV, 547
Rogers, Josiah IV, 56
Rogers, Josiah IV, 158
Rogers, Josiah IV, 349
Rogers, Josiah IV, 433
Rogers, Josiah V, 32
Rogers, Josiah V, 38
Rogers, Josiah V, 115
Rogers, Josiah VI, 370
Rogers, Josiah VI, 440
Rogers, Josiah VI, 553
Rogers, Josiah VI, 774
Rogers, Josiah VI, 986
Rogers, Katharine IV, 271
Rogers, Laura Annie I, 933
Rogers, Leona V, 526
Rogers, Lettice II, 255
Rogers, Lettie A. V, 975
Rogers, Lettis II, 255
Rogers, Levi IV, 56
Rogers, Levi IV, 841
Rogers, Levi IV, 1377
Rogers, Levi V, 310
Rogers, Lewes IV, 56
Rogers, Lewis I, 1161
Rogers, Lewis IV, 56
Rogers, Lewis IV, 547
Rogers, Lindley IV, 56
Rogers, Lindley IV, 57
Rogers, Lindley IV, 107
Rogers, Lindley V, 975
Rogers, Lindley M. IV, 57
Rogers, Lindley M. IV, 101
Rogers, Lindley M. IV, 107
Rogers, Lindley M. V, 973
Rogers, Lindley M. V, 975
Rogers, Lindly M. IV, 107
Rogers, Linley IV, 57
Rogers, Loisa IV, 1377
Rogers, Lottie A. V, 979
Rogers, Louisa IV, 989
Rogers, Louisa IV, 1377
Rogers, Louiza IV, 1377
Rogers, Lucie Saphonia IV, 1221
Rogers, Lucy V, 275
Rogers, Lucy Jane IV, 939
Rogers, Lucy Jane IV, 989
Rogers, Lucy Jane IV, 990
Rogers, Lucy Jane IV, 1204
Rogers, Lucy Jane IV, 1222
Rogers, Lydia II, 182
Rogers, Lydia IV, 547
Rogers, Lydia IV, 957
Rogers, Lydia IV, 990
Rogers, Lydia IV, 1221
Rogers, Lydia IV, 1227
Rogers, Lydia V, 310
Rogers, Lydia VI, 365
Rogers, Lydia VI, 440
Rogers, Lydia VI, 460
Rogers, Lydia VI, 553
Rogers, Lydia Ann IV, 623
Rogers, Lydia Ann IV, 654
Rogers, Lydia Ann Grisel IV, 1377
Rogers, Lydia Ann Grisell IV, 1182
Rogers, Lydia R. V, 525
Rogers, Lydia S. II, 749
Rogers, Lydia S. II, 763
Rogers, Margaret II, 182
Rogers, Margaret II, 255
Rogers, Margaret III, 330
Rogers, Margaret V, 59
Rogers, Margaret V, 115
Rogers, Margaret V, 116
Rogers, Margary IV, 186
Rogers, Marguerite V, 763
Rogers, Marian IV, 56
Rogers, Marion I, 1161
Rogers, Martha I, 569
Rogers, Martha II, 255
Rogers, Martha III, 440
Rogers, Martha III, 446
Rogers, Martha IV, 158
Rogers, Martha V, 116
Rogers, Martha VI, 338
Rogers, Martha VI, 954
Rogers, Martha A. VI, 774
Rogers, Martha Esther II, 182
Rogers, Martha Esther II, 295
Rogers, Martha Esther II, 300
Rogers, Martha J. V, 707
Rogers, Martha Lipponcott IV, 841
Rogers, Mary I, 453
Rogers, Mary I, 933
Rogers, Mary II, 182
Rogers, Mary II, 249
Rogers, Mary II, 255
Rogers, Mary II, 257
Rogers, Mary II, 640
Rogers, Mary II, 818
Rogers, Mary II, 1008
Rogers, Mary II, 1024
Rogers, Mary III, 54
Rogers, Mary III, 274
Rogers, Mary III, 299
Rogers, Mary III, 427
Rogers, Mary III, 440
Rogers, Mary III, 449
Rogers, Mary IV, 43
Rogers, Mary IV, 56
Rogers, Mary IV, 57
Rogers, Mary IV, 107
Rogers, Mary IV, 158
Rogers, Mary IV, 349
Rogers, Mary IV, 433
Rogers, Mary IV, 547
Rogers, Mary IV, 624
Rogers, Mary IV, 816
Rogers, Mary IV, 841
Rogers, Mary V, 71
Rogers, Mary V, 115
Rogers, Mary V, 116
Rogers, Mary V, 818
Rogers, Mary V, 979
Rogers, Mary VI, 440
Rogers, Mary VI, 462
Rogers, Mary VI, 553
Rogers, Mary VI, 986
Rogers, Mary A. II, 858
Rogers, Mary A. II, 916
Rogers, Mary Ann II, 137
Rogers, Mary Ann II, 324
Rogers, Mary Ann II, 818
Rogers, Mary Ann IV, 26
Rogers, Mary Ann IV, 47
Rogers, Mary Ann IV, 57
Rogers, Mary Ann IV, 333
Rogers, Mary Ann IV, 349
Rogers, Mary Ann IV, 547
Rogers, Mary Ann IV, 562
Rogers, Mary C. IV, 96
Rogers, Mary C. IV, 107
Rogers, Mary C. IV, 618
Rogers, Mary C. IV, 654
Rogers, Mary F. V, 707
Rogers, Mary G. III, 102
Rogers, Mary G. III, 274
Rogers, Mary H. IV, 755
Rogers, Mary K. V, 975
Rogers, Mary K. V, 979
Rogers, Mary L. II, 256
Rogers, Mary Olivia II, 1069
Rogers, Mary Olivia II, 1078
Rogers, Mary Perkinson II, 255
Rogers, Mary T. II, 300
Rogers, Mary Virginia I, 899
Rogers, Mary Ward III, 274
Rogers, Maryann IV, 547
Rogers, Massy V, 310
Rogers, Mercy II, 182
Rogers, Mercy II, 255
Rogers, Mercy VI, 440
Rogers, Meriba IV, 1377
Rogers, Meriba IV, 1384
Rogers, Michael V, 275
Rogers, Mocha VI, 812
Rogers, Morris M. III, 440
Rogers, Morris M. III, 446
Rogers, Moses II, 255
Rogers, Moses F. III, 274
Rogers, Muriel R. III, 299
Rogers, Nancy Celora IV, 1222
Rogers, Nannie I, 933
Rogers, Naomi V, 763
Rogers, Nathan IV, 56
Rogers, Nathan IV, 57
Rogers, Nathan IV, 90
Rogers, Nathan IV, 107
Rogers, Nathan IV, 1377
Rogers, Nathan V, 975
Rogers, Nathan H. V, 979
Rogers, Nathan I. IV, 107
Rogers, Nathan J. IV, 56
Rogers, Nathan L. V, 975
Rogers, Nathaniel VI, 839
Rogers, Nathaniel VI, 854
Rogers, Nicholas II, 415
Rogers, Norman Lester V, 763
Rogers, Owen VI, 365
Rogers, Owen VI, 400
Rogers, Owen VI, 440
Rogers, Owen VI, 462
Rogers, Owen VI, 553
Rogers, Owen, Jr. VI, 440
Rogers, Pamela IV, 547
Rogers, Patience II, 182
Rogers, Phebe II, 255
Rogers, Phebe II, 266
Rogers, Philip IV, 56
Rogers, Philip IV, 107
Rogers, Philip B. I, 899
Rogers, Philip Bethea I, 933
Rogers, Philip, Jr. IV, 57
Rogers, Philip, Sr. IV, 57
Rogers, Polly IV, 811
Rogers, Polly IV, 859
Rogers, Priscilla IV, 28
Rogers, Priscilla IV, 56
Rogers, Priscilla IV, 57
Rogers, Priscilla IV, 1162
Rogers, Priscilla IV, 1182
Rogers, Rachel I, 514
Rogers, Rachel II, 415
Rogers, Rachel IV, 547
Rogers, Rachel C. II, 916
Rogers, Ray V, 526
Rogers, Ray V, 707
Rogers, Rebecca II, 182
Rogers, Rebecca II, 232
Rogers, Rebecca II, 255
Rogers, Rebecca II, 275
Rogers, Rebecca Witcraft II, 25
Rogers, Rhoda VI, 440
Rogers, Richard III, 274
Rogers, Richard VI, 129
Rogers, Richard VI, 140
Rogers, Richard VI, 143
Rogers, Robert I, 933
Rogers, Robert VI, 440
Rogers, Rowland IV, 547
Rogers, Rowland Cotton III, 27
Rogers, Roy V, 526
Rogers, Roy V, 707
Rogers, Ruby Faye V, 310
Rogers, Ruth II, 241
Rogers, Ruth II, 255
Rogers, Ruth III, 198
Rogers, Ruth III, 332
Rogers, Ruth III, 427
Rogers, Ruth IV, 56
Rogers, Ruth IV, 59
Rogers, Ruth IV, 841
Rogers, Ruth IV, 859
Rogers, Ruth V, 116
Rogers, Ruth A. V, 973
Rogers, Ruth A. V, 975
Rogers, Ruth F. III, 440
Rogers, Ruth H. IV, 101
Rogers, Ruth H. IV, 107
Rogers, Ruthanna I, 607
Rogers, Sameul II, 763
Rogers, Samuel II, 182
Rogers, Samuel II, 255
Rogers, Samuel II, 256
Rogers, Samuel II, 258
Rogers, Samuel II, 749
Rogers, Samuel II, 858
Rogers, Samuel II, 916
Rogers, Samuel IV, 27
Rogers, Samuel IV, 56
Rogers, Samuel IV, 547
Rogers, Samuel V, 115
Rogers, Samuel VI, 839
Rogers, Samuel G. Morton II, 64
Rogers, Samuel W. IV, 57
Rogers, Samuel, Jr. II, 256
Rogers, Sarah I, 514
Rogers, Sarah I, 569
Rogers, Sarah I, 899
Rogers, Sarah II, 182
Rogers, Sarah II, 255
Rogers, Sarah II, 447
Rogers, Sarah II, 858
Rogers, Sarah II, 916
Rogers, Sarah III, 234
Rogers, Sarah III, 274
Rogers, Sarah III, 440
Rogers, Sarah III, 446
Rogers, Sarah III, 496
Rogers, Sarah III, 508
Rogers, Sarah IV, 27
Rogers, Sarah IV, 56
Rogers, Sarah IV, 57
Rogers, Sarah IV, 158
Rogers, Sarah IV, 349
Rogers, Sarah IV, 547
Rogers, Sarah IV, 1182
Rogers, Sarah IV, 1221

gers, Sarah VI, 384
gers, Sarah VI, 440
gers, Sarah VI, 553
gers, Sarah Alice IV, 433
gers, Sarah Anna II, 324
gers, Sarah Catharine IV, 271
gers, Sarah Eliz. III, 253
gers, Sarah Eliz. III, 274
gers, Sarah Frances IV, 28
gers, Sarah Frances IV, 57
gers, Sarah H. IV, 624
gers, Sarah Louisa IV, 1182
gers, Sarah Louisa IV, 1222
gers, Sarah T. II, 749
gers, Sarah T. II, 763
gers, Sarah T. II, 858
gers, Sarah T. II, 916
gers, Sarah T. III, 419
gers, Sarah T. III, 440
gers, Sarah Taylor II, 818
gers, Sidney VI, 440
gers, Sidney VI, 447
gers, Silas IV, 1221
gers, Silas IV, 1377
gers, Silas R. IV, 1222
gers, Silas R. IV, 1377
gers, Stacey II, 300
gers, Stephen McBride VI, 440
gers, Susan I, 1161
gers, Susan B. I, 1161
gers, Susan Engle II, 817
gers, Susanna IV, 56
gers, Susanna IV, 547
gers, Susanna IV, 560
gers, Susanna IV, 562
gers, Susanna IV, 1221
gers, Susannah IV, 547
gers, Theodor VI, 384
gers, Thernando I, 1161
gers, Thomas II, 255
gers, Thomas II, 266
gers, Thomas II, 415
gers, Thomas II, 447
gers, Thomas II, 503
gers, Thomas II, 604
gers, Thomas II, 640
gers, Thomas IV, 271
gers, Thomas IV, 547
gers, Thomas IV, 1182
gers, Thomas II IV, 547
gers, Thomas, Jr. II, 182
gers, Thomas, Jr. II, 255
gers, Thomas, Sr. II, 182
gers, Thomasine II, 244
gers, Thomasine Mumford II, 255
gers, Thos. IV, 547
gers, Tim VI, 954
gers, Timothy VI, 338
gers, Tomason II, 182
gers, Vernon V, 763
gers, Virginia E. IV, 271
gers, W. III, 440
gers, Wallace V, 357
gers, Walter B. V, 357
gers, Wd. Rachel II, 182
gers, Wd. Rachel C. II, 818
gers, Wesley V, 357
gers, Wesley Earl V, 763
gers, William I, 607
gers, William I, 933
gers, William I, 1161
gers, William II, 255
gers, William II, 300
gers, William II, 312
gers, William II, 324
gers, William V, 116
gers, William D., Jr. III, 274
gers, William, Jr. V, 116
ogers, Willie V, 357
ogers, Winston IV, 57
ogers, Winston D. IV, 57
ogers, Winston D. IV, 107
ogers, Wm. A. V, 357
ogers, Wm. Davis III, 274
ogers, Zettie V, 707
ogerson, Absilla I, 48
ogerson, Absilla I, 71
ogerson, Ann I, 192
ogerson, Anne I, 183
ogerson, Doratha I, 191
ogerson, Doratha I, 199
ogerson, Dorotha I, 199
ogerson, Dorothy I, 928
ogerson, Elisabeth I, 71
ogerson, Elisabeth I, 86
ogerson, Elisabeth P. I, 257
ogerson, Elizabeth I, 254
ogerson, Elizabeth I, 257
ogerson, Gabriel I, 164
ogerson, Gabriel I, 199
Rogerson, Gabriel I, 257
Rogerson, John I, 183
Rogerson, Margaret I, 183
Rogerson, Margaret I, 257
Roggan, Emily II, 314
Rogge, Frederick W. V, 763
Rogge, Lula Lenora V, 763
Rogge, Myrtle May V, 763
Roggie, Henry IV, 1222
Rogstron, Elinor VI, 525
Rogstron, Thomas VI, 525
Roh, Mariah II, 811
Roher, Donald McKinley IV, 755
Roher, George Wayne IV, 756
Roher, Raymond IV, 755
Roher, Raymond IV, 756
Roher, Raymond Paul IV, 755
Roher, Vera IV, 755
Roher, Vera IV, 756
Roher, W. D. IV, 755
Rohly, Ida IV, 1336
Rohr, Jacob VI, 810
Rohr, Jacob VI, 851
Rohr, May IV, 1262
Rohr, Nancy VI, 851
Rohr, Philip VI, 851
Rohr, Sally VI, 851
Rohrback, Goldie V, 200
Rohrback, Susan V, 200
Rohser, Susanna IV, 995
Roice, D. L. V, 1017
Roice, Delilah V, 1017
Roice, Edward C. V, 1017
Roice, Edwin W. V, 1017
Roice, Rebecca V, 1017
Rolalas, James VI, 851
Rolalas, Martha VI, 851
Roland, Ann II, 256
Roland, Hannah VI, 440
Roland, Henry V, 200
Roland, Ishmael II, 415
Roland, James II, 640
Roland, Jane V, 200
Roland, Joseph II, 640
Roland, Margrett II, 415
Roland, Micajah VI, 987
Roland, Sarah II, 640
Roland, Sidney VI, 987
Rolet, Mary II, 640
Rolfe, George VI, 40
Rolfe, Mary I, 164
Rolfe, Mary I, 170
Rolingson, Elizabeth VI, 209
Rolland, Mary A. III, 73
Rolland, Mary E. III, 238
Rolland, Samuel F. V, 1017
Rolland, Wm. V, 1017
Roller, Sarah IV, 634
Roller, Sarah IV, 654
Rollier, Sadie IV, 1262
Rolling, Alfred G. IV, 756
Rollinson, Catherine Parlette V, 526
Rollinson, Thomas V, 273
Rollison, Catherine Parlette V, 707
Rolph, Hana II, 95
Rolph, Sarah II, 95
Romain, Ephraim V, 958
Romain, John VI, 877
Roman, ??? IV, 1085
Roman, ??? IV, 1125
Roman, Abraham IV, 1137
Roman, Amos IV, 433
Roman, Amos IV, 1097
Roman, Amos IV, 1113
Roman, Ann IV, 1113
Roman, Ann IV, 1123
Roman, Ann IV, 1137
Roman, Eli IV, 1137
Roman, Elizabeth IV, 1137
Roman, Ellwood IV, 1137
Roman, Elwood IV, 1137
Roman, Ephraim IV, 433
Roman, Ephraim IV, 1113
Roman, Ephraim IV, 1123
Roman, Ephraim IV, 1137
Roman, Evan IV, 167
Roman, Even IV, 433
Roman, Ezra IV, 433
Roman, Hampton IV, 1113
Roman, Hamton IV, 433
Roman, Hannah II, 447
Roman, Hannah IV, 433
Roman, Isaac IV, 433
Roman, Isaac IV, 1113
Roman, Isaac IV, 1137
Roman, Jane II, 826
Roman, Jesse IV, 1113
Roman, Jesse IV, 1137
Roman, Lydia IV, 1097
Roman, Lydia IV, 1113
Roman, Mary IV, 433
Roman, Mary IV, 1113
Roman, Mary IV, 1137
Roman, Mary Cecille IV, 433
Roman, Mary Jane IV, 1113
Roman, Mary Jane IV, 1137
Roman, Mary W. IV, 1113
Roman, Philip II, 415
Roman, Philip II, 447
Roman, Phillip II, 415
Roman, Rachel II, 640
Roman, Rachel IV, 1113
Roman, Rachel IV, 1137
Roman, Rachel IV, 1140
Roman, Sarah Ann IV, 433
Roman, Sarah Ann IV, 1137
Roman, Sarah Ann IV, 1139
Roman, Sarah Elizabeth IV, 1129
Roman, Sarah Elizabeth IV, 1137
Roman, Susan IV, 433
Roman, Thomas C. IV, 433
Roman, Thomas I. IV, 433
Roman, Thomas J. IV, 433
Roman, Thomas L. IV, 433
Roman, Wd. Dorothy II, 640
Roman, Wd. Mary II, 415
Roman, William IV, 1137
Romans, ??? IV, 547
Romans, Abraham IV, 1075
Romans, Amos IV, 1075
Romans, Ann IV, 514
Romans, Ann IV, 548
Romans, Elisha IV, 349
Romans, Elisha IV, 548
Romans, Elisha IV, 562
Romans, Elizabeth IV, 538
Romans, Elizabeth IV, 548
Romans, Elizabeth IV, 1075
Romans, Elvira R. IV, 538
Romans, Ephraim IV, 1075
Romans, Ephraim IV, 1183
Romans, Evan IV, 349
Romans, Evan IV, 547
Romans, Evan IV, 548
Romans, Evan IV, 550
Romans, Evan D. IV, 547
Romans, Evans IV, 547
Romans, Ezra IV, 1075
Romans, George IV, 547
Romans, Hampton IV, 1075
Romans, Hannah IV, 349
Romans, Hannah IV, 538
Romans, Hannah IV, 547
Romans, Hannah IV, 548
Romans, Hannah H. IV, 547
Romans, Isaac IV, 1075
Romans, Jacob IV, 547
Romans, Jacob IV, 548
Romans, Jane IV, 349
Romans, Jane IV, 514
Romans, Jane IV, 547
Romans, Jane IV, 548
Romans, Jordan IV, 547
Romans, Joseph IV, 547
Romans, Joseph IV, 548
Romans, Joseph IV, 1183
Romans, Joseph IV, 1222
Romans, Joseph T. IV, 538
Romans, Lucinda IV, 1161
Romans, Lucinda IV, 1183
Romans, Lydia IV, 349
Romans, Lydia IV, 542
Romans, Lydia IV, 547
Romans, Lydia IV, 548
Romans, Lydia IV, 1113
Romans, Martha T. IV, 536
Romans, Martha T. IV, 548
Romans, Mary IV, 349
Romans, Mary IV, 378
Romans, Mary IV, 547
Romans, Mary IV, 548
Romans, Mary IV, 1075
Romans, Mary IV, 1113
Romans, Mary Ann IV, 349
Romans, Mary Ann IV, 548
Romans, Mary Cecille IV, 433
Romans, Mary P. IV, 548
Romans, Moses IV, 349
Romans, Moses IV, 548
Romans, Moses, Jr. IV, 562
Romans, Phebe IV, 547
Romans, Phebe S. IV, 548
Romans, Rachel II, 640
Romans, Rachel II, 658
Romans, Richard IV, 1113
Romans, Robert IV, 349
Romans, Robert IV, 548
Romans, Robert IV, 562
Romans, Sally IV, 562
Romans, Sally IV, 1183
Romans, Sally IV, 1222
Romans, Sarah IV, 586
Romans, Sarah Ann IV, 1075
Romans, Susan IV, 452
Romans, Susan H. IV, 548
Romans, Susan W. IV, 547
Romans, Tacy IV, 547
Romans, Tacy IV, 548
Romans, Tacy IV, 550
Romans, Tamar IV, 547
Romans, Thomas IV, 547
Romans, Thomas J. IV, 548
Romans, Thos. J. IV, 452
Romans, Valentine IV, 547
Romans, Viola D. IV, 1262
Romans, William IV, 547
Romer, Maria III, 357
Romick, Lida G. IV, 1183
Romick, Lida G. IV, 1262
Romick, Lida M. IV, 1262
Romine, Dora V, 200
Romine, Emily V, 200
Romine, Hannah IV, 433
Romine, Maria V, 49
Romine, Maria V, 116
Romine, Maria M. V, 116
Romines, Fanny VI, 851
Romines, Jasbon VI, 851
Romman, Phillip II, 415
Rommel, William I, 899
Rommins, Hannah VI, 440
Ronald, Andrew VI, 986
Ronald, Elizabeth VI, 986
Ronald, Emily R. VI, 986
Ronald, George W. VI, 986
Roncer, Hannah VI, 440
Roney, Michael V, 200
Roney, Virginia V, 200
Ronk, Nancy VI, 986
Ronk, Samuel VI, 986
Ronsley, James I, 440
Ronsley, James I, 453
Ronsley, John I, 417
Ronsley, John I, 440
Ronsley, Joseph I, 440
Ronsley, Joseph I, 453
Ronsley, Sarah I, 440
Rood, Abigail IV, 671
Rood, Abigail IV, 756
Rood, Abigail IV, 770
Rood, Abigail IV, 797
Rood, Abigail IV, 841
Rood, Ann Eliza IV, 271
Rood, Augusta IV, 271
Rood, Betty IV, 756
Rood, Betty IV, 915
Rood, Clarissa IV, 271
Rood, Clarissa IV, 735
Rood, Clarissa IV, 756
Rood, Clarissa IV, 768
Rood, Clarissa IV, 915
Rood, Clarissa IV, 990
Rood, Clarissa IV, 1009
Rood, Elizabeth IV, 756
Rood, Emmor IV, 271
Rood, Emmor IV, 292
Rood, Emmor IV, 756
Rood, Emmor IV, 915
Rood, Emmor IV, 990
Rood, Emmor IV, 1183
Rood, Emmore IV, 1183
Rood, Isaiah IV, 756
Rood, Ithamar IV, 756
Rood, Ithamar IV, 915
Rood, Ithamer IV, 990
Rood, Jane L. IV, 756
Rood, Jane L. IV, 780
Rood, Jonathan IV, 271
Rood, Jonathan IV, 735
Rood, Jonathan IV, 756
Rood, Jonathan IV, 768
Rood, Jonathan IV, 770
Rood, Jonathan IV, 915
Rood, Jonathan IV, 990
Rood, Lavina IV, 756
Rood, Lavina IV, 768
Rood, Lavina IV, 915
Rood, Lucina IV, 756
Rood, Lucina IV, 915
Rood, Lusina IV, 735
Rood, Lusina IV, 756
Rood, Luvina IV, 756
Rood, Mary Ann IV, 903
Rood, Mary Ann IV, 915
Rood, Michael IV, 671
Rood, Rhoda IV, 671
Rood, Roger IV, 756
Rood, Roger IV, 915
Rood, Tacy IV, 271
Rood, Tacy IV, 292
Rood, Wd. Abigail IV, 756
Rood, William IV, 271
Roof, Hana II, 95
Rook, George II, 640
Rook, Hannah II, 640
Rook, Thomas II, 415
Rook, Thomas II, 640
Rooke, George II, 640
Rooke, Mary III, 80
Rooke, Mary III, 274
Rooke, Thomas II, 640
Rooker, Pheba V, 763
Rookhill, Joseph II, 95
Rooney, Charles C. V, 200
Rooney, Charley Creighton V, 200
Rooney, Effie A. V, 116
Rooney, Harry V, 200
Rooney, Harry Walter V, 200
Rooney, Michael V, 200
Rooney, Samuel F. V, 200
Rooney, Samuel T. V, 200
Rooney, Virginia V, 200
Roop, Mary Deb II, 763
Rooraback, John O. III, 274
Roorback, ??? III, 274
Roorback, Abigail III, 274
Roorback, Alfred III, 274
Roorback, Benjamin C. III, 274
Roorback, John O. III, 274
Roorback, Mary F. III, 274
Roorback, William III, 274
Roos, Ruth VI, 688
Roos, Ruth VI, 696
Roosa, Claud IV, 433
Roosa, Elizabeth IV, 418
Roosa, Elizabeth IV, 433
Roosa, Ervin IV, 418
Roosa, Ervin IV, 433
Roose, Margaret V, 429
Roose, Mary IV, 756
Roose, Mary N. IV, 676
Roose, Mary N. IV, 756
Roosen, Maria II, 447
Roosen, Paul II, 447
Root, Ann III, 27
Root, Ann III, 93
Root, Fred IV, 1336
Root, Howard Cassin III, 89
Root, Howard Cassin III, 274
Root, Jane III, 89
Root, Jane J. II, 854
Root, Jane J. III, 274
Root, Jane Johnson II, 916
Root, Jane T. II, 916
Root, Louis A. II, 818
Root, Robert C. I, 569
Roots, Rachel I, 164
Roots, Rachel I, 166
Roox, Elizabeth V, 252
Roox, Elizabeth V, 275
Rop, Phineas V, 116
Rop, Sarah Ann V, 840
Rop, Sarah Ann V, 860
Rop, Thomas V, 116
Roper, Abigail II, 210
Roper, Edmund VI, 845
Roper, Elizabeth VI, 851
Roper, Frances VI, 862
Roper, Henry C. VI, 851
Roper, Joshua II, 210
Roper, Joshua II, 233
Roper, Joshua II, 261
Roper, Lewis VI, 926
Roper, Martha II, 196
Roper, Mary II, 233
Roper, Mary II, 245
Roper, Mary II, 640
Roper, Mary II, 651
Roper, Nancy W. VI, 851
Roper, Robert VI, 851
Roper, Robert R. VI, 851
Roper, Sarah II, 210
Roper, Sarah II, 233
Roper, Sarah II, 261
Roper, Thomas II, 196
Roper, Thomas II, 210
Rosamond, Mary II, 871
Rosbrugh, Hilkiah VI, 1002
Rosbrugh, Isabel VI, 1002
Rosco, Luke II, 232
Rosco, Luke II, 256
Rosco, Mary II, 232
Rosco, Mary II, 256
Rosco, Mary III, 274
Rosco, Phebe II, 232
Rosco, Phebe II, 256
Roscoe, Luke II, 256
Roscoe, Mary II, 256
Roscoe, Phebe II, 256
Roscow, Ann II, 1014
Roscow, Ann II, 1024
Rose, Abigail II, 640

Rose, Alice IV, 1336
Rose, Alvina IV, 1328
Rose, Andrew I, 1161
Rose, Andrew V, 526
Rose, Annie I, 227
Rose, Annie V, 275
Rose, Aquilla II, 415
Rose, Atkin II, 415
Rose, Atkinson II, 415
Rose, Atkinson II, 640
Rose, Augusta IV, 1328
Rose, Benjamin II, 415
Rose, Carrie V, 275
Rose, Catharine VI, 987
Rose, David II, 415
Rose, David II, 640
Rose, Deborah II, 640
Rose, Deborah II, 645
Rose, Dialtha I, 1161
Rose, Edward J. V, 707
Rose, Eli II, 415
Rose, Eli II, 640
Rose, Elisabeth H. I, 235
Rose, Elisabeth H. I, 257
Rose, Elizabeth II, 415
Rose, Elizabeth VI, 851
Rose, Elizabeth VI, 986
Rose, Elizabeth H. I, 227
Rose, Elizabeth Harriett I, 211
Rose, Elizabeth M. VI, 987
Rose, George I, 257
Rose, George T. I, 257
Rose, Grace IV, 1262
Rose, Hannah III, 476
Rose, Henry B. I, 317
Rose, Hephsebah II, 828
Rose, Hettie I, 340
Rose, James E. V, 707
Rose, Jennie I, 942
Rose, Jessie V, 275
Rose, John II, 1024
Rose, John V, 1017
Rose, John S. II, 415
Rose, John S. II, 640
Rose, John W. I, 340
Rose, Jonathan II, 640
Rose, Jonnie I, 340
Rose, Joseph V, 275
Rose, Joseph E. V, 275
Rose, Letah IV, 1336
Rose, Letitia VI, 440
Rose, Mamie L. I, 227
Rose, Margaret I, 227
Rose, Margaret V, 707
Rose, Marshal I, 340
Rose, Martha IV, 593
Rose, Martha VI, 99
Rose, Martha VI, 119
Rose, Martha VI, 440
Rose, Mary I, 234
Rose, Mary I, 257
Rose, Mary Ellen IV, 1056
Rose, Mary Ellen IV, 1075
Rose, Mary, Jr. II, 640
Rose, Maud V, 275
Rose, Melcema V, 1017
Rose, Melissa V, 275
Rose, Melissa J. V, 275
Rose, Netta V, 275
Rose, Nettie V, 275
Rose, Nol L. V, 707
Rose, Phebe II, 582
Rose, Phebe II, 640
Rose, Rebecca II, 415
Rose, Rebecca II, 640
Rose, Rebecca II, 645
Rose, Rebecca II, 1024
Rose, Rena I, 340
Rose, Robert VI, 986
Rose, Robert P. I, 257
Rose, Samuel II, 415
Rose, Samuel II, 640
Rose, Samuel Lippincott II, 640
Rose, Sarah II, 1024
Rose, Sarah VI, 987
Rose, Sarah J. I, 317
Rose, Sarah M. I, 340
Rose, Septimus II, 415
Rose, Susan A. I, 340
Rose, Susanah I, 1161
Rose, Susannah VI, 987
Rose, Thomas II, 415
Rose, Thomas II, 640
Rose, Thomas II, 645
Rose, Thomas II, 1024
Rose, Thomas E. VI, 987
Rose, Uriah VI, 987
Rose, Uriah, Jr. VI, 987
Rose, William VI, 813
Rose, William VI, 851
Rose, William VI, 987
Rose, William VI, 1001
Rose, William M. I, 235
Rose, William M. I, 257
Rose, Wm. IV, 1328
Rose, Wm. H. I, 211
Rose, Wm. M. I, 227
Roseberry, Mary V, 496
Roseberry, Mary V, 526
Rosebrough, Isabella VI, 1002
Rosebrough, Janie VI, 1002
Rosebrugh, Hilkiah VI, 987
Rosebrugh, Margaret VI, 1002
Rosebrugh, Susanna VI, 987
Rosecrans, Rebecca III, 245
Rosecrans, Rebecca III, 294
Rosell, William II, 415
Rosenberger, Alonzo A. V, 595
Rosenbower, Herbert V, 464
Rosenbower, J. R. V, 464
Rosenbower, Lydia V, 464
Rosenbower, Nellie V, 464
Roseter, Anne VI, 31
Roseter, Anne VI, 36
Rosher, John V, 275
Rosher, Sarah V, 116
Rosnell, William I, 948
Rosogins, John II, 447
Rosogins, Nicholas II, 447
Ross, Addison Shepherd I, 625
Ross, Albert IV, 1377
Ross, Albert V, 526
Ross, Albert V, 707
Ross, Albert V, 708
Ross, Albert J. V, 708
Ross, Albert L. V, 642
Ross, Alberta V, 526
Ross, Alberta L. V, 708
Ross, Alexander VI, 357
Ross, Alexander VI, 358
Ross, Alexander VI, 359
Ross, Alexander VI, 402
Ross, Alexander VI, 410
Ross, Alexander VI, 440
Ross, Alexander VI, 609
Ross, Alfred VI, 441
Ross, Alfred L. V, 642
Ross, Alfred S. V, 275
Ross, Alfred S. V, 642
Ross, Alfred Simmons V, 275
Ross, Alfred Simmons V, 642
Ross, Alice Josephine I, 625
Ross, Almira Jane V, 275
Ross, Almira Jane V, 642
Ross, Almira Jane V, 707
Ross, Almira Jane V, 708
Ross, Amanda Jane V, 275
Ross, Andrew I, 71
Ross, Andrew, Jr. I, 54
Ross, Andrew, Jr. I, 71
Ross, Ann I, 900
Ross, Ann II, 893
Ross, Ann II, 916
Ross, Ann VI, 440
Ross, Ann Eliza VI, 863
Ross, Ann R. II, 256
Ross, Ann R. II, 267
Ross, Anna I, 71
Ross, Anna III, 209
Ross, Anna III, 275
Ross, Anna IV, 57
Ross, Anna IV, 330
Ross, Anna IV, 349
Ross, Anna B. III, 274
Ross, Anna L. III, 274
Ross, Anna L. III, 275
Ross, Anne III, 275
Ross, Anne IV, 394
Ross, Anne IV, 433
Ross, Augustus W. III, 275
Ross, Barbara II, 640
Ross, Bates IV, 496
Ross, Belle IV, 496
Ross, Berrilla B. VI, 774
Ross, Bessie IV, 496
Ross, Blanch V, 707
Ross, Caroline II, 415
Ross, Caroline II, 763
Ross, Caroline II, 916
Ross, Caroline III, 137
Ross, Caroline III, 274
Ross, Carrie Ellen V, 642
Ross, Catharen VI, 440
Ross, Catharine VI, 521
Ross, Catharine VI, 553
Ross, Catharine VI, 774
Ross, Catherine V, 116
Ross, Catherine VI, 405
Ross, Catherine VI, 440
Ross, Catherine VI, 451
Ross, Catherine VI, 521
Ross, Cephas II, 786
Ross, Cephas III, 274
Ross, Charles V, 839
Ross, Charles V, 860
Ross, Charles VI, 735
Ross, Charles VI, 774
Ross, Chas. V, 1017
Ross, Clara V, 707
Ross, Clara Bell IV, 496
Ross, Clara M. III, 147
Ross, Cleo I, 340
Ross, Cleo M. I, 340
Ross, Cora Leonard V, 526
Ross, Cordelia A. III, 131
Ross, Cordelia A. III, 275
Ross, Daniel I, 71
Ross, David I, 274
Ross, David VI, 374
Ross, David VI, 405
Ross, David VI, 440
Ross, David VI, 451
Ross, David VI, 521
Ross, David VI, 553
Ross, David VI, 554
Ross, David VI, 735
Ross, David VI, 774
Ross, David F. V, 357
Ross, David T. V, 275
Ross, David, Jr. VI, 521
Ross, David, Jr. VI, 774
Ross, Doshia VI, 987
Ross, Edna IV, 496
Ross, Edward II, 763
Ross, Edward III, 274
Ross, Edward H. II, 916
Ross, Edward H. III, 274
Ross, Elden V, 526
Ross, Elden V, 707
Ross, Eldon V, 526
Ross, Eldon V, 708
Ross, Elender VI, 876
Ross, Elenor VI, 987
Ross, Elisa I, 71
Ross, Elisabeth I, 257
Ross, Eliza I, 76
Ross, Elizabeth I, 274
Ross, Elizabeth II, 95
Ross, Elizabeth III, 274
Ross, Elizabeth IV, 19
Ross, Elizabeth IV, 57
Ross, Elizabeth IV, 330
Ross, Elizabeth IV, 349
Ross, Elizabeth IV, 548
Ross, Elizabeth IV, 549
Ross, Elizabeth V, 275
Ross, Elizabeth V, 642
Ross, Elliam Erskine V, 275
Ross, Ellis V, 642
Ross, Ellis V, 707
Ross, Ellis V, 708
Ross, Ellis R. V, 275
Ross, Ellis R. V, 642
Ross, Ellis Rees V, 275
Ross, Ellis Rees V, 642
Ross, Elmira J. Jane V, 275
Ross, Elmira Jane V, 642
Ross, Elsie III, 172
Ross, Elsie III, 274
Ross, Emaline V, 707
Ross, Emeline V, 526
Ross, Emeline VI, 889
Ross, Emma V, 526
Ross, Emma V, 707
Ross, Emmaline V, 707
Ross, Enos V, 275
Ross, Enos V, 642
Ross, Enos VI, 435
Ross, Enos VI, 445
Ross, Enos VI, 774
Ross, Enos Rachel VI, 440
Ross, Ester I, 257
Ross, Esther I, 54
Ross, Esther I, 206
Ross, Eva O. H. V, 642
Ross, Eva O. H. V, 707
Ross, Eva O. H. V, 708
Ross, Frank V, 357
Ross, Frank V, 464
Ross, George VI, 410
Ross, George VI, 440
Ross, Hannah II, 818
Ross, Hannah II, 916
Ross, Hannah VI, 440
Ross, Hannah VI, 441
Ross, Hannah VI, 445
Ross, Hannah VI, 774
Ross, Henry W. II, 916
Ross, Henry W. III, 274
Ross, Hunter IV, 496
Ross, Isaac Buckley II, 640
Ross, Isaiah II, 1003
Ross, Isaiah II, 1024
Ross, Jabez VI, 987
Ross, Jacob IV, 1377
Ross, James I, 71
Ross, James I, 257
Ross, James V, 464
Ross, James VI, 774
Ross, James A. V, 642
Ross, James Albert V, 642
Ross, Jennie V, 526
Ross, Jennie V, 707
Ross, Jessie IV, 496
Ross, Job II, 447
Ross, John II, 256
Ross, John II, 267
Ross, John II, 415
Ross, John VI, 359
Ross, John VI, 402
Ross, John VI, 409
Ross, John VI, 440
Ross, John VI, 876
Ross, John VI, 944
Ross, John VI, 963
Ross, John VI, 987
Ross, John Carroll VI, 774
Ross, John F. VI, 774
Ross, John F., Second VI, 774
Ross, John R. V, 860
Ross, Jonathan VI, 372
Ross, Jonathan VI, 440
Ross, Jonathan VI, 774
Ross, Joseph VI, 987
Ross, Julia I, 618
Ross, Katharine VI, 359
Ross, Katherine VI, 374
Ross, Katherine VI, 440
Ross, Katherine VI, 735
Ross, Katherine VI, 774
Ross, Kenneth Addison I, 625
Ross, Lawrence I, 620
Ross, Lawrence I, 636
Ross, Lawrence I, 640
Ross, Lawrence Calvin I, 625
Ross, Lena B. V, 707
Ross, Levi V, 1017
Ross, Levi VI, 440
Ross, Lillian V, 275
Ross, Lillie V, 357
Ross, Lola I, 625
Ross, Lola Perkins I, 640
Ross, Louella V, 707
Ross, Louella G. V, 707
Ross, Loulu V, 526
Ross, Luella IV, 496
Ross, Lutherland VI, 963
Ross, Lydia VI, 359
Ross, Lydia VI, 402
Ross, Lydia VI, 405
Ross, Lydia VI, 425
Ross, Lydia VI, 435
Ross, Lydia VI, 440
Ross, Lydia VI, 441
Ross, Lydia VI, 445
Ross, Lydia VI, 774
Ross, Margaret IV, 593
Ross, Margaret IV, 1113
Ross, Margaret IV, 1377
Ross, Margaret V, 275
Ross, Margaret H. IV, 1377
Ross, Mariette III, 131
Ross, Mariette III, 310
Ross, Martha II, 379
Ross, Martha VI, 372
Ross, Martha VI, 440
Ross, Martha VI, 445
Ross, Martha A. I, 928
Ross, Martha Ann V, 275
Ross, Martha Ann V, 628
Ross, Martha Ann V, 642
Ross, Martha G. V, 642
Ross, Mary I, 153
Ross, Mary I, 164
Ross, Mary I, 206
Ross, Mary I, 257
Ross, Mary I, 611
Ross, Mary I, 636
Ross, Mary I, 640
Ross, Mary II, 640
Ross, Mary II, 666
Ross, Mary II, 786
Ross, Mary IV, 19
Ross, Mary IV, 57
Ross, Mary IV, 69
Ross, Mary V, 464
Ross, Mary V, 611
Ross, Mary V, 642
Ross, Mary VI, 445
Ross, Mary VI, 521
Ross, Mary VI, 553
Ross, Mary VI, 554
Ross, Mary VI, 774
Ross, Mary A. V, 860
Ross, Mary Ann V, 839
Ross, Mary E. V, 860
Ross, Mary Emily V, 860
Ross, Mary Hinton I, 620
Ross, Mary K. I, 640
Ross, Mary P. VI, 987
Ross, Mary Susannah VI, 774
Ross, Milly VI, 1007
Ross, Milton IV, 1183
Ross, Milton IV, 1377
Ross, Mina IV, 496
Ross, Mina IV, 1183
Ross, Nancy VI, 944
Ross, Nancy VI, 987
Ross, Nannie I, 625
Ross, Nellie V, 642
Ross, Nellie E. V, 708
Ross, Nicholas II, 379
Ross, Oatas V, 526
Ross, Okey D. IV, 1262
Ross, Ollie V, 464
Ross, Ordie L. V, 707
Ross, Oris V, 526
Ross, Orris V, 707
Ross, Patty VI, 987
Ross, Phebe IV, 57
Ross, Phebe IV, 349
Ross, Phebe IV, 541
Ross, Phebe IV, 548
Ross, Phebe VI, 374
Ross, Phebe VI, 440
Ross, Phebe VI, 735
Ross, Phebe VI, 774
Ross, Phineas IV, 271
Ross, Phineas V, 116
Ross, Rachel II, 590
Ross, Rachel II, 640
Ross, Rachel IV, 1377
Ross, Rachel VI, 405
Ross, Rachel VI, 440
Ross, Rebecca IV, 57
Ross, Rebecca IV, 1377
Ross, Rebecca V, 702
Ross, Rebecca V, 707
Ross, Rebecca VI, 774
Ross, Rebecca B. IV, 1377
Ross, Rebecca J. V, 642
Ross, Rebecca J. V, 708
Ross, Rebeckah II, 1024
Ross, Rebekah II, 1003
Ross, Rebekah II, 1024
Ross, Reuben I, 274
Ross, Reuben IV, 19
Ross, Reuben IV, 57
Ross, Reuben IV, 330
Ross, Reuben IV, 349
Ross, Reuben IV, 350
Ross, Rhoda V, 1017
Ross, Robert VI, 987
Ross, Ross V, 708
Ross, Ruben I, 274
Ross, Ruth IV, 93
Ross, Ruth IV, 107
Ross, Ruth Ann II, 893
Ross, Ruth Ann II, 916
Ross, S. J. V, 464
Ross, Sabra A. VI, 774
Ross, Samuel II, 256
Ross, Samuel II, 267
Ross, Samuel II, 415
Ross, Samuel II, 640
Ross, Samuel II, 763
Ross, Samuel II, 818
Ross, Samuel II, 916
Ross, Samuel III, 137
Ross, Samuel III, 274
Ross, Samuel III, 275
Ross, Samuel VI, 774
Ross, Samuel E. V, 275
Ross, Samuel E. V, 642
Ross, Samuel Enos V, 642
Ross, Samuel H. III, 131
Ross, Samuel H. III, 275
Ross, Samuel Holcomb II, 818
Ross, Samuel Holcomb II, 916
Ross, Samuel Holcomb III, 274
Ross, Sarah II, 256
Ross, Sarah II, 267
Ross, Sarah II, 415
Ross, Sarah II, 640
Ross, Sarah II, 763
Ross, Sarah II, 818
Ross, Sarah II, 916
Ross, Sarah III, 137
Ross, Sarah III, 274
Ross, Sarah III, 275
Ross, Sarah V, 43
Ross, Sarah V, 116
Ross, Sarah Ann V, 839
Ross, Sarah Ann VI, 774
Ross, Sarah H. III, 274

ss, Sherman IV, 496
ss, Sinah VI, 963
ss, Stephen VI, 440
ss, Susanna VI, 987
ss, Susannah VI, 987
ss, Sutherland VI, 987
ss, Sutherland VI, 1007
ss, Thomas II, 476
ss, Thomas II, 640
ss, Thomas III, 209
ss, Thomas III, 275
ss, Thomas IV, 271
ss, Thomas IV, 433
ss, Thomas, Jr. II, 640
ss, Uriah VI, 987
ss, Viola V, 915
ss, Wd. Lydia Hollingsworth VI, 409
ss, Wd. Martha Parry II, 786
ss, Webster T. IV, 1377
ss, Wilber IV, 1377
ss, Wilbur IV, 1377
ss, William I, 640
ss, William II, 415
ss, William III, 275
ss, William IV, 496
ss, William VI, 132
ss, William VI, 140
ss, William VI, 863
ss, William Bascom I, 625
ss, William D. IV, 1377
ss, William Erskine V, 642
ss, William L. IV, 1262
ss, Willie V, 464
ss, Wm. II, 640
ss, Wm. E. V, 642
osse, Ann VI, 440
osse, Jonathan VI, 440
osse, Levi VI, 440
osse, Martha VI, 440
osse, Rachel VI, 440
osse, Uriah VI, 987
ossel, Mary II, 231
ossel, Mary II, 256
ossel, Phebe IV, 84
ossel, Phebe IV, 107
ossel, Rachel II, 256
ossel, Rachel II, 264
ossel, Zachary II, 231
ossel, Zachary II, 256
ossell, Hannah IV, 723
ossell, Hannah IV, 756
ossell, Hannah Ann IV, 271
ossell, Joseph IV, 271
ossell, Mary II, 256
ossell, Olive IV, 723
ossell, Rachel II, 256
ossell, Zachary II, 256
osser, Albert G. VI, 812
osser, Ambrose VI, 812
osser, Ambrose VI, 841
osser, Ambrose VI, 851
osser, Ann VI, 818
osser, Ann VI, 841
osser, Ann VI, 861
osser, Ann W. VI, 835
osser, Betsy VI, 842
osser, Catharine VI, 796
osser, Catharine VI, 831
osser, David VI, 850
osser, David VI, 851
osser, David VI, 860
osser, Edmund VI, 851
osser, Edmund W. VI, 851
osser, Elizabeth VI, 851
osser, Elizabeth VI, 987
osser, Elizabeth A. VI, 864
osser, Fanny VI, 819
osser, Frances VI, 851
osser, Gabell VI, 808
osser, James VI, 851
osser, Jesse VI, 851
osser, Joel VI, 851
osser, John VI, 801
osser, John VI, 802
osser, John VI, 808
osser, John VI, 851
osser, John VI, 857
osser, John VI, 861
osser, John VI, 864
osser, John VI, 987
osser, John VI, 1019
osser, John, Jr. VI, 851
osser, John, Jr. VI, 857
osser, Jonathan VI, 819
osser, Jonathan VI, 1019
osser, Judith VI, 851
osser, Judith P. VI, 851
osser, Lavina VI, 820
osser, Lorenzo VI, 851
osser, Lorinza VI, 822
Rosser, Louisa VI, 827
Rosser, Lucy B. VI, 838
Rosser, Malinda VI, 851
Rosser, Margaret VI, 851
Rosser, Martha VI, 849
Rosser, Martha VI, 850
Rosser, Martha VI, 851
Rosser, Martha VI, 860
Rosser, Martha VI, 861
Rosser, Martha J. VI, 857
Rosser, Mary VI, 808
Rosser, Mary VI, 851
Rosser, Mary Ann VI, 851
Rosser, Mary E. VI, 851
Rosser, Mary T. VI, 860
Rosser, Nancy VI, 808
Rosser, Nancy VI, 820
Rosser, Nancy VI, 827
Rosser, Nancy VI, 851
Rosser, Nancy VI, 987
Rosser, Nancy VI, 1019
Rosser, Octavia VI, 801
Rosser, Patty VI, 796
Rosser, Pitman VI, 851
Rosser, Pleasant VI, 796
Rosser, Pleasant VI, 851
Rosser, Pleasant B. VI, 846
Rosser, Pleasant B. VI, 851
Rosser, Pleasant B. VI, 860
Rosser, Pleasant B. VI, 862
Rosser, Polly VI, 862
Rosser, Preston G. VI, 851
Rosser, Robert R. VI, 799
Rosser, Robert S. VI, 864
Rosser, Sally VI, 796
Rosser, Sally VI, 812
Rosser, Sally VI, 851
Rosser, Sarah VI, 841
Rosser, Sarah VI, 851
Rosser, Susanna VI, 861
Rosser, Thirza VI, 802
Rosser, Thomas VI, 834
Rosser, Thomas VI, 851
Rosser, Thomas VI, 860
Rosser, Thomas VI, 862
Rosser, Thos., Sr. VI, 835
Rosser, Visey VI, 851
Rosser, Widower Jonathan VI, 987
Rosser, William VI, 796
Rosser, William VI, 808
Rosser, William VI, 819
Rosser, William VI, 834
Rosser, William VI, 835
Rosser, William VI, 842
Rosser, William VI, 849
Rosser, William VI, 851
Rosser, William VI, 865
Rosser, William VI, 866
Rosser, Winfred VI, 860
Rosser, Wm. VI, 796
Rossiter, Alfred III, 188
Rossiter, Alfred III, 275
Rossiter, Alfred III, 301
Rossiter, Anna Arabella III, 250
Rossiter, Anna Arabella III, 275
Rossiter, Helen III, 188
Rossiter, Helen III, 275
Rossiter, Helena III, 275
Rossiter, Jonathan N. III, 275
Rossiter, Margaret III, 250
Rossiter, Nette III, 301
Rossiter, Sigmond H. III, 275
Rossiter, Thos. III, 250
Roszel, Smith I, 900
Rotch, Ann Waln II, 601
Rotch, Ann Waln II, 641
Rotch, Benjamin II, 641
Rotch, Charity IV, 158
Rotch, Charity IV, 841
Rotch, Elizabeth II, 641
Rotch, Francis II, 601
Rotch, Francis II, 641
Rotch, Joseph II, 641
Rotch, Rebecca II, 640
Rotch, Thomas IV, 158
Rotch, Thomas IV, 841
Rotch, Wm. II, 640
Rotchester, Hannah VI, 211
Rotchford, Dennia II, 415
Rotchford, Dennis II, 415
Rotchford, Denniss II, 415
Rotchford, Elizabeth II, 415
Rotchford, Patience II, 415
Rotchford, Rebecca II, 415
Rotchford, Solomon II, 415
Rotchford, Wd. Elizabeth II, 415
Rotchford, Wd. Mary II, 415
Roth, Ann II, 641
Roth, Dorothy II, 959
Roth, Edward Augustus, Jr. II, 959
Roth, Kenneth V, 1017
Roth, May V, 1017
Roth, Reba Milton II, 959
Rothchild, Alice IV, 654
Rother, Jane V, 429
Rotherford, Adia V, 643
Rotherford, Jannie V, 643
Rotherford, John V, 643
Rotherford, Susannah V, 643
Rotherford, Sylvia V, 643
Rothermell, Nancy V, 929
Rothweiler, Caroline III, 187
Rothweiler, Caroline III, 251
Rothweiler, Wd. Caroline III, 275
Rothweiler, William III, 275
Rothweiler, Wm. III, 187
Rothweiler, Wm. III, 251
Rothwell, Elizabeth II, 415
Rothwell, Henry II, 415
Rothwell, Mary II, 415
Rottmier, Margaretta E. IV, 271
Rottmier, Otto IV, 271
Roughton, Jane VI, 987
Roughton, John VI, 987
Roulling, Polly VI, 845
Roulstone, John II, 447
Round, Wm. E. IV, 1292
Round, Wm. Gilbert IV, 1292
Roundtree, Edward Q. I, 71
Roundtree, Elisabeth I, 71
Roundtree, Elisabeth I, 79
Roundtree, Elizabeth VI, 987
Roundtree, Jesse I, 16
Roundtree, Jesse I, 20
Roundtree, Jesse I, 28
Roundtree, Jesse I, 32
Roundtree, Jesse A. I, 30
Roundtree, Jesse V. I, 16
Roundtree, Jesse V. I, 33
Roundtree, John C. I, 17
Roundtree, John C. I, 29
Roundtree, John C. I, 30
Roundtree, John C. I, 71
Roundtree, Leah I, 29
Roundtree, Leola I, 20
Roundtree, Leota I, 85
Roundtree, Lydia I, 71
Roundtree, Lydia I, 89
Roundtree, Lydia A. I, 17
Roundtree, Lydia Ann I, 30
Roundtree, Martha Jane I, 32
Roundtree, Minerva I, 71
Roundtree, Nathaniel VI, 987
Roundtree, Nettie Lee I, 16
Roundtree, Nettie Lee I, 33
Roundtree, Nina I, 28
Roundtree, Nina A. I, 16
Roundtree, Pleasant I, 16
Roundtree, Pleasant I, 28
Roundtree, Pleasant I, 32
Roundtree, Pleasant A. I, 30
Roundtree, Rebecca Jane I, 29
Roundtree, William A. I, 17
Roundtree, William A. I, 71
Roundtree, Winslow Virginia I, 16
Rountree, Dudley VI, 937
Rountree, Elizabeth III, 275
Rountree, Elizabeth F. III, 217
Rountree, Elizabeth F. III, 275
Rountree, Frederic C. III, 217
Rountree, Frederic E. III, 217
Rountree, Isabella M. III, 275
Rountree, Josephine F. III, 217
Rountree, Julia J. III, 275
Rountree, Maine III, 275
Rountree, Nancy VI, 937
Rountree, P. Francena III, 217
Rountree, Samuel VI, 937
Rountree, Susannah VI, 937
Rountree, Wm. F. III, 275
Rountree, Wm. M. III, 217
Rountree, Wm. M. III, 275
Rouse, Agnes IV, 433
Rouse, Albert IV, 433
Rouse, Albert M. IV, 440
Rouse, Alberta May IV, 433
Rouse, Cloe I, 1011
Rouse, Cloe I, 1012
Rouse, Helen R. IV, 433
Rouse, Helen R. IV, 440
Rouse, Helen Ruth IV, 433
Rouse, James Wilford IV, 433
Rouse, Jane Hanson IV, 433
Rouse, Julia Maud IV, 433
Rouse, Mary IV, 756
Rouse, Mary E. IV, 433
Rouse, Mary H. IV, 428
Rouse, Mary H. IV, 433
Rouse, Mary Hanson IV, 433
Rouse, Mary N. IV, 440
Rouse, Miles IV, 433
Rouse, Miles F. IV, 433
Rouse, Miles Fay IV, 433
Rouse, Robert Miles IV, 433
Rouse, William Henry IV, 433
Roush, Ruth Elizabeth V, 595
Rousse, Laura De II, 901
Routan, Milton V, 1017
Routh, Alice V, 357
Routh, Alice V, 363
Routh, Belle I, 924
Routh, Francis II, 415
Routh, J. Wesley I, 418
Routh, James II, 415
Routh, James II, 642
Routh, Lydia Rotch VI, 266
Routh, Martha VI, 266
Routh, Rebecca I, 924
Routh, William I, 924
Routledge, ??? III, 90
Routledge, ??? III, 275
Routledge, Evelyn C. III, 90
Routledge, Evelyn C. III, 275
Routledge, John II, 968
Routledge, John II, 992
Routledge, John II, 1024
Routledge, Margaret II, 968
Routledge, Margaret II, 992
Routledge, Margaret II, 1024
Routledge, Margarett II, 968
Routledge, Mary II, 1005
Routledge, Mary II, 1024
Routledge, Rachel II, 968
Routledge, Thomas II, 968
Routledge, Thomas II, 1005
Routledge, Thomas II, 1024
Routlidge, John II, 1024
Routlidge, Margaret II, 1024
Routon, Jane VI, 987
Routon, John VI, 987
Routon, Mille VI, 966
Routon, Richard VI, 966
Routsaw, Mary A. V, 429
Rouze, Elizabeth VI, 851
Rouze, Thomas VI, 851
Rovedaf, Rebecca II, 546
Rovedaf, Rebecca II, 641
Row, Abraham II, 447
Row, Anna III, 222
Row, Barberah II, 447
Row, Christopher II, 415
Row, Maggie I, 317
Row, Mary II, 415
Row, Robert II, 415
Row, Sarah M. II, 866
Row, Sarah M. II, 916
Row, Sarah Mason II, 795
Rowan, Ann II, 641
Rowan, Ann II, 655
Rowan, Eliza II, 415
Rowan, Hannah II, 641
Rowan, Hannah II, 655
Rowan, Hannah V, 375
Rowan, Hannah Ann V, 949
Rowan, Hannah Ann V, 958
Rowan, Jeremiah V, 375
Rowan, Lettice II, 300
Rowan, Martha A. V, 375
Rowan, Mary Ann II, 498
Rowan, Mary Ann II, 641
Rowan, Moses II, 641
Rowan, Moses II, 655
Rowan, Sarah II, 809
Rowand, Gilbert W. IV, 1292
Rowand, Wm. IV, 1292
Rowden, Elizabeth II, 641
Rowden, Elizabeth II, 981
Rowden, Elizabeth II, 1024
Rowdon, Elizabeth II, 472
Rowe, Alfred T. III, 17
Rowe, Alfred Tennyson III, 275
Rowe, Anna V, 1017
Rowe, Anne VI, 843
Rowe, Beatrice Alice III, 17
Rowe, Beatrice Alice III, 275
Rowe, Bertha IV, 1336
Rowe, Bertha Jane IV, 1336
Rowe, Bessie V, 358
Rowe, Earl V, 275
Rowe, Effie May IV, 1336
Rowe, Elsie E. III, 17
Rowe, Elsie E. III, 275
Rowe, Fred IV, 1336
Rowe, Frederick IV, 1336
Rowe, Frederick Geo. IV, 1336
Rowe, Harrison VI, 852
Rowe, Henry VI, 85
Rowe, Henry A. VI, 85
Rowe, Ida I, 318
Rowe, J. W. V, 464
Rowe, James VI, 85
Rowe, Julia E. VI, 63
Rowe, Julia E. VI, 85
Rowe, Lizzie V, 357
Rowe, Lizzie V, 358
Rowe, Madeline IV, 1336
Rowe, Magdeline Leigh IV, 1336
Rowe, Maggie I, 317
Rowe, Margaret Logan IV, 1336
Rowe, Mark V, 358
Rowe, Martha III, 275
Rowe, Martha V, 358
Rowe, Martha VI, 63
Rowe, Martha VI, 85
Rowe, Martha VI, 87
Rowe, Martin V, 275
Rowe, Mary G. IV, 1369
Rowe, Mattie I, 317
Rowe, Nelly VI, 852
Rowe, Nettie I, 317
Rowe, Patrick VI, 63
Rowe, Rebecca V, 275
Rowe, Rebecca V, 643
Rowe, Rebecca S. V, 275
Rowe, Rebecca S. V, 643
Rowe, Sarah VI, 85
Rowe, Violet V, 692
Rowe, Violet V, 708
Rowell, ??? II, 641
Rowell, Isaac II, 641
Rowell, Rebecca II, 641
Rowen, Ann II, 641
Rowen, Ann II, 676
Rowen, Eliza II, 641
Rowen, Hannah II, 641
Rowen, Mary II, 641
Rowen, Mary Ann II, 641
Rowen, Mary Ann II, 763
Rowen, Mary K. V, 358
Rowen, Mary R. V, 358
Rowen, Moses II, 641
Rowen, Phebe II, 641
Rowen, Sarah II, 812
Rowen, Walter II, 676
Rowin, Francis VI, 211
Rowin, Mary VI, 211
Rowland, ??? III, 413
Rowland, Abigail II, 86
Rowland, Abigail II, 95
Rowland, Abigail II, 256
Rowland, Alfred I, 484
Rowland, Ann II, 641
Rowland, Ann II, 818
Rowland, Anna VI, 852
Rowland, Benjamin II, 310
Rowland, Caroline R. II, 917
Rowland, Caroline Ridgway II, 818
Rowland, Catherine II, 788
Rowland, Charles J. II, 917
Rowland, Chas. James II, 916
Rowland, Clement II, 844
Rowland, Clement II, 917
Rowland, Daniel John II, 785
Rowland, Drusilla III, 413
Rowland, Drusilla III, 441
Rowland, Effie II, 818
Rowland, Elizabeth II, 804
Rowland, Ethel K. IV, 1183
Rowland, Euphemia II, 818
Rowland, Frances VI, 852
Rowland, Hannah II, 310
Rowland, Hannah II, 1078
Rowland, Hannah II, 1080
Rowland, Hannah S. II, 1078
Rowland, Ida IV, 1262
Rowland, James II, 416
Rowland, James II, 476
Rowland, James II, 586
Rowland, James II, 641
Rowland, James II, 763
Rowland, James II, 818
Rowland, James II, 916
Rowland, James II, 917
Rowland, James, Jr. II, 586
Rowland, James, Jr. II, 641
Rowland, James, Jr. II, 763
Rowland, James, Jr. II, 818
Rowland, James, Jr. II, 916
Rowland, Jennett II, 709
Rowland, John II, 447
Rowland, John II, 641
Rowland, John II, 788
Rowland, John II, 818
Rowland, John II, 916
Rowland, John VI, 852
Rowland, Joseph II, 416
Rowland, Joseph II, 641
Rowland, Joseph II, 917
Rowland, Joseph G. II, 818

Rowland, Joseph Galloway II, 818
Rowland, Joseph W. II, 641
Rowland, Joshua II, 641
Rowland, Mary II, 310
Rowland, Mary II, 818
Rowland, Mary II, 844
Rowland, Mary II, 870
Rowland, Mary II, 917
Rowland, Mary VI, 987
Rowland, Mary L. II, 844
Rowland, Mary L. II, 917
Rowland, Mary L. III, 145
Rowland, Melson Laws II, 818
Rowland, Micajah VI, 987
Rowland, Patsey VI, 987
Rowland, Phebe Ann II, 586
Rowland, Phebe Ann II, 641
Rowland, Phebe Ann II, 763
Rowland, Phebe Ann II, 818
Rowland, Phebe Ann II, 916
Rowland, Rachel II, 416
Rowland, Rachel II, 586
Rowland, Rachel II, 641
Rowland, Rachel II, 763
Rowland, Rachel II, 916
Rowland, Rachel Edwards II, 916
Rowland, Rebecca II, 818
Rowland, Rebecca II, 917
Rowland, Rebecca M. III, 145
Rowland, Rebecca M. III, 241
Rowland, Rebecca Mifflin II, 763
Rowland, Rebecca Mifflin II, 917
Rowland, Reuben VI, 987
Rowland, Richards VI, 597
Rowland, Robert VI, 852
Rowland, Robert VI, 981
Rowland, Robert VI, 987
Rowland, Samuel II, 75
Rowland, Samuel II, 95
Rowland, Samuel III, 145
Rowland, Samuel F. II, 870
Rowland, Samuel F. II, 917
Rowland, Samuel J. II, 917
Rowland, Samuel Johns II, 818
Rowland, Sarah II, 75
Rowland, Sarah II, 93
Rowland, Sarah II, 95
Rowland, Sarah II, 362
Rowland, Sarah II, 641
Rowland, Sarah II, 794
Rowland, Sarah II, 818
Rowland, Sidney VI, 987
Rowland, Susannah II, 788
Rowland, Tabitha B. II, 790
Rowland, Taby VI, 987
Rowland, Thomas VI, 987
Rowland, Thomas Fisher II, 818
Rowland, Thos. Fisher II, 917
Rowland, Wd. Rachel II, 476
Rowland, Wd. Rachel II, 818
Rowles, Elizabeth VI, 531
Rowles, Elizabeth VI, 554
Rowles, Hezekiah VI, 531
Rowles, Hezekiah VI, 554
Rowles, Mary VI, 531
Rowles, Mary VI, 554
Rowles, Ruth V, 247
Rowlet, Abigail II, 1059
Rowlet, Abigail S. II, 1078
Rowlet, Ann II, 1024
Rowlet, Ann II, 1059
Rowlet, David E. II, 1024
Rowlet, Drucilla II, 1024
Rowlet, Drucilla II, 1059
Rowlet, Drucilla II, 1078
Rowlet, Drucilla P. II, 1024
Rowlet, Edwin II, 1059
Rowlet, George II, 917
Rowlet, John II, 1024
Rowlet, John II, 1059
Rowlet, John II, 1078
Rowlet, Mary II, 917
Rowlet, Mary L. II, 1078
Rowlet, Mercy L. II, 1078
Rowlet, Sarah P. II, 1024
Rowlet, Sarah P. II, 1078
Rowlet, Thomas II, 1024
Rowlet, Thomas P. II, 1078
Rowlet, Thomas Phips II, 1024
Rowlett, Abigail II, 1059
Rowlett, Abigail S. II, 1078
Rowlett, Ann II, 1059
Rowlett, Ann II, 1078
Rowlett, Clara II, 917
Rowlett, Clara Eleanor II, 815
Rowlett, David E. II, 1059
Rowlett, David E. II, 1078
Rowlett, Drucilla II, 1059
Rowlett, Drucilla II, 1078
Rowlett, Drucilla P. II, 1024
Rowlett, Edward Elmer II, 917
Rowlett, Edward Elmer II, 919
Rowlett, Edwin II, 1059
Rowlett, Edwin II, 1078
Rowlett, Elizabeth H. II, 917
Rowlett, Florence Mary II, 919
Rowlett, Florence May II, 917
Rowlett, George II, 917
Rowlett, George II, 1078
Rowlett, George B. II, 815
Rowlett, George B. II, 818
Rowlett, Jesse II, 1078
Rowlett, John II, 818
Rowlett, John II, 917
Rowlett, John II, 1024
Rowlett, John II, 1059
Rowlett, John II, 1078
Rowlett, Josephine O. II, 917
Rowlett, Lizzie A. II, 815
Rowlett, Lizzie C. II, 818
Rowlett, Margery II, 917
Rowlett, Margery M. II, 878
Rowlett, Margery Mickle II, 818
Rowlett, Martha II, 1078
Rowlett, Martha W. II, 1078
Rowlett, Mary II, 512
Rowlett, Mary II, 641
Rowlett, Mary II, 818
Rowlett, Mary II, 917
Rowlett, Mary L. II, 1078
Rowlett, Mercy L. II, 1078
Rowlett, Samuel II, 818
Rowlett, Sarah II, 1059
Rowlett, Sarah Ann II, 818
Rowlett, Sarah P. II, 1078
Rowlett, Thomas P. II, 1059
Rowlett, Thomas P. II, 1078
Rowlett, Thomas Phips II, 1024
Rowley, Mary II, 156
Rowley, Miriam II, 199
Rowley, Miriam II, 256
Rowley, Rachel M. II, 818
Rowlings, Ann II, 256
Rowlings, Thomas II, 256
Rowls, Azariah II, 641
Rown, Margrett II, 416
Rownd, James S. IV, 433
Rowne, Hannah IV, 1292
Rowne, John W. IV, 1292
Rowntree, Anna Mary III, 275
Rowntree, Bernard III, 205
Rowntree, Bernard III, 275
Rowntree, Cedric III, 275
Rowntree, Elizabeth III, 275
Rowntree, Elizabeth F. III, 275
Rowntree, Gertrude III, 205
Rowntree, Gertrude E. III, 275
Rowntree, Hannah III, 275
Rowntree, Hannah E. III, 275
Rowntree, Hannah Elizabeth III, 275
Rowntree, Hannah W. III, 275
Rowntree, Henry III, 275
Rowntree, Henry, Jr. III, 275
Rowntree, Isabella M. III, 275
Rowntree, John H. III, 275
Rowntree, Joseph III, 275
Rowntree, Joseph W. III, 275
Rowntree, Julia J. III, 275
Rowntree, Maine III, 275
Rowntree, Mary III, 275
Rowntree, Robert W. III, 275
Rowntree, William B. III, 275
Rowntree, Wm. F. III, 275
Rowntree, Wm. M. III, 275
Roworth, Ann II, 416
Roworth, William II, 416
Roxey, ??? III, 101
Roy, Alice C. III, 275
Roy, Catharine VI, 874
Roy, Catharine VI, 965
Roy, David VI, 992
Roy, Elizabeth VI, 880
Roy, Eugenie III, 275
Roy, Frances J. VI, 924
Roy, Frank A. III, 275
Roy, Frankey VI, 987
Roy, Harold E. III, 275
Roy, James VI, 987
Roy, John VI, 1018
Roy, Joseph VI, 987
Roy, Lincoln III, 275
Roy, Mary VI, 992
Roy, Mary A. VI, 1018
Roy, Mrs. Permelia VI, 987
Roy, Nancy VI, 924
Roy, Nancy VI, 987
Roy, Peggy VI, 919
Roy, Peter VI, 880
Roy, Peter VI, 919
Roy, Samuel B. VI, 987
Roy, Wm. W. VI, 965
Royall, ??? VI, 149
Royall, James T. VI, 901
Royall, Joseph VI, 204
Royall, Joseph VI, 211
Royall, Mary II, 631
Royall, Mary II, 641
Royall, Mary II, 1001
Royall, Mary II, 1024
Royall, Mary S. VI, 987
Royall, Richard VI, 201
Royall, Richard VI, 205
Royall, Richard VI, 211
Royall, Richard VI, 219
Royall, William E. VI, 987
Royall, Wm. II, 631
Royall, Wm. II, 641
Royalty, Elizabeth VI, 809
Royalty, George W. VI, 809
Royalty, John VI, 852
Royalty, Nancy VI, 852
Royalty, Sam. VI, 809
Royar, Unity IV, 756
Royce, Alice III, 100
Royce, Alice III, 183
Royer, Judith VI, 977
Royer, Mary E. IV, 1292
Royer, Unity IV, 756
Roys, Alice C. III, 275
Roys, Lincoln III, 275
Royse, Christian V, 797
Royse, Lulie V, 797
Royse, Wilbur V, 797
Royster, Charles VI, 167
Royster, Charles VI, 192
Royster, Charles VI, 211
Royster, John VI, 211
Royster, John VI, 220
Royster, Peter VI, 168
Royster, Peter, Jr. VI, 211
Rozell, Nancy II, 822
Rozso, Bela III, 419
Rozso, Bela III, 441
Rozso, Lazos III, 441
Rozso, Marguerite III, 441
Rozso, Rosana III, 419
Rozso, Rosana III, 441
Rubel, Henry V, 116
Rubel, Owen V, 116
Rubel, Rachel I, 900
Rubel, Rachel V, 116
Rubel, Samuel I, 1131
Rubel, Samuel V, 116
Rubel, Susannah V, 116
Rubel, Walter V, 116
Rubel, William I, 1131
Rubel, William V, 116
Rubenstock, Peter II, 447
Rubenstock, Sibella II, 447
Rubins, Florence III, 97
Rubins, Florence III, 275
Rubins, Harry W. III, 97
Rubins, Harry W. III, 275
Rubins, Marian III, 97
Rubins, Marian III, 275
Ruble, Earnest IV, 271
Ruble, Elizabeth VI, 441
Ruble, Emma IV, 841
Ruble, Ether V, 709
Ruble, George VI, 441
Ruble, Harriet IV, 37
Ruble, Harriet IV, 57
Ruble, Henry I, 1131
Ruble, Henry V, 595
Ruble, James VI, 441
Ruble, Jane I, 1023
Ruble, Jemima VI, 441
Ruble, Norah IV, 271
Ruble, Owen I, 1131
Ruble, Owen V, 526
Ruble, Peter I, 1015
Ruble, Peter I, 1023
Ruble, Rachel I, 1131
Ruble, Rachel V, 595
Ruble, Rachel V, 606
Ruble, Rosa IV, 271
Ruble, Ruth V, 429
Ruble, Samuel I, 1023
Ruble, Samuel I, 1037
Ruble, Samuel I, 1131
Ruble, Samuel, Jr. V, 526
Ruble, Sarah I, 1023
Ruble, Sarah VI, 441
Ruble, Sarah Haworth VI, 441
Ruble, Stella V, 708
Ruble, Susannah I, 1023
Ruble, Susannah I, 1131
Ruble, Walter I, 1131
Ruble, Walter V, 526
Ruble, William I, 1131
Ruble, William V, 595
Rubottom, ??? I Sup 1, 12
Rubottom, Edith I, 386
Rubottom, Elizabeth I, 417
Rubottom, George I, 386
Rubottom, George I, 417
Rubottom, Hannah I, 417
Rubottom, Jane I, 417
Rubottom, Joseph I, 417
Rubottom, Mary I, 417
Rubottom, Miriam I, 386
Rubottom, Miriam I, 417
Rubottom, Simon I, 417
Rubottom, Thomas I, 386
Rubottom, Thomas I, 417
Ruby, Clementina II, 917
Ruby, Clementine G. II, 883
Ruby, Clementine G. II, 917
Ruck, Alice VI, 729
Ruck, Rev. Sydney VI, 729
Rucker, A. T. B. VI, 852
Rucker, Alfred VI, 951
Rucker, Alfred VI, 988
Rucker, Alfred C. VI, 988
Rucker, Alice VI, 987
Rucker, Ambrose VI, 938
Rucker, Ambrose VI, 1003
Rucker, Ambrose C. VI, 987
Rucker, Ambrose L. VI, 943
Rucker, Ambrose, Jr. VI, 987
Rucker, Ambrosse VI, 987
Rucker, Angeline VI, 902
Rucker, Anthony VI, 887
Rucker, Anthony VI, 970
Rucker, Anthony VI, 982
Rucker, Anthony VI, 987
Rucker, Anthony VI, 1003
Rucker, Bearnard VI, 951
Rucker, Benjamin A. VI, 987
Rucker, Bennett VI, 987
Rucker, Bernard VI, 852
Rucker, Bernard VI, 965
Rucker, Bernard VI, 983
Rucker, Bernard VI, 988
Rucker, Betsey VI, 987
Rucker, Charles H. VI, 848
Rucker, Clifton H. VI, 852
Rucker, Dolly VI, 852
Rucker, Eliza M. VI, 982
Rucker, Elizabeth VI, 970
Rucker, Elizabeth VI, 987
Rucker, Emily Chesterson VI, 940
Rucker, Euphan VI, 987
Rucker, Frances VI, 927
Rucker, George VI, 875
Rucker, George VI, 877
Rucker, George VI, 881
Rucker, George VI, 886
Rucker, George VI, 896
Rucker, George VI, 899
Rucker, George VI, 903
Rucker, George VI, 905
Rucker, George VI, 908
Rucker, George VI, 910
Rucker, George VI, 912
Rucker, George VI, 913
Rucker, George VI, 922
Rucker, George VI, 929
Rucker, George VI, 931
Rucker, George VI, 937
Rucker, George VI, 950
Rucker, George VI, 955
Rucker, George VI, 969
Rucker, George VI, 970
Rucker, George VI, 974
Rucker, George VI, 986
Rucker, George VI, 987
Rucker, George VI, 988
Rucker, George VI, 992
Rucker, George VI, 998
Rucker, George VI, 1002
Rucker, George VI, 1013
Rucker, George VI, 1020
Rucker, Gideon VI, 987
Rucker, James VI, 987
Rucker, James M. VI, 987
Rucker, James W. VI, 987
Rucker, Johanna VI, 987
Rucker, John VI, 838
Rucker, John C. VI, 852
Rucker, John C. VI, 988
Rucker, Jonathan VI, 941
Rucker, Jonathan VI, 987
Rucker, Jordan P. VI, 988
Rucker, Joshua VI, 962
Rucker, Joshua VI, 971
Rucker, Joycy VI, 987
Rucker, Louisa VI, 852
Rucker, Lucy VI, 929
Rucker, Lucy VI, 987
Rucker, Lucy E. VI, 965
Rucker, Lucy M. VI, 988
Rucker, Malinda VI, 987
Rucker, Margaret VI, 902
Rucker, Margarett VI, 987
Rucker, Marinda VI, 987
Rucker, Mary VI, 938
Rucker, Mary Elizabeth VI, 988
Rucker, Mary Jane VI, 852
Rucker, Mary Leake VI, 970
Rucker, Mildred H. VI, 962
Rucker, Nancy VI, 852
Rucker, Nancy VI, 908
Rucker, Nancy VI, 987
Rucker, Nelson D. VI, 852
Rucker, Peggy VI, 987
Rucker, Polly VI, 852
Rucker, Reuben VI, 852
Rucker, Sally VI, 987
Rucker, Sarah VI, 951
Rucker, Sarah F. VI, 887
Rucker, Sarah Jane VI, 987
Rucker, Sophia VI, 1003
Rucker, Susan VI, 971
Rucker, Susan VI, 988
Rucker, Susanna VI, 910
Rucker, Susanna B. VI, 1004
Rucker, Thomas VI, 940
Rucker, Thomas VI, 987
Rucker, William VI, 929
Rucker, William VI, 987
Rucker, Wm. VI, 908
Rucker, Wm. VI, 987
Rucker, Wm. P. VI, 962
Rucker, Wm. P. VI, 965
Rucker, Wm. P. VI, 986
Ruckitt, William, Jr. II, 256
Ruckman, Anna Trego II, 862
Ruckman, Anna Trego II, 917
Ruckman, Eliza II, 862
Ruckman, Eliza II, 917
Ruckman, Hannah I, 537
Ruckman, Hannah I, 569
Ruckman, Isaac I, 569
Ruckman, Isaiah I, 569
Ruckman, Isaiah I, 900
Ruckman, John Horner II, 862
Ruckman, John Horner II, 917
Ruckman, Joseph I, 514
Ruckman, Joseph I, 569
Ruckman, Josiah I, 569
Ruckman, Martha I, 550
Ruckman, Martha I, 569
Ruckman, Samuel IV, 271
Ruckman, Sarah I, 514
Ruckman, Thos. Hart II, 862
Ruckman, Thos. Hart II, 917
Rudd, Charles VI, 334
Rudd, Charles VI, 842
Rudd, Ida V, 988
Rudd, Martha VI, 859
Rudd, Perlina K. VI, 822
Rudd, Sarah II, 641
Rudd, Sarah II, 694
Rudd, Thomas VI, 795
Rudd, Thomas VI, 822
Rudder, ??? VI, 291
Ruddick, Agnes V, 200
Ruddick, Anna V, 708
Ruddick, Eliza J. V, 708
Ruddick, Ida V, 708
Ruddick, Jane I, 865
Ruddick, John V, 200
Ruddick, Rosa V, 200
Ruddick, Ursula V, 200
Ruddick, Urxala V, 200
Ruddick, William V, 708
Ruddock, Alice I, 418
Ruddock, Ann I, 418
Ruddock, Benjamin I, 343
Ruddock, Benjamin I, 418
Ruddock, Benjamin I, 570
Ruddock, John I, 418
Ruddock, Joseph I, 343
Ruddock, Joseph I, 418
Ruddock, Sarah I, 847
Ruddock, William I, 418
Rudduc, Rhoda I, 878
Rudduc, Rhoda I, 900
Rudduck, Alice I, 514
Rudduck, Alice I, 791
Rudduck, Alice I, 900
Rudduck, Alise I, 791
Rudduck, Benjamin I, 487
Rudduck, Benjamin I, 570
Rudduck, Dinah I, 560
Rudduck, Dinah I, 570
Rudduck, Dinah I, 791
Rudduck, Ida V, 708
Rudduck, Jane I, 773
Rudduck, Jane I, 791
Rudduck, Jane I, 835

ıdduck, Jane I, 865
ıdduck, Jane Ruth I, 835
ıdduck, Jemima I, 791
ıdduck, John I, 487
ıdduck, John I, 570
ıdduck, John I, 791
ıdduck, John I, 794
ıdduck, John I, 847
ıdduck, John I, 900
ıdduck, John I Sup 1, 9
ıdduck, John V, 526
ıdduck, John, Jr. I, 773
ıdduck, Joseph I, 514
ıdduck, Joseph I, 570
ıdduck, Joseph I, 688
ıdduck, Joseph I, 786
ıdduck, Joseph I, 791
ıdduck, Martha I, 786
ıdduck, Mary I, 835
ıdduck, Mary I, 865
ıdduck, Phebe I, 560
ıdduck, Phebe I, 570
ıdduck, Phebe I, 688
ıdduck, Pheby I, 791
ıdduck, Rebeccah I, 786
ıdduck, Rhoda I, 900
ıdduck, Sarah I, 570
ıdduck, Sarah I, 773
ıdduck, Sarah I, 791
ıdduck, Sarah I, 900
ıdduck, Sarah V, 310
ıdduck, Sarah V, 526
ıdduck, Solomon I, 570
ıdduck, Ursula V, 526
ıdduck, William I, 514
ıdduck, William I, 570
ıdduck, William I, 791
ıdduck, William I, 835
ıdduck, William I, 865
ıdduck, William I, 953
ıdduck, William I Sup 1, 9
ıddicks, Dinah I, 514
ıddicks, Jeane I, 514
ıddicks, Jemime I, 514
ıdducks, John I, 514
ıdducks, John I, 570
ıdducks, John I, 579
ıdducks, Phebe I, 514
ıdducks, Sarah I, 514
ıdducks, Sarah I, 579
ıdducks, William I, 514
ıdducks, Wm. I, 514
ıddux, Benjamin I, 570
ıddux, Joseph I, 684
ıddux, Joseph I, 688
ıddux, Phebe I, 684
ıddux, Phebe I, 688
ıde, Amanda V, 358
ıde, Elizabeth V, 358
ıde, Elvira V, 708
ıde, Joseph V, 358
ıdell, Edna IV, 1262
ıdibough, Isabel IV, 654
ıdibough, Isabella IV, 666
ıdledge, Elizabeth IV, 433
ıdledge, Elizabeth IV, 445
ıdley, Daniel, Jr. II, 447
ıdman, Joseph II, 416
ıdman, Sarah II, 416
ıdman, Thomas II, 416
ıdolp, Elizabeth F. II, 764
ıdolp, John II, 763
ıdolp, John M. II, 764
ıdolp, Samuel F. II, 764
ıdolp, Thomas II, 763
ıdolph, Anna E. II, 137
ıdolph, Caroline II, 722
ıdolph, Deborah F. II, 949
ıdolph, Elizabeth II, 763
ıdolph, Elizabeth II, 949
ıdolph, Elizabeth F. II, 764
ıdolph, Elwood Z. II, 137
ıdolph, Gladys M. II, 137
ıdolph, Gladys M. III, 275
ıdolph, Gladys M. III, 303
ıdolph, Hannah II, 717
ıdolph, Hannah II, 763
ıdolph, Hannah L. II, 947
ıdolph, John II, 763
ıdolph, John II, 949
ıdolph, John M. II, 717
ıdolph, John M. II, 764
ıdolph, Rachel IV, 1262
ıdolph, Samuel F. II, 764
ıdolph, Samuel F. II, 949
ıdolph, Sarah An II, 717
ıdolph, Sarah Ann II, 717
ıdolph, Sarah Ann II, 763
ıdolph, Sarah Ann II, 949
ıdolph, Thomas II, 717
ıdolph, Thomas II, 763
Rudolph, Thomas II, 949
Rudolph, Wm. Henry III, 275
Rudolph, Wm. Henry III, 303
Rudson, Mary II, 584
Rudson, Mary II, 641
Rudulph, Elizabeth II, 641
Rudulph, George II, 641
Rudulph, John II, 535
Rudulph, John II, 641
Rudulph, Joseph II, 535
Rudulph, Joseph II, 641
Rudulph, Martha II, 598
Rudulph, Martha II, 641
Rudulph, Mary II, 535
Rudulph, Mary II, 641
Rudy, Alice V, 429
Rudy, Elizabeth IV, 1292
Rudy, Elizabeth V, 358
Rudy, Elizabeth V, 429
Rudy, Elizabeth V, 811
Rudy, Frank V, 429
Rudy, John IV, 1292
Rudy, John V, 429
Rudy, Leroy V, 429
Rudy, Lizzie V, 429
Rudy, Mary May V, 429
Rudy, Nichodemus V, 429
Rudy, Samuel IV, 1292
Rue, Elvira II, 1051
Rue, Elvira II, 1059
Rue, Elvira II, 1073
Rue, Elvira II, 1078
Rue, Rebecca V, 643
Rufener, Lena IV, 1042
Ruff, Sally VI, 922
Ruffing, Catherine IV, 1262
Ruffing, Ella IV, 1262
Ruffing, Lillian IV, 1262
Ruffing, Nicholas IV, 1262
Ruffner, Daniel B. II, 831
Ruffner, Daniel B. II, 839
Ruffner, Mary S. II, 917
Rufina, Sarah V, 479
Rufina, Sarah V, 541
Rufina, Sarah V, 605
Rufing, Sarah V, 605
Rufner, Lena IV, 1042
Ruger, Ida T. V, 860
Ruger, Lillian V, 860
Ruger, Lillian Frances V, 855
Ruger, Lillian Frances V, 860
Rugg, Allen M. IV, 1042
Rugg, Anna IV, 1042
Rugg, Anna B. IV, 1042
Rugg, J. L. IV, 1336
Rugg, Leverett J. IV, 1042
Ruggan, L. W. IV, 1336
Ruggby, Alpha IV, 778
Ruggby, Anna IV, 778
Ruggby, Henry IV, 778
Ruggle, Nathaniel II, 416
Ruggles, Aimee III, 138
Ruggles, Aimee III, 275
Ruggles, Augustus G. III, 275
Ruggles, Emily B. III, 275
Ruggles, James Henry III, 138
Ruggles, James Henry III, 275
Ruggles, Loretta IV, 1173
Ruggles, Susan III, 138
Ruggles, Susan III, 275
Ruggly, Alva IV, 990
Ruggly, Alva Fay IV, 990
Ruggly, Anna IV, 990
Ruggly, Elpha Viola IV, 990
Ruggly, Fay IV, 990
Ruggly, Henry IV, 990
Rugley, Alva IV, 990
Rugley, Fay IV, 990
Rugley, Henry IV, 990
Ruher, Ella V, 1017
Ruhl, Anna IV, 726
Ruhl, Edward IV, 726
Ruhl, Eliza Jane IV, 1137
Ruhl, Eliza Jane IV, 1138
Ruhl, Grace IV, 726
Ruhl, J. C. IV, 1222
Ruhl, Mae W. IV, 1262
Ruhl, May IV, 1262
Ruhl, Miller IV, 1262
Ruhle, J. C. IV, 1222
Ruhle, Jeremiah C. IV, 1222
Ruhwidel, Elizabeth VI, 85
Ruhwidel, George VI, 85
Ruith, Jane I, 900
Rulan, Elizabeth III, 275
Ruland, ??? III, 413
Ruland, Drusilla III, 413
Ruland, Drusilla III, 441
Rule, Adam VI, 1005
Rule, Jacob VI, 952
Rule, Jacob VI, 988
Rule, Lydia VI, 952
Rule, Rebecca VI, 988
Rulon, Abel II, 256
Rulon, Abel II, 300
Rulon, Abel II, 312
Rulon, Ann II, 416
Rulon, Ann II, 478
Rulon, Ann II, 641
Rulon, Ann II, 717
Rulon, Ann B. II, 764
Rulon, Anne II, 641
Rulon, Benjamin II, 416
Rulon, Benjamin II, 478
Rulon, Benjamin II, 641
Rulon, Clayton II, 95
Rulon, Eliza Ann II, 280
Rulon, Eliza Ann II, 300
Rulon, Elizabeth Archer II, 416
Rulon, Elizabeth Archer II, 764
Rulon, Ellen II, 139
Rulon, Ephraim II, 195
Rulon, Ephraim II, 256
Rulon, Ephraim II, 300
Rulon, Ephraim II, 324
Rulon, Henry III, 275
Rulon, John II, 717
Rulon, John II, 764
Rulon, John W. II, 416
Rulon, John W. II, 478
Rulon, John W. II, 641
Rulon, Mary Ann II, 324
Rulon, Mary Ann II, 717
Rulon, Mary Ann II, 764
Rulon, Mary W. II, 641
Rulon, Mary W. II, 764
Rulon, Mary W. II, 840
Rulon, Mary W. II, 917
Rulon, Moses II, 77
Rulon, Moses II, 95
Rulon, Moses II, 195
Rulon, Moses II, 256
Rulon, Priscilla II, 95
Rulon, Rose II, 1078
Rulon, Rose II, 1079
Rulon, Samuel II, 717
Rulon, Samuel II, 764
Rulon, Sarah II, 195
Rulon, Sarah II, 256
Rulon, Sarah II, 300
Rulon, Sarah II, 324
Rulon, Sarah II, 478
Rulon, Sarah II, 641
Rulon, Sarah W. II, 416
Rulon, Sarah W. II, 764
Rulon, Susanna II, 95
Rulon, Susanna II, 195
Rulon, Susanna II, 256
Rulon, Susanna II, 312
Rulon, Susannah II, 77
Rulon, Susannah II, 95
Rulon, Susannah II, 300
Rulon, Wd. Sarah II, 416
Rumbard, Daniel II, 522
Rumbard, Eli II, 522
Rumbard, Esther II, 522
Rumbard, Joseph II, 522
Rumbard, Rachel II, 522
Rumbard, Rachel II, 641
Rumbey, Clemmons I, 274
Rumbo, Benjamin V, 356
Rumbo, Deborah Rachel V, 356
Rumbo, Isaac V, 356
Rumbo, Jane V, 356
Rumbo, Jane M. V, 356
Rumbo, Robert V, 356
Rumbolt, Lydia V, 1017
Rumery, Ethel IV, 1292
Rumford, Jonathan II, 641
Rumford, Susanna II, 608
Rumford, Susanna II, 641
Rumford, Susannah II, 641
Rummel, Bell III, 297
Rummel, Bell III, 303
Rummel, J. H. IV, 756
Rummell, Elizabeth IV, 756
Rummell, J. H. IV, 756
Rummery, Ethel IV, 1292
Rummery, Wm. IV, 1292
Rummin, Hannah II, 447
Rummin, Mary II, 447
Rummin, Philip II, 447
Rummin, Phillip II, 447
Rumsey, Maria E. II, 156
Rumsey, Mariah II, 144
Rumsey, Mariah II, 156
Run, Pike IV, 45
Run, Pike IV, 46
Runals, Elizabeth I, 813
Runals, Elizabeth I, 835
Rundal, Esther IV, 644
Rundal, Esther IV, 654
Rundal, Isaac IV, 644
Rundal, Rebecca IV, 644
Rundel, Esther IV, 654
Rundel, Sarah II, 95
Rundel, Warrick II, 95
Runell, Mary I, 835
Runels, Nancy I, 569
Runge, George II, 818
Runk, Charles V, 358
Runk, Clara V, 358
Runk, Dorsey F. V, 358
Runk, John D. H. V, 358
Runk, Leota Mancher V, 429
Runkell, Elizabeth III, 165
Runkell, Elizabeth III, 166
Runkell, John III, 165
Runkle, Bruno W. V, 1017
Runkle, Elizabeth III, 213
Runnells, ??? III, 265
Runnells, Abigail III, 111
Runnells, Abigail III, 265
Runnells, Abigail III, 275
Runnells, Abigail III, 276
Runnells, Abraham III, 265
Runnells, Ann III, 265
Runnells, Ann III, 275
Runnells, Ann Maria III, 265
Runnells, Anna Maria III, 276
Runnells, Cora V, 643
Runnells, Elias III, 275
Runnells, Elijah H. III, 275
Runnells, Elijah H. III, 276
Runnells, Elijah J. III, 111
Runnells, George V, 643
Runnells, Lewis V, 643
Runnells, Robert III, 275
Runnels, Clarissa V, 274
Runnels, Elias III, 275
Runnels, Henry V, 243
Runnels, Henry V, 274
Runnels, Isaac W. Haines V, 243
Runnels, Matilda I, 996
Runnels, Matilda I, 1000
Runnion, Albert V, 1017
Runnion, Dorotha Bell V, 1017
Runnion, Dorothy Bell V, 1017
Runnion, Francis V, 1017
Runnion, Jennie M. V, 1017
Runnion, Rachel V, 1017
Runnion, Susie V, 1017
Runyolds, Josinah V, 858
Runyolds, William V, 858
Rupe, Amanda V, 1017
Rupert, Amanda V, 1017
Rupert, Ann II, 621
Rupert, Ann II, 641
Rupert, Charity V, 1017
Rupert, G. W. V, 1017
Rupert, Henrietta V, 1017
Rupert, James V, 1017
Rupert, John N. V, 1017
Rupert, Mary II, 627
Rupert, Mary II, 641
Rupert, Michael VI, 924
Rupert, Nora E. IV, 1336
Rupert, Sidney V, 1017
Rupert, Wm. B. IV, 1336
Rupill, Hannah Ann IV, 271
Rusco, Charity IV, 1240
Ruse, Aaron V, 429
Ruse, Ann V, 410
Ruse, Ann V, 429
Ruse, Jennie V, 429
Ruse, Margaret V, 323
Ruse, Margaret V, 357
Ruse, Margaret V, 429
Ruse, Michael V, 429
Ruse, Rachel V, 429
Ruse, Rebecca V, 393
Ruse, Rebecca V, 429
Ruse, Ruth V, 429
Ruse, Sarah V, 379
Ruse, Sarah V, 429
Ruse, Thomas V, 429
Ruse, Thos. V, 429
Rusel, Elener I, 607
Rusell, Elizabeth VI, 338
Rusell, William VI, 338
Rush, A. G. I, 733
Rush, Agnes II, 182
Rush, Albert IV, 1262
Rush, Albert T. IV, 1262
Rush, Alta I, 920
Rush, Alta I, 948
Rush, Ann I, 769
Rush, Arabel I, 733
Rush, Arahable F. I, 733
Rush, Asael I, 733
Rush, Azel I, 732
Rush, Azel I, 733
Rush, Azel I, 769
Rush, Azel G. I, 705
Rush, Azel G. I, 733
Rush, Azle I, 733
Rush, Benjamin I, 257
Rush, Benjn. I, 257
Rush, Clyde I, 948
Rush, D. M. I, 733
Rush, Darinda I, 716
Rush, Darinda I, 733
Rush, Darinda I, 769
Rush, Derinda I, 732
Rush, Doctor M. I, 705
Rush, Dorcas I, 722
Rush, Dorcas I, 732
Rush, Dorcas I, 733
Rush, Dorcas I, 769
Rush, Doskie I, 933
Rush, Dougan I, 733
Rush, Dougan I, 769
Rush, Edna IV, 1262
Rush, Effie I, 933
Rush, Eliza I, 733
Rush, Eliza I, 738
Rush, Eliza Jane I, 705
Rush, Elizabeth I, 709
Rush, Elizabeth I, 732
Rush, Elizabeth I, 733
Rush, Elizabeth I, 769
Rush, Elwood I, 733
Rush, Emela I, 733
Rush, Emily I, 733
Rush, Emma IV, 1262
Rush, Eunice I, 927
Rush, Evangeline I, 948
Rush, Frances I, 733
Rush, Frances I, 739
Rush, Francis Elon I, 705
Rush, G. W. I, 733
Rush, George Washington Gwyer I, 705
Rush, H. B. I, 733
Rush, Henery I, 733
Rush, Henry I, 733
Rush, Henry M. I, 705
Rush, Iredel I, 769
Rush, Iredell I, 709
Rush, Iredell I, 732
Rush, Iredell I, 733
Rush, J. M. I, 933
Rush, John M. I, 948
Rush, Joseph E. I, 705
Rush, Joseph E. I, 733
Rush, Joseph N. I, 733
Rush, Julia A. I, 733
Rush, Julian I, 733
Rush, Julian Winfield I, 733
Rush, Marianna III, 407
Rush, Martha Mahulda I, 733
Rush, Mary I, 722
Rush, Mary I, 732
Rush, Mary I, 733
Rush, Mary I, 736
Rush, Mary I, 769
Rush, Milicent I, 705
Rush, Milicent I, 710
Rush, Milicent I, 733
Rush, Nancy I, 724
Rush, Nancy I, 733
Rush, Nellie B. IV, 271
Rush, Nettie IV, 1262
Rush, Nixon I, 733
Rush, Nixon I, 769
Rush, Pamelia III, 407
Rush, Polly I, 733
Rush, Susannah I, 718
Rush, Susannah I, 733
Rush, Thomas Bradford I, 733
Rusher, Ann VI, 973
Rusher, Asenath VI, 902
Rusher, Asenath VI, 997
Rusher, Cena VI, 988
Rusher, Elizabeth VI, 953
Rusher, Elizabeth VI, 988
Rusher, Fanny VI, 923
Rusher, George VI, 935
Rusher, George VI, 988
Rusher, Henry VI, 988
Rusher, James VI, 890
Rusher, James VI, 902
Rusher, James VI, 953
Rusher, James VI, 973
Rusher, James VI, 988
Rusher, James VI, 997
Rusher, Jesse T. VI, 988
Rusher, Jordan P. VI, 902
Rusher, Jordan P. VI, 981
Rusher, Jordan P. VI, 988
Rusher, Judith Ann Elizabeth VI, 988
Rusher, Lucy VI, 935
Rusher, Minerva VI, 902

Rusher, Polly VI, 973
Rusher, Rebecka Ann VI, 997
Rusher, Ruth VI, 997
Rusher, Sally VI, 890
Rusher, Sicily VI, 988
Rusher, William VI, 988
Rushmore, ??? III, 210
Rushmore, Adelaide III, 414
Rushmore, Adelaide III, 441
Rushmore, Adelaide III, 442
Rushmore, Amy III, 431
Rushmore, Amy III, 441
Rushmore, Amy III, 472
Rushmore, Amy III, 496
Rushmore, Amy III, 507
Rushmore, Amy L. III, 442
Rushmore, Amy L. III, 454
Rushmore, Anna III, 113
Rushmore, Anna III, 496
Rushmore, Anna III, 508
Rushmore, Anna M. III, 276
Rushmore, Anna M. III, 331
Rushmore, Anneke III, 441
Rushmore, Annie H. III, 495
Rushmore, Annie H. III, 496
Rushmore, Benj. III, 496
Rushmore, Benj. H. III, 276
Rushmore, Benj. H. III, 331
Rushmore, Beth III, 441
Rushmore, Carly Jackson III, 441
Rushmore, Caroline III, 441
Rushmore, Caroline A. III, 421
Rushmore, Caroline A. III, 441
Rushmore, Charles III, 441
Rushmore, Charles III, 496
Rushmore, Charles III, 505
Rushmore, Clara S. III, 214
Rushmore, Clara S. III, 276
Rushmore, Constance III, 441
Rushmore, David Barker III, 276
Rushmore, Deborah III, 276
Rushmore, Deborah III, 441
Rushmore, Deborah III, 465
Rushmore, Deborah III, 496
Rushmore, Deborah III, 503
Rushmore, Deborah III, 504
Rushmore, Deborah III, 508
Rushmore, Dr. Edward C. III, 163
Rushmore, Dr. Edward C. III, 276
Rushmore, Dr. Mary D. III, 276
Rushmore, Edmond III, 441
Rushmore, Edmund III, 441
Rushmore, Edmund P. III, 441
Rushmore, Edna L. III, 442
Rushmore, Edward III, 214
Rushmore, Edward III, 276
Rushmore, Edward III, 442
Rushmore, Elizabeth III, 442
Rushmore, Elizabeth III, 443
Rushmore, Elizabeth III, 496
Rushmore, Elizabeth III, 505
Rushmore, Ellen III, 214
Rushmore, Ellen III, 276
Rushmore, Emily III, 163
Rushmore, Emily III, 276
Rushmore, Emily III, 439
Rushmore, Emily III, 441
Rushmore, Emily III, 447
Rushmore, Emily W. III, 441
Rushmore, Esther III, 442
Rushmore, Esther III, 481
Rushmore, Esther III, 496
Rushmore, Esther L. III, 441
Rushmore, Esther L. III, 454
Rushmore, Frances III, 210
Rushmore, Frances Gertrude III, 276
Rushmore, Frances Gertrude III, 331
Rushmore, Freddie III, 441
Rushmore, Gertrude III, 276
Rushmore, Gertrude III, 441
Rushmore, Halstead III, 441
Rushmore, Halstead III, 447
Rushmore, Hannah III, 276
Rushmore, Henry III, 439
Rushmore, Henry III, 441
Rushmore, Henry W. III, 442
Rushmore, Isaac III, 276
Rushmore, Isaac III, 408
Rushmore, Isaac III, 411
Rushmore, Isaac III, 434
Rushmore, Isaac III, 441
Rushmore, Isaac III, 442
Rushmore, Isaac III, 451
Rushmore, Isaac III, 455
Rushmore, Isaac III, 462
Rushmore, Isaac W. III, 262
Rushmore, Isaac W. III, 276
Rushmore, Jacob III, 429
Rushmore, Jacob III, 441
Rushmore, Jacob III, 481
Rushmore, Jacob III, 496
Rushmore, Jame III, 462
Rushmore, James III, 441
Rushmore, James III, 465
Rushmore, James III, 496
Rushmore, James III, 504
Rushmore, James III, 508
Rushmore, Jane III, 441
Rushmore, Jane III, 442
Rushmore, Jane III, 461
Rushmore, Jane III, 471
Rushmore, Jemima III, 496
Rushmore, Jericho III, 276
Rushmore, Jno. Howard III, 276
Rushmore, John III, 496
Rushmore, John Howard III, 395
Rushmore, John Howard III, 441
Rushmore, John Howard III, 442
Rushmore, John U. III, 276
Rushmore, Julia A. III, 276
Rushmore, Julia Anna III, 395
Rushmore, Julia Anna III, 441
Rushmore, Leon III, 441
Rushmore, Leon III, 442
Rushmore, Leon A. III, 441
Rushmore, Leon A. III, 444
Rushmore, Leon A., Jr. III, 421
Rushmore, Leon A., Jr. III, 441
Rushmore, Leon Aug. III, 444
Rushmore, Lilian T. III, 442
Rushmore, Lydia III, 434
Rushmore, Lydia III, 441
Rushmore, Lydia M. III, 441
Rushmore, Lydia, Jr. III, 441
Rushmore, Maria III, 441
Rushmore, Marian III, 442
Rushmore, Martha III, 441
Rushmore, Mary III, 411
Rushmore, Mary III, 429
Rushmore, Mary III, 441
Rushmore, Mary III, 442
Rushmore, Mary III, 444
Rushmore, Mary III, 481
Rushmore, Mary III, 496
Rushmore, Mary Jane III, 262
Rushmore, Mary Jane III, 276
Rushmore, Mary Lee III, 441
Rushmore, Mary R. III, 434
Rushmore, Mary W. III, 444
Rushmore, Matilda III, 436
Rushmore, Matilda III, 441
Rushmore, Matilda III, 442
Rushmore, Phebe III, 408
Rushmore, Phebe III, 413
Rushmore, Phebe III, 418
Rushmore, Phebe III, 434
Rushmore, Phebe III, 441
Rushmore, Phebe III, 442
Rushmore, Phebe III, 454
Rushmore, Phebe III, 457
Rushmore, Phebe III, 471
Rushmore, Phebe III, 496
Rushmore, Phebe T. III, 413
Rushmore, Phebe T. III, 441
Rushmore, Rachel III, 442
Rushmore, Rachel W. III, 431
Rushmore, Robert Stephen III, 441
Rushmore, Roslyn III, 441
Rushmore, Samuel III, 441
Rushmore, Samuel III, 442
Rushmore, Samuel W. III, 276
Rushmore, Samuel W. III, 441
Rushmore, Sarah III, 276
Rushmore, Sarah III, 400
Rushmore, Sarah III, 408
Rushmore, Sarah III, 411
Rushmore, Sarah III, 418
Rushmore, Sarah III, 441
Rushmore, Sarah III, 451
Rushmore, Sarah III, 455
Rushmore, Sarah III, 462
Rushmore, Silas III, 441
Rushmore, Silas III, 454
Rushmore, Silas A. III, 210
Rushmore, Silas A. III, 276
Rushmore, Stephen III, 413
Rushmore, Stephen III, 418
Rushmore, Stephen III, 434
Rushmore, Stephen III, 436
Rushmore, Stephen III, 441
Rushmore, Stephen III, 442
Rushmore, Stephen III, 457
Rushmore, Stephen III, 471
Rushmore, Stephen III, 496
Rushmore, Stephen T. III, 414
Rushmore, Stephen T. III, 441
Rushmore, Stephen T. III, 442
Rushmore, Thomas III, 400
Rushmore, Thomas III, 441
Rushmore, Thomas III, 442
Rushmore, Thomas III, 443
Rushmore, Thomas H. III, 495
Rushmore, Thomas H. III, 496
Rushmore, Thos. III, 441
Rushmore, Thos. III, 442
Rushmore, Thos. III, 461
Rushmore, Townsend III, 431
Rushmore, Townsend III, 441
Rushmore, Townsend III, 442
Rushmore, Townsend III, 472
Rushmore, Townsend III, 496
Rushmore, Townsend III, 507
Rushmore, Wd. Elizabeth III, 442
Rushmore, William T. III, 442
Rushmore, Willie III, 441
Rushton, Abraham III, 276
Rushton, Benj. III, 192
Rushton, Benjamin III, 276
Rushton, Benjamin G. III, 276
Rushton, Christiana III, 205
Rushton, Christiana III, 276
Rushton, Christina III, 276
Rushton, David III, 276
Rushton, David T. III, 276
Rushton, Elizabeth III, 102
Rushton, Elizabeth III, 276
Rushton, Hannah III, 205
Rushton, Hannah III, 276
Rushton, Hannah III, 353
Rushton, Harriet E. III, 276
Rushton, James III, 205
Rushton, James III, 276
Rushton, James III, 353
Rushton, Joseph III, 276
Rushton, Mary Ann III, 276
Rushton, Sarah III, 192
Rushton, Sarah III, 276
Rushton, Sarah III, 353
Rushton, Sarah III, 496
Rushton, Sarah III, 505
Rushton, Sarah III, 506
Rusk, John V, 929
Rusk, Maria V, 929
Russel, Abraham, Jr. II, 642
Russel, Ann I, 1037
Russel, Ann II, 512
Russel, Ann II, 642
Russel, Ann V, 116
Russel, Carl I, 640
Russel, Catharine I, 971
Russel, David I, 514
Russel, Elenor I, 570
Russel, Elizabeth V, 116
Russel, Ellener I, 514
Russel, Esther IV, 57
Russel, George I, 514
Russel, George I, 570
Russel, Hannah A. IV, 220
Russel, Hannah Ann IV, 279
Russel, Hepzibah I, 514
Russel, Isaac I, 1037
Russel, Isaac V, 116
Russel, Isaac V, 792
Russel, James V, 116
Russel, Jane R. V, 921
Russel, Jane R. V, 929
Russel, John I, 514
Russel, John I, 570
Russel, John II, 641
Russel, Joseph II, 642
Russel, Joseph IV, 220
Russel, Judith I, 514
Russel, Judith I, 570
Russel, Judith I, 835
Russel, Judith I, 840
Russel, Lottie I, 853
Russel, Martha I, 514
Russel, Martha I, 570
Russel, Mary I, 514
Russel, Mary Ann IV, 756
Russel, Mary Ann IV, 767
Russel, Miriam I, 514
Russel, Miriam I, 570
Russel, Robison I, 514
Russel, Rosanna I, 1037
Russel, Rosanna V, 116
Russel, Ruth I, 514
Russel, Sarah I, 514
Russel, Sarah IV, 1178
Russel, Sarah IV, 1183
Russel, Tamer V, 754
Russel, Timmothy I, 570
Russel, Timothy I, 514
Russel, Timothy I, 570
Russel, William I, 514
Russel, William I, 570
Russel, Wm. P. IV, 1292
Russell, ??? I, 16
Russell, Abbie V, 418
Russell, Abraham III, 276
Russell, Abraham, Jr. II, 642
Russell, Ada II, 890
Russell, Ada II, 917
Russell, Agnes III, 265
Russell, Agnes III, 276
Russell, Agnes III, 277
Russell, Alexandria III, 276
Russell, Alice III, 276
Russell, Alice Englar VI, 775
Russell, Ann I, 1037
Russell, Ann II, 642
Russell, Ann V, 723
Russell, Ann V, 747
Russell, Ann V, 763
Russell, Ann VI, 554
Russell, Ann VI, 633
Russell, Ann VI, 678
Russell, Ann VI, 696
Russell, Ann VI, 851
Russell, Anne VI, 554
Russell, Asa IV, 176
Russell, Asenath IV, 176
Russell, Belle IV, 1240
Russell, Benjamin III, 276
Russell, Benjamin VI, 85
Russell, Benjamin VI, 119
Russell, Benjamin VI, 266
Russell, Benjamin Bailey VI, 119
Russell, Benjamin S. II, 700
Russell, Bertha I, 625
Russell, Bertha I, 630
Russell, Bertha I, 640
Russell, Bertha IV, 882
Russell, Bertha P. III, 277
Russell, Bettie Jane I, 625
Russell, Caleb VI, 623
Russell, Caleb VI, 675
Russell, Caleb VI, 696
Russell, Caleb VI, 775
Russell, Caleb, Jr. VI, 696
Russell, Calvin II, 717
Russell, Carl I, 640
Russell, Carrie IV, 1308
Russell, Catharine I, 996
Russell, Charles I, 570
Russell, Charles I, 971
Russell, Charles I, 996
Russell, Charles VI, 775
Russell, Charles R. III, 276
Russell, Charles R. III, 277
Russell, Charlotte H. III, 276
Russell, Chas. V, 418
Russell, Clara B. III, 108
Russell, Clara B. III, 270
Russell, Clyde I, 625
Russell, Clyde I, 640
Russell, Clyde I, 641
Russell, Clyde E. I, 625
Russell, Clyde F. I, 640
Russell, Curtin IV, 1308
Russell, Curtin IV, 1336
Russell, D. L. VI, 977
Russell, Daniel IV, 756
Russell, Daniel V, 905
Russell, Daniel VI, 858
Russell, Daniel L. VI, 893
Russell, Dolph IV, 882
Russell, Dorothy I, 570
Russell, Dorothy J. I, 514
Russell, Dosia VI, 988
Russell, Dr. Worthington S. III, 309
Russell, Earl I, 640
Russell, Earl V. I, 625
Russell, Earl V. I, 640
Russell, Edgar M. VI, 696
Russell, Edith IV, 1336
Russell, Edwin IV, 1336
Russell, Edwin IV, 1339
Russell, Edwin A. IV, 1336
Russell, Edwin A. VI, 266
Russell, Eleanor VI, 851
Russell, Elener I, 607
Russell, Elenor I, 570
Russell, Eliza I, 1161
Russell, Eliza II, 806
Russell, Eliza II, 890
Russell, Eliza II, 917
Russell, Eliza IV, 756
Russell, Eliza Ann II, 917
Russell, Elizabeth I, 1033
Russell, Elizabeth I, 1037
Russell, Elizabeth II, 717
Russell, Elizabeth III, 276
Russell, Elizabeth IV, 1336
Russell, Elizabeth IV, 1339
Russell, Elizabeth V, 792
Russell, Elizabeth V, 929
Russell, Elizabeth VI, 554
Russell, Elizabeth VI, 623
Russell, Elizabeth VI, 675
Russell, Elizabeth VI, 677
Russell, Elizabeth VI, 692
Russell, Elizabeth VI, 696
Russell, Elizabeth VI, 702
Russell, Elizabeth VI, 812
Russell, Elizabeth VI, 988
Russell, Elizabeth A. IV, 211
Russell, Elizabeth A. IV, 271
Russell, Elizabeth Ann IV, 271
Russell, Elizabeth S. III, 276
Russell, Elizabeth S. VI, 696
Russell, Ellen E. III, 276
Russell, Ellen E. III, 277
Russell, Ellen Eliza III, 277
Russell, Ellen Eliza III, 309
Russell, Emanuel III, 276
Russell, Emily V, 596
Russell, Esther IV, 107
Russell, Esther V, 929
Russell, Esther VI, 604
Russell, Ethel IV, 1262
Russell, Ethel M. IV, 1317
Russell, Ethel M. IV, 1336
Russell, Everett III, 276
Russell, Everett De Witt III, 27
Russell, Faith VI, 119
Russell, Fanny VI, 858
Russell, Florence IV, 1336
Russell, Frances III, 276
Russell, Frances C. IV, 756
Russell, Francis VI, 775
Russell, Frank III, 276
Russell, Frank J. III, 239
Russell, Frank J. III, 276
Russell, Frank J. VI, 775
Russell, George I, 570
Russell, George I, 822
Russell, George I, 835
Russell, George VI, 988
Russell, Gilbert III, 276
Russell, Gilbert E. III, 276
Russell, Gulielma IV, 271
Russell, Hannah I, 1033
Russell, Hannah I, 1037
Russell, Hannah IV, 756
Russell, Hannah VI, 469
Russell, Hannah VI, 522
Russell, Hannah VI, 554
Russell, Hannah VI, 696
Russell, Hannah VI, 758
Russell, Hannah VI, 775
Russell, Hannah A. IV, 271
Russell, Hannah Ann IV, 271
Russell, Hannah Ann IV, 272
Russell, Hannah Ann IV, 279
Russell, Hannah Ann VI, 554
Russell, Hannah Ann VI, 775
Russell, Hannah M. VI, 696
Russell, Hannah Maria VI, 623
Russell, Hannah Maria VI, 627
Russell, Hannah Maria VI, 696
Russell, Hannah R. III, 276
Russell, Harriet Jane VI, 696
Russell, Henry Casshel II, 717
Russell, Henry R. III, 276
Russell, Henry R. VI, 696
Russell, Henry R. VI, 702
Russell, Hephzibah I, 570
Russell, Hepsebeth V, 905
Russell, Hepsibah I, 574
Russell, Hepzebah I, 275
Russell, Hepzibah I, 570
Russell, Hepzibeth I, 275
Russell, Hepzibeth V, 899
Russell, Humphrey III, 276
Russell, Ida VI, 510
Russell, Isaac I, 1037
Russell, Isaac III, 248
Russell, Isaac III, 276
Russell, Isaac V, 792
Russell, Isaac D. III, 53
Russell, Isaac D. III, 276
Russell, Isaac S. III, 277
Russell, J. H. I, 640
Russell, James IV, 211
Russell, James IV, 271
Russell, James V, 929
Russell, James VI, 521
Russell, James VI, 522
Russell, James VI, 554
Russell, James VI, 758
Russell, James VI, 775
Russell, James VI, 812
Russell, James VI, 814
Russell, James VI, 824
Russell, James VI, 852
Russell, James VI, 862
Russell, James VI, 988

ssell, James, Sr. IV, 271
ssell, Jane III, 276
ssell, Jane IV, 196
ssell, Jane IV, 271
ssell, Jane V, 929
ssell, Jane C. III, 53
ssell, Jane C. III, 248
ssell, Jane C. III, 276
ssell, Jane D. IV, 271
ssell, Jane D. IV, 311
ssell, Jane D. IV, 314
ssell, Jane R. V, 929
ssell, Jane Richardson II, 717
ssell, Jason Kirk IV, 756
ssell, Jason Kirk IV, 1336
ssell, Jesse V, 929
ssell, Jessie III, 190
ssell, John I, 340
ssell, John I, 514
ssell, John I, 570
ssell, John II, 447
ssell, John II, 641
ssell, John II, 692
ssell, John II, 806
ssell, John II, 890
ssell, John II, 917
ssell, John II, 1024
ssell, John IV, 271
ssell, John IV, 756
ssell, John VI, 522
ssell, John VI, 554
ssell, John VI, 758
ssell, John VI, 775
ssell, John VI, 976
ssell, John VI, 988
ssell, John Thomas VI, 554
ssell, John Thomas VI, 775
ssell, John W. III, 276
ssell, John Wady III, 276
ssell, John Wady III, 277
ssell, Jonas VI, 696
ssell, Jonathan S. III, 276
ssell, Joseph I, 514
ssell, Joseph II, 416
ssell, Joseph II, 642
ssell, Joseph IV, 211
ssell, Joseph IV, 266
ssell, Joseph IV, 271
ssell, Joseph IV, 272
ssell, Joseph IV, 279
ssell, Joseph VI, 758
ssell, Joseph Janney VI, 554
ssell, Joseph Janney VI, 775
ssell, Joseph Mather II, 1024
ssell, Joshua VI, 554
ssell, Joshua VI, 565
ssell, Joshua VI, 567
ssell, Joshua VI, 696
ssell, Josiah III, 276
ssell, Josiah IV, 1292
ssell, Josie III, 239
ssell, Josie III, 276
ssell, Josie B. VI, 775
ssell, Josie M. III, 276
ssell, Judith I, 570
ssell, Judith I, 822
ssell, Judith I, 835
ssell, Julia III, 248
ssell, Julia III, 264
ssell, Julia F. III, 276
ssell, Julia Frances III, 248
ssell, Julia Frances III, 276
ssell, Laura I, 616
ssell, Lawrence Myers III, 276
ssell, Lawrence Myers VI, 775
ssell, Lela IV, 882
ssell, Lemuel VI, 119
ssell, Lewellyn VI, 696
ssell, Lewis J. III, 276
ssell, Lewis J. III, 277
ssell, Lon V, 643
ssell, Louisa III, 276
ssell, Louise I, 625
ssell, Louise I, 641
ssell, Lucea II, 533
ssell, Lucea II, 642
ssell, Lucie S. III, 277
ssell, Lucy II, 533
ssell, Lucy II, 642
ssell, Lyndon I, 340
ssell, M. N. IV, 1336
ssell, Margaret IV, 1336
ssell, Margaret V, 905
ssell, Margaret S. I, 16
ssell, Maria III, 276
ssell, Marian Edith II, 764
ssell, Marie IV, 1336
ssell, Marion Edith II, 717
ssell, Martha I, 538
ssell, Martha I, 570
ssell, Martha IV, 176
Russell, Martha IV, 211
Russell, Martha IV, 266
Russell, Martha IV, 271
Russell, Martha IV, 678
Russell, Martha IV, 756
Russell, Martha VI, 554
Russell, Martha VI, 814
Russell, Martin I, 1161
Russell, Mary I, 340
Russell, Mary I, 570
Russell, Mary I, 996
Russell, Mary I, 997
Russell, Mary II, 700
Russell, Mary III, 276
Russell, Mary III, 277
Russell, Mary III, 405
Russell, Mary IV, 107
Russell, Mary IV, 113
Russell, Mary IV, 271
Russell, Mary V, 358
Russell, Mary V, 418
Russell, Mary VI, 554
Russell, Mary VI, 689
Russell, Mary VI, 755
Russell, Mary VI, 775
Russell, Mary VI, 776
Russell, Mary VI, 845
Russell, Mary VI, 987
Russell, Mary Adaline II, 806
Russell, Mary Ann IV, 756
Russell, Mary B. III, 277
Russell, Mary Jane I, 514
Russell, Mary Jane V, 358
Russell, Matilda M. IV, 756
Russell, Mildred Grace V, 596
Russell, Minta Belle IV, 1240
Russell, Miriam I, 570
Russell, Miriam I, 576
Russell, Miriam VI, 645
Russell, Miriam VI, 648
Russell, Miriam VI, 667
Russell, Miriam VI, 679
Russell, Miriam VI, 696
Russell, Miriam VI, 702
Russell, Miriam VI, 704
Russell, Miriam VI, 706
Russell, Miriam VI, 707
Russell, Miriam VI, 723
Russell, Mittie I, 625
Russell, Mourning Bailey VI, 119
Russell, Mr. Richard VI, 12
Russell, Mrs. ??? VI, 11
Russell, Mrs. Clyde E. I, 640
Russell, Mrs. Mittie I, 640
Russell, Mrs. Rose M. IV, 1336
Russell, Myrtle IV, 882
Russell, Nancy III, 277
Russell, Nancy VI, 824
Russell, Olive I, 1036
Russell, Olive I, 1037
Russell, Orville D. IV, 1240
Russell, Parvin IV, 1336
Russell, Paul Swain I, 835
Russell, Percy III, 265
Russell, Percy III, 276
Russell, Percy III, 277
Russell, Phebe IV, 107
Russell, Phebe VI, 119
Russell, Phebe Ann III, 277
Russell, Phebe C. IV, 1183
Russell, Phebe C. V, 763
Russell, Phoebe C. V, 763
Russell, Pleasant VI, 988
Russell, Polly VI, 852
Russell, Polly VI, 976
Russell, Priscilla V, 123
Russell, Rachel IV, 756
Russell, Rachel VI, 505
Russell, Rachel VI, 554
Russell, Rachel VI, 561
Russell, Rachel VI, 562
Russell, Rachel VI, 563
Russell, Rachel VI, 565
Russell, Rachel VI, 567
Russell, Rachel VI, 649
Russell, Rachel VI, 650
Russell, Rachel VI, 696
Russell, Rachel VI, 701
Russell, Rachel VI, 702
Russell, Rachel VI, 704
Russell, Rachel A. IV, 211
Russell, Rachel A. IV, 271
Russell, Rebecca II, 956
Russell, Rebecca IV, 1262
Russell, Rebecca VI, 119
Russell, Rebecca VI, 140
Russell, Rebecca VI, 266
Russell, Rebecca VI, 775
Russell, Rebecca Gaskill II, 700
Russell, Rebeckah VI, 119
Russell, Rebeckah VI, 120
Russell, Rebeckah VI, 266
Russell, Rebeckah Gaskill II, 704
Russell, Rebekah VI, 554
Russell, Rhoda VI, 441
Russell, Richard VI, 11
Russell, Richard VI, 12
Russell, Robert VI, 811
Russell, Robert VI, 814
Russell, Robert VI, 988
Russell, Robison I, 570
Russell, Robt. VI, 979
Russell, Roger Sidwell III, 276
Russell, Roger Sidwell VI, 775
Russell, Rosanna I, 1037
Russell, Rosanna V, 792
Russell, Rosanna VI, 988
Russell, Rosannah V, 747
Russell, Rose M. IV, 1336
Russell, Ruth IV, 1336
Russell, Ruth C. IV, 1310
Russell, Ruth C. IV, 1336
Russell, Ruth M. IV, 1336
Russell, Ruth M. IV, 1341
Russell, Samuel I, 1023
Russell, Samuel I, 1033
Russell, Samuel I, 1037
Russell, Samuel IV, 548
Russell, Samuel V, 747
Russell, Samuel VI, 441
Russell, Samuel B. V, 596
Russell, Samuel E. V, 596
Russell, Sarah I, 570
Russell, Sarah I, 582
Russell, Sarah I, 1053
Russell, Sarah II, 416
Russell, Sarah II, 447
Russell, Sarah IV, 211
Russell, Sarah IV, 271
Russell, Sarah IV, 1183
Russell, Sarah IV, 1336
Russell, Sarah V, 792
Russell, Sarah VI, 441
Russell, Sarah VI, 482
Russell, Sarah VI, 554
Russell, Sarah VI, 565
Russell, Sarah VI, 567
Russell, Sarah VI, 675
Russell, Sarah VI, 696
Russell, Sarah VI, 704
Russell, Sarah VI, 852
Russell, Sarah VI, 988
Russell, Sarah A. IV, 271
Russell, Sarah A. IV, 1336
Russell, Sarah Ann VI, 696
Russell, Sarah Ansley IV, 271
Russell, Seth III, 277
Russell, Shubael III, 277
Russell, Solomon B. III, 277
Russell, Sopha VI, 266
Russell, Sophia VI, 119
Russell, Sophia VI, 120
Russell, Sophia VI, 140
Russell, Sophia VI, 266
Russell, Sophia B. VI, 140
Russell, Stanley Seaton III, 277
Russell, Stephen III, 277
Russell, Susanna II, 717
Russell, Susannah II, 675
Russell, Susannah VI, 482
Russell, Susannah VI, 521
Russell, Susannah VI, 522
Russell, Susannah VI, 554
Russell, Susannah VI, 758
Russell, Susannah VI, 775
Russell, Talbot I, 996
Russell, Tamer V, 763
Russell, Theodore IV, 1336
Russell, Theodore VI, 623
Russell, Theodore VI, 627
Russell, Theodore VI, 696
Russell, Theodore A. IV, 1336
Russell, Thomas II, 642
Russell, Thomas VI, 482
Russell, Thomas VI, 554
Russell, Thomas VI, 565
Russell, Thomas VI, 567
Russell, Thomas VI, 675
Russell, Thomas VI, 696
Russell, Thomas VI, 704
Russell, Thomas VI, 852
Russell, Thomas VI, 860
Russell, Thomas Clarkson I, 514
Russell, Thomas John III, 277
Russell, Thomas S. III, 276
Russell, Thomas Stanley IV, 271
Russell, Thomas W. VI, 441
Russell, Thomas W. VI, 775
Russell, Thomas, Jr. VI, 696
Russell, Thos. W. III, 276
Russell, Thos. W. III, 277
Russell, Timmothy I, 570
Russell, Timothy I, 570
Russell, Timothy I, 835
Russell, Timothy I, 840
Russell, Tristrum VI, 441
Russell, Walter III, 277
Russell, Walter T. IV, 1336
Russell, Widow Judith I, 840
Russell, William I, 538
Russell, William I, 570
Russell, William I, 1161
Russell, William II, 416
Russell, William VI, 554
Russell, William C. I, 625
Russell, William Clyde I, 625
Russell, Wm. V, 929
Russell, Wm. VI, 696
Russell, Wm. P. IV, 1292
Russell, Wm. Tallman III, 277
Russell, Worthington III, 276
Russell, Worthington III, 277
Russell, Worthington S. III, 277
Rust, Albert IV, 756
Rust, Albert VI, 852
Rust, Betsy H. VI, 850
Rust, Elizabeth A. V, 94
Rust, Elizabeth A. V, 116
Rust, Elizabeth A. L. V, 929
Rust, Enos VI, 835
Rust, George VI, 807
Rust, George VI, 835
Rust, George VI, 836
Rust, George VI, 850
Rust, George VI, 988
Rust, Lucinda VI, 991
Rust, Marilla V, 200
Rust, Nancy E. VI, 850
Rust, Nannie B. VI, 852
Rust, Phebe VI, 988
Rust, Rebeckah VI, 835
Rustin, John I, 1037
Rustin, Lydia II, 642
Rustin, Samuel II, 642
Rustin, Samuel II, 649
Rustin, Wd. Lydia II, 649
Ruston, Elizabeth I, 1030
Ruston, Elizabeth I, 1037
Ruston, James I, 1037
Ruston, John I, 1037
Rutan, Milton V, 1017
Ruth Ellen, ??? IV, 816
Ruth, Frances, Jr. II, 642
Ruth, Georgia E. I, 418
Ruth, J. Wesley I, 418
Ruth, James II, 642
Ruth, Jane I, 835
Ruth, Jane I, 1131
Ruth, Jane V, 116
Ruth, Lura M. I, 418
Ruth, Martha J. I, 418
Ruth, Mary I, 418
Ruth, Susanna II, 642
Rutherford, Ada B. V, 708
Rutherford, Ada B. V, 929
Rutherford, Adelaide V, 929
Rutherford, Benjamin V, 275
Rutherford, Davidella V, 708
Rutherford, Elizabeth VI, 915
Rutherford, Howard VI, 988
Rutherford, John V, 275
Rutherford, John V, 526
Rutherford, John V, 643
Rutherford, John V, 708
Rutherford, John V, 929
Rutherford, John P. V, 929
Rutherford, Maggie E. V, 275
Rutherford, Maria VI, 988
Rutherford, Mary Ann V, 275
Rutherford, Mary Jane V, 526
Rutherford, Mary Jane V, 708
Rutherford, Rosanna VI, 988
Rutherford, Susanna G. V, 708
Rutherford, Susannah G. V, 526
Rutherford, Sylvia V, 526
Rutherford, Sylvia V, 708
Rutherford, Sylvia V, 893
Rutherford, Sylvia V, 929
Rutherford, Sylvia C. V, 929
Rutherford, William VI, 915
Rutherford, William VI, 988
Ruthledge, John B. VI, 852
Ruthledge, John W. VI, 852
Ruthledge, Julianna VI, 852
Ruthledge, Lucinda VI, 852
Rutledge, Alex VI, 834
Rutledge, Ann VI, 852
Rutledge, Emma V, 924
Rutledge, Emma V, 929
Rutledge, Lucinda D. VI, 863
Rutledge, William VI, 852
Rutlege, Katie V, 526
Rutlidge, Elizabeth IV, 433
Rutlidge, Elizabeth IV, 445
Rutmire, Ella IV, 272
Rutter, Martha II, 570
Rutter, Martha II, 642
Rutter, Nathaniel II, 416
Rutter, Samuel II, 570
Rutter, Samuel II, 642
Rutter, Sarah II, 570
Rutter, Sarah II, 642
Rutter, Solomon II, 416
Rutter, Susan IV, 756
Rutter, Thomas II, 570
Rutter, Thomas II, 642
Rutter, Thomas II, 1024
Rutter, Thomas III, 277
Rutter, Thomas VI, 775
Rutty, ??? III, 207
Rutty, Grace III, 207
Rutty, Grace III, 277
Ryall, Israel II, 416
Ryall, Jeremiah II, 447
Ryall, Jeremy II, 416
Ryall, John II, 416
Ryall, Joseph II, 416
Ryall, Mary II, 416
Ryall, Susanna II, 416
Ryall, Thomas II, 416
Ryall, William II, 416
Ryan, Angelina VI, 940
Ryan, Catherine Ramsey V, 200
Ryan, Elizabeth III, 93
Ryan, Elizabeth III, 277
Ryan, Elizabeth VI, 988
Ryan, Ephraim V, 200
Ryan, Ephraim E. V, 200
Ryan, George W. III, 277
Ryan, Harry E. III, 93
Ryan, Harry E. III, 277
Ryan, John VI, 988
Ryan, Joshua VI, 988
Ryan, Julian VI, 988
Ryan, Margaret V, 497
Ryan, Margaret V, 526
Ryan, Margaret V, 596
Ryan, Martha A. VI, 988
Ryan, Mary VI, 872
Ryan, Mary VI, 1012
Ryan, Mary Balenge VI, 988
Ryan, Nancy VI, 875
Ryan, Nellie W. III, 277
Ryan, Polly VI, 988
Ryan, Preston VI, 988
Ryan, Prudence I, 418
Ryan, Sarah E. VI, 988
Ryan, Whitehead, Jr. VI, 988
Ryan, William VI, 931
Ryan, William VI, 940
Ryan, William VI, 988
Rybecker, Kenneth IV, 1336
Rybecker, Thelma IV, 1336
Ryckman, Rhoda Canada IV, 1336
Ryder, Charles C. III, 277
Ryder, Eliza IV, 1336
Ryder, Emalane C. III, 195
Ryder, Emelane C. III, 277
Ryder, Harvey IV, 1336
Ryder, Herbert IV, 1336
Ryder, James IV, 1336
Ryder, Jane III, 436
Ryder, Jas. L. IV, 1336
Ryder, John IV, 1336
Ryder, Josiah C. III, 195
Ryder, Josiah C. III, 277
Ryder, Margaret IV, 1336
Ryder, Mary Ann III, 277
Ryder, Mary H. III, 277
Ryder, Nelson IV, 1336
Ryerson, Martain II, 642
Rykes, Mary N. IV, 1336
Ryland, Anne VI, 266
Ryland, Anne Elizabeth VI, 266
Ryley, Mary II, 81
Ryley, Mary II, 95
Ryly, Elizabeth I, 378
Ryly, Elizabeth I, 418
Rynor, Elizabeth VI, 1004
Rynor, George VI, 1004
Ryon, Fred L. IV, 990
Ryon, Fred L. IV, 994
Ryon, Geo. L. IV, 990
Ryon, Olive A. IV, 990
Ryon, Olive A. IV, 994
Ryon, Polly M. IV, 990
Rysdick, ??? III, 132
Rysdick, Ann R. III, 132
Rysdyk, Ann III, 277
Ryser, Carol IV, 756
Ryser, Carol Elsie IV, 756
Ryser, Earnest IV, 756
Ryser, Earnest Lewis IV, 756

Ryser, Edith IV, 756
Ryser, Edith Louise IV, 756
Ryser, Ernest IV, 756
Ryser, Lena IV, 756
Ryser, Paul IV, 756
Ryser, Paul Earnest IV, 756

S???, Elizabeth II, 103
Saalfield, Eugenia III, 175
Saalfield, Eugenia III, 277
Saalfield, Lizzie T. III, 175
Saalfield, Lizzie T. III, 277
Saalfield, Richard A. III, 175
Saalfield, Richard A. III, 277
Saber, Cora V, 763
Saber, William V, 763
Saber, William H. V, 763
Sabin, Arnold T. V, 116
Sabin, Bessie M. V, 526
Sabin, Elizabeth V, 116
Sabin, Elizabeth V, 526
Sabin, Geo. W. V, 708
Sabin, George V, 526
Sabin, George V, 596
Sabin, George W. V, 116
Sabin, George W. V, 596
Sabin, Harriet V, 88
Sabin, John M. V, 526
Sabin, Louisa V, 116
Sabin, Louisa V, 144
Sabin, Lydia V, 116
Sabin, Lydia V, 526
Sabin, Lydia V, 571
Sabin, Lydia V, 596
Sabin, Lydia Smith V, 526
Sabin, Margaret V, 83
Sabin, Margaret V, 526
Sabin, Maria V, 65
Sabin, Martha V, 65
Sabin, Martha C. V, 116
Sabin, Martha M. V, 526
Sabin, Mary V, 98
Sabin, Mary V, 116
Sabin, Mary V, 526
Sabin, Mary V, 596
Sabin, Mary Ann V, 526
Sabin, Matilda V, 116
Sabin, Matilda V, 141
Sabin, Matilda V, 526
Sabin, Ora V, 526
Sabin, Ora Louisa V, 526
Sabin, Paul V, 116
Sabin, Paul V, 526
Sabin, Rachel V, 25
Sabin, Rachel V, 477
Sabin, Rachel V, 526
Sabin, Sarah V, 90
Sabin, Sarah V, 116
Sabin, Sarah V, 526
Sabin, Stuart V, 526
Sabin, Warren V, 526
Sabin, William V, 116
Sabin, William V, 526
Sabin, William H. V, 116
Sabine, George V, 526
Sabrell, Benjamin IV, 759
Sabrell, Joseph IV, 759
Sabrell, Matthew IV, 759
Sabrell, Polly IV, 759
Sabrell, Rebecca IV, 759
Sabrell, Sally IV, 759
Sabrell, Susannah IV, 759
Sabrieski, Mary II, 917
Sabriskie, Mary II, 872
Sachavarell, Arthur II, 416
Sachavarell, Daniel II, 416
Sachavarell, Martha II, 416
Sacheverill, Arthur II, 416
Sacheverill, Daniel II, 416
Sacheverill, Eleanor II, 642
Sacheverill, Elizabeth II, 642
Sacket, Ann IV, 158
Sacket, Ann IV, 159
Sacket, Mary V, 1017
Sacket, Phebe III, 277
Sacket, Samuel IV, 159
Sacket, Sarah IV, 149
Sacket, Sarah IV, 159
Sackett, Elizabeth Ball IV, 756
Sackett, Lucinda IV, 756
Sackett, Lucinda IV, 776
Sackett, Samuel IV, 776
Sackett, Sarah IV, 776
Sackrider, Phebe IV, 1377
Sackrider, Sarah I, 923
Sackrider, Sarah I, 924
Sadden, Henry II, 416
Sadders, Abigail V, 200
Saddler, Louise I, 219
Saders, Rebekah II, 509
Sadler, ??? VI, 95
Sadler, Bartley VI, 120
Sadler, Benjamin VI, 120
Sadler, Charles VI, 120
Sadler, Edna Pretlow VI, 85
Sadler, Eliza VI, 120
Sadler, Fanny VI, 120
Sadler, Featherson VI, 120
Sadler, Featherson VI, 140
Sadler, Henry VI, 120
Sadler, James VI, 120
Sadler, John Jordan VI, 85
Sadler, John S. VI, 85
Sadler, John Smith VI, 120
Sadler, Louise IV, 1336
Sadler, Lucy VI, 120
Sadler, Martha VI, 120
Sadler, Mary VI, 120
Sadler, Merianna VI, 120
Sadler, Miriam VI, 120
Sadler, Nathaniel VI, 120
Sadler, Rebecca VI, 120
Sadler, Rhoda VI, 85
Sadler, Rhoda VI, 120
Sadler, Robert VI, 852
Sadler, Rodacy VI, 120
Sadler, Samuel Pretlow VI, 85
Sadler, Sarah VI, 120
Sadler, Sarah, Jr. VI, 120
Sadler, Thomas VI, 120
Sadler, Thomas, Jr. VI, 120
Sadler, William Rose VI, 120
Sadler, Wilmouth VI, 852
Sadler, Zachariah VI, 120
Saeger, Aubrey P. II, 917
Saeger, Carlton E. II, 917
Saeger, John P. II, 917
Saeger, Kate H. II, 917
Saeger, Margaret C. VI, 441
Safely, Henry III, 277
Saferight, Jeremiah I, 668
Saferight, Jeremiah I, 688
Saferight, Nancy I, 514
Safetra, Benjamin V, 116
Safetra, Elizabeth V, 116
Safetra, George W. V, 116
Safetra, James H. V, 116
Safetra, Jane T. V, 116
Safetra, Meribah V, 116
Safetra, Robert V, 116
Saffle, Mary E. IV, 1336
Saffle, Richard H. IV, 1336
Saffle, Walter E. M. IV, 1336
Sagar, Margaret C. VI, 438
Sagar, Silas VI, 438
Sagar, Thomas VI, 438
Sage, Alice IV, 1150
Sager, Edna McPherson V, 275
Sager, Martin B. IV, 1292
Sager, Nanny E. IV, 1292
Sager, Sarah A. IV, 1290
Sager, Sarah A. IV, 1292
Sailer, Elizabeth II, 917
Sailer, Hannah II, 818
Sailer, Thos. II, 818
Sailer, Wm. II, 818
Sailor, Elizabeth II, 917
Sailor, Elizabeth Jackson II, 849
Sailor, Elizabeth Jackson II, 917
Sailor, Josephine II, 917
Sailor, Mary A. II, 840
Sailor, Mary A. II, 917
Sailor, Mary C. II, 849
Sailor, Randolph II, 849
Sailor, Randolph II, 917
Sailor, Thos. H. Powers II, 849
Sailor, Thos. H. Powers II, 917
Saint, Achsa I, 71
Saint, Acsah I, 47
Saint, Acsah I, 71
Saint, Alpheus I, 71
Saint, Benjamin I, 34
Saint, Benjamin I, 71
Saint, Benjamin I, 130
Saint, Benjamin I, 164
Saint, Betsa I, 318
Saint, Betsey I, 733
Saint, Daniel I, 17
Saint, Daniel I, 36
Saint, Daniel I, 55
Saint, Daniel I, 62
Saint, Daniel I, 71
Saint, Daniel I, 733
Saint, Dowdy I, 71
Saint, Easter I, 307
Saint, Easter I, 318
Saint, Elisabeth I, 42
Saint, Elisabeth I, 62
Saint, Elisabeth I, 71
Saint, Elizabeth I, 719
Saint, Elizabeth I, 732
Saint, Elizabeth I, 733
Saint, Emily G. V, 243
Saint, Emily G. V, 275
Saint, Ester I, 318
Saint, Ester I, 733
Saint, Esther I, 318
Saint, Esther I, 733
Saint, Exum I, 71
Saint, Gulielma I, 42
Saint, Gulielma I, 71
Saint, Hannah I, 130
Saint, Hannah I, 164
Saint, Hannah I, 257
Saint, Harkelus I, 36
Saint, Harkelus I, 71
Saint, Hercules I, 17
Saint, Hercules I, 71
Saint, Jane I, 67
Saint, Jane I, 71
Saint, Jane I, 280
Saint, Jane I, 318
Saint, Janiss I, 257
Saint, Jean I, 71
Saint, Jean I, 318
Saint, Jenette I, 71
Saint, Julian I, 71
Saint, Margaret I, 17
Saint, Margaret I, 36
Saint, Margaret I, 55
Saint, Margaret I, 71
Saint, Margaret I, 200
Saint, Margaret Trueblood I, 733
Saint, Mary I, 733
Saint, Penina I, 34
Saint, Penina I, 71
Saint, Rachel I, 71
Saint, Robert I, 705
Saint, Sarah I, 36
Saint, Sarah I, 71
Saint, Thomas I, 67
Saint, Thomas I, 71
Saint, Thomas I, 318
Saint, Thomas I, 733
Saint, Widow Margaret I, 199
Saint, William I, 47
Saint, William I, 71
Sainte, Mary I, 733
Saintmire, Elizabeth V, 116
Saires, Wm. V, 201
Sairls, Beulah V, 53
Sairls, Beulah V, 116
Saiter, Ella IV, 1183
Saladay, Hannah IV, 107
Sale, Ann A. VI, 988
Sale, Charlotte L. VI, 852
Sale, Elizabeth VI, 903
Sale, Emily Frances VI, 965
Sale, John VI, 988
Sale, John F. VI, 852
Sale, John F. VI, 887
Sale, John F. VI, 935
Sale, Mahala S. VI, 988
Sale, Martha L. VI, 988
Sale, Mary VI, 988
Sale, N. VI, 974
Sale, N. VI, 975
Sale, N. VI, 1020
Sale, Nelson VI, 870
Sale, Nelson VI, 891
Sale, Nelson VI, 905
Sale, Nelson VI, 956
Sale, Nelson VI, 970
Sale, Nelson VI, 974
Sale, Nelson VI, 975
Sale, Nelson VI, 988
Sale, Nelson VI, 990
Sale, Nelson VI, 995
Sale, Nelson VI, 1003
Sale, Nelson VI, 1005
Sale, Nelson VI, 1007
Sale, R. A. VI, 1007
Sale, Richard A. VI, 965
Sale, Richard A. VI, 988
Sale, Richard H. VI, 933
Sale, Sally VI, 988
Sale, Thomas VI, 965
Sale, Thomas VI, 988
Sale, Thomas P. VI, 988
Sale, Thos. VI, 903
Saleway, William II, 416
Salisbury, Mamie L. IV, 1262
Salkeld, Barbadoes II, 642
Salkeld, John II, 642
Sallaway, Hannah II, 642
Sallaway, Hannah II, 652
Sallaway, Hannah II, 672
Salling, Elizabeth Jane VI, 988
Salling, Henry VI, 988
Salloman, Polly VI, 811
Sally, Ida IV, 1336
Salmen, Ada IV, 1336
Salmen, Mary Ann IV, 1336
Salmen, Michael IV, 1336
Salmen, Mrs. Maria IV, 1336
Salmen, Samuel IV, 1336
Salmen, Wilhelmina IV, 1336
Salmon, Elizabeth VI, 988
Salmon, Evalina P. VI, 988
Salmon, Evey VI, 988
Salmon, George L. VI, 988
Salmon, Huldah VI, 988
Salmon, Jesse J. VI, 988
Salmon, Joel VI, 961
Salmon, Joel VI, 988
Salmon, John VI, 906
Salmon, John VI, 988
Salmon, John, Junr. VI, 906
Salmon, Nathan VI, 988
Salmon, Rhoda VI, 988
Salmon, Sally VI, 906
Salmon, Sally VI, 988
Salmon, Samuel IV, 1336
Salmon, William VI, 988
Salmons, Ada IV, 1336
Salmons, Calistia VI, 852
Salmons, Geo. W. VI, 813
Salmons, Jemima VI, 903
Salmons, Jesse J. VI, 852
Salmons, Jesse J. VI, 988
Salmons, John VI, 852
Salmons, John D. VI, 808
Salmons, John D. VI, 811
Salmons, John D. VI, 852
Salmons, Mary Ann IV, 1336
Salmons, Nathan VI, 988
Salmons, Panthea F. VI, 852
Salmons, Rhoda VI, 988
Salmons, Ro. VI, 990
Salmons, Robert D. VI, 1001
Salmons, Sally VI, 988
Salsburg, Rebecca II, 642
Salsbury, Elizabeth L. II, 752
Salsbury, Elizabeth L. II, 764
Salsbury, Rebecca II, 483
Salter, Ann C. II, 913
Salter, Ann C. II, 917
Salter, Arthur J. IV, 756
Salter, Arthur John IV, 756
Salter, Frederick IV, 756
Salter, Hannah II, 642
Salter, Hannah II, 690
Salter, Hannah IV, 756
Salter, Joseph IV, 756
Salter, Margaret II, 557
Salter, Margaret II, 642
Salter, Sarah I, 56
Salter, Sarah I, 71
Salter, Sarah II, 416
Salter, Sarah P. V, 929
Salter, William II, 416
Salter, Wm. II, 642
Salters, Ezra V, 1017
Salts, ??? III, 434
Salts, Margery II, 1024
Salts, Margery II, 1030
Salts, Martha III, 434
Salts, Martha III, 442
Saltus, Lloyd III, 277
Saltus, Lloyd III, 282
Saltus, Sarah III, 277
Saltus, Sarah III, 282
Saltzgaber, Elizabeth V, 1017
Saltzgaber, Ella V, 1017
Saltzgaber, Mamie V, 1017
Salway, Christopher II, 642
Salway, Hannah II, 642
Salway, Mary II, 642
Salway, Mary II, 677
Salway, Sarah II, 642
Salway, Wm. II, 642
Salway, Wm. II, 677
Samall, Elizabeth I, 900
Sammond, Francis VI, 852
Sammond, G. W. VI, 852
Sammond, George L. VI, 988
Sammond, Huldah VI, 988
Sammonds, James VI, 12
Sammonds, Jsseph VI, 11
Sammons, Benjamin F. V, 276
Sammons, Charles W. V, 276
Sammons, George B. VI, 817
Sammons, John VI, 907
Sammons, Leonard G. V, 276
Sammons, Lexie V, 708
Sammons, Molley VI, 907
Sammons, Mrs. Maria IV, 1336
Sammow, Rachel VI, 441
Samms, Ann II, 642
Samms, Ann IV, 57
Samms, Ann IV, 654
Samms, Ann IV, 664
Samms, Benj. IV, 654
Samms, Benjamin IV, 57
Samms, Benjamin IV, 654
Samms, Isaac IV, 654
Samms, Jesse IV, 57
Samms, Jesse IV, 654
Samms, John IV, 57
Samms, John IV, 613
Samms, John IV, 654
Samms, John IV, 664
Samms, John, Jr. IV, 654
Samms, John, Jr. IV, 882
Samms, Nathaniel II, 642
Samms, Nathaniel IV, 57
Samms, Nathaniel, Jr. II, 642
Samms, Rachel IV, 613
Samms, Rachel IV, 654
Samms, Rachel IV, 655
Samms, Rebecca IV, 654
Samms, Samuel IV, 655
Samms, Sarah II, 642
Samms, Sarah IV, 57
Samms, Sarah IV, 613
Samms, Sarah IV, 654
Samms, Sarah IV, 655
Samms, Sarah IV, 664
Samms, Susannah IV, 655
Samms, Thomas II, 642
Samms, Thomas IV, 655
Sample, Mary VI, 441
Sample, Nellie I, 12
Sample, Nellie I, 59
Sample, Sarah VI, 487
Sample, Sarah VI, 554
Sampsel, Lydia Ann IV, 760
Sampson, ??? III, 35
Sampson, Alden III, 277
Sampson, Alden III, 315
Sampson, Alfred I, 570
Sampson, Alfred V, 1017
Sampson, Alfred T. I, 625
Sampson, Archibald T. I, 570
Sampson, Archie T. I, 570
Sampson, Benjamin VI, 991
Sampson, Charles W. I, 865
Sampson, Charles W. I, 900
Sampson, David I, 570
Sampson, David E. I, 625
Sampson, David John L. I, 57(
Sampson, Edward H. I, 865
Sampson, Edward H. I, 900
Sampson, Elbert Howard I, 62
Sampson, Elizabeth IV, 272
Sampson, Elizabeth E. I, 570
Sampson, Elizabeth G. I, 865
Sampson, Elizabeth G. I, 900
Sampson, Emma I, 570
Sampson, Emma I, 864
Sampson, Emma I, 899
Sampson, Emma I, 900
Sampson, Emma W. I, 865
Sampson, Esther P. III, 277
Sampson, Ezra I, 625
Sampson, Ezra I, 640
Sampson, Hannah C. III, 35
Sampson, Helen I, 625
Sampson, Herman Arthur I, 6
Sampson, Ida I, 625
Sampson, Ida Thrift I, 640
Sampson, James I, 570
Sampson, John N. I, 570
Sampson, Judah VI, 991
Sampson, Lizzie E. I, 570
Sampson, Maria H. III, 277
Sampson, Maria H. III, 315
Sampson, Maria L. I, 900
Sampson, Maria Lizie I, 865
Sampson, Maria Lizzie I, 900
Sampson, Mary I, 570
Sampson, Mary III, 277
Sampson, Mary Ann IV, 1042
Sampson, Phebe J. III, 277
Sampson, Ruth I, 640
Sampson, Ruth Virginia I, 625
Sampson, Ruth Virginia I, 640
Sampson, Sallie C. M. I, 625
Sampson, Sara I, 640
Sampson, Sarah I, 625
Sampson, Sarah III, 277
Sampson, Sarah III, 315
Sampson, Sarah IV, 1042
Sampson, Sarah C. M. I, 640
Sampson, Sarah E. III, 277
Sampson, Sarah T. III, 277
Sampson, William A. I, 865
Sampson, William A. I, 900
Sampson, Wm. IV, 1042
Sams, Alpharetta IV, 1183
Sams, Ann II, 482
Sams, Ann II, 642
Sams, Edith IV, 756
Sams, Floyd V, 310

ns, Hannah II, 447
ns, Herbert J. IV, 1183
ns, Hubert IV, 1183
ns, John II, 447
ns, John, Jr. IV, 756
ns, Louisa IV, 1183
ns, Louisa M. IV, 1183
ns, Mary II, 447
ns, Mary V, 116
ns, Nathaniel II, 482
ns, Nathaniel II, 642
ns, Nathaniel, Jr. II, 482
ns, Nathaniel, Jr. II, 642
ns, Nettie V, 429
ns, Sarah II, 482
ns, Sarah II, 642
nuel, ??? IV, 816
nuel, Alvina H. IV, 816
nuel, Charles W. IV, 816
nuel, Edward Y. IV, 816
nuel, Irena H. IV, 816
nuel, Jane IV, 350
nuel, Jehu II, 642
nuel, Mary Jane IV, 816
nuel, Mary R. IV, 816
nuel, Phebe Jane IV, 816
nuels, Ada V, 834
nuels, Jane IV, 350
nuels, L. R. V, 116
nuels, Mary IV, 350
nband, Caroline III, 240
nboarn, Daniel VI, 36
nborn, Ann Augusta III, 277
nborn, Caroline V. III, 277
nborn, Daniel VI, 37
nborn, James III, 277
nborn, Lydia III, 277
nborn, Lydia S. III, 216
nborn, Lydia S. III, 277
nborn, Mary VI, 37
nborn, Mary H. III, 277
nborn, Nestor III, 277
nborn, Nestor H. III, 216
nborn, Nestor H. III, 277
nborne, Daniel VI, 41
nbourn, Daniel VI, 27
nbourn, Daniel VI, 35
nbourn, Daniel VI, 36
nbourn, Daniel VI, 37
nbourne, Daniel VI, 8
nbourne, Daniel VI, 17
nbourne, Daniel VI, 18
nbourne, Daniel VI, 41
nbourne, Sarah VI, 8
nburn, Daniel VI, 36
nburn, Daniell VI, 36
nburn, Mary VI, 36
nburn, Sarah VI, 8
nburn, Sarah VI, 17
nd, Elizabeth II, 447
nd, Hannah B. IV, 1273
nd, Hannah B. IV, 1292
nd, John II, 447
nd, Rachel II, 447
ndal, David IV, 272
ndbing, Pauline III, 285
ndefer, Judah I, 1037
ndell, Dama IV, 272
nder, Mary II, 643
nderford, Betsey I, 318
nderford, Charity I, 318
nderford, Cloe I, 318
nderford, Drusilla I, 318
nderford, James I, 315
nderford, James I, 318
nderford, John I, 304
nderford, John I, 318
nderford, Judah I, 318
nderford, Judith I, 315
nderford, Judith I, 318
nderford, Lucrecy I, 318
nderford, Lucresa I, 318
nderford, Sarah I, 304
nderford, Sarah I, 318
nderford, Zilpha I, 318
nders, Aaron I, 116
nders, Aaron I, 164
nders, Aaron, Sr. I, 164
nders, Abigail I, 164
nders, Abigail I, 174
nders, Abigail I, 199
nders, Abisha IV, 841
nders, Abishai IV, 654
nders, Abraham I, 71
nders, Abraham I, 72
nders, Abraham I, 73
nders, Abraham I, 116
nders, Abraham I, 117
nders, Abraham I, 149
nders, Abraham I, 164
nders, Abraham I, 165
Sanders, Abraham I, 199
Sanders, Abraham I, 200
Sanders, Abraham I, 1045
Sanders, Abraham I, 1050
Sanders, Abraham I Sup 1, 8
Sanders, Ada R. I, 73
Sanders, Addison V, 276
Sanders, Addison V, 310
Sanders, Addison V, 358
Sanders, Addison V, 429
Sanders, Addison V, 708
Sanders, Adison V, 708
Sanders, Albert I, 72
Sanders, Albert I, 73
Sanders, Albert I, 257
Sanders, Albert V, 1017
Sanders, Alice V, 149
Sanders, Alice V, 200
Sanders, Allen I, 72
Sanders, Amelia Allison V, 117
Sanders, Amos III, 277
Sanders, Amos III, 278
Sanders, Amy V, 190
Sanders, Amy V, 191
Sanders, Amy V, 200
Sanders, Ann I, 68
Sanders, Ann I, 72
Sanders, Ann I, 87
Sanders, Ann I, 199
Sanders, Ann I, 203
Sanders, Ann I, 373
Sanders, Ann I, 418
Sanders, Ann I, 538
Sanders, Ann I, 570
Sanders, Ann I, 836
Sanders, Ann II, 999
Sanders, Ann II, 1024
Sanders, Ann IV, 211
Sanders, Ann IV, 272
Sanders, Ann IV, 654
Sanders, Ann IV, 915
Sanders, Ann VI, 441
Sanders, Ann S. VI, 852
Sanders, Anna I, 72
Sanders, Anna V, 117
Sanders, Anne I, 117
Sanders, Anne I, 227
Sanders, Anny V, 200
Sanders, Ardel I, 1161
Sanders, Armela I, 968
Sanders, Barbara I, 1045
Sanders, Barbara I, 1050
Sanders, Barbara V, 200
Sanders, Barbara V, 526
Sanders, Barbara V, 541
Sanders, Barbara V, 544
Sanders, Barclay V, 358
Sanders, Barclay V, 359
Sanders, Bathsheba V, 340
Sanders, Bathsheba V, 358
Sanders, Beecher I, 1161
Sanders, Bell V, 464
Sanders, Benj. I, 418
Sanders, Benj. I, 419
Sanders, Benja. I, 164
Sanders, Benjamin I, 46
Sanders, Benjamin I, 65
Sanders, Benjamin I, 71
Sanders, Benjamin I, 72
Sanders, Benjamin I, 87
Sanders, Benjamin I, 164
Sanders, Benjamin I, 199
Sanders, Benjamin I, 418
Sanders, Benjamin I, 1037
Sanders, Benjamin I, 1045
Sanders, Benjamin I, 1050
Sanders, Benjamin IV, 654
Sanders, Benjamin IV, 841
Sanders, Benjamin V, 117
Sanders, Benjm. I, 164
Sanders, Bessie IV, 272
Sanders, Betsey I, 227
Sanders, Betsy V, 112
Sanders, Betsy V, 116
Sanders, Betsy V, 276
Sanders, Betty I, 72
Sanders, Betty I, 80
Sanders, Caroline V, 136
Sanders, Caroline V, 359
Sanders, Caroline Amelia H. V, 310
Sanders, Catharine IV, 915
Sanders, Charity I, 418
Sanders, Charity I, 1045
Sanders, Charity I, 1050
Sanders, Charity I, 1058
Sanders, Charity IV, 654
Sanders, Charity IV, 736
Sanders, Charity IV, 756
Sanders, Charity V, 191
Sanders, Charity V, 200
Sanders, Charles I, 164
Sanders, Charles I, 174
Sanders, Charles I, 199
Sanders, Charles I, 733
Sanders, Charles II, 416
Sanders, Charles II, 643
Sanders, Charles II, 685
Sanders, Charles III, 277
Sanders, Charles Peitsmeyer V, 276
Sanders, Charles R. V, 276
Sanders, Charley V, 1017
Sanders, Chas. W. III, 189
Sanders, Chas. W. III, 216
Sanders, Chas. Walton III, 277
Sanders, Christopher VI, 852
Sanders, Cyrus V, 310
Sanders, Cyrus V, 358
Sanders, Daniel V, 191
Sanders, Daniel V, 200
Sanders, Daniel V, 201
Sanders, Daniel J. VI, 852
Sanders, Daniel Webster V, 117
Sanders, Daniel Webster V, 276
Sanders, David I, 791
Sanders, David I, 800
Sanders, David I, 836
Sanders, David I, 1161
Sanders, David III, 277
Sanders, David V, 276
Sanders, David V, 310
Sanders, David V, 358
Sanders, David V, 359
Sanders, David V, 429
Sanders, David V, 708
Sanders, David V, 929
Sanders, David B. I, 791
Sanders, David B. I, 836
Sanders, David Lewis V, 276
Sanders, David Lewis V, 526
Sanders, Deborah Ann V, 117
Sanders, Deborah Ann V, 276
Sanders, Deborah Ann V, 358
Sanders, Deborah Ann V, 526
Sanders, Dempsey I, 1045
Sanders, Dorcas I, 153
Sanders, Dorcas I, 164
Sanders, Drewsiller VI, 989
Sanders, Droster V, 201
Sanders, Edgar J. IV, 272
Sanders, Edgar J. IV, 1336
Sanders, Edith III, 278
Sanders, Edna V, 359
Sanders, Edwin V, 708
Sanders, Edwin Allen V, 708
Sanders, Edy II, 416
Sanders, Eleanor V, 117
Sanders, Eleanor V, 219
Sanders, Eleanor V, 276
Sanders, Eleanor V, 310
Sanders, Eleanor V, 358
Sanders, Eli V, 200
Sanders, Elihu V, 200
Sanders, Elisabeth I, 62
Sanders, Elisabeth I, 68
Sanders, Elisabeth I, 71
Sanders, Elisabeth I, 72
Sanders, Elisabeth I, 73
Sanders, Elisabeth I, 164
Sanders, Elisabeth I, 167
Sanders, Eliza I, 72
Sanders, Eliza I, 73
Sanders, Eliza A. I, 73
Sanders, Eliza A. V, 276
Sanders, Eliza Ann I, 72
Sanders, Eliza Arbelle V, 276
Sanders, Eliza Ella I, 73
Sanders, Elizabeth I, 257
Sanders, Elizabeth I, 297
Sanders, Elizabeth I, 318
Sanders, Elizabeth I, 705
Sanders, Elizabeth I, 733
Sanders, Elizabeth I, 791
Sanders, Elizabeth I, 799
Sanders, Elizabeth I, 803
Sanders, Elizabeth I, 818
Sanders, Elizabeth I, 836
Sanders, Elizabeth I, 1050
Sanders, Elizabeth II, 643
Sanders, Elizabeth II, 691
Sanders, Elizabeth II, 968
Sanders, Elizabeth V, 117
Sanders, Elizabeth V, 276
Sanders, Elizabeth V, 357
Sanders, Elizabeth V, 358
Sanders, Elizabeth V, 838
Sanders, Elizabeth V, 860
Sanders, Elizabeth V, 885
Sanders, Elizabeth VI, 266
Sanders, Elizabeth VI, 267
Sanders, Elizabeth C. VI, 853
Sanders, Elizabeth F. H. VI, 988
Sanders, Elizabeth Pope V, 358
Sanders, Elizabeth T. VI, 967
Sanders, Ella A. III, 189
Sanders, Ella A. III, 216
Sanders, Ella A. III, 277
Sanders, Ellen V, 276
Sanders, Ellen V, 358
Sanders, Ellen V, 359
Sanders, Elma IV, 272
Sanders, Elma Ann V, 310
Sanders, Elma Ann V, 526
Sanders, Elma Pearl V, 359
Sanders, Elvira V, 359
Sanders, Emily V, 117
Sanders, Emily V, 200
Sanders, Emily V, 276
Sanders, Emily V, 358
Sanders, Emily V, 526
Sanders, Emily N. V, 197
Sanders, Emily N. V, 201
Sanders, Emily N. V, 276
Sanders, Emma I, 1161
Sanders, Emmily V, 276
Sanders, Ephraim II, 968
Sanders, Epsey IV, 899
Sanders, Epsey IV, 915
Sanders, Epsy IV, 915
Sanders, Ermel E. V, 201
Sanders, Ervin I, 1161
Sanders, Ethel V, 359
Sanders, Euclid V, 359
Sanders, Fannie May IV, 990
Sanders, Fanny M. IV, 990
Sanders, Ferrebee I, 1047
Sanders, Ferrebee I, 1050
Sanders, Ferribe I, 1045
Sanders, Florence V, 1017
Sanders, Forrest I, 836
Sanders, Forris I, 791
Sanders, Frances C. V, 358
Sanders, Francis I, 72
Sanders, Fredric I, 72
Sanders, G. M. IV, 1336
Sanders, Garret VI, 852
Sanders, George VI, 961
Sanders, George VI, 988
Sanders, George VI, 989
Sanders, George Duncan II, 1024
Sanders, Gidion J. I, 73
Sanders, Grace I, 1161
Sanders, Grace III, 216
Sanders, Grace III, 277
Sanders, Grace III, 278
Sanders, Grace V, 708
Sanders, Grace A. V, 276
Sanders, Grace Green V, 708
Sanders, Gracy I, 1161
Sanders, Gulielma I, 791
Sanders, Gulielma I, 836
Sanders, Gulielma V, 110
Sanders, Gulielma V, 276
Sanders, Gulielma V, 335
Sanders, Gulielma V, 358
Sanders, Gulielma V, 366
Sanders, Gulielma M. V, 270
Sanders, Gulielma M. V, 276
Sanders, Gulielma M. V, 354
Sanders, Gulielma Maria V, 358
Sanders, Gulielma Sanders V, 117
Sanders, Gulyelmy V, 358
Sanders, Hallowell I Sup 1, 11
Sanders, Hannah I, 69
Sanders, Hannah I, 72
Sanders, Hannah I, 117
Sanders, Hannah I, 199
Sanders, Hannah I, 705
Sanders, Hannah I, 836
Sanders, Hannah I Sup 1, 5
Sanders, Hannah I Sup 1, 6
Sanders, Hannah II, 416
Sanders, Hannah II, 631
Sanders, Hannah II, 643
Sanders, Hannah IV, 211
Sanders, Hannah IV, 253
Sanders, Hannah IV, 272
Sanders, Hannah V, 885
Sanders, Hannah VI, 164
Sanders, Hannah VI, 166
Sanders, Hannah VI, 211
Sanders, Hannah VI, 441
Sanders, Harold III, 278
Sanders, Harold A. III, 277
Sanders, Harold A., Jr. III, 278
Sanders, Henry I, 227
Sanders, Henry V, 929
Sanders, Henry W. IV, 990
Sanders, Hester II, 416
Sanders, Hezekiah I, 418
Sanders, Hezekiah I, 514
Sanders, Hezekiah I, 570
Sanders, Hezekiah I, 773
Sanders, Hezekiah I, 791
Sanders, Hezekiah I, 835
Sanders, Hezekiah I, 836
Sanders, Hezekiah V, 117
Sanders, Hezekiah V, 310
Sanders, Hezekiah V, 358
Sanders, Hezekiah V, 929
Sanders, Hezekiah VI, 267
Sanders, Hezekiah H. IV, 1262
Sanders, Hezekiah H. V, 358
Sanders, Hezekiah H. V, 359
Sanders, Hezikiah VI, 267
Sanders, Hollaway I, 1050
Sanders, Hollorvel I, 1045
Sanders, Hollowell I, 1050
Sanders, Hugh Allen I, 1161
Sanders, Huldah J. V, 1017
Sanders, Isaac V, 117
Sanders, Jacob I, 791
Sanders, Jacob I, 836
Sanders, Jacob W. I, 72
Sanders, Jadiah I, 514
Sanders, James I, 836
Sanders, James II, 416
Sanders, James Edward I, 73
Sanders, James R. VI, 988
Sanders, Jamima I, 791
Sanders, Jane I, 570
Sanders, Jane I, 775
Sanders, Jane I, 781
Sanders, Jane I, 791
Sanders, Jane I, 833
Sanders, Jane I, 836
Sanders, Jane IV, 220
Sanders, Jane IV, 272
Sanders, Jane V, 117
Sanders, Jane V, 141
Sanders, Jane V, 310
Sanders, Jane V, 313
Sanders, Jane V, 526
Sanders, Jane VI, 164
Sanders, Jane VI, 211
Sanders, Jane VI, 267
Sanders, Jane VI, 441
Sanders, Jay I, 72
Sanders, Jean VI, 371
Sanders, Jeane VI, 852
Sanders, Jemima I, 775
Sanders, Jemima I, 791
Sanders, Jemima I, 836
Sanders, Jemima VI, 267
Sanders, Jemime I, 523
Sanders, Jemime I, 570
Sanders, Jeremiah I, 570
Sanders, Jesse I, 514
Sanders, Jesse I, 570
Sanders, Jesse I, 589
Sanders, Jesse I, 596
Sanders, Jesse I, 791
Sanders, Jesse I, 836
Sanders, Jesse IV, 654
Sanders, Jesse V, 117
Sanders, Jesse V, 200
Sanders, Jesse V, 276
Sanders, Jesse V, 310
Sanders, Jesse V, 358
Sanders, Jhon I, 117
Sanders, Joel I, 418
Sanders, Joel I, 514
Sanders, Joel I, 538
Sanders, Joel I, 570
Sanders, Joel I, 773
Sanders, Joel I, 791
Sanders, Joel I, 836
Sanders, Joel I, 1045
Sanders, Joel I, 1050
Sanders, Joel V, 200
Sanders, Joel V, 526
Sanders, Joel V, 544
Sanders, Joel VI, 267
Sanders, Joel, Jr. I, 836
Sanders, Joel, Jr. I, 1045
Sanders, John I, 71
Sanders, John I, 72
Sanders, John I, 74
Sanders, John I, 87
Sanders, John I, 116
Sanders, John I, 117
Sanders, John I, 153
Sanders, John I, 164
Sanders, John I, 165
Sanders, John I, 167
Sanders, John I, 173
Sanders, John I, 200
Sanders, John I, 257
Sanders, John I, 410
Sanders, John I, 418
Sanders, John I, 514
Sanders, John I, 570

Sanders, John I, 773
Sanders, John I, 775
Sanders, John I, 781
Sanders, John I, 791
Sanders, John I, 835
Sanders, John I, 836
Sanders, John I, 968
Sanders, John I, 971
Sanders, John I, 1037
Sanders, John I, 1045
Sanders, John I, 1050
Sanders, John I, 1053
Sanders, John II, 206
Sanders, John II, 256
Sanders, John II, 416
Sanders, John II, 643
Sanders, John II, 691
Sanders, John IV, 272
Sanders, John V, 32
Sanders, John V, 116
Sanders, John V, 117
Sanders, John V, 204
Sanders, John V, 219
Sanders, John V, 276
Sanders, John V, 310
Sanders, John V, 335
Sanders, John V, 358
Sanders, John V, 469
Sanders, John V, 526
Sanders, John VI, 164
Sanders, John VI, 211
Sanders, John VI, 266
Sanders, John VI, 267
Sanders, John VI, 371
Sanders, John VI, 441
Sanders, John VI, 813
Sanders, John VI, 989
Sanders, John C. V, 117
Sanders, John H. I, 1161
Sanders, John H. V, 276
Sanders, John H. V, 310
Sanders, John M. V, 358
Sanders, John R. I, 72
Sanders, John Sanders V, 117
Sanders, John, Jr. I, 570
Sanders, John, Jr. I, 773
Sanders, John, Jr. I, 836
Sanders, John, Jr. I, 1050
Sanders, John, Jr. VI, 211
Sanders, John, Jr. VI, 267
Sanders, John, Sr. VI, 211
Sanders, Jonathan I, 72
Sanders, Jonathan I, 257
Sanders, Jonathan I, 791
Sanders, Jonathan I, 836
Sanders, Jonathan V, 94
Sanders, Jonathan V, 116
Sanders, Jonathan V, 117
Sanders, Jonathan V, 200
Sanders, Jonathan V, 249
Sanders, Jonathan V, 276
Sanders, Jonathan V, 315
Sanders, Jonathan V, 339
Sanders, Jonathan V, 358
Sanders, Jonathan V, 359
Sanders, Jonathan L. V, 359
Sanders, Jonathan, Jr. V, 359
Sanders, Joseph I, 71
Sanders, Joseph I, 72
Sanders, Joseph I, 199
Sanders, Joseph I, 227
Sanders, Joseph I, 257
Sanders, Joseph I, 258
Sanders, Joseph I, 705
Sanders, Joseph I, 733
Sanders, Joseph I, 791
Sanders, Joseph I, 836
Sanders, Joseph II, 631
Sanders, Joseph II, 643
Sanders, Joseph IV, 211
Sanders, Joseph IV, 272
Sanders, Joseph V, 117
Sanders, Joseph VI, 441
Sanders, Joseph A. I, 73
Sanders, Joseph Wells I, 705
Sanders, Joseph Wills V, 885
Sanders, Joshua I, 72
Sanders, Joshua I, 74
Sanders, Josiah I, 72
Sanders, Josiah I, 1045
Sanders, Josiah, Jr. I, 72
Sanders, Judah I Sup 1, 8
Sanders, Judith I, 71
Sanders, Judith I, 514
Sanders, Judith I, 791
Sanders, Judith V, 358
Sanders, Julas VI, 961
Sanders, Julia I, 72
Sanders, Julia I, 257
Sanders, Julia E. I, 72
Sanders, Keziah I, 71
Sanders, Lacey I, 1161
Sanders, Latilda I, 72
Sanders, Latilda I, 73
Sanders, Laura V, 1017
Sanders, Leah I, 71
Sanders, Leah I, 72
Sanders, Leah I, 74
Sanders, Leah I, 116
Sanders, Leah I, 418
Sanders, Leah I, 419
Sanders, Levi IV, 654
Sanders, Levi IV, 841
Sanders, Levi V, 276
Sanders, Levi V, 358
Sanders, Levi H. V, 276
Sanders, Levi H. V, 526
Sanders, Libby V, 200
Sanders, Lindley M. V, 358
Sanders, Lucy V, 929
Sanders, Lucy V, 943
Sanders, Lucy VI, 961
Sanders, Lydia I, 71
Sanders, Lydia I, 85
Sanders, Lydia I, 418
Sanders, Lydia I, 429
Sanders, Lydia I, 1045
Sanders, Lydia I, 1050
Sanders, Lydia V, 94
Sanders, Lydia V, 116
Sanders, Lydia V, 200
Sanders, Lydia V, 201
Sanders, Lydia V, 276
Sanders, Lydia V, 358
Sanders, Lydia E. V, 276
Sanders, Lydia Elma V, 276
Sanders, Mable V, 1017
Sanders, Macy III, 278
Sanders, Mafra E. I, 73
Sanders, Malissa Jane V, 643
Sanders, Malissa Jane V, 647
Sanders, Margaret I, 46
Sanders, Margaret I, 71
Sanders, Margaret I, 72
Sanders, Margaret I, 195
Sanders, Margaret I, 199
Sanders, Margaret I, 705
Sanders, Margaret I, 733
Sanders, Margaret I, 1045
Sanders, Margaret I, 1050
Sanders, Margaret I, 1051
Sanders, Margaret IV, 736
Sanders, Margaret V, 331
Sanders, Margaret V, 358
Sanders, Margaret V, 359
Sanders, Margaret Ada I, 73
Sanders, Margery I, 1050
Sanders, Margott VI, 988
Sanders, Maria L. V, 276
Sanders, Mariah V, 276
Sanders, Mariam I, 705
Sanders, Martha I, 72
Sanders, Martha I, 117
Sanders, Martha I, 140
Sanders, Martha I, 164
Sanders, Martha I, 173
Sanders, Martha I, 199
Sanders, Martha I, 418
Sanders, Martha I, 589
Sanders, Martha I, 596
Sanders, Martha I, 705
Sanders, Martha I, 733
Sanders, Martha I, 773
Sanders, Martha I, 791
Sanders, Martha I, 808
Sanders, Martha I, 814
Sanders, Martha I, 815
Sanders, Martha I, 819
Sanders, Martha I, 835
Sanders, Martha I, 836
Sanders, Martha IV, 272
Sanders, Martha V, 303
Sanders, Martha V, 310
Sanders, Martha V, 358
Sanders, Martha V, 366
Sanders, Martha V, 885
Sanders, Martha VI, 267
Sanders, Martha VI, 441
Sanders, Martha VI, 852
Sanders, Martha B. IV, 990
Sanders, Martha E. I, 73
Sanders, Martha E. IV, 1262
Sanders, Martha E. V, 359
Sanders, Martha J. I, 1161
Sanders, Martha Sanders V, 117
Sanders, Mary I, 35
Sanders, Mary I, 71
Sanders, Mary I, 72
Sanders, Mary I, 74
Sanders, Mary I, 87
Sanders, Mary I, 116
Sanders, Mary I, 149
Sanders, Mary I, 164
Sanders, Mary I, 165
Sanders, Mary I, 199
Sanders, Mary I, 200
Sanders, Mary I, 201
Sanders, Mary I, 202
Sanders, Mary I, 227
Sanders, Mary I, 257
Sanders, Mary I, 413
Sanders, Mary I, 418
Sanders, Mary I, 514
Sanders, Mary I, 538
Sanders, Mary I, 570
Sanders, Mary I, 589
Sanders, Mary I, 705
Sanders, Mary I, 733
Sanders, Mary I, 791
Sanders, Mary I, 800
Sanders, Mary I, 803
Sanders, Mary I, 836
Sanders, Mary I, 1050
Sanders, Mary II, 17
Sanders, Mary II, 968
Sanders, Mary II, 989
Sanders, Mary II, 994
Sanders, Mary II, 1009
Sanders, Mary II, 1024
Sanders, Mary III, 277
Sanders, Mary IV, 272
Sanders, Mary V, 117
Sanders, Mary V, 129
Sanders, Mary V, 190
Sanders, Mary V, 200
Sanders, Mary V, 276
Sanders, Mary V, 358
Sanders, Mary V, 359
Sanders, Mary V, 363
Sanders, Mary V, 469
Sanders, Mary V, 479
Sanders, Mary V, 526
Sanders, Mary V, 830
Sanders, Mary V, 885
Sanders, Mary V, 929
Sanders, Mary VI, 29
Sanders, Mary VI, 36
Sanders, Mary VI, 441
Sanders, Mary VI, 852
Sanders, Mary A. IV, 990
Sanders, Mary Ann IV, 272
Sanders, Mary Ann V, 828
Sanders, Mary Ann V, 860
Sanders, Mary C. V, 359
Sanders, Mary Cannidy V, 526
Sanders, Mary Caroline V, 358
Sanders, Mary E. VI, 813
Sanders, Mary J. I, 73
Sanders, Mary J. I, 257
Sanders, Mary Julia I, 257
Sanders, Masce I, 1063
Sanders, Masse I, 1053
Sanders, Massey I, 1050
Sanders, Massey V, 200
Sanders, Massey V, 204
Sanders, Matthew I, 318
Sanders, Mercy V, 117
Sanders, Merriam V, 117
Sanders, Michael I, 257
Sanders, Milla I, 809
Sanders, Milla I, 836
Sanders, Milley I, 410
Sanders, Milley I, 418
Sanders, Milley I, 836
Sanders, Milley V, 358
Sanders, Milly I, 418
Sanders, Milly I, 791
Sanders, Milly I, 836
Sanders, Milly V, 116
Sanders, Milly V, 117
Sanders, Milly V, 276
Sanders, Milly V, 328
Sanders, Milly V, 335
Sanders, Milly V, 358
Sanders, Milly VI, 988
Sanders, Miriam I, 72
Sanders, Miriam I, 117
Sanders, Miriam I, 137
Sanders, Miriam I, 164
Sanders, Miriam I, 167
Sanders, Miriam I, 393
Sanders, Miriam I, 418
Sanders, Miriam I, 1045
Sanders, Miriam V, 117
Sanders, Miriam V, 200
Sanders, Miriam V, 885
Sanders, Mordecai I, 1045
Sanders, Mordecai I, 1050
Sanders, Mordecai I, 1051
Sanders, Mordecai IV, 736
Sanders, Morris I, 165
Sanders, Myrriam I, 72
Sanders, Myrriam I, 76
Sanders, Nancy I, 165
Sanders, Nancy I, 199
Sanders, Nancy I, 705
Sanders, Nancy I, 733
Sanders, Nancy V, 885
Sanders, Nathan I, 72
Sanders, Nathan I, 227
Sanders, Nathan I, 257
Sanders, Nathan VI, 852
Sanders, Nathaniel V, 276
Sanders, Nathaniel V, 358
Sanders, Nathaniel Pope V, 358
Sanders, Nora Bivins I, 1161
Sanders, Orpha I, 72
Sanders, Patheny I, 72
Sanders, Paul II, 95
Sanders, Paul II, 416
Sanders, Paul, Jr. II, 416
Sanders, Pearl IV, 1262
Sanders, Peninah I, 72
Sanders, Peter VI, 441
Sanders, Pharabe I, 318
Sanders, Pharaby I, 164
Sanders, Pharaby I, 176
Sanders, Pharaby I, 199
Sanders, Phariba I, 1161
Sanders, Pharibe I, 72
Sanders, Phariby I, 72
Sanders, Phebe I, 799
Sanders, Phebe I, 836
Sanders, Pheraby I, 164
Sanders, Pheraby I, 199
Sanders, Pheriba I, 47
Sanders, Pheriba I, 72
Sanders, Philip VI, 965
Sanders, Precillah I, 71
Sanders, Precillah I, 73
Sanders, Priscilla I, 542
Sanders, Priscilla I, 570
Sanders, Priscilla I, 781
Sanders, Priscilla I, 791
Sanders, Priscilla I, 799
Sanders, Priscilla I, 836
Sanders, Prissila I, 227
Sanders, Prudence I, 1050
Sanders, R. Anna III, 277
Sanders, R. Anna III, 278
Sanders, Rachel I, 47
Sanders, Rachel I, 72
Sanders, Rachel I, 80
Sanders, Rachel I, 413
Sanders, Rachel I, 418
Sanders, Rachel V, 191
Sanders, Rachel V, 200
Sanders, Rachel V, 201
Sanders, Rachel V, 276
Sanders, Rachel V, 282
Sanders, Rachel V, 310
Sanders, Rachel M. V, 32
Sanders, Rachel M. V, 117
Sanders, Rachel M. V, 310
Sanders, Rebecah I, 791
Sanders, Rebecah V, 249
Sanders, Rebecca I, 72
Sanders, Rebecca I, 836
Sanders, Rebecca II, 95
Sanders, Rebecca II, 206
Sanders, Rebecca II, 256
Sanders, Rebecca II, 968
Sanders, Rebecca II, 1010
Sanders, Rebecca II, 1024
Sanders, Rebecca V, 200
Sanders, Rebecca V, 201
Sanders, Rebecca V, 276
Sanders, Rebecca V, 282
Sanders, Rebecca V, 310
Sanders, Rebecca V, 356
Sanders, Rebecca V, 358
Sanders, Rebecca V, 359
Sanders, Rebecca V, 860
Sanders, Rebecca VI, 988
Sanders, Rebecca A. V, 200
Sanders, Rebeccah I, 164
Sanders, Rebeccah I, 174
Sanders, Rebeckah IV, 654
Sanders, Rebekah I, 418
Sanders, Rhoda I, 805
Sanders, Rhoda I, 836
Sanders, Rhoda V, 200
Sanders, Richard I, 53
Sanders, Richard I, 71
Sanders, Richard I, 72
Sanders, Richard I, 117
Sanders, Richard I, 199
Sanders, Richard I, 733
Sanders, Richard I Sup 1, 5
Sanders, Richard I Sup 1, 6
Sanders, Richard II, 416
Sanders, Richard V, 310
Sanders, Richard V, 358
Sanders, Richard B. V, 117
Sanders, Richard B. V, 141
Sanders, Richard B. V, 310
Sanders, Richard B. V, 313
Sanders, Richard B. V, 526
Sanders, Richard John V, 708
Sanders, Richard W. VI, 988
Sanders, Robert II, 968
Sanders, Robert II, 1009
Sanders, Robert II, 1010
Sanders, Robert II, 1024
Sanders, Robert IV, 272
Sanders, Robert Bell III, 278
Sanders, Roster V, 201
Sanders, Ruth IV, 912
Sanders, Ruth IV, 915
Sanders, Ruth V, 200
Sanders, Ruth V, 249
Sanders, Ruth V, 276
Sanders, Ruth V, 339
Sanders, Ruth V, 359
Sanders, Sally V, 276
Sanders, Sally V, 358
Sanders, Samuel I, 791
Sanders, Samuel I, 836
Sanders, Samuel I, 900
Sanders, Samuel I, 968
Sanders, Samuel V, 249
Sanders, Samuel V, 276
Sanders, Samuel V, 282
Sanders, Samuel V, 310
Sanders, Samuel V, 358
Sanders, Samuel Sanders V, 1
Sanders, Sarah I, 61
Sanders, Sarah I, 72
Sanders, Sarah I, 74
Sanders, Sarah I, 164
Sanders, Sarah I, 377
Sanders, Sarah I, 418
Sanders, Sarah I, 570
Sanders, Sarah I, 791
Sanders, Sarah I, 800
Sanders, Sarah I, 822
Sanders, Sarah I, 836
Sanders, Sarah I, 1045
Sanders, Sarah I, 1048
Sanders, Sarah I, 1050
Sanders, Sarah I, 1058
Sanders, Sarah II, 55
Sanders, Sarah II, 95
Sanders, Sarah II, 416
Sanders, Sarah II, 447
Sanders, Sarah II, 460
Sanders, Sarah II, 633
Sanders, Sarah II, 643
Sanders, Sarah II, 685
Sanders, Sarah II, 691
Sanders, Sarah IV, 272
Sanders, Sarah IV, 654
Sanders, Sarah IV, 830
Sanders, Sarah IV, 841
Sanders, Sarah IV, 855
Sanders, Sarah V, 117
Sanders, Sarah V, 200
Sanders, Sarah V, 201
Sanders, Sarah V, 204
Sanders, Sarah V, 246
Sanders, Sarah V, 276
Sanders, Sarah V, 304
Sanders, Sarah V, 310
Sanders, Sarah V, 354
Sanders, Sarah V, 358
Sanders, Sarah V, 359
Sanders, Sarah V, 544
Sanders, Sarah VI, 267
Sanders, Sarah VI, 324
Sanders, Sarah VI, 371
Sanders, Sarah VI, 441
Sanders, Sarah E. V, 359
Sanders, Sarah Emily V, 276
Sanders, Sarah Emily V, 358
Sanders, Sarah, Jr. V, 334
Sanders, Sarah, Jr. V, 358
Sanders, Sarah, Sr. V, 359
Sanders, Scott V, 200
Sanders, Seth I, 73
Sanders, Seth W. I, 72
Sanders, Smith I, 165
Sanders, Smith I, 199
Sanders, Stanley V, 464
Sanders, Stephen I, 72
Sanders, Stephen I, 164
Sanders, Stephen VI, 988
Sanders, Susanna I, 773
Sanders, Susanna I, 791
Sanders, Susanna IV, 272
Sanders, Susannah V, 117
Sanders, Susannah V, 198
Sanders, Susannah V, 200
Sanders, Susannah VI, 441
Sanders, Tennyson V, 359
Sanders, Thomas I, 71

lers, Thomas I, 72
lers, Thomas I, 117
lers, Thomas I, 199
lers, Thomas I, 418
lers, Thomas I, 705
lers, Thomas I, 733
lers, Thomas I, 791
lers, Thomas I, 836
lers, Thomas I, 900
lers, Thomas I, 968
lers, Thomas I, 1045
lers, Thomas I, 1050
lers, Thomas V, 112
lers, Thomas V, 116
lers, Thomas V, 117
lers, Thomas V, 197
lers, Thomas V, 200
lers, Thomas V, 201
lers, Thomas V, 215
lers, Thomas V, 276
lers, Thomas V, 354
lers, Thomas V, 358
lers, Thomas V, 526
lers, Thomas V, 885
lers, Thomas VI, 852
lers, Thomas M. V, 334
lers, Thomas M. V, 358
lers, Thomas, Jr. V, 201
lers, Thos. V, 276
lers, Thos. V, 358
lers, Thos. Chalkley V, 358
lers, Ugene I, 1161
lers, Wd. Elizabeth II, 416
lers, Wd. Rebecca II, 1024
lers, Wd. Sarah II, 611
lers, Widow Hannah I, 53
lers, Widow Hannah I, 72
lers, Wilbur V, 359
lers, William I, 72
lers, William I, 257
lers, William I, 297
lers, William I, 570
lers, William I, 791
lers, William I, 836
lers, William I, 1045
lers, William I, 1050
lers, William II, 416
lers, William V, 190
lers, William V, 191
lers, William V, 200
lers, William V, 358
lers, William VI, 22
lers, William VI, 36
lers, William Harrison VI, 988
lers, William J. I, 73
lers, William Jonathan I, 72
lers, William P. V, 358
lers, Winfred VI, 988
lers, Wm. II, 918
lers, Wm. V, 200
lers, Wm. VI, 29
lers, Wm. H. IV, 990
lers, Wm. P. V, 359
derson, Ann I, 836
derson, Ann I, 865
derson, Ann I, 900
derson, Ann I, 1012
derson, Belinda VI, 984
derson, Belinda M. VI, 933
derson, Belinda M. VI, 950
derson, Belinda M. VI, 989
derson, Catharine III, 278
derson, Charles I, 836
derson, Charles I, 900
derson, Charles I, 1012
derson, Elizabeth A. VI, 989
derson, Ellen IV, 1292
derson, Foster V, 643
derson, Frances III, 164
derson, Frances V, 276
derson, Francis V, 201
derson, Frank V, 201
derson, Frank V, 276
derson, Geo. V, 643
derson, George IV, 1292
derson, George V, 643
derson, George E. VI, 878
derson, George E. VI, 921
derson, George E. VI, 989
derson, Ida IV, 1292
derson, J. E. VI, 893
derson, James VI, 950
derson, John IV, 1292
derson, John E. VI, 989
derson, Manerva IV, 1292
derson, Martha J. VI, 989
derson, Mary T. VI, 893
derson, Paulina D. VI, 984
derson, Sarah J. VI, 950
derson, Thomas N. VI, 989
Sandgraves, Charles G. IV, 1292
Sandifer, Dicey VI, 812
Sandifer, Elizabeth VI, 841
Sandifer, James VI, 841
Sandifer, Samuel VI, 841
Sandors, Elizabeth VI, 259
Sandors, Elizabeth VI, 260
Sandors, Elizabeth VI, 266
Sandors, Elizabeth VI, 267
Sandors, John VI, 259
Sandors, John VI, 267
Sandries, Sarah I, 836
Sandries, Sarah I, 837
Sands, ??? VI, 697
Sands, Abraham III, 278
Sands, Agnes III, 278
Sands, Agnes C. III, 201
Sands, Agnes C. III, 278
Sands, Ann II, 823
Sands, Ann IV, 496
Sands, Anna G. III, 278
Sands, Anna P. III, 278
Sands, Benjamin II, 823
Sands, Benjamin VI, 554
Sands, Bensalem II, 256
Sands, Betsy III, 278
Sands, Catharine III, 278
Sands, Clementina III, 269
Sands, Daniel III, 278
Sands, Daniel C. III, 278
Sands, Daniel C. III, 318
Sands, Daniel C. VI, 697
Sands, Daniel C., Jr. III, 278
Sands, David II, 642
Sands, David III, 117
Sands, David III, 278
Sands, David Jerome III, 278
Sands, Dr. David III, 201
Sands, Edmond VI, 553
Sands, Edmund II, 208
Sands, Edmund II, 256
Sands, Edmund VI, 475
Sands, Edmund VI, 483
Sands, Edmund VI, 554
Sands, Edward III, 405
Sands, Edward III, 442
Sands, Eliza VI, 775
Sands, Elizabeth II, 447
Sands, Elizabeth VI, 554
Sands, Elizabeth VI, 564
Sands, Elizabeth Ann III, 278
Sands, Emily Augusta III, 278
Sands, Emma III, 278
Sands, Esther VI, 475
Sands, Esther VI, 520
Sands, Esther VI, 522
Sands, Esther VI, 554
Sands, Esther VI, 664
Sands, Esther VI, 697
Sands, George W. V, 1017
Sands, Gulielma III, 278
Sands, Hannah V, 958
Sands, Hannah VI, 496
Sands, Hannah VI, 552
Sands, Hannah VI, 553
Sands, Hannah VI, 554
Sands, Hannah VI, 579
Sands, Hannah VI, 720
Sands, Hannah B. IV, 1292
Sands, Hannah B. V, 949
Sands, Hannah B. V, 958
Sands, Hettie I, 318
Sands, Hewlett III, 442
Sands, Isaac III, 293
Sands, Isaac VI, 520
Sands, Isaac VI, 554
Sands, Isaac VI, 666
Sands, Isaac VI, 669
Sands, Isaac VI, 697
Sands, Jacob VI, 475
Sands, Jacob VI, 554
Sands, James VI, 483
Sands, John II, 204
Sands, John II, 256
Sands, John II, 416
Sands, John II, 447
Sands, John III, 428
Sands, John III, 442
Sands, John IV, 272
Sands, John IV, 496
Sands, John A. III, 278
Sands, John Q. III, 278
Sands, John Quincy III, 278
Sands, Jonah VI, 441
Sands, Jonah VI, 520
Sands, Jonah VI, 664
Sands, Jonah VI, 666
Sands, Jonah VI, 669
Sands, Jonah VI, 697
Sands, Jonas VI, 522
Sands, Jonas Janney VI, 441
Sands, Jonas, Sr. VI, 441
Sands, Joseph VI, 554
Sands, Katharine III, 428
Sands, Katharine III, 442
Sands, Margaret IV, 496
Sands, Martha II, 447
Sands, Martha III, 278
Sands, Martha IV, 1288
Sands, Martha IV, 1292
Sands, Martha I. III, 117
Sands, Martha I. III, 278
Sands, Martha Jane III, 278
Sands, Martha S. III, 278
Sands, Martha S. III, 318
Sands, Mary II, 204
Sands, Mary II, 208
Sands, Mary II, 256
Sands, Mary III, 278
Sands, Mary III, 405
Sands, Mary III, 437
Sands, Mary III, 442
Sands, Mary III, 496
Sands, Mary VI, 483
Sands, Mary VI, 520
Sands, Mary VI, 553
Sands, Mary VI, 554
Sands, Mary VI, 666
Sands, Mary VI, 669
Sands, Mary VI, 697
Sands, Mary H. III, 278
Sands, Mary M. III, 43
Sands, Mary, Jr. II, 226
Sands, Mary, Jr. II, 256
Sands, Mathew IV, 1288
Sands, Mathew IV, 1292
Sands, Matthew T. V, 958
Sands, Matthew W. V, 958
Sands, Nancy IV, 1240
Sands, Nathaniel D. III, 278
Sands, Pamelia III, 278
Sands, Paulina III, 117
Sands, Paulina III, 201
Sands, Paulina III, 278
Sands, Permelia III, 278
Sands, Phebe Ann III, 278
Sands, Phebe F. III, 278
Sands, Rachel VI, 475
Sands, Rachel VI, 554
Sands, Rachel Wilson II, 781
Sands, Rachel Wilson II, 796
Sands, Rebecca IV, 876
Sands, Rebecca IV, 882
Sands, Reuben III, 278
Sands, Richard II, 226
Sands, Richard II, 256
Sands, Richard III, 278
Sands, Ruth V, 949
Sands, Ruth V, 958
Sands, Ruth VI, 618
Sands, Ruth VI, 697
Sands, Samuel III, 278
Sands, Samuel III, 437
Sands, Samuel IV, 1183
Sands, Samuel V, 958
Sands, Samuel B. V, 929
Sands, Samuel B. V, 958
Sands, Samuel B. VI, 775
Sands, Samuel, Jr. III, 496
Sands, Sarah II, 628
Sands, Sarah II, 642
Sands, Sarah III, 278
Sands, Sarah III, 437
Sands, Sarah VI, 407
Sands, Sarah VI, 410
Sands, Sarah VI, 441
Sands, Sarah VI, 520
Sands, Sarah VI, 554
Sands, Sarah VI, 666
Sands, Sarah VI, 669
Sands, Sarah VI, 697
Sands, Sarah Elizabeth III, 278
Sands, Stephen II, 1024
Sands, Stephen VI, 554
Sands, Stephen VI, 697
Sands, Steven II, 208
Sands, Steven II, 256
Sands, Sybil III, 428
Sands, Sybil III, 442
Sands, Theodocious III, 278
Sands, Thomas II, 416
Sands, Thomas III, 278
Sands, Thomas V, 949
Sands, Thomas V, 958
Sands, Treadwell III, 278
Sands, Wd. Paulina III, 278
Sands, Whitson V, 958
Sands, William III, 278
Sands, William L. III, 278
Sandusky, Abe IV, 1262
Sandusky, J. Gilford IV, 1262
Sandusky, Julia IV, 1262
Sandusky, Susanna IV, 1262
Sandwich, Sarah II, 565
Sandwich, Sarah II, 642
Sandwich, Wm. II, 565
Sandwich, Wm. II, 642
Sandwith, Elizabeth II, 416
Sandwith, Elizabeth II, 508
Sandwith, Elizabeth II, 642
Sandwith, Mary II, 416
Sandwith, Sarah II, 416
Sandwith, Sarah II, 642
Sandwith, William II, 416
Sandwith, Wm. II, 642
Sandyfer, Betsey I, 318
Sandyfer, Judah I, 318
Sanford, Birdie IV, 1336
Sanford, Hannah VI, 510
Sanford, Hannah VI, 554
Sanford, Harry W. IV, 1336
Sanford, Nora IV, 1336
Sanger, Daniel II, 764
Sankee, Martha II, 642
Sankey, Abigail II, 815
Sankey, Martha II, 642
Sanor, Mardie IV, 841
Sanor, Mary IV, 841
Sanor, Perry IV, 841
Sanor, Sarah Elizabeth IV, 839
Sanor, Sarah Elizabeth IV, 841
Sansbury, Sarah IV, 882
Sansherry, Sarah IV, 876
Sansherry, Sarah IV, 882
Sansom, ??? II, 416
Sansom, Beulah II, 643
Sansom, Catherine II, 416
Sansom, Elizabeth II, 416
Sansom, Hannah II, 416
Sansom, Hannah II, 430
Sansom, Hannah II, 480
Sansom, Hannah II, 547
Sansom, Hannah II, 642
Sansom, Hannah II, 717
Sansom, John II, 416
Sansom, John II, 566
Sansom, John II, 642
Sansom, Joseph II, 416
Sansom, Joseph II, 642
Sansom, Mary II, 416
Sansom, Samuel II, 416
Sansom, Samuel II, 480
Sansom, Samuel II, 547
Sansom, Samuel II, 566
Sansom, Samuel II, 642
Sansom, Samuel II, 717
Sansom, Samuel, Jr. II, 416
Sansom, Samuel, Jr. II, 480
Sansom, Samuel, Jr. II, 642
Sansom, Sarah II, 416
Sansom, Sarah II, 566
Sansom, Sarah II, 642
Sansom, Sarah II, 814
Sansom, Susanna II, 547
Sansom, Susanna II, 717
Sansom, Susannah II, 643
Sansom, William II, 416
Sansom, William II, 717
Sansom, Wm. II, 547
Sansom, Wm. II, 643
Sansom, Wm. II, 764
Santee, Ann H. IV, 1183
Santee, Anna IV, 1042
Santee, Christopher C. IV, 1183
Santee, Curtis IV, 1042
Santee, David IV, 1183
Santee, Dean Paul IV, 990
Santee, Deloram IV, 990
Santee, Delorma IV, 990
Santee, Delorma IV, 1042
Santee, Earl Stanley IV, 990
Santee, Elizabeth IV, 1183
Santee, Esek Irving IV, 990
Santee, Evangeline IV, 1042
Santee, Florence E. IV, 990
Santee, Florence E. IV, 1042
Santee, G. E. IV, 1042
Santee, Gideon E. IV, 1042
Santee, Hannah IV, 950
Santee, Hannah IV, 990
Santee, Helen IV, 990
Santee, Herbert Earl IV, 990
Santee, Isaac P. IV, 1183
Santee, Jane IV, 1183
Santee, Kenneth Lee IV, 990
Santee, Leon B. IV, 990
Santee, Looyde IV, 1183
Santee, Loyde IV, 1183
Santee, Luella IV, 986
Santee, Mabel IV, 990
Santee, Margaret IV, 1183
Santee, Margaret Elizabeth IV, 1183
Santee, Margery Beth IV, 990
Santee, Mary IV, 1183
Santee, Mary E. IV, 1042
Santee, Mary P. IV, 1073
Santee, Mary P. IV, 1075
Santee, Phebe Jane IV, 1183
Santee, Philena M. IV, 990
Santee, Ralph Wendell IV, 990
Santee, Sarah IV, 756
Santee, Sarah Ann IV, 1183
Santee, Sarah L. IV, 1183
Santee, Silvester J. IV, 990
Santee, Sylvester J. IV, 990
Santee, Thomas IV, 1042
Santee, Thomas W. IV, 1042
Santee, Washington IV, 1183
Santee, Wm. IV, 1042
Santell, Henry III, 277
Santell, Henry III, 278
Santora, Albert IV, 272
Santora, Lura IV, 272
Sanxton, Ann II, 244
Sanxton, Ann II, 256
Sanyan, Ann II, 95
Sapp, Anna Lou V, 701
Sapp, Anna Lou V, 708
Sapp, Charles V, 708
Sapp, Charley V, 708
Sapp, Chas. V, 705
Sapp, Dora V, 643
Sapp, Emery V, 643
Sapp, Emery J. V, 708
Sapp, Emma V, 708
Sapp, Helen V, 708
Sapp, Mildred V, 705
Sapp, Mildred V, 708
Sapp, Rebecca I, 570
Sarafian, Gadar III, 28
Sarafian, Gadar III, 29
Sarafian, Gadar III, 278
Sarafian, George III, 28
Sarafian, George III, 278
Sarafian, Sarkis III, 29
Sarafian, Sarkis T. III, 29
Sarafian, Solomon III, 28
Sarafian, Solomon III, 278
Sarah, Mary V, 502
Sarah, Pennina I, 195
Sarah???, Sallie VI, 681
Sarah???, Sally VI, 550
Sarber, Ida C. V, 117
Sarber, Jane IV, 272
Sargant, Ann I, 900
Sargent, Ann I, 900
Sargent, Anne I, 900
Sargent, Annie V, 1017
Sargent, Bessie V, 1017
Sargent, Elizabeth I, 900
Sargent, Elizabeth I, 904
Sargent, Florence V, 1017
Sargent, Florine V, 1017
Sargent, Forest V, 1017
Sargent, Jacob I, 900
Sargent, Jeremiah VI, 441
Sargent, John VI, 441
Sargent, Joseph V, 1017
Sargent, Julia E. I, 618
Sargent, Lucile V, 1017
Sargent, Lura V, 1017
Sargent, Martha IV, 520
Sargent, Martha IV, 548
Sargent, Mary V, 1017
Sargent, Matilda V, 1017
Sargent, Ola V, 1017
Sargent, Rachel VI, 441
Sargent, Ralph V, 1017
Sargent, Ruth II, 788
Sargent, Ruth II, 814
Sargent, Viola V, 1017
Sargent, Walter V, 1017
Sargent, Walter A. V, 1017
Sargent, Wm. V, 1017
Sargint, Rachel VI, 441
Sarjant, Jeremiah VI, 441
Sarjeant, Jacob I, 900
Sarles, Leander III, 172
Sarles, Leander III, 278
Sarles, Susan Amelia III, 172
Sarles, Susan Amelia III, 278
Sartain, Amy II, 866
Sartain, Amy II, 917
Sarver, Elizabeth V, 276
Sarver, Frank V, 276
Sarver, Hazel V, 596
Sarver, Ruby V, 596
Sarver, Ruby V, 708
Sarver, Ruth V, 276
Sarver, Viola V, 596
Sashverill, Eleanor II, 642
Sashverill, Elizabeth II, 642
Sassar, Eliza I, 928

Satbler, Edward VI, 511
Satbler, Mary VI, 511
Satcher, Ann II, 968
Satcher, Ann II, 1024
Satcher, Hannah II, 968
Satcher, Hannah II, 1007
Satcher, Hannah II, 1024
Satcher, John II, 968
Satcher, John II, 1007
Satcher, John II, 1024
Satcher, Mary II, 968
Satcher, Mary II, 1007
Satcher, Mary II, 1024
Satcher, Mercy II, 1024
Satcher, Phebe II, 1024
Satcher, Rachel II, 1024
Satcher, Robert II, 968
Satcher, Robert II, 1024
Satcher, Sarah II, 1024
Satcher, Sarah II, 1039
Satel, Henry III, 278
Sater, Ella IV, 1222
Saterthwait, Elizabeth II, 256
Saterthwait, Hannah II, 195
Saterthwait, Hannah II, 256
Saterthwait, Joseph II, 195
Saterthwait, Joseph II, 256
Saterthwait, Phebe IV, 350
Saterthwait, Samuel II, 195
Saterthwait, Samuel II, 256
Saterthwaite, Deborah II, 206
Saterthwaite, Deborah II, 256
Saterthwaite, George II, 256
Saterthwaite, James II, 206
Saterthwaite, James II, 256
Saterthwaite, Margaret II, 252
Saterthwaite, Margaret II, 256
Saterthwaite, Rebecca II, 252
Saterthwaite, Rebecca II, 256
Sathertwait, Emily S. IV, 214
Sathertwait, Isaac H. IV, 214
Satterhwait, Beulah IV, 774
Satterhwait, Isaac H. IV, 774
Satterly, Hannah III, 442
Satterly, John, Jr. III, 442
Satterthwait, ??? IV, 350
Satterthwait, Aaron II, 865
Satterthwait, Aaron II, 917
Satterthwait, Abel II, 1024
Satterthwait, Abigail II, 865
Satterthwait, Abigail II, 917
Satterthwait, Adaline IV, 822
Satterthwait, Adaline IV, 841
Satterthwait, Adaline M. IV, 272
Satterthwait, Adaline M. IV, 692
Satterthwait, Adaline M. IV, 841
Satterthwait, Alfred S. IV, 841
Satterthwait, Alice R. IV, 272
Satterthwait, Alice R. IV, 290
Satterthwait, Alice R. IV, 841
Satterthwait, Alice R. IV, 842
Satterthwait, Amos II, 988
Satterthwait, Amos II, 1025
Satterthwait, Ann II, 202
Satterthwait, Ann II, 256
Satterthwait, Ann II, 977
Satterthwait, Ann II, 1024
Satterthwait, Ann IV, 158
Satterthwait, Ann IV, 272
Satterthwait, Ann IV, 325
Satterthwait, Ann IV, 350
Satterthwait, Ann IV, 355
Satterthwait, Ann IV, 424
Satterthwait, Ann IV, 433
Satterthwait, Ann IV, 434
Satterthwait, Ann B. IV, 822
Satterthwait, Ann B. IV, 842
Satterthwait, Ann S. IV, 325
Satterthwait, Ann S. IV, 350
Satterthwait, Anna II, 256
Satterthwait, Anna IV, 203
Satterthwait, Anna IV, 272
Satterthwait, Anna B. IV, 841
Satterthwait, Anna M. IV, 834
Satterthwait, Anna M. IV, 841
Satterthwait, Anna M. IV, 842
Satterthwait, Anne IV, 433
Satterthwait, Asa M. III, 278
Satterthwait, Barkley A. IV, 841
Satterthwait, Benjamin C. II, 1051
Satterthwait, Benjamin C. II, 1060
Satterthwait, Bessie B. III, 384
Satterthwait, Caroline B. III, 384
Satterthwait, Caroline Jackson III, 377
Satterthwait, Caroline W. IV, 681
Satterthwait, Caroline W. IV, 841
Satterthwait, Carrie J. III, 377
Satterthwait, Carrie J. III, 384
Satterthwait, Charles W. IV, 841
Satterthwait, Charles Waller IV, 842
Satterthwait, Charles Walter IV, 841
Satterthwait, Charles Walter IV, 842
Satterthwait, Charlotte II, 969
Satterthwait, Chas. IV, 822
Satterthwait, Chas. W. IV, 272
Satterthwait, Chas. W. IV, 692
Satterthwait, Chas. W. IV, 841
Satterthwait, Clement III, 377
Satterthwait, David IV, 379
Satterthwait, David IV, 433
Satterthwait, David IV, 841
Satterthwait, Donald Henry IV, 841
Satterthwait, Edith II, 1060
Satterthwait, Edith M. IV, 720
Satterthwait, Edith M. IV, 841
Satterthwait, Edith M. IV, 842
Satterthwait, Edward IV, 272
Satterthwait, Edward IV, 433
Satterthwait, Edward IV, 434
Satterthwait, Edward M. II, 865
Satterthwait, Edward M. II, 917
Satterthwait, Elizabeth II, 256
Satterthwait, Elizabeth II, 264
Satterthwait, Elizabeth II, 788
Satterthwait, Elizabeth II, 988
Satterthwait, Elizabeth II, 999
Satterthwait, Elizabeth II, 1024
Satterthwait, Elizabeth II, 1025
Satterthwait, Elizabeth II, 1079
Satterthwait, Elizabeth IV, 158
Satterthwait, Elizabeth IV, 159
Satterthwait, Elizabeth IV, 433
Satterthwait, Elizabeth C. II, 1025
Satterthwait, Elizabeth C. II, 1051
Satterthwait, Elizabeth C. II, 1060
Satterthwait, Elizabeth J. IV, 433
Satterthwait, Elizabeth J. IV, 440
Satterthwait, Elizabeth T. II, 1060
Satterthwait, Ella F. II, 921
Satterthwait, Ellen IV, 720
Satterthwait, Ellen IV, 758
Satterthwait, Ellen R. IV, 720
Satterthwait, Ellen R. IV, 842
Satterthwait, Ellen Ruth IV, 841
Satterthwait, Emily IV, 841
Satterthwait, Emily S. IV, 272
Satterthwait, Emily S. IV, 841
Satterthwait, Emily S. IV, 842
Satterthwait, Esther A. IV, 841
Satterthwait, Ethel N. IV, 842
Satterthwait, Fannie Vance V, 201
Satterthwait, Fanny Vance V, 201
Satterthwait, Frances Vance V, 201
Satterthwait, Franklin B. IV, 841
Satterthwait, Franklin P. IV, 841
Satterthwait, George II, 1060
Satterthwait, George S. IV, 691
Satterthwait, George T. II, 921
Satterthwait, Giles II, 1024
Satterthwait, Giles II, 1041
Satterthwait, Giles II, 1047
Satterthwait, Giles II, 1059
Satterthwait, Hannah II, 1010
Satterthwait, Hannah II, 1024
Satterthwait, Hannah III, 278
Satterthwait, Hannah A. II, 256
Satterthwait, Hannah B. III, 278
Satterthwait, Hannah M. III, 278
Satterthwait, Harold Walter IV, 842
Satterthwait, Helen IV, 841
Satterthwait, Helen F. IV, 842
Satterthwait, Helen Forsythe IV, 842
Satterthwait, Helen M. IV, 842
Satterthwait, Henry W. II, 966
Satterthwait, Henry W. II, 1060
Satterthwait, Hutchen IV, 792
Satterthwait, Hutchin IV, 433
Satterthwait, Ida IV, 434
Satterthwait, Ida IV, 439
Satterthwait, Ida A. IV, 716
Satterthwait, Ida A. IV, 720
Satterthwait, Ida A. IV, 820
Satterthwait, Ida A. IV, 835
Satterthwait, Ida A. IV, 841
Satterthwait, Ida A. IV, 842
Satterthwait, Isaac II, 1059
Satterthwait, Isaac H. III, 384
Satterthwait, Isaac H. IV, 272
Satterthwait, Isaac H. IV, 841
Satterthwait, James M. IV, 841
Satterthwait, Jane II, 965
Satterthwait, Jane II, 1010
Satterthwait, Jane II, 1024
Satterthwait, Jane III, 38
Satterthwait, Jerusha IV, 421
Satterthwait, Jerusha IV, 433
Satterthwait, Jerusha IV, 434
Satterthwait, Jiles II, 1024
Satterthwait, Job III, 278
Satterthwait, John V, 526
Satterthwait, John W. IV, 711
Satterthwait, John W. IV, 841
Satterthwait, John W. IV, 1025
Satterthwait, Jos. W. IV, 350
Satterthwait, Jos. W. IV, 355
Satterthwait, Joseph II, 256
Satterthwait, Joseph II, 264
Satterthwait, Joseph II, 1024
Satterthwait, Joseph II, 1025
Satterthwait, Joseph II, 1041
Satterthwait, Joseph IV, 158
Satterthwait, Joseph IV, 272
Satterthwait, Joseph IV, 325
Satterthwait, Joseph IV, 350
Satterthwait, Joseph IV, 433
Satterthwait, Joseph W. IV, 350
Satterthwait, Joseph W. IV, 433
Satterthwait, Joseph W. IV, 434
Satterthwait, Joseph W. IV, 841
Satterthwait, Joseph, Jr. IV, 434
Satterthwait, Josepha III, 278
Satterthwait, Josepha Y. III, 278
Satterthwait, Joshua IV, 350
Satterthwait, Joshua IV, 433
Satterthwait, Joshua W. IV, 433
Satterthwait, Judge Mason IV, 433
Satterthwait, Lewis P. II, 1060
Satterthwait, Lizzie H. II, 865
Satterthwait, Lizzie H. II, 917
Satterthwait, Lucy II, 966
Satterthwait, Lucy II, 1060
Satterthwait, Lydia IV, 792
Satterthwait, Lydia Ann IV, 433
Satterthwait, Mabel C. IV, 990
Satterthwait, Mabel H. IV, 687
Satterthwait, Mabel H. IV, 990
Satterthwait, Maraha IV, 350
Satterthwait, Marion II, 1062
Satterthwait, Marjorie Ann IV, 841
Satterthwait, Marjorie Ann IV, 842
Satterthwait, Martha IV, 420
Satterthwait, Martha IV, 433
Satterthwait, Martha IV, 434
Satterthwait, Martha IV, 758
Satterthwait, Martha Marie IV, 841
Satterthwait, Mary II, 256
Satterthwait, Mary II, 264
Satterthwait, Mary II, 966
Satterthwait, Mary II, 1024
Satterthwait, Mary II, 1041
Satterthwait, Mary IV, 158
Satterthwait, Mary IV, 350
Satterthwait, Mary IV, 433
Satterthwait, Mary A. II, 969
Satterthwait, Mary B. II, 917
Satterthwait, Mary E. IV, 820
Satterthwait, Mary E. IV, 841
Satterthwait, Mary E. IV, 842
Satterthwait, Mary E. IV, 1381
Satterthwait, Mary Ellen IV, 716
Satterthwait, Meriba IV, 158
Satterthwait, Merribah IV, 433
Satterthwait, Michael II, 1024
Satterthwait, Michael C. II, 1060
Satterthwait, Mildred E. IV, 841
Satterthwait, Mildred Emily IV, 841
Satterthwait, Mildred Emily IV, 842
Satterthwait, Nathan IV, 325
Satterthwait, Nathan IV, 350
Satterthwait, Nathan IV, 433
Satterthwait, Nathan IV, 440
Satterthwait, Phebe IV, 323
Satterthwait, Phebe IV, 350
Satterthwait, Phebe H. II, 1050
Satterthwait, Phebe H. II, 1059
Satterthwait, Rachel II, 1025
Satterthwait, Rachel IV, 1381
Satterthwait, Rachel S. IV, 709
Satterthwait, Rebecca II, 988
Satterthwait, Rebecca II, 1025
Satterthwait, Rebecca IV, 325
Satterthwait, Rebecca IV, 350
Satterthwait, Rebecca IV, 681
Satterthwait, Rebecca IV, 711
Satterthwait, Rebecca IV, 1025
Satterthwait, Rebecca Carlile II, 1025
Satterthwait, Rebeckah IV, 433
Satterthwait, Reuben IV, 1381
Satterthwait, Richard IV, 158
Satterthwait, Richard IV, 433
Satterthwait, Richard IV, 434
Satterthwait, Richard IV, 681
Satterthwait, Richard IV, 841
Satterthwait, Richard Isaac IV, 841
Satterthwait, Richard Isaac IV, 842
Satterthwait, Robert W. IV, 433
Satterthwait, Robert Whitehill IV, 159
Satterthwait, Ruth IV, 379
Satterthwait, Ruth IV, 433
Satterthwait, Ruth IV, 841
Satterthwait, Ruth C. IV, 692
Satterthwait, Ruth C. IV, 807
Satterthwait, Ruth C. IV, 841
Satterthwait, Ruth C. IV, 842
Satterthwait, S. Clement III, 384
Satterthwait, Samuel II, 256
Satterthwait, Samuel II, 264
Satterthwait, Samuel II, 1010
Satterthwait, Samuel II, 1024
Satterthwait, Samuel II, 1025
Satterthwait, Samuel IV, 350
Satterthwait, Samuel IV, 433
Satterthwait, Sarah II, 1024
Satterthwait, Sarah IV, 433
Satterthwait, Sarah A. II, 954
Satterthwait, Sarah Ann IV, 433
Satterthwait, Sarah Ann IV, 434
Satterthwait, Sarah Ann IV, 439
Satterthwait, Sarah C. II, 921
Satterthwait, Sarah C. IV, 691
Satterthwait, Susan II, 1047
Satterthwait, Susan II, 1059
Satterthwait, Susan B. II, 1059
Satterthwait, Susannah II, 1024
Satterthwait, Thomas II, 1050
Satterthwait, Thomas II, 1059
Satterthwait, Thomas IV, 158
Satterthwait, Thomas IV, 159
Satterthwait, Thomas IV, 433
Satterthwait, Thos. C. II, 921
Satterthwait, W. L. IV, 290
Satterthwait, Watson II, 969
Satterthwait, William II, 202
Satterthwait, William II, 256
Satterthwait, William III, 278
Satterthwait, William IV, 137
Satterthwait, William IV, 350
Satterthwait, William IV, 433
Satterthwait, William IV, 841
Satterthwait, William D. IV, 687
Satterthwait, William D. IV, 720
Satterthwait, William D. IV, 841
Satterthwait, William E. III, 278
Satterthwait, William W. IV, 433
Satterthwait, Wilma IV, 419
Satterthwait, Wilma IV, 433
Satterthwait, Wilma IV, 434
Satterthwait, Wilmer L. IV, 272
Satterthwait, Wilmer L. IV, 841
Satterthwait, Wilmer L. IV, 842
Satterthwait, Wm. II, 988
Satterthwait, Wm. II, 1010
Satterthwait, Wm. II, 1024
Satterthwait, Wm. IV, 158
Satterthwait, Wm. IV, 350
Satterthwait, Wm. D. IV, 716
Satterthwait, Wm. D. IV, 820
Satterthwait, Wm. D. IV, 835
Satterthwait, Wm. D. IV, 841
Satterthwait, Wm. D. IV, 842
Satterthwait, Wm. D. IV, 990
Satterthwait, Wm., Jr. II, 1024
Satterthwaite, ??? IV, 757
Satterthwaite, Aaron II, 917
Satterthwaite, Abagale V, 88
Satterthwaite, Abel II, 416
Satterthwaite, Abel II, 487
Satterthwaite, Abel II, 643
Satterthwaite, Abel II, 969
Satterthwaite, Abel II, 1024
Satterthwaite, Abel V, 117
Satterthwaite, Abi II, 1079
Satterthwaite, Abi W. II, 1079
Satterthwaite, Abi W. II, 1080
Satterthwaite, Abigail II, 917
Satterthwaite, Abigail V, 117
Satterthwaite, Abraham V, 117
Satterthwaite, Adaline M. IV, 757
Satterthwaite, Alice II, 969
Satterthwaite, Alice II, 1060
Satterthwaite, Alice Eppert II, 1066
Satterthwaite, Alice R. IV, 27
Satterthwaite, Amos II, 1025
Satterthwaite, Amos II, 1059
Satterthwaite, Amos II, 1079
Satterthwaite, Amos W. II, 9
Satterthwaite, Amos W. II, 1
Satterthwaite, Amos W. II, 1
Satterthwaite, Ann II, 256
Satterthwaite, Ann II, 416
Satterthwaite, Ann II, 917
Satterthwaite, Ann II, 969
Satterthwaite, Ann II, 1079
Satterthwaite, Ann II, 1080
Satterthwaite, Ann IV, 330
Satterthwaite, Ann IV, 350
Satterthwaite, Ann IV, 757
Satterthwaite, Ann B. IV, 75
Satterthwaite, Ann B. IV, 75
Satterthwaite, Ann F. II, 106
Satterthwaite, Ann F. II, 107
Satterthwaite, Ann F. II, 107
Satterthwaite, Ann F. II, 108
Satterthwaite, Ann S. IV, 35
Satterthwaite, Anna II, 256
Satterthwaite, Anna II, 313
Satterthwaite, Anna II, 1066
Satterthwaite, Anna IV, 330
Satterthwaite, Anna IV, 496
Satterthwaite, Anna V, 118
Satterthwaite, Anna Bryant II, 969
Satterthwaite, Anna E. II, 96
Satterthwaite, Anna H. II, 8
Satterthwaite, Anna M. II, 9
Satterthwaite, Anna R. II, 10
Satterthwaite, Anna R. II, 10
Satterthwaite, Annie II, 1071
Satterthwaite, Annie II, 1079
Satterthwaite, Annie M. IV,
Satterthwaite, Barclay A. IV,
Satterthwaite, Barklay IV, 7
Satterthwaite, Barkley A. IV,
Satterthwaite, Barkly A. IV,
Satterthwaite, Benjamin II,
Satterthwaite, Benjamin II,
Satterthwaite, Benjamin V, 5
Satterthwaite, Benjamin V, 8
Satterthwaite, Benjamin V, 9
Satterthwaite, Benjamin V, 1
Satterthwaite, Benjamin C. II, 1060
Satterthwaite, Benjamin L. V, 117
Satterthwaite, Beulah IV, 75
Satterthwaite, C. Howard II,
Satterthwaite, Caleb II, 256
Satterthwaite, Caleb IV, 137
Satterthwaite, Caleb IV, 137
Satterthwaite, Caleb V, 117
Satterthwaite, Cameron IV,
Satterthwaite, Caroline II, 1
Satterthwaite, Caroline F. IV
Satterthwaite, Caroline P. II,
Satterthwaite, Caroline T. II,
Satterthwaite, Caroline T. II, 1060
Satterthwaite, Caroline W. IV, 757
Satterthwaite, Caroline Wrigh IV, 757
Satterthwaite, Catharine II,
Satterthwaite, Catharine II,
Satterthwaite, Charles II, 10
Satterthwaite, Charles II, 10
Satterthwaite, Charles II, 10
Satterthwaite, Charles IV, 75
Satterthwaite, Charles D. II, 1066
Satterthwaite, Charles D. II, 1079
Satterthwaite, Charles W. IV,
Satterthwaite, Charlotte II, 1
Satterthwaite, Charlotte II, 1
Satterthwaite, Charlotte C. II, 1079
Satterthwaite, Charlotte M. II, 300
Satterthwaite, Clement V, 11
Satterthwaite, Clifford II, 96
Satterthwaite, Clifford II, 10
Satterthwaite, Cornelia IV, 1
Satterthwaite, Cornelius J. IV, 1378
Satterthwaite, Daniel IV, 137
Satterthwaite, Daniel IV, 137
Satterthwaite, David II, 1066
Satterthwaite, David II, 1070

erthwaite, David II, 1079
erthwaite, David II, 1082
erthwaite, David IV, 757
erthwaite, David F. IV, 757
erthwaite, David F. IV, 758
erthwaite, David, Jr. II, 1066
erthwaite, David, Jr. II, 1070
erthwaite, David, Jr. II, 1079
erthwaite, Deborah II, 256
erthwaite, Deborah II, 969
erthwaite, Deborah Celia V, 1378
erthwaite, Dorothy II, 225
erthwaite, Dorothy II, 256
erthwaite, Earnest H. IV, 757
erthwaite, Edgar IV, 757
erthwaite, Edgar IV, 758
erthwaite, Edith II, 968
erthwaite, Edith II, 969
erthwaite, Edith II, 1060
erthwaite, Edith V, 118
erthwaite, Edith M. IV, 757
erthwaite, Edith M. IV, 758
erthwaite, Edward IV, 757
erthwaite, Edward B. V, 1378
erthwaite, Edward M. II, 818
erthwaite, Edward M. II, 917
erthwaite, Edward S. II, 969
erthwaite, Edward S. I, 1060
erthwaite, Edward Sharpless I, 1060
erthwaite, Edward Sharpless I, 1063
erthwaite, Elisabeth R. V, 1377
erthwaite, Eliza V, 53
erthwaite, Eliza V, 118
erthwaite, Elizabeth II, 256
erthwaite, Elizabeth II, 740
erthwaite, Elizabeth II, 764
erthwaite, Elizabeth II, 818
erthwaite, Elizabeth II, 968
erthwaite, Elizabeth II, 969
erthwaite, Elizabeth II, 973
erthwaite, Elizabeth II, 1024
erthwaite, Elizabeth II, 1025
erthwaite, Elizabeth II, 1036
erthwaite, Elizabeth II, 1047
erthwaite, Elizabeth II, 1059
erthwaite, Elizabeth II, 1063
erthwaite, Elizabeth II, 1066
erthwaite, Elizabeth II, 1070
erthwaite, Elizabeth II, 1077
erthwaite, Elizabeth II, 1078
erthwaite, Elizabeth II, 1079
erthwaite, Elizabeth IV, 153
erthwaite, Elizabeth IV, 158
erthwaite, Elizabeth IV, 1350
erthwaite, Elizabeth IV, 1377
erthwaite, Elizabeth IV, 1378
erthwaite, Elizabeth V, 21
erthwaite, Elizabeth V, 53
erthwaite, Elizabeth V, 57
erthwaite, Elizabeth V, 117
erthwaite, Elizabeth V, 510
erthwaite, Elizabeth V, 526
erthwaite, Elizabeth B. I, 1079
erthwaite, Elizabeth B. I, 1080
erthwaite, Elizabeth C. I, 1025
erthwaite, Elizabeth C. I, 1060
erthwaite, Elizabeth G. I, 917
erthwaite, Elizabeth H. I, 865
erthwaite, Elizabeth M. V, 1357
erthwaite, Elizabeth M. V, 1378
erthwaite, Elizabeth P. V, 1357
erthwaite, Elizabeth P. V, 1378
erthwaite, Elizabeth R. V, 1378
erthwaite, Elizabeth T. I, 1060
erthwaite, Elizabeth W. I, 960
erthwaite, Elizabeth W. I, 969
erthwaite, Elizabeth W. I, 1051
erthwaite, Elizabeth W. I, 1060
erthwaite, Ella F. II, 918
Satterthwaite, Ellen R. IV, 757
Satterthwaite, Ellen R. IV, 758
Satterthwaite, Ellis W. IV, 757
Satterthwaite, Elma Adaline IV, 757
Satterthwaite, Elsie II, 969
Satterthwaite, Emily S. IV, 272
Satterthwaite, Emma II, 917
Satterthwaite, Estella IV, 1378
Satterthwaite, Esther V, 118
Satterthwaite, Fanny Vance V, 118
Satterthwaite, Frances Vance V, 118
Satterthwaite, Frank B. II, 1079
Satterthwaite, Franklin II, 1066
Satterthwaite, Franklin P. IV, 757
Satterthwaite, Frederic II, 1060
Satterthwaite, Frederic G. II, 968
Satterthwaite, Frederic G. II, 1060
Satterthwaite, Frederic Gites, Jr. II, 968
Satterthwaite, Frederick G. II, 968
Satterthwaite, George II, 256
Satterthwaite, George II, 968
Satterthwaite, George II, 969
Satterthwaite, George II, 1060
Satterthwaite, George II, 1079
Satterthwaite, George IV, 757
Satterthwaite, George IV, 1030
Satterthwaite, George V, 118
Satterthwaite, George S. IV, 757
Satterthwaite, George T. II, 918
Satterthwaite, George T. IV, 757
Satterthwaite, Georgianna II, 1079
Satterthwaite, Georgianna C. II, 1066
Satterthwaite, Gerardus II, 917
Satterthwaite, Giles II, 968
Satterthwaite, Giles II, 969
Satterthwaite, Giles II, 1024
Satterthwaite, Giles II, 1059
Satterthwaite, Giles V, 117
Satterthwaite, Grace II, 1066
Satterthwaite, Grace E. II, 1079
Satterthwaite, Hannah II, 256
Satterthwaite, Hannah II, 1059
Satterthwaite, Hannah IV, 757
Satterthwaite, Hannah IV, 1357
Satterthwaite, Hannah IV, 1377
Satterthwaite, Hannah IV, 1378
Satterthwaite, Hannah IV, 1381
Satterthwaite, Hannah IV, 1382
Satterthwaite, Hannah V, 140
Satterthwaite, Hannah A. II, 256
Satterthwaite, Hannah A. III, 302
Satterthwaite, Hannah A. IV, 1377
Satterthwaite, Hannah B. II, 917
Satterthwaite, Hannah B. II, 938
Satterthwaite, Hannah B. II, 1079
Satterthwaite, Hannah B. IV, 757
Satterthwaite, Hannah S. IV, 1377
Satterthwaite, Harry V, 118
Satterthwaite, Helen II, 1060
Satterthwaite, Helen Lorene II, 1060
Satterthwaite, Helen Lorene II, 1063
Satterthwaite, Helen Story II, 969
Satterthwaite, Henry V, 117
Satterthwaite, Henry W. II, 968
Satterthwaite, Henry W. II, 969
Satterthwaite, Henry W. II, 1060
Satterthwaite, Henry W., Jr. II, 969
Satterthwaite, Henry Warrington II, 1057
Satterthwaite, Henry Warrington II, 1060
Satterthwaite, Howard II, 1066
Satterthwaite, Howard II, 1079
Satterthwaite, Howard IV, 757
Satterthwaite, Hutchen IV, 757
Satterthwaite, Hutchin IV, 757
Satterthwaite, Ida A. IV, 757
Satterthwaite, Ida A. IV, 758
Satterthwaite, Isaac II, 95
Satterthwaite, Isaac II, 1059
Satterthwaite, Isaac IV, 757
Satterthwaite, Isaac B. II, 1079
Satterthwaite, Isaac H. IV, 272
Satterthwaite, Isaac H. IV, 757
Satterthwaite, Isaac H. IV, 758
Satterthwaite, Isaac W. IV, 757
Satterthwaite, Israel V, 117
Satterthwaite, Jacob IV, 757
Satterthwaite, James II, 191
Satterthwaite, James II, 225
Satterthwaite, James II, 256
Satterthwaite, James II, 416
Satterthwaite, James II, 417
Satterthwaite, James II, 643
Satterthwaite, James II, 917
Satterthwaite, James M. IV, 757
Satterthwaite, James Pearce II, 1060
Satterthwaite, James Peirce II, 968
Satterthwaite, Jane II, 1010
Satterthwaite, Jane II, 1024
Satterthwaite, Jane II, 1066
Satterthwaite, Jane III, 130
Satterthwaite, Jane IV, 1357
Satterthwaite, Jane IV, 1378
Satterthwaite, Jane V, 57
Satterthwaite, Jane V, 117
Satterthwaite, Jane C. IV, 1378
Satterthwaite, Jiles II, 1024
Satterthwaite, Joel II, 256
Satterthwaite, John II, 416
Satterthwaite, John II, 764
Satterthwaite, John II, 969
Satterthwaite, John IV, 757
Satterthwaite, John V, 21
Satterthwaite, John V, 57
Satterthwaite, John V, 117
Satterthwaite, John V, 510
Satterthwaite, John V, 526
Satterthwaite, John B. II, 968
Satterthwaite, John B. II, 969
Satterthwaite, John B. II, 1060
Satterthwaite, John W. IV, 757
Satterthwaite, John W. IV, 1030
Satterthwaite, John Wright IV, 757
Satterthwaite, Jonathan II, 968
Satterthwaite, Joseph II, 256
Satterthwaite, Joseph II, 300
Satterthwaite, Joseph II, 740
Satterthwaite, Joseph II, 764
Satterthwaite, Joseph II, 917
Satterthwaite, Joseph II, 968
Satterthwaite, Joseph II, 969
Satterthwaite, Joseph II, 1024
Satterthwaite, Joseph II, 1025
Satterthwaite, Joseph II, 1059
Satterthwaite, Joseph IV, 1377
Satterthwaite, Joseph V, 118
Satterthwaite, Joseph B. II, 968
Satterthwaite, Joseph C. IV, 1357
Satterthwaite, Joseph C. IV, 1377
Satterthwaite, Joseph C. IV, 1378
Satterthwaite, Joseph H. II, 968
Satterthwaite, Joseph H. II, 969
Satterthwaite, Joseph H. II, 970
Satterthwaite, Joseph H. II, 1047
Satterthwaite, Joseph H. II, 1059
Satterthwaite, Joseph H. II, 1060
Satterthwaite, Joseph H. II, 1062
Satterthwaite, Joseph H., Jr. II, 1060
Satterthwaite, Joseph M. V, 118
Satterthwaite, Joseph W. IV, 330
Satterthwaite, Joseph W. IV, 350
Satterthwaite, Joseph W. IV, 757
Satterthwaite, Joseph, Jr. II, 1059
Satterthwaite, Joshua II, 313
Satterthwaite, Lacy II, 1057
Satterthwaite, Laurence II, 969
Satterthwaite, Leslie J. V, 118
Satterthwaite, Lewis P. II, 1060
Satterthwaite, Lewis P. II, 1063
Satterthwaite, Lizzie H. II, 917
Satterthwaite, Louis II, 968
Satterthwaite, Louis P. II, 969
Satterthwaite, Lucy II, 968
Satterthwaite, Lucy II, 969
Satterthwaite, Lucy II, 1060
Satterthwaite, Lucy S. II, 1060
Satterthwaite, Lydia IV, 757
Satterthwaite, Lydia V, 117
Satterthwaite, Lydia Ann IV, 757
Satterthwaite, M. Virginia III, 302
Satterthwaite, Mabel C. IV, 758
Satterthwaite, Mabel H. IV, 758
Satterthwaite, Mable C. IV, 757
Satterthwaite, Maraha IV, 350
Satterthwaite, Margaret II, 256
Satterthwaite, Margaret II, 1060
Satterthwaite, Margaret S. II, 969
Satterthwaite, Margaretta W. II, 968
Satterthwaite, Margaretta W. II, 1060
Satterthwaite, Martha IV, 757
Satterthwaite, Martha V, 46
Satterthwaite, Martha V, 118
Satterthwaite, Martha A. IV, 757
Satterthwaite, Martha A. V, 118
Satterthwaite, Martha C. II, 1066
Satterthwaite, Martha C. II, 1079
Satterthwaite, Martha C. II, 1084
Satterthwaite, Mary II, 191
Satterthwaite, Mary II, 256
Satterthwaite, Mary II, 643
Satterthwaite, Mary II, 917
Satterthwaite, Mary II, 968
Satterthwaite, Mary II, 969
Satterthwaite, Mary II, 1024
Satterthwaite, Mary II, 1047
Satterthwaite, Mary II, 1059
Satterthwaite, Mary II, 1079
Satterthwaite, Mary II, 1080
Satterthwaite, Mary IV, 350
Satterthwaite, Mary V, 21
Satterthwaite, Mary V, 94
Satterthwaite, Mary V, 117
Satterthwaite, Mary A. II, 969
Satterthwaite, Mary A. II, 1060
Satterthwaite, Mary A. II, 1062
Satterthwaite, Mary A. II, 1063
Satterthwaite, Mary A. II, 1079
Satterthwaite, Mary Anna II, 969
Satterthwaite, Mary Anna II, 970
Satterthwaite, Mary B. II, 764
Satterthwaite, Mary B. II, 843
Satterthwaite, Mary B. II, 917
Satterthwaite, Mary C. II, 970
Satterthwaite, Mary C. II, 1060
Satterthwaite, Mary C. II, 1062
Satterthwaite, Mary C. V, 117
Satterthwaite, Mary E. IV, 757
Satterthwaite, Mary E. IV, 758
Satterthwaite, Mary E. IV, 1378
Satterthwaite, Mary Elizabeth IV, 1378
Satterthwaite, Mary Ella IV, 757
Satterthwaite, Mary G. II, 917
Satterthwaite, Mary Garrigues II, 818
Satterthwaite, Mary Jane IV, 1378
Satterthwaite, Mary L. V, 94
Satterthwaite, Mary S. II, 1059
Satterthwaite, Mary S. II, 1061
Satterthwaite, Mary Sydney II, 1057
Satterthwaite, Mary Sydney II, 1060
Satterthwaite, Mary Viva II, 968
Satterthwaite, Meriba IV, 158
Satterthwaite, Michael II, 964
Satterthwaite, Michael II, 968
Satterthwaite, Michael II, 969
Satterthwaite, Michael II, 1024
Satterthwaite, Michael II, 1048
Satterthwaite, Michael II, 1055
Satterthwaite, Michael II, 1059
Satterthwaite, Michael II, 1060
Satterthwaite, Michael C. II, 1060
Satterthwaite, Michael L. II, 1060
Satterthwaite, Michal II, 969
Satterthwaite, Naomi Cope II, 969
Satterthwaite, Naomi H. V, 117
Satterthwaite, Naomi H. V, 118
Satterthwaite, Nathan IV, 350
Satterthwaite, Phebe II, 95
Satterthwaite, Phebe II, 960
Satterthwaite, Phebe II, 969
Satterthwaite, Phebe II, 1059
Satterthwaite, Phebe II, 1063
Satterthwaite, Phebe II, 1083
Satterthwaite, Phebe Ann II, 1079
Satterthwaite, Phebe Ann II, 1082
Satterthwaite, Phebe H. II, 740
Satterthwaite, Phebe H. II, 764
Satterthwaite, Phebe H. II, 969
Satterthwaite, Phebe H. II, 1051
Satterthwaite, Phebe H. II, 1059
Satterthwaite, Phebe H. II, 1060
Satterthwaite, Rachel II, 969
Satterthwaite, Rachel IV, 757
Satterthwaite, Rachel B. II, 917
Satterthwaite, Rachel S. IV, 757
Satterthwaite, Rachel W. II, 324
Satterthwaite, Rebecca II, 256
Satterthwaite, Rebecca II, 1025
Satterthwaite, Rebecca II, 1059
Satterthwaite, Rebecca II, 1079
Satterthwaite, Rebecca II, 1080
Satterthwaite, Rebecca IV, 756
Satterthwaite, Rebecca IV, 757
Satterthwaite, Rebecca IV, 1030
Satterthwaite, Rebecca V, 31
Satterthwaite, Rebecca V, 117
Satterthwaite, Rebecca V, 118
Satterthwaite, Rebecca V, 137
Satterthwaite, Rebecca B. V, 118
Satterthwaite, Rebecca G. IV, 757
Satterthwaite, Rebecca G. IV, 1030
Satterthwaite, Rebecca M. II, 917
Satterthwaite, Rebecca, Sr. II, 1079
Satterthwaite, Rebecca, Sr. II, 1080
Satterthwaite, Rebeckah II, 81
Satterthwaite, Rebeckah II, 95
Satterthwaite, Reuben IV, 1377
Satterthwaite, Reuben IV, 1378
Satterthwaite, Rhoda S. II, 969
Satterthwaite, Rhoda S. II, 1048
Satterthwaite, Rhoda S. II, 1060
Satterthwaite, Richard IV, 756
Satterthwaite, Richard IV, 757
Satterthwaite, Richard IV, 1030
Satterthwaite, Robert Howard II, 1066
Satterthwaite, Rose II, 1078
Satterthwaite, Rose II, 1079
Satterthwaite, Rose R. II, 1079
Satterthwaite, Rowland IV, 757
Satterthwaite, Rowland T. IV, 757
Satterthwaite, Russell V, 118
Satterthwaite, Ruth IV, 757
Satterthwaite, Ruth V, 52
Satterthwaite, Ruth V, 117
Satterthwaite, Ruth V, 118
Satterthwaite, Ruth C. IV, 757
Satterthwaite, Ruth C. IV, 758
Satterthwaite, Samuel II, 256
Satterthwaite, Samuel II, 764
Satterthwaite, Samuel II, 917
Satterthwaite, Samuel II, 969
Satterthwaite, Samuel II, 1059
Satterthwaite, Samuel III, 302
Satterthwaite, Samuel IV, 1350
Satterthwaite, Samuel IV, 1357
Satterthwaite, Samuel IV, 1377
Satterthwaite, Samuel IV, 1378
Satterthwaite, Samuel IV, 1381
Satterthwaite, Samuel IV, 1382
Satterthwaite, Samuel V, 117
Satterthwaite, Samuel M. IV, 1357
Satterthwaite, Samuel M. IV, 1377
Satterthwaite, Samuel M. IV, 1378
Satterthwaite, Sarah II, 256
Satterthwaite, Sarah II, 964
Satterthwaite, Sarah II, 968
Satterthwaite, Sarah II, 969
Satterthwaite, Sarah II, 1024
Satterthwaite, Sarah II, 1060
Satterthwaite, Sarah IV, 757
Satterthwaite, Sarah IV, 1377
Satterthwaite, Sarah IV, 1382
Satterthwaite, Sarah V, 88
Satterthwaite, Sarah V, 117
Satterthwaite, Sarah V, 118
Satterthwaite, Sarah A. II, 1055
Satterthwaite, Sarah A. II, 1059
Satterthwaite, Sarah A. IV, 1377
Satterthwaite, Sarah A. IV, 1378
Satterthwaite, Sarah Ann II, 969
Satterthwaite, Sarah Ann V, 59
Satterthwaite, Sarah Ann V, 118
Satterthwaite, Sarah Anna II, 969
Satterthwaite, Sarah B. II, 1060
Satterthwaite, Sarah C. II, 918
Satterthwaite, Sarah C. IV, 757
Satterthwaite, Sarah Elizabeth II, 969
Satterthwaite, Susan II, 968
Satterthwaite, Susan II, 1059
Satterthwaite, Susan V, 117
Satterthwaite, Susan V, 144
Satterthwaite, Susan B. II, 968
Satterthwaite, Susan B. II, 1059
Satterthwaite, Susanna II, 416
Satterthwaite, Susanna II, 487

Satterthwaite, Susanna II, 643
Satterthwaite, Susanna II, 1066
Satterthwaite, Susannah II, 969
Satterthwaite, Susannah II, 1027
Satterthwaite, Susannah II, 1059
Satterthwaite, Susannah II, 1063
Satterthwaite, Susannah S. II, 973
Satterthwaite, Tacey II, 1079
Satterthwaite, Tacey II, 1080
Satterthwaite, Tacie II, 1079
Satterthwaite, Tacie II, 1080
Satterthwaite, Tacy II, 964
Satterthwaite, Tacy II, 969
Satterthwaite, Tacy II, 1048
Satterthwaite, Tacy II, 1059
Satterthwaite, Tacy II, 1060
Satterthwaite, Tacy II, 1079
Satterthwaite, Tacy II, 1084
Satterthwaite, Tacy R. II, 969
Satterthwaite, Tacy R. II, 1055
Satterthwaite, Tacy, Jr. II, 1077
Satterthwaite, Tacy, Jr. II, 1078
Satterthwaite, Thelma V, 118
Satterthwaite, Thomas II, 740
Satterthwaite, Thomas II, 764
Satterthwaite, Thomas II, 960
Satterthwaite, Thomas II, 968
Satterthwaite, Thomas II, 969
Satterthwaite, Thomas II, 1051
Satterthwaite, Thomas II, 1059
Satterthwaite, Thomas II, 1060
Satterthwaite, Thomas IV, 153
Satterthwaite, Thomas IV, 158
Satterthwaite, Thos. C. II, 918
Satterthwaite, Viva II, 1060
Satterthwaite, Walter B. II, 968
Satterthwaite, Walter B. II, 1060
Satterthwaite, Walter S. II, 968
Satterthwaite, Walter S. II, 969
Satterthwaite, Walter S. II, 1060
Satterthwaite, Watson II, 1066
Satterthwaite, Watson II, 1079
Satterthwaite, Watson II, 1082
Satterthwaite, William II, 256
Satterthwaite, William II, 968
Satterthwaite, William II, 969
Satterthwaite, William II, 973
Satterthwaite, William II, 1010
Satterthwaite, William II, 1066
Satterthwaite, William IV, 757
Satterthwaite, William IV, 1377
Satterthwaite, William IV, 1378
Satterthwaite, William D. IV, 757
Satterthwaite, William D. IV, 758
Satterthwaite, William, Jr. II, 969
Satterthwaite, William, Jr. II, 1066
Satterthwaite, Willie V, 117
Satterthwaite, Wilmer L. IV, 272
Satterthwaite, Wm. II, 643
Satterthwaite, Wm. II, 764
Satterthwaite, Wm. II, 917
Satterthwaite, Wm. II, 1024
Satterthwaite, Wm. II, 1059
Satterthwaite, Wm. II, 1063
Satterthwaite, Wm. II, 1070
Satterthwaite, Wm. II, 1077
Satterthwaite, Wm. II, 1078
Satterthwaite, Wm. II, 1079
Satterthwaite, Wm. II, 1080
Satterthwaite, Wm. II, 1084
Satterthwaite, Wm. IV, 158
Satterthwaite, Wm. IV, 350
Satterthwaite, Wm. IV, 757
Satterthwaite, Wm. D. IV, 757
Satterthwaite, Wm. E. II, 917
Satterthwaite, Wm. S. II, 1079
Satterthwaite, Wm. T. IV, 757
Satterthwaite, Wm., Jr. II, 1024
Satterthwaite, Wm., Jr. II, 1036
Satterthwaite, Wm., Jr. II, 1059
Satterthwaite, Wm., Jr. II, 1077
Satterthwaite, Wm., Jr. II, 1078
Satterthwaite, Wm., Jr. II, 1079
Satterthwaite, Wm., Jr. II, 1080
Satterthwaite, Wm., Jr. II, 1084
Sattertwait, Mabel H. IV, 934
Sattertwait, Wm. D. IV, 934
Satterwait, Phebe H. II, 1059
Satterwait, Thomas II, 1059
Satterwaite, Benjamin II, 182
Satterwaite, Mary II, 1027
Satterwaite, Sarah II, 182
Satterwaite, Susannah II, 1024
Satterwaite, Wm. II, 1027
Sattheirthwaite, Abel V, 42
Sattherthwaite, Charles II, 1071
Sattherthwaite, Georgianna II, 1071
Sattherthwaite, Lydia V, 42
Sattherthwaite, Tacie II, 1071
Sattherthwaite, Wm. II, 1071
Sattison, Clara IV, 1240
Sattison, Harriet IV, 1240
Sauders, Ann V, 861
Sauders, Hannah IV, 272
Sauders, Joseph IV, 272
Sauders, Mary Ann IV, 272
Sauders, Robert E. IV, 272
Saul, Ann II, 417
Saul, Ann II, 808
Saul, Ann II, 818
Saul, Anthony II, 417
Saul, Hannah II, 417
Saul, Hannah VI, 852
Saul, Isabel II, 417
Saul, Jane II, 417
Saul, John II, 1025
Saul, Joseph II, 417
Saul, Joseph II, 575
Saul, Joseph II, 643
Saul, Joseph Wilkinson IV, 842
Saul, Joshua II, 417
Saul, Louisa V, 276
Saul, Mary II, 417
Saul, Mary II, 643
Saul, Moses II, 764
Saul, Rebecca II, 417
Saul, Samuel VI, 852
Saul, Sarah II, 417
Saul, Sarah II, 575
Saul, Sarah II, 643
Saull, Anthony II, 417
Saull, Joseph II, 643
Saull, Mary II, 643
Saull, Sarah II, 643
Saum, Lida V, 359
Saunder, Elizabeth II, 207
Saunder, Elizabeth II, 256
Saunder, Paul II, 207
Saunder, Paul II, 256
Saunders, ??? I, 30
Saunders, ??? III, 88
Saunders, Abigail I, 199
Saunders, Abraham I, 164
Saunders, Abraham I, 199
Saunders, Abraham I, 200
Saunders, Abraham I Sup 1, 6
Saunders, Abraham II, 95
Saunders, Abraham II, 256
Saunders, Abraham II, 643
Saunders, Ada I, 17
Saunders, Ada R. I, 73
Saunders, Adah R. I, 67
Saunders, Albert I, 17
Saunders, Albert I, 21
Saunders, Albert I, 41
Saunders, Albert I, 72
Saunders, Albert I, 73
Saunders, Albert I, 225
Saunders, Albert I, 252
Saunders, Albert I, 257
Saunders, Albert II, 918
Saunders, Alexandria VI, 140
Saunders, Alexandria VI, 605
Saunders, Alias VI, 852
Saunders, Alice V, 958
Saunders, Amarilla VI, 989
Saunders, Ambrose VI, 592
Saunders, Angeline L. VI, 989
Saunders, Ann I, 17
Saunders, Ann I, 30
Saunders, Ann I, 199
Saunders, Ann II, 417
Saunders, Ann IV, 107
Saunders, Ann V, 860
Saunders, Ann VI, 441
Saunders, Ann D. VI, 963
Saunders, Ann Eliza VI, 989
Saunders, Ann M. VI, 847
Saunders, Ann Perisho I, 17
Saunders, Ann S. VI, 852
Saunders, Anna IV, 107
Saunders, Anna V, 117
Saunders, Anna Perisho I, 21
Saunders, Anne H. II, 918
Saunders, Anthony II, 602
Saunders, Anthony II, 643
Saunders, Ardena VI, 901
Saunders, Benjamin I, 17
Saunders, Benjamin I, 418
Saunders, Benjamin VI, 989
Saunders, Benjamin S. VI, 944
Saunders, Berry VI, 897
Saunders, Berry VI, 989
Saunders, Bessie M. I, 933
Saunders, Bessie M. I, 940
Saunders, Bessie M. I, 948
Saunders, Betsey VI, 852
Saunders, Caleb I, 17
Saunders, Caroline Talbert I, 17
Saunders, Catharine VI, 879
Saunders, Charles II, 643
Saunders, Charles II, 918
Saunders, Charles Francis II, 918
Saunders, Charlotte VI, 989
Saunders, Chas. II, 856
Saunders, Chas. II, 918
Saunders, Clark IV, 107
Saunders, Daniel VI, 879
Saunders, Daniel VI, 887
Saunders, Daniel VI, 901
Saunders, Daniel VI, 902
Saunders, Daniel VI, 929
Saunders, Daniel VI, 931
Saunders, Daniel VI, 964
Saunders, Daniel VI, 965
Saunders, Daniel VI, 989
Saunders, Daniel G. VI, 931
Saunders, David VI, 555
Saunders, David VI, 775
Saunders, David VI, 884
Saunders, David VI, 889
Saunders, David VI, 892
Saunders, David VI, 934
Saunders, David VI, 949
Saunders, David VI, 951
Saunders, David VI, 963
Saunders, David VI, 977
Saunders, David VI, 980
Saunders, David VI, 989
Saunders, David VI, 996
Saunders, Drewsiller VI, 989
Saunders, Edgar IV, 272
Saunders, Edgar J. IV, 1336
Saunders, Edmund I, 17
Saunders, Edward II, 643
Saunders, Edward II, 818
Saunders, Edward II, 918
Saunders, Edward A. III, 278
Saunders, Edward W. III, 278
Saunders, Edward W. VI, 847
Saunders, Edwin III, 278
Saunders, Elijah Johnson VI, 338
Saunders, Elisabeth I, 17
Saunders, Eliza I, 21
Saunders, Eliza I, 72
Saunders, Eliza I, 73
Saunders, Eliza VI, 989
Saunders, Eliza A. I, 17
Saunders, Eliza A. I, 73
Saunders, Eliza Ann I, 41
Saunders, Eliza Ann I, 72
Saunders, Eliza Ella I, 17
Saunders, Eliza Ella I, 73
Saunders, Eliza L. III, 88
Saunders, Eliza L. III, 278
Saunders, Elizabeth I, 227
Saunders, Elizabeth I, 243
Saunders, Elizabeth I, 257
Saunders, Elizabeth II, 38
Saunders, Elizabeth II, 95
Saunders, Elizabeth II, 256
Saunders, Elizabeth II, 643
Saunders, Elizabeth III, 278
Saunders, Elizabeth IV, 107
Saunders, Elizabeth IV, 1336
Saunders, Elizabeth V, 117
Saunders, Elizabeth VI, 802
Saunders, Elizabeth VI, 964
Saunders, Elizabeth VI, 989
Saunders, Elizabeth A. VI, 797
Saunders, Elizabeth Clark III, 278
Saunders, Ella E. I, 22
Saunders, Ellen VI, 755
Saunders, Ellen VI, 989
Saunders, Elma IV, 272
Saunders, Emeline S. VI, 892
Saunders, Emily VI, 955
Saunders, Esther I, 17
Saunders, Esther II, 417
Saunders, Esther II, 643
Saunders, Esther II, 653
Saunders, Eura Emily I, 17
Saunders, Fanny VI, 813
Saunders, Fleming VI, 847
Saunders, Fleming VI, 852
Saunders, Florentine VI, 989
Saunders, Frances VI, 931
Saunders, Frances VI, 989
Saunders, Francis T. I, 17
Saunders, Francis White I, 17
Saunders, Frederick III, 278
Saunders, G. M. IV, 1336
Saunders, George VI, 988
Saunders, George VI, 989
Saunders, George G. VI, 879
Saunders, George G. VI, 901
Saunders, George G. VI, 989
Saunders, George W. VI, 872
Saunders, George W. VI, 925
Saunders, George W. VI, 937
Saunders, George W. VI, 989
Saunders, Gideon Jonathan I, 17
Saunders, Gidion J. I, 73
Saunders, Gustavus A. VI, 989
Saunders, Hannah I Sup 1, 6
Saunders, Hannah II, 22
Saunders, Hannah II, 256
Saunders, Hannah II, 489
Saunders, Hannah II, 580
Saunders, Hannah II, 643
Saunders, Hannah II, 918
Saunders, Hannah II, 923
Saunders, Hannah VI, 211
Saunders, Hannah VI, 421
Saunders, Hannah VI, 441
Saunders, Hannah VI, 541
Saunders, Hannah VI, 605
Saunders, Hannah VI, 739
Saunders, Hannah VI, 763
Saunders, Hannah VI, 775
Saunders, Hannah M. II, 918
Saunders, Hannah McPherson II, 818
Saunders, Hannah P. II, 856
Saunders, Hannah P. II, 918
Saunders, Hannah, Jr. II, 643
Saunders, Henry II, 918
Saunders, Henry V, 929
Saunders, Henry VI, 929
Saunders, Henry VI, 948
Saunders, Henry VI, 989
Saunders, Hezekiah I, 836
Saunders, Hezekiah V, 929
Saunders, Hezekiah VI, 186
Saunders, Hezekiah VI, 211
Saunders, Hezikiah VI, 267
Saunders, Isaac II, 643
Saunders, Isaac IV, 107
Saunders, Isaac V, 117
Saunders, Isaac V, 860
Saunders, Jacob I, 17
Saunders, Jacob I, 836
Saunders, James II, 38
Saunders, James II, 95
Saunders, James II, 256
Saunders, James C. VI, 989
Saunders, James Edward I, 17
Saunders, James Edward I, 73
Saunders, Jane V, 117
Saunders, Jane VI, 172
Saunders, Jane VI, 173
Saunders, Jane VI, 211
Saunders, Jane VI, 267
Saunders, Jane VI, 441
Saunders, Jane VI, 592
Saunders, Jane VI, 884
Saunders, Jane VI, 944
Saunders, Jane VI, 989
Saunders, Jemima VI, 267
Saunders, Jesse I, 17
Saunders, Jesse V, 117
Saunders, Jesse VI, 955
Saunders, Jno VI, 554
Saunders, Jno VI, 555
Saunders, Joel I, 418
Saunders, Joel VI, 592
Saunders, John I, 17
Saunders, John I, 72
Saunders, John I, 200
Saunders, John I, 227
Saunders, John II, 38
Saunders, John II, 95
Saunders, John II, 256
Saunders, John II, 643
Saunders, John II, 818
Saunders, John II, 918
Saunders, John III, 278
Saunders, John IV, 1336
Saunders, John V, 117
Saunders, John VI, 172
Saunders, John VI, 211
Saunders, John VI, 267
Saunders, John VI, 441
Saunders, John VI, 541
Saunders, John VI, 555
Saunders, John VI, 577
Saunders, John VI, 602
Saunders, John VI, 605
Saunders, John VI, 725
Saunders, John VI, 769
Saunders, John VI, 775
Saunders, John VI, 785
Saunders, John VI, 789
Saunders, John VI, 809
Saunders, John VI, 852
Saunders, John VI, 904
Saunders, John VI, 915
Saunders, John VI, 989
Saunders, John Cornwell I, 1
Saunders, John G. VI, 989
Saunders, John M. VI, 775
Saunders, John R. I, 17
Saunders, John, Jr. VI, 211
Saunders, John, Jr. VI, 755
Saunders, John, Sr. VI, 211
Saunders, Jonathan I, 17
Saunders, Jonathan I, 22
Saunders, Jonathan I, 72
Saunders, Jonathan I, 80
Saunders, Joseph I, 71
Saunders, Joseph I, 227
Saunders, Joseph II, 417
Saunders, Joseph II, 489
Saunders, Joseph II, 544
Saunders, Joseph II, 580
Saunders, Joseph II, 631
Saunders, Joseph II, 643
Saunders, Joseph II, 818
Saunders, Joseph II, 918
Saunders, Joseph IV, 107
Saunders, Joseph IV, 1336
Saunders, Joseph V, 117
Saunders, Joseph V, 863
Saunders, Joseph VI, 441
Saunders, Joseph VI, 503
Saunders, Joseph VI, 541
Saunders, Joseph VI, 555
Saunders, Joseph VI, 605
Saunders, Joseph VI, 746
Saunders, Joseph VI, 775
Saunders, Joseph VI, 989
Saunders, Joseph A. I, 73
Saunders, Joseph Albert I, 17
Saunders, Joshua II, 417
Saunders, Judeth I Sup 1, 6
Saunders, Judith I, 36
Saunders, Judith I, 71
Saunders, Judith VI, 211
Saunders, Julia I, 17
Saunders, Julia I, 72
Saunders, Julia I, 225
Saunders, Julia I, 252
Saunders, Julia I, 257
Saunders, Julia E. I, 72
Saunders, Juliess VI, 944
Saunders, Julius VI, 878
Saunders, Julius VI, 925
Saunders, Julius VI, 989
Saunders, Julius, Jr. VI, 989
Saunders, Julous VI, 1001
Saunders, Lavinia VI, 887
Saunders, Lemual H. VI, 938
Saunders, Lemuel VI, 989
Saunders, Lillie III, 278
Saunders, Lockey VI, 989
Saunders, Louisa W. VI, 901
Saunders, Lucinda VI, 852
Saunders, Lucinda VI, 889
Saunders, Lucinda VI, 938
Saunders, Lucy V, 929
Saunders, Lucy VI, 810
Saunders, Lucy VI, 904
Saunders, Lucy VI, 934
Saunders, Lydia II, 489
Saunders, Lydia II, 643
Saunders, Macpherson II, 856
Saunders, Macpherson II, 918
Saunders, Macpherson II, 923
Saunders, Mafra I, 17
Saunders, Mafra E. I, 73
Saunders, Malinda VI, 881
Saunders, Malissa Jane V, 64
Saunders, Mamie V, 643
Saunders, Margaret I, 17
Saunders, Margaret I, 72
Saunders, Margaret I, 80
Saunders, Margaret I, 88
Saunders, Margaret I, 199
Saunders, Margaret V, 860
Saunders, Margaret V, 863
Saunders, Margaret VI, 915
Saunders, Margaret VI, 929
Saunders, Margaret Ada I, 17
Saunders, Margaret Ada I, 73
Saunders, Margaret P. II, 918
Saunders, Margret VI, 915
Saunders, Martha I, 17
Saunders, Martha I, 199
Saunders, Martha V, 863
Saunders, Martha VI, 211
Saunders, Martha VI, 267
Saunders, Martha VI, 441
Saunders, Martha E. I, 73
Saunders, Martha Emily I, 17
Saunders, Martha Jane VI, 98
Saunders, Mary I, 17
Saunders, Mary I, 22
Saunders, Mary I, 62
Saunders, Mary I, 72

nders, Mary I, 80
nders, Mary I, 199
nders, Mary II, 602
nders, Mary II, 643
nders, Mary II, 810
nders, Mary II, 818
nders, Mary II, 918
nders, Mary V, 643
nders, Mary V, 929
nders, Mary VI, 85
nders, Mary VI, 87
nders, Mary VI, 441
nders, Mary VI, 541
nders, Mary VI, 554
nders, Mary VI, 602
nders, Mary VI, 605
nders, Mary VI, 624
nders, Mary VI, 697
nders, Mary VI, 775
nders, Mary VI, 785
nders, Mary VI, 897
nders, Mary VI, 989
nders, Mary A. IV, 226
nders, Mary A. VI, 852
nders, Mary Ann III, 278
nders, Mary Ann VI, 989
nders, Mary C. VI, 1020
nders, Mary F. II, 918
nders, Mary J. I, 73
nders, Mary J. I, 225
nders, Mary J. VI, 852
nders, Mary J. VI, 944
nders, Mary Julia I, 17
nders, Mary Julia I, 255
nders, Mary Julia I, 257
nders, Mary P. II, 918
nders, Mary P. VI, 989
nders, Matilda I, 17
nders, McPherson II, 818
nders, McPherson II, 823
nders, McPherson II, 918
nders, McPherson VI, 775
nders, Michael I, 257
nders, Milla I, 836
nders, Mima VI, 1001
nders, Miriam V, 117
nders, Nancy I, 199
nders, Nancy VI, 802
nders, Nancy VI, 951
nders, Nancy VI, 989
nders, Nancy R. VI, 989
nders, Nathan I, 17
nders, Orpha I, 17
nders, Patsey VI, 878
nders, Paul II, 38
nders, Paul II, 95
nders, Paul II, 256
nders, Paul II, 526
nders, Paul II, 643
nders, Paul IV, 57
nders, Paul IV, 107
nders, Peggy I, 17
nders, Penninah I, 17
nders, Peter II, 818
nders, Peter II, 918
nders, Peter II, 923
nders, Peter VI, 140
nders, Peter VI, 421
nders, Peter VI, 727
nders, Peter VI, 739
nders, Peter VI, 763
nders, Peter VI, 775
nders, Peter VI, 864
nders, Phariba I, 17
nders, Philip VI, 592
nders, Philip VI, 989
nders, Polly VI, 925
nders, Polly VI, 977
nders, Polly VI, 989
nders, Polly VI, 1020
nders, R. H. N. VI, 892
nders, Rachel I, 17
nders, Rachel II, 643
nders, Randolph VI, 901
nders, Rebecca I, 17
nders, Rebecca I, 72
nders, Rebecca I, 80
nders, Rebecca II, 95
nders, Rebecca II, 256
nders, Rebecca II, 1024
nders, Rebecca V, 860
nders, Rebecca VI, 988
nders, Rebecca VI, 989
nders, Rebecca B. VI, 989
nders, Rebeckah II, 38
nders, Rebekah I, 418
nders, Reuben VI, 989
nders, Richard I, 227
nders, Richard I Sup 1, 6
nders, Richard II, 643
nders, Richard II, 659
Saunders, Robert VI, 85
Saunders, Robt. E. IV, 226
Saunders, Sabre VI, 989
Saunders, Sallie G. II, 918
Saunders, Sally VI, 324
Saunders, Sally VI, 338
Saunders, Sally VI, 975
Saunders, Sally VI, 996
Saunders, Samuel II, 38
Saunders, Samuel II, 95
Saunders, Samuel II, 96
Saunders, Samuel II, 256
Saunders, Samuel II, 818
Saunders, Samuel II, 918
Saunders, Sarah I, 1058
Saunders, Sarah II, 95
Saunders, Sarah II, 631
Saunders, Sarah II, 643
Saunders, Sarah II, 659
Saunders, Sarah II, 818
Saunders, Sarah II, 823
Saunders, Sarah II, 856
Saunders, Sarah II, 905
Saunders, Sarah II, 918
Saunders, Sarah II, 923
Saunders, Sarah IV, 107
Saunders, Sarah V, 117
Saunders, Sarah V, 835
Saunders, Sarah V, 860
Saunders, Sarah VI, 267
Saunders, Sarah VI, 541
Saunders, Sarah VI, 555
Saunders, Sarah VI, 569
Saunders, Sarah VI, 775
Saunders, Sarah VI, 785
Saunders, Sarah VI, 989
Saunders, Sarah Pancoast VI, 739
Saunders, Sarah Pancoast VI, 775
Saunders, Seth I, 73
Saunders, Seth W. I, 17
Saunders, Seth W. I, 22
Saunders, Seth W. I, 67
Saunders, Seth W. I, 72
Saunders, Seth William I, 17
Saunders, Smith I, 199
Saunders, Stephen VI, 951
Saunders, Susan VI, 965
Saunders, Susan Ann VI, 970
Saunders, Susanna II, 544
Saunders, Susanna II, 643
Saunders, Susanna VI, 555
Saunders, Susanna VI, 746
Saunders, Susannah V, 117
Saunders, Susannah VI, 441
Saunders, Susannah VI, 503
Saunders, Susannah VI, 535
Saunders, Susannah VI, 746
Saunders, Susannah VI, 766
Saunders, Susannah VI, 775
Saunders, Susannah VI, 781
Saunders, Susannah VI, 934
Saunders, Susannah VI, 989
Saunders, Thomas I, 17
Saunders, Thomas I, 418
Saunders, Thomas II, 918
Saunders, Thomas V, 117
Saunders, Thomas VI, 967
Saunders, Thomas VI, 989
Saunders, Thomas H. II, 818
Saunders, Thomas H. VI, 775
Saunders, Thomas N. VI, 852
Saunders, Thomas T. VI, 989
Saunders, Thos. H. II, 818
Saunders, Thos. H. II, 918
Saunders, Thos. Howland II, 818
Saunders, Uriah I, 17
Saunders, W. F. I, 933
Saunders, W. G. VI, 989
Saunders, Wanton VI, 555
Saunders, Wd. Mary II, 823
Saunders, Wd. Mary Pancoast VI, 775
Saunders, Wd. Sally II, 818
Saunders, Widow Mary VI, 541
Saunders, Widow Mary VI, 555
Saunders, Widow Mary VI, 577
Saunders, Wiley I, 17
Saunders, William I, 227
Saunders, William I, 243
Saunders, William I, 257
Saunders, William IV, 107
Saunders, William VI, 802
Saunders, William VI, 813
Saunders, William VI, 852
Saunders, William VI, 967
Saunders, William VI, 970
Saunders, William VI, 989
Saunders, William VI, 1020
Saunders, William H. VI, 989
Saunders, William J. I, 73
Saunders, William Jonathan I, 17
Saunders, William Jonathan I, 72
Saunders, William M. II, 818
Saunders, William S. I, 940
Saunders, William S. I, 948
Saunders, Williame VI, 926
Saunders, Wm. II, 643
Saunders, Wm. II, 918
Saunders, Wm. VI, 938
Saunders, Wm. H. VI, 938
Saunders, Wm. M. II, 918
Saunderson, Belinda M. VI, 933
Saunderson, Belinda M. VI, 989
Saunderson, Elizabeth A. VI, 989
Saunderson, George E. VI, 989
Saunderson, John E. VI, 989
Saunderson, Martha J. VI, 989
Saunderson, Nancy VI, 901
Saunderson, Nancy F. VI, 933
Saunderson, Thomas N. VI, 989
Sauner, Louisa III, 138
Saurneuf, Celestin III, 96
Saurneuf, Celestin III, 279
Saurneuf, Maria C. III, 96
Saurneuf, Marie C. III, 279
Saurneuf, Marie Louise III, 96
Saurneuf, Marie Louise III, 279
Savage, Caroline IV, 990
Savage, Charity III, 279
Savage, Charity III, 384
Savage, Daniel II, 417
Savage, David IV, 990
Savage, Edw. III, 279
Savage, Eliza D. III, 139
Savage, Eliza D. III, 279
Savage, Eliza Dutton III, 279
Savage, Esther V, 318
Savage, Esther V, 359
Savage, Florence IV, 990
Savage, Florence IV, 1003
Savage, Florence N. IV, 990
Savage, George II, 417
Savage, Hannah II, 643
Savage, Hannah III, 279
Savage, Jno VI, 59
Savage, Jose F. F. III, 181
Savage, Jose R. F. III, 139
Savage, Jose R. F. III, 240
Savage, Jose R. F. III, 279
Savage, Mary II, 61
Savage, Mary II, 96
Savage, Mary III, 240
Savage, Mary E. III, 181
Savage, Mary Eliz. III, 279
Savage, Mary H. III, 139
Savage, Mary H. III, 279
Savage, Ramona T. III, 240
Savage, Ramona T. III, 279
Savage, Ramona Teresa III, 279
Savage, Rebecca II, 417
Savage, Richard VI, 844
Savage, Robert III, 279
Savage, Samuel II, 643
Savage, Samuel III, 279
Savage, Sarah III, 279
Savage, Teresa F. III, 279
Savage, Thomas III, 442
Savary, Rebecca H. II, 717
Savery, Ann II, 417
Savery, Ann II, 625
Savery, Ann II, 643
Savery, Benjamin II, 417
Savery, Edward II, 643
Savery, Elizabeth II, 417
Savery, Elizabeth II, 634
Savery, Elizabeth II, 643
Savery, Elizabeth II, 717
Savery, Elizabeth H. II, 735
Savery, Elizabeth H. II, 764
Savery, Elizabeth H. IV, 135
Savery, John II, 417
Savery, John II, 644
Savery, John Cresson II, 717
Savery, John Cresson II, 764
Savery, Joseph II, 417
Savery, Mary II, 417
Savery, Mary II, 621
Savery, Mary II, 625
Savery, Mary II, 643
Savery, Mary II, 644
Savery, Rachel II, 417
Savery, Rebecca II, 498
Savery, Rebecca II, 643
Savery, Rebecca II, 644
Savery, Rebecca II, 717
Savery, Rebecca II, 735
Savery, Rebecca II, 764
Savery, Rebecca IV, 135
Savery, Rebecca IV, 136
Savery, Rebecca H. IV, 758
Savery, Rebecca W. II, 498
Savery, Rebecca W. II, 644
Savery, Rebecca W. II, 717
Savery, Rebecca W. II, 764
Savery, Sarah II, 519
Savery, Sarah II, 643
Savery, Sarah II, 717
Savery, Thomas II, 417
Savery, Thomas II, 498
Savery, Thomas II, 643
Savery, Thomas II, 644
Savery, Thomas II, 717
Savery, Thomas II, 735
Savery, Thomas II, 764
Savery, William II, 417
Savery, William II, 717
Savery, Wm. II, 621
Savery, Wm. II, 625
Savery, Wm. II, 643
Savery, Wm. II, 735
Savery, Wm. II, 764
Savery, Wm. IV, 135
Savery, Wm. IV, 136
Savery, Wm., Jr. II, 519
Savery, Wm., Jr. II, 643
Savidge, Samuel Warren, Sr. VI, 120
Savidge, William VI, 120
Savil, Benjamin II, 644
Savill, Benjamin II, 644
Savill, Franklin V, 526
Savill, Margaret R. V, 526
Saville, Caldonia V, 526
Saville, Frank V, 526
Saville, Franklin V, 526
Saville, John Franklin V, 526
Saville, Margaret R. V, 526
Savory, Benjamin II, 417
Savory, John II, 417
Savory, Joseph II, 417
Savory, Mary II, 644
Savory, Rachel II, 417
Savory, William II, 417
Savoy, William VI, 157
Sawders, Joseph I, 57
Sawders, Joseph I, 71
Sawders, Mary I, 57
Sawders, Mary I, 71
Sawier, Arthur II, 644
Sawier, Arthur II, 665
Sawier, Elizabeth II, 644
Sawier, Elizabeth II, 665
Sawin, Horace V, 118
Sawyer, Abigail I, 752
Sawyer, Abigail I, 769
Sawyer, Arthur II, 644
Sawyer, Benaiah III, 279
Sawyer, Daisy Gertrude I, 17
Sawyer, Eliphabet I, 165
Sawyer, Eliphal I, 165
Sawyer, Elizabeth II, 51
Sawyer, Elizabeth II, 96
Sawyer, Elizabeth II, 644
Sawyer, Elizabeth IV, 393
Sawyer, Elizabeth IV, 434
Sawyer, Elizabeth Ann IV, 434
Sawyer, Elliott I, 165
Sawyer, Enoch I, 752
Sawyer, Florence III, 140
Sawyer, Florence III, 279
Sawyer, George F. IV, 434
Sawyer, George W. I, 752
Sawyer, George W. I, 769
Sawyer, Grace I, 625
Sawyer, Grace I, 640
Sawyer, Hannah IV, 827
Sawyer, Hattie C. I, 752
Sawyer, James IV, 393
Sawyer, James IV, 434
Sawyer, John T. III, 279
Sawyer, John Tilton III, 140
Sawyer, Julia E. I, 17
Sawyer, Lelia R. I, 752
Sawyer, Lillie I, 948
Sawyer, Lucy Lenora I, 17
Sawyer, Marguerite III, 140
Sawyer, Marguerite III, 279
Sawyer, Mary A. I, 752
Sawyer, Mary Lou I, 625
Sawyer, Mary Louise I, 640
Sawyer, Moses G. III, 279
Sawyer, Nancy I, 752
Sawyer, Nancy I, 760
Sawyer, Nancy I, 769
Sawyer, Polly I, 752
Sawyer, Rebecca I, 625
Sawyer, Rebecca R. I, 769
Sawyer, Rebekah I, 165
Sawyer, Rhoda P. IV, 758
Sawyer, Ruth I, 158
Sawyer, Ruth I, 165
Sawyer, S. O. I, 625
Sawyer, Samuel I, 752
Sawyer, Samuel I, 769
Sawyer, Sarah I, 752
Sawyer, Sarah I, 769
Sawyer, Sarah R. IV, 715
Sawyer, Sarah R. IV, 758
Sawyer, Stephen I, 165
Sawyer, Susanna II, 611
Sawyer, Susanna II, 644
Sawyer, Theo. I, 640
Sawyer, Theodore I, 625
Sawyer, Theodore I, 640
Sawyer, Thomas I, 752
Sawyer, Thomas I, 769
Sawyer, Thomas A. IV, 434
Sawyer, Viola III, 279
Sawyer, Viola III, 309
Sawyer, Walter III, 279
Sawyer, William I, 165
Sawyer, William Edward I, 17
Sawyers, Angeline VI, 989
Sawyers, Lucy VI, 989
Sawyers, Thomas VI, 989
Saxbie, John II, 417
Saxby, Thomas II, 447
Saxon, Betty IV, 758
Saxon, Catharine VI, 605
Saxon, Hannah VI, 605
Saxon, Hannah, Sr. VI, 605
Saxon, Mary VI, 605
Saxton, ??? III, 434
Saxton, Amy III, 493
Saxton, Caleb III, 493
Saxton, Catherine V, 119
Saxton, Catherine VI, 442
Saxton, George VI, 442
Saxton, Hannah V, 201
Saxton, Hannah VI, 442
Saxton, Hannah VI, 447
Saxton, Mary III, 434
Saxton, Mary III, 442
Saxton, Mary V, 129
Saxton, Mary V, 160
Saxton, Mary V, 201
Saxton, Mary VI, 442
Saxton, Mary Moorman V, 201
Saxton, Mashac VI, 442
Saxton, Mashac VI, 447
Saxton, Meshach VI, 442
Saxton, Sarah V, 201
Say, Ann II, 417
Say, Bathsheba VI, 989
Say, Benjamin II, 417
Say, Benjamin II, 644
Say, Elizabeth VI, 970
Say, Mary II, 417
Say, Mary II, 447
Say, Mary II, 644
Say, Mary A. VI, 982
Say, Mary A., Sr. VI, 982
Say, Meriam II, 600
Say, Meriam II, 644
Say, Peter VI, 982
Say, Peter VI, 989
Say, Polly VI, 970
Say, Polly VI, 989
Say, Preston VI, 989
Say, Rebecca II, 256
Say, Rebecca II, 257
Say, Rebecca Ann II, 417
Say, Rebecca Ann II, 494
Say, Rebecca Ann II, 644
Say, Rebekah II, 644
Say, Richard II, 447
Say, Sarah II, 644
Say, Susanna II, 644
Say, Susannah II, 481
Say, Thomas II, 256
Say, Thomas II, 417
Say, Thomas II, 481
Say, Thomas II, 644
Say, William II, 417
Say, William II, 447
Say, Wm. II, 447
Say, Wm. II, 644
Sayer, John H. V, 45
Sayer, Sarah Jane V, 45
Sayer, William II, 257
Sayers, Anna IV, 758
Sayers, Clinton V, 277
Sayers, Emma V, 66
Sayers, Emma V, 118
Sayers, Esther Grace V, 708
Sayers, James Wilbur V, 118
Sayers, John V, 118
Sayers, John H. V, 201
Sayers, L. D. V, 708
Sayers, Lillian V, 277

Sayers, Lillian V, 708
Sayers, Lottie V, 201
Sayers, Mary IV, 758
Sayers, Mary V, 118
Sayers, Phebe V, 218
Sayers, Phebe V, 276
Sayers, Phebe G. V, 277
Sayers, Phebe G. V, 708
Sayers, Robert IV, 758
Sayers, Sarah J. V, 118
Sayers, St. Clair V, 708
Sayers, Wilbur V, 201
Sayers, William IV, 758
Sayers, Wm. V, 118
Sayers, Wm. V, 201
Saylor, Anna III, 103
Saylor, Anna III, 279
Saylor, David S. III, 103
Saylor, David Sutton III, 279
Saylor, Parry Dorland III, 279
Sayman, Abraham III, 279
Saynders, Jane VI, 166
Saynders, Jane VI, 211
Saynders, John VI, 211
Saynders, John, Jr. VI, 166
Saynders, John, Jr. VI, 211
Sayr, Rebekah III, 148
Sayr, Rebekah III, 279
Sayre, Arthenici V, 118
Sayre, Artieneci V, 118
Sayre, David V, 100
Sayre, David V, 118
Sayre, Elizabeth V, 100
Sayre, Elizabeth V, 118
Sayre, Emily V, 114
Sayre, Emily V, 118
Sayre, Emma V, 118
Sayre, Irena V, 105
Sayre, Irena V, 118
Sayre, James Wilbur V, 118
Sayre, John V, 118
Sayre, Mary V, 99
Sayre, Mary V, 118
Sayre, Minerva V, 118
Sayre, Minerva V, 132
Sayre, Rachel II, 96
Sayre, Ruth II, 64
Sayre, Ruth II, 96
Sayre, Sarah V, 118
Sayre, Sarah J. V, 118
Sayre, Silas V, 118
Sayre, William V, 118
Sayre, Wm. V, 118
Sayres, Abigail III, 279
Sayres, David V, 708
Sayres, Davis L. V, 708
Sayres, Esther Grace V, 708
Sayres, Isaac III, 279
Sayres, L. D. V, 708
Sayres, Lillian V, 708
Sayres, Lillian C. V, 526
Sayres, Phebe V, 526
Sayres, Phebe G. V, 708
Sayres, Rebekah III, 279
Sayres, St. Clair V, 708
Sayrs, Arthenici V, 118
Says, Rebecca II, 202
Says, Rebecca II, 256
Says, Thomas II, 202
Says, Thomas II, 256
Scaggs, Christopher VI, 989
Scaggs, Tabitha VI, 989
Scale, Mona IV, 758
Scales, Albert IV, 1262
Scales, Alice Cynthia III, 187
Scales, Alice Cynthia III, 279
Scales, Alice L. III, 65
Scales, Alice L. III, 132
Scales, Alice L. III, 187
Scales, Alice L. III, 279
Scales, Anna III, 96
Scales, Anna III, 279
Scales, Edw. S. III, 132
Scales, Edward S. III, 65
Scales, Edward S. III, 187
Scales, Edward S. III, 279
Scales, Elizabeth III, 279
Scales, Elizabeth VI, 400
Scales, Elizabeth VI, 441
Scales, Elmyra IV, 1262
Scales, Fannie IV, 1262
Scales, Freeman III, 96
Scales, Freeman III, 279
Scales, Georgenie V, 596
Scales, Harold E. III, 279
Scales, Joseph V, 596
Scales, Margaret III, 132
Scales, Margaret L. III, 279
Scales, Martha V, 596
Scales, Maud IV, 1262
Scales, Mollie I, 640
Scales, Myrtle IV, 1262
Scales, Naomi V, 596
Scales, Ruth III, 279
Scales, Ruth V, 596
Scales, Sarah IV, 1262
Scales, Walter VI, 400
Scales, Walter VI, 441
Scales, Wm. W. IV, 1262
Scamahorn, Cora May V, 201
Scammahorn, Cora May V, 201
Scammahorn, Eunice V, 201
Scammahorn, Helen V, 201
Scammahorn, Helen M. V, 214
Scanandore, Ellen II, 707
Scanandore, Elsie II, 707
Scanandore, Joel II, 707
Scannon, Mary III, 273
Scantlebury, ??? III, 280
Scantlebury, Alfred L. III, 279
Scantlebury, Amy T. III, 143
Scantlebury, Amy T. III, 193
Scantlebury, Amy T. III, 279
Scantlebury, Ann III, 279
Scantlebury, Cornelia II, 918
Scantlebury, Edw. III, 279
Scantlebury, Edward III, 193
Scantlebury, Edward III, 279
Scantlebury, Edward III, 302
Scantlebury, Edward T. III, 279
Scantlebury, Elizabeth III, 279
Scantlebury, Emilie L. III, 279
Scantlebury, Enoch III, 279
Scantlebury, John III, 279
Scantlebury, John B. III, 184
Scantlebury, John B. III, 279
Scantlebury, John Barlow III, 279
Scantlebury, Joseph III, 279
Scantlebury, Louisa J. III, 184
Scantlebury, Louisa J. III, 279
Scantlebury, Mary A. III, 279
Scantlebury, Mary Ann III, 302
Scantlebury, Mary Anna III, 193
Scantlebury, Mary Anna III, 279
Scantlebury, Samuel III, 149
Scantlebury, Samuel III, 279
Scantlebury, Samuel III, 280
Scantlebury, Sarah III, 149
Scantlebury, Sarah III, 279
Scantlebury, Sarah III, 280
Scantlebury, Sarah J. III, 279
Scantlebury, Thomas III, 279
Scantlebury, Thomas III, 280
Scantlin, Jeremiah VI, 989
Scantlin, Tabby VI, 989
Scantling, Cain VI, 989
Scantling, Jeremiah VI, 989
Scantling, Peggy VI, 969
Scantling, Sarah VI, 989
Scantling, Tabby VI, 989
Scarberry, Polly VI, 990
Scarberry, Robert VI, 990
Scarboro, Almina E. I, 936
Scarborough, Amy Ann II, 1060
Scarborough, Amy Ann II, 1079
Scarborough, Amyanne Alfred II, 1079
Scarborough, Charles II, 1079
Scarborough, Charles R. II, 1079
Scarborough, Charles Reeder II, 1060
Scarborough, Col. Edmund VI, 11
Scarborough, Cynthia II, 1079
Scarborough, Elizabeth II, 1025
Scarborough, Elizabeth II, 1079
Scarborough, Elizabeth VI, 941
Scarborough, Elizabeth B. II, 918
Scarborough, Hannah II, 1079
Scarborough, Hannah II, 1083
Scarborough, Isaac II, 1079
Scarborough, Isaac K. II, 1079
Scarborough, Isaac K. II, 1083
Scarborough, Isaac Kirk II, 1060
Scarborough, Jane II, 1025
Scarborough, Jane II, 1079
Scarborough, John II, 981
Scarborough, John II, 1025
Scarborough, John II, 1060
Scarborough, John II, 1079
Scarborough, John II, 1083
Scarborough, John III, 280
Scarborough, John W. Hannah II, 1079
Scarborough, Kirk II, 1079
Scarborough, Mary II, 1021
Scarborough, Mary II, 1025
Scarborough, Mary II, 1079
Scarborough, Mary VI, 955
Scarborough, Mary VI, 990
Scarborough, Phebe Ann II, 1079
Scarborough, Phebe Ann II, 1083
Scarborough, Reader II, 1079
Scarborough, Robert VI, 990
Scarborough, Robert VI, 995
Scarborough, Susanna II, 981
Scarborough, Susanna VI, 995
Scarborough, Susannah II, 981
Scarborough, Susannah II, 1025
Scarbourough, Colonel Edmund VI, 11
Scarbrough, Augustin I, 92
Scarbrough, Elizabeth II, 996
Scarbrough, Elizabeth II, 1025
Scarbrough, Elizabeth VI, 437
Scarbrough, Elizabeth VI, 441
Scarbrough, Jane II, 1025
Scarbrough, John II, 996
Scarbrough, John II, 1000
Scarbrough, John II, 1025
Scarbrough, Mary II, 1025
Scarbrough, Ostran I, 92
Scarbrough, Sarah II, 1000
Scarbrough, Sarah II, 1025
Scarbrough, Susannah II, 1025
Scarlet, Annie M. II, 918
Scarlet, Edwin II, 918
Scarlet, Edwin W. II, 918
Scarlet, Ephriam II, 707
Scarlet, James II, 716
Scarlet, James II, 717
Scarlet, John I, 418
Scarlet, Lydia Ann II, 701
Scarlet, Lydia Ann II, 707
Scarlet, Martha S. II, 716
Scarlet, Mary J. II, 918
Scarlet, Orpha I, 717
Scarlet, Orpha I, 733
Scarlet, Rachel Ann II, 716
Scarlet, Ruth I, 733
Scarlet, Sarah Boone II, 707
Scarlet, Sarah F. II, 717
Scarlett, Amanda Elvina II, 818
Scarlett, Annie M. II, 918
Scarlett, Deborah VI, 653
Scarlett, Deborah VI, 718
Scarlett, Deborah VI, 775
Scarlett, Deborah VI, 789
Scarlett, Deborah VI, 790
Scarlett, Edwin II, 918
Scarlett, Edwin W. II, 918
Scarlett, Elizabeth II, 791
Scarlett, Elizabeth II, 818
Scarlett, Ellen Brumfield II, 805
Scarlett, Grace III, 412
Scarlett, Grace III, 442
Scarlett, Hannah I, 349
Scarlett, John II, 791
Scarlett, John II, 818
Scarlett, Joseph II, 918
Scarlett, Joseph P. II, 918
Scarlett, Joseph Pownall II, 818
Scarlett, Levi II, 818
Scarlett, Mary I, 349
Scarlett, Mary A. II, 918
Scarlett, Mary J. II, 791
Scarlett, Mary J. II, 857
Scarlett, Mary J. II, 918
Scarlett, Nathaniel I, 349
Scarlett, Nathaniel VI, 775
Scarlett, Nathaniel VI, 789
Scarlett, Ruth I, 733
Scarlett, Ruth I, 736
Scarlett, Sarah D. II, 739
Scarlett, Sarah D. II, 764
Scarlett, Sir James III, 412
Scarlett, Sir James III, 442
Scarlett, Sophia II, 809
Scarnell, Eliz. III, 46
Scarret, Amy II, 417
Scarret, Emme II, 417
Scarret, Esther II, 417
Scarret, Isaac II, 417
Scarret, James II, 417
Scarret, John II, 417
Scarret, Joseph II, 417
Scarret, Susanna II, 417
Scarret, Susanna II, 644
Scatterday, Laura VI, 528
Scattergood, Abigail II, 193
Scattergood, Abigail II, 257
Scattergood, Alpheus IV, 842
Scattergood, Amelia II, 318
Scattergood, Amelia II, 324
Scattergood, Amelia Ann II, 324
Scattergood, Ann II, 257
Scattergood, Ann II, 259
Scattergood, Ann II, 717
Scattergood, Ann II, 753
Scattergood, Ann II, 764
Scattergood, Anna II, 699
Scattergood, Anna IV, 758
Scattergood, Anna M. II, 147
Scattergood, Anna M. II, 157
Scattergood, Anna Maria II, 137
Scattergood, Anna Maria II, 157
Scattergood, Benjamin II, 257
Scattergood, Caleb II, 157
Scattergood, Caleb II, 212
Scattergood, Caleb II, 257
Scattergood, Caleb II, 313
Scattergood, Caleb II, 324
Scattergood, Caroline II, 717
Scattergood, Caroline C. II, 764
Scattergood, Catharine II, 156
Scattergood, Catharine II, 157
Scattergood, Catharine II, 271
Scattergood, Catharine II, 312
Scattergood, Catharine II, 324
Scattergood, Christopher II, 182
Scattergood, David II, 257
Scattergood, David II, 717
Scattergood, David II, 764
Scattergood, David IV, 758
Scattergood, Edward IV, 758
Scattergood, Elisa II, 240
Scattergood, Elisa II, 257
Scattergood, Elisabeth II, 182
Scattergood, Eliza II, 130
Scattergood, Eliza II, 133
Scattergood, Eliza II, 137
Scattergood, Eliza II, 147
Scattergood, Eliza II, 150
Scattergood, Eliza II, 157
Scattergood, Eliza II, 182
Scattergood, Eliza II, 818
Scattergood, Elizabeth II, 131
Scattergood, Elizabeth II, 182
Scattergood, Elizabeth II, 192
Scattergood, Elizabeth II, 202
Scattergood, Elizabeth II, 257
Scattergood, Elizabeth II, 457
Scattergood, Elizabeth II, 546
Scattergood, Elizabeth II, 643
Scattergood, Elizabeth II, 644
Scattergood, Elizabeth II, 700
Scattergood, Elizabeth IV, 758
Scattergood, Ellen II, 156
Scattergood, Ellen II, 157
Scattergood, Ellen II, 312
Scattergood, Ellen II, 320
Scattergood, Ellen II, 324
Scattergood, Ellen II, 818
Scattergood, Ellen II, 918
Scattergood, Emaline II, 157
Scattergood, Emaline B. II, 137
Scattergood, Emaline B. II, 150
Scattergood, Emaline B. II, 157
Scattergood, Emeline B. II, 133
Scattergood, Estella II, 918
Scattergood, Estelle II, 157
Scattergood, Estelle II, 881
Scattergood, Estelle II, 918
Scattergood, George II, 717
Scattergood, George J. II, 764
Scattergood, Hannah II, 247
Scattergood, Hannah II, 257
Scattergood, Hannah Ann II, 156
Scattergood, Hannah Ann II, 157
Scattergood, Hannah Ann II, 312
Scattergood, Hannah Ann II, 318
Scattergood, Hannah Ann II, 324
Scattergood, Hannah Ann II, 818
Scattergood, Hannah Ann II, 918
Scattergood, Hannah C. II, 300
Scattergood, Hannah C. II, 306
Scattergood, Hannah H. II, 137
Scattergood, Hannah H. II, 146
Scattergood, Hannah H. II, 157
Scattergood, Howard II, 157
Scattergood, Howard II, 313
Scattergood, Howard II, 324
Scattergood, James II, 717
Scattergood, John II, 182
Scattergood, John II, 257
Scattergood, John II, 546
Scattergood, John II, 643
Scattergood, John II, 644
Scattergood, Jonathan II, 130
Scattergood, Jonathan II, 133
Scattergood, Jonathan II, 137
Scattergood, Jonathan II, 147
Scattergood, Jonathan II, 150
Scattergood, Jonathan II, 157
Scattergood, Jonathan II, 257
Scattergood, Jonathan II, 818
Scattergood, Jonathan B. II, 157
Scattergood, Jonathan Barton II, 818
Scattergood, Jonathan Barton II, 918
Scattergood, Joseph II, 182
Scattergood, Joseph II, 233
Scattergood, Joseph II, 257
Scattergood, Joseph II, 271
Scattergood, Joseph II, 300
Scattergood, Joseph II, 457
Scattergood, Joseph II, 546
Scattergood, Joseph II, 644
Scattergood, Joseph II, 700
Scattergood, Joseph II, 712
Scattergood, Joseph II, 717
Scattergood, Joseph II, 753
Scattergood, Joseph II, 754
Scattergood, Joseph II, 764
Scattergood, Joseph IV, 758
Scattergood, Joseph B. II, 71
Scattergood, Joseph H. II, 30
Scattergood, Joseph R. II, 13
Scattergood, Joseph R. II, 15
Scattergood, Joshua II, 257
Scattergood, Lewis H. II, 157
Scattergood, Louis H. II, 918
Scattergood, Martha II, 147
Scattergood, Martha II, 157
Scattergood, Martha II, 257
Scattergood, Martha II, 644
Scattergood, Martha II, 717
Scattergood, Martha A. II, 13
Scattergood, Martha A. II, 15
Scattergood, Mary II, 182
Scattergood, Mary II, 212
Scattergood, Mary II, 257
Scattergood, Mary II, 300
Scattergood, Mary II, 417
Scattergood, Mary II, 644
Scattergood, Mary II, 700
Scattergood, Mary II, 712
Scattergood, Mary II, 717
Scattergood, Mary II, 753
Scattergood, Mary II, 754
Scattergood, Mary II, 764
Scattergood, Mary IV, 534
Scattergood, Mary C. II, 714
Scattergood, Mary C. II, 717
Scattergood, Mary C. II, 764
Scattergood, Mary C. IV, 758
Scattergood, Morris II, 717
Scattergood, Phebe II, 257
Scattergood, Phebe II, 271
Scattergood, Phebe A. II, 764
Scattergood, Phebe Anna II, 71
Scattergood, Rachel II, 324
Scattergood, Rachel II, 712
Scattergood, Rachel II, 754
Scattergood, Rachel II, 764
Scattergood, Rachel H. II, 157
Scattergood, Rachel H. II, 324
Scattergood, Rachel Heaton II, 157
Scattergood, Rachel P. II, 717
Scattergood, Rachel W. II, 313
Scattergood, Rebecca II, 156
Scattergood, Rebecca II, 157
Scattergood, Rebecca II, 182
Scattergood, Rebecca II, 233
Scattergood, Rebecca II, 257
Scattergood, Rebecca II, 270
Scattergood, Rebecca II, 299
Scattergood, Rebecca II, 300
Scattergood, Rebecca II, 309
Scattergood, Rebecca II, 312
Scattergood, Rebecca II, 313
Scattergood, Rebecca II, 314
Scattergood, Rebecca II, 324
Scattergood, Rebecca II, 326
Scattergood, Rebecca II, 457
Scattergood, Rebecca II, 643
Scattergood, Rebecca II, 644
Scattergood, Rebecca II, 745
Scattergood, Rebecca II, 764
Scattergood, Rebecca II, 818
Scattergood, Rebecca II, 874
Scattergood, Rebecca II, 918
Scattergood, Rebecca IV, 535
Scattergood, Rebecca IV, 758
Scattergood, Rebecca H. II, 918
Scattergood, Rebecca Pike II, 257
Scattergood, Rebecca R. II, 257
Scattergood, Rebecca S. IV, 534
Scattergood, Rebekah II, 644
Scattergood, Rebekah II, 679
Scattergood, Samuel II, 182
Scattergood, Samuel II, 240
Scattergood, Samuel II, 257
Scattergood, Samuel II, 714
Scattergood, Samuel II, 717
Scattergood, Samuel II, 764
Scattergood, Samuel IV, 534
Scattergood, Samuel IV, 758
Scattergood, Samuel C. II, 717
Scattergood, Samuel H. II, 717
Scattergood, Samuel H. II, 764
Scattergood, Samuel, Jr. II, 271
Scattergood, Sarah II, 157

ergood, Sarah II, 182
ergood, Sarah II, 222
ergood, Sarah II, 233
ergood, Sarah II, 250
ergood, Sarah II, 257
ergood, Sarah II, 717
ergood, Sarah II, 764
ergood, Sarah IV, 758
ergood, Sarah R. II, 137
ergood, Sarah R. II, 157
ergood, Sarah S. II, 147
ergood, Sarah S. II, 156
tergood, Sarah S. II, 157
tergood, Sarah W. II, 312
tergood, Sarah W. II, 324
tergood, Savery II, 717
tergood, Susan II, 130
tergood, Susan IV, 758
tergood, Susan G. II, 714
tergood, Thomas II, 182
tergood, Thomas II, 192
tergood, Thomas II, 233
tergood, Thomas II, 240
tergood, Thomas II, 247
tergood, Thomas II, 257
tergood, Thomas II, 259
tergood, Thomas II, 457
tergood, Thomas II, 644
tergood, Thomas II, 1025
tergood, Thomas IV, 758
ttergood, Thomas VI, 511
ttergood, Thomas F. II, 644
ttergood, Thomas F. II, 764
ttergood, Thomas H. II, 764
ttergood, Thomas, Jr. II, 257
ttergood, Thomas, Jr. II, 271
ttergood, Thomas, Jr. II, 717
ttergood, Thomasin II, 247
ttergood, Thomasin II, 257
ttergood, Thomasin II, 271
ttergood, Wd. Sarah II, 182
ttergood, William II, 300
ttergood, William II, 324
ttergood, William A. II, 312
ttergood, William A. II, 313
ttergood, William W. II, 313
ttergood, William W. II, 318
ttergood, William W. II, 324
ttergood, Wm. II, 157
attergood, Wm. A. II, 156
attergood, Wm. A. II, 157
attergood, Wm. A. II, 818
attergood, Wm. A. II, 874
attergood, Wm. A. II, 918
attergood, Wm. H. II, 137
attergood, Wm. H. II, 157
attergood, Wm. H. II, 918
attergood, Wm. Hancock II, 818
attergood, Wm. W. II, 157
elly, Norman V, 1019
haab, Nicholas P. IV, 1336
hachtil, Emma W. III, 62
had, Adelaide Hall VI, 762
haeffer, Herbert V, 763
haeffer, Irene L. IV, 1337
haeffer, Mary V, 763
haeffer, Rebecca Anna V, 763
haeffer, Sophia F. III, 106
haffer, Hannah II, 918
haffer, Mary E. V, 861
haiber, Ivan Victor V, 708
halk, Catharine III, 396
halk, Catharine III, 442
haller, Anna II, 717
haller, Anna C. II, 740
haller, Anna C. II, 764
challer, Annie II, 764
challer, Clara II, 717
challer, Clara II, 740
challer, Clara II, 764
challer, Herman A. II, 717
challer, Herman A. II, 740
challer, Herman A. II, 764
chank, Susanna III, 280
chank, Susanna III, 298
chatzle, Mattie V, 763
chatzley, Ira V, 763
Schatzley, Minnie V, 763
Schauer, Grant V, 834
Schauer, Grant V, 860
Schauer, Sarah E. V, 860
Schauer, Sarah Elizabeth V, 834
Schauers, Grant V, 860
Schauers, Sarah E. V, 860
Schauers, Thelma V, 860
Schauers, Vera V, 860
Schavoir, Johanna III, 181
Schavoir, Johanna III, 337
Scheble, Adolphus Edw. III, 420
Scheble, Gertrude S. III, 420
Scheble, Rosita III, 420
Scheckells, Ava I, 945
Scheckells, Ava I, 949
Scheckles, Ava L. I, 930
Scheckles, Laura I, 930
Scheckles, Richard I, 930
Scheetz, Elizabeth II, 805
Scheible, Elizabeth Geboren III, 496
Scheifelin, ??? III, 199
Scheifelin, Hannah III, 199
Schell, Anna M. III, 124
Schell, Anna M. III, 280
Schell, Augustus III, 124
Schell, Augustus III, 280
Schell, Ira V, 201
Schell, Lettie IV, 496
Schenck, ??? III, 301
Schenck, Sarah III, 280
Schenck, Sarah III, 301
Schenck, Susan III, 280
Schenk, Catharine L. VI, 876
Schenk, Catharine L. VI, 990
Schenk, Frances R. VI, 876
Schenk, John W. VI, 876
Schenk, John W. VI, 990
Schertzer, Verty IV, 1292
Scheuer, Charles P. III, 496
Scheuer, Elizabeth III, 496
Scheuer, Margaret E. III, 496
Schiath, Ivan Victor V, 708
Schickedantz, John V, 1017
Schickedantz, Susie V, 1017
Schieffelin, Jacob III, 280
Schilling, Martha IV, 757
Schilling, Martha IV, 758
Schillinger, Philip VI, 267
Schillinger, Philip G. VI, 267
Schisler, Sarah IV, 842
Schissel, Agnes III, 280
Schissel, Agnes V. III, 280
Schissel, Edmund III, 280
Schissel, Francis III, 280
Schissel, Louis III, 280
Schissel, Louisa III, 280
Schissel, Selma III, 280
Schissell, Agnes III, 135
Schissell, Agnes III, 136
Schissell, Arlene III, 136
Schissell, Edmund III, 136
Schissell, Francis III, 136
Schissell, Francis C. III, 136
Schissell, Hazel Arline III, 136
Schissell, Louis III, 135
Schissell, Louisa III, 136
Schissell, Selma III, 136
Schissell, Selma, Jr. III, 136
Schissell, Sophia III, 136
Schissell, Walter III, 136
Schlack, Annie VI, 441
Schlack, Charles VI, 441
Schlack, Charlotte Belle VI, 441
Schlack, Gover H. VI, 441
Schlack, Grover Hauptman VI, 441
Schlack, Helen Louise VI, 441
Schlack, Mary Lou VI, 441
Schlack, Nina VI, 441
Schlack, Nina T. VI, 441
Schlager, Lena III, 347
Schlagle, Faith IV, 1337
Schlagle, Josephine IV, 1337
Schlagle, Ruth IV, 1337
Schlecher, William A. IV, 758
Schlegel, Benj. IV, 1336
Schlegel, Benj. IV, 1337
Schlegel, Clara H. L. II, 764
Schlegel, Faith IV, 1337
Schlegel, Frank M. IV, 1336
Schlegel, Frank Martin IV, 1336
Schlegel, Josephine IV, 1336
Schlegel, Josephine IV, 1337
Schlegel, Nellie IV, 1336
Schlegel, Ruth IV, 1337
Schlegel, Wm. Schwendeman II, 764
Schleicher, William IV, 1337
Schleigle, Frank M. IV, 1336
Schleigle, Nellie IV, 1336
Schlenter, Christian IV, 1337
Schlenter, Eliz. IV, 1337
Schlenter, Nettie IV, 1337
Schlicht, Antonia III, 280
Schlicht, Antonia III, 344
Schlicht, Caroline III, 118
Schlicht, Caroline III, 280
Schlicht, Clara III, 118
Schlicht, Clara III, 280
Schlicht, Julius III, 280
Schlicht, Julius III, 344
Schlicht, Otto III, 118
Schlicht, Otto III, 280
Schlism, Frank IV, 1262
Schlism, Helen IV, 1262
Schlueter, Elizabeth IV, 1337
Schlueter, Fred IV, 1337
Schlueter, Fred J. IV, 1337
Schmalz, Helena III, 275
Schmick, Angela V, 929
Schmick, Ermin J. V, 929
Schmick, Erwin V, 929
Schmick, Erwin J. V, 929
Schmick, Geo. V, 929
Schmick, Jessie Allen V, 929
Schmick, Jessie Wasterman V, 891
Schmick, Jessie Westerman V, 929
Schmick, Johanna V, 929
Schmick, Muriel V, 929
Schmick, Paul V, 929
Schmick, Walter V, 929
Schmick, Walter P. V, 929
Schmick, Walter Philip V, 891
Schmick, Walter Philip V, 929
Schmick, Walter Ringold V, 929
Schmidt, Anna M. III, 293
Schmidt, Cora V, 706
Schmidt, Robert D. V, 706
Schmuch, Abigail II, 644
Schmuck, Abigail II, 644
Schmuck, Edward W. III, 280
Schmucke, Elizabeth II, 257
Schnapp, Allie Ross IV, 1183
Schnapp, Ella IV, 1183
Schneer, Fred'k Hirleman III, 223
Schneer, Frederick Hirlman III, 280
Schneer, Mary III, 280
Schneer, Mary B. III, 280
Schneer, Mary Birdsall III, 223
Schneider, Christopher F. III, 280
Schneider, Christopher F. III, 302
Schneider, Edwin C. III, 442
Schneider, Geo. IV, 1337
Schneider, Louis III, 442
Schneider, Louisa III, 442
Schneider, Louisa IV, 1337
Schneider, Louisa E. III, 280
Schneider, Louisa E. III, 302
Schneider, Louise IV, 1337
Schneider, Louise F. III, 442
Schneider, Magdalena IV, 1337
Schneider, Mamie IV, 1337
Schneider, Margaret III, 280
Schneider, Margaret III, 302
Schneider, Norman IV, 1337
Schneider, Philip IV, 1337
Schneider, Wd. Hannah II, 796
Schnell, Carolina II, 707
Schocke, Alice III, 280
Schocke, Alice E. III, 280
Schocke, Arthur III, 280
Schoeke, ??? III, 325
Schoeke, Alice E. III, 325
Schofield, Abigail IV, 444
Schofield, Andrew IV, 1113
Schofield, Andrew IV, 1114
Schofield, Andrew IV, 1137
Schofield, Andrew IV, 1183
Schofield, Andrew T. IV, 1113
Schofield, Ann II, 1031
Schofield, Anna M. IV, 1113
Schofield, Anne IV, 1098
Schofield, Anne IV, 1114
Schofield, Aron VI, 819
Schofield, Belinda IV, 1109
Schofield, Belinda IV, 1113
Schofield, Belinda IV, 1114
Schofield, Belinda H. IV, 1114
Schofield, Belinda H. IV, 1138
Schofield, Belinda S. IV, 1114
Schofield, Belinda S. IV, 1133
Schofield, Belinda S. IV, 1137
Schofield, Benjamin II, 1060
Schofield, Blanche Edith IV, 1113
Schofield, Clarence I. IV, 1113
Schofield, Clark IV, 314
Schofield, David IV, 314
Schofield, David IV, 350
Schofield, David IV, 842
Schofield, David VI, 605
Schofield, Dortha B. IV, 1110
Schofield, Edith II, 1060
Schofield, Edith III, 280
Schofield, Edith III, 322
Schofield, Edith IV, 1109
Schofield, Edith IV, 1110
Schofield, Edith IV, 1114
Schofield, Edith M. IV, 1114
Schofield, Eliza H. II, 918
Schofield, Elizabeth V, 118
Schofield, Ellen B. III, 280
Schofield, Frank III, 280
Schofield, Frank III, 322
Schofield, Geo. A. IV, 1110
Schofield, Harrietta III, 280
Schofield, Harrietta III, 322
Schofield, Henry, Jr. III, 194
Schofield, Isaac K. II, 644
Schofield, Isaac Knight II, 644
Schofield, Issachar IV, 1113
Schofield, Issachar IV, 1114
Schofield, Jane VI, 605
Schofield, John IV, 548
Schofield, John IV, 1109
Schofield, John IV, 1113
Schofield, John IV, 1114
Schofield, John IV, 1133
Schofield, John IV, 1137
Schofield, John IV, 1183
Schofield, John VI, 605
Schofield, John Robert IV, 1113
Schofield, Jonathan T. II, 1060
Schofield, Jonathan T. IV, 444
Schofield, Joseph I, 1050
Schofield, Joseph II, 1060
Schofield, Joseph IV, 314
Schofield, Joshua IV, 324
Schofield, Joshua IV, 350
Schofield, Joshua IV, 689
Schofield, Lydia II, 1060
Schofield, Lydia IV, 758
Schofield, Lydia A. II, 918
Schofield, Lydia Jane IV, 1098
Schofield, Lydia Jane IV, 1113
Schofield, Lydia Jane IV, 1114
Schofield, Margaret IV, 1183
Schofield, Margaret Ann IV, 314
Schofield, Margaret Ann IV, 324
Schofield, Margaret Ann IV, 350
Schofield, Margaret Ann IV, 689
Schofield, Maria IV, 417
Schofield, Martha II, 1060
Schofield, Mary VI, 744
Schofield, Natilie W. III, 194
Schofield, Natilie W. III, 280
Schofield, Oliver II, 1060
Schofield, Rachel IV, 842
Schofield, Rachel IV, 1114
Schofield, Rachel IV, 1123
Schofield, Rachel IV, 1183
Schofield, Rachel VI, 605
Schofield, Rachel Ann IV, 1114
Schofield, Rachel G. IV, 1113
Schofield, Rachel J. IV, 1137
Schofield, Rebecca II, 644
Schofield, Rebecca IV, 350
Schofield, Rebecca IV, 842
Schofield, Rebecca Jane IV, 314
Schofield, Robert Marcus IV, 314
Schofield, Ruanna IV, 1111
Schofield, Ruanna IV, 1113
Schofield, Ruanna IV, 1114
Schofield, Samuel II, 644
Schofield, Sarah II, 644
Schofield, Sarah Ann II, 644
Schofield, Sarah Jane II, 780
Schofield, Stephen IV, 1113
Schofield, Stephen IV, 1114
Schofield, Stephen H. IV, 1114
Schofield, Susannah I, 1050
Schofield, Thomas IV, 417
Schofield, Thomas IV, 1183
Schofield, William S. IV, 1113
Schofield, Wm. H. III, 280
Schofield, Wm. Henry, Jr. III, 280
Schogin, Rachel IV, 385
Schogin, Rachel IV, 434
Scholefield, George III, 280
Scholes, Edith II, 38
Scholes, John II, 38
Scholes, Rebeckah II, 38
Scholes, Susanna IV, 532
Scholes, Susanna IV, 548
Scholey, Abigail II, 257
Scholey, Ann II, 182
Scholey, Elisabeth II, 257
Scholey, Elisha IV, 759
Scholey, Elizabeth II, 262
Scholey, Esable II, 182
Scholey, Frances II, 182
Scholey, Hannah II, 257
Scholey, Hannah IV, 759
Scholey, Henry IV, 759
Scholey, Isabel II, 257
Scholey, John II, 182
Scholey, John II, 244
Scholey, John II, 257
Scholey, Jonathan II, 182
Scholey, Jonathan II, 257
Scholey, Mary II, 182
Scholey, Mary II, 196
Scholey, Mary II, 253
Scholey, Mary II, 255
Scholey, Mary II, 257
Scholey, Rebecca II, 182
Scholey, Rebecca II, 257
Scholey, Rebeckah II, 182
Scholey, Robert II, 255
Scholey, Robert II, 257
Scholey, Samuel II, 182
Scholey, Sarah II, 182
Scholey, Sarah II, 248
Scholey, Sarah II, 257
Scholey, Susannah II, 182
Scholey, Susannah II, 244
Scholey, Susannah II, 257
Scholey, Thomas II, 182
Scholey, Thomas II, 248
Scholey, Thomas II, 257
Scholfield, ??? VI, 726
Scholfield, Aaron VI, 697
Scholfield, Abigail IV, 272
Scholfield, Abigail IV, 273
Scholfield, Abigail IV, 281
Scholfield, Abigail IV, 430
Scholfield, Abigail IV, 434
Scholfield, Alexandria VI, 442
Scholfield, Andrew IV, 434
Scholfield, Andrew IV, 473
Scholfield, Andrew IV, 496
Scholfield, Andrew IV, 1183
Scholfield, Andrew VI, 442
Scholfield, Andrew VI, 555
Scholfield, Andrew VI, 775
Scholfield, Andrew VI, 776
Scholfield, Ann VI, 401
Scholfield, Ann VI, 441
Scholfield, Ann VI, 442
Scholfield, Ann VI, 462
Scholfield, Ann VI, 538
Scholfield, Ann VI, 555
Scholfield, Ann VI, 697
Scholfield, Ann VI, 710
Scholfield, Ann VI, 711
Scholfield, Ann VI, 713
Scholfield, Ann VI, 776
Scholfield, Ann N. VI, 442
Scholfield, Ann, Jr. VI, 776
Scholfield, Ann, Sr. VI, 441
Scholfield, Anna IV, 434
Scholfield, Anna IV, 439
Scholfield, Anne VI, 403
Scholfield, Anne VI, 441
Scholfield, Aron VI, 697
Scholfield, Belinda H. IV, 1138
Scholfield, Benjamin VI, 555
Scholfield, Benjamin VI, 697
Scholfield, Catherine VI, 441
Scholfield, Cidney IV, 434
Scholfield, Clark IV, 314
Scholfield, David IV, 108
Scholfield, David IV, 273
Scholfield, David IV, 314
Scholfield, David IV, 697
Scholfield, David IV, 758
Scholfield, David VI, 555
Scholfield, David VI, 697
Scholfield, David B. VI, 776
Scholfield, Edith IV, 272
Scholfield, Edith IV, 434
Scholfield, Edith IV, 441
Scholfield, Edith IV, 455
Scholfield, Edith IV, 496
Scholfield, Edith VI, 475
Scholfield, Edith VI, 555
Scholfield, Edith VI, 557
Scholfield, Edith VI, 764
Scholfield, Edith VI, 776
Scholfield, Eleanor VI, 558
Scholfield, Eleanor VI, 733
Scholfield, Eleanor VI, 776
Scholfield, Eleanor VI, 784
Scholfield, Elizabeth VI, 403
Scholfield, Elizabeth VI, 441
Scholfield, Elizabeth VI, 442
Scholfield, Elizabeth VI, 555
Scholfield, Elizabeth VI, 775
Scholfield, Elizabeth VI, 776
Scholfield, Elizabeth W. IV, 758
Scholfield, Enoch VI, 555
Scholfield, Enoch VI, 697
Scholfield, Franklin IV, 434
Scholfield, Frederick IV, 434
Scholfield, George Clark IV, 273
Scholfield, Hannah R. VI, 667
Scholfield, Hannah R. VI, 702
Scholfield, Hannah Russell VI, 755
Scholfield, Hannah Russell VI, 775

Scholfield, Hannah Russell VI, 776
Scholfield, Hugh Clark IV, 758
Scholfield, Isaac K. II, 644
Scholfield, Isaac Knight II, 644
Scholfield, Isaachar IV, 434
Scholfield, Isaachar IV, 1183
Scholfield, Isachar IV, 272
Scholfield, Isachar VI, 555
Scholfield, Isachar VI, 764
Scholfield, Isachar VI, 776
Scholfield, Isacher VI, 776
Scholfield, Issachar IV, 434
Scholfield, Issachar IV, 441
Scholfield, Issachar IV, 455
Scholfield, Issachar IV, 496
Scholfield, Issachar IV, 1183
Scholfield, J. T. IV, 281
Scholfield, James IV, 434
Scholfield, Jane VI, 442
Scholfield, Jane VI, 555
Scholfield, Jane VI, 697
Scholfield, John II, 1025
Scholfield, John IV, 434
Scholfield, John IV, 548
Scholfield, John IV, 1183
Scholfield, John VI, 441
Scholfield, John VI, 555
Scholfield, John VI, 776
Scholfield, John G. IV, 548
Scholfield, Jonathan IV, 430
Scholfield, Jonathan IV, 434
Scholfield, Jonathan VI, 475
Scholfield, Jonathan VI, 557
Scholfield, Jonathan VI, 558
Scholfield, Jonathan VI, 727
Scholfield, Jonathan VI, 733
Scholfield, Jonathan VI, 776
Scholfield, Jonathan VI, 784
Scholfield, Jonathan T. IV, 272
Scholfield, Jonathan T. IV, 273
Scholfield, Jonathan T. IV, 434
Scholfield, Joseph IV, 314
Scholfield, Joseph IV, 434
Scholfield, Joseph IV, 758
Scholfield, Joseph VI, 442
Scholfield, Joseph VI, 755
Scholfield, Joseph VI, 775
Scholfield, Joseph VI, 776
Scholfield, Joseph Clark IV, 273
Scholfield, Joseph Clark IV, 758
Scholfield, Joseph L. VI, 775
Scholfield, Joseph L. VI, 776
Scholfield, Joseph L., Jr. VI, 776
Scholfield, Joseph N. VI, 441
Scholfield, Joshua IV, 272
Scholfield, Joshua IV, 758
Scholfield, Lewis VI, 442
Scholfield, Lewis VI, 776
Scholfield, Lewis N. VI, 442
Scholfield, Lydia IV, 724
Scholfield, Lydia IV, 758
Scholfield, Mahlon VI, 401
Scholfield, Mahlon VI, 403
Scholfield, Mahlon VI, 441
Scholfield, Mahlon VI, 442
Scholfield, Mahlon VI, 462
Scholfield, Mahlon VI, 538
Scholfield, Mahlon VI, 555
Scholfield, Mahlon VI, 727
Scholfield, Mahlon VI, 776
Scholfield, Margaret IV, 434
Scholfield, Margaret IV, 758
Scholfield, Margaret IV, 776
Scholfield, Margaret IV, 1183
Scholfield, Margaret A. VI, 776
Scholfield, Margaret Ann IV, 272
Scholfield, Margaret Ann IV, 314
Scholfield, Margaret Ann IV, 758
Scholfield, Maria Pope VI, 776
Scholfield, Mariah IV, 434
Scholfield, Martha IV, 434
Scholfield, Martha IV, 455
Scholfield, Martha IV, 548
Scholfield, Martha IV, 557
Scholfield, Mary IV, 434
Scholfield, Mary IV, 758
Scholfield, Mary VI, 755
Scholfield, Mary VI, 775
Scholfield, Mary VI, 776
Scholfield, Mary Eliza VI, 776
Scholfield, Phebe Allen VI, 776
Scholfield, Rachel IV, 434
Scholfield, Rachel IV, 441
Scholfield, Rachel IV, 473
Scholfield, Rachel IV, 496
Scholfield, Rachel IV, 548
Scholfield, Rachel IV, 593
Scholfield, Rachel IV, 758
Scholfield, Rachel IV, 1183
Scholfield, Rachel VI, 441
Scholfield, Rachel VI, 442
Scholfield, Rachel VI, 697
Scholfield, Rachel VI, 776
Scholfield, Rachel Ann VI, 776
Scholfield, Rachel G. IV, 434
Scholfield, Rachel J. IV, 496
Scholfield, Rachel N. IV, 593
Scholfield, Rachel N. VI, 401
Scholfield, Rachel N. VI, 441
Scholfield, Rebecca II, 644
Scholfield, Rebecca IV, 273
Scholfield, Rebecca IV, 434
Scholfield, Rebecca IV, 697
Scholfield, Rebecca IV, 758
Scholfield, Rebecca Jane IV, 273
Scholfield, Rebecca Jane IV, 314
Scholfield, Rebecca Jane IV, 758
Scholfield, Rebecca M. IV, 430
Scholfield, Rebecca M. IV, 434
Scholfield, Rebecca, Jr. IV, 758
Scholfield, Robert Marcus IV, 273
Scholfield, Robert Marcus IV, 314
Scholfield, Robert Marcus IV, 758
Scholfield, Samuel II, 644
Scholfield, Samuel IV, 758
Scholfield, Samuel IV, 776
Scholfield, Samuel VI, 475
Scholfield, Samuel VI, 555
Scholfield, Samuel VI, 557
Scholfield, Samuel VI, 697
Scholfield, Samuel Silvester IV, 758
Scholfield, Samuel Sylvester IV, 273
Scholfield, Samuel W. VI, 776
Scholfield, Sarah II, 644
Scholfield, Sarah VI, 555
Scholfield, Sarah VI, 776
Scholfield, Sarah Ann II, 644
Scholfield, Sarah Ann VI, 558
Scholfield, Sarah Ann VI, 776
Scholfield, Sarah Ann VI, 784
Scholfield, Sarah N. VI, 776
Scholfield, Sidney IV, 434
Scholfield, Susanna VI, 776
Scholfield, Susannah VI, 776
Scholfield, Thomas IV, 434
Scholfield, Thomas IV, 1183
Scholfield, Thomas M. IV, 434
Scholfield, Thomas M. VI, 776
Scholfield, Thomas Marshall IV, 434
Scholfield, Thomas Marshall VI, 776
Scholfield, Wd. Rachel VI, 555
Scholfield, William IV, 1183
Scholfield, William VI, 442
Scholfield, William VI, 776
Scholfield, William A. VI, 776
Scholfield, William Davis IV, 273
Scholfield, William Davis IV, 758
Scholfield, William G. IV, 434
Scholfield, William Grubb IV, 434
Scholfield, William Grubb VI, 776
Scholfield, William J. VI, 442
Scholfield, Wm. IV, 758
Scholley, Elizabeth M. VI, 472
School, Nicholas IV, 1337
Schooley, ??? IV, 548
Schooley, ??? IV, 603
Schooley, ??? VI, 348
Schooley, Aaron V, 429
Schooley, Aaron V, 527
Schooley, Aaron VI, 555
Schooley, Aaron VI, 557
Schooley, Aaron VI, 697
Schooley, Abigail II, 262
Schooley, Abigail IV, 548
Schooley, Abigail V, 958
Schooley, Abigail VI, 557
Schooley, Addison IV, 548
Schooley, Agnes IV, 350
Schooley, Agnes IV, 593
Schooley, Agness IV, 409
Schooley, Amos VI, 555
Schooley, Amos VI, 557
Schooley, Amos VI, 697
Schooley, Ann IV, 17
Schooley, Ann IV, 108
Schooley, Ann IV, 548
Schooley, Ann IV, 792
Schooley, Ann V, 118
Schooley, Ann V, 526
Schooley, Ann V, 909
Schooley, Ann V, 929
Schooley, Ann VI, 442
Schooley, Ann VI, 510
Schooley, Ann VI, 531
Schooley, Ann VI, 555
Schooley, Ann VI, 556
Schooley, Ann VI, 557
Schooley, Ann VI, 605
Schooley, Ann VI, 697
Schooley, Ann VI, 701
Schooley, Ann K. V, 929
Schooley, Ann W. V, 929
Schooley, Anna IV, 543
Schooley, Anna IV, 548
Schooley, Anna V, 493
Schooley, Anna V, 527
Schooley, Anna V, 958
Schooley, Anna M. V, 596
Schooley, Anne IV, 548
Schooley, Anne Jane IV, 759
Schooley, Anne Jane IV, 791
Schooley, Archibald IV, 916
Schooley, Asenath IV, 548
Schooley, Asenath V, 527
Schooley, Asenath V, 860
Schooley, Benj. V, 909
Schooley, Benj. V, 929
Schooley, Benjamin I, 792
Schooley, Benjamin IV, 548
Schooley, Benjamin V, 526
Schooley, Benjamin V, 527
Schooley, Benjamin V, 532
Schooley, Benjamin V, 596
Schooley, Benjamin V, 929
Schooley, Betty V, 118
Schooley, Betty VI, 605
Schooley, Catharine V, 917
Schooley, Catharine V, 929
Schooley, Catharine VI, 471
Schooley, Catharine N. V, 929
Schooley, Catherine VI, 556
Schooley, Cecilia V, 118
Schooley, Charles VI, 556
Schooley, Charles S. V, 596
Schooley, Cicily V, 118
Schooley, Cisily V, 958
Schooley, Clare VI, 557
Schooley, Clarkson IV, 273
Schooley, Clarkson IV, 350
Schooley, Clarkson C. IV, 273
Schooley, Daniel VI, 538
Schooley, Daniel VI, 555
Schooley, David IV, 916
Schooley, David V, 494
Schooley, David VI, 555
Schooley, Deborah IV, 57
Schooley, Deborah IV, 759
Schooley, Deborah IV, 769
Schooley, Deborah IV, 793
Schooley, Deborah V, 596
Schooley, Deborah VI, 338
Schooley, Deborah VI, 355
Schooley, Deborah VI, 555
Schooley, Deborah L. V, 498
Schooley, Deborah L. V, 527
Schooley, Deborah L. V, 574
Schooley, Deborah L. V, 596
Schooley, Dillworth IV, 990
Schooley, Dilworth IV, 793
Schooley, Dilworth IV, 990
Schooley, Dorothy IV, 108
Schooley, Dorothy IV, 273
Schooley, Dorothy VI, 555
Schooley, Ebenezer W. IV, 548
Schooley, Effie VI, 557
Schooley, Eli L. VI, 555
Schooley, Eli L. VI, 557
Schooley, Elijah VI, 555
Schooley, Elisabeth II, 257
Schooley, Elisha IV, 57
Schooley, Elisha IV, 273
Schooley, Elisha IV, 610
Schooley, Elisha IV, 655
Schooley, Elisha IV, 659
Schooley, Elisha IV, 667
Schooley, Elisha IV, 722
Schooley, Elisha IV, 759
Schooley, Elisha IV, 769
Schooley, Elisha IV, 793
Schooley, Elisha VI, 338
Schooley, Elisha VI, 355
Schooley, Elisha VI, 508
Schooley, Elisha VI, 555
Schooley, Elisha, Jr. IV, 793
Schooley, Eliza IV, 990
Schooley, Eliza VI, 556
Schooley, Eliza Ann VI, 549
Schooley, Eliza Ann VI, 555
Schooley, Eliza Ann VI, 556
Schooley, Eliza M. VI, 556
Schooley, Elizabeth I, 791
Schooley, Elizabeth I, 792
Schooley, Elizabeth I, 836
Schooley, Elizabeth I, 1012
Schooley, Elizabeth IV, 57
Schooley, Elizabeth IV, 750
Schooley, Elizabeth IV, 759
Schooley, Elizabeth V, 118
Schooley, Elizabeth V, 276
Schooley, Elizabeth V, 282
Schooley, Elizabeth V, 389
Schooley, Elizabeth V, 429
Schooley, Elizabeth V, 484
Schooley, Elizabeth V, 493
Schooley, Elizabeth V, 494
Schooley, Elizabeth V, 527
Schooley, Elizabeth V, 909
Schooley, Elizabeth V, 929
Schooley, Elizabeth V, 958
Schooley, Elizabeth V, 960
Schooley, Elizabeth VI, 355
Schooley, Elizabeth VI, 471
Schooley, Elizabeth VI, 472
Schooley, Elizabeth VI, 475
Schooley, Elizabeth VI, 488
Schooley, Elizabeth VI, 510
Schooley, Elizabeth VI, 512
Schooley, Elizabeth VI, 535
Schooley, Elizabeth VI, 549
Schooley, Elizabeth VI, 555
Schooley, Elizabeth VI, 556
Schooley, Elizabeth VI, 583
Schooley, Elizabeth VI, 622
Schooley, Elizabeth VI, 697
Schooley, Elizabeth C. V, 596
Schooley, Elizabeth H. V, 909
Schooley, Elizabeth Jane IV, 1183
Schooley, Elizabeth Mosher IV, 1183
Schooley, Elizabeth, Jr. VI, 555
Schooley, Elliott C. VI, 557
Schooley, Elmer VI, 557
Schooley, Elmer E. V, 596
Schooley, Emeline V, 958
Schooley, Emeline V, 960
Schooley, Emily IV, 654
Schooley, Emily IV, 793
Schooley, Emily IV, 933
Schooley, Emily IV, 990
Schooley, Emily VI, 555
Schooley, Emily VI, 556
Schooley, Emley IV, 655
Schooley, Emma III, 107
Schooley, Emma III, 180
Schooley, Emma IV, 586
Schooley, Emma IV, 593
Schooley, Emma VI, 488
Schooley, Emma VI, 514
Schooley, Emma VI, 524
Schooley, Emma VI, 534
Schooley, Emma VI, 555
Schooley, Emma VI, 556
Schooley, Emma VI, 565
Schooley, Enoch VI, 371
Schooley, Enoch VI, 442
Schooley, Enoch VI, 477
Schooley, Ephraim VI, 476
Schooley, Ephraim VI, 538
Schooley, Ephraim VI, 556
Schooley, Ephraim VI, 557
Schooley, Ephraim VI, 567
Schooley, Ephraim VI, 624
Schooley, Ephraim VI, 697
Schooley, Esther IV, 548
Schooley, Esther VI, 442
Schooley, Esther VI, 475
Schooley, Esther VI, 477
Schooley, Esther VI, 524
Schooley, Esther VI, 538
Schooley, Esther VI, 555
Schooley, Esther VI, 556
Schooley, Esther VI, 622
Schooley, Esther VI, 697
Schooley, Esther S. IV, 548
Schooley, Ezra V, 527
Schooley, Frances VI, 557
Schooley, Francina IV, 514
Schooley, Frank Wilber V, 596
Schooley, Franklin Edward VI, 557
Schooley, Gabriel I, 792
Schooley, Geo. IV, 548
Schooley, George W. IV, 548
Schooley, Hannah IV, 273
Schooley, Hannah IV, 700
Schooley, Hannah IV, 754
Schooley, Hannah IV, 759
Schooley, Hannah IV, 842
Schooley, Hannah IV, 909
Schooley, Hannah IV, 916
Schooley, Hannah V, 429
Schooley, Hannah V, 432
Schooley, Hannah V, 494
Schooley, Hannah V, 527
Schooley, Hannah V, 860
Schooley, Hannah V, 948
Schooley, Hannah V, 958
Schooley, Hannah VI, 475
Schooley, Hannah VI, 555
Schooley, Hannah VI, 556
Schooley, Hannah VI, 557
Schooley, Hannah VI, 697
Schooley, Hannah VI, 698
Schooley, Hannah R. IV, 759
Schooley, Henry IV, 273
Schooley, Henry IV, 759
Schooley, Henry IV, 842
Schooley, Henry IV, 916
Schooley, Henry VI, 556
Schooley, Henry VI, 557
Schooley, Henry VI, 697
Schooley, Henry B. IV, 793
Schooley, Henry M. VI, 556
Schooley, Henry Moore VI, 557
Schooley, Hervy IV, 916
Schooley, Honor IV, 586
Schooley, Horace VI, 556
Schooley, Horace P. VI, 557
Schooley, Ira V, 527
Schooley, Irene VI, 557
Schooley, Isaac IV, 57
Schooley, Isaac IV, 167
Schooley, Isaac IV, 350
Schooley, Isaac IV, 562
Schooley, Isaac IV, 1183
Schooley, Isaac V, 498
Schooley, Isaac V, 526
Schooley, Isaac V, 527
Schooley, Isaac V, 574
Schooley, Isaac V, 596
Schooley, Isaac V, 860
Schooley, Isaac VI, 442
Schooley, Isaac VI, 557
Schooley, Isaac VI, 697
Schooley, Isaac VI, 698
Schooley, Isaac VI, 701
Schooley, Isaac E. IV, 548
Schooley, Isaac E. IV, 1222
Schooley, Isaac Everett IV, 548
Schooley, Isabel II, 253
Schooley, Israel IV, 57
Schooley, Israel IV, 265
Schooley, Israel IV, 273
Schooley, Israel IV, 654
Schooley, Israel IV, 655
Schooley, Israel IV, 752
Schooley, Israel IV, 759
Schooley, Israel IV, 793
Schooley, Israel IV, 990
Schooley, Israel V, 118
Schooley, Israel VI, 355
Schooley, Israel VI, 555
Schooley, Israel VI, 605
Schooley, Israel M. IV, 655
Schooley, James I, 791
Schooley, James I, 836
Schooley, James I, 1007
Schooley, James I, 1012
Schooley, James IV, 654
Schooley, James IV, 655
Schooley, James IV, 740
Schooley, James IV, 759
Schooley, James IV, 793
Schooley, James IV, 978
Schooley, James IV, 990
Schooley, James V, 929
Schooley, James VI, 556
Schooley, James R. V, 929
Schooley, James Thomas VI, 556
Schooley, Jemima IV, 314
Schooley, Jesse V, 494
Schooley, Joel V, 494
Schooley, Joel V, 958
Schooley, Joel VI, 555
Schooley, John I, 792
Schooley, John I, 836
Schooley, John IV, 57
Schooley, John IV, 610
Schooley, John IV, 667
Schooley, John IV, 759
Schooley, John IV, 792
Schooley, John IV, 842
Schooley, John IV, 916
Schooley, John V, 118
Schooley, John V, 494
Schooley, John V, 507
Schooley, John V, 526
Schooley, John V, 527
Schooley, John V, 596
Schooley, John V, 860
Schooley, John VI, 355
Schooley, John VI, 471
Schooley, John VI, 488
Schooley, John VI, 499
Schooley, John VI, 502
Schooley, John VI, 508
Schooley, John VI, 512
Schooley, John VI, 513
Schooley, John VI, 524

ey, John VI, 555
ey, John VI, 556
ey, John VI, 605
ey, John VI, 697
ey, John, Jr. VI, 442
ey, John, Jr. VI, 472
ey, John, Jr. VI, 474
ey, John, Jr. VI, 510
ey, John, Jr. VI, 555
ey, John, Jr. VI, 556
ey, Jonas P. VI, 471
ey, Jonas P. VI, 555
ey, Jonas P. VI, 556
ey, Jonathan II, 257
ey, Jonathan VI, 556
ey, Joseph VI, 538
ey, Joseph Ephraim
, 556
ey, Joseph Ephraim
, 557
ey, Kate VI, 556
ey, Lambert V, 958
ey, Lambert M. VI, 557
ey, Leah I, 791
ey, Leah I, 834
ey, Leah I, 836
ey, Leah IV, 548
ey, Leah V, 526
ey, Leah V, 527
ey, Leah V, 542
ey, Lewis IV, 916
ey, Lindley IV, 350
ey, Lucinda V, 527
ey, Lucinda V, 532
ey, Lydia IV, 740
ey, Lydia IV, 793
ey, Lydia Ann V, 527
ey, Lydia Ann V, 958
ey, Lydia Ann V, 961
ey, Mahala IV, 548
ey, Mahlon IV, 548
ey, Mahlon IV, 586
ey, Mahlon V, 118
ey, Mahlon V, 958
ey, Mahlon VI, 442
ey, Mahlon VI, 475
ey, Mahlon VI, 549
ey, Mahlon VI, 556
ey, Mahlon VI, 557
ey, Mahlon VI, 622
ey, Mahlon VI, 697
ey, Margaret I, 791
ey, Margaret I, 813
ey, Margaret I, 836
ey, Margaret IV, 220
ey, Margaret IV, 273
ey, Margaret IV, 842
ey, Margaret IV, 916
ey, Margarett V, 526
ey, Margret I, 836
ey, Mariam V, 955
ey, Mariam V, 958
ey, Mariana VI, 556
ey, Marianna VI, 478
ey, Marianna VI, 557
ey, Marianna VI, 734
ey, Marianna VI, 769
ey, Marianna VI, 776
ey, Marshall V, 596
ey, Mary II, 257
ey, Mary IV, 57
ey, Mary IV, 548
ey, Mary IV, 654
ey, Mary IV, 659
ey, Mary IV, 759
ey, Mary V, 417
ey, Mary V, 429
ey, Mary V, 527
ey, Mary V, 530
ey, Mary V, 929
ey, Mary V, 958
ey, Mary VI, 338
ey, Mary VI, 355
ey, Mary VI, 508
ey, Mary VI, 513
ey, Mary VI, 524
ey, Mary VI, 556
ey, Mary Catharine VI, 583
ey, Mary Catherine VI, 556
ey, Mary D. IV, 548
ey, Mary E. IV, 409
ey, Mary E. IV, 434
ey, Mary E. VI, 556
ey, Mary Ellen V, 955
ey, Mary Ellen V, 958
ey, Mary Esther VI, 476
ey, Mary Esther VI, 555
ey, Mary Esther VI, 556
ey, Mary Esther VI, 624
ey, Mary Esther VI, 697
ey, Matilda IV, 759
Schooley, Matilda IV, 792
Schooley, Matilda V, 929
Schooley, Milton VI, 471
Schooley, Milton VI, 556
Schooley, Miriam V, 389
Schooley, Miriam V, 429
Schooley, Miriam V, 527
Schooley, Miriam A. V, 958
Schooley, Miriam A. VI, 557
Schooley, Nancy IV, 350
Schooley, Nancy IV, 543
Schooley, Nancy IV, 548
Schooley, Nancy V, 527
Schooley, Nancy VI, 697
Schooley, Narcissa L. VI, 555
Schooley, Nathan I, 792
Schooley, Nathan V, 417
Schooley, Nathan V, 527
Schooley, Nathan V, 530
Schooley, Nathan V, 596
Schooley, Nelson V, 596
Schooley, Obed IV, 916
Schooley, Omri V, 484
Schooley, Omri V, 527
Schooley, Omry V, 527
Schooley, Paul IV, 548
Schooley, Peter IV, 548
Schooley, Phebe IV, 548
Schooley, Phebe IV, 654
Schooley, Phebe IV, 667
Schooley, Phebe IV, 759
Schooley, Phebe IV, 792
Schooley, Phebe V, 507
Schooley, Phebe V, 527
Schooley, Phebe VI, 469
Schooley, Phebe VI, 537
Schooley, Phebe VI, 538
Schooley, Phebe VI, 556
Schooley, Phebe P. VI, 556
Schooley, Pheby IV, 610
Schooley, Phineas IV, 350
Schooley, Phineas IV, 548
Schooley, Phineas VI, 697
Schooley, Phinehas IV, 562
Schooley, Rachel IV, 57
Schooley, Rachel IV, 273
Schooley, Rachel IV, 610
Schooley, Rachel IV, 654
Schooley, Rachel IV, 655
Schooley, Rachel IV, 659
Schooley, Rachel IV, 667
Schooley, Rachel IV, 722
Schooley, Rachel IV, 740
Schooley, Rachel IV, 759
Schooley, Rachel IV, 769
Schooley, Rachel IV, 793
Schooley, Rachel IV, 823
Schooley, Rachel IV, 842
Schooley, Rachel IV, 916
Schooley, Rachel V, 493
Schooley, Rachel V, 526
Schooley, Rachel V, 527
Schooley, Rachel V, 952
Schooley, Rachel V, 958
Schooley, Rachel VI, 338
Schooley, Rachel VI, 355
Schooley, Rachel VI, 508
Schooley, Rachel VI, 555
Schooley, Rachel Louisa VI, 478
Schooley, Rachel Louisa VI, 555
Schooley, Rachel Louisa VI, 556
Schooley, Rachel Louisa VI, 557
Schooley, Rachel Louisa VI, 566
Schooley, Rachel Louisa VI, 567
Schooley, Rachel Louise VI, 734
Schooley, Rachel Louise VI, 776
Schooley, Rachel T. IV, 548
Schooley, Raymond L. VI, 556
Schooley, Rebecca I, 1012
Schooley, Rebecca II, 257
Schooley, Rebecca II, 277
Schooley, Rebecca IV, 548
Schooley, Rebecca IV, 655
Schooley, Rebecca IV, 978
Schooley, Rebecca IV, 990
Schooley, Rebecca V, 527
Schooley, Rebecca V, 596
Schooley, Rebecca V, 925
Schooley, Rebecca V, 929
Schooley, Rebecca Ann V, 929
Schooley, Rebecca Jane V, 527
Schooley, Rebeccah IV, 654
Schooley, Reuben IV, 759
Schooley, Reuben IV, 792
Schooley, Reuben IV, 916
Schooley, Reuben VI, 442
Schooley, Reuben VI, 475
Schooley, Reuben VI, 477
Schooley, Reuben VI, 524
Schooley, Reuben VI, 538
Schooley, Reuben VI, 555
Schooley, Reuben VI, 556
Schooley, Reuben VI, 557
Schooley, Reuben VI, 622
Schooley, Reuben VI, 697
Schooley, Reuben VI, 725
Schooley, Reuben E. VI, 478
Schooley, Reuben E. VI, 555
Schooley, Reuben E. VI, 556
Schooley, Reuben E. VI, 557
Schooley, Reuben E. VI, 566
Schooley, Reuben E. VI, 567
Schooley, Reuben E. VI, 734
Schooley, Reuben E. VI, 776
Schooley, Reuben L. VI, 556
Schooley, Rheuben, Jr. VI, 557
Schooley, Rhoda C. V, 494
Schooley, Richard IV, 273
Schooley, Richard IV, 759
Schooley, Richard IV, 842
Schooley, Richard IV, 859
Schooley, Richard VI, 557
Schooley, Richard VI, 697
Schooley, Robert V, 494
Schooley, Robert N. V, 929
Schooley, Robert S. IV, 548
Schooley, Ruth VI, 513
Schooley, Ruth VI, 557
Schooley, Ruth Alice V, 958
Schooley, Ruth H. V, 949
Schooley, Ruth H. V, 959
Schooley, Ruth Jesse V, 494
Schooley, Sally IV, 562
Schooley, Samuel I, 791
Schooley, Samuel I, 792
Schooley, Samuel I, 836
Schooley, Samuel I, 1012
Schooley, Samuel IV, 350
Schooley, Samuel IV, 548
Schooley, Samuel V, 118
Schooley, Samuel V, 526
Schooley, Samuel V, 527
Schooley, Samuel V, 958
Schooley, Samuel V, 960
Schooley, Samuel VI, 537
Schooley, Samuel VI, 557
Schooley, Samuel VI, 605
Schooley, Samuel VI, 697
Schooley, Samuel I. V, 929
Schooley, Samuel J. V, 929
Schooley, Sarah II, 233
Schooley, Sarah II, 257
Schooley, Sarah II, 1025
Schooley, Sarah IV, 57
Schooley, Sarah IV, 265
Schooley, Sarah IV, 273
Schooley, Sarah IV, 314
Schooley, Sarah IV, 315
Schooley, Sarah IV, 350
Schooley, Sarah IV, 548
Schooley, Sarah IV, 562
Schooley, Sarah IV, 610
Schooley, Sarah IV, 654
Schooley, Sarah IV, 667
Schooley, Sarah IV, 740
Schooley, Sarah IV, 752
Schooley, Sarah IV, 759
Schooley, Sarah IV, 793
Schooley, Sarah IV, 916
Schooley, Sarah IV, 990
Schooley, Sarah IV, 1183
Schooley, Sarah V, 417
Schooley, Sarah V, 512
Schooley, Sarah V, 527
Schooley, Sarah V, 925
Schooley, Sarah V, 929
Schooley, Sarah V, 958
Schooley, Sarah V, 959
Schooley, Sarah VI, 338
Schooley, Sarah VI, 355
Schooley, Sarah VI, 371
Schooley, Sarah VI, 442
Schooley, Sarah VI, 471
Schooley, Sarah VI, 472
Schooley, Sarah VI, 510
Schooley, Sarah VI, 513
Schooley, Sarah VI, 537
Schooley, Sarah VI, 555
Schooley, Sarah VI, 556
Schooley, Sarah VI, 557
Schooley, Sarah VI, 697
Schooley, Sarah VI, 698
Schooley, Sarah VI, 701
Schooley, Sarah Abigail V, 958
Schooley, Sarah Ann VI, 555
Schooley, Sarah C. IV, 273
Schooley, Sarah C. V, 929
Schooley, Sarah Esther V, 950
Schooley, Sarah Esther V, 958
Schooley, Sarah Jane IV, 654
Schooley, Sarah Jane IV, 655
Schooley, Sarah Jane V, 494
Schooley, Sarah Mercer IV, 654
Schooley, Sarah Mercer IV, 655
Schooley, Sarah Stone VI, 556
Schooley, Sarah, Jr. IV, 548
Schooley, Scisly V, 960
Schooley, Sewell V, 494
Schooley, Sicily VI, 605
Schooley, Susan IV, 548
Schooley, Susanna I, 1007
Schooley, Susanna I, 1012
Schooley, Susannah V, 276
Schooley, Susannah V, 527
Schooley, Tacey VI, 538
Schooley, Tacey VI, 555
Schooley, Tacey VI, 557
Schooley, Tacey VI, 567
Schooley, Tacey Ann VI, 555
Schooley, Tacy VI, 442
Schooley, Tacy VI, 476
Schooley, Tacy VI, 556
Schooley, Tacy VI, 624
Schooley, Tacy VI, 697
Schooley, Thomas V, 526
Schooley, Thomas V, 527
Schooley, Unice V, 527
Schooley, Virginia M. V, 958
Schooley, Virginia M. VI, 557
Schooley, William I, 1012
Schooley, William IV, 57
Schooley, William IV, 108
Schooley, William IV, 350
Schooley, William IV, 548
Schooley, William IV, 593
Schooley, William IV, 759
Schooley, William V, 118
Schooley, William V, 276
Schooley, William V, 527
Schooley, William VI, 355
Schooley, William VI, 442
Schooley, William VI, 475
Schooley, William VI, 555
Schooley, William VI, 557
Schooley, William VI, 605
Schooley, William VI, 698
Schooley, William VI, 701
Schooley, William H. V, 527
Schooley, William H. VI, 556
Schooley, William H. VI, 557
Schooley, William, Jr. VI, 557
Schooley, William, Jr. VI, 697
Schooley, Wm. IV, 273
Schooley, Wm. IV, 409
Schooley, Wm. IV, 754
Schooley, Wm. IV, 759
Schooley, Wm. IV, 792
Schooley, Wm. VI, 510
Schooley, Wm. VI, 531
Schooley, Wm. VI, 556
Schooley, Wm. VI, 697
Schooley, Wm., Jr. VI, 556
Schooley, Wm., Jr. VI, 698
Schoolfied, Samuel VI, 811
Schoolfield, Aaron VI, 832
Schoolfield, Ann VI, 338
Schoolfield, Ann VI, 442
Schoolfield, Ann VI, 852
Schoolfield, B. VI, 852
Schoolfield, Benjamin VI, 338
Schoolfield, Benjamin VI, 852
Schoolfield, David IV, 674
Schoolfield, David VI, 855
Schoolfield, Jane VI, 855
Schoolfield, John VI, 338
Schoolfield, John VI, 605
Schoolfield, John VI, 852
Schoolfield, Judith VI, 312
Schoolfield, Judith VI, 338
Schoolfield, Judith VI, 852
Schoolfield, Rachel VI, 338
Schoolfield, Rebecca IV, 674
Schoolfield, Sally VI, 852
Schoolfield, Samuel VI, 338
Schoolfield, Samuel VI, 852
Schoolly, Ann IV, 71
Schooly, Ann VI, 442
Schooly, Asenath V, 527
Schooly, Benjamin I, 1010
Schooly, Benjamin I, 1012
Schooly, Cisily V, 958
Schooly, Deborah VI, 355
Schooly, Elisha IV, 655
Schooly, Elisha IV, 907
Schooly, Elisha VI, 355
Schooly, Elizabeth I, 1009
Schooly, Elizabeth I, 1012
Schooly, Elizabeth V, 958
Schooly, Elizabeth VI, 355
Schooly, Emily IV, 613
Schooly, Emily IV, 654
Schooly, Emley IV, 655
Schooly, Isaac V, 527
Schooly, Isaac V, 596
Schooly, Isaac VI, 442
Schooly, Israel IV, 613
Schooly, Israel VI, 355
Schooly, James I, 1012
Schooly, James IV, 654
Schooly, John I, 1010
Schooly, John I, 1012
Schooly, John V, 527
Schooly, John V, 860
Schooly, John VI, 355
Schooly, Mahlon V, 958
Schooly, Mahlon VI, 442
Schooly, Mary VI, 355
Schooly, Nelson V, 596
Schooly, Rachel I, 996
Schooly, Rachel I, 1010
Schooly, Rachel I, 1012
Schooly, Rachel IV, 655
Schooly, Rachel IV, 907
Schooly, Rachel IV, 916
Schooly, Rachel VI, 355
Schooly, Rebecca I, 1012
Schooly, Rebeccah IV, 654
Schooly, Rebekah I, 1010
Schooly, Rebekah I, 1012
Schooly, Samuel I, 996
Schooly, Samuel I, 1010
Schooly, Samuel I, 1012
Schooly, Samuel V, 958
Schooly, Sarah II, 1025
Schooly, Sarah IV, 613
Schooly, Sarah VI, 355
Schooly, Sarah Mercer IV, 655
Schooly, Susanna I, 1010
Schooly, Susanna I, 1012
Schooly, Susannah V, 260
Schooly, Susannah V, 276
Schooly, Susannah V, 527
Schooly, Tacy VI, 442
Schooly, William I, 1012
Schooly, William VI, 355
Schooly, William VI, 442
Schoonover, Anna V, 708
Schoonover, Cazy V, 708
Schoonover, Cazy V, 715
Schoonover, Earl V, 708
Schoonover, Earl V, 715
Schoonover, Earle V, 708
Schoonover, Effie V, 708
Schoonover, Ida V, 708
Schoonover, Nicholas V, 708
Schopp, Harry IV, 1337
Schopp, Louis IV, 1337
Schorb, Mary IV, 1222
Schorsten, Esther Sarah IV, 1042
Schorsten, Walter IV, 1042
Schotterbeck, Frederick III, 442
Schouten, Charles M. V, 860
Schouten, Sarah J. V, 860
Schrepper, August V, 929
Schrepper, Helmuth V, 929
Schrepper, Hertha V, 929
Schrepper, Louisa V, 929
Schriber, Grace Oldham IV, 1337
Schroeder, Carl H. II, 717
Schroeder, Carl W. II, 764
Schroeder, Caroline IV, 1337
Schroeder, Henrietta II, 717
Schroeder, Martin IV, 1337
Schroeder, Maximillan II, 717
Schropp, Eugenie II, 705
Schroter, Martin IV, 1337
Schryer, Carolyn Virginia II, 313
Schryer, David Richard II, 313
Schryer, Elizabeth II, 313
Schryer, Ella J. II, 313
Schryer, Robert James II, 313
Schryer, William II, 313
Schryer, William Clyde II, 313
Schryer, William Land II, 313
Schryver, George III, 495
Schryver, George III, 496
Schryver, Julia III, 495
Schryver, Julia III, 496
Schuberg, Alice Emma V, 708
Schuberg, Alice Emma V, 721
Schuberg, Benj. F. V, 721
Schuberg, Benjamin F. V, 708
Schuberg, Benjamin Franklin
V, 708
Schuff, Aaron III, 442
Schul, Ella V, 860
Schuley, Sarah VI, 513
Schulkins, Frank IV, 1337
Schull, Rachel VI, 442
Schull, Rachel H. II, 847
Schull, Rachel H. II, 919
Schullin, Dessy IV, 759
Schulte, Celia S. IV, 1337
Schulte, Geo. IV, 1337

Schulte, Walter P. IV, 1337
Schultz, Anne B. Davis II, 818
Schultz, Ellen II, 818
Schultz, Grace V, 708
Schultz, Josephine Lea II, 818
Schultz, Lindley V, 708
Schultz, Lindley V, 709
Schultz, Mary Richards II, 818
Schultz, Walter P. IV, 1337
Schultz, William V, 708
Schultz, Wm. II, 818
Schultz, Wm., Jr. II, 818
Schume, Anna Maria II, 918
Schume, Joseph II, 918
Schume, Lydia II, 918
Schume, Phebe II, 918
Schumo, Thomas II, 644
Schums, Thomas II, 644
Schureman, Mary III, 119
Schureman, Mary III, 156
Schurman, Charles F. III, 280
Schurman, Frederick III, 280
Schurman, Jane III, 280
Schurtz, Christiana II, 1079
Schurtz, Christianna II, 1068
Schurtz, Christianna II, 1079
Schurz, Christiana II, 1079
Schutzer, Mary IV, 1292
Schutzer, Mary A. IV, 1292
Schutzer, Verty IV, 1292
Schuyler, Elizabeth II, 918
Schuyler, Elizabeth G. II, 918
Schuyler, Elizabeth S. II, 918
Schwab, George V, 763
Schwab, Grace V, 763
Schwarstrauber, Helen Miriam V, 860
Schwarstrauber, Loi Maurise V, 860
Schwartz, Annie III, 280
Schwartz, Paul Otto IV, 1337
Schwartz, Pearl IV, 1337
Schwartztrauber, Helen Miriam V, 860
Schwartztrauber, Loi Maurise V, 860
Schwartztrauber, Lois V, 860
Schwartztrauber, Lois V, 861
Schwartztrauber, William F. V, 860
Schweikert, Emma III, 280
Schweikert, William III, 280
Schweikert, Wm. III, 280
Schweitzer, Jennie V, 930
Schwendeman, Anna II, 699
Schwendeman, Anna II, 708
Schwendeman, Anna II, 714
Schwendeman, Anna II, 764
Schwendeman, Anthony II, 699
Schwendeman, Anthony II, 708
Schwendeman, Anthony II, 714
Schwendeman, Anthony II, 764
Schwendeman, Caroline A. II, 714
Schwendeman, Caroline A. II, 764
Schwendeman, Clara H. L. II, 764
Schwendeman, Daniel II, 764
Schwendeman, Florence II, 699
Schwendeman, Florence II, 764
Schwendeman, Herbert II, 764
Schwendeman, Ida II, 764
Schwendeman, Martha II, 708
Schwendeman, Martha II, 764
Schwendeman, Wm. II, 764
Schwenderman, Anna II, 717
Schwenderman, Anna II, 764
Schwenderman, Anthony II, 717
Schwenderman, Anthony II, 764
Schwenderman, Blanche II, 717
Schwenderman, Caroline A. II, 717
Schwenderman, Caroline A. II, 764
Schwenderman, Clara H. L. II, 764
Schwenderman, Daniel II, 717
Schwenderman, Daniel II, 764
Schwenderman, Florence II, 717
Schwenderman, Florence II, 764
Schwenderman, Herbert II, 717
Schwenderman, Herbert II, 764
Schwenderman, Ida II, 717
Schwenderman, Ida II, 764
Schwenderman, Martha II, 764
Schwenderman, Martha A. II, 717
Schwenderman, William II, 717
Schwenderman, Wm. II, 764
Schwibold, Ethel V, 201
Schwicklick, Mrs. Anna IV, 842
Sciamn, Ann II, 417
Sciamn, Hannah II, 417
Sciamn, John II, 417
Sciffington, George III, 280
Scofield, Ann II, 417
Scofield, Belinda S. IV, 1101
Scofield, Ebenezer III, 207
Scofield, Henry II, 417
Scofield, Henry II, 447
Scofield, Jane VI, 398
Scofield, John II, 447
Scofield, John IV, 1101
Scofield, Mary Ellen III, 207
Scofield, Mary Ellen III, 280
Scofield, Mary Emma III, 147
Scofield, Mary Emma III, 242
Scofield, Mary L. III, 207
Scofield, Mary L. III, 280
Scofield, Perley Picket IV, 1076
Scofield, Rebecca III, 280
Scofield, Rebecca IV, 1073
Scofield, Rebecca IV, 1076
Scofield, Richard II, 417
Scofield, William VI, 398
Scoggin, Rebecca II, 38
Scoggins, Rebecca II, 96
Scoggy, Jesse J. V, 708
Scolds, Almira IV, 1262
Scolds, Fannie IV, 1262
Scolds, Sarah IV, 1262
Scolds, Susan B. IV, 1262
Scolefield, Ann II, 1010
Scolefield, Ann II, 1025
Scolefield, John II, 1010
Scolefield, John II, 1025
Scoles, Elmyra IV, 1262
Scoles, Myrtle IV, 1262
Scolfield, Sarah Ann VI, 785
Scooley, John II, 197
Scooley, John II, 257
Scooley, Rebecca II, 197
Scooley, Rebecca II, 257
Scooly, Isabel II, 257
Scoonover, Eleanor VI, 990
Scoonover, Henry VI, 990
Scot, Deborah I, 1050
Scot, Elizabeth II, 240
Scot, Elizabeth II, 257
Scot, Hannah II, 1025
Scot, Hannah II, 1031
Scot, Jane II, 1031
Scot, Jno VI, 36
Scot, Joan VI, 36
Scot, John II, 1025
Scot, John VI, 36
Scot, Joshua I, 275
Scot, Lydia I, 1050
Scot, Margaret II, 257
Scot, Rebecca II, 258
Scot, Robert IV, 350
Scot, Sarah I, 733
Scot, Sarah II, 1025
Scot, William VI, 36
Scote, Hannah I, 117
Scote, John I, 117
Scote, Ruth I, 117
Scote, Stephen I, 117
Scote, Stephen, Sr. I, 117
Scott, ??? VI, 58
Scott, ??? VI, 726
Scott, Abbie Rebecca W. III, 280
Scott, Abigail II, 183
Scott, Abigail II, 258
Scott, Abigail IV, 759
Scott, Abigail IV, 867
Scott, Abigail IV, 882
Scott, Abigail IV, 991
Scott, Abigail V, 118
Scott, Abigail Ann V, 861
Scott, Abigail Ann V, 885
Scott, Abigail Ann V, 886
Scott, Abner II, 257
Scott, Abner V, 118
Scott, Abner S. V, 861
Scott, Abner S. V, 883
Scott, Abner S. V, 885
Scott, Abraham II, 182
Scott, Abraham II, 257
Scott, Abraham II, 275
Scott, Abraham II, 417
Scott, Abraham II, 644
Scott, Abraham II, 1025
Scott, Abraham, Jr. II, 257
Scott, Adaline VI, 990
Scott, Adam I, 275
Scott, Agnes W. VI, 820
Scott, Albert M. IV, 1183
Scott, Alfred IV, 1293
Scott, Alfred V, 464
Scott, Alice I, 614
Scott, Alice C. VI, 74
Scott, Almira L. VI, 990
Scott, Almira L. VI, 1004
Scott, Alvan V, 959
Scott, Alvernon IV, 1222
Scott, Ama IV, 1273
Scott, Amos IV, 132
Scott, Amos IV, 273
Scott, Amos IV, 466
Scott, Amos IV, 504
Scott, Amos V, 118
Scott, Amos V, 861
Scott, Amos V, 885
Scott, Amy IV, 1293
Scott, Amy V, 190
Scott, Amy J. IV, 175
Scott, Amy J. IV, 273
Scott, Ann I, 73
Scott, Ann I, 165
Scott, Ann I, 167
Scott, Ann I, 245
Scott, Ann I, 257
Scott, Ann II, 182
Scott, Ann II, 257
Scott, Ann II, 976
Scott, Ann II, 1025
Scott, Ann IV, 132
Scott, Ann IV, 174
Scott, Ann IV, 224
Scott, Ann IV, 273
Scott, Ann IV, 655
Scott, Ann IV, 759
Scott, Ann IV, 842
Scott, Ann IV, 865
Scott, Ann IV, 882
Scott, Ann IV, 883
Scott, Ann IV, 990
Scott, Ann IV, 991
Scott, Ann V, 118
Scott, Ann V, 527
Scott, Ann V, 976
Scott, Ann V, 979
Scott, Ann VI, 18
Scott, Ann VI, 84
Scott, Ann VI, 85
Scott, Ann VI, 86
Scott, Ann VI, 120
Scott, Ann VI, 140
Scott, Ann VI, 142
Scott, Ann VI, 442
Scott, Ann VI, 550
Scott, Ann VI, 558
Scott, Ann VI, 698
Scott, Ann VI, 721
Scott, Ann VI, 777
Scott, Ann VI, 806
Scott, Ann Eliza V, 527
Scott, Ann Eliza V, 976
Scott, Ann Eliza V, 979
Scott, Ann H. VI, 839
Scott, Ann M. L. VI, 806
Scott, Ann S. VI, 823
Scott, Anna IV, 199
Scott, Anna IV, 273
Scott, Anna IV, 398
Scott, Anna IV, 434
Scott, Anna IV, 435
Scott, Anna Eliza II, 918
Scott, Anna J. IV, 199
Scott, Anna J. IV, 273
Scott, Anna M. VI, 58
Scott, Anne I, 165
Scott, Anne IV, 159
Scott, Anne IV, 435
Scott, Anne VI, 990
Scott, Annie VI, 834
Scott, Aphfera VI, 851
Scott, Asenath II, 825
Scott, Asenath IV, 408
Scott, Asenath IV, 435
Scott, Asenath IV, 1075
Scott, Austin III, 442
Scott, Austin Allan III, 395
Scott, Austin Allan III, 442
Scott, Austin Allan, Jr. III, 442
Scott, Austin Allen III, 30
Scott, Austin Allen III, 280
Scott, Aveline V, 118
Scott, Azar IV, 1183
Scott, Azor IV, 1183
Scott, Balsaroe VI, 801
Scott, Belinda R. VI, 842
Scott, Ben VI, 990
Scott, Beniamin II, 236
Scott, Beniamin II, 257
Scott, Benj. IV, 882
Scott, Benjamin II, 183
Scott, Benjamin IV, 655
Scott, Benjamin IV, 759
Scott, Benjamin IV, 842
Scott, Benjamin IV, 865
Scott, Benjamin IV, 867
Scott, Benjamin IV, 882
Scott, Benjamin IV, 883
Scott, Benjamin IV, 990
Scott, Benjamin VI, 550
Scott, Benjamin VI, 558
Scott, Benjamin VI, 698
Scott, Benjamin VI, 990
Scott, Benjamin S. IV, 435
Scott, Benjamin S. IV, 1293
Scott, Benjamin, Jr. IV, 882
Scott, Benjamin, Jr. IV, 883
Scott, Bethiel II, 182
Scott, Bethual II, 257
Scott, Betsy VI, 852
Scott, Bettie Lillie I, 614
Scott, Beverly VI, 990
Scott, Bowers VI, 85
Scott, Bridget II, 1012
Scott, Bridget II, 1025
Scott, Caleb I, 117
Scott, Caroline VI, 85
Scott, Caroline B. VI, 85
Scott, Carr VI, 62
Scott, Carr VI, 64
Scott, Carr VI, 85
Scott, Carr VI, 86
Scott, Carrie V, 1017
Scott, Carrie VI, 85
Scott, Carrie VI, 86
Scott, Catharine III, 281
Scott, Catherine VI, 18
Scott, Causby VI, 990
Scott, Charity VI, 958
Scott, Charity VI, 990
Scott, Charles II, 1025
Scott, Charles V, 464
Scott, Charles V, 527
Scott, Charles V, 959
Scott, Charles F. IV, 273
Scott, Charles W. VI, 853
Scott, Charlotte VI, 852
Scott, Charlotte H. VI, 990
Scott, Chas. V, 464
Scott, Chas. V, 948
Scott, Chas. V, 959
Scott, Chas. F. W. IV, 273
Scott, Christian VI, 31
Scott, Christian VI, 32
Scott, Christian VI, 45
Scott, Christian VI, 46
Scott, Clarence Delbert IV, 1042
Scott, Cloey Luella IV, 1042
Scott, Clyde Alvin IV, 273
Scott, Comilla VI, 852
Scott, Cosby VI, 903
Scott, Cozbi VI, 915
Scott, Cyrus II, 1025
Scott, Cyrus IV, 435
Scott, Cyrus IV, 1075
Scott, Daniel V, 118
Scott, Daniel V, 861
Scott, Daniel V, 885
Scott, Daniel J. IV, 124
Scott, Daniel J. IV, 132
Scott, David IV, 273
Scott, David IV, 435
Scott, David IV, 1293
Scott, David V, 118
Scott, David V, 763
Scott, David J. IV, 179
Scott, David J. IV, 273
Scott, David James IV, 273
Scott, David Lawrence VI, 18
Scott, David Williams III, 442
Scott, Deborah II, 640
Scott, Deborah II, 645
Scott, Deborah II, 1025
Scott, Deborah IV, 435
Scott, Deborah IV, 1056
Scott, Deborah IV, 1074
Scott, Deborah IV, 1075
Scott, Dorothy II, 644
Scott, Dorothy II, 692
Scott, Doshia VI, 990
Scott, Drury VI, 990
Scott, Earl Hurford IV, 273
Scott, Easter IV, 496
Scott, Edith IV, 273
Scott, Edith C. IV, 273
Scott, Edith L. IV, 273
Scott, Edith Lukens IV, 273
Scott, Edna V, 276
Scott, Edna V, 464
Scott, Edward I, 165
Scott, Edward VI, 852
Scott, Elcy VI, 990
Scott, Eli IV, 655
Scott, Eli IV, 759
Scott, Eli V, 201
Scott, Eli J. V, 763
Scott, Eliphebet I, 318
Scott, Elisabeth I, 73
Scott, Elisabeth I, 136
Scott, Elisabeth I, 144
Scott, Elisabeth I, 165
Scott, Elisabeth I, 169
Scott, Elisabeth I, 200
Scott, Elisabeth IV, 759
Scott, Eliza IV, 759
Scott, Eliza A. VI, 980
Scott, Eliza Ann IV, 621
Scott, Eliza Ann IV, 655
Scott, Eliza Ann IV, 892
Scott, Eliza Ann IV, 894
Scott, Elizabeth I, 70
Scott, Elizabeth I, 101
Scott, Elizabeth I, 117
Scott, Elizabeth I, 257
Scott, Elizabeth I, 275
Scott, Elizabeth I, 276
Scott, Elizabeth II, 182
Scott, Elizabeth II, 183
Scott, Elizabeth II, 257
Scott, Elizabeth II, 269
Scott, Elizabeth II, 551
Scott, Elizabeth II, 644
Scott, Elizabeth II, 1012
Scott, Elizabeth II, 1025
Scott, Elizabeth IV, 159
Scott, Elizabeth IV, 175
Scott, Elizabeth IV, 199
Scott, Elizabeth IV, 273
Scott, Elizabeth IV, 312
Scott, Elizabeth IV, 314
Scott, Elizabeth IV, 398
Scott, Elizabeth IV, 434
Scott, Elizabeth IV, 435
Scott, Elizabeth IV, 511
Scott, Elizabeth IV, 548
Scott, Elizabeth IV, 655
Scott, Elizabeth IV, 759
Scott, Elizabeth IV, 842
Scott, Elizabeth IV, 991
Scott, Elizabeth IV, 1068
Scott, Elizabeth IV, 1075
Scott, Elizabeth IV, 1293
Scott, Elizabeth V, 118
Scott, Elizabeth V, 464
Scott, Elizabeth V, 959
Scott, Elizabeth VI, 27
Scott, Elizabeth VI, 30
Scott, Elizabeth VI, 36
Scott, Elizabeth VI, 37
Scott, Elizabeth VI, 46
Scott, Elizabeth VI, 86
Scott, Elizabeth VI, 87
Scott, Elizabeth VI, 442
Scott, Elizabeth VI, 553
Scott, Elizabeth VI, 558
Scott, Elizabeth VI, 570
Scott, Elizabeth VI, 583
Scott, Elizabeth VI, 698
Scott, Elizabeth VI, 721
Scott, Elizabeth VI, 722
Scott, Elizabeth VI, 765
Scott, Elizabeth VI, 804
Scott, Elizabeth VI, 809
Scott, Elizabeth VI, 852
Scott, Elizabeth VI, 853
Scott, Elizabeth VI, 930
Scott, Elizabeth Ann IV, 230
Scott, Elizabeth Ann IV, 273
Scott, Elizabeth Cowan VI, 9
Scott, Elizabeth E. IV, 273
Scott, Elizabeth M. V, 952
Scott, Elizabeth M. V, 959
Scott, Elizabeth R. VI, 897
Scott, Elizabeth R. VI, 990
Scott, Elizabeth W. IV, 435
Scott, Elizabeth Whiteside II, 787
Scott, Elizabeth, VI, 558
Scott, Elizabeth, Jr. IV, 435
Scott, Ella V, 276
Scott, Ella V, 763
Scott, Ella Louisa IV, 1074
Scott, Ella Louisa IV, 1075
Scott, Ella R. V, 763
Scott, Ellen VI, 53
Scott, Ellen VI, 85
Scott, Ellen VI, 86
Scott, Ellen VI, 91
Scott, Ellen J. VI, 86
Scott, Ellie V, 464
Scott, Elnora IV, 1183
Scott, Emily VI, 996
Scott, Emily Ann IV, 1074
Scott, Emily Ann IV, 1075
Scott, Emily W. VI, 802
Scott, Emma IV, 263
Scott, Emma IV, 273

Emma E. VI, 834
Enoch IV, 273
Enoch IV, 435
Enoch IV, 1273
Enoch B. V, 930
Enoch M. IV, 435
Enoch M. IV, 1293
Estel V, 276
Estel V, 464
Estell V, 464
Esther IV, 496
Esther IV, 504
Esther IV, 1293
Esther V, 882
Esther V, 951
Esther V, 959
Esther VI, 742
Esther VI, 743
Esther VI, 778
Esther A. VI, 742
Esther E. V, 959
Esther Griffith IV, 273
Esther H. V, 882
Esther H. V, 885
Esther H. VI, 742
Esther H. VI, 776
Esther W. V, 883
Esther W. V, 885
Eva L. VI, 86
Evalina Virginia VI, 85
Evaline IV, 435
Evaline IV, 1293
Eveline V, 90
Eveline V, 118
Evelyn V, 118
Exira V, 1017
Exum I, 245
Exum I, 257
Exum VI, 168
Fannie VI, 864
Fanny IV, 1183
Frances IV, 864
Frances IV, 883
Frances W. VI, 852
Francis W. VI, 844
Frank IV, 1183
Frank V, 596
Frankey VI, 990
Franklin IV, 1183
Franklin VI, 85
Franklin VI, 86
Gabriel VI, 802
Gabriel VI, 864
Gabriel J. VI, 986
Geo. IV, 273
George IV, 273
George VI, 107
George VI, 120
George VI, 777
George VI, 909
George VI, 990
George VI, 1012
George E. IV, 273
George G. VI, 85
George G. VI, 86
George W. VI, 60
George W. VI, 85
George W. VI, 86
Gideon Bloxsom V, 959
Grace II, 182
Grover V, 1017
Hanah II, 644
Hannah I, 157
Hannah I, 165
Hannah I, 275
Hannah I Sup 1, 5
Hannah I Sup 1, 6
Hannah I Sup 1, 8
Hannah II, 236
Hannah II, 257
Hannah II, 417
Hannah II, 644
Hannah II, 918
Hannah II, 1025
Hannah IV, 159
Hannah IV, 434
Hannah IV, 435
Hannah IV, 452
Hannah IV, 593
Hannah IV, 842
Hannah IV, 991
Hannah IV, 1183
Hannah V, 527
Hannah V, 959
Hannah VI, 558
Hannah VI, 698
Hannah A. V, 596
Hannah E. II, 918
Hannah H. II, 858
Hannah H. II, 918
Hannah J. IV, 273
Scott, Hannah S. IV, 1183
Scott, Hariet IV, 1042
Scott, Harriett B. VI, 864
Scott, Harrison Newton IV, 273
Scott, Harry N. IV, 273
Scott, Henrietta VI, 852
Scott, Henry I, 200
Scott, Henry I, 418
Scott, Henry II, 1025
Scott, Henry F. I, 200
Scott, Hester IV, 1277
Scott, Hester IV, 1293
Scott, Hiram IV, 759
Scott, Hiram IV, 991
Scott, Horatio VI, 776
Scott, Howard T. V, 885
Scott, Irena V, 708
Scott, Isaac IV, 883
Scott, Isaac IV, 1183
Scott, Isaac VI, 86
Scott, Isaac VI, 558
Scott, Isaac VI, 698
Scott, Isaac VI, 721
Scott, Isaac V. IV, 1183
Scott, Isaacs VI, 86
Scott, Isabel I, 73
Scott, Isabel I, 77
Scott, Isaiah V, 527
Scott, Israel IV, 635
Scott, Israel IV, 655
Scott, Israel IV, 759
Scott, Israel IV, 892
Scott, Israel IV, 893
Scott, Israel VI, 558
Scott, Israel VI, 698
Scott, Isum V, 201
Scott, J. VI, 864
Scott, J. H. IV, 1293
Scott, Jack VI, 843
Scott, Jacob IV, 655
Scott, Jacob IV, 882
Scott, Jacob VI, 467
Scott, Jacob VI, 553
Scott, Jacob VI, 558
Scott, Jacob VI, 570
Scott, Jacob VI, 583
Scott, Jacob VI, 698
Scott, Jacob VI, 722
Scott, Jacob, Jr. VI, 558
Scott, James II, 417
Scott, James V, 190
Scott, James V, 201
Scott, James V, 959
Scott, James VI, 85
Scott, James VI, 86
Scott, James VI, 129
Scott, James VI, 140
Scott, James VI, 852
Scott, James VI, 853
Scott, James VI, 869
Scott, James VI, 870
Scott, James VI, 872
Scott, James VI, 873
Scott, James VI, 878
Scott, James VI, 886
Scott, James VI, 891
Scott, James VI, 892
Scott, James VI, 897
Scott, James VI, 898
Scott, James VI, 900
Scott, James VI, 902
Scott, James VI, 906
Scott, James VI, 909
Scott, James VI, 916
Scott, James VI, 918
Scott, James VI, 919
Scott, James VI, 920
Scott, James VI, 924
Scott, James VI, 926
Scott, James VI, 929
Scott, James VI, 932
Scott, James VI, 933
Scott, James VI, 937
Scott, James VI, 940
Scott, James VI, 942
Scott, James VI, 948
Scott, James VI, 957
Scott, James VI, 964
Scott, James VI, 966
Scott, James VI, 968
Scott, James VI, 972
Scott, James VI, 985
Scott, James VI, 986
Scott, James VI, 990
Scott, James VI, 991
Scott, James VI, 993
Scott, James VI, 1002
Scott, James VI, 1005
Scott, James VI, 1006
Scott, James VI, 1008
Scott, James VI, 1013
Scott, James VI, 1015
Scott, James VI, 1016
Scott, James VI, 1020
Scott, James C. IV, 991
Scott, James Cowgill IV, 991
Scott, James F. I, 614
Scott, James Henry VI, 85
Scott, James Jordan VI, 85
Scott, James Jordan VI, 86
Scott, James P. VI, 990
Scott, James P. VI, 1014
Scott, James T. VI, 958
Scott, James T. VI, 990
Scott, James Tooke VI, 45
Scott, James Tooke VI, 46
Scott, Jane II, 787
Scott, Jane II, 1025
Scott, Jane III, 280
Scott, Jane IV, 643
Scott, Jane IV, 655
Scott, Jane IV, 833
Scott, Jane IV, 842
Scott, Jane IV, 882
Scott, Jane VI, 578
Scott, Jane VI, 883
Scott, Jane P. III, 281
Scott, Janet VI, 833
Scott, Janet VI, 848
Scott, Janie V, 464
Scott, Jas. Thos. III, 280
Scott, Jasent V, 118
Scott, Jason IV, 1293
Scott, Jason V, 118
Scott, Jeanette VI, 85
Scott, Jehu IV, 991
Scott, Jemima I, 117
Scott, Jemima I, 120
Scott, Jemima I, 165
Scott, Jemima I, 169
Scott, Jemima II, 1009
Scott, Jemima II, 1025
Scott, Jemima II, 1031
Scott, Jennie III, 496
Scott, Jesse IV, 159
Scott, Jesse IV, 273
Scott, Jesse IV, 434
Scott, Jesse IV, 435
Scott, Jesse IV, 452
Scott, Jesse IV, 593
Scott, Jesse M. IV, 273
Scott, Jessy VI, 168
Scott, Jessy VI, 174
Scott, Jessy VI, 211
Scott, Jno VI, 36
Scott, Jno. II, 257
Scott, Joan VI, 36
Scott, Joan VI, 37
Scott, Job I, 73
Scott, Job III, 281
Scott, Job IV, 159
Scott, Job IV, 273
Scott, Job IV, 434
Scott, Job IV, 435
Scott, Job IV, 444
Scott, Job IV, 655
Scott, Job IV, 759
Scott, Job IV, 1293
Scott, Job VI, 194
Scott, Job VI, 211
Scott, Joel VI, 873
Scott, Joel VI, 990
Scott, Joeseph I, 70
Scott, John I, 165
Scott, John II, 257
Scott, John II, 559
Scott, John II, 640
Scott, John II, 644
Scott, John II, 1025
Scott, John II, 1033
Scott, John III, 280
Scott, John IV, 175
Scott, John IV, 199
Scott, John IV, 273
Scott, John IV, 312
Scott, John IV, 314
Scott, John IV, 1056
Scott, John IV, 1074
Scott, John IV, 1075
Scott, John V, 201
Scott, John V, 464
Scott, John VI, 27
Scott, John VI, 30
Scott, John VI, 31
Scott, John VI, 36
Scott, John VI, 37
Scott, John VI, 41
Scott, John VI, 207
Scott, John VI, 208
Scott, John VI, 834
Scott, John VI, 842
Scott, John VI, 852
Scott, John VI, 903
Scott, John VI, 990
Scott, John VI, 1020
Scott, John C. VI, 990
Scott, John Fulsham VI, 120
Scott, John Isum V, 201
Scott, John L. V, 527
Scott, John L. V, 976
Scott, John Lawrence V, 979
Scott, John Townsend II, 1025
Scott, John W. III, 281
Scott, John Watts VI, 990
Scott, John, Jr. II, 640
Scott, John, Sr. V, 763
Scott, Jonathan VI, 698
Scott, Joseph I, 1
Scott, Joseph I, 46
Scott, Joseph I, 73
Scott, Joseph I, 117
Scott, Joseph I, 146
Scott, Joseph I, 165
Scott, Joseph I, 167
Scott, Joseph I, 183
Scott, Joseph I, 200
Scott, Joseph II, 257
Scott, Joseph II, 258
Scott, Joseph II, 417
Scott, Joseph II, 644
Scott, Joseph III, 280
Scott, Joseph III, 281
Scott, Joseph III, 286
Scott, Joseph IV, 643
Scott, Joseph IV, 655
Scott, Joseph IV, 759
Scott, Joseph IV, 833
Scott, Joseph IV, 842
Scott, Joseph IV, 859
Scott, Joseph IV, 882
Scott, Joseph IV, 991
Scott, Joseph IV, 1183
Scott, Joseph IV, 1190
Scott, Joseph VI, 60
Scott, Joseph VI, 85
Scott, Joseph VI, 550
Scott, Joseph VI, 558
Scott, Joseph VI, 698
Scott, Joseph VI, 721
Scott, Joseph VI, 816
Scott, Joseph VI, 852
Scott, Joseph VI, 853
Scott, Joseph VI, 990
Scott, Joseph Lewis II, 787
Scott, Joseph M. VI, 18
Scott, Joseph W. VI, 990
Scott, Joseph, Jr. I, 165
Scott, Joseph, Jr. VI, 558
Scott, Joshua I, 1
Scott, Joshua I, 117
Scott, Joshua I, 139
Scott, Joshua I, 165
Scott, Joshua I, 275
Scott, Joshua I, 276
Scott, Joshua IV, 159
Scott, Joshua IV, 273
Scott, Joshua IV, 398
Scott, Joshua IV, 434
Scott, Joshua IV, 435
Scott, Joshua IV, 1273
Scott, Joshua IV, 1293
Scott, Joshua V, 959
Scott, Joshua VI, 933
Scott, Joshua VI, 990
Scott, Joshua, Jr. IV, 1293
Scott, Joshuah I Sup 1, 6
Scott, Judith VI, 864
Scott, Judith VI, 990
Scott, Julia III, 281
Scott, Julia III, 357
Scott, Julia Matilda III, 281
Scott, Julia Matilda III, 357
Scott, Kathren VI, 36
Scott, Kathryn III, 396
Scott, Lamphear H. III, 281
Scott, Lanphear H. III, 357
Scott, Leah II, 182
Scott, Leah II, 257
Scott, Leah II, 275
Scott, Lee Martha IV, 1293
Scott, Lemuel N. IV, 991
Scott, Lemuel Nelson IV, 991
Scott, Lennaus VI, 990
Scott, Leonard L. VI, 74
Scott, Lewis IV, 991
Scott, Lively Susan VI, 844
Scott, Lizzie V, 464
Scott, Lois V, 276
Scott, Louisa V, 527
Scott, Louisa V, 979
Scott, Louisa VI, 85
Scott, Louisa V. VI, 990
Scott, Louise I, 620
Scott, Lucile R. VI, 86
Scott, Lucretia VI, 805
Scott, Lucy V, 885
Scott, Lucy VI, 975
Scott, Lucy VI, 990
Scott, Luther S. V, 763
Scott, Lydia IV, 435
Scott, Lydia IV, 759
Scott, Lydia IV, 842
Scott, Lydia IV, 991
Scott, Lydia IV, 1293
Scott, Lydia V, 78
Scott, Lydia V, 118
Scott, Lydia V, 190
Scott, Lydia V, 276
Scott, Lydia VI, 958
Scott, Lydia A. V, 276
Scott, Lydia A. V, 464
Scott, Lydia Lee IV, 435
Scott, Lydia Lee V, 118
Scott, Mahlon IV, 273
Scott, Mahlon Hough VI, 476
Scott, Mahlon S. IV, 273
Scott, Mahlon S. VI, 776
Scott, Maime C. V, 763
Scott, Maklin S. VI, 793
Scott, Malinda VI, 933
Scott, Malissa Ann VI, 899
Scott, Marabeth V, 860
Scott, Mareb VI, 686
Scott, Mareb VI, 698
Scott, Margaret I, 123
Scott, Margaret II, 183
Scott, Margaret II, 237
Scott, Margaret II, 257
Scott, Margaret IV, 759
Scott, Margaret IV, 991
Scott, Margaret V, 276
Scott, Margaret V, 464
Scott, Margaret VI, 678
Scott, Margaret VI, 698
Scott, Margaret VI, 990
Scott, Margaret Ann VI, 990
Scott, Margaret I. Lewis VI, 18
Scott, Margrett II, 183
Scott, Mariah B. VI, 833
Scott, Marial L. VI, 806
Scott, Marib VI, 558
Scott, Maribah IV, 435
Scott, Maribah IV, 444
Scott, Marietta IV, 1098
Scott, Marietta IV, 1114
Scott, Marry I, 117
Scott, Marsha R. VI, 86
Scott, Martha IV, 435
Scott, Martha IV, 494
Scott, Martha IV, 496
Scott, Martha V, 118
Scott, Martha V, 123
Scott, Martha V, 359
Scott, Martha VI, 62
Scott, Martha VI, 85
Scott, Martha VI, 86
Scott, Martha VI, 558
Scott, Martha VI, 583
Scott, Martha VI, 679
Scott, Martha VI, 686
Scott, Martha VI, 698
Scott, Martha VI, 721
Scott, Martha VI, 722
Scott, Martha VI, 792
Scott, Martha VI, 804
Scott, Martha VI, 852
Scott, Martha VI, 1014
Scott, Martha Ann III, 214
Scott, Martha W. VI, 820
Scott, Martha Williams V, 118
Scott, Mary I, 1
Scott, Mary I, 61
Scott, Mary I, 73
Scott, Mary I, 117
Scott, Mary I, 127
Scott, Mary I, 146
Scott, Mary I, 165
Scott, Mary I, 612
Scott, Mary II, 183
Scott, Mary II, 257
Scott, Mary II, 300
Scott, Mary II, 559
Scott, Mary II, 644
Scott, Mary II, 992
Scott, Mary II, 1025
Scott, Mary III, 281
Scott, Mary IV, 655
Scott, Mary IV, 759
Scott, Mary IV, 893
Scott, Mary IV, 894
Scott, Mary V, 118
Scott, Mary V, 299
Scott, Mary V, 310
Scott, Mary V, 861

Scott, Mary VI, 18
Scott, Mary VI, 64
Scott, Mary VI, 85
Scott, Mary VI, 86
Scott, Mary VI, 404
Scott, Mary VI, 442
Scott, Mary VI, 476
Scott, Mary VI, 558
Scott, Mary VI, 816
Scott, Mary VI, 852
Scott, Mary VI, 915
Scott, Mary VI, 990
Scott, Mary A. VI, 60
Scott, Mary Ann II, 1025
Scott, Mary Ann IV, 435
Scott, Mary Ann IV, 759
Scott, Mary Ann IV, 842
Scott, Mary Ann IV, 882
Scott, Mary Ann IV, 990
Scott, Mary Ann IV, 991
Scott, Mary Ann IV, 1074
Scott, Mary Ann IV, 1075
Scott, Mary Ann IV, 1112
Scott, Mary Ann IV, 1183
Scott, Mary Ann IV, 1190
Scott, Mary Ann V, 882
Scott, Mary Ann V, 885
Scott, Mary Ann VI, 909
Scott, Mary C. VI, 852
Scott, Mary D. IV, 435
Scott, Mary E. IV, 273
Scott, Mary E. VI, 1004
Scott, Mary Elizabeth IV, 273
Scott, Mary M. VI, 476
Scott, Mary M. VI, 511
Scott, Mary M. VI, 777
Scott, Mary Virginia V, 979
Scott, Mary, Jr. V, 861
Scott, Maryann IV, 842
Scott, Maryann IV, 883
Scott, Matthias VI, 852
Scott, Mattie E. VI, 60
Scott, Maude IV, 1293
Scott, Merab VI, 698
Scott, Meredith Dixon VI, 873
Scott, Meribah IV, 435
Scott, Meribah IV, 1293
Scott, Meribah V, 118
Scott, Meribe V, 44
Scott, Meribe V, 118
Scott, Meriby IV, 435
Scott, Merihab IV, 1293
Scott, Minnie V, 464
Scott, Minor II, 1025
Scott, Miriam I, 165
Scott, Mordacai I, 117
Scott, Nancy VI, 852
Scott, Nancy VI, 853
Scott, Nancy VI, 880
Scott, Nancy VI, 903
Scott, Nancy VI, 909
Scott, Nancy VI, 942
Scott, Nancy VI, 990
Scott, Nancy VI, 1012
Scott, Nancy C. VI, 990
Scott, Nancy E. VI, 1020
Scott, Nancy J. VI, 852
Scott, Naomi V, 930
Scott, Oella V, 104
Scott, Oella V, 118
Scott, Ollie B. IV, 1293
Scott, Oma Grace IV, 1293
Scott, Opal V, 677
Scott, Opal V, 708
Scott, Oral V, 276
Scott, Orville V, 643
Scott, Patience II, 182
Scott, Patience II, 183
Scott, Patience II, 257
Scott, Patience II, 258
Scott, Patsey V, 201
Scott, Patsy V, 190
Scott, Patsy V, 201
Scott, Peggy VI, 805
Scott, Penelope I, 37
Scott, Penelope I, 73
Scott, Pennelope I, 73
Scott, Penninah I, 46
Scott, Penninah I, 73
Scott, Pennington IV, 435
Scott, Pennington IV, 593
Scott, Permelia IV, 1183
Scott, Peter VI, 880
Scott, Peter VI, 990
Scott, Phebe IV, 655
Scott, Phebe IV, 759
Scott, Phebe IV, 842
Scott, Phebe IV, 883
Scott, Phebe IV, 891
Scott, Phebe IV, 894
Scott, Phebe IV, 990
Scott, Phebe IV, 991
Scott, Phebe H. IV, 759
Scott, Pheobe IV, 882
Scott, Pickney VI, 844
Scott, Pinkney VI, 801
Scott, Pinkney VI, 805
Scott, Pinkney VI, 842
Scott, Pinkney VI, 852
Scott, Pinkney VI, 865
Scott, Pleasant VI, 937
Scott, Pleasant VI, 1012
Scott, Polly VI, 852
Scott, Polly VI, 990
Scott, Polly VI, 1000
Scott, Priscilla VI, 990
Scott, Prophet IV, 759
Scott, Prophet IV, 991
Scott, Prophet B. IV, 842
Scott, Prophet B. IV, 882
Scott, Prophet B. IV, 883
Scott, Prophet B. IV, 991
Scott, Quincy V, 596
Scott, Rachel II, 918
Scott, Rachel IV, 49
Scott, Rachel IV, 57
Scott, Rachel IV, 466
Scott, Rachel IV, 496
Scott, Rachel IV, 504
Scott, Rachel IV, 991
Scott, Rachel VI, 698
Scott, Rachel B. II, 918
Scott, Rachel T. II, 858
Scott, Rachel T. II, 918
Scott, Rachel Tomlinson II, 792
Scott, Rachel W. IV, 124
Scott, Rachel W. IV, 132
Scott, Rebecca I, 117
Scott, Rebecca II, 183
Scott, Rebecca II, 258
Scott, Rebecca IV, 273
Scott, Rebecca IV, 434
Scott, Rebecca IV, 435
Scott, Rebecca IV, 477
Scott, Rebecca IV, 496
Scott, Rebecca IV, 892
Scott, Rebecca IV, 894
Scott, Rebecca IV, 1273
Scott, Rebecca IV, 1293
Scott, Rebecca V, 763
Scott, Rebecca V, 794
Scott, Rebecca V, 1017
Scott, Rebecca VI, 53
Scott, Rebecca VI, 76
Scott, Rebecca VI, 85
Scott, Rebecca VI, 86
Scott, Rebecca VI, 91
Scott, Rebecca VI, 442
Scott, Rebecca VI, 558
Scott, Rebecca VI, 843
Scott, Rebecca A. VI, 467
Scott, Rebecca A. VI, 558
Scott, Rebecca K. VI, 92
Scott, Rebekah VI, 553
Scott, Rebekah VI, 558
Scott, Rhoda I, 47
Scott, Rhoda I, 73
Scott, Rhoda I, 183
Scott, Rhoda VI, 990
Scott, Rhoda VI, 998
Scott, Ro. W. VI, 868
Scott, Robert II, 1025
Scott, Robert IV, 435
Scott, Robert IV, 1075
Scott, Robert VI, 36
Scott, Robert VI, 118
Scott, Robert VI, 833
Scott, Robert VI, 852
Scott, Robert VI, 893
Scott, Robert VI, 953
Scott, Robert Elwood V, 464
Scott, Robert Lee VI, 85
Scott, Robert Scott VI, 120
Scott, Robina VI, 818
Scott, Rosa V, 464
Scott, Rosa B. IV, 273
Scott, Rosa C. IV, 273
Scott, Rufus Butler VI, 85
Scott, Ruth I, 117
Scott, Ruth I, 140
Scott, Ruth I, 165
Scott, Ruthanna IV, 191
Scott, Ruthanna IV, 273
Scott, Sabilla Ann V, 471
Scott, Sabilla Ann V, 527
Scott, Salley VI, 926
Scott, Sally VI, 842
Scott, Sally VI, 852
Scott, Sally VI, 853
Scott, Sally VI, 990
Scott, Sally VI, 1012
Scott, Saml. B. VI, 990
Scott, Samuel I, 61
Scott, Samuel I, 73
Scott, Samuel I, 165
Scott, Samuel II, 417
Scott, Samuel II, 1025
Scott, Samuel IV, 435
Scott, Samuel IV, 1075
Scott, Samuel V, 885
Scott, Samuel VI, 802
Scott, Samuel VI, 820
Scott, Samuel VI, 834
Scott, Samuel VI, 842
Scott, Samuel VI, 851
Scott, Samuel VI, 942
Scott, Samuel VI, 986
Scott, Samuel VI, 990
Scott, Samuel Jones VI, 18
Scott, Samuel M. VI, 852
Scott, Sarah I, 56
Scott, Sarah I, 73
Scott, Sarah I, 117
Scott, Sarah I, 129
Scott, Sarah I, 146
Scott, Sarah I, 157
Scott, Sarah I, 165
Scott, Sarah I, 196
Scott, Sarah I, 200
Scott, Sarah I, 733
Scott, Sarah I, 836
Scott, Sarah II, 257
Scott, Sarah II, 640
Scott, Sarah II, 1025
Scott, Sarah II, 1027
Scott, Sarah III, 280
Scott, Sarah IV, 179
Scott, Sarah IV, 273
Scott, Sarah IV, 635
Scott, Sarah IV, 655
Scott, Sarah IV, 759
Scott, Sarah IV, 842
Scott, Sarah IV, 867
Scott, Sarah IV, 882
Scott, Sarah IV, 883
Scott, Sarah IV, 892
Scott, Sarah IV, 893
Scott, Sarah IV, 991
Scott, Sarah IV, 1183
Scott, Sarah IV, 1262
Scott, Sarah V, 118
Scott, Sarah V, 190
Scott, Sarah V, 200
Scott, Sarah V, 201
Scott, Sarah V, 860
Scott, Sarah V, 861
Scott, Sarah V, 948
Scott, Sarah V, 959
Scott, Sarah VI, 36
Scott, Sarah VI, 46
Scott, Sarah VI, 86
Scott, Sarah VI, 92
Scott, Sarah VI, 120
Scott, Sarah VI, 207
Scott, Sarah VI, 208
Scott, Sarah VI, 442
Scott, Sarah VI, 550
Scott, Sarah VI, 558
Scott, Sarah VI, 569
Scott, Sarah VI, 570
Scott, Sarah VI, 698
Scott, Sarah VI, 852
Scott, Sarah Ann II, 645
Scott, Sarah Ann IV, 435
Scott, Sarah Ann IV, 496
Scott, Sarah Ann IV, 499
Scott, Sarah Ann IV, 1056
Scott, Sarah Ann IV, 1075
Scott, Sarah E. VI, 60
Scott, Sarah E. VI, 85
Scott, Sarah E. VI, 86
Scott, Sarah G. IV, 273
Scott, Sarah H. IV, 893
Scott, Sarah Jr. IV, 867
Scott, Sarah Jr. IV, 882
Scott, Sarah M. I, 997
Scott, Sarah M. VI, 990
Scott, Sarah T. IV, 1183
Scott, Savana H. VI, 990
Scott, Stanton IV, 273
Scott, Stanton IV, 435
Scott, Stanton IV, 1277
Scott, Stanton IV, 1293
Scott, Stanton V, 951
Scott, Stanton V, 959
Scott, Steaphen I, 275
Scott, Stephen I, 91
Scott, Stephen I, 92
Scott, Stephen I, 101
Scott, Stephen I, 117
Scott, Stephen I, 140
Scott, Stephen I, 165
Scott, Stephen I Sup 1, 5
Scott, Stephen I Sup 1, 6
Scott, Stephen I Sup 1, 8
Scott, Stephen IV, 1183
Scott, Stephen VI, 287
Scott, Stephen VI, 558
Scott, Stephen VI, 569
Scott, Stephen VI, 570
Scott, Stephen E. IV, 1183
Scott, Stephen Elwood IV, 1183
Scott, Susan V, 596
Scott, Susan V, 708
Scott, Susan VI, 848
Scott, Susan M. VI, 1000
Scott, Susanna VI, 967
Scott, Susanna H. VI, 852
Scott, Susannah E. VI, 845
Scott, T. L. V, 276
Scott, T. W. VI, 86
Scott, T. W. VI, 996
Scott, Tabitha I, 161
Scott, Tabitha I, 165
Scott, Tarleton W. VI, 53
Scott, Tarlton VI, 91
Scott, Tempe VI, 990
Scott, Thelma Elizabeth V, 276
Scott, Thomas II, 183
Scott, Thomas II, 257
Scott, Thomas II, 417
Scott, Thomas II, 992
Scott, Thomas II, 1025
Scott, Thomas IV, 435
Scott, Thomas IV, 1075
Scott, Thomas V, 118
Scott, Thomas V, 861
Scott, Thomas VI, 18
Scott, Thomas VI, 120
Scott, Thomas VI, 835
Scott, Thomas VI, 852
Scott, Thomas VI, 990
Scott, Thomas VI, 993
Scott, Thomas Draper VI, 86
Scott, Thomas H. IV, 1042
Scott, Thomas L. V, 276
Scott, Thomas L. V, 464
Scott, Thomas Leron IV, 1042
Scott, Thomas Ricks VI, 86
Scott, Thomas S. V, 464
Scott, Thomas Smith II, 183
Scott, Thomas W. VI, 897
Scott, Thomas W. VI, 990
Scott, Thomas W. VI, 996
Scott, Thomas W. VI, 1014
Scott, Thos. II, 858
Scott, Thos. II, 918
Scott, Thos. J. II, 918
Scott, Thos. T. VI, 821
Scott, Thos. W. VI, 823
Scott, Timothy V, 527
Scott, Timothy V, 959
Scott, Tom. VI, 806
Scott, Ursley Goode VI, 980
Scott, Virginia VI, 823
Scott, Virginia A. VI, 60
Scott, Virginia A. VI, 85
Scott, Virginia A. VI, 86
Scott, Virginia A. VI, 92
Scott, Wally III, 395
Scott, Wally III, 442
Scott, Wally B. III, 280
Scott, Walter IV, 273
Scott, Walter V, 464
Scott, Walter V, 596
Scott, Walter V, 885
Scott, Walter A. IV, 273
Scott, Watson IV, 435
Scott, Watson IV, 593
Scott, Wd. Hanah II, 550
Scott, Wd. Margaret VI, 36
Scott, Widow Sarah I, 165
Scott, Widow Tabitha I, 139
Scott, Widow Tabitha I, 165
Scott, Willey R. VI, 990
Scott, William I, 257
Scott, William IV, 496
Scott, William IV, 655
Scott, William IV, 759
Scott, William IV, 882
Scott, William IV, 1293
Scott, William V, 190
Scott, William V, 201
Scott, William V, 527
Scott, William VI, 31
Scott, William VI, 36
Scott, William VI, 41
Scott, William VI, 46
Scott, William VI, 48
Scott, William VI, 85
Scott, William VI, 86
Scott, William VI, 87
Scott, William VI, 558
Scott, William VI, 559
Scott, William VI, 698
Scott, William VI, 820
Scott, William VI, 823
Scott, William VI, 845
Scott, William VI, 852
Scott, William VI, 864
Scott, William VI, 896
Scott, William VI, 926
Scott, William VI, 967
Scott, William VI, 975
Scott, William VI, 990
Scott, William B. V, 430
Scott, William C. I, 200
Scott, William E. V, 527
Scott, William I. VI, 18
Scott, William J. VI, 140
Scott, William J. VI, 142
Scott, William P. VI, 823
Scott, William R. VI, 990
Scott, William T. VI, 990
Scott, William, Senior VI, 18
Scott, William, Senior VI, 36
Scott, William, Senior VI, 48
Scott, William, Sr. VI, 8
Scott, Wilson VI, 852
Scott, Wm. IV, 867
Scott, Wm. IV, 882
Scott, Wm. V, 959
Scott, Wm. V, 976
Scott, Wm. VI, 37
Scott, Wm. VI, 46
Scott, Wm. VI, 558
Scott, Wm. A. VI, 777
Scott, Wm. E. V, 976
Scott, Wm. Exum V, 979
Scott, Wm. J. V, 979
Scott, Woodson VI, 60
Scott, Woodson VI, 86
Scotte, William VI, 36
Scotten, Ann II, 417
Scotten, Ann II, 645
Scotten, Emma E. IV, 1262
Scotten, Everett E. IV, 1262
Scotten, Jane II, 645
Scotten, John II, 417
Scotten, John II, 645
Scotten, Mary I, 621
Scotten, Priscilla II, 638
Scotten, Priscilla II, 645
Scotten, Robert II, 645
Scotten, Ruth II, 645
Scotten, Sarah II, 645
Scotten, Stephen II, 645
Scotten, Wd. Ruth II, 645
Scotton, Ann II, 645
Scotton, Ann V, 930
Scotton, Jane II, 645
Scotton, John II, 417
Scotton, John II, 645
Scotton, Priscilla II, 645
Scotton, Robert II, 645
Scotton, Ruth II, 645
Scotton, Sarah II, 645
Scotton, Stephen II, 645
Scotton, Wd. Ruth II, 645
Scotts, John, Sr. V, 763
Scovell, Bell IV, 1262
Scovell, Francis IV, 1262
Scradder, Julia Ann IV, 1378
Scradder, Julia Ann IV, 1383
Scranton, Elizabeth II, 918
Scranton, Elizabeth G. II, 91
Scranton, Elizabeth G. II, 93
Scranton, Elizabeth Garrigues II, 824
Scranton, Frederick II, 865
Scranton, Frederick II, 918
Scranton, Frederick II, 919
Scranton, Frederick II, 932
Scranton, Martha II, 865
Scranton, Martha II, 918
Scranton, Mary M. II, 865
Scranton, Mary M. II, 918
Scranton, Mary M. II, 932
Scranton, Wm. II, 865
Scranton, Wm. II, 918
Screnck, Susan III, 280
Scribner, Maria III, 281
Scribner, Mary Ann III, 281
Scrispe, Thomas VI, 171
Scriven, Alice III, 442
Scriven, Hannah I, 318
Scriven, Hannah I, 319
Scriven, Isaac I, 275
Scriven, Isaac I, 279
Scriven, James III, 281
Scriven, James III, 412
Scriven, James III, 413
Scriven, James III, 442
Scriven, Mary III, 412
Scriven, Mary III, 413

ɜn, Mary III, 442
ɜns, Alie I, 318
ɜns, Isaac I, 318
ens, Patience I, 318
ens, Susannah I, 318
ɜr, Isaac I, 275
g, Charity Ann V, 20
'g, Charity Ann V, 118
gs, Cinthe I, 997
gs, Cinthe I, 999
gs, Cynthia I, 984
gs, Cynthia I, 997
gs, Jane I, 997
gs, Jane Wales I, 997
ggy, Alpha V, 201
ggy, Alpha H. V, 201
ggy, Anna V, 201
ggy, Anna V, 708
ggy, Annie V, 201
ggy, Annie L. V, 708
ggy, Carey D. V, 708
ggy, Carrie V, 201
ggy, Cory D. V, 201
ggy, Elizabeth V, 201
ggy, Francis V, 201
ggy, Francis B. V, 201
ggy, Francis W. V, 201
ggy, Hattie V, 201
ggy, Hazel V, 708
ggy, Herman A. V, 201
ggy, Ira V, 201
ggy, Ira E. V, 201
ggy, Jennie V, 708
ggy, Jennie R. V, 201
ggy, Jennie R. V, 708
ggy, Jesse Edgar V, 201
ggy, Jesse J. V, 201
ggy, Jesse J. V, 708
oggy, Joseph M. V, 708
oggy, Joseph N. V, 201
oggy, Joseph N. V, 708
oggy, Lydia E. V, 201
oggy, Lydia E. V, 708
oggy, Mary E. V, 201
oggy, Naomi V, 708
oggy, Naomi C. V, 201
oggy, Naomi C. V, 708
oggy, Raymond V, 201
oggy, Raymond C. V, 201
oggy, Robert E. V, 201
oggy, Robert E. V, 708
oggy, Sallie V, 201
oggy, Thomas V, 201
oggy, Walter A. V, 201
oggy, Wilber V, 201
oggy, Wilbert V, 201
ous, John II, 417
uggs, Betty VI, 990
uggs, Charlotte VI, 910
uggs, Charlotte VI, 990
uggs, Creed T. VI, 853
uggs, Cross VI, 872
uggs, Drury VI, 819
uggs, Elizabeth VI, 879
uggs, Elizabeth VI, 934
uggs, Elizabeth VI, 990
uggs, Elizabeth C. VI, 853
uggs, Ella Jane VI, 934
ruggs, Gross VI, 948
ruggs, Gross VI, 951
ruggs, Gross VI, 967
ruggs, Gross VI, 974
ruggs, Gross VI, 986
ruggs, Gross VI, 990
ruggs, Gross VI, 991
ruggs, Gross VI, 1001
ruggs, Gross VI, 1014
ruggs, Isaac B. VI, 853
ruggs, James L. VI, 805
ruggs, James L. VI, 853
cruggs, Jane VI, 881
cruggs, John VI, 853
cruggs, John A. VI, 829
cruggs, John M. VI, 853
cruggs, Judith VI, 990
cruggs, Judith A. VI, 844
cruggs, Kessiah VI, 853
cruggs, Langhorne VI, 853
cruggs, Mildred L. VI, 990
cruggs, Minnie F. VI, 853
Scruggs, Nancy VI, 990
Scruggs, Nancy M. VI, 990
Scruggs, Patty VI, 819
Scruggs, Reeves S. VI, 990
Scruggs, Richard M. VI, 990
Scruggs, Richard M. VI, 1019
Scruggs, Samuel VI, 815
Scruggs, Sarah VI, 853
Scruggs, Sarah A. VI, 815
Scruggs, Sarah Ann VI, 1016
Scruggs, Sophia W. VI, 990
Scruggs, T. C. VI, 1016
Scruggs, T. C. VI, 1019
Scruggs, Theophilus C. VI, 1019
Scruggs, Thomas VI, 879
Scruggs, Thomas VI, 990
Scruggs, William VI, 990
Scruggs, William VI, 1016
Scruggs, William B. VI, 990
Scudder, Clara V. II, 1079
Scudder, Clara Virginia II, 919
Scudder, Elizabeth IV, 496
Scudder, Elizabeth IV, 499
Scudder, Harold B. II, 1079
Scudder, Henry III, 281
Scudder, Henry III, 442
Scudder, Henry III, 454
Scudder, Henry III, 472
Scudder, Julia Ann IV, 1378
Scudder, Julia Ann IV, 1383
Scudder, Mary III, 442
Scudder, Mary III, 454
Scudder, Phebe III, 318
Scudder, Phebe III, 451
Scudder, Phebe ??? III, 281
Scudder, Samuel III, 120
Scudder, Samuel III, 281
Scudder, Samuel III, 318
Scudder, Samuel III, 451
Scudder, Wd. Mary III, 442
Scudder, Wd. Mary III, 472
Scudder, Wd. Phebe III, 120
Scuder, Henry III, 436
Scuder, Mary III, 436
Scull, Abigail II, 123
Scull, Abigail II, 417
Scull, Anna M. II, 919
Scull, Benjamin II, 418
Scull, Comfort II, 417
Scull, David II, 123
Scull, David II, 743
Scull, David II, 764
Scull, David II, 765
Scull, David, Jr. II, 764
Scull, Deborah II, 33
Scull, Deborah II, 38
Scull, Deborah II, 120
Scull, Deborah II, 123
Scull, Edward II, 418
Scull, Edward II, 645
Scull, Edward II, 764
Scull, Edward L. II, 765
Scull, Elisabeth II, 549
Scull, Elizabeth II, 418
Scull, Elizabeth II, 645
Scull, Ella Flitcraft II, 919
Scull, Esther II, 418
Scull, Esther II, 599
Scull, Esther II, 645
Scull, Florence D. II, 818
Scull, Gideon II, 38
Scull, Gideon II, 81
Scull, Gideon II, 96
Scull, Gideon D. II, 123
Scull, Gideon D. II, 764
Scull, Hannah II, 123
Scull, Hannah II, 645
Scull, Hannah II, 764
Scull, Hannah II, 765
Scull, Hannah II, 888
Scull, Hannah II, 919
Scull, Hannah W. II, 764
Scull, Hannah W. II, 765
Scull, Henry II, 123
Scull, Hope II, 33
Scull, Hope II, 38
Scull, Hope II, 120
Scull, Hope II, 122
Scull, Hope II, 123
Scull, Hope II, 818
Scull, Isaac II, 123
Scull, Isaac II, 818
Scull, Isaac II, 919
Scull, Isaac II, 942
Scull, Isabella P. II, 919
Scull, James II, 418
Scull, Jane II, 38
Scull, Jane II, 120
Scull, Jane II, 123
Scull, Jane L. II, 123
Scull, Jane L. II, 728
Scull, Jane L. II, 764
Scull, Jaspar II, 582
Scull, Jaspar II, 645
Scull, Jasper II, 417
Scull, Jasper II, 418
Scull, Joseph F. II, 919
Scull, Joseph Folwell II, 919
Scull, Joseph Folwell II, 920
Scull, Joseph W. II, 919
Scull, Josephine II, 818
Scull, Josephine II, 919
Scull, Josephine II, 920
Scull, Josephine F. II, 919
Scull, Laura II, 919
Scull, Laura W. II, 919
Scull, Louisa W. II, 867
Scull, Louisa W. II, 919
Scull, Lydia II, 38
Scull, Lydia L. II, 123
Scull, Lydia L. II, 743
Scull, Lydia L. II, 764
Scull, Mark II, 38
Scull, Mark II, 120
Scull, Mark II, 123
Scull, Mary II, 38
Scull, Mary II, 120
Scull, Mary II, 123
Scull, Mary II, 582
Scull, Mary II, 645
Scull, Mary II, 650
Scull, Mary II, 743
Scull, Mary II, 764
Scull, Mary II, 788
Scull, Nicholas II, 418
Scull, Paul II, 33
Scull, Paul II, 38
Scull, Paul II, 120
Scull, Paul II, 122
Scull, Paul II, 123
Scull, Paul II, 818
Scull, Paul II, 919
Scull, Paul II, 920
Scull, Pauline II, 919
Scull, Paull II, 38
Scull, Rachel II, 784
Scull, Rachel II, 789
Scull, Rachel H. II, 919
Scull, Rebecca II, 418
Scull, Rebecca II, 645
Scull, Rebecca II, 667
Scull, Ruth II, 96
Scull, Sarah II, 38
Scull, Sarah II, 81
Scull, Sarah II, 96
Scull, Sarah II, 122
Scull, Sarah II, 123
Scull, Sarah II, 418
Scull, Susan H. II, 919
Scull, Susan L. II, 818
Scull, Susan L. II, 919
Scull, Susan Louisa II, 818
Scull, Susan W. II, 919
Scull, Susanna II, 418
Scull, Susanna II, 645
Scull, Susannah L. II, 919
Scull, Susannah L. II, 942
Scull, Thomas L. II, 38
Scull, William II, 417
Scull, William II, 418
Scull, William B. II, 717
Scull, Wm. II, 645
Scullion, Bertha Hall IV, 842
Scullion, Cecil IV, 759
Scullion, Dessy IV, 759
Scullion, Harold IV, 759
Scully, Sarah I, 1131
Sddney, Esther IV, 768
Sea, Dellila VI, 830
Sea, Elizabeth VI, 901
Sea, Joseph VI, 830
Seaber, William H. V, 763
Seabold, Ann V, 861
Seabolt, Ann V, 860
Seabolt, Ann V, 861
Seaborne, Nicholas VI, 11
Seaborne, Nicholas VI, 12
Seabright, Arthur Stanley VI, 442
Seabright, Dorothy Taylor VI, 417
Seabright, Dorothy Taylor VI, 442
Seabright, Glenn William VI, 417
Seabright, Glenn William VI, 442
Seabright, Ida VI, 442
Seabright, Winchester VI, 442
Seabury, Emma IV, 1000
Seabury, Harriet III, 108
Seachrist, Jacob IV, 991
Seachrist, John IV, 925
Seachrist, John IV, 991
Seachrist, Mabel IV, 925
Seachrist, Marietta A. IV, 991
Seachrist, Mary Etta IV, 925
Seachrist, Meribas IV, 991
Seacord, Catharine III, 158
Seacord, James III, 158
Seagar, Frederick IV, 1337
Seagerson, Ann II, 418
Seal, Anna May II, 919
Seal, Annie May II, 818
Seal, Elizabeth A. II, 942
Seal, Emilie II, 818
Seal, Emilie T. II, 919
Seal, Emily T. II, 919
Seal, Fannie II, 919
Seal, Fannie A. II, 919
Seal, Florence II, 919
Seal, Florence R. II, 803
Seal, Florence R. II, 919
Seal, Jane H. II, 919
Seal, Joel A. II, 818
Seal, Joel A. II, 919
Seal, Joseph II, 645
Seal, Lewis T. II, 919
Seal, Martin II, 969
Seal, Thos. II, 919
Seal, Thos. II, 942
Seal, Thos. F. II, 919
Seal, Wilmer G. II, 919
Seal, Wm. II, 919
Seale, Elizabeth II, 1025
Seale, Emilie T. II, 883
Seale, Emilie T. II, 919
Seale, Florence R. II, 883
Seale, Florence R. II, 919
Seale, Joel A. II, 883
Seale, Joel A. II, 919
Seale, Martin II, 1025
Sealy, Albert S. IV, 1184
Sealy, Caroline IV, 1184
Sealy, Mary Ann IV, 652
Sealy, Mary Ann IV, 655
Sealy, Robert IV, 1184
Seaman, ??? III, 391
Seaman, ??? III, 471
Seaman, Abigail III, 442
Seaman, Abigail III, 470
Seaman, Abigail III, 487
Seaman, Abigail III, 507
Seaman, Abraham III, 282
Seaman, Abraham III, 442
Seaman, Abram III, 442
Seaman, Abram III, 456
Seaman, Adam III, 282
Seaman, Adam III, 442
Seaman, Alanson III, 442
Seaman, Alanson III, 459
Seaman, Albert III, 511
Seaman, Albert W. III, 414
Seaman, Albert W. III, 420
Seaman, Albert W. III, 442
Seaman, Albert W. III, 496
Seaman, Albert W. III, 511
Seaman, Albert William III, 483
Seaman, Albert William III, 496
Seaman, Albertson III, 443
Seaman, Alfred III, 511
Seaman, Almy III, 442
Seaman, Almy III, 487
Seaman, Almy III, 497
Seaman, Ambrose III, 443
Seaman, Amy III, 46
Seaman, Amy III, 115
Seaman, Amy III, 281
Seaman, Amy III, 282
Seaman, Amy III, 378
Seaman, Amy III, 384
Seaman, Amy III, 423
Seaman, Amy III, 443
Seaman, Andrew III, 489
Seaman, Andries III, 443
Seaman, Andries III, 459
Seaman, Andries III, 460
Seaman, Andries III, 496
Seaman, Andries III, 497
Seaman, Andries III, 502
Seaman, Ann III, 281
Seaman, Ann III, 443
Seaman, Ann III, 497
Seaman, Ann III, 511
Seaman, Ann Louise III, 416
Seaman, Ann Louise III, 443
Seaman, Ann M. III, 281
Seaman, Ann M. III, 300
Seaman, Ann M. III, 482
Seaman, Ann M. III, 497
Seaman, Ann Maria III, 489
Seaman, Ann Maria III, 511
Seaman, Ann R. III, 282
Seaman, Ann R. III, 339
Seaman, Ann R. III, 498
Seaman, Ann R. VI, 777
Seaman, Anna III, 117
Seaman, Anna III, 203
Seaman, Anna III, 281
Seaman, Anna III, 282
Seaman, Anna III, 283
Seaman, Anna III, 497
Seaman, Anna III, 498
Seaman, Anna Amelia III, 283
Seaman, Anna Louisa III, 498
Seaman, Anna Louise III, 445
Seaman, Anna Marie V, 861
Seaman, Anna Matilda III, 443
Seaman, Anna W. III, 512
Seaman, Anne III, 117
Seaman, Anne III, 408
Seaman, Anne III, 423
Seaman, Anne III, 443
Seaman, Anne III, 444
Seaman, Anne III, 445
Seaman, Anne III, 473
Seaman, Anne III, 507
Seaman, Anne III, 508
Seaman, Annie Laurie III, 445
Seaman, Annie Laurie III, 460
Seaman, Arden III, 480
Seaman, Arden III, 482
Seaman, Arden III, 490
Seaman, Arden III, 497
Seaman, Arden III, 498
Seaman, Ardon III, 497
Seaman, Ardon III, 511
Seaman, Armenia III, 511
Seaman, Avis III, 221
Seaman, Avis III, 497
Seaman, Avis C. III, 480
Seaman, Avis C. III, 497
Seaman, Avis L. III, 281
Seaman, Ayree Cromwell III, 281
Seaman, Ayres Cromwell III, 281
Seaman, Ayres Cromwell III, 300
Seaman, Benj. III, 440
Seaman, Benj. III, 442
Seaman, Benj. III, 444
Seaman, Benj. III, 445
Seaman, Benj. III, 451
Seaman, Benj. III, 458
Seaman, Benjamin III, 281
Seaman, Benjamin III, 428
Seaman, Benjamin III, 443
Seaman, Benjamin III, 444
Seaman, Benjamin III, 453
Seaman, Benjamin III, 485
Seaman, Benjamin III, 487
Seaman, Benjamin III, 497
Seaman, Benjamin III, 498
Seaman, Benjamin III, 511
Seaman, Benjamin R. III, 281
Seaman, Benjamin R. III, 378
Seaman, Benjamin R. III, 384
Seaman, Bessie III, 480
Seaman, Bessie III, 497
Seaman, Blanche IV, 1293
Seaman, Caroline III, 282
Seaman, Caroline III, 283
Seaman, Caroline III, 484
Seaman, Caroline III, 497
Seaman, Caroline III, 498
Seaman, Caroline E. III, 497
Seaman, Caroline Elizabeth III, 482
Seaman, Caroline H. III, 32
Seaman, Caroline H. III, 92
Seaman, Caroline H. III, 281
Seaman, Caroline H. III, 282
Seaman, Carrie L. III, 410
Seaman, Carrie Lane III, 445
Seaman, Cath. III, 501
Seaman, Catharine III, 437
Seaman, Catharine III, 443
Seaman, Catharine III, 458
Seaman, Catharine III, 473
Seaman, Charity III, 445
Seaman, Charity III, 457
Seaman, Charles III, 497
Seaman, Charles III, 498
Seaman, Charles C. III, 498
Seaman, Charles P. III, 511
Seaman, Charlotte III, 497
Seaman, Charlotte B. III, 511
Seaman, Chrissie III, 395
Seaman, Chrissie III, 445
Seaman, Christiana III, 445
Seaman, Clarissa III, 281
Seaman, Cora III, 281
Seaman, Daisy Georgia III, 414
Seaman, Daisy Georgia III, 442
Seaman, Daisy Georgia III, 483
Seaman, Daisy Georgia III, 496
Seaman, Daniel III, 511
Seaman, David III, 155
Seaman, David III, 281
Seaman, David III, 408
Seaman, David III, 446
Seaman, David III, 483
Seaman, David III, 487
Seaman, David III, 489
Seaman, David III, 497
Seaman, David III, 498
Seaman, David III, 512
Seaman, David Sands III, 511
Seaman, Deborah III, 435

Seaman, Deborah III, 442
Seaman, Deborah III, 443
Seaman, Deborah III, 456
Seaman, Deborah III, 469
Seaman, Deborah III, 486
Seaman, Deborah III, 497
Seaman, Dr. James V. III, 282
Seaman, Dr. Valentina III, 281
Seaman, Dr. Valentine III, 117
Seaman, Dr. Valentine III, 281
Seaman, Dr. Valentine III, 282
Seaman, Dr. Valentine III, 283
Seaman, Dr. William III, 399
Seaman, Dr. William III, 497
Seaman, Dr. Wm. III, 281
Seaman, Dr. Wm. III, 282
Seaman, Dr. Wm. III, 283
Seaman, Dr. Wm. III, 403
Seaman, Edda Willets III, 443
Seaman, Edgar V, 464
Seaman, Edmond III, 443
Seaman, Edmund III, 281
Seaman, Edmund III, 360
Seaman, Edmund III, 443
Seaman, Edmund III, 445
Seaman, Edmund III, 470
Seaman, Edward III, 497
Seaman, Edward H. III, 442
Seaman, Edward H. III, 496
Seaman, Edward H. III, 497
Seaman, Edward H. III, 498
Seaman, Edward H. III, 511
Seaman, Edwin H. III, 511
Seaman, Elias III, 502
Seaman, Elias H. III, 281
Seaman, Elias H. III, 445
Seaman, Elias H. III, 497
Seaman, Elias H. III, 498
Seaman, Elijah III, 444
Seaman, Elijah III, 445
Seaman, Elijah III, 480
Seaman, Elijah III, 497
Seaman, Elijah III, 506
Seaman, Eliz. III, 326
Seaman, Eliz. III, 443
Seaman, Eliz. III, 444
Seaman, Eliz. III, 452
Seaman, Eliz. III, 482
Seaman, Eliz. III, 484
Seaman, Eliz. III, 497
Seaman, Eliz. III, 498
Seaman, Eliza III, 281
Seaman, Eliza III, 493
Seaman, Eliza III, 497
Seaman, Elizabeth III, 23
Seaman, Elizabeth III, 155
Seaman, Elizabeth III, 189
Seaman, Elizabeth III, 281
Seaman, Elizabeth III, 282
Seaman, Elizabeth III, 401
Seaman, Elizabeth III, 416
Seaman, Elizabeth III, 417
Seaman, Elizabeth III, 422
Seaman, Elizabeth III, 442
Seaman, Elizabeth III, 443
Seaman, Elizabeth III, 444
Seaman, Elizabeth III, 445
Seaman, Elizabeth III, 456
Seaman, Elizabeth III, 458
Seaman, Elizabeth III, 459
Seaman, Elizabeth III, 469
Seaman, Elizabeth III, 470
Seaman, Elizabeth III, 473
Seaman, Elizabeth III, 480
Seaman, Elizabeth III, 482
Seaman, Elizabeth III, 486
Seaman, Elizabeth III, 487
Seaman, Elizabeth III, 490
Seaman, Elizabeth III, 497
Seaman, Elizabeth III, 498
Seaman, Elizabeth III, 510
Seaman, Elizabeth III, 511
Seaman, Elizabeth H. III, 403
Seaman, Elizabeth H. III, 507
Seaman, Elizabeth H. III, 511
Seaman, Ellen A. III, 511
Seaman, Elvira M. III, 155
Seaman, Elvira M. III, 281
Seaman, Emma III, 445
Seaman, Esther III, 153
Seaman, Esther III, 154
Seaman, Esther III, 155
Seaman, Esther III, 157
Seaman, Esther III, 440
Seaman, Esther III, 443
Seaman, Esther III, 445
Seaman, Esther III, 446
Seaman, Esther III, 465
Seaman, Esther III, 466
Seaman, Esther III, 472
Seaman, Esther III, 483
Seaman, Esther III, 495
Seaman, Esther III, 496
Seaman, Esther III, 497
Seaman, Esther III, 511
Seaman, Ethel III, 208
Seaman, Ethel III, 281
Seaman, Ethelene III, 396
Seaman, Ethelene III, 445
Seaman, Ethelinda III, 502
Seaman, Faith Frances III, 445
Seaman, Faith Frances III, 498
Seaman, Florence III, 483
Seaman, Florence III, 497
Seaman, Frances III, 507
Seaman, Frances F. III, 489
Seaman, Francis F. V, 861
Seaman, Frank III, 159
Seaman, Franklin III, 282
Seaman, Fre'k Willits III, 443
Seaman, Frederick III, 443
Seaman, Frederick III, 445
Seaman, Frederick Augustus III, 281
Seaman, Frederick C. III, 208
Seaman, Frederick C. III, 281
Seaman, Frederick W. III, 498
Seaman, Frederick Willits III, 418
Seaman, George III, 281
Seaman, George W. III, 281
Seaman, Gideon III, 189
Seaman, Gideon III, 281
Seaman, Gideon III, 282
Seaman, Gideon III, 416
Seaman, Gideon III, 422
Seaman, Gideon III, 443
Seaman, Gideon III, 444
Seaman, Gideon III, 445
Seaman, Gideon III, 470
Seaman, Gideon III, 497
Seaman, Gilbert III, 115
Seaman, Gilbert III, 281
Seaman, Gilbert III, 434
Seaman, Gilbert III, 443
Seaman, Gilbert III, 511
Seaman, Giles III, 431
Seaman, Giles III, 443
Seaman, Giles III, 444
Seaman, Giles III, 491
Seaman, Giles III, 497
Seaman, Giles III, 498
Seaman, Grace III, 107
Seaman, Grace III, 281
Seaman, H. Bogart III, 445
Seaman, Hannah III, 179
Seaman, Hannah III, 264
Seaman, Hannah III, 277
Seaman, Hannah III, 281
Seaman, Hannah III, 282
Seaman, Hannah III, 407
Seaman, Hannah III, 422
Seaman, Hannah III, 425
Seaman, Hannah III, 431
Seaman, Hannah III, 442
Seaman, Hannah III, 443
Seaman, Hannah III, 444
Seaman, Hannah III, 445
Seaman, Hannah III, 446
Seaman, Hannah III, 456
Seaman, Hannah III, 467
Seaman, Hannah III, 468
Seaman, Hannah III, 471
Seaman, Hannah III, 491
Seaman, Hannah III, 495
Seaman, Hannah III, 497
Seaman, Hannah III, 498
Seaman, Hannah III, 505
Seaman, Hannah III, 506
Seaman, Hannah III, 507
Seaman, Hannah H. III, 281
Seaman, Hannah P. III, 281
Seaman, Hannah W. III, 497
Seaman, Harriet III, 281
Seaman, Harriet III, 445
Seaman, Henrietta III, 282
Seaman, Henry III, 497
Seaman, Henry IV, 1293
Seaman, Henry B. III, 107
Seaman, Henry B. III, 281
Seaman, Henry B., Jr. III, 281
Seaman, Henry O. III, 442
Seaman, Henry William III, 498
Seaman, Hester III, 282
Seaman, Hezekiah III, 282
Seaman, Hezekiah III, 408
Seaman, Hezekiah III, 443
Seaman, Horace III, 155
Seaman, Horace III, 281
Seaman, Ida Willets III, 418
Seaman, Isaac III, 403
Seaman, Isaac III, 443
Seaman, Isaac III, 458
Seaman, Isabella III, 443
Seaman, Isabella III, 444
Seaman, J. J. III, 511
Seaman, Jackson III, 497
Seaman, Jacob III, 281
Seaman, Jacob III, 282
Seaman, Jacob III, 423
Seaman, Jacob III, 436
Seaman, Jacob III, 437
Seaman, Jacob III, 443
Seaman, Jacob III, 444
Seaman, Jacob III, 446
Seaman, Jacob III, 497
Seaman, Jacob III, 498
Seaman, Jacob III, 501
Seaman, Jacob III, 502
Seaman, Jacob III, 507
Seaman, Jacob III, 511
Seaman, Jacob V. III, 497
Seaman, Jacob W. III, 497
Seaman, Jacob, Jr. III, 281
Seaman, James III, 281
Seaman, James III, 282
Seaman, James III, 431
Seaman, James III, 444
Seaman, James III, 511
Seaman, James H. III, 480
Seaman, James H. III, 483
Seaman, James H. III, 497
Seaman, James V. III, 282
Seaman, Jane III, 235
Seaman, Jane III, 282
Seaman, Jane III, 396
Seaman, Jane III, 407
Seaman, Jane III, 422
Seaman, Jane III, 428
Seaman, Jane III, 430
Seaman, Jane III, 440
Seaman, Jane III, 442
Seaman, Jane III, 443
Seaman, Jane III, 444
Seaman, Jane III, 445
Seaman, Jane III, 446
Seaman, Jane III, 447
Seaman, Jane III, 452
Seaman, Jane III, 458
Seaman, Jane III, 487
Seaman, Jane III, 488
Seaman, Jane III, 497
Seaman, Jane III, 498
Seaman, Jane R. III, 445
Seaman, Jane R. III, 469
Seaman, Jarvis III, 504
Seaman, Jecaniah III, 487
Seaman, Jemima III, 281
Seaman, Jemima III, 417
Seaman, Jemima III, 444
Seaman, Jemima III, 484
Seaman, Jemima III, 485
Seaman, Jemima III, 497
Seaman, Jemima III, 498
Seaman, Jemima III, 511
Seaman, Jenkins III, 281
Seaman, Jennie IV, 1293
Seaman, Jericho Mary III, 488
Seaman, John III, 46
Seaman, John III, 282
Seaman, John III, 432
Seaman, John III, 443
Seaman, John III, 444
Seaman, John III, 445
Seaman, John III, 497
Seaman, John F. III, 282
Seaman, John F. III, 283
Seaman, John G. III, 282
Seaman, John G. III, 339
Seaman, John G. III, 498
Seaman, John H. III, 498
Seaman, John J. III, 511
Seaman, John M. III, 498
Seaman, John R. III, 511
Seaman, John Samuel III, 443
Seaman, John W. III, 281
Seaman, John W. III, 498
Seaman, John Wm. III, 446
Seaman, Jonah III, 23
Seaman, Jonathan III, 281
Seaman, Jonathan III, 417
Seaman, Jonathan III, 444
Seaman, Jonathan III, 473
Seaman, Jonathan III, 484
Seaman, Jonathan III, 498
Seaman, Jordan III, 443
Seaman, Jordan III, 446
Seaman, Jordan III, 496
Seaman, Jordan III, 498
Seaman, Joseph H. III, 242
Seaman, Joseph H. III, 282
Seaman, Josephine R. III, 242
Seaman, Josephine R. III, 282
Seaman, Katharine Valine III, 433
Seaman, Kezia III, 282
Seaman, Kezia III, 428
Seaman, Kezia III, 429
Seaman, Kezia III, 444
Seaman, Kezia III, 445
Seaman, Kezia III, 453
Seaman, Latitia III, 443
Seaman, Latitia III, 444
Seaman, Latitia III, 491
Seaman, Latitia III, 498
Seaman, Laura Eliz. III, 281
Seaman, Leah III, 393
Seaman, Leah III, 444
Seaman, Leah III, 446
Seaman, Leah III, 466
Seaman, Leah III, 471
Seaman, Leonard III, 446
Seaman, Letitia III, 431
Seaman, Letitia III, 485
Seaman, Letitia III, 497
Seaman, Letitia III, 498
Seaman, Letitia M. III, 443
Seaman, Louis V. III, 445
Seaman, Lucretia III, 443
Seaman, Lucretia III, 458
Seaman, Lucretia III, 497
Seaman, Lydia III, 281
Seaman, Lydia III, 282
Seaman, Lydia III, 497
Seaman, Lydia III, 498
Seaman, Margaret III, 443
Seaman, Margaret III, 444
Seaman, Margaret III, 460
Seaman, Margaret III, 498
Seaman, Margaret III, 503
Seaman, Margaret J. III, 424
Seaman, Margaret J. III, 489
Seaman, Margaret J. III, 498
Seaman, Margaret L. III, 445
Seaman, Maria III, 406
Seaman, Maria III, 444
Seaman, Maria Louisa III, 512
Seaman, Marianna III, 498
Seaman, Martha III, 23
Seaman, Martha III, 281
Seaman, Martha III, 317
Seaman, Martha III, 384
Seaman, Martha III, 387
Seaman, Martha III, 419
Seaman, Martha III, 432
Seaman, Martha III, 440
Seaman, Martha III, 442
Seaman, Martha III, 443
Seaman, Martha III, 444
Seaman, Martha III, 445
Seaman, Martha III, 446
Seaman, Martha III, 451
Seaman, Martha III, 452
Seaman, Martha III, 453
Seaman, Martha III, 462
Seaman, Martha III, 467
Seaman, Martha III, 487
Seaman, Martha III, 493
Seaman, Martha III, 495
Seaman, Martha III, 497
Seaman, Martha III, 498
Seaman, Martha III, 503
Seaman, Martha III, 511
Seaman, Martha A. III, 442
Seaman, Martha A. III, 496
Seaman, Martha A. III, 497
Seaman, Martha A. III, 498
Seaman, Martha A. III, 511
Seaman, Martha Althouse III, 511
Seaman, Martha H. III, 46
Seaman, Martha H. III, 282
Seaman, Mary III, 115
Seaman, Mary III, 221
Seaman, Mary III, 281
Seaman, Mary III, 282
Seaman, Mary III, 315
Seaman, Mary III, 384
Seaman, Mary III, 395
Seaman, Mary III, 401
Seaman, Mary III, 408
Seaman, Mary III, 411
Seaman, Mary III, 422
Seaman, Mary III, 428
Seaman, Mary III, 429
Seaman, Mary III, 430
Seaman, Mary III, 432
Seaman, Mary III, 434
Seaman, Mary III, 442
Seaman, Mary III, 443
Seaman, Mary III, 444
Seaman, Mary III, 445
Seaman, Mary III, 446
Seaman, Mary III, 470
Seaman, Mary III, 471
Seaman, Mary III, 487
Seaman, Mary III, 488
Seaman, Mary III, 496
Seaman, Mary III, 497
Seaman, Mary III, 498
Seaman, Mary III, 504
Seaman, Mary III, 506
Seaman, Mary III, 508
Seaman, Mary III, 511
Seaman, Mary A. III, 420
Seaman, Mary A. III, 442
Seaman, Mary Ann III, 228
Seaman, Mary Ann III, 282
Seaman, Mary Ann III, 484
Seaman, Mary Ann III, 485
Seaman, Mary Ann III, 490
Seaman, Mary Ann III, 498
Seaman, Mary Atmore III, 49
Seaman, Mary Attmore III, 5
Seaman, Mary B. III, 444
Seaman, Mary B. III, 497
Seaman, Mary D. III, 497
Seaman, Mary E. III, 510
Seaman, Mary E. III, 511
Seaman, Mary E. IV, 423
Seaman, Mary E. IV, 435
Seaman, Mary H. III, 473
Seaman, Mary H. III, 507
Seaman, Mary J. III, 281
Seaman, Mary L. III, 498
Seaman, Mary L. III, 504
Seaman, Mary P. III, 480
Seaman, Mary P. III, 498
Seaman, Mary S. III, 281
Seaman, Mary S. III, 360
Seaman, Mary S. III, 441
Seaman, Mary S. III, 443
Seaman, Mary S. III, 468
Seaman, Mary S. III, 470
Seaman, Mary W. III, 443
Seaman, Mary W. III, 444
Seaman, Mary W. III, 445
Seaman, Mary W. III, 498
Seaman, Mary, Jr. III, 281
Seaman, Matilda III, 445
Seaman, Matilda III, 498
Seaman, Matilda III, 506
Seaman, Matilda M. III, 444
Seaman, Matilda W. III, 416
Seaman, Matilda W. III, 441
Seaman, Matilda W. III, 443
Seaman, Matilda W. III, 444
Seaman, Mercy III, 423
Seaman, Mercy III, 436
Seaman, Mercy III, 437
Seaman, Mercy III, 443
Seaman, Mercy III, 444
Seaman, Mercy III, 497
Seaman, Micah III, 445
Seaman, Miriam III, 440
Seaman, Miriam III, 443
Seaman, Miriam III, 444
Seaman, Miriam III, 495
Seaman, Miriam III, 498
Seaman, Myrtle C. V, 861
Seaman, Nath. III, 445
Seaman, Nath. III, 447
Seaman, Nathaniel III, 282
Seaman, Nathaniel III, 359
Seaman, Nathaniel III, 409
Seaman, Nathaniel III, 428
Seaman, Nathaniel III, 431
Seaman, Nathaniel III, 437
Seaman, Nathaniel III, 442
Seaman, Nathaniel III, 443
Seaman, Nathaniel III, 444
Seaman, Nathaniel III, 445
Seaman, Nathaniel III, 465
Seaman, Nathaniel III, 473
Seaman, Nathaniel III, 474
Seaman, Nellie III, 498
Seaman, Noah III, 493
Seaman, Noah III, 497
Seaman, Noah III, 498
Seaman, Noah III, 503
Seaman, Obadiah III, 281
Seaman, Obadiah III, 282
Seaman, Obadiah III, 406
Seaman, Obadiah III, 437
Seaman, Obadiah III, 443
Seaman, Obediah III, 432
Seaman, Obediah III, 444
Seaman, Obediah III, 445
Seaman, Oliver III, 498
Seaman, Olte III, 498
Seaman, Percival III, 282
Seaman, Phebe III, 154
Seaman, Phebe III, 155
Seaman, Phebe III, 282
Seaman, Phebe III, 387

an, Phebe III, 419
an, Phebe III, 425
an, Phebe III, 443
an, Phebe III, 444
an, Phebe III, 445
an, Phebe III, 446
an, Phebe III, 456
an, Phebe III, 462
an, Phebe III, 467
an, Phebe III, 475
an, Phebe III, 480
an, Phebe III, 483
an, Phebe III, 497
an, Phebe III, 498
an, Phebe III, 502
an, Phebe III, 506
an, Phebe III, 508
an, Phebe III, 511
an, Phebe P. III, 270
an, Phebe P. III, 282
an, Phebe U. III, 498
an, Phila III, 444
an, Phila. III, 414
an, Philadelphia III, 406
an, Philadelphia III, 444
an, Philadelphia III, 445
an, Philadelphia III, 452
an, Philadelphia III, 454
an, Philadelphia III, 498
an, Philadelphia III, 508
an, Polly III, 487
an, Rachel III, 282
an, Rachel III, 359
an, Rachel III, 409
an, Rachel III, 419
an, Rachel III, 429
an, Rachel III, 442
an, Rachel III, 443
an, Rachel III, 444
an, Rachel III, 445
an, Rachel III, 447
an, Rachel III, 465
an, Rachel III, 473
an, Rachel III, 474
an, Rachel C. III, 416
an, Rebecca III, 92
an, Rebecca III, 281
an, Rebecca III, 283
an, Rebecca III, 384
an, Richard III, 235
an, Richard III, 282
an, Richard III, 407
an, Richard III, 430
an, Richard III, 442
an, Richard III, 443
an, Richard III, 444
an, Richard III, 445
an, Richard III, 452
an, Richard III, 498
an, Richard III, 499
an, Richard I. III, 444
an, Richard W. III, 445
an, Richard, Jr. III, 429
an, Richard, Jr. III, 443
an, Richard, Jr. III, 444
an, Richardson III, 282
an, Robert III, 445
an, Robert III, 446
an, Robert III, 472
an, Robert III, 484
an, Robert III, 485
an, Robert III, 487
an, Robert III, 490
an, Robert III, 495
an, Robert III, 497
an, Robert III, 498
an, Robert III, 505
an, Robert III, 507
an, Roslyn III, 441
an, Roslyn III, 445
an, Ruth E. III, 497
an, Sam'l J. III, 416
an, Sam'l J. III, 443
an, Sam'l J. III, 506
an, Samuel III, 270
an, Samuel III, 282
an, Samuel III, 419
an, Samuel III, 440
an, Samuel III, 442
an, Samuel III, 443
an, Samuel III, 444
an, Samuel III, 445
an, Samuel III, 452
an, Samuel III, 453
an, Samuel III, 457
an, Samuel III, 462
an, Samuel III, 470
an, Samuel III, 477
an, Samuel III, 495
an, Samuel III, 498
an, Samuel H. III, 179
Seaman, Samuel H. III, 277
Seaman, Samuel H. III, 282
Seaman, Samuel J. III, 433
Seaman, Samuel J. III, 441
Seaman, Samuel J. III, 444
Seaman, Samuel J. III, 445
Seaman, Samuel J. III, 469
Seaman, Samuel J. III, 497
Seaman, Samuel J. III, 498
Seaman, Samuel J. III, 506
Seaman, Samuel J., Jr. III, 396
Seaman, Samuel J., Jr. III, 445
Seaman, Samuel Jackson III, 445
Seaman, Samuel, Jr. III, 443
Seaman, Samuel, Jr. III, 444
Seaman, Sarah III, 43
Seaman, Sarah III, 92
Seaman, Sarah III, 277
Seaman, Sarah III, 281
Seaman, Sarah III, 282
Seaman, Sarah III, 403
Seaman, Sarah III, 409
Seaman, Sarah III, 414
Seaman, Sarah III, 428
Seaman, Sarah III, 429
Seaman, Sarah III, 437
Seaman, Sarah III, 443
Seaman, Sarah III, 444
Seaman, Sarah III, 445
Seaman, Sarah III, 447
Seaman, Sarah III, 456
Seaman, Sarah III, 459
Seaman, Sarah III, 460
Seaman, Sarah III, 483
Seaman, Sarah III, 489
Seaman, Sarah III, 495
Seaman, Sarah III, 496
Seaman, Sarah III, 497
Seaman, Sarah III, 498
Seaman, Sarah III, 499
Seaman, Sarah III, 502
Seaman, Sarah III, 507
Seaman, Sarah IV, 273
Seaman, Sarah Jane III, 511
Seaman, Sarah R. III, 281
Seaman, Sarah R. III, 282
Seaman, Sarah R. III, 484
Seaman, Sarah R. III, 497
Seaman, Silas III, 456
Seaman, Simeon III, 445
Seaman, Solomon III, 443
Seaman, Solomon III, 445
Seaman, Solomon III, 469
Seaman, Solomon III, 486
Seaman, Solomon III, 497
Seaman, Stephen III, 497
Seaman, Susan III, 511
Seaman, Susan H. III, 269
Seaman, Susan H. III, 270
Seaman, Susan H. III, 282
Seaman, Susan H. III, 362
Seaman, Susanna III, 501
Seaman, Susannah III, 497
Seaman, Susannah III, 502
Seaman, Tamar III, 282
Seaman, Temperance III, 408
Seaman, Thomas III, 281
Seaman, Thomas III, 282
Seaman, Thomas III, 411
Seaman, Thomas III, 414
Seaman, Thomas III, 422
Seaman, Thomas III, 425
Seaman, Thomas III, 443
Seaman, Thomas III, 444
Seaman, Thomas III, 447
Seaman, Thomas III, 454
Seaman, Thomas III, 456
Seaman, Thomas III, 468
Seaman, Thomas III, 473
Seaman, Thomas III, 475
Seaman, Thomas III, 487
Seaman, Thomas III, 497
Seaman, Thomas III, 498
Seaman, Thomas III, 507
Seaman, Thomas M. III, 281
Seaman, Thomas M. III, 282
Seaman, Thomas, Jr. III, 282
Seaman, Thos III, 498
Seaman, Thos. III, 452
Seaman, Thos. III, 508
Seaman, Valentine III, 92
Seaman, Valentine III, 282
Seaman, Valentine III, 445
Seaman, Valentine H. III, 281
Seaman, Valentine H. III, 283
Seaman, W. III, 422
Seaman, Walter III, 282
Seaman, Walter III, 283
Seaman, Walter B. III, 444
Seaman, Wd. Abigail III, 498
Seaman, Wd. Elizabeth III, 399
Seaman, Wd. Elizabeth III, 403
Seaman, Wd. Elizabeth III, 442
Seaman, Wd. Elizabeth III, 487
Seaman, Wd. Elizabeth H. III, 281
Seaman, Wd. Mary III, 423
Seaman, Wheatley III, 445
Seaman, Whitehead III, 498
Seaman, Willet III, 221
Seaman, Willet III, 281
Seaman, Willet III, 282
Seaman, Willet III, 315
Seaman, Willet III, 384
Seaman, Willet III, 401
Seaman, Willet III, 443
Seaman, Willet III, 445
Seaman, Willet III, 498
Seaman, Willet H. III, 508
Seaman, Willet J. III, 283
Seaman, Willet W. III, 498
Seaman, Willets III, 445
Seaman, Willets III, 446
Seaman, William III, 281
Seaman, William III, 443
Seaman, William III, 444
Seaman, William III, 445
Seaman, William III, 447
Seaman, William III, 484
Seaman, William III, 496
Seaman, William III, 497
Seaman, William III, 498
Seaman, William III, 506
Seaman, William B. III, 511
Seaman, William F. III, 282
Seaman, William H. III, 282
Seaman, William H. III, 489
Seaman, William H. III, 498
Seaman, William H. VI, 777
Seaman, William R. III, 497
Seaman, William S. III, 498
Seaman, William S. III, 507
Seaman, William W. III, 443
Seaman, William, Jr. III, 421
Seaman, Williams III, 422
Seaman, Williams III, 423
Seaman, Williams III, 445
Seaman, Williams III, 471
Seaman, Williams III, 488
Seaman, Williams III, 496
Seaman, Williams III, 497
Seaman, Williams, Jr. III, 446
Seaman, Wm. III, 92
Seaman, Wm. III, 282
Seaman, Wm. F. III, 417
Seaman, Wm. H. III, 424
Seaman, Wm. H. III, 445
Seaman, Wm. H. III, 460
Seaman, Wm. H. III, 489
Seaman, Wm. H. III, 502
Seaman, Wm. Henry III, 281
Seaman, Wm. Laurie III, 445
Seaman, Wm. Laurie III, 498
Seaman, Wm. Lawrie III, 395
Seaman, Wm. S. III, 488
Seaman, Wm. W. III, 410
Seaman, Wright III, 446
Seaman, Zeb. III, 497
Seaman, Zebulon III, 282
Seaman, Zebulon III, 387
Seaman, Zebulon III, 446
Seaman, Zebulon III, 497
Seaman, Zebulon III, 498
Seaman, Zebulon III, 504
Seaman, Zebulun III, 444
Seaman, Zebulun III, 446
Seaman, Zebulun III, 462
Seaman, Zebulun III, 467
Seaman, Zebulun III, 477
Seaman, Zebulun III, 498
Seaman, Zebulun III, 511
Seamans, Rebecca F. V, 522
Seamans, Sarah F. IV, 347
Seamans, Sarah F. IV, 350
Seance, Albert V, 763
Search, Eva V, 276
Searchrist, Effie Mable IV, 991
Searing, Amey III, 446
Searing, Amy III, 428
Searing, Amy III, 446
Searing, Ann Maria III, 446
Searing, Anna III, 425
Searing, Anna III, 446
Searing, Cynthia III, 446
Searing, Dr. Valentine III, 445
Searing, Dr. Valentine III, 446
Searing, Elizabeth III, 283
Searing, Esther III, 446
Searing, George E. III, 446
Searing, John III, 283
Searing, John III, 425
Searing, John III, 428
Searing, John III, 438
Searing, John III, 446
Searing, John III, 474
Searing, John III, 475
Searing, John III, 508
Searing, John S. III, 446
Searing, John S. III, 499
Searing, John, Jr. III, 283
Searing, John, Jr. III, 446
Searing, Maria W. VI, 747
Searing, Mary III, 283
Searing, Mary III, 428
Searing, Mary III, 438
Searing, Mary III, 445
Searing, Mary III, 446
Searing, Mary III, 474
Searing, Mary III, 499
Searing, Mary III, 508
Searing, Mary E. III, 413
Searing, Mary E. III, 446
Searing, Mary Esther III, 446
Searing, Mary U. III, 446
Searing, Mary U. III, 475
Searing, Phebe III, 283
Searing, Phebe III, 415
Searing, Phebe III, 446
Searing, Phebe III, 474
Searing, Phebe III, 499
Searing, Phebe III, 507
Searing, Phebe III, 508
Searing, Rachel III, 158
Searing, Rachel III, 283
Searing, Rachel III, 483
Searing, Rebecca III, 415
Searing, Rebecca III, 446
Searing, Rebecca VI, 730
Searing, Rebecca VI, 747
Searing, Richard III, 413
Searing, Richard III, 446
Searing, Robert III, 445
Searing, Ruth III, 446
Searing, Samuel III, 415
Searing, Samuel III, 446
Searing, Samuel III, 483
Searing, Samuel Haines III, 446
Searing, Sarah III, 283
Searing, Sarah III, 444
Searing, Wm., Jr. III, 445
Searing, Zebulon III, 446
Searles, Stephen B. III, 207
Searles, Stephen B. III, 283
Searles, Wendella III, 207
Searles, Wendella III, 283
Sears, Abigail III, 283
Sears, Abigail IV, 436
Sears, Abigail IV, 534
Sears, Abigail IV, 548
Sears, Abner W. V, 976
Sears, Abner Winder IV, 1293
Sears, Abner Winslow V, 979
Sears, Alice V, 66
Sears, Alice V, 118
Sears, Alice E. IV, 435
Sears, Ann IV, 405
Sears, Ann IV, 435
Sears, Ann IV, 548
Sears, Ann VI, 120
Sears, Ann M. VI, 853
Sears, Anna IV, 385
Sears, Anna IV, 421
Sears, Anna IV, 435
Sears, Anna IV, 496
Sears, Anna IV, 1076
Sears, Anna V, 201
Sears, Anna VI, 130
Sears, Anna VI, 140
Sears, Anne IV, 273
Sears, Anne V, 596
Sears, Arthur V, 596
Sears, Benj. V, 976
Sears, Benj. S. IV, 591
Sears, Benjamin IV, 371
Sears, Benjamin IV, 435
Sears, Benjamin IV, 436
Sears, Benjamin IV, 514
Sears, Benjamin S. IV, 427
Sears, Benjamin S. IV, 436
Sears, Benjamin S. IV, 593
Sears, Benjamin S. IV, 1076
Sears, Benjamin Stanton IV, 435
Sears, Charles W. V, 979
Sears, Chas. V, 976
Sears, Christopher V, 118
Sears, Christopher V, 276
Sears, Christopher V, 643
Sears, Clinton V, 277
Sears, David IV, 428
Sears, David IV, 435
Sears, David IV, 436
Sears, David IV, 1071
Sears, David IV, 1076
Sears, David V, 118
Sears, David V, 976
Sears, David V, 979
Sears, David Bailey VI, 140
Sears, Dolly Pleasant V, 276
Sears, Edna M. IV, 435
Sears, Edward IV, 436
Sears, Edward V, 201
Sears, Edwin IV, 273
Sears, Edwin W. IV, 435
Sears, Edwin W. IV, 436
Sears, Edwin W. IV, 1076
Sears, Eliza VI, 107
Sears, Eliza VI, 120
Sears, Elizabeth II, 258
Sears, Elizabeth IV, 435
Sears, Elizabeth IV, 759
Sears, Elizabeth IV, 1293
Sears, Elizabeth V, 643
Sears, Elizabeth V, 976
Sears, Elizabeth V, 979
Sears, Elizabeth V, 981
Sears, Elizabeth V, 1017
Sears, Elizabeth VI, 107
Sears, Elizabeth VI, 120
Sears, Elizabeth VI, 137
Sears, Elizabeth VI, 140
Sears, Elizabeth VI, 259
Sears, Elizabeth L. V, 976
Sears, Elizabeth L. V, 979
Sears, Ella V, 119
Sears, Ellen IV, 427
Sears, Ellen IV, 436
Sears, Ellen IV, 591
Sears, Ellen IV, 593
Sears, Ellen P. IV, 593
Sears, Elva V, 976
Sears, Elvira V, 976
Sears, Esther IV, 273
Sears, Esther IV, 371
Sears, Esther IV, 435
Sears, Esther IV, 436
Sears, Esther IV, 514
Sears, Ethel R. IV, 435
Sears, Florence V, 596
Sears, Frances Lucile V, 596
Sears, Frederick L. IV, 435
Sears, Frederick L. IV, 436
Sears, Harry V, 596
Sears, Hulda V, 979
Sears, Huldah IV, 435
Sears, Huldah IV, 436
Sears, Huldah IV, 593
Sears, Huldah IV, 1293
Sears, Huldah V, 976
Sears, Huldah VI, 18
Sears, Huldah VI, 74
Sears, Huldah VI, 86
Sears, Huldah VI, 121
Sears, Huldah VI, 136
Sears, Huldah VI, 140
Sears, Huldah VI, 141
Sears, Huldah Simmons VI, 120
Sears, Huldah, Jr. VI, 140
Sears, J. M. VI, 853
Sears, Jane IV, 435
Sears, Jane V, 643
Sears, Jane H. II, 1089
Sears, Jane H. IV, 436
Sears, Jane H. IV, 794
Sears, Jane H. IV, 1114
Sears, Jaohn V, 118
Sears, Jemima VI, 120
Sears, Jemima VI, 123
Sears, John IV, 397
Sears, John IV, 399
Sears, John IV, 435
Sears, John IV, 436
Sears, John IV, 473
Sears, John IV, 496
Sears, John IV, 1293
Sears, John V, 83
Sears, John V, 118
Sears, John V, 276
Sears, John V, 527
Sears, John V, 643
Sears, John VI, 117
Sears, John VI, 120
Sears, John VI, 140
Sears, John C. V, 979
Sears, John G. IV, 436
Sears, John G. IV, 1293
Sears, John G. V, 976
Sears, John G. V, 979
Sears, John Gilliam V, 976
Sears, John Stanton, Sr. VI, 140
Sears, John, Sr. VI, 120
Sears, Joseph IV, 273
Sears, Joseph IV, 435
Sears, Joseph IV, 436
Sears, Joseph J. IV, 435

Sears, Lillian V, 277
Sears, Lillian Clinton V, 527
Sears, Lydia IV, 436
Sears, Lydia V, 971
Sears, Lydia V, 976
Sears, Lydia Ladd V, 976
Sears, Margaret IV, 399
Sears, Margaret IV, 435
Sears, Margaret IV, 1114
Sears, Maria IV, 436
Sears, Maria V, 976
Sears, Mariah IV, 436
Sears, Mariah V, 979
Sears, Martha IV, 421
Sears, Martha IV, 435
Sears, Martha IV, 1069
Sears, Martha IV, 1076
Sears, Martha V, 979
Sears, Martha VI, 120
Sears, Martha VI, 131
Sears, Martha VI, 140
Sears, Mary IV, 424
Sears, Mary IV, 436
Sears, Mary V, 948
Sears, Mary V, 959
Sears, Mary V, 969
Sears, Mary V, 976
Sears, Mary VI, 107
Sears, Mary VI, 120
Sears, Mary Ann IV, 273
Sears, Mary Ann IV, 435
Sears, Mary Ann V, 643
Sears, Mary Ann V, 976
Sears, Mary Ann V, 979
Sears, Mary B. IV, 435
Sears, Mary B. IV, 436
Sears, Mary B. IV, 1076
Sears, Mary Elizabeth IV, 1293
Sears, Mary H. IV, 435
Sears, Mary K. IV, 423
Sears, Mary Sears V, 959
Sears, May IV, 273
Sears, Mildred V, 596
Sears, Miriam VI, 120
Sears, Miriam VI, 133
Sears, Miriam VI, 140
Sears, Moses IV, 1293
Sears, Nancy V, 643
Sears, Paul IV, 435
Sears, Paul IV, 436
Sears, Paul IV, 534
Sears, Paul IV, 548
Sears, Paul V, 969
Sears, Paul V, 976
Sears, Paul V, 979
Sears, Paul VI, 107
Sears, Paul VI, 120
Sears, Paul VI, 121
Sears, Paul VI, 129
Sears, Paul VI, 138
Sears, Paul VI, 139
Sears, Paul VI, 140
Sears, Paul VI, 141
Sears, Penelope V, 83
Sears, Penelope V, 118
Sears, Penelope V, 276
Sears, Penelope V, 527
Sears, Penelope V, 613
Sears, Penelope V, 643
Sears, Penelope Bocock V, 959
Sears, Peter IV, 273
Sears, Peter IV, 374
Sears, Peter IV, 385
Sears, Peter IV, 405
Sears, Peter IV, 421
Sears, Peter IV, 435
Sears, Peter IV, 436
Sears, Peter IV, 496
Sears, Peter IV, 548
Sears, Peter IV, 593
Sears, Peter IV, 1076
Sears, Peter Binford VI, 140
Sears, Peter, Jr. IV, 273
Sears, Peter, Jr. IV, 436
Sears, Pharaby IV, 273
Sears, Phariba IV, 436
Sears, Phariba IV, 593
Sears, Phebe IV, 397
Sears, Phebe IV, 399
Sears, Phebe IV, 435
Sears, Phebe IV, 436
Sears, Phebe IV, 473
Sears, Phebe IV, 496
Sears, Phebe V, 276
Sears, Phebe G. V, 277
Sears, Phebe G. V, 527
Sears, Pheriba IV, 374
Sears, Pheriba IV, 435
Sears, Pheriba IV, 1076
Sears, Pheribah IV, 436
Sears, Pleasant V, 276
Sears, Pleasant V, 527
Sears, Polly V, 276
Sears, Polly Pleasant Christopher V, 527
Sears, Prudence II, 82
Sears, Prudence II, 96
Sears, Rachel II, 96
Sears, Rachel II, 108
Sears, Rachel IV, 1076
Sears, Rachel V, 118
Sears, Rachel V, 976
Sears, Rachel V, 979
Sears, Rachel B. IV, 428
Sears, Rachel B. IV, 436
Sears, Rachel B. IV, 1071
Sears, Rachel B. IV, 1076
Sears, Rebecca IV, 436
Sears, Rebecca V, 976
Sears, Richard II, 96
Sears, Ruth II, 96
Sears, Samuel IV, 1293
Sears, Samuel V, 976
Sears, Samuel V, 979
Sears, Samuel Chas. Creighton V, 976
Sears, Sarah IV, 273
Sears, Sarah IV, 372
Sears, Sarah IV, 405
Sears, Sarah IV, 435
Sears, Sarah IV, 436
Sears, Sarah V, 118
Sears, Sarah VI, 86
Sears, Sarah VI, 97
Sears, Sarah VI, 98
Sears, Sarah VI, 117
Sears, Sarah VI, 120
Sears, Sarah VI, 140
Sears, Sarah VI, 142
Sears, Sarah D. IV, 435
Sears, Sarah D. IV, 436
Sears, Sarah D. IV, 1076
Sears, Sarah Jane IV, 1293
Sears, Sarah Jane V, 976
Sears, Sarah Jane V, 979
Sears, Sarah Peebles VI, 120
Sears, Sarah W. IV, 436
Sears, Sarah, Sr. VI, 120
Sears, Tabitha V, 976
Sears, Tabitha VI, 101
Sears, Tabitha VI, 120
Sears, Thomas I, 948
Sears, Thos. I, 948
Sears, Tilman V, 976
Sears, Tilman V, 979
Sears, Walter B. IV, 435
Sears, Walter B. IV, 436
Sears, William V, 979
Sears, William Henry IV, 435
Sears, Wm. V, 118
Sears, Wm. V, 201
Sears, Wm. V, 976
Sears, Wm. Henry IV, 273
Sears, Wm. Henry IV, 423
Sears, Zalinda V, 975
Sears, Zalinda V, 976
Sears, Zillah IV, 435
Seary, Mary II, 543
Seary, Mary II, 645
Seaton, Alexander II, 418
Seaton, Alexander II, 645
Seaton, Jane II, 183
Seaton, Jane II, 258
Seaton, Jane III, 446
Seaton, Jennie IV, 1293
Seaton, Maggie IV, 1293
Seaton, Margery VI, 648
Seaton, Margery VI, 698
Seaton, Rebecca II, 418
Seaton, Rebekah II, 645
Seaton, Ruth II, 645
Seaver, Elizabeth VI, 777
Seaver, Jonathan VI, 777
Seaver, Jonathan Mercer VI, 777
Seaver, Mary P. VI, 777
Seavers, George L. V, 596
Seavers, Margaret V, 596
Seay, Agness VI, 853
Seay, Ann A. VI, 853
Seay, Easy VI, 815
Seay, Eliza R. VI, 853
Seay, Elizabeth VI, 853
Seay, Elizabeth VI, 863
Seay, James L. VI, 856
Seay, Joseph VI, 815
Seay, Joseph VI, 853
Seay, Samuel VI, 825
Seay, Samuel L. VI, 853
Seay, William VI, 853
Seay, William F. VI, 853
Seay, Wilson F. VI, 796
Seay, Wilson F. VI, 822
Sebastian, Hattie V, 849
Sebborn, Benjamin II, 256
Sebborn, Benjamin II, 258
Sebborn, Elisabeth II, 256
Sebborn, Elisabeth II, 258
Sebborn, Elizabeth II, 256
Sebborn, Elizabeth II, 258
Sebborn, James II, 256
Sebborn, James II, 258
Sebek, Chas. IV, 1337
Sebrall, Elizabeth H. IV, 957
Sebrall, Elizabeth H. IV, 991
Sebrall, Joseph IV, 991
Sebrall, Mary IV, 991
Sebrel, Joseph VI, 120
Sebrel, Rebecca VI, 120
Sebrel, Samuel VI, 8
Sebrel, Sarah VI, 121
Sebrell, ??? VI, 95
Sebrell, Abigail IV, 759
Sebrell, Abigail G. IV, 760
Sebrell, Benjamin IV, 759
Sebrell, Benjamin VI, 120
Sebrell, Benjamin VI, 121
Sebrell, Daniel VI, 45
Sebrell, Daniel VI, 46
Sebrell, Elizabeth VI, 46
Sebrell, Elizabeth VI, 121
Sebrell, Hannah IV, 689
Sebrell, Hannah IV, 759
Sebrell, Hannah IV, 893
Sebrell, Hannah IV, 894
Sebrell, Hannah C. IV, 1042
Sebrell, Huldah K. IV, 1042
Sebrell, Joseph IV, 759
Sebrell, Joseph IV, 793
Sebrell, Joseph VI, 107
Sebrell, Joseph VI, 109
Sebrell, Joseph VI, 120
Sebrell, Joseph VI, 121
Sebrell, Joseph, Jr. IV, 759
Sebrell, Josiah VI, 121
Sebrell, Lidia VI, 46
Sebrell, Margaret VI, 45
Sebrell, Margaret VI, 46
Sebrell, Mary IV, 759
Sebrell, Mary IV, 760
Sebrell, Mary IV, 793
Sebrell, Matthew IV, 689
Sebrell, Matthew IV, 759
Sebrell, Matthew VI, 120
Sebrell, Matthew VI, 121
Sebrell, Matthew B. IV, 759
Sebrell, Matthew B. IV, 760
Sebrell, Moses VI, 45
Sebrell, Moses VI, 46
Sebrell, Naomey VI, 45
Sebrell, Naomey VI, 46
Sebrell, Polly IV, 759
Sebrell, Polly VI, 120
Sebrell, Rebecca IV, 759
Sebrell, Rebecca IV, 793
Sebrell, Rebecca VI, 120
Sebrell, Rebecca J. IV, 759
Sebrell, Rebecca J. IV, 760
Sebrell, Rebeckah VI, 121
Sebrell, Sally IV, 759
Sebrell, Sally VI, 120
Sebrell, Sally VI, 121
Sebrell, Samuel VI, 16
Sebrell, Sarah IV, 793
Sebrell, Sarah VI, 45
Sebrell, Sarah VI, 46
Sebrell, Sarah VI, 121
Sebrell, Sarah M. IV, 892
Sebrell, Sarah M. IV, 894
Sebrell, Susan VI, 120
Sebrell, Susan VI, 121
Sebrell, Susannah IV, 759
Sebring, Minnie IV, 1262
Sechrest, Albert A. I, 596
Sechrest, David S. I, 596
Sechrest, Ella I, 900
Sechrest, Henry O. I, 596
Sechrest, James S. I, 596
Sechrest, John I, 596
Sechrest, Louis I, 596
Sechrest, Samuel S. I, 596
Sechrest, Samuel W. I, 596
Sechrest, Sarah L. I, 596
Sechrest, Thomas I, 596
Sechrest, Thomas F. I, 596
Sechrist, John I, 596
Sechrist, Samuel W. I, 596
Sechrist, Thomas I, 596
Seckle, Anna M. III, 283
Seckle, Harry Lee III, 283
Secor, Ann III, 446
Secor, Benjamin III, 283
Secor, Benjamin III, 294
Secor, Benjamin B. III, 283
Secor, Eliza A. III, 428
Secor, Eliza Ann III, 446
Secor, Elizabeth III, 283
Secor, Elizabeth III, 446
Secor, Elizabeth C. III, 284
Secor, Gilbert W. III, 284
Secor, Hannah III, 283
Secor, Hannah III, 284
Secor, Hannah III, 294
Secor, Hannah III, 446
Secor, Hannah III, 499
Secor, Hannah R. III, 283
Secor, Hannah R. III, 284
Secor, Isaac III, 446
Secor, James III, 284
Secor, Joseph III, 283
Secor, Lydia III, 131
Secor, Lydia III, 284
Secor, Mary III, 283
Secor, Mary III, 284
Secor, Obediah W. III, 284
Secor, Phebe III, 284
Secor, Rebecca III, 284
Secor, Sarah III, 283
Secor, Sarah III, 294
Secor, Sarah Ann III, 284
Secor, Thomas III, 283
Secor, Willet III, 283
Secor, Willet III, 284
Secor, Willet III, 499
Secor, Willett III, 131
Secord, Catharine III, 284
Secord, Mary J. III, 213
Secord, Mary Jane III, 213
Secord, Mary Jane III, 284
Secrist, Theresa Ann V, 930
Seddon, Mary II, 97
Seddon, Sarah II, 651
Sedgwick, Anthony III, 284
Sedham, Mary I, 165
Sedham, Sarah I, 37
Sedham, Sarah I, 73
See, Elizabeth VI, 853
See, John III, 284
See, Maria III, 284
See, Marie III, 284
See, Thomas VI, 853
Seebert, Irvin D. IV, 1262
Seebert, Irvine IV, 1262
Seebert, Nora IV, 1262
Seebohm, Jacob II, 645
Seebohm, Julia II, 711
Seebohm, Julia IV, 640
Seebohm, Julia IV, 655
Seebohm, Julia IV, 734
Seebohn, Julia IV, 768
Seed, Elizabeth III, 284
Seed, Emma C. III, 284
Seed, Emma C. III, 338
Seed, John Hartley III, 284
Seed, Joseph III, 284
Seed, Joseph III, 338
Seed, Joseph H. III, 284
Seed, Mary III, 284
Seed, Mary Louisa III, 284
Seed, Mary Louise III, 284
Seed, Sarah III, 284
Seed, Sarah III, 338
Seedon, William II, 418
Seeds, Alice IV, 273
Seeds, Annie L. II, 717
Seeds, Annie May II, 807
Seeds, Bertram G. II, 717
Seeds, Bertram G. II, 765
Seeds, Elizabeth A. II, 807
Seeds, Frances II, 717
Seeds, Frank IV, 273
Seeds, Jesse II, 807
Seeds, Joseph R. D. II, 717
Seeds, Martha V, 1018
Seeds, Osman J. II, 717
Seeds, Osmond J. II, 765
Seeds, Rachel D. II, 717
Seeds, Rachel D. II, 765
Seeds, Thomas V, 1017
Seeds, Victorine E. II, 717
Seekings, Mary V, 708
Seeley, Sands III, 284
Seelig, George W. III, 511
Seely, ??? III, 364
Seely, Caroline IV, 1184
Seely, Hannah II, 96
Seely, Harriet V. S. III, 284
Seely, Harriet V. S. III, 364
Seely, Sands III, 284
Seer, John Hartley III, 17
Seer, Mary Louisa III, 17
Seeres, Richard II, 96
Seeres, Ruth II, 96
Seers, Christopher V, 118
Seers, John V, 215
Seers, Thomas I, 948
Seery, ??? III, 284
Seery, Hannah III, 284
Seery, Hannah B. III, 284
Seery, Hector III, 284
Sees, Florence Mary II, 919
Sees, Florence May II, 917
Segar, Catharine IV, 760
Segar, Climaco III, 284
Segar, Geo. W. III, 264
Segar, George W. III, 284
Segar, Mary E. IV, 760
Segar, Mary R. III, 264
Segar, Mary R. III, 284
Segar, Ormalo III, 284
Segar, Romalie III, 284
Seggerson, Mary II, 258
Seggerson, Mary II, 645
Seifort, Alta V, 708
Seig, Jacob VI, 860
Seigenthaler, Katharine IV,
Seiger, Alice IV, 273
Seiger, Catharine IV, 760
Seiger, Frederick IV, 1337
Seiger, Mary IV, 1337
Seiger, William IV, 273
Seigert, Alta V, 708
Seigler, Harry V, 596
Seigman, Louise IV, 1337
Seiler, Mary V, 32
Seipel, Anna Belle IV, 1262
Seity, Susan IV, 1242
Seitz, Bishop V, 277
Seitz, Charles E. V, 277
Seitz, Melissa V, 277
Seitz, Rhoda V, 277
Seitz, Rhoda A. V, 277
Seitz, Sydney R. V, 277
Seitz, William V, 277
Selber, Ada II, 969
Selber, Elsa Helena II, 969
Selber, Robert Ludwig II, 96
Selby, Emily IV, 1098
Selby, Emily IV, 1114
Selby, Mary IV, 393
Selby, Mary IV, 436
Selby, Rachel IV, 1111
Selby, Rachel IV, 1114
Selby, Sarah IV, 436
Selden, Catharine V, 930
Selden, Hetty V, 907
Selden, Hetty V, 930
Seldom, Jacob VI, 991
Seldom, Peggy VI, 991
Seldom, Robert VI, 991
Seldom, Suckey VI, 991
Self, Dicey VI, 991
Self, Fannie Alice IV, 1262
Self, Ralph IV, 1262
Self, William VI, 991
Sell, Deborah I, 1045
Sell, Deborah I, 1050
Sell, Elizabeth I, 1045
Sell, Elizabeth I, 1049
Sell, Elizabeth I, 1050
Sell, Enos I, 418
Sell, Enos I, 1045
Sell, Enos I, 1050
Sell, Henry I, 418
Sell, John I, 836
Sell, John I, 837
Sell, John I, 1045
Sell, John I, 1050
Sell, Jonathan I, 418
Sell, Jonathan I, 836
Sell, Jonathan I, 1041
Sell, Jonathan I, 1045
Sell, Jonathan I, 1050
Sell, Margarete IV, 1014
Sell, Mary I, 836
Sell, Mary I, 1045
Sell, Mary I, 1050
Sell, Pascience I, 836
Sell, Patience I, 1045
Sell, Patience I, 1050
Sell, Rebecca IV, 1215
Sell, Rebecca IV, 1222
Sell, Sarah I, 418
Sell, Sarah I, 813
Sell, Sarah I, 836
Sell, Sarah I, 837
Sell, Sarah I, 1045
Sell, Sarah I, 1050
Sell, Thomas I, 836
Sell, Thomas I, 837
Sell, Thomas I, 1041
Sell, Thomas I, 1045
Sell, Thomas I, 1050
Sell, Thomas I Sup 1, 11
Sellars, Baxter S. I, 633
Sellars, Baxter S. I, 640

ars, Bertha IV, 1222
ars, Dora V, 119
ars, Drusilla IV, 991
ars, E. V, 277
ars, Elizabeth II, 645
ars, Ella IV, 1183
ars, Esther Hiatt V, 430
ars, George II, 765
ars, George V, 119
ars, Gertrude I, 633
ars, Gertrude I, 640
ars, Mary II, 491
ars, Mary II, 645
ars, Mary V, 119
ars, Nathan II, 645
ars, Rebecca P. II, 837
ars, Samuel II, 765
eck, Alice D. III, 145
eck, Alice D. III, 284
eck, Anna III, 284
eck, Eliz M. III, 145
eck, Eliz M. III, 284
eck, James W. III, 145
eck, James W. III, 284
eck, Nathaniel III, 499
eck, Sands III, 284
ers, Abram II, 852
ers, Abram II, 919
ers, Albert III, 284
ers, Alfred L. II, 919
ers, Alice II, 818
ers, Alice II, 919
ers, Alice P. II, 919
ers, Alvin V, 1018
ers, Alvin T. V, 1018
ers, Ann W. II, 919
ers, Anne S. II, 834
ers, Annie II, 818
ers, Annie W. II, 919
ers, Baxter I, 616
ers, Charles II, 919
ers, Cyrus Cadwallader II, 418
ers, Cyrus Cadwallader II, 645
ers, David II, 418
ers, David II, 491
ers, David II, 645
ers, David II, 987
ers, David II, 1025
ers, Dora V, 119
ers, Dora Lena V, 119
ers, Elizabeth II, 418
ers, Elizabeth II, 491
ers, Elizabeth II, 645
ers, Elizabeth II, 781
ers, Elizabeth II, 987
ers, Elizabeth II, 1025
ers, Ellen II, 418
ers, Ellen II, 645
ers, Frances G. II, 818
ers, Francis G. II, 919
ers, George II, 765
ers, George V, 119
ers, George H. II, 818
ers, George H. II, 919
ers, George Henry V, 119
ers, George W. II, 919
ers, George Wilson II, 818
ers, Gertrude I, 616
ers, Gertrude I, 625
ers, Hannah II, 418
ers, Hannah II, 645
ers, Hannah III, 284
ers, Isabella P. II, 919
ers, Isaiah M. W. II, 919
ers, James II, 418
ers, James II, 645
ers, James II, 987
ers, James II, 1025
ers, John II, 418
ers, John II, 645
ers, John II, 834
ers, John, Jr. II, 781
ers, John, Jr. II, 919
lers, Joseph II, 418
lers, Joseph II, 645
lers, Joseph P. II, 919
lers, Joseph Powell II, 919
lers, Martha I, 1131
ers, Martha Emily V, 119
lers, Mary II, 418
lers, Mary II, 645
lers, Mary V, 119
lers, Mary C. V, 119
lers, Maurice A. III, 196
lers, Maurice A. III, 284
lers, Nathan II, 645
lers, Nathan II, 919
lers, Nellie IV, 1337
lers, Phyllis III, 284
Sellers, Rachel II, 491
Sellers, Rachel II, 645
Sellers, Rachel II, 987
Sellers, Rachel II, 1025
Sellers, Rachel Coleman II, 418
Sellers, Rebecca Jarret II, 645
Sellers, Rebecca Jarrett II, 418
Sellers, Rebecca P. II, 919
Sellers, Rebecca R. II, 919
Sellers, Samuel II, 765
Sellers, Sarah II, 784
Sellers, Sarah A. II, 818
Sellers, Sarah A. II, 919
Sellers, Susan C. II, 789
Sellers, Susan C. II, 852
Sellers, Susan C. II, 919
Sellers, Susannah II, 852
Sellers, Susannah II, 919
Sellers, Wd. Mary II, 781
Sellew, Ashbel Roberts II, 717
Sellew, C. Virginia II, 645
Sellew, C. Virginia II, 717
Sellew, C. Virginia II, 729
Sellew, C. Virginia II, 765
Sellew, Caroline Virginia II, 717
Sellew, Edwin P. II, 645
Sellew, Edwin P. II, 646
Sellew, Edwin P. II, 717
Sellew, Edwin P. II, 729
Sellew, Edwin P. II, 765
Sellew, Edwin Patterson II, 717
Sellew, Jane Maris II, 717
Sellew, Jeanne II, 717
Sellew, John Edwin II, 717
Sellew, Lois II, 700
Sellew, Mable II, 717
Sellew, Mildred Virginia II, 717
Sellew, V. Lois II, 717
Sellew, Virginia Lois II, 645
Sellew, Virginia Lois II, 729
Sellew, Virginia Lois II, 765
Sellew, William Walton II, 717
Sellew, Wm. Walton II, 646
Sellew, Wm. Walton II, 717
Sellick, Anna III, 284
Sellick, Sands III, 284
Sellman, John IV, 273
Sells, Anna R. IV, 273
Sells, James IV, 273
Sells, John C. IV, 273
Sells, John V. IV, 273
Sells, Jonathan I, 836
Sells, Thomas I, 1050
Selman, John IV, 273
Selmon, Alice IV, 496
Selster, Mary VI, 442
Seltzer, Susan F. II, 919
Seltzer, Susan S. II, 873
Seltzer, Wm. Harris II, 873
Seltzer, Wm. Harris II, 919
Selvee, Charles VI, 991
Selvee, Lucinda VI, 991
Semans, Rebecca V, 395
Semans, Rebecca F. V, 527
Semle, Jesse V, 464
Semmler, Alta III, 284
Semmler, Fritz III, 284
Semmler, Henry Charles III, 284
Semonas, Jamima VI, 959
Semones, John VI, 991
Semones, Mary VI, 991
Semones, Polly VI, 991
Semones, Stephen VI, 991
Semones, William VI, 879
Semonies, Mary VI, 935
Semonis, Emily VI, 953
Semonis, Poly VI, 953
Semonis, Thomas VI, 953
Semple, Lincoln IV, 1337
Semster, Eliza VI, 853
Semster, John VI, 853
Senatt, Cecelia II, 919
Senatt, Cecelia II, 943
Senill, Pearson II, 646
Senill, Rachel II, 646
Senman, A. L. V, 688
Senman, A. L. V, 709
Senman, Lula V, 688
Senman, Lula V, 709
Senniett, Symon II, 447
Senter, Anna VI, 876
Senter, Elizabeth VI, 876
Senter, John VI, 876
Senter, Mary VI, 946
Seplee, Thos. B. II, 919
Serbrell, Sarah IV, 759
Sergeant, Anne I, 896
Sergeant, Anne I, 900
Sergeant, Jacob I, 900
Serman, A. J. V, 1018
Sermon, Barbara II, 646
Sermon, Barbary II, 418
Sermon, Hannah II, 418
Sermon, Hannah II, 646
Sermon, Isaac II, 646
Sermon, Jane II, 418
Sermon, Jane II, 646
Sermon, Jane II, 694
Sermon, Joseph II, 418
Sermon, Joseph II, 503
Sermon, Joseph II, 646
Sermon, Joseph II, 694
Sermon, Mary II, 418
Sermon, Mary II, 503
Sermon, Mary II, 646
Sermon, Mary II, 694
Sermon, Richard II, 503
Sermon, Richard II, 646
Sermon, Robert II, 418
Sermon, Robert II, 646
Sermon, Sarah II, 418
Sermon, Wd. Sarah II, 646
Sermon, Wm. II, 646
Sermons, Joseph II, 418
Sermons, Mary II, 418
Sernones, Isaac VI, 991
Sernones, Mary VI, 991
Sernones, William VI, 991
Serrel, Jane II, 618
Serrell, Jane II, 646
Serril, Jacob II, 322
Serril, Jacob II, 324
Serril, Rebecca II, 322
Serril, Rebecca II, 324
Serril, Rebecca M. II, 324
Serrill, Elizabeth II, 646
Serrill, Elizabeth II, 919
Serrill, Elizabeth Wilson II, 818
Serrill, Frances II, 818
Serrill, Frances II, 919
Serrill, Frances III, 121
Serrill, Frances III, 284
Serrill, Hannah II, 646
Serrill, Hannah II, 919
Serrill, Hannah Shallcross II, 811
Serrill, Henry II, 919
Serrill, Isaac Starr II, 919
Serrill, Jacob II, 646
Serrill, Jane II, 646
Serrill, Jane Peterson II, 919
Serrill, John II, 418
Serrill, John II, 646
Serrill, John H. II, 418
Serrill, John H. II, 646
Serrill, Martha II, 418
Serrill, Martha II, 646
Serrill, Martha II, 919
Serrill, Martha Ash II, 919
Serrill, Pearson II, 646
Serrill, Pearson II, 818
Serrill, Pearson II, 919
Serrill, Pearson III, 121
Serrill, Pearson III, 284
Serrill, Rachel II, 646
Serrill, Rachel II, 818
Serrill, Rachel II, 919
Serrill, Rachel III, 121
Serrill, Rachel III, 284
Serrill, Rebecca H. II, 646
Serrill, Thomas II, 818
Serrill, Thos. II, 919
Serven, J. W. IV, 760
Serven, Sarah IV, 760
Servis, Elisabeth II, 504
Servis, Elisabeth II, 646
Servis, Elizabeth II, 591
Servis, Julia A. V, 763
Sesler, Joseph M. V, 643
Sesler, Martin V, 643
Sessions, Charles Marlow IV, 1262
Sessions, Hannah II, 646
Sessions, James II, 646
Sessions, James III, 284
Setta, Albert D. V, 464
Setta, Nancy V, 464
Settel, Fielding VI, 991
Settel, Peggy VI, 991
Settill, Hannah II, 659
Settill, Jacob II, 659
Settill, Pearson II, 659
Settill, Rachel II, 659
Settle, Alice VI, 987
Settle, Celey VI, 910
Settle, Christiana VI, 991
Settle, Diadem VI, 992
Settle, Fielding VI, 922
Settle, Fielding VI, 1004
Settle, Frances VI, 992
Settle, Frances VI, 1010
Settle, Francis VI, 910
Settle, Francis VI, 937
Settle, Francis VI, 976
Settle, Francis VI, 991
Settle, Francis C. VI, 991
Settle, Greenberry VI, 991
Settle, Greenbury VI, 882
Settle, Henrietta VI, 991
Settle, John VI, 991
Settle, Julia Ann VI, 991
Settle, Lewis VI, 991
Settle, Lucinda Jane VI, 991
Settle, Lucy VI, 991
Settle, Mahala VI, 882
Settle, Martha VI, 991
Settle, Mary V, 359
Settle, Mildred Jane VI, 976
Settle, Newman VI, 910
Settle, Newman VI, 987
Settle, William VI, 987
Settle, William VI, 991
Settle, Wm. S. VI, 992
Settle, Wraty VI, 991
Settles, Amizer V, 596
Settles, Archie V, 596
Settles, Cora V, 596
Settles, Eliza V, 596
Settles, Francis VI, 991
Settles, Kelsie V, 596
Settles, Lucy VI, 991
Settles, Mary V, 359
Settles, Mary V, 596
Settles, Minnie V, 119
Settles, Minnie V, 596
Setts, Albert V, 464
Setts, Hattie Ann V, 464
Setty, Albert V, 464
Setty, Albert D. V, 464
Setty, Ann V, 596
Setty, Byron V, 464
Setty, George V, 277
Setty, Gertrude Anna Victoria V, 464
Setty, Hattie A. V, 464
Setty, Hattie Ann V, 464
Setty, Icy Ruth V, 464
Setty, Jacob VI, 991
Setty, Lillie G. V, 277
Setty, Mary Alice Leota V, 464
Setty, Nancy V, 464
Setty, Olive V, 277
Setty, Olive J. V, 277
Setty, Parkey VI, 991
Setty, Violet May Hattie V, 464
Sevan, Sarah A. V, 688
Sever, George V, 709
Sever, George L. V, 596
Sever, George W. V, 596
Sever, Massie V, 596
Sever, Minnie V, 596
Severns, Bell V, 1018
Severns, Chas. V, 1018
Severns, Maria V, 1018
Severs, Eliza II, 825
Severs, George V, 596
Severs, George V, 709
Severs, George L. V, 596
Severs, George W. V, 596
Severs, Lydia V, 201
Severs, Lydia Ann V, 201
Severs, Margaret V, 596
Severs, Massie V, 596
Severs, Minnie V, 596
Sevilla, Sarah V, 384
Sevort, Zella V, 201
Seward, Elizabeth IV, 548
Seward, Elizabeth IV, 549
Seward, Joseph V, 596
Seward, Rebeckah II, 96
Seward, William VI, 93
Sewel, Mary I, 688
Sewel, Mary I, 900
Sewell, Amanda V, 201
Sewell, David V, 387
Sewell, Elizabeth V, 527
Sewell, Elizabeth V, 539
Sewell, Elizabeth Ann V, 643
Sewell, Elizabeth Howell VI, 757
Sewell, Ethel III, 69
Sewell, George IV, 1293
Sewell, James IV, 1293
Sewell, James Monroe VI, 757
Sewell, M. Elisabeth I, 222
Sewell, Martha V, 387
Sewell, Martha V, 596
Sewell, Martha L. V, 562
Sewell, Martha L. V, 596
Sewell, Martha S. V, 387
Sewell, Mary I, 900
Sewell, Sarah A. V, 359
Sewell, Sarah Ann V, 359
Sewell, Sarah Ann V, 430
Sewell, Susan IV, 1293
Sewell, Wm. J. V, 709
Sewer, Esther II, 418
Sewer, Francis II, 418
Sewers, Esther II, 418
Sewers, Francis II, 418
Sexton, ??? I, 1055
Sexton, Amos V, 194
Sexton, Andrew VI, 853
Sexton, Bessie Arminta I, 1161
Sexton, Catharine IV, 350
Sexton, Catharine V, 297
Sexton, Catharine V, 310
Sexton, Catharine V, 527
Sexton, Catharine VI, 442
Sexton, Catherine IV, 57
Sexton, Catherine IV, 108
Sexton, Catherine V, 119
Sexton, Catherine V, 527
Sexton, Catherine VI, 442
Sexton, Charles Edwin V, 277
Sexton, Charles Franklin I, 1161
Sexton, Chas. V, 277
Sexton, Chas. Edwin V, 277
Sexton, Cora V, 277
Sexton, Flora Elizabeth I, 1161
Sexton, Franklin Charles I, 1161
Sexton, George VI, 442
Sexton, Hannah I, 1098
Sexton, Hannah I, 1161
Sexton, Hannah IV, 57
Sexton, Hannah IV, 108
Sexton, Hannah IV, 341
Sexton, Hannah IV, 350
Sexton, Hannah V, 119
Sexton, Hannah V, 201
Sexton, Hannah V, 927
Sexton, Hannah V, 930
Sexton, Hannah VI, 442
Sexton, James I, 1161
Sexton, James Benton I, 1161
Sexton, James H. I, 1098
Sexton, John I, 1161
Sexton, John A. I, 1098
Sexton, Joseph Henry I, 1161
Sexton, Maria V, 527
Sexton, Marion A. V, 277
Sexton, Marion G. V, 277
Sexton, Mary I, 1055
Sexton, Mary IV, 57
Sexton, Mary IV, 108
Sexton, Mary IV, 350
Sexton, Mary V, 194
Sexton, Mary V, 201
Sexton, Mary V, 527
Sexton, Mary V, 533
Sexton, Mary VI, 442
Sexton, Mary VI, 853
Sexton, Mary Moorman V, 201
Sexton, Mashac VI, 442
Sexton, Masheck IV, 57
Sexton, Meshach VI, 442
Sexton, Meshack IV, 108
Sexton, Meshack IV, 341
Sexton, Meshech VI, 605
Sexton, Myrtle Sarah II, 313
Sexton, Nora Geneva V, 277
Sexton, Rachel II, 313
Sexton, Randolph II, 313
Sexton, Rebecca V, 194
Sexton, S. R. I, 1161
Sexton, Samuel VI, 853
Sexton, Sarah V, 201
Sexton, Susanah I, 1161
Sexton, Susannah I, 1161
Sexton, Susannah I, 1163
Sexton, Susannah IV, 341
Sexton, Viola I, 1161
Sexuar, Ernerst III, 284
Sexuar, Hedwig III, 284
Sexuar, William III, 284
Seybold, Alice V, 119
Seybold, Alice V, 861
Seybold, Alice VI, 559
Seybold, Alice VI, 647
Seybold, Alice VI, 698
Seybold, Casper VI, 559
Seybold, Eleanor V, 119
Seybold, Frederick VI, 559
Seybold, Gasper VI, 559
Seybold, Hannah VI, 484
Seybold, Hannah VI, 485
Seybold, Hannah VI, 559
Seybold, Hannah VI, 633
Seybold, Hannah VI, 698
Seybold, Isaac VI, 559
Seybold, Isaac VI, 698
Seybold, James VI, 559
Seybold, Jasper VI, 485
Seybold, Jasper VI, 559
Seybold, Jasper VI, 633
Seybold, Jasper VI, 698

Seybold, Jasper, Jr. VI, 559
Seybold, Jesse VI, 559
Seybold, Jesse VI, 698
Seybold, John V, 119
Seybold, John V, 861
Seybold, John VI, 484
Seybold, John VI, 559
Seybold, John VI, 698
Seybold, Joseph V, 119
Seybold, Joseph VI, 559
Seybold, Rebecca V, 119
Seybold, Rebecca VI, 699
Seybold, Rebeckah VI, 485
Seybold, Rebekah VI, 559
Seybold, Rebekah VI, 633
Seybold, Rebekah VI, 698
Seybold, Robert VI, 559
Seybold, Robert VI, 699
Seybold, Sarah V, 119
Seybold, Sarah VI, 698
Seybold, Silas VI, 559
Seymour, ??? III, 364
Seymour, Ann IV, 1184
Seymour, Anna A. IV, 1184
Seymour, Anna A. IV, 1189
Seymour, Drake III, 284
Seymour, Edward C. IV, 1240
Seymour, Edwin IV, 1184
Seymour, Eliza J. III, 364
Seymour, Ella E. IV, 1240
Seymour, Esther III, 284
Seymour, Esther C. III, 75
Seymour, Esther E. III, 284
Seymour, Esther H. III, 213
Seymour, Henry III, 213
Seymour, Henry III, 284
Seymour, Huldah III, 284
Seymour, Huldah IV, 1184
Seymour, Levi III, 284
Seymour, Levi IV, 1184
Seymour, Levi IV, 1240
Seymour, Manning IV, 1184
Seymour, Manning IV, 1240
Seymour, Manning L. III, 284
Seymour, Manning L. III, 365
Seymour, Martin IV, 1184
Seymour, Martin IV, 1189
Seymour, Mary III, 284
Seymour, Mary III, 365
Seymour, Mary IV, 1162
Seymour, Mary IV, 1184
Seymour, Mary E. III, 213
Seymour, Mary E. III, 284
Seymour, Mary W. III, 284
Seymour, Rhoda IV, 1184
Seymour, Rhoda C. IV, 1189
Seymour, Rhoda C. IV, 1239
Seymour, Rhoda C. IV, 1240
Seymour, Roda IV, 1231
Seymour, Samuel IV, 1184
Seymour, Silas IV, 1184
Seymour, Silas D. IV, 1184
Seymour, Susan A. IV, 1240
Seymour, Waldo W. IV, 1240
Seymour, William III, 284
Seymour, William IV, 1184
Seymour, William W. III, 284
Seymour, William W. IV, 1184
Seymour, Wm. III, 75
Seymour, Wm. III, 284
Seymour, Wm. W. IV, 1162
Seymour, Wm. W. IV, 1184
Seynold, Hannah VI, 698
Shackleford, Edna V, 277
Shackleford, James VI, 853
Shackleford, James VI, 991
Shackleford, John V, 277
Shackleford, John VI, 853
Shackleford, John VI, 991
Shackleford, Julia Wood IV, 273
Shackleford, Mary V, 277
Shackleford, Mary E. V, 277
Shackleford, Nancy VI, 853
Shackleford, Penelope VI, 991
Shackleford, Wilson V, 277
Shackles, ??? II, 96
Shackles, Josiah Ballenger II, 96
Shackles, Thomas II, 52
Shackles, Thomas II, 96
Shackleton, Richard II, 624
Shackleton, Richard II, 646
Shackleton, Sarah Poole II, 646
Shadarack, Agnes I, 572
Shaddock, Eliza IV, 490
Shaddock, Eliza IV, 496
Shaddock, James II, 447
Shaddock, James II, 599
Shaddock, James II, 646
Shaddock, Jane II, 258
Shaddock, Martha II, 447
Shaddock, Martha II, 646
Shaddock, William II, 258
Shadle, Mary G. IV, 1109
Shadle, Mary G. IV, 1114
Shadley, Bessie V, 677
Shadley, Bessie V, 709
Shadoen, Lucy VI, 991
Shadoen, William VI, 991
Shadwell, Paull II, 23
Shaefer, Arthur C. V, 930
Shaeffer, Irene L. IV, 1337
Shaeffer, Lela IV, 1327
Shaeffer, Lela IV, 1337
Shaeffer, Lillian IV, 1337
Shaeffer, Mary A. IV, 1337
Shaeffer, Susanna IV, 88
Shaeffer, Susanna IV, 108
Shafer, A. D. IV, 1293
Shafer, Ada IV, 496
Shafer, Ada R. IV, 496
Shafer, Alice V, 861
Shafer, Alice M. V, 861
Shafer, Arthur C. V, 930
Shafer, Arthur, Jr. V, 930
Shafer, Bobbie Ruth V, 763
Shafer, C. W. IV, 1262
Shafer, Caroline V, 862
Shafer, Christine Lauretta V, 201
Shafer, Daniel VI, 625
Shafer, Daniel VI, 626
Shafer, Daniel VI, 682
Shafer, Daniel VI, 699
Shafer, Ed V, 851
Shafer, Ed V, 861
Shafer, Edith IV, 496
Shafer, Edith M. IV, 496
Shafer, Elizabeth C. V, 277
Shafer, Ellen V, 359
Shafer, Eva IV, 496
Shafer, Eva E. IV, 496
Shafer, Hannah IV, 842
Shafer, Hannah IV, 855
Shafer, Herbert V, 763
Shafer, Lillian IV, 1262
Shafer, Lucinda V, 201
Shafer, Mabel V, 862
Shafer, Margaret V, 359
Shafer, Mary IV, 648
Shafer, Mary IV, 655
Shafer, Mary V, 359
Shafer, Mary V, 763
Shafer, Mary V, 861
Shafer, Mary E. V, 277
Shafer, Mary E. V, 861
Shafer, Mary E. VI, 682
Shafer, Mary E. VI, 699
Shafer, Mary Elizabeth V, 851
Shafer, Mary Esther V, 763
Shafer, Mary Jane V, 201
Shafer, Matilda Jane V, 359
Shafer, May V, 763
Shafer, Ora V, 175
Shafer, Ora V, 201
Shafer, Philip IV, 496
Shafer, Rachel IV, 894
Shafer, Rebecca Ann V, 763
Shafer, Rebecca Anna V, 763
Shafer, Rosina V, 359
Shafer, Ruth V, 861
Shafer, Sarah Elizabeth VI, 625
Shafer, Sarah Elizabeth VI, 626
Shafer, Sarah Elizabeth VI, 682
Shafer, Sarah Elizabeth VI, 699
Shafer, Sarah Ella Ora V, 201
Shafer, Sarah Ellen IV, 734
Shafer, Sarah Ellen IV, 760
Shafer, Susan V, 680
Shafer, Wesley V, 930
Shaffer, ??? I, 29
Shaffer, A. D. IV, 1293
Shaffer, Alice V, 930
Shaffer, Amanda III, 285
Shaffer, Amanda III, 345
Shaffer, Anna V, 1018
Shaffer, Annie V, 1018
Shaffer, Arthur V, 930
Shaffer, Arthur, Jr. V, 930
Shaffer, Blanch Fouty V, 1018
Shaffer, Chas. V, 1018
Shaffer, Chas. D. V, 1018
Shaffer, Cora Geneva I, 29
Shaffer, Ettie IV, 1293
Shaffer, F. M. V, 1018
Shaffer, Frank IV, 1293
Shaffer, Geneva V, 930
Shaffer, George W. IV, 1184
Shaffer, Gladys IV, 760
Shaffer, James IV, 1222
Shaffer, James V, 1018
Shaffer, James M. IV, 273
Shaffer, Jane V, 1018
Shaffer, Joshua V, 930
Shaffer, Leslie D. V, 930
Shaffer, Lillian IV, 760
Shaffer, Lillie IV, 1293
Shaffer, Louie IV, 1293
Shaffer, Louise III, 285
Shaffer, Louise J. III, 345
Shaffer, Lydia V, 930
Shaffer, Lydia Ann IV, 760
Shaffer, Marion V, 1018
Shaffer, Martha V, 1018
Shaffer, Mary IV, 1222
Shaffer, Mary IV, 1293
Shaffer, Mary B. V, 1018
Shaffer, Mary H. IV, 273
Shaffer, Mary M. IV, 1184
Shaffer, Mrs. Clara IV, 760
Shaffer, N. Lavina Corie IV, 1184
Shaffer, Nathan V, 119
Shaffer, Rhuben IV, 760
Shaffer, Russel Eugene V, 930
Shaffer, Sarah Ann II, 813
Shaffer, Sarah E. V, 1018
Shaffer, Sarah Ellen IV, 760
Shaffer, Sarah Ellen V, 1018
Shaffer, Susan V, 930
Shaffer, Susanna IV, 108
Shaffer, Thos. III, 285
Shaffer, Thos. III, 345
Shaffer, Wesley V, 930
Shahl, Eleanor IV, 159
Shahl, Isaac IV, 159
Shahl, John IV, 159
Shahl, Mahlon IV, 159
Shahl, Margaret IV, 159
Shahl, Samuel IV, 159
Shahl, Stacy IV, 159
Shakers, Isaac D. II, 751
Shakers, Jane D. II, 751
Shakers, Sarah II, 751
Shakle, Thomas II, 493
Shakle, Thomas II, 511
Shakle, Thomas II, 514
Shakleford, Simon V, 464
Shakles, Thomas II, 558
Shakles, Thomas II, 646
Shalcross, Ann II, 989
Shalcross, Ann II, 1025
Shalcross, Ruth II, 992
Shalcross, Ruth II, 1025
Shalcross, Sarah P. IV, 313
Shalcross, Sarah P. IV, 314
Shalcross, Wm. II, 1025
Shallcross, Leonard II, 995
Shallcross, Leonard II, 1025
Shallcross, Mary II, 646
Shallcross, Mary II, 674
Shallcross, Mary II, 807
Shallcross, Sarah P. IV, 274
Shallcross, Sarah P. IV, 350
Shallcross, Wm. II, 1025
Shallenberg, Augustus IV, 760
Shallenberg, Faynetta IV, 760
Shallenberg, Grace IV, 760
Shallenberg, Kenneth IV, 760
Shallenberg, Lowell IV, 760
Shallenberg, Marjorie IV, 760
Shallenberg, Robert IV, 760
Shallenberg, Walter IV, 760
Shallenberg, Walter IV, 842
Shalley, Jane II, 646
Shallington, Alice J. I, 318
Shambaugh, Elizabeth V, 202
Shambaugh, Emma V, 202
Shambaugh, Hazel V, 202
Shambaugh, Helen V, 202
Shambaugh, Horace V, 202
Shambaugh, I. N. V, 202
Shambaugh, Levi J. V, 202
Shambaugh, Mildred Esther V, 202
Shambaugh, Sarah A. V, 201
Shambaugh, Sarah Ann V, 202
Shamblain, Rachel IV, 350
Shamel, Elizabeth IV, 549
Shamel, Rachel IV, 527
Shamlin, Rachel IV, 341
Shanck, Alice C. IV, 1337
Shanck, Alice D. IV, 1337
Shanck, H. K. IV, 1337
Shanck, Henry K. IV, 1337
Shands, Missouri VI, 853
Shands, William A. VI, 853
Shane, Fred V, 202
Shane, James IV, 496
Shane, Mary Eva IV, 496
Shane, Samuel IV, 655
Shaner, Allen B. V, 643
Shaner, Amelia V, 1018
Shaner, Annie M. V, 643
Shaner, Caleb IV, 1138
Shaner, Deborah IV, 130
Shaner, Deborah IV, 132
Shaner, Frederick V, 643
Shaner, Hattie V, 643
Shaner, John V, 1018
Shaner, Lewis V, 596
Shaner, Lucy A. V, 1018
Shaner, Lucy Ann V, 1018
Shaner, Mary IV, 1138
Shaner, Mary E. V, 596
Shaner, Mary Elizabeth V, 596
Shaner, Mary M. V, 643
Shaner, Melcenia V, 643
Shaner, Minnie M. V, 643
Shaner, Myrtle V, 596
Shaner, Phebe Catharine IV, 130
Shaner, Phebe Catharine IV, 132
Shaner, Sarah E. IV, 1131
Shaner, Sarah E. IV, 1138
Shaner, Stella May V, 596
Shaner, Stephen J. V, 643
Shaner, Virgin V, 614
Shaner, Virgin V, 643
Shaneyfelt, Bird V, 1018
Shaneyfelt, Della V, 1018
Shaneyfelt, Orra L. V, 1018
Shank, Alice C. IV, 1337
Shank, Arthur V, 596
Shank, C. Leroy V, 430
Shank, E. Ray V, 596
Shank, Earl V, 596
Shank, Florence M. V, 596
Shank, George H. V, 119
Shank, George H. V, 596
Shank, George Henry V, 119
Shank, George Henry V, 596
Shank, Harry W. V, 430
Shank, Harry Waldo V, 430
Shank, Henry V, 430
Shank, Henry K. IV, 1337
Shank, Jacob V, 596
Shank, Jacob D. V, 430
Shank, Jacob D. V, 596
Shank, James V, 596
Shank, John Stump V, 596
Shank, Joseph E. V, 596
Shank, Joseph H. V, 596
Shank, Jzcob V, 430
Shank, Leo V, 596
Shank, Leo V, 597
Shank, Leonard V, 596
Shank, Leroy V, 430
Shank, Lucian V, 596
Shank, Lucius V, 596
Shank, Marie V, 596
Shank, Martha C. V, 596
Shank, Mary V, 430
Shank, Mary V, 596
Shank, Mary A. V, 596
Shank, Mary Alfretta V, 596
Shank, Mary M. V, 596
Shank, Muriel V, 596
Shank, Murrell V, 596
Shank, Ray V, 597
Shank, Raymond V, 596
Shank, Samuel V, 596
Shank, Sarah V, 430
Shank, Sarah V, 596
Shank, Sarah E. V, 430
Shank, Sarah E. V, 596
Shankland, Sarah IV, 417
Shankland, Sarah IV, 436
Shanks, Carl H. V, 709
Shanks, Carl Herman, Jr. V, 709
Shanks, David L. IV, 1263
Shanks, Edith V, 709
Shanks, Martha VI, 377
Shanks, Martha VI, 442
Shannon, Ada V, 597
Shannon, Charles VI, 844
Shannon, Elizabeth II, 717
Shannon, Elizina B. V, 643
Shannon, Elwood III, 285
Shannon, Frances II, 646
Shannon, Francis II, 646
Shannon, Helen III, 92
Shannon, J. C. IV, 274
Shannon, J. C. V, 643
Shannon, James VI, 835
Shannon, James VI, 853
Shannon, James VI, 991
Shannon, Jane II, 646
Shannon, Jene VI, 991
Shannon, John VI, 853
Shannon, John VI, 991
Shannon, John K. III, 92
Shannon, John K. III, 285
Shannon, Lucy V, 643
Shannon, Luella IV, 274
Shannon, Mary III, 285
Shannon, Mary VI, 862
Shannon, Mary VI, 991
Shannon, Nancy VI, 853
Shannon, Polly VI, 835
Shannon, Rachel VI, 846
Shannon, Rachel VI, 853
Shannon, Rachel R. II, 800
Shannon, Sally Ann VI, 853
Shannon, Sarah IV, 174
Shannon, Sarah IV, 274
Shannon, W. Lane II, 717
Shannon, W. Lane II, 765
Shannon, Walter II, 717
Shannon, William VI, 853
Shannon, Wm. II, 646
Shannon, Wm. Allen IV, 274
Shannon, Wm. Lane II, 765
Shanon, Esther IV, 496
Shaon, Ann VI, 991
Shaon, David VI, 991
Shaon, Eli VI, 945
Shaon, Elizabeth VI, 957
Shaon, James K. VI, 973
Shaon, James K. VI, 991
Shaon, Luraner VI, 945
Shaon, Mary VI, 973
Shaon, Mary VI, 991
Shaon, Minerva A. VI, 973
Shaon, Polly VI, 958
Shaon, Rebecca VI, 945
Shaon, Richard VI, 991
Shaon, Richard T. VI, 945
Shaon, Richard T. VI, 957
Shaon, Richard T. VI, 958
Shaon, Susannah VI, 944
Shaper, Abraham V, 430
Shapley, Mary I, 275
Shaps, Lewis IV, 1337
Shapter, Evangeline III, 285
Shapter, Hannah III, 285
Shapter, Hannah B. III, 328
Shapter, John III, 370
Shapter, John S. III, 180
Shapter, John S. III, 285
Shapter, John S. III, 328
Shapter, Rebecca III, 285
Shapter, Wd. Hannah B. III,
Sharcross, John II, 418
Shardon, Mary I, 418
Shariff, Lucinda V, 430
Sharon, Freddie IV, 274
Sharon, Freddy IV, 274
Sharon, Jane II, 786
Sharon, Sarah A. IV, 274
Sharon, Sarah Ann IV, 226
Sharon, Sarah Ann IV, 274
Sharon, Sarah Ann IV, 497
Sharon, Susan IV, 497
Sharon, Susanna IV, 497
Sharp, ??? III, 112
Sharp, Aaron IV, 1293
Sharp, Abbie IV, 549
Sharp, Abigail IV, 159
Sharp, Abigail IV, 328
Sharp, Abigail V, 976
Sharp, Abigail VI, 605
Sharp, Abigail VI, 699
Sharp, Abigail B. V, 886
Sharp, Abraham VI, 991
Sharp, Adaline IV, 916
Sharp, Adaline IV, 991
Sharp, Adaline IV, 1114
Sharp, Adaline IV, 1138
Sharp, Adam VI, 892
Sharp, Addison IV, 1222
Sharp, Aldis V, 277
Sharp, Aldis A. V, 277
Sharp, Alex. III, 446
Sharp, Alpheus P. VI, 443
Sharp, Amos IV, 1138
Sharp, Angelina IV, 734
Sharp, Angelina IV, 760
Sharp, Ann II, 227
Sharp, Ann II, 258
Sharp, Ann IV, 28
Sharp, Ann IV, 57
Sharp, Ann IV, 436
Sharp, Ann IV, 456
Sharp, Ann IV, 535
Sharp, Ann IV, 549
Sharp, Ann IV, 557
Sharp, Ann IV, 916
Sharp, Ann IV, 991
Sharp, Ann IV, 1114
Sharp, Ann L. II, 717
Sharp, Ann L. II, 743
Sharp, Ann L. II, 765
Sharp, Ann Lindsey II, 418
Sharp, Ann Lindsey II, 765
Sharp, Anna II, 96
Sharp, Anna II, 646
Sharp, Anna II, 647
Sharp, Anna II, 717

p, Anne II, 646
p, Anne VI, 991
p, Anne L. II, 706
p, Anthony II, 38
p, Anthony II, 96
p, Anthony II, 300
p, Anthony II, 418
p, Anthony II, 646
p, Anthony II, 647
p, Arthur V, 882
p, Arthur V, 886
p, Arthur V, 888
p, Arthur V, 976
p, Barshaba VI, 895
p, Bathsheba VI, 989
p, Benjamin II, 647
p, Benjamin II, 765
p, Benjamin III, 285
p, Beulah II, 300
p, Bowman V, 277
p, Caleb VI, 991
p, Caleb VI, 1002
p, Carrie IV, 1293
p, Clayton IV, 760
p, Cyrus V, 277
p, Cyrus VI, 991
p, Cyrus B. V, 277
p, Deborah IV, 613
p, Deborah IV, 655
p, Deborah IV, 1114
p, Deborah IV, 1138
p, Delilah V, 527
p, Dellie V, 597
p, Dora III, 409
p, Dora III, 446
p, Dora Flournoy III, 420
p, Dorothy IV, 1114
p, Dorothy M. IV, 1138
p, Edward H. IV, 1222
p, Eli N. V, 359
p, Eliza IV, 916
p, Eliza IV, 991
p, Eliza IV, 1114
p, Eliza Ann VI, 935
p, Eliza M. V, 882
p, Eliza M. V, 886
p, Elizabeth I, 418
p, Elizabeth I, 428
p, Elizabeth II, 38
p, Elizabeth II, 96
p, Elizabeth II, 227
p, Elizabeth II, 247
p, Elizabeth II, 258
p, Elizabeth II, 275
p, Elizabeth II, 535
p, Elizabeth II, 567
p, Elizabeth II, 646
p, Elizabeth II, 647
p, Elizabeth IV, 1144
p, Elizabeth IV, 1184
p, Elizabeth IV, 1222
p, Elizabeth V, 597
p, Elizabeth V, 886
p, Elizabeth V, 888
p, Elizabeth V, 943
p, Elizabeth VI, 371
p, Elizabeth VI, 372
p, Elizabeth VI, 442
p, Elizabeth VI, 888
p, Elizabeth B. VI, 991
p, Elizabeth, Jr. II, 96
p, Emaline IV, 1114
p, Emaline A. IV, 1138
p, Enoch IV, 613
p, Enoch IV, 655
p, Enoch IV, 842
p, Enoch IV, 991
p, Esther II, 96
p, Esther IV, 1177
p, Esther IV, 1184
p, Esther IV, 1219
p, Esther IV, 1222
p, Esther VI, 442
p, Esther Ann V, 886
p, Evalena G. IV, 1293
p, Frances Oglesby VI, 327
p, Frances Oglesby VI, 878
p, Frances W. VI, 798
p, Frances W. VI, 878
p, Frank V, 277
p, George IV, 159
p, George IV, 350
p, George V, 527
p, George V, 886
p, George VI, 371
p, George VI, 372
p, George VI, 442
p, George VI, 443
p, George VI, 605
p, George VI, 699
p, George VI, 888
Sharp, Grace II, 54
Sharp, Grace II, 96
Sharp, Haines V, 886
Sharp, Haines V, 943
Sharp, Haines V, 976
Sharp, Hannah II, 38
Sharp, Hannah II, 96
Sharp, Hannah II, 200
Sharp, Hannah II, 258
Sharp, Hannah II, 418
Sharp, Hannah II, 647
Sharp, Hannah II, 706
Sharp, Hannah II, 717
Sharp, Hannah II, 718
Sharp, Hannah II, 743
Sharp, Hannah II, 765
Sharp, Hannah III, 285
Sharp, Hannah IV, 477
Sharp, Hannah IV, 497
Sharp, Hannah IV, 916
Sharp, Hannah IV, 991
Sharp, Hannah IV, 1114
Sharp, Hannah IV, 1138
Sharp, Hannah IV, 1222
Sharp, Hannah V, 886
Sharp, Hannah V, 888
Sharp, Hannah VI, 442
Sharp, Hannah Ida IV, 1222
Sharp, Hannah, Jr. II, 418
Sharp, Harvey IV, 1222
Sharp, Hervey IV, 1222
Sharp, Hope II, 646
Sharp, Hope II, 647
Sharp, Hugh II, 200
Sharp, Hugh II, 242
Sharp, Hugh II, 258
Sharp, Hugh II, 264
Sharp, Hugh II, 1026
Sharp, Isaac II, 38
Sharp, Isaac II, 58
Sharp, Isaac II, 96
Sharp, Isaac II, 646
Sharp, Isaac IV, 655
Sharp, Isaac IV, 910
Sharp, Isaac IV, 916
Sharp, Isaac IV, 991
Sharp, Isaac IV, 1114
Sharp, Isaac IV, 1138
Sharp, J. C. IV, 1293
Sharp, Jacob II, 96
Sharp, James II, 418
Sharp, James II, 646
Sharp, James V, 119
Sharp, James V, 979
Sharp, James D. VI, 991
Sharp, Jane II, 96
Sharp, Jane VI, 977
Sharp, Jemima II, 646
Sharp, Jemima V, 886
Sharp, Jemima V, 943
Sharp, Jemima V, 976
Sharp, Jemima C. V, 886
Sharp, Jemima E. V, 885
Sharp, Jemima E. V, 888
Sharp, Jephthah IV, 331
Sharp, Jephthah IV, 350
Sharp, Jeptha IV, 159
Sharp, Jeptha IV, 436
Sharp, Jeptha IV, 557
Sharp, Jeptha VI, 699
Sharp, Jesse IV, 159
Sharp, Jesse IV, 436
Sharp, Jesse V, 277
Sharp, Jesse VI, 443
Sharp, Jesse VI, 605
Sharp, Jesse VI, 699
Sharp, Jesse K. IV, 1222
Sharp, Jesse R. IV, 350
Sharp, Job V, 119
Sharp, Joel IV, 680
Sharp, Joel IV, 725
Sharp, Joel IV, 760
Sharp, Joel IV, 1138
Sharp, John II, 227
Sharp, John II, 247
Sharp, John II, 258
Sharp, John II, 300
Sharp, John II, 418
Sharp, John II, 535
Sharp, John II, 646
Sharp, John II, 647
Sharp, John II, 718
Sharp, John II, 765
Sharp, John II, 919
Sharp, John IV, 477
Sharp, John IV, 497
Sharp, John IV, 1144
Sharp, John IV, 1184
Sharp, John IV, 1222
Sharp, John V, 277
Sharp, John V, 709
Sharp, John VI, 895
Sharp, John VI, 907
Sharp, John VI, 991
Sharp, John W. II, 717
Sharp, John W. IV, 1293
Sharp, John W. V, 277
Sharp, John Webster II, 765
Sharp, John, Jr. II, 765
Sharp, John, Jr. VI, 977
Sharp, John, Jr. VI, 991
Sharp, John, Sr. II, 717
Sharp, Johnson IV, 1293
Sharp, Jonathan IV, 1293
Sharp, Joseph II, 96
Sharp, Joseph II, 418
Sharp, Joseph II, 647
Sharp, Joseph II, 706
Sharp, Joseph II, 717
Sharp, Joseph II, 718
Sharp, Joseph II, 743
Sharp, Joseph II, 765
Sharp, Joseph VI, 605
Sharp, Joseph B. V, 277
Sharp, Joseph N. II, 717
Sharp, Joseph W. II, 765
Sharp, Joseph W. IV, 1222
Sharp, Joshua II, 567
Sharp, Joshua II, 647
Sharp, Joshua VI, 878
Sharp, Joshua VI, 991
Sharp, Josiah II, 646
Sharp, Josiah II, 647
Sharp, Kate IV, 1286
Sharp, Kate IV, 1293
Sharp, Kennard IV, 1222
Sharp, Laura V, 597
Sharp, Leta M. V, 665
Sharp, Leta M. V, 709
Sharp, Levi IV, 1222
Sharp, Levi B. IV, 1222
Sharp, Lewis V, 277
Sharp, Lizzie IV, 1293
Sharp, Loduski IV, 1293
Sharp, Lot VI, 935
Sharp, Lot VI, 989
Sharp, Lot VI, 991
Sharp, Lott VI, 989
Sharp, Louis IV, 1293
Sharp, Louis V, 277
Sharp, Louis M. V, 277
Sharp, Lucy B. VI, 327
Sharp, Lucy B. VI, 829
Sharp, Lydia IV, 159
Sharp, Lydia IV, 350
Sharp, Lydia IV, 910
Sharp, Lydia IV, 916
Sharp, Lydia IV, 991
Sharp, Lydia IV, 1114
Sharp, Lydia IV, 1138
Sharp, Lydia VI, 442
Sharp, Lydia VI, 605
Sharp, Lydia VI, 991
Sharp, Margaret II, 38
Sharp, Margaret V, 119
Sharp, Margaret VI, 991
Sharp, Marget II, 96
Sharp, Margret II, 58
Sharp, Margret II, 96
Sharp, Margrett II, 78
Sharp, Margrett II, 96
Sharp, Margrett II, 418
Sharp, Maria G. VI, 991
Sharp, Mark IV, 1114
Sharp, Mark IV, 1138
Sharp, Martha II, 646
Sharp, Martha IV, 159
Sharp, Martha IV, 328
Sharp, Martha IV, 350
Sharp, Martha IV, 355
Sharp, Martha IV, 436
Sharp, Martha IV, 549
Sharp, Martha IV, 725
Sharp, Martha IV, 760
Sharp, Martha VI, 442
Sharp, Martha VI, 460
Sharp, Martha VI, 542
Sharp, Martha VI, 559
Sharp, Martha VI, 605
Sharp, Martha VI, 699
Sharp, Martha VI, 889
Sharp, Martha J. V, 359
Sharp, Martha W. IV, 680
Sharp, Mary II, 38
Sharp, Mary II, 96
Sharp, Mary II, 106
Sharp, Mary II, 646
Sharp, Mary II, 819
Sharp, Mary II, 919
Sharp, Mary III, 285
Sharp, Mary IV, 350
Sharp, Mary IV, 655
Sharp, Mary IV, 808
Sharp, Mary IV, 842
Sharp, Mary IV, 991
Sharp, Mary IV, 1134
Sharp, Mary IV, 1138
Sharp, Mary VI, 844
Sharp, Mary VI, 991
Sharp, Mary A. V, 277
Sharp, Mary A. Gidley IV, 1222
Sharp, Mary Ann IV, 725
Sharp, Mary Ann IV, 760
Sharp, Mary Ann V, 882
Sharp, Mary Ann V, 884
Sharp, Mary Ann V, 886
Sharp, Mary Ann V, 976
Sharp, Mary Esther IV, 1222
Sharp, Mary L. VI, 991
Sharp, Mary V. IV, 350
Sharp, Matty VI, 892
Sharp, Mercy IV, 410
Sharp, Milton VI, 991
Sharp, Miriam II, 418
Sharp, Nancy VI, 846
Sharp, Nancy VI, 991
Sharp, Nehemiah II, 418
Sharp, Nehemiah II, 646
Sharp, Nellie IV, 985
Sharp, Noah VI, 977
Sharp, Oliver IV, 916
Sharp, Oliver IV, 991
Sharp, Oliver IV, 1114
Sharp, Oliver IV, 1138
Sharp, Oliver IV, 1222
Sharp, Patsey VI, 991
Sharp, Peggy VI, 928
Sharp, Pembrook Flitcraft V, 882
Sharp, Pembrook Flitcraft V, 886
Sharp, Phebe II, 829
Sharp, Phebe IV, 1293
Sharp, Phebe V, 119
Sharp, Phebe V, 310
Sharp, Phebe VI, 383
Sharp, Phebe VI, 442
Sharp, Phebie IV, 1293
Sharp, Phebie IV, 1296
Sharp, Phineas IV, 159
Sharp, Phineas IV, 350
Sharp, Phinehas VI, 442
Sharp, Phinihas VI, 605
Sharp, Polly VI, 991
Sharp, Priscilla III, 112
Sharp, Priscilla III, 285
Sharp, R. P. I, 1161
Sharp, Rachel II, 38
Sharp, Rachel II, 96
Sharp, Rachel II, 113
Sharp, Rachel II, 718
Sharp, Rachel II, 765
Sharp, Rachel II, 1026
Sharp, Rachel VI, 991
Sharp, Rebecca II, 96
Sharp, Rebecca II, 300
Sharp, Rebecca II, 647
Sharp, Rebecca II, 765
Sharp, Rebecca IV, 274
Sharp, Rebecca IV, 349
Sharp, Rebecca IV, 350
Sharp, Rebecca IV, 680
Sharp, Rebecca IV, 725
Sharp, Rebecca IV, 760
Sharp, Rebecca IV, 1222
Sharp, Rebecca VI, 991
Sharp, Rebecca Ann IV, 1222
Sharp, Robert IV, 725
Sharp, Robert V, 709
Sharp, Robert VI, 267
Sharp, Roy V, 527
Sharp, Ruth IV, 760
Sharp, Sally VI, 926
Sharp, Samson VI, 889
Sharp, Samson VI, 928
Sharp, Samson VI, 991
Sharp, Samuel II, 38
Sharp, Samuel II, 96
Sharp, Samuel II, 227
Sharp, Samuel II, 258
Sharp, Samuel II, 567
Sharp, Samuel II, 647
Sharp, Samuel IV, 159
Sharp, Samuel IV, 328
Sharp, Samuel IV, 350
Sharp, Samuel IV, 355
Sharp, Samuel IV, 436
Sharp, Samuel V, 359
Sharp, Samuel VI, 442
Sharp, Samuel VI, 443
Sharp, Samuel VI, 605
Sharp, Samuel VI, 699
Sharp, Samuel F. IV, 549
Sharp, Samuel L. IV, 1222
Sharp, Samuel T. IV, 274
Sharp, Samuel T. IV, 350
Sharp, Samuel T. IV, 549
Sharp, Samuth II, 96
Sharp, Sarah II, 38
Sharp, Sarah II, 96
Sharp, Sarah II, 110
Sharp, Sarah II, 418
Sharp, Sarah II, 646
Sharp, Sarah II, 647
Sharp, Sarah II, 765
Sharp, Sarah IV, 159
Sharp, Sarah IV, 331
Sharp, Sarah IV, 350
Sharp, Sarah IV, 355
Sharp, Sarah IV, 410
Sharp, Sarah IV, 436
Sharp, Sarah IV, 535
Sharp, Sarah IV, 549
Sharp, Sarah IV, 557
Sharp, Sarah IV, 613
Sharp, Sarah IV, 655
Sharp, Sarah IV, 799
Sharp, Sarah IV, 808
Sharp, Sarah IV, 842
Sharp, Sarah IV, 991
Sharp, Sarah IV, 1184
Sharp, Sarah IV, 1193
Sharp, Sarah IV, 1222
Sharp, Sarah V, 359
Sharp, Sarah VI, 605
Sharp, Sarah VI, 699
Sharp, Sarah E. VI, 991
Sharp, Sarah S. II, 728
Sharp, Sarah S. II, 765
Sharp, Sarah, Jr. IV, 655
Sharp, Sarah, Jr. IV, 842
Sharp, Sarah, Jr. IV, 991
Sharp, Silas VI, 991
Sharp, Simeon IV, 760
Sharp, Simeon Webster II, 718
Sharp, Simeon Webster II, 765
Sharp, Susan V, 861
Sharp, Susanna IV, 81
Sharp, Susanna IV, 108
Sharp, Susanna V, 359
Sharp, Susannah IV, 132
Sharp, Tacy IV, 1184
Sharp, Thomas II, 258
Sharp, Thomas II, 275
Sharp, Thomas IV, 410
Sharp, Thomas IV, 760
Sharp, Thomas IV, 1177
Sharp, Thomas IV, 1184
Sharp, Thomas IV, 1219
Sharp, Thomas IV, 1222
Sharp, Thomas V, 709
Sharp, Thomas VI, 442
Sharp, Thomas G. I, 1161
Sharp, Thomas J. V, 527
Sharp, Thomas J. V, 709
Sharp, Thomas, Jr. VI, 442
Sharp, Townsend IV, 1184
Sharp, Townsend IV, 1222
Sharp, Wd. Dora F. III, 446
Sharp, William II, 718
Sharp, William IV, 1293
Sharp, William VI, 844
Sharp, William H. IV, 350
Sharp, William Henry IV, 274
Sharp, Willoughby III, 409
Sharp, Willoughby III, 420
Sharp, Willoughby III, 446
Sharp, Wm. II, 765
Sharp, Wm. IV, 1293
Sharp, Wm. H. IV, 349
Sharp, Wm. L. II, 765
Sharpe, Anne VI, 991
Sharpe, Anthony II, 418
Sharpe, Frances VI, 829
Sharpe, Hope II, 647
Sharpe, Hope II, 672
Sharpe, James VI, 189
Sharpe, James VI, 201
Sharpe, James VI, 207
Sharpe, James VI, 211
Sharpe, James D. VI, 991
Sharpe, John VI, 991
Sharpe, Nehemiah II, 418
Sharpe, Sarah E. VI, 991
Sharples, Abraham II, 508
Sharples, Abraham II, 647
Sharples, Adam II, 96
Sharples, Albert IV, 1222
Sharples, Amy IV, 655
Sharples, Andrew Thompson II, 96
Sharples, Benjamin IV, 57
Sharples, Eliza II, 508
Sharples, Eliza II, 647
Sharples, Elizabeth IV, 23
Sharples, Elizabeth IV, 57

Sharples, Ellen IV, 1222
Sharples, Evi IV, 655
Sharples, Hannah II, 647
Sharples, Helen E. II, 841
Sharples, Helen E. II, 920
Sharples, Henry W. Satterthwait II, 1060
Sharples, Isaac IV, 655
Sharples, Joseph II, 647
Sharples, Lavina IV, 655
Sharples, Lucy II, 1060
Sharples, Lydia IV, 655
Sharples, Lydia IV, 1222
Sharples, Martha S. II, 841
Sharples, Martha S. II, 920
Sharples, Mary II, 96
Sharples, Mary II, 647
Sharples, Miriam IV, 655
Sharples, Nathan IV, 655
Sharples, Phebe II, 508
Sharples, Phebe II, 647
Sharples, Philip M. II, 841
Sharples, Philip M. II, 920
Sharples, Robert II, 508
Sharples, Robert II, 647
Sharples, S. Emlen II, 841
Sharples, S. Emlen II, 920
Sharples, Sarah IV, 655
Sharples, Septimus C. IV, 655
Sharples, Wd. Mary II, 104
Sharples, Wm. II, 647
Sharples, Wm. IV, 1222
Sharpless, ??? IV, 132
Sharpless, Aaron II, 293
Sharpless, Aaron II, 300
Sharpless, Aaron II, 718
Sharpless, Aaron II, 750
Sharpless, Aaron II, 765
Sharpless, Aaron II, 1026
Sharpless, Aaron III, 285
Sharpless, Abraham II, 647
Sharpless, Addie IV, 639
Sharpless, Albert IV, 655
Sharpless, Albert IV, 991
Sharpless, Albert IV, 1222
Sharpless, Albert F. IV, 655
Sharpless, Alfred II, 920
Sharpless, Alfred III, 446
Sharpless, Alfred IV, 718
Sharpless, Alfred IV, 760
Sharpless, Alfred H. II, 718
Sharpless, Amy IV, 77
Sharpless, Amy IV, 108
Sharpless, Amy IV, 613
Sharpless, Amy IV, 655
Sharpless, Amy IV, 991
Sharpless, Ann IV, 158
Sharpless, Ann IV, 159
Sharpless, Ann IV, 274
Sharpless, Anna II, 418
Sharpless, Anna II, 716
Sharpless, Anna B. II, 718
Sharpless, Anna B. II, 765
Sharpless, Anna L. II, 730
Sharpless, Anna L. II, 765
Sharpless, Anna M. II, 920
Sharpless, Anna P. II, 718
Sharpless, Anna P. II, 765
Sharpless, Anna P. IV, 760
Sharpless, Anna R. II, 718
Sharpless, Anna R. II, 765
Sharpless, Anne III, 285
Sharpless, Anne G. II, 819
Sharpless, Anne G. II, 920
Sharpless, Annie G. II, 906
Sharpless, Annie G. II, 920
Sharpless, Benj. II, 418
Sharpless, Benj. III, 285
Sharpless, Benj. IV, 655
Sharpless, Benjamin II, 183
Sharpless, Benjamin II, 418
Sharpless, Benjamin II, 647
Sharpless, Benjamin II, 949
Sharpless, Benjamin II, 1086
Sharpless, Benjamin II, 1089
Sharpless, Benjamin IV, 57
Sharpless, Benjamin IV, 77
Sharpless, Benjamin IV, 108
Sharpless, Benjamin IV, 613
Sharpless, Benjamin IV, 655
Sharpless, Benjamin IV, 991
Sharpless, Benjamin IV, 1222
Sharpless, Beulah E. IV, 639
Sharpless, Blakey II, 647
Sharpless, Caroline III, 414
Sharpless, Caroline III, 446
Sharpless, Caroline H. II, 718
Sharpless, Charles II, 718
Sharpless, Charles II, 968
Sharpless, Charles Henry II, 1089
Sharpless, Charles L. II, 418
Sharpless, Charles L. II, 765
Sharpless, Charles L., Jr. II, 718
Sharpless, Deborah IV, 1222
Sharpless, Delbert IV, 1222
Sharpless, Edith II, 418
Sharpless, Edith II, 514
Sharpless, Edith II, 647
Sharpless, Edith II, 718
Sharpless, Edith II, 765
Sharpless, Edith II, 790
Sharpless, Edith III, 285
Sharpless, Edith IV, 108
Sharpless, Edith IV, 131
Sharpless, Edith IV, 132
Sharpless, Edith IV, 155
Sharpless, Edith IV, 159
Sharpless, Edith IV, 718
Sharpless, Edith IV, 760
Sharpless, Edith VI, 605
Sharpless, Edward II, 647
Sharpless, Edwin II, 418
Sharpless, Edwin II, 718
Sharpless, Edwin IV, 655
Sharpless, Edwin A. IV, 655
Sharpless, Eleanor IV, 614
Sharpless, Eleanor IV, 655
Sharpless, Eliz. III, 446
Sharpless, Eliza II, 418
Sharpless, Eliza II, 614
Sharpless, Eliza II, 647
Sharpless, Eliza II, 718
Sharpless, Eliza II, 812
Sharpless, Eliza Ann IV, 983
Sharpless, Eliza H. II, 718
Sharpless, Elizabeth II, 718
Sharpless, Elizabeth IV, 57
Sharpless, Elizabeth IV, 95
Sharpless, Elizabeth IV, 108
Sharpless, Elizabeth IV, 132
Sharpless, Elizabeth VI, 410
Sharpless, Elizabeth VI, 443
Sharpless, Elizabeth S. III, 446
Sharpless, Elizabeth S. III, 448
Sharpless, Ellen IV, 655
Sharpless, Ellen IV, 1222
Sharpless, Ellen T. IV, 613
Sharpless, Ellen T. IV, 655
Sharpless, Ellis IV, 132
Sharpless, Enos II, 704
Sharpless, Esther II, 647
Sharpless, Esther H. II, 718
Sharpless, Eusebius T. II, 718
Sharpless, Evi IV, 655
Sharpless, Frances M. II, 920
Sharpless, Fred Farley III, 414
Sharpless, Fred Farley III, 446
Sharpless, Frederick III, 446
Sharpless, Frederick H. II, 718
Sharpless, Geo. IV, 158
Sharpless, George II, 418
Sharpless, George II, 647
Sharpless, George IV, 159
Sharpless, Griffith IV, 983
Sharpless, Hannah II, 183
Sharpless, Hannah II, 258
Sharpless, Hannah II, 418
Sharpless, Hannah II, 647
Sharpless, Hannah II, 704
Sharpless, Hannah II, 765
Sharpless, Hannah II, 848
Sharpless, Hannah II, 920
Sharpless, Hannah III, 285
Sharpless, Hannah Pennell IV, 132
Sharpless, Helen E. II, 920
Sharpless, Henry II, 716
Sharpless, Henry G. II, 418
Sharpless, Henry H. G. II, 765
Sharpless, Henry W. II, 718
Sharpless, Henry W. II, 765
Sharpless, Hugh Judge IV, 108
Sharpless, Hugh Judge IV, 436
Sharpless, Isaac II, 15
Sharpless, Isaac II, 418
Sharpless, Isaac II, 514
Sharpless, Isaac II, 647
Sharpless, Isaac II, 750
Sharpless, Isaac II, 765
Sharpless, Isaac III, 102
Sharpless, Isaac III, 285
Sharpless, Isaac IV, 108
Sharpless, Isaac IV, 655
Sharpless, Isaac IV, 760
Sharpless, Isaac IV, 991
Sharpless, Isaac D. II, 647
Sharpless, Isaac D. II, 765
Sharpless, Isaac D. III, 285
Sharpless, Israel IV, 655
Sharpless, Israel IV, 983
Sharpless, Jacob II, 647
Sharpless, Jason IV, 983
Sharpless, Jesse II, 614
Sharpless, Jesse II, 647
Sharpless, Jesse II, 718
Sharpless, Jesse II, 765
Sharpless, Jesse II, 819
Sharpless, Jesse II, 821
Sharpless, Jesse II, 823
Sharpless, Jesse II, 919
Sharpless, Jesse IV, 983
Sharpless, Jesse VI, 443
Sharpless, Joanna II, 614
Sharpless, Joanna II, 647
Sharpless, Joanna II, 718
Sharpless, Joanna II, 765
Sharpless, Joanna II, 819
Sharpless, Joanna II, 821
Sharpless, Joanna II, 823
Sharpless, Joanna II, 919
Sharpless, Joanna VI, 443
Sharpless, John III, 285
Sharpless, John IV, 760
Sharpless, John IV, 991
Sharpless, John M. II, 718
Sharpless, Jonathan IV, 108
Sharpless, Jonathan IV, 122
Sharpless, Jonathan IV, 130
Sharpless, Jonathan IV, 132
Sharpless, Jonathan IV, 687
Sharpless, Jonathan, Jr. IV, 132
Sharpless, Joseph II, 183
Sharpless, Joseph II, 258
Sharpless, Joseph II, 647
Sharpless, Joseph II, 765
Sharpless, Joseph II, 819
Sharpless, Joseph II, 848
Sharpless, Joseph II, 919
Sharpless, Joseph II, 920
Sharpless, Joseph III, 285
Sharpless, Joseph IV, 132
Sharpless, Joshua II, 418
Sharpless, Joshua II, 1086
Sharpless, Joshua, Jr. II, 647
Sharpless, Lacy II, 1057
Sharpless, Lavina IV, 655
Sharpless, Lavina IV, 991
Sharpless, Louisa II, 1089
Sharpless, Lucy II, 966
Sharpless, Lucy II, 968
Sharpless, Lucy II, 969
Sharpless, Lucy II, 1060
Sharpless, Lydia II, 300
Sharpless, Lydia II, 780
Sharpless, Lydia IV, 655
Sharpless, Lydia IV, 1222
Sharpless, Lydia H. IV, 991
Sharpless, Lydia Jones II, 418
Sharpless, Lydia Jones II, 747
Sharpless, Lydia Jones II, 765
Sharpless, Margaret II, 514
Sharpless, Margaret II, 647
Sharpless, Margaret III, 102
Sharpless, Margaret III, 285
Sharpless, Margaret IV, 108
Sharpless, Margaret IV, 122
Sharpless, Margaret IV, 130
Sharpless, Margaret IV, 132
Sharpless, Margaret IV, 436
Sharpless, Martha II, 819
Sharpless, Martha IV, 159
Sharpless, Martha IV, 436
Sharpless, Martha S. II, 920
Sharpless, Mary II, 258
Sharpless, Mary II, 293
Sharpless, Mary II, 300
Sharpless, Mary II, 418
Sharpless, Mary II, 647
Sharpless, Mary II, 716
Sharpless, Mary II, 718
Sharpless, Mary II, 765
Sharpless, Mary II, 787
Sharpless, Mary II, 848
Sharpless, Mary II, 919
Sharpless, Mary II, 949
Sharpless, Mary II, 1026
Sharpless, Mary II, 1086
Sharpless, Mary II, 1089
Sharpless, Mary III, 285
Sharpless, Mary IV, 125
Sharpless, Mary IV, 132
Sharpless, Mary Ann II, 968
Sharpless, Mary B. II, 418
Sharpless, Mary B. II, 647
Sharpless, Mary B. II, 718
Sharpless, Mary B. II, 747
Sharpless, Mary B. II, 765
Sharpless, Mary D. II, 647
Sharpless, Mary D. II, 765
Sharpless, Mary D. III, 285
Sharpless, Mary J. II, 718
Sharpless, Mary Jones II, 718
Sharpless, Mary Louisa II, 949
Sharpless, Mary Louisa II, 1089
Sharpless, Mary Louise II, 1086
Sharpless, Mary W. II, 718
Sharpless, Mary W. II, 765
Sharpless, Mira II, 821
Sharpless, Mira II, 823
Sharpless, Miriam IV, 655
Sharpless, Miriam IV, 991
Sharpless, Naomi II, 707
Sharpless, Nathan IV, 655
Sharpless, Nathan IV, 991
Sharpless, Nathan H. II, 920
Sharpless, Nathan Hunt II, 819
Sharpless, Oliver IV, 983
Sharpless, Paul III, 446
Sharpless, Paul III, 448
Sharpless, Phebe II, 647
Sharpless, Phebe VI, 490
Sharpless, Phebe VI, 505
Sharpless, Philadelphia II, 418
Sharpless, Philadelphia II, 947
Sharpless, Philadelphia II, 1086
Sharpless, Philip M. II, 920
Sharpless, Preston IV, 159
Sharpless, Pricella IV, 687
Sharpless, Priscilla H. IV, 122
Sharpless, Priscilla H. IV, 132
Sharpless, Priscilla Hunt IV, 132
Sharpless, Rachel II, 780
Sharpless, Rachel II, 786
Sharpless, Rachel II, 832
Sharpless, Rachel P. II, 813
Sharpless, Rachel P. II, 906
Sharpless, Rachel P. II, 920
Sharpless, Rebecca II, 704
Sharpless, Rebecca II, 786
Sharpless, Rebecca II, 801
Sharpless, Rebecca II, 823
Sharpless, Rebecca III, 285
Sharpless, Rebecca IV, 108
Sharpless, Rebecca IV, 436
Sharpless, Rebecca G. IV, 350
Sharpless, Rebecca Y. IV, 414
Sharpless, Rebecca Y. IV, 436
Sharpless, Rebeckah II, 1026
Sharpless, Robert II, 647
Sharpless, Ruth II, 718
Sharpless, Ruth IV, 983
Sharpless, Ruth H. II, 765
Sharpless, S. Emlen II, 920
Sharpless, Sabina IV, 132
Sharpless, Sabina IV, 760
Sharpless, Samuel IV, 108
Sharpless, Samuel IV, 132
Sharpless, Samuel IV, 159
Sharpless, Samuel IV, 350
Sharpless, Samuel IV, 414
Sharpless, Samuel IV, 436
Sharpless, Samuel IV, 883
Sharpless, Samuel J. II, 765
Sharpless, Samuel Jones II, 418
Sharpless, Sarah II, 258
Sharpless, Sarah II, 293
Sharpless, Sarah II, 300
Sharpless, Sarah II, 750
Sharpless, Sarah II, 765
Sharpless, Sarah II, 949
Sharpless, Sarah II, 1086
Sharpless, Sarah III, 285
Sharpless, Sarah IV, 655
Sharpless, Sarah IV, 744
Sharpless, Sarah IV, 760
Sharpless, Sarah IV, 982
Sharpless, Sarah IV, 991
Sharpless, Sarah IV, 1222
Sharpless, Sarah H. IV, 1222
Sharpless, Sarah I. II, 920
Sharpless, Sarah J. II, 920
Sharpless, Sarah Jones II, 819
Sharpless, Sarah P. II, 947
Sharpless, Sarah P. II, 949
Sharpless, Sarah P. II, 1089
Sharpless, Sarah Talbot VI, 605
Sharpless, Septimus C. IV, 655
Sharpless, Septimus C. IV, 744
Sharpless, Septimus C. IV, 760
Sharpless, Septimus C. IV, 982
Sharpless, Septimus C. IV, 991
Sharpless, Susanna II, 718
Sharpless, Susanna II, 750
Sharpless, Susanna II, 765
Sharpless, Thomas III, 285
Sharpless, Thomas IV, 159
Sharpless, Thomas IV, 436
Sharpless, Townsend II, 418
Sharpless, Townsend II, 647
Sharpless, Townsend II, 718
Sharpless, Townsend II, 747
Sharpless, Townsend II, 765
Sharpless, Townsend VI, 410
Sharpless, Townsend VI, 443
Sharpless, Townsend T. IV, 63
Sharpless, Wd. Hannah II, 81
Sharpless, William II, 183
Sharpless, William II, 258
Sharpless, William II, 718
Sharpless, William IV, 132
Sharpless, William P. II, 819
Sharpless, Wm. II, 647
Sharpless, Wm. II, 765
Sharpless, Wm. II, 919
Sharpless, Wm. IV, 132
Sharpless, Wm. IV, 1222
Sharpless, Wm. E. III, 446
Sharpless, Wm. P. II, 906
Sharpless, Wm. P. II, 920
Sharpless, Zebedie IV, 760
Sharpless, Zillah M. II, 948
Sharpless, Zillah M. II, 949
Sharpley, ??? VI, 495
Sharplis, Albert IV, 655
Sharplis, Albert T. IV, 632
Sharplis, Amy IV, 655
Sharplis, Benjamin IV, 655
Sharplis, Lydia IV, 632
Sharplis, Lydia IV, 655
Sharpnack, Elizabeth M. IV, 7
Sharpnack, Sarah IV, 760
Sharpneck, Hannah IV, 57
Sharpneck, Hannah IV, 64
Sharpnie, Sarah IV, 760
Sharrack, Constant IV, 436
Sharrack, Constant IV, 455
Sharrack, Elizabeth D. IV, 436
Sharrack, Mary Ellen III, 231
Sharrack, Mary Ellen III, 285
Sharrard, D. C. I, 340
Sharrock, Ellen III, 231
Sharrock, Mary Ellen III, 231
Sharrock, Mary Ellen III, 285
Sharron, Sarah II, 157
Sharron, Susan IV, 497
Sharrot, Jane II, 418
Sharski, Mrs. Frances IV, 133
Shartel, Jacob VI, 998
Shartel, Margaret VI, 998
Shartzer, Charlotte VI, 991
Shartzer, Samuel VI, 991
Shaterthwaite, James II, 417
Shaterwite, Isaac II, 83
Shaterwite, Isaac II, 95
Shaterwite, Phebe II, 83
Shaterwite, Phebe II, 95
Shatterwith, James II, 417
Shatzley, Byron Lee V, 763
Shatzley, Elizabeth V, 763
Shatzley, Ira V, 763
Shatzley, Kyle V, 763
Shatzley, Mattie V, 763
Shatzley, Minnie V, 763
Shaudys, Isabella II, 1075
Shaudys, Isabella II, 1079
Shaudys, Marianna T. II, 1075
Shaudys, Marianna T. II, 1079
Shaudys, Stanley II, 1075
Shaudys, Stanley II, 1079
Shaudys, Vincent P. II, 1075
Shaudys, Vincent P. II, 1079
Shaull, Joseph II, 590
Shaull, Mary II, 590
Shaurman, Amanda III, 285
Shaurman, Amanda III, 294
Shaurman, Emily L. III, 285
Shaurman, Emily L. III, 294
Shaurman, Isaac III, 285
Shaurman, Isaac III, 294
Shaver, Carl IV, 1263
Shaver, Charles W. IV, 1263
Shaver, David VI, 972
Shaver, David VI, 1002
Shaver, Guy IV, 1263
Shaver, Hazel D. IV, 1263
Shaver, Rebecca A. IV, 1263
Shaver, Ruth V, 582
Shaver, Ruth V, 597
Shavers, Andrew VI, 984
Shavers, Ann VI, 984
Shavers, Bartlett VI, 816
Shavers, Dolly VI, 992
Shavers, Elizabeth VI, 816
Shavers, Elizabeth VI, 843
Shavers, Ibbey VI, 930
Shavers, James VI, 992
Shavers, Jesse VI, 992
Shavers, Joel VI, 808
Shavers, Joel VI, 816
Shavers, Joel VI, 843
Shavers, Joel VI, 853
Shavers, John VI, 843
Shavers, John VI, 992
Shavers, Keziah VI, 843

vers, Martha A. VI, 853
vers, Milly VI, 856
vers, Milly VI, 984
vers, Nancy VI, 828
vers, Rebecca VI, 843
vers, Violet VI, 992
vers, Winny VI, 992
vous, Rebecca VI, 984
vr, James K. VI, 924
w, ??? II, 819
w, ??? II, 969
w, Aaron I, 570
w, Aaron I, 586
w, Aaron I, 590
w, Aaron I, 596
w, Abigail IV, 683
w, Abigail IV, 760
w, Abner IV, 843
w, Albert H. II, 718
w, Alexander II, 418
w, Alexander II, 544
w, Alexander II, 622
w, Alexander II, 647
w, Alexander II, 648
w, Alexander II, 718
w, Alexander II, 765
w, Alexander II, 779
w, Alexander II, 819
w, Alexander II, 821
w, Alexander II, 855
w, Alexander II, 874
w, Alexander II, 912
w, Alexander II, 916
w, Alexander II, 920
w, Alexander, Jr. II, 819
w, Alexander, Jr. II, 920
w, Amos II, 96
w, Amos II, 969
w, Amos II, 1026
w, Amos V, 119
w, Amy II, 258
w, Ann II, 647
w, Ann II, 974
w, Ann II, 999
w, Ann II, 1026
w, Ann IV, 57
w, Ann IV, 58
w, Ann IV, 64
w, Ann IV, 842
w, Anna II, 969
w, Anna II, 1080
w, Anna IV, 842
w, Anna M. II, 855
w, Anna M. II, 874
w, Anna M. II, 912
w, Anna M. II, 916
w, Anna M. II, 920
w, Anna Margaret II, 819
w, Anna Margaret II, 916
w, Anna Margaret II, 920
w, Anna Margaret, Jr. II, 817
w, Anna S. II, 821
w, Anne II, 258
w, Annie III, 285
w, Annie Elizabeth V, 597
w, Aron I, 596
w, Benjamin I, 570
w, Benjamin I, 590
w, Benjamin IV, 274
w, Benjamin Vore IV, 57
w, Bessie P. II, 855
w, Bessie P. II, 920
w, Catharine II, 823
w, Cessaly I, 596
w, Chamness VI, 992
w, Charles II, 969
w, Charles IV, 656
w, Charles IV, 842
w, Charles IV, 843
w, Ciciley I, 832
w, Ciciley I, 837
w, Claud Coble I, 949
w, Claude C. I, 949
w, Claude Coble I, 933
w, Constance IV, 1263
w, Constantine IV, 1263
w, Deborah II, 482
w, Deborah II, 648
w, Deborah IV, 840
w, Deborah IV, 843
w, Deborah G. II, 897
w, Deborah G. II, 920
w, Deborah P. II, 648
w, Deborah P. II, 765
w, Deborah P. II, 920
w, Deborah Phipps II, 418
w, Dora V, 763
w, Doris IV, 1337
w, E. R. I, 949
w, Edward II, 447
w, Edward V, 119
Shaw, Edward V, 930
Shaw, Edward V, 953
Shaw, Edward V, 959
Shaw, Edward Thos. V, 930
Shaw, Edward W. IV, 1184
Shaw, Effie Marie V, 202
Shaw, Eli IV, 1293
Shaw, Eliza Ann IV, 656
Shaw, Elizabeth I, 570
Shaw, Elizabeth I, 900
Shaw, Elizabeth II, 418
Shaw, Elizabeth II, 622
Shaw, Elizabeth II, 647
Shaw, Elizabeth II, 648
Shaw, Elizabeth II, 718
Shaw, Elizabeth II, 765
Shaw, Elizabeth II, 779
Shaw, Elizabeth II, 819
Shaw, Elizabeth II, 821
Shaw, Elizabeth II, 920
Shaw, Elizabeth IV, 25
Shaw, Elizabeth IV, 57
Shaw, Elizabeth IV, 274
Shaw, Elizabeth IV, 822
Shaw, Elizabeth IV, 843
Shaw, Elizabeth IV, 1030
Shaw, Elizabeth IV, 1184
Shaw, Elizabeth V, 119
Shaw, Elizabeth V, 144
Shaw, Elizabeth V, 930
Shaw, Elizabeth V, 959
Shaw, Elizabeth VI, 777
Shaw, Elizabeth P. II, 648
Shaw, Elizabeth P. II, 765
Shaw, Elizabeth P. II, 857
Shaw, Elizabeth P. II, 874
Shaw, Elizabeth P. II, 920
Shaw, Elizabeth Phipps II, 794
Shaw, Elizabeth Phipps II, 819
Shaw, Elizabeth S. II, 830
Shaw, Elizabeth S. II, 920
Shaw, Elmira V, 643
Shaw, Emma J. V, 1018
Shaw, Eva Josephine V, 202
Shaw, Ezra IV, 656
Shaw, Fradraca II, 1026
Shaw, Frank I, 1161
Shaw, Frank L. I, 1161
Shaw, Frank Stinson III, 285
Shaw, Frank Stinson III, 333
Shaw, Fredrick II, 1026
Shaw, George II, 418
Shaw, George II, 622
Shaw, George II, 647
Shaw, George II, 648
Shaw, George II, 671
Shaw, George II, 819
Shaw, George II, 824
Shaw, George IV, 1184
Shaw, George V, 202
Shaw, Gertrude I, 625
Shaw, Gertrude H. II, 819
Shaw, Gertrude H. II, 912
Shaw, Gertrude H. II, 920
Shaw, Glen A. IV, 1184
Shaw, Glenn Albert IV, 1184
Shaw, Grace M. IV, 1184
Shaw, Grace Mary IV, 1184
Shaw, Gulielma II, 969
Shaw, Hanna V, 202
Shaw, Hannah II, 647
Shaw, Hannah II, 682
Shaw, Hannah II, 875
Shaw, Hannah II, 1026
Shaw, Hannah IV, 633
Shaw, Hannah IV, 656
Shaw, Hannah IV, 760
Shaw, Hannah IV, 842
Shaw, Hannah IV, 843
Shaw, Hannah IV, 1030
Shaw, Hannah IV, 1210
Shaw, Hannah IV, 1222
Shaw, Hannah D. IV, 914
Shaw, Hannah D. IV, 916
Shaw, Hannah H. IV, 1138
Shaw, Harriet IV, 647
Shaw, Harriet IV, 656
Shaw, Heaton II, 819
Shaw, Helen Augusta V, 202
Shaw, Helen Elise III, 285
Shaw, Helen Elise III, 333
Shaw, Henry C. V, 119
Shaw, Hezediah II, 418
Shaw, Hiel IV, 656
Shaw, Hiel IV, 760
Shaw, Hiel IV, 761
Shaw, Huldah IV, 1378
Shaw, I. A. IV, 1184
Shaw, Ida Manker V, 430
Shaw, Isaac Griffith II, 875
Shaw, Isaac M. IV, 1184
Shaw, Isaacher IV, 1184
Shaw, Isaiah II, 1026
Shaw, Iva Marie IV, 1222
Shaw, James I, 570
Shaw, James II, 418
Shaw, James II, 1026
Shaw, James IV, 760
Shaw, James IV, 1030
Shaw, James V, 202
Shaw, James V, 597
Shaw, James V, 643
Shaw, James VI, 777
Shaw, James Muir II, 819
Shaw, Jane I, 596
Shaw, Jane II, 418
Shaw, Jane IV, 274
Shaw, Jason IV, 1114
Shaw, Jemima IV, 760
Shaw, Jemima IV, 1030
Shaw, Jemima IV, 1031
Shaw, Jenet VI, 355
Shaw, Jennet VI, 355
Shaw, Jennett II, 648
Shaw, Jennie R. III, 285
Shaw, Jeremiah Coppock IV, 843
Shaw, Jesse Paul V, 202
Shaw, Jessie Morrison Hamilton V, 930
Shaw, John I, 570
Shaw, John II, 258
Shaw, John II, 418
Shaw, John II, 647
Shaw, John II, 648
Shaw, John II, 682
Shaw, John II, 1026
Shaw, John IV, 57
Shaw, John IV, 274
Shaw, John IV, 760
Shaw, John IV, 843
Shaw, John IV, 1184
Shaw, John IV, 1222
Shaw, John V, 119
Shaw, John V, 144
Shaw, John V, 930
Shaw, John V, 959
Shaw, John H. V, 202
Shaw, John M. V, 643
Shaw, John S. I, 933
Shaw, John, Jr. IV, 1184
Shaw, Jonathan IV, 274
Shaw, Jonathan IV, 883
Shaw, Jonathan IV, 1184
Shaw, Jonathan IV, 1222
Shaw, Jonathan T. IV, 760
Shaw, Jonathan T. IV, 1030
Shaw, Jonathan T. IV, 1031
Shaw, Joseph II, 418
Shaw, Joseph II, 989
Shaw, Joseph II, 1026
Shaw, Joseph IV, 274
Shaw, Joseph IV, 1030
Shaw, Joseph IV, 1184
Shaw, Joseph V, 119
Shaw, Joseph L. IV, 656
Shaw, Joseph L. IV, 883
Shaw, Joseph Lindley IV, 883
Shaw, Joseph O'Neill III, 285
Shaw, Josiah II, 1026
Shaw, Judith W. VI, 992
Shaw, Latitia IV, 35
Shaw, Latitia IV, 57
Shaw, Letitia IV, 57
Shaw, Levi IV, 760
Shaw, Levi IV, 843
Shaw, Levi IV, 914
Shaw, Levi IV, 916
Shaw, Levi IV, 1293
Shaw, Lewis IV, 1293
Shaw, Lindley IV, 656
Shaw, Lindley IV, 760
Shaw, Lindley IV, 842
Shaw, Lindley IV, 843
Shaw, Lindley IV, 1128
Shaw, Lindley IV, 1138
Shaw, Louisa V, 643
Shaw, M. IV, 656
Shaw, M. A. I, 929
Shaw, Margaret I, 933
Shaw, Margaret II, 1026
Shaw, Margaret II, 1027
Shaw, Margaret IV, 57
Shaw, Margaret IV, 65
Shaw, Margaret IV, 760
Shaw, Margaret IV, 842
Shaw, Margaret IV, 849
Shaw, Margaret V, 930
Shaw, Margaret A. I, 618
Shaw, Margaret, Jr. V, 930
Shaw, Maria III, 285
Shaw, Maria IV, 760
Shaw, Maria IV, 894
Shaw, Mariam IV, 656
Shaw, Mariam IV, 883
Shaw, Marietta I, 625
Shaw, Marietta Shaw Hanner I, 640
Shaw, Martha I, 590
Shaw, Martha II, 883
Shaw, Martha II, 920
Shaw, Martha II, 969
Shaw, Martha IV, 608
Shaw, Martha V, 202
Shaw, Martha VI, 992
Shaw, Martha D. IV, 1114
Shaw, Martha J. V, 430
Shaw, Martha S. IV, 656
Shaw, Mary I, 586
Shaw, Mary I, 590
Shaw, Mary I, 595
Shaw, Mary I, 596
Shaw, Mary II, 418
Shaw, Mary II, 588
Shaw, Mary II, 622
Shaw, Mary II, 647
Shaw, Mary II, 648
Shaw, Mary II, 671
Shaw, Mary II, 718
Shaw, Mary II, 765
Shaw, Mary II, 819
Shaw, Mary II, 824
Shaw, Mary II, 920
Shaw, Mary II, 989
Shaw, Mary II, 1026
Shaw, Mary III, 285
Shaw, Mary IV, 274
Shaw, Mary IV, 655
Shaw, Mary IV, 1222
Shaw, Mary V, 763
Shaw, Mary VI, 543
Shaw, Mary VI, 1007
Shaw, Mary Alice IV, 1128
Shaw, Mary Alice IV, 1138
Shaw, Mary Ann II, 819
Shaw, Mary Ann II, 920
Shaw, Mary Anne II, 852
Shaw, Mary Anne II, 920
Shaw, Mary Belle V, 597
Shaw, Mary E. Fawcett IV, 1114
Shaw, Mary Elizabeth V, 119
Shaw, Mary Elizabeth V, 959
Shaw, Mary Etta I, 640
Shaw, Matilda IV, 916
Shaw, Matthew I, 570
Shaw, Max III, 285
Shaw, Melvina V, 430
Shaw, Mildred VI, 995
Shaw, Milton IV, 656
Shaw, Milton IV, 760
Shaw, Milton IV, 843
Shaw, Milton J. IV, 842
Shaw, Minnie V, 202
Shaw, Miriam IV, 656
Shaw, Miriam IV, 827
Shaw, Miriam IV, 842
Shaw, Miriam IV, 874
Shaw, Miriam IV, 883
Shaw, Miriam IV, 991
Shaw, Miriam IV, 1293
Shaw, Mirium IV, 883
Shaw, Mrs. A. A. IV, 1337
Shaw, N. IV, 656
Shaw, Nathan IV, 656
Shaw, Nathan IV, 827
Shaw, Nathan IV, 842
Shaw, Nathan IV, 874
Shaw, Nathan IV, 883
Shaw, Nathan IV, 991
Shaw, Nathan IV, 1293
Shaw, Noble I, 570
Shaw, Noble I, 586
Shaw, Noble I, 590
Shaw, Noble I, 596
Shaw, Oliver W. II, 920
Shaw, Oliver Wilson II, 920
Shaw, Otis V, 1018
Shaw, Parris I, 590
Shaw, Paul I, 640
Shaw, Paul Shaw I, 640
Shaw, Paul T. I, 625
Shaw, Pauline III, 285
Shaw, Penia IV, 883
Shaw, Penina IV, 656
Shaw, Penina IV, 760
Shaw, Penina IV, 872
Shaw, Penina IV, 883
Shaw, Peninah IV, 632
Shaw, Peninah IV, 656
Shaw, Peninah V, 119
Shaw, Peninah V, 953
Shaw, Peninah V, 959
Shaw, Peninnah V, 119
Shaw, Peter T. II, 96
Shaw, Phebe I, 590
Shaw, Phebe I, 596
Shaw, Phebe I, 832
Shaw, Phebe I, 837
Shaw, Phebe II, 991
Shaw, Phebe II, 1026
Shaw, Phebe IV, 632
Shaw, Phebe IV, 656
Shaw, Phebe Ellen IV, 274
Shaw, Phebe Ellen IV, 286
Shaw, Phebe Ellen IV, 656
Shaw, Phebe Ellen IV, 760
Shaw, Phebe Ellen IV, 842
Shaw, Phebe Ellen IV, 843
Shaw, Rachel II, 418
Shaw, Rachel II, 647
Shaw, Rachel IV, 618
Shaw, Rachel IV, 631
Shaw, Rachel IV, 656
Shaw, Rachel IV, 822
Shaw, Rachel IV, 842
Shaw, Rachel IV, 883
Shaw, Rachel IV, 1222
Shaw, Rachel H. IV, 656
Shaw, Rachel H. IV, 883
Shaw, Ralph Robert III, 285
Shaw, Rebecca II, 418
Shaw, Rebecca II, 765
Shaw, Rebecca II, 819
Shaw, Rebecca II, 821
Shaw, Rebecca II, 920
Shaw, Rebecca IV, 618
Shaw, Rebecca IV, 656
Shaw, Rebecca IV, 760
Shaw, Rebecca IV, 777
Shaw, Rebecca IV, 809
Shaw, Rebecca IV, 843
Shaw, Rebecca IV, 916
Shaw, Rebecca V, 119
Shaw, Rebecca V, 930
Shaw, Rebecca V, 959
Shaw, Rebecca A. IV, 760
Shaw, Rebecca L. V, 930
Shaw, Rebecca T. V, 959
Shaw, Rhoda I, 570
Shaw, Rhoda I, 590
Shaw, Richard III, 446
Shaw, Richard IV, 1378
Shaw, Robert II, 969
Shaw, Robert III, 203
Shaw, Robert V, 930
Shaw, Robert H. V, 119
Shaw, Robert H. V, 959
Shaw, Robert Hill V, 119
Shaw, Robert Hill V, 959
Shaw, Rufus V, 597
Shaw, Russell Z. Taber IV, 274
Shaw, Ruth IV, 82
Shaw, Ruth IV, 108
Shaw, Ruth IV, 1184
Shaw, Ruth IV, 1208
Shaw, Ruth IV, 1222
Shaw, Salius I, 1161
Shaw, Samuel II, 418
Shaw, Samuel II, 588
Shaw, Samuel II, 647
Shaw, Samuel IV, 25
Shaw, Samuel IV, 35
Shaw, Samuel IV, 57
Shaw, Samuel IV, 632
Shaw, Samuel IV, 654
Shaw, Samuel IV, 655
Shaw, Samuel IV, 656
Shaw, Samuel IV, 760
Shaw, Samuel IV, 842
Shaw, Samuel IV, 872
Shaw, Samuel IV, 883
Shaw, Samuel V, 119
Shaw, Samuel V, 930
Shaw, Samuel, Jr. IV, 57
Shaw, Sarah I, 539
Shaw, Sarah I, 570
Shaw, Sarah II, 620
Shaw, Sarah II, 647
Shaw, Sarah II, 648
Shaw, Sarah II, 671
Shaw, Sarah II, 765
Shaw, Sarah II, 814
Shaw, Sarah II, 824
Shaw, Sarah II, 920
Shaw, Sarah IV, 57
Shaw, Sarah IV, 274
Shaw, Sarah IV, 654
Shaw, Sarah IV, 655
Shaw, Sarah IV, 760
Shaw, Sarah IV, 833
Shaw, Sarah IV, 843
Shaw, Sarah IV, 883
Shaw, Sarah IV, 1151
Shaw, Sarah IV, 1184
Shaw, Sarah V, 119

Shaw, Sarah Ann IV, 656
Shaw, Sarah Ann IV, 883
Shaw, Sarah Louisa IV, 916
Shaw, Sarah Louiza IV, 760
Shaw, Sarah Martin IV, 1184
Shaw, Sarah P. II, 920
Shaw, Sarah Phipps II, 821
Shaw, Seth IV, 608
Shaw, Seth IV, 656
Shaw, Seth IV, 760
Shaw, Sicily I, 596
Shaw, Silvia IV, 1184
Shaw, Siscily I, 590
Shaw, Spence II, 647
Shaw, Spence II, 648
Shaw, Susan II, 920
Shaw, Susan II, 1086
Shaw, Susan III, 285
Shaw, Susan B. V, 119
Shaw, Susan Barnard V, 119
Shaw, Susan W. II, 920
Shaw, Susanna II, 418
Shaw, Susanna II, 648
Shaw, Susanna II, 765
Shaw, Susanna IV, 25
Shaw, Susanna IV, 35
Shaw, Susanna IV, 57
Shaw, Susanna IV, 656
Shaw, Susanna IV, 842
Shaw, Susanna IV, 843
Shaw, Susanna Watson II, 819
Shaw, Susannah IV, 656
Shaw, Susannah V, 119
Shaw, Susannah V, 930
Shaw, Susie V, 1018
Shaw, Sylvester IV, 1222
Shaw, Sylvia IV, 1184
Shaw, Temperance V, 643
Shaw, Thelma I, 640
Shaw, Thelma B. I, 625
Shaw, Thelma B. I, 640
Shaw, Thelma Wilma V, 202
Shaw, Thomas II, 418
Shaw, Thomas II, 647
Shaw, Thomas IV, 57
Shaw, Thomas IV, 64
Shaw, Thomas IV, 618
Shaw, Thomas IV, 631
Shaw, Thomas IV, 656
Shaw, Thomas IV, 822
Shaw, Thomas IV, 833
Shaw, Thomas IV, 842
Shaw, Thomas IV, 843
Shaw, Thomas IV, 883
Shaw, Thomas IV, 916
Shaw, Thomas IV, 1222
Shaw, Thomas V, 119
Shaw, Thomas V, 959
Shaw, Thomas E. IV, 656
Shaw, Thomas E. V, 430
Shaw, Thomas H. IV, 842
Shaw, Thomas W. V, 119
Shaw, Thos. IV, 883
Shaw, Thos. V, 930
Shaw, Thos. E. IV, 656
Shaw, Thos. H. IV, 656
Shaw, Thos. W. V, 930
Shaw, Thos. W. V, 959
Shaw, Thos. Wright V, 930
Shaw, Viola Susan III, 203
Shaw, Walter IV, 1114
Shaw, Webster IV, 1293
Shaw, William II, 418
Shaw, William II, 419
Shaw, William IV, 632
Shaw, William IV, 656
Shaw, William IV, 760
Shaw, William IV, 842
Shaw, William IV, 916
Shaw, William V, 119
Shaw, William VI, 992
Shaw, William VI, 995
Shaw, William B. VI, 992
Shaw, William Carroll I, 625
Shaw, William Matthew I, 570
Shaw, William T. V, 119
Shaw, William Wilson IV, 656
Shaw, William Wilson IV, 760
Shaw, Williamson VI, 992
Shaw, Williamson VI, 995
Shaw, Wm. II, 647
Shaw, Wm. IV, 656
Shaw, Wm. IV, 843
Shaw, Wm. IV, 1138
Shaw, Wm. IV, 1210
Shaw, Wm. IV, 1222
Shaw, Wm. A. II, 648
Shaw, Wm. C. I, 640
Shaw, Wm. H. C. I, 625
Shaw, Wm. R. III, 285
Shaw, Wm. S. V, 643
Shaw, Wm. Wilson IV, 656
Shaw, Wm. Wilson IV, 842
Shaw, Wm. Wilson IV, 843
Shaw, Wyatt P. V, 643
Shawcross, Joseph II, 419
Shawcross, Stephen II, 419
Shawhorn, Adie V, 597
Shawthorn, Sarah II, 258
Shawver, George IV, 1293
Shay, Francis L. III, 285
Shay, Phebe IV, 108
Shealds, Martha I, 837
Shealey, Allen V, 643
Shealey, Florence V. IV, 1337
Shealey, Geo. V, 643
Shealey, Joseph V, 643
Shealey, Mariah V, 643
Shealey, Mary Elizabeth V, 643
Sheals, H. V, 380
Sheals, Lucinda V, 380
Sheals, Wm. V, 380
Shealy, Amos R. V, 277
Shearback, Rose B. III, 285
Shearer, Andrew VI, 853
Shearer, Ann VI, 857
Shearer, Anna S. II, 718
Shearer, Anna S. II, 765
Shearer, Anna S. II, 770
Shearer, Anne VI, 802
Shearer, David Mathew II, 718
Shearer, Eliza B. VI, 804
Shearer, Elizabeth VI, 841
Shearer, Elizabeth VI, 853
Shearer, Eva Beard V, 763
Shearer, Harriet VI, 853
Shearer, Isabella VI, 953
Shearer, James VI, 805
Shearer, James VI, 824
Shearer, James VI, 831
Shearer, James VI, 841
Shearer, James VI, 849
Shearer, James VI, 853
Shearer, James VI, 857
Shearer, Jane VI, 824
Shearer, John VI, 802
Shearer, John H. VI, 853
Shearer, Margit VI, 853
Shearer, Martha VI, 824
Shearer, Martha VI, 853
Shearer, Mary VI, 831
Shearer, Mary VI, 853
Shearer, Nancy VI, 853
Shearer, Peggy VI, 849
Shearer, Ruth VI, 853
Shearer, Sarah V, 763
Shearer, Sarah VI, 853
Shearer, Thomas VI, 831
Shearer, Thomas VI, 853
Shearer, William VI, 812
Shearer, William VI, 853
Shearer, Wm. VI, 804
Shearer, Zachariah VI, 853
Shearman, Abram H. V, 930
Shearman, Almira III, 285
Shearman, Anna M. V, 930
Shearman, Chas. V, 930
Shearman, Chas. H. V, 930
Shearman, David S. III, 285
Shearman, David S. V, 930
Shearman, Emily V, 930
Shearman, Emma V, 930
Shearman, Emma A. V, 930
Shearman, Hepsa H. II, 300
Shearman, John D. V, 930
Shearman, John Russell V, 930
Shearman, Joseph T. V, 930
Shearman, Joseph T., Jr. V, 930
Shearman, Laura B. V, 930
Shearman, Mabel V, 930
Shearman, Mabel A. V, 930
Shearman, Mary V, 920
Shearman, Mary K. V, 930
Shearman, Samuel M. III, 285
Shearman, Samuel M. V, 930
Shearman, Thomas Stinson IV, 761
Shearon, Elizabeth IV, 108
Shearon, Richard III, 285
Shearwood, David I Sup 1, 7
Shearwood, Elizabeth I Sup 1, 7
Shearwood, Lydia V, 75
Sheats, Jane IV, 1263
Sheats, Lea IV, 1263
Sheats, Leah IV, 1263
Sheats, Lucie IV, 1263
Sheats, Mary E. V, 1018
Sheckler, Delila V, 1018
Sheckler, Lester V, 1018
Sheckles, Ava I, 949
Shed, Isabella II, 648
Shedaker, Elizabeth II, 258
Sheed, Isabella II, 648
Sheehan, Catharine VI, 992
Sheehan, Cornelius VI, 992
Sheehan, Mary E. IV, 991
Sheehan, Mary E. IV, 1010
Sheekler, Lester V, 1018
Sheels, Joanna I, 997
Sheely, Allen V, 643
Sheely, Elizabeth V, 643
Sheely, Geo. V, 643
Sheely, George V, 643
Sheely, Joseph V, 643
Sheely, Joseph Allen V, 643
Sheely, Maria V, 643
Sheely, Mariah V, 643
Sheely, Mary Elizabeth V, 643
Sheerden, Margaret I, 412
Sheerden, Margaret I, 418
Sheerman, Caroline W. VI, 879
Sheete, Edith V, 119
Sheets, Alice IV, 1000
Sheets, Alva IV, 1000
Sheets, Andrew V, 764
Sheets, Ann V, 764
Sheets, Anna V, 764
Sheets, Bertha C. I, 933
Sheets, Bertha C. I, 949
Sheets, Branson J. I, 933
Sheets, Columbus I, 933
Sheets, Elizabeth H. IV, 1240
Sheets, Ernest V, 202
Sheets, Franzy V, 202
Sheets, Genevieve Elizabeth I, 933
Sheets, Hattie C. I, 933
Sheets, Hattie Florence I, 949
Sheets, J. Floyd I, 933
Sheets, J. Floyd I, 949
Sheets, Jacob V, 764
Sheets, Jacob V, 792
Sheets, John Van I, 949
Sheets, John Vann I, 933
Sheets, June V, 202
Sheets, Lottie IV, 992
Sheets, Margaret A. IV, 939
Sheets, Martin V, 764
Sheets, Mary V, 764
Sheets, Mary E. V, 1018
Sheets, Mary Helen V, 202
Sheets, Matilda IV, 1000
Sheets, Mildred I, 949
Sheets, Mirtie V, 1018
Sheets, Pearl S. I, 949
Sheets, Vaun I, 933
Sheets, William IV, 1240
Sheffield, Edward III, 285
Sheffield, George Haviland III, 69
Sheffield, George Haviland III, 285
Sheffield, Henry W. IV, 1337
Sheffield, John III, 285
Sheffield, Otis B. IV, 1337
Sheffield, Rebecca III, 285
Sheffield, Sarah Louise III, 69
Sheffield, Sarah Louise III, 285
Shehan, Anna E. V, 119
Shehan, Lydia V, 971
Shehan, Lydia V, 976
Sheik, Anna V, 764
Sheik, Edna Hines V, 764
Sheik, Jacob V, 764
Sheik, Mary V, 764
Shekerjian, Benjamin III, 224
Shekerjian, Benjamin III, 290
Shekerjian, Rosa III, 224
Shekerjian, Rosa III, 290
Shekeyian, Benjamin III, 224
Shekeyian, Benjamin III, 290
Shekeyian, Rosa III, 224
Shekeyian, Rosa III, 290
Shela, Maria V, 629
Shela, Maria V, 643
Shelby, David I, 689
Shelden, Mary V, 886
Sheldon, Anna M. V, 914
Sheldon, Anna M. V, 930
Sheldon, Benjamin V, 430
Sheldon, Charles V, 430
Sheldon, Frank V, 430
Sheldon, George V, 430
Sheldon, George L. V, 430
Sheldon, Joan V, 430
Sheldon, Joanna V, 430
Sheldon, Leroy V, 430
Sheldon, Lucinda V, 430
Sheldon, Lucy V, 430
Sheldon, Mary V, 861
Sheldon, Mary V, 930
Sheldon, Melissa V, 430
Sheldon, Nora IV, 1240
Sheldon, Oman V, 430
Sheldon, Omar V, 430
Sheldon, Phebe E. III, 128
Sheldon, Ruth V, 430
Sheldon, W. F. IV, 992
Sheley, Amos R. V, 277
Sheley, Carrie Earl V, 277
Sheley, Elizabeth V, 643
Sheley, George V, 643
Sheley, Joseph Allen V, 643
Sheley, Mariah V, 643
Shelley, Esta V, 764
Shelley, H. M. IV, 1293
Shelley, Jane II, 648
Shelley, Mary II, 565
Shelley, Mary II, 648
Shelley, Sarah Elizabeth V, 742
Shellita, Ann IV, 497
Shelly, Abraham II, 419
Shelly, Ann I, 556
Shelly, Ann I, 570
Shelly, Belinda I, 688
Shelly, Deborah II, 648
Shelly, Diana I, 686
Shelly, Diana I, 689
Shelly, Dianna I, 688
Shelly, Eliza I, 668
Shelly, Elizabeth I, 668
Shelly, Elizabeth I, 688
Shelly, Elizabeth II, 419
Shelly, Enoch I, 668
Shelly, Enoch I, 688
Shelly, Enoch I, 689
Shelly, Esta V, 764
Shelly, Herbert A. V, 764
Shelly, Jane II, 648
Shelly, John II, 419
Shelly, Mary II, 648
Shelly, Sarah II, 508
Shelly, Sarah II, 648
Shelly, William I, 688
Shelly, William II, 419
Shelmire, Mary II, 920
Shels, Joanna I, 997
Shelson, John II, 419
Shelton, Abraham VI, 992
Shelton, Anne VI, 992
Shelton, Dinah II, 648
Shelton, Dinah II, 670
Shelton, Eliza M. VI, 992
Shelton, Eliza R. VI, 992
Shelton, Ellen V, 1018
Shelton, Emilia VI, 992
Shelton, George W. VI, 992
Shelton, Hannah II, 419
Shelton, Hassie I, 625
Shelton, James F. VI, 992
Shelton, Jesse II, 1037
Shelton, John VI, 992
Shelton, Joyce II, 648
Shelton, Lurena I, 668
Shelton, Margaret II, 1037
Shelton, Martha I, 689
Shelton, Martha C. I, 668
Shelton, Martha C. I, 677
Shelton, Martha C. I, 689
Shelton, Martha C. I, 759
Shelton, Martha C. I, 769
Shelton, Mary E. VI, 859
Shelton, Mary Jane VI, 992
Shelton, Mr. ??? VI, 42
Shelton, Polly M. VI, 992
Shelton, Samuel W. VI, 823
Shelton, Sarah II, 1037
Shelton, Sarah S. VI, 958
Shelton, Wesley VI, 992
Shelton, William VI, 958
Shelton, William I. VI, 814
Shelton, William W. VI, 992
Shenault, Martha VI, 848
Shenault, Rachel VI, 858
Shenck, ??? III, 285
Shenck, John S. III, 285
Shenton, Hannah II, 419
Shenton, Hannah II, 648
Shenton, Mary II, 576
Shenton, Mary II, 648
Shenton, Mary II, 696
Shenton, Nathan II, 419
Shenton, Nathan II, 648
Shenton, Rachel II, 487
Shenton, Rachel II, 648
Shepard, Bert IV, 1337
Shepard, Catharine VI, 917
Shepard, Easter VI, 879
Shepard, Effie IV, 1337
Shepard, Jacob VI, 917
Shepard, John II, 96
Shepard, John IV, 1378
Shepard, Judeth II, 1026
Shepard, Judith II, 1026
Shepard, Martha II, 96
Shepard, Messer VI, 443
Shepard, Nellie IV, 1337
Shepard, Polly VI, 879
Shepard, Solomon VI, 443
Shepard, Susannah VI, 443
Shepard, Thomas VI, 443
Sheperd, Elisabeth I, 71
Sheperd, Elisabeth I, 73
Sheperd, Emily V, 359
Sheperd, Hannah V, 698
Sheperd, Josiah VI, 800
Sheperd, Lena V, 359
Sheperd, Sarah M. III, 446
Shephard, Anne II, 66
Shephard, Anne II, 96
Shephard, Benjamin VI, 992
Shephard, Betsey VI, 875
Shephard, Frank V, 359
Shephard, Henry VI, 899
Shephard, Ida VI, 784
Shephard, John VI, 559
Shephard, Judith VI, 559
Shephard, Mark II, 66
Shephard, Mark II, 96
Shephard, Mary VI, 992
Shephard, Mary Alice V, 359
Shephard, Ora V, 359
Shephard, Robert II, 419
Shephard, Sarah L. V, 359
Shephard, Sidney E. V, 359
Shephard, William A. VI, 1009
Shephard, Wm. L. V, 359
Shepheard, John II, 648
Shepheard, Priscilla II, 648
Shepheard, Rachel F. II, 648
Shepheard, Rebecca J. II, 648
Shepher, Jacob VI, 945
Shepherd, ??? V, 747
Shepherd, Albert V, 202
Shepherd, Albert G. III, 285
Shepherd, Allen III, 285
Shepherd, Allen IV, 1184
Shepherd, Allen V, 119
Shepherd, Allen V, 528
Shepherd, Allen V, 597
Shepherd, Allen V, 792
Shepherd, Amaziah V, 119
Shepherd, Amaziah V, 528
Shepherd, Amaziah V, 597
Shepherd, Amaziah Thomas V, 792
Shepherd, Amos Wilson V, 202
Shepherd, Angelina V, 528
Shepherd, Ann II, 648
Shepherd, Ann VI, 699
Shepherd, Anna VI, 701
Shepherd, Anne I, 43
Shepherd, Anne I, 73
Shepherd, Anne I, 76
Shepherd, Austin L. VI, 992
Shepherd, Barbie I, 614
Shepherd, Benjamin II, 419
Shepherd, Benjamin II, 496
Shepherd, Benjamin II, 648
Shepherd, Benjamin IV, 58
Shepherd, Benjamin VI, 443
Shepherd, Benjamin VI, 912
Shepherd, Benjamin VI, 992
Shepherd, Benjamin H. F. VI, 992
Shepherd, Betsy VI, 992
Shepherd, Caleb W. III, 285
Shepherd, Caleb W. III, 356
Shepherd, Caleb W. III, 446
Shepherd, Caleb W. III, 471
Shepherd, Catharine P. I, 688
Shepherd, Catharine P. I, 689
Shepherd, Catherine II, 419
Shepherd, Catherine II, 648
Shepherd, Charles II, 718
Shepherd, Charles Randolph V, 202
Shepherd, Ciphrean I, 165
Shepherd, Ciprian I, 165
Shepherd, Cora V, 202
Shepherd, Cora Louisa V, 202
Shepherd, Cyprian I, 117
Shepherd, Cyprian I, 149
Shepherd, Cyprian I, 165
Shepherd, Daniel II, 790
Shepherd, Daniel V, 202
Shepherd, David II, 419
Shepherd, Deborah II, 645
Shepherd, Deborah III, 215
Shepherd, Denitia VI, 992
Shepherd, Edith V, 119
Shepherd, Edith V, 511
Shepherd, Edith V, 528
Shepherd, Edith V, 597
Shepherd, Elisabeth I, 73

epherd, Elisabeth I, 165
epherd, Elisabeth II, 790
epherd, Eliza III, 446
epherd, Eliza Ann III, 285
epherd, Elizabeth I, 544
epherd, Elizabeth I, 570
epherd, Elizabeth II, 419
epherd, Elizabeth II, 496
epherd, Elizabeth II, 627
epherd, Elizabeth II, 648
epherd, Elizabeth IV, 58
epherd, Elizabeth IV, 108
epherd, Elizabeth IV, 132
epherd, Elizabeth V, 62
epherd, Elizabeth V, 119
epherd, Elizabeth V, 416
epherd, Elizabeth V, 490
epherd, Elizabeth V, 527
epherd, Elizabeth V, 528
epherd, Elizabeth V, 597
epherd, Elizabeth V, 792
epherd, Elizabeth VI, 443
epherd, Elizabeth VI, 992
epherd, Elizabeth A. V, 597
epherd, Elizabeth A. VI, 992
epherd, Ella V, 119
epherd, Emily IV, 58
epherd, Emily IV, 132
epherd, Emily V, 359
epherd, Ernest V, 202
epherd, Eshter VI, 992
epherd, Eugene V, 359
epherd, Eva Fondler V, 491
epherd, Eva Fondler V, 528
epherd, Francis J. V, 528
epherd, Frank V, 202
epherd, Frank V, 359
epherd, George II, 419
epherd, Hannah V, 119
epherd, Hannah V, 202
epherd, Hannah V, 421
epherd, Hannah V, 430
epherd, Hannah V, 528
epherd, Hannah V, 597
epherd, Hannah V, 792
epherd, Hannah E. II, 718
epherd, Hannah S. V, 416
epherd, Helen V, 202
epherd, Henry VI, 992
epherd, Ida VI, 771
epherd, Ida VI, 773
epherd, Ida VI, 777
epherd, Isaac II, 419
epherd, Jacob IV, 58
epherd, Jacob IV, 132
epherd, Jacob V, 119
epherd, Jacob V, 528
epherd, Jacob V, 597
epherd, Jacob V, 792
epherd, Jacob VI, 443
epherd, James II, 419
epherd, James VI, 992
epherd, Jane IV, 48
epherd, Jane IV, 58
epherd, Jane VI, 443
epherd, Jesse V, 62
epherd, Jesse V, 119
epherd, Jesse V, 416
epherd, Jesse V, 490
epherd, Jesse V, 527
epherd, Jesse V, 528
epherd, Jesse V, 597
epherd, Jesse V, 792
epherd, Jessy V, 597
epherd, Joel VI, 992
epherd, Joel VI, 1010
epherd, Joel L. V, 491
epherd, Joel L. V, 528
epherd, John I, 73
epherd, John I, 165
epherd, John II, 644
epherd, John II, 645
epherd, John II, 648
epherd, John II, 718
epherd, John IV, 58
epherd, John IV, 132
epherd, John IV, 1378
epherd, John V, 359
epherd, John VI, 86
epherd, John VI, 443
epherd, John VI, 559
epherd, John VI, 992
epherd, John A. VI, 947
epherd, John A. VI, 992
epherd, John F. V, 359
epherd, John Shepard II, 645
epherd, John Woolman II, 819
epherd, John, Jr. II, 645
epherd, Jonathan III, 286
epherd, Joseph II, 645
epherd, Joseph IV, 58
Shepherd, Joseph IV, 108
Shepherd, Joseph IV, 132
Shepherd, Joseph VI, 443
Shepherd, Joseph B. II, 920
Shepherd, Joseph Scott II, 648
Shepherd, Joseph, Jr. IV, 132
Shepherd, Josiah II, 648
Shepherd, Judith VI, 559
Shepherd, Julian VI, 853
Shepherd, Lena V, 202
Shepherd, Lena V, 359
Shepherd, Levi VI, 443
Shepherd, Lizzie V, 202
Shepherd, Louisa IV, 58
Shepherd, Louisa IV, 132
Shepherd, Louiza IV, 132
Shepherd, Lucy V, 359
Shepherd, Lucy W. III, 263
Shepherd, Lydia IV, 132
Shepherd, Lydia Ellen V, 202
Shepherd, Margaret IV, 58
Shepherd, Margaret IV, 108
Shepherd, Margaret IV, 132
Shepherd, Margaret IV, 1198
Shepherd, Margaret VI, 443
Shepherd, Margaret Jane IV, 58
Shepherd, Margaret Jane IV, 132
Shepherd, Mark C. II, 819
Shepherd, Martha II, 419
Shepherd, Martha V, 119
Shepherd, Martha V, 505
Shepherd, Martha V, 527
Shepherd, Martha V, 528
Shepherd, Martha V, 597
Shepherd, Martha V, 786
Shepherd, Martha V, 792
Shepherd, Martha E. V, 359
Shepherd, Mary I, 51
Shepherd, Mary I, 73
Shepherd, Mary I, 117
Shepherd, Mary I, 149
Shepherd, Mary I, 165
Shepherd, Mary I, 168
Shepherd, Mary I, 689
Shepherd, Mary I, 926
Shepherd, Mary II, 645
Shepherd, Mary II, 648
Shepherd, Mary III, 55
Shepherd, Mary III, 286
Shepherd, Mary IV, 19
Shepherd, Mary IV, 35
Shepherd, Mary IV, 58
Shepherd, Mary IV, 132
Shepherd, Mary IV, 843
Shepherd, Mary VI, 59
Shepherd, Mary VI, 86
Shepherd, Mary VI, 443
Shepherd, Mary VI, 992
Shepherd, Mary Alice V, 359
Shepherd, Mary Ann V, 77
Shepherd, Mary Ann V, 119
Shepherd, Mary Ann V, 792
Shepherd, Mary Ann Rebecca VI, 992
Shepherd, Mary J. VI, 992
Shepherd, Mary Jane V, 406
Shepherd, Mary Jane V, 430
Shepherd, Mary Jane V, 528
Shepherd, Mary Jane V, 792
Shepherd, Mary Jane VI, 999
Shepherd, Mary Lena V, 202
Shepherd, Matilda IV, 546
Shepherd, Matilda IV, 549
Shepherd, McKindry I, 926
Shepherd, Micca Sophia IV, 1184
Shepherd, Minna VI, 992
Shepherd, Minney L. VI, 999
Shepherd, Minney L. VI, 1009
Shepherd, Minnie S. I, 926
Shepherd, Mordecai I, 165
Shepherd, Mordecai M. I, 165
Shepherd, Mordecai M. I, 168
Shepherd, Mordecai Morris I, 117
Shepherd, Nancy Dowell VI, 992
Shepherd, Nathan II, 419
Shepherd, Ora V, 359
Shepherd, Pamela VI, 992
Shepherd, Patience W. II, 819
Shepherd, Priscilla I, 43
Shepherd, Priscilla I, 73
Shepherd, Priscilla I, 117
Shepherd, Priscilla I, 165
Shepherd, Priscilla II, 648
Shepherd, Priscilla II, 718
Shepherd, Priscilla VI, 86
Shepherd, Rachel II, 496
Shepherd, Rachel II, 648
Shepherd, Rachel IV, 58
Shepherd, Rachel IV, 132
Shepherd, Rachel F. II, 648
Shepherd, Rachel R. II, 718
Shepherd, Rebecca J. II, 648
Shepherd, Rebekah VI, 361
Shepherd, Reliance II, 783
Shepherd, Rhoda II, 648
Shepherd, Rhoda II, 819
Shepherd, Rhoda II, 920
Shepherd, Rhoda VI, 992
Shepherd, Richard II, 648
Shepherd, Robert II, 419
Shepherd, Sally Jane IV, 1184
Shepherd, Samuel II, 419
Shepherd, Sarah I, 418
Shepherd, Sarah II, 419
Shepherd, Sarah II, 575
Shepherd, Sarah II, 644
Shepherd, Sarah II, 645
Shepherd, Sarah II, 648
Shepherd, Sarah III, 285
Shepherd, Sarah III, 286
Shepherd, Sarah IV, 26
Shepherd, Sarah IV, 58
Shepherd, Sarah VI, 443
Shepherd, Sarah VI, 474
Shepherd, Sarah VI, 559
Shepherd, Sarah L. V, 359
Shepherd, Sarah W. III, 286
Shepherd, Sepian I, 73
Shepherd, Sewell IV, 1184
Shepherd, Sidney E. V, 359
Shepherd, Siprean I, 73
Shepherd, Siprean I, 165
Shepherd, Solomon IV, 58
Shepherd, Solomon IV, 108
Shepherd, Solomon IV, 132
Shepherd, Solomon VI, 443
Shepherd, Solomon VI, 491
Shepherd, Solomon VI, 664
Shepherd, Solomon VI, 699
Shepherd, Solomon VI, 701
Shepherd, Solomon, Jr. IV, 58
Shepherd, Stephen I, 73
Shepherd, Stephen, Jr. I, 73
Shepherd, Susan VI, 992
Shepherd, Susanna V, 62
Shepherd, Susanna V, 119
Shepherd, Susanna V, 131
Shepherd, Susanna V, 528
Shepherd, Susanna V, 564
Shepherd, Susanna V, 597
Shepherd, Susanna VI, 853
Shepherd, Susannah V, 527
Shepherd, Susannah V, 528
Shepherd, Susannah V, 597
Shepherd, Susannah VI, 491
Shepherd, Susannah VI, 699
Shepherd, Susannah VI, 701
Shepherd, Syprean I, 73
Shepherd, Thomas II, 419
Shepherd, Thomas II, 648
Shepherd, Thomas II, 920
Shepherd, Thomas IV, 58
Shepherd, Thomas IV, 108
Shepherd, Thomas IV, 132
Shepherd, Thomas V, 119
Shepherd, Thomas V, 528
Shepherd, Thomas V, 597
Shepherd, Thomas V, 792
Shepherd, Thomas VI, 443
Shepherd, Thomas VI, 699
Shepherd, Thomas VI, 701
Shepherd, Thomas VI, 853
Shepherd, Thomas VI, 992
Shepherd, Thomas VI, 1008
Shepherd, Thos. II, 819
Shepherd, Verne V, 359
Shepherd, Viola M. V, 491
Shepherd, Viola M. V, 528
Shepherd, William II, 419
Shepherd, William III, 286
Shepherd, William IV, 58
Shepherd, William VI, 853
Shepherd, William VI, 909
Shepherd, William VI, 961
Shepherd, William VI, 992
Shepherd, William VI, 1020
Shepherd, William A. VI, 914
Shepherd, William A. VI, 973
Shepherd, William A. VI, 992
Shepherd, William A. VI, 999
Shepherd, William A. VI, 1009
Shepherd, William C. II, 718
Shepherd, William M. I, 769
Shepherd, William W. V, 597
Shepherd, Wilson IV, 58
Shepherd, Wilson IV, 132
Shepherd, Wm. II, 648
Shepherd, Wm. IV, 132
Shepherd, Wm. VI, 559
Shepherd, Wm. L. V, 359
Shepherd, Wm. R. III, 285
Shepherd, Wm. R. III, 446
Shepherd, Wm. W. V, 597
Shepherd, Woolman J. II, 920
Shepler, Amanda D. IV, 274
Shepler, James IV, 274
Shepler, James Albert IV, 274
Shepp, Caroline L. III, 188
Shepp, Caroline L. III, 286
Shepp, Mary III, 188
Shepp, Mary III, 286
Shepp, Samuel III, 188
Shepp, Samuel III, 286
Sheppard, Allen V, 709
Sheppard, Alvanetha II, 863
Sheppard, Alvanetha II, 920
Sheppard, Amy II, 123
Sheppard, Amy II, 765
Sheppard, Angeline V, 709
Sheppard, Angeline D. V, 709
Sheppard, Ann II, 123
Sheppard, Ann II, 147
Sheppard, Ann II, 157
Sheppard, Ann Elizabeth II, 39
Sheppard, Ann Elizabeth II, 97
Sheppard, Anna II, 721
Sheppard, Anne II, 96
Sheppard, Benjamin II, 741
Sheppard, Benjamin II, 765
Sheppard, Benjamin VI, 154
Sheppard, Benjamin VI, 211
Sheppard, Benjamin VI, 443
Sheppard, Catherine II, 648
Sheppard, Charles II, 38
Sheppard, Charles II, 123
Sheppard, Charles II, 718
Sheppard, Charles II, 765
Sheppard, Charles II, 820
Sheppard, Chas. II, 60
Sheppard, Chas. II, 97
Sheppard, Ciphrean I, 165
Sheppard, Clarkson II, 721
Sheppard, Dr. W. W. V, 709
Sheppard, Eleanor Plummer II, 140
Sheppard, Elisabeth I, 151
Sheppard, Elisabeth I, 165
Sheppard, Elizabeth V, 597
Sheppard, Elizabeth V, 709
Sheppard, Elizabeth VI, 443
Sheppard, Elizabeth S. II, 920
Sheppard, Ella II, 919
Sheppard, Ella II, 920
Sheppard, Ella Flitcraft II, 919
Sheppard, Ella Flitcraft II, 920
Sheppard, Francis J. V, 709
Sheppard, Frank V, 709
Sheppard, George W. II, 123
Sheppard, George Wood II, 39
Sheppard, Hannah II, 137
Sheppard, Hannah II, 140
Sheppard, Hannah V, 709
Sheppard, Hannah VI, 387
Sheppard, Hannah VI, 443
Sheppard, Hannah E. II, 718
Sheppard, Hannah E. II, 765
Sheppard, Hannah J. II, 741
Sheppard, Hannah J. II, 765
Sheppard, Jacob VI, 443
Sheppard, James II, 96
Sheppard, Jane VI, 443
Sheppard, Jesse V, 119
Sheppard, Jesse VI, 443
Sheppard, John II, 38
Sheppard, John II, 88
Sheppard, John II, 96
Sheppard, John II, 97
Sheppard, John II, 112
Sheppard, John II, 648
Sheppard, John II, 741
Sheppard, John II, 765
Sheppard, John V, 359
Sheppard, John VI, 443
Sheppard, John E. II, 39
Sheppard, John E. II, 97
Sheppard, John E. II, 123
Sheppard, John E. II, 741
Sheppard, John E. II, 765
Sheppard, John R. II, 765
Sheppard, John R. Carpenter II, 123
Sheppard, John Woolman II, 920
Sheppard, John, Jr. II, 96
Sheppard, Joseph II, 137
Sheppard, Joseph VI, 443
Sheppard, Joseph B. II, 920
Sheppard, Joseph Scott II, 648
Sheppard, Josiah II, 39
Sheppard, Josiah Foster II, 920
Sheppard, Josiah Foster II, 937
Sheppard, Latitia II, 116
Sheppard, Latitia II, 123
Sheppard, Letitia II, 96
Sheppard, Lettitia II, 88
Sheppard, Lettitia II, 96
Sheppard, Levi VI, 443
Sheppard, Louise V, 709
Sheppard, Lydia II, 123
Sheppard, Lydia II, 648
Sheppard, Lydia II, 920
Sheppard, Lydia VI, 405
Sheppard, Lydia VI, 443
Sheppard, Lydia F. II, 571
Sheppard, Margaret II, 741
Sheppard, Margaret II, 765
Sheppard, Margaret VI, 443
Sheppard, Margaret G. II, 765
Sheppard, Mark II, 39
Sheppard, Mark II, 63
Sheppard, Mark II, 96
Sheppard, Mark C. II, 920
Sheppard, Mark E. II, 920
Sheppard, Martha II, 96
Sheppard, Martha II, 137
Sheppard, Martha II, 157
Sheppard, Martha II, 419
Sheppard, Martha VI, 443
Sheppard, Mary I, 689
Sheppard, Mary II, 38
Sheppard, Mary II, 39
Sheppard, Mary II, 63
Sheppard, Mary II, 69
Sheppard, Mary II, 88
Sheppard, Mary II, 96
Sheppard, Mary II, 97
Sheppard, Mary II, 101
Sheppard, Mary II, 131
Sheppard, Mary II, 137
Sheppard, Mary II, 648
Sheppard, Mary II, 721
Sheppard, Mary II, 741
Sheppard, Mary II, 765
Sheppard, Mary II, 920
Sheppard, Mary II, 937
Sheppard, Mary V, 300
Sheppard, Mary V, 310
Sheppard, Mary VI, 443
Sheppard, Mary C II, 123
Sheppard, Mary D. II, 123
Sheppard, Mary R. II, 741
Sheppard, Mary R. II, 765
Sheppard, Mary S. II, 131
Sheppard, Messer VI, 443
Sheppard, Miriam VI, 443
Sheppard, Moses II, 39
Sheppard, Nathan II, 96
Sheppard, Nathan II, 419
Sheppard, Patience W. II, 920
Sheppard, Phebe II, 131
Sheppard, Priscilla II, 38
Sheppard, Priscilla II, 39
Sheppard, Priscilla II, 96
Sheppard, Priscilla II, 112
Sheppard, Priscilla II, 123
Sheppard, Priscilla II, 718
Sheppard, Priscilla S. II, 123
Sheppard, Priscilla W. II, 716
Sheppard, Rachel II, 38
Sheppard, Rachel II, 123
Sheppard, Rachel II, 137
Sheppard, Rachel II, 698
Sheppard, Rachel II, 765
Sheppard, Rachel A. II, 147
Sheppard, Rachel A. II, 157
Sheppard, Rachel Ann II, 157
Sheppard, Rachel R. II, 38
Sheppard, Rachel R. II, 60
Sheppard, Rachel R. II, 97
Sheppard, Rachel R. II, 123
Sheppard, Rachel R. II, 718
Sheppard, Rebecca N. II, 920
Sheppard, Rebecca N. II, 937
Sheppard, Rhoda II, 920
Sheppard, Richard II, 97
Sheppard, Richard II, 147
Sheppard, Richard II, 157
Sheppard, Richard S. II, 137
Sheppard, Richard S. II, 147
Sheppard, Richard S. II, 157
Sheppard, Richard W. II, 123
Sheppard, Richard W., Jr. II, 97
Sheppard, Richard Wood II, 39
Sheppard, Robert II, 131
Sheppard, Ruth II, 137
Sheppard, Samuel II, 38
Sheppard, Samuel C. II, 39
Sheppard, Samuel C. II, 123
Sheppard, Samuel M. II, 741
Sheppard, Samuel M. II, 765
Sheppard, Sarah II, 24
Sheppard, Sarah II, 39
Sheppard, Sarah II, 97
Sheppard, Sarah II, 116
Sheppard, Sarah II, 123

Sheppard, Sarah II, 419
Sheppard, Sarah II, 648
Sheppard, Sarah VI, 443
Sheppard, Sarah Mulford II, 133
Sheppard, Solomon VI, 443
Sheppard, Susanna V, 119
Sheppard, Susannah VI, 443
Sheppard, Sylvanus C. II, 140
Sheppard, Thomas II, 39
Sheppard, Thomas II, 920
Sheppard, Thomas VI, 443
Sheppard, Thomas R. II, 97
Sheppard, Thomas R. II, 123
Sheppard, Thos. R. II, 88
Sheppard, Thos. R. II, 96
Sheppard, Thos. R. II, 116
Sheppard, Thos. R. II, 123
Sheppard, Thos. S. II, 863
Sheppard, Thos. S. II, 920
Sheppard, Thos. Shaw II, 919
Sheppard, Thos. Shaw II, 920
Sheppard, Velna I, 943
Sheppard, Velna I, 949
Sheppard, Wd. Priscilla II, 38
Sheppard, William II, 39
Sheppard, William C. II, 718
Sheppard, William Carpenter II, 38
Sheppard, Wm. II, 96
Sheppard, Wm. II, 123
Sheppard, Wm. II, 137
Sheppard, Wm. II, 648
Sheppard, Wm. II, 765
Sheppard, Wm. C. II, 123
Sheppard, Wm. C. II, 137
Sheppard, Wm. C. II, 765
Sheppard, Wm. Carpenter II, 123
Sheppard, Wm. H. V, 709
Sheppard, Wm. W. V, 597
Sheppard, Wm. W. V, 709
Sheppard, Woolman J. II, 920
Shepperd, Amaziah V, 528
Shepperd, Ann II, 648
Shepperd, Elizabeth IV, 132
Shepperd, Elizabeth V, 527
Shepperd, Hannah V, 528
Shepperd, Jacob V, 528
Shepperd, Jesse V, 527
Shepperd, John I, 73
Shepperd, John Woolman II, 819
Shepperd, John Woolman II, 920
Shepperd, John, Jr. II, 87
Shepperd, Joseph IV, 108
Shepperd, Joseph IV, 132
Shepperd, Judith II, 1026
Shepperd, Lydia II, 122
Shepperd, Mark C. II, 819
Shepperd, Martha V, 527
Shepperd, Mary I, 59
Shepperd, Mary I, 73
Shepperd, Mary II, 87
Shepperd, Mary IV, 806
Shepperd, Mary IV, 843
Shepperd, Patience W. II, 819
Shepperd, Priscilla II, 122
Shepperd, Priscilla II, 648
Shepperd, Rachel F. II, 648
Shepperd, Rebecca J. II, 648
Shepperd, Richard II, 648
Shepperd, Richard W. II, 122
Shepperd, Samuel II, 122
Shepperd, Sarah M. III, 471
Shepperd, Stephen, Jr. I, 73
Shepperd, Susannah V, 527
Shepperd, Syprean I, 73
Shepperd, Wilson IV, 132
Shepperd, Wm. II, 96
Shepperson, J. G. VI, 916
Shepperson, J. G. VI, 927
Shepperson, J. G. VI, 943
Shepperson, J. G. VI, 949
Shepperson, J. G. VI, 952
Shepperson, J. G. VI, 986
Shepperson, John G. VI, 874
Shepperson, John G. VI, 882
Shepperson, John G. VI, 981
Shepperson, Josiah VI, 795
Shepperson, Josiah VI, 853
Shepperson, Martha D. VI, 992
Shepperson, Martha F. VI, 853
Shepperson, Rev. John G. VI, 992
Sheppherd, Hannah V, 528
Sherad, Elezabeath I, 91
Sherberger, Fredericia P. VI, 402
Sherberger, Fredericia P. VI, 443
Sherboon, Maudlin II, 449
Sherboon, Peter II, 449
Sherburn, Catharine V, 1018
Sherburn, D. E. V, 1018
Sherburn, Daniel Edwin V, 1018
Sherburn, Katie L. V, 1018
Sheredan, Margaret V, 120
Sherenger, F. C. V, 709
Sherenger, M. F. V, 709
Sherenger, Wm. Arthur V, 709
Sherer, Jas. VI, 824
Sherick, Rachel IV, 58
Sherick, Rachel IV, 64
Sheridan, Elizabeth V, 528
Sheridan, Elizabeth V, 595
Sheridan, Elizabeth V, 597
Sheridan, Fam V, 597
Sheridan, George V, 528
Sheridan, Hannah V, 528
Sheridan, John I, 364
Sheridan, John I, 418
Sheridan, John V, 528
Sheridan, John V, 597
Sheridan, Margaret I, 418
Sheridan, Margret I, 418
Sheridan, Mary I, 364
Sheridan, Mary I, 418
Sheridan, Mary Edith V, 359
Sheridan, Rachel V, 528
Sheridan, William V, 528
Sheriff, Hannah V, 277
Sheriff, John V, 430
Sheriff, Lucinda V, 430
Sheriff, Lusinda V, 430
Sherk, Mary V, 536
Sherl, Margaret Jane I, 1161
Sherley, Eliza E. VI, 992
Sherley, Elizabeth VI, 992
Sherley, John VI, 992
Sherley, Joseph VI, 992
Sherlock, Eliza VI, 992
Sherlock, Joseph VI, 992
Sherly, Samuel II, 419
Sherman, ??? III, 486
Sherman, Abigail III, 15
Sherman, Abram IV, 274
Sherman, Albert A. VI, 992
Sherman, Almy III, 486
Sherman, Alva V, 1018
Sherman, Amelia V, 1018
Sherman, Ann E. VI, 992
Sherman, Anna III, 414
Sherman, Anna III, 499
Sherman, Anna U. III, 483
Sherman, Benjamin II, 419
Sherman, Charles III, 286
Sherman, Clara V, 1018
Sherman, Cornelia A. VI, 1016
Sherman, David Romanus IV, 274
Sherman, David S. III, 286
Sherman, Davids III, 192
Sherman, Edy R. IV, 1378
Sherman, Elisha J. IV, 1378
Sherman, Elisha Y. IV, 1378
Sherman, Eliza IV, 1184
Sherman, Eliza IV, 1222
Sherman, Eliza IV, 1223
Sherman, Eliza Q. VI, 1002
Sherman, Elizabeth III, 486
Sherman, Elizabeth J. VI, 1004
Sherman, Emma III, 286
Sherman, Emma Frances III, 15
Sherman, Esther III, 485
Sherman, Esther III, 486
Sherman, Esther III, 499
Sherman, Eunice V, 1018
Sherman, Eva May IV, 1184
Sherman, Ezra IV, 1222
Sherman, Ezra IV, 1223
Sherman, Frances A. VI, 992
Sherman, George V, 1018
Sherman, Harriet P. VI, 992
Sherman, Henry D. VI, 885
Sherman, Hepsa H. III, 192
Sherman, Hepsah H. III, 286
Sherman, Hughes, Reuben VI, 885
Sherman, Isaac III, 121
Sherman, Isaac III, 286
Sherman, Isaac III, 483
Sherman, Isaac III, 500
Sherman, Israel III, 499
Sherman, Jackson V, 1018
Sherman, James III, 499
Sherman, James V, 1018
Sherman, Jane VI, 885
Sherman, John IV, 1151
Sherman, John IV, 1184
Sherman, John D. III, 15
Sherman, John D. III, 286
Sherman, John H. VI, 777
Sherman, John Henry IV, 1184
Sherman, John W. VI, 886
Sherman, Joseph M. V, 1018
Sherman, Louisa V, 1018
Sherman, Lucile Peelle V, 709
Sherman, Luella IV, 1151
Sherman, Luella IV, 1184
Sherman, Lydia IV, 1378
Sherman, Mabel Adams III, 286
Sherman, Madison IV, 1223
Sherman, Margaret III, 121
Sherman, Margaret III, 286
Sherman, Margaret III, 483
Sherman, Margaret III, 499
Sherman, Margaret III, 500
Sherman, Mary III, 486
Sherman, Mary V, 1018
Sherman, Mary A. III, 192
Sherman, Mary A. IV, 1378
Sherman, Mary C. V, 1018
Sherman, Mary S. III, 286
Sherman, Mely V, 1018
Sherman, Mexico VI, 992
Sherman, Mrs. ??? V, 1018
Sherman, Nellie V, 1018
Sherman, Newton IV, 1184
Sherman, Obadiah III, 486
Sherman, Permilia VI, 1004
Sherman, Phebe III, 486
Sherman, Polly M. VI, 992
Sherman, Rebecca III, 488
Sherman, Rebecca III, 499
Sherman, Robert C. VI, 866
Sherman, Sam'l III, 485
Sherman, Samuel III, 286
Sherman, Samuel III, 499
Sherman, Sarah III, 286
Sherman, Sarah G. IV, 1378
Sherman, Solomon III, 486
Sherman, Susan B. IV, 1263
Sherman, Susie B. IV, 1263
Sherman, Susie Buffington IV, 1263
Sherman, Thomas III, 486
Sherman, Thomas D. VI, 992
Sherman, Una V, 1018
Sherman, Wesley IV, 1184
Sherman, William VI, 885
Sherman, William N. VI, 992
Sherman, William N. VI, 1002
Shermon, Blanch O. IV, 1337
Shermon, Florence IV, 1337
Shermon, Frank V. IV, 1337
Shermon, Lucretia S. IV, 1337
Shermon, Lydia A. IV, 1337
Shermon, Melissa E. IV, 1337
Shermon, Mrs. Ruth IV, 1337
Shermon, Parley G. IV, 1337
Shermon, Peleg IV, 1337
Shermon, Richard C. IV, 1337
Shermon, Wm. G. IV, 1337
Shernig, Mary VI, 853
Shernig, Wiley VI, 853
Sherod, Nettie V, 1018
Sherodd, D. C. I, 340
Sherpick, Ann Elizabeth III, 286
Sherpick, Eugene A. III, 138
Sherpick, Eugene A. III, 373
Sherpick, Eugene A., Jr. III, 286
Sherpick, Eugene Arthur III, 286
Sherpick, Eugene Arthur III, 373
Sherpick, Eva Ella III, 138
Sherpick, Eva Ella III, 373
Sherpick, Eva Eva Ella III, 138
Sherpick, Nell III, 286
Sherpick, Wm. Edwards III, 286
Sherrard, DeWitt I, 340
Sherrick, Joanna IV, 58
Sherrick, Joanna IV, 64
Sherrick, Rachel IV, 58
Sherrill, Ellen Bernard II, 779
Sherrill, Enos I, 933
Sherrill, Henry A. I, 933
Sherrill, Henry A. I, 949
Sherrill, Margaret Jane I, 1161
Sherrill, Pearson II, 779
Sherrill, Rachel II, 779
Sherrill, Sarah I, 933
Sherron, Sarah II, 157
Sherron, Sarah J. II, 920
Sherron, Sarah Seal II, 920
Sherron, Susanna IV, 482
Sherron, Susanna IV, 497
Sherry, William IV, 1263
Sherry, Wm. IV, 1263
Shertzer, Ally IV, 1293
Shertzer, Jesse IV, 1293
Shertzer, John M. IV, 1293
Sherwood, ??? III, 286
Sherwood, Abigail V, 120
Sherwood, Albert Bartlett V, 120
Sherwood, Alice Palmer V, 120
Sherwood, Anna IV, 1184
Sherwood, Anna H. IV, 1184
Sherwood, Anna L. V, 103
Sherwood, Anna L. V, 120
Sherwood, Catharine III, 286
Sherwood, Catharine J. II, 884
Sherwood, Catherine J. II, 920
Sherwood, Charles H. V, 120
Sherwood, Darcus V, 120
Sherwood, Dorcas V, 74
Sherwood, Dorcas V, 80
Sherwood, Dorcas V, 120
Sherwood, Dorcas V, 128
Sherwood, Dorcas V, 146
Sherwood, Dorcas E. V, 120
Sherwood, Edith Marie V, 120
Sherwood, Eli V, 59
Sherwood, Eliz. III, 76
Sherwood, Eliz. III, 446
Sherwood, Elizabeth III, 286
Sherwood, Elizabeth V, 59
Sherwood, Elizabeth V, 80
Sherwood, Elizabeth V, 120
Sherwood, Elizabeth V, 128
Sherwood, Elizabeth VI, 729
Sherwood, Elizabeth C. V, 120
Sherwood, Elizabeth C. V, 122
Sherwood, Elizabeth D. IV, 436
Sherwood, Elizabeth M. III, 76
Sherwood, Elizabeth M. III, 286
Sherwood, Ellen Edna V, 120
Sherwood, Emily V, 930
Sherwood, Estie IV, 1293
Sherwood, Fred B. V, 120
Sherwood, George III, 286
Sherwood, Hannah V, 120
Sherwood, Helen V, 120
Sherwood, Henery V, 120
Sherwood, Henry III, 286
Sherwood, Henry V, 120
Sherwood, Hester IV, 1293
Sherwood, Howard V, 120
Sherwood, Howard Brown V, 120
Sherwood, Isaac III, 76
Sherwood, Isaac III, 286
Sherwood, Isaac III, 440
Sherwood, Isaac III, 446
Sherwood, Isaac V, 120
Sherwood, Isaac V, 146
Sherwood, Isaac, Jr. III, 286
Sherwood, J. Henry V, 120
Sherwood, James III, 286
Sherwood, Jason IV, 1184
Sherwood, Jason H. IV, 1184
Sherwood, John V, 80
Sherwood, John V, 120
Sherwood, John V, 122
Sherwood, John B. III, 286
Sherwood, John Henry V, 120
Sherwood, Jonathan V, 120
Sherwood, Laurence Thomas V, 120
Sherwood, Leah I, 35
Sherwood, Leah I, 73
Sherwood, Lidia V, 74
Sherwood, Lydia V, 120
Sherwood, Lydia C. III, 286
Sherwood, Lydia Catherine III, 286
Sherwood, Lydia M. V, 120
Sherwood, Malinda V, 35
Sherwood, Malinda V, 120
Sherwood, Malinda V, 202
Sherwood, Margaret A. V, 75
Sherwood, Margaret A. V, 120
Sherwood, Martha III, 440
Sherwood, Martha III, 446
Sherwood, Mary I, 35
Sherwood, Mary I, 73
Sherwood, Mary III, 131
Sherwood, Mary III, 272
Sherwood, Mary III, 286
Sherwood, Mary V, 59
Sherwood, Mary Amanda V, 120
Sherwood, Mary M. III, 286
Sherwood, Morris III, 446
Sherwood, Morris III, 468
Sherwood, Morris III, 471
Sherwood, Nellie V, 120
Sherwood, Peter III, 286
Sherwood, Peter McCarty III, 286
Sherwood, Phebe IV, 1240
Sherwood, Phebe V, 21
Sherwood, Phebe V, 120
Sherwood, Rachel III, 116
Sherwood, Rachel F. III, 286
Sherwood, Robert III, 286
Sherwood, Samuel IV, 1293
Sherwood, Samuel V, 120
Sherwood, Samuel B. V, 120
Sherwood, Sarah III, 286
Sherwood, Sarah V, 120
Sherwood, Sarah A. V, 120
Sherwood, Sarah C. III, 446
Sherwood, Sarah C. III, 468
Sherwood, Sarah C. III, 471
Sherwood, Sattie V, 120
Sherwood, Thomas V, 21
Sherwood, Thomas V, 74
Sherwood, Thomas V, 120
Sherwood, Thomas V, 128
Sherwood, Thomas V, 146
Sherwood, Vernon VI, 729
Sherwood, Vernon Paul IV, 118
Sherwood, William III, 286
Sherwood, William Henry V, 1
Sheton, Lou I, 873
Sheton, Lou I, 900
Shetzer, Charlotte VI, 991
Shetzer, Samuel VI, 991
Sheuping, Sarah I, 933
Sheuster, Mary E. VI, 853
Sheuster, Philip VI, 853
Shewalter, Clarence W. V, 709
Shewalter, Elizabeth V, 709
Shewalter, Mary E. V, 709
Sheward, Ann VI, 559
Sheward, Elizabeth II, 451
Sheward, Elizabeth II, 648
Sheward, Elizabeth D. IV, 436
Sheward, Jane VI, 500
Sheward, Jane VI, 559
Sheward, John IV, 436
Sheward, Lydia II, 451
Sheward, Lydia II, 648
Sheward, Ruth VI, 497
Sheward, Ruth VI, 500
Sheward, Ruth VI, 559
Sheward, Ruth VI, 641
Sheward, Ruth Smith VI, 559
Sheward, Samuel VI, 496
Sheward, Samuel VI, 497
Sheward, Samuel VI, 500
Sheward, Samuel VI, 559
Sheward, Samuel VI, 562
Sheward, Wd. Ruth Smith VI, 562
Sheward, Widow Ruth VI, 497
Shewberry, Nancy VI, 993
Shewberry, Nathan VI, 993
Shewring, David II, 419
Shewster, Philip VI, 956
Shewster, Phillip VI, 992
Shewster, Polly VI, 992
Shey, Francis L. III, 286
Shiall, John VI, 833
Shidaker, Charles H. V, 120
Shidaker, Eliza V, 597
Shidaker, Harter V, 120
Shidaker, Harter J. V, 120
Shidaker, J. W. V, 597
Shidaker, Louisa A. V, 120
Shidaker, Mary E. V, 597
Shieks, Mintie V, 1018
Shield, Elizabeth V, 611
Shield, Mary Jane V, 487
Shield, Mary Jane V, 528
Shields, Adaline I, 418
Shields, Caroline IV, 1056
Shields, Caroline IV, 1076
Shields, Don IV, 1223
Shields, Donnie H. IV, 1184
Shields, Donnie H. IV, 1223
Shields, Edd IV, 1223
Shields, Eddie P. IV, 1184
Shields, Eddie P. IV, 1223
Shields, Edith May IV, 1223
Shields, Elizabeth V, 528
Shields, Elizabeth V, 618
Shields, Elizabeth V, 643
Shields, Elizabeth V, 644
Shields, Ellen I, 919
Shields, Ellen I, 920
Shields, Elma M. V, 430
Shields, Emma V, 430
Shields, Eva IV, 1223
Shields, Frances VI, 853
Shields, Gulia E. V, 430
Shields, Gulielma V, 430
Shields, Hannah V, 120
Shields, Hannah V, 522
Shields, Hannah V, 528
Shields, Hannah V, 610
Shields, Hannah V, 611
Shields, Hannah V, 617
Shields, Hannah V, 618
Shields, Hannah V, 638
Shields, Hannah V, 643
Shields, Hannah V, 644
Shields, Hannah VI, 167
Shields, Jane II, 648
Shields, Jean II, 470
Shields, Jean II, 648
Shields, Joanna I, 997
Shields, John V, 528

ields, John V, 643
ields, John J. VI, 853
ields, John W. I, 418
ields, Joseph IV, 274
ields, Joseph V, 430
ields, Joseph A. V, 430
ields, Josephine V, 430
ields, Lucinda V, 617
ields, Lucinda V, 643
ields, Lucinda V, 644
ields, Lydia I, 418
ields, Lydia V, 528
ields, Lydia V, 610
ields, Lydia V, 643
ields, Maggie C. IV, 274
ields, Maran I, 900
ields, Margaret V, 643
ields, Margaret V, 644
ields, Margaret V, 645
ields, Maria V, 643
ields, Martha I, 837
ields, Mary Ann V, 617
ields, Mary Ann V, 643
ields, Mary Ann V, 644
ields, Mary J. IV, 1184
ields, Mary J. IV, 1223
ields, Maryann V, 528
ields, Mildred IV, 274
ields, Miriam M. I, 816
ields, Miriam M. I, 837
ields, Moses B. V, 430
ields, Moses P. V, 430
ields, Payton B. IV, 1184
ields, Payton B. IV, 1223
ields, Pheriba V, 578
ields, Pheriba V, 597
ields, Priscilla V, 430
ields, Rachel II, 470
ields, Rachel II, 648
ields, Rebecca V, 528
ields, Rebecca V, 643
ields, Rebecca V, 644
ields, Rebecca V, 648
ields, Sabina Jane IV, 274
ields, Sarah I, 418
ields, Sarah I, 836
ields, Sarah I, 837
ields, Sarah V, 430
ields, Sarah V, 559
ields, Sarah E. V, 430
ields, Sarah Jane V, 618
ields, Sarah Jane V, 643
ields, Sarah Jane V, 644
ields, Virginia IV, 274
ields, William V, 528
ields, William V, 618
ields, William V, 643
ields, William VI, 167
ields, Wm. II, 97
ields, Wm. II, 470
ields, Wm. II, 648
ields, Wm. V, 610
ields, Wm. V, 611
ields, Wm. V, 617
ields, Wm. V, 638
iell, Andrew IV, 704
iell, Andrew IV, 761
iell, Euphemia IV, 761
iell, John W. Fawcett IV, 761
iell, Mary G. IV, 704
iell, Mary G. IV, 761
iell, Robert IV, 761
iels, Elenor VI, 992
iels, Elizabeth VI, 992
iers, Anna II, 259
iers, Deborah II, 612
iers, Deborah II, 649
iers, George II, 612
iers, George II, 649
iers, John II, 649
iers, John, Jr. II, 1026
igley, Mary C. V, 956
igley, Mary C. V, 959
ihon, Abel VI, 443
ihon, Abel VI, 605
ihon, Deborah VI, 443
ihon, Deborah VI, 605
ihon, Ebenezer VI, 443
ihon, Ebenezer VI, 605
ihon, Ebonezar VI, 443
ihon, John VI, 443
ihon, John VI, 605
ihon, Jonah VI, 443
ihon, Jonah VI, 605
ihon, Mary VI, 428
ihon, Mary VI, 443
ihon, Mary VI, 605
ihon, Michael VI, 428
ihon, Michael VI, 443
ihon, Michael VI, 605
ihon, Phebe VI, 443
Shihon, Phebe VI, 605
Shihon, Wd. Michal VI, 443
Shilcock, Beulah F. III, 435
Shilcock, Beulah F. III, 446
Shilcock, Clarence III, 446
Shilcock, Clarence J. III, 435
Shilcock, Helen M. III, 435
Shilcock, Helen M. III, 446
Shiletto, Ann IV, 497
Shiletto, Ann, Jr. IV, 497
Shiletto, John IV, 497
Shillin, John II, 447
Shilling, Nancy Oday V, 1018
Shilling, Susan II, 183
Shilling, Susan II, 300
Shimbron, Margaret M. IV, 639
Shimer, Hattie IV, 1338
Shimer, Olive May IV, 1338
Shimer, Samuel IV, 1338
Shimer, Samuel M. IV, 1338
Shimmel, Jemima D. II, 718
Shimmell, Jemima D. II, 749
Shimmell, Jemima D. II, 765
Shin, Abigail II, 648
Shin, Amos II, 258
Shin, Anner VI, 443
Shin, Benjamin V, 120
Shin, David VI, 443
Shin, Elizabeth V, 277
Shin, Esther VI, 374
Shin, Esther VI, 443
Shin, Frances V, 277
Shin, George V, 277
Shin, John VI, 443
Shin, Martha II, 216
Shin, Martha II, 258
Shin, Mary II, 598
Shin, Mary VI, 443
Shin, Samuel VI, 443
Shin, Thomas II, 216
Shin, Thomas II, 258
Shinall, William VI, 839
Shinar, Jane V, 120
Shinault, Martha VI, 853
Shinborn, Margaret M. IV, 656
Shinbron, Margaret M. IV, 656
Shinbron, Margaret Maria IV, 656
Shinee, Ruth II, 54
Shinee, Ruth II, 97
Shingledecker, Cyrus V, 1018
Shinn, Aaron IV, 761
Shinn, Abigail II, 183
Shinn, Abigail II, 228
Shinn, Abigail II, 258
Shinn, Abigail II, 259
Shinn, Abigail II, 300
Shinn, Abigail II, 306
Shinn, Abigail II, 324
Shinn, Abigail II, 648
Shinn, Abigail IV, 58
Shinn, Abigail IV, 656
Shinn, Abigail IV, 759
Shinn, Abigail IV, 761
Shinn, Abigail IV, 843
Shinn, Abigail IV, 853
Shinn, Abigail IV, 992
Shinn, Abigail VI, 420
Shinn, Abigail VI, 600
Shinn, Abigail VI, 605
Shinn, Abraham II, 259
Shinn, Abraham II, 300
Shinn, Abraham II, 324
Shinn, Abraham IV, 761
Shinn, Abraham IV, 1030
Shinn, Ada II, 313
Shinn, Albert II, 313
Shinn, Albert II, 324
Shinn, Albert N. II, 920
Shinn, Albert W. II, 834
Shinn, Albert W. II, 920
Shinn, Albert Woolman II, 819
Shinn, Albina V, 959
Shinn, Alfred II, 183
Shinn, Alfred II, 259
Shinn, Alice II, 258
Shinn, Alice II, 264
Shinn, Alis II, 183
Shinn, Amos II, 206
Shinn, Amos II, 258
Shinn, Amos VI, 598
Shinn, Amy II, 259
Shinn, Ann II, 183
Shinn, Ann II, 206
Shinn, Ann II, 228
Shinn, Ann II, 258
Shinn, Ann II, 259
Shinn, Ann II, 300
Shinn, Ann II, 313
Shinn, Ann IV, 761
Shinn, Ann IV, 992
Shinn, Ann VI, 480
Shinn, Ann VI, 559
Shinn, Ann VI, 573
Shinn, Ann VI, 594
Shinn, Ann VI, 605
Shinn, Ann Eliza II, 295
Shinn, Ann Eliza II, 300
Shinn, Ann F. II, 259
Shinn, Anna II, 291
Shinn, Anna II, 300
Shinn, Anna II, 320
Shinn, Anna II, 324
Shinn, Anna Canby II, 819
Shinn, Anne II, 313
Shinn, Anner VI, 443
Shinn, Asa II, 183
Shinn, Asa II, 211
Shinn, Asa II, 224
Shinn, Asa II, 228
Shinn, Asa II, 259
Shinn, Asa II, 300
Shinn, Asa II, 313
Shinn, Asa G. II, 324
Shinn, Benjamin II, 259
Shinn, Benjamin IV, 992
Shinn, Benjamin V, 120
Shinn, Byron IV, 992
Shinn, Caleb II, 259
Shinn, Caleb II, 300
Shinn, Caleb IV, 656
Shinn, Caleb IV, 761
Shinn, Caleb IV, 793
Shinn, Charles II, 313
Shinn, Charles IV, 761
Shinn, Charles IV, 892
Shinn, Charles IV, 894
Shinn, Charles IV, 992
Shinn, Charles V, 959
Shinn, Clement II, 258
Shinn, David IV, 761
Shinn, David IV, 894
Shinn, David IV, 992
Shinn, David V, 886
Shinn, David VI, 443
Shinn, David R. IV, 761
Shinn, David R. IV, 992
Shinn, David R. V, 886
Shinn, Earl II, 242
Shinn, Earl II, 259
Shinn, Earl II, 706
Shinn, Earl II, 718
Shinn, Eben II, 313
Shinn, Elijah IV, 761
Shinn, Elijah IV, 992
Shinn, Elijah IV, 1030
Shinn, Elin II, 258
Shinn, Elin II, 263
Shinn, Elisabeth II, 183
Shinn, Elizabeth II, 238
Shinn, Elizabeth II, 239
Shinn, Elizabeth II, 240
Shinn, Elizabeth II, 254
Shinn, Elizabeth II, 258
Shinn, Elizabeth II, 259
Shinn, Elizabeth II, 648
Shinn, Elizabeth II, 649
Shinn, Elizabeth II, 706
Shinn, Elizabeth V, 277
Shinn, Elizabeth VI, 443
Shinn, Elizabeth VI, 598
Shinn, Elwood II, 183
Shinn, Elwood II, 300
Shinn, Elwood II, 313
Shinn, Elwood II, 324
Shinn, Emily II, 314
Shinn, Emily Amanda II, 313
Shinn, Emily Amanda II, 324
Shinn, Emily N. II, 313
Shinn, Emily N. II, 324
Shinn, Emily N. II, 327
Shinn, Emily N. II, 819
Shinn, Emily N. II, 834
Shinn, Emily N. II, 920
Shinn, Emma J. II, 834
Shinn, Emma J. II, 920
Shinn, Emma Jane II, 819
Shinn, Esaias II, 199
Shinn, Esaias II, 259
Shinn, Esther VI, 443
Shinn, Eunice Walton VI, 605
Shinn, Francis II, 259
Shinn, Francis VI, 443
Shinn, Francis VI, 605
Shinn, George II, 206
Shinn, George II, 238
Shinn, George II, 247
Shinn, George II, 258
Shinn, George II, 259
Shinn, George II, 267
Shinn, George VI, 443
Shinn, George VI, 597
Shinn, George VI, 600
Shinn, George VI, 605
Shinn, Grace II, 259
Shinn, Grace II, 300
Shinn, Grace II, 324
Shinn, Grace IV, 761
Shinn, Hannah II, 194
Shinn, Hannah II, 199
Shinn, Hannah II, 211
Shinn, Hannah II, 220
Shinn, Hannah II, 236
Shinn, Hannah II, 247
Shinn, Hannah II, 258
Shinn, Hannah II, 259
Shinn, Hannah II, 832
Shinn, Hannah II, 920
Shinn, Hannah IV, 761
Shinn, Hannah IV, 802
Shinn, Hannah IV, 843
Shinn, Hannah IV, 894
Shinn, Hannah IV, 929
Shinn, Hannah IV, 992
Shinn, Hannah V, 959
Shinn, Hannah Ann V, 886
Shinn, Hannah, Jr. II, 259
Shinn, Henrietta B. II, 819
Shinn, Henrietta B. II, 875
Shinn, Henry W. II, 819
Shinn, Hester IV, 930
Shinn, Hester IV, 992
Shinn, Hiram IV, 761
Shinn, Hope II, 194
Shinn, Hope II, 255
Shinn, Hope II, 258
Shinn, Hope II, 259
Shinn, Howard II, 313
Shinn, Howard II, 324
Shinn, Howard G. II, 819
Shinn, Howard G. II, 875
Shinn, Isaac II, 259
Shinn, Isaiah II, 259
Shinn, Israel II, 259
Shinn, Israel V, 886
Shinn, Israel VI, 443
Shinn, Jacob II, 220
Shinn, Jacob II, 259
Shinn, Jacob, Jr. II, 259
Shinn, James II, 192
Shinn, James II, 194
Shinn, James II, 206
Shinn, James II, 223
Shinn, James II, 249
Shinn, James II, 258
Shinn, James II, 259
Shinn, James IV, 761
Shinn, James IV, 999
Shinn, Jane II, 223
Shinn, Jane II, 258
Shinn, Jane II, 718
Shinn, Jane V, 120
Shinn, Jane McKay VI, 605
Shinn, John II, 183
Shinn, John II, 197
Shinn, John II, 206
Shinn, John II, 212
Shinn, John II, 258
Shinn, John II, 259
Shinn, John II, 648
Shinn, John IV, 761
Shinn, John IV, 992
Shinn, John IV, 1021
Shinn, John IV, 1030
Shinn, John VI, 443
Shinn, John C. IV, 761
Shinn, John C. IV, 992
Shinn, John C. IV, 1030
Shinn, John, Jr. II, 258
Shinn, John, Jr. II, 259
Shinn, John, Jr. II, 263
Shinn, John, Jr. IV, 992
Shinn, Jonathan II, 259
Shinn, Jonathan VI, 443
Shinn, Joseph II, 258
Shinn, Joseph II, 259
Shinn, Joseph II, 300
Shinn, Joseph IV, 761
Shinn, Joseph IV, 992
Shinn, Joseph IV, 1005
Shinn, Joseph V, 959
Shinn, Joseph Biddle II, 259
Shinn, Joseph L. II, 324
Shinn, Joshua II, 259
Shinn, Joshua IV, 58
Shinn, Joshua IV, 656
Shinn, Joshua IV, 761
Shinn, Joshua IV, 843
Shinn, Joshua IV, 853
Shinn, Joshua IV, 859
Shinn, Joshua IV, 992
Shinn, Josiah H. II, 259
Shinn, Josiah H. II, 300
Shinn, Josiah H. II, 324
Shinn, Kedar II, 259
Shinn, Laura B. II, 819
Shinn, Laura B. II, 834
Shinn, Lavinia II, 235
Shinn, Lavinia II, 259
Shinn, Levina II, 259
Shinn, Louisa Hill II, 819
Shinn, Lovina II, 259
Shinn, Lyddy Ann II, 324
Shinn, Lydia II, 206
Shinn, Lydia II, 258
Shinn, Lydia II, 787
Shinn, Lydia IV, 992
Shinn, Lydia IV, 1011
Shinn, Lydia VI, 443
Shinn, Lydia A. II, 314
Shinn, Lydia Ann II, 313
Shinn, Lydia Ann II, 324
Shinn, Lydia Ann II, 325
Shinn, Marcy II, 183
Shinn, Margaret II, 97
Shinn, Margaret II, 112
Shinn, Martha II, 223
Shinn, Martha II, 246
Shinn, Martha II, 258
Shinn, Mary II, 183
Shinn, Mary II, 191
Shinn, Mary II, 192
Shinn, Mary II, 197
Shinn, Mary II, 212
Shinn, Mary II, 219
Shinn, Mary II, 248
Shinn, Mary II, 258
Shinn, Mary II, 259
Shinn, Mary II, 264
Shinn, Mary II, 267
Shinn, Mary II, 298
Shinn, Mary II, 300
Shinn, Mary II, 324
Shinn, Mary II, 649
Shinn, Mary IV, 58
Shinn, Mary IV, 656
Shinn, Mary IV, 759
Shinn, Mary IV, 761
Shinn, Mary IV, 777
Shinn, Mary IV, 793
Shinn, Mary IV, 992
Shinn, Mary IV, 999
Shinn, Mary IV, 1005
Shinn, Mary IV, 1024
Shinn, Mary IV, 1030
Shinn, Mary VI, 381
Shinn, Mary VI, 436
Shinn, Mary VI, 443
Shinn, Mary VI, 597
Shinn, Mary VI, 598
Shinn, Mary VI, 605
Shinn, Mary Ann IV, 992
Shinn, Mary Ann IV, 999
Shinn, Mattie II, 722
Shinn, Mercy II, 259
Shinn, Mercy II, 300
Shinn, Mercy II, 313
Shinn, Miriam II, 259
Shinn, Morgan II, 300
Shinn, Morgan E. II, 324
Shinn, Nathaniel Ellicott II, 819
Shinn, Phebe II, 300
Shinn, Phebe II, 313
Shinn, Phebe IV, 892
Shinn, Phebe IV, 894
Shinn, Posthema II, 253
Shinn, Posthema II, 259
Shinn, Rachel II, 259
Shinn, Rachel IV, 761
Shinn, Rachel IV, 894
Shinn, Rachel IV, 992
Shinn, Rachel V, 886
Shinn, Rachel VI, 416
Shinn, Rachel VI, 443
Shinn, Rachel VI, 597
Shinn, Rachel VI, 600
Shinn, Rachel VI, 605
Shinn, Rachel Hollingsworth VI, 605
Shinn, Rebecca II, 295
Shinn, Rebecca II, 300
Shinn, Rebecca II, 419
Shinn, Rebecca II, 547
Shinn, Rebecca II, 648
Shinn, Rebecca II, 649
Shinn, Rebecca II, 718
Shinn, Rebecca II, 780
Shinn, Rebecca II, 832
Shinn, Rebecca II, 920
Shinn, Rebecca IV, 619
Shinn, Rebecca IV, 656
Shinn, Rebecca IV, 761
Shinn, Rebeckah II, 242
Shinn, Rebeckah II, 259

Shinn, Restore II, 197
Shinn, Restore II, 259
Shinn, Roselia IV, 929
Shinn, Roselia IV, 992
Shinn, Sabilla IV, 992
Shinn, Sabilla IV, 1021
Shinn, Sabilla IV, 1030
Shinn, Sally Ann IV, 761
Shinn, Sally Ann IV, 992
Shinn, Samuel II, 183
Shinn, Samuel II, 258
Shinn, Samuel II, 264
Shinn, Samuel II, 300
Shinn, Samuel II, 313
Shinn, Samuel II, 648
Shinn, Samuel II, 832
Shinn, Samuel II, 920
Shinn, Samuel VI, 443
Shinn, Samuel Fenton II, 649
Shinn, Samuel, Jr. VI, 443
Shinn, Sarah II, 183
Shinn, Sarah II, 211
Shinn, Sarah II, 224
Shinn, Sarah II, 228
Shinn, Sarah II, 247
Shinn, Sarah II, 250
Shinn, Sarah II, 258
Shinn, Sarah II, 259
Shinn, Sarah II, 269
Shinn, Sarah II, 285
Shinn, Sarah II, 300
Shinn, Sarah II, 313
Shinn, Sarah II, 706
Shinn, Sarah II, 718
Shinn, Sarah IV, 759
Shinn, Sarah IV, 793
Shinn, Sarah IV, 992
Shinn, Sarah Elizabeth IV, 992
Shinn, Sarah T. II, 766
Shinn, Septima II, 259
Shinn, Shreeve II, 324
Shinn, Shreeve II, 819
Shinn, Shreve II, 300
Shinn, Shreve II, 313
Shinn, Shreve II, 314
Shinn, Shreve II, 324
Shinn, Shreve II, 327
Shinn, Shreve II, 834
Shinn, Shreve II, 920
Shinn, Sibbilla IV, 992
Shinn, Sibilah IV, 761
Shinn, Sibillah IV, 761
Shinn, Solomon II, 192
Shinn, Solomon II, 258
Shinn, Solomon II, 259
Shinn, Solomon II, 300
Shinn, Solomon II, 313
Shinn, Solomon II, 324
Shinn, Susan IV, 761
Shinn, Susan IV, 894
Shinn, Susan IV, 971
Shinn, Susan IV, 992
Shinn, Susan V, 886
Shinn, Susan S. IV, 992
Shinn, Susanna II, 648
Shinn, Susanna II, 649
Shinn, Susanna S. IV, 992
Shinn, Susannah II, 194
Shinn, Susannah II, 258
Shinn, Susannah IV, 761
Shinn, Susannah S. IV, 761
Shinn, Sybella IV, 761
Shinn, Sybilla IV, 992
Shinn, Thomas II, 183
Shinn, Thomas II, 228
Shinn, Thomas II, 258
Shinn, Thomas II, 259
Shinn, Thomas II, 264
Shinn, Thomas II, 269
Shinn, Thomas II, 300
Shinn, Thomas IV, 58
Shinn, Thomas IV, 619
Shinn, Thomas IV, 656
Shinn, Thomas IV, 759
Shinn, Thomas IV, 761
Shinn, Thomas IV, 793
Shinn, Thomas IV, 992
Shinn, Thomas, Jr. II, 259
Shinn, Thos. IV, 759
Shinn, Walter II, 300
Shinn, Walter II, 313
Shinn, Walter II, 324
Shinn, Wd. Sarah II, 183
Shinn, Willet II, 183
Shinn, Willet II, 300
Shinn, Willet II, 313
Shinn, William II, 183
Shinn, William II, 259
Shinn, William II, 300
Shinn, William II, 313
Shinn, William Henry II, 313
Shinn, Wm. Canby II, 819
Shinn, Wm. H. IV, 992
Shion, Deborah VI, 443
Shion, Deborah VI, 605
Shion, Ebenezer VI, 605
Shion, Mary VI, 443
Shion, Mary VI, 605
Shion, Michael VI, 443
Shion, Michael VI, 605
Shion, Phebe VI, 443
Shion, Phebe VI, 605
Ship, Mell V, 1018
Shipes, Edgar Thomas II, 1057
Shipes, Elisha II, 1057
Shipes, Jane Chace II, 1057
Shipes, Louisa II, 1057
Shiplett, Roy I, 949
Shipley, ??? V, 930
Shipley, Abigail II, 766
Shipley, Ann II, 419
Shipley, Ann II, 491
Shipley, Ann II, 649
Shipley, Ann II, 695
Shipley, Ann III, 40
Shipley, Ann III, 286
Shipley, Ann III, 287
Shipley, Ann IV, 436
Shipley, Ann IV, 440
Shipley, Ann V, 493
Shipley, Ann V, 528
Shipley, Ann V, 930
Shipley, Ann V, 931
Shipley, Ann M. III, 286
Shipley, Ann M. V, 930
Shipley, Ann M. V, 931
Shipley, Anna M. V, 931
Shipley, Caleb M. V, 931
Shipley, Caleb Wright V, 931
Shipley, Caroline II, 300
Shipley, Caroline III, 287
Shipley, Caroline V, 528
Shipley, Caroline V, 931
Shipley, Caroline W. V, 897
Shipley, Catharine V, 931
Shipley, Catharine M. II, 766
Shipley, Catharine M. V, 931
Shipley, Catharine Morris II, 766
Shipley, Chas. J. V, 931
Shipley, Daniel Morris Elliott II, 766
Shipley, Elizabeth II, 419
Shipley, Elizabeth II, 509
Shipley, Elizabeth II, 649
Shipley, Elizabeth A. V, 931
Shipley, Elizabeth C. III, 287
Shipley, Elizabeth C. V, 528
Shipley, Elizabeth C. V, 931
Shipley, Elizabeth C. V, 938
Shipley, Eugene Wm. II, 819
Shipley, Hannah II, 419
Shipley, Hannah II, 649
Shipley, Hannah III, 286
Shipley, Hannah III, 287
Shipley, Hannah V, 930
Shipley, Hannah D. V, 912
Shipley, Hannah D. V, 931
Shipley, Hannah D. V, 938
Shipley, Hannah Elliott II, 718
Shipley, Hannah Elliott II, 766
Shipley, Hannah Taylor V, 931
Shipley, Henry III, 287
Shipley, Henry V, 528
Shipley, Henry V, 931
Shipley, Henry H. V, 931
Shipley, Jacob M. III, 287
Shipley, Jael II, 419
Shipley, Jael II, 649
Shipley, Jane II, 419
Shipley, Jane III, 287
Shipley, Joel II, 602
Shipley, John II, 419
Shipley, John II, 590
Shipley, John II, 602
Shipley, John II, 649
Shipley, John W. III, 286
Shipley, John W. III, 287
Shipley, John W. V, 528
Shipley, John W. V, 931
Shipley, Jonathan V, 930
Shipley, Joseph M. II, 718
Shipley, Joseph M. III, 286
Shipley, Joseph Morris III, 286
Shipley, Katharine Morris V, 931
Shipley, Lucy E. III, 108
Shipley, Lucy E. III, 286
Shipley, Lucy Eddy III, 286
Shipley, Lucy H. III, 286
Shipley, Lydia II, 514
Shipley, Lydia II, 649
Shipley, Lydia II, 718
Shipley, Lydia II, 766
Shipley, Margaret II, 419
Shipley, Margaret II, 460
Shipley, Margaret II, 491
Shipley, Margaret II, 514
Shipley, Margaret II, 590
Shipley, Margaret II, 649
Shipley, Margaretta Elliott II, 766
Shipley, Mary II, 1013
Shipley, Mary II, 1026
Shipley, Mary III, 286
Shipley, Mary III, 288
Shipley, Mary C. V, 912
Shipley, Mary C. V, 931
Shipley, Mary Charlote V, 931
Shipley, Mary Emily V, 514
Shipley, Mary Emily V, 528
Shipley, Mary Emily V, 930
Shipley, Mary Emily V, 931
Shipley, Mary P. III, 287
Shipley, Mary P. V, 528
Shipley, Mary P. V, 931
Shipley, Maurice V, 930
Shipley, Maurice V, 931
Shipley, Morris II, 649
Shipley, Morris III, 286
Shipley, Morris III, 288
Shipley, Morris III, 289
Shipley, Morris V, 930
Shipley, Morris V, 931
Shipley, Morris Catharine II, 718
Shipley, Morris J. III, 287
Shipley, Morris Shotwell V, 931
Shipley, Murray V, 912
Shipley, Murray V, 930
Shipley, Murray V, 931
Shipley, Murray V, 938
Shipley, Murray, Jr. V, 931
Shipley, Phebe III, 287
Shipley, Phebe V, 528
Shipley, Phebe V, 930
Shipley, Phebe V, 931
Shipley, Phebe V, 938
Shipley, Phebe Ann III, 287
Shipley, Rachel Ann IV, 25
Shipley, Rachel Ann IV, 58
Shipley, Robert III, 286
Shipley, Robert III, 287
Shipley, Samuel Richards II, 718
Shipley, Samuel Richards II, 766
Shipley, Sarah II, 460
Shipley, Sarah II, 649
Shipley, Sarah II, 1026
Shipley, Sarah III, 286
Shipley, Sarah III, 289
Shipley, Sarah V, 930
Shipley, Sarah V, 931
Shipley, Sarah Ann II, 649
Shipley, Sarah H. III, 286
Shipley, Susan III, 287
Shipley, Susan M. III, 287
Shipley, Thomas II, 419
Shipley, Thomas II, 514
Shipley, Thomas II, 649
Shipley, Thomas II, 718
Shipley, Thomas II, 1013
Shipley, Thomas II, 1026
Shipley, Thomas III, 287
Shipley, Thomas C. III, 287
Shipley, Thomas C. V, 514
Shipley, Thomas C. V, 528
Shipley, Thomas C. V, 930
Shipley, Thomas Eddy III, 286
Shipley, Thos. V, 931
Shipley, Thos. C. V, 931
Shipley, Walter Tatum V, 931
Shipley, Wd. Margaret Long II, 819
Shipley, William II, 419
Shipley, William III, 287
Shipley, William V, 528
Shipley, William Ellis V, 931
Shipley, William L. III, 286
Shipley, William Wickham II, 419
Shipley, Wm. II, 460
Shipley, Wm. II, 514
Shipley, Wm. II, 590
Shipley, Wm. II, 602
Shipley, Wm. II, 649
Shipley, Wm. II, 766
Shipley, Wm. II, 1026
Shipley, Wm. V, 930
Shipley, Wm. V, 931
Shipley, Wm. V, 938
Shipley, Wm. E. V, 931
Shipley, Wm. Ellis V, 897
Shipley, Wm. Ellis V, 931
Shipley, Wm., Jr. V, 931
Shiply, Sarah II, 1026
Shipman, Caroline IV, 637
Shipman, Caroline IV, 656
Shipman, Eunice IV, 1240
Shipman, Georgianna III, 438
Shipman, Gussie IV, 1240
Shipman, Jas. T. III, 438
Shipman, Stella IV, 1223
Shippard, John I, 73
Shippen, Abigail II, 447
Shippen, Ann II, 649
Shippen, Ann II, 661
Shippen, Edward II, 419
Shippen, Edward II, 563
Shippen, Edward II, 633
Shippen, Edward II, 649
Shippen, Edward II, 661
Shippen, Edward, Jr. II, 447
Shippen, Edward, Sr. II, 419
Shippen, Elizabeth II, 447
Shippen, Esther II, 563
Shippen, Esther II, 649
Shippen, Francina II, 447
Shippen, Hester II, 419
Shippen, John II, 419
Shippen, Joseph II, 447
Shippen, Mary II, 447
Shippen, Rebeckah II, 419
Shippen, Rebeckah II, 633
Shippen, Rebeckah II, 649
Shippen, William II, 419
Shire, Caroline II, 1060
Shire, Ida May V, 1018
Shirer, Ida May V, 1018
Shires, Alice II, 1016
Shires, Alice II, 1026
Shires, Anna II, 259
Shires, Anna II, 989
Shires, Anna II, 1026
Shires, Deborah II, 419
Shires, Deborah II, 540
Shires, Deborah II, 649
Shires, Eleanor II, 419
Shires, George II, 419
Shires, George II, 500
Shires, George II, 510
Shires, George II, 649
Shires, Hannah II, 208
Shires, Hannah II, 259
Shires, Hannah II, 500
Shires, Hannah II, 510
Shires, Hannah II, 649
Shires, John II, 649
Shires, John, Jr. II, 1026
Shirk, Almina IV, 1293
Shirk, Anna V, 644
Shirk, Delpha IV, 1293
Shirk, Eva IV, 1293
Shirk, Jane V, 631
Shirk, Orpha IV, 1293
Shirk, Sarah F. V, 644
Shirkler, Earl IV, 761
Shirley, Ann II, 419
Shirley, Lydia II, 631
Shirley, Lydia II, 649
Shirley, Samuel II, 419
Shirley, Thomas II, 419
Shirley, Wd. Lydia II, 649
Shirtliff, Edward V, 1018
Shirtliff, Plimmeth V, 1018
Shirtliff, Plymouth V, 1018
Shisler, Earl IV, 761
Shisler, Earle IV, 761
Shisler, Harold F. IV, 761
Shisler, Jacob IV, 761
Shisler, Jesse IV, 761
Shisler, Jesse L. IV, 761
Shisler, Lydia IV, 761
Shisler, Olive IV, 761
Shisler, Richard IV, 761
Shisler, Sarah IV, 761
Shisler, Sarah E. IV, 761
Shisler, Sarah E. IV, 843
Shivers, John II, 214
Shivers, John II, 259
Shivers, Martha II, 214
Shivers, Martha II, 259
Shivers, Mary II, 68
Shivers, Mary II, 97
Shivers, Rhoda VI, 363
Shivers, Rhoda VI, 444
Shivers, Samuel II, 214
Shivers, Samuel II, 259
Shivers, Sarah II, 802
Shives, Eliza I, 983
Shives, Eliza I, 997
Shivey, Earl C. IV, 1263
Shivey, Flossie E. IV, 1263
Shivler, Hannah V. II, 856
Shivler, Hannah V. II, 921
Shoaf, Ava Cornelia I, 933
Shoaf, Effie I, 933
Shoaf, Eppie I, 947
Shoaf, Eppie I, 949
Shoaf, Frank I, 933
Shoaf, George I, 947
Shoaf, George I, 949
Shoaf, George F. I, 949
Shoaf, George H. I, 933
Shoaf, George H. W. I, 949
Shoaf, Mildred Aleen I, 933
Shoaf, Sarah J. I, 933
Shoaf, Wilma Jane I, 933
Shoards, Mary II, 552
Shoards, Mary II, 649
Shobe, Caroline V, 1018
Shobe, Helen V, 1018
Shockey, Jane V, 277
Shockey, William V, 277
Shockley, Alice V, 464
Shockley, Almedia IV, 1293
Shockley, Amos IV, 1293
Shockley, Catherine IV, 1293
Shockley, Jacob IV, 1293
Shockley, Nancy IV, 1293
Shockley, Naomi V, 338
Shockley, Naomi V, 359
Shockley, Nola V, 202
Shockley, Reuben IV, 1293
Shockley, Richard IV, 1293
Shockley, Sally IV, 1293
Shockley, Susanna IV, 1293
Shockley, Viola V, 202
Shockley, Wm. V, 464
Shockney, Agnes E. Nicklow V, 709
Shockoley, Peggy VI, 922
Shode, Hannah R. IV, 755
Shoe, Anna M. V, 764
Shoe, Gertrude IV, 761
Shoe, Herbert IV, 761
Shoe, Jacob IV, 761
Shoe, Mary Jane IV, 761
Shoe, R. L. V, 764
Shoe, Robert William IV, 761
Shoe, Robert Wm. IV, 761
Shoecraft, Charlotte IV, 1263
Shoemaker, ??? II, 819
Shoemaker, ??? III, 159
Shoemaker, ??? III, 384
Shoemaker, Abi IV, 274
Shoemaker, Abi IV, 314
Shoemaker, Abi V, 311
Shoemaker, Abigail VI, 756
Shoemaker, Abigail VI, 777
Shoemaker, Abigail, Jr. VI, 777
Shoemaker, Abigail, Sr. VI, 777
Shoemaker, Abm. III, 123
Shoemaker, Abm. III, 287
Shoemaker, Abraham II, 650
Shoemaker, Abraham II, 792
Shoemaker, Abraham III, 106
Shoemaker, Abraham III, 287
Shoemaker, Abraham V, 202
Shoemaker, Abraham V, 884
Shoemaker, Abraham V, 886
Shoemaker, Abraham VI, 444
Shoemaker, Abraham VI, 640
Shoemaker, Abraham VI, 699
Shoemaker, Abraham VI, 700
Shoemaker, Abraham VI, 709
Shoemaker, Abraham VI, 714
Shoemaker, Abraham VI, 778
Shoemaker, Alan II, 968
Shoemaker, Alan II, 972
Shoemaker, Alfred IV, 274
Shoemaker, Alfred IV, 314
Shoemaker, Allen II, 785
Shoemaker, Allen II, 1026
Shoemaker, Alvin Haines II, 92
Shoemaker, Amelia II, 718
Shoemaker, Amelia II, 819
Shoemaker, Amelia Bird II, 71
Shoemaker, Amos D. V, 597
Shoemaker, Ann II, 419
Shoemaker, Ann II, 420
Shoemaker, Ann II, 650
Shoemaker, Ann II, 819
Shoemaker, Ann II, 824
Shoemaker, Ann II, 921
Shoemaker, Ann III, 106
Shoemaker, Ann III, 287
Shoemaker, Ann IV, 274
Shoemaker, Ann IV, 314
Shoemaker, Ann V, 311
Shoemaker, Ann VI, 569
Shoemaker, Ann VI, 756
Shoemaker, Ann VI, 777
Shoemaker, Ann M. II, 819
Shoemaker, Ann Martha II, 79
Shoemaker, Anna II, 248
Shoemaker, Anna II, 259
Shoemaker, Anna II, 419
Shoemaker, Anna II, 603
Shoemaker, Anna II, 650

emaker, Anna II, 804
emaker, Anna V, 311
emaker, Anna VI, 658
emaker, Anna VI, 699
emaker, Anna VI, 700
emaker, Anna B. II, 762
emaker, Anna Bailey II, 718
emaker, Anna Bailey II, 762
emaker, Anna Bailey II, 766
emaker, Anna E. VI, 658
emaker, Anna E. VI, 699
emaker, Anna E. VI, 700
emaker, Anna Elizabeth VI, 650
emaker, Anna M. II, 894
emaker, Anna M. II, 918
emaker, Anna M. II, 921
emaker, Anna Maria II, 921
emaker, Anna Maria III, 159
emaker, Anna Maria III, 287
emaker, Anna McIlvain II, 819
emaker, Anne II, 650
emaker, Anne Parry II, 259
emaker, Annie II, 871
emaker, Annie M. II, 860
emaker, Annie M. II, 921
emaker, Anthony II, 650
emaker, Anthony III, 273
emaker, Anthony III, 287
emaker, Augustus Brock II, 1066
emaker, Augustus Brock II, 1080
emaker, Basil W. VI, 650
emaker, Basil W. VI, 679
emaker, Basil W. VI, 699
emaker, Basil W. VI, 714
emaker, Beaulah II, 478
emaker, Beaulah II, 650
emaker, Benj. III, 287
emaker, Benjamin II, 419
emaker, Benjamin II, 420
emaker, Benjamin II, 478
emaker, Benjamin II, 482
emaker, Benjamin II, 489
emaker, Benjamin II, 602
emaker, Benjamin II, 620
emaker, Benjamin II, 649
emaker, Benjamin II, 650
emaker, Benjamin II, 974
emaker, Benjamin II, 1026
emaker, Benjamin III, 287
emaker, Benjamin Green II, 883
emaker, Benjamin H., Jr. II, 921
emaker, Benjamin, Jr. II, 650
emaker, Betsey VI, 732
emaker, Betsey Elizabeth VI, 619
emaker, Betsy VI, 700
emaker, Brock Milton II, 1066
emaker, C. Francis II, 921
emaker, Caroline E. VI, 650
emaker, Caroline E. VI, 679
emaker, Caroline E. VI, 699
emaker, Caroline E. VI, 700
emaker, Caroline E. VI, 714
emaker, Chales VI, 559
emaker, Charles II, 419
emaker, Charles II, 650
emaker, Charles II, 819
emaker, Charles II, 921
emaker, Charles VI, 778
emaker, Charles B. II, 921
emaker, Charles Bird II, 718
emaker, Charles C. II, 921
emaker, Chas. II, 819
emaker, Chas. II, 901
emaker, Chas. II, 914
emaker, Chas. II, 921
emaker, Chas. V, 931
emaker, Chas. V, 938
emaker, Chas. B. II, 835
emaker, Chas. B. II, 894
emaker, Chas. B. II, 918
emaker, Chas. B. II, 921
emaker, Chas. Bartholomew II, 819
emaker, Chas. Bird II, 819
emaker, Chas. Francis II, 819
emaker, Christiana C. II, 835
emaker, Christiana C. II, 921
emaker, Christiana Cadwallader II, 819
emaker, Clara VI, 669
emaker, Claudia C. II, 1066
emaker, Claudia V. II, 1080
Shoemaker, Coates Walton VI, 777
Shoemaker, Comly B. II, 718
Shoemaker, Comly B. II, 762
Shoemaker, Comly B. II, 766
Shoemaker, Cora E. V, 359
Shoemaker, Cornelia J. VI, 700
Shoemaker, Cynthia II, 796
Shoemaker, Cynthia Green II, 819
Shoemaker, Daniel VI, 763
Shoemaker, Daniel VI, 777
Shoemaker, Daniel N. V, 882
Shoemaker, Daniel N. V, 886
Shoemaker, Daniel N. VI, 746
Shoemaker, Daniel N. VI, 777
Shoemaker, David II, 128
Shoemaker, David II, 650
Shoemaker, David L. VI, 777
Shoemaker, David L. VI, 778
Shoemaker, David P. VI, 777
Shoemaker, Dorothy VI, 763
Shoemaker, Dorothy VI, 777
Shoemaker, Earnest Walton VI, 777
Shoemaker, Edith VI, 658
Shoemaker, Edith VI, 699
Shoemaker, Edith VI, 700
Shoemaker, Edith Eliza VI, 700
Shoemaker, Edith M. VI, 649
Shoemaker, Edith M. VI, 700
Shoemaker, Edward II, 420
Shoemaker, Edward II, 766
Shoemaker, Edward III, 287
Shoemaker, Edward V, 597
Shoemaker, Edward Abijah VI, 669
Shoemaker, Edward E. V, 597
Shoemaker, Edward R. VI, 777
Shoemaker, Edward R. VI, 778
Shoemaker, Edward R. VI, 788
Shoemaker, Edward Walton VI, 777
Shoemaker, Edward Warner II, 419
Shoemaker, Edward Warner II, 650
Shoemaker, Edwin II, 819
Shoemaker, Edwin IV, 274
Shoemaker, Edwin IV, 314
Shoemaker, Edwin V, 311
Shoemaker, Edwin George VI, 700
Shoemaker, Eleanor II, 419
Shoemaker, Elisha VI, 669
Shoemaker, Eliz. III, 287
Shoemaker, Eliza II, 650
Shoemaker, Eliza II, 670
Shoemaker, Eliza III, 287
Shoemaker, Eliza VI, 444
Shoemaker, Elizabeth II, 248
Shoemaker, Elizabeth II, 259
Shoemaker, Elizabeth II, 419
Shoemaker, Elizabeth II, 420
Shoemaker, Elizabeth II, 602
Shoemaker, Elizabeth II, 636
Shoemaker, Elizabeth II, 649
Shoemaker, Elizabeth II, 650
Shoemaker, Elizabeth II, 766
Shoemaker, Elizabeth III, 384
Shoemaker, Elizabeth V, 597
Shoemaker, Elizabeth VI, 473
Shoemaker, Elizabeth VI, 508
Shoemaker, Elizabeth VI, 656
Shoemaker, Elizabeth VI, 699
Shoemaker, Elizabeth VI, 732
Shoemaker, Elizabeth VI, 738
Shoemaker, Elizabeth VI, 749
Shoemaker, Elizabeth VI, 762
Shoemaker, Elizabeth VI, 777
Shoemaker, Elizabeth VI, 778
Shoemaker, Elizabeth VI, 788
Shoemaker, Elizabeth VI, 853
Shoemaker, Elizabeth J. VI, 700
Shoemaker, Elizabeth L. VI, 777
Shoemaker, Elizabeth Lukens VI, 778
Shoemaker, Elizabeth R. V, 931
Shoemaker, Elizabeth R. V, 938
Shoemaker, Elizabeth Rachel II, 819
Shoemaker, Elizabeth Rachel II, 835
Shoemaker, Elizabeth Rachel II, 921
Shoemaker, Elizabeth T. IV, 274
Shoemaker, Elizabeth T. IV, 314
Shoemaker, Elizabeth T. V, 311
Shoemaker, Ella II, 921
Shoemaker, Ella F. II, 819
Shoemaker, Ella F. II, 918
Shoemaker, Ella F. II, 921
Shoemaker, Ellen II, 419
Shoemaker, Ellen II, 649
Shoemaker, Ellen F. VI, 679
Shoemaker, Ellen F. VI, 682
Shoemaker, Ellen F. VI, 700
Shoemaker, Ellie II, 910
Shoemaker, Ellie II, 921
Shoemaker, Elwood VI, 700
Shoemaker, Emerson W. V, 597
Shoemaker, Emmerson W. V, 597
Shoemaker, Estella II, 895
Shoemaker, Eve I, 1118
Shoemaker, Eve I, 1131
Shoemaker, Fannie H. II, 901
Shoemaker, Fannie H. II, 921
Shoemaker, Fanny V, 359
Shoemaker, Fanny B. VI, 777
Shoemaker, Fanny B. VI, 778
Shoemaker, Fanny B. VI, 788
Shoemaker, Fay IV, 1263
Shoemaker, Ferdinand Walton VI, 777
Shoemaker, Flora V, 359
Shoemaker, Frances VI, 746
Shoemaker, Frances VI, 763
Shoemaker, Frances VI, 777
Shoemaker, Frances E. V, 882
Shoemaker, Frances E. V, 886
Shoemaker, Frances M. II, 921
Shoemaker, Frances Maria II, 814
Shoemaker, Frances Maria II, 819
Shoemaker, Frances Maria II, 921
Shoemaker, Francis Dodge VI, 778
Shoemaker, Francis Dodge VI, 788
Shoemaker, Frank A. II, 819
Shoemaker, Franklin II, 921
Shoemaker, Franklin A. II, 819
Shoemaker, Franklin A. II, 901
Shoemaker, Franklin A. II, 914
Shoemaker, Franklin A. II, 921
Shoemaker, George II, 419
Shoemaker, George II, 420
Shoemaker, George II, 649
Shoemaker, George II, 650
Shoemaker, George II, 675
Shoemaker, George II, 819
Shoemaker, George II, 921
Shoemaker, George V, 597
Shoemaker, George VI, 762
Shoemaker, George VI, 777
Shoemaker, George VI, 788
Shoemaker, George W. VI, 699
Shoemaker, George Walton VI, 777
Shoemaker, George, Jr. II, 649
Shoemaker, George, Jr. VI, 778
Shoemaker, Georgiana V, 120
Shoemaker, Greta J. III, 222
Shoemaker, Greta, Jr. III, 287
Shoemaker, Hannah II, 482
Shoemaker, Hannah II, 496
Shoemaker, Hannah II, 600
Shoemaker, Hannah II, 636
Shoemaker, Hannah II, 649
Shoemaker, Hannah II, 650
Shoemaker, Hannah II, 796
Shoemaker, Hannah II, 819
Shoemaker, Hannah II, 907
Shoemaker, Hannah II, 921
Shoemaker, Hannah III, 123
Shoemaker, Hannah III, 287
Shoemaker, Hannah IV, 1184
Shoemaker, Hannah VI, 619
Shoemaker, Hannah VI, 634
Shoemaker, Hannah VI, 699
Shoemaker, Hannah VI, 700
Shoemaker, Hannah VI, 724
Shoemaker, Hannah VI, 732
Shoemaker, Hannah VI, 777
Shoemaker, Harriet II, 819
Shoemaker, Harriet II, 921
Shoemaker, Harrison E. II, 804
Shoemaker, Harry H. II, 1079
Shoemaker, Harry J. II, 1079
Shoemaker, Helen II, 819
Shoemaker, Henry II, 419
Shoemaker, Henry M. V, 597
Shoemaker, Herbert Spencer Lewis VI, 777
Shoemaker, Howard VI, 700
Shoemaker, Ida B. II, 1079
Shoemaker, Isaac II, 419
Shoemaker, Isaac II, 420
Shoemaker, Isaac II, 496
Shoemaker, Isaac II, 649
Shoemaker, Isaac II, 766
Shoemaker, Isaac V, 931
Shoemaker, Isaac B. IV, 274
Shoemaker, Isaac B. IV, 314
Shoemaker, Isaac B. V, 311
Shoemaker, Isaac L. III, 287
Shoemaker, Isaiah Lukens II, 902
Shoemaker, Isaiah Lukens II, 921
Shoemaker, Jacob II, 419
Shoemaker, Jacob II, 420
Shoemaker, Jacob II, 471
Shoemaker, Jacob II, 586
Shoemaker, Jacob II, 626
Shoemaker, Jacob II, 636
Shoemaker, Jacob II, 649
Shoemaker, Jacob II, 650
Shoemaker, Jacob, Jr. II, 649
Shoemaker, Jacob, Jr. II, 650
Shoemaker, James IV, 1184
Shoemaker, Jane II, 129
Shoemaker, Jane II, 139
Shoemaker, Jane II, 420
Shoemaker, Jane II, 650
Shoemaker, Jane II, 766
Shoemaker, Jane II, 819
Shoemaker, Jane II, 974
Shoemaker, Jane II, 1026
Shoemaker, Jane III, 287
Shoemaker, Jane VI, 992
Shoemaker, Jane Longstreth II, 799
Shoemaker, Jennie V, 359
Shoemaker, Jerry IV, 1184
Shoemaker, Joan V, 311
Shoemaker, John II, 822
Shoemaker, John III, 287
Shoemaker, John V, 120
Shoemaker, John E. V, 597
Shoemaker, John Elmer V, 597
Shoemaker, John Rodman III, 287
Shoemaker, John W. II, 766
Shoemaker, John, Jr. II, 650
Shoemaker, Jonathan II, 419
Shoemaker, Jonathan II, 420
Shoemaker, Jonathan II, 586
Shoemaker, Jonathan II, 649
Shoemaker, Jonathan II, 650
Shoemaker, Jonathan II, 651
Shoemaker, Jonathan II, 819
Shoemaker, Jonathan VI, 619
Shoemaker, Jonathan VI, 700
Shoemaker, Jonathan VI, 732
Shoemaker, Jonathan VI, 777
Shoemaker, Joseph II, 248
Shoemaker, Joseph II, 259
Shoemaker, Joseph II, 419
Shoemaker, Joseph II, 420
Shoemaker, Joseph II, 650
Shoemaker, Joseph II, 651
Shoemaker, Joseph II, 871
Shoemaker, Joseph VI, 650
Shoemaker, Joseph VI, 756
Shoemaker, Joseph VI, 777
Shoemaker, Joseph, Jr. II, 259
Shoemaker, Joseph, Jr. II, 651
Shoemaker, June Lenore II, 1066
Shoemaker, Kate II, 914
Shoemaker, Kate II, 921
Shoemaker, Lester B. II, 1066
Shoemaker, Lester I. II, 1080
Shoemaker, Levi T. V, 886
Shoemaker, Levi T. VI, 743
Shoemaker, Levi T. VI, 778
Shoemaker, Levi Tate VI, 700
Shoemaker, Lewis II, 921
Shoemaker, Lewis F. II, 894
Shoemaker, Lewis F. II, 921
Shoemaker, Lewis Foulke II, 819
Shoemaker, Lucretia II, 819
Shoemaker, Lucretia II, 894
Shoemaker, Lucretia II, 921
Shoemaker, Lucy VI, 700
Shoemaker, Lydia II, 650
Shoemaker, Lydia II, 766
Shoemaker, Lydia II, 798
Shoemaker, Lydia II, 804
Shoemaker, Lydia II, 806
Shoemaker, Lydia III, 79
Shoemaker, Lydia M. II, 708
Shoemaker, Lydia M. II, 814
Shoemaker, Lydia M. II, 907
Shoemaker, Lydia M. II, 921
Shoemaker, Malachi II, 650
Shoemaker, Margaret II, 420
Shoemaker, Margaret II, 649
Shoemaker, Margaret II, 650
Shoemaker, Margaret II, 792
Shoemaker, Margaret II, 958
Shoemaker, Margaret III, 106
Shoemaker, Margaret III, 123
Shoemaker, Margaret III, 287
Shoemaker, Margaret IV, 1263
Shoemaker, Margaret V, 884
Shoemaker, Margaret V, 886
Shoemaker, Margaret V, 931
Shoemaker, Margaret V, 938
Shoemaker, Margaret K. V, 886
Shoemaker, Margaret Mary II, 718
Shoemaker, Margaret S. II, 972
Shoemaker, Maria II, 819
Shoemaker, Maria II, 921
Shoemaker, Maria Mira II, 766
Shoemaker, Marian G. II, 718
Shoemaker, Martha II, 819
Shoemaker, Martha II, 822
Shoemaker, Martha II, 921
Shoemaker, Martha IV, 108
Shoemaker, Martha VI, 640
Shoemaker, Martha VI, 699
Shoemaker, Martha VI, 700
Shoemaker, Martha VI, 709
Shoemaker, Martha VI, 714
Shoemaker, Martha A. VI, 712
Shoemaker, Martha Ann VI, 700
Shoemaker, Martha Ann VI, 712
Shoemaker, Martha Ann VI, 713
Shoemaker, Martha B. II, 718
Shoemaker, Martha J. V, 359
Shoemaker, Martha L. II, 718
Shoemaker, Martha L. II, 762
Shoemaker, Martha L. II, 766
Shoemaker, Martha P. II, 921
Shoemaker, Martha Paul II, 827
Shoemaker, Martha Paul II, 921
Shoemaker, Mary II, 420
Shoemaker, Mary II, 489
Shoemaker, Mary II, 626
Shoemaker, Mary II, 640
Shoemaker, Mary II, 645
Shoemaker, Mary II, 649
Shoemaker, Mary II, 650
Shoemaker, Mary II, 651
Shoemaker, Mary II, 675
Shoemaker, Mary II, 718
Shoemaker, Mary II, 803
Shoemaker, Mary II, 819
Shoemaker, Mary II, 883
Shoemaker, Mary II, 921
Shoemaker, Mary III, 287
Shoemaker, Mary IV, 274
Shoemaker, Mary IV, 296
Shoemaker, Mary IV, 350
Shoemaker, Mary V, 120
Shoemaker, Mary V, 202
Shoemaker, Mary A. VI, 778
Shoemaker, Mary A. VI, 788
Shoemaker, Mary Ann VI, 667
Shoemaker, Mary Ann VI, 668
Shoemaker, Mary Ann VI, 700
Shoemaker, Mary Ann VI, 758
Shoemaker, Mary G. II, 921
Shoemaker, Mary K. VI, 778
Shoemaker, Mary Kirkbride II, 921
Shoemaker, Mary P. II, 819
Shoemaker, Mary P. II, 921
Shoemaker, Mary Parry II, 259
Shoemaker, Mary R. II, 921
Shoemaker, Mary R. V, 120
Shoemaker, Mary Tate VI, 700
Shoemaker, Mathias II, 819
Shoemaker, Matthias II, 921
Shoemaker, Medora Smith II, 718
Shoemaker, Mercy II, 419
Shoemaker, Mercy II, 650
Shoemaker, Nathan II, 814
Shoemaker, Nathan II, 819
Shoemaker, Nathan II, 851
Shoemaker, Nathan II, 921
Shoemaker, Naylor VI, 444
Shoemaker, Naylor VI, 667
Shoemaker, Naylor VI, 699
Shoemaker, Naylor VI, 709
Shoemaker, Naylor VI, 714
Shoemaker, Noralee Lloyd VI, 700
Shoemaker, Owen II, 819
Shoemaker, Owen II, 907
Shoemaker, Owen II, 921
Shoemaker, Owen III, 222
Shoemaker, Owen III, 287
Shoemaker, Patricia Spencer VI, 700
Shoemaker, Penelope III, 273
Shoemaker, Penelope III, 287
Shoemaker, Penelope III, 384
Shoemaker, Penelope) III, 384

Shoemaker, Peter II, 129
Shoemaker, Phinneas VI, 669
Shoemaker, Rachel II, 458
Shoemaker, Rachel II, 650
Shoemaker, Rachel II, 819
Shoemaker, Rachel II, 851
Shoemaker, Rachel II, 921
Shoemaker, Rachel VI, 639
Shoemaker, Rachel VI, 640
Shoemaker, Rachel VI, 641
Shoemaker, Rachel VI, 676
Shoemaker, Rachel VI, 699
Shoemaker, Rachel VI, 700
Shoemaker, Rachel C. III, 222
Shoemaker, Rachel C. III, 287
Shoemaker, Rachel M. II, 901
Shoemaker, Rachel M. II, 914
Shoemaker, Rachel M. II, 921
Shoemaker, Rachel W. II, 129
Shoemaker, Raymon W. V, 597
Shoemaker, Raymond W. V, 597
Shoemaker, Rebecca II, 496
Shoemaker, Rebecca II, 630
Shoemaker, Rebecca II, 650
Shoemaker, Rebecca II, 789
Shoemaker, Rebecca II, 851
Shoemaker, Rebecca II, 921
Shoemaker, Rebecca III, 287
Shoemaker, Rebecca Albertson VI, 778
Shoemaker, Rebecka II, 420
Shoemaker, Rebekah II, 649
Shoemaker, Richard Bailey II, 718
Shoemaker, Richard M. II, 650
Shoemaker, Richard M. II, 718
Shoemaker, Richard Martin II, 819
Shoemaker, Richard Whitall II, 718
Shoemaker, Robert II, 819
Shoemaker, Robert II, 883
Shoemaker, Robert II, 921
Shoemaker, Robert VI, 569
Shoemaker, Robert Hilles II, 718
Shoemaker, Robt. VI, 569
Shoemaker, Samuel II, 419
Shoemaker, Samuel II, 420
Shoemaker, Samuel II, 482
Shoemaker, Samuel II, 544
Shoemaker, Samuel II, 630
Shoemaker, Samuel II, 649
Shoemaker, Samuel II, 650
Shoemaker, Samuel III, 287
Shoemaker, Samuel IV, 656
Shoemaker, Samuel VI, 669
Shoemaker, Samuel VI, 699
Shoemaker, Samuel VI, 700
Shoemaker, Samuel M. VI, 669
Shoemaker, Samuel, Jr. II, 650
Shoemaker, Sarah II, 128
Shoemaker, Sarah II, 419
Shoemaker, Sarah II, 420
Shoemaker, Sarah II, 489
Shoemaker, Sarah II, 586
Shoemaker, Sarah II, 620
Shoemaker, Sarah II, 631
Shoemaker, Sarah II, 649
Shoemaker, Sarah II, 650
Shoemaker, Sarah II, 819
Shoemaker, Sarah II, 851
Shoemaker, Sarah II, 883
Shoemaker, Sarah II, 902
Shoemaker, Sarah II, 921
Shoemaker, Sarah V, 884
Shoemaker, Sarah V, 886
Shoemaker, Sarah VI, 444
Shoemaker, Sarah VI, 667
Shoemaker, Sarah VI, 669
Shoemaker, Sarah VI, 699
Shoemaker, Sarah VI, 700
Shoemaker, Sarah VI, 709
Shoemaker, Sarah VI, 714
Shoemaker, Sarah Ann II, 921
Shoemaker, Sarah E. II, 921
Shoemaker, Sarah Elizabeth II, 921
Shoemaker, Sarah Mitchell II, 819
Shoemaker, Sarah Parry II, 259
Shoemaker, Sarah T. II, 870
Shoemaker, Sarah T. II, 921
Shoemaker, Solomon IV, 1184
Shoemaker, Stanley Morris II, 1066
Shoemaker, Susan II, 420
Shoemaker, Susan II, 650
Shoemaker, Susan E. II, 819
Shoemaker, Susan E. V, 886
Shoemaker, Susan E. VI, 743
Shoemaker, Susan Esther VI, 743
Shoemaker, Susan Esther VI, 778
Shoemaker, Susan Whitall II, 718
Shoemaker, Susanah II, 471
Shoemaker, Susanah II, 649
Shoemaker, Susanna II, 420
Shoemaker, Susannah II, 420
Shoemaker, Susannah II, 649
Shoemaker, Susannah II, 968
Shoemaker, Susannah II, 972
Shoemaker, Tacy VI, 778
Shoemaker, Tacy Lenox II, 785
Shoemaker, Thomas I, 1075
Shoemaker, Thomas II, 419
Shoemaker, Thomas II, 420
Shoemaker, Thomas II, 626
Shoemaker, Thomas II, 631
Shoemaker, Thomas II, 649
Shoemaker, Thomas II, 650
Shoemaker, Thomas II, 804
Shoemaker, Thomas IV, 274
Shoemaker, Thomas IV, 314
Shoemaker, Thomas V, 311
Shoemaker, Thomas L. III, 287
Shoemaker, Thomas Rodman III, 287
Shoemaker, Thos. II, 796
Shoemaker, Thos. II, 819
Shoemaker, Thos. IV, 274
Shoemaker, Thos. V, 311
Shoemaker, Thos. C. II, 921
Shoemaker, Thos. Chalkley II, 921
Shoemaker, Thos. Mather II, 819
Shoemaker, Wd. Ann II, 792
Shoemaker, Wd. Elizabeth II, 650
Shoemaker, Wd. Jane Longstreth II, 822
Shoemaker, Wd. Margaret II, 968
Shoemaker, Wd. Margrett II, 420
Shoemaker, Wd. Mary II, 819
Shoemaker, Wd. Mary Kirk II, 785
Shoemaker, Wd. Sarah II, 650
Shoemaker, William IV, 108
Shoemaker, William VI, 972
Shoemaker, William VI, 992
Shoemaker, William M. VI, 853
Shoemaker, Wm. II, 650
Shoemaker, Wm. A. II, 921
Shoemaker, Wm. C. II, 766
Shoemaker, Wm. F. II, 921
Shoemaker, Wm. Foulke II, 819
Shoemaker, Wm. Lukens VI, 778
Shoemaker, Wm. T. VI, 668
Shoemaker, Wm. Tate VI, 667
Shoemaker, Wm. Tate VI, 758
Shoemate, ??? VI, 373
Shoemate, Eliza VI, 373
Shoemate, Eliza VI, 444
Shoemate, Williiam H. VI, 373
Sholders, Sarah Catharine I, 213
Sholders, Sarah Catherine I, 227
Shole, Joseph II, 300
Sholl, Amanda II, 294
Sholl, Amanda II, 300
Sholl, Amanda L. II, 300
Sholl, Arthur Lincoln II, 300
Sholl, Elizabeth L. II, 294
Sholl, Elizabeth L. II, 300
Sholl, Elizabeth Lloyd II, 300
Sholl, Harold II, 300
Sholl, John III, 287
Sholl, Joseph II, 294
Sholl, Joseph II, 300
Sholl, Martha M. II, 300
Sholl, Martha Mellor II, 300
Sholl, William Lloyd II, 300
Sholy, Ann II, 257
Sholy, Ann II, 259
Shomo, Hannah H. V, 764
Shon, James K. VI, 991
Shon, Mary VI, 991
Shook, Allen V, 359
Shook, Curtis IV, 992
Shook, Curtis Edward IV, 992
Shook, Edward S. IV, 992
Shook, Joseph V, 1018
Shook, Laura IV, 992
Shook, Mary IV, 992
Shook, Virginia IV, 992
Shook, Virginia Travers IV, 992
Shook, Wm. A. IV, 992
Shoolfield, Rachel IV, 674
Shoomaker, Jacob II, 420
Shoomaker, Jacob II, 649
Shoomaker, Margaret II, 649
Shoomaker, Susannah II, 649
Shoomaker, Thomas II, 649
Shoomaker, Wd. Margrett II, 420
Shoop, Charles V, 644
Shoop, Elizabeth V, 644
Shoop, Joseph V, 1018
Shoop, Martha G. V, 644
Shoop, May V, 709
Shoop, Minnie V, 1018
Shoop, Richard H. V, 709
Shoppart, Douglas IV, 1338
Shoppart, L. Merritt IV, 1338
Shoppart, Lynn M. IV, 1338
Shoppart, Merret K. IV, 1338
Shoppart, Violet IV, 1338
Shore, Alice IV, 656
Shore, Alice IV, 798
Shore, Alice IV, 843
Shore, James IV, 656
Shore, James IV, 916
Shore, James VI, 700
Shore, James, Jr. IV, 843
Shore, Lincoln II, 301
Shore, Marvin I, 949
Shore, Mary II, 554
Shore, Mary II, 651
Shore, Mary IV, 916
Shore, Pansy D. I, 949
Shore, Rachel IV, 656
Shore, Rachel IV, 761
Shore, Rachel IV, 843
Shore, Rachel IV, 916
Shore, Rebekah IV, 656
Shore, Sarah IV, 656
Shore, Sarah VI, 629
Shore, Sarah VI, 700
Shores, Alice IV, 58
Shores, Anna IV, 274
Shores, Clara A. IV, 274
Shores, Cornelius II, 420
Shores, Hannah II, 259
Shores, James IV, 58
Shores, Jemima V, 764
Shores, Joseph V, 764
Shores, Lewis IV, 274
Shores, Lillie Bell IV, 274
Shores, Lonie Martin IV, 274
Shores, Mary IV, 172
Shores, Mary IV, 274
Shores, Mary Shores Baldwin IV, 274
Shores, Philip IV, 274
Shores, Rachel IV, 58
Shores, Rebecca IV, 58
Shores, Robert IV, 274
Shores, Sarah IV, 58
Shores, Sophia II, 420
Shores, William E. IV, 274
Shorkley, John R. IV, 274
Shorsbery, William II, 447
Short, Adaline I, 682
Short, Adaline I, 689
Short, Catherine E. V, 528
Short, Charles H. VI, 992
Short, Chester IV, 1293
Short, Diadem VI, 992
Short, Elizabeth I. II, 921
Short, Elizabeth J. II, 749
Short, Elizabeth J. II, 766
Short, Elizabeth J. II, 884
Short, Elizabeth J. II, 921
Short, Estella IV, 1338
Short, Estella V, 764
Short, Esther A. IV, 1289
Short, Esther A. IV, 1293
Short, Fielding V, 644
Short, G. F. IV, 1293
Short, G. J. IV, 1293
Short, Geo. A. IV, 1338
Short, George A. V, 764
Short, Isabella IV, 916
Short, J. W. IV, 1293
Short, John V, 528
Short, Luella IV, 1338
Short, Luella V, 764
Short, Lulu V, 764
Short, Mabel IV, 1338
Short, Mabel V, 764
Short, Mable V, 764
Short, Mary V, 202
Short, Mary Ann VI, 319
Short, Nora I, 682
Short, Nora I, 689
Short, Phebe IV, 1293
Short, Phebe V, 528
Short, Stella V, 764
Short, William V, 528
Short, William H. V, 528
Shotwell, ??? II, 791
Shotwell, ??? V, 930
Shotwell, Aaron III, 287
Shotwell, Abel III, 287
Shotwell, Abm. III, 211
Shotwell, Abm. III, 288
Shotwell, Abraham II, 651
Shotwell, Abraham III, 89
Shotwell, Abraham III, 124
Shotwell, Abraham III, 146
Shotwell, Abraham III, 257
Shotwell, Abraham III, 287
Shotwell, Alice II, 766
Shotwell, Alice G. III, 181
Shotwell, Alice G. III, 288
Shotwell, Alice H. III, 288
Shotwell, Alice J. II, 766
Shotwell, Amelia III, 112
Shotwell, Amelia III, 288
Shotwell, Amelia E. III, 287
Shotwell, Amy III, 145
Shotwell, Amy III, 287
Shotwell, Amy III, 446
Shotwell, Amy III, 447
Shotwell, Amy T. III, 287
Shotwell, Amy T. III, 289
Shotwell, Ann III, 221
Shotwell, Ann Fitz Randolph III, 288
Shotwell, Ann M. III, 287
Shotwell, Anna H. III, 289
Shotwell, Annie III, 446
Shotwell, Annie III, 447
Shotwell, Annie III, 450
Shotwell, Augustus F. III, 288
Shotwell, Bathsheba IV, 350
Shotwell, Bathsheba IV, 641
Shotwell, Bathsheba IV, 656
Shotwell, Benj. III, 289
Shotwell, Benjamin III, 145
Shotwell, Benjamin III, 287
Shotwell, Benjamin III, 288
Shotwell, Catharine III, 288
Shotwell, Charlotte III, 288
Shotwell, Daniel IV, 58
Shotwell, Daniel IV, 159
Shotwell, David III, 288
Shotwell, Deborah III, 184
Shotwell, Deborah III, 288
Shotwell, Deborah III, 289
Shotwell, Deborah III, 324
Shotwell, Deborah III, 446
Shotwell, Deborah IV, 58
Shotwell, Deborah IV, 150
Shotwell, Deborah IV, 159
Shotwell, Deborah IV, 350
Shotwell, Deborah IV, 436
Shotwell, Ebenezer IV, 1378
Shotwell, Eden II, 420
Shotwell, Eden II, 651
Shotwell, Eden III, 288
Shotwell, Edward III, 288
Shotwell, Edward IV, 58
Shotwell, Edward IV, 108
Shotwell, Eleanor II, 293
Shotwell, Eleanor II, 301
Shotwell, Eleanor II, 420
Shotwell, Eleanor III, 159
Shotwell, Eleanor III, 288
Shotwell, Eleanor K. II, 183
Shotwell, Eleanor K. II, 301
Shotwell, Eliza III, 289
Shotwell, Elizabeth II, 536
Shotwell, Elizabeth II, 651
Shotwell, Elizabeth III, 89
Shotwell, Elizabeth III, 211
Shotwell, Elizabeth III, 287
Shotwell, Elizabeth III, 288
Shotwell, Elizabeth III, 289
Shotwell, Elizabeth Rich II, 803
Shotwell, Esther III, 124
Shotwell, Esther III, 288
Shotwell, George F. III, 288
Shotwell, Haddock VI, 267
Shotwell, Hannah III, 288
Shotwell, Hannah W. III, 239
Shotwell, Hannah W. III, 288
Shotwell, Harvey III, 288
Shotwell, Haydock VI, 267
Shotwell, Henry III, 102
Shotwell, Henry III, 288
Shotwell, Henry R. III, 288
Shotwell, Henry T. III, 287
Shotwell, Henry T. III, 288
Shotwell, Hope IV, 58
Shotwell, Hope IV, 108
Shotwell, Hope IV, 116
Shotwell, Hope IV, 436
Shotwell, Hope IV, 441
Shotwell, Hope IV, 593
Shotwell, Hope IV, 1114
Shotwell, Hugh II, 651
Shotwell, Isaac II, 651
Shotwell, Isaac II, 766
Shotwell, Isaac II, 819
Shotwell, Isaac III, 288
Shotwell, Isaac IV, 108
Shotwell, Isaac IV, 159
Shotwell, Isaac IV, 350
Shotwell, Isaac IV, 436
Shotwell, Isaac IV, 441
Shotwell, Isaac IV, 593
Shotwell, Isaac IV, 1114
Shotwell, Jacob II, 420
Shotwell, Jacob III, 159
Shotwell, Jacob III, 288
Shotwell, Jane IV, 350
Shotwell, Jane E. III, 289
Shotwell, Jane Eliz. III, 288
Shotwell, Jane Elizabeth III, 1
Shotwell, Jeremiah III, 288
Shotwell, John III, 89
Shotwell, John III, 287
Shotwell, John III, 314
Shotwell, John IV, 108
Shotwell, John D. III, 289
Shotwell, John, Jr. III, 288
Shotwell, Jos. D. III, 287
Shotwell, Jos. F. III, 447
Shotwell, Jos. S. III, 288
Shotwell, Joseph II, 536
Shotwell, Joseph II, 651
Shotwell, Joseph III, 75
Shotwell, Joseph III, 288
Shotwell, Joseph III, 289
Shotwell, Joseph III, 419
Shotwell, Joseph III, 446
Shotwell, Joseph IV, 108
Shotwell, Joseph IV, 159
Shotwell, Joseph D. III, 112
Shotwell, Joseph D. III, 288
Shotwell, Joseph F. III, 288
Shotwell, Joseph F. III, 446
Shotwell, Joseph F. III, 450
Shotwell, Joseph H. III, 288
Shotwell, Joseph S. III, 288
Shotwell, Joseph S. III, 289
Shotwell, Joseph S. III, 324
Shotwell, Joseph S. III, 446
Shotwell, Joseph W. III, 289
Shotwell, Joseph W. III, 447
Shotwell, Joseph, Jr. III, 288
Shotwell, Josiah S. III, 446
Shotwell, Louisa III, 288
Shotwell, Lydia III, 146
Shotwell, Lydia III, 287
Shotwell, Lydia III, 288
Shotwell, Mahlon IV, 350
Shotwell, Mahlon IV, 436
Shotwell, Margaret G. III, 288
Shotwell, Marion IV, 108
Shotwell, Marion IV, 159
Shotwell, Marion IV, 350
Shotwell, Marion IV, 368
Shotwell, Mary II, 651
Shotwell, Mary III, 124
Shotwell, Mary III, 211
Shotwell, Mary III, 221
Shotwell, Mary III, 257
Shotwell, Mary III, 287
Shotwell, Mary III, 288
Shotwell, Mary III, 289
Shotwell, Mary III, 314
Shotwell, Mary IV, 350
Shotwell, Mary IV, 593
Shotwell, Mary IV, 1114
Shotwell, Mary IV, 1119
Shotwell, Mary IV, 1356
Shotwell, Mary VI, 267
Shotwell, Mary VI, 778
Shotwell, Mary F. III, 324
Shotwell, Mary Ruth IV, 1114
Shotwell, Mary Titus III, 288
Shotwell, Merion IV, 436
Shotwell, Miriam IV, 58
Shotwell, Morris III, 287
Shotwell, Murray III, 287
Shotwell, Nathan IV, 436
Shotwell, Nathan IV, 593
Shotwell, Nathan IV, 1378
Shotwell, Nathan Chase IV, 13
Shotwell, Newtown III, 287
Shotwell, Phebe III, 185
Shotwell, Phebe III, 288
Shotwell, Phebe III, 289
Shotwell, Phebe T. III, 289
Shotwell, Phebe T. III, 447
Shotwell, Priscilla IV, 350
Shotwell, Rebecca II, 766
Shotwell, Rebecca IV, 350
Shotwell, Rebecca Fox III, 288
Shotwell, Rebeckah IV, 436
Shotwell, Rich'd III, 288
Shotwell, Richard III, 221
Shotwell, Richard III, 287
Shotwell, Richard III, 288
Shotwell, Richard IV, 1356
Shotwell, Robert II, 651

twell, Robert III, 288
twell, Robert VI, 267
twell, Ruth IV, 593
twell, Ruth IV, 1114
twell, Ruth IV, 1119
twell, Ruth Ella IV, 593
twell, Ruth Ella IV, 595
twell, Samuel II, 260
twell, Samuel III, 112
twell, Samuel III, 289
twell, Samuel Emlen II, 803
twell, Samuel Emlen III, 288
twell, Samuel Emlen III, 289
twell, Samuel H. III, 288
twell, Samuel H. III, 289
twell, Samuel T. III, 289
twell, Samuel Wilson III, 289
twell, Sarah II, 293
twell, Sarah II, 301
twell, Sarah III, 75
twell, Sarah III, 102
twell, Sarah III, 239
twell, Sarah III, 287
twell, Sarah III, 288
twell, Sarah III, 289
twell, Sarah IV, 92
twell, Sarah IV, 108
twell, Sarah IV, 350
twell, Sarah IV, 1378
twell, Sarah Ann II, 420
twell, Sarah Carlile II, 803
twell, Sarah H. III, 286
twell, Sarah H. III, 289
twell, Sarah R. III, 288
twell, Susannah III, 287
twell, Thomas III, 289
twell, Thomas IV, 108
twell, Thomas IV, 159
twell, Thomas IV, 350
twell, Thomas IV, 436
twell, Thomas L. III, 289
twell, Titus IV, 58
twell, Titus IV, 108
twell, Titus IV, 150
twell, Titus IV, 159
twell, Titus IV, 350
twell, Titus IV, 436
twell, Titus IV, 593
twell, Titus IV, 1114
twell, Titus, Jr. IV, 108
twell, Walter III, 446
twell, Walter F. III, 287
twell, Walter F. III, 289
twell, Walter F. III, 447
twell, Walter T. III, 288
twell, Wd. Amy III, 419
twell, Willets Haviland III, 288
twell, William II, 293
twell, William II, 301
twell, William III, 170
twell, William III, 185
twell, William III, 287
twell, William III, 288
twell, William III, 289
twell, William III, 446
twell, William, Jr. II, 293
twell, William, Jr. II, 301
twell, Wm. III, 239
twell, Wm. III, 286
twell, Wm. III, 287
twell, Wm. III, 288
twell, Wm. III, 289
ulars, Roxie I, 262
ulders, Ruth I, 237
ulders, Ruth I, 257
up, Carrie IV, 1235
up, Carrie IV, 1240
urds, Ann T. II, 157
urds, Anna II, 157
urds, Anna Thompson II, 819
urds, Benjamin II, 30
urds, Benjamin II, 39
urds, Benjamin II, 51
urds, Benjamin II, 66
urds, Benjamin II, 97
urds, Benjamin II, 98
urds, Benjamin II, 109
urds, Benjamin II, 119
urds, Benjamin II, 123
urds, Benjamin II, 137
urds, Benjamin II, 157
urds, Benjamin, Jr. II, 39
urds, Benjamin, Sr. II, 39
urds, Charlotte IV, 1240
urds, Christian II, 260
urds, Christopher II, 97
urds, Elizabeth II, 30
urds, Elizabeth II, 39
urds, Elizabeth II, 97
urds, Elizabeth II, 109
Shourds, Elizabeth II, 157
Shourds, Hannah II, 97
Shourds, Hannah II, 123
Shourds, John II, 97
Shourds, Martha II, 39
Shourds, Martha II, 51
Shourds, Martha II, 97
Shourds, Martha II, 123
Shourds, Martha II, 137
Shourds, Martha II, 819
Shourds, Martha B. II, 890
Shourds, Martha B. II, 921
Shourds, Martha C. II, 157
Shourds, Mary II, 30
Shourds, Mary II, 39
Shourds, Mary II, 51
Shourds, Mary II, 66
Shourds, Mary II, 97
Shourds, Mary II, 98
Shourds, Mary II, 106
Shourds, Mary II, 119
Shourds, Mary II, 123
Shourds, Mary A. II, 39
Shourds, Mary A. II, 137
Shourds, Mary A. II, 157
Shourds, Mary B. II, 97
Shourds, Mary W. II, 123
Shourds, Mary W. II, 157
Shourds, Mary, Jr. II, 39
Shourds, Mehetable IV, 1240
Shourds, Nathaniel II, 30
Shourds, Rachel II, 30
Shourds, Rachel II, 39
Shourds, Rachel II, 75
Shourds, Rachel II, 97
Shourds, Rachel II, 106
Shourds, Rachel II, 137
Shourds, Rachel II, 157
Shourds, Rachel G. II, 921
Shourds, Rachel G. II, 933
Shourds, Rachel Griffith II, 819
Shourds, Rhoda II, 26
Shourds, Rhoda II, 28
Shourds, Rhoda II, 29
Shourds, Rhoda II, 39
Shourds, Rhoda II, 66
Shourds, Rhoda II, 97
Shourds, Ruth IV, 1240
Shourds, Samuel II, 39
Shourds, Samuel II, 97
Shourds, Samuel II, 109
Shourds, Samuel II, 157
Shourds, Sarah II, 137
Shourds, Sarah II, 157
Shourds, Sarah II, 890
Shourds, Sarah II, 921
Shourds, Sarah II, 933
Shourds, Susan Tyson II, 819
Shourds, Tamson II, 97
Shourds, Thomas II, 18
Shourds, Thomas II, 39
Shourds, Thomas II, 97
Shourds, Thomas II, 137
Shourds, Thomas II, 157
Shourds, Thomas, Jr. II, 137
Shourds, Thomas, Jr. II, 157
Shourds, Thomison II, 97
Shourds, Thompson II, 157
Shourds, Thompson II, 819
Shourds, Thompson II, 890
Shourds, Thompson II, 921
Shourds, Thompson II, 933
Shourds, Thos. II, 890
Shourds, Thos. II, 921
Shourds, Thos. II, 933
Shourds, William II, 39
Shourds, William C. II, 39
Shourds, Wm. II, 51
Shourds, Wm. II, 97
Shourds, Wm. II, 106
Shourds, Wm. II, 137
Shourds, Wm. C. II, 137
Shourds, Wm. C. II, 157
Shourds, Wm. Thompson II, 819
Shourds, Wm., Jr. II, 123
Shours, Cornelius II, 420
Shout, An II, 420
Shout, Elizabeth II, 420
Shout, Isaac II, 420
Shout, Jacob II, 420
Shout, Margrett II, 420
Shout, Thomas II, 420
Shout, William II, 420
Shout, William II, 447
Shouten, Charles M. V, 861
Shouten, M. E. Church V, 861
Shove, Asa III, 289
Shove, Harriet A. III, 289
Showalter, Abraham VI, 954
Showalter, Alberta IV, 1263
Showalter, Alberta Moss IV, 1263
Showalter, Bertha IV, 1338
Showalter, Emma IV, 1263
Showalter, Fay IV, 1263
Showalter, John R. IV, 1263
Showalter, Lois V, 860
Showalter, Lois V, 861
Showalter, Margaret IV, 1263
Showalter, Marguirite IV, 1263
Showalter, Mary E. V, 709
Showalter, Samuel F. IV, 1338
Showalter, Sewart J. IV, 1263
Showalter, Stewart J. IV, 1263
Showalter, Viola IV, 1338
Showls, Conrade VI, 853
Showls, Elizabeth VI, 860
Showls, Jacob VI, 805
Showls, Jacob VI, 860
Showls, Polly VI, 805
Showls, Sarah VI, 853
Showmaker, Amos D. V, 709
Showmaker, Edward E. V, 709
Showmaker, Elizabeth V, 709
Showmaker, Emerson W. V, 709
Showmaker, George V, 709
Showmaker, Henry M. V, 709
Showmaker, John E. V, 709
Showmaker, Raymon W. V, 709
Showrds, Benjamin II, 97
Showrds, Christopher II, 97
Showrds, Mary II, 97
Showrds, Tamson II, 97
Showrds, Thomison II, 97
Shrader, William IV, 1263
Shreck, Chas. V, 1018
Shreeve, Abigail II, 97
Shreeve, Abigail IV, 761
Shreeve, Abraham II, 39
Shreeve, Abraham II, 97
Shreeve, Abraham Zilley II, 97
Shreeve, Amyetta IV, 973
Shreeve, Amyetta IV, 993
Shreeve, Ann II, 39
Shreeve, Ann II, 97
Shreeve, Ann IV, 702
Shreeve, Ann IV, 762
Shreeve, Anna IV, 761
Shreeve, Asenath IV, 761
Shreeve, Asenath IV, 762
Shreeve, Asenith IV, 762
Shreeve, Benj. II, 651
Shreeve, Benjamin II, 222
Shreeve, Benjamin II, 260
Shreeve, Benjamin II, 651
Shreeve, Benjamin VI, 444
Shreeve, Benjamin VI, 560
Shreeve, Benjamin R. IV, 762
Shreeve, Benjamin, Jr. VI, 560
Shreeve, Caleb II, 192
Shreeve, Caleb II, 222
Shreeve, Caleb II, 260
Shreeve, Caleb II, 315
Shreeve, Caleb II, 651
Shreeve, Caleb VI, 560
Shreeve, Caleb, Jr. II, 234
Shreeve, Caleb, Jr. II, 260
Shreeve, David IV, 761
Shreeve, David IV, 762
Shreeve, Edith II, 39
Shreeve, Edith II, 97
Shreeve, Elisabeth IV, 762
Shreeve, Eliza IV, 762
Shreeve, Elizabeth II, 39
Shreeve, Elizabeth II, 97
Shreeve, Elizabeth II, 192
Shreeve, Elizabeth II, 260
Shreeve, Elizabeth II, 268
Shreeve, Elizabeth II, 709
Shreeve, Elizabeth IV, 761
Shreeve, Elizabeth Ann IV, 947
Shreeve, Elizabeth Ann IV, 993
Shreeve, Elvia VI, 560
Shreeve, Enoch IV, 761
Shreeve, Eunice IV, 761
Shreeve, Eunice IV, 762
Shreeve, Eunice IV, 784
Shreeve, George IV, 784
Shreeve, George M. IV, 762
Shreeve, George W. IV, 761
Shreeve, George W. IV, 762
Shreeve, Grace II, 324
Shreeve, Hanah VI, 560
Shreeve, Hannah II, 97
Shreeve, Hannah II, 260
Shreeve, Hannah II, 651
Shreeve, Hannah VI, 444
Shreeve, Hannah VI, 560
Shreeve, Hope II, 39
Shreeve, Hope II, 97
Shreeve, Isaac VI, 444
Shreeve, Isaac VI, 560
Shreeve, James VI, 560
Shreeve, Job II, 97
Shreeve, Job Shreeve II, 97
Shreeve, Job, Jr. II, 97
Shreeve, Joel IV, 761
Shreeve, John IV, 761
Shreeve, John IV, 762
Shreeve, Jonathan II, 234
Shreeve, Jonathan II, 260
Shreeve, Joseph IV, 274
Shreeve, Joseph IV, 762
Shreeve, Joshua IV, 761
Shreeve, Margaret II, 651
Shreeve, Martha IV, 761
Shreeve, Martha IV, 762
Shreeve, Martha IV, 784
Shreeve, Mary II, 260
Shreeve, Mary IV, 761
Shreeve, Mary IV, 762
Shreeve, Mary V, 931
Shreeve, Mary VI, 560
Shreeve, Mary Eliza IV, 761
Shreeve, Mary Eliza IV, 762
Shreeve, Mercy II, 97
Shreeve, Mercy II, 651
Shreeve, Mercy VI, 560
Shreeve, Penelope II, 315
Shreeve, Rebecca II, 97
Shreeve, Rebecca II, 222
Shreeve, Rebecca II, 260
Shreeve, Rebecca VI, 444
Shreeve, Rebecca VI, 560
Shreeve, Reuben VI, 560
Shreeve, Robert II, 39
Shreeve, Robert II, 97
Shreeve, Samuel VI, 560
Shreeve, Samuel B. VI, 560
Shreeve, Solomon IV, 762
Shreeve, Stacey IV, 762
Shreeve, Stacy IV, 761
Shreeve, Susannah VI, 560
Shreeve, Thomas II, 97
Shreeve, Thomas II, 192
Shreeve, Thomas II, 260
Shreeve, Thomas II, 268
Shreeve, Thomas VI, 560
Shreeve, Thomas C. IV, 762
Shreeve, Thos., Jr. V, 931
Shreeve, Unice IV, 993
Shreeve, Unice IV, 1013
Shreeve, Vashti IV, 761
Shreeve, Vashti IV, 762
Shreeve, Wm. IV, 761
Shreeves, Abigail II, 795
Shreeves, Eliza IV, 762
Shreeves, Marcy II, 450
Shreeves, Marcy II, 651
Shreive, Grace V, 931
Shreive, Mary V, 931
Shreive, Thos. V, 931
Shreve, Abi Cecelia P. IV, 1042
Shreve, Abigail II, 192
Shreve, Abigail II, 253
Shreve, Abigail II, 260
Shreve, Abigail IV, 58
Shreve, Abigail IV, 133
Shreve, Abigail IV, 761
Shreve, Abigail IV, 923
Shreve, Abigail IV, 943
Shreve, Abigail IV, 993
Shreve, Abner VI, 992
Shreve, Abraham L. II, 301
Shreve, Abraham Z. II, 324
Shreve, Abraham Z. II, 913
Shreve, Abraham Z. II, 922
Shreve, Abraham Zelly II, 260
Shreve, Albert IV, 993
Shreve, Albert IV, 994
Shreve, Albert IV, 1042
Shreve, Albert V, 931
Shreve, Aletha IV, 993
Shreve, Aletha IV, 994
Shreve, Aletha IV, 1042
Shreve, Alexandria II, 324
Shreve, Alice IV, 993
Shreve, Alice Elizabeth IV, 994
Shreve, Amy II, 223
Shreve, Amy II, 260
Shreve, Amyetta IV, 993
Shreve, Angetta IV, 992
Shreve, Ann II, 182
Shreve, Ann II, 235
Shreve, Ann II, 260
Shreve, Ann II, 263
Shreve, Ann V, 897
Shreve, Ann VI, 778
Shreve, Anna IV, 673
Shreve, Anna IV, 711
Shreve, Anna IV, 994
Shreve, Anna G. II, 301
Shreve, Anna Glover II, 280
Shreve, Anna Glover II, 301
Shreve, Anna M. IV, 923
Shreve, Anna M. IV, 993
Shreve, Anna M. IV, 1042
Shreve, Anna Mary IV, 994
Shreve, Anna Virginia IV, 1042
Shreve, Annar IV, 936
Shreve, Annar IV, 992
Shreve, Annar IV, 993
Shreve, Annie IV, 992
Shreve, Arnold L. IV, 993
Shreve, Arnold L. IV, 994
Shreve, Arnold L. IV, 1042
Shreve, Arthur J. IV, 1042
Shreve, Asenath IV, 761
Shreve, Benj. II, 590
Shreve, Benj. II, 651
Shreve, Benj. R. IV, 133
Shreve, Benjamin II, 260
Shreve, Benjamin II, 590
Shreve, Benjamin II, 651
Shreve, Benjamin IV, 992
Shreve, Benjamin VI, 444
Shreve, Benjamin VI, 503
Shreve, Benjamin VI, 725
Shreve, Benjamin VI, 778
Shreve, Benjamin B. IV, 133
Shreve, Benjamin Davis II, 922
Shreve, Benjamin R. IV, 133
Shreve, Benjamin R. IV, 762
Shreve, Benjamin S. IV, 993
Shreve, Benjamin Scattergood II, 260
Shreve, Benjamin, Jr. VI, 778
Shreve, Bertha Marie IV, 994
Shreve, Bertha Marie IV, 1042
Shreve, Bettie IV, 994
Shreve, Betty IV, 993
Shreve, Betty IV, 1042
Shreve, Binford S. IV, 916
Shreve, Caleb II, 192
Shreve, Caleb II, 235
Shreve, Caleb II, 260
Shreve, Caleb II, 651
Shreve, Caleb, Jr. II, 194
Shreve, Caleb, Jr. II, 260
Shreve, Calvin IV, 673
Shreve, Calvin IV, 923
Shreve, Calvin IV, 993
Shreve, Calvin IV, 994
Shreve, Calvin IV, 1042
Shreve, Caroline F. C. II, 816
Shreve, Caroline F. C. II, 913
Shreve, Caroline F. C. II, 922
Shreve, Carrie IV, 993
Shreve, Catharine R. II, 301
Shreve, Catherine II, 301
Shreve, Catherine R. II, 280
Shreve, Charles IV, 993
Shreve, Charles IV, 994
Shreve, Charles H. IV, 993
Shreve, Charlotte Louise IV, 993
Shreve, Chas. IV, 993
Shreve, Chas. H. IV, 1042
Shreve, Clara IV, 993
Shreve, Clara IV, 994
Shreve, Clara IV, 1042
Shreve, Clara H. IV, 993
Shreve, Clarah H. IV, 1042
Shreve, Clark G. IV, 993
Shreve, Curtis IV, 993
Shreve, Curtis IV, 1042
Shreve, Curtis G. IV, 994
Shreve, Curtis T. IV, 993
Shreve, Curtis T. IV, 1042
Shreve, David IV, 761
Shreve, Delbert B. IV, 1042
Shreve, Donald Merle IV, 993
Shreve, Edith IV, 986
Shreve, Edith IV, 993
Shreve, Edith IV, 1000
Shreve, Edmond IV, 1042
Shreve, Edmund IV, 993
Shreve, Edmund IV, 1042
Shreve, Eli T. IV, 1042
Shreve, Eliza IV, 133
Shreve, Elizabeth II, 260
Shreve, Elizabeth II, 789
Shreve, Elizabeth II, 812
Shreve, Elizabeth IV, 711
Shreve, Elizabeth IV, 712
Shreve, Elizabeth IV, 761
Shreve, Elizabeth IV, 762
Shreve, Elizabeth IV, 913
Shreve, Elizabeth IV, 916
Shreve, Elizabeth IV, 972
Shreve, Elizabeth IV, 987
Shreve, Elizabeth IV, 992
Shreve, Elizabeth IV, 993
Shreve, Elizabeth V, 903
Shreve, Elizabeth V, 931
Shreve, Elizabeth VI, 778

Shreve, Elizabeth Ann IV, 993
Shreve, Elizabeth Anna IV, 1013
Shreve, Elizabeth Annar IV, 992
Shreve, Elizabeth J. II, 922
Shreve, Elizabeth S. IV, 993
Shreve, Elizabeth S. IV, 994
Shreve, Emily IV, 993
Shreve, Emily IV, 1042
Shreve, Emma IV, 993
Shreve, Emma J. IV, 993
Shreve, Emma J. IV, 994
Shreve, Emma J. IV, 1042
Shreve, Enoch IV, 913
Shreve, Enoch IV, 916
Shreve, Enoch IV, 972
Shreve, Enoch IV, 987
Shreve, Enoch IV, 992
Shreve, Enoch IV, 993
Shreve, Enoch C. IV, 1042
Shreve, Eoizabeth IV, 999
Shreve, Ephraim G. II, 301
Shreve, Esther IV, 936
Shreve, Esther IV, 992
Shreve, Esther IV, 993
Shreve, Ethel IV, 673
Shreve, Ethel IV, 923
Shreve, Ethel E. IV, 1042
Shreve, Eunice IV, 761
Shreve, Eunice IV, 762
Shreve, Eunice IV, 993
Shreve, Evan IV, 958
Shreve, Evan IV, 992
Shreve, Evan IV, 993
Shreve, Evan IV, 998
Shreve, Ezra D. IV, 1042
Shreve, Frances VI, 992
Shreve, Geo. IV, 993
Shreve, Geo. W. IV, 133
Shreve, George M. IV, 762
Shreve, George W. IV, 133
Shreve, George W. IV, 703
Shreve, George W. IV, 761
Shreve, George W. IV, 993
Shreve, Glen IV, 994
Shreve, Glenn IV, 993
Shreve, Glenn IV, 1042
Shreve, Grace II, 324
Shreve, Grace V, 894
Shreve, Grace V, 895
Shreve, Grace V, 931
Shreve, Grace VI, 778
Shreve, Hannah II, 260
Shreve, Hannah II, 590
Shreve, Hannah II, 651
Shreve, Hannah IV, 978
Shreve, Hannah IV, 993
Shreve, Hannah VI, 444
Shreve, Hannah VI, 778
Shreve, Harris IV, 993
Shreve, Harris IV, 994
Shreve, Harris IV, 1042
Shreve, Hazel B. IV, 1042
Shreve, Isaac VI, 444
Shreve, Isaac VI, 560
Shreve, Israel IV, 108
Shreve, Israel IV, 133
Shreve, Janet Esther IV, 993
Shreve, Jesse Moshein IV, 993
Shreve, Jesse Moskin IV, 994
Shreve, Job II, 260
Shreve, Job II, 301
Shreve, Job II, 324
Shreve, Joel IV, 992
Shreve, John II, 301
Shreve, John IV, 58
Shreve, John IV, 71
Shreve, John IV, 133
Shreve, John IV, 761
Shreve, John IV, 762
Shreve, John IV, 923
Shreve, John IV, 943
Shreve, John IV, 992
Shreve, John IV, 993
Shreve, John IV, 994
Shreve, John IV, 999
Shreve, John IV, 1042
Shreve, John VI, 778
Shreve, John G. II, 301
Shreve, Jonathan II, 260
Shreve, Joseph II, 280
Shreve, Joseph II, 301
Shreve, Joseph IV, 58
Shreve, Joseph IV, 108
Shreve, Joseph IV, 133
Shreve, Joseph IV, 274
Shreve, Joseph Earl II, 922
Shreve, Joseph J. IV, 993
Shreve, Joseph J. IV, 1042
Shreve, Joseph Newbold II, 301
Shreve, Josephine H. IV, 1042
Shreve, Joshua IV, 711
Shreve, Joshua IV, 992
Shreve, Joshua IV, 993
Shreve, Joshua IV, 998
Shreve, Joshua IV, 999
Shreve, Judith IV, 993
Shreve, Judith IV, 998
Shreve, Judson W. IV, 1042
Shreve, Kezia IV, 58
Shreve, Kezia IV, 61
Shreve, Lavina IV, 993
Shreve, Lavina IV, 994
Shreve, Lavina IV, 999
Shreve, Lena M. IV, 1042
Shreve, Lenara IV, 1042
Shreve, Leonard G. IV, 1042
Shreve, Leroy M. IV, 993
Shreve, Lewis J. IV, 993
Shreve, Lewis J. IV, 994
Shreve, Lewis J. IV, 1042
Shreve, Lizzie IV, 993
Shreve, Lizzie S. IV, 993
Shreve, Lonora B. IV, 993
Shreve, Lorena J. IV, 1042
Shreve, Lucile IV, 994
Shreve, Lucile A. IV, 993
Shreve, Lucile A. IV, 1042
Shreve, Luella IV, 958
Shreve, Luella J. IV, 925
Shreve, Luella J. IV, 993
Shreve, Luella J. IV, 1018
Shreve, Mabel IV, 1042
Shreve, Mabel E. IV, 993
Shreve, Mabel E. IV, 1042
Shreve, Mable E. IV, 993
Shreve, Margaret II, 420
Shreve, Margaret IV, 108
Shreve, Margaret V, 897
Shreve, Margaret V, 931
Shreve, Margaret VI, 778
Shreve, Marie IV, 994
Shreve, Marie L. IV, 993
Shreve, Marie L. IV, 1042
Shreve, Marilla L. IV, 993
Shreve, Martha II, 252
Shreve, Martha II, 257
Shreve, Martha II, 260
Shreve, Martha IV, 703
Shreve, Martha IV, 761
Shreve, Martha IV, 762
Shreve, Martha IV, 993
Shreve, Mary II, 194
Shreve, Mary II, 231
Shreve, Mary II, 260
Shreve, Mary IV, 133
Shreve, Mary IV, 992
Shreve, Mary IV, 993
Shreve, Mary IV, 1042
Shreve, Mary V, 926
Shreve, Mary V, 931
Shreve, Mary VI, 778
Shreve, Mary Ann IV, 913
Shreve, Mary Anna IV, 987
Shreve, Mary B. IV, 133
Shreve, Mary Eliza IV, 761
Shreve, Mary V. IV, 993
Shreve, Meribah IV, 958
Shreve, Meribah IV, 992
Shreve, Meribah IV, 993
Shreve, Meribah IV, 998
Shreve, Meriha IV, 993
Shreve, Merle C. IV, 993
Shreve, Mildred IV, 993
Shreve, Mildred IV, 994
Shreve, Morilla IV, 994
Shreve, Nora IV, 994
Shreve, Olive IV, 993
Shreve, Olive B. IV, 1042
Shreve, Osborn IV, 992
Shreve, Osborn P. IV, 994
Shreve, Oscar P. IV, 993
Shreve, Philena IV, 993
Shreve, Rachel J. VI, 778
Shreve, Rachel J. VI, 779
Shreve, Rebecca II, 260
Shreve, Rebecca II, 301
Shreve, Rebecca II, 324
Shreve, Rebecca II, 794
Shreve, Rebecca II, 922
Shreve, Rebecca VI, 444
Shreve, Rebecca, Jr. II, 301
Shreve, Rebeckah VI, 444
Shreve, Richard IV, 108
Shreve, Richard V, 931
Shreve, Rosa IV, 1042
Shreve, Rosa L. IV, 994
Shreve, Rosetta IV, 994
Shreve, Rosetta L. IV, 993
Shreve, Ruth IV, 993
Shreve, Ruth IV, 994
Shreve, Ruth IV, 1042
Shreve, Samuel VI, 727
Shreve, Samuel B. II, 324
Shreve, Samuel B. VI, 778
Shreve, Samuel B. VI, 779
Shreve, Sarah Ann II, 913
Shreve, Sarah Ann II, 922
Shreve, Savina IV, 1042
Shreve, Solomon IV, 133
Shreve, Solomon IV, 762
Shreve, Solomon IV, 993
Shreve, Stacey IV, 762
Shreve, Stacey IV, 919
Shreve, Stacy IV, 936
Shreve, Stacy IV, 978
Shreve, Stacy IV, 992
Shreve, Stacy IV, 993
Shreve, Stacy B. IV, 992
Shreve, Stacy B. IV, 994
Shreve, Thomas II, 231
Shreve, Thomas II, 260
Shreve, Thomas V, 897
Shreve, Thomas V, 931
Shreve, Thomas VI, 727
Shreve, Thomas VI, 778
Shreve, Thomas C. IV, 133
Shreve, Thomas C. IV, 762
Shreve, Thos. V, 931
Shreve, Thos. H. V, 931
Shreve, Thos., Jr. V, 931
Shreve, Unice IV, 993
Shreve, Unity IV, 923
Shreve, Unity IV, 993
Shreve, Unity IV, 994
Shreve, Unity IV, 1042
Shreve, Vashti IV, 936
Shreve, Vashti IV, 992
Shreve, Vashti IV, 993
Shreve, Vashti R. IV, 992
Shreve, Wd. Susanna Wood VI, 747
Shreve, Wd. Susannah Wood VI, 503
Shreve, William IV, 992
Shreve, William IV, 993
Shreve, William H. IV, 1042
Shreve, Wilson IV, 993
Shreve, Wm. IV, 936
Shreve, Wm. IV, 993
Shreve, Wm. IV, 1042
Shreve, Wm. V, 931
Shreves, Elizabeth III, 289
Shrewbury, Elizabeth VI, 885
Shrewbury, Nathaniel VI, 932
Shrewbury, Nathaniel VI, 941
Shrewbury, Reuel VI, 931
Shrews, Charity III, 309
Shrewsberry, Milley VI, 883
Shrewsberry, Nathaniel VI, 901
Shrewsberry, Nathaniel VI, 908
Shrewsberry, Nathaniel VI, 947
Shrewsberry, Nathaniel VI, 998
Shrewsberry, Nathaniel VI, 1012
Shrewsberry, Nathl. VI, 883
Shrewsburry, Nathaniel VI, 869
Shrewsburry, Nathaniel VI, 874
Shrewsburry, Nathaniel VI, 905
Shrewsburry, Nathaniel VI, 921
Shrewsburry, Nathaniel VI, 923
Shrewsburry, Nathaniel VI, 927
Shrewsburry, Nathaniel VI, 944
Shrewsburry, Nathaniel VI, 1013
Shrewsbury, Charlotte VI, 993
Shrewsbury, Dabney VI, 992
Shrewsbury, Drewey VI, 883
Shrewsbury, Elizabeth VI, 992
Shrewsbury, Elizabeth VI, 993
Shrewsbury, Elizabeth VI, 1007
Shrewsbury, Joel VI, 993
Shrewsbury, John VI, 992
Shrewsbury, Malinda M. VI, 981
Shrewsbury, Nancey VI, 883
Shrewsbury, Nancy VI, 993
Shrewsbury, Nathan VI, 993
Shrewsbury, Nathaniel VI, 873
Shrewsbury, Nathaniel VI, 875
Shrewsbury, Nathaniel VI, 876
Shrewsbury, Nathaniel VI, 879
Shrewsbury, Nathaniel VI, 881
Shrewsbury, Nathaniel VI, 883
Shrewsbury, Nathaniel VI, 885
Shrewsbury, Nathaniel VI, 886
Shrewsbury, Nathaniel VI, 889
Shrewsbury, Nathaniel VI, 895
Shrewsbury, Nathaniel VI, 902
Shrewsbury, Nathaniel VI, 903
Shrewsbury, Nathaniel VI, 905
Shrewsbury, Nathaniel VI, 909
Shrewsbury, Nathaniel VI, 910
Shrewsbury, Nathaniel VI, 915
Shrewsbury, Nathaniel VI, 916
Shrewsbury, Nathaniel VI, 921
Shrewsbury, Nathaniel VI, 926
Shrewsbury, Nathaniel VI, 935
Shrewsbury, Nathaniel VI, 936
Shrewsbury, Nathaniel VI, 939
Shrewsbury, Nathaniel VI, 942
Shrewsbury, Nathaniel VI, 943
Shrewsbury, Nathaniel VI, 946
Shrewsbury, Nathaniel VI, 954
Shrewsbury, Nathaniel VI, 955
Shrewsbury, Nathaniel VI, 956
Shrewsbury, Nathaniel VI, 958
Shrewsbury, Nathaniel VI, 959
Shrewsbury, Nathaniel VI, 965
Shrewsbury, Nathaniel VI, 969
Shrewsbury, Nathaniel VI, 975
Shrewsbury, Nathaniel VI, 978
Shrewsbury, Nathaniel VI, 979
Shrewsbury, Nathaniel VI, 984
Shrewsbury, Nathaniel VI, 985
Shrewsbury, Nathaniel VI, 987
Shrewsbury, Nathaniel VI, 988
Shrewsbury, Nathaniel VI, 989
Shrewsbury, Nathaniel VI, 992
Shrewsbury, Nathaniel VI, 993
Shrewsbury, Nathaniel VI, 994
Shrewsbury, Nathaniel VI, 997
Shrewsbury, Nathaniel VI, 1000
Shrewsbury, Nathaniel VI, 1008
Shrewsbury, Nathaniel VI, 1011
Shrewsbury, Nathaniel VI, 1012
Shrewsbury, Nathaniel VI, 1013
Shrewsbury, Nathaniel VI, 1021
Shrewsbury, Nathankel VI, 1000
Shrewsbury, Nathl. VI, 993
Shrewsbury, Rhoda VI, 993
Shrewsbury, Rhody VI, 885
Shrewsbury, Ruel VI, 993
Shrewsbury, Sally VI, 993
Shrewsbury, Saml. VI, 981
Shrewsbury, Sarah VI, 993
Shrewsbury, William VI, 903
Shrewsbury, William VI, 993
Shrieve, Benjamin VI, 560
Shrieve, Benjamin VI, 583
Shrieve, Benjamin VI, 747
Shrieve, Benjamin VI, 778
Shrieve, Benjamin, Jr. VI, 560
Shrieve, Caleb VI, 560
Shrieve, Elvia VI, 560
Shrieve, Hanah VI, 560
Shrieve, Hannah VI, 560
Shrieve, Isaac VI, 560
Shrieve, James VI, 560
Shrieve, Joseph Earl II, 922
Shrieve, Mary VI, 560
Shrieve, Mercy VI, 560
Shrieve, Mercy VI, 572
Shrieve, Rebecca II, 922
Shrieve, Rebecca VI, 560
Shrieve, Reuben VI, 560
Shrieve, Samuel VI, 560
Shrieve, Samuel B. VI, 560
Shrieve, Susannah VI, 560
Shrieve, Susannah VI, 583
Shrieve, Thomas III, 289
Shrieve, Thomas VI, 560
Shrieves, Reba A. V, 709
Shrigley, Martha VI, 528
Shrigley, Martha VI, 560
Shrigley, Mary ??? III, 289
Shrigley, Rebecca Allen III, 289
Shriner, Olive A. IV, 994
Shriner, Patience IV, 383
Shriner, Patience IV, 437
Shriver, Elizabeth IV, 990
Shriver, Elizabeth IV, 994
Shriver, Geo. IV, 990
Shriver, Geo. IV, 994
Shriver, George IV, 990
Shriver, Martha IV, 414
Shriver, Martha IV, 437
Shriver, Mary IV, 351
Shriver, Mary H. IV, 351
Shriver, Olivada A. IV, 994
Shriver, Olive A. IV, 990
Shriver, Olive A. IV, 994
Shriver, William Henry IV, 351
Shriver, Wm. Henry IV, 351
Shropshire, Harriet II, 922
Shropshire, Harriet II, 935
Shropshire, Joseph B. II, 842
Shropshire, Joseph B. II, 922
Shropshire, Joseph B. II, 935
Shropshire, Laura II, 842
Shropshire, Laura II, 922
Shropshire, Martha II, 922
Shropshire, Martha II, 935
Shropshire, Martha W. II, 842
Shropshire, Martha W. II, 922
Shropshire, Nelson C. II, 922
Shropshire, Nelson C. II, 935
Shrouds, Ruth IV, 1240
Shrouds, Ruth IV, 1241
Shrove, Lucinda V, 1018
Shroyer, Faye Elleman V, 764
Shrum, Washington IV, 1263
Shry, Mary IV, 966
Shry, Mary E. IV, 1010
Shuard, Jane VI, 499
Shuard, Jane VI, 500
Shuard, Jane VI, 511
Shuard, Jane VI, 645
Shuard, Jane VI, 658
Shubert, Bertha V, 709
Shubert, Everett V, 709
Shubert, George V, 709
Shubert, Ida V, 709
Shubert, Mary II, 420
Shubert, Sadie V, 709
Shudam, Mary I, 165
Shuey, Laura VI, 472
Shuey, Laura VI, 560
Shuey, Louis V. VI, 472
Shuey, Louisa V. VI, 560
Shuff, Aaron P. III, 289
Shugart, Amanda I, 621
Shugart, Catharine I, 418
Shugart, Catharine I, 984
Shugart, Catharine I, 997
Shugart, Elizabeth I, 689
Shugart, Elizabeth I, 691
Shugart, Elizabeth I, 997
Shugart, Elizabeth I, 999
Shugart, George I, 384
Shugart, George I, 418
Shugart, George I, 837
Shugart, George I, 978
Shugart, George I, 997
Shugart, Hanna I, 453
Shugart, Hannah I, 447
Shugart, Hannah I, 453
Shugart, Isaac I, 453
Shugart, John I, 689
Shugart, John I, 978
Shugart, Leonard I, 837
Shugart, Leonard I, 996
Shugart, Leonard I, 997
Shugart, Mary I, 384
Shugart, Mary I, 418
Shugart, Mary I, 978
Shugart, Mary I, 996
Shugart, Mary I, 997
Shugart, Mary Keys I, 997
Shugart, Rachel I, 453
Shugart, Rhoda I, 453
Shugart, Rhode I, 453
Shugart, Russel I, 997
Shugart, Ruth I, 997
Shugart, Ruth Marshill I, 997
Shugart, Sarah I, 837
Shugart, Sarah I, 971
Shugart, Sarah I, 978
Shugart, Susanna I, 689
Shugart, Tamer I, 978
Shugart, William I, 997
Shugart, Zachariah I, 418
Shugart, Zachariah I, 837
Shugart, Zachariah I, 971
Shugart, Zachariah I, 978
Shugart, Zachariah I, 997
Shugart, Zecheriah I, 689
Shugart, Zecheriah I, 691
Shugers, Archibald VI, 469
Shugers, Archibald VI, 560
Shugers, Joseph VI, 560
Shugers, Silema VI, 469
Shugers, Silema VI, 560
Shuggart, Elizabeth I, 997
Shuke, Sarah V, 958
Shuke, Sarah V, 959
Shul, John II, 447
Shull, Rachel H. II, 732
Shull, Rachel H. II, 766
Shultz, Clara IV, 1184
Shultz, Eleanor II, 847
Shultz, Eleanor II, 901
Shultz, Eleanor II, 922
Shultz, Geo. A. IV, 1338
Shultz, Grace V, 709
Shultz, Josehine L. II, 901
Shultz, Josephine L. II, 922
Shultz, Lindley V, 709
Shultz, Lizzie IV, 1212
Shultz, Lizzie IV, 1223
Shultz, Maggie IV, 1338
Shultz, Mary R. II, 847
Shultz, Mary R. II, 922
Shultz, Mrs. ??? IV, 1184
Shultz, Paul IV, 1338
Shultz, Paul H. IV, 1338
Shultz, Rebecca IV, 762
Shultz, Rebecca V, 931
Shultz, Richard IV, 1338

ltz, Walter P. IV, 1338
ltz, Wm. II, 847
ltz, Wm. II, 901
ltz, Wm. II, 922
ltz, Wm. IV, 1184
ltz, Wm. V, 709
ltz, Wm., Jr. II, 844
ltz, Wm., Jr. II, 847
ltz, Wm., Jr. II, 901
ltz, Wm., Jr. II, 922
maker, Lindsay VI, 1022
maker, Margaret IV, 1263
maker, Mariah VI, 1022
maker, Mary E. V, 189
mate, Helen E. VI, 700
mate, Helen E. VI, 719
mo, Joseph II, 918
mo, Phebe II, 918
mway, Abigail IV, 1378
mway, Alice IV, 1338
mway, Josiah IV, 1378
mway, Nathan IV, 1378
nk, Frederick William VI, 993
nk, Sarah VI, 993
pe, Walter H. III, 289
pert, Bertha V, 712
pert, George V, 528
pert, Ida V, 528
ping, Mary I, 625
rden, Margret I, 418
rn, Elizabeth IV, 79
rn, Elizabeth IV, 108
rraf, Lusinda V, 430
ster, Elizabeth II, 922
ster, John VI, 854
ster, Philip VI, 872
ster, Philip VI, 882
ster, Sarah E. VI, 882
te, Abraham II, 420
te, Alice B. V, 121
te, Ann II, 420
te, Ann II, 620
te, Ann II, 651
te, Anna I, 1075
te, Anna I, 1076
te, Atwood II, 420
te, Christian II, 651
te, Edith F. V, 120
te, Edith Furnas V, 120
te, Elias H. V, 931
te, Elizabeth I, 1075
te, Elizabeth I, 1076
te, Elizabeth II, 420
te, Elizabeth II, 495
te, Elizabeth II, 625
te, Elizabeth II, 651
te, Elizabeth II, 659
te, Eunice V, 120
te, Hannah II, 97
te, Hannah II, 260
te, Henry II, 195
te, Henry II, 260
te, Henry II, 420
te, Henry II, 513
te, Henry II, 651
te, Isaac II, 97
te, Isaac II, 420
te, Jacob II, 420
te, Jacob II, 470
te, Jacob II, 651
te, James II, 420
te, James V, 120
te, James H. V, 120
te, Jesabel I, 1075
te, John I, 1075
te, John II, 651
te, Joseph I, 1075
te, Joseph I, 1076
te, Joseph II, 420
te, Joseph II, 651
te, Joseph P. I, 1076
te, Lydia II, 53
te, Lydia II, 97
te, Martha II, 632
te, Martha II, 651
te, Mary I, 1075
te, Mary II, 195
te, Mary II, 260
te, Mary II, 420
te, Mary II, 495
te, Mary II, 513
te, Mary II, 651
te, Mary W. I, 1076
te, Rachel II, 97
te, Rebecca II, 552
te, Rebecca II, 607
te, Rebecca II, 651
te, Rebekah II, 651
te, Robert V, 120
te, Robert H. V, 120
Shute, Ruth Anna V, 60
Shute, Ruth Anna V, 120
Shute, Samuel II, 97
Shute, Samuel II, 420
Shute, Samuel V, 931
Shute, Samuel, Jr. II, 97
Shute, Sarah II, 560
Shute, Sarah II, 607
Shute, Sarah II, 651
Shute, Sarah II, 809
Shute, Sarah V, 120
Shute, Sibyl V, 931
Shute, Thomas I, 1075
Shute, Thomas I, 1076
Shute, Thomas II, 420
Shute, Thomas II, 495
Shute, Thomas II, 607
Shute, Thomas II, 625
Shute, Thomas II, 651
Shute, Thomas, Jr. II, 420
Shute, Wd. Elizabeth II, 420
Shute, William II, 420
Shute, Wm. II, 97
Shute, Wm. II, 651
Shute, Wm. II, 659
Shutes, Ann H. III, 411
Shutt, Ina V, 1018
Shutt, L. E. V, 1018
Shuttle, Elizabeth VI, 853
Shuttle, John VI, 853
Shuttle, Sophia VI, 854
Shutts, Alice B. V, 121
Shwesbury, Nathaniel VI, 1003
Shy, Isaac I, 453
Shy, Martha I, 393
Shy, Martha I, 418
Shy, Martha I, 431
Shy, Martha I, 453
Shy, Martha I, 454
Sibell, Elizabeth III, 289
Sibley, John II, 447
Sibthorp, Ann II, 651
Sibthorp, Christopher II, 420
Sibthorp, Christopher II, 523
Sibthorp, Christopher II, 651
Sibthorp, Mary II, 420
Sibthorp, Mary II, 651
Sibthorpe, Christopher II, 651
Sibthorpe, Mary II, 651
Sickels, Anna J. III, 289
Sickels, Ethel May III, 289
Sickels, Jesse S. III, 289
Sickler, Anna M. II, 137
Sickler, Joseph Sheppard II, 137
Sickler, Joseph Sheppard II, 157
Sickler, Ruth II, 137
Sickler, Ruth S. II, 157
Sickler, Wm. B. II, 137
Sickler, Wm. B. II, 157
Sickler, Wm. Burkhardt II, 137
Sickler, Wm. Burkhardt II, 157
Sickler, Zachius B. II, 137
Sickles, Elizabeth IV, 1042
Sickles, Elsie IV, 274
Sickles, Esther III, 48
Sickles, Esther H. III, 48
Sickles, Ethel IV, 274
Sickles, George W. IV, 274
Sickles, Isaac IV, 274
Sickles, Iva IV, 274
Sickles, Izetta Matilda IV, 274
Sickles, John IV, 274
Sickles, Lizzie IV, 274
Sickles, Oscar IV, 274
Sickles, Phebe III, 48
Sickles, Rosie IV, 274
Sickles, Simon R. IV, 274
Sickles, Sylvia IV, 274
Sickles, Thos. H. III, 48
Sickles, William IV, 274
Sickly, Esther III, 48
Sickly, Esther H. III, 48
Sickly, Phebe III, 48
Sickly, Thos. H. III, 48
Siddal, Deborah II, 420
Siddal, Ezekell II, 420
Siddal, Isaac II, 1026
Siddal, Isaac II, 1031
Siddal, James II, 1026
Siddal, James II, 1031
Siddal, Rebecca II, 1026
Siddal, Rebecca II, 1031
Siddal, Sarah II, 420
Siddall, Aden IV, 883
Siddall, Ann IV, 883
Siddall, Atticus IV, 638
Siddall, Atticus IV, 656
Siddall, Atticus IV, 883
Siddall, David IV, 883
Siddall, Deborah II, 420
Siddall, Ezekell II, 420
Siddall, Hannah IV, 656
Siddall, Hannah IV, 883
Siddall, John IV, 883
Siddall, Mary IV, 871
Siddall, Mary IV, 883
Siddall, Samuel II, 420
Siddall, Sarah II, 420
Siddall, Sarah IV, 656
Siddall, Sarah IV, 883
Siddall, Sarah Burke IV, 656
Siddall, Sarah Jr. IV, 638
Siddall, William IV, 656
Siddans, Hannah II, 632
Siddans, Hannah II, 651
Siddans, Jane II, 651
Siddel, Esther II, 980
Siddel, Isaac II, 1026
Siddel, James II, 1026
Siddel, Rebecca II, 1026
Siddel, Sarah II, 260
Siddel, Sarah II, 1026
Siddel, Sarah II, 1039
Siddell, Sarah IV, 871
Siddell, Sarah IV, 883
Siddens, Sarah II, 455
Siddin, Jane II, 260
Siddle, Atticus IV, 656
Siddle, Esther II, 1026
Siddle, Hannah IV, 656
Siddle, James II, 1026
Siddle, Sarah II, 1026
Siddle, Sarah IV, 656
Siddle, William IV, 656
Siddon, Abraham II, 420
Siddon, Abraham II, 652
Siddon, Ann II, 420
Siddon, Anthony II, 420
Siddon, Anthony II, 567
Siddon, Anthony II, 651
Siddon, Deborah II, 97
Siddon, Deborah II, 105
Siddon, Deborah II, 567
Siddon, Deborah II, 651
Siddon, Enis II, 420
Siddon, Hannah II, 61
Siddon, Hannah II, 97
Siddon, Isabella II, 652
Siddon, Job II, 420
Siddon, Lawry II, 420
Siddon, Lowry II, 651
Siddon, Mary II, 97
Siddon, Mary II, 420
Siddon, Mary II, 651
Siddon, Samuel II, 420
Siddon, Sarah II, 420
Siddon, Sarah II, 454
Siddon, Sarah II, 651
Siddon, Susanna II, 420
Siddon, Susanna II, 651
Siddon, Susanna II, 663
Siddon, Thomas II, 420
Siddon, Thomas II, 567
Siddon, Thomas II, 651
Siddon, Thomas II, 663
Siddons, Abigail II, 651
Siddons, Abigail II, 652
Siddons, Abigail III, 289
Siddons, Abraham II, 652
Siddons, Anthony II, 420
Siddons, Anthony II, 651
Siddons, Deborah II, 39
Siddons, Deborah II, 97
Siddons, Deborah II, 651
Siddons, Edward II, 39
Siddons, Edward II, 651
Siddons, Eleanor II, 652
Siddons, Elianor II, 651
Siddons, Elizabeth II, 39
Siddons, Ezekiel II, 39
Siddons, Ezekiel II, 651
Siddons, Hannah II, 39
Siddons, Hannah II, 97
Siddons, Hannah II, 651
Siddons, Isaac II, 39
Siddons, Isabella II, 652
Siddons, Jane II, 39
Siddons, Jane II, 183
Siddons, Jane II, 260
Siddons, Jane II, 651
Siddons, Jane II, 652
Siddons, Josiah II, 820
Siddons, Josiah II, 922
Siddons, Lowry II, 651
Siddons, Mary II, 39
Siddons, Mary II, 97
Siddons, Mary II, 98
Siddons, Mary II, 651
Siddons, Rebecca II, 651
Siddons, Rebecca II, 652
Siddons, Samuel II, 651
Siddons, Sarah II, 39
Siddons, Sarah II, 97
Siddons, Sarah II, 99
Siddons, Sarah II, 539
Siddons, Sarah II, 651
Siddons, Susanna II, 420
Siddons, Susanna II, 651
Siddons, Thomas II, 651
Siddons, William II, 39
Siddons, Wm. II, 97
Siddons, Wm. II, 98
Siddow, Abigail II, 969
Siddow, James II, 969
Siddow, John II, 969
Sidebottom, Catherine II, 447
Sidebottom, Robert II, 447
Sidells, Geo. V, 1018
Sidells, George V, 1018
Sidells, Stella V, 1018
Sidenstricker, Abi M. V, 121
Sidenstricker, Ella V, 121
Sidenstricker, Harry V, 121
Sidenstricker, Ivy V, 121
Sidenstricker, Lila V, 121
Sidenstricker, Miriam V, 121
Siders, Ellsworth V, 1019
Siders, Elsworth V, 1019
Siders, Joseph V, 1019
Siders, Lucy V, 1019
Siders, Robert V, 1019
Sidersticker, Abi M. V, 121
Sides, Amy B. II, 914
Sides, Amy B. II, 922
Sides, Amy Bullock II, 922
Sides, Andrew II, 820
Sides, Anna T. II, 922
Sides, Annah T. II, 922
Sides, Bessie Buckman II, 922
Sides, Clara May II, 922
Sides, Elizabeth B. II, 875
Sides, Elizabeth B. II, 922
Sides, Fanny II, 922
Sides, Frances II, 820
Sides, Hannah II, 820
Sides, Hannah B. II, 875
Sides, Hannah B. II, 922
Sides, Howard B. II, 922
Sides, Howard Buckman II, 922
Sides, Jacob II, 922
Sides, Jacob B. II, 875
Sides, Jacob B. II, 922
Sides, Jacob H. II, 922
Sides, Jacob Herr II, 820
Sides, Sally A. V, 121
Sides, Sarah A. V, 70
Sides, Sarah A. V, 121
Sides, Thomas Borton II, 922
Sides, Thos. B. II, 922
Sidles, Geo. V, 1018
Sidles, Stella V, 1018
Sidney, Elisha V, 269
Sidney, James II, 801
Sidney, John II, 804
Sidney, Margaret V, 269
Sidney, Wd. Hannah II, 804
Sidon, Enis II, 420
Sidon, Job II, 420
Sidon, Samuel II, 651
Sidwel, David V, 861
Sidwel, Frederick VI, 444
Sidwel, Richard VI, 444
Sidwell, Abbie IV, 223
Sidwell, Abbie IV, 534
Sidwell, Abbie H. IV, 549
Sidwell, Abby IV, 275
Sidwell, Abijah Janney VI, 782
Sidwell, Abner IV, 657
Sidwell, Abraham VI, 444
Sidwell, Albert IV, 549
Sidwell, Albert VI, 782
Sidwell, Albert B. IV, 549
Sidwell, Albert E. IV, 275
Sidwell, Amey I, 1047
Sidwell, Amey I, 1050
Sidwell, Amy IV, 108
Sidwell, Amy VI, 414
Sidwell, Amy VI, 444
Sidwell, Ann IV, 157
Sidwell, Ann IV, 159
Sidwell, Ann VI, 444
Sidwell, Ann M. VI, 444
Sidwell, Ann M. VI, 561
Sidwell, Anna E. IV, 549
Sidwell, Anna M. VI, 560
Sidwell, Anne I, 1050
Sidwell, Barbara Ellen IV, 275
Sidwell, Barbary IV, 275
Sidwell, Benjamin VI, 444
Sidwell, Bertha Isabel IV, 843
Sidwell, Branson D. IV, 223
Sidwell, Branson D. IV, 274
Sidwell, Branson D. IV, 275
Sidwell, Branson D. IV, 534
Sidwell, Branson D. IV, 549
Sidwell, Caroline VI, 782
Sidwell, Catharine I, 418
Sidwell, Catharine I, 425
Sidwell, Catharine I, 1041
Sidwell, Catharine I, 1049
Sidwell, Catharine I, 1050
Sidwell, Charity IV, 58
Sidwell, Charity IV, 91
Sidwell, Charity IV, 108
Sidwell, Charity VI, 395
Sidwell, Charity VI, 416
Sidwell, Charity VI, 444
Sidwell, Charity VI, 501
Sidwell, Charity VI, 560
Sidwell, Cinah IV, 159
Sidwell, Cinah IV, 275
Sidwell, Cinah IV, 437
Sidwell, Cinah IV, 632
Sidwell, Cinah IV, 657
Sidwell, Cineh IV, 220
Sidwell, Cineh IV, 274
Sidwell, Cineh IV, 437
Sidwell, Clara E. IV, 275
Sidwell, Clarence J. IV, 275
Sidwell, Cornelia H. VI, 444
Sidwell, Cornelia H. VI, 454
Sidwell, Cornelia H. VI, 560
Sidwell, Cornelia H. VI, 561
Sidwell, Cornelia H. VI, 575
Sidwell, Cornelia H. VI, 576
Sidwell, Cornelia H. VI, 702
Sidwell, Cornelia H. VI, 717
Sidwell, Dallas J. IV, 549
Sidwell, Dallis J. IV, 549
Sidwell, David I, 1050
Sidwell, David V, 861
Sidwell, Deborah IV, 159
Sidwell, Deborah IV, 260
Sidwell, Deborah IV, 274
Sidwell, Deborah IV, 275
Sidwell, Deborah IV, 437
Sidwell, Deborah IV, 494
Sidwell, Deborah IV, 497
Sidwell, Edith IV, 549
Sidwell, Edward Abijah VI, 782
Sidwell, Edwin H. IV, 549
Sidwell, Eleanor IV, 159
Sidwell, Eleanor IV, 265
Sidwell, Eleanor IV, 274
Sidwell, Eleanor IV, 437
Sidwell, Elenor IV, 275
Sidwell, Eli IV, 159
Sidwell, Eli IV, 265
Sidwell, Eli IV, 275
Sidwell, Eli IV, 330
Sidwell, Eli IV, 351
Sidwell, Eli IV, 491
Sidwell, Eli IV, 497
Sidwell, Eli IV, 650
Sidwell, Elisha IV, 159
Sidwell, Elisha IV, 274
Sidwell, Elisha IV, 275
Sidwell, Elisha IV, 304
Sidwell, Elisha IV, 549
Sidwell, Elisha D. IV, 274
Sidwell, Elisha, Sr. IV, 274
Sidwell, Eliza Ann IV, 274
Sidwell, Elizabeth I, 1050
Sidwell, Elizabeth I, 1051
Sidwell, Elizabeth IV, 202
Sidwell, Elizabeth IV, 274
Sidwell, Elizabeth IV, 275
Sidwell, Elizabeth IV, 304
Sidwell, Elizabeth IV, 351
Sidwell, Elizabeth IV, 417
Sidwell, Elizabeth IV, 437
Sidwell, Elizabeth IV, 525
Sidwell, Elizabeth IV, 549
Sidwell, Elizabeth J. VI, 560
Sidwell, Elizabeth Janney VI, 429
Sidwell, Elizabeth Janney VI, 444
Sidwell, Elizabeth Janney VI, 494
Sidwell, Elizabeth Janney VI, 543
Sidwell, Elizabeth Janney VI, 544
Sidwell, Elizabeth Janney VI, 560
Sidwell, Elizabeth Janney VI, 641
Sidwell, Elizabeth Janney VI, 687
Sidwell, Elizabeth Tomlinson IV, 159
Sidwell, Ellen IV, 274
Sidwell, Elma IV, 351

Sidwell, Elma IV, 497
Sidwell, Elwood IV, 351
Sidwell, Emily IV, 843
Sidwell, Emily C. IV, 819
Sidwell, Emily C. H. IV, 843
Sidwell, Emma IV, 274
Sidwell, Emma IV, 950
Sidwell, Emma IV, 993
Sidwell, Emma S. IV, 198
Sidwell, Emma S. IV, 275
Sidwell, Esther V, 861
Sidwell, Florence IV, 549
Sidwell, Florence Olive IV, 843
Sidwell, Floyd H. IV, 843
Sidwell, Floyd Hall IV, 843
Sidwell, Frances I, 350
Sidwell, Frances I, 528
Sidwell, Frances Brown I, 571
Sidwell, Francis I, 418
Sidwell, Frank R. IV, 275
Sidwell, Frank Russell IV, 275
Sidwell, Frederick VI, 444
Sidwell, Gabrial Baker IV, 159
Sidwell, Gabriel B. IV, 437
Sidwell, Hannah I, 350
Sidwell, Hannah I, 536
Sidwell, Hannah I, 571
Sidwell, Hannah I, 1048
Sidwell, Hannah I, 1050
Sidwell, Hannah IV, 108
Sidwell, Hannah IV, 111
Sidwell, Hannah VI, 444
Sidwell, Hannah VI, 560
Sidwell, Hannah W. IV, 274
Sidwell, Harold Oliver IV, 843
Sidwell, Helen Bowne VI, 782
Sidwell, Henry IV, 108
Sidwell, Henry IV, 159
Sidwell, Henry IV, 220
Sidwell, Henry IV, 260
Sidwell, Henry IV, 265
Sidwell, Henry IV, 274
Sidwell, Henry IV, 275
Sidwell, Henry IV, 351
Sidwell, Henry IV, 437
Sidwell, Henry IV, 497
Sidwell, Hugh IV, 58
Sidwell, Hugh IV, 108
Sidwell, Hugh VI, 367
Sidwell, Hugh VI, 396
Sidwell, Hugh VI, 398
Sidwell, Hugh VI, 429
Sidwell, Hugh VI, 444
Sidwell, Hugh VI, 454
Sidwell, Hugh VI, 501
Sidwell, Hugh VI, 544
Sidwell, Hugh VI, 560
Sidwell, Hugh VI, 576
Sidwell, Isaac IV, 657
Sidwell, Isaac VI, 543
Sidwell, Isaac VI, 561
Sidwell, Isabel IV, 843
Sidwell, Isabel C. IV, 202
Sidwell, Isabell C. IV, 275
Sidwell, Isabella IV, 351
Sidwell, Isabella IV, 466
Sidwell, Isabella IV, 497
Sidwell, Israel II, 721
Sidwell, Israel IV, 183
Sidwell, Israel IV, 202
Sidwell, Israel IV, 213
Sidwell, Israel IV, 274
Sidwell, Israel IV, 275
Sidwell, Israel IV, 299
Sidwell, Israel IV, 513
Sidwell, Israel IV, 549
Sidwell, Israel IV, 800
Sidwell, Israel IV, 804
Sidwell, Israel IV, 950
Sidwell, J. Wilson IV, 843
Sidwell, James IV, 108
Sidwell, James IV, 351
Sidwell, James IV, 437
Sidwell, James VI, 414
Sidwell, James VI, 444
Sidwell, James VI, 561
Sidwell, James C. IV, 351
Sidwell, Jane V, 927
Sidwell, Jane VI, 782
Sidwell, Jesse IV, 108
Sidwell, Jesse IV, 437
Sidwell, John I, 418
Sidwell, John I, 425
Sidwell, John I, 1050
Sidwell, John IV, 159
Sidwell, John IV, 351
Sidwell, John IV, 437
Sidwell, John VI, 561
Sidwell, Joseph I, 1050
Sidwell, Joseph IV, 159
Sidwell, Laura E. IV, 275
Sidwell, Lawrence VI, 782
Sidwell, Lemuel V, 277
Sidwell, Levi V, 277
Sidwell, Lindley IV, 351
Sidwell, Lizzie A. IV, 179
Sidwell, Lizzie A. IV, 183
Sidwell, Lizzie A. IV, 275
Sidwell, Lizzie A. IV, 800
Sidwell, Lizzie Ann IV, 274
Sidwell, Lizzie Ann IV, 275
Sidwell, Louisa II, 721
Sidwell, Louisa IV, 274
Sidwell, Louiza J. IV, 275
Sidwell, Louiza J. IV, 299
Sidwell, Lovisa IV, 437
Sidwell, Lovisa IV, 451
Sidwell, Luella W. IV, 275
Sidwell, Lydia IV, 90
Sidwell, Lydia IV, 108
Sidwell, Lydia IV, 213
Sidwell, Lydia VI, 395
Sidwell, Lydia VI, 444
Sidwell, Lydia J. IV, 275
Sidwell, Lydia Jane II, 706
Sidwell, Lydia Jane IV, 214
Sidwell, Lydia Jane IV, 272
Sidwell, Lydia Jane IV, 274
Sidwell, Lydia Jane IV, 275
Sidwell, Margaret IV, 58
Sidwell, Margaret IV, 108
Sidwell, Margaret IV, 110
Sidwell, Margaret VI, 444
Sidwell, Margaret A. III, 276
Sidwell, Margaret Alice III, 239
Sidwell, Margaret Alice VI, 768
Sidwell, Margaret Alice VI, 775
Sidwell, Martha II, 999
Sidwell, Martha II, 1026
Sidwell, Martha A. VI, 368
Sidwell, Martha Ann VI, 416
Sidwell, Martha Ann VI, 444
Sidwell, Martha L. VI, 444
Sidwell, Martha L. VI, 560
Sidwell, Martha L. VI, 561
Sidwell, Mary I, 418
Sidwell, Mary I, 1049
Sidwell, Mary I, 1050
Sidwell, Mary IV, 58
Sidwell, Mary IV, 91
Sidwell, Mary IV, 108
Sidwell, Mary IV, 275
Sidwell, Mary IV, 351
Sidwell, Mary IV, 549
Sidwell, Mary VI, 398
Sidwell, Mary VI, 444
Sidwell, Mary VI, 543
Sidwell, Mary VI, 544
Sidwell, Mary VI, 782
Sidwell, Mary Ella IV, 202
Sidwell, Mary Ella IV, 275
Sidwell, Mary Ellen IV, 275
Sidwell, Mary Ellicott VI, 782
Sidwell, Mary F. VI, 444
Sidwell, Mary M. IV, 351
Sidwell, Nathan I, 1037
Sidwell, Nathan I, 1050
Sidwell, Nathan IV, 159
Sidwell, Nathan IV, 1076
Sidwell, Nathan P. IV, 497
Sidwell, Nathan, Jr. IV, 437
Sidwell, O. W. IV, 275
Sidwell, Oliver IV, 274
Sidwell, Oliver IV, 275
Sidwell, Oliver F. IV, 819
Sidwell, Oliver F. IV, 843
Sidwell, Oliver T. IV, 843
Sidwell, Oliver W. IV, 275
Sidwell, Phebe IV, 108
Sidwell, Phebe IV, 330
Sidwell, Phebe IV, 351
Sidwell, Phebe IV, 497
Sidwell, Plummer IV, 351
Sidwell, Plummer IV, 497
Sidwell, Rachel II, 721
Sidwell, Rachel IV, 274
Sidwell, Rachel IV, 275
Sidwell, Rachel IV, 513
Sidwell, Rachel IV, 549
Sidwell, Rachel IV, 800
Sidwell, Rachel IV, 804
Sidwell, Rachel IV, 950
Sidwell, Rachel B. IV, 183
Sidwell, Rachel B. IV, 202
Sidwell, Rachel B. IV, 275
Sidwell, Rachel B. IV, 299
Sidwell, Rachel R. IV, 176
Sidwell, Rachel R. IV, 213
Sidwell, Rebecca IV, 159
Sidwell, Rebecca IV, 275
Sidwell, Rebecca IV, 303
Sidwell, Rebecca IV, 657
Sidwell, Rebecca IV, 1066
Sidwell, Rebecca IV, 1076
Sidwell, Rebecca VI, 444
Sidwell, Rebecca VI, 450
Sidwell, Rebecca VI, 543
Sidwell, Rebecca VI, 561
Sidwell, Rebecca Jane VI, 444
Sidwell, Rebekah VI, 561
Sidwell, Rees IV, 108
Sidwell, Richard I, 343
Sidwell, Richard I, 350
Sidwell, Richard I, 418
Sidwell, Richard I, 528
Sidwell, Richard I, 570
Sidwell, Richard I, 571
Sidwell, Richard VI, 395
Sidwell, Richard VI, 416
Sidwell, Richard VI, 444
Sidwell, Richard VI, 501
Sidwell, Richard VI, 560
Sidwell, Richard H. VI, 782
Sidwell, Richard Hartsone VI, 782
Sidwell, Richard Rebecca VI, 560
Sidwell, Richard, Sr. VI, 444
Sidwell, Robert E. IV, 351
Sidwell, Robert Miller VI, 782
Sidwell, Robinson VI, 782
Sidwell, Ruth I, 536
Sidwell, Ruth I, 571
Sidwell, Ruth I, 1050
Sidwell, Samuel VI, 395
Sidwell, Samuel VI, 450
Sidwell, Sarah IV, 108
Sidwell, Sarah IV, 113
Sidwell, Sarah IV, 159
Sidwell, Sarah IV, 161
Sidwell, Sarah IV, 265
Sidwell, Sarah IV, 274
Sidwell, Sarah IV, 275
Sidwell, Sarah IV, 330
Sidwell, Sarah IV, 491
Sidwell, Sarah IV, 497
Sidwell, Sarah IV, 650
Sidwell, Sarah VI, 395
Sidwell, Sarah VI, 444
Sidwell, Sarah VI, 450
Sidwell, Sarah VI, 543
Sidwell, Sarah E. VI, 782
Sidwell, Sarah, Jr. VI, 561
Sidwell, Sina IV, 275
Sidwell, Sina IV, 351
Sidwell, Sina IV, 497
Sidwell, Sina IV, 746
Sidwell, Sina IV, 762
Sidwell, Sina IV, 804
Sidwell, Sina H. IV, 183
Sidwell, Sina H. IV, 274
Sidwell, Sina H. IV, 275
Sidwell, Sina W. IV, 497
Sidwell, Sina W. IV, 650
Sidwell, Sina W. IV, 657
Sidwell, Sinah IV, 220
Sidwell, Sinah IV, 260
Sidwell, Sinah IV, 265
Sidwell, Sinah IV, 274
Sidwell, Sinah IV, 497
Sidwell, Tamasin VI, 560
Sidwell, Thamasin VI, 396
Sidwell, Thamasin VI, 444
Sidwell, Thamasin VI, 544
Sidwell, Thamasin VI, 576
Sidwell, Thamsin VI, 560
Sidwell, Thomas IV, 159
Sidwell, Thomas IV, 202
Sidwell, Thomas IV, 275
Sidwell, Thomas IV, 351
Sidwell, Thomas IV, 437
Sidwell, Thomas IV, 525
Sidwell, Thomas IV, 549
Sidwell, Thomas VI, 561
Sidwell, Thomas W. VI, 727
Sidwell, Thomas W. VI, 728
Sidwell, Thomas W. VI, 778
Sidwell, Thomas W. VI, 782
Sidwell, Thomas W. VI, 792
Sidwell, Thomasin VI, 368
Sidwell, Thomasin VI, 429
Sidwell, Thomasin VI, 454
Sidwell, Thomasin VI, 501
Sidwell, Thomazin VI, 368
Sidwell, Walter N. IV, 275
Sidwell, William I, 418
Sidwell, William I, 1131
Sidwell, William VI, 543
Sidwell, William VI, 561
Sidwell, William H. Oliphant IV, 762
Sidwell, William T. IV, 549
Sidwell, Wilson IV, 549
Sidwell, Wilson T. IV, 202
Sidwell, Wilson T. IV, 274
Sidwell, Wilson T. IV, 275
Sidwell, Wilson T. IV, 843
Siemon, Catharine IV, 1338
Siemon, Dr. Lester IV, 1338
Siemon, Lester IV, 1338
Siferd, Rebecca IV, 676
Sifton, Caroline III, 289
Sifton, John III, 289
Sights, Rebecca VI, 1022
Sigman, Abram III, 289
Sigman, Abram III, 299
Sigman, Ida G. III, 289
Sigman, Ida G. III, 299
Sigman, Susan III, 289
Sigman, Susan III, 299
Signey, Mary II, 538
Signy, Mary II, 652
Sikes, Benj. II, 186
Sikes, Ellinor II, 617
Sikes, George I, 1076
Sikes, Hannah II, 186
Sikes, Isabella I, 1076
Sikes, John VI, 36
Sikes, John VI, 48
Sikes, Mary II, 79
Sikes, Mary II, 97
Sikes, Mary II, 976
Sikes, Mary II, 1031
Sikes, Nathaniel II, 617
Sikes, Nathaniel II, 663
Sikes, Rachel I, 1076
Sikes, Rebecca II, 186
Sikes, Thomas I, 1076
Sikes, Thomas VI, 34
Sikes, Thomas VI, 36
Sikes, Thos. VI, 36
Silar, Adam I, 364
Silar, Adam I, 418
Silar, Adam I, 419
Silar, Jeremiah Hadley I, 364
Silar, Mary I, 364
Silar, Philip I, 364
Silar, Sarah I, 419
Silber, Elsa II, 1060
Silcot, Jane VI, 700
Silcot, Jesse VI, 700
Siler, Adam I, 418
Siler, Adam I, 419
Siler, Catharine V, 771
Siler, Elma I, 676
Siler, Elma I, 689
Siler, Hadly I, 418
Siler, Hannah E. I, 689
Siler, Hannah E. I, 691
Siler, Jeremiah I, 418
Siler, Jeremiah H. I, 418
Siler, Margaret I, 689
Siler, Mary I, 418
Siler, Mrs. Lou V, 1019
Siler, Philip I, 418
Siler, Sarah I, 391
Siler, Sarah I, 418
Siler, Sarah I, 419
Silgrave, William I, 73
Silgraves, William I, 275
Silgreave, Mary II, 652
Silioch, Amos VI, 853
Silioch, Sary VI, 853
Silkgrave, William I, 275
Sill, Abigail II, 922
Sill, Abigail II, 941
Sill, Alfred II, 820
Sill, Alfred II, 843
Sill, Alfred II, 922
Sill, Alice II, 922
Sill, Alice II, 941
Sill, Ann II, 820
Sill, Ann Thompson II, 789
Sill, Clarence II, 843
Sill, Clarence II, 922
Sill, Edwin Middleton II, 922
Sill, Enos I, 733
Sill, Florence Middleton II, 922
Sill, Henry III, 289
Sill, Jane II, 820
Sill, Jonathan I, 418
Sill, Joseph II, 820
Sill, Mary II, 843
Sill, May II, 922
Sill, Naomi II, 843
Sill, Naomi P. II, 922
Sill, Naomi Passmore II, 820
Sill, Naomi Passmore II, 922
Sill, Thos. II, 922
Sill, Thos. II, 941
Sill, Wesley II, 922
Sill, Wesley II, 941
Sillavin, Hannah I, 826
Sillavin, Hannah I, 840
Silleck, Nathaniel III, 499
Sillick, Jennie V, 709
Silliers, Thomas II, 420
Sillman, Mary Ellen I, 949
Sills, Emma IV, 275
Sills, James IV, 275
Silor, Frank III, 256
Silor, Frank III, 289
Silor, Helen B. III, 289
Silor, Helen Buckley III, 256
Silver, Aaron II, 97
Silver, Abel II, 39
Silver, Abel II, 88
Silver, Abel II, 98
Silver, Abigail Ann V, 885
Silver, Abigail Ann V, 886
Silver, Abraham II, 98
Silver, Adna IV, 762
Silver, Adna IV, 994
Silver, Adna B. IV, 762
Silver, Adnah B. IV, 762
Silver, Adney B. IV, 762
Silver, Allen IV, 762
Silver, Amey II, 56
Silver, Amey II, 98
Silver, Ann II, 97
Silver, Ann V, 63
Silver, Ann V, 83
Silver, Ann V, 84
Silver, Ann V, 121
Silver, Ann V, 861
Silver, Ann V, 886
Silver, Ann J. V, 886
Silver, Anna II, 39
Silver, Anna II, 98
Silver, Anna V, 63
Silver, Anna V, 121
Silver, Archabel II, 260
Silver, Archibald II, 39
Silver, Archibald II, 88
Silver, Archibald II, 98
Silver, Archibald II, 183
Silver, Archibald II, 235
Silver, Archibald II, 260
Silver, Archible II, 97
Silver, Elizabeth IV, 762
Silver, Esther II, 98
Silver, Eunice II, 98
Silver, Eunice II, 102
Silver, Hannah II, 98
Silver, Hester II, 51
Silver, Hester II, 98
Silver, Hope II, 39
Silver, Hope II, 88
Silver, Hope II, 98
Silver, Horatio V, 976
Silver, Horatio D. V, 976
Silver, James II, 39
Silver, Jane II, 78
Silver, Jane II, 97
Silver, Jessie I, 622
Silver, Joseph IV, 762
Silver, Joseph V, 976
Silver, Joseph E. V, 885
Silver, Joseph E. V, 886
Silver, Joseph E. V, 888
Silver, Joseph E. V, 976
Silver, Joshua J. V, 886
Silver, Leatitia II, 39
Silver, Letitia V, 121
Silver, Lettitia II, 98
Silver, Lettitia V, 93
Silver, Lettitia V, 121
Silver, Lydia II, 214
Silver, Lydia II, 260
Silver, Lydia IV, 762
Silver, Lydia IV, 994
Silver, Lydia A. IV, 762
Silver, Martha Ann V, 880
Silver, Martha Ann V, 886
Silver, Martha Ann V, 976
Silver, Mary II, 32
Silver, Mary II, 39
Silver, Mary II, 68
Silver, Mary II, 88
Silver, Mary II, 90
Silver, Mary II, 91
Silver, Mary II, 97
Silver, Mary II, 98
Silver, Mary II, 260
Silver, Mary IV, 762
Silver, Mary V, 63
Silver, Mary V, 93
Silver, Mary Ann II, 39
Silver, Patience V, 121
Silver, Patience V, 979
Silver, Phebe V, 830
Silver, Phebe V, 861
Silver, Phebe V, 886
Silver, Phebe V, 968
Silver, Phebe V, 976
Silver, Phebe E. V, 880

r, Rachel II, 97
r, Rachel II, 106
r, Rebecca II, 98
r, Rebecca II, 113
r, Rebecca V, 886
r, Rebecca V, 976
r, Rebecca Ann V, 886
r, Rebeckah II, 39
r, Rebeckah II, 65
r, Rebeckah II, 91
r, Rebeckah II, 98
er, Rebekah V, 121
er, Rhoda II, 98
er, Robert V, 886
er, Ruth II, 98
er, Ruth II, 235
er, Ruth II, 260
er, Samuel II, 91
er, Samuel II, 98
er, Samuel II, 113
er, Samuel V, 121
er, Samuel V, 886
er, Samuel V, 976
er, Sarah II, 97
er, Sarah II, 98
er, Sarah IV, 762
er, Sarah IV, 947
er, Sarah IV, 994
er, Sarah A. IV, 762
er, Sarah Ann V, 886
er, Sarah Ann V, 888
er, Seth II, 39
er, Seth II, 90
er, Seth II, 98
er, Seth V, 93
er, Seth V, 121
ver, Silvia II, 62
ver, Silviah II, 39
ver, Susannah II, 39
ver, Susannah II, 98
ver, Tamson V, 121
ver, Tamson V, 886
ver, Thamason V, 886
ver, Thomas II, 123
ver, William II, 39
ver, William V, 121
ver, William B. V, 83
ver, William B. V, 121
ver, William B. V, 886
ver, Wm. II, 68
ver, Wm. II, 91
ver, Wm. II, 97
ver, Wm. II, 98
ver, Wm. V, 886
ver, Wm. V, 976
ver, Wm. B. V, 886
ver, Wm. B. V, 976
vers, Ann V, 845
lvers, Ann V, 861
lvers, Joseph V, 861
lvers, Kitty VI, 993
lvers, Levi VI, 993
lvers, Mary II, 97
lvers, Mary II, 98
lvers, Rebecca II, 98
lvers, Rebeckah II, 98
lvers, Rhoda II, 67
lvers, Rhoda II, 98
lvers, Samuel V, 121
lvers, Sarah II, 975
lvers, Sarah II, 1026
lvers, Sarah IV, 698
lvers, Sarah IV, 762
lvers, Sarah Ann V, 861
lvers, Sarah Ann V, 874
ilvers, Silvia II, 98
ilvers, Susannah II, 74
ilvers, Susannah II, 98
ilvers, Tamson V, 121
ilverthorn, Abraham IV, 58
ilverthorn, Albert IV, 1338
ilverthorn, Elizabeth IV, 46
ilverthorn, Elizabeth IV, 58
ilverthorn, Isaac IV, 58
ilverthorn, James IV, 58
ilverthorn, James IV, 109
ilverthorn, Jane IV, 58
Silverthorn, Thomas IV, 58
Silverthorn, Thomas IV, 109
Silverthorn, William IV, 58
Silvester, Mary II, 420
Silvin, Adnah B. IV, 762
Silvin, Lydia IV, 762
Silvis, Ella W. II, 813
Silvis, Ella W. II, 907
Silvis, Ella W. II, 922
Sim, Andrew II, 420
Sim, Andrew II, 652
Sim, Elizabeth II, 420
Sim, Jane J. IV, 738
Sim, Jane J. IV, 762
Sim, John II, 420
Sim, Mary II, 652
Sim, Mary II, 659
Simbro, Lettie V, 464
Simbro, Zelphia Ann V, 464
Simbro, Zerelda V, 464
Simbro, Zerilda V, 464
Simbro, Zillpha Ann V, 464
Simcock, Aaron I, 968
Simcock, Ann I, 968
Simcock, Ann II, 1026
Simcock, Anne II, 1026
Simcock, Beulah I, 968
Simcock, Catherine V, 595
Simcock, Catherine V, 597
Simcock, Elizabeth II, 822
Simcock, Elizabeth II, 1026
Simcock, Ezekiel Atkinson II, 1026
Simcock, George II, 447
Simcock, Hannah V, 576
Simcock, Hannah V, 597
Simcock, Hope I, 968
Simcock, Jacob II, 652
Simcock, Jacob II, 675
Simcock, James I, 968
Simcock, James V, 931
Simcock, James V, 932
Simcock, Jane I, 968
Simcock, Job V, 576
Simcock, Job V, 595
Simcock, Job V, 597
Simcock, John I, 968
Simcock, John II, 652
Simcock, John II, 675
Simcock, John II, 1026
Simcock, John, Jr. I, 968
Simcock, Joseph II, 1026
Simcock, Mary I, 1011
Simcock, Mary I, 1012
Simcock, Mary II, 652
Simcock, Mary II, 974
Simcock, Mary II, 975
Simcock, Mary II, 1026
Simcock, Mathias II, 1026
Simcock, Matthias II, 1026
Simcock, Sarah II, 652
Simcock, Sarah II, 675
Simcock, Sarah II, 1013
Simcock, Sarah II, 1018
Simcock, Sarah II, 1026
Simcock, William II, 447
Simcok, Ann II, 1026
Simcok, Anne II, 1026
Simcok, Elizabeth II, 1026
Simcok, John II, 991
Simcok, Mary II, 991
Simcok, Mary II, 1026
Simcok, Mathias II, 1026
Simcok, Matthias II, 1026
Simcok, Sarah II, 1026
Simcon, Thomas I, 165
Simcox, Alma Lora V, 431
Simcox, Alvah H. V, 431
Simcox, Annie M. V, 431
Simcox, Betsy V, 430
Simcox, Betsy Jane V, 437
Simcox, Catherine V, 403
Simcox, Catherine V, 430
Simcox, Catherine Elma V, 431
Simcox, Clara Emma V, 430
Simcox, Clara Emma V, 431
Simcox, Elma V, 430
Simcox, Eva V, 431
Simcox, Francis T. V, 430
Simcox, Francis Thomas V, 431
Simcox, Hannah V, 383
Simcox, Hannah V, 430
Simcox, Hannah V, 431
Simcox, Hannah V, 437
Simcox, Harley V, 431
Simcox, Irena V, 386
Simcox, Irena V, 430
Simcox, James V, 932
Simcox, Job V, 383
Simcox, Job V, 403
Simcox, Job V, 430
Simcox, Job V, 431
Simcox, Job V, 437
Simcox, Jobe V, 431
Simcox, John II, 510
Simcox, John II, 663
Simcox, John V, 386
Simcox, John V, 430
Simcox, John V, 431
Simcox, John Henry V, 431
Simcox, Lindley V, 430
Simcox, Lisbon V, 430
Simcox, Louisa V, 431
Simcox, Lydia V, 430
Simcox, Lydia V, 431
Simcox, Lydia Jane V, 431
Simcox, Martha V, 403
Simcox, Martha V, 430
Simcox, Martha V, 431
Simcox, Mary V, 430
Simcox, Milton H. V, 430
Simcox, Milton N. V, 431
Simcox, Sarah V, 431
Simcox, Sarah A. V, 388
Simcox, Sarah A. V, 430
Simcox, Sarah Elizabeth V, 397
Simcox, Sarah Elizabeth V, 431
Simcox, Stover V, 388
Simcox, Stover V, 430
Simcox, Stover V, 431
Simcox, Susanna V, 430
Simcox, Susannah V, 383
Simcox, Susannah V, 431
Simcox, Thomas V, 430
Simcox, Thomas V, 431
Simcox, Thos. V, 397
Simcox, William Owsley V, 430
Simens, Elizabeth II, 98
Simeon, Lester IV, 1338
Simers, Alfred V, 277
Simes, Agness VI, 993
Simes, Jane V, 464
Simes, Joshua VI, 993
Simison, Edward V, 202
Simison, Helen V, 202
Simkin, Margaret L. III, 289
Simkin, Margaret T. III, 289
Simkin, Robert L. III, 289
Simkins, Elizabeth II, 805
Simmerly, Carlie I, 1161
Simmerly, Minnie I, 1161
Simmes, Hannah Jane V, 431
Simmonds, Ann VI, 365
Simmonds, Ann VI, 444
Simmonds, Ann VI, 447
Simmonds, Elias VI, 447
Simmonds, Elisabeth II, 652
Simmonds, Hannah II, 638
Simmonds, Hannah II, 652
Simmonds, James D. VI, 447
Simmonds, Powel VI, 447
Simmonds, Rebecca VI, 447
Simmonds, Ruth VI, 447
Simmonds, Samuel VI, 447
Simmonds, William Powell VI, 447
Simmons, ??? III, 325
Simmons, ??? VI, 95
Simmons, ??? VI, 177
Simmons, Abigail I, 571
Simmons, Abigail I, 574
Simmons, Abigail V, 121
Simmons, Abigail V, 202
Simmons, Agathy VI, 980
Simmons, Alexander VI, 993
Simmons, Alfred R. V, 277
Simmons, Alfred Rees V, 277
Simmons, Alice V, 431
Simmons, Amelia III, 289
Simmons, Amelia III, 325
Simmons, Amelia IV, 275
Simmons, Amour I, 968
Simmons, Anderson VI, 100
Simmons, Anderson VI, 102
Simmons, Anderson VI, 114
Simmons, Anderson VI, 121
Simmons, Anderson VI, 212
Simmons, Ann II, 652
Simmons, Ann II, 826
Simmons, Ann II, 922
Simmons, Ann VI, 110
Simmons, Ann VI, 177
Simmons, Ann VI, 212
Simmons, Ann VI, 435
Simmons, Anna V, 664
Simmons, Anna V, 709
Simmons, Anna VI, 993
Simmons, Anne VI, 111
Simmons, Anne VI, 121
Simmons, Anne VI, 177
Simmons, Anne VI, 211
Simmons, Annie L. V, 709
Simmons, Barsheba VI, 897
Simmons, Barsheba VI, 993
Simmons, Bell V, 431
Simmons, Catharine II, 828
Simmons, Catherine Hill II, 809
Simmons, Charles I, 552
Simmons, Charles I, 571
Simmons, Charles I, 968
Simmons, Charles V, 359
Simmons, Charles VI, 933
Simmons, Christina I, 902
Simmons, David VI, 748
Simmons, David VI, 778
Simmons, David VI, 993
Simmons, Deborah VI, 121
Simmons, Deborah VI, 138
Simmons, Deborah VI, 141
Simmons, Delmar L. IV, 1338
Simmons, Delmer IV, 1338
Simmons, Don V, 709
Simmons, Don W. V, 709
Simmons, Don, Jr. V, 709
Simmons, Dorothea M. VI, 778
Simmons, Dorothea Murray VI, 748
Simmons, Dr. Bert G. III, 150
Simmons, Dr. Bert G. III, 289
Simmons, Dr. Bert G. III, 310
Simmons, Edward II, 627
Simmons, Edward II, 766
Simmons, Edward II, 826
Simmons, Edward II, 915
Simmons, Edward II, 922
Simmons, Edward IV, 1146
Simmons, Edward S. II, 766
Simmons, Edward W. II, 766
Simmons, Edward, Jr. II, 627
Simmons, Edward, Jr. II, 652
Simmons, Eleanor V, 247
Simmons, Elias VI, 447
Simmons, Elisabeth II, 652
Simmons, Elizabeth I, 552
Simmons, Elizabeth I, 571
Simmons, Elizabeth I, 1131
Simmons, Elizabeth II, 538
Simmons, Elizabeth II, 627
Simmons, Elizabeth II, 652
Simmons, Elizabeth II, 801
Simmons, Elizabeth II, 826
Simmons, Elizabeth II, 1027
Simmons, Elizabeth II, 1041
Simmons, Elizabeth III, 310
Simmons, Elizabeth VI, 100
Simmons, Elizabeth VI, 121
Simmons, Elizabeth VI, 177
Simmons, Elizabeth VI, 202
Simmons, Elizabeth VI, 211
Simmons, Elizabeth VI, 212
Simmons, Elizabeth VI, 959
Simmons, Elizabeth VI, 980
Simmons, Elma V, 398
Simmons, Elma V, 431
Simmons, Emma Aldridge V, 644
Simmons, Ephraim IV, 1184
Simmons, Epsey VI, 993
Simmons, Estella V, 709
Simmons, Ethel Ruble V, 709
Simmons, Ether V, 709
Simmons, Eva V, 431
Simmons, Eva M. V, 431
Simmons, Evalina V, 121
Simmons, Evaline V, 121
Simmons, Evelina II, 1026
Simmons, Evelina II, 1027
Simmons, Evelina V, 861
Simmons, Everline II, 1026
Simmons, Everline V, 861
Simmons, Everline V, 886
Simmons, Frances VI, 993
Simmons, Frank IV, 783
Simmons, George VI, 933
Simmons, George VI, 940
Simmons, Gladys V, 431
Simmons, Grace L. IV, 1338
Simmons, Grace Lillian IV, 1338
Simmons, Gulielma V, 277
Simmons, Gulielma V, 398
Simmons, Gulielma V, 431
Simmons, Hannah I, 571
Simmons, Hannah II, 652
Simmons, Henry II, 1026
Simmons, Huldah IV, 392
Simmons, Huldah VI, 15
Simmons, Huldah VI, 99
Simmons, Huldah VI, 114
Simmons, Huldah VI, 120
Simmons, Huldah VI, 121
Simmons, Huldah, Jr. VI, 121
Simmons, Huldah, Sr. VI, 121
Simmons, J. W. V, 709
Simmons, Jacob V, 277
Simmons, Jacob V, 398
Simmons, Jacob V, 431
Simmons, Jacob V, 644
Simmons, James D. VI, 447
Simmons, James K. V, 709
Simmons, Jane V, 277
Simmons, Jane E. V, 277
Simmons, Jane Ellen V, 277
Simmons, Jehu I, 968
Simmons, Jesse I, 571
Simmons, Jno VI, 36
Simmons, Joel VI, 993
Simmons, John II, 652
Simmons, John II, 922
Simmons, John V, 277
Simmons, John V, 398
Simmons, John V, 431
Simmons, John V, 464
Simmons, John V, 644
Simmons, John VI, 36
Simmons, John VI, 121
Simmons, John VI, 149
Simmons, John VI, 172
Simmons, John VI, 202
Simmons, John VI, 211
Simmons, John VI, 212
Simmons, John C. V, 359
Simmons, John G. II, 820
Simmons, John G. II, 922
Simmons, John R. VI, 852
Simmons, John R. VI, 853
Simmons, Joseph II, 826
Simmons, Joseph V, 431
Simmons, Joseph VI, 121
Simmons, Joseph VI, 159
Simmons, Joseph VI, 211
Simmons, Joseph VI, 212
Simmons, Joseph C. V, 431
Simmons, Josephine II, 817
Simmons, Josephine V, 431
Simmons, Joshua VI, 561
Simmons, Josiah W. V, 277
Simmons, Josiah Westly V, 277
Simmons, Katharine IV, 1146
Simmons, Leonard G. IV, 275
Simmons, Lottie M. V, 709
Simmons, Louie V, 121
Simmons, Lucy Ann VI, 853
Simmons, Lydia I, 593
Simmons, Lydia I, 596
Simmons, Lydia V, 277
Simmons, Margaret II, 816
Simmons, Margaret II, 922
Simmons, Margaret III, 310
Simmons, Margaret C. II, 627
Simmons, Margaret C. II, 652
Simmons, Margaret C. II, 915
Simmons, Margaret Jane IV, 783
Simmons, Margaret S. III, 150
Simmons, Margaret S. III, 289
Simmons, Margaret S. III, 310
Simmons, Margaret W. II, 323
Simmons, Margarett W. II, 324
Simmons, Marlie V, 709
Simmons, Marlie C. V, 709
Simmons, Martha VI, 121
Simmons, Martha VI, 933
Simmons, Mary I, 958
Simmons, Mary I, 1131
Simmons, Mary II, 420
Simmons, Mary II, 1017
Simmons, Mary II, 1026
Simmons, Mary II, 1027
Simmons, Mary II, 1038
Simmons, Mary V, 257
Simmons, Mary V, 277
Simmons, Mary VI, 121
Simmons, Mary VI, 124
Simmons, Mary VI, 202
Simmons, Mary VI, 211
Simmons, Mary E. V, 277
Simmons, Mary E. VI, 853
Simmons, Mary I. II, 922
Simmons, Mary T. V, 277
Simmons, Matilda V, 248
Simmons, Matilda V, 277
Simmons, Mellie IV, 1338
Simmons, Minnie V, 702
Simmons, Minnie V, 709
Simmons, Minnie L. V, 709
Simmons, Mordecai II, 809
Simmons, Nathan I, 968
Simmons, Nellie D. V, 709
Simmons, Oney VI, 993
Simmons, Pamelia III, 325
Simmons, Paul VI, 120
Simmons, Pearl V, 431
Simmons, Peter I, 571
Simmons, Peter I, 958
Simmons, Peter I, 1131
Simmons, Polly IV, 1146
Simmons, Polly IV, 1184
Simmons, Prince George VI, 121
Simmons, Rachel II, 1026
Simmons, Rachel II, 1027
Simmons, Rachel V, 79
Simmons, Rachel V, 121
Simmons, Rebecca I, 1132
Simmons, Rebecca II, 1026
Simmons, Rebecca II, 1027
Simmons, Rebecca V, 27
Simmons, Rebecca V, 121
Simmons, Rebecca V, 247
Simmons, Rebecca V, 277
Simmons, Rebecca V, 398

Simmons, Rebecca V, 431
Simmons, Rebecca V, 861
Simmons, Rebecca VI, 447
Simmons, Rebecca Ann V, 277
Simmons, Rebecca Hockett V, 431
Simmons, Rebeckah II, 1026
Simmons, Rebekah I, 1131
Simmons, Robert VI, 959
Simmons, Robert VI, 980
Simmons, Royal I, 953
Simmons, Royal I, 968
Simmons, Royal I, 1131
Simmons, Royal, Jr. I, 1131
Simmons, Rueben VI, 993
Simmons, Ruth I, 545
Simmons, Ruth I, 571
Simmons, Ruth I, 958
Simmons, Ruth I, 1131
Simmons, Ruth VI, 435
Simmons, Ruth VI, 447
Simmons, Ryal I, 545
Simmons, Ryal I, 571
Simmons, Ryals I, 958
Simmons, Samuel I, 968
Simmons, Samuel V, 277
Simmons, Samuel VI, 435
Simmons, Samuel P. V, 277
Simmons, Samuel Powel V, 277
Simmons, Samuel R. II, 766
Simmons, Sarah I, 571
Simmons, Sarah I, 958
Simmons, Sarah I, 1131
Simmons, Sarah II, 1026
Simmons, Sarah V, 860
Simmons, Sarah V, 861
Simmons, Sarah VI, 202
Simmons, Sarah VI, 211
Simmons, Sarah VI, 212
Simmons, Sarah C. II, 766
Simmons, Sarah Mildred V, 277
Simmons, Sarah S. V, 861
Simmons, Sarah S. V, 886
Simmons, Seraphina V, 431
Simmons, Solomon I, 1131
Simmons, Stella A. V, 709
Simmons, Stephen II, 420
Simmons, Stephen II, 538
Simmons, Stephen II, 652
Simmons, Stephen II, 816
Simmons, Stephen VI, 896
Simmons, Surry I, 571
Simmons, Susanna I, 958
Simmons, Susanna I, 1123
Simmons, Susanna I, 1131
Simmons, Susanna I, 1132
Simmons, Susannah I, 1131
Simmons, Sylvester V, 277
Simmons, Tabitha VI, 102
Simmons, Tabitha VI, 121
Simmons, Tabythia VI, 121
Simmons, Thomas I, 571
Simmons, Thomas II, 1026
Simmons, Thomas V, 121
Simmons, Thomas V, 247
Simmons, Thomas V, 861
Simmons, Thomas VI, 162
Simmons, Thomas VI, 177
Simmons, Thomas VI, 211
Simmons, Thomas P. II, 1027
Simmons, Thomas P. V, 121
Simmons, Thomas P. V, 860
Simmons, Thomas P. V, 861
Simmons, Thomas P. V, 886
Simmons, Thomas W. V, 277
Simmons, Thomas William V, 277
Simmons, Turner W. V, 431
Simmons, Wd. Anne VI, 162
Simmons, Wd. Miriam II, 809
Simmons, William I, 958
Simmons, William I, 1131
Simmons, William II, 324
Simmons, William VI, 121
Simmons, William VI, 211
Simmons, William VI, 993
Simmons, William H. IV, 275
Simmons, William P. VI, 853
Simmons, Wilmuth E. V, 277
Simmons, Wm. II, 766
Simmons, Wm. III, 310
Simms, Alice V, 202
Simms, Charles C. V, 202
Simms, Chas. Cliff V, 202
Simms, Elizabeth II, 591
Simms, Elizabeth II, 620
Simms, Elizabeth II, 652
Simms, Frances M. V, 202
Simms, Francis M. V, 202
Simms, G. Val V, 202
Simms, George V. V, 202
Simms, Hannah J. V, 431
Simms, Hannah Jane V, 431
Simms, Helen U. V, 528
Simms, Jane IV, 657
Simms, John II, 420
Simms, Joseph C. V, 202
Simms, Joseph E. V, 202
Simms, Judith VI, 993
Simms, Lawrence V, 202
Simms, Margrett II, 420
Simms, Minnie V, 202
Simms, Nancy Ellen V, 528
Simms, Penelliphy I, 304
Simms, Pennelliphy I, 318
Simms, Rose V, 528
Simms, Rose B. V, 528
Simms, Sally VI, 1016
Simms, Sarah IV, 109
Simms, Sarah IV, 114
Simms, Sarah VI, 1016
Simms, Sarah L. V, 528
Simms, William VI, 993
Simms, William VI, 1016
Simms, William B. V, 202
Simms, William J. V, 528
Simms, Willie B. V, 202
Simms, Wm. B. V, 202
Simock, Hannah V, 597
Simock, John Stover V, 597
Simock, Lydia V, 597
Simock, Martha Jane V, 597
Simock, Susanna V, 597
Simock, Thomas V, 597
Simon, Abraham, Jr. I, 168
Simon, Margaret I, 168
Simon, Mary I, 168
Simon, Mathew I, 168
Simon, Rachel VI, 444
Simon, Thomas I, 168
Simonds, Louie V, 121
Simone, Catharine III, 94
Simone, Catharine III, 289
Simone, Catharine III, 290
Simone, Edw. P. III, 94
Simone, Edw. P. III, 289
Simone, Katherine II, 447
Simone, Margaret III, 94
Simone, Margaret III, 289
Simons, ??? I, 118
Simons, Abigail I, 769
Simons, Abigail I, 772
Simons, Abner Bane VI, 444
Simons, Abraham I, 119
Simons, Ann I, 119
Simons, Ann I, 734
Simons, Ann VI, 162
Simons, Ann VI, 444
Simons, Barbary I, 119
Simons, Charles II, 421
Simons, Charles V, 359
Simons, Damaris I, 118
Simons, Damaris I, 119
Simons, Debborah I, 118
Simons, Deborah I, 134
Simons, Deborah I, 166
Simons, Deborah III, 290
Simons, Deborah III, 354
Simons, Eleanor V, 582
Simons, Eleanor V, 597
Simons, Eliz. III, 290
Simons, Elizabeth I, 119
Simons, Elizabeth I, 769
Simons, Elizabeth III, 354
Simons, Evaline V, 121
Simons, Frances I, 119
Simons, Francis I, 118
Simons, Francis I, 119
Simons, Hannah I, 533
Simons, Hannah I, 571
Simons, Hannah II, 242
Simons, Hannah II, 260
Simons, Henley V, 597
Simons, Jacob I, 118
Simons, Jehosaphat I, 119
Simons, Jeramiah I, 118
Simons, Jno VI, 36
Simons, John I, 118
Simons, John I, 119
Simons, John I Sup 1, 4
Simons, John I Sup 1, 6
Simons, John II, 242
Simons, John II, 260
Simons, John II, 447
Simons, John VI, 212
Simons, Joseph I, 118
Simons, Joseph VI, 211
Simons, Joseph VI, 212
Simons, Joshua I, 119
Simons, Mary I, 119
Simons, Mary I, 1126
Simons, Mary I, 1131
Simons, Mary VI, 202
Simons, Mary VI, 211
Simons, Mathew I, 769
Simons, Matthew I, 457
Simons, Matthew I, 741
Simons, Matthew I, 769
Simons, Miaram I, 119
Simons, Peeter I, 118
Simons, Peeter I, 119
Simons, Priscilla I Sup 1, 4
Simons, Priscilla I Sup 1, 6
Simons, Rachel VI, 362
Simons, Rachel VI, 444
Simons, Rebecca I, 91
Simons, Rebecca V, 121
Simons, Rebeckah I, 118
Simons, Rebeckah I, 119
Simons, Rebekah I, 119
Simons, Ruben VI, 820
Simons, Samuel I, 119
Simons, Samuel IV, 1294
Simons, Samuel S. IV, 1294
Simons, Sarah I, 769
Simons, Sarah III, 290
Simons, Solomon III, 290
Simons, Solomon III, 354
Simons, Tamer I, 131
Simons, Tamer I, 166
Simons, Thamor I, 118
Simons, Thomas I, 110
Simons, Thomas I, 118
Simons, Thomas I, 119
Simons, Thomas I, 533
Simons, Thomas I, 571
Simons, Thomas I, 769
Simons, Thomas I, 772
Simons, Thomas P. V, 121
Simons, Widow Jane I, 110
Simonson, Amie B. III, 447
Simonson, Jacob S. IV, 794
Simonson, Jacob Severn IV, 794
Simonson, John R. III, 447
Simonson, John R. III, 449
Simonson, Julia III, 447
Simonson, Julia III, 449
Simonson, Knuedsine IV, 794
Simonson, Leah III, 446
Simonson, Mary Brown V, 885
Simonson, Mary Brown V, 886
Simonson, Mary F. III, 447
Simonson, Townsend W. III, 447
Simonton, William V, 431
Simpkins, Elizabeth IV, 875
Simpkins, Elizabeth IV, 883
Simpkins, Mary IV, 881
Simpkins, Mary IV, 883
Simpson, ??? III, 302
Simpson, Ada Price IV, 1338
Simpson, Ada Rice IV, 1338
Simpson, Agnes II, 279
Simpson, Agnes II, 301
Simpson, Agnes II, 1077
Simpson, Agnes II, 1080
Simpson, Amelia II, 922
Simpson, Amelia VI, 212
Simpson, Amelia VI, 218
Simpson, Amos Satterthwaite II, 1080
Simpson, Andrew V, 709
Simpson, Ann II, 67
Simpson, Ann II, 98
Simpson, Ann II, 922
Simpson, Ann II, 976
Simpson, Ann II, 1027
Simpson, Ann II, 1060
Simpson, Ann II, 1071
Simpson, Ann II, 1080
Simpson, Ann IV, 1049
Simpson, Ann IV, 1076
Simpson, Ann V, 764
Simpson, Anna II, 39
Simpson, Anna II, 1027
Simpson, Anna IV, 491
Simpson, Anna IV, 497
Simpson, Anna V, 121
Simpson, Anna V, 277
Simpson, Anna M. II, 1080
Simpson, Austen IV, 392
Simpson, Austen IV, 437
Simpson, Austin IV, 1076
Simpson, Austin IV, 1114
Simpson, Austin E. IV, 1114
Simpson, Barbary IV, 275
Simpson, Benjamin II, 39
Simpson, Benjamin II, 98
Simpson, Benjamin II, 1079
Simpson, Benjamin II, 1080
Simpson, Benjamin VI, 854
Simpson, Benjamin W. II, 1080
Simpson, Bridget II, 796
Simpson, Catherine VI, 839
Simpson, Charles II, 1046
Simpson, David II, 1079
Simpson, David II, 1080
Simpson, David B. V, 431
Simpson, David Butler V, 431
Simpson, David Palmer, Jr. II, 1080
Simpson, Delilah V, 664
Simpson, Derbyshire II, 301
Simpson, Edward V, 202
Simpson, Eleazar V, 202
Simpson, Elisha G. I, 3
Simpson, Elizabeth II, 796
Simpson, Elizabeth II, 1060
Simpson, Elizabeth II, 1069
Simpson, Elizabeth II, 1079
Simpson, Elizabeth II, 1080
Simpson, Elizabeth V, 202
Simpson, Elizabeth VI, 841
Simpson, Elizabeth VI, 854
Simpson, Elizabeth VI, 993
Simpson, Elizabeth B. II, 1079
Simpson, Elizabeth B. II, 1080
Simpson, Elsie VI, 816
Simpson, Emma Alderson II, 301
Simpson, Emma Alderson II, 304
Simpson, Emma T. II, 301
Simpson, Ethel VI, 701
Simpson, Ethel VI, 709
Simpson, Etta V, 709
Simpson, Fannie J. III, 302
Simpson, Fred IV, 1338
Simpson, Frederick II, 301
Simpson, Frederick II, 304
Simpson, George II, 279
Simpson, George II, 301
Simpson, George II, 304
Simpson, George L. III, 290
Simpson, George O. IV, 1184
Simpson, Grace II, 796
Simpson, Hannah II, 39
Simpson, Hannah II, 70
Simpson, Hannah II, 98
Simpson, Hannah II, 421
Simpson, Hannah II, 652
Simpson, Hannah II, 1027
Simpson, Hannah II, 1060
Simpson, Hannah II, 1080
Simpson, Hannah S. II, 1078
Simpson, Helen V, 202
Simpson, Henrietta III, 60
Simpson, Henrietta III, 290
Simpson, Henry V, 709
Simpson, James II, 39
Simpson, James II, 98
Simpson, James II, 421
Simpson, James II, 652
Simpson, James II, 976
Simpson, James II, 1024
Simpson, James II, 1027
Simpson, James II, 1060
Simpson, James II, 1069
Simpson, James II, 1071
Simpson, James II, 1076
Simpson, James II, 1077
Simpson, James II, 1080
Simpson, James IV, 765
Simpson, James, Jr. II, 98
Simpson, James, Jr. II, 1027
Simpson, Jane IV, 1073
Simpson, Jane IV, 1076
Simpson, Jane P. III, 290
Simpson, Jeptha E. IV, 1114
Simpson, John II, 39
Simpson, John II, 98
Simpson, John II, 976
Simpson, John II, 1024
Simpson, John II, 1025
Simpson, John II, 1027
Simpson, John II, 1060
Simpson, John II, 1071
Simpson, John II, 1079
Simpson, John II, 1080
Simpson, John IV, 437
Simpson, John IV, 1076
Simpson, John IV, 1114
Simpson, John V, 277
Simpson, John V, 764
Simpson, John VI, 841
Simpson, John VI, 993
Simpson, Joseph II, 39
Simpson, Joseph II, 98
Simpson, Joseph II, 279
Simpson, Joseph II, 301
Simpson, Joseph II, 652
Simpson, Joseph II, 1025
Simpson, Joseph H. II, 124
Simpson, Joseph Hartshorn II, 124
Simpson, Joseph Hartshorn II, 652
Simpson, Joseph Hartshorne II, 766
Simpson, Julia M. II, 902
Simpson, Julia M. II, 922
Simpson, Kesia II, 1080
Simpson, Kezia II, 1080
Simpson, Latilda I, 73
Simpson, Latitia II, 1046
Simpson, Latitia II, 1060
Simpson, Lenna S. V, 431
Simpson, Letitia II, 1079
Simpson, Letitia II, 1080
Simpson, Lillian VI, 633
Simpson, Lindley M. Thompson IV, 275
Simpson, Lucy IV, 765
Simpson, Lula May IV, 1184
Simpson, Lydia I, 73
Simpson, Mabel IV, 1263
Simpson, Mable IV, 1263
Simpson, Maria III, 290
Simpson, Martha I, 837
Simpson, Martha III, 290
Simpson, Martha III, 292
Simpson, Martha V, 431
Simpson, Martha A. V, 431
Simpson, Mary I, 73
Simpson, Mary I, 989
Simpson, Mary II, 98
Simpson, Mary II, 562
Simpson, Mary II, 652
Simpson, Mary II, 766
Simpson, Mary II, 820
Simpson, Mary II, 1027
Simpson, Mary II, 1060
Simpson, Mary II, 1066
Simpson, Mary IV, 1114
Simpson, Mary V, 1019
Simpson, Mary VI, 993
Simpson, Mary Alice V, 431
Simpson, Mary E. I, 39
Simpson, Mary E. I, 73
Simpson, Mary E. I, 989
Simpson, Mary E. I, 997
Simpson, Mary Eliza I, 3
Simpson, Mary Emily V, 378
Simpson, Mary Ingham II, 1027
Simpson, Mary J. II, 902
Simpson, Mary J. II, 922
Simpson, Mary P. IV, 1073
Simpson, Mary P. IV, 1076
Simpson, Mayfield II, 301
Simpson, Maysfield II, 301
Simpson, Minnie V, 861
Simpson, Oliver IV, 1114
Simpson, Pearl VI, 689
Simpson, Pearl VI, 701
Simpson, Rebecca II, 1079
Simpson, Rebecca II, 1080
Simpson, Rebecca IV, 275
Simpson, Rebecca IV, 293
Simpson, Rebecca IV, 1114
Simpson, Rebekah II, 88
Simpson, Rebekah II, 98
Simpson, Richard IV, 1076
Simpson, Richard IV, 1114
Simpson, Robert II, 820
Simpson, Robert II, 902
Simpson, Robert II, 922
Simpson, Robert III, 290
Simpson, Robert III, 292
Simpson, Ruth II, 976
Simpson, Ruth II, 1024
Simpson, Ruth II, 1027
Simpson, Ruth II, 1076
Simpson, Ruth II, 1080
Simpson, Sabilla IV, 1076
Simpson, Sabilla IV, 1114
Simpson, Sabilla F. IV, 437
Simpson, Sabilla F. IV, 1076
Simpson, Sallie III, 440
Simpson, Sally VI, 686
Simpson, Sally VI, 701
Simpson, Samuel II, 39
Simpson, Samuel II, 98
Simpson, Samuel II, 421
Simpson, Samuel II, 652
Simpson, Samuel M. VI, 830
Simpson, Sarah II, 279
Simpson, Sarah II, 301
Simpson, Sarah II, 304
Simpson, Sarah IV, 50
Simpson, Sarah IV, 437
Simpson, Sarah Ann II, 796
Simpson, Sarah E. III, 292
Simpson, Sarah Eliz. III, 290
Simpson, Sarah Eliz. III, 293
Simpson, Sarah Elizabeth III, 292
Simpson, Sibilah IV, 1076
Simpson, Sibilla IV, 392

son, Sibilla IV, 437
son, Simeon V, 431
son, Stacy II, 796
son, Susanna I, 989
son, Susanna II, 1060
son, Susanna II, 1069
son, Susanna II, 1071
son, Susanna II, 1076
son, Susanna II, 1077
son, Susanna II, 1080
son, Susanna G. V, 431
son, Susannah II, 1024
son, Susannah II, 1027
son, Susannah V, 400
son, Susannah V, 431
son, Tacie II, 1079
son, Tacie II, 1080
son, Tacy II, 1080
son, Thelma V, 709
son, Thomas II, 39
son, Thomas II, 98
son, W. R. IV, 1263
son, Wd. Alice II, 421
son, Wd. Alice II, 652
son, William II, 39
son, William VI, 993
son, William A. VI, 839
son, William E. V, 431
son, Wm. II, 98
son, Wm. II, 652
son, Wm. II, 796
son, Wm. II, 1080
son, Wm. F. IV, 1114
son, Wm. N. II, 902
son, Wm. N. II, 922
son, Yeamans II, 796
son, Zurellie V, 709
son, Zurilla V, 709
, Alice Underwood V, 121
Allie May VI, 86
Andrew II, 652
Ann II, 447
, Ann II, 652
, Anslam V, 441
Berlin VI, 86
Catharine IV, 1042
, Chas. Cliff V, 202
, Cleaveland VI, 86
, Conley VI, 86
Delilah V, 528
Eddie VI, 86
, Edward VI, 68
, Edward F. VI, 68
, Edward F. VI, 86
Edward W. VI, 854
Elizabeth II, 652
Elizabeth Irene VI, 86
Francis M. V, 202
G. Val V, 202
George VI, 993
George VI, 1016
George V. V, 202
Hannah J. V, 441
Hedgepeth VI, 86
Helen U. V, 528
James VI, 854
John II, 447
John II, 652
John R. VI, 86
Joseph V, 528
Joseph E. V, 202
Joseph E. V, 528
Judith VI, 993
Luckey VI, 854
Mable IV, 1263
Margaret II, 652
Margaret II, 827
Margaret C. VI, 854
Margaret S. VI, 848
Martha E. V, 528
Mary II, 652
Mary Fitzgerald V, 441
Massey I, 1050
Milley VI, 993
Minnie V, 202
Murphrey VI, 86
Nancy VI, 854
Nancy Ellen V, 528
Nannie VI, 86
Nathe W. VI, 854
Patsy VI, 854
Penelliphy I, 318
Rebecca Jane V, 528
Rose V, 528
Rose B. V, 528
Ruth Ellen V, 528
Sally VI, 1016
Samuel B. VI, 848
Sarah V, 121
Sarah L. V, 528
Serene VI, 848
Sims, Stephen V, 121
Sims, Thomas M. VI, 86
Sims, Victoria VI, 68
Sims, Victoria VI, 86
Sims, Virgie VI, 86
Sims, William V, 528
Sims, William VI, 854
Sims, William VI, 993
Sims, William B. VI, 797
Sims, William J. V, 528
Sims, Willie B. V, 202
Sims, Willis VI, 854
Sims, Wm. V, 441
Sims, Wm. V, 528
Sims, Wm. D. V, 528
Simson, Elizabeth V, 202
Simson, Ethel VI, 709
Simson, John VI, 993
Simson, Latilda I, 72
Simson, Lydia I, 47
Simson, Mary VI, 993
Simson, Thomas I, 165
Sinckler, Edward VI, 993
Sinckler, Joannah VI, 993
Sinclair, Abbina IV, 351
Sinclair, Abijah IV, 1185
Sinclair, Abraham V, 121
Sinclair, Abraham VI, 447
Sinclair, Albina IV, 351
Sinclair, Albina IV, 437
Sinclair, Albina IV, 1185
Sinclair, Albinah IV, 351
Sinclair, Alexander VI, 993
Sinclair, Alice VI, 701
Sinclair, Ann IV, 437
Sinclair, Ann IV, 534
Sinclair, Ann VI, 497
Sinclair, Ann VI, 561
Sinclair, Ann VI, 644
Sinclair, Ann VI, 701
Sinclair, Anna III, 87
Sinclair, Anna III, 290
Sinclair, Anna S. III, 290
Sinclair, Barton IV, 843
Sinclair, Betsey VI, 996
Sinclair, Cath. J. A. III, 290
Sinclair, Cinthia IV, 351
Sinclair, Cynthia IV, 345
Sinclair, Cynthia IV, 351
Sinclair, Cynthia IV, 544
Sinclair, David IV, 843
Sinclair, Eden IV, 351
Sinclair, Eden IV, 549
Sinclair, Edw. P. III, 290
Sinclair, Edward VI, 896
Sinclair, Edward VI, 993
Sinclair, Eliz. III, 260
Sinclair, Elizabeth II, 793
Sinclair, Elizabeth III, 87
Sinclair, Elizabeth III, 112
Sinclair, Elizabeth III, 123
Sinclair, Elizabeth III, 290
Sinclair, Elizabeth IV, 343
Sinclair, Elizabeth IV, 348
Sinclair, Elizabeth IV, 351
Sinclair, Elizabeth IV, 422
Sinclair, Elizabeth IV, 437
Sinclair, Elizabeth IV, 843
Sinclair, Elizabeth IV, 855
Sinclair, Elizabeth IV, 1185
Sinclair, Elizabeth V, 31
Sinclair, Elizabeth V, 121
Sinclair, Elizabeth VI, 561
Sinclair, Elizabeth VI, 992
Sinclair, Ellen VI, 706
Sinclair, Emerson V, 202
Sinclair, Emma III, 290
Sinclair, Esther VI, 639
Sinclair, Esther VI, 701
Sinclair, Esther VI, 767
Sinclair, Esther VI, 778
Sinclair, Frances VI, 993
Sinclair, Geo. IV, 348
Sinclair, Geo. V, 359
Sinclair, George IV, 326
Sinclair, George IV, 345
Sinclair, George IV, 351
Sinclair, George IV, 843
Sinclair, George VI, 355
Sinclair, George VI, 701
Sinclair, Hannah VI, 561
Sinclair, Harry Addison III, 290
Sinclair, Hudson IV, 843
Sinclair, Isaac VI, 932
Sinclair, Isaac VI, 992
Sinclair, Isaac VI, 993
Sinclair, Isaac P. V, 121
Sinclair, Isaac Proctor V, 121
Sinclair, Jacob IV, 843
Sinclair, Jacob Lindley V, 121
Sinclair, Jacob Lindley VI, 778
Sinclair, James IV, 159
Sinclair, James IV, 351
Sinclair, James VI, 497
Sinclair, James VI, 561
Sinclair, James VI, 643
Sinclair, James VI, 644
Sinclair, James VI, 701
Sinclair, James VI, 706
Sinclair, James B. IV, 437
Sinclair, James K., Jr. III, 290
Sinclair, James Kennedy III, 290
Sinclair, James, Jr. VI, 701
Sinclair, Jane IV, 326
Sinclair, Jane IV, 345
Sinclair, Joannah VI, 993
Sinclair, Job VI, 561
Sinclair, John II, 793
Sinclair, John III, 87
Sinclair, John III, 112
Sinclair, John III, 123
Sinclair, John III, 260
Sinclair, John III, 290
Sinclair, John V, 31
Sinclair, John V, 121
Sinclair, John VI, 561
Sinclair, John VI, 633
Sinclair, John VI, 701
Sinclair, John VI, 993
Sinclair, John F. III, 290
Sinclair, John M. V, 121
Sinclair, John Musgrove V, 121
Sinclair, John T. III, 290
Sinclair, John, Jr. V, 121
Sinclair, Jonas VI, 706
Sinclair, Joseph III, 290
Sinclair, Judah VI, 993
Sinclair, Katharine VI, 1022
Sinclair, Keziah V, 121
Sinclair, Keziah VI, 561
Sinclair, Ladonna V, 202
Sinclair, Ladonna L. V, 202
Sinclair, Levi IV, 843
Sinclair, Louella V, 202
Sinclair, Louise V, 202
Sinclair, Louise L. V, 202
Sinclair, Lowell V, 202
Sinclair, Lowell L. V, 202
Sinclair, Lucy IV, 843
Sinclair, Lucy VI, 993
Sinclair, Margaret III, 123
Sinclair, Margaret III, 290
Sinclair, Margaret S. III, 290
Sinclair, Martha V, 359
Sinclair, Mary IV, 159
Sinclair, Mary IV, 275
Sinclair, Mary IV, 351
Sinclair, Mary IV, 375
Sinclair, Mary IV, 437
Sinclair, Mary VI, 497
Sinclair, Mary VI, 561
Sinclair, Mary VI, 644
Sinclair, Mary VI, 701
Sinclair, Mary VI, 706
Sinclair, Mary Ann III, 290
Sinclair, Mary, Jr. VI, 643
Sinclair, Mary, Jr. VI, 701
Sinclair, Mary, Sr. VI, 643
Sinclair, Matilda IV, 843
Sinclair, Matilda IV, 916
Sinclair, Melvina V, 359
Sinclair, Miriam VI, 706
Sinclair, Pearl V, 202
Sinclair, Phebe IV, 193
Sinclair, Phebe IV, 275
Sinclair, Phebe IV, 326
Sinclair, Phebe IV, 351
Sinclair, Phebe IV, 437
Sinclair, Phebe VI, 701
Sinclair, Phebe VI, 706
Sinclair, Rachel V, 31
Sinclair, Rachel V, 121
Sinclair, Rachel VI, 633
Sinclair, Rachel VI, 701
Sinclair, Rebecca II, 826
Sinclair, Rebecca P. V, 121
Sinclair, Rebecca Proctor V, 121
Sinclair, Rebeckah VI, 993
Sinclair, Robert, Junr. VI, 993
Sinclair, Ruth IV, 843
Sinclair, Ruth IV, 859
Sinclair, Ruth IV, 860
Sinclair, Ruth IV, 916
Sinclair, Samuel Croosley IV, 275
Sinclair, Sarah V, 121
Sinclair, Sarah VI, 779
Sinclair, Sarah Louise III, 290
Sinclair, Susan II, 793
Sinclair, Susan III, 112
Sinclair, Susan III, 290
Sinclair, Thomas Russell VI, 706
Sinclair, Wagman VI, 936
Sinclair, Wayman VI, 956
Sinclair, Wayman VI, 993
Sinclair, Wayman VI, 1005
Sinclair, William VI, 701
Sinclair, Wm. II, 652
Sinclaire, Elizabeth VI, 561
Sinclaire, Hannah VI, 561
Sinclaire, James K. III, 19
Sinclaire, Job VI, 561
Sinclaire, John VI, 561
Sinclaire, Keziah VI, 561
Sinclaire, Sara Louise III, 19
Sinclear, George IV, 58
Sinclear, George V, 277
Sinclear, George VI, 338
Sinclear, Martha V, 277
Sindledicker, Pearl IV, 994
Siner, Benjamin VI, 993
Siner, Betsy VI, 943
Siner, Elathian VI, 993
Siner, Elizabeth VI, 950
Siner, George VI, 993
Siner, James VI, 902
Siner, James VI, 993
Siner, Jeremiah VI, 993
Siner, John VI, 993
Siner, John, Jr. VI, 891
Siner, John, Jr. VI, 943
Siner, John, Sr. VI, 891
Siner, John, Sr. VI, 943
Siner, Jonathan VI, 891
Siner, Jonathan VI, 896
Siner, Jonathan VI, 993
Siner, Judith VI, 896
Siner, Kitty VI, 935
Siner, Lucy VI, 896
Siner, Lucy VI, 924
Siner, Lucy VI, 935
Siner, Lucy VI, 993
Siner, Martha Ann VI, 993
Siner, Mary VI, 891
Siner, Mary VI, 993
Siner, Nancy VI, 993
Siner, Polley VI, 993
Siner, Polly VI, 886
Siner, Robert VI, 924
Siner, Robert VI, 947
Siner, Robert VI, 993
Siner, Sally VI, 902
Singer, Cora IV, 1263
Singer, Dorothea IV, 275
Singer, Frances Isabell IV, 275
Singer, Mable IV, 275
Singer, Martha Jane IV, 269
Singer, Martha Jane IV, 275
Singer, Odessa IV, 275
Singer, Rachel IV, 1240
Singer, Walter IV, 275
Singledecker, Pearl IV, 994
Singledecker, Pearl A. IV, 994
Singletary, David I, 1037
Singletary, Ella I, 639
Singletary, Ella I, 640
Singletary, Florence Malone IV, 1338
Singletary, Sarah I, 1026
Singletary, Sarah I, 1037
Singleterry, David I, 1016
Singleton, ??? III, 56
Singleton, Alice B. III, 56
Singleton, Elizabeth II, 421
Singleton, Jane III, 198
Singleton, John II, 421
Singleton, Margaret II, 1026
Singleton, Margaret II, 1027
Singleton, Thomas II, 421
Singletonnise, John I, 733
Singley, Ann II, 137
Singley, Anna L. II, 157
Singley, Edward II, 137
Singley, Edward II, 157
Singley, Edward II, 922
Singley, Hannah II, 755
Singley, Hannah II, 766
Singley, Jesse I. II, 157
Singley, Jesse Iden II, 157
Singley, Mary II, 137
Singley, Mary II, 157
Singley, Maurin II, 137
Singley, Morris G. II, 157
Singley, Samuel L. II, 157
Singley, Samuel Leeds II, 137
Singley, Samuel Leeds II, 157
Singley, Wm. L. II, 137
Singley, Wm. L. II, 157
Sinickson, Mary E. II, 1089
Sinickson, Sennica II, 260
Sinickson, Sinick II, 301
Sinions, ??? III, 45
Sinions, Sarah III, 45
Sinixson, Sinix II, 260
Sink, Andrew IV, 58
Sink, Ann IV, 58
Sink, Eve IV, 58
Sink, George I, 733
Sink, George IV, 58
Sink, Jacob I, 733
Sink, Mary I, 733
Sink, Mary IV, 58
Sink, Sarah IV, 58
Sink, Susanna I, 733
Sinke, George I, 733
Sinke, Susanna I, 711
Sinke???, Susanna I, 733
Sinkler, Alexander VI, 993
Sinkler, Betsey VI, 885
Sinkler, Betsey VI, 993
Sinkler, Betsy VI, 993
Sinkler, Catharine VI, 993
Sinkler, David VI, 887
Sinkler, David VI, 993
Sinkler, Elizabeth VI, 887
Sinkler, Elizabeth VI, 956
Sinkler, Frances VI, 993
Sinkler, George VI, 887
Sinkler, George VI, 913
Sinkler, George VI, 956
Sinkler, George VI, 993
Sinkler, George VI, 1021
Sinkler, Isaac VI, 885
Sinkler, Isaac VI, 956
Sinkler, Isaac VI, 993
Sinkler, James VI, 643
Sinkler, James VI, 993
Sinkler, John VI, 993
Sinkler, John, Jr. VI, 993
Sinkler, Judah VI, 993
Sinkler, Latitia VI, 1021
Sinkler, Lucy VI, 993
Sinkler, Martha VI, 914
Sinkler, Mary, Jr. VI, 643
Sinkler, Mary, Sr. VI, 643
Sinkler, Melinda VI, 956
Sinkler, Nancy VI, 913
Sinkler, Nancy VI, 975
Sinkler, Phebe VI, 704
Sinkler, Polly VI, 1022
Sinkler, Rachel VI, 914
Sinkler, Rebeckah VI, 993
Sinkler, Robert VI, 885
Sinkler, Robert VI, 914
Sinkler, Robert VI, 1022
Sinkler, Robert, Junr. VI, 993
Sinkler, Ruth VI, 933
Sinkler, Sarah VI, 993
Sinkler, Sarah VI, 1005
Sinkler, Wayman VI, 913
Sinkler, Wayman VI, 975
Sinks, ??? V, 774
Sinks, Amelia V, 764
Sinks, Andrew V, 764
Sinks, Anna V, 764
Sinks, George V, 764
Sinks, Mary I, 733
Sinks, Mary I, 739
Sinks, R. V, 764
Sinn, Sarah Ann II, 922
Sinnard, Flora E. V, 202
Sinnard, James V, 202
Sinnard, Nancy E. V, 202
Sinnard, Rebecca V, 202
Sinnard, Sarah J. V, 202
Sinnard, Silas V, 202
Sinnard, William W. V, 202
Sinnard, Wm. W. V, 202
Sinnerd, Margaret I, 1063
Sinnickson, Ann II, 124
Sinnickson, John M. II, 39
Sinnickson, Joseph Copner II, 98
Sinnickson, Rebecca II, 76
Sinnickson, Rebecca II, 98
Sinnickson, Seneca II, 98
Sinnickson, Seneca II, 260
Sinnickson, Sennica II, 260
Sinnickson, Sinix II, 260
Sinnickson, Sinnick II, 39
Sinnickson, Sinnick II, 98
Sinnickson, Wd. Ann D. II, 39
Sinor, Benjamin VI, 993
Sinor, Lucy VI, 935
Sinor, Polley VI, 993
Sinsmith, Julia IV, 497
Sinsmith, Maggie IV, 497
Sinton, Ann VI, 267
Sinton, Anna VI, 212
Sinton, Anna VI, 267
Sinton, Arabella VI, 212
Sinton, David II, 652
Sinton, Edward VI, 212
Sinton, Edward VI, 267
Sinton, Henry VI, 212
Sinton, Hosetta B. IV, 370

Sinton, Hosetta B. IV, 437
Sinton, Jacob II, 652
Sinton, Jacob VI, 212
Sinton, Jacob VI, 267
Sinton, James II, 652
Sinton, James VI, 212
Sinton, Job II, 503
Sinton, Job II, 652
Sinton, John VI, 212
Sinton, Joseph VI, 212
Sinton, Margaret III, 290
Sinton, Margaret VI, 197
Sinton, Margaret VI, 212
Sinton, Martha II, 463
Sinton, Martha II, 652
Sinton, Mary II, 503
Sinton, Mary II, 652
Sinton, Rebecca VI, 212
Sinton, Rebecca VI, 267
Sinton, Rebeckah S. VI, 163
Sinton, Rebeckah S. VI, 212
Sinton, Sarah II, 652
Sinton, Sarah VI, 212
Sinton, Thomas II, 503
Sinton, Thomas II, 652
Sinton, Thomas VI, 212
Sinton, William VI, 212
Sinton, Wm. II, 652
Sioussa, Ida B. VI, 561
Sioussa, Ida B. VI, 566
Sioussa, Iva B. VI, 565
Sipe, Clarence IV, 1223
Sipe, Clint IV, 1223
Sipe, Flora IV, 1185
Sipe, George IV, 1185
Sipe, Gertie IV, 1223
Sipe, Gertrude IV, 1223
Sipe, Lloyd IV, 1223
Sipe, Lydia IV, 1223
Sipe, Mahlon F. IV, 1223
Sipe, Mary IV, 1185
Sipe, Mary IV, 1223
Sipe, Mary E. IV, 1223
Sipe, May B. IV, 1223
Sipe, Nellie IV, 1185
Sipe, Wm. IV, 1223
Sipes, Lydia IV, 1223
Sipes, Mahlon F. IV, 1223
Sipes, Wm. IV, 1223
Sipher, ??? III, 206
Sipher, Owen IV, 1338
Sipher, Ruth IV, 1338
Sipher, Ruth A. IV, 1338
Sipher, Sarah III, 206
Sipher, Sarah III, 290
Siple, Ann Belle IV, 1263
Siples, Clara V, 1019
Siples, Josiah V, 1019
Sipp, Hannah IV, 787
Sipp, Julia Ann IV, 787
Sipp, Michael IV, 787
Sircle, Bertha Ruth V, 558
Sircle, Minnie R. V, 558
Sirket, Hannah II, 1027
Sirket, John II, 1027
Sirket, John II, 1040
Sirkit, Hannah II, 260
Sirkit, Hannah II, 276
Sirkit, John II, 260
Sirkit, John II, 276
Sirl, Tacy II, 1027
Sirles, Elizabeth II, 260
Sirridge, Mary II, 260
Sirridge, Mary II, 272
Sirridge, William II, 260
Sirridge, William II, 272
Sisam, Priscilla II, 652
Sisam, Priscilla II, 653
Sisam, Thomas II, 652
Sisam, Thomas II, 653
Sisney, John I, 571
Sisney, Ruth I, 526
Sisney, Ruth I, 571
Sisom, Hannah II, 998
Sisom, Hannah II, 1027
Sisom, John II, 1027
Sisom, John II, 1031
Sisom, Lydia II, 956
Sisom, Rachel II, 980
Sisom, Rachel II, 1027
Sisom, Rebecca II, 1031
Sisom, Sarah II, 967
Sisom, Thomas II, 980
Sisom, Thomas II, 1027
Sisom, Thomas II, 1031
Sisom, Wm. II, 1031
Sison, Lydia II, 956
Sissle, Mary IV, 536
Sissle, Mary IV, 549
Sisson, Abigail III, 290
Sisson, Ann V, 932
Sisson, Anna R. II, 718
Sisson, Charles II, 718
Sisson, Elizabeth V, 121
Sisson, Elizabeth V, 932
Sisson, Eunice V, 932
Sisson, Geo. V, 932
Sisson, Isaac V, 932
Sisson, John VI, 994
Sisson, Judith VI, 994
Sisson, Mary V, 932
Sisum, John II, 447
Sitch, Joshua II, 421
Sites, Adam II, 909
Sites, Adam II, 922
Sites, Catharine C. II, 922
Sites, Catherine C. II, 909
Sites, Clark E. IV, 1263
Sites, Elizabeth II, 421
Sites, Ella V, 1019
Sites, Ellen V, 1019
Sites, Geo. V, 1019
Sites, Geo., Jr. V, 1019
Sites, George II, 421
Sites, George V, 1019
Sites, George VI, 1022
Sites, Jacob V, 1019
Sites, Jonas V, 1019
Sites, Rachel V, 1019
Sites, Rebecca C. II, 909
Sites, Rebecca C. II, 922
Sites, Rena IV, 1263
Sites, Rhoda V, 277
Sitgreaves, ??? II, 421
Sitgreaves, Garry Loveridge III, 290
Sitgreaves, Helen Burgess III, 290
Sitgreaves, Jessie L. III, 290
Sitgreaves, Mary II, 421
Sitgreaves, Mary II, 652
Sitgreaves, Sarah Ann II, 421
Sitgreaves, Thomas II, 421
Sitgreaves, William II, 421
Sitgreaves, Wm. II, 652
Sitterson, Hannah I, 52
Sitterson, Hannah I, 73
Sittro, Jacob V, 278
Sivers, Elizabeth I, 152
Sivers, Elizabeth I, 165
Siverts, Sophia II, 652
Siveter, Lydia IV, 1185
Siveter, Mary IV, 1185
Siveter, Samuel IV, 1185
Siveter, Thomas IV, 1185
Siveter, Thos. IV, 1185
Sivil, Jane IV, 248
Sivil, Jane IV, 275
Sizemore, Irena I, 997
Sizemore, Malicia I, 997
Sizemore, Mary A. I, 997
Skarats, Isaac II, 417
Skarats, James II, 417
Skean, Mary Lee I, 949
Skeen, Maud V, 464
Skeen, Thomas V, 464
Skelly, Amanda V, 1019
Skelly, Mahala IV, 477
Skelly, Mahala IV, 497
Skelly, Norman V, 1019
Skelly, Wm. V, 1019
Skelton, ??? III, 350
Skelton, Abigail II, 558
Skelton, Abigail II, 652
Skelton, Abraham III, 290
Skelton, Abram III, 290
Skelton, Ann II, 969
Skelton, Geraldus IV, 1185
Skelton, Hannah II, 642
Skelton, Hannah II, 652
Skelton, Hannah III, 290
Skelton, Jane II, 969
Skelton, Jane II, 995
Skelton, Jane II, 1027
Skelton, Jesse II, 1027
Skelton, John II, 969
Skelton, John II, 995
Skelton, John II, 1027
Skelton, Joseph II, 969
Skelton, Margaret II, 969
Skelton, Margaret II, 1027
Skelton, Mary II, 638
Skelton, Mary II, 652
Skelton, Mary II, 969
Skelton, Rhoda II, 806
Skelton, Sarah II, 1027
Skelton, Sarah III, 290
Skelton, Sarah III, 350
Skelton, Susan II, 718
Skelton, Thomas II, 642
Skelton, Thomas II, 652
Skelton, William II, 969
Skerret, Susanna II, 644
Skerrett, Emme II, 417
Skerrett, Esther II, 417
Skerrett, James II, 417
Skerrett, John II, 417
Skerrett, Joseph II, 417
Skerrett, Susanna II, 417
Skidmore, Esther III, 488
Skidmore, Esther III, 499
Skidmore, Joseph III, 488
Skidmore, Joseph III, 499
Skidmore, Mary III, 402
Skidmore, Mary VI, 337
Skidmore, Mary VI, 338
Skidmore, Mary VI, 854
Skidmore, William VI, 338
Skidmore, William VI, 854
Skidmore, William J. III, 447
Skill, Elizabeth II, 1027
Skillern, Hannah Braxton VI, 994
Skillern, William P. VI, 994
Skillman, Eliza VI, 662
Skillman, Eliza VI, 701
Skillman, Eliza VI, 753
Skillman, Eliza VI, 779
Skillman, Isabella VI, 662
Skillman, Isabella VI, 701
Skillman, Isabelle VI, 753
Skillman, Isabelle VI, 755
Skillman, Isabelle VI, 779
Skillman, Jacob VI, 662
Skillman, Jacob VI, 701
Skillman, Jacob VI, 753
Skillman, Jacob VI, 779
Skillman-Janney, Isabelle VI, 780
Skilton, Jennet II, 977
Skilton, Jennet II, 1027
Skimmer, Alexander IV, 843
Skimming, Robert V, 709
Skimmings, Helen V, 528
Skimmings, Robert V, 705
Skimmings, Robert V, 709
Skimmings, Ruth V, 705
Skimmings, Ruth V, 709
Skinnall, Caroline VI, 1010
Skinnall, Sarah Ann VI, 1010
Skinnell, Daniel C. VI, 994
Skinnell, Eleanor VI, 1012
Skinnell, Eliza Ann VI, 994
Skinnell, George E. VI, 994
Skinnell, George E. VI, 1012
Skinnell, James VI, 994
Skinnell, Joseph S. VI, 892
Skinnell, Joseph S. VI, 994
Skinnell, Mary VI, 994
Skinnell, Mary Jane VI, 913
Skinnell, Rebecca VI, 994
Skinnell, Robert VI, 913
Skinnell, Robert VI, 994
Skinnell, Robert VI, 1010
Skinner, Aaron III, 306
Skinner, Charles L. III, 290
Skinner, Charles L. III, 305
Skinner, Chas. L. III, 290
Skinner, Edith J. IV, 407
Skinner, Edith J. IV, 408
Skinner, Edith J. IV, 437
Skinner, Elizabeth II, 421
Skinner, Elizabeth II, 653
Skinner, Evane I, 17
Skinner, Gertrude I. III, 335
Skinner, Gertrude, I. III, 290
Skinner, Hanna H. III, 306
Skinner, James I, 17
Skinner, James I Sup 1, 7
Skinner, Jeremiah I, 17
Skinner, John I, 17
Skinner, Jonathan I, 17
Skinner, Jonathan I Sup 1, 7
Skinner, Joseph I, 17
Skinner, Joseph I, 73
Skinner, Joseph II, 652
Skinner, Joseph II, 653
Skinner, Joshua I, 17
Skinner, Joshua I, 45
Skinner, Joshua I, 73
Skinner, Lloyd I. IV, 407
Skinner, Lura M. V, 597
Skinner, Martha Smith I, 73
Skinner, Mary I, 17
Skinner, Mary I Sup 1, 7
Skinner, Matilda E. III, 305
Skinner, MatildaH, III, 290
Skinner, Millisa III, 306
Skinner, Moses J. III, 306
Skinner, Precillah I, 71
Skinner, Precillah I, 73
Skinner, Priscilla I, 17
Skinner, Richard I, 17
Skinner, Richard I, 66
Skinner, Richard I, 73
Skinner, Richard I Sup 1, 7
Skinner, Samuel I, 17
Skinner, Samuel I, 71
Skinner, Samuel I, 73
Skinner, Sarah I, 17
Skinner, Sarah I, 45
Skinner, Sarah I, 50
Skinner, Sarah I, 55
Skinner, Sarah I, 66
Skinner, Sarah I, 73
Skinner, Sarah I, 78
Skinner, Sarah I Sup 1, 7
Skinner, Thomas III, 290
Skinner, Thomas Edward III, 290
Skinner, Thomas Edward III, 335
Skinner, Widow Sarah I, 56
Skinner, Widow Sarah I, 73
Skinner, William I, 17
Skinner, Wm. II, 653
Skinner, Zachariah I, 17
Skinsley, Esther II, 643
Skinsley, Esther II, 653
Skipper, Archie IV, 1263
Skipper, Archie C. IV, 1263
Skipper, Edward Leroy IV, 1263
Skipper, G. IV, 1263
Skipper, Lillie IV, 1263
Skively, Esther II, 643
Skively, Esther II, 653
Skofield, Henry II, 447
Skoly, Samuel II, 447
Skott, Samuel II, 417
Skull, James II, 447
Skull, Susanna II, 447
Skyler, Elizabeth II, 866
Skyler, Elizabeth S. II, 922
Skyles, Mary I, 212
Skyran, John II, 653
Skyrin, John II, 653
Skyron, Mary V, 899
Skyron, Mary V, 932
Skyson, Ann V, 932
Skyson, Elizabeth V, 932
Skyson, Mary V, 932
Slack, Abraham VI, 957
Slack, Abraham VI, 994
Slack, Ann II, 987
Slack, Ann II, 1027
Slack, Anna III, 290
Slack, Edward L. IV, 1263
Slack, Emma V, 121
Slack, Emma G. V, 38
Slack, Ethel V, 677
Slack, Ethel V, 710
Slack, Fannie V, 861
Slack, Hannah VI, 994
Slack, Harrison III, 290
Slack, Harry Calleston III, 290
Slack, Harry Carleton III, 48
Slack, Jane II, 1060
Slack, John VI, 936
Slack, John VI, 957
Slack, John VI, 994
Slack, Joseph VI, 994
Slack, Lott VI, 994
Slack, Lucinda VI, 994
Slack, Margaret VI, 957
Slack, Mary III, 48
Slack, Mary III, 290
Slack, Mary VI, 870
Slack, Mary VI, 957
Slack, Mary VI, 994
Slack, Mary C. III, 48
Slack, Matilda V, 31
Slack, Matilda V, 121
Slack, Matilda P. V, 121
Slack, Matthias VI, 994
Slack, Sarah VI, 994
Slack, Susanna VI, 936
Slack, Virginia IV, 1263
Slack, Virginia D. IV, 1263
Slack, William VI, 994
Slade, Betty VI, 854
Slade, Florence IV, 1338
Slade, Henry M. VI, 86
Slade, John VI, 854
Slade, Mary VI, 92
Slade, Mary Ann II, 820
Slade, Mrs. C. C. IV, 1338
Slade, Mrs. C. N. IV, 1338
Sladek, James IV, 1338
Slagel, Dick V, 710
Slagle, Dick V, 710
Slain, Gertrude V, 1019
Slanik, Frank III, 290
Slate, Elvira E. II, 872
Slate, Elvira E. II, 922
Slate, George II, 872
Slate, George II, 922
Slate, James Walton II, 872
Slate, James Walton II, 922
Slate, Sarah F. II, 872
Slate, Sarah F. II, 922
Slater, Catharine IV, 894
Slater, Elizabeth IV, 894
Slater, Lavina IV, 894
Slater, Lucinda IV, 894
Slater, Minnie IV, 1294
Slater, Sarah IV, 894
Slater, Tamer IV, 994
Slates, Alexander IV, 275
Slates, Mary E. IV, 275
Slates, Oscar B. IV, 275
Slates, Sophia IV, 275
Slaton, Elizabeth VI, 994
Slaton, John VI, 994
Slaton, Mary IV, 1294
Slatter, Jonathan II, 421
Slaughter, Agniss VI, 994
Slaughter, Ann V, 959
Slaughter, Ann VI, 490
Slaughter, Ann VI, 587
Slaughter, Ann VI, 978
Slaughter, Ann P. VI, 810
Slaughter, Anna V, 278
Slaughter, Anna V, 292
Slaughter, Bertha V, 278
Slaughter, Capt. Joseph VI, 9
Slaughter, Charles V, 278
Slaughter, Charles VI, 810
Slaughter, Charles D. VI, 82
Slaughter, Charles Edward V, 278
Slaughter, Chas. V, 278
Slaughter, Chas. D. VI, 854
Slaughter, Chas. Edward V, 2
Slaughter, Chloe V, 257
Slaughter, Chloe V, 278
Slaughter, Clara V, 278
Slaughter, Eliza VI, 801
Slaughter, Elizabeth V, 283
Slaughter, Emily P. VI, 978
Slaughter, Frances H. VI, 99
Slaughter, Goodrich VI, 894
Slaughter, James C. VI, 891
Slaughter, James C. VI, 896
Slaughter, John VI, 994
Slaughter, John Jackson V, 2
Slaughter, John P. VI, 854
Slaughter, Joseph VI, 891
Slaughter, Joseph VI, 994
Slaughter, Juliet E. VI, 854
Slaughter, Kitty Gissag VI, 9
Slaughter, Marcus V, 278
Slaughter, Marcus A. V, 278
Slaughter, Mary Lightfoot VI, 903
Slaughter, Mary Louise VI, 5
Slaughter, Mary Louise VI, 5
Slaughter, Mary Louise VI, 5
Slaughter, Mary T. VI, 928
Slaughter, Mrs. M. A. V, 431
Slaughter, Paulina A. VI, 827
Slaughter, Reuben VI, 903
Slaughter, Reuben VI, 908
Slaughter, Reuben VI, 962
Slaughter, Richard VI, 994
Slaughter, Sarah VI, 501
Slaughter, Sarah VI, 561
Slaughter, Sarah A. B. VI, 82
Slaughter, Sarah F. VI, 854
Slaughter, Stanley Earl V, 27
Slaughter, Susan VI, 891
Slaughter, Susanna VI, 994
Slaughters, James C. VI, 994
Slaughters, Maria Louisa VI,
Slauik, Frank III, 290
Slavick, Joseph II, 718
Slavick, Winifred II, 718
Slay, Eleanor IV, 275
Slay, Elijah IV, 275
Slayton, Margaret IV, 1338
Slayton, Mary IV, 1338
Slayton, Ray IV, 1338
Slayton, Ray Chas. IV, 1338
Sled, Dadman VI, 853
Sled, Eliza VI, 853
Sled, James VI, 994
Sled, John VI, 994
Sled, Josiah VI, 853
Sled, Milley VI, 994
Sled, Susan VI, 994
Sled, William VI, 994
Sledd, Barksdale VI, 880
Sledd, Elizabeth VI, 966
Sledd, Evelina VI, 880
Sledd, James VI, 924
Sledd, James VI, 951
Sledd, James VI, 966
Sledd, James VI, 994

d, James VI, 1005
d, Jemima VI, 859
d, John VI, 859
d, John VI, 966
d, Jordan VI, 1009
d, Josiah VI, 797
d, Josiah VI, 815
d, Josiah VI, 854
d, Martha VI, 1005
d, Nancy VI, 797
d, Nancy VI, 966
d, Nancy VI, 1005
d, Rebecca VI, 854
d, Susan VI, 1005
d, William VI, 994
ge, Addie I, 900
ge, Benjamin I, 900
ge, Georgie I, 900
ge, Lunettia M. I, 865
ge, Luretta I, 900
ge, Luretta I, 903
m, Elsie III, 24
m, Elsie III, 290
m, Elsie III, 291
m, R. B. III, 24
m, R. B. III, 290
m, R. B. III, 291
per, Abigail II, 653
per, Albert II, 820
per, Amanda V, 959
per, Ann V, 122
per, Ann Eliza II, 796
per, Ann Eliza II, 868
per, Ann Eliza II, 923
per, Anna V, 959
per, Anna H. II, 820
per, Anna H. II, 876
per, Anna H. II, 923
per, Anna W. II, 766
per, Anne V, 202
per, Anne V, 212
per, Anne V, 959
per, Avis V, 88
per, Avis V, 121
per, Avis V, 202
per, Avis V, 954
per, Avis V, 959
per, Barclay II, 820
per, Benjamin II, 183
per, Benjamin II, 653
per, Benjamin Elwood II, 923
per, Buddell V, 121
per, Buddell V, 138
per, Buddell V, 959
per, Budder V, 202
per, Charles II, 455
per, Charles II, 653
per, Charles V, 202
per, Charles V, 945
per, Charles V, 959
per, Chas. V, 212
per, Chas. V, 959
per, Chloe Ann V, 959
per, Deborah II, 653
per, Edith II, 280
per, Edith II, 301
per, Edith A. II, 301
per, Edith A. II, 766
per, Edwin II, 653
per, Edwin II, 766
per, Eliza V, 122
per, Elizabeth II, 766
per, Elizabeth V, 121
per, Elizabeth V, 122
per, Elizabeth V, 202
per, Elizabeth V, 959
per, Elizabeth F. II, 923
per, Elizabeth H. V, 121
per, Elizabeth H. V, 138
per, Elizabeth H. V, 959
per, Elizabeth T. II, 653
per, Emma T. II, 820
per, Emma T. II, 923
eper, Ephraim V, 959
eper, Ephraim Jane Henrietta V, 959
eper, Hannah II, 183
eper, Hannah II, 227
eper, Hannah II, 260
eper, Hannah II, 653
eper, Hannah II, 695
eper, Hannah II, 820
eper, Hannah II, 923
eper, Hannah V, 959
eper, Huldah II, 421
eper, Huldah II, 653
eper, Isaiah V, 959
eper, Israel II, 653
eper, Israel II, 766
eper, Jacob V, 121
eper, Jacob V, 138
Sleeper, Jacob V, 202
Sleeper, Jacob V, 959
Sleeper, James II, 766
Sleeper, Jane V, 959
Sleeper, Jno. II, 260
Sleeper, John II, 183
Sleeper, John II, 227
Sleeper, John II, 260
Sleeper, John II, 653
Sleeper, John II, 923
Sleeper, John V, 959
Sleeper, John R. II, 796
Sleeper, John R. II, 820
Sleeper, John R. II, 923
Sleeper, Jonathan II, 183
Sleeper, Jonathan II, 227
Sleeper, Jonathan II, 260
Sleeper, Jonathan II, 653
Sleeper, Jonathan II, 766
Sleeper, Jonathan II, 890
Sleeper, Jonathan II, 918
Sleeper, Jonathan II, 923
Sleeper, Jonathan II, 930
Sleeper, Jonathan V, 122
Sleeper, Joseph II, 183
Sleeper, Joseph W. II, 766
Sleeper, Keturah V, 202
Sleeper, Keturah V, 211
Sleeper, Keturah V, 959
Sleeper, Lydia II, 796
Sleeper, Lydia II, 820
Sleeper, Lydia II, 923
Sleeper, Martha II, 653
Sleeper, Martha II, 890
Sleeper, Martha II, 918
Sleeper, Martha II, 923
Sleeper, Martha II, 930
Sleeper, Martha V, 959
Sleeper, Martha H. II, 653
Sleeper, Martha H. II, 806
Sleeper, Martha H. II, 890
Sleeper, Martha H. II, 923
Sleeper, Mary II, 183
Sleeper, Mary II, 260
Sleeper, Mary II, 653
Sleeper, Mary II, 766
Sleeper, Mary II, 820
Sleeper, Mary V, 122
Sleeper, Mary Ann II, 898
Sleeper, Mary Ann II, 923
Sleeper, Mary G. II, 653
Sleeper, Mary G. II, 923
Sleeper, Mary G. II, 930
Sleeper, Mary L. II, 742
Sleeper, Mary L. II, 766
Sleeper, Nehemiah II, 421
Sleeper, Nehemiah II, 653
Sleeper, Nehemiah II, 718
Sleeper, Nehemiah II, 820
Sleeper, Nehemiah II, 923
Sleeper, Patience V, 121
Sleeper, Patience V, 202
Sleeper, Patience V, 211
Sleeper, Patience V, 861
Sleeper, Patience V, 954
Sleeper, Patience V, 959
Sleeper, Patience V, 976
Sleeper, Phebe II, 183
Sleeper, Phebe II, 653
Sleeper, Rachel II, 820
Sleeper, Rachel II, 923
Sleeper, Rebecca II, 653
Sleeper, Rebecca II, 766
Sleeper, Rebecca II, 820
Sleeper, Rebecca II, 876
Sleeper, Rebecca II, 923
Sleeper, Rebecca II, 930
Sleeper, Rebecca V, 959
Sleeper, Rebecca P. II, 923
Sleeper, Samuel II, 183
Sleeper, Samuel V, 121
Sleeper, Samuel V, 202
Sleeper, Samuel V, 211
Sleeper, Samuel V, 954
Sleeper, Samuel V, 959
Sleeper, Samuel V, 976
Sleeper, Sarah II, 653
Sleeper, Sarah II, 818
Sleeper, Sarah II, 823
Sleeper, Sarah II, 918
Sleeper, Sarah II, 923
Sleeper, Sarah V, 121
Sleeper, Sarah V, 122
Sleeper, Sarah V, 138
Sleeper, Sarah V, 959
Sleeper, Sarah I. III, 349
Sleeper, Sharon II, 653
Sleeper, Sharon II, 766
Sleeper, Sharon II, 820
Sleeper, Sharon II, 876
Sleeper, Sharon II, 923
Sleeper, Sharon II, 930
Sleeper, Sibil II, 98
Sleeper, Susanna II, 766
Sleeper, Sybel II, 260
Sleeper, Sybella II, 260
Sleeper, Wd. Mary II, 820
Sleeper, Wd. Mary II, 923
Sleeper, William II, 183
Sleeper, William II, 301
Sleeper, William V, 121
Sleeper, William V, 122
Sleeper, William V, 959
Sleeper, William Meridith V, 202
Sleeper, Wm. II, 653
Sleeper, Wm. II, 766
Sleeper, Wm. II, 923
Sleeper, Wm. V, 959
Sleeper, Wm. Ashby II, 653
Sleeper, Wm. H. II, 923
Sleigh, Arthur Hastings III, 447
Sleigh, Arthur Hastings III, 462
Sleigh, Catharine III, 422
Sleigh, Catharine III, 447
Sleigh, Hannah III, 408
Sleigh, Hannah III, 447
Sleigh, Mary Jane III, 447
Sleigh, Mary Jane III, 462
Sleigh, Stephen III, 422
Sleigh, Stephen III, 447
Sleight, Jane III, 193
Sleight, Jane III, 291
Slein, Clyde IV, 497
Sleppy, Anna V, 764
Sleppy, Della V, 764
Sleppy, Harvey V, 764
Slethum, Levi V, 359
Slicer, Albert W. IV, 1294
Slicer, George F. IV, 1294
Slicer, Hannah II, 653
Slicer, Hannah II, 671
Slicer, Julia A. IV, 1294
Slicer, Minie IV, 1294
Slicer, Sallie E. IV, 1294
Slicer, Sarah A. IV, 1294
Sliker, Rose V, 691
Sliker, Rose V, 710
Slinker, Elizabeth VI, 957
Slinker, John VI, 957
Sliter, Chalkley IV, 1223
Sliter, Seth IV, 1223
Sloan, Anna Cora III, 291
Sloan, Charity IV, 1365
Sloan, Charity IV, 1378
Sloan, Charles II, 301
Sloan, Charles B. II, 301
Sloan, Edwin II, 301
Sloan, Elizabeth II, 183
Sloan, Elizabeth II, 301
Sloan, Elizabeth V, 122
Sloan, Elizabeth V, 928
Sloan, Elizabeth V, 932
Sloan, Elizabeth H. II, 280
Sloan, Elizabeth H. II, 301
Sloan, Jeremiah H. II, 301
Sloan, John A. II, 301
Sloan, Joseph II, 98
Sloan, Joseph II, 280
Sloan, Joseph II, 301
Sloan, Joseph III, 291
Sloan, Joseph Swett II, 766
Sloan, Joseph, Jr. II, 766
Sloan, Leonora II, 783
Sloan, Marmaduke II, 301
Sloan, Mary T. IV, 1378
Sloan, Phebe P. IV, 1185
Sloan, Phebe P. IV, 1187
Sloan, Rachel II, 260
Sloan, Rachel II, 301
Sloan, Rachel C. II, 301
Sloan, Rachel S. II, 280
Sloan, Rachel S. II, 301
Sloan, William H. III, 291
Sloanaker, Cora Ellen V, 359
Sloanaker, Phebe J. V, 359
Sloane, Elizabeth V, 122
Sloane, Leonora II, 839
Sloane, Leonora II, 923
Slocum, ??? III, 272
Slocum, Abbie III, 153
Slocum, Abbie III, 291
Slocum, Abigail VI, 697
Slocum, Abigail VI, 701
Slocum, Ada IV, 762
Slocum, Annie IV, 762
Slocum, Caroline III, 291
Slocum, Charles II, 766
Slocum, Charles III, 291
Slocum, Charles M. II, 766
Slocum, Christopher II, 591
Slocum, Christopher III, 291
Slocum, Christopher M. III, 291
Slocum, Christopher Marshall II, 653
Slocum, Dr. John H. III, 291
Slocum, Edward III, 291
Slocum, Edward E. III, 291
Slocum, Edward M. III, 291
Slocum, Eliz. III, 291
Slocum, Elizabeth III, 291
Slocum, Elizabeth Flower II, 591
Slocum, Elizabeth Flower II, 653
Slocum, Elizabeth Flowers III, 291
Slocum, Emeline V, 932
Slocum, Emeline M. III, 291
Slocum, Emeline M. V, 932
Slocum, Emmeline M. III, 291
Slocum, George IV, 762
Slocum, Harriet M. II, 726
Slocum, Harriet M. II, 766
Slocum, Harvey IV, 762
Slocum, Henry N. III, 291
Slocum, Henry Nason III, 153
Slocum, Hypacia M. III, 291
Slocum, John II, 591
Slocum, John II, 653
Slocum, John III, 291
Slocum, Jonathan L. I, 571
Slocum, Marceline III, 291
Slocum, Marshall III, 291
Slocum, Martha II, 591
Slocum, Martha II, 653
Slocum, Mary III, 107
Slocum, Mary III, 219
Slocum, Mary III, 291
Slocum, Mary IV, 641
Slocum, Mary IV, 657
Slocum, Mary Abbie III, 153
Slocum, Mary Abbie III, 291
Slocum, Mary B. II, 766
Slocum, Mary B. III, 272
Slocum, Mary B. III, 291
Slocum, Mary H. III, 291
Slocum, Mary R. II, 766
Slocum, Robert VI, 697
Slocum, Robert VI, 701
Slocum, Robert F. III, 291
Slocum, Sarah VI, 557
Slocum, Sarah VI, 697
Slocum, Sarah VI, 698
Slocum, Sarah VI, 701
Slocum, Sussana III, 291
Slocum, Thomas Stelle III, 291
Slocum, William T. III, 291
Slocum, Wm. L. III, 107
Slocum, Wm. T. III, 291
Sloffreger, David V, 932
Sloffreger, Francis V, 932
Sloffreger, H. Fred, Jr. V, 932
Sloffreger, Ida B. V, 932
Slonaker, Ada V, 764
Slonaker, Guy V, 764
Slonaker, Ruth V, 764
Slone, Bert A. IV, 1263
Slone, Jennie IV, 1263
Sloonaker, Phebe Jane V, 224
Sloonaker, Phebe Jane V, 278
Sluder, Ella I, 620
Sluder, Isaac I, 620
Sluder, Phariba I, 615
Sluder, Phariba I, 620
Sluder, Sarah I, 257
Sluder, Sarah A. I, 257
Slusher, David VI, 854
Slusher, Geo. V, 464
Slusher, George V, 464
Slusher, George V, 644
Slusher, Polly VI, 854
Slutebeck, Maggie V, 1019
Sluterbeck, Jacob V, 1019
Sluterbeck, Maggie V, 1019
Sluterbeck, Mahala V, 1019
Slutes, Edna III, 291
Slutes, Julia III, 291
Slutes, Merrill Clark III, 170
Slutes, Merrill Clark III, 291
Slutes, Wm. Laurence III, 291
Slutts, Sarah IV, 211
Slutts, Sarah IV, 275
Sluyter, Anna Mary IV, 1030
Sluyter, Catharine IV, 892
Sluyter, Catharine IV, 895
Sluyter, Deborah E. IV, 1027
Sluyter, Deborah E. IV, 1030
Sluyter, Deborah Ellen II, 799
Sluyter, Deborah Ellen IV, 1030
Sluyter, Henrietta B. IV, 1030
Sluyter, Henry IV, 895
Sluyter, Marcus IV, 1030
Sluyter, Marcus O. IV, 1030
Sluyter, Margaret IV, 1030
Sluyter, Marquis IV, 1030
Sluyter, Marquis O. IV, 1027
Sluyter, Nancy IV, 895
Sluyter, Rebecca IV, 1030
Sluyter, Sarah IV, 892
Sluyter, Sarah IV, 895
Sluyter, Sarah Ann IV, 895
Sluyter, Sarah Ann IV, 1027
Sluyter, Sarah Ann IV, 1030
Sluyter, Sarah Maria IV, 1030
Sluyter, Sylvester C. IV, 1030
Sluyter, William K. IV, 1030
Sluyter, Wm. K. IV, 892
Sluyter, Wm. K. IV, 895
Sly, Benjamin F. V, 597
Sly, Carle C. V, 597
Sly, Edie R. V, 597
Sly, Jacob S. V, 597
Sly, Minnie May V, 597
Sly, Mollie V, 597
Sly, Ulysses S. V, 597
Sly, Willie H. V, 597
Slycer, Hannah II, 653
Slyter, Amy IV, 1185
Slyter, Chalkley IV, 275
Slyter, Chalkley IV, 1185
Slyter, Chalkley IV, 1223
Slyter, Elizabeth IV, 275
Slyter, Elizabeth IV, 1185
Slyter, Elizabeth Ann IV, 1185
Slyter, Eunice IV, 1168
Slyter, Eunice IV, 1185
Slyter, Eunice IV, 1213
Slyter, Eunice IV, 1223
Slyter, Horton H. IV, 1185
Slyter, Jacob IV, 275
Slyter, Jacob IV, 1185
Slyter, Mila IV, 1150
Slyter, Mila IV, 1185
Slyter, Milia IV, 1150
Slyter, Milia IV, 1185
Slyter, Milla IV, 275
Slyter, Milla IV, 1185
Slyter, Phebe IV, 1185
Slyter, Ruth IV, 1166
Slyter, Ruth IV, 1185
Slyter, Seth IV, 1185
Slyter, Seth IV, 1223
Slyter, Thomas IV, 1185
Slyter, Unice IV, 275
Slyvester, William V, 218
Smack, Charles V, 464
Smack, Chauncey Malcom V, 464
Smack, Ida V, 464
Smack, Marlene V, 464
Smaley, Cora V, 203
Small, Aaron V, 764
Small, Abigail I, 1012
Small, Abner V, 278
Small, Abner V, 764
Small, Abraham I, 705
Small, Abraham I, 733
Small, Abram I, 165
Small, Alce VI, 30
Small, Alce VI, 36
Small, Amay VI, 28
Small, Amos V, 122
Small, Amy VI, 36
Small, Ann I, 900
Small, Ann V, 299
Small, Ann V, 311
Small, Ann VI, 33
Small, Ann VI, 36
Small, Anna I, 266
Small, Anna I, 275
Small, Anna I, 705
Small, Anna I, 733
Small, Anna IV, 58
Small, Anna V, 122
Small, Anna V, 278
Small, Anne I, 55
Small, Anne I, 74
Small, Austie V, 465
Small, Ben VI, 23
Small, Ben VI, 37
Small, Benj. VI, 28
Small, Benjamin I, 73
Small, Benjamin I, 117
Small, Benjamin I, 165
Small, Benjamin I, 263
Small, Benjamin I, 264
Small, Benjamin I, 267
Small, Benjamin I, 275
Small, Benjamin I, 1012
Small, Benjamin V, 764
Small, Benjamin VI, 8
Small, Benjamin VI, 18
Small, Benjamin VI, 28
Small, Benjamin VI, 30
Small, Benjamin VI, 36
Small, Caleb I, 266
Small, Caleb I, 275

Small, Christian I, 36
Small, Christian I, 74
Small, Christian I, 180
Small, Christian I, 186
Small, Clara Jane V, 644
Small, Clarissa V, 122
Small, Clarkey I, 166
Small, Clarkey I, 733
Small, Clarkey I Sup 1, 8
Small, Clarkey V, 311
Small, Clerkey I, 160
Small, Clerkey I, 166
Small, Comfort I, 266
Small, Comfort I, 275
Small, Comfort IV, 58
Small, E. O. V, 465
Small, Edmond VI, 36
Small, Edmund I, 266
Small, Edmund IV, 58
Small, Eli V, 644
Small, Elisabeth I, 165
Small, Elizabeth I, 117
Small, Elizabeth I, 165
Small, Elizabeth I, 167
Small, Elizabeth I, 268
Small, Elizabeth I, 275
Small, Elizabeth I, 695
Small, Elizabeth I, 705
Small, Elizabeth I, 733
Small, Elizabeth I, 895
Small, Elizabeth I, 1012
Small, Elizabeth V, 302
Small, Elizabeth V, 308
Small, Elizabeth V, 311
Small, Elizabeth V, 764
Small, Elizabeth VI, 18
Small, Elizabeth VI, 30
Small, Elizabeth VI, 36
Small, Elizabeth VI, 37
Small, Ephraim V, 311
Small, Ephraim V, 465
Small, Esther I, 198
Small, Esther I, 200
Small, Florence V, 465
Small, Gideon I, 117
Small, Gideon I, 165
Small, Gideon I, 705
Small, Gideon I, 716
Small, Gideon I, 733
Small, Gideon I, 968
Small, Gideon V, 122
Small, Gideon V, 278
Small, Hannah I, 113
Small, Hannah I, 266
Small, Hannah I, 271
Small, Hannah I, 275
Small, Hannah IV, 58
Small, Hannah VI, 36
Small, Isabel V, 311
Small, Jacob I, 968
Small, Jacob V, 278
Small, Jacob V, 529
Small, James I, 36
Small, James I, 74
Small, James H. V, 644
Small, Jane I, 733
Small, Jane I, 900
Small, Jane V, 465
Small, Jeane I, 705
Small, Jesse I, 117
Small, Jesse I, 733
Small, Jesse V, 302
Small, Jesse V, 311
Small, Jesse V, 764
Small, Jno VI, 37
Small, John I, 113
Small, John I, 117
Small, John I, 165
Small, John I, 263
Small, John I, 264
Small, John I, 266
Small, John I, 268
Small, John I, 275
Small, John I, 733
Small, John IV, 58
Small, John VI, 8
Small, John VI, 18
Small, John VI, 30
Small, John VI, 36
Small, John, Jr. I, 60
Small, John, Jr. I, 73
Small, John, Jr. I, 74
Small, Jonas I, 266
Small, Jonas I, 273
Small, Jonas I, 275
Small, Jonas I Sup 1, 8
Small, Jonas IV, 58
Small, Jonathan V, 122
Small, Jonathan Amos V, 311
Small, Joseph I, 117
Small, Joseph I, 160
Small, Joseph I, 166
Small, Joseph I, 275
Small, Joseph I, 733
Small, Joseph I, 968
Small, Joseph V, 122
Small, Joseph V, 215
Small, Joseph V, 295
Small, Joseph V, 311
Small, Joseph VI, 33
Small, Joseph VI, 36
Small, Joshua I, 74
Small, Joshua I, 145
Small, Joshua I, 166
Small, Joshua I, 266
Small, Joshua V, 122
Small, Joshua V, 311
Small, Josiah I, 74
Small, Josiah I, 705
Small, Josiah I, 733
Small, Lemuel I, 165
Small, Lidia I, 705
Small, Lyda I, 117
Small, Lyda I, 165
Small, Lyddia I, 117
Small, Lyddia I, 165
Small, Lyddia I, 733
Small, Lydia I, 132
Small, Lydia I, 165
Small, Lydia I, 733
Small, Lydia I, 900
Small, Marth Jane V, 861
Small, Martha Jane V, 827
Small, Mary I, 34
Small, Mary I, 74
Small, Mary I, 264
Small, Mary I, 269
Small, Mary I, 275
Small, Mary I, 382
Small, Mary I, 419
Small, Mary I, 1012
Small, Mary II, 193
Small, Mary II, 260
Small, Mary II, 813
Small, Mary III, 249
Small, Mary V, 464
Small, Mary V, 465
Small, Mary V, 644
Small, Mary V, 764
Small, Mary VI, 36
Small, Mary E. I, 865
Small, Mary E. I, 900
Small, Mary E. I, 903
Small, Mary, Jr. I, 189
Small, Mary, Jr. I, 200
Small, Matt VI, 23
Small, Matt VI, 37
Small, Matthew I, 74
Small, Meriam I, 275
Small, Meriam I, 1012
Small, Miriam I, 117
Small, Miriam I, 166
Small, Miriam I, 267
Small, Miriam I, 275
Small, Miriam V, 764
Small, Mourning I, 38
Small, Mourning I, 74
Small, Nathan I, 166
Small, Nathan V, 311
Small, Obadiah I, 165
Small, Obadiah I, 705
Small, Obadiah I, 733
Small, Obadiah V, 311
Small, Obediah I, 74
Small, Obediah I, 111
Small, Obediah I, 117
Small, Obediah I, 132
Small, Obediah I, 165
Small, Obediah I, 166
Small, Obediah I, 167
Small, Obediah I, 275
Small, Obediah I, 695
Small, Obediah I, 705
Small, Obediah V, 122
Small, Obediah V, 295
Small, Obediah, Jr. I, 165
Small, Patience I, 55
Small, Patience I, 74
Small, Peninah I, 1012
Small, Peninah V, 764
Small, Rachel I, 68
Small, Rachel I, 74
Small, Rachel I, 111
Small, Rachel I, 113
Small, Rachel I, 117
Small, Rachel I, 157
Small, Rachel I, 165
Small, Rachel V, 122
Small, Rachel V, 255
Small, Rachel V, 278
Small, Rachel V, 303
Small, Rachel V, 311
Small, Rachell I, 275
Small, Rebeckah I, 60
Small, Rebeckah I, 73
Small, Ruth V, 258
Small, Ruth V, 278
Small, Ruth V, 311
Small, Ruth A. V, 278
Small, Samuel I, 117
Small, Samuel I, 165
Small, Samuel I, 167
Small, Samuel V, 122
Small, Samuel V, 311
Small, Samuel V, 359
Small, Sarah I, 117
Small, Sarah I, 145
Small, Sarah I, 161
Small, Sarah I, 165
Small, Sarah I, 166
Small, Sarah I, 167
Small, Sarah I, 266
Small, Sarah I, 275
Small, Sarah I, 705
Small, Sarah I, 716
Small, Sarah I, 733
Small, Sarah IV, 58
Small, Sarah V, 122
Small, Sarah V, 311
Small, Sarah V, 764
Small, Silas I, 266
Small, Silas I, 269
Small, Silas I, 272
Small, Silas I, 275
Small, Silas IV, 58
Small, Solomon I, 275
Small, Solomon Hubbard I, 275
Small, Susan I, 275
Small, Susanah I, 165
Small, Susannah I, 165
Small, Susannah I, 170
Small, Thomas I, 74
Small, Thomas I, 167
Small, Thomas, Jr. I, 74
Small, Timothy I, 266
Small, Timothy I, 275
Small, Timothy IV, 58
Small, Widow Elizabeth I, 900
Small, Widow Sarah I, 273
Small, William I, 117
Small, William I, 266
Small, William I, 275
Small, William S. I, 275
Smalley, Albert V, 1019
Smalley, Anna IV, 1263
Smalley, Benjamin F. IV, 1263
Smalley, Carey IV, 1263
Smalley, Carley IV, 1263
Smalley, Charles III, 229
Smalley, Charles III, 291
Smalley, Clara III, 229
Smalley, Clara III, 291
Smalley, Clara IV, 1263
Smalley, Cora V, 203
Smalley, Daniel C. V, 203
Smalley, Eliza Jane V, 359
Smalley, Ezra IV, 275
Smalley, Ira M. IV, 1263
Smalley, Maggie IV, 1263
Smalley, Margaret IV, 1263
Smalley, Maria IV, 275
Smalley, Mary V, 1019
Smalley, Mont IV, 1263
Smalley, Nellie IV, 1263
Smalley, Rachel V, 359
Smalley, Roy IV, 1263
Smalley, Symantha IV, 1263
Smalley, Wm. IV, 1263
Smallwood, Dellie IV, 1263
Smallwood, Henry L. IV, 1263
Smallwood, Mary II, 600
Smallwood, Mary II, 653
Smallwood, Randoll II, 421
Smallwood, Rosa B. IV, 275
Smally, Benjamin F. IV, 1263
Smally, Margaret IV, 1263
Smally, Mont IV, 1263
Smart, Ann II, 23
Smart, Ann II, 39
Smart, Ann II, 40
Smart, Ann II, 58
Smart, Ann II, 98
Smart, Ann T. II, 124
Smart, Anna II, 40
Smart, Benjamin III, 384
Smart, Carroll V, 710
Smart, Catharine II, 39
Smart, Catharine II, 62
Smart, Catharine II, 98
Smart, Catharine III, 291
Smart, Deborah II, 39
Smart, Deborah II, 40
Smart, Deborah II, 124
Smart, Deborah II, 766
Smart, Deborah IV, 533
Smart, Deborah IV, 549
Smart, E. C. VI, 849
Smart, Edmund VI, 854
Smart, Edward II, 40
Smart, Elizabeth II, 39
Smart, Elizabeth II, 40
Smart, Elizabeth II, 82
Smart, Elizabeth II, 98
Smart, Elizabeth II, 421
Smart, Elizabeth III, 379
Smart, Elizabeth III, 384
Smart, Elizabeth VI, 854
Smart, Elizabeth E. III, 291
Smart, Hannah II, 39
Smart, Hannah II, 40
Smart, Hannah II, 80
Smart, Hannah II, 98
Smart, Hannah III, 291
Smart, Hannah III, 384
Smart, Hannah, Jr. II, 124
Smart, Isaac II, 23
Smart, Isaac II, 39
Smart, Isaac II, 40
Smart, Isaac II, 98
Smart, Isaac IV, 180
Smart, Isaac IV, 706
Smart, Isaac, Jr. II, 40
Smart, Isaac, Jr. II, 98
Smart, Isaac, Jr. II, 105
Smart, Isaac, Jr. II, 124
Smart, Isaac, Sr. II, 39
Smart, Isabell II, 39
Smart, Jane II, 40
Smart, John II, 40
Smart, John II, 99
Smart, John II, 421
Smart, John VI, 849
Smart, John VI, 854
Smart, Joseph III, 384
Smart, Lucy III, 384
Smart, Lucy A. III, 291
Smart, Lydia II, 421
Smart, Lydia II, 628
Smart, Lydia II, 653
Smart, Lydia F. III, 389
Smart, Mable V, 677
Smart, Mable V, 710
Smart, Mable E. V, 710
Smart, Madaline L. V, 710
Smart, Mary II, 39
Smart, Mary II, 40
Smart, Mary II, 97
Smart, Mary II, 98
Smart, Mary II, 124
Smart, Mary III, 291
Smart, Mary III, 384
Smart, Mary E. III, 109
Smart, Mary E. III, 291
Smart, Mary, Jr. II, 40
Smart, Nathan II, 17
Smart, Nathan II, 39
Smart, Nathan II, 40
Smart, Nathan II, 98
Smart, Polly VI, 849
Smart, Rebecca II, 40
Smart, Rebecca II, 98
Smart, Rebecca II, 105
Smart, Rebecca II, 124
Smart, Rebecca IV, 180
Smart, Rebecca IV, 275
Smart, Rebecca IV, 512
Smart, Rebecca IV, 524
Smart, Rebecca IV, 706
Smart, Rebeckah II, 39
Smart, Rebekah II, 98
Smart, Rebekah II, 103
Smart, Robert II, 39
Smart, Roger II, 39
Smart, Roy M. V, 677
Smart, Roy M. V, 710
Smart, Ruth II, 40
Smart, Ruth II, 124
Smart, Ruth IV, 549
Smart, Ruth IV, 706
Smart, Ruth IV, 762
Smart, Ruth IV, 793
Smart, Sally VI, 854
Smart, Sarah II, 39
Smart, Sarah II, 98
Smart, Sarah II, 103
Smart, Thomas C. III, 384
Smart, Thomas Clarke, Jr. III, 384
Smart, Thos. III, 384
Smart, Thos. C. III, 384
Smart, Thos. Clark III, 384
Smart, Thos. Clarke III, 379
Smart, William III, 291
Smart, William III, 384
Smart, William Thompson II
Smart, Wilson II, 39
Smart, Wm. III, 109
Smart, Wm. III, 291
Smart, Wm. T. II, 124
Smarte, Elizabeth II, 98
Smarte, Elizabeth II, 104
Smarte, Isaac II, 98
Smarte, Isaac II, 104
Smathers, Hannah IV, 642
Smathers, Hannah IV, 657
Smedley, ??? II, 820
Smedley, A. Ruth II, 767
Smedley, Alban M. II, 923
Smedley, Albin M. II, 834
Smedley, Albin M. II, 893
Smedley, Albin M. II, 923
Smedley, Albin Matlack II, 8
Smedley, Alvin M. II, 923
Smedley, Amanda R. II, 767
Smedley, Amanda Ruth II, 7
Smedley, Amy II, 421
Smedley, Amy II, 653
Smedley, Ann H. II, 1046
Smedley, Ann H. II, 1060
Smedley, Anna F. II, 923
Smedley, Anna L. II, 834
Smedley, Anna L. II, 923
Smedley, Anna Lukens II, 78
Smedley, Anna Maria II, 820
Smedley, Anna Maria II, 923
Smedley, Arthur C. III, 447
Smedley, Arthur C. III, 475
Smedley, Benjamin IV, 916
Smedley, Bennett L. II, 820
Smedley, Caroline Hallowell II, 820
Smedley, David VI, 447
Smedley, David VI, 778
Smedley, David VI, 779
Smedley, Eleanor Hallowell II, 820
Smedley, Eliza Ann II, 421
Smedley, Elizabeth II, 421
Smedley, Elizabeth II, 820
Smedley, Elizabeth II, 876
Smedley, Elizabeth II, 923
Smedley, Elizabeth III, 447
Smedley, Elizabeth III, 475
Smedley, Elizabeth G. II, 871
Smedley, Elizabeth G. II, 923
Smedley, Elizabeth J. II, 718
Smedley, Elizabeth Kirk II, 8
Smedley, Elizabeth Kirk II, 8
Smedley, Elizabeth Kirk II, 9
Smedley, Esther Ann V, 122
Smedley, Ezra V, 122
Smedley, Fannie E. II, 871
Smedley, Florence Elizabeth II, 820
Smedley, Franklin J. V, 122
Smedley, George II, 534
Smedley, George II, 653
Smedley, Golda III, 447
Smedley, Golda III, 475
Smedley, Hannah II, 740
Smedley, Hannah II, 767
Smedley, Isaac II, 421
Smedley, Isaac II, 653
Smedley, Isaac II, 796
Smedley, Isaac G. II, 923
Smedley, Isaac Garrett II, 82
Smedley, Isaac Garrett II, 87
Smedley, Isaac Garrett II, 92
Smedley, J. Franklin V, 42
Smedley, Jacob II, 421
Smedley, Jacob II, 571
Smedley, Jacob II, 653
Smedley, Jacob II, 718
Smedley, Jacob II, 766
Smedley, Jacob II, 767
Smedley, James II, 767
Smedley, Jeffrey II, 421
Smedley, Jeffrey II, 653
Smedley, John II, 571
Smedley, John II, 653
Smedley, John II, 820
Smedley, John IV, 916
Smedley, Joseph II, 1060
Smedley, Joseph, Jr. II, 1046
Smedley, Joseph, Jr. II, 1060
Smedley, Kersey II, 421
Smedley, Kersey II, 653
Smedley, Lauretta III, 107
Smedley, Lauretta III, 291
Smedley, Lewis II, 1027
Smedley, Lewis V. III, 107
Smedley, Lewis V. III, 291
Smedley, Lillian II, 779
Smedley, Louis B. II, 779
Smedley, Margaret V, 203

lley, Margaret A. II, 834
lley, Margaret A. II, 923
lley, Margaret Anna II, 820
lley, Margaret Anna II, 893
lley, Margaret Anna II, 923
lley, Marianna III, 245
lley, Marianna III, 299
lley, Mary II, 36
lley, Mary II, 122
lley, Mary II, 796
lley, Mary III, 291
lley, Mary IV, 904
lley, Mary IV, 916
lley, Mary A. II, 779
lley, Mary A. II, 923
lley, Mary Ann II, 421
lley, Mary Ann II, 653
lley, Mary Atkinson II, 820
lley, Mary D. II, 923
lley, Mary D. II, 927
lley, Mary H. II, 820
lley, Mary H. II, 893
lley, Mary H. II, 923
lley, Mary H. III, 198
lley, Mary Hewlings II, 820
dley, Nathan II, 820
dley, Nathan II, 893
dley, Nathan II, 923
dley, Nathan II, 927
dley, Nathan Cope II, 820
dley, Phebe II, 793
dley, Philena II, 718
dley, Rachel II, 1046
dley, Rachel II, 1060
dley, Rachel VI, 778
dley, Rachel VI, 779
dley, Rachel J. VI, 778
dley, Rachel J. VI, 779
dley, Rebecca II, 571
dley, Rebecca II, 653
dley, Rebecca II, 718
dley, Rebecca II, 767
dley, Rebecca II, 820
dley, Rebecca III, 291
dley, Rebecca J. II, 766
dley, Rebecca J. II, 767
dley, Ruth II, 718
dley, Ruth V, 42
dley, Ruth V, 122
dley, Ruth C. V, 122
dley, Samuel II, 718
dley, Samuel W. III, 198
dley, Samuel W. III, 291
dley, Sarah II, 653
dley, Sarah A. II, 927
dley, Sarah Ann II, 820
dley, Sarah Ann II, 923
dley, Selina III, 107
dley, Selina III, 291
dley, Susanna II, 571
dley, Susanna II, 653
dley, Susanna IV, 916
dley, Tacy II, 1027
dley, Thomas II, 718
dley, Thomas II, 740
dley, Thomas II, 767
dley, Thomas W. II, 718
dley, Thos. II, 923
dley, Thos. D. II, 820
dley, Thos. G. II, 871
dley, Thos. G. II, 923
dley, Walter II, 718
dley, Walter II, 767
dley, Wd. Deborah Hawley II, 796
dley, Wm. III, 291
dley, Wm. J. II, 718
dley, Wm. J. II, 767
dley, Wm. Jones II, 766
dley, Wm. Jones II, 767
dly, Isaac II, 653
edly, Phebe VI, 456
lger, Harry IV, 1338
lser, Abraham VI, 877
lser, Abraham VI, 895
lser, Abraham VI, 915
lser, Abraham VI, 954
lser, Abraham VI, 985
lser, Abraham VI, 994
lser, Catharine VI, 994
lser, Catherine VI, 924
lser, Cathrine VI, 924
lser, Elizabeth VI, 915
lser, Elizabeth VI, 985
lser, Harry VI, 994
lser, Jane VI, 994
lser, Jesse VI, 984
lser, Jesse VI, 994
lser, Jesse, Jr. VI, 915
lser, John VI, 885
lser, John VI, 924
Smelser, John VI, 954
Smelser, John VI, 985
Smelser, John VI, 994
Smelser, John, Jr. VI, 924
Smelser, John, Jr. VI, 925
Smelser, John, Jr. VI, 994
Smelser, Judith VI, 994
Smelser, Julia VI, 877
Smelser, Letha VI, 994
Smelser, Mary VI, 901
Smelser, Matilda VI, 994
Smelser, Nancy VI, 1003
Smelser, Paschal VI, 966
Smelser, Paulser VI, 877
Smelser, Paulser VI, 924
Smelser, Paulser VI, 991
Smelser, Paulser VI, 994
Smelser, Permelia VI, 985
Smelser, Polly VI, 994
Smelser, Rachel VI, 954
Smelser, Rachel VI, 994
Smelser, Rebecca VI, 885
Smelser, Rebekah VI, 924
Smelser, Sally VI, 994
Smelser, Sarah S. S. VI, 994
Smelser, Sina VI, 895
Smelser, Stephen VI, 994
Smelser, Susanah VI, 994
Smelser, Tabby VI, 994
Smelser, Tamsey VI, 954
Smeltzer, Abraham V, 1019
Smeltzer, Catharine V, 1019
Smeltzer, Harry IV, 1338
Smeltzer, Harry C. IV, 1338
Smeth, Pheby II, 99
Smich, Mary Ann IV, 482
Smich, Mary Ann IV, 497
Smiley, Ada IV, 275
Smiley, Albert K. III, 87
Smiley, Albert K. III, 291
Smiley, Daniel III, 291
Smiley, Edward IV, 275
Smiley, Eliza P. III, 87
Smiley, Eliza P. III, 291
Smiley, James W. VI, 995
Smiley, Jane VI, 995
Smiley, Leslie IV, 276
Smiley, Mary Ann IV, 275
Smiley, Melissa IV, 275
Smiley, Melissa E. IV, 276
Smiley, Phoebe III, 291
Smiley, Rezin IV, 275
Smiley, Robert IV, 275
Smiley, Sarah F. VI, 267
Smilie, Andrew VI, 1002
Smilie, Leslie IV, 276
Smith, ??? I, 11
Smith, ??? I, 12
Smith, ??? I, 26
Smith, ??? II, 421
Smith, ??? II, 447
Smith, ??? II, 815
Smith, ??? III, 281
Smith, ??? III, 294
Smith, ??? III, 308
Smith, ??? III, 394
Smith, ??? III, 414
Smith, ??? III, 447
Smith, ??? III, 449
Smith, ??? III, 457
Smith, ??? III, 503
Smith, ??? IV, 549
Smith, ??? IV, 550
Smith, ??? VI, 59
Smith, ??? VI, 418
Smith, ??? VI, 738
Smith, ??? VI, 784
Smith, A. V, 278
Smith, A. J. I, 1161
Smith, Aaron I, 1037
Smith, Aaron II, 180
Smith, Aaron II, 212
Smith, Aaron II, 261
Smith, Aaron II, 421
Smith, Aaron II, 655
Smith, Aaron IV, 59
Smith, Aaron IV, 109
Smith, Aaron IV, 351
Smith, Aaron VI, 561
Smith, Aaron VI, 562
Smith, Aaron VI, 563
Smith, Aaron VI, 701
Smith, Aaron T. IV, 278
Smith, Aaron T. IV, 285
Smith, Aaron T. IV, 1116
Smith, Aaron Thomas IV, 1115
Smith, Aaron Thomas IV, 1116
Smith, Abbie IV, 278
Smith, Abel III, 291
Smith, Abel S. III, 291
Smith, Abel S. III, 292
Smith, Abi A. V, 710
Smith, Abi W. II, 1066
Smith, Abi W. II, 1079
Smith, Abi W. II, 1080
Smith, Abigail I, 364
Smith, Abigail I, 419
Smith, Abigail II, 40
Smith, Abigail II, 184
Smith, Abigail II, 199
Smith, Abigail II, 251
Smith, Abigail II, 257
Smith, Abigail II, 261
Smith, Abigail II, 262
Smith, Abigail II, 531
Smith, Abigail II, 654
Smith, Abigail III, 128
Smith, Abigail III, 130
Smith, Abigail III, 227
Smith, Abigail III, 291
Smith, Abigail III, 292
Smith, Abigail III, 294
Smith, Abigail III, 385
Smith, Abigail III, 389
Smith, Abigail III, 447
Smith, Abigail IV, 1185
Smith, Abigail V, 241
Smith, Abigail V, 278
Smith, Abigail V, 389
Smith, Abigail B. II, 509
Smith, Abigail B. II, 655
Smith, Abigail Bowne II, 421
Smith, Abner I, 419
Smith, Abner III, 385
Smith, Abner V, 278
Smith, Abner V, 279
Smith, Abner VI, 563
Smith, Abner A. V, 279
Smith, Abner D. V, 279
Smith, Abraham I, 968
Smith, Abraham I, 1077
Smith, Abraham I, 1088
Smith, Abraham I, 1098
Smith, Abraham I, 1132
Smith, Abraham I, 1137
Smith, Abraham I, 1146
Smith, Abraham II, 655
Smith, Abraham II, 687
Smith, Abraham III, 291
Smith, Abraham III, 292
Smith, Abraham III, 294
Smith, Abraham IV, 17
Smith, Abraham IV, 21
Smith, Abraham IV, 59
Smith, Abraham IV, 60
Smith, Abraham IV, 550
Smith, Abraham IV, 594
Smith, Abraham IV, 762
Smith, Abraham IV, 763
Smith, Abraham IV, 843
Smith, Abraham IV, 994
Smith, Abraham V, 976
Smith, Abraham VI, 429
Smith, Abraham VI, 444
Smith, Abraham VI, 445
Smith, Abraham VI, 561
Smith, Abraham VI, 562
Smith, Abraham VI, 995
Smith, Abraham, Jr. III, 291
Smith, Abram I, 1098
Smith, Abram VI, 779
Smith, Achasah R. IV, 549
Smith, Achilles VI, 854
Smith, Achsah IV, 393
Smith, Achsah IV, 442
Smith, Achsah IV, 525
Smith, Achsah IV, 549
Smith, Achsah IV, 550
Smith, Achsah R. IV, 183
Smith, Achsah R. IV, 277
Smith, Achsah R. IV, 515
Smith, Achsah R. IV, 550
Smith, Ada Alberta IV, 276
Smith, Ada Alberta IV, 278
Smith, Ada Alberta IV, 1115
Smith, Ada Alberta IV, 1116
Smith, Ada L. V, 710
Smith, Adaline IV, 366
Smith, Adaline IV, 438
Smith, Addison I, 641
Smith, Adrian III, 294
Smith, Adrian IV, 1379
Smith, Agnes II, 315
Smith, Agnes II, 820
Smith, Agnes III, 293
Smith, Agnes III, 322
Smith, Agnes IV, 1077
Smith, Agnes H. II, 924
Smith, Agnes H. II, 945
Smith, Agness VI, 854
Smith, Ailse III, 67
Smith, Ailse III, 294
Smith, Airs IV, 1185
Smith, Alban II, 655
Smith, Alban G. VI, 779
Smith, Albanus II, 421
Smith, Albanus II, 767
Smith, Albert IV, 843
Smith, Albert IV, 1294
Smith, Albert IV, 1338
Smith, Albert VI, 708
Smith, Albert E. III, 292
Smith, Albert E. III, 295
Smith, Albert H. IV, 214
Smith, Albert H. IV, 276
Smith, Albert H. IV, 277
Smith, Albert H. VI, 704
Smith, Albert H., Jr. IV, 277
Smith, Albert Henry IV, 276
Smith, Albert W. Starbuck IV, 278
Smith, Albin Gilpin II, 655
Smith, Alcinda VI, 705
Smith, Alcora Susan I, 12
Smith, Aletha L. IV, 1338
Smith, Alex III, 291
Smith, Alex H. VI, 984
Smith, Alex. III, 130
Smith, Alex. III, 447
Smith, Alexander III, 311
Smith, Alexander III, 414
Smith, Alexander VI, 981
Smith, Alexander VI, 995
Smith, Alexander A. VI, 995
Smith, Alexander A. VI, 1000
Smith, Alexander H. II, 421
Smith, Alexander H. VI, 996
Smith, Alexander R. VI, 995
Smith, Alexd. H. VI, 981
Smith, Alexr. H. VI, 976
Smith, Alfred II, 421
Smith, Alfred II, 767
Smith, Alfred III, 125
Smith, Alfred V, 597
Smith, Alfred V, 598
Smith, Alfred C. I, 625
Smith, Alfred Carman III, 74
Smith, Alfred Carman III, 292
Smith, Alfred Carman III, 385
Smith, Alfred Carmen III, 378
Smith, Alfred D. III, 292
Smith, Alfred E. V, 598
Smith, Alfred Holbrook III, 294
Smith, Alfred I. IV, 1185
Smith, Alfred J. IV, 1185
Smith, Alfred J. IV, 1240
Smith, Alfred Kirkbride II, 302
Smith, Alfred Kirkbride II, 767
Smith, Alfred V. V, 432
Smith, Alice II, 261
Smith, Alice II, 654
Smith, Alice II, 655
Smith, Alice II, 718
Smith, Alice III, 231
Smith, Alice III, 292
Smith, Alice IV, 351
Smith, Alice IV, 352
Smith, Alice IV, 423
Smith, Alice IV, 438
Smith, Alice IV, 440
Smith, Alice IV, 549
Smith, Alice IV, 550
Smith, Alice IV, 562
Smith, Alice IV, 763
Smith, Alice IV, 1185
Smith, Alice V, 279
Smith, Alice VI, 429
Smith, Alice VI, 444
Smith, Alice VI, 445
Smith, Alice VI, 460
Smith, Alice VI, 485
Smith, Alice VI, 561
Smith, Alice VI, 562
Smith, Alice VI, 563
Smith, Alice VI, 571
Smith, Alice VI, 586
Smith, Alice VI, 644
Smith, Alice VI, 695
Smith, Alice VI, 701
Smith, Alice VI, 702
Smith, Alice VI, 705
Smith, Alice VI, 707
Smith, Alice VI, 710
Smith, Alice VI, 995
Smith, Alice Anna V, 932
Smith, Alice C. III, 23
Smith, Alice C. III, 292
Smith, Alice C. III, 295
Smith, Alice E. V, 279
Smith, Alice E. V, 710
Smith, Alice Hays V, 1019
Smith, Alice M. IV, 277
Smith, Alice M. IV, 278
Smith, Alice M. IV, 440
Smith, Alice Paxton II, 820
Smith, Alice Paxton II, 924
Smith, Alice T. VI, 708
Smith, Alice, Jr. VI, 562
Smith, Aliph G. III, 292
Smith, Aliph Gertrude III, 245
Smith, Allen IV, 549
Smith, Allis Blanch I, 1161
Smith, Alma I, 318
Smith, Alma J. III, 511
Smith, Almira B. V, 290
Smith, Almira R. V, 278
Smith, Alphoretta IV, 1223
Smith, Alta E. V, 432
Smith, Altha A. VI, 995
Smith, Alva IV, 1241
Smith, Alva. IV, 1240
Smith, Alvin IV, 763
Smith, Amanda II, 138
Smith, Amanda IV, 1264
Smith, Amanda V, 573
Smith, Amanda VI, 854
Smith, Amanda J. IV, 1097
Smith, Amanda J. IV, 1115
Smith, Amanda Jane IV, 1114
Smith, Ambrose V, 431
Smith, Ambrose V, 432
Smith, Amelia II, 184
Smith, Amelia II, 262
Smith, Amelia II, 301
Smith, Amelia III, 126
Smith, Amelia III, 293
Smith, Amelia III, 294
Smith, Amelia III, 295
Smith, Amelia IV, 1185
Smith, Amelia IV, 1240
Smith, Amelia IV, 1241
Smith, Ammy VI, 854
Smith, Amos I, 17
Smith, Amos I, 33
Smith, Amos II, 301
Smith, Amos II, 1060
Smith, Amos IV, 59
Smith, Amos IV, 276
Smith, Amos IV, 320
Smith, Amos IV, 351
Smith, Amos IV, 520
Smith, Amos IV, 541
Smith, Amos IV, 549
Smith, Amos IV, 550
Smith, Amos IV, 551
Smith, Amos IV, 1115
Smith, Amos IV, 1294
Smith, Amos V, 278
Smith, Amos V, 447
Smith, Amos VI, 701
Smith, Amos VI, 705
Smith, Amos VI, 706
Smith, Amos Harvey IV, 109
Smith, Amos, Jr. IV, 550
Smith, Amy IV, 60
Smith, Amy IV, 438
Smith, Amy IV, 439
Smith, Amy IV, 1098
Smith, Amy IV, 1114
Smith, Amy IV, 1116
Smith, Amy V, 976
Smith, Amy Eleanor V, 269
Smith, Amy Eleanor V, 278
Smith, Amy Elizabeth IV, 1090
Smith, Amy Elizabeth IV, 1115
Smith, Amy Elizabeth IV, 1116
Smith, Amy T. IV, 277
Smith, Amy T. IV, 290
Smith, Amy T. IV, 549
Smith, Amy T. IV, 550
Smith, Amy T. IV, 551
Smith, Amy T. IV, 553
Smith, Andrew II, 183
Smith, Andrew VI, 984
Smith, Andrew J. V, 465
Smith, Andrew J. V, 874
Smith, Andrew Jackson I, 1161
Smith, Andrew M'Kay VI, 605
Smith, Angelia E. III, 447
Smith, Angeline III, 511
Smith, Angie V, 529
Smith, Angie V, 644
Smith, Ann I, 74
Smith, Ann I, 75
Smith, Ann I, 419
Smith, Ann I, 420
Smith, Ann I, 1024
Smith, Ann II, 40
Smith, Ann II, 55
Smith, Ann II, 66
Smith, Ann II, 89
Smith, Ann II, 90
Smith, Ann II, 99
Smith, Ann II, 103

Smith, Ann II, 104
Smith, Ann II, 183
Smith, Ann II, 184
Smith, Ann II, 185
Smith, Ann II, 206
Smith, Ann II, 261
Smith, Ann II, 262
Smith, Ann II, 421
Smith, Ann II, 422
Smith, Ann II, 530
Smith, Ann II, 557
Smith, Ann II, 573
Smith, Ann II, 616
Smith, Ann II, 641
Smith, Ann II, 653
Smith, Ann II, 655
Smith, Ann II, 656
Smith, Ann II, 708
Smith, Ann II, 714
Smith, Ann II, 849
Smith, Ann II, 879
Smith, Ann II, 923
Smith, Ann II, 969
Smith, Ann III, 139
Smith, Ann III, 292
Smith, Ann III, 294
Smith, Ann III, 413
Smith, Ann III, 447
Smith, Ann III, 453
Smith, Ann III, 491
Smith, Ann IV, 23
Smith, Ann IV, 31
Smith, Ann IV, 39
Smith, Ann IV, 52
Smith, Ann IV, 53
Smith, Ann IV, 59
Smith, Ann IV, 60
Smith, Ann IV, 64
Smith, Ann IV, 76
Smith, Ann IV, 77
Smith, Ann IV, 109
Smith, Ann IV, 159
Smith, Ann IV, 345
Smith, Ann IV, 351
Smith, Ann IV, 416
Smith, Ann IV, 437
Smith, Ann IV, 438
Smith, Ann IV, 439
Smith, Ann IV, 551
Smith, Ann IV, 768
Smith, Ann IV, 994
Smith, Ann IV, 1076
Smith, Ann IV, 1090
Smith, Ann IV, 1097
Smith, Ann IV, 1114
Smith, Ann IV, 1115
Smith, Ann IV, 1185
Smith, Ann IV, 1231
Smith, Ann IV, 1240
Smith, Ann V, 40
Smith, Ann V, 122
Smith, Ann V, 123
Smith, Ann V, 203
Smith, Ann V, 465
Smith, Ann V, 525
Smith, Ann V, 529
Smith, Ann V, 548
Smith, Ann V, 597
Smith, Ann V, 598
Smith, Ann V, 858
Smith, Ann V, 862
Smith, Ann VI, 420
Smith, Ann VI, 444
Smith, Ann VI, 445
Smith, Ann VI, 446
Smith, Ann VI, 496
Smith, Ann VI, 505
Smith, Ann VI, 561
Smith, Ann VI, 562
Smith, Ann VI, 563
Smith, Ann VI, 575
Smith, Ann VI, 579
Smith, Ann VI, 605
Smith, Ann VI, 642
Smith, Ann VI, 650
Smith, Ann VI, 699
Smith, Ann VI, 701
Smith, Ann VI, 703
Smith, Ann VI, 705
Smith, Ann VI, 706
Smith, Ann VI, 707
Smith, Ann VI, 708
Smith, Ann VI, 716
Smith, Ann VI, 720
Smith, Ann VI, 912
Smith, Ann VI, 915
Smith, Ann VI, 949
Smith, Ann VI, 1006
Smith, Ann Dennis II, 100
Smith, Ann E. IV, 994
Smith, Ann Eliza III, 440
Smith, Ann G. II, 421
Smith, Ann Gray IV, 594
Smith, Ann Maria IV, 1240
Smith, Ann Thomas II, 99
Smith, Ann W. II, 454
Smith, Ann W. II, 656
Smith, Ann W. II, 767
Smith, Ann, Jr. VI, 561
Smith, Ann, Jr. VI, 701
Smith, Ann, Jr. VI, 707
Smith, Anna I, 318
Smith, Anna II, 23
Smith, Anna II, 55
Smith, Anna II, 99
Smith, Anna II, 158
Smith, Anna II, 183
Smith, Anna II, 184
Smith, Anna II, 255
Smith, Anna II, 262
Smith, Anna II, 422
Smith, Anna II, 590
Smith, Anna II, 622
Smith, Anna II, 653
Smith, Anna II, 654
Smith, Anna II, 655
Smith, Anna II, 783
Smith, Anna II, 820
Smith, Anna II, 969
Smith, Anna II, 1000
Smith, Anna II, 1027
Smith, Anna II, 1028
Smith, Anna III, 215
Smith, Anna III, 292
Smith, Anna III, 295
Smith, Anna III, 372
Smith, Anna IV, 90
Smith, Anna IV, 109
Smith, Anna IV, 159
Smith, Anna IV, 249
Smith, Anna IV, 276
Smith, Anna IV, 277
Smith, Anna IV, 278
Smith, Anna IV, 320
Smith, Anna IV, 351
Smith, Anna IV, 387
Smith, Anna IV, 434
Smith, Anna IV, 438
Smith, Anna IV, 439
Smith, Anna IV, 550
Smith, Anna IV, 551
Smith, Anna IV, 594
Smith, Anna IV, 735
Smith, Anna IV, 994
Smith, Anna IV, 1185
Smith, Anna IV, 1186
Smith, Anna IV, 1294
Smith, Anna V, 203
Smith, Anna V, 279
Smith, Anna V, 502
Smith, Anna V, 529
Smith, Anna V, 710
Smith, Anna V, 862
Smith, Anna V, 953
Smith, Anna V, 960
Smith, Anna VI, 445
Smith, Anna VI, 505
Smith, Anna VI, 650
Smith, Anna VI, 701
Smith, Anna VI, 703
Smith, Anna VI, 995
Smith, Anna C. II, 923
Smith, Anna C. IV, 762
Smith, Anna Canby II, 924
Smith, Anna D. IV, 439
Smith, Anna D. IV, 551
Smith, Anna D. IV, 762
Smith, Anna D. IV, 763
Smith, Anna E. V, 862
Smith, Anna G. V, 432
Smith, Anna G. V, 932
Smith, Anna Gilpin V, 932
Smith, Anna Hilliard II, 138
Smith, Anna I. II, 783
Smith, Anna Kaighn II, 924
Smith, Anna Leora IV, 843
Smith, Anna Leora IV, 851
Smith, Anna M. III, 293
Smith, Anna M. IV, 278
Smith, Anna M. V, 123
Smith, Anna M. V, 710
Smith, Anna Maria V, 932
Smith, Anna Martitia I, 689
Smith, Anna Mary IV, 438
Smith, Anna Mary IV, 782
Smith, Anna R. II, 739
Smith, Anna R. II, 767
Smith, Anna Rebecca II, 130
Smith, Anna Rebecca II, 146
Smith, Anna Rebecca II, 157
Smith, Anna Ridgway II, 421
Smith, Anna T. VI, 636
Smith, Anna T. VI, 701
Smith, Anna T. VI, 706
Smith, Anna W. III, 292
Smith, Anna W. III, 407
Smith, Anna W. III, 447
Smith, Anna W. IV, 438
Smith, Anna W. IV, 440
Smith, Anna Webster IV, 1338
Smith, Anne II, 184
Smith, Anne IV, 520
Smith, Anne IV, 549
Smith, Anne IV, 550
Smith, Anne V, 529
Smith, Anne VI, 496
Smith, Anne VI, 561
Smith, Anne VI, 562
Smith, Anne VI, 563
Smith, Anne VI, 584
Smith, Anne VI, 631
Smith, Anne VI, 642
Smith, Anne VI, 706
Smith, Anne VI, 899
Smith, Anne VI, 1002
Smith, Anne B. II, 924
Smith, Anne Bartram II, 788
Smith, Anne Elizabeth III, 294
Smith, Anne Maria IV, 1185
Smith, Anney I, 364
Smith, Annie I, 318
Smith, Annie II, 801
Smith, Annie III, 292
Smith, Annie III, 295
Smith, Annie III, 317
Smith, Annie IV, 1241
Smith, Annie C. III, 295
Smith, Annie J. III, 502
Smith, Annie R. VI, 439
Smith, Annie R. VI, 446
Smith, Annie Rebecca VI, 445
Smith, Annie T. III, 120
Smith, Annie T. VI, 615
Smith, Annie T. VI, 636
Smith, Anor V, 279
Smith, Anora Fitzpatrick V, 598
Smith, Anthony IV, 59
Smith, Anthony IV, 109
Smith, Anthony V, 465
Smith, Anzonetta IV, 1223
Smith, Arabella II, 715
Smith, Archibald III, 438
Smith, Archibald III, 447
Smith, Archibald S. III, 447
Smith, Arlando Winfield I, 689
Smith, Arley V, 465
Smith, Arth VI, 445
Smith, Arthur IV, 277
Smith, Arthur IV, 438
Smith, Arthur B. II, 137
Smith, Arthur B. II, 158
Smith, Arthur H. IV, 434
Smith, Arthur H. IV, 439
Smith, Arthur Nathan IV, 276
Smith, Arthur T. V, 432
Smith, Arthur T. V, 710
Smith, Asa III, 292
Smith, Asa IV, 109
Smith, Asa IV, 1379
Smith, Asa B. III, 295
Smith, Asenath IV, 437
Smith, Asenath IV, 439
Smith, Asenath IV, 1115
Smith, Asenath IV, 1240
Smith, Asenath IV, 1241
Smith, Asenath IV, 1379
Smith, Asenath VI, 650
Smith, Asenath E. IV, 1114
Smith, Aseneth II, 1028
Smith, Asher B. V, 122
Smith, Asher B. V, 123
Smith, Atalantic V, 278
Smith, Atilla II, 124
Smith, Atlantic V, 274
Smith, Atlantic V, 279
Smith, Atlantick V, 278
Smith, Attila II, 656
Smith, Attila II, 767
Smith, Attilla II, 41
Smith, Attilla II, 100
Smith, Augustine VI, 995
Smith, Augustus C. III, 295
Smith, Austin V, 710
Smith, Austin VI, 970
Smith, Austin VI, 995
Smith, Austin T. V, 710
Smith, Avice IV, 276
Smith, Avis IV, 277
Smith, Avis IV, 1186
Smith, Avis V, 862
Smith, Azariah III, 499
Smith, Bank VI, 995
Smith, Barak IV, 439
Smith, Barcaiah I, 275
Smith, Barcklay IV, 438
Smith, Barclay II, 138
Smith, Barclay II, 157
Smith, Barclay IV, 277
Smith, Barclay IV, 408
Smith, Barclay IV, 411
Smith, Barclay IV, 437
Smith, Barclay IV, 440
Smith, Barclay V, 278
Smith, Barclay V, 279
Smith, Barclay Arney II, 421
Smith, Barzillai II, 183
Smith, Barzillai II, 263
Smith, Barzillai II, 301
Smith, Barzillai II, 656
Smith, Barzillai C. II, 183
Smith, Beatrice Grandstaff V, 1019
Smith, Benj. III, 163
Smith, Benj. III, 293
Smith, Benj. III, 294
Smith, Benj. III, 310
Smith, Benj. III, 451
Smith, Benj. VI, 993
Smith, Benj. C. III, 295
Smith, Benjamin I, 53
Smith, Benjamin I, 74
Smith, Benjamin I, 227
Smith, Benjamin I, 1024
Smith, Benjamin II, 183
Smith, Benjamin II, 184
Smith, Benjamin II, 261
Smith, Benjamin II, 262
Smith, Benjamin II, 263
Smith, Benjamin II, 421
Smith, Benjamin II, 454
Smith, Benjamin II, 654
Smith, Benjamin II, 655
Smith, Benjamin II, 656
Smith, Benjamin III, 55
Smith, Benjamin III, 163
Smith, Benjamin III, 290
Smith, Benjamin III, 292
Smith, Benjamin III, 293
Smith, Benjamin III, 295
Smith, Benjamin III, 447
Smith, Benjamin III, 454
Smith, Benjamin IV, 59
Smith, Benjamin IV, 60
Smith, Benjamin IV, 159
Smith, Benjamin IV, 278
Smith, Benjamin IV, 438
Smith, Benjamin IV, 544
Smith, Benjamin IV, 549
Smith, Benjamin IV, 550
Smith, Benjamin IV, 843
Smith, Benjamin V, 932
Smith, Benjamin V, 936
Smith, Benjamin VI, 121
Smith, Benjamin VI, 445
Smith, Benjamin VI, 562
Smith, Benjamin H. IV, 434
Smith, Benjamin H. IV, 439
Smith, Benjamin H. IV, 440
Smith, Benjamin P. II, 923
Smith, Benjamin Poultney II, 421
Smith, Benjamin Poultney II, 923
Smith, Benjamin R. II, 421
Smith, Benjamin Raper II, 767
Smith, Benjamin W. IV, 277
Smith, Benjamin W. VI, 433
Smith, Benjamin, Jr. I, 74
Smith, Bernard VI, 571
Smith, Bert V, 1019
Smith, Bertha IV, 1223
Smith, Bertha VI, 616
Smith, Bertha VI, 702
Smith, Bertha E. VI, 686
Smith, Bertha E. VI, 702
Smith, Bertha E. VI, 707
Smith, Bertha J. VI, 622
Smith, Bertha J. VI, 626
Smith, Bertha J. VI, 628
Smith, Bertha J. VI, 631
Smith, Bertha J. VI, 635
Smith, Bertha J. VI, 671
Smith, Bertha J. VI, 702
Smith, Bertram III, 134
Smith, Bertram III, 293
Smith, Bessie IV, 1294
Smith, Bessie V, 710
Smith, Bessie V, 712
Smith, Bethany III, 291
Smith, Bethena V, 862
Smith, Bethia III, 294
Smith, Betsey I, 1146
Smith, Betsey VI, 870
Smith, Betsey VI, 995
Smith, Betsy IV, 722
Smith, Betty IV, 909
Smith, Betty VI, 934
Smith, Beulah II, 41
Smith, Beulah II, 100
Smith, Beulah II, 111
Smith, Bird VI, 899
Smith, Boocajah I, 275
Smith, Booker VI, 936
Smith, Booker F. VI, 822
Smith, Booker F. VI, 854
Smith, Bowker W. VI, 995
Smith, Britan VI, 854
Smith, Bruce V, 203
Smith, Buly I, 1063
Smith, Burgess IV, 1138
Smith, Burt A. III, 499
Smith, Burton VI, 828
Smith, C. N. IV, 1186
Smith, Caleb I, 74
Smith, Caleb I, 705
Smith, Caleb I, 734
Smith, Caleb II, 99
Smith, Caleb V, 122
Smith, Caleb VI, 708
Smith, Caleb H. II, 867
Smith, Caleb H. II, 924
Smith, Caleb Hallowell II, 796
Smith, Caleb Hallowell II, 820
Smith, Caleb R. II, 183
Smith, Caleb R. II, 263
Smith, Caleb Raper II, 183
Smith, Caleb Roper V, 122
Smith, Calista V, 598
Smith, Calista Emiline V, 597
Smith, Calvin VI, 995
Smith, Canby II, 1080
Smith, Candance IV, 550
Smith, Capt. John VI, 93
Smith, Carl H. VI, 703
Smith, Carl L. IV, 763
Smith, Carl Nathan IV, 277
Smith, Carman III, 385
Smith, Carmelite Hernandex VI, 752
Smith, Carmelite Hernandez VI, 779
Smith, Caroline I, 689
Smith, Caroline II, 262
Smith, Caroline II, 263
Smith, Caroline II, 655
Smith, Caroline II, 656
Smith, Caroline II, 719
Smith, Caroline III, 292
Smith, Caroline III, 294
Smith, Caroline III, 295
Smith, Caroline IV, 246
Smith, Caroline IV, 277
Smith, Caroline IV, 1076
Smith, Caroline IV, 1077
Smith, Caroline IV, 1138
Smith, Caroline V, 123
Smith, Caroline VI, 708
Smith, Caroline E. III, 292
Smith, Caroline M. II, 718
Smith, Caroline M. II, 767
Smith, Caroline M. IV, 278
Smith, Caroline McPhail V, 710
Smith, Caroline N. IV, 1076
Smith, Caroline R. II, 767
Smith, Caroline Ridgway II, 421
Smith, Carolyn Bowen II, 138
Smith, Carolyn Elizabeth II, 969
Smith, Carolyn Heacock VI, 703
Smith, Carrie IV, 1186
Smith, Carrie IV, 1264
Smith, Cassius IV, 1186
Smith, Catharine I, 419
Smith, Catharine I, 428
Smith, Catharine II, 183
Smith, Catharine II, 184
Smith, Catharine II, 261
Smith, Catharine II, 262
Smith, Catharine II, 820
Smith, Catharine III, 295
Smith, Catharine III, 380
Smith, Catharine III, 385
Smith, Catharine IV, 109
Smith, Catharine IV, 351
Smith, Catharine IV, 438
Smith, Catharine IV, 465
Smith, Catharine IV, 497
Smith, Catharine IV, 515
Smith, Catharine IV, 540
Smith, Catharine IV, 549
Smith, Catharine IV, 550
Smith, Catharine IV, 553
Smith, Catharine IV, 630
Smith, Catharine IV, 657
Smith, Catharine IV, 762
Smith, Catharine IV, 1042

Catharine V, 136
Catharine VI, 854
Catharine VI, 970
Catharine VI, 1003
Catharine B. IV, 549
Catharine C. II, 1055
Catharine C. II, 1060
Catharine Emeline V, 598
Catharine F. III, 292
Catharine F. III, 370
Catharine F. V, 360
Catharine L. IV, 497
Catharine L. IV, 550
Catharine L. IV, 551
Catharine S. IV, 482
Catharine S. IV, 497
Catharine S. IV, 551
Catherine II, 654
Catherine IV, 109
Catherine IV, 277
Catherine IV, 351
Catherine V, 122
Catherine V, 278
Catherine V, 279
Catherine V, 290
Catherine B. IV, 277
Catherine Ellen II, 824
Catherine L. IV, 550
Catherine S. IV, 277
Catherine Sophia Louisa
cks II, 715
Celia IV, 1240
Celia IV, 1241
Celia E. VI, 995
Chad V, 122
Chamness VI, 992
Chamness VI, 995
Charity II, 99
Charity III, 295
Charity IV, 1241
Charles II, 313
Charles II, 421
Charles III, 292
Charles III, 294
Charles IV, 1077
Charles IV, 1186
Charles IV, 1223
Charles IV, 1379
Charles V, 122
Charles V, 123
Charles V, 598
Charles V, 710
Charles VI, 707
Charles VI, 995
Charles A. III, 292
Charles A. IV, 1379
Charles B. II, 1080
Charles D. V, 710
Charles E. II, 767
Charles E. II, 776
Charles F. III, 292
Charles F. III, 295
Charles F. III, 315
Charles G. V, 123
Charles J. V, 432
Charles L. II, 655
Charles Livesey IV, 594
Charles Newton II, 313
Charles Newton II, 324
Charles P. V, 123
Charles R. V, 123
Charles S. II, 128
Charles S. II, 421
Charles Thomas IV, 1076
Charles Valentine III, 447
Charles Valentine III, 467
Charles W. II, 656
Charles W. II, 767
Charles W. V, 529
Charles W. V, 598
Charlex M. V, 529
Charley V, 465
Charley V, 529
Charlie V, 278
Charlie V, 360
Charlotte III, 292
Charlotte V, 278
Charlotte V, 279
Charlotte V, 284
Charlotte V, 432
Charlotte V, 447
Charlotte VI, 446
Charlotte VI, 939
Charlotte A. VI, 446
Charlotte F. II, 158
Charlotte Fletcher II, 138
Charlotte L. II, 301
Charlotte Lawrence
, 301
Charlotte S. III, 447
Chas F. III, 295

Smith, Chas. V, 932
Smith, Chas. V, 1019
Smith, Chas. D. V, 691
Smith, Chas. D. V, 710
Smith, Chas. F. III, 295
Smith, Chas. F. III, 315
Smith, Chas. Ferdinand IV, 1223
Smith, Chas. H. III, 245
Smith, Chas. H. III, 292
Smith, Chas. H. III, 294
Smith, Chas. V. III, 467
Smith, Chester I, 419
Smith, Chester IV, 1186
Smith, Chester V, 710
Smith, Chloe IV, 159
Smith, Christian II, 421
Smith, Christian IV, 60
Smith, Christiana II, 553
Smith, Christiana IV, 60
Smith, Christiana IV, 69
Smith, Christiana IV, 594
Smith, Christiana IV, 994
Smith, Christianna IV, 580
Smith, Christianna IV, 594
Smith, Christina II, 654
Smith, Christopher II, 23
Smith, Christopher II, 30
Smith, Christopher II, 40
Smith, Christopher II, 76
Smith, Christopher II, 88
Smith, Christopher II, 90
Smith, Christopher II, 99
Smith, Christopher II, 100
Smith, Christopher II, 421
Smith, Christopher II, 654
Smith, Cina V, 431
Smith, Clara V, 203
Smith, Clara V, 466
Smith, Clara V, 529
Smith, Clara V, 710
Smith, Clara V, 764
Smith, Clara V, 1019
Smith, Clara E. V, 432
Smith, Clara Ladd V, 278
Smith, Clara May V, 203
Smith, Clarence V, 360
Smith, Clarence V, 598
Smith, Clarence V, 710
Smith, Clarence W. III, 292
Smith, Clark I, 642
Smith, Clark II, 99
Smith, Clarkson III, 294
Smith, Clarkson VI, 708
Smith, Clement II, 40
Smith, Clement II, 41
Smith, Clement II, 100
Smith, Clement II, 108
Smith, Clement II, 124
Smith, Clement H. II, 767
Smith, Clement W. II, 40
Smith, Clement Wilson II, 820
Smith, Clemsey VI, 936
Smith, Clifford II, 654
Smith, Clifford II, 655
Smith, Clifford V, 278
Smith, Clifford V, 279
Smith, Clinton IV, 278
Smith, Clinton IV, 1185
Smith, Clinton Lindley IV, 276
Smith, Clinton Lindley IV, 278
Smith, Clinton Lindley IV, 1116
Smith, Clyde I, 640
Smith, Clyde IV, 1223
Smith, Clyde V, 598
Smith, Clyde E. I, 625
Smith, Coleman VI, 995
Smith, Conrad V, 465
Smith, Copathite IV, 109
Smith, Coperthraite VI, 445
Smith, Coperthwaite IV, 59
Smith, Coperthwite IV, 109
Smith, Copethite VI, 446
Smith, Copothwait VI, 445
Smith, Copperthwait VI, 605
Smith, Coppertwait IV, 59
Smith, Cora V, 644
Smith, Cora V, 710
Smith, Cora L. IV, 1263
Smith, Cordelia V, 432
Smith, Cordelia B. V, 432
Smith, Cornelia I, 318
Smith, Cornelia III, 295
Smith, Cousins IV, 60
Smith, Craig V, 862
Smith, Curtis W. IV, 277
Smith, Curtis W. IV, 440
Smith, Custis W. IV, 246
Smith, Cuzzy VI, 995
Smith, Cynthia E. I, 899
Smith, Cynthia E. I, 900
Smith, Cyrus V, 123

Smith, Cyrus V, 432
Smith, Cyrus V, 932
Smith, Cyrus N. V, 932
Smith, D??? IV, 549
Smith, Dale Martin IV, 1185
Smith, Daniel I, 364
Smith, Daniel I, 379
Smith, Daniel I, 419
Smith, Daniel I, 997
Smith, Daniel I, 1023
Smith, Daniel I, 1037
Smith, Daniel II, 40
Smith, Daniel II, 59
Smith, Daniel II, 99
Smith, Daniel II, 100
Smith, Daniel II, 183
Smith, Daniel II, 184
Smith, Daniel II, 185
Smith, Daniel II, 205
Smith, Daniel II, 238
Smith, Daniel II, 244
Smith, Daniel II, 249
Smith, Daniel II, 252
Smith, Daniel II, 261
Smith, Daniel II, 262
Smith, Daniel II, 421
Smith, Daniel II, 454
Smith, Daniel II, 457
Smith, Daniel II, 530
Smith, Daniel II, 653
Smith, Daniel II, 654
Smith, Daniel II, 655
Smith, Daniel II, 656
Smith, Daniel II, 660
Smith, Daniel IV, 59
Smith, Daniel IV, 109
Smith, Daniel IV, 1185
Smith, Daniel IV, 1240
Smith, Daniel IV, 1241
Smith, Daniel IV, 1264
Smith, Daniel IV, 1378
Smith, Daniel IV, 1379
Smith, Daniel V, 122
Smith, Daniel V, 598
Smith, Daniel V, 710
Smith, Daniel VI, 562
Smith, Daniel B. II, 262
Smith, Daniel B. II, 421
Smith, Daniel B. II, 655
Smith, Daniel B. II, 656
Smith, Daniel B. II, 718
Smith, Daniel B. II, 767
Smith, Daniel C. V, 631
Smith, Daniel Doughty II, 257
Smith, Daniel Doughty II, 262
Smith, Daniel J. VI, 653
Smith, Daniel W. IV, 437
Smith, Daniel W. IV, 1379
Smith, Daniel William V, 431
Smith, Daniel Wm. V, 432
Smith, Daniel, Jr. I, 1037
Smith, Daniel, Jr. II, 55
Smith, Daniel, Jr. II, 183
Smith, Daniel, Jr. II, 262
Smith, Daniel, Jr. II, 552
Smith, David I, 74
Smith, David I, 419
Smith, David I, 997
Smith, David I, 1015
Smith, David I, 1023
Smith, David I, 1024
Smith, David I, 1037
Smith, David II, 40
Smith, David II, 41
Smith, David II, 55
Smith, David II, 61
Smith, David II, 99
Smith, David II, 100
Smith, David II, 138
Smith, David II, 150
Smith, David II, 157
Smith, David II, 185
Smith, David II, 313
Smith, David II, 654
Smith, David II, 820
Smith, David II, 923
Smith, David II, 1009
Smith, David II, 1028
Smith, David IV, 96
Smith, David IV, 109
Smith, David IV, 159
Smith, David IV, 276
Smith, David IV, 277
Smith, David IV, 314
Smith, David IV, 356
Smith, David IV, 437
Smith, David IV, 438
Smith, David IV, 439
Smith, David IV, 449
Smith, David IV, 883
Smith, David IV, 1057

Smith, David IV, 1066
Smith, David IV, 1076
Smith, David IV, 1077
Smith, David IV, 1114
Smith, David IV, 1115
Smith, David IV, 1116
Smith, David IV, 1138
Smith, David IV, 1181
Smith, David IV, 1185
Smith, David IV, 1186
Smith, David VI, 445
Smith, David VI, 446
Smith, David VI, 459
Smith, David VI, 561
Smith, David VI, 562
Smith, David VI, 586
Smith, David VI, 605
Smith, David VI, 678
Smith, David VI, 702
Smith, David VI, 705
Smith, David VI, 854
Smith, David VI, 899
Smith, David VI, 995
Smith, David B. IV, 1089
Smith, David B. IV, 1114
Smith, David B. IV, 1115
Smith, David B. IV, 1116
Smith, David C. II, 263
Smith, David F. IV, 1115
Smith, David G. IV, 315
Smith, David H. IV, 883
Smith, David H. V, 932
Smith, David M. V, 360
Smith, David P. III, 20
Smith, David P. III, 292
Smith, David P. III, 314
Smith, David R. IV, 1128
Smith, David R. IV, 1138
Smith, David R. VI, 446
Smith, David W. V, 278
Smith, David, Jr. VI, 995
Smith, Dean V, 529
Smith, Deborah II, 57
Smith, Deborah II, 99
Smith, Deborah II, 184
Smith, Deborah II, 209
Smith, Deborah II, 262
Smith, Deborah II, 263
Smith, Deborah II, 421
Smith, Deborah II, 447
Smith, Deborah II, 655
Smith, Deborah III, 292
Smith, Deborah III, 294
Smith, Deborah III, 295
Smith, Deborah III, 444
Smith, Deborah III, 447
Smith, Deborah III, 448
Smith, Deborah III, 498
Smith, Deborah III, 499
Smith, Deborah IV, 59
Smith, Deborah IV, 77
Smith, Deborah IV, 109
Smith, Deborah IV, 277
Smith, Deborah IV, 843
Smith, Deborah V, 123
Smith, Deborah V, 529
Smith, Deborah V, 555
Smith, Deborah V, 597
Smith, Deborah V, 952
Smith, Deborah V, 959
Smith, Deborah V, 962
Smith, Deborah VI, 445
Smith, Deborah VI, 605
Smith, Deborah A. I, 681
Smith, Deborah A. I, 689
Smith, Deborah Ann IV, 438
Smith, Deborah Ann IV, 440
Smith, Deborah Ann IV, 445
Smith, Deborah B. II, 263
Smith, Deborah B. II, 767
Smith, Deborah B. IV, 214
Smith, Deborah B. IV, 277
Smith, Deborah Shaw II, 790
Smith, Deborah T. IV, 497
Smith, Deborah T. IV, 536
Smith, Deborah T. IV, 550
Smith, Delaney R. VI, 796
Smith, Dewannah VI, 854
Smith, Diana IV, 959
Smith, Dill A. III, 293
Smith, Dillwyn II, 183
Smith, Dillwyn II, 296
Smith, Dillwyn II, 301
Smith, Dillwyn II, 302
Smith, Dillwyn R. IV, 438
Smith, Dinah I, 1024
Smith, Dinah I, 1061
Smith, Dinah I, 1063
Smith, Dinah IV, 959
Smith, Donald V, 203
Smith, Donald V, 710

Smith, Donald Wilmer IV, 276
Smith, Dora IV, 1294
Smith, Dora V, 710
Smith, Dorcas II, 40
Smith, Dorcas V, 428
Smith, Dorcas V, 431
Smith, Dorcas V, 432
Smith, Dorcas V, 434
Smith, Doris Ellingwood VI, 628
Smith, Doris Ellingwood VI, 702
Smith, Doroth Ann IV, 300
Smith, Dorotha II, 99
Smith, Dorothy I, 11
Smith, Dorothy I, 18
Smith, Dorothy I, 57
Smith, Dorothy I, 74
Smith, Dorothy II, 40
Smith, Dorothy II, 99
Smith, Dorothy II, 100
Smith, Dorothy II, 197
Smith, Dorothy II, 225
Smith, Dorothy II, 261
Smith, Dorothy III, 467
Smith, Dorothy V, 710
Smith, Dorothy VI, 496
Smith, Dorothy VI, 497
Smith, Dorothy VI, 559
Smith, Dorothy VI, 562
Smith, Dorothy A. IV, 497
Smith, Dorothy Ann IV, 277
Smith, Dorothy J. III, 447
Smith, Dorothy J. III, 467
Smith, Dr. Lucian V, 529
Smith, Drury VI, 976
Smith, Drury H. VI, 921
Smith, Drusilla S. IV, 994
Smith, Duane V, 529
Smith, Dussey V, 465
Smith, E. Anna IV, 278
Smith, E. Lewis, Jr. III, 295
Smith, E. Raymond VI, 703
Smith, Ebaneezer IV, 109
Smith, Ebelina I, 914
Smith, Eber II, 1028
Smith, Eber IV, 1223
Smith, Eber U. V, 123
Smith, Edgar IV, 551
Smith, Edgar IV, 762
Smith, Edgar IV, 763
Smith, Edgar O. V, 279
Smith, Edgar T. IV, 438
Smith, Edgar T. IV, 439
Smith, Edgar T. IV, 550
Smith, Edith IV, 205
Smith, Edith IV, 213
Smith, Edith IV, 246
Smith, Edith IV, 276
Smith, Edith IV, 277
Smith, Edith IV, 482
Smith, Edith IV, 497
Smith, Edith IV, 538
Smith, Edith IV, 550
Smith, Edith IV, 551
Smith, Edith IV, 594
Smith, Edith IV, 994
Smith, Edith IV, 1186
Smith, Edith VI, 561
Smith, Edith VI, 563
Smith, Edith VI, 702
Smith, Edith F. II, 783
Smith, Edith F. II, 924
Smith, Edith H. IV, 536
Smith, Edith K. IV, 497
Smith, Edith K. IV, 550
Smith, Edith Lillian IV, 276
Smith, Edith Lillian IV, 278
Smith, Edith M. IV, 246
Smith, Edith M. IV, 278
Smith, Edith R. IV, 497
Smith, Edith R. IV, 550
Smith, Edith S. II, 783
Smith, Edith S. II, 924
Smith, Edmond III, 498
Smith, Edmond III, 499
Smith, Edmond Louis II, 302
Smith, Edmund II, 421
Smith, Edmund III, 444
Smith, Edmund III, 447
Smith, Edmund IV, 246
Smith, Edmund IV, 277
Smith, Edmund IV, 438
Smith, Edmund IV, 812
Smith, Edmund IV, 883
Smith, Edmund V, 122
Smith, Edmund VI, 446
Smith, Edmund J. IV, 440
Smith, Edmund Louis II, 767
Smith, Edmund S. IV, 214
Smith, Edmund S. IV, 276
Smith, Edmund S. IV, 278
Smith, Edmund S. IV, 438

Smith, Edmund S. IV, 440
Smith, Edna III, 125
Smith, Edna III, 292
Smith, Edna D. III, 125
Smith, Edna Mae I, 18
Smith, Edward II, 214
Smith, Edward II, 261
Smith, Edward II, 421
Smith, Edward III, 67
Smith, Edward III, 69
Smith, Edward III, 292
Smith, Edward III, 294
Smith, Edward IV, 883
Smith, Edward IV, 1338
Smith, Edward V, 597
Smith, Edward V, 710
Smith, Edward Betts II, 820
Smith, Edward J VI, 686
Smith, Edward J. III, 263
Smith, Edward J. III, 294
Smith, Edward J. VI, 625
Smith, Edward J. VI, 626
Smith, Edward J. VI, 628
Smith, Edward J. VI, 693
Smith, Edward J. VI, 702
Smith, Edward J. VI, 704
Smith, Edward J. VI, 707
Smith, Edward J. VI, 723
Smith, Edward Joseph VI, 707
Smith, Edward L. VI, 515
Smith, Edward Lewis II, 302
Smith, Edward Lincoln II, 183
Smith, Edward Lincoln II, 302
Smith, Edward M. II, 183
Smith, Edward M. II, 301
Smith, Edward M. II, 302
Smith, Edward M. II, 719
Smith, Edward Milnor II, 656
Smith, Edward Milnor II, 767
Smith, Edward Rockhill II, 185
Smith, Edward Wade II, 17
Smith, Edward, Jr. VI, 702
Smith, Edwin III, 497
Smith, Edwin Oscar III, 292
Smith, Edwin S. IV, 277
Smith, Edwin S. IV, 439
Smith, Effie V, 432
Smith, Effie M. V, 431
Smith, Effie M. V, 432
Smith, Elbert J. IV, 438
Smith, Elbert J. IV, 439
Smith, Elbert J. IV, 550
Smith, Elbert J. IV, 551
Smith, Eldra E. V, 278
Smith, Eleanor III, 120
Smith, Eleanor III, 137
Smith, Eleanor III, 292
Smith, Eleanor III, 295
Smith, Eleanor IV, 549
Smith, Eleanor V, 236
Smith, Eleanor V, 278
Smith, Eleanor V, 710
Smith, Eleanor VI, 707
Smith, Eleanor Pancoast VI, 702
Smith, Eleanor Pancoast VI, 703
Smith, Electa A. I, 625
Smith, Elener III, 292
Smith, Elgar V, 279
Smith, Eli IV, 1114
Smith, Eli IV, 1116
Smith, Eli V, 120
Smith, Eli V, 300
Smith, Elias III, 293
Smith, Elias IV, 109
Smith, Elias V, 932
Smith, Elias E. II, 1080
Smith, Elihu III, 236
Smith, Elihu III, 292
Smith, Elihu III, 293
Smith, Elihu III, 295
Smith, Elihu III, 380
Smith, Elihu III, 385
Smith, Elihu IV, 438
Smith, Elihu IV, 439
Smith, Elihu IV, 1076
Smith, Elihu IV, 1111
Smith, Elihu IV, 1115
Smith, Elijah I, 1098
Smith, Elijah V, 529
Smith, Elisabeth I, 39
Smith, Elisabeth I, 74
Smith, Elisabeth I, 249
Smith, Elisabeth I, 257
Smith, Elisabeth II, 184
Smith, Elisabeth II, 196
Smith, Elisabeth II, 257
Smith, Elisabeth II, 261
Smith, Elisabeth II, 277
Smith, Elisabeth IV, 657
Smith, Elisabeth IV, 661
Smith, Elisha II, 55
Smith, Elisha II, 100
Smith, Elisha II, 655
Smith, Elisha IV, 379
Smith, Elisha IV, 437
Smith, Elisha IV, 439
Smith, Elisha IV, 549
Smith, Elisha IV, 1115
Smith, Elisha VI, 854
Smith, Eliz. III, 163
Smith, Eliz. M. III, 236
Smith, Eliza I, 613
Smith, Eliza I, 1088
Smith, Eliza I, 1161
Smith, Eliza II, 100
Smith, Eliza II, 820
Smith, Eliza II, 923
Smith, Eliza III, 20
Smith, Eliza III, 295
Smith, Eliza III, 369
Smith, Eliza IV, 276
Smith, Eliza IV, 351
Smith, Eliza IV, 353
Smith, Eliza IV, 417
Smith, Eliza IV, 439
Smith, Eliza IV, 440
Smith, Eliza IV, 812
Smith, Eliza IV, 843
Smith, Eliza IV, 1115
Smith, Eliza IV, 1286
Smith, Eliza IV, 1294
Smith, Eliza VI, 568
Smith, Eliza VI, 911
Smith, Eliza VI, 995
Smith, Eliza Ann II, 655
Smith, Eliza Ann IV, 59
Smith, Eliza Ann V, 905
Smith, Eliza Ann V, 932
Smith, Eliza D. IV, 214
Smith, Eliza D. IV, 276
Smith, Eliza D. IV, 278
Smith, Eliza D. IV, 438
Smith, Eliza E. V, 431
Smith, Eliza Emma V, 431
Smith, Eliza H. II, 923
Smith, Eliza H. II, 924
Smith, Eliza H. VI, 911
Smith, Eliza P. II, 421
Smith, Elizabeth I, 214
Smith, Elizabeth I, 227
Smith, Elizabeth I, 310
Smith, Elizabeth I, 318
Smith, Elizabeth I, 373
Smith, Elizabeth I, 405
Smith, Elizabeth I, 416
Smith, Elizabeth I, 419
Smith, Elizabeth I, 641
Smith, Elizabeth I, 642
Smith, Elizabeth I, 705
Smith, Elizabeth I, 734
Smith, Elizabeth I, 817
Smith, Elizabeth I, 837
Smith, Elizabeth I, 933
Smith, Elizabeth I, 991
Smith, Elizabeth I, 997
Smith, Elizabeth I, 1023
Smith, Elizabeth I, 1060
Smith, Elizabeth I, 1063
Smith, Elizabeth I, 1088
Smith, Elizabeth II, 30
Smith, Elizabeth II, 40
Smith, Elizabeth II, 41
Smith, Elizabeth II, 55
Smith, Elizabeth II, 56
Smith, Elizabeth II, 58
Smith, Elizabeth II, 75
Smith, Elizabeth II, 87
Smith, Elizabeth II, 99
Smith, Elizabeth II, 100
Smith, Elizabeth II, 113
Smith, Elizabeth II, 132
Smith, Elizabeth II, 136
Smith, Elizabeth II, 138
Smith, Elizabeth II, 165
Smith, Elizabeth II, 183
Smith, Elizabeth II, 184
Smith, Elizabeth II, 185
Smith, Elizabeth II, 191
Smith, Elizabeth II, 195
Smith, Elizabeth II, 233
Smith, Elizabeth II, 252
Smith, Elizabeth II, 255
Smith, Elizabeth II, 261
Smith, Elizabeth II, 262
Smith, Elizabeth II, 292
Smith, Elizabeth II, 421
Smith, Elizabeth II, 422
Smith, Elizabeth II, 447
Smith, Elizabeth II, 488
Smith, Elizabeth II, 489
Smith, Elizabeth II, 529
Smith, Elizabeth II, 557
Smith, Elizabeth II, 580
Smith, Elizabeth II, 584
Smith, Elizabeth II, 587
Smith, Elizabeth II, 603
Smith, Elizabeth II, 626
Smith, Elizabeth II, 653
Smith, Elizabeth II, 654
Smith, Elizabeth II, 655
Smith, Elizabeth II, 656
Smith, Elizabeth II, 701
Smith, Elizabeth II, 715
Smith, Elizabeth II, 719
Smith, Elizabeth II, 756
Smith, Elizabeth II, 767
Smith, Elizabeth II, 783
Smith, Elizabeth II, 785
Smith, Elizabeth II, 820
Smith, Elizabeth II, 823
Smith, Elizabeth II, 969
Smith, Elizabeth II, 970
Smith, Elizabeth II, 1002
Smith, Elizabeth II, 1010
Smith, Elizabeth II, 1027
Smith, Elizabeth II, 1028
Smith, Elizabeth II, 1030
Smith, Elizabeth II, 1035
Smith, Elizabeth II, 1060
Smith, Elizabeth II, 1070
Smith, Elizabeth II, 1080
Smith, Elizabeth III, 74
Smith, Elizabeth III, 292
Smith, Elizabeth III, 293
Smith, Elizabeth III, 294
Smith, Elizabeth III, 413
Smith, Elizabeth III, 447
Smith, Elizabeth III, 453
Smith, Elizabeth III, 482
Smith, Elizabeth III, 499
Smith, Elizabeth IV, 47
Smith, Elizabeth IV, 59
Smith, Elizabeth IV, 60
Smith, Elizabeth IV, 85
Smith, Elizabeth IV, 109
Smith, Elizabeth IV, 113
Smith, Elizabeth IV, 276
Smith, Elizabeth IV, 277
Smith, Elizabeth IV, 321
Smith, Elizabeth IV, 351
Smith, Elizabeth IV, 359
Smith, Elizabeth IV, 374
Smith, Elizabeth IV, 386
Smith, Elizabeth IV, 424
Smith, Elizabeth IV, 429
Smith, Elizabeth IV, 437
Smith, Elizabeth IV, 438
Smith, Elizabeth IV, 439
Smith, Elizabeth IV, 443
Smith, Elizabeth IV, 455
Smith, Elizabeth IV, 515
Smith, Elizabeth IV, 525
Smith, Elizabeth IV, 544
Smith, Elizabeth IV, 549
Smith, Elizabeth IV, 550
Smith, Elizabeth IV, 551
Smith, Elizabeth IV, 553
Smith, Elizabeth IV, 562
Smith, Elizabeth IV, 594
Smith, Elizabeth IV, 641
Smith, Elizabeth IV, 762
Smith, Elizabeth IV, 763
Smith, Elizabeth IV, 831
Smith, Elizabeth IV, 874
Smith, Elizabeth IV, 883
Smith, Elizabeth IV, 908
Smith, Elizabeth IV, 994
Smith, Elizabeth IV, 1058
Smith, Elizabeth IV, 1076
Smith, Elizabeth IV, 1114
Smith, Elizabeth IV, 1115
Smith, Elizabeth IV, 1138
Smith, Elizabeth IV, 1181
Smith, Elizabeth IV, 1186
Smith, Elizabeth IV, 1326
Smith, Elizabeth IV, 1379
Smith, Elizabeth IV, 1385
Smith, Elizabeth V, 93
Smith, Elizabeth V, 122
Smith, Elizabeth V, 123
Smith, Elizabeth V, 203
Smith, Elizabeth V, 252
Smith, Elizabeth V, 278
Smith, Elizabeth V, 279
Smith, Elizabeth V, 360
Smith, Elizabeth V, 420
Smith, Elizabeth V, 431
Smith, Elizabeth V, 432
Smith, Elizabeth V, 521
Smith, Elizabeth V, 529
Smith, Elizabeth V, 559
Smith, Elizabeth V, 598
Smith, Elizabeth V, 631
Smith, Elizabeth V, 644
Smith, Elizabeth V, 861
Smith, Elizabeth V, 862
Smith, Elizabeth V, 882
Smith, Elizabeth V, 886
Smith, Elizabeth V, 932
Smith, Elizabeth V, 959
Smith, Elizabeth VI, 381
Smith, Elizabeth VI, 445
Smith, Elizabeth VI, 446
Smith, Elizabeth VI, 561
Smith, Elizabeth VI, 563
Smith, Elizabeth VI, 568
Smith, Elizabeth VI, 679
Smith, Elizabeth VI, 685
Smith, Elizabeth VI, 696
Smith, Elizabeth VI, 702
Smith, Elizabeth VI, 704
Smith, Elizabeth VI, 834
Smith, Elizabeth VI, 835
Smith, Elizabeth VI, 854
Smith, Elizabeth VI, 858
Smith, Elizabeth VI, 865
Smith, Elizabeth VI, 888
Smith, Elizabeth VI, 918
Smith, Elizabeth VI, 979
Smith, Elizabeth VI, 995
Smith, Elizabeth VI, 1005
Smith, Elizabeth A. VI, 801
Smith, Elizabeth A. VI, 865
Smith, Elizabeth Alice M. II, 783
Smith, Elizabeth Ann VI, 947
Smith, Elizabeth B. IV, 214
Smith, Elizabeth B. IV, 276
Smith, Elizabeth B. IV, 277
Smith, Elizabeth B. IV, 408
Smith, Elizabeth B. IV, 438
Smith, Elizabeth B. VI, 695
Smith, Elizabeth B. VI, 702
Smith, Elizabeth B. VI, 721
Smith, Elizabeth B. VI, 723
Smith, Elizabeth Bacon II, 263
Smith, Elizabeth Bacon II, 422
Smith, Elizabeth Bacon II, 656
Smith, Elizabeth Bacon II, 719
Smith, Elizabeth Bacon II, 767
Smith, Elizabeth Black II, 100
Smith, Elizabeth Burr II, 820
Smith, Elizabeth C. V, 120
Smith, Elizabeth C. V, 122
Smith, Elizabeth Emma V, 432
Smith, Elizabeth F. II, 158
Smith, Elizabeth F. II, 924
Smith, Elizabeth G. II, 138
Smith, Elizabeth G. II, 158
Smith, Elizabeth G. II, 866
Smith, Elizabeth G. II, 924
Smith, Elizabeth G. IV, 497
Smith, Elizabeth G. IV, 550
Smith, Elizabeth G. IV, 551
Smith, Elizabeth H. II, 158
Smith, Elizabeth H. II, 159
Smith, Elizabeth H. IV, 37
Smith, Elizabeth H. IV, 60
Smith, Elizabeth H. V, 886
Smith, Elizabeth Hitchings III, 295
Smith, Elizabeth Lee II, 138
Smith, Elizabeth Lee II, 158
Smith, Elizabeth M. II, 296
Smith, Elizabeth M. II, 301
Smith, Elizabeth M. III, 292
Smith, Elizabeth M. III, 295
Smith, Elizabeth Mitchell III, 292
Smith, Elizabeth N. VI, 707
Smith, Elizabeth P. II, 767
Smith, Elizabeth P. II, 864
Smith, Elizabeth P. II, 924
Smith, Elizabeth P. III, 292
Smith, Elizabeth P. III, 295
Smith, Elizabeth R. II, 183
Smith, Elizabeth R. II, 733
Smith, Elizabeth R. II, 767
Smith, Elizabeth R. IV, 1116
Smith, Elizabeth Smith II, 655
Smith, Elizabeth T. III, 378
Smith, Elizabeth T. III, 385
Smith, Elizabeth W. IV, 241
Smith, Elizabeth W. IV, 276
Smith, Elizabeth W. IV, 277
Smith, Elizabeth W. IV, 380
Smith, Elizabeth W. IV, 417
Smith, Elizabeth W. IV, 438
Smith, Elizabeth W. IV, 439
Smith, Elizabeth W. IV, 586
Smith, Elizabeth W. IV, 594
Smith, Elizabeth, Jr. II, 54
Smith, Elizabeth, Jr. II, 99
Smith, Elizabeth, Jr. II, 655
Smith, Elkanah II, 184
Smith, Ella IV, 1338
Smith, Ella V, 710
Smith, Ella V, 1019
Smith, Ella VI, 561
Smith, Ella VI, 575
Smith, Ella VI, 576
Smith, Ella VI, 702
Smith, Ella VI, 717
Smith, Ella E. V, 279
Smith, Ella E. V, 465
Smith, Ella G. VI, 627
Smith, Ella G. VI, 707
Smith, Ella Gardner VI, 622
Smith, Ella Gardner VI, 670
Smith, Ella Gardner VI, 702
Smith, Ella Gardner VI, 703
Smith, Ella J. V, 710
Smith, Ella T. IV, 551
Smith, Ella T. IV, 762
Smith, Ella T. IV, 763
Smith, Ellen II, 820
Smith, Ellen II, 851
Smith, Ellen II, 924
Smith, Ellen IV, 1186
Smith, Ellen IV, 1326
Smith, Ellen V, 432
Smith, Ellen V, 529
Smith, Ellen V, 598
Smith, Ellen V, 764
Smith, Ellen VI, 636
Smith, Ellen VI, 645
Smith, Ellen VI, 652
Smith, Ellen VI, 653
Smith, Ellen VI, 701
Smith, Ellen VI, 703
Smith, Ellen VI, 704
Smith, Ellen VI, 724
Smith, Ellen A. III, 292
Smith, Ellen A. III, 295
Smith, Ellen Augusta III, 29
Smith, Ellen B. II, 138
Smith, Ellen B. II, 158
Smith, Ellen H. VI, 706
Smith, Ellen Haines VI, 662
Smith, Ellen Haines VI, 664
Smith, Ellen Haines VI, 753
Smith, Ellen May IV, 1186
Smith, Ellinor II, 1009
Smith, Ellinor II, 1028
Smith, Ellis C. V, 862
Smith, Ellwood IV, 1115
Smith, Elma IV, 438
Smith, Elma L. V, 278
Smith, Elmer II, 138
Smith, Elmer II, 158
Smith, Elmer IV, 1186
Smith, Elmer V, 278
Smith, Elmer E. V, 360
Smith, Elmer McGrew IV, 10
Smith, Elmer McGrew IV, 11
Smith, Elmer, Jr. II, 138
Smith, Elmer, Jr. II, 158
Smith, Elmore IV, 1186
Smith, Elonar II, 71
Smith, Elonar II, 99
Smith, Elsie III, 493
Smith, Elsie VI, 627
Smith, Elsmer V, 529
Smith, Elton Verner III, 133
Smith, Elton Verner III, 292
Smith, Elvira VI, 655
Smith, Elvira Lowe I, 949
Smith, Elvira P. V, 123
Smith, Elvire P. V, 123
Smith, Elwood I, 18
Smith, Elwood II, 421
Smith, Elwood II, 820
Smith, Elwood IV, 276
Smith, Elwood IV, 437
Smith, Elwood IV, 439
Smith, Elwood IV, 550
Smith, Elwood IV, 551
Smith, Elwood IV, 1115
Smith, Elwood Thomas IV, 49
Smith, Elwood Thomas IV, 55
Smith, Elzy IV, 1185
Smith, Ema Jane V, 431
Smith, Emanuel I, 933
Smith, Emanuel I, 949
Smith, Emanuel II, 184
Smith, Emeline IV, 1375
Smith, Emeline IV, 1379
Smith, Emeline V, 1019
Smith, Emeline M. III, 34
Smith, Emerson V, 432
Smith, Emily II, 820
Smith, Emily II, 923
Smith, Emily III, 45
Smith, Emily III, 441
Smith, Emily III, 447
Smith, Emily IV, 1294

, Emily V, 598
, Emily V, 710
, Emily V, 954
, Emily V, 959
, Emily VI, 679
, Emily B. II, 923
, Emily B. II, 924
, Emily F. II, 158
, Emily F. III, 18
, Emily Fogg II, 138
, Emily L. III, 285
, Emily L. III, 294
, Emily Sophia II, 421
, Emily Sophia II, 767
, Emma III, 292
, Emma III, 367
, Emma III, 499
, Emma IV, 782
, Emma IV, 843
, Emma IV, 850
, Emma IV, 1294
, Emma V, 278
, Emma V, 279
, Emma V, 597
, Emma V, 874
, Emma V, 1019
, Emma H. I, 1161
, Emma J. IV, 438
, Emma J. IV, 440
, Emma Jane V, 432
, Emma Jane V, 710
, Emma L. IV, 278
, Emma L. IV, 491
, Emma L. IV, 497
, Emma Malissa V, 279
, Emma R. IV, 1138
, Emma S. III, 295
, Emma T. VI, 708
, Emmeline V, 1019
, Emmeline M. III, 292
, Enoch VI, 446
, Enos VI, 440
, Ephraim II, 158
, Ephraim II, 159
, Ephraim II, 719
, Ephraim III, 499
, Ephraim IV, 59
, Ephraim IV, 60
, Ephraim IV, 437
, Ephraim IV, 439
, Ephraim V, 278
, Ephraim V, 431
, Ephraim V, 432
, Ephraim V, 861
, Ephraim V, 862
, Ephraim C. II, 130
, Ephraim C. II, 146
, Ephraim C. II, 157
, Ephraim Oliphant IV, 657
, Eri V, 597
, Ernest B. II, 924
, Erwin Hulme II, 820
, Erwin Hulme II, 924
h, Estel V, 279
h, Estel V, 465
h, Esther I, 74
h, Esther I, 227
h, Esther I, 257
h, Esther I, 260
h, Esther I, 364
h, Esther I, 377
h, Esther I, 390
h, Esther I, 419
h, Esther II, 40
h, Esther II, 88
h, Esther II, 100
h, Esther II, 183
h, Esther II, 262
h, Esther II, 421
h, Esther II, 452
h, Esther II, 509
h, Esther II, 568
h, Esther II, 580
h, Esther II, 654
h, Esther II, 655
h, Esther II, 656
h, Esther II, 687
h, Esther II, 719
h, Esther III, 292
h, Esther III, 321
h, Esther IV, 109
h, Esther IV, 133
h, Esther IV, 352
h, Esther IV, 1185
h, Esther IV, 1223
h, Esther V, 54
h, Esther V, 123
h, Esther V, 495
h, Esther V, 529
h, Esther V, 644
h, Esther VI, 639
Smith, Esther VI, 702
Smith, Esther VI, 703
Smith, Esther VI, 910
Smith, Esther F. II, 723
Smith, Esther Fisher II, 263
Smith, Esther Fisher II, 656
Smith, Esther Fisher II, 776
Smith, Esther Louisa VI, 707
Smith, Esther Louise III, 293
Smith, Esther Louise VI, 616
Smith, Esther Louise VI, 702
Smith, Esther M. II, 718
Smith, Esther Morton II, 656
Smith, Esther Morton II, 767
Smith, Esther R. II, 302
Smith, Esther R. II, 767
Smith, Esther S. II, 835
Smith, Esther S. II, 923
Smith, Esther Syng II, 727
Smith, Estil V, 465
Smith, Ethan IV, 159
Smith, Ethel III, 224
Smith, Ethel III, 295
Smith, Ethel C. IV, 278
Smith, Ethel C. IV, 280
Smith, Ethel C. IV, 550
Smith, Ethel C. IV, 551
Smith, Ethel C. IV, 762
Smith, Ethel C. IV, 763
Smith, Ethel C. IV, 768
Smith, Eugene IV, 276
Smith, Eugene IV, 278
Smith, Eugene IV, 763
Smith, Eugene Franklin I, 1161
Smith, Eugenia L. II, 313
Smith, Eunice I, 419
Smith, Eunice I, 837
Smith, Eunice I, 839
Smith, Eunice II, 707
Smith, Eunice V, 203
Smith, Eunice H. IV, 407
Smith, Eunice H. IV, 438
Smith, Eunice H. IV, 439
Smith, Eva V, 764
Smith, Eva D. IV, 551
Smith, Eva Irene IV, 277
Smith, Eva Irene IV, 551
Smith, Eva Irene IV, 763
Smith, Eva Irene IV, 1131
Smith, Eva Irene IV, 1138
Smith, Eva M. IV, 550
Smith, Evalina I, 596
Smith, Evalinah I, 590
Smith, Evaline IV, 278
Smith, Evan II, 719
Smith, Evan IV, 277
Smith, Evan IV, 438
Smith, Evan IV, 594
Smith, Evan IV, 820
Smith, Evan IV, 994
Smith, Evan IV, 1051
Smith, Evan IV, 1076
Smith, Evan IV, 1115
Smith, Evan IV, 1138
Smith, Evan V, 241
Smith, Evan V, 278
Smith, Evan V, 389
Smith, Evan V, 447
Smith, Eve II, 100
Smith, Eve V, 122
Smith, Eve V, 123
Smith, Eve V, 529
Smith, Eve R. III, 292
Smith, Evelina I, 596
Smith, Evelina I, 914
Smith, Eveline IV, 1294
Smith, Even IV, 276
Smith, Everett W. V, 279
Smith, Evi II, 40
Smith, Evi II, 100
Smith, Evi II, 128
Smith, Evi II, 138
Smith, Evi II, 150
Smith, Evi II, 157
Smith, Evi IV, 769
Smith, Ezekiel III, 293
Smith, Ezekiel VI, 561
Smith, Ezra IV, 351
Smith, Ezra IV, 550
Smith, Ezra VI, 703
Smith, F. G. VI, 933
Smith, Fannie I, 689
Smith, Fannie V, 432
Smith, Fannie V, 862
Smith, Fannie C. V, 432
Smith, Fannie J. III, 290
Smith, Fannie M. III, 294
Smith, Fanny V, 32
Smith, Fanny V, 122
Smith, Fanny V, 123
Smith, Fanny C. V, 278
Smith, Fanny C. V, 279
Smith, Fanny C. V, 432
Smith, Fanny G. V, 710
Smith, Fanny Jane I, 689
Smith, Fanny T. II, 719
Smith, Fatima J. I, 681
Smith, Fatima J. I, 689
Smith, Ferris II, 820
Smith, Ferris II, 923
Smith, Florence VI, 708
Smith, Florence Chevy III, 191
Smith, Florence Chevy III, 294
Smith, Florence L. III, 134
Smith, Florence L. III, 293
Smith, Florentine VI, 947
Smith, Florentine VI, 986
Smith, Florentine VI, 995
Smith, Forest IV, 1185
Smith, Forest Dudley IV, 1186
Smith, Frances II, 421
Smith, Frances II, 603
Smith, Frances II, 1008
Smith, Frances III, 115
Smith, Frances III, 293
Smith, Frances III, 410
Smith, Frances III, 447
Smith, Frances IV, 1186
Smith, Frances VI, 649
Smith, Frances VI, 663
Smith, Frances VI, 703
Smith, Frances VI, 819
Smith, Frances A. II, 924
Smith, Frances A. III, 295
Smith, Frances Ashbridge II, 796
Smith, Frances B. III, 163
Smith, Frances B. III, 292
Smith, Frances C. III, 447
Smith, Frances Canby II, 820
Smith, Frances Canby II, 924
Smith, Frances Eliza V, 932
Smith, Francis II, 238
Smith, Francis II, 261
Smith, Francis II, 276
Smith, Francis II, 421
Smith, Francis IV, 895
Smith, Francis V, 764
Smith, Francis V, 1019
Smith, Francis VI, 172
Smith, Francis VI, 212
Smith, Francis VI, 854
Smith, Francis A. II, 867
Smith, Francis D. IV, 550
Smith, Francis H. III, 292
Smith, Francis V. II, 719
Smith, Francis Willard II, 969
Smith, Frank III, 295
Smith, Frank IV, 1294
Smith, Frank V, 1019
Smith, Frank A. V, 710
Smith, Frank B. V, 203
Smith, Frank D. II, 313
Smith, Frank P. II, 144
Smith, Frank P. II, 158
Smith, Frank R. V, 203
Smith, Frank W. III, 294
Smith, Franklin I, 900
Smith, Franklin II, 128
Smith, Franklin II, 656
Smith, Franklin IV, 1294
Smith, Franklin D. V, 278
Smith, Franklin D. V, 279
Smith, Franklin Griscom II, 820
Smith, Franklin R. II, 767
Smith, Fred I, 18
Smith, Fred IV, 763
Smith, Fred V, 710
Smith, Fred E. I, 641
Smith, Fred Ellsworth I, 625
Smith, Fred S. V, 710
Smith, Fred'k D. III, 293
Smith, Fred'k D. III, 322
Smith, Frederick IV, 1115
Smith, Frederick V, 644
Smith, Frederick E. I, 641
Smith, Frederick P. III, 293
Smith, Frederick Stuckey IV, 454
Smith, Freelove IV, 1379
Smith, Freeman IV, 1186
Smith, Garland IV, 1241
Smith, Genesis V, 465
Smith, Geneva V, 1019
Smith, Geo, Jr. IV, 550
Smith, Geo. I, 933
Smith, Geo. IV, 276
Smith, Geo. IV, 351
Smith, Geo. IV, 497
Smith, Geo. IV, 546
Smith, Geo. IV, 550
Smith, Geo. V, 932
Smith, Geo. V, 960
Smith, Geo. VI, 562
Smith, Geo. D. V, 932
Smith, Geo. K. IV, 762
Smith, Geo. K. IV, 768
Smith, George I, 968
Smith, George I, 1024
Smith, George I, 1088
Smith, George I, 1091
Smith, George I, 1098
Smith, George II, 183
Smith, George II, 421
Smith, George II, 654
Smith, George II, 655
Smith, George II, 1080
Smith, George IV, 26
Smith, George IV, 27
Smith, George IV, 43
Smith, George IV, 59
Smith, George IV, 60
Smith, George IV, 69
Smith, George IV, 109
Smith, George IV, 159
Smith, George IV, 538
Smith, George IV, 549
Smith, George IV, 550
Smith, George IV, 580
Smith, George IV, 594
Smith, George V, 278
Smith, George V, 279
Smith, George V, 959
Smith, George VI, 212
Smith, George VI, 445
Smith, George VI, 460
Smith, George VI, 561
Smith, George VI, 562
Smith, George VI, 605
Smith, George VI, 886
Smith, George A. II, 820
Smith, George A. II, 923
Smith, George A. II, 924
Smith, George B. IV, 549
Smith, George B. IV, 550
Smith, George D. II, 262
Smith, George D. II, 263
Smith, George D. V, 932
Smith, George F. II, 820
Smith, George F. II, 924
Smith, George F. II, 1060
Smith, George Ferdinand II, 820
Smith, George G. III, 511
Smith, George H. II, 820
Smith, George J. B. III, 295
Smith, George K. IV, 387
Smith, George K. IV, 438
Smith, George K. IV, 439
Smith, George K. IV, 550
Smith, George K. IV, 551
Smith, George K. IV, 735
Smith, George Peyton II, 820
Smith, George Peyton II, 924
Smith, George R. II, 421
Smith, George R. II, 530
Smith, George R. II, 655
Smith, George W. II, 315
Smith, George W. II, 924
Smith, George W. II, 945
Smith, George W. IV, 1294
Smith, George W. V, 360
Smith, George W. VI, 995
Smith, George, Jr. II, 261
Smith, Gertha I, 949
Smith, Gilbert IV, 1223
Smith, Gilbert V, 710
Smith, Gilbert Badger III, 295
Smith, Gilpin II, 655
Smith, Ginny VI, 995
Smith, Goldie V, 710
Smith, Goldie A. V, 432
Smith, Goldie Ann V, 432
Smith, Goldsmith Chandlee VI, 605
Smith, Grace II, 40
Smith, Grace II, 75
Smith, Grace II, 100
Smith, Grace II, 183
Smith, Grace II, 185
Smith, Grace II, 263
Smith, Grace II, 301
Smith, Grace II, 447
Smith, Grace II, 653
Smith, Grace II, 655
Smith, Grace II, 656
Smith, Grace II, 657
Smith, Grace II, 767
Smith, Grace IV, 1101
Smith, Grace IV, 1115
Smith, Grace Alma IV, 276
Smith, Grace Alma IV, 282
Smith, Grace Ann II, 719
Smith, Grace Carol III, 133
Smith, Grace Carol III, 292
Smith, Grace S. II, 719
Smith, Grizzel II, 719
Smith, Grizzel II, 816
Smith, Grover T. V, 710
Smith, Gulielma I, 705
Smith, Gulielma I, 734
Smith, Gulielma III, 293
Smith, Gulielma IV, 59
Smith, Gulielma IV, 351
Smith, Gulielma IV, 550
Smith, Gulielma V, 122
Smith, Gulielma V, 241
Smith, Gulielma V, 278
Smith, Gulielma V, 389
Smith, Gulielma VI, 703
Smith, Gulielma M. II, 262
Smith, Gulielma Maria II, 99
Smith, Gulielma Maria II, 184
Smith, Gulielma Maria II, 209
Smith, Gulielma Maria II, 243
Smith, Gulielma Maria II, 262
Smith, Gulielma Maria II, 263
Smith, Gulielma Maria II, 719
Smith, Gulielma Matilda III, 281
Smith, Gulielma Matilda III, 293
Smith, Guy VI, 944
Smith, Guy VI, 995
Smith, Guy VI, 1006
Smith, H. E. IV, 1338
Smith, H. Howard V, 932
Smith, H. J. IV, 1264
Smith, H. J. Sterling IV, 1264
Smith, Halla Z. V, 432
Smith, Hallie J. V, 432
Smith, Halsey M. III, 441
Smith, Halsey M. III, 447
Smith, Halsey M. III, 460
Smith, Halstead M. III, 447
Smith, Hannah I, 7
Smith, Hannah I, 11
Smith, Hannah I, 18
Smith, Hannah I, 419
Smith, Hannah I, 968
Smith, Hannah I, 1023
Smith, Hannah I, 1024
Smith, Hannah I, 1053
Smith, Hannah I, 1061
Smith, Hannah I, 1063
Smith, Hannah I, 1088
Smith, Hannah I Sup 1, 4
Smith, Hannah I Sup 1, 6
Smith, Hannah II, 40
Smith, Hannah II, 50
Smith, Hannah II, 55
Smith, Hannah II, 56
Smith, Hannah II, 60
Smith, Hannah II, 65
Smith, Hannah II, 66
Smith, Hannah II, 78
Smith, Hannah II, 99
Smith, Hannah II, 100
Smith, Hannah II, 111
Smith, Hannah II, 124
Smith, Hannah II, 138
Smith, Hannah II, 147
Smith, Hannah II, 150
Smith, Hannah II, 157
Smith, Hannah II, 170
Smith, Hannah II, 183
Smith, Hannah II, 184
Smith, Hannah II, 203
Smith, Hannah II, 211
Smith, Hannah II, 241
Smith, Hannah II, 243
Smith, Hannah II, 244
Smith, Hannah II, 261
Smith, Hannah II, 262
Smith, Hannah II, 421
Smith, Hannah II, 422
Smith, Hannah II, 454
Smith, Hannah II, 484
Smith, Hannah II, 509
Smith, Hannah II, 584
Smith, Hannah II, 617
Smith, Hannah II, 653
Smith, Hannah II, 654
Smith, Hannah II, 655
Smith, Hannah II, 656
Smith, Hannah II, 735
Smith, Hannah II, 767
Smith, Hannah II, 776
Smith, Hannah II, 790
Smith, Hannah II, 815
Smith, Hannah II, 970
Smith, Hannah II, 1028
Smith, Hannah III, 42
Smith, Hannah III, 283
Smith, Hannah III, 293
Smith, Hannah III, 294
Smith, Hannah III, 447
Smith, Hannah III, 451
Smith, Hannah III, 465

Smith, Hannah III, 499
Smith, Hannah III, 503
Smith, Hannah IV, 26
Smith, Hannah IV, 27
Smith, Hannah IV, 30
Smith, Hannah IV, 33
Smith, Hannah IV, 52
Smith, Hannah IV, 59
Smith, Hannah IV, 60
Smith, Hannah IV, 67
Smith, Hannah IV, 95
Smith, Hannah IV, 109
Smith, Hannah IV, 115
Smith, Hannah IV, 133
Smith, Hannah IV, 276
Smith, Hannah IV, 277
Smith, Hannah IV, 408
Smith, Hannah IV, 411
Smith, Hannah IV, 437
Smith, Hannah IV, 438
Smith, Hannah IV, 439
Smith, Hannah IV, 446
Smith, Hannah IV, 550
Smith, Hannah IV, 594
Smith, Hannah IV, 762
Smith, Hannah IV, 773
Smith, Hannah IV, 909
Smith, Hannah IV, 974
Smith, Hannah IV, 994
Smith, Hannah IV, 1057
Smith, Hannah IV, 1076
Smith, Hannah IV, 1077
Smith, Hannah IV, 1111
Smith, Hannah IV, 1114
Smith, Hannah IV, 1115
Smith, Hannah IV, 1138
Smith, Hannah IV, 1151
Smith, Hannah IV, 1156
Smith, Hannah IV, 1186
Smith, Hannah IV, 1379
Smith, Hannah V, 28
Smith, Hannah V, 52
Smith, Hannah V, 122
Smith, Hannah V, 278
Smith, Hannah V, 402
Smith, Hannah V, 429
Smith, Hannah V, 431
Smith, Hannah V, 432
Smith, Hannah V, 503
Smith, Hannah V, 529
Smith, Hannah V, 710
Smith, Hannah V, 843
Smith, Hannah V, 861
Smith, Hannah V, 917
Smith, Hannah V, 959
Smith, Hannah V, 976
Smith, Hannah V, 1019
Smith, Hannah VI, 171
Smith, Hannah VI, 212
Smith, Hannah VI, 440
Smith, Hannah VI, 444
Smith, Hannah VI, 445
Smith, Hannah VI, 446
Smith, Hannah VI, 451
Smith, Hannah VI, 515
Smith, Hannah VI, 562
Smith, Hannah VI, 563
Smith, Hannah VI, 604
Smith, Hannah VI, 605
Smith, Hannah VI, 691
Smith, Hannah VI, 702
Smith, Hannah VI, 774
Smith, Hannah VI, 779
Smith, Hannah VI, 854
Smith, Hannah Ann II, 138
Smith, Hannah Ann II, 150
Smith, Hannah Ann II, 157
Smith, Hannah B. II, 244
Smith, Hannah B. II, 263
Smith, Hannah B. IV, 763
Smith, Hannah B. IV, 994
Smith, Hannah C. I, 681
Smith, Hannah C. I, 689
Smith, Hannah C. II, 124
Smith, Hannah C. II, 157
Smith, Hannah C. II, 302
Smith, Hannah C. II, 719
Smith, Hannah C. II, 767
Smith, Hannah C. III, 295
Smith, Hannah Dickenson II, 99
Smith, Hannah Eliza J. II, 749
Smith, Hannah Eliza J. II, 767
Smith, Hannah Evans V, 133
Smith, Hannah F. IV, 1076
Smith, Hannah G. II, 100
Smith, Hannah G. II, 108
Smith, Hannah G. II, 124
Smith, Hannah H. II, 130
Smith, Hannah H. II, 146
Smith, Hannah H. II, 157
Smith, Hannah H. II, 158
Smith, Hannah H. II, 159
Smith, Hannah H. IV, 440
Smith, Hannah J. IV, 549
Smith, Hannah J. IV, 551
Smith, Hannah Janney VI, 571
Smith, Hannah L. II, 719
Smith, Hannah L. V, 360
Smith, Hannah Logan II, 263
Smith, Hannah Logan II, 656
Smith, Hannah Logan II, 719
Smith, Hannah Logan II, 723
Smith, Hannah Maria V, 932
Smith, Hannah P. II, 128
Smith, Hannah P. II, 923
Smith, Hannah P. IV, 1115
Smith, Hannah P. V, 932
Smith, Hannah Poultney II, 815
Smith, Hannah Poultney II, 911
Smith, Hannah Poultney II, 923
Smith, Hannah R. VI, 446
Smith, Hannah S. II, 117
Smith, Hannah S. II, 124
Smith, Hannah S. II, 263
Smith, Hannah S. IV, 439
Smith, Hannah S. IV, 763
Smith, Hannah S. IV, 1073
Smith, Hannah S. IV, 1077
Smith, Hannah S. IV, 1089
Smith, Hannah S. IV, 1115
Smith, Hannah S. IV, 1128
Smith, Hannah W. IV, 314
Smith, Hannah W. IV, 315
Smith, Hannah W. V, 959
Smith, Hannah W. V, 960
Smith, Hannah W. VI, 446
Smith, Hannay IV, 1064
Smith, Hariet V, 960
Smith, Harriet II, 144
Smith, Harriet II, 158
Smith, Harriet III, 269
Smith, Harriet III, 293
Smith, Harriet IV, 1090
Smith, Harriet IV, 1114
Smith, Harriet IV, 1115
Smith, Harriet VI, 854
Smith, Harriet A. I, 221
Smith, Harriet A. I, 227
Smith, Harriet B. II, 158
Smith, Harriet Hollingsworth V, 529
Smith, Harriet T. III, 82
Smith, Harriet T. III, 293
Smith, Harrison IV, 763
Smith, Harrison V, 279
Smith, Harry IV, 1264
Smith, Harry E. III, 293
Smith, Harry L. IV, 763
Smith, Harvey IV, 109
Smith, Harvey IV, 1378
Smith, Harvey IV, 1379
Smith, Harvey VI, 706
Smith, Harvey W. IV, 551
Smith, Hattie V, 710
Smith, Hattie A. I, 249
Smith, Hattie A. I, 257
Smith, Havilah V, 278
Smith, Havilah V, 279
Smith, Haviland IV, 762
Smith, Hazael D. V, 241
Smith, Hazel IV, 1185
Smith, Hazel IV, 1186
Smith, Hazeltine I, 933
Smith, Hazeltine I, 949
Smith, Helen III, 132
Smith, Helen III, 294
Smith, Helen IV, 276
Smith, Helen IV, 278
Smith, Helen V, 710
Smith, Helen B. II, 313
Smith, Helen Gertrude III, 293
Smith, Helen Gertrude III, 322
Smith, Helen M. II, 138
Smith, Helen Rebecca II, 138
Smith, Helen Rebecca II, 158
Smith, Helen Rebecca IV, 278
Smith, Helena Smith IV, 1076
Smith, Helene IV, 1115
Smith, Helina IV, 1114
Smith, Henery, Jr. VI, 445
Smith, Henrie VI, 854
Smith, Henrietta VI, 649
Smith, Henrietta VI, 702
Smith, Henrietta VI, 703
Smith, Henrietta VI, 706
Smith, Henrietta VI, 707
Smith, Henrietta VI, 724
Smith, Henrietta Stewart VI, 703
Smith, Henry I, 74
Smith, Henry II, 184
Smith, Henry II, 262
Smith, Henry II, 263
Smith, Henry II, 969
Smith, Henry II, 1027
Smith, Henry III, 215
Smith, Henry III, 295
Smith, Henry III, 453
Smith, Henry III, 499
Smith, Henry III, 505
Smith, Henry IV, 17
Smith, Henry IV, 31
Smith, Henry IV, 59
Smith, Henry IV, 60
Smith, Henry IV, 722
Smith, Henry IV, 883
Smith, Henry IV, 1076
Smith, Henry IV, 1114
Smith, Henry IV, 1115
Smith, Henry IV, 1138
Smith, Henry IV, 1185
Smith, Henry IV, 1186
Smith, Henry IV, 1338
Smith, Henry V, 123
Smith, Henry V, 529
Smith, Henry V, 540
Smith, Henry V, 597
Smith, Henry V, 598
Smith, Henry V, 710
Smith, Henry V, 1019
Smith, Henry VI, 444
Smith, Henry VI, 445
Smith, Henry VI, 485
Smith, Henry VI, 497
Smith, Henry VI, 561
Smith, Henry VI, 562
Smith, Henry VI, 563
Smith, Henry VI, 571
Smith, Henry VI, 644
Smith, Henry VI, 651
Smith, Henry VI, 695
Smith, Henry VI, 702
Smith, Henry VI, 705
Smith, Henry VI, 710
Smith, Henry VI, 712
Smith, Henry VI, 995
Smith, Henry A. V, 278
Smith, Henry A. V, 360
Smith, Henry Alice VI, 562
Smith, Henry C. II, 924
Smith, Henry C. II, 931
Smith, Henry Clement II, 790
Smith, Henry H. III, 293
Smith, Henry H. VI, 561
Smith, Henry H. VI, 575
Smith, Henry H. VI, 576
Smith, Henry H. VI, 667
Smith, Henry H. VI, 702
Smith, Henry H. VI, 717
Smith, Henry H. VI, 755
Smith, Henry Hill II, 99
Smith, Henry Howard V, 932
Smith, Henry Mitchell III, 293
Smith, Henry R. VI, 741
Smith, Henry R. VI, 779
Smith, Henry Timmerman IV, 1076
Smith, Henry Zimmerman IV, 1115
Smith, Henry, Jr. IV, 59
Smith, Hepsabeth I, 596
Smith, Hepsebeth V, 899
Smith, Hepzabath V, 932
Smith, Hepzibah V, 898
Smith, Hepzibah V, 932
Smith, Herbert T. III, 292
Smith, Herbert T. III, 293
Smith, Herman III, 293
Smith, Herman H. III, 226
Smith, Herman H. III, 227
Smith, Herman H. III, 293
Smith, Herman H. III, 312
Smith, Herman H. III, 499
Smith, Hesea I, 74
Smith, Hester I, 74
Smith, Hester I, 318
Smith, Hester I, 627
Smith, Hester III, 321
Smith, Hester S. VI, 621
Smith, Hester S. VI, 624
Smith, Hester S. VI, 702
Smith, Hester S. VI, 704
Smith, Hill II, 40
Smith, Hill II, 89
Smith, Hill II, 99
Smith, Hill II, 100
Smith, Holinsworth I, 1098
Smith, Hollensworth I, 1146
Smith, Homer V, 529
Smith, Horace II, 924
Smith, Horace IV, 763
Smith, Horace G. III, 233
Smith, Horace G. III, 293
Smith, Horace J. II, 719
Smith, Horace J. II, 767
Smith, Horace S. Furman II, 924
Smith, Hosea I, 74
Smith, Hosea I, 166
Smith, Hosey I, 74
Smith, Hosey I, 86
Smith, Howard IV, 1338
Smith, Howard V, 932
Smith, Howard VI, 702
Smith, Howard C. II, 924
Smith, Howard Conrad II, 820
Smith, Howard E. III, 511
Smith, Howard M. VI, 653
Smith, Howard Penrose IV, 276
Smith, Hugh II, 421
Smith, Hugh II, 422
Smith, Hugh II, 1060
Smith, Hugh V, 932
Smith, Hugh H. V, 123
Smith, Hugh H. V, 902
Smith, Hugh H. V, 932
Smith, Hulda IV, 550
Smith, Hulda V, 512
Smith, Hulda V, 529
Smith, Huldah I, 86
Smith, Huldah IV, 321
Smith, Huldah IV, 351
Smith, Huldah IV, 549
Smith, Huldah IV, 647
Smith, Huldah IV, 657
Smith, Humphrey IV, 438
Smith, Humphrey IV, 439
Smith, Humphrey IV, 1076
Smith, Humphrey IV, 1115
Smith, Ida IV, 434
Smith, Ida IV, 439
Smith, Ida V, 529
Smith, Ida Clair III, 292
Smith, Ida May V, 279
Smith, Ila H. I, 933
Smith, Ila Hedgecock I, 949
Smith, Imo IV, 1164
Smith, Imo IV, 1186
Smith, Iowa VI, 446
Smith, Ira IV, 1378
Smith, Ira IV, 1379
Smith, Ira IV, 1385
Smith, Ira G. III, 296
Smith, Irena V, 597
Smith, Irene V, 529
Smith, Irene V, 598
Smith, Irvin Edward IV, 1185
Smith, Irving J. III, 293
Smith, Irving J. IV, 278
Smith, Irving James IV, 276
Smith, Irving James IV, 278
Smith, Irving James IV, 1115
Smith, Irving James IV, 1116
Smith, Isaac I, 968
Smith, Isaac I, 1088
Smith, Isaac I, 1098
Smith, Isaac I, 1116
Smith, Isaac I, 1132
Smith, Isaac I, 1146
Smith, Isaac I, 1161
Smith, Isaac II, 55
Smith, Isaac II, 138
Smith, Isaac II, 421
Smith, Isaac II, 422
Smith, Isaac II, 654
Smith, Isaac II, 655
Smith, Isaac II, 1027
Smith, Isaac II, 1028
Smith, Isaac III, 294
Smith, Isaac IV, 549
Smith, Isaac IV, 1185
Smith, Isaac IV, 1186
Smith, Isaac V, 122
Smith, Isaac V, 123
Smith, Isaac V, 279
Smith, Isaac V, 463
Smith, Isaac V, 465
Smith, Isaac V, 466
Smith, Isaac V, 862
Smith, Isaac V, 1019
Smith, Isaac VI, 367
Smith, Isaac VI, 440
Smith, Isaac VI, 444
Smith, Isaac VI, 445
Smith, Isaac VI, 446
Smith, Isaac VI, 462
Smith, Isaac VI, 605
Smith, Isaac VI, 995
Smith, Isaac E. II, 923
Smith, Isaac M. V, 279
Smith, Isaac R. V, 862
Smith, Isaac Smart II, 17
Smith, Isaac, Jr. V, 861
Smith, Isaac, Jr. VI, 446
Smith, Isaac, Sr. VI, 445
Smith, Isabella III, 37
Smith, Isabella IV, 1362
Smith, Isabella IV, 1379
Smith, Isabella W. IV, 1379
Smith, Isabelle III, 295
Smith, Isabelle III, 396
Smith, Isabelle III, 438
Smith, Isabelle III, 447
Smith, Isaiah IV, 549
Smith, Isaiah V, 279
Smith, Isaiah V, 360
Smith, Isaiah V, 529
Smith, Isaiah V, 862
Smith, Israel II, 707
Smith, Israel IV, 59
Smith, Israel IV, 407
Smith, Israel IV, 549
Smith, Israel IV, 1185
Smith, Israel IV, 1223
Smith, Israel VI, 650
Smith, Iva IV, 735
Smith, Iva IV, 763
Smith, Iva V, 278
Smith, Iva D. IV, 550
Smith, Iva D. IV, 735
Smith, Iva D. IV, 762
Smith, Iva D. IV, 763
Smith, J. H. I, 625
Smith, J. Lincoln II, 158
Smith, J. R. IV, 278
Smith, J. Russell VI, 649
Smith, J. Russell VI, 702
Smith, J. Russell VI, 703
Smith, J. Russell VI, 706
Smith, J. Russell VI, 724
Smith, J. Russell VI, 752
Smith, J. Russell VI, 779
Smith, J. Stewart VI, 649
Smith, J. Stewart VI, 703
Smith, J. Walter VI, 406
Smith, J. Walter VI, 514
Smith, J. Walter VI, 622
Smith, J. Walter VI, 627
Smith, J. Walter VI, 660
Smith, J. Walter VI, 670
Smith, J. Walter VI, 702
Smith, J. Walter VI, 703
Smith, J. Walter VI, 707
Smith, Jacob I, 227
Smith, Jacob II, 656
Smith, Jacob III, 292
Smith, Jacob III, 294
Smith, Jacob III, 295
Smith, Jacob III, 444
Smith, Jacob III, 447
Smith, Jacob III, 465
Smith, Jacob III, 469
Smith, Jacob III, 495
Smith, Jacob III, 499
Smith, Jacob IV, 30
Smith, Jacob IV, 59
Smith, Jacob IV, 276
Smith, Jacob IV, 328
Smith, Jacob IV, 351
Smith, Jacob IV, 550
Smith, Jacob V, 122
Smith, Jacob V, 278
Smith, Jacob V, 279
Smith, Jacob V, 311
Smith, Jacob V, 465
Smith, Jacob V, 1019
Smith, Jacob VI, 444
Smith, Jacob VI, 446
Smith, Jacob VI, 636
Smith, Jacob VI, 703
Smith, Jacob VI, 704
Smith, Jacob VI, 705
Smith, Jacob VI, 708
Smith, Jacob VI, 854
Smith, Jacob A. V, 529
Smith, Jacob C. II, 924
Smith, Jacob C. V, 1019
Smith, Jacob L. V, 465
Smith, Jacob R. II, 421
Smith, Jacob R. II, 656
Smith, Jacob R. II, 719
Smith, Jacob R. II, 767
Smith, Jacob, Jr. V, 122
Smith, Jael II, 89
Smith, Jael II, 100
Smith, Jamaica III, 294
Smith, James I, 419
Smith, James I, 1023
Smith, James I, 1037
Smith, James II, 40
Smith, James II, 41
Smith, James II, 50
Smith, James II, 99
Smith, James II, 100
Smith, James II, 124
Smith, James II, 138
Smith, James II, 147

, James II, 157
, James II, 183
, James II, 184
, James II, 185
, James II, 240
, James II, 261
, James II, 262
, James II, 263
, James II, 421
, James II, 422
James II, 452
James II, 625
, James II, 654
, James II, 655
, James II, 656
, James II, 719
, James II, 723
, James II, 735
, James II, 767
, James II, 776
, James II, 790
, James II, 969
, James II, 970
, James III, 252
, James III, 294
, James III, 447
, James III, 453
, James IV, 59
, James IV, 60
, James IV, 109
, James IV, 276
, James IV, 353
, James IV, 550
, James IV, 594
, James IV, 994
, James IV, 1064
, James IV, 1076
, James IV, 1077
, James IV, 1294
, James V, 28
, James V, 122
, James V, 123
, James V, 203
, James V, 274
, James V, 278
, James V, 279
, James V, 290
, James V, 360
, James V, 432
, James V, 567
, James V, 631
, James V, 710
, James V, 862
, James VI, 415
, James VI, 444
, James VI, 446
, James VI, 605
, James VI, 705
, James VI, 706
, James VI, 882
, James A. VI, 995
, James A. McGrew IV, 277
, James Andrew V, 431
, James B. III, 447
, James B. IV, 994
h, James B. IV, 1223
h, James B. IV, 1227
h, James B., Jr. III, 395
h, James B., Jr. III, 447
h, James Bruce V, 203
h, James C. IV, 1186
h, James Charles II, 719
h, James Charles II, 767
h, James E. V, 598
h, James E. V, 710
h, James F. V, 1019
h, James Hulme II, 820
h, James Hulme II, 924
h, James L. I, 933
h, James L. II, 421
h, James L. II, 767
h, James L. III, 447
h, James L. IV, 437
h, James Lincoln II, 138
h, James Matthew I, 74
h, James P. IV, 1223
h, James Parke II, 421
h, James W. II, 421
h, James, Jr. II, 262
h, James, Jr. II, 509
h, James, Jr. II, 580
h, James, Jr. II, 655
h, Jane I, 49
h, Jane I, 74
h, Jane I, 1063
h, Jane II, 45
h, Jane II, 184
h, Jane II, 185
h, Jane II, 261
h, Jane II, 262
h, Jane II, 654
Smith, Jane II, 949
Smith, Jane II, 1007
Smith, Jane II, 1027
Smith, Jane III, 295
Smith, Jane III, 445
Smith, Jane III, 447
Smith, Jane III, 499
Smith, Jane IV, 59
Smith, Jane IV, 71
Smith, Jane IV, 85
Smith, Jane IV, 95
Smith, Jane IV, 109
Smith, Jane IV, 339
Smith, Jane IV, 351
Smith, Jane IV, 415
Smith, Jane IV, 419
Smith, Jane IV, 437
Smith, Jane IV, 438
Smith, Jane IV, 439
Smith, Jane IV, 549
Smith, Jane IV, 550
Smith, Jane IV, 1180
Smith, Jane IV, 1185
Smith, Jane V, 529
Smith, Jane V, 535
Smith, Jane V, 597
Smith, Jane VI, 436
Smith, Jane VI, 445
Smith, Jane VI, 446
Smith, Jane VI, 507
Smith, Jane VI, 563
Smith, Jane VI, 703
Smith, Jane VI, 720
Smith, Jane VI, 995
Smith, Jane B. II, 262
Smith, Jane Burling II, 184
Smith, Jane Harvey IV, 109
Smith, Jane M. V, 463
Smith, Janedis IV, 439
Smith, Jarrett II, 313
Smith, Jarvis L. V, 631
Smith, Jasper III, 293
Smith, Jasper III, 294
Smith, Jeames II, 99
Smith, Jean I, 419
Smith, Jean I, 424
Smith, Jean I, 1018
Smith, Jean I, 1024
Smith, Jean I, 1060
Smith, Jean I, 1063
Smith, Jean VI, 445
Smith, Jehu I, 117
Smith, Jehu IV, 109
Smith, Jemima I, 1091
Smith, Jemima I, 1098
Smith, Jenette I, 318
Smith, Jennetta I, 318
Smith, Jennie I, 617
Smith, Jennie V, 529
Smith, Jennie V, 1019
Smith, Jennie E. III, 228
Smith, Jennie E. III, 293
Smith, Jennie P. IV, 1223
Smith, Jenny VI, 976
Smith, Jenny VI, 1002
Smith, Jeremiah I, 1023
Smith, Jeremiah IV, 909
Smith, Jeremiah V, 465
Smith, Jeremiah Addeson I, 626
Smith, Jeremiah W. V, 279
Smith, Jeretah IV, 277
Smith, Jeretha IV, 314
Smith, Jeretta IV, 276
Smith, Jerimiah II, 40
Smith, Jerry IV, 1294
Smith, Jerusha III, 292
Smith, Jerusha IV, 769
Smith, Jervis S. II, 313
Smith, Jervis S. II, 324
Smith, Jervis S. II, 851
Smith, Jervis S. II, 864
Smith, Jervis S. II, 924
Smith, Jesse I, 1088
Smith, Jesse I, 1090
Smith, Jesse I, 1098
Smith, Jesse III, 293
Smith, Jesse IV, 59
Smith, Jesse IV, 60
Smith, Jesse IV, 109
Smith, Jesse IV, 133
Smith, Jesse IV, 213
Smith, Jesse IV, 1115
Smith, Jesse V, 861
Smith, Jesse V, 862
Smith, Jesse VI, 432
Smith, Jesse VI, 446
Smith, Jesse VI, 563
Smith, Jesse E. II, 263
Smith, Jesse Franklin I, 900
Smith, Jesse H. V, 431
Smith, Jesse James I, 627
Smith, Jesse Kersey I, 900
Smith, Jesse L. IV, 372
Smith, Jesse L. IV, 438
Smith, Jesse P. IV, 549
Smith, Jesse P. IV, 550
Smith, Jessie Carrol V, 710
Smith, Jessie S. III, 292
Smith, Jinney VI, 986
Smith, Jirah IV, 276
Smith, Jirah IV, 277
Smith, Jirah IV, 1185
Smith, Jirah IV, 1186
Smith, Jirah V, 862
Smith, Jno. II, 262
Smith, Jno. III, 499
Smith, Jno., Jr. VI, 995
Smith, Joana IV, 883
Smith, Joanna II, 421
Smith, Joanna II, 465
Smith, Joanna II, 654
Smith, Joanna IV, 657
Smith, Joanna IV, 868
Smith, Joanna IV, 874
Smith, Joanna IV, 883
Smith, Joanna IV, 905
Smith, Joanna IV, 908
Smith, Job I, 74
Smith, Job I, 227
Smith, Job I, 257
Smith, Job I, 260
Smith, Job II, 185
Smith, Job II, 262
Smith, Job II, 263
Smith, Job II, 656
Smith, Job IV, 276
Smith, Job IV, 1185
Smith, Job IV, 1186
Smith, Job V, 278
Smith, Job V, 279
Smith, Job V, 284
Smith, Job V, 432
Smith, Job V, 447
Smith, Job V, 862
Smith, Job V, 868
Smith, Job Bacon II, 184
Smith, Job R. II, 263
Smith, Job R. II, 301
Smith, Job R. II, 767
Smith, Joel IV, 277
Smith, Joel IV, 437
Smith, Joel IV, 445
Smith, Joel VI, 446
Smith, Joel J. IV, 440
Smith, Joel K. IV, 551
Smith, Johanna II, 654
Smith, John I, 7
Smith, John I, 11
Smith, John I, 18
Smith, John I, 39
Smith, John I, 74
Smith, John I, 78
Smith, John I, 110
Smith, John I, 117
Smith, John I, 166
Smith, John I, 167
Smith, John I, 170
Smith, John I, 419
Smith, John I, 668
Smith, John I, 689
Smith, John I, 695
Smith, John I, 705
Smith, John I, 734
Smith, John I, 1024
Smith, John I, 1037
Smith, John I, 1161
Smith, John II, 17
Smith, John II, 28
Smith, John II, 40
Smith, John II, 66
Smith, John II, 78
Smith, John II, 99
Smith, John II, 100
Smith, John II, 103
Smith, John II, 109
Smith, John II, 183
Smith, John II, 184
Smith, John II, 185
Smith, John II, 196
Smith, John II, 209
Smith, John II, 211
Smith, John II, 215
Smith, John II, 243
Smith, John II, 261
Smith, John II, 262
Smith, John II, 263
Smith, John II, 301
Smith, John II, 421
Smith, John II, 422
Smith, John II, 447
Smith, John II, 477
Smith, John II, 584
Smith, John II, 620
Smith, John II, 625
Smith, John II, 653
Smith, John II, 654
Smith, John II, 655
Smith, John II, 815
Smith, John II, 820
Smith, John II, 911
Smith, John II, 923
Smith, John II, 969
Smith, John II, 970
Smith, John II, 1025
Smith, John II, 1027
Smith, John II, 1041
Smith, John III, 294
Smith, John III, 295
Smith, John III, 444
Smith, John III, 447
Smith, John III, 453
Smith, John IV, 59
Smith, John IV, 60
Smith, John IV, 76
Smith, John IV, 109
Smith, John IV, 117
Smith, John IV, 159
Smith, John IV, 276
Smith, John IV, 277
Smith, John IV, 351
Smith, John IV, 355
Smith, John IV, 439
Smith, John IV, 538
Smith, John IV, 550
Smith, John IV, 594
Smith, John IV, 657
Smith, John IV, 763
Smith, John IV, 883
Smith, John IV, 959
Smith, John IV, 994
Smith, John IV, 1180
Smith, John IV, 1185
Smith, John IV, 1186
Smith, John V, 17
Smith, John V, 122
Smith, John V, 123
Smith, John V, 278
Smith, John V, 279
Smith, John V, 396
Smith, John V, 416
Smith, John V, 428
Smith, John V, 431
Smith, John V, 432
Smith, John V, 529
Smith, John V, 597
Smith, John V, 631
Smith, John V, 827
Smith, John V, 861
Smith, John V, 886
Smith, John V, 899
Smith, John V, 1019
Smith, John VI, 97
Smith, John VI, 98
Smith, John VI, 121
Smith, John VI, 212
Smith, John VI, 267
Smith, John VI, 420
Smith, John VI, 445
Smith, John VI, 446
Smith, John VI, 469
Smith, John VI, 497
Smith, John VI, 505
Smith, John VI, 538
Smith, John VI, 559
Smith, John VI, 562
Smith, John VI, 563
Smith, John VI, 605
Smith, John VI, 606
Smith, John VI, 617
Smith, John VI, 622
Smith, John VI, 624
Smith, John VI, 625
Smith, John VI, 633
Smith, John VI, 645
Smith, John VI, 650
Smith, John VI, 658
Smith, John VI, 664
Smith, John VI, 668
Smith, John VI, 696
Smith, John VI, 701
Smith, John VI, 702
Smith, John VI, 705
Smith, John VI, 706
Smith, John VI, 707
Smith, John VI, 754
Smith, John VI, 854
Smith, John VI, 888
Smith, John VI, 911
Smith, John VI, 912
Smith, John VI, 930
Smith, John VI, 955
Smith, John VI, 995
Smith, John C. III, 26
Smith, John C. III, 230
Smith, John C. III, 293
Smith, John C. III, 295
Smith, John C. IV, 439
Smith, John C. V, 1019
Smith, John C. VI, 815
Smith, John C. VI, 817
Smith, John C. VI, 854
Smith, John C. VI, 857
Smith, John Cope IV, 133
Smith, John D. II, 421
Smith, John D. II, 655
Smith, John D. VI, 866
Smith, John E. IV, 994
Smith, John E. IV, 1223
Smith, John Emerson V, 710
Smith, John Emmerson V, 710
Smith, John F. IV, 109
Smith, John F. V, 644
Smith, John Frank II, 138
Smith, John Frederick IV, 1076
Smith, John Frederick IV, 1115
Smith, John G. III, 511
Smith, John H. I, 1161
Smith, John H. I, 1162
Smith, John H. V, 597
Smith, John H. VI, 949
Smith, John H. VI, 990
Smith, John Henry V, 710
Smith, John J. II, 263
Smith, John J. II, 421
Smith, John J. II, 422
Smith, John J. II, 655
Smith, John J. II, 656
Smith, John J. II, 767
Smith, John J. III, 250
Smith, John J. III, 293
Smith, John J., Jr. II, 656
Smith, John J., Jr. II, 719
Smith, John L. II, 719
Smith, John L. IV, 439
Smith, John Lynas II, 767
Smith, John M. II, 641
Smith, John M. II, 655
Smith, John M. III, 293
Smith, John M. IV, 351
Smith, John M. IV, 482
Smith, John M. IV, 497
Smith, John M. IV, 542
Smith, John M. IV, 549
Smith, John M. IV, 550
Smith, John M. IV, 551
Smith, John Morton II, 718
Smith, John Morton II, 767
Smith, John N. IV, 536
Smith, John N. IV, 994
Smith, John P. IV, 277
Smith, John P. IV, 994
Smith, John P. V, 278
Smith, John Powell VI, 446
Smith, John R. IV, 1379
Smith, John R. V, 403
Smith, John R. V, 431
Smith, John R. VI, 704
Smith, John R. VI, 723
Smith, John S. I, 74
Smith, John S. IV, 386
Smith, John S. IV, 424
Smith, John S. IV, 437
Smith, John Scholfield VI, 562
Smith, John Singclair VI, 446
Smith, John Steward IV, 994
Smith, John T. III, 126
Smith, John T. IV, 277
Smith, John T. IV, 278
Smith, John T. V, 431
Smith, John T. S. III, 293
Smith, John T. S. III, 294
Smith, John T. S. III, 295
Smith, John T. Slocum III, 292
Smith, John Thomas IV, 277
Smith, John Thomas VI, 562
Smith, John Thompson I, 1088
Smith, John W. I, 689
Smith, John W. IV, 213
Smith, John W. IV, 276
Smith, John W. IV, 277
Smith, John W. IV, 351
Smith, John W. IV, 437
Smith, John W. IV, 439
Smith, John W. IV, 549
Smith, John W. IV, 550
Smith, John W. IV, 762
Smith, John W. IV, 763
Smith, John W. V, 431
Smith, John W. VI, 950
Smith, John W. VI, 995
Smith, John, Jr. I, 74
Smith, John, Jr. I, 166
Smith, John, Jr. II, 56
Smith, John, Jr. II, 97

Smith, John, Jr. II, 99
Smith, John, Jr. II, 261
Smith, John, Jr. II, 466
Smith, John, Jr. II, 653
Smith, John, Jr. II, 1027
Smith, John, Jr. II, 1030
Smith, John, Jr. III, 453
Smith, John, Jr. VI, 639
Smith, John, Jr. VI, 703
Smith, John, Jr. VI, 854
Smith, John, Jr. VI, 995
Smith, John, Sr. I, 74
Smith, John, Sr. I, 166
Smith, Jonah IV, 59
Smith, Jonah IV, 437
Smith, Jonah IV, 438
Smith, Jonah VI, 446
Smith, Jonas IV, 109
Smith, Jonas VI, 446
Smith, Jonas VI, 562
Smith, Jonas VI, 563
Smith, Jonas VI, 645
Smith, Jonas VI, 648
Smith, Jonas VI, 667
Smith, Jonas VI, 679
Smith, Jonas VI, 702
Smith, Jonas VI, 704
Smith, Jonas VI, 707
Smith, Jonas VI, 723
Smith, Jonathan I, 74
Smith, Jonathan II, 40
Smith, Jonathan II, 93
Smith, Jonathan II, 99
Smith, Jonathan II, 100
Smith, Jonathan II, 110
Smith, Jonathan II, 184
Smith, Jonathan II, 301
Smith, Jonathan II, 654
Smith, Jonathan II, 1009
Smith, Jonathan II, 1028
Smith, Jonathan III, 18
Smith, Jonathan III, 292
Smith, Jonathan III, 453
Smith, Jonathan IV, 59
Smith, Jonathan IV, 205
Smith, Jonathan IV, 276
Smith, Jonathan IV, 277
Smith, Jonathan IV, 439
Smith, Jonathan IV, 594
Smith, Jonathan V, 123
Smith, Jonathan V, 279
Smith, Jonathan V, 465
Smith, Jonathan V, 959
Smith, Jonathan VI, 995
Smith, Jonathan Biles II, 602
Smith, Jonathan Biles II, 654
Smith, Jonathan W. VI, 446
Smith, Jonothan V, 123
Smith, Jordan Zadoc V, 122
Smith, Jordon I, 900
Smith, Jordon P. I, 249
Smith, Jordon P. I, 257
Smith, Jos. VI, 444
Smith, Joseph I, 55
Smith, Joseph I, 74
Smith, Joseph I, 117
Smith, Joseph I, 166
Smith, Joseph I, 1024
Smith, Joseph I, 1037
Smith, Joseph I, 1060
Smith, Joseph I, 1063
Smith, Joseph I, 1088
Smith, Joseph I, 1098
Smith, Joseph I Sup 1, 4
Smith, Joseph I Sup 1, 6
Smith, Joseph I Sup 1, 8
Smith, Joseph II, 55
Smith, Joseph II, 75
Smith, Joseph II, 99
Smith, Joseph II, 132
Smith, Joseph II, 183
Smith, Joseph II, 184
Smith, Joseph II, 185
Smith, Joseph II, 203
Smith, Joseph II, 261
Smith, Joseph II, 262
Smith, Joseph II, 263
Smith, Joseph II, 301
Smith, Joseph II, 421
Smith, Joseph II, 654
Smith, Joseph II, 655
Smith, Joseph II, 656
Smith, Joseph II, 719
Smith, Joseph II, 767
Smith, Joseph II, 969
Smith, Joseph II, 970
Smith, Joseph III, 63
Smith, Joseph III, 283
Smith, Joseph III, 288
Smith, Joseph III, 294
Smith, Joseph IV, 59
Smith, Joseph IV, 60
Smith, Joseph IV, 86
Smith, Joseph IV, 109
Smith, Joseph IV, 117
Smith, Joseph IV, 133
Smith, Joseph IV, 159
Smith, Joseph IV, 392
Smith, Joseph IV, 437
Smith, Joseph IV, 439
Smith, Joseph IV, 874
Smith, Joseph IV, 883
Smith, Joseph IV, 905
Smith, Joseph IV, 908
Smith, Joseph IV, 983
Smith, Joseph IV, 1076
Smith, Joseph IV, 1114
Smith, Joseph IV, 1115
Smith, Joseph IV, 1186
Smith, Joseph IV, 1294
Smith, Joseph IV, 1326
Smith, Joseph V, 28
Smith, Joseph V, 32
Smith, Joseph V, 122
Smith, Joseph V, 133
Smith, Joseph V, 529
Smith, Joseph V, 548
Smith, Joseph V, 827
Smith, Joseph V, 843
Smith, Joseph V, 861
Smith, Joseph V, 932
Smith, Joseph VI, 393
Smith, Joseph VI, 444
Smith, Joseph VI, 445
Smith, Joseph VI, 446
Smith, Joseph VI, 453
Smith, Joseph VI, 462
Smith, Joseph VI, 562
Smith, Joseph VI, 563
Smith, Joseph VI, 854
Smith, Joseph Allen VI, 605
Smith, Joseph B. II, 421
Smith, Joseph B. II, 422
Smith, Joseph B. II, 655
Smith, Joseph D. II, 655
Smith, Joseph D. II, 719
Smith, Joseph Franklin IV, 1138
Smith, Joseph H. II, 184
Smith, Joseph H. II, 301
Smith, Joseph H. II, 656
Smith, Joseph H. II, 767
Smith, Joseph H. V, 597
Smith, Joseph H. V, 598
Smith, Joseph H. V, 710
Smith, Joseph P. II, 301
Smith, Joseph P. II, 735
Smith, Joseph P. II, 767
Smith, Joseph Pancoast II, 263
Smith, Joseph R. II, 184
Smith, Joseph R. II, 262
Smith, Joseph R. II, 263
Smith, Joseph R. II, 301
Smith, Joseph Smith II, 1011
Smith, Joseph T. VI, 440
Smith, Joseph T. VI, 445
Smith, Joseph T. VI, 446
Smith, Joseph T. VI, 597
Smith, Joseph T. VI, 774
Smith, Joseph W. III, 294
Smith, Joseph W. V, 279
Smith, Joseph, Jr. I, 49
Smith, Joseph, Jr. I, 74
Smith, Joseph, Jr. IV, 1116
Smith, Joseph, Jr. V, 529
Smith, Joseph, Jr. VI, 446
Smith, Josephine I, 1161
Smith, Josephine III, 414
Smith, Josephine III, 447
Smith, Josephine A. IV, 440
Smith, Joshua II, 202
Smith, Joshua II, 261
Smith, Joshua IV, 549
Smith, Joshua IV, 1076
Smith, Joshua IV, 1138
Smith, Joshua VI, 648
Smith, Joshua VI, 652
Smith, Joshua VI, 704
Smith, Joshua P. IV, 438
Smith, Joshua R. II, 184
Smith, Joshua R. II, 185
Smith, Joshua R. II, 262
Smith, Joshua Raper II, 183
Smith, Joshua Raper II, 262
Smith, Joshua Reynolds I, 900
Smith, Joshua W. IV, 277
Smith, Joshua W. IV, 551
Smith, Joshua W. IV, 763
Smith, Joshua W. IV, 1131
Smith, Joshua W. IV, 1138
Smith, Joshua Walter IV, 550
Smith, Josiah I, 74
Smith, Josiah I, 200
Smith, Josiah I, 865
Smith, Josiah I, 900
Smith, Josiah II, 55
Smith, Josiah II, 100
Smith, Josiah II, 136
Smith, Josiah II, 138
Smith, Josiah IV, 405
Smith, Josiah IV, 437
Smith, Josiah IV, 549
Smith, Josiah V, 122
Smith, Josiah V, 278
Smith, Josiah VI, 446
Smith, Josiah B. IV, 763
Smith, Josiah Bundy IV, 277
Smith, Josiah L. II, 40
Smith, Josiah L. II, 138
Smith, Josiah S. II, 157
Smith, Joweph VI, 445
Smith, Joyce II, 184
Smith, Joyce II, 210
Smith, Joyce II, 261
Smith, Joyce II, 641
Smith, Joyce II, 655
Smith, Judah VI, 858
Smith, Jude VI, 445
Smith, Judith II, 54
Smith, Judith II, 99
Smith, Judith III, 257
Smith, Judith III, 294
Smith, Judith IV, 59
Smith, Judith IV, 96
Smith, Judith IV, 109
Smith, Judith IV, 159
Smith, Judith IV, 437
Smith, Judith IV, 438
Smith, Judith IV, 439
Smith, Judith IV, 449
Smith, Judith IV, 749
Smith, Judith IV, 1115
Smith, Judith V, 899
Smith, Judith VI, 979
Smith, Judith C. III, 292
Smith, Judith C. III, 294
Smith, Judith C. III, 295
Smith, Judith C. III, 315
Smith, Julia V, 279
Smith, Julia V, 465
Smith, Julia D. V, 932
Smith, Julia Ella V, 279
Smith, Junius L. IV, 276
Smith, Junius L. IV, 278
Smith, Jureta IV, 277
Smith, Katharine II, 184
Smith, Katharine II, 205
Smith, Katharine II, 261
Smith, Katharine IV, 130
Smith, Katharine IV, 133
Smith, Katherine III, 83
Smith, Katherine L. III, 395
Smith, Katherine L. III, 447
Smith, Katie C. V, 548
Smith, Katie M. IV, 278
Smith, Keith III, 132
Smith, Keith III, 294
Smith, Kelley VI, 995
Smith, Kersey IV, 1076
Smith, Kesia II, 1080
Smith, Kezia VI, 706
Smith, Kezia T. VI, 393
Smith, Kezia T. VI, 394
Smith, Kezia T. VI, 445
Smith, Keziah II, 1060
Smith, Keziah V, 862
Smith, Keziah V, 868
Smith, Keziah VI, 445
Smith, Keziah VI, 645
Smith, Keziah VI, 674
Smith, Keziah VI, 704
Smith, Keziah T. VI, 446
Smith, Kittie V, 835
Smith, Kitty III, 499
Smith, Kitty III, 505
Smith, L. I. III, 294
Smith, L. J. IV, 1186
Smith, L. Marlin IV, 762
Smith, Lamar IV, 1264
Smith, Lanore IV, 1264
Smith, Latitia III, 447
Smith, Laura I, 1161
Smith, Laura IV, 1378
Smith, Laura V, 278
Smith, Laura VI, 652
Smith, Laura VI, 704
Smith, Laura B. V, 360
Smith, Laura Bell V, 278
Smith, Laura F. III, 295
Smith, Laura G. V, 932
Smith, Laura Gilpin V, 932
Smith, Laurena IV, 1223
Smith, Lavina IV, 60
Smith, Lavina IV, 762
Smith, Lavina IV, 1042
Smith, Lavina IV, 1372
Smith, Lavina IV, 1379
Smith, Lavina V, 432
Smith, Lavina V, 529
Smith, Lavinah V, 416
Smith, Lavinah V, 431
Smith, Lavinia II, 799
Smith, Lavisa IV, 353
Smith, Lawrence IV, 1223
Smith, Lawrence V, 203
Smith, Leah I, 18
Smith, Leah I, 46
Smith, Leah I, 55
Smith, Leah I, 71
Smith, Leah I, 74
Smith, Leah I, 90
Smith, Leah I, 418
Smith, Leah I, 419
Smith, Leah I Sup 1, 8
Smith, Leah V, 465
Smith, Leah VI, 619
Smith, Leah VI, 621
Smith, Leah VI, 628
Smith, Leah VI, 631
Smith, Leah VI, 650
Smith, Leah VI, 651
Smith, Leah VI, 704
Smith, Leatitie I, 1063
Smith, Leda Diana V, 360
Smith, Lelia M. I, 257
Smith, Lemuel IV, 276
Smith, Lemuel IV, 550
Smith, Lemuel IV, 551
Smith, Lemuel IV, 994
Smith, Lemuel J. IV, 1164
Smith, Lemuel J. IV, 1185
Smith, Lena IV, 1164
Smith, Lena IV, 1185
Smith, Lena IV, 1186
Smith, Lena V, 279
Smith, Lena M. V, 432
Smith, Lena M. V, 710
Smith, Leslie IV, 1264
Smith, Lester Janney VI, 703
Smith, Letisha I, 900
Smith, Letishe I, 865
Smith, Letitia I, 900
Smith, Letitia IV, 59
Smith, Letitia IV, 351
Smith, Letitia IV, 550
Smith, Letitia V, 122
Smith, Letitia VI, 446
Smith, Letitia VI, 703
Smith, Levi I, 1088
Smith, Levi IV, 276
Smith, Levi IV, 277
Smith, Levi IV, 283
Smith, Levi IV, 594
Smith, Levi IV, 1076
Smith, Levi V, 274
Smith, Levi V, 279
Smith, Levi V, 360
Smith, Levi V, 465
Smith, Levi V, 954
Smith, Levi V, 959
Smith, Levi V, 960
Smith, Levi V, 1019
Smith, Levi VI, 429
Smith, Levi VI, 435
Smith, Levi VI, 444
Smith, Levi VI, 445
Smith, Levi VI, 446
Smith, Levi VI, 460
Smith, Levina IV, 60
Smith, Levina V, 431
Smith, Levina V, 509
Smith, Levina V, 529
Smith, Lewis III, 294
Smith, Lewis IV, 549
Smith, Lewis Branson IV, 276
Smith, Lewis S. II, 324
Smith, Lewis T. III, 294
Smith, Lidya II, 40
Smith, Lillian II, 924
Smith, Lillian II, 931
Smith, Lillian III, 414
Smith, Lillian III, 447
Smith, Lillian Holliday V, 710
Smith, Lillie I, 921
Smith, Lillie V, 764
Smith, Lindley II, 820
Smith, Lindley II, 923
Smith, Lindley II, 924
Smith, Lindley V, 279
Smith, Lindley V, 360
Smith, Lindley E. IV, 762
Smith, Lindley M. II, 302
Smith, Lindley M. IV, 1115
Smith, Lindley M. V, 278
Smith, Lindley Murray II, 301
Smith, Linneus IV, 843
Smith, Livina J. I, 922
Smith, Lizzie II, 969
Smith, Lizzie V, 278
Smith, Lizzie V, 279
Smith, Lizzie V, 360
Smith, Lizzie V, 597
Smith, Lizzie V, 598
Smith, Lizzie V, 675
Smith, Lizzie V, 710
Smith, Lizzie M. IV, 180
Smith, Lizzie M. IV, 191
Smith, Lizzie M. IV, 276
Smith, Lizzie M. IV, 278
Smith, Lizzie M. IV, 513
Smith, Lizzie M. IV, 550
Smith, Lizzie M. IV, 551
Smith, Lizzie M. V, 597
Smith, Lizzie May V, 710
Smith, Lloyd P. II, 421
Smith, Lloyd P. II, 767
Smith, Logan II, 215
Smith, Lorana III, 499
Smith, Lou V, 1019
Smith, Louella V, 432
Smith, Louella J. V, 432
Smith, Louisa II, 719
Smith, Louisa II, 767
Smith, Louisa III, 296
Smith, Louisa IV, 439
Smith, Louisa IV, 1076
Smith, Louisa IV, 1138
Smith, Louisa V, 278
Smith, Louisa V, 447
Smith, Louisa VI, 703
Smith, Louisa M. III, 294
Smith, Louisa P. IV, 550
Smith, Louisa P. IV, 551
Smith, Louisa Reeder V, 278
Smith, Louisa S. IV, 679
Smith, Louise I, 625
Smith, Louise I, 640
Smith, Louise I, 641
Smith, Louise II, 969
Smith, Louise A. III, 293
Smith, Louise Piatt IV, 1338
Smith, Louiza II, 767
Smith, Louiza V, 274
Smith, Louiza V, 278
Smith, Lovey I, 57
Smith, Lovey I, 74
Smith, Lovey I, 117
Smith, Lovey I, 166
Smith, Lovina IV, 763
Smith, Lu III, 47
Smith, Lu III, 210
Smith, Lucian V, 529
Smith, Lucille Slade II, 924
Smith, Lucina V, 529
Smith, Lucina F. IV, 1379
Smith, Lucinda IV, 440
Smith, Lucinda IV, 452
Smith, Lucinda IV, 1114
Smith, Lucinda IV, 1122
Smith, Lucinda M. IV, 438
Smith, Lucretia B. III, 295
Smith, Lucretia M. II, 924
Smith, Lucretia M. VI, 741
Smith, Lucretia M. VI, 742
Smith, Lucretia M. VI, 779
Smith, Lucretia M. VI, 793
Smith, Lucy I, 318
Smith, Lucy II, 40
Smith, Lucy II, 124
Smith, Lucy II, 138
Smith, Lucy II, 263
Smith, Lucy II, 923
Smith, Lucy II, 924
Smith, Lucy VI, 797
Smith, Lucy VI, 899
Smith, Lucy VI, 1015
Smith, Lucy A. II, 924
Smith, Luella J. V, 278
Smith, Luella J. V, 432
Smith, Luella M. V, 279
Smith, Luke F. II, 158
Smith, Luke F. II, 159
Smith, Lusinda IV, 1076
Smith, Luther V, 644
Smith, Lycurgas V, 278
Smith, Lydda II, 261
Smith, Lyddia I, 61
Smith, Lyddia I, 74
Smith, Lydia I, 1116
Smith, Lydia I, 1127
Smith, Lydia I, 1132
Smith, Lydia I, 1146
Smith, Lydia II, 138
Smith, Lydia II, 157
Smith, Lydia II, 655
Smith, Lydia III, 292
Smith, Lydia IV, 21

, Lydia IV, 59
, Lydia IV, 102
, Lydia IV, 109
, Lydia IV, 159
, Lydia IV, 276
, Lydia IV, 277
, Lydia IV, 314
, Lydia IV, 315
, Lydia IV, 351
, Lydia IV, 352
, Lydia IV, 355
, Lydia IV, 379
, Lydia IV, 437
, Lydia IV, 438
, Lydia IV, 439
, Lydia IV, 456
, Lydia IV, 483
, Lydia IV, 497
, Lydia IV, 530
, Lydia IV, 542
, Lydia IV, 549
, Lydia IV, 550
, Lydia IV, 551
, Lydia IV, 1076
, Lydia IV, 1114
, Lydia IV, 1115
, Lydia IV, 1294
, Lydia IV, 1350
, Lydia IV, 1372
, Lydia IV, 1378
, Lydia IV, 1379
n, Lydia V, 24
n, Lydia V, 122
n, Lydia V, 123
h, Lydia V, 278
h, Lydia V, 279
h, Lydia V, 360
h, Lydia V, 465
h, Lydia V, 469
h, Lydia V, 529
h, Lydia V, 567
h, Lydia V, 581
h, Lydia V, 594
h, Lydia V, 598
h, Lydia V, 950
h, Lydia V, 960
h, Lydia VI, 440
h, Lydia VI, 444
h, Lydia VI, 445
h, Lydia VI, 446
h, Lydia VI, 453
h, Lydia VI, 521
h, Lydia VI, 562
h, Lydia VI, 563
h, Lydia VI, 605
h, Lydia VI, 649
h, Lydia VI, 652
h, Lydia VI, 664
h, Lydia VI, 666
h, Lydia VI, 668
h, Lydia VI, 704
h, Lydia VI, 707
h, Lydia A. IV, 1379
h, Lydia Ann IV, 277
h, Lydia Ann IV, 497
h, Lydia Ann IV, 505
h, Lydia Ann IV, 539
h, Lydia Ann IV, 1138
h, Lydia Ann IV, 1379
h, Lydia Ann V, 123
h, Lydia Ann V, 278
h, Lydia Ann V, 585
h, Lydia Ann V, 598
h, Lydia Ann VI, 446
h, Lydia B. IV, 550
h, Lydia B. VI, 708
h, Lydia C. III, 294
h, Lydia H. V, 529
h, Lydia J. IV, 372
h, Lydia Jane IV, 1114
h, Lydia Jane IV, 1116
h, Lydia M. IV, 1138
h, Lydia Morris V, 278
h, Lydia P. IV, 549
h, Lydia S. II, 144
th, Lydia S. II, 158
th, Lydia S. IV, 1092
th, Lydia S. IV, 1115
th, Lydia V. IV, 1066
th, Lydia V. IV, 1067
th, Lydia V. IV, 1076
th, Lydia V. IV, 1077
th, Lydia V. IV, 1116
th, Lydia V. Smith IV, 1077
th, Lydia W. V, 529
th, Lydia W., Jr. VI, 515
th, Lydia, Jr. V, 529
th, Lydiann IV, 550
th, Lyman IV, 763
th, Lynnley George II, 924
th, M. Lena IV, 994
Smith, M. S. IV, 762
Smith, Mabel IV, 1223
Smith, Mabel V, 675
Smith, Mabel V, 710
Smith, Mabel V, 764
Smith, Mabel Gertrude IV, 277
Smith, Mabel J. V, 710
Smith, Mable V, 598
Smith, Madge Osborn V, 691
Smith, Madge Osborn V, 710
Smith, Maggie IV, 1186
Smith, Maggie V, 710
Smith, Maggie D. H. I, 641
Smith, Mahala IV, 86
Smith, Mahala IV, 109
Smith, Mahala IV, 117
Smith, Mahala V, 359
Smith, Mahala V, 363
Smith, Mahala V, 932
Smith, Mahala V, 936
Smith, Mahala V, 944
Smith, Mahlon IV, 159
Smith, Mahlon IV, 351
Smith, Mahlon IV, 352
Smith, Mahlon IV, 439
Smith, Mahlon VI, 444
Smith, Mahlon VI, 446
Smith, Mahlon VI, 455
Smith, Mahlon VI, 555
Smith, Mahlon VI, 562
Smith, Mahlon VI, 563
Smith, Mahlon VI, 579
Smith, Mahlon VI, 584
Smith, Mahlon VI, 605
Smith, Mahlon VI, 606
Smith, Mahlon T. VI, 446
Smith, Malvina III, 292
Smith, Manda V, 710
Smith, Marcella W. V, 360
Smith, Marcy I, 1023
Smith, Margare IV, 109
Smith, Margaret I, 101
Smith, Margaret I, 625
Smith, Margaret I, 626
Smith, Margaret I, 641
Smith, Margaret I, 1023
Smith, Margaret II, 138
Smith, Margaret II, 184
Smith, Margaret II, 209
Smith, Margaret II, 262
Smith, Margaret II, 263
Smith, Margaret II, 422
Smith, Margaret II, 447
Smith, Margaret II, 484
Smith, Margaret II, 620
Smith, Margaret II, 653
Smith, Margaret II, 654
Smith, Margaret II, 655
Smith, Margaret II, 707
Smith, Margaret II, 767
Smith, Margaret II, 774
Smith, Margaret II, 776
Smith, Margaret II, 794
Smith, Margaret II, 815
Smith, Margaret II, 1021
Smith, Margaret II, 1027
Smith, Margaret IV, 19
Smith, Margaret IV, 59
Smith, Margaret IV, 121
Smith, Margaret IV, 133
Smith, Margaret IV, 346
Smith, Margaret IV, 351
Smith, Margaret IV, 352
Smith, Margaret IV, 356
Smith, Margaret IV, 407
Smith, Margaret IV, 437
Smith, Margaret IV, 594
Smith, Margaret IV, 762
Smith, Margaret V, 122
Smith, Margaret V, 123
Smith, Margaret V, 311
Smith, Margaret V, 420
Smith, Margaret V, 431
Smith, Margaret V, 447
Smith, Margaret V, 496
Smith, Margaret V, 529
Smith, Margaret V, 631
Smith, Margaret V, 874
Smith, Margaret VI, 396
Smith, Margaret VI, 444
Smith, Margaret VI, 445
Smith, Margaret VI, 446
Smith, Margaret VI, 596
Smith, Margaret VI, 605
Smith, Margaret A. II, 138
Smith, Margaret Ann IV, 1073
Smith, Margaret Ann IV, 1076
Smith, Margaret Ann IV, 1077
Smith, Margaret Ann IV, 1115
Smith, Margaret Ann IV, 1138
Smith, Margaret B. V, 960
Smith, Margaret Edith IV, 276
Smith, Margaret Edith IV, 277
Smith, Margaret F. II, 864
Smith, Margaret F. II, 924
Smith, Margaret L. V, 465
Smith, Margaret M. II, 767
Smith, Margaret Morris II, 262
Smith, Margaret Morris II, 302
Smith, Margaret Morris II, 421
Smith, Margaret Morris II, 767
Smith, Margaret W. II, 421
Smith, Margaret Wharton II, 767
Smith, Margarett I, 1023
Smith, Margaretta II, 656
Smith, Margaretta III, 310
Smith, Margaretta V, 260
Smith, Margaretta V, 278
Smith, Margaretta V, 279
Smith, Margery II, 261
Smith, Margery II, 262
Smith, Margery II, 816
Smith, Margery III, 293
Smith, Margery III, 294
Smith, Margratt II, 422
Smith, Maria II, 263
Smith, Maria II, 299
Smith, Maria II, 301
Smith, Maria III, 295
Smith, Maria IV, 276
Smith, Maria IV, 277
Smith, Maria IV, 439
Smith, Maria IV, 489
Smith, Maria IV, 550
Smith, Maria IV, 1076
Smith, Maria IV, 1114
Smith, Maria IV, 1115
Smith, Maria IV, 1138
Smith, Maria A. III, 511
Smith, Maria Ann V, 122
Smith, Maria Ann V, 279
Smith, Maria Ann V, 512
Smith, Maria Ann V, 529
Smith, Maria E. V, 279
Smith, Maria Ellis V, 465
Smith, Maria F. III, 292
Smith, Maria H. IV, 276
Smith, Maria H. IV, 277
Smith, Maria H. IV, 278
Smith, Maria H. IV, 438
Smith, Maria H. IV, 439
Smith, Maria H. IV, 440
Smith, Maria H. IV, 550
Smith, Maria W. III, 252
Smith, Maria W. III, 294
Smith, Mariah IV, 1361
Smith, Mariah IV, 1379
Smith, Mariah V, 278
Smith, Mariam IV, 1116
Smith, Mariam B. IV, 549
Smith, Marianna III, 263
Smith, Marianna III, 294
Smith, Marianna VI, 693
Smith, Marianna VI, 704
Smith, Marianna VI, 779
Smith, Marianna VI, 784
Smith, Marianna S. III, 263
Smith, Marie III, 499
Smith, Marie V, 529
Smith, Marion III, 294
Smith, Marion IV, 277
Smith, Marion IV, 440
Smith, Marion IV, 1076
Smith, Marium V, 827
Smith, Marium V, 861
Smith, Marjorie III, 294
Smith, Marjorie A. IV, 551
Smith, Marjorie A. IV, 553
Smith, Marjorie Ann IV, 285
Smith, Marjorie Anna IV, 278
Smith, Marjorie Anna IV, 553
Smith, Marjorie Anna IV, 1115
Smith, Marjorie Anna IV, 1116
Smith, Marjorie H. I, 641
Smith, Marjorie Helen I, 625
Smith, Marjory A. IV, 277
Smith, Mark II, 40
Smith, Mark II, 100
Smith, Mark IV, 551
Smith, Marmaduke II, 99
Smith, Marmaduke II, 100
Smith, Marmaduke III, 294
Smith, Marritt S. III, 293
Smith, Marry II, 99
Smith, Marry II, 110
Smith, Marshall V, 203
Smith, Martha I, 7
Smith, Martha I, 18
Smith, Martha I, 43
Smith, Martha I, 74
Smith, Martha I, 318
Smith, Martha I, 340
Smith, Martha I, 968
Smith, Martha I, 1088
Smith, Martha I, 1098
Smith, Martha I, 1132
Smith, Martha II, 17
Smith, Martha II, 40
Smith, Martha II, 184
Smith, Martha II, 185
Smith, Martha II, 262
Smith, Martha II, 302
Smith, Martha II, 421
Smith, Martha II, 477
Smith, Martha II, 654
Smith, Martha II, 767
Smith, Martha II, 1060
Smith, Martha III, 129
Smith, Martha III, 294
Smith, Martha III, 439
Smith, Martha III, 447
Smith, Martha III, 453
Smith, Martha III, 457
Smith, Martha IV, 17
Smith, Martha IV, 59
Smith, Martha IV, 121
Smith, Martha IV, 145
Smith, Martha IV, 159
Smith, Martha IV, 277
Smith, Martha IV, 328
Smith, Martha IV, 342
Smith, Martha IV, 351
Smith, Martha IV, 352
Smith, Martha IV, 383
Smith, Martha IV, 405
Smith, Martha IV, 437
Smith, Martha IV, 438
Smith, Martha IV, 439
Smith, Martha IV, 486
Smith, Martha IV, 549
Smith, Martha IV, 550
Smith, Martha IV, 599
Smith, Martha IV, 763
Smith, Martha IV, 864
Smith, Martha IV, 883
Smith, Martha IV, 916
Smith, Martha V, 19
Smith, Martha V, 123
Smith, Martha V, 126
Smith, Martha V, 465
Smith, Martha V, 644
Smith, Martha V, 858
Smith, Martha V, 861
Smith, Martha V, 862
Smith, Martha VI, 97
Smith, Martha VI, 98
Smith, Martha VI, 121
Smith, Martha VI, 429
Smith, Martha VI, 437
Smith, Martha VI, 440
Smith, Martha VI, 444
Smith, Martha VI, 445
Smith, Martha VI, 446
Smith, Martha VI, 562
Smith, Martha VI, 563
Smith, Martha VI, 606
Smith, Martha VI, 636
Smith, Martha VI, 695
Smith, Martha VI, 703
Smith, Martha VI, 704
Smith, Martha VI, 854
Smith, Martha VI, 995
Smith, Martha A. VI, 854
Smith, Martha Ann II, 1080
Smith, Martha Ann VI, 995
Smith, Martha Baldwin IV, 1186
Smith, Martha Baldwin IV, 1294
Smith, Martha C. IV, 532
Smith, Martha C. IV, 551
Smith, Martha E. V, 1019
Smith, Martha E. VI, 995
Smith, Martha Grace I, 26
Smith, Martha J. I, 257
Smith, Martha J. II, 751
Smith, Martha J. II, 767
Smith, Martha Jane VI, 995
Smith, Martha Kirby II, 100
Smith, Martha L. V, 529
Smith, Martha M. I, 1162
Smith, Martha M. II, 184
Smith, Martha M. II, 302
Smith, Martha M. II, 422
Smith, Martha M. II, 656
Smith, Martha N. IV, 1185
Smith, Martha P. IV, 629
Smith, Martha P. IV, 657
Smith, Martha W. III, 166
Smith, Martha W. III, 294
Smith, Martha, Jr. IV, 439
Smith, Martin VI, 854
Smith, Martin H. VI, 829
Smith, Mary I, 47
Smith, Mary I, 50
Smith, Mary I, 53
Smith, Mary I, 55
Smith, Mary I, 72
Smith, Mary I, 74
Smith, Mary I, 79
Smith, Mary I, 117
Smith, Mary I, 166
Smith, Mary I, 167
Smith, Mary I, 238
Smith, Mary I, 257
Smith, Mary I, 318
Smith, Mary I, 405
Smith, Mary I, 419
Smith, Mary I, 625
Smith, Mary I, 679
Smith, Mary I, 689
Smith, Mary I, 705
Smith, Mary I, 729
Smith, Mary I, 732
Smith, Mary I, 734
Smith, Mary I, 900
Smith, Mary I, 1023
Smith, Mary I, 1024
Smith, Mary I, 1063
Smith, Mary I, 1075
Smith, Mary I, 1088
Smith, Mary I, 1090
Smith, Mary I, 1098
Smith, Mary I, 1161
Smith, Mary I, 1162
Smith, Mary II, 27
Smith, Mary II, 40
Smith, Mary II, 41
Smith, Mary II, 55
Smith, Mary II, 61
Smith, Mary II, 68
Smith, Mary II, 75
Smith, Mary II, 85
Smith, Mary II, 86
Smith, Mary II, 93
Smith, Mary II, 99
Smith, Mary II, 100
Smith, Mary II, 111
Smith, Mary II, 124
Smith, Mary II, 128
Smith, Mary II, 132
Smith, Mary II, 138
Smith, Mary II, 158
Smith, Mary II, 180
Smith, Mary II, 183
Smith, Mary II, 184
Smith, Mary II, 185
Smith, Mary II, 202
Smith, Mary II, 203
Smith, Mary II, 212
Smith, Mary II, 214
Smith, Mary II, 238
Smith, Mary II, 243
Smith, Mary II, 244
Smith, Mary II, 245
Smith, Mary II, 247
Smith, Mary II, 248
Smith, Mary II, 249
Smith, Mary II, 251
Smith, Mary II, 260
Smith, Mary II, 261
Smith, Mary II, 262
Smith, Mary II, 263
Smith, Mary II, 277
Smith, Mary II, 297
Smith, Mary II, 301
Smith, Mary II, 315
Smith, Mary II, 421
Smith, Mary II, 422
Smith, Mary II, 447
Smith, Mary II, 489
Smith, Mary II, 502
Smith, Mary II, 552
Smith, Mary II, 620
Smith, Mary II, 637
Smith, Mary II, 653
Smith, Mary II, 654
Smith, Mary II, 655
Smith, Mary II, 704
Smith, Mary II, 719
Smith, Mary II, 767
Smith, Mary II, 820
Smith, Mary II, 911
Smith, Mary II, 923
Smith, Mary II, 970
Smith, Mary II, 980
Smith, Mary II, 986
Smith, Mary II, 1010
Smith, Mary II, 1027
Smith, Mary II, 1028
Smith, Mary II, 1030
Smith, Mary II, 1050
Smith, Mary II, 1060
Smith, Mary II, 1072
Smith, Mary II, 1080
Smith, Mary III, 63

Smith, Mary III, 67
Smith, Mary III, 130
Smith, Mary III, 145
Smith, Mary III, 184
Smith, Mary III, 185
Smith, Mary III, 226
Smith, Mary III, 236
Smith, Mary III, 291
Smith, Mary III, 292
Smith, Mary III, 293
Smith, Mary III, 294
Smith, Mary III, 295
Smith, Mary III, 316
Smith, Mary III, 402
Smith, Mary III, 407
Smith, Mary III, 447
Smith, Mary III, 448
Smith, Mary III, 452
Smith, Mary III, 453
Smith, Mary III, 454
Smith, Mary III, 495
Smith, Mary III, 499
Smith, Mary III, 507
Smith, Mary III, 508
Smith, Mary IV, 34
Smith, Mary IV, 58
Smith, Mary IV, 59
Smith, Mary IV, 60
Smith, Mary IV, 63
Smith, Mary IV, 106
Smith, Mary IV, 109
Smith, Mary IV, 159
Smith, Mary IV, 205
Smith, Mary IV, 276
Smith, Mary IV, 277
Smith, Mary IV, 278
Smith, Mary IV, 324
Smith, Mary IV, 351
Smith, Mary IV, 352
Smith, Mary IV, 353
Smith, Mary IV, 371
Smith, Mary IV, 392
Smith, Mary IV, 437
Smith, Mary IV, 438
Smith, Mary IV, 439
Smith, Mary IV, 441
Smith, Mary IV, 454
Smith, Mary IV, 520
Smith, Mary IV, 538
Smith, Mary IV, 549
Smith, Mary IV, 550
Smith, Mary IV, 594
Smith, Mary IV, 769
Smith, Mary IV, 820
Smith, Mary IV, 832
Smith, Mary IV, 843
Smith, Mary IV, 895
Smith, Mary IV, 976
Smith, Mary IV, 994
Smith, Mary IV, 1051
Smith, Mary IV, 1057
Smith, Mary IV, 1058
Smith, Mary IV, 1076
Smith, Mary IV, 1114
Smith, Mary IV, 1115
Smith, Mary IV, 1138
Smith, Mary IV, 1182
Smith, Mary IV, 1185
Smith, Mary IV, 1186
Smith, Mary IV, 1236
Smith, Mary IV, 1240
Smith, Mary IV, 1379
Smith, Mary V, 28
Smith, Mary V, 42
Smith, Mary V, 59
Smith, Mary V, 93
Smith, Mary V, 120
Smith, Mary V, 122
Smith, Mary V, 123
Smith, Mary V, 130
Smith, Mary V, 203
Smith, Mary V, 278
Smith, Mary V, 279
Smith, Mary V, 300
Smith, Mary V, 403
Smith, Mary V, 431
Smith, Mary V, 432
Smith, Mary V, 447
Smith, Mary V, 463
Smith, Mary V, 465
Smith, Mary V, 466
Smith, Mary V, 529
Smith, Mary V, 547
Smith, Mary V, 597
Smith, Mary V, 655
Smith, Mary V, 710
Smith, Mary V, 861
Smith, Mary V, 862
Smith, Mary V, 932
Smith, Mary VI, 367
Smith, Mary VI, 378
Smith, Mary VI, 393
Smith, Mary VI, 416
Smith, Mary VI, 435
Smith, Mary VI, 444
Smith, Mary VI, 445
Smith, Mary VI, 446
Smith, Mary VI, 455
Smith, Mary VI, 462
Smith, Mary VI, 476
Smith, Mary VI, 485
Smith, Mary VI, 561
Smith, Mary VI, 562
Smith, Mary VI, 563
Smith, Mary VI, 579
Smith, Mary VI, 584
Smith, Mary VI, 593
Smith, Mary VI, 605
Smith, Mary VI, 606
Smith, Mary VI, 617
Smith, Mary VI, 621
Smith, Mary VI, 626
Smith, Mary VI, 634
Smith, Mary VI, 649
Smith, Mary VI, 650
Smith, Mary VI, 658
Smith, Mary VI, 693
Smith, Mary VI, 703
Smith, Mary VI, 704
Smith, Mary VI, 705
Smith, Mary VI, 706
Smith, Mary VI, 710
Smith, Mary VI, 711
Smith, Mary VI, 712
Smith, Mary VI, 713
Smith, Mary VI, 741
Smith, Mary VI, 779
Smith, Mary VI, 854
Smith, Mary VI, 995
Smith, Mary A. III, 18
Smith, Mary A. III, 129
Smith, Mary A. IV, 959
Smith, Mary A. VI, 834
Smith, Mary Abbarilla V, 431
Smith, Mary Acice IV, 440
Smith, Mary Alenda II, 138
Smith, Mary Alice IV, 453
Smith, Mary Alinda II, 158
Smith, Mary Ann II, 41
Smith, Mary Ann II, 719
Smith, Mary Ann II, 767
Smith, Mary Ann II, 820
Smith, Mary Ann II, 1080
Smith, Mary Ann IV, 228
Smith, Mary Ann IV, 277
Smith, Mary Ann IV, 437
Smith, Mary Ann IV, 439
Smith, Mary Ann IV, 440
Smith, Mary Ann IV, 538
Smith, Mary Ann IV, 549
Smith, Mary Ann IV, 550
Smith, Mary Ann IV, 551
Smith, Mary Ann IV, 554
Smith, Mary Ann IV, 763
Smith, Mary Ann IV, 1115
Smith, Mary Ann V, 36
Smith, Mary Ann V, 123
Smith, Mary Ann V, 300
Smith, Mary Ann V, 311
Smith, Mary Anna II, 1080
Smith, Mary Anna III, 294
Smith, Mary Anna III, 308
Smith, Mary Anna VI, 702
Smith, Mary Annis IV, 594
Smith, Mary Atlantic V, 267
Smith, Mary Atlantic V, 279
Smith, Mary Avice IV, 440
Smith, Mary B. II, 184
Smith, Mary B. II, 263
Smith, Mary B. II, 422
Smith, Mary B. II, 655
Smith, Mary B. II, 656
Smith, Mary B. II, 718
Smith, Mary B. II, 719
Smith, Mary B. II, 767
Smith, Mary B. II, 923
Smith, Mary B. V, 957
Smith, Mary B. V, 960
Smith, Mary Betts II, 820
Smith, Mary C. II, 263
Smith, Mary C. II, 422
Smith, Mary C. III, 293
Smith, Mary C. IV, 376
Smith, Mary C. IV, 440
Smith, Mary C. V, 28
Smith, Mary C. V, 122
Smith, Mary C. V, 1019
Smith, Mary Caleb IV, 438
Smith, Mary Caleb IV, 453
Smith, Mary Catharine Jones II, 703
Smith, Mary D. II, 183
Smith, Mary D. II, 184
Smith, Mary D. VI, 380
Smith, Mary D. VI, 406
Smith, Mary D. VI, 444
Smith, Mary David IV, 1076
Smith, Mary E. II, 40
Smith, Mary E. II, 124
Smith, Mary E. II, 138
Smith, Mary E. II, 158
Smith, Mary E. II, 719
Smith, Mary E. II, 767
Smith, Mary E. II, 776
Smith, Mary E. II, 820
Smith, Mary E. II, 924
Smith, Mary E. IV, 278
Smith, Mary E. IV, 800
Smith, Mary E. IV, 1115
Smith, Mary E. V, 122
Smith, Mary E. V, 203
Smith, Mary E. V, 431
Smith, Mary E. V, 631
Smith, Mary E. V, 710
Smith, Mary E. V, 764
Smith, Mary E. V, 862
Smith, Mary E. VI, 703
Smith, Mary E. J. I, 949
Smith, Mary Edith IV, 276
Smith, Mary Elihu IV, 1115
Smith, Mary Eliz. III, 294
Smith, Mary Elizabeth II, 302
Smith, Mary Elizabeth II, 767
Smith, Mary Elizabeth III, 294
Smith, Mary Elizabeth V, 122
Smith, Mary Elizabeth V, 123
Smith, Mary Elizabeth V, 278
Smith, Mary Elizabeth V, 432
Smith, Mary Elizabeth V, 710
Smith, Mary Elizabeth Emma Jane V, 710
Smith, Mary Ellen II, 138
Smith, Mary Ellen II, 706
Smith, Mary Ellen IV, 277
Smith, Mary Ellen IV, 438
Smith, Mary Ellen IV, 439
Smith, Mary Ellen IV, 1115
Smith, Mary Ellen IV, 1122
Smith, Mary Ellen V, 123
Smith, Mary Ellen V, 203
Smith, Mary Ellen V, 279
Smith, Mary Emily VI, 705
Smith, Mary Emlen II, 735
Smith, Mary Emlen II, 767
Smith, Mary Emma IV, 191
Smith, Mary Emma IV, 276
Smith, Mary Estella V, 529
Smith, Mary F. II, 1066
Smith, Mary F. IV, 818
Smith, Mary F. IV, 843
Smith, Mary F. IV, 1076
Smith, Mary F. IV, 1115
Smith, Mary F. VI, 995
Smith, Mary Garrigus II, 655
Smith, Mary H. II, 924
Smith, Mary H. II, 945
Smith, Mary H. III, 263
Smith, Mary H. III, 294
Smith, Mary H. IV, 741
Smith, Mary H. IV, 763
Smith, Mary H. IV, 832
Smith, Mary H. IV, 1088
Smith, Mary H. IV, 1115
Smith, Mary H. VI, 628
Smith, Mary H. VI, 702
Smith, Mary H. VI, 930
Smith, Mary Hall II, 99
Smith, Mary Hannah VI, 625
Smith, Mary Hannah VI, 626
Smith, Mary Hannah VI, 628
Smith, Mary Hannah VI, 686
Smith, Mary Hannah VI, 693
Smith, Mary Hannah VI, 702
Smith, Mary Hannah VI, 704
Smith, Mary Hannah VI, 707
Smith, Mary Hannah VI, 723
Smith, Mary I. VI, 446
Smith, Mary J. III, 293
Smith, Mary J. IV, 1076
Smith, Mary J. IV, 1115
Smith, Mary J. IV, 1138
Smith, Mary J. IV, 1338
Smith, Mary J. VI, 817
Smith, Mary Jane II, 136
Smith, Mary Jane IV, 521
Smith, Mary Jane IV, 523
Smith, Mary Jane IV, 550
Smith, Mary Jane IV, 551
Smith, Mary Jane VI, 446
Smith, Mary Jane VI, 995
Smith, Mary L. I, 641
Smith, Mary L. II, 183
Smith, Mary L. II, 302
Smith, Mary L. II, 422
Smith, Mary L. II, 704
Smith, Mary L. II, 767
Smith, Mary L. III, 311
Smith, Mary L. T. III, 294
Smith, Mary Loudon VI, 393
Smith, Mary Louise II, 802
Smith, Mary Lownes II, 263
Smith, Mary Lownes II, 422
Smith, Mary Lownes II, 656
Smith, Mary Lydia II, 128
Smith, Mary M. I, 1161
Smith, Mary M. IV, 381
Smith, Mary M. IV, 438
Smith, Mary M. IV, 440
Smith, Mary M. V, 529
Smith, Mary M. V, 598
Smith, Mary M. VI, 708
Smith, Mary M. VI, 779
Smith, Mary Mae III, 292
Smith, Mary Maranda V, 710
Smith, Mary Margaret I, 626
Smith, Mary Margaret VI, 915
Smith, Mary Morton II, 718
Smith, Mary Morton II, 767
Smith, Mary P. II, 1009
Smith, Mary P. II, 1028
Smith, Mary P. IV, 212
Smith, Mary P. IV, 276
Smith, Mary P. IV, 550
Smith, Mary Pleasant VI, 704
Smith, Mary R. IV, 550
Smith, Mary R. IV, 551
Smith, Mary R. IV, 762
Smith, Mary R. IV, 763
Smith, Mary R. IV, 1116
Smith, Mary R. IV, 1138
Smith, Mary R. VI, 417
Smith, Mary R. VI, 418
Smith, Mary R. VI, 445
Smith, Mary R. VI, 446
Smith, Mary S. VI, 59
Smith, Mary S. VI, 86
Smith, Mary S. VI, 561
Smith, Mary S. VI, 575
Smith, Mary S. VI, 576
Smith, Mary S. VI, 667
Smith, Mary S. VI, 702
Smith, Mary S. VI, 717
Smith, Mary Scholfield VI, 755
Smith, Mary T. IV, 438
Smith, Mary T. IV, 439
Smith, Mary T. IV, 1090
Smith, Mary T. IV, 1115
Smith, Mary T. V, 710
Smith, Mary T. V, 862
Smith, Mary T. VI, 446
Smith, Mary V. VI, 704
Smith, Mary V. VI, 723
Smith, Mary W. II, 137
Smith, Mary W. IV, 246
Smith, Mary W. IV, 277
Smith, Mary W. IV, 539
Smith, Mary W. IV, 550
Smith, Mary W. L. II, 158
Smith, Mary, Jr. II, 457
Smith, Mary, Jr. II, 655
Smith, Mary, Jr. VI, 563
Smith, Mary, Jur. VI, 446
Smith, Mary, Sr. VI, 445
Smith, Maryann IV, 276
Smith, Maryann IV, 439
Smith, Mason VI, 995
Smith, Masy IV, 1236
Smith, Masy IV, 1240
Smith, Mathew II, 447
Smith, Matilda IV, 763
Smith, Matilda IV, 994
Smith, Matilda IV, 1004
Smith, Matilda IV, 1014
Smith, Matilda Ruthland III, 294
Smith, Maude IV, 968
Smith, Maude V, 710
Smith, Maude Elizabeth III, 294
Smith, Max C. IV, 1264
Smith, Maximilian I, 74
Smith, May III, 233
Smith, May III, 293
Smith, May V, 597
Smith, May V, 1019
Smith, May VI, 706
Smith, Mazy I, 257
Smith, Md. Elizabeth VI, 469
Smith, Md. Lydia VI, 469
Smith, Melvina H. III, 125
Smith, Mercy II, 221
Smith, Mercy II, 261
Smith, Mercy VI, 641
Smith, Mercy VI, 704
Smith, Meriah V, 1019
Smith, Meriam II, 301
Smith, Meribah II, 184
Smith, Meribah II, 262
Smith, Meribah II, 802
Smith, Meribah IV, 37
Smith, Meribah IV, 59
Smith, Meribah IV, 60
Smith, Meriman II, 100
Smith, Merritt L. III, 499
Smith, Micajah IV, 59
Smith, Micajah IV, 109
Smith, Micajah IV, 133
Smith, Mildred IV, 762
Smith, Mildred IV, 763
Smith, Mildred V, 529
Smith, Mildred VI, 995
Smith, Millisent II, 40
Smith, Millisent II, 99
Smith, Millisent II, 109
Smith, Milly W. VI, 942
Smith, Milnor D. II, 183
Smith, Milnor D. II, 302
Smith, Milton IV, 1114
Smith, Milton IV, 1223
Smith, Minnie IV, 762
Smith, Minnie IV, 763
Smith, Minnie V, 278
Smith, Minnie V, 597
Smith, Minnie V, 598
Smith, Minnie V, 710
Smith, Minnie V, 1019
Smith, Mintie V, 710
Smith, Mira B. IV, 276
Smith, Miriam I, 74
Smith, Miriam II, 820
Smith, Miriam IV, 550
Smith, Miriam VI, 446
Smith, Miriam VI, 645
Smith, Miriam VI, 648
Smith, Miriam VI, 667
Smith, Miriam VI, 679
Smith, Miriam VI, 702
Smith, Miriam VI, 704
Smith, Miriam VI, 707
Smith, Miriam VI, 723
Smith, Miriam B. II, 923
Smith, Miriam B. IV, 277
Smith, Miriam B. IV, 553
Smith, Miriam G. VI, 723
Smith, Miriam W. IV, 1138
Smith, Mollie A. III, 93
Smith, Molllie A. III, 294
Smith, Mordecai V, 122
Smith, Mordecai V, 529
Smith, Mordecai V, 932
Smith, Mordecai VI, 446
Smith, Morley Lyford III, 499
Smith, Morley Lyford III, 502
Smith, Morris II, 55
Smith, Morris II, 184
Smith, Morris II, 263
Smith, Morris II, 719
Smith, Morris II, 767
Smith, Morris III, 294
Smith, Morris C. IV, 550
Smith, Morris C. IV, 551
Smith, Morris, Jr. III, 294
Smith, Morton III, 166
Smith, Morton III, 294
Smith, Moses III, 447
Smith, Mourning VI, 995
Smith, Mrs. Phebe A. III, 312
Smith, Murray L. IV, 551
Smith, Murray L. IV, 763
Smith, Myra E. III, 143
Smith, Myra E. III, 295
Smith, Myra Mae III, 190
Smith, N. VI, 627
Smith, Nancy I, 419
Smith, Nancy I, 628
Smith, Nancy IV, 228
Smith, Nancy IV, 276
Smith, Nancy IV, 277
Smith, Nancy IV, 573
Smith, Nancy IV, 594
Smith, Nancy IV, 895
Smith, Nancy IV, 974
Smith, Nancy IV, 994
Smith, Nancy IV, 1052
Smith, Nancy IV, 1076
Smith, Nancy IV, 1077
Smith, Nancy IV, 1089
Smith, Nancy IV, 1115
Smith, Nancy IV, 1138
Smith, Nancy V, 787
Smith, Nancy V, 792
Smith, Nancy V, 917
Smith, Nancy VI, 854
Smith, Nancy VI, 856
Smith, Nancy VI, 955
Smith, Nancy VI, 981
Smith, Nancy VI, 995

h, Nancy Ann I, 1162
h, Nancy C. V, 278
th, Nancy E. V, 431
th, Nancy Elizabeth V, 432
th, Nancy G. V, 630
h, Nancy G. V, 644
th, Nancy P. VI, 815
th, Nanie B. VI, 854
th, Naomi II, 40
h, Naomi II, 66
h, Naomi II, 100
th, Naomi IV, 21
th, Naomi IV, 59
th, Naomi IV, 276
th, Naomi IV, 277
th, Naomi V, 279
th, Naomi VI, 445
th, Naomi VI, 515
th, Naomi VI, 561
th, Naomi VI, 562
th, Naomi VI, 563
th, Naomi C. V, 241
th, Naomi C. V, 278
th, Naomis VI, 554
th, Naomy IV, 59
th, Narcissa VI, 995
th, Nathan I, 74
th, Nathan I, 419
th, Nathan I, 705
th, Nathan II, 55
th, Nathan III, 447
th, Nathan IV, 59
th, Nathan IV, 60
th, Nathan IV, 276
th, Nathan IV, 277
th, Nathan IV, 351
th, Nathan IV, 439
th, Nathan IV, 497
th, Nathan IV, 515
th, Nathan IV, 540
th, Nathan IV, 549
th, Nathan IV, 550
th, Nathan IV, 553
th, Nathan IV, 594
th, Nathan V, 122
th, Nathan V, 279
th, Nathan V, 311
th, Nathan Allen II, 641
th, Nathan Allen II, 655
th, Nathan H. VI, 707
th, Nathan Haines VI, 670
th, Nathan Haines VI, 703
th, Nathan J. IV, 213
th, Nathan R. IV, 180
th, Nathan R. IV, 191
th, Nathan R. IV, 276
th, Nathan R. IV, 278
th, Nathan R. IV, 513
th, Nathan R. IV, 550
th, Nathan, Jr. IV, 277
th, Nathan, Jr. IV, 550
th, Nathaniel II, 30
th, Nathaniel III, 294
th, Nathaniel III, 385
th, Nathaniel III, 389
th, Nathaniel III, 499
th, Nathaniel White VI, 605
th, Nehemiah III, 294
ith, Nellie M. III, 294
th, Nelson III, 285
th, Nelson III, 294
th, Nelson III, 499
ith, Nelson, Jr. III, 294
ith, Nettie V, 203
th, Nettie VI, 703
ith, Nettie May IV, 278
ith, Nettie Virginia V, 278
ith, Nettie Virginia V, 279
ith, Newlin R. VI, 703
ith, Newton V, 529
ith, Newton Edward V, 529
ith, Nicholas L. I, 1161
ith, Noah II, 54
ith, Noah II, 99
ith, Nolia V, 465
ith, Nora I, 18
ith, Nora I, 882
ith, Nora I, 900
ith, Nora V. I, 11
ith, Norman D. III, 294
ith, Oakford II, 40
ith, Obed III, 294
ith, Olie V, 1019
ith, Olive I, 1024
ith, Olive I, 1053
ith, Olive I, 1060
ith, Olive I, 1063
ith, Olive II, 183
ith, Olive B. V, 432
ith, Olive Blanch V, 432
ith, Olive Geraldine I, 625
Smith, Olive L. IV, 276
Smith, Olive L. IV, 278
Smith, Oliver V, 279
Smith, Oliver V, 957
Smith, Oliver V, 960
Smith, Oliver C. I, 641
Smith, Oliver C. V, 932
Smith, Oliver G. V, 279
Smith, Oliver J. IV, 278
Smith, Oliver Parry II, 313
Smith, Oliver Parry II, 324
Smith, Oliver Thomas IV, 1138
Smith, Onias I, 74
Smith, Ordwa V, 279
Smith, Ordway V, 279
Smith, Oreiania V, 123
Smith, Oren V, 529
Smith, Oriana V, 123
Smith, Orlando V, 278
Smith, Orlando V, 279
Smith, Orlistus R. V, 122
Smith, Orlistus R. V, 123
Smith, Orpha V, 465
Smith, Osborn IV, 1114
Smith, Osborne IV, 1115
Smith, Oscar III, 292
Smith, Oscar C. IV, 1223
Smith, Oscar Stephen IV, 276
Smith, Oscar Stephen IV, 1115
Smith, Oscar Stephen IV, 1116
Smith, Oscar Stephens IV, 278
Smith, Otho E. V, 278
Smith, Otis IV, 1378
Smith, Otto E. V, 279
Smith, P. VI, 815
Smith, Pardon II, 790
Smith, Parke E. IV, 276
Smith, Parks IV, 278
Smith, Parks Eugene IV, 278
Smith, Parrin VI, 839
Smith, Pascal V, 631
Smith, Paschal VI, 834
Smith, Patience III, 294
Smith, Patience V, 122
Smith, Patience V, 843
Smith, Patience V, 861
Smith, Patience V, 862
Smith, Patience VI, 444
Smith, Patience VI, 445
Smith, Paul II, 770
Smith, Paulina V, 278
Smith, Paulina VI, 995
Smith, Paulina C. VI, 893
Smith, Payton VI, 801
Smith, Pearl V, 203
Smith, Pearson IV, 212
Smith, Pearson IV, 276
Smith, Pearson IV, 277
Smith, Pearson IV, 549
Smith, Pearson IV, 550
Smith, Pearson Thomas IV, 277
Smith, Peggy VI, 995
Smith, Pemberton II, 767
Smith, Penina I, 65
Smith, Penina I, 74
Smith, Peninah I, 110
Smith, Peninah I, 155
Smith, Peninah I, 166
Smith, Peninah I, 734
Smith, Peninah IV, 59
Smith, Peninah V, 122
Smith, Penninah I, 705
Smith, Percival C. III, 191
Smith, Percival C. III, 294
Smith, Percival C. III, 295
Smith, Perin VI, 834
Smith, Peter III, 453
Smith, Peter IV, 277
Smith, Peter IV, 843
Smith, Peter IV, 1379
Smith, Peter V, 279
Smith, Peter B. IV, 1379
Smith, Peter E. II, 138
Smith, Phebe I, 419
Smith, Phebe II, 655
Smith, Phebe II, 770
Smith, Phebe II, 923
Smith, Phebe II, 969
Smith, Phebe II, 970
Smith, Phebe II, 987
Smith, Phebe II, 1011
Smith, Phebe II, 1027
Smith, Phebe II, 1028
Smith, Phebe III, 20
Smith, Phebe III, 294
Smith, Phebe III, 314
Smith, Phebe III, 315
Smith, Phebe III, 411
Smith, Phebe III, 428
Smith, Phebe III, 429
Smith, Phebe III, 447
Smith, Phebe III, 459
Smith, Phebe III, 469
Smith, Phebe III, 481
Smith, Phebe III, 499
Smith, Phebe IV, 59
Smith, Phebe IV, 105
Smith, Phebe IV, 109
Smith, Phebe IV, 276
Smith, Phebe IV, 277
Smith, Phebe IV, 386
Smith, Phebe IV, 437
Smith, Phebe IV, 438
Smith, Phebe IV, 439
Smith, Phebe IV, 538
Smith, Phebe IV, 546
Smith, Phebe IV, 549
Smith, Phebe IV, 550
Smith, Phebe IV, 574
Smith, Phebe IV, 657
Smith, Phebe IV, 664
Smith, Phebe IV, 843
Smith, Phebe IV, 850
Smith, Phebe IV, 883
Smith, Phebe IV, 916
Smith, Phebe IV, 1076
Smith, Phebe IV, 1114
Smith, Phebe IV, 1115
Smith, Phebe IV, 1185
Smith, Phebe IV, 1186
Smith, Phebe IV, 1366
Smith, Phebe IV, 1378
Smith, Phebe IV, 1379
Smith, Phebe V, 421
Smith, Phebe V, 431
Smith, Phebe V, 432
Smith, Phebe V, 529
Smith, Phebe VI, 446
Smith, Phebe VI, 562
Smith, Phebe VI, 563
Smith, Phebe VI, 605
Smith, Phebe VI, 639
Smith, Phebe VI, 701
Smith, Phebe VI, 704
Smith, Phebe VI, 706
Smith, Phebe A. III, 227
Smith, Phebe A. III, 293
Smith, Phebe A. III, 449
Smith, Phebe A. III, 499
Smith, Phebe Ann II, 1057
Smith, Phebe Ann II, 1060
Smith, Phebe Ann VI, 446
Smith, Phebe Ann VI, 689
Smith, Phebe B. III, 292
Smith, Phebe B. III, 295
Smith, Phebe C. III, 230
Smith, Phebe C. III, 293
Smith, Phebe C. III, 295
Smith, Phebe D. III, 499
Smith, Phebe Ella III, 499
Smith, Phebe Ella III, 502
Smith, Phebe H. II, 820
Smith, Phebe H. II, 923
Smith, Phebe K. IV, 1185
Smith, Phebe K. IV, 1240
Smith, Phebe K. IV, 1379
Smith, Phebe L. V, 278
Smith, Phebe L. V, 360
Smith, Phebe M. V, 431
Smith, Phebe M. V, 432
Smith, Phebe T. III, 292
Smith, Phebe, Jr. III, 447
Smith, Phebe, Jr. VI, 445
Smith, Phebe, Jr. VI, 462
Smith, Pheby I, 419
Smith, Pheby II, 99
Smith, Phidelia IV, 1379
Smith, Philemon VI, 995
Smith, Philip III, 129
Smith, Philip IV, 1294
Smith, Phoebe V, 676
Smith, Phoebe V, 710
Smith, Pile II, 99
Smith, Piles II, 40
Smith, Pleasant I, 364
Smith, Pleasant I, 379
Smith, Pleasant I, 419
Smith, Pleasant II, 970
Smith, Pleasant II, 1027
Smith, Pleasant VI, 520
Smith, Pleasant VI, 563
Smith, Pleasant VI, 658
Smith, Pleasant VI, 663
Smith, Pleasant VI, 666
Smith, Pleasant VI, 705
Smith, Pleasant VI, 707
Smith, Pleasant Janney VI, 446
Smith, Polly I, 935
Smith, Polly VI, 854
Smith, Polly VI, 932
Smith, Polly VI, 984
Smith, Polly M. VI, 854
Smith, Portia VI, 406
Smith, Portia VI, 622
Smith, Portia VI, 645
Smith, Portia VI, 660
Smith, Portia VI, 703
Smith, Portia VI, 705
Smith, Portia VI, 706
Smith, Portia VI, 707
Smith, Portia H. VI, 707
Smith, Portia Haines VI, 703
Smith, Powell II, 138
Smith, Powell II, 158
Smith, Powell R. II, 138
Smith, Prior I, 1161
Smith, Prior S. I, 1161
Smith, Prior S. IV, 1223
Smith, Priscilla I, 251
Smith, Priscilla I, 257
Smith, Priscilla II, 652
Smith, Priscilla II, 653
Smith, Priscilla II, 820
Smith, Priscilla II, 910
Smith, Priscilla II, 923
Smith, Priscilla VI, 995
Smith, Priscilla Parry II, 313
Smith, Prudence II, 17
Smith, Prudence II, 40
Smith, Prudence II, 54
Smith, Prudence II, 99
Smith, Prudence II, 100
Smith, Prudence IV, 60
Smith, Prudence V, 529
Smith, Pryor IV, 1223
Smith, R. Frederick IV, 763
Smith, R. Hannah VI, 617
Smith, Rachel I, 18
Smith, Rachel I, 39
Smith, Rachel I, 56
Smith, Rachel I, 74
Smith, Rachel I, 78
Smith, Rachel I, 377
Smith, Rachel I, 419
Smith, Rachel I, 705
Smith, Rachel I, 734
Smith, Rachel I, 968
Smith, Rachel I, 1037
Smith, Rachel I, 1088
Smith, Rachel II, 40
Smith, Rachel II, 66
Smith, Rachel II, 68
Smith, Rachel II, 89
Smith, Rachel II, 99
Smith, Rachel II, 100
Smith, Rachel II, 165
Smith, Rachel II, 180
Smith, Rachel II, 184
Smith, Rachel II, 211
Smith, Rachel II, 238
Smith, Rachel II, 239
Smith, Rachel II, 250
Smith, Rachel II, 261
Smith, Rachel II, 262
Smith, Rachel II, 263
Smith, Rachel II, 301
Smith, Rachel II, 422
Smith, Rachel II, 625
Smith, Rachel II, 655
Smith, Rachel II, 719
Smith, Rachel II, 970
Smith, Rachel II, 1015
Smith, Rachel II, 1027
Smith, Rachel II, 1028
Smith, Rachel II, 1030
Smith, Rachel III, 294
Smith, Rachel III, 295
Smith, Rachel III, 444
Smith, Rachel III, 447
Smith, Rachel III, 465
Smith, Rachel III, 469
Smith, Rachel IV, 38
Smith, Rachel IV, 59
Smith, Rachel IV, 60
Smith, Rachel IV, 67
Smith, Rachel IV, 106
Smith, Rachel IV, 109
Smith, Rachel IV, 145
Smith, Rachel IV, 155
Smith, Rachel IV, 159
Smith, Rachel IV, 213
Smith, Rachel IV, 277
Smith, Rachel IV, 323
Smith, Rachel IV, 540
Smith, Rachel IV, 549
Smith, Rachel IV, 550
Smith, Rachel IV, 553
Smith, Rachel IV, 594
Smith, Rachel IV, 610
Smith, Rachel IV, 657
Smith, Rachel IV, 843
Smith, Rachel IV, 845
Smith, Rachel IV, 883
Smith, Rachel IV, 895
Smith, Rachel IV, 983
Smith, Rachel IV, 994
Smith, Rachel IV, 1094
Smith, Rachel IV, 1115
Smith, Rachel IV, 1116
Smith, Rachel IV, 1223
Smith, Rachel V, 32
Smith, Rachel V, 40
Smith, Rachel V, 93
Smith, Rachel V, 122
Smith, Rachel V, 123
Smith, Rachel V, 133
Smith, Rachel V, 134
Smith, Rachel V, 274
Smith, Rachel V, 278
Smith, Rachel V, 279
Smith, Rachel V, 284
Smith, Rachel V, 360
Smith, Rachel V, 396
Smith, Rachel V, 416
Smith, Rachel V, 431
Smith, Rachel V, 432
Smith, Rachel V, 529
Smith, Rachel V, 597
Smith, Rachel V, 605
Smith, Rachel VI, 393
Smith, Rachel VI, 444
Smith, Rachel VI, 445
Smith, Rachel VI, 446
Smith, Rachel VI, 460
Smith, Rachel VI, 462
Smith, Rachel VI, 492
Smith, Rachel VI, 505
Smith, Rachel VI, 554
Smith, Rachel VI, 561
Smith, Rachel VI, 562
Smith, Rachel VI, 563
Smith, Rachel VI, 606
Smith, Rachel VI, 620
Smith, Rachel VI, 631
Smith, Rachel VI, 636
Smith, Rachel VI, 649
Smith, Rachel VI, 650
Smith, Rachel VI, 655
Smith, Rachel VI, 656
Smith, Rachel VI, 667
Smith, Rachel VI, 670
Smith, Rachel VI, 678
Smith, Rachel VI, 701
Smith, Rachel VI, 702
Smith, Rachel VI, 703
Smith, Rachel VI, 704
Smith, Rachel VI, 705
Smith, Rachel VI, 706
Smith, Rachel VI, 707
Smith, Rachel VI, 708
Smith, Rachel VI, 713
Smith, Rachel VI, 779
Smith, Rachel A. I, 1161
Smith, Rachel A. V, 122
Smith, Rachel A. V, 123
Smith, Rachel A. V, 279
Smith, Rachel A. V, 432
Smith, Rachel Amanda V, 432
Smith, Rachel C. II, 292
Smith, Rachel C. II, 301
Smith, Rachel C. III, 250
Smith, Rachel C. III, 293
Smith, Rachel C. IV, 994
Smith, Rachel C. IV, 999
Smith, Rachel C. V, 932
Smith, Rachel Caps I, 419
Smith, Rachel D. IV, 278
Smith, Rachel D. IV, 285
Smith, Rachel E. IV, 278
Smith, Rachel E. V, 529
Smith, Rachel Elizabeth V, 529
Smith, Rachel L. VI, 703
Smith, Rachel M. V, 431
Smith, Rachel N. IV, 323
Smith, Rachel N. IV, 352
Smith, Rachel P. II, 421
Smith, Rachel P. II, 656
Smith, Rachel P. II, 767
Smith, Rachel P. IV, 1089
Smith, Rachel P. IV, 1115
Smith, Rachel R. IV, 1116
Smith, Rachel S. VI, 406
Smith, Rachel S. VI, 660
Smith, Rachel S. VI, 670
Smith, Rachel S. VI, 678
Smith, Rachel S. VI, 702
Smith, Rachel S. VI, 703
Smith, Rachel Steer VI, 514
Smith, Rachel W. III, 145
Smith, Rachel W. III, 294
Smith, Rachel W. III, 295
Smith, Racy II, 313
Smith, Railph I, 596
Smith, Ralph I, 74

Smith, Ralph I, 166
Smith, Ralph I, 1037
Smith, Ralph II, 261
Smith, Ralph II, 262
Smith, Ralph Lindley IV, 276
Smith, Ralph Lindley IV, 277
Smith, Ralph, Jr. VI, 854
Smith, Randal IV, 59
Smith, Randal IV, 109
Smith, Randolph IV, 109
Smith, Raper II, 184
Smith, Raper II, 262
Smith, Raper II, 263
Smith, Raper II, 301
Smith, Raper II, 302
Smith, Raper II, 656
Smith, Raper II, 767
Smith, Ray IV, 1338
Smith, Raymond V, 279
Smith, Raymond Conrad II, 820
Smith, Raymond W. IV, 276
Smith, Rayne II, 99
Smith, Rayne II, 110
Smith, Reba Gertrude II, 820
Smith, Rebecca II, 23
Smith, Rebecca II, 30
Smith, Rebecca II, 76
Smith, Rebecca II, 88
Smith, Rebecca II, 99
Smith, Rebecca II, 100
Smith, Rebecca II, 261
Smith, Rebecca II, 262
Smith, Rebecca II, 275
Smith, Rebecca II, 288
Smith, Rebecca II, 301
Smith, Rebecca II, 421
Smith, Rebecca II, 422
Smith, Rebecca II, 466
Smith, Rebecca II, 625
Smith, Rebecca II, 653
Smith, Rebecca II, 655
Smith, Rebecca II, 656
Smith, Rebecca II, 719
Smith, Rebecca II, 801
Smith, Rebecca II, 815
Smith, Rebecca II, 820
Smith, Rebecca II, 911
Smith, Rebecca II, 923
Smith, Rebecca II, 1060
Smith, Rebecca III, 245
Smith, Rebecca III, 294
Smith, Rebecca IV, 31
Smith, Rebecca IV, 59
Smith, Rebecca IV, 60
Smith, Rebecca IV, 86
Smith, Rebecca IV, 109
Smith, Rebecca IV, 131
Smith, Rebecca IV, 133
Smith, Rebecca IV, 276
Smith, Rebecca IV, 277
Smith, Rebecca IV, 351
Smith, Rebecca IV, 353
Smith, Rebecca IV, 364
Smith, Rebecca IV, 377
Smith, Rebecca IV, 380
Smith, Rebecca IV, 391
Smith, Rebecca IV, 417
Smith, Rebecca IV, 437
Smith, Rebecca IV, 438
Smith, Rebecca IV, 439
Smith, Rebecca IV, 441
Smith, Rebecca IV, 445
Smith, Rebecca IV, 449
Smith, Rebecca IV, 514
Smith, Rebecca IV, 541
Smith, Rebecca IV, 549
Smith, Rebecca IV, 550
Smith, Rebecca IV, 551
Smith, Rebecca IV, 722
Smith, Rebecca IV, 762
Smith, Rebecca IV, 763
Smith, Rebecca IV, 1076
Smith, Rebecca IV, 1110
Smith, Rebecca IV, 1114
Smith, Rebecca IV, 1115
Smith, Rebecca V, 48
Smith, Rebecca V, 122
Smith, Rebecca V, 239
Smith, Rebecca V, 278
Smith, Rebecca V, 932
Smith, Rebecca VI, 372
Smith, Rebecca VI, 406
Smith, Rebecca VI, 422
Smith, Rebecca VI, 438
Smith, Rebecca VI, 439
Smith, Rebecca VI, 445
Smith, Rebecca VI, 706
Smith, Rebecca VI, 785
Smith, Rebecca VI, 995
Smith, Rebecca A. IV, 278
Smith, Rebecca A. VI, 705
Smith, Rebecca Ann II, 421
Smith, Rebecca Ann II, 923
Smith, Rebecca Ann IV, 363
Smith, Rebecca Ann IV, 439
Smith, Rebecca B. VI, 705
Smith, Rebecca Darby II, 263
Smith, Rebecca Darby II, 656
Smith, Rebecca Darby II, 719
Smith, Rebecca E. IV, 438
Smith, Rebecca E. VI, 689
Smith, Rebecca F. III, 310
Smith, Rebecca H. IV, 1115
Smith, Rebecca J. II, 924
Smith, Rebecca Jane V, 279
Smith, Rebecca L. IV, 276
Smith, Rebecca L. IV, 283
Smith, Rebecca L. IV, 1076
Smith, Rebecca L. IV, 1112
Smith, Rebecca L. IV, 1115
Smith, Rebecca M. IV, 551
Smith, Rebecca R. III, 292
Smith, Rebecca Ruth VI, 707
Smith, Rebecca S. IV, 241
Smith, Rebecca S. IV, 276
Smith, Rebecca S. IV, 439
Smith, Rebecca S. V, 360
Smith, Rebecca T. IV, 438
Smith, Rebecca W. II, 421
Smith, Rebecca W. IV, 374
Smith, Rebecca W. IV, 376
Smith, Rebecca W. IV, 439
Smith, Rebecca W. IV, 515
Smith, Rebecca W. IV, 550
Smith, Rebecca Wharton II, 767
Smith, Rebeckah II, 40
Smith, Rebeckah II, 99
Smith, Rebeckah II, 261
Smith, Rebeckah IV, 109
Smith, Rebeckah IV, 437
Smith, Rebeckah VI, 605
Smith, Rebeckah VI, 606
Smith, Rebedca V, 529
Smith, Rebekah I, 364
Smith, Rebekah I, 419
Smith, Rebekah I, 1063
Smith, Rebekah VI, 445
Smith, Rebekah VI, 446
Smith, Rebekah VI, 701
Smith, Reed VI, 995
Smith, Rees IV, 277
Smith, Reese IV, 276
Smith, Remington IV, 1185
Smith, Reuben II, 422
Smith, Reva Marie V, 203
Smith, Richard II, 40
Smith, Richard II, 57
Smith, Richard II, 66
Smith, Richard II, 68
Smith, Richard II, 99
Smith, Richard II, 100
Smith, Richard II, 138
Smith, Richard II, 165
Smith, Richard II, 183
Smith, Richard II, 184
Smith, Richard II, 241
Smith, Richard II, 244
Smith, Richard II, 255
Smith, Richard II, 261
Smith, Richard II, 262
Smith, Richard II, 263
Smith, Richard II, 301
Smith, Richard II, 421
Smith, Richard II, 422
Smith, Richard II, 557
Smith, Richard II, 590
Smith, Richard II, 617
Smith, Richard II, 626
Smith, Richard II, 653
Smith, Richard II, 654
Smith, Richard II, 655
Smith, Richard II, 656
Smith, Richard II, 674
Smith, Richard II, 719
Smith, Richard III, 444
Smith, Richard III, 453
Smith, Richard III, 511
Smith, Richard IV, 109
Smith, Richard IV, 113
Smith, Richard IV, 437
Smith, Richard IV, 497
Smith, Richard IV, 868
Smith, Richard IV, 1114
Smith, Richard IV, 1115
Smith, Richard H. IV, 438
Smith, Richard Howell II, 422
Smith, Richard Howell II, 767
Smith, Richard Laurence II, 656
Smith, Richard Lawrence II, 767
Smith, Richard M. II, 183
Smith, Richard M. II, 184
Smith, Richard M. II, 209
Smith, Richard M. II, 263
Smith, Richard M. II, 292
Smith, Richard M. II, 296
Smith, Richard M. II, 299
Smith, Richard M. II, 301
Smith, Richard M. II, 767
Smith, Richard M. II, 820
Smith, Richard Morris II, 184
Smith, Richard Morris II, 262
Smith, Richard Morris II, 767
Smith, Richard R. II, 262
Smith, Richard R. II, 422
Smith, Richard R. II, 557
Smith, Richard R. II, 655
Smith, Richard S. II, 183
Smith, Richard S. II, 243
Smith, Richard S. II, 262
Smith, Richard Timberlake V, 359
Smith, Richard, Jr. II, 66
Smith, Richard, Jr. II, 99
Smith, Richard, Jr. II, 184
Smith, Richard, Jr. II, 251
Smith, Richard, Jr. II, 261
Smith, Richard, Jr. II, 262
Smith, Richard, Jr. II, 584
Smith, Richard, Jr. II, 654
Smith, Richard, Jr. II, 1007
Smith, Richard, Jr. II, 1027
Smith, Richard, Sr. II, 184
Smith, Richard, Sr. II, 240
Smith, Richard, Sr. II, 261
Smith, Richards II, 203
Smith, Ritchard IV, 59
Smith, Rob II, 183
Smith, Robert I, 74
Smith, Robert I, 705
Smith, Robert I, 732
Smith, Robert I, 734
Smith, Robert II, 40
Smith, Robert II, 99
Smith, Robert II, 113
Smith, Robert II, 183
Smith, Robert II, 184
Smith, Robert II, 191
Smith, Robert II, 195
Smith, Robert II, 252
Smith, Robert II, 261
Smith, Robert II, 262
Smith, Robert II, 263
Smith, Robert II, 277
Smith, Robert II, 421
Smith, Robert II, 422
Smith, Robert II, 653
Smith, Robert II, 654
Smith, Robert II, 655
Smith, Robert II, 656
Smith, Robert II, 660
Smith, Robert II, 704
Smith, Robert II, 718
Smith, Robert II, 969
Smith, Robert II, 970
Smith, Robert II, 980
Smith, Robert II, 987
Smith, Robert II, 1027
Smith, Robert IV, 241
Smith, Robert IV, 278
Smith, Robert IV, 417
Smith, Robert IV, 437
Smith, Robert IV, 438
Smith, Robert IV, 440
Smith, Robert IV, 441
Smith, Robert IV, 455
Smith, Robert IV, 843
Smith, Robert V, 122
Smith, Robert V, 932
Smith, Robert VI, 445
Smith, Robert VI, 446
Smith, Robert VI, 562
Smith, Robert VI, 717
Smith, Robert VI, 801
Smith, Robert VI, 838
Smith, Robert VI, 854
Smith, Robert VI, 995
Smith, Robert VI, 1003
Smith, Robert B. VI, 446
Smith, Robert Barkley VI, 446
Smith, Robert Clinton V, 932
Smith, Robert D. II, 851
Smith, Robert D. II, 924
Smith, Robert D. V, 710
Smith, Robert Dubois II, 313
Smith, Robert Dubois II, 324
Smith, Robert Dubois II, 820
Smith, Robert Grant IV, 959
Smith, Robert H. II, 719
Smith, Robert H. IV, 276
Smith, Robert H. IV, 277
Smith, Robert H. IV, 366
Smith, Robert H. IV, 380
Smith, Robert H. IV, 423
Smith, Robert H. IV, 438
Smith, Robert H. IV, 439
Smith, Robert H. IV, 594
Smith, Robert H. IV, 762
Smith, Robert H. VI, 446
Smith, Robert Harrison I, 689
Smith, Robert J. II, 656
Smith, Robert J. VI, 212
Smith, Robert K. IV, 438
Smith, Robert Lindley II, 767
Smith, Robert M. VI, 708
Smith, Robert P. II, 767
Smith, Robert Pearsall II, 719
Smith, Robert Y. VI, 995
Smith, Robert, Jr. II, 99
Smith, Robert, Jr. II, 262
Smith, Robert, Jr. II, 422
Smith, Robert, Jr. II, 457
Smith, Robert, Jr. II, 655
Smith, Robert, Jr. II, 656
Smith, Robert, Jr. IV, 277
Smith, Robert, Jr. IV, 439
Smith, Robt. IV, 276
Smith, Rody VI, 854
Smith, Roe Petty I, 641
Smith, Roella I, 626
Smith, Roella Jane I, 624
Smith, Roger II, 99
Smith, Roper VI, 267
Smith, Rosanna I, 53
Smith, Rosanna I, 74
Smith, Rosanna V, 122
Smith, Rosannah V, 122
Smith, Rosannah V, 133
Smith, Rose II, 184
Smith, Rose V, 203
Smith, Rose A. II, 907
Smith, Rose A. II, 924
Smith, Rosetta B. IV, 1186
Smith, Ross VI, 446
Smith, Roy IV, 763
Smith, Roy H. I, 1161
Smith, Roy Vernon V, 279
Smith, Ruannah III, 295
Smith, Ruannah III, 343
Smith, Ruath Hannah VI, 702
Smith, Ruben VI, 995
Smith, Ruby K. I, 933
Smith, Rufus I, 318
Smith, Rufus V, 279
Smith, Rufus V, 465
Smith, Rufus V, 631
Smith, Ruhama III, 499
Smith, Ruhama III, 503
Smith, Russell Franklin V, 278
Smith, Ruth I, 993
Smith, Ruth I, 997
Smith, Ruth I, 1024
Smith, Ruth I, 1063
Smith, Ruth I, 1088
Smith, Ruth II, 970
Smith, Ruth II, 988
Smith, Ruth II, 1027
Smith, Ruth II, 1028
Smith, Ruth III, 447
Smith, Ruth IV, 21
Smith, Ruth IV, 43
Smith, Ruth IV, 56
Smith, Ruth IV, 59
Smith, Ruth IV, 60
Smith, Ruth IV, 550
Smith, Ruth IV, 843
Smith, Ruth IV, 853
Smith, Ruth IV, 1064
Smith, Ruth IV, 1076
Smith, Ruth IV, 1077
Smith, Ruth IV, 1175
Smith, Ruth IV, 1185
Smith, Ruth IV, 1186
Smith, Ruth V, 122
Smith, Ruth V, 123
Smith, Ruth V, 133
Smith, Ruth V, 252
Smith, Ruth V, 278
Smith, Ruth V, 279
Smith, Ruth V, 311
Smith, Ruth V, 566
Smith, Ruth V, 567
Smith, Ruth V, 598
Smith, Ruth V, 952
Smith, Ruth V, 959
Smith, Ruth V, 960
Smith, Ruth V, 976
Smith, Ruth VI, 445
Smith, Ruth VI, 446
Smith, Ruth VI, 459
Smith, Ruth VI, 500
Smith, Ruth VI, 559
Smith, Ruth VI, 561
Smith, Ruth VI, 562
Smith, Ruth VI, 586
Smith, Ruth VI, 641
Smith, Ruth VI, 678
Smith, Ruth VI, 702
Smith, Ruth VI, 705
Smith, Ruth A. V, 597
Smith, Ruth A. V, 710
Smith, Ruth Ann V, 591
Smith, Ruth Ann V, 598
Smith, Ruth Ann V, 710
Smith, Ruth B. III, 438
Smith, Ruth B. III, 447
Smith, Ruth E. III, 497
Smith, Ruth F. IV, 1114
Smith, Ruth H. II, 698
Smith, Ruth Hanna VI, 622
Smith, Ruth Hannah VI, 617
Smith, Ruth Hannah VI, 618
Smith, Ruth Hannah VI, 622
Smith, Ruth Hannah VI, 625
Smith, Ruth Hannah VI, 633
Smith, Ruth Hannah VI, 645
Smith, Ruth Hannah VI, 664
Smith, Ruth Hannah VI, 668
Smith, Ruth Hannah VI, 696
Smith, Ruth Hannah VI, 703
Smith, Ruth Hannah VI, 704
Smith, Ruth Hannah VI, 706
Smith, Ruth Hannah VI, 707
Smith, Ruth Hannah VI, 754
Smith, Ruth Hannah, Jr. VI,
Smith, Ruth L. V, 676
Smith, Ruth M. V, 279
Smith, Ruth M. V, 281
Smith, Ruth, Jr. II, 55
Smith, S. Archibald III, 396
Smith, S. W. III, 293
Smith, S??? V, 465
Smith, Sabilla IV, 377
Smith, Sabilla IV, 438
Smith, Sadie Ray I, 949
Smith, Sala IV, 1378
Smith, Sala IV, 1379
Smith, Salley VI, 923
Smith, Sallie V, 764
Smith, Sallie J. VI, 402
Smith, Sallie J. VI, 446
Smith, Sallie L. II, 924
Smith, Sally IV, 437
Smith, Sally IV, 438
Smith, Sally IV, 449
Smith, Sally V, 122
Smith, Sally V, 123
Smith, Sally VI, 445
Smith, Sally VI, 446
Smith, Sally VI, 460
Smith, Sally VI, 858
Smith, Sally VI, 875
Smith, Sally VI, 886
Smith, Sally VI, 949
Smith, Sally VI, 963
Smith, Sally VI, 994
Smith, Sally VI, 995
Smith, Sally VI, 996
Smith, Sally Ann II, 656
Smith, Sally Fisher II, 263
Smith, Sally Fisher II, 656
Smith, Sally Fisher II, 719
Smith, Sally S. C. VI, 995
Smith, Sam VI, 986
Smith, Sam'l W. III, 295
Smith, Sam. VI, 893
Smith, Saml B. IV, 505
Smith, Saml. VI, 942
Smith, Saml. VI, 949
Smith, Samuel I, 55
Smith, Samuel I, 74
Smith, Samuel I, 250
Smith, Samuel I, 257
Smith, Samuel II, 40
Smith, Samuel II, 54
Smith, Samuel II, 78
Smith, Samuel II, 99
Smith, Samuel II, 138
Smith, Samuel II, 183
Smith, Samuel II, 184
Smith, Samuel II, 185
Smith, Samuel II, 199
Smith, Samuel II, 225
Smith, Samuel II, 257
Smith, Samuel II, 260
Smith, Samuel II, 261
Smith, Samuel II, 262
Smith, Samuel II, 313
Smith, Samuel II, 324
Smith, Samuel II, 654
Smith, Samuel II, 655
Smith, Samuel II, 656
Smith, Samuel II, 969
Smith, Samuel II, 970
Smith, Samuel II, 1000
Smith, Samuel II, 1007

h, Samuel II, 1027
h, Samuel III, 145
h, Samuel III, 292
h, Samuel III, 294
h, Samuel III, 295
h, Samuel III, 407
h, Samuel III, 447
h, Samuel III, 448
h, Samuel III, 499
h, Samuel III, 507
h, Samuel III, 508
h, Samuel IV, 23
h, Samuel IV, 59
h, Samuel IV, 91
h, Samuel IV, 109
h, Samuel IV, 159
h, Samuel IV, 276
h, Samuel IV, 277
h, Samuel IV, 351
h, Samuel IV, 359
h, Samuel IV, 374
h, Samuel IV, 438
h, Samuel IV, 439
h, Samuel IV, 482
h, Samuel IV, 515
h, Samuel IV, 525
h, Samuel IV, 549
h, Samuel IV, 550
h, Samuel IV, 551
h, Samuel IV, 553
h, Samuel IV, 594
h, Samuel IV, 630
h, Samuel IV, 657
h, Samuel IV, 762
h, Samuel IV, 763
h, Samuel IV, 883
h, Samuel IV, 994
h, Samuel IV, 1064
h, Samuel IV, 1076
h, Samuel IV, 1114
h, Samuel IV, 1115
h, Samuel IV, 1138
h, Samuel IV, 1185
h, Samuel IV, 1378
h, Samuel IV, 1379
h, Samuel V, 432
h, Samuel V, 529
h, Samuel VI, 358
h, Samuel VI, 366
h, Samuel VI, 444
h, Samuel VI, 445
h, Samuel VI, 446
h, Samuel VI, 463
h, Samuel VI, 485
h, Samuel VI, 515
h, Samuel VI, 554
h, Samuel VI, 561
h, Samuel VI, 562
h, Samuel VI, 563
h, Samuel VI, 631
h, Samuel VI, 636
h, Samuel VI, 655
h, Samuel VI, 667
h, Samuel VI, 701
h, Samuel VI, 703
h, Samuel VI, 705
h, Samuel VI, 706
h, Samuel VI, 708
h, Samuel VI, 713
h, Samuel VI, 801
h, Samuel VI, 854
h, Samuel VI, 888
h, Samuel VI, 995
h, Samuel Archibald III, 37
h, Samuel Archibald III, 295
h, Samuel B. II, 719
h, Samuel B. II, 767
h, Samuel B. III, 295
h, Samuel B. IV, 497
h, Samuel B. IV, 514
h, Samuel B. IV, 539
h, Samuel B. IV, 549
th, Samuel B. IV, 550
th, Samuel B. IV, 551
th, Samuel B. IV, 559
h, Samuel B. IV, 1138
h, Samuel C. IV, 367
h, Samuel C. IV, 438
h, Samuel C. IV, 439
h, Samuel C. IV, 440
th, Samuel C. IV, 509
th, Samuel C. IV, 550
th, Samuel E. III, 295
th, Samuel E. VI, 779
th, Samuel I. III, 295
th, Samuel I. III, 343
th, Samuel J. II, 185
th, Samuel J. III, 499
th, Samuel K. IV, 497
h, Samuel Laurence II, 656
h, Samuel Lawrence II, 767
Smith, Samuel P. II, 144
Smith, Samuel P. II, 158
Smith, Samuel R. II, 183
Smith, Samuel R. II, 301
Smith, Samuel R. IV, 497
Smith, Samuel R. IV, 550
Smith, Samuel R. IV, 551
Smith, Samuel Rolen II, 185
Smith, Samuel S. II, 655
Smith, Samuel S. II, 864
Smith, Samuel S. II, 924
Smith, Samuel S. V, 529
Smith, Samuel, Junior VI, 705
Smith, Sara Elma IV, 551
Smith, Sarah I, 55
Smith, Sarah I, 57
Smith, Sarah I, 65
Smith, Sarah I, 72
Smith, Sarah I, 74
Smith, Sarah I, 110
Smith, Sarah I, 155
Smith, Sarah I, 166
Smith, Sarah I, 257
Smith, Sarah I, 275
Smith, Sarah I, 364
Smith, Sarah I, 705
Smith, Sarah I, 734
Smith, Sarah I, 900
Smith, Sarah I, 997
Smith, Sarah I, 1018
Smith, Sarah I, 1024
Smith, Sarah I, 1088
Smith, Sarah I, 1110
Smith, Sarah I, 1161
Smith, Sarah II, 40
Smith, Sarah II, 41
Smith, Sarah II, 50
Smith, Sarah II, 51
Smith, Sarah II, 54
Smith, Sarah II, 55
Smith, Sarah II, 66
Smith, Sarah II, 69
Smith, Sarah II, 72
Smith, Sarah II, 78
Smith, Sarah II, 86
Smith, Sarah II, 89
Smith, Sarah II, 97
Smith, Sarah II, 99
Smith, Sarah II, 100
Smith, Sarah II, 102
Smith, Sarah II, 138
Smith, Sarah II, 140
Smith, Sarah II, 172
Smith, Sarah II, 183
Smith, Sarah II, 184
Smith, Sarah II, 200
Smith, Sarah II, 220
Smith, Sarah II, 240
Smith, Sarah II, 244
Smith, Sarah II, 249
Smith, Sarah II, 252
Smith, Sarah II, 261
Smith, Sarah II, 262
Smith, Sarah II, 301
Smith, Sarah II, 313
Smith, Sarah II, 324
Smith, Sarah II, 422
Smith, Sarah II, 447
Smith, Sarah II, 457
Smith, Sarah II, 530
Smith, Sarah II, 584
Smith, Sarah II, 637
Smith, Sarah II, 653
Smith, Sarah II, 654
Smith, Sarah II, 655
Smith, Sarah II, 660
Smith, Sarah II, 670
Smith, Sarah II, 674
Smith, Sarah II, 711
Smith, Sarah II, 716
Smith, Sarah II, 719
Smith, Sarah II, 721
Smith, Sarah II, 723
Smith, Sarah II, 782
Smith, Sarah II, 820
Smith, Sarah II, 923
Smith, Sarah II, 969
Smith, Sarah II, 1025
Smith, Sarah II, 1027
Smith, Sarah II, 1028
Smith, Sarah II, 1060
Smith, Sarah II, 1080
Smith, Sarah III, 55
Smith, Sarah III, 69
Smith, Sarah III, 252
Smith, Sarah III, 294
Smith, Sarah III, 295
Smith, Sarah III, 394
Smith, Sarah III, 402
Smith, Sarah III, 441
Smith, Sarah III, 444
Smith, Sarah III, 447
Smith, Sarah III, 453
Smith, Sarah III, 460
Smith, Sarah III, 498
Smith, Sarah III, 499
Smith, Sarah IV, 17
Smith, Sarah IV, 26
Smith, Sarah IV, 51
Smith, Sarah IV, 59
Smith, Sarah IV, 60
Smith, Sarah IV, 62
Smith, Sarah IV, 71
Smith, Sarah IV, 76
Smith, Sarah IV, 86
Smith, Sarah IV, 109
Smith, Sarah IV, 110
Smith, Sarah IV, 117
Smith, Sarah IV, 124
Smith, Sarah IV, 131
Smith, Sarah IV, 133
Smith, Sarah IV, 159
Smith, Sarah IV, 276
Smith, Sarah IV, 277
Smith, Sarah IV, 334
Smith, Sarah IV, 351
Smith, Sarah IV, 354
Smith, Sarah IV, 438
Smith, Sarah IV, 439
Smith, Sarah IV, 458
Smith, Sarah IV, 559
Smith, Sarah IV, 573
Smith, Sarah IV, 594
Smith, Sarah IV, 639
Smith, Sarah IV, 650
Smith, Sarah IV, 657
Smith, Sarah IV, 744
Smith, Sarah IV, 763
Smith, Sarah IV, 820
Smith, Sarah IV, 883
Smith, Sarah IV, 905
Smith, Sarah IV, 916
Smith, Sarah IV, 959
Smith, Sarah IV, 983
Smith, Sarah IV, 985
Smith, Sarah IV, 994
Smith, Sarah IV, 1114
Smith, Sarah IV, 1138
Smith, Sarah IV, 1185
Smith, Sarah IV, 1186
Smith, Sarah IV, 1223
Smith, Sarah IV, 1240
Smith, Sarah IV, 1241
Smith, Sarah IV, 1379
Smith, Sarah V, 53
Smith, Sarah V, 122
Smith, Sarah V, 123
Smith, Sarah V, 278
Smith, Sarah V, 341
Smith, Sarah V, 356
Smith, Sarah V, 359
Smith, Sarah V, 394
Smith, Sarah V, 396
Smith, Sarah V, 416
Smith, Sarah V, 425
Smith, Sarah V, 431
Smith, Sarah V, 432
Smith, Sarah V, 465
Smith, Sarah V, 529
Smith, Sarah V, 540
Smith, Sarah V, 554
Smith, Sarah V, 579
Smith, Sarah V, 597
Smith, Sarah V, 710
Smith, Sarah V, 827
Smith, Sarah V, 861
Smith, Sarah V, 936
Smith, Sarah V, 959
Smith, Sarah V, 960
Smith, Sarah V, 1019
Smith, Sarah VI, 267
Smith, Sarah VI, 415
Smith, Sarah VI, 418
Smith, Sarah VI, 444
Smith, Sarah VI, 445
Smith, Sarah VI, 446
Smith, Sarah VI, 472
Smith, Sarah VI, 475
Smith, Sarah VI, 476
Smith, Sarah VI, 496
Smith, Sarah VI, 505
Smith, Sarah VI, 517
Smith, Sarah VI, 520
Smith, Sarah VI, 521
Smith, Sarah VI, 538
Smith, Sarah VI, 551
Smith, Sarah VI, 562
Smith, Sarah VI, 563
Smith, Sarah VI, 571
Smith, Sarah VI, 572
Smith, Sarah VI, 619
Smith, Sarah VI, 622
Smith, Sarah VI, 624
Smith, Sarah VI, 642
Smith, Sarah VI, 644
Smith, Sarah VI, 651
Smith, Sarah VI, 658
Smith, Sarah VI, 662
Smith, Sarah VI, 664
Smith, Sarah VI, 666
Smith, Sarah VI, 668
Smith, Sarah VI, 694
Smith, Sarah VI, 696
Smith, Sarah VI, 699
Smith, Sarah VI, 701
Smith, Sarah VI, 703
Smith, Sarah VI, 704
Smith, Sarah VI, 705
Smith, Sarah VI, 707
Smith, Sarah VI, 708
Smith, Sarah VI, 710
Smith, Sarah VI, 711
Smith, Sarah VI, 712
Smith, Sarah VI, 713
Smith, Sarah VI, 714
Smith, Sarah VI, 716
Smith, Sarah VI, 717
Smith, Sarah VI, 854
Smith, Sarah VI, 995
Smith, Sarah A. I, 74
Smith, Sarah A. I, 88
Smith, Sarah A. III, 295
Smith, Sarah A. V, 123
Smith, Sarah A. V, 902
Smith, Sarah A. V, 932
Smith, Sarah Amanda V, 432
Smith, Sarah Ann I, 17
Smith, Sarah Ann I, 33
Smith, Sarah Ann II, 40
Smith, Sarah Ann II, 124
Smith, Sarah Ann II, 138
Smith, Sarah Ann II, 147
Smith, Sarah Ann II, 157
Smith, Sarah Ann II, 422
Smith, Sarah Ann II, 790
Smith, Sarah Ann IV, 347
Smith, Sarah Ann IV, 352
Smith, Sarah Ann IV, 434
Smith, Sarah Ann IV, 439
Smith, Sarah Ann IV, 549
Smith, Sarah Ann IV, 550
Smith, Sarah Ann IV, 562
Smith, Sarah Ann VI, 618
Smith, Sarah Ann VI, 621
Smith, Sarah Ann VI, 622
Smith, Sarah Ann VI, 623
Smith, Sarah Ann VI, 706
Smith, Sarah B. II, 138
Smith, Sarah B. III, 23
Smith, Sarah B. III, 292
Smith, Sarah B. III, 294
Smith, Sarah B. III, 295
Smith, Sarah B. V, 31
Smith, Sarah B. V, 123
Smith, Sarah B. V, 582
Smith, Sarah C. IV, 1294
Smith, Sarah D. II, 864
Smith, Sarah D. II, 924
Smith, Sarah D. III, 195
Smith, Sarah E. III, 292
Smith, Sarah E. V, 431
Smith, Sarah E. VI, 653
Smith, Sarah Elen V, 432
Smith, Sarah Eliz. III, 290
Smith, Sarah Eliz. III, 293
Smith, Sarah Eliza IV, 1115
Smith, Sarah Eliza IV, 1138
Smith, Sarah Eliza. IV, 1076
Smith, Sarah Elizabeth III, 292
Smith, Sarah Ellen IV, 406
Smith, Sarah Ellen IV, 439
Smith, Sarah Ellen V, 432
Smith, Sarah Ellen VI, 648
Smith, Sarah Ellen VI, 652
Smith, Sarah Ellen VI, 704
Smith, Sarah Elma IV, 367
Smith, Sarah Elma IV, 439
Smith, Sarah Elma IV, 440
Smith, Sarah Elma IV, 509
Smith, Sarah Elma IV, 550
Smith, Sarah Elsa IV, 1076
Smith, Sarah Emily V, 123
Smith, Sarah Emlen II, 743
Smith, Sarah F. V, 279
Smith, Sarah F. V, 432
Smith, Sarah F. VI, 1019
Smith, Sarah Fisher II, 263
Smith, Sarah Freeman V, 932
Smith, Sarah Goodwin II, 100
Smith, Sarah H. III, 295
Smith, Sarah H. VI, 652
Smith, Sarah H. VI, 653
Smith, Sarah H. VI, 706
Smith, Sarah J. IV, 1223
Smith, Sarah J. IV, 1374
Smith, Sarah J. IV, 1379
Smith, Sarah Jane III, 294
Smith, Sarah Jane IV, 1223
Smith, Sarah Jane IV, 1264
Smith, Sarah Jane IV, 1294
Smith, Sarah Jane IV, 1378
Smith, Sarah Jane IV, 1379
Smith, Sarah L II, 783
Smith, Sarah Logan II, 184
Smith, Sarah Logan II, 262
Smith, Sarah Logan II, 654
Smith, Sarah P. II, 324
Smith, Sarah P. II, 851
Smith, Sarah P. II, 924
Smith, Sarah R. II, 185
Smith, Sarah R. II, 421
Smith, Sarah T. IV, 1223
Smith, Sarah T. IV, 1227
Smith, Sarah T. V, 432
Smith, Sarah U. III, 447
Smith, Sarah W. IV, 439
Smith, Sarah W. IV, 453
Smith, Sarah, Jr. II, 1060
Smith, Sarah, Jr. IV, 439
Smith, Sarah, Jr. VI, 563
Smith, Saray II, 99
Smith, Sary V, 279
Smith, Sarye VI, 886
Smith, Seath II, 185
Smith, Seath II, 248
Smith, Seath II, 260
Smith, Sene IV, 1378
Smith, Sene IV, 1379
Smith, Seneca V, 932
Smith, Senneca V, 932
Smith, Serena II, 719
Smith, Seth I, 1077
Smith, Seth I, 1088
Smith, Seth I, 1098
Smith, Seth II, 185
Smith, Seth II, 247
Smith, Seth II, 263
Smith, Seth II, 302
Smith, Seth II, 422
Smith, Seth II, 656
Smith, Seth II, 767
Smith, Seth III, 295
Smith, Seth V, 93
Smith, Seth V, 122
Smith, Seth V, 203
Smith, Seth V, 252
Smith, Seth V, 502
Smith, Seth V, 503
Smith, Seth V, 529
Smith, Seth V, 945
Smith, Seth V, 952
Smith, Seth V, 959
Smith, Seth V, 962
Smith, Seth V, 976
Smith, Seth VI, 393
Smith, Seth VI, 445
Smith, Seth VI, 446
Smith, Seth VI, 631
Smith, Seth VI, 667
Smith, Seth VI, 706
Smith, Seth VI, 713
Smith, Shannon IV, 278
Smith, Sharron M. IV, 278
Smith, Sheldon W. IV, 741
Smith, Sheldon W. IV, 763
Smith, Shewill II, 422
Smith, Sibbilla IV, 1115
Smith, Sibilla IV, 437
Smith, Sibilla IV, 439
Smith, Sibilla IV, 1110
Smith, Sibilla IV, 1115
Smith, Sibyl II, 185
Smith, Silas III, 294
Smith, Silinda IV, 1241
Smith, Silvanus III, 295
Smith, Simon II, 184
Smith, Simon Alonzo V, 431
Smith, Sina IV, 843
Smith, Sinah V, 432
Smith, Sinclair IV, 381
Smith, Sinclair IV, 437
Smith, Sinclair IV, 438
Smith, Sinclair IV, 439
Smith, Sinclair IV, 550
Smith, Sinclair IV, 581
Smith, Sinclair IV, 594
Smith, Sinia V, 397
Smith, Sinia V, 432
Smith, Smith V, 1019
Smith, Smith Pearson IV, 1115
Smith, Solimon T. VI, 883
Smith, Solomon II, 184
Smith, Solomon II, 185
Smith, Solomon II, 251

Smith, Solomon II, 261
Smith, Solomon II, 275
Smith, Solomon T. VI, 883
Smith, Solomon T. VI, 995
Smith, Sonisa I, 676
Smith, Sonisa I, 689
Smith, Sophia IV, 1379
Smith, Sophia V, 279
Smith, Sophia VI, 995
Smith, Stanley V, 278
Smith, Stella V, 465
Smith, Stephen II, 100
Smith, Stephen III, 291
Smith, Stephen III, 295
Smith, Stephen IV, 438
Smith, Stephen IV, 439
Smith, Stephen IV, 1110
Smith, Stephen IV, 1114
Smith, Stephen IV, 1115
Smith, Stephen IV, 1116
Smith, Stephen V, 861
Smith, Stephen V, 886
Smith, Stephen VI, 854
Smith, Stephen VI, 897
Smith, Stephen VI, 995
Smith, Stephen H. III, 143
Smith, Stephen H. III, 295
Smith, Stephen P. VI, 995
Smith, Stephen R. III, 292
Smith, Stephen R. III, 295
Smith, Sterling IV, 1264
Smith, Susan III, 74
Smith, Susan III, 294
Smith, Susan III, 497
Smith, Susan V, 279
Smith, Susan V, 529
Smith, Susan B. II, 1080
Smith, Susan C. VI, 995
Smith, Susan Caroline V, 431
Smith, Susan Cox II, 820
Smith, Susan M. II, 924
Smith, Susan V. II, 867
Smith, Susan V. II, 924
Smith, Susan Verree II, 796
Smith, Susan Verree II, 820
Smith, Susanah VI, 854
Smith, Susanna I, 571
Smith, Susanna I, 593
Smith, Susanna I, 596
Smith, Susanna II, 183
Smith, Susanna II, 185
Smith, Susanna II, 421
Smith, Susanna IV, 93
Smith, Susanna IV, 109
Smith, Susanna IV, 437
Smith, Susanna IV, 883
Smith, Susanna VI, 633
Smith, Susanna VI, 634
Smith, Susanna VI, 706
Smith, Susanna VI, 949
Smith, Susanna VI, 995
Smith, Susanna B. II, 133
Smith, Susanna D. II, 185
Smith, Susanna Dillwyn II, 452
Smith, Susanna Dillwyn II, 656
Smith, Susanna R. II, 296
Smith, Susanna R. II, 299
Smith, Susanna R. II, 301
Smith, Susannah I, 590
Smith, Susannah I, 1012
Smith, Susannah II, 28
Smith, Susannah II, 40
Smith, Susannah II, 72
Smith, Susannah II, 99
Smith, Susannah II, 100
Smith, Susannah II, 109
Smith, Susannah II, 172
Smith, Susannah II, 184
Smith, Susannah II, 209
Smith, Susannah II, 262
Smith, Susannah II, 263
Smith, Susannah IV, 133
Smith, Susannah IV, 159
Smith, Susannah IV, 341
Smith, Susannah IV, 351
Smith, Susannah IV, 368
Smith, Susannah IV, 438
Smith, Susannah IV, 439
Smith, Susannah IV, 458
Smith, Susannah IV, 762
Smith, Susannah IV, 876
Smith, Susannah VI, 445
Smith, Susannah VI, 562
Smith, Susannah VI, 599
Smith, Susannah VI, 605
Smith, Susannah VI, 633
Smith, Susannah VI, 649
Smith, Susannah VI, 703
Smith, Susannah VI, 738
Smith, Susannah VI, 779
Smith, Susannah VI, 949
Smith, Susannah R. II, 185
Smith, Susannah R. II, 292
Smith, Sussana IV, 351
Smith, Sussanah IV, 351
Smith, Sylinda Ann IV, 1241
Smith, Sylvanus III, 439
Smith, Sylvanus III, 447
Smith, Sylvanus III, 499
Smith, Sylvia Jane IV, 401
Smith, Sylvia Jane IV, 439
Smith, Tabitha II, 185
Smith, Tabitha II, 263
Smith, Tabitha VI, 995
Smith, Tabitha R. II, 185
Smith, Tabitha R. II, 301
Smith, Tabitha R. II, 656
Smith, Tabitha R. II, 767
Smith, Tacie V, 644
Smith, Tacy IV, 59
Smith, Tacy IV, 159
Smith, Tacy IV, 381
Smith, Tacy IV, 438
Smith, Tacy IV, 439
Smith, Tacy IV, 547
Smith, Tacy IV, 548
Smith, Tacy IV, 549
Smith, Tacy IV, 550
Smith, Tacy IV, 594
Smith, Tacy E. IV, 438
Smith, Tacy M. IV, 581
Smith, Tacy M. IV, 594
Smith, Tamer IV, 59
Smith, Tamer VI, 606
Smith, Tamor IV, 159
Smith, Taylor IV, 334
Smith, Taylor IV, 351
Smith, Tedford IV, 1223
Smith, Tedford P. I, 1161
Smith, Tedford P. IV, 1223
Smith, Thamor IV, 551
Smith, Theodore V, 598
Smith, Theodore V, 631
Smith, Theodorie IV, 994
Smith, Theofel I, 74
Smith, Thomas I, 364
Smith, Thomas I, 419
Smith, Thomas I, 900
Smith, Thomas II, 41
Smith, Thomas II, 45
Smith, Thomas II, 99
Smith, Thomas II, 111
Smith, Thomas II, 184
Smith, Thomas II, 185
Smith, Thomas II, 210
Smith, Thomas II, 238
Smith, Thomas II, 261
Smith, Thomas II, 262
Smith, Thomas II, 263
Smith, Thomas II, 275
Smith, Thomas II, 421
Smith, Thomas II, 422
Smith, Thomas II, 451
Smith, Thomas II, 488
Smith, Thomas II, 489
Smith, Thomas II, 653
Smith, Thomas II, 654
Smith, Thomas II, 969
Smith, Thomas II, 970
Smith, Thomas II, 1010
Smith, Thomas II, 1028
Smith, Thomas II, 1030
Smith, Thomas II, 1060
Smith, Thomas II, 1070
Smith, Thomas II, 1080
Smith, Thomas III, 294
Smith, Thomas III, 452
Smith, Thomas IV, 38
Smith, Thomas IV, 59
Smith, Thomas IV, 60
Smith, Thomas IV, 67
Smith, Thomas IV, 77
Smith, Thomas IV, 109
Smith, Thomas IV, 145
Smith, Thomas IV, 159
Smith, Thomas IV, 276
Smith, Thomas IV, 277
Smith, Thomas IV, 415
Smith, Thomas IV, 437
Smith, Thomas IV, 438
Smith, Thomas IV, 439
Smith, Thomas IV, 443
Smith, Thomas IV, 454
Smith, Thomas IV, 573
Smith, Thomas IV, 594
Smith, Thomas IV, 657
Smith, Thomas IV, 883
Smith, Thomas IV, 974
Smith, Thomas IV, 994
Smith, Thomas IV, 1058
Smith, Thomas IV, 1076
Smith, Thomas IV, 1077
Smith, Thomas IV, 1089
Smith, Thomas IV, 1114
Smith, Thomas IV, 1115
Smith, Thomas IV, 1138
Smith, Thomas V, 122
Smith, Thomas V, 123
Smith, Thomas V, 279
Smith, Thomas V, 431
Smith, Thomas V, 529
Smith, Thomas V, 597
Smith, Thomas VI, 437
Smith, Thomas VI, 445
Smith, Thomas VI, 446
Smith, Thomas VI, 462
Smith, Thomas VI, 505
Smith, Thomas VI, 554
Smith, Thomas VI, 561
Smith, Thomas VI, 562
Smith, Thomas VI, 563
Smith, Thomas VI, 605
Smith, Thomas VI, 649
Smith, Thomas VI, 650
Smith, Thomas VI, 695
Smith, Thomas VI, 701
Smith, Thomas VI, 826
Smith, Thomas VI, 835
Smith, Thomas VI, 855
Smith, Thomas VI, 995
Smith, Thomas Arthur II, 820
Smith, Thomas Arthur V, 431
Smith, Thomas E. IV, 1138
Smith, Thomas Fawcett VI, 605
Smith, Thomas Franklin III, 295
Smith, Thomas Janney VI, 627
Smith, Thomas L. II, 767
Smith, Thomas N. VI, 707
Smith, Thomas P. F. IV, 1114
Smith, Thomas Parry II, 313
Smith, Thomas Parry II, 324
Smith, Thomas R. III, 295
Smith, Thomas R. VI, 636
Smith, Thomas R. VI, 701
Smith, Thomas R. VI, 706
Smith, Thomas Russell VI, 636
Smith, Thomas Russell VI, 645
Smith, Thomas Russell VI, 652
Smith, Thomas Russell VI, 653
Smith, Thomas Russell VI, 702
Smith, Thomas Russell VI, 703
Smith, Thomas Russell VI, 704
Smith, Thomas Russell VI, 707
Smith, Thomas Russell VI, 724
Smith, Thomas Smith VI, 605
Smith, Thomas T. III, 294
Smith, Thomas T. III, 295
Smith, Thomas Thorn III, 292
Smith, Thomas W. II, 654
Smith, Thomas W. III, 295
Smith, Thomas W. IV, 438
Smith, Thomas Wilkerson IV, 562
Smith, Thomas Wilkinson IV, 352
Smith, Thomas Wilkinson IV, 549
Smith, Thomas, Jr. IV, 351
Smith, Thomas, Jr. IV, 439
Smith, Thomas, Jr. IV, 454
Smith, Thomas, Jr. IV, 657
Smith, Thomas, Jr. V, 529
Smith, Thomas, Jr. VI, 444
Smith, Thomas, Jr. VI, 446
Smith, Thomas, Jr. VI, 563
Smith, Thompson IV, 438
Smith, Thompson IV, 440
Smith, Thompson IV, 453
Smith, Thos. I, 364
Smith, Thos. II, 54
Smith, Thos. II, 99
Smith, Thos. II, 783
Smith, Thos. II, 816
Smith, Thos. II, 820
Smith, Thos. IV, 159
Smith, Thos. IV, 277
Smith, Thos. IV, 553
Smith, Thos. V, 917
Smith, Thos. L. II, 656
Smith, Thos. Richpole III, 292
Smith, Thos. T. III, 23
Smith, Thos. T. III, 292
Smith, Thos. T. III, 295
Smith, Thos. T. V, 278
Smith, Thos., Jr. IV, 339
Smith, Thos., Jr. IV, 351
Smith, Timothy II, 969
Smith, Timothy II, 970
Smith, Timothy II, 1015
Smith, Timothy II, 1027
Smith, Timothy III, 402
Smith, Timothy IV, 59
Smith, Timothy IV, 60
Smith, Timothy IV, 71
Smith, Timothy IV, 109
Smith, Timothy IV, 115
Smith, Timothy IV, 133
Smith, Timothy, Jr. II, 1027
Smith, Timothy, Jr. IV, 109
Smith, Tishe I, 166
Smith, Tishe I, 170
Smith, Tishe I, 705
Smith, Tishe I, 734
Smith, Tishe V, 122
Smith, Tishey I, 74
Smith, Tristram IV, 277
Smith, Tristram V, 279
Smith, Tristran IV, 277
Smith, Tristrim V, 278
Smith, Truman IV, 1186
Smith, Tryphena II, 184
Smith, Tryphena II, 185
Smith, Tryphena II, 261
Smith, Tryphosa II, 184
Smith, Tryphosa II, 272
Smith, Tryphosia II, 262
Smith, Uelysus Grant I, 1161
Smith, Upton II, 770
Smith, Urshel V, 203
Smith, Ursula VI, 995
Smith, Usley VI, 995
Smith, Vada V, 279
Smith, Vannje C. V, 278
Smith, Velma V, 764
Smith, Vera IV, 763
Smith, Vera E. IV, 762
Smith, Vergil IV, 1223
Smith, Vernon V, 278
Smith, Vesta I, 627
Smith, Vinel VI, 913
Smith, Viola V, 655
Smith, Viola V, 710
Smith, Viola E. IV, 1338
Smith, Viola H. V, 710
Smith, Virgil IV, 1223
Smith, Virginia VI, 446
Smith, Virginia E. IV, 276
Smith, Virginia E. IV, 278
Smith, Virginia R. IV, 276
Smith, Voral VI, 913
Smith, W. H. I, 641
Smith, W. J. IV, 282
Smith, W. Scott II, 138
Smith, W. T. I, 626
Smith, Waite III, 499
Smith, Walker IV, 277
Smith, Walker IV, 1263
Smith, Walker IV, 1264
Smith, Walker V, 710
Smith, Walker B. V, 710
Smith, Walker L. IV, 1264
Smith, Walter IV, 276
Smith, Walter IV, 277
Smith, Walter IV, 551
Smith, Walter IV, 1185
Smith, Walter Lincoln V, 278
Smith, Warren I, 18
Smith, Warren IV, 1186
Smith, Washington VI, 86
Smith, Wat E. IV, 1294
Smith, Wd. Ann II, 180
Smith, Wd. Bethany III, 292
Smith, Wd. Dorcas II, 99
Smith, Wd. Elizabeth II, 183
Smith, Wd. Hannah II, 183
Smith, Wd. Joanna II, 602
Smith, Wd. Laura F. III, 26
Smith, Wd. Letitia II, 783
Smith, Wd. Mary II, 1041
Smith, Wd. Mary VI, 713
Smith, Wd. Mary Woodrow VI, 562
Smith, Wd. Rebecca VI, 785
Smith, Wd. Rebecca Jane II, 820
Smith, Wd. Sallie Levis II, 820
Smith, Wd. Sarah II, 165
Smith, Wd. Susannah II, 185
Smith, Widow Mary VI, 667
Smith, Widow Mary VI, 706
Smith, Widow Rachel I, 39
Smith, Widow Rachel I, 74
Smith, Widow Ruth VI, 497
Smith, Widow Ruth Hannah VI, 633
Smith, Widow Ruth Hannah VI, 705
Smith, Widow Sarah I, 66
Smith, Widow Sarah I, 74
Smith, Wieford B. IV, 1116
Smith, Wil II, 184
Smith, Wil??? II, 184
Smith, Wilfred B. IV, 1115
Smith, Wilkinson IV, 352
Smith, Wilkinson IV, 550
Smith, Will IV, 278
Smith, Will T. IV, 278
Smith, Willet II, 262
Smith, Willet III, 293
Smith, Willet III, 294
Smith, William I, 91
Smith, William I, 275
Smith, William I, 419
Smith, William I, 487
Smith, William I, 571
Smith, William I, 900
Smith, William I, 1018
Smith, William I, 1024
Smith, William I, 1037
Smith, William I, 1063
Smith, William I, 1088
Smith, William I, 1098
Smith, William I, 1132
Smith, William I, 1146
Smith, William I, 1162
Smith, William II, 40
Smith, William II, 41
Smith, William II, 172
Smith, William II, 184
Smith, William II, 209
Smith, William II, 214
Smith, William II, 261
Smith, William II, 262
Smith, William II, 421
Smith, William II, 422
Smith, William II, 447
Smith, William II, 488
Smith, William II, 783
Smith, William III, 295
Smith, William III, 296
Smith, William III, 447
Smith, William III, 499
Smith, William IV, 59
Smith, William IV, 60
Smith, William IV, 109
Smith, William IV, 159
Smith, William IV, 278
Smith, William IV, 351
Smith, William IV, 416
Smith, William IV, 437
Smith, William IV, 438
Smith, William IV, 439
Smith, William IV, 549
Smith, William IV, 762
Smith, William IV, 1090
Smith, William IV, 1097
Smith, William IV, 1114
Smith, William IV, 1115
Smith, William IV, 1240
Smith, William IV, 1294
Smith, William IV, 1379
Smith, William V, 122
Smith, William V, 123
Smith, William V, 431
Smith, William V, 432
Smith, William V, 529
Smith, William V, 710
Smith, William V, 862
Smith, William V, 932
Smith, William VI, 444
Smith, William VI, 445
Smith, William VI, 446
Smith, William VI, 451
Smith, William VI, 496
Smith, William VI, 497
Smith, William VI, 561
Smith, William VI, 562
Smith, William VI, 563
Smith, William VI, 584
Smith, William VI, 605
Smith, William VI, 644
Smith, William VI, 664
Smith, William VI, 668
Smith, William VI, 696
Smith, William VI, 699
Smith, William VI, 701
Smith, William VI, 707
Smith, William VI, 827
Smith, William VI, 854
Smith, William VI, 915
Smith, William VI, 995
Smith, William A. III, 292
Smith, William A. III, 295
Smith, William A. IV, 278
Smith, William A. IV, 1114
Smith, William B. II, 715
Smith, William B. IV, 1378
Smith, William B. VI, 854
Smith, William Brown IV, 59
Smith, William C. II, 185
Smith, William C. III, 295
Smith, William C. IV, 438
Smith, William C. VI, 796
Smith, William C. VI, 995
Smith, William D. IV, 440
Smith, William F. I, 624
Smith, William F. IV, 277
Smith, William F. V, 932
Smith, William G. IV, 550

h, William G. VI, 679
h, William G. VI, 704
h, William G. VI, 707
h, William H. II, 783
h, William H. III, 295
h, William H. IV, 276
h, William H. IV, 1114
h, William H. V, 279
h, William H. V, 529
h, William H. VI, 515
h, William H. VI, 995
h, William Heulings II, 422
h, William I. V, 861
h, William J. VI, 645
h, William J. VI, 664
h, William J. VI, 707
h, William K. IV, 550
h, William K. VI, 854
h, William Lovet II, 261
h, William Lovett II, 184
h, William Orla V, 710
h, William P. II, 421
h, William P. III, 295
h, William P. IV, 550
h, William P. IV, 1379
h, William R. III, 369
h, William R. IV, 497
h, William R. IV, 551
h, William R. V, 431
h, William R. V, 432
h, William R. V, 710
h, William Rockhill II, 185
h, William S. IV, 440
h, William T. III, 295
h, William T. VI, 702
h, William T. VI, 995
h, William Thomas IV, 1115
h, William Thomas VI, 616
h, William W. III, 296
h, William W. IV, 439
h, William, Jr. I, 1098
h, William, Jr. VI, 563
h, Williams IV, 1185
h, Willie IV, 1186
h, Willis I, 257
h, Willis IV, 1223
h, Willis IV, 1241
h, Willis J. IV, 1240
h, Willis R. IV, 1185
h, Willis R. IV, 1198
h, Willis R. IV, 1240
h, Wilma IV, 994
h, Wilmer J. IV, 276
h, Winnamore IV, 278
h, Wm Thomas VI, 702
h, Wm, Jr. II, 100
h, Wm. I, 1110
h, Wm. II, 86
h, Wm. II, 99
h, Wm. II, 100
h, Wm. II, 111
h, Wm. II, 138
h, Wm. II, 447
h, Wm. II, 584
h, Wm. II, 603
h, Wm. II, 653
h, Wm. II, 654
h, Wm. II, 655
th, Wm. II, 767
th, Wm. II, 1000
th, Wm. II, 1021
h, Wm. II, 1027
th, Wm. III, 292
th, Wm. III, 295
th, Wm. IV, 133
th, Wm. IV, 159
h, Wm. IV, 321
th, Wm. IV, 377
th, Wm. IV, 449
h, Wm. IV, 550
h, Wm. IV, 959
h, Wm. IV, 1077
h, Wm. IV, 1114
h, Wm. IV, 1115
th, Wm. IV, 1240
th, Wm. IV, 1338
th, Wm. V, 360
th, Wm. V, 432
th, Wm. V, 465
th, Wm. V, 710
th, Wm. V, 932
th, Wm. V, 959
th, Wm. VI, 497
th, Wm. VI, 520
th, Wm. VI, 521
h, Wm. VI, 579
th, Wm. VI, 627
th, Wm. VI, 642
th, Wm. VI, 666
h, Wm. VI, 701
th, Wm. VI, 703
Smith, Wm. VI, 704
Smith, Wm. VI, 705
Smith, Wm. VI, 707
Smith, Wm. VI, 720
Smith, Wm. A. V, 1019
Smith, Wm. C. II, 923
Smith, Wm. C. II, 924
Smith, Wm. Canby II, 820
Smith, Wm. Clark I, 641
Smith, Wm. D. IV, 762
Smith, Wm. D. IV, 773
Smith, Wm. Drewet II, 654
Smith, Wm. F. IV, 1077
Smith, Wm. F. IV, 1115
Smith, Wm. G. IV, 550
Smith, Wm. G. IV, 554
Smith, Wm. G. VI, 685
Smith, Wm. H. IV, 1116
Smith, Wm. H. V, 598
Smith, Wm. H. Pearman VI, 834
Smith, Wm. Harvey IV, 278
Smith, Wm. Hilliard II, 138
Smith, Wm. Hilliard II, 158
Smith, Wm. Hunter I, 626
Smith, Wm. Irish VI, 703
Smith, Wm. J. V, 644
Smith, Wm. J. VI, 406
Smith, Wm. J. VI, 622
Smith, Wm. J. VI, 645
Smith, Wm. J. VI, 660
Smith, Wm. J. VI, 662
Smith, Wm. J. VI, 696
Smith, Wm. J. VI, 703
Smith, Wm. Janney VI, 753
Smith, Wm. K. VI, 666
Smith, Wm. L. V, 1019
Smith, Wm. McCoy V, 710
Smith, Wm. O. IV, 1338
Smith, Wm. Orla V, 710
Smith, Wm. P. III, 224
Smith, Wm. P. V, 710
Smith, Wm. Pearson IV, 1115
Smith, Wm. Peter IV, 782
Smith, Wm. R. II, 138
Smith, Wm. R. III, 295
Smith, Wm. R. IV, 276
Smith, Wm. R. IV, 550
Smith, Wm. R. IV, 994
Smith, Wm. R. IV, 999
Smith, Wm. R. V, 710
Smith, Wm. R. VI, 416
Smith, Wm. R. VI, 417
Smith, Wm. R. VI, 445
Smith, Wm. S. IV, 1115
Smith, Wm. Silvanus IV, 1114
Smith, Wm. T. III, 120
Smith, Wm. T. III, 292
Smith, Wm. T. III, 295
Smith, Wm. T. III, 317
Smith, Wm. T. IV, 1116
Smith, Wm. T. IV, 1185
Smith, Wm. T. IV, 1241
Smith, Wm. T. VI, 686
Smith, Wm. Thomas II, 783
Smith, Wm. W. IV, 446
Smith, Wm. Wallace II, 719
Smith, Wm., Jr. II, 656
Smith, Wm., Jr. IV, 1114
Smith, Wm., Sr. IV, 1114
Smith, Wraymond V, 278
Smith, Yana IV, 1240
Smith, Yana IV, 1241
Smith, Zachariah Taylor I, 689
Smith, Zeriah III, 292
Smith, Zeruiah III, 385
Smith, Zilpha I, 312
Smith, Zilpha I, 318
Smith, Zimri V, 279
Smith, Zimri V, 432
Smith, Zimry V, 278
Smith, Zodak I, 865
Smith, Zopher I, 1037
Smith, Zopher IV, 1379
Smith-Sheward, Ruth VI, 496
Smith-Sheward, Ruth VI, 497
Smith-Sheward, Ruth VI, 500
Smith-Sheward, Ruth VI, 648
Smith-Sheward, Ruth VI, 705
Smithers, Frances VI, 843
Smithers, L. VI, 843
Smithey, Francis II, 17
Smithey, Francis II, 45
Smithfield, Charles William II, 422
Smithfield, Mary IV, 352
Smithin, Elizabeth V, 279
Smithin, Elizabeth V, 284
Smithly, Ida IV, 1338
Smithly, Wm. IV, 1338
Smithson, Alta V, 279
Smithson, Alta V, 360
Smithson, Alta H. V, 279
Smithson, Bessie V, 710
Smithson, Carter V, 432
Smithson, Celia V, 360
Smithson, Celie V, 360
Smithson, Charles V, 710
Smithson, Della V, 710
Smithson, Dorothy V, 710
Smithson, Drummond VI, 858
Smithson, Elvira VI, 854
Smithson, Frank V, 432
Smithson, Fred V, 710
Smithson, Geo. W. VI, 982
Smithson, Jane V, 432
Smithson, Jane V, 434
Smithson, Jane VI, 811
Smithson, Jemima VI, 858
Smithson, John VI, 854
Smithson, John B. VI, 845
Smithson, John M. VI, 858
Smithson, Josephine V, 360
Smithson, Lewis V, 432
Smithson, Louie V, 432
Smithson, Lucinda E. V, 279
Smithson, Lucy VI, 854
Smithson, Madge V, 710
Smithson, Margaret J. VI, 854
Smithson, Martha J. V, 360
Smithson, Mary V, 279
Smithson, Mary V, 282
Smithson, Mary V, 420
Smithson, Mary V, 432
Smithson, Mary VI, 338
Smithson, Mary VI, 342
Smithson, Mary VI, 854
Smithson, Maud V, 360
Smithson, Samuel VI, 338
Smithson, Samuel VI, 811
Smithson, Samuel VI, 854
Smithson, Samuel VI, 858
Smithson, Seley VI, 854
Smithson, Solomon V, 432
Smithson, Tyre VI, 854
Smithson, William VI, 810
Smithson, Wm. M. VI, 854
Smittle, Cathron V, 203
Smittle, Thomas H. V, 203
Smitz, Wm. V, 1019
Smolk, Abraham IV, 1379
Smolk, Mary IV, 1379
Smoot, Mary J. V, 279
Smoot, Verdie E. V, 279
Smooth, Pauline VI, 854
Smooth, Wilson VI, 854
Smout, Edward II, 447
Smout, Elizabeth II, 447
Smyth, ??? VI, 738
Smyth, ??? VI, 748
Smyth, Abram VI, 779
Smyth, Anna II, 820
Smyth, Anna C. II, 923
Smyth, Anna Canby II, 802
Smyth, Anna Canby II, 819
Smyth, Anna Canby II, 881
Smyth, Anna Canby II, 924
Smyth, David II, 820
Smyth, Edward Betts II, 820
Smyth, Elizabeth F. II, 872
Smyth, Elizabeth F. II, 924
Smyth, Emily II, 803
Smyth, Emily II, 820
Smyth, Emily II, 923
Smyth, Emily B. II, 846
Smyth, Emily B. II, 852
Smyth, Emily B. II, 881
Smyth, Emily B. II, 882
Smyth, Emily B. II, 923
Smyth, Emily B. II, 924
Smyth, Emily Betts II, 803
Smyth, Ferris II, 820
Smyth, Ferris II, 923
Smyth, Frances Canby II, 786
Smyth, Frances Canby II, 820
Smyth, Frances Canby II, 846
Smyth, Frances Canby II, 924
Smyth, Hannah VI, 738
Smyth, Hannah VI, 779
Smyth, Horace II, 872
Smyth, Horace II, 924
Smyth, Jane III, 296
Smyth, Lindley II, 872
Smyth, Lindley II, 923
Smyth, Lindley II, 924
Smyth, Lucy II, 852
Smyth, Lucy II, 923
Smyth, Lucy II, 924
Smyth, Martha II, 815
Smyth, Mary B. II, 923
Smyth, Mary Betts II, 820
Smyth, Mary E. II, 872
Smyth, Mary E. II, 924
Smyth, Mary H. II, 924
Smyth, Mary M. VI, 748
Smyth, Mary M. VI, 779
Smyth, Rachel VI, 779
Smyth, Rebecca III, 296
Smyth, Richard II, 76
Smyth, Richard II, 99
Smyth, Sarah VI, 243
Smyth, Sarah VI, 267
Smyth, Susannah II, 76
Smyth, Susannah II, 99
Smyth, Thomas H. III, 296
Smyth, Wm. C. II, 846
Smyth, Wm. C. II, 852
Smyth, Wm. C. II, 881
Smyth, Wm. C. II, 882
Smyth, Wm. C. II, 923
Smyth, Wm. C. II, 924
Smyth, Wm. Canby II, 803
Smyth, Wm. Canby II, 820
Smythe, Lindley M. II, 302
Smythe, Parks IV, 278
Smythe, Rebecca III, 296
Smythe, Thomas H. III, 296
Smythe, Will IV, 278
Smythers, Rachel II, 463
Smythers, Rachel II, 656
Snapp, Nancy S. VI, 854
Snapp, Philip K., Jr. VI, 854
Snead, Altha A. VI, 995
Snead, Amelia A. VI, 894
Snead, Christine V, 432
Snead, Edward Brooks II, 656
Snead, Elizabeth II, 473
Snead, Elizabeth II, 656
Snead, Elizabeth VI, 840
Snead, Eva V, 432
Snead, Evan VI, 339
Snead, Evan VI, 854
Snead, Evan VI, 889
Snead, Evan VI, 894
Snead, Evan VI, 995
Snead, Frank V, 432
Snead, George T. VI, 995
Snead, Grace II, 489
Snead, Grace II, 656
Snead, Israel VI, 854
Snead, James VI, 854
Snead, James Oran V, 432
Snead, John J. VI, 994
Snead, John Y. VI, 893
Snead, John Y. VI, 995
Snead, Judy F. VI, 889
Snead, Lee V, 432
Snead, Lemira J. VI, 995
Snead, Lizzie V, 432
Snead, Lucinda VI, 854
Snead, M. VI, 995
Snead, Mark V, 432
Snead, Martha D. VI, 995
Snead, Martimer V, 432
Snead, Mary II, 422
Snead, Mary II, 447
Snead, Mary II, 552
Snead, Mary II, 656
Snead, Mary VI, 312
Snead, Mary VI, 339
Snead, Molly VI, 339
Snead, Molly VI, 854
Snead, Nancy VI, 854
Snead, Polly VI, 894
Snead, Polly VI, 995
Snead, Richard II, 422
Snead, Sally VI, 339
Snead, Sally VI, 854
Snead, Sarah V, 123
Snead, Sarah V, 360
Snead, Sarah VI, 331
Snead, Sarah VI, 338
Snead, Sarah VI, 339
Snead, Sophia M. VI, 928
Snead, Thos. H. VI, 964
Snead, William II, 422
Snead, William II, 447
Snead, William VI, 339
Snead, William VI, 854
Snead, Wm. II, 473
Snead, Wm. II, 489
Snead, Wm. II, 656
Sneathen, Elizabeth V, 764
Sneathen, Elizabeth V, 769
Sneathen, Mary V, 764
Sneathen, Sarah V, 764
Sneathen, Sarah V, 769
Sneddon, Charles IV, 763
Sneddon, Janet IV, 763
Sneddon, Ruth Bernice IV, 763
Sneddon, William IV, 763
Snedeker, ??? III, 491
Snedeker, Deborah III, 499
Snedeker, Mary III, 491
Snedeker, Mary III, 499
Snedeker, Sadie IV, 1338
Snee, Rebecca IV, 484
Snee, Rebecca IV, 497
Sneed, Wm. II, 665
Snelgrove, Achsah I, 1030
Snelgrove, Achsah I, 1037
Snell, Angeline II, 947
Snell, J. F. V, 1019
Snell, Joseph II, 947
Snell, Joseph II, 1086
Snell, Nancy V, 1019
Snell, Nancy E. V, 1019
Snell, Nobel VI, 841
Snell, Sophia IV, 1338
Snellen, Carrie V, 203
Snellen, George V, 203
Snellen, Rachel I Sup 1, 4
Snellen, Rachel I Sup 1, 6
Snelley, Carrie V, 203
Snelling, Alemeda V. IV, 995
Snelling, Almeda V. IV, 958
Snelling, Almeda V. IV, 992
Snelling, Almeda V. IV, 994
Snelling, Amelia J. IV, 995
Snelling, Easter I, 90
Snelling, Esther I Sup 1, 6
Snelling, Hannah I, 18
Snelling, Hannah I Sup 1, 3
Snelling, Hannah I Sup 1, 6
Snelling, Hester I, 18
Snelling, Israel I, 18
Snelling, Israel I Sup 1, 6
Snelling, John IV, 994
Snelling, John D. IV, 958
Snelling, Michael IV, 995
Snelling, Michael E. L. IV, 958
Snelling, Michael E. S. IV, 994
Snelling, Michal VI, 195
Snelling, Michal VI, 212
Snelling, Pamelia J. IV, 995
Snelling, Parmelia Jane IV, 994
Snelling, Rachel I, 18
Snelling, Rachel I Sup 1, 6
Snelser, Charles VI, 929
Snelser, Elizabeth VI, 929
Snelson, Allen I, 1162
Snelson, Bula I, 1162
Snelson, Fanny VI, 983
Snelson, Sarah VI, 859
Snidar, Aggy VI, 996
Snidar, Jacob VI, 996
Snider, ??? V, 1019
Snider, Aggy VI, 996
Snider, Amanda V, 1019
Snider, Betsey VI, 996
Snider, Charles V, 279
Snider, Charles V, 465
Snider, Cinthia VI, 914
Snider, Daisy J. I, 933
Snider, Daniel V, 1019
Snider, Earl IV, 1042
Snider, Eliza V, 20
Snider, Eliza V, 123
Snider, Eliza V, 932
Snider, Eliza D. V, 123
Snider, Eliza D. V, 932
Snider, Eliza Jane VI, 949
Snider, Elizabeth I, 734
Snider, Elizabeth IV, 48
Snider, Elizabeth IV, 60
Snider, Ella V, 465
Snider, Emeline VI, 873
Snider, Emily V, 1019
Snider, Etta V, 1019
Snider, Frances VI, 996
Snider, George H. I, 933
Snider, Hannah IV, 748
Snider, Hannah IV, 763
Snider, Henry VI, 884
Snider, Hester Ann V, 502
Snider, Hester Ann V, 514
Snider, Hester Ann V, 529
Snider, Homer V, 279
Snider, Ira V, 1019
Snider, Jacob VI, 996
Snider, James I, 949
Snider, James V, 432
Snider, James P. I, 901
Snider, James P. I, 933
Snider, Jane I, 893
Snider, Jane I, 901
Snider, John H. I, 933
Snider, Joicey VI, 884
Snider, Lovy VI, 897
Snider, Ludy Ann VI, 904
Snider, Mahlin VI, 964
Snider, Mahlon V, 465
Snider, Martha V, 118
Snider, Martha V, 123
Snider, Martha McMillan V, 529

Snider, Martin VI, 904
Snider, Mary I, 933
Snider, Mary V, 853
Snider, Mary V, 862
Snider, Mary Ann V, 1019
Snider, Mary J. E. VI, 996
Snider, Mastin VI, 904
Snider, Mastin VI, 949
Snider, Mastin VI, 996
Snider, Minda V, 1019
Snider, Minnie I, 938
Snider, Minnie I, 949
Snider, Nancy VI, 996
Snider, Nancy Jane I, 933
Snider, Philip V, 432
Snider, Polly VI, 996
Snider, Price VI, 917
Snider, Price VI, 996
Snider, Ray V, 1019
Snider, Rebecca V, 831
Snider, Rebecca V, 862
Snider, Sally V, 123
Snider, Sally VI, 996
Snider, Samuel V, 1019
Snider, Sand V, 432
Snider, Sarah IV, 486
Snider, Sarah IV, 497
Snider, Sarah VI, 917
Snider, Sophronia Ann V, 393
Snider, Sophronia Ann V, 432
Snider, Thomas VI, 996
Snider, Tishie I, 876
Snider, Tishie I, 900
Snider, William I, 901
Snider, William I, 933
Snider, William VI, 884
Snider, William VI, 904
Snider, William VI, 996
Snider, William F. VI, 996
Snider, William Martin VI, 897
Snider, William V. VI, 996
Sniffen, Catharine M. III, 296
Sniffen, John III, 296
Sniffen, Mary J. III, 332
Snipes, Anne Elizabeth II, 970
Snipes, Della Jane I, 227
Snipes, Delphina I, 258
Snipes, E. T. I, 258
Snipes, Edgar Bradshaw II, 970
Snipes, Edgar T. I, 262
Snipes, Edgar Thomas I, 227
Snipes, Edgar Thomas II, 970
Snipes, Edgar Thomas II, 1061
Snipes, Edgar Thomas, Jr. II, 970
Snipes, Elisha II, 1061
Snipes, Elisha Thomas I, 227
Snipes, Elisha Thomas II, 970
Snipes, Elizabeth I, 262
Snipes, Harriet O. I, 247
Snipes, Harriet O. I, 258
Snipes, Harvey Grant I, 227
Snipes, Hattie Omega I, 227
Snipes, Howell Omega I, 258
Snipes, Isaac Finley I, 227
Snipes, Isaac Finley I, 258
Snipes, Jane I, 258
Snipes, Jane II, 970
Snipes, Jane Chace II, 1061
Snipes, Kitda Darah I, 258
Snipes, Kittie Sarah I, 227
Snipes, Loueasa I, 227
Snipes, Louisa I, 258
Snipes, Louisa II, 970
Snipes, Louisa II, 1061
Snipes, Mary V, 849
Snipes, Mary V, 862
Snipes, Miriam I, 231
Snipes, Miriam I, 258
Snipes, Oscar Pennington I, 227
Snipes, Parthenia I, 241
Snipes, Parthenia I, 258
Snipes, Parthenia I, 262
Snipes, Parthenia Henley I, 837
Snipes, Samuel Moon II, 970
Snipes, Thomas I, 258
Snipes, William Elwood I, 227
Snipes, William Elwood I, 258
Snitciff, Thelma IV, 1042
Snoad, Charles S. IV, 995
Snoad, Elizabeth C. IV, 995
Snoad, Esther B. IV, 995
Snoad, Sarah Ann IV, 995
Snoad, Susanna IV, 995
Snoad, Warren W. IV, 995
Snoberger, Rachel IV, 1338
Snoddon, Ann II, 985
Snoddon, Ann II, 1028
Snoddy, Daniel VI, 977
Snoddy, Elizabeth VI, 859
Snoddy, Elizabeth A. VI, 977
Snoddy, J. Cary VI, 859
Snoddy, John VI, 855
Snoddy, Robert VI, 854
Snoddy, Robert VI, 876
Snoddy, Robert VI, 893
Snoddy, Sophia VI, 854
Snode, Esther II, 100
Snode, Esther II, 124
Snode, Hannah R. IV, 763
Snode, John II, 100
Snode, Mabel IV, 1000
Snode, Susannah IV, 683
Snode, Susannah IV, 763
Snode, Wm. IV, 1043
Snoden, Mary W. V, 58
Snoden, Richard V, 58
Snoden, Sarah Amanda V, 58
Snodgrass, Bartley VI, 996
Snodgrass, Betsey VI, 996
Snodgrass, Chas. V, 1019
Snodgrass, Eliza I, 837
Snodgrass, Ella V, 1019
Snodgrass, Frank IV, 278
Snodgrass, George VI, 996
Snodgrass, Jacob V, 598
Snodgrass, May Marie V, 710
Snodgrass, Nancy C. VI, 996
Snodgrass, Orville V, 710
Snodon, Ann II, 247
Snodon, Ann II, 263
Snook, Edward V, 598
Snook, Nathan K. V, 598
Snow, Abner VI, 855
Snow, Asa III, 296
Snow, Bertha Emily I, 923
Snow, Cary VI, 820
Snow, Catharine VI, 803
Snow, Cona VI, 855
Snow, Daniel VI, 839
Snow, Daniel VI, 840
Snow, Daniel VI, 844
Snow, Daniel VI, 855
Snow, Daniel VI, 863
Snow, Eady VI, 996
Snow, Eliza VI, 980
Snow, Elizabeth VI, 810
Snow, Elizabeth VI, 899
Snow, George W. VI, 899
Snow, George W. VI, 996
Snow, Harriet III, 296
Snow, Henry VI, 854
Snow, Jabez VI, 899
Snow, Jabez VI, 967
Snow, Jabez, Jr. VI, 899
Snow, Jane L. I, 923
Snow, Jemima VI, 858
Snow, John II, 422
Snow, John VI, 799
Snow, John VI, 810
Snow, John VI, 820
Snow, John, Jr. VI, 799
Snow, Judith VI, 799
Snow, Martha VI, 854
Snow, Martha B. VI, 899
Snow, Martha D. VI, 845
Snow, Martha E. III, 296
Snow, Mary II, 422
Snow, Mary II, 472
Snow, Mary II, 477
Snow, Mary II, 656
Snow, Mary VI, 922
Snow, Mary VI, 984
Snow, Mary C. VI, 855
Snow, Nancy C. VI, 996
Snow, Peter II, 422
Snow, Polly VI, 845
Snow, Polly VI, 855
Snow, Rachel VI, 996
Snow, Richard VI, 845
Snow, Richard VI, 855
Snow, Sally VI, 840
Snow, Sarah VI, 836
Snow, Sarah VI, 996
Snow, Sarah C. VI, 967
Snow, Terry VI, 820
Snow, Terry VI, 996
Snow, Thomas II, 422
Snow, Thomas VI, 980
Snow, Thomas VI, 996
Snow, Vincent VI, 855
Snow, William H. I, 923
Snowd, Susanna IV, 929
Snowd, Susanna IV, 995
Snowde, Esther II, 124
Snowden, Alta V, 530
Snowden, Alta V, 710
Snowden, Alta V, 711
Snowden, Alton L. V, 529
Snowden, Amanda V, 58
Snowden, Amanda V, 123
Snowden, Amanda V, 530
Snowden, Ann II, 185
Snowden, Ann II, 196
Snowden, Ann II, 263
Snowden, Ann II, 422
Snowden, Anna D. II, 719
Snowden, Anna M. VI, 779
Snowden, Anna M. VI, 786
Snowden, Anna Maria III, 44
Snowden, Arthur V, 530
Snowden, Arthur V, 711
Snowden, Beulah II, 767
Snowden, Beulah II, 865
Snowden, Beulah II, 924
Snowden, Caroline V, 960
Snowden, Celia V, 530
Snowden, Celia V, 711
Snowden, Celia Kite V, 530
Snowden, Charles E. V, 123
Snowden, Charles Edward V, 530
Snowden, Charles Edwin V, 529
Snowden, Deborah VI, 474
Snowden, Deborah VI, 532
Snowden, Edward II, 719
Snowden, Edward II, 767
Snowden, Edward II, 768
Snowden, Edward V, 123
Snowden, Edward V, 529
Snowden, Edward V, 530
Snowden, Edward V, 663
Snowden, Edward V, 710
Snowden, Edward V, 711
Snowden, Edward Arthur V, 711
Snowden, Edward Dixon II, 719
Snowden, Elisha V, 644
Snowden, Elizabeth E. VI, 779
Snowden, Elizabeth E. VI, 786
Snowden, Elizabeth H. VI, 779
Snowden, Elizabeth T. VI, 264
Snowden, Ellen Jane V, 28
Snowden, Ellen Jane V, 530
Snowden, Emily Ann IV, 781
Snowden, Ester Anna V, 598
Snowden, Esther V, 598
Snowden, Esther Anna V, 598
Snowden, Esther Anna V, 710
Snowden, Esther Anna V, 711
Snowden, Flora P. V, 711
Snowden, Hannah B. II, 865
Snowden, Hannah B. II, 924
Snowden, Hannah Briggs II, 820
Snowden, Henry III, 44
Snowden, Henry A. V, 123
Snowden, Henry Allen V, 530
Snowden, Henry H. V, 123
Snowden, Ilo V, 663
Snowden, Ilo V, 710
Snowden, Isaac VI, 779
Snowden, Isaac VI, 786
Snowden, Jane II, 656
Snowden, Jane V, 29
Snowden, Jane V, 123
Snowden, John II, 185
Snowden, John II, 196
Snowden, John II, 263
Snowden, John C. II, 767
Snowden, John C. II, 768
Snowden, John C. II, 820
Snowden, John C. II, 865
Snowden, John C. II, 924
Snowden, Leonard II, 656
Snowden, Leonard, Jr. II, 656
Snowden, Lewis Philip V, 529
Snowden, Lydia V, 598
Snowden, Lydia M. V, 598
Snowden, Lydia M. V, 710
Snowden, M. P. V, 598
Snowden, Malinda V, 598
Snowden, Malinda V, 710
Snowden, Malinda P. V, 598
Snowden, Malinda P. V, 711
Snowden, Mary II, 767
Snowden, Mary V, 123
Snowden, Mary V, 529
Snowden, Mary V, 530
Snowden, Mary V, 711
Snowden, Mary P. V, 705
Snowden, Mary W. V, 529
Snowden, Melinda V, 594
Snowden, Melinda V, 598
Snowden, Myles II, 865
Snowden, Myles II, 924
Snowden, Myrtle V, 530
Snowden, Myrtle V, 711
Snowden, Nancy IV, 781
Snowden, Nettie V, 710
Snowden, Nettie V, 719
Snowden, Patience VI, 447
Snowden, Peter IV, 781
Snowden, Philip VI, 447
Snowden, Rachel II, 656
Snowden, Rachel II, 682
Snowden, Rachel V, 63
Snowden, Rachel V, 123
Snowden, Rachel V, 511
Snowden, Rachel V, 529
Snowden, Rachel V, 530
Snowden, Rachel V, 711
Snowden, Rachel G. V, 123
Snowden, Rachel G. VI, 395
Snowden, Rachel G. VI, 447
Snowden, Rachel L. V, 529
Snowden, Rachel L. V, 530
Snowden, Rebecca II, 656
Snowden, Rebecca II, 767
Snowden, Richard V, 63
Snowden, Richard V, 123
Snowden, Richard V, 529
Snowden, Richard V, 530
Snowden, Richard VI, 395
Snowden, Richard VI, 447
Snowden, Robert V, 598
Snowden, Robert V, 710
Snowden, Robert V, 711
Snowden, Robert P. V, 598
Snowden, Robert P. V, 710
Snowden, Roy Tomkins V, 530
Snowden, Roy Townsend V, 711
Snowden, Ruth L. IV, 1338
Snowden, Samuel VI, 726
Snowden, Sara V, 692
Snowden, Sarah II, 656
Snowden, Sarah II, 719
Snowden, Sarah V, 530
Snowden, Sarah V, 692
Snowden, Sarah V, 711
Snowden, Sarah A. V, 529
Snowden, Sarah A. V, 530
Snowden, Sarah Amanda V, 123
Snowden, Sarah Amanda V, 530
Snowden, Sarah Amanda V, 622
Snowden, Sarah Amanda V, 644
Snowden, Sarah D. VI, 779
Snowden, Sarah M. II, 767
Snowden, Seth V, 529
Snowden, Seth V, 530
Snowden, Seth V, 711
Snowden, Thomas VI, 264
Snowden, William V, 710
Snowden, William F. V, 529
Snowden, William H. V, 598
Snowden, William J. V, 598
Snowden, William J. V, 710
Snowden, Wm. V, 598
Snowden, Wm. V, 719
Snowden, Wm. H. V, 598
Snowden, Wm. J. V, 711
Snowdon, Beulah II, 767
Snowdon, Edward II, 768
Snowdon, Edward V, 123
Snowdon, Jane II, 656
Snowdon, Jane II, 696
Snowdon, John C. II, 768
Snowdon, Leonard II, 656
Snowdon, Leonard II, 696
Snowdon, Mary II, 767
Snowdon, Sarah M. II, 767
Snugg, John II, 447
Snyder, A. T. V, 644
Snyder, Abigail IV, 1379
Snyder, Agnes IV, 278
Snyder, Anna Amelia V, 764
Snyder, Anna Amelia V, 862
Snyder, Anna Imelia V, 862
Snyder, Anna Isabel V, 421
Snyder, Anna Isabel V, 432
Snyder, Anne J. V, 432
Snyder, Annie Amelia V, 764
Snyder, Barbary VI, 921
Snyder, Casius Delmi V, 862
Snyder, Cassius Delmar V, 862
Snyder, Cassius Delmi V, 764
Snyder, Charity A. III, 301
Snyder, Charles E. V, 764
Snyder, Clover IV, 1338
Snyder, Douglas V, 711
Snyder, Earl IV, 1042
Snyder, Earle IV, 1042
Snyder, Eleaner C. V, 764
Snyder, Eleanor V, 840
Snyder, Eleanor V, 862
Snyder, Eleanor C. V, 740
Snyder, Eleanor C. V, 764
Snyder, Eleanor C. V, 862
Snyder, Eliza V, 432
Snyder, Eliza V, 932
Snyder, Elizabeth V, 432
Snyder, Estella V, 432
Snyder, Frances VI, 996
Snyder, Frank K. IV, 278
Snyder, Gertrude Belle V, 599
Snyder, Gurtie IV, 1264
Snyder, Gustie IV, 1264
Snyder, Hannah IV, 763
Snyder, Hannah E. IV, 748
Snyder, Hannah E. IV, 763
Snyder, Harriet III, 119
Snyder, Harriet III, 296
Snyder, Harriett V, 711
Snyder, Helen V, 711
Snyder, Helen V, 764
Snyder, Helen Wright V, 687
Snyder, Helen Wright V, 711
Snyder, Ida E. V, 644
Snyder, J. Earle V, 711
Snyder, J. O. IV, 1338
Snyder, J. Thad V, 711
Snyder, James IV, 574
Snyder, James V, 432
Snyder, James P. I, 901
Snyder, Jane I, 901
Snyder, Jennie V, 432
Snyder, Julia W. V, 599
Snyder, Katharine L. III, 296
Snyder, Lenna V, 764
Snyder, Letha Eloise V, 764
Snyder, Lizzie IV, 278
Snyder, Lovey VI, 964
Snyder, Mahitable H. III, 296
Snyder, Margaret II, 780
Snyder, Mary V, 792
Snyder, Mary V, 862
Snyder, Mary Carpenter III, 2
Snyder, Mastin VI, 996
Snyder, Mrs. C. L. IV, 763
Snyder, Mrs. Clayton IV, 1338
Snyder, Nancy VI, 996
Snyder, Olive IV, 1042
Snyder, Olive L. IV, 1042
Snyder, Perry V, 599
Snyder, Philip V, 432
Snyder, Phillip V, 432
Snyder, Rachel IV, 574
Snyder, Rachel IV, 594
Snyder, Raymond V, 764
Snyder, Rebecca V, 862
Snyder, Richmond F. III, 296
Snyder, Salathiel V, 764
Snyder, Sally V, 122
Snyder, Sally V, 123
Snyder, Sally VI, 996
Snyder, Samuel V, 432
Snyder, Sand V, 432
Snyder, Sophronia Ann V, 432
Snyder, Thomas VI, 996
Snyder, Thos. J. III, 296
Snyder, William I, 901
Snyder, William V. VI, 996
Snyder, Winfield IV, 1264
Snyder, Winfield S. IV, 1264
Snyder, Wm. Halleck III, 119
Snyder, Wm. Halleck III, 296
Snypes, E. T. I, 258
Soale, Bessie V, 311
Soale, Bessie V, 465
Soale, Chas. E. V, 465
Soale, Nancy V, 311
Soale, Nancy P. V, 465
Soale, Phebe V, 465
Soale, Phoebe V, 311
Soane, Henry VI, 204
Soane, Henry VI, 212
Soane, John VI, 212
Sobehart, Andrew IV, 734
Sobehart, E. A. IV, 1339
Sobehart, Francis IV, 734
Sobehart, Lena IV, 734
Soberhart, Baby IV, 1339
Soberhart, E. A. IV, 1339
Sobiehardt, Baby IV, 1339
Sochell, Andrew II, 448
Sockman, John V, 711
Soggerson, Mary II, 656
Sohns, Anna V, 203
Sohns, Elizabeth V, 203
Sohns, Lewis V, 203
Sohns, Lula Belle V, 203
Sohns, Lulu B. V, 203
Solars, Elizabeth V, 1019
Solars, Eva V, 1019
Solars, George V, 1019
Soldan, Julia R. III, 89
Solenberger, Ansel Benjamin VI, 439
Solenberger, Ansel Benjamin VI, 447
Solenberger, B. Franklin VI, 4
Solenberger, Mary Opal VI, 43
Solenberger, Mary Opal VI, 44
Solenberger, Susie S. VI, 447
Solers, Elizabeth V, 1019
Solers, Eva V, 1019
Solers, George V, 1019
Soles, Florence Lucile V, 644
Sollers, George V, 1019

mon, Caroline IV, 1339
mon, Eleanor II, 422
mon, Elizabeth II, 1015
mon, Elizabeth II, 1028
bury, Martha II, 863
arindyck, Sarah III, 403
erndike, Louisa II, 801
ers, Albertus II, 124
ers, Ann II, 128
ers, Ann II, 819
ers, Chas. Edward II, 820
ers, Clarence III, 296
ers, Edward O. V, 123
ers, Eli V, 976
ers, Elizabeth II, 103
ers, Elizabeth II, 116
ers, Elizabeth II, 124
ers, Elizabeth VI, 581
ers, Elizabeth Acton II, 116
ers, Ella V, 976
ers, Emma V, 976
ers, George R. II, 116
ers, George W. II, 116
ers, George Wills II, 116
ers, Helen A. III, 296
ers, Helen Augusta III, 208
ers, Ida V, 976
ers, Jacob II, 124
ers, John II, 103
ers, John V, 976
ers, Joseph III, 208
ers, Joseph III, 296
ers, Laura V, 976
ers, Lewis V, 123
ers, Lewis E. V, 976
ers, Martha II, 120
ers, Martha II, 124
ers, Mary II, 116
ers, Mary VI, 580
ers, Mary S. VI, 483
ers, Mary S. VI, 581
ers, Mary, Jr. II, 116
ers, Omar II, 116
ers, Phebe V, 44
ers, Phebe Ann II, 116
ers, Rachel II, 91
ers, Rachel II, 103
ers, Richard II, 128
ers, Ruth M. V, 976
ers, Samuel II, 103
ers, Susan W. II, 116
ers, Walter III, 296
ers, William VI, 447
erville, Ethel Herbert IV, 278
erville, James IV, 995
erville, James Andrew IV, 278
erville, Mary IV, 995
erville, Orville William IV, 278
erville, Ralph Irvin IV, 278
erville, Susanna IV, 995
mer, Hannah II, 422
mers, Elizabeth II, 103
merville, Mary IV, 995
ner, Thomas II, 422
nonson, Catharine Ann III, 290
ghurst, John II, 422
ghurst, Olive II, 422
ghurst, Sarah II, 656
ghurst, Sarah II, 685
nafrank, Bertha IV, 1241
ntag, Charles II, 422
ntag, William II, 422
s, Lulu B. V, 203
tag, Charles II, 422
tag, Hannah II, 656
tag, Hannah II, 694
tag, Hannah II, 719
tag, Samuel II, 422
tag, William II, 422
ey, Louisa II, 299
ey, Lovisa II, 302
t, Julia IV, 1294
er, Edmond IV, 1043
er, Hanna K. IV, 133
er, John II, 422
er, Joy L. IV, 1339
er, Lydia IV, 133
her, Catharine IV, 133
her, Hanna K. IV, 133
her, Hannah IV, 60
her, Hannah IV, 110
her, Joseph IV, 39
her, Joseph IV, 60
her, Joseph IV, 110
her, Joseph IV, 133
her, Joseph IV, 134
her, Lydia IV, 60
her, Lydia IV, 110
Sopher, Lydia IV, 133
Sopher, Mary IV, 60
Sopher, Phebe IV, 39
Sopher, Phebe IV, 60
Sopher, Ruth IV, 39
Sopher, Ruth IV, 60
Sopher, Sarah IV, 60
Sopher, Sarah IV, 110
Sopher, Sarah IV, 133
Sopher, Sarah IV, 134
Sopher, Susanna IV, 60
Sopher, Susanna IV, 133
Sopher, William IV, 60
Sophia, Hannah V, 82
Sopors, John II, 422
Sorby, Mary IV, 1379
Sorby, Mary IV, 1381
Sorenson, Harriett E. IV, 1339
Sorenson, Ruth M. IV, 1339
Sorrell, Jane II, 656
Sorrow, Eliza Johnson I, 340
Soskky, Mary I, 419
Sotcher, Ann II, 1024
Sotcher, Ann II, 1035
Sotcher, John II, 1035
Sotcher, Mercy II, 976
Sotcher, Phebe II, 1014
Sotcher, Phebe II, 1024
Sotcher, Rachel II, 1024
Sotcher, Rachel II, 1039
Sotcher, Robert II, 1024
Sothie, Matilda V, 48
Sothie, Matilda V, 123
Sotley, Hannah II, 792
Sotley, John II, 792
Sotley, Wd. Phebe II, 792
Souder, Florence J. II, 869
Souder, Florence J. II, 924
Soulby, Harper VI, 779
Soulby, Henry VI, 779
Soulby, Sarah Ann VI, 779
Soule, Benjamin IV, 1379
Soule, Benjamin C. IV, 1379
Soule, George IV, 1379
Soule, Howland IV, 1379
Soule, Joel IV, 1379
Soule, Mabel C. IV, 1379
Soule, Mahala C. IV, 1379
Soule, Mahala L. IV, 1379
Soule, Matilda IV, 1371
Soule, Matilda IV, 1379
Soule, Sarah M. IV, 1379
Soundy, Thomas II, 657
Sousman, Sarah II, 820
South, Arthur W. M. II, 768
South, Edith K. II, 768
South, Enis V, 711
South, Hannah W. II, 1047
South, Hannah W. II, 1061
South, John VI, 939
South, Katy VI, 996
South, Lizzie G. V, 711
South, Martha V, 637
South, Martha V, 644
South, Mary VI, 939
South, Ruth IV, 34
South, Ruth IV, 60
South, William VI, 996
South, Wm. V, 711
Southabee, Elizabeth II, 657
Southabee, Wm. II, 657
Southall, John VI, 167
Southall, John VI, 188
Southall, John VI, 192
Southall, John VI, 212
Southard, Alice V, 465
Southard, Alice C. V, 465
Southard, Alice C. V, 530
Southard, Ann Eliza V, 360
Southard, Dr. S. C. V, 465
Southard, Emeline R. III, 511
Southard, Forester E. V, 432
Southard, Foster E. V, 432
Southard, James V, 432
Southard, John IV, 1294
Southard, John H. III, 511
Southard, Lillian V, 360
Southard, Lillian V, 432
Southard, Lillian A. V, 432
Southard, Louisa IV, 1294
Southard, Louiza IV, 1294
Southard, Lucilla III, 511
Southard, Mary E. III, 511
Southard, Mary J. V, 432
Southard, S. C. V, 465
Southard, S. C. V, 530
Southard, Sarah E. III, 511
Southbe, Joan II, 422
Southbe, John II, 422
Southbe, William II, 422
Southbee, Elizabeth II, 452
Southbee, Wm. II, 452
Southby, John II, 422
Southby, William II, 422
Southeby, Elizabeth II, 657
Southeby, John II, 657
Southeby, Patience II, 657
Southeby, Wm. II, 657
Southerd, Forester E. V, 432
Southerd, James V, 432
Southerd, Lillian A. V, 432
Southerd, Mary J. V, 432
Southerland, Andrew III, 296
Southerland, Andrew III, 365
Southerland, Ann VI, 563
Southerland, James III, 296
Southerland, James, Jr. III, 296
Southerland, John III, 296
Southerland, John P. III, 296
Southerland, Maria III, 296
Southerland, Maria III, 365
Southerland, Phebe III, 296
Southerland, Phebe III, 365
Southerland, Phebe Jane III, 296
Southerland, Sarah R. III, 243
Southerland, Uriah III, 296
Southerland, William III, 296
Southerly, Susanna V, 590
Southerne, Edward VI, 11
Southgate, Esther P. V, 123
Southgate, Esther Welch V, 123
Southwick, Abraham L. IV, 1379
Southwick, Albert IV, 1379
Southwick, Ann II, 260
Southwick, Ann II, 263
Southwick, Ann D. III, 141
Southwick, Anna L. III, 296
Southwick, Deborah IV, 1379
Southwick, Elizabeth II, 224
Southwick, Elizabeth II, 263
Southwick, Elizabeth IV, 1379
Southwick, Elizabeth S. III, 296
Southwick, Elizabeth Smart III, 221
Southwick, Ezra IV, 1379
Southwick, Ford IV, 1379
Southwick, Geo. William III, 296
Southwick, George William III, 296
Southwick, Hannah II, 235
Southwick, Hannah II, 263
Southwick, Hannah Lapham IV, 1379
Southwick, James II, 185
Southwick, James II, 214
Southwick, James II, 263
Southwick, Jonathan II, 263
Southwick, Joseph II, 263
Southwick, Josiah II, 263
Southwick, Josias, Jr. II, 263
Southwick, Julia A. III, 438
Southwick, Julia A. III, 447
Southwick, Julia Ann III, 296
Southwick, Laura IV, 1379
Southwick, Maria IV, 1379
Southwick, Mary II, 185
Southwick, Mary II, 263
Southwick, Mary III, 296
Southwick, Mary III, 309
Southwick, Mary Jane IV, 1379
Southwick, Matilda III, 296
Southwick, Phebe II, 185
Southwick, Phebe II, 263
Southwick, Rachel II, 214
Southwick, Rachel II, 263
Southwick, Rachel II, 277
Southwick, Rebecca II, 263
Southwick, Rebecca II, 534
Southwick, Rebecca II, 657
Southwick, Ruth II, 212
Southwick, Ruth II, 263
Southwick, Samuel II, 263
Southwick, Sarah II, 214
Southwick, Sarah II, 263
Southwick, Smith A. IV, 1379
Southwick, Solomon II, 260
Southwick, Solomon II, 263
Southwick, Solomon II, 277
Southwick, Thos. M. III, 296
Southwood, Edward VI, 447
Southwood, Susannah VI, 437
Southwood, Susannah VI, 447
Southworth, Abram L. IV, 1379
Southworth, Wilbur D. V, 711
Southworth, Wilbur S. V, 711
Soward, Elisha V, 203
Soward, T. J. V, 203
Sowell, Jane VI, 855
Sowell, Mary VI, 841
Sowell, Nancy VI, 841
Sowell, Phillip VI, 855
Sowen, Lydia II, 422
Sower, Lydia II, 422
Sowers, Bell V, 1019
Sowers, Julie V, 1019
Sowers, Thomas V, 1019
Sowle, Eliza M. III, 296
Sowle, Eliza M. III, 352
Sowle, George IV, 1379
Sowle, Jethro III, 296
Sowle, Jethro III, 352
Sowle, Mary III, 296
Sowle, Mary III, 352
Sowles, Florence Lucile V, 644
Sowles, Lucile V, 644
Soxton, Susan M. IV, 1339
Spackman, Adaline II, 820
Spackman, Adaline II, 887
Spackman, Adaline II, 924
Spackman, Ann II, 896
Spackman, Ann II, 924
Spackman, Anna II, 924
Spackman, Anna C. II, 821
Spackman, Catharine II, 887
Spackman, Catharine Moore II, 924
Spackman, Chalkley II, 820
Spackman, Chalkley II, 821
Spackman, Chalkley II, 887
Spackman, Chalkley II, 924
Spackman, Deborah II, 657
Spackman, Deborah II, 820
Spackman, Deborah II, 924
Spackman, Ellis L. II, 924
Spackman, Ellis Leeds II, 887
Spackman, Ellis Leeds II, 924
Spackman, George II, 657
Spackman, George II, 768
Spackman, Henry C. II, 924
Spackman, Henry Clay II, 821
Spackman, Joseph II, 657
Spackman, Martha II, 870
Spackman, Mary M. II, 924
Spackman, Mary Master II, 821
Spackman, Samuel II, 657
Spackman, Samuel II, 821
Spackman, Samuel II, 924
Spackman, Samuel C. II, 924
Spackman, Susan A. II, 924
Spackman, Susan Ann II, 821
Spackman, Thomas II, 657
Spackman, Thos. II, 820
Spackman, Thos. II, 924
Spackman, Wm. M. II, 924
Spackman, Wm. Master II, 821
Spahlinger, Geo. IV, 1339
Spahlinger, George IV, 1339
Spahlinger, Mary IV, 1339
Spahlinger, Walter IV, 1339
Spaid, Mary V, 711
Spain, Clarey I, 997
Spain, Clary I, 989
Spain, Clary I, 997
Spain, Elijah IV, 1294
Spain, Emily I, 997
Spain, Lizie IV, 1294
Spain, Thomas I, 997
Spalding, ??? I, 947
Spalding, ??? I, 949
Spalding, Ann IV, 433
Spalding, Charles W. IV, 434
Spalding, David IV, 434
Spalding, Elizabeth IV, 434
Spalding, Elizabeth J. IV, 433
Spalding, Elizabeth J. IV, 440
Spalding, Huchin IV, 434
Spalding, Lydia Ann IV, 434
Spalding, Maribah IV, 434
Spalding, Rosanna II, 1080
Spalding, Rosanna II, 1081
Spalding, Roxie I, 947
Spalding, Roxie I, 949
Spalding, Ruth IV, 434
Spalding, Sarah IV, 434
Spalding, Thomas IV, 434
Spalding, William IV, 433
Spalding, William IV, 434
Spangler, Jane V, 360
Spar, John V, 1020
Sparger, Allen I, 901
Sparger, Edith Anne I, 901
Sparger, Hiram I, 901
Sparger, Jane I, 901
Sparger, Job I, 901
Sparger, John I, 901
Sparger, Katharine IV, 1146
Sparger, Rachel V, 279
Sparger, Rachel V, 311
Sparger, Wm. Anderson I, 901
Sparks, ??? III, 28
Sparks, ??? III, 296
Sparks, Abi V, 489
Sparks, Abi V, 530
Sparks, Abi V, 711
Sparks, Aby V, 530
Sparks, Anna Irene III, 28
Sparks, Anna Irene III, 296
Sparks, Benjamin V, 530
Sparks, Charles VI, 1006
Sparks, Ethel Rebecca V, 711
Sparks, Frances Farquhar V, 530
Sparks, Francis Farquhar V, 530
Sparks, George IV, 1186
Sparks, Isaac IV, 1294
Sparks, Josiah W. V, 711
Sparks, Julia VI, 996
Sparks, Laura B. V, 711
Sparks, Mary IV, 127
Sparks, Mary IV, 133
Sparks, Rachel II, 100
Sparks, Rachel II, 103
Sparks, Richard II, 448
Sparks, Sarah II, 556
Sparks, Sarah II, 657
Sparks, Sarah IV, 81
Sparks, Sarah IV, 110
Sparks, William VI, 996
Sparrow, Anna Mary IV, 278
Sparrow, Anthony II, 657
Sparrow, Benjamin IV, 278
Sparrow, Clarabelle IV, 278
Sparrow, Eliza B. IV, 278
Sparrow, Elizabeth IV, 278
Sparrow, J. IV, 278
Sparrow, John II, 657
Sparrow, John C. IV, 278
Sparrow, S. Vincent IV, 278
Sparrow, Sarah E. IV, 278
Spauge, Lydia III, 35
Spaugh, G. D. I, 949
Spaulding, C. E. V, 1020
Spaulding, Eugene V, 1020
Spaulding, Hazel V, 1020
Spaulding, John IV, 1264
Spaulding, Louisa P. IV, 551
Spaulding, Mary E. III, 238
Spaulding, Rosa V, 1020
Spaulding, Ruth V, 1020
Spaulding, Tradar V, 1020
Speakman, Ann VI, 339
Speakman, Ann VI, 355
Speakman, Anna J. II, 844
Speakman, Anna J. II, 925
Speakman, Anna Maria II, 867
Speakman, Anna Walter II, 925
Speakman, Bethenia VI, 996
Speakman, Betty IV, 159
Speakman, Betty IV, 278
Speakman, Caroline II, 785
Speakman, Caroline II, 844
Speakman, Caroline II, 924
Speakman, Caroline II, 925
Speakman, Catharine II, 1028
Speakman, Deborah II, 657
Speakman, Ebenezer VI, 339
Speakman, Ebenezer VI, 355
Speakman, Edward II, 924
Speakman, Edward II, 925
Speakman, Eliza R. VI, 417
Speakman, Elizabeth VI, 339
Speakman, Elizabeth VI, 355
Speakman, Emma II, 867
Speakman, Emma II, 925
Speakman, Emma G. II, 925
Speakman, Emma W. II, 867
Speakman, Enoch H. VI, 779
Speakman, Esther II, 657
Speakman, Esther II, 924
Speakman, Esther II, 1028
Speakman, Esther IV, 110
Speakman, Esther IV, 698
Speakman, George II, 657
Speakman, Hannah II, 422
Speakman, Hannah II, 543
Speakman, Hannah II, 657
Speakman, Hannah II, 924
Speakman, Hannah E. II, 865
Speakman, Hannah E. II, 924
Speakman, Hannah E. II, 925
Speakman, Hannah Edwards II, 821
Speakman, Horace II, 821
Speakman, Jacob VI, 339
Speakman, James IV, 1186
Speakman, Jesse VI, 355
Speakman, Jesse VI, 954
Speakman, Jesse VI, 960
Speakman, John II, 544
Speakman, John II, 657
Speakman, John II, 1028
Speakman, John III, 296
Speakman, John A. VI, 960
Speakman, John A. VI, 996
Speakman, John Dennis II, 1028

Speakman, Joseph II, 657
Speakman, Joseph II, 1028
Speakman, Joshua VI, 355
Speakman, Kesiah II, 657
Speakman, Kezia II, 1028
Speakman, Keziah II, 657
Speakman, Keziah II, 1028
Speakman, Lydia II, 422
Speakman, Lydia II, 543
Speakman, Lydia II, 657
Speakman, Lydia II, 1028
Speakman, Malinda VI, 960
Speakman, Martha III, 508
Speakman, Mary II, 422
Speakman, Mary II, 657
Speakman, Mary II, 1028
Speakman, Mary R. VI, 416
Speakman, Mary R. VI, 417
Speakman, Mary R. VI, 447
Speakman, Nancy VI, 954
Speakman, Nettie II, 925
Speakman, Phebe VI, 355
Speakman, Pheby VI, 339
Speakman, Samuel II, 657
Speakman, Sarah II, 422
Speakman, Sarah II, 657
Speakman, Thomas II, 657
Speakman, Thomas VI, 339
Speakman, Thomas H. II, 924
Speakman, Thos. II, 844
Speakman, Thos. A. II, 865
Speakman, Thos. A. II, 925
Speakman, Thos. H. II, 844
Speakman, Thos. H. II, 865
Speakman, Thos. H. II, 924
Speakman, Thos. H. II, 925
Speakman, Thos. Henry II, 821
Speakman, Townsend II, 422
Speakman, Townsend II, 543
Speakman, Townsend II, 657
Speakman, Townsend II, 821
Speakman, Townsend II, 1028
Speakman, Virginia J. II, 865
Speakman, Virginia J. II, 924
Speakman, Virginia J. II, 925
Speakman, Wd. Hannah II, 544
Speakman, Wd. Hannah II, 821
Speakman, Wilson VI, 417
Speakman, Wm. G. II, 867
Speakman, Wm. J., Jr. II, 867
Spear, Ada V, 644
Spear, Ada Emily V, 711
Spear, Almeda V, 644
Spear, Carey V, 644
Spear, Carey V, 711
Spear, Cleo F. V, 644
Spear, Doriene White IV, 1339
Spear, Edna Emily V, 711
Spear, Edna Emily V, 720
Spear, Effie Jane V, 644
Spear, Eli V, 644
Spear, Eliza V, 203
Spear, Eliza V, 637
Spear, Eliza V, 644
Spear, Esther A. V, 644
Spear, Fannie IV, 1339
Spear, Frank V, 644
Spear, Fred V, 711
Spear, Fred V, 716
Spear, Freda V, 711
Spear, Freda Louise V, 711
Spear, Grace Ann V, 644
Spear, Hannah V, 792
Spear, Henry V, 203
Spear, Hugh V, 711
Spear, James V, 203
Spear, James V, 644
Spear, John V, 644
Spear, John Dana V, 711
Spear, John F. V, 644
Spear, Joseph Russell IV, 1339
Spear, Leon Spray V, 644
Spear, Leonedas E. V, 644
Spear, Leonidas E. V, 644
Spear, Louisa V, 711
Spear, Louisa V, 716
Spear, Louise Turner V, 644
Spear, Louise Turner V, 711
Spear, Lydia V, 203
Spear, M. C. IV, 1339
Spear, Martha J. V, 644
Spear, Mary V, 203
Spear, Mary V, 644
Spear, Mary E. V, 644
Spear, Mildred Jeanne V, 711
Spear, Minnie V, 644
Spear, Minnie V, 711
Spear, Paul Stanley V, 644
Spear, Ray Cyrus V, 644
Spear, S. Orricy V, 644
Spear, Samuel V, 203
Spear, Samuel V, 644
Spear, Solomon Carey V, 644
Spear, Thos. L. V, 644
Spear, Wilbur V, 711
Spear, Wm. V, 644
Spear, Zeph V, 644
Spearman, Elizabeth VI, 832
Spearman, John VI, 832
Spears, Abram I, 932
Spears, Ada V, 644
Spears, Ada V, 720
Spears, Ada Emily V, 711
Spears, Betty I, 932
Spears, Carey V, 644
Spears, Carey V, 711
Spears, Elizabeth V, 644
Spears, Elizabeth M. I, 932
Spears, Fannie IV, 497
Spears, Freda V, 711
Spears, Freda Louise V, 667
Spears, Freda Louise V, 711
Spears, Hugh V, 711
Spears, Isaac I, 571
Spears, Isaac I, 1016
Spears, John Dana V, 711
Spears, Leason I, 901
Spears, Lydia I, 539
Spears, Lydia I, 571
Spears, Lydia I, 901
Spears, Lydia I, 1016
Spears, Margery V, 279
Spears, Mary I, 571
Spears, Mary I, 1016
Spears, Mildred Jeanne V, 711
Spears, Minnie V, 644
Spears, Minnie V, 711
Spears, Moses Evans I, 571
Spears, Moses Evans I, 1016
Spears, Nancy I, 932
Spears, Robert I, 571
Spears, Robert I, 1016
Spears, Samuel I, 901
Spears, Wilbur V, 667
Spears, Wilbur V, 711
Spears, Wm. V, 644
Spece, Lewis VI, 815
Specer, Martha VI, 810
Speck, Asenath IV, 787
Speck, Harry IV, 787
Speck, Harry H. IV, 787
Speck, Lillie B. IV, 787
Speck, Lilly IV, 787
Speck, Mary IV, 799
Speck, Mary IV, 843
Speck, Moses S. IV, 787
Speck, Phebe S. IV, 763
Speck, Phebe S. IV, 786
Speck, Vera IV, 787
Speddy, Mable IV, 1339
Speece, Allie IV, 1294
Speece, Archer VI, 828
Speece, Archibald VI, 848
Speece, Archibald VI, 855
Speece, Catharine VI, 855
Speece, Charles VI, 832
Speece, Conrad VI, 858
Speece, Conrad VI, 998
Speece, Conrade VI, 843
Speece, Conrade VI, 855
Speece, Eliza VI, 855
Speece, Emily M. VI, 828
Speece, Frances R. VI, 855
Speece, Frederick VI, 828
Speece, George IV, 1294
Speece, George VI, 855
Speece, George W. VI, 816
Speece, Isabella VI, 828
Speece, Isabella VI, 855
Speece, Jemima VI, 796
Speece, Jemima VI, 855
Speece, Jemima A. VI, 855
Speece, John VI, 855
Speece, Joseph IV, 1294
Speece, Lewis VI, 816
Speece, Lewis VI, 831
Speece, Lewis VI, 855
Speece, Lewis VI, 858
Speece, Lewis VI, 862
Speece, Lewis VI, 956
Speece, Lewis VI, 982
Speece, Lewis VI, 996
Speece, Maggie IV, 1294
Speece, Margaret VI, 843
Speece, Mary VI, 831
Speece, Mary F. VI, 828
Speece, Nathan VI, 855
Speece, Peter VI, 848
Speece, Peter VI, 855
Speece, Rachel VI, 855
Speece, Sally VI, 855
Speece, Sarah VI, 816
Speece, Sarah VI, 996
Speece, Sophia A. VI, 858
Speece, Susannah VI, 998
Speece, Washington VI, 816
Speece, William F. VI, 855
Speed, John VI, 192
Speed, John VI, 212
Speed, Joseph VI, 141
Speed, Joseph VI, 143
Speelman, Elvira V, 764
Speelman, L. D. V, 764
Speelman, Levi Augustus V, 764
Speer, Ann V, 203
Speer, Anna V, 203
Speer, Benjamin H. V, 203
Speer, Cleo F. V, 203
Speer, Eliza V, 203
Speer, Esther A. V, 644
Speer, Frank V, 644
Speer, Grace V, 203
Speer, Grace A. V, 203
Speer, Grace Anna V, 203
Speer, Henry V, 203
Speer, James V, 203
Speer, James V, 644
Speer, John V, 203
Speer, John F. V, 203
Speer, John F. V, 205
Speer, John F. V, 628
Speer, John F. V, 644
Speer, John T. V, 203
Speer, Leason I, 901
Speer, Leon V, 203
Speer, Leon Spray V, 203
Speer, Leonedas E. V, 644
Speer, Leonidas V, 203
Speer, Leonidas E. V, 203
Speer, Lydia I, 901
Speer, Lydia I, 1016
Speer, Lydia V, 203
Speer, Lydia M. V, 203
Speer, Margaret III, 123
Speer, Margaret III, 199
Speer, Martha J. V, 203
Speer, Mary V, 203
Speer, Mary V, 205
Speer, Mary V, 644
Speer, Mary E. V, 203
Speer, Mary E. V, 628
Speer, Mary E. V, 644
Speer, Mattie V, 203
Speer, Mattie E. V, 203
Speer, Nancy V, 203
Speer, Nancy V, 205
Speer, Orricy V, 203
Speer, Paul Stanley V, 203
Speer, Ralph V, 203
Speer, Ray V, 203
Speer, Ray Cyrus V, 203
Speer, S. Orricy V, 203
Speer, Samuel I, 901
Speer, Samuel I, 1016
Speer, Samuel V, 203
Speer, Zeph V, 644
Speers, Samuel I, 1037
Speese, Allie IV, 1294
Speese, Maggie IV, 1294
Speicher, Katharine IV, 1339
Speiden, ??? VI, 761
Speiden, ??? VI, 779
Speiden, John VI, 779
Speiden, Lucy VI, 779
Speiden, Mary P. VI, 779
Spell, August IV, 1043
Spell, Mary IV, 1043
Spellman, Albert V, 465
Spellman, Bertha V, 203
Spellman, Ella V, 203
Spellman, Elsie V, 203
Spellman, Gay V, 465
Spellman, Guy V, 465
Spellman, Hattie V, 203
Spellman, Hugh V, 465
Spellman, James V, 1020
Spellman, Margaret V, 465
Spellman, Mildred V, 675
Spellman, Mildred V, 711
Spellman, Walter V, 675
Spellman, Walter V, 711
Spence, Andrew VI, 1002
Spence, Andrew F. VI, 996
Spence, Edna V, 279
Spence, Elenor VI, 996
Spence, J. F. V, 279
Spence, James VI, 912
Spence, James VI, 996
Spence, John II, 422
Spence, Lucy VI, 996
Spence, Lydia II, 657
Spence, M. Etta V, 279
Spence, M. Etta V, 465
Spence, Mary E. V, 465
Spence, Mary Jessup I, 75
Spence, Minnie V, 279
Spence, Rachel II, 422
Spence, Rachel II, 633
Spence, Rachel II, 657
Spence, Samuel II, 422
Spence, Wm. V, 465
Spencer, ??? III, 192
Spencer, ??? VI, 726
Spencer, Aaron Addison I, 753
Spencer, Abigail I, 75
Spencer, Abigail I, 770
Spencer, Abner IV, 159
Spencer, Abner IV, 325
Spencer, Abner IV, 332
Spencer, Abner IV, 340
Spencer, Abner IV, 352
Spencer, Abner IV, 440
Spencer, Abner IV, 1065
Spencer, Abner IV, 1077
Spencer, Abner VI, 707
Spencer, Abraham II, 422
Spencer, Ada V, 124
Spencer, Ada V, 360
Spencer, Ada Sirona A. I, 753
Spencer, Adeline IV, 935
Spencer, Adeline IV, 995
Spencer, Adeliza I, 923
Spencer, Albert Henry V, 123
Spencer, Albert Sidney I, 753
Spencer, Alex N. III, 31
Spencer, Alice IV, 324
Spencer, Alice IV, 352
Spencer, Alice VI, 779
Spencer, Allan J. I, 75
Spencer, Allen Jay I, 44
Spencer, Allen Jay I, 75
Spencer, Almina J. V, 49
Spencer, Almina J. V, 124
Spencer, Althanissa IV, 1186
Spencer, Amanda J. I, 865
Spencer, Amanda Jane I, 901
Spencer, Amie H. III, 296
Spencer, Amie M. III, 192
Spencer, Amy IV, 352
Spencer, Amy IV, 355
Spencer, Amy IV, 440
Spencer, Amy IV, 763
Spencer, Amy IV, 995
Spencer, Amy D. IV, 1163
Spencer, Amy D. IV, 1186
Spencer, Amy Drucetta IV, 1223
Spencer, Amy Drusilla IV, 1186
Spencer, Amy Drusilla IV, 1209
Spencer, Amy Drusilla IV, 1223
Spencer, Ann I, 752
Spencer, Ann II, 821
Spencer, Ann II, 1080
Spencer, Ann IV, 159
Spencer, Ann IV, 325
Spencer, Ann IV, 330
Spencer, Ann IV, 332
Spencer, Ann IV, 346
Spencer, Ann IV, 352
Spencer, Ann IV, 436
Spencer, Ann IV, 440
Spencer, Ann IV, 546
Spencer, Ann IV, 1077
Spencer, Ann VI, 703
Spencer, Ann VI, 708
Spencer, Ann, Jr. VI, 561
Spencer, Ann, Jr. VI, 701
Spencer, Ann, Jr. VI, 707
Spencer, Anna II, 1087
Spencer, Anna II, 1089
Spencer, Anna IV, 440
Spencer, Anna IV, 551
Spencer, Anna IV, 579
Spencer, Anna IV, 594
Spencer, Anna G. IV, 594
Spencer, Anna Jane I, 753
Spencer, Anna Jane I, 770
Spencer, Anna L. III, 296
Spencer, Anna L. III, 297
Spencer, Anna Louisa III, 296
Spencer, Anna M. IV, 440
Spencer, Anna W. IV, 438
Spencer, Anna W. IV, 440
Spencer, Annie M. III, 296
Spencer, Arthur I, 641
Spencer, Arthur Abram V, 123
Spencer, Arthur T. I, 626
Spencer, Asa II, 821
Spencer, Asa IV, 347
Spencer, Asa IV, 352
Spencer, Asa IV, 440
Spencer, Asenath I, 662
Spencer, Asenath I, 752
Spencer, Asenath I, 768
Spencer, Asenath I, 769
Spencer, Asenath I, 770
Spencer, Asenath IV, 352
Spencer, Asenath IV, 1077
Spencer, Asenath C. I, 612
Spencer, Asenath C. I, 626
Spencer, Asenith I, 770
Spencer, Athamissa IV, 352
Spencer, Athanesa IV, 440
Spencer, Athanisa IV, 1186
Spencer, Athanissa IV, 1186
Spencer, Athanissa IV, 1198
Spencer, Athenissa IV, 1186
Spencer, Augusta E. V, 204
Spencer, Aurie E. I, 641
Spencer, Benjamin I, 769
Spencer, Benjamin I, 770
Spencer, Benjamin I, 865
Spencer, Benjamin I, 901
Spencer, Betcy IV, 159
Spencer, Betsey IV, 324
Spencer, Betsey IV, 352
Spencer, Betsey VI, 707
Spencer, Betsy IV, 352
Spencer, Beverley VI, 855
Spencer, Blanch V, 932
Spencer, Blanche V, 932
Spencer, Bulah E. IV, 1376
Spencer, Callie I, 1162
Spencer, Caroline I, 901
Spencer, Caroline V, 123
Spencer, Caroline V, 124
Spencer, Caroline V, 598
Spencer, Caroline E. I, 865
Spencer, Caroline J. V, 598
Spencer, Charles II, 716
Spencer, Charles II, 1087
Spencer, Charles II, 1089
Spencer, Charles VI, 829
Spencer, Charles A. V, 123
Spencer, Charles L. III, 296
Spencer, Charles S. III, 296
Spencer, Chris V. III, 296
Spencer, Chris. V. III, 297
Spencer, Christopher C. V. III, 296
Spencer, Christopher V. III, 296
Spencer, Clarence III, 297
Spencer, Cornelia D. I, 752
Spencer, Cornelia Delphinia I, 770
Spencer, Cyrus I, 75
Spencer, Cyrus I, 752
Spencer, Cyrus I, 770
Spencer, David IV, 156
Spencer, David IV, 159
Spencer, David IV, 346
Spencer, David IV, 352
Spencer, David VI, 707
Spencer, David VI, 815
Spencer, David VI, 851
Spencer, David VI, 855
Spencer, David P. IV, 159
Spencer, Deborah I, 752
Spencer, Deborah I, 760
Spencer, Deborah I, 769
Spencer, Deborah L. V, 486
Spencer, Deborah L. V, 530
Spencer, Della A. I, 759
Spencer, Della A. I, 770
Spencer, Delphenia Ann I, 753
Spencer, Delphina Cornelia I, 662
Spencer, Delphina Martitia I, 753
Spencer, Delphina Martitia I, 770
Spencer, Dora I, 626
Spencer, Dora I, 627
Spencer, Dora I, 641
Spencer, Dora Edith I, 753
Spencer, Edith Ann IV, 1186
Spencer, Edna V, 280
Spencer, Edwin IV, 159
Spencer, Eleanor IV, 159
Spencer, Eleanor Lee II, 893
Spencer, Eleanor Lee II, 925
Spencer, Elenor IV, 159
Spencer, Elias E. I, 752
Spencer, Elias E. I, 770
Spencer, Elias E. I, 923
Spencer, Elisha IV, 352
Spencer, Elisha IV, 440
Spencer, Eliza Ann I, 766
Spencer, Eliza Ann I, 770
Spencer, Eliza C. I, 258
Spencer, Eliza C. I, 753
Spencer, Eliza S. I, 258
Spencer, Elizabeth I, 752
Spencer, Elizabeth I, 769
Spencer, Elizabeth I, 865
Spencer, Elizabeth IV, 465
Spencer, Elizabeth IV, 497

encer, Elizabeth IV, 551
encer, Elizabeth VI, 851
encer, Elizabeth VI, 855
encer, Elizabeth E. I, 755
encer, Elizabeth E. I, 770
encer, Elizabeth Jane I, 770
encer, Ellen II, 949
encer, Ellen II, 1086
encer, Ellen II, 1089
encer, Ellen P. IV, 380
encer, Ellen P. IV, 440
pencer, Ellis Willets IV, 1186
pencer, Ellwood IV, 1186
pencer, Elmer V, 204
pencer, Elwood IV, 352
pencer, Elwood IV, 440
pencer, Elwood IV, 546
pencer, Elwood IV, 551
pencer, Elwood V, 960
pencer, Elwood R. IV, 1186
pencer, Elwood Ridgeway IV, 1186
pencer, Emily V, 711
pencer, Emma V, 711
pencer, Emma Talbott II, 966
pencer, Enoch I, 752
pencer, Enoch II, 1028
pencer, Enoch F. I, 770
pencer, Enoch Spencer II, 1012
pencer, Enos Christopher I, 753
Spencer, Ester II, 422
Spencer, Esther II, 422
Spencer, Esther II, 565
Spencer, Esther II, 657
Spencer, Eunice IV, 352
Spencer, Eunice IV, 440
Spencer, Eunice IV, 551
Spencer, Eunice IV, 1169
Spencer, Eunice IV, 1186
Spencer, Eunice V, 958
Spencer, Eunice V, 960
Spencer, Eunice Drusilla IV, 1186
Spencer, Eva V, 360
Spencer, Fay V, 204
Spencer, Flora Jane I, 753
Spencer, Florence I, 626
Spencer, Florence I, 641
Spencer, Frances V, 123
Spencer, Frances V, 598
Spencer, Francis V, 123
Spencer, Francis V, 598
Spencer, Frank V, 711
Spencer, Franklin V, 598
Spencer, Friend V, 435
Spencer, Geo. IV, 440
Spencer, Geo. IV, 551
Spencer, Geo. Clarkson IV, 1186
Spencer, Geo. D. III, 296
Spencer, George IV, 352
Spencer, George IV, 440
Spencer, George IV, 551
Spencer, George IV, 1169
Spencer, George IV, 1186
Spencer, George V, 204
Spencer, George V, 530
Spencer, George C. IV, 1186
Spencer, George Clarkson IV, 1186
Spencer, George E. V, 530
Spencer, George T. IV, 579
Spencer, George T. IV, 594
Spencer, George T. IV, 1186
Spencer, George Thomas IV, 1186
Spencer, H. III, 192
Spencer, Hannah I, 752
Spencer, Hannah I, 757
Spencer, Hannah I, 769
Spencer, Hannah I, 770
Spencer, Hannah I, 865
Spencer, Hannah I, 901
Spencer, Hannah IV, 352
Spencer, Hannah V, 435
Spencer, Hannah V, 530
Spencer, Hannah VI, 447
Spencer, Hannah VI, 563
Spencer, Hannah VI, 619
Spencer, Hannah VI, 628
Spencer, Hannah VI, 655
Spencer, Hannah VI, 682
Spencer, Hannah VI, 701
Spencer, Hannah VI, 707
Spencer, Hannah A. V, 360
Spencer, Hannah Ann V, 344
Spencer, Hannah Ann V, 360
Spencer, Hannah C. B. I, 865
Spencer, Hannah J. V, 960
Spencer, Hannah Jane IV, 352
Spencer, Hannah Jane IV, 1186
Spencer, Hannah Jane IV, 1192
Spencer, Harriet IV, 325
Spencer, Harriet IV, 332
Spencer, Harriet IV, 352
Spencer, Harriet IV, 440
Spencer, Harriet A. III, 296
Spencer, Harriett IV, 352
Spencer, Harriett IV, 1077
Spencer, Harry V, 530
Spencer, Harry E. V, 530
Spencer, Hattie E. I, 44
Spencer, Hattie E. I, 75
Spencer, Hattie Ellen I, 626
Spencer, Hattie Ellen I, 627
Spencer, Hester II, 422
Spencer, Hinson Clay IV, 1186
Spencer, Huysen Clay IV, 1186
Spencer, Inez I, 626
Spencer, Ineza Estelle I, 641
Spencer, Iowa May IV, 278
Spencer, Ira IV, 352
Spencer, Ira IV, 1077
Spencer, Ira L. IV, 1077
Spencer, Isaac I, 741
Spencer, Isaac I, 752
Spencer, Isaac I, 768
Spencer, Isaac I, 769
Spencer, Isaac I, 770
Spencer, Isaac IV, 450
Spencer, Isaac V, 432
Spencer, Isaac F. I, 752
Spencer, Isaac F. I, 770
Spencer, Isaac Millikan I, 753
Spencer, Isaac, Jr. I, 770
Spencer, James A. III, 296
Spencer, James T. I, 752
Spencer, James T. I, 770
Spencer, Jane IV, 450
Spencer, Jane C. V, 598
Spencer, Jane Caroline V, 598
Spencer, Jarrett II, 657
Spencer, John I, 752
Spencer, John I, 769
Spencer, John I, 770
Spencer, John II, 422
Spencer, John IV, 324
Spencer, John IV, 352
Spencer, John IV, 440
Spencer, John IV, 594
Spencer, John IV, 1186
Spencer, John V, 960
Spencer, John VI, 544
Spencer, John VI, 563
Spencer, John B. I, 752
Spencer, John B. I, 770
Spencer, John B. V, 530
Spencer, John D. IV, 1186
Spencer, John Edmund VI, 687
Spencer, John F. I, 752
Spencer, John F. I, 770
Spencer, John K. V, 123
Spencer, John K. V, 598
Spencer, John M. II, 893
Spencer, John M. II, 925
Spencer, John Q. IV, 1182
Spencer, John Q. IV, 1186
Spencer, Jonas IV, 352
Spencer, Jonathan II, 966
Spencer, Jonathan IV, 159
Spencer, Jonathan IV, 325
Spencer, Jonathan IV, 352
Spencer, Jonathan IV, 440
Spencer, Jonathan VI, 707
Spencer, Jonathan J. III, 296
Spencer, Joseph I, 752
Spencer, Joseph I, 760
Spencer, Joseph I, 769
Spencer, Joseph I, 770
Spencer, Joseph IV, 352
Spencer, Joseph IV, 355
Spencer, Joseph IV, 440
Spencer, Judeath VI, 851
Spencer, Judith VI, 521
Spencer, Judith VI, 526
Spencer, Judith VI, 563
Spencer, Judith VI, 757
Spencer, Judith VI, 779
Spencer, Judith VI, 794
Spencer, Judith VI, 849
Spencer, Keziah W. I, 865
Spencer, L. J. I, 641
Spencer, Laban I, 612
Spencer, Laban I, 626
Spencer, Laban I, 662
Spencer, Laban I, 752
Spencer, Laban I, 770
Spencer, Laben I, 769
Spencer, Lawrence J. I, 626
Spencer, Lawrence Jerome I, 641
Spencer, Lea IV, 278
Spencer, Leah IV, 156
Spencer, Leah IV, 159
Spencer, Leah IV, 346
Spencer, Leah IV, 352
Spencer, Leigh Thomas V, 598
Spencer, Lemuel I, 752
Spencer, Lemuel I, 753
Spencer, Lemuel I, 770
Spencer, Leonard V, 711
Spencer, Leota M. V, 432
Spencer, Lewis I, 752
Spencer, Lillie I, 626
Spencer, Lillie I, 627
Spencer, Lillie I, 641
Spencer, Lillie I, 642
Spencer, Lotty VI, 855
Spencer, Louisa IV, 352
Spencer, Louisa IV, 1172
Spencer, Louisa IV, 1186
Spencer, Louiza IV, 440
Spencer, Lyda G. IV, 393
Spencer, Lyda G. IV, 440
Spencer, Lydia II, 501
Spencer, Lydia II, 657
Spencer, Lydia IV, 324
Spencer, Lydia IV, 352
Spencer, Lydia IV, 355
Spencer, Lydia IV, 440
Spencer, Lydia IV, 1077
Spencer, Lydia IV, 1169
Spencer, Lydia IV, 1186
Spencer, Lydia VI, 544
Spencer, Lydia VI, 563
Spencer, Lydia VI, 687
Spencer, Lydia Ann IV, 325
Spencer, Lydia Ann IV, 352
Spencer, Lydia Ann IV, 440
Spencer, Lydia Ann IV, 1077
Spencer, Madison L. I, 752
Spencer, Madison L. I, 770
Spencer, Margaret I, 381
Spencer, Margaret I, 419
Spencer, Margaret VI, 539
Spencer, Margaret VI, 563
Spencer, Margaret VI, 682
Spencer, Margaret VI, 707
Spencer, Mariah IV, 440
Spencer, Martha V, 226
Spencer, Martha V, 280
Spencer, Martha Frances I, 770
Spencer, Martha Luezer I, 753
Spencer, Martha R. I, 752
Spencer, Martha Rhodema I, 622
Spencer, Martha Rhodena I, 612
Spencer, Mary I, 741
Spencer, Mary I, 752
Spencer, Mary I, 753
Spencer, Mary I, 762
Spencer, Mary I, 767
Spencer, Mary I, 769
Spencer, Mary I, 770
Spencer, Mary I, 865
Spencer, Mary I, 901
Spencer, Mary II, 422
Spencer, Mary II, 578
Spencer, Mary II, 657
Spencer, Mary II, 716
Spencer, Mary IV, 159
Spencer, Mary IV, 324
Spencer, Mary IV, 346
Spencer, Mary IV, 352
Spencer, Mary IV, 651
Spencer, Mary IV, 657
Spencer, Mary IV, 1182
Spencer, Mary IV, 1186
Spencer, Mary V, 204
Spencer, Mary VI, 561
Spencer, Mary VI, 562
Spencer, Mary VI, 563
Spencer, Mary VI, 707
Spencer, Mary A. I, 770
Spencer, Mary Ann I, 753
Spencer, Mary Ann I, 901
Spencer, Mary Ann IV, 159
Spencer, Mary Ann IV, 439
Spencer, Mary Ann IV, 440
Spencer, Mary Ann VI, 779
Spencer, Mary B. II, 716
Spencer, Mary B. III, 363
Spencer, Mary Carnelia I, 753
Spencer, Mary Caroline I, 753
Spencer, Mary E. III, 126
Spencer, Mary E. III, 296
Spencer, Mary E. V, 123
Spencer, Mary E. V, 598
Spencer, Mary Emma V, 123
Spencer, Mary Emma V, 124
Spencer, Mary F. I, 752
Spencer, Mary Frances I, 770
Spencer, Mary James II, 821
Spencer, Mary K. VI, 855
Spencer, Mary M. IV, 233
Spencer, Mary M. IV, 278
Spencer, Mary P. II, 947
Spencer, Mary P. II, 1087
Spencer, Mary P. II, 1089
Spencer, Mary R. IV, 594
Spencer, Mary R. V, 598
Spencer, Mary S. I, 753
Spencer, Maryan IV, 159
Spencer, Maurice V, 711
Spencer, May I, 770
Spencer, Melissa IV, 432
Spencer, Melissa IV, 440
Spencer, Mercy IV, 159
Spencer, Mercy IV, 352
Spencer, Mercy IV, 358
Spencer, Mercy VI, 707
Spencer, Michael I, 752
Spencer, Michael I, 753
Spencer, Miller IV, 465
Spencer, Morris IV, 352
Spencer, Moses VI, 829
Spencer, Moses VI, 855
Spencer, Mr. ??? IV, 1339
Spencer, Mrs. ??? IV, 1339
Spencer, Mrs. Albert IV, 1339
Spencer, N. L. I, 641
Spencer, Nancy I, 752
Spencer, Nancy I, 770
Spencer, Nancy VI, 855
Spencer, Nancy E. I, 752
Spencer, Nancy Elizabeth I, 770
Spencer, Nannie III, 31
Spencer, Nathan IV, 159
Spencer, Nathan IV, 325
Spencer, Nathan IV, 330
Spencer, Nathan IV, 332
Spencer, Nathan IV, 346
Spencer, Nathan IV, 352
Spencer, Nathan IV, 440
Spencer, Nathan VI, 563
Spencer, Nathan VI, 655
Spencer, Nathan VI, 682
Spencer, Nathan VI, 701
Spencer, Nathan VI, 703
Spencer, Nathan VI, 708
Spencer, Nathan F. I, 752
Spencer, Nathan F. I, 753
Spencer, Nathan F. I, 767
Spencer, Nathan F. I, 769
Spencer, Nathan F. I, 770
Spencer, Nathan L. I, 626
Spencer, Nathan L. I, 627
Spencer, Nathan L. I, 641
Spencer, Nathan L. I, 752
Spencer, Nathan L. I, 770
Spencer, Nathan, Jr. VI, 561
Spencer, Nathan, Jr. VI, 701
Spencer, Nathan, Jr. VI, 707
Spencer, Nathan, Sr. VI, 563
Spencer, Nathan, Sr. VI, 707
Spencer, Nettie II, 904
Spencer, Olive I, 923
Spencer, Oliver VI, 521
Spencer, Oliver VI, 526
Spencer, Oliver VI, 563
Spencer, Oliver VI, 779
Spencer, Oliver VI, 794
Spencer, Oliver M. V, 889
Spencer, Pertima Elmina I, 753
Spencer, Phebe IV, 159
Spencer, Phebe IV, 332
Spencer, Phebe IV, 352
Spencer, Phebe IV, 1175
Spencer, Phebe IV, 1186
Spencer, Phebe VI, 707
Spencer, Phebe Ann III, 296
Spencer, Phebe E. IV, 347
Spencer, Phebe E. IV, 352
Spencer, Polly VI, 829
Spencer, Priscilla IV, 763
Spencer, Priscilla IV, 766
Spencer, Priscilla V, 123
Spencer, Priscilla V, 598
Spencer, Rachel I, 752
Spencer, Rachel I, 769
Spencer, Rachel II, 588
Spencer, Rachel II, 657
Spencer, Rachel IV, 325
Spencer, Rachel IV, 340
Spencer, Rachel IV, 352
Spencer, Rachel IV, 440
Spencer, Rachel IV, 1065
Spencer, Rachel IV, 1077
Spencer, Rachel VI, 267
Spencer, Rachel VI, 669
Spencer, Rachel N. IV, 440
Spencer, Rachell II, 422
Spencer, Rebecca I, 752
Spencer, Rebecca I, 766
Spencer, Rebecca I, 770
Spencer, Rebecca II, 970
Spencer, Rebecca II, 1061
Spencer, Rebecca IV, 159
Spencer, Rebecca IV, 278
Spencer, Rebecca VI, 779
Spencer, Rebecca Luzena I, 753
Spencer, Rebecca Luzena I, 770
Spencer, Rebecca W. E. II, 737
Spencer, Rebecca W. E. II, 768
Spencer, Rheuben H. I, 752
Spencer, Richard II, 422
Spencer, Robert IV, 763
Spencer, Robert IV, 995
Spencer, Robert B. I, 753
Spencer, Robert B. I, 770
Spencer, Robert C. I, 752
Spencer, Robert C. I, 770
Spencer, Robert E. I, 641
Spencer, Robert E. I, 752
Spencer, Robert E. I, 770
Spencer, Robert Elwood I, 626
Spencer, Rodema I, 615
Spencer, Roxana Corrina I, 753
Spencer, Roxanna Corrinna I, 770
Spencer, Russell L. V, 124
Spencer, Russell S. V, 598
Spencer, Russell T. V, 123
Spencer, Russell T. V, 598
Spencer, Ruth I, 759
Spencer, Ruth I, 769
Spencer, Ruth C. I, 752
Spencer, Ruth E. I, 753
Spencer, Ruthanna II, 947
Spencer, S. Elizabeth II, 893
Spencer, S. Elizabeth II, 925
Spencer, Samuel II, 422
Spencer, Samuel II, 565
Spencer, Samuel II, 657
Spencer, Samuel IV, 159
Spencer, Samuel IV, 352
Spencer, Samuel VI, 563
Spencer, Samuel VI, 707
Spencer, Samuel A. III, 296
Spencer, Sarah I, 571
Spencer, Sarah I, 770
Spencer, Sarah I, 901
Spencer, Sarah I, 1037
Spencer, Sarah IV, 159
Spencer, Sarah IV, 325
Spencer, Sarah IV, 330
Spencer, Sarah IV, 352
Spencer, Sarah IV, 355
Spencer, Sarah IV, 357
Spencer, Sarah IV, 440
Spencer, Sarah IV, 450
Spencer, Sarah IV, 479
Spencer, Sarah IV, 497
Spencer, Sarah IV, 1123
Spencer, Sarah V, 764
Spencer, Sarah VI, 539
Spencer, Sarah VI, 563
Spencer, Sarah VI, 621
Spencer, Sarah VI, 640
Spencer, Sarah VI, 648
Spencer, Sarah VI, 667
Spencer, Sarah VI, 680
Spencer, Sarah VI, 682
Spencer, Sarah VI, 683
Spencer, Sarah VI, 685
Spencer, Sarah VI, 690
Spencer, Sarah VI, 703
Spencer, Sarah VI, 707
Spencer, Sarah VI, 708
Spencer, Sarah A. III, 296
Spencer, Sarah Ann II, 966
Spencer, Sarah E. V, 123
Spencer, Sarah E. V, 598
Spencer, Sarah, Jr. II, 1012
Spencer, Sarah, Jr. II, 1028
Spencer, Shubal G. I, 752
Spencer, Shubal G. I, 770
Spencer, Sidney IV, 465
Spencer, Sidney VI, 447
Spencer, Sidney Cornelius I, 626
Spencer, Sidney Cornelius I, 627
Spencer, Sophronia I, 758
Spencer, Sophronia I, 770
Spencer, Sophronia Eliza I, 753
Spencer, Strickland V, 598
Spencer, Susan I, 626
Spencer, Susan I, 627
Spencer, Susan I, 641
Spencer, Susan I, 798
Spencer, Susan I, 837
Spencer, Susan V, 435
Spencer, Susannah VI, 447
Spencer, Thomas VI, 212
Spencer, Thomas VI, 267
Spencer, Thomas VI, 779
Spencer, Thomas A. I, 753
Spencer, Thomas E. IV, 352
Spencer, Thomas F. VI, 855
Spencer, Thomas H. III, 296
Spencer, Thomas O. I, 752

Spencer, Thomas O. I, 770
Spencer, Thomas R. II, 1080
Spencer, Thomas R. V, 123
Spencer, Thomas R. V, 598
Spencer, Thomas R. J. K. V, 598
Spencer, Unice IV, 440
Spencer, Wd. Judith VI, 521
Spencer, Wd. Judith VI, 760
Spencer, Wd. Judith VI, 779
Spencer, Wd. Judith VI, 794
Spencer, Widow Judith VI, 526
Spencer, Widow Margaret VI, 707
Spencer, William I, 571
Spencer, William I, 901
Spencer, William I, 1037
Spencer, William IV, 440
Spencer, William IV, 1186
Spencer, William V, 764
Spencer, William VI, 708
Spencer, William D. III, 447
Spencer, William F. IV, 352
Spencer, William F. IV, 1186
Spencer, William Penn III, 296
Spencer, William T. IV, 438
Spencer, William T. IV, 440
Spencer, Winnie V, 280
Spencer, Wm. IV, 352
Spencer, Wm. VI, 648
Spencer, Wm. F. IV, 1175
Spencer, Wm. F. IV, 1186
Spencer, Wm. Penn III, 297
Spencer, Wyat B. I, 770
Spencer, Wyawt B. I, 752
Spencer-Lawrence, Judith VI, 518
Spencer-Lawrence, Judith VI, 522
Spencer-Lawrence, Judith VI, 579
Spencer-Lawrence, Judith VI, 754
Spencer-Nickols, Magaret VI, 655
Spencert, Eunice IV, 1163
Spencert, George IV, 1163
Spenser, Amanda Jane I, 891
Spenser, Amanda Jane I, 901
Spenser, Ann IV, 325
Spenser, Betsey IV, 325
Spenser, Caroline I, 873
Spenser, Caroline I, 901
Spenser, Hannah I, 882
Spenser, Hannah I, 901
Spenser, Mary I, 882
Spenser, Mary I, 901
Spenser, Mary Ann I, 894
Spenser, Mary Ann I, 901
Spenser, Nathan IV, 325
Speplen, L. E. IV, 1264
Sperey, Nancy I, 38
Sperry, Bertha IV, 1148
Sperry, Charles Herbert IV, 497
Sperry, Clency C. IV, 497
Sperry, Dora IV, 1148
Sperry, Harriett Virginia IV, 497
Sperry, James II, 657
Sperry, Martin IV, 1148
Spey, John II, 448
Spey, Mary II, 448
Sphar, Ann V, 203
Sphon, Jasper N. V, 1020
Spicer, Abigail III, 297
Spicer, Abraham III, 297
Spicer, Abraham VI, 855
Spicer, Dorothy Gladys III, 127
Spicer, Dorothy Gladys III, 297
Spicer, Earl IV, 1264
Spicer, Eber G. III, 297
Spicer, Eber Grant III, 297
Spicer, Ella IV, 1264
Spicer, Esther III, 297
Spicer, J. Lindley III, 127
Spicer, J. Lindley III, 297
Spicer, Jacob II, 84
Spicer, Jacob II, 100
Spicer, Jacob III, 297
Spicer, Lindley M. III, 297
Spicer, Lindley Milton III, 297
Spicer, Margaret IV, 278
Spicer, Martha III, 297
Spicer, Mary II, 84
Spicer, Mary II, 100
Spicer, Mary III, 297
Spicer, Meraler VI, 855
Spicer, Pearl IV, 1264
Spicer, Phebe III, 297
Spicer, Phoebe III, 127
Spicer, Phoebe III, 297
Spicer, R. Barkley IV, 278
Spicer, Samuel III, 297
Spicer, Sarah III, 297
Spicer, Sylvia II, 348
Spicer, William Jones IV, 278
Spickard, ??? VI, 996
Spickard, Henry VI, 996
Spicker, Frederick IV, 763
Spickler, James IV, 763
Spickler, Lulu IV, 763
Spickler, Malisa IV, 763
Spiecher, Katharine IV, 1339
Spiel, Hannah IV, 980
Spiel, Hannah IV, 995
Spielman, Seymore V, 432
Spier, Laura IV, 278
Spier, R. Barklay IV, 278
Spier, Vera III, 196
Spier, Wm. Jones Spier IV, 278
Spies, Laura IV, 278
Spikeman, Ann II, 422
Spikeman, Ann II, 657
Spikeman, Grace II, 422
Spikeman, Grace II, 653
Spikeman, Grace II, 657
Spikeman, Jesse VI, 996
Spikeman, Mary II, 422
Spikeman, Mary II, 490
Spikeman, Mary II, 657
Spikeman, Randal II, 657
Spikeman, Randall II, 657
Spikeman, Randolph II, 422
Spikeman, Randolph II, 490
Spikeman, Randolph II, 653
Spikeman, Randolph II, 657
Spikeman, Sally VI, 996
Spiker, Florence IV, 763
Spiker, Fred IV, 763
Spiker, Frederick IV, 763
Spiker, George IV, 763
Spiker, Margaret IV, 763
Spiker, Mary IV, 763
Spiker, Pearl E. A. IV, 763
Spikman, Ann II, 607
Spikman, Ann II, 657
Spikman, Randal II, 607
Spikman, Randal II, 657
Spikman, Randall II, 657
Spiller, George VI, 855
Spiller, Jemima VI, 855
Spillett, Mary M. III, 265
Spillman, Arnold Dolder II, 1059
Spillman, Arnold Dolder II, 1061
Spillman, E. T. I, 921
Spillman, Emily II, 1059
Spillman, Emily II, 1061
Spillman, Henry J. II, 1059
Spillman, Henry J. II, 1061
Spillman, Marguerite Shoemaker II, 1059
Spillman, Marguerite Shoemaker II, 1061
Spink, Eliza III, 61
Spink, Eliza III, 297
Spink, Katherine III, 61
Spink, Katherine III, 297
Spink, Thomas H. III, 61
Spink, Thomas H. III, 297
Spinks, Martin V, 711
Spinner, Jesse VI, 923
Spinner, Jesse VI, 992
Spinner, Jesse VI, 996
Spinner, Louisa C. VI, 923
Spinner, Lucinda VI, 996
Spinner, Martha D. VI, 995
Spinner, Nancy VI, 996
Spira, Sarah IV, 278
Spitler, Ralph V, 764
Spitler, Viola V, 764
Spivey, Abba I, 297
Spivey, Abba I, 318
Spivey, Abigail I, 297
Spivey, Abigail I, 308
Spivey, Abigail I, 318
Spivey, Becca I, 297
Spivey, Becca I, 318
Spivey, Charity I, 297
Spivey, Charity I, 307
Spivey, Charity I, 318
Spivey, Daughtry Winson I, 18
Spivey, Elizabeth I, 297
Spivey, Elvin L. I, 18
Spivey, Ephraim I, 297
Spivey, Ethel I, 217
Spivey, Exum I, 297
Spivey, John I, 297
Spivey, John I, 308
Spivey, John I, 318
Spivey, Lewis Lee I, 18
Spivey, Lucy Virginia I, 18
Spivey, Margaret E. I, 18
Spivey, Margaret E. I, 29
Spivey, Miriam I, 297
Spivey, Nancy I, 18
Spivey, Nancy I, 75
Spivey, Nancy Marie I, 18
Spivey, Ruth Amelia I, 18
Spivey, Sarah I, 211
Spivey, Warren I, 75
Spivey, Warren W. I, 18
Spivey, Warren W. I, 29
Spivey, William I, 18
Spivey, William Jesse I, 18
Spivy, ??? VI, 86
Spivy, Ann E. VI, 68
Spivy, Ann E. VI, 86
Spivy, Annie VI, 86
Spivy, Dred VI, 86
Spivy, Jeremiah VI, 68
Spivy, Jeremiah VI, 86
Spivy, Jerusha VI, 68
Spivy, Jerusha VI, 86
Spivy, Nancy A. VI, 69
Spivy, Nancy A. VI, 86
Spivy, Nancy A. VI, 91
Spivy, Onnie VI, 86
Splawn, Mary M. VI, 708
Splawn, Mary M. VI, 711
Splawn, Mary M. VI, 713
Splawn, Walter VI, 708
Splawn, Walter M. W. VI, 713
Spohn, Cath. J. A. III, 290
Spohn, Oscar V, 530
Spond, Clara V, 530
Spond, Oscar V, 530
Sponsler, Lucinda V, 862
Spoon, Cylla I, 936
Spoon, E. J. I, 949
Spoon, Elizabeth I, 933
Spoon, Ernest Greeley I, 933
Spoon, James I, 933
Spoon, Olive I, 892
Spoon, Olive I, 901
Spooner, Sarah VI, 673
Spooner, Sarah VI, 681
Spottswood, Gov. ??? VI, 94
Spradlin, Abner VI, 996
Spradlin, Amanda VI, 996
Spradlin, Ann Eliza VI, 958
Spradlin, Calvin VI, 922
Spradlin, Calvin VI, 932
Spradlin, Calvin VI, 996
Spradlin, Charles VI, 990
Spradlin, Charles H. VI, 996
Spradlin, Cleopatra VI, 996
Spradlin, Emily VI, 996
Spradlin, Finetta VI, 951
Spradlin, James VI, 958
Spradlin, John VI, 951
Spradlin, John VI, 960
Spradlin, Julia VI, 997
Spradlin, Mary E. VI, 960
Spradlin, Medon VI, 953
Spradlin, Sarah VI, 996
Spradlin, Sarah F. VI, 953
Spradlin, Silas VI, 996
Spradlin, William VI, 960
Spradlin, William VI, 996
Spradling, Abner VI, 959
Spradling, Abner VI, 996
Spradling, Agness VI, 996
Spradling, Amanda VI, 996
Spradling, Calvin VI, 996
Spradling, Charles H. VI, 996
Spradling, Cleopatra VI, 996
Spradling, Edward VI, 996
Spradling, Edwin VI, 996
Spradling, Emily VI, 996
Spradling, Green B. VI, 960
Spradling, Green B. VI, 996
Spradling, James VI, 960
Spradling, James VI, 996
Spradling, James A. VI, 996
Spradling, Jane VI, 999
Spradling, Jas. VI, 996
Spradling, John, Jr. VI, 996
Spradling, Judith VI, 996
Spradling, Julia VI, 997
Spradling, Julina VI, 960
Spradling, Lemira B. VI, 996
Spradling, Lucy VI, 996
Spradling, Mary Jane VI, 960
Spradling, Meador VI, 996
Spradling, Nancy VI, 996
Spradling, Nehemiah VI, 996
Spradling, Pegga VI, 996
Spradling, Polly VI, 959
Spradling, Polly VI, 996
Spradling, Rachel VI, 959
Spradling, Rhoda E. VI, 996
Spradling, Sally VI, 909
Spradling, Sarah VI, 882
Spradling, Sarah VI, 959
Spradling, Sarah VI, 996
Spradling, Sarah Ann VI, 960
Spradling, Silas VI, 996
Spradling, Thomas VI, 960
Spradling, Thomas VI, 996
Spradling, Thomas VI, 999
Spradling, William VI, 909
Spradling, William VI, 996
Spradling, William H. VI, 996
Sprag, Ralph II, 448
Spragg, Elizabeth S. III, 448
Spragg, Hannah III, 448
Spragg, Micah III, 448
Spragg, Rowland III, 448
Sprague, Alfred III, 434
Sprague, Alfred III, 447
Sprague, Ann III, 322
Sprague, Anna IV, 1294
Sprague, Caroline III, 448
Sprague, Caroline M. III, 322
Sprague, Cornelia V, 711
Sprague, Ebeneezer II, 768
Sprague, Eliza Jane III, 434
Sprague, Eliza Jane III, 447
Sprague, Elizabeth III, 448
Sprague, Elizabeth III, 472
Sprague, Elizabeth S. III, 448
Sprague, Enos T. III, 297
Sprague, Esther V, 711
Sprague, Frankie V, 711
Sprague, Franklin IV, 1294
Sprague, George V, 711
Sprague, George B. V, 711
Sprague, Grace IV, 1294
Sprague, Hannah III, 448
Sprague, Hannah III, 473
Sprague, Hannah III, 474
Sprague, Hannah M. IV, 1294
Sprague, Howard R. V, 711
Sprague, Jacob III, 448
Sprague, Jacob III, 472
Sprague, James IV, 1294
Sprague, John III, 322
Sprague, Karl L. V, 711
Sprague, Louise V, 711
Sprague, Lydia III, 297
Sprague, Matilda IV, 110
Sprague, Matilda IV, 112
Sprague, Maude M. V, 711
Sprague, Micah III, 448
Sprague, Micah III, 473
Sprague, Michael III, 474
Sprague, Myrtle V, 711
Sprague, Rowland III, 448
Spratly, Peggy Margaret VI, 121
Spratly, Peggy Margaret VI, 124
Spray, ??? V, 598
Spray, Abner I, 1058
Spray, Ada May V, 598
Spray, Allen V, 204
Spray, Allen V, 205
Spray, Alva G. V, 204
Spray, Amos V, 204
Spray, Amos V, 205
Spray, Anna I, 1162
Spray, Anna M. I, 1162
Spray, Benjamin V, 205
Spray, Bertha V, 530
Spray, Bertha V, 711
Spray, Catharine C. V, 598
Spray, Catharine C. V, 711
Spray, Catherine C. V, 598
Spray, Charity I, 1058
Spray, Charity V, 166
Spray, Charity V, 182
Spray, Charity V, 204
Spray, Charity V, 205
Spray, Charity V, 598
Spray, Charles Franklin V, 204
Spray, Christopher V, 181
Spray, Christopher V, 204
Spray, Christopher V, 205
Spray, Clara Emma V, 204
Spray, Clara Emma V, 205
Spray, Dinah I, 1024
Spray, Dinah I, 1056
Spray, Dinah I, 1058
Spray, Dinah I, 1059
Spray, Dinah IV, 60
Spray, Dinah V, 42
Spray, Dinah V, 124
Spray, Dinah V, 182
Spray, Dinah V, 204
Spray, Dinah V, 205
Spray, Dinah V, 208
Spray, Dinah V, 211
Spray, Dinah V, 212
Spray, Eli N. V, 204
Spray, Elias V, 205
Spray, Elihu V, 189
Spray, Elihu V, 204
Spray, Elihu V, 205
Spray, Elizabeth I, 1059
Spray, Elizabeth V, 181
Spray, Elizabeth V, 184
Spray, Elizabeth V, 204
Spray, Elizabeth V, 205
Spray, Elizabeth V, 211
Spray, Elizabeth V, 212
Spray, Elizabeth Ellen V, 204
Spray, Elizabeth Ellen V, 205
Spray, Enos V, 862
Spray, Esther I, 1058
Spray, Esther V, 160
Spray, Esther V, 204
Spray, Esther V, 205
Spray, Esther V, 212
Spray, Eunace V, 205
Spray, Eunice V, 124
Spray, Eunice V, 125
Spray, Eunice V, 204
Spray, Eunice Steddom V, 205
Spray, Eva V, 711
Spray, Hannah I, 1024
Spray, Hannah I, 1058
Spray, Hannah V, 164
Spray, Hannah V, 187
Spray, Hannah V, 189
Spray, Hannah V, 204
Spray, Hannah V, 205
Spray, Hannah A. V, 598
Spray, Hannah A. V, 711
Spray, Hannah Ann V, 598
Spray, Harlan V, 204
Spray, Henry I, 1058
Spray, Henry V, 124
Spray, Henry V, 187
Spray, Henry V, 204
Spray, Henry V, 205
Spray, Henry V, 515
Spray, Henry V, 530
Spray, Henry V, 711
Spray, Henry Wilson I, 1162
Spray, Ida M. V, 711
Spray, Ida May V, 598
Spray, Isaac V, 204
Spray, Isaac V, 205
Spray, Isaac V, 598
Spray, Isaac V, 711
Spray, Isaac T. V, 205
Spray, James I, 1058
Spray, James IV, 60
Spray, James V, 166
Spray, James V, 182
Spray, James V, 204
Spray, James V, 205
Spray, James V, 598
Spray, James V, 711
Spray, James, Jr. V, 205
Spray, Jehu V, 191
Spray, Jehu V, 204
Spray, Jehu V, 205
Spray, Jesse I, 1058
Spray, Jesse IV, 60
Spray, Jesse V, 31
Spray, Jesse V, 124
Spray, Jesse V, 125
Spray, Jesse V, 156
Spray, Jesse V, 160
Spray, Jesse V, 204
Spray, Jesse V, 205
Spray, Jesse Milton V, 205
Spray, Jesse, Jr. V, 204
Spray, Jesse, Jr. V, 205
Spray, John I, 1058
Spray, John IV, 60
Spray, John V, 124
Spray, John V, 176
Spray, John V, 196
Spray, John V, 200
Spray, John V, 204
Spray, John V, 205
Spray, John V, 206
Spray, John V, 208
Spray, John C. V, 598
Spray, John C. V, 711
Spray, John Henry Wilson V, 205
Spray, John Jesse James V, 205
Spray, Joseph I, 1059
Spray, Joseph V, 204
Spray, Joseph V, 205
Spray, Joseph V, 212
Spray, Keturah I, 1058
Spray, Lydia Jane V, 204
Spray, Lydia Jane V, 205
Spray, Margery V, 124
Spray, Margery V, 125
Spray, Margery V, 126
Spray, Margery V, 204
Spray, Margery V, 206
Spray, Martha V, 44
Spray, Martha V, 124
Spray, Martin V, 204
Spray, Mary I, 1024
Spray, Mary I, 1058

y, Mary I, 1059
y, Mary IV, 60
y, Mary V, 17
y, Mary V, 42
y, Mary V, 124
y, Mary V, 160
y, Mary V, 164
y, Mary V, 166
y, Mary V, 191
y, Mary V, 196
y, Mary V, 198
y, Mary V, 203
y, Mary V, 204
y, Mary V, 205
y, Mary V, 469
y, Mary V, 711
y, Mary V, 792
y, Mary A. V, 205
y, Mary Ann V, 187
y, Mary Ann V, 205
y, Mary Ann V, 515
y, Mary Ann V, 530
y, Mary Ann V, 711
y, Mary F. V, 598
y, Mary F. V, 711
y, Mary Florence V, 598
y, Mary W. V, 205
y, Maryann V, 204
y, Massey I, 1057
y, Massey V, 176
y, Massey V, 204
y, Massie V, 204
y, Michael V, 836
y, Michael V, 862
y, Mordecai I, 1058
y, Mordecai I, 1063
y, Mordecai V, 124
y, Mordecai V, 204
y, Mordecai V, 205
y, Naomi I, 1037
y, Naomi I, 1063
y, Naomi IV, 60
y, Phebe V, 124
y, Phebe V, 186
y, Phebe V, 204
y, Phebe V, 205
y, Phebe V, 595
y, Phebe V, 598
y, Phebe V, 711
y, Phebe V, 862
y, Phebe J. V, 598
y, Rachel V, 204
y, Rachel V, 205
y, Rachel V, 208
y, Rebecah I, 1024
y, Rebecah V, 205
y, Rebecca V, 31
y, Rebecca V, 124
y, Rebecca V, 187
y, Rebecca V, 191
y, Rebecca V, 204
y, Rebecca V, 205
y, Rebecca V, 598
y, Rebecca L. V, 711
y, Sammie L. V, 598
y, Samuel I, 1024
y, Samuel I, 1058
y, Samuel I, 1059
y, Samuel I, 1063
y, Samuel IV, 60
y, Samuel V, 17
y, Samuel V, 42
y, Samuel V, 124
y, Samuel V, 198
y, Samuel V, 204
y, Samuel V, 205
y, Samuel V, 208
y, Samuel V, 212
y, Samuel V, 469
y, Samuel V, 711
y, Samuel L. V, 711
y, Samuel Lawrence V, 598
y, Samuel, Jr. V, 205
y, Sarah I, 1024
y, Sarah I, 1058
y, Sarah I, 1063
y, Sarah V, 124
y, Sarah V, 176
y, Sarah V, 196
y, Sarah V, 200
y, Sarah V, 204
y, Sarah V, 205
y, Sarah V, 206
y, Sarah V, 208
y, Sarah Ann V, 204
y, Sarah Ann V, 205
y, Susanna V, 154
y, Susanna V, 205
y, Susannah V, 204
y, Thomas I, 1058
y, Uriah V, 191
Spray, Uriah V, 204
Spray, Uriah V, 205
Spray, William I, 1058
Spray, William V, 124
Spray, William V, 204
Spray, William V, 205
Spray, William V, 211
Spray, William W. V, 205
Spray, Wilson I, 1162
Spray, Wm. V, 205
Spray, Wm. W. V, 205
Spreogle, Katherine II, 422
Sprewell, Eleanor I, 571
Spriggs, Joseph VI, 881
Spriggs, Joseph VI, 890
Spriggs, Joseph VI, 905
Spriggs, Joseph VI, 911
Spriggs, Joseph VI, 917
Spriggs, Joseph VI, 926
Spriggs, Joseph VI, 932
Spriggs, Joseph VI, 950
Spriggs, Joseph VI, 968
Spriggs, Joseph VI, 976
Spriggs, Joseph VI, 1011
Spriggs, Joseph VI, 1015
Sprigs, Rebecca IV, 228
Sprigs, Rebecca IV, 278
Sprigs, Sidney IV, 278
Spring, Isabell VI, 9
Spring, Isabelle VI, 7
Spring, Jesse O. IV, 1339
Spring, Mrs. Robert VI, 11
Spring, Rebecca B. II, 730
Spring, Rebecca B. II, 768
Spring, Robart VI, 9
Spring, Robert VI, 11
Spring, Robert VI, 12
Spring, Wortha IV, 1339
Springer, Abigail I, 514
Springer, Abigail I, 792
Springer, Abigail I, 837
Springer, Abram V, 1020
Springer, Anna II, 657
Springer, Anne II, 657
Springer, Barnabas I, 514
Springer, Barnabas I, 792
Springer, Barnabas I, 837
Springer, Bell III, 297
Springer, Bell III, 303
Springer, Benjamin II, 657
Springer, Bess III, 297
Springer, Bess III, 303
Springer, Edward I, 837
Springer, Edward V, 1020
Springer, Elizabeth I, 792
Springer, Franklin II, 925
Springer, Fred G. V, 465
Springer, Freelove I, 514
Springer, Freelove I, 792
Springer, Freelove I, 837
Springer, Frelove I, 837
Springer, George I, 514
Springer, George I, 792
Springer, George I, 837
Springer, George I, 901
Springer, Hannah II, 236
Springer, Hannah II, 263
Springer, James I, 901
Springer, Job I, 514
Springer, Job I, 792
Springer, Job I, 837
Springer, John III, 297
Springer, John III, 303
Springer, Lizzie V, 1020
Springer, Lovina IV, 1241
Springer, Mary II, 92
Springer, Mary II, 100
Springer, Mary Jane II, 131
Springer, Mathew I, 837
Springer, Matthew I, 514
Springer, Matthew I, 792
Springer, Sally I, 792
Springer, Samuel I, 901
Springer, Sarah I, 514
Springer, Sarah I, 571
Springer, Sarah I, 792
Springer, Sarah I, 825
Springer, Sarah I, 837
Springer, Sibyl T. II, 124
Springer, Stephen I, 514
Springer, Stephen I, 571
Springer, Stephen I, 792
Springer, Stephen I, 825
Springer, Stephen I, 837
Springer, William I, 792
Springer, Zelma V, 1020
Sprogle, Christian Lodowick II, 448
Sprogs, Sidney IV, 278
Sproll, Aaron V, 1020
Sproul, Evelyn Irene V, 1020
Sprouse, Charles V, 711
Sprouse, David V, 530
Sprouse, Floyd Carey V, 711
Sprouse, Goldie V, 530
Sprouse, Harold V, 530
Sprouse, Harold Edwin V, 530
Sprouse, James B. V, 530
Sprouse, James Holson V, 530
Sprouse, James Ransom V, 530
Sprouse, Lucile May V, 530
Sprouse, Lucile Way V, 530
Sprouse, Lucille V, 530
Sprouse, Pearl Carey V, 711
Sprouse, Russell V, 530
Sprouse, Russle Leonard V, 530
Sprouse, Samuel VI, 997
Sprouse, Sarah VI, 997
Sprout, Clarence V, 205
Sprout, E. T. V, 205
Sprout, Penn V, 205
Sprunger, Marguerite L. IV, 1339
Spry, Emma IV, 1294
Spry, Emma T. IV, 1294
Spry, Helen Lutta V, 1020
Spry, Samuel IV, 1294
Spry, Wm. Horace V, 1020
Spur, Almeda V, 644
Spur, Cleo F. V, 644
Spur, Grace Ann V, 644
Spur, John F. V, 644
Spur, Leon Spray V, 644
Spur, Leonidas E. V, 644
Spur, Martha J. V, 644
Spur, Mary E. V, 644
Spur, Paul Stanley V, 644
Spur, Ray Cyrus V, 644
Spur, S. Orricy V, 644
Spurgen, Hannah IV, 86
Spurgen, Hannah IV, 110
Spurgeon, Alvin C. V, 712
Spurgeon, Amanda J. V, 644
Spurgeon, Andrew J. V, 644
Spurgeon, Daniel V, 530
Spurgeon, Daniel V, 711
Spurgeon, Daniel V, 712
Spurgeon, Daniel B. V, 530
Spurgeon, Ella V, 711
Spurgeon, Frank V, 712
Spurgeon, Goldie V, 530
Spurgeon, Goldie V, 712
Spurgeon, Goldie F. V, 712
Spurgeon, Jesse A. V, 711
Spurgeon, Lida V, 530
Spurgeon, Lida V, 711
Spurgeon, Lida V, 712
Spurgeon, Lida J. V, 711
Spurgeon, Mary B. V, 712
Spurgeon, Minnie V, 711
Spurrier, Amy IV, 510
Spurrier, Ann IV, 551
Spurrier, Mary IV, 278
Spurrier, Mary IV, 308
Spurrier, Sarah II, 422
Spurrier, Theophilus II, 422
Squeers, Elizabeth I, 113
Squeers, Rogers I, 113
Squerril, Esther II, 657
Squibb, Caleb II, 100
Squibb, Edward II, 925
Squibb, Edward R. II, 768
Squibb, Edward R. II, 925
Squibb, Hannah II, 800
Squibb, John VI, 447
Squibb, Lydia VI, 447
Squibb, Martha II, 805
Squibb, Martha II, 822
Squibb, Mary II, 821
Squibb, Mary II, 925
Squibb, Robert II, 325
Squibb, Robert II, 821
Squibb, Robert II, 925
Squibb, Sarah VI, 447
Squibb, Thos. S. II, 925
Squier, Benjamin B. III, 297
Squier, Bertrand III, 297
Squier, Bertrand Wintringham III, 297
Squier, Caroline M. III, 297
Squier, Ellen III, 173
Squier, Ellen III, 297
Squier, Ellen H. III, 297
Squier, Gardner III, 297
Squier, Helen Eliz. III, 297
Squier, Helen Eliz. III, 362
Squier, Lucien III, 297
Squier, Lucien B. III, 173
Squier, Lucien B. III, 297
Squier, Lucien B., Jr. III, 297
Squier, Lucien B., Jr. III, 362
Squire, Benjamin I, 166
Squire, Charles III, 157
Squire, Charles III, 297
Squire, Charles H. III, 225
Squire, Edward L. III, 297
Squire, Eliza III, 225
Squire, Eliza III, 297
Squire, Elizabeth III, 225
Squire, Emma III, 297
Squire, Eva H. V, 530
Squire, Grace III, 157
Squire, Grace III, 297
Squire, Ida III, 157
Squire, Ida III, 297
Squire, Loatta III, 225
Squire, Mary Ann III, 225
Squire, Mary Ann III, 297
Squire, Mary Emma III, 225
Squire, Samuel III, 225
Squire, Samuel III, 297
Squire, Sarah III, 297
Squire, Thomas III, 297
Squire, William J. III, 225
Squires, Belle V, 205
Squires, Benjamin I, 166
Squires, Betsy VI, 997
Squires, Elisabeth I, 166
Squires, Elizabeth I, 159
Squires, Elizabeth I, 166
Squires, Elizabeth VI, 938
Squires, Isadore V, 205
Squires, Isadore Bell V, 205
Squires, Jemima VI, 997
Squires, John VI, 997
Squires, Levi VI, 965
Squires, Levie VI, 997
Squires, Lewis VI, 955
Squires, Lockey VI, 997
Squires, Margaret I, 75
Squires, Mary I, 40
Squires, Mary I, 75
Squires, Mary I, 166
Squires, Mary VI, 997
Squires, Nancy VI, 997
Squires, Peggy VI, 1007
Squires, Rachel I, 415
Squires, Rachel I, 419
Squires, Roger I, 75
Squires, Roger I, 166
Squires, Rogers I, 166
Squires, Sally T. VI, 901
Squires, Sarah I, 75
Squires, Sarah I, 135
Squires, Sarah I, 166
Squires, Thomas VI, 869
Squires, Thomas VI, 997
Squires, Uriah VI, 901
Squires, Uriah VI, 907
Squires, Uriah VI, 938
Squires, Uriah VI, 997
Squirrel, ??? II, 423
Squirrel, Esther II, 657
Sratton, Dillwyn IV, 214
Sratton, Elizabeth IV, 214
Sratton, Frazier O. VI, 1018
Sreeve, Elizabeth IV, 993
Sreeve, Emily IV, 993
Sreeve, Enoch IV, 993
Sreeve, John IV, 993
Sreeve, Joshua IV, 993
Sreeve, Mary IV, 993
Sreeve, Unity IV, 993
Sreeve, Wm. IV, 993
Sreve, Abigail IV, 895
Sreve, Ann G. IV, 891
Sreve, Ann G. IV, 895
Sreve, Annie IV, 992
Sreve, Enoch IV, 992
Sreve, Evan IV, 992
Sreve, Evan IV, 993
Sreve, Joel IV, 992
Sreve, John IV, 895
Sreve, John IV, 992
Sreve, Joshua IV, 992
Sreve, Mary IV, 992
Sreve, Meribah IV, 993
Sreve, Rachel IV, 891
Sreve, Stacy IV, 992
Sreve, Thomas C. IV, 891
Sreve, Thomas C. IV, 895
Sreve, Vashti IV, 992
Sreve, William IV, 992
Sriver, John IV, 44
Sriver, Mary H. IV, 44
Sriver, Mary H. IV, 60
Sriver, Mary H. IV, 337
Sriver, Mary H. IV, 351
Sriver, Rachel IV, 44
Sriver, William H. IV, 60
Sriver, William Henry IV, 60
Srokes, Mary VI, 637
Sroufe, Andrew V, 598
Sroufe, Edith V, 599
Sroufe, George Delbert V, 598
St Clair, Frances II, 642
St Clair, William VI, 991
St. Aubin, Margaret IV, 1043
St. Aubin, Peter IV, 1043
St. Clair, Ada V, 599
St. Clair, Ada V, 933
St. Clair, Ann IV, 495
St. Clair, Ann IV, 496
St. Clair, Bessie IV, 1224
St. Clair, Bessie B. IV, 1224
St. Clair, Buford W. VI, 994
St. Clair, C. B. VI, 994
St. Clair, Carrol C. VI, 994
St. Clair, Catharine VI, 976
St. Clair, Catharine M. VI, 994
St. Clair, Christopher H. VI, 993
St. Clair, Edward VI, 976
St. Clair, Edward W. VI, 994
St. Clair, Elizabeth VI, 981
St. Clair, Elizabeth VI, 993
St. Clair, Elizabeth VI, 994
St. Clair, Elmira VI, 994
St. Clair, Erwin IV, 1224
St. Clair, Fanny H. L. VI, 896
St. Clair, Frances II, 658
St. Clair, Frances VI, 994
St. Clair, George V, 275
St. Clair, George VI, 952
St. Clair, George VI, 982
St. Clair, George VI, 993
St. Clair, George VI, 1020
St. Clair, Glen IV, 1224
St. Clair, Hannah IV, 1224
St. Clair, Hannah M. IV, 1224
St. Clair, Harry IV, 1224
St. Clair, Harry B. IV, 1224
St. Clair, Henry T. VI, 994
St. Clair, Irwih M. IV, 1224
St. Clair, Isaac VI, 871
St. Clair, Isaac VI, 876
St. Clair, Isaac VI, 908
St. Clair, Isaac VI, 948
St. Clair, Isaac VI, 996
St. Clair, J. T. VI, 892
St. Clair, J. T. VI, 1008
St. Clair, James E. VI, 994
St. Clair, John VI, 981
St. Clair, John VI, 984
St. Clair, John VI, 994
St. Clair, John P. VI, 994
St. Clair, Joseph D. VI, 994
St. Clair, Joseph D. VI, 1010
St. Clair, Katharine VI, 994
St. Clair, Kitturian VI, 994
St. Clair, Lucinda VI, 897
St. Clair, Lucinda VI, 952
St. Clair, Lucinda VI, 994
St. Clair, Lydia VI, 925
St. Clair, Martha V, 275
St. Clair, Martha M. VI, 1020
St. Clair, Mary IV, 281
St. Clair, Mary IV, 1224
St. Clair, Meador VI, 994
St. Clair, Mrs. Katharine VI, 994
St. Clair, Nancy VI, 994
St. Clair, Nancy C. VI, 996
St. Clair, Prudence VI, 993
St. Clair, Rhoda E. VI, 996
St. Clair, Rhoda W. VI, 994
St. Clair, Robert VI, 994
St. Clair, Robert, Jr. VI, 994
St. Clair, Robert, Sr. VI, 994
St. Clair, Ruth IV, 205
St. Clair, Ruth IV, 280
St. Clair, Sarah VI, 976
St. Clair, Sarah Frances VI, 994
St. Clair, Sarah S. S. VI, 994
St. Clair, Skitturian VI, 994
St. Clair, William VI, 897
St. Clair, William VI, 925
St. Clair, William VI, 994
St. Clair, William VI, 996
St. Clair, Wm. H. IV, 1224
St. Clear, Ann IV, 432
St. Clear, Ann IV, 444
St. Clear, Catharine IV, 432
St. Clear, James IV, 432
St. George, Elvina A. IV, 1339
St. George, Elwin A. IV, 1339
St. John, George VI, 823
St. John, George VI, 844
St. John, George VI, 856
St. John, James VI, 856
St. John, Nancy VI, 823
St. John, Nancy VI, 856
St. John, Sarah VI, 856
St. Pier, ??? III, 496
Staats, Margaret IV, 60
Staats, Margaret IV, 80
Staats, Margaret IV, 110

Staats, Margaret IV, 352
Staats, Margaret IV, 562
Staats, Mary Ann V, 862
Stabbiker, Mrs. ??? IV, 1339
Stabeler, Susan VI, 782
Stabler, ??? VI, 779
Stabler, Abram VI, 268
Stabler, Alban G. VI, 780
Stabler, Albert VI, 662
Stabler, Albert VI, 753
Stabler, Albert VI, 755
Stabler, Albert VI, 780
Stabler, Albert VI, 781
Stabler, Albert VI, 782
Stabler, Albert VI, 790
Stabler, Albert, Jr. VI, 729
Stabler, Albert, Jr. VI, 763
Stabler, Albert, Jr. VI, 780
Stabler, Albert, Jr. VI, 781
Stabler, Albert, Sr. VI, 780
Stabler, Alexandria VI, 267
Stabler, Alice VI, 782
Stabler, Alice VI, 792
Stabler, Allen VI, 782
Stabler, Ann III, 298
Stabler, Ann VI, 121
Stabler, Ann VI, 122
Stabler, Ann VI, 510
Stabler, Ann VI, 512
Stabler, Ann VI, 563
Stabler, Ann VI, 564
Stabler, Ann VI, 677
Stabler, Ann VI, 708
Stabler, Ann VI, 711
Stabler, Ann VI, 780
Stabler, Ann VI, 783
Stabler, Ann R. VI, 682
Stabler, Ann R. VI, 782
Stabler, Anna VI, 781
Stabler, Anna Bunker III, 298
Stabler, Anna Ellora III, 85
Stabler, Anna Ellora III, 298
Stabler, Anna M. III, 297
Stabler, Anna M. III, 298
Stabler, Anna R. VI, 564
Stabler, Anna R. VI, 780
Stabler, Anna R. VI, 783
Stabler, Annie VI, 781
Stabler, Arthur Phillips VI, 564
Stabler, Arthur Phillips VI, 708
Stabler, Augustus VI, 782
Stabler, Barbara VI, 733
Stabler, C. Norman III, 229
Stabler, C. Norman III, 297
Stabler, Caleb VI, 677
Stabler, Caleb B. VI, 677
Stabler, Caleb B. VI, 783
Stabler, Caleb Bentley VI, 564
Stabler, Caleb Bentley VI, 711
Stabler, Caleb Bentley VI, 783
Stabler, Caroline H. VI, 781
Stabler, Charles F. VI, 733
Stabler, Charles Franklin Brooks VI, 781
Stabler, Charles Frqnklin VI, 733
Stabler, Charles M. III, 298
Stabler, Charles M. VI, 782
Stabler, Chas. M. III, 297
Stabler, Chas. N., Jr. III, 297
Stabler, Cora Lea II, 782
Stabler, Cornelia III, 298
Stabler, Cornelia VI, 663
Stabler, Cornelia VI, 765
Stabler, Cornelia Janney VI, 781
Stabler, Deborah VI, 18
Stabler, Deborah VI, 264
Stabler, Deborah VI, 267
Stabler, Deborah VI, 268
Stabler, Deborah VI, 564
Stabler, Deborah VI, 748
Stabler, Deborah VI, 771
Stabler, Deborah VI, 780
Stabler, Deborah VI, 781
Stabler, Deborah VI, 783
Stabler, Deborah H. VI, 748
Stabler, Derick B. VI, 543
Stabler, Dr. Richard H. VI, 753
Stabler, Edith Herrick VI, 733
Stabler, Edw. VI, 511
Stabler, Edw. L. III, 298
Stabler, Edw. Russell III, 298
Stabler, Edward III, 23
Stabler, Edward III, 298
Stabler, Edward VI, 121
Stabler, Edward VI, 122
Stabler, Edward VI, 212
Stabler, Edward VI, 213
Stabler, Edward VI, 264
Stabler, Edward VI, 267
Stabler, Edward VI, 268
Stabler, Edward VI, 339
Stabler, Edward VI, 510
Stabler, Edward VI, 512
Stabler, Edward VI, 545
Stabler, Edward VI, 563
Stabler, Edward VI, 564
Stabler, Edward VI, 587
Stabler, Edward VI, 682
Stabler, Edward VI, 708
Stabler, Edward VI, 725
Stabler, Edward VI, 731
Stabler, Edward VI, 741
Stabler, Edward VI, 746
Stabler, Edward VI, 751
Stabler, Edward VI, 758
Stabler, Edward VI, 771
Stabler, Edward VI, 774
Stabler, Edward VI, 780
Stabler, Edward VI, 781
Stabler, Edward VI, 782
Stabler, Edward VI, 783
Stabler, Edward H. III, 119
Stabler, Edward H. III, 247
Stabler, Edward H. III, 298
Stabler, Edward H. VI, 759
Stabler, Edward H. VI, 781
Stabler, Edward L. III, 298
Stabler, Edward L. III, 323
Stabler, Edward Lincoln VI, 732
Stabler, Edward Morgan VI, 733
Stabler, Edward Palmer III, 297
Stabler, Edward R., Jr. III, 85
Stabler, Edward Russell III, 298
Stabler, Edward Stabler VI, 781
Stabler, Edward, Jr. II, 657
Stabler, Edward, Jr. VI, 727
Stabler, Edward, Jr. VI, 781
Stabler, Eleanor M. III, 46
Stabler, Eleanor M. III, 298
Stabler, Eleanor M. VI, 732
Stabler, Eleanor M. VI, 733
Stabler, Eleanor Merit VI, 733
Stabler, Eleanor Merritt VI, 781
Stabler, Eliz. III, 298
Stabler, Eliz. T. III, 298
Stabler, Eliza VI, 783
Stabler, Eliza P. VI, 564
Stabler, Eliza P. VI, 783
Stabler, Elizabeth III, 229
Stabler, Elizabeth III, 297
Stabler, Elizabeth III, 298
Stabler, Elizabeth III, 323
Stabler, Elizabeth VI, 472
Stabler, Elizabeth VI, 564
Stabler, Elizabeth VI, 731
Stabler, Elizabeth VI, 732
Stabler, Elizabeth VI, 763
Stabler, Elizabeth VI, 780
Stabler, Elizabeth VI, 781
Stabler, Elizabeth VI, 782
Stabler, Elizabeth VI, 783
Stabler, Elizabeth Pleasants VI, 18
Stabler, Elzabeth VI, 781
Stabler, Fannie II, 925
Stabler, Fannie Brooke II, 925
Stabler, Frances Miller VI, 731
Stabler, Frances Miller VI, 781
Stabler, Frances Miller VI, 782
Stabler, Francis III, 297
Stabler, Francis III, 298
Stabler, Francis VI, 765
Stabler, Francis VI, 781
Stabler, Frebon VI, 733
Stabler, Frederick B. VI, 544
Stabler, Frederick B. VI, 687
Stabler, Frederick B. VI, 688
Stabler, Frederick B. VI, 708
Stabler, Frederick B., Jr. VI, 564
Stabler, Frona VI, 733
Stabler, George Lea VI, 782
Stabler, George Miller VI, 782
Stabler, George S. Worth VI, 782
Stabler, Griffen Miller III, 297
Stabler, Hannah B. VI, 708
Stabler, Hannah B. VI, 712
Stabler, Hannah B. VI, 780
Stabler, Hannah Brown VI, 708
Stabler, Hannah Brown VI, 711
Stabler, Harold B. VI, 731
Stabler, Harold B. VI, 740
Stabler, Harold B. VI, 781
Stabler, Harold B. Stabler VI, 781
Stabler, Harriett VI, 781
Stabler, Helen VI, 782
Stabler, Helen VI, 790
Stabler, Helen B. J. VI, 781
Stabler, Helen Bowne VI, 662
Stabler, Helen Bowne VI, 753
Stabler, Helen Bowne VI, 755
Stabler, Helen Bowne VI, 780
Stabler, Helen Bowne VI, 781
Stabler, Helen Bowne VI, 782
Stabler, Helen Janney VI, 782
Stabler, Henry VI, 760
Stabler, Henry VI, 781
Stabler, Henry VI, 782
Stabler, Henry Russell VI, 782
Stabler, Howard Parker III, 298
Stabler, Howard Parker III, 334
Stabler, Ida III, 297
Stabler, Ida VI, 782
Stabler, Isabella E. VI, 782
Stabler, Isabella Skillman VI, 782
Stabler, Isabelle Skillman VI, 780
Stabler, Isabelle Skillman VI, 790
Stabler, James Brooke VI, 782
Stabler, James P. VI, 564
Stabler, James P. VI, 783
Stabler, James Pleasants VI, 781
Stabler, James Pleasants VI, 792
Stabler, Jane VI, 753
Stabler, Jane VI, 756
Stabler, Jane VI, 781
Stabler, John Hugh VI, 781
Stabler, John Roberts III, 298
Stabler, Joseph Bond VI, 781
Stabler, Juliet VI, 782
Stabler, Laurence Janney VI, 782
Stabler, Letitia VI, 708
Stabler, Louisa III, 298
Stabler, Louisa M. III, 23
Stabler, Louisa M. III, 119
Stabler, Louisa M. III, 247
Stabler, Louisa M. III, 298
Stabler, Louise M. III, 23
Stabler, Louise M. III, 247
Stabler, Louise M. III, 298
Stabler, Louise Merritt III, 298
Stabler, Mahlon VI, 511
Stabler, Mahlon Janney VI, 781
Stabler, Margaret VI, 18
Stabler, Margaret VI, 733
Stabler, Margaret VI, 746
Stabler, Margaret VI, 782
Stabler, Margaret A. III, 298
Stabler, Margaret A. III, 334
Stabler, Maria Ann VI, 564
Stabler, Marianna VI, 766
Stabler, Marie Ann VI, 708
Stabler, Mary III, 298
Stabler, Mary VI, 121
Stabler, Mary VI, 122
Stabler, Mary VI, 213
Stabler, Mary VI, 264
Stabler, Mary VI, 267
Stabler, Mary VI, 268
Stabler, Mary VI, 476
Stabler, Mary VI, 482
Stabler, Mary VI, 509
Stabler, Mary VI, 510
Stabler, Mary VI, 511
Stabler, Mary VI, 512
Stabler, Mary VI, 543
Stabler, Mary VI, 544
Stabler, Mary VI, 545
Stabler, Mary VI, 558
Stabler, Mary VI, 563
Stabler, Mary VI, 564
Stabler, Mary VI, 587
Stabler, Mary VI, 731
Stabler, Mary VI, 736
Stabler, Mary VI, 741
Stabler, Mary VI, 746
Stabler, Mary VI, 751
Stabler, Mary VI, 760
Stabler, Mary VI, 771
Stabler, Mary VI, 774
Stabler, Mary VI, 780
Stabler, Mary VI, 781
Stabler, Mary VI, 782
Stabler, Mary VI, 783
Stabler, Mary A. VI, 307
Stabler, Mary A. VI, 339
Stabler, Mary Ann VI, 308
Stabler, Mary Ann VI, 339
Stabler, Mary Annie VI, 746
Stabler, Mary Annie VI, 781
Stabler, Mary Annie VI, 782
Stabler, Mary C. III, 298
Stabler, Mary C. VI, 759
Stabler, Mary C. VI, 781
Stabler, Mary Cornelia VI, 681
Stabler, Mary Cornelia VI, 682
Stabler, Mary Cornelia VI, 708
Stabler, Mary Moore VI, 766
Stabler, Mary P. VI, 781
Stabler, Mary Pleasant VI, 781
Stabler, Mary Sidwell VI, 564
Stabler, Mary Sidwell VI, 687
Stabler, Mary Sidwell VI, 688
Stabler, Norah Leland VI, 782
Stabler, Norah Leland VI, 792
Stabler, Norman III, 298
Stabler, Norman Herrick VI, 733
Stabler, Philip T. VI, 681
Stabler, Philip T. VI, 682
Stabler, Philips VI, 708
Stabler, Phillip T. VI, 708
Stabler, Phinneas, Edward VI, 758
Stabler, Raymond IV, 1339
Stabler, Rebecca VI, 708
Stabler, Rebecca VI, 781
Stabler, Rebecca T. VI, 544
Stabler, Rebecca T. VI, 564
Stabler, Rebecca T. VI, 688
Stabler, Richard H. VI, 759
Stabler, Richard Hartshore VI, 781
Stabler, Richard Hartshorne VI, 756
Stabler, Robert Brooke VI, 782
Stabler, Robert M. VI, 708
Stabler, Robert M. VI, 711
Stabler, Robert M. VI, 712
Stabler, Robert M. VI, 780
Stabler, Robert Miller VI, 746
Stabler, Robert Miller VI, 780
Stabler, Robinson VI, 307
Stabler, Robinson VI, 308
Stabler, Robinson VI, 339
Stabler, Robinson VI, 738
Stabler, Robinson VI, 781
Stabler, Sarah VI, 18
Stabler, Sarah VI, 121
Stabler, Sarah VI, 268
Stabler, Sarah VI, 751
Stabler, Sarah VI, 780
Stabler, Sarah VI, 781
Stabler, Sarah VI, 782
Stabler, Sarah Brooke VI, 740
Stabler, Sarah Brooke VI, 782
Stabler, Sarah Brooks VI, 731
Stabler, Sarah Brooks VI, 781
Stabler, Sarah E. VI, 746
Stabler, Sarah E. VI, 780
Stabler, Sarah Marshall VI, 780
Stabler, Sarah Marshall VI, 782
Stabler, Sophia VI, 677
Stabler, Susan VI, 741
Stabler, Susannah VI, 781
Stabler, Sylvia VI, 733
Stabler, T. Brooke VI, 708
Stabler, Tarlton B. VI, 544
Stabler, Tarlton B. VI, 564
Stabler, Tarlton B. VI, 688
Stabler, Tarlton B. VI, 708
Stabler, Tarlton Brook VI, 564
Stabler, Thomas VI, 18
Stabler, Thomas Bartram VI, 781
Stabler, Thomas Moore VI, 782
Stabler, Thomas Pleasants VI, 564
Stabler, Thomas Pleasants VI, 783
Stabler, Thomas S. VI, 781
Stabler, Thomas S. VI, 782
Stabler, Walter III, 298
Stabler, Warwick M. VI, 782
Stabler, Wd. Elizabeth VI, 729
Stabler, Wd. Elizabeth VI, 781
Stabler, William VI, 121
Stabler, William VI, 122
Stabler, William VI, 264
Stabler, William VI, 267
Stabler, William VI, 545
Stabler, William VI, 564
Stabler, William VI, 726
Stabler, William VI, 748
Stabler, William VI, 771
Stabler, William VI, 778
Stabler, William VI, 780
Stabler, William VI, 781
Stabler, William VI, 783
Stabler, William Hartshore VI, 781
Stabler, Wm. VI, 783
Stabler, Wm. Henry VI, 564
Stabler, Wm. Henry VI, 783
Stacey, Alce II, 423
Stacey, Alice II, 263
Stacey, Ann II, 238
Stacey, Ann II, 263
Stacey, Elin II, 258
Stacey, Elin II, 263
Stacey, John II, 163
Stacey, John II, 263
Stacey, Mahlon II, 1007
Stacey, Robert II, 238
Stacey, Robert II, 258
Stacey, Robert II, 263
Stacey, Sarah II, 1007
Stacey, Sarah II, 1029
Stacey, William II, 423
Stack, David I, 596
Stack, John I, 641
Stack, Mary I, 624
Stack, Mary A. II, 925
Stack, Mary Ann II, 925
Stackhous, James II, 657
Stackhous, Job II, 1028
Stackhouse, ??? II, 423
Stackhouse, Agnes II, 1006
Stackhouse, Agnes II, 1028
Stackhouse, Agness II, 1028
Stackhouse, Alice IV, 827
Stackhouse, Alice IV, 844
Stackhouse, Alice V, 360
Stackhouse, Alice D. V, 530
Stackhouse, Alice D. V, 599
Stackhouse, Alsa IV, 844
Stackhouse, Alse IV, 844
Stackhouse, Amos II, 423
Stackhouse, Amos II, 821
Stackhouse, Amos II, 1028
Stackhouse, Amos B. II, 1080
Stackhouse, Ann II, 788
Stackhouse, Ann II, 1014
Stackhouse, Ann II, 1028
Stackhouse, Ann II, 1029
Stackhouse, Ann II, 1079
Stackhouse, Ann II, 1080
Stackhouse, Anna II, 768
Stackhouse, Anna II, 813
Stackhouse, Anna II, 1080
Stackhouse, Anna IV, 908
Stackhouse, Anna IV, 916
Stackhouse, Anna D. II, 768
Stackhouse, Anna D. II, 970
Stackhouse, Anna D. II, 1061
Stackhouse, Anna L. II, 1066
Stackhouse, Anna L. II, 1081
Stackhouse, Anna M. II, 139
Stackhouse, Anna Maud II, 821
Stackhouse, Anna Payson II, 821
Stackhouse, Anna S. II, 821
Stackhouse, Anna S. II, 925
Stackhouse, Benjamin II, 657
Stackhouse, Benjamin II, 658
Stackhouse, Benjamin II, 1028
Stackhouse, Benjamin II, 1029
Stackhouse, Benjamin IV, 763
Stackhouse, C. W. V, 712
Stackhouse, Charles II, 1028
Stackhouse, Charles D. II, 423
Stackhouse, Charles Deas II, 658
Stackhouse, Daniel II, 1028
Stackhouse, Daniel S. II, 756
Stackhouse, David II, 1028
Stackhouse, David II, 1029
Stackhouse, David L. II, 1080
Stackhouse, Delcena V, 599
Stackhouse, Edith II, 423
Stackhouse, Edith II, 658
Stackhouse, Edith II, 719
Stackhouse, Edith II, 756
Stackhouse, Edith II, 768
Stackhouse, Edith II, 821
Stackhouse, Edith II, 823
Stackhouse, Edith D. II, 821
Stackhouse, Edward L. II, 1066
Stackhouse, Edward L. II, 1081
Stackhouse, Eliza V, 599
Stackhouse, Eliza E. V, 530
Stackhouse, Elizabeth II, 249
Stackhouse, Elizabeth II, 263
Stackhouse, Elizabeth II, 657
Stackhouse, Elizabeth II, 1005
Stackhouse, Elizabeth II, 1028
Stackhouse, Elizabeth II, 1043
Stackhouse, Elizabeth II, 1080
Stackhouse, Elizabeth IV, 279
Stackhouse, Elizabeth D. II, 925
Stackhouse, Elizabeth L. II, 1080
Stackhouse, Elizabeth S. II, 1066
Stackhouse, Ella II, 821
Stackhouse, Ellison II, 821
Stackhouse, Ellison II, 925
Stackhouse, Ellison Dilworth II, 925
Stackhouse, Emily A. II, 1066
Stackhouse, Emily Sharpless II, 821
Stackhouse, Esther II, 263
Stackhouse, Esther S. II, 925
Stackhouse, Florence S. II, 139
Stackhouse, Frank V, 360
Stackhouse, Hannah II, 1028
Stackhouse, Hannah II, 1037
Stackhouse, Hannah IV, 279

ckhouse, Hannah IV, 657
ckhouse, Hannah IV, 844
ckhouse, Hasting II, 423
ckhouse, Hastings II, 821
ckhouse, Hastings III, 298
ckhouse, Henry II, 1081
ckhouse, Henry W. II, 1066
ckhouse, Henry W. II, 1079
ckhouse, Henry W. II, 1080
ckhouse, Henry, Jr. II, 1066
ckhouse, Herman V, 599
ckhouse, Hermon V, 530
ckhouse, Isaac II, 1028
ckhouse, Isaac II, 1033
ckhouse, Isaac II, 1037
ckhouse, Isaac II, 1080
ckhouse, Jacob II, 1080
ckhouse, Jacob W. II, 925
ckhouse, Jacob W. II, 1066
ckhouse, Jacob W. II, 1077
ckhouse, Jacob W. II, 1080
ckhouse, Jacob W. II, 1082
ckhouse, James II, 423
ckhouse, James II, 545
ckhouse, James II, 657
ckhouse, James II, 1077
ckhouse, James II, 1079
ckhouse, James II, 1080
ckhouse, James V, 599
ckhouse, James R. II, 1079
ckhouse, James R. II, 1080
ckhouse, James S. II, 139
ckhouse, James W. V, 530
ckhouse, Jesse Walton II, 821
ckhouse, Job II, 1028
ckhouse, John II, 263
ckhouse, John II, 423
ckhouse, John II, 657
ckhouse, John II, 821
ckhouse, John II, 925
ckhouse, John II, 1028
ckhouse, John II, 1029
ckhouse, John II, 1080
ckhouse, John S. II, 1080
ckhouse, John, Jr. II, 1005
ckhouse, John, Jr. II, 1028
ckhouse, Joseph II, 423
ckhouse, Joseph II, 1028
ckhouse, Joseph D. II, 821
ckhouse, Joseph Dilworth II, 821
ckhouse, Joshua II, 1028
ckhouse, Josie V, 360
ckhouse, Kezia II, 1066
ckhouse, Laura Newbold II, 925
ckhouse, Lewis S. II, 925
ckhouse, Lottie V, 530
ckhouse, Lottie V, 599
ckhouse, Marcy II, 1028
ckhouse, Margaret II, 423
ckhouse, Margaret II, 563
ckhouse, Margaret II, 657
ckhouse, Margaret II, 1028
ckhouse, Margaret II, 1033
ckhouse, Margery II, 1028
ckhouse, Margery II, 1029
ckhouse, Maria II, 1066
ckhouse, Maria II, 1077
ckhouse, Maria II, 1080
ckhouse, Maria P. II, 1080
ckhouse, Maria P. II, 1082
ckhouse, Marjorie II, 779
ckhouse, Martha II, 423
ckhouse, Martha II, 545
ckhouse, Martha II, 657
ckhouse, Martha II, 689
ckhouse, Martha II, 1028
ckhouse, Martha II, 1029
ckhouse, Martha II, 1077
ckhouse, Martha II, 1079
ckhouse, Martha II, 1080
ckhouse, Martha II, 1082
ckhouse, Martha IV, 844
ckhouse, Martha P. II, 1066
ckhouse, Mary II, 423
ckhouse, Mary II, 1007
ckhouse, Mary II, 1014
ckhouse, Mary II, 1028
ckhouse, Mary II, 1029
ckhouse, Mary II, 1066
ckhouse, Mary II, 1079
ckhouse, Mary II, 1080
ckhouse, Mary V, 360
ckhouse, Mary Ann II, 1080
ckhouse, Mary Anna II, 1066
ckhouse, Mary Anna II, 1080
ckhouse, Mary L. II, 1080
ckhouse, Mary P. II, 1066
ckhouse, Mary P. II, 1080
ckhouse, Mary R. II, 925
Stackhouse, Mary S. II, 1059
Stackhouse, Mary S. II, 1061
Stackhouse, Mary Shaw II, 925
Stackhouse, Matilda II, 792
Stackhouse, Matilda II, 859
Stackhouse, Matilda II, 925
Stackhouse, Mercy II, 970
Stackhouse, Mercy II, 1012
Stackhouse, Mercy II, 1028
Stackhouse, Mercy II, 1029
Stackhouse, Mercy II, 1086
Stackhouse, Myrtle V, 688
Stackhouse, Myrtle V, 689
Stackhouse, Myrtle V, 712
Stackhouse, Nicholas II, 1043
Stackhouse, Orville V, 360
Stackhouse, Orville C. V, 360
Stackhouse, Oscar M. IV, 1339
Stackhouse, Phoebe K. II, 821
Stackhouse, Powel II, 658
Stackhouse, Powell II, 423
Stackhouse, Powell II, 658
Stackhouse, Powell II, 719
Stackhouse, Powell II, 756
Stackhouse, Powell II, 768
Stackhouse, Powell II, 821
Stackhouse, Powell, Jr. II, 768
Stackhouse, Powell, Jr. II, 821
Stackhouse, Pownell II, 823
Stackhouse, Priscilla II, 984
Stackhouse, Priscilla II, 1028
Stackhouse, Providence II, 423
Stackhouse, Rebecca II, 821
Stackhouse, Rebecca II, 1028
Stackhouse, Rebecca Ann II, 792
Stackhouse, Rebecca Ann II, 859
Stackhouse, Rebecca Ann II, 925
Stackhouse, Rebecca Ann V, 932
Stackhouse, Rebecca S. II, 925
Stackhouse, Rebecca Stockton II, 925
Stackhouse, Rebecca, Jr. II, 1028
Stackhouse, Robert II, 423
Stackhouse, Robert II, 545
Stackhouse, Robert II, 657
Stackhouse, Samuel II, 263
Stackhouse, Samuel II, 925
Stackhouse, Samuel A. II, 1061
Stackhouse, Samuel P. II, 792
Stackhouse, Samuel P. II, 859
Stackhouse, Samuel P. II, 925
Stackhouse, Sarah II, 423
Stackhouse, Sarah II, 823
Stackhouse, Sarah II, 1012
Stackhouse, Sarah II, 1028
Stackhouse, Sarah II, 1036
Stackhouse, Sarah C. II, 1080
Stackhouse, Sarah L. II, 1080
Stackhouse, Sarah Phipps II, 821
Stackhouse, Selva V, 530
Stackhouse, Selva V, 599
Stackhouse, Silas II, 1028
Stackhouse, Silas II, 1029
Stackhouse, Sullivan V, 599
Stackhouse, Susan P. II, 1066
Stackhouse, Susanna II, 657
Stackhouse, Susanna II, 658
Stackhouse, Susanna II, 768
Stackhouse, Susanna L. II, 756
Stackhouse, Susanna L. II, 768
Stackhouse, Tacie II, 1066
Stackhouse, Tacy IV, 844
Stackhouse, Thomas II, 1014
Stackhouse, Thomas II, 1028
Stackhouse, Thomas II, 1033
Stackhouse, Thomas II, 1037
Stackhouse, Thos. II, 821
Stackhouse, Thurman V, 599
Stackhouse, Wilbur V, 360
Stackhouse, William II, 1028
Stackhouse, William II, 1029
Stackhouse, Wm. II, 658
Stackhouse, Wm. II, 1028
Stackhouse, Wm. II, 1029
Stackpole, Mary D. IV, 763
Stacy, Alce II, 423
Stacy, Alice II, 235
Stacy, Alice II, 263
Stacy, Edna IV, 995
Stacy, Elizabeth II, 478
Stacy, Elizabeth II, 658
Stacy, Elizabeth II, 1005
Stacy, Elizabeth II, 1029
Stacy, Elizabeth VI, 516
Stacy, Elizabeth VI, 586
Stacy, John II, 235
Stacy, John II, 263
Stacy, John II, 423
Stacy, John II, 546
Stacy, John II, 658
Stacy, Mahlon II, 185
Stacy, Mahlon II, 1005
Stacy, Mahlon II, 1022
Stacy, Mahlon II, 1029
Stacy, Martin L. IV, 995
Stacy, Mary II, 423
Stacy, Mary II, 546
Stacy, Mary II, 658
Stacy, Mary II, 1022
Stacy, Mary II, 1029
Stacy, Rebecca II, 185
Stacy, Robert II, 163
Stacy, Robert II, 423
Stacy, Ruth II, 185
Stacy, Ruth II, 978
Stacy, Ruth II, 1029
Stacy, Samuel II, 448
Stacy, Sarah II, 1029
Stacy, Susan IV, 995
Stacy, Thomas II, 423
Stacy, Thomas IV, 995
Stacy, Thomas L. IV, 995
Stacy, William II, 423
Staff, Malinda III, 298
Staff, William E. III, 298
Staffe, Ethel Mae III, 183
Staffe, Ethel Mae III, 298
Staffe, Malinda III, 298
Staffe, William E. III, 298
Stafford, ??? V, 315
Stafford, Abigail I, 75
Stafford, Abigail I, 136
Stafford, Abigail I, 166
Stafford, Abigail I, 705
Stafford, Abigail I, 706
Stafford, Abigail I, 734
Stafford, Abraham IV, 916
Stafford, Ann I, 806
Stafford, Ann I, 837
Stafford, Bessie I, 626
Stafford, Caroline V, 862
Stafford, Content IV, 916
Stafford, David IV, 914
Stafford, David B. I, 626
Stafford, Eli I, 706
Stafford, Eli I, 734
Stafford, Elias B. V, 932
Stafford, Elias C. V, 932
Stafford, Elias Clarkson I, 788
Stafford, Elias Clarkson I, 792
Stafford, Elisabeth I, 75
Stafford, Elisabeth I, 166
Stafford, Elizabeth I, 709
Stafford, Elizabeth I, 734
Stafford, Elizabeth I, 837
Stafford, Elizabeth S. I, 828
Stafford, Elizabeth S. I, 837
Stafford, Ellen M. I, 928
Stafford, Ellen M. I, 936
Stafford, Esther IV, 815
Stafford, Esther IV, 844
Stafford, Esther F. IV, 753
Stafford, Esther F. IV, 763
Stafford, Esther T. IV, 914
Stafford, Esther T. IV, 916
Stafford, Gabrel I, 706
Stafford, Gabrel I, 969
Stafford, Gabriel I, 117
Stafford, Gabriel I, 734
Stafford, Gabriel I, 969
Stafford, Garris I, 1066
Stafford, Garvis I, 1071
Stafford, Genette IV, 279
Stafford, Irene IV, 279
Stafford, Isaiah I, 166
Stafford, James V, 124
Stafford, James V, 360
Stafford, Jarvis I, 837
Stafford, Jarvis V, 124
Stafford, Jennie III, 298
Stafford, John I, 166
Stafford, John I, 706
Stafford, John I, 734
Stafford, John I, 969
Stafford, John V, 124
Stafford, John V, 360
Stafford, John V, 852
Stafford, John V, 862
Stafford, John H. V, 852
Stafford, John H. V, 862
Stafford, Joseph I, 117
Stafford, Joseph I, 734
Stafford, Joseph I, 837
Stafford, Joseph C. I, 828
Stafford, Joseph C. I, 837
Stafford, Joseph C. V, 932
Stafford, Joshua IV, 753
Stafford, Joshua IV, 763
Stafford, Joshua IV, 916
Stafford, Josiah I, 143
Stafford, Josiah I, 166
Stafford, Julius V, 932
Stafford, Levan I, 837
Stafford, Levisa I, 837
Stafford, Lydia I, 828
Stafford, Lydia I, 837
Stafford, Lydia V, 932
Stafford, Margaret IV, 279
Stafford, Marmaduke J. V, 862
Stafford, Martha V, 852
Stafford, Martha V, 862
Stafford, Mary I, 166
Stafford, Mary IV, 844
Stafford, Mary J. V, 862
Stafford, Matthew I, 734
Stafford, Miriam I, 166
Stafford, Moses I, 571
Stafford, Mourning I, 837
Stafford, Nathan I, 828
Stafford, Nathan I, 837
Stafford, Nathan D. V, 932
Stafford, Pauline III, 133
Stafford, Pauline III, 298
Stafford, Phebe M. V, 932
Stafford, Rachel V, 862
Stafford, Rebecca I, 837
Stafford, Rebecca V, 124
Stafford, Roy E. III, 298
Stafford, Ruth I, 166
Stafford, Ruth I, 419
Stafford, Samuel I, 75
Stafford, Samuel I, 117
Stafford, Samuel I, 136
Stafford, Samuel I, 166
Stafford, Samuel I, 705
Stafford, Samuel I, 706
Stafford, Samuel I, 734
Stafford, Samuel V, 862
Stafford, Sarah I, 143
Stafford, Sarah I, 166
Stafford, Sarah I, 706
Stafford, Sarah I, 732
Stafford, Sarah I, 734
Stafford, Sarah I, 735
Stafford, Sarah I, 814
Stafford, Sarah I, 837
Stafford, Sarah I, 895
Stafford, Sarah I, 901
Stafford, Sarah V, 530
Stafford, Sarah V, 543
Stafford, Sarah V, 544
Stafford, Sary I, 419
Stafford, Shaderack V, 360
Stafford, Shadrack I, 837
Stafford, Shadrack V, 124
Stafford, Shadrick I, 837
Stafford, Shedrick V, 215
Stafford, Stacy V, 280
Stafford, Tacy V, 124
Stafford, Teecy I, 837
Stafford, Thomas I, 166
Stafford, Thomas I, 706
Stafford, Thomas I, 734
Stafford, Wm. P. V, 932
Stagg, Alfred Lindsey I, 419
Stagg, Dorothy II, 423
Stagg, Hannah V, 902
Stagg, Hannah V, 932
Stagg, Hannah Davis V, 932
Stagg, Hannah Isabella V, 932
Stagg, Jemima I, 398
Stagg, Jemima I, 419
Stagg, Joab I, 419
Stagg, Joab Hodgin I, 419
Stagg, John II, 423
Stagg, Sarah Jane I, 419
Stagg, William Wheeler I, 419
Staggs, Laura V, 870
Stahl, Andrew IV, 844
Stahl, Ella IV, 1294
Stahl, Jennie IV, 1294
Stahl, Lavina IV, 844
Stahl, Lavina IV, 857
Stahl, Lester IV, 844
Stahl, Martha IV, 844
Stahl, Wm. IV, 1294
Stahleker, Elsie IV, 1339
Staiger, A. David III, 298
Staiger, David II, 768
Staiger, David III, 298
Staiger, David La Shell III, 298
Staiger, Gladys Helen III, 298
Staiger, Sophie K. III, 298
Stainback, Ida I, 628
Stainton, Eldora III, 298
Stainton, Henry III, 298
Stainton, John L. III, 298
Stainton, Katherine III, 298
Stainton, Margaret N. III, 298
Stainton, Robt. S. III, 298
Staintor, John L. III, 87
Staintor, Katherine III, 87
Stalcup, Rebecca IV, 860
Staley, Dora IV, 1339
Staley, Frank IV, 1339
Staley, Huldah V, 764
Staley, Huldah V, 772
Staley, James S. VI, 997
Staley, Margaret I, 419
Staley, Martha M. VI, 997
Staley, Mary G. I, 419
Stalhleker, Elsie IV, 1339
Stalion, Kesia I, 997
Stalk, Elizabeth VI, 554
Stalker, Aaron I, 209
Stalker, Aaron I, 258
Stalker, Aaron I, 571
Stalker, Aaron I, 753
Stalker, Aaron I, 760
Stalker, Aaron I, 770
Stalker, Aaron I, 792
Stalker, Alice I, 616
Stalker, Alice I, 753
Stalker, Alice I, 755
Stalker, Alice I, 770
Stalker, Alice I, 792
Stalker, Alice I, 807
Stalker, Alice I, 837
Stalker, Allen I, 865
Stalker, Allice I, 760
Stalker, Allice I, 770
Stalker, Ann V, 225
Stalker, Anna V, 280
Stalker, Bellinda I, 760
Stalker, Bellinda I, 770
Stalker, Benjamin I, 753
Stalker, Betty I, 686
Stalker, Betty I, 689
Stalker, Catherine Stephen IV, 1264
Stalker, Charles IV, 1264
Stalker, Clementine I, 770
Stalker, Daniel V, 280
Stalker, Daniel B. V, 280
Stalker, David I, 770
Stalker, David V, 599
Stalker, Deborah I, 792
Stalker, Deborah V, 124
Stalker, Dillon I, 865
Stalker, Eleanor V, 599
Stalker, Elenor V, 530
Stalker, Eli V, 124
Stalker, Eli V, 217
Stalker, Eli V, 225
Stalker, Eli V, 280
Stalker, Eli V, 552
Stalker, Eli V, 599
Stalker, Eliza I, 753
Stalker, Elizabeth I, 792
Stalker, Elizabeth IV, 1339
Stalker, Elizabeth V, 124
Stalker, Emily V, 280
Stalker, Emily V, 293
Stalker, Esther IV, 1264
Stalker, Eunice I, 753
Stalker, Eve I, 677
Stalker, Eve I, 689
Stalker, Eve I, 753
Stalker, Eve I, 770
Stalker, Eve I, 901
Stalker, Eve I, 997
Stalker, Gennett V, 217
Stalker, George I, 571
Stalker, George I, 674
Stalker, George I, 689
Stalker, George I, 753
Stalker, George I, 770
Stalker, George I, 773
Stalker, George I, 792
Stalker, George I, 837
Stalker, George I, 865
Stalker, George I, 894
Stalker, George I, 901
Stalker, George V, 124
Stalker, George, Jr. I, 837
Stalker, Grace I, 792
Stalker, Grace I, 837
Stalker, Grace I, 838
Stalker, Hannah I, 753
Stalker, Hannah I, 766
Stalker, Hannah I, 769
Stalker, Hannah I, 770
Stalker, Hannah I, 792
Stalker, Hannah I, 811
Stalker, Hannah I, 838
Stalker, Hannah I, 865
Stalker, Hannah I, 894
Stalker, Hannah I, 901
Stalker, Harriet E. I, 571
Stalker, Harriett I, 770
Stalker, Harriett Emeline I, 753
Stalker, Herman IV, 1264
Stalker, Jabez I, 753
Stalker, Jabez I, 770

Stalker, James Addison I, 770
Stalker, Jane I, 209
Stalker, Jane I, 258
Stalker, Jane I, 571
Stalker, Jane I, 753
Stalker, Jane I, 760
Stalker, Jane I, 770
Stalker, Jane I, 838
Stalker, Jane Maria I, 753
Stalker, John I, 741
Stalker, John I, 753
Stalker, John I, 770
Stalker, John I, 792
Stalker, John I, 837
Stalker, John I, 843
Stalker, John V, 225
Stalker, John V, 280
Stalker, John V, 599
Stalker, Jonathan I, 753
Stalker, Jonathan I, 792
Stalker, Jonathan I, 837
Stalker, Jonathan I, 838
Stalker, Joseph I, 689
Stalker, Keziah I, 741
Stalker, Keziah I, 753
Stalker, Keziah I, 770
Stalker, Keziah I, 792
Stalker, Keziah I, 837
Stalker, Keziah I, 843
Stalker, Keziah E. I, 534
Stalker, Keziah E. I, 571
Stalker, Keziah Elma I, 753
Stalker, Louisa I, 770
Stalker, Louisa I, 771
Stalker, Louiza I, 770
Stalker, Luiza I, 865
Stalker, Lydia I, 753
Stalker, Lydia I, 770
Stalker, Lydia I, 792
Stalker, Lydia I, 838
Stalker, Lydia V, 530
Stalker, Lydia V, 599
Stalker, Lydia C. I, 571
Stalker, Lydia E. I, 761
Stalker, Lydia E. I, 770
Stalker, Lydia E. Futrell I, 258
Stalker, Mahala B. V, 217
Stalker, Mahala B. V, 280
Stalker, Mahlon I, 770
Stalker, Martha I, 770
Stalker, Mary I, 838
Stalker, Mary I, 1007
Stalker, Mary I, 1012
Stalker, Mary V, 280
Stalker, Mary V, 530
Stalker, Mary V, 599
Stalker, Mary A. I, 571
Stalker, Mary A. I, 575
Stalker, Mary Ann I, 209
Stalker, Mary Ann I, 753
Stalker, Mary Ann I, 770
Stalker, Mary Ann V, 280
Stalker, Mary Elizabeth IV, 1264
Stalker, Mary Ellen IV, 676
Stalker, Mary Ellen V, 280
Stalker, Nathan I, 770
Stalker, Nathan I, 837
Stalker, Nathan I, 1007
Stalker, Nathan I, 1012
Stalker, Nathan V, 280
Stalker, Nathan V, 294
Stalker, Nathan V, 530
Stalker, Nathan V, 599
Stalker, Rachel I, 674
Stalker, Rachel I, 689
Stalker, Rachel I, 753
Stalker, Rachel I, 770
Stalker, Rachel I, 792
Stalker, Rachel I, 800
Stalker, Rachel I, 837
Stalker, Rachel I, 838
Stalker, Rachel V, 124
Stalker, Rachel Ann I, 770
Stalker, Rebeca I, 770
Stalker, Rebecca I, 753
Stalker, Rebecca I, 767
Stalker, Rebecca I, 770
Stalker, Rebecca I, 792
Stalker, Rebecca I, 811
Stalker, Rebecca I, 837
Stalker, Rhoda V, 599
Stalker, Richard I, 686
Stalker, Richard I, 689
Stalker, Ruth I, 770
Stalker, Ruth V, 280
Stalker, Ruth F. I, 571
Stalker, Ruth F. I, 753
Stalker, Sally I, 753
Stalker, Sally I, 770
Stalker, Sally I, 894
Stalker, Sally I, 901
Stalker, Sarah I, 689
Stalker, Sarah I, 753
Stalker, Sarah I, 773
Stalker, Sarah I, 792
Stalker, Sarah I, 837
Stalker, Sarah I, 838
Stalker, Sarah I, 901
Stalker, Sarah V, 599
Stalker, Sarah Bradley I, 837
Stalker, Sarah Emily V, 280
Stalker, Sarah M. I, 770
Stalker, Tacy Genette V, 280
Stalker, Tacy Jenet V, 231
Stalker, Tacy Jenet V, 280
Stalker, Tacy Jennet V, 225
Stalker, Tacy Jennett V, 280
Stalker, Tacy Jennette V, 280
Stalker, Tacy Jennette V, 552
Stalker, Thomas I, 677
Stalker, Thomas I, 689
Stalker, Thomas I, 753
Stalker, Thomas I, 770
Stalker, Thomas I, 792
Stalker, Thomas I, 837
Stalker, Thomas I, 894
Stalker, Thomas I, 901
Stalker, Thomas I, 997
Stalker, Thomas, Jr. I, 753
Stalker, Zebedee I, 770
Stalks, Elizabeth VI, 564
Stall, Edward II, 658
Stall, Edward H. II, 658
Stall, Elizabeth II, 583
Stall, Elizabeth II, 658
Stall, Frances II, 642
Stall, Frances II, 658
Stall, Francis V, 124
Stall, Jennie IV, 1294
Stall, John II, 658
Stall, John V, 124
Stall, John F. V, 889
Stalling, Rebecca V, 862
Stalling, Sarah Jane I, 75
Stalling, Sarah Jane I, 83
Stallings, ??? I, 27
Stallings, Audry Carrie I, 18
Stallings, Charity I, 30
Stallings, Elias Wilber I, 18
Stallings, James E. I, 24
Stallings, James M. I, 30
Stallings, John I, 8
Stallings, Joseph V. I, 18
Stallings, Joseph Wickliff I, 18
Stallings, Leah E. I, 18
Stallings, Leah Elizabeth I, 27
Stallings, Lillie Bell I, 8
Stallings, Minnie Peele I, 340
Stallings, Sarah Jane I, 24
Stallings, Victoria Odell I, 18
Stalter, Delilah V, 1020
Stalter, Ezra V, 1017
Stalter, Mary V, 1020
Stalter, Ola V, 1020
Stalter, Sarah J. V, 1020
Staly, Margaret I, 397
Staly, Margaret I, 419
Stamater, Peter A. V, 712
Stamates, Artemissa V, 712
Stamates, Arthur V, 712
Stamates, Frank V, 712
Stamates, Peter A. V, 712
Stamats, Artemecia V, 712
Stamats, Artemesa V, 432
Stamats, Artemiss V, 432
Stamats, Artemissa V, 712
Stamats, Arthur V, 432
Stamats, Arthur V, 712
Stamats, Frank V, 432
Stamats, Frank V, 712
Stamats, Peter A. V, 712
Stambrough, James V, 530
Stamets, Frankie IV, 1294
Stamey, Abel I, 1162
Stamey, Minnie I, 1162
Stamey, Perry I, 1162
Stamm, Dr. Fred K. III, 417
Stamp, Clara B. IV, 755
Stamp, Mary IV, 755
Stamp, Wm. IV, 755
Stamper, Ann II, 563
Stamper, Dinah II, 562
Stamper, Dinah II, 658
Stamper, Elizabeth II, 563
Stamper, John II, 448
Stamper, John II, 658
Stamper, Joseph II, 563
Stamper, Margaret II, 563
Stamper, Martha II, 563
Stamper, Mary II, 563
Stamper, Rachel II, 563
Stamper, Samuel II, 563
Stamper, Wm. II, 563
Stamps, Martha P. I, 910
Stanaland, Ann II, 1004
Stanaland, Ann II, 1029
Stanaland, Esther II, 1004
Stanaland, Esther II, 1029
Stanaland, Thomas II, 1004
Stanaland, Thomas II, 1029
Stanbeck, Rachel II, 635
Stanbeck, Rachel II, 658
Stanberry, Mary II, 423
Stanberry, Nathan II, 423
Stanborough, Mary V, 501
Stanborough, Mary V, 530
Stanbrough, Ann V, 530
Stanbrough, Elizabeth V, 432
Stanbrough, Elizabeth V, 500
Stanbrough, Elizabeth V, 530
Stanbrough, Elizabeth V, 531
Stanbrough, Evan V, 500
Stanbrough, Evan V, 530
Stanbrough, Evan V, 531
Stanbrough, Francis V, 531
Stanbrough, Francis Hester V, 530
Stanbrough, Francis Hester V, 531
Stanbrough, Isaac V, 530
Stanbrough, Isaac V, 531
Stanbrough, James V, 530
Stanbrough, James V, 531
Stanbrough, Jane V, 531
Stanbrough, John V, 530
Stanbrough, John V, 531
Stanbrough, Jonathan V, 530
Stanbrough, Leah V, 530
Stanbrough, Leah V, 531
Stanbrough, Malinda V, 220
Stanbrough, Malinda V, 280
Stanbrough, Mary V, 236
Stanbrough, Mary V, 527
Stanbrough, Mary V, 530
Stanbrough, Mary V, 531
Stanbrough, Mary Ann V, 492
Stanbrough, Mary Ann V, 530
Stanbrough, Mary Ann V, 531
Stanbrough, Nehemiah V, 236
Stanbrough, Nehemiah V, 500
Stanbrough, Nehemiah V, 530
Stanbrough, Phebe V, 530
Stanbrough, Rachel V, 236
Stanbrough, Rachel V, 271
Stanbrough, Rachel V, 280
Stanbrough, Rachel V, 530
Stanbrough, Rachel V, 531
Stanbrough, Ruth V, 500
Stanbrough, Ruth V, 530
Stanbrough, Samuel V, 530
Stanbrough, Samuel V, 531
Stanbrough, Sarah V, 530
Stanbrough, Solomon V, 280
Stanbrough, Solomon V, 530
Stanbrough, Solomon V, 531
Stanbrough, Tabitha V, 280
Stanbrough, Tabitha V, 530
Stanbrough, Tabitha V, 531
Stanbrough, Thomas V, 531
Stanbrough, Tobitha V, 530
Stanbrough, William V, 271
Stanbrough, William V, 280
Stanbrough, William V, 524
Stanbrough, William V, 530
Stanbrough, William V, 531
Stanbury, Joseph II, 423
Stanbury, Mary II, 423
Stanbury, Mary II, 549
Stanbury, Mary II, 658
Stanbury, Nathan II, 423
Stanbury, Nathan II, 549
Stanbury, Nathan II, 658
Stanbury, Sarah III, 218
Stancie, Ann II, 201
Stancie, Ann II, 263
Stancombe, Addie I, 616
Stancombe, Addie I, 619
Stancombe, Addie M. I, 618
Stancombe, Charlotte I, 618
Stancombe, John I, 618
Standbury, Mary II, 520
Standbury, Nathan II, 520
Standfield, Charity I, 838
Standfield, David I, 1098
Standfield, David I, 1099
Standfield, Elizabeth I, 1098
Standfield, Elizabeth I, 1099
Standfield, Mary I, 374
Standfield, Mary Biddock I, 419
Standfield, Nathaniel I, 1098
Standfield, Sam'l, Jr. I, 1098
Standfield, Samuel I, 1098
Standfield, Samuel, Jr. I, 1098
Standfield, Thomas I, 1098
Standfield, William I, 1098
Standfield, William Williams I, 1098
Standfield, William Williams I, 1099
Standfield, William, Jr. I, 1132
Standish, Daniell II, 423
Standish, Thomson IV, 1294
Standley, Achsah I, 592
Standley, Achsah I, 597
Standley, Agatha VI, 269
Standley, Alice VI, 250
Standley, Ann VI, 268
Standley, Anthony V, 280
Standley, Archelous I, 997
Standley, Asheley VI, 269
Standley, Barbara VI, 564
Standley, Barbary VI, 564
Standley, Catharine VI, 564
Standley, Delphia VI, 997
Standley, Eliza VI, 270
Standley, Elizabeth VI, 564
Standley, Elizabeth VI, 956
Standley, Esther VI, 997
Standley, George VI, 997
Standley, Hannah I, 989
Standley, Hannah I, 997
Standley, Hannah V, 280
Standley, Harris VI, 997
Standley, James VI, 564
Standley, James C. IV, 844
Standley, John V, 280
Standley, John VI, 250
Standley, John VI, 267
Standley, John VI, 268
Standley, John VI, 269
Standley, John VI, 339
Standley, Jonathan IV, 844
Standley, Leah IV, 844
Standley, Littleberry IV, 844
Standley, Madox VI, 269
Standley, Margaret I, 997
Standley, Martha VI, 235
Standley, Martha VI, 269
Standley, Mary II, 100
Standley, Mary II, 101
Standley, Mary II, 423
Standley, Mary II, 484
Standley, Mary II, 658
Standley, Mary IV, 844
Standley, Mary VI, 997
Standley, Micajah VI, 564
Standley, Micajah VI, 575
Standley, Pleasant VI, 997
Standley, Plesent VI, 300
Standley, Plesent VI, 882
Standley, Priscilla VI, 922
Standley, Rachel VI, 997
Standley, Rebecca II, 264
Standley, Reuben VI, 997
Standley, Rhoda IV, 844
Standley, Sally VI, 990
Standley, Samuel IV, 844
Standley, Samuel VI, 855
Standley, Sarah VI, 855
Standley, Susanna VI, 882
Standley, Thomas VI, 179
Standley, Thomas VI, 213
Standley, Thomas VI, 268
Standley, William I, 907
Standley, William II, 264
Standley, William V, 280
Standley, William VI, 564
Standly, Esther VI, 997
Standly, Huldah I, 838
Standly, Isaac I, 573
Standly, Mary I, 573
Standly, Mary I, 821
Standly, Mary I, 838
Standly, Mary II, 101
Standly, Phebe I, 821
Standly, Phebe I, 838
Standly, Rachel I, 573
Standly, Rachel I, 574
Standly, Reuben VI, 997
Standsbury, Mary IV, 60
Stanely, Dorothy May IV, 844
Stanely, Frances IV, 844
Stanely, Isaac Votaw IV, 844
Stanely, Robert Clarence IV, 844
Stanely, Wilmer Wilid IV, 844
Stanes, John II, 658
Stanfell, Munford VI, 884
Stanfield, ??? IV, 1269
Stanfield, Alice I, 792
Stanfield, Chanty V, 206
Stanfield, Charity I, 838
Stanfield, Charity I, 891
Stanfield, Charity I, 901
Stanfield, Charity V, 124
Stanfield, Charity V, 205
Stanfield, Charity V, 666
Stanfield, Charity S. V, 557
Stanfield, Charles I, 1088
Stanfield, David I, 1088
Stanfield, David I, 1089
Stanfield, David I, 1095
Stanfield, David I, 1097
Stanfield, David I, 1099
Stanfield, David IV, 1294
Stanfield, David S. I, 1088
Stanfield, Deborah I, 571
Stanfield, Deborah I, 838
Stanfield, Elijah I, 1088
Stanfield, Elizabeth I, 1088
Stanfield, Elizabeth I, 1099
Stanfield, Evan J. V, 205
Stanfield, Frances II, 448
Stanfield, Francis II, 561
Stanfield, Francis II, 658
Stanfield, George I, 571
Stanfield, Grace I, 837
Stanfield, Grace I, 838
Stanfield, Grace II, 561
Stanfield, Grace II, 658
Stanfield, Hannah I, 364
Stanfield, Hannah I, 419
Stanfield, Hannah I, 803
Stanfield, Hannah I, 838
Stanfield, Hannah V, 124
Stanfield, Hannah Jones I, 10
Stanfield, Hazel V, 206
Stanfield, Huldah Jane I, 114
Stanfield, Isaac I, 1088
Stanfield, James I, 1162
Stanfield, James II, 448
Stanfield, James II, 561
Stanfield, James II, 658
Stanfield, James V, 206
Stanfield, James V, 599
Stanfield, James C. I, 1146
Stanfield, James C. I, 1162
Stanfield, James, Jr. V, 205
Stanfield, Jane I, 571
Stanfield, Jane I, 801
Stanfield, Jane I, 838
Stanfield, Jane V, 124
Stanfield, Jane V, 165
Stanfield, Jane V, 205
Stanfield, Jesse IV, 1294
Stanfield, Joel I, 838
Stanfield, John I, 364
Stanfield, John I, 419
Stanfield, John I, 571
Stanfield, John I, 792
Stanfield, John I, 837
Stanfield, John I, 838
Stanfield, John I, 971
Stanfield, John IV, 1294
Stanfield, John V, 124
Stanfield, John V, 205
Stanfield, John V, 557
Stanfield, Jonathan I, 792
Stanfield, Joseph M. VI, 800
Stanfield, Lida V, 206
Stanfield, Lidia Jane I, 1088
Stanfield, Lydia I, 545
Stanfield, Lydia I, 571
Stanfield, Lydia I, 838
Stanfield, Lydia I, 997
Stanfield, Lydia I, 1088
Stanfield, Lydia IV, 1294
Stanfield, Margaret IV, 1294
Stanfield, Martha P. I, 1162
Stanfield, Mary I, 561
Stanfield, Mary I, 571
Stanfield, Mary I, 814
Stanfield, Mary I, 838
Stanfield, Mary I, 901
Stanfield, Mary II, 448
Stanfield, Mary II, 561
Stanfield, Mary II, 658
Stanfield, Mary IV, 1294
Stanfield, Mary V, 124
Stanfield, Mary V, 205
Stanfield, Mary V, 557
Stanfield, Mary V, 572
Stanfield, Mary Biddock I, 41
Stanfield, Maryetta I, 1146
Stanfield, Massy V, 205
Stanfield, Nancy V, 203
Stanfield, Nancy V, 205
Stanfield, Naomi IV, 1294
Stanfield, Nathan I, 792
Stanfield, Nathan I, 838
Stanfield, Phillipinia I, 401
Stanfield, Phillipinia I, 419
Stanfield, Philopena I, 838
Stanfield, Philpania I, 997
Stanfield, Philpena I, 419
Stanfield, Rachel I, 792

nfield, Rachel I, 837
nfield, Rachel I, 838
nfield, Rebekah I, 803
nfield, Rebekah I, 838
nfield, Ruth V, 189
nfield, Ruth V, 205
nfield, Samuel I, 419
nfield, Samuel I, 571
nfield, Samuel I, 792
nfield, Samuel I, 837
nfield, Samuel I, 838
nfield, Samuel I, 901
nfield, Samuel I, 997
nfield, Samuel I, 1088
nfield, Samuel I, 1162
nfield, Samuel IV, 1294
nfield, Samuel V, 124
nfield, Samuel V, 205
nfield, Samuel Vernon I, 1088
nfield, Sarah I, 1146
nfield, Sarah I, 1162
nfield, Sarah II, 989
nfield, Sarah II, 1029
nfield, Sarah IV, 1294
nfield, Thomas I, 419
nfield, Thomas I, 571
nfield, Thomas I, 838
nfield, Thomas I, 969
nfield, Thomas I, 1077
nfield, Thomas IV, 1294
nfield, Thomas V, 124
nfield, Widow Mary I, 571
nfield, William I, 419
nfield, William I, 571
nfield, William I, 838
nfield, William I, 891
nfield, William I, 901
nfield, William IV, 1294
nfield, William V, 124
nfield, William V, 205
nfield, William Williams I, 1088
nfield, William Williams I, 1099
nfield, William, Jr. I, 571
nfield, William, Jr. I, 1132
nford, Albert III, 446
nford, Albert III, 448
nford, Elizabeth S. III, 446
nford, Elizabeth S. III, 448
nford, Helen III, 446
nford, Helen III, 448
nger, Ann II, 33
nhope, ??? II, 448
nhope, Hannah II, 448
nhope, Richard II, 448
nle, Archalos VI, 269
nley, ??? IV, 995
nley, ??? IV, 996
nley, ??? IV, 999
nley, ??? IV, 1269
nley, ??? V, 443
nley, ??? VI, 223
nley, ??? VI, 268
nley, ??? VI, 269
nley, Aaron I, 515
nley, Aaron I, 590
nley, Aaron I, 596
nley, Aaron I, 626
nley, Aaron IV, 996
nley, Aaron IV, 1000
nley, Aaron IV, 1001
nley, Abbie I, 618
nley, Abel I, 514
nley, Abel I, 515
nley, Abel I, 516
nley, Abel I, 568
nley, Abel I, 572
nley, Abel I, 573
nley, Abel I, 792
nley, Abel I, 969
nley, Abigail I, 515
nley, Abigail I, 516
nley, Abigail I, 540
nley, Abigail I, 546
nley, Abigail I, 572
nley, Abigail I, 573
nley, Abigail I, 578
nley, Abigail I, 590
nley, Abigail I, 597
nley, Abigail I, 608
nley, Abigail I, 689
nley, Abigail I, 838
nley, Abigail I, 886
nley, Abigail I, 901
nley, Abigail I, 1010
nley, Abigail I, 1012
nley, Abigail IV, 279
nley, Abigail IV, 310
nley, Abigail IV, 690
nley, Abigail IV, 763
Stanley, Abigail IV, 764
Stanley, Abigail IV, 765
Stanley, Abigail IV, 766
Stanley, Abigail IV, 914
Stanley, Abigail IV, 916
Stanley, Abigail IV, 927
Stanley, Abigail IV, 941
Stanley, Abigail IV, 960
Stanley, Abigail IV, 970
Stanley, Abigail IV, 985
Stanley, Abigail IV, 989
Stanley, Abigail IV, 993
Stanley, Abigail IV, 995
Stanley, Abigail IV, 996
Stanley, Abigail IV, 997
Stanley, Abigail IV, 998
Stanley, Abigail IV, 1000
Stanley, Abigail IV, 1001
Stanley, Abigail IV, 1187
Stanley, Abigail VI, 271
Stanley, Abigail VI, 339
Stanley, Abigail H. I, 573
Stanley, Abigail H. I, 668
Stanley, Abigail H. IV, 1001
Stanley, Abigail K. IV, 997
Stanley, Abigal VI, 268
Stanley, Abigal VI, 339
Stanley, Able I, 572
Stanley, Able I, 608
Stanley, Able I, 1012
Stanley, Abner H. IV, 1294
Stanley, Abraham I, 969
Stanley, Abraham IV, 90
Stanley, Abraham IV, 110
Stanley, Abraham IV, 764
Stanley, Abraham IV, 766
Stanley, Abraham IV, 767
Stanley, Abraham IV, 999
Stanley, Abraham VI, 268
Stanley, Abraham VI, 271
Stanley, Abraham VI, 272
Stanley, Abraham VI, 339
Stanley, Abraham, Jr. IV, 765
Stanley, Abram IV, 679
Stanley, Abram IV, 764
Stanley, Abram IV, 766
Stanley, Abram IV, 767
Stanley, Abram IV, 999
Stanley, Abram VI, 272
Stanley, Achsa I, 515
Stanley, Achsa I, 572
Stanley, Achsa I, 597
Stanley, Achsah I, 590
Stanley, Achsah I, 596
Stanley, Achsah I, 597
Stanley, Achsah IV, 1294
Stanley, Achsah IV, 1295
Stanley, Achsah V, 124
Stanley, Ada I, 626
Stanley, Ada Lee I, 641
Stanley, Ada Odessa IV, 963
Stanley, Ada Odissa IV, 999
Stanley, Addison W. IV, 998
Stanley, Adeline V, 206
Stanley, Adeline S. V, 862
Stanley, Adiso W. IV, 1001
Stanley, Adolpheus E. I, 839
Stanley, Adolphius I, 839
Stanley, Adolphus E. I, 792
Stanley, Adora IV, 998
Stanley, Adrian IV, 1003
Stanley, Aechelous VI, 270
Stanley, Agatha IV, 763
Stanley, Agatha IV, 764
Stanley, Agatha IV, 765
Stanley, Agatha IV, 766
Stanley, Agatha IV, 995
Stanley, Agatha IV, 996
Stanley, Agatha VI, 251
Stanley, Agatha VI, 253
Stanley, Agatha VI, 268
Stanley, Agatha VI, 269
Stanley, Agatha VI, 271
Stanley, Agatha VI, 272
Stanley, Aggatha I, 572
Stanley, Agnes I, 553
Stanley, Agnes I, 571
Stanley, Agnes I, 572
Stanley, Agnes VI, 189
Stanley, Agnes VI, 192
Stanley, Agnes VI, 213
Stanley, Agnes VI, 214
Stanley, Agnes VI, 268
Stanley, Agnes VI, 270
Stanley, Agnes VI, 271
Stanley, Agness I, 537
Stanley, Agness I, 571
Stanley, Agness I, 572
Stanley, Agness I, 997
Stanley, Agness I, 998
Stanley, Agness VI, 268
Stanley, Agness VI, 271
Stanley, Agness VI, 272
Stanley, Albert E. IV, 1043
Stanley, Albert G. IV, 1003
Stanley, Albert R. IV, 998
Stanley, Albert R. IV, 1002
Stanley, Alberti Galen IV, 999
Stanley, Alfred E. Warrington IV, 1003
Stanley, Alfred R. Thomas IV, 279
Stanley, Alfred W. IV, 767
Stanley, Alfred W. IV, 1000
Stanley, Alfred W. IV, 1003
Stanley, Alice IV, 996
Stanley, Alice IV, 999
Stanley, Alice IV, 1000
Stanley, Alice VI, 251
Stanley, Alice VI, 268
Stanley, Alice VI, 269
Stanley, Alice A. IV, 1002
Stanley, Alice Ann IV, 997
Stanley, Alice Ann IV, 1001
Stanley, Alice Esther I, 573
Stanley, Allen IV, 766
Stanley, Allen IV, 996
Stanley, Allen IV, 1001
Stanley, Allen IV, 1003
Stanley, Allen F. IV, 1000
Stanley, Almeda V, 1020
Stanley, Almina M. C. IV, 936
Stanley, Almina M. C. IV, 1003
Stanley, Almira IV, 997
Stanley, Almond IV, 765
Stanley, Almond IV, 767
Stanley, Almyra IV, 999
Stanley, Almyra IV, 1003
Stanley, Alphard IV, 1294
Stanley, Alvina IV, 229
Stanley, Alvina IV, 279
Stanley, Alvina IV, 969
Stanley, Alvina IV, 997
Stanley, Alvina IV, 999
Stanley, Amanda I, 515
Stanley, Amelia IV, 765
Stanley, Amelia IV, 1187
Stanley, Amelia V, 206
Stanley, Amelia F. IV, 765
Stanley, Amelia F. IV, 766
Stanley, Amelia F. IV, 767
Stanley, Amelia F. IV, 1147
Stanley, Amelia F. IV, 1187
Stanley, Amelia Felicia IV, 1187
Stanley, Amey VI, 272
Stanley, Amiel I, 515
Stanley, Amos IV, 762
Stanley, Amos IV, 992
Stanley, Amos IV, 996
Stanley, Amos IV, 999
Stanley, Amos IV, 1001
Stanley, Amos IV, 1002
Stanley, Amy IV, 764
Stanley, Amy IV, 765
Stanley, Amy IV, 781
Stanley, Amy IV, 941
Stanley, Amy IV, 984
Stanley, Amy IV, 995
Stanley, Amy IV, 996
Stanley, Amy IV, 1000
Stanley, Amy IV, 1001
Stanley, Amy IV, 1003
Stanley, Amy IV, 1211
Stanley, Amy IV, 1223
Stanley, Amy IV, 1224
Stanley, Amy F. IV, 551
Stanley, Amy J. IV, 921
Stanley, Amy J. IV, 998
Stanley, Amy T. IV, 550
Stanley, Amy T. IV, 551
Stanley, Andrew I, 515
Stanley, Andrew I, 573
Stanley, Andrew II, 720
Stanley, Andrew IV, 694
Stanley, Andrew IV, 722
Stanley, Andrew IV, 764
Stanley, Andrew IV, 765
Stanley, Andrew IV, 766
Stanley, Andrew IV, 767
Stanley, Andrew IV, 770
Stanley, Andrew IV, 845
Stanley, Andrew IV, 998
Stanley, Andrew IV, 999
Stanley, Andrew IV, 1001
Stanley, Andrew VI, 272
Stanley, Angelina IV, 1294
Stanley, Ann I, 590
Stanley, Ann I, 993
Stanley, Ann I, 997
Stanley, Ann IV, 764
Stanley, Ann IV, 765
Stanley, Ann IV, 766
Stanley, Ann IV, 901
Stanley, Ann IV, 937
Stanley, Ann IV, 950
Stanley, Ann IV, 996
Stanley, Ann IV, 998
Stanley, Ann IV, 1001
Stanley, Ann IV, 1116
Stanley, Ann VI, 227
Stanley, Ann VI, 268
Stanley, Ann VI, 269
Stanley, Ann VI, 270
Stanley, Ann Eliza VI, 952
Stanley, Ann W. IV, 955
Stanley, Ann W. IV, 998
Stanley, Anna I, 514
Stanley, Anna I, 515
Stanley, Anna I, 565
Stanley, Anna I, 573
Stanley, Anna I, 592
Stanley, Anna I, 596
Stanley, Anna I, 913
Stanley, Anna I, 914
Stanley, Anna IV, 707
Stanley, Anna IV, 766
Stanley, Anna IV, 995
Stanley, Anna Blanche IV, 986
Stanley, Anna Elizabeth I, 572
Stanley, Anna M. IV, 998
Stanley, Anna M. IV, 1002
Stanley, Anna M. IV, 1003
Stanley, Anna M. IV, 1043
Stanley, Anna Maria IV, 997
Stanley, Anna May IV, 1043
Stanley, Anne IV, 764
Stanley, Anne VI, 268
Stanley, Anne VI, 269
Stanley, Anne VI, 272
Stanley, Anne VI, 273
Stanley, Annie IV, 999
Stanley, Annie IV, 1043
Stanley, Annie V, 1020
Stanley, Annie M. IV, 968
Stanley, Annie M. IV, 1000
Stanley, Annie Margery IV, 1000
Stanley, Ansalem IV, 764
Stanley, Ansalem IV, 996
Stanley, Ansalem IV, 1001
Stanley, Ansalem Tillman IV, 997
Stanley, Anthony I, 515
Stanley, Anthony I, 572
Stanley, Anthony V, 280
Stanley, Anthony V, 531
Stanley, Anzanetta IV, 999
Stanley, Anzonetta IV, 1003
Stanley, Archaldus VI, 270
Stanley, Archalor VI, 270
Stanley, Archalos VI, 269
Stanley, Archalus I, 978
Stanley, Archelaus I, 571
Stanley, Archelaus I, 572
Stanley, Archelaus I, 838
Stanley, Archelaus VI, 189
Stanley, Archelaus VI, 192
Stanley, Archelaus VI, 213
Stanley, Archelaus VI, 214
Stanley, Archelaus VI, 270
Stanley, Archelius I, 990
Stanley, Archelius I, 997
Stanley, Archelous I, 993
Stanley, Archelous I, 997
Stanley, Archelus I, 971
Stanley, Archelus VI, 268
Stanley, Archiles VI, 270
Stanley, Archilleas VI, 269
Stanley, Archilles VI, 268
Stanley, Arthur IV, 1000
Stanley, Arthur Clyde IV, 986
Stanley, Arthur Loren IV, 440
Stanley, Asa I, 515
Stanley, Asa I, 590
Stanley, Asa I, 597
Stanley, Asenath I, 573
Stanley, Asenath I, 608
Stanley, Asenath I, 626
Stanley, Asenath I, 838
Stanley, Asenath IV, 997
Stanley, Asenath IV, 1002
Stanley, Aseneth I, 641
Stanley, Asheley VI, 269
Stanley, Assenath I, 573
Stanley, Barbara I, 572
Stanley, Barbary I, 572
Stanley, Barbery I, 515
Stanley, Barnabas I, 792
Stanley, Benj. IV, 998
Stanley, Benjamin IV, 279
Stanley, Benjamin IV, 690
Stanley, Benjamin IV, 763
Stanley, Benjamin IV, 764
Stanley, Benjamin IV, 765
Stanley, Benjamin IV, 766
Stanley, Benjamin IV, 767
Stanley, Benjamin IV, 901
Stanley, Benjamin IV, 907
Stanley, Benjamin IV, 921
Stanley, Benjamin IV, 925
Stanley, Benjamin IV, 937
Stanley, Benjamin IV, 951
Stanley, Benjamin IV, 964
Stanley, Benjamin IV, 992
Stanley, Benjamin IV, 995
Stanley, Benjamin IV, 996
Stanley, Benjamin IV, 999
Stanley, Benjamin IV, 1002
Stanley, Benjamin IV, 1007
Stanley, Benjamin VI, 268
Stanley, Benjamin VI, 271
Stanley, Benjamin VI, 272
Stanley, Benjamin C. IV, 996
Stanley, Benjamin C. IV, 999
Stanley, Benjamin C. IV, 1002
Stanley, Benjamin C. IV, 1003
Stanley, Benjamin Franklin I, 668
Stanley, Benjamin G. IV, 1003
Stanley, Benjamin V. IV, 352
Stanley, Benjamin W. IV, 1003
Stanley, Benjamin Walker IV, 997
Stanley, Benjamin Walker IV, 1001
Stanley, Bernice IV, 1000
Stanley, Bertha Elvira IV, 1043
Stanley, Bertha Marie IV, 1000
Stanley, Bertha Mertis IV, 1000
Stanley, Bessie Anna IV, 1000
Stanley, Bessie Anna IV, 1003
Stanley, Bessie Estella IV, 999
Stanley, Betsey I, 573
Stanley, Betsey I, 596
Stanley, Betsey I, 838
Stanley, Betsy I, 515
Stanley, Betsy I, 591
Stanley, Betsy I, 806
Stanley, Betsy I, 838
Stanley, Betsy VI, 314
Stanley, Betsy Jane I, 591
Stanley, Betty VI, 270
Stanley, Binford IV, 765
Stanley, Binford IV, 997
Stanley, Binford IV, 1043
Stanley, Binford VI, 272
Stanley, Binford T. IV, 999
Stanley, Birdella V, 206
Stanley, Blanche IV, 1000
Stanley, Blanche IV, 1003
Stanley, Blanche IV, 1043
Stanley, Blanche E. IV, 968
Stanley, Bulah I, 590
Stanley, Bulah VI, 271
Stanley, Buly I, 515
Stanley, Byron IV, 999
Stanley, Byron IV, 1002
Stanley, Caleb IV, 996
Stanley, Caleb IV, 998
Stanley, Caleb IV, 1000
Stanley, Caleb IV, 1001
Stanley, Caleb IV, 1005
Stanley, Caleb IV, 1295
Stanley, Caleb V, 124
Stanley, Caleb VI, 214
Stanley, Caleb VI, 268
Stanley, Caless I, 515
Stanley, Callie I, 615
Stanley, Calvin I, 573
Stanley, Calvin I, 591
Stanley, Calvin I, 597
Stanley, Calvin IV, 998
Stanley, Calvin IV, 1043
Stanley, Carl Van IV, 999
Stanley, Carolina VI, 270
Stanley, Caroline A. IV, 1223
Stanley, Caroline Ann IV, 1224
Stanley, Casper IV, 998
Stanley, Casper IV, 1043
Stanley, Catharine I, 515
Stanley, Catharine I, 792
Stanley, Catharine I, 838
Stanley, Catharine IV, 704
Stanley, Catharine IV, 764
Stanley, Catharine IV, 765
Stanley, Catharine IV, 767
Stanley, Catharine VI, 564
Stanley, Catharine L. IV, 551
Stanley, Catherine I, 515
Stanley, Catherine VI, 184
Stanley, Catherine VI, 213
Stanley, Catherine VI, 268
Stanley, Catherine VI, 269
Stanley, Catherine VI, 270
Stanley, Catherine L. IV, 550
Stanley, Cathron VI, 269
Stanley, Celia VI, 272

Stanley, Charles I, 515
Stanley, Charles I, 573
Stanley, Charles IV, 997
Stanley, Charles IV, 1000
Stanley, Charles IV, 1003
Stanley, Charles E. IV, 999
Stanley, Charles Edward V, 206
Stanley, Charles Joseph IV, 998
Stanley, Charles Joseph IV, 1295
Stanley, Charles Ray IV, 1000
Stanley, Charles Ray IV, 1003
Stanley, Charley E. IV, 1043
Stanley, Charlie L. I, 668
Stanley, Charlotte I, 590
Stanley, Charlotte I, 594
Stanley, Charlotte I, 597
Stanley, Charlotte IV, 973
Stanley, Charlotte IV, 996
Stanley, Charlotte IV, 998
Stanley, Charlotte IV, 1000
Stanley, Charlotte K. IV, 998
Stanley, Charlotte K. IV, 1003
Stanley, Chas. Joseph IV, 1002
Stanley, Chester G. IV, 1043
Stanley, Chlotilda IV, 939
Stanley, Chlotilda IV, 995
Stanley, Chlotilda IV, 997
Stanley, Chlotilda IV, 999
Stanley, Christopher J. IV, 998
Stanley, Christopher J. IV, 1002
Stanley, Clara IV, 986
Stanley, Clara H. IV, 960
Stanley, Clarence IV, 999
Stanley, Clarence IV, 1003
Stanley, Clarence Wilbur IV, 440
Stanley, Clayton Robert IV, 440
Stanley, Clotilda IV, 764
Stanley, Clotilda IV, 937
Stanley, Clotilda IV, 1000
Stanley, Clotilda IV, 1002
Stanley, Clyde M. IV, 1000
Stanley, Clyde M. IV, 1003
Stanley, Clyde M. IV, 1043
Stanley, Collita I, 573
Stanley, Cora I, 626
Stanley, Cora E. IV, 1043
Stanley, Cora L. IV, 1043
Stanley, Cynthia V, 206
Stanley, Cyrus I, 573
Stanley, Cyrus I, 590
Stanley, Cyrus I, 604
Stanley, Cyrus IV, 996
Stanley, Cyrus IV, 1001
Stanley, Daner VI, 167
Stanley, Daner VI, 192
Stanley, Daner VI, 213
Stanley, Daniel IV, 997
Stanley, Daniel H. IV, 279
Stanley, Daniel H. IV, 288
Stanley, Daniel Walker IV, 1001
Stanley, David IV, 998
Stanley, David IV, 1187
Stanley, David M. IV, 765
Stanley, Deborah I, 590
Stanley, Deborah I, 596
Stanley, Deborah I, 597
Stanley, Deborah I, 914
Stanley, Deborah IV, 764
Stanley, Deborah IV, 948
Stanley, Deborah IV, 995
Stanley, Deborah IV, 1001
Stanley, Delphia VI, 339
Stanley, Delphina T. IV, 971
Stanley, Delphina T. IV, 998
Stanley, Diana I, 551
Stanley, Diana I, 573
Stanley, Dianna I, 516
Stanley, Dorcas I, 516
Stanley, Dorcas I, 551
Stanley, Dorcas I, 572
Stanley, Doris Irene IV, 986
Stanley, Dr. T. J. VI, 272
Stanley, Dr. T. J. VI, 273
Stanley, Dresilla VI, 312
Stanley, Drusilla IV, 998
Stanley, Drusilla IV, 999
Stanley, Drusilla IV, 1002
Stanley, Drusilla IV, 1223
Stanley, Drusilla IV, 1224
Stanley, Ede VI, 250
Stanley, Edeth I, 838
Stanley, Edey VI, 250
Stanley, Edey VI, 269
Stanley, Edith I, 838
Stanley, Edith I, 978
Stanley, Edith IV, 696
Stanley, Edith IV, 764
Stanley, Edith IV, 765
Stanley, Edith IV, 781
Stanley, Edith IV, 960
Stanley, Edith IV, 986
Stanley, Edith IV, 995
Stanley, Edith IV, 996
Stanley, Edith IV, 998
Stanley, Edith IV, 1000
Stanley, Edith IV, 1001
Stanley, Edith IV, 1003
Stanley, Edith IV, 1043
Stanley, Edith V, 206
Stanley, Edith VI, 268
Stanley, Edith VI, 269
Stanley, Edith VI, 271
Stanley, Edith VI, 272
Stanley, Edith A. IV, 406
Stanley, Edith A. IV, 440
Stanley, Edith A. IV, 821
Stanley, Edith E. IV, 648
Stanley, Edithy VI, 945
Stanley, Edmond IV, 919
Stanley, Edmond IV, 996
Stanley, Edmond, Jr. IV, 996
Stanley, Edmund IV, 279
Stanley, Edmund IV, 751
Stanley, Edmund IV, 764
Stanley, Edmund IV, 765
Stanley, Edmund IV, 766
Stanley, Edmund IV, 993
Stanley, Edmund IV, 999
Stanley, Edmund VI, 268
Stanley, Edmund VI, 271
Stanley, Edmund VI, 272
Stanley, Edmund VI, 831
Stanley, Edna IV, 940
Stanley, Edna IV, 1001
Stanley, Edna IV, 1043
Stanley, Edna May IV, 1043
Stanley, Edward I, 572
Stanley, Edward I, 578
Stanley, Edward IV, 998
Stanley, Edward IV, 1000
Stanley, Edward IV, 1001
Stanley, Edward IV, 1003
Stanley, Edward VI, 854
Stanley, Edward VI, 855
Stanley, Edward D. VI, 839
Stanley, Edward M. IV, 999
Stanley, Edwin IV, 997
Stanley, Edwin IV, 1001
Stanley, Edwin IV, 1116
Stanley, Edwin IV, 1224
Stanley, Edwin W. IV, 1001
Stanley, Effie IV, 986
Stanley, Eleanor IV, 1000
Stanley, Eleazar IV, 1295
Stanley, Eleazar V, 124
Stanley, Eleazer I, 515
Stanley, Eleazer V, 124
Stanley, Elesar IV, 1294
Stanley, Eli I, 562
Stanley, Eli I, 573
Stanley, Eli IV, 91
Stanley, Eli IV, 767
Stanley, Eli IV, 793
Stanley, Eli IV, 939
Stanley, Eli IV, 943
Stanley, Eli IV, 996
Stanley, Eli IV, 997
Stanley, Eli IV, 998
Stanley, Eli IV, 999
Stanley, Eli IV, 1001
Stanley, Eli G. IV, 1043
Stanley, Eli J. IV, 1043
Stanley, Eli T. IV, 998
Stanley, Eli T. IV, 1001
Stanley, Elias I, 516
Stanley, Elihu IV, 996
Stanley, Elihu IV, 1000
Stanley, Elihu IV, 1001
Stanley, Elihu IV, 1002
Stanley, Elihu B. IV, 236
Stanley, Elihu B. IV, 279
Stanley, Elihu B. IV, 765
Stanley, Elihu B. IV, 766
Stanley, Elihu B. IV, 996
Stanley, Elihu B. IV, 998
Stanley, Elihu B. IV, 1000
Stanley, Elihu B. IV, 1001
Stanley, Elihu B. IV, 1002
Stanley, Elijah I, 562
Stanley, Elijah I, 571
Stanley, Elijah I, 792
Stanley, Elijah I, 838
Stanley, Elijah I, 978
Stanley, Elijah I, 997
Stanley, Elijah IV, 764
Stanley, Elijah IV, 765
Stanley, Elijah IV, 766
Stanley, Elijah IV, 783
Stanley, Elijah IV, 933
Stanley, Elijah IV, 955
Stanley, Elijah IV, 996
Stanley, Elijah IV, 999
Stanley, Elijah IV, 1000
Stanley, Elijah IV, 1003
Stanley, Elijah VI, 268
Stanley, Elijah VI, 269
Stanley, Elijah VI, 271
Stanley, Elijah VI, 272
Stanley, Elijah T. IV, 1002
Stanley, Elijah Thomas IV, 996
Stanley, Elisabeth II, 658
Stanley, Elisha IV, 995
Stanley, Eliza I, 590
Stanley, Eliza I, 597
Stanley, Eliza I, 819
Stanley, Eliza I, 838
Stanley, Eliza IV, 681
Stanley, Eliza IV, 764
Stanley, Eliza IV, 765
Stanley, Eliza IV, 766
Stanley, Eliza IV, 883
Stanley, Eliza IV, 990
Stanley, Eliza IV, 996
Stanley, Eliza IV, 1001
Stanley, Eliza IV, 1002
Stanley, Eliza V, 124
Stanley, Eliza V, 740
Stanley, Eliza VI, 270
Stanley, Eliza C. IV, 767
Stanley, Eliza C. IV, 877
Stanley, Eliza C. IV, 883
Stanley, Eliza C. IV, 979
Stanley, Eliza C. IV, 999
Stanley, Eliza C. IV, 1001
Stanley, Eliza C. IV, 1003
Stanley, Eliza Crenshaw VI, 272
Stanley, Eliza Jane IV, 997
Stanley, Eliza T. IV, 464
Stanley, Eliza T. IV, 497
Stanley, Eliza T. IV, 925
Stanley, Eliza T. IV, 996
Stanley, Eliza T. IV, 998
Stanley, Eliza Terrell IV, 764
Stanley, Elizabeth I, 515
Stanley, Elizabeth I, 516
Stanley, Elizabeth I, 527
Stanley, Elizabeth I, 537
Stanley, Elizabeth I, 567
Stanley, Elizabeth I, 571
Stanley, Elizabeth I, 572
Stanley, Elizabeth I, 573
Stanley, Elizabeth I, 578
Stanley, Elizabeth I, 580
Stanley, Elizabeth I, 590
Stanley, Elizabeth I, 597
Stanley, Elizabeth I, 603
Stanley, Elizabeth I, 604
Stanley, Elizabeth I, 608
Stanley, Elizabeth I, 825
Stanley, Elizabeth I, 838
Stanley, Elizabeth I, 986
Stanley, Elizabeth I, 997
Stanley, Elizabeth II, 552
Stanley, Elizabeth II, 719
Stanley, Elizabeth IV, 279
Stanley, Elizabeth IV, 690
Stanley, Elizabeth IV, 728
Stanley, Elizabeth IV, 764
Stanley, Elizabeth IV, 765
Stanley, Elizabeth IV, 766
Stanley, Elizabeth IV, 787
Stanley, Elizabeth IV, 793
Stanley, Elizabeth IV, 901
Stanley, Elizabeth IV, 907
Stanley, Elizabeth IV, 916
Stanley, Elizabeth IV, 921
Stanley, Elizabeth IV, 925
Stanley, Elizabeth IV, 926
Stanley, Elizabeth IV, 927
Stanley, Elizabeth IV, 933
Stanley, Elizabeth IV, 937
Stanley, Elizabeth IV, 938
Stanley, Elizabeth IV, 941
Stanley, Elizabeth IV, 964
Stanley, Elizabeth IV, 973
Stanley, Elizabeth IV, 984
Stanley, Elizabeth IV, 988
Stanley, Elizabeth IV, 992
Stanley, Elizabeth IV, 993
Stanley, Elizabeth IV, 995
Stanley, Elizabeth IV, 996
Stanley, Elizabeth IV, 997
Stanley, Elizabeth IV, 998
Stanley, Elizabeth IV, 999
Stanley, Elizabeth IV, 1000
Stanley, Elizabeth IV, 1001
Stanley, Elizabeth IV, 1002
Stanley, Elizabeth IV, 1003
Stanley, Elizabeth IV, 1007
Stanley, Elizabeth IV, 1011
Stanley, Elizabeth IV, 1223
Stanley, Elizabeth IV, 1224
Stanley, Elizabeth IV, 1294
Stanley, Elizabeth V, 280
Stanley, Elizabeth V, 360
Stanley, Elizabeth V, 433
Stanley, Elizabeth V, 531
Stanley, Elizabeth V, 830
Stanley, Elizabeth V, 862
Stanley, Elizabeth VI, 166
Stanley, Elizabeth VI, 172
Stanley, Elizabeth VI, 174
Stanley, Elizabeth VI, 189
Stanley, Elizabeth VI, 192
Stanley, Elizabeth VI, 198
Stanley, Elizabeth VI, 213
Stanley, Elizabeth VI, 214
Stanley, Elizabeth VI, 268
Stanley, Elizabeth VI, 269
Stanley, Elizabeth VI, 271
Stanley, Elizabeth VI, 272
Stanley, Elizabeth VI, 564
Stanley, Elizabeth VI, 1017
Stanley, Elizabeth A. I, 573
Stanley, Elizabeth Ann IV, 995
Stanley, Elizabeth Ann IV, 997
Stanley, Elizabeth Ann IV, 999
Stanley, Elizabeth Ann IV, 1001
Stanley, Elizabeth C. IV, 1002
Stanley, Elizabeth E. IV, 1223
Stanley, Elizabeth Jesse VI, 272
Stanley, Elizabeth M. II, 122
Stanley, Elizabeth M. II, 124
Stanley, Elizabeth, Jr. VI, 269
Stanley, Ella IV, 786
Stanley, Ella IV, 1043
Stanley, Ellen I, 574
Stanley, Ellen I, 597
Stanley, Ellen I, 641
Stanley, Ellen II, 700
Stanley, Ellen II, 713
Stanley, Ellen II, 720
Stanley, Ellen IV, 513
Stanley, Ellen IV, 552
Stanley, Ellen IV, 765
Stanley, Ellen IV, 770
Stanley, Ellen IV, 845
Stanley, Ellen IV, 988
Stanley, Ellen IV, 997
Stanley, Ellen IV, 999
Stanley, Ellwood IV, 996
Stanley, Elma IV, 1003
Stanley, Elmer E. IV, 999
Stanley, Elmina I, 516
Stanley, Elmina IV, 941
Stanley, Elmina IV, 963
Stanley, Elmina IV, 999
Stanley, Elmina IV, 1003
Stanley, Elmina M. IV, 936
Stanley, Elmira IV, 930
Stanley, Elmira IV, 1002
Stanley, Elmore E. IV, 1002
Stanley, Elsie IV, 1043
Stanley, Elwood I, 590
Stanley, Elwood IV, 764
Stanley, Elwood IV, 766
Stanley, Elwood IV, 998
Stanley, Elwood IV, 1000
Stanley, Elwood IV, 1001
Stanley, Emaline I, 888
Stanley, Emaline I, 901
Stanley, Emerson L. IV, 767
Stanley, Emerson L. IV, 999
Stanley, Emerson L. IV, 1003
Stanley, Emily IV, 996
Stanley, Emily Jane IV, 933
Stanley, Emily Jane IV, 998
Stanley, Emma IV, 1043
Stanley, Emma C. IV, 1003
Stanley, Emma E. IV, 999
Stanley, Emmerson L. IV, 1000
Stanley, Emmor IV, 997
Stanley, Emmor IV, 1001
Stanley, Emmor IV, 1003
Stanley, Emmor F. IV, 1000
Stanley, Enocy P. IV, 786
Stanley, Enos I, 998
Stanley, Eoizabeth IV, 999
Stanley, Ernest G. IV, 1000
Stanley, Estella IV, 977
Stanley, Estella IV, 1003
Stanley, Ester I, 515
Stanley, Esther I, 515
Stanley, Esther I, 623
Stanley, Esther IV, 279
Stanley, Esther IV, 713
Stanley, Esther IV, 764
Stanley, Esther IV, 765
Stanley, Esther IV, 921
Stanley, Esther IV, 929
Stanley, Esther IV, 964
Stanley, Esther IV, 995
Stanley, Esther IV, 996
Stanley, Esther IV, 997
Stanley, Esther IV, 998
Stanley, Esther IV, 999
Stanley, Esther IV, 1001
Stanley, Esther IV, 1002
Stanley, Esther IV, 1005
Stanley, Esther IV, 1006
Stanley, Esther IV, 1043
Stanley, Esther IV, 1223
Stanley, Esther IV, 1225
Stanley, Esther B. IV, 1043
Stanley, Esther Elma IV, 999
Stanley, Esther Elma IV, 1003
Stanley, Esther Jane IV, 352
Stanley, Ethel IV, 406
Stanley, Ethel A. IV, 407
Stanley, Ethel A. IV, 440
Stanley, Ethel Alice IV, 821
Stanley, Eugenia Ellen I, 573
Stanley, Eunice IV, 933
Stanley, Eunice IV, 1002
Stanley, Eunice IV, 1379
Stanley, Eva V, 206
Stanley, Evan IV, 1002
Stanley, Evan G. IV, 997
Stanley, Evan G. IV, 999
Stanley, Evan G. IV, 1002
Stanley, Evangeline Mosher IV, 1224
Stanley, Everett IV, 1014
Stanley, Ezra IV, 765
Stanley, Ezra IV, 767
Stanley, Ezra IV, 997
Stanley, Ezra IV, 1003
Stanley, F. C. IV, 1224
Stanley, F. C. V, 764
Stanley, Fannie I, 626
Stanley, Fanny IV, 766
Stanley, Fanny VI, 272
Stanley, Felicia A. IV, 767
Stanley, Felicia A. IV, 1187
Stanley, Fleming IV, 466
Stanley, Fleming IV, 497
Stanley, Fleming IV, 764
Stanley, Fleming IV, 766
Stanley, Fleming IV, 1002
Stanley, Fleming VI, 272
Stanley, Fleming A. IV, 997
Stanley, Fleming A. IV, 1002
Stanley, Fleming A. IV, 1379
Stanley, Flemming A. IV, 933
Stanley, Florence A. V, 206
Stanley, Floy O. IV, 784
Stanley, Frances IV, 764
Stanley, Frances IV, 765
Stanley, Frances IV, 781
Stanley, Frances IV, 844
Stanley, Frances VI, 269
Stanley, Francis V, 206
Stanley, Francis VI, 243
Stanley, Francis VI, 272
Stanley, Francis C. IV, 1210
Stanley, Francis C. IV, 1223
Stanley, Francis C. IV, 1224
Stanley, Francis C. V, 764
Stanley, Francis C. V, 1020
Stanley, Frank IV, 1339
Stanley, Frank V, 206
Stanley, Franklin IV, 998
Stanley, Franklin IV, 1001
Stanley, Franklin V, 206
Stanley, Franklin C. IV, 1000
Stanley, Frederick IV, 764
Stanley, Frederick IV, 766
Stanley, Frederick VI, 272
Stanley, Garland IV, 686
Stanley, Garland IV, 764
Stanley, Garland IV, 766
Stanley, Garland IV, 949
Stanley, Garland IV, 995
Stanley, Garland IV, 1000
Stanley, Garland IV, 1001
Stanley, Garland VI, 272
Stanley, Gennetta IV, 1295
Stanley, George I, 997
Stanley, George IV, 765
Stanley, George IV, 767
Stanley, George IV, 998
Stanley, George IV, 1001
Stanley, George V, 360
Stanley, George V, 424
Stanley, George V, 433
Stanley, George VI, 167
Stanley, George VI, 339
Stanley, George VI, 871
Stanley, George VI, 895
Stanley, George VI, 945
Stanley, George VI, 952
Stanley, George VI, 968
Stanley, George VI, 972
Stanley, George VI, 975
Stanley, George VI, 997

ey, George VI, 1004
ey, George VI, 1017
ey, George T. IV, 998
ey, George T. IV, 999
ey, George T. IV, 1002
ey, George T. IV, 1003
ey, George T. IV, 1043
ey, George T. IV, 1223
ey, George T. IV, 1224
ey, George W. VI, 988
ey, George, Jr. VI, 997
ey, Gerard IV, 766
ey, Geroo IV, 1000
ey, Gertrude IV, 766
ey, Gertrude IV, 824
ey, Gertrude IV, 844
ey, Gideon VI, 268
ey, Gideon K. VI, 272
ey, Gillmore IV, 1295
ey, Girtrude IV, 999
ey, Gladys IV, 1043
ey, Goldie IV, 1295
ey, Gourley R. I, 590
ey, Gravener I, 572
ey, Gravener I, 573
ey, Gravner I, 572
ey, Gravner I, 573
ey, Gulielma I, 590
ey, Gurley I, 597
ey, Guy IV, 1043
ey, Guy C. IV, 1043
ey, H. H. V, 1020
ey, Hannah I, 514
ey, Hannah I, 515
ey, Hannah I, 516
ey, Hannah I, 527
ey, Hannah I, 557
ey, Hannah I, 562
ey, Hannah I, 571
ey, Hannah I, 572
ey, Hannah I, 573
ey, Hannah I, 590
ey, Hannah I, 597
ey, Hannah I, 604
ey, Hannah I, 792
ey, Hannah I, 838
ey, Hannah I, 997
ey, Hannah I, 1011
ey, Hannah I, 1012
ey, Hannah IV, 101
ey, Hannah IV, 110
ey, Hannah IV, 279
ey, Hannah IV, 681
ey, Hannah IV, 741
ey, Hannah IV, 765
ey, Hannah IV, 766
ey, Hannah IV, 933
ey, Hannah IV, 967
ey, Hannah IV, 980
ey, Hannah IV, 996
ey, Hannah IV, 997
ey, Hannah IV, 998
ey, Hannah IV, 1000
ey, Hannah IV, 1002
ey, Hannah IV, 1010
ey, Hannah V, 280
ey, Hannah V, 531
ey, Hannah V, 644
ey, Hannah VI, 268
ey, Hannah VI, 287
ey, Hannah Ann IV, 235
ey, Hannah Ann IV, 271
ey, Hannah Ann IV, 272
ey, Hannah Ann IV, 279
ey, Hannah Ann IV, 1043
ey, Hannah G. IV, 997
ey, Hannah G. IV, 1001
ey, Hannah M. IV, 110
ey, Hannah M. IV, 765
ey, Hannah M. IV, 766
ey, Hannah M. IV, 767
ey, Hannah, Jr. I, 1012
ey, Hannah, Sr. I, 838
ey, Harriet IV, 279
ey, Harriet IV, 291
ey, Harriet IV, 767
ey, Harriet IV, 999
ey, Harriet IV, 1002
ey, Harriet VI, 854
ey, Harriet R. IV, 765
ey, Harris O. IV, 1000
ey, Harris O. IV, 1003
ey, Harris O. IV, 1043
ey, Harry IV, 927
ey, Hazel III, 298
ey, Hazel D. III, 152
ey, Helen IV, 1003
ey, Helen IV, 1043
ey, Helen Elvira IV, 1000
ey, Helen Miles IV, 1043
ey, Helen R. IV, 433
Stanley, Helen R. IV, 440
Stanley, Henrietta IV, 764
Stanley, Henrietta IV, 936
Stanley, Henrietta IV, 995
Stanley, Henrietta IV, 997
Stanley, Henrietta IV, 998
Stanley, Henrietta IV, 999
Stanley, Henry I, 515
Stanley, Henry I, 572
Stanley, Henry I, 573
Stanley, Henry IV, 1000
Stanley, Henry IV, 1003
Stanley, Henry Benedict IV, 497
Stanley, Henry G. IV, 998
Stanley, Henry G. IV, 1003
Stanley, Henryette IV, 1014
Stanley, Hezel D. III, 298
Stanley, Hiram V, 1020
Stanley, Homer IV, 1000
Stanley, Homer IV, 1003
Stanley, Homer IV, 1043
Stanley, Homer Raymond IV, 999
Stanley, Homer S. IV, 1000
Stanley, Horace J. IV, 1000
Stanley, Howard V, 206
Stanley, Huldah I, 626
Stanley, Huldah I, 792
Stanley, Huldah I, 804
Stanley, Huldah I, 838
Stanley, Huldah VI, 197
Stanley, Huldah VI, 213
Stanley, Huldah VI, 238
Stanley, Huldah VI, 268
Stanley, Huldah VI, 269
Stanley, Huldah VI, 271
Stanley, Huldah VI, 272
Stanley, Huldah VI, 273
Stanley, Huldah I. I, 681
Stanley, Huldah I. I, 689
Stanley, Huldah J. I, 668
Stanley, Huldah L. J. I, 615
Stanley, Hutchens I, 997
Stanley, Ida IV, 1000
Stanley, Ina M. IV, 999
Stanley, Ira I, 515
Stanley, Ira I, 516
Stanley, Ira I, 590
Stanley, Ira IV, 279
Stanley, Ira IV, 1294
Stanley, Ira V, 124
Stanley, Isaac I, 515
Stanley, Isaac I, 516
Stanley, Isaac I, 572
Stanley, Isaac I, 573
Stanley, Isaac I, 590
Stanley, Isaac I, 596
Stanley, Isaac I, 597
Stanley, Isaac I, 641
Stanley, Isaac I, 819
Stanley, Isaac I, 838
Stanley, Isaac IV, 764
Stanley, Isaac IV, 765
Stanley, Isaac IV, 766
Stanley, Isaac IV, 767
Stanley, Isaac IV, 926
Stanley, Isaac IV, 933
Stanley, Isaac IV, 938
Stanley, Isaac IV, 995
Stanley, Isaac IV, 996
Stanley, Isaac IV, 997
Stanley, Isaac IV, 1000
Stanley, Isaac IV, 1001
Stanley, Isaac IV, 1002
Stanley, Isaac V, 433
Stanley, Isaac V, 531
Stanley, Isaac VI, 269
Stanley, Isaac VI, 271
Stanley, Isaac VI, 272
Stanley, Isaac E. IV, 765
Stanley, Isaac E. IV, 767
Stanley, Isaac F. I, 689
Stanley, Isaac H. I, 573
Stanley, Isaac H. I, 615
Stanley, Isaac H. I, 668
Stanley, Isaac H. I, 689
Stanley, Isaac H. C. I, 626
Stanley, Isaac N. IV, 1001
Stanley, Isaac V. IV, 1002
Stanley, Isaac W. IV, 997
Stanley, Isabel IV, 996
Stanley, Isabella IV, 765
Stanley, Isabella IV, 999
Stanley, Isaiah I, 516
Stanley, Isaiah I, 572
Stanley, Isaiah I, 573
Stanley, Isaiah I, 838
Stanley, Isaiah IV, 696
Stanley, Isaiah IV, 764
Stanley, Isaiah IV, 766
Stanley, Isaiah IV, 946
Stanley, Isaiah IV, 997
Stanley, Isaiah IV, 1001
Stanley, Isaiah IV, 1116
Stanley, Isaiah IV, 1223
Stanley, Isaiah IV, 1224
Stanley, Isaiah V, 206
Stanley, Isareal I, 590
Stanley, Isiah I, 838
Stanley, Israel I, 515
Stanley, Israel I, 527
Stanley, Israel I, 573
Stanley, Israel I, 586
Stanley, Israel I, 596
Stanley, Israel I, 603
Stanley, Israel I, 604
Stanley, Israel IV, 440
Stanley, Israel IV, 765
Stanley, Israel IV, 766
Stanley, Israel IV, 933
Stanley, Israel IV, 939
Stanley, Israel IV, 971
Stanley, Israel IV, 996
Stanley, Israel IV, 998
Stanley, Israel IV, 1000
Stanley, Israel IV, 1002
Stanley, Isrial I, 608
Stanley, Ivey I, 597
Stanley, Jacob IV, 764
Stanley, Jacob IV, 766
Stanley, Jacob IV, 1001
Stanley, Jacob IV, 1077
Stanley, Jacob VI, 213
Stanley, James I, 515
Stanley, James I, 545
Stanley, James I, 571
Stanley, James I, 572
Stanley, James I, 573
Stanley, James I, 792
Stanley, James I, 838
Stanley, James I, 979
Stanley, James I, 997
Stanley, James I, 998
Stanley, James IV, 279
Stanley, James IV, 440
Stanley, James IV, 619
Stanley, James IV, 657
Stanley, James IV, 671
Stanley, James IV, 690
Stanley, James IV, 728
Stanley, James IV, 763
Stanley, James IV, 764
Stanley, James IV, 765
Stanley, James IV, 766
Stanley, James IV, 767
Stanley, James IV, 787
Stanley, James IV, 793
Stanley, James IV, 919
Stanley, James IV, 973
Stanley, James IV, 995
Stanley, James IV, 996
Stanley, James IV, 997
Stanley, James IV, 998
Stanley, James IV, 999
Stanley, James IV, 1000
Stanley, James IV, 1001
Stanley, James IV, 1211
Stanley, James IV, 1294
Stanley, James V, 124
Stanley, James V, 531
Stanley, James VI, 174
Stanley, James VI, 181
Stanley, James VI, 184
Stanley, James VI, 213
Stanley, James VI, 224
Stanley, James VI, 246
Stanley, James VI, 268
Stanley, James VI, 269
Stanley, James VI, 272
Stanley, James VI, 564
Stanley, James VI, 855
Stanley, James B. IV, 1001
Stanley, James C. IV, 440
Stanley, James C. IV, 594
Stanley, James C. IV, 764
Stanley, James C. IV, 766
Stanley, James C. IV, 844
Stanley, James C. IV, 883
Stanley, James C. IV, 995
Stanley, James C. IV, 1000
Stanley, James C. IV, 1001
Stanley, James C. IV, 1002
Stanley, James C. IV, 1223
Stanley, James Crew IV, 657
Stanley, James Crew IV, 766
Stanley, James Crew VI, 272
Stanley, James Edwin V, 531
Stanley, James G. IV, 1224
Stanley, James, Jr. IV, 440
Stanley, James, Jr. IV, 766
Stanley, James, Jr. VI, 172
Stanley, James, Jr. VI, 174
Stanley, James, Jr. VI, 213
Stanley, James, Jr. VI, 214
Stanley, Jamima I, 838
Stanley, Jamima V, 424
Stanley, Jamima V, 433
Stanley, Jane I, 515
Stanley, Jane I, 597
Stanley, Jane IV, 279
Stanley, Jane IV, 930
Stanley, Jane IV, 952
Stanley, Jane IV, 996
Stanley, Jane IV, 997
Stanley, Jane IV, 1000
Stanley, Jane IV, 1001
Stanley, Jane M. IV, 235
Stanley, Janet IV, 996
Stanley, Janet IV, 1001
Stanley, Jared IV, 234
Stanley, Jared IV, 279
Stanley, Jared IV, 766
Stanley, Jared IV, 973
Stanley, Jared IV, 996
Stanley, Jared IV, 999
Stanley, Jared IV, 1000
Stanley, Jared IV, 1002
Stanley, Jason L. IV, 998
Stanley, Jason L. IV, 1003
Stanley, Jean I, 590
Stanley, Jefferson IV, 765
Stanley, Jefferson IV, 767
Stanley, Jefferson IV, 999
Stanley, Jehu IV, 765
Stanley, Jehu IV, 962
Stanley, Jehu IV, 996
Stanley, Jehu IV, 999
Stanley, Jehu IV, 1000
Stanley, Jehu IV, 1043
Stanley, Jehu C. IV, 986
Stanley, Jehu C. IV, 997
Stanley, Jehu C. IV, 1000
Stanley, Jehu C. IV, 1002
Stanley, Jehu C. IV, 1003
Stanley, Jemima I, 516
Stanley, Jemima I, 562
Stanley, Jemima I, 571
Stanley, Jemima I, 572
Stanley, Jemima I, 573
Stanley, Jemima I, 838
Stanley, Jemima V, 124
Stanley, Jemima V, 227
Stanley, Jemima V, 280
Stanley, Jemima V, 433
Stanley, Jemimah I, 572
Stanley, Jemimah V, 433
Stanley, Jene II, 719
Stanley, Jenet IV, 1001
Stanley, Jennet IV, 764
Stanley, Jennet IV, 997
Stanley, Jennie I, 573
Stanley, Jerdon IV, 1002
Stanley, Jeremiah IV, 697
Stanley, Jeremiah IV, 701
Stanley, Jeremiah IV, 764
Stanley, Jeremiah IV, 765
Stanley, Jeremiah IV, 766
Stanley, Jeremiah IV, 767
Stanley, Jeremiah IV, 950
Stanley, Jeremiah IV, 998
Stanley, Jeremiah V, 433
Stanley, Jeremiah Parker V, 433
Stanley, Jesse I, 515
Stanley, Jesse I, 516
Stanley, Jesse I, 542
Stanley, Jesse I, 545
Stanley, Jesse I, 571
Stanley, Jesse I, 572
Stanley, Jesse I, 573
Stanley, Jesse I, 586
Stanley, Jesse I, 590
Stanley, Jesse I, 596
Stanley, Jesse I, 597
Stanley, Jesse I, 600
Stanley, Jesse I, 792
Stanley, Jesse I, 838
Stanley, Jesse I, 979
Stanley, Jesse I, 997
Stanley, Jesse I, 998
Stanley, Jesse II, 122
Stanley, Jesse II, 124
Stanley, Jesse II, 768
Stanley, Jesse IV, 440
Stanley, Jesse IV, 594
Stanley, Jesse IV, 765
Stanley, Jesse IV, 766
Stanley, Jesse IV, 995
Stanley, Jesse IV, 996
Stanley, Jesse IV, 998
Stanley, Jesse IV, 999
Stanley, Jesse IV, 1001
Stanley, Jesse IV, 1187
Stanley, Jesse V, 206
Stanley, Jesse VI, 268
Stanley, Jesse VI, 269
Stanley, Jesse VI, 272
Stanley, Jesse VI, 273
Stanley, Jesse VI, 881
Stanley, Jesse VI, 997
Stanley, Jesse Crew IV, 764
Stanley, Jesse H. I, 574
Stanley, Jesse H. I, 597
Stanley, Jesse H. I, 641
Stanley, Jesse T. IV, 998
Stanley, Jesse T. IV, 999
Stanley, Jesse T. IV, 1002
Stanley, Jesse Thomas IV, 766
Stanley, Jesse Thomas VI, 272
Stanley, Joanna IV, 764
Stanley, Joanna IV, 765
Stanley, Joanna IV, 766
Stanley, Joanna IV, 777
Stanley, Joanna IV, 996
Stanley, Joanna B. IV, 996
Stanley, Joanna B. IV, 998
Stanley, Joanna B. IV, 1007
Stanley, Job IV, 764
Stanley, Joel IV, 764
Stanley, Joel IV, 766
Stanley, Joel IV, 939
Stanley, Joel IV, 995
Stanley, Joel IV, 997
Stanley, Joel IV, 999
Stanley, Joel IV, 1000
Stanley, Joel IV, 1002
Stanley, Joel VI, 269
Stanley, Joel VI, 272
Stanley, John I, 515
Stanley, John I, 537
Stanley, John I, 572
Stanley, John I, 573
Stanley, John I, 586
Stanley, John I, 590
Stanley, John I, 596
Stanley, John I, 597
Stanley, John I, 792
Stanley, John I, 838
Stanley, John I, 914
Stanley, John IV, 110
Stanley, John IV, 279
Stanley, John IV, 679
Stanley, John IV, 718
Stanley, John IV, 763
Stanley, John IV, 764
Stanley, John IV, 765
Stanley, John IV, 766
Stanley, John IV, 767
Stanley, John IV, 789
Stanley, John IV, 952
Stanley, John IV, 970
Stanley, John IV, 995
Stanley, John IV, 997
Stanley, John IV, 999
Stanley, John IV, 1001
Stanley, John IV, 1002
Stanley, John V, 280
Stanley, John V, 447
Stanley, John V, 531
Stanley, John VI, 165
Stanley, John VI, 213
Stanley, John VI, 224
Stanley, John VI, 227
Stanley, John VI, 238
Stanley, John VI, 250
Stanley, John VI, 251
Stanley, John VI, 268
Stanley, John VI, 269
Stanley, John VI, 270
Stanley, John VI, 271
Stanley, John VI, 272
Stanley, John VI, 273
Stanley, John VI, 339
Stanley, John VI, 800
Stanley, John VI, 855
Stanley, John A. IV, 1002
Stanley, John B. IV, 939
Stanley, John B. IV, 995
Stanley, John B. IV, 998
Stanley, John B. IV, 999
Stanley, John B. IV, 1003
Stanley, John C. IV, 1043
Stanley, John H. IV, 766
Stanley, John H. IV, 997
Stanley, John H. IV, 1000
Stanley, John H. IV, 1017
Stanley, John Hutchens I, 838
Stanley, John J. IV, 765
Stanley, John J. IV, 767
Stanley, John J. IV, 998
Stanley, John J. IV, 1001
Stanley, John M. IV, 927
Stanley, John M. IV, 1002
Stanley, John Martin IV, 996
Stanley, John Martin IV, 997
Stanley, John Martin IV, 1000

Stanley, John Milton IV, 1223
Stanley, John N. I, 573
Stanley, John T. VI, 803
Stanley, John W. IV, 784
Stanley, John, Jr. IV, 279
Stanley, John, Jr. IV, 310
Stanley, John, Jr. IV, 960
Stanley, John, Jr. IV, 985
Stanley, John, Jr. IV, 996
Stanley, John, Jr. IV, 1000
Stanley, John, Jr. IV, 1002
Stanley, John, Jr. VI, 270
Stanley, John, Sr. IV, 939
Stanley, Jonah VI, 214
Stanley, Jonathan I, 590
Stanley, Jonathan I, 997
Stanley, Jonathan IV, 101
Stanley, Jonathan IV, 110
Stanley, Jonathan IV, 440
Stanley, Jonathan IV, 497
Stanley, Jonathan IV, 594
Stanley, Jonathan IV, 681
Stanley, Jonathan IV, 728
Stanley, Jonathan IV, 741
Stanley, Jonathan IV, 764
Stanley, Jonathan IV, 765
Stanley, Jonathan IV, 766
Stanley, Jonathan IV, 767
Stanley, Jonathan IV, 844
Stanley, Jonathan IV, 995
Stanley, Jonathan IV, 996
Stanley, Jonathan IV, 1000
Stanley, Jonathan IV, 1001
Stanley, Jonathan IV, 1147
Stanley, Jonathan IV, 1187
Stanley, Jonathan VI, 239
Stanley, Jonathan VI, 269
Stanley, Jonathan VI, 271
Stanley, Jonathan VI, 272
Stanley, Jonathan, Jr. IV, 765
Stanley, Jordan IV, 764
Stanley, Jordan IV, 997
Stanley, Jordan IV, 1002
Stanley, Jordan VI, 272
Stanley, Jorden I, 997
Stanley, Jordon IV, 766
Stanley, Josaiah I, 573
Stanley, Joseph I, 571
Stanley, Joseph I, 572
Stanley, Joseph I, 641
Stanley, Joseph I, 785
Stanley, Joseph I, 792
Stanley, Joseph I, 835
Stanley, Joseph I, 838
Stanley, Joseph I, 979
Stanley, Joseph I, 997
Stanley, Joseph IV, 690
Stanley, Joseph IV, 763
Stanley, Joseph IV, 764
Stanley, Joseph IV, 766
Stanley, Joseph IV, 927
Stanley, Joseph IV, 989
Stanley, Joseph IV, 993
Stanley, Joseph IV, 994
Stanley, Joseph IV, 995
Stanley, Joseph IV, 996
Stanley, Joseph IV, 997
Stanley, Joseph IV, 998
Stanley, Joseph IV, 1001
Stanley, Joseph IV, 1002
Stanley, Joseph IV, 1003
Stanley, Joseph IV, 1015
Stanley, Joseph IV, 1294
Stanley, Joseph IV, 1295
Stanley, Joseph VI, 213
Stanley, Joseph VI, 268
Stanley, Joseph VI, 272
Stanley, Joseph H. IV, 1000
Stanley, Joseph Hinchman IV, 766
Stanley, Joseph M. I, 626
Stanley, Joseph, Jr. IV, 962
Stanley, Joseph, Jr. IV, 1001
Stanley, Josephine I, 573
Stanley, Josephine IV, 1002
Stanley, Joshua I, 516
Stanley, Joshua I, 573
Stanley, Joshua I, 591
Stanley, Joshua I, 596
Stanley, Joshua I, 668
Stanley, Joshua I, 689
Stanley, Joshua I, 886
Stanley, Joshua I, 901
Stanley, Joshua IV, 673
Stanley, Joshua IV, 753
Stanley, Joshua IV, 764
Stanley, Joshua IV, 766
Stanley, Joshua IV, 997
Stanley, Joshua IV, 1002
Stanley, Joshua IV, 1003
Stanley, Joshua IV, 1223
Stanley, Joshua VI, 247
Stanley, Joshua VI, 268
Stanley, Joshua VI, 269
Stanley, Joshua VI, 270
Stanley, Joshua VI, 271
Stanley, Joshua VI, 272
Stanley, Joshua W. IV, 999
Stanley, Joshua W. IV, 1003
Stanley, Joshua, Jr. VI, 271
Stanley, Josiah I, 516
Stanley, Josiah I, 590
Stanley, Josiah I, 597
Stanley, Josiah IV, 765
Stanley, Josiah IV, 766
Stanley, Josiah IV, 996
Stanley, Josiah IV, 1000
Stanley, Josiah IV, 1001
Stanley, Josiah Elwood V, 531
Stanley, Judith I, 572
Stanley, Judith I, 578
Stanley, Judith I, 980
Stanley, Judith I, 998
Stanley, Judith IV, 694
Stanley, Judith IV, 763
Stanley, Judith IV, 765
Stanley, Judith IV, 766
Stanley, Judith IV, 993
Stanley, Judith IV, 995
Stanley, Judith IV, 996
Stanley, Judith IV, 998
Stanley, Judith IV, 1001
Stanley, Judith IV, 1224
Stanley, Judith IV, 1294
Stanley, Judith IV, 1295
Stanley, Judith V, 473
Stanley, Judith V, 531
Stanley, Judith VI, 167
Stanley, Judith Abigail VI, 272
Stanley, Judith Ann IV, 927
Stanley, Judith Ann IV, 997
Stanley, Judith Ann IV, 998
Stanley, Judith Ann IV, 1002
Stanley, Judith C. IV, 230
Stanley, Judith C. IV, 279
Stanley, Judith C. IV, 310
Stanley, Judith C. IV, 764
Stanley, Judith C. IV, 970
Stanley, Judith C. IV, 996
Stanley, Judith C. IV, 999
Stanley, Judith C. IV, 1224
Stanley, Judith C. IV, 1227
Stanley, Julia V, 1020
Stanley, Julia C. IV, 1001
Stanley, Julia Catharine IV, 998
Stanley, Julia E. IV, 1002
Stanley, Juliann I, 515
Stanley, Juliann IV, 1223
Stanley, Juliet IV, 996
Stanley, Juliet IV, 999
Stanley, Juliet IV, 1002
Stanley, Juliet IV, 1003
Stanley, Kalita C. I, 573
Stanley, Kate Gaylord IV, 1187
Stanley, Katharine I, 838
Stanley, Kellita I, 573
Stanley, Keren Newby V, 433
Stanley, Keturah IV, 996
Stanley, Keturah IV, 1001
Stanley, Laura IV, 681
Stanley, Laura IV, 765
Stanley, Laura IV, 767
Stanley, Laura IV, 998
Stanley, Laura IV, 999
Stanley, Laura IV, 1001
Stanley, Laura F. IV, 767
Stanley, Laura F. IV, 999
Stanley, Laura F. IV, 1000
Stanley, Laura F. IV, 1003
Stanley, Laura S. IV, 1000
Stanley, Laura Susan IV, 927
Stanley, Laura T. IV, 1003
Stanley, Lavina I, 573
Stanley, Lavina IV, 762
Stanley, Lavina IV, 993
Stanley, Lavina IV, 996
Stanley, Lavina IV, 999
Stanley, Lavina IV, 1002
Stanley, Lavina IV, 1043
Stanley, Lawrence IV, 1043
Stanley, Leah IV, 766
Stanley, Leah IV, 782
Stanley, Leah IV, 844
Stanley, Leah IV, 850
Stanley, Leah IV, 996
Stanley, Leah IV, 1001
Stanley, Leander IV, 941
Stanley, Leander IV, 963
Stanley, Leander IV, 998
Stanley, Leander M. IV, 999
Stanley, Leander M. IV, 1003
Stanley, Lemiel V, 1020
Stanley, Lemuel IV, 440
Stanley, Lemuel IV, 594
Stanley, Lemuel IV, 766
Stanley, Lemuel IV, 844
Stanley, Lemuel IV, 995
Stanley, Lemuel VI, 272
Stanley, Lena May IV, 1002
Stanley, Lenna Mae IV, 784
Stanley, Lenna Mae IV, 1003
Stanley, Lenna Mae IV, 1013
Stanley, Lesley J. IV, 1000
Stanley, Levi IV, 998
Stanley, Levi IV, 1000
Stanley, Levi IV, 1003
Stanley, Levi, Jr. IV, 1003
Stanley, Levina I, 573
Stanley, Levina I, 838
Stanley, Levina IV, 752
Stanley, Levina IV, 765
Stanley, Levina IV, 766
Stanley, Levinah I, 838
Stanley, Lewis IV, 997
Stanley, Libby VI, 855
Stanley, Lillas Adell IV, 1000
Stanley, Lillian IV, 440
Stanley, Lindsey IV, 996
Stanley, Lindsey IV, 1000
Stanley, Lindsey IV, 1001
Stanley, Littleberry IV, 440
Stanley, Littleberry IV, 594
Stanley, Littleberry IV, 763
Stanley, Littleberry IV, 764
Stanley, Littleberry IV, 765
Stanley, Littleberry IV, 766
Stanley, Littleberry IV, 844
Stanley, Littleberry IV, 967
Stanley, Littleberry IV, 995
Stanley, Littleberry IV, 996
Stanley, Littleberry IV, 998
Stanley, Littleberry IV, 1000
Stanley, Littleberry IV, 1002
Stanley, Littleberry IV, 1010
Stanley, Littleberry VI, 238
Stanley, Littleberry VI, 269
Stanley, Littleberry VI, 272
Stanley, Littleburg IV, 919
Stanley, Littlebury VI, 268
Stanley, Littlebury VI, 270
Stanley, Littlebury VI, 271
Stanley, Lois Aileen IV, 1000
Stanley, Lola S. I, 574
Stanley, Lolo Sophronia I, 597
Stanley, Loran IV, 433
Stanley, Loran A. IV, 440
Stanley, Loran Alverdo IV, 440
Stanley, Loren Alverda IV, 440
Stanley, Lorin C. IV, 1000
Stanley, Louisa IV, 998
Stanley, Louisa IV, 1001
Stanley, Louisa IV, 1002
Stanley, Louisa May IV, 440
Stanley, Louise IV, 976
Stanley, Louiza J. IV, 971
Stanley, Louiza J. IV, 1002
Stanley, Lucina IV, 997
Stanley, Lucina IV, 1002
Stanley, Lucina IV, 1013
Stanley, Lucinda IV, 996
Stanley, Lucinda IV, 1001
Stanley, Lucinda IV, 1002
Stanley, Lucinda IV, 1295
Stanley, Lucy I, 573
Stanley, Lucy IV, 695
Stanley, Lucy IV, 764
Stanley, Lucy IV, 765
Stanley, Lucy IV, 766
Stanley, Lucy IV, 995
Stanley, Lucy IV, 996
Stanley, Lucy IV, 1001
Stanley, Lucy VI, 269
Stanley, Lucy VI, 272
Stanley, Lucy VI, 280
Stanley, Lucy VI, 997
Stanley, Lucy Ann VI, 269
Stanley, Lucy Ann VI, 272
Stanley, Lucy Anne VI, 272
Stanley, Luiza I, 604
Stanley, Lula I, 338
Stanley, Lula I, 340
Stanley, Lurana I, 604
Stanley, Lusena I, 516
Stanley, Lusetta I, 597
Stanley, Lusetta I, 598
Stanley, Luzena I, 531
Stanley, Luzena I, 573
Stanley, Luzena I, 590
Stanley, Luzena I, 604
Stanley, Luzena I, 608
Stanley, Luzetta I, 590
Stanley, Luzetta I, 597
Stanley, Lydia I, 542
Stanley, Lydia I, 572
Stanley, Lydia I, 573
Stanley, Lydia I, 586
Stanley, Lydia I, 590
Stanley, Lydia I, 591
Stanley, Lydia I, 597
Stanley, Lydia I, 604
Stanley, Lydia I, 792
Stanley, Lydia I, 798
Stanley, Lydia I, 838
Stanley, Lydia IV, 90
Stanley, Lydia IV, 110
Stanley, Lydia IV, 739
Stanley, Lydia IV, 750
Stanley, Lydia IV, 766
Stanley, Lydia IV, 869
Stanley, Lydia IV, 883
Stanley, Lydia IV, 936
Stanley, Lydia IV, 962
Stanley, Lydia IV, 984
Stanley, Lydia IV, 996
Stanley, Lydia IV, 998
Stanley, Lydia IV, 999
Stanley, Lydia IV, 1000
Stanley, Lydia IV, 1001
Stanley, Lydia IV, 1002
Stanley, Lydia IV, 1003
Stanley, Lydia IV, 1006
Stanley, Lydia IV, 1015
Stanley, Lydia IV, 1204
Stanley, Lydia IV, 1223
Stanley, Lydia IV, 1224
Stanley, Lydia IV, 1225
Stanley, Lydia IV, 1295
Stanley, Lydia A. IV, 986
Stanley, Lydia Ann IV, 939
Stanley, Lydia Ann IV, 999
Stanley, Lydia E. IV, 967
Stanley, Lydia E. IV, 998
Stanley, Lydia H. IV, 91
Stanley, Lydia K. IV, 37
Stanley, Lydia K. IV, 60
Stanley, Lydia L. V, 862
Stanley, Lydia L. V, 871
Stanley, Lydia Maria IV, 997
Stanley, Lydia Maria IV, 999
Stanley, Lydia Maria IV, 1002
Stanley, Lydia Maria IV, 1003
Stanley, Lydia Maria IV, 1339
Stanley, Lydia Marie IV, 1003
Stanley, Lydia Melvina IV, 1000
Stanley, Lydia Melvina IV, 1003
Stanley, Lydia Rhoda IV, 1002
Stanley, Lydia S. IV, 986
Stanley, Lyeia IV, 883
Stanley, Mabel IV, 279
Stanley, Mabel IV, 767
Stanley, Mabel V, 206
Stanley, Mabel Anna IV, 1000
Stanley, Mabel C. V, 206
Stanley, Mabel Coy IV, 1003
Stanley, Mabel Vonetta IV, 1000
Stanley, Mable L. IV, 986
Stanley, Maddox VI, 197
Stanley, Maddox VI, 213
Stanley, Maddox VI, 268
Stanley, Maddox VI, 269
Stanley, Maddox VI, 270
Stanley, Maddox VI, 271
Stanley, Maddox VI, 272
Stanley, Maddox VI, 287
Stanley, Maddox, Jr. VI, 271
Stanley, Madox VI, 269
Stanley, Madox VI, 270
Stanley, Maggie V, 206
Stanley, Mahala I, 573
Stanley, Mahaly J. I, 538
Stanley, Mahaly J. I, 573
Stanley, Mahlon I, 557
Stanley, Mahlon I, 572
Stanley, Mahlon I, 573
Stanley, Mahlon I, 586
Stanley, Mahlon I, 590
Stanley, Mahlon I, 604
Stanley, Majory VI, 268
Stanley, Majory VI, 269
Stanley, Malinda V, 1020
Stanley, Malon I, 515
Stanley, Margaret I, 590
Stanley, Margaret I, 997
Stanley, Margaret IV, 679
Stanley, Margaret IV, 765
Stanley, Margaret IV, 926
Stanley, Margaret IV, 939
Stanley, Margaret IV, 944
Stanley, Margaret IV, 964
Stanley, Margaret IV, 976
Stanley, Margaret IV, 995
Stanley, Margaret IV, 998
Stanley, Margaret IV, 999
Stanley, Margaret IV, 1001
Stanley, Margaret IV, 1002
Stanley, Margaret IV, 1005
Stanley, Margaret VI, 230
Stanley, Margaret VI, 271
Stanley, Margaret A. IV, 997
Stanley, Margaret Anna IV, 9
Stanley, Margaret B. IV, 234
Stanley, Margaret B. IV, 279
Stanley, Margaret B. IV, 973
Stanley, Margaret B. IV, 999
Stanley, Margaret B. IV, 1000
Stanley, Margaret B. IV, 1002
Stanley, Margaret C. IV, 997
Stanley, Margaret E. IV, 1295
Stanley, Margery VI, 268
Stanley, Maria IV, 673
Stanley, Maria IV, 764
Stanley, Maria IV, 765
Stanley, Maria IV, 766
Stanley, Maria IV, 996
Stanley, Maria IV, 1001
Stanley, Maria VI, 272
Stanley, Mariah VI, 895
Stanley, Mariana IV, 1002
Stanley, Marietta IV, 998
Stanley, Marietta IV, 999
Stanley, Marietta IV, 1002
Stanley, Marietta S. IV, 924
Stanley, Marietta S. IV, 1002
Stanley, Marjory VI, 242
Stanley, Martha I, 515
Stanley, Martha I, 516
Stanley, Martha I, 531
Stanley, Martha I, 572
Stanley, Martha I, 578
Stanley, Martha I, 590
Stanley, Martha I, 792
Stanley, Martha I, 809
Stanley, Martha I, 838
Stanley, Martha I, 979
Stanley, Martha I, 987
Stanley, Martha I, 990
Stanley, Martha I, 997
Stanley, Martha IV, 697
Stanley, Martha IV, 764
Stanley, Martha IV, 765
Stanley, Martha IV, 767
Stanley, Martha IV, 844
Stanley, Martha IV, 847
Stanley, Martha IV, 958
Stanley, Martha IV, 995
Stanley, Martha IV, 997
Stanley, Martha IV, 1000
Stanley, Martha IV, 1002
Stanley, Martha IV, 1003
Stanley, Martha IV, 1295
Stanley, Martha V, 68
Stanley, Martha V, 124
Stanley, Martha V, 360
Stanley, Martha V, 394
Stanley, Martha V, 433
Stanley, Martha VI, 235
Stanley, Martha VI, 268
Stanley, Martha VI, 269
Stanley, Martha VI, 270
Stanley, Martha VI, 272
Stanley, Martha VI, 871
Stanley, Martha Ann IV, 998
Stanley, Martha E. I, 839
Stanley, Martha Emaline I, 792
Stanley, Martha Emily IV, 997
Stanley, Martha J. VI, 839
Stanley, Martha S. IV, 718
Stanley, Martha S. IV, 962
Stanley, Martha S. IV, 996
Stanley, Martha S. IV, 1002
Stanley, Martha W. IV, 999
Stanley, Martha W. IV, 1003
Stanley, Martha W. IV, 1339
Stanley, Marthha W. IV, 1002
Stanley, Marthy VI, 250
Stanley, Marthy VI, 268
Stanley, Martin IV, 764
Stanley, Martin IV, 766
Stanley, Martin IV, 999
Stanley, Martin IV, 1001
Stanley, Martin IV, 1002
Stanley, Martin IV, 1077
Stanley, Martin IV, 1116
Stanley, Mary I, 515
Stanley, Mary I, 516
Stanley, Mary I, 540
Stanley, Mary I, 542
Stanley, Mary I, 572
Stanley, Mary I, 573
Stanley, Mary I, 590
Stanley, Mary I, 591
Stanley, Mary I, 594
Stanley, Mary I, 596
Stanley, Mary I, 597
Stanley, Mary I, 641

ey, Mary I, 785
ey, Mary I, 792
ey, Mary I, 809
ey, Mary I, 838
ey, Mary I, 911
ey, Mary I, 914
ey, Mary I, 979
ey, Mary I, 993
ey, Mary I, 997
ey, Mary II, 41
ey, Mary II, 100
ey, Mary II, 101
ey, Mary II, 423
ey, Mary II, 658
ey, Mary IV, 110
ey, Mary IV, 235
ey, Mary IV, 279
ey, Mary IV, 297
ey, Mary IV, 305
ey, Mary IV, 352
ey, Mary IV, 355
ey, Mary IV, 440
ey, Mary IV, 497
ey, Mary IV, 551
ey, Mary IV, 594
ey, Mary IV, 657
ey, Mary IV, 690
ey, Mary IV, 696
ey, Mary IV, 722
ey, Mary IV, 728
ey, Mary IV, 751
ey, Mary IV, 764
ey, Mary IV, 765
ey, Mary IV, 766
ey, Mary IV, 767
ey, Mary IV, 770
ey, Mary IV, 787
ey, Mary IV, 844
ey, Mary IV, 883
ey, Mary IV, 944
ey, Mary IV, 949
ey, Mary IV, 951
ey, Mary IV, 972
ey, Mary IV, 993
ey, Mary IV, 995
ey, Mary IV, 996
ey, Mary IV, 997
ey, Mary IV, 998
ey, Mary IV, 999
ey, Mary IV, 1000
ey, Mary IV, 1001
ey, Mary IV, 1002
ey, Mary IV, 1043
ey, Mary IV, 1116
ey, Mary IV, 1133
ey, Mary IV, 1138
ey, Mary IV, 1187
ey, Mary IV, 1294
ey, Mary V, 124
ey, Mary VI, 165
ey, Mary VI, 167
ey, Mary VI, 213
ey, Mary VI, 239
ey, Mary VI, 242
ey, Mary VI, 249
ey, Mary VI, 268
ey, Mary VI, 269
ey, Mary VI, 271
ey, Mary VI, 272
ey, Mary VI, 339
ey, Mary VI, 855
ey, Mary VI, 975
ey, Mary A. IV, 1001
ey, Mary A. V, 712
ey, Mary A. VI, 852
ey, Mary A. C. IV, 1000
ey, Mary A. E. IV, 927
ey, Mary A. E. IV, 981
ey, Mary A. E. IV, 1000
ey, Mary A. E. IV, 1003
ey, Mary Ann IV, 279
ey, Mary Ann IV, 756
ey, Mary Ann IV, 764
ey, Mary Ann IV, 765
ey, Mary Ann IV, 767
ey, Mary Ann IV, 789
ey, Mary Ann IV, 939
ey, Mary Ann IV, 952
ey, Mary Ann IV, 985
ey, Mary Ann IV, 992
ey, Mary Ann IV, 995
ey, Mary Ann IV, 996
ey, Mary Ann IV, 997
ey, Mary Ann IV, 999
ey, Mary Ann IV, 1000
ey, Mary Ann IV, 1001
ey, Mary Ann IV, 1002
ey, Mary Ann IV, 1003
ey, Mary Ann IV, 1043
ey, Mary Ann IV, 1116
ey, Mary Ann IV, 1117
Stanley, Mary Ann VI, 915
Stanley, Mary Anna IV, 999
Stanley, Mary Anne IV, 998
Stanley, Mary C. IV, 971
Stanley, Mary C. IV, 1002
Stanley, Mary C. IV, 1223
Stanley, Mary E. IV, 236
Stanley, Mary E. IV, 767
Stanley, Mary E. IV, 939
Stanley, Mary E. IV, 996
Stanley, Mary E. IV, 999
Stanley, Mary E. IV, 1003
Stanley, Mary E. IV, 1043
Stanley, Mary E. IV, 1294
Stanley, Mary Edith V, 206
Stanley, Mary Eliza IV, 1000
Stanley, Mary Elizabeth IV, 765
Stanley, Mary Elizabeth IV, 1223
Stanley, Mary Ellen IV, 962
Stanley, Mary Ellen IV, 998
Stanley, Mary Ellen IV, 1000
Stanley, Mary Ellen IV, 1003
Stanley, Mary Ellen IV, 1043
Stanley, Mary Elvira IV, 1000
Stanley, Mary Emily IV, 279
Stanley, Mary Emily IV, 998
Stanley, Mary Emily IV, 1001
Stanley, Mary Emily IV, 1002
Stanley, Mary Frances VI, 269
Stanley, Mary Frances VI, 272
Stanley, Mary H. IV, 643
Stanley, Mary H. IV, 738
Stanley, Mary H. IV, 767
Stanley, Mary H. IV, 999
Stanley, Mary H. IV, 1002
Stanley, Mary H. IV, 1003
Stanley, Mary Isabella I, 597
Stanley, Mary J. I, 574
Stanley, Mary J. IV, 999
Stanley, Mary J. IV, 1043
Stanley, Mary J. VI, 855
Stanley, Mary J. C. IV, 999
Stanley, Mary Jane I, 623
Stanley, Mary Jane I, 638
Stanley, Mary K. IV, 883
Stanley, Mary K. IV, 997
Stanley, Mary K. IV, 1002
Stanley, Mary K. IV, 1003
Stanley, Mary P. IV, 1002
Stanley, Mary P. V, 862
Stanley, Mary Rayl I, 515
Stanley, Mary Smith IV, 1002
Stanley, Mary V. IV, 279
Stanley, Mary V. IV, 352
Stanley, Mary Viola IV, 999
Stanley, Mary W. IV, 279
Stanley, Matilda IV, 764
Stanley, Matilda IV, 766
Stanley, Matilda IV, 997
Stanley, Matilda VI, 272
Stanley, Matilda VI, 973
Stanley, Matthew I, 514
Stanley, Matthew I, 572
Stanley, Matthew I, 608
Stanley, Matthew I, 969
Stanley, Maud IV, 941
Stanley, Maud Lemina IV, 1000
Stanley, Maude IV, 1003
Stanley, May E. IV, 1043
Stanley, Mehale I, 591
Stanley, Melvina IV, 1003
Stanley, Mercy IV, 235
Stanley, Meribah IV, 764
Stanley, Meribah IV, 992
Stanley, Meribah IV, 998
Stanley, Merihab IV, 996
Stanley, Merlin D. IV, 1003
Stanley, Merlin David IV, 1000
Stanley, Mervin IV, 824
Stanley, Mervin IV, 844
Stanley, Mervin T. IV, 766
Stanley, Micajah I, 515
Stanley, Micajah I, 571
Stanley, Micajah I, 572
Stanley, Micajah IV, 279
Stanley, Micajah IV, 764
Stanley, Micajah IV, 766
Stanley, Micajah IV, 943
Stanley, Micajah IV, 969
Stanley, Micajah IV, 988
Stanley, Micajah IV, 995
Stanley, Micajah IV, 997
Stanley, Micajah IV, 1000
Stanley, Micajah IV, 1043
Stanley, Micajah V, 531
Stanley, Micajah VI, 268
Stanley, Micajah VI, 269
Stanley, Micajah VI, 270
Stanley, Micajah VI, 272
Stanley, Micajah VI, 575
Stanley, Micajah B. IV, 968
Stanley, Micajah B. IV, 997
Stanley, Micajah B. IV, 1000
Stanley, Micajah B. IV, 1003
Stanley, Micajah B. IV, 1043
Stanley, Micajah C. IV, 996
Stanley, Micajah C. IV, 1002
Stanley, Michael I, 586
Stanley, Michael I, 590
Stanley, Michael I, 597
Stanley, Michael I, 911
Stanley, Michael I, 914
Stanley, Michal I, 516
Stanley, Michel I, 515
Stanley, Michel I, 516
Stanley, Michel I, 542
Stanley, Michel I, 572
Stanley, Mildred IV, 1003
Stanley, Mildred VI, 271
Stanley, Mildred Elizabeth IV, 986
Stanley, Mildred Elizabeth IV, 1000
Stanley, Milicent IV, 1001
Stanley, Milicent IV, 1116
Stanley, Milicent V, 933
Stanley, Miliscent IV, 753
Stanley, Miliscent IV, 764
Stanley, Milisient I, 573
Stanley, Milla I, 796
Stanley, Milla I, 838
Stanley, Millah I, 838
Stanley, Milley VI, 268
Stanley, Milley VI, 270
Stanley, Milley VI, 271
Stanley, Milley Crew IV, 997
Stanley, Milley Crew IV, 1001
Stanley, Milley Crew IV, 1116
Stanley, Milley Crew IV, 1224
Stanley, Millicent IV, 1077
Stanley, Millie C. IV, 1224
Stanley, Milly IV, 696
Stanley, Milly IV, 728
Stanley, Milly IV, 764
Stanley, Milly IV, 765
Stanley, Milly IV, 766
Stanley, Milly VI, 238
Stanley, Milly VI, 268
Stanley, Milly VI, 269
Stanley, Milly VI, 272
Stanley, Milton I, 573
Stanley, Milton IV, 764
Stanley, Milton IV, 995
Stanley, Milton IV, 1001
Stanley, Milton IV, 1223
Stanley, Milton P. IV, 1294
Stanley, Missouri IV, 997
Stanley, Morris IV, 550
Stanley, Morris IV, 551
Stanley, Morris J. IV, 1000
Stanley, Morris J. IV, 1003
Stanley, Morris J. IV, 1043
Stanley, Moses I, 515
Stanley, Moses I, 590
Stanley, Moses IV, 704
Stanley, Moses IV, 713
Stanley, Moses IV, 723
Stanley, Moses IV, 763
Stanley, Moses IV, 764
Stanley, Moses IV, 765
Stanley, Moses IV, 766
Stanley, Moses IV, 995
Stanley, Moses IV, 997
Stanley, Moses IV, 998
Stanley, Moses IV, 1001
Stanley, Moses IV, 1116
Stanley, Moses IV, 1224
Stanley, Moses VI, 268
Stanley, Moses VI, 272
Stanley, Mrs. Harris O. IV, 1003
Stanley, Mrs. Mayme IV, 1339
Stanley, Mrs. Violet IV, 1043
Stanley, Naddy IV, 919
Stanley, Nancy I, 572
Stanley, Nancy I, 573
Stanley, Nancy I, 586
Stanley, Nancy I, 590
Stanley, Nancy I, 595
Stanley, Nancy I, 597
Stanley, Nancy I, 603
Stanley, Nancy I, 997
Stanley, Nancy IV, 696
Stanley, Nancy IV, 764
Stanley, Nancy IV, 766
Stanley, Nancy IV, 946
Stanley, Nancy IV, 995
Stanley, Nancy IV, 997
Stanley, Nancy IV, 1000
Stanley, Nancy IV, 1001
Stanley, Nancy IV, 1116
Stanley, Nancy IV, 1223
Stanley, Nancy IV, 1224
Stanley, Nancy V, 360
Stanley, Nancy V, 373
Stanley, Nancy V, 433
Stanley, Nancy VI, 272
Stanley, Nancy VI, 972
Stanley, Nancy VI, 997
Stanley, Nancy C. V, 792
Stanley, Nancy C. V, 793
Stanley, Nancy M. II, 719
Stanley, Nancy M. II, 768
Stanley, Naomy I, 515
Stanley, Nathan I, 515
Stanley, Nathan I, 516
Stanley, Nathan I, 571
Stanley, Nathan I, 573
Stanley, Nathan I, 590
Stanley, Nathan I, 591
Stanley, Nathan I, 594
Stanley, Nathan I, 596
Stanley, Nathan I, 597
Stanley, Nathan I, 626
Stanley, Nathan I, 668
Stanley, Nathan I, 689
Stanley, Nathan IV, 765
Stanley, Nathan IV, 996
Stanley, Nathan IV, 1000
Stanley, Nathan IV, 1001
Stanley, Nathan IV, 1003
Stanley, Nathan VI, 268
Stanley, Nathan VI, 270
Stanley, Nathan Dicks I, 516
Stanley, Nathan H. IV, 1003
Stanley, Nathan Harrison IV, 997
Stanley, Nathan Harrison IV, 1000
Stanley, Nathan Harrison IV, 1001
Stanley, Nathaniel IV, 766
Stanley, Nathaniel IV, 996
Stanley, Nathaniel IV, 1001
Stanley, Nathaniel Gerard VI, 272
Stanley, Nathaniel J. IV, 766
Stanley, Nathaniel J. IV, 869
Stanley, Nathaniel J. IV, 883
Stanley, Nathaniel J. IV, 1000
Stanley, Nathaniel J. IV, 1002
Stanley, Nathaniel Jared IV, 995
Stanley, Nettie IV, 1003
Stanley, Newton IV, 1294
Stanley, Nora IV, 765
Stanley, Obediah VI, 268
Stanley, Obediah VI, 270
Stanley, Olive A. IV, 1002
Stanley, Olive Abigail IV, 998
Stanley, Olive T. V, 206
Stanley, Oliver IV, 998
Stanley, Oliver V, 206
Stanley, Osborn IV, 764
Stanley, Osborn IV, 964
Stanley, Osborn IV, 976
Stanley, Osborn IV, 996
Stanley, Osborn IV, 997
Stanley, Osborn IV, 999
Stanley, Osborn IV, 1001
Stanley, Osborn IV, 1002
Stanley, Overton IV, 764
Stanley, Overton IV, 765
Stanley, Overton IV, 766
Stanley, Overton IV, 767
Stanley, Overton IV, 770
Stanley, Overton IV, 997
Stanley, Overton IV, 1000
Stanley, Overton IV, 1002
Stanley, Overton VI, 272
Stanley, Parthena J. VI, 881
Stanley, Paul Leland IV, 1000
Stanley, Pearl IV, 1000
Stanley, Pearl IV, 1003
Stanley, Pearl B. III, 19
Stanley, Pearl B. III, 298
Stanley, Percy C. IV, 1000
Stanley, Permelia VI, 973
Stanley, Peter L. IV, 1002
Stanley, Peter Ladd IV, 998
Stanley, Phebe I, 514
Stanley, Phebe I, 515
Stanley, Phebe I, 516
Stanley, Phebe I, 571
Stanley, Phebe I, 572
Stanley, Phebe I, 573
Stanley, Phebe I, 578
Stanley, Phebe I, 590
Stanley, Phebe I, 591
Stanley, Phebe I, 594
Stanley, Phebe I, 596
Stanley, Phebe I, 597
Stanley, Phebe I, 626
Stanley, Phebe I, 785
Stanley, Phebe I, 792
Stanley, Phebe I, 835
Stanley, Phebe I, 838
Stanley, Phebe IV, 765
Stanley, Phebe IV, 996
Stanley, Phebe IV, 1001
Stanley, Phebe VI, 268
Stanley, Phebe Murrow I, 573
Stanley, Phebe P. IV, 1185
Stanley, Phebe P. IV, 1187
Stanley, Phebe P. IV, 1198
Stanley, Phebe Vansyoc IV, 786
Stanley, Philena IV, 1001
Stanley, Philena Ann IV, 998
Stanley, Philena M. IV, 990
Stanley, Philena M. IV, 999
Stanley, Pinkney F. I, 626
Stanley, Pinkney F. I, 641
Stanley, Pleasant IV, 764
Stanley, Pleasant IV, 781
Stanley, Pleasant IV, 941
Stanley, Pleasant IV, 999
Stanley, Pleasant VI, 268
Stanley, Pleasant VI, 269
Stanley, Pleasant VI, 270
Stanley, Pleasant VI, 339
Stanley, Pleasant VI, 870
Stanley, Pleasant VI, 889
Stanley, Pleasant VI, 973
Stanley, Pleasant VI, 975
Stanley, Pleasant VI, 997
Stanley, Pleasant VI, 1001
Stanley, Pleasant T. IV, 973
Stanley, Pleasant T. IV, 996
Stanley, Pleasant T. IV, 998
Stanley, Pleasant T. IV, 1002
Stanley, Pleasant, Jr. VI, 339
Stanley, Pleasants VI, 197
Stanley, Pleasants VI, 213
Stanley, Pleasants VI, 270
Stanley, Plesant VI, 915
Stanley, Polly VI, 804
Stanley, Polly VI, 1001
Stanley, Preston I, 573
Stanley, Preston I, 626
Stanley, Priscilla IV, 466
Stanley, Priscilla IV, 497
Stanley, Priscilla IV, 498
Stanley, Priscilla IV, 763
Stanley, Priscilla IV, 764
Stanley, Priscilla IV, 766
Stanley, Priscilla IV, 936
Stanley, Priscilla IV, 995
Stanley, Priscilla IV, 996
Stanley, Priscilla IV, 997
Stanley, Priscilla IV, 1000
Stanley, Priscilla IV, 1001
Stanley, Priscilla IV, 1017
Stanley, Priscilla VI, 191
Stanley, Priscilla VI, 194
Stanley, Priscilla VI, 213
Stanley, Priscilla VI, 214
Stanley, Priscilla VI, 269
Stanley, Priscilla VI, 272
Stanley, Priscilla VI, 312
Stanley, Priscilla VI, 339
Stanley, Prudence I, 515
Stanley, Prudence I, 545
Stanley, Prudence I, 572
Stanley, Prudence I, 573
Stanley, Prudence V, 124
Stanley, Prudence Hunt I, 668
Stanley, Prudence, Jr. I, 515
Stanley, R. Edward IV, 1003
Stanley, Rachel I, 514
Stanley, Rachel I, 515
Stanley, Rachel I, 568
Stanley, Rachel I, 572
Stanley, Rachel I, 573
Stanley, Rachel I, 579
Stanley, Rachel I, 590
Stanley, Rachel I, 594
Stanley, Rachel I, 597
Stanley, Rachel I, 608
Stanley, Rachel I, 989
Stanley, Rachel I, 997
Stanley, Rachel I, 998
Stanley, Rachel I, 1012
Stanley, Rachel IV, 440
Stanley, Rachel IV, 619
Stanley, Rachel IV, 657
Stanley, Rachel IV, 673
Stanley, Rachel IV, 762
Stanley, Rachel IV, 764
Stanley, Rachel IV, 765
Stanley, Rachel IV, 766
Stanley, Rachel IV, 973
Stanley, Rachel IV, 996
Stanley, Rachel IV, 997
Stanley, Rachel IV, 998
Stanley, Rachel IV, 1000
Stanley, Rachel IV, 1001
Stanley, Rachel IV, 1002

Stanley, Rachel IV, 1077
Stanley, Rachel IV, 1103
Stanley, Rachel IV, 1116
Stanley, Rachel IV, 1148
Stanley, Rachel IV, 1187
Stanley, Rachel V, 124
Stanley, Rachel V, 249
Stanley, Rachel V, 280
Stanley, Rachel VI, 247
Stanley, Rachel VI, 268
Stanley, Rachel VI, 269
Stanley, Rachel VI, 271
Stanley, Rachel VI, 272
Stanley, Rachel A. IV, 1037
Stanley, Rachel A. IV, 1043
Stanley, Rachel Ann IV, 1043
Stanley, Rachel C. IV, 994
Stanley, Rachel C. IV, 999
Stanley, Rachel Ella IV, 235
Stanley, Rachel G. IV, 235
Stanley, Rachel Melinda I, 997
Stanley, Rachel P. IV, 989
Stanley, Rachel P. IV, 999
Stanley, Ralph Ernest IV, 440
Stanley, Raymond IV, 1043
Stanley, Rea IV, 1003
Stanley, Rea M. IV, 1003
Stanley, Rebeca Jane I, 792
Stanley, Rebecah I, 516
Stanley, Rebecah I, 792
Stanley, Rebecca I, 532
Stanley, Rebecca I, 572
Stanley, Rebecca I, 573
Stanley, Rebecca I, 579
Stanley, Rebecca I, 592
Stanley, Rebecca I, 597
Stanley, Rebecca I, 604
Stanley, Rebecca II, 202
Stanley, Rebecca IV, 695
Stanley, Rebecca IV, 764
Stanley, Rebecca IV, 765
Stanley, Rebecca IV, 766
Stanley, Rebecca IV, 939
Stanley, Rebecca IV, 943
Stanley, Rebecca IV, 944
Stanley, Rebecca IV, 960
Stanley, Rebecca IV, 982
Stanley, Rebecca IV, 993
Stanley, Rebecca IV, 995
Stanley, Rebecca IV, 997
Stanley, Rebecca IV, 998
Stanley, Rebecca IV, 999
Stanley, Rebecca IV, 1001
Stanley, Rebecca IV, 1003
Stanley, Rebecca IV, 1043
Stanley, Rebecca IV, 1223
Stanley, Rebecca IV, 1224
Stanley, Rebecca V, 124
Stanley, Rebecca V, 531
Stanley, Rebecca VI, 194
Stanley, Rebecca VI, 214
Stanley, Rebecca VI, 269
Stanley, Rebecca VI, 271
Stanley, Rebecca VI, 272
Stanley, Rebecca Ann IV, 996
Stanley, Rebecca C. IV, 999
Stanley, Rebecca H. I, 997
Stanley, Rebecca J. I, 803
Stanley, Rebecca J. I, 839
Stanley, Rebecca Tamson IV, 996
Stanley, Rebecka Ann VI, 997
Stanley, Rebeckah I, 515
Stanley, Rebeckah VI, 190
Stanley, Rebeckah VI, 213
Stanley, Rebeckah VI, 214
Stanley, Rebekah I, 516
Stanley, Rebekah I, 590
Stanley, Rhea M. IV, 1000
Stanley, Rhea M. IV, 1043
Stanley, Rhoda I, 590
Stanley, Rhoda I, 596
Stanley, Rhoda I, 597
Stanley, Rhoda I, 626
Stanley, Rhoda IV, 440
Stanley, Rhoda IV, 594
Stanley, Rhoda IV, 690
Stanley, Rhoda IV, 764
Stanley, Rhoda IV, 765
Stanley, Rhoda IV, 781
Stanley, Rhoda IV, 823
Stanley, Rhoda IV, 844
Stanley, Rhoda IV, 928
Stanley, Rhoda IV, 956
Stanley, Rhoda IV, 996
Stanley, Rhoda IV, 998
Stanley, Rhoda IV, 999
Stanley, Rhoda IV, 1000
Stanley, Rhoda IV, 1001
Stanley, Rhoda IV, 1211
Stanley, Rhoda IV, 1223
Stanley, Rhoda IV, 1224
Stanley, Rhoda IV, 1294
Stanley, Rhoda M. IV, 1043
Stanley, Rhoda M. IV, 1241
Stanley, Rhodah I, 515
Stanley, Richard I, 515
Stanley, Richard I, 516
Stanley, Richard I, 540
Stanley, Richard I, 572
Stanley, Richard I, 573
Stanley, Richard I, 590
Stanley, Richard I, 595
Stanley, Richard I, 597
Stanley, Richard I, 598
Stanley, Richard I, 608
Stanley, Richard IV, 998
Stanley, Richard IV, 1294
Stanley, Richard Edward IV, 1002
Stanley, Richard Edward IV, 1295
Stanley, Richard H. I, 572
Stanley, Rittitha I, 515
Stanley, Robert I, 572
Stanley, Robert IV, 750
Stanley, Robert IV, 764
Stanley, Robert IV, 928
Stanley, Robert IV, 936
Stanley, Robert IV, 960
Stanley, Robert IV, 984
Stanley, Robert IV, 986
Stanley, Robert IV, 995
Stanley, Robert IV, 998
Stanley, Robert IV, 999
Stanley, Robert IV, 1001
Stanley, Robert IV, 1002
Stanley, Robert IV, 1006
Stanley, Robert IV, 1014
Stanley, Robert IV, 1204
Stanley, Robert IV, 1223
Stanley, Robert IV, 1224
Stanley, Robert IV, 1225
Stanley, Robert V, 206
Stanley, Robert C. IV, 767
Stanley, Robert Clarence IV, 766
Stanley, Robert Leslie IV, 1000
Stanley, Robert Leslie IV, 1003
Stanley, Robert Miles IV, 1043
Stanley, Robert Wade IV, 1000
Stanley, Rosanna IV, 1002
Stanley, Roscoe Irving IV, 999
Stanley, Roscoe R. IV, 766
Stanley, Roscoe R. IV, 767
Stanley, Roscoe R. IV, 844
Stanley, Roy IV, 1000
Stanley, Roy C. IV, 1003
Stanley, Rufus I, 641
Stanley, Rufus K. I, 626
Stanley, Russell IV, 1043
Stanley, Ruth I, 515
Stanley, Ruth I, 524
Stanley, Ruth I, 545
Stanley, Ruth I, 572
Stanley, Ruth I, 573
Stanley, Ruth I, 590
Stanley, Ruth I, 597
Stanley, Ruth II, 720
Stanley, Ruth IV, 91
Stanley, Ruth IV, 694
Stanley, Ruth IV, 722
Stanley, Ruth IV, 764
Stanley, Ruth IV, 765
Stanley, Ruth IV, 770
Stanley, Ruth IV, 845
Stanley, Ruth IV, 999
Stanley, Ruth IV, 1133
Stanley, Ruth IV, 1294
Stanley, Ruth V, 280
Stanley, Ruth V, 519
Stanley, Ruth V, 531
Stanley, Ruth VI, 997
Stanley, Ruth A. IV, 608
Stanley, Ruthanna IV, 988
Stanley, Ruthanna IV, 997
Stanley, Ruthanna IV, 999
Stanley, Sadie F. IV, 1224
Stanley, Sally I, 590
Stanley, Sally I, 595
Stanley, Sally I, 597
Stanley, Sally VI, 1004
Stanley, Samantha IV, 933
Stanley, Samantha IV, 998
Stanley, Samantha IV, 1000
Stanley, Sammuel I, 572
Stanley, Sammuel I, 582
Stanley, Samuel I, 515
Stanley, Samuel I, 516
Stanley, Samuel I, 571
Stanley, Samuel I, 572
Stanley, Samuel I, 573
Stanley, Samuel I, 586
Stanley, Samuel I, 590
Stanley, Samuel I, 596
Stanley, Samuel I, 792
Stanley, Samuel I, 838
Stanley, Samuel I, 901
Stanley, Samuel I, 914
Stanley, Samuel I, 997
Stanley, Samuel II, 122
Stanley, Samuel II, 124
Stanley, Samuel IV, 279
Stanley, Samuel IV, 355
Stanley, Samuel IV, 551
Stanley, Samuel IV, 689
Stanley, Samuel IV, 764
Stanley, Samuel IV, 765
Stanley, Samuel IV, 766
Stanley, Samuel IV, 844
Stanley, Samuel IV, 995
Stanley, Samuel IV, 996
Stanley, Samuel IV, 998
Stanley, Samuel IV, 1000
Stanley, Samuel IV, 1001
Stanley, Samuel V, 360
Stanley, Samuel V, 373
Stanley, Samuel V, 394
Stanley, Samuel V, 433
Stanley, Samuel V, 531
Stanley, Samuel V, 1020
Stanley, Samuel VI, 268
Stanley, Samuel VI, 269
Stanley, Samuel VI, 272
Stanley, Samuel VI, 339
Stanley, Samuel VI, 817
Stanley, Samuel VI, 855
Stanley, Samuel VI, 922
Stanley, Samuel B. IV, 235
Stanley, Samuel N. IV, 995
Stanley, Samuel W. IV, 279
Stanley, Samuel W. IV, 297
Stanley, Samuel W. IV, 352
Stanley, Samuel W. IV, 551
Stanley, Samuel W. IV, 764
Stanley, Samuel W. IV, 1001
Stanley, Samuel, Jr. I, 592
Stanley, Samuel, Jr. I, 596
Stanley, Samuel, Jr. I, 597
Stanley, Sarah I, 515
Stanley, Sarah I, 516
Stanley, Sarah I, 534
Stanley, Sarah I, 545
Stanley, Sarah I, 550
Stanley, Sarah I, 567
Stanley, Sarah I, 571
Stanley, Sarah I, 572
Stanley, Sarah I, 573
Stanley, Sarah I, 575
Stanley, Sarah I, 581
Stanley, Sarah I, 582
Stanley, Sarah I, 586
Stanley, Sarah I, 590
Stanley, Sarah I, 593
Stanley, Sarah I, 594
Stanley, Sarah I, 596
Stanley, Sarah I, 597
Stanley, Sarah I, 792
Stanley, Sarah I, 838
Stanley, Sarah I, 901
Stanley, Sarah II, 122
Stanley, Sarah II, 124
Stanley, Sarah IV, 498
Stanley, Sarah IV, 671
Stanley, Sarah IV, 679
Stanley, Sarah IV, 686
Stanley, Sarah IV, 689
Stanley, Sarah IV, 750
Stanley, Sarah IV, 764
Stanley, Sarah IV, 765
Stanley, Sarah IV, 767
Stanley, Sarah IV, 928
Stanley, Sarah IV, 945
Stanley, Sarah IV, 949
Stanley, Sarah IV, 960
Stanley, Sarah IV, 986
Stanley, Sarah IV, 995
Stanley, Sarah IV, 996
Stanley, Sarah IV, 997
Stanley, Sarah IV, 998
Stanley, Sarah IV, 999
Stanley, Sarah IV, 1000
Stanley, Sarah IV, 1001
Stanley, Sarah IV, 1002
Stanley, Sarah IV, 1006
Stanley, Sarah IV, 1014
Stanley, Sarah IV, 1017
Stanley, Sarah IV, 1223
Stanley, Sarah IV, 1224
Stanley, Sarah IV, 1225
Stanley, Sarah IV, 1294
Stanley, Sarah V, 206
Stanley, Sarah V, 280
Stanley, Sarah V, 501
Stanley, Sarah V, 531
Stanley, Sarah VI, 165
Stanley, Sarah VI, 168
Stanley, Sarah VI, 197
Stanley, Sarah VI, 213
Stanley, Sarah VI, 214
Stanley, Sarah VI, 268
Stanley, Sarah VI, 269
Stanley, Sarah VI, 270
Stanley, Sarah VI, 271
Stanley, Sarah VI, 272
Stanley, Sarah VI, 314
Stanley, Sarah VI, 339
Stanley, Sarah VI, 800
Stanley, Sarah VI, 855
Stanley, Sarah VI, 997
Stanley, Sarah A. I, 668
Stanley, Sarah A. IV, 1223
Stanley, Sarah A. V, 764
Stanley, Sarah A. V, 1020
Stanley, Sarah Ann IV, 765
Stanley, Sarah Ann IV, 996
Stanley, Sarah Ann IV, 1210
Stanley, Sarah Ann VI, 997
Stanley, Sarah Elizabeth IV, 999
Stanley, Sarah F. IV, 1224
Stanley, Sarah H. IV, 279
Stanley, Sarah H. IV, 288
Stanley, Sarah J. IV, 1002
Stanley, Sarah K. IV, 1223
Stanley, Sarah Mills V, 124
Stanley, Sarah N. IV, 1001
Stanley, Sarah R. IV, 998
Stanley, Sarah R. IV, 1002
Stanley, Sarah R. IV, 1003
Stanley, Sarah R. IV, 1224
Stanley, Sarah T. IV, 995
Stanley, Sarah T. IV, 1043
Stanley, Sarah T. IV, 1295
Stanley, Sarah Talitha IV, 998
Stanley, Sarah Talitha IV, 1002
Stanley, Sarah Talitha IV, 1295
Stanley, Sarah V. IV, 963
Stanley, Sarah V. IV, 1002
Stanley, Sary I, 572
Stanley, Saryan VI, 997
Stanley, Shadick I, 572
Stanley, Shadrach VI, 270
Stanley, Shadrack I, 572
Stanley, Shadrack VI, 190
Stanley, Shadrack VI, 192
Stanley, Shadrack VI, 213
Stanley, Shadrack VI, 214
Stanley, Shadrack VI, 270
Stanley, Shadrack VI, 271
Stanley, Shadrick I, 516
Stanley, Shadrick I, 572
Stanley, Shadrick VI, 270
Stanley, Sharon V, 206
Stanley, Sibyl IV, 998
Stanley, Sibyl IV, 1002
Stanley, Sibyl IV, 1003
Stanley, Sibyl IV, 1223
Stanley, Sibyl IV, 1224
Stanley, Sidney IV, 998
Stanley, Simeon IV, 765
Stanley, Simon IV, 767
Stanley, Sina E. IV, 767
Stanley, Sina Emily IV, 766
Stanley, Sina Emily IV, 844
Stanley, Soloman IV, 919
Stanley, Soloman VI, 270
Stanley, Soloman VI, 271
Stanley, Soloman VI, 272
Stanley, Solomon I, 515
Stanley, Solomon I, 590
Stanley, Solomon I, 596
Stanley, Solomon I, 597
Stanley, Solomon IV, 690
Stanley, Solomon IV, 763
Stanley, Solomon IV, 765
Stanley, Solomon IV, 766
Stanley, Solomon IV, 995
Stanley, Solomon IV, 996
Stanley, Solomon IV, 998
Stanley, Solomon IV, 1002
Stanley, Solomon IV, 1116
Stanley, Solomon VI, 268
Stanley, Solomon VI, 271
Stanley, Strangeman I, 515
Stanley, Strangeman I, 516
Stanley, Strangeman I, 562
Stanley, Strangeman I, 571
Stanley, Strangeman I, 572
Stanley, Strangeman I, 590
Stanley, Strangeman I, 830
Stanley, Strangeman I, 838
Stanley, Strangeman I, 847
Stanley, Strangeman V, 124
Stanley, Strangeman V, 215
Stanley, Strangeman V, 280
Stanley, Strangeman VI, 268
Stanley, Strangeman VI, 27
Stanley, Strangman V, 124
Stanley, Susan I, 564
Stanley, Susan I, 573
Stanley, Susan IV, 767
Stanley, Susanna I, 515
Stanley, Susanna I, 540
Stanley, Susanna I, 561
Stanley, Susanna I, 563
Stanley, Susanna I, 571
Stanley, Susanna I, 572
Stanley, Susanna I, 573
Stanley, Susanna I, 997
Stanley, Susanna IV, 713
Stanley, Susanna IV, 767
Stanley, Susanna IV, 997
Stanley, Susanna IV, 998
Stanley, Susanna IV, 1224
Stanley, Susanna V, 360
Stanley, Susanna V, 433
Stanley, Susanna VI, 300
Stanley, Susanna VI, 339
Stanley, Susannah I, 571
Stanley, Susannah I, 997
Stanley, Susannah I, 1012
Stanley, Susannah IV, 704
Stanley, Susannah IV, 723
Stanley, Susannah IV, 764
Stanley, Susannah IV, 765
Stanley, Susannah IV, 1116
Stanley, Susannah V, 373
Stanley, Susannah V, 394
Stanley, Susannah V, 433
Stanley, Susannah V, 531
Stanley, Susannah VI, 268
Stanley, Susannah VI, 270
Stanley, Susannah VI, 271
Stanley, Susannah, Jr. IV, 7
Stanley, Sybil IV, 999
Stanley, Tace IV, 996
Stanley, Tacy IV, 765
Stanley, Tacy IV, 957
Stanley, Tacy IV, 998
Stanley, Tacy IV, 1001
Stanley, Talitha IV, 994
Stanley, Talitha IV, 996
Stanley, Talitha IV, 998
Stanley, Talitha IV, 1000
Stanley, Temperance VI, 26
Stanley, Temple I, 516
Stanley, Temple I, 608
Stanley, Temple I, 914
Stanley, Thelma Leah IV, 8
Stanley, Theodore IV, 999
Stanley, Theodore IV, 1043
Stanley, Thomas I, 515
Stanley, Thomas I, 571
Stanley, Thomas I, 573
Stanley, Thomas I, 590
Stanley, Thomas I, 597
Stanley, Thomas I, 623
Stanley, Thomas I, 1050
Stanley, Thomas IV, 279
Stanley, Thomas IV, 763
Stanley, Thomas IV, 764
Stanley, Thomas IV, 765
Stanley, Thomas IV, 766
Stanley, Thomas IV, 781
Stanley, Thomas IV, 919
Stanley, Thomas IV, 936
Stanley, Thomas IV, 995
Stanley, Thomas IV, 997
Stanley, Thomas IV, 1000
Stanley, Thomas IV, 1017
Stanley, Thomas VI, 147
Stanley, Thomas VI, 191
Stanley, Thomas VI, 194
Stanley, Thomas VI, 213
Stanley, Thomas VI, 214
Stanley, Thomas VI, 223
Stanley, Thomas VI, 227
Stanley, Thomas VI, 239
Stanley, Thomas VI, 247
Stanley, Thomas VI, 256
Stanley, Thomas VI, 267
Stanley, Thomas VI, 268
Stanley, Thomas VI, 269
Stanley, Thomas VI, 271
Stanley, Thomas VI, 272
Stanley, Thomas VI, 1002
Stanley, Thomas B. IV, 883
Stanley, Thomas B. IV, 972
Stanley, Thomas B. IV, 996
Stanley, Thomas B. IV, 997
Stanley, Thomas B. IV, 100
Stanley, Thomas B. IV, 100
Stanley, Thomas Benford I
Stanley, Thomas Binford I
Stanley, Thomas C. IV, 763
Stanley, Thomas C. IV, 766
Stanley, Thomas C. IV, 782

ley, Thomas C. IV, 844
ley, Thomas C. IV, 850
ley, Thomas C. IV, 860
ley, Thomas C. IV, 996
ley, Thomas C. IV, 1001
ley, Thomas Crew IV, 764
ley, Thomas E. IV, 551
ley, Thomas E. IV, 844
ley, Thomas E. IV, 847
ley, Thomas Elwood IV, 998
ley, Thomas Elwood IV, 1002
ley, Thomas Gerard IV, 765
ley, Thomas H. IV, 279
ley, Thomas H. IV, 995
ley, Thomas H. IV, 1001
ley, Thomas J. VI, 272
ley, Thomas Jared IV, 996
ley, Thomas Jared IV, 1001
ley, Thomas L. IV, 981
ley, Thomas Lindley IV, 997
ley, Thomas Lindley IV, 1000
ley, Thomas P. IV, 764
ley, Thomas P. IV, 766
ley, Thomas P. IV, 997
ley, Thomas P. IV, 1001
ley, Thomas P. VI, 973
ley, Thomas S. IV, 1003
ley, Thomas, Jr. IV, 1001
ley, Thomas, Jr. VI, 166
ley, Thomas, Jr. VI, 213
ley, Thomas, Jr. VI, 269
ley, Thomas, Jr. VI, 271
ley, Thomas, Sr. VI, 213
ley, Thomas, Sr. VI, 272
ley, Thomasson IV, 1001
ley, Thomasson P. IV, 997
ley, Thos. I, 515
ley, Thos. IV, 271
ley, Thos. IV, 279
ley, Thos. IV, 694
ley, Thos. IV, 696
ley, Thos. IV, 764
ley, Thos. IV, 993
ley, Thos. IV, 1000
ley, Thos. VI, 213
ley, Thos. VI, 268
ley, Thos. Binford IV, 764
ley, Thos. Binford VI, 269
ley, Thos. E. IV, 550
ley, Thos. H. IV, 279
ley, Thos. H. IV, 305
ley, Thos. L. IV, 927
ley, Thos. L. IV, 1000
ley, Timothy IV, 764
ley, Timothy IV, 916
ley, Timothy IV, 941
ley, Timothy IV, 996
ley, Timothy IV, 997
ley, Timothy IV, 1001
ley, Townsen IV, 1294
ley, Townsend P. IV, 1295
ley, Unity I, 515
ley, Unity I, 536
ley, Unity I, 573
ley, Unity IV, 279
ley, Unity IV, 694
ley, Unity IV, 756
ley, Unity IV, 764
ley, Unity IV, 766
ley, Unity IV, 939
ley, Unity IV, 943
ley, Unity IV, 969
ley, Unity IV, 988
ley, Unity IV, 993
ley, Unity IV, 995
ley, Unity IV, 997
ley, Unity IV, 999
ley, Unity IV, 1000
ley, Unity IV, 1002
ley, Unity VI, 239
ley, Unity VI, 268
ley, Unity VI, 271
ley, Unity VI, 272
ley, Unity C. IV, 764
ley, Unity C. IV, 907
ley, Unity C. IV, 964
ley, Unity C. IV, 996
ley, Unity C. IV, 997
ley, Unity C. IV, 998
ley, Unity Crew IV, 996
ley, Unity, Jr. IV, 764
ley, Uree IV, 765
ley, Uree IV, 783
ley, Uree IV, 933
ley, Uree IV, 939
ley, Uree IV, 955
ley, Uree IV, 996
ley, Uree IV, 998
ley, Uree IV, 999
ley, Uree IV, 1002
ley, Uree C. IV, 933
Stanley, Uree C. IV, 971
Stanley, Uree C. IV, 1002
Stanley, Uree C. IV, 1003
Stanley, Uriah I, 515
Stanley, Uriah I, 573
Stanley, Ursley VI, 272
Stanley, Ursula VI, 270
Stanley, Valentine IV, 1002
Stanley, Valentine M. IV, 997
Stanley, Valentine M. IV, 1002
Stanley, Valentine M. IV, 1003
Stanley, Vera Fay IV, 1000
Stanley, Verna Marie IV, 440
Stanley, Vernon IV, 1043
Stanley, Viola C. IV, 1000
Stanley, Viola Chlotilda IV, 981
Stanley, Voluntine IV, 999
Stanley, Waddy IV, 764
Stanley, Waddy IV, 766
Stanley, Waddy IV, 995
Stanley, Waddy IV, 997
Stanley, Waddy IV, 1001
Stanley, Waddy VI, 190
Stanley, Waddy VI, 194
Stanley, Waddy VI, 213
Stanley, Waddy VI, 214
Stanley, Waddy VI, 269
Stanley, Waddy VI, 270
Stanley, Waddy VI, 271
Stanley, Waddy VI, 272
Stanley, Waldy IV, 765
Stanley, Walker IV, 997
Stanley, Walter IV, 765
Stanley, Walter IV, 996
Stanley, Walter IV, 998
Stanley, Walter IV, 1001
Stanley, Walter IV, 1116
Stanley, Walter IV, 1117
Stanley, Waren E. IV, 1003
Stanley, Warren IV, 1003
Stanley, Warren E. IV, 999
Stanley, Wayne V, 206
Stanley, Wd. Elizabeth VI, 214
Stanley, Wd. Sarah VI, 272
Stanley, Widow Elizabeth I, 515
Stanley, Widow Jemima I, 830
Stanley, Willard Lorain IV, 999
Stanley, William I, 515
Stanley, William I, 516
Stanley, William I, 532
Stanley, William I, 534
Stanley, William I, 540
Stanley, William I, 563
Stanley, William I, 571
Stanley, William I, 572
Stanley, William I, 573
Stanley, William I, 574
Stanley, William I, 580
Stanley, William I, 590
Stanley, William I, 596
Stanley, William I, 597
Stanley, William I, 600
Stanley, William I, 792
Stanley, William I, 838
Stanley, William I, 847
Stanley, William I, 997
Stanley, William I, 1053
Stanley, William II, 202
Stanley, William II, 423
Stanley, William IV, 765
Stanley, William V, 280
Stanley, William V, 531
Stanley, William VI, 18
Stanley, William VI, 214
Stanley, William VI, 246
Stanley, William VI, 268
Stanley, William VI, 269
Stanley, William VI, 270
Stanley, William VI, 271
Stanley, William VI, 272
Stanley, William VI, 564
Stanley, William VI, 852
Stanley, William B. IV, 440
Stanley, William B. IV, 883
Stanley, William C. Johnson IV, 279
Stanley, William F. IV, 279
Stanley, William Franklin I, 792
Stanley, William P. IV, 767
Stanley, William P. IV, 996
Stanley, William P. IV, 999
Stanley, William Penn I, 573
Stanley, Willis IV, 765
Stanley, Willis IV, 767
Stanley, Wilma Louelva IV, 1000
Stanley, Wilmer C. IV, 999
Stanley, Wilmer W. IV, 767
Stanley, Wilmer Wilid IV, 766
Stanley, Wilson IV, 998
Stanley, Wilson J. IV, 1003
Stanley, Wm. I, 516
Stanley, Wm. IV, 406
Stanley, Wm. IV, 440
Stanley, Wm. IV, 498
Stanley, Wm. IV, 821
Stanley, Wm. VI, 213
Stanley, Wm. VI, 271
Stanley, Wm. B. IV, 877
Stanley, Wm. Cattell IV, 1000
Stanley, Wm. H. M. IV, 235
Stanley, Wm. P. II, 768
Stanley, Wm. P. IV, 979
Stanley, Wm. P. IV, 990
Stanley, Wm. P. IV, 1001
Stanley, Wm. P. IV, 1002
Stanley, Wm. P. IV, 1003
Stanley, Wm. Penn II, 768
Stanley, Woddy IV, 695
Stanley, Zach. I, 515
Stanley, Zachariah I, 571
Stanley, Zachariah I, 969
Stanley, Zachariah VI, 18
Stanley, Zachariah VI, 268
Stanley, Zachariah VI, 270
Stanley, Zachariah VI, 271
Stanley, Zachariah VI, 339
Stanley, Zacharias I, 561
Stanley, Zacharias I, 571
Stanley, Zacheriah VI, 165
Stanley, Zacheriah VI, 168
Stanley, Zacheriah VI, 213
Stanley, Zacheriah VI, 214
Stanley, Zacheriah VI, 268
Stanley, Zacheriah VI, 270
Stanley, Zacheriah VI, 271
Stanley, Zimri I, 590
Stanley, Zimri I, 591
Stanley, Zimri I, 596
Stanley, Zimri I, 806
Stanley, Zimri I, 838
Stanley, Zimry I, 515
Stanleyetta, Jos. III, 318
Stanleyetta, Ruth Amelia III, 318
Stanly, Abel I, 600
Stanly, Abigail I, 600
Stanly, Abigail I, 838
Stanly, Abigail IV, 916
Stanly, Able I, 608
Stanly, Archelaus I, 773
Stanly, Eli IV, 767
Stanly, Elizabeth I, 802
Stanly, Elizabeth V, 862
Stanly, Elizabeth J. V, 831
Stanly, Eunice IV, 1352
Stanly, Eunice IV, 1379
Stanly, Fleming IV, 1379
Stanly, Fleming A. IV, 1352
Stanly, Gertrude IV, 1379
Stanly, James VI, 855
Stanly, Josephine IV, 1352
Stanly, Josephine IV, 1379
Stanly, Libby VI, 855
Stanly, Lydia I, 600
Stanly, Martha E. I, 827
Stanly, Martha E. I, 839
Stanly, Mary P. V, 862
Stanly, Mary P. V, 873
Stanly, Matthew I, 608
Stanly, Prudence I, 600
Stanly, Richard I, 600
Stanly, Sarah I, 600
Stannard, Mary IV, 1295
Stannton, Amy II, 1022
Stannup, Lydia II, 448
Stannup, Thomas II, 448
Stansbury, Frances III, 298
Stansbury, Joseph II, 423
Stansbury, Joseph A. III, 298
Stansbury, Joseph Albert III, 298
Stansbury, Sarah III, 71
Stansbury, Sarah III, 298
Stansbury, Susanna III, 280
Stansbury, Susanna III, 298
Stanton, ??? IV, 1269
Stanton, ??? V, 965
Stanton, Aaron I, 668
Stanton, Aaron IV, 767
Stanton, Aaron VI, 340
Stanton, Aaron VI, 855
Stanton, Abel V, 977
Stanton, Abigail I, 266
Stanton, Abigail I, 267
Stanton, Abigail I, 269
Stanton, Abigail I, 275
Stanton, Abigail I, 276
Stanton, Abigail I, 558
Stanton, Abigail I, 574
Stanton, Abigail II, 423
Stanton, Abigail IV, 60
Stanton, Abigail IV, 160
Stanton, Abigail IV, 238
Stanton, Abigail IV, 251
Stanton, Abigail IV, 279
Stanton, Abigail IV, 352
Stanton, Abigail IV, 391
Stanton, Abigail IV, 441
Stanton, Abigail IV, 442
Stanton, Abigail IV, 498
Stanton, Abigail IV, 594
Stanton, Abigail IV, 597
Stanton, Abigail IV, 767
Stanton, Abigail, Jr. IV, 279
Stanton, Abigail, Jr. IV, 442
Stanton, Abigale IV, 60
Stanton, Abigale Roberson I, 276
Stanton, Achsah IV, 442
Stanton, Acsah II, 1029
Stanton, Addison I, 18
Stanton, Agnes VI, 340
Stanton, Agness VI, 133
Stanton, Agness VI, 141
Stanton, Alabama I, 622
Stanton, Albert V, 978
Stanton, Alfred IV, 767
Stanton, Alfred IV, 768
Stanton, Alfred V, 977
Stanton, Alfred V, 979
Stanton, Alfred Hodgin IV, 442
Stanton, Alice I, 266
Stanton, Alice I, 267
Stanton, Alice I, 272
Stanton, Alice I, 275
Stanton, Alice I, 276
Stanton, Allie V, 1020
Stanton, Almeda V, 977
Stanton, Almeda V, 979
Stanton, Almeda V, 1020
Stanton, Almedia V, 976
Stanton, Almedia VI, 130
Stanton, Almedia VI, 141
Stanton, Almedia VI, 142
Stanton, Almira V, 978
Stanton, Amee II, 207
Stanton, Amee II, 264
Stanton, Amor IV, 767
Stanton, Amos IV, 767
Stanton, Amos V, 124
Stanton, Amy I, 668
Stanton, Amy II, 264
Stanton, Amy II, 1029
Stanton, Angelina IV, 279
Stanton, Angelina IV, 280
Stanton, Angelina IV, 300
Stanton, Angelina V, 977
Stanton, Angelina V, 978
Stanton, Angeline IV, 1295
Stanton, Ann I, 658
Stanton, Ann I, 668
Stanton, Ann I, 687
Stanton, Ann I, 689
Stanton, Ann I, 770
Stanton, Ann II, 264
Stanton, Ann IV, 279
Stanton, Ann IV, 442
Stanton, Ann IV, 594
Stanton, Ann V, 93
Stanton, Ann V, 124
Stanton, Ann V, 360
Stanton, Ann V, 531
Stanton, Ann V, 974
Stanton, Ann V, 977
Stanton, Ann V, 978
Stanton, Ann V, 979
Stanton, Ann VI, 85
Stanton, Ann VI, 86
Stanton, Ann VI, 87
Stanton, Ann VI, 103
Stanton, Ann VI, 122
Stanton, Ann VI, 141
Stanton, Ann VI, 142
Stanton, Ann VI, 339
Stanton, Ann L. V, 979
Stanton, Anna I, 268
Stanton, Anna I, 276
Stanton, Anna I, 668
Stanton, Anna I, 673
Stanton, Anna I, 689
Stanton, Anna IV, 374
Stanton, Anna IV, 441
Stanton, Anna VI, 340
Stanton, Anna C. IV, 425
Stanton, Anna C. IV, 442
Stanton, Anna Clara IV, 441
Stanton, Anna M. V, 125
Stanton, Anne I, 266
Stanton, Anne II, 207
Stanton, Anne II, 264
Stanton, Anne D. V, 977
Stanton, Annie IV, 441
Stanton, Aron VI, 339
Stanton, Arthur E. IV, 366
Stanton, Arthur E. IV, 441
Stanton, Arthur E. IV, 442
Stanton, Avis I, 276
Stanton, Benj. IV, 238
Stanton, Benj. IV, 262
Stanton, Benj. IV, 279
Stanton, Benj. IV, 352
Stanton, Benj. IV, 767
Stanton, Benj. V, 977
Stanton, Benj. Franklin V, 978
Stanton, Benj., Sr. IV, 279
Stanton, Benjamin I, 117
Stanton, Benjamin I, 144
Stanton, Benjamin I, 166
Stanton, Benjamin I, 266
Stanton, Benjamin I, 274
Stanton, Benjamin I, 275
Stanton, Benjamin I, 558
Stanton, Benjamin I, 574
Stanton, Benjamin I, 668
Stanton, Benjamin I, 689
Stanton, Benjamin IV, 60
Stanton, Benjamin IV, 61
Stanton, Benjamin IV, 110
Stanton, Benjamin IV, 167
Stanton, Benjamin IV, 251
Stanton, Benjamin IV, 279
Stanton, Benjamin IV, 280
Stanton, Benjamin IV, 374
Stanton, Benjamin IV, 401
Stanton, Benjamin IV, 431
Stanton, Benjamin IV, 441
Stanton, Benjamin IV, 442
Stanton, Benjamin IV, 498
Stanton, Benjamin IV, 676
Stanton, Benjamin IV, 715
Stanton, Benjamin IV, 767
Stanton, Benjamin IV, 768
Stanton, Benjamin IV, 778
Stanton, Benjamin IV, 844
Stanton, Benjamin IV, 909
Stanton, Benjamin IV, 916
Stanton, Benjamin IV, 1295
Stanton, Benjamin V, 979
Stanton, Benjamin C. V, 976
Stanton, Benjamin C. V, 979
Stanton, Benjamin C. VI, 87
Stanton, Benjamin Franklin V, 978
Stanton, Benjamin H. IV, 441
Stanton, Benjamin W. IV, 280
Stanton, Benjamin, Jr. I, 272
Stanton, Benjamin, Jr. I, 275
Stanton, Benjamin, Jr. I, 276
Stanton, Benjamin, Sr. IV, 279
Stanton, Bessie V, 712
Stanton, Betey I, 327
Stanton, Betsy IV, 498
Stanton, Betsy IV, 909
Stanton, Betsy IV, 916
Stanton, Betsy IV, 1295
Stanton, Blanch D. IV, 442
Stanton, Borden I, 266
Stanton, Borden I, 276
Stanton, Borden I, 308
Stanton, Borden I, 318
Stanton, Borden IV, 60
Stanton, Borden IV, 160
Stanton, Borden IV, 365
Stanton, Borden IV, 436
Stanton, Borden IV, 441
Stanton, Borden IV, 442
Stanton, Borden IV, 594
Stanton, Borden, Jr. IV, 160
Stanton, Borden, Jr. IV, 442
Stanton, Bordon IV, 52
Stanton, Bordon IV, 60
Stanton, Bordon IV, 137
Stanton, Bordon IV, 442
Stanton, Bordon IV, 594
Stanton, Byron IV, 767
Stanton, Carlton V, 712
Stanton, Carlton W. V, 712
Stanton, Caroline I, 276
Stanton, Caroline IV, 767
Stanton, Caroline IV, 768
Stanton, Caroline IV, 844
Stanton, Caroline V, 977
Stanton, Catharine I, 275
Stanton, Catharine I, 277
Stanton, Catharine I, 419
Stanton, Catharine IV, 441
Stanton, Catharine IV, 447
Stanton, Catharine IV, 594
Stanton, Catharine IV, 596
Stanton, Catharine Ann V, 968
Stanton, Catharine Ann V, 976
Stanton, Catharine Ann V, 979
Stanton, Catharine M. II, 719
Stanton, Catherine V, 124
Stanton, Catherine V, 973
Stanton, Catherine VI, 339
Stanton, Catherine VI, 340

Stanton, Catherine VI, 606
Stanton, Catherine Ann V, 38
Stanton, Catherine Ann V, 125
Stanton, Catherine Ann VI, 87
Stanton, Chalkley V, 976
Stanton, Chalkley V, 977
Stanton, Chalkly VI, 141
Stanton, Charity IV, 374
Stanton, Charity IV, 441
Stanton, Charity IV, 442
Stanton, Charles V, 124
Stanton, Charles F. V, 977
Stanton, Charles Osborn IV, 279
Stanton, Charles Osborn IV, 916
Stanton, Charlotta IV, 436
Stanton, Charlotte IV, 52
Stanton, Charlotte IV, 60
Stanton, Charlotte IV, 160
Stanton, Charlotte IV, 441
Stanton, Charlotte IV, 442
Stanton, Chas. W. V, 978
Stanton, Christian I, 689
Stanton, Christian VI, 42
Stanton, Christian VI, 122
Stanton, Clara IV, 441
Stanton, Clarey IV, 441
Stanton, Clary IV, 260
Stanton, Clary IV, 279
Stanton, Clary IV, 383
Stanton, Clary IV, 441
Stanton, Clary IV, 442
Stanton, Dalton IV, 767
Stanton, Daniel I, 266
Stanton, Daniel II, 355
Stanton, Daniel II, 423
Stanton, Daniel II, 508
Stanton, Daniel II, 583
Stanton, Daniel II, 658
Stanton, Daniel III, 298
Stanton, Daniel IV, 279
Stanton, Daniel IV, 280
Stanton, Daniel IV, 300
Stanton, Daniel IV, 375
Stanton, Daniel IV, 441
Stanton, Daniel IV, 551
Stanton, Daniel IV, 1295
Stanton, Daniel V, 124
Stanton, Daniel V, 280
Stanton, Daniel V, 977
Stanton, Daniel V, 978
Stanton, Daniel VI, 23
Stanton, Daniel VI, 95
Stanton, Daniel VI, 122
Stanton, Daniel VI, 291
Stanton, Daniel VI, 339
Stanton, Daniel VI, 340
Stanton, Daniel E. IV, 441
Stanton, Daniel E. IV, 442
Stanton, Daniel Wm. V, 977
Stanton, Daniell II, 423
Stanton, David I, 266
Stanton, David I, 658
Stanton, David I, 668
Stanton, David I, 687
Stanton, David I, 689
Stanton, David I, 690
Stanton, David I, 770
Stanton, David IV, 60
Stanton, David IV, 279
Stanton, David IV, 441
Stanton, David IV, 550
Stanton, David IV, 551
Stanton, David IV, 558
Stanton, David IV, 594
Stanton, David IV, 657
Stanton, David IV, 767
Stanton, David IV, 768
Stanton, David V, 124
Stanton, David V, 977
Stanton, David VI, 340
Stanton, David A. I, 949
Stanton, David Absolom I, 690
Stanton, David T. V, 979
Stanton, Davis I, 276
Stanton, Dean II, 768
Stanton, Deborah I, 516
Stanton, Deborah IV, 441
Stanton, Deborah IV, 442
Stanton, Deborah IV, 767
Stanton, Deborah V, 977
Stanton, Deborah VI, 142
Stanton, Deborah VI, 339
Stanton, Deborah VI, 340
Stanton, Deborah A. V, 973
Stanton, Deborah A. V, 976
Stanton, Deborah Ann V, 979
Stanton, Deborah Bundy IV, 375
Stanton, Deborah I. IV, 280
Stanton, Deborah J. V, 93
Stanton, Deborah J. V, 124
Stanton, Deborah J. V, 977
Stanton, Deborah Jane V, 125
Stanton, Deborah Jane V, 976
Stanton, Deborah Jane VI, 87
Stanton, Deborah T. IV, 242
Stanton, Deborah W. IV, 1295
Stanton, Dinah V, 176
Stanton, Dinah V, 206
Stanton, Dinah V, 531
Stanton, Dinah V, 645
Stanton, Dorcas IV, 61
Stanton, Dorcas IV, 110
Stanton, E. Dean II, 719
Stanton, E. Dean II, 768
Stanton, E. E. IV, 1116
Stanton, Edith IV, 374
Stanton, Edith IV, 441
Stanton, Edith Mary IV, 380
Stanton, Edith Mary IV, 442
Stanton, Edith Rebecca IV, 442
Stanton, Edmond IV, 441
Stanton, Edmond IV, 1116
Stanton, Edmund IV, 382
Stanton, Edmund IV, 438
Stanton, Edmund IV, 441
Stanton, Edmund IV, 442
Stanton, Edmund C. IV, 441
Stanton, Edmund C. IV, 442
Stanton, Edna V, 976
Stanton, Edna V, 979
Stanton, Edna VI, 142
Stanton, Edna E. V, 977
Stanton, Edna E. V, 979
Stanton, Edna M. IV, 441
Stanton, Edna M. IV, 442
Stanton, Edward II, 207
Stanton, Edward II, 264
Stanton, Edward II, 1029
Stanton, Edward V, 124
Stanton, Edward V, 977
Stanton, Eleanor I, 668
Stanton, Eli II, 719
Stanton, Eli IV, 280
Stanton, Eli IV, 374
Stanton, Eli IV, 375
Stanton, Eli IV, 441
Stanton, Eli IV, 442
Stanton, Eli IV, 453
Stanton, Eli IV, 767
Stanton, Elias IV, 61
Stanton, Elias IV, 110
Stanton, Elias IV, 279
Stanton, Elias IV, 304
Stanton, Elias IV, 916
Stanton, Elijah IV, 767
Stanton, Elijah V, 124
Stanton, Elisabeth I, 166
Stanton, Eliza V, 124
Stanton, Eliza V, 976
Stanton, Elizabeth I, 265
Stanton, Elizabeth I, 266
Stanton, Elizabeth I, 267
Stanton, Elizabeth I, 275
Stanton, Elizabeth I, 276
Stanton, Elizabeth I, 287
Stanton, Elizabeth I, 308
Stanton, Elizabeth I, 318
Stanton, Elizabeth I, 689
Stanton, Elizabeth I, 692
Stanton, Elizabeth II, 528
Stanton, Elizabeth II, 658
Stanton, Elizabeth IV, 60
Stanton, Elizabeth IV, 160
Stanton, Elizabeth IV, 310
Stanton, Elizabeth IV, 365
Stanton, Elizabeth IV, 366
Stanton, Elizabeth IV, 375
Stanton, Elizabeth IV, 401
Stanton, Elizabeth IV, 416
Stanton, Elizabeth IV, 428
Stanton, Elizabeth IV, 431
Stanton, Elizabeth IV, 441
Stanton, Elizabeth IV, 442
Stanton, Elizabeth IV, 715
Stanton, Elizabeth IV, 767
Stanton, Elizabeth IV, 768
Stanton, Elizabeth V, 124
Stanton, Elizabeth V, 280
Stanton, Elizabeth V, 977
Stanton, Elizabeth V, 978
Stanton, Elizabeth V, 979
Stanton, Elizabeth VI, 103
Stanton, Elizabeth VI, 122
Stanton, Elizabeth VI, 142
Stanton, Elizabeth VI, 337
Stanton, Elizabeth VI, 339
Stanton, Elizabeth VI, 340
Stanton, Elizabeth VI, 847
Stanton, Elizabeth Ann IV, 1295
Stanton, Elizabeth Ann V, 712
Stanton, Elizabeth M. V, 38
Stanton, Elizabeth M. V, 124
Stanton, Elizabeth M. V, 968
Stanton, Elizabeth M. V, 976
Stanton, Elizabeth M. V, 979
Stanton, Elizabeth M. VI, 87
Stanton, Elizabeth, Jr. I, 276
Stanton, Elizabeth, Sr. I, 276
Stanton, Ellen V, 979
Stanton, Ellen D. IV, 441
Stanton, Ellen D. IV, 442
Stanton, Ellen J. V, 125
Stanton, Elma C. IV, 442
Stanton, Elmira V, 978
Stanton, Elsie H. IV, 442
Stanton, Elwood IV, 768
Stanton, Elwood V, 976
Stanton, Elwood V, 977
Stanton, Elwood V, 979
Stanton, Elwood VI, 141
Stanton, Elwood VI, 142
Stanton, Elwood Dean II, 768
Stanton, Elwood Dean IV, 441
Stanton, Elwood Dean IV, 442
Stanton, Elwood Dean IV, 704
Stanton, Elwood Dean IV, 767
Stanton, Emaline V, 979
Stanton, Emeline V, 977
Stanton, Emely V, 977
Stanton, Emily V, 712
Stanton, Emma V, 977
Stanton, Emma A. IV, 442
Stanton, Emma A. IV, 453
Stanton, Emma C. IV, 441
Stanton, Emma C. IV, 453
Stanton, Enoch I, 266
Stanton, Enoch II, 264
Stanton, Enoch IV, 60
Stanton, Enoch IV, 160
Stanton, Enoch IV, 352
Stanton, Enoch IV, 441
Stanton, Enoch IV, 442
Stanton, Enoch IV, 594
Stanton, Ephraim IV, 1116
Stanton, Esther IV, 768
Stanton, Esther S. II, 768
Stanton, Esther Sidney II, 719
Stanton, Esther Sidney II, 768
Stanton, Esther Sidney IV, 704
Stanton, Esther Sidney IV, 767
Stanton, Eunice I, 668
Stanton, Eunice I, 678
Stanton, Eunice I, 689
Stanton, Eunice IV, 441
Stanton, Eunice Maude I, 18
Stanton, Eva B. III, 50
Stanton, Eva T. II, 719
Stanton, Eva T. II, 768
Stanton, Eva T. IV, 441
Stanton, Eva T. IV, 442
Stanton, Everette G. IV, 442
Stanton, Faith VI, 102
Stanton, Faith VI, 103
Stanton, Faith VI, 122
Stanton, Francis I, 689
Stanton, Francis W. IV, 441
Stanton, Frederick V, 124
Stanton, Frederick V, 125
Stanton, Frederick V, 129
Stanton, Frederick V, 531
Stanton, Frederick V, 977
Stanton, Frederick VI, 141
Stanton, Fredrec VI, 122
Stanton, Fredrick V, 124
Stanton, Fredrick V, 977
Stanton, George Elwood I, 690
Stanton, George F. I, 689
Stanton, George F. I, 690
Stanton, George Fox I, 668
Stanton, Gulielma V, 124
Stanton, Gulielma V, 280
Stanton, Gulielma VI, 339
Stanton, Gulielma VI, 340
Stanton, Hannah I, 266
Stanton, Hannah I, 267
Stanton, Hannah I, 274
Stanton, Hannah I, 275
Stanton, Hannah I, 276
Stanton, Hannah I, 277
Stanton, Hannah I, 419
Stanton, Hannah I, 668
Stanton, Hannah I, 758
Stanton, Hannah I, 770
Stanton, Hannah IV, 60
Stanton, Hannah IV, 160
Stanton, Hannah IV, 262
Stanton, Hannah IV, 279
Stanton, Hannah IV, 442
Stanton, Hannah IV, 550
Stanton, Hannah IV, 594
Stanton, Hannah IV, 598
Stanton, Hannah IV, 767
Stanton, Hannah IV, 1295
Stanton, Hannah V, 124
Stanton, Hannah V, 125
Stanton, Hannah V, 129
Stanton, Hannah V, 531
Stanton, Hannah V, 621
Stanton, Hannah V, 644
Stanton, Hannah V, 977
Stanton, Hannah V, 978
Stanton, Hannah VI, 339
Stanton, Hannah VI, 340
Stanton, Hannah J. IV, 551
Stanton, Hanson V, 977
Stanton, Harriet M. V, 243
Stanton, Harriet M. V, 280
Stanton, Henry I, 117
Stanton, Henry I, 263
Stanton, Henry I, 264
Stanton, Henry I, 266
Stanton, Henry I, 267
Stanton, Henry I, 274
Stanton, Henry I, 275
Stanton, Henry I, 276
Stanton, Henry I, 318
Stanton, Henry I, 327
Stanton, Henry I, 689
Stanton, Henry III, 86
Stanton, Henry III, 298
Stanton, Henry IV, 60
Stanton, Henry IV, 260
Stanton, Henry IV, 279
Stanton, Henry IV, 365
Stanton, Henry IV, 383
Stanton, Henry IV, 441
Stanton, Henry IV, 442
Stanton, Henry IV, 551
Stanton, Henry E. IV, 442
Stanton, Henry Edmund IV, 442
Stanton, Henry H. I, 331
Stanton, Henry J. I, 275
Stanton, Henry, Jr. I, 263
Stanton, Henry, Jr. I, 264
Stanton, Henry, Jr. I, 275
Stanton, Henry, Jr. IV, 280
Stanton, Henry, Sr. I, 131
Stanton, Henry, Sr. I, 166
Stanton, Henry, Sr. I, 263
Stanton, Henry, Sr. I, 267
Stanton, Henry, Sr. I, 275
Stanton, Henry, Sr. IV, 280
Stanton, Hephsabeth V, 280
Stanton, Hephsibah I, 684
Stanton, Hephsibah I, 689
Stanton, Hephzabah VI, 339
Stanton, Hepsibah I, 266
Stanton, Hepsibah I, 574
Stanton, Hepsibah V, 124
Stanton, Hepsibah VI, 340
Stanton, Hepzabah VI, 314
Stanton, Hepzebah VI, 339
Stanton, Hepzibah I, 516
Stanton, Hepzibah I, 678
Stanton, Hepzibah I, 689
Stanton, Hepzibah VI, 339
Stanton, Hiram V, 531
Stanton, Hiram V, 977
Stanton, Hiram V, 978
Stanton, Hope I, 267
Stanton, Hope I, 275
Stanton, Hope I, 276
Stanton, Hope IV, 160
Stanton, Hope IV, 436
Stanton, Hope IV, 441
Stanton, Hope IV, 442
Stanton, Howard A. IV, 441
Stanton, Howard Arden IV, 442
Stanton, Huldah I, 685
Stanton, Huldah I, 689
Stanton, Huldah I, 732
Stanton, Huldah I, 734
Stanton, Huldah V, 124
Stanton, Huldah VI, 301
Stanton, Huldah VI, 339
Stanton, Huldah VI, 340
Stanton, Hulday V, 280
Stanton, Hunnicut V, 124
Stanton, Hunnicutt V, 280
Stanton, Hunnicutt VI, 339
Stanton, Ida IV, 402
Stanton, Ida IV, 715
Stanton, Ida J. IV, 215
Stanton, Ida J. IV, 280
Stanton, Ida J. IV, 401
Stanton, Ida J. IV, 442
Stanton, Ida Jane IV, 441
Stanton, Ira V, 977
Stanton, Isaac IV, 594
Stanton, Isaac V, 978
Stanton, Isaac F. I, 668
Stanton, Isaac F. I, 770
Stanton, Isaac Hays V, 978
Stanton, J. VI, 87
Stanton, J. C. V, 1020
Stanton, Jackson E. V, 1020
Stanton, James I, 258
Stanton, James I, 276
Stanton, James I, 287
Stanton, James I, 308
Stanton, James I, 318
Stanton, James I, 327
Stanton, James I, 419
Stanton, James I, 516
Stanton, James I, 770
Stanton, James IV, 160
Stanton, James IV, 279
Stanton, James IV, 374
Stanton, James IV, 434
Stanton, James IV, 441
Stanton, James IV, 442
Stanton, James IV, 551
Stanton, James IV, 767
Stanton, James V, 93
Stanton, James V, 124
Stanton, James V, 176
Stanton, James V, 206
Stanton, James V, 280
Stanton, James V, 360
Stanton, James V, 531
Stanton, James V, 621
Stanton, James V, 644
Stanton, James V, 645
Stanton, James V, 974
Stanton, James V, 976
Stanton, James V, 979
Stanton, James VI, 18
Stanton, James VI, 85
Stanton, James VI, 86
Stanton, James VI, 87
Stanton, James VI, 122
Stanton, James VI, 133
Stanton, James VI, 141
Stanton, James VI, 304
Stanton, James VI, 339
Stanton, James VI, 340
Stanton, James VI, 997
Stanton, James A. V, 979
Stanton, James Albert V, 979
Stanton, James D. IV, 1295
Stanton, James E. V, 599
Stanton, James E. V, 977
Stanton, James Edwin V, 976
Stanton, James Edwin VI, 122
Stanton, James Edwin Daniel William VI, 142
Stanton, James F. V, 125
Stanton, James Franklin V, 712
Stanton, James H. V, 969
Stanton, James H. V, 976
Stanton, James H. V, 979
Stanton, James, Jr. VI, 103
Stanton, James, Jr. VI, 122
Stanton, James, Jr. VI, 141
Stanton, Jane II, 719
Stanton, Jane IV, 382
Stanton, Jane IV, 425
Stanton, Jane IV, 441
Stanton, Jane IV, 1295
Stanton, Jane D. II, 768
Stanton, Jane D. IV, 767
Stanton, Jane Davis II, 719
Stanton, Jehu V, 645
Stanton, Jehu L. V, 645
Stanton, Jesse I, 668
Stanton, Jesse I, 689
Stanton, Jesse I, 874
Stanton, Jesse I, 901
Stanton, Jesse V, 531
Stanton, Jesse F. V, 531
Stanton, Job IV, 60
Stanton, John I, 266
Stanton, John I, 275
Stanton, John I, 276
Stanton, John I, 419
Stanton, John I, 574
Stanton, John I, 668
Stanton, John I, 684
Stanton, John I, 689
Stanton, John I, 839
Stanton, John I, 901
Stanton, John II, 423
Stanton, John III, 298
Stanton, John IV, 594
Stanton, John IV, 767
Stanton, John IV, 1295
Stanton, John V, 124
Stanton, John V, 280
Stanton, John V, 531
Stanton, John V, 969
Stanton, John V, 970
Stanton, John V, 976
Stanton, John V, 977
Stanton, John VI, 18
Stanton, John VI, 66

ton, John VI, 86
ton, John VI, 87
ton, John VI, 104
ton, John VI, 122
ton, John VI, 135
ton, John VI, 141
ton, John VI, 339
ton, John VI, 340
ton, John A. V, 976
ton, John F. V, 712
ton, John F. V, 970
ton, John F. V, 977
ton, John Fleming V, 979
ton, John Lindley IV, 441
ton, John Oliver V, 979
ton, John Oliver VI, 142
ton, John T. V, 712
ton, John W. IV, 1295
ton, John W. V, 979
ton, John, Jr. VI, 129
ton, John, Jr. VI, 141
ton, John, Sr. VI, 141
ton, Jonah D. V, 977
ton, Jonah D. V, 978
ton, Jonathan I, 266
ton, Jonathan I, 276
ton, Jonathan IV, 594
ton, Jonathan V, 976
ton, Jonathan V, 979
ton, Jonathan VI, 130
ton, Jonathan VI, 141
ton, Jonathan VI, 142
ton, Jonathan H. III, 298
ton, Jonathan L. I, 668
ton, Jordon IV, 441
ton, Joseph I, 275
ton, Joseph I, 276
ton, Joseph I, 318
ton, Joseph I, 668
ton, Joseph IV, 60
ton, Joseph IV, 279
ton, Joseph IV, 352
ton, Joseph IV, 354
ton, Joseph IV, 365
ton, Joseph IV, 374
ton, Joseph IV, 409
ton, Joseph IV, 441
ton, Joseph IV, 442
ton, Joseph IV, 598
ton, Joseph IV, 767
ton, Joseph IV, 768
ton, Joseph IV, 844
ton, Joseph V, 38
ton, Joseph V, 124
ton, Joseph V, 125
ton, Joseph V, 133
ton, Joseph V, 968
ton, Joseph V, 973
ton, Joseph V, 976
ton, Joseph V, 977
ton, Joseph V, 979
ton, Joseph VI, 142
ton, Joseph E. IV, 441
ton, Joseph E. IV, 442
ton, Joseph F. V, 977
ton, Joseph Fleming V, 979
ton, Josiah II, 423
ton, Julia V, 979
ton, Julius Porgan I, 690
ton, Katharine VI, 606
ton, Katherine VI, 598
ton, Katherine M. II, 768
ton, Lantham VI, 850
ton, Latham I, 516
ton, Latham V, 124
ton, Latham V, 280
ton, Latham V, 531
ton, Latham VI, 301
ton, Latham VI, 339
ton, Latham VI, 340
ton, Laura IV, 676
ton, Laura IV, 767
ton, Laura IV, 768
ton, Laura IV, 844
ton, Laura IV, 1095
ton, Laura IV, 1116
ton, Laura Edgerton IV, 1116
ton, Lemuel VI, 122
ton, Lemuel VI, 141
ton, Levi I, 668
ton, Levi I, 689
ton, Levi I, 732
ton, Levi I, 734
ton, Levisa IV, 1132
ton, Levisa IV, 1138
ton, Lewis J. V, 645
ton, Lewis Jehu V, 645
ton, Liddy I, 267
ton, Liddy I, 275
ton, Lindley IV, 441
ton, Lindley IV, 442
Stanton, Lotte IV, 160
Stanton, Lotte IV, 442
Stanton, Louis V, 645
Stanton, Louis J. V, 645
Stanton, Louisa V, 712
Stanton, Louise III, 97
Stanton, Louise III, 298
Stanton, Lucinda V, 645
Stanton, Lucy VI, 122
Stanton, Lundy IV, 767
Stanton, Lusindya I, 668
Stanton, Lydia I, 266
Stanton, Lydia I, 267
Stanton, Lydia I, 270
Stanton, Lydia I, 275
Stanton, Lydia I, 276
Stanton, Lydia I, 574
Stanton, Lydia I, 668
Stanton, Lydia I, 689
Stanton, Lydia I, 839
Stanton, Lydia I, 901
Stanton, Lydia IV, 60
Stanton, Lydia IV, 151
Stanton, Lydia IV, 160
Stanton, Lydia IV, 238
Stanton, Lydia IV, 279
Stanton, Lydia IV, 391
Stanton, Lydia IV, 441
Stanton, Lydia IV, 479
Stanton, Lydia IV, 498
Stanton, Lydia IV, 579
Stanton, Lydia IV, 594
Stanton, Lydia IV, 767
Stanton, Lydia IV, 1295
Stanton, Lydia V, 976
Stanton, Lydia V, 978
Stanton, Lydia VI, 104
Stanton, Lydia VI, 122
Stanton, Lydia VI, 141
Stanton, Lydia VI, 340
Stanton, Lydia VI, 855
Stanton, Lydia B. V, 976
Stanton, Lydia B. V, 979
Stanton, Lydia C. V, 979
Stanton, Lydia G. V, 599
Stanton, Lydia G. V, 970
Stanton, Lydia G. V, 977
Stanton, Lydia H. III, 216
Stanton, Lydia M. III, 298
Stanton, Mahlon IV, 279
Stanton, Mahlon IV, 916
Stanton, Mahlon VI, 339
Stanton, Mahlon VI, 340
Stanton, Maranda IV, 365
Stanton, Maranda IV, 441
Stanton, Maranda IV, 442
Stanton, Margaret I, 689
Stanton, Margaret I, 874
Stanton, Margaret I, 901
Stanton, Margaret III, 298
Stanton, Margaret IV, 594
Stanton, Margaret V, 206
Stanton, Margaret V, 356
Stanton, Margaret V, 360
Stanton, Margaret V, 531
Stanton, Margaret V, 644
Stanton, Margaret N. III, 86
Stanton, Mariam I, 272
Stanton, Mariam I, 276
Stanton, Mariella V, 712
Stanton, Marietta V, 712
Stanton, Martha I, 852
Stanton, Martha III, 298
Stanton, Martha IV, 279
Stanton, Martha IV, 304
Stanton, Martha IV, 442
Stanton, Martha IV, 551
Stanton, Martha IV, 558
Stanton, Martha IV, 594
Stanton, Martha IV, 600
Stanton, Martha IV, 676
Stanton, Martha IV, 768
Stanton, Martha IV, 844
Stanton, Martha IV, 1344
Stanton, Martha V, 531
Stanton, Martha V, 976
Stanton, Martha VI, 61
Stanton, Martha VI, 87
Stanton, Martha VI, 114
Stanton, Martha VI, 122
Stanton, Martha Ann I, 690
Stanton, Martha Ann V, 979
Stanton, Martha Emily V, 591
Stanton, Martha Emily V, 599
Stanton, Martha Emly V, 701
Stanton, Martha I. VI, 87
Stanton, Martha M. IV, 767
Stanton, Martha M. IV, 778
Stanton, Mary I, 263
Stanton, Mary I, 264
Stanton, Mary I, 266
Stanton, Mary I, 267
Stanton, Mary I, 269
Stanton, Mary I, 274
Stanton, Mary I, 275
Stanton, Mary I, 276
Stanton, Mary I, 419
Stanton, Mary I, 668
Stanton, Mary I, 678
Stanton, Mary I, 684
Stanton, Mary I, 689
Stanton, Mary I, 734
Stanton, Mary I, 1037
Stanton, Mary III, 298
Stanton, Mary IV, 61
Stanton, Mary IV, 110
Stanton, Mary IV, 160
Stanton, Mary IV, 175
Stanton, Mary IV, 279
Stanton, Mary IV, 280
Stanton, Mary IV, 352
Stanton, Mary IV, 354
Stanton, Mary IV, 365
Stanton, Mary IV, 374
Stanton, Mary IV, 409
Stanton, Mary IV, 441
Stanton, Mary IV, 442
Stanton, Mary IV, 456
Stanton, Mary IV, 551
Stanton, Mary IV, 579
Stanton, Mary IV, 585
Stanton, Mary IV, 594
Stanton, Mary IV, 767
Stanton, Mary IV, 1295
Stanton, Mary V, 124
Stanton, Mary V, 125
Stanton, Mary V, 133
Stanton, Mary V, 525
Stanton, Mary V, 531
Stanton, Mary V, 979
Stanton, Mary VI, 87
Stanton, Mary VI, 97
Stanton, Mary VI, 98
Stanton, Mary VI, 122
Stanton, Mary VI, 134
Stanton, Mary VI, 141
Stanton, Mary VI, 142
Stanton, Mary VI, 339
Stanton, Mary VI, 340
Stanton, Mary VI, 997
Stanton, Mary Alma IV, 366
Stanton, Mary Alma IV, 442
Stanton, Mary Ann IV, 1295
Stanton, Mary Ann V, 974
Stanton, Mary Ann V, 976
Stanton, Mary Ann VI, 122
Stanton, Mary Ann VI, 142
Stanton, Mary D. IV, 441
Stanton, Mary E. V, 979
Stanton, Mary Emma V, 125
Stanton, Mary H. V, 125
Stanton, Mary H. V, 969
Stanton, Mary H. V, 976
Stanton, Mary J. IV, 594
Stanton, Mary Jane IV, 442
Stanton, Mary Katharine I, 327
Stanton, Mary L. V, 968
Stanton, Mary L. V, 977
Stanton, Mary P. II, 719
Stanton, Mary P. IV, 374
Stanton, Mary P. IV, 383
Stanton, Mary P. IV, 441
Stanton, Mary P. IV, 453
Stanton, Mary P. V, 531
Stanton, Mary Ruth V, 977
Stanton, Mary Ruth V, 978
Stanton, Mary S. I, 684
Stanton, Mary S. I, 690
Stanton, Mary S. V, 124
Stanton, Mary Susanna I, 690
Stanton, Melinda I, 668
Stanton, Meriam I, 275
Stanton, Merion Daniel IV, 442
Stanton, Micajah IV, 442
Stanton, Michael V, 976
Stanton, Michael VI, 141
Stanton, Michal V, 969
Stanton, Michal VI, 135
Stanton, Mildred Leroy IV, 441
Stanton, Miriam I, 266
Stanton, Mollie I, 929
Stanton, Mollie I, 931
Stanton, Nancy IV, 594
Stanton, Nathan I, 668
Stanton, Nathan I, 689
Stanton, Nathan I, 805
Stanton, Nathan I, 839
Stanton, Nathan IV, 441
Stanton, Nathan IV, 594
Stanton, Nathan IV, 1295
Stanton, Nathan E. IV, 441
Stanton, Nathan E. IV, 442
Stanton, Nelly I, 270
Stanton, Nelly I, 274
Stanton, Nelly I, 276
Stanton, Oliver IV, 767
Stanton, Oliver IV, 768
Stanton, Oliver IV, 844
Stanton, Oliver H. V, 977
Stanton, Oliver Henry V, 979
Stanton, Owen I, 266
Stanton, Owen I, 267
Stanton, Owen I, 269
Stanton, Owen I, 276
Stanton, Owen I, 318
Stanton, Owen, Jr. I, 276
Stanton, Owen, Sr. I, 276
Stanton, Owin I, 266
Stanton, Patience VI, 97
Stanton, Patience VI, 98
Stanton, Patience VI, 122
Stanton, Pauline B. IV, 442
Stanton, Penina I, 276
Stanton, Peninah IV, 160
Stanton, Peninah IV, 442
Stanton, Peninah IV, 594
Stanton, Peninah IV, 598
Stanton, Pharaby VI, 66
Stanton, Pharaby VI, 86
Stanton, Pharaby VI, 87
Stanton, Pheba VI, 340
Stanton, Phebe I, 318
Stanton, Phebe I, 516
Stanton, Phebe I, 839
Stanton, Phebe V, 977
Stanton, Phebe V, 978
Stanton, Phebe VI, 339
Stanton, Phebe VI, 606
Stanton, Phebey VI, 339
Stanton, Pheby I, 305
Stanton, Pheby I, 318
Stanton, Pheraba VI, 141
Stanton, Pheraby VI, 141
Stanton, Pheriba VI, 66
Stanton, Pheriba VI, 86
Stanton, Pheriba VI, 87
Stanton, Polly I, 327
Stanton, Rachel I, 668
Stanton, Rachel II, 1029
Stanton, Rachel IV, 374
Stanton, Rachel IV, 434
Stanton, Rachel IV, 441
Stanton, Rachel IV, 551
Stanton, Rachel V, 506
Stanton, Rachel V, 531
Stanton, Rachel Ann IV, 584
Stanton, Rachel Ann IV, 594
Stanton, Rachel S. I, 683
Stanton, Rachel S. I, 689
Stanton, Rebecah I, 276
Stanton, Rebecca I, 276
Stanton, Rebecca IV, 417
Stanton, Rebecca IV, 438
Stanton, Rebecca IV, 441
Stanton, Rebecca IV, 442
Stanton, Rebecca IV, 767
Stanton, Rebecca IV, 768
Stanton, Rebecca IV, 785
Stanton, Rebecca IV, 844
Stanton, Rebecca IV, 1116
Stanton, Rebecca V, 970
Stanton, Rebecca D. IV, 375
Stanton, Rebecca D. IV, 441
Stanton, Rebecca D. IV, 442
Stanton, Rebecca H. V, 978
Stanton, Rebecca M. V, 599
Stanton, Rebecca M. V, 977
Stanton, Rebecca M. V, 978
Stanton, Rebecca M. V, 979
Stanton, Rebecca R. V, 978
Stanton, Rebecca W. IV, 442
Stanton, Rhoda V, 568
Stanton, Rhoda V, 599
Stanton, Rhoda V, 969
Stanton, Rhoda V, 970
Stanton, Rhoda V, 976
Stanton, Rhoda V, 979
Stanton, Rhoda VI, 340
Stanton, Rhoda G. V, 599
Stanton, Rhoda G. V, 977
Stanton, Richard IV, 279
Stanton, Richard IV, 1077
Stanton, Robert I, 166
Stanton, Robert III, 50
Stanton, Robert V, 933
Stanton, Robert V, 977
Stanton, Robert VI, 87
Stanton, Robert VI, 122
Stanton, Robert, Jr. V, 933
Stanton, Robinson V, 976
Stanton, Ruhama I, 690
Stanton, Ruth I, 266
Stanton, Ruth I, 271
Stanton, Ruth I, 275
Stanton, Ruth I, 276
Stanton, Ruth I, 574
Stanton, Ruth I, 689
Stanton, Ruth IV, 279
Stanton, Ruth IV, 916
Stanton, Ruth V, 490
Stanton, Ruth V, 531
Stanton, Ruth V, 599
Stanton, Ruth V, 601
Stanton, Ruth V, 977
Stanton, Ruth V, 979
Stanton, Ruth VI, 122
Stanton, Ruth Ann V, 977
Stanton, Ruth Annah IV, 420
Stanton, Ruth Annah IV, 442
Stanton, Ruth E. II, 768
Stanton, Ruth Elizabeth II, 719
Stanton, Ruth H. I, 689
Stanton, Ruth H. I, 805
Stanton, Ruth H. I, 839
Stanton, Salley VI, 339
Stanton, Salley VI, 340
Stanton, Sally VI, 301
Stanton, Sally VI, 340
Stanton, Sampson VI, 18
Stanton, Sampson VI, 122
Stanton, Sampson VI, 141
Stanton, Samson VI, 122
Stanton, Samuel I, 264
Stanton, Samuel I, 574
Stanton, Samuel I, 668
Stanton, Samuel I, 689
Stanton, Samuel I, 734
Stanton, Samuel I, 1032
Stanton, Samuel I, 1037
Stanton, Samuel II, 423
Stanton, Samuel V, 124
Stanton, Samuel V, 506
Stanton, Samuel V, 531
Stanton, Samuel V, 977
Stanton, Samuel VI, 339
Stanton, Samuel VI, 340
Stanton, Samuel Lloyd IV, 280
Stanton, Samuel Milnor I, 690
Stanton, Samuel, Sr. I, 668
Stanton, Sarah I, 266
Stanton, Sarah I, 274
Stanton, Sarah I, 275
Stanton, Sarah I, 276
Stanton, Sarah I, 277
Stanton, Sarah I, 516
Stanton, Sarah I, 574
Stanton, Sarah I, 618
Stanton, Sarah I, 668
Stanton, Sarah I, 680
Stanton, Sarah I, 682
Stanton, Sarah I, 687
Stanton, Sarah I, 689
Stanton, Sarah I, 760
Stanton, Sarah I, 770
Stanton, Sarah I, 810
Stanton, Sarah I, 839
Stanton, Sarah I, 1032
Stanton, Sarah I, 1037
Stanton, Sarah II, 355
Stanton, Sarah II, 423
Stanton, Sarah II, 508
Stanton, Sarah II, 583
Stanton, Sarah II, 658
Stanton, Sarah II, 792
Stanton, Sarah IV, 61
Stanton, Sarah IV, 110
Stanton, Sarah IV, 279
Stanton, Sarah IV, 287
Stanton, Sarah IV, 322
Stanton, Sarah IV, 352
Stanton, Sarah IV, 374
Stanton, Sarah IV, 382
Stanton, Sarah IV, 402
Stanton, Sarah IV, 411
Stanton, Sarah IV, 438
Stanton, Sarah IV, 441
Stanton, Sarah IV, 442
Stanton, Sarah IV, 578
Stanton, Sarah IV, 594
Stanton, Sarah IV, 767
Stanton, Sarah IV, 1116
Stanton, Sarah V, 124
Stanton, Sarah V, 531
Stanton, Sarah V, 644
Stanton, Sarah V, 648
Stanton, Sarah VI, 122
Stanton, Sarah Ann IV, 1295
Stanton, Sarah B. IV, 280
Stanton, Sarah B. IV, 400
Stanton, Sarah B. IV, 411
Stanton, Sarah B. IV, 441
Stanton, Sarah Burr IV, 442
Stanton, Sarah E. IV, 442
Stanton, Sarah Elma IV, 441

Stanton, Sarah R. A. I, 668
Stanton, Sarah S. IV, 594
Stanton, Schooley IV, 442
Stanton, Sidney F. II, 719
Stanton, Sidney F. II, 768
Stanton, Sina M. IV, 442
Stanton, Smith V, 712
Stanton, Stephen IV, 1295
Stanton, Stephen V, 124
Stanton, Stephen Butler V, 280
Stanton, Stephen Butler VI, 339
Stanton, Stephen Butler VI, 340
Stanton, Susanna I, 266
Stanton, Susanna I, 273
Stanton, Susanna I, 276
Stanton, Susanna IV, 60
Stanton, Susanna IV, 279
Stanton, Susannah I, 276
Stanton, Susannah I, 308
Stanton, Susannah I, 318
Stanton, Susannah IV, 160
Stanton, Susannah IV, 767
Stanton, Susannah V, 124
Stanton, Susannah V, 531
Stanton, Susannah V, 645
Stanton, Sylvanus VI, 122
Stanton, Tabitha IV, 280
Stanton, Tabitha IV, 374
Stanton, Tabitha IV, 382
Stanton, Tabitha IV, 441
Stanton, Theodocia V, 599
Stanton, Theodocia V, 977
Stanton, Theodocia V, 978
Stanton, Theodosia V, 567
Stanton, Theodosia V, 599
Stanton, Theodosia V, 601
Stanton, Thomas I, 327
Stanton, Thomas IV, 279
Stanton, Thomas IV, 441
Stanton, Thomas IV, 594
Stanton, Thomas IV, 767
Stanton, Thomas IV, 916
Stanton, Thomas V, 977
Stanton, Thomas VI, 142
Stanton, Thomas Elwood V, 979
Stanton, Thomas H. I, 305
Stanton, Thomas H. I, 318
Stanton, Thomas H. I, 331
Stanton, Thomas L. I, 668
Stanton, Thomas N. V, 979
Stanton, Thomas, Jr. II, 1029
Stanton, Tillie V, 1020
Stanton, Virginia V, 977
Stanton, Virginia Ann V, 979
Stanton, W. Macy IV, 442
Stanton, Walter V, 979
Stanton, Widow Elisabeth I, 144
Stanton, Widow Elisabeth I, 166
Stanton, Widow Elizabeth I, 117
Stanton, Widow Nelly I, 276
Stanton, Widow Sarah I, 658
Stanton, Wilford T. IV, 442
Stanton, William I, 266
Stanton, William I, 267
Stanton, William I, 276
Stanton, William I, 419
Stanton, William I, 516
Stanton, William I, 574
Stanton, William I, 668
Stanton, William I, 683
Stanton, William I, 689
Stanton, William I, 760
Stanton, William I, 770
Stanton, William I, 839
Stanton, William I Sup 1, 10
Stanton, William II, 719
Stanton, William IV, 60
Stanton, William IV, 160
Stanton, William IV, 352
Stanton, William IV, 382
Stanton, William IV, 391
Stanton, William IV, 425
Stanton, William IV, 441
Stanton, William IV, 594
Stanton, William IV, 767
Stanton, William IV, 1295
Stanton, William V, 124
Stanton, William V, 206
Stanton, William V, 280
Stanton, William V, 360
Stanton, William V, 469
Stanton, William V, 490
Stanton, William V, 531
Stanton, William V, 599
Stanton, William V, 644
Stanton, William VI, 87
Stanton, William VI, 122
Stanton, William VI, 141
Stanton, William VI, 298
Stanton, William VI, 339
Stanton, William VI, 340
Stanton, William VI, 598
Stanton, William VI, 606
Stanton, William C. I, 668
Stanton, William E. V, 979
Stanton, William F. V, 125
Stanton, William Hanson IV, 442
Stanton, William Henry IV, 441
Stanton, William Macy IV, 441
Stanton, William R. V, 599
Stanton, William R. VI, 87
Stanton, William T. IV, 1295
Stanton, William, Jr. VI, 339
Stanton, William, Jr. VI, 340
Stanton, William, Sr. IV, 310
Stanton, Wilmer L. Hall IV, 280
Stanton, Wm. II, 719
Stanton, Wm. IV, 280
Stanton, Wm. IV, 322
Stanton, Wm. IV, 585
Stanton, Wm. IV, 767
Stanton, Wm. V, 356
Stanton, Wm. V, 601
Stanton, Wm. V, 712
Stanton, Wm. V, 977
Stanton, Wm. V, 978
Stanton, Wm. E. V, 712
Stanton, Wm. F. V, 933
Stanton, Wm. G. V, 712
Stanton, Wm. H. II, 719
Stanton, Wm. H. II, 768
Stanton, Wm. Henry II, 768
Stanton, Wm. Henry IV, 442
Stanton, Wm. Macy IV, 380
Stanton, Wm. Macy IV, 442
Stanton, Wm. R. V, 601
Stanton, Wm. R. V, 976
Stanton, Wm. R. V, 977
Stanton, Wm. R. V, 978
Stanton, Wm. R. V, 979
Stanton, Zaccheus IV, 767
Stanton, Zacheus I, 516
Stanton, Zacheus IV, 767
Stanton, Zacheus IV, 919
Stanton, Zacheus VI, 301
Stanton, Zacheus VI, 339
Stanton, Zacheus VI, 340
Stanton, Zebulon A. I, 18
Stantons, Henry I, 263
Stanup, Richard II, 448
Stanworth, Mary II, 448
Stapler, ??? II, 423
Stapler, Abigail II, 1061
Stapler, Achsah II, 1042
Stapler, Acsah II, 970
Stapler, Acsah II, 987
Stapler, Acsah II, 1023
Stapler, Acsah II, 1029
Stapler, Ann II, 970
Stapler, Ann II, 1061
Stapler, Ann B. II, 768
Stapler, Anna Miller II, 807
Stapler, Anna P. K. II, 152
Stapler, Anna P. K. II, 158
Stapler, Charles II, 970
Stapler, Charles II, 1029
Stapler, Charles II, 1061
Stapler, Chas. II, 878
Stapler, Chas. II, 925
Stapler, Christian II, 1061
Stapler, Christiana II, 325
Stapler, Christianna II, 325
Stapler, Christianna II, 1081
Stapler, Edwin II, 152
Stapler, Edwin II, 158
Stapler, Elizabeth II, 423
Stapler, Elizabeth II, 1061
Stapler, Elizabeth G. II, 878
Stapler, Elizabeth G. II, 925
Stapler, Esther II, 970
Stapler, Esther II, 1029
Stapler, Esther II, 1061
Stapler, George II, 448
Stapler, Hannah II, 325
Stapler, Hannah II, 423
Stapler, Hannah II, 658
Stapler, Hannah II, 821
Stapler, Hannah II, 970
Stapler, Hannah II, 1023
Stapler, Hannah II, 1029
Stapler, Hannah II, 1042
Stapler, Hannah II, 1061
Stapler, Hannah B. K. II, 158
Stapler, Hannah Bullock II, 152
Stapler, Hannah Bullock II, 158
Stapler, Hannah M. II, 925
Stapler, Hannah, Jr. II, 1061
Stapler, Hester II, 987
Stapler, Hester II, 1029
Stapler, Horace Elias Kirk II, 152
Stapler, Horace Elias Kirk II, 158
Stapler, James B. II, 768
Stapler, John II, 423
Stapler, John II, 531
Stapler, John II, 546
Stapler, John II, 658
Stapler, John II, 970
Stapler, John II, 987
Stapler, John II, 1023
Stapler, John II, 1029
Stapler, John II, 1042
Stapler, John II, 1061
Stapler, John II, 1076
Stapler, John II, 1081
Stapler, John Thomas II, 1081
Stapler, John W. II, 768
Stapler, John White II, 658
Stapler, John, Jr. II, 658
Stapler, John, Jr. II, 1029
Stapler, Joseph B. II, 1076
Stapler, Joseph B. II, 1081
Stapler, Joseph Betts II, 807
Stapler, Latitia II, 970
Stapler, Latitia II, 1061
Stapler, Margaret II, 423
Stapler, Martha II, 514
Stapler, Martha II, 658
Stapler, Martha II, 1022
Stapler, Martha II, 1029
Stapler, Mary II, 423
Stapler, Mary II, 531
Stapler, Mary II, 543
Stapler, Mary II, 658
Stapler, Mary II, 807
Stapler, Mary II, 970
Stapler, Mary II, 1061
Stapler, Mary II, 1076
Stapler, Mary II, 1081
Stapler, Mary B. II, 768
Stapler, Mary M. II, 1056
Stapler, Mary M. II, 1061
Stapler, Rachel II, 970
Stapler, Rachel II, 975
Stapler, Rachel II, 1029
Stapler, Rachel II, 1042
Stapler, Rodman Russell II, 925
Stapler, Sarah II, 658
Stapler, Sarah II, 821
Stapler, Sarah II, 970
Stapler, Sarah II, 1029
Stapler, Sarah II, 1061
Stapler, Sarah II, 1081
Stapler, Sarah F. II, 768
Stapler, Sarah Fisher II, 768
Stapler, Sarah J. II, 878
Stapler, Sarah J. II, 925
Stapler, Stephen II, 423
Stapler, Stephen II, 531
Stapler, Stephen II, 658
Stapler, Stephen II, 970
Stapler, Stephen II, 1022
Stapler, Stephen II, 1029
Stapler, Susannah II, 423
Stapler, Susannah II, 448
Stapler, Susannah II, 970
Stapler, Susannah II, 987
Stapler, Susannah II, 1029
Stapler, Thomas II, 423
Stapler, Thomas II, 658
Stapler, Thomas II, 970
Stapler, Thomas II, 975
Stapler, Thomas II, 987
Stapler, Thomas II, 1029
Stapler, Thomas II, 1042
Stapler, Thomas II, 1061
Stapler, Thomas Vaughn II, 925
Stapler, Thomas W. II, 925
Stapler, Thomas, Jr. II, 658
Stapler, Thomas, Jr. II, 1061
Stapler, Thos. II, 821
Stapler, Thos. W. II, 878
Stapler, Thos. W. II, 925
Stapler, William II, 423
Stapler, William II, 448
Stapler, William II, 821
Stapler, William II, 970
Stapler, Wm. II, 448
Stapler, Wm. II, 925
Stapler, Wm. II, 1061
Staples, Amelia III, 298
Staples, Amey VI, 850
Staples, Betsy VI, 855
Staples, Charles VI, 823
Staples, Charles VI, 840
Staples, David VI, 881
Staples, Elizabeth VI, 831
Staples, Elizabeth VI, 836
Staples, Elizabeth VI, 855
Staples, Frances VI, 855
Staples, Frances VI, 867
Staples, Franky VI, 855
Staples, Garland VI, 855
Staples, George W. VI, 855
Staples, Hannah W. III, 298
Staples, Isaac VI, 855
Staples, Jacob IV, 1379
Staples, James VI, 855
Staples, James M. VI, 855
Staples, Jane VI, 855
Staples, Jefferson VI, 855
Staples, Jerome W. VI, 997
Staples, John II, 255
Staples, John VI, 855
Staples, John VI, 881
Staples, John VI, 997
Staples, John J. III, 212
Staples, John J. III, 298
Staples, John, Jr. III, 298
Staples, Judith VI, 855
Staples, Judith VI, 997
Staples, Julian R. VI, 997
Staples, Lavinia M. VI, 855
Staples, Louisey L. VI, 997
Staples, Lucy J. VI, 855
Staples, Malinda B. VI, 844
Staples, Martha VI, 855
Staples, Martha VI, 997
Staples, Mary II, 264
Staples, Mary II, 270
Staples, Mary VI, 971
Staples, Mercy II, 255
Staples, Myra VI, 840
Staples, Orreana VI, 855
Staples, Pauline VI, 854
Staples, Polly VI, 857
Staples, Powhatan VI, 855
Staples, Prudence VI, 881
Staples, Rebecca VI, 828
Staples, Rebeckah II, 1024
Staples, Rosalie III, 212
Staples, Rosalie III, 298
Staples, Samuel VI, 854
Staples, Samuel VI, 855
Staples, Samuel VI, 971
Staples, Susan VI, 867
Staples, Thomas II, 264
Staples, Thomas II, 270
Staples, William VI, 836
Staples, William VI, 855
Staples, William J. III, 298
Staples, William L. VI, 832
Staples, William T. VI, 997
Staples, Wm. J. III, 298
Staples, Wm. T. III, 298
Stapleton, Adaline IV, 632
Stapleton, Adaline IV, 657
Stapleton, Ann II, 453
Stapleton, Ann II, 658
Stapleton, David IV, 632
Stapleton, Grace II, 423
Stapleton, Joshua IV, 61
Stapleton, Joshua IV, 657
Stapleton, Martha IV, 632
Stapleton, Mary II, 658
Stapleton, Rachel II, 640
Stapleton, Rachel II, 658
Stapleton, Reginald II, 453
Stapleton, Reginald II, 658
Stapleton, Samuel IV, 61
Stapleton, Samuel IV, 657
Stapleton, Samuel IV, 883
Stapleton, Susanna IV, 61
Stapleton, Susannah IV, 61
Stapleton, Susannah IV, 657
Stapleton, Thomas II, 453
Stapleton, Thomas II, 658
Star, Elizabeth V, 206
Star, Elizabeth V, 863
Star, Elizabeth V, 933
Star, Esther V, 863
Star, Esther V, 933
Star, Eva IV, 768
Star, George IV, 498
Star, Henry V, 863
Star, Henry V, 933
Star, Jesse V, 863
Star, Jesse V, 933
Star, Joshua V, 863
Star, Joshua V, 933
Star, Lydia IV, 937
Star, Mary V, 863
Star, Mary V, 933
Star, Moses VI, 447
Star, Nehemiah V, 863
Star, Nehemiah V, 933
Star, William V, 863
Star, William V, 933
Starbert, Charity I, 1030
Starbert, Charity I, 1037
Starbuck, Abbie H. VI, 196
Starbuck, Abbie S. IV, 169
Starbuck, Abbie S. IV, 214
Starbuck, Abbie S. IV, 280
Starbuck, Abbie S. IV, 575
Starbuck, Abigail I, 516
Starbuck, Abigail I, 517
Starbuck, Abigail I, 571
Starbuck, Abigail I, 574
Starbuck, Abigail I, 591
Starbuck, Abigail I, 594
Starbuck, Abigail I, 597
Starbuck, Abigail I, 779
Starbuck, Abigail I, 806
Starbuck, Abigail I, 839
Starbuck, Abigail V, 531
Starbuck, Abigail V, 544
Starbuck, Abigail W. I, 792
Starbuck, Abraham IV, 443
Starbuck, Abram IV, 443
Starbuck, Achsah I, 516
Starbuck, Achsah V, 491
Starbuck, Achsah V, 531
Starbuck, Addison IV, 280
Starbuck, Adelbert W. IV, 443
Starbuck, Aden V, 712
Starbuck, Aden Charles V, 64
Starbuck, Aden L. V, 645
Starbuck, Aden, Jr. V, 645
Starbuck, Adin V, 645
Starbuck, Adin L. V, 599
Starbuck, Adin L. V, 645
Starbuck, Adin L. V, 712
Starbuck, Aiden V, 645
Starbuck, Albert IV, 280
Starbuck, Albert IV, 762
Starbuck, Albert V, 645
Starbuck, Albert V, 712
Starbuck, Albert W. IV, 280
Starbuck, Albert W. IV, 768
Starbuck, Alexander V, 125
Starbuck, Alfred IV, 443
Starbuck, Alice IV, 280
Starbuck, Alice V, 666
Starbuck, Alice V, 712
Starbuck, Alice B. IV, 196
Starbuck, Alice B. IV, 280
Starbuck, Alice B. IV, 575
Starbuck, Alice Bertha IV, 57
Starbuck, Alice J. IV, 280
Starbuck, Almeda IV, 595
Starbuck, Almedia IV, 567
Starbuck, Almedia IV, 595
Starbuck, Almira III, 53
Starbuck, Almira III, 323
Starbuck, Almira V, 125
Starbuck, Almyra V, 40
Starbuck, Almyra V, 125
Starbuck, Amy V, 645
Starbuck, Ann I, 517
Starbuck, Ann I, 552
Starbuck, Ann I, 574
Starbuck, Ann I, 912
Starbuck, Ann I, 914
Starbuck, Ann IV, 280
Starbuck, Ann IV, 443
Starbuck, Ann IV, 594
Starbuck, Ann IV, 595
Starbuck, Anna I, 559
Starbuck, Anna I, 574
Starbuck, Anna I, 830
Starbuck, Anna I, 839
Starbuck, Anna II, 703
Starbuck, Anna IV, 160
Starbuck, Anna IV, 280
Starbuck, Anna IV, 443
Starbuck, Anna IV, 455
Starbuck, Anna IV, 1066
Starbuck, Anna IV, 1077
Starbuck, Anna V, 645
Starbuck, Anna D. IV, 280
Starbuck, Anna L. IV, 280
Starbuck, Anna L. IV, 768
Starbuck, Anna M. IV, 628
Starbuck, Anna M. IV, 715
Starbuck, Anna M. IV, 768
Starbuck, Anna Mae IV, 768
Starbuck, Anne IV, 442
Starbuck, Aris I, 839
Starbuck, Arthur V, 645
Starbuck, Arthur V, 712
Starbuck, Asa V, 645
Starbuck, Asenath IV, 409
Starbuck, Asenath IV, 438
Starbuck, Asenath IV, 443
Starbuck, B. F. IV, 280
Starbuck, B. Franklin IV, 280
Starbuck, Bazabeel I, 597
Starbuck, Bazabel I, 597
Starbuck, Benj. III, 299
Starbuck, Benj. IV, 280
Starbuck, Benj. F. IV, 715
Starbuck, Benjamin I, 591
Starbuck, Benjamin I, 839
Starbuck, Benjamin III, 299
Starbuck, Benjamin IV, 280

uck, Benjamin IV, 1069
uck, Benjamin B. I, 597
uck, Benjamin F. I, 591
uck, Benjamin F. IV, 252
uck, Benjamin F. IV, 280
uck, Benjamin F. IV, 628
uck, Benjamin F. IV, 768
uck, Benjamin F. IV, 1066
uck, Benjamin F. IV, 1077
uck, Benjamin F. V, 125
uck, Benjamin Franklin
V, 768
uck, Bertha V, 712
uck, Bertha Shugart V, 645
uck, Betha Shupert V, 712
uck, Bezabeel I, 591
uck, Bezabel I, 591
uck, Bezebel I, 597
uck, Caleb B. IV, 444
uck, Caleb L. IV, 443
uck, Carlton Franklin
V, 768
uck, Charles I, 779
uck, Charles I, 792
uck, Charles I, 810
uck, Charles I, 839
uck, Charles V, 125
uck, Charles V, 531
uck, Charles V, 532
uck, Charles V, 599
uck, Charles V, 645
uck, Charles V, 669
uck, Charles V, 712
uck, Charles B. I, 839
uck, Chas. R. V, 712
uck, Chas. Richard V, 712
uck, Clara V, 712
uck, Clara A. V, 645
uck, Clara A. V, 712
uck, Clara E. IV, 768
uck, Clara Esther IV, 768
uck, Clara L. IV, 443
uck, Clarissa I, 563
uck, Clarissa I, 574
uck, Clarissa I, 839
uck, Clarissa V, 531
uck, Clarissa V, 640
uck, Clarissa V, 645
uck, Clarisse I, 574
uck, Clarkson I, 591
uck, Clarkson I, 597
uck, Clary Ann V, 645
uck, Clinton IV, 280
uck, Clinton J. IV, 280
uck, Clyde L. IV, 443
uck, Damaras I, 517
uck, Damaris I, 539
uck, Damaris I, 574
uck, Daniel I, 574
uck, Daniel I, 597
uck, Daniel IV, 280
uck, Daniel IV, 595
uck, Darius I, 591
uck, Darius I, 597
uck, Deborah I, 804
uck, Deborah I, 839
uck, Deborah Ann IV, 443
uck, Deborah Ann IV, 768
uck, Delilah V, 125
uck, Dinah I, 559
uck, Dinah I, 574
uck, Dinah I, 839
uck, Donald Edward IV, 768
uck, Dorcas I, 516
uck, Dorcas I, 574
uck, Dorcas V, 125
uck, Dorothy IV, 768
uck, Dorothy Jean IV, 768
uck, Earl C. V, 702
uck, Earl C. V, 712
uck, Earnest V, 531
uck, Earnest V, 532
uck, Edith IV, 280
uck, Edith IV, 1295
uck, Edith V, 217
uck, Edith V, 280
uck, Edith M. IV, 443
uck, Edmund IV, 443
uck, Edward I, 517
uck, Edward I, 574
uck, Eleaner I, 597
uck, Eleanor I, 574
uck, Eleanor I, 597
uck, Elihu I, 586
uck, Elihu I, 591
uck, Elihu I, 597
uck, Elisha IV, 160
uck, Elisha IV, 431
uck, Elisha IV, 443
uck, Elisha IV, 595
uck, Elisha, Jr. IV, 443
Starbuck, Eliza IV, 1114
Starbuck, Eliza V, 125
Starbuck, Eliza Adams V, 280
Starbuck, Elizabeth I, 516
Starbuck, Elizabeth I, 574
Starbuck, Elizabeth I, 810
Starbuck, Elizabeth I, 839
Starbuck, Elizabeth IV, 160
Starbuck, Elizabeth IV, 280
Starbuck, Elizabeth IV, 426
Starbuck, Elizabeth IV, 428
Starbuck, Elizabeth IV, 438
Starbuck, Elizabeth IV, 442
Starbuck, Elizabeth IV, 443
Starbuck, Elizabeth IV, 594
Starbuck, Elizabeth IV, 595
Starbuck, Elizabeth IV, 768
Starbuck, Elizabeth V, 125
Starbuck, Ella I, 926
Starbuck, Ella I, 930
Starbuck, Ellwood I, 591
Starbuck, Elwood I, 597
Starbuck, Emily I, 591
Starbuck, Emily I, 597
Starbuck, Emily I, 598
Starbuck, Emily IV, 280
Starbuck, Emily IV, 768
Starbuck, Ernest V, 645
Starbuck, Estella V, 531
Starbuck, Ester I, 574
Starbuck, Esther I, 533
Starbuck, Esther I, 574
Starbuck, Esther V, 669
Starbuck, Esther V, 712
Starbuck, Ethel C. IV, 280
Starbuck, Ethel C. IV, 762
Starbuck, Ethel C. IV, 768
Starbuck, Eunice I, 516
Starbuck, Eunice I, 517
Starbuck, Eunice I, 591
Starbuck, Eunice I, 597
Starbuck, Eunice I, 598
Starbuck, Eunice I, 810
Starbuck, Eunice I, 837
Starbuck, Eunice I, 839
Starbuck, Eunice IV, 366
Starbuck, Eunice IV, 427
Starbuck, Eunice IV, 442
Starbuck, Eunice IV, 443
Starbuck, Eunice IV, 592
Starbuck, Eunice IV, 595
Starbuck, Eunice R. IV, 280
Starbuck, Eva B. IV, 197
Starbuck, Eva B. IV, 280
Starbuck, Everett V, 709
Starbuck, Everett V, 712
Starbuck, Ezra V, 645
Starbuck, Florence IV, 1003
Starbuck, Frankie V, 531
Starbuck, Franklin V, 645
Starbuck, Franklin V, 712
Starbuck, Gayer I, 516
Starbuck, Gayer I, 537
Starbuck, Gayer I, 574
Starbuck, Gayer I, 591
Starbuck, Gayer I, 839
Starbuck, Gayer V, 206
Starbuck, Gayer V, 531
Starbuck, Gayer V, 544
Starbuck, Gayer V, 645
Starbuck, Gayer, Jr. I, 574
Starbuck, Gaynor V, 625
Starbuck, Gaynor V, 640
Starbuck, Gayr I, 516
Starbuck, Gear I, 574
Starbuck, George I, 559
Starbuck, George I, 574
Starbuck, George I, 839
Starbuck, George IV, 160
Starbuck, George IV, 280
Starbuck, George IV, 367
Starbuck, George IV, 426
Starbuck, George IV, 427
Starbuck, George IV, 442
Starbuck, George IV, 443
Starbuck, George IV, 445
Starbuck, George IV, 565
Starbuck, George IV, 595
Starbuck, George IV, 768
Starbuck, George IV, 770
Starbuck, George V, 125
Starbuck, George W. I, 591
Starbuck, Gladys V, 532
Starbuck, Goldie V, 645
Starbuck, Granville A. V, 712
Starbuck, Hannah I, 516
Starbuck, Hannah III, 298
Starbuck, Hannah V, 531
Starbuck, Harman I, 597
Starbuck, Harnet D. I, 591
Starbuck, Hazel V, 531
Starbuck, Hepsibah I, 574
Starbuck, Hepzabeth I, 907
Starbuck, Hepzebah I, 839
Starbuck, Hepzibah I, 570
Starbuck, Hepzibah I, 574
Starbuck, Hepzibah I, 839
Starbuck, Hepzibah III, 299
Starbuck, Hepzibeth I, 517
Starbuck, Herbert V, 532
Starbuck, Herbert V, 599
Starbuck, Hezekiah I, 559
Starbuck, Hezekiah I, 574
Starbuck, Hezekiah I, 586
Starbuck, Hezekiah I, 591
Starbuck, Hezekiah I, 597
Starbuck, Hezekiah I, 839
Starbuck, Hezekiah I, 971
Starbuck, Hezekiah IV, 160
Starbuck, Hezekiah IV, 442
Starbuck, Hezekiah IV, 443
Starbuck, Hezekiah IV, 594
Starbuck, Hezekiah IV, 595
Starbuck, Hezekiah IV, 1269
Starbuck, Hezekiah IV, 1295
Starbuck, Hezekiah V, 531
Starbuck, Hezekiah V, 645
Starbuck, Hezekiah V, 788
Starbuck, Hezekiah, Jr. I, 574
Starbuck, Heziah IV, 1295
Starbuck, Hilda IV, 442
Starbuck, Hobert V, 645
Starbuck, Howland V, 125
Starbuck, Hubert V, 531
Starbuck, Huldah IV, 443
Starbuck, Hussey IV, 442
Starbuck, Irena IV, 443
Starbuck, J. Clinton II, 719
Starbuck, J. Clinton II, 768
Starbuck, James Harper I, 597
Starbuck, James M. I, 591
Starbuck, Jane I, 517
Starbuck, Jane I, 533
Starbuck, Jane I, 574
Starbuck, Jane I, 586
Starbuck, Jane I, 591
Starbuck, Jane I, 597
Starbuck, Jean I, 591
Starbuck, Jeane I, 574
Starbuck, Jeane I, 576
Starbuck, Jesse I, 597
Starbuck, Jesse II, 719
Starbuck, Jesse IV, 280
Starbuck, Jesse IV, 374
Starbuck, Jesse IV, 443
Starbuck, Jesse IV, 768
Starbuck, Jesse V, 360
Starbuck, Jesse V, 645
Starbuck, Jesse C. V, 360
Starbuck, Jesse C. V, 645
Starbuck, Jesse G. V, 531
Starbuck, Jesse H. V, 645
Starbuck, Jesse R. IV, 677
Starbuck, Jesse R. IV, 768
Starbuck, Jethro I, 516
Starbuck, Jethro I, 574
Starbuck, Jethro I, 830
Starbuck, Jethro I, 839
Starbuck, Jethro IV, 160
Starbuck, Jethro IV, 442
Starbuck, Jethro IV, 443
Starbuck, Joel V, 531
Starbuck, Joel V, 645
Starbuck, John I, 517
Starbuck, John I, 591
Starbuck, John I, 839
Starbuck, John IV, 160
Starbuck, John IV, 182
Starbuck, John IV, 190
Starbuck, John IV, 197
Starbuck, John IV, 280
Starbuck, John IV, 443
Starbuck, John IV, 594
Starbuck, John IV, 595
Starbuck, John IV, 768
Starbuck, John IV, 1077
Starbuck, John V, 125
Starbuck, John V, 645
Starbuck, John F. V, 645
Starbuck, John L. V, 712
Starbuck, John T. V, 607
Starbuck, John T. V, 645
Starbuck, John, Jr. IV, 280
Starbuck, John, Jr. IV, 570
Starbuck, John, Jr. IV, 595
Starbuck, Joseph IV, 443
Starbuck, Joseph IV, 1295
Starbuck, Joseph V, 645
Starbuck, Joseph Clinton II, 768
Starbuck, Joseph Clinton IV, 443
Starbuck, Joseph Earle IV, 443
Starbuck, Josephine V, 645
Starbuck, Josephine V, 712
Starbuck, Judith I, 559
Starbuck, Judith I, 574
Starbuck, Judith I, 586
Starbuck, Judith I, 591
Starbuck, Judith I, 597
Starbuck, Judith V, 645
Starbuck, Judith V, 788
Starbuck, Judith V, 793
Starbuck, Latham I, 516
Starbuck, Latham I, 574
Starbuck, Latham I, 586
Starbuck, Latham I, 591
Starbuck, Latham I, 597
Starbuck, Lelilah V, 125
Starbuck, Leo V, 360
Starbuck, Leo V, 645
Starbuck, Lewis I, 591
Starbuck, Lewis I, 872
Starbuck, Lewis I, 901
Starbuck, Lewis C. IV, 280
Starbuck, Lidia I, 839
Starbuck, Lillian V, 702
Starbuck, Lillian V, 712
Starbuck, Lizzie V, 645
Starbuck, Lizzie V, 712
Starbuck, Lois Catherine IV, 768
Starbuck, Lorena IV, 280
Starbuck, Louis C. IV, 280
Starbuck, Louisa V, 355
Starbuck, Louisa V, 360
Starbuck, Louisa V, 599
Starbuck, Louisa V, 645
Starbuck, Louisa M. V, 712
Starbuck, Lucile R. IV, 768
Starbuck, Lucinda I, 591
Starbuck, Lucinda I, 595
Starbuck, Lucinda I, 597
Starbuck, Luzena I, 926
Starbuck, Lydai B. I, 792
Starbuck, Lydia I, 516
Starbuck, Lydia I, 517
Starbuck, Lydia I, 557
Starbuck, Lydia I, 574
Starbuck, Lydia I, 839
Starbuck, Lydia I, 843
Starbuck, Lydia I, 844
Starbuck, Lydia III, 52
Starbuck, Lydia III, 215
Starbuck, Lydia III, 357
Starbuck, Lydia IV, 367
Starbuck, Lydia IV, 426
Starbuck, Lydia IV, 427
Starbuck, Lydia IV, 442
Starbuck, Lydia IV, 443
Starbuck, Lydia IV, 565
Starbuck, Lydia IV, 595
Starbuck, Lydia IV, 1276
Starbuck, Lydia IV, 1295
Starbuck, Lydia V, 125
Starbuck, Lydia V, 611
Starbuck, Lydia V, 645
Starbuck, Lydia A. III, 299
Starbuck, Lydia B. I, 720
Starbuck, Lydia B. I, 734
Starbuck, Lydia B. I, 816
Starbuck, Lydia B. I, 839
Starbuck, Lydia Ellen IV, 443
Starbuck, Mabel IV, 280
Starbuck, Mabel D. IV, 443
Starbuck, Mabel Loretta IV, 169
Starbuck, Mabel Loretta IV, 280
Starbuck, Mahalah I, 574
Starbuck, Margaret IV, 443
Starbuck, Margaret V, 644
Starbuck, Margaret V, 645
Starbuck, Margaret V, 712
Starbuck, Marietta IV, 190
Starbuck, Marietta IV, 280
Starbuck, Marion V, 645
Starbuck, Martha IV, 280
Starbuck, Martha IV, 424
Starbuck, Martha IV, 443
Starbuck, Martha IV, 629
Starbuck, Martha IV, 657
Starbuck, Martha IV, 715
Starbuck, Martha IV, 768
Starbuck, Martha V, 645
Starbuck, Martha S. IV, 628
Starbuck, Martha, Jr. V, 712
Starbuck, Mary I, 516
Starbuck, Mary I, 517
Starbuck, Mary I, 551
Starbuck, Mary I, 574
Starbuck, Mary I, 586
Starbuck, Mary I, 591
Starbuck, Mary I, 600
Starbuck, Mary I, 799
Starbuck, Mary I, 823
Starbuck, Mary I, 839
Starbuck, Mary I, 901
Starbuck, Mary I, 912
Starbuck, Mary I, 914
Starbuck, Mary I, 1132
Starbuck, Mary III, 298
Starbuck, Mary IV, 160
Starbuck, Mary IV, 280
Starbuck, Mary IV, 377
Starbuck, Mary IV, 379
Starbuck, Mary IV, 406
Starbuck, Mary IV, 431
Starbuck, Mary IV, 442
Starbuck, Mary IV, 443
Starbuck, Mary V, 531
Starbuck, Mary V, 625
Starbuck, Mary V, 645
Starbuck, Mary D. V, 645
Starbuck, Mary E. I, 597
Starbuck, Mary E. I, 872
Starbuck, Mary E. I, 901
Starbuck, Mary Edwards V, 125
Starbuck, Mary Elizabeth I, 901
Starbuck, Mary Jane II, 719
Starbuck, Mary Jane IV, 374
Starbuck, Mary Jane IV, 443
Starbuck, Mary Jane IV, 444
Starbuck, Mary P. IV, 443
Starbuck, Mary P. IV, 445
Starbuck, Mary P. IV, 768
Starbuck, Mary P. IV, 770
Starbuck, Mary Rebecca II, 973
Starbuck, Mary T. IV, 280
Starbuck, Mary T. IV, 768
Starbuck, Mathew I, 839
Starbuck, Matilda I, 591
Starbuck, Matthew I, 517
Starbuck, Matthew I, 559
Starbuck, Matthew I, 574
Starbuck, Matthew I, 839
Starbuck, Maurice B. V, 645
Starbuck, Maurice B. V, 712
Starbuck, Melinda I, 591
Starbuck, Melissa T. IV, 443
Starbuck, Merab III, 298
Starbuck, Milton I, 591
Starbuck, Milton IV, 393
Starbuck, Milton IV, 443
Starbuck, Moses I, 516
Starbuck, Moses V, 531
Starbuck, Moses V, 645
Starbuck, Nathan IV, 442
Starbuck, Nathan Hussey IV, 443
Starbuck, Nathan I. V, 645
Starbuck, Nathan L. V, 712
Starbuck, Nathan T. V, 645
Starbuck, Nathan T. V, 712
Starbuck, Nathaniel III, 52
Starbuck, Nathaniel III, 215
Starbuck, Nathaniel III, 298
Starbuck, Nathaniel III, 299
Starbuck, Nathaniel III, 357
Starbuck, Nellie V, 645
Starbuck, Nellie M. V, 712
Starbuck, Osee V, 645
Starbuck, Osie V, 360
Starbuck, Osie V, 645
Starbuck, Pamela I, 516
Starbuck, Parmelia I, 534
Starbuck, Parmelia I, 574
Starbuck, Paul I, 516
Starbuck, Paul I, 517
Starbuck, Paul I, 570
Starbuck, Paul I, 574
Starbuck, Paul I, 839
Starbuck, Paul I, 907
Starbuck, Paul V, 125
Starbuck, Paul, Jr. I, 839
Starbuck, Pauline V, 531
Starbuck, Pauline V, 532
Starbuck, Pauline V, 599
Starbuck, Pauline V, 645
Starbuck, Peter I, 516
Starbuck, Peter I, 574
Starbuck, Phebe I, 517
Starbuck, Phebe I, 533
Starbuck, Phebe I, 574
Starbuck, Phebe III, 215
Starbuck, Polly Ann V, 624
Starbuck, Polly Ann V, 645
Starbuck, Rachel I, 516
Starbuck, Rachel I, 557
Starbuck, Rachel I, 573
Starbuck, Rachel I, 574
Starbuck, Rachel I, 591
Starbuck, Rachel I, 597
Starbuck, Rachel I, 839
Starbuck, Rachel IV, 160
Starbuck, Rachel IV, 426
Starbuck, Rachel IV, 427
Starbuck, Rachel IV, 443
Starbuck, Rachel IV, 1077
Starbuck, Rachel IV, 1284

Starbuck, Rachel IV, 1295
Starbuck, Rachel V, 125
Starbuck, Rachel V, 141
Starbuck, Rachel V, 280
Starbuck, Ralph John IV, 768
Starbuck, Ray Leo V, 645
Starbuck, Raymond V, 360
Starbuck, Raymond V, 645
Starbuck, Raymond V, 666
Starbuck, Raymond V, 712
Starbuck, Raymond Leo V, 645
Starbuck, Rebecca I, 516
Starbuck, Rebecca I, 586
Starbuck, Rebecca I, 597
Starbuck, Rebecca I, 839
Starbuck, Rebecca I, 1057
Starbuck, Rebecca IV, 160
Starbuck, Rebecca IV, 414
Starbuck, Rebecca IV, 442
Starbuck, Rebecca IV, 443
Starbuck, Rebecca IV, 572
Starbuck, Rebecca IV, 595
Starbuck, Rebecca IV, 1295
Starbuck, Rebecca V, 171
Starbuck, Rebecca V, 206
Starbuck, Rebecca V, 626
Starbuck, Rebecca V, 645
Starbuck, Rebekah I, 574
Starbuck, Rebekah I, 591
Starbuck, Rebekah I, 830
Starbuck, Rebekah I, 839
Starbuck, Reuben I, 516
Starbuck, Reuben I, 573
Starbuck, Reuben I, 586
Starbuck, Reuben I, 591
Starbuck, Reuben I, 799
Starbuck, Reuben I, 839
Starbuck, Reuben I, 901
Starbuck, Rhoda I, 517
Starbuck, Rhoda IV, 416
Starbuck, Rhoda IV, 442
Starbuck, Rhoda IV, 443
Starbuck, Robert IV, 443
Starbuck, Robert IV, 594
Starbuck, Robert IV, 595
Starbuck, Robert IV, 1077
Starbuck, Robert Geo. IV, 768
Starbuck, Rohda I, 542
Starbuck, Rohda I, 574
Starbuck, Ruth I, 516
Starbuck, Ruth I, 556
Starbuck, Ruth I, 574
Starbuck, Ruth I, 779
Starbuck, Ruth I, 792
Starbuck, Ruth I, 810
Starbuck, Ruth I, 839
Starbuck, Ruth Ann IV, 595
Starbuck, Ruth Ella IV, 593
Starbuck, Ruth Ella IV, 595
Starbuck, Ruth Ellen IV, 595
Starbuck, Ruth Emily IV, 768
Starbuck, Ruthanna IV, 280
Starbuck, Ruthanna IV, 595
Starbuck, Sabilla IV, 443
Starbuck, Salem IV, 768
Starbuck, Salley I, 804
Starbuck, Salley I, 839
Starbuck, Sally I, 517
Starbuck, Sally I, 839
Starbuck, Samuel I, 574
Starbuck, Samuel I, 926
Starbuck, Samuel I, 1057
Starbuck, Samuel IV, 438
Starbuck, Samuel IV, 443
Starbuck, Samuel IV, 594
Starbuck, Samuel IV, 595
Starbuck, Samuel V, 171
Starbuck, Samuel V, 206
Starbuck, Samuel V, 531
Starbuck, Samuel V, 645
Starbuck, Sarah I, 517
Starbuck, Sarah IV, 160
Starbuck, Sarah IV, 182
Starbuck, Sarah IV, 190
Starbuck, Sarah IV, 197
Starbuck, Sarah IV, 252
Starbuck, Sarah IV, 280
Starbuck, Sarah IV, 422
Starbuck, Sarah IV, 442
Starbuck, Sarah IV, 443
Starbuck, Sarah IV, 595
Starbuck, Sarah IV, 768
Starbuck, Sarah IV, 1069
Starbuck, Sarah IV, 1077
Starbuck, Sarah V, 645
Starbuck, Sarah Crew IV, 595
Starbuck, Sarah M. IV, 280
Starbuck, Sarah T. IV, 570
Starbuck, Sarah T. IV, 595
Starbuck, Seth I, 517
Starbuck, Seth I, 804
Starbuck, Seth I, 839
Starbuck, Shubal I, 839
Starbuck, Sibilla IV, 443
Starbuck, Sidney IV, 443
Starbuck, Stella V, 532
Starbuck, Stella V, 599
Starbuck, Stella V, 645
Starbuck, Stephen III, 298
Starbuck, Susan I, 612
Starbuck, Susan Eliza I, 591
Starbuck, Susana I, 574
Starbuck, Susanna I, 516
Starbuck, Susanna I, 537
Starbuck, Susanna I, 574
Starbuck, Susanna V, 206
Starbuck, Susannah V, 531
Starbuck, Susannah V, 544
Starbuck, Susannah V, 625
Starbuck, Susannah V, 631
Starbuck, Susannah V, 637
Starbuck, Susannah V, 640
Starbuck, Susannah V, 645
Starbuck, Susannah, Jr. V, 645
Starbuck, Sydney Ann IV, 1295
Starbuck, Tacy IV, 393
Starbuck, Tacy IV, 443
Starbuck, Temple I, 591
Starbuck, Thomas I, 516
Starbuck, Thomas I, 574
Starbuck, Thomas I, 586
Starbuck, Thomas I, 591
Starbuck, Thomas I, 595
Starbuck, Thomas I, 597
Starbuck, Thomas IV, 196
Starbuck, Thomas IV, 214
Starbuck, Thomas IV, 280
Starbuck, Thomas IV, 575
Starbuck, Thomas IV, 595
Starbuck, Thomas Arthur V, 712
Starbuck, Thomas C. I, 591
Starbuck, Thomas Hawes V, 125
Starbuck, Thos. S. IV, 169
Starbuck, Tristam I, 839
Starbuck, Tristram I, 517
Starbuck, Trustram I, 839
Starbuck, Uriah I, 597
Starbuck, Uriah V, 125
Starbuck, Urieh I, 591
Starbuck, Uriel I, 591
Starbuck, Viola C. IV, 443
Starbuck, Virginia V, 712
Starbuck, William I, 517
Starbuck, William I, 574
Starbuck, William I, 576
Starbuck, William I, 586
Starbuck, William I, 591
Starbuck, William I, 597
Starbuck, William I, 839
Starbuck, William IV, 594
Starbuck, William IV, 595
Starbuck, William V, 125
Starbuck, William V, 645
Starbuck, William V, 712
Starbuck, William A. V, 645
Starbuck, William A. V, 712
Starbuck, William H. I, 591
Starbuck, William, Jr. I, 574
Starbuck, Willie V, 645
Starbuck, Willie A. V, 360
Starbuck, Willie A. V, 645
Starbuck, Wm. IV, 572
Starbuck, Wm. IV, 595
Starbuck, Wm. V, 645
Starbuck, Wm. A. V, 645
Starbuck, Wm. A. V, 712
Starbuck, Wm. Marianna V, 712
Starbuck, Wm. R. V, 645
Starcher, Earl E. IV, 280
Stargle, S. M. IV, 280
Stark, Hannah H. IV, 1003
Stark, Hannah H. IV, 1019
Stark, Ora V, 1020
Starke, Mary Jane VI, 852
Starkey, Alice S. V, 599
Starkey, Eli V, 599
Starkey, Elijah VI, 997
Starkey, Elizabeth VI, 997
Starkey, Frances B. V, 599
Starkey, Frances Belle V, 599
Starkey, Frank V, 599
Starkey, Frank P. V, 599
Starkey, Frank Pierce V, 599
Starkey, Gertrude B. V, 599
Starkey, Gertrude Belle V, 599
Starkey, Judith VI, 997
Starkey, Mildred VI, 997
Starkey, Sharrod G. VI, 997
Starkey, Shederick VI, 997
Starkey, William A. VI, 997
Starkins, Abigail III, 448
Starkins, Julia III, 440
Starkins, Julia E. III, 158
Starkins, Julia E. III, 299
Starky, Judith VI, 997
Starky, Mary II, 1015
Starky, Mary II, 1029
Starky, Mercy II, 1015
Starky, Sharrod G. VI, 997
Starky, Shederick VI, 997
Starlen, Mary D. IV, 1067
Starlen, Mary D. IV, 1077
Starlo, Peter II, 448
Starner, Mary IV, 1224
Starner, Mary IV, 1226
Starns, Mrs. Mary V, 280
Starns, Ruth V, 243
Starns, Ruth V, 280
Starns, William V, 280
Starr, ??? V, 877
Starr, ??? VI, 646
Starr, Abner V, 125
Starr, Ann II, 423
Starr, Ann II, 659
Starr, Ann IV, 280
Starr, Ann IV, 296
Starr, Anna II, 870
Starr, Anna II, 925
Starr, Anna M. V, 933
Starr, Arthur II, 423
Starr, Ashbridge II, 659
Starr, Benjamin II, 423
Starr, Caroline III, 225
Starr, Caroline IV, 1177
Starr, Catherine IV, 1192
Starr, Charles V, 863
Starr, Chas. W. V, 933
Starr, Chas. West V, 933
Starr, Clarence Raymond V, 712
Starr, Deborah II, 714
Starr, Edwin Albert IV, 1030
Starr, Eleanor V, 863
Starr, Eli T. II, 925
Starr, Elisha II, 659
Starr, Elizabeth II, 659
Starr, Elizabeth II, 690
Starr, Elizabeth IV, 1030
Starr, Elizabeth V, 862
Starr, Elizabeth V, 863
Starr, Elizabeth V, 933
Starr, Elma IV, 246
Starr, Elma IV, 280
Starr, Elma M. IV, 280
Starr, Elmer IV, 246
Starr, Elmer IV, 280
Starr, Elmer IV, 1264
Starr, Elmer A. IV, 1264
Starr, Esther V, 863
Starr, Esther V, 886
Starr, Esther V, 933
Starr, Francis IV, 280
Starr, Francis Cist V, 933
Starr, George IV, 498
Starr, George IV, 657
Starr, George Dilwyn II, 659
Starr, George L. IV, 657
Starr, Hannah II, 659
Starr, Hannah IV, 280
Starr, Hannah U. IV, 1187
Starr, Harriet F. IV, 280
Starr, Helen IV, 1264
Starr, Henry IV, 1030
Starr, Henry V, 863
Starr, Henry V, 933
Starr, Hillas IV, 1030
Starr, Horace Chipman V, 933
Starr, Isaac II, 423
Starr, Isaac II, 458
Starr, Isaac II, 646
Starr, Isaac II, 659
Starr, Isaac Walter II, 659
Starr, Jacob II, 659
Starr, James II, 423
Starr, James II, 531
Starr, James II, 658
Starr, James II, 659
Starr, James IV, 1030
Starr, James V, 862
Starr, James V, 863
Starr, Jane II, 658
Starr, Jane II, 659
Starr, Jane IV, 1030
Starr, Jeremiah II, 658
Starr, Jeremiah II, 659
Starr, Jesse V, 862
Starr, Jesse V, 863
Starr, Jesse V, 933
Starr, John II, 423
Starr, John II, 467
Starr, John II, 531
Starr, John II, 658
Starr, John II, 659
Starr, John III, 299
Starr, John V, 862
Starr, John V, 863
Starr, Joseph II, 423
Starr, Joseph II, 659
Starr, Joshua V, 862
Starr, Joshua V, 863
Starr, Joshua V, 933
Starr, Katherine II, 423
Starr, Lewis II, 906
Starr, Lewis II, 925
Starr, Lydia II, 423
Starr, Lydia II, 531
Starr, Lydia II, 658
Starr, Lydia II, 659
Starr, Lydia, Jr. II, 423
Starr, Margaret Hall II, 659
Starr, Martha IV, 280
Starr, Mary II, 423
Starr, Mary II, 600
Starr, Mary II, 659
Starr, Mary II, 906
Starr, Mary II, 925
Starr, Mary V, 862
Starr, Mary V, 863
Starr, Mary V, 933
Starr, Mary A. IV, 498
Starr, Mary Ann II, 659
Starr, Mary Etta V, 712
Starr, Mary Etta Timberlake V, 532
Starr, Mary L. IV, 1030
Starr, Mary M. III, 299
Starr, Merrick IV, 280
Starr, Merrick IV, 296
Starr, Metta V, 712
Starr, Mordecai F. IV, 280
Starr, Moses II, 423
Starr, Moses II, 658
Starr, Moses II, 659
Starr, Moses IV, 280
Starr, Moses VI, 447
Starr, Nathan IV, 280
Starr, Nathan W. IV, 280
Starr, Nehemiah IV, 1030
Starr, Nehemiah V, 863
Starr, Nehemiah V, 933
Starr, Nehemkah V, 863
Starr, Phebe II, 715
Starr, Phebe V, 862
Starr, Rachel II, 423
Starr, Rachel II, 458
Starr, Rachel II, 646
Starr, Rachel II, 659
Starr, Rachel II, 779
Starr, Rachel II, 818
Starr, Rachel III, 121
Starr, Rachel III, 284
Starr, Raymond V, 712
Starr, Rebecca II, 659
Starr, Rebecca IV, 657
Starr, Robert IV, 1030
Starr, Ruth Emma V, 712
Starr, Samuel II, 658
Starr, Samuel II, 659
Starr, Samuel II, 925
Starr, Sarah II, 423
Starr, Sarah II, 467
Starr, Sarah V, 862
Starr, Sarah VI, 447
Starr, Sarah VI, 997
Starr, Susanna P. II, 709
Starr, Tacy Ann VI, 646
Starr, Tacy Ann VI, 708
Starr, Thomas II, 423
Starr, Thomas II, 659
Starr, Wd. Rachel II, 423
Starr, Wd. Sarah II, 467
Starr, Wd. Sarah II, 659
Starr, William IV, 1030
Starr, William V, 862
Starr, William V, 863
Starr, William V, 933
Starr, William Cooper V, 933
Starr, William H. VI, 997
Starr, Willits V, 863
Starr, Wilson II, 423
Starr, Wilson II, 659
Starr, Wm. II, 658
Starr, Wm. C. V, 933
Starr, Wm. H. VI, 895
Starr, Wm. H. VI, 1010
Start, Minerva IV, 1224
Starta, Benjamin IV, 137
Statham, Caroline VI, 849
Statham, Charles VI, 977
Statham, Richmond VI, 859
Statler, Bessie V, 682
Statler, Bessie M. V, 712
Statler, Celia IV, 574
Statler, Celia IV, 595
Statler, Delila V, 1020
Statler, Delilah V, 1020
Statler, Della V, 599
Statler, Della V, 712
Statler, Emma G. V, 599
Statler, Emma T. V, 712
Statler, Lydia V, 599
Statler, Lydia V, 601
Statler, Lydia V, 712
Statler, Mary V, 599
Statler, Mary V, 712
Statler, Mary V, 1020
Statler, Ola V, 1020
Statler, Samuel V, 599
Statler, Sarah J. V, 1020
Statler, Sarah Jane V, 1020
Staton, Elizabeth VI, 855
Staton, Reuben H. VI, 855
Staton, Sarah J. VI, 855
Staton, William W. VI, 855
Stats, Mary Ann V, 831
Stats, Mary Ann V, 862
Stattem, William VI, 840
Statton, Isaac IV, 1043
Statton, Sarah B. IV, 1043
Stauffer, Elizabeth II, 130
Stauffer, J. N. II, 130
Stauffer, S. A. II, 130
Stauffer, Sophia IV, 943
Staunton, Andrew VI, 816
Staunton, Elizabeth VI, 337
Staunton, Frederick V, 33
Staunton, Hannah V, 33
Staunton, Louisa V, 712
Staunton, Mary V, 33
Staunton, Mary Frances II,
Staunton, Mary Frances II,
Staunton, Match VI, 814
Staunton, Wm. F. V, 933
Staut, Lula Mae IV, 957
Stead, Cecil I, 1162
Steadham, Alice V, 766
Steadham, John V, 765
Steadham, John V, 766
Steadham, Rebecca V, 161
Steadham, Rebecca V, 206
Steadman, Arthur IV, 1077
Steadman, Daniel IV, 1077
Steadman, Daniel IV, 1078
Steadman, Ellen IV, 1187
Steadman, Esther IV, 1128
Steadman, Esther IV, 1138
Steadman, Esther H. IV, 11
Steadman, Hannah IV, 1077
Steadman, James F. IV, 107
Steadman, Jefferson IV, 107
Steadman, John IV, 1077
Steadman, John S. IV, 1077
Steadman, Lewis Elmer IV,
Steadman, Louisa D. IV, 10
Steadman, Louisa J. IV, 107
Steadman, Louisa W. IV, 10
Steafferd, Mariam I, 117
Steal, Andrew VI, 967
Stean, Mary VI, 447
Steaphenson, Martha VI, 12
Steaphenson, Peter VI, 122
Steargeon, Barbara V, 756
Steargeon, Phebe V, 756
Steargeon, Wm. V, 756
Stearns, Ann IV, 768
Stearns, Barbara III, 299
Stearns, Catharine III, 299
Stearns, Emma L. II, 786
Stearns, Isaac H. III, 299
Stearns, J. Milton III, 299
Stearns, Lutie B. III, 299
Stearns, Marie III, 299
Stearns, Mary III, 411
Stearns, Nella III, 299
Stearns, Nella III, 351
Stearns, Paul Adams III, 29
Stearns, Rev. Charles III, 41
Stearns, Susan III, 411
Stearns, Whitney Kneeland III, 299
Stearns, William V, 280
Stearns, Winthrop III, 299
Stearns, Winthrop III, 351
Steavens, Enoch I, 575
Steavenson, Asenath I, 565
Steavenson, Asenath I, 575
Stebbins, Alfred III, 122
Stebbins, Alfred III, 299
Stebbins, Edith III, 122
Stebbins, Edith III, 299
Stebbins, Londa III, 122
Stebbins, Londa III, 299
Stebbins, Nora IV, 1339
Stebbins, Nora May IV, 133
Steckneck, Dora IV, 1182
Steddom, Abijah V, 98

dom, Abijah V, 125
dom, Abijah V, 126
dom, Abijah V, 189
dom, Abijah V, 206
dom, Albert V, 126
dom, Albert W. V, 126
dom, Alice V, 40
dom, Alice V, 113
dom, Alice V, 124
dom, Alice V, 125
dom, Alice V, 126
dom, Alice V, 206
dom, Alice V, 765
dom, Alice V, 766
dom, Alice C. V, 125
dom, Alice T. V, 126
dom, Alpheus V, 125
dom, Ann I, 1038
dom, Ann C. V, 126
dom, Ann C. V, 206
dom, Anna I, 1024
dom, Anna V, 89
dom, Anna V, 125
dom, Anna V, 126
dom, Anna T. V, 125
dom, Anna T. V, 126
dom, Anna T. V, 141
dom, Anna W. V, 126
dom, Annie V, 126
dom, Carrie C. V, 126
dom, Carrie E. V, 126
dom, Charity V, 125
dom, Charles V, 126
dom, Christan V, 126
dom, Christianna V, 40
dom, Christianna V, 125
dom, Christianna V, 732
dom, Cornelia V, 126
dom, Cornelia A. V, 933
dom, Cornelia A. P. V, 933
dom, Deborah V, 98
dom, Deborah V, 126
dom, Deborah V, 189
dom, Deborah V, 206
dom, Edward R. V, 126
dom, Edward R. V, 206
dom, Elizabeth Adaline
V, 125
dom, Elizabeth C. V, 90
dom, Elizabeth C. V, 126
dom, Ella C. V, 126
dom, Emily V, 126
dom, Emma H. V, 99
dom, Emma H. V, 126
dom, Esther V, 109
dom, Esther V, 113
dom, Esther V, 125
dom, Esther V, 126
dom, Esther V, 599
dom, Esther V, 819
dom, Esther P. V, 126
dom, Eunace V, 206
dom, Eunice I, 1031
dom, Eunice I, 1038
dom, Eunice V, 124
dom, Eunice V, 125
dom, Eunice M. V, 125
dom, Eunice M. V, 126
dom, Francis W. V, 125
dom, George V, 126
dom, Hanry I, 1038
dom, Henry I, 1024
dom, Henry I, 1038
dom, Henry V, 40
dom, Henry V, 70
dom, Henry V, 81
dom, Henry V, 125
dom, Henry V, 126
dom, Henry V, 741
dom, Henry V, 765
dom, Henry, Jr. V, 35
dom, Henry, Jr. V, 126
dom, Horace T. V, 125
dom, Isaac V, 126
dom, Isaac K. V, 112
dom, Isaac K. V, 125
dom, Isaac K. V, 126
dom, Isaac Kelly V, 125
dom, Isaac P. V, 126
dom, Isaac P. C. V, 112
dom, Isaac P. C. V, 126
dom, J. J. G. V, 126
dom, Jason W. V, 125
dom, Jesse Spray, Jr. V, 206
dom, John I, 1024
dom, John I, 1038
dom, John V, 40
dom, John V, 113
dom, John V, 124
dom, John V, 125
dom, John V, 126
Steddom, John V, 206
Steddom, John V, 765
Steddom, John V, 766
Steddom, John Compton V, 206
Steddom, John D. V, 125
Steddom, John F. IV, 281
Steddom, John F. IV, 288
Steddom, John F. V, 41
Steddom, John F. V, 126
Steddom, John F. V, 130
Steddom, John Furnas V, 125
Steddom, John Furnas V, 159
Steddom, John Furnas V, 206
Steddom, John H. V, 125
Steddom, John H. V, 126
Steddom, Joseph V, 125
Steddom, Joseph V, 126
Steddom, Joseph V, 933
Steddom, Joseph J. V, 125
Steddom, Laura V, 125
Steddom, Lucinda V, 112
Steddom, Lucinda V, 126
Steddom, Lurana V, 97
Steddom, Lurana V, 125
Steddom, Lydia IV, 281
Steddom, Lydia IV, 288
Steddom, Lydia V, 125
Steddom, Lydia V, 126
Steddom, Lydia V, 130
Steddom, Margery V, 108
Steddom, Margery V, 124
Steddom, Margery V, 125
Steddom, Margery V, 126
Steddom, Margery V, 204
Steddom, Margery V, 206
Steddom, Martha I, 1038
Steddom, Martha V, 40
Steddom, Martha V, 81
Steddom, Martha V, 123
Steddom, Martha V, 125
Steddom, Martha V, 126
Steddom, Martha L. V, 126
Steddom, Mary I, 318
Steddom, Mary I, 1024
Steddom, Mary I, 1035
Steddom, Mary I, 1038
Steddom, Mary V, 81
Steddom, Mary V, 125
Steddom, Mary V, 126
Steddom, Mary V, 808
Steddom, Mary Ann V, 41
Steddom, Mary Ann V, 125
Steddom, Mary Ann V, 126
Steddom, Mary Ann V, 159
Steddom, Mary Ann V, 206
Steddom, Mary H. V, 125
Steddom, Mary K. V, 126
Steddom, Mary T. V, 126
Steddom, Maurice P. V, 126
Steddom, Moses V, 113
Steddom, Moses V, 125
Steddom, Moses V, 126
Steddom, Moses V, 594
Steddom, Moses V, 599
Steddom, Myron V, 125
Steddom, Narcissa V, 112
Steddom, Narcissa V, 125
Steddom, Narcissa V, 126
Steddom, Newton V, 126
Steddom, Oscar F. V, 125
Steddom, Rachel V, 126
Steddom, Rebecca I, 1055
Steddom, Rebecca V, 40
Steddom, Rebecca V, 108
Steddom, Rebecca V, 125
Steddom, Rebecca V, 126
Steddom, Rebecca V, 206
Steddom, Rebecca T. V, 125
Steddom, Rhoda V, 103
Steddom, Rhoda V, 125
Steddom, Rhoda V, 126
Steddom, Rhoda V, 741
Steddom, Rhoda V, 757
Steddom, Rhoda V, 765
Steddom, Rice V, 125
Steddom, Ruth V, 70
Steddom, Ruth V, 125
Steddom, Sallie V, 35
Steddom, Sallie V, 126
Steddom, Samuel IV, 281
Steddom, Samuel V, 97
Steddom, Samuel V, 125
Steddom, Samuel V, 126
Steddom, Samuel V, 130
Steddom, Samuel V, 206
Steddom, Samuel V, 765
Steddom, Samuel T. V, 109
Steddom, Samuel T. V, 124
Steddom, Samuel T. V, 126
Steddom, Samuel T. V, 204
Steddom, Samuel T. V, 206
Steddom, Samuel T. V, 819
Steddom, Sarah V, 113
Steddom, Sarah V, 126
Steddom, Sarah V, 130
Steddom, Sarah V, 594
Steddom, Sarah V, 599
Steddom, Sarah Ann V, 125
Steddom, Sarah F. V, 55
Steddom, Sarah F. V, 125
Steddom, Sarah J. IV, 281
Steddom, Sarah J. IV, 288
Steddom, Sarah J. V, 126
Steddom, Sarah P. V, 126
Steddom, Seth V, 125
Steddom, Susanna V, 97
Steddom, Susanna V, 125
Steddom, Susanna V, 130
Steddom, Susanna V, 206
Steddom, Susannah IV, 281
Steddom, Susannah V, 765
Steddom, Sylvan V, 126
Steddom, Terrill V, 126
Steddom, Thomas Terrell IV, 281
Steddom, Viola V, 126
Steddom, Widow Mary I, 1038
Steddom, William C. V, 126
Steddon, Annie V, 142
Steddon, Cornelia A. P. V, 933
Stedham, Andrew I, 166
Stedham, Henry I, 1015
Stedman, Ellen IV, 1187
Stedman, James I, 1038
Stedman, Mary IV, 185
Stedman, Mary IV, 281
Stedman, Salie V, 793
Stedman, Susannah I, 1038
Stedom, Anna V, 125
Stedom, Christianna V, 125
Stedom, David S. V, 594
Stedom, Esther V, 594
Stedom, Esther V, 599
Stedom, Esther Ann V, 594
Stedom, Esther S. V, 594
Stedom, Eunace V, 205
Stedom, Eunace V, 206
Stedom, Eunice V, 125
Stedom, Henry V, 125
Stedom, Jehu Evan V, 594
Stedom, John V, 125
Stedom, Lydia V, 594
Stedom, Martha V, 125
Stedom, Mary V, 125
Stedom, Mary T. V, 594
Stedom, Samuel V, 125
Stedom, Sarah T. V, 594
Stedom, William V, 594
Stedom, Wm. T. V, 594
Stedom, Wm., Jr. V, 594
Stedson, Cynthia II, 719
Stedson, George II, 719
Steed, Martha I, 949
Steed, Mattie M. I, 933
Steed, Mattie M. I, 934
Steed, Neola Elizabeth I, 934
Steed, Robert L. I, 641
Steed, Thomas J. I, 933
Steed, Thomas J. I, 934
Steedom, Mary I, 300
Steedom, Mary I, 318
Steel, ??? IV, 929
Steel, Abigail IV, 259
Steel, Abigail IV, 281
Steel, Agnes IV, 409
Steel, Alexander VI, 835
Steel, Alexander VI, 837
Steel, Alexander VI, 855
Steel, Andrew II, 899
Steel, Andrew II, 925
Steel, Andrew VI, 997
Steel, Ann II, 632
Steel, Ann II, 659
Steel, Banajah I, 268
Steel, Benajah I, 276
Steel, Benajah IV, 61
Steel, Benjamin IV, 137
Steel, Clifton VI, 820
Steel, Deborah II, 423
Steel, Eleanor II, 637
Steel, Eleanor II, 659
Steel, Elijah IV, 61
Steel, Eliza I, 597
Steel, Elizabeth II, 651
Steel, Elizabeth II, 659
Steel, Elizabeth II, 675
Steel, Elizabeth II, 899
Steel, Elizabeth II, 925
Steel, Elizabeth IV, 844
Steel, Elizabeth IV, 855
Steel, Elizabeth VI, 837
Steel, Elizabeth VI, 855
Steel, Elizabeth VI, 997
Steel, Francis VI, 875
Steel, Francis VI, 967
Steel, Francis VI, 971
Steel, Francis VI, 997
Steel, George VI, 802
Steel, George VI, 822
Steel, George VI, 997
Steel, Hannah II, 423
Steel, Hannah II, 659
Steel, Harriett J. V, 360
Steel, Henry II, 423
Steel, Henry II, 652
Steel, Henry II, 659
Steel, James II, 370
Steel, James II, 423
Steel, James II, 470
Steel, James II, 620
Steel, James II, 659
Steel, James II, 667
Steel, James II, 684
Steel, James, Jr. II, 423
Steel, Jane VI, 997
Steel, Jary IV, 1003
Steel, John II, 659
Steel, John VI, 835
Steel, John VI, 1008
Steel, Leah IV, 409
Steel, Lucinda IV, 1102
Steel, Lucinda IV, 1116
Steel, Martha II, 423
Steel, Martha II, 620
Steel, Martha II, 659
Steel, Martha II, 684
Steel, Martha IV, 409
Steel, Mary II, 423
Steel, Mary II, 632
Steel, Mary II, 652
Steel, Mary II, 659
Steel, Mary II, 684
Steel, Mary II, 899
Steel, Mary II, 925
Steel, Mary IV, 61
Steel, Mary IV, 409
Steel, Mary IV, 844
Steel, Mary IV, 855
Steel, Mary IV, 929
Steel, Mary IV, 1091
Steel, Mary IV, 1116
Steel, Mary IV, 1308
Steel, Mary V, 1020
Steel, Mary VI, 835
Steel, Mary VI, 853
Steel, Mary VI, 967
Steel, Mary VI, 971
Steel, Mary J. II, 925
Steel, Mary Lucy IV, 533
Steel, Nancy IV, 409
Steel, Peter I, 276
Steel, Peter IV, 61
Steel, Philip M. II, 1029
Steel, Polly VI, 997
Steel, Rebecca, Sr. II, 684
Steel, Rebeccah II, 423
Steel, Rebekah II, 659
Steel, Robert II, 659
Steel, Ruth II, 667
Steel, Ruth Thompson II, 659
Steel, Sally VI, 997
Steel, Sarah I, 268
Steel, Sarah I, 276
Steel, Sarah I, 373
Steel, Sarah I, 419
Steel, Sarah II, 423
Steel, Sarah II, 643
Steel, Sarah II, 659
Steel, Sarah IV, 61
Steel, Thomas III, 299
Steel, Thoms II, 620
Steel, Thos. II, 899
Steel, Thos. II, 925
Steel, Wd. Martha II, 470
Steel, Wd. Mary II, 423
Steel, Wd. Mary II, 659
Steel, William B. II, 821
Steel, William, Jr. IV, 409
Steel, Wm. II, 659
Steel, Wm. II, 684
Steel, Wm. IV, 533
Steele, Ada L. IV, 768
Steele, Alec. VI, 805
Steele, Alex. VI, 846
Steele, Alexander VI, 828
Steele, Alexander VI, 835
Steele, Alexander VI, 855
Steele, Bessie I, 923
Steele, Carl S. IV, 768
Steele, Catharine III, 299
Steele, Catharine VI, 828
Steele, Catharine VI, 855
Steele, Earl V, 206
Steele, Elijah IV, 160
Steele, Elizabeth VI, 805
Steele, Elizabeth VI, 855
Steele, Fernie IV, 1339
Steele, George VI, 796
Steele, George VI, 855
Steele, George VI, 916
Steele, George VI, 954
Steele, James VI, 855
Steele, Jane VI, 855
Steele, Jennie I, 617
Steele, John VI, 797
Steele, John VI, 820
Steele, John VI, 822
Steele, John VI, 837
Steele, John VI, 851
Steele, Lydia IV, 154
Steele, Lydia IV, 160
Steele, Maggie IV, 768
Steele, Margaret VI, 820
Steele, Martha IV, 444
Steele, Mary II, 549
Steele, Mary VI, 447
Steele, Mary VI, 456
Steele, Mary A. I, 641
Steele, Mary A. VI, 828
Steele, Mary J. I, 617
Steele, Moses VI, 855
Steele, Nancy VI, 855
Steele, Olive M. IV, 768
Steele, Peter IV, 160
Steele, Rachel VI, 855
Steele, Ruth IV, 150
Steele, Ruth IV, 160
Steele, Sally VI, 855
Steele, Samuel VI, 820
Steele, Sarah VI, 797
Steele, Sarah VI, 822
Steele, Sarah A. VI, 846
Steele, Stephen I, 617
Steele, Susan W. VI, 844
Steele, Susanna W. VI, 855
Steele, Thomas III, 299
Steele, William VI, 846
Steele, William VI, 855
Steelman, John II, 659
Steelman, Susanna II, 659
Steelmon, Sinthy I, 998
Steen, Abigal VI, 825
Steen, Archibald VI, 855
Steen, Hannah VI, 997
Steen, Jane VI, 855
Steen, John VI, 855
Steen, Judith VI, 815
Steen, Judith S. VI, 855
Steen, Mary VI, 447
Steen, Mary VI, 855
Steen, Paulina P. VI, 869
Steen, Polly VI, 903
Steen, Polly VI, 989
Steen, Thomas VI, 831
Steen, Thomas VI, 997
Steen, William VI, 855
Steen, Wm. VI, 869
Steer, ??? IV, 137
Steer, Abbie L. IV, 281
Steer, Abbie Loretta IV, 281
Steer, Abbie Loretta IV, 283
Steer, Abbie Loretta IV, 552
Steer, Abby IV, 444
Steer, Abby Loretta IV, 552
Steer, Abigail IV, 144
Steer, Abigail IV, 272
Steer, Abigail IV, 281
Steer, Abigail IV, 434
Steer, Abigail IV, 444
Steer, Abigail VI, 379
Steer, Abigail VI, 380
Steer, Abigail VI, 384
Steer, Abigail VI, 447
Steer, Abigail VI, 448
Steer, Abigail VI, 462
Steer, Abigail VI, 489
Steer, Abigail VI, 551
Steer, Abigail VI, 566
Steer, Abigail VI, 567
Steer, Abigail VI, 603
Steer, Abza J. IV, 176
Steer, Abzie Jane IV, 281
Steer, Abzie Ladd IV, 283
Steer, Achsah IV, 283
Steer, Achsah P. IV, 243
Steer, Achsah P. IV, 281
Steer, Adrian IV, 1380
Steer, Adrian P. IV, 1380
Steer, Albert IV, 282
Steer, Albert I. IV, 283
Steer, Albert I. IV, 844
Steer, Albert J. IV, 844
Steer, Albert J. IV, 945
Steer, Albert J. IV, 1004
Steer, Alexandria III, 299

Steer, Alfred G. II, 768
Steer, Alfred G. IV, 282
Steer, Alfred G. IV, 283
Steer, Alfred G. Steer II, 769
Steer, Alfred Gilbert IV, 444
Steer, Alfred Gilbert IV, 446
Steer, Alice B. IV, 282
Steer, Alice M. IV, 282
Steer, Alice Mary IV, 235
Steer, Alice Mary IV, 282
Steer, Alice Mary IV, 640
Steer, Alice May IV, 657
Steer, Alice R. II, 702
Steer, Alice R. II, 735
Steer, Alice R. II, 768
Steer, Alice R. IV, 192
Steer, Alice R. IV, 282
Steer, Alza J. IV, 282
Steer, Alzie Jane IV, 552
Steer, Amos IV, 160
Steer, Amos IV, 249
Steer, Amos IV, 281
Steer, Amos IV, 282
Steer, Amos IV, 756
Steer, Amos IV, 768
Steer, Amos IV, 839
Steer, Amos IV, 1004
Steer, Amos IV, 1380
Steer, Amos VI, 448
Steer, Amos R. IV, 1380
Steer, Ana Caroline IV, 1004
Steer, Ann IV, 243
Steer, Ann IV, 281
Steer, Ann IV, 551
Steer, Ann VI, 416
Steer, Ann VI, 447
Steer, Ann VI, 448
Steer, Ann VI, 471
Steer, Ann VI, 490
Steer, Ann VI, 510
Steer, Ann VI, 512
Steer, Ann VI, 529
Steer, Ann VI, 547
Steer, Ann VI, 564
Steer, Ann VI, 565
Steer, Ann VI, 566
Steer, Ann VI, 567
Steer, Ann VI, 576
Steer, Ann VI, 578
Steer, Ann VI, 618
Steer, Ann VI, 708
Steer, Ann Jr. IV, 249
Steer, Ann L. VI, 448
Steer, Ann M. IV, 281
Steer, Ann M. IV, 282
Steer, Ann Maule, Jr. IV, 282
Steer, Ann, Jr. VI, 547
Steer, Ann, Jr. VI, 548
Steer, Ann, Jr. VI, 565
Steer, Anna IV, 444
Steer, Anna IV, 844
Steer, Anna B. IV, 444
Steer, Anna B. IV, 768
Steer, Anna B. IV, 844
Steer, Anna Caroline IV, 1004
Steer, Anna D. IV, 296
Steer, Anna M. IV, 223
Steer, Anna M. IV, 281
Steer, Anna M. IV, 282
Steer, Anna M. IV, 283
Steer, Anna M. IV, 410
Steer, Anna M. IV, 444
Steer, Anna Mary IV, 281
Steer, Anna Mary IV, 444
Steer, Anne IV, 283
Steer, Anne VI, 448
Steer, Anne VI, 490
Steer, Anne VI, 565
Steer, Anne E. VI, 567
Steer, Benjamin IV, 160
Steer, Benjamin IV, 281
Steer, Benjamin IV, 282
Steer, Benjamin VI, 448
Steer, Benjamin VI, 471
Steer, Benjamin VI, 490
Steer, Benjamin VI, 492
Steer, Benjamin VI, 529
Steer, Benjamin VI, 547
Steer, Benjamin VI, 565
Steer, Benjamin VI, 567
Steer, Benjamin VI, 576
Steer, Benjamin VI, 618
Steer, Benjamin VI, 708
Steer, Benjamin W. IV, 282
Steer, Benjamin W. IV, 1367
Steer, Benjamin W. IV, 1368
Steer, Benjamin W. IV, 1380
Steer, Bertha M. IV, 444
Steer, Beulah VI, 448
Steer, Beulah VI, 460
Steer, Beulah VI, 566
Steer, Beulah VI, 584
Steer, Beulah W. VI, 448
Steer, Beulah W. VI, 584
Steer, Caroline B. VI, 567
Steer, Catharine IV, 1380
Steer, Catherine IV, 1380
Steer, Charles IV, 444
Steer, Charles A. IV, 281
Steer, Charles L. IV, 281
Steer, Clara B. IV, 281
Steer, Clara Ellen IV, 281
Steer, Daniel VI, 593
Steer, David IV, 154
Steer, David IV, 160
Steer, David IV, 243
Steer, David IV, 252
Steer, David IV, 281
Steer, David IV, 282
Steer, David IV, 1354
Steer, David IV, 1380
Steer, David IV, 1382
Steer, David VI, 448
Steer, David Quincey IV, 1380
Steer, David Quincy IV, 282
Steer, David Quincy IV, 1380
Steer, Davis, Sr. VI, 593
Steer, Deb. IV, 1380
Steer, Deborah IV, 255
Steer, Deborah IV, 281
Steer, Deborah IV, 282
Steer, Deborah IV, 283
Steer, Deborah VI, 592
Steer, Deborah A. I, 901
Steer, Deborah Ann IV, 281
Steer, Deborah H. IV, 174
Steer, Deborah H. IV, 281
Steer, Deborah H. IV, 282
Steer, Deborah H. IV, 1380
Steer, Deborah M. IV, 844
Steer, Donald Ralph IV, 1004
Steer, Dorothy IV, 282
Steer, Dorothy IV, 1004
Steer, Dorothy A. IV, 254
Steer, Dorothy A. IV, 282
Steer, E. C. IV, 281
Steer, Edgar H. VI, 561
Steer, Edgar H. VI, 565
Steer, Edgar H. VI, 567
Steer, Edith IV, 282
Steer, Edith IV, 444
Steer, Edith T. IV, 176
Steer, Edith T. IV, 282
Steer, Edmon M. IV, 283
Steer, Edward Nathan IV, 1004
Steer, Edwin IV, 1004
Steer, Edwin M. IV, 281
Steer, Edwin M. IV, 1004
Steer, Edwin N. IV, 1004
Steer, Edwin Nathan IV, 1004
Steer, Elenor VI, 593
Steer, Elese Nadine IV, 1004
Steer, Elgar VI, 593
Steer, Elise Nadine IV, 1004
Steer, Elisha IV, 281
Steer, Elisha IV, 283
Steer, Elisha B. II, 702
Steer, Elisha B. IV, 183
Steer, Elisha B. IV, 192
Steer, Elisha B. IV, 200
Steer, Elisha B. IV, 205
Steer, Elisha B. IV, 240
Steer, Elisha B. IV, 243
Steer, Elisha B. IV, 281
Steer, Elisha B. IV, 282
Steer, Elisha B. IV, 283
Steer, Elisha B. IV, 444
Steer, Elisha B. IV, 768
Steer, Elisha B. IV, 815
Steer, Elisha B. IV, 817
Steer, Elisha B. IV, 844
Steer, Elisha B. IV, 1097
Steer, Elisha B. IV, 1380
Steer, Elisha Brackin IV, 281
Steer, Elisha P. IV, 734
Steer, Elisha P. IV, 768
Steer, Eliza IV, 444
Steer, Eliza C. IV, 419
Steer, Eliza C. IV, 444
Steer, Eliza H. IV, 246
Steer, Eliza H. IV, 282
Steer, Eliza H. IV, 283
Steer, Eliza H. IV, 444
Steer, Elizabeth IV, 165
Steer, Elizabeth IV, 281
Steer, Elizabeth IV, 283
Steer, Elizabeth IV, 375
Steer, Elizabeth IV, 444
Steer, Elizabeth IV, 1358
Steer, Elizabeth IV, 1380
Steer, Elizabeth V, 933
Steer, Elizabeth VI, 488
Steer, Elizabeth VI, 493
Steer, Elizabeth VI, 509
Steer, Elizabeth VI, 510
Steer, Elizabeth VI, 541
Steer, Elizabeth VI, 561
Steer, Elizabeth VI, 565
Steer, Elizabeth VI, 566
Steer, Elizabeth VI, 567
Steer, Elizabeth VI, 593
Steer, Elizabeth Ann IV, 1004
Steer, Elizabeth E. IV, 676
Steer, Elizabeth E. IV, 768
Steer, Elizabeth M. II, 904
Steer, Elizabeth M. II, 925
Steer, Elizabeth M. VI, 509
Steer, Elizabeth M. VI, 567
Steer, Ella T. IV, 444
Steer, Ellen IV, 183
Steer, Ellen IV, 282
Steer, Ellen IV, 1097
Steer, Ellen VI, 493
Steer, Ellen VI, 566
Steer, Ellen VI, 567
Steer, Ellen C. II, 702
Steer, Ellen C. IV, 205
Steer, Ellen C. IV, 283
Steer, Ellen C. IV, 817
Steer, Ellen C. IV, 844
Steer, Ellen G. IV, 192
Steer, Ellen G. IV, 200
Steer, Ellen G. IV, 282
Steer, Ellen G. IV, 283
Steer, Ellen G. IV, 444
Steer, Ellen G. IV, 844
Steer, Ellis D. IV, 1004
Steer, Elma IV, 225
Steer, Elma IV, 281
Steer, Elma IV, 282
Steer, Elmira IV, 444
Steer, Elmira T. IV, 394
Steer, Elmira T. IV, 444
Steer, Elmira T. IV, 768
Steer, Emily IV, 1368
Steer, Emily IV, 1380
Steer, Emily H. IV, 1367
Steer, Emma IV, 146
Steer, Emma IV, 160
Steer, Emma IV, 282
Steer, Emma IV, 394
Steer, Emma IV, 444
Steer, Emma E. VI, 478
Steer, Emma E. VI, 565
Steer, Emma E. VI, 566
Steer, Emma E. VI, 783
Steer, Emma F. VI, 565
Steer, Emma R. IV, 281
Steer, Enoch V, 933
Steer, Esther VI, 548
Steer, Florence H. IV, 200
Steer, Florence H. IV, 282
Steer, Florence H. IV, 1097
Steer, Florence H. IV, 1098
Steer, Florence H. IV, 1116
Steer, Frank Isaac IV, 1004
Steer, Franklin VI, 565
Steer, Franklin M. III, 299
Steer, Franklin M. VI, 478
Steer, Franklin M. VI, 488
Steer, Franklin M. VI, 561
Steer, Franklin M. VI, 566
Steer, Franklin M. VI, 567
Steer, Franklin M. VI, 783
Steer, Frederick B. VI, 567
Steer, Grace IV, 160
Steer, Grace IV, 231
Steer, Grace IV, 269
Steer, Grace IV, 281
Steer, Grace IV, 282
Steer, Grace IV, 444
Steer, Grace IV, 768
Steer, Grace V, 933
Steer, Grace VI, 379
Steer, Grace VI, 415
Steer, Grace VI, 447
Steer, Grace VI, 448
Steer, Grace VI, 472
Steer, Grace VI, 507
Steer, Grace VI, 565
Steer, Grace VI, 566
Steer, Grace VI, 592
Steer, Grace VI, 597
Steer, Grace Alma IV, 276
Steer, Grace Alma IV, 282
Steer, Greenberry IV, 160
Steer, Greenberry IV, 282
Steer, Greenberry P. IV, 281
Steer, Greenberry P. IV, 1368
Steer, Greenberry P. IV, 1380
Steer, Greenbury P. IV, 282
Steer, Greenbury P. IV, 1380
Steer, Hanna IV, 178
Steer, Hanna S. IV, 181
Steer, Hannah IV, 204
Steer, Hannah IV, 282
Steer, Hannah IV, 844
Steer, Hannah V, 933
Steer, Hannah VI, 442
Steer, Hannah VI, 447
Steer, Hannah VI, 448
Steer, Hannah VI, 462
Steer, Hannah VI, 471
Steer, Hannah VI, 497
Steer, Hannah VI, 565
Steer, Hannah VI, 566
Steer, Hannah VI, 567
Steer, Hannah VI, 593
Steer, Hannah VI, 617
Steer, Hannah VI, 618
Steer, Hannah VI, 619
Steer, Hannah VI, 640
Steer, Hannah VI, 643
Steer, Hannah VI, 708
Steer, Hannah C. IV, 768
Steer, Hannah M. IV, 281
Steer, Hannah M. IV, 282
Steer, Hannah M. IV, 1354
Steer, Hannah M. IV, 1380
Steer, Hannah P. IV, 276
Steer, Hannah P. IV, 282
Steer, Hannah P. IV, 283
Steer, Hannah P. IV, 1077
Steer, Hannah S. IV, 262
Steer, Hannah S. IV, 283
Steer, Hannah S. IV, 1072
Steer, Hannah S. IV, 1077
Steer, Hariett A. VI, 510
Steer, Harold James IV, 444
Steer, Harriet IV, 281
Steer, Harriet IV, 282
Steer, Harriet IV, 1380
Steer, Harriet V, 933
Steer, Harriet A. III, 299
Steer, Harriet A. IV, 282
Steer, Harriet A. IV, 404
Steer, Harriet A. IV, 444
Steer, Harriet A. VI, 506
Steer, Harriet A. VI, 567
Steer, Harriet A. VI, 568
Steer, Harriet T. VI, 567
Steer, Harriett A. VI, 571
Steer, Harriett A. VI, 576
Steer, Helen Elizabeth IV, 1004
Steer, Horace W. IV, 281
Steer, Horace W. IV, 282
Steer, Ida IV, 1367
Steer, Ida IV, 1380
Steer, Ida B. IV, 281
Steer, Ida B. VI, 561
Steer, Ida B. VI, 566
Steer, Ida G. III, 289
Steer, Ida G. III, 299
Steer, Irving M. IV, 1004
Steer, Isaac IV, 160
Steer, Isaac IV, 281
Steer, Isaac IV, 282
Steer, Isaac IV, 768
Steer, Isaac IV, 1358
Steer, Isaac IV, 1380
Steer, Isaac VI, 402
Steer, Isaac VI, 416
Steer, Isaac VI, 421
Steer, Isaac VI, 447
Steer, Isaac VI, 448
Steer, Isaac VI, 472
Steer, Isaac VI, 482
Steer, Isaac VI, 492
Steer, Isaac VI, 493
Steer, Isaac VI, 507
Steer, Isaac VI, 512
Steer, Isaac VI, 536
Steer, Isaac VI, 554
Steer, Isaac VI, 565
Steer, Isaac VI, 566
Steer, Isaac VI, 567
Steer, Isaac VI, 568
Steer, Isaac VI, 583
Steer, Isaac VI, 584
Steer, Isaac VI, 725
Steer, Isaac VI, 767
Steer, Isaac E. III, 289
Steer, Isaac E. III, 299
Steer, Isaac E. VI, 448
Steer, Isaac E. VI, 529
Steer, Isaac E. VI, 565
Steer, Isaac E. VI, 566
Steer, Isaac E. VI, 568
Steer, Isaac E. VI, 571
Steer, Isaac E. VI, 576
Steer, Isaac H. VI, 448
Steer, Isaac H. VI, 783
Steer, Isaac Hollingsworth VI, 566
Steer, Isaac Hollingsworth VI, 783
Steer, Isaac Nevitt VI, 566
Steer, Isabel IV, 1380
Steer, Israel IV, 179
Steer, Israel IV, 255
Steer, Israel IV, 264
Steer, Israel IV, 281
Steer, Israel IV, 282
Steer, Israel IV, 283
Steer, Israel IV, 299
Steer, Israel IV, 430
Steer, Israel IV, 444
Steer, Israel IV, 451
Steer, Israel IV, 768
Steer, Israel IV, 844
Steer, Israel IV, 1077
Steer, Iva B. VI, 565
Steer, James III, 299
Steer, James IV, 144
Steer, James IV, 160
Steer, James IV, 171
Steer, James IV, 243
Steer, James IV, 272
Steer, James IV, 281
Steer, James IV, 282
Steer, James IV, 375
Steer, James IV, 410
Steer, James IV, 434
Steer, James IV, 444
Steer, James IV, 551
Steer, James IV, 552
Steer, James IV, 558
Steer, James IV, 1077
Steer, James VI, 379
Steer, James VI, 380
Steer, James VI, 384
Steer, James VI, 425
Steer, James VI, 447
Steer, James VI, 448
Steer, James VI, 462
Steer, James VI, 489
Steer, James VI, 551
Steer, James VI, 566
Steer, James VI, 567
Steer, James VI, 603
Steer, James D. III, 299
Steer, James D. VI, 565
Steer, James D. VI, 772
Steer, James D. VI, 783
Steer, James M. VI, 416
Steer, James M. VI, 448
Steer, James M. VI, 488
Steer, James M. VI, 509
Steer, James M. VI, 529
Steer, James M. VI, 565
Steer, James M. VI, 566
Steer, James M. VI, 567
Steer, James M. VI, 783
Steer, James M., Jr. VI, 566
Steer, James Moore VI, 541
Steer, James Moore VI, 565
Steer, James Moore VI, 566
Steer, James Moore VI, 783
Steer, James O. III, 265
Steer, James W. IV, 282
Steer, James W. IV, 283
Steer, James W. IV, 844
Steer, James, Jr. IV, 160
Steer, James, Jr. IV, 164
Steer, James, Jr. IV, 208
Steer, James, Jr. IV, 282
Steer, James, Jr. IV, 283
Steer, James, Jr. IV, 396
Steer, James, Jr. IV, 444
Steer, James, Sr. IV, 283
Steer, Jane IV, 160
Steer, Jane IV, 282
Steer, Jane IV, 1380
Steer, Jane M. IV, 281
Steer, Jane M. IV, 282
Steer, Jane M. IV, 768
Steer, Jane M. IV, 780
Steer, Jane M. IV, 1380
Steer, Jane M. IV, 1382
Steer, Jas. IV, 281
Steer, Jason P. IV, 281
Steer, Jason P. IV, 282
Steer, Jennie VI, 565
Steer, Jesse Leah C. IV, 835
Steer, Jessie C. IV, 255
Steer, Jessie C. IV, 283
Steer, Jessie Leah IV, 844
Steer, Jessie Leah IV, 945
Steer, Jessie Leah IV, 1004
Steer, Jessie Leah C. IV, 844
Steer, Joel VI, 593
Steer, John VI, 493
Steer, John VI, 565
Steer, John VI, 566
Steer, John VI, 567

r, John B. VI, 565
r, John B. VI, 566
, John B. VI, 783
r, John B. Crawford II, 768
r, John Ogden IV, 444
r, John S. VI, 561
r, Jonah VI, 448
r, Jonah VI, 565
r, Jonah VI, 566
r, Jos. VI, 541
r, Joseph IV, 146
r, Joseph IV, 160
r, Joseph IV, 174
r, Joseph IV, 231
r, Joseph IV, 269
r, Joseph IV, 281
r, Joseph IV, 282
r, Joseph IV, 283
r, Joseph IV, 394
r, Joseph IV, 444
r, Joseph IV, 768
r, Joseph IV, 1380
r, Joseph V, 933
r, Joseph VI, 377
r, Joseph VI, 384
r, Joseph VI, 415
r, Joseph VI, 442
r, Joseph VI, 447
r, Joseph VI, 448
r, Joseph VI, 460
r, Joseph VI, 472
r, Joseph VI, 492
r, Joseph VI, 493
r, Joseph VI, 507
r, Joseph VI, 529
r, Joseph VI, 548
r, Joseph VI, 553
r, Joseph VI, 557
r, Joseph VI, 565
r, Joseph VI, 566
r, Joseph VI, 567
r, Joseph VI, 584
r, Joseph VI, 593
r, Joseph VI, 767
r, Joseph B. IV, 283
r, Joseph G. IV, 394
r, Joseph G. IV, 444
r, Joseph G. IV, 768
r, Joseph H. VI, 482
r, Joseph H. VI, 536
r, Joseph H. VI, 565
r, Joseph H. VI, 566
r, Joseph H. VI, 584
r, Joseph H. VI, 767
r, Joseph H. VI, 783
r, Joseph, Jr. IV, 282
r, Joseph, Jr. IV, 1380
r, Joseph, Jr. VI, 591
r, Joshua IV, 281
r, Joshua IV, 282
r, Joshua IV, 933
r, Joshua IV, 1004
r, Joshua VI, 448
r, Joshua R. IV, 1004
r, Josie IV, 283
r, Kinard IV, 1380
r, L. Ellis IV, 844
r, Laura IV, 366
r, Laura E. IV, 171
r, Laura E. IV, 281
r, Laura E. IV, 282
r, Laura E. IV, 368
r, Laura E. IV, 444
r, Lavina IV, 281
r, Lavina IV, 282
r, Lavina IV, 756
r, Lavina IV, 768
r, Leah VI, 416
r, Leah VI, 448
r, Leah VI, 565
r, Leah VI, 566
r, Leah VI, 567
r, Leah VI, 571
er, Leah W. II, 925
er, Leah W. VI, 566
er, Leah W. VI, 567
er, Leah Walker II, 904
er, Leah Walker II, 925
er, Lena Irena IV, 1004
er, Lerura Ann VI, 548
er, Lewis W. II, 904
er, Lewis W. II, 925
er, Lewis W. VI, 506
er, Lewis W. VI, 509
er, Lewis W. VI, 510
er, Lewis W. VI, 561
er, Lewis W. VI, 565
er, Lewis W. VI, 566
er, Lewis W. VI, 567
er, Lewis W. VI, 568
er, Lindley IV, 283
Steer, Lindley IV, 844
Steer, Lindley IV, 1072
Steer, Lindley IV, 1077
Steer, Lindley B. IV, 178
Steer, Lindley B. IV, 181
Steer, Lindley B. IV, 204
Steer, Lindley B. IV, 262
Steer, Lindley B. IV, 276
Steer, Lindley B. IV, 281
Steer, Lindley B. IV, 282
Steer, Lindley B. IV, 283
Steer, Lindley B. IV, 375
Steer, Lindley B. IV, 444
Steer, Lindley Ellis IV, 282
Steer, Lindley Ellis IV, 283
STeer, Lindley Ellis IV, 801
Steer, Lindley Ellis IV, 844
Steer, Lois Marie IV, 1004
Steer, Louesia VI, 448
Steer, Louis IV, 176
Steer, Louis C. IV, 183
Steer, Louis C. IV, 235
Steer, Louis C. IV, 254
Steer, Louis C. IV, 282
Steer, Louis Clarence IV, 281
Steer, Louisa IV, 430
Steer, Louisa IV, 444
Steer, Louisa IV, 1073
Steer, Louisa VI, 371
Steer, Louisa VI, 448
Steer, Louisa VI, 476
Steer, Louisa VI, 565
Steer, Louisa VI, 568
Steer, Louisa D. IV, 183
Steer, Louisa D. IV, 282
Steer, Louisa D. IV, 444
Steer, Louisa D. IV, 1077
Steer, Louiza D. IV, 282
Steer, Lusine IV, 1004
Steer, Lydia IV, 768
Steer, Lydia VI, 447
Steer, Lydia VI, 448
Steer, Lydia VI, 565
Steer, Lydia VI, 567
Steer, Lydia VI, 583
Steer, Lydia A. IV, 282
Steer, Lydia A. IV, 310
Steer, Lydia Ann IV, 281
Steer, Lydia Ann VI, 438
Steer, Lydia Ann VI, 553
Steer, Lydia Ann VI, 566
Steer, Lydia Ann VI, 567
Steer, Lydia Ann VI, 783
Steer, Lydia K. IV, 283
Steer, Lydie VI, 556
Steer, M Ella VI, 568
Steer, M. Ella VI, 576
Steer, Margaret III, 178
Steer, Margaret III, 299
Steer, Margaret IV, 165
Steer, Margaret IV, 826
Steer, Margaret IV, 844
Steer, Margaret R. IV, 282
Steer, Margaret R. IV, 283
Steer, Margaret R. IV, 844
Steer, Marget VI, 597
Steer, Marjorie Jean IV, 1004
Steer, Mark VI, 567
Steer, Martha IV, 171
Steer, Martha IV, 281
Steer, Martha IV, 584
Steer, Martha IV, 797
Steer, Mary III, 178
Steer, Mary III, 299
Steer, Mary IV, 144
Steer, Mary IV, 160
Steer, Mary IV, 178
Steer, Mary IV, 208
Steer, Mary IV, 281
Steer, Mary IV, 282
Steer, Mary IV, 283
Steer, Mary IV, 396
Steer, Mary IV, 410
Steer, Mary IV, 444
Steer, Mary IV, 575
Steer, Mary IV, 595
Steer, Mary IV, 933
Steer, Mary IV, 1004
Steer, Mary IV, 1077
Steer, Mary VI, 377
Steer, Mary VI, 421
Steer, Mary VI, 428
Steer, Mary VI, 447
Steer, Mary VI, 448
Steer, Mary VI, 482
Steer, Mary VI, 493
Steer, Mary VI, 565
Steer, Mary VI, 566
Steer, Mary VI, 567
Steer, Mary A. III, 299
Steer, Mary A. IV, 844
Steer, Mary A. VI, 565
Steer, Mary Alcie VI, 783
Steer, Mary Alice III, 265
Steer, Mary Alice VI, 772
Steer, Mary Alice VI, 783
Steer, Mary C. IV, 171
Steer, Mary C. IV, 213
Steer, Mary C. IV, 282
Steer, Mary C. IV, 283
Steer, Mary C. IV, 797
Steer, Mary C. IV, 815
Steer, Mary C. IV, 839
Steer, Mary C. IV, 844
Steer, Mary Elizabeth IV, 1004
Steer, Mary Esther VI, 476
Steer, Mary Esther VI, 567
Steer, Mary F. III, 299
Steer, Mary F. VI, 478
Steer, Mary F. VI, 488
Steer, Mary F. VI, 561
Steer, Mary F. VI, 565
Steer, Mary F. VI, 566
Steer, Mary F. VI, 567
Steer, Mary F. VI, 783
Steer, Mary Frances VI, 488
Steer, Mary G. IV, 282
Steer, Mary G. IV, 283
Steer, Mary G. IV, 375
Steer, Mary G. IV, 444
Steer, Mary I. VI, 509
Steer, Mary I. VI, 567
Steer, Mary Isabel VI, 566
Steer, Mary J. IV, 176
Steer, Mary J. IV, 282
Steer, Mary J. IV, 310
Steer, Mary Jane IV, 171
Steer, Mary Jane IV, 180
Steer, Mary Jane IV, 225
Steer, Mary Jane IV, 281
Steer, Mary Jane IV, 282
Steer, Mary Jane IV, 283
Steer, Mary Jane IV, 366
Steer, Mary Jane IV, 513
Steer, Mary Jane IV, 552
Steer, Mary Louise VI, 561
Steer, Mary Louise VI, 565
Steer, Mary Louise VI, 567
Steer, Mary M. VI, 492
Steer, Mary M. VI, 567
Steer, Mary McP VI, 566
Steer, Mary McPherson VI, 566
Steer, Mary McPherson VI, 783
Steer, Mary S. IV, 181
Steer, Mary S. IV, 366
Steer, Mary T. VI, 567
Steer, Mary T. VI, 568
Steer, Mary W. IV, 243
Steer, Mary W. IV, 281
Steer, Mary W. IV, 283
Steer, Meribah IV, 1004
Steer, Millicent IV, 815
Steer, Millicent IV, 844
Steer, Millicent H. IV, 282
Steer, Millicent H. IV, 283
Steer, Millicent H. IV, 815
Steer, Millicent H. IV, 844
Steer, Miriam Ellen VI, 567
Steer, Miriam Ellen VI, 568
Steer, Moses IV, 1004
Steer, Naomi VI, 592
Steer, Nathan IV, 171
Steer, Nathan IV, 176
Steer, Nathan IV, 180
Steer, Nathan IV, 225
Steer, Nathan IV, 281
Steer, Nathan IV, 282
Steer, Nathan IV, 283
Steer, Nathan IV, 310
Steer, Nathan IV, 366
Steer, Nathan IV, 513
Steer, Nathan IV, 551
Steer, Nathan IV, 552
Steer, Nathan IV, 1004
Steer, Nellie IV, 1004
Steer, Nicholas VI, 490
Steer, Nicholas VI, 565
Steer, Nicholas VI, 567
Steer, Noami VI, 593
Steer, Obed VI, 548
Steer, Phebe IV, 154
Steer, Phebe IV, 160
Steer, Phebe IV, 204
Steer, Phebe IV, 252
Steer, Phebe IV, 281
Steer, Phebe IV, 282
Steer, Phebe IV, 283
Steer, Phebe IV, 1354
Steer, Phebe IV, 1380
Steer, Phebe IV, 1382
Steer, Phebe VI, 402
Steer, Phebe VI, 421
Steer, Phebe VI, 447
Steer, Phebe VI, 448
Steer, Phebe VI, 482
Steer, Phebe VI, 507
Steer, Phebe VI, 512
Steer, Phebe VI, 536
Steer, Phebe VI, 554
Steer, Phebe VI, 565
Steer, Phebe VI, 567
Steer, Phebe VI, 568
Steer, Phebe VI, 583
Steer, Phebe VI, 584
Steer, Phebe VI, 767
Steer, Phebe A. IV, 283
Steer, Phebe Anna IV, 281
Steer, Phebe Elma IV, 281
Steer, Phebe M. VI, 783
Steer, Phebe Moore VI, 566
Steer, Phebe Moore VI, 783
Steer, Phebe S. IV, 204
Steer, Phineas J. VI, 567
Steer, Phineas J. VI, 783
Steer, Phinneas VI, 418
Steer, Phinneas J. VI, 566
Steer, Rachel IV, 160
Steer, Rachel IV, 231
Steer, Rachel IV, 243
Steer, Rachel IV, 281
Steer, Rachel IV, 282
Steer, Rachel IV, 283
Steer, Rachel VI, 448
Steer, Rachel VI, 493
Steer, Rachel VI, 523
Steer, Rachel VI, 551
Steer, Rachel VI, 554
Steer, Rachel VI, 565
Steer, Rachel VI, 566
Steer, Rachel VI, 567
Steer, Rachel VI, 592
Steer, Rachel VI, 593
Steer, Rachel VI, 603
Steer, Rachel VI, 604
Steer, Rachel VI, 696
Steer, Rachel VI, 702
Steer, Rachel G. IV, 281
Steer, Rachel G. IV, 283
Steer, Rachel G. IV, 444
Steer, Rachel Jane VI, 568
Steer, Rachel Louisa VI, 478
Steer, Rachel Louisa VI, 555
Steer, Rachel Louisa VI, 557
Steer, Rachel Louisa VI, 566
Steer, Rachel Louisa VI, 567
Steer, Rachel Louise VI, 734
Steer, Rachel Louise VI, 776
Steer, Ralph C. IV, 1004
Steer, Rebecca IV, 171
Steer, Rebecca IV, 179
Steer, Rebecca IV, 281
Steer, Rebecca IV, 283
Steer, Rebecca IV, 368
Steer, Rebecca IV, 430
Steer, Rebecca IV, 444
Steer, Rebecca IV, 451
Steer, Rebecca IV, 768
Steer, Rebecca IV, 797
Steer, Rebecca IV, 844
Steer, Rebecca IV, 1077
Steer, Rebecca B. IV, 255
Steer, Rebecca B. IV, 264
Steer, Rebecca B. IV, 282
Steer, Rebecca B. IV, 283
Steer, Rebecca B. IV, 299
Steer, Rebecca B. IV, 844
Steer, Rebecca Elizabeth VI, 566
Steer, Rebecca S. IV, 366
Steer, Rebecka VI, 497
Steer, Rebeka VI, 567
Steer, Richard IV, 281
Steer, Richard A. IV, 283
Steer, Richard Arthur IV, 282
Steer, Robert M. VI, 565
Steer, Robert M. VI, 566
Steer, Robert M. VI, 567
Steer, Robert M. VI, 783
Steer, Ruanna IV, 281
Steer, Ruanna IV, 283
Steer, Ruanna IV, 375
Steer, Ruanna IV, 444
Steer, Ruanna Bundy IV, 444
Steer, Rue Ann VI, 548
Steer, Ruth II, 659
Steer, Ruth IV, 160
Steer, Ruth IV, 164
Steer, Ruth IV, 171
Steer, Ruth IV, 243
Steer, Ruth IV, 272
Steer, Ruth IV, 281
Steer, Ruth IV, 282
Steer, Ruth IV, 434
Steer, Ruth IV, 444
Steer, Ruth IV, 552
Steer, Ruth IV, 558
Steer, Ruth VI, 448
Steer, Ruth VI, 565
Steer, Ruth VI, 566
Steer, Ruth VI, 567
Steer, S. Louisa IV, 254
Steer, S. Louiza IV, 176
Steer, S. Louiza IV, 235
Steer, Samuel IV, 160
Steer, Samuel IV, 281
Steer, Samuel IV, 282
Steer, Samuel IV, 404
Steer, Samuel IV, 444
Steer, Samuel V, 933
Steer, Samuel VI, 529
Steer, Samuel VI, 593
Steer, Samuel L. III, 299
Steer, Samuel L. VI, 506
Steer, Samuel L. VI, 510
Steer, Samuel L. VI, 567
Steer, Samuel L. VI, 568
Steer, Samuel L. VI, 571
Steer, Samuel L. VI, 576
Steer, Samuel R. VI, 565
Steer, Sara Mildred IV, 1004
Steer, Sarah IV, 160
Steer, Sarah IV, 165
Steer, Sarah IV, 269
Steer, Sarah IV, 281
Steer, Sarah IV, 282
Steer, Sarah V, 933
Steer, Sarah VI, 379
Steer, Sarah VI, 448
Steer, Sarah VI, 492
Steer, Sarah VI, 529
Steer, Sarah VI, 536
Steer, Sarah VI, 541
Steer, Sarah VI, 553
Steer, Sarah VI, 557
Steer, Sarah VI, 565
Steer, Sarah VI, 566
Steer, Sarah VI, 567
Steer, Sarah VI, 767
Steer, Sarah VI, 783
Steer, Sarah A. VI, 568
Steer, Sarah A. VI, 576
Steer, Sarah Ann VI, 565
Steer, Sarah Ann VI, 567
Steer, Sarah Ann VI, 568
Steer, Sarah Ann VI, 576
Steer, Sarah Anne VI, 448
Steer, Sarah E. IV, 264
Steer, Sarah E. IV, 282
Steer, Sarah E. IV, 430
Steer, Sarah E. IV, 444
Steer, Sarah Jane IV, 1368
Steer, Sarah Jane IV, 1380
Steer, Sarah L. IV, 183
Steer, Sarah Louisa IV, 282
Steer, Sarah Louisa IV, 283
Steer, Sarah M. IV, 1004
Steer, Sarah R. IV, 281
Steer, Sarah W. II, 925
Steer, Selina Taber IV, 444
Steer, Selma L. II, 768
Steer, Selma L. II, 769
Steer, Selma L. IV, 444
Steer, Selma L. IV, 446
Steer, Sina IV, 283
Steer, Sina IV, 299
Steer, Sina R. IV, 281
Steer, Sina R. IV, 282
Steer, Sina R. IV, 283
Steer, Sina R. IV, 299
Steer, Sina R. IV, 451
Steer, Susanna IV, 165
Steer, Susanna VI, 380
Steer, Susanna VI, 448
Steer, Virginia VI, 506
Steer, Virginia H. VI, 567
Steer, Walter J. IV, 281
Steer, Walter J. IV, 283
Steer, Wd. Elizabeth Moore VI, 472
Steer, Wd. Grace VI, 384
Steer, Widow Leah VI, 529
Steer, Wilda June IV, 1004
Steer, William III, 178
Steer, William IV, 281
Steer, William IV, 282
Steer, William IV, 283
Steer, William VI, 448
Steer, William VI, 565
Steer, William VI, 566
Steer, William VI, 567
Steer, William VI, 593
Steer, William B. VI, 371
Steer, William B. VI, 448
Steer, William B. VI, 476
Steer, William B. VI, 565

Steer, William B. VI, 783
Steer, William B., Jr. VI, 565
Steer, William E. IV, 281
Steer, William E. VI, 566
Steer, William G. IV, 281
Steer, William G. IV, 283
Steer, William G. IV, 419
Steer, William G. IV, 444
Steer, William H. IV, 283
Steer, William M. IV, 282
Steer, William M. IV, 1380
Steer, Wilmer IV, 282
Steer, Wilmer I. IV, 283
Steer, Wilson IV, 283
Steer, Wilson J. IV, 171
Steer, Wilson J. IV, 213
Steer, Wilson J. IV, 281
Steer, Wilson J. IV, 282
Steer, Wilson J. IV, 283
Steer, Wilson J. IV, 366
Steer, Wilson J. IV, 797
Steer, Wilson J. IV, 815
Steer, Wilson J. IV, 844
Steer, Wm. III, 299
Steer, Wm. VI, 568
Steer, Wm. B. VI, 568
Steer, Wm. G. IV, 246
Steer, Wm. G. IV, 282
Steer, Wm. G. IV, 430
Steer, Wm. G. IV, 444
Steer, Wm. G. IV, 1073
Steer, Wm. G. IV, 1077
Steere, Benjamin VI, 741
Steere, Elizabeth II, 953
Steere, Jonathan M. I, 75
Steerman, John VI, 997
Steerman, Nancy VI, 997
Steerman, Vintner VI, 1013
Steerman, Vintner C. VI, 997
Steerman, William VI, 997
Steers, ??? IV, 915
Steers, Lavina IV, 915
Steet, Rachel Louisa VI, 556
Steeves, Alfred J. IV, 768
Steeves, Edith IV, 768
Steeves, Edith L. IV, 769
Steeves, Elma T. IV, 769
Steeves, Elmer T. IV, 768
Steeves, Flora IV, 768
Steeves, Isabel Edith IV, 769
Steeves, Isabelle IV, 768
Steffenson, Helen V, 206
Steffenson, Maggie V, 206
Steffenson, Marshal V, 206
Steffey, Julia Ann IV, 833
Steffey, Julia Ann IV, 844
Stehl, Edward Rich III, 299
Stehl, George III, 299
Stehl, George Christopher III, 299
Stehl, Richard E. III, 299
Stehl, Wilhelmine III, 299
Stehle, Margaret E. II, 703
Stehle, Margaret E. II, 738
Stehle, Margaret E. II, 768
Steiger, Caroline III, 152
Steiger, Caroline III, 339
Steiger, David II, 768
Steigle, George IV, 61
Stein, Anna IV, 1004
Stein, Caroline II, 1061
Stein, Freda IV, 1004
Stein, Freda E. IV, 1004
Stein, Henry VI, 997
Stein, John II, 1061
Stein, Lewis A. IV, 1004
Stein, Lydia A. IV, 1004
Stein, Mary A. III, 511
Stein, Mary Ann VI, 997
Steinbarger, John G. V, 765
Steinberger, Laura IV, 1339
Steinberger, Ralph IV, 1339
Steinberger, Ralph D. IV, 1339
Steiner, C. Charles IV, 283
Steiner, Ina III, 299
Steiner, Ina F. III, 51
Steiner, Jesse IV, 283
Steiner, Martha III, 222
Steiner, Martha III, 299
Steiner, Violet IV, 283
Steinhauser, ??? III, 274
Steinhauser, Henry B. III, 299
Steinhauser, Mary III, 274
Steinhauser, Mary III, 299
Steinhauser, Muriel III, 274
Steinhauser, Muriel R. III, 299
Steiniger, Clara II, 717
Steinman, Edith V, 206
Stell, Frances VI, 928
Stelling, Lydia III, 299
Stells, John II, 448
Stells, Priscilla II, 448
Stells, Robert II, 448
Steman, Belle V, 1020
Steman, Hertha V, 1020
Steman, Luca V, 1020
Stemmons, Jacob VI, 304
Stemmons, Jacob VI, 803
Stemmons, Jacob VI, 855
Stemmons, Nancy VI, 855
Stemp, Louisa V, 1020
Stemple, John II, 1029
Stemple, Rose IV, 1339
Step, Elizabeth VI, 866
Step, Morrica VI, 824
Step, Patsey VI, 824
Step, Sarah VI, 866
Stephanian, Acabe III, 224
Stephanian, Acabe III, 299
Stephans, Hannah V, 490
Stephen, Abigail IV, 552
Stephen, Addie IV, 284
Stephen, Alexander IV, 283
Stephen, Amos L. IV, 283
Stephen, Ann IV, 283
Stephen, Ann IV, 1077
Stephen, Anna IV, 526
Stephen, Anna IV, 541
Stephen, Anna IV, 552
Stephen, Anna IV, 1077
Stephen, Anna D. IV, 284
Stephen, Anna D. IV, 1078
Stephen, Anna M. IV, 552
Stephen, Barclay IV, 444
Stephen, Barclay IV, 552
Stephen, Catharine IV, 160
Stephen, Catharine IV, 283
Stephen, Catharine IV, 284
Stephen, Catharine IV, 552
Stephen, Clarence IV, 283
Stephen, Clarence M. IV, 284
Stephen, David I, 575
Stephen, David IV, 283
Stephen, David IV, 284
Stephen, David IV, 444
Stephen, David IV, 514
Stephen, David IV, 526
Stephen, David IV, 541
Stephen, David IV, 542
Stephen, David IV, 552
Stephen, David IV, 554
Stephen, David IV, 1077
Stephen, David IV, 1116
Stephen, Deborah IV, 284
Stephen, Deborah IV, 1078
Stephen, Elenor IV, 284
Stephen, Eliza IV, 283
Stephen, Eliza IV, 444
Stephen, Eliza IV, 514
Stephen, Eliza IV, 542
Stephen, Eliza IV, 552
Stephen, Eliza M. IV, 526
Stephen, Eliza M. IV, 552
Stephen, Eliza M. IV, 580
Stephen, Eliza M. IV, 595
Stephen, Elizabeth II, 610
Stephen, Elizabeth IV, 276
Stephen, Elizabeth IV, 283
Stephen, Elizabeth IV, 284
Stephen, Elizabeth IV, 552
Stephen, Elizabeth IV, 1077
Stephen, Elizabeth IV, 1116
Stephen, Ella V, 206
Stephen, Ellenor IV, 283
Stephen, Elsworth IV, 284
Stephen, Elwood IV, 1077
Stephen, Esther IV, 283
Stephen, Even I, 575
Stephen, Florence E. IV, 284
Stephen, Florence Lukens IV, 283
Stephen, Francina IV, 284
Stephen, Francina IV, 538
Stephen, Francina IV, 552
Stephen, Grace M. IV, 283
Stephen, Grace M. IV, 284
Stephen, Harry W. IV, 283
Stephen, Isaac IV, 283
Stephen, J. William IV, 284
Stephen, James IV, 284
Stephen, John II, 423
Stephen, Jonah IV, 284
Stephen, Jonathan I, 575
Stephen, Jonathan IV, 283
Stephen, Joseph IV, 283
Stephen, Josiah IV, 284
Stephen, Josiah IV, 1078
Stephen, Julia IV, 284
Stephen, Laura IV, 283
Stephen, Lemuel IV, 284
Stephen, Lewis IV, 283
Stephen, Louis IV, 284
Stephen, Lydia IV, 1077
Stephen, Lydia T. IV, 1077
Stephen, Mahala IV, 284
Stephen, Margaret Anna IV, 283
Stephen, Margaret Anna IV, 284
Stephen, Mary I, 575
Stephen, Mary IV, 283
Stephen, Mary J. IV, 552
Stephen, Mary Jane IV, 552
Stephen, Mrs. Anna IV, 284
Stephen, Mrs. Maggie IV, 284
Stephen, Phancinah IV, 283
Stephen, Phebe IV, 284
Stephen, Phebe IV, 1078
Stephen, Rachel D. IV, 1077
Stephen, Rachel E. IV, 542
Stephen, Rachel E. IV, 552
Stephen, Rachel Esther IV, 552
Stephen, Rebecca IV, 284
Stephen, Rebecca IV, 1077
Stephen, Rebecca IV, 1078
Stephen, Rebecca L. IV, 276
Stephen, Rebecca L. IV, 283
Stephen, Robert IV, 284
Stephen, Sadie IV, 284
Stephen, Samuel IV, 276
Stephen, Samuel IV, 283
Stephen, Samuel IV, 284
Stephen, Samuel IV, 552
Stephen, Samuel IV, 1078
Stephen, Samuel VI, 644
Stephen, Samuel C. IV, 284
Stephen, Sarah IV, 283
Stephen, Sarah IV, 284
Stephen, Sarah IV, 552
Stephen, Sarah IV, 554
Stephen, Sarah IV, 1116
Stephen, Sarah A. IV, 284
Stephen, Sarah Elizabeth IV, 284
Stephen, Sarah T. IV, 552
Stephen, Silas IV, 160
Stephen, Silas IV, 283
Stephen, Silas IV, 284
Stephen, Silas IV, 552
Stephen, Sylas IV, 552
Stephen, Texana IV, 284
Stephen, Thos. IV, 283
Stephen, Ursilla I, 575
Stephen, Viley IV, 283
Stephen, William IV, 283
Stephen, William IV, 284
Stephen, William IV, 444
Stephen, William D. IV, 1077
Stephen, William H. IV, 284
Stephen, William M. IV, 284
Stephen, Wilson IV, 444
Stephen, Wilson IV, 552
Stephen, Wm. M. IV, 1078
Stephen, Zachariah IV, 283
Stephen, Zachariah IV, 552
Stephen, Zachariah IV, 1077
Stephen, Zachariah IV, 1116
Stephens, ??? III, 299
Stephens, Abel I, 517
Stephens, Abel I, 575
Stephens, Abigail IV, 552
Stephens, Alice V, 465
Stephens, Allie V, 1020
Stephens, Alonzo V, 127
Stephens, Alonzo V, 206
Stephens, Alpha V, 127
Stephens, Alpha V, 206
Stephens, Alpheus V, 433
Stephens, Amos L. IV, 1077
Stephens, Amos L. IV, 1078
Stephens, Amy II, 768
Stephens, Ann II, 264
Stephens, Ann II, 925
Stephens, Ann II, 926
Stephens, Ann IV, 283
Stephens, Ann IV, 298
Stephens, Ann IV, 1077
Stephens, Ann IV, 1078
Stephens, Ann V, 933
Stephens, Ann B. V, 465
Stephens, Ann T. V, 837
Stephens, Ann T. V, 863
Stephens, Anna IV, 552
Stephens, Anna IV, 1069
Stephens, Anna IV, 1077
Stephens, Anna D. IV, 1078
Stephens, Anna M. IV, 1078
Stephens, Augusta V, 465
Stephens, Barclay IV, 552
Stephens, Barlow V, 127
Stephens, Benjamin II, 660
Stephens, Bertha B. V, 465
Stephens, Bessie E. V, 467
Stephens, Bethania W. VI, 998
Stephens, Caroline IV, 1078
Stephens, Caroline IV, 1079
Stephens, Cary V, 1020
Stephens, Cassius V, 280
Stephens, Cassius V, 465
Stephens, Catharine IV, 518
Stephens, Catharine IV, 552
Stephens, Catharine IV, 1116
Stephens, Catharine VI, 998
Stephens, Catherine IV, 1116
Stephens, Charles II, 719
Stephens, Charles II, 768
Stephens, Charley V, 465
Stephens, Chlo V, 465
Stephens, Chloe V, 465
Stephens, Cloyd V, 1020
Stephens, Cornelius II, 423
Stephens, Cornelius V, 280
Stephens, Cornelius V, 465
Stephens, Daniel B. VI, 1018
Stephens, David I, 517
Stephens, David I, 575
Stephens, David I, 668
Stephens, David IV, 519
Stephens, David IV, 552
Stephens, David IV, 1069
Stephens, David IV, 1077
Stephens, David IV, 1116
Stephens, David IV, 1117
Stephens, David James V, 433
Stephens, Deborah IV, 1078
Stephens, Deborah V, 342
Stephens, Deborah V, 360
Stephens, Deborah V, 433
Stephens, Dennis V, 645
Stephens, Donald L. V, 645
Stephens, Earl V, 1020
Stephens, Earle V, 1020
Stephens, Edmond II, 423
Stephens, Elam I, 1162
Stephens, Eleanor V, 424
Stephens, Eleanor V, 433
Stephens, Eliza I, 575
Stephens, Eliza IV, 519
Stephens, Elizabeth II, 423
Stephens, Elizabeth II, 660
Stephens, Elizabeth II, 821
Stephens, Elizabeth II, 926
Stephens, Elizabeth IV, 218
Stephens, Elizabeth IV, 220
Stephens, Elizabeth IV, 283
Stephens, Elizabeth IV, 552
Stephens, Elizabeth IV, 1063
Stephens, Elizabeth IV, 1077
Stephens, Elizabeth IV, 1078
Stephens, Elizabeth IV, 1080
Stephens, Elizabeth IV, 1116
Stephens, Elizabeth V, 465
Stephens, Elizabeth VI, 729
Stephens, Elizabeth VI, 805
Stephens, Elizabeth VI, 882
Stephens, Elizabeth VI, 998
Stephens, Ella V, 127
Stephens, Ella V, 206
Stephens, Ella V, 280
Stephens, Ellen II, 793
Stephens, Elwood IV, 1077
Stephens, Elwood IV, 1078
Stephens, Elwood V, 465
Stephens, Emily II, 660
Stephens, Emily III, 299
Stephens, Enoch I, 575
Stephens, Ester I, 839
Stephens, Esther I, 517
Stephens, Esther I, 575
Stephens, Esther IV, 1077
Stephens, Esther V, 357
Stephens, Esther V, 360
Stephens, Eva B. V, 933
Stephens, Evan I, 517
Stephens, Evan I, 544
Stephens, Evan I, 575
Stephens, Evan I, 839
Stephens, Evan II, 448
Stephens, Evan V, 360
Stephens, Evan V, 374
Stephens, Evan V, 433
Stephens, Even I, 517
Stephens, Even, Jr. I, 575
Stephens, Evin I, 839
Stephens, Francina IV, 552
Stephens, Francina IV, 1116
Stephens, Francinah IV, 1116
Stephens, Frederick S. III, 299
Stephens, Gedion I, 517
Stephens, George I, 517
Stephens, George I, 575
Stephens, George II, 660
Stephens, Gideon I, 575
Stephens, Gideon I, 804
Stephens, Gideon I, 839
Stephens, Gideon V, 126
Stephens, Gideon V, 280
Stephens, Gideon V, 342
Stephens, Gideon V, 357
Stephens, Gideon V, 360
Stephens, Gideon V, 433
Stephens, Grant V, 1020
Stephens, Hallie A. V, 127
Stephens, Hannah I, 991
Stephens, Hannah I, 998
Stephens, Hannah II, 264
Stephens, Hannah V, 490
Stephens, Hannah V, 532
Stephens, Hannah V, 933
Stephens, Harry V, 127
Stephens, Henry II, 768
Stephens, Henry VI, 1019
Stephens, Howard Wilson V, (
Stephens, Hulda A. V, 433
Stephens, Huldah Ann V, 433
Stephens, Ida V, 933
Stephens, Ida M. V, 933
Stephens, Ira P. I, 1162
Stephens, Isaac II, 264
Stephens, Isaac IV, 1077
Stephens, Isaac IV, 1078
Stephens, Isaac V, 933
Stephens, Isaac, Jr. V, 921
Stephens, Isaac, Jr. V, 933
Stephens, Jabez I, 839
Stephens, Jacob II, 264
Stephens, Jacob V, 933
Stephens, Jacob VI, 797
Stephens, James II, 423
Stephens, James II, 612
Stephens, James II, 660
Stephens, James II, 685
Stephens, James VI, 848
Stephens, Jane II, 423
Stephens, Jesse II, 821
Stephens, John I, 517
Stephens, John I, 575
Stephens, John II, 101
Stephens, John II, 423
Stephens, John V, 433
Stephens, John V, 465
Stephens, John VI, 847
Stephens, John VI, 998
Stephens, John VI, 1009
Stephens, John M. VI, 998
Stephens, John W. V, 465
Stephens, Jonathan I, 517
Stephens, Jonathan I, 668
Stephens, Jonathan I, 1038
Stephens, Jonathan IV, 220
Stephens, Jonathan IV, 1077
Stephens, Joseph IV, 1078
Stephens, Josiah IV, 1078
Stephens, Judith V, 933
Stephens, Judith G. V, 933
Stephens, Julia IV, 284
Stephens, Julia V, 280
Stephens, Leo M. V, 712
Stephens, Lewis V, 645
Stephens, Lucinda V, 712
Stephens, Lydia I, 575
Stephens, Lydia I, 579
Stephens, Lydia IV, 1077
Stephens, Lydia V, 280
Stephens, Lydia V, 360
Stephens, Lydia V, 921
Stephens, Lydia V, 933
Stephens, Lydia Elva V, 433
Stephens, Lydia M. V, 933
Stephens, Lydia T. IV, 1077
Stephens, Madge V, 465
Stephens, Martha V, 886
Stephens, Martha V, 888
Stephens, Mary I, 575
Stephens, Mary I, 804
Stephens, Mary I, 839
Stephens, Mary I, 1162
Stephens, Mary II, 423
Stephens, Mary II, 660
Stephens, Mary II, 685
Stephens, Mary V, 126
Stephens, Mary V, 280
Stephens, Mary V, 342
Stephens, Mary V, 357
Stephens, Mary V, 360
Stephens, Mary V, 433
Stephens, Mary V, 465
Stephens, Mary VI, 1018
Stephens, Mary Alma V, 433
Stephens, Mary Ann II, 768
Stephens, Mary B. VI, 877
Stephens, Mary J. II, 926
Stephens, Mary J. IV, 220
Stephens, Mary J. IV, 519
Stephens, Mary James II, 821
Stephens, Mary Jane IV, 552
Stephens, Matilda VI, 998
Stephens, Moses C. IV, 942
Stephens, Myrtla Stout V, 465

ens, Myrtle V, 465
ens, Nancy I, 575
ens, Nancy VI, 848
ens, Naomi I, 575
ens, Naomi I, 839
ens, Neoma I, 517
ens, Neomi I, 575
ens, Noah V, 1020
ens, Norma Pearl V, 465
ens, Paulina V, 433
ens, Paulina Ann V, 433
ens, Peggy VI, 797
ens, Pelena V, 407
ens, Pelena V, 433
ens, Permelia J. V, 433
ens, Permelia Jane V, 433
ens, Phebe I, 575
ens, Phebe I, 580
ens, Phebe IV, 1078
ens, Phebe B. VI, 888
ens, Polly VI, 933
ens, Polly VI, 1009
ens, Priscilla V, 374
ens, Priscilla V, 433
ens, Prudence I, 575
ens, Prudence I, 668
ens, Rachel IV, 423
ens, Rachel D. IV, 1077
ens, Ralph II, 448
ens, Rebecca IV, 314
ens, Rebecca IV, 315
ens, Rebecca IV, 1077
ens, Rebecca IV, 1078
ens, Rebecca S. IV, 1077
ens, Robert I, 575
ens, Robert VI, 847
ens, Robert VI, 998
ens, Sally VI, 855
ens, Samuel IV, 552
ens, Samuel IV, 1077
ens, Samuel IV, 1078
ens, Samuel IV, 1116
ens, Samuel V, 126
ens, Samuel V, 280
ens, Samuel V, 360
ens, Sarah I, 839
ens, Sarah II, 264
ens, Sarah II, 612
hens, Sarah II, 660
hens, Sarah II, 812
hens, Sarah IV, 523
hens, Sarah IV, 552
hens, Sarah IV, 1116
hens, Sarah IV, 1117
hens, Sarah T. IV, 552
hens, Sarah T. IV, 1116
hens, Sarah W. II, 264
hens, Silas I, 517
hens, Silas IV, 552
hens, Silas IV, 1116
hens, Simon I, 419
hens, Sophia VI, 847
hens, Stella V, 712
hens, Susannah II, 813
hens, Susannah II, 816
hens, Thomas V, 360
hens, Thomas VI, 855
hens, Thomas VI, 1011
hens, Urcily I, 839
hens, Uriah I, 517
hens, Uriah I, 575
hens, Ursilla I, 839
hens, Ursula I, 517
hens, Ursula I, 544
hens, Ursula I, 575
hens, Vadie V, 1020
hens, Velma V, 1020
hens, Vernon V, 465
hens, Vilee IV, 188
hens, Vilee IV, 283
hens, Vincent V, 360
hens, Vincent T. V, 360
hens, Violet B. VI, 877
hens, Webster V, 645
hens, Webster E. V, 645
hens, William I, 517
hens, William I, 575
hens, William II, 719
hens, William V, 433
hens, William VI, 11
hens, William VI, 998
hens, William A. V, 360
hens, William D. IV, 1077
hens, William L. V, 433
hens, William W. II, 821
hens, William W. VI, 882
hens, Wilson IV, 552
hens, Wm. VI, 729
hens, Wm. A. V, 360
hens, Wm. M. IV, 1078
hens, Wm. W. II, 926
Stephens, Wm. W. VI, 933
Stephens, Zachariah IV, 1077
Stephens, Zachariah IV, 1116
Stephenson, Adelia B. IV, 1264
Stephenson, Amelia II, 101
Stephenson, Ann II, 660
Stephenson, Arthur VI, 87
Stephenson, B. W. I, 575
Stephenson, Belle V, 679
Stephenson, Berny I, 575
Stephenson, Briner L. IV, 1264
Stephenson, Christian VI, 62
Stephenson, Christian VI, 87
Stephenson, Conley VI, 87
Stephenson, Curtis S. IV, 1264
Stephenson, Daniel II, 101
Stephenson, Dorcas I, 770
Stephenson, Dorcus I, 770
Stephenson, Dwight V, 678
Stephenson, Dwight V, 712
Stephenson, Edward II, 424
Stephenson, Emily I, 575
Stephenson, Emma V, 433
Stephenson, Emma V, 712
Stephenson, Gawen II, 660
Stephenson, Hannah II, 745
Stephenson, Hannah II, 768
Stephenson, Ibba I, 575
Stephenson, Isabelle I, 559
Stephenson, Isabelle I, 575
Stephenson, James V, 280
Stephenson, James VI, 82
Stephenson, James VI, 388
Stephenson, James H. IV, 1264
Stephenson, James R. VI, 57
Stephenson, James R. VI, 87
Stephenson, John I, 575
Stephenson, John I, 597
Stephenson, John II, 101
Stephenson, John V, 280
Stephenson, John V, 645
Stephenson, John VI, 87
Stephenson, John H. VI, 87
Stephenson, John R. V, 645
Stephenson, John Robert I, 597
Stephenson, Josiah II, 264
Stephenson, Lafayette VI, 68
Stephenson, Lafayette VI, 82
Stephenson, Lafayette VI, 87
Stephenson, Levina VI, 82
Stephenson, Ludia I, 575
Stephenson, Lydia I, 575
Stephenson, Maggie VI, 87
Stephenson, Maggie A. VI, 82
Stephenson, Maggie A. VI, 91
Stephenson, Mahlon I, 1132
Stephenson, Mahlon I, 1137
Stephenson, Mahlon I, 1162
Stephenson, Mahlon I, 1163
Stephenson, Margaret II, 155
Stephenson, Margaret II, 158
Stephenson, Margaret A. VI, 68
Stephenson, Margaret A. VI, 87
Stephenson, Margaret H. II, 158
Stephenson, Marshall IV, 1264
Stephenson, Martha VI, 85
Stephenson, Martha VI, 87
Stephenson, Mary I, 596
Stephenson, Mary I, 597
Stephenson, Mary I, 1099
Stephenson, Mary II, 101
Stephenson, Mary IV, 24
Stephenson, Mary V, 599
Stephenson, Mary V, 645
Stephenson, Mary V, 678
Stephenson, Mary V, 712
Stephenson, Mary VI, 87
Stephenson, Mary A. VI, 57
Stephenson, Mary A. VI, 87
Stephenson, Melvina I, 597
Stephenson, Milly VI, 821
Stephenson, Milly VI, 855
Stephenson, Nancy I, 575
Stephenson, Nancy I, 597
Stephenson, Nicholas I, 1099
Stephenson, Nicholas I, 1162
Stephenson, Owen C. Williams I, 1162
Stephenson, Phebe I, 575
Stephenson, Priscilla II, 264
Stephenson, Prudence I, 690
Stephenson, Rebecca I, 575
Stephenson, Rebecca VI, 87
Stephenson, Richmond VI, 87
Stephenson, Robert I, 575
Stephenson, Robert V, 599
Stephenson, Ruth Hodgin I, 641
Stephenson, Ruth Sarah VI, 708
Stephenson, Ruth Sarah VI, 717
Stephenson, Samuel VI, 855
Stephenson, Sarah I, 419
Stephenson, Sarah II, 984
Stephenson, Sarah II, 1029
Stephenson, Sarah VI, 87
Stephenson, Sarah VI, 448
Stephenson, Sarah VI, 821
Stephenson, Sarah Edna VI, 388
Stephenson, Seth II, 302
Stephenson, Sophia VI, 856
Stephenson, Wiley VI, 855
Stephenson, Wiley VI, 856
Stephenson, William II, 264
Stephenson, William T. VI, 87
Stephenson, Winny A. VI, 855
Stephenson, Wm. II, 101
Stephenson, Wm. T. VI, 85
Stephinson, John I, 597
Stepley, Annie M. VI, 377
Stepley, Annie M. VI, 437
Stepp, Dicey VI, 823
Stepp, Elizabeth VI, 845
Stepp, James VI, 856
Stepp, Jane VI, 845
Stepp, Jenny VI, 862
Stepp, John VI, 853
Stepp, John VI, 854
Stepp, John VI, 856
Stepp, Joseph VI, 823
Stepp, Joseph VI, 855
Stepp, Joseph VI, 856
Stepp, Joseph VI, 862
Stepp, Martha VI, 856
Stepp, Martin VI, 856
Stepp, Mary VI, 862
Stepp, Mary S. VI, 856
Stepp, Mourning VI, 856
Stepp, Nancy VI, 855
Stepp, Nancy VI, 856
Stepp, Patsy VI, 856
Stepp, Soloman VI, 856
Steppe, Anne VI, 801
Steppe, Elizabeth VI, 849
Steppe, John VI, 801
Steppen, John VI, 849
Steptoe, Catharine Louisa VI, 998
Steptoe, E. D. VI, 938
Steptoe, Elizabeth VI, 998
Steptoe, Elizabeth J. VI, 916
Steptoe, Elizabeth P. VI, 325
Steptoe, Elizabeth P. VI, 829
Steptoe, Elizabeth R. VI, 981
Steptoe, Fanny VI, 998
Steptoe, Frances VI, 832
Steptoe, Frances C. VI, 887
Steptoe, George VI, 325
Steptoe, George VI, 829
Steptoe, George VI, 916
Steptoe, J. C. VI, 913
Steptoe, J. C. VI, 947
Steptoe, James VI, 325
Steptoe, James VI, 832
Steptoe, James VI, 839
Steptoe, James VI, 846
Steptoe, James VI, 883
Steptoe, James VI, 920
Steptoe, James VI, 961
Steptoe, James VI, 977
Steptoe, James VI, 990
Steptoe, James VI, 998
Steptoe, James VI, 1021
Steptoe, James C. VI, 887
Steptoe, James C. VI, 966
Steptoe, James C. VI, 971
Steptoe, James C. VI, 985
Steptoe, James L. VI, 326
Steptoe, James P. VI, 893
Steptoe, James, Sr. VI, 977
Steptoe, Jas. C. VI, 931
Steptoe, Jno. D. VI, 935
Steptoe, Jno. R. VI, 912
Steptoe, Jno. R. VI, 916
Steptoe, Jno. R. VI, 918
Steptoe, Jno. R. VI, 919
Steptoe, Jno. R. VI, 931
Steptoe, Jno. R. VI, 933
Steptoe, Jno. R. VI, 950
Steptoe, Jno. R. VI, 952
Steptoe, Jno. R. VI, 954
Steptoe, Jno. R. VI, 955
Steptoe, Jno. R. VI, 975
Steptoe, Jno. R. VI, 981
Steptoe, Jno. R. VI, 1003
Steptoe, Jno. R. VI, 1018
Steptoe, Jno. R. VI, 1019
Steptoe, John W. VI, 326
Steptoe, Lucy VI, 846
Steptoe, Lucy VI, 977
Steptoe, Mary Ann VI, 893
Steptoe, Milly VI, 326
Steptoe, Moorman VI, 326
Steptoe, Robert C. VI, 839
Steptoe, Robert C. VI, 981
Steptoe, Robert C. VI, 998
Steptoe, Sarah VI, 839
Steptoe, Thomas VI, 884
Steptoe, Thomas VI, 998
Sterardson, Rachel II, 660
Sterart, Grace II, 739
Stergion, Levi V, 765
Sterle, Mary II, 448
Sterling, Ann E. VI, 983
Sterling, Ann Eliza II, 822
Sterling, Anne B. II, 926
Sterling, Caroline IV, 284
Sterling, Dallas M. IV, 284
Sterling, Edith II, 926
Sterling, Edith II, 940
Sterling, Edith Weatherby II, 311
Sterling, Elizabeth VI, 998
Sterling, Floyd IV, 284
Sterling, George II, 424
Sterling, Hannah II, 821
Sterling, Hannah II, 926
Sterling, Hannah II, 940
Sterling, Homer IV, 1295
Sterling, James Smith II, 821
Sterling, James Smith II, 926
Sterling, James Smith II, 940
Sterling, Louisa IV, 284
Sterling, Mabel V, 1020
Sterling, Margaret IV, 284
Sterling, Margaret J. IV, 284
Sterling, Martha II, 424
Sterling, Montgomery IV, 284
Sterling, Nancy VI, 983
Sterling, Otto IV, 1295
Sterling, Rebecca II, 313
Sterling, Rebecca B. II, 807
Sterling, Samuel IV, 1295
Sterling, Sarah IV, 1295
Sterling, Sarah Ann V, 1020
Sterling, Thomas VI, 998
Sterling, Thos. II, 926
Sterling, Thos. II, 940
Sterling, Trenton II, 926
Sterling, William Harry IV, 284
Sterman, Frances VI, 998
Sterman, Robert VI, 998
Stern, Ann IV, 61
Stern, B. VI, 824
Stern, Bessie B. II, 843
Stern, Bessie B. II, 926
Stern, Dorothy VI, 824
Stern, Frances A. VI, 856
Stern, Francis VI, 856
Stern, Hettie III, 299
Stern, Hettie III, 338
Stern, L. VI, 825
Stern, Lawrence B. VI, 856
Stern, Louis III, 299
Stern, Louis III, 338
Stern, Lucy VI, 856
Stern, Nancy VI, 825
Stern, Nancy VI, 856
Stern, Peter VI, 831
Stern, Polly VI, 903
Stern, Robert D. VI, 827
Stern, Rosalie III, 299
Stern, Rosalie III, 338
Stern, Susanna VI, 831
Sterne, Ann VI, 110
Sterner, Maud IV, 1187
Sterr, Abigail VI, 606
Sterr, Andrew M'Kay VI, 606
Sterr, David VI, 606
Sterr, Grace VI, 606
Sterr, Isaac VI, 606
Sterr, James VI, 606
Sterr, John Garwood VI, 606
Sterr, Joseph VI, 606
Sterr, Joseph Allen VI, 606
Sterr, Joseph, Jr. VI, 606
Sterr, Joshua VI, 606
Sterr, Lindley B. IV, 184
Sterr, Martha Fearnley VI, 606
Sterr, Mary VI, 606
Sterr, Mary Pusey VI, 606
Sterr, Patience M'Kay VI, 606
Sterr, Phebe VI, 606
Sterr, Rachel VI, 606
Sterr, Ruanna IV, 184
Sterr, Sarah VI, 606
Sterren, Anne IV, 133
Sterrett, Florence III, 245
Sterrett, Florence III, 299
Sterrett, Frank Meade III, 245
Sterrett, Frank Meade III, 299
Sterrett, James W. III, 299
Sterrett, James Woods III, 299
Sterrett, Jas. W. III, 299
Sterrett, Margaret W. III, 299
Sterrit, Francene IV, 1187
Stethen, Levi V, 360
Stetson, Cynthia II, 719
Stetson, Elizabeth III, 121
Stetson, Jennie K. III, 158
Stetson, Jennie K. III, 299
Stetson, John III, 299
Stetson, John B. II, 926
Stetson, John S. III, 158
Stetson, John S. III, 299
Stetson, Sherman Hawxhurst III, 299
Stetson, Walter Kissam III, 299
Steuart, Lorenzo R. VI, 998
Steuart, Sarah Ann VI, 998
Steven, Earl V, 1020
Steven, Elizabeth IV, 514
Steven, Elizabeth IV, 552
Steven, Francina IV, 514
Steven, Jesse IV, 514
Stevenens, Thomas VI, 967
Stevens, Abel I, 517
Stevens, Alice V, 250
Stevens, Alpheus V, 433
Stevens, Amos L. IV, 1078
Stevens, Ann II, 264
Stevens, Ann II, 302
Stevens, Ann II, 925
Stevens, Ann II, 926
Stevens, Ann III, 119
Stevens, Ann III, 248
Stevens, Anna M. IV, 552
Stevens, Asseneth I, 517
Stevens, Beatrice IV, 1339
Stevens, Benjamin II, 660
Stevens, Benjamin III, 299
Stevens, Bethania W. VI, 998
Stevens, Betsey VI, 998
Stevens, Betsy IV, 1236
Stevens, Betsy IV, 1241
Stevens, Caroline C. VI, 856
Stevens, Cassius V, 280
Stevens, Catharine VI, 998
Stevens, Charles VI, 975
Stevens, Charles VI, 998
Stevens, Charles E. Cooper IV, 1004
Stevens, Charles J. III, 299
Stevens, Charles W. VI, 938
Stevens, Charles W. VI, 998
Stevens, Charley IV, 769
Stevens, Chas. Eli IV, 1004
Stevens, Cona VI, 856
Stevens, Cooper IV, 769
Stevens, Cornelius V, 280
Stevens, Daniel B. VI, 998
Stevens, Danl. B. VI, 966
Stevens, David I, 517
Stevens, David I, 534
Stevens, David I, 575
Stevens, Deborah IV, 1064
Stevens, Deborah IV, 1078
Stevens, Deborah V, 406
Stevens, Deborah V, 433
Stevens, Edith IV, 1004
Stevens, Edmond II, 423
Stevens, Edward III, 299
Stevens, Edward Gaskill II, 264
Stevens, Edward, Jr. III, 299
Stevens, Elam I, 1132
Stevens, Elisabeth VI, 955
Stevens, Elizabeth II, 660
Stevens, Elizabeth II, 812
Stevens, Elizabeth VI, 856
Stevens, Elizabeth VI, 998
Stevens, Ella V, 250
Stevens, Ella V, 280
Stevens, Elmira II, 797
Stevens, Elvirah F. VI, 998
Stevens, Emily II, 660
Stevens, Ester I, 839
Stevens, Esther I, 517
Stevens, Esther I, 535
Stevens, Esther I, 575
Stevens, Eva B. V, 933
Stevens, Evan I, 822
Stevens, Evan I, 839
Stevens, Evan V, 360
Stevens, Evelyn III, 431
Stevens, Evelyn III, 448
Stevens, Even I, 575
Stevens, Even, Jr. I, 575
Stevens, Fanny III, 300
Stevens, Frances Eleanor II, 703
Stevens, Frederick W. III, 448
Stevens, George II, 660
Stevens, Guian II, 660
Stevens, Hallie A. V, 127
Stevens, Hannah II, 264
Stevens, Hannah II, 302
Stevens, Hannah II, 325
Stevens, Harry IV, 769

Stevens, Harry V, 127
Stevens, Harry J. IV, 1004
Stevens, Harry J. Cooper IV, 1004
Stevens, Henry V, 250
Stevens, Henry VI, 985
Stevens, Henry VI, 998
Stevens, Henry J. VI, 856
Stevens, Hulda A. V, 433
Stevens, Ida V, 933
Stevens, Ida M. V, 933
Stevens, Ira P. I, 1132
Stevens, Isaac II, 264
Stevens, Isaac II, 302
Stevens, Isaac II, 325
Stevens, Isaac IV, 1078
Stevens, Isaac V, 933
Stevens, Jacob II, 264
Stevens, Jacob II, 302
Stevens, Jacob II, 325
Stevens, Jacob II, 1061
Stevens, Jacob V, 933
Stevens, James II, 423
Stevens, James II, 660
Stevens, James III, 448
Stevens, James VI, 808
Stevens, James VI, 809
Stevens, James VI, 998
Stevens, Jane L. VI, 998
Stevens, Jeremiah P. VI, 796
Stevens, John I, 575
Stevens, John II, 101
Stevens, John II, 423
Stevens, John II, 660
Stevens, John III, 256
Stevens, John III, 300
Stevens, John VI, 856
Stevens, John VI, 877
Stevens, John VI, 998
Stevens, John Campbell III, 448
Stevens, John Henry VI, 1019
Stevens, John M. VI, 998
Stevens, John M. B. VI, 856
Stevens, Judith V, 933
Stevens, Judith G. V, 933
Stevens, Julia V, 280
Stevens, Kezia IV, 58
Stevens, Kezia IV, 61
Stevens, Leo M. V, 712
Stevens, Leota V, 631
Stevens, Loretta E. VI, 998
Stevens, Lucretia II, 264
Stevens, Lydia I, 517
Stevens, Lydia V, 340
Stevens, Lydia V, 360
Stevens, Lydia V, 933
Stevens, M. Wills VI, 998
Stevens, Margaret VI, 998
Stevens, Margaret VI, 1015
Stevens, Margaret M. VI, 856
Stevens, Marie III, 418
Stevens, Marie III, 448
Stevens, Martha VI, 998
Stevens, Martha D. IV, 769
Stevens, Martha D. IV, 1004
Stevens, Mary I, 517
Stevens, Mary I, 534
Stevens, Mary I, 575
Stevens, Mary I, 1132
Stevens, Mary II, 423
Stevens, Mary II, 462
Stevens, Mary II, 628
Stevens, Mary II, 660
Stevens, Mary V, 360
Stevens, Mary VI, 886
Stevens, Mary VI, 998
Stevens, Mary VI, 1009
Stevens, Mary Alma V, 381
Stevens, Mary Alma V, 433
Stevens, Mary B. VI, 998
Stevens, Mary E. IV, 769
Stevens, Mary E. IV, 1004
Stevens, Mary Elizabeth IV, 1004
Stevens, Mary Ella II, 703
Stevens, Mary Emeline VI, 998
Stevens, Mary J. II, 926
Stevens, Mary W. III, 448
Stevens, Matilda VI, 998
Stevens, Mehitabebel VI, 753
Stevens, Mehitabel VI, 733
Stevens, Minnie IV, 1339
Stevens, Moses C. IV, 769
Stevens, Moses C. IV, 942
Stevens, Moses C. IV, 1004
Stevens, Mrs. Maggie IV, 284
Stevens, Nancy I, 517
Stevens, Nancy VI, 998
Stevens, Nancy VI, 1014
Stevens, Naomi I, 822
Stevens, Naomi I, 839
Stevens, Neil Campbell III, 431
Stevens, Neil Campbell III, 448
Stevens, Neoma I, 792
Stevens, Noah V, 1020
Stevens, Paulina VI, 998
Stevens, Pheby I, 517
Stevens, Rebecca IV, 347
Stevens, Rebecca IV, 1078
Stevens, Richard II, 660
Stevens, Robert I, 575
Stevens, Robert VI, 830
Stevens, Robert VI, 920
Stevens, Robert VI, 954
Stevens, Robert VI, 955
Stevens, Robert VI, 998
Stevens, Rollin Howard II, 703
Stevens, Samuel IV, 1078
Stevens, Sarah I, 839
Stevens, Sarah II, 264
Stevens, Sarah II, 573
Stevens, Sarah II, 654
Stevens, Sarah II, 660
Stevens, Sarah III, 256
Stevens, Sarah III, 300
Stevens, Sarah IV, 692
Stevens, Sarah IV, 769
Stevens, Sarah VI, 844
Stevens, Sarah M. IV, 769
Stevens, Sarah M. IV, 1004
Stevens, Sarah T. IV, 1116
Stevens, Sarah W. II, 264
Stevens, Solomon B. VI, 998
Stevens, Stella V, 712
Stevens, Stephen B. VI, 998
Stevens, Stevens IV, 769
Stevens, Susannah VI, 998
Stevens, Theresa IV, 1339
Stevens, Thomas V, 360
Stevens, Thomas VI, 998
Stevens, Ursilla I, 575
Stevens, Vincent V, 360
Stevens, Violet B. VI, 877
Stevens, William VI, 964
Stevens, William VI, 998
Stevens, William A. V, 360
Stevens, William H. VI, 998
Stevens, William M. VI, 952
Stevens, William M. VI, 998
Stevens, William M. VI, 1015
Stevens, William W. VI, 1014
Stevens, William W. VI, 1015
Stevens, Wm. A. V, 360
Stevens, Zilly VI, 998
Stevenson, Alice II, 258
Stevenson, Alice II, 264
Stevenson, Allen II, 448
Stevenson, Amanda V, 599
Stevenson, Amelia II, 41
Stevenson, Amelia II, 58
Stevenson, Amelia II, 79
Stevenson, Amelia II, 101
Stevenson, Amelia II, 111
Stevenson, Ann II, 41
Stevenson, Ann II, 185
Stevenson, Ann II, 235
Stevenson, Ann II, 237
Stevenson, Ann II, 264
Stevenson, Ann II, 298
Stevenson, Ann II, 302
Stevenson, Ann II, 313
Stevenson, Ann II, 323
Stevenson, Ann II, 325
Stevenson, Ann II, 660
Stevenson, Ann III, 300
Stevenson, Ann III, 314
Stevenson, Ann III, 353
Stevenson, Anna II, 185
Stevenson, Anna II, 228
Stevenson, Anna II, 264
Stevenson, Anna II, 313
Stevenson, Anna V, 127
Stevenson, Anna Amelia II, 101
Stevenson, Anna R. V, 127
Stevenson, Anna W. II, 58
Stevenson, Anna W. II, 101
Stevenson, Anna, Jr. II, 302
Stevenson, Anne II, 246
Stevenson, Anne II, 264
Stevenson, Annie L. V, 599
Stevenson, Ashfield II, 264
Stevenson, Bathsheba II, 264
Stevenson, Bathsheba II, 302
Stevenson, Bathsheba II, 313
Stevenson, Bathsheba N. II, 185
Stevenson, Bernice II, 291
Stevenson, Bernice II, 302
Stevenson, Caleb II, 264
Stevenson, Carrie V, 599
Stevenson, Catharine II, 228
Stevenson, Catherine V, 127
Stevenson, Charles II, 41
Stevenson, Charles II, 101
Stevenson, Charlotte V, 127
Stevenson, Charlotte V, 137
Stevenson, Chas. II, 79
Stevenson, Chas. II, 101
Stevenson, Clayton V, 127
Stevenson, Cornel II, 185
Stevenson, Cornel II, 213
Stevenson, Cornel II, 228
Stevenson, Cornel II, 256
Stevenson, Cornel II, 313
Stevenson, Cornell II, 185
Stevenson, Cornell II, 264
Stevenson, Cornell II, 325
Stevenson, Cornwel II, 313
Stevenson, Cornwell II, 264
Stevenson, Daniel II, 41
Stevenson, Daniel II, 101
Stevenson, David II, 302
Stevenson, David II, 313
Stevenson, Deborah II, 185
Stevenson, Deborah II, 213
Stevenson, Deborah II, 264
Stevenson, Edgar V, 599
Stevenson, Edward II, 424
Stevenson, Edward II, 660
Stevenson, Edward III, 170
Stevenson, Edward III, 300
Stevenson, Eliakim II, 185
Stevenson, Elisabeth II, 185
Stevenson, Elizabeth II, 24
Stevenson, Elizabeth II, 185
Stevenson, Elizabeth II, 246
Stevenson, Elizabeth II, 256
Stevenson, Elizabeth II, 264
Stevenson, Elizabeth II, 302
Stevenson, Elizabeth II, 424
Stevenson, Elizabeth II, 784
Stevenson, Elizabeth III, 300
Stevenson, Elizabeth H. II, 313
Stevenson, Elizabeth H. II, 325
Stevenson, Elizabeth Osbourn II, 264
Stevenson, Elizabeth S. II, 313
Stevenson, Elizabeth S. II, 316
Stevenson, Elizabeth S. II, 325
Stevenson, Elnathan II, 185
Stevenson, Elnathan II, 231
Stevenson, Elnathan II, 258
Stevenson, Elnathan II, 264
Stevenson, Elnathan II, 313
Stevenson, Emela II, 41
Stevenson, Emeline F. II, 325
Stevenson, Emeline T. II, 313
Stevenson, Emily I, 575
Stevenson, Emily L. II, 101
Stevenson, Emma V, 433
Stevenson, Ezra II, 302
Stevenson, Ezra II, 313
Stevenson, Gawen II, 660
Stevenson, George V, 127
Stevenson, George V, 137
Stevenson, Grace II, 660
Stevenson, Grace III, 399
Stevenson, Grace W. III, 67
Stevenson, Hannah II, 548
Stevenson, Hannah III, 170
Stevenson, Hepsabah V, 52
Stevenson, Hepsibah V, 127
Stevenson, Isaac II, 185
Stevenson, James II, 41
Stevenson, James II, 101
Stevenson, James II, 424
Stevenson, James V, 127
Stevenson, James B. V, 127
Stevenson, James M. V, 599
Stevenson, Jane VI, 882
Stevenson, John I, 597
Stevenson, John I, 934
Stevenson, John II, 24
Stevenson, John II, 41
Stevenson, John II, 47
Stevenson, John II, 58
Stevenson, John II, 79
Stevenson, John II, 101
Stevenson, John II, 111
Stevenson, John II, 235
Stevenson, John II, 264
Stevenson, John II, 424
Stevenson, John III, 300
Stevenson, John III, 353
Stevenson, John R. V, 599
Stevenson, John, Jr. II, 58
Stevenson, John, Jr. II, 101
Stevenson, Jonathan II, 264
Stevenson, Joseph II, 185
Stevenson, Joseph II, 302
Stevenson, Joseph II, 313
Stevenson, Joseph V, 127
Stevenson, Joshua II, 302
Stevenson, Joshua II, 313
Stevenson, Joshua II, 325
Stevenson, Josiah II, 264
Stevenson, Josiah II, 302
Stevenson, Lydia II, 185
Stevenson, Lydia II, 302
Stevenson, Lydia II, 313
Stevenson, Lydia III, 67
Stevenson, Lydia III, 300
Stevenson, Lydia Ann II, 313
Stevenson, Lydia Ann II, 325
Stevenson, Lydia W. III, 399
Stevenson, M. Morris III, 399
Stevenson, Maggie Daisy I, 934
Stevenson, Mahlon I, 1118
Stevenson, Mahlon I, 1132
Stevenson, Margaret II, 86
Stevenson, Margaret II, 101
Stevenson, Margaret IV, 108
Stevenson, Margaret IV, 110
Stevenson, Margaret H. II, 158
Stevenson, Margaretta II, 158
Stevenson, Marmaduke II, 185
Stevenson, Mary I, 597
Stevenson, Mary I, 1132
Stevenson, Mary II, 24
Stevenson, Mary II, 41
Stevenson, Mary II, 47
Stevenson, Mary II, 86
Stevenson, Mary II, 101
Stevenson, Mary II, 111
Stevenson, Mary II, 185
Stevenson, Mary II, 213
Stevenson, Mary II, 228
Stevenson, Mary II, 256
Stevenson, Mary II, 264
Stevenson, Mary II, 302
Stevenson, Mary II, 313
Stevenson, Mary II, 325
Stevenson, Mary II, 424
Stevenson, Mary IV, 61
Stevenson, Mary IV, 797
Stevenson, Mary IV, 844
Stevenson, Mary V, 599
Stevenson, Mary A. IV, 844
Stevenson, Mary Ann V, 127
Stevenson, Melvina I, 597
Stevenson, Mercy II, 235
Stevenson, Mercy II, 264
Stevenson, Micajah II, 264
Stevenson, Miner V, 599
Stevenson, Morris III, 67
Stevenson, Morris III, 300
Stevenson, Nannie I, 934
Stevenson, Nathan II, 325
Stevenson, Nathan M. II, 302
Stevenson, Nathan M. II, 313
Stevenson, Nicolas I, 1132
Stevenson, Priscilla II, 185
Stevenson, Priscilla II, 264
Stevenson, Priscilla II, 302
Stevenson, Rachel II, 79
Stevenson, Rachel II, 101
Stevenson, Rachel II, 226
Stevenson, Rachel II, 256
Stevenson, Rachel II, 264
Stevenson, Rachel II, 660
Stevenson, Rebecak VI, 933
Stevenson, Rebecca II, 185
Stevenson, Rebecca II, 264
Stevenson, Rebecca V, 127
Stevenson, Rebecca V, 136
Stevenson, Richard II, 101
Stevenson, Robert V, 599
Stevenson, Ruth I, 1118
Stevenson, Ruth I, 1132
Stevenson, Ruth Hodgin I, 641
Stevenson, Sadie V, 1020
Stevenson, Samuel II, 101
Stevenson, Samuel II, 185
Stevenson, Samuel V, 52
Stevenson, Samuel V, 127
Stevenson, Samuel V, 136
Stevenson, Samuel, Jr. V, 127
Stevenson, Sarah II, 185
Stevenson, Sarah II, 209
Stevenson, Sarah II, 231
Stevenson, Sarah II, 249
Stevenson, Sarah II, 264
Stevenson, Sarah II, 302
Stevenson, Sarah II, 313
Stevenson, Sarah II, 325
Stevenson, Sarah II, 660
Stevenson, Sarah II, 828
Stevenson, Sarah V, 127
Stevenson, Sarah V, 136
Stevenson, Seth II, 302
Stevenson, Stacy II, 185
Stevenson, Stacy II, 313
Stevenson, Stacy II, 325
Stevenson, Stevenson II, 185
Stevenson, Susanna II, 185
Stevenson, Susannah III, 33
Stevenson, Susannah III, 30
Stevenson, Thomas II, 249
Stevenson, Thomas II, 258
Stevenson, Thomas II, 264
Stevenson, Thomas III, 300
Stevenson, Thomas III, 314
Stevenson, Thomas Minor V,
Stevenson, Thomas, Jr. III, 3
Stevenson, Thomas, Sr. III, 3
Stevenson, Wd. Anne II, 185
Stevenson, Wd. Hannah II, 5
Stevenson, Wd. Hannah II, 6
Stevenson, Wd. Susan Allebon II, 784
Stevenson, William II, 185
Stevenson, William II, 226
Stevenson, William II, 264
Stevenson, William III, 300
Stevenson, William V, 127
Stevenson, William B. II, 41
Stevenson, William Lawrie II
Stevenson, Wm. II, 86
Stevenson, Wm. II, 101
Stevenson, Wm. II, 235
Stevenson, Wm. II, 784
Steves, Edith IV, 741
Steves, Edith L. IV, 769
Steves, Egbert O. III, 300
Steves, Egbert O. III, 357
Steves, Egbert O. III, 363
Steves, Elma T. IV, 769
Steves, Isabel Edith IV, 769
Steves, Jennie M. III, 300
Steves, Jennie M. III, 357
Steves, Jennie M. III, 363
Steveson, Martha VI, 104
Steveson, Peter VI, 104
Stevins, Barlow V, 127
Steward, Aaron IV, 657
Steward, Aaron IV, 1004
Steward, Aaron IV, 1005
Steward, Aaron A. IV, 1004
Steward, Adessa T. IV, 1147
Steward, Adessa T. IV, 1187
Steward, Albert J. IV, 1147
Steward, Albert J. IV, 1187
Steward, Alice V, 1020
Steward, Caleb II, 660
Steward, Calvin IV, 1004
Steward, Caroline IV, 1187
Steward, Catharine I, 734
Steward, Catharine VI, 448
Steward, David Holloway IV,
Steward, Edwin II, 325
Steward, Eliza IV, 657
Steward, Eliza IV, 923
Steward, Eliza IV, 1004
Steward, Eliza IV, 1005
Steward, Eliza V, 228
Steward, Eliza V, 280
Steward, Eliza P. IV, 1004
Steward, Eliza P. IV, 1005
Steward, Eliza P. IV, 1010
Steward, Elizabeth I, 734
Steward, Elizabeth II, 660
Steward, Elizabeth H. II, 325
Steward, Elnora S. IV, 657
Steward, Emaline IV, 1004
Steward, Emaline IV, 1017
Steward, Emaline H. IV, 1005
Steward, Emeline IV, 769
Steward, Emeline IV, 965
Steward, Emeline IV, 1004
Steward, George Wm. V, 433
Steward, Hamilton V, 1020
Steward, Hannah II, 660
Steward, Henry J. V, 433
Steward, Isaac IV, 923
Steward, Isaac IV, 1004
Steward, Isaac IV, 1005
Steward, John IV, 657
Steward, John IV, 1004
Steward, John IV, 1005
Steward, Joseph IV, 657
Steward, Joseph IV, 769
Steward, Joseph IV, 965
Steward, Joseph IV, 1004
Steward, Joseph IV, 1017
Steward, Littleberry VI, 998
Steward, Lydia II, 660
Steward, Lydia IV, 621
Steward, Lydia IV, 657
Steward, Margaret VI, 961
Steward, Martha I, 1162
Steward, Martha II, 660
Steward, Martha VI, 966
Steward, Mary I, 734
Steward, Mary VI, 998
Steward, Mary Ann II, 325
Steward, Mary Ann V, 1020
Steward, Mary Anna II, 325

ward, Massey IV, 657
ward, Massey IV, 1004
ward, Matilda IV, 1004
ward, Matilda IV, 1005
ward, Mercy IV, 657
ward, Mercy IV, 1004
ward, Mercy Mariah IV, 1004
ward, Mercy Mariah IV, 1005
ward, Merium II, 158
ward, Miriam II, 158
ward, Patience V, 433
ward, Rachel IV, 769
ward, Rachel IV, 1004
eward, Rachel IV, 1017
eward, Rachel P. IV, 1004
eward, Rachel P. IV, 1005
eward, Rebecca V, 469
eward, Robert IV, 1187
eward, Robert V, 433
eward, Robert VI, 448
eward, Samuel IV, 657
eward, Samuel IV, 1004
eward, Sarah II, 185
eward, Sarah VI, 1006
eward, Talitha IV, 589
eward, Talitha IV, 595
eward, Thomas II, 325
eward, William IV, 657
eward, William IV, 1004
eward, Wm. V, 646
ewardson, Ann II, 660
ewardson, Ann II, 719
ewardson, Anna II, 430
ewardson, Anna II, 475
ewardson, Anna II, 547
ewardson, Anna II, 660
tewardson, Anna II, 719
tewardson, Dorothy II, 547
tewardson, Dorothy II, 660
tewardson, Elizabeth II, 475
tewardson, Elizabeth II, 660
tewardson, George II, 547
tewardson, George II, 660
tewardson, George II, 719
tewardson, George II, 768
tewardson, George, Jr. II, 719
tewardson, Gulielma Maria II, 719
Stewardson, John II, 719
Stewardson, John H. II, 424
Stewardson, John Head II, 660
Stewardson, Margaret II, 430
Stewardson, Margaret II, 719
Stewardson, Margaret II, 768
Stewardson, Rachel II, 660
Stewardson, Rachel II, 719
Stewardson, Robert II, 430
Stewardson, Thomas II, 424
Stewardson, Thomas II, 475
Stewardson, Thomas II, 547
Stewardson, Thomas II, 660
Stewardson, Thomas II, 719
Stewardson, Thomas II, 768
Stewardson, Thomas, Jr. II, 768
Stewart, Aaron IV, 1005
Stewart, Abbe V, 944
Stewart, Abbe L. V, 944
Stewart, Abigail V, 944
Stewart, Abigail L. I, 453
Stewart, Addessa T. IV, 1187
Stewart, Adessa T. IV, 1187
Stewart, Albert J. IV, 1187
Stewart, Alcanser H. I, 901
Stewart, Alexander I, 421
Stewart, Alexander V, 944
Stewart, Alexander H. V, 944
Stewart, Alexander Stanton V, 944
Stewart, Alfred IV, 284
Stewart, Alice II, 1029
Stewart, Alice II, 1041
Stewart, Alice V, 944
Stewart, Almer IV, 1224
Stewart, Amariah II, 41
Stewart, Anita I, 937
Stewart, Anita I, 949
Stewart, Ann II, 29
Stewart, Ann II, 41
Stewart, Ann II, 73
Stewart, Ann II, 84
Stewart, Ann II, 101
Stewart, Ann II, 706
Stewart, Ann II, 707
Stewart, Ann II, 718
Stewart, Ann M. III, 281
Stewart, Ann M. III, 300
Stewart, Anna I, 724
Stewart, Anna I, 734
Stewart, Anna II, 132
Stewart, Anna V, 360
Stewart, Anna E. IV, 1264
Stewart, Annie V, 280
Stewart, Annie L. V, 944
Stewart, Arthur V, 532
Stewart, Arthur V, 713
Stewart, Asenath I, 793
Stewart, Benjamin I, 422
Stewart, Betsy VI, 904
Stewart, Blanche E. I, 618
Stewart, C. W. I, 949
Stewart, Caleb II, 660
Stewart, Carl L. V, 713
Stewart, Caroline IV, 1187
Stewart, Caroline A. II, 926
Stewart, Caroline Alberta IV, 1187
Stewart, Caroline Ann IV, 1187
Stewart, Caroline Ann V, 977
Stewart, Catharine I, 724
Stewart, Catharine III, 170
Stewart, Catharine III, 300
Stewart, Charles I, 447
Stewart, Charles I, 453
Stewart, Charles II, 424
Stewart, Charles H. VI, 989
Stewart, Charlotte VI, 998
Stewart, Constantine VI, 911
Stewart, Cora V, 713
Stewart, D. W. I, 949
Stewart, Daniel IV, 1187
Stewart, Daniel V, 977
Stewart, David C. V, 280
Stewart, David Holloway IV, 769
Stewart, Donald V, 713
Stewart, Edna IV, 1264
Stewart, Eldon Frank V, 280
Stewart, Eliza IV, 1005
Stewart, Eliza V, 280
Stewart, Elizabeth I, 421
Stewart, Elizabeth I, 792
Stewart, Elizabeth II, 41
Stewart, Elizabeth II, 57
Stewart, Elizabeth II, 101
Stewart, Elizabeth II, 660
Stewart, Elizabeth V, 280
Stewart, Elizabeth VI, 856
Stewart, Elizabeth VI, 964
Stewart, Elizabeth A. V, 360
Stewart, Elizabeth D. IV, 352
Stewart, Elizabeth J. V, 280
Stewart, Elizabeth M. III, 74
Stewart, Elizabeth M. III, 300
Stewart, Elizabeth M. III, 400
Stewart, Ella V, 713
Stewart, Elnora S. IV, 633
Stewart, Elnora S. IV, 657
Stewart, Elsie V, 280
Stewart, Elsie V, 360
Stewart, Emeline IV, 769
Stewart, Emeline H. IV, 769
Stewart, Emma V, 675
Stewart, Emma V, 712
Stewart, Esther V, 280
Stewart, Eveline III, 269
Stewart, Evelyn III, 269
Stewart, Flora E. V, 646
Stewart, Frank V, 280
Stewart, Fred V, 713
Stewart, George II, 41
Stewart, George IV, 1187
Stewart, George V, 646
Stewart, George V, 712
Stewart, George W. V, 977
Stewart, George Wm. V, 433
Stewart, Grace V, 712
Stewart, Grace Kirk V, 713
Stewart, Gravener I, 1050
Stewart, Gulielma I, 793
Stewart, Gwendolyn III, 427
Stewart, Gwendolyn III, 448
Stewart, Hannah II, 41
Stewart, Hannah II, 59
Stewart, Hannah II, 101
Stewart, Hannah II, 660
Stewart, Hannah II, 719
Stewart, Hannah III, 171
Stewart, Hannah III, 300
Stewart, Hannah Ann II, 158
Stewart, Hannah M. V, 879
Stewart, Hannah M. V, 886
Stewart, Harold IV, 1264
Stewart, Helen IV, 1264
Stewart, Henrietta VI, 649
Stewart, Henrietta VI, 702
Stewart, Henrietta VI, 703
Stewart, Henrietta VI, 706
Stewart, Henrietta VI, 707
Stewart, Henrietta VI, 724
Stewart, Henry I, 421
Stewart, Henry I, 734
Stewart, Henry VI, 856
Stewart, Henry J. V, 433
Stewart, Hester A. V, 433
Stewart, Hugh III, 281
Stewart, Hugh III, 300
Stewart, Huldah II, 424
Stewart, Ida II, 869
Stewart, Irena V, 646
Stewart, Isaac I, 575
Stewart, Isaac I, 792
Stewart, Isaac II, 424
Stewart, Isaac IV, 1005
Stewart, Isabel III, 300
Stewart, James II, 41
Stewart, James II, 96
Stewart, James II, 101
Stewart, James II, 132
Stewart, James VI, 812
Stewart, James VI, 856
Stewart, James VI, 998
Stewart, James W. VI, 998
Stewart, Jehu I, 575
Stewart, Jehu I, 792
Stewart, Jennie C. V, 646
Stewart, Jennie Crumley V, 646
Stewart, Jennie Crumley V, 713
Stewart, John I, 421
Stewart, John I, 453
Stewart, John I, 734
Stewart, John II, 41
Stewart, John II, 66
Stewart, John II, 101
Stewart, John II, 660
Stewart, John IV, 1004
Stewart, John IV, 1005
Stewart, John V, 280
Stewart, John V, 360
Stewart, John VI, 856
Stewart, John F. I, 901
Stewart, John T. I, 1162
Stewart, John, Jr. II, 59
Stewart, John, Jr. II, 101
Stewart, Joseph II, 41
Stewart, Joseph II, 101
Stewart, Joseph II, 138
Stewart, Joseph II, 1029
Stewart, Joseph II, 1041
Stewart, Joseph IV, 769
Stewart, Joseph V, 532
Stewart, Joseph V, 712
Stewart, Joseph V, 713
Stewart, Joseph E. V, 646
Stewart, Laura I, 1162
Stewart, Leslie IV, 1264
Stewart, Lidya II, 41
Stewart, Littleberry VI, 998
Stewart, Lorenzo R. VI, 998
Stewart, Lydia II, 66
Stewart, Lydia II, 101
Stewart, Lydia II, 660
Stewart, Mable V, 713
Stewart, Margaret II, 132
Stewart, Margaret II, 424
Stewart, Margaret II, 660
Stewart, Margaret II, 678
Stewart, Mark II, 41
Stewart, Mark II, 101
Stewart, Mark II, 158
Stewart, Martha I, 792
Stewart, Martha I, 793
Stewart, Martha I, 1162
Stewart, Martha II, 660
Stewart, Martha IV, 1264
Stewart, Martha Ann VI, 998
Stewart, Mary I, 453
Stewart, Mary I, 724
Stewart, Mary I, 734
Stewart, Mary II, 41
Stewart, Mary II, 51
Stewart, Mary II, 66
Stewart, Mary II, 96
Stewart, Mary II, 101
Stewart, Mary IV, 1264
Stewart, Mary Ann II, 815
Stewart, Mary B. II, 41
Stewart, Mary B. II, 790
Stewart, Mary Jane II, 138
Stewart, Mary Jane II, 158
Stewart, Mary L. IV, 284
Stewart, Mary Lancaster V, 646
Stewart, Mary Verita V, 280
Stewart, Matilda IV, 1004
Stewart, Matilda IV, 1005
Stewart, Matilda IV, 1264
Stewart, Melisent II, 41
Stewart, Mercy Mariah IV, 1005
Stewart, Merium II, 158
Stewart, Milly VI, 856
Stewart, Milly VI, 1021
Stewart, Minor V, 280
Stewart, Minor V, 360
Stewart, Miriam II, 158
Stewart, Mylasent II, 41
Stewart, Nancy III, 70
Stewart, Nancy III, 122
Stewart, Nancy VI, 904
Stewart, Nancy VI, 998
Stewart, Nathaniel VI, 1021
Stewart, Ora V, 280
Stewart, Ora V, 360
Stewart, Parthena VI, 998
Stewart, Patience IV, 1187
Stewart, Patience V, 977
Stewart, Pearl V, 712
Stewart, Phebe I, 792
Stewart, Polly VI, 856
Stewart, Polly VI, 964
Stewart, Rachel II, 41
Stewart, Rachel II, 101
Stewart, Rachel IV, 769
Stewart, Rachel IV, 1005
Stewart, Rachel IV, 1018
Stewart, Rachel P. IV, 769
Stewart, Rachel P. IV, 790
Stewart, Rebecca I, 901
Stewart, Rebecca II, 41
Stewart, Rebecca IV, 528
Stewart, Rebecca IV, 552
Stewart, Rebecca IV, 561
Stewart, Rebecca IV, 562
Stewart, Rebecca V, 532
Stewart, Robert I, 575
Stewart, Robert I, 792
Stewart, Robert I, 793
Stewart, Robert II, 424
Stewart, Robert IV, 1187
Stewart, Robert V, 433
Stewart, Robert J. V, 713
Stewart, Rose V, 646
Stewart, Ruth I, 447
Stewart, Ruth I, 453
Stewart, Samuel I, 734
Stewart, Samuel II, 29
Stewart, Samuel II, 41
Stewart, Samuel II, 73
Stewart, Samuel II, 101
Stewart, Samuel II, 158
Stewart, Samuel, Jr. II, 101
Stewart, Samuel, Jr. II, 660
Stewart, Sarah I, 453
Stewart, Sarah I, 734
Stewart, Sarah I, 792
Stewart, Sarah I, 812
Stewart, Sarah I, 839
Stewart, Sarah I, 840
Stewart, Sarah II, 29
Stewart, Sarah II, 41
Stewart, Sarah II, 73
Stewart, Sarah II, 101
Stewart, Sarah II, 264
Stewart, Sarah III, 171
Stewart, Sarah III, 300
Stewart, Sarah V, 280
Stewart, Sarah Ann VI, 998
Stewart, Sarah E. I, 1162
Stewart, Sarah E. V, 280
Stewart, Sarah Elizabeth VI, 887
Stewart, Sarah H. VI, 1021
Stewart, Solomon I, 421
Stewart, Sophia IV, 284
Stewart, Stanton Alexander V, 944
Stewart, Susanna II, 702
Stewart, Susanna III, 281
Stewart, Susanna III, 300
Stewart, Susannah I, 575
Stewart, Susannah I, 577
Stewart, Susannah V, 584
Stewart, Susannah V, 599
Stewart, Tabitha I, 720
Stewart, Tabitha I, 734
Stewart, Tamer IV, 769
Stewart, Tamer IV, 792
Stewart, Thadeus V. I, 901
Stewart, Therman B. V, 646
Stewart, Thomas II, 41
Stewart, Thomas III, 74
Stewart, Thomas III, 300
Stewart, Thomas IV, 284
Stewart, Thomas VI, 936
Stewart, Thomas VI, 977
Stewart, Thomas VI, 978
Stewart, Thomas VI, 998
Stewart, Thos. III, 400
Stewart, Vereta V, 280
Stewart, W. G. I, 937
Stewart, W. G. I, 949
Stewart, Wendell E. V, 713
Stewart, William II, 41
Stewart, William IV, 1004
Stewart, William IV, 1187
Stewart, William V, 646
Stewart, William VI, 974
Stewart, William VI, 998
Stewart, William W. VI, 820
Stewart, Wm. II, 101
Stewart, Wm. IV, 1187
Stewart, Wm. V, 646
Stewart, Wm. H. IV, 1187
Stewart, Wm. I. V, 712
Stewart, Wm. Lee I, 949
Stewart, Wm. Paul I, 949
Stewart, Wm., Jr. IV, 1187
Stewart, Zimry I, 734
Steweard, Abigail L. I, 453
Stewert, David C. IV, 1241
Stewrt, Nathaniel VI, 1014
Steymets, Mary III, 300
Sthrother, Eliza VI, 372
Stickel, George IV, 133
Stickel, Jane IV, 133
Stickel, Sina IV, 869
Stickel, Sina IV, 883
Stickle, Callie V, 765
Stickle, Clinton V, 765
Stickle, George IV, 61
Stickle, George IV, 110
Stickle, Jane IV, 61
Stickle, Jane IV, 110
Stickle, Paul Markley V, 765
Stickle, Rachel V, 765
Stickle, Ralph V, 765
Stickle, Wd. Sallie V, 765
Stickney, Adaline III, 60
Stickney, Adaline III, 300
Stickney, Byron III, 300
Stickney, Edith III, 300
Stickney, Edith G. III, 94
Stickney, Frank III, 60
Stickney, Frank III, 300
Stickney, Mary A. III, 94
Stickney, Mary A. III, 300
Stickney, Phebe III, 300
Stickney, Samuel C. III, 300
Stickney, Walter III, 300
Sticlle, Jane IV, 133
Stiddom, Anna I, 1024
Stiddom, Christian I, 1024
Stiddom, Eunice I, 1024
Stiddom, Hanry I, 1038
Stiddom, Henry I, 1024
Stiddom, Henry I, 1035
Stiddom, John I, 1024
Stiddom, John I, 1038
Stiddom, Martha I, 1024
Stiddom, Martha I, 1035
Stiddom, Martha I, 1038
Stiddom, Mary I, 1024
Stiddom, Mary I, 1038
Stiddom, Samuel I, 1024
Stidham, Ann I, 1035
Stidham, Ann I, 1038
Stidman, Susannah I, 1038
Stiff, Amey VI, 998
Stiff, Barsheba VI, 998
Stiff, Betsy VI, 892
Stiff, Burwell VI, 999
Stiff, Delilah VI, 999
Stiff, Eney VI, 998
Stiff, Harrison VI, 999
Stiff, Henry VI, 968
Stiff, Henry VI, 978
Stiff, Henry VI, 998
Stiff, Jacob VI, 886
Stiff, Jacob VI, 892
Stiff, Jacob VI, 923
Stiff, Jacob VI, 974
Stiff, Jacob VI, 998
Stiff, James VI, 968
Stiff, James VI, 998
Stiff, James VI, 1010
Stiff, James M. VI, 962
Stiff, James M. VI, 975
Stiff, James M. VI, 999
Stiff, James, Sr. VI, 998
Stiff, Jesse VI, 998
Stiff, John VI, 886
Stiff, John VI, 998
Stiff, John B. VI, 886
Stiff, Juley Ann VI, 999
Stiff, Katey VI, 998
Stiff, Lewis VI, 878
Stiff, Lewis VI, 998
Stiff, Lucinda VI, 886
Stiff, Lucy Ann VI, 999
Stiff, Mary VI, 999
Stiff, Nancy VI, 880
Stiff, Polly VI, 968
Stiff, Polly VI, 974
Stiff, Polly VI, 998
Stiff, Priscilla V, 713
Stiff, Rhoda VI, 998
Stiff, Richard VI, 998
Stiff, Sally VI, 923
Stiff, Sally VI, 998

Stiff, Sally Lewis VI, 978
Stiff, Sarah VI, 1010
Stiff, Washington VI, 999
Stiff, William VI, 998
Stiffler, Mary Griffith IV, 769
Stigleman, Olive V, 963
Stiles, Aaron B. II, 308
Stiles, Alice May V, 206
Stiles, Amy V, 599
Stiles, Amyann V, 599
Stiles, Ann V, 599
Stiles, Ann M. VI, 783
Stiles, Benj. II, 129
Stiles, Benjamin II, 660
Stiles, Caroline V, 599
Stiles, Charles VI, 783
Stiles, Elisabeth II, 621
Stiles, Elisabeth II, 660
Stiles, Eliza Ann II, 926
Stiles, Elizabeth II, 129
Stiles, Elizabeth Ann II, 926
Stiles, Elva Lucile V, 206
Stiles, George II, 719
Stiles, Hannah B. VI, 783
Stiles, Henry R. VI, 783
Stiles, Hilbe D. V, 206
Stiles, Isaac V, 206
Stiles, Jane E. II, 308
Stiles, Joseph II, 461
Stiles, Joseph II, 593
Stiles, Joseph II, 660
Stiles, Kate W. II, 131
Stiles, Kathryn II, 131
Stiles, Leora Isabelle V, 206
Stiles, Levi B. VI, 783
Stiles, Levi R. VI, 783
Stiles, Lucy II, 461
Stiles, Lucy II, 660
Stiles, M. E. II, 706
Stiles, Martha II, 129
Stiles, Mary II, 593
Stiles, Mary II, 660
Stiles, Mary Belle V, 206
Stiles, Mary S. IV, 1295
Stiles, Nancy V, 206
Stiles, Nellie II, 308
Stiles, Rachel IV, 843
Stiles, Rachel IV, 845
Stiles, Rachel V, 599
Stiles, Renton R. VI, 783
Stiles, Robert IV, 1187
Stiles, Robert V, 599
Stiles, Samuel R. VI, 783
Stiles, Wm. F. II, 131
Still, Benjamin VI, 910
Still, Benjamin VI, 999
Still, Catherine VI, 881
Still, Dashe VI, 826
Still, Elizabeth VI, 843
Still, Henry VI, 999
Still, Jacob VI, 826
Still, Jacob VI, 843
Still, Jacob VI, 881
Still, Martha VI, 826
Still, Mary I, 379
Still, Mary I, 419
Still, Nancy VI, 933
Still, Nancy VI, 999
Still, Thomas F. VI, 933
Stille, Anniebelle II, 821
Stiller, John VI, 999
Stiller, Mary Ann VI, 999
Stillings, Emma Reed V, 599
Stillings, James V, 599
Stillings, James V, 713
Stillings, John V, 713
Stillings, Mary A. V, 595
Stillings, Mary A. V, 599
Stillings, Mary A. V, 713
Stillings, Sarah V, 713
Stillion, Anna M. IV, 402
Stillion, Anna M. IV, 444
Stillion, Annie M. IV, 444
Stillion, George C. IV, 444
Stillwagon, Cretia IV, 284
Stillwagon, Henry IV, 284
Stillwagon, Hettie IV, 284
Stillwagon, Isaac IV, 284
Stillwagon, Peter IV, 284
Stillwagon, Sarah Ann IV, 284
Stillwagoner, George V, 1020
Stillwagoner, Sarah V, 1020
Stillwell, Abigail III, 494
Stillwell, Eliza IV, 1005
Stillwell, Lemuel V, 361
Stillwell, Mary III, 499
Stillwell, Mary V, 361
Stillwell, William III, 499
Stilwagon, Mary C. II, 910
Stilwagon, Mary C. II, 926
Stilwell, Eliza IV, 1012
Stilwell, Elizabeth II, 101
Stilwell, Martha II, 630
Stilwell, Martha II, 646
Stilwell, Martha II, 660
Stilwell, Mary III, 300
Stilwell, William III, 300
Stim, Louis A. III, 132
Stim, Louis A. III, 300
Stim, Lucile E. III, 132
Stim, Lucille E. III, 300
Stim, Natalia M. III, 132
Stim, Natalia M. III, 300
Stimemetz, Mabel V, 1020
Stimets, Mary III, 304
Stimson, Lydia C. VI, 999
Stimson, Nelson VI, 833
Stimson, Nelson B. VI, 999
Stinard, Emily III, 300
Stinard, Lucy Velma IV, 498
Stine, Caroline II, 1061
Stiner, Chris IV, 284
Stiner, Erma IV, 1187
Stiner, Jesse IV, 283
Stiner, Mary IV, 1224
Stiner, Sarah V, 750
Stiner, Sarah V, 765
Stingley, Albert V, 206
Stingley, Albert V, 532
Stingley, Alice V, 532
Stingley, Alie V, 532
Stingley, Calvin V, 532
Stingley, Charles V, 532
Stingley, Clarence V, 532
Stingley, Elizabeth V, 532
Stingley, Gilead V, 532
Stingley, Luther V, 532
Stingley, Mary J. V, 206
Stingley, Mary J. V, 532
Stingley, Nancy V, 532
Stingley, Rose V, 206
Stingley, William V, 532
Stingley, William Allison V, 532
Stingly, Albert V, 532
Stingly, Alice V, 532
Stingly, William Allison V, 532
Stinnard, Elisabeth II, 660
Stinnett, Alexander VI, 999
Stinnett, Annah VI, 999
Stinnett, Catharine J. VI, 999
Stinnett, Charles VI, 999
Stinnett, Charles A. VI, 999
Stinnett, Elizabeth VI, 999
Stinnett, Elizabeth B. VI, 999
Stinnett, Frances VI, 999
Stinnett, Joel M. VI, 999
Stinnett, John L. VI, 999
Stinnett, John T. VI, 999
Stinnett, Judith VI, 999
Stinnett, Lindsay VI, 891
Stinnett, Lindsey VI, 999
Stinnett, Linesey VI, 999
Stinnett, Linsey VI, 999
Stinnett, Margaret VI, 999
Stinnett, Martha Jane VI, 999
Stinnett, Mary VI, 891
Stinnett, Mary Jane VI, 999
Stinnett, Nancy VI, 999
Stinnett, Pleasant VI, 999
Stinnett, Rebecca VI, 999
Stinnett, Reubin VI, 999
Stinnett, Sally VI, 999
Stinnett, Sandy L. VI, 999
Stinnett, Thomas VI, 999
Stinnett, William VI, 999
Stinnitt, Mary Jane VI, 999
Stinnitt, Sandy L. VI, 999
Stinson, Ann II, 811
Stinson, Edgar V, 127
Stinson, Edgar V, 646
Stinson, Edgar S. C. V, 646
Stinson, Effie V, 646
Stinson, Elizabeth VI, 448
Stinson, Jefferson V, 646
Stinson, Jennie R. III, 285
Stinson, Mary II, 811
Stinson, Rebecca V, 646
Stinson, Samuel II, 811
Stinson, Thos. V, 646
Stinson, Thos. J. V, 646
Stintell, William VI, 891
Stintett, Tabitha VI, 891
Stinton, Elisabeth II, 528
Stinton, Elisabeth II, 660
Stinton, William VI, 25
Stinton, William VI, 29
Stinton, William VI, 32
Stinyard, Elizabeth II, 424
Stipe, Helen Irene VI, 451
Stipe, Irene Maurice VI, 448
Stipe, Irene Maurice VI, 457
Stipe, Irene W. VI, 448
Stipe, James Leslie VI, 448
Stipe, James Leslie VI, 451
Stipe, James William VI, 448
Stipe, James William VI, 457
Stirridge, James III, 300
Stirridge, Zachariah III, 300
Stirridge, Zachary III, 300
Stitchworth, Ann V, 646
Stites, George II, 768
Stites, Minnie IV, 1339
Stith, Ann VI, 927
Stith, Benjamin VI, 840
Stith, Benjamin VI, 852
Stith, Betsy VI, 856
Stith, Catherine VI, 830
Stith, Elizabeth Ann VI, 999
Stith, Elizabeth B. VI, 842
Stith, Eveline VI, 856
Stith, Harriett B. VI, 999
Stith, John VI, 825
Stith, John VI, 830
Stith, John VI, 856
Stith, Joseph VI, 856
Stith, Joseph VI, 927
Stith, Joseph VI, 999
Stith, Lucy VI, 943
Stith, Lucy A. VI, 856
Stith, Martha VI, 852
Stith, Mary VI, 910
Stith, Nancy VI, 856
Stith, Polly VI, 825
Stith, Rhoda VI, 856
Stith, Richard VI, 825
Stith, Richard VI, 830
Stith, Richard VI, 842
Stith, Richard VI, 856
Stith, Richard VI, 943
Stith, Richard VI, 999
Stith, Susanna VI, 856
Stith, Thomas VI, 856
Stith, William VI, 856
Stith, William B. VI, 999
Stith, William J. VI, 856
Stitsworth, Ann V, 646
Stitt, Mary IV, 697
Stitt, William III, 300
Stiven, Sarah II, 573
Stiven, Sarah II, 660
Stiver, Blanche Pettit IV, 769
Stiver, Joseph IV, 769
Stiver, Lydia S. IV, 769
Stivers, ??? III, 103
Stivers, ??? III, 408
Stivers, Ann III, 103
Stivers, Jos. C. III, 103
Stivers, Kesiah III, 102
Stivers, Kesiah III, 300
Stivers, Kezia III, 103
Stivers, Kezia III, 448
Stivers, Keziah III, 408
Stivers, Martha III, 102
Stivers, Martha III, 300
Stivers, Martha III, 448
Stivers, Phebe W. III, 103
Stivers, Rosanna B. III, 103
Stivers, Sarah E. III, 103
Stivers, Thomas III, 102
Stivers, Thomas III, 103
Stivers, Thomas III, 300
Stivers, Thomas, Jr. III, 300
Stives, Edith IV, 768
Stoakes, Deliverance II, 233
Stoakes, Deliverance II, 265
Stoakes, Emiline I. VI, 856
Stoakes, Jas. R. VI, 856
Stoakes, Mary II, 233
Stoakes, Mary II, 265
Stoakes, Polly VI, 856
Stoakes, Thomas II, 234
Stoakes, Thomas II, 265
Stoakes, Thomas VI, 856
Stoakes, Thomas, Jr. II, 233
Stoakes, Thomas, Jr. II, 265
Stoaks, Hannah II, 264
Stoaks, John II, 244
Stoaks, John II, 255
Stoaks, John II, 265
Stoaks, John, Jr. II, 264
Stoaks, Mary II, 244
Stoaks, Mary II, 265
Stoaks, Rachel III, 448
Stoaks, Sarah II, 242
Stoaks, Sarah II, 255
Stoaks, Sarah II, 265
Stoaks, Thomas III, 448
Stoan, Catherine I, 690
Stoan, Huldah I, 679
Stoan, Huldah I, 690
Stoan, John I, 690
Stocdaile, Ruth II, 424
Stocdaile, William II, 424
Stocdale, David II, 1038
Stocdale, Jane II, 1038
Stock, Eliza IV, 657
Stock, Eliza IV, 864
Stock, Eliza IV, 883
Stock, Elza IV, 769
Stock, Jesse IV, 1224
Stock, Jessie M. IV, 1224
Stockdal, Mary II, 242
Stockdal, Mary II, 264
Stockdale, Amy IV, 19
Stockdale, Amy IV, 61
Stockdale, Amy IV, 883
Stockdale, David II, 1029
Stockdale, Dorothy II, 985
Stockdale, Dorothy II, 1029
Stockdale, Elizabeth IV, 366
Stockdale, Fairbank B. III, 300
Stockdale, Geo. Maychim III, 100
Stockdale, George Fairbanks III, 300
Stockdale, George Maychim III, 300
Stockdale, Hannah II, 1029
Stockdale, Jane II, 1029
Stockdale, John II, 424
Stockdale, John II, 660
Stockdale, John IV, 110
Stockdale, Mercy II, 1029
Stockdale, Phebe II, 1022
Stockdale, Phebe II, 1029
Stockdale, Ruth II, 424
Stockdale, Sarah Ann III, 300
Stockdale, Sarah Lavada IV, 366
Stockdale, Susannah II, 264
Stockdale, Susannah II, 270
Stockdale, William II, 424
Stockdale, William II, 1005
Stockdale, William II, 1029
Stockdale, Winifred III, 300
Stockdale, Winifred M. III, 100
Stockdale, Winifred M. III, 300
Stockdale, Wm. II, 1022
Stockdale, Wm. IV, 366
Stockdalle, Dorothy II, 1029
Stockdell, Abigail II, 264
Stockdell, David II, 1029
Stockdell, Elizabeth II, 264
Stockdell, Hannah II, 264
Stockdell, Hannah II, 984
Stockdell, Hannah II, 1029
Stockdell, Henry II, 264
Stockdell, Hudson II, 264
Stockdell, Jane II, 1029
Stockdell, Joseph II, 264
Stockdell, Mary II, 264
Stockdell, Samuel II, 264
Stockden, Richard II, 424
Stockden, Susanna II, 264
Stockdol, Abigail II, 264
Stockdol, Elizabeth II, 264
Stockdol, Henry II, 264
Stockdol, Hudson II, 264
Stockdol, Joseph II, 264
Stockdol, Samuel II, 264
Stockdon, Daniel VI, 272
Stockdon, Jehu VI, 273
Stockdon, John VI, 273
Stockdon, Mary I, 839
Stockdon, Newberry VI, 272
Stockdon, Prudence VI, 272
Stockdon, Thomas VI, 272
Stocker, Anne III, 398
Stockes, Susannah II, 1012
Stockey, Eliza H. II, 926
Stockey, Nehemiah II, 926
Stockhouse, Hannah IV, 619
Stocking, Edgar E. Stocking VI, 783
Stocking, Emily VI, 783
Stocking, Fanny H. VI, 783
Stocking, Mary E. VI, 783
Stockley, Eliza H. II, 886
Stockley, Harriet E. II, 886
Stockley, Harriet E. II, 926
Stockley, Nehemiah II, 886
Stockly, Harriet E. II, 926
Stockman, Mary V, 206
Stockman, Mary V, 207
Stocks, Elizabeth VI, 568
Stocks, John H. VI, 568
Stocks, Mary VI, 568
Stockton, Abigail II, 185
Stockton, Abigail II, 264
Stockton, Abigail II, 265
Stockton, Abigail II, 284
Stockton, Abigail II, 285
Stockton, Abigail II, 302
Stockton, Abigail II, 424
Stockton, Abigail II, 719
Stockton, Abigail II, 768
Stockton, Abraham II, 185
Stockton, Abraham II, 265
Stockton, Abraham II, 274
Stockton, Abraham II, 302
Stockton, Abraham, Jr. II, 185
Stockton, Abraham, Jr. II, 265
Stockton, Abraham, Jr. II, 274
Stockton, Abram II, 185
Stockton, Ann I, 839
Stockton, Ann I, 971
Stockton, Ann I, 998
Stockton, Ann II, 101
Stockton, Ann II, 185
Stockton, Ann II, 254
Stockton, Ann II, 264
Stockton, Ann II, 265
Stockton, Ann II, 793
Stockton, Ann II, 1030
Stockton, Ann Eliza I, 793
Stockton, Bethshabah VI, 999
Stockton, Burr II, 264
Stockton, Burr II, 265
Stockton, Dan VI, 310
Stockton, Dan VI, 932
Stockton, Dan. VI, 913
Stockton, Daniel I, 998
Stockton, Daniel D. I, 901
Stockton, Daniel D. I, 914
Stockton, Daniel Doughty I, 793
Stockton, Daughty I, 839
Stockton, David II, 264
Stockton, David II, 970
Stockton, Doughty I, 793
Stockton, Doughty I, 839
Stockton, Doughty I, 910
Stockton, Doughty I, 914
Stockton, Doughty V, 127
Stockton, Edith II, 185
Stockton, Edith II, 302
Stockton, Edith II, 1030
Stockton, Edith B. II, 1025
Stockton, Edith B. II, 1030
Stockton, Edith D. II, 302
Stockton, Eliza VI, 448
Stockton, Eliza VI, 457
Stockton, Elizabeth I, 575
Stockton, Elizabeth I, 591
Stockton, Elizabeth I, 793
Stockton, Elizabeth I, 839
Stockton, Elizabeth I, 907
Stockton, Elizabeth I, 910
Stockton, Elizabeth I, 914
Stockton, Elizabeth I, 998
Stockton, Elizabeth II, 255
Stockton, Elizabeth II, 264
Stockton, Elizabeth II, 265
Stockton, Elizabeth II, 285
Stockton, Elizabeth II, 302
Stockton, Elizabeth II, 424
Stockton, Elizabeth II, 825
Stockton, Elizabeth II, 828
Stockton, Elizabeth II, 970
Stockton, Elizabeth II, 1029
Stockton, Elizabeth II, 1041
Stockton, Elizabeth Woolston II, 1029
Stockton, G. IV, 1263
Stockton, George II, 185
Stockton, George II, 302
Stockton, Hannah II, 185
Stockton, Hannah II, 238
Stockton, Hannah II, 264
Stockton, Hannah II, 790
Stockton, Henry II, 264
Stockton, Henry II, 265
Stockton, Hudson II, 264
Stockton, Hudson II, 265
Stockton, Hudson II, 424
Stockton, Hudson II, 660
Stockton, Israel II, 660
Stockton, Jane II, 1029
Stockton, Jane II, 1041
Stockton, Jane II, 1061
Stockton, Jane II, 1075
Stockton, Jane II, 1081
Stockton, Job II, 200
Stockton, Job II, 264
Stockton, Job V, 127
Stockton, John I, 998
Stockton, Joseph I, 998
Stockton, Joseph II, 264
Stockton, Joseph II, 265
Stockton, Joseph W. I, 914
Stockton, Joseph Wilson I, 793
Stockton, Lucretia II, 264
Stockton, Margaret VI, 913
Stockton, Martha P. I, 914
Stockton, Mary I, 839
Stockton, Mary I, 998
Stockton, Mary II, 200
Stockton, Mary II, 264

kton, Mary II, 284
kton, Mary II, 302
kton, Mary Ann I, 793
kton, Mary Ann I, 913
kton, Mary Ann I, 914
kton, Nancy D. I, 912
kton, Nancy D. I, 914
kton, Nancy Dougharthy I, 793
kton, Newberry VI, 888
kton, Newbury VI, 913
kton, Newbury VI, 999
kton, Patty VI, 881
kton, Rachel II, 185
kton, Rachel A. II, 265
kton, Rachel A. II, 274
kton, Rachel A. II, 302
kton, Rachel R. II, 294
kton, Rachel R. II, 302
kton, Richard II, 660
kton, Richard V, 127
kton, Richard, Jr. II, 660
kton, Robert Jarvis II, 970
kton, Sally B. I, 912
kton, Sally B. I, 914
kton, Sally Bell I, 793
kton, Samuel II, 185
kton, Samuel II, 264
kton, Samuel II, 265
kton, Samuel II, 284
kton, Samuel II, 285
kton, Samuel II, 302
kton, Samuel II, 1030
kton, Sarah I, 995
kton, Sarah I, 998
kton, Sarah II, 185
kton, Sarah II, 264
kton, Sarah W. II, 185
kton, Sarah W. II, 302
kton, Susan II, 185
kton, Susan II, 265
kton, Susan II, 274
kton, Susanna II, 264
kton, Susannah II, 185
kton, Thomas VI, 214
kton, Thomas VI, 275
kton, Thomas Clayton I, 793
kton, Wd. Rachel A. II, 185
kton, William I, 998
kton, William II, 185
kton, William II, 200
kton, William II, 264
kton, William II, 265
kton, William Franklin I, 793
kton, Wm. II, 264
kwell, Etta IV, 1339
kwell, Etta M. IV, 1043
kwell, Sarah IV, 109
kwell, Sarah IV, 110
cton, Ann II, 264
cton, Catherine VI, 310
cton, Catherine VI, 340
cton, Dan VI, 340
cton, David II, 264
cton, Edith B. II, 1030
cton, Eliza I, 591
cton, Israel II, 660
cton, John I, 591
cton, Thomas I, 598
cton, William I, 591
cton, William I, 598
cton, William II, 264
cton, Wm. II, 264
dard, Mary II, 424
ddard, Clarissa V, 713
ddard, Clarissa D. V, 713
ddard, Eliz P. III, 146
ddard, Harry A. V, 713
ddard, Harry C. V, 713
ddard, Henry P. V, 713
ddard, James E. V, 713
ddard, James Edwin V, 713
ddard, Jane III, 16
ddard, Jane III, 190
ddard, Nathan IV, 1380
ddard, Rhoda IV, 1380
ddard, Sarah VI, 919
ddard, Solomon VI, 919
ddard, Virginia B. V, 713
ddard, Zimrada IV, 1380
ddart, Amy III, 249
ddart, Amy III, 300
ffer, Anna Mary IV, 782
ffer, Caroline V, 934
ffner, John IV, 1264
ffregen, David Miller V, 713
ffregen, Frances T. V, 713
ffregen, Francis Turpin V, 713
ffregen, H. Frederick, Jr. V, 713
Stoffregen, Harry Frederick, Jr. V, 713
Stoffregen, Ida B. V, 713
Stoffregen, Ida Belle V, 713
Stogdell, Elizabeth II, 186
Stogden, Ada Belle V, 433
Stogden, Anna J. V, 433
Stogden, Daniel I, 998
Stogden, Jeanetta V, 433
Stogden, John I, 998
Stogden, John W. V, 433
Stogden, Joseph I, 998
Stogden, Margaret V, 433
Stogden, Margaret E. V, 433
Stogden, Margaret Emily V, 433
Stogden, Mary II, 264
Stogden, Mary Emily V, 392
Stogden, Mary Emily V, 433
Stogden, Thomas V, 433
Stogden, William I, 998
Stogden, William V, 433
Stogden, Wm. V, 433
Stogdill, Elizabeth II, 265
Stogdon, Ann I, 839
Stogdon, Elizabeth I, 839
Stogdon, Hannah II, 264
Stogdon, Hannah II, 265
Stogdon, Margaret V, 433
Stogdon, William V, 433
Stoker, Cora V, 765
Stoker, Elizabeth V, 765
Stoker, Peter John V, 765
Stokes, ??? II, 313
Stokes, ??? III, 301
Stokes, Abigail II, 185
Stokes, Abigail II, 265
Stokes, Abigail II, 274
Stokes, Abigail II, 276
Stokes, Abigail II, 313
Stokes, Abigail II, 315
Stokes, Abigail II, 325
Stokes, Abigail II, 661
Stokes, Abigail II, 828
Stokes, Abigail W. II, 265
Stokes, Abigail W. II, 302
Stokes, Abigail, Jr. II, 661
Stokes, Abraham III, 301
Stokes, Abraham Z. II, 313
Stokes, Abraham Z. II, 325
Stokes, Agnes II, 719
Stokes, Agnes II, 757
Stokes, Agnes II, 769
Stokes, Albert II, 719
Stokes, Alcesta K. II, 876
Stokes, Alcesta K. II, 926
Stokes, Alcesta Kinsey II, 821
Stokes, Alexander II, 265
Stokes, Alfred E. II, 424
Stokes, Alfred E. II, 661
Stokes, Alfred E. V, 127
Stokes, Alice II, 298
Stokes, Alice II, 302
Stokes, Alice II, 313
Stokes, Alice II, 323
Stokes, Alice II, 325
Stokes, Alice R. II, 302
Stokes, Alice R. IV, 658
Stokes, Amanda II, 424
Stokes, Amanda II, 661
Stokes, Amanda V, 127
Stokes, Amy II, 307
Stokes, Amy C. II, 303
Stokes, Ann II, 185
Stokes, Ann II, 186
Stokes, Ann II, 265
Stokes, Ann II, 286
Stokes, Ann II, 302
Stokes, Ann II, 303
Stokes, Ann II, 307
Stokes, Ann II, 313
Stokes, Ann II, 314
Stokes, Ann II, 316
Stokes, Ann II, 325
Stokes, Ann Eliza II, 926
Stokes, Ann L. II, 313
Stokes, Ann L. II, 318
Stokes, Ann L. II, 325
Stokes, Ann Lancaster II, 796
Stokes, Ann W. II, 303
Stokes, Anna II, 265
Stokes, Anna II, 303
Stokes, Anna II, 313
Stokes, Anna II, 314
Stokes, Anna II, 719
Stokes, Anna II, 738
Stokes, Anna II, 821
Stokes, Anna II, 904
Stokes, Anna II, 926
Stokes, Anna E. II, 314
Stokes, Anna E. II, 322
Stokes, Anna E. II, 325
Stokes, Anna G. II, 318
Stokes, Anna G. II, 325
Stokes, Anna Naomi II, 719
Stokes, Annie II, 309
Stokes, Annie II, 314
Stokes, Asher II, 302
Stokes, Asher II, 307
Stokes, Asher II, 314
Stokes, Asher W. II, 325
Stokes, B. Howard II, 325
Stokes, Barclay II, 138
Stokes, Benjamin II, 302
Stokes, Benjamin II, 313
Stokes, Benjamin Howard II, 313
Stokes, Benjamin R. II, 325
Stokes, Beulah A. IV, 660
Stokes, Beulah Ann IV, 657
Stokes, Beulah Ann IV, 658
Stokes, Blanche II, 863
Stokes, Blanche II, 926
Stokes, Caleb IV, 658
Stokes, Caleb IV, 660
Stokes, Carleton P. II, 763
Stokes, Carleton P. II, 769
Stokes, Carlton P. II, 757
Stokes, Carlton P. II, 769
Stokes, Caroline II, 309
Stokes, Caroline II, 313
Stokes, Caroline II, 314
Stokes, Caroline II, 325
Stokes, Catherine W. II, 739
Stokes, Catherine W. II, 769
Stokes, Chalkley II, 281
Stokes, Chalkley II, 303
Stokes, Charles II, 185
Stokes, Charles II, 265
Stokes, Charles II, 290
Stokes, Charles II, 302
Stokes, Charles II, 303
Stokes, Charles II, 307
Stokes, Charles II, 313
Stokes, Charles II, 314
Stokes, Charles II, 325
Stokes, Chas. II, 827
Stokes, David II, 185
Stokes, David II, 186
Stokes, David II, 265
Stokes, David II, 302
Stokes, David II, 313
Stokes, David II, 314
Stokes, David II, 325
Stokes, Deborah V, 59
Stokes, Deborah V, 127
Stokes, Deliverance II, 265
Stokes, Edward II, 265
Stokes, Edward II, 302
Stokes, Edward II, 314
Stokes, Edward II, 325
Stokes, Edward V, 933
Stokes, Edward D. II, 926
Stokes, Edwin II, 661
Stokes, Eliza S. II, 890
Stokes, Eliza S. II, 926
Stokes, Eliza Stow II, 821
Stokes, Elizabeth II, 185
Stokes, Elizabeth II, 186
Stokes, Elizabeth II, 228
Stokes, Elizabeth II, 265
Stokes, Elizabeth II, 275
Stokes, Elizabeth II, 276
Stokes, Elizabeth II, 285
Stokes, Elizabeth II, 302
Stokes, Elizabeth II, 309
Stokes, Elizabeth II, 314
Stokes, Elizabeth II, 323
Stokes, Elizabeth II, 325
Stokes, Elizabeth II, 661
Stokes, Elizabeth II, 821
Stokes, Elizabeth IV, 61
Stokes, Elizabeth IV, 883
Stokes, Elizabeth IV, 1336
Stokes, Elizabeth IV, 1339
Stokes, Elizabeth VI, 568
Stokes, Elizabeth B. II, 313
Stokes, Elizabeth B. II, 318
Stokes, Elizabeth B. II, 325
Stokes, Elizabeth C. II, 711
Stokes, Elizabeth D. II, 314
Stokes, Elizabeth D. II, 325
Stokes, Elizabeth D. II, 326
Stokes, Elizabeth J. II, 757
Stokes, Elizabeth J. II, 769
Stokes, Elizabeth K. II, 763
Stokes, Elizabeth K. II, 769
Stokes, Elizabeth R. II, 313
Stokes, Elizabeth R. II, 769
Stokes, Elizabeth W. II, 314
Stokes, Elizabeth W. II, 325
Stokes, Ella II, 786
Stokes, Ella II, 845
Stokes, Ella II, 926
Stokes, Ellis II, 424
Stokes, Ellis II, 661
Stokes, Ellis V, 127
Stokes, Ellis A. V, 127
Stokes, Emiline I. VI, 856
Stokes, Emma II, 822
Stokes, Esther II, 204
Stokes, Esther II, 265
Stokes, Eva II, 311
Stokes, Frances II, 719
Stokes, Frances D. II, 738
Stokes, Frances D. II, 769
Stokes, Francis II, 739
Stokes, Francis II, 769
Stokes, Francis B. II, 311
Stokes, Francis C. II, 719
Stokes, Francis C. II, 757
Stokes, Francis C. II, 769
Stokes, Francis Collins II, 719
Stokes, Franklin II, 313
Stokes, Franklin II, 325
Stokes, George II, 926
Stokes, George T. II, 821
Stokes, Hannah II, 185
Stokes, Hannah II, 186
Stokes, Hannah II, 228
Stokes, Hannah II, 264
Stokes, Hannah II, 265
Stokes, Hannah II, 275
Stokes, Hannah II, 302
Stokes, Hannah II, 305
Stokes, Hannah II, 313
Stokes, Hannah II, 325
Stokes, Hannah II, 326
Stokes, Hannah II, 424
Stokes, Hannah II, 661
Stokes, Hannah II, 769
Stokes, Hannah II, 1000
Stokes, Hannah II, 1030
Stokes, Hannah III, 301
Stokes, Hannah V, 79
Stokes, Hannah V, 127
Stokes, Hannah Ann II, 138
Stokes, Hannah M. V, 127
Stokes, Hannah R. II, 661
Stokes, Helen V, 127
Stokes, Helen C. V, 127
Stokes, Henry II, 302
Stokes, Henry II, 314
Stokes, Henry II, 821
Stokes, Henry II, 904
Stokes, Henry II, 926
Stokes, Herbert II, 302
Stokes, Herbert N. II, 313
Stokes, Herbert N. II, 314
Stokes, Herbert N. II, 325
Stokes, Hilliard II, 325
Stokes, Hilyard II, 314
Stokes, Hope II, 821
Stokes, Horace M. II, 424
Stokes, Horace M. II, 661
Stokes, Horace M. V, 127
Stokes, Hovan M. V, 127
Stokes, Hovan??? M. V, 127
Stokes, Isaac II, 281
Stokes, Isaac II, 290
Stokes, Isaac II, 303
Stokes, Isaac II, 661
Stokes, Isaac II, 711
Stokes, Isaac II, 757
Stokes, Isaac II, 769
Stokes, Isaac B. II, 926
Stokes, Isaac C. II, 719
Stokes, Isaac C. II, 769
Stokes, Isabella II, 661
Stokes, Israel II, 185
Stokes, Israel II, 186
Stokes, Israel II, 265
Stokes, Israel II, 302
Stokes, Israel II, 309
Stokes, Israel II, 313
Stokes, Israel II, 314
Stokes, Israel L. II, 314
Stokes, Israel L. II, 325
Stokes, Israel, Jr. II, 303
Stokes, Jacob II, 661
Stokes, James II, 311
Stokes, James II, 313
Stokes, James II, 314
Stokes, James II, 1030
Stokes, James G. II, 325
Stokes, James M. II, 314
Stokes, James M. II, 325
Stokes, Jane II, 661
Stokes, Jane II, 719
Stokes, Jarret II, 185
Stokes, Jarrett II, 302
Stokes, Jarrett II, 313
Stokes, Jarrett II, 314
Stokes, Jarrett II, 325
Stokes, Jarvis II, 186
Stokes, Jarvis II, 265
Stokes, Jas. R. VI, 856
Stokes, Jervis II, 186
Stokes, Jervis II, 265
Stokes, Jervis II, 275
Stokes, Jervis II, 309
Stokes, Jervis II, 314
Stokes, Jervis II, 315
Stokes, Jno. II, 186
Stokes, John II, 138
Stokes, John II, 186
Stokes, John II, 194
Stokes, John II, 227
Stokes, John II, 228
Stokes, John II, 264
Stokes, John II, 265
Stokes, John II, 302
Stokes, John II, 313
Stokes, John II, 314
Stokes, John II, 325
Stokes, John II, 661
Stokes, John II, 821
Stokes, John II, 1000
Stokes, John II, 1010
Stokes, John II, 1030
Stokes, John IV, 658
Stokes, John VI, 214
Stokes, John H. II, 719
Stokes, John H. II, 749
Stokes, John H. II, 769
Stokes, John H. VI, 568
Stokes, John Hinchman II, 660
Stokes, John Hinksman II, 660
Stokes, John L. II, 185
Stokes, John L. II, 265
Stokes, John L. II, 313
Stokes, John L. II, 314
Stokes, John L. II, 904
Stokes, John L. II, 926
Stokes, John Lancaster II, 265
Stokes, John Lancaster II, 821
Stokes, John Lancaster II, 926
Stokes, John S. II, 186
Stokes, John S. II, 302
Stokes, John S. IV, 657
Stokes, John S. IV, 658
Stokes, John Stoaks II, 265
Stokes, John W. II, 303
Stokes, John W. II, 307
Stokes, John W. II, 314
Stokes, John W. II, 325
Stokes, John W. II, 890
Stokes, John W. II, 926
Stokes, John Woolman II, 821
Stokes, John, Jr. II, 265
Stokes, Joseph II, 265
Stokes, Joseph II, 274
Stokes, Joseph II, 302
Stokes, Joseph II, 314
Stokes, Joseph II, 738
Stokes, Joseph II, 769
Stokes, Joseph II, 821
Stokes, Joseph II, 1000
Stokes, Joseph II, 1030
Stokes, Joseph, Jr. II, 719
Stokes, Joseph, Jr. II, 738
Stokes, Joseph, Jr. II, 769
Stokes, Joshua II, 186
Stokes, Joshua II, 314
Stokes, Joshua II, 424
Stokes, Joshua II, 661
Stokes, Joshua II, 926
Stokes, Joshua B. II, 313
Stokes, Josiah II, 821
Stokes, Josiah II, 926
Stokes, Julia II, 325
Stokes, Katherine E. II, 704
Stokes, Kesia II, 661
Stokes, Kezia II, 661
Stokes, Lena IV, 1264
Stokes, Lewis II, 763
Stokes, Lewis II, 769
Stokes, Lewis II, 926
Stokes, Lewis Knight II, 926
Stokes, Louis II, 769
Stokes, Lydia II, 281
Stokes, Lydia II, 290
Stokes, Lydia II, 302
Stokes, Lydia II, 303
Stokes, Lydia II, 314
Stokes, Lydia II, 325
Stokes, Lydia II, 711
Stokes, Lydia II, 757
Stokes, Lydia II, 769
Stokes, Lydia II, 926
Stokes, Lydia V, 933
Stokes, Lydia L. II, 719
Stokes, Lydia L. II, 749
Stokes, Lydia M. V, 933
Stokes, Lydia S. II, 316
Stokes, Lydia S. II, 325

Stokes, Lydia W. II, 763
Stokes, Lydia W. II, 769
Stokes, Malvina F. II, 302
Stokes, Malvina F. IV, 658
Stokes, Margaret II, 786
Stokes, Maria II, 265
Stokes, Maria II, 276
Stokes, Maria II, 314
Stokes, Maria V, 127
Stokes, Martha II, 228
Stokes, Martha II, 265
Stokes, Martha II, 284
Stokes, Martha II, 302
Stokes, Martha II, 314
Stokes, Martha II, 317
Stokes, Martha II, 325
Stokes, Martha B. II, 314
Stokes, Martha B. II, 325
Stokes, Martha B. II, 926
Stokes, Martha E. II, 926
Stokes, Martha H. II, 320
Stokes, Martha H. II, 325
Stokes, Mary II, 158
Stokes, Mary II, 186
Stokes, Mary II, 194
Stokes, Mary II, 265
Stokes, Mary II, 302
Stokes, Mary II, 314
Stokes, Mary II, 660
Stokes, Mary II, 678
Stokes, Mary II, 805
Stokes, Mary II, 926
Stokes, Mary II, 1010
Stokes, Mary II, 1030
Stokes, Mary II, 1031
Stokes, Mary VI, 387
Stokes, Mary VI, 568
Stokes, Mary VI, 571
Stokes, Mary VI, 669
Stokes, Mary VI, 704
Stokes, Mary VI, 706
Stokes, Mary VI, 712
Stokes, Mary VI, 713
Stokes, Mary Ann II, 926
Stokes, Mary Ann VI, 999
Stokes, Mary E. II, 738
Stokes, Mary H. II, 138
Stokes, Mary H. II, 158
Stokes, Mary Hewes II, 150
Stokes, Mary J. II, 281
Stokes, Mary J. II, 303
Stokes, Mary K. II, 719
Stokes, Melvina F. IV, 658
Stokes, Milton II, 313
Stokes, Milton II, 325
Stokes, Milton W. II, 325
Stokes, Mona V, 127
Stokes, Mordecai II, 186
Stokes, Mordecai II, 265
Stokes, Mordecai II, 456
Stokes, Mordecai II, 539
Stokes, Mordecai II, 661
Stokes, Nancy E. II, 749
Stokes, Nathan H. II, 302
Stokes, Nathan H. II, 314
Stokes, Nathan H. II, 325
Stokes, Nathaniel II, 1030
Stokes, Nathaniel II, 1031
Stokes, Nathaniel VI, 571
Stokes, Nathaniel N. II, 749
Stokes, Nathaniel Newlin II, 719
Stokes, Nathaniel Newlin, Jr. II, 769
Stokes, Phebe P. II, 290
Stokes, Phebe P. II, 303
Stokes, Rachael II, 315
Stokes, Rachel II, 186
Stokes, Rachel II, 227
Stokes, Rachel II, 265
Stokes, Rachel II, 302
Stokes, Rachel II, 307
Stokes, Rachel II, 314
Stokes, Rachel II, 821
Stokes, Rachel II, 904
Stokes, Rachel II, 926
Stokes, Rachel III, 301
Stokes, Rachel III, 370
Stokes, Rachel III, 448
Stokes, Rachel III, 476
Stokes, Rachel IV, 658
Stokes, Rachel E. II, 307
Stokes, Rachel V. II, 186
Stokes, Rachel V. II, 302
Stokes, Rachel V. IV, 657
Stokes, Rachel V. IV, 658
Stokes, Rachel W. II, 313
Stokes, Rachel W. II, 325
Stokes, Rachel W. II, 327
Stokes, Rebecca IV, 657
Stokes, Rebecca L. II, 186
Stokes, Rebecca L. II, 302
Stokes, Rebecca L. II, 313
Stokes, Rebecca L. II, 318
Stokes, Rebecca L. II, 325
Stokes, Rebecca W. II, 313
Stokes, Rebecca W. II, 320
Stokes, Rebecca W. II, 325
Stokes, Richard II, 786
Stokes, Richard II, 926
Stokes, Rowland II, 314
Stokes, Rowland II, 325
Stokes, Ruth IV, 658
Stokes, Ruth IV, 660
Stokes, Ruth Anna IV, 221
Stokes, Ruth Anna IV, 658
Stokes, Ruthanna IV, 658
Stokes, Samuel II, 186
Stokes, Samuel II, 265
Stokes, Samuel II, 661
Stokes, Samuel II, 719
Stokes, Samuel II, 926
Stokes, Samuel III, 301
Stokes, Samuel V, 933
Stokes, Samuel H. VI, 999
Stokes, Samuel, Jr. II, 217
Stokes, Samuel, Jr. II, 265
Stokes, Sarah II, 186
Stokes, Sarah II, 217
Stokes, Sarah II, 229
Stokes, Sarah II, 265
Stokes, Sarah II, 302
Stokes, Sarah II, 313
Stokes, Sarah II, 314
Stokes, Sarah II, 325
Stokes, Sarah II, 661
Stokes, Sarah II, 821
Stokes, Sarah IV, 1336
Stokes, Sarah B. II, 313
Stokes, Sarah B. II, 321
Stokes, Sarah B. II, 325
Stokes, Sarah R. II, 229
Stokes, Sarah R. II, 265
Stokes, Sarah Rodgers II, 265
Stokes, Sarah W. II, 769
Stokes, Selano II, 661
Stokes, Serena III, 301
Stokes, Silvanus VI, 214
Stokes, Stogdel II, 265
Stokes, Stogdell II, 186
Stokes, Stogdell II, 265
Stokes, Stogdill II, 265
Stokes, Susan II, 302
Stokes, Susan II, 305
Stokes, Susan II, 719
Stokes, Susan W. II, 224
Stokes, Susan W. II, 265
Stokes, Susan W. II, 314
Stokes, Susan W. II, 325
Stokes, Susan W. II, 326
Stokes, Susanna II, 661
Stokes, Susannah II, 265
Stokes, Susannah II, 1010
Stokes, Susannah II, 1030
Stokes, Sylania II, 926
Stokes, Sylvania II, 821
Stokes, Sylvia II, 719
Stokes, Tacy II, 185
Stokes, Tacy II, 265
Stokes, Tacy II, 302
Stokes, Tacy II, 313
Stokes, Thomas II, 661
Stokes, Thomas III, 301
Stokes, Thomas III, 370
Stokes, Thomas III, 448
Stokes, Thomas III, 476
Stokes, Thomas, Jr. II, 265
Stokes, Thos. II, 821
Stokes, Thos., Sr. II, 821
Stokes, Thos., Sr. II, 926
Stokes, Walter P. II, 719
Stokes, Walter P., Jr. II, 719
Stokes, William II, 303
Stokes, William II, 313
Stokes, William II, 314
Stokes, William II, 322
Stokes, William II, 325
Stokes, William F. II, 424
Stokes, William J. II, 314
Stokes, William J. II, 325
Stokes, Wm. II, 138
Stokes, Wm. II, 158
Stokes, Wm. II, 265
Stokes, Wm. II, 660
Stokes, Wm. II, 661
Stokes, Wm. F. II, 661
Stokes, Woolman II, 302
Stokes, Woolman II, 314
Stokes, Woolman II, 325
Stokesberry, Emma M. IV, 658
Stokesberry, Henry IV, 658
Stokesberry, Inetta P. IV, 658
Stokesberry, Inetta Pearl IV, 658
Stokesberry, Isaac IV, 658
Stokesberry, John IV, 658
Stokesberry, John, Jr. IV, 658
Stokesberry, Maria Elma IV, 658
Stokesberry, Rachel IV, 658
Stokesberry, Ruth IV, 658
Stokesberry, Sarah IV, 658
Stokesberry, Susannah IV, 658
Stokesberry, William IV, 658
Stokesbery, Emma M. IV, 658
Stokesbury, Sarah VI, 606
Stokey, ??? III, 301
Stokey, Catharine III, 301
Stokey, Isaac III, 301
Stokler, John II, 448
Stokler, Richard II, 448
Stokton, Mary II, 258
Stokton, Mary II, 264
Stoler, Adam II, 424
Stoley, Thomas II, 17
Stoll, Jennie Reams V, 600
Stoll, Mary Chamberlain IV, 284
Stolts, Abigail V, 765
Stolts, Daniel V, 765
Stolts, John, Jr. V, 765
Stolts, Martha Ellen V, 765
Stoltz, Abigail V, 765
Stoltz, Charles W. V, 713
Stoltz, Daniel V, 765
Stoltz, David A. V, 765
Stoltz, Eloise IV, 1339
Stoltz, Geo. W. IV, 1339
Stoltz, Jane V, 675
Stoltz, Jane V, 713
Stoltz, John V, 765
Stoltz, John, Jr. V, 765
Stoltz, Martha Ellen V, 765
Stoltz, Rufus IV, 1339
Stoltz, Sarah IV, 1339
Stonaker, May V, 465
Stone, ??? VI, 508
Stone, Abbie T. I, 612
Stone, Abigail I, 52
Stone, Abigail I, 75
Stone, Abraham J. V, 646
Stone, Admire VI, 888
Stone, Admire VI, 929
Stone, Admire VI, 945
Stone, Admire VI, 999
Stone, Admire H. VI, 1014
Stone, Agnes VI, 233
Stone, Agnes VI, 238
Stone, Agnes VI, 239
Stone, Agnes VI, 273
Stone, Agness VI, 273
Stone, Albert G. VI, 838
Stone, Alonza VI, 273
Stone, Alonzo VI, 273
Stone, Ann B. VI, 838
Stone, Anna VI, 272
Stone, Anna E. II, 833
Stone, Anna E. II, 926
Stone, Anna L. III, 149
Stone, Annie L. III, 213
Stone, Annie L. III, 214
Stone, Annie L. III, 301
Stone, Anthony VI, 273
Stone, Apphia VI, 945
Stone, Apphia VI, 962
Stone, Apphia VI, 998
Stone, Armsbe VI, 239
Stone, Asbury I, 612
Stone, B. F. VI, 273
Stone, Barsheba VI, 998
Stone, Benjamin F. VI, 273
Stone, Bernard Fenelon VI, 710
Stone, Caroline V, 646
Stone, Caroline VI, 273
Stone, Carrie I, 624
Stone, Catharine I, 75
Stone, Catharine I, 668
Stone, Catharine I, 669
Stone, Catharine I, 690
Stone, Catherine I, 690
Stone, Center I, 690
Stone, Charles M. VI, 432
Stone, Christian I, 568
Stone, Christian I, 575
Stone, Christian I, 668
Stone, Christian VI, 234
Stone, Christian VI, 273
Stone, Christopher VI, 856
Stone, Clementine VI, 916
Stone, Cordelia D. VI, 568
Stone, Daniel VI, 507
Stone, Daniel VI, 512
Stone, Daniel VI, 539
Stone, Daniel VI, 568
Stone, Daniel Edwin VI, 568
Stone, David VI, 448
Stone, Deborah II, 533
Stone, Deborah II, 661
Stone, Edna T. VI, 708
Stone, Edna T. VI, 783
Stone, Edward Walker VI, 432
Stone, Eleanor H. IV, 110
Stone, Eleanor H. IV, 116
Stone, Eleanor H. VI, 568
Stone, Eleanor H. VI, 583
Stone, Eliza V, 465
Stone, Eliza V, 713
Stone, Eliza VI, 568
Stone, Eliza C. VI, 432
Stone, Elizabeth VI, 234
Stone, Elizabeth VI, 273
Stone, Elizabeth VI, 561
Stone, Elizabeth VI, 568
Stone, Elizabeth VI, 856
Stone, Elizabeth VI, 944
Stone, Elizabeth VI, 989
Stone, Elizabeth VI, 999
Stone, Elma I, 612
Stone, Elma I, 641
Stone, Emily Elizabeth VI, 273
Stone, Eusebius VI, 886
Stone, Eusebius VI, 967
Stone, Eusebius VI, 1013
Stone, Eusebius VI, 1018
Stone, Faustine I, 895
Stone, Faustine I, 901
Stone, Frank IV, 1339
Stone, Frank IV, 1340
Stone, Geo. VI, 1013
Stone, George II, 1030
Stone, George VI, 944
Stone, George VI, 963
Stone, George VI, 999
Stone, George VI, 1009
Stone, Geraldine IV, 1339
Stone, Geraldine E. IV, 1339
Stone, Gladys H. I, 624
Stone, Grace VI, 856
Stone, Granville VI, 568
Stone, Hannah V, 839
Stone, Hannah V, 863
Stone, Helen IV, 1143
Stone, Helen IV, 1187
Stone, Helen VI, 708
Stone, Henry VI, 999
Stone, Hezekiah VI, 848
Stone, Hugh Exton II, 833
Stone, Hugh Exton II, 926
Stone, Hugh M. I, 1162
Stone, Huldah I, 669
Stone, Huldah I, 690
Stone, Huldah VI, 272
Stone, Huldah VI, 273
Stone, Isaac I, 901
Stone, Isaac VI, 708
Stone, Isaac S VI, 710
Stone, Isaac S. VI, 708
Stone, Isaac S. VI, 713
Stone, Isaac S. VI, 784
Stone, Isaac S. Stone VI, 783
Stone, J. A. VI, 273
Stone, J. Austin VI, 708
Stone, James VI, 998
Stone, James VI, 999
Stone, James Austin VI, 708
Stone, James Austin VI, 742
Stone, James Austin VI, 784
Stone, James H. VI, 372
Stone, James H. VI, 448
Stone, James H. VI, 568
Stone, James H. VI, 708
Stone, James H. VI, 713
Stone, Jane VI, 708
Stone, Jane VI, 999
Stone, Jas. H. III, 214
Stone, Jemima VI, 512
Stone, Jemimah VI, 568
Stone, Jenny IV, 1241
Stone, Jesse Calvert VI, 448
Stone, John I, 75
Stone, John I, 575
Stone, John I, 668
Stone, John I, 669
Stone, John I, 690
Stone, John I, 865
Stone, John I, 901
Stone, John II, 833
Stone, John II, 926
Stone, John VI, 234
Stone, John VI, 273
Stone, John VI, 856
Stone, John VI, 999
Stone, Joseph Crew I, 420
Stone, Joseph Crew VI, 273
Stone, Joseph H. VI, 568
Stone, Joseph H. VI, 857
Stone, Joshua VI, 273
Stone, Joshua VI, 856
Stone, Laura V, 713
Stone, Laura A. VI, 273
Stone, Laura M. V, 713
Stone, Leo IV, 1339
Stone, Leo IV, 1340
Stone, Lewellyn P. VI, 568
Stone, Lewis VI, 432
Stone, Lewis D. VI, 508
Stone, Littleberry VI, 999
Stone, Louisa II, 833
Stone, Louisa II, 926
Stone, Louisa VI, 273
Stone, Lucinda VI, 999
Stone, Lucy VI, 234
Stone, Lucy VI, 273
Stone, Lucy VI, 848
Stone, Lucy Ann VI, 999
Stone, Luse VI, 239
Stone, Lydia I, 57
Stone, Lydia I, 75
Stone, Margaret VI, 742
Stone, Margaret VI, 784
Stone, Margaret H. VI, 857
Stone, Marietta VI, 509
Stone, Martha VI, 856
Stone, Martha VI, 891
Stone, Martha VI, 999
Stone, Martha Ann III, 214
Stone, Martha Ann VI, 708
Stone, Martha Ann VI, 713
Stone, Mary I, 1162
Stone, Mary IV, 61
Stone, Mary IV, 65
Stone, Mary VI, 18
Stone, Mary VI, 273
Stone, Mary VI, 431
Stone, Mary VI, 448
Stone, Mary VI, 888
Stone, Mary VI, 1013
Stone, Mary C. VI, 999
Stone, Mary E. I, 1152
Stone, Mary E. I, 1162
Stone, Mary E. V, 933
Stone, Mary Eugenia VI, 568
Stone, Menoah VI, 962
Stone, Micajah VI, 838
Stone, Micajah VI, 863
Stone, Micajah VI, 885
Stone, Micajah VI, 999
Stone, Milley VI, 962
Stone, Miriam I, 63
Stone, Miriam I, 75
Stone, Moses VI, 979
Stone, Moses VI, 999
Stone, N. C. VI, 923
Stone, Nancy VI, 972
Stone, Nancy VI, 999
Stone, Nicholas I, 383
Stone, Nicholas I, 419
Stone, Nicholas I, 420
Stone, Nicholas VI, 18
Stone, Nicholas VI, 234
Stone, Nicholas VI, 238
Stone, Nicholas VI, 239
Stone, Nicholas VI, 273
Stone, Nicholas VI, 275
Stone, Nicholas VI, 276
Stone, Nicolas VI, 273
Stone, Nicols VI, 273
Stone, Polly VI, 856
Stone, Rachel VI, 507
Stone, Rachel VI, 628
Stone, Rachel VI, 655
Stone, Rachel J. VI, 477
Stone, Rachel J. VI, 507
Stone, Rachel Jane VI, 402
Stone, Richard Ballard VI, 273
Stone, Ruth IV, 1264
Stone, Salathial I, 687
Stone, Salathial I, 690
Stone, Salathiel I, 669
Stone, Sallie Ann VI, 508
Stone, Sally I, 1006
Stone, Sally VI, 999
Stone, Samuel IV, 110
Stone, Samuel L. VI, 432
Stone, Samuel S. VI, 568
Stone, Sarah I, 556
Stone, Sarah I, 575
Stone, Sarah I, 668
Stone, Sarah VI, 448
Stone, Sarah VI, 507
Stone, Sarah VI, 512
Stone, Sarah VI, 539
Stone, Sarah VI, 568
Stone, Sarah VI, 891
Stone, Sarah Ann VI, 539
Stone, Sarah Ann VI, 568
Stone, Sarah H. VI, 372
Stone, Sarah H. VI, 448
Stone, Sarah H. VI, 568

e, Sarah M. VI, 432
e, Sarah, Jr. VI, 568
e, Stella VI, 1014
e, Stephen VI, 999
e, Susan T. VI, 432
e, Susanah VI, 273
e, Susanna I, 687
e, Susanna I, 690
e, Susanna VI, 941
e, Susanna VI, 999
e, Susannah VI, 227
e, Susie IV, 1340
e, Tabitha VI, 856
e, Thamasin VI, 783
e, Thamasin J. VI, 708
e, Thamasin J. VI, 713
e, Thamasin J. VI, 784
e, Thamasin Jane VI, 710
e, Thomas VI, 272
e, Thomas VI, 512
e, Thomas VI, 561
e, Thomas VI, 568
e, Thomas A. VI, 999
e, Thomas P. VI, 568
e, W. H. I, 624
e, Wd. Sarah VI, 272
e, William VI, 808
e, William VI, 814
e, William VI, 835
e, William VI, 837
e, William VI, 856
e, William VI, 907
e, William VI, 944
e, William VI, 999
e, William H. VI, 540
e, William H. VI, 568
e, Wm. IV, 1241
ebank, Susannah II, 101
ebridg, Mary VI, 397
ebridg, Mary VI, 448
ehill, E. Daisy III, 301
ehill, John III, 301
ehill, Sarah III, 301
ehill, William M. III, 301
eking, Eliza V, 465
eking, Eliza H. V, 465
eking, May V, 465
eman, Charlotte I, 958
eman, Charlotte I, 1006
eman, David Wm. V, 765
eman, Elizabeth I, 420
eman, Elizabeth I, 958
eman, Elizabeth I, 961
eman, Elizabeth I, 969
eman, Elizabeth I, 980
eman, Elizabeth I, 998
eman, Elizabeth I, 1005
eman, Elizabeth I, 1006
eman, Elizabeth I, 1009
eman, Elizabeth I, 1012
eman, Elizabeth Davis I, 998
eman, Elizabeth T. V, 765
eman, Elizabeth, Sr. I, 1006
eman, Emely I, 983
eman, Emely I, 998
eman, Emily I, 958
eman, Emily I, 1006
eman, Emma Jane V, 765
eman, Evelyn I, 1006
eman, Evlyn I, 998
eman, Henston Floyd V, 765
eman, James I, 958
eman, James, Sr. I, 1012
eman, Janny Alice I, 980
eman, Janny Alice I, 998
eman, Jeams I, 969
eman, Jenney Alice I, 1006
eman, Jenny I, 1006
eman, John Watson V, 765
eman, Joshua I, 420
eman, Joshua I, 958
eman, Joshua I, 961
eman, Joshua I, 969
eman, Joshua I, 1006
eman, Joshua I, 1008
eman, Joshua I, 1012
eman, Joshua F. I, 1006
eman, Joshua Freeman
I, 1006
eman, Julia Anne I, 1006
eman, Levi James I, 958
eman, Lewis I, 998
eman, Lucinda I, 958
eman, Lydia I, 958
eman, Lydia I, 1006
eman, Lydia I, 1007
eman, Lydia I, 1012
eman, Mark I, 1006
eman, Mark D. I, 998
eman, Mark D. I, 1006
eman, Martin I, 998
Stoneman, Mary I, 958
Stoneman, Mary I, 1006
Stoneman, Mary I, 1010
Stoneman, Mary I, 1012
Stoneman, Milton I, 998
Stoneman, Nancy I, 958
Stoneman, Nancy I, 998
Stoneman, Nancy I, 1006
Stoneman, Newel I, 998
Stoneman, Sally I, 958
Stoneman, Sally I, 1006
Stoneman, Sally I, 1008
Stoneman, Sally I, 1012
Stoneman, Sarah I, 389
Stoneman, Sarah I, 420
Stoneman, Sarah I, 958
Stoneman, Sarah I, 969
Stoneman, Sarah I, 1001
Stoneman, Sarah I, 1012
Stoneman, William I, 998
Stoner, David VI, 940
Stoner, David VI, 999
Stoner, John VI, 856
Stoner, Martha A. VI, 999
Stoner, Mary E. VI, 856
Stonerock, Mattie IV, 1264
Stonerock, Sarah IV, 1264
Stookesberry, Inetta Pearl
IV, 658
Stooksberry, Harriet IV, 877
Stooksberry, Harriet IV, 884
Stooksberry, Henry IV, 884
Stooksberry, Isaac IV, 884
Stooksberry, John IV, 883
Stooksberry, John IV, 884
Stooksberry, Maria Elma IV, 618
Stooksberry, Maria Elma IV, 658
Stooksberry, Rachel IV, 884
Stooksberry, Ruth IV, 869
Stooksberry, Ruth IV, 884
Stooksberry, Sarah IV, 883
Stooksberry, Sarah IV, 884
Stooksberry, Susannah IV, 884
Stooksberry, William IV, 884
Stooksbetty, Isaac IV, 884
Stoopes, Sina V, 532
Stoops, Alta V, 465
Stoops, Cora IV, 1264
Stoops, Cora Ethel IV, 1264
Stoops, Edna May IV, 1264
Stoops, Fred V, 713
Stoops, Frederick V, 713
Stoops, Lizzie V, 207
Stoops, Lucinda IV, 1264
Stoops, Luetrel IV, 1264
Stoops, Margaret V, 713
Stoops, Myrtle V, 465
Stoops, Samuel V, 465
Stoops, Sarah Alcinda V, 532
Stoops, Sina V, 532
Stoops, Sina V, 713
Stoops, Walter V, 713
Stoops, Zot V, 465
Stoors, Hannah VI, 214
Stora, John V, 886
Storch, Caroline V, 934
Storch, Charles Raymond V, 933
Storch, Chas. Raymond V, 934
Storch, Cora V, 934
Storch, Dayton V, 934
Storch, Dayton T. V, 934
Storch, Dayton Townsend V, 933
Storch, Dorotha Laura V, 934
Storch, Dorothy Laura V, 934
Storch, Ella V, 934
Storch, Elleanor V, 934
Storch, Geo. A. V, 934
Storch, Geo. Anderson V, 933
Storch, Geo. Anderson V, 944
Storch, Gustavus F. V, 933
Storch, John Oliver V, 934
Storch, Mary C. V, 934
Storch, Mary Catharine V, 933
Storch, Mary Catharine V, 944
Storch, Oliver V, 934
Storch, Robert V, 934
Storch, Robert C. V, 934
Storch, Robert Chester V, 933
Storch, Sarah Elizabeth V, 933
Storch, Vergie Lee V, 934
Storer, Archibald VI, 856
Storer, Bartlet VI, 856
Storer, Bartlett VI, 829
Storer, Edward VI, 818
Storer, Edward VI, 826
Storer, Elizabeth VI, 818
Storer, Elizabeth VI, 829
Storer, Elizabeth VI, 856
Storer, Elva V, 351
Storer, Elva V, 361
Storer, Glenn V, 351
Storer, Glenn V, 361
Storer, Henrietta VI, 856
Storer, John B. VI, 856
Storer, Kitty F. VI, 856
Storer, Patty VI, 856
Storer, Pleasant VI, 856
Storer, Polly VI, 826
Storer, Sally VI, 856
Storer, Samuel VI, 856
Storey, Creighton R. III, 190
Storey, Creighton R. III, 301
Storey, Dorothea III, 190
Storey, Dorothea III, 301
Storey, Edward II, 448
Storey, Elizabeth III, 71
Storey, Jane VI, 856
Storey, Joseph E. VI, 856
Storey, Peter III, 190
Storey, Sadie III, 190
Storey, Sadie III, 301
Stork, Mary II, 235
Stork, Mary II, 266
Stork, Robert II, 266
Storker, Lydia I, 838
Storm, Annie L. III, 377
Storm, Annie L. III, 385
Storm, Elizabeth E. III, 385
Storm, Frederic III, 385
Storm, Frederick III, 377
Storm, Frederick III, 385
Storm, George III, 385
Storm, Mary III, 385
Storm, Thos. C. III, 385
Stormes, W. H. IV, 1295
Stormes, Willie IV, 1295
Storrs, Hannah VI, 214
Storrs, Joseph III, 301
Storrs, Joshua VI, 98
Storrs, Joshua VI, 106
Storrs, Joshua VI, 122
Storrs, Joshua VI, 203
Storrs, Joshua VI, 206
Storrs, Joshua VI, 214
Storrs, Patience III, 301
Storrs, Robert III, 301
Storrs, Samuel VI, 122
Storrs, Susanna VI, 203
Storrs, Susanna VI, 206
Storrs, Susanna VI, 214
Storrs, Susanna, Junior VI, 214
Storrs, Wd. Patience III, 301
Storrs, William VI, 214
Story, ??? III, 87
Story, ??? III, 301
Story, ??? VI, 42
Story, Ann II, 424
Story, Ann II, 649
Story, Ann II, 661
Story, Caleb E. I, 223
Story, Elizabeth I, 690
Story, Elizabeth II, 1008
Story, Elizabeth II, 1030
Story, Ella E. I, 222
Story, Ella E. I, 223
Story, Emigin I, 215
Story, Enoch III, 301
Story, Garnetta D. I, 222
Story, Hannah II, 661
Story, Hannah II, 687
Story, Helen II, 1060
Story, John II, 424
Story, John II, 661
Story, Kaleb E. I, 222
Story, Margaret II, 1060
Story, Martha C. III, 87
Story, Martha C. III, 301
Story, Mary II, 479
Story, Mary II, 661
Story, Mary II, 687
Story, Mary III, 301
Story, Nannie E. I, 223
Story, Patience II, 583
Story, Patience III, 211
Story, Patience III, 301
Story, Rachel II, 969
Story, Rachel II, 1030
Story, Robert III, 211
Story, Robert III, 301
Story, Samuel II, 424
Story, Samuel II, 661
Story, Samuel II, 970
Story, Samuel II, 1030
Story, Sarah II, 687
Story, Thomas II, 424
Story, Thomas II, 649
Story, Thomas II, 661
Story, Thomas II, 970
Story, Thomas II, 1030
Story, Thomas VI, 11
Story, Thomas VI, 12
Story, Thomas VI, 13
Story, Thomas VI, 23
Story, Thomas VI, 24
Stotesbury, Martha II, 758
Stotesbury, Martha II, 769
Stothard, ??? III, 301
Stothard, Eliza III, 301
Stothard, James III, 301
Stotler, Leota V, 361
Stotler, Martha V, 361
Stott, Elizabeth VI, 915
Stott, John VI, 915
Stott, Malinda VI, 999
Stott, Nathan VI, 999
Stotts, J. R. IV, 1241
Stotz, Margaret IV, 552
Stoud, Edna Mae V, 127
Stoud, Frederick D. V, 127
Stoud, Mary C. V, 127
Stoud, Maybelle L. V, 127
Stoud, Peter S. V, 127
Stoud, Sadie V, 127
Stoud, Wm. V, 127
Stouffer, Evelin IV, 1264
Stouffer, Evelyn IV, 1264
Stouffer, Margaret IV, 1264
Stouffer, May IV, 1264
Stoughtenburg, Parmelia III, 280
Stoughtenburg, Peter III, 280
Stoughtenburg, Sarah III, 280
Stoughtenburgh, David III, 301
Stoughtenburgh, Edwin III, 301
Stoughtenburgh, Jacob F. III, 301
Stoughtenburgh, James V.
III, 301
Stoughtenburgh, Joseph III, 301
Stoughtenburgh, Mary III, 301
Stoughtenburgh, Mary Ann
III, 301
Stoughtenburgh, Pamelia
III, 301
Stoughtenburgh, Parmelia
III, 301
Stoughtenburgh, Peter III, 301
Stoughtenburgh, Peter L. III, 301
Stoughtenburgh, Samuel V.
III, 301
Stoughtenburgh, Sarah III, 301
Stoughtenburgh, Wright F.
III, 301
Stoughton, Ada R. III, 301
Stoughton, Bradley III, 301
Stoughton, Bradley III, 335
Stoughton, Chas. B. III, 301
Stoughton, Grace A. III, 301
Stoughton, Grace Abbie III, 301
Stoughton, Grace Abbie III, 335
Stoughton, Lenore III, 37
Stoughton, Lenore III, 301
Stoughton, Lenore M. III, 301
Stoughton, Lenore Maple III, 301
Stoughton, Philip Van Everen
III, 37
Stoughton, Philip Van Everen
III, 301
Stoup, Isaac II, 424
Stout, Aaron I, 364
Stout, Aaron I, 420
Stout, Achsah I, 893
Stout, Achsah I, 901
Stout, Ada L. I, 934
Stout, Ada Lou I, 949
Stout, Addison T. I, 421
Stout, Adonijah I, 470
Stout, Adonijah I, 471
Stout, Adonijah I, 485
Stout, Alexander I, 420
Stout, Alida May V, 281
Stout, Allen I. V, 281
Stout, Alvin H. V, 281
Stout, Amanda I, 421
Stout, Amanda E. I, 421
Stout, Amanda Ellen I, 421
Stout, Amey I, 471
Stout, Amy I, 484
Stout, Ann I, 365
Stout, Ann I, 397
Stout, Ann I, 409
Stout, Ann I, 419
Stout, Ann I, 420
Stout, Ann IV, 1380
Stout, Ann V, 127
Stout, Ann V, 469
Stout, Ann V, 532
Stout, Ann V, 646
Stout, Ann E. VI, 831
Stout, Anna I, 420
Stout, Anna I, 471
Stout, Anna I, 482
Stout, Anna I, 485
Stout, Anna I, 615
Stout, Anna V, 532
Stout, Anna V, 646
Stout, Anna Elizabeth I, 471
Stout, Anne I, 364
Stout, Anne V, 497
Stout, Anne V, 532
Stout, Anne V, 544
Stout, Annie Luella I, 626
Stout, Asenath I, 421
Stout, Benjamin F. VI, 831
Stout, Benoni J. I, 485
Stout, Benoni Joseph I, 471
Stout, Calvin IV, 1187
Stout, Calvin C. I, 485
Stout, Calvin T. I, 472
Stout, Catharine I, 472
Stout, Catharine I, 477
Stout, Catharine I, 485
Stout, Charity I, 350
Stout, Charity I, 361
Stout, Charity I, 364
Stout, Charity I, 365
Stout, Charity I, 420
Stout, Charity I, 421
Stout, Charity II, 947
Stout, Charles I, 364
Stout, Charles I, 365
Stout, Charles I, 412
Stout, Charles I, 420
Stout, Charles I, 421
Stout, Charles I, 470
Stout, Charles I, 471
Stout, Charles I, 472
Stout, Charles I, 479
Stout, Charles I, 484
Stout, Charles I, 641
Stout, Charles Henry I, 626
Stout, Charles T. I, 471
Stout, Charlotte V, 600
Stout, Charlotte V, 866
Stout, Charlotte, V, 863
Stout, Clara Ella I, 934
Stout, Connie I, 615
Stout, Connie I, 641
Stout, Connie J. I, 632
Stout, Connie J. I, 641
Stout, Cynthia I, 485
Stout, Cyrus I, 421
Stout, Cyrus C. I, 471
Stout, Daniel H. I, 485
Stout, David I, 364
Stout, David I, 365
Stout, David I, 420
Stout, David I, 421
Stout, David I, 471
Stout, David I, 473
Stout, David I, 485
Stout, David I, 1132
Stout, David V, 127
Stout, David V, 532
Stout, David A. I, 421
Stout, David O. I, 421
Stout, David W. I, 421
Stout, Deborah Ann V, 127
Stout, Deborah F. I, 471
Stout, Dina V, 542
Stout, Dinah I, 364
Stout, Dinah V, 127
Stout, Dinah V, 532
Stout, Drucella V, 713
Stout, Edith I, 421
Stout, Edith I, 460
Stout, Edith I, 471
Stout, Edith I, 485
Stout, Eleanor I, 683
Stout, Eleanor I, 690
Stout, Eleanor I, 969
Stout, Eleanor I, 1132
Stout, Eleazor I, 484
Stout, Elener I, 420
Stout, Elenor I, 420
Stout, Eli N. I, 641
Stout, Eli Newlin I, 472
Stout, Eli Newlin I, 626
Stout, Elihu V, 532
Stout, Elijah V, 600
Stout, Elijah V, 863
Stout, Eliza V, 532
Stout, Eliza V, 646
Stout, Eliza Jane V, 646
Stout, Elizabeth I, 351
Stout, Elizabeth I, 361
Stout, Elizabeth I, 362
Stout, Elizabeth I, 365
Stout, Elizabeth I, 387
Stout, Elizabeth I, 410
Stout, Elizabeth I, 412
Stout, Elizabeth I, 420
Stout, Elizabeth I, 471
Stout, Elizabeth I, 485
Stout, Elizabeth I, 969
Stout, Elizabeth I, 1129

Stout, Elizabeth I, 1132
Stout, Elizabeth IV, 1295
Stout, Elizabeth V, 646
Stout, Elizabeth Moon I, 420
Stout, Emma L. I, 471
Stout, Enoch I, 626
Stout, Enoch I, 641
Stout, Enoch L. I, 615
Stout, Enoch L. I, 641
Stout, Enos I, 471
Stout, Enos Lewis I, 471
Stout, Epharium I, 969
Stout, Ephraim I, 365
Stout, Ephraim I, 1099
Stout, Ephraim I, 1132
Stout, Esther C. V, 127
Stout, Ethel I, 626
Stout, Ethel I, 641
Stout, Etta I, 641
Stout, Etta IV, 1241
Stout, Flora J. I, 421
Stout, Florence V, 713
Stout, Frances I, 364
Stout, Frances I, 420
Stout, Geo. V, 532
Stout, George I, 364
Stout, George V, 127
Stout, George V, 532
Stout, George V, 646
Stout, George M. I, 471
Stout, George Monroe I, 471
Stout, Gertrude I, 641
Stout, Gertrude Lilliam I, 626
Stout, Hannah I, 351
Stout, Hannah I, 361
Stout, Hannah I, 364
Stout, Hannah I, 365
Stout, Hannah I, 375
Stout, Hannah I, 386
Stout, Hannah I, 409
Stout, Hannah I, 412
Stout, Hannah I, 420
Stout, Hannah I, 421
Stout, Hannah I, 423
Stout, Hannah I, 470
Stout, Hannah I, 471
Stout, Hannah I, 472
Stout, Hannah I, 479
Stout, Hannah I, 483
Stout, Hannah I, 484
Stout, Hannah I, 485
Stout, Hannah I, 626
Stout, Hannah I, 685
Stout, Hannah I, 690
Stout, Hannah V, 532
Stout, Hannah V, 646
Stout, Hannah C. I, 421
Stout, Hannah E. I, 421
Stout, Hannah Jane I, 421
Stout, Hannah Jane I, 471
Stout, Harmon J. I, 485
Stout, Harmon Z. I, 472
Stout, Harmon Z. I, 734
Stout, Ida F. I, 471
Stout, Ina A. IV, 957
Stout, Irvin Taber I, 485
Stout, Isaac I, 365
Stout, Isaac I, 420
Stout, Isaac I, 969
Stout, Isaac I, 1101
Stout, Isaac I, 1110
Stout, Isaac I, 1132
Stout, Isaac V, 127
Stout, Isaac V, 207
Stout, Isaac V, 485
Stout, Isaac V, 532
Stout, Isaac V, 600
Stout, Isaac V, 863
Stout, Isaac H. V, 532
Stout, Isaac Jones I, 1132
Stout, Isaac M. V, 127
Stout, Isaac M., Jr. V, 127
Stout, Isaac Newton I, 901
Stout, Isaac, Jr. V, 532
Stout, Isaac, Jr. V, 600
Stout, Isac I, 420
Stout, Isaiah V, 532
Stout, Isaiah V, 600
Stout, Isam I, 420
Stout, J. B. VI, 831
Stout, J. Nereus I, 471
Stout, Jacob I, 365
Stout, Jacob I, 420
Stout, Jacob I, 1132
Stout, Jacob Andrew I, 421
Stout, Jane I, 378
Stout, Jane I, 420
Stout, Jane I, 421
Stout, Jane V, 127
Stout, Jane V, 600
Stout, Jane V, 646
Stout, Jane V, 968
Stout, Jane V, 977
Stout, Jane D. V, 127
Stout, Jane D. V, 600
Stout, Jane D. V, 977
Stout, Jesse I, 365
Stout, Jesse I, 420
Stout, Jesse I, 1110
Stout, Jesse I, 1132
Stout, Jesse V, 127
Stout, Jesse V, 178
Stout, Jesse V, 207
Stout, Jesse V, 532
Stout, Jesse V, 600
Stout, Jesse V, 863
Stout, Job I, 365
Stout, Job I, 421
Stout, John I, 364
Stout, John I, 365
Stout, John I, 420
Stout, John I, 421
Stout, John I, 485
Stout, John V, 127
Stout, John V, 465
Stout, John V, 466
Stout, John V, 469
Stout, John V, 532
Stout, John V, 544
Stout, John V, 610
Stout, John V, 646
Stout, John C. I, 471
Stout, John C. I, 483
Stout, John C. I, 485
Stout, John J. I, 421
Stout, John S. I, 421
Stout, John T. I, 421
Stout, John W. III, 301
Stout, John, Jr. V, 473
Stout, John, Jr. V, 508
Stout, John, Jr. V, 532
Stout, Jonathan I, 365
Stout, Jonathan I, 420
Stout, Joseph I, 361
Stout, Joseph I, 364
Stout, Joseph I, 365
Stout, Joseph I, 420
Stout, Joseph I, 457
Stout, Joseph I, 471
Stout, Joseph I, 482
Stout, Joseph I, 483
Stout, Joseph I, 484
Stout, Joseph I, 485
Stout, Joseph I, 685
Stout, Joseph I, 690
Stout, Joseph I, 969
Stout, Joseph Alen I, 484
Stout, Joseph E. I, 471
Stout, Joseph, Sr. I, 485
Stout, Joshua I, 421
Stout, Josiah Clarkson I, 471
Stout, Julianna I, 1132
Stout, Kelita C. I, 485
Stout, Ketita I, 471
Stout, Leah I, 471
Stout, Leah I, 483
Stout, Leah I, 485
Stout, Lena Emma I, 934
Stout, Levi I, 484
Stout, Levi N. I, 459
Stout, Lew Wallace IV, 957
Stout, Lewis I, 485
Stout, Lidya I, 1110
Stout, Louisa II, 947
Stout, Louisa IV, 1187
Stout, Lucetta III, 301
Stout, Lucetta V, 465
Stout, Lucetta V, 466
Stout, Lucetta T. V, 465
Stout, Lucinda I, 934
Stout, Lucinda V, 527
Stout, Lucinda V, 532
Stout, Lucinda V, 646
Stout, Luzena I, 485
Stout, Luzena Mirium I, 471
Stout, Lyda I, 365
Stout, Lydia I, 1132
Stout, Lydia V, 127
Stout, Lydia V, 532
Stout, Lydia V, 600
Stout, Lydia H. IV, 1380
Stout, Mahlon I, 421
Stout, Malissa J. I, 471
Stout, Margaret I, 345
Stout, Margaret I, 362
Stout, Margaret I, 364
Stout, Margaret I, 365
Stout, Margaret I, 412
Stout, Margaret I, 420
Stout, Margaret I, 471
Stout, Margaret I, 662
Stout, Margaret I, 690
Stout, Margaret I, 1110
Stout, Margaret V, 127
Stout, Margaret V, 469
Stout, Margaret V, 532
Stout, Margaret V, 542
Stout, Margaret V, 544
Stout, Margaret Lavina I, 485
Stout, Margery I, 465
Stout, Margery I, 471
Stout, Margery I, 477
Stout, Margery I, 485
Stout, Margret I, 364
Stout, Margret I, 365
Stout, Maria V, 127
Stout, Martha V, 46
Stout, Martha V, 485
Stout, Martha V, 532
Stout, Martha V, 600
Stout, Martha L. IV, 1187
Stout, Martha Leuevina I, 471
Stout, Martitia I, 470
Stout, Martitia I, 471
Stout, Martitia I, 485
Stout, Mary I, 361
Stout, Mary I, 364
Stout, Mary I, 365
Stout, Mary I, 393
Stout, Mary I, 407
Stout, Mary I, 411
Stout, Mary I, 412
Stout, Mary I, 420
Stout, Mary I, 421
Stout, Mary I, 430
Stout, Mary I, 464
Stout, Mary I, 471
Stout, Mary I, 477
Stout, Mary I, 485
Stout, Mary I, 934
Stout, Mary I, 969
Stout, Mary I, 1132
Stout, Mary II, 821
Stout, Mary V, 127
Stout, Mary V, 532
Stout, Mary V, 533
Stout, Mary V, 600
Stout, Mary V, 863
Stout, Mary V, 866
Stout, Mary Ann I, 421
Stout, Mary Ann I, 472
Stout, Mary B. V, 532
Stout, Mary B. V, 610
Stout, Mary B. V, 646
Stout, Mary E. I, 471
Stout, Mary E. I, 472
Stout, Mary F. I, 485
Stout, Mary G. IV, 1380
Stout, Mary Gray IV, 1358
Stout, Mary J. I, 421
Stout, Mary L. I, 471
Stout, Mary L. V, 127
Stout, Matilda I, 1132
Stout, Matilda V, 127
Stout, Matilda V, 532
Stout, Matilda V, 555
Stout, Matilda V, 600
Stout, Matthew V, 646
Stout, Melvin V, 1020
Stout, Metelde I, 1110
Stout, Micajah V, 532
Stout, Michal I, 420
Stout, Minnie IV, 1264
Stout, Molcy I, 472
Stout, Molsy June I, 472
Stout, Nancy I, 421
Stout, Nancy I, 471
Stout, Nancy I, 485
Stout, Nancy A. I, 471
Stout, Nancy A. I, 483
Stout, Nancy A. I, 485
Stout, Naoma I, 471
Stout, Naoma V, 646
Stout, Naomi I, 471
Stout, Naomi I, 485
Stout, Naomi V, 532
Stout, Naomi V, 646
Stout, Naomy I, 471
Stout, Naomy I, 484
Stout, Nathan I, 365
Stout, Nathan I, 421
Stout, Neomi I, 420
Stout, Nereus I, 421
Stout, Nette III, 301
Stout, Nettie E. I, 471
Stout, Noah Webster I, 626
Stout, Noah Webster I, 641
Stout, Nora Edna V, 127
Stout, Obed V. I, 421
Stout, Orpah Jane V, 281
Stout, Patience I, 485
Stout, Patience F. I, 471
Stout, Penelope E. I, 471
Stout, Peninah I, 463
Stout, Peninah I, 471
Stout, Peninah I, 477
Stout, Peninah I, 485
Stout, Permelig L. I, 470
Stout, Peter I, 345
Stout, Peter I, 350
Stout, Peter I, 351
Stout, Peter I, 361
Stout, Peter I, 362
Stout, Peter I, 364
Stout, Peter I, 365
Stout, Peter I, 375
Stout, Peter I, 407
Stout, Peter I, 420
Stout, Peter I, 421
Stout, Peter I, 471
Stout, Peter I, 662
Stout, Peter I, 683
Stout, Peter I, 690
Stout, Peter I, 969
Stout, Phebe I, 365
Stout, Phebe I, 371
Stout, Phebe I, 421
Stout, Phebe I, 1110
Stout, Phebe I, 1132
Stout, Phebe V, 127
Stout, Phebe V, 532
Stout, Phebe V, 600
Stout, Phebe V, 646
Stout, Phebe J. I, 421
Stout, Phebe Jane I, 421
Stout, Phebe L. V, 646
Stout, Rachel I, 345
Stout, Rachel I, 365
Stout, Rachel I, 370
Stout, Rachel I, 372
Stout, Rachel I, 379
Stout, Rachel I, 410
Stout, Rachel I, 420
Stout, Rachel I, 421
Stout, Rachel I, 470
Stout, Rachel I, 471
Stout, Rachel I, 472
Stout, Rachel I, 479
Stout, Rachel I, 483
Stout, Rachel I, 484
Stout, Rachel I, 485
Stout, Rachel I, 690
Stout, Rachel I, 1110
Stout, Rachel I, 1132
Stout, Rachel IV, 1187
Stout, Rachel IV, 1241
Stout, Rachel C. IV, 1187
Stout, Rachel J. I, 471
Stout, Rebecca V, 127
Stout, Rebecca V, 600
Stout, Rebecca V, 602
Stout, Rebeckah V, 532
Stout, Rebecke I, 1110
Stout, Rebekah I, 1132
Stout, Reece I, 934
Stout, Reece Cox I, 949
Stout, Robert R. I, 421
Stout, Rosanna V, 207
Stout, Rosanna V, 532
Stout, Rosanna V, 600
Stout, Rosanna V, 863
Stout, Rosannah I, 471
Stout, Rosannah I, 483
Stout, Rosannah I, 485
Stout, Rosannah V, 178
Stout, Rosannah V, 207
Stout, Roxanah E. I, 471
Stout, Roxanna I, 421
Stout, Roxanna V. I, 421
Stout, Ruth I, 365
Stout, Ruth I, 372
Stout, Ruth I, 420
Stout, Ruth I, 471
Stout, Ruth I, 473
Stout, Ruth I, 485
Stout, Ruth V, 281
Stout, Ruth M. V, 279
Stout, Ruth M. V, 281
Stout, Samuel I, 365
Stout, Samuel I, 379
Stout, Samuel I, 420
Stout, Samuel I, 690
Stout, Samuel I, 1110
Stout, Samuel IV, 687
Stout, Samuel IV, 769
Stout, Samuel, Jr. I, 1099
Stout, Sarah I, 350
Stout, Sarah I, 364
Stout, Sarah I, 365
Stout, Sarah I, 386
Stout, Sarah I, 387
Stout, Sarah I, 410
Stout, Sarah I, 420
Stout, Sarah I, 421
Stout, Sarah I, 1110
Stout, Sarah I, 1132
Stout, Sarah IV, 687
Stout, Sarah IV, 769
Stout, Sarah V, 127
Stout, Sarah V, 517
Stout, Sarah V, 532
Stout, Sarah V, 600
Stout, Sarah V, 646
Stout, Sarah A. I, 421
Stout, Sarah Ann I, 421
Stout, Silas I, 934
Stout, Silas V, 1020
Stout, Silas C. I, 472
Stout, Silas C. I, 485
Stout, Simon I, 420
Stout, Simon I, 421
Stout, Simon V, 281
Stout, Solomon I, 364
Stout, Solomon I, 365
Stout, Solomon I, 372
Stout, Solomon I, 407
Stout, Solomon I, 420
Stout, Solomon I, 471
Stout, Solomon I, 482
Stout, Solomon I, 485
Stout, Solomon A. I, 421
Stout, Sophia I, 452
Stout, Sophia I, 453
Stout, Sophia I, 485
Stout, Stephen I, 364
Stout, Stephen V, 127
Stout, Stephen V, 532
Stout, Stephen V, 600
Stout, Stephen V, 646
Stout, Stephen V, 863
Stout, Susan I, 421
Stout, Susanna I, 421
Stout, Susanna I, 471
Stout, Susanna V, 207
Stout, Susanna V, 485
Stout, Susanna V, 600
Stout, Susanna V, 863
Stout, Susannah I, 482
Stout, Susannah I, 485
Stout, Susannah I, 1101
Stout, Susannah I, 1110
Stout, Susannah I, 1132
Stout, Susannah V, 127
Stout, Susannah V, 508
Stout, Susannah V, 532
Stout, Susannah V, 600
Stout, Thomas I, 364
Stout, Thomas I, 365
Stout, Thomas I, 410
Stout, Thomas I, 420
Stout, Thomas I, 421
Stout, Thomas B. I, 421
Stout, Thomas Lindley I, 934
Stout, Thomas Lindley I, 94
Stout, Viola C. I, 421
Stout, Walter I, 949
Stout, Walter V, 1020
Stout, Walter Howard I, 934
Stout, Walter M. I, 471
Stout, William I, 364
Stout, William I, 420
Stout, William I, 421
Stout, William I, 471
Stout, William I, 472
Stout, William I, 479
Stout, William I, 485
Stout, William I, 626
Stout, William II, 947
Stout, William V, 1020
Stout, William Addison I, 62
Stout, William Addison I, 64
Stout, William B. V, 600
Stout, Wm. I, 365
Stout, Wm. I, 371
Stout, Wm. IV, 1187
Stout, Wm. V, 1020
Stout, Wm. Patterson I, 421
Stout, Z. Walter I, 934
Stout, Zachariah I, 969
Stout, Zeno I, 471
Stout, Zimri I, 471
Stout, Zimri I, 472
Stout, Zimri I, 477
Stout, Zimri I, 485
Stout, Zimri C. I, 471
Stout, Zimri Walter I, 949
Stout, Zimry C. I, 471
Stoutenburgh, David III, 301
Stoutenburgh, Mary Ann III
Stoval, Bartholomew VI, 865
Stoval, Elizabeth VI, 865
Stoval, Thomas VI, 865
Stovall, Bartholomew VI, 84
Stovall, Delilah VI, 949
Stovall, Dorothy VI, 304

ll, Dorothy VI, 803
ll, Elizabeth VI, 304
ll, Elizabeth VI, 803
ll, Elizabeth VI, 855
ll, Elizabeth VI, 948
ll, Elizabeth VI, 999
ll, George VI, 856
ll, George, Jr. VI, 997
ll, Jenny VI, 856
ll, John VI, 826
ll, John VI, 856
ll, Linda R. VI, 856
ll, Martha VI, 846
ll, Martha VI, 997
ll, Nancy VI, 855
ll, Penelope VI, 826
ll, Sarah VI, 856
ll, Terisha VI, 856
r, Adam J. III, 301
r, Amy Jane III, 269
r, Amy Jane III, 301
r, Anna VI, 896
r, Anna E. III, 269
r, Anna E. III, 301
r, Anne V, 559
r, Charity A. III, 301
r, Egbert P. III, 269
r, Egbert P. III, 301
r, Egbert P., Jr. III, 301
r, George VI, 896
r, Marget VI, 977
r, S. Elizabeth III, 301
r, Sally VI, 977
r, William B. VI, 896
Charles II, 424
Charles II, 661
Charles II, 674
Charles II, 769
Charles II, 821
Chas II, 489
Chas. II, 926
Esther II, 424
Esther II, 661
Esther II, 674
Esther II, 719
Hannah II, 661
Isaac II, 424
Isaac II, 489
Isaac II, 769
Isaac II, 926
John II, 424
Lydia II, 424
Lydia II, 489
Lydia II, 661
Lydia II, 674
Mary II, 424
Mary II, 489
Mary II, 661
Merdy II, 424
Peter II, 424
Samuel II, 661
Sarah II, 424
Wd. Mary II, 489
e, Bertha Louise I, 934
e, Carrie Genevieve V, 281
e, Emeline V, 958
e, Emeline V, 960
e, Genevieve V, 281
e, Nellie V, 281
e, Nellie Karnes V, 465
e, Nellie Kearns V, 281
e, Rodema V, 281
e, Ruth V, 713
e, Ruth Todhunter V, 281
e, Ruthanna V, 713
e, Ruthanna V, 715
e, Stanley V, 281
e, Stanley B. V, 281
e, Willard V, 713
e, Willard V, 715
e, Willard H. V, 281
ell, Bell IV, 1264
ell, Francis IV, 1264
ers, Margaret G. IV, 284
er, Alma IV, 1264
Hannah II, 661
Patience II, 508
Patience II, 661
Thomas II, 424
er, Wm. B. IV, 1264
ley, David IV, 939
ley, Mary II, 1027
ley, Mary II, 1030
ley, Mary IV, 939
ley, Rachel A. IV, 939
ling, Ann II, 1081
ling, Ann H. II, 1081
ling, Caroline II, 786
ling, Louisa II, 137
ling, Mary II, 1046
ling, Mary II, 1061
Stradling, Rachel II, 1052
Stradling, Rachel II, 1061
Stradling, Samuel II, 137
Stradling, Sarah Elizabeth II, 137
Stradling, Thomas II, 1030
Stradling, Thomas II, 1061
Stradling, Wm. II, 1061
Strahl, ??? IV, 1047
Strahl, Abdon IV, 595
Strahl, Abdon??? IV, 595
Strahl, Alfred IV, 595
Strahl, Amos IV, 445
Strahl, Amos V, 127
Strahl, Amos G. IV, 444
Strahl, Amos G. IV, 445
Strahl, Angelina IV, 371
Strahl, Angelina IV, 445
Strahl, Angelina IV, 1078
Strahl, Ann IV, 160
Strahl, Ann IV, 284
Strahl, Ann IV, 365
Strahl, Ann IV, 391
Strahl, Ann IV, 444
Strahl, Ann IV, 445
Strahl, Ann IV, 507
Strahl, Ann IV, 566
Strahl, Ann IV, 595
Strahl, Ann IV, 684
Strahl, Ann W. IV, 445
Strahl, Ann W. V, 90
Strahl, Ann W. V, 127
Strahl, Anna IV, 284
Strahl, Anna IV, 353
Strahl, Anna IV, 517
Strahl, Anna IV, 552
Strahl, Anne IV, 552
Strahl, Caspar IV, 284
Strahl, Caspar IV, 445
Strahl, Casper IV, 445
Strahl, Casper IV, 449
Strahl, Cibilla IV, 1078
Strahl, Daniel IV, 284
Strahl, Daniel IV, 445
Strahl, Daniel IV, 595
Strahl, David IV, 284
Strahl, David IV, 445
Strahl, Edmond IV, 445
Strahl, Edmund IV, 284
Strahl, Edmund IV, 444
Strahl, Edmund IV, 445
Strahl, Eleanor IV, 284
Strahl, Eleanor IV, 1116
Strahl, Elen IV, 451
Strahl, Eli IV, 444
Strahl, Eli IV, 445
Strahl, Eli V, 127
Strahl, Elinor IV, 284
Strahl, Elizabeth IV, 284
Strahl, Elizabeth IV, 430
Strahl, Elizabeth IV, 433
Strahl, Elizabeth IV, 445
Strahl, Ellen IV, 284
Strahl, Ellen IV, 398
Strahl, Ellen IV, 445
Strahl, Ellen IV, 595
Strahl, Ellen, Jr. IV, 595
Strahl, Elmer IV, 552
Strahl, Elmer IV, 1078
Strahl, Elmer IV, 1116
Strahl, Elmor IV, 160
Strahl, Elmor IV, 595
Strahl, Eunice IV, 409
Strahl, Eunice IV, 445
Strahl, Hannah IV, 284
Strahl, Hannah IV, 321
Strahl, Hannah IV, 353
Strahl, Hannah IV, 371
Strahl, Hannah IV, 445
Strahl, Hannah IV, 451
Strahl, Hannah IV, 552
Strahl, Hannah IV, 595
Strahl, Ira IV, 595
Strahl, Isaac IV, 284
Strahl, Isaac IV, 398
Strahl, Isaac IV, 445
Strahl, Isaac IV, 451
Strahl, Isaac IV, 595
Strahl, Isaac, Jr. IV, 595
Strahl, Jane IV, 284
Strahl, Jane IV, 353
Strahl, Jane IV, 445
Strahl, Jane IV, 552
Strahl, Jason IV, 595
Strahl, Jesse IV, 284
Strahl, Jesse IV, 353
Strahl, Jesse IV, 445
Strahl, Jesse IV, 552
Strahl, Joel IV, 365
Strahl, Joel IV, 445
Strahl, Joel IV, 595
Strahl, John IV, 160
Strahl, John IV, 284
Strahl, John IV, 391
Strahl, John IV, 595
Strahl, John IV, 684
Strahl, John, Jr. IV, 595
Strahl, Jonathan IV, 353
Strahl, Joseph IV, 284
Strahl, Joseph IV, 353
Strahl, Joseph IV, 445
Strahl, Joseph IV, 552
Strahl, Lavina IV, 353
Strahl, Lavisa IV, 552
Strahl, Levina IV, 353
Strahl, Lovisa IV, 284
Strahl, Lovisa IV, 445
Strahl, Lydia IV, 595
Strahl, Lydia IV, 597
Strahl, Mahlon IV, 284
Strahl, Mahlon IV, 595
Strahl, Mahlon IV, 599
Strahl, Margaret IV, 284
Strahl, Margaret IV, 445
Strahl, Margaret IV, 451
Strahl, Margaret IV, 595
Strahl, Maribah IV, 435
Strahl, Maribah IV, 444
Strahl, Marinda IV, 595
Strahl, Martha IV, 284
Strahl, Martha IV, 353
Strahl, Martha IV, 445
Strahl, Martha IV, 517
Strahl, Martha IV, 552
Strahl, Mary IV, 160
Strahl, Mary IV, 284
Strahl, Mary IV, 445
Strahl, Mary IV, 449
Strahl, Mary IV, 595
Strahl, Mary IV, 599
Strahl, Mary IV, 684
Strahl, Mary IV, 769
Strahl, Mary IV, 1078
Strahl, Mary Jane IV, 445
Strahl, Mary Jane IV, 1078
Strahl, Meriba IV, 445
Strahl, Merihab IV, 284
Strahl, Osborh IV, 1078
Strahl, Osborn IV, 445
Strahl, Osborn IV, 1078
Strahl, Phebe IV, 587
Strahl, Phebe IV, 595
Strahl, Philip IV, 284
Strahl, Philip IV, 394
Strahl, Philip IV, 430
Strahl, Philip IV, 435
Strahl, Philip IV, 444
Strahl, Philip IV, 445
Strahl, Philip IV, 455
Strahl, Philip IV, 1078
Strahl, Philip V, 127
Strahl, Philip, Jr. IV, 445
Strahl, Phillip IV, 284
Strahl, Rachel IV, 284
Strahl, Rachel IV, 428
Strahl, Rachel IV, 445
Strahl, Rebecca IV, 160
Strahl, Rebecca IV, 284
Strahl, Rebecca IV, 351
Strahl, Rebecca IV, 353
Strahl, Rebecca IV, 391
Strahl, Rebecca IV, 439
Strahl, Rebecca IV, 444
Strahl, Rebecca IV, 445
Strahl, Rebecca IV, 552
Strahl, Rebecca Ann IV, 445
Strahl, Rebecca Ann IV, 1078
Strahl, Rhoda Ann IV, 394
Strahl, Rhoda Ann IV, 445
Strahl, Samuel IV, 284
Strahl, Samuel IV, 445
Strahl, Samuel IV, 451
Strahl, Samuel IV, 595
Strahl, Sarah IV, 160
Strahl, Sarah IV, 284
Strahl, Sarah IV, 370
Strahl, Sarah IV, 430
Strahl, Sarah IV, 435
Strahl, Sarah IV, 444
Strahl, Sarah IV, 445
Strahl, Sarah IV, 455
Strahl, Sarah V, 127
Strahl, Sarah Lee IV, 1078
Strahl, Sibbila IV, 445
Strahl, Sibella IV, 1078
Strahl, Stacy IV, 284
Strahl, Stacy IV, 595
Strahl, Stashey IV, 284
Strahl, Stephen IV, 445
Strahl, Stephen IV, 1078
Strahl, Thomas IV, 284
Strahl, Thomas IV, 353
Strahl, Thomas IV, 444
Strahl, Thomas IV, 517
Strahl, Thomas IV, 552
Strahl, William IV, 284
Strahl, William IV, 353
Strahl, William IV, 445
Strahl, William IV, 552
Straight, Anna V, 433
Straight, Francis V, 433
Straight, James C. V, 433
Straight, Maria IV, 876
Straight, Maria IV, 884
Straight, Mary R. V, 433
Strain, David V, 433
Strain, Emma V, 465
Strait, Annie V, 433
Strait, Francis M. V, 433
Strait, Mary R. V, 433
Strall, Rebecca IV, 329
Strall, Stephen IV, 1078
Stranahan, Edgar V, 713
Stranahan, Edgar H. V, 713
Stranahan, Esther V, 713
Stranahan, Irene V, 713
Stranahan, Irene D. V, 713
Strand, Abraham II, 17
Strand, Abraham II, 65
Strand, Abraham II, 89
Strand, Abraham II, 101
Strand, Isabell II, 65
Strand, Rachel II, 89
Strand, Rachel II, 101
Strange, Eliza VI, 951
Strange, Elizabeth VI, 831
Strange, Elizabeth VI, 856
Strange, Elizabeth VI, 987
Strange, Elizabeth VI, 1000
Strange, Elizabeth A. VI, 950
Strange, Frances VI, 829
Strange, Frances VI, 866
Strange, George VI, 856
Strange, Jane VI, 123
Strange, Jane VI, 124
Strange, Jane VI, 1000
Strange, John VI, 987
Strange, John VI, 1000
Strange, Littlebury VI, 340
Strange, Martha D. VI, 848
Strange, Mary VI, 831
Strange, Mary VI, 856
Strange, Mary L. VI, 954
Strange, Nathaniel VI, 842
Strange, Nathaniel VI, 856
Strange, Nathaniel VI, 866
Strange, Nathaniel S. VI, 926
Strange, Patsey VI, 813
Strange, Robert VI, 813
Strange, Robert VI, 824
Strange, Robert VI, 829
Strange, Robert VI, 848
Strange, Robert VI, 856
Strange, Robert VI, 903
Strange, Robert VI, 953
Strange, Robert VI, 1000
Strange, Robt. VI, 951
Strange, Sophia W. VI, 903
Strange, Thomas VI, 954
Strangely, Athaliah V, 237
Strangely, Athaliah V, 281
Strangman, William III, 302
Strantton, Charles V, 713
Strantton, David J. V, 713
Strantton, Helen V, 713
Strantton, Helen Frances V, 713
Strars, Hester V, 1020
Stratan, Bathsheba V, 886
Stratan, Daniel IV, 658
Stratan, Esther IV, 658
Stratan, Hester IV, 658
Stratan, John IV, 658
Stratan, Mary IV, 658
Stratan, Sarah V, 886
Stratan, Wm. L. V, 886
Strate, Ann V, 76
Strate, Ann V, 127
Strate, Anna V, 433
Strate, Annie V, 433
Strate, Francis V, 433
Strate, Francis M. V, 433
Strate, Francis W. V, 433
Strate, James C. V, 433
Strate, Mary R. V, 433
Strate, Sarah V, 433
Strate, Seth V, 433
Strathdon, Clementina III, 137
Straton, Amy IV, 613
Straton, Amy IV, 667
Straton, Aron IV, 771
Straton, Daniel IV, 613
Straton, Elias VI, 449
Straton, Eliza Jane IV, 1295
Straton, Evi IV, 771
Straton, Jacob IV, 658
Straton, Jacob VI, 449
Straton, Jerusha IV, 771
Straton, John II, 424
Straton, Joseph, Jr. IV, 658
Straton, Margaret IV, 658
Straton, Mary IV, 613
Straton, Naomi IV, 658
Straton, Rebecca D. VI, 702
Straton, Rebekah IV, 658
Strattan, Amos II, 76
Strattan, Amos II, 102
Strattan, Amy III, 302
Strattan, Amy T. III, 302
Strattan, Ann II, 821
Strattan, Ann II, 926
Strattan, Benjamin II, 821
Strattan, Benjamin II, 926
Strattan, Benjamin III, 302
Strattan, Benjamin W. III, 302
Strattan, Caroline O. V, 128
Strattan, Charlotte L. III, 302
Strattan, Clara Hayes III, 213
Strattan, Clara Hayes III, 302
Strattan, Clayton II, 926
Strattan, Clement T. III, 302
Strattan, David V, 128
Strattan, Deborah II, 926
Strattan, Deborah II, 941
Strattan, Deborah III, 117
Strattan, Deborah III, 302
Strattan, Edward III, 302
Strattan, Edward L. V, 128
Strattan, Edward Rudolph III, 213
Strattan, Edward Rudolph III, 302
Strattan, Elizabeth II, 821
Strattan, Elizabeth III, 302
Strattan, Elizabeth A. II, 926
Strattan, Elizabeth A. II, 941
Strattan, Elizabeth D. II, 781
Strattan, Emilie L. III, 302
Strattan, Emily L. III, 302
Strattan, Enoch III, 302
Strattan, Enoch, Jr. III, 302
Strattan, Evi IV, 771
Strattan, Fannie J. III, 302
Strattan, G. Edmund III, 117
Strattan, G. Edmund III, 302
Strattan, Geo. W. III, 302
Strattan, George W. III, 280
Strattan, George W. III, 302
Strattan, Gideon II, 821
Strattan, Hallie III, 302
Strattan, Hannah II, 76
Strattan, Hannah II, 102
Strattan, Hannah II, 823
Strattan, Harriet V, 128
Strattan, Isabella M. III, 302
Strattan, Isaiah II, 84
Strattan, Israel II, 823
Strattan, Jacob II, 661
Strattan, John II, 926
Strattan, John II, 941
Strattan, Jonathan V, 863
Strattan, Jos. P. III, 302
Strattan, Judith III, 302
Strattan, Latham III, 302
Strattan, Lydia II, 796
Strattan, Lydia II, 820
Strattan, M. Virginia III, 302
Strattan, Margaret III, 280
Strattan, Margaret III, 302
Strattan, Martha W. III, 302
Strattan, Mary II, 65
Strattan, Mary II, 84
Strattan, Mary II, 102
Strattan, Mary Ann III, 302
Strattan, Mary Anna III, 302
Strattan, Melecent Ann V, 863
Strattan, Phebe III, 302
Strattan, Phebe Ann III, 302
Strattan, Prudence V, 863
Strattan, Rachel II, 41
Strattan, Rachel II, 76
Strattan, Rachel II, 102
Strattan, Robert M. III, 302
Strattan, Sallie Brick II, 823
Strattan, Sarah II, 821
Strattan, Virgina III, 33
Strattan, Virginia M. III, 302
Strattan, Virginia T. III, 302
Strattan, William III, 302
Strattan, William Irvine III, 302
Strattan, Wm. Irvine III, 302
Stratten, Amos II, 41
Stratten, Amy II, 266
Stratten, Amy IV, 110
Stratten, Ann VI, 606

Stratten, Benjamin IV, 110
Stratten, Edward V, 533
Stratten, Elias VI, 448
Stratten, Enoch II, 266
Stratten, Ephraim IV, 110
Stratten, Frank IV, 772
Stratten, Hannah II, 1030
Stratten, Joseph VI, 448
Stratten, Joseph VI, 449
Stratten, Levi IV, 110
Stratten, Mary II, 101
Stratten, Naomi IV, 110
Stratten, Naomi VI, 448
Stratten, Rachel II, 41
Stratten, Rebecca IV, 110
Stratten, Sarah IV, 1295
Stratten, Sarah IV, 1301
Stratten, Sarah VI, 449
Stratten, Stephen V, 533
Stratten, Wm. II, 102
Strattin, Naomi VI, 449
Stratton, ??? III, 68
Stratton, ??? III, 219
Stratton, ??? III, 303
Stratton, ??? III, 349
Stratton, ??? V, 877
Stratton, Aaron IV, 769
Stratton, Aaron IV, 770
Stratton, Aaron IV, 771
Stratton, Aaron IV, 778
Stratton, Aaron IV, 1005
Stratton, Aaron, Jr. IV, 770
Stratton, Aaron, Jr. IV, 945
Stratton, Aaron, Jr. IV, 1005
Stratton, Abagail IV, 771
Stratton, Abby IV, 678
Stratton, Abi IV, 769
Stratton, Abi IV, 771
Stratton, Abi IV, 822
Stratton, Abi IV, 845
Stratton, Abi IV, 846
Stratton, Abigail II, 711
Stratton, Abigail IV, 552
Stratton, Abigail IV, 756
Stratton, Abigail IV, 769
Stratton, Abigail IV, 770
Stratton, Abigail IV, 771
Stratton, Abigail IV, 797
Stratton, Abigail IV, 831
Stratton, Abigail IV, 833
Stratton, Abigail IV, 845
Stratton, Abigail IV, 846
Stratton, Abigail IV, 1066
Stratton, Abigail IV, 1078
Stratton, Abigail V, 882
Stratton, Abigail V, 886
Stratton, Abraham IV, 771
Stratton, Abraham IV, 1005
Stratton, Abram II, 715
Stratton, Abram II, 720
Stratton, Abram II, 730
Stratton, Abram II, 760
Stratton, Abram II, 769
Stratton, Abram IV, 553
Stratton, Abram IV, 771
Stratton, Abram IV, 803
Stratton, Abram IV, 845
Stratton, Abram IV, 846
Stratton, Adda V, 361
Stratton, Alban VI, 857
Stratton, Albert V, 600
Stratton, Albert B. IV, 845
Stratton, Albert B. IV, 846
Stratton, Albert C. II, 720
Stratton, Albert C. IV, 552
Stratton, Albert Clifton IV, 553
Stratton, Albert E. V, 601
Stratton, Albert J. IV, 215
Stratton, Alexander III, 302
Stratton, Alfred IV, 659
Stratton, Alfred IV, 772
Stratton, Alfred IV, 802
Stratton, Alfred IV, 845
Stratton, Alfred C. V, 600
Stratton, Alfred H. IV, 770
Stratton, Alfred H. IV, 772
Stratton, Alice IV, 846
Stratton, Alice A. IV, 846
Stratton, Alice A. IV, 851
Stratton, Alice Ann IV, 846
Stratton, Alice E. II, 720
Stratton, Alice E. II, 769
Stratton, Alice E. IV, 845
Stratton, Alice E. IV, 846
Stratton, Alice Elizabeth II, 720
Stratton, Alice Sylvania IV, 771
Stratton, Allen J. IV, 845
Stratton, Allice Ann IV, 845
Stratton, Almina A. V, 600
Stratton, Almira IV, 659
Stratton, Almira A. V, 713
Stratton, Alta E. IV, 808
Stratton, Alta E. IV, 845
Stratton, Alta E. IV, 846
Stratton, Amanda V, 487
Stratton, Amanda V, 532
Stratton, Amanda V, 533
Stratton, Amanda F. V, 600
Stratton, Amanda F. V, 713
Stratton, Amelia Falicia IV, 772
Stratton, Amos II, 102
Stratton, Amy II, 266
Stratton, Amy III, 279
Stratton, Amy IV, 61
Stratton, Amy IV, 110
Stratton, Amy IV, 616
Stratton, Amy IV, 658
Stratton, Amy IV, 659
Stratton, Amy IV, 667
Stratton, Amy VI, 306
Stratton, Amy VI, 340
Stratton, Amy VI, 341
Stratton, Amy I. III, 177
Stratton, Ann II, 1019
Stratton, Ann II, 1028
Stratton, Ann II, 1030
Stratton, Ann III, 302
Stratton, Ann III, 358
Stratton, Ann IV, 616
Stratton, Ann IV, 658
Stratton, Ann IV, 768
Stratton, Ann IV, 769
Stratton, Ann IV, 770
Stratton, Ann IV, 771
Stratton, Ann IV, 802
Stratton, Ann IV, 845
Stratton, Ann IV, 846
Stratton, Ann IV, 916
Stratton, Ann VI, 606
Stratton, Ann Eliza IV, 845
Stratton, Ann Eliza IV, 1005
Stratton, Ann Eliza V, 882
Stratton, Ann Eliza V, 887
Stratton, Anna III, 143
Stratton, Anna III, 358
Stratton, Anna IV, 215
Stratton, Anna IV, 801
Stratton, Anna E. V, 600
Stratton, Anna Elizabeth IV, 845
Stratton, Anna Elizabeth IV, 846
Stratton, Anna M. IV, 183
Stratton, Anna M. IV, 285
Stratton, Anna M. IV, 686
Stratton, Anna M. IV, 769
Stratton, Anna M. IV, 770
Stratton, Anna M. IV, 771
Stratton, Anna M. IV, 772
Stratton, Anna M. IV, 802
Stratton, Anna M. IV, 813
Stratton, Anna M. IV, 845
Stratton, Anna M. IV, 846
Stratton, Anna Mary IV, 698
Stratton, Anna Mary IV, 749
Stratton, Anna R. IV, 728
Stratton, Anne III, 358
Stratton, Annie IV, 846
Stratton, Archa VI, 1000
Stratton, Archd. VI, 901
Stratton, Archibald VI, 1000
Stratton, Aron IV, 771
Stratton, Arrena V, 433
Stratton, Arrena V, 600
Stratton, Arrena V, 601
Stratton, Arrena V, 713
Stratton, Arthur J. IV, 544
Stratton, Arthur J. IV, 553
Stratton, Arthur John IV, 430
Stratton, Arthur John IV, 445
Stratton, Arthur John IV, 552
Stratton, Barclay IV, 285
Stratton, Barclay IV, 445
Stratton, Barclay IV, 531
Stratton, Barclay IV, 552
Stratton, Barclay IV, 770
Stratton, Barclay IV, 771
Stratton, Barclay IV, 845
Stratton, Barclay IV, 846
Stratton, Barclay W. IV, 803
Stratton, Barclay W. IV, 845
Stratton, Barcley W. IV, 846
Stratton, Barkley IV, 802
Stratton, Barkly IV, 771
Stratton, Bathsheba V, 880
Stratton, Bathsheba V, 886
Stratton, Benj. III, 302
Stratton, Benj. IV, 552
Stratton, Benj. IV, 770
Stratton, Benj. D. IV, 770
Stratton, Benj. D. IV, 1138
Stratton, Benj., Jr. III, 358
Stratton, Benjam VI, 449
Stratton, Benjamin II, 303
Stratton, Benjamin II, 926
Stratton, Benjamin II, 1028
Stratton, Benjamin II, 1030
Stratton, Benjamin III, 223
Stratton, Benjamin III, 302
Stratton, Benjamin IV, 61
Stratton, Benjamin IV, 110
Stratton, Benjamin IV, 513
Stratton, Benjamin IV, 552
Stratton, Benjamin IV, 616
Stratton, Benjamin IV, 658
Stratton, Benjamin IV, 831
Stratton, Benjamin V, 532
Stratton, Benjamin V, 600
Stratton, Benjamin VI, 306
Stratton, Benjamin VI, 340
Stratton, Benjamin VI, 606
Stratton, Benjamin VI, 708
Stratton, Benjamin VI, 721
Stratton, Benjamin Clark V, 532
Stratton, Benjamin D. II, 700
Stratton, Benjamin D. II, 713
Stratton, Benjamin D. II, 720
Stratton, Benjamin D. IV, 765
Stratton, Benjamin D. IV, 770
Stratton, Benjamin D. IV, 771
Stratton, Benjamin D. IV, 845
Stratton, Benjamin D. IV, 846
Stratton, Benjamin Laurance IV, 553
Stratton, Benjamin W. III, 302
Stratton, Benjamin, Jr. III, 302
Stratton, Bethuel II, 101
Stratton, Bethuel II, 102
Stratton, Blanch IV, 838
Stratton, Blanch IV, 845
Stratton, Blanch IV, 846
Stratton, Blanche IV, 751
Stratton, Booker VI, 844
Stratton, Caleb III, 302
Stratton, Caleb V, 490
Stratton, Caleb V, 533
Stratton, Caroline III, 68
Stratton, Caroline O. V, 128
Stratton, Charity IV, 215
Stratton, Charles II, 303
Stratton, Charles II, 720
Stratton, Charles IV, 445
Stratton, Charles IV, 552
Stratton, Charles IV, 553
Stratton, Charles IV, 708
Stratton, Charles IV, 751
Stratton, Charles IV, 769
Stratton, Charles IV, 770
Stratton, Charles IV, 771
Stratton, Charles IV, 845
Stratton, Charles IV, 846
Stratton, Charles IV, 916
Stratton, Charles Brown II, 720
Stratton, Charles H. IV, 772
Stratton, Charles H. IV, 845
Stratton, Charles H. IV, 1005
Stratton, Charles W. IV, 845
Stratton, Charles, Jr. IV, 769
Stratton, Charlotte III, 257
Stratton, Charlotte VI, 1000
Stratton, Charlotte L. III, 257
Stratton, Charlotte L. III, 302
Stratton, Chas. IV, 697
Stratton, Chas. W. IV, 846
Stratton, Cinthia III, 302
Stratton, Clara IV, 771
Stratton, Clara V, 433
Stratton, Clara V, 600
Stratton, Clara V, 601
Stratton, Clara V, 713
Stratton, Clara E. IV, 393
Stratton, Clara E. IV, 445
Stratton, Clara E. IV, 707
Stratton, Clara E. IV, 772
Stratton, Clara E. V, 713
Stratton, Clara F. IV, 445
Stratton, Clarence Victor V, 600
Stratton, Clarence Victor V, 713
Stratton, Clarrie E. V, 600
Stratton, Clayton II, 424
Stratton, Clayton II, 661
Stratton, Clifton D. IV, 215
Stratton, Daniel III, 87
Stratton, Daniel III, 303
Stratton, Daniel IV, 61
Stratton, Daniel IV, 552
Stratton, Daniel IV, 616
Stratton, Daniel IV, 625
Stratton, Daniel IV, 658
Stratton, Daniel IV, 659
Stratton, Daniel IV, 769
Stratton, Daniel IV, 770
Stratton, Daniel IV, 771
Stratton, Daniel IV, 833
Stratton, Daniel IV, 845
Stratton, Daniel IV, 846
Stratton, Daniel IV, 1078
Stratton, Daniel VI, 340
Stratton, Daniel VI, 341
Stratton, Daniel VI, 822
Stratton, Daniel VI, 833
Stratton, Daniel VI, 856
Stratton, David IV, 625
Stratton, David IV, 658
Stratton, David IV, 659
Stratton, David IV, 765
Stratton, David IV, 768
Stratton, David IV, 769
Stratton, David IV, 771
Stratton, David IV, 802
Stratton, David IV, 1295
Stratton, David V, 128
Stratton, David V, 433
Stratton, David V, 532
Stratton, David V, 533
Stratton, David V, 534
Stratton, David V, 600
Stratton, David V, 601
Stratton, David V, 713
Stratton, David V, 934
Stratton, David VI, 340
Stratton, David VI, 341
Stratton, David Harvey V, 600
Stratton, David P. IV, 236
Stratton, David P. IV, 285
Stratton, David P. IV, 770
Stratton, David P. IV, 771
Stratton, David P. IV, 916
Stratton, David William V, 532
Stratton, David, Jr. V, 600
Stratton, Davis IV, 770
Stratton, Davis Harvey V, 128
Stratton, Debora IV, 846
Stratton, Deborah IV, 769
Stratton, Deborah IV, 770
Stratton, Deborah IV, 793
Stratton, Deborah IV, 836
Stratton, Deborah IV, 845
Stratton, Deborah IV, 846
Stratton, Deborah IV, 916
Stratton, Deborah A. IV, 770
Stratton, Deborah Ann IV, 438
Stratton, Deborah Ann IV, 445
Stratton, Deborah Ann IV, 768
Stratton, Deborah Ann IV, 771
Stratton, Deborah Ann IV, 916
Stratton, Deborh IV, 749
Stratton, Dillwyn IV, 285
Stratton, Dillwyn IV, 445
Stratton, Dillwyn IV, 692
Stratton, Dillwyn IV, 771
Stratton, Dillwyn IV, 807
Stratton, Dillwyn IV, 838
Stratton, Dillwyn IV, 846
Stratton, Dillwyn IV, 851
Stratton, Dillwyn E. IV, 215
Stratton, Dilwin IV, 285
Stratton, Dilwyn IV, 771
Stratton, Dilwyn IV, 836
Stratton, Dilwyn IV, 845
Stratton, Dolores Jean IV, 772
Stratton, Doris IV, 772
Stratton, Dorothy IV, 552
Stratton, Dorothy IV, 845
Stratton, Dorothy IV, 846
Stratton, Dorothy IV, 1133
Stratton, Dorothy IV, 1138
Stratton, Dorothy H. IV, 797
Stratton, Dorothy H. IV, 1138
Stratton, Dorothy S. IV, 553
Stratton, Dorothy S. IV, 846
Stratton, Dosha V, 532
Stratton, Dosha V, 676
Stratton, Dosha V, 698
Stratton, Dosha V, 705
Stratton, Dosha VI, 332
Stratton, Dosha VI, 333
Stratton, Dosha VI, 340
Stratton, Dosha VI, 341
Stratton, Doshy VI, 340
Stratton, Dusannah V, 532
Stratton, E. D. VI, 808
Stratton, Ed IV, 771
Stratton, Edith II, 720
Stratton, Edith II, 760
Stratton, Edith II, 769
Stratton, Edith IV, 553
Stratton, Edith IV, 658
Stratton, Edith IV, 845
Stratton, Edith IV, 846
Stratton, Edith IV, 1005
Stratton, Edith IV, 1009
Stratton, Edith R. IV, 430
Stratton, Edith R. IV, 445
Stratton, Edith R. IV, 544
Stratton, Edith R. IV, 553
Stratton, Edith S. II, 715
Stratton, Edney VI, 1000
Stratton, Edward IV, 266
Stratton, Edward IV, 285
Stratton, Edward IV, 445
Stratton, Edward IV, 621
Stratton, Edward IV, 653
Stratton, Edward IV, 658
Stratton, Edward IV, 659
Stratton, Edward IV, 727
Stratton, Edward IV, 769
Stratton, Edward IV, 770
Stratton, Edward IV, 771
Stratton, Edward IV, 772
Stratton, Edward IV, 802
Stratton, Edward IV, 813
Stratton, Edward IV, 908
Stratton, Edward IV, 917
Stratton, Edward V, 128
Stratton, Edward V, 533
Stratton, Edward V, 600
Stratton, Edward F. IV, 393
Stratton, Edward F. IV, 445
Stratton, Edward F. IV, 707
Stratton, Edward F. IV, 770
Stratton, Edward F. IV, 771
Stratton, Edward F. IV, 772
Stratton, Edward L. V, 128
Stratton, Edward Linch V, 5
Stratton, Edward Stratton V
Stratton, Edwin IV, 215
Stratton, Edwin IV, 770
Stratton, Eleanor IV, 771
Stratton, Eleanor IV, 846
Stratton, Eleanor Louise IV,
Stratton, Eli V, 128
Stratton, Eli V, 863
Stratton, Elias II, 102
Stratton, Elias IV, 61
Stratton, Elias IV, 638
Stratton, Elias IV, 658
Stratton, Elias IV, 659
Stratton, Elias IV, 769
Stratton, Elias VI, 341
Stratton, Elias VI, 448
Stratton, Elias VI, 449
Stratton, Elisabeth IV, 771
Stratton, Elisha IV, 285
Stratton, Elisha IV, 748
Stratton, Elisha IV, 769
Stratton, Elisha IV, 770
Stratton, Elisha IV, 771
Stratton, Elisha IV, 845
Stratton, Elisha IV, 916
Stratton, Elisha IV, 1078
Stratton, Eliz. III, 243
Stratton, Eliza III, 302
Stratton, Eliza IV, 770
Stratton, Eliza IV, 771
Stratton, Eliza V, 533
Stratton, Eliza Jane IV, 1295
Stratton, Elizabeth II, 101
Stratton, Elizabeth II, 424
Stratton, Elizabeth II, 661
Stratton, Elizabeth III, 243
Stratton, Elizabeth III, 302
Stratton, Elizabeth IV, 285
Stratton, Elizabeth IV, 698
Stratton, Elizabeth IV, 748
Stratton, Elizabeth IV, 769
Stratton, Elizabeth IV, 770
Stratton, Elizabeth IV, 771
Stratton, Elizabeth IV, 803
Stratton, Elizabeth IV, 836
Stratton, Elizabeth IV, 838
Stratton, Elizabeth IV, 845
Stratton, Elizabeth IV, 846
Stratton, Elizabeth IV, 903
Stratton, Elizabeth IV, 916
Stratton, Elizabeth IV, 1295
Stratton, Elizabeth VI, 856
Stratton, Elizabeth VI, 1000
Stratton, Elizabeth Agester II, 827
Stratton, Elizabeth B. IV, 44
Stratton, Elizabeth B. IV, 77
Stratton, Elizabeth B. IV, 77
Stratton, Elizabeth B. IV, 81
Stratton, Elizabeth B. IV, 84
Stratton, Elizabeth B. IV, 84
Stratton, Elizabeth E. IV, 10
Stratton, Elizabeth H. IV, 21
Stratton, Elizabeth H. IV, 84
Stratton, Elizabeth H. VI, 10
Stratton, Elizabeth R. IV, 84
Stratton, Elizabeth Rachel IV, 846
Stratton, Ella IV, 772
Stratton, Ella B. IV, 770
Stratton, Ella Lillian IV, 692
Stratton, Ella Lillian IV, 771

tton, Ella Lillian IV, 807
tton, Ella Lillian IV, 845
tton, Ella Lillian IV, 846
tton, Ellan IV, 876
tton, Ellan IV, 884
tton, Ellen II, 700
tton, Ellen II, 713
tton, Ellen II, 720
tton, Ellen IV, 513
tton, Ellen IV, 552
tton, Ellen IV, 765
tton, Ellen IV, 769
tton, Ellen IV, 770
tton, Ellen IV, 771
tton, Ellen IV, 831
tton, Ellen IV, 845
atton, Ellen IV, 846
atton, Ellen IV, 909
atton, Ellen IV, 916
atton, Ellen IV, 1138
atton, Elma IV, 803
atton, Elma IV, 846
atton, Elma B. IV, 846
atton, Elma E. IV, 215
atton, Emeline VI, 822
atton, Emily IV, 770
atton, Emily IV, 966
atton, Emily IV, 1005
atton, Emily VI, 708
atton, Emily VI, 721
atton, Emily C. IV, 215
atton, Emily L. III, 177
atton, Emly IV, 771
atton, Emma Julia IV, 772
atton, Emma Kelley IV, 846
atton, Enoch II, 266
atton, Enoch III, 177
atton, Enoch III, 213
atton, Enoch III, 279
atton, Enos Alley III, 302
atton, Ephraim II, 1019
atton, Ephraim II, 1030
ratton, Ephraim IV, 110
ratton, Esther II, 700
ratton, Esther IV, 625
ratton, Esther IV, 658
ratton, Esther IV, 659
ratton, Esther IV, 684
ratton, Esther IV, 738
ratton, Esther IV, 770
ratton, Esther IV, 771
ratton, Esther IV, 833
ratton, Esther IV, 846
ratton, Esther IV, 999
ratton, Esther IV, 1005
ratton, Esther IV, 1067
ratton, Esther IV, 1078
ratton, Esther V, 532
ratton, Esther V, 593
ratton, Esther V, 600
ratton, Esther V, 705
ratton, Esther VI, 340
ratton, Esther F. IV, 1043
ratton, Esther T. IV, 772
tratton, Esther T. IV, 1005
tratton, Esther T. IV, 1043
tratton, Eunice V, 128
tratton, Eunice V, 863
tratton, Evi IV, 659
tratton, Evi IV, 769
tratton, Evi IV, 770
tratton, Evi IV, 771
tratton, Evi IV, 1005
tratton, Fannie J. III, 290
tratton, Flora V, 361
tratton, Flora V, 433
tratton, Flora E. V, 361
tratton, Flora E. V, 600
tratton, Flora E. V, 601
tratton, Flora E. V, 713
tratton, Flora Ellen V, 433
Stratton, Flora Ellen V, 600
Stratton, Frances IV, 770
Stratton, Frances IV, 771
Stratton, Frances V, 433
Stratton, Frances J. V, 600
Stratton, Frances Rachel IV, 771
Stratton, Francis IV, 770
Stratton, Francis IV, 771
Stratton, Francis V, 361
Stratton, Francis V, 601
Stratton, Francis Irvin V, 433
Stratton, Francis Irvin V, 600
Stratton, Francis J. V, 713
Stratton, Frank IV, 772
Stratton, Frank J. IV, 215
Stratton, Franklin IV, 772
Stratton, Franklin IV, 845
Stratton, Franklin IV, 846
Stratton, Franklin IV, 1005
Stratton, Franklin IV, 1043
Stratton, Fraz. O. VI, 966
Stratton, Frazier O. VI, 963
Stratton, Frazier O. VI, 1000
Stratton, Geo. W. III, 257
Stratton, Geo. W. IV, 285
Stratton, Geo. W. IV, 445
Stratton, Geo. W. IV, 534
Stratton, Geo. W. IV, 797
Stratton, Geo. W. IV, 846
Stratton, George IV, 702
Stratton, George IV, 769
Stratton, George IV, 771
Stratton, George IV, 772
Stratton, George IV, 802
Stratton, George IV, 984
Stratton, George IV, 992
Stratton, George IV, 1005
Stratton, George W. IV, 509
Stratton, George W. IV, 552
Stratton, George W. IV, 553
Stratton, Gertrude IV, 1223
Stratton, Gertrude Sipe IV, 1224
Stratton, Giddeon II, 102
Stratton, Gideon II, 101
Stratton, Gideon II, 186
Stratton, Hannah II, 102
Stratton, Hannah II, 266
Stratton, Hannah II, 303
Stratton, Hannah II, 1019
Stratton, Hannah II, 1030
Stratton, Hannah III, 302
Stratton, Hannah III, 303
Stratton, Hannah III, 349
Stratton, Hannah IV, 61
Stratton, Hannah IV, 445
Stratton, Hannah IV, 531
Stratton, Hannah IV, 552
Stratton, Hannah IV, 658
Stratton, Hannah IV, 697
Stratton, Hannah IV, 733
Stratton, Hannah IV, 769
Stratton, Hannah IV, 770
Stratton, Hannah IV, 771
Stratton, Hannah IV, 778
Stratton, Hannah IV, 802
Stratton, Hannah IV, 845
Stratton, Hannah IV, 1005
Stratton, Hannah IV, 1295
Stratton, Hannah V, 128
Stratton, Hannah VI, 341
Stratton, Hannah VI, 449
Stratton, Hannah VI, 606
Stratton, Hannah D. II, 715
Stratton, Hannah D. II, 720
Stratton, Hannah D. II, 730
Stratton, Hannah D. II, 760
Stratton, Hannah D. II, 769
Stratton, Hannah D. IV, 803
Stratton, Hannah D. IV, 846
Stratton, Hannah F. III, 219
Stratton, Hannah F. III, 302
Stratton, Hannah F. IV, 771
Stratton, Hannah H. IV, 285
Stratton, Hannah H. IV, 553
Stratton, Hannah H. IV, 770
Stratton, Hannah H. IV, 771
Stratton, Hannah H. IV, 845
Stratton, Hannah H. IV, 846
Stratton, Hannah M. III, 302
Stratton, Hannah M. IV, 771
Stratton, Hannah T. IV, 1005
Stratton, Harriet V, 128
Stratton, Harriet V, 533
Stratton, Harriet V, 713
Stratton, Harriett V, 532
Stratton, Harriett V, 600
Stratton, Hattie IV, 1264
Stratton, Helen II, 720
Stratton, Helen II, 769
Stratton, Henry VI, 903
Stratton, Henry VI, 1018
Stratton, Herman IV, 772
Stratton, Hester IV, 658
Stratton, Hope II, 101
Stratton, Hope IV, 658
Stratton, Hope IV, 686
Stratton, Hope IV, 769
Stratton, Hope IV, 771
Stratton, Howard IV, 285
Stratton, Howard IV, 302
Stratton, Howard E. IV, 553
Stratton, Howard Ephraim IV, 552
Stratton, Ida J. IV, 215
Stratton, Isaac IV, 769
Stratton, Isaac IV, 771
Stratton, Isaac IV, 845
Stratton, Isaac IV, 846
Stratton, Isaac IV, 1005
Stratton, Isaac IV, 1187
Stratton, Isaac IV, 1264
Stratton, Isaac V, 128
Stratton, Isaac V, 600
Stratton, Isaac VI, 881
Stratton, Isabella III, 214
Stratton, Isabella M. III, 213
Stratton, Isadora E. II, 720
Stratton, Isadora Elizabeth Platt II, 769
Stratton, Isaiah II, 101
Stratton, Isaiah II, 303
Stratton, Isaiah IV, 658
Stratton, Israel II, 303
Stratton, Iwadora Elizabeth Platt II, 730
Stratton, J. Russell IV, 770
Stratton, Jack VI, 949
Stratton, Jack VI, 952
Stratton, Jack VI, 1000
Stratton, Jacob II, 661
Stratton, Jacob II, 769
Stratton, Jacob IV, 61
Stratton, Jacob IV, 658
Stratton, Jacob IV, 1295
Stratton, Jacob V, 128
Stratton, Jacob VI, 306
Stratton, Jacob VI, 449
Stratton, Jacob VI, 606
Stratton, James IV, 697
Stratton, James IV, 769
Stratton, James IV, 770
Stratton, James IV, 802
Stratton, James IV, 845
Stratton, James IV, 1264
Stratton, James E. V, 600
Stratton, James Edward IV, 553
Stratton, James Erwin IV, 658
Stratton, James H. IV, 728
Stratton, James Hervey IV, 802
Stratton, Jane III, 302
Stratton, Jane III, 303
Stratton, Jane V, 490
Stratton, Jane V, 533
Stratton, Jane VI, 948
Stratton, Jane W. III, 303
Stratton, Janice V, 863
Stratton, Jennet VI, 949
Stratton, Jerusha IV, 658
Stratton, Jerusha IV, 769
Stratton, Jerusha IV, 770
Stratton, Jerusha IV, 771
Stratton, Jerusha IV, 1005
Stratton, Jesse F. V, 533
Stratton, Joel IV, 61
Stratton, Joel IV, 658
Stratton, Joel IV, 770
Stratton, Joel IV, 771
Stratton, Joel IV, 1005
Stratton, Joel IV, 1295
Stratton, Joel V, 113
Stratton, Joel V, 128
Stratton, Joel VI, 341
Stratton, Joel VI, 606
Stratton, John II, 1019
Stratton, John II, 1030
Stratton, John IV, 61
Stratton, John IV, 625
Stratton, John IV, 658
Stratton, John IV, 681
Stratton, John IV, 769
Stratton, John IV, 770
Stratton, John IV, 771
Stratton, John V, 207
Stratton, John V, 433
Stratton, John V, 600
Stratton, John V, 601
Stratton, John V, 713
Stratton, John VI, 340
Stratton, John VI, 808
Stratton, John VI, 810
Stratton, John VI, 814
Stratton, John VI, 1000
Stratton, John VI, 1007
Stratton, John VI, 1018
Stratton, John A. II, 720
Stratton, John A. II, 769
Stratton, John A. IV, 845
Stratton, John A. IV, 846
Stratton, John A., Jr. II, 720
Stratton, John Alfred II, 720
Stratton, John Alfred II, 730
Stratton, John Alfred II, 769
Stratton, John B. VI, 838
Stratton, John B. VI, 1000
Stratton, John Cope IV, 658
Stratton, John E. IV, 365
Stratton, John E. IV, 445
Stratton, John E. IV, 770
Stratton, John E. IV, 771
Stratton, John F. IV, 552
Stratton, John F. IV, 845
Stratton, John F. IV, 846
Stratton, John F. IV, 1133
Stratton, John F. IV, 1138
Stratton, John H. V, 361
Stratton, John H. V, 433
Stratton, John H. V, 601
Stratton, John H. V, 713
Stratton, John Haines V, 433
Stratton, John Haines V, 600
Stratton, John Haynes V, 600
Stratton, John M. IV, 728
Stratton, John M. IV, 771
Stratton, John Mickle IV, 769
Stratton, John Mickle IV, 770
Stratton, John T. IV, 845
Stratton, John T. IV, 846
Stratton, John W. V, 600
Stratton, John W. VI, 833
Stratton, John W. VI, 861
Stratton, John William IV, 728
Stratton, Jonah IV, 770
Stratton, Jonathan IV, 772
Stratton, Jonathan V, 863
Stratton, Jonathan D. V, 863
Stratton, Jonathan D. V, 882
Stratton, Jonathan D. V, 886
Stratton, Jonathan D. V, 888
Stratton, Jonothan V, 128
Stratton, Jos. D. VI, 951
Stratton, Jos. R. IV, 183
Stratton, Joseph III, 302
Stratton, Joseph IV, 61
Stratton, Joseph IV, 243
Stratton, Joseph IV, 658
Stratton, Joseph IV, 723
Stratton, Joseph IV, 769
Stratton, Joseph IV, 770
Stratton, Joseph IV, 771
Stratton, Joseph IV, 772
Stratton, Joseph IV, 775
Stratton, Joseph IV, 793
Stratton, Joseph IV, 801
Stratton, Joseph IV, 802
Stratton, Joseph IV, 845
Stratton, Joseph IV, 846
Stratton, Joseph IV, 1295
Stratton, Joseph V, 128
Stratton, Joseph V, 433
Stratton, Joseph V, 532
Stratton, Joseph V, 573
Stratton, Joseph V, 600
Stratton, Joseph V, 601
Stratton, Joseph V, 705
Stratton, Joseph V, 713
Stratton, Joseph VI, 306
Stratton, Joseph VI, 332
Stratton, Joseph VI, 340
Stratton, Joseph VI, 344
Stratton, Joseph VI, 448
Stratton, Joseph VI, 449
Stratton, Joseph VI, 606
Stratton, Joseph VI, 809
Stratton, Joseph VI, 862
Stratton, Joseph C. IV, 445
Stratton, Joseph C. IV, 770
Stratton, Joseph C. IV, 771
Stratton, Joseph C. IV, 803
Stratton, Joseph C. IV, 813
Stratton, Joseph C. IV, 845
Stratton, Joseph Cope IV, 658
Stratton, Joseph Curle VI, 306
Stratton, Joseph D. VI, 1000
Stratton, Joseph Daniel V, 532
Stratton, Joseph E. V, 863
Stratton, Joseph H. IV, 285
Stratton, Joseph H. IV, 772
Stratton, Joseph H. IV, 1043
Stratton, Joseph H. Branson IV, 553
Stratton, Joseph Henry IV, 845
Stratton, Joseph Henry IV, 846
Stratton, Joseph Henry IV, 999
Stratton, Joseph Henry IV, 1005
Stratton, Joseph Henry IV, 1043
Stratton, Joseph R. IV, 285
Stratton, Joseph R. IV, 686
Stratton, Joseph R. IV, 698
Stratton, Joseph R. IV, 749
Stratton, Joseph R. IV, 770
Stratton, Joseph R. IV, 772
Stratton, Joseph W. IV, 770
Stratton, Joseph Whittier IV, 1005
Stratton, Joseph, Jr. IV, 658
Stratton, Joseph, Jr. IV, 769
Stratton, Joseph, Jr. V, 600
Stratton, Joseph, Jr. VI, 333
Stratton, Joseph, Jr. VI, 341
Stratton, Josephine III, 87
Stratton, Josephine III, 303
Stratton, Joshua IV, 285
Stratton, Joshua IV, 627
Stratton, Joshua IV, 658
Stratton, Joshua IV, 659
Stratton, Joshua IV, 660
Stratton, Joshua IV, 715
Stratton, Joshua IV, 769
Stratton, Joshua IV, 770
Stratton, Joshua IV, 771
Stratton, Joshua, Jr. IV, 770
Stratton, Josiah II, 101
Stratton, Josiah IV, 769
Stratton, Josiah IV, 771
Stratton, Josiah IV, 845
Stratton, Josiah IV, 846
Stratton, Josiah IV, 916
Stratton, Judah VI, 903
Stratton, Judith III, 223
Stratton, Judith III, 302
Stratton, Judith V, 281
Stratton, Judith V, 283
Stratton, Judith V, 600
Stratton, Judith V, 713
Stratton, L??? III, 302
Stratton, Latham III, 76
Stratton, Latham III, 223
Stratton, Latham III, 302
Stratton, Latham III, 303
Stratton, Laura M. IV, 836
Stratton, Laura M. IV, 845
Stratton, Laura M. IV, 846
Stratton, Laurance IV, 552
Stratton, Lemira IV, 658
Stratton, Letitia Emaline V, 532
Stratton, Levi IV, 61
Stratton, Levi IV, 110
Stratton, Levi IV, 658
Stratton, Levy V, 533
Stratton, Levy VI, 341
Stratton, Lewis IV, 770
Stratton, Lewis IV, 771
Stratton, Lillian A. IV, 215
Stratton, Lorena V, 433
Stratton, Lorena V, 600
Stratton, Lorena V, 713
Stratton, Louisa III, 216
Stratton, Louisa III, 303
Stratton, Louisa IV, 770
Stratton, Louisa IV, 771
Stratton, Louisa IV, 845
Stratton, Louisa VI, 814
Stratton, Louiza IV, 697
Stratton, Lucinda IV, 838
Stratton, Lucinda IV, 845
Stratton, Lucinda IV, 846
Stratton, Lucy D. VI, 833
Stratton, Lydia III, 76
Stratton, Lydia III, 302
Stratton, Lydia III, 303
Stratton, Lydia IV, 686
Stratton, Lydia IV, 769
Stratton, Lydia IV, 770
Stratton, Lydia IV, 771
Stratton, Lydia IV, 802
Stratton, Lydia IV, 846
Stratton, Lydia IV, 916
Stratton, Lydia IV, 1005
Stratton, Lydia V, 207
Stratton, Lydia V, 433
Stratton, Lydia V, 601
Stratton, Lydia V, 713
Stratton, Lydia L. V, 600
Stratton, M. Virginia III, 257
Stratton, Mabel IV, 285
Stratton, Mabel IV, 302
Stratton, Mabel IV, 553
Stratton, Maggie IV, 772
Stratton, Mahlon V, 533
Stratton, Mahlon V, 600
Stratton, Mahlon V, 713
Stratton, Mahlon VI, 332
Stratton, Mahlon VI, 333
Stratton, Mahlon, Jr. V, 600
Stratton, Margaret IV, 21
Stratton, Margaret IV, 61
Stratton, Margaret IV, 649
Stratton, Margaret IV, 658
Stratton, Margaret IV, 772
Stratton, Margaret IV, 1043
Stratton, Margaret VI, 340
Stratton, Margaret VI, 341
Stratton, Margaret VI, 1000
Stratton, Margaret L. IV, 772
Stratton, Margaret L. IV, 1043
Stratton, Mariah IV, 802
Stratton, Mariam C. IV, 215
Stratton, Marjorie A. IV, 551
Stratton, Marjorie A. IV, 553
Stratton, Marjorie Ann IV, 285
Stratton, Marjorie Anna IV, 553
Stratton, Marjory A. IV, 277
Stratton, Mark IV, 658
Stratton, Mark IV, 769

Stratton, Mark IV, 771
Stratton, Mark IV, 822
Stratton, Mark IV, 845
Stratton, Mark IV, 846
Stratton, Mark IV, 1005
Stratton, Mark Townsend II, 424
Stratton, Mark Townsend II, 661
Stratton, Martha IV, 552
Stratton, Martha IV, 557
Stratton, Martha IV, 697
Stratton, Martha IV, 751
Stratton, Martha IV, 769
Stratton, Martha IV, 770
Stratton, Martha IV, 771
Stratton, Martha IV, 788
Stratton, Martha IV, 1005
Stratton, Martha VI, 810
Stratton, Martha D. IV, 681
Stratton, Martha D. IV, 701
Stratton, Martha D. IV, 728
Stratton, Martha D. IV, 770
Stratton, Martha D. IV, 771
Stratton, Martha D. IV, 772
Stratton, Martha E. IV, 770
Stratton, Martha E. IV, 916
Stratton, Martha Emily V, 532
Stratton, Martha J. IV, 845
Stratton, Martha J. IV, 846
Stratton, Martha J. IV, 854
Stratton, Martha W. IV, 285
Stratton, Martha W. IV, 553
Stratton, Martha W. IV, 771
Stratton, Marthy Emily V, 532
Stratton, Mary II, 101
Stratton, Mary II, 102
Stratton, Mary II, 104
Stratton, Mary II, 303
Stratton, Mary II, 720
Stratton, Mary II, 1028
Stratton, Mary II, 1030
Stratton, Mary IV, 61
Stratton, Mary IV, 445
Stratton, Mary IV, 553
Stratton, Mary IV, 621
Stratton, Mary IV, 625
Stratton, Mary IV, 638
Stratton, Mary IV, 658
Stratton, Mary IV, 659
Stratton, Mary IV, 675
Stratton, Mary IV, 708
Stratton, Mary IV, 727
Stratton, Mary IV, 748
Stratton, Mary IV, 764
Stratton, Mary IV, 765
Stratton, Mary IV, 769
Stratton, Mary IV, 770
Stratton, Mary IV, 771
Stratton, Mary IV, 813
Stratton, Mary IV, 845
Stratton, Mary IV, 846
Stratton, Mary IV, 908
Stratton, Mary IV, 916
Stratton, Mary IV, 917
Stratton, Mary IV, 992
Stratton, Mary IV, 1005
Stratton, Mary IV, 1295
Stratton, Mary V, 207
Stratton, Mary V, 533
Stratton, Mary V, 600
Stratton, Mary V, 606
Stratton, Mary VI, 340
Stratton, Mary VI, 341
Stratton, Mary VI, 344
Stratton, Mary VI, 606
Stratton, Mary VI, 862
Stratton, Mary VI, 1000
Stratton, Mary Ann IV, 771
Stratton, Mary Ann VI, 1000
Stratton, Mary Anna III, 279
Stratton, Mary C. IV, 813
Stratton, Mary C. IV, 846
Stratton, Mary C. IV, 949
Stratton, Mary C. IV, 1005
Stratton, Mary C. V, 63
Stratton, Mary E. V, 600
Stratton, Mary E. V, 713
Stratton, Mary Eleanor IV, 698
Stratton, Mary Eleanor IV, 770
Stratton, Mary Elizabeth V, 600
Stratton, Mary Ellen II, 720
Stratton, Mary Ellen IV, 845
Stratton, Mary F. II, 949
Stratton, Mary F. IV, 552
Stratton, Mary F. IV, 553
Stratton, Mary F. IV, 772
Stratton, Mary H. IV, 266
Stratton, Mary H. IV, 285
Stratton, Mary H. IV, 445
Stratton, Mary H. IV, 653
Stratton, Mary H. IV, 658
Stratton, Mary H. IV, 659
Stratton, Mary H. IV, 770
Stratton, Mary H. IV, 771
Stratton, Mary H. IV, 772
Stratton, Mary H. IV, 846
Stratton, Mary H. IV, 1005
Stratton, Mary Jane IV, 772
Stratton, Mary Jane IV, 1005
Stratton, Mary Jane IV, 1012
Stratton, Mary L. VI, 856
Stratton, Mary Lois III, 303
Stratton, Mary M. V, 881
Stratton, Mary M. V, 887
Stratton, Mary P. IV, 438
Stratton, Mary P. IV, 443
Stratton, Mary P. IV, 445
Stratton, Mary P. IV, 768
Stratton, Mary P. IV, 770
Stratton, Mary P. IV, 771
Stratton, Mary P. Starbruck IV, 445
Stratton, Mary Sarah V, 600
Stratton, Mary, Jr. IV, 769
Stratton, Mattie I, 217
Stratton, May E. V, 713
Stratton, Melecent Ann V, 863
Stratton, Melva W. IV, 285
Stratton, Melva W. IV, 445
Stratton, Micajah V, 532
Stratton, Micajah V, 600
Stratton, Michael IV, 675
Stratton, Michael IV, 698
Stratton, Michael IV, 756
Stratton, Michael IV, 769
Stratton, Michael IV, 770
Stratton, Michael IV, 771
Stratton, Michael IV, 797
Stratton, Michael IV, 845
Stratton, Michael IV, 846
Stratton, Michael IV, 903
Stratton, Michael IV, 1005
Stratton, Michael T. IV, 769
Stratton, Michael T. IV, 771
Stratton, Michael T. IV, 846
Stratton, Michael, Jr. IV, 552
Stratton, Michael, Jr. IV, 557
Stratton, Michael, Jr. IV, 770
Stratton, Michael, Jr. IV, 771
Stratton, Michael, Jr. IV, 788
Stratton, Michal IV, 658
Stratton, Minerva W. IV, 534
Stratton, Minerva W. IV, 552
Stratton, Minerva W. IV, 553
Stratton, Morton Brown II, 720
Stratton, Myra S. IV, 728
Stratton, Nancy III, 233
Stratton, Nancy V, 518
Stratton, Nancy V, 532
Stratton, Nancy V, 533
Stratton, Nancy V, 587
Stratton, Nancy VI, 340
Stratton, Naomi IV, 61
Stratton, Naomi IV, 110
Stratton, Naomi IV, 658
Stratton, Naomi IV, 1295
Stratton, Naomi V, 63
Stratton, Naomi V, 128
Stratton, Naomi VI, 340
Stratton, Naomi VI, 341
Stratton, Naomi VI, 448
Stratton, Naomi VI, 449
Stratton, Naomi VI, 606
Stratton, Naomy IV, 61
Stratton, Naomy VI, 606
Stratton, Narcissa V, 600
Stratton, Nathaniel M. III, 302
Stratton, Nellie V, 700
Stratton, Neomi VI, 341
Stratton, Neomi VI, 449
Stratton, Nettie V, 700
Stratton, Nettie V, 713
Stratton, Oliver B. IV, 772
Stratton, Oliver B. IV, 1043
Stratton, Owen IV, 658
Stratton, Paul E. IV, 770
Stratton, Pemelia VI, 1014
Stratton, Phebe III, 76
Stratton, Phebe III, 223
Stratton, Phebe III, 302
Stratton, Phebe III, 303
Stratton, Phebe Ann III, 302
Stratton, Phebe Mead III, 302
Stratton, Philena IV, 772
Stratton, Philena IV, 1043
Stratton, Polly VI, 1000
Stratton, Priscilla IV, 365
Stratton, Priscilla IV, 445
Stratton, Prudence V, 863
Stratton, Prudence V, 882
Stratton, Prudence V, 888
Stratton, R. J. IV, 1340
Stratton, R. M. III, 303
Stratton, Rachel II, 102
Stratton, Rachel II, 122
Stratton, Rachel II, 124
Stratton, Rachel IV, 285
Stratton, Rachel IV, 627
Stratton, Rachel IV, 658
Stratton, Rachel IV, 660
Stratton, Rachel IV, 715
Stratton, Rachel IV, 769
Stratton, Rachel IV, 770
Stratton, Rachel IV, 771
Stratton, Rachel IV, 802
Stratton, Rachel IV, 845
Stratton, Rachel IV, 846
Stratton, Rachel IV, 1005
Stratton, Rachel IV, 1295
Stratton, Rachel Ann V, 588
Stratton, Rachel Ann V, 600
Stratton, Rachel C. IV, 770
Stratton, Rachel W. IV, 681
Stratton, Rachel W. IV, 728
Stratton, Rachel W. IV, 770
Stratton, Rachel W. IV, 771
Stratton, Rachel, Jr. II, 102
Stratton, Rebecca III, 122
Stratton, Rebecca III, 361
Stratton, Rebecca IV, 61
Stratton, Rebecca IV, 110
Stratton, Rebecca IV, 616
Stratton, Rebecca IV, 658
Stratton, Rebecca IV, 769
Stratton, Rebecca IV, 770
Stratton, Rebecca IV, 771
Stratton, Rebecca IV, 802
Stratton, Rebecca IV, 975
Stratton, Rebecca IV, 1005
Stratton, Rebecca IV, 1295
Stratton, Rebecca V, 68
Stratton, Rebecca V, 128
Stratton, Rebecca V, 573
Stratton, Rebecca V, 600
Stratton, Rebecca D. IV, 723
Stratton, Rebecca D. IV, 770
Stratton, Rebecca D. IV, 845
Stratton, Rebecca D. VI, 708
Stratton, Rebecca D. VI, 721
Stratton, Rebecca D. VI, 723
Stratton, Rebecca H. IV, 845
Stratton, Rebecca S. IV, 1005
Stratton, Rebeccah IV, 658
Stratton, Rebeckah VI, 306
Stratton, Rebeckah VI, 341
Stratton, Rebekah IV, 110
Stratton, Rebekah IV, 658
Stratton, Rebekah V, 113
Stratton, Rebekah V, 128
Stratton, Rhoda IV, 491
Stratton, Rhoda IV, 498
Stratton, Rhoda IV, 658
Stratton, Rhoda IV, 671
Stratton, Rhoda IV, 675
Stratton, Rhoda IV, 698
Stratton, Rhoda IV, 756
Stratton, Rhoda IV, 769
Stratton, Rhoda IV, 770
Stratton, Rhoda IV, 771
Stratton, Rhoda IV, 797
Stratton, Rhoda IV, 802
Stratton, Rhoda IV, 845
Stratton, Rhoda IV, 903
Stratton, Rhoda IV, 1005
Stratton, Rhoda S. IV, 984
Stratton, Rhoda S. IV, 1005
Stratton, Rhoda, Jr. IV, 769
Stratton, Robert Lee IV, 772
Stratton, Robert M. III, 290
Stratton, Robert M. III, 302
Stratton, Robert M. III, 303
Stratton, Robert S. IV, 802
Stratton, Robt. M. III, 303
Stratton, Ross IV, 438
Stratton, Ross IV, 445
Stratton, Ross IV, 748
Stratton, Ross IV, 769
Stratton, Ross IV, 770
Stratton, Ross IV, 771
Stratton, Ross IV, 916
Stratton, Ross J. IV, 445
Stratton, Ruth III, 448
Stratton, Ruth III, 456
Stratton, Ruth IV, 658
Stratton, Ruth IV, 659
Stratton, Ruth V, 532
Stratton, Ruth V, 533
Stratton, Ruth V, 534
Stratton, Ruth V, 557
Stratton, Ruth V, 600
Stratton, Ruth Ann IV, 771
Stratton, Ruth Ann V, 600
Stratton, Ruthann IV, 846
Stratton, Ruthanna II, 700
Stratton, Ruthanna II, 708
Stratton, Ruthanna II, 712
Stratton, Ruthanna IV, 445
Stratton, Ruthanna IV, 513
Stratton, Ruthanna IV, 553
Stratton, Ruthanna IV, 771
Stratton, Ruthanna IV, 801
Stratton, Ruthanna IV, 845
Stratton, Sabina IV, 658
Stratton, Sadie IV, 1187
Stratton, Salina Ann V, 713
Stratton, Sally VI, 325
Stratton, Sally VI, 333
Stratton, Sally VI, 341
Stratton, Samira IV, 401
Stratton, Samira IV, 771
Stratton, Samira IV, 813
Stratton, Samuel W. III, 302
Stratton, Sara IV, 802
Stratton, Sara IV, 845
Stratton, Sarah II, 186
Stratton, Sarah III, 483
Stratton, Sarah III, 499
Stratton, Sarah IV, 243
Stratton, Sarah IV, 244
Stratton, Sarah IV, 285
Stratton, Sarah IV, 658
Stratton, Sarah IV, 659
Stratton, Sarah IV, 723
Stratton, Sarah IV, 769
Stratton, Sarah IV, 775
Stratton, Sarah IV, 831
Stratton, Sarah IV, 845
Stratton, Sarah IV, 846
Stratton, Sarah IV, 904
Stratton, Sarah IV, 916
Stratton, Sarah IV, 917
Stratton, Sarah IV, 1187
Stratton, Sarah IV, 1264
Stratton, Sarah IV, 1295
Stratton, Sarah V, 128
Stratton, Sarah V, 533
Stratton, Sarah V, 600
Stratton, Sarah V, 863
Stratton, Sarah V, 886
Stratton, Sarah VI, 306
Stratton, Sarah VI, 332
Stratton, Sarah VI, 341
Stratton, Sarah VI, 449
Stratton, Sarah VI, 606
Stratton, Sarah VI, 809
Stratton, Sarah VI, 1018
Stratton, Sarah A. V, 887
Stratton, Sarah A. VI, 808
Stratton, Sarah A. VI, 857
Stratton, Sarah Ann IV, 236
Stratton, Sarah Ann IV, 285
Stratton, Sarah B. IV, 769
Stratton, Sarah B. IV, 1005
Stratton, Sarah B. IV, 1264
Stratton, Sarah B. V, 533
Stratton, Sarah B. V, 536
Stratton, Sarah B. V, 887
Stratton, Sarah C. V, 863
Stratton, Sarah C. V, 886
Stratton, Sarah E. V, 701
Stratton, Sarah S. IV, 845
Stratton, Sarah, Jr. V, 600
Stratton, Semira IV, 621
Stratton, Semira IV, 658
Stratton, Semira IV, 659
Stratton, Semira IV, 742
Stratton, Semira IV, 771
Stratton, Semira IV, 960
Stratton, Semira IV, 981
Stratton, Semyra IV, 770
Stratton, Shady IV, 61
Stratton, Shady IV, 625
Stratton, Shady IV, 658
Stratton, Shady IV, 659
Stratton, Shady VI, 340
Stratton, Shady VI, 341
Stratton, Simeon IV, 770
Stratton, Simon IV, 771
Stratton, Sina II, 720
Stratton, Sina IV, 215
Stratton, Sina IV, 285
Stratton, Sina IV, 553
Stratton, Sina IV, 627
Stratton, Sina IV, 715
Stratton, Sina IV, 769
Stratton, Sina IV, 770
Stratton, Sina IV, 771
Stratton, Sina IV, 802
Stratton, Sina IV, 845
Stratton, Sina IV, 1005
Stratton, Sina S. II, 713
Stratton, Sorena V, 601
Stratton, Stanley W. IV, 277
Stratton, Stanley W. IV, 285
Stratton, Stanley W. IV, 551
Stratton, Stanley W. IV, 553
Stratton, Stanley Willits IV, 5
Stratton, Stanley Willits IV, 5
Stratton, Stephen V, 533
Stratton, Stephen V, 600
Stratton, Stephen T. V, 532
Stratton, Susan VI, 898
Stratton, Susanna IV, 984
Stratton, Susanna IV, 992
Stratton, Susanna IV, 1005
Stratton, Susanna IV, 1295
Stratton, Susanna V, 533
Stratton, Susanna VI, 340
Stratton, Susannah IV, 616
Stratton, Susannah IV, 702
Stratton, Susannah IV, 770
Stratton, Susannah IV, 771
Stratton, Susannah IV, 772
Stratton, Susannah IV, 1295
Stratton, Susannah V, 532
Stratton, Susannah V, 533
Stratton, Susannah V, 706
Stratton, Susannah VI, 341
Stratton, Terrissa VI, 1000
Stratton, Theodocia V, 600
Stratton, Thomas IV, 658
Stratton, Thomas VI, 1000
Stratton, Thomas A. V, 533
Stratton, Thomas Leech IV, 88
Stratton, Thos. VI, 995
Stratton, Unity IV, 770
Stratton, Unity IV, 771
Stratton, Unity IV, 945
Stratton, Unity IV, 1005
Stratton, Virgina T. III, 33
Stratton, Virginia III, 87
Stratton, Virginia III, 303
Stratton, W. T. IV, 770
Stratton, Walloby IV, 846
Stratton, Walter B. IV, 845
Stratton, Walter B. IV, 846
Stratton, Walter C. IV, 808
Stratton, Walter G. Edgerton IV, 1005
Stratton, Walter N. IV, 215
Stratton, Wd. Rebecca D. VI, 72
Stratton, Wilford H. IV, 845
Stratton, William III, 302
Stratton, William IV, 771
Stratton, William IV, 802
Stratton, William V, 128
Stratton, William V, 863
Stratton, William VI, 903
Stratton, William VI, 1000
Stratton, William Ashton IV, 55
Stratton, William D. IV, 771
Stratton, William D. IV, 772
Stratton, William D. VI, 799
Stratton, William D. VI, 822
Stratton, William L. V, 863
Stratton, William M. IV, 771
Stratton, William M. VI, 810
Stratton, William W. III, 302
Stratton, William W. IV, 659
Stratton, William W. IV, 770
Stratton, William W. IV, 772
Stratton, Willie T. IV, 1043
Stratton, Willis T. IV, 772
Stratton, Willobee IV, 845
Stratton, Willoughby IV, 846
Stratton, Wilmer Joseph IV, 553
Stratton, Wilmer L. IV, 215
Stratton, Wm. II, 102
Stratton, Wm. II, 661
Stratton, Wm. III, 243
Stratton, Wm. IV, 769
Stratton, Wm. IV, 770
Stratton, Wm. Brantingham IV, 845
Stratton, Wm. Bratingham IV, 846
Stratton, Wm. D. IV, 770
Stratton, Wm. I. III, 243
Stratton, Wm. L. V, 880
Stratton, Wm. L. V, 886
Stratton, Wm. M. IV, 770
Stratton, Wm. M. VI, 856
Stratton, Wm. R. II, 1081
Stratton, Wm. W. II, 661
Stratton, Wm. W. III, 302
Stratton, Wm. Willis II, 1028
Stratton, Wm. Willis II, 1030
Stratton, Zaccheus IV, 769
Stratton, Zacheus IV, 771
Stratton, Zacheus IV, 845
Stratton, Zacheus IV, 846
Straub, John V, 1020
Straub, Mary V, 1020
Straugh, Esther IV, 946
Straughan, Ann IV, 285
Straughan, Daniel IV, 285

ghan, Job IV, 110
ghan, John IV, 256
ghan, John IV, 285
ghan, Margaret IV, 772
ghan, Martha L. IV, 256
ghan, Martha L. IV, 285
ghan, Martha L. IV, 772
ghan, Rebecca IV, 675
ghan, Rebecca IV, 772
ghen, Daniel IV, 775
ghen, Margaret IV, 772
ghen, Margaret IV, 775
ghn, Ann IV, 772
ghn, Annie M. I, 626
ghn, Arminta I, 641
ghn, Arminta Pritchard
, 626
ghn, Hannah IV, 772
ghn, Hannah M. IV, 772
ghn, Jacob IV, 772
ghn, Job IV, 110
ghn, John IV, 745
ghn, John IV, 772
ghn, Lydia J. IV, 772
ghn, Lydia Jane IV, 772
ghn, Margaret IV, 772
ghn, Martha IV, 772
ghn, Martha L. IV, 285
ghn, Martha L. IV, 745
ghn, Martha L. IV, 772
ghn, Mary IV, 772
ghn, Mary R. IV, 772
ghn, Maurice I, 626
ghn, Rebecca IV, 772
ghn, Thomas IV, 110
ghn, Townsend IV, 772
sburg, Elias M. V, 128
v, Charles V, 433
v, Elizabeth V, 433
v, John V, 433
v, Lindley V, 433
v, Melvin V, 433
v, Patience V, 433
v, Sylvester V, 433
vbridge, Ann II, 327
vbridge, Daniel L. II, 720
vbridge, Edward R. II, 720
vbridge, Edward R. II, 769
vbridge, Frederick H. II, 720
vbridge, Frederick H. II, 769
vbridge, J??? II, 720
vbridge, Justis II, 720
vbridge, Justus C. II, 769
vbridge, Mary L. II, 720
vhan, Job IV, 110
vhen, Thomas IV, 61
vhen, Thomas IV, 110
vl, Elmer IV, 1116
vn, Ann IV, 772
vn, Anna I, 1063
vn, Anna V, 99
vn, Anna V, 128
vn, Anne I, 1063
vn, Esther IV, 38
vn, Esther IV, 61
vn, Esther IV, 946
vn, Esther IV, 1005
vn, George V, 99
vn, Hannah IV, 772
vn, Hannah M. IV, 772
vn, Jacob IV, 772
vn, John IV, 772
vn, Judith IV, 61
vn, Lydia J. IV, 772
vn, Lydia J. IV, 777
vn, Lydia Jane IV, 772
vn, Mary I, 1061
vn, Mary I, 1063
vn, Mary IV, 772
vn, Mary R. IV, 772
vn, Matilda Ann II, 718
vn, Sarah V, 99
vn, Sarah V, 196
vn, Thomas IV, 61
vn, Townsend IV, 772
ker, Rebecca II, 266
t, Elizabeth II, 102
ter, James II, 661
h, Ann IV, 700
h, Ann IV, 774
h, Charles II, 158
h, Joshua B. II, 158
h, Lydia V, 327
h, Lydia V, 361
h, Lydia L. II, 158
h, Rachel Ann II, 158
ker, Rebecca II, 219
t, Aaron II, 41
t, Aaron II, 102
t, Aaron IV, 701
t, Aaron IV, 772
Street, Aaron IV, 1005
Street, Aaron V, 128
Street, Agnes II, 1030
Street, Agnes II, 1039
Street, Agnes IV, 285
Street, Agnes IV, 445
Street, Agness IV, 285
Street, Agness IV, 314
Street, Alfred Earnest IV, 773
Street, Ann II, 102
Street, Ann IV, 110
Street, Ann IV, 772
Street, Ann IV, 773
Street, Ann IV, 1005
Street, Ann, Jr. IV, 772
Street, Anna II, 41
Street, Anna II, 102
Street, Anna IV, 110
Street, Anna IV, 707
Street, Anna IV, 772
Street, Anna IV, 773
Street, Anna Rachel V, 765
Street, Anthony VI, 857
Street, Ardell V, 713
Street, Aron II, 41
Street, Balinda IV, 285
Street, Balinda IV, 1005
Street, Belinda IV, 160
Street, Belinda IV, 773
Street, Charles IV, 772
Street, Charles Clifford IV, 1187
Street, Clement F. IV, 773
Street, Clifford IV, 1187
Street, David IV, 704
Street, David IV, 772
Street, David IV, 773
Street, David VI, 1000
Street, Edna V, 713
Street, Elizabeth I, 485
Street, Elizabeth II, 49
Street, Elizabeth II, 102
Street, Elizabeth IV, 160
Street, Elizabeth IV, 173
Street, Elizabeth IV, 285
Street, Elizabeth IV, 1005
Street, Elma IV, 314
Street, Esther IV, 773
Street, Esther B. IV, 724
Street, Eunice II, 41
Street, Eunice II, 98
Street, Eunice II, 102
Street, Eunice IV, 110
Street, Eunice IV, 704
Street, Eunice IV, 707
Street, Eunice IV, 772
Street, Eunice IV, 773
Street, Eunice V, 128
Street, Eunice F. IV, 773
Street, George IV, 724
Street, George IV, 772
Street, George IV, 773
Street, Griffith IV, 173
Street, Griffith IV, 285
Street, Gulia Elma IV, 315
Street, Gulielma IV, 285
Street, Hannah II, 661
Street, Hannah IV, 285
Street, Hannah IV, 307
Street, Hannah IV, 439
Street, Hannah IV, 446
Street, Hannah IV, 762
Street, Hannah IV, 773
Street, Hezekiah VI, 857
Street, Isaac II, 41
Street, Isaac II, 102
Street, Isaac IV, 160
Street, Isaac IV, 285
Street, Isaac IV, 739
Street, Isaac IV, 743
Street, Isaac IV, 772
Street, Isaac IV, 773
Street, Isaac IV, 1005
Street, Isaac V, 128
Street, Isaac Mather IV, 773
Street, Jessie V, 713
Street, John II, 41
Street, John II, 102
Street, John IV, 110
Street, John IV, 772
Street, John IV, 773
Street, John IV, 1005
Street, John V, 128
Street, John Ellison IV, 1005
Street, John G. III, 303
Street, John G. III, 370
Street, John W. IV, 772
Street, John W. IV, 773
Street, John, Jr. IV, 692
Street, John, Jr. IV, 772
Street, Joseph IV, 773
Street, Joseph J. IV, 772
Street, Judith C. VI, 1000
Street, Lavina IV, 773
Street, Lewis IV, 772
Street, Lewis IV, 773
Street, Lewis V, 934
Street, Lola V, 713
Street, Louis IV, 704
Street, Louis IV, 773
Street, Lydia II, 41
Street, Lydia II, 102
Street, Lydia IV, 110
Street, Lydia IV, 701
Street, Lydia IV, 772
Street, Lydia IV, 773
Street, Lydia IV, 950
Street, Lydia IV, 1005
Street, Lydia V, 128
Street, Lydia B. IV, 773
Street, Lydia S. III, 303
Street, Lydia S. III, 370
Street, Lydia S. IV, 846
Street, Margaret P. V, 765
Street, Martha IV, 773
Street, Martha Jr. IV, 692
Street, Mary II, 41
Street, Mary II, 102
Street, Mary II, 661
Street, Mary IV, 701
Street, Mary IV, 772
Street, Mary IV, 773
Street, Mary V, 128
Street, Mary Ann IV, 160
Street, Mary Ann IV, 173
Street, Mary Ann IV, 285
Street, Mary Ann IV, 510
Street, Mary Ann IV, 553
Street, Mary Ann IV, 773
Street, Mary Ann IV, 1005
Street, Maryann IV, 773
Street, Mildred Ardella V, 713
Street, Nancy VI, 857
Street, Ogden IV, 773
Street, Peter W. VI, 1000
Street, Polly VI, 1000
Street, Rachel IV, 160
Street, Rachel IV, 285
Street, Rachel IV, 314
Street, Rachel IV, 1005
Street, Rebecca IV, 160
Street, Rebecca IV, 285
Street, Rebecca IV, 312
Street, Rebecca IV, 314
Street, Rebecca IV, 743
Street, Rebecca IV, 772
Street, Rebecca IV, 1005
Street, Rose V, 713
Street, Samuel II, 41
Street, Samuel II, 102
Street, Samuel IV, 762
Street, Samuel IV, 772
Street, Samuel IV, 773
Street, Samuel IV, 932
Street, Samuel IV, 1005
Street, Samuel V, 128
Street, Samuel J. IV, 773
Street, Samuel S. IV, 773
Street, Samuel S. V, 128
Street, Samuel Scotton IV, 772
Street, Samuel W. IV, 773
Street, Samuel, Jr. IV, 772
Street, Sarah IV, 739
Street, Sarah IV, 762
Street, Sarah IV, 772
Street, Sarah IV, 773
Street, Sarah IV, 932
Street, Sarah IV, 1005
Street, Sarah L. IV, 704
Street, Sarah L. IV, 773
Street, Sarah T. IV, 705
Street, Sarah T. IV, 773
Street, Sarah, Jr. IV, 773
Street, Sibyl IV, 772
Street, Sibyl IV, 773
Street, Sibyl IV, 774
Street, Sibyl IV, 1005
Street, Sibyl IV, 1006
Street, Sibyl T. IV, 772
Street, Sibyl Tatum IV, 773
Street, Susan M. VI, 1000
Street, Triphena VI, 857
Street, Unice IV, 773
Street, Unice V, 128
Street, Webster IV, 773
Street, William II, 41
Street, William D. VI, 1000
Street, William J. IV, 773
Street, Wm. II, 661
Street, Wm. IV, 772
Street, Wm. J. IV, 773
Street, Zadock II, 41
Street, Zadock II, 98
Street, Zadock II, 102
Street, Zadock IV, 772
Street, Zadock IV, 1006
Street, Zadok IV, 707
Street, Zadok IV, 772
Street, Zadok IV, 773
Street, Zadok IV, 774
Street, Zadok IV, 1005
Street, Zadok, Jr. IV, 772
Street, Zadok, Jr. IV, 773
Streeter, Ann F. II, 155
Streeter, Ann F. II, 158
Streeter, Carrie IV, 1187
Streeter, Catharine III, 303
Streeter, Catherine III, 448
Streeter, Daniel III, 303
Streeter, Daniel III, 448
Streeter, Daniel D. III, 275
Streeter, Daniel D., Jr. III, 303
Streeter, Daniel Denison III, 303
Streeter, Daniel Denison III, 448
Streeter, Daniel Denison, Jr.
III, 448
Streeter, Elias H. II, 155
Streeter, Elias H. II, 158
Streeter, Florence III, 140
Streeter, Florence III, 279
Streeter, Gladys M. III, 275
Streeter, Gladys M. III, 303
Streeter, Gladys M. III, 448
Streeter, Hannah II, 155
Streeter, Hannah II, 158
Streeter, Harrison II, 155
Streeter, Harrison II, 158
Streeter, James II, 1030
Streeter, Leonard II, 803
Streeter, Mariah III, 448
Streeter, Mary II, 803
Streeter, Milford B. III, 303
Streeter, Milford B. III, 448
Streeter, S. Maria III, 303
Streeter, Samuel Schuyler
III, 303
Streeter, Samuel Schuyler
III, 448
Streeter, Sarah Ann III, 303
Streeter, William IV, 1187
Streeter, Wm. IV, 1187
Streetley, Charlotte A. II, 825
Streetly, Charlotte A. II, 926
Streetly, Charlotte A. II, 934
Streight, Eliz. III, 303
Streight, Elizabeth III, 187
Streight, Elizabeth III, 303
Streight, John III, 187
Streight, John III, 303
Streight, Margaret III, 187
Streight, Margaret III, 303
Streight, Sarah Catharine
IV, 285
Stresh, Debrah II, 102
Stresh, Esther II, 102
Stretch, Aaron II, 41
Stretch, Aaron V, 281
Stretch, Abner II, 158
Stretch, Abner IV, 773
Stretch, Abner B. IV, 773
Stretch, Agnes II, 424
Stretch, Agnes II, 661
Stretch, Alice IV, 1380
Stretch, Ann II, 81
Stretch, Ann II, 102
Stretch, Ann II, 103
Stretch, Ann II, 158
Stretch, Ann II, 424
Stretch, Ann II, 662
Stretch, Ann IV, 773
Stretch, Anna IV, 773
Stretch, Anne IV, 1380
Stretch, Bashabe II, 102
Stretch, Beulah II, 103
Stretch, Bradway II, 41
Stretch, Charles II, 138
Stretch, Charles II, 158
Stretch, Charles IV, 773
Stretch, David II, 41
Stretch, David Wilson V, 281
Stretch, Deborah II, 41
Stretch, Debrah II, 102
Stretch, Elisha II, 41
Stretch, Elisha II, 57
Stretch, Elisha II, 102
Stretch, Elisha II, 103
Stretch, Elizabeth II, 41
Stretch, Elizabeth II, 69
Stretch, Elizabeth II, 102
Stretch, Elizabeth II, 103
Stretch, Elizabeth II, 109
Stretch, Elizabeth II, 138
Stretch, Elizabeth II, 424
Stretch, Elizabeth II, 588
Stretch, Elizabeth II, 661
Stretch, Elizabeth B. II, 103
Stretch, Elonar II, 68
Stretch, Elonar II, 102
Stretch, Eloner II, 102
Stretch, Esther II, 102
Stretch, Etta May V, 281
Stretch, Hannah II, 41
Stretch, Hannah II, 102
Stretch, Hannah II, 109
Stretch, Hannah II, 424
Stretch, Hannah II, 579
Stretch, Hannah II, 661
Stretch, Hester II, 41
Stretch, Isaac II, 661
Stretch, Jael II, 41
Stretch, Jael II, 69
Stretch, Jael II, 102
Stretch, James L. II, 158
Stretch, James L. IV, 773
Stretch, James Lewis II, 662
Stretch, Joanna II, 156
Stretch, Job II, 41
Stretch, Job II, 102
Stretch, Job II, 103
Stretch, Job II, 124
Stretch, John II, 424
Stretch, Jonathan II, 41
Stretch, Jonathan II, 69
Stretch, Jonathan II, 102
Stretch, Jonathan II, 109
Stretch, Joseph II, 41
Stretch, Joseph II, 102
Stretch, Joseph II, 109
Stretch, Joseph II, 424
Stretch, Joseph II, 575
Stretch, Joseph II, 661
Stretch, Joseph II, 662
Stretch, Joseph VI, 880
Stretch, Joseph VI, 1000
Stretch, Joseph, Jr. II, 41
Stretch, Joseph, Jr. II, 69
Stretch, Joseph, Jr. II, 102
Stretch, Joseph, Jr. II, 109
Stretch, Joshua II, 41
Stretch, Joshua II, 66
Stretch, Joshua II, 102
Stretch, Joshua II, 103
Stretch, Joshua II, 138
Stretch, Joshua B. II, 158
Stretch, Lidya II, 41
Stretch, Luke II, 102
Stretch, Lydia II, 66
Stretch, Lydia II, 102
Stretch, Lydia II, 424
Stretch, Lydia II, 575
Stretch, Lydia II, 661
Stretch, Lydia V, 361
Stretch, Lydia L. II, 158
Stretch, Lydia T. II, 138
Stretch, Lydia T. II, 158
Stretch, Margery II, 424
Stretch, Margery II, 661
Stretch, Mark II, 41
Stretch, Mark II, 102
Stretch, Martha II, 41
Stretch, Martha V, 281
Stretch, Martha V, 327
Stretch, Martha V, 361
Stretch, Mary II, 41
Stretch, Mary II, 66
Stretch, Mary II, 83
Stretch, Mary II, 102
Stretch, Mary II, 103
Stretch, Mary II, 424
Stretch, Mary II, 661
Stretch, Mary B. II, 57
Stretch, Mary B. II, 102
Stretch, Mary D. II, 102
Stretch, Mary Hildreth II, 135
Stretch, Millisent II, 41
Stretch, Nathan II, 41
Stretch, Nathan II, 102
Stretch, Peter II, 99
Stretch, Peter II, 102
Stretch, Peter II, 424
Stretch, Peter II, 575
Stretch, Peter II, 661
Stretch, Rachel Ann II, 138
Stretch, Rachel Ann II, 158
Stretch, Rebecca II, 117
Stretch, Rebecca II, 124
Stretch, Rebecca VI, 1000
Stretch, Rebecca G. IV, 773
Stretch, Rebeckah II, 41
Stretch, Rebeckah II, 102
Stretch, Ruth II, 83
Stretch, Ruth II, 662
Stretch, Sally VI, 889
Stretch, Samuel II, 41
Stretch, Samuel II, 102

Stretch, Samuel II, 424
Stretch, Samuel II, 677
Stretch, Samuel IV, 773
Stretch, Samuel Levis II, 661
Stretch, Sarah II, 41
Stretch, Sarah II, 57
Stretch, Sarah II, 69
Stretch, Sarah II, 92
Stretch, Sarah II, 99
Stretch, Sarah II, 102
Stretch, Sarah II, 104
Stretch, Sarah II, 109
Stretch, Sarah II, 424
Stretch, Sarah II, 556
Stretch, Sarah II, 661
Stretch, Sarah VI, 894
Stretch, Sarah Smith II, 102
Stretch, Susanah VI, 889
Stretch, Sybil II, 662
Stretch, Thomas II, 424
Stretch, Thomas II, 661
Stretch, Thomas Wesley V, 281
Stretch, Wd. Agnes II, 677
Stretch, William II, 424
Stretch, Wm. II, 102
Stretch, Wm. II, 662
Stretch, Wm. B. II, 102
Stretch, Wm. B. II, 103
Stretcher, Mary V, 960
Stretcher, Mary V, 961
Strettell, Amos II, 662
Strettell, Ann II, 662
Strettell, Frances II, 662
Strettell, Robert II, 424
Strettell, Robert II, 662
Strettell, Robert, Jr. II, 662
Stretter, Harrison II, 158
Strettle, Amos II, 662
Strettle, Ann II, 424
Strettle, Ann II, 662
Strettle, Frances II, 662
Strettle, Robert II, 424
Strettle, Robert II, 662
Strettle, Robert, Jr. II, 424
Strettle, Robert, Jr. II, 662
Strettle, Wd. Philititia II, 424
Strickel, Rebecca V, 489
Strickel, Rebecca V, 533
Strickland, ??? I, 641
Strickland, ??? III, 174
Strickland, Amos II, 425
Strickland, Ann II, 794
Strickland, Charlotte I, 295
Strickland, Frances II, 425
Strickland, John I, 295
Strickland, John II, 662
Strickland, John II, 794
Strickland, John II, 1024
Strickland, John II, 1030
Strickland, Marenda I, 295
Strickland, Margery II, 1024
Strickland, Margery II, 1030
Strickland, Mary II, 662
Strickland, Maude I, 213
Strickland, Miles II, 425
Strickland, Miles II, 549
Strickland, Miles II, 662
Strickland, Rachel II, 549
Strickland, Rachel II, 662
Strickland, Rachel II, 1027
Strickland, Rachel II, 1030
Strickland, S. Olivia III, 174
Strickland, Sarah II, 788
Strickland, Simeon III, 499
Strickland, Thomas II, 425
Strickland, Thomas II, 662
Strickle, George V, 207
Strickle, Kate V, 207
Strickle, Katie V, 207
Strickle, Rebecca V, 533
Stricklen, Anna I, 734
Stricklen, Mary I, 734
Strickling, Lucy I, 393
Strickling, Lucy I, 421
Strickling, Sarah I, 316
Strickling, Sarah I, 318
Stricth, Jesse IV, 1380
Striker, Philip II, 816
Striker, Rebecca II, 816
Striker, Wd. Elizabeth Ann II, 816
Strimple, Nettie M. IV, 1241
Strine, Lemuel V, 1020
Strine, Mahala V, 1020
String, Gertrude III, 220
String, Norman D. III, 220
Stringer, Hannah II, 761
Stringer, Hannah II, 769
Stringer, Mary II, 1030
Stringer, Mary II, 1042
Stringham, Adis H. III, 303
Stringham, Adis H. III, 338
Stringham, Altheas III, 303
Stringham, Ann Eliza III, 26
Stringham, Ann Eliza III, 303
Stringham, Anna III, 61
Stringham, Anna H. III, 61
Stringham, Annie E. III, 430
Stringham, Annie E. III, 448
Stringham, Bess III, 297
Stringham, Bess III, 303
Stringham, David III, 303
Stringham, Eleanor III, 100
Stringham, Eleanor III, 303
Stringham, Eleanor III, 407
Stringham, Eleanor III, 448
Stringham, Eleanor Caroline III, 189
Stringham, Eleanor Caroline III, 303
Stringham, Eleonor III, 463
Stringham, Elliot Barnes III, 303
Stringham, Ernest III, 303
Stringham, Ernest J. III, 303
Stringham, Ernest J. III, 338
Stringham, Eugene H. III, 189
Stringham, Eugene H. III, 303
Stringham, Florence III, 90
Stringham, Florence III, 303
Stringham, Gertrude III, 303
Stringham, Gertrude III, 335
Stringham, Gertrude M. III, 303
Stringham, Hannah III, 303
Stringham, Irene III, 430
Stringham, Irene III, 448
Stringham, Irving III, 303
Stringham, Irving J. III, 100
Stringham, Irving J. III, 303
Stringham, Irving J. III, 407
Stringham, Irving J. III, 448
Stringham, Irving J. III, 463
Stringham, Irving, Jr. III, 407
Stringham, James C. III, 303
Stringham, James C. III, 335
Stringham, Jas. C. III, 303
Stringham, John III, 26
Stringham, John III, 303
Stringham, John III, 430
Stringham, John III, 448
Stringham, Leroy Marshall III, 303
Stringham, Lydia III, 303
Stringham, Lydia III, 407
Stringham, Lydia III, 448
Stringham, Marion III, 303
Stringham, Marion III, 448
Stringham, Marion III, 463
Stringham, Norman III, 303
Stringham, Norman D. III, 303
Stringham, Norris III, 303
Stringham, Norris B. III, 297
Stringham, Norris B. III, 303
Stringham, Ralph Irving III, 303
Stringham, Samuel III, 40
Stringham, Samuel III, 303
Stringham, Sarah III, 40
Stringham, Sarah III, 303
Stringham, Willis III, 303
Stringham, Willis T. III, 90
Stringham, Willis T. III, 303
Stringham, Winifrid III, 303
Stringham, Winnifred III, 303
Stripley, Ann III, 335
Stripley, Hannah III, 335
Stripley, Morris III, 335
Stripp, Charlie V, 1020
Stripp, Lizzie V, 1020
Stripp, Wm. V, 1020
Strode, Ann VI, 449
Strode, Elizabeth II, 662
Strode, Rachel II, 662
Strohl, Amos V, 127
Stroke, Mary VI, 710
Strokes, Albert II, 768
Strokes, Beulah Ann II, 769
Strokes, Caleb II, 769
Strokes, Edwin II, 768
Strokes, Elizabeth II, 768
Strokes, Ellwood H. II, 769
Strokes, Elwood H. II, 769
Strokes, Hannah R. II, 768
Strokes, Henry II, 768
Strokes, Isaac Collins II, 768
Strokes, Isaac Collins II, 769
Strokes, Isabella II, 768
Strokes, Jane II, 768
Strokes, John H. II, 769
Strokes, Lydia L. II, 769
Strokes, Mary VI, 667
Strokes, Nancy E. II, 769
Strokes, Nathaniel N. II, 769
Strokes, Ruth II, 769
Strokes, Ruthanna II, 769
Strokes, Samuel II, 768
Strokes, Sarah II, 768
Strokes, Sarah II, 769
Strokes, Selano II, 768
Strokes, Susan II, 768
Stroman, Scott V, 863
Strong, ??? VI, 269
Strong, Abner Early VI, 838
Strong, Anna Mary IV, 1380
Strong, Anne VI, 269
Strong, Anne VI, 273
Strong, Asa W. IV, 1380
Strong, Catharine VI, 836
Strong, Clifton VI, 857
Strong, Dally VI, 841
Strong, Daniel IV, 1380
Strong, David VI, 857
Strong, Edna D. VI, 857
Strong, Edward VI, 273
Strong, Elizabeth III, 385
Strong, Elizabeth VI, 815
Strong, Emily VI, 861
Strong, Enoch D. IV, 1368
Strong, Enoch D. IV, 1380
Strong, Esther A. V, 646
Strong, Esther Ann V, 646
Strong, Gabriel VI, 857
Strong, Georgina III, 418
Strong, Georgina III, 448
Strong, Gulielma IV, 726
Strong, Gulielma IV, 774
Strong, Hannah III, 448
Strong, Hannah III, 470
Strong, Hannah Richard III, 470
Strong, Isabella III, 424
Strong, Jesse VI, 273
Strong, Judith Wingfee VI, 273
Strong, Keturah VI, 863
Strong, Lucinda VI, 857
Strong, Lucretia VI, 857
Strong, Lucy III, 385
Strong, Martha VI, 857
Strong, Mary VI, 817
Strong, Mercy IV, 1380
Strong, Peggy VI, 857
Strong, Sally VI, 838
Strong, Sarah J. IV, 1380
Strong, Sarah Jane IV, 1368
Strong, Sarah Jane IV, 1380
Strong, Selah III, 448
Strong, Selah III, 470
Strong, Susan VI, 273
Strong, Tarlton VI, 857
Strong, Thomas VI, 857
Strong, Thomas VI, 861
Strong, Thos. C. III, 385
Strong, William VI, 273
Strong, William VI, 324
Strong, William VI, 839
Strong, William VI, 845
Strong, William VI, 966
Strongitham, ??? III, 394
Strongitham, Anna III, 448
Strongitham, Catharine III, 394
Strongitham, Catharine III, 448
Strongitham, Henry III, 448
Stronn, Judith IV, 34
Stronn, Judith IV, 61
Strope, ??? III, 303
Strope, Diana III, 303
Strope, Julia III, 303
Strothers, J. C. P. IV, 1187
Strothers, James IV, 1224
Strothers, James P. IV, 1224
Strothers, Jennie IV, 1224
Strothers, Lenora J. IV, 1224
Stroud, Ann II, 812
Stroud, Ann IV, 207
Stroud, Ann IV, 285
Stroud, Ann V, 544
Stroud, Ann VI, 449
Stroud, Ann VI, 568
Stroud, Ann M. IV, 285
Stroud, Ann M. V, 533
Stroud, Caroline V, 977
Stroud, Charles IV, 1295
Stroud, Charles V, 128
Stroud, Charles V, 967
Stroud, Charles V, 972
Stroud, Charles V, 977
Stroud, Charles V, 979
Stroud, Chas. V, 934
Stroud, Chas. V, 972
Stroud, Chas. V, 977
Stroud, Daniel II, 744
Stroud, Daniel II, 769
Stroud, Deborah Ann IV, 480
Stroud, Deborah Ann IV, 498
Stroud, Edward B. V, 977
Stroud, Edward B. V, 979
Stroud, Eleanor II, 720
Stroud, Eleanor II, 744
Stroud, Eleanor V, 533
Stroud, Eleanor H. II, 769
Stroud, Eliza D. II, 744
Stroud, Eliza D. II, 769
Stroud, Eliza D. V, 84
Stroud, Eliza D. V, 128
Stroud, Eliza D. V, 972
Stroud, Eliza D. V, 977
Stroud, Elizabeth II, 42
Stroud, Elizabeth II, 103
Stroud, Elizabeth II, 303
Stroud, Ellen V, 533
Stroud, Ellen V, 544
Stroud, Emily H. IV, 285
Stroud, Emily H. V, 533
Stroud, Emma II, 303
Stroud, Emma IV, 1340
Stroud, Emma E. II, 303
Stroud, Emma Elizabeth II, 303
Stroud, Ethel VI, 701
Stroud, Ethel VI, 709
Stroud, Evalina B. V, 128
Stroud, Evaline IV, 1295
Stroud, Evaline V, 977
Stroud, Eveline V, 977
Stroud, Eveline B. V, 128
Stroud, Fannie VI, 709
Stroud, George M. II, 662
Stroud, George M. II, 720
Stroud, George M. II, 744
Stroud, George M. II, 769
Stroud, George M. V, 977
Stroud, Hannah, Sr. IV, 103
Stroud, Hannah, Sr. IV, 110
Stroud, Hazel V, 601
Stroud, Isaac II, 42
Stroud, Isaac II, 103
Stroud, Isaac II, 662
Stroud, Jacob II, 186
Stroud, Jacob IV, 207
Stroud, Jacob IV, 285
Stroud, Jacob V, 533
Stroud, Jacob V, 544
Stroud, Jane II, 425
Stroud, Jane VI, 632
Stroud, Jane VI, 701
Stroud, Jane VI, 709
Stroud, Jane C. VI, 632
Stroud, John Hallowell II, 720
Stroud, Letitia II, 425
Stroud, Lidia II, 103
Stroud, Lidya II, 42
Stroud, Lidya II, 103
Stroud, Lydia B. V, 967
Stroud, Lydia B. V, 977
Stroud, Margaret II, 711
Stroud, Mary II, 42
Stroud, Mary II, 103
Stroud, Mary IV, 285
Stroud, Mary VI, 477
Stroud, Mary VI, 484
Stroud, Mary VI, 546
Stroud, Mary VI, 547
Stroud, Mary VI, 568
Stroud, Mary B. IV, 285
Stroud, Mary B. IV, 308
Stroud, Mary B. V, 533
Stroud, Mary N. II, 303
Stroud, Mary P. V, 972
Stroud, Mary P. V, 977
Stroud, Mary Paul V, 977
Stroud, Maurice K. VI, 701
Stroud, Maurice K. VI, 709
Stroud, Mrs. ??? IV, 1340
Stroud, Myrtle IV, 1340
Stroud, Rebecca II, 303
Stroud, Rebecca Hallowell II, 720
Stroud, Rebecca R. II, 303
Stroud, Sally Ann IV, 285
Stroud, Sally Ann IV, 309
Stroud, Sally Ann V, 977
Stroud, Sally Ann V, 979
Stroud, Sally B. IV, 207
Stroud, Sally B. IV, 285
Stroud, Sally B. V, 533
Stroud, Samuel VI, 568
Stroud, Sarah B. V, 533
Stroud, Susan II, 720
Stroud, Susan II, 769
Stroud, Susan V, 979
Stroud, Susan B. IV, 1295
Stroud, Susan B. V, 128
Stroud, Susan B. V, 967
Stroud, Susan B. V, 972
Stroud, Susan B. V, 977
Stroud, Susannah VI, 568
Stroud, Thomas II, 42
Stroud, Thomas II, 103
Stroud, Thomas II, 662
Stroud, Thomas II, 720
Stroud, Wd. Mary N. II, 186
Stroud, Wd. Susan B. V, 934
Stroud, William II, 425
Stroud, William IV, 285
Stroud, William V, 533
Stroud, William A. VI, 701
Stroud, William A. VI, 709
Stroud, Wm. VI, 709
Stroug, Jane C. VI, 632
Stroup, Bertha IV, 1264
Stroup, Charles F. IV, 1264
Stroup, Chas. IV, 1264
Stroup, Chas. F. IV, 1264
Stroup, Ella V, 646
Stroup, Lawrence IV, 1005
Stroup, Lester Wilson IV, 10
Stroup, Lida IV, 1005
Stroup, Lida IV, 1006
Stroup, Mary IV, 1264
Stroup, Mary Esther IV, 1264
Stroup, Mary M. IV, 1264
Stroup, Patience V, 128
Stroup, Samuel IV, 1264
Stroup, Sarah Pauline IV, 12
Stroup, William V, 361
Strouse, Robert V, 128
Strowd, Wd. Martha II, 448
Struthers, Flora May IV, 118
Struthers, J. C. P. IV, 1187
Struthers, James IV, 1224
Struthers, James C. P. IV, 11
Struthers, Jennie IV, 1224
Struthers, Lenora Jane IV, 1
Strwabridge, Ann II, 325
Stuard, Calvin VI, 449
Stuard, Elizabeth I, 826
Stuard, Elizabeth I, 839
Stuard, Jehu I, 839
Stuard, Mary I, 134
Stuard, Mary I, 166
Stuard, Sarah I, 453
Stuart, Aaron I, 770
Stuart, Aaron IV, 659
Stuart, Abbe V, 944
Stuart, Abigail I, 365
Stuart, Abigail I, 386
Stuart, Abigail I, 421
Stuart, Abigail V, 944
Stuart, Abigail L. I, 453
Stuart, Abigail L. I, 455
Stuart, Absolem I, 840
Stuart, Aggy VI, 998
Stuart, Alcanser H. I, 901
Stuart, Alex I, 421
Stuart, Alexander I, 365
Stuart, Alexander I, 415
Stuart, Alexander I, 421
Stuart, Alexander I, 734
Stuart, Alexander V, 944
Stuart, Alexander Stanton V,
Stuart, Alexandrew I, 734
Stuart, Alfred I, 422
Stuart, Alice V, 944
Stuart, Amos I, 392
Stuart, Amos I, 422
Stuart, Amos I, 575
Stuart, Amos I, 793
Stuart, Amos I, 840
Stuart, Amos I, 1050
Stuart, Amos I Sup 1, 11
Stuart, Amos Elbridge I, 793
Stuart, Amy I, 397
Stuart, Amy I, 422
Stuart, Amy C. I, 422
Stuart, Amy C. I, 428
Stuart, Anita I, 934
Stuart, Anita I, 949
Stuart, Anita Anderson I, 949
Stuart, Ann I, 365
Stuart, Ann I, 421
Stuart, Ann II, 101
Stuart, Anna I, 734
Stuart, Anne VI, 857
Stuart, Annie I, 949
Stuart, Annie Florence I, 922
Stuart, Annie Florence I, 934
Stuart, Annie L. V, 944
Stuart, Asenath I, 365
Stuart, Asenath I, 840
Stuart, Benjamin I, 422
Stuart, Bertha A. I, 422
Stuart, Besse VI, 998
Stuart, Betsy VI, 1017
Stuart, C. W. I, 949
Stuart, Caroline I, 422
Stuart, Catharine I, 366
Stuart, Catharine I, 421
Stuart, Catharine I, 469
Stuart, Catharine I, 575
Stuart, Catharine I, 734

rt, Celia VI, 998
rt, Charles I, 365
rt, Charles I, 422
rt, Charles H. VI, 998
rt, Charlotte VI, 998
rt, Clarence I, 934
rt, Cora E. I, 936
rt, D. W. I, 949
rt, David I, 793
rt, David M. I, 422
rt, David M. I, 427
art, David M. I, 428
rt, Delphina I, 793
art, Dinah I, 345
art, Dinah I, 370
art, Dinah I, 421
art, Eddie I, 422
art, Elexander I, 365
art, Elias I, 422
art, Elihu I, 422
art, Elisa IV, 659
art, Elisabeth I, 840
art, Eliza Ann VI, 974
art, Eliza M. I, 793
art, Eliza P. IV, 1005
art, Eliza P. IV, 1010
art, Elizabeth I, 345
art, Elizabeth I, 365
art, Elizabeth I, 366
art, Elizabeth I, 373
art, Elizabeth I, 387
art, Elizabeth I, 415
art, Elizabeth I, 421
art, Elizabeth I, 422
art, Elizabeth I, 461
art, Elizabeth I, 471
art, Elizabeth I, 734
art, Elizabeth I, 793
art, Elizabeth I, 803
art, Elizabeth I, 828
art, Elizabeth I, 839
art, Elizabeth I, 840
art, Elizabeth I, 928
art, Elizabeth I, 1048
art, Elizabeth I, 1050
art, Elizabeth VI, 857
art, Elizabeth VI, 998
art, Elizabeth Ann I, 422
art, Elizabeth, II I, 840
art, Elizbeth Smith VI, 1017
art, Ellixander I, 365
art, Elsie I, 949
art, Elsie Ellen I, 934
uart, Emma I, 422
uart, Erasmus J. I, 840
uart, Essie M. I, 933
uart, Essie M. I, 949
uart, Essie May I, 934
uart, Eunice I, 366
uart, Eunice I, 401
uart, Eunice I, 422
uart, Flossie I, 949
uart, Flossie Alma I, 934
uart, Gasner I, 575
uart, Gravener I, 1050
uart, Guli I, 840
uart, Hannah I, 373
uart, Hannah I, 415
uart, Hannah I, 421
uart, Hannah I, 422
uart, Hannah I, 457
tuart, Hannah I, 460
tuart, Hannah I, 470
tuart, Hannah I, 472
tuart, Hannah I, 485
tuart, Hannah I, 575
tuart, Hannah I, 734
tuart, Hannah I, 1047
tuart, Hannah I, 1050
tuart, Hannah VI, 998
tuart, Harper F. I, 571
tuart, Harper F. I, 575
tuart, Harper F. I, 840
tuart, Harper Franklin I, 793
Stuart, Harrison I, 422
Stuart, Henry I, 365
Stuart, Henry I, 421
Stuart, Henry I, 422
Stuart, Henry I, 734
Stuart, Henry I, 840
Stuart, Henry, Jr. I, 734
Stuart, Huldah I, 365
Stuart, Isaac I, 575
Stuart, Isaac I, 840
Stuart, Isaac II, 424
Stuart, Isaack I, 840
Stuart, Ivy I, 365
Stuart, James I, 934
Stuart, James II, 101
Stuart, James VI, 835
Stuart, James VI, 857
Stuart, James W. VI, 998
Stuart, Jane I, 770
Stuart, Jane E. I, 934
Stuart, Jehu I, 365
Stuart, Jehu I, 421
Stuart, Jehu I, 422
Stuart, Jehu I, 517
Stuart, Jehu I, 571
Stuart, Jehu I, 575
Stuart, Jehu I, 716
Stuart, Jehu I, 734
Stuart, Jehu I, 773
Stuart, Jehu I, 793
Stuart, Jehu I, 839
Stuart, Jehu I, 840
Stuart, Jehu H. I, 840
Stuart, Jehu W. I, 840
Stuart, Jehu, Jr. I, 839
Stuart, Jehu, Jr. I, 840
Stuart, Jesse VI, 998
Stuart, Job I, 365
Stuart, Job I, 422
Stuart, Joel I, 365
Stuart, John I, 345
Stuart, John I, 365
Stuart, John I, 366
Stuart, John I, 420
Stuart, John I, 421
Stuart, John I, 422
Stuart, John I, 470
Stuart, John I, 471
Stuart, John I, 734
Stuart, John I, 793
Stuart, John I, 840
Stuart, John II, 101
Stuart, John II, 108
Stuart, John II, 660
Stuart, John IV, 659
Stuart, John VI, 857
Stuart, John F. I, 901
Stuart, John Sidney I, 793
Stuart, Jonathan H. I, 793
Stuart, Joseph II, 41
Stuart, Joseph IV, 659
Stuart, Joseph Gurney I, 365
Stuart, Joshua I, 365
Stuart, Josiah E. VI, 998
Stuart, Julia A. I, 258
Stuart, Julia Ann I, 241
Stuart, Julia Ann I, 258
Stuart, Julia Ann I, 365
Stuart, Katharine I, 815
Stuart, Katharine I, 840
Stuart, Littleberry VI, 998
Stuart, Lorenzo R. VI, 998
Stuart, Loruhama I, 840
Stuart, Louisa I, 793
Stuart, Louisa I, 813
Stuart, Louisa I, 840
Stuart, Luiza I, 803
Stuart, Luiza I, 840
Stuart, Luke VI, 839
Stuart, Luke VI, 998
Stuart, Lydia II, 73
Stuart, Lydia II, 101
Stuart, Margaret Anita I, 920
Stuart, Mark II, 101
Stuart, Martha I, 365
Stuart, Martha I, 366
Stuart, Martha I, 421
Stuart, Martha I, 734
Stuart, Martha I, 799
Stuart, Martha I, 802
Stuart, Martha I, 839
Stuart, Martha I, 840
Stuart, Martha I, 933
Stuart, Martha I, 934
Stuart, Martha IV, 1264
Stuart, Martha Ann VI, 998
Stuart, Martisia Jane I, 793
Stuart, Martitia J. I, 802
Stuart, Martitia J. I, 840
Stuart, Mary I, 365
Stuart, Mary I, 411
Stuart, Mary I, 420
Stuart, Mary I, 421
Stuart, Mary I, 422
Stuart, Mary I, 723
Stuart, Mary I, 734
Stuart, Mary I, 793
Stuart, Mary II, 101
Stuart, Mary II, 108
Stuart, Mary IV, 1376
Stuart, Mary VI, 998
Stuart, Mary A. I, 571
Stuart, Mary A. I, 575
Stuart, Mary A. I, 756
Stuart, Mary A. I, 770
Stuart, Mary J. I, 365
Stuart, Mary J. I, 949
Stuart, Mary Jane I, 922
Stuart, Mary Jane I, 934
Stuart, Mary Jane I, 949
Stuart, Mary Wade II, 808
Stuart, Matilda I, 392
Stuart, Matilda I, 422
Stuart, Matilda I, 575
Stuart, Matilda I, 793
Stuart, Matilda I, 840
Stuart, Matilda H. I, 840
Stuart, Mattie I, 422
Stuart, Mercy IV, 659
Stuart, Meriam I, 793
Stuart, Michael I, 422
Stuart, Miriam I, 798
Stuart, Miriam I, 840
Stuart, Morris I, 422
Stuart, Nancy II, 797
Stuart, Nancy VI, 998
Stuart, Nancy B. VI, 857
Stuart, Nancy H. VI, 947
Stuart, Naomi I, 365
Stuart, Naomi I, 421
Stuart, Naomi I, 471
Stuart, Nathan I, 422
Stuart, Neomi I, 365
Stuart, Neomi I, 420
Stuart, Neomi I, 421
Stuart, Parthena VI, 998
Stuart, Patrick I, 422
Stuart, Paul I, 949
Stuart, Peter I, 365
Stuart, Peter I, 422
Stuart, Phebe I, 365
Stuart, Phebe I, 800
Stuart, Phebe I, 840
Stuart, Polly Alice VI, 998
Stuart, Pricilla VI, 926
Stuart, Rachel I, 421
Stuart, Rachel I, 422
Stuart, Rachel I, 575
Stuart, Rachel I, 793
Stuart, Rachel I, 809
Stuart, Rachel I, 840
Stuart, Rachel II, 73
Stuart, Rachel II, 101
Stuart, Rebecca I, 901
Stuart, Rebecca V, 481
Stuart, Rebecca V, 532
Stuart, Rebecca E. I, 365
Stuart, Richard VI, 998
Stuart, Riley I, 365
Stuart, Robert I, 365
Stuart, Robert I, 421
Stuart, Robert I, 517
Stuart, Robert I, 575
Stuart, Robert I, 734
Stuart, Robert I, 799
Stuart, Robert I, 839
Stuart, Robert I, 840
Stuart, Robert I, 1050
Stuart, Robert Adison I, 793
Stuart, Robert Stuart Hiatt I, 840
Stuart, Rogina I, 422
Stuart, Ruth I, 365
Stuart, Ruth I, 394
Stuart, Ruth I, 422
Stuart, Ruth IV, 61
Stuart, Ruth Ellen I, 422
Stuart, Ruth Ellen I, 427
Stuart, Ruth Herin I, 422
Stuart, Sallie I, 920
Stuart, Samuel I, 366
Stuart, Samuel I, 373
Stuart, Samuel I, 421
Stuart, Samuel I, 457
Stuart, Samuel I, 485
Stuart, Samuel I, 734
Stuart, Samuel IV, 659
Stuart, Sarah I, 422
Stuart, Sarah I, 517
Stuart, Sarah I, 571
Stuart, Sarah I, 575
Stuart, Sarah I, 716
Stuart, Sarah I, 734
Stuart, Sarah I, 773
Stuart, Sarah I, 793
Stuart, Sarah I, 800
Stuart, Sarah I, 805
Stuart, Sarah I, 806
Stuart, Sarah I, 839
Stuart, Sarah I, 840
Stuart, Sarah II, 101
Stuart, Sarah A. I, 806
Stuart, Sarah A. I, 840
Stuart, Sarah Ann I, 422
Stuart, Sarah Ann I, 793
Stuart, Sarah Ann VI, 998
Stuart, Simon I, 366
Stuart, Simon I, 401
Stuart, Simon I, 422
Stuart, Simon G. I, 422
Stuart, Solomon I, 421
Stuart, Solomon I, 422
Stuart, Solomon I, 922
Stuart, Solomon I, 933
Stuart, Solomon I, 934
Stuart, Solomon I, 949
Stuart, Solomon M. I, 934
Stuart, Solomon M. I, 949
Stuart, Stanton Alexander V, 944
Stuart, Susan H. I, 422
Stuart, Susanna V, 584
Stuart, Susannah I, 575
Stuart, Tabitha I, 734
Stuart, Temple I, 840
Stuart, Thadeus V. I, 901
Stuart, Thomas VI, 998
Stuart, W. G. I, 949
Stuart, Walter G. I, 920
Stuart, Walter G. I, 934
Stuart, William VI, 998
Stuart, William Paul I, 934
Stuart, Wm. II, 101
Stuart, Wm. IV, 659
Stuart, Wm. Lee I, 949
Stuart, Wm. Paul I, 949
Stuart, Wm. Zeno I, 365
Stuart, Zimri I, 366
Stuart, Zimri I, 734
Stuart, Zimri I, 793
Stuart, Zimri I, 840
Stuart, Zimri I, 901
Stuart, Zimry I, 734
Stubb, Alden V, 865
Stubb, Alden V, 867
Stubb, Alice V, 867
Stubb, Alma V, 867
Stubb, Amy V, 866
Stubb, Amy E. V, 867
Stubb, Benj. V, 867
Stubb, Bertha A. V, 867
Stubb, Bessie V, 867
Stubb, Calvin V, 867
Stubb, Celia V, 866
Stubb, Charles V, 867
Stubb, Charles H. V, 865
Stubb, Charles W. V, 865
Stubb, Charles W. V, 867
Stubb, Charlotte V, 866
Stubb, Clarence B. V, 867
Stubb, Clayton V, 867
Stubb, Clayton S. V, 867
Stubb, Cora V, 867
Stubb, Daniel V, 866
Stubb, David F. V, 867
Stubb, Davis T. V, 867
Stubb, Dedan V, 867
Stubb, Delilah V, 867
Stubb, Della M. V, 867
Stubb, Dukie V, 867
Stubb, Edith V, 867
Stubb, Edwin V, 865
Stubb, Edwin V, 867
Stubb, Eleanor V, 865
Stubb, Eli V, 867
Stubb, Elihu V, 867
Stubb, Elijah M. V, 867
Stubb, Enoch V, 865
Stubb, Enoch V, 867
Stubb, Enoch D. V, 867
Stubb, Estella V, 865
Stubb, Estella E. V, 867
Stubb, Esther V, 867
Stubb, Esther A. V, 867
Stubb, Esther Ann V, 867
Stubb, Flora B. V, 867
Stubb, Grace V, 867
Stubb, Hebert V, 867
Stubb, Henry V, 866
Stubb, Hiram V, 867
Stubb, Ira S. V, 867
Stubb, Ira, Jr. V, 867
Stubb, Irma V, 867
Stubb, Irvin V, 867
Stubb, Irvin Talbert V, 867
Stubb, Isaac Alvadore V, 867
Stubb, Jacob V, 866
Stubb, Jemima V, 866
Stubb, Jesse G. V, 867
Stubb, John C. V, 867
Stubb, John F. V, 865
Stubb, John F. V, 867
Stubb, Jonathan E. V, 867
Stubb, Joseph V, 866
Stubb, Joseph H. V, 867
Stubb, Laura V, 865
Stubb, Laura A. V, 867
Stubb, Laura Ann V, 867
Stubb, Lorenzo V, 865
Stubb, Lura C. V, 867
Stubb, Lydia V, 866
Stubb, Lydia A. V, 867
Stubb, Lydia Ann V, 867
Stubb, Mahlon V, 866
Stubb, Marmaduke V, 867
Stubb, Martha J. V, 867
Stubb, Martha Jane V, 867
Stubb, Mary V, 865
Stubb, Mary V, 866
Stubb, Mary V, 867
Stubb, Mary Emma V, 867
Stubb, Mary H. V, 867
Stubb, Mary Jane V, 867
Stubb, Mary Luanna V, 865
Stubb, Matilda V, 867
Stubb, Naomi T. Randall V, 865
Stubb, Nathan V, 866
Stubb, Orando V, 867
Stubb, Oscar V, 867
Stubb, Phebe Lillian V, 867
Stubb, Rachel C. V, 865
Stubb, Rachel C. V, 867
Stubb, Rachel H. V, 867
Stubb, Raymond V, 867
Stubb, Raymond K. V, 867
Stubb, Robert Edwin V, 867
Stubb, Rue Ann V, 867
Stubb, Russel A. V, 867
Stubb, Russell V, 867
Stubb, Samuel A. V, 867
Stubb, Sarah V, 865
Stubb, Sarah V, 866
Stubb, Sarah E. V, 867
Stubb, Sarah Jane V, 867
Stubb, Slyvanus V, 867
Stubb, Stephen V, 866
Stubb, Susan H. V, 867
Stubb, Susannah V, 867
Stubb, Thomas J. V, 867
Stubb, Tressa V, 867
Stubb, William C. V, 867
Stubb, William P. V, 867
Stubb, Zimri V, 865
Stubbines, Elizabeth II, 42
Stubbines, Henry II, 42
Stubbings, Henry II, 17
Stubbins, Catharine IV, 469
Stubbins, Elizabeth II, 103
Stubbins, Elizabeth IV, 469
Stubbins, Henry II, 42
Stubbins, Henry II, 64
Stubbins, Henry II, 103
Stubbins, Henry II, 108
Stubbins, Mary II, 103
Stubbins, Mary II, 108
Stubbins, Rebeckah II, 64
Stubbins, Rebeckah II, 103
Stubbins, Samuel II, 103
Stubbins, Sarah II, 103
Stubbins, Thomas IV, 469
Stubbs, ??? V, 823
Stubbs, ??? V, 877
Stubbs, Abraham I, 1045
Stubbs, Abraham IV, 446
Stubbs, Achsah V, 88
Stubbs, Achsah V, 128
Stubbs, Adaline V, 864
Stubbs, Albert V, 128
Stubbs, Albert V, 281
Stubbs, Albert V, 864
Stubbs, Albert V, 865
Stubbs, Albert V, 866
Stubbs, Albert L. V, 865
Stubbs, Albert M. V, 281
Stubbs, Alden V, 832
Stubbs, Alden V, 864
Stubbs, Alden V, 867
Stubbs, Alice V, 865
Stubbs, Allen V, 864
Stubbs, Allen V, 866
Stubbs, Allen V, 867
Stubbs, Alma V, 864
Stubbs, Alma V, 865
Stubbs, Alpheus V, 865
Stubbs, Alva Elisha V, 865
Stubbs, Alvadore V, 864
Stubbs, Alvan V, 864
Stubbs, Alvan V, 867
Stubbs, Alvin V, 866
Stubbs, Amanda V, 128
Stubbs, Amanda V, 863
Stubbs, Amanda V, 868
Stubbs, Amy V, 863
Stubbs, Amy V, 864
Stubbs, Amy V, 866
Stubbs, Amy Evalena V, 865
Stubbs, Ann V, 128
Stubbs, Ann V, 839
Stubbs, Ann V, 851
Stubbs, Ann V, 852
Stubbs, Ann V, 864
Stubbs, Ann V, 865

Stubbs, Ann V, 866
Stubbs, Ann V, 870
Stubbs, Ann Miller I, 422
Stubbs, Anna V, 864
Stubbs, Anna V, 865
Stubbs, Anna F. V, 853
Stubbs, Anna F. V, 866
Stubbs, Anne II, 662
Stubbs, Arthur T. V, 865
Stubbs, Asenath IV, 1078
Stubbs, Asenath IV, 1099
Stubbs, Benjamin V, 865
Stubbs, Bertha IV, 498
Stubbs, Bertha V, 865
Stubbs, Bertha Anna V, 865
Stubbs, Bessie L. V, 865
Stubbs, Beulah V, 848
Stubbs, Beulah A. V, 865
Stubbs, Beulah Ann V, 864
Stubbs, Beulah Ann V, 870
Stubbs, Calvin V, 864
Stubbs, Calvin V, 865
Stubbs, Caroline V, 864
Stubbs, Celia V, 863
Stubbs, Celia V, 866
Stubbs, Charles V, 863
Stubbs, Charles Moffit V, 865
Stubbs, Charles Moffitt V, 864
Stubbs, Charlotte V, 601
Stubbs, Charlotte V, 765
Stubbs, Charlotte V, 864
Stubbs, Charlotte V, 866
Stubbs, Charlotte, V, 863
Stubbs, Clara V, 864
Stubbs, Clarence B. V, 865
Stubbs, Claud B. V, 865
Stubbs, Clayton S. V, 865
Stubbs, Clifford V, 865
Stubbs, Coretta V, 865
Stubbs, Daniel V, 863
Stubbs, Daniel V, 866
Stubbs, Daniel P. V, 866
Stubbs, Darcas V, 128
Stubbs, David T. V, 864
Stubbs, David T. V, 865
Stubbs, Deborah I, 406
Stubbs, Deborah I, 422
Stubbs, Deborah I, 1041
Stubbs, Deborah I, 1045
Stubbs, Deborah IV, 446
Stubbs, Deborah IV, 450
Stubbs, Dedan A. V, 865
Stubbs, Delila V, 865
Stubbs, Delilah V, 851
Stubbs, Delilah V, 863
Stubbs, Delilah V, 864
Stubbs, Delilah V, 874
Stubbs, Edith III, 69
Stubbs, Edith V, 584
Stubbs, Edith V, 601
Stubbs, Edith V, 865
Stubbs, Edith V, 866
Stubbs, Edith B. III, 303
Stubbs, Edith B. III, 304
Stubbs, Edwin V, 865
Stubbs, Effa Luella V, 865
Stubbs, Eleanor V, 832
Stubbs, Eleanor V, 864
Stubbs, Eleanor V, 865
Stubbs, Eleanor V, 866
Stubbs, Elenor C. V, 864
Stubbs, Eli V, 845
Stubbs, Eli V, 853
Stubbs, Eli V, 864
Stubbs, Eli V, 866
Stubbs, Elihu V, 856
Stubbs, Elihu V, 863
Stubbs, Elihu V, 864
Stubbs, Elihu V, 865
Stubbs, Elihu V, 867
Stubbs, Elijah V, 848
Stubbs, Elijah V, 866
Stubbs, Elijah M. V, 863
Stubbs, Elijah M. V, 865
Stubbs, Elijah M. V, 870
Stubbs, Elisha V, 844
Stubbs, Elisha V, 851
Stubbs, Elisha V, 863
Stubbs, Elisha V, 864
Stubbs, Elisha V, 865
Stubbs, Elisha V, 866
Stubbs, Eliza I, 1045
Stubbs, Eliza IV, 403
Stubbs, Eliza IV, 441
Stubbs, Eliza IV, 446
Stubbs, Eliza Ann V, 840
Stubbs, Eliza Ann V, 867
Stubbs, Elizabeth I, 402
Stubbs, Elizabeth I, 422
Stubbs, Elizabeth I, 1045
Stubbs, Elizabeth I, 1051
Stubbs, Elizabeth IV, 381
Stubbs, Elizabeth IV, 446
Stubbs, Elizabeth IV, 1064
Stubbs, Elizabeth IV, 1078
Stubbs, Elizabeth V, 120
Stubbs, Elizabeth V, 128
Stubbs, Elizabeth V, 601
Stubbs, Elizabeth V, 832
Stubbs, Elizabeth V, 833
Stubbs, Elizabeth V, 836
Stubbs, Elizabeth V, 844
Stubbs, Elizabeth V, 851
Stubbs, Elizabeth V, 854
Stubbs, Elizabeth V, 855
Stubbs, Elizabeth V, 863
Stubbs, Elizabeth V, 864
Stubbs, Elizabeth V, 865
Stubbs, Elizabeth V, 866
Stubbs, Elizabeth V, 868
Stubbs, Elizabeth V, 873
Stubbs, Elizabeth V, 874
Stubbs, Elizabeth Ann V, 864
Stubbs, Elizabeth Ann V, 866
Stubbs, Elizabeth J. V, 863
Stubbs, Elizabeth M. V, 578
Stubbs, Elizabeth M. V, 601
Stubbs, Elizabeth M. V, 867
Stubbs, Elizabeth R. III, 304
Stubbs, Elizabeth T. V, 864
Stubbs, Elizabeth, Jr. IV, 1078
Stubbs, Elvira V, 856
Stubbs, Elvira V, 863
Stubbs, Elvira V, 864
Stubbs, Elvira V, 865
Stubbs, Elvira V, 866
Stubbs, Elvira E. V, 864
Stubbs, Elvira Elizabeth V, 866
Stubbs, Elvira Elizabeth V, 867
Stubbs, Enoch V, 863
Stubbs, Enoch V, 864
Stubbs, Enoch V, 866
Stubbs, Enoch Albert V, 867
Stubbs, Enos P. V, 578
Stubbs, Enos P. V, 601
Stubbs, Enos P. V, 844
Stubbs, Enos P. V, 864
Stubbs, Enos P. V, 867
Stubbs, Esther I, 422
Stubbs, Esther I, 1045
Stubbs, Esther IV, 1078
Stubbs, Esther V, 105
Stubbs, Esther V, 128
Stubbs, Esther V, 589
Stubbs, Esther V, 765
Stubbs, Esther V, 844
Stubbs, Esther V, 856
Stubbs, Esther V, 857
Stubbs, Esther V, 863
Stubbs, Esther V, 864
Stubbs, Esther V, 865
Stubbs, Esther V, 866
Stubbs, Esther A. V, 864
Stubbs, Esther Alma V, 864
Stubbs, Esther Anna V, 865
Stubbs, Esther Elma V, 837
Stubbs, Esther T. V, 578
Stubbs, Esther T. V, 844
Stubbs, Esther T. V, 865
Stubbs, Etta M. V, 867
Stubbs, Eunice F. V, 128
Stubbs, Eva Keziah V, 864
Stubbs, Frederic Austin V, 865
Stubbs, George E. V, 865
Stubbs, Hannah I, 1045
Stubbs, Hannah IV, 1078
Stubbs, Hannah IV, 1083
Stubbs, Hannah V, 48
Stubbs, Hannah V, 51
Stubbs, Hannah V, 128
Stubbs, Hannah V, 487
Stubbs, Hannah V, 533
Stubbs, Hannah V, 864
Stubbs, Hannah V, 866
Stubbs, Harriet C. V, 865
Stubbs, Harriet Emma V, 852
Stubbs, Helia V, 866
Stubbs, Henry IV, 446
Stubbs, Henry IV, 1078
Stubbs, Henry V, 856
Stubbs, Henry V, 864
Stubbs, Henry V, 866
Stubbs, Henry V, 887
Stubbs, Herbert V, 865
Stubbs, Hiram V, 845
Stubbs, Hiram V, 866
Stubbs, Horace III, 304
Stubbs, Horace R. III, 69
Stubbs, Horace R. III, 303
Stubbs, Horace R. III, 304
Stubbs, Horace R. III, 358
Stubbs, Howard L. III, 304
Stubbs, Idalla M. V, 865
Stubbs, Idda IV, 446
Stubbs, Iddo I, 1045
Stubbs, Iddo IV, 446
Stubbs, Irvin V, 865
Stubbs, Irvin Talbert V, 869
Stubbs, Isaac I, 377
Stubbs, Isaac I, 422
Stubbs, Isaac I, 840
Stubbs, Isaac I, 1045
Stubbs, Isaac I, 1050
Stubbs, Isaac I, 1051
Stubbs, Isaac I Sup 1, 11
Stubbs, Isaac IV, 446
Stubbs, Isaac IV, 1064
Stubbs, Isaac IV, 1078
Stubbs, Isaac V, 48
Stubbs, Isaac V, 88
Stubbs, Isaac V, 120
Stubbs, Isaac V, 128
Stubbs, Isaac V, 765
Stubbs, Isaac V, 863
Stubbs, Isaac V, 866
Stubbs, Isaac Alvadore V, 865
Stubbs, Isaac C. V, 865
Stubbs, Isaac, Jr. IV, 1078
Stubbs, Isaac, Jr. V, 128
Stubbs, Jacob I, 1045
Stubbs, Jacob IV, 446
Stubbs, Jacob V, 863
Stubbs, Jacob V, 866
Stubbs, Jane I, 1045
Stubbs, Jane I, 1049
Stubbs, Jane I, 1050
Stubbs, Jane V, 105
Stubbs, Jane V, 128
Stubbs, Jane V, 854
Stubbs, Jane V, 863
Stubbs, Jane V, 866
Stubbs, Jean V, 829
Stubbs, Jean W. III, 304
Stubbs, Jemima V, 863
Stubbs, Jemima V, 866
Stubbs, Jesse V, 866
Stubbs, Jesse G. V, 865
Stubbs, Joel V, 864
Stubbs, Joel V, 866
Stubbs, John I, 422
Stubbs, John I, 840
Stubbs, John I, 1041
Stubbs, John I, 1045
Stubbs, John I, 1049
Stubbs, John I, 1050
Stubbs, John I, 1051
Stubbs, John IV, 1077
Stubbs, John IV, 1078
Stubbs, John V, 105
Stubbs, John V, 128
Stubbs, John V, 829
Stubbs, John V, 832
Stubbs, John V, 854
Stubbs, John V, 859
Stubbs, John V, 863
Stubbs, John V, 864
Stubbs, John V, 865
Stubbs, John V, 866
Stubbs, John V, 887
Stubbs, John C. V, 865
Stubbs, John C. V, 867
Stubbs, John Clinton V, 864
Stubbs, John F. V, 846
Stubbs, John, Jr. V, 866
Stubbs, John, Jr. V, 887
Stubbs, John, Sr. V, 887
Stubbs, Jonathan V, 849
Stubbs, Jonathan V, 863
Stubbs, Jonathan V, 864
Stubbs, Jonathan V, 865
Stubbs, Jonathan V, 866
Stubbs, Jonathan V, 867
Stubbs, Jonathan Elijah V, 864
Stubbs, Joseph I, 422
Stubbs, Joseph I, 1045
Stubbs, Joseph I, 1050
Stubbs, Joseph IV, 403
Stubbs, Joseph IV, 428
Stubbs, Joseph IV, 446
Stubbs, Joseph IV, 450
Stubbs, Joseph IV, 1078
Stubbs, Joseph V, 128
Stubbs, Joseph V, 584
Stubbs, Joseph V, 601
Stubbs, Joseph V, 851
Stubbs, Joseph V, 860
Stubbs, Joseph V, 863
Stubbs, Joseph V, 864
Stubbs, Joseph V, 865
Stubbs, Joseph V, 866
Stubbs, Joseph V, 867
Stubbs, Joseph V, 868
Stubbs, Joseph V, 887
Stubbs, Joseph H. V, 866
Stubbs, Joseph, Sr. V, 866
Stubbs, Kezia V, 855
Stubbs, Kezia V, 863
Stubbs, Keziah V, 128
Stubbs, Keziah V, 831
Stubbs, Keziah V, 832
Stubbs, Keziah V, 845
Stubbs, Keziah V, 864
Stubbs, Keziah V, 866
Stubbs, Keziah V, 868
Stubbs, Keziah V, 879
Stubbs, Keziah V, 887
Stubbs, Laura Ann V, 835
Stubbs, Lauretta III, 69
Stubbs, Laurette III, 358
Stubbs, Laurette W. III, 304
Stubbs, Levi V, 833
Stubbs, Lindley V, 765
Stubbs, Lindley H. V, 864
Stubbs, Lindly V, 866
Stubbs, Lizzie III, 304
Stubbs, Lizzie V, 281
Stubbs, Lorenzo V, 864
Stubbs, Lorenzo V, 865
Stubbs, Lorenzo V, 867
Stubbs, Louisa D. IV, 1077
Stubbs, Louisa W. IV, 1078
Stubbs, Louise R. III, 304
Stubbs, Luana V, 859
Stubbs, Lucretia III, 303
Stubbs, Luiza IV, 1078
Stubbs, Luna E. V, 865
Stubbs, Lura G. V, 865
Stubbs, Lydia V, 863
Stubbs, Lydia V, 865
Stubbs, Lydia V, 866
Stubbs, Lydia V, 887
Stubbs, Lydia A. V, 864
Stubbs, Lydia A. V, 865
Stubbs, Lydia Elvira V, 865
Stubbs, Mabel Wernland V, 865
Stubbs, Mahlon V, 863
Stubbs, Mahlon V, 866
Stubbs, Margaret I, 377
Stubbs, Margaret I, 422
Stubbs, Margaret I, 840
Stubbs, Margaret I, 1045
Stubbs, Margaret I, 1051
Stubbs, Margaret IV, 446
Stubbs, Margaret IV, 1078
Stubbs, Margaret IV, 1079
Stubbs, Margaret V, 48
Stubbs, Margaret V, 88
Stubbs, Margaret V, 128
Stubbs, Margaret V, 829
Stubbs, Margaret V, 859
Stubbs, Margaret V, 860
Stubbs, Margaret V, 863
Stubbs, Margaret V, 864
Stubbs, Margaret V, 866
Stubbs, Margret I, 840
Stubbs, Maria IV, 1078
Stubbs, Mariah V, 830
Stubbs, Mariah V, 864
Stubbs, Marian V, 866
Stubbs, Marmaduke V, 859
Stubbs, Marmaduke V, 864
Stubbs, Marmaduke M. V, 846
Stubbs, Marmaduke M. V, 865
Stubbs, Marmaduke Nathan V, 865
Stubbs, Martha V, 128
Stubbs, Martha V, 829
Stubbs, Martha V, 851
Stubbs, Martha V, 863
Stubbs, Martha V, 864
Stubbs, Martha Ann V, 848
Stubbs, Martha Ann V, 863
Stubbs, Martha Ann V, 864
Stubbs, Martha Ann V, 870
Stubbs, Mary I, 575
Stubbs, Mary I, 1045
Stubbs, Mary I, 1049
Stubbs, Mary I, 1051
Stubbs, Mary II, 456
Stubbs, Mary II, 662
Stubbs, Mary IV, 446
Stubbs, Mary IV, 1064
Stubbs, Mary IV, 1068
Stubbs, Mary IV, 1078
Stubbs, Mary V, 532
Stubbs, Mary V, 533
Stubbs, Mary V, 578
Stubbs, Mary V, 601
Stubbs, Mary V, 750
Stubbs, Mary V, 765
Stubbs, Mary V, 826
Stubbs, Mary V, 829
Stubbs, Mary V, 839
Stubbs, Mary V, 845
Stubbs, Mary V, 851
Stubbs, Mary V, 863
Stubbs, Mary V, 864
Stubbs, Mary V, 865
Stubbs, Mary V, 866
Stubbs, Mary V, 867
Stubbs, Mary V, 868
Stubbs, Mary Anna V, 864
Stubbs, Mary E. V, 867
Stubbs, Mary Elmina V, 864
Stubbs, Mary Emma V, 864
Stubbs, Mary H. V, 601
Stubbs, Mary H. V, 864
Stubbs, Mary Hannah V, 856
Stubbs, Mary Hannah V, 865
Stubbs, Mary Jane V, 864
Stubbs, Mary K. V, 867
Stubbs, Mary S. V, 832
Stubbs, Mary, Sr. V, 866
Stubbs, Matilda V, 865
Stubbs, Melissa V, 865
Stubbs, Melissa J. V, 865
Stubbs, Melva Edger V, 864
Stubbs, Milton V, 837
Stubbs, Milton V, 863
Stubbs, Milton V, 866
Stubbs, Natha M. V, 864
Stubbs, Nathan I, 402
Stubbs, Nathan I, 422
Stubbs, Nathan I, 1041
Stubbs, Nathan I, 1050
Stubbs, Nathan I, 1051
Stubbs, Nathan I Sup 1, 11
Stubbs, Nathan V, 128
Stubbs, Nathan V, 852
Stubbs, Nathan V, 854
Stubbs, Nathan V, 855
Stubbs, Nathan V, 864
Stubbs, Nathan V, 865
Stubbs, Nathan V, 866
Stubbs, Nathan V, 868
Stubbs, Nathan V, 870
Stubbs, Nathan, Jr. V, 866
Stubbs, Newton I, 1045
Stubbs, Newton V, 128
Stubbs, Newton V, 863
Stubbs, Newton V, 868
Stubbs, Orla L. V, 865
Stubbs, Orlando Clinton V, 865
Stubbs, Oscar M. V, 865
Stubbs, Patcey I, 1045
Stubbs, Phebe Lilian V, 864
Stubbs, Priscilla II, 813
Stubbs, Rachel I, 1045
Stubbs, Rachel IV, 446
Stubbs, Rachel IV, 1068
Stubbs, Rachel IV, 1077
Stubbs, Rachel IV, 1078
Stubbs, Rachel V, 128
Stubbs, Rachel V, 849
Stubbs, Rachel V, 854
Stubbs, Rachel V, 856
Stubbs, Rachel V, 859
Stubbs, Rachel V, 863
Stubbs, Rachel V, 864
Stubbs, Rachel V, 866
Stubbs, Rachel V, 867
Stubbs, Rachel A. V, 865
Stubbs, Rachel Alma V, 864
Stubbs, Rachel C. V, 846
Stubbs, Rachel H. V, 847
Stubbs, Rachel H. V, 851
Stubbs, Rachel P. II, 813
Stubbs, Rebecca IV, 428
Stubbs, Rebecca IV, 446
Stubbs, Rebecca IV, 1075
Stubbs, Rebecca IV, 1078
Stubbs, Rebecca V, 128
Stubbs, Rebecca V, 868
Stubbs, Rebekah I, 1045
Stubbs, Rebekah V, 863
Stubbs, Rhoda I, 1045
Stubbs, Rhoda IV, 446
Stubbs, Rhoda IV, 450
Stubbs, Rhoda IV, 595
Stubbs, Rilda C. V, 864
Stubbs, Riley V, 864
Stubbs, Riley V, 866
Stubbs, Robert V, 864
Stubbs, Robert V, 866
Stubbs, Rosanna V, 866
Stubbs, Rosannah V, 864
Stubbs, Ruth Alma V, 865
Stubbs, Ruth Emma V, 864
Stubbs, Samuel I, 1045
Stubbs, Samuel I, 1049
Stubbs, Samuel I, 1051
Stubbs, Samuel IV, 1068
Stubbs, Samuel IV, 1078
Stubbs, Samuel V, 128
Stubbs, Samuel V, 829

bs, Samuel V, 839
bs, Samuel V, 845
bs, Samuel V, 863
bs, Samuel V, 864
bs, Samuel V, 865
bs, Samuel V, 866
bs, Samuel A. V, 864
bs, Samuel A. V, 865
bs, Samuel, Jr. V, 866
bs, Sarah I, 1045
bs, Sarah IV, 401
bbs, Sarah IV, 446
bbs, Sarah IV, 451
bs, Sarah IV, 1078
bs, Sarah V, 95
bbs, Sarah V, 128
bbs, Sarah V, 851
bbs, Sarah V, 859
bbs, Sarah V, 863
bbs, Sarah V, 864
bbs, Sarah V, 866
bbs, Sarah E. V, 865
bbs, Sarah Elizabeth V, 865
bbs, Sarah Ellen V, 865
bbs, Sarah F. V, 865
bbs, Sarah J. V, 837
bbs, Sarah Jane V, 866
bbs, Sarah Jane V, 869
bbs, Sarah, Jr. V, 866
bbs, Stephen V, 863
bbs, Stephen V, 866
bbs, Susan V, 845
bbs, Susan V, 846
bbs, Susan V, 859
bbs, Susan V, 865
bbs, Susan H. V, 847
ubbs, Susan J. V, 864
ubbs, Susan L. V, 864
ubbs, Susanah V, 865
ubbs, Susannah V, 765
ubbs, Susannah V, 840
ubbs, Susannah V, 856
ubbs, Susannah V, 865
ubbs, Susannah V, 867
ubbs, Susannah C. II, 814
ubbs, Susannah S. V, 864
ubbs, T. V, 833
ubbs, Tabitha I, 1045
ubbs, Tabitha V, 128
ubbs, Tabitha V, 845
ubbs, Tabitha V, 863
ubbs, Tabitha V, 864
ubbs, Thomas I, 406
ubbs, Thomas I, 422
ubbs, Thomas I, 1050
ubbs, Thomas I Sup 1, 11
tubbs, Thomas II, 456
tubbs, Thomas II, 662
tubbs, Thomas V, 859
tubbs, Thomas V, 865
tubbs, Thomas W. IV, 1078
tubbs, Treva V, 865
tubbs, Verona V, 859
tubbs, Verona V, 865
tubbs, Vincent V, 864
tubbs, William I, 1045
tubbs, William I, 1051
tubbs, William IV, 1078
tubbs, William V, 128
tubbs, William V, 765
tubbs, William V, 851
Stubbs, William V, 852
Stubbs, William V, 863
Stubbs, William V, 864
Stubbs, William V, 865
Stubbs, William V, 866
Stubbs, William V, 874
Stubbs, William C. V, 865
Stubbs, William I. V, 864
Stubbs, William M. V, 863
Stubbs, William P. V, 864
Stubbs, William P. V, 865
Stubbs, William Riley V, 865
Stubbs, William S. V, 857
Stubbs, William, Jr. V, 865
Stubbs, William, Sr. V, 866
Stubbs, Wm. IV, 1078
Stubbs, Wm. V, 856
Stubbs, Wm. V, 864
Stubbs, Wm. V, 887
Stubbs, Zilpah IV, 403
Stubbs, Zilpah IV, 428
Stubbs, Zilpah IV, 446
Stubbs, Zilpah IV, 450
Stubbs, Zilpha I, 1045
Stubbs, Zilpha IV, 446
Stubbs, Zimri V, 128
Stubbs, Zimri V, 864
Stubbs, Zimri V, 866
Stubbs, Zimri V, 869
Stubbs, Zimri Alvin V, 865
Stubes, Thomas I, 422
Stubings, Elizabeth II, 27
Stubings, Elizabeth II, 42
Stubings, Elizabeth II, 103
Stubings, Henry II, 27
Stubings, Henry II, 42
Stubings, Henry II, 103
Stubings, Samuel II, 42
Stubings, Sarah II, 42
Stubins, Samuel II, 98
Stubins, Samuel II, 103
Stubins, Sarah II, 70
Stubins, Sarah II, 98
Stubins, Sarah II, 103
Stubs, Abraham IV, 160
Stubs, Deborah I, 422
Stubs, Deborah IV, 160
Stubs, Eliza IV, 160
Stubs, Elizabeth I, 422
Stubs, Elizabeth IV, 160
Stubs, Elizabeth IV, 1080
Stubs, Elizabeth, Jr. IV, 1078
Stubs, Emma V, 207
Stubs, Esther I, 422
Stubs, Hannah IV, 1078
Stubs, Iddo IV, 160
Stubs, Isaac I, 840
Stubs, Isaac IV, 160
Stubs, Isaac IV, 1080
Stubs, Jacob IV, 160
Stubs, John I, 422
Stubs, John IV, 1078
Stubs, John V, 469
Stubs, Joseph IV, 148
Stubs, Joseph IV, 160
Stubs, Luiza IV, 1078
Stubs, Margaret I, 422
Stubs, Margret I, 840
Stubs, Mary I, 1016
Stubs, Rachel IV, 148
Stubs, Rachel IV, 160
Stubs, Rachel IV, 1078
Stubs, Rebecca IV, 160
Stubs, Rhoda IV, 160
Stubs, Sarah IV, 160
Stubs, Sarah IV, 1080
Stubs, Wm. IV, 1078
Stubs, Zilpha IV, 148
Stubs, Zilphah IV, 160
Stuck, Pemela Maria IV, 610
Stuck, Pemela Maria IV, 659
Stuckert, George T. II, 821
Stuckert, Priscilla II, 926
Stuckert, Priscilla II, 929
Stuckert, Wd. Priscilla II, 821
Stuckey, Eli V, 1021
Stuckey, Elihu V, 1021
Stuckey, Elizabeth V, 1021
Stuckey, Ira V, 1021
Stuckey, Ira P. V, 1021
Stuckey, J. Marion I, 340
Stuckey, Lila I, 340
Stuckey, Lou I, 337
Stuckey, Lou I, 340
Stuckey, Louvinia I, 340
Stuckey, Lucy Demint V, 1021
Stuckey, Ora E. I, 340
Stuckey, Segal V, 1021
Stuckey, Seigle V, 1020
Stuckey, Susan V, 1021
Stuckey, Susanna V, 1020
Stuckey, Thos. V, 1021
Studavin, Aseneth V, 639
Studavin, Aseneth V, 646
Studwan, Sarah V, 533
Studwell, Edwin A. III, 226
Studwell, Edwin A. III, 304
Studwell, Hannah B. III, 304
Studwell, John, Jr. III, 304
Studwell, Mary III, 226
Studwell, Mary III, 304
Studyvin, Abigail V, 885
Studyvin, Abigail V, 887
Stueart, Jehu, Jr. I, 839
Stuert, Henry, Jr. I, 734
Stuhlman, Eva V, 765
Stukey, Ordie IV, 1264
Stuller, Catherine IV, 774
Stuller, Elizabeth IV, 774
Stuller, Harry IV, 774
Stuller, Henry IV, 774
Stuller, James IV, 774
Stuller, Jane IV, 774
Stuller, Mrs. Henry IV, 774
Stults, Christinia V, 765
Stults, David V, 765
Stults, Elizabeth Gene V, 713
Stults, Homer V, 713
Stults, Jno. S. V, 765
Stults, John V, 765
Stults, Martha Ellen V, 765
Stults, Mary Katharine V, 713
Stults, Susan IV, 1295
Stults, Wd. Abigail V, 765
Stultz, Abigail V, 727
Stultz, Elizabeth Gene V, 713
Stultz, Homer V, 677
Stultz, John V, 727
Stultz, Martha Ellen V, 727
Stultz, Mary Katharine V, 677
Stultz, Mary Margaret V, 311
Stumm, Erwin C. VI, 784
Stump, Anna VI, 980
Stump, Clara V, 1021
Stump, Daniel P. V, 128
Stump, Edey VI, 1000
Stump, Edward VI, 1000
Stump, Elenor VI, 873
Stump, Eliza VI, 955
Stump, Elizabeth VI, 504
Stump, Elizabeth VI, 569
Stump, Ethel V, 1021
Stump, Florence V, 1021
Stump, Florence L. V, 128
Stump, Ford L. V, 1021
Stump, Francis V, 1021
Stump, Grace V, 1021
Stump, Icadore V, 1021
Stump, Isadore V, 1021
Stump, John V, 601
Stump, John VI, 955
Stump, John VI, 980
Stump, John VI, 1000
Stump, Leighfee V, 207
Stump, Lucian Shank V, 601
Stump, Lucrettia VI, 1000
Stump, Luella V, 207
Stump, Lydia V, 501
Stump, Lydia V, 533
Stump, Mag V, 1021
Stump, Margaret V, 601
Stump, Margaret VI, 980
Stump, Martha Ann VI, 1000
Stump, Mary V, 128
Stump, Mary V, 601
Stump, Mary VI, 1000
Stump, Mary Charlotte V, 533
Stump, Mary E. V, 1021
Stump, Mary Emily V, 128
Stump, Melvina V, 207
Stump, Nettie V, 1021
Stump, Orla V, 1021
Stump, Perly V, 1021
Stump, Peter V, 1021
Stump, Polly VI, 1000
Stump, Rachel V, 533
Stump, Sally VI, 1000
Stump, Samuel V, 1021
Stump, Samuel J. V, 1021
Stump, Samuel T. V, 1021
Stump, Thomas VI, 886
Stump, Thomas VI, 955
Stump, Thomas VI, 1000
Stump, William VI, 1000
Stump, William B. VI, 917
Stump, William B. VI, 1000
Stumps, Mary Emily V, 128
Stuot, Ann I, 421
Stuot, Joseph I, 421
Stuot, Mary I, 421
Stuot, Neomi I, 421
Stupp, Catharine A. V, 1021
Stupp, Chas. V, 1021
Stupp, Edward V, 1021
Stupp, G. W. V, 1021
Stupp, Josephine V, 1021
Stupp, Lizzie V, 1021
Sturdevant, ??? III, 304
Sturdevant, Augusta III, 304
Sturdevant, Edgar D. III, 304
Sturdevant, Harry E. III, 102
Sturdevant, Harry E. III, 304
Sturdevant, Jennie III, 102
Sturdevant, Jennie D. III, 304
Sturdevant, Lewis III, 204
Sturdevant, Mary III, 204
Sturdevant, Mary III, 304
Sturdwart, Matthew P. VI, 906
Sturdwart, Matthew P. VI, 990
Sturge, Edw. Pease III, 304
Sturge, Edward P. III, 342
Sturge, Grace III, 304
Sturge, Grace Lower III, 304
Sturge, Grace Lower III, 342
Sturge, Sara III, 304
Sturge, Wilson III, 304
Sturgeon, Cora V, 646
Sturgeon, Ella V, 646
Sturgeon, George V, 765
Sturgeon, Jeremiah V, 646
Sturgeon, Jesse V, 646
Sturgeon, John V, 646
Sturgeon, Letitia B. V, 714
Sturgeon, Levi V, 765
Sturgeon, Lewis V, 601
Sturgeon, Lou M. V, 646
Sturgeon, Margaret V, 646
Sturgeon, Phebe IV, 61
Sturgeon, Phebe IV, 66
Sturgeon, Phebe V, 765
Sturgeon, Susannah V, 759
Sturgeon, Susannah V, 765
Sturges, Ann II, 448
Sturges, Anthony II, 448
Sturges, Cornelius II, 425
Sturgion, George V, 765
Sturgion, Levi V, 765
Sturgion, Phebe V, 765
Sturgion, Susannah V, 765
Sturgis, Anthony II, 425
Sturgis, Cornelius II, 425
Sturgiss, Jane II, 703
Sturgiss, Jane II, 707
Sturman, Anne VI, 885
Sturman, Elizabeth VI, 857
Sturman, Margaret VI, 1000
Sturman, Penelope VI, 1000
Sturman, Triphena VI, 857
Sturman, Valentine VI, 857
Sturman, Valentine VI, 1000
Sturman, Vintner VI, 985
Sturman, Vintner VI, 1000
Sturman, Vintnier VI, 1014
Sturman, William VI, 857
Sturman, William VI, 885
Sturtavant, ??? III, 304
Sturtavant, Augusta III, 304
Sturtavant, Edgar D. III, 304
Sturtavant, Harry E. III, 304
Sturtavant, Jennie D. III, 304
Sturtavant, Mary III, 304
Stutlemire, Sarah V, 1021
Stutsman, Nancy V, 765
Stutsman, Nancy V, 769
Stuyvesant, Annie III, 73
Stuyvesant, Charles W. III, 73
Stuyvesant, Charles W. III, 238
Styer, Chalkley II, 831
Styer, Chankley II, 893
Styer, Chas. II, 821
Styer, Chas. II, 926
Styer, Hannah II, 821
Styer, Mary II, 821
Styer, Sarah II, 831
Styer, Sarah II, 893
Styles, Amy Ann IV, 1187
Styles, Ann IV, 1187
Styles, Anna F. II, 973
Styles, Caroline IV, 1187
Styles, Caroline IV, 1380
Styles, Caroline S. IV, 1351
Styles, Caroline S. IV, 1380
Styles, John IV, 1187
Styles, Martha II, 973
Styles, Mary W. II, 963
Styles, Rachel IV, 1146
Styles, Rachel IV, 1187
Styles, Rachel V, 727
Styles, Rachel V, 765
Styles, Reuben II, 973
Styles, Robert IV, 1146
Styles, Robert IV, 1187
Styles, Robert IV, 1380
Styles, Robert V, 727
Styles, Robert V, 765
Stymets, Mary III, 304
Stymus, Jonah P. III, 499
Stymus, Rachel III, 494
Stymus, Rachel III, 499
Stymus, Sarah H. III, 499
Stymus, Smith III, 494
Stymus, Smith III, 499
Styre, Isla Willis I, 627
Styre, Walter J. I, 627
Sublet, Jacob VI, 829
Sublet, Mathew VI, 829
Sublet, Nancy VI, 821
Sublet, Nancy VI, 829
Sublet, Wm. VI, 955
Sublett, Benj. VI, 857
Sublett, Benj. B. VI, 857
Sublett, Edmund W. VI, 1000
Sublett, Elizabeth VI, 831
Sublett, Elizabeth VI, 857
Sublett, Elizabeth VI, 1000
Sublett, Frances VI, 857
Sublett, Frankey VI, 857
Sublett, George A. VI, 857
Sublett, Harriett P. VI, 1016
Sublett, Isabella VI, 857
Sublett, Jacob VI, 857
Sublett, Lucy A. VI, 813
Sublett, Martha VI, 806
Sublett, Martha VI, 857
Sublett, Mary VI, 812
Sublett, Mary VI, 857
Sublett, Mathew VI, 806
Sublett, Mathew VI, 831
Sublett, Mathew VI, 857
Sublett, Nancy VI, 857
Sublett, Sally VI, 857
Sublett, Sarah VI, 857
Sublett, Susan VI, 1000
Sublett, Thomas VI, 812
Sublett, Thomas VI, 831
Sublett, Thomas VI, 857
Sublett, Thomas C. VI, 1000
Sublett, Thos. C. VI, 911
Sublett, William VI, 857
Subley, Fanny VI, 857
Subley, Samuel VI, 857
Suddarth, Dorothy Helen I, 626
Suddarth, Edward I, 631
Suddarth, Edward I, 641
Suddarth, Elizabeth Ann I, 626
Suddarth, Helen I, 613
Suddarth, Helen I, 626
Suddarth, Helen I, 631
Suddarth, Helen I, 641
Suddarth, Kenneth Edward I, 626
Suddarth, Rufus Edward I, 613
Suddarth, Rufus Edward I, 626
Sudeth, Benjamin IV, 1295
Sudler, John W. E. II, 926
Sudler, Virginia II, 926
Suffrance, Mary V, 117
Suffrance, Mary V, 129
Suffrin, David I, 1012
Suffrin, Deborah I, 1012
Suffrins, Alfred V, 129
Suffrins, Charles V, 129
Suffrins, David I, 1006
Suffrins, David I, 1012
Suffrins, David V, 124
Suffrins, David V, 128
Suffrins, David V, 129
Suffrins, David VI, 214
Suffrins, Deborah I, 1006
Suffrins, Deborah I, 1012
Suffrins, Deborah V, 124
Suffrins, Deborah V, 128
Suffrins, Deborah V, 129
Suffrins, Deborah VI, 214
Suffrins, Elizabeth I, 1010
Suffrins, Elizabeth I, 1012
Suffrins, Elizabeth VI, 214
Suffrins, Hannah I, 1012
Suffrins, Hannah V, 124
Suffrins, Hannah V, 129
Suffrins, Hannah VI, 214
Suffrins, Harriet V, 129
Suffrins, Jesse I, 1006
Suffrins, Jesse V, 129
Suffrins, John V, 129
Suffrins, John V, 934
Suffrins, John VI, 214
Suffrins, Mary I, 1012
Suffrins, Mary V, 129
Suffrins, Mary VI, 214
Suffrins, Samuel V, 128
Suffrins, Samuel V, 129
Suffrins, Sarah I, 1012
Suffrins, Sarah V, 98
Suffrins, Sarah V, 129
Suffrins, Sarah VI, 214
Suffrins, Thomas V, 129
Suffrins, Thomas VI, 214
Sugar, Ann II, 425
Sugar, Elizabeth II, 503
Sugar, Elizabeth II, 662
Sugar, Mary II, 622
Sugar, Mary II, 662
Sugar, Sarah II, 425
Sugar, Thomas II, 425
Sugar, Thomas II, 503
Sugar, Thomas II, 622
Sugar, Thomas II, 662
Sugar, Thomas, Jr. II, 622
Sugar, Thomas, Jr. II, 662
Sugars, Mary II, 662
Sugars, Sarah I, 837
Sugars, Sarah II, 425
Sugars, Thomas II, 662
Sugart, George I, 837
Sugert, Isaac I, 453
Sugget, Jane IV, 774
Sugget, Mary Ann IV, 774
Sugget, Thomas IV, 774
Suggs, Edith I, 627
Suggs, Elizabeth I, 934
Suggs, Exeline I, 318
Suggs, Trecy E. I, 318
Suisfelt, Maria V, 934

Suit, Julia IV, 1295
Sulivan, Elizabeth II, 194
Sulivan, Elizabeth II, 266
Sulliavant, Ruffine I, 318
Sullivan, Amos G. III, 499
Sullivan, Charity V, 765
Sullivan, Dionitia VI, 1000
Sullivan, Emily I, 597
Sullivan, Emily I, 598
Sullivan, Emily I, 840
Sullivan, Eugenia A. I, 840
Sullivan, Giles F. I, 949
Sullivan, Hannah I, 840
Sullivan, J. W. I, 318
Sullivan, Jacob III, 499
Sullivan, Jennie I, 626
Sullivan, Jennie I, 628
Sullivan, Jennie I, 641
Sullivan, John R. I, 318
Sullivan, John W. I, 318
Sullivan, Larry I, 318
Sullivan, Lou I, 318
Sullivan, Lou E. I, 318
Sullivan, Margaret I, 318
Sullivan, Margaret Ann III, 499
Sullivan, Mary Victoria III, 499
Sullivan, Minnie I, 318
Sullivan, Patsy I, 318
Sullivan, Ruffine I, 318
Sullivan, T. Avery I, 626
Sullivan, T. Avery I, 628
Sullivan, Thomas IV, 1043
Sullivan, William VI, 1000
Sullivan, William A. J. I, 318
Sullivant, Larry I, 297
Sullivant, Larry I, 318
Sullivant, Mary I, 297
Sumers, Rachil VI, 1000
Sumers, Sarah VI, 1000
Sumers, Zachariah VI, 1000
Sumersalt, Cora Small IV, 1295
Sumleader, Sophia III, 136
Sumleader, Sophia III, 304
Summer, Abigail I, 961
Summer, Adaline V, 601
Summer, Allen V, 129
Summer, Bowwater V, 129
Summer, Edward O. V, 129
Summer, Ellenor Mendenhall V, 129
Summer, Esther V, 129
Summer, Eugene V, 601
Summer, Eugene F. V, 601
Summer, Eunice V. V, 129
Summer, Harriet Emma V, 601
Summer, Isaac V, 129
Summer, John IV, 1340
Summer, John V, 129
Summer, Laura V, 129
Summer, Mary V, 129
Summer, Oliver V, 129
Summer, Phebe V, 129
Summer, Rebecca V, 129
Summer, Robert I, 575
Summer, Ruth V, 129
Summer, Ruth Mendenhall V, 129
Summer, Stephen V, 601
Summer, Thomas V, 129
Summer, William V, 601
Summerhayes, Henry Geo. V, 934
Summerhayes, Jane Emma V, 934
Summers, Abinah VI, 516
Summers, Adeline V, 361
Summers, Agnes Jane VI, 1000
Summers, Albertus II, 124
Summers, Albinah VI, 569
Summers, Ann VI, 569
Summers, Blanch V, 361
Summers, Castlereigh VI, 1000
Summers, Cathren II, 103
Summers, Daniel Brandreth II, 103
Summers, David II, 42
Summers, Deborah IV, 498
Summers, Edward O. V, 129
Summers, Elizabeth II, 42
Summers, Elizabeth II, 71
Summers, Elizabeth II, 103
Summers, Elizabeth II, 124
Summers, Eunice V. V, 129
Summers, Hannah II, 53
Summers, Hannah II, 103
Summers, Isaac II, 42
Summers, Isaac II, 103
Summers, Isaac V, 311
Summers, Jacob II, 42
Summers, Jacob II, 103
Summers, Jacob II, 124
Summers, John II, 103
Summers, John V, 129
Summers, John J. VI, 569
Summers, John Janney VI, 569
Summers, Laura V, 94
Summers, Laura V, 129
Summers, Lewis Preston VI, 309
Summers, Martha II, 124
Summers, Mary VI, 540
Summers, Mary VI, 569
Summers, Mary Albina VI, 569
Summers, Melvina V, 646
Summers, Paul Taulbott VI, 1000
Summers, Phebe I, 343
Summers, Phebe V, 129
Summers, Rachel II, 100
Summers, Rachel II, 103
Summers, Rachil VI, 1000
Summers, Rebeckah II, 42
Summers, Robert I, 343
Summers, Robert I, 422
Summers, Robert VI, 569
Summers, Ruth V, 129
Summers, Ruth Albinah VI, 754
Summers, Samuel II, 103
Summers, Sarah VI, 1000
Summers, Wd. Phebe VI, 569
Summers, William VI, 516
Summers, William VI, 569
Summers, Wm. V, 361
Summers, Wm. VI, 569
Summers, Wm. VI, 754
Summers, Wm. Morris V, 361
Summers, Zachariah VI, 1000
Summersett, Leah V, 1021
Summersett, Mary C. V, 1021
Summersett, Rachel E. V, 1021
Summersett, Tish V, 1021
Summersett, Wm. V, 1021
Sumnar, Elenor I, 575
Sumnar, William I, 575
Sumner, Abigail I, 958
Sumner, Abigail I, 965
Sumner, Abigail I, 969
Sumner, Abigail I, 1012
Sumner, Abigail V, 281
Sumner, Abigail V, 311
Sumner, Absalom I, 969
Sumner, Absalom V, 311
Sumner, Absalom V, 465
Sumner, Adaline V, 714
Sumner, Agnes I, 614
Sumner, Allen V, 129
Sumner, Allen V, 311
Sumner, Amy I, 969
Sumner, Amy V, 311
Sumner, Ann V, 281
Sumner, Ann V, 311
Sumner, Anna V, 302
Sumner, Anne I, 1012
Sumner, Bowater I, 517
Sumner, Bowater I, 529
Sumner, Bowater I, 575
Sumner, Bowater I, 969
Sumner, Bowater I, 971
Sumner, Bowater V, 215
Sumner, Bowater V, 292
Sumner, Bowater, Jr. V, 311
Sumner, Bowwater V, 129
Sumner, Caleb I, 517
Sumner, Caleb I, 530
Sumner, Caleb I, 575
Sumner, Caleb I, 969
Sumner, Caleb V, 281
Sumner, Caleb V, 295
Sumner, Caleb V, 311
Sumner, Charles IV, 774
Sumner, Edward O. V, 129
Sumner, Eleanor I, 538
Sumner, Eleanor I, 575
Sumner, Eleanor I, 1101
Sumner, Eleanor I, 1126
Sumner, Eleanor I, 1132
Sumner, Elenor I, 575
Sumner, Elenor I, 969
Sumner, Elenor I, 1101
Sumner, Elenor I, 1111
Sumner, Elizabeth I, 901
Sumner, Elizabeth V, 281
Sumner, Elizabeth V, 311
Sumner, Ellenor Mendenhall V, 129
Sumner, Emma Agnes I, 614
Sumner, Esther I, 517
Sumner, Esther V, 129
Sumner, Esther V, 311
Sumner, Eunice V. V, 129
Sumner, Frances V, 934
Sumner, Hannah I, 545
Sumner, Hannah I, 575
Sumner, Hannah I, 958
Sumner, Hannah I, 969
Sumner, Hannah V, 281
Sumner, Hannah V, 311
Sumner, Hannah V, 312
Sumner, Hannah Lydia Rebecca V, 281
Sumner, Harriet E. V, 714
Sumner, Isaac V, 129
Sumner, Isaac V, 311
Sumner, John I, 517
Sumner, John V, 129
Sumner, Jonathan I, 1011
Sumner, Jonathan I, 1012
Sumner, Joseph I, 614
Sumner, Joseph I, 958
Sumner, Joseph I, 965
Sumner, Joseph I, 969
Sumner, Joseph V, 281
Sumner, Joseph V, 311
Sumner, Joshua I, 575
Sumner, Joshua I, 1012
Sumner, Laura V, 129
Sumner, Lydia V, 305
Sumner, Martha V, 281
Sumner, Martha V, 289
Sumner, Martha V, 311
Sumner, Martha V, 313
Sumner, Martha V, 934
Sumner, Martin V, 311
Sumner, Marton V, 311
Sumner, Mary I, 517
Sumner, Mary I, 575
Sumner, Mary V, 129
Sumner, Mary V, 281
Sumner, Mary V, 298
Sumner, Mary V, 311
Sumner, Mary Elizabeth IV, 774
Sumner, Matilda V, 311
Sumner, Olive V, 311
Sumner, Oliver V, 129
Sumner, Phebe I, 517
Sumner, Phebe I, 958
Sumner, Phebe I, 963
Sumner, Phebe I, 969
Sumner, Phebe I, 1012
Sumner, Phebe I, 1111
Sumner, Phebe I, 1126
Sumner, Phebe I, 1132
Sumner, Phebe V, 129
Sumner, Phebe V, 281
Sumner, Phebe V, 298
Sumner, Phebe V, 304
Sumner, Phebe V, 309
Sumner, Phebe V, 311
Sumner, Priscilla V, 465
Sumner, Rachel V, 311
Sumner, Rebecca V, 129
Sumner, Rebecca V, 215
Sumner, Rebecca V, 301
Sumner, Rebecka V, 311
Sumner, Rebeckah I, 529
Sumner, Rebeckah I, 575
Sumner, Rebeckah V, 281
Sumner, Rebeckah V, 292
Sumner, Rebeckah V, 303
Sumner, Rebeckah V, 311
Sumner, Rebekah I, 517
Sumner, Robert I, 517
Sumner, Robert I, 575
Sumner, Robert V, 281
Sumner, Robert V, 465
Sumner, Ruth V, 129
Sumner, Ruth Mendenhall I, 1132
Sumner, Ruth Mendenhall V, 129
Sumner, Samuel I, 901
Sumner, Samuel I, 958
Sumner, Samuel I, 969
Sumner, Samuel V, 281
Sumner, Samuel V, 311
Sumner, Sarah I, 575
Sumner, Sarah I, 885
Sumner, Sarah I, 901
Sumner, Sarah I, 969
Sumner, Sarah I, 1012
Sumner, Sarah I, 1132
Sumner, Sarah E. V, 465
Sumner, Sarah E. V, 714
Sumner, Sarah Emma IV, 774
Sumner, Stephen J. V, 714
Sumner, Susanna I, 1011
Sumner, Susanna I, 1012
Sumner, Tabitha V, 226
Sumner, Tabitha V, 281
Sumner, Thomas I, 575
Sumner, Thomas I, 958
Sumner, Thomas I, 969
Sumner, Thomas V, 129
Sumner, Thomas V, 281
Sumner, Thomas V, 289
Sumner, Thomas V, 311
Sumner, Thomas V, 313
Sumner, Thos. I, 545
Sumner, Tobitha V, 465
Sumner, Widow Mary I, 530
Sumner, Widow Phebe I, 517
Sumner, William I, 538
Sumner, William I, 575
Sumner, William I, 969
Sumner, William I, 1101
Sumner, William I, 1132
Sumner, William V, 714
Sumner, Wm. I, 1111
Sumner, Wm. M. V, 714
Sumners, Abigail V, 311
Sumners, Adaline V, 714
Sumners, Phebe V, 129
Sumners, Robert VI, 480
Sumners, Robert VI, 569
Sumners, Sarah I, 1132
Sumners, Wd. Phebe VI, 480
Sumners, Wd. Phebe VI, 569
Sumners, William V, 714
Sumpter, Edmund VI, 857
Sumpter, Jane VI, 857
Sumption, Amos R. V, 281
Sumption, Benjamin V, 281
Sumption, Hannah M. V, 281
Sumption, James T. V, 281
Sumption, John L. V, 281
Sumption, Joseph A. V, 281
Sumption, Mary Ann V, 281
Sumption, Rachel IV, 225
Sumption, Rachel IV, 285
Sumption, Samuel II, 662
Sumption, Susan V, 281
Sunbury, Sarah IV, 876
Sunby, Richard II, 662
Sunderland, Isaac VI, 449
Sunderland, Louisa V, 1021
Sunderland, Margaret V, 1021
Sunderland, Richard V, 1021
Sunderlin, Abigail VI, 449
Sunderlin, Isaac VI, 449
Sunders, Fredric I, 72
Suple, Elizabeth II, 927
Suplee, ??? II, 826
Suplee, Andrew II, 826
Suplee, Anna P. II, 907
Suplee, Anna P. II, 927
Suplee, Anna Pickering II, 821
Suplee, Caroline P. II, 927
Suplee, Caroline Stepney II, 927
Suplee, Chalkley J. II, 927
Suplee, Chalkley Jones II, 821
Suplee, Charles Jones II, 821
Suplee, Chas. J. II, 927
Suplee, Edward Betts II, 822
Suplee, Elizabeth II, 927
Suplee, Emily II, 821
Suplee, Emily J. II, 907
Suplee, Emily J. II, 927
Suplee, Emily Jones II, 927
Suplee, Frederick Paxson II, 822
Suplee, Helen Marot II, 927
Suplee, Lydia II, 926
Suplee, Lydia S. II, 821
Suplee, Marjorie Ellinwood II, 927
Suplee, Mary Emily II, 821
Suplee, Thomas B. II, 927
Suplee, Thomas B., Jr. II, 821
Suplee, Thomas B., Jr. II, 927
Suplee, Thomas Baker II, 821
Suplee, Thornton Pike II, 927
Suplee, Thos. II, 821
Suplee, Thos. B. II, 907
Suplee, Thos. B. II, 927
Suplee, Thos. Baker II, 821
Suplee, Wd. Lydia II, 821
Suplee, Wd. Rachel II, 826
Suplee, William Jones II, 821
Suplee, Wm. J. II, 907
Suplee, Wm. J. II, 927
Suplee, Wm. Jones II, 821
Supler, George II, 425
Supler, Susan II, 425
Supplee, Caroline Stepney II, 910
Supplee, Caroline Stepney II, 927
Supplee, Chas. J. II, 910
Supplee, Chas. J. II, 927
Supplee, Elizabeth II, 927
Supplee, Emily J. II, 910
Supplee, Emily J. II, 927
Supplee, Jane II, 819
Supplee, Sarah II, 829
Supplee, Thomas B. II, 927
Supplee, Thos. B. II, 910
Surface, Alice D. IV, 1337
Surface, Bertha M. V, 714
Surface, Charles V, 129
Surface, Cynthia V, 793
Surface, Edward V, 207
Surface, Emma V, 129
Surface, George Harold V, 12
Surface, Ida Marie V, 129
Surface, Jacob IV, 1337
Surface, Jacob V, 765
Surface, Margaret IV, 1337
Surface, Mary V, 129
Surface, Russell Daniel V, 12
Surgeon, Susannah V, 759
Surgeon, Susannah V, 765
Surket, John II, 970
Surket, Sarah II, 970
Surket, William II, 970
Surkett, John II, 970
Surkett, Sarah II, 970
Surl, Tacy II, 1030
Surl, Tacy II, 1036
Surman, Barbara II, 646
Surman, Wd. Sarah II, 646
Surman, Wm. II, 646
Susan, D. VI, 808
Sutcliff, Abm. III, 304
Sutcliff, Elizabeth III, 96
Sutcliff, Elizabeth III, 304
Sutcliff, John III, 96
Sutcliff, John III, 304
Sutcliff, Joshua II, 662
Sutcliff, Marian Elizabeth IV, 1043
Sutcliff, Pascha II, 662
Sutcliff, Robert II, 425
Sutcliff, Robert II, 662
Sutcliff, Sarah III, 304
Sutcliff, Viola IV, 1043
Sutcliffe, Ann S. III, 157
Sutcliffe, Joshua II, 662
Suthard, John IV, 1295
Sutherland, ??? III, 304
Sutherland, Anna III, 304
Sutherland, Anna Ella III, 304
Sutherland, Caroline Anna III, 304
Sutherland, Charlotte III, 304
Sutherland, Charlotte P. III, 30
Sutherland, Donald III, 304
Sutherland, Donald Grant III, 304
Sutherland, Frank V, 661
Sutherland, Frank V, 714
Sutherland, Herman G. III, 304
Sutherland, Janet III, 100
Sutherland, Judith VI, 901
Sutherland, Minnie E. I, 340
Sutherland, Ransom B. VI, 995
Sutherland, Ruth IV, 1240
Sutherland, Ruth IV, 1241
Sutherland, Sarah VI, 1000
Sutherland, Thomas VI, 1000
Sutherland, Vedith V, 661
Sutherland, Vedith V, 714
Sutliff, Martha III, 304
Sutliff, Mary L. III, 304
Sutliff, Timothy M. III, 304
Sutmiller, Emma Ploger IV, 1187
Sutphen, Henry VI, 938
Sutphin, Christopher VI, 1000
Sutphin, Hendrick VI, 1000
Sutphin, James VI, 857
Sutphin, Margaret H. VI, 857
Sutphin, Melinda VI, 1000
Sutphin, Rachel VI, 1000
Sutphin, William VI, 1000
Suttenfield, Edith VI, 809
Suttenfield, Edith VI, 857
Suttenfield, James VI, 853
Suttenfield, James VI, 857
Suttenfield, Mary VI, 824
Suttenfield, Mary VI, 836
Suttenfield, Nancy VI, 823
Sutter, Ann Catherine II, 816
Sutter, Mary II, 816
Sutter, Samuel II, 816
Suttin, Rachel II, 1023
Suttin, Rachel II, 1030
Suttle, Elizabeth VI, 971
Sutton, ??? III, 306
Sutton, Aaron III, 131
Sutton, Aaron III, 137
Sutton, Aaron III, 304
Sutton, Aaron III, 306
Sutton, Aaron IV, 1381
Sutton, Aaron Fraklin VI, 784
Sutton, Aaron Franklin III, 304
Sutton, Abby III, 61
Sutton, Abby Jane III, 304
Sutton, Abby Jane III, 314
Sutton, Abigail III, 304
Sutton, Abraham III, 304
Sutton, Abraham III, 305
Sutton, Adrea H. III, 304
Sutton, Albert III, 304

n, Albert III, 306
n, Alfred III, 304
n, Alfred III, 305
n, Alice M. VI, 736
n, Alice M. VI, 784
n, Amelia III, 305
n, Amy III, 153
n, Amy III, 304
n, Amy III, 306
n, Ann II, 266
n, Ann III, 304
n, Ann III, 305
n, Ann L. III, 17
n, Ann Louisa III, 305
n, Ann M. III, 304
n, Anna III, 131
n, Anna III, 256
n, Anna III, 304
n, Anna III, 305
n, Anna B. III, 241
n, Anna B. III, 305
n, Anna B. III, 306
n, Anna H. III, 131
n, Anna H. III, 217
n, Anna H. III, 306
n, Anna Louisa III, 305
n, Anna Louise III, 306
n, Anne H. III, 304
n, Ardena V, 601
n, Asa III, 305
n, Asa IV, 1381
on, Asa U. IV, 1374
on, Asa W. IV, 1377
on, Asa W. IV, 1380
on, Asa W. IV, 1381
on, Asa W. IV, 1382
on, Burnis I, 340
on, Caleb III, 304
on, Caleb U. III, 304
on, Caleb U., Jr. III, 304
on, Caroline III, 306
on, Carrie III, 47
on, Carrie III, 304
on, Catharine VI, 569
ton, Charles III, 208
ton, Charles III, 304
ton, Charles VI, 736
ton, Charles VI, 779
ton, Charles VI, 784
ton, Charles T. III, 304
ton, Charlotte III, 290
ton, Charlotte III, 305
ton, Chenoa III, 232
ton, Chris'r. VI, 982
ton, Christopher VI, 1000
ton, Clara IV, 285
ton, Clarissa M. III, 335
ton, Daniel VI, 569
ton, Daniel H. III, 304
ton, Daniel H. III, 305
ton, Daniel H. VI, 784
ton, Daniel Isaac VI, 569
ton, David III, 305
ton, David IV, 1381
ton, Deborah III, 325
ton, Don Franklin VI, 773
ton, Don Franklin VI, 784
tton, Edgar III, 305
tton, Edgar III, 306
tton, Edgar Ardel V, 601
tton, Edmund III, 305
tton, Edward III, 305
tton, Edward IV, 1381
tton, Eliphalet W. III, 305
tton, Elisabeth I, 135
tton, Elisabeth I, 166
tton, Eliza III, 64
tton, Elizabeth III, 253
tton, Elizabeth III, 305
tton, Elizabeth Ann III, 96
tton, Elizabeth Ann III, 97
tton, Elizabeth Ann III, 305
tton, Elizabeth Ann III, 306
tton, Elizabeth B. VI, 784
utton, Elizabeth P. II, 908
utton, Elizabeth P. II, 927
utton, Elizabeth R. IV, 1374
utton, Elizabeth R. IV, 1381
utton, Emeline III, 305
utton, Emma I, 616
utton, Eugene III, 306
utton, Fabel V, 601
utton, Florence K. III, 305
utton, Franklin III, 305
utton, Freelove III, 305
utton, Geo. T. III, 305
utton, George I Sup 1, 5
utton, George I Sup 1, 6
utton, George III, 153
utton, George III, 304
Sutton, George III, 306
Sutton, George III, 335
Sutton, George A. III, 305
Sutton, George A. III, 315
Sutton, George E. III, 266
Sutton, George E. III, 305
Sutton, George Thomas III, 256
Sutton, George Thomas III, 304
Sutton, George Thomas III, 305
Sutton, George W. III, 306
Sutton, Hannah III, 173
Sutton, Hannah III, 304
Sutton, Hannah III, 305
Sutton, Hannah III, 306
Sutton, Hannah III, 345
Sutton, Hannah III, 368
Sutton, Hannah A. IV, 1381
Sutton, Hannah W. III, 305
Sutton, Hannah W. VI, 784
Sutton, Harley V, 601
Sutton, Harriett S. VI, 773
Sutton, Harriett Shepherd VI, 773
Sutton, Harriett Shepherd VI, 784
Sutton, Hazel Blossom III, 415
Sutton, Hazel Blossom III, 448
Sutton, Helen III, 305
Sutton, Helen S. III, 151
Sutton, Helen S. III, 305
Sutton, Henry III, 173
Sutton, Henry III, 304
Sutton, Henry III, 305
Sutton, Henry III, 306
Sutton, Henry III, 345
Sutton, Henry VI, 784
Sutton, Hetty Jane II, 788
Sutton, Hope VI, 894
Sutton, Hope VI, 982
Sutton, Horace III, 30
Sutton, Isaac I, 902
Sutton, Isaac III, 304
Sutton, Isaac III, 305
Sutton, Isaac IV, 1377
Sutton, Isaac IV, 1380
Sutton, Isaac IV, 1381
Sutton, Isaac VI, 569
Sutton, Isaac M. III, 151
Sutton, Isaac M. III, 305
Sutton, Izita V, 601
Sutton, Jacob III, 306
Sutton, Jacob H. III, 17
Sutton, Jacob H. III, 305
Sutton, James III, 305
Sutton, James IV, 1241
Sutton, James VI, 784
Sutton, James America VI, 569
Sutton, Jane M. III, 304
Sutton, Jean Evelyn VI, 784
Sutton, Jeannette III, 232
Sutton, Jeannette III, 305
Sutton, Jesse III, 306
Sutton, John II, 425
Sutton, John VI, 214
Sutton, John VI, 569
Sutton, John VI, 725
Sutton, John Joseph III, 306
Sutton, John M. III, 304
Sutton, John, Jr. VI, 569
Sutton, Joseph III, 448
Sutton, Joseph W. III, 17
Sutton, Josephine VI, 784
Sutton, Joshua III, 304
Sutton, Joshua III, 306
Sutton, Joshua III, 368
Sutton, Joshua W. III, 63
Sutton, Leila N. III, 305
Sutton, Lizzie M. I, 901
Sutton, Louisa M. III, 305
Sutton, Louisa M. VI, 784
Sutton, Lucretia III, 305
Sutton, Margaret III, 256
Sutton, Margaret III, 304
Sutton, Margaret III, 305
Sutton, Margaret III, 335
Sutton, Margaret R. III, 306
Sutton, Maria Louisa III, 63
Sutton, Marianna VI, 779
Sutton, Marianna VI, 784
Sutton, Martha III, 304
Sutton, Martha III, 368
Sutton, Martha H. III, 227
Sutton, Martha H. III, 306
Sutton, Mary I, 75
Sutton, Mary II, 425
Sutton, Mary II, 482
Sutton, Mary II, 555
Sutton, Mary II, 601
Sutton, Mary II, 602
Sutton, Mary II, 662
Sutton, Mary III, 232
Sutton, Mary III, 253
Sutton, Mary III, 305
Sutton, Mary III, 326
Sutton, Mary III, 328
Sutton, Mary IV, 1187
Sutton, Mary IV, 1191
Sutton, Mary VI, 784
Sutton, Mary Ann III, 305
Sutton, Mary B. III, 305
Sutton, Mary B. VI, 784
Sutton, Mary D. III, 306
Sutton, Mary E. IV, 1378
Sutton, Mary E. IV, 1381
Sutton, Mary Gough VI, 784
Sutton, Mary H. I, 902
Sutton, Mary H. III, 137
Sutton, Mary H. III, 304
Sutton, Mary Jane III, 305
Sutton, Mary Jane III, 306
Sutton, Mary R. III, 306
Sutton, Mary W. III, 305
Sutton, Matilda E. III, 305
Sutton, MatildaH, III, 290
Sutton, Melissa III, 304
Sutton, Millie Elma I, 340
Sutton, Minnie I, 340
Sutton, Moses IV, 1381
Sutton, Nancy VI, 1000
Sutton, Nathaniel I, 90
Sutton, Nathaniel I, 135
Sutton, Nathaniel I, 166
Sutton, Nathaniel VI, 894
Sutton, Nehemiah IV, 1378
Sutton, Nehemiah IV, 1381
Sutton, Nehemiah M. IV, 1381
Sutton, Nellie III, 305
Sutton, Nellie III, 315
Sutton, Olive III, 305
Sutton, Peninah I, 189
Sutton, Peninah I, 200
Sutton, Phebe II, 266
Sutton, Phebe III, 96
Sutton, Phebe III, 208
Sutton, Phebe III, 304
Sutton, Phebe III, 306
Sutton, Phebe IV, 1187
Sutton, Phebe IV, 1191
Sutton, Phebe VI, 779
Sutton, Phebe VI, 784
Sutton, Phebe F. III, 97
Sutton, Phebe F. III, 305
Sutton, Phebe H. III, 173
Sutton, Phebe H. III, 305
Sutton, Phebe H. III, 306
Sutton, Phebe H. VI, 784
Sutton, Phebe Jane III, 225
Sutton, Phebe Jane III, 306
Sutton, Philena II, 927
Sutton, Rebecca I, 90
Sutton, Rebecca III, 153
Sutton, Rebecca III, 304
Sutton, Rebecca III, 306
Sutton, Rebecca VI, 784
Sutton, Rebecca K. III, 306
Sutton, Richard II, 425
Sutton, Richard II, 555
Sutton, Richard II, 601
Sutton, Richard II, 662
Sutton, Richard VI, 87
Sutton, Richard B. III, 306
Sutton, Robert II, 662
Sutton, Robert III, 306
Sutton, Robert Franklin VI, 784
Sutton, Roxie Lucile V, 601
Sutton, Sadie V, 714
Sutton, Sallie E. I, 340
Sutton, Samuel VI, 784
Sutton, Samuel A. III, 306
Sutton, Samuel B. III, 306
Sutton, Sarah I, 90
Sutton, Sarah I Sup 1, 5
Sutton, Sarah I Sup 1, 6
Sutton, Sarah III, 304
Sutton, Sarah III, 305
Sutton, Sarah III, 306
Sutton, Sarah IV, 1377
Sutton, Sarah IV, 1380
Sutton, Sarah V, 27
Sutton, Sarah V, 129
Sutton, Sarah A. IV, 1374
Sutton, Sarah A. IV, 1377
Sutton, Sarah A. IV, 1381
Sutton, Sarah A. IV, 1382
Sutton, Sarah A. M. III, 195
Sutton, Sarah Eliz III, 306
Sutton, Sarah Elizabeth III, 131
Sutton, Sarah Jane III, 304
Sutton, Sarah Jane III, 305
Sutton, Sarah Jane III, 306
Sutton, Sarah M. III, 305
Sutton, Sarah U. III, 305
Sutton, Sarah U. IV, 1381
Sutton, Selina III, 266
Sutton, Selina R. III, 305
Sutton, Silas III, 96
Sutton, Silas III, 97
Sutton, Silas III, 253
Sutton, Silas III, 305
Sutton, Silas III, 306
Sutton, Silas H. III, 232
Sutton, Silas H. III, 305
Sutton, Stephen III, 305
Sutton, Stephen III, 306
Sutton, Stephen I. III, 306
Sutton, Susanna VI, 994
Sutton, Thomas II, 927
Sutton, Thomas III, 305
Sutton, Thomas U. III, 306
Sutton, Thos. C. II, 908
Sutton, Thos. G. III, 305
Sutton, Thos. U. III, 225
Sutton, Thos. U. III, 306
Sutton, Townsend III, 305
Sutton, Walton R. I, 340
Sutton, Widow Rebecca I, 90
Sutton, William III, 305
Sutton, William IV, 1381
Sutton, William A. III, 306
Sutton, William Henry III, 305
Sutton, Winnie V, 601
Sutton, Wm. II, 927
Sutton, Wm. III, 290
Sutton, Wm. III, 305
Suydam, Gulielma V, 129
Suydam, Jacobus III, 499
Suydam, Martha III, 385
Suydam, Phebe III, 306
Suydam, Phebe III, 499
Suydam, Rebecca III, 499
Swabdjo, James IV, 285
Swabdjo, Mary IV, 285
Swabdjo, Mike IV, 285
Swadner, Ada V, 207
Swadner, Blanche V, 765
Swadner, Blanche Virginia V, 765
Swadner, Frances V, 765
Swadner, Frances V. V, 765
Swadner, Owen V, 207
Swaffer, Jacob II, 425
Swaffer, James II, 662
Swagart, Edith V, 207
Swagart, Margaret V, 207
Swager, Mattie IV, 1295
Swaggard, William V, 1021
Swaim, Amy V, 846
Swaim, Cornelia I, 882
Swaim, Cornelia I, 902
Swaim, Cornelia I, 922
Swaim, Elkanah I, 934
Swaim, Elnathan I, 902
Swaim, Elzahhan V. I, 865
Swaim, Elzathan V. I, 934
Swaim, Gabriel V, 868
Swaim, Gurney I, 949
Swaim, Gurney Allen I, 934
Swaim, Henry E. I, 770
Swaim, Joseph S. I, 770
Swaim, Mamie I, 949
Swaim, Margaret I, 770
Swaim, Margret I, 770
Swaim, Mary I, 934
Swaim, Mary R. I, 922
Swaim, Mary Regina I, 934
Swaim, Rachel I, 770
Swaim, Rachel I, 934
Swaim, Sanford I, 934
Swaim, Shubal I, 922
Swain, ??? III, 307
Swain, Aaron III, 306
Swain, Abraham II, 103
Swain, Abraham II, 970
Swain, Abraham II, 1030
Swain, Abraham II, 1041
Swain, Abraham II, 1043
Swain, Abraham Benjamin II, 1043
Swain, Abram II, 103
Swain, Agnes III, 212
Swain, Agnes III, 306
Swain, Alice V, 925
Swain, Alice V, 934
Swain, Amey VI, 945
Swain, Amy V, 832
Swain, Amy V, 841
Swain, Amy V, 868
Swain, Angelina I, 518
Swain, Ann I, 1111
Swain, Ann I, 1123
Swain, Ann I, 1132
Swain, Ann II, 1030
Swain, Ann III, 306
Swain, Ann C. III, 306
Swain, Ann Eliza I, 576
Swain, Anna I, 517
Swain, Anna I, 576
Swain, Anna I, 669
Swain, Anna I, 676
Swain, Anna I, 690
Swain, Anna II, 1030
Swain, Anna V, 107
Swain, Anna V, 129
Swain, Anna V, 281
Swain, Anna V, 971
Swain, Anna V, 974
Swain, Anna V, 977
Swain, Anna Jane I, 576
Swain, Anne VI, 1000
Swain, Anny V, 251
Swain, Anny V, 281
Swain, Antrim V, 868
Swain, Antrim R. V, 868
Swain, Anuel I, 690
Swain, Asher V, 868
Swain, Augusta S. III, 123
Swain, Augusta S. III, 306
Swain, Benjamin II, 266
Swain, Benjamin II, 970
Swain, Benjamin II, 1030
Swain, Benjamin II, 1043
Swain, Bertrand E. III, 306
Swain, Bethiah I, 690
Swain, Bethiah I, 840
Swain, Bethiah I, 1111
Swain, Betsy Ann I, 576
Swain, Beulah I, 598
Swain, Buley I, 576
Swain, Calahill M. VI, 1001
Swain, Calohill M. VI, 909
Swain, Charles II, 1081
Swain, Charles VI, 908
Swain, Charles VI, 948
Swain, Charles VI, 982
Swain, Charles VI, 984
Swain, Charles VI, 1000
Swain, Charles E. III, 306
Swain, Charles F. III, 123
Swain, Charles W. VI, 776
Swain, Charles W. VI, 784
Swain, Charles W. VI, 785
Swain, Charlotte E. VI, 1001
Swain, Chas. F. III, 256
Swain, Chas. F. III, 306
Swain, Chas. M. II, 923
Swain, Chas. M. II, 927
Swain, Chrales VI, 558
Swain, Custy VI, 1001
Swain, Cyntha I, 690
Swain, Cynthia I, 669
Swain, Cyrus V, 868
Swain, Cyrus T. V, 868
Swain, David I, 517
Swain, David I, 518
Swain, David I, 559
Swain, David I, 576
Swain, David II, 970
Swain, David II, 1030
Swain, David II, 1043
Swain, David V, 281
Swain, David V, 788
Swain, David M. I, 576
Swain, Deborah I, 517
Swain, Deborah I, 576
Swain, Deborah I, 684
Swain, Deborah I, 690
Swain, Deborah I, 840
Swain, Deborah II, 266
Swain, Deborah II, 662
Swain, Deborah II, 769
Swain, Demandy VI, 899
Swain, Dr. George I, 576
Swain, E. Randolph II, 314
Swain, E. Randolph II, 325
Swain, Ebe VI, 972
Swain, Edith Neal III, 306
Swain, Edmond Randolph II, 324
Swain, Edmond Randolph II, 325
Swain, Edmund R. II, 314
Swain, Edmund R. II, 325
Swain, Edward III, 306
Swain, Edwin J. III, 306
Swain, Elias H. V, 129
Swain, Elihu I, 576
Swain, Elihu I, 669
Swain, Elihu I, 685
Swain, Elihu I, 690
Swain, Elihu I, 969
Swain, Elihu I, 1077
Swain, Elihu I, 1099
Swain, Elihu I, 1101
Swain, Elihu I, 1111
Swain, Elihu I, 1132
Swain, Elihu I, 1137
Swain, Elihu, Jr. I, 672
Swain, Elijah VI, 857

Swain, Elijah VI, 958
Swain, Eliza I, 690
Swain, Eliza M. I, 669
Swain, Elizabeth I, 576
Swain, Elizabeth I, 669
Swain, Elizabeth I, 979
Swain, Elizabeth I, 995
Swain, Elizabeth I, 998
Swain, Elizabeth II, 662
Swain, Elizabeth II, 781
Swain, Elizabeth II, 970
Swain, Elizabeth II, 998
Swain, Elizabeth II, 1001
Swain, Elizabeth II, 1030
Swain, Elizabeth II, 1043
Swain, Elizabeth III, 306
Swain, Elizabeth V, 298
Swain, Elizabeth V, 311
Swain, Elizabeth VI, 958
Swain, Elizabeth VI, 1000
Swain, Elizabeth VI, 1001
Swain, Elvira I, 686
Swain, Elvira I, 690
Swain, Emily VI, 880
Swain, Emily Alberta II, 314
Swain, Emily Ann I, 682
Swain, Emily Ann I, 690
Swain, Emily B. III, 122
Swain, Emily B. III, 306
Swain, Eunice I, 529
Swain, Eunice I, 576
Swain, Eunice I, 669
Swain, Eunice I, 690
Swain, Eunice I, 998
Swain, Ezra I, 1111
Swain, Forrest Woolman II, 314
Swain, Francis V, 207
Swain, Francis V, 765
Swain, Gabriel V, 832
Swain, Gabriel V, 868
Swain, George I, 517
Swain, George I, 518
Swain, George I, 576
Swain, George I, 684
Swain, George I, 690
Swain, George I, 840
Swain, George III, 307
Swain, George VI, 945
Swain, George VI, 958
Swain, George VI, 1000
Swain, George VI, 1001
Swain, George B. I, 518
Swain, George B. V, 129
Swain, George F. III, 306
Swain, George Franklin I, 518
Swain, George John VI, 978
Swain, George R. I, 576
Swain, George. R. I, 608
Swain, Gilbert II, 325
Swain, Gilbert II, 1030
Swain, Gilbert II, 1081
Swain, Gilbert L. II, 314
Swain, Gilbert L. II, 325
Swain, Gilbert L. II, 327
Swain, Gorg R. I, 608
Swain, Hannah I, 669
Swain, Hannah I, 840
Swain, Hannah I, 969
Swain, Hannah I, 1111
Swain, Hannah I, 1130
Swain, Hannah I, 1132
Swain, Hannah II, 91
Swain, Hannah II, 103
Swain, Hannah II, 970
Swain, Hannah II, 1030
Swain, Hannah II, 1043
Swain, Hannah Lawrence II, 995
Swain, Hannah Lawrence Fetter II, 1030
Swain, Harriet V, 832
Swain, Harriet V, 846
Swain, Harriet V, 868
Swain, Haskin C. VI, 873
Swain, Henrietta B. V, 714
Swain, Henry I, 517
Swain, Henry I, 518
Swain, Henry I, 576
Swain, Henry Elliot I, 753
Swain, Hephzibah I, 793
Swain, Hepsabah V, 207
Swain, Hepzibah V, 765
Swain, Howlan I, 576
Swain, Howland I, 517
Swain, Howland I, 518
Swain, Howland I, 576
Swain, Howland I, 600
Swain, Howland I, 690
Swain, Huldah I, 992
Swain, Huldah I, 998
Swain, Huldah I, 1111
Swain, Huldah I, 1123
Swain, Huldah I, 1132
Swain, Ira I, 669
Swain, Ira I, 1111
Swain, Irene I, 669
Swain, Irene I, 690
Swain, Isaac II, 103
Swain, Isaac II, 1030
Swain, Isaiah V, 281
Swain, Jacob II, 103
Swain, Jacob II, 1030
Swain, James Harvey III, 306
Swain, James O. B. VI, 958
Swain, James O. B. VI, 1000
Swain, Jane Emeline VI, 1001
Swain, Jedidah I, 576
Swain, Jedidah I, 669
Swain, Jedidah I, 690
Swain, Jefferson I, 1132
Swain, Jemima I, 517
Swain, Jemima I, 518
Swain, Jemima I, 576
Swain, Jemima I, 581
Swain, Jemimah I, 690
Swain, Jeremiah VI, 880
Swain, Jeremiah VI, 945
Swain, Jeremiah VI, 972
Swain, Jeremiah VI, 984
Swain, Jeremiah VI, 1000
Swain, Jesse F. H. I, 576
Swain, Jessee F. H. I, 576
Swain, Jethro I, 669
Swain, Jethro I, 682
Swain, Jethro I, 683
Swain, Jethro I, 685
Swain, Jethro I, 686
Swain, Jethro I, 690
Swain, Job I, 669
Swain, Job I, 1111
Swain, John I, 517
Swain, John I, 669
Swain, John I, 969
Swain, John I, 1111
Swain, John I, 1123
Swain, John I, 1132
Swain, John II, 970
Swain, John VI, 1002
Swain, John G. I, 518
Swain, John G. I, 576
Swain, John N. VI, 1001
Swain, John R. I, 979
Swain, John Turner I, 517
Swain, John Turner I, 576
Swain, Jonathan I, 518
Swain, Jonathan I, 576
Swain, Jonathan II, 970
Swain, Jonathan II, 1030
Swain, Jonathan II, 1043
Swain, Jonathan V, 281
Swain, Jonathan V, 868
Swain, Jonathan I. V, 281
Swain, Joseph I, 576
Swain, Joseph I, 669
Swain, Joseph I, 690
Swain, Joseph I, 753
Swain, Joseph I, 840
Swain, Joseph I, 1111
Swain, Joseph I Sup 1, 9
Swain, Joseph V, 465
Swain, Joseph Paterson I, 979
Swain, Joseph Sylvester I, 753
Swain, Joshua IV, 160
Swain, Joshua IV, 285
Swain, Joshua VI, 449
Swain, Joshua VI, 591
Swain, Joshua VI, 596
Swain, Joshua VI, 600
Swain, Judah V, 207
Swain, Judida I, 840
Swain, Judith I, 576
Swain, Judith I, 793
Swain, Judith I, 835
Swain, Judith I, 840
Swain, Judith V, 765
Swain, Judy Ann VI, 909
Swain, Keziah I, 518
Swain, Keziah I, 576
Swain, Lawrence P. III, 306
Swain, Lemuel VI, 880
Swain, Letitia II, 1030
Swain, Lewis I, 1111
Swain, Lidia I, 576
Swain, Lola Katherine V, 433
Swain, Lousina I, 608
Swain, Lucien B. III, 306
Swain, Luzena I, 576
Swain, Luzena I, 608
Swain, Lydia I, 517
Swain, Lydia I, 576
Swain, Lydia I, 669
Swain, Lydia I, 673
Swain, Lydia I, 690
Swain, Lydia I, 692
Swain, Lydia I, 693
Swain, Lydia I, 809
Swain, Lydia I, 840
Swain, Lydia I, 1111
Swain, Lydia I, 1132
Swain, Lydia I, 1134
Swain, Lydia V, 782
Swain, Lydia V, 868
Swain, Lydia A. II, 314
Swain, Lydia Ann II, 324
Swain, Lydia Ann II, 325
Swain, Mahala M. V, 129
Swain, Margaret VI, 857
Swain, Maria L. III, 256
Swain, Maria Louisa III, 306
Swain, Mariam I, 576
Swain, Mariam I, 998
Swain, Martha II, 1030
Swain, Martha V, 868
Swain, Martha VI, 784
Swain, Martha VI, 945
Swain, Martha VI, 978
Swain, Martha H. V, 868
Swain, Mary I, 669
Swain, Mary I, 672
Swain, Mary I, 979
Swain, Mary II, 103
Swain, Mary II, 266
Swain, Mary II, 1030
Swain, Mary IV, 285
Swain, Mary V, 207
Swain, Mary V, 765
Swain, Mary V, 862
Swain, Mary V, 868
Swain, Mary V, 977
Swain, Mary Ann I, 984
Swain, Mary Ann I, 998
Swain, Mary Ann III, 174
Swain, Mary Ann III, 306
Swain, Mary Ann Rebecca VI, 992
Swain, Mary B. IV, 446
Swain, Mary B. IV, 457
Swain, Mary D. II, 923
Swain, Mary D. II, 927
Swain, Mary D. III, 306
Swain, Mary Ingham V, 281
Swain, Mary T. III, 123
Swain, Mary T. III, 256
Swain, Mary T. III, 306
Swain, Mary T. V, 868
Swain, Mary W. II, 1081
Swain, Matilda I, 685
Swain, Matilda I, 690
Swain, Meraby D. II, 1081
Swain, Meriba II, 1081
Swain, Meriba D. II, 325
Swain, Meriba D. II, 327
Swain, Meribe D. II, 314
Swain, Meribe D. II, 325
Swain, Mildred VI, 909
Swain, Milly VI, 982
Swain, Miriam I, 518
Swain, Miriam I, 570
Swain, Miriam I, 576
Swain, Miriam I, 608
Swain, Miriam I, 810
Swain, Miriam I, 840
Swain, Miriam I, 998
Swain, Miriam V, 782
Swain, Nancy VI, 899
Swain, Nancy VI, 909
Swain, Nancy VI, 984
Swain, Nancy VI, 992
Swain, Nancy VI, 1000
Swain, Narcissa I, 669
Swain, Narcissa I, 690
Swain, Nathan I, 518
Swain, Nathan I, 576
Swain, Nathan I, 979
Swain, Nathan I, 998
Swain, Nathan II, 425
Swain, Nathan Carter I, 979
Swain, Nathan W. I, 995
Swain, Nathan W. I, 998
Swain, Nathaniel I, 575
Swain, Nathaniel I, 576
Swain, Nathaniel I, 669
Swain, Nathaniel I, 690
Swain, Nathaniel I, 840
Swain, Nathaniel I, 969
Swain, Nathaniel I, 1111
Swain, Nathaniel I Sup 1, 9
Swain, Patty VI, 1000
Swain, Paul I, 518
Swain, Paul I, 529
Swain, Paul I, 576
Swain, Paul I, 793
Swain, Paul I, 840
Swain, Paul I, 998
Swain, Paul V, 207
Swain, Paul V, 765
Swain, Phebe I, 517
Swain, Phebe I, 518
Swain, Phebe I, 549
Swain, Phebe I, 559
Swain, Phebe I, 576
Swain, Phebe I, 600
Swain, Phebe I, 628
Swain, Phebe I, 690
Swain, Phebe I, 693
Swain, Phebe I, 936
Swain, Phebe V, 788
Swain, Phebe E. I, 517
Swain, Phebe Emila I, 518
Swain, Pleasant VI, 910
Swain, Rachel I, 669
Swain, Rachel I, 1111
Swain, Rachel I, 1132
Swain, Rachel V, 465
Swain, Rachel L. I, 686
Swain, Rachel L. I, 690
Swain, Reading W. V, 868
Swain, Rebecca V, 207
Swain, Rebeckah V, 765
Swain, Reuben I, 517
Swain, Reuel I, 517
Swain, Reuel I, 518
Swain, Reuel I, 570
Swain, Reuel I, 576
Swain, Reuel I, 840
Swain, Rewel I, 840
Swain, Rhoda I, 669
Swain, Rhoda I, 690
Swain, Rhoda I, 693
Swain, Rhoda W. I, 690
Swain, Rhuel I, 576
Swain, Richard III, 306
Swain, Robert B. III, 306
Swain, Robert G. VI, 899
Swain, Robert G. VI, 1001
Swain, Ruben I, 576
Swain, Ruel I, 576
Swain, Ruel I, 608
Swain, Ruel I, 793
Swain, Ruel I, 998
Swain, Ruth I, 518
Swain, Ruth I, 983
Swain, Ruth I, 998
Swain, Ruth J. III, 306
Swain, Sally I, 517
Swain, Sally I, 518
Swain, Sally Ann I, 1111
Swain, Samuel I, 669
Swain, Samuel I, 1111
Swain, Samuel I, 1132
Swain, Samuel II, 91
Swain, Samuel II, 103
Swain, Samuel II, 970
Swain, Samuel II, 1030
Swain, Samuel II, 1043
Swain, Samuel VI, 784
Swain, Samuel E. V, 129
Swain, Sarah I, 518
Swain, Sarah I, 549
Swain, Sarah I, 576
Swain, Sarah I, 669
Swain, Sarah I, 683
Swain, Sarah I, 685
Swain, Sarah I, 690
Swain, Sarah I, 693
Swain, Sarah I, 969
Swain, Sarah I, 1101
Swain, Sarah I, 1111
Swain, Sarah I, 1132
Swain, Sarah II, 923
Swain, Sarah II, 927
Swain, Sarah II, 970
Swain, Sarah II, 1030
Swain, Sarah II, 1041
Swain, Sarah III, 306
Swain, Sarah V, 920
Swain, Sarah V, 934
Swain, Sarah VI, 948
Swain, Sarah Ann VI, 558
Swain, Sarah Ann VI, 776
Swain, Sarah Ann VI, 784
Swain, Sarah Ann VI, 785
Swain, Sarah M. I, 979
Swain, Sarah M. I, 998
Swain, Silvanus I, 669
Swain, Silvanus I, 672
Swain, Silvanus I, 690
Swain, Silvanus I, 693
Swain, Silvanus I, 810
Swain, Silvanus I, 840
Swain, Susa I, 517
Swain, Susan I, 576
Swain, Susan III, 306
Swain, Susan Elizabeth I, 518
Swain, Susanna I, 683
Swain, Susanna I, 690
Swain, Susannah I, 1111
Swain, Sylvanus V, 782
Swain, Thomas I, 517
Swain, Thomas I, 576
Swain, Thomas I, 669
Swain, Thomas I, 683
Swain, Thomas I, 690
Swain, Thomas I, 692
Swain, Thomas I, 809
Swain, Thomas I, 840
Swain, Thomas V, 129
Swain, Thomas V, 146
Swain, Thomas V, 207
Swain, Thomas V, 765
Swain, Thomas Clarkson I,
Swain, Thomas More I, 518
Swain, Timothy I, 518
Swain, Timothy I, 576
Swain, Timothy V, 868
Swain, Unice V, 207
Swain, Unice V, 765
Swain, Valentine III, 306
Swain, Wd. Mary III, 306
Swain, Widow Anna Jane I,
Swain, Widow Judith I, 840
Swain, William I, 518
Swain, William I, 576
Swain, William I, 669
Swain, William I, 979
Swain, William I, 1111
Swain, William A. III, 306
Swain, William A. III, 307
Swain, William T. I, 690
Swain, Wm. M. II, 923
Swain, Wm. M. II, 927
Swaine, Abraham II, 1030
Swaine, Benjamin II, 993
Swaine, Benjamin II, 1030
Swaine, Charles VI, 1002
Swaine, Charles, Sr. VI, 956
Swaine, Dr. George I, 576
Swaine, Elizabeth VI, 984
Swaine, Elizabeth VI, 1002
Swaine, Hannah Lawrence Fetter II, 1030
Swaine, Jeremiah VI, 832
Swaine, Mary II, 993
Swaine, Mary II, 1030
Swaine, Peggy VI, 956
Swaine, Samuel II, 927
Swaine, Widow Anna Jane I, 5
Swainey, Frances I, 366
Swainey, Jos. I, 366
Swainey, Joseph I, 366
Swainey, Joseph I, 422
Swainey, Lydia I, 366
Swainy, Frances I, 422
Swainy, Jos. I, 366
Swainy, Joseph I, 422
Swainy, Lydia I, 366
Swainy, Lydia I, 384
Swainy, Lydia I, 422
Swainy, Mary I, 366
Swainy, William I, 422
Swallow, Alberta V, 1021
Swallow, Caroline V, 788
Swallow, Caroline V, 793
Swallow, Catharine V, 765
Swallow, Catherine V, 733
Swallow, Catherine V, 781
Swallow, Catherine V, 793
Swallow, Daniel V, 793
Swallow, Elizabeth I, 980
Swallow, Elizabeth I, 998
Swallow, Elizabeth V, 793
Swallow, Emily IV, 536
Swallow, Emily IV, 553
Swallow, Fanny V, 794
Swallow, James V, 793
Swallow, James V, 1021
Swallow, James O. V, 793
Swallow, Jas. V, 782
Swallow, John I, 840
Swallow, John V, 129
Swallow, John V, 793
Swallow, Judith V, 782
Swallow, Judith V, 793
Swallow, Lula Elizabeth V, 765
Swallow, Lydda V, 765
Swallow, Lydia I, 840
Swallow, Lydia V, 794
Swallow, Mary J. V, 1021
Swallow, Mary Jane V, 1021
Swallow, Priscilla V, 788
Swallow, Priscilla V, 793
Swallow, Rosa May V, 1021
Swallow, Sarah V, 765
Swallow, Sarah V, 769
Swallow, Silvanus V, 793
Swallow, Silvenius V, 765

ow, Silvenus I, 980
ow, Silvenus I, 998
ow, Simpson V, 793
, Benjamin IV, 1381
Elma IV, 53
Elma IV, 61
Frederic IV, 1381
, Frederick IV, 1381
Frederick Asa III, 307
Hannah A. IV, 1381
Harriet V, 833
, Harriet V, 868
Helen III, 307
Lydia B. IV, 1381
Patience D. IV, 1381
, Ruth IV, 61
der, Blanche V, 765
der, Blanche Virginia V, 765
der, Charles V, 765
der, Charles W. V, 765
der, Elsie V, 766
der, Elsie B. V, 868
der, Elvin V, 766
der, Elvin W. V, 868
der, Etta V, 765
der, Frances V, 765
der, Frances V. V, 765
der, Frankie V, 766
der, Frankie R. V, 868
der, James V, 765
der, James V, 766
der, James M. V, 868
der, Lester V, 766
der, Minnie V, 765
der, T. Lester V, 868
ders, Charles V, 765
ders, Etta V, 765
e, Betty IV, 498
e, Francis IV, 498
e, Hannah I, 810
e, Hannah I, 840
e, Henry I, 576
e, Joshua IV, 498
e, Judith I, 840
e, Mary II, 1030
e, Mary IV, 498
e, Sarah I, 810
ey, Charles Baumer VI, 784
ey, Charles Baumer VI, 786
ey, Charlotte Ellen VI, 784
ey, David Roy VI, 784
ey, John I, 969
ey, Joseph I, 690
ey, Joseph I, 969
ey, Lucy Ellen VI, 784
ey, Lydia I, 690
ey, Lydia, Jr. I, 753
ey, Lydia, Sr. I, 753
ey, Mary Eda VI, 784
ey, Mary Eda VI, 786
ey, Mary Gertrude VI, 784
ey, Ruth I, 969
ey, Susanna I, 687
ey, Susanna I, 690
ey, William I, 969
go, Alce VI, 449
son, John IV, 1043
son, Mary IV, 1043
y, Franceis I, 366
y, James I, 366
y, Jane I, 366
y, John I, 969
y, Joseph I, 366
y, Lyda I, 366
y, Lydia I, 366
y, Margaret I, 366
y, Mary I, 366
y, Ruth I, 969
y, Susannah I, 366
n, Anna V, 129
n, David V, 129
n, Isarah V, 129
n, Jonothan V, 129
t, Carrie III, 307
t, Deborah III, 54
t, Deborah III, 307
t, John III, 54
t, John III, 307
t, Mary IV, 1109
t, Mary IV, 1116
t, Wm. King III, 307
thmore, ??? III, 263
thmore, Margaret III, 263
twout, Hannah II, 782
tz, Carrie III, 66
tz, Harriet III, 420
tz, Harriet III, 448
tz, John VI, 87
tz, King III, 66
tz, Mildred III, 93
tz, Mildred III, 363
Swartz, Roberta III, 66
Swartz, Roberta T. III, 66
Swartz, Roberta T. III, 307
Swartz, Vera White IV, 774
Swatland, J. V. VI, 1005
Swavely, Esther II, 720
Swavely, Franklin G. II, 720
Swavely, Jeremiah II, 720
Swayn, Anna V, 281
Swayn, David V, 281
Swayn, Isaiah V, 281
Swayn, Jonathan I. V, 281
Swayne, Albanus II, 720
Swayne, Albanus R. II, 769
Swayne, Albanus R. II, 927
Swayne, Albanus Rest II, 822
Swayne, Amanda IV, 1295
Swayne, Amanda V, 960
Swayne, Amanda Ann IV, 1187
Swayne, Ann II, 804
Swayne, Ann V, 960
Swayne, Benj. IV, 221
Swayne, Benjamin P. II, 927
Swayne, Benjamin Pennock II, 822
Swayne, Benjamin W. II, 834
Swayne, Benjamin W. II, 927
Swayne, Bertrand E. III, 306
Swayne, Betty VI, 606
Swayne, Caleb II, 822
Swayne, Caleb II, 927
Swayne, Charles W. VI, 784
Swayne, Charles W. VI, 785
Swayne, Chas. M. II, 927
Swayne, Clarissa R. IV, 1093
Swayne, Clarissa R. IV, 1116
Swayne, Deborah II, 266
Swayne, Deborah II, 662
Swayne, Deborah II, 769
Swayne, Edith Neal III, 306
Swayne, Edward III, 306
Swayne, Edwin J. III, 306
Swayne, Elias IV, 595
Swayne, Elias H. V, 129
Swayne, Elias M. IV, 446
Swayne, Eliza IV, 351
Swayne, Eliza IV, 353
Swayne, Eliza IV, 553
Swayne, Eliza IV, 562
Swayne, Eliza V, 960
Swayne, Elizabeth II, 662
Swayne, Elizabeth II, 769
Swayne, Elizabeth II, 822
Swayne, Elizabeth III, 306
Swayne, Frances VI, 606
Swayne, George B. V, 129
Swayne, Hannah VI, 606
Swayne, Huson II, 822
Swayne, Isaac IV, 446
Swayne, Isaac IV, 595
Swayne, Isaac B. IV, 446
Swayne, Isaac B. IV, 595
Swayne, Isaac B. IV, 1187
Swayne, Isaac B. V, 960
Swayne, Isaac B. VI, 449
Swayne, Isaac B. VI, 450
Swayne, Isaac P. IV, 1295
Swayne, Jacob II, 822
Swayne, Jane McKay VI, 606
Swayne, Jedidah I, 558
Swayne, Jedidah I, 576
Swayne, John IV, 446
Swayne, John IV, 595
Swayne, John VI, 449
Swayne, John VI, 542
Swayne, John VI, 569
Swayne, John VI, 606
Swayne, John VI, 785
Swayne, John Thomas IV, 446
Swayne, John Thomas VI, 449
Swayne, John Thomas VI, 785
Swayne, Joseph I, 558
Swayne, Joseph I, 576
Swayne, Joshua IV, 110
Swayne, Joshua IV, 353
Swayne, Joshua IV, 420
Swayne, Joshua IV, 446
Swayne, Joshua IV, 498
Swayne, Joshua IV, 553
Swayne, Joshua IV, 562
Swayne, Joshua IV, 595
Swayne, Joshua V, 960
Swayne, Joshua VI, 449
Swayne, Joshua VI, 542
Swayne, Joshua VI, 569
Swayne, Joshua VI, 605
Swayne, Joshua VI, 606
Swayne, Joshua VI, 785
Swayne, Joshua W. VI, 449
Swayne, Lawrence P. III, 306
Swayne, Mahala M. V, 23
Swayne, Mahala M. V, 129
Swayne, Margaret IV, 390
Swayne, Margaret IV, 420
Swayne, Margaret IV, 446
Swayne, Margaret IV, 595
Swayne, Margaret VI, 371
Swayne, Margaret VI, 449
Swayne, Margaret B. II, 834
Swayne, Margaret B. II, 927
Swayne, Maria IV, 1187
Swayne, Maria IV, 1295
Swayne, Maria V, 960
Swayne, Maria VI, 449
Swayne, Maria VI, 450
Swayne, Mariah IV, 1187
Swayne, Martha VI, 784
Swayne, Mary II, 792
Swayne, Mary IV, 221
Swayne, Mary IV, 285
Swayne, Mary IV, 446
Swayne, Mary IV, 498
Swayne, Mary IV, 530
Swayne, Mary IV, 553
Swayne, Mary IV, 595
Swayne, Mary V, 960
Swayne, Mary Ann II, 834
Swayne, Mary Ann II, 927
Swayne, Mary Ann IV, 353
Swayne, Mary Ann IV, 553
Swayne, Mary Ann IV, 562
Swayne, Mary Ann VI, 785
Swayne, Mary B. IV, 446
Swayne, Mary B. VI, 449
Swayne, Mary Clevenger VI, 606
Swayne, Mary D. II, 927
Swayne, Mary D. III, 306
Swayne, Noah IV, 446
Swayne, Noah IV, 595
Swayne, Noah VI, 449
Swayne, Noah VI, 785
Swayne, Phebe VI, 606
Swayne, Rachel II, 822
Swayne, Rachel IV, 446
Swayne, Rachel IV, 595
Swayne, Rachel VI, 449
Swayne, Rachel B. IV, 446
Swayne, Rebecca IV, 353
Swayne, Rebecca IV, 446
Swayne, Rebecca IV, 553
Swayne, Rebecca IV, 562
Swayne, Rebecca V, 960
Swayne, Rebecca VI, 449
Swayne, Rebecca VI, 542
Swayne, Rebecca VI, 569
Swayne, Rebecca VI, 785
Swayne, Rebecca B. IV, 420
Swayne, Rebeckah IV, 553
Swayne, Rebeckah VI, 605
Swayne, Rebeckah VI, 606
Swayne, Rebekah VI, 449
Swayne, Ruth J. III, 306
Swayne, Samuel II, 822
Swayne, Samuel II, 927
Swayne, Samuel IV, 390
Swayne, Samuel IV, 420
Swayne, Samuel IV, 446
Swayne, Samuel IV, 595
Swayne, Samuel VI, 371
Swayne, Samuel VI, 449
Swayne, Samuel VI, 606
Swayne, Samuel VI, 784
Swayne, Samuel E. V, 129
Swayne, Samuel F. IV, 446
Swayne, Samuel F. V, 960
Swayne, Samuel F. VI, 449
Swayne, Sarah II, 927
Swayne, Sarah IV, 595
Swayne, Sarah V, 920
Swayne, Sarah V, 934
Swayne, Sarah VI, 785
Swayne, Sarah A. IV, 390
Swayne, Sarah A. IV, 446
Swayne, Sarah Ann IV, 446
Swayne, Sarah Ann IV, 595
Swayne, Sarah Ann V, 951
Swayne, Sarah Ann V, 960
Swayne, Sarah Ann VI, 449
Swayne, Sarah Ann VI, 784
Swayne, Sarah Ann VI, 785
Swayne, Sarah Brown VI, 606
Swayne, Sarah H. VI, 542
Swayne, Sarah H. VI, 569
Swayne, Susanna IV, 221
Swayne, Susannah II, 822
Swayne, Thomas IV, 353
Swayne, Thomas IV, 446
Swayne, Thomas IV, 562
Swayne, Thomas V, 129
Swayne, Thomas V, 960
Swayne, Thomas VI, 449
Swayne, Thomas VI, 569
Swayne, Thomas VI, 785
Swayne, Thomas, Jr. IV, 562
Swayne, Thomas, Jr. V, 960
Swayne, Thos. IV, 351
Swayne, Wd. Rebecca VI, 569
Swayne, Wd. Rebecca VI, 785
Swayne, Wm. II, 834
Swayne, Wm. II, 927
Swayne, Wm. M. II, 927
Swayne, Wm. P. II, 769
Swayne, Wm. P. II, 927
Swayze, Cecile I, 949
Swayze, Cecile I, 951
Swayze, Hayes Prentise I, 949
Swayze, Hayes Prentise I, 951
Swayze, Lillie III, 172
Swayzee, Cecile I, 949
Swayzee, Hayes Prentise I, 949
Sweany, John I, 576
Sweany, Joseph I, 576
Sweany, Lydia I, 741
Sweany, Ruth I, 576
Sweany, Susanah I, 576
Sweany, William I, 576
Swearinger, Thomas V, 465
Swearinger, Thos. W. V, 465
Swecord, Catharine III, 284
Swecord, James III, 284
Sweeney, Anna V, 281
Sweeney, Anna V, 361
Sweeney, James V, 281
Sweeney, James V, 361
Sweeney, Jane I, 771
Sweeney, John VI, 857
Sweeney, Joseph I, 771
Sweeney, Joseph A. VI, 857
Sweeney, Lucy A. VI, 857
Sweeney, Maria S. IV, 659
Sweeney, Martha VI, 857
Sweeney, Moses VI, 857
Sweeney, Nancy VI, 857
Sweeney, Susannah VI, 832
Sweeney, Wm. D. VI, 857
Sweeny, James V, 281
Sweeny, Martha VI, 1001
Sweeny, Moses VI, 1001
Sweet, ??? III, 68
Sweet, ??? III, 307
Sweet, Abiah III, 400
Sweet, Abiah III, 448
Sweet, Abigail I, 728
Sweet, Abigail I, 734
Sweet, Ada IV, 1340
Sweet, Ada D. IV, 1340
Sweet, Almond E. III, 214
Sweet, Almond E. III, 307
Sweet, Amelia IV, 1241
Sweet, Ann I, 576
Sweet, Ann V, 789
Sweet, Anna I, 576
Sweet, Anna I, 825
Sweet, Anna I, 840
Sweet, Anna V, 753
Sweet, Anna V, 788
Sweet, Anna V, 793
Sweet, Betsey II, 927
Sweet, Betsey III, 307
Sweet, Betsy II, 822
Sweet, Catharine III, 400
Sweet, Catharine V, 793
Sweet, Catharine V, 794
Sweet, Charles T. IV, 285
Sweet, Charles T. IV, 1340
Sweet, Charles W. IV, 1241
Sweet, Charlotte Bartlett Wilhelmina II, 798
Sweet, Chas. W. IV, 1340
Sweet, Daniel IV, 1381
Sweet, Dodge III, 307
Sweet, Edith I, 734
Sweet, Edith I, 840
Sweet, Edith V, 794
Sweet, Elizabeth V, 1021
Sweet, Elnathan III, 400
Sweet, Elnathan III, 448
Sweet, Garner I, 734
Sweet, George W. III, 307
Sweet, Hermes IV, 1381
Sweet, Hermes M. III, 307
Sweet, Imogene III, 214
Sweet, Imogene III, 307
Sweet, Irene IV, 1241
Sweet, Isaac I, 734
Sweet, Jemima I, 887
Sweet, Jemima I, 902
Sweet, Jervis III, 307
Sweet, Jervis C. II, 927
Sweet, Jervis C. III, 307
Sweet, John I, 576
Sweet, John I, 773
Sweet, John I, 840
Sweet, John I, 902
Sweet, John I Sup 1, 10
Sweet, John V, 788
Sweet, John, Jr. I, 576
Sweet, John, Jr. I, 902
Sweet, Jonathan III, 440
Sweet, Jonathan III, 448
Sweet, Lettie IV, 1241
Sweet, Lucius IV, 1381
Sweet, Lydia IV, 1381
Sweet, Lydia V, 793
Sweet, Margaret III, 68
Sweet, Margaret III, 307
Sweet, Mary I, 734
Sweet, Mary I, 840
Sweet, Mary I, 902
Sweet, Mary III, 440
Sweet, Mary III, 448
Sweet, Mary V, 788
Sweet, Mary Ann V, 207
Sweet, Mary E. II, 822
Sweet, Mary, Jr. I, 734
Sweet, Maryann V, 789
Sweet, Maryann V, 793
Sweet, Rachel II, 822
Sweet, Rachel II, 927
Sweet, Rachel III, 307
Sweet, Rebecca V, 780
Sweet, Rebecca V, 793
Sweet, Rhoda I, 734
Sweet, Richard V, 789
Sweet, Sarah A. III, 214
Sweet, Sarah A. III, 307
Sweet, Solomon V, 793
Sweet, Stephen I, 734
Sweet, Wd. Rachel II, 822
Sweet, William IV, 1241
Sweet, Wright IV, 1340
Sweet, Wright J. IV, 1340
Sweetland, Experience IV, 1381
Sweetman, Eliza V, 934
Sweetman, Eliza, Jr. V, 934
Sweetman, Elizabeth V, 934
Sweetman, Wm. V, 934
Sweetman, Wm., Jr. V, 934
Sweezy, Hannah III, 385
Swemley, Jane VI, 400
Swemley, Jane VI, 449
Sweney, Ann IV, 55
Sweney, Ann IV, 61
Sweney, Anna V, 281
Sweney, David VI, 948
Sweney, Isaac I, 117
Sweney, Jane I, 771
Sweney, Joseph I, 422
Sweney, Polly VI, 948
Swenson, Dorothy III, 224
Swenson, Dorothy W. III, 307
Swenson, Magnus III, 224
Swenson, Magnus III, 307
Swerts, Sophia II, 662
Swetman, Eliza V, 934
Swetman, Elizabeth V, 934
Swetman, Wm. V, 934
Swett, Ann II, 663
Swett, Benjamin II, 266
Swett, Benjamin II, 651
Swett, Benjamin II, 663
Swett, Benjamin, Jr. II, 266
Swett, Benjamin, Jr. II, 556
Swett, Benjamin, Jr. II, 663
Swett, Charlotte B. II, 871
Swett, Charlotte B. II, 927
Swett, Charlotte B. W. II, 871
Swett, Charlotte B. W. II, 927
Swett, John II, 663
Swett, Mary II, 266
Swett, Mary II, 556
Swett, Mary II, 663
Swett, Mary Dawson II, 266
Swett, Susanna II, 266
Swett, Susanna II, 651
Swett, Susanna II, 663
Swett, Susannah II, 266
Swett, Susannah II, 663
Swett, Wm. Gray II, 871
Swett, Wm. Gray II, 927
Swezey, Hannah III, 499
Swezey, Hannah III, 500
Swicard, Ann Elizabeth IV, 1111
Swick, Peter E. V, 1021
Swick, Rachel VI, 694
Swick, Rachel VI, 709
Swickard, Ann Elizabeth IV, 429
Swift, Abial V, 934
Swift, Abigail II, 266
Swift, Calvin V, 934
Swift, Deborah V, 934
Swift, Eliza V, 934
Swift, Elizabeth V, 891
Swift, Elizabeth V, 934

Swift, Latitia II, 633
Swift, Latitia II, 663
Swift, Letitia II, 663
Swift, Lidia V, 934
Swift, Louisa I, 923
Swift, Lydia V, 905
Swift, Lydia V, 934
Swift, Rachel Alice V, 361
Swift, Reuben, Jr. V, 934
Swift, Rueben V, 934
Swift, Ruth V, 934
Swift, Silvanus V, 934
Swift, Stephen V, 934
Swift, Sylvanus V, 934
Swift, Verlinda V, 113
Swift, Verlinda V, 129
Swift, William V, 934
Swift, Zebulon III, 307
Swigart, Margaret V, 207
Swigart, Mary IV, 570
Swigert, Cynthia IV, 606
Swigert, Cynthia IV, 659
Swiggett, Henrietta II, 186
Swiggett, Henrietta II, 303
Swihart, Frank V, 1021
Swihart, Lucinda V, 1021
Swihart, Sarah V, 1021
Swillivant, John II, 448
Swimney, Lillie III, 56
Swimney, Lillie III, 253
Swindel, Gulia E. I, 690
Swindel, Gulia E. I, 692
Swindel, Huldah I, 690
Swindell, Gulia E. I, 690
Swinden, Elizabeth II, 1009
Swinden, Elizabeth II, 1030
Swinden, Robert II, 1009
Swinden, Robert II, 1030
Swindler, Elizabeth IV, 73
Swindler, Elizabeth IV, 110
Swineden, Robert II, 1030
Swinerton, John III, 190
Swiney, Martha VI, 1001
Swiney, Moses VI, 1001
Swing, D. J. I, 934
Swing, D. Robert I, 949
Swing, David Robert I, 934
Swing, Dorothy I, 934
Swing, Dorothy I, 949
Swing, Edith I, 934
Swing, Elizabeth II, 70
Swing, Elizabeth II, 103
Swing, Lillie I, 922
Swing, Margaret I, 934
Swing, Margaret Lillian I, 934
Swing, Myrtle I, 949
Swing, Myrtle Roberta I, 934
Swing, Ora Helena I, 934
Swing, Ora J. I, 949
Swing, Pauline I, 949
Swing, Pauline Reynolds I, 934
Swing, Robert I, 949
Swingler, Elizabeth IV, 110
Swink, Sarah V, 714
Swinnerton, ??? III, 307
Swinnerton, Elizabeth III, 307
Swinnerton, John III, 307
Swinnerton, John W. III, 307
Swinnerton, John William III, 307
Swinnerton, Joseph III, 307
Swinnerton, Richard III, 307
Swinnerton, Robert III, 307
Swinnerton, Sarah III, 307
Swinney, Ann II, 55
Swinney, Ann II, 103
Swinney, Betsy VI, 1001
Swinney, Catharine VI, 857
Swinney, Celina F. VI, 857
Swinney, Chas. VI, 857
Swinney, Daniel VI, 810
Swinney, Delitha E. VI, 817
Swinney, Elizabeth VI, 857
Swinney, Emily VI, 954
Swinney, Emily A. VI, 857
Swinney, Garland VI, 954
Swinney, Garland VI, 1001
Swinney, George W. VI, 857
Swinney, Jane VI, 817
Swinney, Jane VI, 857
Swinney, Jas. G. VI, 857
Swinney, John E. VI, 857
Swinney, John H. VI, 842
Swinney, John H. VI, 857
Swinney, Lucy H. E. VI, 862
Swinney, Lydia VI, 325
Swinney, Lydia VI, 341
Swinney, Martha VI, 801
Swinney, Martha J. VI, 857
Swinney, Mary C. VI, 857
Swinney, Melvina VI, 842
Swinney, Milly VI, 866
Swinney, Milton VI, 954
Swinney, Nancy VI, 857
Swinney, Nancy R. VI, 866
Swinney, Octavia Burge VI, 857
Swinney, Polly VI, 857
Swinney, Robert M. VI, 857
Swinney, Sarah W. VI, 862
Swinney, Susanna VI, 833
Swinney, Thomas VI, 857
Swinney, William VI, 848
Swinney, William VI, 862
Swinney, William VI, 866
Swinney, William H. VI, 817
Swinney, Wj. D. VI, 857
Swinney, Wm. Garland VI, 974
Swinney, Wm. H. VI, 857
Swinny, Betsy VI, 1001
Swinny, Garland VI, 1001
Swinny, John P. VI, 1001
Swinny, Lydia VI, 1001
Swinny, Martha VI, 1001
Swinny, Moses VI, 1001
Swinny, Polly VI, 1001
Swinny, Sally VI, 1001
Swinny, William VI, 1001
Swishelm, George W. V, 281
Swishelm, Rosa V, 281
Swisher, Amanda V, 1021
Swisher, C. Brinton II, 318
Swisher, C. Brinton II, 326
Swisher, Enos V, 1021
Swisher, Louisa V, 1021
Swisher, Mary IV, 1295
Swisher, Mary H. II, 318
Swisher, Mary H. II, 326
Swisshelm, Cora V, 361
Swisshelm, Ellen V, 714
Swisshelm, George V, 281
Swisshelm, George W. V, 281
Swisshelm, Jennie V, 281
Swisshelm, Mabel V, 311
Swisshelm, Rosa V, 281
Swisshelm, Susie V, 466
Switzer, ??? VI, 681
Switzer, Augustus II, 908
Switzer, Augustus II, 927
Switzer, Catharine A. II, 908
Switzer, Catharine A. II, 927
Switzer, J. Augustus II, 908
Switzer, Mary Ellen II, 908
Switzer, Mary Ellen II, 927
Switzer, Viola IV, 1264
Switzer, Wm. IV, 1264
Swonger, Anna V, 281
Swonger, Henry V, 281
Swonger, Henry E. V, 281
Swonger, Louie V, 281
Swonger, Maud V, 281
Swonger, Robert V, 281
Swope, Anna C. II, 927
Swope, Rachel V, 868
Swope, Sarah V, 533
Sybell, Frederick III, 307
Sybell, Wd. Elizabeth W. III, 307
Syddons, Mary II, 97
Syddons, Mary II, 98
Syddons, Wm. II, 97
Syddons, Wm. II, 98
Sydner, Sarah Elizabeth VI, 196
Sydnor, Blanch VI, 273
Sydnor, Blanche VI, 273
Sydnor, Charles VI, 273
Sydnor, Charles Edward VI, 273
Sydnor, Edmund Bacon VI, 237
Sydnor, Edw VI, 236
Sydnor, Edward VI, 237
Sydnor, Edward VI, 273
Sydnor, Foster VI, 915
Sydnor, Isabella VI, 273
Sydnor, J. Isabella VI, 273
Sydnor, Judith Isabella VI, 236
Sydnor, Judith Isabella VI, 237
Sydnor, Judith Isabella VI, 273
Sydnor, M. Josephine VI, 273
Sydnor, Sarah VI, 273
Sydnor, Sarah Elizabeth VI, 196
Sydnor, Thomas W. VI, 273
Sydnor, Walter Crew VI, 237
Sydwell, Esther V, 861
Syferd, Adaline V, 281
Syferd, Amy V, 282
Syferd, Araminta V, 281
Syferd, Araminta J. V, 281
Syferd, Belle V, 282
Syferd, Corda V, 282
Syferd, Cordelia Keith V, 281
Syferd, Cordelia N. V, 281
Syferd, Jane V, 281
Syferd, Jer. V, 281
Syferd, Martha V, 281
Syferd, Martha V, 282
Syferd, Martha Keith V, 281
Syferd, Phillip J. V, 281
Syferd, Thomas V, 281
Syferd, Virginia V, 247
Syferd, Virginia V, 281
Syferd, William W. V, 281
Syford, Thomas V, 281
Sykes, Ann II, 186
Sykes, Ann II, 266
Sykes, Ann II, 268
Sykes, Ann II, 425
Sykes, Ann II, 588
Sykes, Ann II, 663
Sykes, Ann V, 937
Sykes, Anna III, 25
Sykes, Anna III, 307
Sykes, Anna V, 937
Sykes, Barclay IV, 286
Sykes, Benj. II, 186
Sykes, Benj. V, 937
Sykes, Benjamin II, 186
Sykes, Benjamin II, 266
Sykes, Benjamin II, 303
Sykes, Elizabeth II, 266
Sykes, Elizabeth II, 303
Sykes, Elizabeth II, 588
Sykes, Elizabeth II, 663
Sykes, Elizabeth II, 1031
Sykes, Hannah II, 186
Sykes, Hannah II, 266
Sykes, Hannah II, 303
Sykes, Hannah II, 769
Sykes, Hannah II, 976
Sykes, Hannah II, 1031
Sykes, Hannah V, 934
Sykes, James II, 588
Sykes, Joanna II, 663
Sykes, John II, 663
Sykes, Joseph II, 663
Sykes, Mary II, 204
Sykes, Mary II, 266
Sykes, Mary II, 425
Sykes, Mary II, 663
Sykes, Mary II, 1031
Sykes, Mary, Jr. II, 663
Sykes, Nathaniel II, 663
Sykes, Pearl I, 637
Sykes, Pearl I, 641
Sykes, Rachel II, 588
Sykes, Rachel II, 663
Sykes, Rachel II, 671
Sykes, Rachel II, 694
Sykes, Rebecca II, 186
Sykes, Rebeckah II, 266
Sykes, Robert W. II, 663
Sykes, Robert W. II, 769
Sykes, Samuel II, 204
Sykes, Samuel II, 266
Sykes, Samuel II, 425
Sykes, Samuel II, 588
Sykes, Samuel II, 663
Sykes, Samuel II, 1031
Sykes, Thomas II, 663
Sykes, William II, 186
Sykes, William II, 266
Sykes, William II, 425
Sykes, Wm. II, 588
Sykes, Wm. II, 663
Sykes, Wm. II, 1031
Sylavant, Larry I, 297
Sylavant, Mary I, 297
Sylavent, Chelley I, 286
Sylavent, Jesse I, 286
Sylavent, Priscilla I, 286
Sylven, Judith III, 448
Sylvester, Ann IV, 353
Sylvester, Rachel M. III, 307
Sylvester, William T. III, 307
Symcock, John V, 533
Symmes, Ernest L. I, 75
Symmes, Ernest L. III, 307
Symmes, Ernest Lewis I, 18
Symmes, Herbert Austin I, 18
Symmes, Lewis I, 18
Symmes, Lewis I, 75
Symmes, Margaret I, 75
Symmes, Margaret W. I, 18
Symmes, Margaret W. I, 20
Symmes, Margaret W. I, 75
Symmes, Margaret W. I, 83
Symmes, Margaret W. I, 641
Symmes, Margaret W. III, 307
Symmes, Margaret Wilson I, 626
Symmes, Sarah H. I, 18
Symmes, Sarah H. I, 75
Symmes, William I, 626
Symmes, William A. I, 18
Symmes, William A. I, 75
Symmes, William A. I, 83
Symmes, William A. III, 307
Symmes, William Edward III, 307
Symmes, Wm. A. I, 20
Symnes, Margaret I, 902
Symnes, Wm. A. I, 902
Symonds, Lonie V, 129
Symonds, Milicent I, 75
Symonds, Nathan I, 902
Symons, ??? I, 25
Symons, Aaron Lynn I, 167
Symons, Aaron Morris, Sr. I, 167
Symons, Abel Trueblood I, 167
Symons, Abigail I, 769
Symons, Abraham I, 117
Symons, Abraham I, 118
Symons, Abraham I, 135
Symons, Abraham I, 167
Symons, Abraham I, 168
Symons, Abraham I, 706
Symons, Abraham I, 734
Symons, Abraham, Jr. I, 168
Symons, Abraham, Jr. I, 734
Symons, Abram I, 734
Symons, Abram V, 766
Symons, Absala I, 167
Symons, Absilla I, 75
Symons, Absilla I, 86
Symons, Absole I, 168
Symons, Absylla I, 119
Symons, Achsah V, 766
Symons, Ann I, 117
Symons, Ann I, 118
Symons, Ann I, 120
Symons, Ann I, 130
Symons, Ann I, 148
Symons, Ann I, 151
Symons, Ann I, 153
Symons, Ann I, 156
Symons, Ann I, 158
Symons, Ann I, 165
Symons, Ann I, 166
Symons, Ann I, 167
Symons, Ann I, 168
Symons, Ann I, 669
Symons, Ann I, 706
Symons, Ann I, 734
Symons, Ann, Sr. I, 92
Symons, Anne I, 131
Symons, Arnould I, 91
Symons, Barbary I, 117
Symons, Benjamin F. V, 747
Symons, Benjamin F. V, 766
Symons, Benjeaman I, 119
Symons, Betsy I, 120
Symons, Betty I, 148
Symons, Betty I, 167
Symons, Caleb I, 118
Symons, Caleb I, 133
Symons, Caleb I, 168
Symons, Caleb Trueblood I, 167
Symons, Caroline E. I, 118
Symons, Chalkley I, 119
Symons, Charles I, 706
Symons, Christina I, 902
Symons, Cyntha Ann I, 118
Symons, Cynthia Ann I, 69
Symons, Cynthia Ann I, 75
Symons, Damaras I, 167
Symons, Damaris I, 166
Symons, Damaris I, 172
Symons, Deborah I, 166
Symons, Elisabeth I, 25
Symons, Elisabeth I, 35
Symons, Elisabeth I, 69
Symons, Elisabeth I, 75
Symons, Elisabeth I, 118
Symons, Elisabeth I, 124
Symons, Elisabeth I, 140
Symons, Elisabeth I, 151
Symons, Elisabeth I, 154
Symons, Elisabeth I, 164
Symons, Elisabeth I, 166
Symons, Elisabeth I, 167
Symons, Elisabeth I, 168
Symons, Elisabeth I, 173
Symons, Elizabeth I, 91
Symons, Elizabeth I, 118
Symons, Elizabeth I, 120
Symons, Elizabeth I, 124
Symons, Elizabeth I, 165
Symons, Elizabeth I, 167
Symons, Elizabeth I, 669
Symons, Elizabeth I, 685
Symons, Elizabeth I, 690
Symons, Elizabeth I, 741
Symons, Elizabeth I, 902
Symons, Elva I, 118
Symons, Elvy I, 128
Symons, Elvy I, 168
Symons, Gertrude E. IV, 286
Symons, Gulielma I, 118
Symons, Gulielma I, 168
Symons, Gulielma I, 706
Symons, Henery I, 706
Symons, Henry I, 91
Symons, Jacob I, 118
Symons, Jacob I, 119
Symons, Jacob I, 133
Symons, Jacob I, 168
Symons, Jacob Wilson I, 118
Symons, James I, 118
Symons, James I, 168
Symons, Jane I, 119
Symons, Jane I, 120
Symons, Jane I, 132
Symons, Jane I, 155
Symons, Jane I, 167
Symons, Jane I, 902
Symons, Jehosaphat I, 96
Symons, Jehosaphat I, 118
Symons, Jehosephat I, 118
Symons, Jehoshaphat I, 118
Symons, Jehoshaphat I, 119
Symons, Jehoshaphat I, 131
Symons, Jehoshaphat I, 132
Symons, Jehoshaphat I, 137
Symons, Jehoshaphat I, 153
Symons, Jehoshaphat I, 167
Symons, Jehoshaphat I, 168
Symons, Jehosphaphat I, 11[illegible]
Symons, Jehosphaphat I, 11[illegible]
Symons, Jeremiah I, 92
Symons, Jeremiah I, 120
Symons, Jeremiah I, 164
Symons, Jeremiah I, 166
Symons, Jeremiah, Jr. I, 166
Symons, Jeremiah, Sr. I, 92
Symons, Jesa I, 118
Symons, Jesse I, 118
Symons, Jesse I, 132
Symons, Jesse I, 149
Symons, Jesse I, 167
Symons, Jesse I, 168
Symons, Jesse, Jr. I, 168
Symons, Jesse, Sr. I, 168
Symons, John I, 69
Symons, John I, 75
Symons, John I, 79
Symons, John I, 92
Symons, John I, 117
Symons, John I, 118
Symons, John I, 119
Symons, John I, 120
Symons, John I, 127
Symons, John I, 148
Symons, John I, 162
Symons, John I, 166
Symons, John I, 167
Symons, John I, 168
Symons, John I, 669
Symons, John I, 690
Symons, John I, 706
Symons, John Symons, Sr. I,
Symons, John, Jr. I, 167
Symons, John, Jr. I, 168
Symons, John, Sr. I, 140
Symons, John, Sr. I, 169
Symons, Joseph I, 119
Symons, Joseph I, 120
Symons, Joseph I, 124
Symons, Joseph I, 167
Symons, Joseph I, 169
Symons, Joseph I, 669
Symons, Joseph Henley I, 16[illegible]
Symons, Joshua I, 119
Symons, Josiah I, 118
Symons, Ledia I, 118
Symons, Lydda I, 118
Symons, Lyddea I, 118
Symons, Lyddia I, 137
Symons, Lyddia I, 167
Symons, Lydia I, 118
Symons, Lydia I, 119
Symons, Lydia I, 129
Symons, Lydia I, 131
Symons, Lydia I, 167
Symons, Lydia I, 168
Symons, Lydia I, 850
Symons, Margaret I, 118
Symons, Margaret I, 159
Symons, Margaret I, 168
Symons, Margaret I, 685
Symons, Margaret I, 690
Symons, Margaret I, 706
Symons, Margaret I, 734
Symons, Marget I, 118
Symons, Martha I, 118
Symons, Martha I, 162
Symons, Martha I, 166
Symons, Mary I, 96
Symons, Mary I, 104
Symons, Mary I, 117

ns, Mary I, 118
ns, Mary I, 119
ns, Mary I, 120
ns, Mary I, 127
ns, Mary I, 132
ns, Mary I, 133
ns, Mary I, 135
ns, Mary I, 136
ns, Mary I, 146
ns, Mary I, 148
ns, Mary I, 157
ns, Mary I, 164
ns, Mary I, 165
ns, Mary I, 166
ns, Mary I, 167
ns, Mary I, 168
ns, Mary I, 170
ns, Mary I, 706
ns, Mary I, 734
ns, Mary Ann I, 118
ns, Mathew I, 168
ns, Matthew I, 118
ns, Matthew I, 119
ns, Matthew I, 168
ns, Matthew I, 669
ns, Matthew I, 706
ns, Matthew I, 734
ns, Milicent I, 75
ns, Milisant I, 149
ns, Milisant I, 168
ns, Miliscent I, 119
ns, Miliscent I, 168
ns, Milisent I, 60
ns, Milisent I, 75
ns, Milisent I, 147
ns, Milisent I, 167
ns, Millecent I, 118
ns, Millisant I, 103
ns, Miriam I, 118
ns, Miriam I, 162
ns, Miriam I, 164
ns, Miriam I, 167
ns, Miriam I, 169
ns, Moorning I, 168
ns, Mourning I, 118
ns, Nathan I, 75
ns, Nathan I, 86
ns, Nathan I, 118
ns, Nathan I, 119
ns, Nathan I, 167
ns, Nathan I, 168
ns, Nathan I, 902
ns, Penellepy I, 118
ns, Penelope I, 149
ns, Penelope I, 168
ns, Peninah I, 119
ns, Peninah I, 133
ns, Peninah I, 168
ns, Penninah I, 118
ns, Penninah I, 168
ns, Peter I, 92
ns, Peter I, 119
ns, Peter I, 131
ns, Peter I, 146
ns, Peter I, 162
ns, Peter I, 166
ns, Peter I, 167
ns, Pharebe I, 119
ns, Phebey I, 706
ns, Pleasant I, 119
ns, Priscilla I, 119
ns, Priscilla I, 131
ns, Priscilla I, 167
ns, Prudence I, 669
ns, Rachel I, 164
ns, Rachel I, 166
ns, Rebacah I, 119
ns, Rebecah I, 105
ns, Rebecca I, 92
ns, Rebecca I, 104
ns, Rebecca I, 110
ns, Rebeckah I, 167
ns, Rebekah I, 145
ns, Rebekah I, 148
ns, Rebekah I, 167
ns, Robert IV, 286
ns, Samuel I, 117
ns, Samuel I, 167
ns, Samuel I, 168
ns, Samuel I, 706
ns, Samuel I, 734
ns, Sarah I, 75
ns, Sarah I, 79
ns, Sarah I, 117
ns, Sarah I, 118
ns, Sarah I, 119
ns, Sarah I, 132
ns, Sarah I, 143
ns, Sarah I, 144
ns, Sarah I, 145
ns, Sarah I, 153
Symons, Sarah I, 154
Symons, Sarah I, 165
Symons, Sarah I, 167
Symons, Sarah I, 168
Symons, Sarah I, 669
Symons, Sarah I, 706
Symons, Sarah I, 734
Symons, Sarah I, 741
Symons, Sarah I, 769
Symons, Silas I, 118
Symons, Tamer I, 166
Symons, Thomas I, 60
Symons, Thomas I, 75
Symons, Thomas I, 91
Symons, Thomas I, 92
Symons, Thomas I, 104
Symons, Thomas I, 110
Symons, Thomas I, 118
Symons, Thomas I, 119
Symons, Thomas I, 120
Symons, Thomas I, 131
Symons, Thomas I, 132
Symons, Thomas I, 158
Symons, Thomas I, 166
Symons, Thomas I, 167
Symons, Thomas I, 168
Symons, Thomas I, 706
Symons, Thomas I, 734
Symons, Thomas I, 902
Symons, Thomas C. I, 168
Symons, Thomas Newby I, 118
Symons, Verlinda V, 747
Symons, Verlinda V, 766
Symons, Widow Elizabeth I, 118
Symons, Widow Elizabeth I, 132
Symons, Widow Jane I, 167
Symons, Widow Lyddia I, 137
Symons, William I, 118
Symons, William I, 119
Symons, William I, 120
Symons, William I, 124
Symons, William I, 129
Symons, William I, 136
Symons, William I, 148
Symons, William I, 167
Symons, William I, 168
Symons, Williamson I, 119
Symons, Wilson I, 168
Symons, Zachariah I, 110
Syms, Alice V, 202
Synder, Sarah Elizabeth VI, 214
Synestodt, Geo. V, 934
Synestodt, Maria V, 934
Syng, Daniel II, 425
Syng, Elizabeth II, 425
Syng, Esther II, 767
Synisvedt, Thos. I. V, 934
Synnesstredt, Agusta Louisa V, 934
Synnesstredt, Augusta Louisa V, 934
Synnesstredt, Frank K. Andrew V, 934
Synnesstredt, Frederick Andrew V, 934
Synnesstredt, Geo. V, 934
Synnesstredt, Geo. C. V, 934
Synnesstredt, George V, 934
Synnesstredt, Georgianna Maria V, 934
Synnesstredt, Margaretta Elizabeth V, 934
Synnesstredt, Maria V, 934
Synnesstredt, Nancy Harvey V, 934
Synnesstredt, Otho Christian V, 934
Synnesstredt, Otto Christian V, 934
Synnesstredt, Thomas V, 934
Synnesstredt, Thos. I. V, 934
Synnestoedt, Mariah E. V, 129
Synnestvedt, Augusta Louisa V, 934
Synnestvedt, Frederick Andrew V, 934
Synnestvedt, Geo. C. V, 934
Synnestvedt, Georgianna Maria V, 934
Synnestvedt, Margaretta Elizabeth V, 934
Synnestvedt, Maria V, 934
Synnestvedt, Nancy Harvey V, 934
Synnestvedt, Otto Christian V, 934
Synor, John VI, 945
Synor, Nancy VI, 945
Synor, Sophia VI, 935
Synton, William VI, 163
Syoms, John, Jr. I, 167
Sypes, John C. V, 766
Sypes, Lizzie F. I, 950
Sypes, Tom A. I, 950
Sysom, Hannah II, 1027
Sysom, John II, 1027
Sysom, John II, 1031
Sysom, Rachel II, 1027
Sysom, Rebecca II, 1026
Sysom, Rebecca II, 1031
Sysom, Thomas II, 1026
Sysom, Thomas II, 1027
Sysom, Thomas II, 1031
Sysom, Wm. II, 1031
Sytz, Elizabeth II, 421

T???, Mary III, 24
T???, Mary III, 124
Tabb, Evalina VI, 753
Tabb, Evelina VI, 407
Tabb, Evelina VI, 417
Tabb, Mary E. VI, 517
Tabbot, Thomas I, 841
Tabener, Justice ??? VI, 41
Taber, Abby IV, 535
Taber, Abby IV, 553
Taber, Abby T. IV, 533
Taber, Abigail IV, 1188
Taber, Adelbert E. IV, 1224
Taber, Adelbert Eugene IV, 1225
Taber, Alice II, 822
Taber, Allen IV, 1188
Taber, Allen J. I, 902
Taber, Amanda M. IV, 1225
Taber, Amanda Mahina IV, 1224
Taber, Ann IV, 1224
Taber, Ann IV, 1374
Taber, Ann IV, 1381
Taber, Ann V, 935
Taber, Anna III, 80
Taber, Anna III, 308
Taber, Anna III, 336
Taber, Anna IV, 349
Taber, Anna IV, 353
Taber, Anna IV, 1201
Taber, Anna IV, 1221
Taber, Anna IV, 1224
Taber, Anna IV, 1225
Taber, Anna F. III, 248
Taber, Anna F. III, 308
Taber, Anna H. III, 117
Taber, Anna H. III, 307
Taber, Anna Keese III, 308
Taber, Anna Matilda II, 822
Taber, Anna R. IV, 286
Taber, Anna R. IV, 388
Taber, Anna R. IV, 446
Taber, Anna R. IV, 577
Taber, Anna R. IV, 595
Taber, Anna Ruse III, 308
Taber, Antipas II, 822
Taber, Augustus III, 117
Taber, Augustus III, 248
Taber, Augustus III, 307
Taber, Augustus III, 308
Taber, Augustus Frederick III, 308
Taber, Benj. IV, 286
Taber, Benj. IV, 353
Taber, Benj. Phillips V, 935
Taber, Benjamin IV, 1224
Taber, Benjamin IV, 1225
Taber, Benjamin F. I, 865
Taber, Benjamin F. I, 902
Taber, Benjamin J. IV, 1225
Taber, Benjamin S. IV, 1224
Taber, Carol E. III, 307
Taber, Caroline III, 106
Taber, Caroline L. III, 29
Taber, Caroline L. III, 307
Taber, Caroline L. III, 308
Taber, Carrie III, 308
Taber, Carrol Emma III, 308
Taber, Charles R. IV, 774
Taber, Charlotte III, 308
Taber, Charlotte Bliss III, 308
Taber, Clarkson III, 307
Taber, Clarkson III, 308
Taber, Clarkson III, 447
Taber, Clarkson III, 448
Taber, Cornelia III, 307
Taber, Daniel III, 448
Taber, David S. III, 308
Taber, David S. III, 364
Taber, David Shearman III, 308
Taber, David Shearman, Jr. III, 308
Taber, Deborah III, 294
Taber, Deborah III, 307
Taber, Deborah III, 308
Taber, Deborah III, 447
Taber, Deborah III, 448
Taber, Deborah C. III, 308
Taber, Dora B. I, 1162
Taber, Edmund B. III, 308
Taber, Edna A. IV, 446
Taber, Edna Russel III, 308
Taber, Edna Russell III, 210
Taber, Edna Russell III, 308
Taber, Eliza III, 162
Taber, Eliza III, 210
Taber, Eliza III, 308
Taber, Eliza Ann IV, 1188
Taber, Eliza H. III, 16
Taber, Eliza H. III, 308
Taber, Eliza S. III, 308
Taber, Elizabeth II, 425
Taber, Elizabeth III, 308
Taber, Elizabeth D. III, 308
Taber, Elizabeth M. IV, 389
Taber, Elizabeth O. III, 106
Taber, Elizabeth U. III, 308
Taber, Elizabeth U. III, 364
Taber, Ellen Elizabeth V, 935
Taber, Emma L. I, 1162
Taber, Ervin I, 1162
Taber, Ervin G. I, 1162
Taber, Ervin Guiotto IV, 1225
Taber, Erwin G. I, 1162
Taber, Evelyn Alice III, 308
Taber, Florence III, 243
Taber, Florence IV, 389
Taber, Florence R. III, 308
Taber, Francis IV, 533
Taber, Francis IV, 1225
Taber, Francis Bailey IV, 446
Taber, Francis Wm. IV, 1224
Taber, Frank III, 308
Taber, Franklin M. IV, 774
Taber, Freeman IV, 1188
Taber, Freeman IV, 1224
Taber, Geo. Derwin V, 935
Taber, Geo. Dowin V, 935
Taber, George II, 822
Taber, George IV, 1188
Taber, George M. IV, 1188
Taber, George N. IV, 1188
Taber, Gertrude Townsend III, 423
Taber, Guli Elma M. IV, 1188
Taber, Gulielma IV, 1197
Taber, Gulielma IV, 1198
Taber, Hannah T. III, 307
Taber, Hannah T. III, 308
Taber, Harold Earl III, 308
Taber, Harold Earle III, 308
Taber, Helen IV, 446
Taber, Henry Allen V, 935
Taber, Horace IV, 1188
Taber, Horace IV, 1224
Taber, Ida Rosella IV, 1224
Taber, Isaac IV, 1188
Taber, J. Oscar IV, 774
Taber, James IV, 1188
Taber, James IV, 1225
Taber, James C. IV, 1224
Taber, James C. IV, 1225
Taber, James R. III, 16
Taber, James R. III, 308
Taber, James Russell III, 162
Taber, James Russell III, 308
Taber, Jas. R. III, 16
Taber, Jas. R. III, 210
Taber, Jethro W. V, 935
Taber, Joel Oscar IV, 774
Taber, John III, 117
Taber, John R. III, 80
Taber, John R. III, 308
Taber, John R. III, 336
Taber, Jonathan III, 308
Taber, Jonathan Clarkson III, 308
Taber, Joseph J. IV, 286
Taber, Joseph J. IV, 446
Taber, Joseph John IV, 286
Taber, Joseph John IV, 388
Taber, Joseph John IV, 444
Taber, Joseph John IV, 1073
Taber, Joseph John IV, 1078
Taber, Joseph John H. IV, 264
Taber, Joseph John H. IV, 446
Taber, Joseph John J. IV, 286
Taber, Joseph Paul IV, 446
Taber, Josephine C. III, 308
Taber, Josephine C. III, 336
Taber, Julia IV, 1225
Taber, Katherine H. III, 448
Taber, Keziah VI, 123
Taber, Leamon IV, 1224
Taber, Lenion IV, 1224
Taber, Lewis III, 16
Taber, Lewis IV, 221
Taber, Lewis IV, 286
Taber, Lewis IV, 446
Taber, Lewis IV, 1224
Taber, Lois I, 1162
Taber, Lois C. III, 29
Taber, Lois C. III, 308
Taber, Louis IV, 409
Taber, Louis IV, 980
Taber, Louis IV, 1078
Taber, Louis J. IV, 286
Taber, Louis J. IV, 389
Taber, Louis J. IV, 446
Taber, Lucy Ann IV, 687
Taber, Lucy Ann IV, 774
Taber, Lydia IV, 533
Taber, Lysander O. IV, 1224
Taber, Mabel S. IV, 389
Taber, Maranda A. IV, 1225
Taber, Marian H. III, 308
Taber, Marion H. III, 16
Taber, Marion Russell III, 308
Taber, Martha I, 902
Taber, Martha III, 308
Taber, Martha III, 448
Taber, Martha III, 472
Taber, Martha IV, 1188
Taber, Martha IV, 1229
Taber, Martha A. I, 902
Taber, Martha Jane IV, 1162
Taber, Martha Jane IV, 1188
Taber, Martha T. III, 356
Taber, Mary III, 80
Taber, Mary IV, 388
Taber, Mary IV, 446
Taber, Mary IV, 1073
Taber, Mary IV, 1078
Taber, Mary A. I, 902
Taber, Mary A. IV, 446
Taber, Mary Ann IV, 221
Taber, Mary Ann IV, 286
Taber, Mary Ann IV, 409
Taber, Mary Ann IV, 446
Taber, Mary Ann IV, 980
Taber, Mary Ann IV, 1078
Taber, Mary Anna III, 307
Taber, Mary Anna III, 308
Taber, Mary C. III, 308
Taber, Mary D. I, 902
Taber, Mary Elizabeth IV, 1188
Taber, Mary F. III, 248
Taber, Mary F. III, 307
Taber, Mary F. III, 308
Taber, Mary H. III, 308
Taber, Mary H. IV, 264
Taber, Mary H. IV, 286
Taber, Mary Jane IV, 1224
Taber, Mary Jane IV, 1225
Taber, Mary Lewis IV, 286
Taber, Mary P. IV, 286
Taber, Mary P. IV, 444
Taber, Mary P. IV, 446
Taber, Mary P. IV, 774
Taber, Mary P. IV, 1078
Taber, Mary R. IV, 1201
Taber, Mary R. IV, 1224
Taber, May Alice I, 865
Taber, Mellie III, 308
Taber, Melvin Louis IV, 286
Taber, Meriam IV, 1224
Taber, Miriam IV, 1182
Taber, Miriam IV, 1188
Taber, Miriam IV, 1229
Taber, Miriam Almina IV, 1224
Taber, Mirium IV, 1224
Taber, Moses IV, 774
Taber, Moses Franklin IV, 774
Taber, Nancy I, 998
Taber, Nathan IV, 1188
Taber, Nathan IV, 1224
Taber, Nathan IV, 1225
Taber, Nellie III, 308
Taber, Ollie IV, 1225
Taber, Orianna IV, 1201
Taber, Orianna IV, 1225
Taber, Orianna M. IV, 1224
Taber, Orson L. IV, 1225
Taber, Paul Hoag III, 308
Taber, Phebe III, 448
Taber, Phebe III, 454
Taber, Phebe IV, 286
Taber, Phebe IV, 353
Taber, Phebe IV, 1225
Taber, Phebe E. IV, 1224
Taber, Phebe Ellen IV, 286
Taber, Phebe Jane IV, 1224
Taber, Phebe Jane IV, 1225
Taber, Phebe P. IV, 774
Taber, Rachel IV, 286
Taber, Rachel IV, 409
Taber, Rachel H. IV, 221
Taber, Rachel H. IV, 286

Taber, Rachel Hannah IV, 286
Taber, Rebecca III, 448
Taber, Reuben IV, 1224
Taber, Reuben IV, 1225
Taber, Reuben R. V, 868
Taber, Robert D. I, 902
Taber, Roslyn III, 448
Taber, Russell IV, 286
Taber, Russell Z. IV, 286
Taber, Russell Zeno IV, 286
Taber, S. Phebe III, 471
Taber, Salma Lizzie IV, 286
Taber, Samuel C. III, 448
Taber, Samuel S. III, 307
Taber, Samuel S. III, 308
Taber, Samuel T. III, 308
Taber, Samuel T. III, 356
Taber, Samuel T. III, 448
Taber, Samuel T. III, 472
Taber, Sara D. IV, 255
Taber, Sara Debora IV, 286
Taber, Sarah IV, 446
Taber, Sarah IV, 1188
Taber, Sarah IV, 1224
Taber, Sarah Ann IV, 1225
Taber, Sarah D. IV, 423
Taber, Sarah D. IV, 446
Taber, Sarah Matilda IV, 1224
Taber, Selma IV, 959
Taber, Selma L. IV, 444
Taber, Selma L. IV, 446
Taber, Selma Lizzie IV, 286
Taber, Selma Lizzie IV, 446
Taber, Selma P. IV, 253
Taber, Selma P. IV, 286
Taber, Selma P. IV, 397
Taber, Selma P. IV, 980
Taber, Selma Phebe IV, 286
Taber, Silas IV, 349
Taber, Silas IV, 353
Taber, Silas IV, 1188
Taber, Silas IV, 1201
Taber, Silas IV, 1221
Taber, Silas IV, 1224
Taber, Silas IV, 1225
Taber, Stephen III, 448
Taber, Susana W. IV, 1224
Taber, Susannah W. L. IV, 1225
Taber, Thomas III, 448
Taber, Thomas III, 454
Taber, Thomas IV, 1188
Taber, Thomas IV, 1224
Taber, Thomas Elwood IV, 1188
Taber, Thomas Elwood IV, 1225
Taber, Thos. V, 935
Taber, W. L. G. IV, 1225
Taber, Walter IV, 1224
Taber, William II, 425
Taber, William IV, 1188
Taber, William IV, 1224
Taber, William Battey III, 308
Taber, William C. III, 29
Taber, William Henry III, 308
Taber, William P. IV, 286
Taber, William P. IV, 446
Taber, William P., Jr. IV, 446
Taber, William R. I, 902
Taber, Wm. IV, 1224
Taber, Wm. IV, 1225
Taber, Wm. C III, 307
Taber, Wm. C. III, 106
Taber, Wm. C. III, 307
Taber, Wm. C. III, 308
Taber, Wm. Clarkson III, 308
Taber, Wm. Garretson IV, 1224
Taber, Wm. H. III, 448
Taber, Wm. Lloyd Garrison IV, 1225
Taber, Wm. P. IV, 255
Taber, Wm. P. IV, 286
Taber, Wm. P. IV, 423
Taber, Zeno C. IV, 1225
Taberer, ??? VI, 39
Taberer, Christian VI, 29
Taberer, Christian VI, 33
Taberer, Christian VI, 37
Taberer, Elizabeth VI, 33
Taberer, Elizabeth VI, 37
Taberer, Hugh VI, 37
Taberer, Justice ??? VI, 41
Taberer, Justiss VI, 37
Taberer, Major ??? VI, 24
Taberer, Margaret VI, 37
Taberer, Tho. VI, 37
Taberer, Thomas VI, 33
Taberer, Thomas VI, 37
Taberer, Thomas VI, 41
Tabitha, Rebecca V, 976
Table, Frances VI, 1001
Table, William F. VI, 1001
Tabler, Margaret I, 1121
Tabler, Margaret I, 1132
Tabor, Amanda Mahina IV, 1224
Tabor, Ann IV, 1224
Tabor, Anna IV, 1224
Tabor, Anna IV, 1225
Tabor, Anna R. IV, 446
Tabor, Benjamin IV, 1225
Tabor, Benjamin S. IV, 1224
Tabor, Betty IV, 1221
Tabor, Caroline III, 82
Tabor, Edna A. IV, 366
Tabor, Edna A. IV, 446
Tabor, Elizabeth II, 510
Tabor, Elizabeth II, 663
Tabor, Ervin I, 1162
Tabor, Eva A. III, 82
Tabor, Evelyn Alice III, 82
Tabor, Francis Bailey IV, 446
Tabor, George II, 927
Tabor, Helen IV, 446
Tabor, Hezekiah VI, 123
Tabor, Isaac IV, 1188
Tabor, Isaac V, 361
Tabor, James C. IV, 1224
Tabor, James C. IV, 1225
Tabor, Joseph J. IV, 446
Tabor, Joseph John H. IV, 446
Tabor, Joseph Paul IV, 446
Tabor, Keziah VI, 123
Tabor, Lewis IV, 286
Tabor, Lewis IV, 446
Tabor, Louis J. IV, 366
Tabor, Louis J. IV, 446
Tabor, Lysander O. IV, 1224
Tabor, Martha IV, 1208
Tabor, Martha IV, 1229
Tabor, Mary IV, 446
Tabor, Mary A. IV, 446
Tabor, Mary Ann IV, 446
Tabor, Mary Jane IV, 1219
Tabor, Mary Jane IV, 1224
Tabor, Mary P. IV, 446
Tabor, Mary R. IV, 1224
Tabor, May Alice I, 865
Tabor, Melvin Louis IV, 286
Tabor, Miriam IV, 1208
Tabor, Miriam IV, 1221
Tabor, Miriam IV, 1229
Tabor, Miriam Almina IV, 1224
Tabor, Mirium IV, 1224
Tabor, Nathan IV, 1219
Tabor, Nathan IV, 1224
Tabor, Ollie IV, 1225
Tabor, Phebe IV, 1225
Tabor, Phebe E. IV, 1224
Tabor, Phebe Ellen IV, 286
Tabor, Reuben IV, 1224
Tabor, Reuben IV, 1225
Tabor, Russell IV, 286
Tabor, Sarah IV, 446
Tabor, Sarah IV, 1188
Tabor, Sarah V, 361
Tabor, Sarah Ann IV, 1225
Tabor, Sarah D. IV, 446
Tabor, Sarah Matilda IV, 1224
Tabor, Selma L. II, 768
Tabor, Selma L. II, 769
Tabor, Selma Lizzie IV, 446
Tabor, Silas IV, 1224
Tabor, Silas IV, 1225
Tabor, Stephen III, 385
Tabor, Susana W. IV, 1224
Tabor, Thomas IV, 1208
Tabor, Thomas IV, 1224
Tabor, W. C. III, 82
Tabor, W. L. G. IV, 1225
Tabor, W. Worth IV, 1221
Tabor, William P. IV, 446
Tabor, William P., Jr. IV, 446
Taborer, Rachel VI, 338
Taborer, Rachel VI, 341
Taborn, Samuel IV, 1296
Tabour, Hezekiah VI, 123
Tace, Sadie V, 749
Tackler, James V, 1021
Tackler, Schuman G. V, 207
Tacy, Fanny VI, 873
Tadhunter, Milton V, 646
Tadlock, Aaron I, 120
Tadlock, Aaron I, 735
Tadlock, Ann I, 120
Tadlock, Chalkley I, 735
Tadlock, Deborough I, 120
Tadlock, Demsey I, 120
Tadlock, Edward I, 120
Tadlock, Elisabeth I, 120
Tadlock, Elisabeth I, 169
Tadlock, Elizabeth I, 331
Tadlock, Jesse I, 120
Tadlock, John I, 120
Tadlock, Joseph I, 120
Tadlock, Joshua I, 120
Tadlock, Joshua I, 331
Tadlock, Mary I, 120
Tadlock, Mary I, 710
Tadlock, Mary I, 735
Tadlock, Miles I, 120
Tadlock, Susannah I, 120
Tadlock, Thomas I, 200
Taffan, ??? III, 135
Taft, Elizabeth II, 425
Taft, Jane II, 425
Taft, Samuel II, 42
Tagart, John II, 663
Tagart, Mary II, 663
Tagart, Sarah Noble II, 663
Tage, Jane VI, 729
Tagg, Adrian III, 308
Tagg, Ann II, 822
Tagg, Ann II, 927
Tagg, Ann C. II, 784
Tagg, Ann C. II, 842
Tagg, Anna III, 237
Tagg, Anna III, 308
Tagg, Anna C. II, 927
Tagg, Bertha II, 927
Tagg, Eliza III, 308
Tagg, Eliza IV, 1381
Tagg, Geo. III, 308
Tagg, George II, 822
Tagg, George II, 927
Tagg, George III, 237
Tagg, George III, 308
Tagg, George IV, 1381
Tagg, George, Jr. III, 308
Tagg, Henry II, 842
Tagg, Henry II, 927
Tagg, John IV, 1381
Tagg, John M. III, 308
Tagg, John Turnpenny II, 822
Tagg, John Turnpenny II, 927
Tagg, Martha J. II, 842
Tagg, Martha J. II, 927
Tagg, Mary II, 927
Tagg, Mary III, 308
Tagg, Mary IV, 1381
Tagg, Susanna III, 308
Tagg, Susannah IV, 1381
Tagg, Tabitha III, 237
Tagg, Tabitha III, 308
Tagg, Tabitha Turnpenny II, 927
Tagg, Wilmot III, 308
Tagg, Wilmot IV, 1381
Taggart, Alice V, 714
Taggart, Asenath II, 822
Taggart, Calvin II, 822
Taggart, Calvin II, 838
Taggart, Calvin II, 927
Taggart, Edward B. II, 927
Taggart, Edward Betts II, 822
Taggart, John II, 42
Taggart, John II, 103
Taggart, John II, 663
Taggart, Jonathan II, 425
Taggart, Mary II, 608
Taggart, Mary II, 663
Taggart, Mary II, 838
Taggart, Mary II, 899
Taggart, Mary B. II, 838
Taggart, Mary B. II, 927
Taggart, Mary B. III, 33
Taggart, Mary Betts II, 783
Taggart, Mary E. II, 822
Taggart, Mary F. IV, 1340
Taggart, Nancy IV, 353
Taggart, Reuben II, 822
Taggart, Ruth IV, 1340
Taggart, Ruth E. IV, 1340
Taggart, Sarah K. II, 838
Taggart, Sarah K. II, 927
Taggart, Sarah Kirk II, 822
Taggart, Sarah Noble II, 663
Taggart, Wd. Asenath II, 822
Taggart, William H. II, 822
Taggart, Wm. W. II, 927
Taggert, Asenath II, 927
Taggert, Calvin II, 927
Taggert, Edward B. II, 927
Taggert, John II, 927
Taggert, Mary B. II, 927
Taggert, Nancy IV, 349
Taggert, Sarah K. II, 927
Taggert, William H. II, 822
Taggert, Wm. W. II, 927
Tahammont, John Johnson V, 1021
Tailer, George I, 91
Tailer, Moorning I, 169
Tailler, Elinor I, 91
Tailler, George I, 91
Taillor, Jonathan I, 91
Tailor, Mary I, 155
Tailor, Mary I, 169
Tailor, Mary II, 425
Tait, Charles H. VI, 815
Take, Mary V, 1021
Talbert, ??? V, 823
Talbert, Aaron V, 868
Talbert, Aaron V, 869
Talbert, Aaron V, 935
Talbert, Aaron S. V, 935
Talbert, Aaron V. V, 869
Talbert, Abby Ann II, 186
Talbert, Abraham Merrit II, 186
Talbert, Allen IV, 1188
Talbert, Amanda V, 826
Talbert, Amanda V, 862
Talbert, Amanda V, 863
Talbert, Amanda V, 868
Talbert, Amanda V, 869
Talbert, Anderson V, 869
Talbert, Anna V, 129
Talbert, Anna V, 869
Talbert, Anna Margaret II, 186
Talbert, Asa V, 865
Talbert, Asa V, 868
Talbert, Asa V, 869
Talbert, Asa V, 872
Talbert, Asa V, 875
Talbert, Asia V, 869
Talbert, Benjamin II, 186
Talbert, Benjamin B. II, 186
Talbert, Burgess Dewitt V, 869
Talbert, Caleb V, 869
Talbert, Catherine V, 869
Talbert, Charity I, 690
Talbert, Charity V, 869
Talbert, Charles II, 186
Talbert, Charles Clifford II, 186
Talbert, Charles S. II, 186
Talbert, Charles T. V, 869
Talbert, Chastine V, 869
Talbert, Clara V, 869
Talbert, Clara May V, 869
Talbert, Corwin V, 869
Talbert, David IV, 353
Talbert, David V, 935
Talbert, David L. V, 935
Talbert, Deborah II, 186
Talbert, Dorinda V, 869
Talbert, Durinda V, 869
Talbert, Earnest L. V, 869
Talbert, Edith V, 869
Talbert, Elijah V, 857
Talbert, Elijah V, 868
Talbert, Elijah V, 869
Talbert, Elizabeth V, 129
Talbert, Elizabeth V, 825
Talbert, Elizabeth V, 826
Talbert, Elizabeth V, 836
Talbert, Elizabeth V, 863
Talbert, Elizabeth V, 868
Talbert, Elizabeth V, 869
Talbert, Elizabeth Ann V, 869
Talbert, Elizabeth D. II, 186
Talbert, Elvira V, 868
Talbert, Elvira V, 869
Talbert, Elvira V, 875
Talbert, Emeline V, 846
Talbert, Emeline V, 868
Talbert, Emma V, 869
Talbert, Emmeline V, 869
Talbert, Enoch V, 868
Talbert, Enoch V, 869
Talbert, Enos V, 868
Talbert, Ervin M. V, 869
Talbert, Esther V, 841
Talbert, Esther V, 868
Talbert, Esther V, 869
Talbert, Eunice V, 868
Talbert, Eunice V, 869
Talbert, Flora Zella E. V, 869
Talbert, Florazelle V, 869
Talbert, George B. II, 186
Talbert, Grace II, 186
Talbert, Grace II, 266
Talbert, Helah V, 846
Talbert, Helah V, 868
Talbert, Helah V, 869
Talbert, Helen V, 827
Talbert, Isaac IV, 353
Talbert, Isaac V, 868
Talbert, Isaac V, 869
Talbert, Isaiah V, 868
Talbert, Isaiah V, 869
Talbert, Isiah V, 869
Talbert, J. IV, 491
Talbert, James II, 186
Talbert, Jesse V, 868
Talbert, Jesse V, 869
Talbert, Jesse, Jr. V, 869
Talbert, Job V, 129
Talbert, Job V, 826
Talbert, Job V, 862
Talbert, Job V, 863
Talbert, Job V, 868
Talbert, Job V, 869
Talbert, John V, 129
Talbert, John V, 868
Talbert, John V, 869
Talbert, John H. II, 186
Talbert, John R. IV, 1188
Talbert, Jonathan V, 868
Talbert, Jonathan V, 869
Talbert, Jonothan V, 129
Talbert, Joseph V, 868
Talbert, Joseph V, 869
Talbert, Joseph A. V, 869
Talbert, Joseph Brantingham II, 186
Talbert, Joseph W. II, 186
Talbert, Keziah V, 862
Talbert, Keziah V, 868
Talbert, Lee V, 869
Talbert, Lee R. V, 869
Talbert, Lindley V, 868
Talbert, Lindley V, 869
Talbert, Lydia V, 868
Talbert, Lydia V, 869
Talbert, Lydia Ellen V, 869
Talbert, Margaret I, 690
Talbert, Margaret I, 841
Talbert, Margaret V, 869
Talbert, Marianna II, 186
Talbert, Maris V, 868
Talbert, Maris V, 869
Talbert, Martha II, 186
Talbert, Mary I, 841
Talbert, Mary I, 998
Talbert, Mary IV, 353
Talbert, Mary IV, 491
Talbert, Mary IV, 1188
Talbert, Mary V, 129
Talbert, Mary V, 856
Talbert, Mary V, 863
Talbert, Mary V, 868
Talbert, Mary V, 869
Talbert, Mary Esther V, 869
Talbert, Mary Eveline V, 868
Talbert, Mary H. V, 857
Talbert, Mary H. V, 868
Talbert, Mary H. V, 869
Talbert, Mary S. V, 868
Talbert, Melissa J. V, 865
Talbert, Melissa Jane V, 868
Talbert, Melva E. V, 869
Talbert, Merriam V, 129
Talbert, Miriam I, 802
Talbert, Miriam I, 810
Talbert, Miriam I, 841
Talbert, Miriam V, 129
Talbert, Nathan V, 836
Talbert, Nathan V, 868
Talbert, Nathan V, 869
Talbert, Obadiah V, 868
Talbert, Obediah V, 869
Talbert, Paris V, 869
Talbert, Patience V, 869
Talbert, Phebe V, 72
Talbert, Phebe V, 129
Talbert, Rachel II, 266
Talbert, Rachel IV, 353
Talbert, Rachel V, 868
Talbert, Rachel V, 869
Talbert, Rahab I, 690
Talbert, Rahab V, 869
Talbert, Rebecca IV, 1188
Talbert, Rebecca V, 859
Talbert, Rebecca V, 868
Talbert, Rebecca V, 869
Talbert, Rebecca H. II, 186
Talbert, Rebekah V, 863
Talbert, Rhoda V, 868
Talbert, Rhoda V, 869
Talbert, Richard I, 841
Talbert, Richard V, 129
Talbert, Richard V, 868
Talbert, Richard V, 869
Talbert, Ruth V, 826
Talbert, Ruth V, 868
Talbert, Ruth V, 869
Talbert, Samuel V, 868
Talbert, Samuel V, 869
Talbert, Samuel V, 935
Talbert, Samuel VI, 449
Talbert, Samuel W. II, 186
Talbert, Sarah II, 186
Talbert, Sarah V, 834
Talbert, Sarah V, 865
Talbert, Sarah V, 868
Talbert, Sarah V, 869
Talbert, Sarah V, 872
Talbert, Sarah VI, 798
Talbert, Sarah Ann V, 831

rt, Sarah Ann V, 869
rt, Sarah Anna V, 869
rt, Sarah Ellen V, 868
rt, Sarah Ellen V, 869
rt, Sarah Jane V, 869
rt, Sarah M. IV, 1116
rt, Solomon V, 827
rt, Solomon V, 846
rt, Solomon V, 868
rt, Solomon V, 869
rt, Susanna V, 868
rt, Susannah V, 868
rt, Susannah VI, 454
rt, Sussana IV, 353
rt, Sylvanus V, 72
rt, Sylvanus V, 129
rt, Sylvanus V, 793
rt, Thomas II, 186
rt, Thomas V, 129
rt, Thomas V, 863
rt, Thomas V, 868
rt, Thomas V, 869
rt, Thomas K. II, 186
rt, Wd. Rebecca V, 836
rt, William I, 810
rt, William V, 129
rt, William V, 863
rt, William V, 868
rt, William V, 869
rt, William Bull I, 802
rt, William Bull I, 841
rt, Z. E. V, 869
rt, Zell E. V, 869
rt, Zimri V, 868
t, ??? I, 840
t, Abigail F. IV, 286
t, Addison VI, 804
t, Allen VI, 832
t, Allen VI, 857
t, Ann II, 663
t, Ann IV, 1071
t, Ann VI, 857
t, Anna IV, 1006
t, Anniee S. III, 500
t, Benjamin IV, 286
t, Benjamin I. IV, 659
t, Betsey VI, 801
t, Charles VI, 865
t, Charles VI, 1005
t, Charles M. VI, 857
t, David VI, 830
t, David B. IV, 553
t, David G. VI, 866
t, Edmund VI, 812
t, Elbert A. VI, 815
t, Elbert A. VI, 1001
t, Eliza VI, 815
t, Eliza Jane IV, 1070
t, Eliza Jane IV, 1078
t, Elizabeth I, 841
t, Elizabeth IV, 286
t, Elizabeth V, 869
t, Elizabeth VI, 1001
t, Emily IV, 287
t, Frances VI, 866
t, Haidee IV, 696
t, Haile VI, 1001
t, Hannah II, 663
t, Hannah T. IV, 479
t, Harry IV, 696
t, Hillery VI, 796
t, Hillery VI, 815
t, I. VI, 910
t, Isaham VI, 1001
t, Ish. VI, 906
t, Isham VI, 330
t, Isham VI, 332
t, Isham VI, 875
t, Isham VI, 885
t, Isham VI, 896
t, Isham VI, 962
t, Isham VI, 965
t, Isham VI, 984
t, Isham VI, 990
t, Isham VI, 1001
t, Isham VI, 1010
t, Isham VI, 1021
t, Jacob I, 969
t, Jacob I, 1012
t, Jacob I, 1162
t, James IV, 111
t, James VI, 935
t, Jane IV, 1071
t, Jane VI, 830
t, Jane VI, 857
t, Jesse I, 841
t, Joanoh VI, 804
t, John I, 576
t, John I, 773
t, John I, 841
t, John I, 847
Talbot, John I, 953
Talbot, John I, 969
Talbot, John I, 971
Talbot, John I, 1162
Talbot, John II, 663
Talbot, John IV, 111
Talbot, John IV, 286
Talbot, John IV, 553
Talbot, John IV, 1225
Talbot, John V, 129
Talbot, John V, 601
Talbot, John VI, 302
Talbot, John VI, 304
Talbot, John VI, 341
Talbot, John VI, 871
Talbot, John VI, 876
Talbot, John VI, 915
Talbot, John VI, 1001
Talbot, Jos. A. IV, 286
Talbot, Joseph IV, 61
Talbot, Joseph IV, 167
Talbot, Joseph IV, 1117
Talbot, Julia III, 500
Talbot, Kinsey IV, 479
Talbot, L. G. VI, 815
Talbot, Levicy VI, 818
Talbot, Lydia I, 1007
Talbot, Lydia I, 1008
Talbot, Lydia I, 1012
Talbot, Margaret I, 841
Talbot, Margaret IV, 286
Talbot, Maria S. VI, 1001
Talbot, Martha VI, 847
Talbot, Martha VI, 857
Talbot, Martha VI, 872
Talbot, Martha A. VI, 865
Talbot, Mary I, 773
Talbot, Mary I, 841
Talbot, Mary I, 1010
Talbot, Mary I, 1012
Talbot, Mary I, 1013
Talbot, Mary I, 1053
Talbot, Mary II, 663
Talbot, Mary IV, 61
Talbot, Mary IV, 286
Talbot, Mary IV, 696
Talbot, Mary V, 129
Talbot, Mary V, 601
Talbot, Mary VI, 876
Talbot, Mary VI, 1005
Talbot, Mary Ann IV, 286
Talbot, Mary J. I, 1162
Talbot, Mathew VI, 857
Talbot, Mathew VI, 876
Talbot, Matthew VI, 980
Talbot, May J. I, 1162
Talbot, Melvill VI, 865
Talbot, Melville H. VI, 1001
Talbot, Merritt VI, 815
Talbot, Mildred A. VI, 815
Talbot, Miriam I, 841
Talbot, Nancy I, 1162
Talbot, Nancy VI, 815
Talbot, Nancy VI, 836
Talbot, Nancy VI, 935
Talbot, Nathan IV, 286
Talbot, Paulina M. VI, 830
Talbot, Pleasant VI, 818
Talbot, Pleasant VI, 837
Talbot, Pleasant VI, 851
Talbot, Pleasent VI, 801
Talbot, Rachel IV, 553
Talbot, Rachel VI, 414
Talbot, Rebecca I, 1012
Talbot, Rebecca II, 425
Talbot, Rebecca II, 603
Talbot, Rebecca II, 663
Talbot, Richard I, 841
Talbot, Robert Delbert IV, 286
Talbot, Sally VI, 837
Talbot, Samuel I, 969
Talbot, Samuel IV, 111
Talbot, Samuel VI, 414
Talbot, Sarah I, 1012
Talbot, Sarah VI, 1001
Talbot, Sarah VI, 1021
Talbot, Sarah R. IV, 1079
Talbot, Susan VI, 513
Talbot, Susan VI, 812
Talbot, Susan C. VI, 1001
Talbot, Susanna I, 1012
Talbot, Susanna IV, 286
Talbot, Susannah I, 1001
Talbot, Susannah II, 797
Talbot, Sylvanus V, 129
Talbot, Thomas I, 841
Talbot, Thomas III, 500
Talbot, Thomas V, 869
Talbot, Walter R. VI, 458
Talbot, William I, 841
Talbot, William IV, 286
Talbot, William IV, 287
Talbot, William IV, 1071
Talbot, William Bull I, 841
Talbot, Williston VI, 801
Talbot, Williston VI, 818
Talbot, Williston VI, 837
Talbot, Williston VI, 857
Talbot, Williston VI, 1001
Talbott, Abigail IV, 201
Talbott, Abigail IV, 286
Talbott, Abigail IV, 472
Talbott, Abigail IV, 499
Talbott, Abigail F. IV, 286
Talbott, Abner IV, 1078
Talbott, Abner IV, 1079
Talbott, Adaline IV, 499
Talbott, Adaline IV, 500
Talbott, Adaline IV, 659
Talbott, Adaline IV, 660
Talbott, Addison IV, 286
Talbott, Addison M. IV, 498
Talbott, Adelbert R. IV, 1225
Talbott, Adeline IV, 659
Talbott, Alen IV, 499
Talbott, Allen IV, 110
Talbott, Allen IV, 111
Talbott, Allen IV, 160
Talbott, Allen IV, 498
Talbott, Allen IV, 499
Talbott, Allen IV, 1078
Talbott, Allen IV, 1079
Talbott, Allen IV, 1188
Talbott, Allen IV, 1203
Talbott, Allen IV, 1225
Talbott, Allen VI, 843
Talbott, Almon IV, 499
Talbott, Alvin, Jr. IV, 1225
Talbott, Ann II, 663
Talbott, Ann IV, 499
Talbott, Ann IV, 1078
Talbott, Ann IV, 1079
Talbott, Ann IV, 1082
Talbott, Ann VI, 374
Talbott, Ann VI, 541
Talbott, Ann VI, 558
Talbott, Ann VI, 569
Talbott, Ann VI, 570
Talbott, Ann VI, 761
Talbott, Ann VI, 785
Talbott, Ann E. V, 935
Talbott, Ann Eliza IV, 286
Talbott, Ann Eliza IV, 498
Talbott, Ann H. VI, 449
Talbott, Ann P. IV, 1078
Talbott, Anna IV, 978
Talbott, Anna IV, 1006
Talbott, Anna VI, 569
Talbott, Anna VI, 570
Talbott, Anna VI, 671
Talbott, Anna VI, 709
Talbott, Anna VI, 785
Talbott, Anna A. III, 309
Talbott, Anna A. IV, 286
Talbott, Anna A. IV, 287
Talbott, Anna A. IV, 1006
Talbott, Anna Alice III, 197
Talbott, Anna Alice IV, 1006
Talbott, Anna M. IV, 1006
Talbott, Anna R. IV, 287
Talbott, Benj. IV, 498
Talbott, Benj. T. IV, 497
Talbott, Benjamin IV, 61
Talbott, Benjamin IV, 71
Talbott, Benjamin IV, 111
Talbott, Benjamin IV, 286
Talbott, Benjamin IV, 471
Talbott, Benjamin IV, 498
Talbott, Benjamin IV, 659
Talbott, Benjamin IV, 1381
Talbott, Benjamin I. IV, 498
Talbott, Benjamin I. IV, 499
Talbott, Benjamin I. IV, 659
Talbott, Benjamin I. IV, 1381
Talbott, Benjamin T. IV, 498
Talbott, Beulah IV, 61
Talbott, Beulah IV, 111
Talbott, Beulah IV, 471
Talbott, Beulah IV, 498
Talbott, Caleb IV, 498
Talbott, Caleb IV, 499
Talbott, Caleb S. IV, 286
Talbott, Caroline IV, 286
Talbott, Caroline IV, 498
Talbott, Caroline E. IV, 286
Talbott, Caroline E. IV, 499
Talbott, Caroline E. IV, 1006
Talbott, Caroline E. IV, 1225
Talbott, Caroline K. IV, 1006
Talbott, Caroline Kinsey IV, 1225
Talbott, Casander IV, 499
Talbott, Cassandra IV, 463
Talbott, Cassandra IV, 498
Talbott, Chandler IV, 1381
Talbott, Charles E. IV, 286
Talbott, Charles Russel V, 935
Talbott, Chas. B. IV, 287
Talbott, Chas. R. V, 935
Talbott, David IV, 61
Talbott, David IV, 286
Talbott, David IV, 353
Talbott, David IV, 553
Talbott, David IV, 1116
Talbott, David V, 935
Talbott, David VI, 857
Talbott, David B. IV, 553
Talbott, David B. IV, 1381
Talbott, David L. V, 935
Talbott, Deborah IV, 286
Talbott, Deborah IV, 471
Talbott, Deborah IV, 498
Talbott, Deborah IV, 499
Talbott, Deborah A. IV, 499
Talbott, Deborah Ann IV, 498
Talbott, Deborah P. IV, 498
Talbott, Delbert IV, 1225
Talbott, Delbert R. IV, 1006
Talbott, Eli P. IV, 286
Talbott, Eli P. IV, 498
Talbott, Elihu H. IV, 1078
Talbott, Elijah IV, 498
Talbott, Elijah IV, 499
Talbott, Elisha IV, 498
Talbott, Elisha IV, 499
Talbott, Elisha IV, 1079
Talbott, Elisha VI, 569
Talbott, Elisha VI, 775
Talbott, Elisha VI, 785
Talbott, Elisha H. IV, 1078
Talbott, Elisha S. V, 935
Talbott, Elisha Saunders V, 935
Talbott, Elisha, Jr. VI, 785
Talbott, Eliza Jane IV, 499
Talbott, Eliza Jane IV, 1078
Talbott, Elizabeth IV, 110
Talbott, Elizabeth IV, 111
Talbott, Elizabeth IV, 160
Talbott, Elizabeth IV, 286
Talbott, Elizabeth IV, 472
Talbott, Elizabeth IV, 496
Talbott, Elizabeth IV, 498
Talbott, Elizabeth IV, 499
Talbott, Elizabeth IV, 1225
Talbott, Elizabeth VI, 558
Talbott, Elizabeth VI, 569
Talbott, Elizabeth VI, 570
Talbott, Elizabeth VI, 761
Talbott, Elizabeth VI, 785
Talbott, Elizabeth C. IV, 286
Talbott, Elizabeth C. IV, 499
Talbott, Emily IV, 287
Talbott, Emily B. IV, 286
Talbott, Emily B. IV, 846
Talbott, Emily B. IV, 1006
Talbott, Emma M. IV, 446
Talbott, Erving IV, 499
Talbott, Esther IV, 286
Talbott, Esther IV, 287
Talbott, Esther IV, 1006
Talbott, Esther IV, 1223
Talbott, Esther IV, 1225
Talbott, Esther Matilda IV, 499
Talbott, Esther S. IV, 1225
Talbott, Ethel IV, 287
Talbott, Findlay M. IV, 111
Talbott, Finley IV, 499
Talbott, Finley M. IV, 499
Talbott, Finly IV, 111
Talbott, George C. IV, 498
Talbott, Hannah II, 425
Talbott, Hannah IV, 111
Talbott, Hannah IV, 160
Talbott, Hannah IV, 286
Talbott, Hannah IV, 471
Talbott, Hannah IV, 499
Talbott, Hannah IV, 1071
Talbott, Hannah IV, 1078
Talbott, Hannah IV, 1079
Talbott, Hannah VI, 570
Talbott, Hannah Maria IV, 1188
Talbott, Hannah T. IV, 498
Talbott, Hannah, Jr. VI, 761
Talbott, Hannah, Jr. VI, 785
Talbott, Isaac IV, 353
Talbott, Isabella IV, 487
Talbott, Isabella IV, 498
Talbott, Jacob VI, 449
Talbott, James IV, 111
Talbott, James VI, 709
Talbott, Jane IV, 98
Talbott, Jane IV, 111
Talbott, Jane IV, 486
Talbott, Jane IV, 499
Talbott, Jesse VI, 761
Talbott, Jesse VI, 785
Talbott, Jesse T. VI, 570
Talbott, John II, 425
Talbott, John IV, 61
Talbott, John IV, 110
Talbott, John IV, 111
Talbott, John IV, 160
Talbott, John IV, 286
Talbott, John IV, 353
Talbott, John IV, 463
Talbott, John IV, 498
Talbott, John IV, 499
Talbott, John IV, 553
Talbott, John IV, 1078
Talbott, John IV, 1079
Talbott, John IV, 1225
Talbott, John IV, 1360
Talbott, John IV, 1381
Talbott, John V, 935
Talbott, John VI, 449
Talbott, John VI, 569
Talbott, John C. IV, 487
Talbott, John C. IV, 498
Talbott, John C. IV, 499
Talbott, John H. VI, 570
Talbott, John H. VI, 709
Talbott, John L. V, 935
Talbott, John R. IV, 499
Talbott, John R. IV, 1188
Talbott, John R. IV, 1225
Talbott, John Roberts IV, 1188
Talbott, John Samuel IV, 286
Talbott, John Saunders VI, 785
Talbott, John T. V, 935
Talbott, Jonathan IV, 1116
Talbott, Jos. IV, 472
Talbott, Jos. IV, 498
Talbott, Jos. VI, 502
Talbott, Jos. A. IV, 286
Talbott, Jos. F. IV, 473
Talbott, Joseph IV, 61
Talbott, Joseph IV, 110
Talbott, Joseph IV, 111
Talbott, Joseph IV, 160
Talbott, Joseph IV, 286
Talbott, Joseph IV, 287
Talbott, Joseph IV, 498
Talbott, Joseph IV, 499
Talbott, Joseph IV, 1006
Talbott, Joseph IV, 1071
Talbott, Joseph IV, 1078
Talbott, Joseph IV, 1079
Talbott, Joseph IV, 1116
Talbott, Joseph IV, 1117
Talbott, Joseph IV, 1188
Talbott, Joseph IV, 1225
Talbott, Joseph V, 935
Talbott, Joseph VI, 449
Talbott, Joseph VI, 505
Talbott, Joseph VI, 536
Talbott, Joseph VI, 541
Talbott, Joseph VI, 558
Talbott, Joseph VI, 569
Talbott, Joseph VI, 570
Talbott, Joseph VI, 576
Talbott, Joseph VI, 671
Talbott, Joseph VI, 688
Talbott, Joseph VI, 709
Talbott, Joseph VI, 761
Talbott, Joseph VI, 785
Talbott, Joseph A. IV, 286
Talbott, Joseph A. IV, 498
Talbott, Joseph A. IV, 499
Talbott, Joseph A. IV, 1006
Talbott, Joseph A. IV, 1223
Talbott, Joseph A. IV, 1225
Talbott, Joseph C. VI, 785
Talbott, Joseph E. IV, 286
Talbott, Joseph F. IV, 498
Talbott, Joseph F. IV, 1078
Talbott, Joseph F. IV, 1116
Talbott, Joseph M. IV, 499
Talbott, Joseph Talbott VI, 709
Talbott, Joseph W. IV, 499
Talbott, Joseph, Jr. VI, 569
Talbott, Joseph, Jr. VI, 570
Talbott, Kelly IV, 499
Talbott, Kinsey IV, 286
Talbott, Kinsey IV, 471
Talbott, Kinsey IV, 498
Talbott, Kinsey IV, 499
Talbott, Kinsey IV, 1006
Talbott, Kinsey IV, 1078
Talbott, Kinsey M. IV, 286
Talbott, Kinsey M. IV, 499
Talbott, Kinsey M. IV, 1006
Talbott, Kinsey M. IV, 1225
Talbott, Kinsey P. IV, 498
Talbott, Kinsey, Jr. IV, 498
Talbott, Kinsey, Jr. IV, 499

Talbott, Laura IV, 978
Talbott, Laura IV, 1006
Talbott, Laura A. IV, 1006
Talbott, Lewis IV, 1078
Talbott, Louis IV, 1079
Talbott, Lydia IV, 1116
Talbott, Lydia VI, 449
Talbott, M. Elizabeth IV, 287
Talbott, M. Elizabeth IV, 1006
Talbott, M. Kelley IV, 498
Talbott, Mahala IV, 467
Talbott, Mahala IV, 498
Talbott, Mahala IV, 499
Talbott, Margaret IV, 111
Talbott, Margaret IV, 286
Talbott, Margaret IV, 473
Talbott, Margaret IV, 498
Talbott, Margaret IV, 499
Talbott, Margaret IV, 1078
Talbott, Margaret IV, 1079
Talbott, Margaret IV, 1116
Talbott, Margaret Logan VI, 449
Talbott, Margret IV, 499
Talbott, Martha IV, 499
Talbott, Mary IV, 61
Talbott, Mary IV, 99
Talbott, Mary IV, 110
Talbott, Mary IV, 111
Talbott, Mary IV, 160
Talbott, Mary IV, 286
Talbott, Mary IV, 353
Talbott, Mary IV, 467
Talbott, Mary IV, 472
Talbott, Mary IV, 491
Talbott, Mary IV, 498
Talbott, Mary IV, 499
Talbott, Mary IV, 553
Talbott, Mary IV, 1116
Talbott, Mary IV, 1188
Talbott, Mary IV, 1203
Talbott, Mary IV, 1225
Talbott, Mary IV, 1379
Talbott, Mary IV, 1381
Talbott, Mary V, 935
Talbott, Mary VI, 449
Talbott, Mary VI, 541
Talbott, Mary VI, 569
Talbott, Mary VI, 570
Talbott, Mary Ann IV, 172
Talbott, Mary Ann IV, 286
Talbott, Mary Ann IV, 463
Talbott, Mary Ann IV, 498
Talbott, Mary Ann IV, 499
Talbott, Mary Ann IV, 1078
Talbott, Mary Ann IV, 1082
Talbott, Mary Ann VI, 785
Talbott, Mary C. IV, 1006
Talbott, Mary E. III, 197
Talbott, Mary E. III, 309
Talbott, Mary E. IV, 286
Talbott, Mary E. IV, 1006
Talbott, Mary Elizabeth IV, 286
Talbott, Mary Elizabeth IV, 498
Talbott, Mary Elizabeth IV, 1006
Talbott, Mary Elizabeth IV, 1225
Talbott, Mary F. IV, 498
Talbott, Mary F. IV, 1203
Talbott, Mary F. IV, 1225
Talbott, Mary Farquhar IV, 1188
Talbott, Mary J. IV, 499
Talbott, Mary Jane IV, 499
Talbott, Mary R. V, 935
Talbott, Mary S. IV, 206
Talbott, Mary S. IV, 286
Talbott, Mary S. IV, 553
Talbott, Mary S. IV, 1381
Talbott, Mary Samantha IV, 286
Talbott, Mary T. IV, 471
Talbott, Mary T. IV, 498
Talbott, Mary, Jr. IV, 499
Talbott, Matilda IV, 498
Talbott, Matilda IV, 499
Talbott, Matilda IV, 834
Talbott, Matilda IV, 846
Talbott, Matilda M. IV, 499
Talbott, Nancy VI, 857
Talbott, Nathan IV, 61
Talbott, Nathan IV, 111
Talbott, Nathan IV, 201
Talbott, Nathan IV, 286
Talbott, Nathan IV, 472
Talbott, Nathan IV, 498
Talbott, Nathan IV, 499
Talbott, Nathan V, 935
Talbott, Nathan VI, 449
Talbott, Phebe IV, 1078
Talbott, Phebe IV, 1079
Talbott, Phebe R. V, 935
Talbott, Precilla IV, 1381
Talbott, Priscilla IV, 497
Talbott, Priscilla IV, 498
Talbott, Priscilla IV, 499
Talbott, Priscilla IV, 1381
Talbott, Rachel IV, 61
Talbott, Rachel IV, 286
Talbott, Rachel IV, 353
Talbott, Rachel IV, 463
Talbott, Rachel IV, 498
Talbott, Rachel IV, 499
Talbott, Rachel IV, 553
Talbott, Rachel IV, 1360
Talbott, Rachel IV, 1381
Talbott, Rachel V, 935
Talbott, Rachel VI, 449
Talbott, Rachel VI, 569
Talbott, Rachel VI, 671
Talbott, Rachel VI, 709
Talbott, Rachel A. IV, 498
Talbott, Rachel Ann IV, 499
Talbott, Rebecca II, 425
Talbott, Rebecca IV, 61
Talbott, Rebecca IV, 286
Talbott, Rebecca IV, 476
Talbott, Rebecca IV, 479
Talbott, Rebecca IV, 499
Talbott, Rebecca IV, 1188
Talbott, Rebecca V, 935
Talbott, Rebecca VI, 449
Talbott, Rebecca VI, 558
Talbott, Rebecca VI, 576
Talbott, Rebecca VI, 785
Talbott, Rebecca L. IV, 498
Talbott, Rebecca W. V, 935
Talbott, Rebekah IV, 477
Talbott, Rebekah IV, 499
Talbott, Rebekah VI, 449
Talbott, Rebekah VI, 505
Talbott, Rebekah VI, 569
Talbott, Rebekah VI, 570
Talbott, Rebekah VI, 651
Talbott, Rebekah VI, 709
Talbott, Richard Litle VI, 785
Talbott, Robert IV, 111
Talbott, Robert IV, 160
Talbott, Robert IV, 498
Talbott, Robert IV, 499
Talbott, Robert IV, 834
Talbott, Robert IV, 846
Talbott, Robert Delbert IV, 286
Talbott, Ruth A. V, 935
Talbott, Sam'l C. V, 935
Talbott, Sameul VI, 709
Talbott, Samuel IV, 61
Talbott, Samuel IV, 99
Talbott, Samuel IV, 110
Talbott, Samuel IV, 111
Talbott, Samuel IV, 286
Talbott, Samuel V, 935
Talbott, Samuel VI, 449
Talbott, Samuel VI, 569
Talbott, Samuel VI, 570
Talbott, Samuel VI, 709
Talbott, Samuel, Jr. V, 935
Talbott, Sarah IV, 110
Talbott, Sarah IV, 111
Talbott, Sarah IV, 160
Talbott, Sarah IV, 498
Talbott, Sarah IV, 1006
Talbott, Sarah IV, 1071
Talbott, Sarah IV, 1078
Talbott, Sarah IV, 1079
Talbott, Sarah IV, 1188
Talbott, Sarah IV, 1225
Talbott, Sarah IV, 1381
Talbott, Sarah VI, 449
Talbott, Sarah VI, 558
Talbott, Sarah VI, 569
Talbott, Sarah VI, 570
Talbott, Sarah VI, 775
Talbott, Sarah VI, 785
Talbott, Sarah A. IV, 498
Talbott, Sarah A. IV, 1116
Talbott, Sarah Ann IV, 496
Talbott, Sarah Ann IV, 499
Talbott, Sarah E. IV, 287
Talbott, Sarah E. IV, 498
Talbott, Sarah E. IV, 1006
Talbott, Sarah Elizabeth V, 935
Talbott, Sarah Jane V, 935
Talbott, Sarah M. IV, 286
Talbott, Sarah M. IV, 1116
Talbott, Sarah R. IV, 1079
Talbott, Sarah R. IV, 1099
Talbott, Sarahann IV, 499
Talbott, Susan II, 803
Talbott, Susan IV, 498
Talbott, Susan VI, 365
Talbott, Susan VI, 520
Talbott, Susan VI, 570
Talbott, Susan VI, 576
Talbott, Susan VI, 659
Talbott, Susan VI, 717
Talbott, Susan T. VI, 582
Talbott, Susanna IV, 61
Talbott, Susanna IV, 111
Talbott, Susanna IV, 286
Talbott, Susanna IV, 353
Talbott, Susanna IV, 498
Talbott, Susanna IV, 553
Talbott, Susanna C. IV, 553
Talbott, Susannah IV, 286
Talbott, Susannah IV, 471
Talbott, Susannah IV, 498
Talbott, Susannah IV, 659
Talbott, Susannah IV, 1360
Talbott, Susannah IV, 1381
Talbott, Susannah VI, 449
Talbott, Susannah VI, 560
Talbott, Susannah VI, 568
Talbott, Susannah VI, 570
Talbott, Susannah VI, 576
Talbott, Susannah VI, 582
Talbott, Susannah C. IV, 553
Talbott, Susannah C. IV, 1381
Talbott, Sussana IV, 353
Talbott, Thomas IV, 499
Talbott, Thomas IV, 1225
Talbott, Thomas C. IV, 498
Talbott, Thomas C. IV, 499
Talbott, Thomas M. IV, 499
Talbott, Wallace Pierson V, 935
Talbott, Walter VI, 449
Talbott, Wd. Elizabeth B. VI, 785
Talbott, Wd. Rebekah VI, 570
Talbott, Widower Joseph VI, 651
Talbott, William IV, 110
Talbott, William IV, 111
Talbott, William IV, 160
Talbott, William IV, 286
Talbott, William IV, 287
Talbott, William IV, 498
Talbott, William IV, 500
Talbott, William IV, 659
Talbott, William IV, 660
Talbott, William IV, 1078
Talbott, William IV, 1381
Talbott, William A. IV, 499
Talbott, William A. IV, 1006
Talbott, William B. IV, 1381
Talbott, William J. IV, 286
Talbott, William J. IV, 498
Talbott, William M. IV, 286
Talbott, William M. IV, 499
Talbott, William W. VI, 785
Talbott, Wm. IV, 286
Talbott, Wm. IV, 499
Talbott, Wm. IV, 1079
Talbott, Wm. A. IV, 499
Talbott, Wm. A. IV, 1078
Talbott, Wm. A. IV, 1082
Talbott, Wm. A. IV, 1099
Talbott, Wm. A. IV, 1116
Talbott, Wm. H. V, 935
Talbott, Wm. K. IV, 286
Talbott, Wm. K. IV, 978
Talbott, Wm. M. III, 197
Talbott, Wm. M. III, 309
Talbott, Wm. M. IV, 1006
Talbott, Wm., Jr. IV, 1006
Talbott, Wm., Jr. IV, 1079
Talbut, John I, 969
Talbutt, Mary I, 422
Talcott, Daniel III, 309
Talcott, George III, 309
Talcott, Joseph III, 309
Talcott, Mary III, 309
Talcott, Mary III, 333
Talcott, Rebecca III, 309
Talcott, Richard III, 309
Talcott, Richard III, 333
Talcott, Sarah III, 309
Taler, Elizabeth VI, 916
Taler, John VI, 916
Taley, Sarah II, 192
Taley, Sarah II, 266
Talitha, Margaret VI, 240
Tallburt, ??? IV, 1085
Tallcot, M. Ida III, 328
Talle, Rogert VI, 810
Talleaferro, Roderick VI, 857
Talleaferro, Susannah VI, 857
Tallmage, Clementina III, 309
Tallman, ??? III, 141
Tallman, Charity III, 309
Tallman, Eliza III, 142
Tallman, Eliza III, 309
Tallman, Elizabeth III, 141
Tallman, Elizabeth III, 309
Tallman, Hannah III, 309
Tallman, J. IV, 1296
Tallman, James III, 309
Tallman, Mary III, 309
Tallman, Sam'l III, 309
Tallman, Samuel III, 309
Tallman, Sarah II, 266
Tally, Benoni Carter VI, 863
Tally, Betsy VI, 857
Tally, Carter VI, 857
Tally, Clabern VI, 857
Tally, Dashia VI, 802
Tally, David VI, 857
Tally, Edith Spencer I, 950
Tally, Patty VI, 857
Tally, Polly VI, 857
Tally, Ray I, 950
Talmadge, Clementina III, 309
Talmadge, Daniel III, 309
Talmadge, Daniel III, 332
Talmadge, Emeline III, 239
Talmadge, Hanna III, 309
Talmadge, Huston V, 656
Talmadge, Huston V, 714
Talmadge, Lena V, 656
Talmadge, Lena V, 714
Talmadge, Mary III, 309
Talmadge, Mary B. III, 309
Talmadge, Mary B. III, 332
Talman, ??? III, 381
Talman, ??? III, 385
Talman, Elizabeth II, 911
Talman, Elizabeth II, 927
Talman, Henry S. II, 911
Talman, Henry S. II, 927
Talman, James III, 309
Talman, Marion L. II, 1072
Talman, Marion L. II, 1081
Talman, Mary III, 309
Talman, Mary III, 381
Talman, Mary III, 385
Talman, Sarah II, 266
Talor, Ann VI, 606
Talor, Elisabeth I, 258
Talor, Israel VI, 606
Talor, James VI, 606
Talor, Jane VI, 606
Talor, Jesse VI, 606
Talor, Joel VI, 606
Talor, Jonathan VI, 606
Talor, Joseph VI, 606
Talor, Martin Fearnley VI, 606
Talor, Mary I, 998
Talor, Nancy VI, 915
Talor, Rebecca VI, 606
Talor, Sarah VI, 606
Talton, Christian I, 258
Talton, Christian P. I, 258
Talton, Christian P. I, 319
Talton, Christiana I, 258
Tamer, Rosa IV, 1265
Tampath, Branch VI, 857
Tampath, Elizabeth VI, 857
Tamplin, Agness VI, 1001
Tamplin, John VI, 1001
Tamplin, Mary IV, 1296
Tampset, Martha Ann V, 129
Tampset, Martha Ann V, 137
Tamson, ??? VI, 424
Tanguy, Alfred II, 822
Tanguy, Henry G. II, 927
Tanguy, Henry Gilpen II, 822
Tanguy, Mary A. II, 822
Tanguy, Mary A. II, 927
Tanguy, Ruthanna II, 822
Tanguy, Samuel L. II, 927
Tankersley, Ann VI, 974
Tankersley, Elizabeth VI, 974
Tankersley, George VI, 857
Tankersley, James VI, 898
Tankersley, James VI, 965
Tankersley, Mary VI, 965
Tankersley, Mary Jane VI, 1001
Tankersley, Permelia VI, 898
Tankersley, Polly VI, 857
Tankersley, Richard VI, 947
Tankersley, Richard VI, 1001
Tankersley, Winston VI, 880
Tankersly, Ann VI, 864
Tankersly, Winston W. VI, 1001
Tankesley, James VI, 948
Tankesly, Winston VI, 898
Tankiman, Isaac IV, 499
Tannar, Rebecca IV, 1265
Tannar, Rosa IV, 1265
Tanner, Arthur VI, 1001
Tanner, Benjamin VI, 796
Tanner, Benjamin VI, 809
Tanner, Benjamin VI, 810
Tanner, Benjamin VI, 836
Tanner, Benjamin VI, 858
Tanner, Benjamin VI, 993
Tanner, Betsy VI, 796
Tanner, Branch VI, 858
Tanner, Caleb VI, 1001
Tanner, Deborah IV, 147
Tanner, Deborah IV, 160
Tanner, Dolly VI, 849
Tanner, Edward William III,
Tanner, Edward Wm. III, 30
Tanner, Eliza I, 927
Tanner, Elizabeth VI, 858
Tanner, Elizabeth VI, 1001
Tanner, Elizabeth N. R. VI,
Tanner, Ellen III, 309
Tanner, Ellen E. III, 276
Tanner, Ellen E. III, 277
Tanner, Ellen E. III, 309
Tanner, Ellen Eliza III, 277
Tanner, Ellen Eliza III, 309
Tanner, Emma Louisa III, 3
Tanner, Frederick K. VI, 809
Tanner, James VI, 820
Tanner, James VI, 858
Tanner, Janes VI, 858
Tanner, Jemima VI, 858
Tanner, Joel VI, 858
Tanner, John II, 663
Tanner, John VI, 858
Tanner, John H. VI, 858
Tanner, Levicy VI, 809
Tanner, Leviney VI, 858
Tanner, Lucy VI, 858
Tanner, Lucy VI, 1001
Tanner, Lydia IV, 446
Tanner, Lydia IV, 1079
Tanner, Manuel VI, 1001
Tanner, Martha VI, 858
Tanner, Mary II, 663
Tanner, Mary VI, 836
Tanner, Mary VI, 858
Tanner, Mary Ann VI, 893
Tanner, Mary Benj. Randolph VI, 1001
Tanner, Mary J. VI, 858
Tanner, Minerva VI, 1001
Tanner, N. R. VI, 867
Tanner, Nancy VI, 820
Tanner, Nancy VI, 836
Tanner, Nancy VI, 858
Tanner, Nancy C. VI, 858
Tanner, Nathan VI, 796
Tanner, Nathan VI, 804
Tanner, Nathan VI, 809
Tanner, Nathan VI, 811
Tanner, Nathan VI, 820
Tanner, Nathan VI, 824
Tanner, Nathan VI, 829
Tanner, Nathan VI, 830
Tanner, Nathan VI, 836
Tanner, Nathan VI, 837
Tanner, Nathan VI, 841
Tanner, Nathan VI, 846
Tanner, Nathan VI, 847
Tanner, Nathan VI, 856
Tanner, Nathan VI, 858
Tanner, Nathan VI, 866
Tanner, Nathaniel VI, 809
Tanner, Nathaniel VI, 858
Tanner, Phebe VI, 836
Tanner, Phillip H. VI, 858
Tanner, Rachel VI, 503
Tanner, Rachel VI, 570
Tanner, Susanna VI, 836
Tanner, Susannah VI, 810
Tanner, Tilden IV, 1381
Tanner, Tildon IV, 1381
Tanner, Vincent VI, 858
Tanner, Vincent G. VI, 810
Tanner, William III, 309
Tanner, William IV, 499
Tanner, William VI, 858
Tanner, William J. III, 309
Tanner, Wm. Albert IV, 847
Tanner, Wm. J. III, 277
Tanner, Wm. J. III, 309
Tanner, Wm. Joseph, Jr. III,
Tanner, Wm., Jr. III, 309
Tanner, Woodson VI, 858
Tannon, Ola V, 207
Tanquary, Lydia VI, 395
Tanquary, Lydia VI, 449
Tanquery, Abigail VI, 427
Tanquery, Abigail VI, 449
Tanquery, Bulah VI, 428
Tanquery, Lydia VI, 449
Tanquery, Unice VI, 428
Tansey, Alexander I, 422
Tansey, Catharine I, 422
Tansey, Leah I, 422
Tansey, Leah I, 430
Tantardini, Antonia III, 254
Tanzey, Alexander I, 422
Tanzey, Alexander VI, 570
Tanzey, Alexander, Jr. I, 576
Tanzey, Alexander, Jr. VI, 57
Tanzey, Alexander, Sr. VI, 57

, Catharine I, 422
, Catharine VI, 570
, Catherine VI, 570
, Cathrine, Jr. VI, 570
y, Edward VI, 570
y, Mary VI, 580
y, Mary VI, 581
y, William I, 422
Alexander I, 422
Catharine I, 422
Charity I, 422
Leah I, 422
Martha I, 377
Martha I, 422
Martha Carson I, 422
William I, 422
Rebekah II, 663
y, Sarah I, 710
y, Sarah I, 735
n, ??? III, 135
n, Lydia III, 309
n, Mary III, 309
n, Shadrach III, 309
n, Susan III, 309
n, Theodore III, 309
en, Caroline III, 450
en, Caroline A. III, 448
en, Caroline R. III, 452
en, Isaac III, 448
en, Jeremiah III, 448
en, Jeremiah III, 450
en, John B. C. III, 448
en, John B. C. III, 450
en, Leonard III, 448
en, Lydia III, 500
en, Lydia III, 506
en, Mary III, 448
en, Mary III, 450
en, Mary Ann III, 448
en, Mary Ann III, 450
en, Phebe Ann III, 448
en, Philena III, 448
en, Susan III, 267
en, Theodore III, 267
en, Willet U. III, 448
in, Priscilla IV, 1176
in, Rhoda IV, 1176
in, Rhoda IV, 1188
in, Samuel IV, 1176
et, Delight Jane IV, 982
et, Nora IV, 982
et, Wm. IV, 982
orough, H. H. VI, 141
orough, H. N. VI, 132
orough, Hartwell H. VI, 142
y, Catharine L. VI, 1001
y, William H. VI, 1001
dy, Elisha VI, 872
dy, Jane VI, 858
dy, Paul J. VI, 1020
dy, Samuel VI, 858
dy, Samuel C. VI, 816
ent, Mary II, 425
ton, Christian P. I, 319
lton, Christian Pike I, 319
r, Hannah IV, 131
r, Hannah IV, 133
am, David IV, 774
e, Alice VI, 843
e, Amanda Jane VI, 1001
e, Ann I, 576
e, Ann VI, 709
e, Ann VI, 871
e, Caleb VI, 809
e, Caleb VI, 858
e, Caleb VI, 944
e, Caleb VI, 987
e, Caleb VI, 1008
e, Caleb VI, 1020
te, Caleb, Jr. VI, 966
te, Caleb, Jr. VI, 1000
te, Catharine VI, 903
te, Charlotte Q. VI, 1001
te, Edith VI, 449
te, Edith VI, 638
te, Edith VI, 679
te, Edith VI, 700
te, Edith VI, 709
te, Edith, Jr. VI, 709
te, Edmund VI, 811
te, Edmund VI, 823
te, Edmund VI, 843
te, Edmund VI, 987
te, Elizabeth VI, 449
te, Elizabeth VI, 709
ate, Elizabeth VI, 928
ate, Elizabeth VI, 1001
ate, Euphan VI, 987
ate, Fanny VI, 951
ate, Hannah II, 448
ate, Hannah III, 500
Tate, Hannah III, 507
Tate, Hannah VI, 543
Tate, Hannah VI, 570
Tate, Harriet C. VI, 823
Tate, Henry VI, 316
Tate, Henry VI, 796
Tate, Henry VI, 858
Tate, Henry VI, 871
Tate, Henry VI, 962
Tate, Henry VI, 987
Tate, Henry F. VI, 914
Tate, Henry F. VI, 1001
Tate, Henry T. VI, 923
Tate, James VI, 287
Tate, Jane VI, 923
Tate, Jesse VI, 316
Tate, Jesse VI, 709
Tate, Jesse VI, 796
Tate, Jesse VI, 871
Tate, Jesse VI, 928
Tate, Jesse VI, 1001
Tate, Jesse VI, 1010
Tate, Joan II, 448
Tate, John VI, 951
Tate, Levi VI, 449
Tate, Levi VI, 570
Tate, Levi VI, 638
Tate, Levi VI, 679
Tate, Levi VI, 700
Tate, Levi VI, 709
Tate, Louisa VI, 1001
Tate, Lucy VI, 979
Tate, Margaret VI, 1001
Tate, Martha VI, 570
Tate, Mary IV, 95
Tate, Mary IV, 111
Tate, Mary VI, 449
Tate, Mary VI, 570
Tate, Mary VI, 709
Tate, Mary O. VI, 1001
Tate, Matilda A. VI, 887
Tate, Milton VI, 887
Tate, Milton VI, 903
Tate, Mima VI, 1001
Tate, Nancy VI, 858
Tate, Nancy VI, 979
Tate, Nancy VI, 1001
Tate, Nathan VI, 843
Tate, Nathaniel VI, 903
Tate, Nathaniel VI, 1001
Tate, Obadiah VI, 887
Tate, Obadiah VI, 903
Tate, Obadiah VI, 922
Tate, Obadiah VI, 1001
Tate, Pamelia VI, 922
Tate, Patsey C. VI, 858
Tate, Polly VI, 1001
Tate, Polly Henry VI, 903
Tate, Pricilla VI, 638
Tate, Priscilla VI, 388
Tate, Priscilla VI, 449
Tate, Priscilla VI, 637
Tate, Priscilla VI, 709
Tate, Rachel II, 448
Tate, Rebecca E. V, 53
Tate, Rebecca E. V, 129
Tate, Rhoda VI, 1001
Tate, Robert II, 448
Tate, Ruth VI, 570
Tate, Sally VI, 871
Tate, Sally VI, 1001
Tate, Sally VI, 1010
Tate, Sally M. VI, 811
Tate, Samuel VI, 1001
Tate, Sarah IV, 133
Tate, Sarah VI, 316
Tate, Sarah VI, 667
Tate, Sarah VI, 700
Tate, Sarah VI, 709
Tate, Sarah VI, 714
Tate, Sarah VI, 888
Tate, Sarah H. VI, 796
Tate, Serena IV, 1265
Tate, Susanna VI, 709
Tate, Susanna VI, 1001
Tate, Susannah IV, 95
Tate, Susannah IV, 111
Tate, Tabitha VI, 888
Tate, William VI, 388
Tate, William VI, 449
Tate, William VI, 638
Tate, William VI, 709
Tate, William H. VI, 1001
Tate, William N. VI, 1001
Tate, William N. VI, 1016
Tate, Wm. VI, 570
Tate, Wm. VI, 637
Tate, Wm. J. VI, 1001
Tate, Zachariah VI, 1001
Tate, Zachariah G. VI, 969
Tatem, Amy V, 935
Tatem, David II, 828
Tatem, Eleanor V, 935
Tatem, Elizabeth V, 935
Tatem, Elizabeth P. II, 1061
Tatem, Hephsebah II, 828
Tatem, Martha II, 828
Tatem, Mary III, 124
Tatem, Mary C. V, 935
Tatem, Rachel II, 588
Tatem, Rachel II, 663
Tatem, Rachel V, 935
Tatem, Ruth III, 254
Tatem, Ruth III, 309
Tatem, Samuel III, 124
Tatem, Samuel V, 935
Tatem, Samuel C., Jr. V, 935
Tatem, Susanna II, 588
Tatem, Wm. II, 588
Tatham, Anne II, 663
Tatham, Benj., Jr. III, 309
Tatham, Benjamin, Jr. III, 81
Tatham, Benjamin, Jr. III, 309
Tatham, Charles III, 309
Tatham, Edwin III, 309
Tatham, Fanny III, 309
Tatham, Francis III, 309
Tatham, Hannah H. III, 309
Tatham, James II, 663
Tatham, James III, 309
Tatham, John II, 663
Tatham, Mary II, 663
Tatham, Mary III, 309
Tatham, Rachel II, 663
Tatham, Rebecca III, 81
Tatham, Rebecca III, 309
Tatham, Sarah II, 663
Tatham, Susanna II, 663
Tatham, William III, 309
Tatham, Wm. II, 663
Tatlock, Aaron I, 75
Tatlock, Aaron I, 168
Tatlock, Aaron I, 200
Tatlock, Absalom I, 168
Tatlock, Absalom I, 200
Tatlock, Ann I, 75
Tatlock, Ann I, 200
Tatlock, Anna I, 168
Tatlock, Benjamin I, 187
Tatlock, Benjamin I, 200
Tatlock, Chalkley I, 187
Tatlock, Chalkley I, 200
Tatlock, Chalkley I, 735
Tatlock, Deborah I, 168
Tatlock, Deborough I, 75
Tatlock, Deborough I, 189
Tatlock, Deborough I, 200
Tatlock, Demcy I, 200
Tatlock, Dempsey I, 75
Tatlock, Demsey I, 168
Tatlock, Edward I, 75
Tatlock, Edward I, 168
Tatlock, Edward I, 169
Tatlock, Edward I, 180
Tatlock, Edward I, 186
Tatlock, Edward I, 200
Tatlock, Elisabeth I, 140
Tatlock, Elisabeth I, 143
Tatlock, Elisabeth I, 168
Tatlock, Elisabeth I, 169
Tatlock, Elisabeth I, 188
Tatlock, Elisabeth I, 200
Tatlock, Elizabeth I, 169
Tatlock, Gemima I, 141
Tatlock, Gemima I, 168
Tatlock, James I, 75
Tatlock, James I, 120
Tatlock, James I, 168
Tatlock, James I, 169
Tatlock, Jemima I, 168
Tatlock, Jesse I, 75
Tatlock, Jesse I, 143
Tatlock, Jesse I, 168
Tatlock, Jesse I, 200
Tatlock, John I, 75
Tatlock, John I, 120
Tatlock, John I, 127
Tatlock, John I, 168
Tatlock, John I, 169
Tatlock, Joseph I, 75
Tatlock, Joseph I, 168
Tatlock, Joshua I, 75
Tatlock, Joshua I, 168
Tatlock, Joshua I, 169
Tatlock, Joshua I, 200
Tatlock, Kezia I, 127
Tatlock, Kezia I, 168
Tatlock, Kezia I, 176
Tatlock, Keziah I, 120
Tatlock, Keziah I, 168
Tatlock, Mary I, 75
Tatlock, Mary I, 120
Tatlock, Mary I, 168
Tatlock, Mary I, 169
Tatlock, Mary I, 200
Tatlock, Melicent I, 195
Tatlock, Melicent I, 200
Tatlock, Miles I, 75
Tatlock, Miles I, 168
Tatlock, Miles I, 200
Tatlock, Milisin I, 120
Tatlock, Mourning I, 187
Tatlock, Mourning I, 200
Tatlock, Pegga I, 120
Tatlock, Peggy I, 168
Tatlock, Penina I, 120
Tatlock, Pininah I, 200
Tatlock, Pinnah I, 193
Tatlock, Sarah I, 168
Tatlock, Susanna I, 75
Tatlock, Susanna I, 168
Tatlock, Susanna I, 180
Tatlock, Susanna I, 200
Tatlock, Susannah I, 155
Tatlock, Susannah I, 168
Tatlock, Susannah I, 169
Tatlock, Susannah I, 186
Tatlock, Susannah I, 197
Tatlock, Susannah I, 200
Tatlock, Thomas I, 120
Tatlock, Thomas I, 200
Tatnall, Ann II, 425
Tatnall, Ann II, 663
Tatnall, Ashton R. IV, 499
Tatnall, Dorothy II, 425
Tatnall, Edward II, 1056
Tatnall, Edward II, 1061
Tatnall, Margery II, 1056
Tatnall, Margery II, 1061
Tatnall, Mary R. II, 700
Tatnall, Rachel II, 1056
Tatnall, Rachel II, 1061
Tatnall, Thomas II, 425
Tatnall, Thomas II, 663
Tatnall, Wm. II, 1056
Tatnall, Wm. II, 1061
Tatnel, Rachel II, 1061
Tatnell, Ann II, 425
Tatnell, Thomas II, 425
Tatom, Elizabeth VI, 821
Tatum, ??? I, 27
Tatum, ??? IV, 1303
Tatum, Allen II, 103
Tatum, Amy V, 935
Tatum, Anna III, 309
Tatum, Anna P. II, 970
Tatum, Anna P. II, 1061
Tatum, Anne II, 465
Tatum, Anne II, 663
Tatum, Beulah II, 51
Tatum, Beulah II, 103
Tatum, Beulah IV, 446
Tatum, Beulah IV, 757
Tatum, Beulah IV, 772
Tatum, Beulah IV, 774
Tatum, Beulah IV, 932
Tatum, Beulah IV, 964
Tatum, Beulah IV, 1005
Tatum, Beulah IV, 1006
Tatum, Charles III, 309
Tatum, Charles Albert III, 309
Tatum, David III, 309
Tatum, David IV, 774
Tatum, David IV, 933
Tatum, David IV, 1006
Tatum, David IV, 1340
Tatum, David S. III, 279
Tatum, David S. III, 309
Tatum, Edward III, 80
Tatum, Edward III, 81
Tatum, Edward III, 308
Tatum, Edward III, 309
Tatum, Edward, Jr. III, 309
Tatum, Eleanor V, 935
Tatum, Elizabeth II, 51
Tatum, Elizabeth II, 103
Tatum, Elizabeth II, 970
Tatum, Elizabeth II, 1058
Tatum, Elizabeth II, 1061
Tatum, Elizabeth III, 309
Tatum, Elizabeth IV, 932
Tatum, Elizabeth IV, 1006
Tatum, Elizabeth V, 935
Tatum, Elizabeth C. II, 927
Tatum, Elizabeth L. IV, 480
Tatum, Elizabeth L. IV, 499
Tatum, Elizabeth P. II, 1061
Tatum, Geo. IV, 999
Tatum, Geo. M. IV, 480
Tatum, Geo. M. IV, 499
Tatum, George II, 51
Tatum, George II, 103
Tatum, George IV, 287
Tatum, George IV, 446
Tatum, George IV, 595
Tatum, George IV, 757
Tatum, George IV, 932
Tatum, George IV, 964
Tatum, George IV, 1005
Tatum, George IV, 1006
Tatum, George IV, 1016
Tatum, George, Jr. IV, 396
Tatum, George, Jr. IV, 446
Tatum, George, Jr. IV, 1006
Tatum, Hannah IV, 287
Tatum, Hannah IV, 396
Tatum, Hannah IV, 446
Tatum, Hannah IV, 595
Tatum, Hannah IV, 933
Tatum, Hannah IV, 1006
Tatum, Hannah IV, 1016
Tatum, Hannah IV, 1340
Tatum, Hannah B. IV, 774
Tatum, Hannah B. IV, 1006
Tatum, Hannah L. III, 309
Tatum, Harry IV, 774
Tatum, Isaac IV, 1006
Tatum, Jane IV, 774
Tatum, Jennie F. I, 27
Tatum, John II, 51
Tatum, John II, 103
Tatum, John II, 465
Tatum, John II, 663
Tatum, John VI, 1001
Tatum, John R. II, 970
Tatum, John R. II, 1058
Tatum, John R. II, 1061
Tatum, John W. II, 970
Tatum, John W. II, 1058
Tatum, John W. II, 1061
Tatum, John W., Jr. II, 970
Tatum, John W., Jr. II, 1061
Tatum, Josiah III, 309
Tatum, Laura IV, 1006
Tatum, Laurie IV, 1006
Tatum, Lawrence IV, 1006
Tatum, Lawrence W. IV, 774
Tatum, Lawrie IV, 811
Tatum, Lawrie IV, 847
Tatum, Lucy II, 970
Tatum, Lucy R. II, 1058
Tatum, Lucy R. II, 1061
Tatum, Lucy R., Jr. II, 970
Tatum, Lucy Richardson II, 1047
Tatum, Lydia IV, 999
Tatum, Lydia IV, 1006
Tatum, Lydia IV, 1016
Tatum, Maria II, 785
Tatum, Martha M. IV, 705
Tatum, Martha M. IV, 774
Tatum, Mary III, 80
Tatum, Mary III, 296
Tatum, Mary III, 309
Tatum, Mary Ann IV, 847
Tatum, Mary C. V, 935
Tatum, Mary Taber III, 81
Tatum, Mary Taber III, 309
Tatum, Maryann IV, 811
Tatum, Patience III, 309
Tatum, Patience III, 352
Tatum, Rachel II, 717
Tatum, Rachel III, 309
Tatum, Rachel V, 935
Tatum, Rebecca IV, 222
Tatum, Rebecca IV, 287
Tatum, Rebecca IV, 964
Tatum, Rebecca IV, 1006
Tatum, Ruth III, 309
Tatum, Samuel III, 296
Tatum, Samuel III, 309
Tatum, Samuel III, 352
Tatum, Samuel V, 935
Tatum, Samuel C. V, 935
Tatum, Samuel C., Jr. V, 935
Tatum, Sarah II, 465
Tatum, Sarah II, 663
Tatum, Sarah II, 812
Tatum, Sarah III, 171
Tatum, Sarah IV, 986
Tatum, Sarah IV, 999
Tatum, Sarah IV, 1006
Tatum, Sarah IV, 1223
Tatum, Sarah IV, 1224
Tatum, Sarah IV, 1225
Tatum, Sarah M. IV, 499
Tatum, Sebyl IV, 1006
Tatum, Sibyl IV, 772
Tatum, Sibyl IV, 774
Tatum, Sibyl IV, 1005
Tatum, Sibyl IV, 1006
Tatum, Susannah VI, 1001
Tatum, Viola III, 279
Tatum, Viola III, 309
Tatum, Wm. E. III, 309

Tatum, Wm. R. IV, 499
Taube, Emil II, 822
Taube, Sarah II, 822
Taube, Sarah S. II, 927
Tauntum, Benjamin T. III, 309
Tavener, Miriam VI, 449
Tavener, Tabitha VI, 553
Tavener, Tabitha VI, 570
Tavenner, Ann VI, 647
Tavenner, Ann VI, 709
Tavenner, Elizabeth VI, 522
Tavenner, Elizabeth VI, 664
Tavenner, Elizabeth VI, 709
Tavenner, Jonah VI, 522
Tavenner, Miriam VI, 640
Tavenner, Miriam VI, 709
Tavenner, Phebe VI, 689
Tavenner, Phebe VI, 709
Tavenner, Pleasant VI, 692
Tavenner, Pleasant VI, 709
Tavenner, Rebecca VI, 710
Tavenner, Rebecca M. VI, 683
Tavenner, Rebecca M. VI, 709
Tavenner, Sarah VI, 674
Tavenner, Sarah VI, 710
Tavenner, Stacy Janney VI, 691
Tawner, Emma IV, 287
Tawner, George IV, 287
Tawner, Grace IV, 287
Tawner, Henry IV, 287
Tawner, Lurenda IV, 287
Tawner, Nellie IV, 287
Tawner, William IV, 287
Tawner, Wm. J. B. IV, 287
Tayler, Elizabeth II, 586
Tayler, Elizabeth II, 664
Taylor, ??? II, 822
Taylor, ??? III, 309
Taylor, ??? III, 310
Taylor, ??? III, 347
Taylor, ??? V, 129
Taylor, ??? V, 965
Taylor, Aaron V, 870
Taylor, Abby Ann II, 295
Taylor, Abby Ann II, 303
Taylor, Abby B. II, 124
Taylor, Abby B. II, 293
Taylor, Abby B. II, 303
Taylor, Abert V, 433
Taylor, Abiah, Jr. II, 664
Taylor, Abigail I, 200
Taylor, Abigail I, 203
Taylor, Abigail II, 42
Taylor, Abigail II, 200
Taylor, Abigail II, 267
Taylor, Abigail II, 326
Taylor, Abigail II, 425
Taylor, Abigail II, 634
Taylor, Abigail II, 664
Taylor, Abigail V, 870
Taylor, Abigail V, 871
Taylor, Abigail V, 873
Taylor, Abigail C. V. II, 928
Taylor, Abigail Canby II, 822
Taylor, Abijah IV, 61
Taylor, Abijah V, 129
Taylor, Abijah V, 130
Taylor, Abijah V, 977
Taylor, Abijah V, 979
Taylor, Abijah VI, 450
Taylor, Abijah VI, 462
Taylor, Abner II, 266
Taylor, Abraham II, 1062
Taylor, Abraham V, 938
Taylor, Abraham VI, 450
Taylor, Abraham M. II, 279
Taylor, Abraham M. II, 303
Taylor, Abraham M. II, 304
Taylor, Abraham M. V, 931
Taylor, Abraham M. V, 938
Taylor, Abraham Merritt II, 304
Taylor, Abraham Warner II, 1081
Taylor, Abram VI, 449
Taylor, Abram M. II, 186
Taylor, Abram M. V, 938
Taylor, Adam VI, 1002
Taylor, Adin IV, 1225
Taylor, Agnes V, 870
Taylor, Agnes L. V, 871
Taylor, Albert Henry VI, 1002
Taylor, Alexander VI, 881
Taylor, Alfred B. II, 928
Taylor, Alice II, 314
Taylor, Alice III, 337
Taylor, Alice IV, 1225
Taylor, Alice M. IV, 1030
Taylor, Alice S. III, 310
Taylor, Alice W. II, 326
Taylor, Alida French III, 309
Taylor, Allen VI, 450
Taylor, Allen D. IV, 596
Taylor, Allsup VI, 1001
Taylor, Almeda V, 361
Taylor, Almoria IV, 774
Taylor, Alonzo A. V, 870
Taylor, Alpheus V, 870
Taylor, Alpheus V, 871
Taylor, Alsup VI, 987
Taylor, Alva May II, 785
Taylor, Alvan V, 870
Taylor, Alvin V, 870
Taylor, Alvin V, 871
Taylor, Amanda II, 720
Taylor, Amanda A. II, 770
Taylor, Amanda Jackson VI, 956
Taylor, Ambrose IV, 61
Taylor, Ambrose V, 130
Taylor, Ambrose V, 977
Taylor, Ambrose VI, 408
Taylor, Ambrose VI, 449
Taylor, Ambrose VI, 450
Taylor, Amos II, 425
Taylor, Amos II, 720
Taylor, Amos II, 816
Taylor, Amos II, 1032
Taylor, Amos IV, 659
Taylor, Amos IV, 774
Taylor, Amos V, 870
Taylor, Amos V, 871
Taylor, Amos V, 938
Taylor, Amos Moore II, 425
Taylor, Amy VI, 408
Taylor, Amy VI, 449
Taylor, Amy VI, 571
Taylor, Angelina V, 835
Taylor, Angelina V, 870
Taylor, Angelina D. V, 871
Taylor, Angelina P. IV, 595
Taylor, Angelina P. IV, 596
Taylor, Angelina T. V, 844
Taylor, Angelina T. V, 871
Taylor, Angeline V, 870
Taylor, Angeline V, 871
Taylor, Anita III, 309
Taylor, Anita W. III, 310
Taylor, Ann I, 543
Taylor, Ann I, 576
Taylor, Ann I, 1024
Taylor, Ann I, 1038
Taylor, Ann I, 1103
Taylor, Ann II, 267
Taylor, Ann II, 448
Taylor, Ann II, 970
Taylor, Ann II, 971
Taylor, Ann II, 978
Taylor, Ann II, 987
Taylor, Ann II, 1008
Taylor, Ann II, 1025
Taylor, Ann II, 1031
Taylor, Ann II, 1032
Taylor, Ann II, 1061
Taylor, Ann II, 1081
Taylor, Ann III, 500
Taylor, Ann IV, 62
Taylor, Ann IV, 111
Taylor, Ann IV, 160
Taylor, Ann IV, 287
Taylor, Ann IV, 295
Taylor, Ann IV, 447
Taylor, Ann IV, 457
Taylor, Ann IV, 1027
Taylor, Ann IV, 1030
Taylor, Ann IV, 1031
Taylor, Ann V, 533
Taylor, Ann V, 938
Taylor, Ann V, 973
Taylor, Ann V, 977
Taylor, Ann V, 979
Taylor, Ann VI, 123
Taylor, Ann VI, 376
Taylor, Ann VI, 403
Taylor, Ann VI, 449
Taylor, Ann VI, 450
Taylor, Ann VI, 494
Taylor, Ann VI, 530
Taylor, Ann VI, 550
Taylor, Ann VI, 563
Taylor, Ann VI, 567
Taylor, Ann VI, 571
Taylor, Ann VI, 572
Taylor, Ann VI, 606
Taylor, Ann VI, 697
Taylor, Ann VI, 710
Taylor, Ann VI, 711
Taylor, Ann VI, 713
Taylor, Ann Amanda VI, 713
Taylor, Ann Eliza II, 822
Taylor, Ann Eliza II, 928
Taylor, Ann Eliza V, 533
Taylor, Ann R. II, 256
Taylor, Ann R. II, 267
Taylor, Ann, Jr. II, 1061
Taylor, Anna I, 227
Taylor, Anna II, 186
Taylor, Anna II, 266
Taylor, Anna II, 705
Taylor, Anna II, 719
Taylor, Anna II, 842
Taylor, Anna II, 1005
Taylor, Anna II, 1031
Taylor, Anna II, 1032
Taylor, Anna II, 1051
Taylor, Anna II, 1061
Taylor, Anna IV, 353
Taylor, Anna IV, 987
Taylor, Anna IV, 1006
Taylor, Anna IV, 1007
Taylor, Anna V, 130
Taylor, Anna V, 900
Taylor, Anna V, 938
Taylor, Anna B. V, 870
Taylor, Anna B. V, 871
Taylor, Anna D. II, 928
Taylor, Anna D. II, 941
Taylor, Anna E. II, 842
Taylor, Anna E. II, 880
Taylor, Anna E. II, 887
Taylor, Anna E. II, 928
Taylor, Anna Haines V, 938
Taylor, Anna M. II, 297
Taylor, Anna M. II, 304
Taylor, Anna M. II, 928
Taylor, Anna M. V, 913
Taylor, Anna M. V, 938
Taylor, Anna Maria VI, 713
Taylor, Anna S. II, 718
Taylor, Anna S. II, 720
Taylor, Anna S. II, 765
Taylor, Anna S. II, 770
Taylor, Anna T. II, 291
Taylor, Anna T. II, 303
Taylor, Anna W. II, 928
Taylor, Anne II, 664
Taylor, Anne II, 971
Taylor, Anne II, 1062
Taylor, Anne IV, 987
Taylor, Anne IV, 1007
Taylor, Anne IV, 1027
Taylor, Annie IV, 287
Taylor, Annie B. II, 304
Taylor, Annie B. II, 971
Taylor, Annie B. II, 1062
Taylor, Annie Dewees II, 822
Taylor, Annie Gertrude II, 822
Taylor, Annie Gertrude II, 841
Taylor, Annie Gertrude II, 928
Taylor, Annie K. II, 928
Taylor, Anthony II, 120
Taylor, Anthony II, 124
Taylor, Anthony II, 267
Taylor, Anthony II, 293
Taylor, Anthony II, 303
Taylor, Anthony II, 425
Taylor, Anthony II, 448
Taylor, Anthony II, 664
Taylor, Anthony II, 728
Taylor, Anthony II, 770
Taylor, Anthony V, 889
Taylor, Anthony VI, 1002
Taylor, Anthony N. II, 267
Taylor, Anthony N. II, 303
Taylor, Anthony Newbold II, 425
Taylor, Anthony, Jr. II, 664
Taylor, Archibald VI, 858
Taylor, Arthur Kirkbride VI, 712
Taylor, Arthur Kirkbride VI, 713
Taylor, Asa VI, 858
Taylor, Asher II, 266
Taylor, Athony VI, 1002
Taylor, Banner II, 1002
Taylor, Banner II, 1031
Taylor, Banner II, 1032
Taylor, Barnard II, 971
Taylor, Barnard II, 1008
Taylor, Barnard II, 1031
Taylor, Barnard, Jr. VI, 454
Taylor, Barshaba VI, 898
Taylor, Belle V, 870
Taylor, Benjamin II, 200
Taylor, Benjamin II, 208
Taylor, Benjamin II, 267
Taylor, Benjamin II, 295
Taylor, Benjamin II, 297
Taylor, Benjamin II, 303
Taylor, Benjamin II, 304
Taylor, Benjamin II, 664
Taylor, Benjamin II, 970
Taylor, Benjamin II, 971
Taylor, Benjamin II, 978
Taylor, Benjamin II, 982
Taylor, Benjamin II, 986
Taylor, Benjamin II, 987
Taylor, Benjamin II, 1003
Taylor, Benjamin II, 1008
Taylor, Benjamin II, 1012
Taylor, Benjamin II, 1031
Taylor, Benjamin II, 1032
Taylor, Benjamin II, 1033
Taylor, Benjamin II, 1035
Taylor, Benjamin II, 1037
Taylor, Benjamin II, 1042
Taylor, Benjamin II, 1046
Taylor, Benjamin II, 1061
Taylor, Benjamin IV, 25
Taylor, Benjamin IV, 45
Taylor, Benjamin IV, 62
Taylor, Benjamin IV, 652
Taylor, Benjamin IV, 1269
Taylor, Benjamin V, 977
Taylor, Benjamin VI, 444
Taylor, Benjamin VI, 450
Taylor, Benjamin VI, 570
Taylor, Benjamin VI, 858
Taylor, Benjamin F. VI, 710
Taylor, Benjamin F. VI, 713
Taylor, Benjamin H. II, 304
Taylor, Benjamin H. II, 971
Taylor, Benjamin H. II, 1062
Taylor, Benjamin S. IV, 1296
Taylor, Benjamin, Jr. II, 1031
Taylor, Benjamin, Jr. II, 1061
Taylor, Bernard II, 970
Taylor, Bernard II, 978
Taylor, Bernard II, 1031
Taylor, Bernard II, 1032
Taylor, Bernard VI, 450
Taylor, Bernard VI, 472
Taylor, Bernard VI, 475
Taylor, Bernard VI, 517
Taylor, Bernard VI, 563
Taylor, Bernard VI, 571
Taylor, Bernard VI, 572
Taylor, Bernard VI, 619
Taylor, Bernard VI, 622
Taylor, Bernard VI, 624
Taylor, Bernard VI, 662
Taylor, Bernard VI, 671
Taylor, Bernard VI, 705
Taylor, Bernard VI, 710
Taylor, Bernard VI, 711
Taylor, Bernard VI, 712
Taylor, Bernard VI, 713
Taylor, Bernard VI, 714
Taylor, Bernard VI, 717
Taylor, Bernard Fenelon VI, 712
Taylor, Bernard, Jr. VI, 450
Taylor, Bernard, Jr. VI, 708
Taylor, Bernard, Jr. VI, 710
Taylor, Bernard, Jr. VI, 713
Taylor, Bernard, Jr. VI, 714
Taylor, Bernard, Jr. VI, 717
Taylor, Bertha II, 970
Taylor, Betsey VI, 1002
Taylor, Betsy VI, 928
Taylor, Betsy A. VI, 858
Taylor, Bettie IV, 287
Taylor, Betty I, 227
Taylor, Beulah V, 870
Taylor, Beulah V, 887
Taylor, Beulah V, 888
Taylor, Beulah Ann V, 864
Taylor, Beulah Ann V, 870
Taylor, Beulah W. V, 871
Taylor, Blanche Barker IV, 1340
Taylor, Calbe VI, 537
Taylor, Caleb II, 425
Taylor, Caleb II, 664
Taylor, Caleb II, 688
Taylor, Caleb V, 938
Taylor, Caleb VI, 480
Taylor, Caleb VI, 545
Taylor, Caleb VI, 572
Taylor, Caleb VI, 587
Taylor, Caleb M. II, 822
Taylor, Caleb M. II, 928
Taylor, Caleb M. III, 310
Taylor, Caleb W. V, 870
Taylor, Caleb W. V, 871
Taylor, Caleb W. V, 902
Taylor, Caleb W. V, 913
Taylor, Caleb W. V, 931
Taylor, Caleb W. V, 938
Taylor, Calvin H. V, 871
Taylor, Calvin W. V, 871
Taylor, Carl V, 534
Taylor, Caroline II, 316
Taylor, Caroline II, 326
Taylor, Caroline III, 106
Taylor, Caroline III, 309
Taylor, Caroline III, 310
Taylor, Caroline V, 938
Taylor, Caroline VI, 712
Taylor, Caroline VI, 714
Taylor, Caroline B. II, 326
Taylor, Carrie A. IV, 1296
Taylor, Carrie A. V, 870
Taylor, Carrie A. V, 871
Taylor, Catharine II, 208
Taylor, Catharine II, 267
Taylor, Catharine II, 664
Taylor, Catherine II, 664
Taylor, Cathrine II, 613
Taylor, Cathrine II, 664
Taylor, Cecelia H. VI, 621
Taylor, Cecelia H. VI, 627
Taylor, Cecelia H. VI, 710
Taylor, Cecelia H. VI, 712
Taylor, Charity Cornelia II
Taylor, Charles II, 303
Taylor, Charles II, 970
Taylor, Charles II, 1005
Taylor, Charles II, 1031
Taylor, Charles II, 1032
Taylor, Charles A. V, 870
Taylor, Charles A. V, 871
Taylor, Charles Clifford II,
Taylor, Charles E. V, 714
Taylor, Charles Emmot V,
Taylor, Charles M. II, 822
Taylor, Charles M. II, 928
Taylor, Charles M. IV, 447
Taylor, Charles S. I, 934
Taylor, Charles S. II, 303
Taylor, Charles S. II, 304
Taylor, Charles S. V, 938
Taylor, Charles Shoemaker II, 304
Taylor, Charles W. II, 769
Taylor, Charles W. II, 770
Taylor, Charles Yardley VI,
Taylor, Charles Yardley VI,
Taylor, Charlotte VI, 623
Taylor, Charlotte VI, 651
Taylor, Charlotte VI, 710
Taylor, Charlotte H. II, 852
Taylor, Charlotte H. II, 928
Taylor, Chas. H. V, 938
Taylor, Chas. J. II, 822
Taylor, Chas. M. II, 842
Taylor, Chas. M. II, 880
Taylor, Chas. M. II, 887
Taylor, Chas. M. II, 928
Taylor, Chas. M. V, 938
Taylor, Chas. M., Jr. II, 887
Taylor, Chas. M., Jr. II, 928
Taylor, Chas. Mause II, 822
Taylor, Chesley VI, 819
Taylor, Chloe Douglas V, 71
Taylor, Christopher I, 227
Taylor, Christopher I, 252
Taylor, Christopher I, 258
Taylor, Christopher II, 479
Taylor, Christopher II, 664
Taylor, Christopher IV, 170
Taylor, Christopher IV, 287
Taylor, Christopher IV, 446
Taylor, Christopher VI, 123
Taylor, Christopher A. V, 93
Taylor, Cinthy Ann IV, 659
Taylor, Clara IV, 287
Taylor, Clara Bell V, 870
Taylor, Clara Bell V, 871
Taylor, Clarence M. II, 782
Taylor, Clayton II, 266
Taylor, Clayton II, 425
Taylor, Clayton V, 870
Taylor, Clayton V, 871
Taylor, Clifford D. V, 714
Taylor, Cornelia II, 303
Taylor, Cornelia II, 314
Taylor, Cornelia II, 326
Taylor, Cornelia S. II, 303
Taylor, Cornelius VI, 123
Taylor, Crispen II, 928
Taylor, Crispen II, 933
Taylor, Crispin II, 822
Taylor, Curtis II, 664
Taylor, Cyrus II, 970
Taylor, Daniel I, 227
Taylor, Daniel II, 266
Taylor, Daniel IV, 287
Taylor, Daniel G. IV, 596
Taylor, Daniel H. VI, 710
Taylor, Daniel W. VI, 710
Taylor, David I, 75
Taylor, David II, 970
Taylor, David II, 971
Taylor, David II, 1031
Taylor, David IV, 774
Taylor, David IV, 924
Taylor, David IV, 1010
Taylor, David V, 533
Taylor, David V, 864
Taylor, David V, 870
Taylor, David VI, 858

, David VI, 1002
, David B. II, 1032
, David B. II, 1061
, David Barton II, 802
, David Barton II, 806
, David Barton II, 1032
, David Walton V, 870
, Deborah II, 970
, Deborah II, 971
, Deborah II, 988
, Deborah II, 1020
, Deborah II, 1031
, Deborah II, 1032
, Deborah IV, 606
, Deborah IV, 659
, Deborah V, 514
, Deborah V, 533
, Deborah V, 534
, Deborah E. V, 488
, Deborah E. V, 533
, Deborah E. V, 534
, Delila VI, 979
, Diana I, 576
, Dianah VI, 898
, Dillon IV, 287
, Dora I, 615
, Dorcas I, 8
, Dorcas I, 18
, Doshia VI, 1002
, Dr. Franklin II, 822
, Dr. Wm. H. V, 938
, Drusilla Anna IV, 1006
, Dynisia VI, 1002
, E. Lewis II, 928
, Ed. Lawrence II, 425
, Edgar J. III, 309
, Edgar J. III, 351
, Edgar J. III, 466
, Edgar Jefferson III, 448
, Edgar Jefferson III, 466
, Edith VI, 390
, Edith VI, 450
, Edith S. II, 928
, Edith S. IV, 447
, Edith S. IV, 1030
, Edith S. V, 938
, Edith Sterling II, 822
r, Edmond VI, 1002
r, Edmund VI, 848
r, Edmund VI, 858
r, Edmund VI, 956
r, Edward II, 303
r, Edward II, 1062
r, Edward III, 310
r, Edward V, 938
r, Edward VI, 848
r, Edward VI, 866
r, Edward VI, 1002
r, Edward Allison II, 304
, Edward B. II, 970
r, Edward B. II, 1060
r, Edward B. II, 1062
r, Edward Lawrence II, 664
r, Edward Stabler VI, 710
r, Edward Stabler VI, 713
r, Edward W. VI, 710
r, Edwd VI, 995
r, Edwin IV, 1381
r, Edwin C. IV, 1381
, Elbina L. IV, 596
r, Elbina S. IV, 595
r, Eleneor I, 1024
r, Eli VI, 891
, Eliner VI, 898
, Elisabeth I, 169
r, Elisabeth I, 258
r, Elisabeth II, 664
r, Elisabeth Peninah I, 230
r, Elisabeth Peninah I, 258
r, Elisha V, 433
r, Elisha B. VI, 1002
r, Eliz. N. III, 89
r, Eliz. N. III, 274
r, Eliza II, 186
r, Eliza II, 304
r, Eliza II, 425
r, Eliza II, 928
r, Eliza II, 1032
r, Eliza II, 1061
r, Eliza IV, 62
r, Eliza IV, 287
r, Eliza Ann IV, 943
r, Eliza Ann IV, 1006
r, Eliza Ann IV, 1007
r, Eliza Arabella I, 18
r, Eliza Edna I, 902
r, Eliza Henry II, 266
r, Eliza J. I, 75
r, Eliza Jane I, 8
r, Eliza Jane I, 75
r, Eliza V. VI, 1002
Taylor, Eliza W. II, 971
Taylor, Eliza W. II, 990
Taylor, Eliza W. II, 1032
Taylor, Eliza W. II, 1061
Taylor, Elizabeth I, 227
Taylor, Elizabeth I, 252
Taylor, Elizabeth I, 258
Taylor, Elizabeth I, 1024
Taylor, Elizabeth II, 303
Taylor, Elizabeth II, 425
Taylor, Elizabeth II, 484
Taylor, Elizabeth II, 586
Taylor, Elizabeth II, 613
Taylor, Elizabeth II, 638
Taylor, Elizabeth II, 664
Taylor, Elizabeth II, 802
Taylor, Elizabeth II, 970
Taylor, Elizabeth II, 986
Taylor, Elizabeth II, 1002
Taylor, Elizabeth II, 1003
Taylor, Elizabeth II, 1009
Taylor, Elizabeth II, 1031
Taylor, Elizabeth II, 1032
Taylor, Elizabeth II, 1035
Taylor, Elizabeth II, 1061
Taylor, Elizabeth II, 1073
Taylor, Elizabeth II, 1077
Taylor, Elizabeth II, 1081
Taylor, Elizabeth III, 150
Taylor, Elizabeth III, 309
Taylor, Elizabeth III, 310
Taylor, Elizabeth IV, 25
Taylor, Elizabeth IV, 45
Taylor, Elizabeth IV, 62
Taylor, Elizabeth IV, 170
Taylor, Elizabeth IV, 263
Taylor, Elizabeth IV, 287
Taylor, Elizabeth IV, 353
Taylor, Elizabeth IV, 446
Taylor, Elizabeth IV, 595
Taylor, Elizabeth IV, 596
Taylor, Elizabeth IV, 652
Taylor, Elizabeth IV, 924
Taylor, Elizabeth IV, 1006
Taylor, Elizabeth IV, 1007
Taylor, Elizabeth IV, 1010
Taylor, Elizabeth IV, 1050
Taylor, Elizabeth V, 533
Taylor, Elizabeth V, 544
Taylor, Elizabeth V, 837
Taylor, Elizabeth V, 870
Taylor, Elizabeth V, 938
Taylor, Elizabeth V, 943
Taylor, Elizabeth VI, 123
Taylor, Elizabeth VI, 373
Taylor, Elizabeth VI, 449
Taylor, Elizabeth VI, 450
Taylor, Elizabeth VI, 572
Taylor, Elizabeth VI, 618
Taylor, Elizabeth VI, 621
Taylor, Elizabeth VI, 622
Taylor, Elizabeth VI, 623
Taylor, Elizabeth VI, 626
Taylor, Elizabeth VI, 655
Taylor, Elizabeth VI, 696
Taylor, Elizabeth VI, 703
Taylor, Elizabeth VI, 710
Taylor, Elizabeth VI, 714
Taylor, Elizabeth VI, 833
Taylor, Elizabeth VI, 858
Taylor, Elizabeth VI, 860
Taylor, Elizabeth VI, 916
Taylor, Elizabeth VI, 1002
Taylor, Elizabeth A. II, 314
Taylor, Elizabeth A. II, 326
Taylor, Elizabeth C. II, 186
Taylor, Elizabeth C. II, 294
Taylor, Elizabeth C. II, 301
Taylor, Elizabeth C. II, 304
Taylor, Elizabeth C. V, 931
Taylor, Elizabeth C. V, 938
Taylor, Elizabeth J. II, 303
Taylor, Elizabeth K. II, 1061
Taylor, Elizabeth L. II, 720
Taylor, Elizabeth L. V, 902
Taylor, Elizabeth L. V, 938
Taylor, Elizabeth M. II, 720
Taylor, Elizabeth M. II, 770
Taylor, Elizabeth Neal II, 787
Taylor, Elizabeth R. II, 279
Taylor, Elizabeth R. II, 304
Taylor, Elizabeth R. V, 938
Taylor, Elizabeth S. I, 258
Taylor, Elizabeth S. II, 769
Taylor, Elizabeth S. II, 770
Taylor, Elizabeth T. II, 928
Taylor, Elizabeth T. II, 1081
Taylor, Ella M. II, 887
Taylor, Ella M. II, 928
Taylor, Ellen II, 965
Taylor, Ellen M. II, 966
Taylor, Elma IV, 130
Taylor, Elma IV, 133
Taylor, Elmira IV, 62
Taylor, Elvira VI, 1001
Taylor, Elvira VI, 1018
Taylor, Elwood III, 309
Taylor, Ely VI, 1002
Taylor, Emelia L. III, 347
Taylor, Emelie III, 357
Taylor, Emelina F. VI, 802
Taylor, Emily II, 880
Taylor, Emily II, 928
Taylor, Emily IV, 944
Taylor, Emily IV, 1007
Taylor, Emily V, 533
Taylor, Emily V, 534
Taylor, Emily V, 646
Taylor, Emily VI, 624
Taylor, Emily Alice VI, 621
Taylor, Emily Alice VI, 710
Taylor, Emily Alice VI, 712
Taylor, Emily J. III, 310
Taylor, Emily R. IV, 944
Taylor, Emma II, 303
Taylor, Emma VI, 713
Taylor, Emma Alderson II, 301
Taylor, Emma Alderson II, 304
Taylor, Emma Alderson V, 938
Taylor, Emma D. VI, 637
Taylor, Emma D. VI, 740
Taylor, Emma Dutton VI, 710
Taylor, Emma Dutton VI, 711
Taylor, Emma Dutton VI, 713
Taylor, Emma E. VI, 768
Taylor, Emma L. VI, 712
Taylor, Emma P. V, 870
Taylor, Emmaretta V, 871
Taylor, Enoch II, 425
Taylor, Enoch II, 664
Taylor, Enoch II, 720
Taylor, Enoch V, 870
Taylor, Enoch R. V, 870
Taylor, Enoch R. V, 871
Taylor, Ephrath II, 425
Taylor, Estella Helen IV, 1340
Taylor, Estelle III, 337
Taylor, Estelle IV, 1241
Taylor, Estelle IV, 1340
Taylor, Estelle V. III, 309
Taylor, Esther II, 425
Taylor, Esther II, 816
Taylor, Esther IV, 636
Taylor, Esther IV, 659
Taylor, Esther Ann V, 29
Taylor, Esther Ann V, 130
Taylor, Esther E. II, 303
Taylor, Esther E. II, 304
Taylor, Esther Elizabeth II, 186
Taylor, Eunice IV, 943
Taylor, Evan VI, 571
Taylor, Evan P. VI, 727
Taylor, Evan P. VI, 785
Taylor, F. IV, 741
Taylor, F. R. I, 950
Taylor, Fannie C. VI, 645
Taylor, Fannie C. VI, 687
Taylor, Fannie C. VI, 710
Taylor, Fannie C. VI, 711
Taylor, Fanny IV, 774
Taylor, Fanny IV, 780
Taylor, Fanny IV, 1030
Taylor, Fanny IV, 1031
Taylor, Fanny V, 960
Taylor, Fanny VI, 857
Taylor, Fanny VI, 858
Taylor, Fanny VI, 1002
Taylor, Flora Ellen V, 870
Taylor, Florence Estelle III, 309
Taylor, Flushing III, 310
Taylor, Frances I, 343
Taylor, Frances I, 423
Taylor, Frances II, 1032
Taylor, Frances V, 39
Taylor, Frances V, 130
Taylor, Frances V, 977
Taylor, Frances VI, 450
Taylor, Frances VI, 687
Taylor, Frances VI, 712
Taylor, Frances VI, 1002
Taylor, Frances Ann VI, 710
Taylor, Frances, Jr. V, 977
Taylor, Francis II, 326
Taylor, Francis V, 130
Taylor, Francis J. III, 500
Taylor, Frank V, 466
Taylor, Frank V, 870
Taylor, Frank H. V, 938
Taylor, Frank H. V, 939
Taylor, Fred W. II, 880
Taylor, Fred W. II, 928
Taylor, Frederick II, 928
Taylor, Frederick Harvey I, 950
Taylor, Frederick Raymond I, 934
Taylor, Frederick Raymond I, 950
Taylor, Frederick Raymond II, 304
Taylor, Frederick Walter II, 822
Taylor, Garrett IV, 1006
Taylor, Garrott VI, 826
Taylor, Geo. V, 392
Taylor, Geo. R. V, 938
Taylor, George V, 714
Taylor, George V, 837
Taylor, George VI, 273
Taylor, George VI, 287
Taylor, George VI, 858
Taylor, George VI, 862
Taylor, George VI, 1002
Taylor, George A. Hance II, 1081
Taylor, George Clarence III, 309
Taylor, George Clarence III, 337
Taylor, George Dean V, 938
Taylor, George E. II, 303
Taylor, George Edwin III, 500
Taylor, George Herbert II, 186
Taylor, George Herbert II, 304
Taylor, George J. II, 928
Taylor, George Jones II, 822
Taylor, George R. IV, 447
Taylor, George R. V, 938
Taylor, George W. II, 303
Taylor, George W. II, 664
Taylor, George W. II, 769
Taylor, George W. II, 770
Taylor, George W. III, 385
Taylor, George W. VI, 911
Taylor, George W. VI, 982
Taylor, George W. VI, 1002
Taylor, George W., Jr. II, 720
Taylor, Gerald Kirkbride II, 304
Taylor, Gertrude II, 279
Taylor, Gertrude II, 304
Taylor, Gilbert I, 576
Taylor, Gooing VI, 123
Taylor, Grace III, 500
Taylor, Grace IV, 1030
Taylor, Grace VI, 546
Taylor, Grace Anna IV, 774
Taylor, Grace Anna IV, 1029
Taylor, Grace Anna IV, 1030
Taylor, Granville S. II, 314
Taylor, Greenberry VI, 1002
Taylor, Greenbury VI, 916
Taylor, Gretchen Arnold I, 618
Taylor, Griffith IV, 62
Taylor, Gulielma V, 129
Taylor, Gulielma V, 130
Taylor, Gulielma V, 977
Taylor, Gulielma VI, 450
Taylor, H. Agnes II, 782
Taylor, Hannah II, 116
Taylor, Hannah II, 124
Taylor, Hannah II, 186
Taylor, Hannah II, 266
Taylor, Hannah II, 267
Taylor, Hannah II, 425
Taylor, Hannah II, 448
Taylor, Hannah II, 597
Taylor, Hannah II, 664
Taylor, Hannah II, 782
Taylor, Hannah II, 970
Taylor, Hannah II, 971
Taylor, Hannah II, 983
Taylor, Hannah II, 996
Taylor, Hannah II, 1012
Taylor, Hannah II, 1025
Taylor, Hannah II, 1031
Taylor, Hannah II, 1032
Taylor, Hannah II, 1033
Taylor, Hannah II, 1037
Taylor, Hannah II, 1083
Taylor, Hannah III, 309
Taylor, Hannah IV, 62
Taylor, Hannah IV, 636
Taylor, Hannah IV, 659
Taylor, Hannah IV, 774
Taylor, Hannah IV, 1006
Taylor, Hannah IV, 1007
Taylor, Hannah V, 22
Taylor, Hannah V, 32
Taylor, Hannah V, 130
Taylor, Hannah V, 473
Taylor, Hannah V, 474
Taylor, Hannah V, 533
Taylor, Hannah V, 544
Taylor, Hannah V, 601
Taylor, Hannah V, 646
Taylor, Hannah V, 840
Taylor, Hannah V, 870
Taylor, Hannah V, 871
Taylor, Hannah V, 938
Taylor, Hannah VI, 475
Taylor, Hannah VI, 572
Taylor, Hannah VI, 587
Taylor, Hannah VI, 622
Taylor, Hannah VI, 639
Taylor, Hannah VI, 646
Taylor, Hannah VI, 691
Taylor, Hannah VI, 692
Taylor, Hannah VI, 710
Taylor, Hannah VI, 712
Taylor, Hannah VI, 713
Taylor, Hannah VI, 714
Taylor, Hannah Ann VI, 711
Taylor, Hannah B. II, 1062
Taylor, Hannah B. VI, 708
Taylor, Hannah B. VI, 712
Taylor, Hannah B. VI, 780
Taylor, Hannah Brown VI, 708
Taylor, Hannah Brown VI, 711
Taylor, Hannah D. V, 931
Taylor, Hannah D. V, 938
Taylor, Hannah Davis V, 938
Taylor, Hannah J. V, 870
Taylor, Hannah J. V, 871
Taylor, Hannah J. VI, 450
Taylor, Hannah J. VI, 637
Taylor, Hannah J. VI, 710
Taylor, Hannah Janney VI, 475
Taylor, Hannah Janney VI, 622
Taylor, Hannah Janney VI, 641
Taylor, Hannah Janney VI, 652
Taylor, Hannah Janney VI, 653
Taylor, Hannah Janney VI, 689
Taylor, Hannah Janney VI, 711
Taylor, Hannah Janney VI, 713
Taylor, Hannah L. V, 479
Taylor, Hannah L. V, 533
Taylor, Hannah L. V, 534
Taylor, Hannah Maria V, 938
Taylor, Hannah N. V, 533
Taylor, Hannah S. II, 288
Taylor, Hannah S. II, 303
Taylor, Hannah, Jr. II, 1031
Taylor, Hannay VI, 626
Taylor, Hanney VI, 668
Taylor, Hariett A. VI, 472
Taylor, Hariett A. VI, 510
Taylor, Harriet II, 42
Taylor, Harriet III, 347
Taylor, Harriet V, 871
Taylor, Harriet V, 937
Taylor, Harriet V, 938
Taylor, Harriet VI, 858
Taylor, Harriet A. III, 299
Taylor, Harriet A. VI, 506
Taylor, Harriet A. VI, 566
Taylor, Harriet A. VI, 567
Taylor, Harriet A. VI, 568
Taylor, Harriet Eliza V, 870
Taylor, Harriett V, 938
Taylor, Harriett VI, 571
Taylor, Harriett A. VI, 571
Taylor, Harriett A. VI, 576
Taylor, Harvey P. VI, 1002
Taylor, Helen M. A. V, 939
Taylor, Helen Mary V, 938
Taylor, Henrietta VI, 641
Taylor, Henrietta VI, 711
Taylor, Henrietta Jay VI, 711
Taylor, Henrietta Jay VI, 716
Taylor, Henry II, 266
Taylor, Henry III, 310
Taylor, Henry V, 870
Taylor, Henry VI, 450
Taylor, Henry VI, 494
Taylor, Henry VI, 530
Taylor, Henry VI, 567
Taylor, Henry VI, 571
Taylor, Henry VI, 572
Taylor, Henry VI, 700
Taylor, Henry VI, 1002
Taylor, Henry B. II, 1061
Taylor, Henry B. VI, 686
Taylor, Henry B. VI, 708
Taylor, Henry B. VI, 711
Taylor, Henry B. VI, 713
Taylor, Henry B. VI, 716
Taylor, Henry Clayton VI, 713
Taylor, Henry L. V, 870
Taylor, Henry L. V, 871
Taylor, Henry M. III, 310
Taylor, Henry M. VI, 711
Taylor, Henry Madison VI, 645
Taylor, Henry Madison VI, 677
Taylor, Henry Madison VI, 687
Taylor, Henry Madison VI, 695
Taylor, Henry Madison VI, 711
Taylor, Henry Madison VI, 712
Taylor, Henry Madison VI, 713
Taylor, Henry S. VI, 637
Taylor, Henry S. VI, 710
Taylor, Henry Smith VI, 475

Taylor, Henry Smith VI, 587
Taylor, Henry Smith VI, 622
Taylor, Henry Smith VI, 641
Taylor, Henry Smith VI, 652
Taylor, Henry Smith VI, 653
Taylor, Henry Smith VI, 689
Taylor, Henry Smith VI, 710
Taylor, Henry Smith VI, 711
Taylor, Henry Smith VI, 713
Taylor, Herbert K. II, 928
Taylor, Hester I, 518
Taylor, Hezekiah I, 576
Taylor, Hezekiah VI, 858
Taylor, Howard IV, 1030
Taylor, Hudson B. II, 303
Taylor, Hudson B. II, 304
Taylor, Ida IV, 847
Taylor, Ida V, 870
Taylor, Ida A. I, 75
Taylor, Ida Arabella I, 75
Taylor, Ida M. II, 928
Taylor, Inez IV, 1265
Taylor, Ira S. V, 870
Taylor, Ira S. V, 871
Taylor, Irmgard II, 720
Taylor, Isaac I, 423
Taylor, Isaac I, 1024
Taylor, Isaac I, 1038
Taylor, Isaac II, 60
Taylor, Isaac II, 103
Taylor, Isaac II, 303
Taylor, Isaac II, 425
Taylor, Isaac II, 664
Taylor, Isaac III, 106
Taylor, Isaac III, 309
Taylor, Isaac III, 310
Taylor, Isaac IV, 287
Taylor, Isaac IV, 774
Taylor, Isaac IV, 1006
Taylor, Isaac IV, 1007
Taylor, Isaac V, 533
Taylor, Isaac V, 869
Taylor, Isaac V, 870
Taylor, Isaac V, 977
Taylor, Isaac VI, 449
Taylor, Isaac VI, 450
Taylor, Isaac VI, 495
Taylor, Isaac Jesse IV, 1006
Taylor, Isaac L. V, 870
Taylor, Isaac L. V, 871
Taylor, Isaac Lindley V, 870
Taylor, Isaac P. II, 769
Taylor, Israel II, 664
Taylor, Israel II, 782
Taylor, Israel II, 822
Taylor, Israel II, 928
Taylor, Israel IV, 369
Taylor, Israel IV, 447
Taylor, Israel V, 130
Taylor, Israel V, 473
Taylor, Israel V, 527
Taylor, Israel V, 533
Taylor, Israel V, 870
Taylor, Israel VI, 450
Taylor, Israel VI, 606
Taylor, Israel W. IV, 447
Taylor, Israel W. V, 938
Taylor, Isral V, 533
Taylor, Iva V, 601
Taylor, J. Hibberd III, 123
Taylor, J. Hibberd III, 310
Taylor, J. Virginia VI, 372
Taylor, J. W. III, 500
Taylor, Jabez II, 782
Taylor, Jaccob V, 130
Taylor, Jacob I, 1103
Taylor, Jacob II, 303
Taylor, Jacob II, 782
Taylor, Jacob II, 970
Taylor, Jacob IV, 61
Taylor, Jacob IV, 659
Taylor, Jacob IV, 774
Taylor, Jacob IV, 847
Taylor, Jacob IV, 1006
Taylor, Jacob IV, 1007
Taylor, Jacob IV, 1027
Taylor, Jacob V, 489
Taylor, Jacob V, 533
Taylor, Jacob V, 544
Taylor, Jacob V, 973
Taylor, Jacob V, 977
Taylor, Jacob V, 979
Taylor, Jacob VI, 449
Taylor, Jacob VI, 450
Taylor, James I, 343
Taylor, James I, 423
Taylor, James II, 200
Taylor, James II, 267
Taylor, James II, 294
Taylor, James II, 301
Taylor, James II, 303
Taylor, James II, 304
Taylor, James II, 484
Taylor, James II, 664
Taylor, James II, 769
Taylor, James IV, 353
Taylor, James IV, 447
Taylor, James IV, 500
Taylor, James IV, 774
Taylor, James IV, 1188
Taylor, James V, 931
Taylor, James V, 938
Taylor, James VI, 260
Taylor, James VI, 606
Taylor, James VI, 810
Taylor, James VI, 850
Taylor, James VI, 858
Taylor, James VI, 1002
Taylor, James A. VI, 799
Taylor, James Albert V, 870
Taylor, James D. VI, 798
Taylor, James D. VI, 1002
Taylor, James E. VI, 1002
Taylor, James Gurney II, 186
Taylor, James Gurney II, 304
Taylor, James Newton III, 500
Taylor, James S. I, 902
Taylor, James S. II, 928
Taylor, James Silas I, 902
Taylor, James Sterling II, 822
Taylor, Jamima IV, 447
Taylor, Jane I, 18
Taylor, Jane I, 45
Taylor, Jane I, 75
Taylor, Jane I, 1024
Taylor, Jane I, 1034
Taylor, Jane I, 1038
Taylor, Jane II, 208
Taylor, Jane II, 229
Taylor, Jane II, 267
Taylor, Jane II, 425
Taylor, Jane II, 782
Taylor, Jane II, 822
Taylor, Jane II, 829
Taylor, Jane II, 837
Taylor, Jane II, 928
Taylor, Jane II, 1025
Taylor, Jane II, 1031
Taylor, Jane III, 106
Taylor, Jane III, 309
Taylor, Jane III, 310
Taylor, Jane IV, 25
Taylor, Jane IV, 61
Taylor, Jane IV, 62
Taylor, Jane IV, 130
Taylor, Jane IV, 133
Taylor, Jane IV, 447
Taylor, Jane IV, 924
Taylor, Jane IV, 1006
Taylor, Jane IV, 1188
Taylor, Jane V, 130
Taylor, Jane V, 899
Taylor, Jane V, 938
Taylor, Jane VI, 449
Taylor, Jane VI, 450
Taylor, Jane VI, 592
Taylor, Jane VI, 593
Taylor, Jane VI, 606
Taylor, Jane VI, 708
Taylor, Jane VI, 843
Taylor, Jane VI, 1002
Taylor, Jane C. II, 1062
Taylor, Jane C. II, 1074
Taylor, Jane E. I, 18
Taylor, Jane E. II, 928
Taylor, Jane Virginia VI, 618
Taylor, Jane Virginia VI, 622
Taylor, Jane Virginia VI, 625
Taylor, Jane Virginia VI, 626
Taylor, Jane Virginia VI, 627
Taylor, Jane Virginia VI, 628
Taylor, Jane Virginia VI, 702
Taylor, Jane Virginia VI, 711
Taylor, Jane Virginia VI, 712
Taylor, Janie VI, 1002
Taylor, Jean VI, 450
Taylor, Jeane I, 574
Taylor, Jeane I, 576
Taylor, Jeanette V, 656
Taylor, Jeanette V, 714
Taylor, Jediah II, 267
Taylor, Jehu IV, 1225
Taylor, Jehu Lloyd IV, 1006
Taylor, Jemima II, 1025
Taylor, Jemima II, 1031
Taylor, Jemima IV, 261
Taylor, Jemima IV, 287
Taylor, Jemima IV, 426
Taylor, Jemima IV, 446
Taylor, Jennie V, 870
Taylor, Jennie E. II, 928
Taylor, Jennie L. II, 928
Taylor, Jeremiah VI, 963
Taylor, Jesse II, 966
Taylor, Jesse IV, 111
Taylor, Jesse IV, 133
Taylor, Jesse IV, 1006
Taylor, Jesse IV, 1007
Taylor, Jesse V, 514
Taylor, Jesse V, 533
Taylor, Jesse V, 534
Taylor, Jesse VI, 450
Taylor, Jesse VI, 571
Taylor, Jesse VI, 572
Taylor, Jesse VI, 606
Taylor, Jesse Frank V, 533
Taylor, Jesse W. II, 719
Taylor, Jesse W. II, 720
Taylor, Jesse W. II, 822
Taylor, Jesse, Jr. V, 533
Taylor, Jessie III, 310
Taylor, Jno. M. III, 309
Taylor, Joe IV, 1225
Taylor, Joel VI, 355
Taylor, Joel VI, 606
Taylor, Joel C. V, 870
Taylor, John I, 423
Taylor, John I, 576
Taylor, John II, 256
Taylor, John II, 266
Taylor, John II, 267
Taylor, John II, 274
Taylor, John II, 276
Taylor, John II, 425
Taylor, John II, 634
Taylor, John II, 659
Taylor, John II, 663
Taylor, John II, 664
Taylor, John II, 736
Taylor, John II, 769
Taylor, John II, 782
Taylor, John II, 970
Taylor, John II, 1012
Taylor, John II, 1031
Taylor, John IV, 287
Taylor, John IV, 659
Taylor, John IV, 774
Taylor, John IV, 1006
Taylor, John IV, 1007
Taylor, John V, 130
Taylor, John V, 534
Taylor, John V, 870
Taylor, John V, 938
Taylor, John VI, 273
Taylor, John VI, 450
Taylor, John VI, 571
Taylor, John VI, 572
Taylor, John VI, 692
Taylor, John VI, 711
Taylor, John VI, 848
Taylor, John VI, 858
Taylor, John VI, 911
Taylor, John VI, 919
Taylor, John VI, 928
Taylor, John VI, 985
Taylor, John VI, 986
Taylor, John VI, 1001
Taylor, John VI, 1002
Taylor, John A. V, 870
Taylor, John Ambrose V, 129
Taylor, John Ambrose V, 130
Taylor, John Ambrose V, 979
Taylor, John Ambrose VI, 450
Taylor, John Ambrose VI, 571
Taylor, John B. VI, 877
Taylor, John C. V, 870
Taylor, John C. V, 871
Taylor, John Comfort II, 1081
Taylor, John Gardiner II, 1060
Taylor, John Gardiner II, 1062
Taylor, John M. II, 124
Taylor, John M. IV, 596
Taylor, John Marshall VI, 711
Taylor, John Marshall VI, 712
Taylor, John Meader II, 42
Taylor, John Palmer II, 1032
Taylor, John R. II, 425
Taylor, John R. II, 928
Taylor, John W. IV, 287
Taylor, John W. V, 938
Taylor, John W. VI, 1002
Taylor, John, Jr. II, 266
Taylor, John, Jr. II, 1031
Taylor, John, Jr. VI, 801
Taylor, John, Jr. VI, 858
Taylor, Jonah IV, 62
Taylor, Jonathan I, 1015
Taylor, Jonathan I, 1024
Taylor, Jonathan I, 1038
Taylor, Jonathan II, 971
Taylor, Jonathan II, 1025
Taylor, Jonathan II, 1031
Taylor, Jonathan IV, 62
Taylor, Jonathan IV, 111
Taylor, Jonathan IV, 137
Taylor, Jonathan IV, 167
Taylor, Jonathan IV, 287
Taylor, Jonathan IV, 295
Taylor, Jonathan IV, 1188
Taylor, Jonathan V, 533
Taylor, Jonathan V, 793
Taylor, Jonathan V, 960
Taylor, Jonathan V, 977
Taylor, Jonathan VI, 376
Taylor, Jonathan VI, 449
Taylor, Jonathan VI, 450
Taylor, Jonathan VI, 571
Taylor, Jonathan VI, 587
Taylor, Jonathan VI, 606
Taylor, Jonathan VI, 624
Taylor, Jonathan VI, 646
Taylor, Jonathan VI, 686
Taylor, Jonathan VI, 697
Taylor, Jonathan VI, 700
Taylor, Jonathan VI, 710
Taylor, Jonathan VI, 711
Taylor, Jonathan VI, 712
Taylor, Jonathan VI, 713
Taylor, Jonathan VI, 714
Taylor, Jonathan K. VI, 712
Taylor, Jonathan Kirkbride VI, 712
Taylor, Jonathan, Jr. VI, 712
Taylor, Joseph II, 124
Taylor, Joseph II, 266
Taylor, Joseph II, 425
Taylor, Joseph II, 523
Taylor, Joseph II, 664
Taylor, Joseph II, 712
Taylor, Joseph II, 718
Taylor, Joseph II, 720
Taylor, Joseph II, 728
Taylor, Joseph II, 770
Taylor, Joseph II, 822
Taylor, Joseph II, 868
Taylor, Joseph II, 928
Taylor, Joseph II, 967
Taylor, Joseph II, 971
Taylor, Joseph II, 983
Taylor, Joseph II, 985
Taylor, Joseph II, 987
Taylor, Joseph II, 990
Taylor, Joseph II, 1008
Taylor, Joseph II, 1031
Taylor, Joseph II, 1032
Taylor, Joseph II, 1061
Taylor, Joseph II, 1081
Taylor, Joseph IV, 62
Taylor, Joseph IV, 160
Taylor, Joseph IV, 287
Taylor, Joseph IV, 353
Taylor, Joseph IV, 447
Taylor, Joseph IV, 553
Taylor, Joseph IV, 616
Taylor, Joseph IV, 659
Taylor, Joseph IV, 774
Taylor, Joseph IV, 780
Taylor, Joseph IV, 884
Taylor, Joseph IV, 1030
Taylor, Joseph IV, 1031
Taylor, Joseph V, 534
Taylor, Joseph V, 938
Taylor, Joseph VI, 450
Taylor, Joseph VI, 571
Taylor, Joseph VI, 572
Taylor, Joseph VI, 606
Taylor, Joseph VI, 712
Taylor, Joseph VI, 1002
Taylor, Joseph B. II, 303
Taylor, Joseph B. II, 304
Taylor, Joseph B. II, 971
Taylor, Joseph B. II, 1046
Taylor, Joseph B. II, 1058
Taylor, Joseph B. II, 1061
Taylor, Joseph E. II, 303
Taylor, Joseph Franklin II, 769
Taylor, Joseph Freeman II, 267
Taylor, Joseph G. II, 822
Taylor, Joseph G. II, 928
Taylor, Joseph H. II, 822
Taylor, Joseph H. II, 928
Taylor, Joseph H. II, 1061
Taylor, Joseph H. VI, 711
Taylor, Joseph K. II, 971
Taylor, Joseph K. II, 1077
Taylor, Joseph K. II, 1081
Taylor, Joseph N. V, 969
Taylor, Joseph N. V, 977
Taylor, Joseph Neill V, 129
Taylor, Joseph Neill V, 130
Taylor, Joseph Neill VI, 450
Taylor, Joseph Neill VI, 571
Taylor, Joseph W. II, 303
Taylor, Joseph W. V, 938
Taylor, Joseph Wright II, 3(
Taylor, Joseph, Jr. II, 1032
Taylor, Joseph, Jr. II, 1061
Taylor, Joseph, Sr. IV, 659
Taylor, Joshua II, 267
Taylor, Joshua II, 303
Taylor, Joshua IV, 353
Taylor, Joshua IV, 652
Taylor, Joshua IV, 774
Taylor, Joshua IV, 1006
Taylor, Joshua IV, 1357
Taylor, Joshua IV, 1375
Taylor, Joshua IV, 1381
Taylor, Joshua VI, 988
Taylor, Joshua VI, 1002
Taylor, Judith VI, 911
Taylor, Juley Ann VI, 999
Taylor, Julia II, 304
Taylor, Julia III, 309
Taylor, Julia III, 486
Taylor, Julia A. I, 538
Taylor, Julia A. I, 576
Taylor, Julia C. II, 294
Taylor, Julia C. II, 304
Taylor, Julia C. III, 486
Taylor, Julia C. III, 500
Taylor, Julia K. II, 186
Taylor, Katherine VI, 858
Taylor, Katy VI, 1001
Taylor, Keziah IV, 287
Taylor, Keziah IV, 326
Taylor, Keziah IV, 353
Taylor, Keziah IV, 847
Taylor, Kinchin V, 533
Taylor, Kirkbride VI, 710
Taylor, Kirkbride VI, 713
Taylor, Kitturah VI, 898
Taylor, Kizia I, 227
Taylor, Latitia II, 971
Taylor, Latitia II, 985
Taylor, Latitia II, 1008
Taylor, Latitia II, 1031
Taylor, Latitia II, 1032
Taylor, Laura V, 870
Taylor, Laura A. V, 870
Taylor, Laura B. V, 871
Taylor, Laura M. V, 871
Taylor, Laurance H. VI, 645
Taylor, Laurence H. VI, 621
Taylor, Laurence H. VI, 631
Taylor, Laurence H. VI, 687
Taylor, Laurence H. VI, 710
Taylor, Laurence H. VI, 711
Taylor, Laurence H. VI, 712
Taylor, Laurence Lee VI, 631
Taylor, Laurence Lee VI, 712
Taylor, Lauretta M. V, 871
Taylor, Lavica V, 646
Taylor, Lavicia V, 648
Taylor, Lavina IV, 659
Taylor, Lawrence H. VI, 695
Taylor, Lawrence Newbold II, 3
Taylor, Leatitia II, 971
Taylor, Leatitia VI, 667
Taylor, Leatitia VI, 668
Taylor, Leatitia VI, 669
Taylor, Leatitia VI, 712
Taylor, Leila V, 433
Taylor, Lemuel IV, 287
Taylor, Lena D. V, 871
Taylor, Letitia II, 970
Taylor, Letitia VI, 563
Taylor, Letitia VI, 570
Taylor, Letitia VI, 571
Taylor, Letitia VI, 650
Taylor, Letitia VI, 665
Taylor, Letitia VI, 697
Taylor, Letitia VI, 705
Taylor, Letitia VI, 710
Taylor, Letitia VI, 711
Taylor, Levi S. VI, 712
Taylor, Levi S. VI, 714
Taylor, Lewis I, 625
Taylor, Lewis I, 902
Taylor, Lewis II, 186
Taylor, Lewis II, 267
Taylor, Lewis V, 130
Taylor, Lewis V, 864
Taylor, Lewis V, 869
Taylor, Lewis V, 870
Taylor, Lewis V, 977
Taylor, Lewis VI, 691
Taylor, Lewis VI, 713
Taylor, Lewis A. V, 870
Taylor, Lewis A. V, 871
Taylor, Lewis Whitaker II, 42
Taylor, Lewyn II, 425
Taylor, Lida V, 870
Taylor, Lissie S. II, 928
Taylor, Lizzie II, 928
Taylor, Llewellyn II, 425

Loretha May V, 870
Louella V, 361
Louisa I, 902
Louisa V, 918
Louisa V, 938
Louisa C. VI, 711
Louisa C. VI, 716
Louisa E. VI, 708
Louisa E. VI, 711
Louisa E. VI, 713
Louisa F. VI, 710
Louisa Wright II, 799
Louise E. VI, 686
Lucinda VI, 1002
Lucinda A. VI, 1002
Luckey VI, 858
Lucy II, 304
Lucy II, 971
Lucy II, 1062
Lucy V, 477
Lucy V, 533
Lucy V, 601
Lucy V, 646
Lucy VI, 1001
Lucy M. IV, 595
Lucy Mason IV, 587
Lucy Mason IV, 596
Lucy May VI, 631
Lucy May VI, 712
Luella V, 361
Lyda I, 1103
Lydia II, 267
Lydia II, 274
Lydia II, 425
Lydia II, 664
Lydia II, 688
Lydia II, 806
Lydia II, 970
Lydia II, 1061
Lydia III, 123
Lydia III, 310
Lydia IV, 819
Lydia IV, 847
Lydia IV, 1006
Lydia IV, 1007
Lydia V, 870
Lydia VI, 387
Lydia VI, 388
Lydia VI, 449
Lydia VI, 450
Lydia VI, 571
Lydia VI, 587
Lydia VI, 624
Lydia VI, 637
Lydia VI, 686
Lydia VI, 708
Lydia VI, 710
Lydia VI, 711
Lydia VI, 712
Lydia A. IV, 353
Lydia Alice VI, 686
Lydia Alice VI, 712
Lydia Ann IV, 344
Lydia Ann IV, 353
Lydia Ann V, 130
Lydia B. IV, 1381
Lydia F. VI, 712
Lydia F. VI, 713
Lydia F. VI, 714
Lydia L. V, 862
Lydia L. V, 871
Lydia S. IV, 447
Lydia S. V, 938
Lydia W. VI, 700
Lydia W. VI, 713
M. Bessie II, 928
M. Evalyn V, 433
Mabel VI, 631
Mabel A. VI, 621
Mabel A. VI, 710
Mabel A. VI, 711
Mabel A. VI, 712
Mabel Arbutus VI, 687
Mabel Arbutus VI, 695
Mabel Arbutus VI, 712
Maggie IV, 774
Mahlon II, 664
Mahlon II, 970
Mahlon II, 971
Mahlon II, 990
Mahlon II, 1030
Mahlon II, 1031
Mahlon II, 1032
Mahlon II, 1061
Mahlon II, 1081
Mahlon VI, 387
Mahlon VI, 450
Mahlon VI, 568
Mahlon VI, 571
Mahlon VI, 651
Mahlon VI, 667
Taylor, Mahlon VI, 669
Taylor, Mahlon VI, 671
Taylor, Mahlon VI, 687
Taylor, Mahlon VI, 712
Taylor, Mahlon VI, 713
Taylor, Mahlon VI, 725
Taylor, Mahlon Clayton VI, 713
Taylor, Mahlon H. II, 1032
Taylor, Mahlon K. II, 1003
Taylor, Mahlon K. II, 1061
Taylor, Mahlon K. VI, 626
Taylor, Mahlon K. VI, 637
Taylor, Mahlon K. VI, 645
Taylor, Mahlon K. VI, 669
Taylor, Mahlon K. VI, 704
Taylor, Mahlon K. VI, 710
Taylor, Mahlon K. VI, 711
Taylor, Mahlon K. VI, 712
Taylor, Mahlon K. VI, 713
Taylor, Mahlon K., Jr. VI, 621
Taylor, Mahlon K., Jr. VI, 704
Taylor, Mahlon K., Jr. VI, 710
Taylor, Mahlon K., Jr. VI, 711
Taylor, Mahlon K., Jr. VI, 712
Taylor, Mahlon S. VI, 712
Taylor, Malinda C. V, 282
Taylor, Marcy II, 971
Taylor, Marcy II, 1008
Taylor, Marcy II, 1031
Taylor, Margaret I, 576
Taylor, Margaret II, 267
Taylor, Margaret II, 288
Taylor, Margaret II, 303
Taylor, Margaret II, 304
Taylor, Margaret II, 1061
Taylor, Margaret II, 1064
Taylor, Margaret III, 310
Taylor, Margaret IV, 1362
Taylor, Margaret IV, 1381
Taylor, Margaret V, 870
Taylor, Margaret V, 938
Taylor, Margaret VI, 1002
Taylor, Margaret A. II, 326
Taylor, Margaret Ann II, 326
Taylor, Margaret C. I, 208
Taylor, Margaret C. I, 232
Taylor, Margaret C. I, 258
Taylor, Margaret E. VI, 645
Taylor, Margaret E. VI, 677
Taylor, Margaret E. VI, 687
Taylor, Margaret E. VI, 695
Taylor, Margaret E. VI, 711
Taylor, Margaret E. VI, 712
Taylor, Margaret E. VI, 713
Taylor, Margaret S. III, 150
Taylor, Margaret S. III, 310
Taylor, Marguerite H. II, 304
Taylor, Maria II, 267
Taylor, Maria II, 276
Taylor, Maria II, 719
Taylor, Maria II, 720
Taylor, Maria II, 822
Taylor, Maria IV, 54
Taylor, Maria IV, 62
Taylor, Maria V, 533
Taylor, Maria VI, 449
Taylor, Maria VI, 450
Taylor, Maria VI, 988
Taylor, Maria A. IV, 369
Taylor, Maria A. IV, 447
Taylor, Maria Ann II, 782
Taylor, Maria Ann IV, 447
Taylor, Maria B. II, 966
Taylor, Maria Jane VI, 710
Taylor, Maria Jane VI, 713
Taylor, Maria W. VI, 517
Taylor, Maria W. VI, 663
Taylor, Maria W. VI, 667
Taylor, Maria W. VI, 754
Taylor, Maria Wilson VI, 518
Taylor, Maria Wilson VI, 572
Taylor, Maria Wilson VI, 621
Taylor, Maria Wilson VI, 662
Taylor, Maria Wilson VI, 683
Taylor, Maria Wilson VI, 701
Taylor, Maria Wilson VI, 710
Taylor, Maria Wilson VI, 712
Taylor, Maria Wilson VI, 754
Taylor, Mariah V, 513
Taylor, Mariah V, 533
Taylor, Mariah Ann IV, 447
Taylor, Marian S. II, 970
Taylor, Marietta I, 625
Taylor, Marietta IV, 774
Taylor, Marietta IV, 1043
Taylor, Marietta S. VI, 712
Taylor, Marietta S. VI, 713
Taylor, Marion II, 1062
Taylor, Mark II, 720
Taylor, Mark B. II, 770
Taylor, Mark Hughes I, 934
Taylor, Marmaduk II, 267
Taylor, Marmaduk II, 274
Taylor, Marmaduke II, 267
Taylor, Marshall II, 1061
Taylor, Martha I, 1024
Taylor, Martha I, 1038
Taylor, Martha II, 60
Taylor, Martha II, 75
Taylor, Martha II, 103
Taylor, Martha II, 168
Taylor, Martha II, 169
Taylor, Martha II, 195
Taylor, Martha II, 229
Taylor, Martha II, 267
Taylor, Martha II, 283
Taylor, Martha II, 288
Taylor, Martha II, 303
Taylor, Martha II, 304
Taylor, Martha II, 314
Taylor, Martha II, 712
Taylor, Martha II, 928
Taylor, Martha II, 933
Taylor, Martha II, 987
Taylor, Martha II, 1015
Taylor, Martha II, 1031
Taylor, Martha II, 1032
Taylor, Martha II, 1046
Taylor, Martha II, 1061
Taylor, Martha IV, 200
Taylor, Martha IV, 287
Taylor, Martha IV, 353
Taylor, Martha IV, 1362
Taylor, Martha IV, 1381
Taylor, Martha V, 766
Taylor, Martha V, 769
Taylor, Martha V, 848
Taylor, Martha V, 864
Taylor, Martha V, 870
Taylor, Martha VI, 881
Taylor, Martha VI, 975
Taylor, Martha VI, 1002
Taylor, Martha A. V, 870
Taylor, Martha A. VI, 712
Taylor, Martha Ann V, 864
Taylor, Martha Ann V, 870
Taylor, Martha Ann V, 871
Taylor, Martha Ann VI, 700
Taylor, Martha Ann VI, 712
Taylor, Martha Ann VI, 713
Taylor, Martha B. II, 303
Taylor, Martha B. II, 304
Taylor, Martha B. II, 967
Taylor, Martha B. II, 971
Taylor, Martha B. II, 1058
Taylor, Martha J. VI, 858
Taylor, Martha L. IV, 749
Taylor, Martha L. IV, 774
Taylor, Martha L. V, 871
Taylor, Martha R. I, 950
Taylor, Martha Rebecca I, 934
Taylor, Martha Viretta V, 871
Taylor, Martha W. II, 718
Taylor, Martha W. II, 720
Taylor, Martha W. II, 728
Taylor, Martha W. II, 770
Taylor, Marthanna IV, 1375
Taylor, Marthanna IV, 1381
Taylor, Martin V, 870
Taylor, Martin Fearnley VI, 606
Taylor, Martin M. V, 871
Taylor, Mary I, 169
Taylor, Mary I, 423
Taylor, Mary I, 427
Taylor, Mary I, 902
Taylor, Mary I, 998
Taylor, Mary I, 1024
Taylor, Mary I, 1030
Taylor, Mary I, 1033
Taylor, Mary I, 1034
Taylor, Mary I, 1035
Taylor, Mary I, 1038
Taylor, Mary II, 122
Taylor, Mary II, 124
Taylor, Mary II, 195
Taylor, Mary II, 266
Taylor, Mary II, 267
Taylor, Mary II, 314
Taylor, Mary II, 326
Taylor, Mary II, 425
Taylor, Mary II, 479
Taylor, Mary II, 634
Taylor, Mary II, 664
Taylor, Mary II, 720
Taylor, Mary II, 820
Taylor, Mary II, 928
Taylor, Mary II, 957
Taylor, Mary II, 958
Taylor, Mary II, 970
Taylor, Mary II, 971
Taylor, Mary II, 978
Taylor, Mary II, 983
Taylor, Mary II, 985
Taylor, Mary II, 987
Taylor, Mary II, 1008
Taylor, Mary II, 1030
Taylor, Mary II, 1031
Taylor, Mary II, 1032
Taylor, Mary II, 1061
Taylor, Mary III, 310
Taylor, Mary III, 361
Taylor, Mary IV, 61
Taylor, Mary IV, 62
Taylor, Mary IV, 97
Taylor, Mary IV, 111
Taylor, Mary IV, 133
Taylor, Mary IV, 220
Taylor, Mary IV, 287
Taylor, Mary IV, 353
Taylor, Mary IV, 500
Taylor, Mary IV, 616
Taylor, Mary IV, 634
Taylor, Mary IV, 659
Taylor, Mary IV, 774
Taylor, Mary IV, 847
Taylor, Mary IV, 904
Taylor, Mary IV, 1030
Taylor, Mary IV, 1225
Taylor, Mary IV, 1357
Taylor, Mary IV, 1381
Taylor, Mary V, 39
Taylor, Mary V, 122
Taylor, Mary V, 129
Taylor, Mary V, 130
Taylor, Mary V, 473
Taylor, Mary V, 527
Taylor, Mary V, 533
Taylor, Mary V, 837
Taylor, Mary V, 869
Taylor, Mary V, 870
Taylor, Mary V, 908
Taylor, Mary V, 938
Taylor, Mary V, 965
Taylor, Mary V, 977
Taylor, Mary V, 979
Taylor, Mary VI, 260
Taylor, Mary VI, 387
Taylor, Mary VI, 408
Taylor, Mary VI, 449
Taylor, Mary VI, 450
Taylor, Mary VI, 462
Taylor, Mary VI, 518
Taylor, Mary VI, 545
Taylor, Mary VI, 568
Taylor, Mary VI, 571
Taylor, Mary VI, 572
Taylor, Mary VI, 621
Taylor, Mary VI, 626
Taylor, Mary VI, 637
Taylor, Mary VI, 651
Taylor, Mary VI, 667
Taylor, Mary VI, 669
Taylor, Mary VI, 692
Taylor, Mary VI, 704
Taylor, Mary VI, 710
Taylor, Mary VI, 711
Taylor, Mary VI, 712
Taylor, Mary VI, 713
Taylor, Mary VI, 808
Taylor, Mary VI, 858
Taylor, Mary VI, 891
Taylor, Mary VI, 916
Taylor, Mary VI, 986
Taylor, Mary VI, 987
Taylor, Mary VI, 991
Taylor, Mary VI, 1002
Taylor, Mary A. II, 267
Taylor, Mary A. II, 1060
Taylor, Mary A. II, 1062
Taylor, Mary A. S. VI, 1002
Taylor, Mary Ann II, 169
Taylor, Mary Ann II, 186
Taylor, Mary Ann II, 283
Taylor, Mary Ann II, 303
Taylor, Mary Ann II, 802
Taylor, Mary Ann II, 1053
Taylor, Mary Ann II, 1061
Taylor, Mary Ann IV, 62
Taylor, Mary Ann IV, 963
Taylor, Mary Ann IV, 1006
Taylor, Mary Ann IV, 1007
Taylor, Mary Ann V, 870
Taylor, Mary Ann V, 871
Taylor, Mary Ann V, 872
Taylor, Mary Ann VI, 710
Taylor, Mary Anna II, 928
Taylor, Mary Anna II, 970
Taylor, Mary Anna V, 871
Taylor, Mary Annie V, 870
Taylor, Mary Annie V, 871
Taylor, Mary B. II, 720
Taylor, Mary C. II, 186
Taylor, Mary C. II, 303
Taylor, Mary C. II, 1075
Taylor, Mary C. II, 1081
Taylor, Mary C. IV, 1381
Taylor, Mary C. V, 534
Taylor, Mary C. V, 542
Taylor, Mary D. II, 326
Taylor, Mary E. II, 304
Taylor, Mary E. II, 720
Taylor, Mary E. II, 770
Taylor, Mary E. II, 928
Taylor, Mary E. III, 48
Taylor, Mary E. III, 223
Taylor, Mary E. III, 309
Taylor, Mary E. III, 351
Taylor, Mary E. IV, 1375
Taylor, Mary E. V, 870
Taylor, Mary E. V, 871
Taylor, Mary Edna I, 576
Taylor, Mary Elizabeth II, 303
Taylor, Mary Elizabeth II, 782
Taylor, Mary Elizabeth V, 870
Taylor, Mary Elizabeth V, 887
Taylor, Mary Ellen V, 870
Taylor, Mary Ellen V, 871
Taylor, Mary Ellen VI, 645
Taylor, Mary Ellen VI, 652
Taylor, Mary Ellen VI, 653
Taylor, Mary Ellen VI, 654
Taylor, Mary Ellen VI, 670
Taylor, Mary Ellen VI, 677
Taylor, Mary Ellen VI, 711
Taylor, Mary Ellen VI, 712
Taylor, Mary Ellen VI, 713
Taylor, Mary Esther III, 448
Taylor, Mary Esther III, 466
Taylor, Mary Eva V, 871
Taylor, Mary F. V, 871
Taylor, Mary F. V, 913
Taylor, Mary Frances V, 871
Taylor, Mary I. V, 902
Taylor, Mary I. V, 938
Taylor, Mary J. IV, 741
Taylor, Mary J. V, 361
Taylor, Mary J. V, 931
Taylor, Mary Jane IV, 955
Taylor, Mary Jane IV, 1007
Taylor, Mary Jane V, 130
Taylor, Mary Jane V, 601
Taylor, Mary Jane V, 938
Taylor, Mary Jane VI, 686
Taylor, Mary Jane VI, 688
Taylor, Mary Jane VI, 689
Taylor, Mary Jane VI, 711
Taylor, Mary Jane VI, 713
Taylor, Mary Jane VI, 1002
Taylor, Mary Janney VI, 691
Taylor, Mary Janney VI, 692
Taylor, Mary Janney VI, 713
Taylor, Mary Jordan V, 902
Taylor, Mary Jordon V, 938
Taylor, Mary L. V, 533
Taylor, Mary Louisa IV, 659
Taylor, Mary M. VI, 708
Taylor, Mary M. VI, 711
Taylor, Mary Mann VI, 760
Taylor, Mary Mann VI, 785
Taylor, Mary Margaret VI, 915
Taylor, Mary S. VI, 626
Taylor, Mary S. VI, 712
Taylor, Mary S. VI, 714
Taylor, Mary T. II, 754
Taylor, Mary T. II, 770
Taylor, Mary Wilson VI, 517
Taylor, Mary, Jr. II, 982
Taylor, Mary, Jr. VI, 669
Taylor, Mary, Jr. VI, 712
Taylor, Massee VI, 848
Taylor, Matilda II, 782
Taylor, Matilda IV, 45
Taylor, Matilda IV, 46
Taylor, Matilda IV, 61
Taylor, Matilda IV, 62
Taylor, Matilda VI, 879
Taylor, Matthew II, 664
Taylor, Mattie IV, 287
Taylor, Mattie L. IV, 774
Taylor, Mattie V. V, 870
Taylor, Mattie V. V, 871
Taylor, Maud IV, 287
Taylor, Maud V, 871
Taylor, Maude V, 870
Taylor, Maude V, 871
Taylor, Maurine V, 714
Taylor, May VI, 706
Taylor, Mayme V, 714
Taylor, Melinda VI, 915
Taylor, Melva A. V, 871
Taylor, Merciana II, 304
Taylor, Merciana Y. II, 304
Taylor, Mercianna Y. II, 1062
Taylor, Mercy II, 970

Taylor, Mercy II, 987
Taylor, Mercy II, 990
Taylor, Mercy II, 1000
Taylor, Mercy II, 1031
Taylor, Mercy II, 1032
Taylor, Mercy II, 1061
Taylor, Mercy II, 1081
Taylor, Mercy Ann VI, 712
Taylor, Messiah I, 576
Taylor, Mildred VI, 816
Taylor, Milton IV, 774
Taylor, Milton IV, 974
Taylor, Milton IV, 1006
Taylor, Milton IV, 1007
Taylor, Milton V, 533
Taylor, Milton M. V, 493
Taylor, Milton M. V, 534
Taylor, Milton S. V, 870
Taylor, Milton S. V, 871
Taylor, Minnie V, 534
Taylor, Miriam VI, 495
Taylor, Miriam VI, 531
Taylor, Miriam G. VI, 494
Taylor, Miriam G. VI, 495
Taylor, Miriam G. VI, 532
Taylor, Miriam G. VI, 542
Taylor, Miriam G. VI, 571
Taylor, Miriam G. VI, 572
Taylor, Moorning I, 169
Taylor, Mordecai IV, 61
Taylor, Mordecai V, 39
Taylor, Mordecai V, 130
Taylor, Mordecai V, 977
Taylor, Mordecai VI, 450
Taylor, Mordecai, Jr. V, 130
Taylor, Mordica, Jr. V, 977
Taylor, Mordicay VI, 450
Taylor, Morris H. II, 42
Taylor, Morris H. II, 124
Taylor, Mouning VI, 1002
Taylor, Mourning I, 169
Taylor, N. H. V, 466
Taylor, Nancy I, 998
Taylor, Nancy VI, 450
Taylor, Nancy VI, 500
Taylor, Nancy VI, 550
Taylor, Nancy VI, 572
Taylor, Nancy VI, 638
Taylor, Nancy VI, 639
Taylor, Nancy VI, 645
Taylor, Nancy VI, 692
Taylor, Nancy VI, 710
Taylor, Nancy VI, 713
Taylor, Nancy VI, 714
Taylor, Nancy VI, 810
Taylor, Nancy VI, 858
Taylor, Nancy VI, 916
Taylor, Nancy VI, 1002
Taylor, Nancy A. VI, 1002
Taylor, Nancy Ann VI, 1002
Taylor, Nancy C. VI, 990
Taylor, Nancy E. I, 902
Taylor, Nancy W. I, 998
Taylor, Nanne IV, 287
Taylor, Nanny IV, 170
Taylor, Nanny IV, 287
Taylor, Naomi V, 533
Taylor, Nathan I, 576
Taylor, Nathan II, 266
Taylor, Nathan VI, 571
Taylor, Nathan S. V, 870
Taylor, Nathan S. V, 871
Taylor, Nathaniel I, 18
Taylor, Nathaniel I, 75
Taylor, Nathaniel II, 266
Taylor, Nathaniel VI, 568
Taylor, Natty I, 8
Taylor, Newbold II, 664
Taylor, Nicholas G. II, 822
Taylor, Nicholas G. II, 928
Taylor, Noble IV, 287
Taylor, Ola IV, 287
Taylor, Olive I, 576
Taylor, Olive M. V, 870
Taylor, Oliver I, 576
Taylor, Oliver II, 970
Taylor, Oliver II, 1062
Taylor, Oliver IV, 659
Taylor, Oliver IV, 774
Taylor, Oliver IV, 1006
Taylor, Oliver IV, 1007
Taylor, Oliver VI, 714
Taylor, Oliver E. V, 870
Taylor, Olover IV, 659
Taylor, Orpheus V, 870
Taylor, Orpheus V, 871
Taylor, Osa V, 433
Taylor, Page VI, 760
Taylor, Page VI, 785
Taylor, Pamela VI, 744
Taylor, Pamelia VI, 858
Taylor, Pamelia VI, 1002
Taylor, Patience II, 194
Taylor, Patience II, 266
Taylor, Patience VI, 449
Taylor, Patry VI, 1002
Taylor, Patsy VI, 801
Taylor, Pattison VI, 123
Taylor, Penelope VI, 1013
Taylor, Permiela VI, 979
Taylor, Peter II, 970
Taylor, Peter II, 1025
Taylor, Peter II, 1031
Taylor, Peter IV, 61
Taylor, Peter IV, 353
Taylor, Peter IV, 447
Taylor, Peter IV, 500
Taylor, Peter V, 130
Taylor, Peter VI, 450
Taylor, Peter T. VI, 805
Taylor, Peter, Jr. II, 1031
Taylor, Pharaby P. IV, 287
Taylor, Phebe II, 186
Taylor, Phebe II, 215
Taylor, Phebe II, 255
Taylor, Phebe II, 256
Taylor, Phebe II, 266
Taylor, Phebe II, 267
Taylor, Phebe II, 274
Taylor, Phebe II, 276
Taylor, Phebe II, 314
Taylor, Phebe II, 425
Taylor, Phebe II, 655
Taylor, Phebe II, 664
Taylor, Phebe II, 988
Taylor, Phebe II, 1062
Taylor, Phebe III, 310
Taylor, Phebe V, 969
Taylor, Phebe V, 977
Taylor, Phebe A. II, 822
Taylor, Phebe A. II, 928
Taylor, Phebe G. V, 977
Taylor, Phebe, Jr. II, 267
Taylor, Philena IV, 974
Taylor, Philena IV, 1006
Taylor, Philena IV, 1007
Taylor, Philip II, 970
Taylor, Polly VI, 858
Taylor, Polly VI, 898
Taylor, Polly VI, 916
Taylor, Polly VI, 1002
Taylor, Polly A. VI, 805
Taylor, Priscilla I, 625
Taylor, Priscilla F. I, 902
Taylor, Priscilla H. II, 868
Taylor, Priscilla H. II, 928
Taylor, Prudence I, 1024
Taylor, Rachel I, 556
Taylor, Rachel I, 576
Taylor, Rachel I, 934
Taylor, Rachel I, 950
Taylor, Rachel II, 425
Taylor, Rachel II, 555
Taylor, Rachel II, 598
Taylor, Rachel II, 664
Taylor, Rachel II, 970
Taylor, Rachel II, 971
Taylor, Rachel II, 992
Taylor, Rachel II, 1005
Taylor, Rachel II, 1031
Taylor, Rachel II, 1032
Taylor, Rachel II, 1033
Taylor, Rachel V, 130
Taylor, Rachel VI, 543
Taylor, Rachel VI, 544
Taylor, Rachel VI, 571
Taylor, Rachel VI, 572
Taylor, Rachel VI, 587
Taylor, Rachel VI, 710
Taylor, Rachel VI, 802
Taylor, Rachel VI, 858
Taylor, Rachel Bettie II, 782
Taylor, Rachel Farlow I, 950
Taylor, Rachel I. II, 782
Taylor, Ralph IV, 774
Taylor, Ralph S. I, 208
Taylor, Ralph S. I, 232
Taylor, Ralph S. I, 258
Taylor, Rebecah H. VI, 717
Taylor, Rebecca I, 934
Taylor, Rebecca II, 425
Taylor, Rebecca II, 769
Taylor, Rebecca II, 1008
Taylor, Rebecca II, 1032
Taylor, Rebecca II, 1061
Taylor, Rebecca IV, 54
Taylor, Rebecca IV, 62
Taylor, Rebecca IV, 111
Taylor, Rebecca IV, 129
Taylor, Rebecca IV, 133
Taylor, Rebecca IV, 287
Taylor, Rebecca IV, 295
Taylor, Rebecca IV, 652
Taylor, Rebecca IV, 659
Taylor, Rebecca IV, 944
Taylor, Rebecca IV, 1006
Taylor, Rebecca IV, 1007
Taylor, Rebecca IV, 1029
Taylor, Rebecca IV, 1030
Taylor, Rebecca IV, 1188
Taylor, Rebecca V, 835
Taylor, Rebecca V, 869
Taylor, Rebecca V, 870
Taylor, Rebecca V, 939
Taylor, Rebecca VI, 444
Taylor, Rebecca VI, 450
Taylor, Rebecca VI, 606
Taylor, Rebecca VI, 708
Taylor, Rebecca VI, 710
Taylor, Rebecca VI, 713
Taylor, Rebecca VI, 714
Taylor, Rebecca Ann V, 433
Taylor, Rebecca E. V, 870
Taylor, Rebecca E. V, 871
Taylor, Rebecca E. VI, 646
Taylor, Rebecca E. VI, 712
Taylor, Rebecca E. VI, 714
Taylor, Rebecca Emily IV, 1006
Taylor, Rebecca Emily IV, 1007
Taylor, Rebecca H. II, 304
Taylor, Rebecca H. II, 928
Taylor, Rebecca H. II, 1060
Taylor, Rebecca H. II, 1062
Taylor, Rebecca H. VI, 450
Taylor, Rebecca H. VI, 454
Taylor, Rebecca H. VI, 710
Taylor, Rebecca Hughes II, 304
Taylor, Rebecca J. II, 1046
Taylor, Rebecca J. II, 1061
Taylor, Rebecca M. I, 998
Taylor, Rebecca N. V, 939
Taylor, Rebecca P. II, 770
Taylor, Rebecca T. II, 1046
Taylor, Rebecca W. II, 970
Taylor, Rebekah VI, 711
Taylor, Reuben I, 258
Taylor, Reuben IV, 261
Taylor, Reuben IV, 287
Taylor, Reuben VI, 123
Taylor, Reubin I, 227
Taylor, Rev. Geo. F. III, 381
Taylor, Rhoda I, 1024
Taylor, Rhoda I, 1026
Taylor, Rhoda I, 1038
Taylor, Rhody VI, 450
Taylor, Richard I, 1024
Taylor, Richard I, 1030
Taylor, Richard I, 1038
Taylor, Richard IV, 904
Taylor, Richard V, 533
Taylor, Richard V, 601
Taylor, Richard V, 646
Taylor, Richard VI, 450
Taylor, Richard VI, 572
Taylor, Richard VI, 988
Taylor, Richard VI, 1001
Taylor, Richard A. II, 928
Taylor, Richard Baker II, 822
Taylor, Richard H. VI, 712
Taylor, Richard Henry VI, 710
Taylor, Richard Henry VI, 712
Taylor, Richard Henry VI, 713
Taylor, Richard Henry VI, 714
Taylor, Richard W. II, 720
Taylor, Robert I, 343
Taylor, Robert I, 423
Taylor, Robert II, 195
Taylor, Robert II, 267
Taylor, Robert II, 314
Taylor, Robert II, 326
Taylor, Robert II, 425
Taylor, Robert II, 664
Taylor, Robert II, 782
Taylor, Robert III, 310
Taylor, Robert VI, 830
Taylor, Robert VI, 979
Taylor, Robert VI, 987
Taylor, Robert VI, 1002
Taylor, Robert Gray II, 720
Taylor, Rosa V, 466
Taylor, Rosco V, 534
Taylor, Roscoe V, 534
Taylor, Rouse IV, 353
Taylor, Rouse IV, 447
Taylor, Rouse IV, 500
Taylor, Rowse IV, 500
Taylor, Roy V, 534
Taylor, Ruben IV, 446
Taylor, Rusha V, 130
Taylor, Ruth I, 576
Taylor, Ruth II, 736
Taylor, Ruth V, 977
Taylor, Ruth VI, 571
Taylor, Ruth VI, 572
Taylor, Ruth Alice VI, 710
Taylor, Ruth Alice VI, 713
Taylor, Ruth Ann V, 392
Taylor, Ruth Ann V, 977
Taylor, Ruth Anna II, 868
Taylor, Ruth Anna II, 928
Taylor, Ruth Anna IV, 659
Taylor, Ruth Elizabeth VI, 713
Taylor, Ruth H. VI, 713
Taylor, Ruth Hannah VI, 714
Taylor, Ruth L. II, 770
Taylor, Ruth Lynds II, 769
Taylor, Salley VI, 898
Taylor, Salley VI, 916
Taylor, Sallie G. II, 720
Taylor, Sally IV, 287
Taylor, Sally IV, 447
Taylor, Sally VI, 530
Taylor, Sally VI, 858
Taylor, Sally VI, 982
Taylor, Sally VI, 986
Taylor, Sally VI, 988
Taylor, Sally VI, 1002
Taylor, Sally B. IV, 595
Taylor, Sally E. VI, 858
Taylor, Samuel I, 1024
Taylor, Samuel I, 1038
Taylor, Samuel II, 124
Taylor, Samuel II, 208
Taylor, Samuel II, 266
Taylor, Samuel II, 267
Taylor, Samuel II, 425
Taylor, Samuel II, 448
Taylor, Samuel II, 634
Taylor, Samuel II, 638
Taylor, Samuel II, 664
Taylor, Samuel II, 970
Taylor, Samuel II, 1031
Taylor, Samuel II, 1032
Taylor, Samuel III, 310
Taylor, Samuel VI, 858
Taylor, Samuel B. II, 928
Taylor, Samuel C. II, 720
Taylor, Samuel Leiper II, 720
Taylor, Samuel Townsend VI, 712
Taylor, Samuel W. II, 303
Taylor, Sarah I, 423
Taylor, Sarah I, 453
Taylor, Sarah I, 930
Taylor, Sarah II, 120
Taylor, Sarah II, 124
Taylor, Sarah II, 200
Taylor, Sarah II, 266
Taylor, Sarah II, 267
Taylor, Sarah II, 293
Taylor, Sarah II, 303
Taylor, Sarah II, 425
Taylor, Sarah II, 467
Taylor, Sarah II, 523
Taylor, Sarah II, 659
Taylor, Sarah II, 664
Taylor, Sarah II, 688
Taylor, Sarah II, 728
Taylor, Sarah II, 770
Taylor, Sarah II, 928
Taylor, Sarah II, 970
Taylor, Sarah II, 971
Taylor, Sarah II, 981
Taylor, Sarah II, 988
Taylor, Sarah II, 990
Taylor, Sarah II, 997
Taylor, Sarah II, 1008
Taylor, Sarah II, 1031
Taylor, Sarah II, 1032
Taylor, Sarah II, 1042
Taylor, Sarah II, 1046
Taylor, Sarah II, 1058
Taylor, Sarah II, 1061
Taylor, Sarah II, 1081
Taylor, Sarah III, 118
Taylor, Sarah III, 310
Taylor, Sarah III, 500
Taylor, Sarah IV, 279
Taylor, Sarah IV, 287
Taylor, Sarah IV, 587
Taylor, Sarah IV, 596
Taylor, Sarah IV, 622
Taylor, Sarah IV, 659
Taylor, Sarah IV, 847
Taylor, Sarah IV, 868
Taylor, Sarah IV, 877
Taylor, Sarah IV, 884
Taylor, Sarah V, 129
Taylor, Sarah V, 130
Taylor, Sarah V, 392
Taylor, Sarah V, 489
Taylor, Sarah V, 533
Taylor, Sarah V, 870
Taylor, Sarah V, 938
Taylor, Sarah VI, 28
Taylor, Sarah VI, 387
Taylor, Sarah VI, 430
Taylor, Sarah VI, 450
Taylor, Sarah VI, 472
Taylor, Sarah VI, 475
Taylor, Sarah VI, 480
Taylor, Sarah VI, 517
Taylor, Sarah VI, 530
Taylor, Sarah VI, 531
Taylor, Sarah VI, 537
Taylor, Sarah VI, 563
Taylor, Sarah VI, 571
Taylor, Sarah VI, 572
Taylor, Sarah VI, 606
Taylor, Sarah VI, 619
Taylor, Sarah VI, 622
Taylor, Sarah VI, 624
Taylor, Sarah VI, 662
Taylor, Sarah VI, 705
Taylor, Sarah VI, 706
Taylor, Sarah VI, 710
Taylor, Sarah VI, 711
Taylor, Sarah VI, 712
Taylor, Sarah VI, 713
Taylor, Sarah VI, 714
Taylor, Sarah VI, 717
Taylor, Sarah VI, 975
Taylor, Sarah VI, 1001
Taylor, Sarah A. II, 120
Taylor, Sarah A. II, 124
Taylor, Sarah A. II, 949
Taylor, Sarah A. II, 1088
Taylor, Sarah A. II, 1089
Taylor, Sarah A. VI, 473
Taylor, Sarah A. VI, 513
Taylor, Sarah A. VI, 858
Taylor, Sarah A. VI, 1002
Taylor, Sarah Alice VI, 472
Taylor, Sarah Alice VI, 572
Taylor, Sarah Alice VI, 619
Taylor, Sarah Alice VI, 710
Taylor, Sarah Alice VI, 713
Taylor, Sarah Ann II, 1032
Taylor, Sarah Ann II, 1081
Taylor, Sarah Ann II, 1082
Taylor, Sarah Ann VI, 713
Taylor, Sarah Ann VI, 714
Taylor, Sarah Ann VI, 718
Taylor, Sarah B. II, 304
Taylor, Sarah B. II, 971
Taylor, Sarah B. II, 1062
Taylor, Sarah E. IV, 659
Taylor, Sarah E. IV, 774
Taylor, Sarah E. VI, 636
Taylor, Sarah E. VI, 652
Taylor, Sarah E. VI, 653
Taylor, Sarah E. VI, 706
Taylor, Sarah E. VI, 713
Taylor, Sarah Elizabeth VI, 652
Taylor, Sarah Elizabeth VI, 704
Taylor, Sarah Elizabeth VI, 711
Taylor, Sarah Elizabeth VI, 713
Taylor, Sarah F. V, 871
Taylor, Sarah G. II, 712
Taylor, Sarah G. II, 754
Taylor, Sarah G. II, 770
Taylor, Sarah J. V, 870
Taylor, Sarah Kirkbride VI, 710
Taylor, Sarah Kirkbride VI, 713
Taylor, Sarah L. VI, 858
Taylor, Sarah M. II, 186
Taylor, Sarah M. II, 295
Taylor, Sarah M. II, 297
Taylor, Sarah M. II, 303
Taylor, Sarah M. II, 304
Taylor, Sarah M. II, 1088
Taylor, Sarah M. II, 1089
Taylor, Sarah M. IV, 774
Taylor, Sarah M. V, 938
Taylor, Sarah Morris II, 304
Taylor, Sarah R. II, 267
Taylor, Sarah S. III, 310
Taylor, Sarah, Jr. IV, 659
Taylor, Sarah, Senior VI, 706
Taylor, Savoury VI, 933
Taylor, Seth IV, 943
Taylor, Sheppard II, 42
Taylor, Sheppard II, 124
Taylor, Sheppard II, 293
Taylor, Sheppard II, 303
Taylor, Shotwell III, 310
Taylor, Sidewell V, 130
Taylor, Sidwell V, 977
Taylor, Silas V, 870
Taylor, Silas V, 871
Taylor, Silas VI, 908
Taylor, Silas VI, 1002
Taylor, Silas VI, 1010
Taylor, Simeon I, 227
Taylor, Simeon I, 230
Taylor, Simeon I, 258

Simeon IV, 287
Simeon IV, 595
Simeon IV, 596
Simeon VI, 123
Simeon VI, 357
Simeon VI, 450
Simon I, 576
Sophia II, 186
Sophia II, 304
Sophia II, 971
Sophia II, 1058
Sophia II, 1062
Sophia III, 309
Sophia T. II, 967
Spencer I, 576
Spicy VI, 848
Stace IV, 287
Stacy I, 576
Stacy II, 971
Stacy II, 1031
Stephan II, 1062
Stephen II, 425
Stephen IV, 61
Stephen IV, 659
Stephen VI, 387
Stephen VI, 408
Stephen VI, 449
Stephen VI, 450
Steven IV, 659
Stevens Mason VI, 760
Stevens Mason VI, 785
Susan I, 576
Susan II, 326
Susan II, 327
Susan II, 782
Susan II, 822
Susan II, 928
Susan IV, 369
Susan IV, 447
Susan V, 130
Susan V, 533
Susan V, 938
Susan VI, 804
Susan VI, 821
Susan VI, 1002
Susan B. II, 326
Susan Carr VI, 641
Susan Carr VI, 711
Susan Carr VI, 713
Susan D. II, 314
Susan E. V, 870
Susan M. VI, 858
Susan V. V, 870
Susan W. II, 822
Susan W. II, 928
Susan W. III, 310
Susanna I, 423
Susanna I, 430
Susanna VI, 713
Susanna VI, 723
Susanna VI, 987
Susanna Carr VI, 712
Susannah I, 986
Susannah I, 998
Susannah II, 971
Susannah II, 1019
Susannah II, 1032
Susannah IV, 447
Susannah V, 484
Susannah V, 533
Susannah V, 977
Susannah VI, 816
Sylvia Laird II, 720
Synthania I, 576
Tabbith I, 998
Tacie IV, 353
Tacy IV, 287
Tacy IV, 353
Temperance I, 998
Thamasin VI, 783
Thamasin J. VI, 708
Thamasin J. VI, 713
Thamasin J. VI, 784
Thamasin Jane VI, 710
Theodore III, 310
Theodore III, 337
Theodore M. V, 870
Theodore M. V, 871
Thomas I, 576
Thomas II, 168
Thomas II, 169
Thomas II, 195
Thomas II, 229
Thomas II, 267
Thomas II, 283
Thomas II, 288
Thomas II, 303
Thomas II, 314
Thomas II, 425
Thomas II, 598
Thomas II, 613
Taylor, Thomas II, 664
Taylor, Thomas II, 688
Taylor, Thomas II, 1088
Taylor, Thomas II, 1089
Taylor, Thomas III, 309
Taylor, Thomas IV, 622
Taylor, Thomas IV, 659
Taylor, Thomas IV, 774
Taylor, Thomas IV, 884
Taylor, Thomas IV, 1381
Taylor, Thomas V, 870
Taylor, Thomas V, 871
Taylor, Thomas VI, 123
Taylor, Thomas VI, 450
Taylor, Thomas VI, 480
Taylor, Thomas VI, 533
Taylor, Thomas VI, 537
Taylor, Thomas VI, 545
Taylor, Thomas VI, 547
Taylor, Thomas VI, 571
Taylor, Thomas VI, 572
Taylor, Thomas VI, 587
Taylor, Thomas VI, 879
Taylor, Thomas VI, 915
Taylor, Thomas VI, 916
Taylor, Thomas VI, 1002
Taylor, Thomas B. I, 258
Taylor, Thomas B. II, 303
Taylor, Thomas Clarkson VI, 712
Taylor, Thomas Clarkson VI, 713
Taylor, Thomas E. IV, 1381
Taylor, Thomas E. VI, 686
Taylor, Thomas E. VI, 688
Taylor, Thomas E. VI, 711
Taylor, Thomas Edward VI, 708
Taylor, Thomas Edward VI, 711
Taylor, Thomas Edward VI, 713
Taylor, Thomas Eppa VI, 713
Taylor, Thomas G. II, 770
Taylor, Thomas Leiper II, 720
Taylor, Thomas T. VI, 858
Taylor, Thomas W. VI, 1002
Taylor, Thomas, Jr. II, 267
Taylor, Thomas, Jr. II, 303
Taylor, Thomas, Jr. VI, 537
Taylor, Thomas, Jr. VI, 572
Taylor, Thos. IV, 868
Taylor, Thos. VI, 986
Taylor, Thos. Chalkley II, 822
Taylor, Thos. Edward VI, 689
Taylor, Thos. Ellwood II, 782
Taylor, Tillie IV, 774
Taylor, Timothey VI, 570
Taylor, Timothy II, 970
Taylor, Timothy II, 971
Taylor, Timothy II, 981
Taylor, Timothy II, 987
Taylor, Timothy II, 988
Taylor, Timothy II, 996
Taylor, Timothy II, 1008
Taylor, Timothy II, 1030
Taylor, Timothy II, 1031
Taylor, Timothy II, 1032
Taylor, Timothy II, 1042
Taylor, Timothy VI, 563
Taylor, Timothy VI, 568
Taylor, Timothy VI, 571
Taylor, Timothy VI, 697
Taylor, Timothy VI, 705
Taylor, Timothy VI, 710
Taylor, Timothy VI, 711
Taylor, Timothy, Jr. II, 1031
Taylor, Titus II, 782
Taylor, Ursely VI, 123
Taylor, Ursula II, 970
Taylor, Ursula IV, 244
Taylor, Ursula IV, 287
Taylor, Usley VI, 995
Taylor, Victoria S. III, 310
Taylor, Viola IV, 287
Taylor, Viola M. V, 870
Taylor, W. Garrett II, 928
Taylor, W. S. IV, 1340
Taylor, Walter F. IV, 1340
Taylor, Walter Francis IV, 1340
Taylor, Walter W. V, 938
Taylor, Washington VI, 1001
Taylor, Wd. Deborah II, 736
Taylor, Wd. Deborah II, 769
Taylor, Wd. Eliza Wickersham II, 816
Taylor, Wd. Elizabeth II, 187
Taylor, Wd. Elizabeth Neal II, 790
Taylor, Wd. Jane II, 448
Taylor, Wd. Martha II, 822
Taylor, Wd. Priscilla II, 822
Taylor, Wd. Rachel VI, 481
Taylor, Wd. Sarah II, 1031
Taylor, Wesley Allen V, 870
Taylor, Widow Mary I, 1038
Taylor, Widow Mary VI, 667
Taylor, Widow Mary VI, 706
Taylor, Widow Rachel VI, 572
Taylor, William I, 1024
Taylor, William I, 1035
Taylor, William I, 1038
Taylor, William II, 266
Taylor, William II, 425
Taylor, William II, 971
Taylor, William II, 1025
Taylor, William II, 1031
Taylor, William III, 150
Taylor, William III, 309
Taylor, William III, 310
Taylor, William IV, 62
Taylor, William IV, 287
Taylor, William V, 848
Taylor, William V, 869
Taylor, William V, 870
Taylor, William VI, 123
Taylor, William VI, 214
Taylor, William VI, 450
Taylor, William VI, 572
Taylor, William VI, 710
Taylor, William VI, 857
Taylor, William VI, 858
Taylor, William VI, 916
Taylor, William VI, 999
Taylor, William VI, 1001
Taylor, William VI, 1002
Taylor, William Alex. III, 310
Taylor, William Alexander III, 310
Taylor, William Charles II, 186
Taylor, William Charles II, 304
Taylor, William E. V, 870
Taylor, William E. V, 871
Taylor, William Elwood V, 871
Taylor, William H. VI, 858
Taylor, William Henry V, 938
Taylor, William Henry VI, 712
Taylor, William Henry VI, 713
Taylor, William P. VI, 714
Taylor, William S. II, 186
Taylor, William S. II, 267
Taylor, William S. II, 294
Taylor, William S. II, 303
Taylor, William S. II, 304
Taylor, William S. V, 870
Taylor, William S. V, 871
Taylor, William Shipley II, 303
Taylor, William Stubbs V, 870
Taylor, William Yardley VI, 714
Taylor, William, Jr. VI, 572
Taylor, Wilmer L. IV, 659
Taylor, Wilson J. II, 928
Taylor, Wm. II, 664
Taylor, Wm. II, 928
Taylor, Wm. II, 983
Taylor, Wm. II, 987
Taylor, Wm. II, 1008
Taylor, Wm. II, 1031
Taylor, Wm. II, 1032
Taylor, Wm. II, 1061
Taylor, Wm. IV, 426
Taylor, Wm. V, 938
Taylor, Wm. VI, 197
Taylor, Wm. VI, 706
Taylor, Wm. Alex III, 289
Taylor, Wm. Alexander III, 150
Taylor, Wm. B. II, 1061
Taylor, Wm. Field VI, 710
Taylor, Wm. G. II, 928
Taylor, Wm. G., Jr. II, 928
Taylor, Wm. Garrett II, 928
Taylor, Wm. H. V, 714
Taylor, Wm. H. V, 908
Taylor, Wm. H. V, 938
Taylor, Wm. H. VI, 700
Taylor, Wm. Henry VI, 712
Taylor, Wm. J. V, 938
Taylor, Wm. Jordon V, 938
Taylor, Wm. S. IV, 1340
Taylor, Wm. Shipley V, 938
Taylor, Yardley II, 1083
Taylor, Yardley VI, 475
Taylor, Yardley VI, 572
Taylor, Yardley VI, 622
Taylor, Yardley VI, 626
Taylor, Yardley VI, 639
Taylor, Yardley VI, 646
Taylor, Yardley VI, 710
Taylor, Yardley VI, 712
Taylor, Yardley VI, 713
Taylor, Yardley VI, 714
Taylor, Yardly VI, 450
Taylor, Zachariah I, 576
Taylor, Zana VI, 904
Taylor, Zimri V, 870
Taylor-Janney, Maria Wilson VI, 753
Taylour, Ann VI, 449
Taylour, Jacob VI, 449
Tayloy, Widow Mary I, 1038
Taymor, Mary IV, 1265
Taymor, Rosa IV, 1265
Taymor, Roy IV, 1265
Taynor, Roy IV, 1265
Tayson, Jesse VI, 787
Tayson, Margaret VI, 787
Teag, Penticost II, 664
Teage, Samuel P. I, 1162
Teague, Alce I, 1024
Teague, Alce V, 130
Teague, Alice V, 125
Teague, Alice V, 765
Teague, Alice V, 766
Teague, Ann I, 377
Teague, Ann I, 423
Teague, Arria V, 766
Teague, Arrie L. V, 766
Teague, Banks I, 423
Teague, Charles Howell I, 423
Teague, Chester V, 766
Teague, Chester Wayne V, 766
Teague, Clarence Wade I, 423
Teague, David B. V, 766
Teague, David M. V, 730
Teague, Delia Ethel V, 766
Teague, Delilah V, 858
Teague, Delilah V, 871
Teague, Duane W. V, 766
Teague, Duane West V, 766
Teague, Ed. I, 628
Teague, Edward I, 423
Teague, Edward Morris I, 423
Teague, Elijah I, 1024
Teague, Elizabeth II, 426
Teague, Elizabeth II, 564
Teague, Elizabeth II, 664
Teague, Erastus I, 423
Teague, Esther V, 130
Teague, Esther V, 730
Teague, Esther V, 766
Teague, Esther V, 799
Teague, Furnas V, 130
Teague, Isaac V, 793
Teague, Isaac V, 799
Teague, Isaac C. V, 749
Teague, Isaac C. V, 766
Teague, Isaac C. V, 793
Teague, Isaac C. V, 816
Teague, Israel V, 816
Teague, Jane II, 426
Teague, Jane V, 730
Teague, Jane V, 800
Teague, Jane V, 816
Teague, Joanna V, 816
Teague, John Quincy A. I, 841
Teague, Jonathan V, 799
Teague, Joseph V, 130
Teague, Joseph C. V, 749
Teague, Joseph C. V, 766
Teague, Joseph C. V, 793
Teague, Joshua V, 799
Teague, Keturah V, 816
Teague, Lemuel C. V, 788
Teague, Lucy I, 628
Teague, Lucy Ann I, 423
Teague, Lurana V, 799
Teague, Lurana V, 813
Teague, Luranah V, 723
Teague, Luranah V, 730
Teague, Luranah V, 766
Teague, Luranah V, 799
Teague, Lurannah V, 130
Teague, Lydia V, 756
Teague, Martha I, 878
Teague, Martha I, 902
Teague, Martha V, 749
Teague, Martha V, 766
Teague, Martha V, 788
Teague, Martha V, 793
Teague, Martha J. V, 793
Teague, Mary I, 1033
Teague, Mary I, 1038
Teague, Mary V, 130
Teague, Mary V, 730
Teague, Mary V, 731
Teague, Mary V, 799
Teague, Mary V, 800
Teague, Mary V, 814
Teague, Mary V, 815
Teague, Mary T. V, 730
Teague, Maurice E. I, 423
Teague, Minnie I, 628
Teague, Minnie I, 643
Teague, Minnie Lauvenia I, 423
Teague, Minnie Williams I, 641
Teague, Moses V, 130
Teague, Moses V, 730
Teague, Moses V, 800
Teague, Mrs. Arrie L. V, 766
Teague, Nancy I, 423
Teague, Nancy I, 453
Teague, Octavia I, 950
Teague, Pentecost II, 564
Teague, Pentecost II, 664
Teague, Penticost II, 426
Teague, Penticost II, 664
Teague, Prudence V, 766
Teague, Prudence V, 775
Teague, Prudence V, 780
Teague, Prudence V, 793
Teague, Prudence V, 803
Teague, Rebecca V, 723
Teague, Rebecca V, 730
Teague, Rebecca V, 749
Teague, Rebecca V, 766
Teague, Rebecca V, 793
Teague, Rebecca V, 795
Teague, Rebecca V, 799
Teague, Rebecca V, 806
Teague, Rebecca V, 811
Teague, Rebecca V, 818
Teague, Rebeccah V, 130
Teague, Rebekah V, 125
Teague, Rhoda V, 130
Teague, Rhoda V, 756
Teague, Rhoda V, 766
Teague, Rhoda V, 818
Teague, Richard Q. A. I, 841
Teague, Sam'l V, 799
Teague, Samuel I, 690
Teague, Samuel I, 1024
Teague, Samuel I, 1162
Teague, Samuel V, 125
Teague, Samuel V, 130
Teague, Samuel V, 723
Teague, Samuel V, 730
Teague, Samuel V, 756
Teague, Samuel V, 765
Teague, Samuel V, 766
Teague, Samuel V, 775
Teague, Samuel V, 780
Teague, Samuel V, 793
Teague, Samuel V, 795
Teague, Samuel V, 799
Teague, Samuel V, 811
Teague, Samuel V, 814
Teague, Samuel V, 818
Teague, Samuel P. I, 1162
Teague, Samuel T. V, 799
Teague, Samuel, Jr. V, 803
Teague, Sarah I, 902
Teague, Susanna V, 125
Teague, Susanna V, 130
Teague, Susannah V, 130
Teague, Sybil A. I, 397
Teague, Sybil A. I, 423
Teague, T. Elwood V, 799
Teal, Ann I, 626
Teal, Anna I, 640
Teal, Anna I, 641
Teal, Chas. A. II, 911
Teal, Chas. A. II, 928
Teal, Chas. Albert II, 822
Teal, Harriet II, 911
Teal, Harriet II, 928
Teal, J. L. I, 626
Teal, J. L. I, 640
Teal, J. L. I, 641
Teal, Martha R. II, 911
Teal, Martha R. II, 928
Teal, Martha Roberts II, 822
Teal, Peter II, 911
Teal, Peter II, 928
Teale, Carrie III, 66
Teale, Carrie III, 307
Teaple, Henry H. IV, 1225
Teaple, Mary IV, 1225
Teaple, Sarahann IV, 1225
Teaple, Thomas IV, 1225
Tearl, Joanna IV, 353
Teas, Anna V, 829
Teas, Anna V, 871
Teas, Anne V, 871
Teas, Charles II, 103
Teas, Charles V, 871
Teas, Cora V, 766
Teas, Edward V, 871
Teas, Edward V, 887
Teas, John II, 103
Teas, John V, 887
Teas, John Carter V, 871
Teas, Joseph L. V, 871
Teas, Martha II, 103
Teas, Mary II, 103
Teas, Mary II, 665
Teas, Mary V, 871
Teas, Mary VI, 729
Teas, Mary VI, 762
Teas, Miriam Hough V, 361

Teas, Phebe Ann V, 871
Teas, Rachel II, 103
Teas, Rachel II, 485
Teas, Rachel II, 665
Teas, Rebecca II, 665
Teas, Rebecca II, 1081
Teas, Sarah V, 361
Teas, Sarah V, 871
Teas, Sarah V, 887
Teas, Sarah A. V, 887
Teas, Sarah C. V, 886
Teas, Sarah C. V, 887
Teas, Stephen V, 871
Teas, Stephen W. V, 829
Teas, Stephen W. V, 871
Teas, Susan C. V, 339
Teas, Susan C. V, 361
Teas, Susannah V, 871
Teas, Thomas V, 871
Teas, Thomas C. IV, 500
Teas, Thomas L. V, 887
Teas, Thomas S. II, 665
Teas, Thomas S. V, 886
Teas, Thomas S. V, 887
Teas, William V, 871
Teas, Zeri V, 361
Teasdale, John IV, 287
Teasdale, John G. IV, 287
Teass, Catherine VI, 858
Teass, Eleanor VI, 858
Teass, Elizabeth VI, 866
Teass, John VI, 821
Teass, John VI, 858
Teass, John VI, 866
Teass, John VI, 1002
Teass, John, Jr. VI, 858
Teass, Lucy VI, 821
Teass, Malinda VI, 858
Teass, Mary VI, 858
Teass, Nancy VI, 1002
Teass, Thomas VI, 821
Teass, Thomas VI, 866
Teass, William VI, 866
Teass, William J. VI, 858
Tebbets, Charles E. III, 310
Tedder, Mary II, 610
Tedder, Mary II, 665
Teegarden, Mary IV, 634
Teegarden, Mary IV, 659
Teeple, Benjamin L. IV, 493
Teeple, Elizabeth IV, 493
Teeple, Hannah Maria IV, 493
Teeple, John IV, 493
Teeple, Joseph IV, 493
Teeple, Joshua IV, 493
Teeple, Juli Ann IV, 493
Teeple, Mary IV, 492
Teeple, Mary IV, 493
Teeple, Rebecca IV, 493
Teeple, Richard IV, 493
Teeple, Susanna Mary T. IV, 493
Teeple, Susanna T. IV, 493
Teeple, Susannah W. IV, 493
Teeple, Thomas IV, 493
Teeple, William IV, 493
Teeples, Henry IV, 500
Tees, John II, 103
Teetars, Ann IV, 679
Teetars, Ann IV, 776
Teetars, John IV, 758
Teetars, Margaret IV, 758
Teetars, Margaret IV, 776
Teetars, Martha IV, 776
Teetars, Mary IV, 758
Teeter, Jacob VI, 858
Teeter, Sophia A. VI, 858
Teeters, Ann IV, 776
Teeters, Elisha IV, 776
Teeters, John IV, 776
Teeters, John IV, 1007
Teeters, Jonathan IV, 776
Teeters, Margaret IV, 776
Teeters, Mary IV, 776
Teeters, Mary IV, 1007
Teeters, Mary, Jr. IV, 776
Teeters, Rebecca IV, 776
Teetors, Elisha IV, 776
Teetors, Job IV, 776
Teetors, John IV, 776
Teetors, Jonathan IV, 776
Teetors, Martha W. IV, 776
Teetors, Susannah IV, 734
Teetors, Susannah IV, 776
Teft, Sarah III, 131
Tegethoff, Carrie Sophia IV, 1340
Tegethoff, Florence IV, 1340
Tegethoff, Florence Ada IV, 1340
Tegue, Alice V, 130
Tegue, Esther V, 130
Tegue, Joseph V, 130
Tegue, Lurannah V, 130
Tegue, Moses V, 130
Tegue, Rebecca V, 130
Tegue, Rhoda V, 130
Teillier, Letitia II, 426
Teillier, Sarah II, 426
Telbram, Richard II, 971
Telfair, Alice G. V, 646
Telfair, Alice Green V, 646
Telfair, John Peyton V, 714
Telfair, Peyton V, 714
Telfair, Wm. B. V, 646
Telitha, Harriet I, 301
Tellier, Sarah II, 426
Tellis, Elizabeth VI, 335
Tellis, Elizabeth VI, 971
Tellis, Richard VI, 335
Tellis, Richard VI, 971
Tellis, Ruth V, 872
Tellous, Jane VI, 343
Telner, Jacob III, 310
Telner, Susanna, Jr. III, 45
Telner, Susannah III, 310
Telner, Susannah, Jr. III, 310
Temanus, Margery IV, 112
Temanus, Margery IV, 115
Temberlake, Hannah VI, 795
Temberlake, Mary VI, 795
Tempas, Joseph II, 426
Temperance, Jane VI, 240
Tempest, James II, 426
Tempest, Joseph II, 426
Tempest, Rachel II, 426
Tempest, Rachel II, 550
Tempest, Rachel II, 665
Tempest, Robert II, 426
Templar, Emily Catharine VI, 652
Templar, Emily Catharine VI, 662
Templar, Emily Catharine VI, 665
Temple, Abraham Parker II, 822
Temple, Abram P. II, 822
Temple, Ada III, 449
Temple, Ada U. III, 399
Temple, Ada U. III, 449
Temple, Alcora Susan I, 18
Temple, Alexander W. IV, 1265
Temple, Allen VI, 130
Temple, Allen VI, 136
Temple, Allen VI, 142
Temple, Allen VI, 144
Temple, Anna II, 426
Temple, Anna II, 770
Temple, Charles III, 310
Temple, Charles III, 372
Temple, Chas. II, 835
Temple, Chas. II, 928
Temple, Chas. III, 449
Temple, Daniel II, 665
Temple, Daniel II, 770
Temple, Daniel G. II, 665
Temple, Edna III, 449
Temple, Edna III, 465
Temple, Edward B. II, 928
Temple, Edward B. III, 310
Temple, Edward Brinton II, 835
Temple, Edward Brinton II, 928
Temple, Elizabeth P. II, 928
Temple, Elizabeth Pratt II, 822
Temple, Emily G. III, 310
Temple, Emily Grace III, 310
Temple, Emily Grace III, 372
Temple, Emily M. III, 449
Temple, Emma II, 822
Temple, Emmett IV, 1296
Temple, Frances M. III, 310
Temple, George IV, 1296
Temple, Glen III, 449
Temple, Hannah II, 822
Temple, Ida IV, 1296
Temple, Ida V, 1021
Temple, Jacob III, 449
Temple, Jacob P. III, 449
Temple, Jacob Paxson III, 449
Temple, Jacob Paxson III, 458
Temple, James VI, 130
Temple, James VI, 142
Temple, Jane II, 770
Temple, Jane V, 1021
Temple, Jane B. II, 770
Temple, Jane Bettle II, 665
Temple, John H. IV, 1296
Temple, John M. II, 928
Temple, John Malin II, 822
Temple, Joseph E. II, 665
Temple, Joseph E. II, 770
Temple, Keturah II, 665
Temple, Keturah II, 770
Temple, Louisa V, 1021
Temple, Lucy B. III, 310
Temple, Lucy Bartram II, 928
Temple, Lucy Taylor II, 835
Temple, Lucy Taylor II, 928
Temple, Mariah IV, 1296
Temple, Martha IV, 847
Temple, Mary I, 374
Temple, Mary I, 423
Temple, Mary II, 426
Temple, Mary II, 665
Temple, Mary A. III, 139
Temple, Mary K. III, 399
Temple, Mira E. II, 665
Temple, Mira E. II, 770
Temple, N. C. V, 1021
Temple, Nathaniel IV, 62
Temple, Neuten C. V, 1021
Temple, Philena III, 449
Temple, Philena M. II, 835
Temple, Philena M. II, 928
Temple, Richard III, 399
Temple, Richard U. III, 449
Temple, Richard Underhill III, 465
Temple, Samuel B. II, 426
Temple, Samuel Bettle II, 426
Temple, Sarah I, 423
Temple, Sarah C. IV, 1265
Temple, Solomon II, 426
Temple, Solomon II, 665
Temple, William VI, 785
Temple, Wm. V, 1021
Templen, Margaret H. V, 466
Templer, Balsena VI, 664
Templer, Balsena VI, 714
Templer, Emily Catharine VI, 664
Templer, Emily Catharine VI, 667
Templer, Emily Catharine VI, 674
Templer, Emily Catharine VI, 714
Templer, Emily Catherine VI, 615
Templer, Emily Catherine VI, 753
Templer, Hannah VI, 714
Templer, Jacob VI, 714
Templer, James VI, 664
Templer, James VI, 714
Temples, Mary I, 594
Temples, Mary I, 598
Temples, Sarah I, 373
Temples, Sarah I, 423
Templeton, Harriet IV, 847
Templeton, Harriet IV, 853
Templeton, Harriot IV, 847
Templeton, Martin VI, 832
Templin, Caroline V, 282
Templin, Caroline V, 466
Templin, Ella V, 466
Templin, Ellen M. V, 466
Templin, Euphemia V, 457
Templin, J. M. V, 466
Templin, James V, 677
Templin, James V, 714
Templin, Joel V, 466
Templin, Letitia V, 282
Templin, Letitia V, 466
Templin, Lettice Reames V, 466
Templin, Lettie V, 282
Templin, Lorena V, 714
Templin, Louise V, 677
Templin, Louise V, 714
Templin, Margaret V, 457
Templin, Margaret V, 466
Templin, Margaret H. V, 466
Templin, Martha IV, 955
Templin, Martha IV, 1007
Templin, Milton V, 457
Templin, Oscar V, 282
Templin, Oscar V, 466
Templin, Russell V, 714
Templin, Sylvanus V, 466
Templin, Unice V, 24
Templin, Unice V, 130
Templin, William W. V, 282
Templin, Wm. V, 466
Tendale, Rachel II, 103
Tender, Maggie V, 207
Tener, Herman V, 714
Tenison, Christopher VI, 953
Tenison, Sarah VI, 341
Tennant, Alfred A. IV, 1357
Tennant, Fannie L. IV, 1357
Tennant, Olivia C. IV, 1357
Tennant, Olivia C. IV, 1382
Tennel, Isabelle Bidgood IV, 1340
Tenney, Anna F. V, 766
Tennis, Laura V, 1021
Tennis, Matilda IV, 774
Tennis, Moses IV, 774
Tennison, Ann VI, 328
Tennison, Ann VI, 341
Tennison, Christopher VI, 941
Tennison, Fanny VI, 922
Tennison, John VI, 328
Tennison, John VI, 341
Tennison, Sarah VI, 328
Tennison, Sarah VI, 341
Tennyson, Sarah VI, 329
Tentham, Mary II, 663
Teples, Henry IV, 500
Teples, Mary IV, 500
Teples, Sarah Ann IV, 500
Teples, Sarah Ann T. IV, 500
Teples, Thomas IV, 500
Teppance, James VI, 842
Teppance, Patty VI, 842
Terel, Anna I, 557
Terel, Anna I, 577
Terell, Cety VI, 260
Terell, Charles VI, 835
Terell, David VI, 841
Terell, Mary W. VI, 803
Terell, Sarah VI, 305
Terell, Winefred VI, 841
Terhune, Frances M. III, 131
Terhune, James III, 131
Terhune, James III, 310
Terhune, Mariette III, 131
Terhune, Mariette III, 310
Terrel, Amanda V, 207
Terrel, Benjamin V, 434
Terrel, Catharine V, 434
Terrel, Christopher V, 130
Terrel, David V, 130
Terrel, David V, 207
Terrel, David, Jr. V, 282
Terrel, David, Jr. V, 447
Terrel, Deborah I, 577
Terrel, Edward VI, 1004
Terrel, Elizabeth V, 207
Terrel, Elizabeth V, 434
Terrel, Esther V, 173
Terrel, Esther V, 207
Terrel, Hampton W. V, 207
Terrel, Harriet M. V, 207
Terrel, James V, 434
Terrel, Jane V, 434
Terrel, John V, 434
Terrel, John H. V, 207
Terrel, Joseph V, 130
Terrel, Judith V, 130
Terrel, Lois A. V, 207
Terrel, Mary V, 130
Terrel, Mary V, 207
Terrel, Mary S. V, 207
Terrel, Nancy M. V, 207
Terrel, Pleasant V, 130
Terrel, Pleasant V, 173
Terrel, Pleasant V, 207
Terrel, Rebecca V, 434
Terrel, Robert W. V, 207
Terrel, Sarah V, 130
Terrel, Sarah V, 434
Terrel, Susannah V, 434
Terrel, Thomas V, 130
Terrel, William V, 434
Terrell, ??? IV, 1303
Terrell, ??? V, 466
Terrell, ??? VI, 223
Terrell, ??? VI, 293
Terrell, Abagail VI, 274
Terrell, Ada V, 361
Terrell, Adaline E. V, 283
Terrell, Adalyne V, 282
Terrell, Agatha I, 536
Terrell, Agatha I, 577
Terrell, Agatha VI, 275
Terrell, Agatha VI, 319
Terrell, Agatha VI, 341
Terrell, Agatha VI, 342
Terrell, Agga VI, 274
Terrell, Aggatha I, 577
Terrell, Albert V, 714
Terrell, Alexander Watkins VI, 342
Terrell, Alice IV, 1340
Terrell, Alice V, 361
Terrell, Alice V, 935
Terrell, Alice E. V, 348
Terrell, Alice E. V, 361
Terrell, Allen J. V, 361
Terrell, Allen McKay V, 714
Terrell, Allen P. V, 283
Terrell, Amos H. IV, 227
Terrell, Amos H. IV, 288
Terrell, Amos H. IV, 1007
Terrell, Amos H. V, 872
Terrell, Amy VI, 235
Terrell, Amy VI, 274
Terrell, Amy VI, 276
Terrell, Ann IV, 287
Terrell, Ann V, 282
Terrell, Ann VI, 275
Terrell, Ann VI, 341
Terrell, Ann VI, 342
Terrell, Ann L. IV, 227
Terrell, Ann L. IV, 288
Terrell, Ann L. VI, 258
Terrell, Ann L. VI, 275
Terrell, Ann L. VI, 812
Terrell, Ann M. V, 261
Terrell, Anna I, 577
Terrell, Anna V, 282
Terrell, Anna VI, 275
Terrell, Anna VI, 319
Terrell, Anna E. V, 283
Terrell, Anna E. V, 361
Terrell, Anna L. VI, 258
Terrell, Anna L. VI, 277
Terrell, Anna Lynch VI, 27
Terrell, Anna M. V, 64
Terrell, Anna M. V, 361
Terrell, Anne VI, 258
Terrell, Anne VI, 273
Terrell, Anne VI, 274
Terrell, Anne VI, 275
Terrell, Anne VI, 342
Terrell, Arthur IV, 1340
Terrell, Asenath V, 434
Terrell, Asenith V, 434
Terrell, B. J. V, 434
Terrell, Bailey VI, 187
Terrell, Beecher V, 434
Terrell, Benjamin V, 434
Terrell, Benjamin VI, 274
Terrell, Benjamin VI, 276
Terrell, Benjamin VI, 342
Terrell, Betsy VI, 858
Terrell, Betsy H. VI, 842
Terrell, Betty VI, 274
Terrell, Bety VI, 260
Terrell, Bety VI, 274
Terrell, Caleb VI, 274
Terrell, Caleb VI, 277
Terrell, Caroline VI, 214
Terrell, Caroline VI, 230
Terrell, Caroline VI, 274
Terrell, Caroline VI, 277
Terrell, Catey VI, 276
Terrell, Catharine V, 434
Terrell, Catherine V, 434
Terrell, Catherine VI, 274
Terrell, Caty IV, 288
Terrell, Caty VI, 238
Terrell, Caty VI, 274
Terrell, Caty VI, 277
Terrell, Celesta Jane V, 434
Terrell, Cety VI, 275
Terrell, Charity VI, 858
Terrell, Charity Ann V, 283
Terrell, Charles V, 361
Terrell, Charles VI, 274
Terrell, Charles E. V, 283
Terrell, Charles Earnice V,
Terrell, Charles L. VI, 276
Terrell, Charles L. VI, 858
Terrell, Charles L. VI, 863
Terrell, Charles Linch VI, 2
Terrell, Charles Lynch VI, 2
Terrell, Charles Lynch VI, 3
Terrell, Charles Warren V, 4
Terrell, Chas. E. V, 361
Terrell, Chiles VI, 274
Terrell, Chiles VI, 276
Terrell, Chris. V, 407
Terrell, Christopher IV, 227
Terrell, Christopher V, 276
Terrell, Christopher V, 282
Terrell, Christopher VI, 319
Terrell, Christopher VI, 341
Terrell, Christopher VI, 342
Terrell, Christopher VI, 343
Terrell, Christopher VI, 355
Terrell, Christopher C. V, 28
Terrell, Christopher Cornelius V, 283
Terrell, Christopher J. VI, 3
Terrell, Christopher M. V, 28
Terrell, Christopher M. V, 4
Terrell, Clara V, 466
Terrell, Clara A. V, 466
Terrell, Clara A. V, 714
Terrell, Clara B. V, 714
Terrell, Clarai V, 282
Terrell, Clarinda V, 282
Terrell, Clarinda V, 283
Terrell, Clarinda V, 291
Terrell, Clarinda V, 455
Terrell, Clarinda V, 456
Terrell, Clarinda V, 466

ll, Clark IV, 192
ll, Clark IV, 208
ll, Clark IV, 227
ll, Clark IV, 228
ll, Clark IV, 281
ll, Clark IV, 287
ll, Clark IV, 288
ll, Clark VI, 274
ll, Clark M. I, 258
ll, Clark, Jr. IV, 288
ll, Clark, Sr. IV, 288
ell, Clarke VI, 277
ell, Clayton V, 283
ell, Clayton V, 361
ell, Clinton S. V, 714
ell, Clyde V, 466
ell, Collins VI, 319
ell, David V, 243
ell, David V, 282
ell, David V, 283
ell, David V, 292
ell, David VI, 215
ell, David VI, 232
ell, David VI, 234
rell, David VI, 235
rell, David VI, 239
rell, David VI, 240
rell, David VI, 246
rell, David VI, 249
rell, David VI, 256
rell, David VI, 274
rell, David VI, 275
rell, David VI, 276
rell, David VI, 279
rell, David VI, 295
rell, David VI, 312
rell, David VI, 319
rell, David VI, 341
rell, David VI, 342
rell, David VI, 1020
rell, David E. V, 282
rrell, David E. V, 283
rrell, David E. V, 361
rrell, David Edgar V, 282
rrell, David F. V, 282
rrell, David F. V, 283
rrell, David Terrell VI, 319
rrell, David W. V, 283
rrell, David, Jr. V, 282
rrell, David, Jr. VI, 275
rrell, David, Jr. VI, 280
rrell, David, Sr. VI, 342
rrell, Deborah I, 577
rrell, Deborah I, 841
rrell, Deborah I, 902
rrell, Deborah VI, 276
rrell, Deborah VI, 342
rrell, Deborough I, 577
rrell, Dudley VI, 812
rrell, Dudley VI, 836
rrell, Dudley VI, 842
rrell, Dudley VI, 858
errell, Dudley VI, 867
errell, Duff VI, 275
errell, E. Annetta V, 466
errell, E. Everett V, 714
errell, E??? VI, 277
errell, Edith I, 927
errell, Edith H. V, 352
errell, Edith H. V, 361
errell, Edna V, 262
errell, Edna V, 282
errell, Edna V, 283
errell, Edna VI, 187
errell, Edward VI, 274
errell, Edward VI, 276
Terrell, Edward VI, 318
Terrell, Edward VI, 324
Terrell, Edward VI, 341
Terrell, Edward VI, 342
Terrell, Edward VI, 355
Terrell, Edward VI, 832
Terrell, Edward Everett V, 434
Terrell, Edward Everett, Jr. V, 714
Terrell, Edward, Jr. VI, 355
Terrell, Edwin V, 282
Terrell, Edwin V, 283
Terrell, Edwin VI, 277
Terrell, Elias V, 534
Terrell, Elisabeth V, 244
Terrell, Elisabeth V, 283
Terrell, Eliza IV, 774
Terrell, Eliza A. V, 282
Terrell, Eliza Ann VI, 274
Terrell, Eliza Ann VI, 277
Terrell, Elizabeth IV, 279
Terrell, Elizabeth IV, 287
Terrell, Elizabeth IV, 288
Terrell, Elizabeth V, 276
Terrell, Elizabeth V, 282
Terrell, Elizabeth V, 283
Terrell, Elizabeth V, 289
Terrell, Elizabeth V, 331
Terrell, Elizabeth V, 361
Terrell, Elizabeth V, 365
Terrell, Elizabeth V, 407
Terrell, Elizabeth V, 434
Terrell, Elizabeth V, 466
Terrell, Elizabeth VI, 179
Terrell, Elizabeth VI, 210
Terrell, Elizabeth VI, 215
Terrell, Elizabeth VI, 241
Terrell, Elizabeth VI, 265
Terrell, Elizabeth VI, 274
Terrell, Elizabeth VI, 276
Terrell, Elizabeth VI, 277
Terrell, Elizabeth VI, 319
Terrell, Elizabeth VI, 320
Terrell, Elizabeth VI, 328
Terrell, Elizabeth VI, 341
Terrell, Elizabeth VI, 342
Terrell, Elizabeth VI, 355
Terrell, Elizabeth VI, 832
Terrell, Elizabeth VI, 833
Terrell, Elizabeth VI, 863
Terrell, Elizabeth A. IV, 288
Terrell, Elizabeth Ann IV, 288
Terrell, Elizabeth Ann IV, 305
Terrell, Elizabeth Ann IV, 1007
Terrell, Elizabeth C. IV, 288
Terrell, Elizabeth D. IV, 256
Terrell, Elizabeth D. IV, 305
Terrell, Elizabeth D. IV, 1007
Terrell, Elizabeth D. VI, 182
Terrell, Elizabeth D. VI, 215
Terrell, Elizabeth W. V, 361
Terrell, Elva R. V, 361
Terrell, Elva R. V, 466
Terrell, Emma Ann V, 283
Terrell, Estella V, 434
Terrell, Esther I, 258
Terrell, Esther IV, 288
Terrell, Esther V, 282
Terrell, Esther V, 361
Terrell, Esther Gladys M. I, 258
Terrell, Esther Inez V, 434
Terrell, Esther P. I, 258
Terrell, Eva V, 720
Terrell, Everett V, 714
Terrell, Faith V, 656
Terrell, Faith Austin V, 714
Terrell, Flora A. V, 283
Terrell, Flora A. V, 361
Terrell, Flora Annis V, 282
Terrell, Florence Asenath V, 434
Terrell, Florence Morrow V, 434
Terrell, Florence Russell IV, 1340
Terrell, Francis Robert V, 434
Terrell, Frank V, 283
Terrell, George IV, 287
Terrell, George V, 282
Terrell, George VI, 274
Terrell, George VI, 277
Terrell, George M. V, 714
Terrell, George T. VI, 327
Terrell, Gerrard VI, 342
Terrell, Gladys M. I, 258
Terrell, Glen V, 361
Terrell, Glenn L. IV, 1340
Terrell, Gurney V, 656
Terrell, Hampton V, 361
Terrell, Hampton W. V, 196
Terrell, Hampton W. V, 282
Terrell, Hampton W. V, 283
Terrell, Hannah IV, 287
Terrell, Hannah K. IV, 208
Terrell, Hannah K. IV, 288
Terrell, Harriet M. V, 196
Terrell, Harriet M. V, 282
Terrell, Harriet M. V, 283
Terrell, Harriett M. V, 361
Terrell, Harrison IV, 1340
Terrell, Harry V, 283
Terrell, Harry E. V, 283
Terrell, Hattie M. V, 283
Terrell, Helen Avelyne V, 282
Terrell, Helen E. V, 283
Terrell, Henry VI, 214
Terrell, Henry VI, 215
Terrell, Henry VI, 218
Terrell, Henry VI, 219
Terrell, Henry VI, 232
Terrell, Henry VI, 258
Terrell, Henry VI, 260
Terrell, Henry VI, 273
Terrell, Henry VI, 274
Terrell, Henry VI, 275
Terrell, Henry VI, 276
Terrell, Henry VI, 278
Terrell, Henry VI, 338
Terrell, Henry VI, 342
Terrell, Henry VI, 854
Terrell, Henry VI, 858
Terrell, Henry, Jr. VI, 275
Terrell, Hester IV, 288
Terrell, Hester G. IV, 226
Terrell, Hester G. IV, 288
Terrell, Hester G. IV, 775
Terrell, Hester G. IV, 1340
Terrell, Hezekiah IV, 1340
Terrell, Hezekiah V, 361
Terrell, Hezekiah V, 935
Terrell, Hezekiah M. IV, 1340
Terrell, Hezekiah M. V, 935
Terrell, Homer Clark I, 258
Terrell, Howard V. V, 714
Terrell, Howard Vincent V, 714
Terrell, Hoyt Brooks I, 258
Terrell, Ira IV, 287
Terrell, Isabella IV, 256
Terrell, Isabella IV, 288
Terrell, Isabella VI, 250
Terrell, Israel V, 249
Terrell, Israel V, 282
Terrell, Israel V, 714
Terrell, Israel A. V, 282
Terrell, Israel A. V, 283
Terrell, Israel A. V, 361
Terrell, Israel A. V, 363
Terrell, Israel Allen V, 282
Terrell, Israel, Jr. V, 283
Terrell, James V, 434
Terrell, James VI, 250
Terrell, James VI, 858
Terrell, James H. I, 927
Terrell, James H. V, 282
Terrell, James H. V, 283
Terrell, James H. V, 352
Terrell, James H. V, 361
Terrell, James H. VI, 277
Terrell, James J. V, 283
Terrell, James L. V, 282
Terrell, Jane IV, 288
Terrell, Jane V, 233
Terrell, Jane V, 282
Terrell, Jane V, 283
Terrell, Jane V, 361
Terrell, Jane V, 417
Terrell, Jane V, 432
Terrell, Jane V, 434
Terrell, Jane VI, 324
Terrell, Jane VI, 341
Terrell, Jane VI, 342
Terrell, Jane VI, 355
Terrell, Jean VI, 341
Terrell, Jean VI, 342
Terrell, Jemima VI, 858
Terrell, Jesse VI, 185
Terrell, Jesse VI, 187
Terrell, Jesse VI, 190
Terrell, Jesse VI, 194
Terrell, Jesse VI, 214
Terrell, Jesse VI, 215
Terrell, Jesse VI, 274
Terrell, Jesse VI, 276
Terrell, Jesse VI, 277
Terrell, Joana IV, 288
Terrell, Joanna IV, 287
Terrell, Joanna IV, 288
Terrell, Joanna VI, 230
Terrell, Joanna VI, 274
Terrell, Joanna VI, 276
Terrell, Joanna VI, 277
Terrell, Joel Albert V, 872
Terrell, John IV, 287
Terrell, John IV, 288
Terrell, John IV, 1340
Terrell, John V, 361
Terrell, John V, 365
Terrell, John V, 417
Terrell, John V, 434
Terrell, John VI, 232
Terrell, John VI, 240
Terrell, John VI, 250
Terrell, John VI, 274
Terrell, John VI, 277
Terrell, John VI, 858
Terrell, John A. VI, 277
Terrell, John H. V, 282
Terrell, John H. V, 283
Terrell, John H. V, 289
Terrell, John H. V, 331
Terrell, John H. V, 361
Terrell, John J. VI, 342
Terrell, John Lasley VI, 342
Terrell, Johnson VI, 341
Terrell, Johnson VI, 342
Terrell, Johnson VI, 355
Terrell, Jonathan VI, 250
Terrell, Jonathan VI, 274
Terrell, Jonathan VI, 276
Terrell, Jonathan VI, 277
Terrell, Joseph IV, 288
Terrell, Joseph IV, 1007
Terrell, Joseph V, 261
Terrell, Joseph V, 282
Terrell, Joseph V, 283
Terrell, Joseph VI, 19
Terrell, Joseph VI, 258
Terrell, Joseph VI, 272
Terrell, Joseph VI, 274
Terrell, Joseph VI, 275
Terrell, Joseph VI, 277
Terrell, Joseph Christopher VI, 342
Terrell, Joseph W. VI, 277
Terrell, Joseph Walker VI, 274
Terrell, Judith V, 243
Terrell, Judith V, 281
Terrell, Judith V, 282
Terrell, Judith V, 283
Terrell, Judith VI, 187
Terrell, Judith VI, 274
Terrell, Judith VI, 318
Terrell, Judith VI, 341
Terrell, Judith VI, 342
Terrell, Judith VI, 355
Terrell, Kitty VI, 274
Terrell, Kitty VI, 276
Terrell, Kitty VI, 277
Terrell, Kitty Pleasant IV, 774
Terrell, Kitty Pleasants VI, 277
Terrell, Lemmel IV, 919
Terrell, Lemuel IV, 774
Terrell, Lemuel VI, 274
Terrell, Lemuel VI, 276
Terrell, Lemuel VI, 277
Terrell, Leona V, 466
Terrell, Letitia W. VI, 812
Terrell, Letty VI, 858
Terrell, Lewis Horton V, 282
Terrell, Lewis Horton V, 283
Terrell, Lewis P. V, 283
Terrell, Lewis P. V, 466
Terrell, Lois V, 173
Terrell, Lois A. V, 173
Terrell, Lorana M. V, 601
Terrell, Louisa VI, 274
Terrell, Lucy VI, 244
Terrell, Lucy VI, 256
Terrell, Lucy VI, 274
Terrell, Lucy VI, 275
Terrell, Lucy VI, 276
Terrell, Lucy VI, 277
Terrell, Lucy VI, 305
Terrell, Lucy VI, 327
Terrell, Lucy VI, 341
Terrell, Lucy VI, 342
Terrell, Lucy W. IV, 288
Terrell, Lucy W. IV, 305
Terrell, Lucy Winston IV, 288
Terrell, Lycurgus V, 283
Terrell, Lydia IV, 267
Terrell, Lydia IV, 288
Terrell, Lydia IV, 562
Terrell, Lydia V, 126
Terrell, Lydia J. IV, 288
Terrell, Lydia J. IV, 1296
Terrell, Lydia J. IV, 1299
Terrell, Lydia Jane IV, 775
Terrell, M. V, 282
Terrell, Mabel IV, 1340
Terrell, Mahala IV, 260
Terrell, Mahala IV, 287
Terrell, Mahala VI, 274
Terrell, Mahala VI, 277
Terrell, Mahala VI, 867
Terrell, Mahlon IV, 288
Terrell, Mahlon VI, 274
Terrell, Malinda V, 282
Terrell, Malinda V, 283
Terrell, Manson V, 276
Terrell, Manson V, 282
Terrell, Manson V, 283
Terrell, Margaret VI, 250
Terrell, Margaret VI, 274
Terrell, Margaret VI, 276
Terrell, Maria VI, 274
Terrell, Marianna I, 927
Terrell, Martha IV, 774
Terrell, Martha V, 361
Terrell, Martha VI, 251
Terrell, Martha A. V, 283
Terrell, Martha E. V, 283
Terrell, Martha E. VI, 816
Terrell, Martha Elma V, 282
Terrell, Martha M. V, 466
Terrell, Martha M. VI, 858
Terrell, Mary I, 577
Terrell, Mary IV, 192
Terrell, Mary IV, 208
Terrell, Mary IV, 227
Terrell, Mary IV, 228
Terrell, Mary IV, 287
Terrell, Mary V, 239
Terrell, Mary V, 243
Terrell, Mary V, 246
Terrell, Mary V, 282
Terrell, Mary V, 292
Terrell, Mary V, 613
Terrell, Mary V, 646
Terrell, Mary V, 714
Terrell, Mary V, 872
Terrell, Mary VI, 190
Terrell, Mary VI, 194
Terrell, Mary VI, 214
Terrell, Mary VI, 215
Terrell, Mary VI, 235
Terrell, Mary VI, 257
Terrell, Mary VI, 274
Terrell, Mary VI, 275
Terrell, Mary VI, 276
Terrell, Mary VI, 277
Terrell, Mary VI, 308
Terrell, Mary VI, 330
Terrell, Mary VI, 338
Terrell, Mary VI, 341
Terrell, Mary VI, 342
Terrell, Mary VI, 355
Terrell, Mary VI, 858
Terrell, Mary Ann VI, 250
Terrell, Mary Ann VI, 265
Terrell, Mary Ann VI, 266
Terrell, Mary Ann VI, 274
Terrell, Mary Ann VI, 277
Terrell, Mary Ann Hunnicutt VI, 277
Terrell, Mary Bailey VI, 185
Terrell, Mary Bailey VI, 215
Terrell, Mary Bailey VI, 274
Terrell, Mary Bailey VI, 276
Terrell, Mary Brackney V, 646
Terrell, Mary Davis V, 282
Terrell, Mary E. V, 223
Terrell, Mary E. V, 282
Terrell, Mary E. V, 283
Terrell, Mary E. V, 714
Terrell, Mary Edna V, 282
Terrell, Mary F. IV, 288
Terrell, Mary H. V, 361
Terrell, Mary J. IV, 281
Terrell, Mary J. IV, 288
Terrell, Mary J. VI, 845
Terrell, Mary Louise V, 714
Terrell, Mary Matilda V, 714
Terrell, Mary T. IV, 227
Terrell, Mary T. IV, 288
Terrell, Mary T. V, 872
Terrell, Mary T. Ladd VI, 215
Terrell, Mary W. IV, 272
Terrell, Mary W. IV, 288
Terrell, Mathew IV, 260
Terrell, Mathew IV, 287
Terrell, Mathew IV, 288
Terrell, Mathew IV, 1007
Terrell, Mathew VI, 276
Terrell, Matilda V, 714
Terrell, Matilda VI, 274
Terrell, Matilda VI, 277
Terrell, Matilda C. V, 361
Terrell, Matthew IV, 226
Terrell, Matthew IV, 256
Terrell, Matthew IV, 279
Terrell, Matthew IV, 287
Terrell, Matthew IV, 288
Terrell, Matthew IV, 305
Terrell, Matthew IV, 774
Terrell, Matthew IV, 775
Terrell, Matthew VI, 182
Terrell, Matthew VI, 210
Terrell, Matthew VI, 215
Terrell, Matthew VI, 274
Terrell, Matthew VI, 277
Terrell, Matthew P. VI, 182
Terrell, Matthew P. VI, 215
Terrell, Matthew P. VI, 261
Terrell, Matthew P. VI, 274
Terrell, Matthew P. VI, 276
Terrell, Matthew Peatross VI, 274
Terrell, Matthew W. IV, 227
Terrell, Matthew, Jr. IV, 288
Terrell, Mattie C. V, 714
Terrell, Maty W. IV, 288
Terrell, Micajah I, 541
Terrell, Micajah I, 577
Terrell, Micajah VI, 187
Terrell, Micajah VI, 258
Terrell, Micajah VI, 274
Terrell, Micajah VI, 275
Terrell, Micajah VI, 276
Terrell, Micajah VI, 290
Terrell, Micajah VI, 341
Terrell, Micajah VI, 342

Terrell, Micajah T. VI, 327
Terrell, Micajah, Jr. I, 577
Terrell, Michael IV, 288
Terrell, Mildred VI, 233
Terrell, Mildred VI, 234
Terrell, Milla VI, 234
Terrell, Milla VI, 274
Terrell, Milla VI, 275
Terrell, Milley VI, 275
Terrell, Millicent VI, 275
Terrell, Millie V, 173
Terrell, Millie V, 361
Terrell, Millie V, 434
Terrell, Milly V, 434
Terrell, Milly VI, 277
Terrell, Minnie V, 466
Terrell, Miriam VI, 274
Terrell, Miriam VI, 276
Terrell, Miriam Murdaugh VI, 250
Terrell, Miriam Murdaugh VI, 274
Terrell, Miriam Murdock VI, 250
Terrell, Mishael IV, 287
Terrell, Molley VI, 295
Terrell, Molley VI, 342
Terrell, Molly VI, 295
Terrell, Molly VI, 341
Terrell, Nancy V, 455
Terrell, Nancy VI, 238
Terrell, Nancy VI, 239
Terrell, Nancy VI, 274
Terrell, Nancy VI, 276
Terrell, Nancy VI, 277
Terrell, Nancy VI, 319
Terrell, Nancy VI, 342
Terrell, Nancy VI, 803
Terrell, Nancy VI, 858
Terrell, Nancy E. V, 283
Terrell, Nancy Thomas IV, 774
Terrell, Nancy Thomas VI, 277
Terrell, Nannie V, 361
Terrell, Nanny VI, 274
Terrell, Narcissa V, 282
Terrell, Nathan IV, 1007
Terrell, Nicey L. VI, 277
Terrell, Nicy Lynch IV, 774
Terrell, Nicy Lynch VI, 277
Terrell, Nisa Linch IV, 774
Terrell, Olive IV, 288
Terrell, Olive B. IV, 256
Terrell, Olive B. IV, 288
Terrell, Olive Margaret I, 258
Terrell, Olive P. IV, 256
Terrell, Oliver C. I, 258
Terrell, Orlando V, 466
Terrell, Parmelia VI, 274
Terrell, Patsy VI, 342
Terrell, Patty V, 361
Terrell, Patty VI, 256
Terrell, Patty VI, 274
Terrell, Patty VI, 276
Terrell, Patty VI, 343
Terrell, Penelope VI, 858
Terrell, Peter VI, 858
Terrell, Phebe J. V, 249
Terrell, Phebe J. V, 250
Terrell, Phebe J. V, 283
Terrell, Phebe Jane V, 282
Terrell, Pleasant V, 282
Terrell, Pleasant V, 361
Terrell, Pleasant VI, 19
Terrell, Pleasant VI, 215
Terrell, Pleasant VI, 235
Terrell, Pleasant VI, 238
Terrell, Pleasant VI, 244
Terrell, Pleasant VI, 257
Terrell, Pleasant VI, 274
Terrell, Pleasant VI, 275
Terrell, Pleasant VI, 276
Terrell, Pleasant VI, 277
Terrell, Pleasant VI, 342
Terrell, Pleasant A. V, 283
Terrell, Pleasant M. V, 283
Terrell, Pleasant M. V, 348
Terrell, Pleasant M. V, 361
Terrell, Pleasant M. V, 935
Terrell, Pleasants VI, 214
Terrell, Pleasants VI, 274
Terrell, Pleasants VI, 276
Terrell, Pleasants VI, 341
Terrell, Polly VI, 319
Terrell, Polly VI, 341
Terrell, Polly VI, 342
Terrell, Polly VI, 835
Terrell, Polly VI, 836
Terrell, Polly VI, 858
Terrell, R. V, 282
Terrell, Rachel IV, 260
Terrell, Rachel IV, 287
Terrell, Rachel IV, 288
Terrell, Rachel V, 276
Terrell, Rachel V, 282
Terrell, Rachel V, 283
Terrell, Rachel VI, 244
Terrell, Rachel VI, 245
Terrell, Rachel VI, 274
Terrell, Rachel VI, 276
Terrell, Rachel VI, 277
Terrell, Rachel VI, 319
Terrell, Rachel M. IV, 192
Terrell, Rachel M. IV, 288
Terrell, Randal H. V, 714
Terrell, Randall V, 714
Terrell, Rebecca IV, 172
Terrell, Rebecca IV, 287
Terrell, Rebecca IV, 288
Terrell, Rebecca IV, 774
Terrell, Rebecca V, 283
Terrell, Rebecca V, 434
Terrell, Rebecca V, 456
Terrell, Rebecca VI, 19
Terrell, Rebecca VI, 235
Terrell, Rebecca VI, 274
Terrell, Rebecca VI, 276
Terrell, Rebecca VI, 277
Terrell, Rebecca B. IV, 267
Terrell, Rebecca B. IV, 288
Terrell, Rebecca B. IV, 500
Terrell, Rebecca J. V, 283
Terrell, Rebeckah VI, 276
Terrell, Rebeckah VI, 858
Terrell, Rhoda VI, 274
Terrell, Rhoda VI, 276
Terrell, Rhoda VI, 277
Terrell, Richmond VI, 147
Terrell, Richmond VI, 215
Terrell, Richmond VI, 277
Terrell, Robert VI, 215
Terrell, Robert VI, 274
Terrell, Robert VI, 276
Terrell, Robert VI, 277
Terrell, Robert VI, 341
Terrell, Robert S. VI, 277
Terrell, Robert Samuel IV, 774
Terrell, Robert Samuel VI, 277
Terrell, Roy V, 283
Terrell, Ruth V, 282
Terrell, Ruth A. V, 283
Terrell, Ruth A. V, 331
Terrell, Ruth A. V, 361
Terrell, Ruth Ann V, 282
Terrell, Ruth E. V, 224
Terrell, Ruth E. V, 283
Terrell, Rutherford V, 282
Terrell, Rutherford V, 283
Terrell, Salley VI, 261
Terrell, Salley VI, 274
Terrell, Salley VI, 276
Terrell, Salley VI, 277
Terrell, Sally IV, 260
Terrell, Sally IV, 269
Terrell, Sally IV, 287
Terrell, Sally IV, 288
Terrell, Sally VI, 275
Terrell, Sally VI, 277
Terrell, Sally VI, 319
Terrell, Sally VI, 342
Terrell, Sally VI, 858
Terrell, Samuel V, 282
Terrell, Samuel V, 283
Terrell, Samuel VI, 179
Terrell, Samuel VI, 215
Terrell, Samuel VI, 265
Terrell, Samuel VI, 274
Terrell, Samuel VI, 275
Terrell, Samuel VI, 277
Terrell, Samuel VI, 341
Terrell, Samuel VI, 342
Terrell, Samuel VI, 822
Terrell, Samuel VI, 832
Terrell, Samuel VI, 858
Terrell, Samuel C. V, 282
Terrell, Samuel C. V, 283
Terrell, Samuel H. V, 283
Terrell, Samuel S. V, 282
Terrell, Samuel S. V, 283
Terrell, Sarah I, 577
Terrell, Sarah I, 582
Terrell, Sarah IV, 287
Terrell, Sarah IV, 288
Terrell, Sarah V, 282
Terrell, Sarah V, 292
Terrell, Sarah V, 361
Terrell, Sarah V, 429
Terrell, Sarah V, 434
Terrell, Sarah VI, 214
Terrell, Sarah VI, 215
Terrell, Sarah VI, 218
Terrell, Sarah VI, 219
Terrell, Sarah VI, 258
Terrell, Sarah VI, 274
Terrell, Sarah VI, 275
Terrell, Sarah VI, 276
Terrell, Sarah VI, 296
Terrell, Sarah VI, 312
Terrell, Sarah VI, 341
Terrell, Sarah VI, 342
Terrell, Sarah VI, 355
Terrell, Sarah VI, 867
Terrell, Sarah VI, 1004
Terrell, Sarah A. VI, 814
Terrell, Sarah H. IV, 279
Terrell, Sarah H. IV, 288
Terrell, Sarah H. V, 282
Terrell, Sarah H. V, 283
Terrell, Sarah H. V, 361
Terrell, Sarah H. V, 363
Terrell, Sarah J. IV, 281
Terrell, Sarah J. IV, 288
Terrell, Sarah V. V, 282
Terrell, Sarah V. V, 283
Terrell, Sicily V, 282
Terrell, Sidney H. V, 249
Terrell, Sidney H. V, 282
Terrell, Sidney H. V, 361
Terrell, Sidney H. V, 363
Terrell, Sisley V, 407
Terrell, Sisley A. V, 282
Terrell, Susan VI, 342
Terrell, Susanna V, 434
Terrell, Susanna V, 714
Terrell, Susanna VI, 319
Terrell, Susanna VI, 324
Terrell, Susanna VI, 342
Terrell, Susannah V, 417
Terrell, Susannah V, 434
Terrell, Susannah C. V, 714
Terrell, Sydney H. V, 283
Terrell, T. P. V, 456
Terrell, Tarlton VI, 274
Terrell, Tasso V, 173
Terrell, Thomas IV, 287
Terrell, Thomas IV, 288
Terrell, Thomas IV, 774
Terrell, Thomas V, 126
Terrell, Thomas V, 283
Terrell, Thomas VI, 230
Terrell, Thomas VI, 235
Terrell, Thomas VI, 244
Terrell, Thomas VI, 273
Terrell, Thomas VI, 274
Terrell, Thomas VI, 276
Terrell, Thomas VI, 277
Terrell, Thomas H. IV, 288
Terrell, Thomas M. VI, 858
Terrell, Thomas P. V, 466
Terrell, Thomas Scattergood VI, 277
Terrell, Thos. H. IV, 172
Terrell, Thos. H. IV, 272
Terrell, Thos. H. IV, 287
Terrell, Thos. P. V, 455
Terrell, Thos. P. V, 466
Terrell, Thos. Pretlow VI, 250
Terrell, Timothy VI, 250
Terrell, Timothy VI, 274
Terrell, Timothy VI, 276
Terrell, Timothy VI, 858
Terrell, Timothy VI, 865
Terrell, Ursula VI, 274
Terrell, Ursula VI, 275
Terrell, Virginia III, 91
Terrell, Walter VI, 277
Terrell, Widow Deborah I, 541
Terrell, William V, 434
Terrell, William VI, 214
Terrell, William VI, 277
Terrell, William VI, 319
Terrell, William VI, 817
Terrell, William VI, 867
Terrell, William C. IV, 288
Terrell, William F. VI, 277
Terrell, William G. V, 282
Terrell, William G. V, 283
Terrell, William H. V, 714
Terrell, William M. V, 282
Terrell, William Manson V, 283
Terrell, William Penn VI, 274
Terrell, Willie A. V, 283
Terrell, Winiford VI, 342
Terrell, Winifred VI, 274
Terrell, Winifred VI, 342
Terrell, Winifred VI, 1020
Terrell, Winneford VI, 342
Terrell, Wm. IV, 267
Terrell, Wm. V, 714
Terrell, Wm. G. V, 361
Terrey, Elizabeth V, 283
Terrey, Sarah V, 283
Terril, Amos H. V, 844
Terril, Amos H. V, 872
Terril, Elizabeth V, 872
Terril, Henry VI, 291
Terril, Mahala IV, 590
Terril, Mary T. V, 844
Terril, Mary T. V, 872
Terril, Matthew IV, 500
Terril, Matthew V, 872
Terril, Rebecca IV, 464
Terril, Rebecca IV, 500
Terril, Rebecca B. IV, 500
Terril, Sarah IV, 500
Terril, Thomas H. IV, 500
Terril, Thos. H. IV, 464
Terrill, Adaline E. V, 283
Terrill, Amos H. V, 872
Terrill, Anna V, 26
Terrill, Anna V, 130
Terrill, Anna M. V, 130
Terrill, Annie V, 130
Terrill, Benjamin V, 434
Terrill, Benjamin VI, 920
Terrill, Catherine V, 434
Terrill, Catherine E. VI, 797
Terrill, Christopher V, 130
Terrill, Christopher V, 958
Terrill, Christopher V, 960
Terrill, Clark V, 130
Terrill, Cornelia V, 130
Terrill, David V, 130
Terrill, David V, 960
Terrill, David VI, 286
Terrill, David VI, 287
Terrill, David Edgar V, 282
Terrill, Dudley VI, 798
Terrill, Edward VI, 252
Terrill, Edward VI, 254
Terrill, Edward VI, 338
Terrill, Edward VI, 854
Terrill, Elizabeth V, 282
Terrill, Elizabeth V, 428
Terrill, Elizabeth V, 434
Terrill, Elizabeth V, 872
Terrill, Elizabeth V, 958
Terrill, Elizabeth V, 960
Terrill, Flora Annis V, 282
Terrill, Hampton W. V, 282
Terrill, Henry VI, 855
Terrill, James V, 434
Terrill, Jane V, 428
Terrill, Jane V, 434
Terrill, Joel Albert V, 872
Terrill, John V, 428
Terrill, John V, 434
Terrill, John H. V, 282
Terrill, Joseph V, 130
Terrill, Judith V, 130
Terrill, Louisa VI, 252
Terrill, Lurana V, 130
Terrill, Lurana M. V, 130
Terrill, Lydia V, 130
Terrill, Mary V, 130
Terrill, Mary V, 279
Terrill, Mary V, 282
Terrill, Mary V, 872
Terrill, Mary V, 960
Terrill, Mary VI, 252
Terrill, Mary VI, 254
Terrill, Mary VI, 338
Terrill, Mary VI, 850
Terrill, Mary VI, 854
Terrill, Mary Edna V, 282
Terrill, Mary S. V, 130
Terrill, Mary T. V, 872
Terrill, Matthew V, 872
Terrill, Nancy VI, 798
Terrill, Narcissa V, 282
Terrill, Narcissa V, 293
Terrill, Pearson II, 665
Terrill, Phebe Jane V, 282
Terrill, Pleasant V, 130
Terrill, Pleasant V, 282
Terrill, Rebecca V, 237
Terrill, Rebecca V, 283
Terrill, Rebecca V, 429
Terrill, Rebecca V, 434
Terrill, Ruth Ann V, 282
Terrill, Samuel V, 130
Terrill, Samuel S. V, 130
Terrill, Sarah V, 126
Terrill, Sarah V, 130
Terrill, Sarah V, 233
Terrill, Sarah V, 282
Terrill, Sarah V, 434
Terrill, Sarah VI, 286
Terrill, Sarah VI, 287
Terrill, Sarah VI, 872
Terrill, Sisley A. V, 255
Terrill, Susanna V, 434
Terrill, Thomas V, 130
Terrill, William V, 434
Terrill, William VI, 338
Terrill, William VI, 797
Terrill, William VI, 854
Terrills, ??? VI, 283
Terrol, Sarah V, 909
Terroll, Lemuel IV, 774
Terry, ??? III, 99
Terry, ??? III, 164
Terry, ??? V, 857
Terry, Addie V, 283
Terry, Addie A. V, 283
Terry, Amey II, 665
Terry, Ann Henry VI, 889
Terry, Anna H. III, 310
Terry, Anna H. III, 366
Terry, Annie V, 283
Terry, Benjamin II, 1032
Terry, Betsy VI, 295
Terry, Betsy VI, 343
Terry, Calohill VI, 1003
Terry, Caroline V, 283
Terry, Caroline V, 293
Terry, Caroline E. V, 283
Terry, Caroline P. II, 969
Terry, Carolus G. VI, 818
Terry, Carolus G. VI, 845
Terry, Carolus G. VI, 859
Terry, Carolus G. VI, 935
Terry, Charles III, 310
Terry, Charles M. III, 310
Terry, Chas. M. III, 366
Terry, David IV, 1188
Terry, David V, 283
Terry, David D. III, 157
Terry, David Jeremiah V, 283
Terry, Edward Eugene V, 283
Terry, Edward F. V, 283
Terry, Eleanor II, 665
Terry, Eleanor A. III, 157
Terry, Eleanor Hortense III, 15
Terry, Eliza V, 275
Terry, Eliza V, 283
Terry, Eliza Q. VI, 1002
Terry, Elizabeth II, 969
Terry, Elizabeth V, 283
Terry, Elizabeth VI, 930
Terry, Ellinor II, 1032
Terry, Enoch VI, 874
Terry, Enoch VI, 875
Terry, Enoch VI, 929
Terry, Enoch VI, 953
Terry, Enoch VI, 973
Terry, Enoch VI, 981
Terry, Enoch VI, 995
Terry, Enoch VI, 1002
Terry, Enoch VI, 1013
Terry, Enoch W. VI, 885
Terry, Enoch W. VI, 886
Terry, Enoch W. VI, 888
Terry, Enoch W. VI, 889
Terry, Enoch W. VI, 893
Terry, Enoch W. VI, 895
Terry, Enoch W. VI, 896
Terry, Enoch W. VI, 905
Terry, Enoch W. VI, 906
Terry, Enoch W. VI, 909
Terry, Enoch W. VI, 913
Terry, Enoch W. VI, 915
Terry, Enoch W. VI, 921
Terry, Enoch W. VI, 923
Terry, Enoch W. VI, 928
Terry, Enoch W. VI, 929
Terry, Enoch W. VI, 930
Terry, Enoch W. VI, 940
Terry, Enoch W. VI, 941
Terry, Enoch W. VI, 942
Terry, Enoch W. VI, 945
Terry, Enoch W. VI, 953
Terry, Enoch W. VI, 961
Terry, Enoch W. VI, 965
Terry, Enoch W. VI, 966
Terry, Enoch W. VI, 973
Terry, Enoch W. VI, 978
Terry, Enoch W. VI, 981
Terry, Enoch W. VI, 982
Terry, Enoch W. VI, 987
Terry, Enoch W. VI, 997
Terry, Enoch W. VI, 1001
Terry, Enoch W. VI, 1003
Terry, Enoch W. VI, 1004
Terry, Enoch W. VI, 1005
Terry, Enoch W. VI, 1007
Terry, Enoch W. VI, 1013
Terry, Enoch W. VI, 1018
Terry, Ephraim IV, 1225
Terry, Eugene F. V, 283
Terry, Ezra Wharton II, 1032
Terry, Florence Cordelia V, 283
Terry, Frances VI, 883
Terry, Frank III, 310
Terry, Frant F. V, 283
Terry, Fred V, 283
Terry, Freddie V, 283

, Grant Frederic V, 283
, Harold V, 283
, Henrietta VI, 859
, Henry VI, 963
, Henry VI, 1002
, Hezekiah F. VI, 859
, James VI, 799
, James VI, 859
, James VI, 1002
, James E. VI, 859
, Jane II, 1017
, Jane II, 1032
, Jasper II, 1017
, Jasper II, 1032
, Jeduthan V, 283
, Jeduthen V, 283
, Jenny VI, 1002
, Jeremiah IV, 1188
, Jeremiah IV, 1225
, Jeremiah V, 283
, Jesper II, 1010
, Jesper II, 1032
, John II, 1032
, John V, 283
, John VI, 859
, John VI, 930
, John VI, 1003
, John A. V, 935
, John B. IV, 1188
, John P. IV, 1188
, John P. V, 283
, John P. VI, 989
, Jonathan IV, 1188
, Joseph VI, 859
, Julia A. V, 857
, Julia A. V, 872
, Juriah VI, 800
, Keziah III, 488
, Laura III, 67
, Laura V, 283
, Letty III, 67
, Louisa J. VI, 859
, Lucy II, 1010
, Lucy II, 1032
, Lucy VI, 1013
, Lucy W. VI, 941
, Margaret III, 164
, Margaret III, 310
, Margaret III, 366
y, Margaret H. III, 310
, Maria A. VI, 859
, Marion H. III, 99
y, Martha II, 1032
y, Martha II, 1037
, Martha A. VI, 1002
, Martha M. VI, 851
y, Mary V, 283
y, Mary A. V, 283
y, Mary A. E. V, 283
y, Mary Ann V, 246
y, Mary E. VI, 859
y, Mary E. VI, 894
y, Mary M. C. VI, 859
y, Melvina I, 423
y, Milton VI, 941
y, Morris II, 969
y, Nancy VI, 889
y, Nancy L. VI, 859
y, Nancy L. VI, 942
y, Nathaniel VI, 799
y, Nathaniel VI, 800
y, Ophelia V, 246
y, Ophelia V, 283
y, Peggy VI, 1002
y, Polly VI, 883
y, Polly VI, 1002
y, Rebecca II, 267
y, Rebecca II, 665
y, Rebecca III, 310
y, Rebecca F. III, 310
y, Rebeckah II, 267
y, Rebeckah III, 310
y, Rebeckah III, 316
y, Rhoda VI, 1001
y, Ruth II, 529
y, Ruth II, 665
y, Sarah IV, 1188
y, Sarah V, 283
y, Sarah VI, 313
y, Sarah VI, 314
y, Sarah VI, 343
y, Sarah VI, 859
ry, Sarah Willets III, 310
ry, Stashy VI, 1002
ry, Stephen VI, 818
ry, Stephen VI, 859
ry, Stephen VI, 1002
ry, Susan VI, 1003
ry, Susanna VI, 922
ry, Susannah VI, 1019
ry, Thomas I, 423
Terry, Thomas I, 577
Terry, Thomas II, 1010
Terry, Thomas II, 1017
Terry, Thomas II, 1032
Terry, Thomas IV, 1188
Terry, Thomas V, 283
Terry, Thomas VI, 313
Terry, Thomas VI, 314
Terry, Thomas VI, 343
Terry, Thomas VI, 1002
Terry, Thomas VI, 1013
Terry, Thomas B. I, 423
Terry, Thomas F. V, 283
Terry, Thomas J. V, 283
Terry, Thos. Carlton V, 283
Terry, Vista F. V, 283
Terry, William VI, 880
Terry, William VI, 881
Terry, William VI, 889
Terry, William VI, 894
Terry, William VI, 930
Terry, William VI, 953
Terry, William VI, 982
Terry, William VI, 1002
Terry, William VI, 1008
Terry, William B. VI, 800
Terry, William B. VI, 859
Terry, William P. V, 283
Terry, William, Jr. VI, 889
Terry, Winston VI, 859
Terry, Wm. II, 665
Terry, Wm. V, 283
Terry, Wm. P. V, 246
Terry, Zelah III, 67
Terwilkger, Lizzie II, 969
Terwiller, Joseph II, 426
Terwillinger, Amy IV, 847
Terwillinger, Amy IV, 856
Teryl, Deborah I, 902
Tesimer, Emil G. IV, 775
Tesmer, Cathern L. IV, 775
Tesmer, Emil G. IV, 775
Tesmer, Gattlieb IV, 775
Tesmer, La Vern Catharine IV, 775
Tesmer, Lavern C. IV, 775
Tesmer, Lois I. IV, 775
Tesmer, Melvin Leroy IV, 775
Tesmer, Rose IV, 775
Test, ??? IV, 603
Test, Abel IV, 848
Test, Abner II, 42
Test, Abner IV, 848
Test, Albert B. IV, 775
Test, Albert B. IV, 776
Test, Albert B. IV, 847
Test, Albert B. IV, 848
Test, Alfred IV, 847
Test, Alfred L., Jr. II, 720
Test, Alfred Langstaff II, 720
Test, Alfred Langstaff II, 770
Test, Alfred Langstaff IV, 847
Test, Ann II, 81
Test, Ann II, 99
Test, Ann II, 103
Test, Ann II, 104
Test, Ann II, 105
Test, Ann II, 124
Test, Ann II, 138
Test, Ann II, 426
Test, Ann II, 573
Test, Ann II, 665
Test, Ann II, 887
Test, Ann II, 928
Test, Ann IV, 775
Test, Ann IV, 798
Test, Ann IV, 801
Test, Ann IV, 847
Test, Ann IV, 1007
Test, Ann IV, 1127
Test, Ann IV, 1138
Test, Ann D. IV, 237
Test, Ann D. IV, 288
Test, Ann D. IV, 775
Test, Ann D. IV, 776
Test, Ann D. IV, 847
Test, Ann J. IV, 732
Test, Ann J. IV, 775
Test, Ann J. IV, 847
Test, Ann J. IV, 1007
Test, Ann J. IV, 1043
Test, Ann L. IV, 775
Test, Ann L. IV, 798
Test, Ann L. IV, 847
Test, Anna II, 135
Test, Benjamin II, 42
Test, Benjamin II, 67
Test, Benjamin II, 104
Test, Benjamin II, 665
Test, Benjamin IV, 288
Test, Benjamin IV, 447
Test, Benjamin IV, 654
Test, Benjamin IV, 659
Test, Benjamin IV, 775
Test, Benjamin IV, 776
Test, Benjamin IV, 781
Test, Benjamin IV, 848
Test, Benjamin A. IV, 776
Test, Benjamin A. IV, 793
Test, Benjamin A. IV, 847
Test, Benjamin B. IV, 775
Test, Benjamin B. IV, 776
Test, Benjamin B. IV, 847
Test, Beulah S. II, 132
Test, Clayton II, 104
Test, Clayton II, 124
Test, Clayton II, 138
Test, Clayton II, 158
Test, Daniel IV, 775
Test, Daniel IV, 776
Test, Daniel IV, 847
Test, Daniel IV, 848
Test, Daniel D. II, 720
Test, Daniel D. II, 770
Test, Daniel D. IV, 802
Test, Daniel D. IV, 847
Test, Daniel D., Jr. II, 770
Test, David II, 42
Test, David II, 104
Test, David IV, 775
Test, David IV, 847
Test, David IV, 848
Test, Deborah II, 42
Test, Deborah II, 104
Test, Deborah IV, 775
Test, Deborah IV, 776
Test, Deborah IV, 825
Test, Deborah IV, 847
Test, Deborah IV, 848
Test, Dorcas II, 42
Test, Dorcas IV, 848
Test, Drucilla IV, 847
Test, Drusilla II, 959
Test, Drusilla II, 967
Test, Drusilla IV, 775
Test, Drusilla IV, 776
Test, Drusilla IV, 793
Test, Drusilla IV, 830
Test, Drusilla IV, 847
Test, Edith IV, 704
Test, Edith IV, 775
Test, Edith M. IV, 792
Test, Eleanor IV, 848
Test, Eleanor Ann II, 104
Test, Eleanor Ann II, 138
Test, Eli IV, 848
Test, Elisha IV, 288
Test, Elisha IV, 775
Test, Elizabeth II, 42
Test, Elizabeth II, 51
Test, Elizabeth II, 67
Test, Elizabeth II, 74
Test, Elizabeth II, 84
Test, Elizabeth II, 101
Test, Elizabeth II, 103
Test, Elizabeth II, 104
Test, Elizabeth II, 138
Test, Elizabeth II, 267
Test, Elizabeth II, 426
Test, Elizabeth II, 592
Test, Elizabeth II, 644
Test, Elizabeth II, 665
Test, Elizabeth II, 870
Test, Elizabeth II, 928
Test, Elizabeth IV, 288
Test, Elizabeth IV, 447
Test, Elizabeth IV, 704
Test, Elizabeth IV, 775
Test, Elizabeth IV, 840
Test, Elizabeth IV, 847
Test, Elizabeth IV, 848
Test, Elizabeth IV, 1137
Test, Elizabeth V, 130
Test, Elizabeth V, 935
Test, Elizabeth D. IV, 215
Test, Elizabeth D. IV, 288
Test, Elizabeth D. IV, 848
Test, Elizabeth R. IV, 703
Test, Elizabeth R. IV, 775
Test, Elizabeth Test IV, 1138
Test, Ellanor IV, 848
Test, Ellen R. IV, 848
Test, Emily II, 967
Test, Emily IV, 793
Test, Emily C. IV, 848
Test, Esther IV, 848
Test, Frances II, 51
Test, Frances II, 103
Test, Francis II, 42
Test, Francis II, 59
Test, Francis II, 67
Test, Francis II, 98
Test, Francis II, 103
Test, Francis II, 104
Test, Grace II, 448
Test, Hammond IV, 848
Test, Hannah II, 64
Test, Hannah II, 85
Test, Hannah II, 92
Test, Hannah II, 104
Test, Hannah II, 124
Test, Hannah II, 138
Test, Hannah II, 158
Test, Hannah II, 665
Test, Hannah IV, 161
Test, Hannah IV, 288
Test, Hannah IV, 447
Test, Hannah IV, 659
Test, Hannah IV, 703
Test, Hannah IV, 704
Test, Hannah IV, 732
Test, Hannah IV, 775
Test, Hannah IV, 847
Test, Hannah IV, 848
Test, Hannah E. II, 928
Test, Hannah E. VI, 743
Test, Hannah Elizabeth II, 158
Test, Hannah Elizabeth II, 928
Test, Hannah Elizabeth VI, 785
Test, Hannah, Jr. II, 124
Test, Hanry II, 426
Test, Harmon IV, 1138
Test, Henry II, 426
Test, Henry II, 665
Test, Hiram IV, 848
Test, Hope II, 42
Test, Hope II, 50
Test, Hope II, 104
Test, Huldah IV, 1367
Test, Huldah IV, 1382
Test, Isaac II, 42
Test, Isaac IV, 161
Test, Isaac IV, 659
Test, Isaac IV, 732
Test, Isaac IV, 772
Test, Isaac IV, 775
Test, Isaac IV, 847
Test, Isaac IV, 848
Test, Isaac B. IV, 775
Test, Isaac B. IV, 798
Test, Isaac B. IV, 808
Test, Isaac B. IV, 847
Test, Israel IV, 848
Test, Jacob IV, 848
Test, Jane IV, 775
Test, Jane IV, 821
Test, Jane IV, 847
Test, Jean II, 89
Test, Jean II, 103
Test, John II, 42
Test, John II, 50
Test, John II, 84
Test, John II, 85
Test, John II, 104
Test, John II, 138
Test, John II, 426
Test, John II, 448
Test, John II, 592
Test, John II, 665
Test, John IV, 775
Test, John IV, 847
Test, John IV, 848
Test, John V, 130
Test, John V, 935
Test, John S. IV, 775
Test, John S. IV, 776
Test, John S. IV, 847
Test, John S. IV, 848
Test, John, Jr. IV, 848
Test, Joseph II, 42
Test, Joseph II, 64
Test, Joseph II, 81
Test, Joseph II, 92
Test, Joseph II, 103
Test, Joseph II, 104
Test, Joseph II, 105
Test, Joseph II, 107
Test, Joseph II, 124
Test, Joseph II, 138
Test, Joseph II, 158
Test, Joseph II, 426
Test, Joseph II, 592
Test, Joseph II, 665
Test, Joseph IV, 161
Test, Joseph IV, 659
Test, Joseph IV, 775
Test, Joseph IV, 848
Test, Joseph C. V, 887
Test, Joseph D. II, 138
Test, Joseph D. II, 158
Test, Joseph, Jr. II, 104
Test, Kersey IV, 848
Test, Latitia M. II, 158
Test, Leatitia II, 42
Test, Leatitia II, 74
Test, Leatitia II, 104
Test, Lemuel IV, 776
Test, Lemuel IV, 793
Test, Lemuel IV, 848
Test, Letitia II, 65
Test, Letitia II, 104
Test, Letitia M. II, 138
Test, Letitia M., Jr. II, 158
Test, Lidya II, 42
Test, Lidya II, 49
Test, Lidya II, 104
Test, Lucina IV, 775
Test, Lucina IV, 847
Test, Lucy II, 142
Test, Lucy II, 158
Test, Luella L. IV, 847
Test, Lusina IV, 775
Test, Lusina IV, 821
Test, Lusine IV, 821
Test, Lusine IV, 847
Test, Lydia II, 42
Test, Lydia II, 720
Test, Lydia IV, 775
Test, Lydia V, 935
Test, Lydia M. II, 138
Test, Lydia Smedley II, 770
Test, M. Alice V, 887
Test, Margaret II, 138
Test, Margaret II, 158
Test, Margaret IV, 732
Test, Margaret IV, 772
Test, Margaret IV, 775
Test, Margaret IV, 793
Test, Margaret IV, 798
Test, Margaret IV, 808
Test, Margaret IV, 847
Test, Margaret IV, 848
Test, Maria IV, 848
Test, Martha II, 42
Test, Martha II, 124
Test, Martha II, 138
Test, Martha II, 158
Test, Martha II, 886
Test, Martha II, 928
Test, Martha IV, 775
Test, Martha IV, 776
Test, Martha IV, 844
Test, Martha IV, 847
Test, Martha Emily IV, 848
Test, Martha Virginia II, 870
Test, Martha Virginia II, 928
Test, Mary II, 42
Test, Mary II, 59
Test, Mary II, 103
Test, Mary II, 104
Test, Mary II, 138
Test, Mary II, 426
Test, Mary II, 448
Test, Mary II, 720
Test, Mary IV, 288
Test, Mary IV, 447
Test, Mary IV, 654
Test, Mary IV, 659
Test, Mary IV, 775
Test, Mary IV, 781
Test, Mary IV, 847
Test, Mary A. IV, 821
Test, Mary Ann IV, 675
Test, Mary Ann IV, 775
Test, Mary Ann IV, 821
Test, Mary Ann IV, 847
Test, Mary B. II, 770
Test, Mary B. IV, 848
Test, Mary Brantingham II, 770
Test, Mary C. II, 720
Test, Mary C. IV, 802
Test, Mary C. IV, 847
Test, Mary Jane II, 720
Test, Mary L. IV, 775
Test, Mary L. IV, 776
Test, Mary L. IV, 847
Test, Mary S. IV, 848
Test, Mary W. II, 928
Test, Mary W. V, 935
Test, Mary, Jr. IV, 775
Test, Maryann IV, 847
Test, Mildred IV, 848
Test, Mode IV, 848
Test, Nathaniel IV, 848
Test, Ner II, 50
Test, Phebe IV, 848
Test, Priscilla IV, 733
Test, Rachel II, 42
Test, Rachel II, 103
Test, Rachel II, 104
Test, Rachel II, 107
Test, Rachel IV, 288
Test, Rachel IV, 447
Test, Rachel IV, 775

Test, Rachel IV, 848
Test, Rachel V, 130
Test, Rachel V, 935
Test, Rebecca II, 104
Test, Rebecca IV, 288
Test, Rebecca IV, 447
Test, Rebecca IV, 769
Test, Rebecca IV, 775
Test, Rebecca IV, 808
Test, Rebecca IV, 845
Test, Rebecca IV, 847
Test, Rebecca D. IV, 775
Test, Rebecca D. IV, 781
Test, Rebeccah II, 104
Test, Rebekah II, 64
Test, Rebekah II, 98
Test, Rebekah II, 103
Test, Rebekah II, 104
Test, Richard II, 138
Test, Richard II, 448
Test, Robert Leland IV, 847
Test, Ruth II, 31
Test, Ruth II, 42
Test, Ruth II, 77
Test, Ruth II, 104
Test, Ruth Ann II, 158
Test, Ruth Ann II, 928
Test, Ruth Ann VI, 743
Test, Sallie IV, 848
Test, Samuel II, 42
Test, Samuel II, 49
Test, Samuel II, 102
Test, Samuel II, 104
Test, Samuel II, 105
Test, Samuel II, 124
Test, Samuel II, 138
Test, Samuel II, 158
Test, Samuel IV, 161
Test, Samuel IV, 659
Test, Samuel IV, 675
Test, Samuel IV, 775
Test, Samuel IV, 821
Test, Samuel IV, 847
Test, Samuel IV, 1007
Test, Samuel IV, 1043
Test, Samuel V, 130
Test, Samuel V, 935
Test, Samuel, Jr. II, 42
Test, Samuel, Jr. IV, 732
Test, Samuel, Jr. IV, 775
Test, Samuel, Jr. IV, 847
Test, Samuel, Jr. IV, 1007
Test, Samuel, Jr. V, 130
Test, Samuel, Jr. V, 935
Test, Sara IV, 845
Test, Sarah II, 42
Test, Sarah II, 67
Test, Sarah II, 80
Test, Sarah II, 102
Test, Sarah II, 103
Test, Sarah II, 104
Test, Sarah II, 105
Test, Sarah II, 426
Test, Sarah II, 542
Test, Sarah II, 665
Test, Sarah II, 694
Test, Sarah II, 928
Test, Sarah IV, 769
Test, Sarah IV, 775
Test, Sarah V, 130
Test, Sarah V, 935
Test, Sarah A. II, 85
Test, Sarah A. II, 104
Test, Sarah A. II, 870
Test, Sarah A. II, 959
Test, Sarah Ann IV, 848
Test, Sarah Antram II, 959
Test, Sarah M. II, 928
Test, Sarahann IV, 848
Test, Temperance IV, 848
Test, Thomas II, 42
Test, Thomas II, 104
Test, Thomas II, 426
Test, Willard IV, 848
Test, William B. II, 720
Test, William Emily IV, 776
Test, Wm. II, 104
Test, Wm. II, 132
Test, Wm. II, 870
Test, Wm. II, 928
Test, Wm. IV, 793
Test, Wm. IV, 847
Test, Wm. IV, 848
Test, Wm. B. II, 770
Test, Wm. P. II, 870
Test, Wm. P. II, 928
Test, Zaccheus II, 959
Test, Zaccheus II, 967
Test, Zaccheus IV, 161
Test, Zaccheus IV, 659
Test, Zaccheus IV, 733
Test, Zaccheus IV, 775
Test, Zaccheus IV, 776
Test, Zaccheus, Jr. IV, 775
Test, Zaccheus, Jr. IV, 793
Test, Zacheus II, 42
Test, Zacheus II, 104
Test, Zacheus IV, 703
Test, Zacheus IV, 704
Test, Zacheus IV, 769
Test, Zacheus IV, 775
Test, Zacheus IV, 776
Test, Zacheus IV, 830
Test, Zacheus IV, 845
Test, Zacheus IV, 847
Test, Zacheus IV, 848
Test, Zackeus IV, 776
Tetars, Ann IV, 776
Tetars, Elisha IV, 776
Tetars, Elisha, Jr. IV, 776
Tetars, Jane IV, 776
Tetars, Jesse IV, 776
Tetars, Job IV, 776
Tetars, John IV, 776
Tetars, John C. IV, 776
Tetars, Jonathan IV, 776
Tetars, Margaret IV, 776
Tetars, Martha IV, 776
Tetars, Martha W. IV, 776
Tetars, Mary IV, 776
Tetars, Mary, Jr. IV, 776
Tetars, Rebecca IV, 776
Tetars, Susanna IV, 776
Tetars, Susannah IV, 776
Teter, Allie V, 283
Teter, Edward V, 283
Teter, Howard V, 283
Teters, Martha IV, 748
Tetley, Martha I, 629
Tetley, Martha I, 641
Tever, Herman V, 714
Tew, ??? II, 426
Tew, Dr. Samuel II, 426
Tew, Edward II, 448
Tew, Elizabeth II, 448
Tew, Henry II, 426
Tew, Lydia II, 448
Tew, Mary II, 426
Tew, Samuel II, 426
Tewley, John VI, 1015
Tewley, Sarah VI, 1015
Tews, Edward II, 448
Tews, Samuel II, 448
Texana, Martha I, 1154
Thacary, Hannah II, 665
Thacher, David V, 534
Thacher, David VI, 451
Thacher, Elizabeth V, 534
Thacher, Hannah V, 534
Thacher, Jesse V, 534
Thacher, Jesse VI, 451
Thacher, John V, 534
Thacher, Jonathan VI, 451
Thacher, Joseph V, 534
Thacher, Joseph VI, 451
Thacher, Martha VI, 451
Thacher, Mary V, 1021
Thacher, Mary VI, 450
Thacher, Mary VI, 451
Thacher, Richard VI, 451
Thacher, Ruth V, 534
Thacher, Ruth VI, 451
Thacher, Stephen V, 534
Thacher, Susanna V, 601
Thacher, Thomas V, 534
Thacher, Thomas VI, 451
Thacher, William V, 534
Thackary, Sarah II, 158
Thacker, ??? III, 310
Thacker, Harriet VI, 859
Thacker, John III, 310
Thacker, Lucy Ann III, 310
Thacker, Samuel VI, 859
Thackeray, Jacob II, 104
Thackery, Elizabeth II, 42
Thackery, Ester II, 1032
Thackery, Esther II, 981
Thackery, Hannah II, 42
Thackery, Hannah II, 73
Thackery, Hannah II, 104
Thackery, Jacob II, 42
Thackery, Jacob II, 104
Thackery, James II, 1032
Thackery, James, Jr. II, 981
Thackery, James, Jr. II, 1032
Thackery, Joseph II, 42
Thackery, Joshua II, 1032
Thackery, Rachel II, 1032
Thackery, Sarah II, 158
Thackery, Sarah II, 1006
Thackery, Sarah II, 1032
Thackery, Stephen II, 42
Thackery, Stephen II, 104
Thackery, Thomas II, 42
Thackery, Thomas II, 104
Thackery, William II, 42
Thackray, James II, 1018
Thackray, James II, 1032
Thackray, Margaret E. II, 843
Thackray, Mary II, 785
Thackray, Mary II, 843
Thackray, Rachel II, 1018
Thackray, Rachel II, 1032
Thackray, Sarah II, 138
Thackry, Joshua II, 1032
Thackston, Mary VI, 990
Thain, ??? III, 310
Thain, David III, 310
Thain, Deborah III, 310
Thain, Jethro III, 310
Thain, Lydia III, 310
Thain, Lydia V, 935
Thain, Samuel III, 310
Thamazin, Mary VI, 401
Thane, Deborah III, 310
Thane, Jethro III, 310
Thane, Samuel III, 310
Tharp, Anna V, 362
Tharp, Annie V, 362
Tharp, Arthur V, 362
Tharp, Cora V, 361
Tharp, Cora V, 362
Tharp, Eli N. V, 361
Tharp, Eli Wm. V, 361
Tharp, Elizabeth I, 1071
Tharp, Maud V, 361
Tharp, Maud V, 362
Tharp, Miriam V, 560
Tharp, Miriam V, 601
Tharp, Samuel V, 362
Tharp, Ursley I, 608
Tharpe, Louisa I, 579
Thatcher, Ann V, 33
Thatcher, Ann V, 130
Thatcher, Ann V, 601
Thatcher, Anna V, 590
Thatcher, Anna V, 702
Thatcher, Anna V, 1021
Thatcher, Anna F. V, 601
Thatcher, Anna J. V, 601
Thatcher, Anna Letitia II, 822
Thatcher, Annie J. V, 591
Thatcher, Annie J. V, 601
Thatcher, Cassie V, 1021
Thatcher, Clyde V, 1021
Thatcher, David V, 130
Thatcher, David V, 534
Thatcher, David V, 601
Thatcher, David V, 935
Thatcher, David VI, 450
Thatcher, David VI, 451
Thatcher, Deborah V, 567
Thatcher, Deborah V, 601
Thatcher, Edith I, 518
Thatcher, Edith I, 577
Thatcher, Edward V, 131
Thatcher, Electa III, 310
Thatcher, Eliza II, 798
Thatcher, Elizabeth I, 518
Thatcher, Elizabeth I, 577
Thatcher, Elizabeth II, 426
Thatcher, Elizabeth II, 586
Thatcher, Elizabeth II, 665
Thatcher, Elizabeth II, 822
Thatcher, Elizabeth V, 510
Thatcher, Elizabeth V, 534
Thatcher, Elizabeth V, 601
Thatcher, Elizabeth B. II, 843
Thatcher, Elizabeth B. II, 928
Thatcher, Emily V, 579
Thatcher, Emily V, 601
Thatcher, Eva V, 1021
Thatcher, George V, 646
Thatcher, George V, 714
Thatcher, Gordon Estell V, 1021
Thatcher, Hannah I, 518
Thatcher, Hannah I, 577
Thatcher, Hannah V, 534
Thatcher, Hannah V, 601
Thatcher, Hannah VI, 450
Thatcher, Hannah VI, 451
Thatcher, Harry V, 714
Thatcher, Harvey S. III, 310
Thatcher, Hazel V, 702
Thatcher, Hazel V, 714
Thatcher, Hazel V, 722
Thatcher, Insam V, 601
Thatcher, Isaac V, 131
Thatcher, Jesse V, 130
Thatcher, Jesse V, 534
Thatcher, Jesse V, 601
Thatcher, Jesse V, 714
Thatcher, Jesse VI, 387
Thatcher, Jesse VI, 450
Thatcher, Jesse VI, 451
Thatcher, Jesse Karl II, 822
Thatcher, Jesse W. II, 822
Thatcher, Jesse W. II, 843
Thatcher, Jesse W. II, 928
Thatcher, Jesse W., Jr. II, 822
Thatcher, John II, 426
Thatcher, John II, 665
Thatcher, John V, 534
Thatcher, John V, 601
Thatcher, John V, 960
Thatcher, Jonathan VI, 450
Thatcher, Jonathan VI, 451
Thatcher, Joseph I, 518
Thatcher, Joseph I, 577
Thatcher, Joseph V, 130
Thatcher, Joseph V, 510
Thatcher, Joseph V, 534
Thatcher, Joseph V, 601
Thatcher, Joseph VI, 451
Thatcher, Joseph J. V, 601
Thatcher, Joseph, Jr. V, 534
Thatcher, Joseph, Jr. V, 601
Thatcher, Joseph, Sr. V, 534
Thatcher, Joshua IV, 1296
Thatcher, Letitia A. II, 843
Thatcher, Letitia A. II, 928
Thatcher, Lillian II, 822
Thatcher, Lon V, 1021
Thatcher, Lucinda V, 601
Thatcher, Lucretia V, 662
Thatcher, Lucretia V, 714
Thatcher, Lucretia V, 722
Thatcher, Lydia V, 131
Thatcher, Lydia V, 599
Thatcher, Lydia V, 601
Thatcher, Lydia Maria V, 601
Thatcher, Lydia Mariah V, 601
Thatcher, Mark VI, 450
Thatcher, Mark VI, 451
Thatcher, Martha V, 601
Thatcher, Martha V, 714
Thatcher, Martha VI, 425
Thatcher, Martha VI, 450
Thatcher, Martha VI, 451
Thatcher, Martha Emma V, 559
Thatcher, Mary II, 426
Thatcher, Mary V, 130
Thatcher, Mary V, 131
Thatcher, Mary V, 469
Thatcher, Mary V, 471
Thatcher, Mary V, 534
Thatcher, Mary V, 714
Thatcher, Mary V, 1021
Thatcher, Mary VI, 450
Thatcher, Mary VI, 451
Thatcher, Mary VI, 459
Thatcher, Mary E. V, 714
Thatcher, Mary Ellen V, 601
Thatcher, Mary Hannah V, 714
Thatcher, Mary M. V, 1021
Thatcher, Mary Ruth V, 977
Thatcher, Mary Ruth V, 978
Thatcher, Mary, Sr. VI, 450
Thatcher, Nancy V, 714
Thatcher, Nannie V, 714
Thatcher, Oliver J. V, 601
Thatcher, Oliver J. V, 714
Thatcher, Paxson Blakey II, 822
Thatcher, Richard I, 518
Thatcher, Richard II, 426
Thatcher, Richard II, 586
Thatcher, Richard II, 665
Thatcher, Richard VI, 451
Thatcher, Robert Fraleigh II, 822
Thatcher, Royal II, 822
Thatcher, Rufus V, 1021
Thatcher, Ruth II, 426
Thatcher, Ruth V, 130
Thatcher, Ruth V, 533
Thatcher, Ruth V, 534
Thatcher, Ruth V, 558
Thatcher, Ruth V, 599
Thatcher, Ruth V, 601
Thatcher, Ruth VI, 387
Thatcher, Ruth VI, 450
Thatcher, Ruth VI, 451
Thatcher, Samuel VI, 450
Thatcher, Samuel VI, 459
Thatcher, Sarah I, 518
Thatcher, Sarah V, 601
Thatcher, Sarah V, 693
Thatcher, Sarah M. II, 928
Thatcher, Sarah M. V, 559
Thatcher, Sarah M. V, 601
Thatcher, Stephen V, 534
Thatcher, Stephen V, 601
Thatcher, Stephen V, 1021
Thatcher, Stephen VI, 450
Thatcher, Susan V, 515
Thatcher, Susan V, 534
Thatcher, Susan V, 583
Thatcher, Susan V, 601
Thatcher, Susan V, 694
Thatcher, Susanna V, 533
Thatcher, Susanna V, 601
Thatcher, Susannah V, 567
Thatcher, Theodocia V, 977
Thatcher, Theodocia V, 978
Thatcher, Theodosia V, 599
Thatcher, Theodosia V, 601
Thatcher, Thomas V, 130
Thatcher, Thomas V, 533
Thatcher, Thomas V, 534
Thatcher, Thomas V, 601
Thatcher, Thomas VI, 450
Thatcher, Thomas VI, 451
Thatcher, Thomas Stephen Joh
V, 601
Thatcher, Thos. Jackson III, 3
Thatcher, Wd. Sarah II, 822
Thatcher, William I, 518
Thatcher, William I, 577
Thatcher, William V, 534
Thatcher, William V, 601
Thatcher, William VI, 450
Thatcher, William H. V, 601
Thatcher, Wm. V, 601
Thatcher, Wm. David V, 601
Thatcher, Wm. Penn II, 822
Thawait, Lucy Gray VI, 452
Thaxton, David T. VI, 1003
Thaxton, Elizabeth VI, 1003
Thaxton, Frances VI, 889
Thaxton, Henry C. VI, 1003
Thaxton, James C. VI, 1003
Thaxton, John VI, 892
Thaxton, John F. VI, 1003
Thaxton, Lucy Ann Mary
VI, 1003
Thaxton, Mary Ann VI, 892
Thaxton, Matilda VI, 1003
Thaxton, Matilda VI, 1016
Thaxton, Nathaniel VI, 1003
Thaxton, Nathaniel F. VI, 889
Thaxton, Nathaniel F. VI, 100
Thaxton, Permelia E. VI, 1003
Thaxton, Sophia VI, 1003
Thaxton, Susan VI, 1003
Thaxton, Susan Jane VI, 1003
Thaxton, William VI, 889
Thaxton, William VI, 892
Thaxton, William VI, 940
Thaxton, William VI, 1003
Thaxton, William H. VI, 987
Thayer, Aline Arden III, 311
Thayer, Almeida V, 749
Thayer, Amy IV, 1382
Thayer, Ann Maria III, 311
Thayer, Anna V, 766
Thayer, Anna Maria V, 749
Thayer, Arthur E. V, 749
Thayer, Blanche F. III, 127
Thayer, Blanche F. III, 311
Thayer, Carolina Matilda
IV, 1382
Thayer, Caroline III, 428
Thayer, Caroline III, 449
Thayer, Caroline M. III, 311
Thayer, Charlotte B. V, 748
Thayer, Chas. Henry III, 311
Thayer, Chas. W. V, 749
Thayer, Davis James V, 766
Thayer, Davis W. V, 748
Thayer, Davis W. V, 766
Thayer, Dorah Elizabeth V, 74
Thayer, Elisha V, 748
Thayer, Elisha Davis V, 749
Thayer, Eliz. H. III, 449
Thayer, Eliza Rebecca V, 749
Thayer, Elizabeth V, 748
Thayer, Elizabeth V, 754
Thayer, Elizabeth V, 766
Thayer, Elizabeth V, 794
Thayer, Elizabeth H. III, 449
Thayer, Elizabeth M. V, 766
Thayer, Emma Luella V, 749
Thayer, Enes Thayer V, 748
Thayer, Enoch V, 749
Thayer, Enos V, 766
Thayer, Erasmus V, 766
Thayer, Erasmus M. V, 766
Thayer, Etta Reed III, 311
Thayer, Eunice V, 748
Thayer, Eunice V, 766
Thayer, Eunice Ann V, 749
Thayer, Francis III, 428
Thayer, Francis Kendall III, 44
Thayer, Geo. A. III, 449
Thayer, Geo. A., Jr. III, 449
Thayer, George III, 449

er, George A. III, 449
er, George A. III, 463
er, George A., Jr. III, 449
er, Ichabod V, 766
er, Jane III, 449
er, Jane V, 766
er, Jane J. III, 449
er, Jean III, 449
yer, Jean III, 463
yer, John V, 749
yer, John V, 766
yer, Lambert Jefferson V, 748
yer, Lambert Jefferson V, 749
yer, Lydia V, 793
yer, Lydia Ann V, 749
yer, Marcy IV, 1382
yer, Martha Ellen V, 749
yer, Mary III, 311
yer, Mary V, 749
yer, Mary J. V, 766
yer, Mary Jane V, 748
yer, Miriam V, 749
yer, Nathaniel III, 127
yer, Nathaniel III, 311
yer, Phebe C. IV, 1382
yer, Robert Warren III, 449
yer, Sarah V, 749
yer, Sarah Elizabeth V, 749
yer, Susan E. V, 749
yer, Wait Almina IV, 1382
yer, Willard III, 311
yer, Willett III, 311
yer, Wm. Allen V, 748
yer, Wm. Frederick III, 449
each, Rebecca II, 665
each, Rebecca II, 670
eale, Harriet E. III, 439
eall, Amy III, 506
eall, Eleazer III, 506
ekstine, Elizabeth IV, 776
ems, Marcy I, 276
eobold, H. L. Johnson I, 641
eobold, Louise I, 635
eobold, Louise I, 641
eobold, Minnie I, 641
eobold, Phillis Louise I, 641
es, David V, 646
es, Hannah V, 646
ew, ??? III, 311
ew, Ada Hepzibah III, 167
ew, Ada Hepzibah III, 311
ew, Friend A. III, 311
ew, Gilmore E. III, 167
ew, Gilmore E. III, 311
ew, Mary Ann III, 311
ew, Parmelia III, 311
ibon, Gabriel II, 448
ibon, Jane II, 448
imm, Curt III, 449
imm, Eliz. III, 449
imm, Elizabeth III, 449
imm, Morley III, 449
hirman, Hick V, 466
istle, Maud III, 240
histlethwaite, Anna M. IV, 32
histlethwaite, Anna M. IV, 62
histlethwaite, Anne M. IV, 62
histlethwaite, Anthony IV, 111
histlethwaite, Eleanor II, 928
histlethwaite, Elizabeth II, 928
histlethwaite, Elizabeth W. II, 929
histlethwaite, John II, 928
histlethwaite, Mary IV, 31
histlethwaite, Mary IV, 62
histlethwaite, Mary Ann IV, 46
histlethwaite, Mary Ann IV, 62
histlethwaite, Mary Anne IV, 62
histlethwaite, Mary B. V, 477
Thistlethwaite, Mary B. V, 534
Thistlethwaite, Sarah IV, 60
Thistlethwaite, Sarah IV, 62
Thistlethwaite, Theodosius III, 311
Thistlethwaite, Wm. II, 928
Thistlethwaite, Wm. II, 929
Thistlewait, Elizabeth W. II, 929
Thistlewait, Wm. II, 929
Thistlewaite, Eleanor II, 935
Thistlewaite, Elizabeth II, 935
Thistlewaite, John II, 935
Thistlewaite, Thos. V, 935
Thistlewaite, Wm. II, 935
Thoben, Ada III, 135
Thoben, Ada III, 311
Thoben, Caroline III, 311
Thoben, Frederick H. III, 311
Thobin, Ada III, 135
Thobin, Ada III, 311
Thobin, Caroline III, 311
Thobin, Frederick H. III, 311
Thom, Elizabeth P. VI, 785
Thom, Elizabeth Preston VI, 786
Thom, Judith Preston VI, 786
Thom, Rachel VI, 750
Thom, Rachel Trimble VI, 749
Thom, Rachel Trimble VI, 785
Thom, Rachel Trimbles VI, 786
Thom, Stephen VI, 277
Thom, William Taylor III VI, 786
Thom, Wm. Taylor VI, 785
Thom, Wm. Taylor, Jr. VI, 749
Thom, Wm. Taylor, Jr. VI, 785
Thom, Wm. Taylor, Jr. VI, 786
Thomaon, Mary II, 528
Thomas, ??? I, 1068
Thomas, ??? II, 426
Thomas, ??? III, 41
Thomas, ??? III, 311
Thomas, Aaron IV, 290
Thomas, Aaron IV, 1079
Thomas, Aaron IV, 1110
Thomas, Aaron IV, 1117
Thomas, Aaron V, 760
Thomas, Aaron VI, 606
Thomas, Aaron Frame IV, 553
Thomas, Abel I, 169
Thomas, Abel I, 297
Thomas, Abel I, 577
Thomas, Abel I, 1024
Thomas, Abel I, 1036
Thomas, Abel I, 1038
Thomas, Abel II, 267
Thomas, Abel II, 277
Thomas, Abel II, 564
Thomas, Abel II, 666
Thomas, Abel IV, 62
Thomas, Abel IV, 80
Thomas, Abel IV, 111
Thomas, Abel IV, 290
Thomas, Abel IV, 596
Thomas, Abel IV, 660
Thomas, Abel IV, 777
Thomas, Abel IV, 848
Thomas, Abel V, 131
Thomas, Abel V, 738
Thomas, Abel V, 766
Thomas, Abel V, 768
Thomas, Abel V, 769
Thomas, Abel V, 935
Thomas, Abel J. V, 131
Thomas, Abel Thomas IV, 62
Thomas, Abel, Jr. V, 766
Thomas, Abel, Sr. V, 767
Thomas, Abigail I, 423
Thomas, Abigail I, 948
Thomas, Abigail II, 823
Thomas, Abigail III, 449
Thomas, Abigail IV, 161
Thomas, Abigail IV, 288
Thomas, Abigail IV, 290
Thomas, Abigail V, 96
Thomas, Abigail V, 131
Thomas, Abigail V, 767
Thomas, Abigail V, 769
Thomas, Abigail V, 773
Thomas, Abigail M. IV, 312
Thomas, Abigail M. IV, 314
Thomas, Abigail R. I, 934
Thomas, Abigail Robbins I, 950
Thomas, Abijhai I, 1045
Thomas, Abisha IV, 161
Thomas, Abisha IV, 353
Thomas, Abisha IV, 447
Thomas, Abishae I, 1051
Thomas, Abishai IV, 447
Thomas, Able IV, 111
Thomas, Abner IV, 776
Thomas, Abner IV, 777
Thomas, Abner IV, 1008
Thomas, Abner V, 978
Thomas, Abraham V, 771
Thomas, Absillet V, 563
Thomas, Absillet V, 602
Thomas, Absolam V, 769
Thomas, Absolom V, 767
Thomas, Achsa I, 793
Thomas, Achsa I, 1068
Thomas, Ada IV, 1265
Thomas, Ada V, 768
Thomas, Ada J. V, 768
Thomas, Adaline IV, 1105
Thomas, Adaline T. IV, 1117
Thomas, Addie III, 224
Thomas, Addie III, 311
Thomas, Addison J. IV, 1117
Thomas, Adeline IV, 1117
Thomas, Adella B. IV, 291
Thomas, Adrian IV, 290
Thomas, Aelty II, 665
Thomas, Agga I, 793
Thomas, Agga I, 841
Thomas, Agnes I, 841
Thomas, Agnes I, 1072
Thomas, Agnes III, 449
Thomas, Agnes V, 612
Thomas, Agnes A. III, 449
Thomas, Agness I, 423
Thomas, Agness I, 1071
Thomas, Agnis I, 1068
Thomas, Agnis, Sr. I, 1068
Thomas, Airs IV, 290
Thomas, Albert III, 449
Thomas, Albert V, 131
Thomas, Albert V, 936
Thomas, Alce VI, 451
Thomas, Alexander V, 647
Thomas, Alexandria II, 666
Thomas, Alfred II, 822
Thomas, Alfred V, 131
Thomas, Alfred V, 978
Thomas, Alfred V, 1021
Thomas, Alfred R. IV, 289
Thomas, Alfred R. IV, 291
Thomas, Alice I, 577
Thomas, Alice II, 426
Thomas, Alice II, 622
Thomas, Alice II, 665
Thomas, Alice IV, 111
Thomas, Alice VI, 399
Thomas, Alice VI, 451
Thomas, Alice Ann III, 449
Thomas, Alice Haworth V, 647
Thomas, Alice R. IV, 272
Thomas, Alice R. IV, 290
Thomas, Alice R. IV, 841
Thomas, Alice R. IV, 842
Thomas, Alice Rosella IV, 289
Thomas, Alisha IV, 353
Thomas, Allen VI, 859
Thomas, Allen Alexander Mode IV, 776
Thomas, Allen J. V, 767
Thomas, Alma IV, 848
Thomas, Alma IV, 1296
Thomas, Almeda I, 543
Thomas, Almeda I, 577
Thomas, Almeda V, 473
Thomas, Almeda V, 647
Thomas, Almedia V, 534
Thomas, Almedia V, 646
Thomas, Almedia V, 647
Thomas, Almeidia V, 768
Thomas, Almeta I, 577
Thomas, Almira V, 131
Thomas, Almira Jane IV, 697
Thomas, Almira Jane IV, 777
Thomas, Alpha V, 534
Thomas, Alva IV, 1225
Thomas, Alva Curtis V, 647
Thomas, Alvin IV, 448
Thomas, Amanda V, 768
Thomas, Amanda I. II, 785
Thomas, Amanda P. VI, 1003
Thomas, Amelia II, 186
Thomas, Amelia II, 297
Thomas, Amelia II, 304
Thomas, Amelia IV, 1340
Thomas, Amelia L. II, 296
Thomas, Amelia L. II, 304
Thomas, Amos II, 720
Thomas, Amy T. IV, 214
Thomas, Amy T. IV, 290
Thomas, Amy T. IV, 528
Thomas, Amy T. IV, 550
Thomas, Amy T. IV, 553
Thomas, Anderson E. IV, 291
Thomas, Angeline G. IV, 1030
Thomas, Ann I, 276
Thomas, Ann I, 518
Thomas, Ann I, 523
Thomas, Ann I, 577
Thomas, Ann I, 1036
Thomas, Ann I, 1038
Thomas, Ann I, 1071
Thomas, Ann II, 42
Thomas, Ann II, 81
Thomas, Ann II, 104
Thomas, Ann II, 267
Thomas, Ann II, 426
Thomas, Ann II, 564
Thomas, Ann II, 665
Thomas, Ann II, 666
Thomas, Ann II, 687
Thomas, Ann II, 770
Thomas, Ann II, 822
Thomas, Ann II, 827
Thomas, Ann II, 929
Thomas, Ann II, 1032
Thomas, Ann III, 31
Thomas, Ann III, 202
Thomas, Ann IV, 173
Thomas, Ann IV, 207
Thomas, Ann IV, 288
Thomas, Ann IV, 289
Thomas, Ann IV, 290
Thomas, Ann IV, 305
Thomas, Ann IV, 596
Thomas, Ann IV, 848
Thomas, Ann IV, 865
Thomas, Ann IV, 884
Thomas, Ann IV, 892
Thomas, Ann IV, 895
Thomas, Ann IV, 1008
Thomas, Ann IV, 1030
Thomas, Ann V, 131
Thomas, Ann V, 534
Thomas, Ann V, 612
Thomas, Ann V, 635
Thomas, Ann V, 646
Thomas, Ann V, 743
Thomas, Ann V, 766
Thomas, Ann V, 769
Thomas, Ann V, 935
Thomas, Ann V, 936
Thomas, Ann VI, 56
Thomas, Ann VI, 87
Thomas, Ann VI, 207
Thomas, Ann VI, 451
Thomas, Ann VI, 548
Thomas, Ann VI, 974
Thomas, Ann VI, 1003
Thomas, Ann C. II, 899
Thomas, Ann C. II, 929
Thomas, Ann Eliza IV, 270
Thomas, Ann Eliza IV, 290
Thomas, Ann Eliza IV, 314
Thomas, Ann G. II, 720
Thomas, Ann H. IV, 884
Thomas, Ann L. II, 752
Thomas, Ann L. II, 770
Thomas, Ann L. IV, 180
Thomas, Ann Maria V, 647
Thomas, Ann T. IV, 290
Thomas, Ann W. II, 929
Thomas, Anna I, 75
Thomas, Anna I, 187
Thomas, Anna I, 793
Thomas, Anna I, 841
Thomas, Anna I, 1068
Thomas, Anna I, 1071
Thomas, Anna I, 1072
Thomas, Anna II, 186
Thomas, Anna II, 267
Thomas, Anna II, 666
Thomas, Anna III, 69
Thomas, Anna III, 285
Thomas, Anna IV, 236
Thomas, Anna IV, 244
Thomas, Anna IV, 288
Thomas, Anna IV, 289
Thomas, Anna IV, 290
Thomas, Anna IV, 291
Thomas, Anna V, 131
Thomas, Anna V, 767
Thomas, Anna V, 768
Thomas, Anna V, 1021
Thomas, Anna VI, 792
Thomas, Anna VI, 1003
Thomas, Anna E. IV, 1296
Thomas, Anna L. II, 893
Thomas, Anna L. II, 929
Thomas, Anna L. IV, 190
Thomas, Anna L. IV, 196
Thomas, Anna L. IV, 231
Thomas, Anna L. IV, 289
Thomas, Anna L. IV, 291
Thomas, Anna M. V, 633
Thomas, Anna M. V, 647
Thomas, Anna Mary IV, 208
Thomas, Anna R. IV, 291
Thomas, Annaliza IV, 288
Thomas, Anne I, 187
Thomas, Anne I, 276
Thomas, Anne I, 841
Thomas, Anne I, 1068
Thomas, Anne V, 771
Thomas, Anne VI, 1003
Thomas, Anne R. IV, 289
Thomas, Anne T. IV, 834
Thomas, Anne T. IV, 848
Thomas, Annie A. III, 449
Thomas, Annie E. IV, 1340
Thomas, Aquilla IV, 424
Thomas, Aquilla IV, 447
Thomas, Aquilla IV, 596
Thomas, Archd. VI, 1003
Thomas, Archibald VI, 1003
Thomas, Arloff IV, 448
Thomas, Arthur II, 509
Thomas, Arthur II, 666
Thomas, Arthur H. IV, 660
Thomas, Arthur Richard IV, 1007
Thomas, Arvine IV, 1030
Thomas, Asa II, 720
Thomas, Asa II, 770
Thomas, Asa IV, 447
Thomas, Asa IV, 596
Thomas, Asa V, 769
Thomas, Asael IV, 161
Thomas, Asahel I, 1045
Thomas, Asahel IV, 353
Thomas, Asahel IV, 414
Thomas, Asahel IV, 447
Thomas, Ascenath IV, 1030
Thomas, Asenath IV, 201
Thomas, Asenath IV, 290
Thomas, Asenath IV, 291
Thomas, Asenath IV, 302
Thomas, Asenath IV, 583
Thomas, Asenath IV, 719
Thomas, Asenath IV, 776
Thomas, Asenath IV, 1030
Thomas, Asenath V, 767
Thomas, Asenath V, 935
Thomas, Asenath H. IV, 289
Thomas, Ashel IV, 353
Thomas, Ashley II, 426
Thomas, Augusta V, 714
Thomas, Avice IV, 161
Thomas, Avis I, 276
Thomas, Avis IV, 288
Thomas, Avis IV, 290
Thomas, Avis IV, 314
Thomas, Avis V, 960
Thomas, Azael IV, 448
Thomas, Barbara II, 1009
Thomas, Barbara II, 1032
Thomas, Barbara Ann V, 768
Thomas, Bathsheba IV, 895
Thomas, Bathshebe IV, 891
Thomas, Beniamin I, 277
Thomas, Benj. I, 518
Thomas, Benj. II, 580
Thomas, Benj. II, 666
Thomas, Benj. IV, 287
Thomas, Benj. V, 767
Thomas, Benj. V, 768
Thomas, Benj. F. V, 936
Thomas, Benj. F. V, 978
Thomas, Benjamin I, 187
Thomas, Benjamin I, 200
Thomas, Benjamin I, 518
Thomas, Benjamin I, 523
Thomas, Benjamin I, 577
Thomas, Benjamin I, 793
Thomas, Benjamin I, 841
Thomas, Benjamin I, 1068
Thomas, Benjamin I, 1071
Thomas, Benjamin I, 1072
Thomas, Benjamin I Sup 1, 10
Thomas, Benjamin II, 231
Thomas, Benjamin II, 267
Thomas, Benjamin II, 270
Thomas, Benjamin II, 665
Thomas, Benjamin II, 666
Thomas, Benjamin IV, 161
Thomas, Benjamin IV, 288
Thomas, Benjamin IV, 290
Thomas, Benjamin IV, 353
Thomas, Benjamin IV, 357
Thomas, Benjamin IV, 448
Thomas, Benjamin V, 131
Thomas, Benjamin V, 283
Thomas, Benjamin V, 762
Thomas, Benjamin V, 769
Thomas, Benjamin V, 771
Thomas, Benjamin Franklin IV, 1007
Thomas, Benjamin Franklin IV, 1008
Thomas, Benjamin Franklin V, 131
Thomas, Benjamin J. IV, 289
Thomas, Benjamin J. IV, 291
Thomas, Benjamin J. IV, 660
Thomas, Bertha IV, 1008
Thomas, Bertha A. IV, 660
Thomas, Bessie IV, 1265
Thomas, Betha H. IV, 930
Thomas, Betsey VI, 877
Thomas, Betsey VI, 937
Thomas, Betsey VI, 1003
Thomas, Betsey Ann VI, 1003
Thomas, Betsy VI, 1003
Thomas, Betta I, 577
Thomas, Betty I, 518
Thomas, Betty I, 561
Thomas, Betty I, 577
Thomas, Betty I, 793
Thomas, Betty I, 1068
Thomas, Beulah II, 402
Thomas, Beulah II, 812
Thomas, Beulah VI, 757
Thomas, Beulah A. IV, 289

Thomas, Beulah A. IV, 291
Thomas, Beulah A. IV, 660
Thomas, Beulah Ann IV, 657
Thomas, Beulah Ann IV, 660
Thomas, Beulah E. IV, 289
Thomas, Beulah E. IV, 305
Thomas, Beulah Elma II, 770
Thomas, Beulah Elma IV, 289
Thomas, Beulah M. IV, 660
Thomas, Beulah May IV, 660
Thomas, Birtha H. IV, 1007
Thomas, Bradaway IV, 212
Thomas, Bradaway IV, 289
Thomas, Bradway IV, 205
Thomas, Bradway IV, 288
Thomas, Bradway IV, 290
Thomas, Bradway IV, 579
Thomas, Brodowa IV, 290
Thomas, Buelah IV, 776
Thomas, Buelah IV, 777
Thomas, Bula E. IV, 289
Thomas, Bulah IV, 289
Thomas, Bulah Almeda IV, 289
Thomas, Bulahelma II, 666
Thomas, Byron G. IV, 289
Thomas, C. Frank II, 929
Thomas, C. Jane V, 243
Thomas, C. Jane V, 283
Thomas, Caleb V, 767
Thomas, Caleb V, 769
Thomas, Caleb Eyre II, 722
Thomas, Calvin IV, 777
Thomas, Calvin V, 647
Thomas, Calvin H. IV, 777
Thomas, Calvin W. V, 767
Thomas, Camilla A. VI, 975
Thomas, Camm I, 1045
Thomas, Camm I, 1051
Thomas, Camm IV, 396
Thomas, Camm IV, 412
Thomas, Camm IV, 447
Thomas, Camm IV, 454
Thomas, Camm IV, 596
Thomas, Camm V, 59
Thomas, Camm, Jr. IV, 447
Thomas, Camm, Jr. IV, 448
Thomas, Cammuel VI, 1003
Thomas, Camuel VI, 1003
Thomas, Caroline II, 822
Thomas, Caroline V, 978
Thomas, Caroline E. VI, 650
Thomas, Caroline E. VI, 679
Thomas, Caroline E. VI, 699
Thomas, Caroline E. VI, 700
Thomas, Caroline E. VI, 714
Thomas, Caroline Elizabeth V, 612
Thomas, Caroline Elizabeth V, 646
Thomas, Caroline Elizabeth V, 647
Thomas, Caroline L. II, 929
Thomas, Carrie Augusta II, 822
Thomas, Carrie E. IV, 660
Thomas, Catharine I, 386
Thomas, Catharine I, 423
Thomas, Catharine II, 221
Thomas, Catharine II, 267
Thomas, Catharine IV, 441
Thomas, Catharine IV, 447
Thomas, Catharine IV, 528
Thomas, Catharine IV, 594
Thomas, Catharine IV, 596
Thomas, Catharine VI, 521
Thomas, Catharine VI, 553
Thomas, Catharine VI, 774
Thomas, Catharine VI, 1003
Thomas, Catharine E. V, 769
Thomas, Catharine Elizabeth V, 768
Thomas, Catharine L. I, 902
Thomas, Catharine M. IV, 776
Thomas, Catharine M. IV, 777
Thomas, Catherine VI, 435
Thomas, Catherine VI, 440
Thomas, Catherine VI, 451
Thomas, Catherine VI, 521
Thomas, Catherine Dare Vickers VI, 786
Thomas, Caty I, 1045
Thomas, Caty IV, 161
Thomas, Caty IV, 447
Thomas, Chalkley IV, 289
Thomas, Chalkley IV, 291
Thomas, Chalkley IV, 1030
Thomas, Chalkley V, 131
Thomas, Chalkley V, 534
Thomas, Chalkley V, 646
Thomas, Chalkley V, 647
Thomas, Charity V, 131
Thomas, Charity V, 134
Thomas, Charles I, 1069
Thomas, Charles II, 426
Thomas, Charles III, 449
Thomas, Charles IV, 1340
Thomas, Charles VI, 1003
Thomas, Charles B. IV, 1030
Thomas, Charles C. IV, 776
Thomas, Charles E. II, 929
Thomas, Charles Ebenezer VI, 142
Thomas, Charles F. I, 902
Thomas, Charles O. IV, 917
Thomas, Charles Oscar IV, 1007
Thomas, Charles Oscar IV, 1008
Thomas, Charles W. V, 131
Thomas, Charles W. V, 978
Thomas, Chas. II, 929
Thomas, Chas. IV, 1340
Thomas, Chas. E. IV, 1340
Thomas, Chas. W. V, 923
Thomas, Chas. W. V, 935
Thomas, Chas. W. V, 936
Thomas, Chester IV, 1340
Thomas, Chester H. IV, 1340
Thomas, Chloe V, 768
Thomas, Chole VI, 1003
Thomas, Christan I, 841
Thomas, Christan I, 1068
Thomas, Christan I, 1071
Thomas, Christian I, 518
Thomas, Christian V, 767
Thomas, Christian V, 769
Thomas, Christian P. V, 769
Thomas, Christian Thomas V, 767
Thomas, Christina IV, 1265
Thomas, Christopher H. IV, 353
Thomas, Christopher H. IV, 448
Thomas, Christopher M. V, 131
Thomas, Cidney IV, 448
Thomas, Clara V, 647
Thomas, Clara V, 735
Thomas, Clara V, 768
Thomas, Clarence E. II, 929
Thomas, Clark Willcuts I, 793
Thomas, Clarkson IV, 289
Thomas, Clarkson IV, 290
Thomas, Clarkson V, 646
Thomas, Clarkson V, 647
Thomas, Clarkson V, 768
Thomas, Clarkson B. IV, 289
Thomas, Clarkson B. IV, 291
Thomas, Cloe VI, 974
Thomas, Cloey VI, 1003
Thomas, Clyde IV, 1265
Thomas, Clyde V, 768
Thomas, Colvin Henry IV, 776
Thomas, Cora A. I, 902
Thomas, Cynthia P. VI, 1003
Thomas, D. V, 730
Thomas, Daniel I, 276
Thomas, Daniel I, 1071
Thomas, Daniel II, 426
Thomas, Daniel II, 622
Thomas, Daniel II, 665
Thomas, Daniel II, 666
Thomas, Daniel II, 697
Thomas, Daniel II, 726
Thomas, Daniel II, 770
Thomas, Daniel IV, 1007
Thomas, Daniel IV, 1008
Thomas, Daniel V, 767
Thomas, Daniel V, 771
Thomas, Daniel I. II, 908
Thomas, Daniel I. II, 927
Thomas, David I, 276
Thomas, David I, 297
Thomas, David I, 318
Thomas, David I, 319
Thomas, David II, 186
Thomas, David II, 217
Thomas, David II, 231
Thomas, David II, 267
Thomas, David II, 426
Thomas, David II, 823
Thomas, David II, 929
Thomas, David IV, 62
Thomas, David IV, 111
Thomas, David IV, 113
Thomas, David IV, 117
Thomas, David IV, 180
Thomas, David IV, 288
Thomas, David IV, 289
Thomas, David IV, 290
Thomas, David IV, 291
Thomas, David IV, 660
Thomas, David IV, 803
Thomas, David IV, 848
Thomas, David IV, 1008
Thomas, David IV, 1079
Thomas, David V, 131
Thomas, David V, 733
Thomas, David V, 762
Thomas, David V, 765
Thomas, David V, 767
Thomas, David V, 769
Thomas, David VI, 922
Thomas, David VI, 983
Thomas, David VI, 1003
Thomas, David VI, 1015
Thomas, David B. IV, 1008
Thomas, David Blackburn IV, 1007
Thomas, David Blackburn IV, 1008
Thomas, David H. V, 1021
Thomas, David Hall IV, 290
Thomas, David Johnson V, 768
Thomas, Davis III, 311
Thomas, Debora IV, 1079
Thomas, Deborah II, 426
Thomas, Deborah III, 167
Thomas, Deborah IV, 236
Thomas, Deborah IV, 290
Thomas, Deborah IV, 447
Thomas, Deborah IV, 1008
Thomas, Deborah IV, 1012
Thomas, Deborah IV, 1079
Thomas, Deborah IV, 1117
Thomas, Deborah IV, 1120
Thomas, Deborah V, 771
Thomas, Deborah VI, 474
Thomas, Deborah C. III, 311
Thomas, Delilah VI, 1003
Thomas, Dinah II, 426
Thomas, Dorcas I, 277
Thomas, Dorcas IV, 290
Thomas, Dorcas IV, 596
Thomas, Dorcas IV, 777
Thomas, Dorcas IV, 1008
Thomas, Dorcas IV, 1296
Thomas, Dorcas Ann IV, 989
Thomas, Dorcas Ann IV, 1007
Thomas, Dorcas Ann IV, 1008
Thomas, Dorothy IV, 884
Thomas, Dr. ??? II, 343
Thomas, Drusilla R. II, 929
Thomas, E. V, 730
Thomas, E. V, 768
Thomas, E. A. V, 534
Thomas, E. W. I, 1162
Thomas, Earnest B. IV, 291
Thomas, Ebeneezer IV, 1188
Thomas, Ebenezar IV, 1188
Thomas, Ebenezar VI, 19
Thomas, Ebenezer II, 426
Thomas, Ebenezer VI, 130
Thomas, Ebenezer VI, 142
Thomas, Edgar B. IV, 289
Thomas, Edgar B. IV, 291
Thomas, Edith IV, 213
Thomas, Edith IV, 288
Thomas, Edith IV, 289
Thomas, Edith IV, 353
Thomas, Edith IV, 431
Thomas, Edith IV, 447
Thomas, Edith J. IV, 291
Thomas, Edna IV, 196
Thomas, Edna IV, 289
Thomas, Edna IV, 290
Thomas, Edna Vickers VI, 770
Thomas, Edna Vickers VI, 786
Thomas, Edward I, 1024
Thomas, Edward I, 1038
Thomas, Edward I, 1039
Thomas, Edward II, 426
Thomas, Edward II, 448
Thomas, Edward II, 540
Thomas, Edward II, 665
Thomas, Edward II, 666
Thomas, Edward III, 311
Thomas, Edward IV, 884
Thomas, Edward V, 21
Thomas, Edward V, 33
Thomas, Edward V, 100
Thomas, Edward V, 134
Thomas, Edward V, 362
Thomas, Edward V, 506
Thomas, Edward V, 534
Thomas, Edward V, 646
Thomas, Edward V, 647
Thomas, Edward V, 767
Thomas, Edward V, 768
Thomas, Edward V, 769
Thomas, Edward V, 770
Thomas, Edward VI, 8
Thomas, Edward VI, 12
Thomas, Edward VI, 13
Thomas, Edward VI, 19
Thomas, Edward VI, 35
Thomas, Edward VI, 36
Thomas, Edward VI, 37
Thomas, Edward A. IV, 1340
Thomas, Edward L. V, 131
Thomas, Edward R. V, 534
Thomas, Edward S. V, 131
Thomas, Edward, Jr. V, 131
Thomas, Edward, Jr. V, 768
Thomas, Edward, Jr. V, 769
Thomas, Edwd VI, 215
Thomas, Edwd, Junior VI, 215
Thomas, Edwin II, 186
Thomas, Edwin IV, 776
Thomas, Edwin IV, 848
Thomas, Elam V, 767
Thomas, Eldridge VI, 1003
Thomas, Eleanor II, 186
Thomas, Eleanor II, 665
Thomas, Eleanor IV, 289
Thomas, Eleanor IV, 290
Thomas, Eleanor IV, 1008
Thomas, Eleanor IV, 1043
Thomas, Eleanor Jane IV, 777
Thomas, Eleanor Jane IV, 1007
Thomas, Eleanor Jane IV, 1008
Thomas, Eleanor Mildred IV, 776
Thomas, Eleanor Miller IV, 1008
Thomas, Eleazer III, 311
Thomas, Elen R. IV, 1021
Thomas, Elenor IV, 777
Thomas, Elenor V, 935
Thomas, Elenor G. IV, 291
Thomas, Eli IV, 447
Thomas, Eli IV, 727
Thomas, Eli IV, 776
Thomas, Eli IV, 777
Thomas, Eli IV, 1079
Thomas, Eli IV, 1105
Thomas, Eli IV, 1117
Thomas, Eli V, 768
Thomas, Eli V, 769
Thomas, Elias V, 767
Thomas, Elias V, 769
Thomas, Elihu V, 131
Thomas, Elihu V, 936
Thomas, Elijah I, 518
Thomas, Elijah I, 577
Thomas, Elijah I, 841
Thomas, Elijah I, 1068
Thomas, Elijah I, 1071
Thomas, Elijah I, 1072
Thomas, Elijah II, 799
Thomas, Elijah II, 822
Thomas, Elijah IV, 660
Thomas, Elijah V, 33
Thomas, Elijah V, 131
Thomas, Elijah V, 767
Thomas, Elijah V, 769
Thomas, Elisabeth I, 141
Thomas, Elisabeth I, 165
Thomas, Elisabeth I, 169
Thomas, Elisabeth II, 186
Thomas, Elisabeth II, 665
Thomas, Elisha II, 1057
Thomas, Elisha II, 1061
Thomas, Elisha IV, 1296
Thomas, Elisha V, 131
Thomas, Elisha V, 146
Thomas, Elisha V, 352
Thomas, Elisha V, 362
Thomas, Eliza IV, 448
Thomas, Eliza IV, 718
Thomas, Eliza IV, 719
Thomas, Eliza IV, 776
Thomas, Eliza IV, 777
Thomas, Eliza V, 131
Thomas, Eliza VI, 783
Thomas, Eliza Ann V, 362
Thomas, Eliza B. VI, 1003
Thomas, Eliza Jane IV, 417
Thomas, Eliza Jane IV, 448
Thomas, Eliza Jane IV, 989
Thomas, Eliza Jane IV, 1007
Thomas, Eliza Jane IV, 1008
Thomas, Eliza Jane IV, 1137
Thomas, Eliza Jane IV, 1138
Thomas, Elizabeth I, 120
Thomas, Elizabeth I, 277
Thomas, Elizabeth I, 841
Thomas, Elizabeth I, 1024
Thomas, Elizabeth I, 1028
Thomas, Elizabeth I, 1038
Thomas, Elizabeth I, 1045
Thomas, Elizabeth I, 1051
Thomas, Elizabeth I, 1068
Thomas, Elizabeth II, 54
Thomas, Elizabeth II, 66
Thomas, Elizabeth II, 104
Thomas, Elizabeth II, 267
Thomas, Elizabeth II, 426
Thomas, Elizabeth II, 512
Thomas, Elizabeth II, 665
Thomas, Elizabeth II, 722
Thomas, Elizabeth II, 784
Thomas, Elizabeth II, 802
Thomas, Elizabeth II, 823
Thomas, Elizabeth II, 827
Thomas, Elizabeth III, 31
Thomas, Elizabeth IV, 111
Thomas, Elizabeth IV, 161
Thomas, Elizabeth IV, 180
Thomas, Elizabeth IV, 190
Thomas, Elizabeth IV, 218
Thomas, Elizabeth IV, 288
Thomas, Elizabeth IV, 289
Thomas, Elizabeth IV, 290
Thomas, Elizabeth IV, 314
Thomas, Elizabeth IV, 393
Thomas, Elizabeth IV, 396
Thomas, Elizabeth IV, 412
Thomas, Elizabeth IV, 447
Thomas, Elizabeth IV, 454
Thomas, Elizabeth IV, 553
Thomas, Elizabeth IV, 578
Thomas, Elizabeth IV, 596
Thomas, Elizabeth IV, 727
Thomas, Elizabeth IV, 776
Thomas, Elizabeth IV, 777
Thomas, Elizabeth IV, 836
Thomas, Elizabeth IV, 848
Thomas, Elizabeth IV, 884
Thomas, Elizabeth IV, 999
Thomas, Elizabeth IV, 1056
Thomas, Elizabeth IV, 1079
Thomas, Elizabeth IV, 1113
Thomas, Elizabeth IV, 1188
Thomas, Elizabeth IV, 1340
Thomas, Elizabeth V, 56
Thomas, Elizabeth V, 59
Thomas, Elizabeth V, 78
Thomas, Elizabeth V, 131
Thomas, Elizabeth V, 362
Thomas, Elizabeth V, 473
Thomas, Elizabeth V, 534
Thomas, Elizabeth V, 612
Thomas, Elizabeth V, 727
Thomas, Elizabeth V, 728
Thomas, Elizabeth V, 733
Thomas, Elizabeth V, 735
Thomas, Elizabeth V, 738
Thomas, Elizabeth V, 752
Thomas, Elizabeth V, 762
Thomas, Elizabeth V, 764
Thomas, Elizabeth V, 766
Thomas, Elizabeth V, 767
Thomas, Elizabeth V, 768
Thomas, Elizabeth V, 769
Thomas, Elizabeth V, 770
Thomas, Elizabeth V, 771
Thomas, Elizabeth V, 774
Thomas, Elizabeth V, 793
Thomas, Elizabeth V, 821
Thomas, Elizabeth VI, 509
Thomas, Elizabeth VI, 519
Thomas, Elizabeth VI, 520
Thomas, Elizabeth VI, 521
Thomas, Elizabeth VI, 714
Thomas, Elizabeth VI, 749
Thomas, Elizabeth VI, 756
Thomas, Elizabeth VI, 859
Thomas, Elizabeth VI, 870
Thomas, Elizabeth VI, 976
Thomas, Elizabeth VI, 988
Thomas, Elizabeth VI, 1003
Thomas, Elizabeth A. II, 905
Thomas, Elizabeth A. II, 929
Thomas, Elizabeth A. IV, 848
Thomas, Elizabeth Ann IV, 596
Thomas, Elizabeth Ann V, 975
Thomas, Elizabeth Ann V, 978
Thomas, Elizabeth Archer II, 812
Thomas, Elizabeth H. IV, 660
Thomas, Elizabeth H. IV, 1110
Thomas, Elizabeth H. IV, 1112
Thomas, Elizabeth H. IV, 1117
Thomas, Elizabeth Houston IV, 848
Thomas, Elizabeth M. II, 186
Thomas, Elizabeth M. II, 286
Thomas, Elizabeth M. II, 304
Thomas, Elizabeth S. IV, 180
Thomas, Elizabeth S. IV, 289
Thomas, Elizabeth S. IV, 448
Thomas, Elizabeth T. V, 765
Thomas, Elizabeth, Jr. IV, 447
Thomas, Elizabeth, Jr. V, 769
Thomas, Ella IV, 901
Thomas, Ella W. II, 893
Thomas, Ella W. II, 929
Thomas, Elleanor IV, 1079
Thomas, Ellen II, 929
Thomas, Ellen IV, 777
Thomas, Ellen IV, 1117
Thomas, Ellen V, 978

nas, Ellen F. VI, 679
nas, Ellenor V, 935
nas, Elliott J. II, 929
nas, Ellis V, 534
nas, Ellis R. V, 646
nas, Ellmer A. V, 534
nas, Ellsworth V, 1021
nas, Ellwood II, 929
nas, Ellwood IV, 660
nas, Elma IV, 205
nas, Elma IV, 289
nas, Elma IV, 290
nas, Elma IV, 579
nas, Elma IV, 580
nas, Elma IV, 596
nas, Elma V, 647
nas, Elma Luella IV, 1007
nas, Elma Luella IV, 1008
nas, Elmer H. IV, 660
nas, Elmira IV, 289
nas, Elmira IV, 448
nas, Elmira V, 131
nas, Elmira V, 936
nas, Elmirah Jane IV, 776
nas, Elmore A. V, 534
nas, Elton II, 186
nas, Elton II, 304
nas, Elva V, 767
nas, Elva V, 769
nas, Elvira V, 767
nas, Elwood II, 893
nas, Elwood IV, 289
nas, Elwood IV, 291
nas, Elwood IV, 657
nas, Elwood IV, 660
nas, Elwood IV, 776
nas, Elwood IV, 777
nas, Elwood C. V, 768
nas, Emily II, 722
nas, Emily V, 767
nas, Emily V, 978
nas, Emily V, 979
nas, Emma V, 405
nas, Emma V, 434
nas, Emma V, 768
nas, Emma V, 774
nas, Emma V, 1021
nas, Emma B. IV, 289
nas, Emma B. IV, 290
nas, Emma E. IV, 848
nas, Emma H. V, 434
nas, Enoch, Jr. II, 666
nas, Enos II, 744
nas, Enos II, 770
nas, Enos IV, 596
nas, Enos V, 767
nas, Enos V, 769
nas, Enos VI, 440
nas, Enos VI, 451
nas, Enos E. V, 769
nas, Ephraim IV, 1056
nas, Ephraim W. IV, 1056
nas, Erastus V, 362
nas, Erastus N. V, 362
nas, Ernest B. IV, 289
nas, Ernest B. IV, 291
nas, Ester IV, 289
nas, Esther II, 666
nas, Esther II, 720
nas, Esther II, 770
nas, Esther IV, 111
nas, Esther IV, 776
nas, Esther IV, 777
nas, Esther IV, 821
nas, Esther IV, 848
nas, Esther IV, 980
nas, Esther IV, 1007
nas, Esther IV, 1008
nas, Esther IV, 1043
nas, Esther V, 207
nas, Esther V, 362
nas, Esther V, 534
nas, Esther V, 646
nas, Esther V, 762
nas, Esther V, 765
nas, Esther V, 767
nas, Esther V, 769
nas, Esther A. V, 768
nas, Esther Ann V, 734
nas, Esther Ann V, 769
nas, Esther H. IV, 291
nas, Esther H. IV, 1007
nas, Esther H. IV, 1008
nas, Esther L. II, 827
nas, Etta A. VI, 714
nas, Eunice IV, 999
nas, Eunice V, 768
nas, Eva V, 768
nas, Eva May IV, 1043
nas, Evan I, 577
nas, Evan I, 1024
Thomas, Evan II, 426
Thomas, Evan II, 448
Thomas, Evan II, 666
Thomas, Evan III, 311
Thomas, Evan IV, 660
Thomas, Evan V, 131
Thomas, Evan V, 766
Thomas, Evan VI, 357
Thomas, Evan VI, 358
Thomas, Evan VI, 399
Thomas, Evan VI, 435
Thomas, Evan VI, 451
Thomas, Evan VI, 548
Thomas, Evan VI, 606
Thomas, Evan VI, 726
Thomas, Evan Barker III, 311
Thomas, Evan D. IV, 660
Thomas, Evan Morrison II, 426
Thomas, Evan Morrison II, 666
Thomas, Evan, Jr. V, 769
Thomas, Evan, Jr. VI, 451
Thomas, Evan, Sr. V, 769
Thomas, Evans V, 733
Thomas, Evin V, 768
Thomas, Evin VI, 215
Thomas, Ezekiel V, 541
Thomas, Ezekiel VI, 404
Thomas, Ezekiel VI, 450
Thomas, Ezekiel VI, 451
Thomas, Ezekiel VI, 591
Thomas, Ezekiel VI, 606
Thomas, Fanny III, 311
Thomas, Filena IV, 1079
Thomas, Fleming VI, 1003
Thomas, Flemming A. IV, 999
Thomas, Frances V, 647
Thomas, Frances J. V, 647
Thomas, Frances M. III, 311
Thomas, Francis I, 319
Thomas, Francis I, 518
Thomas, Francis I, 577
Thomas, Francis I, 841
Thomas, Francis I, 1066
Thomas, Francis I, 1068
Thomas, Francis I, 1071
Thomas, Francis V, 283
Thomas, Francis V, 768
Thomas, Francis M. VI, 1003
Thomas, Franklin IV, 848
Thomas, Frederick I, 577
Thomas, Frederick IV, 448
Thomas, Geo. V, 766
Thomas, George II, 426
Thomas, George II, 666
Thomas, George II, 812
Thomas, George II, 905
Thomas, George II, 929
Thomas, George II, 1062
Thomas, George V, 131
Thomas, George V, 602
Thomas, George V, 767
Thomas, George V, 768
Thomas, George V, 769
Thomas, George V, 807
Thomas, George VI, 869
Thomas, George VI, 886
Thomas, George VI, 949
Thomas, George VI, 975
Thomas, George VI, 1003
Thomas, George Henry IV, 1188
Thomas, George Thomas II, 666
Thomas, George W. VI, 1003
Thomas, Gertrude V, 612
Thomas, Gilbert E. IV, 183
Thomas, Gilbert E. IV, 289
Thomas, Gilbert E. IV, 291
Thomas, Gilbert E. IV, 660
Thomas, Gillie Ann VI, 1003
Thomas, Gladys T. III, 91
Thomas, Gladys T. III, 311
Thomas, Grace II, 202
Thomas, Grace II, 267
Thomas, Grace II, 448
Thomas, Grace IV, 1265
Thomas, Grace V, 207
Thomas, Grace V, 754
Thomas, Grace V, 767
Thomas, Gulay I, 1068
Thomas, Gulielma IV, 288
Thomas, Gulielma V, 767
Thomas, Gwenlin II, 665
Thomas, Halford IV, 291
Thomas, Hammond IV, 776
Thomas, Hammond IV, 777
Thomas, Hannah I, 276
Thomas, Hannah I, 277
Thomas, Hannah I, 297
Thomas, Hannah I, 318
Thomas, Hannah I, 319
Thomas, Hannah I, 625
Thomas, Hannah I, 793
Thomas, Hannah I, 827
Thomas, Hannah I, 841
Thomas, Hannah I, 843
Thomas, Hannah I, 1068
Thomas, Hannah I, 1069
Thomas, Hannah I, 1072
Thomas, Hannah II, 267
Thomas, Hannah II, 426
Thomas, Hannah II, 452
Thomas, Hannah II, 509
Thomas, Hannah II, 665
Thomas, Hannah II, 666
Thomas, Hannah II, 744
Thomas, Hannah II, 770
Thomas, Hannah II, 822
Thomas, Hannah II, 823
Thomas, Hannah IV, 108
Thomas, Hannah IV, 111
Thomas, Hannah IV, 161
Thomas, Hannah IV, 210
Thomas, Hannah IV, 290
Thomas, Hannah IV, 596
Thomas, Hannah IV, 777
Thomas, Hannah IV, 884
Thomas, Hannah IV, 1008
Thomas, Hannah V, 647
Thomas, Hannah V, 738
Thomas, Hannah V, 767
Thomas, Hannah V, 768
Thomas, Hannah V, 807
Thomas, Hannah VI, 450
Thomas, Hannah VI, 451
Thomas, Hannah VI, 521
Thomas, Hannah VI, 533
Thomas, Hannah VI, 572
Thomas, Hannah C. IV, 776
Thomas, Hannah C. IV, 1021
Thomas, Hannah C. V, 767
Thomas, Hannah Heaton II, 231
Thomas, Hannah Heaton II, 267
Thomas, Hannah J. VI, 714
Thomas, Hannah P. II, 886
Thomas, Hannah P. II, 929
Thomas, Hannah T. IV, 777
Thomas, Hannah T. IV, 884
Thomas, Hannah T. IV, 1007
Thomas, Hannah, Jr. IV, 777
Thomas, Hannah, Jr. V, 769
Thomas, Hanson V, 978
Thomas, Harding VI, 798
Thomas, Harley A. IV, 1043
Thomas, Harriet III, 31
Thomas, Harriet IV, 291
Thomas, Harriet IV, 363
Thomas, Harriet IV, 447
Thomas, Harriet IV, 596
Thomas, Harriet V, 767
Thomas, Harriet V, 769
Thomas, Harriet S. IV, 291
Thomas, Harriett VI, 1003
Thomas, Harry II, 822
Thomas, Harry C. II, 893
Thomas, Harry C. II, 929
Thomas, Harry K. IV, 1043
Thomas, Harvard VI, 1003
Thomas, Harvey II, 770
Thomas, Harvey IV, 289
Thomas, Harvey IV, 303
Thomas, Harvey IV, 660
Thomas, Harvey IV, 1008
Thomas, Hattie IV, 1338
Thomas, Hattie IV, 1340
Thomas, Hays V, 131
Thomas, Hazel V, 768
Thomas, Helen B. II, 838
Thomas, Helen B. II, 929
Thomas, Helen Irene VI, 451
Thomas, Hendin VI, 859
Thomas, Hendley I, 1068
Thomas, Hendley V, 283
Thomas, Henrietta V, 752
Thomas, Henrietta V, 768
Thomas, Henrietta V, 769
Thomas, Henrietta VI, 471
Thomas, Henrietta VI, 1003
Thomas, Henry II, 666
Thomas, Henry IV, 777
Thomas, Henry IV, 827
Thomas, Henry IV, 848
Thomas, Henry IV, 875
Thomas, Henry IV, 884
Thomas, Henry V, 767
Thomas, Henry V, 768
Thomas, Henry V, 769
Thomas, Henry Camm IV, 447
Thomas, Henry P. V, 767
Thomas, Henry P. V, 769
Thomas, Herbert II, 929
Thomas, Herbert G. IV, 1265
Thomas, Hester VI, 656
Thomas, Hester VI, 714
Thomas, Hezekiah I, 1045
Thomas, Hezekiah IV, 161
Thomas, Hezekiah IV, 384
Thomas, Hezekiah IV, 447
Thomas, Hezekiah IV, 596
Thomas, Hiram IV, 190
Thomas, Hiram IV, 1117
Thomas, Hiram A. IV, 776
Thomas, Hiram A. IV, 777
Thomas, Howard IV, 291
Thomas, Howard D. V, 131
Thomas, Howard D. V, 936
Thomas, Howard D. V, 978
Thomas, Hubert IV, 1265
Thomas, Hugh II, 511
Thomas, Hugh II, 665
Thomas, Hugh II, 666
Thomas, Hugh IV, 448
Thomas, Hugh J. IV, 353
Thomas, Hugh Judge IV, 353
Thomas, Hugh Judge IV, 448
Thomas, Hugh Martin V, 767
Thomas, Hulda I, 267
Thomas, Hulda I, 276
Thomas, Huldah I, 276
Thomas, Huldah I, 1068
Thomas, Huldah V, 506
Thomas, Huldah V, 534
Thomas, Huldah V, 647
Thomas, Huldah V, 767
Thomas, Huldy IV, 62
Thomas, Humphrey V, 612
Thomas, Huntington IV, 1188
Thomas, I. C. V, 768
Thomas, I. Hannah IV, 1040
Thomas, I. Hannah IV, 1043
Thomas, Ida I, 950
Thomas, Ida IV, 848
Thomas, Ida V, 612
Thomas, Ida Gray I, 934
Thomas, Ida Virginia II, 822
Thomas, Increase IV, 447
Thomas, Ira V, 769
Thomas, Irena V, 1021
Thomas, Irene IV, 1340
Thomas, Irene E. IV, 1340
Thomas, Irvin V, 767
Thomas, Irvin V, 769
Thomas, Isaac I, 518
Thomas, Isaac I, 556
Thomas, Isaac I, 577
Thomas, Isaac I, 793
Thomas, Isaac I, 841
Thomas, Isaac I, 1024
Thomas, Isaac I, 1038
Thomas, Isaac I, 1066
Thomas, Isaac I, 1068
Thomas, Isaac I, 1070
Thomas, Isaac I, 1071
Thomas, Isaac I, 1072
Thomas, Isaac II, 426
Thomas, Isaac II, 899
Thomas, Isaac II, 929
Thomas, Isaac IV, 180
Thomas, Isaac IV, 190
Thomas, Isaac IV, 196
Thomas, Isaac IV, 203
Thomas, Isaac IV, 204
Thomas, Isaac IV, 231
Thomas, Isaac IV, 236
Thomas, Isaac IV, 288
Thomas, Isaac IV, 289
Thomas, Isaac IV, 290
Thomas, Isaac IV, 447
Thomas, Isaac IV, 448
Thomas, Isaac IV, 776
Thomas, Isaac IV, 777
Thomas, Isaac IV, 884
Thomas, Isaac IV, 999
Thomas, Isaac IV, 1008
Thomas, Isaac IV, 1117
Thomas, Isaac IV, 1362
Thomas, Isaac IV, 1382
Thomas, Isaac V, 146
Thomas, Isaac V, 362
Thomas, Isaac V, 567
Thomas, Isaac V, 602
Thomas, Isaac V, 647
Thomas, Isaac V, 714
Thomas, Isaac V, 738
Thomas, Isaac V, 754
Thomas, Isaac V, 766
Thomas, Isaac V, 767
Thomas, Isaac V, 768
Thomas, Isaac V, 769
Thomas, Isaac V, 770
Thomas, Isaac V, 793
Thomas, Isaac V, 936
Thomas, Isaac VI, 451
Thomas, Isaac VI, 521
Thomas, Isaac VI, 859
Thomas, Isaac VI, 937
Thomas, Isaac VI, 966
Thomas, Isaac VI, 976
Thomas, Isaac VI, 1003
Thomas, Isaac B. V, 534
Thomas, Isaac B. VI, 416
Thomas, Isaac B. VI, 451
Thomas, Isaac G. IV, 777
Thomas, Isaac Green IV, 777
Thomas, Isaac Green IV, 1007
Thomas, Isaac Green IV, 1008
Thomas, Isaac H. V, 131
Thomas, Isaac H. V, 936
Thomas, Isaac H. V, 978
Thomas, Isaac Hays V, 131
Thomas, Isaac J. V, 611
Thomas, Isaac J. V, 647
Thomas, Isaac L. V, 534
Thomas, Isaac, Jr. V, 767
Thomas, Isaac, Sr. V, 768
Thomas, Isaah V, 131
Thomas, Isadore Cobbs IV, 1043
Thomas, Isaiah V, 131
Thomas, Isaiah V, 733
Thomas, Isaiah V, 766
Thomas, Isaiah V, 768
Thomas, Isaiah V, 769
Thomas, Isaiah V, 793
Thomas, Isaiah F. V, 768
Thomas, Isaiah, Jr. V, 769
Thomas, Isom V, 793
Thomas, Isom C. V, 760
Thomas, Isom C. V, 767
Thomas, Isom C. V, 768
Thomas, Isom C. V, 769
Thomas, Isom C. V, 791
Thomas, Israel IV, 180
Thomas, Israel IV, 289
Thomas, Israel IV, 777
Thomas, Isral IV, 776
Thomas, J. C. I, 626
Thomas, J. Horace IV, 1340
Thomas, J. Howard IV, 289
Thomas, Jacob II, 666
Thomas, Jacob II, 1062
Thomas, Jacob IV, 290
Thomas, Jacob IV, 682
Thomas, Jacob IV, 704
Thomas, Jacob IV, 776
Thomas, Jacob IV, 777
Thomas, Jacob IV, 778
Thomas, Jacob IV, 884
Thomas, Jacob IV, 1021
Thomas, Jacob V, 131
Thomas, Jacob V, 771
Thomas, Jacob R. VI, 451
Thomas, Jacob W. V, 767
Thomas, Jacob W. V, 769
Thomas, Jacob, Jr. V, 131
Thomas, James I, 423
Thomas, James I, 577
Thomas, James I, 793
Thomas, James I, 795
Thomas, James I, 1068
Thomas, James I, 1071
Thomas, James I Sup 1, 10
Thomas, James II, 42
Thomas, James II, 267
Thomas, James II, 426
Thomas, James II, 665
Thomas, James II, 666
Thomas, James II, 677
Thomas, James II, 929
Thomas, James III, 449
Thomas, James IV, 431
Thomas, James IV, 447
Thomas, James IV, 1188
Thomas, James IV, 1296
Thomas, James V, 752
Thomas, James V, 767
Thomas, James VI, 816
Thomas, James VI, 859
Thomas, James VI, 999
Thomas, James VI, 1003
Thomas, James VI, 1022
Thomas, James Arthur V, 647
Thomas, James Carey II, 720
Thomas, James Carey II, 770
Thomas, James Christopher IV, 1188
Thomas, James Christopher VI, 142
Thomas, James F. IV, 1008
Thomas, James H. V, 131
Thomas, James M. II, 426
Thomas, James M. II, 666
Thomas, James M. IV, 1007
Thomas, Jane I, 577
Thomas, Jane II, 426
Thomas, Jane II, 665
Thomas, Jane II, 770

Thomas, Jane II, 825
Thomas, Jane II, 929
Thomas, Jane IV, 596
Thomas, Jane V, 131
Thomas, Jane V, 534
Thomas, Jane V, 612
Thomas, Jane V, 635
Thomas, Jane V, 646
Thomas, Jane V, 647
Thomas, Jane VI, 416
Thomas, Jane VI, 451
Thomas, Jane VI, 1003
Thomas, Jane L. II, 929
Thomas, Jane Longstreth II, 799
Thomas, Jane M. V, 534
Thomas, Jane Owen V, 769
Thomas, Jane W. V, 611
Thomas, Jane W. V, 647
Thomas, Jane Walker II, 787
Thomas, Jane, Jr. V, 131
Thomas, Jehu IV, 596
Thomas, Jemima III, 311
Thomas, Jemima V, 733
Thomas, Jemima VI, 859
Thomas, Jennie IV, 1007
Thomas, Jennie V, 207
Thomas, Jennie G. III, 449
Thomas, Jesse I, 267
Thomas, Jesse I, 268
Thomas, Jesse I, 276
Thomas, Jesse I, 277
Thomas, Jesse I, 319
Thomas, Jesse I, 577
Thomas, Jesse I, 1038
Thomas, Jesse I, 1068
Thomas, Jesse I, 1071
Thomas, Jesse IV, 117
Thomas, Jesse IV, 161
Thomas, Jesse IV, 229
Thomas, Jesse IV, 288
Thomas, Jesse IV, 289
Thomas, Jesse IV, 290
Thomas, Jesse IV, 447
Thomas, Jesse IV, 776
Thomas, Jesse IV, 777
Thomas, Jesse IV, 989
Thomas, Jesse IV, 998
Thomas, Jesse IV, 1007
Thomas, Jesse IV, 1008
Thomas, Jesse IV, 1056
Thomas, Jesse IV, 1079
Thomas, Jesse IV, 1116
Thomas, Jesse IV, 1117
Thomas, Jesse IV, 1120
Thomas, Jesse V, 131
Thomas, Jesse V, 283
Thomas, Jesse V, 646
Thomas, Jesse V, 733
Thomas, Jesse V, 766
Thomas, Jesse P. IV, 290
Thomas, Jesse, Jr. IV, 1079
Thomas, Jesse, Sr. I, 276
Thomas, Jesse, Sr. IV, 290
Thomas, Jessey I, 277
Thomas, Jno. F. VI, 844
Thomas, Joanna IV, 287
Thomas, Joanna IV, 288
Thomas, Joanna IV, 290
Thomas, Joanna IV, 353
Thomas, Joanna IV, 357
Thomas, Joanna IV, 447
Thomas, Joanna IV, 448
Thomas, Joanna IV, 777
Thomas, Joanna IV, 989
Thomas, Joanna IV, 1007
Thomas, Joanna IV, 1008
Thomas, Joanna IV, 1079
Thomas, Joanna IV, 1117
Thomas, Joanna IV, 1138
Thomas, Joanna V, 768
Thomas, Joanna B. IV, 998
Thomas, Joanna B. IV, 1007
Thomas, Joanna B. IV, 1008
Thomas, Joanna Owen V, 766
Thomas, John I, 258
Thomas, John I, 276
Thomas, John I, 277
Thomas, John I, 319
Thomas, John I, 518
Thomas, John I, 577
Thomas, John I, 793
Thomas, John I, 841
Thomas, John I, 1024
Thomas, John I, 1036
Thomas, John I, 1038
Thomas, John I, 1066
Thomas, John I, 1068
Thomas, John I, 1071
Thomas, John I Sup 1, 10
Thomas, John II, 42
Thomas, John II, 81
Thomas, John II, 104
Thomas, John II, 426
Thomas, John II, 509
Thomas, John II, 666
Thomas, John II, 713
Thomas, John II, 744
Thomas, John II, 770
Thomas, John II, 823
Thomas, John II, 1062
Thomas, John IV, 111
Thomas, John IV, 161
Thomas, John IV, 288
Thomas, John IV, 290
Thomas, John IV, 448
Thomas, John IV, 550
Thomas, John IV, 553
Thomas, John IV, 596
Thomas, John IV, 719
Thomas, John IV, 776
Thomas, John IV, 777
Thomas, John IV, 860
Thomas, John IV, 884
Thomas, John IV, 891
Thomas, John IV, 892
Thomas, John IV, 895
Thomas, John IV, 1007
Thomas, John IV, 1008
Thomas, John IV, 1079
Thomas, John IV, 1084
Thomas, John IV, 1117
Thomas, John IV, 1225
Thomas, John IV, 1382
Thomas, John V, 131
Thomas, John V, 283
Thomas, John V, 362
Thomas, John V, 534
Thomas, John V, 612
Thomas, John V, 635
Thomas, John V, 646
Thomas, John V, 647
Thomas, John V, 733
Thomas, John V, 738
Thomas, John V, 754
Thomas, John V, 766
Thomas, John V, 768
Thomas, John V, 769
Thomas, John V, 935
Thomas, John VI, 56
Thomas, John VI, 399
Thomas, John VI, 451
Thomas, John VI, 587
Thomas, John VI, 786
Thomas, John VI, 873
Thomas, John VI, 971
Thomas, John VI, 1003
Thomas, John A. V, 647
Thomas, John B. IV, 289
Thomas, John B. IV, 1007
Thomas, John C. III, 311
Thomas, John C. IV, 917
Thomas, John C. IV, 1008
Thomas, John C. VI, 943
Thomas, John C. VI, 1003
Thomas, John D. II, 666
Thomas, John D. V, 766
Thomas, John D. V, 769
Thomas, John F. VI, 862
Thomas, John H. IV, 660
Thomas, John H. VI, 815
Thomas, John Henry I, 423
Thomas, John L. V, 935
Thomas, John M. II, 426
Thomas, John M. II, 666
Thomas, John M. W. II, 720
Thomas, John Martin IV, 999
Thomas, John R. VI, 1003
Thomas, John S. II, 666
Thomas, John W. VI, 142
Thomas, John, II I, 1072
Thomas, John, III I, 1072
Thomas, John, Jr. I, 577
Thomas, John, Jr. I, 841
Thomas, John, Jr. IV, 777
Thomas, John, Jr. V, 353
Thomas, John, Jr. V, 362
Thomas, John, Jr. V, 647
Thomas, John, Sr. I, 1066
Thomas, John, Sr. I, 1068
Thomas, John, Sr. V, 743
Thomas, Jonah IV, 288
Thomas, Jonah IV, 448
Thomas, Jonathan I, 187
Thomas, Jonathan II, 426
Thomas, Jonathan II, 665
Thomas, Jonathan II, 666
Thomas, Jonathan II, 770
Thomas, Jonathan II, 822
Thomas, Jonathan II, 828
Thomas, Jonathan IV, 288
Thomas, Jonathan IV, 290
Thomas, Jonathan IV, 848
Thomas, Jonathan IV, 884
Thomas, Jonathan IV, 1079
Thomas, Jonathan IV, 1117
Thomas, Jonathan IV, 1269
Thomas, Jonathan IV, 1296
Thomas, Jonathan V, 612
Thomas, Jonathan V, 771
Thomas, Jonathan H. IV, 447
Thomas, Jonathan H. IV, 1079
Thomas, Jonathan J. II, 666
Thomas, Jonathan, Jr. V, 733
Thomas, Josep I, 277
Thomas, Joseph I, 169
Thomas, Joseph I, 276
Thomas, Joseph I, 277
Thomas, Joseph I, 793
Thomas, Joseph I, 841
Thomas, Joseph I, 843
Thomas, Joseph I, 958
Thomas, Joseph I, 969
Thomas, Joseph I, 1038
Thomas, Joseph I, 1068
Thomas, Joseph I, 1071
Thomas, Joseph I Sup 1, 4
Thomas, Joseph II, 231
Thomas, Joseph II, 426
Thomas, Joseph II, 448
Thomas, Joseph II, 512
Thomas, Joseph II, 665
Thomas, Joseph II, 666
Thomas, Joseph II, 929
Thomas, Joseph IV, 288
Thomas, Joseph IV, 289
Thomas, Joseph IV, 290
Thomas, Joseph IV, 447
Thomas, Joseph IV, 596
Thomas, Joseph IV, 777
Thomas, Joseph IV, 1007
Thomas, Joseph IV, 1079
Thomas, Joseph IV, 1108
Thomas, Joseph IV, 1117
Thomas, Joseph IV, 1138
Thomas, Joseph V, 647
Thomas, Joseph V, 727
Thomas, Joseph V, 733
Thomas, Joseph V, 735
Thomas, Joseph V, 762
Thomas, Joseph V, 767
Thomas, Joseph V, 768
Thomas, Joseph V, 769
Thomas, Joseph V, 771
Thomas, Joseph V, 774
Thomas, Joseph V, 935
Thomas, Joseph VI, 343
Thomas, Joseph VI, 355
Thomas, Joseph VI, 451
Thomas, Joseph VI, 522
Thomas, Joseph VI, 656
Thomas, Joseph VI, 714
Thomas, Joseph E. V, 362
Thomas, Joseph Franklin IV, 776
Thomas, Joseph G. IV, 777
Thomas, Joseph G. IV, 1008
Thomas, Joseph Garretson IV, 1007
Thomas, Joseph Garritson IV, 777
Thomas, Joseph H. IV, 1030
Thomas, Joseph P. V, 768
Thomas, Joseph Thomas II, 267
Thomas, Joseph, Jr. II, 426
Thomas, Joseph, Jr. II, 929
Thomas, Josephine IV, 660
Thomas, Joshua II, 666
Thomas, Joshua VI, 870
Thomas, Joshua VI, 951
Thomas, Joshua VI, 960
Thomas, Joshua VI, 1003
Thomas, Josiah V, 345
Thomas, Josiah Walton IV, 1008
Thomas, Judith II, 666
Thomas, Judith Ann IV, 999
Thomas, Julia II, 426
Thomas, Julia Ann VI, 943
Thomas, Katherine VI, 735
Thomas, Katherine VI, 774
Thomas, Kersey IV, 1030
Thomas, Kersey G. IV, 777
Thomas, Kersey G. IV, 1007
Thomas, Kersey G. IV, 1008
Thomas, Keziah V, 53
Thomas, Keziah V, 131
Thomas, Keziah Edith VI, 606
Thomas, Lafayette VI, 859
Thomas, Laura Elizabeth V, 768
Thomas, Lavina IV, 999
Thomas, Lelia I, 634
Thomas, Lelia I, 641
Thomas, Lelia Mable I, 626
Thomas, Lemuel II, 822
Thomas, Lemuel II, 929
Thomas, Lemuel VI, 1003
Thomas, Leona IV, 1265
Thomas, Leona V, 768
Thomas, Leonard IV, 1030
Thomas, Leonard Patterson VI, 142
Thomas, Leonard V. H. II, 770
Thomas, Leonard W. H. II, 720
Thomas, Leslie B. IV, 289
Thomas, Leslie Binns IV, 289
Thomas, Levi I, 841
Thomas, Levi IV, 660
Thomas, Levi V, 767
Thomas, Levi V, 769
Thomas, Levi L. IV, 448
Thomas, Levi L. V, 131
Thomas, Levi S. IV, 777
Thomas, Levi S. V, 131
Thomas, Levi Stokes IV, 660
Thomas, Levina V, 767
Thomas, Levinia VI, 859
Thomas, Lewin Hartley III, 311
Thomas, Lewis I, 793
Thomas, Lewis I, 841
Thomas, Lewis I, 1066
Thomas, Lewis I, 1068
Thomas, Lewis I, 1071
Thomas, Lewis I, 1072
Thomas, Lewis IV, 776
Thomas, Lewis IV, 1030
Thomas, Lewis V, 534
Thomas, Lewis V, 647
Thomas, Lewis V, 767
Thomas, Lewis V, 769
Thomas, Lewis V, 872
Thomas, Lewis B. IV, 448
Thomas, Lewis Hartley III, 91
Thomas, Lewis Huckeby I, 1071
Thomas, Lewis Thomas I, 1071
Thomas, Lewis, Jr. I, 1068
Thomas, Lewis, Jr. I, 1072
Thomas, Lewis, Sr. I, 1068
Thomas, Libbie III, 449
Thomas, Lidia V, 146
Thomas, Lileas Adell IV, 1007
Thomas, Liles Adell IV, 1008
Thomas, Lillian V, 768
Thomas, Lilly I, 1068
Thomas, Lilly I, 1070
Thomas, Lilly I, 1072
Thomas, Lindley C. V, 768
Thomas, Lindley Murray V, 768
Thomas, Lizzie IV, 1007
Thomas, Lizzie IV, 1265
Thomas, Lizzie V, 760
Thomas, Louella V, 131
Thomas, Louisa IV, 1132
Thomas, Louisa V, 751
Thomas, Louisa V, 767
Thomas, Louisa V, 769
Thomas, Louisa Ann II, 793
Thomas, Louisa Doan V, 714
Thomas, Louisa G. IV, 963
Thomas, Louisa G. IV, 1007
Thomas, Louisa G. IV, 1008
Thomas, Louisa H. VI, 1022
Thomas, Louisa Jane V, 647
Thomas, Louise IV, 1138
Thomas, Louiza V, 767
Thomas, Louiza G. IV, 1008
Thomas, Louiza Jane V, 647
Thomas, Louvisa V, 768
Thomas, Lovice IV, 161
Thomas, Lovicey I, 276
Thomas, Lovicey I, 277
Thomas, Lovina V, 948
Thomas, Lovina V, 960
Thomas, Lucetta V, 951
Thomas, Lucille V, 768
Thomas, Lucinda IV, 149
Thomas, Lucinda IV, 161
Thomas, Lucinda IV, 290
Thomas, Lucinda IV, 407
Thomas, Lucinda IV, 448
Thomas, Lucinda IV, 756
Thomas, Lucinda IV, 776
Thomas, Lucinda IV, 777
Thomas, Lucy I, 340
Thomas, Lucy IV, 180
Thomas, Lucy IV, 289
Thomas, Lucy IV, 290
Thomas, Lucy IV, 928
Thomas, Lucy IV, 1008
Thomas, Lucy VI, 1003
Thomas, Lucy Ann V, 612
Thomas, Lucy Ann VI, 960
Thomas, Lucy P. IV, 1007
Thomas, Lucy P. IV, 1008
Thomas, Ludlow III, 311
Thomas, Luella IV, 848
Thomas, Luella L. IV, 216
Thomas, Luella L. IV, 289
Thomas, Luella L. IV, 291
Thomas, Luella L. IV, 819
Thomas, Luella L. IV, 848
Thomas, Luke V, 283
Thomas, Lulu IV, 1265
Thomas, Luvena VI, 1003
Thomas, Lydda I, 1068
Thomas, Lydia I, 206
Thomas, Lydia I, 319
Thomas, Lydia I, 924
Thomas, Lydia I, 1068
Thomas, Lydia II, 267
Thomas, Lydia II, 426
Thomas, Lydia II, 666
Thomas, Lydia II, 770
Thomas, Lydia II, 929
Thomas, Lydia IV, 53
Thomas, Lydia IV, 62
Thomas, Lydia IV, 111
Thomas, Lydia IV, 180
Thomas, Lydia IV, 289
Thomas, Lydia IV, 290
Thomas, Lydia IV, 660
Thomas, Lydia IV, 803
Thomas, Lydia IV, 848
Thomas, Lydia V, 131
Thomas, Lydia V, 525
Thomas, Lydia V, 534
Thomas, Lydia V, 759
Thomas, Lydia V, 767
Thomas, Lydia V, 769
Thomas, Lydia VI, 389
Thomas, Lydia VI, 451
Thomas, Lydia B. IV, 290
Thomas, Lydia B. IV, 291
Thomas, Lydia B. IV, 848
Thomas, Lydia H. IV, 553
Thomas, Lydia J. IV, 772
Thomas, Lydia J. IV, 777
Thomas, Lydia Jane IV, 776
Thomas, Lydia Jane IV, 777
Thomas, Lydia K. IV, 660
Thomas, Lydia S. II, 813
Thomas, Lydia S. IV, 289
Thomas, Lydia S. IV, 290
Thomas, Lydia S. IV, 303
Thomas, Mabel IV, 1008
Thomas, Mabel Clare I, 950
Thomas, Mabel S. IV, 289
Thomas, Mabell I, 950
Thomas, Mable Clair I, 934
Thomas, Maggie IV, 1008
Thomas, Maggie V, 612
Thomas, Maggie Daisy I, 934
Thomas, Mahala VI, 958
Thomas, Mahala G. V, 602
Thomas, Mahala J. V, 567
Thomas, Mahama J. V, 602
Thomas, Mahlon V, 405
Thomas, Mahlon V, 434
Thomas, Mahlon VI, 619
Thomas, Mahlon VI, 630
Thomas, Mahlon VI, 689
Thomas, Mahlon VI, 714
Thomas, Manlove I, 793
Thomas, Manlove I, 841
Thomas, Manlove I, 1068
Thomas, Manlove I, 1071
Thomas, Margaret I, 75
Thomas, Margaret I, 187
Thomas, Margaret I, 882
Thomas, Margaret I, 902
Thomas, Margaret I, 950
Thomas, Margaret I, 1050
Thomas, Margaret I, 1051
Thomas, Margaret II, 255
Thomas, Margaret II, 267
Thomas, Margaret II, 277
Thomas, Margaret II, 426
Thomas, Margaret II, 448
Thomas, Margaret II, 548
Thomas, Margaret II, 665
Thomas, Margaret II, 666
Thomas, Margaret II, 697
Thomas, Margaret III, 311
Thomas, Margaret IV, 399
Thomas, Margaret IV, 447
Thomas, Margaret IV, 596
Thomas, Margaret IV, 884
Thomas, Margaret IV, 1007
Thomas, Margaret IV, 1008
Thomas, Margaret IV, 1021
Thomas, Margaret IV, 1030
Thomas, Margaret IV, 1296
Thomas, Margaret IV, 1340
Thomas, Margaret V, 733
Thomas, Margaret VI, 617
Thomas, Margaret VI, 618
Thomas, Margaret Elizabeth IV, 289

omas, Margaret Ellenor I, 626
omas, Margaret S. IV, 324
omas, Margaret S. IV, 353
omas, Margaret T. VI, 619
omas, Margaret T. VI, 657
omas, Margaret T. VI, 714
omas, Margaretta II, 186
omas, Margaretta II, 296
omas, Margaretta II, 304
omas, Maria II, 1062
omas, Maria III, 41
omas, Maria III, 311
omas, Maria IV, 776
omas, Maria IV, 901
omas, Maria IV, 917
omas, Maria IV, 1056
omas, Maria B. III, 311
omas, Maria L. IV, 682
omas, Maria L. IV, 777
omas, Maria S. III, 157
omas, Maria S. III, 158
omas, Maria S. III, 299
omas, Maria S. VI, 747
omas, Maria Shoemaker II, 799
omas, Mariah IV, 917
omas, Mariah IV, 1056
omas, Mariah Emily V, 647
omas, Mariam V, 768
omas, Marianna IV, 289
omas, Marie V, 768
omas, Marjorie E. V, 872
omas, Marjorie N. II, 770
omas, Marjorie Nicholson II, 720
omas, Mark I, 258
omas, Martha I, 268
omas, Martha I, 276
omas, Martha I, 841
omas, Martha II, 548
omas, Martha II, 666
omas, Martha II, 806
omas, Martha II, 809
omas, Martha II, 822
omas, Martha IV, 176
omas, Martha IV, 190
omas, Martha IV, 289
omas, Martha IV, 1117
omas, Martha IV, 1122
omas, Martha V, 766
omas, Martha V, 767
omas, Martha V, 769
omas, Martha VI, 435
omas, Martha VI, 451
omas, Martha VI, 800
omas, Martha VI, 859
omas, Martha VI, 886
omas, Martha A. IV, 448
omas, Martha Ann IV, 289
omas, Martha Ann IV, 290
omas, Martha Ann V, 612
omas, Martha Ann V, 768
omas, Martha B. IV, 272
omas, Martha J. IV, 198
omas, Martha J. IV, 289
omas, Martha J. IV, 290
omas, Martha J. IV, 291
omas, Martha Parry II, 810
omas, Martin V, 767
omas, Martin V, 769
omas, Mary I, 258
omas, Mary I, 276
omas, Mary I, 277
omas, Mary I, 319
omas, Mary I, 340
omas, Mary I, 518
omas, Mary I, 544
omas, Mary I, 577
omas, Mary I, 626
omas, Mary I, 831
omas, Mary I, 841
omas, Mary I, 958
omas, Mary I, 960
omas, Mary I, 969
omas, Mary I, 1013
omas, Mary I, 1024
omas, Mary I, 1038
omas, Mary I, 1039
omas, Mary I, 1068
omas, Mary I, 1069
omas, Mary I, 1071
omas, Mary II, 104
omas, Mary II, 109
omas, Mary II, 186
omas, Mary II, 203
omas, Mary II, 217
omas, Mary II, 221
omas, Mary II, 231
omas, Mary II, 253
omas, Mary II, 254
omas, Mary II, 267
Thomas, Mary II, 426
Thomas, Mary II, 448
Thomas, Mary II, 640
Thomas, Mary II, 656
Thomas, Mary II, 665
Thomas, Mary II, 666
Thomas, Mary II, 720
Thomas, Mary II, 770
Thomas, Mary II, 929
Thomas, Mary II, 1032
Thomas, Mary II, 1041
Thomas, Mary III, 30
Thomas, Mary III, 282
Thomas, Mary III, 311
Thomas, Mary IV, 111
Thomas, Mary IV, 113
Thomas, Mary IV, 117
Thomas, Mary IV, 190
Thomas, Mary IV, 199
Thomas, Mary IV, 208
Thomas, Mary IV, 212
Thomas, Mary IV, 213
Thomas, Mary IV, 214
Thomas, Mary IV, 217
Thomas, Mary IV, 231
Thomas, Mary IV, 236
Thomas, Mary IV, 238
Thomas, Mary IV, 276
Thomas, Mary IV, 288
Thomas, Mary IV, 289
Thomas, Mary IV, 290
Thomas, Mary IV, 291
Thomas, Mary IV, 444
Thomas, Mary IV, 448
Thomas, Mary IV, 553
Thomas, Mary IV, 596
Thomas, Mary IV, 660
Thomas, Mary IV, 682
Thomas, Mary IV, 704
Thomas, Mary IV, 776
Thomas, Mary IV, 819
Thomas, Mary IV, 972
Thomas, Mary IV, 1007
Thomas, Mary IV, 1008
Thomas, Mary IV, 1015
Thomas, Mary IV, 1030
Thomas, Mary IV, 1079
Thomas, Mary IV, 1117
Thomas, Mary IV, 1122
Thomas, Mary IV, 1138
Thomas, Mary IV, 1188
Thomas, Mary IV, 1265
Thomas, Mary IV, 1296
Thomas, Mary IV, 1382
Thomas, Mary V, 21
Thomas, Mary V, 33
Thomas, Mary V, 34
Thomas, Mary V, 42
Thomas, Mary V, 100
Thomas, Mary V, 131
Thomas, Mary V, 134
Thomas, Mary V, 283
Thomas, Mary V, 286
Thomas, Mary V, 362
Thomas, Mary V, 534
Thomas, Mary V, 541
Thomas, Mary V, 612
Thomas, Mary V, 733
Thomas, Mary V, 738
Thomas, Mary V, 740
Thomas, Mary V, 766
Thomas, Mary V, 767
Thomas, Mary V, 768
Thomas, Mary V, 769
Thomas, Mary V, 770
Thomas, Mary V, 771
Thomas, Mary VI, 142
Thomas, Mary VI, 451
Thomas, Mary VI, 619
Thomas, Mary VI, 630
Thomas, Mary VI, 689
Thomas, Mary VI, 714
Thomas, Mary VI, 1003
Thomas, Mary Adaline IV, 776
Thomas, Mary Ann I, 619
Thomas, Mary Ann II, 822
Thomas, Mary Ann IV, 289
Thomas, Mary Ann IV, 290
Thomas, Mary Ann IV, 291
Thomas, Mary Ann IV, 447
Thomas, Mary Ann IV, 1001
Thomas, Mary Ann IV, 1008
Thomas, Mary Ann IV, 1079
Thomas, Mary Ann IV, 1116
Thomas, Mary Ann IV, 1117
Thomas, Mary Ann IV, 1188
Thomas, Mary Ann V, 534
Thomas, Mary Ann V, 646
Thomas, Mary Ann V, 647
Thomas, Mary Anna IV, 972
Thomas, Mary B. II, 426
Thomas, Mary B. II, 929
Thomas, Mary B. IV, 448
Thomas, Mary Brown V, 771
Thomas, Mary C. II, 770
Thomas, Mary C. III, 449
Thomas, Mary C. VI, 971
Thomas, Mary C. VI, 999
Thomas, Mary E. II, 713
Thomas, Mary E. IV, 776
Thomas, Mary E. IV, 777
Thomas, Mary E. IV, 778
Thomas, Mary E. V, 614
Thomas, Mary E. V, 647
Thomas, Mary Eldora IV, 1007
Thomas, Mary Eldora IV, 1008
Thomas, Mary Elizabeth IV, 1007
Thomas, Mary Elizabeth K. II, 929
Thomas, Mary Eva IV, 289
Thomas, Mary Eva IV, 291
Thomas, Mary Evans V, 646
Thomas, Mary F. II, 929
Thomas, Mary F. IV, 1021
Thomas, Mary G. IV, 1008
Thomas, Mary G. IV, 1108
Thomas, Mary G. IV, 1117
Thomas, Mary H. II, 899
Thomas, Mary H. II, 929
Thomas, Mary Irene I, 626
Thomas, Mary Irene I, 641
Thomas, Mary J. IV, 1007
Thomas, Mary J. V, 663
Thomas, Mary Jane I, 902
Thomas, Mary Jane IV, 660
Thomas, Mary Jane V, 714
Thomas, Mary Jane VI, 686
Thomas, Mary Jane VI, 688
Thomas, Mary Jane VI, 689
Thomas, Mary Jane VI, 714
Thomas, Mary L. II, 186
Thomas, Mary L. III, 292
Thomas, Mary L. III, 311
Thomas, Mary L. IV, 777
Thomas, Mary L. IV, 1079
Thomas, Mary L. W. III, 311
Thomas, Mary Lewin III, 31
Thomas, Mary Lloyd II, 827
Thomas, Mary M. IV, 289
Thomas, Mary M. IV, 291
Thomas, Mary M. IV, 660
Thomas, Mary M. IV, 777
Thomas, Mary M. VI, 1003
Thomas, Mary M. T. II, 929
Thomas, Mary P. IV, 290
Thomas, Mary P. M. V, 767
Thomas, Mary S. II, 929
Thomas, Mary S. III, 311
Thomas, Mary S. IV, 777
Thomas, Mary S. IV, 892
Thomas, Mary S. IV, 895
Thomas, Mary S. IV, 1030
Thomas, Mary T. IV, 289
Thomas, Mary T. IV, 290
Thomas, Mary T. IV, 291
Thomas, Mary T. IV, 1008
Thomas, Mary T. V, 949
Thomas, Mary T. V, 960
Thomas, Mary Thomas VI, 471
Thomas, Mary W. II, 770
Thomas, Mary, Jr. V, 676
Thomas, Maude V, 872
Thomas, Melissa V, 730
Thomas, Melissa V, 767
Thomas, Melissa Alice IV, 1030
Thomas, Mercy II, 426
Thomas, Mercy II, 666
Thomas, Mercy II, 770
Thomas, Mercy II, 929
Thomas, Mercy L. IV, 777
Thomas, Meriam B. IV, 290
Thomas, Merle V, 768
Thomas, Micah II, 665
Thomas, Micajah V, 769
Thomas, Micajah C. V, 767
Thomas, Micajah W. V, 362
Thomas, Michael II, 426
Thomas, Michaner V, 771
Thomas, Michener V, 771
Thomas, Michoes V, 771
Thomas, Milard IV, 777
Thomas, Mildred IV, 884
Thomas, Miley I Sup 1, 10
Thomas, Milley I, 793
Thomas, Milly I, 577
Thomas, Milly VI, 816
Thomas, Milo V, 767
Thomas, Milo V, 769
Thomas, Minerva IV, 1338
Thomas, Minerva V, 768
Thomas, Miriam IV, 550
Thomas, Miriam V, 767
Thomas, Miriam V, 768
Thomas, Miriam B. IV, 290
Thomas, Miriam B. IV, 448
Thomas, Miriam B. IV, 553
Thomas, Missouri I, 1162
Thomas, Moley I, 1068
Thomas, Molley I, 841
Thomas, Molley I, 1068
Thomas, Molley I, 1071
Thomas, Molly I, 379
Thomas, Molly I, 423
Thomas, Molly I, 518
Thomas, Molly I, 577
Thomas, Molly I, 793
Thomas, Molly I, 841
Thomas, Molly I, 1066
Thomas, Molly VI, 859
Thomas, Morris I, 1071
Thomas, Moses II, 426
Thomas, Moses II, 665
Thomas, Moses VI, 606
Thomas, Mr. ??? IV, 1340
Thomas, Mr. E. A. IV, 1340
Thomas, Mrs. ??? IV, 1340
Thomas, Mrs. Emma A. IV, 1340
Thomas, Myrtle IV, 917
Thomas, Myrtle IV, 1007
Thomas, Myrtle IV, 1008
Thomas, Nancey VI, 982
Thomas, Nancy I, 902
Thomas, Nancy I, 1068
Thomas, Nancy V, 765
Thomas, Nancy V, 766
Thomas, Nancy V, 767
Thomas, Nancy V, 769
Thomas, Nancy V, 771
Thomas, Nancy VI, 929
Thomas, Nancy VI, 937
Thomas, Nancy VI, 1003
Thomas, Nancy VI, 1015
Thomas, Nanna V, 646
Thomas, Nanney I, 1068
Thomas, Nannie I. III, 31
Thomas, Naomi II, 793
Thomas, Naomi II, 816
Thomas, Naomi II, 821
Thomas, Naomi II, 825
Thomas, Naomi V, 33
Thomas, Naomi V, 131
Thomas, Naomi V, 771
Thomas, Naomy V, 771
Thomas, Nathan I, 276
Thomas, Nathan IV, 288
Thomas, Nathan IV, 290
Thomas, Nathan IV, 528
Thomas, Nathan IV, 596
Thomas, Nathan IV, 719
Thomas, Nathan IV, 776
Thomas, Nathan IV, 777
Thomas, Nathan IV, 848
Thomas, Nathan IV, 1007
Thomas, Nathan IV, 1008
Thomas, Nathan IV, 1021
Thomas, Nathan IV, 1030
Thomas, Nathan IV, 1382
Thomas, Nathan M. IV, 288
Thomas, Nathaniel I, 276
Thomas, Nathaniel I, 277
Thomas, Nathaniel IV, 161
Thomas, Nathaniel IV, 290
Thomas, Nathaniel IV, 596
Thomas, Nathaniel IV, 777
Thomas, Nathaniel IV, 1269
Thomas, Nathaniel VI, 357
Thomas, Nathaniel VI, 872
Thomas, Nathaniel VI, 888
Thomas, Nathaniel VI, 928
Thomas, Nathaniel VI, 965
Thomas, Nathaniel VI, 995
Thomas, Nathaniel VI, 999
Thomas, Nathaniel VI, 1001
Thomas, Nathaniel VI, 1003
Thomas, Nathaniel VI, 1010
Thomas, Nehemiah I, 1024
Thomas, Nehemiah V, 131
Thomas, Nehemiah V, 767
Thomas, Nehemiah V, 768
Thomas, Nehemiah V, 821
Thomas, Nehemiah, Jr. V, 768
Thomas, Nehemiah, Jr. V, 769
Thomas, Nehemiah, Sr. V, 767
Thomas, Nellie IV, 1340
Thomas, Nellie M. IV, 1340
Thomas, Newton IV, 892
Thomas, Newton IV, 895
Thomas, Newton IV, 1030
Thomas, Nicholas V, 771
Thomas, Nicolas V, 771
Thomas, Nixon W. VI, 917
Thomas, Nixson VI, 1003
Thomas, Noah V, 767
Thomas, Noah V, 769
Thomas, Nuton IV, 777
Thomas, Olive Myra IV, 291
Thomas, Oliver II, 426
Thomas, Oliver IV, 198
Thomas, Oliver IV, 289
Thomas, Oliver IV, 291
Thomas, Oliver IV, 660
Thomas, Oliver A. IV, 777
Thomas, Oliver Abel IV, 1008
Thomas, Oliver Able IV, 777
Thomas, Oliver F. IV, 660
Thomas, Opeckon I, 577
Thomas, Orma V, 207
Thomas, Orynthee V, 923
Thomas, Owen IV, 848
Thomas, Owen IV, 1021
Thomas, Owen IV, 1030
Thomas, Parmelia P. V, 767
Thomas, Patience I, 297
Thomas, Patience I, 319
Thomas, Patience IV, 111
Thomas, Patience IV, 112
Thomas, Patience IV, 688
Thomas, Patience IV, 777
Thomas, Paul IV, 848
Thomas, Pauline L. II, 929
Thomas, Peachy Ann VI, 1003
Thomas, Pearly IV, 1117
Thomas, Pearson IV, 288
Thomas, Pearson IV, 289
Thomas, Pearson IV, 290
Thomas, Pearson IV, 448
Thomas, Pearson IV, 550
Thomas, Pearson IV, 553
Thomas, Permelia V, 769
Thomas, Peter II, 823
Thomas, Peter II, 929
Thomas, Peter IV, 180
Thomas, Peter IV, 190
Thomas, Peter IV, 212
Thomas, Peter IV, 213
Thomas, Peter IV, 236
Thomas, Peter IV, 238
Thomas, Peter IV, 288
Thomas, Peter IV, 289
Thomas, Peter IV, 290
Thomas, Peter IV, 291
Thomas, Peter IV, 448
Thomas, Peter IV, 553
Thomas, Peter IV, 1382
Thomas, Peter L. IV, 208
Thomas, Peter L. IV, 289
Thomas, Peter L. IV, 290
Thomas, Peter L. IV, 291
Thomas, Peter L. IV, 972
Thomas, Peter, Jr. IV, 290
Thomas, Pheba V, 771
Thomas, Phebe I, 958
Thomas, Phebe II, 426
Thomas, Phebe II, 666
Thomas, Phebe II, 770
Thomas, Phebe II, 796
Thomas, Phebe II, 929
Thomas, Phebe III, 70
Thomas, Phebe III, 311
Thomas, Phebe IV, 353
Thomas, Phebe IV, 414
Thomas, Phebe IV, 424
Thomas, Phebe IV, 447
Thomas, Phebe IV, 448
Thomas, Phebe IV, 452
Thomas, Phebe IV, 453
Thomas, Phebe IV, 727
Thomas, Phebe IV, 776
Thomas, Phebe IV, 777
Thomas, Phebe IV, 1008
Thomas, Phebe V, 131
Thomas, Phebe V, 612
Thomas, Phebe V, 733
Thomas, Phebe V, 766
Thomas, Phebe V, 767
Thomas, Phebe V, 768
Thomas, Phebe V, 769
Thomas, Phebe V, 936
Thomas, Phebe VI, 451
Thomas, Phebe Ann IV, 776
Thomas, Phebe D. IV, 393
Thomas, Phebe G. IV, 290
Thomas, Phebe G. IV, 1362
Thomas, Phebe G. IV, 1382
Thomas, Phebe W. II, 929
Thomas, Pheeby II, 666
Thomas, Philena IV, 447
Thomas, Philena IV, 1079
Thomas, Philena IV, 1117
Thomas, Philena IV, 1120
Thomas, Philena C. II, 929
Thomas, Philip III, 311
Thomas, Philip VI, 862
Thomas, Philip VI, 929

Thomas, Philip E. III, 31
Thomas, Philip Mason IV, 448
Thomas, Phillip VI, 859
Thomas, Phillip VI, 1018
Thomas, Phineas II, 426
Thomas, Phinehas II, 426
Thomas, Pleasant IV, 764
Thomas, Pluma Ellen IV, 448
Thomas, Polley VI, 976
Thomas, Polly I, 841
Thomas, Polly I, 1068
Thomas, Polly VI, 1003
Thomas, Precilla IV, 447
Thomas, Precilla IV, 454
Thomas, Priscilla I, 877
Thomas, Priscilla I, 902
Thomas, Priscilla I, 1045
Thomas, Priscilla II, 426
Thomas, Priscilla II, 926
Thomas, Priscilla II, 929
Thomas, Priscilla IV, 161
Thomas, Priscilla IV, 399
Thomas, Priscilla IV, 447
Thomas, Priscilla IV, 596
Thomas, Priscilla IV, 776
Thomas, Priscilla IV, 777
Thomas, Priscilla V, 131
Thomas, Priscilla V, 140
Thomas, Priscilla V, 728
Thomas, Priscilla V, 767
Thomas, Priscilla V, 769
Thomas, Priscilla VI, 56
Thomas, Priscilla VI, 87
Thomas, Priscilla Gulielma II, 781
Thomas, Priscilla H. II, 770
Thomas, Priscilla H. II, 929
Thomas, Prisy VI, 56
Thomas, Prisy VI, 87
Thomas, Prudence I, 1024
Thomas, Prudence II, 666
Thomas, Prudence II, 1008
Thomas, Prudence II, 1032
Thomas, Prudence IV, 1296
Thomas, Prudence V, 100
Thomas, Prudence V, 131
Thomas, Prudence VI, 951
Thomas, Quintilly VI, 1003
Thomas, R. E. V, 1021
Thomas, R. Leland IV, 216
Thomas, R. Leland IV, 291
Thomas, R. Orynthee V, 936
Thomas, Rachel I, 556
Thomas, Rachel I, 577
Thomas, Rachel I, 793
Thomas, Rachel I, 841
Thomas, Rachel I, 1068
Thomas, Rachel I, 1070
Thomas, Rachel I, 1071
Thomas, Rachel I, 1072
Thomas, Rachel II, 186
Thomas, Rachel II, 231
Thomas, Rachel II, 267
Thomas, Rachel II, 448
Thomas, Rachel II, 580
Thomas, Rachel II, 665
Thomas, Rachel II, 666
Thomas, Rachel II, 683
Thomas, Rachel II, 929
Thomas, Rachel II, 1062
Thomas, Rachel IV, 50
Thomas, Rachel IV, 62
Thomas, Rachel IV, 180
Thomas, Rachel IV, 184
Thomas, Rachel IV, 203
Thomas, Rachel IV, 205
Thomas, Rachel IV, 212
Thomas, Rachel IV, 238
Thomas, Rachel IV, 288
Thomas, Rachel IV, 289
Thomas, Rachel IV, 290
Thomas, Rachel IV, 579
Thomas, Rachel IV, 596
Thomas, Rachel IV, 660
Thomas, Rachel IV, 864
Thomas, Rachel IV, 884
Thomas, Rachel IV, 1138
Thomas, Rachel IV, 1340
Thomas, Rachel V, 21
Thomas, Rachel V, 131
Thomas, Rachel V, 283
Thomas, Rachel V, 345
Thomas, Rachel V, 362
Thomas, Rachel V, 749
Thomas, Rachel V, 767
Thomas, Rachel V, 768
Thomas, Rachel VI, 548
Thomas, Rachel B. IV, 290
Thomas, Rachel E. IV, 183
Thomas, Rachel E. IV, 289
Thomas, Rachel E. IV, 1241
Thomas, Rachel E. IV, 1340
Thomas, Rachel Elma IV, 289
Thomas, Rachel Emma VI, 291
Thomas, Rachel H. IV, 290
Thomas, Rachel W. IV, 1021
Thomas, Rachil I, 1068
Thomas, Ramona V, 612
Thomas, Rebeca, Sr. I, 1045
Thomas, Rebecca I, 934
Thomas, Rebecca I, 1051
Thomas, Rebecca II, 186
Thomas, Rebecca II, 267
Thomas, Rebecca II, 426
Thomas, Rebecca II, 448
Thomas, Rebecca II, 665
Thomas, Rebecca II, 666
Thomas, Rebecca II, 812
Thomas, Rebecca II, 822
Thomas, Rebecca II, 905
Thomas, Rebecca II, 929
Thomas, Rebecca IV, 161
Thomas, Rebecca IV, 288
Thomas, Rebecca IV, 363
Thomas, Rebecca IV, 393
Thomas, Rebecca IV, 399
Thomas, Rebecca IV, 403
Thomas, Rebecca IV, 424
Thomas, Rebecca IV, 441
Thomas, Rebecca IV, 447
Thomas, Rebecca IV, 448
Thomas, Rebecca IV, 553
Thomas, Rebecca IV, 596
Thomas, Rebecca IV, 682
Thomas, Rebecca IV, 719
Thomas, Rebecca IV, 760
Thomas, Rebecca IV, 776
Thomas, Rebecca IV, 777
Thomas, Rebecca IV, 778
Thomas, Rebecca IV, 848
Thomas, Rebecca IV, 895
Thomas, Rebecca IV, 989
Thomas, Rebecca IV, 1007
Thomas, Rebecca IV, 1008
Thomas, Rebecca IV, 1056
Thomas, Rebecca IV, 1079
Thomas, Rebecca IV, 1116
Thomas, Rebecca IV, 1117
Thomas, Rebecca IV, 1120
Thomas, Rebecca IV, 1138
Thomas, Rebecca V, 131
Thomas, Rebecca V, 541
Thomas, Rebecca V, 767
Thomas, Rebecca V, 935
Thomas, Rebecca VI, 450
Thomas, Rebecca VI, 451
Thomas, Rebecca VI, 862
Thomas, Rebecca A. IV, 289
Thomas, Rebecca A. IV, 987
Thomas, Rebecca A. IV, 1008
Thomas, Rebecca Ann IV, 290
Thomas, Rebecca Ann IV, 713
Thomas, Rebecca Ann IV, 777
Thomas, Rebecca Ann IV, 848
Thomas, Rebecca Ann IV, 850
Thomas, Rebecca Ann IV, 1007
Thomas, Rebecca Ann IV, 1008
Thomas, Rebecca Ann IV, 1137
Thomas, Rebecca Ann IV, 1138
Thomas, Rebecca Ellin IV, 776
Thomas, Rebecca H. V, 131
Thomas, Rebecca H. V, 936
Thomas, Rebecca Jr. IV, 776
Thomas, Rebecca S. IV, 777
Thomas, Rebecca S. IV, 895
Thomas, Rebecca, Jr. IV, 777
Thomas, Rebeckah I, 1068
Thomas, Rebeckah II, 267
Thomas, Rebeckah VI, 606
Thomas, Rebekah VI, 591
Thomas, Rebekah VI, 606
Thomas, Rebkah I, 841
Thomas, Rees II, 665
Thomas, Rees II, 687
Thomas, Reese II, 665
Thomas, Reese D. IV, 660
Thomas, Reuben II, 1062
Thomas, Reuben IV, 776
Thomas, Reuben V, 767
Thomas, Reuben V, 768
Thomas, Rhoda V, 762
Thomas, Rhoda V, 767
Thomas, Rhoda V, 768
Thomas, Rhoda V, 769
Thomas, Rhoda J. V, 767
Thomas, Richard I, 141
Thomas, Richard I, 169
Thomas, Richard II, 426
Thomas, Richard II, 540
Thomas, Richard II, 665
Thomas, Richard II, 666
Thomas, Richard II, 1032
Thomas, Richard IV, 1056
Thomas, Richard VI, 474
Thomas, Richard VI, 726
Thomas, Richard H. III, 70
Thomas, Richard H. III, 167
Thomas, Richard L. II, 1062
Thomas, Richard Lindsay II, 720
Thomas, Ridgway II, 666
Thomas, Roberet P. IV, 452
Thomas, Robert II, 179
Thomas, Robert II, 186
Thomas, Robert II, 217
Thomas, Robert II, 231
Thomas, Robert II, 267
Thomas, Robert II, 296
Thomas, Robert II, 297
Thomas, Robert II, 304
Thomas, Robert II, 512
Thomas, Robert II, 665
Thomas, Robert II, 666
Thomas, Robert II, 1009
Thomas, Robert II, 1032
Thomas, Robert IV, 161
Thomas, Robert IV, 288
Thomas, Robert IV, 290
Thomas, Robert IV, 756
Thomas, Robert IV, 776
Thomas, Robert IV, 777
Thomas, Robert IV, 884
Thomas, Robert V, 131
Thomas, Robert V, 473
Thomas, Robert V, 534
Thomas, Robert V, 646
Thomas, Robert V, 647
Thomas, Robert VI, 1018
Thomas, Robert Elsworth V, 1021
Thomas, Robert J. II, 770
Thomas, Robert L. IV, 289
Thomas, Robert Leland IV, 289
Thomas, Robert Leland IV, 819
Thomas, Robert Leland IV, 848
Thomas, Robert P. II, 726
Thomas, Robert P. II, 770
Thomas, Robert P. IV, 246
Thomas, Robert P. IV, 289
Thomas, Robert P. IV, 291
Thomas, Robert P. IV, 447
Thomas, Robert P. IV, 596
Thomas, Robert P. IV, 643
Thomas, Robert P. IV, 660
Thomas, Robert P. IV, 777
Thomas, Robert S. II, 929
Thomas, Robert Swan II, 823
Thomas, Roberta V, 714
Thomas, Rollin V, 771
Thomas, Rosa A. V, 1021
Thomas, Rose IV, 928
Thomas, Ross IV, 448
Thomas, Ruanna IV, 236
Thomas, Ruanna IV, 288
Thomas, Ruanna IV, 289
Thomas, Ruanna IV, 290
Thomas, Ruannah IV, 203
Thomas, Ruannah IV, 288
Thomas, Rueben V, 769
Thomas, Ruelien V, 769
Thomas, Rufus VI, 943
Thomas, Rufus VI, 1003
Thomas, Ruth I, 1036
Thomas, Ruth I, 1038
Thomas, Ruth I, 1068
Thomas, Ruth IV, 62
Thomas, Ruth IV, 111
Thomas, Ruth IV, 396
Thomas, Ruth IV, 447
Thomas, Ruth IV, 448
Thomas, Ruth IV, 596
Thomas, Ruth IV, 877
Thomas, Ruth IV, 884
Thomas, Ruth IV, 895
Thomas, Ruth IV, 1281
Thomas, Ruth IV, 1296
Thomas, Ruth V, 353
Thomas, Ruth V, 362
Thomas, Ruth V, 632
Thomas, Ruth V, 647
Thomas, Ruth V, 738
Thomas, Ruth V, 766
Thomas, Ruth V, 768
Thomas, Ruth V, 769
Thomas, Ruth VI, 404
Thomas, Ruth VI, 451
Thomas, Ruth VI, 522
Thomas, Ruth VI, 656
Thomas, Ruth VI, 668
Thomas, Ruth VI, 714
Thomas, Ruth Ann II, 792
Thomas, Ruth E. I, 423
Thomas, Ruth K. VI, 760
Thomas, Ruth K. VI, 773
Thomas, Ruth, Jr. V, 769
Thomas, Sadie Russell IV, 1340
Thomas, Salley V, 767
Thomas, Samuel I, 950
Thomas, Samuel II, 426
Thomas, Samuel II, 822
Thomas, Samuel II, 1032
Thomas, Samuel IV, 149
Thomas, Samuel IV, 199
Thomas, Samuel IV, 289
Thomas, Samuel IV, 596
Thomas, Samuel IV, 660
Thomas, Samuel VI, 471
Thomas, Samuel VI, 958
Thomas, Samuel B. II, 770
Thomas, Samuel B. II, 929
Thomas, Samuel Baldwin II, 426
Thomas, Samuel C. IV, 660
Thomas, Samuel C. IV, 777
Thomas, Samuel Caleb IV, 660
Thomas, Samuel Clark IV, 62
Thomas, Samuel Clark IV, 111
Thomas, Samuel E. IV, 289
Thomas, Samuel M. VI, 1003
Thomas, Samuel S. IV, 448
Thomas, Samuel S. IV, 553
Thomas, Samuel T. IV, 290
Thomas, Samuel T. S. IV, 553
Thomas, Samuel Tilden I, 934
Thomas, Sarah I, 187
Thomas, Sarah I, 276
Thomas, Sarah I, 277
Thomas, Sarah I, 297
Thomas, Sarah I, 831
Thomas, Sarah I, 841
Thomas, Sarah I, 958
Thomas, Sarah I, 969
Thomas, Sarah I, 1024
Thomas, Sarah I, 1036
Thomas, Sarah I, 1038
Thomas, Sarah I, 1051
Thomas, Sarah I, 1068
Thomas, Sarah I, 1069
Thomas, Sarah I, 1070
Thomas, Sarah I, 1071
Thomas, Sarah II, 267
Thomas, Sarah II, 270
Thomas, Sarah II, 402
Thomas, Sarah II, 426
Thomas, Sarah II, 448
Thomas, Sarah II, 509
Thomas, Sarah II, 511
Thomas, Sarah II, 540
Thomas, Sarah II, 665
Thomas, Sarah II, 666
Thomas, Sarah II, 713
Thomas, Sarah II, 744
Thomas, Sarah II, 770
Thomas, Sarah II, 818
Thomas, Sarah II, 823
Thomas, Sarah II, 828
Thomas, Sarah II, 829
Thomas, Sarah III, 449
Thomas, Sarah IV, 117
Thomas, Sarah IV, 149
Thomas, Sarah IV, 161
Thomas, Sarah IV, 204
Thomas, Sarah IV, 212
Thomas, Sarah IV, 229
Thomas, Sarah IV, 288
Thomas, Sarah IV, 289
Thomas, Sarah IV, 290
Thomas, Sarah IV, 291
Thomas, Sarah IV, 307
Thomas, Sarah IV, 308
Thomas, Sarah IV, 447
Thomas, Sarah IV, 448
Thomas, Sarah IV, 585
Thomas, Sarah IV, 596
Thomas, Sarah IV, 703
Thomas, Sarah IV, 777
Thomas, Sarah IV, 827
Thomas, Sarah IV, 828
Thomas, Sarah IV, 848
Thomas, Sarah IV, 875
Thomas, Sarah IV, 884
Thomas, Sarah IV, 933
Thomas, Sarah IV, 1007
Thomas, Sarah IV, 1008
Thomas, Sarah IV, 1056
Thomas, Sarah IV, 1079
Thomas, Sarah IV, 1110
Thomas, Sarah IV, 1117
Thomas, Sarah IV, 1138
Thomas, Sarah IV, 1265
Thomas, Sarah V, 131
Thomas, Sarah V, 352
Thomas, Sarah V, 362
Thomas, Sarah V, 647
Thomas, Sarah V, 648
Thomas, Sarah V, 727
Thomas, Sarah V, 733
Thomas, Sarah V, 738
Thomas, Sarah V, 739
Thomas, Sarah V, 743
Thomas, Sarah V, 764
Thomas, Sarah V, 765
Thomas, Sarah V, 766
Thomas, Sarah V, 767
Thomas, Sarah V, 768
Thomas, Sarah V, 769
Thomas, Sarah V, 770
Thomas, Sarah V, 771
Thomas, Sarah V, 794
Thomas, Sarah V, 935
Thomas, Sarah V, 936
Thomas, Sarah VI, 372
Thomas, Sarah VI, 451
Thomas, Sarah VI, 493
Thomas, Sarah VI, 495
Thomas, Sarah VI, 547
Thomas, Sarah VI, 617
Thomas, Sarah VI, 641
Thomas, Sarah VI, 766
Thomas, Sarah Ann II, 1062
Thomas, Sarah ann IV, 111
Thomas, Sarah Ann IV, 776
Thomas, Sarah Ann IV, 777
Thomas, Sarah Ann V, 766
Thomas, Sarah B. IV, 690
Thomas, Sarah B. IV, 776
Thomas, Sarah B. IV, 777
Thomas, Sarah B. IV, 1056
Thomas, Sarah C. IV, 353
Thomas, Sarah C. IV, 357
Thomas, Sarah E. II, 726
Thomas, Sarah E. II, 770
Thomas, Sarah E. V, 936
Thomas, Sarah E. V, 941
Thomas, Sarah Elizabeth IV,
Thomas, Sarah Elizabeth IV,
Thomas, Sarah Ellen V, 131
Thomas, Sarah Ellen V, 936
Thomas, Sarah G. II, 726
Thomas, Sarah G. II, 770
Thomas, Sarah G. II, 929
Thomas, Sarah H. II, 770
Thomas, Sarah Hoofman V, 1
Thomas, Sarah J. IV, 917
Thomas, Sarah J. IV, 1008
Thomas, Sarah Jane IV, 1007
Thomas, Sarah M. II, 426
Thomas, Sarah M. II, 666
Thomas, Sarah M. III, 449
Thomas, Sarah M. IV, 660
Thomas, Sarah W. V, 936
Thomas, Sarah, Sr. V, 769
Thomas, Saray V, 767
Thomas, Sareptah V, 131
Thomas, Scatten IV, 500
Thomas, Scotten IV, 290
Thomas, Scytha VI, 859
Thomas, Selah I, 1069
Thomas, Seth V, 767
Thomas, Sidna IV, 596
Thomas, Sidney IV, 447
Thomas, Sidney V, 59
Thomas, Sidney V, 131
Thomas, Sidney B. III, 311
Thomas, Silvester L. V, 362
Thomas, Silvester S. V, 362
Thomas, Simeon I, 1071
Thomas, Smithson VI, 1003
Thomas, Soloman I, 793
Thomas, Solomon I, 841
Thomas, Solomon I, 1068
Thomas, Solomon I, 1071
Thomas, Solomon I, 1072
Thomas, Solomon II, 186
Thomas, Solomon II, 221
Thomas, Solomon II, 253
Thomas, Solomon II, 267
Thomas, Spencer II, 1062
Thomas, Stanley IV, 1008
Thomas, Stella Janice V, 207
Thomas, Stephen I, 518
Thomas, Stephen I, 577
Thomas, Stephen I, 793
Thomas, Stephen I, 827
Thomas, Stephen I, 831
Thomas, Stephen I, 841
Thomas, Stephen I, 1066
Thomas, Stephen I, 1068
Thomas, Stephen I, 1069
Thomas, Stephen I, 1070
Thomas, Stephen I, 1071
Thomas, Stephen I, 1072
Thomas, Stephen V, 767
Thomas, Stephen V, 769
Thomas, Stephen V, 793
Thomas, Suckey VI, 1003
Thomas, Sue R. II, 929
Thomas, Susan II, 186

mas, Susan II, 297
mas, Susan II, 304
mas, Susan II, 709
mas, Susan IV, 246
mas, Susan IV, 289
mas, Susan IV, 596
mas, Susan IV, 643
mas, Susan IV, 660
mas, Susan IV, 1079
mas, Susan V, 767
mas, Susan Jane IV, 589
mas, Susan Jane IV, 596
mas, Susan L. II, 793
mas, Susan L. II, 929
mas, Susan Longstreth II, 823
mas, Susan M. IV, 199
mas, Susan M. IV, 289
mas, Susan M. IV, 290
mas, Susan M. IV, 291
mas, Susan M. IV, 660
mas, Susan T. II, 179
mas, Susann IV, 353
mas, Susanna I, 518
mas, Susanna I, 841
mas, Susanna IV, 204
mas, Susanna IV, 269
mas, Susanna IV, 288
mas, Susanna IV, 290
mas, Susanna IV, 353
mas, Susanna IV, 370
mas, Susanna IV, 448
mas, Susanna IV, 596
mas, Susanna IV, 895
mas, Susanna IV, 1079
mas, Susanna V, 473
mas, Susanna V, 534
mas, Susanna V, 760
mas, Susanna V, 768
mas, Susanna V, 936
mas, Susannah I, 1068
mas, Susannah II, 665
mas, Susannah IV, 290
mas, Susannah IV, 448
mas, Susannah IV, 596
mas, Susannah IV, 776
mas, Susannah IV, 1117
mas, Susannah IV, 1122
mas, Susannah V, 738
mas, Susannah V, 766
mas, Susannah V, 767
mas, Susannah V, 768
mas, Susannah V, 952
mas, Susannah V, 960
mas, Susannah VI, 859
mas, Sussanah IV, 353
mas, Sylvester V, 362
mas, Tabitha IV, 553
mas, Tacy II, 807
mas, Tacy II, 828
mas, Tacy Edith IV, 290
mas, Tacy Elizabeth IV, 289
mas, Tacy Jane IV, 1030
mas, Tamar V, 754
mas, Tamar V, 767
mas, Tamer V, 754
mas, Tamson M. V, 534
mas, Temperance IV, 596
mas, Temperance IV, 777
mas, Temperance IV, 860
mas, Temperance IV, 1007
mas, Temperance IV, 1008
mas, Temperance IV, 1296
mas, Temperance V, 767
mas, Teressa V, 534
mas, Terrell IV, 353
mas, Terresa V, 647
mas, Terressa V, 534
mas, Thamsin V, 534
mas, Thamzin II, 1032
mas, Thomas I, 793
mas, Thomas I Sup 1, 6
mas, Thomas II, 66
mas, Thomas II, 186
mas, Thomas II, 426
mas, Thomas IV, 848
mas, Thomas IV, 1188
mas, Thomas V, 131
mas, Thomas French IV, 111
mas, Thomas French IV, 777
mas, Thomasin II, 666
mas, Thomzin II, 1032
mas, Thos. Gilbert V, 767
mas, Tilden I, 841
mas, Tilden I, 1072
mas, Timothy II, 186
mas, Townsend IV, 173
mas, Townsend IV, 289
mas, Townsend IV, 305
mas, Una V, 794
mas, Uriah V, 534
Thomas, Uriah V, 646
Thomas, Uriah V, 647
Thomas, Valentine IV, 901
Thomas, Valentine IV, 917
Thomas, Vashti V, 33
Thomas, Vashti V, 131
Thomas, Vicey IV, 184
Thomas, Vicey IV, 290
Thomas, Vildan I, 1068
Thomas, Virginia IV, 1340
Thomas, Virginia VI, 451
Thomas, Virginia VI, 452
Thomas, Walter I, 626
Thomas, Walter I, 634
Thomas, Walter I, 641
Thomas, Walter IV, 289
Thomas, Walter IV, 291
Thomas, Walter IV, 848
Thomas, Walter S. IV, 176
Thomas, Walter S. IV, 272
Thomas, Walter S. IV, 289
Thomas, Walter S. IV, 291
Thomas, Walter S. IV, 660
Thomas, Walter T. IV, 660
Thomas, Wd. Hannah II, 343
Thomas, Wd. Hannah II, 828
Thomas, Wd. Jane Longstreth II, 822
Thomas, Wd. Mary Elizabeth II, 822
Thomas, Wd. Priscilla II, 821
Thomas, Wd. Rachel II, 231
Thomas, Wd. Rachel II, 267
Thomas, Wd. Sarah II, 426
Thomas, Wd. Sarah II, 666
Thomas, Wesley I, 934
Thomas, Wethered B. III, 224
Thomas, Wethered B. III, 311
Thomas, Widow Beulah VI, 521
Thomas, Widow Beulah VI, 533
Thomas, William I, 841
Thomas, William I, 902
Thomas, William I, 958
Thomas, William I, 960
Thomas, William I, 969
Thomas, William I, 1024
Thomas, William I, 1036
Thomas, William I, 1038
Thomas, William I, 1045
Thomas, William II, 186
Thomas, William II, 254
Thomas, William II, 267
Thomas, William II, 304
Thomas, William II, 426
Thomas, William III, 449
Thomas, William IV, 161
Thomas, William IV, 288
Thomas, William IV, 290
Thomas, William IV, 353
Thomas, William IV, 393
Thomas, William IV, 399
Thomas, William IV, 441
Thomas, William IV, 447
Thomas, William IV, 448
Thomas, William IV, 553
Thomas, William IV, 596
Thomas, William IV, 777
Thomas, William IV, 1008
Thomas, William IV, 1079
Thomas, William IV, 1117
Thomas, William IV, 1188
Thomas, William V, 131
Thomas, William V, 733
Thomas, William V, 738
Thomas, William V, 768
Thomas, William V, 769
Thomas, William VI, 142
Thomas, William VI, 786
Thomas, William VI, 800
Thomas, William VI, 816
Thomas, William VI, 832
Thomas, William VI, 850
Thomas, William VI, 859
Thomas, William VI, 910
Thomas, William VI, 912
Thomas, William VI, 937
Thomas, William VI, 974
Thomas, William VI, 976
Thomas, William VI, 982
Thomas, William VI, 1003
Thomas, William VI, 1006
Thomas, William A. IV, 290
Thomas, William A. V, 534
Thomas, William A. VI, 1003
Thomas, William Albert IV, 289
Thomas, William E. II, 304
Thomas, William G. III, 311
Thomas, William M. I, 948
Thomas, William M. I, 950
Thomas, William, Jr. II, 720
Thomas, William, Sr. V, 769
Thomas, Winney VI, 1003
Thomas, Winnifred II, 426
Thomas, Wm. II, 666
Thomas, Wm. II, 770
Thomas, Wm. II, 793
Thomas, Wm. II, 821
Thomas, Wm. IV, 363
Thomas, Wm. IV, 393
Thomas, Wm. IV, 399
Thomas, Wm. IV, 424
Thomas, Wm. IV, 447
Thomas, Wm. IV, 1117
Thomas, Wm. IV, 1122
Thomas, Wm. IV, 1338
Thomas, Wm. V, 766
Thomas, Wm. V, 767
Thomas, Wm. V, 768
Thomas, Wm. V, 793
Thomas, Wm. A. V, 534
Thomas, Wm. B. II, 770
Thomas, Wm. F. V, 612
Thomas, Wm. G. III, 31
Thomas, Wm. Geo. III, 311
Thomas, Wm. George III, 292
Thomas, Wm. George III, 311
Thomas, Wm. J. IV, 1079
Thomas, Wm. J. V, 767
Thomas, Wm. Jolliff, Jr. VI, 451
Thomas, Wm. Jolliffe, Jr. VI, 451
Thomas, Wm. Laribee V, 612
Thomas, Wm. Mode IV, 776
Thomas, Wm. Mode IV, 1008
Thomas, Wm. R. II, 929
Thomas, Zachariah I, 1071
Thomas, Zadoc Willis IV, 1007
Thomas, Zadock Willis IV, 1008
Thomas, Zebulon II, 426
Thomas, Zebulon II, 666
Thomas, Zebulon II, 770
Thomas, Zebulon II, 929
Thomas, Zella IV, 1340
Thomas, Zilla II, 666
Thomas, Zillah II, 426
Thomas, Zillah II, 564
Thomas, Zillah II, 666
Thomas, Zilpah V, 768
Thomas, Zilpah V, 791
Thomas, Zilpah V, 793
Thomas, Zilpha V, 769
Thomas, Zilphah V, 769
Thomason, Ann IV, 291
Thomason, Arthur VI, 1003
Thomason, Bartlett VI, 880
Thomason, Caroline M. VI, 1003
Thomason, Catherine VI, 909
Thomason, Christopher VI, 1003
Thomason, Eunice IV, 354
Thomason, James VI, 884
Thomason, James VI, 1003
Thomason, John VI, 909
Thomason, John VI, 974
Thomason, John VI, 1004
Thomason, Lydia B. V, 978
Thomason, Maria IV, 291
Thomason, Mariah IV, 413
Thomason, Mariah IV, 448
Thomason, Mary II, 787
Thomason, Nancy VI, 880
Thomason, Nancy VI, 1003
Thomason, Nancy VI, 1004
Thomason, Nancy L. VI, 974
Thomason, Nelson A. VI, 916
Thomason, Rebecca L. V, 655
Thomason, Samuel IV, 300
Thomason, Sarah IV, 387
Thomason, Sarah IV, 448
Thomason, Sarah Ann VI, 1004
Thomason, Thomas IV, 291
Thomason, Thomas IV, 413
Thomason, Thomas J. VI, 1004
Thomason, Thomas, Jr. IV, 448
Thomasson, Abigail IV, 291
Thomasson, Abigail IV, 297
Thomasson, Abigail IV, 353
Thomasson, Abigail IV, 354
Thomasson, Abigail IV, 596
Thomasson, Abigail IV, 598
Thomasson, Amerrilla VI, 876
Thomasson, Ann IV, 211
Thomasson, Ann IV, 291
Thomasson, Anna M. IV, 291
Thomasson, Annie IV, 291
Thomasson, Arthur E. IV, 596
Thomasson, Arthur Everett IV, 596
Thomasson, Elizabeth IV, 300
Thomasson, Eunice II, 720
Thomasson, Eunice IV, 291
Thomasson, Eunice IV, 328
Thomasson, Eunice IV, 353
Thomasson, Eunice IV, 354
Thomasson, Eunice IV, 574
Thomasson, Eunice IV, 576
Thomasson, Eunice IV, 596
Thomasson, Eunice IV, 598
Thomasson, Eunice IV, 1138
Thomasson, James IV, 596
Thomasson, Jesse J. IV, 596
Thomasson, John II, 720
Thomasson, John IV, 291
Thomasson, John IV, 328
Thomasson, John IV, 353
Thomasson, John IV, 354
Thomasson, John IV, 574
Thomasson, John IV, 576
Thomasson, John IV, 596
Thomasson, John IV, 598
Thomasson, John IV, 1138
Thomasson, John VI, 876
Thomasson, John VI, 905
Thomasson, John VI, 1004
Thomasson, John J. IV, 596
Thomasson, John, Jr. IV, 291
Thomasson, Jones IV, 291
Thomasson, Joseph II, 720
Thomasson, Joseph II, 770
Thomasson, Joseph IV, 291
Thomasson, Joseph IV, 353
Thomasson, Joseph IV, 354
Thomasson, Joseph Earl IV, 596
Thomasson, Josiah V, 295
Thomasson, Lydia IV, 349
Thomasson, Lydia IV, 354
Thomasson, Maria IV, 231
Thomasson, Maria IV, 291
Thomasson, Maria IV, 353
Thomasson, Maria IV, 354
Thomasson, Maria IV, 500
Thomasson, Maria IV, 502
Thomasson, Mariah IV, 291
Thomasson, Mariah IV, 300
Thomasson, Mary IV, 291
Thomasson, Mary IV, 307
Thomasson, Mary IV, 500
Thomasson, Mary IV, 505
Thomasson, Mary IV, 596
Thomasson, Mary A. IV, 596
Thomasson, Mary A. IV, 1134
Thomasson, Mary A. IV, 1138
Thomasson, Mary B. IV, 291
Thomasson, Mary B. IV, 296
Thomasson, Mary E. IV, 596
Thomasson, Mary S. IV, 291
Thomasson, Mary W. IV, 291
Thomasson, Mary W. IV, 500
Thomasson, Myra IV, 291
Thomasson, Nancy VI, 1004
Thomasson, Nathan IV, 291
Thomasson, Nathan IV, 596
Thomasson, Nathan IV, 1134
Thomasson, Nathan IV, 1138
Thomasson, Sally VI, 905
Thomasson, Samuel IV, 291
Thomasson, Samuel IV, 300
Thomasson, Samuel IV, 354
Thomasson, Samuel IV, 596
Thomasson, Samuel G. IV, 500
Thomasson, Samuel J. IV, 211
Thomasson, Samuel J. IV, 291
Thomasson, Samuel J. IV, 296
Thomasson, Samuel J. IV, 307
Thomasson, Samuel J. IV, 353
Thomasson, Samuel J. IV, 500
Thomasson, Samuel J. IV, 505
Thomasson, Sara IV, 574
Thomasson, Sara IV, 596
Thomasson, Sarah IV, 291
Thomasson, Sarah IV, 353
Thomasson, Sarah IV, 354
Thomasson, Sarah IV, 596
Thomasson, Thomas IV, 291
Thomasson, Thomas IV, 353
Thomasson, Thomas IV, 354
Thomasson, Thomas IV, 596
Thomasson, Thomas W. IV, 291
Thomasson, Thomas, Jr. IV, 291
Thomasson, Thomas, Jr. IV, 353
Thomasson, Thos. IV, 231
Thomasson, Thos. IV, 291
Thomasson, Thos. IV, 500
Thomasson, Thos. IV, 596
Thomasson, Virginia IV, 291
Thomasson, Will IV, 291
Thomers, Sally VI, 1012
Thomerson, Arthur VI, 1003
Thomerson, Caroline M. VI, 1003
Thomerson, Sally VI, 1012
Thomes, Francis I, 90
Thomlinson, Abel II, 326
Thomlinson, Mary II, 326
Thomlinson, Rebecca IV, 877
Thompkins, James VI, 859
Thompkins, Martha II, 124
Thompkins, Mercy VI, 560
Thompkins, Mercy VI, 572
Thompkins, Polly VI, 859
Thompsom, John C. IV, 187
Thompsom, Rebecca IV, 187
Thompson, ??? II, 427
Thompson, ??? III, 227
Thompson, ??? III, 312
Thompson, ??? III, 341
Thompson, ??? V, 887
Thompson, Aaron II, 42
Thompson, Aaron II, 44
Thompson, Aaron II, 76
Thompson, Aaron II, 91
Thompson, Aaron II, 105
Thompson, Aaron IV, 177
Thompson, Aaron IV, 188
Thompson, Aaron IV, 208
Thompson, Aaron IV, 228
Thompson, Aaron IV, 291
Thompson, Aaron IV, 292
Thompson, Aaron IV, 293
Thompson, Aaron, Jr. IV, 292
Thompson, Aaron, Sr. IV, 292
Thompson, Abel I, 440
Thompson, Abel I, 446
Thompson, Abel I, 454
Thompson, Abi IV, 293
Thompson, Abigail I, 386
Thompson, Abigail I, 423
Thompson, Abigail II, 44
Thompson, Abigail II, 91
Thompson, Abigail II, 105
Thompson, Abigail II, 124
Thompson, Abigail II, 139
Thompson, Abigail V, 811
Thompson, Abraham II, 42
Thompson, Abraham II, 43
Thompson, Abraham II, 44
Thompson, Abraham V, 936
Thompson, Abrose III, 312
Thompson, Absolom VI, 859
Thompson, Ada V, 434
Thompson, Ada C. III, 64
Thompson, Ada L. IV, 777
Thompson, Adam II, 104
Thompson, Adam II, 667
Thompson, Adam VI, 931
Thompson, Adeline Enfield IV, 293
Thompson, Albert IV, 777
Thompson, Alex II, 311
Thompson, Alex VI, 1016
Thompson, Alexander II, 314
Thompson, Alexander II, 324
Thompson, Alexander II, 326
Thompson, Alexander II, 1081
Thompson, Alexander VI, 859
Thompson, Alfred I, 423
Thompson, Alfred I, 424
Thompson, Alfred II, 138
Thompson, Alfred V, 132
Thompson, Alfred V, 362
Thompson, Alfred V, 1021
Thompson, Alfred Haughton V, 936
Thompson, Alfred McDuffry I, 454
Thompson, Alice II, 894
Thompson, Alice III, 153
Thompson, Alice III, 311
Thompson, Alice D. I, 262
Thompson, Alice H. III, 312
Thompson, Allen IV, 293
Thompson, Almara VI, 859
Thompson, Almira V, 207
Thompson, Alta III, 341
Thompson, Alta R. IV, 1265
Thompson, Alvin E. IV, 292
Thompson, Alvin E. IV, 293
Thompson, Amanda IV, 197
Thompson, Amanda V, 1021
Thompson, Amanda Bell IV, 293
Thompson, Amelia IV, 1340
Thompson, Amos Hiatt V, 715
Thompson, Amos J. Hiatt V, 362
Thompson, Amos V. IV, 292
Thompson, Amsey IV, 884
Thompson, Amy I, 378
Thompson, Amy I, 423
Thompson, Amy I, 425
Thompson, Amy II, 426
Thompson, Amy V, 284
Thompson, Amy V, 373
Thompson, Amy V, 434
Thompson, Amy C. I, 424
Thompson, Anderson VI, 932
Thompson, Anderson VI, 1014
Thompson, Andrew II, 17
Thompson, Andrew II, 39

Thompson, Andrew II, 42
Thompson, Andrew II, 43
Thompson, Andrew II, 44
Thompson, Andrew II, 45
Thompson, Andrew II, 49
Thompson, Andrew II, 56
Thompson, Andrew II, 89
Thompson, Andrew II, 91
Thompson, Andrew II, 104
Thompson, Andrew II, 105
Thompson, Andrew II, 106
Thompson, Andrew II, 124
Thompson, Andrew II, 128
Thompson, Andrew II, 132
Thompson, Andrew II, 138
Thompson, Andrew II, 139
Thompson, Andrew II, 140
Thompson, Andrew II, 144
Thompson, Andrew II, 150
Thompson, Andrew II, 158
Thompson, Andrew II, 159
Thompson, Andrew II, 667
Thompson, Andrew V, 434
Thompson, Andrew VI, 837
Thompson, Andrew VI, 863
Thompson, Andrew VI, 866
Thompson, Andrew B. VI, 859
Thompson, Ann I, 407
Thompson, Ann I, 423
Thompson, Ann I, 454
Thompson, Ann I, 1038
Thompson, Ann I, 1079
Thompson, Ann II, 43
Thompson, Ann II, 44
Thompson, Ann II, 75
Thompson, Ann II, 82
Thompson, Ann II, 85
Thompson, Ann II, 86
Thompson, Ann II, 104
Thompson, Ann II, 105
Thompson, Ann II, 106
Thompson, Ann II, 134
Thompson, Ann II, 139
Thompson, Ann II, 448
Thompson, Ann II, 667
Thompson, Ann II, 794
Thompson, Ann II, 1032
Thompson, Ann III, 311
Thompson, Ann IV, 27
Thompson, Ann IV, 62
Thompson, Ann IV, 208
Thompson, Ann IV, 228
Thompson, Ann IV, 249
Thompson, Ann IV, 291
Thompson, Ann IV, 292
Thompson, Ann IV, 293
Thompson, Ann IV, 298
Thompson, Ann IV, 306
Thompson, Ann IV, 354
Thompson, Ann IV, 697
Thompson, Ann IV, 1079
Thompson, Ann VI, 115
Thompson, Ann VI, 123
Thompson, Ann VI, 215
Thompson, Ann VI, 387
Thompson, Ann VI, 415
Thompson, Ann VI, 451
Thompson, Ann VI, 498
Thompson, Ann VI, 551
Thompson, Ann VI, 559
Thompson, Ann VI, 572
Thompson, Ann VI, 573
Thompson, Ann C. VI, 1014
Thompson, Ann D. C. II, 138
Thompson, Ann Dallas Clark II, 138
Thompson, Ann E. II, 129
Thompson, Ann E. II, 139
Thompson, Ann Eliza III, 311
Thompson, Ann Eliza III, 312
Thompson, Ann Elizabeth II, 147
Thompson, Ann Elizabeth II, 159
Thompson, Ann H. VI, 509
Thompson, Ann H. VI, 512
Thompson, Ann H. VI, 573
Thompson, Ann L. VI, 1004
Thompson, Ann Meriwether VI, 870
Thompson, Ann, Jr. II, 43
Thompson, Anna I, 298
Thompson, Anna II, 135
Thompson, Anna II, 138
Thompson, Anna IV, 293
Thompson, Anna IV, 1340
Thompson, Anna B. II, 159
Thompson, Anna Craft IV, 292
Thompson, Anna D. C. II, 158
Thompson, Anna L. I, 424
Thompson, Anna L. II, 127
Thompson, Anna L. II, 131
Thompson, Anna L. II, 158
Thompson, Anna L. II, 159
Thompson, Anna L. V, 434
Thompson, Anna Lewis IV, 293
Thompson, Anna S. VI, 786
Thompson, Anne II, 44
Thompson, Anne M. II, 138
Thompson, Annie I, 319
Thompson, Annie II, 150
Thompson, Annie II, 159
Thompson, Annie Bullock II, 138
Thompson, Annie L. IV, 292
Thompson, Annie S. II, 144
Thompson, Annie S. II, 159
Thompson, Annie T. II, 132
Thompson, Annie W. I, 950
Thompson, Annis IV, 884
Thompson, Arminda IV, 293
Thompson, Asaph IV, 1083
Thompson, Austin B. IV, 293
Thompson, Avis R. VI, 859
Thompson, B. O. V, 715
Thompson, Benjamin II, 43
Thompson, Benjamin II, 44
Thompson, Benjamin II, 105
Thompson, Benjamin II, 109
Thompson, Benjamin II, 426
Thompson, Benjamin II, 823
Thompson, Benjamin II, 929
Thompson, Benjamin II, 1032
Thompson, Benjamin II, 1062
Thompson, Benjamin II, 1081
Thompson, Benoni IV, 291
Thompson, Berney IV, 293
Thompson, Bernice IV, 1188
Thompson, Bertha I, 934
Thompson, Bessie VI, 695
Thompson, Bethnea I, 424
Thompson, Billie Howard IV, 777
Thompson, Birney IV, 293
Thompson, Birtsel V, 715
Thompson, Birtzel V, 714
Thompson, Bismark IV, 1008
Thompson, Blake I, 621
Thompson, Blake T. I, 626
Thompson, Blake T. I, 638
Thompson, Blake T. I, 642
Thompson, Blake T. I, 950
Thompson, Blanch Meredith I, 627
Thompson, Boyd IV, 293
Thompson, Bradbury IV, 292
Thompson, Bradway IV, 62
Thompson, Bradway IV, 249
Thompson, Bradway IV, 291
Thompson, Bradway IV, 292
Thompson, Bradway IV, 298
Thompson, Bradway IV, 354
Thompson, Bradways IV, 27
Thompson, Bradways IV, 62
Thompson, C. Wistar II, 125
Thompson, Calvin I, 386
Thompson, Calvin I, 423
Thompson, Caroline I, 454
Thompson, Caroline II, 139
Thompson, Caroline II, 770
Thompson, Caroline IV, 930
Thompson, Caroline IV, 1008
Thompson, Caroline IV, 1083
Thompson, Caroline VI, 755
Thompson, Caroline VI, 859
Thompson, Caroline Miller II, 131
Thompson, Carrie IV, 293
Thompson, Carrie IV, 777
Thompson, Carrie V, 434
Thompson, Carver IV, 291
Thompson, Carver IV, 293
Thompson, Casper W. II, 43
Thompson, Casper W. II, 124
Thompson, Casper W. II, 125
Thompson, Casper W. II, 126
Thompson, Catharine I, 424
Thompson, Catharine I, 427
Thompson, Catharine I, 440
Thompson, Catharine I, 448
Thompson, Catharine I, 451
Thompson, Catharine I, 453
Thompson, Catharine I, 454
Thompson, Catharine II, 43
Thompson, Catharine II, 106
Thompson, Catharine III, 312
Thompson, Catharine IV, 292
Thompson, Catharine T. III, 148
Thompson, Catherine I, 1079
Thompson, Catherine III, 148
Thompson, Charles I, 934
Thompson, Charles I, 950
Thompson, Charles III, 312
Thompson, Charles IV, 293
Thompson, Charles V, 434
Thompson, Charles V, 872
Thompson, Charles D. IV, 292
Thompson, Charles E. II, 929
Thompson, Charles Samuel I, 934
Thompson, Charles T. II, 770
Thompson, Charles Trotter II, 720
Thompson, Charlie IV, 293
Thompson, Charlotte A. II, 138
Thompson, Charlotte Hannah VI, 786
Thompson, Charlotte Q. VI, 1001
Thompson, Chas. Evans II, 823
Thompson, Christopher II, 426
Thompson, Christopher II, 427
Thompson, Christopher III, 311
Thompson, Clara V, 715
Thompson, Clara A. I, 627
Thompson, Clarence IV, 292
Thompson, Clarence IV, 293
Thompson, Clarence W. I, 262
Thompson, Clarissa V, 915
Thompson, Clark H. II, 127
Thompson, Clark H. II, 131
Thompson, Clark H. II, 135
Thompson, Clark H. II, 138
Thompson, Clark H. II, 158
Thompson, Clark H. II, 159
Thompson, Clark L. II, 159
Thompson, Cora Amanda V, 132
Thompson, Cornelia II, 131
Thompson, Cornelia III, 249
Thompson, Cornelia III, 311
Thompson, Cornelia Frances I, 934
Thompson, D. J. VI, 808
Thompson, Daisy D. I, 424
Thompson, Daniel II, 44
Thompson, Daniel II, 314
Thompson, Daniel II, 427
Thompson, Daniel II, 1032
Thompson, Daniel VI, 859
Thompson, Daniel B. III, 312
Thompson, Daniel D. VI, 779
Thompson, Daniel D. VI, 786
Thompson, Daniel R. I, 319
Thompson, Daniel W. I, 454
Thompson, Danyeal R. I, 298
Thompson, David I, 934
Thompson, David II, 43
Thompson, David II, 73
Thompson, David II, 106
Thompson, David III, 311
Thompson, David IV, 292
Thompson, David IV, 1079
Thompson, David VI, 859
Thompson, David VI, 863
Thompson, David A. II, 44
Thompson, David A. II, 106
Thompson, David A. II, 138
Thompson, David A. II, 159
Thompson, David Allen II, 138
Thompson, David J. VI, 1004
Thompson, David L. VI, 832
Thompson, David Waddy, Jr. VI, 1004
Thompson, David, Sr. VI, 1004
Thompson, Deborah II, 44
Thompson, Deborah II, 90
Thompson, Deborah II, 97
Thompson, Deborah II, 105
Thompson, Decatur V, 132
Thompson, Delphina I, 424
Thompson, Dinah I, 356
Thompson, Dinah I, 366
Thompson, Dinah I, 398
Thompson, Dinah I, 423
Thompson, Dinah II, 267
Thompson, Dixon I, 298
Thompson, Dora I, 626
Thompson, Dora I, 627
Thompson, Dorithy II, 44
Thompson, Dorothy II, 67
Thompson, Dorothy II, 104
Thompson, Dorrothy II, 67
Thompson, Dougan I, 424
Thompson, Dr. Leonard Ramsay III, 449
Thompson, Dr. Leonard Ramsey III, 427
Thompson, Dr. Percy Beecher III, 156
Thompson, Dr. Percy Beecher III, 312
Thompson, Dunham II, 43
Thompson, Dunham II, 106
Thompson, E. W. H. IV, 1188
Thompson, Edgar IV, 1265
Thompson, Edith I, 440
Thompson, Edith I, 454
Thompson, Edith I, 627
Thompson, Edith I, 642
Thompson, Edith II, 20
Thompson, Edith II, 31
Thompson, Edith II, 44
Thompson, Edith II, 77
Thompson, Edith II, 105
Thompson, Edith II, 106
Thompson, Edith II, 107
Thompson, Edith IV, 206
Thompson, Edith IV, 291
Thompson, Edith IV, 292
Thompson, Edith IV, 1068
Thompson, Edith IV, 1079
Thompson, Edith IV, 1315
Thompson, Edith C. V, 207
Thompson, Edith Virginia III, 369
Thompson, Edna I, 454
Thompson, Edna V, 872
Thompson, Edna V, 884
Thompson, Edna V, 887
Thompson, Edward II, 97
Thompson, Edward II, 667
Thompson, Edward III, 311
Thompson, Edward IV, 292
Thompson, Edward IV, 293
Thompson, Edward VI, 859
Thompson, Edward, Jr. VI, 573
Thompson, Edward, Jr. VI, 582
Thompson, Edwin V, 362
Thompson, Edwin V, 936
Thompson, Edwin S. IV, 293
Thompson, Edwin Stanton IV, 293
Thompson, Effie IV, 293
Thompson, Effie V, 434
Thompson, Effie V, 714
Thompson, Effie V, 715
Thompson, Egbert Arnold VI, 786
Thompson, Egbert Williams VI, 748
Thompson, Egbert Williams VI, 786
Thompson, Elanor VI, 837
Thompson, Elda Margaret IV, 1265
Thompson, Eleanor I, 449
Thompson, Eleanor I, 453
Thompson, Eleanor VI, 837
Thompson, Elenor VI, 831
Thompson, Elenor VI, 837
Thompson, Elenor VI, 859
Thompson, Eli IV, 292
Thompson, Eli V, 132
Thompson, Eli V, 207
Thompson, Eli V, 434
Thompson, Elihu IV, 1083
Thompson, Elijah V, 887
Thompson, Elisha II, 43
Thompson, Elisha II, 106
Thompson, Elisha IV, 292
Thompson, Elisha IV, 293
Thompson, Eliza II, 44
Thompson, Eliza II, 138
Thompson, Eliza II, 139
Thompson, Eliza III, 312
Thompson, Eliza IV, 291
Thompson, Eliza IV, 292
Thompson, Eliza V, 1021
Thompson, Eliza A. VI, 932
Thompson, Eliza Ann IV, 292
Thompson, Eliza L. VI, 851
Thompson, Eliza T. VI, 1004
Thompson, Elizabeth I, 298
Thompson, Elizabeth I, 348
Thompson, Elizabeth I, 356
Thompson, Elizabeth I, 366
Thompson, Elizabeth I, 391
Thompson, Elizabeth I, 398
Thompson, Elizabeth I, 405
Thompson, Elizabeth I, 423
Thompson, Elizabeth I, 440
Thompson, Elizabeth I, 449
Thompson, Elizabeth I, 451
Thompson, Elizabeth I, 453
Thompson, Elizabeth I, 454
Thompson, Elizabeth I, 934
Thompson, Elizabeth II, 24
Thompson, Elizabeth II, 36
Thompson, Elizabeth II, 39
Thompson, Elizabeth II, 42
Thompson, Elizabeth II, 43
Thompson, Elizabeth II, 44
Thompson, Elizabeth II, 56
Thompson, Elizabeth II, 60
Thompson, Elizabeth II, 71
Thompson, Elizabeth II, 81
Thompson, Elizabeth II, 97
Thompson, Elizabeth II, 98
Thompson, Elizabeth II, 104
Thompson, Elizabeth II, 105
Thompson, Elizabeth II, 106
Thompson, Elizabeth II, 109
Thompson, Elizabeth II, 124
Thompson, Elizabeth II, 131
Thompson, Elizabeth II, 138
Thompson, Elizabeth II, 139
Thompson, Elizabeth II, 150
Thompson, Elizabeth II, 158
Thompson, Elizabeth II, 159
Thompson, Elizabeth II, 212
Thompson, Elizabeth II, 268
Thompson, Elizabeth II, 448
Thompson, Elizabeth II, 667
Thompson, Elizabeth II, 704
Thompson, Elizabeth II, 800
Thompson, Elizabeth II, 808
Thompson, Elizabeth II, 809
Thompson, Elizabeth II, 929
Thompson, Elizabeth III, 215
Thompson, Elizabeth III, 312
Thompson, Elizabeth IV, 292
Thompson, Elizabeth IV, 314
Thompson, Elizabeth IV, 412
Thompson, Elizabeth IV, 429
Thompson, Elizabeth IV, 448
Thompson, Elizabeth IV, 610
Thompson, Elizabeth IV, 660
Thompson, Elizabeth IV, 1008
Thompson, Elizabeth IV, 1068
Thompson, Elizabeth IV, 1079
Thompson, Elizabeth IV, 1083
Thompson, Elizabeth IV, 1265
Thompson, Elizabeth IV, 1382
Thompson, Elizabeth V, 207
Thompson, Elizabeth V, 602
Thompson, Elizabeth V, 887
Thompson, Elizabeth VI, 399
Thompson, Elizabeth VI, 444
Thompson, Elizabeth VI, 451
Thompson, Elizabeth VI, 498
Thompson, Elizabeth VI, 573
Thompson, Elizabeth VI, 805
Thompson, Elizabeth VI, 837
Thompson, Elizabeth VI, 859
Thompson, Elizabeth VI, 877
Thompson, Elizabeth VI, 1004
Thompson, Elizabeth Ann IV, 1083
Thompson, Elizabeth B. II, 43
Thompson, Elizabeth B. II, 11
Thompson, Elizabeth B. II, 12
Thompson, Elizabeth C. III, 3
Thompson, Elizabeth D. II, 1
Thompson, Elizabeth E. II, 89
Thompson, Elizabeth E. II, 92
Thompson, Elizabeth E. VI, 7
Thompson, Elizabeth E. VI, 7
Thompson, Elizabeth Evans II, 807
Thompson, Elizabeth H. II, 1
Thompson, Elizabeth H. II, 1
Thompson, Elizabeth H. II, 72
Thompson, Elizabeth H. II, 7
Thompson, Elizabeth H. II, 77
Thompson, Elizabeth J. VI, 10
Thompson, Elizabeth L. VI, 9
Thompson, Elizabeth M. VI, 7
Thompson, Elizabeth P. IV, 10
Thompson, Elizabeth Sharp II, 138
Thompson, Elizabeth U. III, 3
Thompson, Elizabeth W. II, 12
Thompson, Elizabeth W. II, 12
Thompson, Elizabeth W. II, 66
Thompson, Elizabeth W. II, 72
Thompson, Elizabeth W. VI, 9
Thompson, Ella II, 138
Thompson, Ella II, 149
Thompson, Ella II, 159
Thompson, Ella V, 434
Thompson, Ella V, 715
Thompson, Ellen IV, 777
Thompson, Ellen V, 602
Thompson, Ellen VI, 786
Thompson, Ellen E. II, 929
Thompson, Ellsworth V, 602
Thompson, Elmer H. V, 434
Thompson, Elmina I, 413
Thompson, Elmina I, 423
Thompson, Elvira II, 1072
Thompson, Elvira II, 1081
Thompson, Elwood I, 366
Thompson, Elwood I, 423
Thompson, Elwood IV, 292
Thompson, Elwood IV, 293
Thompson, Emilie II, 818
Thompson, Emma II, 127
Thompson, Emma II, 142
Thompson, Emma II, 159
Thompson, Emma J. II, 127
Thompson, Emma J. II, 138

mpson, Emma J. II, 139
mpson, Emma J. IV, 293
mpson, Emma L. III, 312
mpson, Emmor IV, 1083
mpson, Enoch I, 440
mpson, Enoch I, 454
mpson, Ernest I, 642
mpson, Essie I, 642
mpson, Essie W. I, 642
mpson, Esther I, 1062
mpson, Esther I, 1063
mpson, Esther II, 43
mpson, Esther II, 89
mpson, Esther II, 106
mpson, Esther II, 116
mpson, Esther II, 124
mpson, Esther II, 126
mpson, Esther II, 667
mpson, Esther IV, 177
mpson, Esther IV, 291
mpson, Esther IV, 292
mpson, Esther IV, 1079
ompson, Esther C. IV, 1079
ompson, Etta IV, 293
ompson, Evelyn I, 626
ompson, Evelyn I, 638
ompson, Evelyn I, 642
ompson, Evelyn M. I, 950
ompson, Ezekiel II, 97
ompson, Ezra IV, 291
ompson, Ezra IV, 292
ompson, Ezra IV, 293
ompson, Fanny VI, 884
ompson, Farlin IV, 884
ompson, Florence E. V, 336
ompson, Florence E. V, 362
ompson, Floyd IV, 1008
ompson, Frances II, 770
ompson, Frances III, 312
ompson, Frances D. VI, 859
ompson, Frances J. VI, 970
ompson, Francis II, 427
ompson, Francis II, 720
ompson, Francis II, 770
hompson, Francis III, 249
hompson, Francis III, 311
hompson, Francis III, 312
hompson, Francis III, 338
hompson, Francis III, 370
hompson, Francis O. II, 138
hompson, Francis, Jr. II, 585
hompson, Francis, Jr. II, 668
hompson, Francis, Jr. III, 311
hompson, Frank V, 207
hompson, Franklin V, 715
hompson, Franklin S. IV, 293
hompson, Freddie T. V, 362
hompson, Geo G. III, 293
hompson, Geo. III, 312
hompson, Geo. G. III, 312
hompson, Geo. S. III, 312
hompson, George I, 423
hompson, George I, 1162
hompson, George II, 427
hompson, George II, 448
Thompson, George II, 770
Thompson, George III, 215
Thompson, George III, 312
Thompson, George IV, 293
Thompson, George H. IV, 292
Thompson, George W. VI, 859
Thompson, Gerard IV, 1083
Thompson, Gerhardus III, 312
Thompson, Gilbert II, 427
Thompson, Gladys IV, 1340
Thompson, Grace II, 42
Thompson, Grace II, 43
Thompson, Grace II, 44
Thompson, Grace II, 45
Thompson, Grace II, 57
Thompson, Grace II, 89
Thompson, Grace II, 105
Thompson, Grace II, 109
Thompson, Grace V, 434
Thompson, Grace V, 872
Thompson, Grove III, 449
Thompson, Grove G. III, 312
Thompson, Grove G. III, 427
Thompson, Grove G. III, 449
Thompson, Grove G. III, 500
Thompson, Gulia Elma M. I, 424
Thompson, Guliaelma M. I, 402
Thompson, Guliaelma M. I, 423
Thompson, Hannah I, 420
Thompson, Hannah I, 423
Thompson, Hannah I, 424
Thompson, Hannah I, 440
Thompson, Hannah I, 453
Thompson, Hannah I, 454
Thompson, Hannah I, 741
Thompson, Hannah I, 1162
Thompson, Hannah II, 42
Thompson, Hannah II, 43
Thompson, Hannah II, 44
Thompson, Hannah II, 66
Thompson, Hannah II, 76
Thompson, Hannah II, 78
Thompson, Hannah II, 95
Thompson, Hannah II, 104
Thompson, Hannah II, 105
Thompson, Hannah II, 187
Thompson, Hannah II, 304
Thompson, Hannah II, 426
Thompson, Hannah II, 427
Thompson, Hannah II, 585
Thompson, Hannah II, 667
Thompson, Hannah II, 668
Thompson, Hannah II, 720
Thompson, Hannah II, 770
Thompson, Hannah II, 786
Thompson, Hannah III, 311
Thompson, Hannah IV, 62
Thompson, Hannah IV, 232
Thompson, Hannah IV, 291
Thompson, Hannah IV, 292
Thompson, Hannah IV, 298
Thompson, Hannah IV, 777
Thompson, Hannah IV, 884
Thompson, Hannah V, 132
Thompson, Hannah V, 207
Thompson, Hannah V, 602
Thompson, Hannah V, 647
Thompson, Hannah V, 715
Thompson, Hannah VI, 415
Thompson, Hannah VI, 444
Thompson, Hannah VI, 451
Thompson, Hannah VI, 573
Thompson, Hannah VI, 748
Thompson, Hannah VI, 769
Thompson, Hannah Ann II, 124
Thompson, Hannah Ann II, 128
Thompson, Hannah Ann II, 138
Thompson, Hannah Ann II, 144
Thompson, Hannah Ann II, 158
Thompson, Hannah Eayre VI, 748
Thompson, Hannah Eayre VI, 786
Thompson, Hannah G. II, 122
Thompson, Hannah G. II, 124
Thompson, Hannah M. II, 929
Thompson, Hannah, Jr. II, 106
Thompson, Hannah, Jr. VI, 534
Thompson, Hannah, Jr. VI, 573
Thompson, Harrie IV, 1265
Thompson, Harrison Morton I, 424
Thompson, Harry IV, 1265
Thompson, Harry V, 534
Thompson, Harry L. IV, 777
Thompson, Harry Lee IV, 777
Thompson, Harvey IV, 293
Thompson, Hattie IV, 1265
Thompson, Hayes I, 424
Thompson, Hazel III, 312
Thompson, Hazel III, 449
Thompson, Hazel E. III, 500
Thompson, Hector II, 1032
Thompson, Hector II, 1062
Thompson, Hector, Jr. II, 1062
Thompson, Helen Ware III, 24
Thompson, Helen Ware III, 312
Thompson, Henry II, 427
Thompson, Henry II, 667
Thompson, Henry Harvey II, 1081
Thompson, Herbert I, 209
Thompson, Hester I, 1024
Thompson, Horace D. II, 720
Thompson, Horace D. II, 770
Thompson, Howard V, 132
Thompson, Hugh II, 427
Thompson, Hugh II, 667
Thompson, Ida IV, 293
Thompson, Ida Evelyn I, 621
Thompson, Ida May V, 770
Thompson, Isaac I, 298
Thompson, Isaac I, 319
Thompson, Isaac I, 1024
Thompson, Isaac II, 44
Thompson, Isaac II, 78
Thompson, Isaac II, 105
Thompson, Isaac IV, 292
Thompson, Isaac V, 132
Thompson, Isaac V, 815
Thompson, Isaac VI, 573
Thompson, Isaac H. I, 950
Thompson, Isaac Nixon II, 105
Thompson, Isaac, Jr. V, 770
Thompson, Isaac, Jr. VI, 573
Thompson, Isabel II, 39
Thompson, Isabel II, 42
Thompson, Isabella III, 312
Thompson, Isla Willis I, 627
Thompson, Israel II, 667
Thompson, Israel IV, 291
Thompson, Israel IV, 292
Thompson, Israel IV, 293
Thompson, Israel VI, 500
Thompson, Israel VI, 509
Thompson, Israel VI, 551
Thompson, Israel VI, 573
Thompson, Israel H. VI, 509
Thompson, Israel H. VI, 512
Thompson, Israel H. VI, 573
Thompson, Israel Jenkins IV, 292
Thompson, Israel Jenkins IV, 293
Thompson, Issabell II, 42
Thompson, J. B. IV, 1008
Thompson, J. Leroy V, 715
Thompson, J. Leslie V, 362
Thompson, J. Walter I, 937
Thompson, J. Walter I, 950
Thompson, Jacob II, 43
Thompson, Jacob II, 44
Thompson, Jacob II, 77
Thompson, Jacob II, 106
Thompson, Jacob II, 139
Thompson, Jacob R. V, 1021
Thompson, James I, 348
Thompson, James I, 423
Thompson, James I, 453
Thompson, James I, 1079
Thompson, James II, 43
Thompson, James II, 44
Thompson, James II, 77
Thompson, James II, 104
Thompson, James II, 106
Thompson, James II, 427
Thompson, James II, 738
Thompson, James II, 807
Thompson, James II, 810
Thompson, James II, 823
Thompson, James III, 144
Thompson, James III, 311
Thompson, James III, 312
Thompson, James IV, 1188
Thompson, James IV, 1315
Thompson, James V, 602
Thompson, James B. II, 427
Thompson, James B. II, 625
Thompson, James B. II, 667
Thompson, James B. II, 720
Thompson, James B. II, 770
Thompson, James Beaton II, 720
Thompson, James Eli IV, 293
Thompson, James H. VI, 1004
Thompson, James Howard IV, 1265
Thompson, James Howard IV, 1340
Thompson, James M. I, 424
Thompson, Jane I, 1033
Thompson, Jane I, 1038
Thompson, Jane II, 43
Thompson, Jane II, 44
Thompson, Jane II, 89
Thompson, Jane II, 104
Thompson, Jane II, 667
Thompson, Jane III, 249
Thompson, Jane III, 311
Thompson, Jane III, 312
Thompson, Jane IV, 219
Thompson, Jane IV, 292
Thompson, Jane IV, 293
Thompson, Jane V, 434
Thompson, Jane V, 815
Thompson, Jane VI, 866
Thompson, Jane Alexandria VI, 786
Thompson, Jane Emeline I, 424
Thompson, Jane Peirce II, 808
Thompson, Jane W. VI, 786
Thompson, Jas. III, 311
Thompson, Jaspar V, 434
Thompson, Jasper C. VI, 878
Thompson, Jasper C. VI, 1004
Thompson, Jemima VI, 859
Thompson, Jemimah II, 78
Thompson, Jemimah II, 105
Thompson, Jenkins IV, 292
Thompson, Jenny VI, 866
Thompson, Jenny VI, 931
Thompson, Jeremiah III, 312
Thompson, Jeremiah IV, 1382
Thompson, Jesse I, 454
Thompson, Jesse L. VI, 1004
Thompson, Jesse M. I, 402
Thompson, Jesse M. I, 424
Thompson, Joanna V, 434
Thompson, John I, 298
Thompson, John I, 356
Thompson, John I, 366
Thompson, John I, 386
Thompson, John I, 398
Thompson, John I, 423
Thompson, John II, 17
Thompson, John II, 40
Thompson, John II, 42
Thompson, John II, 43
Thompson, John II, 44
Thompson, John II, 52
Thompson, John II, 57
Thompson, John II, 104
Thompson, John II, 105
Thompson, John II, 106
Thompson, John II, 116
Thompson, John II, 124
Thompson, John II, 126
Thompson, John II, 138
Thompson, John II, 426
Thompson, John II, 427
Thompson, John II, 580
Thompson, John II, 625
Thompson, John II, 667
Thompson, John II, 808
Thompson, John II, 823
Thompson, John II, 893
Thompson, John II, 929
Thompson, John II, 1062
Thompson, John III, 312
Thompson, John III, 492
Thompson, John III, 500
Thompson, John IV, 131
Thompson, John IV, 260
Thompson, John IV, 291
Thompson, John IV, 292
Thompson, John IV, 293
Thompson, John IV, 697
Thompson, John IV, 884
Thompson, John IV, 1083
Thompson, John V, 602
Thompson, John V, 872
Thompson, John V, 887
Thompson, John VI, 797
Thompson, John VI, 837
Thompson, John VI, 851
Thompson, John VI, 859
Thompson, John VI, 884
Thompson, John VI, 912
Thompson, John VI, 913
Thompson, John VI, 1004
Thompson, John A. VI, 1004
Thompson, John C. IV, 203
Thompson, John C. IV, 211
Thompson, John C. IV, 219
Thompson, John C. IV, 271
Thompson, John C. IV, 291
Thompson, John C. IV, 292
Thompson, John C. IV, 293
Thompson, John C. IV, 323
Thompson, John C. IV, 354
Thompson, John C. V, 434
Thompson, John Couzens IV, 62
Thompson, John Cozens IV, 291
Thompson, John E. II, 135
Thompson, John E. II, 138
Thompson, John E. II, 159
Thompson, John F. I, 424
Thompson, John H. IV, 291
Thompson, John H. IV, 293
Thompson, John J. II, 720
Thompson, John J. II, 738
Thompson, John J. II, 770
Thompson, John J. VI, 1004
Thompson, John J., Jr. II, 720
Thompson, John N. II, 43
Thompson, John P. IV, 1083
Thompson, John S. IV, 292
Thompson, John Thompson II, 738
Thompson, John W. I, 454
Thompson, John W. II, 1032
Thompson, John W. II, 1081
Thompson, John W. IV, 293
Thompson, John Wesley I, 627
Thompson, John, Jr. II, 106
Thompson, John, Jr. II, 667
Thompson, Jonah II, 427
Thompson, Jonah II, 667
Thompson, Jonah II, 668
Thompson, Jonah V, 872
Thompson, Jonah VI, 573
Thompson, Jonathan I, 423
Thompson, Jonathan II, 42
Thompson, Jonathan IV, 777
Thompson, Jonathan H. I, 454
Thompson, Joseph I, 423
Thompson, Joseph I, 440
Thompson, Joseph I, 453
Thompson, Joseph I, 454
Thompson, Joseph I, 1024
Thompson, Joseph I, 1033
Thompson, Joseph I, 1038
Thompson, Joseph I, 1062
Thompson, Joseph II, 43
Thompson, Joseph II, 44
Thompson, Joseph II, 62
Thompson, Joseph II, 67
Thompson, Joseph II, 68
Thompson, Joseph II, 72
Thompson, Joseph II, 104
Thompson, Joseph II, 105
Thompson, Joseph II, 106
Thompson, Joseph II, 667
Thompson, Joseph II, 770
Thompson, Joseph IV, 292
Thompson, Joseph IV, 660
Thompson, Joseph IV, 884
Thompson, Joseph IV, 1079
Thompson, Joseph V, 131
Thompson, Joseph V, 770
Thompson, Joseph V, 793
Thompson, Joseph V, 872
Thompson, Joseph VI, 415
Thompson, Joseph VI, 451
Thompson, Joseph VI, 512
Thompson, Joseph VI, 573
Thompson, Joseph VI, 1004
Thompson, Joseph Addison IV, 1083
Thompson, Joseph B. II, 43
Thompson, Joseph B. II, 124
Thompson, Joseph D. V, 362
Thompson, Joseph D. V, 936
Thompson, Joseph M. IV, 292
Thompson, Joseph M. IV, 1079
Thompson, Joseph, Jr. I, 1038
Thompson, Josephine I, 262
Thompson, Josephine I, 1153
Thompson, Josephine I, 1162
Thompson, Josephine H. I, 424
Thompson, Josephine H. I, 1162
Thompson, Joshua II, 36
Thompson, Joshua II, 42
Thompson, Joshua II, 43
Thompson, Joshua II, 44
Thompson, Joshua II, 71
Thompson, Joshua II, 85
Thompson, Joshua II, 97
Thompson, Joshua II, 105
Thompson, Joshua II, 106
Thompson, Joshua II, 124
Thompson, Joshua II, 127
Thompson, Joshua II, 129
Thompson, Joshua II, 134
Thompson, Joshua II, 138
Thompson, Joshua II, 139
Thompson, Joshua II, 144
Thompson, Joshua II, 569
Thompson, Joshua II, 667
Thompson, Joshua III, 385
Thompson, Joshua IV, 292
Thompson, Joshua IV, 1079
Thompson, Joshua V, 936
Thompson, Joshua G. II, 44
Thompson, Joshua L. II, 720
Thompson, Joshua Longstreth II, 427
Thompson, Joshua Longstreth II, 770
Thompson, Joshua, Jr. II, 50
Thompson, Joshua, Jr. II, 86
Thompson, Joshua, Jr. II, 105
Thompson, Joshua, Jr. II, 106
Thompson, Joshua, Jr. II, 109
Thompson, Joshua, Jr. IV, 1079
Thompson, Josiah II, 427
Thompson, Julia IV, 292
Thompson, Julia IV, 293
Thompson, Katharine E. I, 454
Thompson, Katie IV, 1265
Thompson, Kersey IV, 293
Thompson, Kesiah VI, 859
Thompson, Keziah VI, 1004
Thompson, L. Joshua III, 312
Thompson, Laura II, 311
Thompson, Laura II, 314
Thompson, Laura II, 322
Thompson, Laura II, 326
Thompson, Laura IV, 293
Thompson, Laura V, 434
Thompson, Lawrence V, 434
Thompson, Lawrence V, 715
Thompson, Lela I, 262
Thompson, Leroy V, 661
Thompson, Leroy V, 715
Thompson, Leslie V, 715
Thompson, Lester IV, 292
Thompson, Lester IV, 293
Thompson, Levi IV, 292
Thompson, Levi VI, 859
Thompson, Lewis II, 44
Thompson, Lewis II, 124
Thompson, Lewis II, 139

Thompson, Lewis II, 159
Thompson, Lewis II, 929
Thompson, Lewis IV, 291
Thompson, Lewis IV, 292
Thompson, Lewis V, 715
Thompson, Lewis Elwood V, 714
Thompson, Lida Lucile V, 715
Thompson, Lidia II, 44
Thompson, Lidia Ann IV, 1083
Thompson, Lindley I, 366
Thompson, Lindley I, 423
Thompson, Lindley IV, 292
Thompson, Lindley IV, 293
Thompson, Lindley M. IV, 292
Thompson, Lindley M. IV, 293
Thompson, Lindly I, 424
Thompson, Linley Murray IV, 292
Thompson, Liza J. V, 1021
Thompson, Lockey VI, 797
Thompson, Lorene IV, 293
Thompson, Louisa T. VI, 928
Thompson, Louisa W. I, 454
Thompson, Louise IV, 500
Thompson, Louiza IV, 777
Thompson, Lucinda VI, 955
Thompson, Lucy I, 627
Thompson, Lucy II, 127
Thompson, Lucy III, 148
Thompson, Lucy III, 311
Thompson, Lucy III, 312
Thompson, Lucy IV, 1188
Thompson, Lucy V, 362
Thompson, Lucy V, 936
Thompson, Lucy VI, 859
Thompson, Lucy Jane III, 312
Thompson, Lula Esther IV, 1008
Thompson, Lulu V, 534
Thompson, Lulu Esther IV, 1008
Thompson, Lutie A. V, 715
Thompson, Lydia I, 440
Thompson, Lydia I, 444
Thompson, Lydia I, 454
Thompson, Lydia I, 1062
Thompson, Lydia II, 427
Thompson, Lydia II, 625
Thompson, Lydia II, 667
Thompson, Lydia II, 720
Thompson, Lydia V, 131
Thompson, Lydia V, 967
Thompson, Lydia V, 978
Thompson, Lydia VI, 1004
Thompson, Lydia Ann IV, 1083
Thompson, Lydia B. V, 132
Thompson, Lydia B. V, 978
Thompson, Lydia Haines II, 106
Thompson, Lydia J. IV, 293
Thompson, Lydia Jane I, 424
Thompson, Lydia P. II, 667
Thompson, M. Adaline II, 929
Thompson, M. J. II, 129
Thompson, Maggie IV, 1008
Thompson, Mahala VI, 1004
Thompson, Mahlon V, 434
Thompson, Mahlon J. I, 423
Thompson, Malinda I, 356
Thompson, Malinda I, 366
Thompson, Margaret I, 409
Thompson, Margaret I, 423
Thompson, Margaret I, 454
Thompson, Margaret I, 934
Thompson, Margaret II, 43
Thompson, Margaret II, 427
Thompson, Margaret II, 572
Thompson, Margaret II, 667
Thompson, Margaret II, 1032
Thompson, Margaret II, 1062
Thompson, Margaret III, 144
Thompson, Margaret III, 312
Thompson, Margaret IV, 293
Thompson, Margaret IV, 777
Thompson, Margaret IV, 1008
Thompson, Margaret IV, 1083
Thompson, Margaret IV, 1265
Thompson, Margaret V, 284
Thompson, Margaret V, 290
Thompson, Margaret VI, 837
Thompson, Margaret VI, 859
Thompson, Margaret VI, 863
Thompson, Margaret VI, 1004
Thompson, Margaret E. I, 627
Thompson, Margarett II, 106
Thompson, Margaretta II, 1062
Thompson, Margaretta II, 1081
Thompson, Maria I, 929
Thompson, Maria III, 215
Thompson, Maria III, 312
Thompson, Maria V, 362
Thompson, Maria V, 936
Thompson, Maria B. III, 312
Thompson, Maria Jane III, 312
Thompson, Marianna II, 135
Thompson, Marie V, 434
Thompson, Marie V, 872
Thompson, Marietta I, 626
Thompson, Marietta I, 627
Thompson, Marion Beck IV, 1340
Thompson, Mark II, 43
Thompson, Mark II, 106
Thompson, Mark II, 139
Thompson, Mark Bradway II, 106
Thompson, Martha I, 423
Thompson, Martha I, 446
Thompson, Martha I, 450
Thompson, Martha I, 453
Thompson, Martha I, 454
Thompson, Martha II, 43
Thompson, Martha II, 106
Thompson, Martha II, 502
Thompson, Martha II, 667
Thompson, Martha IV, 111
Thompson, Martha IV, 292
Thompson, Martha IV, 697
Thompson, Martha IV, 777
Thompson, Martha IV, 1083
Thompson, Martha V, 311
Thompson, Martha V, 534
Thompson, Martha V, 535
Thompson, Martha V, 770
Thompson, Martha V, 1021
Thompson, Martha VI, 859
Thompson, Martha A. I, 402
Thompson, Martha A. I, 424
Thompson, Martha E. V, 770
Thompson, Martichia I, 424
Thompson, Mary I, 262
Thompson, Mary I, 366
Thompson, Mary I, 415
Thompson, Mary I, 423
Thompson, Mary I, 448
Thompson, Mary I, 453
Thompson, Mary I, 454
Thompson, Mary I, 829
Thompson, Mary I, 841
Thompson, Mary I, 1024
Thompson, Mary I, 1038
Thompson, Mary II, 40
Thompson, Mary II, 43
Thompson, Mary II, 44
Thompson, Mary II, 52
Thompson, Mary II, 57
Thompson, Mary II, 62
Thompson, Mary II, 67
Thompson, Mary II, 68
Thompson, Mary II, 69
Thompson, Mary II, 72
Thompson, Mary II, 74
Thompson, Mary II, 76
Thompson, Mary II, 77
Thompson, Mary II, 90
Thompson, Mary II, 97
Thompson, Mary II, 105
Thompson, Mary II, 106
Thompson, Mary II, 124
Thompson, Mary II, 126
Thompson, Mary II, 127
Thompson, Mary II, 128
Thompson, Mary II, 132
Thompson, Mary II, 138
Thompson, Mary II, 150
Thompson, Mary II, 159
Thompson, Mary II, 212
Thompson, Mary II, 267
Thompson, Mary II, 426
Thompson, Mary II, 427
Thompson, Mary II, 463
Thompson, Mary II, 551
Thompson, Mary II, 552
Thompson, Mary II, 667
Thompson, Mary II, 802
Thompson, Mary II, 816
Thompson, Mary II, 1062
Thompson, Mary III, 221
Thompson, Mary III, 249
Thompson, Mary III, 311
Thompson, Mary III, 312
Thompson, Mary III, 338
Thompson, Mary III, 370
Thompson, Mary IV, 62
Thompson, Mary IV, 111
Thompson, Mary IV, 131
Thompson, Mary IV, 133
Thompson, Mary IV, 291
Thompson, Mary IV, 292
Thompson, Mary IV, 293
Thompson, Mary IV, 761
Thompson, Mary IV, 777
Thompson, Mary IV, 1079
Thompson, Mary IV, 1083
Thompson, Mary IV, 1117
Thompson, Mary IV, 1129
Thompson, Mary IV, 1139
Thompson, Mary V, 131
Thompson, Mary V, 132
Thompson, Mary V, 142
Thompson, Mary V, 715
Thompson, Mary V, 872
Thompson, Mary V, 880
Thompson, Mary V, 887
Thompson, Mary VI, 415
Thompson, Mary VI, 451
Thompson, Mary VI, 593
Thompson, Mary VI, 606
Thompson, Mary VI, 694
Thompson, Mary VI, 714
Thompson, Mary VI, 944
Thompson, Mary VI, 957
Thompson, Mary VI, 1004
Thompson, Mary Adaline II, 823
Thompson, Mary Ann III, 311
Thompson, Mary Ann IV, 1079
Thompson, Mary Ann IV, 1082
Thompson, Mary Ann IV, 1083
Thompson, Mary B. II, 667
Thompson, Mary B. IV, 293
Thompson, Mary C. II, 138
Thompson, Mary C. II, 159
Thompson, Mary C. II, 1062
Thompson, Mary C. II, 1075
Thompson, Mary C. II, 1081
Thompson, Mary C. D. II, 135
Thompson, Mary Catharine IV, 217
Thompson, Mary Catharine IV, 293
Thompson, Mary D. II, 159
Thompson, Mary E. IV, 236
Thompson, Mary E. IV, 292
Thompson, Mary E. IV, 293
Thompson, Mary E. V, 362
Thompson, Mary E. VI, 786
Thompson, Mary E. VI, 1004
Thompson, Mary Elizabeth III, 156
Thompson, Mary Elizabeth III, 312
Thompson, Mary Elizabeth IV, 293
Thompson, Mary Elizabeth VI, 1022
Thompson, Mary Ella II, 703
Thompson, Mary Etta I, 950
Thompson, Mary Frances II, 823
Thompson, Mary Frances II, 925
Thompson, Mary Frances II, 929
Thompson, Mary H. III, 312
Thompson, Mary Harriett V, 715
Thompson, Mary I. II, 140
Thompson, Mary I. II, 929
Thompson, Mary J. II, 929
Thompson, Mary Jane II, 127
Thompson, Mary Jane II, 129
Thompson, Mary Jane II, 138
Thompson, Mary Jane II, 139
Thompson, Mary Jane II, 144
Thompson, Mary Joyce II, 823
Thompson, Mary L. VI, 973
Thompson, Mary Martha V, 715
Thompson, Mary N. II, 43
Thompson, Mary S. II, 44
Thompson, Mary S. III, 311
Thompson, Mary S. III, 312
Thompson, Mary Smart III, 312
Thompson, Mary Tacy IV, 293
Thompson, Mary W. II, 124
Thompson, Mary W. II, 125
Thompson, Mary Weaver VI, 786
Thompson, Mary Wistar II, 43
Thompson, Maryh II, 138
Thompson, Mathew VI, 859
Thompson, Matilda IV, 1083
Thompson, Matthew VI, 798
Thompson, Matthew VI, 859
Thompson, Matthew VI, 1004
Thompson, Mattie I, 424
Thompson, Mattie IV, 1265
Thompson, Maude III, 190
Thompson, Maude III, 312
Thompson, May V, 704
Thompson, May V, 715
Thompson, Maynard V, 715
Thompson, McClelland V, 715
Thompson, Melinda I, 398
Thompson, Melinda I, 423
Thompson, Mellicent II, 43
Thompson, Mildred IV, 293
Thompson, Miles G. VI, 786
Thompson, Milicent II, 77
Thompson, Milicent II, 106
Thompson, Millicent II, 77
Thompson, Milliscent II, 69
Thompson, Milliscent II, 105
Thompson, Millisent II, 44
Thompson, Minney Lea I, 424
Thompson, Minnie IV, 292
Thompson, Miriam VI, 714
Thompson, Miriam VI, 722
Thompson, Miriam VI, 723
Thompson, Mortimer VI, 714
Thompson, Mortimer VI, 722
Thompson, Mortimer VI, 723
Thompson, Mr. ??? IV, 777
Thompson, Mr. ??? VI, 695
Thompson, Mrs. ??? IV, 777
Thompson, Mrs. Allen IV, 293
Thompson, Mrs. Phebe A. III, 312
Thompson, Myrtle IV, 232
Thompson, Nancey VI, 1004
Thompson, Nancy I, 1024
Thompson, Nancy IV, 131
Thompson, Nancy V, 635
Thompson, Nancy V, 872
Thompson, Nancy V, 884
Thompson, Nancy V, 887
Thompson, Nancy VI, 512
Thompson, Nancy VI, 859
Thompson, Nancy Eayre VI, 786
Thompson, Naomi IV, 293
Thompson, Nathan IV, 1083
Thompson, Nathaniel II, 44
Thompson, Nathaniel IV, 62
Thompson, Nathaniel W. VI, 1004
Thompson, Nellie R. I, 934
Thompson, Nelson A. VI, 1004
Thompson, Noah A. V, 770
Thompson, Olive C. III, 312
Thompson, Ora L. I, 209
Thompson, Oscar IV, 293
Thompson, Oscar V, 362
Thompson, Oscar A. V, 715
Thompson, Pamelia H. II, 789
Thompson, Parmelia Henly II, 851
Thompson, Parmelia Henly II, 929
Thompson, Patsey VI, 859
Thompson, Patsy VI, 1004
Thompson, Paul IV, 293
Thompson, Pearl IV, 292
Thompson, Pearl VI, 382
Thompson, Peggy VI, 991
Thompson, Penelope Elizabeth I, 319
Thompson, Permilia VI, 1004
Thompson, Peter II, 131
Thompson, Peter II, 427
Thompson, Peter II, 667
Thompson, Peter II, 720
Thompson, Peter II, 770
Thompson, Peter II, 823
Thompson, Peter VI, 856
Thompson, Phebe I, 423
Thompson, Phebe I, 425
Thompson, Phebe I, 427
Thompson, Phebe II, 720
Thompson, Phebe II, 807
Thompson, Phebe II, 823
Thompson, Phebe II, 893
Thompson, Phebe II, 929
Thompson, Phebe II, 1032
Thompson, Phebe II, 1051
Thompson, Phebe II, 1062
Thompson, Phebe II, 1073
Thompson, Phebe II, 1081
Thompson, Phebe III, 312
Thompson, Phebe III, 492
Thompson, Phebe III, 500
Thompson, Phebe IV, 354
Thompson, Phebe IV, 1083
Thompson, Phebe A. III, 227
Thompson, Phebe A. III, 312
Thompson, Phebe A. III, 426
Thompson, Phebe A. III, 449
Thompson, Phebe Ellen IV, 337
Thompson, Phebe J. I, 424
Thompson, Phebe M. II, 1081
Thompson, Pleasant VI, 573
Thompson, Pleasant VI, 575
Thompson, Pleasant VI, 955
Thompson, Pleasy IV, 884
Thompson, Polly I, 298
Thompson, Polly I, 424
Thompson, Polly IV, 344
Thompson, Polly IV, 354
Thompson, Polly VI, 828
Thompson, Priscilla I, 423
Thompson, Prudence II, 43
Thompson, Prudence II, 72
Thompson, Prudence II, 105
Thompson, R. J. V, 1021
Thompson, Rachel II, 43
Thompson, Rachel II, 44
Thompson, Rachel II, 51
Thompson, Rachel II, 62
Thompson, Rachel II, 103
Thompson, Rachel II, 105
Thompson, Rachel II, 106
Thompson, Rachel II, 107
Thompson, Rachel II, 427
Thompson, Rachel II, 525
Thompson, Rachel II, 667
Thompson, Rachel II, 823
Thompson, Rachel IV, 292
Thompson, Rachel IV, 297
Thompson, Rachel IV, 660
Thompson, Rachel R. II, 929
Thompson, Ralph V, 715
Thompson, Ralph H. I, 262
Thompson, Ralph H., Jr. I, 262
Thompson, Raymond V, 872
Thompson, Reasin IV, 291
Thompson, Reazin IV, 293
Thompson, Rebeca II, 104
Thompson, Rebecca II, 20
Thompson, Rebecca II, 40
Thompson, Rebecca II, 43
Thompson, Rebecca II, 44
Thompson, Rebecca II, 49
Thompson, Rebecca II, 50
Thompson, Rebecca II, 73
Thompson, Rebecca II, 85
Thompson, Rebecca II, 98
Thompson, Rebecca II, 105
Thompson, Rebecca II, 106
Thompson, Rebecca II, 128
Thompson, Rebecca II, 134
Thompson, Rebecca II, 138
Thompson, Rebecca II, 144
Thompson, Rebecca II, 158
Thompson, Rebecca II, 159
Thompson, Rebecca II, 160
Thompson, Rebecca II, 311
Thompson, Rebecca II, 314
Thompson, Rebecca II, 324
Thompson, Rebecca II, 326
Thompson, Rebecca II, 427
Thompson, Rebecca II, 569
Thompson, Rebecca II, 580
Thompson, Rebecca II, 625
Thompson, Rebecca II, 645
Thompson, Rebecca II, 667
Thompson, Rebecca II, 668
Thompson, Rebecca II, 713
Thompson, Rebecca II, 1032
Thompson, Rebecca II, 1062
Thompson, Rebecca II, 1078
Thompson, Rebecca IV, 203
Thompson, Rebecca IV, 211
Thompson, Rebecca IV, 271
Thompson, Rebecca IV, 291
Thompson, Rebecca IV, 292
Thompson, Rebecca IV, 293
Thompson, Rebecca IV, 354
Thompson, Rebecca V, 647
Thompson, Rebecca VI, 849
Thompson, Rebecca VI, 859
Thompson, Rebecca B. II, 667
Thompson, Rebecca B. II, 721
Thompson, Rebecca Chalkley II, 427
Thompson, Rebecca Chalkley II, 580
Thompson, Rebecca Chalkley II, 667
Thompson, Rebecca I. II, 140
Thompson, Rebecca M. IV, 293
Thompson, Rebecca O. II, 770
Thompson, Rebecca Owen II, 667
Thompson, Rebecca W. II, 43
Thompson, Rebecca W. II, 124
Thompson, Rebecca W. II, 125
Thompson, Rebeccah II, 69
Thompson, Rebeccah II, 105
Thompson, Rebeck II, 91
Thompson, Rebeck II, 104
Thompson, Rebeckah II, 42
Thompson, Rebeckah II, 43
Thompson, Rebeckah II, 44
Thompson, Rebeckah II, 50
Thompson, Rebeckah II, 105
Thompson, Rebeckah VI, 582
Thompson, Rebekah II, 85
Thompson, Rebekah II, 105
Thompson, Rebekah II, 667
Thompson, Rebekah IV, 323
Thompson, Rebekah IV, 354
Thompson, Rebekah VI, 573
Thompson, Rezan IV, 62
Thompson, Rezin IV, 292
Thompson, Rhoda IV, 293
Thompson, Rhoda Hazelton VI, 786

mpson, Rhoda M. VI, 1004
mpson, Richard I, 1016
mpson, Richard I, 1024
mpson, Richard I, 1038
mpson, Richard I, 1142
mpson, Richard II, 43
mpson, Richard II, 106
mpson, Richard II, 138
mpson, Richard II, 159
mpson, Richard II, 585
mpson, Richard II, 668
mpson, Richard V, 132
mpson, Richard V, 811
mpson, Richard A. VI, 1004
mpson, Richard R. V, 1021
mpson, Robert I, 642
mpson, Robert II, 427
mpson, Robert II, 525
mpson, Robert II, 547
mpson, Robert II, 590
mpson, Robert II, 667
mpson, Robert IV, 1083
mpson, Robert V, 872
mpson, Robert V, 887
mpson, Robert B. IV, 293
mpson, Robert E. L. I, 642
mpson, Rosalie I, 627
mpson, Rosanna II, 1062
mpson, Rosanna II, 1081
mpson, Rose IV, 1008
mpson, Rosey Pearl I, 424
mpson, Rozen IV, 291
mpson, Ruanna IV, 393
mpson, Rufus I, 423
mpson, Rufus N. I, 424
mpson, Ruth I, 386
mpson, Ruth I, 423
mpson, Ruth II, 43
mpson, Ruth II, 52
mpson, Ruth II, 67
mpson, Ruth II, 106
mpson, Ruth II, 427
mpson, Ruth II, 667
mpson, Ruth IV, 188
mpson, Ruth IV, 291
mpson, Ruth IV, 292
mpson, Ruth V, 845
mpson, Ruth V, 872
mpson, Ruth V, 887
mpson, Ruth Anna IV, 292
mpson, Ruth Ella I, 937
mpson, Ruth Ella I, 950
mpson, Ruth Esther V, 661
mpson, Ruth Esther V, 715
mpson, Ruth Rogers III, 427
mpson, Ruth Rogers III, 449
mpson, S. III, 148
mpson, S. Grant I, 424
mpson, Sallie Taylor I, 950
mpson, Sallie Thompson I, 934
mpson, Sally I, 378
mpson, Sally I, 423
mpson, Sally V, 915
mpson, Sally VI, 913
mpson, Sally VI, 1004
mpson, Sally Ann IV, 236
mpson, Sally P. VI, 1004
mpson, Sam'l III, 148
mpson, Samuel I, 642
mpson, Samuel I, 934
mpson, Samuel II, 20
mpson, Samuel II, 43
mpson, Samuel II, 44
mpson, Samuel II, 105
mpson, Samuel II, 106
mpson, Samuel II, 107
mpson, Samuel II, 427
mpson, Samuel II, 668
mpson, Samuel III, 148
mpson, Samuel III, 311
mpson, Samuel III, 312
mpson, Samuel IV, 62
mpson, Samuel IV, 291
mpson, Samuel IV, 292
mpson, Samuel IV, 293
mpson, Samuel IV, 1079
mpson, Samuel IV, 1117
mpson, Samuel V, 132
mpson, Samuel V, 872
mpson, Samuel V, 887
ompson, Samuel VI, 573
ompson, Samuel VI, 859
ompson, Samuel B. V, 132
ompson, Samuel Brown I, 1024
ompson, Samuel H. I, 627
ompson, Samuel P. II, 667
ompson, Samuel S. III, 145
ompson, Samuel S. III, 211
ompson, Samuel S. III, 312
Thompson, Sara Lois I, 627
Thompson, Sarah I, 348
Thompson, Sarah I, 423
Thompson, Sarah I, 440
Thompson, Sarah I, 453
Thompson, Sarah I, 884
Thompson, Sarah I, 902
Thompson, Sarah I, 1038
Thompson, Sarah II, 36
Thompson, Sarah II, 42
Thompson, Sarah II, 43
Thompson, Sarah II, 44
Thompson, Sarah II, 45
Thompson, Sarah II, 67
Thompson, Sarah II, 69
Thompson, Sarah II, 76
Thompson, Sarah II, 92
Thompson, Sarah II, 95
Thompson, Sarah II, 103
Thompson, Sarah II, 104
Thompson, Sarah II, 105
Thompson, Sarah II, 106
Thompson, Sarah II, 109
Thompson, Sarah II, 118
Thompson, Sarah II, 124
Thompson, Sarah II, 129
Thompson, Sarah II, 138
Thompson, Sarah II, 139
Thompson, Sarah II, 148
Thompson, Sarah II, 158
Thompson, Sarah II, 314
Thompson, Sarah II, 426
Thompson, Sarah II, 427
Thompson, Sarah II, 547
Thompson, Sarah II, 590
Thompson, Sarah II, 592
Thompson, Sarah II, 613
Thompson, Sarah II, 627
Thompson, Sarah II, 667
Thompson, Sarah II, 785
Thompson, Sarah II, 823
Thompson, Sarah III, 213
Thompson, Sarah III, 214
Thompson, Sarah III, 311
Thompson, Sarah III, 312
Thompson, Sarah III, 338
Thompson, Sarah IV, 62
Thompson, Sarah IV, 177
Thompson, Sarah IV, 188
Thompson, Sarah IV, 208
Thompson, Sarah IV, 249
Thompson, Sarah IV, 260
Thompson, Sarah IV, 291
Thompson, Sarah IV, 292
Thompson, Sarah IV, 293
Thompson, Sarah V, 845
Thompson, Sarah V, 872
Thompson, Sarah V, 883
Thompson, Sarah V, 887
Thompson, Sarah VI, 500
Thompson, Sarah VI, 509
Thompson, Sarah VI, 573
Thompson, Sarah VI, 674
Thompson, Sarah VI, 714
Thompson, Sarah VI, 854
Thompson, Sarah VI, 856
Thompson, Sarah VI, 859
Thompson, Sarah VI, 1004
Thompson, Sarah A. II, 810
Thompson, Sarah A. VI, 859
Thompson, Sarah Ann IV, 211
Thompson, Sarah Ann IV, 291
Thompson, Sarah Ann IV, 292
Thompson, Sarah Ann IV, 1117
Thompson, Sarah Ann IV, 1137
Thompson, Sarah Ann IV, 1139
Thompson, Sarah Biddle II, 667
Thompson, Sarah Biddle II, 770
Thompson, Sarah D. VI, 1004
Thompson, Sarah E. I, 937
Thompson, Sarah E. I, 950
Thompson, Sarah E. II, 929
Thompson, Sarah E. V, 434
Thompson, Sarah E. VI, 991
Thompson, Sarah Eleanor VI, 573
Thompson, Sarah Eleanor VI, 578
Thompson, Sarah Elizabeth IV, 293
Thompson, Sarah L. II, 720
Thompson, Sarah Longstreth II, 770
Thompson, Sarah P. II, 138
Thompson, Sarah P. II, 139
Thompson, Sarah Piggott I, 454
Thompson, Sarah T. II, 144
Thompson, Sarah T. II, 159
Thompson, Scattergood II, 314
Thompson, Sicily VI, 988
Thompson, Sidney IV, 1340
Thompson, Sidney H. II, 827
Thompson, Silas M. I, 626
Thompson, Silas M. I, 627
Thompson, Silas Milton I, 642
Thompson, Simeon I, 423
Thompson, Sinah VI, 451
Thompson, Sinah VI, 454
Thompson, Sophia V, 142
Thompson, Sophia V, 567
Thompson, Sophia V, 602
Thompson, Sophronia E. I, 424
Thompson, Spencer M. I, 627
Thompson, Spotswood A. VI, 1004
Thompson, Stacy Snowden VI, 786
Thompson, Stephen I, 319
Thompson, Stephen IV, 292
Thompson, Susan I, 1038
Thompson, Susan II, 44
Thompson, Susan II, 133
Thompson, Susan II, 139
Thompson, Susan II, 427
Thompson, Susan II, 704
Thompson, Susan II, 720
Thompson, Susan IV, 1083
Thompson, Susan VI, 859
Thompson, Susan VI, 943
Thompson, Susan G. II, 119
Thompson, Susan G. II, 124
Thompson, Susan G. II, 150
Thompson, Susan G. II, 158
Thompson, Susan M. II, 585
Thompson, Susan M. II, 668
Thompson, Susan T. II, 720
Thompson, Susan T. II, 738
Thompson, Susan T. II, 770
Thompson, Susanna II, 453
Thompson, Susanna II, 667
Thompson, Susanna II, 885
Thompson, Susanna VI, 1004
Thompson, Susanna B. VI, 1004
Thompson, Susanna H. II, 929
Thompson, Susanna Kelly II, 929
Thompson, Susanna Morris II, 770
Thompson, Susannah I, 450
Thompson, Susannah I, 454
Thompson, Susannah I, 1024
Thompson, Susannah I, 1038
Thompson, Susannah II, 43
Thompson, Susannah II, 44
Thompson, Susannah II, 86
Thompson, Susannah II, 105
Thompson, Susannah II, 106
Thompson, Susannah II, 823
Thompson, Susannah V, 872
Thompson, Susannah V, 887
Thompson, Sydney IV, 1340
Thompson, Tabitha IV, 443
Thompson, Tabitha IV, 444
Thompson, Tabitha IV, 525
Thompson, Tabitha IV, 553
Thompson, Tabitha IV, 686
Thompson, Tacy IV, 224
Thompson, Tacy IV, 271
Thompson, Tacy IV, 291
Thompson, Tacy IV, 292
Thompson, Talitha II, 705
Thompson, Talitha IV, 281
Thompson, Talitha IV, 291
Thompson, Talitha IV, 534
Thompson, Telitha IV, 203
Thompson, Telitha IV, 292
Thompson, Temple I, 423
Thompson, Thekla IV, 1320
Thompson, Thelma I, 627
Thompson, Theron VI, 786
Thompson, Thomas I, 440
Thompson, Thomas I, 454
Thompson, Thomas II, 42
Thompson, Thomas II, 43
Thompson, Thomas II, 44
Thompson, Thomas II, 67
Thompson, Thomas II, 69
Thompson, Thomas II, 74
Thompson, Thomas II, 95
Thompson, Thomas II, 104
Thompson, Thomas II, 105
Thompson, Thomas II, 106
Thompson, Thomas II, 427
Thompson, Thomas II, 667
Thompson, Thomas III, 312
Thompson, Thomas V, 434
Thompson, Thomas VI, 931
Thompson, Thomas VI, 1004
Thompson, Thomas E. IV, 293
Thompson, Thomas Elwood IV, 292
Thompson, Thomas M. II, 139
Thompson, Thomas, Jr. II, 106
Thompson, Thos. II, 77
Thompson, Thos. II, 90
Thompson, Thos. II, 106
Thompson, Thos. V, 936
Thompson, Thos. E. IV, 236
Thompson, Thos. E. IV, 292
Thompson, Uldrich III, 153
Thompson, Uldrick III, 311
Thompson, Uldrick III, 312
Thompson, Vesper V, 647
Thompson, Viola IV, 292
Thompson, Viola R. IV, 293
Thompson, Virginia III, 342
Thompson, Virginia C. III, 312
Thompson, Virginia Grace I, 934
Thompson, Virginia Grace I, 950
Thompson, W. II, 106
Thompson, W. C. I, 950
Thompson, W. E. I, 642
Thompson, W. Jasper I, 262
Thompson, W. Jasper I, 424
Thompson, W. Jasper I, 1153
Thompson, W. Jasper I, 1162
Thompson, W. T. I, 626
Thompson, Waddy VI, 870
Thompson, Waddy VI, 973
Thompson, Waddy VI, 1004
Thompson, Walter IV, 1265
Thompson, Walter F. IV, 293
Thompson, Walter J. I, 627
Thompson, Wd. Edith II, 43
Thompson, Wd. Emma L. III, 145
Thompson, Wd. Mary II, 104
Thompson, Wd. Phebe II, 823
Thompson, Willard L. IV, 292
Thompson, William I, 366
Thompson, William I, 423
Thompson, William II, 42
Thompson, William II, 43
Thompson, William II, 44
Thompson, William II, 268
Thompson, William II, 314
Thompson, William II, 427
Thompson, William III, 24
Thompson, William III, 311
Thompson, William III, 312
Thompson, William III, 342
Thompson, William III, 369
Thompson, William IV, 291
Thompson, William IV, 292
Thompson, William IV, 293
Thompson, William V, 142
Thompson, William V, 284
Thompson, William V, 872
Thompson, William VI, 415
Thompson, William VI, 444
Thompson, William VI, 451
Thompson, William VI, 818
Thompson, William VI, 859
Thompson, William VI, 1001
Thompson, William VI, 1004
Thompson, William VI, 1022
Thompson, William A. II, 314
Thompson, William C. I, 934
Thompson, William Clarence I, 627
Thompson, William Ernest I, 627
Thompson, William Graser I, 950
Thompson, William H. II, 43
Thompson, William J. I, 423
Thompson, William Penn II, 823
Thompson, William W. III, 312
Thompson, William, Jr. IV, 293
Thompson, William, Jr. VI, 805
Thompson, William, Jr. VI, 818
Thompson, William, Jr. VI, 853
Thompson, William, Sr. IV, 293
Thompson, Winfred Huston I, 627
Thompson, Wm. I, 423
Thompson, Wm. II, 67
Thompson, Wm. II, 69
Thompson, Wm. II, 81
Thompson, Wm. II, 89
Thompson, Wm. II, 95
Thompson, Wm. II, 104
Thompson, Wm. II, 105
Thompson, Wm. II, 106
Thompson, Wm. II, 124
Thompson, Wm. II, 138
Thompson, Wm. II, 139
Thompson, Wm. II, 150
Thompson, Wm. II, 158
Thompson, Wm. II, 667
Thompson, Wm. II, 929
Thompson, Wm. II, 1062
Thompson, Wm. II, 1081
Thompson, Wm. III, 312
Thompson, Wm. IV, 232
Thompson, Wm. IV, 297
Thompson, Wm. IV, 1083
Thompson, Wm. V, 887
Thompson, Wm. VI, 955
Thompson, Wm. Albert IV, 293
Thompson, Wm. D. IV, 1083
Thompson, Wm. D. V, 362
Thompson, Wm. J. I, 424
Thompson, Wm. Jasper I, 424
Thompson, Wm. Jesse I, 424
Thompson, Wm. M. IV, 1083
Thompson, Wm., Jr. II, 60
Thompson, Wm., Jr. II, 105
Thompson, Wm., Jr. II, 124
Thompson, Wm., Sr. IV, 293
Thompson, Zilpah T. IV, 864
Thompson, Zilpah T. IV, 884
Thompson, Zilpha IV, 884
Thompson, Zolda IV, 884
Thoms, Mary Ann VI, 953
Thomson, ??? III, 312
Thomson, Ada V, 434
Thomson, Adam II, 468
Thomson, Adam II, 667
Thomson, Alma IV, 1296
Thomson, Anderson VI, 970
Thomson, Andrew II, 667
Thomson, Ann II, 540
Thomson, Ann II, 667
Thomson, Ann II, 1032
Thomson, Ann IV, 161
Thomson, Ann IV, 288
Thomson, Ann L. VI, 1004
Thomson, Benjamin II, 426
Thomson, Bradway IV, 161
Thomson, Bradway IV, 288
Thomson, Caroline II, 770
Thomson, Carrie V, 434
Thomson, Couzens IV, 161
Thomson, Daniel II, 427
Thomson, David Waddy, Jr. VI, 1004
Thomson, Dinah II, 233
Thomson, Dinah II, 267
Thomson, Edward II, 667
Thomson, Elisha IV, 1296
Thomson, Elizabeth I, 577
Thomson, Elizabeth II, 212
Thomson, Elizabeth II, 268
Thomson, Elizabeth II, 667
Thomson, Elizabeth IV, 1008
Thomson, Elizabeth H. II, 770
Thomson, Elizabeth W. II, 667
Thomson, Elmer H. V, 434
Thomson, Esther II, 106
Thomson, Esther II, 453
Thomson, Esther II, 667
Thomson, Gustava S. III, 94
Thomson, Hannah I, 431
Thomson, Hannah I, 577
Thomson, Hannah II, 105
Thomson, Hannah II, 465
Thomson, Hannah II, 667
Thomson, Hannah II, 770
Thomson, Hannah IV, 161
Thomson, Hannah V, 207
Thomson, Hannah V, 607
Thomson, Hannah V, 611
Thomson, Hannah V, 647
Thomson, Henry II, 233
Thomson, Hester II, 453
Thomson, Hugh II, 667
Thomson, Isaac I, 577
Thomson, Isaac I, 1016
Thomson, Isaac, Jr. V, 770
Thomson, Isabella III, 230
Thomson, Isabella III, 312
Thomson, J. B. IV, 1008
Thomson, James III, 230
Thomson, James M. V, 466
Thomson, Jane II, 667
Thomson, Jasper C. VI, 928
Thomson, Jesse L. VI, 1004
Thomson, Joanna V, 434
Thomson, John II, 426
Thomson, John II, 427
Thomson, John II, 448
Thomson, John II, 503
Thomson, John II, 667
Thomson, John II, 823
Thomson, John IV, 161
Thomson, John J. II, 770
Thomson, Jonah II, 668
Thomson, Jonah V, 872
Thomson, Joseph I, 577
Thomson, Joshua II, 667
Thomson, Keziah VI, 1004
Thomson, Louiza IV, 748
Thomson, Louiza IV, 777
Thomson, Lydia B. V, 132
Thomson, Maggie IV, 1008
Thomson, Margaretta II, 1081
Thomson, Margaretta II, 1082

Thomson, Martha II, 667
Thomson, Mary II, 427
Thomson, Mary II, 503
Thomson, Mary II, 667
Thomson, Mary III, 230
Thomson, Mary IV, 161
Thomson, Mary IV, 288
Thomson, Mary IV, 291
Thomson, Mary IV, 553
Thomson, Mary Adaline II, 823
Thomson, Mary B. II, 667
Thomson, N. A. VI, 942
Thomson, N. A. VI, 1001
Thomson, N. A. VI, 1014
Thomson, Nathaniel W. VI, 1004
Thomson, Nelson A. VI, 1020
Thomson, Peter II, 465
Thomson, Peter II, 503
Thomson, Peter II, 667
Thomson, Peter II, 720
Thomson, Peter II, 770
Thomson, Peter II, 772
Thomson, Phebe II, 1001
Thomson, Phebe II, 1032
Thomson, Rachel II, 427
Thomson, Reason IV, 161
Thomson, Rebecca II, 559
Thomson, Rebecca II, 667
Thomson, Rebecca IV, 1296
Thomson, Rebecca B. II, 667
Thomson, Rebecca B. II, 721
Thomson, Rebecca J. I, 735
Thomson, Rebecca O. II, 772
Thomson, Rebecca Owen II, 465
Thomson, Rebecca Owen II, 667
Thomson, Rhoda M. VI, 1004
Thomson, Richard I, 577
Thomson, Richard II, 159
Thomson, Richard A. VI, 1004
Thomson, Robert II, 427
Thomson, Robert II, 540
Thomson, Rosanna II, 1080
Thomson, Rosanna II, 1081
Thomson, Ruth V, 960
Thomson, Samuel IV, 161
Thomson, Samuel B. IV, 553
Thomson, Samuel P. II, 667
Thomson, Sarah I, 404
Thomson, Sarah I, 423
Thomson, Sarah II, 105
Thomson, Sarah II, 427
Thomson, Sarah II, 468
Thomson, Sarah II, 540
Thomson, Sarah II, 667
Thomson, Sarah II, 823
Thomson, Sarah IV, 161
Thomson, Sarah VI, 1004
Thomson, Sarah Ann IV, 1117
Thomson, Sarah Biddle II, 667
Thomson, Sarah Biddle II, 770
Thomson, Sarah Biddle II, 772
Thomson, Sarah D. VI, 1004
Thomson, Scattergood II, 314
Thomson, Sherman IV, 1296
Thomson, Susanna II, 667
Thomson, Tabitha IV, 553
Thomson, Thomas I, 577
Thomson, Thomas II, 667
Thomson, Thomas III, 312
Thomson, Thomas VI, 1004
Thomson, Waddy VI, 973
Thomson, William II, 427
Thomson, William VI, 859
Thomspson, Margaret IV, 193
Thomspson, Mary VI, 387
Thomspson, William VI, 387
Thonlow, Perry I, 642
Thoos, Christopher IV, 1340
Thoos, Christopher M. IV, 1340
Thoos, Margaret IV, 1340
Thoos, Margaret M. IV, 1340
Thorbury, Ruth V, 302
Thorn, ??? III, 312
Thorn, ??? IV, 1382
Thorn, Abigail III, 20
Thorn, Abigail III, 292
Thorn, Abigail III, 403
Thorn, Abraham III, 79
Thorn, Abraham III, 312
Thorn, Albert M. II, 930
Thorn, Albert Middleton II, 823
Thorn, Alfred V, 132
Thorn, Alfred M. V, 132
Thorn, Alfred M. V, 715
Thorn, Amy III, 33
Thorn, Amy III, 279
Thorn, Amy III, 302
Thorn, Amy III, 312
Thorn, Amy T. III, 302
Thorn, Ann III, 300
Thorn, Ann III, 312
Thorn, Ann III, 314
Thorn, Ann III, 449
Thorn, Ann IV, 210
Thorn, Ann IV, 293
Thorn, Ann V, 182
Thorn, Ann W. II, 806
Thorn, Anna III, 312
Thorn, Anna IV, 62
Thorn, Anna M. V, 132
Thorn, Anne III, 312
Thorn, Anthony II, 1033
Thorn, Benjamin II, 1033
Thorn, Benjamin V, 132
Thorn, Benjamin Harry II, 930
Thorn, Catharine IV, 293
Thorn, Catharine IV, 500
Thorn, Catherine IV, 62
Thorn, Catherine IV, 111
Thorn, Catherine V, 132
Thorn, Catherine V, 825
Thorn, Catherine V, 872
Thorn, Chalkey N. II, 771
Thorn, Chalkley II, 770
Thorn, Charity III, 312
Thorn, Charles III, 402
Thorn, Charles III, 449
Thorn, Charlotte S. II, 889
Thorn, Charlotte S. II, 930
Thorn, Charlotte Smith II, 805
Thorn, Charlotte T. III, 249
Thorn, Charlotte T. III, 313
Thorn, Chas. III, 449
Thorn, Chester III, 313
Thorn, Clark V, 960
Thorn, Cornelia III, 408
Thorn, Cornelia III, 449
Thorn, Cornelia V, 715
Thorn, Daniel III, 206
Thorn, Daniel III, 312
Thorn, Daniel III, 450
Thorn, Daniel Hill V, 362
Thorn, Daniel S. III, 115
Thorn, Daniel S. III, 312
Thorn, Diadamia II, 268
Thorn, Dorcas V, 132
Thorn, Edgar III, 313
Thorn, Edgar IV, 111
Thorn, Edith Ann II, 929
Thorn, Edward V, 962
Thorn, Edwin III, 249
Thorn, Edwin III, 313
Thorn, Elbert H. III, 408
Thorn, Elbert H. III, 449
Thorn, Elihu V, 207
Thorn, Elihu V, 960
Thorn, Elijah V, 207
Thorn, Elijah V, 960
Thorn, Eliz. III, 312
Thorn, Eliza III, 315
Thorn, Eliza V, 715
Thorn, Eliza F. III, 225
Thorn, Eliza F. III, 226
Thorn, Elizabeth II, 823
Thorn, Elizabeth II, 930
Thorn, Elizabeth III, 98
Thorn, Elizabeth III, 245
Thorn, Elizabeth III, 314
Thorn, Elizabeth III, 402
Thorn, Elizabeth III, 403
Thorn, Elizabeth III, 450
Thorn, Elizabeth IV, 62
Thorn, Elizabeth IV, 111
Thorn, Elizabeth IV, 161
Thorn, Elizabeth IV, 210
Thorn, Elizabeth IV, 293
Thorn, Elizabeth V, 132
Thorn, Elizabeth V, 207
Thorn, Elizabeth V, 574
Thorn, Elizabeth V, 602
Thorn, Elizabeth V, 715
Thorn, Elizabeth V, 960
Thorn, Elizabeth H. V, 602
Thorn, Elizabeth H. V, 961
Thorn, Emma II, 930
Thorn, Esther IV, 1296
Thorn, Esther V, 207
Thorn, Esther V, 960
Thorn, Ezra V, 132
Thorn, Freelove III, 124
Thorn, Freelove III, 313
Thorn, George III, 314
Thorn, Hannah II, 268
Thorn, Hannah III, 72
Thorn, Hannah III, 79
Thorn, Hannah III, 115
Thorn, Hannah III, 313
Thorn, Hannah III, 314
Thorn, Hannah III, 396
Thorn, Hannah III, 449
Thorn, Hannah III, 450
Thorn, Hannah IV, 62
Thorn, Hannah IV, 111
Thorn, Hannah IV, 113
Thorn, Hannah IV, 161
Thorn, Hannah IV, 210
Thorn, Hannah IV, 238
Thorn, Hannah IV, 293
Thorn, Hannah IV, 1296
Thorn, Hannah V, 182
Thorn, Hannah V, 207
Thorn, Hannah V, 955
Thorn, Hannah V, 960
Thorn, Hannah V, 962
Thorn, Hannah V, 978
Thorn, Hannah W. V, 959
Thorn, Hannah W. V, 960
Thorn, Hannah W. V, 961
Thorn, Isaac II, 889
Thorn, Isaac II, 930
Thorn, Isaac II, 1033
Thorn, Isaac III, 450
Thorn, Isaac IV, 62
Thorn, Isaac IV, 71
Thorn, Isaac IV, 111
Thorn, Isaac IV, 113
Thorn, Isaac IV, 161
Thorn, Isaac IV, 210
Thorn, Isaac IV, 238
Thorn, Isaac IV, 293
Thorn, Isaac V, 132
Thorn, Isaac V, 207
Thorn, Isaac V, 825
Thorn, Isaac V, 959
Thorn, Isaac V, 960
Thorn, Isaac V, 961
Thorn, Isaac V, 978
Thorn, Isaac G. V, 960
Thorn, Isaac Thomas IV, 1382
Thorn, Jacob III, 315
Thorn, James III, 115
Thorn, James III, 200
Thorn, James III, 313
Thorn, James III, 314
Thorn, James III, 402
Thorn, James III, 449
Thorn, James III, 450
Thorn, Jemima III, 450
Thorn, Jemima III, 452
Thorn, Joanna III, 313
Thorn, John III, 250
Thorn, John III, 313
Thorn, John III, 403
Thorn, John III, 449
Thorn, John IV, 293
Thorn, John V, 132
Thorn, John V, 715
Thorn, John V, 960
Thorn, John W. V, 715
Thorn, John Williams V, 960
Thorn, John, Jr. III, 313
Thorn, John, Jr. V, 132
Thorn, Jonathan III, 88
Thorn, Jonathan III, 124
Thorn, Jonathan III, 226
Thorn, Jonathan III, 313
Thorn, Jonathan III, 315
Thorn, Jordan III, 313
Thorn, Jos. III, 450
Thorn, Joseph II, 268
Thorn, Joseph III, 41
Thorn, Joseph III, 288
Thorn, Joseph III, 313
Thorn, Joseph III, 314
Thorn, Joseph III, 315
Thorn, Joseph, Jr. II, 929
Thorn, Lavinia II, 786
Thorn, Leonard III, 403
Thorn, Levi V, 960
Thorn, Linton III, 314
Thorn, Lucy M. V, 715
Thorn, Lydia III, 88
Thorn, Lydia A. III, 315
Thorn, Lydia Ann III, 313
Thorn, Margaret IV, 62
Thorn, Margaret IV, 111
Thorn, Margaret IV, 161
Thorn, Maria III, 449
Thorn, Maria III, 450
Thorn, Marmaduke Eale Phiany III, 449
Thorn, Martha III, 314
Thorn, Martha J. III, 450
Thorn, Martha Johanna III, 41
Thorn, Martha Johanna III, 313
Thorn, Martin M. IV, 1382
Thorn, Mary II, 889
Thorn, Mary II, 1033
Thorn, Mary III, 200
Thorn, Mary III, 250
Thorn, Mary III, 288
Thorn, Mary III, 313
Thorn, Mary III, 314
Thorn, Mary III, 344
Thorn, Mary III, 402
Thorn, Mary III, 449
Thorn, Mary III, 450
Thorn, Mary IV, 111
Thorn, Mary IV, 161
Thorn, Mary IV, 238
Thorn, Mary IV, 293
Thorn, Mary IV, 1382
Thorn, Mary V, 132
Thorn, Mary V, 715
Thorn, Mary V, 956
Thorn, Mary V, 960
Thorn, Mary Anna II, 1081
Thorn, Mary L. II, 1066
Thorn, Mary L. II, 1076
Thorn, Mary M. V, 132
Thorn, Mercy III, 313
Thorn, Nancy V, 960
Thorn, Nancy Maria V, 961
Thorn, Nancy Williams V, 960
Thorn, Nathan II, 929
Thorn, Nathan II, 930
Thorn, Nathaniel III, 314
Thorn, Oakleigh III, 313
Thorn, Ophelia III, 63
Thorn, Penelope III, 79
Thorn, Penelope III, 314
Thorn, Penelope III, 396
Thorn, Penelope III, 401
Thorn, Penelope III, 404
Thorn, Penelope III, 450
Thorn, Penelope III, 456
Thorn, Peter IV, 1382
Thorn, Peter M. IV, 660
Thorn, Phebe III, 20
Thorn, Phebe III, 313
Thorn, Phebe III, 314
Thorn, Phebe III, 315
Thorn, Phebe III, 401
Thorn, Phebe III, 449
Thorn, Phebe III, 450
Thorn, Phebe G. IV, 1362
Thorn, Phebe G. IV, 1382
Thorn, Phiany III, 402
Thorn, Rachel II, 929
Thorn, Rachel II, 930
Thorn, Rachel IV, 293
Thorn, Rachel IV, 303
Thorn, Rachel IV, 1296
Thorn, Rachel V, 132
Thorn, Rachel V, 207
Thorn, Rachel V, 284
Thorn, Rachel V, 488
Thorn, Rachel V, 534
Thorn, Rachel V, 953
Thorn, Rachel V, 954
Thorn, Rachel V, 960
Thorn, Rebecca II, 771
Thorn, Rebecca II, 929
Thorn, Rebecca III, 315
Thorn, Rebecca T. II, 721
Thorn, Ruth IV, 1362
Thorn, Ruth IV, 1382
Thorn, Ruth V, 132
Thorn, Ruth V, 241
Thorn, Ruth V, 284
Thorn, Ruth V, 955
Thorn, Ruth V, 956
Thorn, Ruth V, 960
Thorn, Samuel III, 115
Thorn, Samuel III, 300
Thorn, Samuel III, 313
Thorn, Samuel III, 314
Thorn, Samuel III, 449
Thorn, Samuel C. III, 450
Thorn, Samuel Collins II, 668
Thorn, Samuel Collins II, 770
Thorn, Sarah II, 53
Thorn, Sarah II, 106
Thorn, Sarah II, 771
Thorn, Sarah III, 115
Thorn, Sarah III, 206
Thorn, Sarah III, 313
Thorn, Sarah III, 403
Thorn, Sarah IV, 62
Thorn, Sarah IV, 111
Thorn, Sarah IV, 113
Thorn, Sarah IV, 293
Thorn, Sarah IV, 1296
Thorn, Sarah V, 87
Thorn, Sarah V, 132
Thorn, Sarah V, 207
Thorn, Sarah V, 825
Thorn, Sarah V, 954
Thorn, Sarah V, 960
Thorn, Sarah D. III, 115
Thorn, Sarah D. III, 312
Thorn, Sarah Emma V, 961
Thorn, Sarah, Jr. V, 207
Thorn, Stephen III, 312
Thorn, Stephen III, 402
Thorn, Stephen III, 403
Thorn, Stephen III, 450
Thorn, Stephen V, 132
Thorn, Stephen V, 715
Thorn, Stephen M. V, 132
Thorn, Susanah II, 1032
Thorn, Susannah II, 1032
Thorn, Susannah V, 715
Thorn, Tacy II, 268
Thorn, Tamar V, 336
Thorn, Tamar V, 362
Thorn, Tamer V, 960
Thorn, Thamar V, 953
Thorn, Thomas II, 770
Thorn, Thomas III, 20
Thorn, Thomas III, 79
Thorn, Thomas III, 98
Thorn, Thomas III, 245
Thorn, Thomas III, 313
Thorn, Thomas III, 396
Thorn, Thomas III, 401
Thorn, Thomas III, 404
Thorn, Thomas III, 449
Thorn, Thomas III, 450
Thorn, Thomas IV, 62
Thorn, Thomas IV, 111
Thorn, Thomas IV, 161
Thorn, Thomas IV, 293
Thorn, Thomas V, 182
Thorn, Thomas V, 207
Thorn, Thomas V, 241
Thorn, Thomas V, 284
Thorn, Thomas V, 953
Thorn, Thomas V, 955
Thorn, Thomas V, 960
Thorn, Thomas P. III, 313
Thorn, Thos. IV, 210
Thorn, Thos. V, 956
Thorn, Thos. V, 960
Thorn, Wd. Sarah III, 314
Thorn, Webster IV, 1362
Thorn, Webster IV, 1382
Thorn, William III, 313
Thorn, William III, 314
Thorn, William III, 315
Thorn, William III, 450
Thorn, William III, 452
Thorn, William IV, 62
Thorn, William IV, 111
Thorn, William IV, 293
Thorn, William V, 207
Thorn, William V, 284
Thorn, William V, 488
Thorn, William V, 534
Thorn, William V, 602
Thorn, William V, 960
Thorn, William P. V, 960
Thorn, Wm. IV, 161
Thorn, Wm. V, 207
Thorn, Wm. V, 574
Thorn, Wm. V, 953
Thorn, Wm. V, 954
Thorn, Wm. V, 960
Thorn, Wm. V, 961
Thorn, Wm. V, 962
Thorn, Wm. F. V, 960
Thorn, Wm. H. III, 63
Thorn, Woodbridge III, 315
Thornberry, Abel V, 284
Thornberry, Abel V, 285
Thornberry, Abel V, 466
Thornberry, Abel V, 602
Thornberry, Abigail V, 535
Thornberry, Ann I, 690
Thornberry, Isaac I, 681
Thornberry, Isaac I, 690
Thornberry, Jane Thomas Judith V, 535
Thornberry, Jemimah V, 535
Thornberry, Jemimah V, 602
Thornberry, Joel V, 535
Thornberry, Joseph I, 690
Thornberry, Judith V, 535
Thornberry, Lydia V, 602
Thornberry, Martha I, 682
Thornberry, Martha I, 690
Thornberry, Mary IV, 500
Thornberry, Mary A. IV, 848
Thornberry, Mary A. V, 232
Thornberry, Mary A. V, 284
Thornberry, Mary Ann V, 588
Thornberry, Mary Ann V, 602
Thornberry, Nathan V, 602
Thornberry, Rachel V, 602
Thornberry, Rebecca V, 602
Thornberry, Rebeccah I, 681
Thornberry, Rebeccah I, 690
Thornberry, Rhoda IV, 500
Thornberry, Rhoda V, 284
Thornberry, Rhoda V, 602

ıberry, Rhoda D. IV, 848
ıberry, Richard V, 535
ıberry, Risher W. IV, 500
ıberry, Shadrick V, 535
nberry, Susanna V, 602
nberry, Susannah J. V, 602
ıberry, Thomas V, 535
nberry, William I, 690
nberry, William V, 232
nberry, William V, 602
nberry, William J. IV, 500
nberry, William J. V, 284
nberry, William J. V, 285
nberry, William J. V, 602
nberry, Wm. G. V, 602
nberry, Wm. J. IV, 848
nberry, Wm. J. V, 602
nborough, Abel V, 602
nborough, Abraham VI, 452
nborough, Ann I, 870
nborough, Ann I, 902
rnborough, Ann V, 445
rnborough, Ann V, 447
rnborough, Ann V, 448
rnborough, Edward IV, 448
rnborough, Edward V, 447
rnborough, Elizabeth I, 771
rnborough, Elizabeth I, 1013
rnborough, Elizabeth V, 132
rnborough, Elizabeth V, 446
rnborough, Elizabeth V, 447
rnborough, Eunice V, 132
rnborough, Hannah I, 1013
rnborough, Hannah V, 132
rnborough, Henry V, 132
rnborough, Isaac, Jr. V, 447
rnborough, James I, 542
rnborough, James I, 578
rnborough, Jane I, 1013
ornborough, Joab V, 446
ornborough, Joab V, 447
ornborough, John I, 578
ornborough, John V, 132
ornborough, Joseph I, 969
ornborough, Joseph I, 1101
ornborough, Joseph V, 447
ornborough, Joseph, Jr. I, 578
ornborough, Lydia I, 1013
ornborough, Lydia V, 602
ornborough, Mallachi I, 542
ornborough, Margaret I, 1013
ornborough, Margaret V, 447
ornborough, Milton V, 132
ornborough, Morgin I, 969
ornborough, Nathan V, 447
ornborough, Nathan V, 448
ornborough, Norton I, 771
ornborough, Rachel I, 424
ornborough, Rachel I, 959
ornborough, Rachel V, 446
ornborough, Rebecca I, 1101
ornborough, Rebecca V, 132
ornborough, Rebecca V, 166
ornborough, Rebecca V, 207
hornborough, Rhoda V, 505
hornborough, Rhoda V, 535
hornborough, Rhoda V, 602
hornborough, Richard I, 578
hornborough, Sarah I, 741
hornborough, Sarah I, 1013
hornborough, William I, 902
hornborough, William I, 959
hornborough, William I, 969
hornborough, William I, 1101
hornbourgh, Phebe I, 735
hornbroug, Rebeckah I, 578
hornbrough, Abel V, 284
hornbrough, Abigail I, 577
hornbrough, Abigail I, 793
hornbrough, Abraham VI, 451
hornbrough, Abraham VI, 452
Thornbrough, Achsa I, 902
Thornbrough, Achsah I, 874
Thornbrough, Albanah VI, 451
Thornbrough, Alexander V, 284
Thornbrough, Amos VI, 452
Thornbrough, Ann I, 578
Thornbrough, Ann I, 690
Thornbrough, Ann I, 793
Thornbrough, Ann I, 902
Thornbrough, Ann V, 132
Thornbrough, Ann V, 284
Thornbrough, Ann V, 447
Thornbrough, Ann VI, 451
Thornbrough, Anna Jessop I, 578
Thornbrough, Anna Jessop I, 582
Thornbrough, Asahel I, 793
Thornbrough, Benjamin VI, 362
Thornbrough, Benjamin VI, 384
Thornbrough, Benjamin VI, 451
Thornbrough, Benjamin, Jr. VI, 452
Thornbrough, Benjamin, Sr. VI, 452
Thornbrough, Charity I, 793
Thornbrough, Charity I, 902
Thornbrough, Charity I, 969
Thornbrough, Charity VI, 452
Thornbrough, Daniel I, 547
Thornbrough, Daniel I, 578
Thornbrough, Edward I, 578
Thornbrough, Edward I, 902
Thornbrough, Edward I Sup 1, 9
Thornbrough, Edward IV, 414
Thornbrough, Edward IV, 448
Thornbrough, Edward V, 132
Thornbrough, Edward V, 284
Thornbrough, Elizabeth I, 577
Thornbrough, Elizabeth I, 669
Thornbrough, Elizabeth I, 706
Thornbrough, Elizabeth I, 771
Thornbrough, Elizabeth I, 829
Thornbrough, Elizabeth I, 841
Thornbrough, Elizabeth I, 847
Thornbrough, Elizabeth I, 902
Thornbrough, Elizabeth I, 969
Thornbrough, Elizabeth I, 1009
Thornbrough, Elizabeth I, 1013
Thornbrough, Elizabeth IV, 414
Thornbrough, Elizabeth IV, 448
Thornbrough, Elizabeth V, 221
Thornbrough, Elizabeth V, 284
Thornbrough, Elizabeth VI, 362
Thornbrough, Elizabeth VI, 451
Thornbrough, George I, 657
Thornbrough, George I, 669
Thornbrough, George I, 685
Thornbrough, George I, 690
Thornbrough, George I, 969
Thornbrough, Hannah I, 671
Thornbrough, Hannah I, 793
Thornbrough, Hannah I, 796
Thornbrough, Hannah I, 841
Thornbrough, Hannah I, 1013
Thornbrough, Hannah V, 132
Thornbrough, Hannah VI, 452
Thornbrough, Henry I, 793
Thornbrough, Henry I, 841
Thornbrough, Henry I, 902
Thornbrough, Henry I, 969
Thornbrough, Henry I, 1101
Thornbrough, Henry, Jr. I, 969
Thornbrough, Isaac I, 690
Thornbrough, Isaac V, 284
Thornbrough, Isaac V, 362
Thornbrough, Isaac Edward V, 284
Thornbrough, Jacob V, 132
Thornbrough, Jane I, 793
Thornbrough, Jane I, 969
Thornbrough, Jane V, 132
Thornbrough, Jane V, 244
Thornbrough, Jane V, 284
Thornbrough, Joab V, 284
Thornbrough, Job V, 284
Thornbrough, Joel I, 578
Thornbrough, Joel I, 582
Thornbrough, Joel VI, 452
Thornbrough, John I, 969
Thornbrough, John V, 221
Thornbrough, John V, 284
Thornbrough, John V, 319
Thornbrough, John V, 362
Thornbrough, John V, 443
Thornbrough, Joseph I, 577
Thornbrough, Joseph I, 690
Thornbrough, Joseph I, 793
Thornbrough, Joseph I, 902
Thornbrough, Joseph I, 969
Thornbrough, Joseph I, 1013
Thornbrough, Joseph IV, 448
Thornbrough, Joseph V, 132
Thornbrough, Joseph V, 252
Thornbrough, Joseph V, 284
Thornbrough, Judith VI, 451
Thornbrough, Keziah V, 132
Thornbrough, Lourath I, 793
Thornbrough, Lowery I, 902
Thornbrough, Lowery I, 969
Thornbrough, Lydia V, 252
Thornbrough, Margaret I, 547
Thornbrough, Margaret V, 284
Thornbrough, Margaret V, 447
Thornbrough, Margret I, 793
Thornbrough, Martha I, 578
Thornbrough, Martha I, 690
Thornbrough, Mary I, 577
Thornbrough, Mary I, 669
Thornbrough, Mary I, 685
Thornbrough, Mary I, 690
Thornbrough, Mary I, 793
Thornbrough, Mary I, 873
Thornbrough, Mary I, 902
Thornbrough, Mary V, 132
Thornbrough, Mary VI, 362
Thornbrough, Mary VI, 451
Thornbrough, Miriam I, 690
Thornbrough, Miriam I, 692
Thornbrough, Miriam I, 706
Thornbrough, Morgan I, 793
Thornbrough, Morgin I, 969
Thornbrough, Nathan I, 771
Thornbrough, Nathan V, 132
Thornbrough, Norton I, 771
Thornbrough, Phebe V, 132
Thornbrough, Phebe V, 244
Thornbrough, Phebe V, 284
Thornbrough, Phebe VI, 451
Thornbrough, Rachel I, 657
Thornbrough, Rachel I, 793
Thornbrough, Rachel I, 841
Thornbrough, Rachel I, 902
Thornbrough, Rachel I, 969
Thornbrough, Rachel I, 1101
Thornbrough, Rachel IV, 448
Thornbrough, Rachel V, 221
Thornbrough, Rachel V, 284
Thornbrough, Rebecca I, 793
Thornbrough, Rebecca I, 841
Thornbrough, Rebecca V, 284
Thornbrough, Rebecca V, 362
Thornbrough, Rebeccah I, 690
Thornbrough, Richard I, 793
Thornbrough, Richard I, 902
Thornbrough, Richard I, 969
Thornbrough, Robert II, 668
Thornbrough, Ruth I, 690
Thornbrough, Ruth I, 706
Thornbrough, Saphira I, 793
Thornbrough, Sarah I, 669
Thornbrough, Sarah I, 706
Thornbrough, Sarah I, 771
Thornbrough, Sarah II, 668
Thornbrough, Sarah VI, 384
Thornbrough, Sarah VI, 451
Thornbrough, Sophir I, 902
Thornbrough, Sophir I, 969
Thornbrough, Susannah I, 873
Thornbrough, Susannah I, 902
Thornbrough, Susannah V, 284
Thornbrough, Susannah V, 319
Thornbrough, Susannah V, 362
Thornbrough, Thomas I, 690
Thornbrough, Thomas I, 692
Thornbrough, Thomas I, 706
Thornbrough, Thomas II, 668
Thornbrough, Thomas VI, 451
Thornbrough, Thomas, Sr. I, 706
Thornbrough, Walter I, 793
Thornbrough, Walter I, 969
Thornbrough, Walter I, 1101
Thornbrough, Wellmett I, 793
Thornbrough, William I, 669
Thornbrough, William I, 690
Thornbrough, William I, 735
Thornbrough, William I, 902
Thornbrough, William I, 969
Thornbrough, William I, 1132
Thornbrough, William VI, 451
Thornbrough, William VI, 452
Thornbrough, Winslow I, 706
Thornbrug, Ann I, 518
Thornbrug, Edward I, 518
Thornbrug, Elizabeth I, 518
Thornbrug, Jacob I, 518
Thornbrug, Jane I, 518
Thornbrug, Joseph I, 518
Thornbrug, Margaret I, 518
Thornbrug, Nathan I, 518
Thornbrug, Phebe I, 518
Thornbrug, Sarah I, 518
Thornbrug, Thomas I, 577
Thornbrug, Thomas, III I, 578
Thornbrugh, Abigail I, 503
Thornbrugh, Abigail I, 518
Thornbrugh, Abigail I, 519
Thornbrugh, Abigail I, 528
Thornbrugh, Abigail I, 572
Thornbrugh, Abigail I, 577
Thornbrugh, Abigail I, 578
Thornbrugh, Abraham VI, 383
Thornbrugh, Albanah VI, 383
Thornbrugh, Ann I, 518
Thornbrugh, Ann I, 519
Thornbrugh, Ann I, 547
Thornbrugh, Ann I, 577
Thornbrugh, Ann I, 578
Thornbrugh, Ann VI, 451
Thornbrugh, Anna I, 579
Thornbrugh, Anna Jessop I, 578
Thornbrugh, Anne J. I, 579
Thornbrugh, Asael I, 518
Thornbrugh, Ballinger I, 578
Thornbrugh, Benjamin I, 519
Thornbrugh, Benjamin I, 578
Thornbrugh, Benjamin VI, 405
Thornbrugh, Benjamin VI, 451
Thornbrugh, Daniel I, 578
Thornbrugh, Edward I, 518
Thornbrugh, Edward I, 519
Thornbrugh, Edward I, 577
Thornbrugh, Edward I, 578
Thornbrugh, Edward I, 584
Thornbrugh, Edward I, 902
Thornbrugh, Elizabeth I, 518
Thornbrugh, Elizabeth I, 519
Thornbrugh, Elizabeth I, 546
Thornbrugh, Elizabeth I, 572
Thornbrugh, Elizabeth I, 577
Thornbrugh, Elizabeth I, 578
Thornbrugh, Elizabeth I, 793
Thornbrugh, Elizabeth I, 841
Thornbrugh, Elizabeth I, 865
Thornbrugh, Elizabeth I, 902
Thornbrugh, George I, 518
Thornbrugh, Grace I, 579
Thornbrugh, Hannah I, 518
Thornbrugh, Hannah I, 519
Thornbrugh, Hannah I, 578
Thornbrugh, Hannah I, 841
Thornbrugh, Hannah I, 865
Thornbrugh, Henry I, 518
Thornbrugh, Henry I, 519
Thornbrugh, Henry I, 552
Thornbrugh, Henry I, 563
Thornbrugh, Henry I, 572
Thornbrugh, Henry I, 577
Thornbrugh, Henry I, 773
Thornbrugh, Henry I, 841
Thornbrugh, Henry I, 1133
Thornbrugh, Isaac I, 518
Thornbrugh, Isaac I, 519
Thornbrugh, Isaac I, 578
Thornbrugh, Isaac I, 579
Thornbrugh, James I, 518
Thornbrugh, James I, 519
Thornbrugh, James I, 563
Thornbrugh, James I, 577
Thornbrugh, James I, 578
Thornbrugh, James I, 579
Thornbrugh, James I, 971
Thornbrugh, James I, 1053
Thornbrugh, Jane I, 518
Thornbrugh, Jane I, 519
Thornbrugh, Jane I, 560
Thornbrugh, Jane I, 577
Thornbrugh, Jane I, 793
Thornbrugh, Jane I, 841
Thornbrugh, Jane I, 865
Thornbrugh, Jeane I, 518
Thornbrugh, Jemima I, 540
Thornbrugh, Joel I, 519
Thornbrugh, Joel I, 578
Thornbrugh, John I, 518
Thornbrugh, John I, 519
Thornbrugh, John I, 578
Thornbrugh, Joseph I, 519
Thornbrugh, Joseph I, 526
Thornbrugh, Joseph I, 563
Thornbrugh, Joseph I, 577
Thornbrugh, Joseph I, 578
Thornbrugh, Joseph I, 579
Thornbrugh, Joseph I, 773
Thornbrugh, Joseph I, 793
Thornbrugh, Joseph I, 841
Thornbrugh, Joseph I, 865
Thornbrugh, Joseph, Jr. I, 578
Thornbrugh, Joseph, Jr. I, 1133
Thornbrugh, Joshua I, 519
Thornbrugh, Judeth I, 578
Thornbrugh, Judith I, 519
Thornbrugh, Judith I, 572
Thornbrugh, Judith I, 578
Thornbrugh, Judith I, 579
Thornbrugh, Judith Unthank I, 578
Thornbrugh, Kezia I, 578
Thornbrugh, Kezia I, 584
Thornbrugh, Keziah I, 578
Thornbrugh, Lowry I, 518
Thornbrugh, Lydda I, 519
Thornbrugh, Lydia I, 578
Thornbrugh, Lydia I, 582
Thornbrugh, Lydia I, 865
Thornbrugh, Mahala I, 608
Thornbrugh, Mallachi I, 578
Thornbrugh, Margaret I, 518
Thornbrugh, Margaret I, 519
Thornbrugh, Margaret I, 530
Thornbrugh, Margaret I, 544
Thornbrugh, Margaret I, 577
Thornbrugh, Margaret I, 578
Thornbrugh, Margaret I, 793
Thornbrugh, Margaret I, 1104
Thornbrugh, Margret I, 841
Thornbrugh, Margret I, 865
Thornbrugh, Martha I, 519
Thornbrugh, Martha I, 524
Thornbrugh, Martha I, 531
Thornbrugh, Martha I, 572
Thornbrugh, Martha I, 577
Thornbrugh, Martha I, 578
Thornbrugh, Mary I, 518
Thornbrugh, Mary I, 519
Thornbrugh, Mary I, 523
Thornbrugh, Mary I, 545
Thornbrugh, Mary I, 563
Thornbrugh, Mary I, 577
Thornbrugh, Mary I, 578
Thornbrugh, Mary I, 793
Thornbrugh, Mary I, 817
Thornbrugh, Mary I, 841
Thornbrugh, Mary I, 865
Thornbrugh, Mary Ann I, 519
Thornbrugh, Miriam I, 695
Thornbrugh, Miriam I, 700
Thornbrugh, Morgan I, 1133
Thornbrugh, Nancy I, 519
Thornbrugh, Nancy I, 579
Thornbrugh, Nathan I, 519
Thornbrugh, Phebe I, 572
Thornbrugh, Phebe I, 578
Thornbrugh, Prudence I, 503
Thornbrugh, Prudence I, 519
Thornbrugh, Prudence I, 550
Thornbrugh, Prudence I, 578
Thornbrugh, Prudence Hunt I, 519
Thornbrugh, Rachel I, 518
Thornbrugh, Rachel I, 519
Thornbrugh, Rachel I, 561
Thornbrugh, Rachel I, 563
Thornbrugh, Rachel I, 577
Thornbrugh, Rachel I, 578
Thornbrugh, Rachel I, 773
Thornbrugh, Rachel I, 835
Thornbrugh, Rachel I, 841
Thornbrugh, Rachel I, 1133
Thornbrugh, Rebecca I, 552
Thornbrugh, Rebecca I, 578
Thornbrugh, Rebecca I, 841
Thornbrugh, Rebeccah I, 578
Thornbrugh, Rebeckah I, 578
Thornbrugh, Rebekah I, 1132
Thornbrugh, Richard I, 518
Thornbrugh, Richard I, 519
Thornbrugh, Richard I, 572
Thornbrugh, Richard I, 578
Thornbrugh, Richard I, 841
Thornbrugh, Richard I, 1133
Thornbrugh, Ruth I, 519
Thornbrugh, Ruth I, 549
Thornbrugh, Ruth I, 553
Thornbrugh, Ruth I, 577
Thornbrugh, Ruth I, 578
Thornbrugh, Samuel I, 519
Thornbrugh, Sarah I, 519
Thornbrugh, Sarah I, 548
Thornbrugh, Sarah I, 578
Thornbrugh, Sarah I, 735
Thornbrugh, Sarah I, 865
Thornbrugh, Sarah VI, 405
Thornbrugh, Sarah VI, 451
Thornbrugh, Stephen I, 540
Thornbrugh, Susanah I, 519
Thornbrugh, Susanna I, 578
Thornbrugh, Susanna I, 793
Thornbrugh, Susanna I, 841
Thornbrugh, Susannah I, 519
Thornbrugh, Susannah I, 575
Thornbrugh, Susannah I, 577
Thornbrugh, Susannah I, 865
Thornbrugh, Thomas I, 424
Thornbrugh, Thomas I, 503
Thornbrugh, Thomas I, 518
Thornbrugh, Thomas I, 519
Thornbrugh, Thomas I, 528
Thornbrugh, Thomas I, 549
Thornbrugh, Thomas I, 572
Thornbrugh, Thomas I, 577
Thornbrugh, Thomas I, 578
Thornbrugh, Thomas I, 579
Thornbrugh, Thomas I, 695
Thornbrugh, Thomas I, 700
Thornbrugh, Thomas I, 735
Thornbrugh, Thomas I, 841
Thornbrugh, Thomas I, 1133
Thornbrugh, Thomas, III I, 578
Thornbrugh, Thomas, Jr. I, 540
Thornbrugh, Thomas, Jr. I, 578
Thornbrugh, Thos. I, 487
Thornbrugh, Thos. I, 519
Thornbrugh, Thos. I, 577
Thornbrugh, Thos., Jr. I, 524

Thornbrugh, Thos., Jr. I, 577
Thornbrugh, Thos., Sr. I, 572
Thornbrugh, Thos., Sr. I, 578
Thornbrugh, Walter I, 518
Thornbrugh, Walter I, 523
Thornbrugh, Walter I, 577
Thornbrugh, Walter I, 578
Thornbrugh, Walter I, 841
Thornbrugh, Walter I, 865
Thornbrugh, Walter I, 1133
Thornbrugh, Welmet I, 519
Thornbrugh, Welmet I, 526
Thornbrugh, Welmet I, 577
Thornbrugh, Widow Martha I, 578
Thornbrugh, Widow Rebeckah I, 563
Thornbrugh, William I, 424
Thornbrugh, William I, 519
Thornbrugh, William I, 563
Thornbrugh, William I, 578
Thornbrugh, William I, 579
Thornbrugh, William I, 582
Thornbrugh, William I, 735
Thornbrugh, William I, 793
Thornbrugh, William I, 841
Thornbrugh, William I, 865
Thornbrugh, Winslow I, 735
Thornburg, Aaron Carson I, 950
Thornburg, Abel V, 285
Thornburg, Abel V, 602
Thornburg, Adda V, 362
Thornburg, Addie V, 285
Thornburg, Albena IV, 62
Thornburg, Allie V, 362
Thornburg, Alonzo V, 647
Thornburg, Alonzo E. V, 278
Thornburg, Alonzo E. V, 647
Thornburg, America V, 285
Thornburg, Ann I, 424
Thornburg, Ann I, 552
Thornburg, Ann I, 578
Thornburg, Ann V, 285
Thornburg, Ann V, 293
Thornburg, Ann V, 468
Thornburg, Ann V, 978
Thornburg, Anna I, 579
Thornburg, Annie Ethel V, 285
Thornburg, Benjamin IV, 62
Thornburg, Benjamin VI, 371
Thornburg, Carrie M. V, 285
Thornburg, Carrie M. V, 715
Thornburg, Catharine I, 750
Thornburg, Charity VI, 414
Thornburg, Charity VI, 452
Thornburg, Charles H. V, 285
Thornburg, Christopher V, 362
Thornburg, Clarence V, 285
Thornburg, Clarence V, 362
Thornburg, Clarence E. V, 285
Thornburg, Clinton V, 285
Thornburg, Cyrus V, 362
Thornburg, Dinah V, 535
Thornburg, Dinah V, 647
Thornburg, Dinah V, 978
Thornburg, Dinah P. V, 979
Thornburg, Dosha D. V, 647
Thornburg, Dosha Dinah V, 647
Thornburg, Edward IV, 62
Thornburg, Edward V, 282
Thornburg, Edward V, 285
Thornburg, Edward V, 362
Thornburg, Eli V, 535
Thornburg, Eli V, 978
Thornburg, Eli V, 979
Thornburg, Elizabeth I, 1013
Thornburg, Elizabeth V, 266
Thornburg, Elizabeth V, 284
Thornburg, Elizabeth V, 362
Thornburg, Elizabeth V, 393
Thornburg, Elizabeth V, 434
Thornburg, Emmazetta V, 535
Thornburg, Frances E. V, 285
Thornburg, Frances E. V, 362
Thornburg, George I, 750
Thornburg, Hannah I, 1013
Thornburg, Hannah V, 362
Thornburg, Hannah VI, 415
Thornburg, Hannah VI, 452
Thornburg, Hannah W. V, 285
Thornburg, Hannah W. V, 362
Thornburg, Hariet E. V, 285
Thornburg, Harriet E. V, 285
Thornburg, Harriet E. V, 362
Thornburg, Harriet M. V, 282
Thornburg, Herbert V, 285
Thornburg, Howard Paul V, 285
Thornburg, Imogene V, 285
Thornburg, Isaac I, 579
Thornburg, Isaac V, 362
Thornburg, Isaac N. V, 285
Thornburg, Jacob V, 132
Thornburg, Jacob V, 285
Thornburg, Jacob V, 311
Thornburg, James I, 579
Thornburg, James Brooks V, 978
Thornburg, James Brooks V, 979
Thornburg, Jamimy V, 978
Thornburg, Jane I, 1013
Thornburg, Jane W. V, 362
Thornburg, Jemima V, 978
Thornburg, Jemima Ann V, 535
Thornburg, Jesse V, 285
Thornburg, Jesse V, 362
Thornburg, Joel I, 578
Thornburg, Joel V, 132
Thornburg, Joel V, 311
Thornburg, Joel V, 535
Thornburg, Joel V, 647
Thornburg, Joel Thomas V, 647
Thornburg, Joel Thos. V, 647
Thornburg, John V, 362
Thornburg, John Milton V, 285
Thornburg, John Milton V, 362
Thornburg, John W. V, 362
Thornburg, Joseph I, 375
Thornburg, Joseph I, 424
Thornburg, Joseph I, 579
Thornburg, Joseph I, 1013
Thornburg, Joseph V, 311
Thornburg, Josiah V, 1022
Thornburg, Judeth I, 578
Thornburg, Judith M. V, 647
Thornburg, Judith Mary V, 647
Thornburg, Keziah I, 578
Thornburg, Lamar V, 362
Thornburg, Lewis V, 362
Thornburg, Lydia I, 1013
Thornburg, Lydia V, 132
Thornburg, Lydia V, 311
Thornburg, Lydia V, 362
Thornburg, Lydia V, 468
Thornburg, Lydia A. V, 285
Thornburg, Lydia A. V, 362
Thornburg, Lydia J. V, 362
Thornburg, Mahala I, 608
Thornburg, Malinda V, 249
Thornburg, Malissa Jane V, 643
Thornburg, Malissa Jane V, 647
Thornburg, Margaret I, 1013
Thornburg, Mariam I, 735
Thornburg, Marium I, 735
Thornburg, Martha V, 534
Thornburg, Marvin V, 285
Thornburg, Marvin V, 362
Thornburg, Mary I, 566
Thornburg, Mary I, 578
Thornburg, Mary IV, 62
Thornburg, Mary VI, 371
Thornburg, Mary A. V, 285
Thornburg, Mary Ann V, 222
Thornburg, Mary Ann V, 285
Thornburg, Mary Ann V, 362
Thornburg, Mary S. V, 285
Thornburg, Mary Stella V, 285
Thornburg, Matilda Ann V, 362
Thornburg, Matilda Jane V, 285
Thornburg, Matilda Jane V, 362
Thornburg, Melissa Jane V, 647
Thornburg, Meriam I, 735
Thornburg, Milton V, 285
Thornburg, Minnie V, 285
Thornburg, N. R. I, 950
Thornburg, Nancy I, 579
Thornburg, Nancy V, 285
Thornburg, Nancy V, 647
Thornburg, Nancy Ann V, 647
Thornburg, Nancy E. V, 647
Thornburg, Nancy Elizabeth V, 647
Thornburg, Naomi V, 535
Thornburg, Naomi V, 978
Thornburg, Naomi P. V, 978
Thornburg, Nellie V, 285
Thornburg, Nellie E. V, 285
Thornburg, Nellie E. V, 715
Thornburg, Phebe I, 578
Thornburg, Phebe I, 735
Thornburg, Phebe Jane V, 362
Thornburg, Rachel I, 375
Thornburg, Rachel I, 424
Thornburg, Rachel V, 278
Thornburg, Rachel V, 282
Thornburg, Rachel V, 285
Thornburg, Rachel V, 362
Thornburg, Rachel A. V, 362
Thornburg, Rachel Ann V, 285
Thornburg, Rachel Anna V, 362
Thornburg, Rachel E. V, 362
Thornburg, Rachel Emma V, 285
Thornburg, Rachel Emma V, 362
Thornburg, Rachel M. V, 285
Thornburg, Rachel May V, 285
Thornburg, Ralph V, 208
Thornburg, Ralph V, 285
Thornburg, Ralph W. V, 285
Thornburg, Raymond V, 285
Thornburg, Raymond V, 715
Thornburg, Raymond B. V, 285
Thornburg, Rebecca I, 578
Thornburg, Rebecca V, 362
Thornburg, Rebeccah I, 578
Thornburg, Rhoda V, 362
Thornburg, Rhoda V, 456
Thornburg, Rhoda V, 602
Thornburg, Russel W. V, 285
Thornburg, Ruth I, 735
Thornburg, Ruth I, 737
Thornburg, Ruth V, 96
Thornburg, Ruth V, 132
Thornburg, Ruth V, 235
Thornburg, Ruth V, 285
Thornburg, Ruth V, 311
Thornburg, S. H. V, 285
Thornburg, Samuel V, 362
Thornburg, Samuel C. V, 285
Thornburg, Samuel C. V, 362
Thornburg, Samuel Charles V, 285
Thornburg, Samuel Chas. V, 362
Thornburg, Samuel W. V, 285
Thornburg, Sarah I, 728
Thornburg, Sarah I, 735
Thornburg, Sarah I, 750
Thornburg, Sarah I, 1013
Thornburg, Sarah V, 285
Thornburg, Sarah V, 362
Thornburg, Sarah V, 535
Thornburg, Sarah V, 715
Thornburg, Sarah V, 978
Thornburg, Sarah V, 979
Thornburg, Sarah B. V, 285
Thornburg, Sarah E. V, 647
Thornburg, Sarah Emily V, 647
Thornburg, Sarah J. V, 224
Thornburg, Sarah J. V, 285
Thornburg, Silas V, 285
Thornburg, Silas V, 362
Thornburg, Silas V, 715
Thornburg, Silas H. V, 285
Thornburg, Silas H. V, 362
Thornburg, Silas H. V, 715
Thornburg, Susannah V, 362
Thornburg, Thomas I, 424
Thornburg, Thomas I, 735
Thornburg, Thomas V, 647
Thornburg, Victoria V, 285
Thornburg, Victoria V, 362
Thornburg, Victoria A. V, 285
Thornburg, W. W. V, 285
Thornburg, W. W. V, 1022
Thornburg, William I, 424
Thornburg, William I, 735
Thornburg, William V, 362
Thornburg, William G. V, 362
Thornburg, William J. V, 285
Thornburg, William W. V, 285
Thornburg, William W. V, 362
Thornburg, Winslow I, 735
Thornburg, Wm. V, 468
Thornburg, Wm. W. V, 362
Thornburg, Wm. W. V, 1022
Thornburgh, Abel V, 132
Thornburgh, Abel V, 284
Thornburgh, Abel V, 602
Thornburgh, Abigail I, 1117
Thornburgh, Abigail I, 1133
Thornburgh, Abigail V, 524
Thornburgh, Abigail V, 534
Thornburgh, Abigail V, 535
Thornburgh, Achsa I, 902
Thornburgh, Albena IV, 62
Thornburgh, Alexander V, 284
Thornburgh, Alonzo E. V, 284
Thornburgh, America V, 284
Thornburgh, Ann I, 1111
Thornburgh, Ann I, 1133
Thornburgh, Ann V, 132
Thornburgh, Ann V, 284
Thornburgh, Ann V, 447
Thornburgh, Anna Jessop V, 284
Thornburgh, Bessie Mae V, 284
Thornburgh, Betsy V, 535
Thornburgh, Brown IV, 448
Thornburgh, Charity I, 1111
Thornburgh, Charity I, 1126
Thornburgh, Charity I, 1133
Thornburgh, Charlotte E. V, 284
Thornburgh, Charritty I, 1130
Thornburgh, Charritty I, 1132
Thornburgh, Chas. V, 284
Thornburgh, Cyrus V, 284
Thornburgh, Cyrus V, 362
Thornburgh, Daniel V, 132
Thornburgh, Dempsy I, 1111
Thornburgh, Dinah I, 1130
Thornburgh, Dinah I, 1133
Thornburgh, Dinah V, 132
Thornburgh, Dinah V, 534
Thornburgh, Dinah V, 535
Thornburgh, Dinah V, 647
Thornburgh, Dinah V, 978
Thornburgh, Dorcas V, 432
Thornburgh, Dorcas V, 434
Thornburgh, Edith M. V, 284
Thornburgh, Edna IV, 448
Thornburgh, Edward I, 561
Thornburgh, Edward I, 578
Thornburgh, Edward IV, 425
Thornburgh, Edward IV, 448
Thornburgh, Edward V, 24
Thornburgh, Edward V, 132
Thornburgh, Edward V, 284
Thornburgh, Edward V, 447
Thornburgh, Eleanor I, 1111
Thornburgh, Eli V, 522
Thornburgh, Eli V, 535
Thornburgh, Eli V, 978
Thornburgh, Eli P. V, 534
Thornburgh, Elinor I, 1133
Thornburgh, Elizabeth I, 561
Thornburgh, Elizabeth I, 591
Thornburgh, Elizabeth I, 598
Thornburgh, Elizabeth I, 1111
Thornburgh, Elizabeth I, 1126
Thornburgh, Elizabeth I, 1133
Thornburgh, Elizabeth IV, 425
Thornburgh, Elizabeth IV, 448
Thornburgh, Elizabeth V, 132
Thornburgh, Elizabeth V, 284
Thornburgh, Elizabeth V, 362
Thornburgh, Elizabeth V, 423
Thornburgh, Elizabeth V, 434
Thornburgh, Elizabeth V, 447
Thornburgh, Elizabeth VI, 451
Thornburgh, Elizabeth Ann V, 535
Thornburgh, Emmazetta V, 535
Thornburgh, Ephraim Smith V, 434
Thornburgh, Erma V, 208
Thornburgh, Eunice V, 132
Thornburgh, Frances Elizabeth V, 284
Thornburgh, George I, 1099
Thornburgh, Grace I, 579
Thornburgh, Hannah I, 578
Thornburgh, Hannah I, 582
Thornburgh, Hannah V, 132
Thornburgh, Hannah V, 284
Thornburgh, Hannah V, 362
Thornburgh, Hannah VI, 393
Thornburgh, Hannah VI, 452
Thornburgh, Hannah W. V, 284
Thornburgh, Harriet Ellen V, 284
Thornburgh, Henry I, 1111
Thornburgh, Henry I, 1132
Thornburgh, Henry I, 1133
Thornburgh, Henry V, 132
Thornburgh, Henry, Sr. I, 1111
Thornburgh, Isaac V, 284
Thornburgh, Isaac V, 362
Thornburgh, Isaac Edward V, 284
Thornburgh, Isaac Norton V, 284
Thornburgh, Isaac, Jr. V, 447
Thornburgh, Isaac, Jr. V, 448
Thornburgh, Jacob I, 1111
Thornburgh, Jacob I, 1133
Thornburgh, Jacob V, 132
Thornburgh, Jacob V, 284
Thornburgh, Jacob V, 311
Thornburgh, James A. V, 534
Thornburgh, Jane V, 132
Thornburgh, Jane V, 284
Thornburgh, Jane V, 529
Thornburgh, Jane V, 535
Thornburgh, Jane Thomas Judith V, 535
Thornburgh, Jane W. V, 362
Thornburgh, Jemima V, 535
Thornburgh, Jemima V, 538
Thornburgh, Jemima V, 603
Thornburgh, Jemima V, 978
Thornburgh, Jemima Ann V, 535
Thornburgh, Jemimah V, 535
Thornburgh, Jemimah V, 602
Thornburgh, Jemimah Ann V, 535
Thornburgh, Jesse I, 1111
Thornburgh, Jesse V, 423
Thornburgh, Jessop V, 284
Thornburgh, Joab V, 284
Thornburgh, Joab V, 447
Thornburgh, Job V, 284
Thornburgh, Job V, 447
Thornburgh, Joel V, 132
Thornburgh, Joel V, 284
Thornburgh, Joel V, 311
Thornburgh, Joel V, 534
Thornburgh, Joel V, 535
Thornburgh, Joel V, 647
Thornburgh, Joel VI, 452
Thornburgh, Joel Judkins IV
Thornburgh, John I, 1111
Thornburgh, John V, 132
Thornburgh, John V, 284
Thornburgh, John Beals V, 1
Thornburgh, John Milton V, 2
Thornburgh, John, Jr. V, 447
Thornburgh, Jonathan V, 534
Thornburgh, Jonathan V, 535
Thornburgh, Joseph I, 577
Thornburgh, Joseph I, 578
Thornburgh, Joseph I, 841
Thornburgh, Joseph I, 1077
Thornburgh, Joseph I, 1099
Thornburgh, Joseph I, 1111
Thornburgh, Joseph I, 1133
Thornburgh, Joseph IV, 448
Thornburgh, Joseph V, 132
Thornburgh, Joseph V, 284
Thornburgh, Joseph V, 311
Thornburgh, Joseph V, 447
Thornburgh, Joseph V, 448
Thornburgh, Joseph V, 775
Thornburgh, Joseph, Jr. I, 113
Thornburgh, Joseph, Jr. V, 447
Thornburgh, Joseph, Sr. V, 770
Thornburgh, Josiah V, 522
Thornburgh, Josiah V, 535
Thornburgh, Judith I, 578
Thornburgh, Judith V, 534
Thornburgh, Judith V, 535
Thornburgh, Judith VI, 387
Thornburgh, Judith VI, 451
Thornburgh, Keziah V, 132
Thornburgh, Keziah V, 284
Thornburgh, Kinsey I, 1111
Thornburgh, L. A. V, 284
Thornburgh, Larkin I, 1111
Thornburgh, Larkin I, 1133
Thornburgh, Lettie V, 434
Thornburgh, Lettie S. V, 423
Thornburgh, Lewis I, 1111
Thornburgh, Lewis I, 1133
Thornburgh, Lewis V, 362
Thornburgh, Lindsey I, 568
Thornburgh, Louisa V, 284
Thornburgh, Louisa V, 291
Thornburgh, Louisa J. V, 284
Thornburgh, Lowrethe I, 1130
Thornburgh, Lowrethe I, 1132
Thornburgh, Lucy Stanton IV, 448
Thornburgh, Lydia I, 1111
Thornburgh, Lydia I, 1118
Thornburgh, Lydia I, 1133
Thornburgh, Lydia V, 132
Thornburgh, Lydia V, 284
Thornburgh, Lydia V, 311
Thornburgh, Lydia V, 362
Thornburgh, Lydia Ann V, 284
Thornburgh, Lydia J. V, 352
Thornburgh, Lydia J. V, 362
Thornburgh, Lydia Jane IV, 259
Thornburgh, Lydia Jane IV, 293
Thornburgh, Lydia Jane IV, 425
Thornburgh, Lydia Jane IV, 448
Thornburgh, Lydia Jane V, 284
Thornburgh, Lydia S. V, 522
Thornburgh, Malinda V, 284
Thornburgh, Malissa Jane V, 535
Thornburgh, Margaret V, 284
Thornburgh, Margaret V, 447
Thornburgh, Marium I, 735
Thornburgh, Martha I, 526
Thornburgh, Martha I, 578
Thornburgh, Martha V, 534
Thornburgh, Martha V, 535
Thornburgh, Marvin V, 284
Thornburgh, Mary I, 1111
Thornburgh, Mary I, 1133
Thornburgh, Mary V, 24
Thornburgh, Mary V, 132
Thornburgh, Mary V, 284
Thornburgh, Mary V, 501
Thornburgh, Mary V, 534
Thornburgh, Mary V, 535
Thornburgh, Mary A. V, 284
Thornburgh, Mary Ann V, 284
Thornburgh, Matilda Ann V, 362
Thornburgh, Matilda Jane V, 284
Thornburgh, Melissa Jane V, 535
Thornburgh, Melissa Jane V, 647

...burgh, Meriam I, 720
...burgh, Meriam I, 735
...burgh, Milton V, 132
...burgh, Milton V, 284
...burgh, Morgan I, 1133
...burgh, Nancy I, 560
...burgh, Nancy I, 579
...burgh, Nancy V, 284
...burgh, Nancy V, 519
...burgh, Nancy V, 535
...burgh, Nancy V, 635
...burgh, Nancy V, 647
...burgh, Nancy Ann V, 535
...burgh, Naomi V, 535
...burgh, Naomi P. V, 535
...burgh, Naomi P. V, 978
...burgh, Nathan V, 132
...burgh, Nathan V, 284
...burgh, Nathan V, 447
...burgh, Nathan V, 600
...burgh, Nathan V, 602
...burgh, Phebe I, 735
...burgh, Phebe V, 24
...burgh, Phebe V, 132
...burgh, Phebe V, 284
...burgh, Phebe VI, 384
...burgh, Phebe VI, 451
...burgh, Phebe Jane V, 362
...burgh, Rachel I, 578
...burgh, Rachel I, 1111
...burgh, Rachel I, 1132
...burgh, Rachel I, 1133
...burgh, Rachel IV, 448
...burgh, Rachel V, 207
...burgh, Rachel V, 284
...burgh, Rachel V, 341
...burgh, Rachel V, 362
...burgh, Rachel V, 448
...burgh, Rachel V, 775
...burgh, Rachel Ann V, 284
...burgh, Rachel B. V, 284
...burgh, Rachel Emma V, 284
...burgh, Ralph V, 208
...burgh, Reachel I, 1132
...burgh, Rebecca V, 132
...burgh, Rebecca V, 207
...burgh, Rebecca V, 284
...burgh, Rebecca V, 600
...burgh, Rebecca V, 602
...burgh, Rebecca V, 770
...burgh, Rebecca V, 775
...burgh, Rebeckah V, 775
...burgh, Rebekah I, 1132
...burgh, Rebekah I, 1133
...burgh, Rhoda V, 284
...burgh, Rhoda V, 535
...burgh, Richard I, 1133
...burgh, Richard V, 534
...burgh, Richard V, 535
...burgh, Ruth V, 132
...burgh, Ruth V, 311
...burgh, Samuel V, 284
...burgh, Samuel V, 362
...burgh, Samuel Charles V, 284
...burgh, Samuel W. V, 285
...burgh, Sarah I, 591
...burgh, Sarah I, 598
...burgh, Sarah I, 718
...burgh, Sarah I, 734
...burgh, Sarah I, 735
...burgh, Sarah I, 1111
...burgh, Sarah V, 284
...burgh, Sarah V, 522
...burgh, Sarah V, 535
...burgh, Sarah V, 978
...burgh, Sarah Beals V, 132
...burgh, Sarah Emely V, 535
...burgh, Sarah Emily V, 535
...burgh, Sarah Emily V, 647
...burgh, Shadrach V, 534
...burgh, Shadrack V, 535
...burgh, Shadrick V, 535
...burgh, Silas H. V, 284
...burgh, Simon I, 1111
...burgh, Sophia I, 1111
...burgh, Sophia I, 1132
...burgh, Sophia I, 1133
...burgh, Sophia I, 1134
...burgh, Susanna I, 568
...burgh, Susannah V, 284
...burgh, Thomas I, 343
...burgh, Thomas I, 718
...burgh, Thomas I, 735
...burgh, Thomas I, 1133
...burgh, Thomas V, 132
...burgh, Thomas V, 207
...burgh, Thomas V, 284
...burgh, Thomas V, 519
...burgh, Thomas V, 534
Thornburgh, Thomas V, 535
Thornburgh, Thomas V, 647
Thornburgh, Thomas V, 775
Thornburgh, Thomas, Jr. I, 578
Thornburgh, Thos. I, 847
Thornburgh, Thos. V, 635
Thornburgh, Walter I, 577
Thornburgh, Walter I, 1111
Thornburgh, Walter I, 1133
Thornburgh, Wellmett I, 1111
Thornburgh, Welmet I, 1130
Thornburgh, Welmet Patten I, 1133
Thornburgh, William I, 343
Thornburgh, William I, 579
Thornburgh, William I, 1111
Thornburgh, William I, 1132
Thornburgh, William I, 1133
Thornburgh, William V, 207
Thornburgh, William V, 284
Thornburgh, William V, 362
Thornburgh, William V, 535
Thornburgh, William V, 775
Thornburgh, William J. V, 284
Thornburgh, William Maulsby I, 1133
Thornburgh, William N. V, 535
Thornburgh, William W. V, 284
Thornburgh, Winslow I, 735
Thornburgh, Wm. I, 1111
Thornburhg, Elizabeth Ann V, 482
Thornburhg, Nancy V, 482
Thornbury, Benjamin I, 578
Thornbury, Benjamin, Jr. VI, 452
Thornbury, Elizabeth V, 279
Thornbury, Elizabeth V, 284
Thornbury, Elizabeth Manerva V, 650
Thornbury, Grace I, 579
Thornbury, Hannah V, 621
Thornbury, Hannah V, 647
Thornbury, Isaac V, 621
Thornbury, Isaac V, 647
Thornbury, Mary A. IV, 778
Thornbury, Mary Jane V, 622
Thornbury, Nathan V, 647
Thornbury, Rebecca V, 647
Thornbury, Rhoda D. IV, 778
Thornbury, Rishie W. IV, 778
Thornbury, Ruth V, 311
Thornbury, Susannah J. V, 602
Thornbury, Susannah J. V, 605
Thornbury, Thomas I, 841
Thornbury, William J. IV, 778
Thorne, ??? III, 312
Thorne, ??? III, 313
Thorne, Abby Jane III, 304
Thorne, Abby Jane III, 314
Thorne, Abigail III, 312
Thorne, Abigail III, 313
Thorne, Abigail III, 314
Thorne, Abigail III, 357
Thorne, Abraham III, 312
Thorne, Abraham III, 314
Thorne, Adison C. III, 449
Thorne, Albert M. II, 930
Thorne, Albert Middleton II, 823
Thorne, Alfred V, 715
Thorne, Alfred M. V, 715
Thorne, Alida III, 312
Thorne, Amy III, 312
Thorne, Ann III, 314
Thorne, Ann III, 449
Thorne, Anna III, 312
Thorne, Anna C. III, 449
Thorne, Anna C. III, 450
Thorne, Anna C. III, 462
Thorne, Anna K. V, 936
Thorne, Anna Lippincott VI, 759
Thorne, Anna Lippincott VI, 786
Thorne, Anna M. V, 83
Thorne, Anna R. III, 313
Thorne, Anna R. III, 314
Thorne, Anna R. III, 347
Thorne, Anna Rosella III, 314
Thorne, Anna Rosella V, 936
Thorne, Anne III, 312
Thorne, Benj. III, 449
Thorne, Benjamin III, 313
Thorne, Benjamin III, 314
Thorne, Benjamin V, 132
Thorne, Benjamin Harry II, 930
Thorne, Benjamin Henry II, 823
Thorne, Catharin H. III, 312
Thorne, Chalkey N. II, 771
Thorne, Charity III, 312
Thorne, Charles III, 449
Thorne, Charlotte III, 314
Thorne, Charlotte S. II, 930
Thorne, Charlotte T. III, 313
Thorne, Chas. III, 449
Thorne, Chester III, 313
Thorne, Cornelia III, 449
Thorne, Cornelia V, 715
Thorne, Daniel III, 312
Thorne, Daniel III, 450
Thorne, Daniel S. III, 312
Thorne, Delilah III, 313
Thorne, Edgar III, 313
Thorne, Edgar IV, 111
Thorne, Edith A. V, 936
Thorne, Edith Ann II, 823
Thorne, Edith Ann II, 929
Thorne, Edith Ann II, 930
Thorne, Edith Ann V, 936
Thorne, Edward Carpenter III, 137
Thorne, Edward Carpenter III, 313
Thorne, Edward Carpenter III, 315
Thorne, Edwin III, 313
Thorne, Edwin III, 314
Thorne, Elbert H. III, 449
Thorne, Elbert H. III, 450
Thorne, Eliz. III, 312
Thorne, Eliz. III, 427
Thorne, Eliza II, 852
Thorne, Eliza II, 930
Thorne, Eliza III, 312
Thorne, Eliza III, 315
Thorne, Eliza V, 715
Thorne, Eliza T. III, 313
Thorne, Elizabeth II, 427
Thorne, Elizabeth II, 668
Thorne, Elizabeth II, 823
Thorne, Elizabeth II, 930
Thorne, Elizabeth III, 313
Thorne, Elizabeth III, 314
Thorne, Elizabeth III, 450
Thorne, Elizabeth V, 83
Thorne, Elizabeth V, 715
Thorne, Elnathan III, 313
Thorne, Elnathan III, 314
Thorne, Elwood E. II, 823
Thorne, Elwood E. II, 930
Thorne, Elwood E. V, 936
Thorne, Emily III, 394
Thorne, Emily III, 447
Thorne, Emily III, 449
Thorne, Emily B. III, 394
Thorne, Emily B. III, 412
Thorne, Emily B. III, 449
Thorne, Emily B. III, 450
Thorne, Emily B. III, 486
Thorne, Emily B. III, 500
Thorne, Emily C. III, 449
Thorne, Emma II, 823
Thorne, Emma II, 930
Thorne, Emma III, 486
Thorne, Emma III, 500
Thorne, Esther II, 823
Thorne, Esther II, 923
Thorne, Esther II, 930
Thorne, Ezra V, 132
Thorne, Florence L. III, 412
Thorne, Florence L. III, 449
Thorne, Frances III, 449
Thorne, Franklin Palmer II, 1081
Thorne, Frederick V, 936
Thorne, Freelove III, 313
Thorne, Freelove III, 314
Thorne, George III, 313
Thorne, George III, 314
Thorne, George White III, 313
Thorne, Grace Anna V, 936
Thorne, Hallock IV, 133
Thorne, Hannah II, 930
Thorne, Hannah III, 313
Thorne, Hannah III, 314
Thorne, Hannah III, 405
Thorne, Hannah III, 449
Thorne, Hannah III, 450
Thorne, Hannah A. II, 930
Thorne, Helen A. III, 314
Thorne, Helen H. III, 39
Thorne, Henry II, 823
Thorne, Howard Ellsworth III, 313
Thorne, Howard Ellsworth III, 315
Thorne, Howard Ellworth III, 71
Thorne, Ida III, 72
Thorne, Ida III, 315
Thorne, Isaac II, 930
Thorne, Isaac III, 313
Thorne, Isaac III, 314
Thorne, Isaac III, 394
Thorne, Isaac III, 447
Thorne, Isaac III, 449
Thorne, Isaac III, 450
Thorne, Isaac III, 486
Thorne, Isaac III, 500
Thorne, Isaac C. III, 394
Thorne, Isaac C. III, 412
Thorne, Isaac C. III, 449
Thorne, Isaac C. III, 450
Thorne, Isaac C. III, 486
Thorne, Isabel II, 1081
Thorne, Jacob III, 313
Thorne, Jacob III, 314
Thorne, Jacob III, 315
Thorne, Jacob M. VI, 773
Thorne, Jacob M. VI, 786
Thorne, James III, 313
Thorne, James III, 314
Thorne, James III, 449
Thorne, James III, 450
Thorne, James V, 936
Thorne, James Frederick III, 313
Thorne, James Frederick III, 314
Thorne, James H. III, 314
Thorne, James P. III, 39
Thorne, James P. III, 314
Thorne, Jane III, 314
Thorne, Jane D. III, 313
Thorne, Jemima III, 450
Thorne, Joanna III, 313
Thorne, John III, 313
Thorne, John III, 314
Thorne, John III, 405
Thorne, John III, 449
Thorne, John III, 464
Thorne, John V, 83
Thorne, John V, 715
Thorne, John W. V, 715
Thorne, John, Jr. III, 313
Thorne, Jonathan III, 313
Thorne, Jonathan III, 314
Thorne, Jonathan III, 315
Thorne, Jonathan, Jr. III, 313
Thorne, Jordan III, 313
Thorne, Jos. III, 450
Thorne, Joseph II, 136
Thorne, Joseph II, 268
Thorne, Joseph II, 820
Thorne, Joseph II, 823
Thorne, Joseph II, 923
Thorne, Joseph II, 929
Thorne, Joseph II, 930
Thorne, Joseph III, 205
Thorne, Joseph III, 313
Thorne, Joseph III, 314
Thorne, Joseph III, 315
Thorne, Joseph V, 936
Thorne, Joseph Howard II, 823
Thorne, Joseph Howard II, 930
Thorne, Joseph Howard V, 936
Thorne, Joseph, Jr. II, 929
Thorne, Joseph, Sr. III, 312
Thorne, Josephine V, 936
Thorne, Josephine A. III, 314
Thorne, Josephine A. III, 347
Thorne, Josephine Allen III, 314
Thorne, Julia III, 447
Thorne, Julia III, 449
Thorne, Julia J. III, 449
Thorne, Landon Ketcham III, 449
Thorne, Landon Ketcham, Jr. III, 409
Thorne, Leonard III, 449
Thorne, Leonard III, 450
Thorne, Leonard D. III, 314
Thorne, Levi V, 936
Thorne, Levi E. III, 313
Thorne, Levi E. III, 314
Thorne, Levi E. III, 347
Thorne, Levi E. V, 936
Thorne, Lilian III, 39
Thorne, Lilian III, 314
Thorne, Linton III, 314
Thorne, Lizzie III, 449
Thorne, Louisa III, 313
Thorne, Louise Francis III, 71
Thorne, Louise Francis III, 313
Thorne, Lovisa II, 427
Thorne, Lucy L. III, 449
Thorne, Lucy M. V, 715
Thorne, Lucy R. II, 930
Thorne, Lydia III, 205
Thorne, Lydia III, 313
Thorne, Lydia III, 314
Thorne, Lydia A. III, 315
Thorne, Lydia Ann III, 313
Thorne, Lydia Ann III, 314
Thorne, Margaret Hayes III, 59
Thorne, Margaret Hayes III, 314
Thorne, Margrett Elizabeth V, 715
Thorne, Maria III, 315
Thorne, Maria III, 420
Thorne, Maria III, 449
Thorne, Maria III, 450
Thorne, Maria III, 500
Thorne, Maria C. VI, 759
Thorne, Maria C. VI, 786
Thorne, Maria H. III, 401
Thorne, Maria H. III, 449
Thorne, Maria H. III, 450
Thorne, Maria H. III, 462
Thorne, Marmaduke Eale Phiany III, 449
Thorne, Martha III, 105
Thorne, Martha III, 314
Thorne, Martha B. II, 1081
Thorne, Martha J. III, 314
Thorne, Martha J. III, 450
Thorne, Martha Johanna III, 313
Thorne, Martha S. II, 1077
Thorne, Mary II, 930
Thorne, Mary III, 261
Thorne, Mary III, 313
Thorne, Mary III, 314
Thorne, Mary III, 405
Thorne, Mary III, 449
Thorne, Mary III, 450
Thorne, Mary III, 464
Thorne, Mary V, 132
Thorne, Mary V, 715
Thorne, Mary Ann II, 813
Thorne, Mary Anna II, 1081
Thorne, Mary Anna III, 314
Thorne, Mary Annah III, 314
Thorne, Mary Annah III, 329
Thorne, Mary Eliz. III, 450
Thorne, Mary Elizabeth III, 313
Thorne, Mary Elizabeth III, 401
Thorne, Mary Elizabeth III, 450
Thorne, Mary Ella VI, 773
Thorne, Mary Ella VI, 786
Thorne, Mary H. II, 815
Thorne, Mary L. II, 1081
Thorne, Mary M. V, 715
Thorne, Mary W. III, 394
Thorne, Mary W. III, 449
Thorne, Mary W. III, 450
Thorne, May III, 137
Thorne, May III, 313
Thorne, Mercy III, 313
Thorne, Morris VI, 759
Thorne, Morris VI, 786
Thorne, Moses III, 314
Thorne, Nathan II, 823
Thorne, Nathan II, 929
Thorne, Nathan II, 930
Thorne, Nathan VI, 786
Thorne, Nathaniel III, 314
Thorne, Nehemiah II, 930
Thorne, Oakleigh III, 313
Thorne, Oakleigh III, 314
Thorne, Ophelia III, 313
Thorne, Ophelia III, 315
Thorne, Parmelia III, 314
Thorne, Penelope III, 314
Thorne, Penelope III, 449
Thorne, Penelope III, 450
Thorne, Peter III, 314
Thorne, Peter I. III, 326
Thorne, Peter J. III, 314
Thorne, Peter J. III, 329
Thorne, Phebe III, 313
Thorne, Phebe III, 314
Thorne, Phebe III, 315
Thorne, Phebe III, 405
Thorne, Phebe III, 449
Thorne, Phebe III, 450
Thorne, Phebe Anna III, 313
Thorne, Phebe Anna III, 314
Thorne, Rachel II, 823
Thorne, Rachel II, 930
Thorne, Rebecca II, 771
Thorne, Rebecca II, 820
Thorne, Rebecca II, 923
Thorne, Rebecca II, 929
Thorne, Rebecca II, 930
Thorne, Rebecca III, 315
Thorne, Rebecca T. II, 721
Thorne, Richard III, 405
Thorne, Sam'l C. III, 401
Thorne, Sam'l C. III, 450
Thorne, Samuel II, 721
Thorne, Samuel III, 313
Thorne, Samuel III, 314
Thorne, Samuel III, 449
Thorne, Samuel C. III, 315
Thorne, Samuel C. III, 420
Thorne, Samuel C. III, 449
Thorne, Samuel C. III, 450
Thorne, Samuel C. III, 462
Thorne, Samuel C. III, 500
Thorne, Samuel Collins II, 668
Thorne, Samuel, Jr. III, 313
Thorne, Sarah II, 106

Thorne, Sarah II, 136
Thorne, Sarah II, 721
Thorne, Sarah II, 771
Thorne, Sarah III, 182
Thorne, Sarah III, 313
Thorne, Sarah III, 314
Thorne, Sarah D. III, 312
Thorne, Sarah L. II, 823
Thorne, Sharon II, 930
Thorne, Stephen III, 312
Thorne, Stephen III, 450
Thorne, Stephen V, 715
Thorne, Susanah II, 1032
Thorne, Susannah III, 314
Thorne, Susannah V, 715
Thorne, Thomas III, 304
Thorne, Thomas III, 313
Thorne, Thomas III, 314
Thorne, Thomas III, 449
Thorne, Thomas III, 450
Thorne, Thomas J. III, 314
Thorne, Thomas P. III, 313
Thorne, Thomas, Jr. III, 314
Thorne, Thos. II, 668
Thorne, Thos. III, 314
Thorne, Veronica III, 409
Thorne, Veronica III, 449
Thorne, Walter T. V, 936
Thorne, Walter Thomas III, 314
Thorne, Wd. Elizabeth Hutchins II, 786
Thorne, Wd. Sarah III, 314
Thorne, Webster III, 314
Thorne, William II, 427
Thorne, William III, 313
Thorne, William III, 314
Thorne, William III, 315
Thorne, William III, 450
Thorne, William B. II, 823
Thorne, William H. III, 315
Thorne, William H. III, 450
Thorne, William J. III, 313
Thorne, William Lincoln III, 315
Thorne, Wm. II, 668
Thorne, Wm. II, 721
Thorne, Wm. Byles II, 786
Thorne, Wm. H. III, 72
Thorne, Wm. H. III, 313
Thorne, Wm. H. III, 315
Thorne, Woodbridge III, 315
Thornecraft, Derick III, 421
Thornecraft, Temperance III, 421
Thornell, Nellie III, 305
Thornell, Nellie III, 315
Thornhill, Ann V, 434
Thornhill, Edna VI, 904
Thornhill, Eliza VI, 918
Thornhill, Elizabeth VI, 870
Thornhill, Elizabeth VI, 884
Thornhill, Emma Zerilda V, 434
Thornhill, Ezekiel VI, 1004
Thornhill, Homer V, 434
Thornhill, James VI, 904
Thornhill, Jennie V, 434
Thornhill, Jesse VI, 805
Thornhill, Jesse VI, 821
Thornhill, Jesse VI, 859
Thornhill, Jesse, Jr. VI, 821
Thornhill, Joshua VI, 859
Thornhill, Judy VI, 859
Thornhill, Leonard VI, 1004
Thornhill, Martha Ann VI, 950
Thornhill, Mary V, 434
Thornhill, Mary A. VI, 821
Thornhill, Mary C. VI, 859
Thornhill, Nancey VI, 1004
Thornhill, Permelia VI, 968
Thornhill, Rachel VI, 890
Thornhill, Reuben VI, 998
Thornhill, Sally VI, 907
Thornhill, Sally VI, 919
Thornhill, Susanna VI, 1004
Thornhill, Wilber V, 434
Thornhill, William VI, 884
Thornhill, William VI, 907
Thornhill, William VI, 950
Thornhill, William VI, 995
Thornhill, William VI, 1004
Thornicraft, Achsah III, 406
Thornicraft, Adah III, 393
Thornicraft, Adah III, 450
Thornicraft, Ann III, 405
Thornicraft, Anne III, 450
Thornicraft, Benjamin III, 450
Thornicraft, Derick III, 393
Thornicraft, Derick III, 450
Thornicraft, Elizabeth III, 450
Thornicraft, Francis III, 450
Thornicraft, Hannah III, 450
Thornicraft, Helen III, 450
Thornicraft, Peter III, 450
Thornicraft, Temperance III, 393
Thornicraft, Temperance III, 450
Thornicraft, Thomas III, 393
Thornicraft, Thomas III, 450
Thornicraft, William III, 450
Thornicraft, Willmett III, 393
Thornicraft, Willmett III, 450
Thornicraft, Wilmot III, 450
Thornlin, Wm. A. V, 1022
Thornlow, Capelia I, 642
Thornlow, Capelia Beatrice I, 627
Thornlow, Charles C. I, 621
Thornlow, Charles C. I, 627
Thornlow, Fetna I, 628
Thornlow, Fetney I, 627
Thornlow, Fetney I, 642
Thornlow, Fetnie I, 642
Thornlow, Kenneth I, 642
Thornlow, Margaret Lucile I, 642
Thornlow, Mrs. C. C. I, 627
Thornlow, Percie R. I, 627
Thornlow, Perry I, 642
Thornlow, Velma H. I, 621
Thornlow, Velna I, 637
Thornlow, Zilpha I, 627
Thornlow, Zilpha I, 628
Thornlow, Zilphia I, 621
Thornlow, Zilphy I, 642
Thornsbrough, Robert II, 492
Thornsbrough, Robert II, 668
Thornsbrough, Sarah II, 492
Thornsbrough, Sarah II, 668
Thornten, Hannah II, 1033
Thornten, James II, 1033
Thornten, Joseph II, 1033
Thornton, ??? III, 166
Thornton, ??? V, 794
Thornton, Abigail V, 770
Thornton, Abraham I, 424
Thornton, Alfred I, 842
Thornton, Alfred W. I, 794
Thornton, Alice Emily III, 166
Thornton, Alice Emily III, 315
Thornton, Alwilda IV, 500
Thornton, Ann I, 74
Thornton, Ann I, 75
Thornton, Ann II, 427
Thornton, Ann II, 668
Thornton, Ann W. II, 828
Thornton, Ann Walker II, 828
Thornton, Anna V, 770
Thornton, Anna V, 794
Thornton, Anna VI, 857
Thornton, Bartlett I, 75
Thornton, Bartlett I, 842
Thornton, Bartlett Y. I, 794
Thornton, Bartlett Y. I, 842
Thornton, Boyd IV, 1296
Thornton, Charles Buckman II, 1033
Thornton, Charles J. III, 315
Thornton, Cora I, 842
Thornton, Cornelia I, 842
Thornton, Cornelia G. VI, 680
Thornton, Daniel II, 721
Thornton, Daniel II, 771
Thornton, Daniel III, 315
Thornton, David I, 424
Thornton, E. S. I, 842
Thornton, Edward V, 936
Thornton, Eli I, 424
Thornton, Eli I, 841
Thornton, Eli I, 842
Thornton, Eli I, 1038
Thornton, Eli V, 770
Thornton, Elias S. I, 794
Thornton, Eliz. R. III, 315
Thornton, Elizabeth II, 721
Thornton, Elizabeth II, 788
Thornton, Elizabeth II, 823
Thornton, Elizabeth II, 979
Thornton, Elizabeth II, 989
Thornton, Elizabeth II, 1033
Thornton, Elizabeth V, 770
Thornton, Elizabeth B. V, 936
Thornton, Elizabeth C. II, 721
Thornton, Elizabeth F. VI, 837
Thornton, Elizabeth M. II, 771
Thornton, Elizabeth M. III, 315
Thornton, Elizabeth P. II, 983
Thornton, Elizabeth P. II, 1033
Thornton, Elizabeth Pearson II, 826
Thornton, Emeline IV, 1296
Thornton, Emma II, 823
Thornton, Emma III, 315
Thornton, Emma A. IV, 500
Thornton, Evan C. V, 132
Thornton, Evan C. V, 715
Thornton, Francis III, 315
Thornton, Francis VI, 837
Thornton, Geo. D. III, 315
Thornton, Hannah II, 986
Thornton, Hannah II, 1033
Thornton, Hannah V, 936
Thornton, Harley IV, 1296
Thornton, Henry I, 75
Thornton, Henry I, 794
Thornton, Henry I, 842
Thornton, Henry III, 315
Thornton, James II, 427
Thornton, James II, 823
Thornton, James II, 989
Thornton, James II, 1028
Thornton, James II, 1033
Thornton, James III, 315
Thornton, James M. II, 721
Thornton, Jesse I, 277
Thornton, John II, 1020
Thornton, John II, 1033
Thornton, John C. III, 295
Thornton, John C. III, 315
Thornton, Joseph I, 75
Thornton, Joseph I, 579
Thornton, Joseph II, 828
Thornton, Joseph II, 1033
Thornton, Joseph Alson I, 794
Thornton, Joshua I, 794
Thornton, Joshua I, 842
Thornton, Joshua V, 770
Thornton, Julia A. III, 315
Thornton, Keziah I, 811
Thornton, Keziah I, 842
Thornton, Keziah D. I, 794
Thornton, Letitia IV, 1296
Thornton, Lucy I, 532
Thornton, Lucy I, 579
Thornton, Lucy I, 842
Thornton, Lydia I, 393
Thornton, Lydia I, 424
Thornton, Lydia V, 770
Thornton, Lydia M. II, 721
Thornton, Lydia M. II, 771
Thornton, Lydia M. III, 315
Thornton, Margaret II, 1028
Thornton, Margaret II, 1033
Thornton, Margrett II, 1033
Thornton, Martha I, 343
Thornton, Martha I, 424
Thornton, Martha V, 132
Thornton, Martha VI, 857
Thornton, Martha VI, 859
Thornton, Martha B. V, 715
Thornton, Mary I, 75
Thornton, Mary I, 85
Thornton, Mary I, 276
Thornton, Mary I, 277
Thornton, Mary I, 424
Thornton, Mary II, 828
Thornton, Mary II, 1017
Thornton, Mary II, 1033
Thornton, Mary V, 770
Thornton, Mary Abby Rebecca V, 794
Thornton, Mary Thornton V, 770
Thornton, Nancy I, 579
Thornton, Nansey I, 75
Thornton, Nathan V, 770
Thornton, Nelson IV, 1296
Thornton, Paulina A. VI, 1004
Thornton, Phebe III, 315
Thornton, Phebe B. III, 295
Thornton, Pleasant VI, 859
Thornton, R. S. VI, 817
Thornton, Rachel I, 394
Thornton, Rachel I, 424
Thornton, Rachel II, 721
Thornton, Rachel III, 315
Thornton, Rebecca IV, 193
Thornton, Rebecca IV, 293
Thornton, Rebecca IV, 500
Thornton, Rebecca V, 770
Thornton, Rebeccah I, 394
Thornton, Rebeccah I, 424
Thornton, Rhoda IV, 1349
Thornton, Rhoda IV, 1382
Thornton, S. M. VI, 1014
Thornton, Sally Ann I, 794
Thornton, Sampson IV, 500
Thornton, Samuel III, 315
Thornton, Samuel VI, 680
Thornton, Samuel Y. V, 936
Thornton, Sarah I, 793
Thornton, Sarah I, 842
Thornton, Sarah I, 887
Thornton, Sarah I, 902
Thornton, Sarah I, 990
Thornton, Sarah I, 998
Thornton, Sarah II, 427
Thornton, Sarah II, 475
Thornton, Sarah II, 570
Thornton, Sarah II, 668
Thornton, Sarah II, 1020
Thornton, Sarah II, 1033
Thornton, Sarah V, 767
Thornton, Sarah V, 768
Thornton, Sarah V, 770
Thornton, Sarah V, 794
Thornton, Sarah J. VI, 859
Thornton, Sarah, Jr. II, 668
Thornton, Shubal C. I, 794
Thornton, Sterling C. VI, 857
Thornton, Subel I, 842
Thornton, Thomas I, 75
Thornton, Thomas I, 85
Thornton, Thomas I, 343
Thornton, Thomas I, 424
Thornton, Thomas I, 793
Thornton, Thomas I, 794
Thornton, Thomas I, 842
Thornton, Thomas V, 767
Thornton, Thomas V, 768
Thornton, Thomas V, 770
Thornton, Thomas V, 794
Thornton, Thomas, Jr. I, 842
Thornton, William I, 842
Thornton, William I, 902
Thornton, William I, 998
Thornton, William J. VI, 1004
Thornton, William L. VI, 859
Thornton, Willis I, 75
Thornton, Willis I, 532
Thornton, Willis I, 579
Thornton, Willis I, 735
Thornton, Willis I, 842
Thornton, Willis I, 998
Thornton, Willis P. I, 794
Thornton, Wm. II, 668
Thornton, Wm. V, 936
Thornton, Wm. Bidgood, Jr. II, 1033
Thorntown, Abraham I, 1024
Thorntown, Sarah I, 998
Thorntown, William I, 998
Thorntown, Willis I, 998
Thornye, Oakleigh III, 59
Thorp, ??? IV, 448
Thorp, ??? VI, 95
Thorp, Ann IV, 354
Thorp, Ann V, 132
Thorp, Ann V, 957
Thorp, Ann V, 961
Thorp, Ann F. IV, 347
Thorp, Ann F. IV, 354
Thorp, Ann F. V, 961
Thorp, Anna I, 826
Thorp, Anna I, 842
Thorp, Anna R. V, 132
Thorp, David VI, 1004
Thorp, Delia V, 285
Thorp, Doshia VI, 928
Thorp, Edwin II, 971
Thorp, Edwina Gertrude II, 971
Thorp, Eleanor IV, 354
Thorp, Eleanor IV, 448
Thorp, Eleanor VI, 1004
Thorp, Elizabeth I, 579
Thorp, Elizabeth IV, 354
Thorp, Elizabeth IV, 448
Thorp, Elizabeth VI, 830
Thorp, Elizabeth VI, 861
Thorp, Elizabeth VI, 887
Thorp, Elizabeth VI, 919
Thorp, Elizabeth VI, 1004
Thorp, Elvira VI, 1004
Thorp, Elvira Lee VI, 949
Thorp, Emma IV, 1296
Thorp, Ersley I, 579
Thorp, Fan. VI, 849
Thorp, Florence R. III, 315
Thorp, Frances VI, 861
Thorp, Frances VI, 942
Thorp, Frances VI, 1004
Thorp, Francis VI, 1004
Thorp, Francis T. VI, 1004
Thorp, George V, 132
Thorp, George R. V, 132
Thorp, Gertrude L. II, 971
Thorp, Hannah IV, 354
Thorp, Hannah IV, 430
Thorp, Hannah IV, 448
Thorp, Henry F. IV, 354
Thorp, Huldah V, 647
Thorp, Iran VI, 809
Thorp, J. Laurence, Jr. II, 971
Thorp, J. Lawrence II, 971
Thorp, Jabes IV, 1117
Thorp, Jabes V, 132
Thorp, Jabesh IV, 448
Thorp, Jabez IV, 354
Thorp, Jabez IV, 1117
Thorp, Jabez V, 132
Thorp, James IV, 354
Thorp, James IV, 448
Thorp, James IV, 1117
Thorp, James VI, 859
Thorp, Jane VI, 1004
Thorp, Jesse IV, 354
Thorp, Jesse IV, 448
Thorp, John VI, 1004
Thorp, Joseph V, 647
Thorp, Joseph VI, 123
Thorp, Joseph VI, 124
Thorp, Joseph E. V, 647
Thorp, Louisa I, 579
Thorp, Lucy VI, 859
Thorp, Mabel III, 197
Thorp, Mabel L. III, 315
Thorp, Malcolm R. III, 197
Thorp, Malcolm R. III, 315
Thorp, Margaret IV, 354
Thorp, Maria IV, 778
Thorp, Maria IV, 914
Thorp, Maria IV, 917
Thorp, Maria IV, 1029
Thorp, Maria IV, 1030
Thorp, Maria V, 132
Thorp, Maria V, 961
Thorp, Maria R. IV, 1030
Thorp, Mary IV, 354
Thorp, Mary IV, 448
Thorp, Mary IV, 1030
Thorp, Mary V, 132
Thorp, Mary L. VI, 949
Thorp, Mary P. V, 132
Thorp, Mary, Jr. V, 132
Thorp, Mildred Katherine II
Thorp, Minerva V, 132
Thorp, Nancy VI, 928
Thorp, Nathan VI, 925
Thorp, Pamelia VI, 809
Thorp, Pamelia VI, 975
Thorp, Patsey VI, 925
Thorp, Permelia VI, 900
Thorp, Polly VI, 925
Thorp, Rebecca S. II, 971
Thorp, Rebecca Shoemaker, Jr II, 971
Thorp, Rutth VI, 1004
Thorp, Samuel IV, 354
Thorp, Samuel IV, 448
Thorp, Samuel V, 961
Thorp, Sophia VI, 849
Thorp, Susannah VI, 123
Thorp, Thomas II, 268
Thorp, Thomas IV, 354
Thorp, Thomas IV, 448
Thorp, Thomas IV, 778
Thorp, Thomas IV, 1029
Thorp, Thomas IV, 1030
Thorp, Thomas IV, 1117
Thorp, Thomas V, 132
Thorp, Thomas V, 961
Thorp, Thomas VI, 1004
Thorp, Thomas, Jr. IV, 778
Thorp, Tomsey VI, 881
Thorp, Viola V. V, 647
Thorp, Walter III, 315
Thorp, William VI, 881
Thorp, William VI, 887
Thorp, William VI, 1004
Thorp, Zerinda G. VI, 1004
Thorp., Elvira VI, 948
Thorpe, Edna W. II, 1055
Thorpe, Edna W. II, 1062
Thorpe, Edwina Gertrude II, 1062
Thorpe, Eva V, 693
Thorpe, George R. V, 108
Thorpe, George R. V, 132
Thorpe, Gertrude L. II, 1062
Thorpe, J. Lawrence II, 1062
Thorpe, Lawrence II, 1062
Thorpe, Margaret II, 668
Thorpe, Margaret Talbert V, 8
Thorpe, Mary V, 132
Thorpe, Mary P. V, 132
Thorpe, Mary, Jr. V, 108
Thorpe, Mary, Jr. V, 132
Thorpe, Mildred Katherine II, 1062
Thorpe, Thomas II, 268
Thorpe, Wm. S. Lovett II, 106
Thorton, Jane IV, 467
Thorton, Laura B. IV, 1265
Thorton, Moses IV, 467
Thorton, Rebecca IV, 467
Thorton, Sampson IV, 467
Thrailkill, Catherine Elizabeth IV, 1265
Thrailkill, Elsie IV, 1265
Thrailkill, Elsie E. IV, 1265
Thrailkill, Ostra IV, 1265
Thrailkill, Tolford IV, 1265

ailkill, Walter IV, 1265
all, Anna IV, 1241
all, Frank IV, 1241
asher, Elizabeth VI, 573
asher, Gilbert V, 602
asher, Hannah V, 602
asher, John V, 602
asher, John VI, 926
asher, Lydia V, 602
asher, Martha V, 602
asher, Sarah E. V, 602
esher, Gilbert V, 602
esher, John V, 602
esher, Lydia V, 602
esher, Martha V, 602
esher, Sarah E. V, 602
ift, Bertha I, 842
ift, Bessie Virginia I, 627
ift, Bessie Virginia I, 642
ift, Bethel I, 842
ift, D. B. I, 642
ift, David I, 842
ift, David Bethel I, 627
ift, David Bethel, Jr. I, 627
ift, David Bethel, Jr. I, 642
ift, Elizabeth I, 902
ift, Elizabeth I, 905
ift, Ellen I, 627
ift, Elma I, 842
ift, Emma I, 842
rift, Hester I, 627
rift, Hester I, 642
rift, Ida I, 625
rift, Ida I, 842
rift, Obed I, 627
rift, Obed A. I, 625
rift, Obed A. I, 842
rift, Ottis Winfield I, 842
rift, Pearl I, 842
rift, S. Ellen I, 625
rift, Sarah E. I, 842
rocatt, Jno. James VI, 844
rockmorton, David William VI, 451
rockmorton, David William VI, 452
rockmorton, Foster Sheridan V, 362
rockmorton, Iva V, 362
rockmorton, J. Mellon VI, 452
rockmorton, James Mellon VI, 452
rockmorton, Jane V, 132
rockmorton, Jefferson V, 362
rockmorton, Job V, 132
hrockmorton, Job VI, 412
hrockmorton, Job VI, 452
hrockmorton, Leah VI, 452
hrockmorton, Leah H. VI, 412
hrockmorton, Leah H. VI, 452
hrockmorton, Rebecca VI, 452
hrockmorton, Sarah Ann VI, 452
hrockmorton, Thomas Lee VI, 452
hrockmorton, Virginia VI, 451
hrockmorton, Virginia VI, 452
hrockmorton, William VI, 452
hrogmorton, Jane V, 132
hrop, Sarah IV, 1265
hrossell, Emily C. III, 202
hrossell, Emily C. III, 315
Throssell, Helen III, 202
Throssell, Helen III, 315
Throssell, Jos. E. III, 202
Throssell, Jos. E. III, 315
Thrusher, Gilbert V, 647
Thrusher, Gilbert T. V, 647
Thrusher, Hannah V, 647
Thrusher, Hannah Ella V, 647
Thrusher, John Emery V, 647
Thrusher, Maggie V, 434
Thrusher, Maggie C. V, 434
Thrusher, Mary Martha Anna V, 647
Thrusher, Sarah Edna V, 647
Thuerwaechter, Christina II, 705
Thurman, Alexander VI, 859
Thurman, Ann VI, 338
Thurman, Ann VI, 852
Thurman, Ann Mariah VI, 1004
Thurman, Augustine L. VI, 1004
Thurman, Augustine S. VI, 934
Thurman, Baze VI, 1004
Thurman, Betsey VI, 1004
Thurman, Catharine VI, 1007
Thurman, Elizabeth VI, 859
Thurman, Elizabeth VI, 904
Thurman, Elizabeth VI, 914
Thurman, Elizabeth VI, 1004
Thurman, George B. VI, 859
Thurman, Henry VI, 968
Thurman, Henry VI, 1004
Thurman, James VI, 1004
Thurman, John VI, 859
Thurman, John VI, 984
Thurman, John VI, 1017
Thurman, Joseph VI, 908
Thurman, Joseph VI, 913
Thurman, Joseph VI, 959
Thurman, Joseph VI, 1004
Thurman, Joseph VI, 1017
Thurman, Lydda VI, 959
Thurman, Lydia VI, 215
Thurman, Margaret VI, 1004
Thurman, Martha VI, 859
Thurman, Molley VI, 984
Thurman, Nancey VI, 1004
Thurman, Nancy VI, 859
Thurman, Nancy VI, 1017
Thurman, Nathan VI, 859
Thurman, Peyton VI, 1004
Thurman, Polly VI, 1017
Thurman, Priscilla VI, 904
Thurman, Rhoda VI, 795
Thurman, Richard VI, 338
Thurman, Richard VI, 795
Thurman, Richard VI, 852
Thurman, Richard VI, 859
Thurman, Richard VI, 912
Thurman, Richard VI, 978
Thurman, Richard VI, 1004
Thurman, Robert J. VI, 1004
Thurman, Robert W. VI, 849
Thurman, Ruth VI, 1017
Thurman, Sally VI, 852
Thurman, Sally VI, 859
Thurman, Sally VI, 1004
Thurman, Samuel VI, 859
Thurman, Sarah VI, 355
Thurman, Sarah VI, 859
Thurman, Sarah VI, 1004
Thurman, Sophia S. VI, 1004
Thurman, Susan N. VI, 859
Thurman, Vintner VI, 900
Thurman, William VI, 859
Thurmon, Catharine VI, 1007
Thurmon, Matilda VI, 1007
Thurmon, Robert J. VI, 1004
Thurmon, Sophia S. VI, 1004
Thurmond, Elizabeth VI, 1009
Thurmond, John VI, 1009
Thurmond, Philip VI, 876
Thurrowgood, Mr. Adam VI, 9
Thurst, Giles II, 448
Thurston, Abigail II, 823
Thurston, Abigail III, 113
Thurston, Abigail III, 315
Thurston, Abigail III, 385
Thurston, Abigail E. III, 389
Thurston, Amelia V, 132
Thurston, Amelia V, 978
Thurston, Amelia V, 979
Thurston, Amy III, 315
Thurston, Anna D. III, 315
Thurston, Anna Day III, 315
Thurston, Anna U. III, 385
Thurston, Dora V, 978
Thurston, Dora V, 979
Thurston, Edward III, 315
Thurston, Edward D. III, 204
Thurston, Edward D. III, 315
Thurston, Edward Day III, 315
Thurston, Eleanor III, 192
Thurston, Eleanor III, 315
Thurston, Eliza IV, 1188
Thurston, Hetty Wharton II, 823
Thurston, Hetty Wharton II, 930
Thurston, Hetty Wharton III, 385
Thurston, Jane III, 315
Thurston, Jane R. III, 97
Thurston, Jane R. III, 315
Thurston, John W. I, 929
Thurston, John W. III, 385
Thurston, Jos. D. II, 823
Thurston, Joseph D. II, 930
Thurston, Joseph D. III, 385
Thurston, Joseph Delaplaine II, 823
Thurston, Joseph Delaplaine III, 315
Thurston, Lucy I, 929
Thurston, Marcia VI, 828
Thurston, Maria H. III, 277
Thurston, Maria H. III, 315
Thurston, Mary II, 823
Thurston, Mary III, 282
Thurston, Mary III, 315
Thurston, Mary VI, 1005
Thurston, Mary Day III, 315
Thurston, Mary Jane IV, 1188
Thurston, Mary U. III, 385
Thurston, Pearl Edna I, 929
Thurston, Peleg III, 315
Thurston, Phebe IV, 1188
Thurston, Philip Wanton III, 315
Thurston, Plummer VI, 1005
Thurston, Portsmouth III, 315
Thurston, Ruth L. IV, 1340
Thurston, Sara F. III, 204
Thurston, Sara F. III, 315
Thurston, Thomas VI, 5
Thurston, Thomas VI, 6
Thurston, Thomas VI, 37
Thurston, Thos. C. Bell III, 385
Thurston, Vinal IV, 1188
Thurston, Wd. Abigail III, 315
Thurston, William III, 315
Thurston, William III, 385
Thurston, William R. III, 192
Thurston, William R. III, 315
Thurston, William R., Jr. III, 315
Thurston, William Richardson III, 315
Thurston, William Wharton III, 385
Thurston, Wm. R. II, 823
Thurston, Wm. R. III, 97
Thurston, Wm. R. III, 113
Thurston, Wm. R. III, 315
Thurston, Wm. R. III, 389
Thurston, Wm. R., Jr. III, 277
Thurston, Wm. R., Jr. III, 315
Thurston, Wm. Richardson III, 315
Thurston, Wm. W. II, 930
Thurston, Wm. Wharton II, 930
Thuspane, Jno. I, 1
Thuspane???, Jno. I, 1
Thuston, Hannah II, 448
Thwait, Amelia IV, 500
Thwait, Edward IV, 500
Thwait, Edward IV, 554
Thwait, Gover Schlack VI, 452
Thwait, Grover Hauptman Schlack VI, 452
Thwait, Ida VI, 365
Thwait, Ida VI, 441
Thwait, Ida VI, 452
Thwait, James IV, 500
Thwait, James IV, 554
Thwait, John VI, 365
Thwait, John VI, 441
Thwait, John VI, 452
Thwait, Lucy VI, 392
Thwait, Maria IV, 500
Thwait, Mary Ann IV, 500
Thwait, Nina VI, 441
Thwait, Nina VI, 452
Thwait, Sophia IV, 500
Thwaite, Amelia IV, 500
Thwaite, Amelia IV, 554
Thwaite, Edward IV, 500
Thwaite, Edward IV, 554
Thwaite, Isabel IV, 553
Thwaite, Isabella IV, 554
Thwaite, James IV, 500
Thwaite, James IV, 550
Thwaite, James IV, 553
Thwaite, James IV, 554
Thwaite, James T. IV, 553
Thwaite, Jane IV, 554
Thwaite, John IV, 554
Thwaite, Lucy IV, 527
Thwaite, Lucy IV, 554
Thwaite, Maria IV, 500
Thwaite, Maria IV, 554
Thwaite, Mary Ann IV, 500
Thwaite, Mary Ann IV, 550
Thwaite, Mary Ann IV, 553
Thwaite, Mary Ann IV, 554
Thwaite, Richard IV, 500
Thwaite, Richard IV, 554
Thwaite, Richard V, 936
Thwaite, Sophia IV, 500
Thwaite, Sophia IV, 554
Thwaith, Gover Schlack VI, 452
Thwaith, Grover Hauptman Schlack VI, 452
Thwaith, Ida VI, 452
Thwaith, James VI, 452
Thwaith, James L. VI, 452
Thwaith, James T. VI, 452
Thwaith, Jennie VI, 452
Thwaith, John VI, 452
Thwaith, Lucy Gray VI, 452
Thwaith, Nina VI, 452
Thwaith, Sophia VI, 452
Thwaith, Sophie VI, 452
Thweat, James VI, 199
Thweat, James VI, 215
Tibbals, Louisa IV, 1037
Tibbals, Louisa IV, 1043
Tibbits, Sarah I, 277
Tibbits], ??? III, 316
Tibbits], Howard D. III, 316
Tibbits], John III, 316
Tibbits], John B. III, 316
Tibbles, Mary Ann V, 523
Tibbles, Mary Ann V, 535
Tibbs, Elizabeth VI, 798
Tibbs, Elizabeth VI, 858
Tibbs, Elizabeth VI, 859
Tibbs, Frances D. VI, 859
Tibbs, John VI, 859
Tibbs, John VI, 861
Tibbs, Judy VI, 859
Tibbs, Martha VI, 858
Tibbs, Mary J. VI, 858
Tibbs, Nancy VI, 861
Tibbs, Philadelphia VI, 798
Tibbs, William VI, 859
Tibbs, William H. VI, 818
Tibby, Thomas II, 448
Tibout, Susanna II, 556
Tibout, Susanna II, 668
Tiby, Elizabeth II, 448
Tiby, John II, 427
Tiby, John II, 448
Tiby, Wd. Elizabeth II, 427
Tice, Albert V, 602
Tice, Amy V, 602
Tice, Amy Loretta V, 602
Tice, Anna Jane V, 133
Tice, Maggie Edith V, 602
Tice, Nathan V, 602
Tice, Nathan Grant V, 133
Tice, Olga III, 316
Tice, Olga M. III, 265
Tice, R. Solomon III, 265
Tice, R. Solomon III, 316
Tice, Wallace V, 133
Tice, Wallace V, 602
Tickenor, Adalaide II, 817
Tidball, Martha IV, 319
Tidball, Martha IV, 354
Tidd, Oscar V, 648
Tidd, Versie V, 648
Tidmarsh, Hannah II, 427
Tidmarsh, Hannah II, 668
Tidmarsh, Rose II, 489
Tidmarsh, Rose II, 668
Tidmarsh, Sarah II, 586
Tidmarsh, Sarah II, 668
Tidmarsh, Wd. Hannah II, 515
Tidmarsh, William II, 427
Tidmarsh, Wm. II, 515
Tidmarsh, Wm. II, 668
Tidrick, Mary IV, 371
Tidrick, Mary IV, 448
Tidwell, James VI, 87
Tidwell, Pressie VI, 87
Tidwell, Robert VI, 87
Tierney, Anna II, 279
Tierney, Anna II, 304
Tierney, Bertha III, 324
Tierney, Bertha H. III, 324
Tierney, Bertha Hazard III, 316
Tierney, Margaret II, 279
Tierney, Margaret II, 304
Tierney, Thomas II, 279
Tierney, Thomas II, 304
Tierney, Thomas Leo II, 279
Tierney, Thomas Leo II, 304
Tiffany, ??? III, 125
Tiffany, Caroline C. III, 316
Tiffany, Charlotte III, 316
Tiffany, Mary L. III, 125
Tiffany, Mary L. III, 316
Tiffany, Wm. W. III, 316
Tiffin, Eunice V, 250
Tiffin, Eunice V, 285
Tighlman, Ann R. II, 721
Tigue, John Quincy A. I, 841
Tilar, Mary II, 89
Tilar, Mary II, 107
Tilar, Wm. II, 107
Tilbary, Ann II, 427
Tilbury, Ann II, 427
Tilbury, Ann II, 668
Tilbury, Ann II, 678
Tilbury, Elizabeth II, 427
Tilbury, Elizabeth II, 583
Tilbury, Elizabeth II, 668
Tilbury, Thomas II, 427
Tilbury, Thomas II, 583
Tilbury, Thomas II, 668
Tilbury, Thomas II, 678
Tilden, Jane III, 316
Tiler, Daniel VI, 953
Tiler, Martha I, 1162
Tiler, Peggy VI, 966
Tiler, Polly VI, 953
Tiler, Polly VI, 966
Tiley, Elizabeth II, 268
Tilford, Samuel VI, 820
Till, Ann II, 427
Till, Ann II, 668
Till, Ann II, 677
Till, John II, 668
Till, Mary II, 427
Till, Rosamond II, 668
Till, Wd. Ann II, 624
Till, William II, 427
Till, Wm. II, 668
Till, Wm. II, 677
Tillas, John VI, 334
Tillas, John VI, 343
Tillas, Nancy VI, 343
Tillas, Richard VI, 277
Tillas, Richard VI, 343
Tillas, Sarah VI, 334
Tillas, Sarah VI, 343
Tillbury, Thomas II, 427
Tiller, Margaret VI, 277
Tiller, Margaret F. VI, 277
Tiller, Maria Ann VI, 277
Tiller, T. VI, 277
Tilless, Richard VI, 277
Tilley, Bessie Marion III, 316
Tilley, Elizabeth IV, 778
Tilley, John III, 316
Tilley, John Llewellen III, 129
Tilley, John Llewellen III, 316
Tilley, John Llewellen III, 337
Tilley, Joyce Llewellen III, 316
Tilley, Mrs. Elizabeth IV, 778
Tilley, Sarah IV, 778
Tilley, Thos. Humphries IV, 778
Tillier, Hannah II, 427
Tillier, John II, 427
Tillier, Thomas II, 427
Tillinghast, Mary V, 715
Tillious, Jane VI, 343
Tillis, Elizabeth VI, 1014
Tillis, Sary VI, 1014
Tillman, Edward VI, 322
Tillman, Mary I, 935
Tillman, Mary VI, 322
Tillman, Mary VI, 343
Tillotson, Nancy M. III, 133
Tillotson, Nancy M. III, 265
Tillous, David VI, 1005
Tillous, Sarah VI, 1005
Tillson, Anah III, 316
Tillson, Annah III, 316
Tillson, Carrie III, 316
Tillson, Edward Hosmer III, 316
Tillson, Lydia III, 316
Tillson, Mary Smith III, 316
Tillson, Phebe R. III, 316
Tillson, Sarah H. III, 316
Tillson, Timothy III, 316
Tillson, William E. S. III, 316
Tillson, William P. C. III, 316
Tillson, Winfield Scott III, 316
Tillson, Wm. E. S. III, 316
Tillton, Daniel II, 196
Tillton, Daniel II, 268
Tillton, Elizabeth II, 196
Tillton, Elizabeth II, 268
Tillton, Sarah II, 196
Tillton, Sarah II, 268
Tillyer, Latitia II, 472
Tillyer, Latitia II, 668
Tilman, Edward VI, 343
Tilman, Edward VI, 1005
Tilman, Molly VI, 343
Tilman, Molly VI, 1005
Tilson, ??? III, 316
Tilson, Anah III, 316
Tilson, Annah III, 316
Tilson, Bethany III, 165
Tilson, Bethany III, 316
Tilson, Carrie III, 316
Tilson, Edward Hosmer III, 316
Tilson, Isaiah III, 316
Tilson, Isaiah S. III, 316
Tilson, Lydia III, 316
Tilson, Lydia W. III, 184
Tilson, Martha S. III, 316
Tilson, Mary Smith III, 316
Tilson, Phebe R. III, 316
Tilson, Sarah III, 165
Tilson, Sarah III, 316
Tilson, Sarah H. III, 316
Tilson, Timothy III, 316
Tilson, William E. S. III, 316
Tilson, William F. III, 184
Tilson, William F. III, 316
Tilson, William P. C. III, 316
Tilson, Winfield Scott III, 316
Tilson, Wm. E. S. III, 316
Tilton, Abraham III, 316

Tilton, Amos III, 316
Tilton, Ann II, 230
Tilton, Ann II, 268
Tilton, Ann IV, 133
Tilton, Ann IV, 134
Tilton, Benj. W. III, 316
Tilton, Benjamin Combs II, 268
Tilton, Caroline L. III, 316
Tilton, Caroline S. L. III, 316
Tilton, Catharine III, 224
Tilton, Catharine III, 317
Tilton, Catharine V, 936
Tilton, Charity II, 268
Tilton, Charles IV, 62
Tilton, Charles IV, 111
Tilton, Charles IV, 133
Tilton, Charles Edward III, 316
Tilton, Daniel II, 106
Tilton, Daniel II, 253
Tilton, Daniel II, 268
Tilton, Daniel III, 316
Tilton, David II, 209
Tilton, David II, 268
Tilton, Edw. L. III, 316
Tilton, Edward III, 316
Tilton, Edward L. III, 316
Tilton, Eliz. III, 316
Tilton, Eliz. B. III, 317
Tilton, Elizabeth II, 268
Tilton, Elizabeth IV, 62
Tilton, Elizabeth IV, 111
Tilton, Elizabeth IV, 133
Tilton, Elizabeth V, 936
Tilton, Elizabeth B. III, 316
Tilton, Elizabeth B. III, 317
Tilton, Elizabeth B. V, 936
Tilton, Enoch IV, 62
Tilton, Enoch IV, 111
Tilton, Enoch IV, 133
Tilton, Enoch, Jr. IV, 133
Tilton, Esther III, 297
Tilton, Esther III, 316
Tilton, Hannah II, 239
Tilton, Hannah II, 268
Tilton, Hester III, 316
Tilton, James IV, 62
Tilton, James IV, 111
Tilton, James IV, 133
Tilton, Job IV, 133
Tilton, Jobe IV, 133
Tilton, John II, 268
Tilton, John III, 297
Tilton, John III, 316
Tilton, John IV, 62
Tilton, John IV, 111
Tilton, John IV, 133
Tilton, John, Jr. III, 310
Tilton, John, Jr. III, 316
Tilton, John, Sr. III, 316
Tilton, Joseph IV, 62
Tilton, Joseph IV, 111
Tilton, Joseph IV, 133
Tilton, Joseph W. III, 316
Tilton, Joseph White III, 233
Tilton, Joseph White III, 316
Tilton, Josephine H. III, 316
Tilton, Lydia II, 230
Tilton, Lydia II, 268
Tilton, Mary II, 253
Tilton, Mary II, 268
Tilton, Mary III, 233
Tilton, Mary III, 316
Tilton, Mary IV, 62
Tilton, Mary IV, 111
Tilton, Mary IV, 133
Tilton, Mary IV, 134
Tilton, Mary Ann II, 268
Tilton, Mary B. III, 316
Tilton, Mary Eastman III, 316
Tilton, Mary Elizabeth III, 316
Tilton, Mary S. III, 317
Tilton, Mathias IV, 111
Tilton, Mathias IV, 133
Tilton, Matthias IV, 62
Tilton, Mellis III, 316
Tilton, Mellis S. III, 317
Tilton, Millis V, 936
Tilton, Minnie H. V, 362
Tilton, Morgan IV, 133
Tilton, Rebeckah III, 310
Tilton, Rebeckah III, 316
Tilton, Samuel III, 316
Tilton, Samuel IV, 133
Tilton, Sarah II, 268
Tilton, Sarah III, 316
Tilton, Sarah IV, 62
Tilton, Sarah IV, 111
Tilton, Sarah IV, 133
Tilton, Sarah V, 936
Tilton, Sarah M. III, 316
Tilton, Sarah M. III, 317
Tilton, Thomas III, 316
Tilton, Thomas III, 317
Tilton, Thomas V, 936
Tilton, Thos. V, 936
Tilton, Wd. Catharine III, 316
Tilton, William II, 268
Tilton, William III, 224
Tilton, William III, 316
Tilton, William V, 362
Tilton, William V, 936
Tilton, Wm. V, 936
Timberlake, ??? IV, 161
Timberlake, ??? V, 315
Timberlake, Acquilla V, 363
Timberlake, Agnes VI, 343
Timberlake, Agness V, 285
Timberlake, Agness VI, 343
Timberlake, Alfred V, 328
Timberlake, Alfred V, 362
Timberlake, Alfred V, 363
Timberlake, Alfred V, 487
Timberlake, Alfred V, 518
Timberlake, Alfred V, 535
Timberlake, Alfred V, 648
Timberlake, Amelia V, 602
Timberlake, Amy IV, 754
Timberlake, Amy IV, 778
Timberlake, Amy V, 133
Timberlake, Amy V, 312
Timberlake, Amy V, 363
Timberlake, Anna Eliza V, 602
Timberlake, Annie Elizabeth V, 535
Timberlake, Aquilla V, 363
Timberlake, Arthur V, 602
Timberlake, Asenath V, 312
Timberlake, Betsy VI, 343
Timberlake, Betty VI, 323
Timberlake, C. J. VI, 829
Timberlake, Caroline V, 363
Timberlake, Caroline V, 535
Timberlake, Caroline V, 648
Timberlake, Catharine V, 584
Timberlake, Catharine V, 602
Timberlake, Catharine F. V, 515
Timberlake, Catharine F. V, 535
Timberlake, Catherine V, 602
Timberlake, Charles V, 535
Timberlake, Charles VI, 815
Timberlake, Charles VI, 818
Timberlake, Charles VI, 823
Timberlake, Charles VI, 828
Timberlake, Charlotte C. VI, 750
Timberlake, Chas. VI, 813
Timberlake, Chris VI, 860
Timberlake, Chris. VI, 343
Timberlake, Christopher VI, 323
Timberlake, Christopher VI, 343
Timberlake, Deborah Ann V, 363
Timberlake, Edward V, 363
Timberlake, Edward V, 535
Timberlake, Eliza D. V, 363
Timberlake, Eliza D. V, 481
Timberlake, Eliza D. V, 535
Timberlake, Eliza D. V, 648
Timberlake, Elizabeth V, 285
Timberlake, Elizabeth V, 362
Timberlake, Elizabeth V, 363
Timberlake, Elizabeth V, 567
Timberlake, Elizabeth V, 602
Timberlake, Elizabeth VI, 296
Timberlake, Elizabeth VI, 343
Timberlake, Elizabeth VI, 859
Timberlake, Evaline V, 535
Timberlake, Gennette VI, 864
Timberlake, Hannah V, 363
Timberlake, Harmon V, 312
Timberlake, John IV, 754
Timberlake, John IV, 778
Timberlake, John IV, 1296
Timberlake, John V, 133
Timberlake, John V, 285
Timberlake, John V, 312
Timberlake, John V, 317
Timberlake, John V, 345
Timberlake, John V, 363
Timberlake, John V, 936
Timberlake, John VI, 298
Timberlake, John VI, 322
Timberlake, John VI, 343
Timberlake, John VI, 798
Timberlake, John VI, 850
Timberlake, John B. V, 363
Timberlake, John Bateman V, 363
Timberlake, John P. V, 312
Timberlake, John Phillip V, 363
Timberlake, John W. V, 319
Timberlake, John W. V, 362
Timberlake, John W. V, 363
Timberlake, John W. V, 967
Timberlake, John W. V, 978
Timberlake, John, Jr. IV, 778
Timberlake, Jonathan V, 133
Timberlake, Jonathan V, 285
Timberlake, Jonathan V, 362
Timberlake, Jonathan V, 363
Timberlake, Jonathan V, 515
Timberlake, Jonathan V, 535
Timberlake, Jonathan V, 584
Timberlake, Jonathan V, 602
Timberlake, Joseph R. V, 363
Timberlake, Joseph Rhoads V, 312
Timberlake, Judith V, 285
Timberlake, Judith V, 317
Timberlake, Judith V, 363
Timberlake, Judith VI, 343
Timberlake, Lydia V, 312
Timberlake, Lydia V, 363
Timberlake, Mahala V, 363
Timberlake, Mahala V, 936
Timberlake, Mahala V, 944
Timberlake, Mahlon V, 363
Timberlake, Marietta V, 535
Timberlake, Martha V, 335
Timberlake, Martha V, 363
Timberlake, Martha R. V, 303
Timberlake, Martha R. V, 312
Timberlake, Mary IV, 778
Timberlake, Mary V, 285
Timberlake, Mary V, 317
Timberlake, Mary V, 330
Timberlake, Mary V, 358
Timberlake, Mary V, 362
Timberlake, Mary V, 363
Timberlake, Mary V, 535
Timberlake, Mary V, 543
Timberlake, Mary V, 544
Timberlake, Mary V, 978
Timberlake, Mary VI, 298
Timberlake, Mary VI, 322
Timberlake, Mary VI, 343
Timberlake, Mary VI, 802
Timberlake, Mary VI, 823
Timberlake, Mary VI, 860
Timberlake, Mary Ann V, 312
Timberlake, Mary Ann V, 363
Timberlake, Mary B. V, 363
Timberlake, Mary B. V, 518
Timberlake, Mary B. V, 535
Timberlake, Mary B. V, 648
Timberlake, Mary E. V, 363
Timberlake, Mary Elizabeth V, 363
Timberlake, Mary Etta V, 712
Timberlake, Mary W. V, 330
Timberlake, Mary W. V, 363
Timberlake, Maryann V, 363
Timberlake, Matthew Charles V, 535
Timberlake, Mildred VI, 813
Timberlake, Milly VI, 322
Timberlake, Milton V, 363
Timberlake, Molley V, 363
Timberlake, Mollie V, 345
Timberlake, Molly V, 936
Timberlake, Mourning IV, 354
Timberlake, Mourning V, 345
Timberlake, Mourning V, 363
Timberlake, Mourning VI, 324
Timberlake, Mourning VI, 343
Timberlake, Mourning VI, 1005
Timberlake, Nancy V, 285
Timberlake, Nancy VI, 818
Timberlake, Nancy VI, 847
Timberlake, Phebe V, 328
Timberlake, Phebe V, 363
Timberlake, Phebe V, 487
Timberlake, Phebe V, 518
Timberlake, Phebe V, 535
Timberlake, Phebe V, 648
Timberlake, Philip VI, 942
Timberlake, Phillip VI, 323
Timberlake, Phillip VI, 859
Timberlake, Pleasant V, 312
Timberlake, Polly VI, 298
Timberlake, Polly VI, 798
Timberlake, Rachel IV, 1296
Timberlake, Rachel V, 363
Timberlake, Rachel V, 967
Timberlake, Rachel V, 978
Timberlake, Rachel B. V, 363
Timberlake, Rachel B. V, 978
Timberlake, Rachel J. V, 363
Timberlake, Rebecca V, 362
Timberlake, Rebecca Emily IV, 1296
Timberlake, Rebecca Emily V, 535
Timberlake, Rebecca Mary V, 602
Timberlake, Richard V, 285
Timberlake, Richard V, 330
Timberlake, Richard V, 362
Timberlake, Richard V, 363
Timberlake, Richard V, 535
Timberlake, Richard V, 543
Timberlake, Richard V, 544
Timberlake, Richard V, 602
Timberlake, Richard V, 936
Timberlake, Richard V, 944
Timberlake, Richard V, 978
Timberlake, Richard VI, 343
Timberlake, Richard VI, 802
Timberlake, Richard VI, 1005
Timberlake, Sallie V, 285
Timberlake, Sally V, 343
Timberlake, Sally V, 363
Timberlake, Sally VI, 343
Timberlake, Sarah V, 602
Timberlake, Sarah VI, 802
Timberlake, Sarah VI, 1005
Timberlake, Sarah Matilda V, 602
Timberlake, Susan IV, 239
Timberlake, Susan IV, 293
Timberlake, Susannah V, 330
Timberlake, Susannah V, 362
Timberlake, Susannah V, 363
Timberlake, Susannah E. V, 363
Timberlake, Susannah E. V, 535
Timberlake, Thomas VI, 860
Timberlake, William V, 363
Timberlake, William VI, 324
Timberlake, William VI, 343
Timberlake, William VI, 994
Timberlake, William VI, 1005
Timberleek, John IV, 1296
Timberleek, Rachel IV, 1296
Timberleek, Rebecca Emily IV, 1296
Timmerman, Helene Smith IV, 1079
Timmerman, Henry IV, 1079
Timmerman, Henry Timmerman IV, 1079
Timmerman, John Frederick IV, 1079
Timmerman, Maria IV, 1079
Timmerman, Wm. IV, 1079
Timmis, Eleanor III, 427
Timmis, Eleanor III, 450
Timmis, Eleanor Patracia III, 450
Timmis, Mary G. III, 450
Timmis, Mary Garetta III, 450
Timmis, Walter Stott III, 450
Timmis, Wm. Walter III, 427
Timmis, Wm. Walter III, 450
Timmis, Wm. Walter, Jr. III, 450
Timmons, Azariah V, 285
Timmons, Charity V, 285
Timmons, Mary V, 285
Timmons, Mary Ann V, 285
Timmons, Rachel V, 285
Timmons, Shadrock R. V, 285
Timmons, Tillie V, 1022
Timmons, Wm. V, 1022
Tinbrook, Sarah A. I, 533
Tinbrook, Sarah A. I, 579
Tindal, Benj. II, 45
Tindal, Esther II, 45
Tindal, Mary II, 45
Tindall, Benjamin II, 44
Tindall, Benjamin II, 90
Tindall, Benjamin II, 106
Tindall, Daniel VI, 1005
Tindall, Elizabeth II, 61
Tindall, Elizabeth II, 106
Tindall, Esther II, 44
Tindall, Esther II, 90
Tindall, Esther II, 106
Tindall, Hester II, 44
Tindall, Joseph II, 44
Tindall, Joseph II, 106
Tindall, Mary II, 44
Tindall, Mary II, 106
Tindall, Mary II, 109
Tindall, Rachel II, 105
Tindall, Rachel II, 106
Tindall, Rhode VI, 1005
Tinder, Mary F. IV, 394
Tinder, Mary F. IV, 448
Tindol, Miles V, 1022
Tines, Frances H. VI, 860
Tines, Samuel VI, 860
Tinges, Mary II, 549
Tinges, Mary II, 668
Tingle, Mary A. II, 822
Tingle, Mary A. II, 927
Tingley, Harriet II, 598
Tingley, Harriet II, 668
Tingram, Mary I, 828
Tinker, ??? III, 317
Tinker, Arena I, 1162
Tinker, Catharine III, 317
Tinker, Edith IV, 1265
Tinker, Glenn IV, 1265
Tinker, Willis L. IV, 1341
Tinnerson, Nancy VI, 883
Tinney, Eliza Ann IV, 1152
Tinney, Eliza Ann IV, 1198
Tinny, Loved II, 448
Tinny, Mary II, 448
Tinny, Richard II, 448
Tinsely, Nancy VI, 1005
Tinsely, Rucker J. VI, 1005
Tinsely, William VI, 1007
Tinsley, Absalom VI, 1005
Tinsley, Absolom VI, 886
Tinsley, Addison VI, 1005
Tinsley, Agnes Jane VI, 1000
Tinsley, Anthony G. VI, 860
Tinsley, Anthony G. VI, 903
Tinsley, Anthony G. VI, 923
Tinsley, Anthony G. VI, 1005
Tinsley, Anthony G. VI, 1006
Tinsley, Arthur L. VI, 860
Tinsley, Betsy VI, 997
Tinsley, Cassandra D. VI, 100[illegible]
Tinsley, Celina E. VI, 1000
Tinsley, Celina E. VI, 1005
Tinsley, Charlotte A. VI, 925
Tinsley, Cleopatra Albertine VI, 956
Tinsley, Edward VI, 973
Tinsley, Edward VI, 997
Tinsley, Elisha W. VI, 1005
Tinsley, Eliza VI, 1007
Tinsley, Eliza M. VI, 1013
Tinsley, Elizabeth VI, 860
Tinsley, Elizabeth VI, 1005
Tinsley, Elizabeth F. VI, 860
Tinsley, Elizabeth R. VI, 967
Tinsley, Emily VI, 903
Tinsley, Harriett C. VI, 899
Tinsley, Henrietta E. VI, 1005
Tinsley, Isaac VI, 1020
Tinsley, James VI, 883
Tinsley, James VI, 956
Tinsley, James VI, 1005
Tinsley, John I. VI, 930
Tinsley, Joseph VI, 1005
Tinsley, Joseph VI, 1013
Tinsley, Joshua VI, 1005
Tinsley, Judith VI, 886
Tinsley, Judith C. VI, 899
Tinsley, Lafayette VI, 956
Tinsley, Lafayette VI, 1005
Tinsley, Lilly Clarinda I, 1133
Tinsley, Louisa M. VI, 928
Tinsley, Louisa M. VI, 1005
Tinsley, Lucretia VI, 956
Tinsley, Martha VI, 860
Tinsley, Martha VI, 1005
Tinsley, Mary VI, 923
Tinsley, Mary VI, 982
Tinsley, Mary VI, 1005
Tinsley, Mary A. G. VI, 979
Tinsley, Mary Jane VI, 995
Tinsley, Mary L. VI, 1005
Tinsley, Mary T. VI, 860
Tinsley, Milly VI, 886
Tinsley, Nancy VI, 1006
Tinsley, Oliver VI, 979
Tinsley, Palatine R. VI, 1005
Tinsley, Peggy VI, 883
Tinsley, Polly VI, 1005
Tinsley, Robert VI, 860
Tinsley, Robert VI, 886
Tinsley, Rodney VI, 995
Tinsley, Rodney VI, 1005
Tinsley, Ruth VI, 973
Tinsley, Saml. G. VI, 1006
Tinsley, Saml. G. VI, 1009
Tinsley, Samuel VI, 860
Tinsley, Samuel G. VI, 967
Tinsley, Samuel G. VI, 1005
Tinsley, Sarah VI, 1005
Tinsley, Susan VI, 1005
Tinsley, William VI, 846
Tinsley, William VI, 860
Tinsley, William VI, 886
Tinsley, William VI, 954
Tinsley, William VI, 956
Tinsley, William VI, 971
Tinsley, William VI, 1005
Tinsley, Wm. P. VI, 899
Tinsley, Zachariah D. VI, 1005
Tinucane, Margaret III, 428
Tippin, Hattie IV, 1265
Tipping, Robert III, 317
Tipton, Abigail IV, 293
Tipton, Abigail IV, 596

on, Abijah IV, 448
on, Abijah IV, 458
on, Abijah IV, 573
on, Abijah IV, 597
on, Abijahk Elihu IV, 294
on, Albert IV, 1265
on, Ann Elizabeth IV, 597
on, Cisney IV, 597
on, David IV, 293
on, David IV, 294
on, David IV, 585
on, David IV, 596
on, David IV, 597
on, David IV, 1188
on, Elihu IV, 293
on, Elihu IV, 597
on, Elisha IV, 294
on, Elizabeth IV, 294
on, Esther IV, 293
on, Esther IV, 294
on, Esther IV, 569
on, Esther IV, 597
on, Esther W. IV, 573
on, Esther W. IV, 597
on, Hannah IV, 293
on, Hannah IV, 294
on, Hannah IV, 597
on, Hannah Ann IV, 581
on, Hannah Ann IV, 597
on, Ira I, 1162
on, J. Henderson Farr I, 1162
on, Jane IV, 597
on, John IV, 293
on, John IV, 294
on, John IV, 569
on, John IV, 597
on, Joseph IV, 294
on, Joseph IV, 597
on, Joseph Lindley IV, 1188
on, Levi IV, 294
on, Levi K. IV, 597
on, Luke IV, 293
on, Luke IV, 294
on, Luke IV, 448
on, Luke IV, 500
on, Luke IV, 570
on, Luke IV, 596
on, Luke IV, 597
on, Luke IV, 1188
on, Mary IV, 293
on, Mary IV, 294
on, Mary IV, 570
on, Mary IV, 573
on, Mary IV, 585
on, Mary IV, 596
on, Mary IV, 597
on, Mary IV, 1188
on, Mary Ann IV, 597
on, Mollie Farr I, 1162
on, Phebe IV, 294
on, Phebe IV, 596
on, Phebe IV, 597
on, Phebe Ann IV, 294
on, Phebe Jane IV, 1188
on, Priscilla IV, 293
on, Priscilla IV, 294
on, Priscilla IV, 448
on, Priscilla IV, 500
on, Priscilla IV, 570
ton, Priscilla IV, 596
ton, Priscilla IV, 597
ton, Priscilla H. IV, 1188
ton, Rachel IV, 293
ton, Rachel IV, 294
ton, Rachel IV, 565
ton, Rachel IV, 597
ton, Rebecca I, 1162
ton, Rebecca IV, 577
ton, Rebecca IV, 596
ton, Rebecca IV, 597
ton, Samuel IV, 596
ton, Samuel IV, 597
ton, Sarah IV, 569
ton, Sarah IV, 596
ton, Sarah IV, 597
ton, Sarah Ann IV, 294
ton, Sidney IV, 376
ton, Sidney IV, 448
ton, Sidney IV, 458
ton, Sidney IV, 569
ton, Sidney IV, 573
ton, Sidney IV, 597
ton, Stephen IV, 597
ton, Susan IV, 294
ton, Susanna IV, 596
ton, Susannah IV, 294
ton, Tacy IV, 597
ton, Tacy Ann IV, 294
ton, Tacy Ann IV, 596
ton, Tacy Ann IV, 597
ton, Tacy Ann IV, 1188
Tipton, William IV, 294
Tipton, William IV, 596
Tipton, William B. IV, 597
Tipton, William K. IV, 1188
Tipton, Wm. IV, 597
Tipton, Wm. K. IV, 597
Tipton, Wm. K. IV, 1188
Tire, Milly VI, 308
Tirrence, Eleanor II, 427
Tisdale, Elias I, 175
Tisdale, Elisabeth I, 169
Tisdale, Elisabeth I, 175
Tisdale, Jennie VI, 565
Tisdale, John M. I, 175
Tisdale, Joseph M. I, 175
Tisdale, Lewis I, 175
Tisdale, Lydia I, 175
Tisdale, Martha I, 175
Tisdale, Melia I, 175
Tisdale, Nixon I, 175
Tisdale, Priscilla I, 175
Tisdale, Samuel I, 175
Tisdale, Thaddeus I, 175
Tison, Ann I, 408
Tison, Ann I, 424
Tison, Arcada I, 374
Tison, Arcada I, 424
Tison, Benjamin I, 408
Tison, Benjamin I, 424
Tison, Cornelius I, 374
Tison, Cornelius I, 424
Tison, Elizabeth VI, 1008
Tison, Jane I, 424
Tison, Jane I, 709
Tison, Jane I, 735
Tison, Jean I, 424
Tison, Macklon VI, 1008
Tison, Seberah I, 390
Tison, Seberah I, 424
Titermary, Mary II, 106
Titis, Annie III, 295
Titis, John V. III, 295
Titis, Phebe W. III, 295
Titley, Joseph II, 668
Titley, Thomas III, 317
Titter, Henry II, 427
Titter, Mary II, 427
Tittermary, Mary II, 44
Tittery, Cicely II, 668
Tittery, Cicely II, 693
Tittery, Daniel II, 427
Tittery, Joshua II, 427
Tittery, Joshua II, 668
Tittery, Joshua II, 693
Tittery, Wd. Cicely II, 534
Titus, ??? III, 317
Titus, ??? III, 318
Titus, ??? III, 319
Titus, ??? III, 455
Titus, ??? III, 506
Titus, Abigail II, 311
Titus, Abigail III, 317
Titus, Abigail III, 318
Titus, Abigail III, 333
Titus, Abigail III, 334
Titus, Abigail III, 381
Titus, Abigail III, 385
Titus, Abigail III, 426
Titus, Abigail III, 430
Titus, Abigail III, 434
Titus, Abigail III, 450
Titus, Abigail III, 452
Titus, Abigail III, 454
Titus, Abigail III, 456
Titus, Abigail III, 470
Titus, Abigail III, 471
Titus, Abigail III, 473
Titus, Abigail III, 476
Titus, Abigail III, 500
Titus, Abigail III, 507
Titus, Adeline C. III, 318
Titus, Adrienne III, 405
Titus, Agnes III, 244
Titus, Agnes III, 317
Titus, Agnes III, 319
Titus, Agnes J. III, 317
Titus, Albert III, 318
Titus, Albert III, 319
Titus, Albertine V, 770
Titus, Alice Mary III, 451
Titus, Alice W. III, 317
Titus, Alice W. III, 451
Titus, Allen Gilbert V, 770
Titus, Alonzo III, 318
Titus, Amelia III, 456
Titus, Amelia M. III, 317
Titus, Amelia M. III, 319
Titus, Amy III, 73
Titus, Amy III, 317
Titus, Amy III, 450
Titus, Amy III, 452
Titus, Amy III, 467
Titus, Amy III, 500
Titus, Ancil III, 511
Titus, Ann III, 90
Titus, Ann III, 91
Titus, Ann III, 139
Titus, Ann III, 317
Titus, Ann III, 318
Titus, Ann III, 319
Titus, Ann III, 369
Titus, Ann III, 395
Titus, Ann III, 399
Titus, Ann III, 450
Titus, Ann III, 452
Titus, Ann III, 453
Titus, Ann III, 455
Titus, Ann III, 456
Titus, Ann III, 462
Titus, Ann C. III, 194
Titus, Ann C. III, 317
Titus, Ann Elizabeth III, 318
Titus, Ann H. III, 413
Titus, Ann H. III, 453
Titus, Ann H. III, 454
Titus, Ann H. III, 456
Titus, Ann T. III, 334
Titus, Anna III, 450
Titus, Anna III, 452
Titus, Anna III, 463
Titus, Anna III, 469
Titus, Anna III, 470
Titus, Anna III, 500
Titus, Anna IV, 1382
Titus, Anna C. III, 319
Titus, Anna C. III, 450
Titus, Anna C. III, 469
Titus, Anna K. III, 333
Titus, Anna W. III, 451
Titus, Anne III, 318
Titus, Anne III, 385
Titus, Anne III, 413
Titus, Anne III, 437
Titus, Anne III, 450
Titus, Anne III, 467
Titus, Annie III, 292
Titus, Annie III, 295
Titus, Annie III, 317
Titus, Annie III, 446
Titus, Annie III, 447
Titus, Annie III, 450
Titus, Annie III, 451
Titus, Annie III, 486
Titus, Annie III, 500
Titus, Annie L. III, 319
Titus, Annie S. III, 244
Titus, Annie W. III, 454
Titus, Arthur IV, 1296
Titus, Augustin III, 454
Titus, Austin III, 317
Titus, Benj. III, 393
Titus, Benj. III, 443
Titus, Benjamin III, 317
Titus, Benjamin III, 319
Titus, Benjamin III, 450
Titus, Benjamin III, 454
Titus, Benjamin III, 456
Titus, Benjamin IV, 778
Titus, Bertha III, 317
Titus, Betsey III, 452
Titus, Caroline III, 450
Titus, Caroline III, 451
Titus, Caroline III, 452
Titus, Caroline III, 460
Titus, Caroline A. III, 448
Titus, Caroline B. III, 318
Titus, Caroline J. III, 319
Titus, Caroline R. III, 452
Titus, Caroline V. III, 448
Titus, Caroline V. III, 450
Titus, Caroline V. III, 451
Titus, Catharine III, 426
Titus, Catharine III, 451
Titus, Charity III, 406
Titus, Charity III, 415
Titus, Charity III, 450
Titus, Charity III, 456
Titus, Charles III, 317
Titus, Charles III, 400
Titus, Charles III, 408
Titus, Charles III, 448
Titus, Charles III, 450
Titus, Charles III, 451
Titus, Charles III, 453
Titus, Charles F. III, 317
Titus, Charles F. III, 397
Titus, Charles F. III, 450
Titus, Charles F. III, 451
Titus, Charles F. III, 467
Titus, Charles H. V, 770
Titus, Charles T. III, 455
Titus, Chas. III, 453
Titus, Chas. F. III, 467
Titus, Coles III, 317
Titus, Cornelius Bertram III, 317
Titus, Cornelius Bertram III, 133
Titus, Cornelius Bertram III, 319
Titus, Daniel III, 317
Titus, Daniel III, 450
Titus, Daniel III, 451
Titus, Daniel III, 452
Titus, Daniel III, 467
Titus, Daniel III, 500
Titus, David III, 318
Titus, David III, 379
Titus, David III, 385
Titus, David III, 418
Titus, David III, 451
Titus, David III, 455
Titus, David, Jr. III, 385
Titus, Deborah III, 317
Titus, Deborah III, 385
Titus, Deborah III, 454
Titus, Deborah C. III, 455
Titus, Deborah T. III, 202
Titus, Dewitt C. III, 511
Titus, Edmond III, 317
Titus, Edmond III, 319
Titus, Edmond IV, 1382
Titus, Edmund III, 120
Titus, Edmund III, 144
Titus, Edmund III, 317
Titus, Edmund III, 318
Titus, Edmund III, 319
Titus, Edmund III, 408
Titus, Edmund III, 413
Titus, Edmund III, 423
Titus, Edmund III, 434
Titus, Edmund III, 438
Titus, Edmund III, 441
Titus, Edmund III, 443
Titus, Edmund III, 447
Titus, Edmund III, 451
Titus, Edmund III, 452
Titus, Edmund III, 453
Titus, Edmund III, 454
Titus, Edmund III, 455
Titus, Edmund III, 456
Titus, Edmund III, 474
Titus, Edmund IV, 1382
Titus, Edward III, 451
Titus, Edward III, 456
Titus, Edward Francis III, 451
Titus, Edward P. III, 385
Titus, Edward P. III, 452
Titus, Edward S. III, 426
Titus, Edward S. III, 451
Titus, Eliz S. III, 148
Titus, Eliz. III, 91
Titus, Eliz. III, 346
Titus, Eliz. III, 406
Titus, Eliz. III, 451
Titus, Eliz. III, 452
Titus, Eliz. S. III, 210
Titus, Eliza III, 318
Titus, Eliza III, 385
Titus, Eliza III, 386
Titus, Eliza III, 451
Titus, Eliza T. IV, 1382
Titus, Elizabeth III, 18
Titus, Elizabeth III, 40
Titus, Elizabeth III, 257
Titus, Elizabeth III, 319
Titus, Elizabeth III, 379
Titus, Elizabeth III, 381
Titus, Elizabeth III, 385
Titus, Elizabeth III, 386
Titus, Elizabeth III, 389
Titus, Elizabeth III, 396
Titus, Elizabeth III, 398
Titus, Elizabeth III, 402
Titus, Elizabeth III, 404
Titus, Elizabeth III, 407
Titus, Elizabeth III, 416
Titus, Elizabeth III, 419
Titus, Elizabeth III, 422
Titus, Elizabeth III, 425
Titus, Elizabeth III, 430
Titus, ELizabeth III, 430
Titus, Elizabeth III, 431
Titus, Elizabeth III, 437
Titus, Elizabeth III, 443
Titus, Elizabeth III, 451
Titus, Elizabeth III, 452
Titus, Elizabeth III, 453
Titus, Elizabeth III, 454
Titus, Elizabeth III, 455
Titus, Elizabeth III, 456
Titus, Elizabeth III, 457
Titus, Elizabeth III, 465
Titus, Elizabeth III, 468
Titus, Elizabeth III, 475
Titus, Elizabeth III, 500
Titus, Elizabeth Ann III, 317
Titus, Elizabeth Ann III, 318
Titus, Elizabeth Ann III, 451
Titus, Elizabeth C. III, 317
Titus, Elizabeth C. III, 394
Titus, Elizabeth C. III, 451
Titus, Elizabeth I. III, 318
Titus, Elizabeth P. III, 451
Titus, Elizabeth P. III, 472
Titus, Elizabeth R. III, 318
Titus, Ellwood V. III, 401
Titus, Ellwood V. III, 451
Titus, Elwood V. III, 452
Titus, Emily III, 451
Titus, Emily III, 454
Titus, Emily N. III, 452
Titus, Emma III, 318
Titus, Emma III, 343
Titus, Emma III, 452
Titus, Emma C. III, 456
Titus, Esther III, 317
Titus, Esther III, 319
Titus, Esther III, 351
Titus, Esther III, 406
Titus, Esther III, 451
Titus, Esther C. III, 317
Titus, Esther C. III, 318
Titus, Esther L. III, 441
Titus, Esther L. III, 454
Titus, Esther L. III, 456
Titus, Francis III, 406
Titus, Francis III, 450
Titus, Francis III, 451
Titus, Francis III, 455
Titus, Franklin III, 317
Titus, Frederick E. III, 469
Titus, Geo. B. III, 468
Titus, Geo. P. III, 450
Titus, Geo. P. III, 457
Titus, Geo. P. III, 463
Titus, George III, 317
Titus, George III, 318
Titus, George B. III, 317
Titus, George B. III, 450
Titus, George B. III, 451
Titus, George B. III, 470
Titus, George I. III, 318
Titus, George P. III, 451
Titus, George P. III, 454
Titus, George P. III, 457
Titus, Georgiana III, 317
Titus, Georgiana III, 451
Titus, Gilbert III, 451
Titus, Gilbert III, 476
Titus, Hannah III, 317
Titus, Hannah III, 318
Titus, Hannah III, 319
Titus, Hannah III, 385
Titus, Hannah III, 396
Titus, Hannah III, 406
Titus, Hannah III, 412
Titus, Hannah III, 413
Titus, Hannah III, 418
Titus, Hannah III, 423
Titus, Hannah III, 430
Titus, Hannah III, 447
Titus, Hannah III, 449
Titus, Hannah III, 451
Titus, Hannah III, 452
Titus, Hannah III, 453
Titus, Hannah III, 454
Titus, Hannah III, 456
Titus, Hannah III, 459
Titus, Hannah III, 466
Titus, Hannah III, 467
Titus, Hannah III, 469
Titus, Hannah III, 500
Titus, Hannah III, 502
Titus, Hannah B. III, 317
Titus, Hannah B. III, 450
Titus, Hannah B. III, 452
Titus, Hannah S. III, 319
Titus, Helen Edith III, 347
Titus, Helen L. III, 451
Titus, Henrietta III, 452
Titus, Henrietta III, 455
Titus, Henrietta III, 465
Titus, Henrietta III, 468
Titus, Henrietta IV, 1341
Titus, Henrietta E. III, 194
Titus, Henrietta E. III, 317
Titus, Henrietta E. III, 319
Titus, Henry III, 73
Titus, Henry III, 317
Titus, Henry III, 378
Titus, Henry III, 385
Titus, Henry III, 396
Titus, Henry III, 399
Titus, Henry III, 413
Titus, Henry III, 434
Titus, Henry III, 450

Titus, Henry III, 451
Titus, Henry III, 454
Titus, Henry III, 465
Titus, Henry III, 469
Titus, Henry III, 500
Titus, Henry B. III, 444
Titus, Henry E. III, 452
Titus, Henry P. III, 452
Titus, Henry T. III, 469
Titus, Henry W. III, 500
Titus, Howland III, 500
Titus, I. T. III, 452
Titus, Ida III, 318
Titus, Isaac III, 404
Titus, Isaac III, 406
Titus, Isaac III, 411
Titus, Isaac III, 412
Titus, Isaac III, 451
Titus, Isaac III, 452
Titus, Isaac III, 456
Titus, Isaac III, 464
Titus, Isaac IV, 1382
Titus, Isaac C. III, 317
Titus, Isaac D. III, 454
Titus, Israel III, 452
Titus, Israel D. IV, 778
Titus, Jacob III, 317
Titus, Jacob III, 318
Titus, Jacob III, 385
Titus, Jacob III, 451
Titus, Jacob III, 452
Titus, Jacob III, 456
Titus, Jacob III, 500
Titus, Jacob S. III, 317
Titus, Jacob S. III, 318
Titus, Jacob S. III, 455
Titus, James III, 317
Titus, James III, 399
Titus, James III, 407
Titus, James III, 413
Titus, James III, 421
Titus, James III, 435
Titus, James III, 437
Titus, James III, 444
Titus, James III, 448
Titus, James III, 450
Titus, James III, 451
Titus, James III, 452
Titus, James III, 456
Titus, James III, 500
Titus, James IV, 1382
Titus, James C. III, 317
Titus, James V. III, 318
Titus, Jane III, 318
Titus, Jane III, 379
Titus, Jane III, 385
Titus, Jane III, 421
Titus, Jane III, 434
Titus, Jane III, 435
Titus, Jane III, 444
Titus, Jane III, 451
Titus, Jane III, 452
Titus, Jane III, 453
Titus, Jane C. III, 434
Titus, Jane C. III, 452
Titus, Jane C. III, 453
Titus, Jane Elizabeth III, 407
Titus, Jean III, 452
Titus, Jemima III, 317
Titus, Jemima III, 318
Titus, Jemima III, 406
Titus, Jemima III, 450
Titus, Jemima III, 451
Titus, Jemima III, 452
Titus, Jemima III, 455
Titus, Jericho III, 319
Titus, Jerusha III, 385
Titus, Jerusia III, 318
Titus, Jno. III, 460
Titus, Joanna III, 452
Titus, Joanna III, 469
Titus, Johanna III, 452
Titus, John III, 73
Titus, John III, 317
Titus, John III, 318
Titus, John III, 359
Titus, John III, 385
Titus, John III, 395
Titus, John III, 402
Titus, John III, 404
Titus, John III, 408
Titus, John III, 421
Titus, John III, 432
Titus, John III, 434
Titus, John III, 435
Titus, John III, 439
Titus, John III, 440
Titus, John III, 445
Titus, John III, 451
Titus, John III, 452
Titus, John III, 454
Titus, John III, 455
Titus, John III, 456
Titus, John III, 459
Titus, John III, 462
Titus, John III, 471
Titus, John III, 473
Titus, John III, 500
Titus, John C. III, 456
Titus, John J. III, 452
Titus, John V. III, 317
Titus, John V. III, 330
Titus, John V. III, 453
Titus, John V. III, 459
Titus, John, Jr. III, 318
Titus, John, Jr. III, 319
Titus, John, Jr. III, 435
Titus, John, Jr. III, 452
Titus, John, Jr. III, 456
Titus, John, Jr. III, 500
Titus, John, Sr. III, 444
Titus, John, Sr. III, 452
Titus, John, Sr. III, 454
Titus, Jonathan III, 318
Titus, Jonathan III, 466
Titus, Jonathan III, 500
Titus, Jonathan III, 504
Titus, Jos. III, 347
Titus, Joseph III, 318
Titus, Joseph III, 319
Titus, Joseph Lee III, 317
Titus, Joseph R. III, 318
Titus, Joshua III, 318
Titus, Joshua III, 406
Titus, Joshua III, 423
Titus, Joshua III, 452
Titus, Joshua III, 453
Titus, Joshua III, 454
Titus, Joshua, Jr. III, 453
Titus, Keturah III, 278
Titus, Keturah III, 318
Titus, Kezia III, 445
Titus, Kezia III, 453
Titus, Kezia III, 456
Titus, Lizzie III, 317
Titus, Lizzie III, 318
Titus, Louise Jane III, 318
Titus, Lydia III, 354
Titus, Lydia III, 385
Titus, Lydia III, 394
Titus, Lydia III, 400
Titus, Lydia III, 434
Titus, Lydia III, 453
Titus, Lydia III, 454
Titus, Lydia III, 471
Titus, Lydia Ann III, 245
Titus, Lydia L. III, 379
Titus, Lydia L. III, 385
Titus, Lydia T. III, 18
Titus, Lydia T. III, 318
Titus, Margaret III, 165
Titus, Margaret III, 317
Titus, Margaret III, 318
Titus, Margaret III, 400
Titus, Margaret III, 408
Titus, Margaret III, 411
Titus, Margaret III, 415
Titus, Margaret III, 450
Titus, Margaret III, 452
Titus, Margaret III, 453
Titus, Margaret III, 456
Titus, Margery III, 454
Titus, Maria III, 380
Titus, Maria III, 413
Titus, Maria III, 453
Titus, Maria III, 456
Titus, Maria III, 471
Titus, Maria F. III, 386
Titus, Maria Louise III, 451
Titus, Marie Josephine III, 133
Titus, Marie Josephine III, 317
Titus, Marie Louise III, 401
Titus, Marietta III, 317
Titus, Marietta III, 451
Titus, Marietta III, 468
Titus, Marietta III, 470
Titus, Martha III, 73
Titus, Martha III, 144
Titus, Martha III, 164
Titus, Martha III, 317
Titus, Martha III, 318
Titus, Martha III, 319
Titus, Martha III, 333
Titus, Martha III, 378
Titus, Martha III, 385
Titus, Martha III, 399
Titus, Martha III, 411
Titus, Martha III, 413
Titus, Martha III, 436
Titus, Martha III, 437
Titus, Martha III, 443
Titus, Martha III, 444
Titus, Martha III, 447
Titus, Martha III, 451
Titus, Martha III, 452
Titus, Martha III, 453
Titus, Martha III, 454
Titus, Martha III, 455
Titus, Martha III, 456
Titus, Martha III, 461
Titus, Martha III, 474
Titus, Martha III, 494
Titus, Martha III, 500
Titus, Martha III, 511
Titus, Martha C. III, 318
Titus, Martha C. III, 319
Titus, Martha Esther V, 770
Titus, Martha P. III, 317
Titus, Martha P. III, 318
Titus, Martha S. III, 278
Titus, Martha S. III, 318
Titus, Mary II, 311
Titus, Mary II, 781
Titus, Mary III, 73
Titus, Mary III, 250
Titus, Mary III, 252
Titus, Mary III, 317
Titus, Mary III, 319
Titus, Mary III, 340
Titus, Mary III, 359
Titus, Mary III, 378
Titus, Mary III, 385
Titus, Mary III, 398
Titus, Mary III, 399
Titus, Mary III, 402
Titus, Mary III, 404
Titus, Mary III, 423
Titus, Mary III, 426
Titus, Mary III, 429
Titus, Mary III, 432
Titus, Mary III, 433
Titus, Mary III, 434
Titus, Mary III, 442
Titus, Mary III, 444
Titus, Mary III, 445
Titus, Mary III, 446
Titus, Mary III, 447
Titus, Mary III, 450
Titus, Mary III, 451
Titus, Mary III, 452
Titus, Mary III, 453
Titus, Mary III, 454
Titus, Mary III, 455
Titus, Mary III, 456
Titus, Mary III, 457
Titus, Mary III, 459
Titus, Mary III, 464
Titus, Mary III, 465
Titus, Mary III, 466
Titus, Mary III, 469
Titus, Mary III, 470
Titus, Mary III, 471
Titus, Mary III, 473
Titus, Mary III, 474
Titus, Mary III, 476
Titus, Mary III, 500
Titus, Mary III, 501
Titus, Mary III, 504
Titus, Mary IV, 778
Titus, Mary IV, 1382
Titus, Mary Ann III, 317
Titus, Mary Ann III, 448
Titus, Mary Ann III, 450
Titus, Mary F. III, 317
Titus, Mary F. III, 319
Titus, Mary F. III, 386
Titus, Mary F. III, 397
Titus, Mary F. III, 450
Titus, Mary F. III, 451
Titus, Mary F. III, 467
Titus, Mary Frances III, 231
Titus, Mary Jenet V, 770
Titus, Mary L. III, 451
Titus, Mary P. III, 319
Titus, Mary P. III, 451
Titus, Mary P. III, 457
Titus, Mary P. III, 472
Titus, Mary P. III, 492
Titus, Mary P. III, 500
Titus, Mary T. III, 450
Titus, Mary T. III, 453
Titus, Mary T. III, 463
Titus, Mary V. III, 452
Titus, Mary W. III, 317
Titus, Mary W. III, 420
Titus, Mary W. III, 450
Titus, Mary W. III, 451
Titus, Mary W. III, 453
Titus, Mary W. III, 456
Titus, Mary W. III, 469
Titus, Melle Stanleyetta III, 318
Titus, Melle Stanleyetta III, 347
Titus, Mercy W. III, 105
Titus, Mercy W. III, 318
Titus, Michael III, 385
Titus, Michael III, 389
Titus, Michael M. III, 318
Titus, Nancy III, 393
Titus, Nancy III, 450
Titus, Nelson IV, 1382
Titus, Obad. III, 500
Titus, Obadiah III, 500
Titus, Obadiah III, 501
Titus, Oliver III, 453
Titus, Oliver III, 468
Titus, Oliver C. III, 318
Titus, Oliver C. III, 319
Titus, Oliver C. III, 343
Titus, Orsin IV, 1382
Titus, Orson IV, 1382
Titus, Patience III, 144
Titus, Patience III, 317
Titus, Patience III, 318
Titus, Patience III, 413
Titus, Patience III, 451
Titus, Patience III, 454
Titus, Peggy III, 318
Titus, Peggy III, 419
Titus, Peggy III, 454
Titus, Peter III, 266
Titus, Peter III, 318
Titus, Peter III, 385
Titus, Peter III, 398
Titus, Peter III, 419
Titus, Peter III, 430
Titus, Peter III, 451
Titus, Peter III, 452
Titus, Peter III, 454
Titus, Peter S. III, 278
Titus, Peter S. III, 318
Titus, Peter, Jr. III, 442
Titus, Peter, Jr. III, 454
Titus, Phebe III, 144
Titus, Phebe III, 317
Titus, Phebe III, 318
Titus, Phebe III, 385
Titus, Phebe III, 398
Titus, Phebe III, 412
Titus, Phebe III, 413
Titus, Phebe III, 416
Titus, Phebe III, 425
Titus, Phebe III, 438
Titus, Phebe III, 439
Titus, Phebe III, 441
Titus, Phebe III, 448
Titus, Phebe III, 450
Titus, Phebe III, 451
Titus, Phebe III, 452
Titus, Phebe III, 453
Titus, Phebe III, 454
Titus, Phebe III, 455
Titus, Phebe III, 456
Titus, Phebe III, 461
Titus, Phebe III, 462
Titus, Phebe III, 464
Titus, Phebe III, 465
Titus, Phebe III, 469
Titus, Phebe III, 500
Titus, Phebe III, 506
Titus, Phebe III, 507
Titus, Phebe B. III, 105
Titus, Phebe B. III, 318
Titus, Phebe C. III, 451
Titus, Phebe J. III, 470
Titus, Phebe L. III, 385
Titus, Phebe L. III, 389
Titus, Phebe W. III, 318
Titus, Phebe W. III, 319
Titus, Phebe W. III, 330
Titus, Phebe W. III, 398
Titus, Phebe W. III, 446
Titus, Phebe W. III, 450
Titus, Phebe W. III, 453
Titus, Phebe W. III, 459
Titus, Phebe W. III, 460
Titus, Phila. III, 453
Titus, Philadelphia III, 318
Titus, Philadelphia III, 445
Titus, Philadelphia III, 452
Titus, Philadelphia III, 454
Titus, Rachel III, 454
Titus, Rachel W. III, 270
Titus, Rachel W. III, 439
Titus, Rachel W. III, 454
Titus, Rachel W. III, 495
Titus, Rachel W. III, 500
Titus, Rebecca III, 453
Titus, Rhoda III, 111
Titus, Richard II, 311
Titus, Richard III, 202
Titus, Richard III, 317
Titus, Richard III, 318
Titus, Richard III, 319
Titus, Richard III, 385
Titus, Richard III, 426
Titus, Richard III, 431
Titus, Richard III, 447
Titus, Richard III, 451
Titus, Richard III, 452
Titus, Richard III, 453
Titus, Richard III, 454
Titus, Richard III, 455
Titus, Richard III, 458
Titus, Richard III, 469
Titus, Richard III, 475
Titus, Richard III, 476
Titus, Richard III, 501
Titus, Richard A. III, 317
Titus, Richard A. III, 318
Titus, Richard A. III, 319
Titus, Richard D. III, 317
Titus, Richard R. III, 318
Titus, Richard U. III, 318
Titus, Richard W. III, 319
Titus, Richard W. III, 454
Titus, Richard W. III, 492
Titus, Richard W. III, 500
Titus, Richard, Jr. III, 318
Titus, Robert III, 319
Titus, Robert III, 420
Titus, Robert III, 450
Titus, Robert III, 451
Titus, Robert III, 454
Titus, Robert III, 456
Titus, Robert III, 469
Titus, Robert Franklin III, 454
Titus, Robert P. III, 453
Titus, Robert S. III, 319
Titus, Robert W. III, 441
Titus, Robert W. III, 454
Titus, Robert W. III, 456
Titus, Robt. III, 420
Titus, Rosetta III, 434
Titus, Rosetta III, 454
Titus, Rowland III, 18
Titus, Rowland III, 318
Titus, Rowland III, 394
Titus, Rowland III, 439
Titus, Rowland III, 451
Titus, Rowland III, 453
Titus, Rowland III, 461
Titus, Ruth III, 406
Titus, Ruth III, 448
Titus, Ruth III, 450
Titus, Ruth III, 451
Titus, Ruth III, 455
Titus, Ruth III, 456
Titus, Ruth A. III, 318
Titus, Ruth Amelia III, 318
Titus, Ruth Amelia III, 319
Titus, Ruth Amelia III, 347
Titus, Sam'l III, 437
Titus, Samuel III, 40
Titus, Samuel III, 144
Titus, Samuel III, 250
Titus, Samuel III, 257
Titus, Samuel III, 317
Titus, Samuel III, 319
Titus, Samuel III, 333
Titus, Samuel III, 334
Titus, Samuel III, 381
Titus, Samuel III, 385
Titus, Samuel III, 396
Titus, Samuel III, 412
Titus, Samuel III, 430
Titus, Samuel III, 434
Titus, Samuel III, 436
Titus, Samuel III, 438
Titus, Samuel III, 450
Titus, Samuel III, 451
Titus, Samuel III, 452
Titus, Samuel III, 455
Titus, Samuel III, 457
Titus, Samuel III, 470
Titus, Samuel III, 471
Titus, Samuel III, 472
Titus, Samuel III, 500
Titus, Samuel IV, 1377
Titus, Samuel IV, 1382
Titus, Samuel B. III, 450
Titus, Samuel C. III, 319
Titus, Samuel C. III, 385
Titus, Samuel C. III, 451
Titus, Samuel G. III, 405
Titus, Samuel G. III, 455
Titus, Samuel J. III, 318
Titus, Samuel J. III, 319
Titus, Samuel L. III, 317
Titus, Samuel L. III, 319
Titus, Samuel P. III, 185
Titus, Samuel P. III, 318
Titus, Samuel P. III, 319
Titus, Samuel R. III, 462
Titus, Samuel S. IV, 1382
Titus, Samuel, Jr. III, 455

Sarah III, 18
Sarah III, 43
Sarah III, 82
Sarah III, 91
Sarah III, 92
Sarah III, 141
Sarah III, 144
Sarah III, 172
Sarah III, 185
Sarah III, 202
Sarah III, 252
Sarah III, 266
Sarah III, 317
Sarah III, 318
Sarah III, 319
Sarah III, 359
Sarah III, 381
Sarah III, 385
Sarah III, 393
Sarah III, 394
Sarah III, 396
Sarah III, 402
Sarah III, 404
Sarah III, 406
Sarah III, 408
Sarah III, 412
Sarah III, 413
Sarah III, 416
Sarah III, 419
Sarah III, 421
, Sarah III, 429
, Sarah III, 432
, Sarah III, 433
, Sarah III, 434
, Sarah III, 435
, Sarah III, 439
, Sarah III, 440
, Sarah III, 441
, Sarah III, 445
, Sarah III, 450
s, Sarah III, 451
s, Sarah III, 452
s, Sarah III, 453
s, Sarah III, 454
s, Sarah III, 455
s, Sarah III, 456
s, Sarah III, 457
s, Sarah III, 458
s, Sarah III, 459
s, Sarah III, 461
s, Sarah III, 462
s, Sarah III, 463
s, Sarah III, 464
s, Sarah III, 468
s, Sarah III, 469
s, Sarah III, 473
s, Sarah III, 475
s, Sarah III, 500
s, Sarah III, 501
s, Sarah III, 507
s, Sarah IV, 1377
s, Sarah IV, 1382
s, Sarah A. IV, 1377
s, Sarah A. IV, 1381
s, Sarah A. IV, 1382
s, Sarah C. III, 319
s, Sarah O. III, 319
s, Sarah P. III, 404
s, Sarah P. III, 451
s, Sarah P. III, 452
s, Sarah P. III, 471
s, Sarah P. IV, 1341
s, Sarah R. III, 318
s, Sarah R. III, 319
s, Sarah W. III, 317
us, Sarah W. III, 465
us, Silas III, 144
us, Silas III, 317
us, Silas III, 319
us, Silas III, 379
us, Silas III, 381
us, Silas III, 385
us, Silas III, 386
us, Silas III, 399
us, Silas III, 416
us, Silas III, 419
us, Silas III, 451
us, Silas III, 452
us, Silas III, 453
us, Silas III, 454
us, Silas III, 455
us, Silas III, 457
us, Silas III, 464
us, Silas III, 465
us, Silas C. III, 455
us, Stanley H. III, 318
us, Stanleyetta III, 318
us, Stephen III, 244
us, Stephen III, 317
us, Stephen III, 318
us, Stephen III, 319
Titus, Stephen III, 429
Titus, Stephen III, 455
Titus, Stephen III, 456
Titus, Stephen III, 470
Titus, Stephen III, 500
Titus, Stephen III, 502
Titus, Stephen III, 506
Titus, Stephen III, 507
Titus, Stephen IV, 1377
Titus, Stephen IV, 1382
Titus, Stephen R. III, 451
Titus, Stephen V. III, 318
Titus, Stephen W. III, 412
Titus, Stephen W. III, 454
Titus, Stephen W. III, 455
Titus, Stephen W. III, 456
Titus, Stephen W. III, 459
Titus, Stephen W. III, 500
Titus, Stephen Wm. III, 319
Titus, Susan III, 318
Titus, Susan III, 385
Titus, Susan III, 454
Titus, Susan III, 456
Titus, Susannah III, 385
Titus, T. III, 495
Titus, Temperance III, 419
Titus, Temperance III, 451
Titus, Temperance III, 455
Titus, Thomas III, 318
Titus, Thomas III, 385
Titus, Thomas III, 445
Titus, Thomas III, 454
Titus, Thomas III, 456
Titus, Thomas Everett III, 469
Titus, Thomas U. III, 456
Titus, Thomas W. III, 317
Titus, Thomas W. III, 319
Titus, Timothy III, 406
Titus, Timothy III, 411
Titus, Timothy III, 415
Titus, Timothy III, 450
Titus, Timothy III, 453
Titus, Timothy III, 456
Titus, Timothy, Jr. III, 456
Titus, Townsend III, 318
Titus, Waller III, 456
Titus, Walter III, 454
Titus, Walter R. III, 456
Titus, Wd. Elizabeth III, 438
Titus, Wd. Hannah III, 456
Titus, Wd. Jane III, 462
Titus, Wd. Phebe III, 500
Titus, Wd. Sarah III, 408
Titus, Willet III, 448
Titus, Willet III, 456
Titus, William III, 43
Titus, William III, 252
Titus, William III, 318
Titus, William III, 319
Titus, William III, 359
Titus, William III, 385
Titus, William III, 396
Titus, William III, 398
Titus, William III, 402
Titus, William III, 416
Titus, William III, 425
Titus, William III, 433
Titus, William III, 443
Titus, William III, 446
Titus, William III, 449
Titus, William III, 450
Titus, William III, 451
Titus, William III, 452
Titus, William III, 453
Titus, William III, 454
Titus, William III, 456
Titus, William III, 469
Titus, William III, 470
Titus, William III, 473
Titus, William III, 475
Titus, William III, 500
Titus, William C. III, 319
Titus, William C. III, 451
Titus, William E. III, 451
Titus, William L. III, 317
Titus, William L. III, 319
Titus, William L. III, 380
Titus, William L. III, 386
Titus, William L. III, 454
Titus, William L., Jr. III, 386
Titus, William Mudge III, 319
Titus, William P. III, 413
Titus, William P. III, 453
Titus, William P. III, 456
Titus, William T. III, 105
Titus, William T. III, 318
Titus, William W. III, 319
Titus, William W. III, 456
Titus, Wm. III, 319
Titus, Wm. III, 396
Titus, Wm. III, 451
Titus, Wm. III, 507
Titus, Wm. L. III, 91
Titus, Wm. L. III, 194
Titus, Wm. L. III, 318
Titus, Wm. L. III, 319
Titus, Wm. L. III, 389
Titus, Wm. M. III, 318
Titus, Wm. Mudge III, 231
Titus, Wm. P. III, 453
Titus, Wm. W. III, 244
Titus, Wm. W. III, 245
Titus, Wm. W. III, 317
Titus, Zilpha III, 456
Tjaden, Florence S. II, 139
Tjaden, John C. II, 139
Tobey, Samuel R., Jr. III, 319
Tobias, Jacob III, 456
Tobias, Jacob III, 464
Tobias, Margaret III, 456
Tobias, Margaret III, 464
Tobias, Phyllis III, 319
Tobias, Priscilla III, 319
Tobias, Rebecca III, 456
Tobias, Rebecca III, 464
Tobin, Emma V, 648
Toby, Alise IV, 1296
Tod, Mary I, 998
Tod, Mary I, 1000
Todd, ??? IV, 448
Todd, ??? IV, 1047
Todd, Alice II, 625
Todd, Alice II, 668
Todd, Alice II, 930
Todd, Ann IV, 448
Todd, Ann IV, 449
Todd, Ann IV, 1067
Todd, Ann IV, 1079
Todd, Anna E. IV, 1043
Todd, Asenath IV, 428
Todd, Asenath IV, 448
Todd, Asenath IV, 449
Todd, Caroline IV, 1078
Todd, Caroline IV, 1079
Todd, Caroline E. IV, 1079
Todd, Daniel IV, 448
Todd, David VI, 136
Todd, David VI, 142
Todd, Deborah II, 427
Todd, Deborah II, 597
Todd, Deborah II, 669
Todd, Deborah Mary II, 668
Todd, Dolley II, 427
Todd, Dolly II, 589
Todd, Dolly II, 668
Todd, Elihu IV, 448
Todd, Elihu IV, 449
Todd, Elihu IV, 1111
Todd, Elihu IV, 1117
Todd, Elisha IV, 438
Todd, Elisha IV, 448
Todd, Elisha IV, 449
Todd, Elisha IV, 1090
Todd, Elisha IV, 1117
Todd, Eliza IV, 1114
Todd, Eliza B. II, 427
Todd, Elizabeth V, 363
Todd, Elizabeth Blair II, 668
Todd, Emily IV, 449
Todd, Emily IV, 1090
Todd, Emily IV, 1117
Todd, Esther V, 479
Todd, Eunice IV, 422
Todd, Eunice IV, 1100
Todd, Eunice IV, 1116
Todd, Eunice IV, 1117
Todd, Eunis IV, 1107
Todd, Frank IV, 778
Todd, Gertrude Glenn IV, 778
Todd, Harry IV, 778
Todd, Harry S. IV, 778
Todd, Humphrey IV, 448
Todd, James II, 427
Todd, James II, 625
Todd, James II, 668
Todd, James II, 823
Todd, James IV, 449
Todd, James IV, 1079
Todd, James V, 363
Todd, John II, 427
Todd, John II, 625
Todd, John II, 668
Todd, John IV, 448
Todd, John IV, 449
Todd, John IV, 778
Todd, John IV, 1117
Todd, John Payne II, 427
Todd, John Payne II, 668
Todd, John W. V, 363
Todd, John, Jr. II, 427
Todd, John, Jr. II, 510
Todd, John, Jr. II, 668
Todd, Josephine IV, 778
Todd, Lillian IV, 1117
Todd, Lindley IV, 449
Todd, Lindley IV, 1117
Todd, Lydia IV, 449
Todd, Lydia IV, 1117
Todd, Mabel IV, 778
Todd, Mabel Lillian IV, 778
Todd, Maranda IV, 449
Todd, Maranda IV, 1079
Todd, Margaret J. V, 1022
Todd, Maria IV, 1117
Todd, Mariah IV, 1117
Todd, Marinda IV, 1079
Todd, Mary II, 96
Todd, Mary II, 106
Todd, Mary II, 427
Todd, Mary II, 496
Todd, Mary II, 510
Todd, Mary II, 625
Todd, Mary II, 668
Todd, Mary IV, 161
Todd, Mary IV, 445
Todd, Mary IV, 448
Todd, Mary IV, 449
Todd, Mary IV, 917
Todd, Mary IV, 1117
Todd, Mary E. IV, 422
Todd, Mary E. IV, 1107
Todd, Mary E. IV, 1117
Todd, Mary H. IV, 1117
Todd, Nancy IV, 449
Todd, Nancy V, 363
Todd, Oliver IV, 1117
Todd, Rebecca I, 424
Todd, Rebecca I, 1041
Todd, Rebecca IV, 437
Todd, Rebecca IV, 448
Todd, Rebecca IV, 449
Todd, Rebecca IV, 1079
Todd, Rebecka I, 1051
Todd, Rebeckah IV, 161
Todd, Rebeckah IV, 449
Todd, Rebekah I, 424
Todd, Richard IV, 778
Todd, Robert I, 1051
Todd, Robert IV, 422
Todd, Robert IV, 448
Todd, Robert IV, 449
Todd, Robert IV, 778
Todd, Robert IV, 1079
Todd, Robert IV, 1100
Todd, Robert IV, 1107
Todd, Robert IV, 1116
Todd, Robert IV, 1117
Todd, Robert, Jr. IV, 1079
Todd, Sallie IV, 1117
Todd, Sally IV, 438
Todd, Sally IV, 449
Todd, Sally IV, 1090
Todd, Sally IV, 1117
Todd, Samuel P. II, 669
Todd, Samuel Poultney II, 668
Todd, Sarah IV, 159
Todd, Sarah IV, 161
Todd, Sarah IV, 449
Todd, Sarah IV, 552
Todd, Sarah IV, 554
Todd, Sarah IV, 1079
Todd, Sarah IV, 1111
Todd, Sarah IV, 1114
Todd, Sarah IV, 1116
Todd, Sarah IV, 1117
Todd, Shannon IV, 449
Todd, Shannon IV, 1117
Todd, Sibbella IV, 445
Todd, Sibbella IV, 1117
Todd, Sibbilla IV, 449
Todd, Sibbilla IV, 1117
Todd, Sibilla IV, 161
Todd, Sibilla IV, 428
Todd, Sibilla IV, 437
Todd, Sibilla IV, 448
Todd, Sibilla IV, 449
Todd, Sibilla IV, 1110
Todd, Sibilla IV, 1117
Todd, Stephen I, 1051
Todd, Stephen IV, 161
Todd, Stephen IV, 428
Todd, Stephen IV, 437
Todd, Stephen IV, 445
Todd, Stephen IV, 448
Todd, Stephen IV, 449
Todd, Stephen IV, 1117
Todd, Susanna IV, 1051
Todd, Susanna IV, 1079
Todd, Theodate I, 1051
Todd, Theodate IV, 449
Todd, Theodate IV, 1057
Todd, Theodate IV, 1079
Todd, Thomas William IV, 1117
Todd, Thos. K. IV, 1114
Todd, Tillman IV, 1117
Todd, Tilman IV, 1117
Todd, Wd. Alice II, 823
Todd, William I, 1051
Todd, William IV, 448
Todd, William IV, 449
Todd, William IV, 1117
Todd, Willie V, 1022
Todd, Wm. IV, 161
Todd, Wm. IV, 1117
Todhunter, Aaron V, 286
Todhunter, Aaron V, 466
Todhunter, Abner I, 1099
Todhunter, Abner V, 133
Todhunter, Abner V, 453
Todhunter, Abner V, 466
Todhunter, Abner, Jr. V, 285
Todhunter, Abner, Sr. V, 286
Todhunter, Abraham VI, 573
Todhunter, Alice V, 715
Todhunter, Alice M. V, 466
Todhunter, Allise M. V, 286
Todhunter, Amos V, 286
Todhunter, Amos V, 451
Todhunter, Amos V, 466
Todhunter, Amos V, 715
Todhunter, Anna M. V, 285
Todhunter, Anna M. V, 286
Todhunter, Bell V, 466
Todhunter, Bessie IV, 1306
Todhunter, Bessie C. V, 715
Todhunter, Bessie C. E. V, 466
Todhunter, Caroline V, 286
Todhunter, Charles V, 286
Todhunter, Clara V, 715
Todhunter, Clara E. V, 286
Todhunter, Clara E. V, 466
Todhunter, Clara E. V, 715
Todhunter, Clayton Vincent V, 286
Todhunter, Edith Rebecca III, 320
Todhunter, Eleanor V, 133
Todhunter, Eleanor V, 285
Todhunter, Eleanor V, 466
Todhunter, Elenor V, 285
Todhunter, Elizabeth V, 286
Todhunter, Elizabeth V, 453
Todhunter, Elizabeth V, 466
Todhunter, Ellen Frances III, 320
Todhunter, Emiline V, 285
Todhunter, Emiline V, 453
Todhunter, Emily V, 286
Todhunter, Emily V, 451
Todhunter, Emily V, 715
Todhunter, Emily E. V, 286
Todhunter, Emily E. V, 466
Todhunter, Evan VI, 573
Todhunter, Frances Ann III, 320
Todhunter, George F. V, 286
Todhunter, Hannah VI, 436
Todhunter, Hannah VI, 452
Todhunter, Hannah VI, 523
Todhunter, Hannah VI, 573
Todhunter, Henry M. V, 285
Todhunter, Henry M. V, 286
Todhunter, Horace Scott V, 286
Todhunter, Ida M. V, 285
Todhunter, Ida M. V, 286
Todhunter, Ida M. V, 453
Todhunter, Isaac I, 1099
Todhunter, Isaac V, 133
Todhunter, Isaac V, 215
Todhunter, Isaac V, 285
Todhunter, Isaac V, 466
Todhunter, Isaac VI, 452
Todhunter, Isaac VI, 573
Todhunter, Isaac Newton V, 286
Todhunter, Isaac, Jr. V, 286
Todhunter, Jacob I, 1099
Todhunter, Jacob V, 133
Todhunter, Jacob V, 286
Todhunter, Jacob V, 466
Todhunter, Jacob VI, 573
Todhunter, Jane II, 820
Todhunter, Jephthah V, 285
Todhunter, Jephthat V, 286
Todhunter, Jerusha V, 252
Todhunter, Jerusha V, 285
Todhunter, Jerusha V, 286
Todhunter, John V, 286
Todhunter, John V, 936
Todhunter, John VI, 573
Todhunter, Joseph VI, 573
Todhunter, Joseph Massey Howey III, 320
Todhunter, Joshua Edmundson III, 320
Todhunter, Julianna V, 453
Todhunter, July V, 133

Todhunter, Jury I, 1099
Todhunter, Jury V, 252
Todhunter, Jury V, 285
Todhunter, Jury V, 286
Todhunter, Laura C. V, 286
Todhunter, Laura C. V, 466
Todhunter, Laura C. V, 715
Todhunter, Lauretta V, 286
Todhunter, Lavena V, 451
Todhunter, Layton W. V, 466
Todhunter, Layton W. V, 715
Todhunter, Layton Wilson V, 286
Todhunter, Lewis V, 286
Todhunter, Lucetta V, 465
Todhunter, Lucetta V, 466
Todhunter, Lucetta E. V, 286
Todhunter, Lucy E. V, 466
Todhunter, Lucy E. V, 715
Todhunter, Margaret V, 133
Todhunter, Margaret V, 286
Todhunter, Margaret V, 291
Todhunter, Margaret VI, 496
Todhunter, Margaret VI, 573
Todhunter, Margaret VI, 578
Todhunter, Marguerite V, 701
Todhunter, Marguerite V, 715
Todhunter, Martha A. V, 285
Todhunter, Mary V, 659
Todhunter, Mary V, 715
Todhunter, Mary VI, 523
Todhunter, Mary VI, 573
Todhunter, Mary L. V, 286
Todhunter, Melissa V, 466
Todhunter, Milton V, 286
Todhunter, Milton V, 466
Todhunter, Milton V, 648
Todhunter, Minnie V, 285
Todhunter, Ora V, 715
Todhunter, Ora V, 716
Todhunter, Oscar B. V, 286
Todhunter, Oscar B. V, 466
Todhunter, Oscar B. V, 936
Todhunter, Rebecca V, 240
Todhunter, Rebecca V, 286
Todhunter, Rebecca V, 466
Todhunter, Rebecca V, 468
Todhunter, Rebecca V, 936
Todhunter, Ruth V, 713
Todhunter, Ruth V, 715
Todhunter, Ruthanna V, 713
Todhunter, Ruthanna V, 715
Todhunter, Sarah V, 286
Todhunter, Virgie V, 715
Todhunter, Walter V, 715
Todhunter, Walter V, 716
Todhunter, William V, 286
Toedteberg, Miss Emma III, 477
Toel, Elvira VI, 854
Toel, Mary VI, 854
Toland, Charles IV, 1341
Toland, Chas. IV, 1341
Toland, Hannah S. II, 749
Toland, Hannah S. II, 771
Toland, Mary IV, 1341
Toland, Mrs. Jennie V, 1022
Toland, W. E. IV, 1341
Tolbat, John V, 535
Tolbat, Mary V, 535
Tolbert, Abigail IV, 294
Tolbert, David IV, 294
Tolbert, Hannah II, 450
Tolbert, Hannah II, 663
Tolbert, Hannah II, 1019
Tolbert, Hannah II, 1033
Tolbert, John IV, 294
Tolbert, Mary II, 663
Tolbert, Nathan IV, 294
Tolbert, Rachel IV, 294
Tolbert, Rebecca IV, 294
Tolbert, Samuel IV, 294
Tolbert, Sarah I, 998
Tolbert, William V, 869
Tolbot, Jacob VI, 449
Tolbot, John VI, 449
Tolbot, Lydia VI, 449
Tolbot, Mary VI, 449
Tolbot, Rachel VI, 449
Tolbot, Rebecca VI, 449
Tolbot, Sarah II, 427
Tolbot, Sarah VI, 449
Tolbot, Susannah VI, 449
Tolbot, Thomas II, 427
Tolbott, Joseph IV, 794
Tolbott, Margaret IV, 794
Tolefree, Maria Amelia III, 44
Tolefree, Wm. III, 44
Toler, Betsey Ann VI, 1005
Toler, Chesley VI, 1005
Toler, Chesley, Jr. VI, 1005
Toler, Christopher VI, 1005
Toler, Edmund VI, 820
Toler, Edy VI, 1005
Toler, Elizabeth VI, 1005
Toler, Garland H. VI, 1005
Toler, John VI, 1005
Toler, Juley VI, 820
Toler, July VI, 922
Toler, Lizzie I, 340
Toler, Mary Ann VI, 931
Toler, Nancy VI, 922
Toler, Sally VI, 922
Toler, Sally VI, 1005
Toler, Stephen VI, 922
Tolerton, Alexander IV, 778
Tolerton, Ann IV, 778
Tolerton, Ann IV, 848
Tolerton, Esther IV, 731
Tolerton, Esther IV, 778
Tolerton, Frances IV, 778
Tolerton, Frances IV, 848
Tolerton, Francis IV, 848
Tolerton, Hill IV, 778
Tolerton, James IV, 500
Tolerton, James IV, 778
Tolerton, James IV, 848
Tolerton, Mary E. IV, 777
Tolerton, Mary E. IV, 778
Tolerton, Robert IV, 778
Tolerton, Wm. IV, 778
Tolfree, John S. III, 320
Tolfree, Maria III, 320
Tolfree, Maria Amelia III, 320
Tolfree, Mary Bowron III, 320
Tolfree, Sarah III, 320
Tolfree, Sarah A. III, 320
Tolfree, William III, 195
Tolfree, William III, 320
Tolfrey, William III, 195
Tolier, Rebecca II, 427
Toll, Delila VI, 826
Toll, Eliza V, 286
Toll, Harry V, 286
Toll, Lida V, 286
Toll, Louise V, 286
Toll, Mary VI, 826
Toll, Paul V, 286
Tollerton, ??? III, 320
Tollerton, Charlotte Ann III, 320
Tollerton, Robert III, 320
Tollerton, Robert IV, 778
Tolleson, Hannah I, 1061
Tolleson, Hannah I, 1063
Tolley, Christopher VI, 1005
Tolley, Elizabeth VI, 1005
Tolley, Ezekiel VI, 983
Tolley, Ezekiel VI, 1005
Tolley, Ezekiel D. VI, 1005
Tolley, Jemima VI, 1005
Tolley, Joseph VI, 1005
Tolley, Joseph H. VI, 1005
Tolley, Lucy VI, 1005
Tolley, Martha VI, 1005
Tolley, Mary VI, 869
Tolley, Mary VI, 1005
Tolley, Owen VI, 970
Tolley, Owen VI, 1005
Tolley, Owen P. VI, 983
Tolley, Polly VI, 1005
Tolley, Priscilla VI, 1005
Tolley, Samuel VI, 1005
Tolley, Susanna L. VI, 885
Tolley, Thomas VI, 869
Tolley, Thomas VI, 885
Tolley, Thomas VI, 1005
Tollis, Ann IV, 63
Tollis, Jason IV, 63
Tollis, Richard IV, 63
Tollis, William IV, 63
Tolly, Bertha Anne V, 648
Tolly, Catharine V, 648
Tolly, Christopher VI, 1005
Tolly, Church V, 648
Tolly, Eliza V, 648
Tolly, Elizabeth VI, 1005
Tolly, Lottie Naomi V, 648
Tolly, Mary VI, 944
Tolly, Perthena VI, 983
Tolly, Priscilla VI, 1005
Tolly, Rebecca V, 648
Tolly, Samuel V, 648
Tolly, Samuel VI, 1005
Tom, Catharine III, 320
Tom, Catherine III, 114
Tom, Penninah I, 63
Tom, Thomas III, 114
Tom, Thomas III, 320
Tomas, Elizabeth IV, 314
Tomas, Sarah I, 200
Tomas, Thomas VI, 94
Tombaugh, Addie J. IV, 1031
Tombaugh, Ruth IV, 1031
Tombaugh, Solomon IV, 1031
Tombaugh, William IV, 1031
Tombling, Elizabeth VI, 87
Tombough, Addis J. IV, 1031
Tombough, Wm. IV, 1031
Tombs, Mary I, 151
Tombs, Mary I, 169
Tome, Ella IV, 1341
Tome, Ethel IV, 1341
Tome, Ethel M. IV, 1341
Tome, Sophia IV, 1341
Tome, Wilburt W. IV, 1341
Tomee, Rebekah I, 76
Tomelnson, Joseph, Jr. II, 975
Tomelnson, Margaret II, 975
Tomelson, Mary Ann IV, 42
Tomes, Abigail I Sup 1, 4
Tomes, Abigail I Sup 1, 6
Tomes, Benjamin I, 200
Tomes, Elizabeth I, 90
Tomes, Elizabeth I Sup 1, 5
Tomes, Elizabeth I Sup 1, 6
Tomes, Francis I, 50
Tomes, Francis I, 59
Tomes, Francis I, 62
Tomes, Francis I, 64
Tomes, Francis I, 76
Tomes, Francis I, 87
Tomes, Francis I, 90
Tomes, Francis I Sup 1, 4
Tomes, Francis I Sup 1, 5
Tomes, Francis I Sup 1, 6
Tomes, Francis I Sup 1, 7
Tomes, John A. I, 200
Tomes, Joshua I, 50
Tomes, Joshua I, 76
Tomes, Joshua I, 90
Tomes, Joshua I Sup 1, 6
Tomes, Margaret I, 76
Tomes, Margaret I Sup 1, 4
Tomes, Margaret I Sup 1, 7
Tomes, Mary I, 61
Tomes, Mary I, 76
Tomes, Mary I, 90
Tomes, Mary I Sup 1, 5
Tomes, Mary I Sup 1, 6
Tomes, Penelope I, 90
Tomes, Pharibe I, 200
Tomes, Pleasant I, 76
Tomes, Pleasant I, 87
Tomes, Priscila I, 64
Tomes, Priscila I, 76
Tomes, Prisela I, 90
Tomes, Rebecca I Sup 1, 5
Tomes, Rebecca I Sup 1, 6
Tomes, Rebeckah I Sup 1, 5
Tomes, Rebeckah I Sup 1, 6
Tomes, Sarah I, 50
Tomes, Sarah I, 76
Tomes, Widow Margaret I, 59
Tomes, Widow Rebecca I, 90
Tomeses, Joshua I, 90
Tomkin, Ann IV, 354
Tomkins, ??? III, 386
Tomkins, Benjamin II, 669
Tomkins, Elizabeth II, 427
Tomkins, Elizabeth II, 781
Tomkins, Elizabeth II, 784
Tomkins, Elizabeth II, 827
Tomkins, Elizabeth III, 386
Tomkins, Hannah II, 821
Tomkins, Hannah II, 827
Tomkins, Jacob II, 771
Tomkins, Jacob II, 784
Tomkins, Jacob II, 827
Tomkins, Jacob, Jr. II, 669
Tomkins, Jane Edge II, 823
Tomkins, John II, 427
Tomkins, John V, 133
Tomkins, Joshua II, 268
Tomkins, Joshua II, 448
Tomkins, Kezia II, 669
Tomkins, Lydia II, 781
Tomkins, Lydia V, 133
Tomkins, Mary VI, 9
Tomkins, Robert II, 448
Tomkins, Robert II, 781
Tomkins, Sarah II, 669
Tomkins, Sarah V, 133
Tomkins, Wd. Elizabeth II, 784
Tomlenson, Joseph, Jr. II, 1033
Tomlenson, Margaret II, 1033
Tomlin, Elizabeth II, 216
Tomlin, Harriett V, 434
Tomlin, Harriett V, 715
Tomlin, Isabel V, 602
Tomlin, Margaret Ann VI, 215
Tomlin, Margaret Ann VI, 218
Tomlin, Peter V, 715
Tomlins, Elisabeth II, 268
Tomlinson, ??? II, 177
Tomlinson, Aaron IV, 294
Tomlinson, Aaron P. IV, 294
Tomlinson, Abel H. II, 314
Tomlinson, Abner II, 1033
Tomlinson, Abner II, 1062
Tomlinson, Adaliza I, 874
Tomlinson, Adaliza K. I, 903
Tomlinson, Adaliza R. I, 865
Tomlinson, Adalize I, 903
Tomlinson, Addie I, 903
Tomlinson, Addie I, 906
Tomlinson, Adeson Jerome I, 865
Tomlinson, Adliza I, 865
Tomlinson, Agnes II, 707
Tomlinson, Alberta S. IV, 1341
Tomlinson, Alesanna IV, 449
Tomlinson, Alesanna IV, 456
Tomlinson, Aletta IV, 294
Tomlinson, Aletta IV, 314
Tomlinson, Alice I, 642
Tomlinson, Alice I, 865
Tomlinson, Alice I, 895
Tomlinson, Alice I, 903
Tomlinson, Alice T. I, 622
Tomlinson, Alina I, 926
Tomlinson, Allazanna IV, 294
Tomlinson, Allen I, 929
Tomlinson, Allen I, 935
Tomlinson, Allen IV, 500
Tomlinson, Allen IV, 1008
Tomlinson, Allen IV, 1265
Tomlinson, Allen J. I, 865
Tomlinson, Allen J. I, 926
Tomlinson, Allen J. I, 931
Tomlinson, Allen J. I, 935
Tomlinson, Allen U. I, 865
Tomlinson, Allen U. I, 866
Tomlinson, Allen U. I, 877
Tomlinson, Allen U. I, 903
Tomlinson, Allen U. I, 950
Tomlinson, Allen Unthank I, 935
Tomlinson, Allette IV, 294
Tomlinson, Allison I, 866
Tomlinson, Alva Curtis V, 133
Tomlinson, Alvira I, 866
Tomlinson, Amanda I, 866
Tomlinson, Amos L. IV, 354
Tomlinson, Andrew D. V, 936
Tomlinson, Ann I, 842
Tomlinson, Ann I, 866
Tomlinson, Ann I, 903
Tomlinson, Ann II, 117
Tomlinson, Ann II, 125
Tomlinson, Ann II, 232
Tomlinson, Ann II, 268
Tomlinson, Ann II, 427
Tomlinson, Ann Jane I, 903
Tomlinson, Anna I, 865
Tomlinson, Anna I, 891
Tomlinson, Anna I, 903
Tomlinson, Anna I, 926
Tomlinson, Anna I, 929
Tomlinson, Anna I, 931
Tomlinson, Anna I, 935
Tomlinson, Anna IV, 812
Tomlinson, Anna IV, 848
Tomlinson, Anna IV, 849
Tomlinson, Anna IV, 917
Tomlinson, Anna Cary II, 791
Tomlinson, Anna F. I, 903
Tomlinson, Anna F. I, 950
Tomlinson, Anna F. IV, 953
Tomlinson, Anna F. IV, 1008
Tomlinson, Anna Faucette I, 950
Tomlinson, Anna Francette I, 935
Tomlinson, Anna L. II, 1081
Tomlinson, Anne I, 866
Tomlinson, Annie I, 624
Tomlinson, Annie I, 942
Tomlinson, Annie I, 950
Tomlinson, Annie T. I, 926
Tomlinson, Benjamin II, 187
Tomlinson, Benjamin II, 232
Tomlinson, Benjamin II, 268
Tomlinson, Benjamin II, 427
Tomlinson, Benjamin II, 669
Tomlinson, Benjamin II, 1033
Tomlinson, Benjamin J. IV, 848
Tomlinson, Benjamin J. IV, 849
Tomlinson, Benjamin J. IV, 917
Tomlinson, Benjamin Kenderdine II, 823
Tomlinson, Benjamin P. II, 1033
Tomlinson, Benjamin P. II, 1062
Tomlinson, Benjamin P. II, 1081
Tomlinson, Benjamin Palmer II, 1033
Tomlinson, Bertha M. VI, 786
Tomlinson, Billy I, 866
Tomlinson, Birdie V, 1022
Tomlinson, Caroline IV, 294
Tomlinson, Caroline IV, 388
Tomlinson, Carroll VI, 581
Tomlinson, Carroll M. VI, 45[illegible]
Tomlinson, Carroll M. VI, 58[illegible]
Tomlinson, Carroll Merrick VI, 457
Tomlinson, Carter IV, 294
Tomlinson, Carvar IV, 294
Tomlinson, Carven IV, 294
Tomlinson, Catharine II, 106
Tomlinson, Catharine II, 108
Tomlinson, Catharine II, 823
Tomlinson, Catharine Waddington II, 106
Tomlinson, Chalkley IV, 294
Tomlinson, Charity I, 827
Tomlinson, Charity I, 842
Tomlinson, Charity I, 866
Tomlinson, Charity I, 903
Tomlinson, Charity V, 133
Tomlinson, Charity V, 297
Tomlinson, Charity V, 312
Tomlinson, Charles F. I, 935
Tomlinson, Charles F. I, 950
Tomlinson, Charles Faucette I, 935
Tomlinson, Clarkson I, 903
Tomlinson, Comley IV, 294
Tomlinson, Comly IV, 294
Tomlinson, Comly IV, 778
Tomlinson, Cornelia I, 771
Tomlinson, Curtis V, 133
Tomlinson, Curtis V, 135
Tomlinson, Daniel IV, 597
Tomlinson, David M. I, 771
Tomlinson, David Marshall I, [illegible]
Tomlinson, Deborah I, 931
Tomlinson, Deborah I, 947
Tomlinson, Deborah I, 950
Tomlinson, Deborah W. IV, 314
Tomlinson, Delacy I, 866
Tomlinson, Dinah I, 866
Tomlinson, Dinah I, 903
Tomlinson, Dinah V, 133
Tomlinson, Dinah V, 312
Tomlinson, Earl J. IV, 1341
Tomlinson, Ebeneezer II, 427
Tomlinson, Ebenezer II, 427
Tomlinson, Eber J. V, 536
Tomlinson, Edward V, 1022
Tomlinson, Edwin IV, 294
Tomlinson, Elisabeth I, 169
Tomlinson, Elisabeth I, 622
Tomlinson, Eliza II, 826
Tomlinson, Eliza II, 930
Tomlinson, Eliza II, 937
Tomlinson, Eliza IV, 849
Tomlinson, Eliza IV, 917
Tomlinson, Eliza C. IV, 848
Tomlinson, Eliza C. IV, 849
Tomlinson, Elizabeth I, 277
Tomlinson, Elizabeth I, 794
Tomlinson, Elizabeth I, 863
Tomlinson, Elizabeth I, 866
Tomlinson, Elizabeth I, 871
Tomlinson, Elizabeth I, 886
Tomlinson, Elizabeth I, 895
Tomlinson, Elizabeth I, 903
Tomlinson, Elizabeth II, 232
Tomlinson, Elizabeth II, 268
Tomlinson, Elizabeth II, 427
Tomlinson, Elizabeth II, 539
Tomlinson, Elizabeth II, 669
Tomlinson, Elizabeth II, 971
Tomlinson, Elizabeth II, 1043
Tomlinson, Elizabeth IV, 161
Tomlinson, Elizabeth IV, 294
Tomlinson, Elizabeth IV, 554
Tomlinson, Elizabeth IV, 597
Tomlinson, Elizabeth IV, 812
Tomlinson, Elizabeth IV, 848
Tomlinson, Elizabeth IV, 849
Tomlinson, Elizabeth IV, 917
Tomlinson, Elizabeth E. IV, 294
Tomlinson, Ella E. IV, 1341
Tomlinson, Ellen I, 753
Tomlinson, Ellen I, 771
Tomlinson, Ellwood I, 771
Tomlinson, Ellwood II, 721
Tomlinson, Ellwood II, 771
Tomlinson, Elvira I, 882
Tomlinson, Elvira Hayworth I, 903
Tomlinson, Emeline J. IV, 294
Tomlinson, Emily II, 304
Tomlinson, Emily IV, 294
Tomlinson, Emily IV, 974
Tomlinson, Emily IV, 1008
Tomlinson, Emily IV, 1023
Tomlinson, Emily IV, 1031
Tomlinson, Emily H. II, 292
Tomlinson, Emily H. II, 304

linson, Emily J. IV, 1008
linson, Emily J. IV, 1043
linson, English I, 903
linson, Enos I, 771
linson, Enos I, 865
linson, Enos I, 903
linson, Enos Addison I, 753
linson, Enos Addison I, 771
linson, Ephraim II, 232
linson, Ephraim II, 268
linson, Erastus D. I, 903
linson, Ester II, 427
linson, Esther II, 669
linson, Esther IV, 835
linson, Esther IV, 848
linson, Ethel D. I, 935
linson, Ethel Diffie I, 950
linson, Faith Miriam V, 133
linson, Frances A. I, 865
nlinson, Francis King I, 642
nlinson, Francis King I, 903
nlinson, Fred H. V, 1022
nlinson, Gaston I, 903
nlinson, Gelia I, 865
nlinson, George P. IV, 312
nlinson, Gertrude I, 935
nlinson, Gilbert II, 1043
nlinson, Griffith S. IV, 294
nlinson, Halstead I, 950
nlinson, Hannah II, 232
nlinson, Hannah II, 268
nlinson, Hannah II, 1033
nlinson, Hannah II, 1043
mlinson, Hannah II, 1062
mlinson, Hannah II, 1081
mlinson, Hannah IV, 199
mlinson, Hannah IV, 294
mlinson, Hannah IV, 312
mlinson, Hannah IV, 314
mlinson, Hannah C. VI, 452
mlinson, Hannah Conrow VI, 457
mlinson, Hannah I. IV, 311
mlinson, Hannah I. IV, 314
mlinson, Hannah W. VI, 452
mlinson, Hattie Ellen I, 626
mlinson, Hattie Ellen I, 627
mlinson, Henry II, 971
mlinson, Henry II, 1021
mlinson, Henry II, 1033
mlinson, Henry B. I, 866
mlinson, Henry Stackhouse II, 1081
mlinson, Hiram I, 866
mlinson, Ida I, 903
mlinson, Ida H. I, 642
mlinson, Isaac I, 866
mlinson, Isaac I, 903
mlinson, Isaac IV, 294
mlinson, Isaac L. I, 903
mlinson, Isaac S. I, 866
mlinson, Isaac S. I, 903
mlinson, Israel II, 1043
omlinson, J. M. I, 865
omlinson, J. M. I, 903
omlinson, Jacob I, 866
omlinson, Jacob V, 133
omlinson, Jacob V, 312
omlinson, James II, 427
omlinson, James II, 1033
omlinson, James B. I, 771
omlinson, James Barzilla I, 753
omlinson, James Copic I, 866
omlinson, Jane I, 794
omlinson, Jane I, 866
omlinson, Jane I, 871
omlinson, Jane I, 903
omlinson, Jane II, 1033
omlinson, Jemima I, 866
omlinson, Jemima I, 872
omlinson, Jemima I, 902
omlinson, Jemimah I, 903
omlinson, Jennie I, 865
omlinson, Jennie E. IV, 500
Tomlinson, Jerome I, 903
Tomlinson, Jesiah I, 1038
Tomlinson, John I, 267
Tomlinson, John I, 277
Tomlinson, John I, 866
Tomlinson, John I, 903
Tomlinson, John II, 244
Tomlinson, John II, 268
Tomlinson, John II, 669
Tomlinson, John II, 823
Tomlinson, John II, 826
Tomlinson, John II, 930
Tomlinson, John II, 937
Tomlinson, John II, 1033
Tomlinson, John V, 312
Tomlinson, John M. I, 865
Tomlinson, John N. IV, 294
Tomlinson, John R. IV, 1341
Tomlinson, Jonathan II, 721
Tomlinson, Jonathan IV, 917
Tomlinson, Joseph I, 794
Tomlinson, Joseph I, 866
Tomlinson, Joseph I, 872
Tomlinson, Joseph I, 902
Tomlinson, Joseph I, 903
Tomlinson, Joseph II, 106
Tomlinson, Joseph II, 108
Tomlinson, Joseph II, 791
Tomlinson, Joseph II, 823
Tomlinson, Joseph II, 971
Tomlinson, Joseph II, 997
Tomlinson, Joseph II, 1019
Tomlinson, Joseph II, 1033
Tomlinson, Joseph II, 1043
Tomlinson, Joseph IV, 294
Tomlinson, Joseph IV, 917
Tomlinson, Joseph, Jr. II, 1033
Tomlinson, Josephine II, 791
Tomlinson, Josiah I, 579
Tomlinson, Josiah I, 753
Tomlinson, Josiah I, 794
Tomlinson, Josiah I, 827
Tomlinson, Josiah I, 842
Tomlinson, Josiah I, 847
Tomlinson, Josiah I, 866
Tomlinson, Josiah I, 871
Tomlinson, Josiah I, 902
Tomlinson, Josiah I, 903
Tomlinson, Josiah V, 133
Tomlinson, Josiah V, 215
Tomlinson, Josiah V, 286
Tomlinson, Josiah V, 312
Tomlinson, Josiah Clarkson I, 771
Tomlinson, Josiah, Jr. V, 312
Tomlinson, Julius L. I, 865
Tomlinson, Kezia II, 304
Tomlinson, Keziah I, 866
Tomlinson, Keziah I, 903
Tomlinson, Keziah II, 177
Tomlinson, Keziah II, 291
Tomlinson, Keziah II, 304
Tomlinson, Laura B. IV, 294
Tomlinson, Lizzie IV, 849
Tomlinson, Lizzie Irene V, 536
Tomlinson, Lois E. IV, 1341
Tomlinson, Louis Joseph II, 791
Tomlinson, Louisa I, 770
Tomlinson, Louisa I, 771
Tomlinson, Luce II, 427
Tomlinson, Lucia II, 669
Tomlinson, Lucinda I, 882
Tomlinson, Lucinda I, 903
Tomlinson, Luretta I, 900
Tomlinson, Luretta I, 903
Tomlinson, Lydia I, 888
Tomlinson, Lydia I, 903
Tomlinson, Lydia II, 106
Tomlinson, Lydia II, 108
Tomlinson, Lydia II, 427
Tomlinson, Lydia II, 566
Tomlinson, Lydia II, 669
Tomlinson, Lydia II, 826
Tomlinson, Lydia II, 930
Tomlinson, Lydia II, 937
Tomlinson, Lydia V, 133
Tomlinson, Lydia V, 434
Tomlinson, Lydia A. V, 133
Tomlinson, Lydia Ann V, 961
Tomlinson, M. J. N. I, 865
Tomlinson, Mahlon II, 1033
Tomlinson, Mahlon II, 1062
Tomlinson, Mahlon II, 1081
Tomlinson, Mahlon Y. II, 1033
Tomlinson, Malvina I, 866
Tomlinson, Margaret I, 277
Tomlinson, Margaret I, 794
Tomlinson, Margaret II, 1019
Tomlinson, Margaret II, 1033
Tomlinson, Margaret IV, 560
Tomlinson, Margaret IV, 562
Tomlinson, Mariah Josephine I, 865
Tomlinson, Mariam IV, 449
Tomlinson, Mariam M. I, 866
Tomlinson, Mariam M. I, 888
Tomlinson, Mariam M. I, 903
Tomlinson, Mark I, 866
Tomlinson, Mark V, 133
Tomlinson, Mark V, 312
Tomlinson, Martha I, 794
Tomlinson, Martha I, 842
Tomlinson, Martha I, 847
Tomlinson, Martha I, 865
Tomlinson, Martha I, 866
Tomlinson, Martha I, 871
Tomlinson, Martha I, 887
Tomlinson, Martha I, 902
Tomlinson, Martha I, 903
Tomlinson, Martha II, 1033
Tomlinson, Martha II, 1062
Tomlinson, Martha IV, 294
Tomlinson, Martha IV, 500
Tomlinson, Martha IV, 835
Tomlinson, Martha IV, 848
Tomlinson, Martha IV, 1008
Tomlinson, Martha E. I, 865
Tomlinson, Martha Helen V, 1022
Tomlinson, Martha M. I, 903
Tomlinson, Martha N. IV, 294
Tomlinson, Martha S. I, 865
Tomlinson, Marther I, 1028
Tomlinson, Marther I, 1038
Tomlinson, Mary I, 865
Tomlinson, Mary I, 866
Tomlinson, Mary I, 894
Tomlinson, Mary I, 898
Tomlinson, Mary I, 903
Tomlinson, Mary II, 86
Tomlinson, Mary II, 106
Tomlinson, Mary II, 107
Tomlinson, Mary II, 427
Tomlinson, Mary II, 669
Tomlinson, Mary II, 971
Tomlinson, Mary II, 1043
Tomlinson, Mary IV, 294
Tomlinson, Mary IV, 917
Tomlinson, Mary VI, 573
Tomlinson, Mary VI, 714
Tomlinson, Mary A. I, 903
Tomlinson, Mary A. II, 314
Tomlinson, Mary Ann I, 877
Tomlinson, Mary Ann I, 903
Tomlinson, Mary Ann IV, 62
Tomlinson, Mary Ann IV, 312
Tomlinson, Mary Ann IV, 314
Tomlinson, Mary Catharine IV, 418
Tomlinson, Mary Catharine IV, 449
Tomlinson, Mary E. I, 624
Tomlinson, Mary E. I, 900
Tomlinson, Mary E. I, 903
Tomlinson, Mary Edwards II, 106
Tomlinson, Mary Elizabeth II, 669
Tomlinson, Mary Elizabeth II, 791
Tomlinson, Mary Elizabeth II, 1048
Tomlinson, Mary Elizabeth II, 1062
Tomlinson, Mary Elizabeth IV, 294
Tomlinson, Mary J. I, 865
Tomlinson, Mary Jane V, 536
Tomlinson, Mary K. II, 1062
Tomlinson, Mary K. II, 1081
Tomlinson, Mary L. IV, 848
Tomlinson, Mary L. IV, 849
Tomlinson, Mary Malvina I, 771
Tomlinson, Mary P. IV, 312
Tomlinson, Mary S. IV, 849
Tomlinson, Mary Wildman II, 791
Tomlinson, Mary, Jr. II, 997
Tomlinson, Mary, Jr. II, 1033
Tomlinson, May L. I, 935
Tomlinson, May L. I, 950
Tomlinson, Menerva IV, 294
Tomlinson, Milcah VI, 573
Tomlinson, Mildred I, 617
Tomlinson, Mildred I, 866
Tomlinson, Mildred I, 926
Tomlinson, Mildred L. I, 865
Tomlinson, Mildred R. I, 877
Tomlinson, Mildred R. I, 903
Tomlinson, Milley V, 286
Tomlinson, Milley V, 312
Tomlinson, Milly V, 312
Tomlinson, Milton I, 903
Tomlinson, Milton V, 434
Tomlinson, Minerva I, 622
Tomlinson, Minerva I, 903
Tomlinson, Mira IV, 294
Tomlinson, Mira M. IV, 500
Tomlinson, Moses I, 794
Tomlinson, Moses I, 863
Tomlinson, Moses I, 866
Tomlinson, Moses I, 903
Tomlinson, Moses V, 122
Tomlinson, Moses V, 133
Tomlinson, Moses V, 311
Tomlinson, Moses V, 312
Tomlinson, Moses L. I, 903
Tomlinson, Myra IV, 1008
Tomlinson, Myra IV, 1043
Tomlinson, Myra M. IV, 500
Tomlinson, Naomi I, 866
Tomlinson, Naomi I, 883
Tomlinson, Naomi I, 888
Tomlinson, Naomi I, 903
Tomlinson, Naomi P. II, 880
Tomlinson, Nellie E. V, 536
Tomlinson, Neomi I, 888
Tomlinson, Neomi I, 903
Tomlinson, O. C. IV, 500
Tomlinson, O. C. IV, 1008
Tomlinson, O. C. IV, 1043
Tomlinson, Olive I, 794
Tomlinson, Olive I, 842
Tomlinson, Olive I, 866
Tomlinson, Olive I, 903
Tomlinson, Olive IV, 1265
Tomlinson, Olive V, 133
Tomlinson, Olive V, 312
Tomlinson, Orland IV, 974
Tomlinson, Orlando IV, 294
Tomlinson, Orlando C. IV, 294
Tomlinson, Orlando C. IV, 500
Tomlinson, Orlando C. IV, 1008
Tomlinson, Orlando C. IV, 1043
Tomlinson, Othniel II, 86
Tomlinson, Othniel II, 106
Tomlinson, Palmer II, 1033
Tomlinson, Pamela II, 1019
Tomlinson, Pamela II, 1033
Tomlinson, Pamela Ambler II, 823
Tomlinson, Pamelia II, 1033
Tomlinson, Pamelia II, 1081
Tomlinson, Paul V, 133
Tomlinson, Paul V, 312
Tomlinson, Paul V, 536
Tomlinson, Peirson II, 1043
Tomlinson, Permelia II, 1055
Tomlinson, Permelia II, 1062
Tomlinson, Phebe II, 721
Tomlinson, Phebe IV, 917
Tomlinson, Phebe A. III, 65
Tomlinson, Phenihas A. I, 866
Tomlinson, Priscilla II, 971
Tomlinson, R. Anna V, 135
Tomlinson, Rachel I, 753
Tomlinson, Rachel I, 771
Tomlinson, Rachel I, 865
Tomlinson, Rachel I, 877
Tomlinson, Rachel I, 903
Tomlinson, Rachel IV, 294
Tomlinson, Rachel IV, 314
Tomlinson, Rachel V, 312
Tomlinson, Rachel V, 485
Tomlinson, Rachel V, 536
Tomlinson, Rachel H. II, 187
Tomlinson, Rachel L. I, 865
Tomlinson, Rebecca II, 268
Tomlinson, Rebecca II, 273
Tomlinson, Rebecca II, 304
Tomlinson, Rebecca II, 721
Tomlinson, Rebecca II, 1062
Tomlinson, Rebecca IV, 294
Tomlinson, Rebecca IV, 313
Tomlinson, Rebecca IV, 314
Tomlinson, Rebecca E. II, 771
Tomlinson, Rebecca J. II, 1081
Tomlinson, Rebecca Sidwell IV, 161
Tomlinson, Rebecca Sidwell IV, 294
Tomlinson, Regina I, 903
Tomlinson, Ressina I, 866
Tomlinson, Richard II, 268
Tomlinson, Richard II, 669
Tomlinson, Robert I, 771
Tomlinson, Robert I, 866
Tomlinson, Robert I, 903
Tomlinson, Robert V, 434
Tomlinson, Robert A. I, 771
Tomlinson, Robert Allen I, 753
Tomlinson, Robert K. II, 1081
Tomlinson, Robert W. I, 903
Tomlinson, Roberta I, 945
Tomlinson, Roberta I, 950
Tomlinson, Roberta T. I, 929
Tomlinson, Ruth V, 122
Tomlinson, Ruth V, 133
Tomlinson, Ruth V, 311
Tomlinson, Ruth V, 312
Tomlinson, Ruth V, 1022
Tomlinson, Ruth M. V, 133
Tomlinson, Ruth Matilda V, 133
Tomlinson, Ruthanna IV, 940
Tomlinson, Ruthanna IV, 1008
Tomlinson, Ruthanna V, 133
Tomlinson, Ruthanna V, 135
Tomlinson, Samira I, 876
Tomlinson, Samira I, 903
Tomlinson, Samuel I, 579
Tomlinson, Samuel I, 622
Tomlinson, Samuel I, 794
Tomlinson, Samuel I, 842
Tomlinson, Samuel I, 866
Tomlinson, Samuel I, 903
Tomlinson, Samuel II, 1019
Tomlinson, Samuel II, 1033
Tomlinson, Samuel IV, 294
Tomlinson, Samuel IV, 314
Tomlinson, Samuel F. I, 865
Tomlinson, Samuel M. I, 903
Tomlinson, Samuel S. IV, 294
Tomlinson, Samuel Y. II, 1033
Tomlinson, Samuel Yardley II, 1033
Tomlinson, Samuel, Jr. I, 866
Tomlinson, Sara V, 715
Tomlinson, Sarah I, 570
Tomlinson, Sarah I, 579
Tomlinson, Sarah I, 791
Tomlinson, Sarah I, 794
Tomlinson, Sarah I, 866
Tomlinson, Sarah I, 903
Tomlinson, Sarah II, 971
Tomlinson, Sarah II, 1033
Tomlinson, Sarah II, 1043
Tomlinson, Sarah IV, 294
Tomlinson, Sarah IV, 333
Tomlinson, Sarah IV, 354
Tomlinson, Sarah V, 133
Tomlinson, Sarah V, 312
Tomlinson, Sarah V, 678
Tomlinson, Sarah Ann IV, 397
Tomlinson, Sarah Ann IV, 449
Tomlinson, Sarah D. IV, 312
Tomlinson, Sarah D. IV, 314
Tomlinson, Sarah Emeline I, 753
Tomlinson, Sarah Emeline I, 771
Tomlinson, Sarah H. II, 292
Tomlinson, Sarah H. II, 304
Tomlinson, Sarah Lacy I, 935
Tomlinson, Sibyl IV, 294
Tomlinson, Sibyl IV, 1008
Tomlinson, Sibyl E. IV, 500
Tomlinson, Sibyl E. IV, 974
Tomlinson, Sidney I, 340
Tomlinson, Sidney I, 642
Tomlinson, Sidney I, 935
Tomlinson, Sidney Halstead I, 935
Tomlinson, Sidney Halstead, Jr. I, 935
Tomlinson, Sina V, 936
Tomlinson, Sue V. I, 635
Tomlinson, Sue V. I, 642
Tomlinson, Sue V. I, 903
Tomlinson, Susan I, 865
Tomlinson, Susanna IV, 294
Tomlinson, Susannah II, 930
Tomlinson, Susannah IV, 311
Tomlinson, Susannah IV, 314
Tomlinson, Susie V, 1022
Tomlinson, Syble E. IV, 500
Tomlinson, Tabitha I, 863
Tomlinson, Tabitha I, 903
Tomlinson, Thomas I, 794
Tomlinson, Thomas I, 842
Tomlinson, Thomas I, 866
Tomlinson, Thomas I, 894
Tomlinson, Thomas I, 903
Tomlinson, Thomas II, 971
Tomlinson, Thomas II, 1033
Tomlinson, Thomas IV, 294
Tomlinson, Thomas D. IV, 311
Tomlinson, Thomas D. IV, 314
Tomlinson, Virginia E. I, 903
Tomlinson, Virginia Estella I, 642
Tomlinson, Walter M. IV, 294
Tomlinson, Warner II, 106
Tomlinson, Wd. Catharine II, 823
Tomlinson, Wd. Kesiah II, 187
Tomlinson, Wd. Mary II, 539
Tomlinson, Wd. Mary Elizabeth II, 823
Tomlinson, Weymond IV, 294
Tomlinson, Widow Elizabeth I, 267
Tomlinson, Widow Elizabeth I, 277
Tomlinson, William I, 257
Tomlinson, William I, 258
Tomlinson, William I, 771
Tomlinson, William I, 794
Tomlinson, William I, 842
Tomlinson, William I, 847
Tomlinson, William I, 866
Tomlinson, William I, 902
Tomlinson, William I, 903
Tomlinson, William I, 953
Tomlinson, William I, 1028
Tomlinson, William I, 1038
Tomlinson, William II, 187
Tomlinson, William V, 133

Tomlinson, William VI, 714
Tomlinson, William Allen I, 935
Tomlinson, William B. I, 753
Tomlinson, William Edwood I, 753
Tomlinson, William S. I, 865
Tomlinson, William Sidney I, 642
Tomlinson, William, Jr. I, 866
Tomlinson, Wm. II, 273
Tomlinson, Wm. V, 312
Tomlinson, Wm. Elwood I, 624
Tomlinson, Wm. Francis IV, 294
Tomlinson, Wm. Gaston I, 865
Tomlinson, Wm. P. II, 1081
Tomlinson, Wymond IV, 294
Tomlinson, Wymond IV, 1008
Tomlinson, Wymond IV, 1043
Tomlinson, Wymond J. IV, 500
Tomlinson, Yardley II, 1033
Tomlinson, Zachariah I, 866
Tomlinson, Zachariah I, 903
Tomlinson, Zebulon J. I, 865
Tommerson, John VI, 1004
Tommerson, Nancy VI, 1004
Tommerson, W. W. VI, 988
Tommerson, William VI, 1004
Tomohlen, Fred H. V, 1022
Tompkins, ??? III, 369
Tompkins, Addie E. V, 466
Tompkins, Addie Elvira V, 286
Tompkins, Ann IV, 336
Tompkins, Ann IV, 354
Tompkins, Benjamin II, 669
Tompkins, Carrie Belle III, 220
Tompkins, Carrie Belle III, 320
Tompkins, Catharine III, 320
Tompkins, Charity III, 320
Tompkins, Charles V, 466
Tompkins, Charles E. V, 466
Tompkins, Charles Ellsworth V, 286
Tompkins, Coles III, 320
Tompkins, Daniel VI, 1005
Tompkins, Daniel H. III, 320
Tompkins, Elijah III, 320
Tompkins, Eliza III, 320
Tompkins, Eliza III, 369
Tompkins, Elizabeth II, 669
Tompkins, Elizabeth V, 286
Tompkins, Elizabeth V, 466
Tompkins, Elizabeth VI, 862
Tompkins, Elizabeth VI, 1005
Tompkins, Elizabeth S. III, 320
Tompkins, Enoch V, 133
Tompkins, Florence III, 220
Tompkins, Florence E. V, 459
Tompkins, Frank III, 320
Tompkins, Frank IV, 1265
Tompkins, Franklin III, 320
Tompkins, Gertrude V, 466
Tompkins, Hannah II, 825
Tompkins, Jacob V, 133
Tompkins, Jacob V, 286
Tompkins, Jacob V, 312
Tompkins, Jacob V, 466
Tompkins, Jacob E. II, 930
Tompkins, Jacob Edge II, 930
Tompkins, Jacob, Jr. II, 669
Tompkins, James III, 320
Tompkins, Jane III, 320
Tompkins, Jannet VI, 814
Tompkins, John II, 669
Tompkins, John V, 133
Tompkins, John V, 286
Tompkins, John V, 466
Tompkins, John VI, 894
Tompkins, John H. III, 320
Tompkins, Joseph III, 320
Tompkins, Joseph V, 133
Tompkins, Julian III, 320
Tompkins, Kezia II, 669
Tompkins, Libbie V, 462
Tompkins, Lidia P. VI, 1005
Tompkins, Lillie I. V, 466
Tompkins, Lindley V, 466
Tompkins, Lottie Belle III, 320
Tompkins, Lottiebelle III, 220
Tompkins, Lydia II, 669
Tompkins, Lydia V, 46
Tompkins, Lydia V, 133
Tompkins, Marley V, 466
Tompkins, Mary II, 669
Tompkins, Mary III, 320
Tompkins, Mary IV, 1265
Tompkins, Mary V, 133
Tompkins, Mary V, 283
Tompkins, Mary V, 286
Tompkins, Mary VI, 7
Tompkins, Mary E. V, 466
mpkins, Mary F. II, 846
kins, Mary F. II, 930
Tompkins, May V, 458
Tompkins, Nancy III, 506
Tompkins, Nancy V, 133
Tompkins, Nancy V, 286
Tompkins, Nancy V, 458
Tompkins, Nannie C. V, 466
Tompkins, Noah III, 320
Tompkins, Phebe III, 320
Tompkins, Phebe Ann III, 320
Tompkins, Pluma V, 466
Tompkins, Rachel V, 133
Tompkins, Rachel V, 246
Tompkins, Rachel V, 286
Tompkins, Rachel V, 304
Tompkins, Rachel V, 312
Tompkins, Rachel V, 466
Tompkins, Robert II, 669
Tompkins, Ruth V, 466
Tompkins, Sally VI, 814
Tompkins, Samuel D. VI, 921
Tompkins, Sarah II, 669
Tompkins, Sarah III, 65
Tompkins, Sarah V, 133
Tompkins, Sarah V, 312
Tompkins, Sarah V, 466
Tompkins, Sarah VI, 846
Tompkins, Sarah VI, 862
Tompkins, Sarah E. V, 466
Tompkins, Stanby III, 320
Tompkins, Stanley III, 220
Tompkins, William V, 133
Tompkins, William V, 466
Tompkins, William VI, 1005
Tompkins, William E. V, 466
Tompkins, William Edgar V, 286
Tompkins, Wm. III, 320
Tompkins, Wm. V, 466
Tompson, B. O. V, 602
Tompson, Daniel II, 1032
Tompson, Effie V, 602
Tompson, Elvira II, 1081
Tompson, Hannah IV, 777
Tompson, Lewis V, 602
Tompson, Mary II, 258
Tompson, Mary II, 267
Tompson, Mary-Martha V, 602
Tompson, Mynard V, 602
Tompt, Ada IV, 1341
Toms, Anderson I, 169
Toms, Anderson I, 189
Toms, Anderson I, 200
Toms, Benjamin I, 200
Toms, Benjamin I, 203
Toms, Caleb I, 18
Toms, Caleb I, 76
Toms, Catharine III, 320
Toms, Elisabeth I, 34
Toms, Elisabeth I, 35
Toms, Elisabeth I, 76
Toms, Elisabeth I, 169
Toms, Elizabeth I, 90
Toms, Elizabeth III, 164
Toms, Elizabeth III, 320
Toms, Elvira I, 154
Toms, Elvira I, 169
Toms, Foster I, 55
Toms, Foster I, 76
Toms, Foster I, 187
Toms, Foster I, 200
Toms, Francis I, 1
Toms, Francis I, 18
Toms, Francis I, 35
Toms, Francis I, 64
Toms, Francis I, 76
Toms, Francis I, 90
Toms, Francis I, 91
Toms, Francis I, 92
Toms, Francis I, 109
Toms, Francis I, 120
Toms, Gansbey I, 76
Toms, Gansby I, 35
Toms, Gansby I, 76
Toms, Gosbey I, 76
Toms, Isabella I, 177
Toms, Jemima I, 200
Toms, Jemima Toms I, 201
Toms, Jesse I, 177
Toms, John I, 35
Toms, John I, 76
Toms, John I, 187
Toms, John I, 200
Toms, John VI, 1005
Toms, John A. I, 169
Toms, John A. I, 200
Toms, John Anderson I, 189
Toms, John Anderson I, 200
Toms, John, Jr. I, 76
Toms, Joseph I, 18
Toms, Joseph I, 76
Toms, Joseph I, 169
Toms, Joseph I, 177
Toms, Joseph I, 200
Toms, Joshua I, 18
Toms, Joshua I, 35
Toms, Joshua I, 63
Toms, Joshua I, 76
Toms, Joshua I, 90
Toms, Margaret I, 49
Toms, Margaret I, 76
Toms, Margaret I, 78
Toms, Martha I, 65
Toms, Martha I, 76
Toms, Martha I, 169
Toms, Martha I, 197
Toms, Martha I, 200
Toms, Martha I, 203
Toms, Mary I, 18
Toms, Mary I, 35
Toms, Mary I, 55
Toms, Mary I, 59
Toms, Mary I, 76
Toms, Mary I, 90
Toms, Mary I, 151
Toms, Mary I, 169
Toms, Mary I, 185
Toms, Mary I, 187
Toms, Mary I, 189
Toms, Mary I, 197
Toms, Mary I, 200
Toms, Milicent I, 63
Toms, Milicent I, 76
Toms, Miriam I, 76
Toms, Miriam I, 79
Toms, Miriam I, 169
Toms, Myrriam I, 72
Toms, Myrriam I, 76
Toms, Penelope I, 18
Toms, Penelope I, 90
Toms, Penninah I, 76
Toms, Pharaba I, 169
Toms, Pharaba I, 177
Toms, Phariba I, 76
Toms, Pharibe I, 187
Toms, Pharibe I, 200
Toms, Phariby I, 189
Toms, Phariby I, 200
Toms, Pleasant I, 76
Toms, Priscila I, 18
Toms, Priscila I, 76
Toms, Priscile I, 1
Toms, Prisela I, 90
Toms, Rebecca I, 43
Toms, Rebecca I, 76
Toms, Rebecca I, 78
Toms, Rebecca I, 90
Toms, Rebekah I, 76
Toms, Sally Ann I, 76
Toms, Sarah I, 76
Toms, Sarah I, 192
Toms, Sarah I, 200
Toms, Sarah VI, 1005
Toms, Sarah Ann S. VI, 1005
Toms, Sarah E. V, 133
Toms, Sarah E. V, 144
Toms, Thomas III, 320
Toms, Widow Margaret I, 55
Toms, Widow Margaret I, 76
Toms, Widow Mary I, 200
Toms, Z. I, 76
Toms, Zachariah I, 76
Toms, Zachariah I, 78
Tomson, Christopher II, 427
Tomson, Elizabeth I, 527
Tomson, Elizabeth I, 577
Tomson, Elizabeth II, 448
Tomson, Gilbert II, 427
Tomson, Hannah I, 577
Tomson, Hannah II, 427
Tomson, Henry II, 427
Tomson, John II, 69
Tomson, John II, 104
Tomson, John II, 427
Tomson, Joseph I, 577
Tomson, Joseph II, 92
Tomson, Joseph II, 104
Tomson, Lidia II, 448
Tomson, Lydia II, 427
Tomson, Mary II, 427
Tomson, Sarah II, 69
Tomson, Sarah II, 92
Tomson, Sarah II, 104
Tomson, Thomas I, 527
Tomson, Thomas I, 577
Tomson, Thomas II, 427
Toney, Charles VI, 1006
Toney, Charles W. VI, 1006
Toney, Elizabeth VI, 860
Toney, Elizabeth Ann VI, 1006
Toney, Harris VI, 945
Toney, James VI, 859
Toney, Mahaley VI, 983
Toney, Nancey VI, 1006
Toney, Nancy L. VI, 859
Toney, William VI, 983
Toney, William H. C. VI, 860
Toney, Zelpah VI, 1006
Tong, Eliza V, 489
Tong, Eliza V, 536
Tong, Jow III, 320
Tong, Yet III, 320
Tongrell, Allie I, 622
Tongrell, Allie Arnett I, 622
Tongrell, Samuel K. I, 622
Tongue, Mary II, 427
Tongue, Mary II, 464
Tongue, Mary II, 669
Tonkin, George W. II, 721
Tonkin, Kezia II, 669
Tonkin, Martha II, 125
Tonkin, Martha II, 771
Tonkins, Martha II, 125
Tonkins, Mary II, 60
Tonkins, Mary II, 107
Tonkins, Samuel II, 60
Tonkins, Samuel II, 107
Tonkins, Sibyl II, 268
Tonkins, Sibylla II, 304
Took, James I, 131
Took, James I, 169
Took, Joan VI, 36
Took, Joan VI, 37
Took, Tho VI, 36
Tooke, ??? VI, 39
Tooke, Caleb Bundy I, 169
Tooke, James I, 92
Tooke, James I, 169
Tooke, Jeams I, 120
Tooke, Joan VI, 30
Tooke, Joan VI, 36
Tooke, Joan VI, 37
Tooke, John VI, 93
Tooke, Mary VI, 27
Tooke, Mary VI, 28
Tooke, Mary VI, 37
Tooke, Tho. VI, 37
Tooke, Thomas VI, 34
Tooke, Thomas VI, 37
Tooke, Thomas VI, 41
Tool, Alpha IV, 778
Tool, C. Lamoine IV, 778
Tool, Clarence IV, 1044
Tool, David IV, 778
Tool, Elpha Rugley IV, 1008
Tool, Hannah IV, 1044
Tool, Horner IV, 1044
Tool, Isaac IV, 778
Tool, Levi P. IV, 1044
Tool, Marrella IV, 778
Tool, Walter IV, 1044
Tooley, Elizabeth II, 199
Tooley, Elizabeth II, 268
Tooley, Nancy VI, 890
Toomes, Alpheus I, 669
Toomes, Nereus Eugene I, 669
Toomes, Patience I, 669
Toomes, Sarah I, 669
Toomes, Sarah Ruby I, 669
Tooms, Francis I, 91
Tope, Rebecca IV, 406
Topham, Ann II, 427
Topham, Catharine II, 428
Topham, Catherine II, 427
Topham, Christopher II, 669
Topham, Daniel II, 428
Topham, Hannah II, 428
Topham, Mary II, 428
Topham, Mathew II, 428
Topham, William II, 427
Topham, William II, 428
Topham, Wm. II, 669
Topliff, Ann II, 428
Topliff, Hannah II, 567
Topliff, Hannah II, 669
Topliff, Hannah II, 806
Topliff, John II, 428
Topliff, Martha II, 486
Topliff, Mary II, 486
Topliff, Richard II, 428
Topliff, Richard II, 485
Topliff, Richard II, 567
Topliff, Richard II, 669
Topliff, Sarah II, 485
Topliff, Sarah II, 567
Topliff, Sarah II, 669
Topliff, Sarah II, 678
Topliff, Thomas II, 428
Topliff, William II, 428
Toplin, Mary II, 819
Toplin, Mary II, 824
Toppen, Christopher II, 669
Toppen, Theodore III, 19
Toppen, Wd. Susan III, 19
Topping, David III, 320
Topping, Dorothy I, 76
Topping, Dorothy I, 78
Torbert, Elaline G. II, 893
Torbet, Emaline G. II, 930
Tormohlen, F. H. IV, 1341
Tormohlen, Fred H. IV, 1341
Tormohlen, Martha IV, 1341
Tormohlen, Martha Helen IV, 1341
Tormohlen, Ruth IV, 1341
Tormohlen, Ruth E. IV, 1341
Tormohlen, Susie J. IV, 1341
Torner, Ruth I, 91
Torner, William I, 91
Torner, William I, 120
Torr, Charlotte II, 428
Torr, Elizabeth II, 428
Torr, Elizabeth II, 669
Torr, Elizabeth II, 771
Torr, Isabel II, 268
Torr, Jabell II, 268
Torr, John II, 428
Torr, John II, 669
Torr, Josiah II, 268
Torr, Lambert II, 428
Torr, Mary II, 428
Torr, Richard II, 428
Torrance, Andrew VI, 860
Torrance, David VI, 819
Torrance, David VI, 860
Torrance, Elizabeth VI, 860
Torrance, Joseph VI, 860
Torrance, Mary VI, 860
Torrance, Mildred VI, 860
Torrance, Nancy VI, 860
Torrance, Samuel VI, 841
Torrance, Samuel VI, 860
Torrance, William VI, 830
Torrance, William VI, 849
Torrance, William VI, 860
Torrance, Winfred VI, 860
Torrence, Hattie VI, 784
Torrence, Hattie VI, 786
Torrence, Mary Eda VI, 784
Torrence, Mary Eda VI, 786
Torrence, Nancy VI, 831
Torrence, Rebecca VI, 831
Torrence, Samuel VI, 812
Torrence, Wm. Wilson VI, 784
Torrence, Wm. Wilson VI, 786
Torrey, Arthur H. III, 320
Torrey, Lucien E. III, 320
Torrey, Mary M. III, 347
Torrey, Mary W. III, 76
Torrey, Maude III, 320
Torrey, Therese Marie III, 320
Torriance, Rebecca VI, 827
Torriance, Winney VI, 827
Torry, Amy II, 428
Torry, Arthur H. III, 169
Torry, Rebeckah II, 428
Torry, Therese Marie III, 169
Torson, Knud Sina IV, 794
Torson, Knuedsine IV, 794
Tortenson, Malene II, 304
Tortenson, Malina II, 304
Tosh, Amanda VI, 1006
Tosh, Andrew VI, 876
Tosh, George VI, 1006
Tosh, John VI, 1006
Tosh, Lucy VI, 1006
Tosteven, David III, 320
Tosteven, John III, 320
Tosteven, Malene III, 320
Tosteven, Martha III, 320
Tosteven, Peter III, 320
Tosteven, Rachel III, 320
Tosteven, Thomas III, 320
Tostevin, John III, 327
Tostevin, Martha III, 327
Tostevin, Rachel III, 327
Tostinson, Malina II, 304
Tothill, Charles, Jr. III, 320
Tothill, Edward III, 320
Totten, Hannah III, 320
Totten, Martha III, 497
Totten, Richard III, 511
Totten, Robert III, 320
Toughmen, John VI, 875
Tounhuson, Cale V, 1022
Tounhuson, Flo V, 1022
Tounhuson, Gertie V, 1022
Tounhuson, Oral V, 1022
Tounsen, Richard I, 90
Tounson, Mary II, 107
Tours, Belle V, 1022
Toussaint, Eugenie Lecordier III, 78
Toussaint, Eugenie Lecordier III, 320
Tove, John II, 448

l, Dinah I, 440
l, Dorothy I, 454
l, Edith I, 440
l, Edith I, 454
l, Elizabeth I, 440
l, George I, 440
l, Hannah I, 440
l, Hannah I, 454
l, Henry I, 440
l, Henry I, 454
l, Henry V, 133
l, Isaac I, 440
l, Isaac V, 133
l, Jesse I, 424
l, Jesse I, 440
l, Jesse I, 453
l, Jesse I, 454
l, Jesse I, 741
l, Jesse V, 133
l, John I, 440
l, John I, 454
l, Margaret I, 446
l, Margaret I, 454
l, Margret I, 454
l, Martha I, 440
l, Martha I, 453
l, Martha I, 454
l, Martha, Jr. I, 454
l, Martha, Sr. I, 454
l, Mary I, 453
l, Mary I, 454
l, Mary Rebekah I, 454
l, Rachel I, 440
l, Rebecca V, 495
l, Rebecca V, 536
l, Ruth V, 133
l, Ruth V, 498
l, Ruth V, 536
l, Sarah I, 440
l, Sarah I, 447
l, Sarah I, 454
l, Sarah V, 569
ll, Joseph III, 320
er, ??? III, 320
er, Ambrose III, 320
er, Franklin F. III, 320
ers, Hannah II, 428
ers, Robert II, 428
ers, Robert, Jr. II, 428
ers, Robert, Jr. II, 669
e, Percivale II, 268
er, Ann VI, 955
ler, Barnabas VI, 1006
ler, Betsey VI, 1006
ler, Caleb VI, 1006
ler, Elvira VI, 924
ler, Frances VI, 1010
ler, James VI, 924
ler, James VI, 931
ler, James VI, 955
ler, James VI, 1006
ler, James VI, 1010
ler, Joseph VI, 902
ler, Nancy VI, 1006
ler, Robert VI, 1006
ler, Sally VI, 1006
lerton, James IV, 500
les, Margaret C. VI, 854
les, Mariah VI, 850
les, Thomas H. VI, 842
ley, Charley G. V, 1022
ley, Chloe I. V, 1022
ley, Chloie V, 1022
ley, Clifford Towey V, 1022
ley, Lucy Eveline V, 1022
ley, Luni I. V, 1022
ley, Nellie V, 1022
ley, Philips V, 1022
n, ??? II, 428
n, Deborah II, 1003
n, Deborah II, 1033
n, Hannah II, 1031
n, Hannah II, 1033
n, James VI, 40
n, John II, 980
n, John II, 1033
n, Joseph II, 428
n, Rosanna IV, 1361
n, Rosanna IV, 1382
n, Sarah II, 428
n, Sarah II, 978
n, Sarah II, 1033
ne, James VI, 29
ne, James VI, 32
nley, Kalita B. VI, 343
nley, Mary III, 41
ns, Jeanette IV, 972
nsand, Elizabeth I, 1038
nsand, James I, 1027
nsand, James I, 1038
nsand, John I, 1038
Townsand, Mary I, 1027
Townsand, Mary I, 1038
Townsen, Elizabeth II, 107
Townsen, Mary C. I, 76
Townsend, ??? III, 320
Townsend, ??? III, 321
Townsend, ??? III, 385
Townsend, ??? III, 386
Townsend, ??? III, 408
Townsend, ??? III, 443
Townsend, ??? IV, 1141
Townsend, ??? IV, 1341
Townsend, A. Gilbert IV, 849
Townsend, Aaron II, 268
Townsend, Aaron IV, 63
Townsend, Aaron IV, 161
Townsend, Aaron IV, 500
Townsend, Aaron IV, 779
Townsend, Aaron VI, 462
Townsend, Aaron VI, 574
Townsend, Abel IV, 63
Townsend, Abel IV, 660
Townsend, Abel IV, 661
Townsend, Abel T. IV, 778
Townsend, Abel T. IV, 849
Townsend, Abel W. IV, 661
Townsend, Abel W. IV, 664
Townsend, Abigail II, 44
Townsend, Abigail II, 107
Townsend, Abigail II, 428
Townsend, Abigail II, 669
Townsend, Abigail II, 823
Townsend, Abigail II, 930
Townsend, Abigail III, 321
Townsend, Abigail III, 501
Townsend, Abigail III, 507
Townsend, Abigail IV, 449
Townsend, Abigail IV, 594
Townsend, Abigail IV, 597
Townsend, Abigail IV, 1189
Townsend, Abigail IV, 1195
Townsend, Abigail IV, 1296
Townsend, Abigail IV, 1300
Townsend, Abigail V, 363
Townsend, Abigail V, 414
Townsend, Abigail V, 434
Townsend, Abigail V, 435
Townsend, Abigail E. V, 908
Townsend, Abigail Emaly V, 435
Townsend, Abigail Emily V, 363
Townsend, Abigail Emily V, 435
Townsend, Abigail Emily V, 908
Townsend, Abigail Emily V, 937
Townsend, Able F. IV, 779
Townsend, Abner IV, 1296
Townsend, Abner Gilbert IV, 778
Townsend, Abner W. IV, 449
Townsend, Abraham III, 320
Townsend, Ada V, 435
Townsend, Adaline IV, 499
Townsend, Adaline IV, 500
Townsend, Adaline IV, 659
Townsend, Adaline IV, 660
Townsend, Adam IV, 1030
Townsend, Adella May IV, 1296
Townsend, Alfred IV, 660
Townsend, Alice Ann IV, 639
Townsend, Alice Ann IV, 661
Townsend, Alizan IV, 660
Townsend, Allie V, 581
Townsend, Almey III, 321
Townsend, Amelia III, 433
Townsend, Amelia IV, 63
Townsend, Amelia IV, 340
Townsend, Amelia IV, 354
Townsend, Amos IV, 112
Townsend, Amos IV, 294
Townsend, Amos IV, 295
Townsend, Amos VI, 462
Townsend, Amos VI, 574
Townsend, Amos, Jr. IV, 112
Townsend, Ann II, 44
Townsend, Ann II, 107
Townsend, Ann II, 669
Townsend, Ann II, 670
Townsend, Ann III, 456
Townsend, Ann IV, 63
Townsend, Ann IV, 93
Townsend, Ann IV, 112
Townsend, Ann IV, 141
Townsend, Ann IV, 161
Townsend, Ann IV, 182
Townsend, Ann IV, 232
Townsend, Ann IV, 294
Townsend, Ann IV, 295
Townsend, Ann IV, 597
Townsend, Ann IV, 660
Townsend, Ann IV, 661
Townsend, Ann IV, 778
Townsend, Ann IV, 779
Townsend, Ann IV, 884
Townsend, Ann IV, 954
Townsend, Ann IV, 1008
Townsend, Ann IV, 1009
Townsend, Ann IV, 1026
Townsend, Ann V, 915
Townsend, Ann V, 936
Townsend, Ann V, 937
Townsend, Ann V, 944
Townsend, Ann Albertson II, 823
Townsend, Ann C. III, 145
Townsend, Ann C. III, 321
Townsend, Ann Eliza II, 823
Townsend, Ann Eliza III, 363
Townsend, Ann Elizabeth IV, 1189
Townsend, Ann R. IV, 1009
Townsend, Ann U. IV, 202
Townsend, Anna III, 484
Townsend, Anna III, 500
Townsend, Anna IV, 294
Townsend, Anna IV, 311
Townsend, Anna IV, 314
Townsend, Anna B. IV, 1189
Townsend, Anna D. IV, 1009
Townsend, Anna E. III, 79
Townsend, Anna E. III, 321
Townsend, Anna Mary VI, 755
Townsend, Anna W. II, 129
Townsend, Anna W. III, 457
Townsend, Annabella II, 802
Townsend, Annabella II, 930
Townsend, Annabella L. II, 889
Townsend, Annabella L. II, 931
Townsend, Annabella W. II, 930
Townsend, Anne III, 320
Townsend, Anne III, 416
Townsend, Anne B. IV, 1189
Townsend, Anne M. II, 825
Townsend, Anne M. III, 341
Townsend, Anne R. IV, 1009
Townsend, Annette R. L. IV, 1189
Townsend, Anthony IV, 562
Townsend, Arabella II, 881
Townsend, Arabella II, 930
Townsend, Arthur III, 320
Townsend, Arvine IV, 660
Townsend, Arvine IV, 1009
Townsend, Arvine V, 936
Townsend, Asa M. IV, 1189
Townsend, Asa M. IV, 1196
Townsend, Asa M. IV, 1225
Townsend, Asa M. IV, 1227
Townsend, Audrey III, 442
Townsend, Audry III, 457
Townsend, Austin D. V, 435
Townsend, Avis II, 823
Townsend, Avis II, 931
Townsend, Avis II, 932
Townsend, Avis M. III, 241
Townsend, Avis M. III, 263
Townsend, Barbara V, 133
Townsend, Barbary V, 775
Townsend, Barclay B. II, 308
Townsend, Benj. III, 321
Townsend, Benj. IV, 235
Townsend, Benj. IV, 500
Townsend, Benjamin III, 320
Townsend, Benjamin IV, 17
Townsend, Benjamin IV, 63
Townsend, Benjamin IV, 161
Townsend, Benjamin IV, 255
Townsend, Benjamin IV, 294
Townsend, Benjamin IV, 644
Townsend, Benjamin IV, 661
Townsend, Benjamin IV, 849
Townsend, Benjamin IV, 860
Townsend, Benjamin IV, 910
Townsend, Benjamin G. IV, 778
Townsend, Benjamin G. IV, 779
Townsend, Benjamin G. IV, 849
Townsend, Benjamin, Jr. IV, 63
Townsend, Bethia M. IV, 1197
Townsend, Bethia M. IV, 1198
Townsend, Bethiah M. IV, 1189
Townsend, Betty I, 39
Townsend, Betty I, 76
Townsend, Beulah II, 44
Townsend, Beulah II, 107
Townsend, Beulah II, 669
Townsend, Beulah II, 835
Townsend, Beulah II, 931
Townsend, Beulah P. II, 121
Townsend, Beulah P. II, 125
Townsend, Beulah P. II, 930
Townsend, Beulah P. II, 931
Townsend, Beulah Pancoast II, 823
Townsend, Caleb II, 44
Townsend, Caleb II, 107
Townsend, Calvin I, 76
Townsend, Cammie M. V, 378
Townsend, Cammie M. V, 435
Townsend, Caroline IV, 653
Townsend, Caroline IV, 660
Townsend, Caroline IV, 661
Townsend, Caroline IV, 849
Townsend, Catharine II, 77
Townsend, Catharine II, 107
Townsend, Catharine II, 669
Townsend, Catharine II, 932
Townsend, Catharine III, 394
Townsend, Catharine III, 457
Townsend, Catharine IV, 779
Townsend, Catharine T. III, 321
Townsend, Catherine II, 669
Townsend, Catherine III, 456
Townsend, Catherine B. V, 414
Townsend, Catherine B. V, 441
Townsend, Catherine H. II, 931
Townsend, Catherine Hickman II, 823
Townsend, Catherine T. II, 931
Townsend, Cathrine II, 107
Townsend, Caturah IV, 779
Townsend, Celia V, 133
Townsend, Celicia IV, 660
Townsend, Celicia IV, 710
Townsend, Celicia IV, 779
Townsend, Celicia L. IV, 625
Townsend, Celicia L. IV, 661
Townsend, Charles I, 76
Townsend, Charles II, 428
Townsend, Charles II, 546
Townsend, Charles II, 595
Townsend, Charles II, 633
Townsend, Charles II, 669
Townsend, Charles II, 670
Townsend, Charles II, 823
Townsend, Charles IV, 661
Townsend, Charles IV, 779
Townsend, Charles IV, 1189
Townsend, Charlotte V, 844
Townsend, Charlotte V, 872
Townsend, Charlotte T. V, 735
Townsend, Chas. II, 823
Townsend, Chas. II, 930
Townsend, Chas. L. IV, 1009
Townsend, Chas. W. VI, 873
Townsend, Chas., Jr. II, 930
Townsend, Christopher III, 320
Townsend, Clara F. V, 908
Townsend, Clara T. II, 931
Townsend, Clara T. V, 908
Townsend, Clayton W. IV, 1170
Townsend, Clayton W. IV, 1189
Townsend, Clifford V, 908
Townsend, Clinton H. V, 435
Townsend, Cole I, 1063
Townsend, Comley IV, 779
Townsend, Cumly IV, 779
Townsend, Dana V, 435
Townsend, Daniel II, 44
Townsend, Daniel III, 321
Townsend, Daniel III, 408
Townsend, David II, 57
Townsend, David II, 107
Townsend, David II, 801
Townsend, David II, 823
Townsend, David IV, 62
Townsend, David IV, 63
Townsend, David IV, 65
Townsend, David IV, 294
Townsend, David IV, 615
Townsend, David IV, 642
Townsend, David IV, 659
Townsend, David IV, 660
Townsend, David IV, 661
Townsend, David IV, 779
Townsend, David C. II, 931
Townsend, David Cooper II, 823
Townsend, David W. IV, 661
Townsend, David W. IV, 895
Townsend, Dayton H. V, 435
Townsend, Deborah III, 320
Townsend, Deborah III, 442
Townsend, Deborah III, 456
Townsend, Deborah III, 457
Townsend, Deborah III, 459
Townsend, Dillon IV, 778
Townsend, Dillon IV, 779
Townsend, Dillon IV, 1009
Townsend, Dinah III, 470
Townsend, Dinah V, 133
Townsend, Dinah Creek V, 854
Townsend, Dinah Creek V, 872
Townsend, Donald Eugene V, 936
Townsend, Donald Eugene V, 937
Townsend, Edith II, 1025
Townsend, Edith II, 1030
Townsend, Edith IV, 63
Townsend, Edith IV, 98
Townsend, Edith IV, 111
Townsend, Edith IV, 112
Townsend, Edith IV, 161
Townsend, Edith IV, 294
Townsend, Edith IV, 644
Townsend, Edith IV, 660
Townsend, Edith IV, 661
Townsend, Edith IV, 664
Townsend, Edith IV, 778
Townsend, Edith IV, 779
Townsend, Edith IV, 783
Townsend, Edith IV, 833
Townsend, Edith IV, 849
Townsend, Edith IV, 910
Townsend, Edith IV, 1005
Townsend, Edith IV, 1009
Townsend, Edith B. II, 1025
Townsend, Edith B. II, 1030
Townsend, Edith Elizabeth IV, 1189
Townsend, Edith W. IV, 661
Townsend, Edna H. II, 308
Townsend, Edward II, 428
Townsend, Edward II, 669
Townsend, Edward II, 670
Townsend, Edward II, 823
Townsend, Edward II, 930
Townsend, Edward II, 931
Townsend, Edward III, 145
Townsend, Edward III, 321
Townsend, Edward O. III, 386
Townsend, Edward O. III, 389
Townsend, Edward Y. II, 771
Townsend, Edwin III, 320
Townsend, Edwin III, 321
Townsend, Eldora V, 286
Townsend, Eldora V, 363
Townsend, Eleanor III, 121
Townsend, Eleanor III, 242
Townsend, Eleanor III, 320
Townsend, Eli I, 258
Townsend, Eli IV, 63
Townsend, Eli IV, 161
Townsend, Eli IV, 295
Townsend, Eli IV, 354
Townsend, Eli IV, 449
Townsend, Eli IV, 500
Townsend, Eli IV, 554
Townsend, Eli IV, 597
Townsend, Eli IV, 1189
Townsend, Eli IV, 1195
Townsend, Eli IV, 1296
Townsend, Eli IV, 1300
Townsend, Eli V, 133
Townsend, Eli William W. IV, 1296
Townsend, Elipha III, 456
Townsend, Elisa I, 71
Townsend, Elisa Ann V, 872
Townsend, Elisabeth I, 76
Townsend, Elisabeth I, 78
Townsend, Elisabeth II, 669
Townsend, Elisabeth IV, 657
Townsend, Elisabeth IV, 661
Townsend, Elisha II, 428
Townsend, Elisha II, 546
Townsend, Elisha II, 670
Townsend, Elisha II, 771
Townsend, Eliz. III, 455
Townsend, Eliz. III, 457
Townsend, Eliz. F. III, 223
Townsend, Eliza I, 76
Townsend, Eliza III, 457
Townsend, Eliza III, 468
Townsend, Eliza IV, 51
Townsend, Eliza IV, 62
Townsend, Eliza IV, 63
Townsend, Eliza IV, 295
Townsend, Eliza IV, 354
Townsend, Eliza IV, 588
Townsend, Eliza IV, 597
Townsend, Eliza IV, 613
Townsend, Eliza IV, 625
Townsend, Eliza IV, 660
Townsend, Eliza IV, 661
Townsend, Eliza IV, 778
Townsend, Eliza IV, 1008
Townsend, Eliza IV, 1009
Townsend, Eliza A. II, 823
Townsend, Eliza Ann V, 872
Townsend, Eliza May IV, 1296
Townsend, Elizabeth I, 1027
Townsend, Elizabeth I, 1038
Townsend, Elizabeth I, 1060
Townsend, Elizabeth I, 1063
Townsend, Elizabeth II, 44
Townsend, Elizabeth II, 57
Townsend, Elizabeth II, 107
Townsend, Elizabeth II, 142
Townsend, Elizabeth II, 428
Townsend, Elizabeth II, 487
Townsend, Elizabeth II, 669

Townsend, Elizabeth II, 670
Townsend, Elizabeth II, 823
Townsend, Elizabeth II, 866
Townsend, Elizabeth II, 923
Townsend, Elizabeth II, 930
Townsend, Elizabeth III, 40
Townsend, Elizabeth III, 104
Townsend, Elizabeth III, 126
Townsend, Elizabeth III, 206
Townsend, Elizabeth III, 321
Townsend, Elizabeth III, 385
Townsend, Elizabeth III, 386
Townsend, Elizabeth III, 400
Townsend, Elizabeth III, 443
Townsend, Elizabeth III, 451
Townsend, Elizabeth III, 456
Townsend, Elizabeth III, 457
Townsend, Elizabeth IV, 63
Townsend, Elizabeth IV, 181
Townsend, Elizabeth IV, 255
Townsend, Elizabeth IV, 294
Townsend, Elizabeth IV, 340
Townsend, Elizabeth IV, 352
Townsend, Elizabeth IV, 354
Townsend, Elizabeth IV, 449
Townsend, Elizabeth IV, 500
Townsend, Elizabeth IV, 554
Townsend, Elizabeth IV, 562
Townsend, Elizabeth IV, 597
Townsend, Elizabeth IV, 620
Townsend, Elizabeth IV, 660
Townsend, Elizabeth IV, 661
Townsend, Elizabeth IV, 663
Townsend, Elizabeth IV, 779
Townsend, Elizabeth IV, 849
Townsend, Elizabeth IV, 1189
Townsend, Elizabeth IV, 1192
Townsend, Elizabeth IV, 1225
Townsend, Elizabeth IV, 1296
Townsend, Elizabeth IV, 1300
Townsend, Elizabeth V, 133
Townsend, Elizabeth V, 868
Townsend, Elizabeth V, 937
Townsend, Elizabeth V, 978
Townsend, Elizabeth VI, 1018
Townsend, Elizabeth F. II, 823
Townsend, Elizabeth F. II, 889
Townsend, Elizabeth F. II, 898
Townsend, Elizabeth F. II, 931
Townsend, Elizabeth F. III, 321
Townsend, Elizabeth G. IV, 1189
Townsend, Elizabeth G. IV, 1196
Townsend, Elizabeth G. IV, 1225
Townsend, Elizabeth G. IV, 1227
Townsend, Elizabeth N. IV, 660
Townsend, Elizabeth W. II, 546
Townsend, Elizabeth W. II, 670
Townsend, Elizabeth W. II, 771
Townsend, Elizabeth W. IV, 1144
Townsend, Elizabeth W. IV, 1189
Townsend, Ella III, 223
Townsend, Ella V. II, 898
Townsend, Ella V. II, 931
Townsend, Ella Virginia II, 823
Townsend, Ellen B. II, 931
Townsend, Ellen Baldwin II, 823
Townsend, Ellin IV, 1026
Townsend, Ellin IV, 1031
Townsend, Elma III, 79
Townsend, Elmer V, 936
Townsend, Elmer D. V, 937
Townsend, Elmer D., Jr. V, 936
Townsend, Elmina IV, 615
Townsend, Elmina IV, 661
Townsend, Elmina T. IV, 615
Townsend, Elmira IV, 467
Townsend, Elmira IV, 500
Townsend, Elsie II, 931
Townsend, Elva V, 435
Townsend, Elve I, 1063
Townsend, Elvi IV, 63
Townsend, Elvira V, 770
Townsend, Elvira V, 869
Townsend, Elvira V, 872
Townsend, Elvira V, 875
Townsend, Elvira C. V, 872
Townsend, Elviry V, 67
Townsend, Elvy V, 133
Townsend, Elvy V, 775
Townsend, Emely IV, 1296
Townsend, Emer IV, 884
Townsend, Emily IV, 597
Townsend, Emily IV, 1274
Townsend, Emily IV, 1296
Townsend, Emily Sharpless II, 821
Townsend, Emma Frances IV, 1296
Townsend, Emma G. II, 931
Townsend, Emma R. V, 435
Townsend, Emma R. V, 937
Townsend, Emma S. V, 363
Townsend, Emma Spencer V, 363
Townsend, Emma Spencer V, 435
Townsend, Emma W. V, 928
Townsend, Emma W. V, 937
Townsend, Emmor IV, 661
Townsend, Emmor IV, 778
Townsend, Emmor IV, 779
Townsend, Emmor IV, 884
Townsend, Emmor IV, 1009
Townsend, Emmor V, 936
Townsend, Emor V, 937
Townsend, Epinetus III, 321
Townsend, Ernest Hartley IV, 1296
Townsend, Ervine IV, 661
Townsend, Ervine IV, 1009
Townsend, Ervine V, 937
Townsend, Ester III, 321
Townsend, Esther I, 1038
Townsend, Esther II, 791
Townsend, Esther III, 145
Townsend, Esther III, 321
Townsend, Esther III, 457
Townsend, Esther IV, 50
Townsend, Esther IV, 63
Townsend, Esther IV, 112
Townsend, Esther IV, 779
Townsend, Esther IV, 1189
Townsend, Esther IV, 1296
Townsend, Esther V, 378
Townsend, Esther Ann II, 712
Townsend, Esther H. IV, 1296
Townsend, Esther J. V, 435
Townsend, Esther J. V, 566
Townsend, Esther Jane V, 438
Townsend, Esther W. IV, 1163
Townsend, Ethel G. V, 937
Townsend, Ethelanna III, 456
Townsend, Ethelene III, 445
Townsend, Eugene V, 435
Townsend, Evan II, 823
Townsend, Evi S. IV, 778
Townsend, Evi S. IV, 779
Townsend, Evi S. IV, 849
Townsend, Florance Effie IV, 1296
Townsend, Floyd V, 435
Townsend, Frances III, 121
Townsend, Frances III, 320
Townsend, Frances Ann IV, 597
Townsend, Frances Anna IV, 1296
Townsend, Francis IV, 23
Townsend, Francis IV, 62
Townsend, Francis IV, 63
Townsend, Francis IV, 158
Townsend, Francis IV, 161
Townsend, Francis IV, 500
Townsend, Francis IV, 660
Townsend, Francis IV, 661
Townsend, Francis IV, 778
Townsend, Francis IV, 884
Townsend, Francis IV, 1009
Townsend, Francis V, 936
Townsend, Francis VI, 462
Townsend, Francis A. III, 321
Townsend, Francis I. IV, 779
Townsend, Francis J. IV, 954
Townsend, Francis J. IV, 1009
Townsend, Franklin II, 823
Townsend, Franklin II, 930
Townsend, Franklin III, 321
Townsend, Frederick E. III, 321
Townsend, Frederick E. III, 456
Townsend, Geo. III, 321
Townsend, George III, 40
Townsend, George III, 74
Townsend, George III, 121
Townsend, George III, 320
Townsend, George III, 321
Townsend, George III, 484
Townsend, George III, 500
Townsend, George III, 501
Townsend, George III, 506
Townsend, George III, 507
Townsend, George A. V, 435
Townsend, George Craft II, 823
Townsend, George E. II, 930
Townsend, George J. V, 872
Townsend, Georgiana IV, 1009
Townsend, Georgianna IV, 1009
Townsend, Gilbert G. III, 321
Townsend, Griffith Levering IV, 1189
Townsend, Gulia Ann IV, 554
Townsend, Guliann IV, 161
Townsend, Gulielma Maria II, 801
Townsend, Hannah II, 107
Townsend, Hannah II, 428
Townsend, Hannah II, 487
Townsend, Hannah II, 545
Townsend, Hannah II, 633
Townsend, Hannah II, 669
Townsend, Hannah II, 670
Townsend, Hannah II, 817
Townsend, Hannah II, 821
Townsend, Hannah II, 823
Townsend, Hannah II, 862
Townsend, Hannah II, 930
Townsend, Hannah II, 931
Townsend, Hannah III, 321
Townsend, Hannah III, 456
Townsend, Hannah III, 458
Townsend, Hannah III, 461
Townsend, Hannah III, 502
Townsend, Hannah IV, 63
Townsend, Hannah IV, 73
Townsend, Hannah IV, 111
Townsend, Hannah IV, 112
Townsend, Hannah IV, 295
Townsend, Hannah IV, 578
Townsend, Hannah IV, 597
Townsend, Hannah IV, 661
Townsend, Hannah IV, 770
Townsend, Hannah IV, 778
Townsend, Hannah IV, 779
Townsend, Hannah IV, 1031
Townsend, Hannah IV, 1079
Townsend, Hannah IV, 1139
Townsend, Hannah IV, 1169
Townsend, Hannah IV, 1189
Townsend, Hannah V, 508
Townsend, Hannah V, 536
Townsend, Hannah VI, 462
Townsend, Hannah VI, 574
Townsend, Hannah G. IV, 589
Townsend, Hannah G. IV, 597
Townsend, Hannah S. II, 930
Townsend, Hannah W. III, 451
Townsend, Hannah W. III, 457
Townsend, Hannah W. III, 500
Townsend, Hannah W. III, 501
Townsend, Hannah W. III, 503
Townsend, Hannah W. IV, 1189
Townsend, Hannah, Jr. II, 931
Townsend, Hannah, Jr. IV, 295
Townsend, Harold V, 435
Townsend, Harriet III, 321
Townsend, Harriet IV, 63
Townsend, Harriet IV, 354
Townsend, Harriet V, 133
Townsend, Harriet V, 937
Townsend, Harriet Marie V, 435
Townsend, Harriet T. III, 145
Townsend, Harriett IV, 354
Townsend, Harriett V, 938
Townsend, Hattie Rand V, 435
Townsend, Helen IV, 1009
Townsend, Hellen IV, 1009
Townsend, Hellen Romina V, 936
Townsend, Henry II, 823
Townsend, Henry II, 930
Townsend, Henry III, 321
Townsend, Henry III, 451
Townsend, Henry III, 456
Townsend, Henry III, 457
Townsend, Henry VI, 946
Townsend, Henry H. IV, 1009
Townsend, Henry H. IV, 1189
Townsend, Henry Isaac V, 937
Townsend, Henry J. V, 936
Townsend, Henry W. II, 931
Townsend, Henryetta IV, 1296
Townsend, Herbert H. V, 435
Townsend, Hester III, 321
Townsend, Hester V, 133
Townsend, Hewlett III, 416
Townsend, Hewlett III, 422
Townsend, Horace V, 435
Townsend, Horace V, 681
Townsend, Horace V, 715
Townsend, Howard V, 908
Townsend, Ida May V, 908
Townsend, Ines V, 466
Townsend, Inez M. V, 378
Townsend, Isaac II, 107
Townsend, Isaac II, 428
Townsend, Isaac II, 669
Townsend, Isaac II, 821
Townsend, Isaac II, 823
Townsend, Isaac II, 881
Townsend, Isaac II, 889
Townsend, Isaac II, 931
Townsend, Isaac IV, 63
Townsend, Isaac IV, 111
Townsend, Isaac IV, 620
Townsend, Isaac IV, 660
Townsend, Isaac IV, 661
Townsend, Isaac IV, 849
Townsend, Isaac V, 40
Townsend, Isaac V, 133
Townsend, Isaac V, 363
Townsend, Isaac V, 367
Townsend, Isaac V, 435
Townsend, Isaac V, 908
Townsend, Isaac V, 933
Townsend, Isaac V, 937
Townsend, Isaac, Jr. II, 802
Townsend, Isaac, Jr. II, 823
Townsend, Isaac, Jr. II, 930
Townsend, Isaac, Jr. II, 931
Townsend, Isabel I, 66
Townsend, Isabel I, 76
Townsend, Isabel B. V, 936
Townsend, Israel L. IV, 1189
Townsend, Israel Lewis IV, 1189
Townsend, J. M. V, 378
Townsend, J. Wilson II, 931
Townsend, Ja. II, 428
Townsend, Jackson S. III, 459
Townsend, Jacob II, 66
Townsend, Jacob II, 107
Townsend, Jacob II, 542
Townsend, Jacob II, 669
Townsend, Jacob III, 457
Townsend, Jacob IV, 63
Townsend, James I, 1038
Townsend, James I, 1063
Townsend, James I Sup 1, 11
Townsend, James II, 428
Townsend, James III, 320
Townsend, James III, 442
Townsend, James III, 457
Townsend, James III, 501
Townsend, James III, 507
Townsend, James IV, 63
Townsend, James IV, 562
Townsend, James IV, 778
Townsend, James IV, 779
Townsend, James IV, 849
Townsend, James IV, 1189
Townsend, James V, 122
Townsend, James V, 133
Townsend, James V, 735
Townsend, James V, 770
Townsend, James V, 872
Townsend, James V, 915
Townsend, James V, 936
Townsend, James B. IV, 779
Townsend, James B. N. Y. III, 321
Townsend, James D. IV, 661
Townsend, James Dallas IV, 661
Townsend, James W. II, 931
Townsend, James Wood II, 823
Townsend, Jane Anna IV, 1296
Townsend, Jemima IV, 63
Townsend, Jemima IV, 161
Townsend, Jemima IV, 779
Townsend, Jemima IV, 910
Townsend, Jemima IV, 1030
Townsend, Jemima IV, 1031
Townsend, Jemima T. III, 459
Townsend, Jemimah IV, 235
Townsend, Jesse II, 107
Townsend, Jesse II, 771
Townsend, Jesse II, 930
Townsend, Jesse IV, 63
Townsend, Jesse IV, 98
Townsend, Jesse IV, 111
Townsend, Jesse IV, 112
Townsend, Jesse IV, 779
Townsend, Jesse V, 133
Townsend, Jesse VI, 462
Townsend, Jesse B. IV, 1189
Townsend, Jesse B. R. IV, 1189
Townsend, Jesse Townsend IV, 779
Townsend, Jesse W. II, 931
Townsend, Jessie II, 931
Townsend, Joan II, 541
Townsend, Joan II, 669
Townsend, Joanna II, 819
Townsend, Joanna II, 823
Townsend, Joanna III, 321
Townsend, Job Ridgway IV, 161
Townsend, Joel IV, 1026
Townsend, John I, 76
Townsend, John I, 1038
Townsend, John I, 1063
Townsend, John I Sup 1, 11
Townsend, John II, 44
Townsend, John II, 49
Townsend, John II, 107
Townsend, John II, 428
Townsend, John II, 448
Townsend, John II, 487
Townsend, John II, 669
Townsend, John II, 819
Townsend, John II, 823
Townsend, John II, 862
Townsend, John II, 930
Townsend, John II, 1030
Townsend, John III, 258
Townsend, John III, 321
Townsend, John III, 408
Townsend, John III, 437
Townsend, John III, 456
Townsend, John IV, 17
Townsend, John IV, 47
Townsend, John IV, 62
Townsend, John IV, 63
Townsend, John IV, 111
Townsend, John IV, 112
Townsend, John IV, 141
Townsend, John IV, 142
Townsend, John IV, 161
Townsend, John IV, 294
Townsend, John IV, 660
Townsend, John IV, 661
Townsend, John IV, 849
Townsend, John IV, 1008
Townsend, John IV, 1009
Townsend, John V, 67
Townsend, John V, 133
Townsend, John V, 770
Townsend, John V, 845
Townsend, John V, 872
Townsend, John VI, 462
Townsend, John VI, 574
Townsend, John B. III, 457
Townsend, John Dixon IV, 661
Townsend, John Dixon IV, 849
Townsend, John Fares IV, 111
Townsend, John Ferris IV, 63
Townsend, John G. III, 321
Townsend, John K. II, 670
Townsend, John K. II, 930
Townsend, John P. II, 931
Townsend, John P. III, 321
Townsend, John Peckham II, 82
Townsend, John Rebekah VI, 57
Townsend, John T. II, 823
Townsend, John T. V, 937
Townsend, John Thomas V, 435
Townsend, John Thomas V, 936
Townsend, John Thomas V, 937
Townsend, John Wilson II, 823
Townsend, John, Jr. I, 1038
Townsend, John, Jr. I Sup 1, 11
Townsend, Jon I, 76
Townsend, Jonathan IV, 63
Townsend, Jonathan IV, 230
Townsend, Jonathan IV, 778
Townsend, Jonathan IV, 779
Townsend, Jonathan IV, 1008
Townsend, Jonathan IV, 1009
Townsend, Jonathan IV, 1031
Townsend, Jonathan V, 133
Townsend, Jonathan V, 770
Townsend, Jos. L. III, 451
Townsend, Jos. L. III, 499
Townsend, Joseph II, 428
Townsend, Joseph II, 487
Townsend, Joseph II, 669
Townsend, Joseph II, 670
Townsend, Joseph II, 791
Townsend, Joseph II, 923
Townsend, Joseph II, 930
Townsend, Joseph III, 145
Townsend, Joseph III, 321
Townsend, Joseph III, 503
Townsend, Joseph IV, 63
Townsend, Joseph IV, 111
Townsend, Joseph IV, 161
Townsend, Joseph IV, 182
Townsend, Joseph IV, 294
Townsend, Joseph IV, 354
Townsend, Joseph IV, 449
Townsend, Joseph IV, 562
Townsend, Joseph IV, 597
Townsend, Joseph IV, 609
Townsend, Joseph IV, 658
Townsend, Joseph IV, 660
Townsend, Joseph IV, 661
Townsend, Joseph IV, 767
Townsend, Joseph IV, 770
Townsend, Joseph IV, 778
Townsend, Joseph IV, 779
Townsend, Joseph IV, 884
Townsend, Joseph IV, 1009
Townsend, Joseph IV, 1139
Townsend, Joseph IV, 1296
Townsend, Joseph V, 936
Townsend, Joseph V, 937
Townsend, Joseph VI, 453
Townsend, Joseph VI, 462
Townsend, Joseph B. IV, 661
Townsend, Joseph C. II, 931
Townsend, Joseph L. III, 457
Townsend, Joseph L. III, 499
Townsend, Joseph L. III, 500

send, Joseph L. III, 501
send, Joseph Lawrence
III, 500
send, Joseph T. IV, 661
send, Joseph T. IV, 1382
send, Joseph Talbott IV, 660
nsend, Joseph W. I, 76
nsend, Joseph Watson
IV, 1189
nsend, Joseph, Jr. IV, 111
nsend, Joseph, Jr. IV, 294
nsend, Josiah I, 39
nsend, Josiah I, 76
nsend, Josiah I, 162
nsend, Josiah I, 169
nsend, Josiah I, 258
nsend, Josiah II, 88
nsend, Josiah II, 107
nsend, Josiah II, 244
nsend, Josiah II, 268
nsend, Josiah IV, 779
nsend, Josiah V, 133
nsend, Josiah V, 363
nsend, Josiah V, 414
nsend, Josiah V, 434
nsend, Josiah V, 435
nsend, Josiah V, 978
nsend, Josiah Dayton V, 435
nsend, Josiah Dayton V, 937
nsend, Josiah M. V, 435
nsend, Josiah M. V, 566
nsend, Josiah, Jr. V, 435
nsend, Judah II, 107
nsend, Judith II, 107
nsend, Judith IV, 161
nsend, Judith IV, 749
nsend, Judith IV, 778
nsend, Judith IV, 779
nsend, Juditha Douglass
IV, 230
nsend, Juli Ann IV, 161
nsend, Juli Ann IV, 449
nsend, Juli Ann IV, 1079
nsend, Julia Ann IV, 554
nsend, Julia Ann IV, 571
nsend, Julia Ann IV, 597
nsend, Julia Penniman
II, 823
nsend, Juliann IV, 142
nsend, Juliann IV, 449
nsend, Juliann IV, 1079
nsend, Ketturah II, 107
nsend, Keturah II, 107
nsend, Keturah IV, 779
nsend, Keturah V, 47
nsend, Keturah V, 133
nsend, Lavenia II, 930
nsend, Lavina V, 435
nsend, Lavinia II, 159
nsend, Lavinia II, 913
nsend, Lavinia II, 930
nsend, Lazetta IV, 660
nsend, Leander III, 363
nsend, Leander W. III, 79
nsend, Leander W. III, 321
nsend, Lemuel J. G. IV, 660
nsend, Leroy W. II, 931
nsend, Letitia III, 457
nsend, Letitia III, 458
nsend, Letitia III, 459
nsend, Letitia IV, 1189
nsend, Letitia Ann IV, 1189
wnsend, Levi IV, 294
wnsend, Levi IV, 295
wnsend, Levi IV, 311
wnsend, Levi IV, 314
wnsend, Levi IV, 354
wnsend, Levi IV, 356
wnsend, Levi IV, 449
wnsend, Levi IV, 554
wnsend, Levi IV, 597
wnsend, Levi IV, 1139
wnsend, Levi IV, 1189
wnsend, Levi IV, 1296
wnsend, Lewis IV, 661
wnsend, Lewis IV, 697
wnsend, Lewis IV, 778
wnsend, Lewis IV, 779
wnsend, Lewis IV, 884
wnsend, Lewis IV, 974
wnsend, Lewis IV, 1008
wnsend, Lewis IV, 1009
wnsend, Lewis V, 937
wnsend, Lewis VI, 462
wnsend, Lillie V, 937
wnsend, Lilly H. V, 937
wnsend, Lloyd V, 435
wnsend, Louis IV, 919
wnsend, Louisa IV, 1026
wnsend, Lovisa IV, 1189
wnsend, Lowis V, 936
Townsend, Loyd M. V, 435
Townsend, Lucile V, 378
Townsend, Luke II, 448
Townsend, Lydia II, 428
Townsend, Lydia II, 633
Townsend, Lydia II, 669
Townsend, Lydia II, 823
Townsend, Lydia II, 930
Townsend, Lydia III, 430
Townsend, Lydia III, 457
Townsend, Lydia IV, 63
Townsend, Lydia IV, 509
Townsend, Lydia IV, 554
Townsend, Lydia IV, 609
Townsend, Lydia IV, 642
Townsend, Lydia IV, 644
Townsend, Lydia IV, 660
Townsend, Lydia IV, 661
Townsend, Lydia IV, 849
Townsend, Lydia V, 853
Townsend, Lydia V, 872
Townsend, Lydia Ann IV, 647
Townsend, Lydia Ann IV, 648
Townsend, Lydia Ann IV, 661
Townsend, Lydia Ann IV, 895
Townsend, Lydia B. IV, 849
Townsend, Lydia M. III, 457
Townsend, Lydia Margaret V, 435
Townsend, Lydia Margaret V, 937
Townsend, Lydia P. IV, 778
Townsend, Lydia P. IV, 779
Townsend, Lydia W. IV, 1189
Townsend, M. Amelia III, 457
Townsend, Marah IV, 23
Townsend, Marah IV, 62
Townsend, Marah IV, 63
Townsend, Marah IV, 161
Townsend, Margaret I, 76
Townsend, Margaret I, 1032
Townsend, Margaret I, 1038
Townsend, Margaret II, 930
Townsend, Margaret III, 422
Townsend, Margaret III, 499
Townsend, Margaret III, 500
Townsend, Margaret S. II, 914
Townsend, Margaret S. II, 931
Townsend, Margaret Shoemaker
II, 816
Townsend, Maria IV, 229
Townsend, Maria IV, 661
Townsend, Mariah IV, 849
Townsend, Mark II, 866
Townsend, Marrah IV, 500
Townsend, Martha I, 1063
Townsend, Martha II, 428
Townsend, Martha III, 164
Townsend, Martha III, 165
Townsend, Martha III, 258
Townsend, Martha III, 321
Townsend, Martha III, 447
Townsend, Martha III, 457
Townsend, Martha III, 501
Townsend, Martha III, 507
Townsend, Martha IV, 63
Townsend, Martha IV, 92
Townsend, Martha IV, 112
Townsend, Martha IV, 161
Townsend, Martha IV, 235
Townsend, Martha IV, 294
Townsend, Martha IV, 661
Townsend, Martha IV, 778
Townsend, Martha IV, 779
Townsend, Martha IV, 849
Townsend, Martha IV, 971
Townsend, Martha IV, 1009
Townsend, Martha IV, 1028
Townsend, Martha IV, 1031
Townsend, Martha V, 40
Townsend, Martha V, 133
Townsend, Martha V, 845
Townsend, Martha V, 872
Townsend, Martha M. IV, 767
Townsend, Martha M. IV, 778
Townsend, Mary I, 1038
Townsend, Mary II, 49
Townsend, Mary II, 66
Townsend, Mary II, 107
Townsend, Mary II, 428
Townsend, Mary II, 542
Townsend, Mary II, 627
Townsend, Mary II, 669
Townsend, Mary II, 670
Townsend, Mary II, 823
Townsend, Mary II, 862
Townsend, Mary II, 930
Townsend, Mary III, 397
Townsend, Mary III, 406
Townsend, Mary III, 408
Townsend, Mary III, 416
Townsend, Mary III, 421
Townsend, Mary III, 422
Townsend, Mary III, 426
Townsend, Mary III, 451
Townsend, Mary III, 454
Townsend, Mary III, 455
Townsend, Mary III, 456
Townsend, Mary III, 457
Townsend, Mary III, 474
Townsend, Mary III, 475
Townsend, Mary III, 487
Townsend, Mary III, 500
Townsend, Mary III, 501
Townsend, Mary III, 507
Townsend, Mary IV, 62
Townsend, Mary IV, 63
Townsend, Mary IV, 65
Townsend, Mary IV, 66
Townsend, Mary IV, 161
Townsend, Mary IV, 182
Townsend, Mary IV, 249
Townsend, Mary IV, 294
Townsend, Mary IV, 352
Townsend, Mary IV, 354
Townsend, Mary IV, 356
Townsend, Mary IV, 449
Townsend, Mary IV, 554
Townsend, Mary IV, 597
Townsend, Mary IV, 615
Townsend, Mary IV, 629
Townsend, Mary IV, 642
Townsend, Mary IV, 659
Townsend, Mary IV, 660
Townsend, Mary IV, 661
Townsend, Mary IV, 779
Townsend, Mary IV, 849
Townsend, Mary IV, 1030
Townsend, Mary IV, 1189
Townsend, Mary IV, 1296
Townsend, Mary V, 40
Townsend, Mary V, 124
Townsend, Mary V, 133
Townsend, Mary V, 435
Townsend, Mary V, 681
Townsend, Mary V, 715
Townsend, Mary V, 872
Townsend, Mary V, 915
Townsend, Mary VI, 382
Townsend, Mary VI, 462
Townsend, Mary VI, 574
Townsend, Mary Ann IV, 562
Townsend, Mary Ann IV, 597
Townsend, Mary Ann IV, 778
Townsend, Mary Ann IV, 849
Townsend, Mary Ann IV, 1296
Townsend, Mary Ann V, 936
Townsend, Mary Ann Gilbert
IV, 779
Townsend, Mary B. IV, 615
Townsend, Mary B. IV, 661
Townsend, Mary B. IV, 779
Townsend, Mary C. I, 76
Townsend, Mary Catharine
V, 933
Townsend, Mary Catharine
V, 937
Townsend, Mary Catharine
V, 944
Townsend, Mary Catherine
V, 435
Townsend, Mary D. IV, 778
Townsend, Mary D. IV, 974
Townsend, Mary D. IV, 1008
Townsend, Mary D. IV, 1009
Townsend, Mary E. III, 456
Townsend, Mary Elizabeth V, 937
Townsend, Mary Ellen IV, 1189
Townsend, Mary Ellen V, 936
Townsend, Mary Ellen V, 937
Townsend, Mary Elma III, 78
Townsend, Mary Elma III, 321
Townsend, Mary G. II, 923
Townsend, Mary G. II, 930
Townsend, Mary G. IV, 597
Townsend, Mary Hester Sarah
Elizabeth V, 775
Townsend, Mary Isabella
IV, 1189
Townsend, Mary K. II, 931
Townsend, Mary L. II, 930
Townsend, Mary P. III, 457
Townsend, Mary P. IV, 982
Townsend, Mary P. IV, 1009
Townsend, Mary S. II, 931
Townsend, Mary Shipley II, 823
Townsend, Mary T. IV, 648
Townsend, Mary T. IV, 661
Townsend, Mary Way IV, 660
Townsend, Maryann IV, 295
Townsend, Matilda IV, 110
Townsend, Matilda IV, 111
Townsend, Matilda IV, 112
Townsend, May V, 435
Townsend, Melville V, 435
Townsend, Merle V, 936
Townsend, Merle K. V, 937
Townsend, Mildred V, 435
Townsend, Mill John III, 321
Townsend, Milo A. IV, 660
Townsend, Milo N. IV, 661
Townsend, Milo. A. IV, 663
Townsend, Milton IV, 660
Townsend, Milton IV, 661
Townsend, Minerva S. II, 931
Townsend, Minerva Sarah II, 823
Townsend, Minnie V, 936
Townsend, Minnie B. V, 937
Townsend, Mira II, 821
Townsend, Mira II, 823
Townsend, Mira IV, 660
Townsend, Mira H. IV, 661
Townsend, Morris IV, 63
Townsend, Morris IV, 354
Townsend, Moses IV, 63
Townsend, Moses IV, 111
Townsend, Moses IV, 112
Townsend, Moses IV, 777
Townsend, Moses IV, 778
Townsend, Moses IV, 779
Townsend, Moses IV, 1009
Townsend, Moses IV, 1031
Townsend, Moses Bundy IV, 161
Townsend, Moses J. IV, 1009
Townsend, Nancy I, 76
Townsend, Nancy I, 233
Townsend, Nancy I, 258
Townsend, Nancy IV, 92
Townsend, Nancy IV, 93
Townsend, Nancy IV, 111
Townsend, Nancy IV, 112
Townsend, Nathan IV, 645
Townsend, Nathan IV, 660
Townsend, Nathan IV, 661
Townsend, Nathan IV, 779
Townsend, Nathan IV, 895
Townsend, Nathan H. IV, 778
Townsend, Nathan H. IV, 779
Townsend, Nathan H. IV, 849
Townsend, Nathaniel III, 164
Townsend, Nathaniel III, 165
Townsend, Nathaniel III, 321
Townsend, Nathaniel III, 408
Townsend, Nathaniel III, 421
Townsend, Nathaniel III, 457
Townsend, Nettie V, 908
Townsend, Nicholas III, 105
Townsend, Nicholas III, 321
Townsend, Nicholas III, 408
Townsend, Nicholas III, 457
Townsend, Noah II, 88
Townsend, Noah IV, 749
Townsend, Noah Murphy II, 268
Townsend, Obadiah III, 424
Townsend, Obadiah III, 430
Townsend, Obadiah III, 457
Townsend, Oblinger IV, 1079
Townsend, Ogden II, 930
Townsend, Ogden II, 931
Townsend, Oliver J. V, 435
Townsend, Orland V, 435
Townsend, Orlando V, 435
Townsend, Oscar IV, 1009
Townsend, Oscar IV, 1341
Townsend, Pamela IV, 661
Townsend, Pamelia III, 457
Townsend, Pamelia III, 460
Townsend, Penina V, 435
Townsend, Peninah V, 363
Townsend, Peninah V, 435
Townsend, Peninah V, 908
Townsend, Peninah V, 937
Townsend, Peninah Ann V, 908
Townsend, Peninnah V, 933
Townsend, Peninnah V, 937
Townsend, Penninah V, 363
Townsend, Penninah V, 367
Townsend, Penninnah Ann V, 908
Townsend, Permelia IV, 48
Townsend, Permelia IV, 63
Townsend, Peter II, 44
Townsend, Peter II, 107
Townsend, Phebe II, 795
Townsend, Phebe II, 804
Townsend, Phebe III, 138
Townsend, Phebe III, 257
Townsend, Phebe III, 320
Townsend, Phebe III, 321
Townsend, Phebe III, 424
Townsend, Phebe III, 437
Townsend, Phebe III, 441
Townsend, Phebe III, 456
Townsend, Phebe III, 457
Townsend, Phebe III, 484
Townsend, Phebe III, 500
Townsend, Phebe III, 501
Townsend, Phebe III, 506
Townsend, Phebe III, 507
Townsend, Phebe IV, 63
Townsend, Phebe IV, 1296
Townsend, Phebe VI, 462
Townsend, Phebe VI, 574
Townsend, Phebe Ann III, 399
Townsend, Phebe Ann III, 457
Townsend, Phebe Ann III, 459
Townsend, Phebe Anna S.
III, 457
Townsend, Phebe Shotwell
II, 791
Townsend, Phebie IV, 1293
Townsend, Phebie IV, 1296
Townsend, Philadelphia III, 105
Townsend, Philadelphia III, 321
Townsend, Philadelphia III, 408
Townsend, Philadelphia III, 457
Townsend, Philena IV, 1296
Townsend, Philip Pedrick IV, 779
Townsend, Pres. Minister
Letitia III, 326
Townsend, Prior III, 456
Townsend, Prior III, 461
Townsend, Priscilla II, 428
Townsend, Priscilla II, 546
Townsend, Priscilla II, 670
Townsend, Priscilla II, 823
Townsend, Priscilla II, 930
Townsend, Priscilla IV, 1009
Townsend, Priscilla IV, 1018
Townsend, R. III, 321
Townsend, Rachel I, 76
Townsend, Rachel I, 78
Townsend, Rachel I, 87
Townsend, Rachel I, 1063
Townsend, Rachel II, 428
Townsend, Rachel II, 931
Townsend, Rachel III, 458
Townsend, Rachel IV, 62
Townsend, Rachel IV, 63
Townsend, Rachel IV, 658
Townsend, Rachel IV, 660
Townsend, Rachel IV, 661
Townsend, Rachel IV, 697
Townsend, Rachel IV, 770
Townsend, Rachel IV, 778
Townsend, Rachel IV, 779
Townsend, Rachel IV, 849
Townsend, Rachel IV, 974
Townsend, Rachel IV, 1008
Townsend, Rachel IV, 1009
Townsend, Rachel V, 67
Townsend, Rachel V, 75
Townsend, Rachel V, 133
Townsend, Rachel V, 435
Townsend, Rachel VI, 462
Townsend, Rachel Annet IV, 1170
Townsend, Rachel Annet IV, 1189
Townsend, Rachel B. II, 823
Townsend, Rachel B. IV, 661
Townsend, Rachel W. IV, 1189
Townsend, Rachel W. IV, 1190
Townsend, Rachel Wilson II, 823
Townsend, Ralph II, 448
Townsend, Ray Dayton V, 937
Townsend, Rebecca II, 49
Townsend, Rebecca II, 107
Townsend, Rebecca II, 801
Townsend, Rebecca II, 823
Townsend, Rebecca II, 835
Townsend, Rebecca II, 931
Townsend, Rebecca III, 126
Townsend, Rebecca III, 321
Townsend, Rebecca IV, 62
Townsend, Rebecca IV, 67
Townsend, Rebecca IV, 660
Townsend, Rebecca IV, 661
Townsend, Rebecca IV, 664
Townsend, Rebecca IV, 849
Townsend, Rebecca IV, 1031
Townsend, Rebecca V, 936
Townsend, Rebecca Gracey
III, 456
Townsend, Rebecca H. II, 308
Townsend, Rebecca W. II, 881
Townsend, Rebecca W. II, 930
Townsend, Rebecca W. IV, 661
Townsend, Rebecca W. IV, 779
Townsend, Rebecca Willson
II, 802
Townsend, Rebeccah VI, 462
Townsend, Rebeckah II, 44
Townsend, Rebekah VI, 574
Townsend, Rees Cadwalader
IV, 112
Townsend, Rees Cadwallader
IV, 63
Townsend, Reese IV, 112

Townsend, Rhoda V, 297
Townsend, Rhoda V, 312
Townsend, Richard II, 44
Townsend, Richard II, 107
Townsend, Richard II, 135
Townsend, Richard II, 428
Townsend, Richard II, 542
Townsend, Richard II, 669
Townsend, Richard III, 416
Townsend, Richard III, 455
Townsend, Richard III, 457
Townsend, Richard III, 459
Townsend, Richard III, 501
Townsend, Richard III, 507
Townsend, Richard M. III, 321
Townsend, Richard Mott III, 321
Townsend, Robert II, 107
Townsend, Robert IV, 63
Townsend, Robert IV, 112
Townsend, Robert IV, 161
Townsend, Robert IV, 500
Townsend, Robert V, 937
Townsend, Robert C. V, 937
Townsend, Robert George II, 823
Townsend, Roger II, 428
Townsend, Rosanna V, 735
Townsend, Rosanna V, 835
Townsend, Rosannah III, 74
Townsend, Rosannah III, 321
Townsend, Rosannah III, 500
Townsend, Rosannah III, 501
Townsend, Rosannah V, 122
Townsend, Rosannah V, 133
Townsend, Rose IV, 562
Townsend, Roseannah III, 400
Townsend, Roseannah III, 449
Townsend, Roseannah III, 457
Townsend, Ross IV, 562
Townsend, Rossiter II, 1025
Townsend, Rossiter II, 1030
Townsend, Rozilla IV, 1296
Townsend, Ruemourn III, 474
Townsend, Ruth I, 1063
Townsend, Ruth II, 670
Townsend, Ruth II, 771
Townsend, Ruth II, 866
Townsend, Ruth II, 930
Townsend, Ruth IV, 63
Townsend, Ruth IV, 112
Townsend, Ruth IV, 141
Townsend, Ruth IV, 142
Townsend, Ruth IV, 161
Townsend, Ruth IV, 294
Townsend, Ruth IV, 449
Townsend, Ruth IV, 554
Townsend, Ruth IV, 597
Townsend, Ruth IV, 660
Townsend, Ruth IV, 1079
Townsend, Ruth IV, 1144
Townsend, Ruth IV, 1163
Townsend, Ruth IV, 1171
Townsend, Ruth IV, 1189
Townsend, Ruth IV, 1190
Townsend, Ruth IV, 1225
Townsend, Ruth V, 133
Townsend, Ruth V, 854
Townsend, Ruth V, 872
Townsend, Ruth B. V, 937
Townsend, Sabina IV, 63
Townsend, Sabina IV, 98
Townsend, Sabina IV, 111
Townsend, Sabina IV, 112
Townsend, Salem IV, 112
Townsend, Sallie B., Jr. II, 931
Townsend, Sallie Brick II, 823
Townsend, Sally III, 457
Townsend, Sam'l W. III, 223
Townsend, Samuel II, 107
Townsend, Samuel II, 428
Townsend, Samuel II, 670
Townsend, Samuel II, 821
Townsend, Samuel II, 823
Townsend, Samuel II, 835
Townsend, Samuel II, 923
Townsend, Samuel II, 931
Townsend, Samuel III, 206
Townsend, Samuel III, 320
Townsend, Samuel III, 321
Townsend, Samuel III, 455
Townsend, Samuel III, 457
Townsend, Samuel IV, 294
Townsend, Samuel IV, 661
Townsend, Samuel IV, 778
Townsend, Samuel IV, 849
Townsend, Samuel IV, 1009
Townsend, Samuel IV, 1026
Townsend, Samuel IV, 1189
Townsend, Samuel A. III, 321
Townsend, Samuel Sharpless II, 823
Townsend, Samuel Sharpless II, 931
Townsend, Samuel W. II, 889
Townsend, Samuel W. II, 898
Townsend, Samuel W. II, 931
Townsend, Samuel Willson II, 930
Townsend, Samuel Wilson II, 823
Townsend, Sarah I, 39
Townsend, Sarah I, 46
Townsend, Sarah I, 76
Townsend, Sarah I, 78
Townsend, Sarah I, 162
Townsend, Sarah I, 169
Townsend, Sarah I, 1060
Townsend, Sarah I, 1063
Townsend, Sarah II, 36
Townsend, Sarah II, 44
Townsend, Sarah II, 89
Townsend, Sarah II, 107
Townsend, Sarah II, 135
Townsend, Sarah II, 428
Townsend, Sarah II, 669
Townsend, Sarah II, 821
Townsend, Sarah II, 823
Townsend, Sarah III, 393
Townsend, Sarah III, 397
Townsend, Sarah III, 416
Townsend, Sarah III, 422
Townsend, Sarah III, 432
Townsend, Sarah III, 455
Townsend, Sarah III, 456
Townsend, Sarah III, 457
Townsend, Sarah III, 458
Townsend, Sarah III, 461
Townsend, Sarah III, 487
Townsend, Sarah III, 500
Townsend, Sarah III, 501
Townsend, Sarah IV, 47
Townsend, Sarah IV, 54
Townsend, Sarah IV, 62
Townsend, Sarah IV, 63
Townsend, Sarah IV, 67
Townsend, Sarah IV, 85
Townsend, Sarah IV, 91
Townsend, Sarah IV, 111
Townsend, Sarah IV, 112
Townsend, Sarah IV, 175
Townsend, Sarah IV, 294
Townsend, Sarah IV, 295
Townsend, Sarah IV, 597
Townsend, Sarah IV, 613
Townsend, Sarah IV, 645
Townsend, Sarah IV, 658
Townsend, Sarah IV, 660
Townsend, Sarah IV, 661
Townsend, Sarah IV, 778
Townsend, Sarah IV, 895
Townsend, Sarah IV, 1009
Townsend, Sarah V, 133
Townsend, Sarah V, 868
Townsend, Sarah V, 872
Townsend, Sarah VI, 462
Townsend, Sarah VI, 574
Townsend, Sarah A. V, 134
Townsend, Sarah A. V, 435
Townsend, Sarah A. V, 566
Townsend, Sarah Ann III, 321
Townsend, Sarah B. IV, 613
Townsend, Sarah B. IV, 661
Townsend, Sarah G. V, 937
Townsend, Sarah H. IV, 295
Townsend, Sarah K. IV, 229
Townsend, Sarah K. IV, 294
Townsend, Sarah Shotwell II, 798
Townsend, Sarah T. IV, 1079
Townsend, Sarah, Jr. IV, 63
Townsend, Selah IV, 63
Townsend, Seneca IV, 294
Townsend, Seth IV, 1008
Townsend, Seth IV, 1009
Townsend, Silvanus II, 669
Townsend, Silvanus III, 326
Townsend, Sina IV, 63
Townsend, Sina IV, 661
Townsend, Sina IV, 767
Townsend, Sina IV, 770
Townsend, Sina IV, 778
Townsend, Sina IV, 779
Townsend, Sina IV, 1009
Townsend, Sina V, 936
Townsend, Sina V, 937
Townsend, Sina VI, 462
Townsend, Sina Ellen IV, 661
Townsend, Sinah IV, 63
Townsend, Sinah IV, 609
Townsend, Sinah IV, 660
Townsend, Sinah IV, 661
Townsend, Sinah IV, 779
Townsend, Sinah VI, 453
Townsend, Sinah VI, 462
Townsend, Smith IV, 778
Townsend, Smith IV, 779
Townsend, Smith IV, 1009
Townsend, Smith Wm. IV, 1009
Townsend, Solomon III, 321
Townsend, Solomon III, 394
Townsend, Solomon III, 457
Townsend, Sophia III, 457
Townsend, Stephen II, 823
Townsend, Stephen II, 931
Townsend, Stephen II, 932
Townsend, Stephen III, 321
Townsend, Stephen IV, 232
Townsend, Stephen IV, 294
Townsend, Stephen IV, 295
Townsend, Stephen IV, 578
Townsend, Stephen IV, 597
Townsend, Stephen IV, 1079
Townsend, Susan III, 214
Townsend, Susan IV, 1189
Townsend, Susanna II, 428
Townsend, Susanna II, 595
Townsend, Susanna II, 605
Townsend, Susanna II, 669
Townsend, Susanna III, 258
Townsend, Susanna III, 321
Townsend, Susanna Coale IV, 661
Townsend, Susannah III, 321
Townsend, Susannah III, 326
Townsend, Susannah III, 457
Townsend, Susannah III, 458
Townsend, Susannah III, 459
Townsend, Susannah IV, 1189
Townsend, Susannah Coal IV, 661
Townsend, Sylvanus III, 457
Townsend, Sylvanus III, 458
Townsend, Sylvanus III, 459
Townsend, Talbert IV, 63
Townsend, Talbert IV, 661
Townsend, Talbert IV, 664
Townsend, Talbot IV, 613
Townsend, Talbot IV, 660
Townsend, Talbot IV, 661
Townsend, Talbot IV, 778
Townsend, Talbot IV, 783
Townsend, Talbot B. IV, 661
Townsend, Tappen III, 321
Townsend, Tazetta IV, 661
Townsend, Tazetta IV, 664
Townsend, Tazette IV, 779
Townsend, Tazette IV, 783
Townsend, Temperance III, 74
Townsend, Temperance III, 321
Townsend, Thomas II, 428
Townsend, Thomas III, 321
Townsend, Thomas III, 397
Townsend, Thomas III, 430
Townsend, Thomas III, 432
Townsend, Thomas III, 441
Townsend, Thomas III, 455
Townsend, Thomas III, 456
Townsend, Thomas III, 458
Townsend, Thomas III, 460
Townsend, Thomas III, 475
Townsend, Thomas IV, 51
Townsend, Thomas IV, 54
Townsend, Thomas IV, 62
Townsend, Thomas IV, 67
Townsend, Thomas IV, 112
Townsend, Thomas IV, 161
Townsend, Thomas IV, 294
Townsend, Thomas IV, 352
Townsend, Thomas IV, 354
Townsend, Thomas IV, 1144
Townsend, Thomas IV, 1163
Townsend, Thomas IV, 1171
Townsend, Thomas IV, 1189
Townsend, Thomas IV, 1190
Townsend, Thomas IV, 1225
Townsend, Thomas V, 133
Townsend, Thomas V, 434
Townsend, Thomas VI, 462
Townsend, Thomas VI, 574
Townsend, Thomas French IV, 112
Townsend, Thomas French IV, 779
Townsend, Thomas J. III, 457
Townsend, Thomas M. IV, 661
Townsend, Thomas M. IV, 895
Townsend, Thomas Parker II, 669
Townsend, Thomas Townsend IV, 230
Townsend, Thomas W. III, 457
Townsend, Thos. III, 456
Townsend, Thos. IV, 229
Townsend, Thos. IV, 340
Townsend, Thos. V, 937
Townsend, Timothy III, 422
Townsend, Timothy III, 457
Townsend, Timothy III, 487
Townsend, Timothy III, 501
Townsend, Timothy W. IV, 1189
Townsend, Timothy Westley IV, 1189
Townsend, Tolbert IV, 660
Townsend, Virgil V, 435
Townsend, Walter B. III, 321
Townsend, Warren B. V, 435
Townsend, Warren B. V, 928
Townsend, Warren B. V, 937
Townsend, Warren Ringgold V, 937
Townsend, Watson IV, 1296
Townsend, Wd. Ann II, 428
Townsend, Wd. Annabella L. II, 823
Townsend, Wd. Elizabeth III, 437
Townsend, Wd. Hannah Smith II, 823
Townsend, Wd. Mary II, 428
Townsend, Wd. Mary II, 823
Townsend, Wd. Phebe III, 500
Townsend, Widow Elisabeth I, 63
Townsend, Widow Elisabeth I, 76
Townsend, Widow Rachel I, 76
Townsend, Widow Rachel I, 85
Townsend, Willard V, 378
Townsend, William I, 76
Townsend, William I, 78
Townsend, William I, 87
Townsend, William I, 233
Townsend, William I, 258
Townsend, William I, 1038
Townsend, William I Sup 1, 11
Townsend, William II, 428
Townsend, William II, 823
Townsend, William III, 104
Townsend, William III, 321
Townsend, William IV, 63
Townsend, William IV, 597
Townsend, William IV, 661
Townsend, William IV, 779
Townsend, William IV, 1009
Townsend, William IV, 1189
Townsend, William V, 133
Townsend, William V, 770
Townsend, William D. IV, 1008
Townsend, William E. III, 457
Townsend, William E. IV, 1189
Townsend, William H. III, 321
Townsend, William H. V, 872
Townsend, William W. IV, 449
Townsend, Wilson H. II, 931
Townsend, Wm. II, 930
Townsend, Wm. II, 931
Townsend, Wm. III, 400
Townsend, Wm. III, 457
Townsend, Wm. IV, 778
Townsend, Wm. IV, 1009
Townsend, Wm. IV, 1189
Townsend, Wm. IV, 1192
Townsend, Wm. V, 435
Townsend, Wm. V, 868
Townsend, Wm. Columbus IV, 111
Townsend, Wm. D. IV, 1009
Townsend, Wm. E. IV, 1189
Townsend, Wm. Ivan IV, 1044
Townsend, Wm. M. IV, 1296
Townsend, Wm. S. II, 930
Townsend, Wm. Smith II, 823
Townsend, Wm. W. IV, 1296
Townsend, Zelinda E. D. IV, 230
Townsend, Zerviah III, 457
Townsent, Esther I Sup 1, 11
Towsend, Adaline IV, 500
Towsend, Mary II, 547
Towsent, Elizabeth I, 1038
Towsent, Esther I, 1035
Towsent, Esther I, 1038
Towsent, John I, 1038
Toy, Patience II, 428
Toy, Sarah V, 286
Trace, Clara III, 32
Trace, Clara III, 321
Tracey, Clark II, 107
Tracey, Jeremiah II, 44
Tracey, Jeremiah II, 107
Tracey, Kitty Miller VI, 1006
Tracey, Margaret II, 44
Tracey, Soloman VI, 1006
Tracy, Akeley III, 457
Tracy, Capt. Jirah III, 457
Tracy, Cena VI, 988
Tracy, Charles V, 208
Tracy, Clark II, 107
Tracy, Daniel III, 457
Tracy, Dora V, 1022
Tracy, Frederick V, 1022
Tracy, Ida V, 1022
Tracy, Jeremiah II, 90
Tracy, Jeremiah II, 107
Tracy, John VI, 884
Tracy, John VI, 985
Tracy, John VI, 988
Tracy, John VI, 1006
Tracy, Keziah VI, 920
Tracy, Kitty Miller VI, 1006
Tracy, Laura V, 208
Tracy, Margaret II, 90
Tracy, Margaret II, 107
Tracy, Martha G. VI, 884
Tracy, Mary II, 107
Tracy, Nancy VI, 985
Tracy, Nancy VI, 1006
Tracy, Peggy VI, 1006
Tracy, Rebecca IV, 479
Tracy, Rebecca IV, 500
Tracy, Sally VI, 928
Tracy, Sarah III, 500
Tracy, Sarah VI, 1006
Tracy, Sol. VI, 971
Tracy, Soloman VI, 1006
Tracy, Solomon VI, 967
Tracy, William VI, 920
Tracy, William VI, 928
Tracy, William VI, 1006
Tracy, Xemena IV, 884
Tracy, Xermena IV, 884
Trader, Ada N. V, 1022
Trader, Oscar H. V, 1022
Trader, Reta Ruth V, 1022
Trader, Rev. Oscar V, 1022
Trafford, Elizabeth II, 670
Trafford, Elizabeth II, 688
Trafford, Rachel II, 670
Trago, ??? IV, 779
Trago, Elizabeth II, 613
Trago, Elizabeth II, 670
Trago, Hannah A. IV, 751
Trago, Hannah A. IV, 779
Trago, Hannah A. IV, 1031
Trago, John IV, 741
Trago, John IV, 751
Trago, John IV, 779
Trago, John IV, 1021
Trago, John IV, 1031
Trago, John, Jr. IV, 716
Trago, John, Jr. IV, 779
Trago, Mary IV, 779
Trago, Mary IV, 1009
Trago, Sarah IV, 741
Trago, Sarah IV, 1031
Trago, Sarah Ann IV, 716
Trago, Sarah Ann IV, 741
Trago, Sarah Ann IV, 751
Trago, Sarah Ann IV, 779
Trago, Sarah Ann IV, 1031
Trago, Sarah E. IV, 741
Trago, Sarah E. IV, 1031
Trago, Sarah Emily IV, 779
Trags, Elizabeth II, 670
Trahern, Amy IV, 337
Trahern, Amy IV, 354
Trahern, Amy VI, 714
Trahern, Asa IV, 161
Trahern, Asa IV, 295
Trahern, Asa V, 134
Trahern, Asa VI, 714
Trahern, Asa VI, 715
Trahern, Asa VI, 716
Trahern, Dinah IV, 337
Trahern, Dinah VI, 642
Trahern, Dinah VI, 674
Trahern, Dinah VI, 714
Trahern, Dinah VI, 715
Trahern, Dinah VI, 716
Trahern, Elizabeth IV, 161
Trahern, Elizabeth IV, 295
Trahern, Elizabeth V, 134
Trahern, Elizabeth VI, 715
Trahern, Elizabeth VI, 716
Trahern, Enos VI, 715
Trahern, Isaac VI, 715
Trahern, Israel IV, 354
Trahern, Israel VI, 715
Trahern, James IV, 337
Trahern, James VI, 574
Trahern, James VI, 642
Trahern, James VI, 674
Trahern, James VI, 714
Trahern, James VI, 715
Trahern, James VI, 716
Trahern, Jesse VI, 715
Trahern, Lena V, 34
Trahern, Lena V, 134
Trahern, Linah V, 134
Trahern, Mary VI, 693
Trahern, Mary VI, 715

ern, Rebecca VI, 715
ern, Rebekah VI, 574
ern, Rebekah VI, 642
ern, Ruth VI, 715
ern, Samuel IV, 1189
ern, Samuel VI, 715
ern, Sarah VI, 574
ern, Sarah VI, 715
ern, Sina IV, 161
ern, Sina VI, 715
ern, Sinah IV, 295
ern, Thomas VI, 674
ern, Thomas VI, 715
hern, William VI, 574
hern, William VI, 642
hern, William VI, 715
hern, Wm. VI, 715
horn, Israel IV, 354
il, Frances VI, 860
il, Jarrett VI, 860
il, Perlina VI, 860
inor, Augusta B. V, 715
inor, Augusta Barrett V, 664
nor, Augusta Barrett V, 715
nor, Dr. W. J. V, 664
nor, Dr. W. J. V, 715
mer, Elizabeth IV, 98
mer, Elizabeth IV, 112
mmell, Thomas VI, 574
mmell, Widow Mary C.
VI, 574
nam, Presilla VI, 840
nan, Anderson VI, 860
nan, Elizabeth VI, 860
ner, Mrs. John R. IV, 1341
p, Eliza IV, 1382
pnell, John II, 428
sel, Hannah II, 670
sel, Jacob II, 670
sel, Joseph II, 670
sel, Martha II, 670
sel, Mary II, 670
sell, Hannah II, 428
sell, Jacob II, 428
sell, Joseph II, 428
sell, Martha II, 428
sell, Mary II, 428
sey, Mary II, 107
sk, John IV, 779
sk, Ruth IV, 779
venner, Sarah VI, 673
ver, Miranda M. IV, 1341
ver, Mrs. John IV, 1341
ver, Walter J. IV, 1341
vers, Daniel III, 492
vers, Daniel III, 501
vers, Elizabeth III, 232
vers, Elizabeth III, 492
vers, Elizabeth III, 501
vers, Hannah III, 492
vers, Hannah III, 501
viller, Mary II, 612
viller, Mary II, 670
vis, Abbie A. III, 167
vis, Abbie A. III, 321
vis, Abbie A. III, 322
vis, Alfred M. III, 457
vis, Amy J. III, 322
vis, Anna III, 83
vis, Anna III, 322
vis, Anna Edith III, 322
vis, Caroline M. III, 322
vis, Charles IV, 1241
vis, Daisy IV, 1241
vis, Danell I, 120
vis, Deborah I, 120
vis, Edmund D. III, 457
vis, Elizabeth III, 166
vis, Elizabeth III, 322
vis, Elizabeth III, 404
vis, Elizabeth III, 457
vis, Emma III, 322
vis, Gideon Baxter III, 167
vis, Gideon Baxter III, 321
vis, Hannah III, 244
vis, Hannah III, 322
vis, Hannah M. III, 83
vis, Harriett IV, 1237
vis, Harriett IV, 1241
vis, Ira W. III, 321
vis, Jane I, 391
vis, Jane I, 424
vis, Jesse Heaton III, 322
vis, John I, 120
vis, John Alexander III, 325
vis, John Wm. III, 166
vis, John Wm. III, 322
vis, Josiah III, 322
vis, Josiah III, 325
vis, Margory I, 120
vis, Martha III, 322
Travis, Martha E. III, 244
Travis, Martha E. III, 322
Travis, Martha Elizabeth III, 322
Travis, Martha P. III, 84
Travis, Martha P. III, 322
Travis, Martin Wm. III, 83
Travis, Mary A. III, 457
Travis, Mary Eugenia III, 322
Travis, Mary Eugenia III, 325
Travis, Matilda III, 322
Travis, Mortimer J. III, 84
Travis, Mortimer J. III, 322
Travis, Mortimer Josiah III, 322
Travis, Mortimer W. III, 244
Travis, Mortimer W. III, 322
Travis, Mortimer Wm. III, 322
Travis, Nehemiah III, 322
Travis, Phebe III, 322
Travis, Phebe III, 404
Travis, Phebe III, 457
Travis, Phebe G. III, 322
Travis, Ralph M. III, 322
Travis, Ruth Clara III, 322
Travis, Samuel III, 404
Travis, Samuel III, 457
Travis, Sarah IV, 1241
Travis, Sarah Ann III, 176
Travis, Sarah I. III, 321
Travis, Sarah Maria III, 457
Travis, Sary I, 91
Travis, Sary I, 120
Travis, William I, 91
Travis, William I, 120
Travis, William I Sup 1, 4
Travis, William I Sup 1, 5
Trayen, Lydia Ann IV, 1189
Trayer, Elizabeth IV, 84
Trayer, Elizabeth IV, 112
Trayer, Elizabeth IV, 161
Trayer, Lucretia IV, 1341
Trayer, Lydia Ann IV, 1189
Trayer, Parthenia IV, 1189
Trayhern, Dinah VI, 715
Trayhern, Isaac VI, 715
Trayhern, Israel VI, 574
Trayhern, James VI, 574
Trayhern, James VI, 715
Trayhern, James VI, 725
Trayhern, Rebecca VI, 715
Trayhern, Rebekah VI, 574
Trayhern, Sarah VI, 574
Trayhern, William VI, 574
Trayhern, William VI, 715
Trayhorn, Asa V, 134
Trayhorn, Rebecca VI, 715
Trayhorn, William VI, 452
Trayhorn, Wm. VI, 715
Traylor, Boswell VI, 860
Traylor, Boswell VI, 862
Traylor, Elizabeth VI, 860
Traylor, John VI, 860
Traylor, Lucy VI, 860
Traylor, Martha VI, 862
Traylor, Peggy VI, 860
Traylor, Robert VI, 860
Treadgold, Alexander IV, 1341
Treadgold, Alexander S. IV, 1341
Treadway, Anna B. III, 73
Treadwell, ??? III, 322
Treadwell, Adrian U. III, 280
Treadwell, Adrian U. III, 322
Treadwell, Anna III, 322
Treadwell, Augusta III, 322
Treadwell, Dorothy III, 322
Treadwell, Edith III, 280
Treadwell, Edith III, 322
Treadwell, Ellsworth III, 322
Treadwell, Joseph III, 322
Treadwell, Leman B. III, 322
Treadwell, Letitia III, 322
Treadwell, Mary III, 322
Treadwell, Mary III, 386
Treadwell, Samuel III, 322
Trebbe, Elizabeth VI, 540
Trebe, Rebekah VI, 486
Trebe, Rebekah VI, 574
Tredwell, ??? III, 61
Tredwell, Charity III, 445
Tredwell, Charity III, 457
Tredwell, Charity III, 501
Tredwell, Daniel T. III, 457
Tredwell, Dorothy III, 61
Tredwell, Dorothy III, 322
Tredwell, James III, 501
Tredwell, John III, 445
Tredwell, John III, 457
Tredwell, Letitia III, 322
Tredwell, Margaret III, 458
Tredwell, Margaret A. III, 457
Tredwell, Rachel III, 458
Treeman, Maria I, 882
Treeman, Maria I, 903
Treftz, Etta V, 363
Trefz, Alice V, 715
Trefz, Alice V, 720
Trefz, Oren V, 715
Trego, Charles II, 1033
Trego, Elizabeth II, 1033
Trego, John Laycock II, 1033
Trego, Lewis II, 1033
Trego, Mahlon II, 1033
Trego, Mahlon II, 1069
Trego, Mahlon II, 1081
Trego, Martha II, 862
Trego, Martha II, 917
Trego, Mary II, 1033
Trego, Mary IV, 1009
Trego, Phineas II, 1033
Trego, Phinehas II, 1033
Trego, Rachel II, 1033
Trego, Rachel II, 1069
Trego, Rachel II, 1081
Trego, Rachel Anna II, 931
Trego, Rebecca B. II, 1081
Trego, Robert S. II, 1069
Trego, Robert S. II, 1081
Trego, Sarah Ann IV, 1021
Trego, Sarah T. II, 1069
Trego, Sarah T. II, 1081
Trego, William II, 1033
Trehorn, Asa VI, 452
Trehorn, William VI, 452
Tremble, Ann II, 1033
Tremble, Charity IV, 112
Tremble, Daniel II, 1033
Tremble, George Thomas II, 1033
Tremble, John IV, 112
Tremble, John VI, 452
Tremble, John Roberts II, 1033
Tremble, Joseph II, 670
Tremble, Rachel IV, 112
Tremble, Richard II, 1033
Tremble, Samuel II, 670
Tremble, Tamzin II, 1033
Tremble, William IV, 112
Tremble, William Roberts
II, 1033
Tremble, Wm. II, 670
Trenary, Cazy V, 708
Trenary, Cazy V, 715
Trenary, Frank V, 435
Trenary, John L. V, 435
Trenary, Louise V, 435
Trenary, Martha V, 435
Trenary, Nancy V, 435
Trenary, Susan V, 435
Trenile, Thomas II, 428
Trenor, Elizabeth VI, 860
Trenor, James VI, 860
Trent, A. VI, 860
Trent, Abner W. VI, 860
Trent, Alexander VI, 860
Trent, Ann VI, 860
Trent, Ann Elizabeth VI, 1006
Trent, Archibald VI, 1006
Trent, Benjamin VI, 795
Trent, Benjamin VI, 860
Trent, Benjamin B. VI, 860
Trent, Benjamin W. VI, 860
Trent, Benjamin, Jr. VI, 860
Trent, Betsy VI, 874
Trent, Candall VI, 860
Trent, Caroline VI, 795
Trent, Catherine VI, 860
Trent, David A. VI, 860
Trent, Edward W. VI, 860
Trent, Elijah VI, 799
Trent, Elijah VI, 810
Trent, Elijah VI, 822
Trent, Elijah VI, 843
Trent, Elijah VI, 848
Trent, Eliza A. VI, 860
Trent, Elizabeth VI, 799
Trent, Elizabeth VI, 800
Trent, Elizabeth VI, 822
Trent, Elizabeth VI, 860
Trent, Elizabeth A. VI, 860
Trent, Elizabeth Ann VI, 897
Trent, Elizabeth H. VI, 860
Trent, Elizabeth W. VI, 958
Trent, Fanny VI, 829
Trent, Fanny B. VI, 829
Trent, Florence V. V, 286
Trent, Frances VI, 860
Trent, Harvey VI, 822
Trent, Henrietta VI, 860
Trent, Henry VI, 809
Trent, Henry VI, 860
Trent, Henry VI, 888
Trent, Henry VI, 935
Trent, Hessie VI, 813
Trent, Hezekiah VI, 860
Trent, James VI, 860
Trent, Jane VI, 860
Trent, Jesse VI, 1006
Trent, John VI, 795
Trent, John VI, 821
Trent, John VI, 860
Trent, John VI, 958
Trent, John VI, 1005
Trent, Keturah VI, 860
Trent, Lucy VI, 864
Trent, Lurany VI, 843
Trent, Marshall VI, 860
Trent, Martha VI, 860
Trent, Mary VI, 860
Trent, Mary A. VI, 860
Trent, Mary J. VI, 860
Trent, Mildred VI, 860
Trent, Monroe VI, 860
Trent, Nancy VI, 799
Trent, Nancy VI, 860
Trent, Nancy VI, 1005
Trent, Nicholas VI, 1006
Trent, Ob. H. VI, 874
Trent, Obediah VI, 860
Trent, Obediah H. VI, 874
Trent, Olympus VI, 1006
Trent, Pamelia VI, 1006
Trent, Patty VI, 888
Trent, Peggy VI, 860
Trent, Permelia VI, 1006
Trent, Pheba VI, 860
Trent, Polly VI, 815
Trent, Polly VI, 843
Trent, Polly VI, 860
Trent, Polly VI, 1006
Trent, Priscilla VI, 809
Trent, Rachel VI, 1006
Trent, Rebeckah VI, 860
Trent, Reuben VI, 1006
Trent, Robert C. VI, 848
Trent, Robert C. VI, 860
Trent, Sally VI, 810
Trent, Sally VI, 860
Trent, Sally G. VI, 935
Trent, Sarah VI, 824
Trent, Sarah VI, 860
Trent, Sarah A. VI, 848
Trent, Susan VI, 826
Trent, Susan VI, 897
Trent, Thomas VI, 855
Trent, Thomas VI, 860
Trent, William VI, 824
Trent, William VI, 860
Trent, William VI, 1006
Trent, William B. VI, 799
Trent, William B. VI, 860
Trent, William H. VI, 860
Trent, Wyatt VI, 860
Trent, Z. VI, 800
Trent, Zachariah VI, 800
Trenten, Elma V, 961
Trescot, Phebe IV, 946
Trescott, Ann IV, 780
Trescott, Benjamin IV, 780
Trescott, Clark IV, 779
Trescott, Clark IV, 780
Trescott, David IV, 779
Trescott, David S. IV, 780
Trescott, Deborah B. IV, 755
Trescott, Deborah B. IV, 780
Trescott, Ella IV, 692
Trescott, Ella IV, 780
Trescott, Isaac IV, 779
Trescott, Isaac IV, 780
Trescott, Isaac IV, 1380
Trescott, Isaac IV, 1382
Trescott, Isaac L. IV, 779
Trescott, Jane IV, 779
Trescott, Jane IV, 780
Trescott, Jane L. IV, 756
Trescott, Jane L. IV, 780
Trescott, Jane M. IV, 780
Trescott, Jane M. IV, 1380
Trescott, Jane M. IV, 1382
Trescott, Lola G. IV, 780
Trescott, Mary IV, 717
Trescott, Mary IV, 779
Trescott, Mary IV, 780
Trescott, Phebe IV, 780
Trescott, Phebe Jane IV, 696
Trescott, Phebe Jane IV, 780
Trescott, Ruth Anna IV, 717
Trescott, Ruth Anna IV, 780
Trescott, Samuel IV, 780
Trescott, Samuel C. IV, 779
Trescott, Samuel C. IV, 780
Trescott, Samuel C. IV, 1382
Trescott, Sibyl IV, 730
Trescott, Sibyl IV, 780
Trescott, Sophia IV, 779
Trescott, Sophia IV, 780
Trescott, Sophia IV, 1382
Trescott, Syble IV, 780
Tresham, Jane V, 286
Tresham, Mary Jane V, 286
Tresham, Mary Jane V, 293
Tresham, Robert VI, 1006
Tresham, Sarah Ann VI, 1006
Tresto, Ida IV, 1265
Trevalla, Jane II, 425
Treviler, Mary II, 670
Treviller, Joseph II, 428
Treviller, Thomas II, 428
Trewblood, Mary I, 319
Tribba, Ruth V, 134
Tribbee, Asahel VI, 574
Tribbee, Elizabeth VI, 540
Tribbee, Elizabeth VI, 574
Tribbee, George VI, 574
Tribbee, Joseph VI, 574
Tribbee, Margaret VI, 574
Tribbee, Margaret VI, 581
Tribbee, Mary VI, 574
Tribbee, Rebekah VI, 574
Tribbee, Ruth VI, 574
Tribbee, Sarah VI, 574
Tribbee, William VI, 574
Tribbee, Wm. VI, 581
Tribble, Isabella VI, 855
Tribble, John VI, 855
Tribby, Abigail IV, 225
Tribby, Ann IV, 250
Tribby, Ann IV, 295
Tribby, Ann IV, 302
Tribby, Ann IV, 1117
Tribby, Asa IV, 225
Tribby, Charles IV, 225
Tribby, Charles IV, 295
Tribby, Charles H. IV, 295
Tribby, Chas. H. IV, 295
Tribby, Elisha B. IV, 225
Tribby, Elizabeth V, 134
Tribby, Ella IV, 295
Tribby, Ella J. IV, 295
Tribby, Ella T. IV, 295
Tribby, George V, 134
Tribby, Hannah IV, 224
Tribby, Hannah IV, 225
Tribby, Hannah Mary IV, 295
Tribby, Hannah May IV, 295
Tribby, Hannah R. IV, 224
Tribby, Horton J. IV, 224
Tribby, Horton, Jr. IV, 224
Tribby, Isaac IV, 225
Tribby, Isaac B. IV, 295
Tribby, James IV, 225
Tribby, James IV, 269
Tribby, James IV, 295
Tribby, James IV, 1113
Tribby, James IV, 1117
Tribby, Jane IV, 224
Tribby, Jane IV, 225
Tribby, Jane IV, 295
Tribby, Jane IV, 917
Tribby, Jane H. IV, 295
Tribby, John IV, 225
Tribby, John IV, 250
Tribby, John IV, 295
Tribby, John IV, 302
Tribby, John IV, 1117
Tribby, John W. IV, 224
Tribby, John W. IV, 295
Tribby, John W. IV, 917
Tribby, Joseph IV, 225
Tribby, Joseph V, 387
Tribby, Juliet IV, 295
Tribby, Juliett IV, 295
Tribby, Lewis L. IV, 295
Tribby, Lindley IV, 295
Tribby, Lindley IV, 917
Tribby, Lois S. IV, 295
Tribby, Louisa V, 134
Tribby, Louisa V, 387
Tribby, Malissa IV, 295
Tribby, Martha IV, 295
Tribby, Martha Ann IV, 295
Tribby, Mary M. IV, 224
Tribby, Melissa B. IV, 295
Tribby, Pharaby IV, 225
Tribby, Rachel IV, 225
Tribby, Rebecca IV, 269
Tribby, Rebecca IV, 295
Tribby, Rebecca IV, 1112
Tribby, Rebecca IV, 1113
Tribby, Rebecca IV, 1117
Tribby, Ruth IV, 224
Tribby, Ruth V, 134
Tribby, Ruth V, 387
Tribby, Samuel IV, 295
Tribby, Sandy IV, 295
Tribby, Sarah V, 134
Tribby, Sarah J. IV, 295

Tribby, Sarah Jane IV, 250
Tribby, Sarah Jane IV, 295
Tribe, John VI, 574
Tribee, Asahel VI, 574
Tribee, Elizabeth VI, 574
Tribee, George VI, 574
Tribee, John VI, 574
Tribee, John, Jr. VI, 574
Tribee, Jonathan VI, 574
Tribee, Louisa VI, 574
Tribee, Lydia VI, 574
Tribee, Sarah VI, 537
Tribee, Sarah VI, 574
Trible, Aurelia C. VI, 1006
Trible, Austin M. VI, 1006
Trick, Arthur IV, 1341
Trick, Arthur S. IV, 1341
Trick, Elvina IV, 1341
Trick, Elvira IV, 1341
Trick, Lois IV, 1341
Trickey, Lewis V, 1022
Tricky, Hazel V, 715
Trigg, Alason VI, 1006
Trigg, Ann VI, 1006
Trigg, Daniel VI, 1006
Trigg, Dianna VI, 1006
Trigg, Doshia VI, 949
Trigg, Elizabeth VI, 903
Trigg, Elizabeth VI, 1006
Trigg, Haiden VI, 1006
Trigg, John IV, 524
Trigg, John IV, 554
Trigg, John VI, 925
Trigg, John VI, 949
Trigg, John VI, 966
Trigg, John VI, 1006
Trigg, John VI, 1013
Trigg, Locky VI, 931
Trigg, Lucy VI, 1006
Trigg, Martha VI, 1006
Trigg, Mary IV, 554
Trigg, Mary VI, 931
Trigg, Mary VI, 966
Trigg, Nancy IV, 524
Trigg, Nancy IV, 554
Trigg, Nancy VI, 966
Trigg, Polley VI, 981
Trigg, Sarah VI, 860
Trigg, Stephen VI, 949
Trigg, Stephen VI, 1006
Trigg, William VI, 860
Trigg, William VI, 903
Trigg, William VI, 981
Trigg, William VI, 1006
Trigg, William, Jr. VI, 981
Trimble, ??? III, 322
Trimble, ??? III, 330
Trimble, ??? IV, 449
Trimble, Ann II, 971
Trimble, Ann II, 993
Trimble, Ann II, 1033
Trimble, Ann II, 1034
Trimble, Ann II, 1062
Trimble, Ann II, 1081
Trimble, Ann III, 322
Trimble, Ann VI, 452
Trimble, Ann VI, 606
Trimble, Anna F. II, 704
Trimble, Anna F. II, 738
Trimble, Anna F. II, 771
Trimble, Audrey IV, 1265
Trimble, Caleb Harlan IV, 449
Trimble, Caleb Harlan IV, 1079
Trimble, Catharine VI, 452
Trimble, Catherine IV, 112
Trimble, Catherine V, 286
Trimble, Catherine VI, 452
Trimble, Charity IV, 112
Trimble, Charity V, 261
Trimble, Charity V, 286
Trimble, Charity VI, 452
Trimble, Dan'l III, 155
Trimble, Daniel II, 993
Trimble, Daniel II, 1033
Trimble, Daniel II, 1034
Trimble, Daniel III, 156
Trimble, Daniel III, 158
Trimble, Daniel III, 322
Trimble, David II, 931
Trimble, David VI, 452
Trimble, David B. II, 931
Trimble, Edward IV, 1080
Trimble, Edwards IV, 1079
Trimble, Elisha IV, 449
Trimble, Elisha IV, 1079
Trimble, Elisha VI, 452
Trimble, Elisha I. IV, 449
Trimble, Eliza V, 134
Trimble, Eliza G. V, 937
Trimble, Eliza V. V, 937
Trimble, Elizabeth II, 824
Trimble, Elizabeth VI, 408
Trimble, Elizabeth VI, 452
Trimble, Esther Jane II, 931
Trimble, George II, 1033
Trimble, George III, 322
Trimble, George F. III, 322
Trimble, George T. III, 322
Trimble, George Thomas II, 971
Trimble, George Thomas II, 1033
Trimble, Harlen IV, 1080
Trimble, Isaac IV, 112
Trimble, Isaac IV, 1079
Trimble, Isaac V, 134
Trimble, Isaac P. II, 771
Trimble, James II, 931
Trimble, James IV, 449
Trimble, James IV, 1079
Trimble, James V, 134
Trimble, James VI, 452
Trimble, James W. V, 286
Trimble, James W. VI, 395
Trimble, James W. VI, 452
Trimble, Jane II, 931
Trimble, Jno. VI, 452
Trimble, John II, 824
Trimble, John II, 931
Trimble, John II, 1033
Trimble, John IV, 112
Trimble, John IV, 449
Trimble, John IV, 1079
Trimble, John V, 134
Trimble, John V, 286
Trimble, John VI, 437
Trimble, John VI, 452
Trimble, John Roberts II, 1033
Trimble, Joseph II, 670
Trimble, Joseph II, 806
Trimble, Joseph II, 824
Trimble, Joseph II, 855
Trimble, Joseph II, 931
Trimble, Joseph V, 134
Trimble, Joseph VI, 452
Trimble, Joseph G. V, 134
Trimble, Joseph Gilpin V, 134
Trimble, Joseph Gilpin V, 937
Trimble, Joseph H. VI, 452
Trimble, Joseph M. V, 937
Trimble, Joseph, Jr. II, 931
Trimble, Laura M. V, 134
Trimble, Laura M. V, 937
Trimble, Lydia IV, 449
Trimble, Lydia IV, 1079
Trimble, Mary II, 670
Trimble, Mary II, 1033
Trimble, Mary IV, 449
Trimble, Mary IV, 1079
Trimble, Mary IV, 1080
Trimble, Mary Ann VI, 395
Trimble, Mary Ann VI, 452
Trimble, Mary B. III, 155
Trimble, Mary B. III, 156
Trimble, Mary B. III, 158
Trimble, Mary B. III, 322
Trimble, Mary S. III, 330
Trimble, Minnie II, 795
Trimble, Phebe VI, 304
Trimble, Rachel II, 1033
Trimble, Rachel IV, 112
Trimble, Rachel V, 122
Trimble, Rachel V, 134
Trimble, Rachel V, 286
Trimble, Rachel V, 291
Trimble, Rachel VI, 437
Trimble, Rachel VI, 452
Trimble, Rebecca II, 806
Trimble, Rebecca F. II, 931
Trimble, Richard II, 971
Trimble, Richard II, 1033
Trimble, Richard III, 322
Trimble, Samuel II, 670
Trimble, Samuel VI, 452
Trimble, Sarah V, 134
Trimble, Sarah VI, 452
Trimble, Sarah Ann II, 824
Trimble, Sarah Ann II, 855
Trimble, Sarah Ann II, 931
Trimble, Sarah M. V, 937
Trimble, Tamson II, 1033
Trimble, Tamzin II, 1006
Trimble, Tamzin II, 1033
Trimble, Thamazin II, 1033
Trimble, Thamzin II, 1033
Trimble, Thomas VI, 452
Trimble, Wd. Esther Jane II, 806
Trimble, Wd. Rebecca II, 824
Trimble, William IV, 112
Trimble, William V, 134
Trimble, William V, 937
Trimble, William VI, 452
Trimble, William D. VI, 452
Trimble, William Roberts II, 1033
Trimble, Wm. II, 670
Trimble, Wm. II, 771
Trimble, Wm. II, 1033
Trimble, Wm. II, 1034
Trimble, Wm., Jr. II, 670
Trimm, Madella H. III, 322
Trimmer, Alice V, 699
Trimmer, Frances V, 937
Trimmer, Francis V, 937
Trimmer, H. V. V, 602
Trimmer, Homer V. V, 715
Trimmer, Jane V, 602
Trimmer, Jane V, 699
Trimmer, Jane V, 715
Trimmer, Mary Alice V, 602
Trimmer, Mary Alice V, 715
Trimmer, Samuel V, 602
Trimmer, Samuel V, 699
Trimmer, Samuel V, 715
Trine, David V, 872
Trine, David B. V, 872
Trip, Fannie IV, 895
Trip, Fanny IV, 774
Trip, Fanny IV, 895
Trip, George F. IV, 895
Trip, Laban IV, 895
Trip, Mary IV, 895
Trip, Mary Ann IV, 903
Trip, Mary Ann IV, 917
Trip, Samuel IV, 895
Trip, Stephen IV, 895
Triplett, Burr VI, 860
Triplett, Eliza A. VI, 860
Tripp, Anthony III, 396
Tripp, Elizabeth III, 322
Tripp, Eunice III, 322
Tripp, Fannie IV, 849
Tripp, Fannie IV, 895
Tripp, Fanny IV, 780
Tripp, Fanny IV, 798
Tripp, Fanny IV, 849
Tripp, Fanny IV, 895
Tripp, Fanny IV, 1030
Tripp, Fanny IV, 1031
Tripp, George F. IV, 849
Tripp, George F. IV, 895
Tripp, George Fox IV, 917
Tripp, James III, 322
Tripp, Laban IV, 849
Tripp, Laban IV, 895
Tripp, Labon IV, 849
Tripp, Labon IV, 917
Tripp, Lot III, 322
Tripp, Mary III, 396
Tripp, Mary IV, 849
Tripp, Mary IV, 895
Tripp, Mary IV, 917
Tripp, Mary Ann IV, 917
Tripp, Mrs. Ora IV, 1341
Tripp, Peleg III, 322
Tripp, Samuel IV, 780
Tripp, Samuel IV, 798
Tripp, Samuel IV, 849
Tripp, Samuel IV, 860
Tripp, Samuel IV, 895
Tripp, Samuel IV, 917
Tripp, Stephen IV, 849
Tripp, Stephen IV, 895
Tripp, Stephen IV, 917
Tripp, Susanna III, 195
Tripp, Susannah III, 322
Tripp, Tabitha III, 322
Tripp, William Penn IV, 780
Tritt, Mary IV, 908
Tritt, Mary IV, 917
Trivette, Clementine I, 614
Troath, Henry II, 670
Troeger, Amelia III, 322
Troeger, Amelia Louise III, 30
Troeger, Amelia Louise III, 323
Troeger, Anna III, 323
Troeger, Catharine III, 323
Troeger, Ernest III, 323
Troeger, Ernest Anton III, 293
Troeger, Ernest Anton III, 322
Troeger, Ernest Anton III, 323
Troeger, Frederick III, 322
Troeger, George III, 323
Troeger, Helen Gertrude III, 293
Troeger, Helen Gertrude III, 322
Troeger, John F. R. III, 30
Troeger, John F. R. III, 322
Troeger, John F. R. III, 323
Troeger, Mary M. III, 323
Troeger, Robert Ernest III, 322
Troeger, Wilhelmina W. III, 322
Trogden, Abijah I, 485
Trogden, Catharine I, 467
Trogden, Francis Virginia I, 627
Trogden, Harvey I, 627
Trogden, Lovicy I, 485
Trogden, Luben M. I, 424
Trogden, Lyndon I, 424
Trogden, Olive V. I, 424
Trogden, Rebecca I, 424
Trogden, Sarah R. I, 424
Trogden, Susanna I, 424
Trogdon, Ezekiel I, 1102
Trogdon, Ezekiel I, 1133
Trogler, Godfrey IV, 902
Trogmorton, Jane V, 27
Tromer, Nancy VI, 861
Tromer, Robert VI, 861
Tromicker, Hilda IV, 1265
Trood, Eliza II, 650
Trood, Eliza II, 670
Troth, Abel II, 314
Troth, Alice II, 295
Troth, Alice II, 304
Troth, Ann II, 295
Troth, Ann II, 304
Troth, Ann II, 721
Troth, Ann II, 824
Troth, Ann VI, 729
Troth, Ann VI, 788
Troth, Ann B. II, 931
Troth, Ann Berry II, 824
Troth, Anna VI, 751
Troth, Anna VI, 786
Troth, Anna VI, 787
Troth, Anna VI, 788
Troth, Anna S. II, 931
Troth, Asenith II, 959
Troth, Bessie Ione V, 300
Troth, Bessie Ione V, 466
Troth, David II, 959
Troth, Deborah II, 716
Troth, Deborah II, 959
Troth, Elizabeth IV, 112
Troth, Elizabeth B. VI, 787
Troth, Elizabeth D. II, 314
Troth, Elizabeth D. II, 325
Troth, Elizabeth D. II, 326
Troth, Elizabeth T. II, 295
Troth, Elizabeth T. II, 304
Troth, Elizabeth T. II, 931
Troth, Florence Bell V, 466
Troth, Florence Belle V, 312
Troth, George Dillwynn II, 824
Troth, Hannah IV, 104
Troth, Hannah IV, 112
Troth, Hannah IV, 117
Troth, Hannah Maria VI, 786
Troth, Hannah Maria VI, 787
Troth, Hannah Maria VI, 790
Troth, Hannah S. IV, 112
Troth, Hannah S. IV, 117
Troth, Henry II, 428
Troth, Henry II, 670
Troth, Henry IV, 104
Troth, Henry IV, 112
Troth, Henry IV, 117
Troth, Henry C. II, 314
Troth, Henry Clothier II, 326
Troth, Henry H. II, 314
Troth, Henry H. II, 326
Troth, Henry Morris II, 428
Troth, Henry W. VI, 786
Troth, Henry, Jr. II, 670
Troth, Jacob VI, 786
Troth, Jacob M. VI, 729
Troth, Jacob M. VI, 751
Troth, Jacob M. VI, 786
Troth, Jacob M. VI, 787
Troth, Jacob M. VI, 788
Troth, James II, 1081
Troth, James VI, 786
Troth, Jane IV, 112
Troth, Jennie V, 466
Troth, Jessie V, 413
Troth, Jessie V, 435
Troth, Jessie V, 466
Troth, Jessie C. V, 312
Troth, Jno. T. II, 187
Troth, John IV, 112
Troth, John J. II, 304
Troth, John T. II, 187
Troth, John T. II, 295
Troth, John T. II, 304
Troth, Joseph J. VI, 786
Troth, Lillian II, 326
Troth, Lillian II, 924
Troth, Lillian II, 931
Troth, Lillian H. II, 314
Troth, Lizie D. II, 326
Troth, Lizzie T. II, 931
Troth, Louisa II, 912
Troth, Louisa II, 931
Troth, Louisa A. II, 825
Troth, Lydia III, 88
Troth, Lydia A. II, 314
Troth, Margaret IV, 112
Troth, Maria VI, 791
Troth, Martha R. VI, 742
Troth, Martha R. VI, 743
Troth, Martha R. VI, 786
Troth, Mary II, 295
Troth, Mary II, 304
Troth, Mary II, 824
Troth, Mary II, 886
Troth, Mary II, 931
Troth, Mary IV, 104
Troth, Mary IV, 112
Troth, Mary Berry II, 780
Troth, Mary Berry II, 791
Troth, Mary H. VI, 786
Troth, Mary H. VI, 787
Troth, Mary H. VI, 789
Troth, Mary H. VI, 790
Troth, Mary J. V, 300
Troth, Mary J. V, 312
Troth, Mary S. II, 319
Troth, Mary S. II, 326
Troth, Nathan V, 300
Troth, Nathan V, 312
Troth, Nathan V, 466
Troth, P. Hillman VI, 785
Troth, P. Hillman VI, 786
Troth, P. Hillman VI, 790
Troth, Paul Hillman VI, 786
Troth, Paul Hillman VI, 787
Troth, Rachel V, 883
Troth, Rachel V, 887
Troth, Rachel F. V, 887
Troth, Rebecca VI, 751
Troth, Rebecca VI, 786
Troth, Rebecca VI, 787
Troth, Rebecca Louisa II, 721
Troth, Rebecca Nicholson VI, 7
Troth, Samuel II, 295
Troth, Samuel II, 304
Troth, Samuel II, 824
Troth, Samuel F. II, 187
Troth, Samuel F. II, 295
Troth, Samuel F. II, 304
Troth, Samuel F. II, 771
Troth, Samuel F. II, 782
Troth, Samuel Fothergill II, 67
Troth, Samuel N. II, 721
Troth, Samuel N. II, 771
Troth, Sarah IV, 112
Troth, Sarah E. VI, 729
Troth, Sarah E. VI, 786
Troth, Sarah E. VI, 787
Troth, Susan W. II, 318
Troth, Susan W. II, 326
Troth, Wd. Ann II, 824
Troth, Wd. Elizabeth II, 187
Troth, Wd. Elizabeth B. VI, 78
Troth, Wd. Elizabeth B. VI, 78
Troth, William III, 88
Troth, William IV, 112
Troth, William D. II, 314
Troth, Wm. II, 670
Troth, Wm. IV, 112
Troth, Wm. V, 883
Troth, Wm. V, 887
Troth, Wm. H. V, 887
Troth-Gillingham, Martha R. VI, 748
Trotter, ??? VI, 48
Trotter, Adaline V, 978
Trotter, Adaline VI, 87
Trotter, Ann V, 978
Trotter, Ann VI, 87
Trotter, Ann VI, 140
Trotter, Ann VI, 142
Trotter, Ann VI, 215
Trotter, Ann VI, 220
Trotter, Ann B. V, 978
Trotter, Ann B. V, 979
Trotter, Ann B. VI, 87
Trotter, Ann B. VI, 133
Trotter, Ann B. VI, 142
Trotter, Anna VI, 87
Trotter, Anna VI, 142
Trotter, Anne VI, 37
Trotter, Armiger II, 670
Trotter, Arminger VI, 232
Trotter, Arminger VI, 278
Trotter, Benjamin II, 428
Trotter, Benjamin II, 495
Trotter, Benjamin II, 670
Trotter, Charles II, 552
Trotter, Charles II, 670
Trotter, Clarence IV, 780
Trotter, Clarence P. IV, 780
Trotter, Dinah II, 428
Trotter, Dinah II, 648
Trotter, Dinah II, 670
Trotter, Elisabeth II, 552
Trotter, Elisabeth II, 670
Trotter, Eliza V, 978

ter, Eliza V, 979
ter, Eliza VI, 87
ter, Elizabeth II, 428
ter, Elizabeth VI, 37
ter, Elizabeth VI, 86
ter, Elizabeth VI, 87
ter, Elizabeth H. II, 720
ter, Elizabeth Jordan I, 120
ter, Emily V, 979
ter, Hannah II, 513
ter, Hannah II, 670
ter, James II, 428
ter, James Bates VI, 19
ter, John I, 76
ter, John VI, 77
ter, John VI, 87
ter, Joseph II, 428
ter, Joseph II, 457
ter, Joseph II, 513
ter, Joseph II, 648
ter, Joseph II, 670
ter, Joseph VI, 37
ter, Joseph Scott VI, 87
ter, Joseph, Jr. II, 429
ter, Joseph, Jr. II, 670
ter, Joshua V, 978
ter, Joshua V, 979
ter, Joshua VI, 87
ter, Joshua VI, 133
ter, Joshua VI, 135
ter, Joshua VI, 139
ter, Joshua VI, 142
ter, Margaret II, 428
ter, Margaret II, 670
tter, Mary I, 90
tter, Mary I Sup 1, 5
tter, Mary I Sup 1, 6
tter, Mary I Sup 1, 8
tter, Mary II, 428
tter, Mary II, 457
tter, Mary II, 474
tter, Mary II, 670
tter, Mary VI, 85
tter, Mary VI, 87
tter, Milicent VI, 87
tter, Millicent VI, 232
tter, Millicent Cheadle VI, 278
tter, Mr. ??? IV, 780
tter, Mrs. Jessie IV, 780
tter, Nathan II, 428
tter, Nathan II, 670
ter, Nathan II, 720
tter, Penninah VI, 99
tter, Penninah VI, 123
ter, Rachel II, 428
ter, Rachel II, 552
tter, Rachel II, 670
tter, Rebecca II, 429
tter, Rebecca II, 665
ter, Rebecca II, 670
ter, Sarah II, 429
tter, Sarah II, 654
tter, Sarah II, 670
tter, Spencer II, 428
tter, Spencer II, 429
tter, Spencer II, 670
tter, Susan II, 720
tter, Susannah II, 552
tter, Susannah II, 670
tter, Thomas I, 101
tter, Thomas I, 120
tter, Thomas I, 148
tter, Thomas I, 164
tter, Thomas II, 670
tter, Thomas VI, 19
tter, Thomas VI, 37
tter, Thomas VI, 47
tter, Thomas VI, 85
tter, Thomas VI, 87
tter, Thomas VI, 142
tter, Thomas VI, 215
tter, Thomas VI, 219
tter, Thomas Newby VI, 87
tter, Thos. VI, 37
tter, Thos. VI, 87
tter, Viola IV, 1265
tter, Wd. Mary II, 495
tter, Wd. Mary II, 670
tter, Wd. Sarah II, 429
tter, William I, 90
tter, William I, 120
tter, William I Sup 1, 8
tter, William II, 428
tter, William II, 429
tter, William V, 979
tter, William VI, 13
tter, William VI, 19
tter, William VI, 87
tter, William VI, 123
tter, William VI, 142
Trotter, Wm. II, 552
Trotter, Wm. II, 665
Trotter, Wm. II, 670
Trotter, Wm. VI, 99
Trotter, Wm. Benjamin V, 979
Troup, Frank IV, 1241
Troup, John V, 1022
Troup, Maria IV, 1241
Troup, Mary IV, 1241
Troup, Sarah V, 1022
Troup, Susan IV, 1241
Troup, William IV, 1241
Trout, Abraham II, 849
Trout, Abraham II, 931
Trout, Abraham IV, 1296
Trout, Ada M. IV, 1341
Trout, Adda IV, 1341
Trout, Alfred V, 715
Trout, Eliza II, 849
Trout, Eliza II, 931
Trout, Eliza J. V, 555
Trout, Elizabeth IV, 1341
Trout, Ethel II, 721
Trout, Irene II, 824
Trout, Irene II, 849
Trout, Irene II, 931
Trout, Job II, 721
Trout, John IV, 1296
Trout, John V, 555
Trout, Julia A. V, 555
Trout, Mary II, 721
Trout, Mary Eva II, 824
Trout, Matilda IV, 1296
Trout, W. Alfred V, 536
Trout, William Wesley II, 824
Trout, Wm. Wesley II, 849
Trout, Wm. Wesley II, 931
Trout, Zillah V, 363
Trout, Zillah V, 365
Troute, Eliza V, 664
Trover, Maranda IV, 1341
Trowbridge, Electa III, 310
Trowbridge, Seymour IV, 1341
Troxwell, Robert V, 770
Troy, Mary Elisabeth I, 614
Truax, Lydia IV, 595
Truax, Lydia IV, 597
Trubee, Bessie V, 208
Trublod, Elizabeth I, 121
Trublood, Aaron I, 171
Trublood, Aaron I, 258
Trublood, Abel I, 161
Trublood, Abel I, 170
Trublood, Abigail I, 122
Trublood, Abigail I, 170
Trublood, Amos I, 121
Trublood, Ann I, 170
Trublood, Asenath I, 122
Trublood, Caleb I, 121
Trublood, Caleb I, 129
Trublood, Caleb I, 170
Trublood, Caleb I, 171
Trublood, Caleb VI, 123
Trublood, Daniel I, 170
Trublood, Elisabeth I, 170
Trublood, Elizabeth I, 161
Trublood, James I, 170
Trublood, James W. I, 122
Trublood, Jemima I, 77
Trublood, Jesse I, 170
Trublood, John I, 140
Trublood, John I, 170
Trublood, John, Jr. I, 170
Trublood, Jonathan I, 170
Trublood, Jonathan I, 177
Trublood, Joshua I, 122
Trublood, Joshua I, 159
Trublood, Joshua I, 171
Trublood, Lovey I, 170
Trublood, Margaret I, 150
Trublood, Mariam I, 158
Trublood, Mariam I, 170
Trublood, Mary I, 121
Trublood, Mary I, 122
Trublood, Mary I, 140
Trublood, Mary I, 149
Trublood, Mary I, 170
Trublood, Mary I, 171
Trublood, Milisent I, 122
Trublood, Miriam I, 170
Trublood, Miriam I, 177
Trublood, Mourning VI, 123
Trublood, Phebe I, 122
Trublood, Pinninah I, 129
Trublood, Pinninah I, 170
Trublood, Rebeca I, 122
Trublood, Ruth I, 158
Trublood, Ruth I, 170
Trublood, Sarah I, 122
Trublood, Thomas I, 150
Trublood, William I, 122
Trucks, Fanny VI, 1012
Trucks, Henry VI, 988
Trucks, Henry VI, 1006
Trucks, Henry VI, 1012
Trucks, Julian VI, 988
Trucks, Nancy VI, 1006
True, Ann V, 208
True, Ann V, 213
True, Ann V, 544
Trueblood, Aaron I, 120
Trueblood, Aaron I, 129
Trueblood, Aaron I, 170
Trueblood, Aaron I, 171
Trueblood, Aaron I, 201
Trueblood, Aaron I, 230
Trueblood, Aaron I, 258
Trueblood, Abel I, 120
Trueblood, Abel I, 121
Trueblood, Abel I, 144
Trueblood, Abel I, 165
Trueblood, Abel I, 168
Trueblood, Abel I, 169
Trueblood, Abel I, 170
Trueblood, Abel I, 171
Trueblood, Abigail I, 120
Trueblood, Abigail I, 122
Trueblood, Abigail I, 142
Trueblood, Abigail I, 158
Trueblood, Abigail I, 170
Trueblood, Abigail I, 171
Trueblood, Abigail V, 134
Trueblood, Adeline I, 23
Trueblood, Almeda V, 716
Trueblood, Alpheus I, 122
Trueblood, Alpheus V, 716
Trueblood, Amie I, 77
Trueblood, Amos I, 76
Trueblood, Amos I, 121
Trueblood, Amos I, 122
Trueblood, Amos I, 169
Trueblood, Amphineas I, 122
Trueblood, Amy IV, 975
Trueblood, Amy IV, 1009
Trueblood, Amy L. IV, 1009
Trueblood, Ann I, 45
Trueblood, Ann I, 76
Trueblood, Ann I, 120
Trueblood, Ann I, 122
Trueblood, Ann I, 147
Trueblood, Ann I, 170
Trueblood, Ann I, 171
Trueblood, Ann Eliza IV, 641
Trueblood, Ann Eliza IV, 662
Trueblood, Anna I, 113
Trueblood, Anna I, 120
Trueblood, Anna I, 122
Trueblood, Anna I, 171
Trueblood, Anne I, 73
Trueblood, Anne I, 76
Trueblood, Anne I, 121
Trueblood, Aron I, 122
Trueblood, Arrenia I, 579
Trueblood, Asa I, 121
Trueblood, Asa I, 169
Trueblood, Asenath I, 171
Trueblood, Benjamin I, 120
Trueblood, Benjamin I, 121
Trueblood, Benjamin I, 165
Trueblood, Benjamin I, 170
Trueblood, Benjamin I, 171
Trueblood, Benjamin IV, 1382
Trueblood, Benjamin V, 361
Trueblood, Benjamin V, 363
Trueblood, Benjamin V, 716
Trueblood, Betsey I, 171
Trueblood, Betsy I, 122
Trueblood, Betty I, 121
Trueblood, Betty I, 171
Trueblood, Caleb I, 45
Trueblood, Caleb I, 76
Trueblood, Caleb I, 120
Trueblood, Caleb I, 121
Trueblood, Caleb I, 136
Trueblood, Caleb I, 169
Trueblood, Caleb I, 170
Trueblood, Caleb I, 171
Trueblood, Caleb I, 200
Trueblood, Caleb I, 230
Trueblood, Caleb I, 258
Trueblood, Caleb, Jr. I, 170
Trueblood, Caleb, Sr. I, 171
Trueblood, Charles V, 591
Trueblood, Charles V, 602
Trueblood, Charles E. V, 602
Trueblood, Clarke I, 113
Trueblood, Daniel I, 121
Trueblood, Daniel I, 148
Trueblood, Daniel I, 169
Trueblood, Daniel I, 170
Trueblood, Deborough Darby I, 122
Trueblood, Edmund I, 122
Trueblood, Edna Winifred V, 716
Trueblood, Edward Borough I, 120
Trueblood, Edward Borough I, 171
Trueblood, Edwin I, 171
Trueblood, Effie V, 716
Trueblood, Elisabeth I, 63
Trueblood, Elisabeth I, 76
Trueblood, Elisabeth I, 121
Trueblood, Elisabeth I, 122
Trueblood, Elisabeth I, 139
Trueblood, Elisabeth I, 153
Trueblood, Elisabeth I, 169
Trueblood, Elisabeth I, 170
Trueblood, Elisabeth I, 171
Trueblood, Elisabeth I, 201
Trueblood, Elisabeth E. I, 77
Trueblood, Elius I, 121
Trueblood, Eliza Ann V, 591
Trueblood, Eliza Ann V, 602
Trueblood, Eliza Ann Osborn V, 602
Trueblood, Elizabeth I, 113
Trueblood, Elizabeth I, 120
Trueblood, Elizabeth I, 121
Trueblood, Elizabeth I, 122
Trueblood, Elizabeth I, 128
Trueblood, Elizabeth I, 169
Trueblood, Elizabeth I, 171
Trueblood, Elizabeth I, 197
Trueblood, Elizabeth I, 200
Trueblood, Elizabeth I, 669
Trueblood, Elizabeth I, 706
Trueblood, Elizabeth Ann I, 122
Trueblood, Elizabeth E. I, 18
Trueblood, Ephraim I, 121
Trueblood, Ephraim I, 171
Trueblood, Ephraim Overman I, 121
Trueblood, Esther V, 363
Trueblood, Fisher I, 36
Trueblood, Fisher I, 76
Trueblood, Fisher I, 121
Trueblood, Fisher I, 169
Trueblood, Fisher I, 170
Trueblood, Fisher I, 258
Trueblood, Foshe I, 121
Trueblood, Francis IV, 975
Trueblood, Francis IV, 1009
Trueblood, Gabril Newby I, 121
Trueblood, George I, 18
Trueblood, George I, 33
Trueblood, George I, 77
Trueblood, George Matthew I, 19
Trueblood, George W. I, 18
Trueblood, Gracie May I, 18
Trueblood, Gulielma I, 122
Trueblood, Gulielma I, 171
Trueblood, Henrietta I, 18
Trueblood, Irena I, 579
Trueblood, Irena I, 842
Trueblood, Irvin K. V, 716
Trueblood, Irving I, 18
Trueblood, Isaac I, 121
Trueblood, Isaac I, 170
Trueblood, Isaac I, 171
Trueblood, Isaac I, 201
Trueblood, Isaac I, 227
Trueblood, Isaac I, 248
Trueblood, Isaac I, 258
Trueblood, Isaac I, 259
Trueblood, Isaac I, 519
Trueblood, Isaac I, 579
Trueblood, Isaac O. I, 171
Trueblood, Isaac O. I, 201
Trueblood, Isaac O. I, 202
Trueblood, Isaac Overman I, 120
Trueblood, Isabel I, 171
Trueblood, Isabel I, 319
Trueblood, Isabelle I, 579
Trueblood, Isbel I, 121
Trueblood, Isbel I, 158
Trueblood, Isbel I, 169
Trueblood, Isbel I, 170
Trueblood, Isbell I, 121
Trueblood, Isiak I, 122
Trueblood, Izbel I, 36
Trueblood, Izbel I, 76
Trueblood, Jacob I, 121
Trueblood, James I, 121
Trueblood, James I, 122
Trueblood, James I, 147
Trueblood, James I, 170
Trueblood, James I, 171
Trueblood, James I, 706
Trueblood, James W. I, 171
Trueblood, James, Jr. I, 171
Trueblood, Jemima I, 57
Trueblood, Jemima I, 77
Trueblood, Jemima I, 120
Trueblood, Jemima I, 121
Trueblood, Jemima I, 122
Trueblood, Jemima I, 155
Trueblood, Jemima I, 165
Trueblood, Jemima I, 169
Trueblood, Jemima I, 170
Trueblood, Jemima I, 171
Trueblood, Jemima I, 193
Trueblood, Jemima I, 201
Trueblood, Jesse I, 121
Trueblood, Jesse I, 170
Trueblood, Jesse I, 227
Trueblood, Jesse I, 319
Trueblood, Jesse I, 519
Trueblood, Jesse I, 579
Trueblood, Jesse I, 842
Trueblood, Jessee I, 120
Trueblood, Jessee I, 579
Trueblood, John I, 51
Trueblood, John I, 76
Trueblood, John I, 120
Trueblood, John I, 121
Trueblood, John I, 122
Trueblood, John I, 155
Trueblood, John I, 170
Trueblood, John I, 171
Trueblood, John IV, 1009
Trueblood, John William I, 18
Trueblood, John, Jr. I, 170
Trueblood, Jonah I, 170
Trueblood, Jonathan I, 76
Trueblood, Jonathan I, 86
Trueblood, Jonathan I, 121
Trueblood, Jonathan I, 170
Trueblood, Jonathan I, 171
Trueblood, Jonathan I, 319
Trueblood, Jonathan I, 519
Trueblood, Jonathan I, 579
Trueblood, Jordan I, 122
Trueblood, Jordan I, 171
Trueblood, Joseph I, 73
Trueblood, Joseph I, 76
Trueblood, Joseph I, 113
Trueblood, Joseph I, 120
Trueblood, Joseph I, 121
Trueblood, Joseph I, 122
Trueblood, Joseph I, 144
Trueblood, Joseph I, 170
Trueblood, Joseph I, 171
Trueblood, Joseph I, 706
Trueblood, Joseph Charles I, 18
Trueblood, Joseph Henley I, 122
Trueblood, Joseph, Jr. I, 169
Trueblood, Joshua I, 18
Trueblood, Joshua I, 23
Trueblood, Joshua I, 57
Trueblood, Joshua I, 77
Trueblood, Joshua I, 113
Trueblood, Joshua I, 120
Trueblood, Joshua I, 121
Trueblood, Joshua I, 122
Trueblood, Joshua I, 142
Trueblood, Joshua I, 148
Trueblood, Joshua I, 169
Trueblood, Joshua I, 170
Trueblood, Joshua I, 171
Trueblood, Joshua I, 193
Trueblood, Joshua I, 201
Trueblood, Joshua V, 363
Trueblood, Joshua, Jr. I, 171
Trueblood, Josiah I, 111
Trueblood, Josiah I, 121
Trueblood, Josiah I, 122
Trueblood, Josiah I, 128
Trueblood, Josiah I, 158
Trueblood, Josiah I, 169
Trueblood, Josiah I, 170
Trueblood, Josiah I, 171
Trueblood, Josiah I, 706
Trueblood, Josiah V, 134
Trueblood, Josiah, Jr. I, 122
Trueblood, Lancaster I, 171
Trueblood, Lancaster V, 134
Trueblood, Lillie Mae I, 18
Trueblood, Lillie Mae I, 19
Trueblood, Lillie Mae I, 77
Trueblood, Louisa IV, 1009
Trueblood, Lovey I, 170
Trueblood, Lula I, 18
Trueblood, Lyddia I, 169
Trueblood, Lydia I, 34
Trueblood, Lydia I, 76
Trueblood, Lydia I, 121
Trueblood, Lydia I Sup 1, 7
Trueblood, Lyra D. V, 716
Trueblood, Madison I, 18
Trueblood, Maggie Belle I, 18
Trueblood, Manny I, 77
Trueblood, Margaret I, 23
Trueblood, Margaret I, 77

Trueblood, Margaret I, 88
Trueblood, Margaret I, 121
Trueblood, Margaret I, 122
Trueblood, Margaret I, 144
Trueblood, Margaret I, 170
Trueblood, Margaret I, 171
Trueblood, Margaret I, 200
Trueblood, Margaret I, 706
Trueblood, Margaret I, 735
Trueblood, Margaret Adeline I, 77
Trueblood, Margaret Adeline I, 83
Trueblood, Margaret J. I, 18
Trueblood, Margaret Jane I, 33
Trueblood, Margaret, Jr. I, 170
Trueblood, Margret I, 200
Trueblood, Mariam I, 122
Trueblood, Mariam I, 170
Trueblood, Mark I, 122
Trueblood, Mark I, 706
Trueblood, Martha I, 227
Trueblood, Martha I, 259
Trueblood, Martha I, 308
Trueblood, Martha I, 319
Trueblood, Martha I, 519
Trueblood, Martha I, 579
Trueblood, Martha Ann I, 19
Trueblood, Martha H. V, 716
Trueblood, Mary I, 51
Trueblood, Mary I, 76
Trueblood, Mary I, 121
Trueblood, Mary I, 122
Trueblood, Mary I, 136
Trueblood, Mary I, 142
Trueblood, Mary I, 148
Trueblood, Mary I, 158
Trueblood, Mary I, 164
Trueblood, Mary I, 168
Trueblood, Mary I, 169
Trueblood, Mary I, 170
Trueblood, Mary I, 171
Trueblood, Mary I, 220
Trueblood, Mary I, 227
Trueblood, Mary I, 248
Trueblood, Mary I, 258
Trueblood, Mary I, 259
Trueblood, Mary I, 319
Trueblood, Mary I, 519
Trueblood, Mary I, 573
Trueblood, Mary I, 579
Trueblood, Mary I, 580
Trueblood, Mary I, 826
Trueblood, Mary I, 842
Trueblood, Mary V, 716
Trueblood, Mary E. I, 579
Trueblood, Mary E. I, 842
Trueblood, Mary E. V, 716
Trueblood, Mary Eliza I, 58
Trueblood, Mary Eliza I, 77
Trueblood, Mary Eliza I, 122
Trueblood, Mary Ellen I, 579
Trueblood, Mary Ellen I, 842
Trueblood, Mary Saint I, 735
Trueblood, Melinda I, 121
Trueblood, Meriam V, 312
Trueblood, Miles I, 121
Trueblood, Milicent I, 120
Trueblood, Milicent I, 171
Trueblood, Milicent I, 201
Trueblood, Milicent I, 319
Trueblood, Milisant I, 170
Trueblood, Miliscent I, 129
Trueblood, Miliscent I, 170
Trueblood, Milisent I, 170
Trueblood, Milisent I, 171
Trueblood, Milisent I, 177
Trueblood, Milisent I, 258
Trueblood, Millicent I, 120
Trueblood, Millicent I, 230
Trueblood, Millicent I, 258
Trueblood, Milly I, 319
Trueblood, Miram I, 121
Trueblood, Miriam I, 76
Trueblood, Miriam I, 86
Trueblood, Miriam I, 111
Trueblood, Miriam I, 113
Trueblood, Miriam I, 120
Trueblood, Miriam I, 121
Trueblood, Miriam I, 122
Trueblood, Miriam I, 148
Trueblood, Miriam I, 159
Trueblood, Miriam I, 160
Trueblood, Miriam I, 162
Trueblood, Miriam I, 167
Trueblood, Miriam I, 169
Trueblood, Miriam I, 170
Trueblood, Miriam I, 171
Trueblood, Miriam I, 706
Trueblood, Miriam V, 312
Trueblood, Mordecai I, 122
Trueblood, Morgan I, 171
Trueblood, Morning I, 706
Trueblood, Morris I, 122
Trueblood, Morris I, 171
Trueblood, Mournen I, 735
Trueblood, Mourning I, 121
Trueblood, Mourning I, 122
Trueblood, Mourning I, 169
Trueblood, Nancie A. U. I, 77
Trueblood, Nancy A. V. I, 18
Trueblood, Naomi I, 120
Trueblood, Naomi I, 171
Trueblood, Nathan I, 77
Trueblood, Nathan I, 121
Trueblood, Nathan I, 122
Trueblood, Nathan I, 154
Trueblood, Nathan I, 171
Trueblood, Nathan E. I, 18
Trueblood, Nathan E. I, 77
Trueblood, Nathan E. I, 122
Trueblood, Nathan S. I, 121
Trueblood, Patience I, 122
Trueblood, Patience I, 154
Trueblood, Patience I, 171
Trueblood, Pegg I, 122
Trueblood, Peggy I, 122
Trueblood, Peggy I, 150
Trueblood, Peggy I, 171
Trueblood, Peggy I, 706
Trueblood, Peggy I, 735
Trueblood, Peggy V, 134
Trueblood, Peninah I, 230
Trueblood, Peninah I, 258
Trueblood, Penninah I, 121
Trueblood, Penninah I, 170
Trueblood, Penny I, 171
Trueblood, Phinehas I, 121
Trueblood, Phinehas I, 171
Trueblood, Pinninah I, 170
Trueblood, Queen I, 18
Trueblood, Rachel I, 319
Trueblood, Rachel I, 519
Trueblood, Rachel I, 573
Trueblood, Rachel I, 579
Trueblood, Rebeckah I, 150
Trueblood, Rebeckah I, 171
Trueblood, Rebekah I, 121
Trueblood, Robert I, 121
Trueblood, Ruth I, 111
Trueblood, Ruth I, 121
Trueblood, Ruth I, 122
Trueblood, Ruth I, 170
Trueblood, Ruth I, 171
Trueblood, Samuel I, 120
Trueblood, Samuel I, 121
Trueblood, Samuel I, 122
Trueblood, Samuel I, 170
Trueblood, Samuel I, 171
Trueblood, Sarah I, 120
Trueblood, Sarah I, 121
Trueblood, Sarah I, 122
Trueblood, Sarah I, 136
Trueblood, Sarah I, 170
Trueblood, Sarah I, 171
Trueblood, Sarah I, 201
Trueblood, Sarah I, 202
Trueblood, Sarah I, 319
Trueblood, Sarah I, 519
Trueblood, Sarah V, 716
Trueblood, Sarah E. I, 18
Trueblood, Sarah H. V, 361
Trueblood, Sarah H. V, 363
Trueblood, Serena I, 842
Trueblood, Stephen I, 122
Trueblood, Stephen I, 171
Trueblood, Susanna I, 122
Trueblood, Susannah I, 128
Trueblood, Susannah I, 165
Trueblood, Susannah I, 170
Trueblood, Thomas I, 34
Trueblood, Thomas I, 76
Trueblood, Thomas I, 120
Trueblood, Thomas I, 122
Trueblood, Thomas I, 169
Trueblood, Thomas I, 170
Trueblood, Thomas I, 171
Trueblood, Thomas I, 579
Trueblood, Thomas I Sup 1, 7
Trueblood, Timothy I, 170
Trueblood, Tishe I, 166
Trueblood, Tishe I, 170
Trueblood, Widow Elisabeth I, 121
Trueblood, Widow Margaret I, 199
Trueblood, Widow Miriam I, 113
Trueblood, William I, 63
Trueblood, William I, 76
Trueblood, William I, 122
Trueblood, William I, 153
Trueblood, William I, 169
Trueblood, William I, 170
Trueblood, William I, 171
Trueblood, William I, 197
Trueblood, William I, 199
Trueblood, William I, 200
Trueblood, William I, 706
Trueblood, William I, 735
Trueblood, William V, 134
Trueblood, William E. I, 77
Trueblood, William Elias I, 18
Trueblood, William Elias I, 19
Trueblood, William P. I, 122
Trueblood, William Rantorn I, 200
Trueblood, William, Jr. I, 170
Truefit, Emily V. II, 771
Truefit, Emily V. II, 772
Trueman, Abigail II, 517
Trueman, Abigail II, 671
Trueman, Ann II, 670
Trueman, Benajah II, 671
Trueman, Benjamin Andrews II, 671
Trueman, Caroline VI, 1006
Trueman, Catharine H. II, 671
Trueman, Evan II, 671
Trueman, George II, 671
Trueman, Hannah II, 671
Trueman, James II, 517
Trueman, James II, 670
Trueman, James II, 671
Trueman, James VI, 1006
Trueman, James, Jr. II, 671
Trueman, Jeffery V, 134
Trueman, Jeffrey II, 671
Trueman, John II, 429
Trueman, Joseph II, 671
Trueman, Joseph VI, 1006
Trueman, Joseph M. II, 671
Trueman, Joseph M. II, 721
Trueman, Joseph Moore II, 671
Trueman, Joseph Moore II, 721
Trueman, Judith VI, 996
Trueman, Margaret II, 429
Trueman, Martha II, 670
Trueman, Martha VI, 966
Trueman, Martha Ann VI, 966
Trueman, Martha Ann VI, 1006
Trueman, Mary II, 517
Trueman, Mary II, 670
Trueman, Mary II, 671
Trueman, Mary VI, 1006
Trueman, Morris II, 671
Trueman, Nancey VI, 1006
Trueman, Nancey Emeline VI, 1006
Trueman, Phebe II, 671
Trueman, Rachel II, 663
Trueman, Rachel II, 671
Trueman, Rebecca II, 671
Trueman, Richard II, 517
Trueman, Richard II, 670
Trueman, Richard II, 671
Trueman, Robert VI, 1006
Trueman, Sally VI, 937
Trueman, Sarah II, 671
Trueman, Sarah II, 721
Trueman, Susanna II, 671
Trueman, Susannah II, 538
Trueman, Susannah II, 670
Trueman, Thomas II, 670
Trueman, Thomas II, 671
Trueman, Thomas S. II, 671
Trueman, Thomas S. II, 771
Trueman, Wyatt W. VI, 966
Trueman, Wyatt W. VI, 1006
Truett, Hetty II, 932
Truhit, Frances C. VI, 843
Truhit, Wm. VI, 843
Truitt, George VI, 11
Truitt, Ora V, 715
Truitt, Ora V, 716
Truman, ??? III, 323
Truman, Alex Shaw II, 429
Truman, Alexander II, 771
Truman, Alexander S. II, 932
Truman, Alexander Shaw II, 771
Truman, Alexander Shaw II, 824
Truman, Ann II, 670
Truman, Ann II, 771
Truman, Anna II, 805
Truman, Anna II, 887
Truman, Anna II, 924
Truman, Anna II, 932
Truman, Catharine II, 932
Truman, Catharine VI, 880
Truman, Catharine H. II, 671
Truman, Catharine H. II, 887
Truman, Catharine H. II, 933
Truman, Catharine Hickman II, 805
Truman, Catherine VI, 920
Truman, Catherine H. II, 593
Truman, Catherine H. II, 931
Truman, Catherine H. II, 932
Truman, Catherine Hickman II, 823
Truman, Catherine Hickman II, 824
Truman, Elizabeth VI, 891
Truman, Elizabeth G. II, 918
Truman, Elizabeth G. II, 932
Truman, Elizabeth Garrigues II, 824
Truman, Elizabeth Phillips II, 824
Truman, Evalena III, 244
Truman, Evalena III, 323
Truman, Evan II, 509
Truman, Evan II, 671
Truman, George II, 593
Truman, George II, 671
Truman, George II, 771
Truman, George II, 805
Truman, George II, 824
Truman, George II, 887
Truman, George II, 931
Truman, George II, 932
Truman, George II, 933
Truman, George S. II, 932
Truman, George S. VI, 715
Truman, George Shaw II, 429
Truman, George Shaw II, 771
Truman, George, Jr. II, 824
Truman, Hannah II, 509
Truman, Hannah II, 671
Truman, Howard J. II, 918
Truman, Howard J. II, 932
Truman, Howard James II, 824
Truman, J. L. V, 679
Truman, J. L. V, 716
Truman, James II, 429
Truman, James II, 509
Truman, James II, 593
Truman, James II, 648
Truman, James II, 670
Truman, James II, 671
Truman, James II, 771
Truman, James II, 781
Truman, James II, 824
Truman, James II, 918
Truman, James II, 932
Truman, James IV, 112
Truman, James, Jr. II, 600
Truman, James, Jr. II, 671
Truman, Jeffery V, 134
Truman, Jeffrey II, 671
Truman, John II, 429
Truman, John III, 323
Truman, John VI, 880
Truman, John Jackson VI, 715
Truman, Joseph IV, 112
Truman, Joseph VI, 715
Truman, Joseph VI, 878
Truman, Joseph L. VI, 715
Truman, Joseph M. II, 429
Truman, Joseph M. II, 648
Truman, Joseph M. II, 671
Truman, Joseph M. II, 771
Truman, Joseph M. II, 865
Truman, Joseph M. II, 932
Truman, Joseph Moore II, 429
Truman, Joseph Moore II, 671
Truman, Joseph Moore II, 771
Truman, Joseph Moore II, 824
Truman, Joseph Moore, Jr. II, 824
Truman, Joseph N. II, 932
Truman, Josiah T. III, 323
Truman, Lila V, 679
Truman, Lila V, 716
Truman, Lita H. V, 716
Truman, Lita Lucile V, 716
Truman, Llewellyn II, 824
Truman, Lydia Ann IV, 234
Truman, Lydia Ann IV, 295
Truman, Lydia S. II, 932
Truman, Lydia Smith II, 824
Truman, Margaret II, 429
Truman, Margaret IV, 112
Truman, Marianna B. VI, 715
Truman, Martha II, 429
Truman, Mary II, 509
Truman, Mary II, 671
Truman, Mary II, 771
Truman, Mary II, 918
Truman, Mary II, 932
Truman, Mary III, 323
Truman, Mary IV, 112
Truman, Mary A. II, 932
Truman, Mary Ann II, 824
Truman, Mary M. II, 932
Truman, Mary Master II, 824
Truman, Mary S. II, 429
Truman, Mary S. II, 932
Truman, Mary Shaw II, 824
Truman, Morris IV, 63
Truman, Morris IV, 112
Truman, Nancy VI, 891
Truman, Phebe II, 593
Truman, Phebe II, 600
Truman, Phebe II, 648
Truman, Phebe II, 671
Truman, Phebe II, 781
Truman, Phebe II, 824
Truman, Phebe Anna III, 323
Truman, Phebe M. II, 429
Truman, Polly E. VI, 878
Truman, Rebecca II, 671
Truman, Richard II, 429
Truman, Richard II, 671
Truman, Robert VI, 878
Truman, Robert VI, 920
Truman, Sarah II, 429
Truman, Sarah II, 648
Truman, Sarah II, 671
Truman, Sarah II, 771
Truman, Sarah II, 824
Truman, Sarah V, 57
Truman, Sarah Josephine II, 8
Truman, Sarah N. II, 932
Truman, Sarah P. II, 932
Truman, Sarah P. II, 933
Truman, Sarah Pearson II, 82
Truman, Sarah S. II, 429
Truman, Sarah S. II, 932
Truman, Sarah S. V, 58
Truman, Sarah S. V, 134
Truman, Sarah Shaw, Jr. II, 82
Truman, Shaw II, 771
Truman, Susan Y. VI, 715
Truman, Susanna II, 671
Truman, Thomas II, 429
Truman, Thomas II, 670
Truman, Thomas S. II, 671
Truman, Thomas S. II, 771
Truman, Wd. Mary II, 824
Truman, Wd. Susannah T. II, 7
Truman, William II, 429
Truman, William III, 244
Truman, Wyatt VI, 879
Truman, Wyatt VI, 884
Truman, Wyatt W. VI, 955
Trumball, John II, 448
Trumble, Francis II, 429
Trumble, Sarah II, 429
Trumon, Robert VI, 1006
Trump, Abby Ann II, 121
Trump, Abby Ann II, 125
Trump, Catharine M. II, 855
Trump, Catharine M. II, 932
Trump, Chas. N. II, 855
Trump, Chas. N. II, 932
Trump, Daniel II, 672
Trump, Daniel II, 824
Trump, Daniel II, 864
Trump, Daniel II, 932
Trump, David II, 671
Trump, David Furman II, 824
Trump, Edward N. II, 855
Trump, Edward N. II, 932
Trump, Helen M. II, 855
Trump, Helen M. II, 932
Trump, Howard W. II, 824
Trump, Jesse, Jr. II, 671
Trump, Maggie V, 843
Trump, Margaret L. II, 864
Trump, Margaret L. II, 932
Trump, Margaret Longstreth II, 824
Trump, Mary II, 824
Trump, Mary Elizabeth II, 787
Trump, Mary Elizabeth II, 932
Trump, Mary M. II, 864
Trump, Mary M. II, 932
Trump, Watson M. II, 864
Trump, Watson M. II, 932
Trump, Watson Malone II, 824
Truner, James VI, 919
Truss, John V, 208
Trustam, Frederick III, 165
Trustam, Frederick III, 323
Trustam, Jane III, 165
Trustam, Jane III, 323
Trustam, Mary L. III, 165
Trustam, Mary L. III, 323
Trux, Henry VI, 988
Trux, Julian VI, 988
Tryian, David V, 872
Tryon, Lillian III, 94
Tryphena, Benjamin VI, 683
Tryphena, Rachel VI, 683
Tubby, Almira B. III, 323

y, Daniel B. III, 323
y, Edward J. III, 323
y, Eliz. III, 298
y, Elizabeth III, 298
y, Elizabeth III, 323
y, Elizabeth VI, 781
y, Elsie III, 323
y, Josiah T. III, 53
y, Josiah T. III, 252
y, Josiah T. III, 298
y, Josiah T. III, 323
y, Josiah T., Jr. III, 323
y, Mary III, 252
y, Mary III, 323
y, Phebe III, 323
y, Phebe A. III, 323
y, Phebe Anna III, 53
y, Phebe Anna III, 298
y, Phebe Anna III, 323
y, Wm. G. III, 323
t, William I, 998
Friend VI, 278
George VI, 1006
John VI, 8
John VI, 42
John VI, 93
Marietta VI, 278
Mary VI, 1006
Nancy VI, 931
Sarah VI, 861
Thomas VI, 861
Thos. VI, 931
er, ??? VI, 622
er, A. C. I, 946
er, A. C. I, 950
er, Aaron Waller V, 716
er, Abe V, 803
er, Abigail G. V, 134
er, Abraham V, 134
er, Abraham V, 748
er, Abraham V, 770
er, Abraham V, 813
er, Adeline VI, 861
er, Allie V, 771
er, Alphonzo G. I, 866
er, Alphonzo G. I, 903
er, Amanda VI, 835
er, Amanda VI, 861
er, Amanda Jane V, 771
er, Amy V, 716
er, Ann I, 903
er, Ann II, 266
er, Ann II, 268
er, Ann II, 429
er, Ann II, 671
er, Ann II, 771
er, Ann II, 824
er, Ann II, 932
er, Ann V, 937
er, Ann S. II, 268
er, Ann S. III, 323
er, Ann S. V, 937
er, Ann, Jr. II, 771
er, Anna V, 770
er, Anna V, 771
er, Anna B. V, 536
er, Anna S. III, 323
er, Anne B. V, 536
er, Armistead VI, 861
er, Benj. V, 770
er, Benj. V, 937
er, Benj. Sykes V, 937
er, Benjamin II, 268
er, Benjamin II, 429
er, Benjamin II, 671
er, Benjamin II, 771
er, Benjamin II, 808
er, Benjamin II, 824
er, Benjamin II, 865
er, Benjamin II, 895
er, Benjamin II, 932
er, Benjamin Craig II, 429
er, Benjamin Craig II, 671
er, Benjamin S. III, 323
er, Benjamin S. V, 937
er, Betsey III, 370
er, Caleb II, 671
er, Capt. Samuel VI, 145
er, Catherine W. VI, 817
er, Charity II, 932
er, Charity V, 134
er, Charity V, 816
er, Charles V, 716
er, Charles VI, 861
er, Clarice V, 716
er, Creed VI, 973
er, Dandridge VI, 921
er, Daniel II, 721
er, Daniel V, 770
er, Daniel B. IV, 1382
er, David VI, 574
Tucker, Davis L. V, 771
Tucker, Deborah V, 770
Tucker, Deborah V, 810
Tucker, Delania IV, 1341
Tucker, Eber V, 716
Tucker, Edward VI, 809
Tucker, Edward VI, 817
Tucker, Edward VI, 831
Tucker, Edward VI, 857
Tucker, Edward VI, 861
Tucker, Eleanor V, 716
Tucker, Elijah V, 716
Tucker, Elijah N. V, 716
Tucker, Elizabeth I, 823
Tucker, Elizabeth I, 842
Tucker, Elizabeth II, 429
Tucker, Elizabeth II, 671
Tucker, Elizabeth II, 721
Tucker, Elizabeth II, 742
Tucker, Elizabeth II, 771
Tucker, Elizabeth II, 795
Tucker, Elizabeth II, 865
Tucker, Elizabeth II, 932
Tucker, Elizabeth III, 323
Tucker, Elizabeth IV, 679
Tucker, Elizabeth IV, 780
Tucker, Elizabeth V, 730
Tucker, Elizabeth V, 768
Tucker, Elizabeth V, 770
Tucker, Elizabeth V, 937
Tucker, Elizabeth VI, 262
Tucker, Elizabeth VI, 264
Tucker, Elizabeth VI, 831
Tucker, Elizabeth VI, 937
Tucker, Elizabeth B. IV, 780
Tucker, Elizabeth M. II, 429
Tucker, Elizabeth M. II, 671
Tucker, Elizabeth M. II, 721
Tucker, Elizabeth M. II, 771
Tucker, Emily VI, 861
Tucker, Erasmus V, 770
Tucker, Esther III, 124
Tucker, Esther III, 323
Tucker, Eva V, 134
Tucker, Fannie Laura V, 716
Tucker, Florence III, 423
Tucker, Florence Rasche I, 627
Tucker, Frances VI, 992
Tucker, Frances VI, 1007
Tucker, Frances C. V, 771
Tucker, Frances Ellen V, 768
Tucker, Francis Marie V, 716
Tucker, Frederica VI, 622
Tucker, George III, 323
Tucker, George V, 937
Tucker, Granville VI, 933
Tucker, Granville VI, 1006
Tucker, Hannah I, 1088
Tucker, Hannah II, 268
Tucker, Hannah III, 323
Tucker, Hannah V, 911
Tucker, Hannah V, 937
Tucker, Hannah VI, 932
Tucker, Harvey V, 771
Tucker, Henry V, 768
Tucker, Henry L. VI, 1006
Tucker, Howard W. V, 937
Tucker, Ida M. V, 602
Tucker, Isaac V, 602
Tucker, Isaac Hammer I, 1088
Tucker, Jacob V, 730
Tucker, Jacob V, 770
Tucker, Jacob V, 810
Tucker, James II, 429
Tucker, James II, 448
Tucker, James III, 323
Tucker, James W. III, 124
Tucker, James W. III, 323
Tucker, Jane II, 448
Tucker, Jane II, 460
Tucker, Jane Maris II, 717
Tucker, Jesse IV, 780
Tucker, Jesse VI, 973
Tucker, Jesse VI, 1007
Tucker, Jesse R. IV, 679
Tucker, Jesse R. IV, 780
Tucker, Joana I, 1133
Tucker, Joanna I, 1133
Tucker, John I, 1088
Tucker, John I, 1099
Tucker, John I, 1111
Tucker, John I, 1133
Tucker, John II, 448
Tucker, John V, 716
Tucker, John VI, 574
Tucker, John VI, 861
Tucker, John H. VI, 817
Tucker, John I. I, 1133
Tucker, John Ira I, 1088
Tucker, John W. IV, 1241
Tucker, John Wesley IV, 1341
Tucker, Jonathan II, 932
Tucker, Jonathan V, 770
Tucker, Joseph II, 671
Tucker, Joseph V, 770
Tucker, Joseph VI, 452
Tucker, Joseph VI, 453
Tucker, Joshua VI, 902
Tucker, Lucy VI, 1006
Tucker, Lydia I, 579
Tucker, Lydia I, 1088
Tucker, Lydia I, 1133
Tucker, Lydia VI, 545
Tucker, Lydia VI, 574
Tucker, Lydia M. II, 671
Tucker, Lydia M. II, 771
Tucker, Lydia W. II, 771
Tucker, M. L. I, 866
Tucker, Mabel IV, 1341
Tucker, Margaret I, 903
Tucker, Margaret I, 1091
Tucker, Margaret I, 1099
Tucker, Margaret II, 429
Tucker, Margaret II, 671
Tucker, Margaret II, 721
Tucker, Margaret II, 771
Tucker, Margaret II, 932
Tucker, Margaret V, 536
Tucker, Margaret V, 716
Tucker, Margaret V, 771
Tucker, Margaret V, 803
Tucker, Margaret Elizabeth I, 1133
Tucker, Marie V, 716
Tucker, Martha I. I, 903
Tucker, Martha J. I, 866
Tucker, Martha Jane I, 903
Tucker, Martha R. VI, 937
Tucker, Mary I, 903
Tucker, Mary I, 1088
Tucker, Mary I, 1133
Tucker, Mary II, 266
Tucker, Mary II, 268
Tucker, Mary II, 429
Tucker, Mary II, 671
Tucker, Mary II, 771
Tucker, Mary II, 824
Tucker, Mary II, 932
Tucker, Mary III, 405
Tucker, Mary III, 458
Tucker, Mary V, 134
Tucker, Mary V, 730
Tucker, Mary V, 748
Tucker, Mary V, 770
Tucker, Mary V, 798
Tucker, Mary V, 804
Tucker, Mary V, 937
Tucker, Mary VI, 545
Tucker, Mary VI, 574
Tucker, Mary A. I, 866
Tucker, Mary A. I, 903
Tucker, Mary Ann IV, 780
Tucker, Mary B. V, 134
Tucker, Mary B. V, 816
Tucker, Mary E. III, 323
Tucker, Mary E. V, 900
Tucker, Mary E. V, 937
Tucker, Mary Ellis V, 937
Tucker, Mary Emily V, 716
Tucker, Mildred VI, 817
Tucker, Mildred VI, 861
Tucker, Mitchener V, 770
Tucker, Myrtie V, 771
Tucker, Nancy V, 729
Tucker, Nancy VI, 937
Tucker, Nancy VI, 946
Tucker, Nancy VI, 973
Tucker, Nancy B. VI, 1006
Tucker, Nancy King VI, 931
Tucker, Nancy L. VI, 946
Tucker, Naomi I, 1088
Tucker, Naomi I, 1133
Tucker, Naomi V, 740
Tucker, Naomi V, 748
Tucker, Naomi V, 770
Tucker, Naomi V, 771
Tucker, Naomi V, 813
Tucker, Naomi G. V, 134
Tucker, Nellie I. V, 536
Tucker, Nellie J. V, 536
Tucker, Newton V, 716
Tucker, Nicholas V, 134
Tucker, Nicholas V, 770
Tucker, Nicholas V, 816
Tucker, Nicholas VI, 574
Tucker, Nora IV, 295
Tucker, Olfonzo I, 903
Tucker, Pamelia A. VI, 973
Tucker, Phebe III, 323
Tucker, Phebe Ann II, 1081
Tucker, Polly VI, 946
Tucker, Priscilla V, 716
Tucker, Rebecca II, 429
Tucker, Rebecca II, 671
Tucker, Rebecca II, 771
Tucker, Rebecca II, 824
Tucker, Rebecca II, 932
Tucker, Rebecca S. Spray V, 602
Tucker, Rebeccah VI, 1006
Tucker, Rebeckah I, 1088
Tucker, Rhoda V, 770
Tucker, Richard II, 448
Tucker, Richard II, 460
Tucker, Richard II, 671
Tucker, Robert VI, 545
Tucker, Robert VI, 574
Tucker, Rollin V, 770
Tucker, Ronald V, 716
Tucker, Ruth VI, 921
Tucker, Samuel W. V, 937
Tucker, Samuel Wood V, 937
Tucker, Sarah I, 935
Tucker, Sarah I, 946
Tucker, Sarah I, 950
Tucker, Sarah I, 1088
Tucker, Sarah I, 1111
Tucker, Sarah I, 1133
Tucker, Sarah II, 429
Tucker, Sarah II, 671
Tucker, Sarah IV, 1109
Tucker, Sarah IV, 1110
Tucker, Sarah IV, 1118
Tucker, Sarah V, 748
Tucker, Sarah V, 770
Tucker, Sarah V, 813
Tucker, Sarah A. III, 323
Tucker, Sarah C. V, 134
Tucker, Sarah C. V, 800
Tucker, Solomon Beals I, 1088
Tucker, Sophrony W. VI, 931
Tucker, Stith VI, 142
Tucker, Susan III, 323
Tucker, Susan VI, 931
Tucker, Susanna V, 770
Tucker, Susannah V, 770
Tucker, Talbot VI, 932
Tucker, Theodisia II, 865
Tucker, Theodosia II, 429
Tucker, Theodosia II, 671
Tucker, Theodosia II, 771
Tucker, Theodosia II, 808
Tucker, Theodosia II, 824
Tucker, Theodosia II, 895
Tucker, Theodosia II, 932
Tucker, Theodosia, Jr. II, 771
Tucker, Theodosia, Jr. II, 895
Tucker, Theodosia, Jr. II, 932
Tucker, Thomas II, 266
Tucker, Thomas II, 268
Tucker, Thomas II, 429
Tucker, Thomas II, 671
Tucker, Thomas III, 323
Tucker, Thomas V, 937
Tucker, Thomas VI, 344
Tucker, Thomas VI, 536
Tucker, Thomas VI, 574
Tucker, Thomas VI, 805
Tucker, Thomas VI, 841
Tucker, Thomas VI, 862
Tucker, Thomas VI, 932
Tucker, Thomas VI, 1006
Tucker, Thomas L. II, 671
Tucker, Thomas L. II, 721
Tucker, Thomas S. II, 429
Tucker, Thomas S. II, 671
Tucker, Thomas S. II, 771
Tucker, Thomas S. III, 323
Tucker, Thos. II, 824
Tucker, Thos. II, 932
Tucker, Thos. V, 770
Tucker, Thos. V, 937
Tucker, Valentine VI, 833
Tucker, Walter V, 716
Tucker, Walter V, 937
Tucker, Walter Brown V, 937
Tucker, Wd. Jane VI, 145
Tucker, Widow Elizabeth I, 1099
Tucker, William III, 323
Tucker, William V, 937
Tucker, William VI, 215
Tucker, William VI, 921
Tucker, William VI, 992
Tucker, William Ellis II, 429
Tucker, William M. I, 866
Tucker, William M. I, 903
Tucker, William Monroe I, 903
Tucker, William, Jr. II, 268
Tucker, Wm. Ellis II, 671
Tucker, Wm. Ellis II, 721
Tucket, Charity V, 131
Tucket, Nicholas V, 131
Tuckett, Daniel II, 429
Tuckmiss, Ann II, 553
Tuckness, Abraham II, 671
Tuckness, Ann II, 671
Tuckness, Elizabeth II, 671
Tuckness, Elizabeth II, 684
Tuckness, Jane II, 510
Tuckness, Jane II, 671
Tuckness, John II, 107
Tuckness, John II, 429
Tuckness, John II, 671
Tuckness, Lydia II, 671
Tuckness, Mary II, 562
Tuckness, Mary II, 671
Tuckness, Robert II, 510
Tuckness, Robert II, 562
Tuckness, Robert II, 671
Tuckniss, Abraham II, 671
Tuckniss, Ann II, 671
Tuckniss, Elizabeth II, 429
Tuckniss, Henry II, 429
Tuckniss, James II, 429
Tuckniss, John II, 429
Tuckniss, Mary II, 429
Tuckniss, Mary II, 671
Tuckniss, R??? II, 429
Tuckniss, Robert II, 429
Tuckniss, Robert II, 671
Tucness, Henry II, 429
Tuder, Abraham IV, 354
Tuder, Elizabeth IV, 335
Tuder, Elizabeth IV, 354
Tuder, Hannah IV, 319
Tuder, Hannah IV, 354
Tuder, Isaac IV, 354
Tuder, Martha IV, 338
Tuder, Martha IV, 354
Tuder, William IV, 354
Tudor, Martha IV, 338
Tudor, Martha IV, 354
Tudor, Martha IV, 449
Tueder, Isaac IV, 354
Tuft, Mary II, 44
Tuft, Mary II, 107
Tuft, Mary II, 112
Tuft, Mary II, 125
Tufts, Henrietta H. III, 342
Tuggle, Henry L. VI, 861
Tuggle, Martha E. VI, 861
Tuider, Abraham IV, 354
Tuider, Elizabeth IV, 354
Tuider, Hannah IV, 354
Tuider, Isaac IV, 354
Tuider, Martha IV, 354
Tuider, William IV, 354
Tuke, Thomas VI, 15
Tulbert, Elizabeth I, 998
Tulbert, James L. I, 981
Tulbert, James L. I, 998
Tulbert, Mary I, 998
Tulbert, Mary Ann I, 998
Tulbert, Rachel I, 998
Tulbert, Rachel A. I, 981
Tulbert, Rachel A. I, 998
Tulbert, Rachel Ann I, 998
Tulbert, Sarah I, 998
Tulbert, William I, 979
Tulbert, William I, 998
TulbertTulburt, Mary I, 998
TulbertTulburt, William I, 998
Tulburt, Elizabeth I, 989
Tulburt, Elizabeth I, 998
Tulburt, Sarah I, 987
Tulburt, Sarah I, 998
Tuley, George VI, 1006
Tuley, John, Jr. VI, 1006
Tuley, Mary VI, 1006
Tuley, Patsey VI, 1006
Tulga, Albert C. IV, 1341
Tulin, Elizabeth I, 690
Tull, James II, 671
Tull, Mary II, 671
Tull, Mary II, 691
Tull, Rachell II, 671
Tull, Rachell II, 691
Tulla, Mary III, 230
Tullas, ??? VI, 293
Tullas, Elizabeth VI, 335
Tullas, Elizabeth VI, 343
Tullas, Jane VI, 343
Tullas, John VI, 343
Tullas, Martha VI, 343
Tullas, Richard VI, 343
Tuller, Myrtle I, 619
Tulles, Elizabeth VI, 335
Tullis, ??? VI, 293
Tullis, Ann IV, 63
Tullis, Ann IV, 662
Tullis, Ann IV, 884
Tullis, Ann VI, 353
Tullis, Ann VI, 354
Tullis, Ann VI, 355
Tullis, Catharine IV, 662

Tullis, Catharine IV, 884
Tullis, Eliza IV, 662
Tullis, Eliza Ann IV, 662
Tullis, Elizabeth IV, 662
Tullis, Elizabeth IV, 884
Tullis, Elizabeth VI, 343
Tullis, Elizabeth J. IV, 662
Tullis, Err IV, 662
Tullis, Hannah IV, 662
Tullis, Jane IV, 63
Tullis, Jane IV, 662
Tullis, Jane IV, 876
Tullis, Jane IV, 884
Tullis, Jane VI, 334
Tullis, Jane VI, 343
Tullis, Jane VI, 355
Tullis, Jason IV, 63
Tullis, Jason IV, 662
Tullis, Jason IV, 884
Tullis, Jason VI, 355
Tullis, Jason Morlan VI, 355
Tullis, John IV, 63
Tullis, John IV, 662
Tullis, John IV, 884
Tullis, John VI, 334
Tullis, John VI, 343
Tullis, John VI, 355
Tullis, Jonathan IV, 662
Tullis, Joseph IV, 662
Tullis, Joseph IV, 884
Tullis, Laura V, 1022
Tullis, Lewis IV, 662
Tullis, Martha VI, 334
Tullis, Martha VI, 343
Tullis, Martha VI, 354
Tullis, Martha VI, 355
Tullis, Martha A. IV, 662
Tullis, Marthew VI, 334
Tullis, Marthew VI, 343
Tullis, Nancy IV, 63
Tullis, Nancy IV, 662
Tullis, Nancy VI, 343
Tullis, Naomi IV, 662
Tullis, Nathan IV, 662
Tullis, Rachel IV, 662
Tullis, Rebecca IV, 63
Tullis, Rebecca IV, 662
Tullis, Rebeckah VI, 355
Tullis, Rebekah IV, 662
Tullis, Rhoda IV, 662
Tullis, Rhoda IV, 876
Tullis, Rhoda IV, 884
Tullis, Richard IV, 63
Tullis, Richard IV, 662
Tullis, Richard IV, 884
Tullis, Richard VI, 321
Tullis, Richard VI, 334
Tullis, Richard VI, 343
Tullis, Richard VI, 353
Tullis, Richard VI, 354
Tullis, Richard VI, 355
Tullis, Richard, Jr. IV, 662
Tullis, Richard, Jr. VI, 343
Tullis, Richard, Jr. VI, 355
Tullis, Sarah IV, 63
Tullis, Sarah IV, 662
Tullis, Sarah IV, 884
Tullis, Sarah VI, 334
Tullis, Sarah VI, 343
Tullis, Sarah Ann IV, 662
Tullis, Sard IV, 884
Tullis, Smith IV, 662
Tullis, Walter V, 363
Tullis, William IV, 63
Tullis, William IV, 662
Tullis, William IV, 884
Tullis, William VI, 355
Tullis, Wm. IV, 662
Tulliss, Elizabeth J. IV, 643
Tulliss, Smith IV, 662
Tullo, Mary III, 312
Tullos, Martha A. IV, 648
Tullos, Martha A. IV, 662
Tulloss, Ann IV, 864
Tulloss, Ann IV, 881
Tulloss, Ann IV, 884
Tulloss, Catharine IV, 869
Tulloss, Catharine IV, 884
Tulloss, Eliza IV, 662
Tulloss, Eliza Ann IV, 662
Tulloss, Eliza Ann IV, 879
Tulloss, Eliza Ann IV, 884
Tulloss, Eliza Ann IV, 1108
Tulloss, Eliza Ann IV, 1118
Tulloss, Eliza Ann IV, 1135
Tulloss, Elizabeth IV, 884
Tulloss, Er H. IV, 884
Tulloss, Hannah IV, 662
Tulloss, Hannah IV, 872
Tulloss, Hannah IV, 879
Tulloss, Hannah IV, 884
Tulloss, Jane IV, 662
Tulloss, Jane IV, 884
Tulloss, Jason IV, 662
Tulloss, Jason IV, 872
Tulloss, Jason IV, 879
Tulloss, Jason IV, 884
Tulloss, John IV, 662
Tulloss, John IV, 884
Tulloss, Jonathan IV, 662
Tulloss, Jonathan IV, 884
Tulloss, Joseph IV, 884
Tulloss, Lewis IV, 662
Tulloss, Lewis IV, 884
Tulloss, Lindley H. IV, 884
Tulloss, Martha A. IV, 884
Tulloss, Nancy IV, 662
Tulloss, Nathan IV, 662
Tulloss, Nathan IV, 884
Tulloss, Rachel IV, 662
Tulloss, Rachel IV, 798
Tulloss, Rachel IV, 849
Tulloss, Rachel IV, 884
Tulloss, Rebecca IV, 662
Tulloss, Rhoda IV, 662
Tulloss, Rhoda IV, 884
Tulloss, Richard IV, 662
Tulloss, Richard IV, 881
Tulloss, Richard IV, 884
Tulloss, Richard J. IV, 884
Tulloss, Richard, Jr. IV, 662
Tulloss, Sarah IV, 662
Tulloss, Sarah IV, 884
Tulloss, Sarah Ann IV, 662
Tulloss, Sarah Ann IV, 884
Tulloss, Sard IV, 884
Tulloss, Smith IV, 884
Tulloss, William IV, 884
Tully, Hannah II, 653
Tully, Hannah II, 671
Tully, Mary VI, 1007
Tully, Polly VI, 1007
Tuloss, Eliza Ann IV, 884
Tuloss, Hannah IV, 884
Tuloss, Jason IV, 884
Tuloss, Jonathan IV, 884
Tuloss, Joseph IV, 884
Tuloss, Nathan IV, 884
Tuloss, Sarah Ann IV, 884
Tulus, Elizabeth IV, 780
Tulus, Hannah IV, 780
Tulus, Jane IV, 780
Tulus, Jason IV, 780
Tulus, Lindley M. IV, 780
Tulus, Martha IV, 780
Tulus, Richard IV, 780
Tuly, Elizabeth II, 268
Tuly, Mary II, 268
Tumbleson, Aletta IV, 490
Tumbleson, Aletta IV, 501
Tumbleson, Lola V, 1022
Tumbleson, Mary Ann IV, 42
Tumbleson, Mary Ann IV, 62
Tumbleson, Zala V, 1022
Tumlin, Ann II, 429
Tummelson, Lydia IV, 354
Tunis, Ann II, 429
Tunis, Anne Callendar II, 771
Tunis, Anne Callender II, 761
Tunis, Charles II, 671
Tunis, Elizabeth II, 429
Tunis, Hannah II, 671
Tunis, Hannah II, 672
Tunis, Jane II, 429
Tunis, Richard II, 429
Tunis, Sarah II, 429
Tunis, Wm. II, 671
Tunis, Wm. II, 672
Tunison, Hardenburg III, 323
Tunison, Hardenburg III, 367
Tunison, Mary V. III, 323
Tunison, Mary V. III, 367
Tunison, Sarah III, 323
Tunison, Sarah J. III, 367
Tunstall, Frances VI, 1006
Tunstall, John VI, 1006
Tupham, Sarah II, 721
Tupman, Emily II, 824
Tupman, Mary II, 824
Tupman, Mary II, 831
Tupman, Mary II, 932
Tupman, Mary A. II, 932
Tupman, Wm. II, 824
Tupman, Wm. II, 831
Tupman, Wm. II, 932
Tuppence, Amanda VI, 867
Tuppence, Jas. VI, 815
Tuppence, Mary A. VI, 867
Tuppence, Susanna VI, 815
Tupper, Josephine IV, 1341
Turck, Annabel III, 323
Turck, Annabell III, 78
Turck, Charlotte III, 78
Turck, Charlotte III, 323
Turck, Solomon III, 78
Turck, Solomon III, 323
Turk, Sarah IV, 354
Turley, Betsy VI, 843
Turley, Catharine VI, 636
Turley, Catharine VI, 716
Turley, James VI, 798
Turley, James VI, 823
Turley, James VI, 828
Turley, James VI, 843
Turley, James VI, 1007
Turley, James, Jr. VI, 798
Turley, Martha Susan VI, 663
Turley, Martha Susan VI, 667
Turley, Mary VI, 1007
Turley, Ruth VI, 798
Turley, Ruth VI, 877
Turmond, Mary VI, 965
Turnas, John P. II, 932
Turnbull, Emily VI, 494
Turnbull, John VI, 494
Turner, Abraham I, 866
Turner, Abraham I, 903
Turner, Abraham I, 904
Turner, Admire VI, 892
Turner, Admire VI, 901
Turner, Admire VI, 905
Turner, Admire VI, 924
Turner, Admire VI, 949
Turner, Admire VI, 989
Turner, Admire VI, 1000
Turner, Admire, Jr. VI, 1007
Turner, Admmire VI, 931
Turner, Adrian IV, 1296
Turner, Alderson VI, 959
Turner, Alfred VI, 1008
Turner, Alice VI, 355
Turner, Ambrose VI, 936
Turner, Amy V, 536
Turner, Ann I, 866
Turner, Ann V, 506
Turner, Ann V, 536
Turner, Ann VI, 1007
Turner, Ann J. VI, 278
Turner, Anna III, 16
Turner, Anna III, 94
Turner, Anna V, 536
Turner, Anna VI, 993
Turner, Archibald VI, 1007
Turner, Arlo V, 1022
Turner, Artheme VI, 1008
Turner, Bartholomew VI, 278
Turner, Bell V, 435
Turner, Benjamin VI, 896
Turner, Benjamin VI, 985
Turner, Benjamin VI, 1007
Turner, Benjamin B. VI, 1008
Turner, Benjamin, Sr. VI, 980
Turner, Benjn. F. VI, 1000
Turner, Bernice IV, 1296
Turner, Betsey VI, 1007
Turner, C. W. V, 435
Turner, Calvin V, 1022
Turner, Capt. ??? VI, 215
Turner, Capt. John B. VI, 892
Turner, Capt. John B. VI, 1008
Turner, Caroline VI, 1008
Turner, Catharine II, 458
Turner, Catharine II, 482
Turner, Catharine II, 672
Turner, Catharine VI, 1007
Turner, Catharine VI, 1008
Turner, Catherine II, 672
Turner, Catherine C. III, 255
Turner, Catherine C. III, 323
Turner, Charity VI, 1008
Turner, Charles W. V, 435
Turner, Charlotte III, 248
Turner, Charlotte III, 323
Turner, Charlotte III, 458
Turner, Charlotte VI, 1000
Turner, Charlotte C. III, 323
Turner, Charlotte H. III, 67
Turner, Charlotte H. III, 323
Turner, Chas. IV, 1341
Turner, Clarence V, 312
Turner, Clarice V, 660
Turner, Clarice V, 716
Turner, Clement VI, 974
Turner, Cora A. V, 435
Turner, Cyrus C. III, 323
Turner, Cyrus C., Jr. III, 141
Turner, Cyrus C., Jr. III, 323
Turner, David I, 340
Turner, David IV, 1265
Turner, David H. I, 440
Turner, Dorothy T. III, 125
Turner, Dorothy T. III, 323
Turner, Doshia VI, 987
Turner, Eber W. V, 536
Turner, Eber Walter V, 536
Turner, Edith I, 440
Turner, Edith I, 454
Turner, Edith I, 866
Turner, Edward II, 482
Turner, Edward II, 672
Turner, Edward Jones V, 466
Turner, Eleanor C. V, 50
Turner, Eleanor C. V, 134
Turner, Elijah V, 536
Turner, Elijah VI, 348
Turner, Elijah VI, 355
Turner, Elijah VI, 904
Turner, Elijah VI, 930
Turner, Elijah VI, 933
Turner, Elijah VI, 966
Turner, Elijah VI, 971
Turner, Elijah VI, 1007
Turner, Elijah VI, 1008
Turner, Elijah H. V, 536
Turner, Elijah H. VI, 928
Turner, Eliza VI, 861
Turner, Eliza VI, 1008
Turner, Elizabeth I Sup 1, 3
Turner, Elizabeth I Sup 1, 6
Turner, Elizabeth II, 736
Turner, Elizabeth II, 771
Turner, Elizabeth V, 648
Turner, Elizabeth VI, 543
Turner, Elizabeth VI, 812
Turner, Elizabeth VI, 875
Turner, Elizabeth VI, 935
Turner, Elizabeth VI, 1007
Turner, Elizabeth VI, 1019
Turner, Elizabeth Johnson VI, 687
Turner, Elizabeth P. VI, 1007
Turner, Ella F. III, 125
Turner, Ella Frances III, 323
Turner, Ellen VI, 85
Turner, Ellen J. VI, 87
Turner, Emily I, 893
Turner, Emily I, 904
Turner, Emma V, 134
Turner, Emma B. VI, 574
Turner, Emma B. VI, 584
Turner, Esther I, 129
Turner, Esther I, 171
Turner, Eudosa VI, 1008
Turner, Eva I, 621
Turner, Eva V, 435
Turner, Eva Lindley I, 642
Turner, Ezekel I, 77
Turner, Ezekieh I, 77
Turner, Ezekiel I, 172
Turner, Ezekiel I, 454
Turner, Ezekiel I, 866
Turner, Ezekiel I, 903
Turner, Ezekiel I, 904
Turner, Fannie Leura V, 536
Turner, Flaves G. IV, 1241
Turner, Flavis IV, 1241
Turner, Flo V, 602
Turner, Frances VI, 860
Turner, Frances VI, 861
Turner, Frances VI, 946
Turner, Frances VI, 949
Turner, Frances VI, 980
Turner, Frances VI, 1007
Turner, Frances L. V, 536
Turner, Frances Marie V, 678
Turner, Frances Marie V, 716
Turner, Francis III, 323
Turner, Frank III, 125
Turner, Frank III, 323
Turner, Franklin VI, 900
Turner, Franklin VI, 1007
Turner, George VI, 917
Turner, George VI, 975
Turner, Gideon VI, 904
Turner, Goodwin VI, 1007
Turner, H. A. VI, 982
Turner, Hannah I, 440
Turner, Hannah V, 1022
Turner, Hardaway A. VI, 905
Turner, Harriett II, 721
Turner, Henderson IV, 1296
Turner, Henry III, 323
Turner, Henry V, 602
Turner, Henry C. III, 67
Turner, Henry C. III, 248
Turner, Henry C. III, 323
Turner, Henry C. III, 458
Turner, Henry Chandlee, Jr. III, 224
Turner, Henry Chandlee, Jr. III, 323
Turner, Herbert VI, 543
Turner, Herbert VI, 687
Turner, Howard H. III, 255
Turner, Howard H. III, 323
Turner, Howard Haines III, 3
Turner, Isabel V, 1022
Turner, Isabell V, 1022
Turner, Isaiah VI, 932
Turner, J. Pinkney I, 621
Turner, Jabez F. I, 440
Turner, Jacob II, 429
Turner, Jacob II, 470
Turner, Jacob II, 672
Turner, Jain I, 866
Turner, James I, 866
Turner, James I, 904
Turner, James IV, 295
Turner, James IV, 501
Turner, James V, 1022
Turner, James VI, 85
Turner, James VI, 861
Turner, James VI, 869
Turner, James VI, 870
Turner, James VI, 873
Turner, James VI, 874
Turner, James VI, 875
Turner, James VI, 876
Turner, James VI, 877
Turner, James VI, 879
Turner, James VI, 880
Turner, James VI, 882
Turner, James VI, 884
Turner, James VI, 885
Turner, James VI, 887
Turner, James VI, 888
Turner, James VI, 889
Turner, James VI, 890
Turner, James VI, 896
Turner, James VI, 899
Turner, James VI, 903
Turner, James VI, 906
Turner, James VI, 907
Turner, James VI, 908
Turner, James VI, 910
Turner, James VI, 911
Turner, James VI, 913
Turner, James VI, 914
Turner, James VI, 915
Turner, James VI, 916
Turner, James VI, 917
Turner, James VI, 919
Turner, James VI, 922
Turner, James VI, 925
Turner, James VI, 927
Turner, James VI, 928
Turner, James VI, 935
Turner, James VI, 939
Turner, James VI, 940
Turner, James VI, 941
Turner, James VI, 942
Turner, James VI, 944
Turner, James VI, 945
Turner, James VI, 946
Turner, James VI, 949
Turner, James VI, 951
Turner, James VI, 952
Turner, James VI, 953
Turner, James VI, 954
Turner, James VI, 955
Turner, James VI, 956
Turner, James VI, 957
Turner, James VI, 958
Turner, James VI, 959
Turner, James VI, 961
Turner, James VI, 962
Turner, James VI, 964
Turner, James VI, 966
Turner, James VI, 971
Turner, James VI, 973
Turner, James VI, 974
Turner, James VI, 975
Turner, James VI, 976
Turner, James VI, 977
Turner, James VI, 981
Turner, James VI, 982
Turner, James VI, 984
Turner, James VI, 986
Turner, James VI, 987
Turner, James VI, 988
Turner, James VI, 990
Turner, James VI, 991
Turner, James VI, 993
Turner, James VI, 995
Turner, James VI, 996
Turner, James VI, 997
Turner, James VI, 998
Turner, James VI, 999
Turner, James VI, 1000
Turner, James VI, 1001
Turner, James VI, 1002
Turner, James VI, 1003
Turner, James VI, 1005
Turner, James VI, 1007
Turner, James VI, 1009

er, James VI, 1011
er, James VI, 1012
er, James VI, 1016
er, James VI, 1017
er, James VI, 1019
er, James VI, 1022
er, James B. VI, 861
er, James D. VI, 973
er, James G. VI, 1007
er, James Sinclair III, 323
er, James, Sr. VI, 344
er, Jane I, 454
er, Jane I, 903
er, Jane II, 787
er, Jane IV, 295
er, Jane IV, 501
er, Jane IV, 1296
er, Jane VI, 1008
er, Jesse V, 648
er, Jesse VI, 938
er, Jesse VI, 1007
er, Jesse H. VI, 920
er, Jesse T. I, 440
er, John I, 123
er, John I, 129
er, John I, 171
er, John II, 1033
er, John IV, 1296
er, John V, 466
er, John V, 536
er, John VI, 87
er, John VI, 215
er, John VI, 355
er, John VI, 798
er, John VI, 861
er, John VI, 867
er, John VI, 875
er, John VI, 876
er, John VI, 906
er, John VI, 913
er, John VI, 943
er, John VI, 946
er, John VI, 959
er, John VI, 963
er, John VI, 974
er, John VI, 992
er, John VI, 1008
er, John B. VI, 892
er, John B. VI, 973
er, John B. VI, 1007
er, John E. III, 501
er, John H. VI, 961
er, John H. VI, 1007
er, John H. VI, 1008
er, Jonas VI, 1008
er, Joseph I, 454
er, Joseph I, 866
er, Joseph I, 903
er, Joseph I, 904
er, Joseph II, 826
er, Joseph W. VI, 1008
er, Josiah VI, 1007
er, Jubal VI, 1007
er, Judith VI, 1007
er, Judy Ann E. VI, 906
er, Juliann VI, 1008
er, Katharine III, 248
er, Katharine III, 323
er, Katharine III, 324
er, Katherine II, 672
er, Keziah VI, 842
er, Laura J. III, 84
er, Laura J. III, 197
er, Laura J. VI, 736
er, Laura J. VI, 790
er, Lela V, 1022
er, Leo VI, 1007
er, Leonard VI, 867
er, Lewis VI, 875
er, Lewis VI, 959
er, Lewis VI, 1007
er, Lewis VI, 1008
er, Lida V, 550
er, Louisa V, 711
er, Louisa V, 716
er, Lucie III, 501
er, Lucy II, 470
er, Lucy II, 672
er, Lucy VI, 892
er, Lucy VI, 963
er, Lucy VI, 1007
er, Lucy C. VI, 1007
er, Lucy Lea II, 825
er, Lurena Margaret VI, 891
er, Luther V, 602
er, Lydia I, 524
er, Lydia I, 579
er, Lydia II, 530
er, Lydia II, 672
er, Lydia V, 398
er, Lydia V, 435
Turner, Lydia V, 1022
Turner, Mabel VI, 215
Turner, Mabel VI, 278
Turner, Magdalene VI, 1007
Turner, Mahala VI, 1007
Turner, Malinda H. VI, 904
Turner, Mamie V, 648
Turner, Margaret IV, 1265
Turner, Margaret V, 716
Turner, Margaret E. V, 536
Turner, Maria IV, 1296
Turner, Mariah VI, 867
Turner, Marian Chapman III, 458
Turner, Mark VI, 1008
Turner, Martha II, 630
Turner, Martha II, 672
Turner, Martha VI, 906
Turner, Martha VI, 948
Turner, Martha VI, 1008
Turner, Martha VI, 1016
Turner, Martha A. VI, 1008
Turner, Martha Ann VI, 973
Turner, Martha E. III, 323
Turner, Mary I, 577
Turner, Mary I, 579
Turner, Mary I, 866
Turner, Mary I, 903
Turner, Mary I, 904
Turner, Mary I, 906
Turner, Mary I, 1101
Turner, Mary I, 1102
Turner, Mary I, 1133
Turner, Mary II, 470
Turner, Mary II, 573
Turner, Mary II, 672
Turner, Mary IV, 295
Turner, Mary IV, 568
Turner, Mary IV, 598
Turner, Mary V, 208
Turner, Mary V, 536
Turner, Mary VI, 215
Turner, Mary VI, 344
Turner, Mary VI, 875
Turner, Mary VI, 905
Turner, Mary VI, 948
Turner, Mary VI, 957
Turner, Mary VI, 1007
Turner, Mary Ann VI, 1000
Turner, Mary Charlotte III, 323
Turner, Mary Emily V, 536
Turner, Mary H. III, 323
Turner, Mary J. VI, 948
Turner, Mary P. V, 648
Turner, Mary S. VI, 974
Turner, Mary S. H. VI, 892
Turner, Mary Thornbrough I, 579
Turner, Mary Turner V, 466
Turner, Matilda VI, 1007
Turner, Matilda V. VI, 961
Turner, Matthew VI, 215
Turner, Meador VI, 971
Turner, Meador VI, 1007
Turner, Melvina IV, 1341
Turner, Micajah VI, 1007
Turner, Mildred O. VI, 949
Turner, Miles I, 866
Turner, Miles I, 904
Turner, Milley VI, 949
Turner, Milley VI, 1007
Turner, Milley Key VI, 1007
Turner, Milly VI, 1007
Turner, Miriam I, 866
Turner, Miriam I, 903
Turner, Molly VI, 919
Turner, Moses I, 735
Turner, Musedora A. VI, 878
Turner, Nancy I, 873
Turner, Nancy I, 904
Turner, Nancy V, 771
Turner, Nancy VI, 87
Turner, Nancy VI, 812
Turner, Nancy VI, 876
Turner, Nancy VI, 900
Turner, Nancy VI, 925
Turner, Nancy VI, 931
Turner, Nancy VI, 946
Turner, Nancy VI, 948
Turner, Nancy VI, 959
Turner, Nancy VI, 1006
Turner, Nancy VI, 1007
Turner, Nancy VI, 1008
Turner, Nancy VI, 1021
Turner, Nancy A. VI, 985
Turner, Nancy J. VI, 877
Turner, Nancy J. VI, 973
Turner, Nancy M. VI, 990
Turner, Nellie V, 208
Turner, Nellie J. V, 187
Turner, Obadiah W. VI, 1008
Turner, Obediah W. VI, 891
Turner, Parthena VI, 1008
Turner, Patsey VI, 1007
Turner, Patsy VI, 1007
Turner, Peggy VI, 1007
Turner, Percy VI, 85
Turner, Phebe E. III, 501
Turner, Piety VI, 1007
Turner, Polly VI, 861
Turner, Polly VI, 935
Turner, Polly VI, 1007
Turner, Polly VI, 1008
Turner, Priscilla V, 536
Turner, Rachel II, 545
Turner, Rachel II, 672
Turner, Rachel VI, 1007
Turner, Rebecca II, 672
Turner, Rebecca II, 826
Turner, Rebecca IV, 449
Turner, Rebecca IV, 451
Turner, Rebecca VI, 87
Turner, Rebecca VI, 818
Turner, Rebecca VI, 938
Turner, Rebecca VI, 971
Turner, Rebecca B. VI, 989
Turner, Rev. James VI, 949
Turner, Rhoda VI, 932
Turner, Rhoda VI, 992
Turner, Richard VI, 344
Turner, Richard VI, 948
Turner, Richard VI, 987
Turner, Richard VI, 1007
Turner, Richard T., Jr. III, 323
Turner, Richd. I, 90
Turner, Robert II, 429
Turner, Robert II, 448
Turner, Robert II, 672
Turner, Robert VI, 87
Turner, Robert VI, 812
Turner, Robert Chapman III, 323
Turner, Ruth I, 451
Turner, Ruth I, 454
Turner, Ruth I, 866
Turner, Ruth I, 883
Turner, Ruth I, 904
Turner, Sallie III, 323
Turner, Sallie V, 435
Turner, Sally VI, 924
Turner, Sally VI, 933
Turner, Sally VI, 1007
Turner, Samuel S. VI, 1008
Turner, Sarah VI, 355
Turner, Sarah VI, 896
Turner, Sarah VI, 901
Turner, Sarah VI, 949
Turner, Sarah VI, 1008
Turner, Sarah A. III, 141
Turner, Sarah A. III, 323
Turner, Sarah B. VI, 928
Turner, Sarah E. VI, 85
Turner, Sophia IV, 1152
Turner, Sophia IV, 1189
Turner, Stanley IV, 1241
Turner, Stockley VI, 1007
Turner, Sucky VI, 964
Turner, Susan V, 435
Turner, Susan V, 602
Turner, Susanna II, 429
Turner, Susanna VI, 993
Turner, Susanna Jones V, 466
Turner, Tabitha VI, 930
Turner, Thamer I, 172
Turner, Theodosha VI, 966
Turner, Thomas VI, 275
Turner, Thomas VI, 278
Turner, Thomas W. VI, 1008
Turner, Virginia A. III, 224
Turner, Virginia A. III, 323
Turner, Virginia Ann III, 323
Turner, Walter I, 842
Turner, Walter I, 903
Turner, Wililam VI, 1007
Turner, William I, 440
Turner, William I, 454
Turner, William I, 866
Turner, William I, 903
Turner, William VI, 964
Turner, William VI, 1006
Turner, William VI, 1008
Turner, William VI, 1016
Turner, William G. VI, 1008
Turner, William H. VI, 961
Turner, William P. M. VI, 1019
Turner, Willie III, 501
Turner, Wilson VI, 1007
Turner, Zachariah VI, 87
Turney, Vashti E. IV, 501
Turney, William IV, 501
Turney, William B. IV, 501
Turning, Elizabeth W. VI, 787
Turning, Elizabeth W. VI, 791
Turnpenny, Ann II, 822
Turnpenny, Frederick II, 932
Turnpenny, John II, 824
Turnpenny, John II, 932
Turnpenny, Joseph C. II, 932
Turnpenny, Joseph Clarbour II, 932
Turnpenny, Margaret II, 824
Turnpenny, Tabitha II, 824
Turnpenny, Tabitha II, 932
Turpin, ??? C. VI, 903
Turpin, Betsey VI, 926
Turpin, Betsey VI, 1007
Turpin, Calohill VI, 1007
Turpin, Calvin VI, 1007
Turpin, Celinda VI, 1007
Turpin, Daniel VI, 1007
Turpin, David VI, 861
Turpin, Elisha VI, 1007
Turpin, Elisha G. VI, 939
Turpin, Elisha G. VI, 961
Turpin, Elivira VI, 1007
Turpin, Eliza VI, 1007
Turpin, Eliza W. VI, 1007
Turpin, Elizabeth IV, 501
Turpin, Elizabeth V, 937
Turpin, Elizabeth VI, 983
Turpin, Elizabeth A. VI, 930
Turpin, Fannie V, 363
Turpin, Frances V, 349
Turpin, Frances V, 363
Turpin, Frances VI, 1007
Turpin, Ida B. V, 713
Turpin, Ida Belle V, 363
Turpin, Ida Belle V, 713
Turpin, Ida Belle V, 716
Turpin, John VI, 883
Turpin, John VI, 930
Turpin, John VI, 964
Turpin, John VI, 970
Turpin, John VI, 991
Turpin, John VI, 995
Turpin, John VI, 996
Turpin, John VI, 1007
Turpin, John D. VI, 1007
Turpin, John W. VI, 930
Turpin, John W. VI, 1007
Turpin, Josiah VI, 1007
Turpin, Lucetta S. VI, 1007
Turpin, Lucy VI, 869
Turpin, Lucy VI, 892
Turpin, Margaret VI, 1007
Turpin, Martha VI, 816
Turpin, Martha A. VI, 1014
Turpin, Mary VI, 861
Turpin, Mary VI, 1018
Turpin, Mary Ann Eliza VI, 983
Turpin, Mary M. VI, 1007
Turpin, Matilda VI, 1007
Turpin, Meador VI, 1007
Turpin, Mildred A. VI, 1007
Turpin, Nancy VI, 861
Turpin, Philip VI, 998
Turpin, Philip VI, 1007
Turpin, Philip VI, 1014
Turpin, Phillip VI, 930
Turpin, Phillip VI, 1018
Turpin, Polly VI, 1007
Turpin, Richd. L. VI, 1007
Turpin, Roland VI, 1007
Turpin, Rolin G. VI, 903
Turpin, Sarah VI, 902
Turpin, Sarah VI, 1007
Turpin, Sarah A. VI, 903
Turpin, Sarah P. VI, 1018
Turpin, Spotwood H. VI, 1007
Turpin, Thomas VI, 869
Turpin, Thomas VI, 926
Turpin, Thomas VI, 983
Turpin, Thomas VI, 1007
Turpin, Thomas VI, 1018
Turpin, Vincent VI, 1007
Turpin, William III, 324
Turpin, William VI, 983
Turpin, William A. VI, 869
Turpin, William A. VI, 983
Turpin, William C. VI, 930
Turpin, Willis C. VI, 861
Turpin, Willis C. VI, 1018
Turrell, Frances E. III, 458
Turrell, Franklin S. III, 458
Turrell, Henry VI, 215
Turrell, Huldah C. III, 458
Turrell, Jesse M. III, 458
Turrell, Jonathan III, 458
Turrell, Lucy III, 458
Turrell, Sarah VI, 215
Turrell, Stephen H. III, 458
Turrence, Sarah VI, 797
Turtle, Alfred III, 324
Turtle, Arabella III, 324
Turtle, Elizabeth VI, 453
Turtle, Emily III, 324
Turtle, Emily L. III, 324
Turtle, Henry F. III, 324
Turtle, Herbert III, 324
Turtle, Herbert S. III, 324
Turtle, Lancelot James III, 324
Tustin, John II, 672
Tustin, Sarah II, 524
Tustin, Sarah II, 672
Tuthill, Elma W. III, 324
Tuthill, Elma Willets III, 29
Tuthill, Sylvester Davis III, 29
Tuthill, Sylvester Davis III, 324
Tutness, Robert II, 671
Tutney, Mary II, 1033
Tutterow, Rebecca I, 990
Tutterow, Rebecca I, 999
Tuttle, ??? I, 30
Tuttle, Asa C. II, 771
Tuttle, Asa C. IV, 780
Tuttle, Clara Alberta I, 19
Tuttle, Clara Alberta I, 30
Tuttle, Cornelia III, 315
Tuttle, Daniel III, 393
Tuttle, Daniel III, 458
Tuttle, Daniel IV, 1341
Tuttle, Donald V, 674
Tuttle, Donald V, 716
Tuttle, Dora V, 1022
Tuttle, Eliza Ann V, 1022
Tuttle, Ella V, 1022
Tuttle, Esther B. IV, 1189
Tuttle, Esther B. IV, 1196
Tuttle, Harry Walter IV, 780
Tuttle, James V, 1022
Tuttle, Joseph V, 1022
Tuttle, Lucy V, 1022
Tuttle, Lydia IV, 780
Tuttle, Mark I, 26
Tuttle, Martha V, 1022
Tuttle, Mary V, 1022
Tuttle, Mary E. I, 26
Tuttle, Mrs. Nancy IV, 1341
Tuttle, Nancy IV, 1341
Tuttle, Nancy V, 1022
Tuttle, Nancy E. V, 1022
Tuttle, Priscilla V, 1022
Tuttle, Ruth V, 674
Tuttle, Ruth V, 716
Tuttle, Ruth G. V, 938
Tuttle, Samuel V, 1022
Tuttle, Sarah H. III, 393
Tuttle, Sarah H. III, 458
Tuttle, Thomas S. IV, 780
Tuttle, William V, 1022
Tuze, Lydia II, 672
Twaddell, Eliza E. II, 932
Twaddell, Eliza Emily II, 932
Twaddell, Frances D. II, 932
Twaddle, Frances D. II, 932
Twedy, Allen VI, 860
Twedy, Ann VI, 813
Twedy, Bennett VI, 861
Twedy, John VI, 811
Twedy, Robert VI, 818
Twedy, Robert VI, 865
Twedy, Robert VI, 866
Twedy, Robert VI, 867
Twedy, Sally W. IV, 295
Twedy, Sally W. IV, 307
Twedy, Samuel VI, 813
Twedy, Smith B. VI, 851
Tweed, W. W. IV, 1265
Tweed, Wm. M. IV, 1265
Tweed, Wm. M. IV, 1341
Tweedy, Alice IV, 295
Tweedy, Allen VI, 853
Tweedy, Allen VI, 861
Tweedy, Ann M. VI, 853
Tweedy, Barnett VI, 861
Tweedy, Bennett VI, 801
Tweedy, Bennett VI, 857
Tweedy, David III, 324
Tweedy, David III, 338
Tweedy, Elizabeth VI, 861
Tweedy, Elizabeth Ann III, 324
Tweedy, Elizabeth Ann III, 338
Tweedy, Fanny VI, 803
Tweedy, George IV, 295
Tweedy, Hannah G. IV, 295
Tweedy, John VI, 805
Tweedy, John VI, 861
Tweedy, John R. VI, 861
Tweedy, Joseph VI, 851
Tweedy, Joseph VI, 861
Tweedy, Kisiah VI, 803
Tweedy, Mabel III, 324
Tweedy, Martha VI, 861
Tweedy, Mary VI, 807
Tweedy, Mary VI, 861
Tweedy, Mary Ann III, 324

Tweedy, Mary F. VI, 829
Tweedy, Nancy VI, 851
Tweedy, Polly VI, 861
Tweedy, Richard III, 324
Tweedy, Robert VI, 807
Tweedy, Robert VI, 849
Tweedy, Robert VI, 851
Tweedy, Robert VI, 861
Tweedy, Robert C. VI, 861
Tweedy, Sally W. IV, 295
Tweedy, Sarah IV, 295
Tweedy, Sarah IV, 307
Tweedy, Sarah W. IV, 229
Tweedy, Sarah W. IV, 295
Tweedy, Smith G. VI, 861
Tweedy, Smith I. VI, 853
Tweedy, Susanna VI, 861
Tweedy, Thomas I, 92
Tweedy, Visey VI, 851
Tweedy, Wilmer IV, 295
Tweedy, Wilmer J. IV, 295
Tweedy, Winford IV, 295
Tweedy, Winifred IV, 295
Twine, Mary I, 77
Twine, Mary R. I, 77
Twine???, Martha R. I, 54
Twine???, Mary I, 49
Twine???, Mary I, 77
Twine???, Mary R. I, 77
Twining, Abigail VI, 453
Twining, Charles II, 1082
Twining, David Palmer II, 1034
Twining, Elias B. II, 824
Twining, Elias B. II, 932
Twining, Elizabeth II, 1082
Twining, Hannah II, 971
Twining, Hannah II, 1045
Twining, Hannah II, 1062
Twining, Hannah A. II, 932
Twining, Hannah Ann II, 932
Twining, Hannah B. II, 971
Twining, Hannah B. II, 1062
Twining, Hannah C. II, 852
Twining, Hannah C. II, 932
Twining, Henry II, 672
Twining, Henry II, 932
Twining, Jacob II, 971
Twining, Jacob II, 1045
Twining, Jacob II, 1062
Twining, Jane II, 971
Twining, Jane S. II, 932
Twining, Jesse II, 971
Twining, Jesse B. II, 1045
Twining, Jesse B. II, 1062
Twining, Letitia II, 1082
Twining, Letitia W. II, 1082
Twining, Marcy VI, 429
Twining, Marcy VI, 453
Twining, Mary Ann II, 1075
Twining, Mary Anna II, 1082
Twining, Mary Elizabeth II, 954
Twining, Priscilla II, 971
Twining, Priscilla II, 1045
Twining, Priscilla II, 1062
Twining, Rebecca Estella II, 1075
Twining, Rebecca Estella II, 1082
Twining, Stephen VI, 453
Twining, Stephen B. II, 1082
Twining, Susannah II, 1034
Twining, Tamer II, 1019
Twining, Tamer II, 1034
Twining, Wm. W. II, 1075
Twining, Wm. W. II, 1082
Twinning, Henry II, 771
Twitchel, Sarah IV, 1382
Twitchell, Hannah IV, 780
Twomey, Sarah G. II, 771
Twopence, Patsey Mosely VI, 816
Twopence, Rocksinancey VI, 816
Twyford, Elizabeth IV, 354
Tylar, Rebecca II, 107
Tyle, Thomas V, 1022
Tylee, Eliz. III, 324
Tylee, Elizabeth II, 268
Tylee, Elizabeth III, 324
Tylee, James II, 268
Tylee, Mary II, 268
Tylee, Nathaniel II, 268
Tylee, Thomas II, 672
Tylee, Thomas III, 324
Tyler, Abbie II, 932
Tyler, Abbie Woolman II, 824
Tyler, Abigail II, 84
Tyler, Abigail II, 108
Tyler, Alice Ann II, 932
Tyler, Alice Anna II, 932
Tyler, Amanda II, 159
Tyler, Ann II, 45
Tyler, Ann II, 107
Tyler, Ann II, 138
Tyler, Ann II, 932
Tyler, Ann VI, 923
Tyler, Ann Cash VI, 974
Tyler, Anna II, 127
Tyler, Anna II, 149
Tyler, Anna II, 159
Tyler, Anne II, 107
Tyler, Anne VI, 861
Tyler, Benj. II, 138
Tyler, Benj. VI, 898
Tyler, Benjamin II, 44
Tyler, Benjamin II, 45
Tyler, Benjamin II, 65
Tyler, Benjamin II, 106
Tyler, Benjamin II, 107
Tyler, Benjamin II, 108
Tyler, Benjamin II, 138
Tyler, Benjamin II, 149
Tyler, Benjamin II, 156
Tyler, Benjamin II, 159
Tyler, Benjamin A. II, 139
Tyler, Benjamin A. II, 156
Tyler, Benjamin A. II, 159
Tyler, Benjamin Allen II, 139
Tyler, Benjamin Allen II, 159
Tyler, Benjamin Allen, III II, 139
Tyler, Benjamin H. II, 159
Tyler, Benjamin Howard II, 824
Tyler, Benjamin L. II, 127
Tyler, Bertha IV, 1265
Tyler, Beulah II, 127
Tyler, Beulah II, 133
Tyler, Beulah II, 138
Tyler, Beulah II, 139
Tyler, Beulah A. II, 139
Tyler, Beulah Ann II, 125
Tyler, Beulah Ann II, 149
Tyler, Beulah Ann II, 159
Tyler, Catharine II, 45
Tyler, Catharine II, 100
Tyler, Catharine II, 108
Tyler, Catrin II, 79
Tyler, Catrin II, 107
Tyler, Charles H. II, 139
Tyler, Charles H. II, 159
Tyler, Charles H. II, 824
Tyler, Charles H. II, 932
Tyler, Chas. II, 932
Tyler, Daniel VI, 884
Tyler, Daniel VI, 974
Tyler, Dorothea II, 45
Tyler, Dorothea II, 125
Tyler, Dosa VI, 900
Tyler, Doshia VI, 1008
Tyler, Edith II, 105
Tyler, Edith II, 107
Tyler, Edith W. II, 159
Tyler, Edward B. III, 324
Tyler, Elizabeth II, 44
Tyler, Elizabeth II, 45
Tyler, Elizabeth II, 67
Tyler, Elizabeth II, 107
Tyler, Elizabeth II, 108
Tyler, Elizabeth II, 139
Tyler, Elizabeth C. II, 159
Tyler, Elizabeth C. II, 932
Tyler, Elizabeth F. VI, 900
Tyler, Elizabeth H. II, 824
Tyler, Elizabeth M. III, 324
Tyler, Emma II, 824
Tyler, Emma Dudley II, 824
Tyler, Emma H. II, 824
Tyler, Emma H. II, 932
Tyler, Frances VI, 1017
Tyler, Geo. H. II, 932
Tyler, George II, 159
Tyler, George H. II, 139
Tyler, George H. II, 159
Tyler, George H. II, 824
Tyler, George H. II, 932
Tyler, George W. II, 139
Tyler, George W. II, 159
Tyler, George W. II, 824
Tyler, George W. II, 932
Tyler, Grace II, 108
Tyler, Hannah II, 40
Tyler, Hannah II, 45
Tyler, Hannah II, 93
Tyler, Hannah II, 108
Tyler, Hannah Ann II, 138
Tyler, Hannah Ann II, 818
Tyler, Hannah B. II, 159
Tyler, Hannah Buzby II, 139
Tyler, Hannah Buzby II, 156
Tyler, Hannah Buzby II, 159
Tyler, Hannah G. II, 100
Tyler, Hannah G. II, 108
Tyler, Hannah Gillasphey II, 45
Tyler, Hariet I, 1162
Tyler, Harriet I, 1162
Tyler, Hope II, 647
Tyler, Hope II, 672
Tyler, James II, 45
Tyler, James II, 107
Tyler, James Walker II, 824
Tyler, James Walker II, 932
Tyler, James, Jr. II, 108
Tyler, Job II, 44
Tyler, Job II, 45
Tyler, Job II, 52
Tyler, Job II, 108
Tyler, Job, Jr. II, 108
Tyler, Job, Sr. II, 45
Tyler, Johanna II, 45
Tyler, John II, 44
Tyler, John II, 45
Tyler, John II, 84
Tyler, John II, 107
Tyler, John II, 108
Tyler, John II, 109
Tyler, John II, 127
Tyler, John II, 133
Tyler, John II, 138
Tyler, John II, 139
Tyler, John II, 149
Tyler, John II, 159
Tyler, John VI, 874
Tyler, John VI, 947
Tyler, John VI, 950
Tyler, John VI, 1008
Tyler, Jonathan II, 932
Tyler, Joseph VI, 345
Tyler, Joseph VI, 1022
Tyler, Joseph B. II, 139
Tyler, Joseph B. II, 159
Tyler, Joseph B. II, 824
Tyler, Joseph B. II, 932
Tyler, Joseph W. VI, 896
Tyler, Juana VI, 884
Tyler, Katrine II, 45
Tyler, Leatitia II, 44
Tyler, Leatitia II, 73
Tyler, Leatitia II, 107
Tyler, Lidya II, 83
Tyler, Louisa VI, 898
Tyler, Lucy A. II, 139
Tyler, Lucy A. H. II, 159
Tyler, Lydia II, 45
Tyler, Lydia II, 108
Tyler, Lydia II, 139
Tyler, Lydia K. II, 159
Tyler, Margaret II, 139
Tyler, Margaret E. II, 127
Tyler, Margaret H. II, 159
Tyler, Maria IV, 1296
Tyler, Martha I, 1162
Tyler, Martha II, 45
Tyler, Martha II, 107
Tyler, Martha Ann I, 1162
Tyler, Martha J. V, 758
Tyler, Martha J. V, 771
Tyler, Martha P. I, 579
Tyler, Mary II, 44
Tyler, Mary II, 45
Tyler, Mary II, 52
Tyler, Mary II, 106
Tyler, Mary II, 107
Tyler, Mary II, 108
Tyler, Mary A. II, 125
Tyler, Mary A. II, 721
Tyler, Mary Amanda II, 139
Tyler, Mary Amanda II, 159
Tyler, Mary Amanda II, 824
Tyler, Mary Amanda II, 932
Tyler, Mary Anna II, 932
Tyler, Mary D. II, 139
Tyler, Mary H. II, 133
Tyler, Mary H. II, 138
Tyler, Mary Haines II, 139
Tyler, Mary S. II, 159
Tyler, Maryh II, 138
Tyler, Melicent II, 156
Tyler, Melicent II, 159
Tyler, Mercy II, 65
Tyler, Mercy II, 107
Tyler, Milicent II, 139
Tyler, Millicent B. II, 159
Tyler, Mrs. Doshia VI, 975
Tyler, Mrs. Eudotia VI, 923
Tyler, Nancy I, 1162
Tyler, Naomi II, 45
Tyler, Naomi II, 65
Tyler, Naomi II, 107
Tyler, Naomy II, 44
Tyler, Naomy II, 84
Tyler, Naomy II, 107
Tyler, Nelson C. VI, 1008
Tyler, Philip II, 45
Tyler, Philip II, 65
Tyler, Philip II, 107
Tyler, Phillip II, 107
Tyler, Polly E. VI, 1008
Tyler, Rachel II, 44
Tyler, Rachel II, 52
Tyler, Rachel II, 93
Tyler, Rachel II, 96
Tyler, Rachel II, 107
Tyler, Rachel II, 108
Tyler, Rebecca II, 19
Tyler, Rebecca II, 107
Tyler, Rebeckah II, 45
Tyler, Rebekah II, 107
Tyler, Rhoda VI, 975
Tyler, Richard II, 45
Tyler, Robert H. II, 159
Tyler, Robert Haines II, 139
Tyler, Ruth II, 45
Tyler, Ruth II, 107
Tyler, Ruth II, 109
Tyler, Samuel II, 45
Tyler, Samuel II, 107
Tyler, Samuel VI, 861
Tyler, Sarah II, 108
Tyler, Sherman I, 1162
Tyler, Susan III, 501
Tyler, Susannah VI, 950
Tyler, Temperance II, 107
Tyler, Temperance II, 110
Tyler, W. Russell III, 324
Tyler, Walter Dudley II, 824
Tyler, William II, 45
Tyler, William Buzby II, 824
Tyler, William Penn II, 824
Tyler, Wilson M. III, 324
Tyler, Wm. II, 100
Tyler, Wm. II, 107
Tyler, Wm. II, 108
Tyler, Wm. II, 932
Tyler, Wm. B. II, 932
Tyler, Wm. F. II, 159
Tyler, Wm. Fogg II, 139
Tyler, Wm. Penn II, 932
Tyles, Elizabeth II, 260
Tyles, Elizabeth II, 268
Tyles, James II, 260
Tyles, James II, 268
Tyles, Nathaniel II, 260
Tyles, Nathaniel II, 268
Tyley, Edward II, 73
Tyley, Edward II, 108
Tyley, Edward II, 429
Tyley, James II, 268
Tyley, Margaret II, 108
Tyley, Margret II, 108
Tyley, Naomy II, 84
Tyley, Naomy II, 108
Tyley, Rebecca II, 73
Tyley, Rebecca II, 108
Tyllier, Thomas II, 427
Tylor, Martha P. I, 579
Tylor, Mary II, 49
Tylor, Phillip II, 105
Tylor, Phillip II, 107
Tylor, Rachel II, 103
Tylor, Rachel II, 105
Tylor, Rachel II, 107
Tylor, Rebekah II, 49
Tylor, Wm. II, 49
Tylor, Wm. II, 107
Tyman, Elizabeth VI, 329
Tyman, Elizabeth VI, 338
Tyman, Lyman VI, 344
Tymanus, Margery IV, 112
Tymanus, Margery IV, 115
Tyndale, Mary II, 846
Tyndale, Mary II, 933
Tynes, Edith VI, 861
Tynes, Obediah VI, 861
Tynes, Samuel T. VI, 816
Tyo, S. M. V, 286
Tyo, Thomas V, 1022
Tyre, Elizabeth II, 117
Tyre, Elizabeth II, 125
Tyree, Benjamin VI, 861
Tyree, Cora V. VI, 830
Tyree, David VI, 836
Tyree, Elizabeth VI, 861
Tyree, John H. VI, 830
Tyree, Mary VI, 861
Tyree, Matilda VI, 861
Tyree, Mildred VI, 319
Tyree, Mildred VI, 327
Tyree, Mildred VI, 344
Tyree, Mildred VI, 861
Tyree, Milly VI, 344
Tyree, Pleasant VI, 861
Tyree, Polly VI, 861
Tyree, Richard VI, 344
Tyree, Richard VI, 861
Tyree, Richmond VI, 861
Tyree, Samuel C. VI, 861
Tyrel, Deborah I, 902
Tyrrell, Deborah I, 577
Tysen, Samuel IV, 112
Tyser, George Councilman I,
Tyser, Harris I, 424
Tyser, Joseph Allen I, 424
Tyser, Lydia I, 424
Tyson, Aaron I, 424
Tyson, Aaron I, 673
Tyson, Aaron I, 690
Tyson, Abigail II, 933
Tyson, Abigail C. II, 933
Tyson, Abigail R. II, 933
Tyson, Abigail R. II, 935
Tyson, Ann I, 366
Tyson, Ann I, 424
Tyson, Ann II, 429
Tyson, Ann II, 672
Tyson, Ann IV, 112
Tyson, Ann VI, 738
Tyson, Ann VI, 787
Tyson, Anna Gertrude II, 82
Tyson, Anna L. II, 933
Tyson, Anthony Morris II, 8
Tyson, Arcada I, 424
Tyson, Benj. I, 366
Tyson, Benjamin I, 424
Tyson, Benjamin II, 672
Tyson, Bertha III, 414
Tyson, Bertha III, 458
Tyson, Calvin II, 824
Tyson, Caroline II, 860
Tyson, Caroline II, 933
Tyson, Catharine Ellen II, 9
Tyson, Catherine Ellen II, 8
Tyson, Charles II, 429
Tyson, Charles B. II, 933
Tyson, Charles J. II, 933
Tyson, Charles M. IV, 112
Tyson, Charles S. VI, 787
Tyson, Chas. B. II, 933
Tyson, Chas. Barclay II, 824
Tyson, Chas. J. II, 933
Tyson, Chas. J. III, 458
Tyson, Chas. Parry II, 933
Tyson, Chester J. III, 414
Tyson, Chester J. III, 458
Tyson, Comley II, 921
Tyson, Comly II, 819
Tyson, Comly II, 914
Tyson, Comly II, 921
Tyson, Comly II, 933
Tyson, Cornelius I, 366
Tyson, Cornelius I, 424
Tyson, Cornelius I, 690
Tyson, Daniel II, 429
Tyson, Daniel II, 672
Tyson, Daniel II, 933
Tyson, Daniel C. II, 933
Tyson, Daniel T. IV, 112
Tyson, Deborah II, 429
Tyson, Deborah II, 704
Tyson, Derrick II, 672
Tyson, Edwin C. III, 415
Tyson, Edwin C. III, 458
Tyson, Edwin Comly II, 824
Tyson, Eleanor II, 772
Tyson, Eleanor VI, 752
Tyson, Eleanor L. II, 763
Tyson, Eleanor L. II, 772
Tyson, Eleanor Richards II, 8
Tyson, Elenor II, 734
Tyson, Elenor II, 772
Tyson, Elijah II, 780
Tyson, Elijah II, 822
Tyson, Elijah II, 824
Tyson, Elisha II, 591
Tyson, Elisha II, 672
Tyson, Elisha II, 782
Tyson, Elisha, Jr. II, 825
Tyson, Eliza II, 824
Tyson, Eliza II, 933
Tyson, Elizabeth I, 401
Tyson, Elizabeth I, 424
Tyson, Elizabeth II, 474
Tyson, Elizabeth II, 543
Tyson, Elizabeth II, 672
Tyson, Elizabeth II, 802
Tyson, Elizabeth II, 821
Tyson, Elizabeth VI, 787
Tyson, Elizabeth VI, 1008
Tyson, Elizabeth Jane II, 796
Tyson, Emily II, 856
Tyson, Emily II, 933
Tyson, Emma II, 825
Tyson, Emma II, 933
Tyson, Emma II, 935
Tyson, Esther II, 429
Tyson, Esther F. II, 772
Tyson, Esther F. IV, 112
Tyson, Ezekial II, 933
Tyson, Ezekiel II, 860
Tyson, Ezekiel II, 933
Tyson, George II, 429

n, George II, 594
n, George II, 672
n, George II, 772
n, George II, 933
n, George W. II, 933
n, Hannah II, 429
n, Hannah II, 594
n, Hannah II, 672
n, Hannah II, 823
n, Harper VI, 738
n, Harper VI, 787
n, Isaac II, 591
n, Isaac II, 618
n, Isaac II, 672
n, Isaac II, 802
n, Isaac II, 824
n, Isaac G. II, 933
n, Jacob I, 424
n, Jacob II, 672
n, Jacob II, 772
n, Jacob II, 824
n, Jacob II, 933
n, James II, 618
n, James II, 672
n, James IV, 112
n, James, Jr. IV, 112
n, Jane I, 366
n, Jane I, 397
n, Jane I, 410
n, Jane I, 424
n, Jane I, 430
n, Jane I, 690
n, Jane VI, 787
n, Jean I, 419
n, Jean I, 424
n, Jesse VI, 756
n, Job II, 429
n, Job R. II, 734
n, Job R. II, 772
n, Job R. IV, 112
n, John I, 424
n, John II, 824
n, John Kirk II, 824
n, John R. II, 933
n, Jonathan II, 721
n, Jonathan II, 824
n, Joseph II, 429
n, Joseph II, 672
n, Joseph II, 734
n, Joseph II, 772
n, Joseph IV, 112
n, Joseph, Jr. IV, 112
n, Lena I, 628
n, Lena V, 716
n, Letitia E. VI, 787
n, Levi II, 429
n, Levi II, 594
n, Levi II, 672
n, Levi II, 772
n, Levi II, 777
n, Lucretia II, 828
n, Lydia I, 424
n, Lydia I, 673
n, Lydia I, 690
n, Lydia II, 860
n, Lydia II, 933
n, Macklon VI, 1008
n, Margaret II, 813
n, Margaret VI, 756
n, Margaret C. II, 734
n, Mariah E. III, 458
n, Marion II, 824
n, Marshall II, 824
n, Marshall II, 933
n, Martha II, 780
n, Martha II, 822
n, Martha II, 824
n, Martha II, 928
n, Martha II, 933
n, Martha Ann VI, 787
n, Martha H. II, 721
n, Martha H. II, 772
n, Mary II, 591
n, Mary II, 672
n, Mary II, 734
n, Mary II, 772
n, Mary II, 824
n, Mary II, 871
n, Mary II, 933
n, Mary A. II, 824
n, Mary A. VI, 787
n, Mary Ann II, 429
n, Mary Ann II, 772
n, Mary Elizabeth VI, 738
n, Mary Elizabeth VI, 787
n, Mary J. II, 933
n, Mary J. III, 324
n, Mary Jones II, 824
n, Mary Morris II, 933
n, Mary S. II, 933
n, Mary Shoemaker II, 824

Tyson, Mary W. III, 415
Tyson, Mary W. III, 458
Tyson, Matthew S. II, 933
Tyson, Matthew Smith II, 824
Tyson, Nathan C. II, 933
Tyson, Nathan C. II, 935
Tyson, Nathaniel E. VI, 787
Tyson, Oswald E. IV, 1080
Tyson, Patience II, 672
Tyson, Patience, Jr. II, 591
Tyson, Patience, Jr. II, 672
Tyson, Phebe V, 341
Tyson, Phebe V, 363
Tyson, Priscilla II, 797
Tyson, Rachel I, 375
Tyson, Rachel I, 424
Tyson, Rachel II, 824
Tyson, Rachel VI, 763
Tyson, Rachel VI, 787
Tyson, Rachel A. II, 933
Tyson, Rachel G. II, 921
Tyson, Rachel G. II, 933
Tyson, Rachel Griffith II, 819
Tyson, Rachel Thomas II, 802
Tyson, Rebecca I, 424
Tyson, Rebecca II, 780
Tyson, Rebecca II, 824
Tyson, Rebecca II, 933
Tyson, Rebecca J. II, 869
Tyson, Rebecca J. II, 933
Tyson, Rebecca L. II, 933
Tyson, Rebecca T. II, 833
Tyson, Rebecca T. II, 933
Tyson, Rebecca W. II, 933
Tyson, Rebecca Webster II, 797
Tyson, Rebeckah I, 366
Tyson, Richard I, 424
Tyson, Richard II, 429
Tyson, Robert II, 824
Tyson, Ruth Anna B. II, 914
Tyson, Ruth Anna B. II, 933
Tyson, Ruth Anna Brown II, 817
Tyson, Ruth Anna S. II, 933
Tyson, Ruthanna B. II, 933
Tyson, Samuel II, 429
Tyson, Samuel IV, 112
Tyson, Samuel E. VI, 763
Tyson, Samuel E. VI, 787
Tyson, Samuel H. IV, 112
Tyson, Sarah II, 618
Tyson, Sarah II, 672
Tyson, Sarah II, 772
Tyson, Sarah II, 807
Tyson, Sarah II, 824
Tyson, Sarah II, 838
Tyson, Sarah II, 933
Tyson, Sarah Ann II, 933
Tyson, Sarah Ann II, 1034
Tyson, Sarah Ann III, 324
Tyson, Sarah Ann, Jr. II, 933
Tyson, Sarah B. II, 429
Tyson, Sarah B. II, 594
Tyson, Sarah B. II, 672
Tyson, Sarah Harper II, 807
Tyson, Sarah Knight II, 824
Tyson, Sarah Morris II, 825
Tyson, Sarah Morris II, 933
Tyson, Sarah S. II, 825
Tyson, Sarah S. II, 838
Tyson, Sarah S. II, 933
Tyson, Seberah I, 424
Tyson, Susan II, 819
Tyson, Susan II, 824
Tyson, Susan G. II, 326
Tyson, Susan G. II, 921
Tyson, Susan G. II, 933
Tyson, Susan J. II, 914
Tyson, Susan J. II, 933
Tyson, Susan S. II, 933
Tyson, Tacy VI, 662
Tyson, Tacy VI, 739
Tyson, Tacy VI, 752
Tyson, Tacy VI, 767
Tyson, Thomas I, 424
Tyson, Thomas, Jr. I, 424
Tyson, Thos. II, 838
Tyson, Thos. II, 933
Tyson, Wd. Deborah II, 618
Tyson, Wd. Deborah II, 672
Tyson, Wd. Martha II, 822
Tyson, William I, 424
Tyson, William II, 429
Tyson, William VI, 787
Tyson, William R. IV, 112
Tyson, Wm. I, 424
Tyson, Wm. II, 672
Tyson, Wm. VI, 787

Ubderhill, Capt. John III, 196
Ubderhill, Helena III, 196

Udall, Annie T. III, 410
Udall, Annie T. III, 458
Udall, Cath. III, 501
Udall, Catharine III, 324
Udall, Catharine III, 443
Udall, Catharine III, 458
Udall, Charles III, 324
Udall, Charles III, 443
Udall, Charles III, 458
Udall, Charles III, 501
Udall, Deborah III, 324
Udall, Deborah III, 411
Udall, Deborah III, 435
Udall, Deborah III, 458
Udall, Deborah III, 468
Udall, Deborah III, 469
Udall, Deborah III, 501
Udall, Deborah III, 505
Udall, Hannah III, 324
Udall, Hannah III, 505
Udall, Jacob III, 497
Udall, James III, 458
Udall, Jericho III, 324
Udall, John C. III, 324
Udall, Joseph III, 458
Udall, Joseph III, 501
Udall, Joseph III, 505
Udall, Margaret A. III, 458
Udall, Maria III, 324
Udall, Mary III, 497
Udall, Phebe III, 458
Udall, Phebe III, 501
Udall, Phebe III, 505
Udall, Richard III, 410
Udall, Richard III, 435
Udall, Richard III, 458
Udall, Richard III, 501
Udall, Richard III, 505
Udall, Sarah III, 202
Udall, Sarah III, 324
Udall, Sarah III, 454
Udall, Sarah III, 458
Udall, Sarah III, 501
Udall, Susan III, 324
Udall, Susanna III, 454
Udall, Susanna III, 458
Udall, Susanna III, 501
Udall, Susannah III, 497
Udall, Thomas III, 454
Udall, Thomas III, 458
Udall, Thomas III, 501
Udall, Thomas P. III, 458
Udell, Phebe III, 501
Ufford, Bertha III, 324
Ufford, Bertha H. III, 324
Ufford, Bertha Hazard III, 316
Ufford, Charles III, 324
Ufford, Charles Wilbur III, 324
Ufford, Elizabeth III, 324
Ufford, Frank P. III, 316
Ufford, Frank P. III, 324
Ufing, William G. VI, 259
Uhl, Frederick VI, 1008
Uhl, Jacob VI, 1008
Uhl, Pheeby VI, 1008
Uhl, Polly VI, 1008
Uhlan, Bessie E. V, 467
Uhle, Jacob VI, 878
Uhle, Janny VI, 878
Uhle, Mary VI, 878
Uhlen, Bessie E. V, 467
Uhlen, Ellie S. V, 466
Uhlich, Edith IV, 1189
Ulery, Lewulla IV, 849
Ullery, Christinia V, 765
Ullery, Emelina IV, 825
Ullery, Emelina IV, 849
Ullery, Lewulla IV, 849
Ullery, Vera V, 771
Ullery, Virginia V, 771
Ullom, Seymore V, 134
Ullum, Anna M. V, 134
Ullum, Helen V, 134
Ullum, Lenore V, 134
Ullum, Seymore V, 134
Ulmun, Anna M. V, 134
Umbors, Leonora IV, 295
Umphreville, Fanny IV, 295
Umphreville, Henry Lewis IV, 295
Umphreville, Sarah IV, 226
Umphreville, Sarah IV, 295
Umphreville, William IV, 226
Umphreville, William IV, 295
Umphrey, Daniel IV, 1296
Umphrey, David IV, 1282
Umphrey, Joseph II, 429
Umphrey, Mary Jane IV, 1282
Umphrey, Sophia VI, 877
Umphries, Richard V. II, 1082
Umphris, Rebeckah I, 579

Umpleby, Hannah B. II, 835
Umpleby, Hannah B. II, 933
Umstead, Nancy IV, 449
Uncapher, Dora V, 1022
Uncapher, Katie V, 1022
Uncapher, Lydia V, 1022
Unckles, Hannah VI, 493
Unckles, Hannah VI, 574
Unckles, Hannah VI, 586
Unckles, Sarah VI, 575
Uncles, Sarah IV, 679
Uncles, Sarah VI, 575
Uncles, Sarah VI, 586
Underhill, ??? III, 45
Underhill, ??? III, 206
Underhill, ??? III, 309
Underhill, ??? III, 326
Underhill, ??? III, 328
Underhill, ??? III, 391
Underhill, ??? VI, 726
Underhill, Aaron III, 324
Underhill, Aaron C. III, 324
Underhill, Aaron J. III, 328
Underhill, Aaron T. III, 324
Underhill, Abbie III, 338
Underhill, Abby Jane III, 329
Underhill, Abigail I, 424
Underhill, Abigail II, 294
Underhill, Abigail II, 304
Underhill, Abigail III, 326
Underhill, Abigail III, 402
Underhill, Abigail III, 458
Underhill, Abigail K. II, 304
Underhill, Abigail K. III, 324
Underhill, Abigail K. III, 328
Underhill, Abigail K. III, 332
Underhill, Abijah III, 328
Underhill, Abm. C. III, 60
Underhill, Abm. C. III, 325
Underhill, Abm. C. III, 329
Underhill, Abm. S. III, 109
Underhill, Abrah III, 458
Underhill, Abraham III, 324
Underhill, Abraham III, 329
Underhill, Abraham III, 330
Underhill, Abraham III, 393
Underhill, Abraham III, 410
Underhill, Abraham III, 414
Underhill, Abraham III, 457
Underhill, Abraham III, 458
Underhill, Abraham III, 459
Underhill, Abraham III, 467
Underhill, Abraham C. III, 162
Underhill, Abraham C. III, 324
Underhill, Abraham C. III, 328
Underhill, Abraham C. III, 372
Underhill, Abraham C. III, 400
Underhill, Abraham C. III, 422
Underhill, Abraham C. III, 458
Underhill, Abraham I. III, 329
Underhill, Abraham S. III, 238
Underhill, Abraham S. III, 288
Underhill, Abraham S. III, 324
Underhill, Abraham S. III, 326
Underhill, Abraham S. III, 332
Underhill, Abram III, 90
Underhill, Abram III, 329
Underhill, Abram III, 330
Underhill, Abram S. III, 324
Underhill, Abram S. III, 325
Underhill, Abrm. III, 501
Underhill, Abrm. III, 503
Underhill, Ada III, 208
Underhill, Ada III, 274
Underhill, Ada III, 325
Underhill, Ada III, 327
Underhill, Ada III, 449
Underhill, Ada III, 458
Underhill, Ada III, 460
Underhill, Ada A. III, 280
Underhill, Ada L. III, 97
Underhill, Ada L. III, 325
Underhill, Ada U. III, 449
Underhill, Adelia A. III, 325
Underhill, Adelia Augusta III, 60
Underhill, Adeline E. III, 162
Underhill, Adeline E. III, 324
Underhill, Adeline E. III, 325
Underhill, Adna III, 325
Underhill, Adna III, 328
Underhill, Adonijah III, 89
Underhill, Adonijah III, 197
Underhill, Adonijah III, 215
Underhill, Adonijah III, 325
Underhill, Adonijah III, 326
Underhill, Adonijah III, 327
Underhill, Adonijah III, 328
Underhill, Adonijah III, 329
Underhill, Adonijah III, 330
Underhill, Adonijah III, 354
Underhill, Adonijah III, 458

Underhill, Adonijah III, 459
Underhill, Adonijah III, 467
Underhill, Adonijah III, 470
Underhill, Adonijah III, 484
Underhill, Adonijah III, 486
Underhill, Adonijah III, 501
Underhill, Adonijah III, 505
Underhill, Adonijah III, 506
Underhill, Adonijah J. III, 325
Underhill, Adonijah J. III, 501
Underhill, Adonijah, Jr. III, 325
Underhill, Albert III, 322
Underhill, Albert III, 325
Underhill, Alex III, 325
Underhill, Alex. III, 197
Underhill, Alex. III, 331
Underhill, Alex. John III, 97
Underhill, Alex. John III, 327
Underhill, Alexander III, 208
Underhill, Alexander III, 280
Underhill, Alexander III, 325
Underhill, Alexander III, 393
Underhill, Alexander III, 458
Underhill, Alexander, Jr. III, 325
Underhill, Alexandria III, 329
Underhill, Alexandria III, 332
Underhill, Alfred I, 1111
Underhill, Alfred III, 229
Underhill, Alfred III, 325
Underhill, Alfred III, 330
Underhill, Alfred III, 331
Underhill, Alice III, 199
Underhill, Alice III, 327
Underhill, Alice III, 328
Underhill, Alice III, 329
Underhill, Alice E. III, 280
Underhill, Alice E. III, 325
Underhill, Alice Eugenia III, 325
Underhill, Alice H. III, 325
Underhill, Alice H. III, 330
Underhill, Alice Howes III, 102
Underhill, Alice J. III, 490
Underhill, Alice J. III, 501
Underhill, Alonzo III, 324
Underhill, Amanda M. III, 324
Underhill, Amanda M. III, 325
Underhill, Amee III, 330
Underhill, Amelia III, 325
Underhill, Amelia III, 354
Underhill, Amelia III, 502
Underhill, Amelia Augusta III, 60
Underhill, Amery III, 458
Underhill, Amos III, 324
Underhill, Amos III, 325
Underhill, Amos III, 326
Underhill, Amos III, 327
Underhill, Amos III, 330
Underhill, Amos III, 407
Underhill, Amos III, 443
Underhill, Amos III, 458
Underhill, Amos III, 459
Underhill, Amos III, 460
Underhill, Amos, Jr. III, 326
Underhill, Amy III, 326
Underhill, Amy III, 400
Underhill, Amy III, 407
Underhill, Amy III, 413
Underhill, Amy III, 423
Underhill, Amy III, 459
Underhill, Amy III, 501
Underhill, Amy III, 505
Underhill, Amy III, 506
Underhill, Andrew II, 429
Underhill, Andrew II, 672
Underhill, Andrew III, 144
Underhill, Andrew III, 326
Underhill, Andrew III, 327
Underhill, Andrew III, 330
Underhill, Andrew III, 331
Underhill, Andrew III, 332
Underhill, Andrew III, 458
Underhill, Andrew III, 460
Underhill, Andrew III, 467
Underhill, Andrew IV, 1233
Underhill, Andrew IV, 1241
Underhill, Andrew VI, 215
Underhill, Andrew H. IV, 1241
Underhill, Andrew Harvey IV, 1241
Underhill, Andries III, 497
Underhill, Ann III, 326
Underhill, Ann III, 330
Underhill, Ann III, 331
Underhill, Ann III, 384
Underhill, Ann III, 386
Underhill, Ann III, 398
Underhill, Ann III, 401
Underhill, Ann III, 428
Underhill, Ann III, 458
Underhill, Ann III, 460
Underhill, Ann III, 467

Underhill, Ann VI, 536
Underhill, Ann VI, 575
Underhill, Ann VI, 586
Underhill, Ann Eliza II, 805
Underhill, Ann Eliza III, 197
Underhill, Ann Eliza III, 325
Underhill, Ann Eliza III, 326
Underhill, Anna III, 216
Underhill, Anna III, 325
Underhill, Anna III, 328
Underhill, Anna III, 329
Underhill, Anna III, 330
Underhill, Anna III, 386
Underhill, Anna III, 501
Underhill, Anna III, 507
Underhill, Anna IV, 1241
Underhill, Anna A. IV, 1184
Underhill, Anna A. IV, 1189
Underhill, Anna C. III, 325
Underhill, Anna C. III, 327
Underhill, Anna Elizabeth III, 331
Underhill, Anna T. III, 90
Underhill, Anna T. III, 238
Underhill, Anna T. III, 324
Underhill, Anna T. III, 325
Underhill, Anna T. III, 329
Underhill, Anna T. III, 330
Underhill, Anne III, 329
Underhill, Anne III, 407
Underhill, Anne III, 458
Underhill, Anne III, 461
Underhill, Anne III, 501
Underhill, Anne III, 508
Underhill, Anne T. III, 459
Underhill, Annie III, 326
Underhill, Annie III, 331
Underhill, Annie III, 460
Underhill, Annie III, 508
Underhill, Annie T. III, 411
Underhill, Annie T. III, 458
Underhill, Armina I, 1111
Underhill, Augusta III, 326
Underhill, Augusta III, 327
Underhill, Augustus III, 326
Underhill, Augustus III, 327
Underhill, B. III, 232
Underhill, Belinda I, 1111
Underhill, Benjamin II, 932
Underhill, Benjamin II, 933
Underhill, Benjamin III, 126
Underhill, Benjamin III, 326
Underhill, Benjamin III, 329
Underhill, Benjamin III, 456
Underhill, Benjamin III, 457
Underhill, Benjamin III, 458
Underhill, Benjamin C. III, 331
Underhill, Benjamin R. III, 460
Underhill, Bertha III, 501
Underhill, C. III, 229
Underhill, Caleb III, 232
Underhill, Caleb III, 326
Underhill, Caleb III, 328
Underhill, Caleb III, 332
Underhill, Capt. John III, 328
Underhill, Caroline III, 93
Underhill, Caroline III, 325
Underhill, Caroline III, 326
Underhill, Caroline III, 328
Underhill, Caroline III, 329
Underhill, Caroline III, 331
Underhill, Caroline III, 393
Underhill, Caroline III, 433
Underhill, Caroline III, 458
Underhill, Caroline III, 459
Underhill, Caroline III, 492
Underhill, Caroline III, 502
Underhill, Caroline E. III, 231
Underhill, Caroline E. III, 327
Underhill, Caroline E. III, 329
Underhill, Caroline S. III, 327
Underhill, Caroline, Jr. III, 458
Underhill, Carrie J. III, 495
Underhill, Carrie J. III, 499
Underhill, Carrie, Jr. III, 490
Underhill, Carry J. III, 501
Underhill, Catharine III, 424
Underhill, Catharine III, 433
Underhill, Catharine III, 459
Underhill, Catharine III, 466
Underhill, Catharine III, 467
Underhill, Catharine III, 501
Underhill, Catherine III, 459
Underhill, Catherine J. III, 501
Underhill, Celia F. III, 325
Underhill, Charity III, 467
Underhill, Charles III, 326
Underhill, Charles III, 459
Underhill, Charles III, 460
Underhill, Charles V, 134
Underhill, Charles F. III, 326
Underhill, Charles F. III, 330
Underhill, Charles Matthew III, 330
Underhill, Charles R. IV, 1241
Underhill, Charles W. III, 326
Underhill, Charlotte III, 325
Underhill, Charlotte III, 326
Underhill, Charlotte III, 328
Underhill, Charlotte III, 330
Underhill, Charlotte III, 482
Underhill, Charlotte M. III, 61
Underhill, Chas. A. III, 216
Underhill, Chas. F. III, 108
Underhill, Chas. R. III, 329
Underhill, Chas. W. III, 330
Underhill, Clarissa III, 328
Underhill, Clarkson I, 1111
Underhill, Clarkson III, 326
Underhill, Clarkson III, 328
Underhill, Clementina III, 325
Underhill, Clementine III, 501
Underhill, Clementine III, 503
Underhill, Cornelia III, 109
Underhill, Cornelia W. III, 324
Underhill, Cornelia W. III, 326
Underhill, Cyrus III, 326
Underhill, Daniel I, 735
Underhill, Daniel I, 904
Underhill, Daniel III, 324
Underhill, Daniel III, 326
Underhill, Daniel III, 329
Underhill, Daniel III, 331
Underhill, Daniel III, 395
Underhill, Daniel III, 402
Underhill, Daniel III, 433
Underhill, Daniel III, 458
Underhill, Daniel III, 459
Underhill, Daniel III, 486
Underhill, Daniel III, 492
Underhill, Daniel III, 501
Underhill, Daniel III, 505
Underhill, Daniel VI, 787
Underhill, Daniel C. III, 326
Underhill, Daniel H. III, 326
Underhill, Daniel H. III, 331
Underhill, David III, 255
Underhill, David III, 314
Underhill, David III, 326
Underhill, David III, 327
Underhill, David III, 329
Underhill, David III, 330
Underhill, David III, 332
Underhill, David III, 428
Underhill, David III, 458
Underhill, David III, 459
Underhill, David C. III, 459
Underhill, David L. III, 60
Underhill, David L. III, 325
Underhill, David R. III, 95
Underhill, David R. III, 119
Underhill, David R. III, 229
Underhill, David R. III, 326
Underhill, David R. III, 327
Underhill, David R. III, 334
Underhill, Deb. III, 144
Underhill, Deborah III, 144
Underhill, Deborah III, 215
Underhill, Deborah III, 325
Underhill, Deborah III, 326
Underhill, Deborah III, 327
Underhill, Deborah III, 328
Underhill, Deborah III, 329
Underhill, Deborah III, 330
Underhill, Deborah III, 331
Underhill, Deborah III, 457
Underhill, Deborah III, 458
Underhill, Deborah III, 459
Underhill, Deborah III, 467
Underhill, Deborah III, 470
Underhill, Deborah III, 504
Underhill, Deborah S. III, 49
Underhill, Deborah S. III, 89
Underhill, Deborah S. III, 197
Underhill, Deborah S. III, 215
Underhill, Deborah S. III, 326
Underhill, Deborah S. III, 327
Underhill, Deborah, Jr. III, 325
Underhill, Dinah III, 41
Underhill, Dinah III, 330
Underhill, Dinah III, 396
Underhill, Dinah III, 457
Underhill, Dinah III, 458
Underhill, Dinah III, 459
Underhill, Dinah III, 467
Underhill, Dorothy III, 501
Underhill, Dorothy III, 503
Underhill, Edith III, 328
Underhill, Edith III, 330
Underhill, Edith III, 331
Underhill, Edith Lilian III, 174
Underhill, Edmund III, 325
Underhill, Edmund III, 327
Underhill, Edmund III, 328
Underhill, Edmund III, 329
Underhill, Edmund III, 386
Underhill, Edmund Clarence III, 330
Underhill, Edmund R. III, 327
Underhill, Edward III, 328
Underhill, Edward III, 331
Underhill, Edward Albert III, 325
Underhill, Edward C. III, 266
Underhill, Edward C. III, 327
Underhill, Edward W. III, 489
Underhill, Edward W. III, 501
Underhill, Edwin III, 327
Underhill, Edwin III, 331
Underhill, Eleanor III, 212
Underhill, Eleanor III, 330
Underhill, Eleonor III, 327
Underhill, Elias III, 62
Underhill, Elias III, 327
Underhill, Elias III, 329
Underhill, Elias H. III, 326
Underhill, Elias H. III, 327
Underhill, Elias H. III, 330
Underhill, Elias Milton III, 330
Underhill, Elijah Ferris III, 327
Underhill, Eliz. III, 162
Underhill, Eliz. III, 233
Underhill, Eliz. III, 326
Underhill, Eliz. III, 327
Underhill, Eliz. III, 329
Underhill, Eliz. III, 331
Underhill, Eliz. III, 332
Underhill, Eliz. B. III, 325
Underhill, Eliz. B. III, 329
Underhill, Eliz. B. III, 372
Underhill, Eliz. C. III, 329
Underhill, Eliz. D. III, 95
Underhill, Eliz. D. III, 229
Underhill, Eliz. D. III, 326
Underhill, Eliz. G. III, 231
Underhill, Eliz. G. III, 326
Underhill, Eliza III, 40
Underhill, Eliza III, 180
Underhill, Eliza III, 285
Underhill, Eliza III, 325
Underhill, Eliza III, 327
Underhill, Eliza III, 377
Underhill, Eliza III, 386
Underhill, Eliza B. III, 60
Underhill, Eliza B. III, 109
Underhill, Eliza B. III, 328
Underhill, Eliza B. III, 329
Underhill, Eliza B. III, 331
Underhill, Eliza B. III, 370
Underhill, Eliza S. III, 324
Underhill, Elizabeth II, 932
Underhill, Elizabeth II, 933
Underhill, Elizabeth III, 138
Underhill, Elizabeth III, 208
Underhill, Elizabeth III, 293
Underhill, Elizabeth III, 313
Underhill, Elizabeth III, 326
Underhill, Elizabeth III, 327
Underhill, Elizabeth III, 329
Underhill, Elizabeth III, 330
Underhill, Elizabeth III, 331
Underhill, Elizabeth III, 344
Underhill, Elizabeth III, 358
Underhill, Elizabeth III, 359
Underhill, Elizabeth III, 386
Underhill, Elizabeth III, 428
Underhill, Elizabeth III, 435
Underhill, Elizabeth III, 436
Underhill, Elizabeth III, 438
Underhill, Elizabeth III, 442
Underhill, Elizabeth III, 443
Underhill, Elizabeth III, 458
Underhill, Elizabeth III, 459
Underhill, Elizabeth III, 460
Underhill, Elizabeth IV, 1341
Underhill, Elizabeth VI, 787
Underhill, Elizabeth ??? III, 326
Underhill, Elizabeth A. III, 327
Underhill, Elizabeth A. III, 328
Underhill, Elizabeth Anne III, 407
Underhill, Elizabeth B. III, 324
Underhill, Elizabeth B. III, 328
Underhill, Elizabeth G. III, 327
Underhill, Elizabeth G. IV, 1341
Underhill, Elizabeth J. III, 501
Underhill, Elizabeth Livingston III, 327
Underhill, Elizabeth W. II, 672
Underhill, Elizabeth W. II, 748
Underhill, Elizabeth W. II, 772
Underhill, Elizabeth W. III, 51
Underhill, Elizabeth W. III, 327
Underhill, Elizabeth W. III, 330
Underhill, Elizabeth Yeates III, 329
Underhill, Elizabeth Yeats III, 327
Underhill, Elvira I, 1111
Underhill, Emeline III, 489
Underhill, Emeline A. IV, 1241
Underhill, Emeline C. III, 45
Underhill, Emeline C. III, 327
Underhill, Emeline S. III, 501
Underhill, Emily I, 1111
Underhill, Emily III, 460
Underhill, Emily D. IV, 1241
Underhill, Emily H. III, 139
Underhill, Emily H. III, 332
Underhill, Emline A. IV, 1241
Underhill, Emma II, 873
Underhill, Emma II, 933
Underhill, Emma III, 263
Underhill, Emma III, 326
Underhill, Emma III, 327
Underhill, Emma III, 328
Underhill, Emma III, 334
Underhill, Emma III, 479
Underhill, Emma III, 502
Underhill, Emma A. III, 501
Underhill, Emma A. III, 508
Underhill, Emma C. III, 325
Underhill, Emmeline III, 325
Underhill, Ephraim III, 327
Underhill, Esther III, 266
Underhill, Esther H. III, 213
Underhill, Esther R. III, 327
Underhill, Ethel III, 326
Underhill, Ethel III, 327
Underhill, Ethel P. III, 108
Underhill, Etta Foster III, 330
Underhill, Eugene III, 327
Underhill, Eugenie P. III, 400
Underhill, Eugenie P. III, 458
Underhill, Euphemia III, 327
Underhill, Frances A. III, 330
Underhill, Frances Gertrude III, 331
Underhill, Francis VI, 787
Underhill, Francis L. III, 329
Underhill, Francis Lawrence III, 327
Underhill, Francis, H., Jr. III, 216
Underhill, Frank III, 331
Underhill, Franklin II, 933
Underhill, Franklin III, 327
Underhill, Frederick III, 327
Underhill, Frederick A. III, 327
Underhill, Frederick Augustus III, 330
Underhill, Frederick H. III, 330
Underhill, Frederick Shotwell III, 324
Underhill, Freelove III, 393
Underhill, Geo. III, 326
Underhill, Geo. III, 328
Underhill, Geo. III, 329
Underhill, Geo. III, 332
Underhill, George II, 429
Underhill, George III, 320
Underhill, George III, 327
Underhill, George III, 330
Underhill, George III, 342
Underhill, George Calvin IV, 1241
Underhill, George Colvin IV, 1241
Underhill, George S. III, 394
Underhill, George S. III, 459
Underhill, George S. III, 460
Underhill, George W. III, 327
Underhill, George, Jr. III, 327
Underhill, Grace III, 97
Underhill, Grace III, 325
Underhill, Grace III, 327
Underhill, Grace III, 330
Underhill, Grace D. III, 89
Underhill, Grace D. III, 330
Underhill, Hannah I, 735
Underhill, Hannah I, 842
Underhill, Hannah I, 904
Underhill, Hannah I, 1111
Underhill, Hannah I, 1133
Underhill, Hannah II, 672
Underhill, Hannah III, 41
Underhill, Hannah III, 43
Underhill, Hannah III, 129
Underhill, Hannah III, 165
Underhill, Hannah III, 182
Underhill, Hannah III, 199
Underhill, Hannah III, 206
Underhill, Hannah III, 232
Underhill, Hannah III, 285
Underhill, Hannah III, 326
Underhill, Hannah III, 327
Underhill, Hannah III, 328
Underhill, Hannah III, 329
Underhill, Hannah III, 330
Underhill, Hannah III, 354
Underhill, Hannah III, 372
Underhill, Hannah III, 397
Underhill, Hannah III, 419
Underhill, Hannah III, 456
Underhill, Hannah III, 458
Underhill, Hannah III, 459
Underhill, Hannah III, 460
Underhill, Hannah III, 500
Underhill, Hannah III, 501
Underhill, Hannah III, 502
Underhill, Hannah III, 505
Underhill, Hannah III, 506
Underhill, Hannah V, 771
Underhill, Hannah B. III, 32
Underhill, Hannah B. III, 33
Underhill, Hannah Louisa III, 328
Underhill, Hannah Louisa III, 372
Underhill, Hannah M. III, 3
Underhill, Hannah S. III, 32
Underhill, Hannah W. III, 3
Underhill, Hannah W. III, 3
Underhill, Hannah W. III, 3
Underhill, Hannah W. III, 4
Underhill, Hannah W. III, 5
Underhill, Harriet III, 327
Underhill, Harriet G. III, 32
Underhill, Harriet L. III, 10
Underhill, Harriet L. III, 21
Underhill, Harriet L. III, 21
Underhill, Harriet L. III, 32
Underhill, Harriet L. III, 33
Underhill, Harvey IV, 1184
Underhill, Harvey IV, 1189
Underhill, Harvey IV, 1241
Underhill, Helen III, 501
Underhill, Helen III, 503
Underhill, Helen III, 508
Underhill, Helena III, 326
Underhill, Helena III, 328
Underhill, Henrietta III, 50
Underhill, Henrietta III, 50
Underhill, Henry III, 328
Underhill, Henry III, 460
Underhill, Henry F. III, 501
Underhill, Henry H. III, 328
Underhill, Henry H. III, 329
Underhill, Henry S. III, 325
Underhill, Henry S. III, 328
Underhill, Henry T. III, 460
Underhill, Henry T. III, 501
Underhill, Henry T. III, 502
Underhill, Henry W. III, 331
Underhill, Henry W. III, 459
Underhill, Henry W. III, 460
Underhill, Henry W. III, 501
Underhill, Henry W. III, 503
Underhill, Henry Willets, Jr. III, 501
Underhill, Howard L. III, 32
Underhill, Howard Lawrence III, 328
Underhill, Hubert III, 327
Underhill, Ira II, 304
Underhill, Ira III, 329
Underhill, Ira B. II, 187
Underhill, Ira B. II, 294
Underhill, Ira B. II, 304
Underhill, Ira B. III, 324
Underhill, Ira B. III, 328
Underhill, Ira B. III, 332
Underhill, Isaac III, 269
Underhill, Isaac III, 325
Underhill, Isaac III, 327
Underhill, Isaac III, 328
Underhill, Isaac III, 329
Underhill, Isaac III, 330
Underhill, Isaac III, 386
Underhill, Isaac III, 402
Underhill, Isaac III, 460
Underhill, Isaac III, 501
Underhill, Isaac A. III, 305
Underhill, Isaac A. III, 327
Underhill, Isaac Q. III, 326
Underhill, Isaac Q. III, 328
Underhill, Isaac, Sr. III, 328
Underhill, Isabella B. III, 4
Underhill, Israel III, 61
Underhill, Israel III, 64
Underhill, Israel III, 325
Underhill, Israel III, 326
Underhill, Israel III, 328
Underhill, Israel III, 330
Underhill, Israel III, 394
Underhill, Israel III, 402

hill, Israel III, 406
hill, Israel III, 442
hill, Israel III, 443
hill, Israel III, 456
hill, Israel III, 458
hill, Israel III, 459
hill, Israel III, 476
hill, Israel III, 497
hill, Israel III, 500
hill, Jackson III, 501
hill, Jacob III, 329
hill, Jacob III, 407
hill, Jacob III, 413
hill, Jacob III, 424
hill, Jacob III, 457
hill, Jacob III, 460
hill, Jacob III, 466
hill, Jacob III, 467
hill, Jacob III, 502
hill, Jacob IV, 1189
hill, Jacob V, 134
hill, Jacob V, 141
hill, Jacob S. III, 400
hill, Jacob S. III, 411
hill, Jacob S. III, 423
hill, Jacob S. III, 457
hill, Jacob S. III, 458
hill, Jacob S. III, 459
hill, Jacob Smith III, 399
hill, James III, 326
hill, James III, 327
hill, James III, 330
hill, James III, 331
hill, James III, 404
hill, James III, 453
hill, James III, 460
hill, James III, 501
hill, James III, 504
hill, James Edward
I, 327
hill, James Edward
I, 328
hill, Jane I, 1111
hill, Jane I, 1133
hill, Jane III, 38
hill, Jane III, 62
hill, Jane III, 117
hill, Jane III, 229
hill, Jane III, 325
hill, Jane III, 327
hill, Jane III, 328
hill, Jane III, 329
hill, Jane III, 330
hill, Jane III, 465
hill, Jane E. IV, 1233
hill, Jane E. IV, 1241
hill, Jane Elizabeth
I, 328
hill, Jane Elizabeth
I, 332
hill, Jane S. III, 325
hill, Jane S. III, 328
hill, Jane W. III, 394
hill, Jane W. III, 459
hill, Jarvis III, 504
hill, Jay Hoyt III, 328
hill, Jay Hoyt III, 331
hill, Jemima III, 459
hill, Jemima III, 460
hill, Jemima U. III, 461
hill, Jennie IV, 1241
hill, Jesse I, 1111
hill, Jesse B. I, 1111
hill, Jesse H. III, 324
hill, Jessie III, 502
hill, John I, 735
hill, John I, 904
hill, John I, 1133
hill, John III, 43
hill, John III, 99
hill, John III, 251
hill, John III, 324
hill, John III, 326
hill, John III, 327
hill, John III, 328
hill, John III, 329
hill, John III, 330
hill, John III, 332
hill, John III, 386
hill, John III, 393
hill, John III, 397
hill, John III, 412
hill, John III, 432
hill, John III, 438
hill, John III, 458
hill, John III, 470
hill, John III, 504
hill, John V, 771
hill, John C. II, 825
hill, John E. IV, 1241
hill, John Eddy IV, 1241
Underhill, John F. III, 329
Underhill, John T. III, 326
Underhill, John, Jr. I, 735
Underhill, John, Jr. I, 904
Underhill, John, Jr. I, 1111
Underhill, John, Jr. III, 260
Underhill, John, Jr. III, 386
Underhill, John, Sr. I, 1133
Underhill, Jonathan III, 465
Underhill, Jonathan T. IV, 295
Underhill, Jordan III, 505
Underhill, Jordan III, 506
Underhill, Jordan W. III, 502
Underhill, Joseph III, 329
Underhill, Joseph III, 330
Underhill, Joseph III, 460
Underhill, Joseph III, 461
Underhill, Josh. S. III, 327
Underhill, Joshua II, 187
Underhill, Joshua II, 294
Underhill, Joshua II, 304
Underhill, Joshua III, 93
Underhill, Joshua III, 117
Underhill, Joshua III, 324
Underhill, Joshua III, 326
Underhill, Joshua III, 327
Underhill, Joshua III, 329
Underhill, Joshua III, 330
Underhill, Joshua III, 331
Underhill, Joshua III, 359
Underhill, Joshua III, 366
Underhill, Joshua B. III, 138
Underhill, Joshua B. III, 329
Underhill, Joshua L. III, 329
Underhill, Joshua Lawrence
III, 329
Underhill, Joshua S. III, 328
Underhill, Joshua S. III, 329
Underhill, Joshua Sutton III, 329
Underhill, Joshua T. III, 199
Underhill, Josiah J. III, 326
Underhill, Josiah J. III, 328
Underhill, Josiah J. III, 330
Underhill, Josiah J. III, 372
Underhill, Josiah T. III, 327
Underhill, Josiah T. III, 331
Underhill, Julia A. I, 1111
Underhill, Kezia III, 504
Underhill, Keziah III, 410
Underhill, Keziah III, 458
Underhill, Keziah III, 501
Underhill, Lemuel I, 1111
Underhill, Leslie III, 330
Underhill, Letitia III, 329
Underhill, Letitia III, 457
Underhill, Letitia III, 458
Underhill, Letitia III, 459
Underhill, Levi III, 326
Underhill, Levi III, 327
Underhill, Levi III, 329
Underhill, Levi III, 331
Underhill, Levi III, 332
Underhill, Levi VI, 765
Underhill, Levi VI, 787
Underhill, Levi Athan VI, 787
Underhill, Libbie III, 233
Underhill, Libbie III, 330
Underhill, Lindley III, 329
Underhill, Lindley III, 331
Underhill, Lot III, 332
Underhill, Louisa III, 215
Underhill, Louisa III, 324
Underhill, Louisa III, 329
Underhill, Louisa III, 332
Underhill, Louisa S. III, 89
Underhill, Louisa S. III, 329
Underhill, Louise S. III, 325
Underhill, Lucy III, 329
Underhill, Lydia III, 327
Underhill, Lydia III, 331
Underhill, Lydia III, 342
Underhill, Lydia III, 386
Underhill, Lydia III, 429
Underhill, Lydia III, 460
Underhill, Lydia Ann IV, 1241
Underhill, Lydia E. III, 329
Underhill, Lydia E. III, 331
Underhill, Lydia E. III, 370
Underhill, Lydia Green III, 331
Underhill, Lydia Willis III, 327
Underhill, Lydia Willis III, 329
Underhill, M. Ida III, 328
Underhill, Margaret III, 27
Underhill, Margaret III, 329
Underhill, Margaret III, 330
Underhill, Margaret B. III, 324
Underhill, Maria III, 325
Underhill, Maria III, 326
Underhill, Maria III, 329
Underhill, Maria III, 332
Underhill, Maria III, 336
Underhill, Maria III, 386
Underhill, Maria C. III, 329
Underhill, Maria C. III, 331
Underhill, Mariam II, 933
Underhill, Marian II, 933
Underhill, Marianna III, 327
Underhill, Marianna III, 400
Underhill, Marianna III, 459
Underhill, Marietta III, 422
Underhill, Marietta III, 458
Underhill, Marion D. III, 330
Underhill, Martha III, 326
Underhill, Martha III, 329
Underhill, Martha III, 330
Underhill, Mary II, 187
Underhill, Mary II, 294
Underhill, Mary II, 304
Underhill, Mary III, 47
Underhill, Mary III, 93
Underhill, Mary III, 117
Underhill, Mary III, 173
Underhill, Mary III, 206
Underhill, Mary III, 216
Underhill, Mary III, 251
Underhill, Mary III, 260
Underhill, Mary III, 288
Underhill, Mary III, 305
Underhill, Mary III, 324
Underhill, Mary III, 325
Underhill, Mary III, 326
Underhill, Mary III, 327
Underhill, Mary III, 328
Underhill, Mary III, 329
Underhill, Mary III, 330
Underhill, Mary III, 331
Underhill, Mary III, 332
Underhill, Mary III, 334
Underhill, Mary III, 338
Underhill, Mary III, 355
Underhill, Mary III, 359
Underhill, Mary III, 364
Underhill, Mary III, 366
Underhill, Mary III, 386
Underhill, Mary III, 394
Underhill, Mary III, 397
Underhill, Mary III, 402
Underhill, Mary III, 406
Underhill, Mary III, 412
Underhill, Mary III, 424
Underhill, Mary III, 425
Underhill, Mary III, 428
Underhill, Mary III, 432
Underhill, Mary III, 443
Underhill, Mary III, 453
Underhill, Mary III, 456
Underhill, Mary III, 459
Underhill, Mary III, 460
Underhill, Mary III, 470
Underhill, Mary III, 476
Underhill, Mary III, 486
Underhill, Mary III, 497
Underhill, Mary III, 500
Underhill, Mary III, 501
Underhill, Mary III, 502
Underhill, Mary III, 505
Underhill, Mary III, 506
Underhill, Mary A. III, 327
Underhill, Mary A. V, 134
Underhill, Mary A. V, 141
Underhill, Mary Amelia V, 134
Underhill, Mary Ann III, 328
Underhill, Mary Ann III, 329
Underhill, Mary Ann III, 331
Underhill, Mary Anna III, 329
Underhill, Mary Annah III, 314
Underhill, Mary Annah III, 329
Underhill, Mary Augusta III, 327
Underhill, Mary B. II, 667
Underhill, Mary B. II, 672
Underhill, Mary B. II, 748
Underhill, Mary B. II, 772
Underhill, Mary B. III, 329
Underhill, Mary B. III, 330
Underhill, Mary C. III, 327
Underhill, Mary C. III, 329
Underhill, Mary E. III, 325
Underhill, Mary E. IV, 1241
Underhill, Mary Eugenia III, 322
Underhill, Mary Eugenia III, 325
Underhill, Mary F. III, 109
Underhill, Mary F. III, 324
Underhill, Mary F. III, 326
Underhill, Mary F. III, 328
Underhill, Mary F. III, 366
Underhill, Mary J. III, 395
Underhill, Mary J. III, 459
Underhill, Mary J. III, 502
Underhill, Mary Jane III, 327
Underhill, Mary Jane III, 364
Underhill, Mary Jenkins III, 330
Underhill, Mary K. III, 399
Underhill, Mary K. III, 440
Underhill, Mary K. III, 447
Underhill, Mary K. III, 449
Underhill, Mary K. III, 458
Underhill, Mary K. III, 460
Underhill, Mary M. III, 330
Underhill, Mary M. III, 331
Underhill, Mary S. III, 327
Underhill, Mary S. III, 330
Underhill, Mary S. III, 331
Underhill, Mary S. III, 366
Underhill, May I, 735
Underhill, Merriam III, 326
Underhill, Minnie III, 232
Underhill, Mira III, 330
Underhill, Miriam III, 332
Underhill, Morris III, 328
Underhill, Morris III, 330
Underhill, Moses III, 330
Underhill, Nantucket Mary
III, 331
Underhill, Naomi I, 723
Underhill, Naomi I, 735
Underhill, Nathaniel III, 117
Underhill, Nathaniel III, 330
Underhill, Neomy I, 904
Underhill, Pamela III, 325
Underhill, Pamela III, 330
Underhill, Pamela III, 507
Underhill, Pamela T. III, 502
Underhill, Pamelia III, 108
Underhill, Pamelia III, 325
Underhill, Pamelia III, 457
Underhill, Pamelia III, 459
Underhill, Pamelia III, 460
Underhill, Pamelia III, 502
Underhill, Pamelia P. III, 426
Underhill, Parmelia III, 325
Underhill, Parmelia III, 326
Underhill, Parmelia III, 327
Underhill, Parmelia III, 330
Underhill, Perlina A. IV, 1241
Underhill, Perline A. IV, 1241
Underhill, Permelia III, 325
Underhill, Peter Thomson II, 672
Underhill, Phebe III, 47
Underhill, Phebe III, 64
Underhill, Phebe III, 119
Underhill, Phebe III, 228
Underhill, Phebe III, 327
Underhill, Phebe III, 328
Underhill, Phebe III, 329
Underhill, Phebe III, 330
Underhill, Phebe III, 331
Underhill, Phebe III, 332
Underhill, Phebe III, 395
Underhill, Phebe III, 399
Underhill, Phebe III, 407
Underhill, Phebe III, 411
Underhill, Phebe III, 414
Underhill, Phebe III, 458
Underhill, Phebe III, 459
Underhill, Phebe III, 467
Underhill, Phebe III, 470
Underhill, Phebe III, 484
Underhill, Phebe III, 486
Underhill, Phebe III, 497
Underhill, Phebe III, 501
Underhill, Phebe III, 502
Underhill, Phebe III, 506
Underhill, Phebe III, 507
Underhill, Phebe A. III, 197
Underhill, Phebe A. III, 331
Underhill, Phebe Ann III, 457
Underhill, Phebe Ann III, 458
Underhill, Phebe C. III, 122
Underhill, Phebe C. III, 243
Underhill, Phebe C. III, 326
Underhill, Phebe C. III, 327
Underhill, Phebe C. III, 330
Underhill, Phebe C. III, 331
Underhill, Phebe E. III, 329
Underhill, Phebe Ella III, 499
Underhill, Phebe Ella III, 502
Underhill, Phebe F. III, 326
Underhill, Phebe F. III, 327
Underhill, Phebe F. III, 334
Underhill, Phebe G. III, 332
Underhill, Phebe H. III, 229
Underhill, Phebe H. III, 325
Underhill, Phebe H. III, 331
Underhill, Phebe J. III, 327
Underhill, Phebe J. III, 329
Underhill, Phebe J. III, 330
Underhill, Phebe Jane III, 326
Underhill, Phebe S. III, 114
Underhill, Phebe S. III, 325
Underhill, Phebe T. III, 328
Underhill, Phebe T. III, 330
Underhill, Phebe T. III, 372
Underhill, Phebe W. III, 318
Underhill, Phebe W. III, 330
Underhill, Phebe W. III, 453
Underhill, Phebe W. III, 459
Underhill, Phebe W. III, 460
Underhill, Phebe W. III, 501
Underhill, Phebe W. IV, 295
Underhill, Phebe W. IV, 296
Underhill, Phebe, Jr. III, 327
Underhill, Pheby III, 501
Underhill, Philo III, 328
Underhill, Pres. Minister
Letitia III, 326
Underhill, Rachel III, 320
Underhill, Rachel III, 326
Underhill, Rachel III, 327
Underhill, Rachel III, 330
Underhill, Rachel III, 486
Underhill, Rachel III, 501
Underhill, Rachel III, 502
Underhill, Rachel IV, 1189
Underhill, Rachel A. IV, 1241
Underhill, Rachel Singer IV, 1241
Underhill, Rachel W. III, 108
Underhill, Rachel W. III, 326
Underhill, Rachel W. III, 327
Underhill, Rachel W. III, 330
Underhill, Ralph Irving III, 326
Underhill, Ralph Irving III, 330
Underhill, Rebecca III, 402
Underhill, Rebecca III, 459
Underhill, Rebecca B. II, 672
Underhill, Rebeckah I, 709
Underhill, Rebeckah I, 735
Underhill, Rebekah I, 735
Underhill, Reuben III, 325
Underhill, Reuben III, 330
Underhill, Reuben H. III, 102
Underhill, Reuben H. III, 212
Underhill, Reuben H. III, 327
Underhill, Reuben H. W. III, 211
Underhill, Reuben H. W. III, 330
Underhill, Reuben L. III, 330
Underhill, Rhoda M. IV, 1241
Underhill, Richard III, 325
Underhill, Richard III, 440
Underhill, Richard III, 447
Underhill, Richard III, 449
Underhill, Richard III, 457
Underhill, Richard III, 458
Underhill, Richard III, 460
Underhill, Richard III, 507
Underhill, Richard Henry
III, 460
Underhill, Richard L. III, 329
Underhill, Richard T. III, 330
Underhill, Richard W. III, 330
Underhill, Richardson III, 330
Underhill, Robert III, 89
Underhill, Robert III, 233
Underhill, Robert III, 325
Underhill, Robert III, 326
Underhill, Robert III, 327
Underhill, Robert III, 330
Underhill, Robert III, 331
Underhill, Robert III, 332
Underhill, Robert III, 364
Underhill, Robert III, 460
Underhill, Robert Wales III, 331
Underhill, Robt. Wales III, 330
Underhill, Roslyn III, 460
Underhill, Ruith I, 904
Underhill, Ruth I, 735
Underhill, Ruth I, 1118
Underhill, Ruth I, 1133
Underhill, Ruth III, 90
Underhill, Ruth M. III, 324
Underhill, Ruth M. III, 330
Underhill, Ruth S. III, 324
Underhill, S. III, 329
Underhill, S. Louisa III, 330
Underhill, Sam'l III, 500
Underhill, Sam'l J. III, 506
Underhill, Sam'l S. III, 499
Underhill, Sam'l, Jr. III, 501
Underhill, Samuel II, 748
Underhill, Samuel II, 772
Underhill, Samuel III, 40
Underhill, Samuel III, 41
Underhill, Samuel III, 47
Underhill, Samuel III, 51
Underhill, Samuel III, 109
Underhill, Samuel III, 180
Underhill, Samuel III, 285
Underhill, Samuel III, 325
Underhill, Samuel III, 326
Underhill, Samuel III, 327
Underhill, Samuel III, 328
Underhill, Samuel III, 329
Underhill, Samuel III, 330
Underhill, Samuel III, 354
Underhill, Samuel III, 370

Underhill, Samuel III, 377
Underhill, Samuel III, 386
Underhill, Samuel III, 398
Underhill, Samuel III, 428
Underhill, Samuel III, 458
Underhill, Samuel III, 460
Underhill, Samuel III, 467
Underhill, Samuel III, 497
Underhill, Samuel III, 500
Underhill, Samuel III, 501
Underhill, Samuel III, 502
Underhill, Samuel III, 508
Underhill, Samuel B. III, 331
Underhill, Samuel J. III, 459
Underhill, Samuel J. III, 479
Underhill, Samuel J. III, 508
Underhill, Samuel P. II, 672
Underhill, Samuel P. III, 331
Underhill, Samuel P. III, 355
Underhill, Samuel R. III, 331
Underhill, Samuel S. III, 331
Underhill, Samuel S. III, 482
Underhill, Samuel S. III, 501
Underhill, Samuel S. III, 502
Underhill, Samuel S., Jr. III, 490
Underhill, Samuel, Jr. III, 330
Underhill, Sarah I, 735
Underhill, Sarah III, 165
Underhill, Sarah III, 206
Underhill, Sarah III, 251
Underhill, Sarah III, 261
Underhill, Sarah III, 318
Underhill, Sarah III, 325
Underhill, Sarah III, 326
Underhill, Sarah III, 328
Underhill, Sarah III, 329
Underhill, Sarah III, 330
Underhill, Sarah III, 331
Underhill, Sarah III, 332
Underhill, Sarah III, 342
Underhill, Sarah III, 351
Underhill, Sarah III, 393
Underhill, Sarah III, 400
Underhill, Sarah III, 402
Underhill, Sarah III, 412
Underhill, Sarah III, 419
Underhill, Sarah III, 425
Underhill, Sarah III, 432
Underhill, Sarah III, 436
Underhill, Sarah III, 441
Underhill, Sarah III, 443
Underhill, Sarah III, 447
Underhill, Sarah III, 458
Underhill, Sarah III, 459
Underhill, Sarah III, 460
Underhill, Sarah III, 466
Underhill, Sarah III, 494
Underhill, Sarah III, 501
Underhill, Sarah III, 502
Underhill, Sarah III, 504
Underhill, Sarah III, 505
Underhill, Sarah V, 134
Underhill, Sarah V, 141
Underhill, Sarah VI, 787
Underhill, Sarah Ann III, 326
Underhill, Sarah Ann III, 327
Underhill, Sarah Ann III, 328
Underhill, Sarah Ann III, 329
Underhill, Sarah Ann III, 330
Underhill, Sarah Ann III, 332
Underhill, Sarah Ann III, 342
Underhill, Sarah Biddle II, 672
Underhill, Sarah F. III, 329
Underhill, Sarah I. III, 504
Underhill, Sarah Jane III, 331
Underhill, Sarah L. III, 216
Underhill, Sarah P. II, 932
Underhill, Sarah P. II, 933
Underhill, Sarah P. III, 109
Underhill, Sarah P. III, 331
Underhill, Sarah P. III, 458
Underhill, Sarah P. III, 460
Underhill, Sarah R. II, 933
Underhill, Sarah S. III, 329
Underhill, Sarah T. III, 63
Underhill, Sarah T. III, 502
Underhill, Sarah U. III, 325
Underhill, Sarah U. III, 331
Underhill, Sarah U. III, 354
Underhill, Sarah W. III, 255
Underhill, Sarah W. III, 314
Underhill, Sarah W. III, 326
Underhill, Sarah W. III, 329
Underhill, Sarah W. III, 331
Underhill, Sarah W. III, 453
Underhill, Sarah W. III, 459
Underhill, Sarah W. III, 460
Underhill, Silas A. III, 210
Underhill, Silas A. III, 276
Underhill, Silas A. III, 325
Underhill, Silas A. III, 331
Underhill, Silas Albertson III, 331
Underhill, Solomon III, 325
Underhill, Solomon III, 327
Underhill, Solomon III, 331
Underhill, Solomon III, 342
Underhill, Solomon III, 386
Underhill, Solomon III, 429
Underhill, Solomon III, 458
Underhill, Solomon III, 460
Underhill, Sophia III, 221
Underhill, Sophia III, 325
Underhill, Sophia III, 328
Underhill, Sophia III, 329
Underhill, Sophia III, 330
Underhill, Sophia III, 331
Underhill, Sophia III, 354
Underhill, Sophia III, 505
Underhill, Sophia III, 506
Underhill, Stepehn III, 331
Underhill, Stephen III, 326
Underhill, Stephen III, 329
Underhill, Stephen III, 331
Underhill, Stephen III, 459
Underhill, Stephen III, 460
Underhill, Stephen III, 507
Underhill, Stephen C. III, 331
Underhill, Stephen C. III, 458
Underhill, Stephen C. III, 460
Underhill, Stephen J. III, 501
Underhill, Stephen J. III, 502
Underhill, Stephen M. III, 328
Underhill, Stephen M. III, 330
Underhill, Stephen Maurice III, 174
Underhill, Stephen Maurice III, 331
Underhill, Stephen T. III, 502
Underhill, Stephen W. III, 501
Underhill, Stephen, Jr. III, 331
Underhill, Stephen, Jr. III, 501
Underhill, Susan III, 197
Underhill, Susan III, 325
Underhill, Susan III, 331
Underhill, Susan III, 420
Underhill, Susan III, 459
Underhill, Susan III, 460
Underhill, Susannah III, 401
Underhill, Theodore III, 326
Underhill, Thomas II, 429
Underhill, Thomas III, 165
Underhill, Thomas III, 206
Underhill, Thomas III, 326
Underhill, Thomas III, 328
Underhill, Thomas III, 329
Underhill, Thomas III, 351
Underhill, Thomas III, 386
Underhill, Thomas III, 393
Underhill, Thomas III, 419
Underhill, Thomas III, 459
Underhill, Thomas III, 460
Underhill, Thomas III, 466
Underhill, Thomas III, 504
Underhill, Thos. III, 318
Underhill, Thos. III, 326
Underhill, Thos. III, 330
Underhill, Thos. III, 425
Underhill, Thos. III, 436
Underhill, Thos. III, 453
Underhill, Thos. III, 501
Underhill, Thos. III, 504
Underhill, Townsend III, 331
Underhill, Townsend III, 459
Underhill, Townsend N. III, 331
Underhill, Wallace II, 933
Underhill, Walter III, 325
Underhill, Walter III, 329
Underhill, Walter III, 330
Underhill, Walter III, 331
Underhill, Walter III, 332
Underhill, Walter M. III, 331
Underhill, Walter M. III, 332
Underhill, Wd. Hannah III, 328
Underhill, Wd. Hannah B. III, 180
Underhill, Wd. Letitia III, 126
Underhill, Wd. Mary III, 393
Underhill, Wd. Phebe III, 406
Underhill, Wd. Sarah R. II, 825
Underhill, Wd. Sarah W. III, 331
Underhill, Willets III, 420
Underhill, Willets III, 459
Underhill, Willets III, 460
Underhill, William I, 735
Underhill, William I, 904
Underhill, William II, 304
Underhill, William III, 332
Underhill, William III, 460
Underhill, William VI, 215
Underhill, William A. III, 332
Underhill, William Francis III, 332
Underhill, William G. III, 332
Underhill, William H. V, 134
Underhill, William Henry V, 134
Underhill, William Penn III, 328
Underhill, William Waring III, 327
Underhill, William Wilson II, 304
Underhill, William Wilson III, 328
Underhill, William, Jr. III, 332
Underhill, Winifred III, 501
Underhill, Wm. III, 332
Underhill, Wm. III, 338
Underhill, Wm. Francis III, 329
Underhill, Wm. Francis VI, 787
Underhill, Wm. G. III, 495
Underhill, Wm. Wilson III, 139
Underhill, Wm. Wilson III, 332
Underhill, Zerriah III, 64
Underhill, Zerriah III, 330
Underhill, Zeruiah III, 61
Underhill, Zeruiah III, 326
Underhill, Zerviah III, 328
Underhill, Zerviah III, 331
Underwood, Abigail I, 415
Underwood, Abigail I, 425
Underwood, Abigail I, 735
Underwood, Abigail I, 1133
Underwood, Abraham IV, 112
Underwood, Ada Grace V, 135
Underwood, Alexander I, 425
Underwood, Alexander I, 735
Underwood, Alexander IV, 64
Underwood, Alexander VI, 469
Underwood, Alexander VI, 575
Underwood, Alexander VI, 586
Underwood, Alexander, Jr. I, 424
Underwood, Alice V, 357
Underwood, Alice V, 363
Underwood, Alice M. V, 135
Underwood, Alice W. V, 135
Underwood, Allis W. V, 135
Underwood, Amos IV, 64
Underwood, Amos IV, 662
Underwood, Amos IV, 780
Underwood, Amos IV, 885
Underwood, Amos V, 134
Underwood, Amos V, 135
Underwood, Amos V, 306
Underwood, Amos V, 312
Underwood, Amos V, 518
Underwood, Amos V, 536
Underwood, Andrew IV, 1240
Underwood, Ann I, 348
Underwood, Ann I, 376
Underwood, Ann I, 424
Underwood, Ann IV, 663
Underwood, Ann Eliza IV, 1383
Underwood, Anna V, 437
Underwood, Anna V, 536
Underwood, Anna C. IV, 1383
Underwood, Anna H. IV, 662
Underwood, Anna H. IV, 663
Underwood, Anna M. V, 135
Underwood, Anne I, 424
Underwood, Anne V, 537
Underwood, Annie M. V, 135
Underwood, Arthama V, 648
Underwood, Asenath V, 134
Underwood, Asenath V, 473
Underwood, Asenath V, 536
Underwood, Asenath H. V, 536
Underwood, Beaulah IV, 63
Underwood, Benjamin I, 424
Underwood, Benjamin III, 332
Underwood, Benjamin IV, 44
Underwood, Benjamin IV, 63
Underwood, Benjamin IV, 64
Underwood, Benjamin IV, 112
Underwood, Benjamin IV, 662
Underwood, Benjamin V, 135
Underwood, Betty IV, 63
Underwood, Betty IV, 64
Underwood, Betty IV, 112
Underwood, Betty IV, 662
Underwood, Beulah IV, 44
Underwood, Beulah IV, 64
Underwood, Caroline V, 134
Underwood, Caroline V, 135
Underwood, Caroline H. V, 135
Underwood, Catharine IV, 1364
Underwood, Catharine V, 628
Underwood, Catharine V, 648
Underwood, Catherine IV, 1383
Underwood, Catherine V, 134
Underwood, Cemantha IV, 1189
Underwood, Charles I, 935
Underwood, Charles IV, 1383
Underwood, Charles V, 135
Underwood, Charles D. V, 135
Underwood, Charles O. V, 135
Underwood, Chas. D. V, 135
Underwood, Clarkson V, 648
Underwood, Cornelius M. IV, 1382
Underwood, Cornelius M. IV, 1383
Underwood, Cynthia IV, 662
Underwood, Cynthia IV, 895
Underwood, Cynthia M. IV, 894
Underwood, Cynthia M. IV, 895
Underwood, Cyrus IV, 113
Underwood, Cyruss IV, 112
Underwood, Daniel B. V, 135
Underwood, Daniel Baily V, 135
Underwood, Daniel Matthew VI, 586
Underwood, Daniel Matthews VI, 575
Underwood, David W. V, 134
Underwood, David W. V, 135
Underwood, Deborah IV, 64
Underwood, Deborah IV, 662
Underwood, Deborah IV, 885
Underwood, Deborah V, 536
Underwood, Deborah V, 537
Underwood, Deborah V, 544
Underwood, Edward IV, 1383
Underwood, Edwin IV, 1383
Underwood, Eli V, 135
Underwood, Elias IV, 662
Underwood, Elias IV, 885
Underwood, Elihu IV, 112
Underwood, Elihu V, 57
Underwood, Elihu V, 134
Underwood, Elihu V, 135
Underwood, Elihu V, 536
Underwood, Elisabeth M. IV, 663
Underwood, Elisha IV, 112
Underwood, Elizabeth IV, 620
Underwood, Elizabeth IV, 662
Underwood, Elizabeth IV, 864
Underwood, Elizabeth IV, 885
Underwood, Elizabeth IV, 1364
Underwood, Elizabeth IV, 1382
Underwood, Elizabeth IV, 1383
Underwood, Elizabeth V, 1022
Underwood, Elizabeth M. IV, 662
Underwood, Elizabeth R. IV, 1383
Underwood, Ella I, 935
Underwood, Ellen V, 602
Underwood, Esli V, 1022
Underwood, Esther V, 581
Underwood, Esther V, 602
Underwood, Esther Ruth V, 135
Underwood, Eunice V, 341
Underwood, Eunice V, 363
Underwood, Evan V, 648
Underwood, Ezekiel V, 437
Underwood, Ezekiel V, 536
Underwood, Fanny IV, 662
Underwood, Fanny IV, 833
Underwood, Fanny IV, 849
Underwood, Fanny IV, 885
Underwood, George II, 314
Underwood, George IV, 1383
Underwood, George T. V, 135
Underwood, George W. IV, 113
Underwood, Hannah I, 396
Underwood, Hannah I, 425
Underwood, Hannah I, 579
Underwood, Hannah IV, 112
Underwood, Hannah IV, 662
Underwood, Hannah IV, 885
Underwood, Hannah IV, 1189
Underwood, Hannah IV, 1194
Underwood, Hannah V, 135
Underwood, Hannah V, 536
Underwood, Hannah V, 543
Underwood, Hannah V, 544
Underwood, Hannah M. V, 135
Underwood, Hannah P. IV, 1383
Underwood, Harriet V, 57
Underwood, Harriet E. V, 135
Underwood, Harriett E. V, 135
Underwood, Henry I, 425
Underwood, Henry V, 648
Underwood, Henry Ballinger VI, 575
Underwood, Henry Ballinger VI, 586
Underwood, Hester V, 57
Underwood, Hester V, 135
Underwood, Ida M. IV, 1189
Underwood, Ida Mary II, 314
Underwood, Irma V, 135
Underwood, Isaac IV, 662
Underwood, Isaac IV, 877
Underwood, Isaac IV, 885
Underwood, Isaac V, 134
Underwood, Isaac V, 135
Underwood, Isaac V, 536
Underwood, Isaac V, 537
Underwood, James I, 424
Underwood, James IV, 113
Underwood, James V, 363
Underwood, James F. IV, 13
Underwood, James F. IV, 13
Underwood, Jane I, 406
Underwood, Jane I, 424
Underwood, Jane IV, 99
Underwood, Jane IV, 112
Underwood, Jane V, 520
Underwood, Jane V, 536
Underwood, Jane Eva V, 13
Underwood, Jane W. V, 48
Underwood, Jennie E. V, 20
Underwood, Jephaniah IV, 8
Underwood, Jesse Deborah IV, 885
Underwood, John IV, 63
Underwood, John IV, 64
Underwood, John IV, 112
Underwood, John IV, 662
Underwood, John IV, 885
Underwood, John IV, 1364
Underwood, John IV, 1383
Underwood, John V, 21
Underwood, John V, 134
Underwood, John V, 135
Underwood, John V, 536
Underwood, John G. V, 135
Underwood, John H. IV, 118
Underwood, John H. IV, 138
Underwood, Joseph I, 425
Underwood, Joseph IV, 63
Underwood, Joseph IV, 64
Underwood, Joseph IV, 112
Underwood, Joseph IV, 662
Underwood, Joseph IV, 833
Underwood, Joseph IV, 849
Underwood, Joseph IV, 885
Underwood, Joseph IV, 1189
Underwood, Joseph V, 135
Underwood, Julia V, 135
Underwood, Julia A. V, 21
Underwood, Kelly V, 648
Underwood, Laura B. V, 135
Underwood, Laura G. V, 135
Underwood, Laura J. V, 135
Underwood, Leah II, 314
Underwood, Lenora II, 159
Underwood, Leona V, 134
Underwood, Leonard IV, 662
Underwood, Leonard IV, 663
Underwood, Levi IV, 885
Underwood, Lewis IV, 885
Underwood, Lewis V, 134
Underwood, Lewis V, 533
Underwood, Lewis V, 536
Underwood, Lewis V, 887
Underwood, Louisa V, 437
Underwood, Lydia IV, 1383
Underwood, Lydia Jane IV, 1
Underwood, Margaret G. III
Underwood, Marietta V, 135
Underwood, Martha IV, 122
Underwood, Martha IV, 122
Underwood, Martha V, 251
Underwood, Martha V, 286
Underwood, Mary I, 424
Underwood, Mary I, 425
Underwood, Mary IV, 36
Underwood, Mary IV, 59
Underwood, Mary IV, 63
Underwood, Mary IV, 613
Underwood, Mary IV, 623
Underwood, Mary IV, 662
Underwood, Mary IV, 663
Underwood, Mary IV, 780
Underwood, Mary IV, 864
Underwood, Mary IV, 885
Underwood, Mary IV, 895
Underwood, Mary IV, 1189
Underwood, Mary IV, 1296
Underwood, Mary IV, 1370
Underwood, Mary IV, 1383
Underwood, Mary V, 134
Underwood, Mary V, 135
Underwood, Mary V, 518
Underwood, Mary V, 536
Underwood, Mary Ann IV, 1
Underwood, Mary Ann V, 13
Underwood, Mary Ann V, 53
Underwood, Mary Earl I, 34
Underwood, Mary Frances V
Underwood, Matilda V, 135
Underwood, Matilda Jane V,
Underwood, Matilda Jane V,
Underwood, Mordecai P. IV,

rwood, Mordecai P. IV, 598
rwood, Mordecai T. IV, 354
rwood, Myrtle V, 135
rwood, Myrtle J. V, 135
rwood, Nathan IV, 885
rwood, Olive V, 135
rwood, Phebe A. V, 537
rwood, Priscilla V, 134
rwood, Priscilla V, 135
rwood, Priscilla V, 306
rwood, Priscilla V, 312
rwood, Priscilla V, 536
rwood, Priscilla Jane V, 134
rwood, Priscilla Jane V, 518
rwood, Priscilla Jane V, 536
rwood, R. Anna V, 135
rwood, Rachel I, 424
rwood, Rachel I, 425
rwood, Rachel I, 427
rwood, Rachel IV, 642
rwood, Rachel IV, 662
rwood, Rachel IV, 780
rwood, Rachel IV, 885
rwood, Rachel IV, 895
rwood, Rachel IV, 1382
rwood, Rachel IV, 1383
rwood, Rebecca IV, 662
rwood, Rebecca IV, 885
rwood, Rebecca V, 312
rwood, Rebecca V, 536
rwood, Rebecca Jane V, 135
rwood, Rebecca Jane V, 536
rwood, Reuben V, 134
rwood, Reuben V, 536
rwood, Russell E. II, 314
rwood, Ruth I, 373
rwood, Ruth I, 424
rwood, Ruth V, 133
rwood, Ruthanna V, 133
rwood, Ruthanna V, 135
rwood, Sabina IV, 36
rwood, Sabina IV, 63
rwood, Sabina IV, 64
rwood, Sally I, 412
rwood, Sally I, 425
rwood, Sam'l I, 348
rwood, Samuel I, 424
rwood, Samuel I, 425
rwood, Samuel V, 135
rwood, Sarah I, 424
rwood, Sarah IV, 63
rwood, Sarah IV, 64
rwood, Sarah IV, 112
rwood, Sarah IV, 620
rwood, Sarah IV, 631
rwood, Sarah IV, 662
rwood, Sarah IV, 663
rwood, Sarah IV, 780
rwood, Sarah IV, 885
rwood, Sarah IV, 895
rwood, Sarah IV, 1296
rwood, Sarah VI, 453
rwood, Sarah VI, 469
rwood, Sarah VI, 575
rwood, Sarah VI, 586
rwood, Sarah B. V, 533
rwood, Sarah B. V, 887
rwood, Sarah C. IV, 1383
rwood, Sarah Cecelia V, 135
rwood, Stephen IV, 662
rwood, Stephen IV, 663
rwood, Stephen IV, 1296
rwood, Susanna IV, 63
rwood, Susanna IV, 64
rwood, Susanna IV, 885
rwood, Susannah IV, 64
rwood, Susannah IV, 112
rwood, Susannah IV, 662
rwood, Thomas IV, 1383
rwood, Thomas E. V, 536
erwood, Thomas Elwood
V, 134
erwood, Thomas Elwood
V, 536
erwood, Toner V, 208
erwood, Toner M. V, 135
erwood, Vanwyck IV, 1383
erwood, Walter B. V, 135
erwood, Warren V, 134
erwood, Warren V, 135
erwood, Wd. Sarah VI, 575
erwood, Wilber IV, 895
erwood, Wilhelmina V, 135
erwood, Willen IV, 642
erwood, Willen IV, 662
erwood, William III, 332
erwood, William IV, 112
erwood, William IV, 885
erwood, William V, 134
erwood, William V, 135
erwood, William V, 536
Underwood, William M. IV, 663
Underwood, Willin IV, 63
Underwood, Willin IV, 64
Underwood, Willin IV, 112
Underwood, Willin IV, 620
Underwood, Willin IV, 662
Underwood, Willin IV, 780
Underwood, Willin, Jr. IV, 885
Underwood, Willing IV, 63
Underwood, Willing IV, 112
Underwood, Wm. II, 159
Underwood, Wm. IV, 1189
Underwood, Wm. V, 544
Underwood, Wm. E. IV, 1189
Underwood, Wm. Griest II, 933
Underwood, Wm. Luther V, 1022
Underwood, Wm. M. IV, 662
Underwood, Zephaniah IV, 885
Underwood, Zephaniah V, 49
Underwood, Zephaniah V, 133
Underwood, Zephaniah V, 134
Underwood, Zephaniah V, 135
Underwood, Zephaniah V, 312
Underwood, Zephaniah V, 536
Underwood, Zephariah V, 536
Underwood, Zillah IV, 877
Underwood, Zillah IV, 885
Unger, Rose Marie IV, 1265
Unity, Susanna VI, 240
Unquhart, Mary III, 460
Unthank, ??? I, 520
Unthank, Achilles I, 582
Unthank, Allen I, 493
Unthank, Allen I, 519
Unthank, Allen I, 550
Unthank, Allen I, 579
Unthank, Allen I, 580
Unthank, Allen I, 847
Unthank, Allen I, 971
Unthank, Ann I, 519
Unthank, Ann I, 520
Unthank, Ann V, 618
Unthank, Ann V, 648
Unthank, Anna I, 395
Unthank, Anna I, 425
Unthank, Anna I, 520
Unthank, Anna I, 546
Unthank, Anna I, 550
Unthank, Anna I, 579
Unthank, Anna I, 580
Unthank, Anny I, 580
Unthank, Betcey I, 520
Unthank, Beulah I, 520
Unthank, Beulah V, 648
Unthank, Buley I, 579
Unthank, Buley I, 582
Unthank, Dinah I, 425
Unthank, Dinah V, 467
Unthank, Dinah K. V, 231
Unthank, Dinah K. V, 286
Unthank, Dinah K. V, 467
Unthank, Dinah K. V, 716
Unthank, Elam I, 520
Unthank, Eli I, 520
Unthank, Eli I, 546
Unthank, Eli I, 579
Unthank, Eli I, 580
Unthank, Elizabeth I, 425
Unthank, Elizabeth V, 486
Unthank, Elizabeth V, 537
Unthank, Elizabeth V, 648
Unthank, Elizabeth Mary V, 648
Unthank, Emma V, 716
Unthank, Emma H. V, 716
Unthank, Hannah I, 520
Unthank, Hannah I, 535
Unthank, Hannah I, 579
Unthank, James B. V, 716
Unthank, James R. V, 716
Unthank, James Russell V, 716
Unthank, Jemima I, 493
Unthank, Jemima I, 519
Unthank, Jemima I, 549
Unthank, Jemima I, 554
Unthank, Jemima I, 579
Unthank, John I, 277
Unthank, John I, 425
Unthank, John I, 519
Unthank, John I, 549
Unthank, John I, 575
Unthank, John I, 579
Unthank, John I, 580
Unthank, John I, 773
Unthank, John V, 467
Unthank, John V, 648
Unthank, John V, 716
Unthank, John Allen V, 648
Unthank, John C. V, 716
Unthank, Jonathan I, 519
Unthank, Jonathan I, 520
Unthank, Jonathan I, 579
Unthank, Jonathan V, 648
Unthank, Joseph I, 425
Unthank, Joseph I, 487
Unthank, Joseph I, 520
Unthank, Joseph I, 572
Unthank, Joseph I, 578
Unthank, Joseph I, 579
Unthank, Joseph V, 648
Unthank, Joseph C. V, 467
Unthank, Joseph John Allen
V, 648
Unthank, Josiah I, 520
Unthank, Josiah I, 579
Unthank, Josiah I, 580
Unthank, Josiah I, 600
Unthank, Judith I, 520
Unthank, Judith I, 548
Unthank, Judith I, 578
Unthank, Judith I, 579
Unthank, Judith I Sup 1, 9
Unthank, Julius I, 425
Unthank, Lavica V, 646
Unthank, Lavica V, 648
Unthank, Lavicia V, 648
Unthank, Leveicy V, 648
Unthank, Lydia I, 520
Unthank, Lydia I, 575
Unthank, Lydia I, 579
Unthank, Lydia, Jr. I, 520
Unthank, Mahala I, 520
Unthank, Martha C. V, 467
Unthank, Mary I, 425
Unthank, Mary I, 520
Unthank, Mary I, 545
Unthank, Mary I, 579
Unthank, Mary V, 648
Unthank, Mary Rebecca V, 648
Unthank, Nathan I, 425
Unthank, Pleasant I, 520
Unthank, Pleasant I, 580
Unthank, Rachel I, 519
Unthank, Rachel V, 648
Unthank, Rebecah I, 520
Unthank, Rebecca I, 425
Unthank, Rebecca I, 520
Unthank, Rebecca I, 546
Unthank, Rebecca I, 572
Unthank, Rebecca I, 580
Unthank, Rebecca V, 648
Unthank, Rebeckah I, 546
Unthank, Rebeckah I, 580
Unthank, Ruth I, 493
Unthank, Ruth I, 519
Unthank, Ruth I, 520
Unthank, Sarah I, 520
Unthank, Sarah I, 545
Unthank, Sarah I, 549
Unthank, Sarah I, 579
Unthank, Sarah V, 644
Unthank, Sarah V, 648
Unthank, Sarah Elizabeth V, 648
Unthank, Temple I, 395
Unthank, Temple I, 425
Unthank, Temple I, 520
Unthank, Temple I, 580
Unthank, William I, 519
Unthank, William I, 520
Unthank, William I, 546
Unthank, William I, 579
Unthank, William I, 580
Unthank, William I, 969
Unthank, William V, 648
Unthank, William M. V, 648
Unthank, Wm. M. V, 648
Upchurch, Josephine I, 921
Updegraff, Abner IV, 113
Updegraff, Alexander IV, 161
Updegraff, Alice M. IV, 296
Updegraff, Ann IV, 96
Updegraff, Ann IV, 113
Updegraff, Ann IV, 201
Updegraff, Ann IV, 234
Updegraff, Ann IV, 259
Updegraff, Ann IV, 280
Updegraff, Ann IV, 295
Updegraff, Ann IV, 296
Updegraff, Ann IV, 501
Updegraff, Ann IV, 1009
Updegraff, Ann VI, 453
Updegraff, Ann VI, 600
Updegraff, Ann VI, 606
Updegraff, Ann VI, 607
Updegraff, Ann T. IV, 296
Updegraff, Anna E. IV, 296
Updegraff, Anna T. IV, 250
Updegraff, Anna T. IV, 296
Updegraff, Anna T. IV, 645
Updegraff, Anna T. IV, 663
Updegraff, Anna U. IV, 296
Updegraff, Anne U. IV, 221
Updegraff, Casandra IV, 234
Updegraff, Cassander IV, 291
Updegraff, Cassander IV, 501
Updegraff, Cassandra IV, 172
Updegraff, Cassandra IV, 296
Updegraff, Cassandra IV, 464
Updegraff, Cassandra IV, 501
Updegraff, Charles Taylor IV, 296
Updegraff, D. B. IV, 296
Updegraff, David IV, 228
Updegraff, David IV, 250
Updegraff, David IV, 287
Updegraff, David IV, 295
Updegraff, David IV, 296
Updegraff, David IV, 501
Updegraff, David VI, 453
Updegraff, David VI, 606
Updegraff, David VI, 607
Updegraff, David B. IV, 265
Updegraff, David B. IV, 296
Updegraff, David B. IV, 493
Updegraff, David B. IV, 501
Updegraff, David Benjamin
IV, 296
Updegraff, David, Jr. IV, 296
Updegraff, David, Jr. IV, 501
Updegraff, Edith IV, 106
Updegraff, Edith IV, 113
Updegraff, Edward Jessop
IV, 161
Updegraff, Edwin IV, 468
Updegraff, Eli IV, 113
Updegraff, Eliza IV, 295
Updegraff, Eliza IV, 554
Updegraff, Eliza J. IV, 296
Updegraff, Eliza Jane IV, 296
Updegraff, Eliza Jane IV, 501
Updegraff, Eliza Jane IV, 505
Updegraff, Elizabeth IV, 151
Updegraff, Elizabeth IV, 161
Updegraff, Elizabeth IV, 165
Updegraff, Elizabeth IV, 296
Updegraff, Elizabeth IV, 305
Updegraff, Elizabeth IV, 354
Updegraff, Elizabeth IV, 468
Updegraff, Elizabeth P. IV, 296
Updegraff, Frederick Clark
IV, 296
Updegraff, Grace IV, 175
Updegraff, Hannah IV, 161
Updegraff, Hannah IV, 259
Updegraff, Hannah IV, 296
Updegraff, Hannah VI, 606
Updegraff, Hannah VI, 607
Updegraff, Israel IV, 144
Updegraff, Israel IV, 146
Updegraff, Israel IV, 154
Updegraff, Israel IV, 161
Updegraff, Israel IV, 296
Updegraff, James IV, 113
Updegraff, James IV, 295
Updegraff, James VI, 453
Updegraff, James VI, 606
Updegraff, Jane IV, 154
Updegraff, Jane IV, 161
Updegraff, Jane IV, 296
Updegraff, Jane IV, 554
Updegraff, Jonathan IV, 296
Updegraff, Jonathan T. IV, 296
Updegraff, Joseph IV, 95
Updegraff, Joseph IV, 161
Updegraff, Joseph IV, 233
Updegraff, Joseph IV, 295
Updegraff, Joseph IV, 296
Updegraff, Joseph VI, 453
Updegraff, Joseph VI, 606
Updegraff, Joseph VI, 607
Updegraff, Josiah IV, 151
Updegraff, Josiah IV, 161
Updegraff, Josiah IV, 295
Updegraff, Josiah IV, 296
Updegraff, Juliana D. IV, 161
Updegraff, Juliann IV, 203
Updegraff, Juliann IV, 296
Updegraff, Julianna D. IV, 146
Updegraff, Lance IV, 501
Updegraff, Laura IV, 296
Updegraff, Laura A. IV, 296
Updegraff, Lewis W. IV, 296
Updegraff, Lucina IV, 296
Updegraff, Lucina IV, 977
Updegraff, Lucina IV, 1009
Updegraff, Lucina IV, 1044
Updegraff, Lusina IV, 1009
Updegraff, Mary IV, 95
Updegraff, Mary IV, 161
Updegraff, Mary IV, 274
Updegraff, Mary IV, 295
Updegraff, Mary IV, 296
Updegraff, Mary IV, 311
Updegraff, Mary IV, 314
Updegraff, Mary Ada IV, 296
Updegraff, Mary Ann IV, 144
Updegraff, Mary Ann IV, 146
Updegraff, Mary Ann IV, 154
Updegraff, Mary Ann IV, 161
Updegraff, Mary Ann IV, 295
Updegraff, Mary Ann IV, 296
Updegraff, Mary Ann, Jr. IV, 296
Updegraff, Mary B. IV, 291
Updegraff, Mary B. IV, 296
Updegraff, Mary L. IV, 201
Updegraff, Mary L. IV, 296
Updegraff, Mollie IV, 468
Updegraff, Nathan IV, 137
Updegraff, Nathan IV, 172
Updegraff, Nathan IV, 201
Updegraff, Nathan IV, 234
Updegraff, Nathan IV, 259
Updegraff, Nathan IV, 280
Updegraff, Nathan IV, 291
Updegraff, Nathan IV, 295
Updegraff, Nathan IV, 296
Updegraff, Nathan IV, 298
Updegraff, Nathan IV, 464
Updegraff, Nathan IV, 501
Updegraff, Nathan IV, 977
Updegraff, Nathan IV, 1009
Updegraff, Nathan VI, 453
Updegraff, Nathan VI, 600
Updegraff, Nathan VI, 602
Updegraff, Nathan VI, 606
Updegraff, Nathan VI, 607
Updegraff, Oliver Price IV, 296
Updegraff, Phebe IV, 296
Updegraff, Phebe W. IV, 296
Updegraff, R. Blanche IV, 296
Updegraff, Rachel IV, 221
Updegraff, Rachel IV, 295
Updegraff, Rachel IV, 296
Updegraff, Rachel IV, 298
Updegraff, Rachel VI, 453
Updegraff, Rachel VI, 607
Updegraff, Rebecca IV, 287
Updegraff, Rebecca IV, 295
Updegraff, Rebecca IV, 296
Updegraff, Rebecca A. IV, 296
Updegraff, Rebecca B. IV, 265
Updegraff, Rebecca B. IV, 296
Updegraff, Rebecca B. IV, 493
Updegraff, Rebecca B. IV, 501
Updegraff, Rebecca T. IV, 228
Updegraff, Rebecca T. IV, 250
Updegraff, Rebecca T. IV, 296
Updegraff, Rebecca T. IV, 501
Updegraff, Rebecca, Jr. IV, 296
Updegraff, Robert D. IV, 296
Updegraff, Robert W. IV, 296
Updegraff, Russell Taylor IV, 296
Updegraff, Ruthana IV, 295
Updegraff, Samuel IV, 95
Updegraff, Sarah IV, 161
Updegraff, Sarah IV, 228
Updegraff, Sarah IV, 295
Updegraff, Sarah IV, 296
Updegraff, Sarah IV, 313
Updegraff, Sarah IV, 314
Updegraff, Sarah E. IV, 295
Updegraff, Susan V, 939
Updegraff, Susana IV, 233
Updegraff, Susana IV, 295
Updegraff, Susanna IV, 94
Updegraff, Susanna IV, 113
Updegraff, Susanna IV, 181
Updegraff, Susanna IV, 295
Updegraff, Susanna IV, 296
Updegraff, Susannah IV, 296
Updegraff, Susannah V, 939
Updegraff, Susannah VI, 606
Updegraff, Thomas IV, 295
Updegraff, William IV, 296
Updegraff, William B. IV, 296
Updegraff, William D. IV, 296
Updegraff, William R. IV, 296
Updegraff, William Ross IV, 296
Updegraft, Abner IV, 113
Updegraft, Ann IV, 64
Updegraft, Ann IV, 113
Updegraft, Betty IV, 64
Updegraft, David IV, 64
Updegraft, Edith IV, 64
Updegraft, Edith IV, 113
Updegraft, Eli IV, 64
Updegraft, Eli IV, 113
Updegraft, Hannah IV, 64
Updegraft, James IV, 113
Updegraft, Joseph IV, 64
Updegraft, Josiah IV, 64
Updegraft, Nathan IV, 64
Updegraft, Rachel IV, 64
Updegraph, Hannah VI, 491
Updegraph, Joseph VI, 491
Updegraph, Josiah VI, 491

Updegraph, Mary VI, 491
Updegraph, Nathan IV, 167
Updegraph, Sarah VI, 490
Updegrove, Glenn V, 1022
Updegrove, Margaret Ann V, 1022
Updegrove, Mary Ellen V, 1022
Updegrove, Minnie V, 1022
Updegrove, Richard V, 1022
Updegrove, Robert V, 1022
Updegrove, Sally Ann V, 1022
Updegrove, Sally Mae V, 1022
Updike, Amon VI, 870
Updike, Amon VI, 969
Updike, Amon VI, 1006
Updike, Amon VI, 1008
Updike, Caroline F. VI, 1008
Updike, Christopher VI, 1008
Updike, Daniel VI, 1008
Updike, Daniel VI, 1019
Updike, Elizabeth VI, 992
Updike, Elizabeth VI, 1008
Updike, Hannah VI, 502
Updike, Hannah VI, 575
Updike, Hannah VI, 586
Updike, Hannah VI, 969
Updike, Hannah VI, 1008
Updike, Hannah VI, 1019
Updike, Jemima VI, 1008
Updike, Joel VI, 925
Updike, Joel VI, 1008
Updike, Joel VI, 1019
Updike, John VI, 1008
Updike, Jordan VI, 1008
Updike, Louisa W. VI, 1008
Updike, Lucy A. VI, 1008
Updike, Matilda VI, 1008
Updike, Milley VI, 876
Updike, Milly VI, 1008
Updike, Nancy VI, 1008
Updike, Phebe VI, 873
Updike, Polly VI, 969
Updike, Rebecca II, 1034
Updike, Rebecca II, 1036
Updike, Rebecca VI, 1008
Updike, Rebeccah VI, 1006
Updike, Samuel VI, 1008
Updike, Sarah VI, 1008
Updike, Selina VI, 936
Updike, Stephen VI, 1008
Updike, Susan VI, 876
Updike, Thomas VI, 1008
Updike, William VI, 873
Updike, William VI, 1008
Updike, William, Jr. VI, 1008
Updyke, Phebe VI, 870
Upfould, Jane II, 429
Upp, Agatha V, 254
Upp, Agatha V, 286
Upp, Catharine V, 1022
Upp, Charley B. V, 716
Upp, Chas. B. V, 716
Upp, James B. V, 716
Upp, James E. V, 716
Upp, Jennie V, 716
Upp, Jennie S. V, 716
Upp, Martha V, 208
Upp, Mary V, 135
Upp, May J. V, 208
Upp, Nannie V, 208
Upp, Samuel V, 1022
Uprummey, Rose III, 202
Uprumney, Rose III, 367
Upsike, Sarah VI, 1010
Upson, Henrietta IV, 1341
Uptigraff, Ann VI, 606
Uptigraff, James VI, 606
Uptigraff, Joseph VI, 606
Uptigraff, Nathan VI, 606
Upton, Adonijah IV, 1383
Upton, Anes I, 390
Upton, Anes I, 425
Upton, Ann I, 396
Upton, Ann I, 425
Upton, Ann I, 485
Upton, Benjamin VI, 856
Upton, Benjamin VI, 861
Upton, Benjamin VI, 867
Upton, Bessie V, 603
Upton, Charlotte IV, 1383
Upton, Daniel IV, 1383
Upton, Dorothy I, 425
Upton, Dorothy I, 430
Upton, Edmund IV, 1383
Upton, Edward I, 425
Upton, Elizabeth I, 486
Upton, Freborn IV, 1383
Upton, Freeborn IV, 1383
Upton, Gulielma IV, 1383
Upton, Harvey IV, 1383
Upton, James IV, 1383
Upton, Jane I, 485
Upton, Jesse I, 396
Upton, Jesse I, 425
Upton, Jesse I, 485
Upton, Jesse I, 904
Upton, John I, 425
Upton, John I, 472
Upton, John I, 485
Upton, John I, 486
Upton, John I, 904
Upton, John IV, 1383
Upton, John W. V, 602
Upton, Malinda V, 603
Upton, Margaret VI, 867
Upton, Martha I, 425
Upton, Mary V, 603
Upton, Newton V, 603
Upton, Orphan I, 485
Upton, Paul II, 772
Upton, Phebe II, 772
Upton, Richard I, 425
Upton, Samuel IV, 1383
Upton, Samuel S. IV, 1383
Upton, Sarah I, 406
Upton, Sarah I, 425
Upton, Sarah B. II, 772
Upton, Sarah Biddle II, 770
Upton, Sarah Biddle II, 772
Upton, Smith II, 772
Upton, Stephen IV, 1383
Upton, Susan VI, 861
Urich, Cyrus V, 1022
Urich, Mary V, 1022
Urich, Mary A. V, 1022
Uring, Elizabeth II, 448
Uring, Joshua II, 448
Uring, Tregany II, 448
Urmson, Abigail IV, 958
Urmson, Ralph IV, 958
Urnshaw, Hannah IV, 296
Urquahart, Mary III, 332
Urquart, Mary VI, 818
Urquart, Sarah VI, 818
Urquart, Walter VI, 861
Urquhart, Elizabeth VI, 861
Urquhart, James VI, 861
Urquhart, James W. VI, 805
Urquhart, John III, 129
Urquhart, John III, 332
Urquhart, John VI, 990
Urquhart, Kenneth VI, 861
Urquhart, Mary III, 129
Urquhart, Mary III, 412
Urquhart, Mary VI, 861
Urquhart, Nancy VI, 861
Urquhart, Susan VI, 805
Urquhart, Walter VI, 861
Urquhart, William VI, 861
Urton, Alida V, 1023
Urton, Bennett V, 716
Urton, Charles V, 716
Urton, Charles V, 1023
Urton, Charles A. V, 603
Urton, Chas V, 1023
Urton, Chas. IV, 949
Urton, Cleo V, 603
Urton, David V, 1023
Urton, Ezra V, 603
Urton, Ezra V, 716
Urton, Flora V, 1023
Urton, George V, 603
Urton, George W. V, 603
Urton, George W. V, 716
Urton, Isaac V, 1023
Urton, Isabel IV, 949
Urton, John V, 1023
Urton, John K. V, 1023
Urton, John K., Jr. V, 1023
Urton, John W. V, 603
Urton, John W. V, 716
Urton, Julia A. V, 1023
Urton, Louisa V, 716
Urton, Louise V, 670
Urton, Louise V, 716
Urton, Louise M. IV, 949
Urton, Malissa V, 603
Urton, Malissa J. V, 603
Urton, Malissa J. V, 716
Urton, Manta V, 1023
Urton, Mary A. V, 603
Urton, Mary A. V, 716
Urton, Mary Ann V, 603
Urton, Mary Ann V, 716
Urton, Melissa V, 603
Urton, Melissa V, 716
Urton, Oliver V, 603
Urton, Serepta V, 603
Urton, Stella V, 1023
Urton, Tilla V, 1023
Urton, Wm. V, 1023
Usher, Hannah II, 642
Usher, Hannah II, 672
Usher, Jacob II, 429
Usher, Jacob II, 457
Usher, Jacob II, 642
Usher, Jacob II, 672
Usher, Jacob II, 691
Usher, Joseph II, 429
Usher, Mary II, 429
Usher, Mary II, 457
Usher, Mary II, 672
Usher, Ruth II, 429
Usher, Sarah II, 448
Usher, Sarah II, 526
Usher, Sarah II, 672
Usher, Thomas II, 429
Usher, Wm. II, 448
Ussnum, Henry VI, 802
Ussnum, Patsey VI, 802
Utkey, Julia Ann IV, 1383
Utley, Julia Ann IV, 1378
Utley, Sarah D. III, 332
Utman, Stella V, 435
Utter, Alice V, 1023
Utter, Sarah V, 1023
Utter, Vic V, 1023

V. B., William VI, 90
Va Cott, Elizabeth III, 462
Vahn, Charles R. V, 771
Vail, Aaron IV, 64
Vail, Aaron IV, 113
Vail, Aaron V, 135
Vail, Aaron V, 872
Vail, Abigail IV, 297
Vail, Abigail IV, 327
Vail, Abigail IV, 355
Vail, Abigail IV, 449
Vail, Abigail IV, 554
Vail, Abigail IV, 576
Vail, Abigail IV, 598
Vail, Abigail IV, 780
Vail, Abigail, Jr. IV, 297
Vail, Abraham IV, 64
Vail, Abraham IV, 73
Vail, Abraham IV, 113
Vail, Abraham IV, 134
Vail, Abraham IV, 296
Vail, Abraham IV, 354
Vail, Abram IV, 134
Vail, Addison III, 332
Vail, Agnes IV, 35
Vail, Agnes IV, 64
Vail, Agnes IV, 113
Vail, Agnes IV, 123
Vail, Agnes IV, 125
Vail, Agnes IV, 134
Vail, Agness IV, 64
Vail, Agness IV, 113
Vail, Albert L. IV, 1383
Vail, Alice IV, 410
Vail, Alice IV, 411
Vail, Alice IV, 450
Vail, Alice J. IV, 449
Vail, Alice Jane IV, 449
Vail, Anna IV, 113
Vail, Anna IV, 297
Vail, Anna IV, 321
Vail, Anna IV, 354
Vail, Araminta D. III, 332
Vail, Aranna M. II, 869
Vail, Aranna M. II, 933
Vail, Benj. IV, 319
Vail, Benj. IV, 329
Vail, Benj. IV, 337
Vail, Benj. IV, 351
Vail, Benj. IV, 352
Vail, Benj. IV, 357
Vail, Benj. IV, 358
Vail, Benjamin III, 332
Vail, Benjamin IV, 113
Vail, Benjamin IV, 297
Vail, Benjamin IV, 321
Vail, Benjamin IV, 328
Vail, Benjamin IV, 348
Vail, Benjamin IV, 354
Vail, Benjamin IV, 449
Vail, Benjamin IV, 598
Vail, Catharine IV, 83
Vail, Catharine IV, 113
Vail, Catherine IV, 64
Vail, Catherine IV, 113
Vail, Catherine V, 135
Vail, Charles II, 672
Vail, Charles III, 332
Vail, Charles IV, 113
Vail, Charlotte IV, 1383
Vail, Chas. IV, 134
Vail, Clara M. III, 147
Vail, Dan. S. III, 425
Vail, Darvey IV, 355
Vail, David II, 429
Vail, David III, 332
Vail, David IV, 297
Vail, David L. II, 869
Vail, David L. II, 933
Vail, Deborah IV, 449
Vail, Deborah IV, 534
Vail, Deborah IV, 554
Vail, Deborah H. IV, 554
Vail, Delphine IV, 296
Vail, Dingee IV, 453
Vail, Dorinda A. III, 332
Vail, Edward IV, 113
Vail, Edward IV, 134
Vail, Edward G. IV, 135
Vail, Egbert III, 332
Vail, Eleanor V, 872
Vail, Eli III, 332
Vail, Eli A. IV, 64
Vail, Elisha IV, 355
Vail, Eliza IV, 64
Vail, Eliza IV, 74
Vail, Eliza IV, 113
Vail, Elizabeth IV, 113
Vail, Elizabeth IV, 126
Vail, Elizabeth IV, 134
Vail, Elizabeth IV, 209
Vail, Elizabeth IV, 296
Vail, Elizabeth IV, 334
Vail, Elizabeth IV, 355
Vail, Elizabeth IV, 449
Vail, Elizabeth A. IV, 64
Vail, Elma IV, 124
Vail, Elma IV, 134
Vail, Esther IV, 296
Vail, Esther IV, 354
Vail, Esther IV, 357
Vail, Esther IV, 466
Vail, Esther IV, 501
Vail, Esther IV, 598
Vail, Esther IV, 1009
Vail, Esther IV, 1080
Vail, Esther IV, 1081
Vail, Esther C. IV, 598
Vail, Ezeal W. IV, 64
Vail, Geo. D. III, 20
Vail, Geo. F. III, 147
Vail, George D. III, 332
Vail, Georgie S. III, 213
Vail, Georgie S. III, 332
Vail, Hannah IV, 113
Vail, Hannah IV, 132
Vail, Hannah IV, 134
Vail, Hannah IV, 329
Vail, Hannah IV, 337
Vail, Hannah IV, 351
Vail, Hannah IV, 352
Vail, Hannah IV, 354
Vail, Hannah IV, 355
Vail, Hannah IV, 358
Vail, Hannah IV, 449
Vail, Hannah IV, 598
Vail, Hannah Dingy IV, 399
Vail, Hannah Dingy IV, 432
Vail, Hannah, Jr. IV, 449
Vail, Harvey IV, 297
Vail, Hudson III, 332
Vail, Hugh IV, 64
Vail, Hugh IV, 113
Vail, Hugh V, 135
Vail, Hugh D. III, 332
Vail, Isaac III, 332
Vail, Isaac IV, 64
Vail, Isaac IV, 113
Vail, Isaac IV, 297
Vail, Isaac IV, 449
Vail, Isaac E. IV, 64
Vail, Isaac N. IV, 355
Vail, Isaac N. IV, 358
Vail, Isaac N. IV, 380
Vail, Isaac N. IV, 449
Vail, Isaac N. IV, 693
Vail, Isaac N. IV, 780
Vail, Isaac W. IV, 449
Vail, Isaac W. IV, 457
Vail, Isabel Mary III, 332
Vail, Jacob G. IV, 501
Vail, James G. IV, 1336
Vail, James G. IV, 1341
Vail, James H. III, 213
Vail, James H. III, 332
Vail, Jesse IV, 113
Vail, Jesse IV, 124
Vail, Jesse IV, 134
Vail, Jesse IV, 297
Vail, Jesse IV, 355
Vail, Jesse IV, 449
Vail, Jesse IV, 1118
Vail, Jesse D. IV, 135
Vail, Joel IV, 113
Vail, Joel IV, 134
Vail, John III, 198
Vail, John III, 332
Vail, John IV, 296
Vail, John IV, 297
Vail, John IV, 327
Vail, John IV, 449
Vail, John IV, 466
Vail, John IV, 501
Vail, John IV, 554
Vail, John IV, 576
Vail, John IV, 598
Vail, John IV, 780
Vail, John IV, 1009
Vail, John IV, 1080
Vail, John C. IV, 64
Vail, John Lawrence IV, 1009
Vail, John, Jr. IV, 297
Vail, Joseph III, 332
Vail, Joseph IV, 358
Vail, Joseph S. II, 772
Vail, Joseph S. IV, 297
Vail, Josephine III, 147
Vail, Josephine III, 332
Vail, Lemira S. IV, 355
Vail, Lewis IV, 780
Vail, Lot III, 332
Vail, Louis Willets IV, 134
Vail, Louis Willets IV, 780
Vail, Lydia IV, 113
Vail, Lydia IV, 130
Vail, Lydia IV, 134
Vail, Lydia IV, 351
Vail, Lydia IV, 355
Vail, Lydia IV, 449
Vail, Lydia IV, 501
Vail, Lydia C. IV, 449
Vail, Margaret IV, 64
Vail, Margaret IV, 73
Vail, Margaret IV, 113
Vail, Margaret IV, 129
Vail, Margaret IV, 134
Vail, Margaret IV, 296
Vail, Margaret IV, 348
Vail, Margaret IV, 354
Vail, Margaret IV, 726
Vail, Margaret K. II, 869
Vail, Margaret K. II, 933
Vail, Margaret K. III, 151
Vail, Margaret R. II, 869
Vail, Margaret R. II, 933
Vail, Margrat IV, 354
Vail, Maria L. III, 332
Vail, Martha III, 20
Vail, Martha III, 332
Vail, Martha IV, 64
Vail, Martha IV, 134
Vail, Mary III, 20
Vail, Mary III, 332
Vail, Mary IV, 64
Vail, Mary IV, 107
Vail, Mary IV, 113
Vail, Mary IV, 279
Vail, Mary IV, 297
Vail, Mary IV, 352
Vail, Mary IV, 355
Vail, Mary IV, 449
Vail, Mary V, 135
Vail, Mary V, 872
Vail, Mary Ann IV, 64
Vail, Mary Anna III, 425
Vail, Mary B. III, 332
Vail, Mary C. IV, 449
Vail, Mary C. IV, 780
Vail, Mary D. III, 213
Vail, Mary Dell III, 213
Vail, Mary Dell III, 332
Vail, Mary J. III, 332
Vail, Mary M. IV, 380
Vail, Mary M. IV, 449
Vail, Mary M. IV, 693
Vail, Mary M. IV, 780
Vail, Melissa D. IV, 134
Vail, Mercy IV, 20
Vail, Mercy IV, 64
Vail, Mercy IV, 73
Vail, Mercy IV, 113
Vail, Mercy IV, 123
Vail, Mercy IV, 134
Vail, Mercy IV, 449
Vail, Mercy IV, 693
Vail, Nathan IV, 113
Vail, Nathan IV, 355
Vail, Nathan IV, 449
Vail, Nathan C. IV, 64
Vail, Olton IV, 296
Vail, Orpah IV, 598
Vail, Orpha IV, 1009
Vail, Orpha IV, 1080
Vail, Phebe IV, 64
Vail, Phebe IV, 296
Vail, Phebe IV, 598

Phebe IV, 1009
Phebe IV, 1080
Priscilla IV, 113
Priscilla IV, 132
Priscilla IV, 134
Rachel IV, 113
Rachel IV, 115
Rachel IV, 328
Rachel IV, 354
Rachel IV, 449
Rachel D. IV, 355
Rachel D. IV, 449
Rachel D. IV, 457
Randal IV, 449
Randall IV, 64
Randolph IV, 113
Randolph V, 135
Rebecca IV, 64
Rebecca IV, 113
Rebecca IV, 319
Rebecca IV, 321
Rebecca IV, 348
Rebecca IV, 354
Rebecca IV, 357
Rebecca IV, 449
Rebeckah IV, 449
Rebekah IV, 328
Robert IV, 64
Robert IV, 111
Robert IV, 113
Robert IV, 334
Robert IV, 355
Robert IV, 449
Robert A. IV, 64
Robert, Jr. IV, 355
Ruth III, 198
Ruth III, 332
Ruth M. IV, 1336
Ruth M. IV, 1341
Ruth Russell IV, 1341
S. Delphine IV, 297
Samuel III, 115
Samuel III, 332
Samuel IV, 35
Samuel IV, 64
Samuel IV, 90
Samuel IV, 113
Samuel IV, 123
Samuel IV, 126
Samuel IV, 134
Samuel IV, 209
Samuel IV, 296
Samuel IV, 501
Samuel IV, 1009
Samuel V, 872
Samuel C. IV, 134
Sarah III, 72
Sarah III, 115
Sarah III, 332
Sarah IV, 64
Sarah IV, 77
Sarah IV, 111
Sarah IV, 113
Sarah IV, 128
Sarah IV, 134
Sarah IV, 135
Sarah IV, 334
Sarah IV, 355
Sarah IV, 358
Sarah IV, 449
Sarah IV, 501
Sarah IV, 504
Sarah Jane IV, 355
Semantha III, 198
Semantha III, 332
Semira IV, 297
Shubal IV, 113
Shubel IV, 64
Stephen IV, 64
Stephen IV, 113
Stephen V, 135
Stephen, Jr. IV, 113
Susan I, 865
Taylor IV, 64
Taylor IV, 113
Thomas III, 332
Thomas Carr IV, 1009
Thomas Carr IV, 1080
Timothy D. III, 332
Walter C. IV, 449
Walter E. IV, 449
Walter E. IV, 534
Walter E. IV, 554
Webster II, 429
Webster II, 672
William H. IV, 1009
Wm. II, 672
, Aaron V, 872
, Agnes IV, 1068
, Anne IV, 162
, Benjamin IV, 137
Vaile, Benjamin IV, 162
Vaile, Eleanor V, 872
Vaile, Elizabeth IV, 1076
Vaile, Isaac IV, 162
Vaile, Jesse IV, 1139
Vaile, Nathan IV, 162
Vaile, Rachel IV, 162
Vaile, Rebecca IV, 162
Vaile, Robert IV, 162
Vaile, Sarah IV, 162
Vaill, Hannah IV, 355
Vaill, Isabel Mary III, 309
Vaill, Isabel Mary III, 332
Vaill, Mary B. III, 309
Vaill, Mary B. III, 332
Vaill, Timothy D. III, 309
Vaill, Timothy D. III, 332
Vale, Aaron V, 872
Vale, Ann IV, 663
Vale, Ann IV, 885
Vale, Ann P. IV, 885
Vale, Anna IV, 140
Vale, Anna IV, 141
Vale, Anna IV, 885
Vale, Beulah IV, 865
Vale, Beulah IV, 885
Vale, Caroline IV, 663
Vale, Caroline IV, 885
Vale, Deborah IV, 663
Vale, Deborah IV, 863
Vale, Deborah IV, 885
Vale, Edith IV, 885
Vale, Eli IV, 663
Vale, Eli IV, 885
Vale, Eli A. IV, 64
Vale, Eliza IV, 64
Vale, Eliza IV, 885
Vale, Elizabeth A. IV, 64
Vale, Esther VI, 607
Vale, Ezeal W. IV, 64
Vale, Guli Elma IV, 885
Vale, Hiram P. IV, 885
Vale, Isaac IV, 64
Vale, Isaac E. IV, 64
Vale, Jacob IV, 663
Vale, Jacob IV, 876
Vale, Jacob IV, 885
Vale, Jane IV, 885
Vale, John IV, 663
Vale, John IV, 885
Vale, John C. IV, 64
Vale, John T. IV, 885
Vale, John Thomas IV, 885
Vale, John, Jr. IV, 885
Vale, Lewis W. IV, 663
Vale, Louisa IV, 881
Vale, Louisa IV, 885
Vale, Maria IV, 868
Vale, Marian IV, 885
Vale, Martha IV, 64
Vale, Martha IV, 882
Vale, Martha IV, 885
Vale, Martha H. IV, 885
Vale, Mary Ann IV, 64
Vale, Mary Ann IV, 885
Vale, Morton IV, 885
Vale, Nathan C. IV, 64
Vale, Olivia W. IV, 876
Vale, Olivia W. IV, 885
Vale, Phebe IV, 30
Vale, Phebe IV, 64
Vale, Phebe IV, 663
Vale, Phebe IV, 868
Vale, Phebe IV, 885
Vale, Robert IV, 64
Vale, Robert A. IV, 64
Vale, S. Delphine IV, 199
Vale, S. Delphine IV, 297
Vale, Sarah W. IV, 663
Vale, Susan IV, 864
Vale, Susan IV, 885
Vale, Susanna IV, 885
Vale, Wilmer P. IV, 663
Valeart, Anna V, 716
Valenta, Louise F. III, 442
Valentin, Deborah III, 464
Valentine, ??? III, 333
Valentine, Abigail III, 423
Valentine, Alan Chester III, 461
Valentine, Alice III, 333
Valentine, Amelia M. III, 333
Valentine, Amy III, 472
Valentine, Ann II, 721
Valentine, Ann III, 139
Valentine, Ann III, 317
Valentine, Ann III, 333
Valentine, Ann III, 404
Valentine, Ann III, 450
Valentine, Ann III, 460
Valentine, Ann III, 462
Valentine, Ann III, 508
Valentine, Ann C. II, 721
Valentine, Ann C. II, 772
Valentine, Ann E. III, 460
Valentine, Ann Eliza III, 462
Valentine, Ann Elizabeth III, 425
Valentine, Ann Elizabeth III, 461
Valentine, Ann H. II, 429
Valentine, Ann H. II, 498
Valentine, Ann H. II, 673
Valentine, Ann H. II, 721
Valentine, Ann L. III, 337
Valentine, Ann T. III, 333
Valentine, Ann T. III, 334
Valentine, Ann T. III, 362
Valentine, Ann T. III, 462
Valentine, Ann V. III, 222
Valentine, Anna I, 1124
Valentine, Anna III, 222
Valentine, Anna III, 333
Valentine, Anna III, 334
Valentine, Anna III, 423
Valentine, Anna III, 461
Valentine, Anna III, 462
Valentine, Anna C. II, 698
Valentine, Anna C. II, 699
Valentine, Anna C. III, 449
Valentine, Anna C. III, 462
Valentine, Anna K. III, 225
Valentine, Anna K. III, 333
Valentine, Anna K. III, 334
Valentine, Anna K. III, 360
Valentine, Anna Laurie III, 461
Valentine, Anna Maria IV, 780
Valentine, Anne III, 412
Valentine, Anne L. III, 460
Valentine, Annie III, 206
Valentine, Annie III, 223
Valentine, Annie III, 285
Valentine, Annie III, 332
Valentine, Annie III, 334
Valentine, Annie III, 489
Valentine, Annie III, 502
Valentine, Annie K. III, 332
Valentine, Annie K. III, 469
Valentine, Annie L. III, 333
Valentine, Annie L. III, 360
Valentine, Annie L. III, 425
Valentine, Annie L. III, 469
Valentine, Annie Laurie III, 460
Valentine, Asenath II, 825
Valentine, Augusta Erickson III, 461
Valentine, Benajah III, 472
Valentine, Benjamin II, 721
Valentine, Benjamin III, 472
Valentine, Benjamin E. II, 269
Valentine, Benjamin E. II, 429
Valentine, Benjamin E. II, 498
Valentine, Benjamin E. II, 673
Valentine, Benjamin E. II, 721
Valentine, Benjamin E. II, 772
Valentine, Benjamin E. III, 332
Valentine, Benjamin E. III, 333
Valentine, Beulah S. II, 516
Valentine, Beulah S. II, 673
Valentine, Beulah S. III, 333
Valentine, Blanche E. III, 333
Valentine, Blanche E. III, 363
Valentine, Caroline III, 452
Valentine, Caroline III, 460
Valentine, Caroline III, 461
Valentine, Catharine III, 460
Valentine, Catharine S. III, 425
Valentine, Catharine S. III, 461
Valentine, Charles III, 333
Valentine, Charles III, 404
Valentine, Charles III, 408
Valentine, Charles III, 412
Valentine, Charles III, 420
Valentine, Charles III, 460
Valentine, Charles III, 461
Valentine, Charles III, 462
Valentine, Charles III, 471
Valentine, Charles III, 472
Valentine, Charles III, 480
Valentine, Charles III, 502
Valentine, Charles Lowell III, 460
Valentine, Charles Morton II, 269
Valentine, Charles Morton II, 673
Valentine, Charles Morton II, 721
Valentine, Charles Morton II, 772
Valentine, Charles Morton III, 333
Valentine, Charles P. III, 426
Valentine, Charles P. III, 489
Valentine, Charles P. III, 502
Valentine, Charles Post III, 460
Valentine, Charles Post III, 461
Valentine, Charles Post, Jr. III, 461
Valentine, Charlotte B. III, 511
Valentine, Chas. III, 334
Valentine, Chas. III, 420
Valentine, Chas. Edward III, 461
Valentine, Chas. P. III, 489
Valentine, Cloyd Hampton III, 244
Valentine, Cloyd Hampton III, 333
Valentine, Cornelia III, 412
Valentine, Cornelia III, 461
Valentine, Daniel III, 434
Valentine, Daniel III, 459
Valentine, Daniel III, 460
Valentine, Daniel III, 461
Valentine, Daniel III, 511
Valentine, Daniel K. III, 333
Valentine, David III, 333
Valentine, David III, 334
Valentine, David III, 386
Valentine, David III, 400
Valentine, David III, 405
Valentine, David III, 425
Valentine, David III, 456
Valentine, David III, 460
Valentine, David III, 461
Valentine, David III, 502
Valentine, Deborah III, 404
Valentine, Deborah III, 460
Valentine, Deborah III, 461
Valentine, Eleanor Harriet III, 334
Valentine, Elias Lewis III, 334
Valentine, Eliz. III, 333
Valentine, Eliz. III, 447
Valentine, Eliz. III, 461
Valentine, Eliz. III, 462
Valentine, Eliz. A. III, 333
Valentine, Eliza II, 269
Valentine, Eliza II, 673
Valentine, Eliza III, 333
Valentine, Elizabeth III, 21
Valentine, Elizabeth III, 333
Valentine, Elizabeth III, 334
Valentine, ELizabeth III, 430
Valentine, Elizabeth III, 430
Valentine, Elizabeth III, 460
Valentine, Elizabeth III, 461
Valentine, Elizabeth III, 462
Valentine, Elizabeth A. III, 100
Valentine, Elizabeth Ann II, 269
Valentine, Elizabeth Ann II, 498
Valentine, Elizabeth Ann II, 516
Valentine, Elizabeth Ann II, 673
Valentine, Elizabeth Ann II, 721
Valentine, Elizabeth Ann II, 772
Valentine, Elizabeth Ann III, 333
Valentine, Elizabeth Ann III, 334
Valentine, Elizabeth Ann III, 409
Valentine, Elizabeth Ann III, 461
Valentine, Elizabeth H. III, 403
Valentine, Elizabeth H. III, 461
Valentine, Elizabeth P. III, 472
Valentine, Elizabeth R. II, 721
Valentine, Elizabeth R. II, 772
Valentine, Elizabeth V. III, 362
Valentine, Ella III, 225
Valentine, Ella III, 333
Valentine, Elliott III, 333
Valentine, Ellwood III, 384
Valentine, Ellwood III, 386
Valentine, Ellwood III, 434
Valentine, Ellwood III, 461
Valentine, Elwood III, 434
Valentine, Elwood III, 452
Valentine, Elwood III, 460
Valentine, Emily III, 433
Valentine, Emily III, 462
Valentine, Emily N. III, 461
Valentine, Emily T. III, 502
Valentine, Emma III, 46
Valentine, Emma J. I, 1162
Valentine, Ephraim III, 461
Valentine, Ephraim C. III, 461
Valentine, Esther III, 462
Valentine, Esther III, 464
Valentine, Ethel V, 467
Valentine, Ethelinda III, 489
Valentine, Eugene III, 462
Valentine, Florence III, 34
Valentine, Florence E. III, 334
Valentine, Florence N. III, 333
Valentine, Florence N. III, 334
Valentine, Florence N. III, 337
Valentine, Freelove III, 406
Valentine, Freelove III, 461
Valentine, Freelove III, 494
Valentine, Frieda III, 426
Valentine, Frieda III, 461
Valentine, Frieda Harriet III, 461
Valentine, Geo. III, 333
Valentine, Geo. III, 370
Valentine, Geo. III, 454
Valentine, Geo. V, 939
Valentine, Geo. W. I, 1162
Valentine, George III, 333
Valentine, George III, 462
Valentine, George III, 472
Valentine, George VI, 1008
Valentine, George W. I, 1162
Valentine, George W. III, 461
Valentine, Gilbert C. III, 333
Valentine, Hannah I, 1162
Valentine, Hannah III, 264
Valentine, Hannah III, 334
Valentine, Hannah III, 386
Valentine, Hannah III, 400
Valentine, Hannah III, 405
Valentine, Hannah III, 425
Valentine, Hannah III, 456
Valentine, Hannah III, 460
Valentine, Hannah III, 461
Valentine, Hannah III, 462
Valentine, Hannah III, 472
Valentine, Hannah III, 502
Valentine, Hannah E. III, 333
Valentine, Hannah E. III, 461
Valentine, Hannah K. III, 333
Valentine, Hannah T. III, 264
Valentine, Hannah T. III, 333
Valentine, Hannah T. III, 461
Valentine, Harriet III, 333
Valentine, Helen A. III, 461
Valentine, Helen Elise III, 285
Valentine, Helen Elise III, 333
Valentine, Helen Elise III, 334
Valentine, Henry III, 434
Valentine, Henry C. III, 461
Valentine, Henry E. III, 333
Valentine, Henry R. III, 461
Valentine, Isaac R. III, 333
Valentine, Isaac R. III, 406
Valentine, Isaac R. III, 461
Valentine, Jacob II, 498
Valentine, Jacob II, 516
Valentine, Jacob II, 673
Valentine, Jacob II, 721
Valentine, Jacob II, 772
Valentine, Jacob III, 309
Valentine, Jacob III, 318
Valentine, Jacob III, 333
Valentine, Jacob III, 334
Valentine, Jacob III, 409
Valentine, Jacob III, 425
Valentine, Jacob III, 453
Valentine, Jacob III, 460
Valentine, Jacob III, 461
Valentine, Jacob III, 462
Valentine, Jacob III, 472
Valentine, Jacob III, 481
Valentine, Jacob III, 489
Valentine, Jacob III, 501
Valentine, Jacob III, 502
Valentine, Jacob III, 506
Valentine, Jacob VI, 218
Valentine, Jacob D. III, 333
Valentine, Jacob Doty III, 333
Valentine, Jacob L. III, 333
Valentine, Jacob L. III, 502
Valentine, Jacob S. III, 472
Valentine, Jame III, 462
Valentine, James C. II, 673
Valentine, James C. II, 772
Valentine, James Cresson II, 429
Valentine, James Cresson II, 772
Valentine, Jane III, 333
Valentine, Jane III, 334
Valentine, Jane III, 434
Valentine, Jane III, 435
Valentine, Jane III, 441
Valentine, Jane III, 442
Valentine, Jane III, 452
Valentine, Jane III, 461
Valentine, Jane III, 462
Valentine, Jane V, 939
Valentine, Jemima III, 459
Valentine, Jemima III, 461
Valentine, Jemima U. III, 461
Valentine, Jerusha III, 333
Valentine, John II, 825
Valentine, John V, 939
Valentine, John H. II, 933
Valentine, John H. III, 333
Valentine, John H. III, 334
Valentine, John H. F. Matz III, 461
Valentine, John Hampton III, 21
Valentine, John Hampton III, 333
Valentine, John K. II, 913
Valentine, John K. II, 933
Valentine, John King II, 825

Valentine, John T. III, 430
Valentine, John T. III, 447
Valentine, John T. III, 461
Valentine, John T. III, 462
Valentine, Jos. A. III, 100
Valentine, Jos. A. III, 333
Valentine, Jos. U. III, 400
Valentine, Joseph III, 403
Valentine, Joseph III, 472
Valentine, Joseph C. III, 461
Valentine, Joseph L. IV, 1297
Valentine, Joseph U. III, 461
Valentine, Joseph V. III, 402
Valentine, Julia I, 904
Valentine, Kezia III, 480
Valentine, Kezia III, 502
Valentine, Kezia W. III, 460
Valentine, Keziah III, 404
Valentine, Keziah H. III, 333
Valentine, Keziah W. III, 334
Valentine, Latitia III, 461
Valentine, Latitia III, 471
Valentine, Leonard III, 461
Valentine, Lewis III, 333
Valentine, Lewis III, 434
Valentine, Lewis III, 435
Valentine, Lewis III, 441
Valentine, Lewis III, 449
Valentine, Lewis III, 452
Valentine, Lewis III, 460
Valentine, Lewis III, 461
Valentine, Lewis III, 462
Valentine, Lewis VI, 820
Valentine, Louise E. III, 333
Valentine, Lucy VI, 1008
Valentine, Lydia III, 433
Valentine, Lydia P. III, 462
Valentine, Margery H. III, 334
Valentine, Margery Hill III, 38
Valentine, Maria III, 462
Valentine, Maria A. III, 190
Valentine, Maria A. III, 334
Valentine, Martha III, 139
Valentine, Martha III, 318
Valentine, Martha III, 333
Valentine, Martha III, 353
Valentine, Martha III, 360
Valentine, Martha III, 436
Valentine, Martha III, 445
Valentine, Martha III, 446
Valentine, Martha III, 453
Valentine, Martha III, 460
Valentine, Martha III, 462
Valentine, Martha III, 472
Valentine, Martha III, 502
Valentine, Martha III, 506
Valentine, Martha A. III, 333
Valentine, Martha Ann III, 334
Valentine, Mary III, 309
Valentine, Mary III, 333
Valentine, Mary III, 370
Valentine, Mary III, 400
Valentine, Mary III, 408
Valentine, Mary III, 412
Valentine, Mary III, 423
Valentine, Mary III, 425
Valentine, Mary III, 434
Valentine, Mary III, 452
Valentine, Mary III, 460
Valentine, Mary III, 461
Valentine, Mary III, 462
Valentine, Mary III, 471
Valentine, Mary III, 472
Valentine, Mary III, 481
Valentine, Mary III, 497
Valentine, Mary III, 501
Valentine, Mary III, 502
Valentine, Mary III, 505
Valentine, Mary III, 506
Valentine, Mary A. III, 461
Valentine, Mary Ann III, 462
Valentine, Mary Anna III, 222
Valentine, Mary Anna III, 333
Valentine, Mary C. III, 405
Valentine, Mary C. III, 461
Valentine, Mary Jane III, 447
Valentine, Mary Jane III, 461
Valentine, Mary Jane III, 462
Valentine, Mary L. III, 223
Valentine, Mary L. III, 333
Valentine, Mary L. III, 334
Valentine, Mary T. III, 384
Valentine, Mary T. III, 386
Valentine, Mary T. III, 434
Valentine, Mary T. III, 461
Valentine, Milton C. III, 333
Valentine, Obad III, 436
Valentine, Obadiah III, 333
Valentine, Obadiah III, 360
Valentine, Obadiah III, 445
Valentine, Obadiah III, 446
Valentine, Obadiah III, 462
Valentine, Obadiah III, 464
Valentine, Obadiah W. III, 462
Valentine, Oliver III, 442
Valentine, Oliver III, 461
Valentine, Oliver III, 462
Valentine, Oliver T. III, 461
Valentine, Peggy III, 462
Valentine, Phebe II, 672
Valentine, Phebe III, 309
Valentine, Phebe III, 333
Valentine, Phebe III, 425
Valentine, Phebe III, 446
Valentine, Phebe III, 454
Valentine, Phebe III, 461
Valentine, Phebe III, 462
Valentine, Phebe III, 472
Valentine, Phebe V, 939
Valentine, Pheebe II, 672
Valentine, Rachel II, 672
Valentine, Rachel III, 420
Valentine, Rachel III, 460
Valentine, Rachel III, 462
Valentine, Richard III, 423
Valentine, Richard III, 462
Valentine, Richard Arnold III, 333
Valentine, Richard Kirk III, 333
Valentine, Richard, Jr. III, 462
Valentine, Robert II, 672
Valentine, Robert III, 472
Valentine, Robert Barclay III, 333
Valentine, Robert Packard III, 333
Valentine, Rosetta III, 434
Valentine, Samuel III, 404
Valentine, Samuel III, 460
Valentine, Samuel VI, 453
Valentine, Samuel Rhoads II, 721
Valentine, Samuel Rhoads II, 772
Valentine, Samuel T. III, 222
Valentine, Samuel T. III, 225
Valentine, Samuel T. III, 264
Valentine, Samuel T. III, 333
Valentine, Samuel T. III, 334
Valentine, Samuel T. III, 363
Valentine, Samuel T. III, 462
Valentine, Samuel Y. III, 423
Valentine, Sarah III, 333
Valentine, Sarah III, 370
Valentine, Sarah III, 462
Valentine, Sarah A. I, 1162
Valentine, Sarah A. III, 139
Valentine, Sarah A. III, 333
Valentine, Sarah A. III, 338
Valentine, Sarah Ann III, 334
Valentine, Sarah E. III, 100
Valentine, Sarah E. III, 333
Valentine, Sarah T. III, 462
Valentine, Sidney III, 511
Valentine, Silas III, 333
Valentine, Silas III, 462
Valentine, Silas T. III, 462
Valentine, Stephen III, 139
Valentine, Stephen III, 223
Valentine, Stephen III, 285
Valentine, Stephen III, 317
Valentine, Stephen III, 332
Valentine, Stephen III, 333
Valentine, Stephen III, 334
Valentine, Stephen III, 337
Valentine, Stephen III, 338
Valentine, Stephen III, 360
Valentine, Stephen III, 362
Valentine, Stephen III, 462
Valentine, Stephen III, 469
Valentine, Stephen III, 472
Valentine, Stephen Lewis III, 334
Valentine, Stephen, Jr. III, 38
Valentine, Stephen, Jr. III, 206
Valentine, Stephen, Jr. III, 334
Valentine, Susan III, 461
Valentine, Susan D. III, 461
Valentine, Susanna III, 501
Valentine, Susannah III, 502
Valentine, Theodosia III, 408
Valentine, Theodosia III, 462
Valentine, Thomas III, 334
Valentine, Thomas A. III, 472
Valentine, Thomas Edgar III, 190
Valentine, Thomas Edgar III, 333
Valentine, Thomas Edgar III, 334
Valentine, Townsend III, 334
Valentine, Townsend III, 412
Valentine, Townsend III, 450
Valentine, Townsend III, 462
Valentine, Valentine III, 472
Valentine, Vandewater III, 462
Valentine, Virginia II, 825
Valentine, Virginia P. II, 913
Valentine, Virginia P. II, 933
Valentine, Walter Birdsall III, 334
Valentine, Warren III, 34
Valentine, Warren III, 334
Valentine, Wd. Jane III, 462
Valentine, Willet III, 333
Valentine, William II, 269
Valentine, William III, 333
Valentine, William III, 334
Valentine, William III, 462
Valentine, William III, 472
Valentine, William M. III, 461
Valentine, William M. III, 462
Valentine, William, Jr. III, 462
Valentine, Winney VI, 842
Valentine, Winnie III, 244
Valentine, Winnie III, 333
Valentine, Wm, Jr. III, 462
Valentine, Wm. II, 673
Valentine, Wm. III, 462
Valentine, Wm. Augustus III, 462
Valentine, Wm. Henry I, 1162
Valentine, Wm. M. III, 429
Valentine, Wm. M. III, 433
Valentine, Wm. M. III, 502
Valintine, George W. III, 454
Valintine, Phebe III, 454
Vallecoat, William II, 448
Vallentine, Benjamin E. II, 673
Vallentine, Beulah S. II, 673
Vallentine, Charles Morton II, 673
Vallentine, Eliza II, 673
Vallentine, Elizabeth Ann II, 673
Vallentine, Pheebe II, 672
Vallentine, Rachel II, 672
Vallentine, Robert I, 425
Vallentine, Wm. II, 673
Vallicoat, Margrett II, 448
Vallicoat, Sarah II, 448
Vallicoat, Wm. II, 448
Valory, Eugenia L. III, 22
Van Aken, Elizabeth II, 575
Van Aken, Elizabeth II, 673
Van Aken, Henry II, 534
Van Aken, Henry II, 673
Van Aken, Jane II, 534
Van Aken, Wd. Jane II, 673
Van Allen, Margaretta II, 1062
Van Allen, Margaretta II, 1067
Van Allen, Margaretta II, 1081
Van Allen, Margaretta II, 1082
Van Alstine, Mary Ann III, 334
Van Alstyne, Harriet III, 298
Van Alstyne, Harriet III, 334
Van Alstyne, Margaret A. III, 298
Van Alstyne, Margaret A. III, 334
Van Alstyne, Mary Ann III, 334
Van Alstyne, Wm. B. III, 298
Van Alstyne, Wm. B. III, 334
Van Blarcom, Ann III, 462
Van Blarcom, Ella M. III, 462
Van Blarcom, Herman III, 462
Van Blarcom, Herman L. III, 462
Van Brunt, Edw. K. III, 334
Van Brunt, Edward K. III, 234
Van Brunt, Elizabeth III, 234
Van Brunt, Wd. Elizabeth III, 234
Van Brunt, Wd. Elizabeth III, 334
Van Burkirk, Anchor III, 94
Van Burkirk, Andrew III, 263
Van Burkirk, Andrew III, 334
Van Burkirk, Arline III, 82
Van Burkirk, Arline III, 334
Van Burkirk, Bertha III, 334
Van Burkirk, Bertha C. III, 263
Van Burkirk, Bertha C. III, 334
Van Burkirk, Charles Harold III, 334
Van Burkirk, Emma III, 94
Van Burkirk, Emma III, 263
Van Burkirk, Emma III, 334
Van Burkirk, Evelyn III, 334
Van Burkirk, Hilah Ann III, 334
Van Burkirk, Howard U. III, 82
Van Burkirk, Howard U. III, 152
Van Burkirk, Howard U. III, 334
Van Burkirk, Marian III, 94
Van Burkirk, Marian III, 334
Van Burkirk, Martin III, 334
Van Burkirk, Nellie E. III, 152
Van Burkirk, Nellie E. III, 334
Van Buskirk, Alonzo IV, 1297
Van Buskirk, Andrew III, 327
Van Buskirk, Arnold IV, 1297
Van Buskirk, Charles Harold III, 58
Van Buskirk, Emma III, 327
Van Buskirk, Evelyn III, 58
Van Buskirk, Lola IV, 1297
Van Buyleart, John II, 673
Van Buyleart, Mariana II, 673
Van Buyleart, Meriana II, 673
Van Clacke, Ann III, 199
Van Clacke, Ann III, 334
Van Cleaf, Luther V, 1023
Van Cleve, Luther V, 603
Van Cleve, Retta V, 603
Van Clief, Daniel III, 193
Van Clief, Daniel III, 334
Van Clief, Mary M. III, 193
Van Clief, Mary M. III, 334
Van Cot, ??? III, 480
Van Cot, Elizabeth III, 480
Van Cott, Alanson III, 502
Van Cott, Cornelius III, 462
Van Cott, Elford III, 502
Van Cott, Eliza III, 334
Van Cott, Eliza Ann III, 334
Van Cott, Elizabeth III, 334
Van Cott, Elizabeth III, 394
Van Cott, Elizabeth III, 414
Van Cott, Elizabeth III, 415
Van Cott, Elizabeth III, 462
Van Cott, Elizabeth III, 502
Van Cott, Florence III, 502
Van Cott, Gussie III, 502
Van Cott, Jane III, 462
Van Cott, Nicholas III, 462
Van Cott, Oliver III, 414
Van Cott, Oliver III, 462
Van Cott, Peter III, 334
Van Culin, John II, 108
Van Devort, Maud V, 939
Van Devort, Maude E. V, 939
Van Dewall, Nathaniel VI, 215
Van Dolsen, Gertrude I. III, 335
Van Dolsen, Gertrude, I. III, 290
Van Doren, Elizabeth V, 709
Van Duren, James III, 335
Van Dyke, Sarah I, 1122
Van Dyke, Sarah I, 1133
Van Etten, ??? III, 159
Van Etten, Charlotte Louisa III, 159
Van Etten, Charlotte Louisa III, 335
Van Etten, Gertrude III, 335
Van Etten, John III, 335
Van Etten, June III, 335
Van Everen, Eliz. J. III, 116
Van Everen, Eliz. J. III, 301
Van Everen, Eliz. J. III, 335
Van Everen, Elizabeth J. III, 116
Van Everen, Elizabeth J. III, 335
Van Everen, Grace Abbie III, 301
Van Everen, Grace Abbie III, 335
Van Everen, Harriet III, 335
Van Everen, John III, 335
Van Everen, Mary E. III, 116
Van Everen, Mary Effie III, 116
Van Everen, Mary Effie III, 335
Van Everen, Philip III, 116
Van Everen, Philip E. III, 335
Van Everen, Philip F. III, 116
Van Everen, Philip F. III, 301
Van Everen, Philip F. III, 335
Van Every, ??? III, 79
Van Every, Maria III, 79
Van Every, Maria III, 335
Van Fossan, Harry IV, 780
Van Fossen, Harry IV, 849
Van Grundy, Edwin V, 286
Van Grundy, Etna V, 286
Van Helden, Adrian III, 335
Van Helden, Adrian III, 347
Van Helden, Caroline III, 335
Van Helden, Caroline III, 347
Van Hoesen, ??? III, 335
Van Hoesen, Anna III, 335
Van Hoesen, Catharine III, 335
Van Hoesen, Elizabeth II, 713
Van Hoesen, Elizabeth III, 241
Van Hoesen, Elizabeth III, 335
Van Hoesen, Leonard II, 713
Van Hoesen, Mary II, 713
Van Hoesen, Mary III, 335
Van Hoesen, Mary Ann III, 335
Van Hoesen, Thomas III, 335
Van Hoose, James M. VI, 861
Van Hoose, Susan VI, 861
Van Horn, ??? III, 335
Van Horn, Betsy V, 771
Van Horn, Catharine IV, 1297
Van Horn, Charles E. III, 335
Van Horn, Duriah V, 771
Van Horn, James V, 135
Van Horn, Joanna V, 135
Van Horn, John III, 335
Van Horn, John V, 135
Van Horn, Lydia III, 15
Van Horn, Lydia III, 335
Van Horn, Mary Ann III, 33
Van Horn, Mary Sarah V, 77
Van Horn, Rebecca V, 135
Van Horn, Rebecca V, 771
Van Horn, Rebeccah V, 60
Van Horn, Rebeccah V, 135
Van Horn, Robert V, 135
Van Horne, Edward Maria Theresa III, 245
Van Hostein, Cora IV, 404
Van Hostein, Cora IV, 450
Van Houton, ??? III, 54
Van Houton, ??? III, 335
Van Houton, Mary III, 335
Van Houton, Mary Ann III, 5
Van Houton, Mary Ann III, 3
Van Houton, Mary Ella III, 5
Van Houton, Mary Ella III, 3
Van Husan, Caleb III, 79
Van Husan, Flora B. III, 79
Van Hyning, Anna IV, 1277
Van Hyning, Grover IV, 1297
Van Hyning, Hazel Marie IV, 1297
Van Hyning, James IV, 1297
Van Hyning, Levitha Geho IV, 1297
Van Ingen, Abraham III, 335
Van Ingen, Adele III, 335
Van Ingen, Clarissa M. III, 33
Van Ingen, Dudley W. III, 202
Van Ingen, Dudley W. III, 335
Van Ingen, Eliz. S. III, 202
Van Ingen, Eliz. S. III, 335
Van Ingen, Helen III, 202
Van Ingen, Helen III, 335
Van Ingen, Mary III, 335
Van Ingen, William III, 335
Van Ingen, Wm. III, 335
Van Inger, Adele III, 39
Van Keuren, Benj. III, 303
Van Keuren, Gertrude III, 303
Van Keuren, Gertrude III, 335
Van Keuren, Mary Ann III, 303
Van Kleeck, Albert Van Nostrand III, 463
Van Kleeck, Florence III, 463
Van Kleeck, Geo. B. III, 463
Van Kleeck, George Baltus III, 463
Van Kleeck, Grace III, 463
Van Kleeck, Jacob III, 463
Van Kleeck, Louis A. III, 463
Van Kleeck, Louis Ashley III, 4
Van Kleeck, Martha Louise III, 463
Van Kleeck, Phebe III, 463
Van Law, Amy B. IV, 663
Van Law, Joseph S. IV, 635
Van Law, Joseph S. IV, 663
Van Law, Margaret IV, 635
Van Law, Margaret IV, 663
Van Law, Margaret H. IV, 663
Van Law, Thomas E. IV, 663
Van Lindley, John I, 534
Van Lindley, Lysandra Lindley I, 534
Van Loan, John S. III, 335
Van Lude, George Wm. II, 673
Van Lude, Johanna Dorothy II, 673
Van Luden, George Wm. II, 467
Van Luden, George Wm. II, 673
Van Luden, Johanna II, 673
Van Luden, Johanna Dorothy II, 467
Van Luden, Johanna Dorothy II, 673
Van Mannierck, Anthony II, 673
Van Matre, Leona IV, 1155
Van Matre, Leora IV, 1155
Van Matre, Leora IV, 1190
Van Matre, Loren IV, 1155
Van Nessley, Gladys V, 655
Van Nessley, Gladys V, 717
Van Nessley, Wm. V, 655
Van Nice, Mary III, 335
Van Noppen, C. M. I, 580
Van Noppen, Charles L. I, 580
Van Noppen, Johanna Maria I, 580
Van Noppen, John J. I, 580
Van Noppen, Leonard C. I, 580
Van Norsdal, Sarah Harvey III, 114
Van Norsdal, Sarah Harvey III, 335
Van North, Margaret VI, 801

ostrand, ??? III, 429
ostrand, Albert III, 463
ostrand, Anna III, 450
ostrand, Anna III, 463
ostrand, Anna W. III, 451
ostrand, Benj. III, 451
ostrand, Benjamin III, 450
ostrand, Benjamin eadwell III, 463
ostrand, Bertha III, 335
ostrand, Beth III, 503
ostrand, Daniel III, 503
ostrand, Grace III, 463
ostrand, Harriett III, 384
ostrand, Phebe III, 429
ostrand, Phebe III, 463
ostrand, Phebe Amelia I, 484
ostrand, Phebe Amelia I, 503
ostrand, Phebe E. III, 463
ostrand, Phebe Eliza I, 463
ostrand, Richard III, 503
ostrand, Sidney III, 484
ostrand, Sidney J. III, 503
ostrand, Susannah III, 503
ostrans, Bertha III, 223
ote, ??? III, 336
ote, Clementine III, 190
ote, Clementine III, 336
ote, Henry III, 336
ote, James III, 190
ote, James III, 336
ote, Peter T. III, 336
ote, Samuel III, 336
ote, Sarah III, 190
ote, William III, 336
oy, Permelia R. III, 336
elt, Elender VI, 1008
elt, John V, 286
elt, Joseph VI, 1008
elt, Mary V, 286
elt, Phebe V, 287
elt, Phebe V, 290
iper, Jacob III, 336
iper, Matilda III, 336
iper, Sallie III, 336
ubenstock, Gartrue II, 448
ubenstock, Sibilla II, 448
haak, Eliza III, 20
haak, Margaret III, 20
haak, Samuel III, 20
ickle, Alexina III, 215
ickle, Alexina III, 336
ickle, Ella III, 215
ickle, Ella III, 336
ickle, John III, 215
ickle, John III, 336
ickle, Josie IV, 1241
icklin, ??? III, 52
icklin, Eunice III, 336
icklin, Phebe III, 52
icklin, Phebe III, 336
icklin, Timothy III, 336
ise, Charles III, 503
ise, Elbert III, 511
ise, Maria A. III, 511
on, Arthur Leveinus I, 336
on, Leveinus III, 336
on, Maria III, 336
assel, Dorinda E. III, 346
assel, Dorinda Eloise I, 336
assel, Howard III, 336
assel, Phebe III, 336
assel, Phebe III, 346
assel, Wright III, 336
assel, Wright III, 346
rump, Mary Ann V, 871
rump, Mary Ann V, 872
alkenburg, Horace III, 336
alkenburg, Sarah Jane I, 336
echten Waring, J. III, 190
echten, Harriet H. III, 190
elson, Amy III, 463
elson, Losee III, 463
inshitter, Anna IV, 1190
leet, Abby Jane III, 336
leet, John B. III, 336
olkenburg, Howard III, 130
olkenburg, Sarah Jane I, 130
oorhees, ??? III, 336
oorhees, Asa III, 336
oorhis, Eleanor IV, 1383
Way, Pamelia R. III, 336
Winkle, Clarinda V, 371
Winkle, Elizabeth V, 371
Van Winkle, Henry V, 287
Van Winkle, Martha V, 287
Van Winkle, Martha V, 942
Van Winkle, Wm. V, 371
Van Wyck, Deborah III, 54
Van Wyck, Deborah III, 336
Van Wyck, Hannah III, 120
Van Wyck, Hannah III, 336
Van Wyck, John III, 336
Van Wyck, Martha III, 54
Van Wyck, Martha III, 336
Van Wyck, Mary III, 336
Van Wyck, Phebe III, 55
Van Wyck, Phebe III, 336
Van Wyck, Richard P. III, 511
Van Wyck, William III, 54
Van Wyck, William III, 336
Van Zandt, ??? III, 336
Van Zandt, Maria III, 329
Van Zandt, Maria III, 336
Van Zandt, Theodore III, 336
Vanabald, Vincent IV, 781
Vanaken, Elizabeth II, 673
Vanaken, Henry II, 429
Vanaken, Henry II, 673
Vanaken, Jane II, 429
Vanaken, Marcellus V, 648
Vanaken, Paul II, 673
Vanaken, Rebecca II, 673
Vanaken, Rebekah II, 673
Vanaken, Sally A. IV, 1369
Vanaken, Sally A. IV, 1383
Vanaken, Wd. Jane II, 673
Vanaman, Clara M. II, 858
Vanausdel, Ida IV, 1189
Vanausdel, Mrs. F. A. IV, 1189
Vanausdle, Amanda IV, 1297
Vanausdle, Elisha IV, 1297
Vanausdle, Frank IV, 1297
Vanausdle, Margaret IV, 1297
Vanback, Elinor II, 448
Vanback, John II, 448
Vanbibber, Henry II, 429
VanBuskirt, Lola IV, 1297
Vancamp, Ann IV, 134
Vance, Agnes Grace V, 939
Vance, Amanda V, 435
Vance, Amanda S. V, 435
Vance, Anna V, 716
Vance, Anna E. V, 716
Vance, Belva V, 603
Vance, Cecil V, 716
Vance, Edward Alexander V, 939
Vance, Ella H. IV, 543
Vance, Ella H. IV, 554
Vance, Elma V, 435
Vance, Emery V, 435
Vance, Emery H. V, 435
Vance, Emma IV, 1265
Vance, Ethel Anna V, 716
Vance, Fannie V, 208
Vance, Fanny M. V, 208
Vance, Florence Anthony V, 939
Vance, Florence Johnson V, 939
Vance, Florency Anthony V, 913
Vance, Harry D. V, 684
Vance, Harry D. V, 716
Vance, Hugh V, 364
Vance, Hugh S. V, 364
Vance, Jane V, 716
Vance, John V, 716
Vance, Kathryn V, 716
Vance, Linnie V, 716
Vance, Lucy V, 716
Vance, Lynn F. V, 682
Vance, Lynn F. V, 716
Vance, Mary VI, 880
Vance, Samuel Edward V, 913
Vance, Samuel Edward V, 939
Vance, Sarah IV, 1080
Vance, Shirley Maude V, 684
Vance, Shirley Maude V, 716
Vance, Susan V, 716
Vance, Susan J. V, 716
Vancil, Elizabeth I, 900
Vancil, Elizabeth I, 904
Vanclave, Luther V, 1023
Vanclave, Retta V, 1023
Vanculan, John II, 108
Vanculan, Margaret II, 108
Vanculin, John II, 90
Vanculin, John II, 108
Vanculin, Margaret II, 90
Vandagrift, Rebecca VI, 832
Vandegriff, Charity II, 269
Vandegrift, Abraham VI, 861
Vandegrift, Jane VI, 861
Vandegrift, John VI, 861
Vandegrift, Nancy VI, 861
Vandenburgh, Abram P. III, 438
Vandenburgh, Abram P. III, 463
Vandenburgh, Henrietta M. III, 438
Vandenburgh, Henrietta W. III, 463
Vandenwall, Martha VI, 204
Vandenwall, Nathaniel VI, 204
Vandenwall, Nathaniel VI, 215
Vanderbilt, Carrie III, 148
Vanderbilt, Carrie III, 334
Vanderbilt, Carrie S. III, 334
Vanderbilt, Carrie S. III, 335
Vanderbilt, Carrie S. III, 353
Vanderbilt, Chester Willets III, 95
Vanderbilt, Chester Willets III, 334
Vanderbilt, Corinne Lucille III, 334
Vanderbilt, Donald Haddock III, 334
Vanderbilt, Doris Eleanor III, 334
Vanderbilt, Dorothea III, 95
Vanderbilt, Dorothea III, 334
Vanderbilt, Duncan Stevens III, 335
Vanderbilt, Edith III, 148
Vanderbilt, Edith III, 334
Vanderbilt, Edith Judson III, 334
Vanderbilt, Elizabeth III, 483
Vanderbilt, Elizabeth III, 503
Vanderbilt, Isaac III, 334
Vanderbilt, Isaac S. III, 334
Vanderbilt, Isaac S., Jr. III, 148
Vanderbilt, Isaac S., Jr. III, 334
Vanderbilt, Isaac S., Jr. III, 335
Vanderbilt, Isaac S., Jr. III, 353
Vanderbilt, Jane III, 334
Vanderbilt, Jane Patricia III, 334
Vanderbilt, Laura Judith III, 334
Vanderbilt, Margaret III, 482
Vanderbilt, Margaret III, 503
Vanderbilt, Marjorie Gordon III, 334
Vanderbilt, Ralph Petty III, 334
Vanderbilt, Sarah J. III, 334
Vanderburg, Mary B. V, 135
Vanderburgh, Ann Maria IV, 1383
Vanderburgh, Caroline IV, 1383
Vanderburgh, Charlotte IV, 1383
Vanderburgh, Clayman IV, 1383
Vanderburgh, Ellen V, 208
Vanderburgh, George Warren IV, 1383
Vanderburgh, Isaac IV, 1383
Vanderburgh, Jane IV, 1383
Vanderburgh, John IV, 1383
Vanderburgh, Natella V, 208
Vanderburgh, Robert IV, 1383
Vanderburgh, Roxana IV, 1383
Vanderburgh, William D. IV, 1383
Vanderen, Susanna II, 673
Vanderford, Sarah I, 380
Vanderford, Sarah I, 425
Vandergrift, Ally A. VI, 837
Vandergrift, Ann II, 971
Vandergrift, Benjamin Franklin II, 825
Vandergrift, John Hampton II, 825
Vandergrift, Mary Lamb II, 825
Vandergroph, Charity II, 269
Vanderin, Susanna II, 673
Vanderslice, Mary Ann II, 792
Vandervoort, Eunice III, 335
Vandervoort, Mary V, 671
Vandervoort, Mary V, 716
Vandervoort, Maud V, 717
Vandervoort, Maude E. V, 939
Vandervoort, Veda V, 704
Vandervoort, Veda V, 716
VanDervoorte, Eva V, 550
VanDervoorte, John V, 550
VanDervoorte, Lida V, 550
Vandervort, Delitha V, 585
Vandervort, Delitha V, 603
Vandervort, Fannie V, 717
Vandervort, John V, 717
Vandervort, Lucius V, 717
Vandervort, Margaret V, 717
Vandervort, Mary V, 717
Vandervort, Maud V, 717
Vandervort, Mora V, 717
Vandervort, Pauline V, 717
Vandervort, Veda V, 717
Vandervort, Virginia V, 717
Vanderwater, George III, 498
Vanderwater, Margaret III, 498
Vanderwoort, Eva V, 550
Vanderwort, Fannie V, 717
Vanderwort, John V, 717
Vanderwort, Lucius V, 648
Vanderwort, Lucius V, 717
Vanderwort, Margaret V, 648
Vanderwort, Margaret V, 717
Vanderwort, Mary V, 717
Vanderwort, Minnie V, 208
Vanderwort, Myra Pagett V, 648
Vanderwort, Pauline V, 648
Vanderwort, Pauline V, 717
Vanderwort, Veda V, 717
Vanderwort, Virginia V, 717
Vandeveer, ??? III, 286
Vandeveer, ??? III, 335
Vandeveer, Adelaide III, 335
Vandeveer, Hannah III, 286
Vandeveer, Hannah III, 335
Vandever, Charlotte A. II, 825
Vandever, Charlotte A. II, 926
Vandever, Charlotte A. II, 934
Vandever, Keziah II, 825
Vandever, Margaret II, 857
Vandever, Margaret II, 933
Vandever, Thomas II, 673
Vandever, Thos. B. II, 926
Vandever, Thos. B. II, 933
Vandever, Thos. B. II, 934
Vandever, Thos. Ballenger II, 825
Vandever, Wm. II, 825
Vandever, Wm. II, 857
Vandever, Wm. II, 933
Vandevert, Sarah IV, 108
Vandevert, Sarah IV, 113
Vandevoort, Catherine III, 463
Vandevoort, Charles Augustus III, 463
Vandevoort, Eunice III, 17
Vandevoort, G. M. III, 463
Vandevoorter, Sarah VI, 518
Vandevort, Edith Clark V, 716
Vandevort, Mary V, 716
Vandevort, Veda V, 716
Vandewater, Charlotte III, 463
Vandewater, Clarence W. III, 503
Vandewater, David III, 463
Vandewater, Geo. III, 487
Vandewater, Geo. III, 503
Vandewater, George III, 503
Vandewater, Harriet III, 487
Vandewater, Harriet III, 503
Vandewater, James III, 463
Vandewater, Jessie III, 463
Vandewater, John III, 503
Vandewater, John, Jr. III, 503
Vandewater, Margaret III, 487
Vandewater, Margaret III, 503
Vandewater, Naomi III, 463
Vandewater, Naomi C. III, 463
Vandewater, Oakley III, 463
Vandewater, Oscar III, 463
Vandewater, Peter III, 463
Vandewater, Phebe III, 463
Vandewater, Phebe III, 503
Vandewater, Pleasant VI, 575
Vandewater, Robert III, 463
Vandewater, Silas T. III, 503
Vandewater, Susan, Jr. III, 503
Vandigrift, Ann II, 1062
Vandigrift, Joseph II, 1062
Vandiver, Thomas II, 673
Vandoren, Anna M. V, 603
Vandoren, Tarinda V, 677
Vanduzer, John IV, 1383
Vanduzer, Margaret IV, 1383
Vandyke, James V, 1023
Vandyke, Jno., Jr. V, 1023
Vandyke, Pleasant V, 1023
Vandyke, Sarah IV, 573
Vandyke, Sarah IV, 598
Vandyne, Phebe Anna IV, 575
Vandyne, Phebe Anna IV, 598
Vanfassan, Anna IV, 1265
Vanfassan, Wilda IV, 1265
Vanfassan, Wildie IV, 1265
Vanfassan, William IV, 1265
Vanfassan, Wm. IV, 1265
Vanfessen, Rebecca M. IV, 1009
Vanfoson, Elizabeth IV, 1078
Vanfoson, Elizabeth IV, 1080
Vanfossen, Anna IV, 1000
Vanfossen, Anna IV, 1265
Vanfossen, Anna Margarete IV, 1014
Vanfossen, Jacob IV, 1009
Vanfossen, Jacob IV, 1014
Vanfossen, Margaret IV, 1009
Vanfossen, Margarete IV, 1014
VanFossen, Rebecca IV, 993
Vanfossen, Rebecca M. IV, 1009
Vanfossen, Wm. IV, 1265
Vanfosson, Harry IV, 849
Vangaver, Blaizing II, 448
Vangordon, Lodusky Sharp IV, 1297
Vangrundy, Etna V, 286
Vangundy, Chas. E. V, 1023
Vangundy, Daniel V, 1023
Vangundy, Myrtle V, 1023
Vanhooten, Micajah Davis VI, 215
Vanhooten, Susanna VI, 171
Vanhooten, Susanna VI, 215
Vanhorn, Ann II, 1062
Vanhorn, Ann Eliza II, 721
Vanhorn, Benja. I, 1028
Vanhorn, Benja. I, 1034
Vanhorn, Benja. I, 1038
Vanhorn, Benjamin I, 1038
Vanhorn, Benjamin I, 1039
Vanhorn, Charles II, 1062
Vanhorn, Charles IV, 314
Vanhorn, Eleanor II, 1034
Vanhorn, Elizabeth IV, 205
Vanhorn, Elizabeth IV, 297
Vanhorn, Elizabeth IV, 501
Vanhorn, Elizabeth IV, 554
Vanhorn, Elizabeth IV, 1080
Vanhorn, Elizabeth IV, 1118
Vanhorn, Elizabeth VI, 453
Vanhorn, George W. IV, 314
Vanhorn, Hannah II, 673
Vanhorn, Hannah II, 1034
Vanhorn, James V, 135
Vanhorn, James M. IV, 314
Vanhorn, Jane I, 1038
Vanhorn, Jane I, 1039
Vanhorn, Joanna I, 1028
Vanhorn, Joanna I, 1038
Vanhorn, Joanna V, 135
Vanhorn, Joanna V, 469
Vanhorn, Joanna V, 499
Vanhorn, Joanna V, 537
Vanhorn, Lydia II, 1016
Vanhorn, Lydia II, 1034
Vanhorn, Mary II, 1013
Vanhorn, Mary II, 1034
Vanhorn, Mary IV, 314
Vanhorn, Rebecca I, 1039
Vanhorn, Rebecca V, 537
Vanhorn, Robert I, 1039
Vanhorn, Robert IV, 314
Vanhorn, Roberts I, 1039
Vanhorn, Sarah II, 1016
Vanhorn, Sarah II, 1034
Vanhorn, Sarah IV, 314
Vanhorn, Sarah V, 806
Vanhorn, Uriah C. II, 721
Vanhorn, Widow Jane I, 1034
Vanhorne, Eleanor II, 1016
Vanhorne, Hannah II, 992
Vanhorne, Hannah II, 1034
Vanhorne, Mary II, 1034
Vanhorne, Robert V, 135
Vanhusten, Martha II, 430
Vanlaid, Jacob II, 448
Vanlaid, John II, 448
Vanlaw, ??? IV, 450
Vanlaw, Amy IV, 321
Vanlaw, Amy IV, 352
Vanlaw, Amy IV, 355
Vanlaw, Amy IV, 554
Vanlaw, Amy IV, 1099
Vanlaw, Amy IV, 1118
Vanlaw, Amy B. IV, 355
Vanlaw, Amy B. IV, 1118
Vanlaw, Amy B. IV, 1123
Vanlaw, Amy S. IV, 1118
Vanlaw, Amy S. IV, 1123
Vanlaw, Ann II, 269
Vanlaw, Ann IV, 337
Vanlaw, Ann IV, 350
Vanlaw, Ann IV, 355
Vanlaw, Ann IV, 450
Vanlaw, Ann IV, 554
Vanlaw, Ann IV, 1067
Vanlaw, Ann IV, 1080
Vanlaw, Ann IV, 1102
Vanlaw, Ann IV, 1118
Vanlaw, Ann H. IV, 1118
Vanlaw, Ann S. IV, 1118
Vanlaw, Ann S. Vanlaw IV, 355
Vanlaw, Ann W. Maris IV, 1080
Vanlaw, Anna IV, 359
Vanlaw, Anna IV, 450
Vanlaw, Anna IV, 1080
Vanlaw, Anna IV, 1083
Vanlaw, Anna W. IV, 1080
Vanlaw, Anna W. IV, 1118
Vanlaw, Anne II, 187
Vanlaw, Anne IV, 162
Vanlaw, Anne IV, 357

Vanlaw, Anne IV, 554
Vanlaw, Anne IV, 1101
Vanlaw, Anne IV, 1118
Vanlaw, Annie Elvyan IV, 1118
Vanlaw, Carlos T. IV, 1118
Vanlaw, Charles W. IV, 1118
Vanlaw, David B. IV, 1118
Vanlaw, Elisha IV, 355
Vanlaw, Elisha IV, 359
Vanlaw, Elisha IV, 450
Vanlaw, Elisha IV, 1080
Vanlaw, Elisha IV, 1083
Vanlaw, Elisha IV, 1118
Vanlaw, Eliza IV, 355
Vanlaw, Eliza IV, 450
Vanlaw, Eliza IV, 1088
Vanlaw, Eliza IV, 1118
Vanlaw, Elizabeth IV, 297
Vanlaw, Elizabeth L. IV, 1088
Vanlaw, Elizabeth L. IV, 1118
Vanlaw, Elizabeth S. IV, 1088
Vanlaw, Geo. IV, 357
Vanlaw, Geo. IV, 1190
Vanlaw, George II, 187
Vanlaw, George II, 269
Vanlaw, George IV, 162
Vanlaw, George IV, 355
Vanlaw, George IV, 450
Vanlaw, George, Jr. IV, 355
Vanlaw, Hannah IV, 355
Vanlaw, Hannah Ann IV, 1104
Vanlaw, Hannah Ann IV, 1118
Vanlaw, Hannahann IV, 1118
Vanlaw, Isaac IV, 355
Vanlaw, Isaac W. IV, 450
Vanlaw, J. IV, 1106
Vanlaw, Jane IV, 1118
Vanlaw, Jephtha IV, 1118
Vanlaw, Jephtha S. IV, 1118
Vanlaw, Jephthah S. IV, 352
Vanlaw, Jephthah S. IV, 355
Vanlaw, Jeptha Sharp IV, 450
Vanlaw, Jesse IV, 355
Vanlaw, Jesse IV, 450
Vanlaw, Jesse IV, 1109
Vanlaw, Jesse IV, 1118
Vanlaw, Jesse M. IV, 1118
Vanlaw, John II, 187
Vanlaw, John II, 269
Vanlaw, John IV, 162
Vanlaw, John IV, 321
Vanlaw, John IV, 337
Vanlaw, John IV, 350
Vanlaw, John IV, 355
Vanlaw, John IV, 386
Vanlaw, John IV, 440
Vanlaw, John IV, 450
Vanlaw, John IV, 1080
Vanlaw, John IV, 1088
Vanlaw, John IV, 1094
Vanlaw, John IV, 1118
Vanlaw, John, Jr. IV, 1104
Vanlaw, John, Jr. IV, 1118
Vanlaw, Jos. IV, 350
Vanlaw, Jos. IV, 355
Vanlaw, Joseph II, 187
Vanlaw, Joseph II, 211
Vanlaw, Joseph II, 269
Vanlaw, Joseph IV, 162
Vanlaw, Joseph IV, 355
Vanlaw, Joseph IV, 450
Vanlaw, Joseph IV, 554
Vanlaw, Joseph IV, 1123
Vanlaw, Joseph IV, 1190
Vanlaw, Joseph A. IV, 355
Vanlaw, Joseph H. IV, 554
Vanlaw, Joseph L. IV, 1118
Vanlaw, Joseph P. IV, 1190
Vanlaw, Joseph S. IV, 1102
Vanlaw, Joseph S. IV, 1118
Vanlaw, Judah II, 211
Vanlaw, Judah II, 269
Vanlaw, Louisa IV, 355
Vanlaw, Louisa M. IV, 450
Vanlaw, Louisa M. IV, 1094
Vanlaw, Louisa M. IV, 1118
Vanlaw, Lucinda IV, 328
Vanlaw, Lucinda IV, 355
Vanlaw, Lucinda IV, 450
Vanlaw, Lucinda IV, 1118
Vanlaw, Lucinda IV, 1120
Vanlaw, Lydia IV, 321
Vanlaw, Lydia IV, 345
Vanlaw, Lydia IV, 355
Vanlaw, Lydia IV, 450
Vanlaw, Lydia IV, 535
Vanlaw, Lydia IV, 554
Vanlaw, Lydia IV, 1118
Vanlaw, Lydia IV, 1190
Vanlaw, Lydia V, 961
Vanlaw, Lydia Jane IV, 1102
Vanlaw, Lydia Jane IV, 1118
Vanlaw, Lydia Jane Branson IV, 355
Vanlaw, Lydia Jane Branson IV, 1118
Vanlaw, Lydia S. IV, 337
Vanlaw, Lydia S. IV, 533
Vanlaw, Lydia Sharp IV, 450
Vanlaw, Margaret IV, 1102
Vanlaw, Margaret IV, 1118
Vanlaw, Margaret H. IV, 1118
Vanlaw, Martha D. IV, 1118
Vanlaw, Mary II, 187
Vanlaw, Mary II, 211
Vanlaw, Mary II, 269
Vanlaw, Mary II, 946
Vanlaw, Mary IV, 162
Vanlaw, Mary IV, 334
Vanlaw, Mary IV, 350
Vanlaw, Mary IV, 355
Vanlaw, Mary IV, 386
Vanlaw, Mary IV, 450
Vanlaw, Mary Ann IV, 340
Vanlaw, Mary Ann IV, 355
Vanlaw, Mary Ann IV, 450
Vanlaw, Pearson L. IV, 355
Vanlaw, Preston II, 211
Vanlaw, Preston II, 269
Vanlaw, Rachel IV, 1118
Vanlaw, Rachel F. IV, 1109
Vanlaw, Rachel F. IV, 1118
Vanlaw, Reasin IV, 450
Vanlaw, Reason IV, 355
Vanlaw, Reason IV, 1190
Vanlaw, Reason L. IV, 1190
Vanlaw, Rebecca IV, 170
Vanlaw, Rebecca IV, 355
Vanlaw, Rebecca IV, 554
Vanlaw, Rebecca IV, 557
Vanlaw, Rebecca W. IV, 1118
Vanlaw, Rebecca W. IV, 1123
Vanlaw, Resin L. IV, 355
Vanlaw, Samuel II, 187
Vanlaw, Samuel II, 269
Vanlaw, Samuel IV, 162
Vanlaw, Samuel IV, 345
Vanlaw, Samuel IV, 355
Vanlaw, Samuel IV, 450
Vanlaw, Samuel IV, 1118
Vanlaw, Samuel IV, 1190
Vanlaw, Samuel V, 961
Vanlaw, Samuel C. IV, 355
Vanlaw, Samuel C. IV, 1118
Vanlaw, Samuel C. IV, 1139
Vanlaw, Sarah IV, 327
Vanlaw, Sarah IV, 337
Vanlaw, Sarah IV, 350
Vanlaw, Sarah IV, 355
Vanlaw, Sarah IV, 386
Vanlaw, Sarah IV, 440
Vanlaw, Sarah IV, 450
Vanlaw, Sarah IV, 1080
Vanlaw, Sarah IV, 1088
Vanlaw, Sarah IV, 1094
Vanlaw, Sarah IV, 1118
Vanlaw, Sarah IV, 1123
Vanlaw, Sarah IV, 1190
Vanlaw, Sarah Louisa IV, 1118
Vanlaw, Sarah P. IV, 355
Vanlaw, Sarah P. IV, 1190
Vanlaw, Smith IV, 355
Vanlaw, Smith IV, 1118
Vanlaw, Thomas II, 187
Vanlaw, Thomas II, 269
Vanlaw, Thomas IV, 162
Vanlaw, Thomas IV, 337
Vanlaw, Thomas IV, 355
Vanlaw, Thomas IV, 450
Vanlaw, Thomas IV, 1118
Vanlaw, Thomas E. IV, 554
Vanlaw, Thomas E. IV, 1101
Vanlaw, Thomas E. IV, 1118
Vanlaw, Thomas E. IV, 1123
Vanlaw, Thomas Elwood IV, 554
Vanlaw, Thos. IV, 321
Vanlaw, Thos. IV, 355
Vanlaw, Thos. IV, 554
Vanlaw, Wd. Amy S. IV, 1106
Vanlaw, William IV, 355
Vanlaw, Wm. IV, 1190
Vanlaw, Zenas IV, 1067
Vanlear, John II, 448
Vanlear, Mary II, 448
Vanlear, Samuel II, 448
Vanleer, Dr. ??? II, 430
Vanleer, Mary II, 430
Vanmenerick, Anthony II, 673
Vanmeter, Hannah Ann V, 489
Vanmeter, Hannah Ann V, 537
Vanmeter, Martha V, 951
Vanmeter, Martha V, 961
Vann, Ada I, 77
Vann, Andrew J. I, 77
Vann, Andrew P. I, 19
Vann, Andrew W. P. I, 77
Vann, Bert IV, 1341
Vann, Fannie E. I, 19
Vann, Fannie E. I, 77
Vann, George I, 77
Vann, George G. I, 77
Vann, George W. I, 19
Vann, Ida I, 19
Vann, James I, 77
Vann, James W. I, 19
Vann, James W. I, 77
Vann, John A. I, 19
Vann, John A. I, 77
Vann, Louise IV, 1341
Vann, Margaret I, 77
Vann, Minnie I, 52
Vann, Minnie I, 77
Vann, Minnie A. R. I, 19
Vann, Minnie A. R. I, 77
Vann, Mrs. Louise IV, 1341
Vann, William J. I, 19
Vann, William John I, 77
Vann, William K. I, 340
Vannay, Amanda V, 648
Vannay, Daniel V, 648
Vanneman, Andrew II, 139
Vanneman, Ann II, 139
Vanneman, Annie II, 139
Vanneman, Margaret E. II, 159
Vanneman, Mary Harris II, 136
Vannemen, Margaret E. II, 159
Vannersdoll, Elsie V, 609
Vannersdoll, Elsie V, 648
Vannerson, Betty IV, 297
Vannerson, Elizabeth VI, 861
Vannerson, William VI, 861
Vanney, W. J. V, 648
Vannoy, Amanda V, 648
Vannoy, Daniel V, 648
Vannoy, W. J. V, 648
Vannoy, Wm. J. V, 648
Vannuy, Permelia R. III, 336
Vanover, Henry VI, 1008
Vanover, Nancy VI, 1008
Vanpelt, Abner J. V, 717
Vanpelt, Agness V, 255
Vanpelt, Ann IV, 355
Vanpelt, Ann V, 310
Vanpelt, Ann V, 312
Vanpelt, Catharine IV, 162
Vanpelt, Catharine V, 312
Vanpelt, Catharine V, 648
Vanpelt, Catherine V, 448
Vanpelt, Elisha IV, 355
Vanpelt, Elisha IV, 554
Vanpelt, Elisha V, 312
Vanpelt, Hannah IV, 355
Vanpelt, Hannah V, 305
Vanpelt, Hannah V, 312
Vanpelt, John IV, 162
Vanpelt, John IV, 355
Vanpelt, John V, 312
Vanpelt, Jonathan IV, 162
Vanpelt, Jonathan IV, 355
Vanpelt, Jonathan V, 312
Vanpelt, Katy IV, 355
Vanpelt, Lena M. Spear V, 648
Vanpelt, Lydia IV, 509
Vanpelt, Lydia IV, 532
Vanpelt, Lydia IV, 554
Vanpelt, Lydia V, 304
Vanpelt, Lydia V, 312
Vanpelt, Mahlon IV, 355
Vanpelt, Mahlon V, 312
Vanpelt, Mary IV, 162
Vanpelt, Mary IV, 355
Vanpelt, Mary V, 312
Vanpelt, Mary Katy V, 312
Vanpelt, Mary, Jr. V, 312
Vanpelt, Nancy IV, 162
Vanpelt, Nancy V, 302
Vanpelt, Nancy V, 312
Vanpelt, Phebe IV, 355
Vanpelt, Phebe V, 312
Vanpelt, Phebe V, 313
Vanpelt, Rebecca V, 717
Vanpelt, Sarah IV, 328
Vanpelt, Sarah IV, 355
Vanpelt, Sarah IV, 554
Vanpelt, Sarah V, 312
Vansandt, Isaiah II, 1034
Vansandt, Rachel II, 1034
Vansant, Ann I. II, 1071
Vansant, Ann I. II, 1082
Vansant, Ann W. II, 1074
Vansant, Ann W. II, 1082
Vansant, Catharine V, 939
Vansant, Cornelius V, 939
Vansant, Elisabeth II, 1034
Vansant, Grace V, 939
Vansant, Grace P. V, 939
Vansant, Isaiah II, 1034
Vansant, James E. V, 939
Vansant, Jane II, 1000
Vansant, Jane II, 1034
Vansant, John II, 430
Vansant, John V, 364
Vansant, Joseph T. V, 939
Vansant, Joshua II, 1034
Vansant, Mary II, 1082
Vansant, Mary Anna II, 1082
Vansant, Mary Elizabeth V, 939
Vansant, Rachel II, 1014
Vansant, Rachel II, 1034
Vansant, Rebecca P. V, 939
Vansant, Rena V, 364
Vansant, Richard R. V, 939
Vansant, Samuel V, 939
Vansant, Sarah P. V, 939
Vansant, Stephen C. II, 1082
Vansant, Tacy Ann V, 939
Vanschihoc, Abraham IV, 64
Vanschihoc, Ann IV, 64
Vanschihoc, Enoch IV, 64
Vanschihoc, Joanna IV, 64
Vanschihoc, Lydia IV, 64
Vanschihoc, Mary IV, 64
Vanschihoc, Moses IV, 64
Vanschihoc, Rebecca IV, 64
Vanschuiver, Elizabeth V, 829
Vanschuyler, Elizabeth V, 887
Vanschuyler, Wm. V, 887
Vanschuyner, Elizabeth V, 880
Vanschuyner, Elizabeth V, 887
Vanschuyner, Elizabeth J. V, 887
Vanschuyner, Samuel V, 880
Vanschuyner, Samuel V, 887
Vanschuyver, Eliza V, 872
Vanschuyver, Elizabeth V, 872
Vanschuyver, John B. V, 872
Vanschuyver, Joseph V, 887
Vanschuyver, Martha V, 872
Vanschuyver, Martha V, 883
Vanschuyver, Martha V, 887
Vanschuyver, Rebecca V, 872
Vanschuyver, Samuel V, 872
Vanschuyver, Walter V, 872
Vanschuyver, William V, 872
Vanschuyver, William, Jr. V, 872
Vanschuyver, Wm. V, 887
Vansciner, Elizabeth V, 887
Vansciner, Samuel V, 887
Vansciner, Susanna B. V, 888
Vansciner, Wm. V, 887
Vansciner, Wm. A. V, 888
Vanscioc, Abraham IV, 30
Vanscioc, Abraham IV, 64
Vanscioc, Joanna IV, 58
Vanscioc, Joanna IV, 64
Vanscioc, Rachel IV, 30
Vanscioc, Rachel IV, 64
Vanscioch, Moses IV, 64
Vansciock, Aaron IV, 64
Vansciock, Enoch IV, 64
Vansciock, Rachel IV, 58
Vansciock, Rachel IV, 64
Vansciock, Ruth IV, 64
Vansciver, Elizabeth V, 887
Vansciver, Elizabeth J. V, 887
Vansciver, Hannah J. V, 885
Vansciver, Hannah J. V, 887
Vansciver, John B. V, 887
Vansciver, Joseph V, 887
Vansciver, Lydia H. II, 281
Vansciver, Lydia H. II, 304
Vansciver, Martha V, 887
Vansciver, Mary Elizabeth V, 887
Vansciver, Samuel V, 887
Vansciver, Sarah B. V, 887
Vansciver, Susanna B. V, 887
Vansciver, Uriah V, 887
Vansciver, Wm. V, 887
Vansciver, Wm. A. V, 887
Vanscoy, Rebecca IV, 64
Vanscoyoc, Aaron IV, 64
Vanscoyoc, Aaron IV, 123
Vanscoyoc, Aaron IV, 134
Vanscoyoc, Abraham IV, 30
Vanscoyoc, Abraham IV, 64
Vanscoyoc, Albert A. IV, 1009
Vanscoyoc, Albert A. IV, 1010
Vanscoyoc, Amos Emmett IV, 1010
Vanscoyoc, Ann IV, 57
Vanscoyoc, Ann IV, 64
Vanscoyoc, Ann IV, 842
Vanscoyoc, Ann IV, 849
Vanscoyoc, Anna IV, 1010
Vanscoyoc, Aron IV, 64
Vanscoyoc, Eldora IV, 1010
Vanscoyoc, Enoch IV, 51
Vanscoyoc, Enoch IV, 57
Vanscoyoc, Enoch IV, 64
Vanscoyoc, Enoch IV, 134
Vanscoyoc, Enoch IV, 1010
Vanscoyoc, Enoch P. IV, 100
Vanscoyoc, Enoch P. IV, 101
Vanscoyoc, Enoch Willis IV,
Vanscoyoc, Hannah IV, 30
Vanscoyoc, Hannah IV, 64
Vanscoyoc, Harrison IV, 64
Vanscoyoc, Isaac IV, 64
Vanscoyoc, Jane Anna IV, 6
Vanscoyoc, Jesse IV, 64
Vanscoyoc, Joanna IV, 64
Vanscoyoc, Lydia IV, 51
Vanscoyoc, Lydia IV, 57
Vanscoyoc, Lydia IV, 64
Vanscoyoc, Lydia IV, 134
Vanscoyoc, Martha J. IV, 10
Vanscoyoc, Martha Jane IV,
Vanscoyoc, Mary IV, 64
Vanscoyoc, Mary IV, 1010
Vanscoyoc, Moses IV, 64
Vanscoyoc, Oliver IV, 1010
Vanscoyoc, Phebe IV, 1010
Vanscoyoc, Phebe C. IV, 100
Vanscoyoc, Rachel IV, 64
Vanscoyoc, Rebecca IV, 53
Vanscoyoc, Rebecca IV, 64
Vanscoyoc, Ruth IV, 64
Vanscoyoc, Ruth IV, 123
Vanscoyoc, Ruth IV, 134
Vanscoyoc, Ruth Emma IV,
Vanscoyoc, Ruth Emma IV,
Vanscoyoc, Sarah IV, 64
Vanscoyoc, Simeon IV, 64
Vanscoyock, Enoch IV, 69
Vanscoyock, Lydia IV, 69
Vanscoyock, Mary IV, 69
Vanscuyvar, Elizabeth V, 82
Vanscuyvar, Mary V, 829
Vanscuyvar, William J. V, 8
Vansel, Elizabeth I, 904
Vanshiver, Mary Elizabeth
Vanshiver, Sarah V, 870
Vanshiver, William V, 870
Vansickle, Charles IV, 1190
Vansickle, Charley IV, 1190
Vansickle, Chas. IV, 1190
Vansickle, Elnora IV, 1190
Vansickle, Esther D. IV, 119
Vansickle, Mary Ann IV, 11
Vansickle, Walter Filmore IV, 1190
Vansickler, ??? III, 53
Vansickler, Phebe J. III, 53
Vanskiver, Mary Elizabeth
Vanskiver, Sarah B. V, 140
Vanskiver, Sarah B. V, 887
Vanskiver, Uriah V, 887
Vanstiver, Aaron II, 430
Vanstiver, Cornelius II, 430
Vanstiver, William II, 430
Vansycle, Mary Ann V, 961
Vansykle, Abraham IV, 1183
Vansykle, Hannah IV, 1183
Vansykle, Mary Ann IV, 118
Vansykle, Mary Ann IV, 119
Vansyoc, Aaron Emlen IV, 1
Vansyoc, Abraham IV, 892
Vansyoc, Abraham IV, 895
Vansyoc, Albert A. IV, 1009
Vansyoc, Albert A. IV, 1010
Vansyoc, Amos IV, 895
Vansyoc, Amos Emmett IV,
Vansyoc, Ann IV, 849
Vansyoc, Anna IV, 780
Vansyoc, Anna IV, 1010
Vansyoc, Anna Mary IV, 101
Vansyoc, Anna V. IV, 966
Vansyoc, Eldora IV, 780
Vansyoc, Eldora IV, 1010
Vansyoc, Emma IV, 955
Vansyoc, Enoch IV, 780
Vansyoc, Enoch IV, 810
Vansyoc, Enoch IV, 849
Vansyoc, Enoch IV, 895
Vansyoc, Enoch IV, 1010
Vansyoc, Enoch P. IV, 1009
Vansyoc, Enoch P. IV, 1010
Vansyoc, Enoch Willet IV, 7
Vansyoc, Enoch Willis IV, 10
Vansyoc, Enoch Willit IV, 10
Vansyoc, Florence J. IV, 570
Vansyoc, Harrison IV, 895
Vansyoc, Harrison IV, 1031
Vansyoc, Isaac IV, 895
Vansyoc, Jesse IV, 895
Vansyoc, John Oliver IV, 78

c, John Oliver IV, 1010
c, Lydia IV, 895
c, Lydia IV, 1031
c, Martha IV, 956
c, Martha IV, 1010
c, Martha J. IV, 1009
c, Martha Jane IV, 1010
c, Mary IV, 780
c, Mary IV, 1010
c, Mary E. IV, 991
c, Mary E. IV, 1010
c, Oliver IV, 1010
c, Oliver IV, 1031
c, Phebe IV, 810
c, Phebe IV, 849
c, Phebe IV, 1010
c, Phebe C. IV, 780
c, Phebe C. IV, 1009
c, Phebe C. IV, 1010
c, Phebe Eva IV, 780
c, Phebe Eva IV, 1010
c, Rachel IV, 892
c, Rachel IV, 895
c, Ruth IV, 895
c, Ruth IV, 1031
c, Ruth Emma IV, 1009
c, Ruth Emma IV, 1010
c, Sarah Jane IV, 895
c, Simeon IV, 895
c, Thomas Shaw IV, 849
sen, Anna IV, 1265
sen, Wildie IV, 1265
sen, Wm. IV, 1265
pool, Sarah II, 430
s, Deborah V, 537
ss, Calvin V, 537
ss, Calvin V, 717
ss, Calvin R. V, 537
ss, Calvin R. V, 717
ss, Deborah V, 537
ss, Lydia V, 537
ss, Nancy V, 537
ss, Nancy H. V, 537
ss, Willie R. V, 537
ce, Sarah IV, 44
ce, Sarah IV, 64
em, Esther II, 721
ım, Mary Ann II, 971
shitter, Anna IV, 1176
ns, Naomi V, 1023
ees, Mary II, 269
kle, Bessie V, 208
kle, Clarinda V, 364
kle, Clarinda V, 435
kle, Elizabeth V, 338
kle, Elizabeth V, 364
kle, Martha V, 287
kle, Martha V, 939
t, Mary Elizabeth V, 891
t, Mary Elizabeth V, 939
, Lucinda V, 733
Emma V, 467
Grace V, 287
Mary Elizabeth V, 287
Parry V, 467
Percell V, 287
Perry V, 287
Stella Blanche V, 287
n, Abigail II, 673
n, Grace VI, 384
n, Martha I, 1039
n-Edgerton, Grace VI, 472
n-Edgerton, Grace VI, 507
n-Edgerton, Grace VI, 565
n, Grace VI, 567
, Sarah II, 1034
n, Grace VI, 566
, Ann V, 135
Ann V, 571
, Ann V, 603
, Content I, 999
, Grace V, 135
, Hattie L. I, 735
, Irena IV, 565
, Irene IV, 598
, James I, 999
, John M. I, 735
, Lucy IV, 565
, Lucy IV, 598
, Lydia V, 135
, Malinda IV, 565
, Malinda IV, 598
, Margaret V, 135
, Maud I, 735
, Nancy V, 135
, Nathaniel V, 135
, Samuel V, 135
, Sarah Ann V, 20
, Sarah Ann V, 135
, Theodate I, 981
Theodate I, 999
Varner, Thomas V, 135
Varner, William A. I, 735
Varney, Abel IV, 297
Varney, Abel IV, 780
Varney, Able IV, 297
Varney, Anna III, 89
Varney, Anna IV, 297
Varney, Anna IV, 717
Varney, Anna IV, 780
Varney, Anna IV, 781
Varney, Anna C. III, 336
Varney, Charles Arthur III, 336
Varney, Charles C. III, 89
Varney, Charles C. III, 336
Varney, Edith III, 336
Varney, Hannah IV, 297
Varney, Hannah IV, 780
Varney, Hannah IV, 781
Varney, Isaac IV, 297
Varney, Isaac IV, 780
Varney, Isaac IV, 781
Varney, Mary IV, 297
Varney, Permelia R. III, 336
Varney, William IV, 297
Varney, William IV, 780
Varnom, Hannah I, 425
Varnon, Content I, 394
Varnon, Content I, 425
Varnon, Content I, 979
Varnon, Hannah I, 425
Varnon, James I, 979
Varnon, Jonathan II, 430
Varnon, Lydia I, 1051
Varnon, Nathaniel I, 1051
Varnon, Phebe I, 374
Varnon, Phebe I, 408
Varnon, Phebe I, 425
Varnon, Solomon I, 826
Varnon, Solomon I, 842
Varnon, Theodate I, 425
Varnon, Theodate I, 979
Varnum, Ann II, 430
Varnum, David II, 430
Varnum, Eleanor II, 430
Varnum, Elizabeth II, 430
Varnum, Elizabeth VI, 1008
Varnum, Eugene III, 336
Varnum, Hannah I, 425
Varnum, Jacob II, 430
Varnum, Jonathan II, 430
Varnum, Mary VI, 1008
Varnum, Robert II, 430
Varnum, William VI, 1008
Varrelman, Ferdinand A. VI, 759
Varrelman, Ferdinand A. VI, 787
Varrelman, Ferdinand F. VI, 787
Varrelman, Ferdinand Kapper VI, 787
Varrelman, Sallie Belle VI, 759
Varrelman, Sallie Belle VI, 787
Varrelman, Wilhelmina VI, 787
Varssey, Rachel IV, 1245
Vartooguian, Heipsime III, 336
Vartooguian, Lucy III, 336
Vartooguian, Parsegh H. III, 336
Varvel, Ellen Miley V, 648
Vase, Sarah VI, 575
Vass, Ambrose II, 673
Vass, Mary VI, 453
Vass, Mary VI, 458
Vass, Sarah II, 673
Vasse, Ambrose II, 430
Vasse, Eliz. III, 449
Vasse, Mary II, 430
Vasse, Sarah II, 673
Vasse, Sarah VI, 787
Vasser, Rebecca VI, 1008
Vasser, Robert VI, 1008
Vaugh, Frances VI, 858
Vaugh, Harriet VI, 858
Vaugh, Katherine II, 430
Vaugh, Kitty II, 430
Vaugh, Lucinda P. VI, 861
Vaugh, Samuel H. VI, 861
Vaughan, ??? VI, 191
Vaughan, Ann VI, 61
Vaughan, Ann VI, 88
Vaughan, Ann VI, 200
Vaughan, Ann VI, 216
Vaughan, Ann VI, 278
Vaughan, Anna L. VI, 278
Vaughan, Anna Ladd VI, 278
Vaughan, Ares VI, 839
Vaughan, Arthur L. IV, 1119
Vaughan, Benjamin VI, 190
Vaughan, Benjamin VI, 194
Vaughan, Benjamin VI, 215
Vaughan, Benjamin VI, 216
Vaughan, Benjamin VI, 272
Vaughan, Benjamin VI, 278
Vaughan, Benjamin VI, 1008
Vaughan, Benjamin, Jr. VI, 216
Vaughan, Benjamin, Jr. VI, 278
Vaughan, Bowling VI, 278
Vaughan, C. H. VI, 278
Vaughan, Catherine VI, 57
Vaughan, Catherine VI, 88
Vaughan, Charles IV, 781
Vaughan, Charles H. VI, 278
Vaughan, Charles Henry VI, 278
Vaughan, David VI, 88
Vaughan, Dicey VI, 991
Vaughan, Elizabeth VI, 199
Vaughan, Elizabeth VI, 215
Vaughan, Elizabeth VI, 216
Vaughan, Elizabeth VI, 1008
Vaughan, Elizabeth Huntington VI, 142
Vaughan, Fanny VI, 942
Vaughan, Frances Ann VI, 215
Vaughan, Frances Ann VI, 216
Vaughan, George VI, 861
Vaughan, George Henry VI, 142
Vaughan, Hannah VI, 165
Vaughan, Hannah VI, 200
Vaughan, Hannah VI, 215
Vaughan, Hannah VI, 216
Vaughan, James IV, 765
Vaughan, James VI, 66
Vaughan, James VI, 88
Vaughan, James VI, 139
Vaughan, James VI, 191
Vaughan, James VI, 195
Vaughan, James VI, 215
Vaughan, James VI, 216
Vaughan, James VI, 278
Vaughan, Jenny VI, 861
Vaughan, John VI, 157
Vaughan, John L. VI, 278
Vaughan, John Ladd VI, 278
Vaughan, John W. VI, 142
Vaughan, Joseph IV, 1118
Vaughan, Joseph VI, 278
Vaughan, Lemuel VI, 142
Vaughan, Lemuel VI, 278
Vaughan, Lucy VI, 231
Vaughan, Lucy A. VI, 278
Vaughan, Lucy Dabney VI, 278
Vaughan, Mahala VI, 861
Vaughan, Margaret IV, 781
Vaughan, Margaret VI, 190
Vaughan, Margaret VI, 194
Vaughan, Margaret VI, 216
Vaughan, Margaret VI, 278
Vaughan, Margaretta B. VI, 278
Vaughan, Martha M. IV, 1118
Vaughan, Martha Millhouse IV, 1118
Vaughan, Martha T. VI, 801
Vaughan, Mary VI, 66
Vaughan, Mary VI, 88
Vaughan, Mary VI, 142
Vaughan, Mary VI, 157
Vaughan, Mary VI, 158
Vaughan, Mary VI, 191
Vaughan, Mary VI, 195
Vaughan, Mary VI, 216
Vaughan, Mary Ann VI, 142
Vaughan, Mary L. VI, 216
Vaughan, Mary M. VI, 278
Vaughan, Matilda VI, 278
Vaughan, Matthew IV, 749
Vaughan, Matthew IV, 781
Vaughan, Matthew VI, 88
Vaughan, Molley VI, 165
Vaughan, Molly VI, 169
Vaughan, Molly VI, 215
Vaughan, Molly VI, 216
Vaughan, Nicholas VI, 861
Vaughan, Obediah VI, 1008
Vaughan, Peter VI, 131
Vaughan, Peter VI, 132
Vaughan, Peter VI, 141
Vaughan, Peter VI, 142
Vaughan, Phebe IV, 749
Vaughan, Phebe IV, 781
Vaughan, Phillip II, 448
Vaughan, Polly Maria IV, 679
Vaughan, Polly Maria IV, 781
Vaughan, Polly Maria IV, 849
Vaughan, Rebecca IV, 781
Vaughan, Rhoda IV, 765
Vaughan, Robert VI, 88
Vaughan, Salley VI, 1022
Vaughan, Sarah II, 108
Vaughan, Sarah VI, 216
Vaughan, Shadrach VI, 278
Vaughan, Shadrack VI, 216
Vaughan, Shadrack VI, 278
Vaughan, Shadrick VI, 216
Vaughan, Shields VI, 215
Vaughan, Shields VI, 216
Vaughan, Susanna VI, 1008
Vaughan, Unity VI, 157
Vaughan, William VI, 215
Vaughan, William VI, 991
Vaughan, William S. VI, 200
Vaughan, William S. VI, 216
Vaughan, William Shields VI, 165
Vaughan, William Shields VI, 215
Vaughan, William Shields VI, 216
Vaughan, Wm. Shields VI, 216
Vaughn, ??? IV, 929
Vaughn, Abe V, 364
Vaughn, Amy Bailey V, 364
Vaughn, Anna IV, 1062
Vaughn, Anna IV, 1080
Vaughn, Anna V, 135
Vaughn, Anna VI, 885
Vaughn, Anna Mary IV, 1226
Vaughn, Arthur L. IV, 1080
Vaughn, Arthur L. IV, 1226
Vaughn, Benjamin IV, 781
Vaughn, Benjamin VI, 885
Vaughn, Charles I, 211
Vaughn, Charles I, 227
Vaughn, Charles IV, 781
Vaughn, Charles R. V, 771
Vaughn, Chas. I, 227
Vaughn, Clary VI, 935
Vaughn, Clinton C. IV, 1225
Vaughn, Clinton C. IV, 1226
Vaughn, David II, 430
Vaughn, Edgar J. IV, 1225
Vaughn, Edith D. IV, 1226
Vaughn, Elizabeth II, 430
Vaughn, Elizabeth VI, 1008
Vaughn, Elizabeth R. IV, 1226
Vaughn, Ella D. I, 259
Vaughn, Elmer I, 227
Vaughn, Elmer G. I, 259
Vaughn, Elsie IV, 929
Vaughn, Elsie IV, 1010
Vaughn, Elsie V, 364
Vaughn, Errol V, 364
Vaughn, G. C. I, 227
Vaughn, Griffith II, 430
Vaughn, Hannah II, 559
Vaughn, Hannah II, 583
Vaughn, Hannah II, 673
Vaughn, Herbert IV, 1226
Vaughn, Ida V, 364
Vaughn, James IV, 781
Vaughn, James IV, 1010
Vaughn, James IV, 1080
Vaughn, James IV, 1214
Vaughn, James IV, 1217
Vaughn, James IV, 1225
Vaughn, James IV, 1227
Vaughn, James W. IV, 1225
Vaughn, James W. IV, 1227
Vaughn, Joana IV, 1225
Vaughn, Joana Rhoda IV, 1010
Vaughn, Joanna IV, 1010
Vaughn, Joanna IV, 1226
Vaughn, John I, 259
Vaughn, John II, 430
Vaughn, John IV, 781
Vaughn, Joseph IV, 1010
Vaughn, Joseph IV, 1069
Vaughn, Joseph IV, 1080
Vaughn, Joseph IV, 1225
Vaughn, Kate I, 227
Vaughn, Lettice VI, 880
Vaughn, Lindley J. IV, 1010
Vaughn, Lindley J. IV, 1225
Vaughn, Lindley James IV, 1010
Vaughn, Lindley James IV, 1225
Vaughn, Louis IV, 1226
Vaughn, Lula I, 208
Vaughn, Lula I, 209
Vaughn, Maggie IV, 1226
Vaughn, Marcelles IV, 781
Vaughn, Margaret I, 246
Vaughn, Margaret I, 259
Vaughn, Margaret IV, 781
Vaughn, Marguerite V, 364
Vaughn, Mariam E. I, 227
Vaughn, Martha IV, 1069
Vaughn, Martha IV, 1080
Vaughn, Martha S. I, 227
Vaughn, Martha S. I, 259
Vaughn, Martha Sarah I, 211
Vaughn, Mary IV, 1226
Vaughn, Mary A. IV, 1010
Vaughn, Mary Ann IV, 1010
Vaughn, Mary Ann IV, 1225
Vaughn, Mary Anne IV, 1217
Vaughn, Mary Anne IV, 1225
Vaughn, Mary Nettie IV, 1225
Vaughn, Mathew IV, 1225
Vaughn, Matthew IV, 781
Vaughn, Matthew IV, 1225
Vaughn, Miriam E. I, 249
Vaughn, Miriam E. I, 259
Vaughn, Nancy VI, 940
Vaughn, Naomi I, 256
Vaughn, Naomi I, 259
Vaughn, Naomy I, 259
Vaughn, Nellie V, 364
Vaughn, Obediah VI, 1008
Vaughn, Ozella I, 227
Vaughn, Patsy VI, 801
Vaughn, Phebe IV, 781
Vaughn, Phebe IV, 1225
Vaughn, Pollie Maria IV, 1010
Vaughn, Polly Maria IV, 781
Vaughn, Polly Maria IV, 802
Vaughn, Polly Maria IV, 849
Vaughn, Polly Maria IV, 1010
Vaughn, Rachel Ann IV, 1225
Vaughn, Rachel Ann IV, 1227
Vaughn, Rebecca IV, 781
Vaughn, Rebecca F. IV, 1010
Vaughn, Rebecca T. IV, 1010
Vaughn, Rebecca T. IV, 1214
Vaughn, Rebecca T. IV, 1225
Vaughn, Rebecca Terrell IV, 781
Vaughn, Rhoda IV, 781
Vaughn, Rhoda IV, 1010
Vaughn, Rhoda IV, 1080
Vaughn, Rhoda IV, 1214
Vaughn, Rhoda IV, 1217
Vaughn, Rhoda IV, 1225
Vaughn, Rhoda IV, 1226
Vaughn, Rhoda IV, 1227
Vaughn, Richard VI, 822
Vaughn, Ruth I, 259
Vaughn, Sally VI, 964
Vaughn, Samuel II, 430
Vaughn, Sarah I, 259
Vaughn, Unity IV, 1010
Vaughn, Unity IV, 1225
Vaughn, Walter IV, 1225
Vaughn, William II, 430
Vaughn, William P. IV, 1225
Vaughn, Wm. IV, 781
Vaughon, John II, 430
Vaught, Christina VI, 861
Vaught, Harrison VI, 861
Vaun, Eunice I, 597
Vaun, Eunice I, 598
Vaun, Sarah I, 259
Vaux, Ann II, 637
Vaux, Ann II, 673
Vaux, Anna II, 430
Vaux, Anna Stewardson II, 772
Vaux, Eliza II, 430
Vaux, Eliza II, 673
Vaux, Eliza H. II, 772
Vaux, Elizabeth II, 430
Vaux, Elizabeth II, 721
Vaux, Elizabeth V. II, 743
Vaux, Elizabeth V. II, 772
Vaux, Emily II, 430
Vaux, Emily V. II, 771
Vaux, Emily V. II, 772
Vaux, Frances II, 430
Vaux, Frances II, 637
Vaux, Frances II, 673
Vaux, Frances II, 677
Vaux, Frances II, 772
Vaux, George II, 430
Vaux, George II, 637
Vaux, George II, 673
Vaux, George II, 677
Vaux, George II, 721
Vaux, George II, 772
Vaux, George, Jr. II, 721
Vaux, Hannah II, 430
Vaux, Hannah S. V. II, 732
Vaux, Hannah S. V. II, 772
Vaux, Henry VI, 6
Vaux, Henry VI, 11
Vaux, James II, 430
Vaux, James II, 673
Vaux, James II, 677
Vaux, James II, 721
Vaux, Margaret II, 673
Vaux, Mary Emlen II, 430
Vaux, Richard II, 637
Vaux, Richard II, 673
Vaux, Robert II, 673
Vaux, Susan V. II, 735
Vaux, Susan V. II, 772
Vaux, Susanna II, 430
Vaux, Susanna II, 673
Vaux, Susanna II, 677
Vaux, William Sansom II, 430
Vaux, Wm. S. II, 772
Vawn, Elizabeth II, 430

Vawn, Griffith II, 430
Vawn, William II, 430
Vawter, Martha B. VI, 861
Vawter, Silas P. VI, 861
Veach, Rachel I, 622
Veal, Abraham IV, 113
Veal, Benjamin IV, 113
Veal, Catharine V, 136
Veal, Catherine IV, 113
Veal, Elizabeth VI, 1009
Veal, Esther VI, 604
Veal, Esther VI, 607
Veal, Joseph VI, 1009
Veal, Margaret IV, 113
Veal, Mercy IV, 113
Veal, Randal V, 136
Veal, Robert IV, 113
Veal, Samuel IV, 113
Veal, Stephen IV, 113
Veal, Taylor IV, 113
Veal, William VI, 1009
Veale, Catharine V, 136
Veale, Catherine V, 122
Vealey, Harriett VI, 882
Vealey, Isaac VI, 882
Veder, Enos V, 287
Veditae, Oce I, 963
Veditae, Oce I, 969
Veditoe, Oce I, 969
Veditoe, Stephen I, 969
Veere, Ann II, 673
Veil, Ann IV, 885
Veil, Edith IV, 885
Veil, Guli Elma IV, 885
Veil, Morton IV, 885
Velie, Mary Eugenia VI, 729
Velle, Sarah I, 201
Velle, Sarah I, 203
Vellmer, Annie G. III, 172
Vellmer, Annie G. III, 336
Vellmer, Arthur N. III, 336
Vellmer, Horsnal III, 336
Velson, Eugene III, 488
Velsor, Arthur III, 463
Velsor, Cornelius III, 463
Velsor, Eugene III, 488
Velsor, Eugene III, 503
Velsor, Francis Augustus III, 463
Velsor, John III, 463
Velsor, Libbie III, 463
Velsor, Margaret III, 463
Velsor, Mary Lavinia III, 463
Velsor, Ruth III, 463
Velsor, Ruth III, 471
Velsor, Ruth W. III, 503
Velsor, Ruth W. III, 506
Velsor, Sarah III, 463
Velsor, Sarah M. III, 412
Velsor, Sarah M. III, 463
Velsor, Stephen T. III, 412
Velsor, Stephen T. III, 463
Velsor, Susie III, 488
Velsor, Susie III, 503
Velsor, Valentine III, 463
Velsor, Valentine III, 471
Velsor, Valentine III, 503
Velsor, Valentine III, 506
Veltman, ??? III, 178
Veltman, Hester III, 336
Veltman, Lot III, 336
Veltman, Phebe Jane III, 178
Veltman, Phebe Jane III, 336
Venabal, Jane IV, 675
Venabal, Jane IV, 781
Venable, Abraham VI, 260
Venable, Abraham VI, 861
Venable, Agatha VI, 260
Venable, Arthur V, 136
Venable, Bertha IV, 781
Venable, Capt. John VI, 260
Venable, Charles V, 136
Venable, Della V, 136
Venable, Elizabeth VI, 843
Venable, Elizabeth VI, 861
Venable, Elizabeth Ann VI, 1009
Venable, Jacob VI, 861
Venable, Jacob VI, 1009
Venable, Jane IV, 781
Venable, Jane E. VI, 843
Venable, Jno. VI, 861
Venable, John V, 136
Venable, Joseph V, 136
Venable, Lewis IV, 781
Venable, Maria V, 136
Venable, Maria V, 145
Venable, Mary VI, 260
Venable, Mary VI, 861
Venable, Mr. ??? IV, 781
Venable, Mrs. ??? IV, 781
Venable, Nancy VI, 1009
Venable, Nancy S. V, 136
Venable, Nathaniel VI, 861
Venable, Paul C. VI, 1009
Venable, Rachel V, 24
Venable, Rachel V, 136
Venable, Rachel V, 145
Venable, Thomas V, 136
Venable, Vincent IV, 781
Venable, Vincent IV, 1010
Venable, Vincent IV, 1080
Venable, Vincent IV, 1119
Venable, Vincent IV, 1297
Venable, William V, 136
Venable, Wm. V, 145
Vendine, Doshia VI, 1009
Vendine, John VI, 1009
Vendine, Nancy VI, 1009
Venicom, Rachel II, 235
Venicom, Rachel II, 269
Venicom, William II, 235
Venicomb, Elizabeth II, 239
Venicomb, Francis II, 238
Venicomb, Francis II, 269
Venicomb, Hannah II, 673
Venicomb, Rachel II, 238
Venicomb, Rachel II, 269
Venicomb, Sarah II, 269
Venicomb, Sarah II, 270
Venicomb, William II, 269
Venicomb, William II, 270
Venicomb, Zilpha II, 269
Vennable, John II, 269
Venscoyoe, Rebecca VI, 984
Ventress, Nancy I, 711
Ventress, Nancy I, 735
Ventress, Rebeckah I, 735
Venvoras, Mary II, 245
Veon, John IV, 781
Veon, Margaret IV, 781
Veon, Mrs. ??? IV, 781
Veon, Sarah IV, 781
Veon, Sarah Jane IV, 781
Verhurst, Elizabeth II, 448
Verhurst, William II, 448
Verity, Abigail III, 503
Verity, Alonzo III, 511
Verity, Ann Maria III, 511
Verity, Edward III, 511
Verity, Elizabeth II, 994
Verity, Elizabeth II, 1034
Verity, Hannah III, 511
Verity, Jacob J. III, 511
Verity, John II, 994
Verity, John II, 1034
Verity, Mary E. III, 511
Verity, Samuel III, 503
Verity, Samuel III, 511
Verity, Sarah M. III, 511
Verity, Smith III, 511
Verity, Stephen III, 511
Verity, Stephen H. III, 511
Verity, Walter J. III, 463
Vermelion, Flora IV, 297
Vermilian, Ella V, 537
Vermilion, George VI, 863
Vermilion, Robert VI, 955
Vermillian, Blanche Elizabeth VI, 786
Vermillion, Ann I, 1116
Vermillion, Blanche Elizabeth VI, 748
Vermillion, Ella V, 537
Verner, Hannah I, 842
Vernon, ??? IV, 450
Vernon, Abigail IV, 297
Vernon, Abigail IV, 596
Vernon, Abigail IV, 598
Vernon, Abigail T. IV, 598
Vernon, Abijah Edgerton IV, 1119
Vernon, Abner IV, 450
Vernon, Abner IV, 451
Vernon, Abner IV, 1074
Vernon, Abner IV, 1080
Vernon, Abner IV, 1081
Vernon, Addison IV, 1119
Vernon, Addison IV, 1139
Vernon, Agnes Martilda IV, 1080
Vernon, Alice IV, 297
Vernon, Amos I, 425
Vernon, Amos I, 842
Vernon, Amos I, 1045
Vernon, Amos I, 1046
Vernon, Amos I, 1051
Vernon, Amos IV, 162
Vernon, Amos IV, 221
Vernon, Amos IV, 292
Vernon, Amos IV, 373
Vernon, Amos IV, 426
Vernon, Amos IV, 450
Vernon, Amos IV, 451
Vernon, Amos IV, 598
Vernon, Amos IV, 599
Vernon, Amos IV, 1049
Vernon, Amos IV, 1069
Vernon, Amos IV, 1080
Vernon, Amos IV, 1081
Vernon, Amos IV, 1119
Vernon, Amos IV, 1139
Vernon, Andrew III, 501
Vernon, Angeline IV, 1080
Vernon, Ann I, 1045
Vernon, Ann I, 1046
Vernon, Ann I, 1099
Vernon, Ann II, 269
Vernon, Ann II, 430
Vernon, Ann III, 411
Vernon, Ann IV, 60
Vernon, Ann IV, 64
Vernon, Ann IV, 415
Vernon, Ann V, 771
Vernon, Anna II, 108
Vernon, Anna Alwilda IV, 1080
Vernon, Anne II, 269
Vernon, Anne IV, 162
Vernon, Anne IV, 450
Vernon, Asa IV, 450
Vernon, Asa IV, 1119
Vernon, Asenath IV, 1080
Vernon, Asenath IV, 1081
Vernon, Benjamin IV, 64
Vernon, Benjamin IV, 113
Vernon, Benjamin IV, 392
Vernon, Benjamin IV, 450
Vernon, Benjamin IV, 451
Vernon, Benjamin IV, 1080
Vernon, Benjamin IV, 1081
Vernon, Benjamin IV, 1139
Vernon, Caleb II, 430
Vernon, Catharine I, 418
Vernon, Catharine I, 425
Vernon, Catharine IV, 392
Vernon, Catharine IV, 426
Vernon, Catharine IV, 450
Vernon, Catharine IV, 598
Vernon, Catherine Patterson IV, 450
Vernon, Charles D. IV, 297
Vernon, Charles D. IV, 598
Vernon, Charles D. IV, 1119
Vernon, Charles D. IV, 1139
Vernon, Charles Edgar IV, 297
Vernon, Chas. D. IV, 297
Vernon, Chas. D. IV, 596
Vernon, Chas. D. IV, 1119
Vernon, Content I, 425
Vernon, Content I, 958
Vernon, Content I, 969
Vernon, Content I, 1045
Vernon, Content I, 1046
Vernon, Content I, 1051
Vernon, Content IV, 162
Vernon, Content IV, 415
Vernon, Content IV, 450
Vernon, Cynthia Alice IV, 1139
Vernon, Daniel VI, 640
Vernon, Daniel VI, 716
Vernon, David IV, 1080
Vernon, David IV, 1119
Vernon, David IV, 1139
Vernon, Deborah IV, 388
Vernon, Deborah IV, 390
Vernon, Deborah IV, 403
Vernon, Deborah IV, 408
Vernon, Deborah IV, 446
Vernon, Deborah IV, 450
Vernon, Deborah IV, 451
Vernon, Deborah IV, 1119
Vernon, Deborah IV, 1135
Vernon, Deborah IV, 1139
Vernon, Deborah H. IV, 450
Vernon, Dempsey IV, 297
Vernon, Dempsey IV, 1119
Vernon, Dempsey B. IV, 1119
Vernon, Denny IV, 1080
Vernon, Dorothy III, 501
Vernon, Dorothy III, 503
Vernon, E. Alonzo IV, 1139
Vernon, Edith IV, 1080
Vernon, Edith IV, 1081
Vernon, Edna IV, 1139
Vernon, Edna IV, 1140
Vernon, Eleanor II, 430
Vernon, Eleanor II, 673
Vernon, Eli IV, 403
Vernon, Eli IV, 450
Vernon, Eli IV, 451
Vernon, Eli IV, 1119
Vernon, Eli IV, 1133
Vernon, Eli IV, 1139
Vernon, Elijah IV, 450
Vernon, Elijah IV, 451
Vernon, Elijah IV, 598
Vernon, Elijah IV, 1119
Vernon, Elinor II, 430
Vernon, Elisha IV, 598
Vernon, Elisha IV, 1080
Vernon, Elisha IV, 1119
Vernon, Eliza IV, 403
Vernon, Eliza IV, 450
Vernon, Eliza IV, 451
Vernon, Eliza IV, 1119
Vernon, Eliza IV, 1133
Vernon, Eliza IV, 1139
Vernon, Eliza P. IV, 1005
Vernon, Eliza P. IV, 1010
Vernon, Elizabeth I, 1046
Vernon, Elizabeth I, 1133
Vernon, Elizabeth IV, 162
Vernon, Elizabeth IV, 365
Vernon, Elizabeth IV, 450
Vernon, Elizabeth IV, 1049
Vernon, Elizabeth IV, 1080
Vernon, Elizabeth IV, 1081
Vernon, Elizabeth IV, 1095
Vernon, Elizabeth IV, 1100
Vernon, Elizabeth IV, 1105
Vernon, Elizabeth IV, 1119
Vernon, Elizabeth IV, 1139
Vernon, Elizabeth VI, 715
Vernon, Elizabeth VI, 716
Vernon, Elizabeth E. IV, 1119
Vernon, Elizabeth Ellen IV, 1080
Vernon, Elizabeth Jane IV, 1139
Vernon, Ella IV, 1272
Vernon, Ella IV, 1297
Vernon, Elma IV, 20
Vernon, Elma IV, 64
Vernon, Elmy IV, 64
Vernon, Elwood IV, 1119
Vernon, Emily Ann IV, 1139
Vernon, Emily N. IV, 1139
Vernon, Emma Lucy IV, 1139
Vernon, Emma Olive IV, 297
Vernon, Enoch IV, 1119
Vernon, Estella IV, 297
Vernon, Estella IV, 598
Vernon, Esther IV, 392
Vernon, Evaline IV, 1119
Vernon, Evaline IV, 1123
Vernon, Evaline IV, 1139
Vernon, George W. IV, 598
Vernon, George William IV, 1139
Vernon, Giana IV, 162
Vernon, Grace I, 827
Vernon, Grace I, 842
Vernon, Grace I, 1046
Vernon, Grace I, 1051
Vernon, Grace V, 723
Vernon, Grace V, 771
Vernon, Hannah I, 425
Vernon, Hannah I, 794
Vernon, Hannah I, 842
Vernon, Hannah I, 1051
Vernon, Hannah IV, 57
Vernon, Hannah IV, 64
Vernon, Hannah IV, 1069
Vernon, Hannah IV, 1080
Vernon, Hannah IV, 1081
Vernon, Hannah IV, 1139
Vernon, Hannah F. IV, 1119
Vernon, Henry IV, 1080
Vernon, Iddo L. IV, 1139
Vernon, Isaac I, 425
Vernon, Isaac I, 794
Vernon, Isaac I, 1046
Vernon, Isaac I, 1051
Vernon, Isaac I, 1133
Vernon, Isaac IV, 446
Vernon, Isaac IV, 450
Vernon, Isaac IV, 451
Vernon, Isaac IV, 1078
Vernon, Isaac IV, 1080
Vernon, Isaac IV, 1081
Vernon, Jacob II, 430
Vernon, Jacob II, 673
Vernon, Jacob IV, 64
Vernon, James I, 425
Vernon, James I, 842
Vernon, James I, 958
Vernon, James I, 961
Vernon, James I, 969
Vernon, James I, 1013
Vernon, James I, 1039
Vernon, James I, 1041
Vernon, James I, 1045
Vernon, James I, 1046
Vernon, James I, 1051
Vernon, James III, 411
Vernon, James IV, 162
Vernon, James IV, 365
Vernon, James IV, 446
Vernon, James IV, 450
Vernon, James IV, 451
Vernon, James IV, 598
Vernon, James IV, 1052
Vernon, James IV, 1080
Vernon, James IV, 1089
Vernon, James IV, 1119
Vernon, James IV, 1139
Vernon, James IV, 1190
Vernon, James IV, 1195
Vernon, James VI, 716
Vernon, James E. IV, 1119
Vernon, James E. IV, 1139
Vernon, James L. IV, 1119
Vernon, Jane II, 934
Vernon, Jane IV, 451
Vernon, Jane IV, 598
Vernon, Jane IV, 599
Vernon, Jane IV, 1119
Vernon, Jane IV, 1139
Vernon, Jane W. IV, 1139
Vernon, Janney IV, 450
Vernon, Jeams I, 969
Vernon, Jena I, 958
Vernon, Jenny IV, 372
Vernon, Jenny IV, 450
Vernon, Jesse IV, 450
Vernon, Jesse IV, 451
Vernon, Jesse IV, 1119
Vernon, Jesse IV, 1139
Vernon, Jesse IV, 1160
Vernon, Jesse IV, 1190
Vernon, Jesse V, 364
Vernon, Jesse Craft IV, 113
Vernon, John I, 1099
Vernon, John IV, 1080
Vernon, John IV, 1081
Vernon, John IV, 1095
Vernon, John IV, 1119
Vernon, John IV, 1139
Vernon, John VI, 715
Vernon, John VI, 716
Vernon, John Albert IV, 11
Vernon, John E. IV, 1119
Vernon, John T. IV, 598
Vernon, Jonathan VI, 862
Vernon, Joseph II, 430
Vernon, Joseph IV, 408
Vernon, Joseph IV, 450
Vernon, Joseph IV, 451
Vernon, Joseph IV, 598
Vernon, Joseph IV, 794
Vernon, Joseph IV, 1069
Vernon, Joseph IV, 1080
Vernon, Joseph IV, 1081
Vernon, Joseph IV, 1095
Vernon, Joseph IV, 1119
Vernon, Joseph VI, 716
Vernon, Joseph Middleton
Vernon, Joshua II, 430
Vernon, Laura I, 1013
Vernon, Lauretta Asenath IV, 1080
Vernon, Lucy Jane IV, 1080
Vernon, Lydda V, 771
Vernon, Lydia I, 1046
Vernon, Lydia I, 1051
Vernon, Lydia IV, 598
Vernon, Lydia IV, 1119
Vernon, Lydia V, 771
Vernon, Lydia VI, 691
Vernon, Lydia M. IV, 1089
Vernon, Lydia M. IV, 1119
Vernon, Manoah IV, 1119
Vernon, Manoah H. IV, 113
Vernon, Margaret I, 1046
Vernon, Margaret I, 1051
Vernon, Margaret V, 771
Vernon, Martha I, 425
Vernon, Martha I, 1039
Vernon, Martha I, 1041
Vernon, Martha IV, 408
Vernon, Martha IV, 450
Vernon, Martha IV, 451
Vernon, Martha IV, 598
Vernon, Martha Ann IV, 45
Vernon, Mary I, 398
Vernon, Mary I, 425
Vernon, Mary I, 1034
Vernon, Mary I, 1039
Vernon, Mary I, 1044
Vernon, Mary I, 1045
Vernon, Mary I, 1046
Vernon, Mary I, 1133
Vernon, Mary III, 411
Vernon, Mary IV, 87
Vernon, Mary IV, 113
Vernon, Mary IV, 162
Vernon, Mary IV, 221
Vernon, Mary IV, 292
Vernon, Mary IV, 297
Vernon, Mary IV, 373
Vernon, Mary IV, 450
Vernon, Mary IV, 451

on, Mary IV, 598
on, Mary IV, 1052
on, Mary IV, 1069
on, Mary IV, 1080
on, Mary IV, 1081
on, Mary IV, 1095
on, Mary IV, 1101
on, Mary IV, 1119
on, Mary IV, 1129
on, Mary IV, 1139
non, Mary IV, 1140
non, Mary VI, 716
non, Mary Adalaide IV, 1080
non, Mary Ann IV, 390
non, Mary Ann IV, 450
non, Matilda IV, 1080
non, Miles I, 1099
non, Mordecai IV, 1119
non, Mordecai IV, 1139
non, Morgan IV, 1119
non, Nathaniel I, 842
non, Nathaniel I, 1039
non, Nathaniel I, 1046
non, Nathaniel I, 1051
non, Nathaniel V, 723
non, Nathaniel V, 771
non, Osborn IV, 1119
non, Patience IV, 1119
non, Patience IV, 1160
non, Patience IV, 1190
non, Peninah IV, 594
non, Peninah IV, 598
non, Peninah IV, 1080
non, Peninah IV, 1119
rnon, Pennina IV, 1119
rnon, Penninah IV, 1095
rnon, Phebe IV, 1074
rnon, Phebe IV, 1080
rnon, Phebe VI, 715
rnon, Phebe VI, 716
rnon, Rachel I, 1045
rnon, Rachel IV, 77
rnon, Rachel IV, 113
rnon, Rachel IV, 162
rnon, Rachel IV, 292
rnon, Rachel IV, 297
rnon, Rachel IV, 450
rnon, Rachel IV, 451
rnon, Rachel IV, 598
rnon, Rachel IV, 599
rnon, Rachel IV, 674
rnon, Rachel IV, 781
rnon, Rachel IV, 1080
rnon, Rachel IV, 1119
rnon, Rachel IV, 1139
rnon, Rachel IV, 1190
rnon, Rachel IV, 1195
ernon, Rachel Ann IV, 1190
ernon, Rachel E. IV, 1134
ernon, Rachel E. IV, 1139
ernon, Rebecca IV, 449
ernon, Rebecca IV, 450
ernon, Rebecca IV, 451
ernon, Rebekah VI, 640
ernon, Rebekah VI, 716
ernon, Rhoda IV, 388
ernon, Rhoda IV, 446
ernon, Rhoda IV, 450
ernon, Rhoda IV, 451
ernon, Rhoda IV, 1052
ernon, Rhoda IV, 1080
ernon, Rhoda IV, 1081
ernon, Rhoda IV, 1095
ernon, Rhoda IV, 1119
ernon, Rhoda Ann IV, 1080
ernon, Rhoda Ann IV, 1081
ernon, Rhoda Ann IV, 1119
ernon, Rhoda Ann IV, 1139
ernon, Robert I, 425
ernon, Robert I, 842
ernon, Robert I, 1045
ernon, Robert I, 1046
ernon, Robert I, 1051
ernon, Robert II, 430
Vernon, Robert IV, 162
Vernon, Robert IV, 388
Vernon, Robert IV, 390
Vernon, Robert IV, 408
Vernon, Robert IV, 415
Vernon, Robert IV, 446
Vernon, Robert IV, 450
Vernon, Robert IV, 451
Vernon, Robert IV, 598
Vernon, Robert IV, 1080
Vernon, Robert IV, 1119
Vernon, Robert IV, 1134
Vernon, Robert IV, 1139
Vernon, Robert N. IV, 598
Vernon, Robert, Jr. IV, 451
Vernon, Roda IV, 1080
Vernon, Ruthanna IV, 221
Vernon, Ruthanna IV, 297
Vernon, Ruthanna IV, 450
Vernon, Ruthanna IV, 583
Vernon, Ruthanna IV, 598
Vernon, Samuel I, 1046
Vernon, Samuel II, 825
Vernon, Samuel V, 771
Vernon, Sarah IV, 64
Vernon, Sarah IV, 113
Vernon, Sarah IV, 373
Vernon, Sarah IV, 446
Vernon, Sarah IV, 450
Vernon, Sarah IV, 451
Vernon, Sarah IV, 1078
Vernon, Sarah IV, 1080
Vernon, Sarah IV, 1092
Vernon, Sarah IV, 1095
Vernon, Sarah IV, 1119
Vernon, Sarah IV, 1134
Vernon, Sarah IV, 1139
Vernon, Sarah IV, 1190
Vernon, Sarah L. IV, 1092
Vernon, Sarah L. IV, 1119
Vernon, Solomon I, 425
Vernon, Solomon I, 842
Vernon, Solomon I, 1046
Vernon, Solomon I, 1051
Vernon, Solomon I, 1095
Vernon, Solomon I, 1133
Vernon, Sukey VI, 862
Vernon, Tamar I, 961
Vernon, Tamar I, 969
Vernon, Tamar IV, 598
Vernon, Tamar IV, 1095
Vernon, Tamar IV, 1119
Vernon, Tamar IV, 1190
Vernon, Tamar E. IV, 1139
Vernon, Tamer I, 958
Vernon, Tamer IV, 365
Vernon, Tamer IV, 383
Vernon, Tamer IV, 408
Vernon, Tamer IV, 450
Vernon, Tamer IV, 451
Vernon, Tamer IV, 598
Vernon, Tamer IV, 1119
Vernon, Tamer D. IV, 1133
Vernon, Tamir D. IV, 964
Vernon, Tamor I, 1046
Vernon, Tamor IV, 162
Vernon, Tamour I, 1051
Vernon, Theodate I, 425
Vernon, Theodate I, 842
Vernon, Theodate I, 958
Vernon, Theodate I, 1046
Vernon, Theodate I, 1051
Vernon, Theodate IV, 297
Vernon, Theodate IV, 418
Vernon, Theodate IV, 450
Vernon, Theodate IV, 451
Vernon, Theodate IV, 554
Vernon, Theodate IV, 1069
Vernon, Theodate IV, 1080
Vernon, Thisdate IV, 162
Vernon, Thomas I, 1046
Vernon, Thomas I, 1099
Vernon, Thomas IV, 450
Vernon, Thomas IV, 451
Vernon, Thomas IV, 1190
Vernon, Thomas V, 771
Vernon, Thomas L. IV, 1190
Vernon, Thomas Marshal I, 1099
Vernon, Thomas Marshall I, 842
Vernon, Townsend I, 425
Vernon, W. O. V, 467
Vernon, Wallace W. IV, 297
Vernon, William I, 958
Vernon, William I, 1046
Vernon, William II, 430
Vernon, William IV, 450
Vernon, William IV, 594
Vernon, William IV, 598
Vernon, William IV, 1095
Vernon, William IV, 1119
Vernon, William G. IV, 1190
Vernon, William H. IV, 1119
Vernon, William T. IV, 1119
Vernon, Wm. IV, 162
Vernon, Wm. IV, 403
Vernon, Wm. IV, 598
Vernon, Wm. IV, 1080
Vernon, Wm. IV, 1119
Vernon, Wm. IV, 1139
Vernon, Wm. G. IV, 1190
Vernon, Wm. H. IV, 1119
Vernon, Wm. P. IV, 1139
Vernon, Zilpah IV, 450
Vernon, Zilpha IV, 408
Vernon, Zilpha IV, 450
Vernon, Zilpha IV, 1080
Vernon, Zilpha IV, 1119
Vernum, Edmond II, 430
Vernum, Sarah II, 673
Verre, Robert II, 673
Verree, Anne II, 187
Verree, Anne II, 269
Verree, Mary II, 230
Verree, Mary II, 269
Vert, Jacob II, 430
Vesey, Elizabeth II, 674
Vesey, Elizabeth II, 934
Vest, Amy VI, 1009
Vest, Betsy VI, 862
Vest, Charlotte VI, 1009
Vest, Edward VI, 1009
Vest, Elizabeth VI, 894
Vest, Elizabeth VI, 956
Vest, James VI, 836
Vest, Jane VI, 1009
Vest, John VI, 863
Vest, John VI, 869
Vest, John VI, 894
Vest, John VI, 903
Vest, John VI, 928
Vest, John VI, 1009
Vest, John, Jr. VI, 1009
Vest, Joshua VI, 1009
Vest, Keziah VI, 1009
Vest, Margaret C. VI, 863
Vest, Mary VI, 862
Vest, Nancy VI, 903
Vest, Polly VI, 869
Vest, Robert VI, 862
Vest, Stelley VI, 1009
Vest, Thomas VI, 803
Vest, William VI, 1009
Vest., Rebecca VI, 928
Vestal, Achas I, 395
Vestal, Achas I, 426
Vestal, Achsa I, 366
Vestal, Achsa I, 985
Vestal, Achsa I, 999
Vestal, Achsah I, 366
Vestal, Achsah I, 411
Vestal, Achsah I, 426
Vestal, Alfred I, 366
Vestal, Alfred I, 426
Vestal, Alfred Newby I, 426
Vestal, Amy I, 423
Vestal, Amy I, 425
Vestal, Ann I, 366
Vestal, Ann I, 372
Vestal, Ann I, 395
Vestal, Ann I, 408
Vestal, Ann I, 426
Vestal, Ann I, 580
Vestal, Ann I, 999
Vestal, Ann VI, 364
Vestal, Ann VI, 453
Vestal, Ann VI, 716
Vestal, Ann, Jr. VI, 546
Vestal, Ann, Jr. VI, 716
Vestal, Anna I, 950
Vestal, Anna I, 982
Vestal, Anna I, 999
Vestal, Anne I, 842
Vestal, Annie I, 950
Vestal, Arthur I, 950
Vestal, Arthur Lee I, 935
Vestal, Asenath I, 986
Vestal, Asenath I, 999
Vestal, Benj. I, 366
Vestal, Benj. Elwood I, 366
Vestal, Benjamin I, 366
Vestal, Benjamin I, 426
Vestal, Benjamin I, 451
Vestal, Benjamin I, 454
Vestal, Bettie I, 426
Vestal, Clark V, 537
Vestal, Daniel I, 366
Vestal, Daniel I, 414
Vestal, Daniel I, 425
Vestal, Daniel I, 426
Vestal, Daniel I, 979
Vestal, Daniel I, 999
Vestal, Daniel, Jr. I, 999
Vestal, David I, 366
Vestal, David I, 367
Vestal, David I, 378
Vestal, David I, 425
Vestal, David I, 426
Vestal, David I, 454
Vestal, David I, 680
Vestal, David I, 690
Vestal, David I, 842
Vestal, David I, 999
Vestal, David VI, 453
Vestal, Delphina I, 842
Vestal, Dinah I, 979
Vestal, Edith I, 366
Vestal, Edith I, 398
Vestal, Edith I, 426
Vestal, Edith V, 474
Vestal, Edith V, 537
Vestal, Eli I, 366
Vestal, Eli I, 426
Vestal, Eli I, 608
Vestal, Eli I, 842
Vestal, Elizabeth I, 343
Vestal, Elizabeth I, 351
Vestal, Elizabeth I, 360
Vestal, Elizabeth I, 362
Vestal, Elizabeth I, 366
Vestal, Elizabeth I, 377
Vestal, Elizabeth I, 380
Vestal, Elizabeth I, 384
Vestal, Elizabeth I, 405
Vestal, Elizabeth I, 425
Vestal, Elizabeth I, 426
Vestal, Elizabeth I, 486
Vestal, Elizabeth I, 728
Vestal, Elizabeth I, 735
Vestal, Elizabeth I, 842
Vestal, Elizabeth I, 975
Vestal, Elizabeth I, 999
Vestal, Elizabeth V, 136
Vestal, Elizabeth V, 486
Vestal, Elizabeth V, 488
Vestal, Elizabeth V, 537
Vestal, Elizabeth VI, 453
Vestal, Elizabeth C. V, 537
Vestal, Estella I, 611
Vestal, Esther I, 680
Vestal, Esther I, 690
Vestal, Esther I, 867
Vestal, Esther I, 904
Vestal, Esther I, 930
Vestal, Eunce I, 999
Vestal, Eunice I, 986
Vestal, Hannah I, 362
Vestal, Hannah I, 366
Vestal, Hannah I, 413
Vestal, Hannah I, 425
Vestal, Hannah I, 979
Vestal, Hannah I, 990
Vestal, Hannah I, 999
Vestal, Hannah VI, 575
Vestal, Hester I, 904
Vestal, Hilsey I, 999
Vestal, Irena I, 888
Vestal, Irena I, 904
Vestal, Irene I, 928
Vestal, J. E. I, 950
Vestal, Jabin I, 366
Vestal, James I, 425
Vestal, James I, 950
Vestal, James I Sup 1, 9
Vestal, James D. I, 904
Vestal, James E. I, 932
Vestal, James Elijah I, 935
Vestal, Jemima I, 351
Vestal, Jemima I, 366
Vestal, Jemima I, 387
Vestal, Jemima I, 425
Vestal, Jemima I, 608
Vestal, Jemima I, 819
Vestal, Jemima I, 842
Vestal, Jemima I, 999
Vestal, Jemima V, 136
Vestal, Jennie V, 717
Vestal, Jeremiah I, 999
Vestal, Jesse I, 366
Vestal, Jesse I, 426
Vestal, Jesse I, 999
Vestal, John I, 366
Vestal, John I, 425
Vestal, John I, 426
Vestal, John I, 976
Vestal, John I, 979
Vestal, John I, 988
Vestal, John I, 999
Vestal, John I Sup 1, 9
Vestal, John V, 537
Vestal, John VI, 453
Vestal, John VI, 546
Vestal, John VI, 716
Vestal, Jonathan I, 979
Vestal, Joseph I, 366
Vestal, Joseph I, 426
Vestal, Joshua I, 426
Vestal, Ludah E. I, 366
Vestal, Lydia I, 366
Vestal, Lydia I, 409
Vestal, Lydia I, 426
Vestal, Lydia I, 989
Vestal, Lydia I, 999
Vestal, Mae B. I, 950
Vestal, Margaret I, 680
Vestal, Margaret I, 690
Vestal, Margaret I, 976
Vestal, Margaret I, 988
Vestal, Margaret I, 999
Vestal, Margret I, 982
Vestal, Margret I, 999
Vestal, Martha I, 366
Vestal, Martha I, 405
Vestal, Martha I, 426
Vestal, Martin V. I, 935
Vestal, Mary I, 360
Vestal, Mary I, 366
Vestal, Mary I, 367
Vestal, Mary I, 379
Vestal, Mary I, 393
Vestal, Mary I, 398
Vestal, Mary I, 407
Vestal, Mary I, 414
Vestal, Mary I, 425
Vestal, Mary I, 426
Vestal, Mary I, 690
Vestal, Mary I, 735
Vestal, Mary I, 976
Vestal, Mary I, 979
Vestal, Mary I, 986
Vestal, Mary I, 987
Vestal, Mary I, 999
Vestal, Mary V, 136
Vestal, Mary V, 572
Vestal, Mary VI, 366
Vestal, Mary VI, 453
Vestal, Mary Ann I, 426
Vestal, Mary Ann I, 454
Vestal, Mary Ann I, 611
Vestal, Minerva Jane V, 475
Vestal, Minerva Jane V, 537
Vestal, Nancy I, 999
Vestal, Nathan I, 366
Vestal, Nathan I, 426
Vestal, Nellie I, 948
Vestal, Nellie I, 950
Vestal, Nellie Gertrude I, 935
Vestal, Nellie V. I, 932
Vestal, Olive E. V, 537
Vestal, Olive Emily V, 537
Vestal, Phebe I, 423
Vestal, Phebe I, 425
Vestal, Phebe I, 842
Vestal, Phineas I, 366
Vestal, Polly I, 426
Vestal, Polly I, 935
Vestal, Rachel I, 366
Vestal, Rachel I, 397
Vestal, Rachel I, 425
Vestal, Rachel I, 975
Vestal, Rachel I, 979
Vestal, Rachel I, 987
Vestal, Rachel I, 994
Vestal, Rachel I, 999
Vestal, Rachel V, 136
Vestal, Rachel V, 537
Vestal, Rebecca I, 407
Vestal, Rebecca I, 426
Vestal, Rebecca I, 950
Vestal, Rebecca Frances I, 935
Vestal, Rhoda I, 392
Vestal, Rhoda I, 426
Vestal, Rhoda I, 828
Vestal, Rhoda I, 842
Vestal, Rhoda M. I, 366
Vestal, Rhody I, 999
Vestal, Riley I, 486
Vestal, Rosa I, 950
Vestal, Ruth I, 366
Vestal, Ruth I, 411
Vestal, Ruth I, 426
Vestal, Ruth I, 451
Vestal, Ruth I, 454
Vestal, Sally I, 366
Vestal, Sally I, 608
Vestal, Sally I, 842
Vestal, Samuel I, 426
Vestal, Samuel I, 771
Vestal, Samuel V, 136
Vestal, Samuel V, 537
Vestal, Sarah I, 366
Vestal, Sarah I, 378
Vestal, Sarah I, 425
Vestal, Sarah I, 426
Vestal, Sarah I, 428
Vestal, Sarah I, 454
Vestal, Sarah I, 950
Vestal, Sarah I, 999
Vestal, Sarah V, 537
Vestal, Sarah M. I, 932
Vestal, Sarah M. I, 935
Vestal, Silas I, 366
Vestal, Silas I, 426
Vestal, Solomon I, 366
Vestal, Solomon I, 407
Vestal, Solomon I, 426
Vestal, Solomon I, 680
Vestal, Solomon I, 690
Vestal, Solomon I, 867
Vestal, Solomon I, 904
Vestal, Solomon I, 930
Vestal, Spencer V, 537

Vestal, Spencer H. V, 537
Vestal, Spencer W. V, 537
Vestal, Susannah I, 979
Vestal, Tabitha Curris I, 930
Vestal, Telitha I, 894
Vestal, Telitha I, 904
Vestal, Thomas I, 343
Vestal, Thomas I, 360
Vestal, Thomas I, 366
Vestal, Thomas I, 384
Vestal, Thomas I, 425
Vestal, Thomas I, 426
Vestal, Thomas I, 487
Vestal, Thomas I, 580
Vestal, Thomas I, 971
Vestal, Thomas I, 975
Vestal, Thomas I, 999
Vestal, Thomas, Jr. I, 425
Vestal, Thomas, Jr. I, 842
Vestal, Thos. I, 351
Vestal, Thos. I, 362
Vestal, Thos. I, 366
Vestal, W. T. I, 426
Vestal, William I, 343
Vestal, William I, 366
Vestal, William I, 367
Vestal, William I, 425
Vestal, William I, 426
Vestal, William I, 611
Vestal, William I, 690
Vestal, William I, 728
Vestal, William I, 735
Vestal, William I, 904
Vestal, William I, 999
Vestal, William I Sup 1, 9
Vestal, William VI, 453
Vestal, Wm. I, 366
Vestal, Wm. I, 367
Vestal, Wm. I, 425
Vestal, Zimri I, 426
Vestel, Amy V, 782
Vestel, Hannah V, 782
Vestel, Mary VI, 408
Vestel, Thos. V, 782
Vestell, David I, 407
Vestle, Albert E. I, 866
Vestle, Esther I, 866
Vestle, Gustavus A. I, 867
Vestle, Irena I, 866
Vestle, James D. I, 866
Vestle, Leonidis M. I, 867
Vestle, Mariam I, 866
Vestle, Solomon I, 866
Vestle, Talitha C. I, 866
Vestle, William H. I, 866
Vethake, ??? III, 336
Vethake, Chas. Henry III, 336
Vethake, Frederick G. III, 336
Vethake, John III, 336
Vetter, Chas. V, 208
Vetters, Chas. V, 208
Vetters, Chas. Edward V, 208
Veyhl, Fred IV, 1265
Veyhl, Minnie IV, 1265
Vezey, Eliza II, 281
Vezey, Eliza II, 305
Vezey, Elizabeth II, 304
Vezey, Elizabeth II, 934
Vezy, Elizabeth II, 674
Via, Joseph Stratton IV, 117
Via, Mary IV, 65
Via, Mary IV, 113
Via, Mary IV, 117
Via, Mary VI, 341
Via, Mary VI, 344
Via, Nancy VI, 344
Via, Naomi IV, 117
Viar, Littleberry VI, 344
Viar, Littleberry VI, 862
Viar, Mary VI, 344
Viar, Mary VI, 862
Vibber, Alice IV, 1353
Vibber, Alice IV, 1383
Vibber, Amy IV, 1354
Vibber, Benjamin IV, 1354
Vibber, Elijah IV, 1354
Vibber, Elizabeth Dillingham IV, 1354
Vibber, Joseph IV, 1354
Vibber, Maria IV, 1354
Vibber, Mary Odell IV, 1354
Vibber, Polly IV, 1354
Viber, Alice IV, 1383
Viber, Esther IV, 1383
Vichary, Sarah II, 430
Vick, ??? VI, 48
Vick, Achsah I, 259
Vick, Achsah I, 319
Vick, Ann I, 259
Vick, Ann I, 319
Vick, Ann VI, 88
Vick, Asa I, 227
Vick, Benja. I, 259
Vick, Benjamin I, 227
Vick, Benjamin I, 259
Vick, Charity I, 227
Vick, Christian I, 244
Vick, Christian I, 259
Vick, Chritsan I, 319
Vick, Cielia I, 242
Vick, Cielia I, 259
Vick, Cloah I, 319
Vick, Elisabeth I, 259
Vick, Elizabeth I, 319
Vick, Elizabeth VI, 88
Vick, Elly I, 227
Vick, Henry I, 259
Vick, Jacob I, 259
Vick, Jacob VI, 88
Vick, Jacob, Jr. I, 244
Vick, Jacob, Jr. I, 259
Vick, Jacob, Jr. VI, 88
Vick, Jesse I, 244
Vick, Jesse I, 259
Vick, Jesse VI, 88
Vick, Jessey VI, 88
Vick, John I, 227
Vick, John I, 259
Vick, Joseph I, 227
Vick, Marthy I, 304
Vick, Marthy I, 319
Vick, Mary I, 227
Vick, Mary I, 244
Vick, Mary I, 259
Vick, Mary I, 306
Vick, Mary I, 319
Vick, Michal I, 259
Vick, Michal I, 304
Vick, Michal I, 319
Vick, Nancy I, 227
Vick, Nancy I, 259
Vick, Nathan I, 259
Vick, Nathan I, 306
Vick, Nathan I, 319
Vick, Patience I, 259
Vick, Patience I, 315
Vick, Patience I, 319
Vick, Patience VI, 73
Vick, Patience VI, 84
Vick, Patience VI, 88
Vick, Priscilla I, 227
Vick, Richard I, 227
Vick, Richard I, 259
Vick, Richard I, 319
Vick, Richard VI, 88
Vick, Rosabelle I, 259
Vick, Sally I, 259
Vick, Sally I, 319
Vick, Saphira I, 259
Vick, Sapphira I, 319
Vick, Sarah I, 259
Vick, Sophia I, 259
Vick, Tabitha I, 259
Vick, Wilson I, 227
Vick, Wilson I, 259
Vickary, Edward II, 45
Vickary, Hannah II, 45
Vickary, John II, 430
Vickary, Mary II, 430
Vickary, Rebeckah II, 45
Vickary, Sarah II, 45
Vickary, Sarah II, 430
Vickers, Abigail V, 287
Vickers, Abigail V, 364
Vickers, Abigail V, 872
Vickers, Abigail V, 873
Vickers, Abigail Canby II, 822
Vickers, Abraham VI, 575
Vickers, Abraham VI, 716
Vickers, Amanda IV, 156
Vickers, Amanda M. IV, 162
Vickers, Amanda M. IV, 297
Vickers, Amelia V, 136
Vickers, Amelia V, 537
Vickers, Amelia V, 961
Vickers, Amos IV, 297
Vickers, Amos H. IV, 162
Vickers, Amos H. IV, 297
Vickers, Amy VI, 716
Vickers, Ann II, 661
Vickers, Ann II, 674
Vickers, Ann IV, 146
Vickers, Ann IV, 156
Vickers, Ann V, 961
Vickers, Ann VI, 694
Vickers, Ann VI, 716
Vickers, Ann G. IV, 162
Vickers, Anna V, 947
Vickers, Armelia V, 208
Vickers, Barcklay IV, 162
Vickers, Barclay IV, 162
Vickers, Barclay IV, 1119
Vickers, Barclay L. IV, 297
Vickers, Ben V, 208
Vickers, Benjamin Dutton II, 674
Vickers, C. C. V, 208
Vickers, Calvin C. V, 136
Vickers, Calvin C. V, 208
Vickers, Calvin E. V, 136
Vickers, Catherine Dare VI, 770
Vickers, Celia V, 136
Vickers, Celia V, 208
Vickers, Celia V, 537
Vickers, Celia V, 947
Vickers, Celia V, 961
Vickers, Chalkley IV, 162
Vickers, Chalkley IV, 297
Vickers, Chalkley IV, 1119
Vickers, Clara IV, 356
Vickers, Edwin V, 287
Vickers, Edwin V, 364
Vickers, Edwin V, 872
Vickers, Edwin V, 873
Vickers, Elijah IV, 1139
Vickers, Elijah L. IV, 162
Vickers, Eliza IV, 332
Vickers, Eliza IV, 356
Vickers, Elizabeth IV, 146
Vickers, Elizabeth IV, 162
Vickers, Elizabeth IV, 297
Vickers, Elizabeth IV, 816
Vickers, Elizabeth IV, 849
Vickers, Elizabeth VI, 503
Vickers, Elizabeth VI, 575
Vickers, Elizabeth Emily V, 961
Vickers, Elizabeth P. IV, 315
Vickers, Elizabeth P. IV, 816
Vickers, Elizabeth P. IV, 849
Vickers, Elwood IV, 162
Vickers, Elwood IV, 781
Vickers, Emily V, 961
Vickers, Esther II, 661
Vickers, Esther II, 674
Vickers, Eugene II, 934
Vickers, Eugene IV, 297
Vickers, George IV, 162
Vickers, Hannah II, 510
Vickers, Hannah II, 674
Vickers, Hannah IV, 140
Vickers, Hannah IV, 162
Vickers, Hannah IV, 297
Vickers, Hannah IV, 1119
Vickers, Hannah P. IV, 162
Vickers, Helen II, 674
Vickers, Isaac IV, 356
Vickers, Isaac V, 287
Vickers, Isaac M. IV, 162
Vickers, Isaac M. V, 287
Vickers, Isaac M. V, 364
Vickers, Isaac M. V, 872
Vickers, Isaac M. V, 873
Vickers, James III, 336
Vickers, Jemima IV, 162
Vickers, Jemima IV, 258
Vickers, Jemima IV, 297
Vickers, Jemima IV, 315
Vickers, Jemima N. IV, 144
Vickers, Jemima N. IV, 162
Vickers, Jesse IV, 162
Vickers, Jesse Elijah IV, 297
Vickers, Jesse Elijah IV, 1119
Vickers, Jesse H. IV, 162
Vickers, Jesse K. IV, 356
Vickers, John IV, 162
Vickers, John IV, 356
Vickers, John V, 136
Vickers, John V, 208
Vickers, John V, 537
Vickers, John V, 961
Vickers, Jonathan IV, 297
Vickers, Jonathan IV, 315
Vickers, Joseph IV, 297
Vickers, Joseph IV, 315
Vickers, Joseph IV, 781
Vickers, Joseph V, 136
Vickers, Joseph V, 208
Vickers, Joseph V, 537
Vickers, Joseph V, 961
Vickers, Joseph P. IV, 315
Vickers, Joshua II, 674
Vickers, Joshua V, 136
Vickers, Joshua V, 961
Vickers, Kezia II, 674
Vickers, Keziah II, 430
Vickers, Leander IV, 342
Vickers, Leander IV, 356
Vickers, Lena IV, 501
Vickers, Letitia IV, 1135
Vickers, Letitia IV, 1139
Vickers, Lucinda IV, 356
Vickers, Lucinda B. IV, 162
Vickers, Lydia Ann IV, 297
Vickers, M. Cornelia IV, 342
Vickers, M. Cornelia IV, 356
Vickers, Mamie IV, 501
Vickers, Margaret IV, 162
Vickers, Margaret VI, 575
Vickers, Margaretta IV, 356
Vickers, Martha H. IV, 140
Vickers, Martha H. IV, 162
Vickers, Martha H. IV, 297
Vickers, Mary II, 788
Vickers, Mary II, 817
Vickers, Mary IV, 356
Vickers, Mary IV, 1114
Vickers, Mary IV, 1119
Vickers, Mary V, 955
Vickers, Mary V, 961
Vickers, Mary VI, 575
Vickers, Mary VI, 716
Vickers, Mary Ann IV, 162
Vickers, Mary Ann V, 208
Vickers, Mary Ann V, 537
Vickers, Maryann V, 961
Vickers, Mercy VI, 649
Vickers, Mercy VI, 716
Vickers, Milly V, 185
Vickers, Milly V, 208
Vickers, Morris IV, 356
Vickers, Mrs. Susie IV, 781
Vickers, Nettie IV, 501
Vickers, Nixon V, 873
Vickers, Peter II, 661
Vickers, Peter II, 674
Vickers, Phebe Ann IV, 146
Vickers, Phebe Ann IV, 162
Vickers, Phebe Ann IV, 297
Vickers, Rachel IV, 65
Vickers, Rachel IV, 150
Vickers, Rachel IV, 162
Vickers, Rachel IV, 228
Vickers, Rachel IV, 297
Vickers, Rachel IV, 356
Vickers, Rachel VI, 716
Vickers, Rebecca IV, 113
Vickers, Rebecca IV, 162
Vickers, Rebecca IV, 1096
Vickers, Rebecca IV, 1119
Vickers, Rebecca VI, 549
Vickers, Rebecca L. IV, 162
Vickers, Rebecca L. IV, 297
Vickers, Rebecca L. IV, 1119
Vickers, Richard V, 961
Vickers, Roxiana IV, 781
Vickers, Ruth IV, 1114
Vickers, Ruth IV, 1119
Vickers, Ruth V, 947
Vickers, Ruth V, 957
Vickers, Ruth V, 961
Vickers, Ruth Hannah VI, 648
Vickers, Ruth Hannah VI, 716
Vickers, Ruth Jane V, 208
Vickers, Ruth Jane V, 537
Vickers, Samuel IV, 162
Vickers, Samuel N. V, 287
Vickers, Samuel N. V, 364
Vickers, Samuel N. V, 872
Vickers, Samuel Nixon V, 873
Vickers, Samuel P. IV, 332
Vickers, Samuel P. IV, 356
Vickers, Sanford IV, 162
Vickers, Sarah II, 674
Vickers, Sarah V, 961
Vickers, Sarah VI, 706
Vickers, Sarah VI, 716
Vickers, Susan A. IV, 781
Vickers, Susannah VI, 575
Vickers, Thomas IV, 140
Vickers, Thomas IV, 146
Vickers, Thomas IV, 156
Vickers, Thomas IV, 162
Vickers, Thomas IV, 297
Vickers, Thomas IV, 501
Vickers, Thomas V, 287
Vickers, Thomas V, 364
Vickers, Thomas V, 872
Vickers, Thomas V, 873
Vickers, Thomas VI, 716
Vickers, Thomas E. IV, 816
Vickers, Thomas E. IV, 849
Vickers, Thomas Elwood IV, 146
Vickers, Thomas Elwood IV, 162
Vickers, Thomas Elwood IV, 297
Vickers, Thomas Elwood IV, 781
Vickers, Thos. IV, 297
Vickers, Thos. IV, 1119
Vickers, Thos. Elwood IV, 297
Vickers, William IV, 162
Vickers, William IV, 297
Vickers, William V, 136
Vickers, William V, 537
Vickers, William V, 872
Vickers, William V, 873
Vickers, William V, 961
Vickers, William VI, 575
Vickers, William VI, 716
Vickers, William M. V, 287
Vickers, William M. V, 364
Vickers, Wm. V, 947
Vickers, Wm. V, 961
Vickers, Wm. VI, 694
Vickers, Zeba IV, 162
Vickers, Ziba IV, 162
Vickery, Edward II, 82
Vickery, Edward II, 108
Vickery, Esther II, 108
Vickery, Hannah II, 61
Vickery, Hannah II, 71
Vickery, Hannah II, 108
Vickery, Martha II, 82
Vickery, Martha II, 108
Vickery, Mary I, 921
Vickery, Mary II, 103
Vickery, Mary II, 108
Vickery, Phebe II, 108
Vickery, Rachel I, 771
Vickery, Rachel II, 91
Vickery, Rachel II, 92
Vickery, Rachel II, 108
Vickery, Rebecca II, 108
Vickery, Rebeckah II, 64
Vickery, Rebeckah II, 108
Vickery, Richard II, 61
Vickery, Richard II, 108
Vickery, Samuel II, 108
Vickery, Sarah II, 108
Vickors, Joseph IV, 781
Vickors, Roxiana IV, 781
Vickors, Susan A. IV, 781
Vickory, John II, 430
Vickory, Martha I, 876
Vickory, Mary I, 924
Vickory, Mary II, 430
Vickory, Rachel I, 771
Vickrey, Edward II, 69
Vickrey, Edward II, 108
Vickrey, Harmon I, 691
Vickrey, Jesse I, 691
Vickrey, Phebe II, 53
Vickrey, Richard II, 53
Vickrey, Richard II, 108
Vickrey, Sarah II, 69
Vickry, Rachel I, 753
Vickry, Rebecca II, 108
Vicks, Patience VI, 19
Vicktory, Martha I, 904
Vicory, Bernice Newman I, 627
Vicory, Eunice I, 681
Vicory, Eunice I, 683
Vicory, Eunice I, 691
Vicory, Harmon I, 691
Vicory, Jesse I, 691
Vicory, Jesse S. I, 691
Vicory, Luzena I, 690
Vicory, Rachel I, 690
Victery, Martha I, 1113
Viddeto, Stephen I, 847
Vidito, Oce I, 904
Vidito, Ocee I, 904
Vidito, Stephen I, 842
Vidito, Stephen I, 904
Vidito, Stephen I, 1013
Vie, Mary VI, 344
Viele, Dorr III, 308
Viele, Dorr III, 336
Viele, Josephine III, 336
Viele, Josephine C. III, 308
Viele, Josephine C. III, 336
Vieley, Lucy VI, 1009
Vieley, Michael VI, 1009
Vigier, Bernard II, 448
Villars, Laura V, 603
Villars, Wm. V, 603
Vinage, Eunice V, 841
Vinage, Eunice V, 873
Vincent, Daniel V, 901
Vincent, Eliza V, 899
Vincent, Eliza V, 939
Vincent, Elizabeth IV, 451
Vincent, Elizabeth IV, 1190
Vincent, Elizabeth IV, 1274
Vincent, Elizabeth IV, 1297
Vincent, Hannah V, 901
Vincent, Harry IV, 849
Vincent, Jane N. V, 901
Vincent, Mary I, 340
Vincent, May I, 1163
Vincent, Olive IV, 781
Vine, Keturah IV, 140
Vine, Keturah IV, 162
Vinecomb, Ann II, 269
Vinecomb, Anna II, 239
Vinecomb, Anna II, 269
Vinecomb, Elisabeth II, 269
Vinecomb, Francis II, 269

omb, Hannah II, 674
omb, Mary II, 207
omb, Mary II, 269
omb, Rachel II, 269
omb, Sarah II, 259
omb, Sarah II, 269
omb, William II, 269
omb, Zilpha II, 269
ng, Ann II, 448
ng, Benjamin II, 448
ard, Kitty VI, 1009
ard, Martin VI, 1009
ard, Nicholas B. VI, 1009
ard, Polly VI, 1009
om, Ann II, 269
om, Sarah II, 235
om, William II, 235
om, William II, 269
omb, Rachel II, 269
omb, Sarah II, 269
omb, William II, 269
ome, Wm. II, 1034
ratos, Jane II, 721
ratos, Spiros Dionisios
I, 721
g, Angie IV, 1190
g, Angie Kenneth IV, 1190
g, Carl IV, 1190
g, Ella IV, 1190
g, Emma IV, 1190
g, Flora E. IV, 1241
g, Frank IV, 1190
g, Hal IV, 1190
g, Halet IV, 1190
g, Hallet IV, 1190
g, Harriet IV, 1190
g, Hazel IV, 1190
g, Kenneth IV, 1190
g, Love II, 430
g, Maggie IV, 1190
g, Marion IV, 1241
g, Simeon IV, 1190
er, Catharine IV, 992
comb, Anna II, 269
cum, Hannah II, 430
comb, William II, 269
n, Ella I, 214
n, Mary I, 340
n, Mary C. III, 159
n, Nancy I, 340
n, Sarah I, 319
rd, Nicholas B. VI, 1009
rd, Polly VI, 1009
, Etta Irena IV, 1251
, Martha IV, 243
, Ora IV, 1251
n, James II, 430
n, Emily IV, 781
n, Emily R. IV, 781
n, Nancy IV, 781
n, Rebecca IV, 781
n, Ruth E. IV, 781
n, Ruth Elizabeth IV, 781
n, Thomas IV, 781
n, Thos. C. IV, 781
elli, Edna VI, 711
elli, Edna VI, 716
elli, Henrietta Jay VI, 711
elli, Henrietta Jay VI, 716
elli, Robert VI, 711
elli, Robert VI, 716
elli, William V. VI, 716
elli, Wm. V. VI, 711
o, Ocee I, 904
o, Oce I, 904
n, Elizabeth II, 305
om, Ann II, 213
om, William II, 213
Ann IV, 1190
Blackburn IV, 1190
Jesse IV, 1190
Joseph IV, 1190
Maria IV, 1190
Sarah IV, 1190
Susanna IV, 1190
s, Dr. ??? V, 939
s, Laura M. V, 939
s, Mary S. V, 939
r, Catherine III, 189
r, Catherine III, 337
as, Mary II, 646
as, Mary II, 674
tine, Thomas Jefferson
II, 337
rt, Anna V, 717
r, Catherine III, 189
r, Catherine III, 337
nar, Anna III, 337
nar, Daniel III, 337
nar, Daniel Peter III, 337
nar, Daniel S. III, 337

Volkmar, Nina III, 337
Voltz, Lauretta IV, 1266
Voltz, Loretta IV, 1266
Voluntine, Duke M. VI, 862
Voluntine, Wd. Milly VI, 862
Von Brunt, Edw. K. III, 218
Von Buyleart, Meriana II, 673
Von Der Gumeter, Maria III, 336
Von Der Smith, Alice May
III, 137
Von Der Smith, Samuel B.
III, 137
Von Hoegler, Charle III, 337
Von Hoegler, Johanna III, 337
Von Hoegler, Joseph III, 337
Von Hoegler, Louise III, 337
Von K., Paula III, 263
Von Nordroff, Adelaide III, 256
Vonder Smith, Alice S. III, 310
Vonder Smith, Caroline III, 127
Vonder Smith, Caroline III, 309
Vonder Smith, Caroline III, 310
Vonder Smith, Carrie L. III, 127
Vonder Smith, William III, 127
Vonder Smith, Wm. B. III, 309
Vonder Smith, Wm. B. III, 310
Vondersmith, Alice III, 337
Vondersmith, Alice May III, 337
Vondersmith, Carolina III, 337
Vondersmith, Caroline III, 34
Vondersmith, Caroline III, 337
Vondersmith, Carrie III, 337
Vondersmith, Carrie L. III, 337
Vondersmith, Estelle III, 337
Vondersmith, Estelle V. III, 309
Vondersmith, Samuel B. III, 337
Vondersmith, William III, 34
Vondersmith, William B. III, 337
Vondersmith, Wm. III, 337
Vondersmith, Wm. B. III, 337
Vonessen, Matilda V, 364
Voorhees, Elizabeth II, 269
Vorce, Phebe II, 1055
Vorce, Phebe II, 1056
Vorce, Phebe II, 1062
Vore, Abi IV, 406
Vore, Abner V, 771
Vore, Amanda Melvina IV, 1191
Vore, Ann IV, 21
Vore, Ann IV, 65
Vore, Ann IV, 382
Vore, Ann IV, 451
Vore, Ann IV, 501
Vore, Ann IV, 1144
Vore, Ann IV, 1190
Vore, Ann Maria IV, 1190
Vore, Anna J. V, 771
Vore, Anne IV, 501
Vore, Asael V, 287
Vore, Avi IV, 451
Vore, Azel V, 364
Vore, Benjamin IV, 65
Vore, Benjamin IV, 113
Vore, Benjamin IV, 849
Vore, Benjamin IV, 860
Vore, Blackburn IV, 501
Vore, Blackburn IV, 1189
Vore, Blackburn IV, 1190
Vore, Blackburn IV, 1191
Vore, Catharine V, 771
Vore, Christian II, 674
Vore, Deborah V, 536
Vore, Deborah V, 537
Vore, Delbert V, 771
Vore, Delilah Jane IV, 1190
Vore, Edmund IV, 65
Vore, Eleanor IV, 162
Vore, Eleanor IV, 269
Vore, Eleanor IV, 297
Vore, Eleanor IV, 356
Vore, Eli V, 287
Vore, Eli V, 364
Vore, Eliza IV, 1149
Vore, Eliza IV, 1190
Vore, Eliza V, 59
Vore, Elizabeth IV, 21
Vore, Elizabeth IV, 65
Vore, Elizabeth V, 364
Vore, Georgia V, 771
Vore, Gideon II, 674
Vore, Hannah V, 771
Vore, Hazael V, 287
Vore, Isaac IV, 65
Vore, Isaac IV, 113
Vore, Isaac IV, 162
Vore, Isaac IV, 297
Vore, Isaac IV, 356
Vore, Isaac IV, 1190
Vore, Isaac VI, 787
Vore, Isaac, Jr. IV, 1190
Vore, Jacob IV, 65

Vore, Jane V, 60
Vore, Jane V, 136
Vore, Jane V, 537
Vore, Jane V, 542
Vore, Jesse IV, 501
Vore, Jesse IV, 1144
Vore, Jesse IV, 1190
Vore, Jesse IV, 1191
Vore, Jesse T. IV, 1191
Vore, Jesse W. IV, 1191
Vore, John V, 287
Vore, John V, 364
Vore, Joseph IV, 501
Vore, Joseph IV, 1149
Vore, Joseph IV, 1190
Vore, Judd V, 771
Vore, Judson F. V, 771
Vore, Lena V, 771
Vore, Lydia Jane IV, 1190
Vore, Lydia Jane IV, 1191
Vore, Malvina IV, 1191
Vore, Malvina Amanda IV, 1190
Vore, Margaret IV, 65
Vore, Margaret IV, 849
Vore, Maria IV, 501
Vore, Maria IV, 1190
Vore, Mary IV, 103
Vore, Mary IV, 113
Vore, Mary V, 771
Vore, Monroe Freeman IV, 1190
Vore, Mordecai IV, 162
Vore, Mordecai IV, 297
Vore, Mordecai IV, 356
Vore, Mordecai IV, 1190
Vore, Nelson V, 771
Vore, Rachel IV, 1190
Vore, Rachel W. IV, 1189
Vore, Rachel W. IV, 1190
Vore, Rachel W. IV, 1191
Vore, Rebecca IV, 162
Vore, Rebecca IV, 451
Vore, Rebecca IV, 1081
Vore, Rose V, 771
Vore, Ruth Ann IV, 1190
Vore, Ruthanna IV, 1191
Vore, Sarah II, 674
Vore, Sarah IV, 501
Vore, Sarah IV, 1144
Vore, Sarah IV, 1190
Vore, Sarah V, 287
Vore, Sarah V, 364
Vore, Sarah E. IV, 1191
Vore, Sarah Elizabeth IV, 1190
Vore, Sarah R. IV, 1190
Vore, Sarah Rebecca IV, 1190
Vore, Susanna IV, 501
Vore, Susanna IV, 1190
Vore, Susanna V, 287
Vore, Susanna Maria IV, 1191
Vore, Susannah IV, 501
Vore, Susannah V, 364
Vore, W. Wesley V, 771
Vore, William IV, 162
Vore, William IV, 297
Vore, William IV, 356
Vore, William T. IV, 1191
Vorell, Jonathan II, 430
Vorell, Robert II, 430
Vorhees, Elizabeth V, 939
Vorhees, Elizabeth V, 940
Vorhies, Elsie B. IV, 371
Vorhies, Elsie B. IV, 451
Vorr, Eli V, 364
Vosburg, Mable Falkner V, 771
Vose, Harry V, 1023
Votah, Mary VI, 636
Votan, John IV, 740
Votan, Mary M. IV, 740
Votaw, ??? IV, 795
Votaw, Aaron IV, 850
Votaw, Abner IV, 850
Votaw, Adaline IV, 782
Votaw, Albert H. II, 721
Votaw, Albert H. II, 772
Votaw, Alice Ann IV, 850
Votaw, Alice K. IV, 850
Votaw, Ann IV, 65
Votaw, Ann IV, 69
Votaw, Ann IV, 663
Votaw, Ann IV, 781
Votaw, Ann IV, 782
Votaw, Ann IV, 783
Votaw, Ann IV, 834
Votaw, Ann IV, 850
Votaw, Ann IV, 956
Votaw, Ann IV, 1010
Votaw, Ann VI, 575
Votaw, Ann VI, 629
Votaw, Ann VI, 716
Votaw, Anna IV, 782
Votaw, Anna Leora IV, 843

Votaw, Anna M. II, 721
Votaw, Anne IV, 65
Votaw, Argus IV, 850
Votaw, Benjamin IV, 663
Votaw, Benjamin IV, 775
Votaw, Benjamin IV, 781
Votaw, Benjamin IV, 782
Votaw, Benjamin IV, 1010
Votaw, Benjamin IV, 1011
Votaw, Benjamin V, 537
Votaw, Chalkley IV, 849
Votaw, Charles IV, 781
Votaw, Charles IV, 782
Votaw, Clara IV, 843
Votaw, Clara V. IV, 843
Votaw, Clarence J. IV, 1010
Votaw, Clarence J. IV, 1011
Votaw, Curtis IV, 782
Votaw, Daniel IV, 65
Votaw, Daniel IV, 663
Votaw, Daniel IV, 782
Votaw, Daniel IV, 823
Votaw, Daniel IV, 850
Votaw, Daniel V, 136
Votaw, Daniel VI, 716
Votaw, David IV, 781
Votaw, David IV, 1010
Votaw, David IV, 1011
Votaw, Deborah IV, 849
Votaw, Deborah IV, 850
Votaw, Dorothy IV, 849
Votaw, Dorothy IV, 850
Votaw, Edward Courtney IV, 850
Votaw, Elisabeth IV, 663
Votaw, Elisan IV, 984
Votaw, Elisan IV, 1011
Votaw, Eliza Ann IV, 1010
Votaw, Eliza Ann IV, 1011
Votaw, Elizabeth IV, 65
Votaw, Elizabeth IV, 782
Votaw, Elizabeth IV, 832
Votaw, Elizabeth IV, 849
Votaw, Elizabeth IV, 909
Votaw, Elizabeth IV, 921
Votaw, Elizabeth IV, 938
Votaw, Elizabeth IV, 956
Votaw, Elizabeth IV, 998
Votaw, Elizabeth IV, 1006
Votaw, Elizabeth IV, 1010
Votaw, Elizabeth V, 65
Votaw, Elizabeth V, 136
Votaw, Elmore IV, 849
Votaw, Elnore IV, 850
Votaw, Emma IV, 782
Votaw, Emma IV, 843
Votaw, Emma IV, 850
Votaw, Emma M. IV, 782
Votaw, Ernest N. II, 721
Votaw, Ernest Nicholson II, 772
Votaw, Esther IV, 973
Votaw, Esther IV, 1010
Votaw, Esther IV, 1011
Votaw, Frances IV, 765
Votaw, Frances IV, 781
Votaw, Frances IV, 782
Votaw, Gail Walter IV, 782
Votaw, Geo. E. IV, 782
Votaw, George IV, 1010
Votaw, Guli Elma IV, 967
Votaw, Guli Elma IV, 1011
Votaw, Gulielma IV, 1010
Votaw, Gulielma IV, 1011
Votaw, Hannah IV, 675
Votaw, Hannah IV, 781
Votaw, Hannah IV, 782
Votaw, Hannah IV, 924
Votaw, Hannah IV, 998
Votaw, Hannah IV, 1010
Votaw, Hannah IV, 1011
Votaw, Hannah IV, 1044
Votaw, Hannah V, 537
Votaw, Hannah D. V, 537
Votaw, Hannah G. IV, 782
Votaw, Hannah G. IV, 1011
Votaw, Harriet IV, 782
Votaw, Isaac II, 721
Votaw, Isaac IV, 65
Votaw, Isaac IV, 663
Votaw, Isaac IV, 695
Votaw, Isaac IV, 765
Votaw, Isaac IV, 781
Votaw, Isaac IV, 789
Votaw, Isaac IV, 856
Votaw, Isaac IV, 919
Votaw, Isaac IV, 969
Votaw, Isaac IV, 1010
Votaw, Isaac IV, 1011
Votaw, Isaac V, 482
Votaw, Isaac V, 537
Votaw, Isaac VI, 464
Votaw, Isaac VI, 575

Votaw, Isaac VI, 629
Votaw, Isaac VI, 716
Votaw, Isaac B. IV, 675
Votaw, Isaac B. IV, 782
Votaw, Isaac B. IV, 924
Votaw, Isaac B. IV, 1010
Votaw, Isaac B. IV, 1011
Votaw, Isaac, Jr. IV, 65
Votaw, Isaac, Jr. IV, 750
Votaw, Isaac, Jr. IV, 781
Votaw, Isaac, Jr. IV, 782
Votaw, Isaac, Jr. IV, 1010
Votaw, Isaac, Jr. IV, 1011
Votaw, Isaac, Sr. IV, 1010
Votaw, James IV, 65
Votaw, James IV, 663
Votaw, James IV, 828
Votaw, James IV, 849
Votaw, James IV, 850
Votaw, James IV, 1011
Votaw, James IV, 1044
Votaw, James Johnson IV, 850
Votaw, James T. IV, 1010
Votaw, Jane IV, 1010
Votaw, Jane IV, 1011
Votaw, Jemima IV, 65
Votaw, Jemima IV, 781
Votaw, Jemima IV, 782
Votaw, Jemima IV, 1010
Votaw, Jemima IV, 1011
Votaw, John IV, 65
Votaw, John IV, 781
Votaw, John IV, 849
Votaw, John IV, 850
Votaw, John VI, 575
Votaw, John VI, 716
Votaw, John A. IV, 1010
Votaw, John E. IV, 850
Votaw, John Green, Jr. V, 287
Votaw, Jonas IV, 850
Votaw, Jonathan IV, 782
Votaw, Jonathan V, 65
Votaw, Jonathan V, 136
Votaw, Jonothan V, 136
Votaw, Joseph IV, 65
Votaw, Joseph IV, 69
Votaw, Joseph IV, 663
Votaw, Joseph IV, 781
Votaw, Joseph IV, 782
Votaw, Joseph IV, 783
Votaw, Joseph IV, 849
Votaw, Joseph IV, 1011
Votaw, Joseph VI, 575
Votaw, Joseph VI, 716
Votaw, Joshua IV, 781
Votaw, Joshua IV, 1011
Votaw, Joshua W. IV, 782
Votaw, Joshua W. IV, 1010
Votaw, Joshua W. IV, 1011
Votaw, Judith IV, 828
Votaw, Judith IV, 849
Votaw, Judith IV, 850
Votaw, Lawrence IV, 782
Votaw, Lawrence, Jr. IV, 782
Votaw, Lawrence, Jr. IV, 793
Votaw, Leah IV, 65
Votaw, Leah IV, 663
Votaw, Leah IV, 766
Votaw, Leah IV, 782
Votaw, Leah IV, 844
Votaw, Leah IV, 850
Votaw, Leroy IV, 850
Votaw, Levi IV, 849
Votaw, Lewis IV, 1011
Votaw, Lewis H. IV, 850
Votaw, Lindley George IV, 1010
Votaw, Lindley George IV, 1011
Votaw, Louis H. IV, 850
Votaw, Louis H. IV, 1010
Votaw, Lydia IV, 65
Votaw, Lydia IV, 663
Votaw, Lydia IV, 803
Votaw, Lydia IV, 825
Votaw, Lydia IV, 850
Votaw, Lydia IV, 992
Votaw, Lydia IV, 1010
Votaw, Lydia IV, 1011
Votaw, Mahlon IV, 850
Votaw, Martha IV, 781
Votaw, Martha IV, 782
Votaw, Martha IV, 793
Votaw, Martha IV, 849
Votaw, Martha IV, 850
Votaw, Martha IV, 921
Votaw, Martha IV, 1010
Votaw, Martha IV, 1011
Votaw, Mary IV, 22
Votaw, Mary IV, 65
Votaw, Mary IV, 663
Votaw, Mary IV, 781
Votaw, Mary IV, 799

Votaw, Mary IV, 818
Votaw, Mary IV, 849
Votaw, Mary IV, 850
Votaw, Mary IV, 909
Votaw, Mary IV, 917
Votaw, Mary IV, 938
Votaw, Mary IV, 1010
Votaw, Mary V, 136
Votaw, Mary VI, 575
Votaw, Mary VI, 636
Votaw, Mary VI, 716
Votaw, Mary Ann IV, 781
Votaw, Mary Ann V, 242
Votaw, Mary Ann V, 287
Votaw, Mary Ann V, 537
Votaw, Mary B. IV, 782
Votaw, Mary E. IV, 782
Votaw, Mary E. IV, 843
Votaw, Mary Emma IV, 1010
Votaw, Mary Esther IV, 1010
Votaw, Matilda IV, 781
Votaw, Matilda IV, 954
Votaw, Matilda IV, 1010
Votaw, Matilda IV, 1011
Votaw, Melissa IV, 782
Votaw, Melissa IV, 793
Votaw, Millie IV, 782
Votaw, Minnie IV, 782
Votaw, Minnie IV, 793
Votaw, Minnie IV, 850
Votaw, Morris IV, 849
Votaw, Mose IV, 909
Votaw, Moses IV, 22
Votaw, Moses IV, 65
Votaw, Moses IV, 663
Votaw, Moses IV, 781
Votaw, Moses IV, 834
Votaw, Moses IV, 849
Votaw, Moses IV, 850
Votaw, Moses IV, 860
Votaw, Moses IV, 917
Votaw, Moses VI, 575
Votaw, Moses VI, 716
Votaw, Olive May IV, 1010
Votaw, Olive May IV, 1011
Votaw, Pearl Anna IV, 1010
Votaw, Pearl Anna IV, 1011
Votaw, Peirce IV, 781
Votaw, Phebe II, 721
Votaw, Phebe IV, 65
Votaw, Phebe IV, 69
Votaw, Phebe IV, 663
Votaw, Phebe IV, 781
Votaw, Phebe IV, 782
Votaw, Phebe IV, 783
Votaw, Phebe IV, 843
Votaw, Phebe IV, 850
Votaw, Phebe IV, 1010
Votaw, Phebe V, 482
Votaw, Phebe V, 537
Votaw, Phebe C. V, 537
Votaw, Phebe G. IV, 695
Votaw, Phebe G. IV, 781
Votaw, Phebe Nicholson II, 772
Votaw, Phebe Y. IV, 781
Votaw, Phebe Y. IV, 809
Votaw, Phebe, Jr. IV, 782
Votaw, Quinby IV, 850
Votaw, Rachel IV, 65
Votaw, Rachel IV, 663
Votaw, Rachel IV, 781
Votaw, Rachel IV, 782
Votaw, Rachel IV, 783
Votaw, Rachel IV, 800
Votaw, Rachel IV, 850
Votaw, Rachel IV, 1010
Votaw, Rachel IV, 1011
Votaw, Rebecca IV, 65
Votaw, Rebecca IV, 663
Votaw, Rebecca IV, 750
Votaw, Rebecca IV, 781
Votaw, Rebecca IV, 850
Votaw, Rebecca IV, 1010
Votaw, Rebecca IV, 1011
Votaw, Rebecca Ann IV, 848
Votaw, Rebecca Ann IV, 849
Votaw, Rebecca Ann IV, 850
Votaw, Rebecca D. IV, 775
Votaw, Rebecca D. IV, 781
Votaw, Rebeccah IV, 65
Votaw, Rebekah VI, 629
Votaw, Rebekah VI, 716
Votaw, Robert IV, 782
Votaw, Robert IV, 849
Votaw, Robert IV, 850
Votaw, Roscoe IV, 782
Votaw, Roscoe IV, 793
Votaw, Rosella IV, 850
Votaw, Rosella IV, 1011
Votaw, Rosella M. IV, 850
Votaw, Rosella M. IV, 1010
Votaw, Rosella M. IV, 1011
Votaw, Ruth IV, 849
Votaw, Ruth IV, 850
Votaw, Ruth Ann IV, 730
Votaw, Ruth Ann IV, 782
Votaw, Samuel IV, 65
Votaw, Samuel IV, 782
Votaw, Samuel IV, 849
Votaw, Samuel IV, 1010
Votaw, Samuel IV, 1011
Votaw, Samuel IV, 1012
Votaw, Samuel VI, 716
Votaw, Sarah IV, 65
Votaw, Sarah IV, 69
Votaw, Sarah IV, 663
Votaw, Sarah IV, 695
Votaw, Sarah IV, 781
Votaw, Sarah IV, 782
Votaw, Sarah IV, 805
Votaw, Sarah IV, 810
Votaw, Sarah IV, 814
Votaw, Sarah IV, 823
Votaw, Sarah IV, 828
Votaw, Sarah IV, 849
Votaw, Sarah IV, 850
Votaw, Sarah IV, 969
Votaw, Sarah IV, 1010
Votaw, Sarah IV, 1011
Votaw, Sarah IV, 1012
Votaw, Sarah V, 136
Votaw, Sarah VI, 575
Votaw, Sarah, Jr. IV, 781
Votaw, Sibyl IV, 924
Votaw, Sibyl IV, 1011
Votaw, Susanna IV, 781
Votaw, Susanna IV, 850
Votaw, Susanna IV, 856
Votaw, Susannah IV, 782
Votaw, Susannah IV, 789
Votaw, Susannah IV, 850
Votaw, Sybil IV, 1010
Votaw, Sybil IV, 1011
Votaw, Tamer IV, 850
Votaw, Thomas IV, 65
Votaw, Thomas IV, 782
Votaw, Thomas IV, 921
Votaw, Thomas IV, 938
Votaw, Thomas IV, 956
Votaw, Thomas IV, 998
Votaw, Thomas IV, 1006
Votaw, Thomas IV, 1010
Votaw, Thomas VI, 575
Votaw, Thomas VI, 716
Votaw, Thomas Edgar IV, 850
Votaw, Thomas, Jr. IV, 967
Votaw, Thomas, Jr. IV, 1010
Votaw, Thomas, Jr. IV, 1011
Votaw, Virgil IV, 782
Votaw, Virgil IV, 793
Votaw, Wanda IV, 782
Votaw, Wanda IV, 793
Votaw, Warren IV, 782
Votaw, Warren IV, 793
Votaw, Wm. IV, 782
Votow, William T. III, 337
Vox Arx, Marie III, 280
Voxarx, Marie III, 30
Voze, Gideon II, 674
Vredenburgh, ??? III, 337
Vredenburgh, Harriet III, 445
Vredenburgh, John III, 337
Vredenburgh, Zipporah III, 337
Vucapher, Catie V, 1023
Vucapher, Dora V, 1022
Vucapher, Katie V, 1022
Vucapher, Lydia V, 1022
Vuncannon, James C. I, 642
Vuncannon, Kate I, 642
Vuncannon, Lydia I, 486
Vuncanon, Addie A. I, 736
Vuncanon, Alfred I, 736
Vuncanon, Anna I, 714
Vuncanon, Anna I, 736
Vuncanon, Annie Eunice I, 706
Vuncanon, Baraba J. I, 736
Vuncanon, Bessie Elverta I, 706
Vuncanon, Bessie Elverta I, 736
Vuncanon, Bethany I, 736
Vuncanon, Callie Branson I, 706
Vuncanon, Crissia A. I, 736
Vuncanon, Edward Everett I, 706
Vuncanon, Edward Everett I, 736
Vuncanon, Elizabeth I, 736
Vuncanon, Elma B. I, 736
Vuncanon, Emily I, 736
Vuncanon, Emily J. I, 736
Vuncanon, Emma C. I, 736
Vuncanon, Fannie Pearl I, 706
Vuncanon, Fannie Pearl I, 736
Vuncanon, Hattie L. I, 736
Vuncanon, Ida A. I, 736
Vuncanon, Ira I, 736
Vuncanon, Ira I. I, 736
Vuncanon, J. C. I, 706
Vuncanon, James Carl I, 627
Vuncanon, James Carl I, 706
Vuncanon, James Carl, Jr. I, 627
Vuncanon, James M. I, 627
Vuncanon, James M. I, 736
Vuncanon, James Madison I, 706
Vuncanon, John C. I, 736
Vuncanon, Kate I, 627
Vuncanon, Lewella I, 724
Vuncanon, Lewella I, 736
Vuncanon, Lydia I, 736
Vuncanon, Margurite Flay I, 706
Vuncanon, Mary I, 627
Vuncanon, Mary I, 706
Vuncanon, Mary I, 717
Vuncanon, Mary I, 736
Vuncanon, Mary Ann I, 736
Vuncanon, Molsie I, 736
Vuncanon, Molsie J. I, 736
Vuncanon, Monroe Lewis I, 736
Vuncanon, Nancy I, 736
Vuncanon, Nettie J. I, 736
Vuncanon, Rossie Peter I, 706
Vuncanon, Sarah I, 736
Vuncanon, Sarah E. I, 736
Vuncanon, Thomas J. I, 736
Vuncanon, Tyson I, 736
Vuncanon, William I, 736
Vuncanon, Willie H. I, 736
Vuncanon, Wm. Jeremiah I, 706
Vunkanon, Nancy I, 717
Vunkanon, Nancy I, 736

W???, Pauline III, 225
W???, Pauline III, 362
Wachsmith, Ada Hermina IV, 782
Wachsmith, Bobby IV, 782
Wachsmith, Ed. IV, 782
Wachsmith, Edward IV, 782
Wachsmith, Joyce E. IV, 782
Wachsmith, Leo IV, 782
Wachsmith, Mary IV, 782
Wachsmith, Opal L. IV, 782
Wacksmith, Mrs. Mary IV, 785
Waddell, Wm. F. V, 717
Waddelow, Comfort VI, 11
Waddelow, Nicholas VI, 11
Waddelow, Patience VI, 11
Waddelow, Temperance VI, 11
Waddington, Aaron II, 139
Waddington, Ann II, 54
Waddington, Ann II, 108
Waddington, Ann II, 159
Waddington, Anna II, 134
Waddington, Anna B. II, 140
Waddington, Anne II, 151
Waddington, Anne II, 159
Waddington, Annie II, 139
Waddington, Catharine II, 108
Waddington, Deborah Jane I, 580
Waddington, Edith II, 159
Waddington, Edith D. II, 139
Waddington, Edith J. II, 139
Waddington, Edward C. II, 130
Waddington, Edwin Borton II, 139
Waddington, Edwin Borton II, 160
Waddington, Elizabeth II, 57
Waddington, Elizabeth II, 108
Waddington, Elizabeth II, 139
Waddington, Elizabeth Goodwin II, 139
Waddington, Elizabeth W. II, 128
Waddington, Elizabeth W. II, 139
Waddington, Elizabeth W. II, 143
Waddington, Elizabeth W. II, 159
Waddington, Elizabeth W. II, 160
Waddington, Elizabeth W. II, 161
Waddington, Elmer II, 160
Waddington, Emma L. II, 139
Waddington, Emma L. II, 159
Waddington, Emma S. II, 155
Waddington, Emma S. II, 159
Waddington, Florence II, 139
Waddington, Florence II, 159
Waddington, George G. II, 159
Waddington, Georgianna II, 139
Waddington, Georgianna II, 159
Waddington, Helen II, 127
Waddington, Helen Elizabeth II, 139
Waddington, Helen Elizabeth II, 143
Waddington, Helen Elizabeth II, 159
Waddington, Helen Elizabeth II, 160
Waddington, Henry Goodwin II, 139
Waddington, J. Elmer, Jr. II, 160
Waddington, Jane II, 108
Waddington, Jane II, 159
Waddington, Jeane II, 108
Waddington, Jennie F. II, 139
Waddington, John Elmer II, 139
Waddington, Jos. K. II, 139
Waddington, Joseph II, 135
Waddington, Joseph II, 139
Waddington, Joseph II, 155
Waddington, Joseph II, 159
Waddington, Joseph K. II, 127
Waddington, Joseph K. II, 128
Waddington, Joseph K. II, 139
Waddington, Joseph K. II, 143
Waddington, Joseph K. II, 160
Waddington, Joseph K., Jr. II, 139
Waddington, Joshua II, 134
Waddington, Joshua II, 139
Waddington, Joshua II, 151
Waddington, Joshua II, 159
Waddington, Lewella II, 159
Waddington, Louella II, 139
Waddington, Louella II, 159
Waddington, Louise II, 139
Waddington, Louise II, 160
Waddington, Lydia Keasby II, 135
Waddington, Mabel II, 139
Waddington, Mabel B. II, 160
Waddington, Mable B. II, 160
Waddington, Mary II, 130
Waddington, Mary Ann II, 140
Waddington, Mary B. II, 118
Waddington, Mary B. II, 159
Waddington, Mildred II, 130
Waddington, Pauline II, 139
Waddington, Pauline II, 151
Waddington, Pauline II, 159
Waddington, Pauline W. II, 134
Waddington, Richard II, 140
Waddington, Ruth II, 139
Waddington, Ruth W. II, 143
Waddington, Ruth W. II, 155
Waddington, Ruth W. II, 159
Waddington, Ruth Wright II, 135
Waddington, Sarah II, 57
Waddington, Sarah II, 108
Waddington, Sarah II, 139
Waddington, Tacie II, 159
Waddington, Tacy II, 139
Waddington, Tacy II, 159
Waddington, Wm. II, 139
Waddington, Wm. Finlaw II, 127
Waddington, Wm. Morris II, 139
Waddington, Wm. Morris, Jr. II, 139
Waddle, Alexander VI, 750
Waddle, Jacob VI, 176
Waddle, Jacob VI, 216
Waddle, Phebe V, 717
Waddle, Phebe Jane V, 364
Waddle, Rebecca Jane VI, 750
Waddle, Wm. F. V, 717
Waddonton, Elizabeth II, 108
Waddonton, Jeane II, 108
Waddy, Henry II, 674
Wade, Alexander VI, 875
Wade, Alexander VI, 887
Wade, Alexander VI, 898
Wade, Alexander VI, 967
Wade, Alexander VI, 1009
Wade, Allen VI, 865
Wade, Amanda VI, 972
Wade, America VI, 874
Wade, Ann VI, 844
Wade, Ann VI, 1009
Wade, Anna VI, 995
Wade, Anna Louisa VI, 788
Wade, Anne T. II, 45
Wade, Archd. VI, 998
Wade, Archd., Sr. VI, 904
Wade, Archd., Sr. VI, 1009
Wade, Archibald VI, 869
Wade, Archibald VI, 898
Wade, Archibald VI, 1009
Wade, Archibald, Jr. VI, 871
Wade, Archibald, Jr. VI, 1009
Wade, Archibald, Sr. VI, 1009
Wade, Archibald, Sr. VI, 1016
Wade, Archibald, Sr. VI, 1019
Wade, Avaline VI, 887
Wade, Calahill VI, 1019
Wade, Capt. Robert VI, 309
Wade, Catharine R. VI, 958
Wade, Celia Ann VI, 904
Wade, Charity B. VI, 1009
Wade, Charles III, 337
Wade, Chas. V, 1023
Wade, Cora V, 1023
Wade, David VI, 931
Wade, David VI, 985
Wade, David VI, 1009
Wade, Dove V, 208
Wade, Edith V, 287
Wade, Edmund VI, 844
Wade, Edmund VI, 862
Wade, Edmund VI, 1009
Wade, Edward II, 45
Wade, Eliza VI, 1009
Wade, Elizabeth I, 266
Wade, Elizabeth IV, 65
Wade, Elizabeth IV, 162
Wade, Elizabeth IV, 637
Wade, Elizabeth IV, 663
Wade, Elizabeth VI, 838
Wade, Elizabeth VI, 862
Wade, Elizabeth VI, 880
Wade, Elizabeth VI, 970
Wade, Elizabeth VI, 985
Wade, Elizabeth VI, 1009
Wade, Elizabeth W. VI, 1009
Wade, Ellen IV, 598
Wade, Ellen IV, 601
Wade, Esther II, 53
Wade, Esther II, 108
Wade, Fanny VI, 878
Wade, Fanny VI, 985
Wade, Fereba V, 771
Wade, Frances VI, 931
Wade, Frances VI, 1009
Wade, Frances H. VI, 871
Wade, Frank C. IV, 1297
Wade, George L. V, 287
Wade, H. A. VI, 874
Wade, Hannah II, 45
Wade, Hannah II, 674
Wade, Hannah IV, 162
Wade, Hannah IV, 356
Wade, Hannah IV, 445
Wade, Hannah IV, 451
Wade, Hannah VI, 537
Wade, Hannah VI, 587
Wade, Harcourt VI, 788
Wade, Harry V, 1023
Wade, Henrietta Barron II, 785
Wade, Henry II, 45
Wade, Henry VI, 830
Wade, Henry VI, 838
Wade, Henry VI, 856
Wade, Henry VI, 862
Wade, Henry S. I, 426
Wade, Isaac VI, 869
Wade, Isaac VI, 920
Wade, Isaac VI, 932
Wade, Isaac VI, 952
Wade, Isaac VI, 962
Wade, Isaac VI, 967
Wade, Isaac VI, 970
Wade, Isaac VI, 998
Wade, Isaac VI, 1001
Wade, Isaac VI, 1009
Wade, Isaac VI, 1018
Wade, Isaac VI, 1022
Wade, Isaac, Sr. VI, 875
Wade, Isabel VI, 390
Wade, Isabel VI, 462
Wade, Isabella W. I, 625
Wade, Ishum V, 1023
Wade, Isom V, 1023
Wade, Jacob VI, 884
Wade, Jacob VI, 902
Wade, Jacob VI, 979
Wade, Jacob VI, 1009
Wade, James V, 537
Wade, James VI, 862
Wade, James VI, 960
Wade, James VI, 985
Wade, James VI, 995
Wade, James VI, 1009
Wade, James A. V, 537
Wade, James C. IV, 1297
Wade, James G. IV, 1297
Wade, Jane II, 45
Wade, Jane II, 108
Wade, Jane VI, 972
Wade, Jane H. VI, 862
Wade, Jane L. VI, 998
Wade, Jefferson VI, 871
Wade, Jemima VI, 1009
Wade, Jennie V, 1023
Wade, Jeremiah VI, 985
Wade, Jeremiah VI, 1004
Wade, Jeremiah VI, 1009
Wade, Jno. H. VI, 808
Wade, John II, 45
Wade, John II, 430

John VI, 830
John VI, 859
John VI, 958
John VI, 960
John VI, 1009
John VI, 1020
John A. VI, 952
John H. VI, 862
John T. VI, 862
Joseph II, 45
Joshua VI, 1009
Kintchen I, 319
Kitty VI, 962
Lindley IV, 598
Louis F. III, 37
Louis Francis III, 337
Lucinda VI, 862
Lucinda VI, 1009
Lucy VI, 985
Lucy Ann G. VI, 816
Lucy H. E. VI, 862
Luke VI, 862
Lydia II, 106
Lydia II, 108
Lydia IV, 162
Lydia IV, 356
Lydia IV, 451
Lydia IV, 598
Lydia IV, 601
Lydia Ann V, 958
Lydia Ann V, 961
Margaret IV, 445
Margaret IV, 451
Margaret IV, 598
Margaret C. VI, 1019
Marling II, 430
Martha VI, 862
Martha Ann VI, 1022
Martha G. VI, 958
Martha W. VI, 960
Mary I, 266
Mary I, 842
Mary I, 843
Mary II, 45
Mary II, 93
Mary II, 101
Mary II, 108
Mary II, 430
Mary III, 337
Mary IV, 65
Mary IV, 162
Mary IV, 356
Mary IV, 451
Mary IV, 580
Mary IV, 598
Mary VI, 931
Mary VI, 1009
Mary VI, 1012
Mary Ann V, 287
Mary Ann VI, 862
Mary Ann VI, 1009
Mary B. VI, 1020
Mary Balenge VI, 988
Mary E. VI, 874
Mary F. III, 337
Mary H. III, 37
Mary H. III, 337
Mary L. VI, 808
Matilda VI, 1009
Matilda VI, 1016
Maude V, 1023
Mildred B. VI, 1009
Mildred E. H. VI, 862
Milisent II, 45
Millisent II, 674
Minney L. VI, 1009
Mylicent II, 93
Mylicent II, 108
Nancy VI, 960
Nancy VI, 998
Nancy VI, 1009
Nancy E. I, 426
Nathan I, 266
Nathan IV, 65
Nathan IV, 162
Nathan IV, 356
Nora E. V, 1023
Orender VI, 830
Owen I, 266
Owen IV, 65
Owen IV, 162
Owen IV, 356
Owen IV, 445
Owen IV, 451
Owen IV, 598
Paschal B. VI, 1009
Patsy VI, 869
Patsy VI, 1004
Pearin VI, 829
Peggy VI, 1009
Phebe I, 266
Wade, Phebe I, 267
Wade, Phebe I, 277
Wade, Phebe IV, 65
Wade, Phebe IV, 162
Wade, Phebe IV, 356
Wade, Phebe IV, 445
Wade, Phebe IV, 451
Wade, Phebe IV, 598
Wade, Phebe IV, 601
Wade, Pierce VI, 1009
Wade, Polly VI, 856
Wade, Polly VI, 862
Wade, Polly VI, 920
Wade, Polly VI, 1009
Wade, Polly A. VI, 967
Wade, Polly E. VI, 1009
Wade, Prudence II, 17
Wade, Prudence II, 45
Wade, Rachel IV, 162
Wade, Rachel IV, 356
Wade, Rachel IV, 451
Wade, Rachel IV, 598
Wade, Rebecca IV, 598
Wade, Rebecca VI, 862
Wade, Rebekah I, 1013
Wade, Rhoda I, 266
Wade, Rhoda IV, 65
Wade, Rhoda IV, 162
Wade, Rhoda IV, 346
Wade, Rhoda IV, 356
Wade, Rial I, 277
Wade, Richard V, 287
Wade, Robert II, 17
Wade, Robert V, 1023
Wade, Royal I, 266
Wade, Royal I, 267
Wade, Royal I, 277
Wade, Royal IV, 65
Wade, Royal IV, 137
Wade, Royal IV, 162
Wade, Royal IV, 356
Wade, Royal IV, 445
Wade, Royal IV, 451
Wade, Royal IV, 601
Wade, Ruth I, 266
Wade, Ruth IV, 162
Wade, Ruth IV, 356
Wade, Ruth IV, 416
Wade, Ruth IV, 451
Wade, Sally VI, 875
Wade, Sally VI, 1009
Wade, Samuel II, 17
Wade, Samuel II, 45
Wade, Samuel II, 93
Wade, Samuel II, 108
Wade, Sarah I, 266
Wade, Sarah IV, 65
Wade, Sarah IV, 162
Wade, Sarah IV, 356
Wade, Sarah IV, 598
Wade, Sarah V, 969
Wade, Sarah V, 978
Wade, Sarah W. VI, 862
Wade, Silas G. VI, 1009
Wade, Susan V, 1023
Wade, Susanna VI, 952
Wade, Susanna G. VI, 898
Wade, Theodosia F. VI, 958
Wade, Thomas VI, 1009
Wade, Thomas L. VI, 1009
Wade, Thos. V, 287
Wade, Urzilla V, 1023
Wade, Valentine I, 277
Wade, Velma V, 1023
Wade, William VI, 862
Wade, William VI, 1009
Wade, William H. VI, 862
Wade, William W. VI, 948
Wade, Wm. VI, 810
Wade, Zachariah VI, 838
Wade, Zachfield VI, 806
Wade, Zachfield VI, 856
Wade, Zackfield VI, 862
Wadington, Jane II, 82
Wadington, Jane II, 108
Wadington, Margrett II, 448
Wadkins, Angeline VI, 989
Wadkins, Benjamin VI, 279
Wadkins, Cloah I, 319
Wadkins, Elizabeth VI, 253
Wadkins, Martha Ann V, 630
Wadkins, Martha Ann V, 648
Wadkins, Nancy VI, 989
Wadkins, Sally V, 288
Wadsworth, Des demona III, 103
Wadsworth, Thomas I, 1039
Wady, Humphrey II, 1034
Wady, Wd. Sarah II, 1034
Wagar, Elizabeth IV, 1341
Wager, Elizabeth IV, 1266
Wager, Emma III, 337
Wager, Mary VI, 741
Wagers, Rosa V, 1023
Wagginer, Barbara V, 771
Wagginer, Hannah V, 771
Wagginer, Hannah V, 772
Wagginer, Jacob V, 771
Wagginer, John V, 771
Wagginer, Mary V, 771
Wagginer, Nancy V, 771
Wagginer, Susanna V, 771
Waggle, Mary IV, 1297
Waggoner, Anna IV, 1241
Waggoner, Barbara V, 771
Waggoner, Barbara V, 772
Waggoner, Barbary V, 771
Waggoner, Chas. IV, 1241
Waggoner, Elizabeth I, 1050
Waggoner, Elizabeth I, 1051
Waggoner, Hannah V, 771
Waggoner, Hannah V, 772
Waggoner, Jacob V, 771
Waggoner, Jacob VI, 946
Waggoner, John I, 736
Waggoner, John V, 756
Waggoner, John V, 771
Waggoner, John V, 772
Waggoner, Mary I, 1051
Waggoner, Mary V, 730
Waggoner, Mary V, 771
Waggoner, Milton IV, 1044
Waggoner, Mirtie IV, 1241
Waggoner, Molly V, 771
Waggoner, Myrtle IV, 1241
Waggoner, Nancy V, 756
Waggoner, Nancy V, 758
Waggoner, Nancy V, 771
Waggoner, Rose IV, 1241
Waggoner, Susanna V, 771
Waggoner, Tommy IV, 1241
Wagner, Ann II, 430
Wagner, Anna IV, 1241
Wagner, Bernice IV, 782
Wagner, Carlton IV, 1341
Wagner, Charles IV, 1241
Wagner, Charles IV, 1266
Wagner, Chas. IV, 1241
Wagner, Daniel IV, 782
Wagner, Ella IV, 782
Wagner, Flora IV, 782
Wagner, Harriet V. II, 859
Wagner, Harriet V. II, 934
Wagner, Harry IV, 782
Wagner, Henry IV, 782
Wagner, Ida B. IV, 1341
Wagner, John IV, 782
Wagner, John T. IV, 782
Wagner, Louella II, 934
Wagner, Louella S. II, 859
Wagner, Louvina IV, 782
Wagner, Marie IV, 782
Wagner, Mark II, 859
Wagner, Mark II, 934
Wagner, Mark S. II, 859
Wagner, Mark S. II, 934
Wagner, Mary V, 1023
Wagner, Mary Margaret II, 825
Wagner, Mary Margaret II, 934
Wagner, Mirtie IV, 1241
Wagner, Myrtle IV, 1241
Wagner, Rose IV, 1241
Wagner, Tommy IV, 1241
Wagner, Troy O. II, 934
Wagnor, Emma V, 1023
Wagnor, Fred V, 1023
Wagoner, Barbara V, 733
Wagoner, Barbara V, 772
Wagoner, Clara J. V, 939
Wagoner, Emma V, 1023
Wagoner, Fred V, 1023
Wagoner, Harry V, 1023
Wagoner, Jesse V, 1023
Wagoner, John A. V, 1023
Wagoner, Mary V, 1023
Wagoner, Milton IV, 1044
Wagoner, Peter VI, 879
Wagoner, Rosa V, 1023
Wagoner, Sallie I, 924
Wagoner, Sarah V, 1023
Wagstaff, Alexander III, 337
Wagstaff, Amelia III, 142
Wagstaff, Amelia III, 337
Wagstaff, Ann III, 142
Wagstaff, Ann III, 337
Wagstaff, Anna III, 337
Wagstaff, Enphraisah I, 935
Wagstaff, Francis III, 337
Wagstaff, George W. III, 337
Wagstaff, Hannah II, 674
Wagstaff, Hannah M. III, 337
Wagstaff, James II, 430
Wagstaff, James II, 674
Wagstaff, John II, 430
Wagstaff, John Cheeseman III, 337
Wagstaff, John F. I, 935
Wagstaff, Joseph Alexander III, 337
Wagstaff, Mary II, 430
Wagstaff, Mary Elizabeth I, 935
Wagstaff, Myrtle Eva I, 935
Wagstaff, Rachel Maria III, 337
Wagstaff, Rebecca II, 674
Wagstaff, Robert L. I, 928
Wagstaff, Robert Lee I, 935
Wagstaff, Robert Lee I, 950
Wagstaff, Ruth I, 928
Wagstaff, Ruth Evans I, 935
Wagstaff, Ruth Evans I, 950
Wagstaff, Samuel Harford III, 337
Wagstaff, Sarah II, 430
Wagstaff, Sarah II, 674
Wagstaff, Selena Jane I, 928
Wagstaff, Selma Jane I, 950
Wagstaff, Thomas Henry III, 337
Wagstaff, William III, 142
Wagstaff, William III, 337
Wagstaff, William R. III, 337
Wagstaff, Wm. III, 337
Wagstaffe, Hannah II, 674
Wagstaffe, James II, 430
Wagstaffe, James II, 621
Wagstaffe, James II, 674
Wagstaffe, John II, 430
Wagstaffe, Martha II, 674
Wagstaffe, Mary II, 558
Wagstaffe, Mary II, 674
Wagstaffe, Rebecca II, 674
Wagstaffe, Richard II, 674
Wagstaffe, Sarah II, 430
Wagstaffe, Sarah II, 621
Wagstaffe, Sarah II, 674
Wagstaffe, Thomas II, 674
Wah, King III, 337
Wahl, Mary Ann VI, 787
Wahu, Yoo V, 717
Waibel, ??? III, 129
Waibel, Bessie M. III, 337
Waibel, Bessie Marion III, 316
Waibel, Bessie Marion III, 337
Waibel, Margherita Olivia III, 337
Waibel, Marion III, 129
Waibel, Marion III, 316
Waibel, Marion III, 337
Waibel, Wd. Bessie M. III, 129
Waid, Jane II, 108
Waid, Mary I, 580
Waid, Mary I, 842
Waid, Milisent II, 45
Waid, Phebe I, 277
Waid, Rial I, 277
Waight, Maudlin II, 462
Waight, Maudlin II, 674
Waightman, Elizabeth II, 108
Waightman, Wm. II, 108
Wail, J. M. V, 1023
Wailes, Elizabeth I, 999
Wailes, George I, 999
Wailes, Mary V, 136
Wails, Elizabeth V, 287
Wails, George V, 287
Wails, Jane I, 999
Wails, Mary I, 999
Wainman, Hannah II, 81
Wainman, Hannah II, 108
Wainright, Henry II, 430
Wainright, J. W. II, 430
Wainright, Mary II, 430
Wainright, Thomas B. IV, 113
Wainwright, Angeline W. VI, 929
WainWright, F. VI, 1009
Wainwright, Isaac VI, 1009
Wainwright, James II, 139
Wainwright, James E. II, 772
Wainwright, James E. II, 934
Wainwright, James Ellet II, 108
Wainwright, James Ellett II, 125
Wainwright, James Ellett II, 139
Wainwright, James Ellett II, 772
Wainwright, James Elliott II, 160
Wainwright, James Elliott II, 934
Wainwright, Lucinda VI, 327
Wainwright, Lucinda VI, 344
Wainwright, Lucinda H. VI, 1009
Wainwright, Mack VI, 1009
Wainwright, Mary C. VI, 972
Wainwright, Mary C. VI, 1009
Wainwright, Matilda II, 674
Wainwright, Matilda II, 688
Wainwright, Rachel II, 125
Wainwright, Rachel II, 139
Wainwright, Rachel II, 825
Wainwright, Rachel C. II, 108
Wainwright, Rachel C. II, 160
Wainwright, Rachel C. II, 934
Wainwright, Sarah II, 825
Wainwright, Sarah S. VI, 1009
Wainwright, Thomas VI, 1009
Wainwright, Thomas B. II, 108
Wainwright, Thomas B. II, 772
Wainwright, Thomas B. IV, 113
Wainwright, Thomas Berry II, 108
Wainwright, Thos B. II, 674
Wainwright, Wd. Sarah II, 825
Wainwright, William J. II, 825
Wainwright, Wm. J. II, 934
Wainwright, Wm. Josiah II, 674
Wainwright, Wm. Josiah II, 772
Wainwright, Wm. Josiah II, 825
Wair, Joseph II, 109
Wair, Joseph II, 111
Wair, Mary II, 111
Wait, Elizabeth III, 463
Wait, Harold III, 463
Wait, Harold Van A. III, 463
Wait, Harold Van Alden III, 448
Wait, Harold Van Alden III, 463
Wait, Irving S. III, 463
Wait, Irving V. A. III, 463
Wait, John II, 601
Wait, John II, 674
Wait, Lillian III, 463
Wait, Magdalen II, 601
Wait, Magdalen II, 674
Wait, Marion III, 448
Wait, Marion III, 463
Wait, Peninah IV, 202
Wait, Peninah IV, 297
Wait, Sarah II, 653
Wait, Sarah II, 674
Waite, Benjamin II, 608
Waite, Benjamin II, 674
Waite, Hannah II, 448
Waite, Jane II, 608
Waite, Jane II, 674
Waite, John II, 448
Waite, John II, 465
Waite, John II, 674
Waite, Joseph II, 465
Waite, Joseph II, 674
Waite, Magdalen II, 674
Waite, Martha II, 674
Waite, Maudlin II, 674
Waite, Peninah IV, 202
Waite, Peninah IV, 297
Waite, Sarah II, 674
Waite, Wd. Martha II, 465
Waite, William II, 430
Waite, William II, 448
Waites, Clara Bell V, 603
Waites, Edith Marie V, 603
Waites, Goldie V, 603
Waites, Hazel Mary V, 603
Waites, Ida Bell V, 603
Waites, Samuel V, 603
Waites, Sarah IV, 103
Waites, Sarah IV, 113
Waites, Verne Edward V, 603
Waites, Vernie Edward V, 603
Waitham, Hazel IV, 782
Waithhorn, Elizabeth II, 430
Waithman, Mr. ??? IV, 782
Waithman, Mrs. ??? IV, 782
Waitman, Hazel IV, 782
Waitman, Melbourne IV, 782
Waitman, Mr. ??? IV, 782
Waitman, Mrs. ??? IV, 782
Waits, Mary IV, 37
Waits, Mary IV, 66
Waits, Sarah IV, 19
Waits, Sarah IV, 66
Wakefield, Almeda V, 963
Wakefield, B. F. V, 717
Wakefield, Benjamin Frank V, 717
Wakefield, Charlotte V, 894
Wakefield, E. H. V, 717
Wakefield, Eben H. V, 717
Wakefield, Eber IV, 1226
Wakefield, Eber V, 717
Wakefield, Eber H. IV, 1226
Wakefield, Eber H. V, 717
Wakefield, Elizabeth II, 109
Wakefield, Esther I, 611
Wakefield, Frank V, 717
Wakefield, Jane C. V, 717
Wakefield, Jane C. S. W. K. V, 717
Wakefield, Jane S. C. W. K. IV, 1226
Wakefield, Jennie V, 717

Wakefield, Jennie C. IV, 1226
Wakefield, Joseph IV, 1226
Wakefield, Joseph V, 717
Wakefield, Joseph V, 1023
Wakefield, Joseph J. IV, 1226
Wakefield, Joseph J. V, 717
Wakefield, Joseph J. V, 772
Wakefield, Joseph J. V, 963
Wakefield, Louise Ruth III, 465
Wakefield, Louise Ruth F. III, 463
Wakefield, Lydia V, 717
Wakefield, Lydia A. IV, 1226
Wakefield, Lydia A. V, 717
Wakefield, Mary IV, 1226
Wakefield, Mary V, 717
Wakefield, Mary A. V, 717
Wakefield, Mary Ann V, 717
Wakefield, Mary L. V, 717
Wakefield, Mary Louisa V, 717
Wakefield, Robert III, 463
Wakefield, Robert III, 465
Wakelee, Frank IV, 1342
Wakelee, Frank Drew IV, 1341
Wakeley, Charles C. III, 337
Wakeley, Charles C. III, 341
Wakeley, Elizabeth III, 337
Wakeley, Elizabeth B. III, 337
Wakeley, Elizabeth B. III, 341
Wakeley, Frank IV, 1342
Wakeley, J. B. III, 337
Wakeley, Truman III, 337
Wakely, Elizabeth III, 337
Waker, Elizabeth II, 109
Walbridge, Mary H. III, 87
Walbridge, Nelson III, 87
Walch, Domnick VI, 985
Walcott, Dexter VI, 1009
Walcott, Sarah E. VI, 1009
Walcut, Daisy Ethel IV, 1266
Walcut, Ethel V, 1023
Walcut, Ethel Marie IV, 1266
Walcut, Eugene Wilford IV, 1266
Walcut, Ida V, 1023
Walcut, Mattie V, 1023
Walcut, Nathan IV, 1266
Walcut, Ralph Lewis IV, 1266
Walcut, Verna Alice IV, 1266
Walcutt, Arthur V, 1023
Walcutt, E. V, 1023
Walcutt, Erastus V, 1023
Walcutt, Ethel V, 1023
Walcutt, Hattie V, 1023
Walcutt, Ida V, 1023
Walcutt, Janet V, 1023
Walcutt, Mattie V, 1023
Walde, Gincy VI, 1010
Walden, Bevley VI, 1010
Walden, Charles VI, 862
Walden, Elizabeth II, 45
Walden, Elizabeth VI, 862
Walden, Frances VI, 1010
Walden, Hannah II, 45
Walden, Harriett VI, 927
Walden, Jacob VI, 1010
Walden, Jenny VI, 831
Walden, Jenny VI, 894
Walden, Jno. VI, 922
Walden, Jno. VI, 928
Walden, John VI, 894
Walden, John VI, 1010
Walden, Joshua VI, 1010
Walden, Levina VI, 862
Walden, Lewis VI, 855
Walden, Lucinda Jane VI, 991
Walden, Patsey VI, 1010
Walden, Pattsy VI, 855
Walden, Patty VI, 831
Walden, Polly VI, 855
Walden, Polly VI, 922
Walden, Richard VI, 862
Walden, Sally VI, 1010
Walden, Thomas D. VI, 1010
Walden, William II, 45
Waldenburg, Annie Lewis III, 338
Waldenburg, Augustus F. III, 333
Waldenburg, Augustus F. III, 337
Waldenburg, Augustus F., Jr. III, 337
Waldenburg, Eleanor III, 338
Waldenburg, Florence III, 338
Waldenburg, Florence N. III, 333
Waldenburg, Florence N. III, 337
Waldenburg, Julia F. III, 337
Waldenburg, Stephen III, 338
Waldenburg, William III, 337
Waldenburg, Wm. III, 337
Walder, Edward VI, 369
Walder, Mary VI, 369
Waldmeier, Alfred Henry III, 299
Waldmeier, Alfred Henry III, 338
Waldmeier, Alfred Ilma III, 338
Waldmeier, Hettie III, 299
Waldmeier, Hettie III, 338
Waldmeier, Lily III, 338
Waldmeier, Susanna B. III, 338
Waldmeier, Theophilus III, 338
Waldmeier, Viola III, 338
Waldon, Rachel IV, 315
Waldraven, Mary I, 924
Waldresse, Harrison R. IV, 297
Waldron, Angie IV, 297
Waldron, Beverly VI, 1010
Waldron, Cornelius III, 463
Waldron, Cornelius H. III, 463
Waldron, Ella IV, 297
Waldron, Hane IV, 297
Waldron, Harrison R. IV, 297
Waldron, Harrison Riley IV, 297
Waldron, Jinsey VI, 917
Waldron, John, Jr. III, 463
Waldron, Mable IV, 298
Waldron, Moses VI, 1013
Waldron, Nancy Jane IV, 297
Waldron, Nancy M. VI, 1010
Waldron, Rhoda III, 463
Waldron, Robert IV, 297
Waldron, Samuel VI, 1013
Waldron, Sarah VI, 1013
Waldron, Velma IV, 298
Waldron, Winfield IV, 298
Waldrond, Amanda VI, 1006
Waldrond, Ann Mariah VI, 974
Waldrond, Benjamin VI, 1006
Wale, John II, 430
Wale, Joseph II, 430
Wale, Martha II, 430
Walen, Anta May V, 287
Walen, Cora B. V, 287
Walen, Effie Pearl V, 287
Walen, Laura Cademy V, 287
Wales, Caroline V, 136
Wales, Caroline A. V, 136
Wales, Caroline M. V, 96
Wales, Caroline M. V, 136
Wales, Chloe V, 25
Wales, Elizabeth I, 843
Wales, Elizabeth I, 999
Wales, Elizabeth V, 208
Wales, Elizabeth V, 287
Wales, Geo. V, 208
Wales, George I, 834
Wales, George I, 843
Wales, George I, 979
Wales, George I, 999
Wales, George V, 287
Wales, Harriett V, 54
Wales, Harriett V, 136
Wales, Iredell I, 999
Wales, Isaac I, 979
Wales, Isaac I, 999
Wales, Isaac I, 1000
Wales, Isaac V, 32
Wales, Isaac V, 96
Wales, Isaac V, 105
Wales, Isaac V, 136
Wales, Isaac V, 287
Wales, Jacob I, 979
Wales, Jacob I, 999
Wales, Jane I, 999
Wales, Jane V, 136
Wales, Jane S. V, 105
Wales, Jean I, 999
Wales, Margaret I, 979
Wales, Margaret I, 999
Wales, Margret I, 999
Wales, Mary I, 979
Wales, Mary I, 999
Wales, Mary V, 30
Wales, Mary V, 136
Wales, Mary Jane V, 287
Wales, Nancy V, 32
Wales, Nancy V, 136
Wales, Nancy V, 287
Wales, Richard F. V, 136
Wales, Ruth I, 979
Wales, Ruth I, 999
Wales, Ruth I, 1000
Wales, Ruth V, 25
Wales, Ruth V, 32
Wales, Ruth V, 96
Wales, Ruth V, 105
Wales, Ruth V, 136
Wales, Ruth V, 287
Wales, Ruth V, 537
Wales, Sabra I, 979
Wales, Samuel I, 979
Wales, Samuel I, 999
Wales, Samuel V, 25
Wales, Sarah I, 979
Wales, Sarah I, 999
Wales, Sarah V, 127
Wales, Sarah V, 136
Wales, Thomas I, 319
Wales, Thomas V, 136
Wales, Thomas M. V, 127
Wales, Thomas M. V, 136
Wales, Thomas Montgomery V, 136
Wales, Thomas Montgomery V, 287
Wales, W. W. I, 979
Wales, Widow Elizabeth I, 834
Wales, William W. I, 999
Walford, Adis H. III, 303
Walford, Adis H. III, 338
Walford, Alice III, 95
Walford, Alice III, 338
Walford, Edward W. III, 338
Walford, Elizabeth F. III, 338
Walford, Robert III, 303
Walford, Robert III, 338
Walford, Robert M. G. III, 95
Walford, Robt. M. G. III, 338
Walford, Sadie III, 303
Walford, Sadie III, 338
Walk, Charlotte V, 939
Walka, Carl IV, 1342
Walka, Chas. IV, 1342
Walka, Elizabeth IV, 1342
Walker, ??? III, 338
Walker, ??? V, 603
Walker, Aaron IV, 56
Walker, Aaron IV, 65
Walker, Aaron IV, 555
Walker, Abel IV, 113
Walker, Abel IV, 298
Walker, Abel IV, 315
Walker, Abel IV, 522
Walker, Abel IV, 525
Walker, Abel IV, 537
Walker, Abel IV, 554
Walker, Abel IV, 555
Walker, Abel IV, 663
Walker, Abel IV, 708
Walker, Abel IV, 782
Walker, Abel IV, 850
Walker, Abel IV, 1011
Walker, Abel V, 136
Walker, Abel V, 537
Walker, Abel V, 538
Walker, Abel V, 961
Walker, Abel VI, 364
Walker, Abel VI, 369
Walker, Abel VI, 410
Walker, Abel VI, 416
Walker, Abel VI, 431
Walker, Abel VI, 453
Walker, Abel VI, 454
Walker, Abel VI, 457
Walker, Abel VI, 460
Walker, Abel VI, 462
Walker, Abel VI, 570
Walker, Abel VI, 576
Walker, Abel M. IV, 298
Walker, Abel M. IV, 312
Walker, Abel M. IV, 315
Walker, Abel, Jr. VI, 453
Walker, Abel, Jr. VI, 454
Walker, Able IV, 850
Walker, Ada IV, 783
Walker, Ada Hermina IV, 782
Walker, Addison J. V, 717
Walker, Adeline II, 849
Walker, Adeline II, 934
Walker, Adrian IV, 1383
Walker, Agnes Hicks I, 950
Walker, Albert IV, 1044
Walker, Albina VI, 626
Walker, Alex V, 467
Walker, Alexander V, 467
Walker, Alexander VI, 863
Walker, Alfred V, 1023
Walker, Alice IV, 298
Walker, Alice M. IV, 298
Walker, Alice M. IV, 511
Walker, Alice M. IV, 555
Walker, Alpha V, 538
Walker, Alpheus D. V, 538
Walker, Alva V, 467
Walker, Amanda IV, 298
Walker, Amanda IV, 1120
Walker, Amelia IV, 782
Walker, Amelia J. V, 717
Walker, Amelia Jane V, 717
Walker, Amey G. IV, 298
Walker, Amos J. V, 603
Walker, Amos J. V, 717
Walker, Amy IV, 312
Walker, Amy IV, 315
Walker, Amy G. IV, 298
Walker, Ann II, 430
Walker, Ann II, 542
Walker, Ann II, 674
Walker, Ann II, 1034
Walker, Ann III, 324
Walker, Ann IV, 283
Walker, Ann IV, 298
Walker, Ann IV, 663
Walker, Ann VI, 862
Walker, Ann VI, 1010
Walker, Ann Booker VI, 1010
Walker, Ann Carey II, 674
Walker, Ann D. II, 430
Walker, Ann E. V, 435
Walker, Anna I, 999
Walker, Anna III, 181
Walker, Anna III, 338
Walker, Anna III, 339
Walker, Anna IV, 33
Walker, Anna IV, 65
Walker, Anna IV, 113
Walker, Anna IV, 162
Walker, Anna IV, 298
Walker, Anna IV, 356
Walker, Anna IV, 554
Walker, Anna V, 287
Walker, Anna Bashabe IV, 298
Walker, Anna Bathsheba IV, 298
Walker, Anna G. III, 181
Walker, Anna G. III, 338
Walker, Anna M. IV, 850
Walker, Anna T. V. III, 139
Walker, Anna T. V. III, 338
Walker, Anne I, 979
Walker, Anne II, 1034
Walker, Anne IV, 548
Walker, Anne M. IV, 555
Walker, Archibald IV, 1297
Walker, Arthur Edward III, 338
Walker, Arthur H. V, 961
Walker, Asa V, 208
Walker, Asa V, 537
Walker, Asa V, 538
Walker, Asa V, 603
Walker, Asa V, 604
Walker, Asa V, 717
Walker, Asa D. VI, 862
Walker, Asahel II, 825
Walker, Augusta III, 185
Walker, Augusta III, 338
Walker, Avery I, 598
Walker, Avis M. III, 26
Walker, Avis M. III, 338
Walker, Azael V, 537
Walker, Azel V, 136
Walker, Azel V, 208
Walker, Azel V, 275
Walker, Azel V, 287
Walker, Azel V, 525
Walker, Azel V, 537
Walker, Azel V, 538
Walker, Azel V, 545
Walker, Azel V, 603
Walker, Azel V, 604
Walker, Azel V, 717
Walker, Azel VI, 406
Walker, Azel VI, 453
Walker, Azel VI, 454
Walker, Azel, Jr. V, 538
Walker, Azel, Jr. V, 603
Walker, Azel, Jr. V, 604
Walker, Barbara VI, 564
Walker, Barbara VI, 575
Walker, Barbary VI, 564
Walker, Benj. V, 264
Walker, Benjamin II, 249
Walker, Benjamin II, 269
Walker, Benjamin II, 792
Walker, Benjamin V, 287
Walker, Benjamin VI, 626
Walker, Benjamin VI, 834
Walker, Benjamin VI, 846
Walker, Benjamin VI, 863
Walker, Benjamin G. IV, 1383
Walker, Benjamin G. IV, 1385
Walker, Benjamin Garrett VI, 717
Walker, Benjamin L. V, 603
Walker, Benjamin Lewis V, 208
Walker, Benjamin R. V, 287
Walker, Bertha M. IV, 554
Walker, Bertha Mary IV, 522
Walker, Bertha Mary IV, 555
Walker, Betsey R. VI, 798
Walker, Betsy V, 538
Walker, Betsy Ann V, 136
Walker, Betsy Ann V, 537
Walker, Betty VI, 575
Walker, Beulah II, 598
Walker, Beulah II, 674
Walker, Beulah II, 1034
Walker, Beverley VI, 859
Walker, Beverly VI, 852
Walker, Beverly VI, 862
Walker, Beverly VI, 866
Walker, Bruce V, 717
Walker, Bruce Mack V, 604
Walker, Bruce Mc. V, 603
Walker, Buckley VI, 802
Walker, Buckley VI, 846
Walker, Buckley VI, 863
Walker, Buckley VI, 1010
Walker, Bur Smith VI, 717
Walker, Burkley VI, 834
Walker, Burr Smith VI, 717
Walker, Calender II, 431
Walker, Callandar II, 674
Walker, Calvin V, 603
Walker, Calvin B. V, 717
Walker, Caroline IV, 1383
Walker, Caroline VI, 1010
Walker, Caroline A. VI, 827
Walker, Catharine VI, 957
Walker, Catherine VI, 862
Walker, Catherine L. V, 961
Walker, Chapley VI, 838
Walker, Charles III, 34
Walker, Charles III, 273
Walker, Charles III, 338
Walker, Charles III, 339
Walker, Charles V, 717
Walker, Charles VI, 717
Walker, Charles VI, 804
Walker, Charles VI, 818
Walker, Charles VI, 830
Walker, Charles VI, 834
Walker, Charles VI, 838
Walker, Charles VI, 839
Walker, Charles VI, 841
Walker, Charles VI, 847
Walker, Charles VI, 862
Walker, Charles VI, 864
Walker, Charles A. V, 604
Walker, Charles Janney VI,
Walker, Charles Janney VI,
Walker, Charles Janney VI,
Walker, Charles Janney VI,
Walker, Charles Janney VI,
Walker, Charles S. III, 338
Walker, Charlotte IV, 663
Walker, Charlotte VI, 822
Walker, Charlotte Jane IV, 1
Walker, Chas. A. V, 717
Walker, Clara V, 467
Walker, Claude III, 410
Walker, Cleveland III, 338
Walker, Clinton IV, 501
Walker, Cora I, 611
Walker, Cora I, 619
Walker, Cora IV, 204
Walker, Cornelia VI, 717
Walker, Cornelia H. VI, 444
Walker, Cornelia H. VI, 454
Walker, Cornelia H. VI, 560
Walker, Cornelia H. VI, 561
Walker, Cornelia H. VI, 575
Walker, Cornelia H. VI, 576
Walker, Cornelia H. VI, 702
Walker, Cornelia H. VI, 717
Walker, Cornelia N. VI, 635
Walker, Cornelia N. VI, 717
Walker, Cornelia Needles VI
Walker, Cornelia Needles VI
Walker, Cornelia Needles VI
Walker, Cornelia T. III, 215
Walker, Cornelia T. III, 338
Walker, Cynthia VI, 841
Walker, Cyrus V, 538
Walker, Cyrus V, 603
Walker, Cyrus M. V, 604
Walker, Cyrus M. V, 717
Walker, Cyrus W. V, 717
Walker, Daid VI, 795
Walker, Daniel IV, 501
Walker, Daniel IV, 554
Walker, Daniel IV, 555
Walker, Daniel IV, 632
Walker, Daniel IV, 663
Walker, Daniel IV, 1120
Walker, Daniel IV, 1226
Walker, Daniel VI, 438
Walker, Daniel VI, 453
Walker, Daniel VI, 454
Walker, Daniel VI, 456
Walker, Daniel VI, 575
Walker, David V, 538
Walker, David VI, 1010
Walker, David F. V, 208
Walker, David F. V, 537
Walker, David N. III, 26
Walker, Deborah IV, 554
Walker, Deborah V, 538
Walker, Deborah L. V, 522

ker, Deborah S. V, 537
ker, Deborah S. V, 538
ker, Delina VI, 862
ker, Delphia VI, 848
ker, Diana I, 607
ker, Dianna IV, 65
ker, Dinah V, 204
ker, Dinah V, 208
ker, Donald IV, 298
ker, Donald Evaret IV, 298
ker, Dorothy II, 431
ker, Dorothy VI, 787
ker, Dorothy VI, 790
ker, Doshia VI, 1010
ker, Dr. ??? I, 319
ker, Dr. Claude III, 463
ker, E. W. VI, 806
ker, Ebeneazer IV, 298
ker, Ebeneezer IV, 109
ker, Ebeneezer IV, 292
ker, Ebeneezer IV, 298
ker, Ebenezar IV, 113
ker, Ebenezar IV, 162
ker, Ebenezer IV, 17
ker, Ebenezer IV, 65
ker, Ebenezer IV, 71
ker, Ebenezer IV, 162
ker, Ebenezer IV, 298
ker, Ebenezer IV, 356
ker, Ebenezer IV, 555
ker, Ebenezer VI, 454
ker, Ebinazer VI, 453
ker, Edith III, 338
ker, Edith VI, 717
ker, Edith B. VI, 576
ker, Edith Lillian I, 950
ker, Edmond W. VI, 862
ker, Edmund VI, 843
ker, Edmund W. VI, 823
ker, Edmund W. VI, 831
ker, Edward III, 338
er, Edward V, 961
er, Edward VI, 396
er, Edward VI, 416
er, Edward VI, 450
er, Edward VI, 453
er, Edward VI, 454
er, Edward VI, 576
er, Edward VI, 710
er, Edward B. V, 538
er, Edward B. V, 603
er, Edward M. VI, 717
er, Edward M. Needles
VI, 717
er, Edward W. V, 603
er, Effie M. IV, 298
er, Elanor VI, 575
er, Eleanor V, 537
er, Eleanor V, 603
er, Eleanor V, 604
er, Eleanor VI, 546
er, Eleanor VI, 548
er, Eleanor VI, 1010
er, Elenor R. IV, 298
er, Eli IV, 555
er, Eli V, 208
er, Eli V, 435
er, Eli V, 537
er, Eli V, 538
er, Eli J. IV, 799
er, Eli J. IV, 850
er, Elias H. IV, 315
er, Elias Hicks IV, 298
er, Elijah V, 136
er, Elijah V, 537
er, Elinor VI, 548
er, Elisabeth II, 674
er, Elisabeth IV, 783
er, Elisha VI, 717
er, Elisha H. II, 934
er, Elisha H. VI, 575
er, Elisha Hunt II, 852
er, Elisha Hunt II, 934
er, Elisha Hunt VI, 576
er, Eliz. III, 338
er, Eliz. III, 339
er, Eliza I, 598
er, Eliza I, 1133
er, Eliza IV, 356
er, Eliza IV, 525
er, Eliza IV, 555
er, Eliza IV, 663
er, Eliza V, 717
er, Eliza VI, 513
er, Eliza VI, 538
er, Eliza VI, 544
er, Eliza VI, 575
er, Eliza VI, 576
er, Eliza VI, 577
er, Eliza VI, 659
er, Eliza VI, 677
Walker, Eliza VI, 717
Walker, Eliza VI, 843
Walker, Eliza A. II, 852
Walker, Eliza Ann IV, 555
Walker, Eliza Ann IV, 1119
Walker, Eliza Ann IV, 1120
Walker, Eliza Ann V, 538
Walker, Eliza Ann V, 603
Walker, Eliza Ann V, 717
Walker, Eliza H. II, 903
Walker, Eliza H. II, 934
Walker, Eliza H. IV, 554
Walker, Eliza Henderson
VI, 1010
Walker, Eliza J. II, 903
Walker, Eliza J. II, 934
Walker, Eliza J. III, 339
Walker, Eliza J. V, 287
Walker, Eliza J. V, 717
Walker, Eliza J. VI, 488
Walker, Eliza J. VI, 538
Walker, Eliza J. VI, 577
Walker, Eliza J. VI, 635
Walker, Eliza J. VI, 677
Walker, Eliza J. VI, 717
Walker, Eliza Jane V, 287
Walker, Eliza Needles II, 934
Walker, Elizabeth I, 319
Walker, Elizabeth I, 571
Walker, Elizabeth I, 580
Walker, Elizabeth II, 430
Walker, Elizabeth II, 431
Walker, Elizabeth II, 601
Walker, Elizabeth II, 674
Walker, Elizabeth III, 173
Walker, Elizabeth III, 339
Walker, Elizabeth IV, 109
Walker, Elizabeth IV, 113
Walker, Elizabeth IV, 298
Walker, Elizabeth IV, 606
Walker, Elizabeth IV, 651
Walker, Elizabeth IV, 660
Walker, Elizabeth IV, 663
Walker, Elizabeth IV, 783
Walker, Elizabeth IV, 785
Walker, Elizabeth IV, 1226
Walker, Elizabeth V, 208
Walker, Elizabeth V, 287
Walker, Elizabeth V, 436
Walker, Elizabeth V, 538
Walker, Elizabeth V, 603
Walker, Elizabeth V, 717
Walker, Elizabeth VI, 278
Walker, Elizabeth VI, 362
Walker, Elizabeth VI, 410
Walker, Elizabeth VI, 431
Walker, Elizabeth VI, 453
Walker, Elizabeth VI, 454
Walker, Elizabeth VI, 564
Walker, Elizabeth VI, 575
Walker, Elizabeth VI, 576
Walker, Elizabeth VI, 802
Walker, Elizabeth VI, 804
Walker, Elizabeth VI, 816
Walker, Elizabeth VI, 834
Walker, Elizabeth VI, 847
Walker, Elizabeth VI, 849
Walker, Elizabeth VI, 856
Walker, Elizabeth VI, 862
Walker, Elizabeth VI, 910
Walker, Elizabeth VI, 1010
Walker, Elizabeth A. VI, 994
Walker, Elizabeth Ann III, 324
Walker, Elizabeth Ann III, 338
Walker, Elizabeth Ann III, 339
Walker, Elizabeth M. V, 538
Walker, Elizabeth M. V, 603
Walker, Elizabeth P. V, 275
Walker, Elizabeth P. V, 287
Walker, Elizabeth P. V, 538
Walker, Elizabeth P. V, 603
Walker, Elizabeth Prichet VI, 795
Walker, Elizabeth S. VI, 985
Walker, Ella VI, 561
Walker, Ella VI, 575
Walker, Ella VI, 576
Walker, Ella VI, 702
Walker, Ella VI, 717
Walker, Ella D. V, 538
Walker, Ella Dell V, 538
Walker, Ella W. V, 264
Walker, Ellen VI, 548
Walker, Ellen VI, 575
Walker, Ellis Lewis VI, 717
Walker, Elva V, 538
Walker, Elva V, 717
Walker, Elwood T. IV, 298
Walker, Ely J. IV, 850
Walker, Emanuel II, 431
Walker, Emanuel II, 593
Walker, Emanuel II, 674
Walker, Emanuel II, 1034
Walker, Emeline III, 410
Walker, Emeline III, 463
Walker, Emma II, 431
Walker, Emma II, 674
Walker, Emma II, 797
Walker, Emma II, 826
Walker, Emma II, 934
Walker, Emma II, 936
Walker, Emma C. III, 284
Walker, Emma C. III, 338
Walker, Emma T. IV, 850
Walker, Emmanuel II, 1034
Walker, Emmer IV, 511
Walker, Emza V, 287
Walker, Enoch P. II, 431
Walker, Enoch P. II, 674
Walker, Enoch, Jr. II, 721
Walker, Ephraim VI, 862
Walker, Ernest IV, 298
Walker, Ernest R. IV, 298
Walker, Ethel M. IV, 204
Walker, Eugenia V, 718
Walker, Eva IV, 850
Walker, Evan T. III, 338
Walker, Evan Thomas II, 934
Walker, Eve V, 538
Walker, Evelyn IV, 850
Walker, Felix I, 736
Walker, Florence Litchfield
III, 338
Walker, Florence Litchfield
III, 339
Walker, Frances VI, 799
Walker, Frances VI, 806
Walker, Frances VI, 862
Walker, Frances L. VI, 806
Walker, Frances Matilda V, 103
Walker, Francis II, 431
Walker, Francis VI, 834
Walker, Francis VI, 839
Walker, Francis H. VI, 1010
Walker, Francis Thompson
III, 338
Walker, Frank W. V, 538
Walker, Gabriel G. VI, 845
Walker, Gardner IV, 1044
Walker, Garrett VI, 717
Walker, Geo. IV, 162
Walker, Geo. IV, 298
Walker, Geo. Edmondson III, 338
Walker, Geo. H. S. V, 717
Walker, George I, 829
Walker, George I, 843
Walker, George II, 431
Walker, George II, 448
Walker, George II, 1018
Walker, George II, 1034
Walker, George II, 1062
Walker, George IV, 33
Walker, George IV, 65
Walker, George IV, 113
Walker, George IV, 162
Walker, George IV, 298
Walker, George IV, 356
Walker, George IV, 554
Walker, George IV, 1120
Walker, George V, 717
Walker, George VI, 13
Walker, George VI, 804
Walker, George VI, 862
Walker, George Bruce IV, 113
Walker, George Bruce IV, 162
Walker, George Edmondson
III, 339
Walker, George H. S. V, 717
Walker, George J. VI, 862
Walker, George M. A. VI, 1010
Walker, Gertie IV, 501
Walker, Gertrude IV, 501
Walker, Gertrude D. IV, 501
Walker, Goldie V, 718
Walker, Grace V, 467
Walker, Gulielma III, 185
Walker, Gulielma III, 338
Walker, Gwendolyn III, 143
Walker, Gwendolyn III, 339
Walker, H. F. V, 435
Walker, Hananiah II, 674
Walker, Hannah II, 69
Walker, Hannah II, 109
Walker, Hannah II, 111
Walker, Hannah II, 431
Walker, Hannah II, 792
Walker, Hannah III, 185
Walker, Hannah IV, 192
Walker, Hannah IV, 265
Walker, Hannah IV, 292
Walker, Hannah IV, 298
Walker, Hannah IV, 555
Walker, Hannah V, 136
Walker, Hannah V, 537
Walker, Hannah V, 538
Walker, Hannah V, 961
Walker, Hannah VI, 406
Walker, Hannah VI, 453
Walker, Hannah VI, 454
Walker, Hannah Ann IV, 312
Walker, Hannah Ann IV, 315
Walker, Hannah Craven IV, 298
Walker, Hannah H. III, 199
Walker, Hannah H. IV, 1139
Walker, Hannah L. III, 339
Walker, Hannah L. IV, 522
Walker, Hannah L. IV, 525
Walker, Hannah L. IV, 537
Walker, Hannah L. IV, 554
Walker, Hannah L. IV, 555
Walker, Hannah L. IV, 708
Walker, Hannah L. IV, 782
Walker, Hannah L. IV, 783
Walker, Hannah M. IV, 298
Walker, Hannah N. I, 843
Walker, Hannah U. IV, 298
Walker, Hannah U. IV, 663
Walker, Hannah W. IV, 493
Walker, Hannah W. IV, 501
Walker, Hannah W. VI, 416
Walker, Hannah W. VI, 454
Walker, Harold L. III, 338
Walker, Harriet III, 339
Walker, Harriet VI, 862
Walker, Harriette III, 410
Walker, Harriette V. III, 463
Walker, Hattie S. V, 603
Walker, Helen IV, 298
Walker, Helen Irene IV, 298
Walker, Henry II, 305
Walker, Henry III, 166
Walker, Henry III, 338
Walker, Henry V, 538
Walker, Henry Edmund III, 248
Walker, Henry Edmund III, 338
Walker, Hilton D. VI, 862
Walker, Hope III, 273
Walker, Hope III, 338
Walker, Hugh S. II, 934
Walker, Hugh S. VI, 576
Walker, Imanuel II, 431
Walker, Inez Channing IV, 298
Walker, Irene IV, 298
Walker, Irene V, 717
Walker, Irene S. IV, 298
Walker, Irene Samaria IV, 298
Walker, Isaac II, 934
Walker, Isaac III, 185
Walker, Isaac III, 338
Walker, Isaac IV, 65
Walker, Isaac IV, 113
Walker, Isaac IV, 162
Walker, Isaac IV, 356
Walker, Isaac IV, 554
Walker, Isaac IV, 555
Walker, Isaac IV, 663
Walker, Isaac IV, 835
Walker, Isaac IV, 850
Walker, Isaac IV, 983
Walker, Isaac IV, 1011
Walker, Isaac IV, 1119
Walker, Isaac IV, 1120
Walker, Isaac V, 538
Walker, Isaac V, 603
Walker, Isaac V, 604
Walker, Isaac VI, 453
Walker, Isaac VI, 454
Walker, Isaac VI, 513
Walker, Isaac VI, 520
Walker, Isaac VI, 560
Walker, Isaac VI, 568
Walker, Isaac VI, 570
Walker, Isaac VI, 576
Walker, Isaac VI, 582
Walker, Isaac VI, 659
Walker, Isaac VI, 717
Walker, Isaac VI, 754
Walker, Isaac C. V, 538
Walker, Isaac E. IV, 114
Walker, Isaac E. IV, 356
Walker, Isaac E. IV, 554
Walker, Isaac Henry III, 215
Walker, Isaac Henry III, 338
Walker, Isaac John IV, 315
Walker, Isaac W. VI, 576
Walker, Israel IV, 554
Walker, Israel IV, 555
Walker, Israel IV, 1119
Walker, Israel IV, 1120
Walker, Israel N. IV, 1120
Walker, J. E. IV, 204
Walker, J. Edward VI, 560
Walker, J. Edward VI, 567
Walker, J. Edward VI, 576
Walker, J. Edward VI, 702
Walker, J. Edward VI, 717
Walker, J. R. V, 287
Walker, J. Wallace IV, 298
Walker, Jacob Reese VI, 493
Walker, Jacob Reese VI, 576
Walker, James II, 431
Walker, James II, 674
Walker, James IV, 298
Walker, James IV, 606
Walker, James IV, 651
Walker, James IV, 782
Walker, James VI, 513
Walker, James VI, 577
Walker, James VI, 717
Walker, James VI, 989
Walker, James VI, 1011
Walker, James A. VI, 1010
Walker, James B. II, 934
Walker, James F. IV, 511
Walker, James F. IV, 555
Walker, James French IV, 555
Walker, James M. II, 852
Walker, James M. II, 903
Walker, James M. II, 934
Walker, James M. VI, 538
Walker, James M. VI, 544
Walker, James M. VI, 575
Walker, James M. VI, 576
Walker, James M. VI, 577
Walker, James M. VI, 659
Walker, James M. VI, 677
Walker, James M. VI, 717
Walker, James Murray IV, 298
Walker, James Murry IV, 298
Walker, Jamima I, 979
Walker, Jane II, 431
Walker, Jane III, 338
Walker, Jane IV, 65
Walker, Jane IV, 632
Walker, Jane IV, 663
Walker, Jane IV, 1120
Walker, Jane IV, 1226
Walker, Jane VI, 435
Walker, Jane VI, 454
Walker, Jane VI, 493
Walker, Jane VI, 551
Walker, Jane VI, 576
Walker, Jane VI, 582
Walker, Jane VI, 584
Walker, Jane H. IV, 663
Walker, Jas. A. VI, 1002
Walker, Jedidah V, 717
Walker, Jehu V, 208
Walker, Jehu V, 603
Walker, Jehu H. V, 208
Walker, Jehu H. V, 603
Walker, Jemima I, 999
Walker, Jemima V, 535
Walker, Jemima V, 537
Walker, Jemima V, 538
Walker, Jemima V, 603
Walker, Jemima VI, 846
Walker, Jemimah V, 602
Walker, Jennie V, 718
Walker, Jenny VI, 1010
Walker, Jeremiah C. IV, 298
Walker, Jeremiah C. IV, 313
Walker, Jeremiah C. IV, 315
Walker, Jesse IV, 65
Walker, Jesse IV, 298
Walker, Jesse IV, 555
Walker, Jesse IV, 562
Walker, Jesse VI, 862
Walker, Jessie V, 717
Walker, Job II, 431
Walker, Joel IV, 298
Walker, Joel IV, 315
Walker, Joel VI, 908
Walker, Joel VI, 1010
Walker, Joel A. IV, 298
Walker, Joel Aaron IV, 315
Walker, John II, 49
Walker, John II, 109
Walker, John II, 431
Walker, John II, 576
Walker, John II, 674
Walker, John II, 934
Walker, John III, 284
Walker, John III, 338
Walker, John V, 538
Walker, John V, 717
Walker, John VI, 822
Walker, John VI, 862
Walker, John VI, 1010
Walker, John B. III, 339
Walker, John B. V, 604
Walker, John Edward VI, 444
Walker, John Edward VI, 454
Walker, John Edward VI, 560
Walker, John Edward VI, 561

Walker, John Edward VI, 568
Walker, John Edward VI, 575
Walker, John Edward VI, 576
Walker, John Gibson VI, 576
Walker, John J. III, 338
Walker, John Jackson II, 934
Walker, John Jackson III, 338
Walker, John Jackson III, 339
Walker, John L. V, 176
Walker, John L. V, 208
Walker, John L. V, 603
Walker, John Palmer, Jr. II, 1034
Walker, John Paxton II, 1034
Walker, John R. V, 538
Walker, John R. V, 603
Walker, John R. V, 717
Walker, John S. V, 208
Walker, John S. V, 603
Walker, John Simpson V, 538
Walker, John Simpson Lewis V, 208
Walker, John T. VI, 994
Walker, John T. VI, 1010
Walker, John, Jr. VI, 795
Walker, Johnson V, 467
Walker, Jos. IV, 554
Walker, Joseph II, 104
Walker, Joseph II, 109
Walker, Joseph II, 269
Walker, Joseph II, 270
Walker, Joseph II, 431
Walker, Joseph II, 448
Walker, Joseph II, 500
Walker, Joseph II, 612
Walker, Joseph II, 674
Walker, Joseph II, 826
Walker, Joseph II, 1034
Walker, Joseph III, 312
Walker, Joseph III, 338
Walker, Joseph III, 339
Walker, Joseph III, 373
Walker, Joseph IV, 356
Walker, Joseph IV, 501
Walker, Joseph IV, 534
Walker, Joseph IV, 535
Walker, Joseph IV, 554
Walker, Joseph IV, 555
Walker, Joseph IV, 663
Walker, Joseph IV, 782
Walker, Joseph IV, 850
Walker, Joseph IV, 1226
Walker, Joseph V, 136
Walker, Joseph V, 718
Walker, Joseph VI, 453
Walker, Joseph Daniel IV, 1226
Walker, Joseph Henry I, 843
Walker, Joseph Henry III, 338
Walker, Joseph Lupton V, 961
Walker, Joseph Lupton VI, 454
Walker, Joseph M. V, 718
Walker, Joseph P. II, 431
Walker, Joseph P. II, 674
Walker, Joseph P. VI, 1002
Walker, Joseph P. VI, 1010
Walker, Joseph S. IV, 555
Walker, Joseph S. V, 136
Walker, Joseph S. V, 537
Walker, Joseph S. V, 538
Walker, Joseph Townsend IV, 65
Walker, Joshua VI, 659
Walker, Joshua R. V, 287
Walker, Joshua R. V, 603
Walker, Joshua R. V, 604
Walker, Joshua R. V, 717
Walker, Josiah VI, 835
Walker, Josiah J. V, 538
Walker, Josiah Jackson V, 136
Walker, Josiah Jackson V, 537
Walker, Josiah Jackson V, 538
Walker, Judah VI, 1010
Walker, Judith VI, 862
Walker, Judith C. VI, 862
Walker, Julia I, 598
Walker, Julia V, 873
Walker, Julia Ann V, 873
Walker, Julia Ann VI, 1010
Walker, Julia M. IV, 555
Walker, Kissiah VI, 801
Walker, Kitty VI, 804
Walker, Leah IV, 114
Walker, Leah VI, 416
Walker, Leah VI, 453
Walker, Leah VI, 520
Walker, Leah VI, 529
Walker, Leah VI, 576
Walker, Leah VI, 665
Walker, Leah VI, 673
Walker, Leonidas V, 287
Walker, Letitia VI, 717
Walker, Lewen W. III, 339
Walker, Lewis II, 431
Walker, Lewis II, 612
Walker, Lewis II, 674
Walker, Lewis II, 804
Walker, Lewis II, 809
Walker, Lewis II, 825
Walker, Lewis II, 826
Walker, Lewis II, 934
Walker, Lewis II, 936
Walker, Lewis IV, 65
Walker, Lewis IV, 231
Walker, Lewis IV, 265
Walker, Lewis IV, 295
Walker, Lewis IV, 298
Walker, Lewis IV, 356
Walker, Lewis IV, 555
Walker, Lewis IV, 660
Walker, Lewis IV, 663
Walker, Lewis V, 204
Walker, Lewis V, 208
Walker, Lewis V, 424
Walker, Lewis V, 538
Walker, Lewis V, 603
Walker, Lewis VI, 374
Walker, Lewis VI, 406
Walker, Lewis VI, 416
Walker, Lewis VI, 453
Walker, Lewis VI, 454
Walker, Lewis VI, 456
Walker, Lewis VI, 529
Walker, Lewis VI, 565
Walker, Lewis VI, 576
Walker, Lewis B. IV, 90
Walker, Lewis B. IV, 113
Walker, Lewis B. IV, 555
Walker, Lewis B. IV, 850
Walker, Lewis B. VI, 453
Walker, Lewis C. V, 717
Walker, Lewis J. IV, 298
Walker, Lewis J. IV, 663
Walker, Lewis J. V, 717
Walker, Lewis James IV, 663
Walker, Lewis M. IV, 315
Walker, Lewis M. V, 537
Walker, Lewis M. V, 538
Walker, Lewis P. IV, 850
Walker, Lewis T. IV, 554
Walker, Lewis, Jr. VI, 454
Walker, Lewis, Sr. IV, 298
Walker, Linda IV, 298
Walker, Lizzie Bell V, 717
Walker, Lizzie Bue V, 717
Walker, Lloyd V, 467
Walker, Lloyd J. IV, 782
Walker, Lora M. V, 538
Walker, Lorenzo Dow VI, 717
Walker, Lotta IV, 1226
Walker, Louis V, 136
Walker, Louis V, 603
Walker, Louis M. V, 136
Walker, Louis M. V, 538
Walker, Louisa III, 338
Walker, Louisa VI, 862
Walker, Louise I, 598
Walker, Loyal IV, 298
Walker, Lucy II, 852
Walker, Lucy II, 934
Walker, Lucy VI, 717
Walker, Lucy VI, 804
Walker, Lucy VI, 822
Walker, Lucy VI, 859
Walker, Luella L. IV, 554
Walker, Luella Letitia IV, 537
Walker, Luella Letitia IV, 555
Walker, Lydia IV, 554
Walker, Lydia IV, 555
Walker, Lydia IV, 606
Walker, Lydia IV, 663
Walker, Lydia IV, 835
Walker, Lydia IV, 850
Walker, Lydia IV, 983
Walker, Lydia IV, 1011
Walker, Lydia IV, 1119
Walker, Lydia IV, 1120
Walker, Lydia IV, 1383
Walker, Lydia VI, 406
Walker, Lydia VI, 416
Walker, Lydia VI, 417
Walker, Lydia VI, 444
Walker, Lydia VI, 453
Walker, Lydia VI, 454
Walker, Lydia VI, 514
Walker, Lydia VI, 529
Walker, Lydia VI, 660
Walker, Lydia VI, 673
Walker, Lydia N. IV, 555
Walker, Lydia N. IV, 1011
Walker, Lydia N. IV, 1120
Walker, Lydia S. V, 535
Walker, Maggie IV, 501
Walker, Maggy VI, 1011
Walker, Mahlon M. IV, 298
Walker, Manuell II, 431
Walker, Margaret II, 187
Walker, Margaret II, 269
Walker, Margaret II, 270
Walker, Margaret II, 500
Walker, Margaret II, 593
Walker, Margaret II, 826
Walker, Margaret II, 899
Walker, Margaret V, 264
Walker, Margaret V, 287
Walker, Margaret V, 436
Walker, Margaret V, 538
Walker, Margaret VI, 862
Walker, Margaret E. III, 339
Walker, Margaret H. III, 248
Walker, Margaret H. III, 338
Walker, Margaret L. V, 287
Walker, Margarett II, 431
Walker, Maria IV, 501
Walker, Maria IV, 534
Walker, Maria IV, 535
Walker, Maria IV, 554
Walker, Maria IV, 555
Walker, Maria IV, 782
Walker, Maria IV, 850
Walker, Maria V, 603
Walker, Maria V, 604
Walker, Maria V, 717
Walker, Maria Ann V, 538
Walker, Maria Louisa III, 338
Walker, Maria Louisa III, 339
Walker, Mariah IV, 799
Walker, Mariah IV, 850
Walker, Mariam J. IV, 1120
Walker, Marian II, 809
Walker, Marian II, 898
Walker, Marian II, 934
Walker, Marion II, 674
Walker, Martha II, 431
Walker, Martha II, 674
Walker, Martha IV, 65
Walker, Martha IV, 356
Walker, Martha IV, 501
Walker, Martha IV, 516
Walker, Martha IV, 555
Walker, Martha IV, 663
Walker, Martha IV, 828
Walker, Martha IV, 850
Walker, Martha V, 204
Walker, Martha V, 208
Walker, Martha V, 287
Walker, Martha V, 403
Walker, Martha V, 435
Walker, Martha V, 469
Walker, Martha V, 537
Walker, Martha V, 538
Walker, Martha V, 603
Walker, Martha V, 717
Walker, Martha VI, 387
Walker, Martha VI, 453
Walker, Martha VI, 454
Walker, Martha VI, 862
Walker, Martha VI, 1010
Walker, Martha B. IV, 1119
Walker, Martha B. IV, 1120
Walker, Martha H. IV, 534
Walker, Martha H. IV, 554
Walker, Martha J. VI, 836
Walker, Martha Jane V, 603
Walker, Martha Jane V, 717
Walker, Martha W. V, 492
Walker, Martha W. V, 538
Walker, Mary I, 580
Walker, Mary I, 979
Walker, Mary I, 999
Walker, Mary II, 104
Walker, Mary II, 109
Walker, Mary II, 160
Walker, Mary II, 269
Walker, Mary II, 431
Walker, Mary II, 448
Walker, Mary II, 569
Walker, Mary II, 612
Walker, Mary II, 674
Walker, Mary II, 804
Walker, Mary II, 809
Walker, Mary II, 825
Walker, Mary II, 826
Walker, Mary II, 934
Walker, Mary II, 936
Walker, Mary II, 1018
Walker, Mary II, 1034
Walker, Mary II, 1038
Walker, Mary III, 28
Walker, Mary III, 58
Walker, Mary III, 338
Walker, Mary III, 339
Walker, Mary IV, 61
Walker, Mary IV, 65
Walker, Mary IV, 106
Walker, Mary IV, 109
Walker, Mary IV, 113
Walker, Mary IV, 162
Walker, Mary IV, 298
Walker, Mary IV, 315
Walker, Mary IV, 356
Walker, Mary IV, 545
Walker, Mary IV, 554
Walker, Mary IV, 651
Walker, Mary IV, 663
Walker, Mary IV, 782
Walker, Mary IV, 850
Walker, Mary IV, 1011
Walker, Mary IV, 1052
Walker, Mary IV, 1081
Walker, Mary V, 42
Walker, Mary V, 43
Walker, Mary V, 136
Walker, Mary V, 424
Walker, Mary V, 467
Walker, Mary V, 493
Walker, Mary V, 538
Walker, Mary V, 563
Walker, Mary V, 591
Walker, Mary V, 603
Walker, Mary V, 961
Walker, Mary VI, 364
Walker, Mary VI, 369
Walker, Mary VI, 396
Walker, Mary VI, 416
Walker, Mary VI, 431
Walker, Mary VI, 438
Walker, Mary VI, 450
Walker, Mary VI, 453
Walker, Mary VI, 454
Walker, Mary VI, 456
Walker, Mary VI, 457
Walker, Mary VI, 570
Walker, Mary VI, 576
Walker, Mary VI, 710
Walker, Mary VI, 717
Walker, Mary VI, 787
Walker, Mary VI, 790
Walker, Mary VI, 827
Walker, Mary VI, 862
Walker, Mary A. IV, 298
Walker, Mary A. V, 537
Walker, Mary A. V, 716
Walker, Mary A. VI, 862
Walker, Mary A. S. VI, 1002
Walker, Mary Ada IV, 782
Walker, Mary Ann II, 431
Walker, Mary Ann II, 792
Walker, Mary Ann II, 934
Walker, Mary Ann IV, 231
Walker, Mary Ann IV, 298
Walker, Mary Ann IV, 511
Walker, Mary Ann IV, 1383
Walker, Mary Ann IV, 1385
Walker, Mary Ann V, 538
Walker, Mary Ann V, 603
Walker, Mary Ann V, 604
Walker, Mary Ann VI, 576
Walker, Mary Craven IV, 1081
Walker, Mary D. IV, 356
Walker, Mary D. IV, 548
Walker, Mary D. IV, 555
Walker, Mary E. III, 131
Walker, Mary E. VI, 581
Walker, Mary E. VI, 582
Walker, Mary Elizabeth VI, 483
Walker, Mary Elizabeth VI, 576
Walker, Mary Elizabeth VI, 581
Walker, Mary Elizabeth VI, 582
Walker, Mary Frances V, 718
Walker, Mary H. II, 305
Walker, Mary H. IV, 298
Walker, Mary H. IV, 803
Walker, Mary H. IV, 804
Walker, Mary H. IV, 850
Walker, Mary H. VI, 576
Walker, Mary H. Walker II, 292
Walker, Mary J. VI, 839
Walker, Mary L. V, 436
Walker, Mary N. III, 338
Walker, Mary R. VI, 454
Walker, Mary R. VI, 456
Walker, Mary Ruth VI, 454
Walker, Mary Ruth VI, 576
Walker, Mary Ruth VI, 581
Walker, Mary Ruth VI, 582
Walker, Mary S. VI, 493
Walker, Mary S. VI, 576
Walker, Mary S. VI, 951
Walker, Mary T. II, 160
Walker, Mary T. III, 166
Walker, Mary T. III, 338
Walker, Mary T. IV, 1120
Walker, Mary T. E. III, 338
Walker, Mary Ten Eyck III, 208
Walker, Mary Ten Eyck III, 339
Walker, Mary Virginia I, 619
Walker, Micajah VI, 575
Walker, Micajah VI, 1010
Walker, Mildred Rosser VI, 7
Walker, Milicent I, 736
Walker, Milicent I, 738
Walker, Millisent I, 771
Walker, Minnie V, 436
Walker, Miriam IV, 56
Walker, Miriam IV, 65
Walker, Miriam IV, 554
Walker, Miriam IV, 1119
Walker, Miriam IV, 1120
Walker, Mordecai IV, 65
Walker, Mordecai V, 136
Walker, Mordecai V, 208
Walker, Mordecai V, 469
Walker, Mordecai V, 535
Walker, Mordecai V, 537
Walker, Mordecai V, 538
Walker, Mordecai V, 563
Walker, Mordecai V, 591
Walker, Mordecai V, 602
Walker, Mordecai V, 603
Walker, Mordecai V, 604
Walker, Mordecai VI, 362
Walker, Mordecai VI, 430
Walker, Mordecai VI, 444
Walker, Mordecai VI, 453
Walker, Mordecai VI, 454
Walker, Mordecai D. V, 538
Walker, Mordecai J. V, 522
Walker, Mordecai J. V, 538
Walker, Mordecai, Jr. V, 136
Walker, Mordecai, Jr. V, 493
Walker, Mordecai, Jr. V, 538
Walker, Mordicai V, 603
Walker, Nancey I, 979
Walker, Nancy I, 999
Walker, Nancy VI, 839
Walker, Nancy VI, 852
Walker, Nancy VI, 862
Walker, Nancy VI, 863
Walker, Nancy VI, 965
Walker, Nancy VI, 1010
Walker, Nancy J. M. VI, 1010
Walker, Naomi II, 793
Walker, Naomi II, 821
Walker, Naomi May IV, 783
Walker, Nathan VI, 435
Walker, Nathan VI, 453
Walker, Nathan VI, 454
Walker, Nathan VI, 493
Walker, Nathan VI, 551
Walker, Nathan VI, 576
Walker, Nathan VI, 582
Walker, Nathan M. IV, 298
Walker, Nathan U. IV, 298
Walker, Nathan U. IV, 663
Walker, Nellie B. V, 603
Walker, Olive E. IV, 1226
Walker, Ollie M. V, 424
Walker, Ollin Myron I, 950
Walker, Otis III, 339
Walker, Patience Alvira Marshall II, 934
Walker, Pearl L. I, 829
Walker, Pearl L. I, 843
Walker, Peggy VI, 862
Walker, Peletiah Jones VI, 91
Walker, Penias L. V, 961
Walker, Percy Williams III, 3
Walker, Pete R. VI, 1002
Walker, Peter VI, 1010
Walker, Peter R. II, 269
Walker, Peter R. VI, 915
Walker, Peter R. VI, 916
Walker, Peter R. VI, 920
Walker, Peter R. VI, 985
Walker, Phebe II, 249
Walker, Phebe II, 269
Walker, Phebe V, 187
Walker, Phebe V, 208
Walker, Phebe V, 404
Walker, Phebe V, 435
Walker, Phebe F. V, 208
Walker, Phebe F. V, 504
Walker, Phebe F. V, 537
Walker, Phebe F. V, 538
Walker, Phebe H. V, 208
Walker, Philip Thomas III, 33
Walker, Philip Thomas III, 33
Walker, Plesent VI, 811
Walker, Polina I, 598
Walker, Polly VI, 862
Walker, Polly C. VI, 1010
Walker, Precilla I, 999
Walker, Precilla I, 1000
Walker, R. W. I, 950
Walker, R. W., Jr. I, 950
Walker, R., Sr. VI, 985
Walker, Rachel II, 674

er, Rachel II, 686
er, Rachel IV, 231
er, Rachel IV, 265
er, Rachel IV, 295
er, Rachel IV, 298
er, Rachel IV, 308
er, Rachel IV, 660
er, Rachel IV, 663
er, Rachel IV, 882
er, Rachel IV, 885
er, Rachel V, 136
er, Rachel V, 204
er, Rachel V, 208
er, Rachel V, 537
er, Rachel V, 538
er, Rachel V, 603
er, Rachel V, 698
er, Rachel VI, 362
er, Rachel VI, 406
er, Rachel VI, 444
er, Rachel VI, 453
er, Rachel VI, 454
er, Rachel M. IV, 315
er, Rachel T. II, 934
er, Rachel T. III, 338
er, Ralph IV, 782
er, Ralph IV, 783
er, Ralph V, 961
er, Ralph O. IV, 782
er, Raymond B. V, 535
er, Ready VI, 849
er, Rebecah H. VI, 717
er, Rebecca II, 269
er, Rebecca II, 270
er, Rebecca II, 785
er, Rebecca II, 825
er, Rebecca II, 826
er, Rebecca II, 934
er, Rebecca IV, 554
er, Rebecca IV, 1297
er, Rebecca IV, 1298
er, Rebecca V, 436
er, Rebecca V, 538
er, Rebecca V, 644
er, Rebecca V, 648
er, Rebecca V, 717
er, Rebecca VI, 708
er, Rebecca VI, 710
er, Rebecca VI, 713
er, Rebecca VI, 714
er, Rebecca H. VI, 450
er, Rebecca H. VI, 453
er, Rebecca H. VI, 454
er, Rebecca H. VI, 710
er, Rebecca Jane VI, 518
er, Rebecca Jane VI, 520
er, Rebecca Jane VI, 576
er, Rebecca Jane VI, 666
er, Rebecca Jane Walker VI, 754
er, Rebekah II, 674
er, Reva E. V, 538
er, Rhoda G. V, 538
er, Rhoda G. V, 603
er, Rhoda G. V, 693
er, Rich'd L. III, 181
er, Rich. L. III, 339
er, Rich., Jr. III, 338
er, Richard I, 999
er, Richard L. III, 139
er, Richard L. III, 338
er, Richard L. III, 339
er, Richard L., Jr. III, 208
er, Richard L., Jr. III, 338
er, Richard L., Jr. III, 339
er, Ritchard I, 979
er, Robert I, 999
er, Robert III, 338
er, Robert III, 339
er, Robert VI, 575
er, Robert VI, 1010
er, Robert H. VI, 587
er, Robert I. III, 28
er, Robert I. III, 143
er, Robert I. III, 338
er, Robert I. III, 339
er, Robert J. III, 199
er, Robert J. III, 339
ker, Robert M. VI, 910
ker, Robert M. VI, 915
ker, Robert M. VI, 957
ker, Robert M. VI, 1010
ker, Robert R. II, 903
ker, Robert R. II, 934
ker, Robert R. VI, 488
ker, Robert R. VI, 538
ker, Robert R. VI, 576
ker, Robert R. VI, 577
ker, Robert R. VI, 635
ker, Robert R. VI, 677
ker, Robert R. VI, 717

Walker, Robert Roberts VI, 488
Walker, Robert, Jr. I, 979
Walker, Robert, Sr. I, 979
Walker, Robt. I. III, 338
Walker, Rosa V, 1023
Walker, Rosanna VI, 787
Walker, Roy V, 604
Walker, Roy V, 717
Walker, Ruffin I, 598
Walker, Russel V, 717
Walker, Russell V, 603
Walker, Ruth IV, 134
Walker, Ruth IV, 850
Walker, Ruth V, 136
Walker, Ruth V, 176
Walker, Ruth V, 208
Walker, Ruth V, 537
Walker, Ruth V, 538
Walker, Ruth V, 603
Walker, Ruth VI, 717
Walker, Ruth Ann IV, 1226
Walker, Ruth Anna IV, 298
Walker, Ruth E. IV, 850
Walker, Ruth Hanna IV, 313
Walker, Ruth Hannah IV, 298
Walker, Ruth Hannah IV, 315
Walker, Ruth Madona V, 1023
Walker, Ruth Sarah VI, 708
Walker, Ruth Sarah VI, 717
Walker, Ruthanna IV, 221
Walker, Ruthanna IV, 298
Walker, Ruthanna IV, 1120
Walker, Ruthanna IV, 1139
Walker, Ruthannah IV, 298
Walker, Sally VI, 834
Walker, Sally VI, 1010
Walker, Sally Maria V, 603
Walker, Sam'l. VI, 965
Walker, Samantha V, 435
Walker, Samantha M. V, 435
Walker, Samuel II, 430
Walker, Samuel II, 431
Walker, Samuel II, 674
Walker, Samuel II, 675
Walker, Samuel II, 1034
Walker, Samuel IV, 298
Walker, Samuel IV, 555
Walker, Samuel V, 136
Walker, Samuel V, 537
Walker, Samuel V, 873
Walker, Samuel VI, 849
Walker, Samuel VI, 861
Walker, Samuel VI, 862
Walker, Samuel VI, 942
Walker, Samuel G. IV, 298
Walker, Samuel G. IV, 1383
Walker, Samuel P. VI, 1010
Walker, Samuel Pancoast II, 431
Walker, Samuel T. IV, 298
Walker, Samuel T. IV, 555
Walker, Sara G. III, 338
Walker, Sarah I, 396
Walker, Sarah I, 426
Walker, Sarah I, 580
Walker, Sarah II, 269
Walker, Sarah II, 431
Walker, Sarah II, 576
Walker, Sarah II, 612
Walker, Sarah II, 674
Walker, Sarah II, 797
Walker, Sarah II, 804
Walker, Sarah II, 825
Walker, Sarah II, 849
Walker, Sarah II, 885
Walker, Sarah II, 934
Walker, Sarah II, 1019
Walker, Sarah II, 1034
Walker, Sarah II, 1062
Walker, Sarah III, 312
Walker, Sarah III, 338
Walker, Sarah III, 339
Walker, Sarah III, 373
Walker, Sarah IV, 651
Walker, Sarah IV, 663
Walker, Sarah IV, 1120
Walker, Sarah V, 467
Walker, Sarah V, 717
Walker, Sarah V, 718
Walker, Sarah VI, 373
Walker, Sarah VI, 374
Walker, Sarah VI, 406
Walker, Sarah VI, 416
Walker, Sarah VI, 448
Walker, Sarah VI, 453
Walker, Sarah VI, 454
Walker, Sarah VI, 529
Walker, Sarah VI, 546
Walker, Sarah VI, 548
Walker, Sarah VI, 564
Walker, Sarah VI, 565
Walker, Sarah VI, 575

Walker, Sarah VI, 576
Walker, Sarah VI, 577
Walker, Sarah VI, 609
Walker, Sarah VI, 831
Walker, Sarah VI, 862
Walker, Sarah VI, 864
Walker, Sarah Ann VI, 567
Walker, Sarah Ann VI, 568
Walker, Sarah Ann VI, 576
Walker, Sarah Ann VI, 1010
Walker, Sarah C. II, 896
Walker, Sarah C. II, 934
Walker, Sarah C. III, 34
Walker, Sarah C. III, 339
Walker, Sarah E. VI, 839
Walker, Sarah J. V, 208
Walker, Sarah J. V, 603
Walker, Sarah J. V, 717
Walker, Sarah Jane V, 467
Walker, Sarah Jane V, 591
Walker, Sarah Jane V, 604
Walker, Sarah Jane V, 717
Walker, Sarah M. III, 34
Walker, Sarah M. III, 339
Walker, Sarah S. V, 208
Walker, Sarah T. III, 338
Walker, Sarah T. III, 339
Walker, Sheapley VI, 814
Walker, Simpson V, 537
Walker, Sina IV, 114
Walker, Sina VI, 453
Walker, Sinah IV, 63
Walker, Sinah IV, 65
Walker, Sinah VI, 410
Walker, Sinah VI, 451
Walker, Sinah VI, 453
Walker, Sinah VI, 454
Walker, Sinah VI, 462
Walker, Sinah VI, 577
Walker, Sinia VI, 453
Walker, Sophia VI, 717
Walker, Sophia VI, 1010
Walker, Sophia Mary VI, 717
Walker, Stacy IV, 555
Walker, Stanley VI, 576
Walker, Stephen IV, 1383
Walker, Stephen A. IV, 1383
Walker, Susan VI, 454
Walker, Susan VI, 513
Walker, Susan VI, 520
Walker, Susan VI, 544
Walker, Susan VI, 570
Walker, Susan VI, 576
Walker, Susan VI, 577
Walker, Susan VI, 659
Walker, Susan VI, 717
Walker, Susan VI, 833
Walker, Susan, Sr. IV, 1297
Walker, Susanna II, 431
Walker, Susanna VI, 454
Walker, Susanna VI, 830
Walker, Susannah VI, 454
Walker, Susannah VI, 560
Walker, Susannah VI, 568
Walker, Susannah VI, 570
Walker, Susannah VI, 576
Walker, Susannah VI, 582
Walker, Tace IV, 882
Walker, Tace IV, 885
Walker, Tacy IV, 298
Walker, Tacy IV, 555
Walker, Tacy IV, 663
Walker, Tacy IV, 783
Walker, Tacy IV, 885
Walker, Tacy IV, 1120
Walker, Tacy IV, 1121
Walker, Tamer I, 1008
Walker, Tamer I, 1013
Walker, Tamson IV, 90
Walker, Tamson IV, 113
Walker, Tamson IV, 114
Walker, Tamson IV, 555
Walker, Tamson IV, 850
Walker, Thaddeus H. III, 339
Walker, Thamasin H. VI, 369
Walker, Thamasin H. VI, 454
Walker, Thamison H. VI, 453
Walker, Thamzin S. VI, 576
Walker, Theodore III, 338
Walker, Thomas II, 431
Walker, Thomas III, 173
Walker, Thomas III, 339
Walker, Thomas IV, 501
Walker, Thomas IV, 555
Walker, Thomas IV, 663
Walker, Thomas IV, 1226
Walker, Thomas VI, 862
Walker, Thomas VI, 1010
Walker, Thomas E. III, 339
Walker, Thomas Elwood IV, 298
Walker, Thomas H. IV, 1139

Walker, Thomas H. VI, 787
Walker, Thomas H. VI, 790
Walker, Thomas Jerman II, 674
Walker, Thompson IV, 221
Walker, Thompson IV, 298
Walker, Thompson IV, 1081
Walker, Thompson IV, 1120
Walker, Thompson IV, 1139
Walker, Thos. E. III, 324
Walker, Thos. E. III, 338
Walker, Uriah IV, 511
Walker, W. S. I, 319
Walker, Wallace IV, 298
Walker, Walter Edwin V, 1023
Walker, Watson A. IV, 298
Walker, Watson I. VI, 862
Walker, Wd. Ann II, 448
Walker, Wd. Elizabeth II, 49
Walker, Wd. Elizabeth II, 109
Walker, Wd. Elizabeth II, 431
Walker, Wd. Leah VI, 565
Walker, Wd. Phebe II, 789
Walker, Will J. V, 137
Walker, William I, 580
Walker, William I, 736
Walker, William I, 979
Walker, William I, 999
Walker, William II, 431
Walker, William IV, 65
Walker, William IV, 554
Walker, William IV, 555
Walker, William IV, 1011
Walker, William IV, 1119
Walker, William V, 17
Walker, William V, 136
Walker, William V, 204
Walker, William V, 208
Walker, William V, 287
Walker, William V, 469
Walker, William V, 535
Walker, William V, 537
Walker, William V, 538
Walker, William V, 603
Walker, William VI, 453
Walker, William VI, 454
Walker, William VI, 564
Walker, William VI, 575
Walker, William VI, 577
Walker, William VI, 827
Walker, William VI, 847
Walker, William VI, 856
Walker, William VI, 862
Walker, William VI, 865
Walker, William VI, 1010
Walker, William H. I, 736
Walker, William H. V, 603
Walker, William H. V, 604
Walker, William H. V, 717
Walker, William H. VI, 809
Walker, William H. VI, 862
Walker, William I. VI, 1010
Walker, William I., Jr. VI, 951
Walker, William I., Jr. VI, 1010
Walker, William Standley VI, 576
Walker, William Thomas III, 339
Walker, Willie D. V, 435
Walker, Willie D. V, 436
Walker, Willis IV, 850
Walker, Willis J. IV, 850
Walker, Willliam VI, 387
Walker, Wilmoth VI, 915
Walker, Winifred IV, 510
Walker, Winifred IV, 555
Walker, Wm. II, 601
Walker, Wm. II, 674
Walker, Wm. II, 849
Walker, Wm. II, 934
Walker, Wm. IV, 1011
Walker, Wm. IV, 1120
Walker, Wm. V, 208
Walker, Wm. V, 312
Walker, Wm. V, 403
Walker, Wm. V, 435
Walker, Wm. V, 467
Walker, Wm. VI, 548
Walker, Wm. Franklin I, 619
Walker, Wm. H. V, 591
Walker, Wm. H. V, 603
Walker, Wm. H. V, 604
Walker, Wm. H. V, 717
Walker, Wm. I. VI, 949
Walker, Wm. L. II, 1082
Walker, Wm. M. III, 338
Walker, Wm. Smith VI, 836
Walker, Wm. W. VI, 815
Walker-Lupton, Leah VI, 566
Walker-Lupton, Leah VI, 567
Walker-Lupton, Leah VI, 571
Walkers, Elizabeth I, 319
Walkir, Anna I, 980
Walkir, Anna I, 999

Walkup, Anderson V, 436
Walkup, Daniel V, 436
Walkup, Emma V, 436
Walkup, Martha V, 436
Walkup, Rachel V, 436
Walkup, Susanna V, 420
Walkup, Susanna V, 436
Walkup, Susannah V, 436
Wall, ??? III, 339
Wall, Abigail III, 339
Wall, Absalom V, 538
Wall, Absolam V, 538
Wall, Achsa I, 771
Wall, Agness I, 410
Wall, Agness I, 426
Wall, Alexander J. III, 152
Wall, Alexander J. III, 339
Wall, Alexander J., Jr. III, 339
Wall, Alice V, 539
Wall, Alice V, 718
Wall, Alphonso V, 539
Wall, Alphronso O. V, 538
Wall, Alson I, 771
Wall, Amy Christina V, 539
Wall, Ann C. V, 515
Wall, Ann C. V, 538
Wall, Ann C. V, 539
Wall, Ann R. III, 282
Wall, Ann R. III, 339
Wall, Ann R. III, 498
Wall, Anna Frances III, 346
Wall, Augusta III, 339
Wall, Azariah V, 538
Wall, Azariah V, 539
Wall, Azariah Leech V, 538
Wall, Azariah, Jr. V, 538
Wall, B. Frank V, 538
Wall, Bayard T. V, 538
Wall, Bessie V, 718
Wall, Britain I, 771
Wall, Brittain I, 771
Wall, Bulie I, 626
Wall, Burlie I, 627
Wall, Burlie I, 641
Wall, Burlie I, 642
Wall, Charles B. VI, 862
Wall, Christina V, 538
Wall, Comfort I, 580
Wall, Delilah I, 580
Wall, Edith III, 282
Wall, Edith III, 339
Wall, Edith V, 681
Wall, Edith V, 718
Wall, Elizabeth V, 631
Wall, Elizabeth V, 648
Wall, Elizabeth VI, 862
Wall, Emily III, 339
Wall, Emma E. III, 339
Wall, Ethel May V, 498
Wall, Eunice V, 538
Wall, Eunice V, 539
Wall, Eunice O. V, 538
Wall, Franklin V, 539
Wall, Franklin R. I, 771
Wall, George VI, 881
Wall, George R. V, 539
Wall, George R. V, 718
Wall, George Robert V, 718
Wall, Grace M. V, 1026
Wall, Granville V, 539
Wall, Hannah I, 691
Wall, Hannah V, 539
Wall, Hannah V, 718
Wall, Hannah B. V, 539
Wall, Hannah P. V, 718
Wall, Henry I, 771
Wall, Henry V, 718
Wall, Henry Ann VI, 862
Wall, Henry M. V, 538
Wall, Humphrey III, 282
Wall, Humphrey III, 339
Wall, Isaac III, 339
Wall, Isaac V, 538
Wall, Isaac C. III, 339
Wall, James III, 339
Wall, James B. III, 339
Wall, Jane V, 472
Wall, Jane V, 538
Wall, Jereter I, 691
Wall, Jesse I, 753
Wall, Joana IV, 623
Wall, Joana IV, 663
Wall, John I, 580
Wall, John I, 753
Wall, John I, 771
Wall, John I, 843
Wall, John II, 27
Wall, John II, 42
Wall, John II, 43
Wall, John V, 538
Wall, John A. I, 771

Wall, Joseph I, 580
Wall, Joseph I, 753
Wall, Joseph W. I, 771
Wall, Joshua I, 580
Wall, Lillian B. III, 152
Wall, Lillian B. III, 339
Wall, Lillie I, 626
Wall, Lillie I, 627
Wall, Lillie I, 641
Wall, Lillie I, 642
Wall, Lorenz Wohlager III, 339
Wall, Lucy Alice V, 539
Wall, M. Henry V, 539
Wall, M. Henry V, 718
Wall, Mahlon V, 539
Wall, Mahlon Henry V, 538
Wall, Margaret V, 539
Wall, Margaret V, 718
Wall, Mariam I, 759
Wall, Mariam I, 771
Wall, Martha I, 569
Wall, Martha I, 580
Wall, Martha I, 771
Wall, Martha VI, 881
Wall, Mary II, 786
Wall, Mary V, 539
Wall, Mary V, 648
Wall, Mary Ann I, 616
Wall, Mary Ann VI, 454
Wall, Mary Ann VI, 717
Wall, Mary Ann VI, 787
Wall, Matthias III, 339
Wall, Milly VI, 895
Wall, Minnie V, 648
Wall, Nellie E. V, 539
Wall, Nelson I, 771
Wall, Orville V, 681
Wall, Orville V, 718
Wall, Phebe I, 580
Wall, Phebe I, 843
Wall, Phebe V, 487
Wall, Phebe V, 538
Wall, Phebe V, 539
Wall, Philip III, 346
Wall, Poly Bott VI, 895
Wall, Rebecca V, 538
Wall, Rebecca V, 539
Wall, Rebecca Ann V, 609
Wall, Rebecca Ann V, 648
Wall, Rebeccah V, 538
Wall, Rebeckah V, 538
Wall, Renee III, 339
Wall, Renee III, 346
Wall, Renee III, 347
Wall, Richard I, 580
Wall, Richard II, 431
Wall, Richard II, 528
Wall, Richard II, 675
Wall, Robert D. V, 538
Wall, Robert D. V, 539
Wall, Ruth V, 538
Wall, Samuel I, 771
Wall, Sarah I, 771
Wall, Sarah II, 1034
Wall, Sarah III, 191
Wall, Sarah III, 339
Wall, Sarah V, 647
Wall, Sarah V, 648
Wall, Sarah Ann III, 339
Wall, Thomas V, 538
Wall, Thomas Leaton V, 498
Wall, Thomas Leighton V, 538
Wall, Vinnie Corene V, 539
Wall, Viola V, 718
Wall, Viola K. V, 539
Wall, William III, 339
Wall, William V, 538
Wall, William H. III, 339
Wall, William M. III, 339
Wall, William U. III, 339
Wall, Willy VI, 895
Wall, Zelta V. V, 538
Wallace, Abraham V, 1023
Wallace, Achsah Ann III, 339
Wallace, Adaline S. V, 772
Wallace, Albert V, 1023
Wallace, Allen III, 339
Wallace, Ann E. IV, 486
Wallace, Ann E. IV, 501
Wallace, Ann F. VI, 862
Wallace, Anna Barnes II, 934
Wallace, Anna E. V, 758
Wallace, Anna E. V, 772
Wallace, Annie P. III, 26
Wallace, Annie P. III, 339
Wallace, Annie Pancoast III, 339
Wallace, B. Proctor IV, 1191
Wallace, Bell D. V, 1023
Wallace, Bertha IV, 850
Wallace, Bertha V, 1023
Wallace, Bessie IV, 783
Wallace, Carey V, 287
Wallace, Carey M. V, 287
Wallace, Carrie A. V, 1023
Wallace, Cassandra II, 675
Wallace, Catherine V, 718
Wallace, Chanie V, 1023
Wallace, Chas. V, 388
Wallace, Deborah IV, 501
Wallace, Easther II, 431
Wallace, Edna V, 718
Wallace, Edward II, 675
Wallace, Edward Lew II, 934
Wallace, Edward Lew III, 339
Wallace, Eleanor III, 449
Wallace, Eliza VI, 1013
Wallace, Eliza W. VI, 844
Wallace, Elizabeth II, 431
Wallace, Elizabeth II, 587
Wallace, Elizabeth II, 659
Wallace, Elizabeth II, 675
Wallace, Elizabeth V, 287
Wallace, Elizabeth V, 1023
Wallace, Elizabeth VI, 1010
Wallace, Elizabeth E. IV, 850
Wallace, Elsie Barnes II, 934
Wallace, Emma V, 388
Wallace, Emma Barnes II, 934
Wallace, Esther II, 431
Wallace, Eva V, 1023
Wallace, Everett V, 718
Wallace, Fay V, 287
Wallace, Flossie V, 1023
Wallace, Geo. V, 1023
Wallace, George Grier II, 934
Wallace, Grace V, 718
Wallace, Hannah II, 675
Wallace, Hannah VI, 1010
Wallace, Harrison V, 1023
Wallace, Hudson V, 1023
Wallace, Huldah V, 1023
Wallace, John II, 675
Wallace, John II, 934
Wallace, John III, 26
Wallace, John III, 339
Wallace, John S. I, 624
Wallace, John W. VI, 862
Wallace, Joseph Jacob II, 587
Wallace, Leslie V, 467
Wallace, Lesta V, 287
Wallace, Luke VI, 1010
Wallace, Lydia II, 675
Wallace, Margaret III, 206
Wallace, Marian Coe IV, 1342
Wallace, Martha J. V, 1023
Wallace, Mary II, 91
Wallace, Mary II, 109
Wallace, Mary II, 675
Wallace, Mary V, 1023
Wallace, Mary VI, 862
Wallace, Mary A. V, 604
Wallace, Mary L. V, 718
Wallace, Milicent I, 51
Wallace, Milicent I, 77
Wallace, Milisant I, 77
Wallace, Mollie V, 1023
Wallace, Mrs. Belle V, 1023
Wallace, Mrs. Bessie IV, 783
Wallace, Mrs. Coe IV, 1342
Wallace, Nellie V, 1023
Wallace, Pearl L. I, 624
Wallace, Polly VI, 829
Wallace, Proctor IV, 1191
Wallace, Rebecca VI, 1013
Wallace, Richard W. VI, 862
Wallace, Robert II, 431
Wallace, Rose Jenett V, 1023
Wallace, S. V, 388
Wallace, Samuel II, 431
Wallace, Samuel II, 675
Wallace, Sarah II, 675
Wallace, Sarah VI, 829
Wallace, Sarah F. IV, 380
Wallace, Sarah F. IV, 451
Wallace, William IV, 850
Wallace, William IV, 1297
Wallace, William V, 287
Wallace, William VI, 829
Wallace, William VI, 1010
Wallace, William A. IV, 298
Wallace, William B. V, 981
Wallace, Winfield V, 604
Wallace, Wm. V, 1023
Wallack, Martha J. V, 1023
Wallader, Rees IV, 51
Wallader, Ruth IV, 51
Wallbank, Agness II, 675
Wallbank, Edward II, 675
Wallby, John II, 675
Wallby, Susannah II, 675
Wallen, Mary E. II, 139
Wallens, Elizabeth M. II, 293
Wallens, Elizabeth M. II, 305
Waller, Charlotte IV, 1342
Waller, Charlotte P. IV, 1342
Waller, Edward Mintor V, 939
Waller, Edwin V, 939
Waller, Effie IV, 298
Waller, James IV, 298
Waller, Mrs. Mildred IV, 783
Waller, Phebe E. V, 1023
Waller, Rev. Harry IV, 783
Waller, Sylvia V, 1023
Walles, Elizabeth I, 1039
Walley, Naomi II, 978
Walley, Naomi II, 1034
Wallheimer, John II, 431
Wallice, Easther II, 431
Wallice, Elizabeth II, 431
Wallice, Robert II, 431
Wallick, Martha J. V, 1023
Wallin, ??? III, 339
Wallin, Edward III, 339
Wallin, Huldah S. IV, 298
Wallin, Thomas II, 269
Walling, Geo. V, 1023
Walling, Sarah V, 1023
Wallington, Mary II, 489
Wallington, Mary II, 675
Wallis, ??? III, 339
Wallis, Cassandra II, 675
Wallis, Edward II, 675
Wallis, Edward III, 339
Wallis, Elizabeth II, 587
Wallis, Elizabeth II, 675
Wallis, Elizabeth II, 676
Wallis, Ester II, 448
Wallis, Esther II, 448
Wallis, Hannah II, 675
Wallis, John II, 675
Wallis, Joseph II, 448
Wallis, Joseph Jacob II, 675
Wallis, Lydia II, 675
Wallis, Mary II, 448
Wallis, Mary II, 675
Wallis, Milisant I, 77
Wallis, Robert II, 448
Wallis, Samuel II, 675
Wallis, Sarah II, 675
Wallis, Thomas II, 675
Walliss, Esther II, 448
Walliss, Robert II, 448
Wallman, Annie V, 1024
Walln, Hannah II, 550
Walln, Hannah II, 675
Walln, Jane II, 675
Walln, John II, 675
Walln, Mary II, 652
Walln, Mary II, 675
Walln, Richard II, 675
Walln, Sarah II, 675
Wallon, Emma V, 1024
Wallon, Hiram V, 1024
Wallon, Martha VI, 855
Wallon, Michael V, 1024
Wallon, Robert VI, 855
Wallower, Helen III, 503
Walls, Comfort I, 555
Walls, Comfort I, 580
Walls, Comfort VI, 251
Walls, Delilah I, 580
Walls, Dorothy V, 1024
Walls, Emma V, 1026
Walls, Ethel V, 1026
Walls, Grace M. V, 1026
Walls, Hannah I, 691
Walls, Jessie V, 1026
Walls, John II, 448
Walls, John V, 1024
Walls, Joshua I, 580
Walls, Mary VI, 858
Walls, Minnie V, 1024
Walls, Peggy VI, 966
Walls, Sarah II, 1034
Wally, Naomi II, 1034
Walmley, Edward M. II, 305
Walmsbury, Thomas II, 187
Walmsbury, Wd. Elizabeth H. II, 187
Walmsley, Abby L. II, 1086
Walmsley, Abby L. II, 1087
Walmsley, Abby L. II, 1089
Walmsley, Agnes II, 592
Walmsley, Agnes II, 675
Walmsley, Asa II, 1056
Walmsley, Asa II, 1062
Walmsley, Edward H. Foster II, 950
Walmsley, Eliza II, 971
Walmsley, Eliza H. II, 1056
Walmsley, Eliza H. II, 1062
Walmsley, Eliza H. II, 1063
Walmsley, Eliza H. II, 1086
Walmsley, Emma J. II, 948
Walmsley, Emma J. II, 950
Walmsley, Emma J. II, 1087
Walmsley, Emma J. II, 1089
Walmsley, Emma Jane II, 1062
Walmsley, Emma Jane IV, 417
Walmsley, Emma W. II, 1050
Walmsley, Emma W. II, 1063
Walmsley, Janes II, 971
Walmsley, Marianna II, 1089
Walmsley, Marianna W. II, 1057
Walmsley, Marianna W. II, 1063
Walmsley, Mary II, 1056
Walmsley, Mary II, 1062
Walmsley, Mary III, 463
Walmsley, Mary Anna II, 1062
Walmsley, Morton A. II, 971
Walmsley, Morton A. II, 1056
Walmsley, Morton A. II, 1062
Walmsley, Morton A. II, 1063
Walmsley, Morton A. II, 1086
Walmsley, Morton A. II, 1087
Walmsley, Morton A. II, 1089
Walmsley, Richard II, 772
Walmsley, Sarah III, 455
Walmsley, Sarah III, 463
Walmsley, Silas III, 463
Walmsley, Thomas II, 592
Walmsley, Thomas II, 675
Walmsley, Thomas III, 463
Walmsley, William III, 455
Walmsley, William III, 463
Walmsley, Wm. II, 592
Walmsley, Wm. II, 675
Walmsley, Wm. Mason II, 675
Waln, Ann II, 431
Waln, Ann II, 675
Waln, Ann V, 467
Waln, Eliza II, 675
Waln, Elizabeth II, 431
Waln, Elizabeth II, 454
Waln, Elizabeth II, 509
Waln, Elizabeth II, 675
Waln, Elizabeth II, 693
Waln, Ellen II, 772
Waln, Ellin II, 431
Waln, Emma II, 934
Waln, Emma C. II, 934
Waln, Hannah II, 431
Waln, Hannah II, 550
Waln, Hannah II, 632
Waln, Hannah II, 675
Waln, Jacob II, 431
Waln, Jacob S. II, 676
Waln, Jacob Shoemaker II, 676
Waln, Jacob Simcock II, 675
Waln, Jane II, 431
Waln, Jane II, 596
Waln, Jane II, 675
Waln, Jane, Jr. II, 675
Waln, Jesse III, 340
Waln, John II, 431
Waln, John II, 596
Waln, John II, 675
Waln, John II, 693
Waln, Joseph II, 431
Waln, Joseph II, 676
Waln, Joseph VI, 454
Waln, Joseph Wm. V, 467
Waln, Lewis II, 676
Waln, Martha V, 467
Waln, Mary II, 431
Waln, Mary II, 649
Waln, Mary II, 675
Waln, Mary II, 676
Waln, Mary III, 340
Waln, Mary B. II, 886
Waln, Mary B. II, 934
Waln, Millie V, 467
Waln, Nicholas II, 431
Waln, Nicholas II, 454
Waln, Nicholas II, 634
Waln, Nicholas II, 649
Waln, Nicholas II, 652
Waln, Nicholas II, 675
Waln, Patterson Hartshorne II, 1034
Waln, Phebe II, 676
Waln, Rachel II, 431
Waln, Rebecca II, 415
Waln, Rebecca II, 639
Waln, Rebecca II, 676
Waln, Rebecca III, 340
Waln, Richard II, 431
Waln, Richard II, 649
Waln, Richard II, 675
Waln, Richard, Jr. II, 431
Waln, Richard, Jr. II, 454
Waln, Richard, Jr. II, 675
Waln, Robert II, 431
Waln, Robert II, 675
Waln, Robert II, 676
Waln, Robert II, 1000
Waln, Robert II, 1034
Waln, Sarah II, 634
Waln, Sarah II, 652
Waln, Sarah II, 675
Waln, Sarah II, 1014
Waln, Sarah II, 1034
Waln, Sarah III, 340
Waln, Susan II, 639
Waln, Susanna II, 431
Waln, Susanna II, 579
Waln, Susanna II, 675
Waln, Susannah II, 675
Waln, Susannah II, 1000
Waln, Susannah II, 1034
Waln, Thomas V, 467
Waln, Wd. Hannah II, 675
Waln, William II, 431
Walne, Ann II, 431
Walne, Ann II, 675
Walne, Ellin II, 431
Walne, Jane II, 431
Walne, Mary II, 474
Walne, Mary II, 490
Walne, Mary II, 675
Walne, Mary II, 693
Walne, Nicholas II, 431
Walne, Richard II, 431
Walne, Richard II, 448
Walne, Richard, Jr. II, 675
Walne, Susannah II, 579
Walne, Susannah II, 675
Walner, Rachel II, 567
Walner, Rachel II, 676
Walpert, Hazel IV, 1044
Walpole, Gregory II, 53
Walpole, Sarah II, 53
Walrond, Anna VI, 940
Walrond, Benj., Jr. VI, 1010
Walrond, Benja. VI, 940
Walrond, Benjamin VI, 1006
Walrond, Benjamin, Jr. VI, 94
Walrond, Benjamin, Jr. VI, 10
Walrond, Bevaly VI, 1010
Walrond, Calvin VI, 902
Walrond, Calvin VI, 915
Walrond, Calvin VI, 1010
Walrond, Catharine VI, 1010
Walrond, Elizabeth VI, 1010
Walrond, John P. VI, 921
Walrond, Lydia A. VI, 948
Walrond, Mary Jane VI, 921
Walrond, Moses VI, 974
Walrond, Moses VI, 991
Walrond, Moses VI, 1010
Walrond, Nancy VI, 1010
Walrond, Pattsey VI, 1010
Walrond, Rebecca VI, 940
Walrond, Sally VI, 1010
Walrond, Samuel VI, 1010
Walrond, Thomas VI, 1010
Walroud, Elizabeth VI, 820
Walroud, John VI, 820
Wals, Pokehunters VI, 922
Walsh, ??? III, 340
Walsh, Catherine VI, 862
Walsh, Edward V, 208
Walsh, Emily III, 340
Walsh, James VI, 862
Walsheid, ??? III, 207
Walsheid, ??? III, 340
Walsheid, Dorothy Selma III,
Walsheid, Dorothy Selma III,
Walston, ??? I, 19
Walston, Sarah E. I, 19
Waltear, Walter II, 448
Walten, Abi II, 721
Walten, Charles II, 772
Walten, Francis L. II, 721
Walten, George Thomson II, 8
Walten, Lucy Lea II, 825
Walten, Margery II, 825
Walten, Mary V, 209
Walten, Rodman II, 825
Walter, Abigail IV, 322
Walter, Abigail IV, 356
Walter, Agnes III, 340
Walter, Alfred III, 194
Walter, Alfred III, 340
Walter, Alfred W. III, 340
Walter, Ann II, 641
Walter, Ann II, 676
Walter, Anna II, 676
Walter, Anna III, 77
Walter, Anna III, 224
Walter, Anna III, 340
Walter, Anna III, 348
Walter, Anna V, 1024
Walter, Anna M. III, 153
Walter, Anna Maria II, 714

er, Anna S. VI, 788
er, Anna Walter III, 148
er, B. Franklin III, 449
er, Bennett G. IV, 356
er, Branson Hollowell
IV, 356
er, Caroline E. III, 340
er, Charles F. V, 506
er, Chas. IV, 815
er, Chlotilda IV, 946
er, Christy IV, 677
er, Deborah III, 77
er, Deborah III, 147
er, Deborah III, 340
er, Eleanor III, 449
er, Eleanor V, 603
er, Eleanor V, 604
er, Eliz. III, 340
er, Eliza H. III, 40
er, Elizabeth II, 528
er, Elizabeth II, 676
er, Elizabeth III, 148
er, Elizabeth III, 340
er, Elizabeth Ann II, 935
er, Elizabeth H. III, 40
er, Elizabeth H. III, 340
er, Ellwood III, 40
er, Ellwood III, 77
er, Ellwood III, 147
er, Ellwood III, 153
er, Ellwood III, 340
er, Ellwood, Jr. III, 340
er, Emilie III, 340
er, Emily IV, 356
er, Emma II, 934
er, Emma W. II, 957
er, Esther II, 431
er, Esther II, 676
er, Eva May II, 934
er, George T. II, 934
er, Gertrude II, 935
er, Hannah II, 676
er, Hannah IV, 356
er, Hannah V, 311
er, Hannah V, 312
er, Helen III, 340
er, Helen M. IV, 815
er, Henrietta II, 741
er, Henrietta II, 772
er, Henrietta D. II, 934
er, Henry II, 708
er, Henry III, 340
ter, Hiram II, 934
ter, Israel II, 934
ter, Iva Catherine IV, 677
ter, J. Alfred II, 935
ter, J. Thompkins II, 934
ter, Jame M. IV, 299
ter, James IV, 677
ter, Jane IV, 299
ter, Jane H. II, 957
ter, Jane M. IV, 299
ter, Jean III, 449
ter, Jemima II, 676
ter, John Alfred II, 935
ter, Joseph II, 957
ter, Joseph Horace II, 935
ter, Joseph Warner II, 934
ter, Julia T. II, 708
ter, Katharine V, 304
ter, Katharine V, 312
ter, Lena III, 340
ter, Lewis IV, 946
ter, Luetta IV, 299
ter, Lydia II, 676
ter, Marianna III, 77
ter, Martha V, 1024
ter, Mary I, 625
ter, Mary II, 351
ter, Mary V, 208
ter, Mary V, 539
ter, Mary Anna II, 802
ter, Mary E. IV, 299
ter, Mary J. II, 934
ter, Mary J. II, 938
ter, Mary Jeanes II, 827
ter, Mary Luella V, 1024
ter, Naomi II, 934
ter, Phebe II, 676
ter, Phebe IV, 322
ter, Phebe IV, 356
ter, Phebe IV, 1081
ter, Rachel P. II, 934
ter, Rachel S. II, 708
ter, Rebecca II, 351
ter, Rebecca II, 641
ter, Regina Henrietta III, 194
ter, Regina Henrietta III, 340
ter, Roger II, 676
ter, Sarah II, 431
ter, Sarah II, 676
Walter, Sarah II, 825
Walter, Sarah III, 147
Walter, Sarah III, 148
Walter, Sarah III, 340
Walter, Sarah IV, 253
Walter, Sarah IV, 299
Walter, Sarah IV, 741
Walter, Sarah IV, 783
Walter, Sarah R. II, 825
Walter, Sarah R. II, 934
Walter, Sarah R. II, 938
Walter, Sidney IV, 253
Walter, Thomas II, 934
Walter, Thomas III, 340
Walter, Thomas IV, 114
Walter, Thomas IV, 253
Walter, Thomas B. III, 148
Walter, Thomas Burling III, 148
Walter, Thomas, Jr. III, 340
Walter, Thomas, Jr. IV, 65
Walter, Thos. II, 825
Walter, Thos. III, 340
Walter, Viola V, 1024
Walter, Walter IV, 356
Walter, Wm. IV, 322
Walter, Wm. E. II, 935
Walter, Wm. Emley II, 935
Walter, Wm. P. II, 934
Walter, Wm. P. II, 938
Walter, Wm. Penn II, 825
Walters, A. J. IV, 1044
Walters, Albert IV, 1342
Walters, Albert J. IV, 1044
Walters, Alice I, 636
Walters, Alice I, 642
Walters, Alice Cordelia I, 620
Walters, Alice F. I, 642
Walters, Alice L. I, 627
Walters, Ann II, 480
Walters, Ann II, 676
Walters, Ann III, 340
Walters, Ann VI, 685
Walters, Ann VI, 717
Walters, Anna II, 676
Walters, Anna M. II, 811
Walters, Anthony III, 340
Walters, Anthony Lockwood
III, 340
Walters, Benajah VI, 1010
Walters, Bennett G. IV, 356
Walters, Branson Hollowell
IV, 356
Walters, Caroline III, 340
Walters, Caroline P. III, 463
Walters, Catharine III, 340
Walters, Celine V, 939
Walters, Charles E. I, 642
Walters, Charles Elliott I, 627
Walters, Charles Elliott I, 642
Walters, Charles F. I, 620
Walters, Charles F. I, 627
Walters, Charles Stephen I, 636
Walters, Charles Stephen I, 642
Walters, Daniel III, 340
Walters, Daniel D. III, 340
Walters, Dinah VI, 577
Walters, Dinah VI, 607
Walters, Dinah VI, 623
Walters, Dinah VI, 680
Walters, Dinah VI, 717
Walters, Dinah VI, 718
Walters, Dola I, 625
Walters, Dorothy IV, 1342
Walters, Edward III, 340
Walters, Eileen Alice IV, 1044
Walters, Eleonor III, 463
Walters, Elisabeth I, 614
Walters, Elisabeth Rosa I, 614
Walters, Elisabeth Swain I, 627
Walters, Elizabeth I, 641
Walters, Elizabeth I, 642
Walters, Elizabeth I, 933
Walters, Elizabeth III, 340
Walters, Elizabeth III, 415
Walters, Elizabeth III, 463
Walters, Elizabeth IV, 1180
Walters, Elizabeth IV, 1191
Walters, Elizabeth VI, 691
Walters, Elizabeth VI, 717
Walters, Elizabeth VI, 1010
Walters, Ellen Rose IV, 1044
Walters, Emily IV, 356
Walters, Emily VI, 454
Walters, Esther II, 431
Walters, Esther IV, 494
Walters, Esther IV, 501
Walters, Felix III, 340
Walters, Felix M. III, 75
Walters, Felix M. III, 340
Walters, Felix M. III, 463
Walters, Florence Alice I, 627
Walters, Florence Alice I, 642
Walters, Franklin III, 463
Walters, George VI, 577
Walters, George VI, 607
Walters, George VI, 623
Walters, George VI, 680
Walters, George VI, 717
Walters, George VI, 718
Walters, George W. IV, 1191
Walters, George W. VI, 718
Walters, Hannah II, 676
Walters, Henrietta D. II, 318
Walters, Henrietta D. II, 326
Walters, Isaac VI, 607
Walters, Isaac VI, 717
Walters, James VI, 577
Walters, James VI, 607
Walters, James VI, 717
Walters, Jane II, 822
Walters, Jean III, 463
Walters, Jemima II, 676
Walters, Joel B. I, 627
Walters, John IV, 1191
Walters, John B. IV, 1191
Walters, John James IV, 1191
Walters, John James VI, 718
Walters, Joseph III, 340
Walters, Joseph III, 437
Walters, Joseph III, 463
Walters, Judith VI, 577
Walters, Judith VI, 607
Walters, Judith VI, 623
Walters, Judith VI, 625
Walters, Judith VI, 717
Walters, Judith VI, 718
Walters, Judith VI, 721
Walters, Lanta I, 642
Walters, Lanta F. I, 627
Walters, Libbie IV, 1266
Walters, Lyddia II, 326
Walters, Lydia I, 542
Walters, Lydia I, 580
Walters, Lydia II, 676
Walters, Lydia III, 340
Walters, Lydia IV, 1191
Walters, Lydia VI, 577
Walters, Lydia VI, 602
Walters, Lydia VI, 607
Walters, Lydia VI, 656
Walters, Lydia VI, 679
Walters, Lydia VI, 680
Walters, Lydia VI, 685
Walters, Lydia VI, 718
Walters, Lydia VI, 722
Walters, Lydia F. IV, 1191
Walters, Lydia F. VI, 718
Walters, Mahlon IV, 1180
Walters, Mahlon IV, 1191
Walters, Mahlon VI, 607
Walters, Mahlon VI, 691
Walters, Mahlon VI, 717
Walters, Margery F. II, 326
Walters, Maria Jane II, 787
Walters, Martha III, 75
Walters, Martha III, 340
Walters, Martha III, 463
Walters, Martha T. III, 340
Walters, Mary III, 340
Walters, Mary V, 137
Walters, Mary V, 200
Walters, Mary V, 287
Walters, Mary V, 539
Walters, Mary Ann IV, 395
Walters, Mary Ann IV, 451
Walters, Mary C. IV, 1170
Walters, Mary C. IV, 1191
Walters, Mary E. IV, 1191
Walters, Mary Elizabeth IV, 1191
Walters, Mary Elizabeth VI, 718
Walters, Mary Ella I, 627
Walters, Mary N. VI, 718
Walters, Mary N. VI, 722
Walters, Mr. ??? IV, 1342
Walters, Mrs. ??? IV, 1342
Walters, Myrtle I, 627
Walters, Myrtle I, 642
Walters, Nancy N. IV, 1180
Walters, Nancy N. IV, 1191
Walters, Nancy N. VI, 691
Walters, Nancy N. VI, 718
Walters, Nellie IV, 1044
Walters, Phebe III, 340
Walters, Phebe IV, 451
Walters, Reuben III, 340
Walters, Roger II, 676
Walters, Rosa I, 625
Walters, Rosa I, 627
Walters, Rosa Ellen I, 642
Walters, Ruth I, 627
Walters, Ruth III, 340
Walters, Ruth, Jr. III, 340
Walters, Sarah III, 437
Walters, Sarah III, 464
Walters, Sarah VI, 477
Walters, Sarah VI, 577
Walters, Sarah VI, 607
Walters, Sarah VI, 626
Walters, Sarah VI, 718
Walters, Sarah C. IV, 1191
Walters, Sophia IV, 1342
Walters, Stephen III, 340
Walters, Stephen L. III, 340
Walters, Thomas IV, 114
Walters, Thomas IV, 1191
Walters, Thomas VI, 577
Walters, Thomas VI, 607
Walters, Thomas VI, 718
Walters, Thomas VI, 722
Walters, Thomas H. IV, 1191
Walters, William I, 642
Walters, William A. III, 340
Walters, William P. IV, 1191
Walters, William P. VI, 718
Walters, Wm. I, 614
Walters, Wm. I, 625
Walters, Wm. I, 627
Walters, Wm. IV, 1191
Walters, Wm. P. IV, 1191
Walthal, Eliza P. V, 718
Walthal, Francis V, 978
Walthal, John VI, 830
Walthal, Margaret V, 161
Walthal, Margaret V, 209
Walthal, Margaret V, 539
Walthal, Maria E. V, 718
Walthal, Sarah V, 539
Walthal, Sarah V, 978
Walthal, Thomas V, 539
Walthal, Thomas V, 718
Walthall, Alex. B. VI, 862
Walthall, Alta V, 649
Walthall, Ann V, 649
Walthall, Bailey V, 649
Walthall, Celina VI, 862
Walthall, Daniel V, 649
Walthall, Daniel B. V, 491
Walthall, Daniel B. V, 539
Walthall, Daniel B. V, 649
Walthall, Daniel B. VI, 143
Walthall, David V, 615
Walthall, David V, 649
Walthall, David VI, 143
Walthall, Edith V, 649
Walthall, Edith E. V, 649
Walthall, Elijah D. V, 649
Walthall, Eliza P. V, 649
Walthall, Elizabeth V, 624
Walthall, Elizabeth V, 648
Walthall, Elizabeth V, 649
Walthall, Elizabeth VI, 101
Walthall, Elizabeth VI, 123
Walthall, Elizabeth VI, 143
Walthall, Elizabeth VI, 862
Walthall, Elizabeth Ann V, 616
Walthall, Elizabeth Ann V, 631
Walthall, Elizabeth H. V, 539
Walthall, Ellen V, 649
Walthall, Ezra A. V, 649
Walthall, Ezra Allen V, 649
Walthall, Francis V, 979
Walthall, Francis VI, 140
Walthall, Francis VI, 142
Walthall, Francis VI, 143
Walthall, Frederick IV, 1342
Walthall, Gurney V, 649
Walthall, Hannah V, 649
Walthall, Henry VI, 862
Walthall, Isaac G. VI, 862
Walthall, Jane VI, 136
Walthall, Jane VI, 142
Walthall, John V, 649
Walthall, John F. V, 649
Walthall, John G. V, 649
Walthall, Josiah F. V, 649
Walthall, Josiah T. V, 649
Walthall, Judith A. J. VI, 862
Walthall, Levi F. V, 649
Walthall, Louisa V, 615
Walthall, Louisa V, 649
Walthall, Louisa C. V, 649
Walthall, Louisa V. VI, 862
Walthall, Margaret V, 539
Walthall, Margaret V, 616
Walthall, Margaret V, 649
Walthall, Maria E. V, 488
Walthall, Maria E. V, 539
Walthall, Maria E. V, 649
Walthall, Mariah E. V, 649
Walthall, Marie E. V, 649
Walthall, Marion E. V, 488
Walthall, Marion E. V, 539
Walthall, Martha V, 611
Walthall, Martha V, 624
Walthall, Martha V, 628
Walthall, Martha V, 648
Walthall, Martha VI, 130
Walthall, Martha VI, 142
Walthall, Martha VI, 143
Walthall, Martha A. V, 611
Walthall, Martha A. V, 649
Walthall, Martha A. VI, 862
Walthall, Martha Ann VI, 143
Walthall, Mary VI, 819
Walthall, Mary F. VI, 824
Walthall, Mary Martha V, 649
Walthall, Micajah VI, 140
Walthall, Robert VI, 862
Walthall, Robert H. VI, 862
Walthall, Robert M. V, 649
Walthall, Samuel V, 649
Walthall, Sarah V, 539
Walthall, Sarah V, 628
Walthall, Sarah V, 648
Walthall, Sarah V, 649
Walthall, Sarah V, 979
Walthall, Sarah VI, 140
Walthall, Sarah VI, 142
Walthall, Sarah VI, 143
Walthall, Sarah E. V, 649
Walthall, Sarah Emily V, 649
Walthall, Susannah VI, 117
Walthall, Susannah VI, 118
Walthall, Thomas V, 488
Walthall, Thomas V, 539
Walthall, Thomas V, 616
Walthall, Thomas V, 649
Walthall, Thomas VI, 101
Walthall, Thomas VI, 117
Walthall, Thomas VI, 118
Walthall, Thomas VI, 123
Walthall, Thomas VI, 142
Walthall, Thomas VI, 143
Walthall, Thos. V, 631
Walthall, Thos. V, 649
Walthall, Thos. VI, 811
Walthall, William V, 624
Walthall, William V, 648
Walthall, William V, 649
Walthall, William VI, 142
Walthall, William B. V, 649
Walthall, William B. VI, 130
Walthall, William B. VI, 142
Walthall, William B. VI, 143
Walthall, Wm. V, 611
Walthall, Wm. V, 628
Walthall, Wm. V, 649
Walthall, Wm. A. V, 649
Walthall, Wm. B. V, 649
Waltin, Eunice IV, 480
Waltin, James Joseph II, 721
Waltin, Samuel II, 721
Waltin, Sarah J. II, 721
Walton, ??? I, 13
Walton, ??? VI, 778
Walton, ??? VI, 788
Walton, A. V, 539
Walton, Abbie II, 711
Walton, Abbie Rebecca W.
III, 280
Walton, Abby II, 703
Walton, Abby II, 704
Walton, Abby II, 709
Walton, Abby IV, 389
Walton, Abby IV, 451
Walton, Abel John IV, 851
Walton, Abi II, 431
Walton, Abi II, 574
Walton, Abi II, 676
Walton, Abi II, 711
Walton, Abi II, 721
Walton, Abi II, 730
Walton, Abi II, 752
Walton, Abi II, 772
Walton, Abi II, 773
Walton, Abi IV, 451
Walton, Abi IV, 598
Walton, Abigail IV, 53
Walton, Abigail IV, 65
Walton, Abigail IV, 66
Walton, Abigail Hunt VI, 607
Walton, Abraham IV, 42
Walton, Abraham IV, 53
Walton, Abraham IV, 65
Walton, Abraham IV, 66
Walton, Abraham IV, 69
Walton, Abraham IV, 70
Walton, Abraham IV, 607
Walton, Abraham IV, 663
Walton, Abraham IV, 783
Walton, Abraham IV, 827
Walton, Abraham IV, 851
Walton, Abraham IV, 915
Walton, Abraham V, 539

Walton, Abraham, Jr. IV, 66
Walton, Abraham, Jr. IV, 782
Walton, Abraham, Jr. IV, 783
Walton, Abraham, Jr. IV, 851
Walton, Abraham, Sr. IV, 851
Walton, Abram IV, 663
Walton, Abram V, 539
Walton, Achsa II, 676
Walton, Achsah II, 825
Walton, Achsah II, 871
Walton, Achsah II, 928
Walton, Achsah II, 935
Walton, Achsah IV, 663
Walton, Achsah IV, 783
Walton, Acksa II, 676
Walton, Ada L. I, 934
Walton, Addie IV, 639
Walton, Adelaide Y. II, 800
Walton, Albert G. V, 939
Walton, Alexandria III, 341
Walton, Alfred II, 431
Walton, Alfred II, 676
Walton, Alice V, 209
Walton, Allen II, 825
Walton, Allen II, 935
Walton, Amos III, 340
Walton, Amos III, 341
Walton, Amos IV, 65
Walton, Amos IV, 114
Walton, Amos IV, 663
Walton, Amos IV, 783
Walton, Amos IV, 1011
Walton, Amos IV, 1012
Walton, Amos V, 539
Walton, Andrew VI, 600
Walton, Ann II, 269
Walton, Ann II, 276
Walton, Ann IV, 42
Walton, Ann IV, 114
Walton, Ann IV, 299
Walton, Ann IV, 690
Walton, Ann IV, 765
Walton, Ann IV, 782
Walton, Ann IV, 783
Walton, Ann IV, 827
Walton, Ann IV, 851
Walton, Ann IV, 885
Walton, Ann IV, 989
Walton, Ann IV, 1011
Walton, Ann IV, 1019
Walton, Ann V, 539
Walton, Ann VI, 729
Walton, Ann VI, 788
Walton, Ann B. II, 1082
Walton, Ann J. IV, 42
Walton, Ann J. IV, 66
Walton, Ann S. III, 92
Walton, Ann S. III, 341
Walton, Ann W. II, 269
Walton, Anna II, 431
Walton, Anna II, 676
Walton, Anna II, 721
Walton, Anna II, 773
Walton, Anna IV, 451
Walton, Anna IV, 607
Walton, Anna IV, 663
Walton, Anna IV, 1012
Walton, Anna V, 539
Walton, Anna VI, 751
Walton, Anna VI, 786
Walton, Anna VI, 787
Walton, Anna VI, 788
Walton, Anna Barnitz VI, 755
Walton, Anna E. V, 209
Walton, Anna L. IV, 371
Walton, Anna L. IV, 451
Walton, Anna Louisa VI, 788
Walton, Anna Maria IV, 1012
Walton, Anna Mariah IV, 1139
Walton, Anna Marie IV, 1011
Walton, Anna S. IV, 555
Walton, Anna S. VI, 789
Walton, Anna S. VI, 793
Walton, Anne IV, 663
Walton, Anne IV, 1011
Walton, Anne Garrett II, 721
Walton, Anne M. II, 825
Walton, Anne M. II, 935
Walton, Anne M. III, 341
Walton, Anne Mariah IV, 1012
Walton, Annie II, 773
Walton, Annie II, 825
Walton, Annie L. IV, 451
Walton, Annie L. IV, 513
Walton, Annie L. IV, 555
Walton, Anzanetta IV, 88
Walton, Anzanette IV, 114
Walton, Anzonetta IV, 1011
Walton, Anzonetta IV, 1012
Walton, Asenath I, 867
Walton, Asenath I, 876
Walton, Asenath I, 904
Walton, Atlantic Ocean VI, 424
Walton, Atlantic Ocean VI, 454
Walton, Attie V, 209
Walton, Bathsheba IV, 29
Walton, Bathsheba IV, 65
Walton, Bathsheba IV, 66
Walton, Bathsheba IV, 783
Walton, Bathsheba IV, 812
Walton, Bathsheba IV, 851
Walton, Bathsheba IV, 858
Walton, Bathsheba IV, 860
Walton, Bathsheba IV, 917
Walton, Benj. IV, 1011
Walton, Benjamin I, 904
Walton, Benjamin II, 431
Walton, Benjamin II, 676
Walton, Benjamin II, 825
Walton, Benjamin II, 933
Walton, Benjamin II, 935
Walton, Benjamin IV, 42
Walton, Benjamin IV, 62
Walton, Benjamin IV, 65
Walton, Benjamin IV, 66
Walton, Benjamin IV, 69
Walton, Benjamin IV, 114
Walton, Benjamin IV, 783
Walton, Benjamin IV, 865
Walton, Benjamin IV, 885
Walton, Benjamin IV, 932
Walton, Benjamin IV, 1011
Walton, Benjamin IV, 1012
Walton, Benjamin IV, 1031
Walton, Benjamin Ferris II, 676
Walton, Benjamin O. II, 935
Walton, Benjamin Tomkins II, 676
Walton, Bernard III, 155
Walton, Bernard III, 341
Walton, Bertha VI, 788
Walton, Bessie Louella V, 209
Walton, Bessie R. V, 209
Walton, Betsey Ann I, 904
Walton, Betsy Ann I, 878
Walton, Betty V, 188
Walton, Betty V, 209
Walton, Betty VI, 454
Walton, Beulah II, 701
Walton, Brewer Gehley II, 825
Walton, Caroline II, 1082
Walton, Caroline H. II, 935
Walton, Catharine VI, 841
Walton, Catherine V, 189
Walton, Catherine V, 191
Walton, Catherine V, 209
Walton, Charles II, 305
Walton, Charles II, 431
Walton, Charles II, 676
Walton, Charles II, 721
Walton, Charles II, 772
Walton, Charles II, 773
Walton, Charles II, 935
Walton, Charles II, 1074
Walton, Charles II, 1082
Walton, Charles V, 539
Walton, Charles J. II, 773
Walton, Charles James II, 676
Walton, Charles Joseph II, 721
Walton, Charles Morris II, 825
Walton, Charles, Jr. II, 935
Walton, Chlotilda IV, 1011
Walton, Choltilda IV, 1012
Walton, Clara H. II, 935
Walton, Clarkson I, 867
Walton, Clarkson I, 904
Walton, Daniel II, 488
Walton, Daniel II, 676
Walton, David II, 269
Walton, David II, 276
Walton, David II, 676
Walton, David III, 341
Walton, David IV, 65
Walton, David IV, 66
Walton, David IV, 851
Walton, David IV, 885
Walton, David IV, 917
Walton, David VI, 729
Walton, David VI, 730
Walton, David VI, 732
Walton, David VI, 786
Walton, David VI, 788
Walton, David VI, 789
Walton, David G. III, 341
Walton, Deborah II, 322
Walton, Deborah II, 676
Walton, Deborah II, 721
Walton, Deborah IV, 1011
Walton, Deborah IV, 1012
Walton, Deborah IV, 1117
Walton, Deborah IV, 1120
Walton, Deborah IV, 1139
Walton, Deborah V, 159
Walton, Deborah V, 163
Walton, Deborah V, 188
Walton, Deborah V, 209
Walton, Deborah V, 253
Walton, Deborah V, 287
Walton, Deborah VI, 454
Walton, Deborah C. IV, 1012
Walton, Deborah Catherine V, 209
Walton, Deborah D. IV, 1012
Walton, Deborah L. II, 326
Walton, Deborah L. II, 772
Walton, Deborah L. II, 773
Walton, Deborah Lundy II, 326
Walton, Deborah T. IV, 1120
Walton, Deida I, 867
Walton, Didah I, 875
Walton, Didah I, 904
Walton, Dinah V, 196
Walton, Dinah V, 209
Walton, Dora E. II, 935
Walton, Dora E. III, 341
Walton, Dorothy V, 209
Walton, Dorothy VI, 788
Walton, Dr. Alfred G. III, 417
Walton, Eber IV, 663
Walton, Eber Achsah IV, 663
Walton, Edith IV, 851
Walton, Edith IV, 917
Walton, Edith V, 209
Walton, Edith Echo V, 209
Walton, Edward II, 935
Walton, Edward V, 137
Walton, Edward V, 159
Walton, Edward V, 163
Walton, Edward V, 188
Walton, Edward V, 209
Walton, Edward V, 287
Walton, Edward VI, 454
Walton, Edward VI, 767
Walton, Edward VI, 788
Walton, Edward VI, 789
Walton, Edward H. II, 935
Walton, Edward H. IV, 664
Walton, Edward Haviland III, 341
Walton, Edward Hicks II, 825
Walton, Edward Hicks III, 341
Walton, Edward R. V, 209
Walton, Edward Reed V, 209
Walton, Edward T. V, 209
Walton, Edward U. IV, 664
Walton, Edward, Jr. IV, 664
Walton, Edward, Jr. V, 209
Walton, Eli IV, 1011
Walton, Eli IV, 1012
Walton, Elias IV, 917
Walton, Elias H. V, 939
Walton, Eliz. III, 464
Walton, Eliza II, 825
Walton, Eliza IV, 925
Walton, Eliza IV, 962
Walton, Eliza IV, 1011
Walton, Eliza IV, 1012
Walton, Eliza Ann IV, 1012
Walton, Eliza Ann IV, 1015
Walton, Eliza Mifflin II, 825
Walton, Elizabeth II, 257
Walton, Elizabeth II, 269
Walton, Elizabeth II, 431
Walton, Elizabeth II, 488
Walton, Elizabeth II, 600
Walton, Elizabeth II, 676
Walton, Elizabeth II, 721
Walton, Elizabeth II, 750
Walton, Elizabeth II, 772
Walton, Elizabeth II, 783
Walton, Elizabeth II, 825
Walton, Elizabeth II, 928
Walton, Elizabeth II, 935
Walton, Elizabeth III, 341
Walton, Elizabeth IV, 299
Walton, Elizabeth IV, 851
Walton, Elizabeth IV, 1011
Walton, Elizabeth V, 209
Walton, Elizabeth V, 214
Walton, Elizabeth V, 963
Walton, Elizabeth VI, 749
Walton, Elizabeth VI, 755
Walton, Elizabeth VI, 788
Walton, Elizabeth VI, 789
Walton, Elizabeth VI, 862
Walton, Elizabeth A. I, 753
Walton, Elizabeth A. I, 853
Walton, Elizabeth Amanda I, 771
Walton, Elizabeth Ann V, 209
Walton, Elizabeth B. IV, 851
Walton, Elizabeth D. VI, 772
Walton, Elizabeth Hopkins VI, 765
Walton, Elizabeth L. II, 773
Walton, Elizabeth R. III, 92
Walton, Elizabeth R. III, 341
Walton, Ella II, 821
Walton, Ellen III, 228
Walton, Ellen III, 341
Walton, Ellen V, 209
Walton, Ellen VI, 755
Walton, Ellen VI, 765
Walton, Ellen VI, 788
Walton, Ellen H. II, 861
Walton, Ellen T. IV, 1031
Walton, Ellwood II, 772
Walton, Ellwood II, 773
Walton, Emeline IV, 1241
Walton, Emily II, 794
Walton, Emma II, 825
Walton, Emma II, 933
Walton, Emma II, 935
Walton, Emma III, 318
Walton, Emma VI, 788
Walton, Emma J. II, 825
Walton, Emma L. II, 935
Walton, Emma L. II, 1067
Walton, Emma L. II, 1074
Walton, Emma L. II, 1082
Walton, Emmer C. IV, 1012
Walton, Emmor C. IV, 1011
Walton, Esther I, 77
Walton, Esther III, 341
Walton, Esther V, 939
Walton, Esther C. V, 939
Walton, Esther H. IV, 895
Walton, Ethen A. V, 209
Walton, Eunice I, 1055
Walton, Eunice V, 159
Walton, Eunice V, 209
Walton, Eunice VI, 454
Walton, Eunice VI, 592
Walton, Eunice VI, 593
Walton, Eunice VI, 603
Walton, Eunice VI, 607
Walton, Eva May II, 825
Walton, Ezra II, 322
Walton, Ezra II, 326
Walton, Fanny II, 676
Walton, Fanny B. VI, 777
Walton, Fanny B. VI, 778
Walton, Fanny B. VI, 788
Walton, Ferris Price II, 861
Walton, Frances Janney II, 935
Walton, Francis II, 721
Walton, Francis II, 773
Walton, Francis II, 825
Walton, Francis IV, 275
Walton, Francis L. II, 721
Walton, Francis Lightfoot II, 721
Walton, Francis S. IV, 437
Walton, Franklin I, 867
Walton, Gabriel II, 431
Walton, Gabriel IV, 65
Walton, George I, 19
Walton, George I, 64
Walton, George I, 73
Walton, George I, 77
Walton, George I, 87
Walton, George I, 172
Walton, George I, 173
Walton, George I, 177
Walton, George I, 201
Walton, George I, 234
Walton, George I, 259
Walton, George A. II, 935
Walton, George A. VI, 841
Walton, George A. VI, 862
Walton, George Arthur II, 935
Walton, George C. II, 935
Walton, George F. I, 77
Walton, George T. II, 935
Walton, George Thomson II, 825
Walton, Gilpen F. II, 933
Walton, Gilpen F. II, 935
Walton, Grace V, 209
Walton, Hannah II, 469
Walton, Hannah II, 518
Walton, Hannah II, 574
Walton, Hannah II, 676
Walton, Hannah II, 773
Walton, Hannah II, 825
Walton, Hannah III, 228
Walton, Hannah III, 341
Walton, Hannah IV, 663
Walton, Hannah IV, 865
Walton, Hannah IV, 885
Walton, Hannah IV, 932
Walton, Hannah IV, 1011
Walton, Hannah IV, 1012
Walton, Hannah V, 149
Walton, Hannah V, 163
Walton, Hannah V, 209
Walton, Hannah VI, 454
Walton, Hannah VI, 591
Walton, Hannah VI, 607
Walton, Hannah VI, 755
Walton, Hannah Ann II, 721
Walton, Hannah Chandlee VI, 607
Walton, Hannah K. II, 469
Walton, Hannah K. II, 676
Walton, Hannah K. II, 772
Walton, Harriet Disher II, 8
Walton, Harriet Maria IV, 10
Walton, Harriett Emily IV, 1
Walton, Helen Marie V, 209
Walton, Henry I, 867
Walton, Henry I, 904
Walton, Henry II, 431
Walton, Henry B. I, 753
Walton, Henry B. I, 771
Walton, Henry T. V, 209
Walton, Herman V, 209
Walton, Hettie V, 187
Walton, Hettie V, 209
Walton, Hiram II, 750
Walton, Hiram II, 772
Walton, Hiram II, 935
Walton, Homer V, 209
Walton, Howard VI, 788
Walton, Howard T. II, 935
Walton, Irene I, 867
Walton, Isaac III, 341
Walton, Isaac III, 370
Walton, Isaac L. V, 209
Walton, Isaac Marion III, 341
Walton, Isabel I, 73
Walton, Isabel I, 77
Walton, Isabel I, 201
Walton, Isabella I, 64
Walton, Isabella I, 77
Walton, Isabella I, 86
Walton, Isabella I, 139
Walton, Isabella I, 177
Walton, Israel II, 825
Walton, J. Barnard II, 935
Walton, J. Bernard III, 341
Walton, Jacob II, 825
Walton, Jacob II, 887
Walton, Jacob II, 935
Walton, Jacob II, 976
Walton, Jacob II, 1034
Walton, Jacob, Jr. II, 976
Walton, Jacob, Jr. II, 1034
Walton, Jacob, Jr. IV, 1383
Walton, James I, 904
Walton, James II, 469
Walton, James II, 574
Walton, James II, 676
Walton, James II, 722
Walton, James II, 772
Walton, James II, 773
Walton, James II, 825
Walton, James II, 871
Walton, James II, 928
Walton, James II, 935
Walton, James IV, 282
Walton, James IV, 299
Walton, James IV, 371
Walton, James IV, 451
Walton, James IV, 513
Walton, James IV, 555
Walton, James IV, 783
Walton, James V, 939
Walton, James Edward II, 82
Walton, James Edward II, 93
Walton, James Edward IV, 66
Walton, James Joseph II, 721
Walton, James L. III, 81
Walton, James L. III, 341
Walton, James L. V, 939
Walton, James M. II, 935
Walton, James M. III, 341
Walton, James Morris II, 825
Walton, James W. IV, 851
Walton, James, Jr. II, 469
Walton, James, Jr. II, 676
Walton, Jane II, 721
Walton, Jane II, 752
Walton, Jane II, 773
Walton, Jane II, 825
Walton, Jane II, 1074
Walton, Jane II, 1082
Walton, Jane IV, 851
Walton, Jane VI, 600
Walton, Jane Kirkbride II, 82
Walton, Jehu IV, 114
Walton, Jehu IV, 783
Walton, Jehu IV, 989
Walton, Jehu IV, 1011
Walton, Jemima I, 200
Walton, Jemima Ann VI, 732
Walton, Jemima Toms I, 201
Walton, Jeremiah III, 464

ton, Jesse IV, 114
ton, Jesse IV, 690
ton, Jesse IV, 765
ton, Jesse IV, 783
ton, Jesse IV, 851
ton, Jesse IV, 885
ton, Jesse IV, 1011
ton, Jesse IV, 1012
ton, Jesse IV, 1019
ton, Jesse IV, 1120
ton, Jesse P. II, 935
ton, Jesse Pusey II, 935
ton, Job McCarty IV, 851
ton, John I, 867
ton, John I, 904
ton, John II, 825
ton, John II, 935
ton, John III, 341
ton, John IV, 65
ton, John IV, 66
ton, John IV, 851
ton, John IV, 860
ton, John IV, 885
ton, John IV, 917
ton, John IV, 1241
ton, John V, 209
ton, John Dingee IV, 66
ton, John E. V, 209
ton, John Edward V, 209
ton, John F. II, 861
ton, John F. III, 92
ton, John F. III, 341
ton, John T. II, 676
ton, John T. II, 825
ton, John T. II, 935
ton, John Tomkins II, 935
ton, John Tompkins II, 825
ton, John Tompkins, Sr. II, 825
ton, Jonathan II, 1074
ton, Jonathan II, 1082
ton, Jonathan IV, 66
ton, Jonathan IV, 783
ton, Jonathan IV, 851
ton, Jonathan IV, 943
ton, Jonathan IV, 962
ton, Jonathan IV, 1011
ton, Jonathan IV, 1012
ton, Jonathan IV, 1120
ton, Jonathan C. IV, 783
ton, Jonathan C. IV, 935
ton, Jonathan C. IV, 1011
ton, Jonathan T. IV, 1012
ton, Jonathan Walton IV, 1012
ton, Joseph I, 867
ton, Joseph I, 904
ton, Joseph II, 431
ton, Joseph II, 574
ton, Joseph II, 676
ton, Joseph II, 721
ton, Joseph II, 730
ton, Joseph II, 752
ton, Joseph II, 772
ton, Joseph II, 773
ton, Joseph IV, 65
ton, Joseph IV, 299
ton, Joseph IV, 451
ton, Joseph IV, 598
ton, Joseph IV, 851
ton, Joseph IV, 885
ton, Joseph IV, 917
ton, Joseph IV, 1383
ton, Joseph Barnard II, 935
ton, Joseph Elias IV, 885
ton, Joseph Haviland III, 341
ton, Joseph Hefford V, 209
ton, Joseph J. II, 721
ton, Joseph J. II, 773
ton, Joseph J. IV, 451
lton, Joseph James II, 773
ton, Joseph James III, 341
ton, Joseph Marsh IV, 851
ton, Joseph Paxton IV, 851
lton, Joseph S. II, 935
ton, Joseph T. III, 341
ton, Joseph Townsend IV, 851
ton, Joseph V. IV, 783
lton, Joseph, Jr. II, 772
lton, Joshua P. V, 939
ton, Josiah II, 825
ton, Josiah II, 826
lton, Josiah II, 922
lton, Josiah II, 935
lton, Josiah IV, 783
lton, Josiah IV, 1011
ton, Josiah IV, 1012
lton, Josiah IV, 1117
lton, Josiah IV, 1120
lton, Josiah IV, 1139
lton, Judson Todd V, 209
Walton, Julia II, 935
Walton, Julia II, 944
Walton, Julia V, 718
Walton, Juliette V, 649
Walton, Jullietta V, 649
Walton, July Etta V, 639
Walton, July Etta V, 649
Walton, Katherine Litty IV, 783
Walton, Leander IV, 1011
Walton, Leander IV, 1012
Walton, Levi II, 431
Walton, Lewis I, 867
Walton, Lewis I, 904
Walton, Lewis II, 825
Walton, Lewis II, 935
Walton, Lewis IV, 783
Walton, Lewis IV, 1011
Walton, Lewis B. II, 935
Walton, Lewis Brosius Walton II, 935
Walton, Lewis Phillip VI, 755
Walton, Lindley H. I, 904
Walton, Lindley M. I, 771
Walton, Lindley M. H. I, 753
Walton, Louisa II, 721
Walton, Louisa S. II, 773
Walton, Louisa S. IV, 299
Walton, Louisa S. IV, 451
Walton, Louisa S. VI, 767
Walton, Louisa S. VI, 789
Walton, Louise III, 155
Walton, Louise III, 341
Walton, Louise S. VI, 767
Walton, Louiza J. IV, 275
Walton, Louiza J. IV, 299
Walton, Lovisa IV, 437
Walton, Lovisa IV, 451
Walton, Lucy III, 341
Walton, Lucy VI, 788
Walton, Lucy Lea II, 825
Walton, Lutitia I, 753
Walton, Lutitia I, 764
Walton, Lutitia I, 771
Walton, Lututia I, 771
Walton, Luzena I, 867
Walton, Luzena I, 893
Walton, Luzena I, 904
Walton, Lydia II, 825
Walton, Lydia II, 976
Walton, Lydia II, 1034
Walton, Lydia III, 67
Walton, Lydia III, 300
Walton, Lydia IV, 114
Walton, Lydia IV, 738
Walton, Lydia IV, 783
Walton, Lydia IV, 851
Walton, Lydia IV, 885
Walton, Lydia IV, 917
Walton, Lydia IV, 1011
Walton, Lydia IV, 1012
Walton, Lydia V, 939
Walton, Lydia Ann IV, 851
Walton, Lydia Ann IV, 917
Walton, Lydia L. II, 773
Walton, Lydia M. I, 753
Walton, Lydia Martitia I, 771
Walton, Lydia R. II, 326
Walton, LydiaThornton II, 825
Walton, Margaret I, 77
Walton, Margaret I, 221
Walton, Margaret I, 259
Walton, Margaret II, 804
Walton, Margaret II, 825
Walton, Margaret II, 935
Walton, Margaret IV, 66
Walton, Margaret IV, 299
Walton, Margaret IV, 798
Walton, Margaret IV, 851
Walton, Margery II, 326
Walton, Margery II, 825
Walton, Margery F. II, 935
Walton, Maria IV, 962
Walton, Maria IV, 1011
Walton, Maria IV, 1120
Walton, Mariah IV, 1012
Walton, Marietta IV, 1011
Walton, Marietta E. III, 161
Walton, Martha II, 922
Walton, Martha II, 935
Walton, Martha II, 1082
Walton, Martha IV, 42
Walton, Martha IV, 65
Walton, Martha IV, 66
Walton, Martha IV, 663
Walton, Martha IV, 783
Walton, Martha IV, 851
Walton, Martha IV, 885
Walton, Martha IV, 917
Walton, Martha VI, 862
Walton, Martha A. I, 904
Walton, Martha E. V, 209
Walton, Martha L. IV, 851
Walton, Mary I, 13
Walton, Mary I, 19
Walton, Mary I, 36
Walton, Mary I, 77
Walton, Mary I, 87
Walton, Mary I, 234
Walton, Mary II, 431
Walton, Mary II, 676
Walton, Mary II, 721
Walton, Mary II, 799
Walton, Mary II, 825
Walton, Mary II, 826
Walton, Mary II, 922
Walton, Mary II, 935
Walton, Mary III, 341
Walton, Mary III, 453
Walton, Mary III, 464
Walton, Mary IV, 62
Walton, Mary IV, 63
Walton, Mary IV, 65
Walton, Mary IV, 66
Walton, Mary IV, 69
Walton, Mary IV, 70
Walton, Mary IV, 607
Walton, Mary IV, 663
Walton, Mary IV, 783
Walton, Mary IV, 827
Walton, Mary IV, 828
Walton, Mary IV, 851
Walton, Mary IV, 914
Walton, Mary IV, 915
Walton, Mary IV, 917
Walton, Mary V, 163
Walton, Mary V, 196
Walton, Mary V, 209
Walton, Mary V, 214
Walton, Mary VI, 454
Walton, Mary VI, 600
Walton, Mary VI, 1010
Walton, Mary A. I, 884
Walton, Mary A. VI, 778
Walton, Mary Abby III, 341
Walton, Mary Ann II, 788
Walton, Mary Ann II, 824
Walton, Mary Ann IV, 783
Walton, Mary Ann IV, 851
Walton, Mary Ann IV, 852
Walton, Mary Ann IV, 962
Walton, Mary Ann IV, 1011
Walton, Mary C. II, 887
Walton, Mary C. II, 935
Walton, Mary D. III, 306
Walton, Mary Eleanor III, 72
Walton, Mary Emily IV, 851
Walton, Mary Foster III, 81
Walton, Mary H. II, 730
Walton, Mary H. II, 773
Walton, Mary Jamima II, 772
Walton, Mary Jane IV, 1005
Walton, Mary Jane IV, 1011
Walton, Mary Jane IV, 1012
Walton, Mary Jane IV, 1120
Walton, Mary Jane IV, 1139
Walton, Mary Jemima II, 773
Walton, Mary John IV, 66
Walton, Mary John IV, 851
Walton, Mary Lydia V, 209
Walton, Mary Parkings VI, 607
Walton, Mary R. II, 935
Walton, Mary S. II, 773
Walton, Mary S. II, 935
Walton, Mary Shaw II, 825
Walton, Maryann IV, 1100
Walton, Maryann IV, 1120
Walton, Michael II, 431
Walton, Michael II, 600
Walton, Michael II, 676
Walton, Michal II, 518
Walton, Michal II, 676
Walton, Milo V, 209
Walton, Milo V, 718
Walton, Morris VI, 788
Walton, Moses IV, 851
Walton, Moses V, 163
Walton, Moses V, 196
Walton, Moses V, 198
Walton, Moses V, 209
Walton, Moses V, 211
Walton, Moses V, 214
Walton, Moses V, 253
Walton, Moses V, 287
Walton, Moses VI, 454
Walton, Moses VI, 591
Walton, Moses VI, 607
Walton, Nancie I, 934
Walton, Nancy VI, 862
Walton, Nancy C. I, 753
Walton, Nancy Corrinna I, 771
Walton, Nathan IV, 66
Walton, Nathan IV, 783
Walton, Nathan IV, 851
Walton, Nathan IV, 1011
Walton, Nathan IV, 1012
Walton, Nathaniel II, 470
Walton, Nathaniel II, 676
Walton, Oliver C. IV, 851
Walton, Oliver Edward VI, 755
Walton, Penelope I, 931
Walton, Penninah I, 77
Walton, Phebe II, 269
Walton, Phebe II, 276
Walton, Phebe IV, 663
Walton, Phebe V, 939
Walton, Phebe VI, 788
Walton, Phebe A. IV, 851
Walton, Polly V, 209
Walton, Priscilla II, 560
Walton, Priscilla S. IV, 299
Walton, Prudence III, 341
Walton, Prudence III, 370
Walton, Rach Barrett IV, 66
Walton, Rachel II, 804
Walton, Rachel II, 976
Walton, Rachel II, 1034
Walton, Rachel II, 1082
Walton, Rachel IV, 53
Walton, Rachel IV, 65
Walton, Rachel IV, 66
Walton, Rachel IV, 663
Walton, Rachel IV, 782
Walton, Rachel IV, 783
Walton, Rachel V, 198
Walton, Rachel V, 209
Walton, Rachel B. IV, 664
Walton, Rachel Barrett IV, 851
Walton, Rachel Hollingsworth VI, 607
Walton, Rachel P. II, 825
Walton, Rachel P. II, 892
Walton, Rachel P. II, 935
Walton, Rachel Shinn VI, 607
Walton, Rachel W. II, 1082
Walton, Rebecca II, 431
Walton, Rebecca II, 565
Walton, Rebecca II, 710
Walton, Rebecca II, 721
Walton, Rebecca II, 750
Walton, Rebecca II, 772
Walton, Rebecca II, 964
Walton, Rebecca IV, 299
Walton, Rebecca IV, 451
Walton, Rebecca IV, 989
Walton, Rebecca VI, 729
Walton, Rebecca VI, 730
Walton, Rebecca VI, 788
Walton, Rebecca A. IV, 989
Walton, Rebecca A. IV, 1012
Walton, Rebecca Ann IV, 1011
Walton, Rebecca Ann IV, 1012
Walton, Rebecca Ann IV, 1120
Walton, Rebecca Ann IV, 1139
Walton, Rebecca Catherine V, 209
Walton, Rebecca J. II, 933
Walton, Rebecca J. II, 935
Walton, Rebecca S. II, 971
Walton, Rebecca W. II, 861
Walton, Rebecca W. III, 259
Walton, Rebecca Walmsley II, 816
Walton, Rebeccah II, 676
Walton, Rhoda IV, 851
Walton, Richard W. VI, 865
Walton, Ridgway S. II, 935
Walton, Ridgway Stockton II, 825
Walton, Robert III, 341
Walton, Robert V, 539
Walton, Robert VI, 862
Walton, Robert J. II, 935
Walton, Robert James II, 825
Walton, Robert Jeanes II, 935
Walton, Robert R. VI, 828
Walton, Rodman II, 825
Walton, Rosella V, 209
Walton, Rufus I, 904
Walton, Rufus P. I, 867
Walton, Rufus P. I, 904
Walton, Ruth IV, 42
Walton, Ruth IV, 62
Walton, Ruth IV, 65
Walton, Ruth IV, 66
Walton, Ruth IV, 69
Walton, Ruth IV, 663
Walton, Ruth IV, 943
Walton, Ruth IV, 1011
Walton, Ruth V, 191
Walton, Ruth V, 209
Walton, Ruth V, 939
Walton, Ruth Etta V, 209
Walton, S. Francis IV, 299
Walton, S. Francis IV, 451
Walton, Saml. II, 703
Walton, Samuel I, 867
Walton, Samuel I, 904
Walton, Samuel II, 440
Walton, Samuel II, 448
Walton, Samuel II, 721
Walton, Samuel II, 773
Walton, Samuel IV, 299
Walton, Samuel IV, 389
Walton, Samuel IV, 451
Walton, Samuel IV, 555
Walton, Samuel IV, 576
Walton, Samuel IV, 598
Walton, Samuel V, 189
Walton, Samuel V, 191
Walton, Samuel V, 209
Walton, Samuel VI, 420
Walton, Samuel VI, 454
Walton, Samuel VI, 600
Walton, Samuel VI, 607
Walton, Samuel B. VI, 749
Walton, Samuel B. VI, 765
Walton, Samuel B. VI, 788
Walton, Samuel B. VI, 789
Walton, Samuel Francis IV, 451
Walton, Samuel Moses V, 209
Walton, Samuel White I, 172
Walton, Sara IV, 851
Walton, Sarah I, 77
Walton, Sarah I, 234
Walton, Sarah I, 259
Walton, Sarah II, 431
Walton, Sarah II, 448
Walton, Sarah II, 676
Walton, Sarah II, 703
Walton, Sarah II, 887
Walton, Sarah II, 935
Walton, Sarah IV, 299
Walton, Sarah IV, 389
Walton, Sarah IV, 451
Walton, Sarah IV, 935
Walton, Sarah IV, 1011
Walton, Sarah IV, 1012
Walton, Sarah VI, 420
Walton, Sarah VI, 600
Walton, Sarah VI, 607
Walton, Sarah VI, 786
Walton, Sarah VI, 788
Walton, Sarah VI, 789
Walton, Sarah Alice V, 209
Walton, Sarah Ann III, 341
Walton, Sarah Brown VI, 607
Walton, Sarah E. VI, 789
Walton, Sarah J. II, 721
Walton, Sarah J. II, 773
Walton, Sarah J. III, 106
Walton, Sarah J. IV, 299
Walton, Sarah J. IV, 451
Walton, Sarah J. IV, 555
Walton, Sarah J. IV, 576
Walton, Sarah J. IV, 598
Walton, Sarah Jane III, 85
Walton, Sarah Jane III, 341
Walton, Sarah Jane III, 370
Walton, Sarah L. V, 209
Walton, Sarah M. V, 939
Walton, Silas II, 269
Walton, Silas II, 276
Walton, Silas II, 1034
Walton, Silas VI, 788
Walton, Sina IV, 299
Walton, Sina R. IV, 282
Walton, Sina R. IV, 283
Walton, Sina R. IV, 299
Walton, Sina R. IV, 451
Walton, Stacy P. III, 341
Walton, Susan Cadwaller II, 783
Walton, Susan M. II, 871
Walton, Susan M. II, 935
Walton, Susan M. III, 341
Walton, Susan Morris II, 744
Walton, Susan T. II, 825
Walton, Susan T. II, 935
Walton, Susana I, 905
Walton, Susanna I, 867
Walton, Susanna I, 904
Walton, Susannah Morris II, 825
Walton, Sydney M. II, 828
Walton, T. Blakey II, 1082
Walton, Tace IV, 1011
Walton, Tacy IV, 114
Walton, Tacy IV, 690
Walton, Tacy IV, 783
Walton, Talton I, 934
Walton, Tazetta IV, 661
Walton, Tazetta IV, 664
Walton, Tazette IV, 779
Walton, Tazette IV, 783
Walton, Thomas II, 560
Walton, Thomas II, 676
Walton, Thomas III, 341
Walton, Thomas III, 453

Walton, Thomas III, 464
Walton, Thomas VI, 836
Walton, Thomas C. I, 904
Walton, Thomas C. F. I, 867
Walton, Thomas Heston IV, 851
Walton, Thornton IV, 664
Walton, Thornton IV, 783
Walton, Timothy IV, 1383
Walton, Unice VI, 591
Walton, Unice VI, 607
Walton, Unis VI, 598
Walton, Unis VI, 600
Walton, Unis VI, 607
Walton, Uree IV, 114
Walton, Uree IV, 765
Walton, Uree IV, 783
Walton, Uree IV, 1011
Walton, Urie IV, 783
Walton, Virginia IV, 783
Walton, Virginia VI, 788
Walton, Virginia Blanche II, 721
Walton, Virginia Blanche II, 773
Walton, Walter IV, 299
Walton, Walter VI, 788
Walton, Walter VI, 789
Walton, Walter VI, 793
Walton, Walton IV, 851
Walton, Wd Ann IV, 65
Walton, Wd. Caroline II, 825
Walton, Widow Isabella I, 177
Walton, Widower David VI, 788
Walton, Wilhelmina H. M. IV, 1011
Walton, Wilhelmina Henrietta Maria IV, 783
Walton, Wilhelmina K. M. IV, 783
Walton, William II, 431
Walton, William II, 825
Walton, William III, 341
Walton, William IV, 451
Walton, William IV, 664
Walton, William IV, 1011
Walton, William IV, 1012
Walton, William V, 209
Walton, William VI, 862
Walton, William VI, 1010
Walton, William E. III, 341
Walton, William E. VI, 788
Walton, William F. II, 722
Walton, William K. II, 721
Walton, William Marsh III, 341
Walton, Wilmer II, 772
Walton, Wilmer II, 773
Walton, Wilmer II, 935
Walton, Wilmer IV, 664
Walton, Wilmer IV, 783
Walton, Wm. II, 676
Walton, Wm. II, 772
Walton, Wm. II, 871
Walton, Wm. II, 935
Walton, Wm. III, 341
Walton, Wm. E. III, 228
Walton, Wm. E. III, 341
Walton, Wm. E. V, 209
Walton, Wm. Ellis VI, 755
Walton, Wm. Henry II, 825
Walton, Wm. Henry VI, 755
Waltz, Amanuel V, 1024
Waltz, Edward V, 1024
Waltz, Emanuel V, 1024
Waltz, Henry V, 1024
Waltz, Jennie V, 1024
Waltz, Mary A. V, 421
Waltz, Mary A. V, 436
Waltz, Mary A. V, 1024
Waltz, Mary S. V, 1024
Waltz, Naomi V, 1024
Waltzer, Edward IV, 1297
Waltzer, Floyd IV, 1297
Waltzer, Mary IV, 1297
Wamlin, William VI, 123
Wamsley, Ann II, 45
Wamsley, Ann II, 109
Wamsley, Ann II, 112
Wamsley, Dynah II, 45
Wamsley, Edward M. II, 305
Wamsley, Elisabeth II, 305
Wamsley, Elizabeth II, 82
Wamsley, Elizabeth II, 109
Wamsley, George II, 45
Wamsley, Henry II, 45
Wamsley, Henry II, 82
Wamsley, Henry II, 104
Wamsley, Henry II, 109
Wamsley, Jonathan II, 45
Wamsley, Joseph T. II, 305
Wamsley, Joseph Trotter II, 305
Wamsley, Mary E. II, 305
Wamsley, Morris II, 305
Wamsley, Nathaniel II, 45
Wamsley, Rachel II, 109
Wamsley, Sarah II, 104
Wamsley, Sarah II, 109
Wamsley, Thomas II, 305
Wander, Anne W. II, 139
Wander, Annie II, 160
Wander, Annie W. II, 134
Wander, Elizabeth H. II, 139
Wander, Florence II, 139
Wander, Florence S. II, 134
Wander, John II, 139
Wander, John II, 160
Wander, John M. II, 139
Wander, John M. II, 160
Wander, Robert II, 160
Wander, Robert B. II, 139
Wander, Robert B. II, 160
Wander, Sophia II, 139
Wander, Wm. II, 134
Wander, Wm. II, 139
Wander, Wm. II, 160
Wanders, Wm. II, 160
Waney, Patience IV, 114
Wanger, Abram IV, 1297
Wanger, Charles M. IV, 1297
Wanger, Chas. M. IV, 1297
Wanger, David IV, 1297
Wanger, E. P. IV, 1297
Wanger, Edwin P. IV, 1297
Wanger, Emily IV, 1297
Wanger, Hannah IV, 1297
Wanger, Lavina IV, 1297
Wanger, Michael IV, 1297
Wank, Donald J. IV, 783
Wank, Edith IV, 783
Wank, Edith Melvina IV, 783
Wank, Emma IV, 783
Wank, Lloyd IV, 783
Wank, Lloyd Kenneth IV, 783
Wank, Lois Ilene IV, 783
Wank, Margaret IV, 783
Wank, Margaret Jane IV, 783
Wank, Mr. William IV, 783
Wank, Mrs. ??? IV, 783
Wank, Orlan Clyde IV, 783
Wank, Orlin IV, 783
Wank, Robert Eldine IV, 783
Wank, Wm. IV, 783
Wannamaker, Louisa IV, 1337
Wansbrough, John, Jr. III, 341
Wanser, Abbey III, 464
Wanser, Isaac III, 464
Wanser, Jane VI, 278
Wanton, Hannah VI, 789
Wanton, Mary III, 341
Wanton, Mary VI, 771
Wanton, Mary VI, 789
Wanton, Mary H. VI, 548
Wanton, Mary H. VI, 771
Wanton, Mary H. VI, 789
Wanton, Philip VI, 541
Wanton, Philip VI, 555
Wanton, Philip VI, 577
Wanton, Philip VI, 725
Wanton, Philip VI, 771
Wanton, Philip VI, 775
Wanton, Philip VI, 789
Wanton, Sarah VI, 555
Wanton, Sarah VI, 577
Wanton, Stephen III, 341
Wanton, Wd. Mary VI, 769
Wanton, Wd. Mary VI, 789
Wanton, Wd. Mary Pancoast VI, 775
Wanton, Widow Mary VI, 555
Wanton, William R. VI, 789
Wanton, Wm. R. V, 939
Wanzer, Abraham III, 152
Wanzer, Abraham III, 156
Wanzer, Abraham III, 341
Wanzer, Benjamin Hathaway III, 341
Wanzer, Benoni III, 341
Wanzer, Daniel B. III, 511
Wanzer, Ebenezer L. III, 337
Wanzer, Ebenezer L. III, 341
Wanzer, Elizabeth III, 337
Wanzer, Elizabeth III, 341
Wanzer, Elizabeth B. III, 337
Wanzer, Elizabeth B. III, 341
Wanzer, Emily IV, 1374
Wanzer, Emily IV, 1383
Wanzer, Esther III, 337
Wanzer, Esther III, 341
Wanzer, Geo. V, 939
Wanzer, Geo. Henry V, 939
Wanzer, Geo. Hussey V, 939
Wanzer, George V, 137
Wanzer, George H. V, 539
Wanzer, George Henry V, 137
Wanzer, George Henry V, 539
Wanzer, Grace III, 341
Wanzer, Hannah IV, 1272
Wanzer, Jane VI, 278
Wanzer, John III, 341
Wanzer, John V, 137
Wanzer, John V, 539
Wanzer, John V, 939
Wanzer, John Jay III, 341
Wanzer, Lavinia IV, 1374
Wanzer, Malinda V, 137
Wanzer, Malinda V, 539
Wanzer, Margaret III, 169
Wanzer, Margaret III, 341
Wanzer, Melinda V, 137
Wanzer, Melinda V, 939
Wanzer, Michael IV, 1374
Wanzer, Phebe III, 156
Wanzer, Phebe III, 341
Wanzer, Phebe H. III, 341
Wanzer, Sarah III, 341
Wanzer, William H. V, 539
Wanzer, William Haviland V, 137
Wanzer, William Haviland V, 539
Wanzer, Willliam V, 137
Wanzer, Wm. Haviland V, 939
Wappner, George H. V, 1024
Ward Rees, Margaret VI, 652
Ward, ??? II, 825
Ward, ??? III, 25
Ward, ??? VI, 95
Ward, Aaron V, 137
Ward, Aaron Ivins II, 1082
Ward, Abel IV, 969
Ward, Abigail IV, 1051
Ward, Abigail IV, 1081
Ward, Abigail C. I, 227
Ward, Abigail C. I, 249
Ward, Abigail C. I, 259
Ward, Abigail P. II, 722
Ward, Abigail P. IV, 1120
Ward, Addison W. VI, 1010
Ward, Alice M. V, 718
Ward, Allas I, 340
Ward, Allen V, 137
Ward, Allen C. I, 227
Ward, Allen C. I, 259
Ward, Alpha T. V, 210
Ward, Alpheus I, 220
Ward, Alpheus V, 210
Ward, Alpheus A. I, 227
Ward, Alpheus A. I, 249
Ward, Alpheus A. I, 259
Ward, Alpheus C. V, 210
Ward, Alpheus E. V, 138
Ward, Alphoes I, 259
Ward, Alta III, 341
Ward, Ann I, 36
Ward, Ann I, 77
Ward, Ann II, 86
Ward, Ann II, 109
Ward, Ann II, 154
Ward, Ann II, 160
Ward, Ann II, 1034
Ward, Ann V, 37
Ward, Ann V, 137
Ward, Ann V, 138
Ward, Ann VI, 952
Ward, Ann Hendrick VI, 863
Ward, Ann N. II, 139
Ward, Ann N. II, 155
Ward, Ann N. II, 160
Ward, Ann, Jr. V, 137
Ward, Anna III, 341
Ward, Anna H. B. III, 25
Ward, Anna Hazard III, 341
Ward, Annie I, 340
Ward, Anthony I, 367
Ward, Asenath V, 112
Ward, Asenath V, 138
Ward, Atlas I, 340
Ward, Augusta III, 322
Ward, B. E. VI, 797
Ward, Barton B. III, 341
Ward, Benjamin I, 340
Ward, Betty Jane V, 1024
Ward, Beulah V, 27
Ward, Beulah V, 137
Ward, Caroline I, 138
Ward, Caroline I, 172
Ward, Catharine V, 138
Ward, Catherine V, 81
Ward, Catherine V, 137
Ward, Charles II, 431
Ward, Charles IV, 1266
Ward, Charles V, 364
Ward, Charlotte I, 674
Ward, Charlotte I, 691
Ward, Charlotte V, 127
Ward, Charlotte V, 137
Ward, Clayton II, 779
Ward, Colwell V, 137
Ward, Daniel V, 772
Ward, David II, 825
Ward, David V, 807
Ward, Deborah V, 127
Ward, Deborah V, 137
Ward, Dr. Chas. V, 604
Ward, Edith II, 311
Ward, Edward A. II, 139
Ward, Edward Eugene V, 1024
Ward, Edward H. II, 935
Ward, Edward H. Townsend II, 935
Ward, Eliza II, 825
Ward, Eliza III, 341
Ward, Eliza IV, 834
Ward, Eliza IV, 851
Ward, Eliza V, 137
Ward, Eliza VI, 123
Ward, Elizabeth I, 220
Ward, Elizabeth II, 109
Ward, Elizabeth II, 676
Ward, Elizabeth II, 712
Ward, Elizabeth II, 872
Ward, Elizabeth II, 935
Ward, Elizabeth IV, 1266
Ward, Elizabeth IV, 1342
Ward, Elizabeth V, 25
Ward, Elizabeth V, 45
Ward, Elizabeth V, 137
Ward, Elizabeth V, 807
Ward, Elizabeth VI, 374
Ward, Elizabeth VI, 455
Ward, Elizabeth VI, 863
Ward, Elizabeth Crispin V, 939
Ward, Elizabeth W. IV, 1266
Ward, Elizabeth Wager IV, 1044
Ward, Ella V, 1024
Ward, Ellis V, 105
Ward, Ellis V, 137
Ward, Elva V, 718
Ward, Elva V, 720
Ward, Emaline IV, 969
Ward, Emily W. V, 55
Ward, Emily W. V, 138
Ward, Emma V, 138
Ward, Emma L. II, 139
Ward, Emma L. II, 152
Ward, Emma L. II, 160
Ward, Emma Louisa II, 804
Ward, Emma S. II, 160
Ward, Eneas I, 367
Ward, Eneas I, 426
Ward, Enoch II, 779
Ward, Enos I, 426
Ward, Ervin Harold V, 1024
Ward, Eva V, 718
Ward, Evan V, 81
Ward, Evan V, 137
Ward, Evan M. V, 138
Ward, Evan Moris V, 137
Ward, Flora B. IV, 839
Ward, Flora B. IV, 851
Ward, Florence IV, 1266
Ward, Frances VI, 1010
Ward, Gala Ann V, 364
Ward, Geo. W. V, 1024
Ward, George II, 109
Ward, George II, 155
Ward, George II, 311
Ward, George II, 676
Ward, George V, 127
Ward, George V, 137
Ward, George V, 364
Ward, George C. V, 137
Ward, George M. II, 139
Ward, George M. II, 155
Ward, George M. II, 160
Ward, George M. III, 341
Ward, George N. II, 154
Ward, George N. II, 160
Ward, Gideon I, 319
Ward, Giles VI, 843
Ward, Giles VI, 990
Ward, Grace I, 691
Ward, Grace I, 692
Ward, Grace I, 736
Ward, Grace V, 364
Ward, Green V, 137
Ward, Guli Marah II, 109
Ward, Hannah I, 426
Ward, Hannah I, 678
Ward, Hannah I, 691
Ward, Hannah II, 86
Ward, Hannah II, 109
Ward, Hannah II, 139
Ward, Hannah II, 154
Ward, Hannah II, 160
Ward, Hannah II, 676
Ward, Hannah II, 677
Ward, Hannah II, 779
Ward, Hannah II, 825
Ward, Hannah II, 961
Ward, Hannah IV, 799
Ward, Hannah IV, 851
Ward, Hannah V, 37
Ward, Hannah V, 52
Ward, Hannah V, 60
Ward, Hannah V, 137
Ward, Hannah VI, 419
Ward, Hannah VI, 455
Ward, Hannah Ann II, 935
Ward, Hannah Ann III, 341
Ward, Hannah Ann V, 137
Ward, Hannah K. IV, 969
Ward, Hannah Maria IV, 105
Ward, Hannah Maria IV, 108
Ward, Hardy I, 19
Ward, Harriett Cornell I, 227
Ward, Harry V, 718
Ward, Harry V, 720
Ward, Henry VI, 795
Ward, Henry P. III, 341
Ward, Henry Paul III, 341
Ward, Hester II, 431
Ward, Hester VI, 551
Ward, Hester VI, 577
Ward, Hester VI, 653
Ward, Hester VI, 694
Ward, Hesther VI, 506
Ward, Hesther VI, 694
Ward, Hesther VI, 718
Ward, Hiram I, 340
Ward, Ichabod I, 340
Ward, Ichabud I, 340
Ward, Isaac II, 64
Ward, Isaac II, 86
Ward, Isaac II, 109
Ward, Isaac II, 431
Ward, Isaac V, 37
Ward, Isaac V, 137
Ward, Isaac V, 604
Ward, Isaac V, 911
Ward, Isaac V, 939
Ward, Isaac H. V, 137
Ward, Isaac, Jr. V, 137
Ward, Isaiah V, 604
Ward, J. E. H. VI, 863
Ward, J. H. I, 340
Ward, J. W. IV, 969
Ward, Jacob III, 341
Ward, Jacob VI, 506
Ward, Jacob VI, 577
Ward, Jacob VI, 653
Ward, Jacob VI, 694
Ward, Jacob VI, 718
Ward, James I, 77
Ward, James Streeter II, 103
Ward, Jason V, 137
Ward, Jason V, 138
Ward, Jehu II, 431
Ward, Jehu II, 677
Ward, Jehu II, 825
Ward, Jehu II, 935
Ward, Jeremiah Healy II, 106
Ward, Jno. VI, 1010
Ward, Job II, 125
Ward, Joel VI, 455
Ward, John I, 426
Ward, John I, 691
Ward, John II, 86
Ward, John II, 109
Ward, John II, 139
Ward, John II, 154
Ward, John II, 160
Ward, John II, 773
Ward, John II, 779
Ward, John II, 825
Ward, John IV, 969
Ward, John IV, 1242
Ward, John V, 52
Ward, John V, 137
Ward, John VI, 123
Ward, John VI, 330
Ward, John VI, 344
Ward, John VI, 454
Ward, John VI, 455
Ward, John VI, 827
Ward, John VI, 840
Ward, John VI, 952
Ward, John VI, 1010
Ward, John B. II, 677
Ward, John H. I, 7
Ward, John Henry I, 340
Ward, John J. V, 210
Ward, John, Jr. V, 137
Ward, John, Jr. V, 939
Ward, John, Jr. VI, 455
Ward, Jonathan G. I, 77
Ward, Joseph II, 448
Ward, Joseph IV, 1242
Ward, Joseph Parrish II, 935
Ward, Josephine I, 340
Ward, Joshua V, 137

d, Joshua V, 939
d, Joshua G. V, 939
d, Josiah V, 137
d, Josiah V, 138
d, Josie IV, 969
d, Julia A. I, 227
d, Julia A. I, 259
d, Julia M. I, 220
d, Kezia I, 679
d, Kezia I, 691
d, Laney IV, 969
d, Laura W. I, 7
d, Laura W. I, 77
d, Leonard VI, 863
d, Letitia II, 779
d, Lewis II, 935
d, Lewis C. Parrish II, 935
d, Louis C. II, 935
d, Louisa II, 139
d, Louisa II, 152
d, Louisa II, 160
d, Louisa II, 935
d, Louisa II, 1082
d, Louisa II, 1084
d, Louisa A. II, 825
d, Louisa A. II, 935
d, Lucinda I, 691
d, Lucius A. I, 19
d, Lucius A. I, 77
d, Lucy Ann VI, 863
d, Lydia I, 378
d, Lydia I, 426
d, Lydia II, 961
d, Lydia II, 1052
d, Lydia II, 1063
d, Lydia V, 98
d, Lydia V, 137
d, Lydia V, 1024
d, Lydia VI, 455
d, Mabel C. IV, 783
d, Margaret I, 77
d, Margaret V, 736
d, Margaret V, 772
d, Margaret V, 807
d, Margaret V, 820
d, Margaret VI, 653
d, Margaret VI, 694
d, Margaret VI, 718
d, Margaret Kalbren V, 1024
d, Margaret S. I, 19
d, Margaret S. I, 77
d, Margret II, 448
d, Margrett II, 448
d, Maria III, 341
d, Maria V, 37
d, Maria V, 137
d, Maria Ohio V, 137
d, Mark V, 137
d, Mark Wright II, 1082
d, Marshall V, 364
d, Martha I, 77
d, Martha IV, 150
d, Martha IV, 969
d, Martha Ann V, 129
d, Martha Ann V, 137
d, Martha L. I, 77
d, Martha N. VI, 797
d, Mary I, 200
d, Mary I, 201
d, Mary I, 340
d, Mary I, 682
d, Mary I, 691
d, Mary I, 736
d, Mary II, 109
d, Mary II, 431
d, Mary II, 711
d, Mary II, 722
d, Mary II, 773
d, Mary III, 274
d, Mary IV, 638
d, Mary IV, 664
d, Mary IV, 969
d, Mary V, 26
d, Mary V, 27
d, Mary V, 30
d, Mary V, 45
d, Mary V, 85
d, Mary V, 137
d, Mary V, 138
d, Mary V, 210
d, Mary V, 364
d, Mary V, 604
d, Mary V, 915
d, Mary VI, 123
d, Mary VI, 455
d, Mary Abigail I, 227
d, Mary Ann V, 137
d, Mary B. V, 137
d, Mary C. VI, 1010
d, Mary E. V, 210
d, Mary Earl V, 105
Ward, Mary Earl V, 137
Ward, Mary Elizabeth IV, 366
Ward, Mary Head I, 340
Ward, Mary V. IV, 1266
Ward, Mary W. II, 311
Ward, Mason II, 139
Ward, Mason II, 961
Ward, Mat Ransom I, 340
Ward, Matilda C. VI, 795
Ward, Mattie IV, 851
Ward, Mattie B. IV, 783
Ward, May V, 604
Ward, Mildred A. IV, 783
Ward, Minnie I, 340
Ward, Minnie G. III, 341
Ward, Mrs. Guy I, 340
Ward, Mrs. Mamje I, 336
Ward, Nancy I, 143
Ward, Nancy I, 172
Ward, Nancy T. II, 1074
Ward, Nancy T. II, 1082
Ward, Norman III, 341
Ward, Obed I, 682
Ward, Obed I, 691
Ward, Obed I, 736
Ward, Obed V, 364
Ward, Obed VI, 123
Ward, Owen V, 137
Ward, Phebe IV, 879
Ward, Phebe IV, 885
Ward, Phebe IV, 969
Ward, Priscilla I, 367
Ward, Rachel II, 779
Ward, Rachel II, 935
Ward, Rachel II, 1082
Ward, Rachel II, 1084
Ward, Rachel IV, 969
Ward, Rachel V, 29
Ward, Rachel V, 137
Ward, Rachel V, 138
Ward, Rachel V, 364
Ward, Rachel VI, 455
Ward, Rachel S. II, 139
Ward, Rachel S. II, 160
Ward, Ralph II, 448
Ward, Raymond Richard V, 1024
Ward, Rebecca II, 64
Ward, Rebecca II, 109
Ward, Rebecca IV, 833
Ward, Rebecca IV, 851
Ward, Rebecca V, 101
Ward, Rebecca V, 117
Ward, Rebecca V, 137
Ward, Rebecca V, 911
Ward, Rebecca J. V, 137
Ward, Rebeccah II, 109
Ward, Rebecka II, 431
Ward, Rebeckah II, 109
Ward, Rebekah I, 1013
Ward, Richard II, 139
Ward, Richard II, 448
Ward, Richard VI, 204
Ward, Richard VI, 216
Ward, Richard J. II, 825
Ward, Richard J. II, 935
Ward, Robert V, 1024
Ward, Robert A. VI, 863
Ward, Ruth I, 733
Ward, Ruth I, 736
Ward, Ruth II, 676
Ward, Ruth II, 773
Ward, Ruth II, 825
Ward, Ruth II, 935
Ward, Ruth VI, 123
Ward, Ruth Anna II, 779
Ward, Samuel E. IV, 969
Ward, Samuel H. IV, 969
Ward, Sarah I, 172
Ward, Sarah I, 174
Ward, Sarah I, 426
Ward, Sarah II, 109
Ward, Sarah III, 341
Ward, Sarah IV, 156
Ward, Sarah IV, 162
Ward, Sarah IV, 356
Ward, Sarah IV, 1242
Ward, Sarah V, 44
Ward, Sarah V, 137
Ward, Sarah V, 138
Ward, Sarah VI, 278
Ward, Sarah VI, 287
Ward, Sarah VI, 344
Ward, Sarah VI, 363
Ward, Sarah VI, 455
Ward, Sarah VI, 1010
Ward, Sarah Chambless II, 139
Ward, Sarah P. IV, 163
Ward, Sarah P. IV, 356
Ward, Sarah T. II, 139
Ward, Sarah T. II, 155
Ward, Sarah T. II, 160
Ward, Sarah T. II, 815
Ward, Seth J. VI, 863
Ward, Seth, Jr. VI, 800
Ward, Seth, Jr. VI, 862
Ward, Smith J. I, 319
Ward, Stephen I, 426
Ward, Stephen I, 678
Ward, Stephen I, 691
Ward, Stephen VI, 123
Ward, Susan V, 1024
Ward, Susanna I, 426
Ward, Susanna I, 691
Ward, Susanna I, 736
Ward, Susanna V, 364
Ward, Susanna VI, 123
Ward, Susannah I, 367
Ward, Susannah I, 691
Ward, Tacy IV, 968
Ward, Tacy IV, 1012
Ward, Tailor V. V, 137
Ward, Taylor V, 137
Ward, Thlmas H. II, 160
Ward, Thomas II, 139
Ward, Thomas II, 722
Ward, Thomas IV, 1120
Ward, Thomas V, 312
Ward, Thomas H. II, 139
Ward, Thomas H. II, 152
Ward, Thomas H. II, 160
Ward, Timothy I, 691
Ward, Timothy I, 692
Ward, Timothy I, 706
Ward, Timothy V, 364
Ward, Timothy VI, 123
Ward, Townsend II, 935
Ward, Wd. Sarah VI, 330
Ward, Widow Margaret VI, 694
Ward, Widow Margaret Reese VI, 577
Ward, Wilbert W. V, 718
Ward, William I, 691
Ward, William II, 431
Ward, William V, 210
Ward, William Allen I, 227
Ward, Winfield II, 935
Ward, Winfield II, 1082
Ward, Winfield II, 1084
Ward, Winfield S. II, 1082
Ward, Wm. E. II, 935
Ward, Wm. M. VI, 970
Ward, Wm. W. II, 935
Ward, Zadick VI, 863
Ward-Rees, Margaret VI, 632
Ward-Rees, Margaret VI, 694
Warde, Robert V, 1024
Warde, Susan V, 1024
Wardel, James II, 677
Wardell, ??? III, 341
Wardell, ??? III, 342
Wardell, Anthony III, 341
Wardell, Charles II, 269
Wardell, Charles II, 432
Wardell, Charles III, 341
Wardell, Charles VI, 278
Wardell, Constance III, 182
Wardell, Constance III, 341
Wardell, Daniel II, 677
Wardell, Elizabeth III, 341
Wardell, Ella L. III, 341
Wardell, Hannah III, 341
Wardell, Hannah M. III, 341
Wardell, James II, 677
Wardell, Jane III, 341
Wardell, John III, 341
Wardell, John N. III, 341
Wardell, John Southeby II, 677
Wardell, Jos. N. III, 341
Wardell, Joseph II, 269
Wardell, Joseph II, 677
Wardell, Julia A. III, 367
Wardell, Lavinia III, 342
Wardell, Levinus III, 341
Wardell, Mary II, 439
Wardell, Patience II, 657
Wardell, Patience II, 677
Wardell, Raymond W. III, 182
Wardell, Raymond Wesley III, 341
Wardell, Rebecca II, 677
Wardell, Rebecca III, 341
Wardell, William II, 432
Wardell, William Henry III, 342
Warden, Allie I, 642
Warden, Ann A. V, 961
Warden, Anna R. V, 467
Warden, Anne VI, 455
Warden, Arthur Winston I, 642
Warden, Belinda V, 467
Warden, Benson J. V, 939
Warden, Croasdel VI, 455
Warden, Dallas V, 467
Warden, Dallis V, 467
Warden, Edwin V, 939
Warden, Eli I, 627
Warden, Eliza Johnson V, 939
Warden, Elizabet A. V, 961
Warden, Elizabeth V, 963
Warden, Elizabeth Lawrence V, 939
Warden, Emily V, 939
Warden, Emily H. V, 939
Warden, George Ashton V, 961
Warden, H. M. I, 642
Warden, Henrietta I, 614
Warden, Henrietta I, 627
Warden, Isaac V, 364
Warden, Isaac V, 467
Warden, Isaac V, 939
Warden, Jeremiah V, 961
Warden, John V, 963
Warden, John A. V, 961
Warden, John A. V, 963
Warden, Joseph VI, 455
Warden, Joseph VI, 607
Warden, Laura I, 642
Warden, Laura Jane I, 614
Warden, Laura Jane I, 627
Warden, Mary VI, 455
Warden, Mary A. V, 961
Warden, Mary P. V, 961
Warden, Olive V, 939
Warden, Phebe V, 939
Warden, Phebe L. V, 917
Warden, Phebe L. V, 939
Warden, Phoebe V, 939
Warden, Rachel I, 627
Warden, Rebecca V, 467
Warden, Rosanna V, 364
Warden, Sally Paul V, 961
Warden, Sarah V, 950
Warden, Sarah V, 961
Warden, Sarah Aston V, 961
Warden, Van Eaton I, 614
Warden, Van Eaton I, 627
Warden, Van Eaton I, 642
Warder, Agnes II, 432
Warder, Agnes II, 635
Warder, Agnes II, 661
Warder, Agnes II, 677
Warder, Ann II, 432
Warder, Ann II, 578
Warder, Ann II, 668
Warder, Ann II, 677
Warder, Ann II, 971
Warder, Ann V, 939
Warder, Ann VI, 519
Warder, Ann VI, 755
Warder, Ann VI, 789
Warder, Ann A. V, 963
Warder, Anna II, 991
Warder, Anna II, 1034
Warder, Anna V, 940
Warder, Anna Aston V, 940
Warder, Benjamin II, 432
Warder, Benjamin V, 963
Warder, Claudia M. Dorland V, 940
Warder, Deborah II, 637
Warder, Deborah II, 677
Warder, Edward V, 963
Warder, Elizabeth II, 432
Warder, Elizabeth II, 677
Warder, Elizabeth II, 698
Warder, Elizabeth II, 971
Warder, Elizabeth II, 1034
Warder, Elizabeth II, 1041
Warder, Elizabeth V, 939
Warder, Elizabeth V, 940
Warder, Elizabeth V, 963
Warder, Elizabeth VI, 519
Warder, Elizabeth VI, 755
Warder, Elizabeth VI, 789
Warder, Elizabeth Aston V, 963
Warder, Elizabeth B. V, 940
Warder, George II, 432
Warder, George II, 677
Warder, George Ashton V, 961
Warder, George Aston V, 963
Warder, Gulielma V, 940
Warder, Gulielma D. V, 940
Warder, Gulielma M. V, 903
Warder, Gulielma M. V, 940
Warder, Hannah II, 432
Warder, Hannah II, 677
Warder, James T. V, 963
Warder, Jane B. V, 940
Warder, Jeremiah II, 432
Warder, Jeremiah II, 516
Warder, Jeremiah II, 546
Warder, Jeremiah II, 595
Warder, Jeremiah II, 602
Warder, Jeremiah II, 613
Warder, Jeremiah II, 637
Warder, Jeremiah II, 673
Warder, Jeremiah II, 677
Warder, Jeremiah V, 939
Warder, Jeremiah V, 963
Warder, Jeremiah, Jr. II, 637
Warder, Jeremiah, Jr. II, 677
Warder, John II, 432
Warder, John II, 534
Warder, John II, 635
Warder, John II, 677
Warder, John II, 971
Warder, John V, 963
Warder, John VI, 519
Warder, John VI, 755
Warder, John VI, 789
Warder, John A. V, 939
Warder, John A. V, 940
Warder, John A. V, 961
Warder, John A. V, 963
Warder, John H. V, 940
Warder, John R. II, 722
Warder, John, Jr. II, 677
Warder, Joseph II, 432
Warder, Joseph II, 971
Warder, Joseph II, 1034
Warder, Joseph II, 1041
Warder, Lidya II, 613
Warder, Lidya II, 677
Warder, Lydia II, 432
Warder, Lydia II, 677
Warder, Martha II, 677
Warder, Mary II, 432
Warder, Mary II, 516
Warder, Mary II, 546
Warder, Mary II, 556
Warder, Mary II, 602
Warder, Mary II, 630
Warder, Mary II, 637
Warder, Mary II, 673
Warder, Mary II, 677
Warder, Mary II, 971
Warder, Mary Aston V, 963
Warder, Mary P. V, 961
Warder, Mary P. V, 963
Warder, Mary, Jr. II, 516
Warder, Mary, Jr. II, 677
Warder, Meriam II, 677
Warder, Miriam II, 677
Warder, Rachel II, 971
Warder, Rachel II, 975
Warder, Rachel II, 1034
Warder, Rebecca II, 432
Warder, Rebecca II, 595
Warder, Rebecca II, 624
Warder, Rebecca II, 677
Warder, Rebecka II, 432
Warder, Richard II, 432
Warder, Richard II, 578
Warder, Richard II, 624
Warder, Richard II, 630
Warder, Richard II, 635
Warder, Richard II, 668
Warder, Richard II, 677
Warder, Robert V, 940
Warder, Robert B. V, 903
Warder, Robert B. V, 940
Warder, Rueben H. V, 940
Warder, Sally Paul V, 961
Warder, Sarah II, 432
Warder, Sarah II, 470
Warder, Sarah II, 602
Warder, Sarah II, 677
Warder, Solomon II, 556
Warder, Solomon II, 677
Warder, Solomon II, 971
Warder, Solomon II, 991
Warder, Solomon II, 1034
Warder, Solomon II, 1041
Warder, Susanna II, 432
Warder, Susanna II, 673
Warder, Susanna II, 677
Warder, Wd. Agnes II, 677
Warder, William V, 940
Warder, William S. II, 269
Warder, William S. II, 722
Warder, William Savory II, 269
Warder, Willoughby II, 470
Warder, Willoughby II, 677
Warder, Willoughby II, 971
Warder, Willoughby II, 1034
Warder, Willoughby, Jr. II, 1034
Warder, Wm. II, 677
Warder, Wm. V, 963
Warder, Wm. S. II, 773
Warder, Wm., Jr. V, 940
Wardrees, Margaret VI, 652
Wardsworth, Edward VI, 1008
Wardwell, Helen IV, 1342
Ware, Abigail IV, 784
Ware, Abigail IV, 1012

Ware, Adolphus Gus VI, 1012
Ware, Alfred F. IV, 299
Ware, Alfred Raymond IV, 299
Ware, Alfred T. IV, 299
Ware, Amos IV, 783
Ware, Amos IV, 784
Ware, Anna B. II, 140
Ware, Anna B. II, 160
Ware, Anna C. II, 140
Ware, Anna May II, 140
Ware, Anna May II, 160
Ware, Anney Cammil VI, 1002
Ware, Asa IV, 778
Ware, Asa IV, 783
Ware, Asa IV, 784
Ware, Asa IV, 1012
Ware, Asa, Jr. IV, 696
Ware, Asa, Jr. IV, 783
Ware, Bathsheba II, 45
Ware, Beesley II, 110
Ware, Benjamin II, 432
Ware, Benjamin IV, 784
Ware, Benjamin IV, 1012
Ware, Benjamin F. IV, 784
Ware, Beulah II, 135
Ware, Beulah II, 136
Ware, Beulah II, 140
Ware, Beulah II, 155
Ware, Beulah II, 160
Ware, Charles II, 140
Ware, Charles II, 305
Ware, Charles II, 432
Ware, Charles W. II, 305
Ware, David II, 45
Ware, David II, 109
Ware, David II, 110
Ware, Deborah II, 825
Ware, Deborah II, 936
Ware, Dorcas VI, 981
Ware, Edith II, 269
Ware, Edith IV, 661
Ware, Edith IV, 664
Ware, Edith IV, 778
Ware, Edith IV, 783
Ware, Edith IV, 784
Ware, Eleanor II, 160
Ware, Eleanor Plummer II, 140
Ware, Elijah II, 45
Ware, Elijah II, 106
Ware, Elijah II, 109
Ware, Elijah II, 110
Ware, Elijah II, 125
Ware, Elijah II, 135
Ware, Elijah II, 136
Ware, Elijah II, 140
Ware, Elijah II, 155
Ware, Elijah II, 160
Ware, Elisha II, 45
Ware, Eliz. Bancker III, 342
Ware, Eliza Ann IV, 696
Ware, Eliza Ann IV, 784
Ware, Eliza Ann IV, 1012
Ware, Elizabeth II, 39
Ware, Elizabeth II, 45
Ware, Elizabeth II, 55
Ware, Elizabeth II, 56
Ware, Elizabeth II, 60
Ware, Elizabeth II, 69
Ware, Elizabeth II, 76
Ware, Elizabeth II, 97
Ware, Elizabeth II, 102
Ware, Elizabeth II, 105
Ware, Elizabeth II, 109
Ware, Elizabeth II, 110
Ware, Elizabeth IV, 778
Ware, Elizabeth IV, 783
Ware, Elizabeth IV, 784
Ware, Elizabeth V, 879
Ware, Elizabeth V, 887
Ware, Elizabeth VI, 524
Ware, Elizabeth VI, 577
Ware, Elizabeth VI, 718
Ware, Elizabeth B. III, 94
Ware, Ellin II, 432
Ware, Emmor IV, 784
Ware, Emmor IV, 1012
Ware, Grace II, 105
Ware, Grace II, 109
Ware, Hannah II, 32
Ware, Hannah II, 45
Ware, Hannah II, 53
Ware, Hannah II, 57
Ware, Hannah II, 70
Ware, Hannah II, 81
Ware, Hannah II, 94
Ware, Hannah II, 102
Ware, Hannah II, 109
Ware, Hannah II, 623
Ware, Hannah II, 677
Ware, Hannah III, 342
Ware, Henry III, 342
Ware, Henry, Jr. III, 94
Ware, Henry, Jr. III, 342
Ware, Hieskaell S. III, 342
Ware, Hope II, 677
Ware, Isabel III, 312
Ware, Isabel III, 342
Ware, Jacob II, 39
Ware, Jacob II, 45
Ware, Jacob II, 97
Ware, Jacob II, 105
Ware, Jacob II, 109
Ware, Jacob II, 110
Ware, Jane IV, 860
Ware, Jane VI, 577
Ware, Jane VI, 718
Ware, Jane E. III, 342
Ware, Job II, 45
Ware, Job II, 55
Ware, Job II, 100
Ware, Job II, 105
Ware, Job II, 109
Ware, Job II, 110
Ware, Job II, 140
Ware, Job II, 160
Ware, Joel IV, 784
Ware, Joel IV, 1012
Ware, John II, 45
Ware, John II, 55
Ware, John II, 69
Ware, John II, 109
Ware, John II, 110
Ware, John II, 202
Ware, John II, 269
Ware, John II, 788
Ware, John II, 825
Ware, John IV, 783
Ware, John IV, 784
Ware, John IV, 831
Ware, John IV, 851
Ware, John IV, 860
Ware, John, Jr. II, 269
Ware, Joseph II, 17
Ware, Joseph II, 45
Ware, Joseph II, 53
Ware, Joseph II, 55
Ware, Joseph II, 109
Ware, Joseph II, 522
Ware, Joseph IV, 784
Ware, Joseph, Jr. II, 56
Ware, Joseph, Jr. II, 109
Ware, Latitia IV, 784
Ware, Letitia VI, 440
Ware, Lillie H. IV, 299
Ware, Louisa F. III, 342
Ware, Lydia II, 45
Ware, Lydia II, 114
Ware, Lydia II, 125
Ware, Marion II, 140
Ware, Marion II, 160
Ware, Martha II, 45
Ware, Martha II, 55
Ware, Martha II, 109
Ware, Martha VI, 1012
Ware, Mary II, 39
Ware, Mary II, 45
Ware, Mary II, 55
Ware, Mary II, 57
Ware, Mary II, 97
Ware, Mary II, 106
Ware, Mary II, 109
Ware, Mary II, 110
Ware, Mary II, 125
Ware, Mary II, 140
Ware, Mary II, 153
Ware, Mary II, 160
Ware, Mary II, 788
Ware, Mary Ann IV, 783
Ware, Mary Ann IV, 784
Ware, Mary M. II, 135
Ware, Milisent II, 109
Ware, Millicent II, 45
Ware, Millicent II, 110
Ware, Millisent II, 45
Ware, Millisent II, 99
Ware, Millisent II, 109
Ware, Miriam IV, 895
Ware, Mirian IV, 892
Ware, Naomi II, 45
Ware, Patience II, 45
Ware, Peter II, 45
Ware, Polly VI, 1002
Ware, Rebecca II, 32
Ware, Rebecca II, 75
Ware, Rebecca II, 109
Ware, Rebecca II, 110
Ware, Rebeckah II, 45
Ware, Rebeckah II, 76
Ware, Rebeckah II, 109
Ware, Richard II, 32
Ware, Richard II, 45
Ware, Richard II, 57
Ware, Richard II, 109
Ware, Richard III, 342
Ware, Richard Waddington II, 140
Ware, Richard Waddington II, 160
Ware, Robert VI, 577
Ware, Robert VI, 718
Ware, Ruth II, 107
Ware, Ruth II, 109
Ware, Samuel II, 110
Ware, Samuel IV, 783
Ware, Samuel IV, 784
Ware, Samuel IV, 1012
Ware, Samuel Thompson II, 45
Ware, Sarah II, 45
Ware, Sarah II, 49
Ware, Sarah II, 75
Ware, Sarah II, 102
Ware, Sarah II, 105
Ware, Sarah II, 109
Ware, Sarah II, 110
Ware, Sarah II, 202
Ware, Sarah II, 269
Ware, Sarah II, 522
Ware, Sarah II, 677
Ware, Sarah II, 722
Ware, Sarah IV, 784
Ware, Sarah IV, 831
Ware, Sarah IV, 851
Ware, Sarah VI, 577
Ware, Sarah VI, 718
Ware, Sarah F. II, 136
Ware, Sarah F. II, 140
Ware, Sarah F. II, 155
Ware, Sarah F. II, 160
Ware, Sarah Jane IV, 891
Ware, Sarah Jane IV, 895
Ware, Solomon II, 45
Ware, Solomon II, 102
Ware, Solomon II, 109
Ware, Solomon, Jr. II, 45
Ware, Stephen IV, 784
Ware, Susanna II, 109
Ware, Susannah II, 100
Ware, Susannah II, 109
Ware, Talbert IV, 784
Ware, Talbot IV, 784
Ware, Thomas II, 110
Ware, Virginia III, 342
Ware, Virginia C. III, 312
Ware, Wd. Rebecca A. II, 788
Ware, William VI, 577
Ware, William VI, 718
Ware, Wm. II, 110
Ware, Wm. Hadley IV, 299
Ware, Wm. P. II, 140
Ware, Wm. P. II, 160
Ware, Wm. P. III, 312
Ware, Wm. P. III, 342
Ware, Wm. Pettit II, 140
Ware, Wm. Pettit II, 160
Wareham, Margaret V, 734
Waren, Sarah I, 580
Warf, Martha IV, 163
Warfield, Isaac V, 772
Warfield, Jane IV, 567
Warfield, Jane IV, 598
Warfield, John IV, 299
Warfield, John IV, 555
Warfield, Jonathan IV, 223
Warfield, Mariah IV, 299
Warfield, Martha IV, 223
Warfield, Martha IV, 299
Warfield, Martha IV, 554
Warfield, Mary IV, 223
Warfield, Mary IV, 535
Warfield, Mary IV, 555
Warfield, Mary V, 772
Warfield, Mary Bye IV, 555
Warfield, Mary E. V, 772
Waring, ??? III, 342
Waring, Adelaide L. III, 342
Waring, Adelia L. III, 342
Waring, Alethia Portia III, 342
Waring, Alice A. IV, 846
Waring, Alice A. IV, 851
Waring, Amelia III, 342
Waring, Amelia L. III, 342
Waring, Ann III, 327
Waring, Ann III, 342
Waring, Anna II, 950
Waring, Anna III, 342
Waring, Arthur III, 342
Waring, Arthur B. III, 342
Waring, Arthur N. III, 138
Waring, Arthur W. III, 342
Waring, Deborah III, 342
Waring, Edward III, 342
Waring, Elijah II, 305
Waring, Elijah II, 677
Waring, Elizabeth I, 172
Waring, Frances III, 342
Waring, Frances L. III, 66
Waring, Frances L. III, 342
Waring, Frances W. III, 66
Waring, Harriet III, 342
Waring, Harriet H. III, 342
Waring, Henrietta H. III, 342
Waring, J. Van Vechten III, 342
Waring, James Parsons III, 342
Waring, John Burger III, 342
Waring, John Monroe III, 342
Waring, John Monroe L. III, 342
Waring, Junius Van Vechten III, 342
Waring, Lydia III, 342
Waring, Lydia III, 359
Waring, Meta Louisa Beatrice III, 342
Waring, N. III, 342
Waring, Samuel F. III, 342
Waring, Sarah III, 331
Waring, Sarah III, 342
Waring, Sarah Ann III, 327
Waring, Sarah Ann III, 342
Waring, Sarah W. III, 359
Waring, Thaddeus III, 342
Waring, Thomas II, 950
Waring, Thomas II, 1089
Waring, Thomas III, 342
Waring, Wd. Lydia II, 947
Waring, William II, 947
Waring, William III, 342
Waring, William III, 359
Waring, William F. III, 342
Waring, Wm. II, 677
Waring, Wm. III, 327
Waring, Wm. III, 331
Waring, Wm. III, 342
Waring, Wm. F. III, 342
Warington, Elizabeth V, 833
Warington, Elizabeth V, 873
Warmack, Fanny VI, 836
Warmack, Rebecca VI, 834
Warmack, Richard VI, 836
Warman, Ethel V, 924
Warmock, Nancey VI, 1019
Warmock, Robert VI, 1019
Warner, ??? III, 342
Warner, Abigail II, 45
Warner, Abigail II, 110
Warner, Abigail II, 545
Warner, Abigail II, 678
Warner, Abner V, 210
Warner, Abner V, 287
Warner, Abner V, 288
Warner, Abner V, 312
Warner, Abner V, 961
Warner, Abraham II, 1008
Warner, Abraham II, 1032
Warner, Abraham II, 1033
Warner, Abraham II, 1034
Warner, Abraham II, 1042
Warner, Abraham II, 1069
Warner, Abraham II, 1078
Warner, Abraham II, 1082
Warner, Abraham VI, 713
Warner, Abraham VI, 714
Warner, Abraham VI, 718
Warner, Abraham, Jr. II, 1063
Warner, Allen I, 904
Warner, Amos II, 1034
Warner, Amos P. V, 961
Warner, Ann II, 432
Warner, Ann II, 448
Warner, Ann II, 453
Warner, Ann II, 491
Warner, Ann II, 497
Warner, Ann II, 624
Warner, Ann II, 665
Warner, Ann II, 668
Warner, Ann II, 677
Warner, Ann II, 678
Warner, Ann II, 1008
Warner, Ann II, 1032
Warner, Ann II, 1033
Warner, Ann II, 1034
Warner, Ann II, 1035
Warner, Ann II, 1063
Warner, Ann II, 1082
Warner, Ann II, 1084
Warner, Ann IV, 1297
Warner, Ann V, 287
Warner, Ann VI, 378
Warner, Ann Elizabeth II, 305
Warner, Ann Elizabeth V, 961
Warner, Anna IV, 784
Warner, Anne II, 1034
Warner, Anne II, 1042
Warner, Anne IV, 299
Warner, Anne V, 268
Warner, Anne V, 288
Warner, Anne E. I, 904
Warner, Annie Elizabeth I, 90
Warner, Arnold II, 432
Warner, Arnold II, 678
Warner, Asaph IV, 114
Warner, Bell IV, 1226
Warner, Benjamin II, 432
Warner, Benjamin II, 678
Warner, Benjamin II, 701
Warner, Benjamin IV, 1226
Warner, Benjamin IV, 1297
Warner, Benjamin II IV, 1226
Warner, Benjamin P. II, 678
Warner, Benjamin, Sr. IV, 122
Warner, Bill IV, 1226
Warner, Catharine II, 678
Warner, Catherine II, 556
Warner, Catherine II, 678
Warner, Charles I, 904
Warner, Charles II, 187
Warner, Charles II, 552
Warner, Charles II, 678
Warner, Charles II, 773
Warner, Charles A. IV, 299
Warner, Charles Hoover I, 90
Warner, Charles L. II, 773
Warner, Clifton Moore VI, 718
Warner, Croasdel VI, 378
Warner, Croazdale II, 1034
Warner, Daniel II, 432
Warner, Deborah II, 432
Warner, Dorothy I, 950
Warner, Edith III, 342
Warner, Edith W. II, 326
Warner, Edith W. III, 342
Warner, Edmond II, 432
Warner, Edward II, 432
Warner, Edward II, 491
Warner, Edward II, 678
Warner, Edwin VI, 718
Warner, Eliza III, 266
Warner, Eliza V, 312
Warner, Elizabeth II, 432
Warner, Elizabeth II, 557
Warner, Elizabeth II, 678
Warner, Elizabeth II, 1032
Warner, Elizabeth II, 1035
Warner, Elizabeth IV, 114
Warner, Elizabeth IV, 1226
Warner, Elizabeth IV, 1342
Warner, Elizabeth V, 210
Warner, Elizabeth V, 287
Warner, Elizabeth V, 288
Warner, Elizabeth V, 312
Warner, Elizabeth V, 772
Warner, Elizabeth V, 956
Warner, Elizabeth V, 961
Warner, Emma A. I, 950
Warner, Emma Allen I, 950
Warner, Emma B. V, 962
Warner, Emma W. V, 958
Warner, Emma W. V, 962
Warner, Ester II, 432
Warner, Esther II, 432
Warner, Esther II, 433
Warner, Esther II, 555
Warner, Esther II, 559
Warner, Esther II, 677
Warner, Esther II, 678
Warner, Ethel V, 604
Warner, Ettie IV, 1297
Warner, Fairlanab Harrison V, 963
Warner, Francis II, 936
Warner, George II, 45
Warner, George II, 110
Warner, George II, 326
Warner, George II, 432
Warner, George II, 545
Warner, George II, 678
Warner, George II, 682
Warner, George II, 1063
Warner, George II, 1082
Warner, George III, 342
Warner, George F. II, 1082
Warner, George Mahlon IV, 29
Warner, George Malin IV, 299
Warner, George, Jr. II, 110
Warner, George, Jr. II, 825
Warner, George, Jr. II, 936
Warner, George, Jr. II, 1082
Warner, Georgianna III, 342
Warner, Grace IV, 1226
Warner, Hannah II, 281
Warner, Hannah II, 305
Warner, Hannah II, 432
Warner, Hannah II, 433
Warner, Hannah II, 678
Warner, Hannah II, 692
Warner, Hannah II, 698

er, Hannah II, 1063
er, Hannah II, 1082
er, Hannah IV, 299
er, Hannah VI, 718
er, Hannah A. II, 125
er, Hannah Ann II, 125
er, Hannah F. II, 1082
er, Hannah Head II, 678
er, Hannah T. II, 1069
er, Hannah T. II, 1082
er, Hannah Woodward
I, 678
er, Hariet IV, 1226
er, Harriott IV, 1226
er, Henry H. II, 187
er, Hugh V, 961
er, Isaac II, 432
er, Isaac II, 448
er, Isaac II, 483
er, Isaac II, 497
er, Isaac II, 642
er, Isaac II, 677
er, Isaac II, 678
er, Isaac IV, 66
er, Isaac IV, 114
er, Isaac V, 210
er, Isaac V, 287
er, Isaac V, 288
er, Isaac V, 961
er, Isaac V, 962
er, Isaac VI, 488
er, Isaac W. II, 678
er, Isaac W. V, 962
er, Isaiah II, 432
er, J. Woodro V, 138
er, Jabez VI, 1010
er, Jacob II, 448
er, Jacob II, 678
er, Jacob VI, 1010
er, James II, 432
er, James II, 678
er, James IV, 114
er, Jane II, 432
er, Jane II, 579
er, Jane II, 678
er, Jennie IV, 1191
er, Jennie T. II, 1078
er, Jennie T. II, 1082
er, John II, 432
er, John II, 433
er, John II, 448
er, John II, 535
er, John II, 678
er, John II, 773
er, John II, 936
er, John II, 1000
er, John II, 1034
er, John IV, 114
er, John IV, 356
er, John V, 138
er, John V, 210
er, John V, 287
er, John V, 288
er, John V, 961
er, John VI, 684
er, John VI, 718
er, John G. V, 961
er, John H. IV, 1191
er, John H. IV, 1226
er, John Redwood Fisher
I, 678
er, John Redwood Fisher
I, 773
er, John Samuel IV, 1226
er, John, Sr. II, 432
er, Joicey VI, 1010
er, Jonathan II, 1000
er, Jonathan II, 1034
ner, Joseph I, 904
ner, Joseph II, 305
ner, Joseph II, 432
ner, Joseph II, 470
ner, Joseph II, 552
ner, Joseph II, 624
ner, Joseph II, 678
ner, Joseph II, 682
ner, Joseph II, 974
ner, Joseph II, 993
ner, Joseph II, 1032
ner, Joseph II, 1034
ner, Joseph II, 1042
ner, Joseph IV, 1226
ner, Joseph V, 287
ner, Joseph V, 288
ner, Joseph V, 961
ner, Joseph V, 962
ner, Joseph T. II, 678
ner, Joseph Tatnal II, 678
ner, Joseph, Jr. II, 432
ner, Joshua W. V, 539
ner, Joshua W. V, 961
Warner, Joshua Woodrow V, 312
Warner, Katharine II, 448
Warner, Latitia II, 996
Warner, Latitia II, 1034
Warner, Latitia VI, 718
Warner, Laura E. V, 962
Warner, Letitia II, 1063
Warner, Letitia II, 1082
Warner, Letitia II, 1084
Warner, Levi IV, 351
Warner, Levi IV, 356
Warner, Levi V, 210
Warner, Levi V, 287
Warner, Levi V, 288
Warner, Levi V, 312
Warner, Levi V, 956
Warner, Levi V, 961
Warner, Levi W. V, 961
Warner, Levi Woodrow V, 312
Warner, Levina IV, 1226
Warner, Louisa IV, 1214
Warner, Louisa IV, 1226
Warner, Lucy IV, 565
Warner, Lucy IV, 598
Warner, Lyda V, 287
Warner, Lydia II, 432
Warner, Lydia II, 502
Warner, Lydia II, 678
Warner, Lydia II, 773
Warner, Lydia IV, 356
Warner, Lydia IV, 1286
Warner, Lydia IV, 1297
Warner, Lydia V, 138
Warner, Lydia V, 210
Warner, Lydia V, 287
Warner, Lydia V, 288
Warner, Lydia V, 312
Warner, Lydia V, 956
Warner, Lydia V, 961
Warner, Lydia V, 962
Warner, Lydia F. II, 432
Warner, Lydia F. II, 773
Warner, Lydia J. II, 1082
Warner, Lydia Y. II, 936
Warner, Lydia Yardley II, 825
Warner, Mahala V, 138
Warner, Mahala H. V, 138
Warner, Mahala H. V, 539
Warner, Mahala H. V, 567
Warner, Mahala H. V, 604
Warner, Margaret II, 140
Warner, Margaret II, 432
Warner, Margaret II, 632
Warner, Margaret II, 660
Warner, Margaret II, 677
Warner, Margaret II, 678
Warner, Margaret IV, 351
Warner, Margaret IV, 356
Warner, Margaret Parvin II, 701
Warner, Margaret S. V, 961
Warner, Margaret V. IV, 784
Warner, Margery II, 432
Warner, Margery II, 678
Warner, Martha II, 351
Warner, Martha II, 552
Warner, Martha II, 678
Warner, Martha II, 803
Warner, Martha IV, 1225
Warner, Martha IV, 1226
Warner, Martha V, 772
Warner, Mary II, 187
Warner, Mary II, 195
Warner, Mary II, 269
Warner, Mary II, 280
Warner, Mary II, 305
Warner, Mary II, 432
Warner, Mary II, 554
Warner, Mary II, 624
Warner, Mary II, 642
Warner, Mary II, 660
Warner, Mary II, 677
Warner, Mary II, 678
Warner, Mary II, 682
Warner, Mary II, 695
Warner, Mary II, 817
Warner, Mary II, 974
Warner, Mary II, 993
Warner, Mary II, 1000
Warner, Mary II, 1008
Warner, Mary II, 1034
Warner, Mary II, 1035
Warner, Mary IV, 66
Warner, Mary IV, 114
Warner, Mary IV, 1224
Warner, Mary IV, 1226
Warner, Mary V, 210
Warner, Mary V, 287
Warner, Mary V, 288
Warner, Mary V, 960
Warner, Mary V, 961
Warner, Mary VI, 378
Warner, Mary VI, 488
Warner, Mary VI, 718
Warner, Mary Ann II, 993
Warner, Mary Ann II, 1035
Warner, Mary Ann IV, 114
Warner, Mary Ann IV, 116
Warner, Mary E. II, 701
Warner, Mary E. V, 950
Warner, Mary E. V, 962
Warner, Mary J. M. V, 962
Warner, Mary M. II, 936
Warner, Mary Martha II, 936
Warner, Mary R. IV, 420
Warner, Massey II, 473
Warner, Massey II, 678
Warner, Massey V, 287
Warner, Massey V, 288
Warner, Massey V, 312
Warner, Massy V, 288
Warner, Massy V, 310
Warner, Massy V, 961
Warner, Massy Rogers V, 312
Warner, Matilda VI, 476
Warner, Matilda VI, 577
Warner, Mercy II, 535
Warner, Mercy II, 678
Warner, Mercy V, 288
Warner, Mercy V, 956
Warner, Miers II, 432
Warner, Miers Fisher II, 773
Warner, Mollie V, 772
Warner, Moore VI, 679
Warner, Mrs. John VI, 683
Warner, Myers Fisher II, 678
Warner, Myers Fisher II, 773
Warner, Nancy V, 288
Warner, Nellie III, 342
Warner, Nellie VI, 718
Warner, Nellie Grace VI, 679
Warner, Netta VI, 718
Warner, Netta Hannah VI, 683
Warner, Netta Hannah VI, 684
Warner, Nicholas II, 281
Warner, Nicholas II, 305
Warner, Ollie IV, 1226
Warner, Oney VI, 1010
Warner, Osborne VI, 1010
Warner, Pearson II, 432
Warner, Pennington V, 312
Warner, Phebe II, 45
Warner, Phebe II, 110
Warner, Phebe II, 545
Warner, Phebe II, 678
Warner, Phebe IV, 1226
Warner, Prudence II, 552
Warner, Prudence II, 678
Warner, Prudence II, 682
Warner, Rachel II, 432
Warner, Rachel V, 287
Warner, Rachel V, 288
Warner, Rebecca II, 140
Warner, Rebecca II, 432
Warner, Rebecca II, 678
Warner, Rebecca IV, 299
Warner, Rebecca P. V, 953
Warner, Rebecca P. V, 961
Warner, Rebecca P. V, 963
Warner, Rebeccah II, 432
Warner, Rebeckah II, 678
Warner, Rebekah II, 470
Warner, Rebekah II, 678
Warner, Redwood Fisher II, 432
Warner, Redwood Fisher II, 773
Warner, Rhoda IV, 114
Warner, Robert K. IV, 1226
Warner, Robert Kirkbride
IV, 1226
Warner, Ruth IV, 114
Warner, Sallie VI, 718
Warner, Samuel II, 678
Warner, Samuel VI, 1010
Warner, Samuel H. IV, 1226
Warner, Sarah I Sup 1, 6
Warner, Sarah II, 283
Warner, Sarah II, 305
Warner, Sarah II, 432
Warner, Sarah II, 433
Warner, Sarah II, 669
Warner, Sarah II, 678
Warner, Sarah II, 773
Warner, Sarah II, 796
Warner, Sarah II, 829
Warner, Sarah II, 895
Warner, Sarah II, 974
Warner, Sarah II, 981
Warner, Sarah II, 1034
Warner, Sarah II, 1035
Warner, Sarah IV, 1226
Warner, Sarah VI, 328
Warner, Sarah VI, 344
Warner, Sarah VI, 982
Warner, Sarah VI, 1010
Warner, Sarah A. II, 281
Warner, Sarah A. II, 305
Warner, Sarah A. II, 1078
Warner, Sarah A. II, 1082
Warner, Sarah A. V, 962
Warner, Sarah Ann II, 1069
Warner, Sarah Ann II, 1082
Warner, Sarah Ann II, 1083
Warner, Sarah Ann V, 961
Warner, Sarah Ann V, 962
Warner, Sarah Ann VI, 713
Warner, Sarah Ann VI, 714
Warner, Sarah Ann VI, 718
Warner, Sarah F. II, 678
Warner, Scott IV, 784
Warner, Seymour Yardley II, 825
Warner, Silas II, 187
Warner, Silas II, 305
Warner, Simeon II, 432
Warner, Simeon II, 678
Warner, Simeon V, 287
Warner, Simeon V, 953
Warner, Simeon V, 956
Warner, Simeon V, 961
Warner, Simeor II, 432
Warner, Simion V, 312
Warner, Sivan II, 432
Warner, Stafford I, 904
Warner, Stafford Allen II, 305
Warner, Susan II, 433
Warner, Susanna II, 432
Warner, Susanna II, 678
Warner, Susanna IV, 1213
Warner, Susanna IV, 1226
Warner, Swan II, 432
Warner, T. J. Nichols VI, 718
Warner, Thomas II, 433
Warner, Thomas II, 678
Warner, Thomas IV, 114
Warner, Thomas E. IV, 114
Warner, Thomas Ellicott IV, 114
Warner, Thomas Ellicott IV, 116
Warner, Uronica II, 432
Warner, Veronica II, 432
Warner, Veronica II, 483
Warner, Veronica II, 677
Warner, Virginia IV, 784
Warner, Walter L. III, 503
Warner, William II, 45
Warner, William II, 432
Warner, William II, 433
Warner, William II, 448
Warner, William V, 210
Warner, William V, 287
Warner, William V, 288
Warner, William V, 961
Warner, William G. IV, 299
Warner, William Y. II, 1067
Warner, William Y. IV, 299
Warner, Wm. II, 110
Warner, Wm. II, 140
Warner, Wm. II, 448
Warner, Wm. II, 642
Warner, Wm. II, 677
Warner, Wm. II, 678
Warner, Wm. II, 682
Warner, Wm. II, 996
Warner, Wm. II, 1034
Warner, Wm. II, 1063
Warner, Wm. II, 1082
Warner, Wm. II, 1084
Warner, Wm. IV, 1226
Warner, Wm. V, 961
Warner, Wm. VI, 718
Warner, Wm. F. II, 1063
Warner, Wm. F. II, 1082
Warner, Wm. Y. II, 1078
Warner, Wm. Y. II, 1082
Warner, Wm. Y. II, 1083
Warner, Wm., Jr. II, 678
Warner, Woodrow V, 138
Warner, Yardley I, 867
Warner, Yardley I, 904
Warner, Yardley II, 305
Warner, Yardley II, 1063
Warner, Yardley IV, 299
Warner, Yardley VI, 718
Warner, Yardley Taylor II, 1082
Warning, Benj. V, 288
Warning, Benjamin V, 288
Warning, Clarence Ladd V, 288
Warning, Retta V, 288
Warnock, David K. III, 271
Warnock, David K. III, 342
Warnock, James III, 342
Warnock, Martha III, 342
Warnock, Mary III, 271
Warnock, Mary III, 342
Warnock, Robert VI, 974
Warran, Rebekah I, 818
Warrell, Kezia VI, 459
Warrell, Rebecca E. II, 936
Warrelow, Elizabeth II, 978
Warrelow, Elizabeth II, 1035
Warrelow, Jane II, 1035
Warrelow, Thomas II, 978
Warrelow, Thomas II, 1035
Warrelow, Wm. Beakes II, 1035
Warren, ??? III, 185
Warren, ??? III, 342
Warren, Abigail IV, 809
Warren, Abigail IV, 1181
Warren, Abigail IV, 1191
Warren, Adaline IV, 851
Warren, Adaline IV, 1012
Warren, Allen IV, 1384
Warren, Ann I, 580
Warren, Annie VI, 733
Warren, Austin A. IV, 1384
Warren, Barton D. IV, 809
Warren, Benjamin II, 678
Warren, Benjamin II, 679
Warren, Caroline II, 791
Warren, Clifton J. V, 604
Warren, Daniel I, 736
Warren, Daniel I, 907
Warren, Daniel I, 914
Warren, David I, 843
Warren, David I, 1133
Warren, Eliza IV, 1005
Warren, Eliza IV, 1012
Warren, Elizabeth I, 997
Warren, Elizabeth I, 999
Warren, Elizabeth VI, 123
Warren, Elizabeth VI, 124
Warren, Elizabeth Jane IV, 809
Warren, Elizabeth Storey III, 185
Warren, Emma I, 935
Warren, Esther IV, 784
Warren, Eunice II, 605
Warren, Eunice II, 678
Warren, Eva V, 604
Warren, Eva A. V, 718
Warren, Eva H. V, 718
Warren, Eva N. V, 436
Warren, Geo. W. III, 304
Warren, Geo. W. III, 342
Warren, George V, 436
Warren, George Cooke III, 185
Warren, Grace Lower III, 304
Warren, Grace Lower III, 342
Warren, Hannah IV, 1165
Warren, Hannah IV, 1173
Warren, Hannah IV, 1191
Warren, Hannah IV, 1242
Warren, Hannah VI, 123
Warren, Hannah VI, 124
Warren, Harlen L. IV, 809
Warren, Henry I, 1133
Warren, Isaac I, 580
Warren, Isaac II, 433
Warren, Isaac II, 678
Warren, Isaac L. IV, 809
Warren, Iven IV, 299
Warren, Jacob II, 605
Warren, Jacob II, 678
Warren, James I, 1111
Warren, James I, 1133
Warren, James I Sup 1, 9
Warren, James V, 604
Warren, James, Sr. I, 1111
Warren, Jemima Pike V, 718
Warren, Jeremiah IV, 809
Warren, Job IV, 808
Warren, Job IV, 851
Warren, Job IV, 1012
Warren, John IV, 1165
Warren, John IV, 1191
Warren, John IV, 1242
Warren, John V, 436
Warren, John VI, 123
Warren, John VI, 124
Warren, John VI, 1010
Warren, John, Jr. IV, 1191
Warren, Joseph I, 736
Warren, Joseph IV, 784
Warren, Josephine J. III, 185
Warren, Josephine J. III, 342
Warren, Josephine, Jr. III, 185
Warren, Lucile Starkey V, 604
Warren, Lucinda IV, 1384
Warren, Luther V, 604
Warren, Luther V, 670
Warren, Luther V, 718
Warren, Luther E. V, 604
Warren, Mary I, 580
Warren, Mary I, 736
Warren, Mary I, 843
Warren, Mary I, 914
Warren, Mary II, 433
Warren, Mary IV, 1191

Warren, Mary IV, 1342
Warren, Mary A. III, 342
Warren, Mary A. IV, 851
Warren, Mary Alice III, 304
Warren, Nancy I, 580
Warren, Nancy IV, 1191
Warren, Nicholas Cooke III, 185
Warren, Pearl E. V, 604
Warren, Peggy Margaret VI, 121
Warren, Peggy Margaret VI, 124
Warren, Peter VI, 216
Warren, Phebe IV, 1191
Warren, Phebe C. IV, 1165
Warren, Phebe C. IV, 1191
Warren, Phebe Jane IV, 1012
Warren, Phebe Jane IV, 1014
Warren, Preserved IV, 1191
Warren, Priscilla II, 474
Warren, Priscilla II, 678
Warren, Priscilla III, 185
Warren, Rachel I, 736
Warren, Rachel I, 1133
Warren, Rachel V, 718
Warren, Ralph T. V, 604
Warren, Randolph III, 185
Warren, Rebecca I, 934
Warren, Rebecca II, 779
Warren, Rebecca IV, 808
Warren, Rebecca IV, 809
Warren, Rebecca IV, 851
Warren, Rebecca IV, 1012
Warren, Rebekah I, 843
Warren, Ruth I, 843
Warren, Ruth I, 911
Warren, Ruth I, 914
Warren, Samuel IV, 809
Warren, Samuel IV, 851
Warren, Samuel IV, 1012
Warren, Samuel IV, 1383
Warren, Samuel IV, 1384
Warren, Samuel VI, 123
Warren, Samuel VI, 124
Warren, Samuel S. IV, 851
Warren, Samuel, Sr. VI, 123
Warren, Sarah I, 426
Warren, Sarah I, 429
Warren, Sarah I, 543
Warren, Sarah I, 580
Warren, Sarah I, 1133
Warren, Sarah I Sup 1, 9
Warren, Sarah V, 604
Warren, Sarah VI, 123
Warren, Sarah VI, 1010
Warren, Saretta V, 670
Warren, Saretta V, 718
Warren, Susanna II, 264
Warren, Susannah II, 264
Warren, Susannah II, 270
Warren, Tabitha I, 1133
Warren, Thomas IV, 809
Warren, William II, 433
Warren, William III, 185
Warren, William V, 604
Warren, Wilshire V, 436
Warren, Wm. III, 185
Warren, Wm. V, 604
Warren, Wm. V, 718
Warren, Wm. G. IV, 809
Warrenton, Henry II, 270
Warrick, Caroline L. II, 314
Warrick, Elizabeth L. II, 314
Warrick, Fanny VI, 800
Warrick, George II, 314
Warrick, Hannah II, 45
Warrick, John B. II, 320
Warrick, John B. II, 326
Warrick, Lillie V, 772
Warrick, Mary II, 45
Warrick, Mary IV, 569
Warrick, Mary IV, 598
Warrick, Mary Ann II, 320
Warrick, Mary Ann II, 326
Warrick, Mary Hancock II, 314
Warrick, Thomas II, 45
Warrin, Jacob II, 448
Warrin, Mary II, 448
Warriner, William VI, 845
Warring, Alice A. IV, 851
Warring, Alletta Bement III, 199
Warring, Daniel I, 721
Warring, Daniel I, 736
Warring, Elisabeth I, 188
Warring, Joseph I, 736
Warring, Mary I, 721
Warring, Mary I, 736
Warring, Rachel I, 736
Warrington, Abigail IV, 784
Warrington, Abraham IV, 114
Warrington, Abraham IV, 664
Warrington, Abraham IV, 680
Warrington, Abraham IV, 706
Warrington, Abraham IV, 717
Warrington, Abraham IV, 725
Warrington, Abraham IV, 784
Warrington, Abraham IV, 789
Warrington, Abraham IV, 919
Warrington, Abraham IV, 981
Warrington, Abraham IV, 983
Warrington, Abraham IV, 1012
Warrington, Abraham IV, 1013
Warrington, Abraham, Jr. IV, 784
Warrington, Abram IV, 1010
Warrington, Albert IV, 815
Warrington, Albert IV, 836
Warrington, Albert IV, 851
Warrington, Albert IV, 1012
Warrington, Albert IV, 1013
Warrington, Alfred E. IV, 784
Warrington, Alfred E. IV, 785
Warrington, Alfred E. IV, 1012
Warrington, Alfred E. IV, 1013
Warrington, Ann II, 326
Warrington, Ann IV, 725
Warrington, Ann IV, 784
Warrington, Anna H. II, 699
Warrington, Anna Leora IV, 843
Warrington, Anna Leora IV, 851
Warrington, Anna Mary II, 773
Warrington, Atlantic II, 890
Warrington, Atlantic II, 936
Warrington, Charles IV, 851
Warrington, Charles IV, 1012
Warrington, Charles IV, 1013
Warrington, Charles W. II, 125
Warrington, Chas. W. II, 114
Warrington, Chas. W. II, 125
Warrington, Clara Esther IV, 1013
Warrington, Curtis H. II, 773
Warrington, Cyrus J. IV, 451
Warrington, Cyrus J. IV, 851
Warrington, David IV, 784
Warrington, David IV, 1012
Warrington, David IV, 1013
Warrington, Deborah II, 936
Warrington, Edgar IV, 664
Warrington, Edgar IV, 809
Warrington, Edgar IV, 851
Warrington, Edgar IV, 985
Warrington, Edgar IV, 1012
Warrington, Edgar IV, 1013
Warrington, Edith L. IV, 851
Warrington, Edward II, 773
Warrington, Elizabeth II, 270
Warrington, Elizabeth II, 788
Warrington, Elizabeth II, 916
Warrington, Elizabeth IV, 1012
Warrington, Elizabeth V, 873
Warrington, Elizabeth C. II, 916
Warrington, Elizabeth C. II, 936
Warrington, Elizabeth L. II, 773
Warrington, Elizabeth M. IV, 836
Warrington, Elizabeth M. IV, 851
Warrington, Elizabeth M. IV, 1013
Warrington, Enoch II, 270
Warrington, Erving IV, 1013
Warrington, Eunice IV, 762
Warrington, Eunice IV, 784
Warrington, Evan IV, 784
Warrington, Evan IV, 1012
Warrington, Evan IV, 1013
Warrington, Gilbert IV, 183
Warrington, Gilbert IV, 299
Warrington, Gilbert IV, 784
Warrington, Gilbert IV, 931
Warrington, Gilbert IV, 1012
Warrington, Gilbert IV, 1013
Warrington, Hannah II, 168
Warrington, Hannah II, 466
Warrington, Hannah II, 679
Warrington, Hannah IV, 664
Warrington, Hannah IV, 717
Warrington, Hannah IV, 784
Warrington, Hannah IV, 809
Warrington, Hannah IV, 851
Warrington, Hannah IV, 985
Warrington, Hannah IV, 1012
Warrington, Hannah IV, 1013
Warrington, Hannah IV, 1081
Warrington, Hannah C. IV, 664
Warrington, Hannah C. IV, 851
Warrington, Hannah C. IV, 1012
Warrington, Hannah C. IV, 1013
Warrington, Henry II, 114
Warrington, Henry II, 125
Warrington, Henry II, 270
Warrington, Henry IV, 664
Warrington, Henry IV, 784
Warrington, Henry IV, 1012
Warrington, Henry IV, 1013
Warrington, Henry IV, 1081
Warrington, Irving IV, 784
Warrington, Irving IV, 1012
Warrington, Irving IV, 1013
Warrington, Irving IV, 1081
Warrington, James II, 936
Warrington, James A. IV, 784
Warrington, Jane IV, 784
Warrington, Jane IV, 981
Warrington, Jane IV, 1012
Warrington, Jesse IV, 1012
Warrington, Jesse IV, 1013
Warrington, John II, 679
Warrington, John II, 890
Warrington, John II, 936
Warrington, John IV, 784
Warrington, John A. IV, 744
Warrington, John R. IV, 114
Warrington, John R. IV, 117
Warrington, John R. IV, 784
Warrington, John R. IV, 1012
Warrington, John R. IV, 1013
Warrington, Joseph II, 168
Warrington, Josephine IV, 183
Warrington, Josephine IV, 299
Warrington, Josephine IV, 784
Warrington, Josephine IV, 931
Warrington, Josephine IV, 1013
Warrington, Josephine B. IV, 184
Warrington, Josephine B. IV, 1012
Warrington, Josephine B. IV, 1013
Warrington, Joshua IV, 762
Warrington, Joshua IV, 784
Warrington, Joshua IV, 993
Warrington, Joshua IV, 1012
Warrington, Joshua IV, 1013
Warrington, Keziah IV, 114
Warrington, Keziah IV, 664
Warrington, Keziah IV, 784
Warrington, Keziah IV, 789
Warrington, Keziah IV, 981
Warrington, Keziah IV, 983
Warrington, Keziah IV, 1010
Warrington, Keziah IV, 1012
Warrington, Keziah VI, 737
Warrington, Keziah VI, 742
Warrington, Keziah VI, 789
Warrington, Lawrence E. IV, 1013
Warrington, Leneus Henry IV, 1013
Warrington, Lenna Mae IV, 784
Warrington, Lenna Mae IV, 785
Warrington, Lenna Mae IV, 1013
Warrington, Lineas IV, 664
Warrington, Lineus IV, 784
Warrington, Lineus IV, 1013
Warrington, Linnaeas IV, 664
Warrington, Linneas IV, 299
Warrington, Linneaus IV, 451
Warrington, Linneaus IV, 1013
Warrington, Linneous IV, 851
Warrington, Linneus IV, 451
Warrington, Linneus IV, 851
Warrington, Linneus IV, 1012
Warrington, Linneus IV, 1081
Warrington, Linnoeus IV, 803
Warrington, Lizzie J. IV, 784
Warrington, Lydia IV, 299
Warrington, Lydia IV, 851
Warrington, Lydia IV, 1012
Warrington, Lydia IV, 1013
Warrington, Margaret C. II, 114
Warrington, Margaret C. II, 125
Warrington, Margery C. IV, 1012
Warrington, Martha IV, 784
Warrington, Martha IV, 1012
Warrington, Martha IV, 1013
Warrington, Mary IV, 620
Warrington, Mary IV, 664
Warrington, Mary IV, 784
Warrington, Mary IV, 851
Warrington, Mary IV, 1012
Warrington, Mary IV, 1013
Warrington, Mary IV, 1017
Warrington, Mary IV, 1081
Warrington, Mary D. IV, 1012
Warrington, Mary D. IV, 1013
Warrington, Mary D. IV, 1081
Warrington, Mary E. IV, 985
Warrington, Mary E. IV, 1012
Warrington, Mary Elizabeth IV, 985
Warrington, Mary Elizabeth IV, 1013
Warrington, Mary Ellen IV, 299
Warrington, Mary Elma IV, 451
Warrington, Mary Elma IV, 822
Warrington, Mary Elma IV, 851
Warrington, Mary Elma IV, 1101
Warrington, Mary I. IV, 743
Warrington, Mary I. IV, 784
Warrington, Mary Sara IV, 815
Warrington, Mary Sara IV, 851
Warrington, Melva L. IV, 451
Warrington, Melva L. IV, 851
Warrington, Melva S. IV, 851
Warrington, Melva W. IV, 822
Warrington, Melva W. IV, 852
Warrington, Morris J. IV, 1013
Warrington, Nathan IV, 620
Warrington, Nathan IV, 664
Warrington, Nathan IV, 784
Warrington, Nathan IV, 851
Warrington, Nathan IV, 1012
Warrington, Nathan IV, 1013
Warrington, Nathan IV, 1081
Warrington, Paul A. IV, 1012
Warrington, Phebe Ellen IV, 451
Warrington, Phebe Ellen IV, 851
Warrington, Priscilla IV, 706
Warrington, Priscilla IV, 784
Warrington, Rachel IV, 114
Warrington, Rachel IV, 117
Warrington, Rachel IV, 178
Warrington, Rachel IV, 531
Warrington, Rachel IV, 664
Warrington, Rachel IV, 680
Warrington, Rachel IV, 706
Warrington, Rachel IV, 717
Warrington, Rachel IV, 725
Warrington, Rachel IV, 744
Warrington, Rachel IV, 770
Warrington, Rachel IV, 784
Warrington, Rachel IV, 1012
Warrington, Rachel IV, 1013
Warrington, Rebecca IV, 744
Warrington, Rebecca IV, 784
Warrington, Rebecca IV, 1012
Warrington, Rebecca IV, 1013
Warrington, Rebecca W. II, 114
Warrington, Rebecca W. II, 125
Warrington, Ruth IV, 784
Warrington, Ruth IV, 983
Warrington, Ruth IV, 1012
Warrington, Samuel D. IV, 664
Warrington, Samuel D. IV, 1012
Warrington, Sara Etta IV, 833
Warrington, Sara Etta IV, 851
Warrington, Sara Mabel IV, 1013
Warrington, Saraetta IV, 451
Warrington, Sarah II, 809
Warrington, Sarah IV, 784
Warrington, Sarah IV, 1010
Warrington, Sarah IV, 1012
Warrington, Sarah Ann IV, 664
Warrington, Sarah Ann IV, 784
Warrington, Sarah Ann IV, 1012
Warrington, Sarah Ann IV, 1013
Warrington, Sarah Ann IV, 1081
Warrington, Sarah H. II, 679
Warrington, Sarah Mabel IV, 664
Warrington, Sarah Mabel IV, 961
Warrington, Sarah Mable IV, 628
Warrington, Sarah Mable IV, 664
Warrington, Sarah Mable IV, 1012
Warrington, Sarahetta IV, 299
Warrington, Saretta IV, 833
Warrington, Saretta IV, 851
Warrington, Sina IV, 299
Warrington, Sina IV, 451
Warrington, Sina IV, 803
Warrington, Sina IV, 822
Warrington, Sina IV, 843
Warrington, Sina IV, 851
Warrington, Sina B. IV, 451
Warrington, Sina B. IV, 851
Warrington, Susannah II, 825
Warrington, Susannah II, 890
Warrington, Susannah II, 936
Warrington, Susannah, Jr. II, 936
Warrington, Thomas II, 773
Warrington, Thomas IV, 299
Warrington, Thomas IV, 784
Warrington, Thomas IV, 851
Warrington, Thomas IV, 1012
Warrington, Thomas IV, 1013
Warrington, Thomas C. IV, 628
Warrington, Thomas C. IV, 664
Warrington, Thomas C. IV, 961
Warrington, Thomas C. IV, 1012
Warrington, Thomas C. IV, 1013
Warrington, Unice IV, 993
Warrington, Unice IV, 1013
Warrington, Walter H. IV, 1013
Warrington, Wilson IV, 784
Warrington, Wilson IV, 1012
Warrington, Wilson IV, 1013
Warrington, Wilson IV, 1081
Warrington, Wm. II, 936
Warrman, Adah V, 604
Warrman, Ethel V, 604
Warrman, George W. V, 604
Warrman, Mary A. V, 604
Warson, Calvin V, 364
Warson, Eliza Ann V, 364
Warson, Elizabeth V, 364
Warson, Mary V, 364
Warson, Mary Jane V, 364
Warson, Nathan V, 364
Warson, Sarah V, 364
Warson, William V, 364
Warson, Wm. V, 364
Wartenbary, Elizabeth II, 27
Wartenby, Edward II, 683
Wartenby, Elizabeth II, 683
Warterman, Jesse II, 679
Warters, Clandeon I, 319
Warters, Rebeck II, 110
Wartman, John H. III, 425
Wartman, John H. III, 464
Wartman, Louisa J. III, 425
Wartman, Louisa J. III, 464
Wartman, Mary E. III, 464
Warton, Dixon V, 210
Warton, James Dixon V, 210
Warton, John II, 1036
Warton, Sarah Jane V, 210
Warts, Isaac V, 1024
Warwick, Ann Eliza VI, 863
Warwick, Daniel VI, 1010
Warwick, Fanny VI, 801
Warwick, Henry D. VI, 863
Warwick, James VI, 801
Warwick, James VI, 806
Warwick, James VI, 857
Warwick, Lillian V, 772
Warwick, Lillie V, 772
Warwick, Luanna VI, 863
Warwick, Nancy VI, 1010
Warwick, Nancy B. VI, 857
Warwick, Raymond V, 772
Warwick, Sally B. VI, 806
Warwick, William VI, 863
Warwicke, Daniel VI, 1010
Warwicke, Elizabeth VI, 101
Warwicke, James VI, 1010
Warwicke, Nancy VI, 1010
Washborn, Anna IV, 1191
Washborn, Benjamin IV, 1191
Washborn, Charles A. IV, 119
Washborn, Henry IV, 1191
Washborn, Huldah IV, 1191
Washborn, James IV, 1191
Washborn, Jane III, 360
Washborn, Jane III, 470
Washborn, Joseph IV, 1191
Washborn, Joseph C. IV, 1191
Washborn, Mary III, 470
Washborn, Mary IV, 1191
Washborn, Phebe IV, 1191
Washborn, Philena IV, 1191
Washborn, William III, 470
Washborn, William IV, 1191
Washborn, Wm. III, 360
Washborne, Jane III, 451
Washborne, Martha III, 451
Washborne, William III, 451
Washburn, ??? III, 343
Washburn, Abel III, 342
Washburn, Amelia V, 288
Washburn, Amelia Ann V, 288
Washburn, Andrew Goold III,
Washburn, Ann IV, 1191
Washburn, Anna III, 342
Washburn, Anna III, 343
Washburn, Anna IV, 1149
Washburn, Anna IV, 1191
Washburn, Annah III, 342
Washburn, Annah III, 343
Washburn, Benjamin IV, 1191
Washburn, Charles IV, 1191
Washburn, Charles A. IV, 119
Washburn, Daniel III, 342
Washburn, Elijah III, 342
Washburn, Elijah III, 343
Washburn, Eliza Ann III, 342
Washburn, Elizabeth III, 342
Washburn, Elkanah III, 342
Washburn, Ethel V, 210
Washburn, Frances H. III, 34
Washburn, Frank V, 288
Washburn, George V, 288
Washburn, Hannah III, 342
Washburn, Henry IV, 1191
Washburn, Henry C. IV, 1191
Washburn, Henry Craft IV, 11
Washburn, Huldah IV, 1191
Washburn, James IV, 1191
Washburn, James IV, 1236

burn, James IV, 1242
burn, Jessie Florence V, 467
burn, Joseph III, 342
burn, Joseph IV, 1191
burn, Joseph IV, 1242
burn, Joseph C. IV, 1191
burn, Joseph, Jr. IV, 1191
burn, Josephine E. V, 594
burn, Josephine E. V, 604
burn, Lavinia B. IV, 1191
burn, Levinia IV, 1191
burn, Loisa IV, 1191
burn, Louisa IV, 1197
burn, Louisa IV, 1198
burn, Lydia IV, 699
burn, Lydia IV, 785
burn, Manerva IV, 1266
burn, Margarum III, 343
burn, Maria Louise III, 223
burn, Mary III, 342
burn, Mary III, 360
burn, Mary IV, 1191
burn, Mary T. IV, 1191
burn, Minerva IV, 1266
burn, Miriam Margaret
, 87
burn, Miriam Margaret
, 138
burn, Nancy Arabella
II, 71
burn, Phebe III, 297
burn, Phebe IV, 1187
burn, Phebe IV, 1191
burn, Philena IV, 1191
burn, Philener IV, 1191
burn, Phoebe III, 127
burn, Phoebe III, 297
burn, Rachel IV, 1236
burn, Rachel IV, 1242
burn, Rachel H. IV, 785
burn, Rebecca III, 342
burn, Richard III, 342
burn, Robert III, 342
burn, Robert IV, 1191
burn, Samson B. V, 467
burn, Sarah III, 343
burn, Sarah III, 371
burn, Stanley Wynne
Keever V, 138
burn, Tamar III, 342
burn, Tamar III, 343
burn, Thomas W. III, 342
burn, Thomas W. III, 343
burn, William IV, 1191
burn, Wm. III, 342
burn, Zelia IV, 1242
ington, Annabel B. III, 89
ington, Benjamin V, 649
ington, Col. George VI, 16
ington, Col. George VI, 18
ington, Col. George VI, 225
ington, Geo. III, 89
ington, George VI, 466
ington, Henrietta IV, 1191
ington, Henry IV, 1191
ington, John VI, 124
ington, Lavina V. V, 614
ington, Levina V. V, 649
ington, Sadler VI, 124
son, Asa V, 288
son, Asa V, 364
son, Asa V, 436
son, Asa B. V, 436
son, Calvin V, 288
son, Calvin V, 364
son, Calvin V, 375
son, Calvin V, 396
son, Calvin V, 436
son, Calvin H. V, 436
son, Eliza Ann V, 288
son, Eliza Ann V, 364
son, Eliza Ann V, 436
son, Elizabeth I, 931
son, Elizabeth V, 236
son, Elizabeth V, 288
son, Elizabeth V, 364
son, Elizabeth V, 396
son, Elizabeth V, 436
son, Emily V, 288
son, Hannah Ann V, 288
son, Maria V, 326
son, Maria V, 364
son, Mary I, 617
son, Mary V, 288
son, Mary V, 364
son, Mary V, 375
son, Mary V, 396
son, Mary V, 436
son, Mary Jane V, 288
son, Mary Jane V, 364
son, Mary Jane V, 375
Wasson, Mary Jane V, 436
Wasson, Nathan V, 326
Wasson, Nathan V, 364
Wasson, Nathan V, 436
Wasson, P. Alwilda V, 288
Wasson, Priscilla Alwilda V, 288
Wasson, Sarah V, 364
Wasson, Sarah V, 436
Wasson, Thomas Elwood V, 288
Wasson, William V, 236
Wasson, William V, 288
Wasson, William V, 364
Wasson, William V, 436
Wasson, Wm. V, 364
Waston, Martha A. VI, 967
Waston, William O. VI, 967
Wastre, Achsah I, 319
Water, White I, 387
Water, White V, 599
Waterbury, Azariah III, 295
Waterbury, Azariah III, 343
Waterbury, Azariah III, 437
Waterbury, Azariah III, 464
Waterbury, Azariah III, 503
Waterbury, Esther A. IV, 1328
Waterbury, Harriet A. III, 343
Waterbury, John III, 464
Waterbury, Martha III, 464
Waterbury, Mary III, 295
Waterbury, Mary III, 343
Waterbury, Nellie P. VI, 789
Waterbury, Nellie Sylvia IV, 1342
Waterbury, Phebe III, 503
Waterbury, Ralph IV, 1328
Waterbury, Ralph H. IV, 1342
Waterbury, Ruannah III, 295
Waterbury, Ruannah III, 343
Waterbury, Ruhama III, 503
Waterbury, Sarah III, 437
Waterbury, Sarah III, 464
Waterbury, Wm. H. IV, 1342
Waterman, Almina Jane IV, 1226
Waterman, Amos II, 679
Waterman, Amy IV, 193
Waterman, Amy IV, 263
Waterman, Amy IV, 300
Waterman, Amy Phebus IV, 300
Waterman, Ann IV, 226
Waterman, Ann IV, 299
Waterman, Ann IV, 300
Waterman, Ann IV, 555
Waterman, Ann T. IV, 299
Waterman, Barclay II, 679
Waterman, Caleb IV, 1226
Waterman, Charles IV, 299
Waterman, Charles A. IV, 299
Waterman, Charles Johnson
IV, 300
Waterman, Chas. IV, 299
Waterman, Elizabeth II, 679
Waterman, Fanny II, 679
Waterman, Fanny II, 936
Waterman, George IV, 1226
Waterman, Hannah II, 466
Waterman, Hannah II, 615
Waterman, Hannah II, 679
Waterman, Hannah II, 936
Waterman, Hannah IV, 299
Waterman, Hannah IV, 300
Waterman, Hannah IV, 555
Waterman, Hannah W. IV, 314
Waterman, Hannah W. IV, 315
Waterman, Henry Paxon II, 679
Waterman, Henry Paxson II, 679
Waterman, Humphrey II, 433
Waterman, Humphrey II, 567
Waterman, Humphrey II, 679
Waterman, Humphrey II, 936
Waterman, Humphrey J. II, 936
Waterman, Humphrey John
II, 826
Waterman, Isaac IV, 226
Waterman, Isaac IV, 299
Waterman, Isaac IV, 300
Waterman, Isaac IV, 555
Waterman, Isaac Smith II, 826
Waterman, James IV, 251
Waterman, Jane II, 549
Waterman, Jane II, 679
Waterman, Jesse II, 433
Waterman, Jesse II, 615
Waterman, Jesse II, 679
Waterman, John II, 463
Waterman, John II, 466
Waterman, John II, 615
Waterman, John II, 679
Waterman, John II, 825
Waterman, John II, 936
Waterman, John IV, 235
Waterman, John IV, 299
Waterman, John IV, 300
Waterman, John IV, 555
Waterman, John IV, 1226
Waterman, Joseph II, 433
Waterman, Joseph II, 936
Waterman, Joseph IV, 300
Waterman, Leanna IV, 195
Waterman, Leanna IV, 300
Waterman, Leannah IV, 300
Waterman, Leannah IV, 555
Waterman, Lewis II, 679
Waterman, Lewis II, 936
Waterman, Margaret II, 567
Waterman, Margaret II, 679
Waterman, Margaretta II, 936
Waterman, Margaretta C. II, 936
Waterman, Margaretta Carey
II, 826
Waterman, Mary II, 433
Waterman, Mary IV, 235
Waterman, Mary IV, 251
Waterman, Mary IV, 299
Waterman, Mary IV, 1226
Waterman, Mary Paul II, 679
Waterman, Molly Paul II, 547
Waterman, Molly Paul II, 679
Waterman, Phebe II, 433
Waterman, Phebe II, 615
Waterman, Phebe II, 679
Waterman, Phebe II, 826
Waterman, Phebe II, 936
Waterman, Phebe III, 499
Waterman, Phebe IV, 270
Waterman, Phebe IV, 300
Waterman, Phebe IV, 314
Waterman, Phebe IV, 315
Waterman, Phineas IV, 299
Waterman, Rebecca IV, 188
Waterman, Rebecca IV, 251
Waterman, Rebecca IV, 299
Waterman, Rebecca IV, 300
Waterman, Rebecca Ann IV, 299
Waterman, Rebecca Michener
IV, 300
Waterman, Rebeckah IV, 555
Waterman, Robert H. II, 936
Waterman, Robert Hilborne
II, 679
Waterman, Robert L. II, 936
Waterman, Sarah Rebecca
IV, 1226
Waterman, Wd. Fanny II, 825
Waterman, William II, 433
Waterman, William IV, 299
Waterman, William IV, 300
Waterman, Wm. II, 679
Waters, ??? III, 343
Waters, Ann II, 433
Waters, Ann III, 343
Waters, Ann Eliza II, 433
Waters, Artridge VI, 546
Waters, Artridge VI, 577
Waters, Bennet G. VI, 455
Waters, Clandeon I, 319
Waters, Daniel III, 343
Waters, Dinah VI, 602
Waters, Dinah VI, 608
Waters, Dora P. I, 950
Waters, Dora Padgett I, 950
Waters, Edward IV, 356
Waters, Elizabeth II, 433
Waters, Elizabeth II, 605
Waters, Elizabeth II, 679
Waters, Elizabeth VI, 1011
Waters, Ernest W. III, 338
Waters, Florence Litchfield
III, 338
Waters, Fred M. I, 950
Waters, Fred Monroe I, 950
Waters, George IV, 852
Waters, George VI, 602
Waters, George VI, 608
Waters, George Sinclaie II, 773
Waters, George Sinclair II, 433
Waters, Hanson II, 433
Waters, Hanson II, 679
Waters, Hanson II, 773
Waters, Jane IV, 299
Waters, Jane VI, 1011
Waters, Jane M. IV, 269
Waters, Jane M. V, 772
Waters, John VI, 1011
Waters, Joseph VI, 546
Waters, Lydia VI, 602
Waters, Lydia VI, 607
Waters, Lydia VI, 608
Waters, Maggie I, 319
Waters, Margaret VI, 506
Waters, Marry Susannah VI, 577
Waters, Martha II, 433
Waters, Mary II, 433
Waters, Mary II, 745
Waters, Mary II, 773
Waters, Mary VI, 33
Waters, Mary VI, 37
Waters, Mildred I, 319
Waters, Rebecca II, 110
Waters, Rebeck II, 110
Waters, Rebekah II, 110
Waters, Richard VI, 11
Waters, Rodger I, 580
Waters, Roger I, 580
Waters, Roger II, 433
Waters, Roger II, 679
Waters, Rogers I, 580
Waters, Ruth III, 343
Waters, Ruth, Jr. III, 343
Waters, Samuel VI, 546
Waters, Samuel VI, 577
Waters, Sarah II, 433
Waters, Sarah II, 679
Waters, Sarah II, 757
Waters, Sarah II, 773
Waters, Sarah VI, 455
Waters, Sarah VI, 546
Waters, Susannah VI, 546
Waters, Thomas II, 433
Waters, Virginia I, 319
Waters, Walter VI, 33
Waters, Walter VI, 37
Waters, William II, 433
Waters, William II, 448
Waters, Wm. II, 679
Waterson, Abner IV, 570
Waterson, Ann IV, 570
Waterson, Elizabeth IV, 570
Waterworth, Elisabeth IV, 697
Waterworth, Elizabeth IV, 671
Waterworth, Elizabeth IV, 785
Waterworth, Elizabeth IV, 885
Waterworth, James IV, 785
Waterworth, Margaret IV, 785
Waterworth, William IV, 785
Waterworth, William IV, 885
Waterworth, Wm. IV, 697
Waterworth, Wm. IV, 785
Waterworth, Wm. IV, 852
Wathal, Henry VI, 806
Wathall, Jemima VI, 120
Wathall, Thomas VI, 120
Watkin, ??? II, 826
Watkin, Cornelia II, 936
Watkin, Cornelia W. II, 859
Watkin, Cornelia W. II, 936
Watkin, Edith Sharpless II, 826
Watkin, Emma II, 826
Watkin, Emma W. II, 936
Watkin, Enoch II, 826
Watkin, Hannah I, 761
Watkin, Hannah II, 826
Watkin, Hannah B. II, 826
Watkin, Isaac II, 826
Watkins, ??? IV, 1269
Watkins, ??? VI, 95
Watkins, ??? VI, 223
Watkins, ??? VI, 747
Watkins, Aaron VI, 862
Watkins, Adille IV, 1191
Watkins, Agnes VI, 344
Watkins, Agness VI, 131
Watkins, Agness VI, 143
Watkins, Agness VI, 344
Watkins, Albert IV, 1298
Watkins, Aldren III, 343
Watkins, Alice IV, 1342
Watkins, Alida IV, 1298
Watkins, Almeda IV, 1297
Watkins, Almeda IV, 1298
Watkins, Amelia IV, 1297
Watkins, Amos VI, 143
Watkins, Angalina IV, 1298
Watkins, Angelina IV, 279
Watkins, Angelina IV, 300
Watkins, Angelina V, 977
Watkins, Angelina V, 978
Watkins, Angelina VI, 143
Watkins, Ann I, 253
Watkins, Ann I, 259
Watkins, Ann IV, 1298
Watkins, Ann VI, 45
Watkins, Ann VI, 46
Watkins, Ann VI, 119
Watkins, Ann VI, 124
Watkins, Ann VI, 138
Watkins, Ann VI, 143
Watkins, Ann Eliza IV, 1298
Watkins, Anna I, 253
Watkins, Anna I, 259
Watkins, Anna IV, 451
Watkins, Anna IV, 452
Watkins, Anna IV, 501
Watkins, Anna IV, 598
Watkins, Anna V, 397
Watkins, Anna V, 436
Watkins, Anna Jennette IV, 1298
Watkins, Anna Maria VI, 747
Watkins, Anna Maria VI, 789
Watkins, Anne VI, 143
Watkins, Anzonetta IV, 1297
Watkins, Anzonetta Rebecca
IV, 1298
Watkins, Aron VI, 863
Watkins, Asenath IV, 1298
Watkins, Ashley VI, 279
Watkins, Belle I, 950
Watkins, Benj. IV, 505
Watkins, Benj. VI, 279
Watkins, Benjamin IV, 452
Watkins, Benjamin IV, 501
Watkins, Benjamin IV, 1297
Watkins, Benjamin IV, 1298
Watkins, Benjamin VI, 124
Watkins, Benjamin VI, 143
Watkins, Benjamin VI, 159
Watkins, Benjamin VI, 217
Watkins, Benjamin VI, 251
Watkins, Benjamin VI, 252
Watkins, Benjamin VI, 278
Watkins, Benjamin VI, 279
Watkins, Benjamin VI, 863
Watkins, Benjamin, Jr. VI, 279
Watkins, Benjamin, Sr. VI, 279
Watkins, Bennet IV, 452
Watkins, Bennet IV, 1297
Watkins, Bennett IV, 598
Watkins, Bennett VI, 143
Watkins, Bernice IV, 1298
Watkins, Betsy VI, 252
Watkins, Betsy VI, 256
Watkins, Betsy VI, 279
Watkins, C. A. G. VI, 843
Watkins, Caroline IV, 1298
Watkins, Carrie IV, 204
Watkins, Carrie IV, 1280
Watkins, Carrie IV, 1298
Watkins, Catherine Melissa
IV, 1298
Watkins, Chas. IV, 1298
Watkins, Christiana B. IV, 1298
Watkins, Clara IV, 204
Watkins, Cloah I, 319
Watkins, Corenia I, 340
Watkins, Corinna I, 340
Watkins, Cornelia II, 792
Watkins, Cornelia II, 936
Watkins, Creighton IV, 300
Watkins, D. J. I, 950
Watkins, David B. IV, 1298
Watkins, David H. IV, 1298
Watkins, David John I, 935
Watkins, Deborah IV, 206
Watkins, Deborah IV, 300
Watkins, Deborah A. IV, 1280
Watkins, Deborah A. IV, 1298
Watkins, Deborah Ann IV, 1298
Watkins, Deborah D. IV, 1281
Watkins, Deborah D. IV, 1297
Watkins, Deborah D. IV, 1298
Watkins, Delenah VI, 143
Watkins, Delphina IV, 1298
Watkins, Dora I, 340
Watkins, Dorothy I, 56
Watkins, Dorothy I, 77
Watkins, Dorothy VI, 88
Watkins, Edgar J. IV, 1297
Watkins, Edith S. II, 792
Watkins, Edward Horace
IV, 1298
Watkins, Edwin IV, 452
Watkins, Edwin IV, 1297
Watkins, Edwin VI, 143
Watkins, Edwin Lanson IV, 1298
Watkins, Eleanor VI, 863
Watkins, Eli IV, 203
Watkins, Elijah VI, 251
Watkins, Elisabeth I, 259
Watkins, Eliza IV, 1298
Watkins, Eliza J. IV, 1297
Watkins, Eliza Jane IV, 1295
Watkins, Eliza Jane IV, 1297
Watkins, Eliza Jane IV, 1298
Watkins, Elizabeth I, 669
Watkins, Elizabeth I, 678
Watkins, Elizabeth I, 691
Watkins, Elizabeth I, 771
Watkins, Elizabeth I, 794
Watkins, Elizabeth IV, 218
Watkins, Elizabeth IV, 239
Watkins, Elizabeth IV, 279
Watkins, Elizabeth IV, 300
Watkins, Elizabeth IV, 1297
Watkins, Elizabeth IV, 1298
Watkins, Elizabeth V, 569
Watkins, Elizabeth VI, 88

Watkins, Elizabeth VI, 89
Watkins, Elizabeth VI, 143
Watkins, Elizabeth VI, 216
Watkins, Elizabeth VI, 251
Watkins, Elizabeth VI, 252
Watkins, Elizabeth VI, 279
Watkins, Elizabeth VI, 845
Watkins, Elizabeth VI, 862
Watkins, Elizabeth VI, 863
Watkins, Elizabeth B. IV, 1298
Watkins, Elizabeth D. IV, 1274
Watkins, Elizabeth D. IV, 1298
Watkins, Elizabeth Hadley V, 604
Watkins, Elizzbeth VI, 88
Watkins, Elma IV, 1297
Watkins, Emma II, 934
Watkins, Emma II, 936
Watkins, Emma W. II, 936
Watkins, Enoch II, 934
Watkins, Enoch II, 936
Watkins, Enoch VI, 841
Watkins, Enoch VI, 863
Watkins, Enos IV, 1298
Watkins, Ernest IV, 1298
Watkins, Ernest W. III, 343
Watkins, Ethel I, 340
Watkins, Ethel III, 93
Watkins, Ethel III, 343
Watkins, Ethel M. IV, 204
Watkins, Eunice B. I, 761
Watkins, Eunice B. I, 771
Watkins, Eva M. III, 343
Watkins, Evie M. IV, 1298
Watkins, Ezekiel IV, 1297
Watkins, Ezra IV, 1297
Watkins, Ezra IV, 1298
Watkins, Flora IV, 297
Watkins, Flora IV, 300
Watkins, Floyd IV, 1298
Watkins, Francis IV, 1342
Watkins, Francis E. IV, 1342
Watkins, Franklin I, 669
Watkins, G. P. IV, 1191
Watkins, Genito VI, 279
Watkins, Geo. Washington IV, 1298
Watkins, George I, 340
Watkins, George VI, 48
Watkins, George Edward I, 340
Watkins, Gulielma IV, 1297
Watkins, Hanna VI, 863
Watkins, Hannah I, 686
Watkins, Hannah I, 688
Watkins, Hannah I, 691
Watkins, Hannah I, 771
Watkins, Hannah I, 794
Watkins, Hannah I, 843
Watkins, Hannah II, 934
Watkins, Hannah II, 936
Watkins, Hannah IV, 1298
Watkins, Hannah VI, 810
Watkins, Harriet E. IV, 204
Watkins, Harriet E. VI, 863
Watkins, Harriett VI, 1003
Watkins, Harry IV, 300
Watkins, Henery I, 669
Watkins, Henery I, 691
Watkins, Henry I, 259
Watkins, Henry I, 319
Watkins, Henry I, 678
Watkins, Henry I, 691
Watkins, Henry I, 771
Watkins, Henry I, 794
Watkins, Henry VI, 204
Watkins, Henry VI, 216
Watkins, Henry C. IV, 1298
Watkins, Henry, Jr. VI, 148
Watkins, Henry, Jr. VI, 181
Watkins, Henry, Jr. VI, 216
Watkins, Henry, Sr. VI, 148
Watkins, Henry, Sr. VI, 216
Watkins, Hiram Hough V, 963
Watkins, Hoadley A. IV, 1342
Watkins, Howard IV, 1298
Watkins, Ira IV, 598
Watkins, Irven IV, 1298
Watkins, Iry IV, 452
Watkins, Iry IV, 1297
Watkins, Iry VI, 143
Watkins, Isaac II, 792
Watkins, Isaac II, 934
Watkins, Isaac II, 936
Watkins, Jacob VI, 848
Watkins, James I, 259
Watkins, James IV, 451
Watkins, James IV, 598
Watkins, James IV, 1297
Watkins, James IV, 1298
Watkins, James VI, 19
Watkins, James VI, 119
Watkins, James VI, 124
Watkins, James VI, 131
Watkins, James VI, 143
Watkins, James R. IV, 204
Watkins, Jamima IV, 1297
Watkins, Jane I, 259
Watkins, Jane VI, 124
Watkins, Jane VI, 279
Watkins, Jane VI, 797
Watkins, Jane, Jr. VI, 279
Watkins, Jas. IV, 501
Watkins, Jenny VI, 890
Watkins, Jeremiah I, 691
Watkins, Jesse I, 691
Watkins, Jesse I, 753
Watkins, Jesse I, 762
Watkins, Jesse I, 771
Watkins, Jesse VI, 88
Watkins, Job VI, 789
Watkins, Joel I, 688
Watkins, Joel I, 691
Watkins, Joel I, 794
Watkins, Joel I, 843
Watkins, Joel IV, 452
Watkins, Joel IV, 598
Watkins, Joel IV, 1298
Watkins, John I, 259
Watkins, John I, 340
Watkins, John I, 935
Watkins, John IV, 218
Watkins, John IV, 1298
Watkins, John VI, 70
Watkins, John VI, 88
Watkins, John VI, 123
Watkins, John VI, 124
Watkins, John VI, 143
Watkins, John VI, 161
Watkins, John VI, 199
Watkins, John VI, 217
Watkins, John VI, 334
Watkins, John VI, 1003
Watkins, John VI, 1011
Watkins, John Elwood IV, 1297
Watkins, John Hare VI, 88
Watkins, John T. IV, 1297
Watkins, John W. I, 340
Watkins, John W. IV, 279
Watkins, John W. IV, 1298
Watkins, John W. VI, 143
Watkins, Joseph IV, 1342
Watkins, Joseph VI, 217
Watkins, Joseph VI, 279
Watkins, Joseph H. IV, 1297
Watkins, Joseph S. VI, 824
Watkins, Josephine IV, 204
Watkins, Josiah J. VI, 88
Watkins, Judith VI, 253
Watkins, Judith VI, 279
Watkins, Lambert VI, 143
Watkins, Ledy VI, 253
Watkins, Ledy VI, 279
Watkins, Lelia Belle I, 935
Watkins, Lemuel IV, 452
Watkins, Lemuel IV, 598
Watkins, Lemuel IV, 1297
Watkins, Lemuel VI, 143
Watkins, Leroy IV, 204
Watkins, Lewis VI, 1011
Watkins, Lillian IV, 1342
Watkins, Lindley IV, 1298
Watkins, Littleberry I, 259
Watkins, Louisa IV, 1298
Watkins, Luarky I, 753
Watkins, Lucinda I, 691
Watkins, Lucinda IV, 598
Watkins, Lucinda IV, 1297
Watkins, Lucinda VI, 143
Watkins, Lucinda D. VI, 863
Watkins, Lurana ??? IV, 1297
Watkins, Lurena Jane IV, 1298
Watkins, Lusinda IV, 218
Watkins, Lusinda IV, 300
Watkins, Luza VI, 143
Watkins, Lydea VI, 252
Watkins, Lydea VI, 279
Watkins, Lydia I, 691
Watkins, Lydia I, 771
Watkins, Lydia IV, 266
Watkins, Lydia IV, 300
Watkins, Lydia IV, 1298
Watkins, Lydia VI, 143
Watkins, Lydia VI, 318
Watkins, Lydia Alice IV, 1298
Watkins, Margaret IV, 1298
Watkins, Maria W. VI, 789
Watkins, Martha IV, 1298
Watkins, Martha Ann IV, 1297
Watkins, Martha J. IV, 203
Watkins, Martin M. IV, 1297
Watkins, Mary I, 237
Watkins, Mary I, 259
Watkins, Mary I, 753
Watkins, Mary I, 762
Watkins, Mary I, 771
Watkins, Mary II, 613
Watkins, Mary II, 679
Watkins, Mary IV, 1298
Watkins, Mary IV, 1342
Watkins, Mary VI, 46
Watkins, Mary VI, 124
Watkins, Mary VI, 184
Watkins, Mary VI, 199
Watkins, Mary VI, 216
Watkins, Mary VI, 217
Watkins, Mary VI, 251
Watkins, Mary VI, 278
Watkins, Mary VI, 279
Watkins, Mary VI, 841
Watkins, Mary VI, 845
Watkins, Mary VI, 848
Watkins, Mary VI, 863
Watkins, Mary VI, 1011
Watkins, Mary A. VI, 863
Watkins, Mary Ann IV, 1297
Watkins, Mary Ann V, 563
Watkins, Mary Ann V, 604
Watkins, Mary Asenath IV, 1298
Watkins, Mary E. IV, 1342
Watkins, Mary Eliza IV, 1297
Watkins, Mary Jane IV, 1298
Watkins, Mary S. IV, 1297
Watkins, Matilda IV, 1297
Watkins, Matilda A. IV, 1298
Watkins, Matilda Ann IV, 1297
Watkins, Melissa Ann IV, 1297
Watkins, Moses VI, 823
Watkins, Moses VI, 824
Watkins, Moses VI, 841
Watkins, Moses VI, 863
Watkins, Moses VI, 867
Watkins, Nancy VI, 1011
Watkins, Naomi A. IV, 1298
Watkins, Nathan IV, 1298
Watkins, Obedience IV, 1285
Watkins, Obedience IV, 1297
Watkins, Obedience IV, 1298
Watkins, Patty VI, 823
Watkins, Penelope I, 77
Watkins, Penelope VI, 66
Watkins, Penelope VI, 88
Watkins, Phenehas IV, 1298
Watkins, Pheraba IV, 1278
Watkins, Pheraba A. IV, 1298
Watkins, Pheriba Ann IV, 1297
Watkins, Priscilla VI, 159
Watkins, Priscilla VI, 252
Watkins, Priscilla VI, 279
Watkins, Rachel I, 259
Watkins, Rachel I, 319
Watkins, Rachel IV, 1298
Watkins, Rachel V, 79
Watkins, Rachel V, 138
Watkins, Rachel VI, 216
Watkins, Rachel VI, 219
Watkins, Rachel VI, 863
Watkins, Rachel C. IV, 1298
Watkins, Rebecca IV, 1297
Watkins, Rebecca IV, 1298
Watkins, Rebecca A. E. IV, 203
Watkins, Reece VI, 863
Watkins, Reuben I, 253
Watkins, Reuben I, 259
Watkins, Reuben IV, 451
Watkins, Reuben IV, 452
Watkins, Reuben IV, 598
Watkins, Reuben IV, 1297
Watkins, Reuben VI, 124
Watkins, Reuben VI, 131
Watkins, Reuben VI, 143
Watkins, Reubin VI, 143
Watkins, Robert I, 56
Watkins, Robert I, 77
Watkins, Robert IV, 1297
Watkins, Robert IV, 1298
Watkins, Robert VI, 88
Watkins, Robert VI, 131
Watkins, Robert VI, 143
Watkins, Robert VI, 279
Watkins, Robert VI, 810
Watkins, Robert VI, 845
Watkins, Robert VI, 848
Watkins, Robert VI, 863
Watkins, Robert J. III, 343
Watkins, Robert J. IV, 1298
Watkins, Robert K. VI, 863
Watkins, Robert, Jr. VI, 216
Watkins, Robert, Jr. VI, 863
Watkins, Rosa Lee V, 963
Watkins, Ruby Jane I, 340
Watkins, Ruth IV, 1342
Watkins, Ruth Ann IV, 1297
Watkins, Ruth N. I, 761
Watkins, Ruth N. I, 771
Watkins, Sally V, 288
Watkins, Samuel D. VI, 863
Watkins, Samuel M. IV, 1297
Watkins, Sarah I, 935
Watkins, Sarah VI, 102
Watkins, Sarah VI, 104
Watkins, Sarah VI, 124
Watkins, Sarah VI, 161
Watkins, Sarah VI, 279
Watkins, Sarah VI, 824
Watkins, Sarah VI, 867
Watkins, Sarah VI, 1011
Watkins, Sarah A. IV, 204
Watkins, Sarah Ann IV, 1297
Watkins, Sarah Ann IV, 1298
Watkins, Sarah Delphina IV, 1298
Watkins, Sarah Elma IV, 1298
Watkins, Sarah Evaline IV, 1298
Watkins, Sarah T. V, 963
Watkins, Silas I, 691
Watkins, Stanley IV, 1342
Watkins, Susanna I, 691
Watkins, Susanna IV, 598
Watkins, Susanna IV, 1298
Watkins, Susanna VI, 116
Watkins, Susanna VI, 124
Watkins, Susanna A. IV, 501
Watkins, Susanna A. IV, 505
Watkins, Susanna A. IV, 1298
Watkins, Susannah IV, 452
Watkins, Susannah IV, 1297
Watkins, Susannah VI, 115
Watkins, Susannah VI, 143
Watkins, Susannah VI, 279
Watkins, Thelma IV, 1298
Watkins, Theodora I, 340
Watkins, Thomas IV, 1298
Watkins, Thomas VI, 216
Watkins, Thomas VI, 279
Watkins, Thomas VI, 323
Watkins, Thomas VI, 1011
Watkins, Thomas H. VI, 863
Watkins, Unity IV, 452
Watkins, Unity IV, 598
Watkins, Uriah IV, 1297
Watkins, Uriah IV, 1298
Watkins, W. M. VI, 850
Watkins, Wallace D. IV, 1266
Watkins, Wd. Jane VI, 124
Watkins, Wilford IV, 1298
Watkins, William I, 691
Watkins, William I, 771
Watkins, William II, 433
Watkins, William IV, 452
Watkins, William IV, 598
Watkins, William IV, 1297
Watkins, William VI, 143
Watkins, William D. IV, 1297
Watkins, Willie T. I, 340
Watkins, Winefred VI, 119
Watkins, Winifred VI, 124
Watkins, Winna VI, 119
Watkins, Winna VI, 124
Watkins, Winney VI, 124
Watkins, Winona IV, 1298
Watkins, Wm. IV, 1298
Watkins, Wm. V, 963
Watkins, Zilpah IV, 1298
Watkins, Zilpha IV, 1283
Watlin, Eunice IV, 501
Watlin, Joan II, 581
Watlin, Joan II, 679
Watrous, Walter IV, 1266
Watskins, Pauline VI, 807
Watson, ??? III, 343
Watson, Aaron II, 679
Watson, Abigail II, 433
Watson, Abigail II, 604
Watson, Abigail II, 679
Watson, Abigail IV, 183
Watson, Abigail IV, 300
Watson, Abner II, 198
Watson, Abner II, 270
Watson, Abner II, 1035
Watson, Abner II, 1036
Watson, Abner IV, 354
Watson, Abner IV, 356
Watson, Abner IV, 390
Watson, Abner IV, 398
Watson, Abner IV, 435
Watson, Abner IV, 452
Watson, Abner IV, 664
Watson, Achsa I, 843
Watson, Achsa I, 846
Watson, Addie M. IV, 852
Watson, Agness Harriet VI, 973
Watson, Alex. P. VI, 863
Watson, Amos II, 270
Watson, Amos II, 969
Watson, Amos II, 972
Watson, Amos II, 979
Watson, Amos II, 992
Watson, Amos II, 1035
Watson, Amos II, 1036
Watson, Amy IV, 300
Watson, Ann II, 680
Watson, Ann II, 971
Watson, Ann II, 972
Watson, Ann II, 1016
Watson, Ann II, 1021
Watson, Ann II, 1024
Watson, Ann II, 1035
Watson, Ann II, 1036
Watson, Ann III, 148
Watson, Ann IV, 210
Watson, Ann IV, 300
Watson, Ann IV, 356
Watson, Ann IV, 452
Watson, Ann IV, 501
Watson, Ann IV, 502
Watson, Ann IV, 555
Watson, Ann IV, 599
Watson, Ann IV, 664
Watson, Ann VI, 974
Watson, Ann E. VI, 1011
Watson, Ann F. II, 1079
Watson, Ann F. II, 1082
Watson, Ann Jane IV, 502
Watson, Ann Jane IV, 555
Watson, Ann M. IV, 477
Watson, Ann M. IV, 502
Watson, Ann M. IV, 555
Watson, Ann, Jr. II, 1035
Watson, Anna II, 497
Watson, Anna II, 679
Watson, Anna V, 254
Watson, Anna V, 288
Watson, Anna M. IV, 478
Watson, Anna Mary IV, 300
Watson, Anna Mary IV, 502
Watson, Anna Mary IV, 852
Watson, Anna Mary IV, 1266
Watson, Anna Needles II, 72
Watson, Anna Needles II, 77
Watson, Anna Tatum I, 1163
Watson, Anne II, 773
Watson, Anne II, 826
Watson, Anne II, 936
Watson, Anne VI, 882
Watson, Anne M. IV, 300
Watson, Anne M. IV, 502
Watson, Annie I, 923
Watson, Annie IV, 762
Watson, Annie M. IV, 480
Watson, Annie M. IV, 486
Watson, B. W. I, 1163
Watson, Barclay IV, 502
Watson, Barclay IV, 1013
Watson, Barclay S. IV, 300
Watson, Barclay S. IV, 502
Watson, Barclay S. IV, 1013
Watson, Barclay Seebohm IV, 1013
Watson, Barkley Seebohm IV, 1013
Watson, Barnett VI, 1011
Watson, Beatrice IV, 1342
Watson, Benezett IV, 300
Watson, Benezett IV, 502
Watson, Benjamin II, 433
Watson, Benjamin II, 627
Watson, Benjamin II, 679
Watson, Benjamin II, 971
Watson, Benjamin II, 972
Watson, Benjamin II, 980
Watson, Benjamin II, 989
Watson, Benjamin II, 1035
Watson, Benjamin II, 1036
Watson, Benjamin IV, 300
Watson, Benjamin IV, 1167
Watson, Benjamin IV, 1191
Watson, Benjamin IV, 1192
Watson, Benjamin IV, 1242
Watson, Benjamin P. IV, 502
Watson, Benjamin R. VI, 101
Watson, Betsey VI, 871
Watson, Betsy II, 971
Watson, Beulah II, 971
Watson, Branch J. VI, 863
Watson, Bridget II, 197
Watson, Bridget II, 270
Watson, Caleb Maris IV, 101
Watson, Calvin V, 649
Watson, Caroline VI, 863
Watson, Caroline M. II, 936
Watson, Caroline M. II, 939
Watson, Catharine IV, 1192
Watson, Charles II, 680
Watson, Charles II, 971
Watson, Charles II, 1056
Watson, Charles II, 1082

on, Charles V, 539
on, Charles V, 649
on, Charles B. II, 1080
on, Charles C. IV, 502
on, Charles Henry II, 1067
on, Charles Henry II, 1082
son, Charlotte II, 969
son, Charlotte II, 1079
son, Charlotte II, 1082
son, Charlotte V, 649
son, Chas. L. V, 649
son, Clyde O. V, 718
son, Cynthia VI, 1011
son, David II, 971
son, David II, 1013
son, David II, 1035
son, David II, 1036
son, David II, 1056
son, David Satterthwaite II, 1082
son, Deborah II, 975
son, Deborah II, 977
son, Deborah II, 994
son, Deborah II, 1035
son, Deborah IV, 356
tson, Deborah IV, 390
tson, Deborah IV, 405
tson, Deborah IV, 452
tson, Deborah IV, 486
tson, Deborah IV, 502
tson, Deborah IV, 664
tson, Deborah IV, 978
tson, Deborah IV, 1013
tson, Doroth Ann IV, 300
tson, Dorothy IV, 502
tson, Dorothy Ann IV, 277
tson, Dorothy Ann IV, 502
tson, Edith Stoops V, 718
tson, Edith W. II, 826
tson, Edward II, 679
tson, Edward VI, 577
tson, Eleanor II, 479
tson, Elias E. II, 1080
tson, Elinor II, 971
atson, Elisabeth II, 247
atson, Elisabeth II, 270
atson, Elisabeth IV, 452
atson, Eliz. III, 367
atson, Eliza III, 217
atson, Eliza IV, 300
atson, Eliza IV, 502
atson, Eliza IV, 835
atson, Eliza IV, 852
atson, Eliza IV, 1013
atson, Eliza H. VI, 1011
atson, Eliza J. IV, 502
atson, Eliza Jane II, 722
atson, Eliza Jane II, 773
atson, Eliza T. IV, 502
atson, Eliza T. IV, 852
atson, Eliza T. IV, 1266
atson, Elizabeth II, 198
atson, Elizabeth II, 270
atson, Elizabeth II, 433
atson, Elizabeth II, 577
atson, Elizabeth II, 596
atson, Elizabeth II, 601
Vatson, Elizabeth II, 679
Vatson, Elizabeth II, 722
Vatson, Elizabeth II, 773
Vatson, Elizabeth II, 936
Vatson, Elizabeth II, 939
Vatson, Elizabeth II, 969
Vatson, Elizabeth II, 971
Vatson, Elizabeth II, 980
Vatson, Elizabeth II, 992
Vatson, Elizabeth II, 1027
Vatson, Elizabeth II, 1035
Watson, Elizabeth II, 1036
Watson, Elizabeth IV, 354
Watson, Elizabeth IV, 356
Watson, Elizabeth IV, 390
Watson, Elizabeth IV, 398
Watson, Elizabeth IV, 435
Watson, Elizabeth IV, 452
Watson, Elizabeth IV, 495
Watson, Elizabeth IV, 501
Watson, Elizabeth IV, 502
Watson, Elizabeth IV, 599
Watson, Elizabeth IV, 664
Watson, Elizabeth IV, 1189
Watson, Elizabeth IV, 1191
Watson, Elizabeth IV, 1192
Watson, Elizabeth IV, 1242
Watson, Elizabeth V, 718
Watson, Elizabeth VI, 856
Watson, Elizabeth VI, 863
Watson, Elizabeth VI, 1011
Watson, Elizabeth Catharine IV, 1242
Watson, Ellen M. II, 936
Watson, Ellen M. II, 1056
Watson, Elma Caroline IV, 852
Watson, Elma Caroline IV, 1266
Watson, Elziabeth IV, 1165
Watson, Emily IV, 1266
Watson, Emily V, 210
Watson, Emma III, 343
Watson, Emma Jane IV, 502
Watson, Enoch VI, 825
Watson, Esther IV, 180
Watson, Esther IV, 300
Watson, Esther Ann V, 392
Watson, Esther Ann V, 436
Watson, Esther Hannah IV, 502
Watson, Eva IV, 300
Watson, Eva M. III, 343
Watson, Eveny II, 433
Watson, Everett W. III, 343
Watson, Ezraetta II, 1056
Watson, Fanny VI, 1011
Watson, Florence V, 718
Watson, Flounder IV, 502
Watson, Flounders IV, 300
Watson, Frances II, 433
Watson, Frances II, 549
Watson, Frances II, 573
Watson, Frances II, 679
Watson, Frances II, 680
Watson, George II, 773
Watson, George II, 936
Watson, George J. II, 826
Watson, George J. II, 936
Watson, Grace II, 971
Watson, Grace II, 989
Watson, Grace II, 1036
Watson, Grace IV, 502
Watson, Grace IV, 555
Watson, Grainger IV, 1191
Watson, Grainger IV, 1192
Watson, Granger IV, 1165
Watson, Granger IV, 1189
Watson, Granger IV, 1192
Watson, Green VI, 1011
Watson, Gulielma F. II, 826
Watson, Gulielma Maria II, 758
Watson, Gulielma Maria II, 773
Watson, Gulielma S. II, 936
Watson, Hannah II, 241
Watson, Hannah II, 247
Watson, Hannah II, 270
Watson, Hannah II, 579
Watson, Hannah II, 616
Watson, Hannah II, 679
Watson, Hannah II, 956
Watson, Hannah II, 971
Watson, Hannah II, 978
Watson, Hannah II, 986
Watson, Hannah II, 1035
Watson, Hannah IV, 300
Watson, Hannah IV, 356
Watson, Hannah IV, 435
Watson, Hannah IV, 452
Watson, Hannah IV, 502
Watson, Hannah IV, 664
Watson, Hattie V, 604
Watson, Henry II, 936
Watson, Henry II, 939
Watson, Henry Wm. II, 936
Watson, Hettie F. II, 826
Watson, Hettie F. II, 936
Watson, Ibba VI, 1011
Watson, Ira I, 935
Watson, Isaac II, 680
Watson, Isabell V, 649
Watson, Isabella V, 649
Watson, Iva D. IV, 300
Watson, J. Jay III, 343
Watson, Jacob II, 1035
Watson, Jacob II, 1079
Watson, Jacob II, 1080
Watson, Jacob II, 1082
Watson, Jacob Nieper II, 1082
Watson, James II, 679
Watson, James IV, 1013
Watson, James VI, 887
Watson, James VI, 904
Watson, James VI, 1011
Watson, James F. VI, 871
Watson, James F. VI, 905
Watson, James F. VI, 1011
Watson, James H. IV, 300
Watson, James H. IV, 502
Watson, James H. IV, 1013
Watson, James M. II, 1056
Watson, James W. IV, 502
Watson, Jane II, 703
Watson, Jane II, 1023
Watson, Jane II, 1035
Watson, Jane IV, 480
Watson, Jane IV, 502
Watson, Jemima III, 154
Watson, Jemima III, 343
Watson, Jenny VI, 861
Watson, Jesse VI, 861
Watson, Jesse, Jr. VI, 1011
Watson, Joel IV, 183
Watson, John I, 1051
Watson, John II, 187
Watson, John II, 194
Watson, John II, 241
Watson, John II, 270
Watson, John II, 433
Watson, John II, 552
Watson, John II, 679
Watson, John II, 972
Watson, John II, 980
Watson, John II, 1003
Watson, John II, 1035
Watson, John II, 1067
Watson, John II, 1082
Watson, John III, 343
Watson, John IV, 300
Watson, John IV, 476
Watson, John IV, 501
Watson, John IV, 502
Watson, John IV, 555
Watson, John IV, 835
Watson, John IV, 852
Watson, John IV, 1120
Watson, John IV, 1242
Watson, John V, 649
Watson, John V, 718
Watson, John VI, 877
Watson, John VI, 1011
Watson, John D. II, 936
Watson, John D. II, 939
Watson, John Davis II, 826
Watson, John F. VI, 871
Watson, John F. VI, 1011
Watson, John Grainger IV, 1191
Watson, John Granger IV, 1242
Watson, John Gregg II, 1035
Watson, John Jay III, 254
Watson, John Jay III, 343
Watson, John L. II, 1082
Watson, John Lincoln II, 1082
Watson, John M. IV, 852
Watson, John M. V, 718
Watson, John N. IV, 1266
Watson, John S. IV, 502
Watson, John, Jr. IV, 502
Watson, Johnson VI, 874
Watson, Johnson VI, 892
Watson, Johnson VI, 945
Watson, Johnson VI, 974
Watson, Johnson VI, 1011
Watson, Joice VI, 1011
Watson, Jonathan II, 971
Watson, Jonathan V, 940
Watson, Jonathan I. V, 288
Watson, Jonathan J. V, 288
Watson, Jonathan L. V, 940
Watson, Jos. IV, 502
Watson, Joseph II, 270
Watson, Joseph II, 433
Watson, Joseph II, 549
Watson, Joseph II, 573
Watson, Joseph II, 679
Watson, Joseph II, 680
Watson, Joseph II, 826
Watson, Joseph II, 936
Watson, Joseph II, 971
Watson, Joseph II, 972
Watson, Joseph II, 994
Watson, Joseph II, 1035
Watson, Joseph II, 1063
Watson, Joseph III, 343
Watson, Joseph IV, 356
Watson, Joseph IV, 478
Watson, Joseph IV, 501
Watson, Joseph IV, 502
Watson, Joseph IV, 851
Watson, Joseph IV, 852
Watson, Joseph IV, 860
Watson, Joseph IV, 1120
Watson, Joseph VI, 1011
Watson, Joseph Henry II, 773
Watson, Joseph W. IV, 502
Watson, Joseph Wm. Henry II, 826
Watson, Joseph, Jr. II, 1035
Watson, Jude II, 433
Watson, Judith VI, 892
Watson, L. M. VI, 890
Watson, Leila V, 539
Watson, Lena B. V, 718
Watson, Lenna R. V, 718
Watson, Levi II, 971
Watson, Levi II, 1036
Watson, Lindley IV, 300
Watson, Louisa VI, 1011
Watson, Louisa A. VI, 905
Watson, Lucy II, 971
Watson, Lucy II, 1063
Watson, Luella IV, 917
Watson, M. E. IV, 917
Watson, Mahlon II, 971
Watson, Malcon S. II, 1082
Watson, Marcy II, 971
Watson, Margaret II, 255
Watson, Margaret II, 270
Watson, Margaret V, 718
Watson, Margaret Stoop V, 668
Watson, Margarett VI, 904
Watson, Maria IV, 300
Watson, Maria IV, 500
Watson, Maria IV, 502
Watson, Mariah IV, 291
Watson, Mariah IV, 300
Watson, Mariah L. VI, 1011
Watson, Mark II, 198
Watson, Mark II, 270
Watson, Mark II, 972
Watson, Mark II, 975
Watson, Mark II, 980
Watson, Mark II, 991
Watson, Mark II, 992
Watson, Mark II, 997
Watson, Mark II, 1018
Watson, Mark II, 1021
Watson, Mark II, 1024
Watson, Mark II, 1035
Watson, Mark II, 1036
Watson, Mark IV, 356
Watson, Mark IV, 452
Watson, Mark IV, 599
Watson, Mark IV, 664
Watson, Mark A. IV, 1013
Watson, Marmaduk II, 247
Watson, Marmaduk II, 270
Watson, Marshall VI, 957
Watson, Marsia Anne III, 259
Watson, Marsia Anne III, 343
Watson, Martha II, 1035
Watson, Martha II, 1063
Watson, Martha II, 1080
Watson, Martha II, 1082
Watson, Martha IV, 502
Watson, Martha IV, 648
Watson, Martha IV, 664
Watson, Martha VI, 957
Watson, Martha A. VI, 825
Watson, Martha C. II, 936
Watson, Martha Ellis II, 826
Watson, Martha R. II, 1056
Watson, Mary II, 187
Watson, Mary II, 194
Watson, Mary II, 198
Watson, Mary II, 270
Watson, Mary II, 433
Watson, Mary II, 489
Watson, Mary II, 579
Watson, Mary II, 627
Watson, Mary II, 679
Watson, Mary II, 722
Watson, Mary II, 773
Watson, Mary II, 813
Watson, Mary II, 936
Watson, Mary II, 942
Watson, Mary II, 980
Watson, Mary II, 985
Watson, Mary II, 991
Watson, Mary II, 992
Watson, Mary II, 1013
Watson, Mary II, 1020
Watson, Mary II, 1021
Watson, Mary II, 1035
Watson, Mary II, 1036
Watson, Mary III, 254
Watson, Mary III, 343
Watson, Mary III, 386
Watson, Mary IV, 294
Watson, Mary IV, 354
Watson, Mary IV, 356
Watson, Mary IV, 477
Watson, Mary IV, 478
Watson, Mary IV, 501
Watson, Mary IV, 502
Watson, Mary IV, 664
Watson, Mary IV, 1165
Watson, Mary IV, 1192
Watson, Mary IV, 1242
Watson, Mary V, 718
Watson, Mary VI, 483
Watson, Mary VI, 974
Watson, Mary Ann II, 1067
Watson, Mary Ann II, 1082
Watson, Mary Ann IV, 476
Watson, Mary Ann IV, 502
Watson, Mary Ann IV, 851
Watson, Mary Ann IV, 852
Watson, Mary Ann IV, 1120
Watson, Mary C. II, 1056
Watson, Mary Elizabeth III, 343
Watson, Mary G. IV, 1167
Watson, Mary G. IV, 1191
Watson, Mary G. IV, 1242
Watson, Mary H. IV, 300
Watson, Mary H. IV, 502
Watson, Mary H. IV, 1013
Watson, Mary Jane V, 684
Watson, Mary Jane VI, 1011
Watson, Mary P. III, 343
Watson, Mary R. II, 1082
Watson, Mary W. II, 1013
Watson, Mathew II, 433
Watson, Mathew IV, 300
Watson, Mathew IV, 502
Watson, Matilda VI, 1011
Watson, Matilda J. IV, 736
Watson, Matilda J. IV, 785
Watson, Matthew II, 247
Watson, Matthew II, 270
Watson, Matthew IV, 300
Watson, Matthew IV, 478
Watson, Matthew IV, 480
Watson, Matthew IV, 486
Watson, Matthew IV, 502
Watson, Matthew IV, 555
Watson, Merlin A. III, 259
Watson, Merlin A. III, 343
Watson, Michael IV, 300
Watson, Michael IV, 502
Watson, Michal IV, 300
Watson, Millie IV, 1342
Watson, Nancy VI, 882
Watson, Nancy VI, 956
Watson, Nancy VI, 1011
Watson, Nathan II, 1035
Watson, Nathan IV, 300
Watson, Nathaniel II, 433
Watson, Nicholas W. VI, 1011
Watson, Oliver IV, 502
Watson, Oliver J. IV, 502
Watson, Palmer II, 1082
Watson, Paulina A. VI, 1011
Watson, Phebe II, 971
Watson, Phebe II, 978
Watson, Phebe II, 979
Watson, Phebe II, 980
Watson, Phebe II, 989
Watson, Phebe II, 1035
Watson, Phebe II, 1036
Watson, Phebe IV, 300
Watson, Phebe IV, 356
Watson, Phebe IV, 398
Watson, Phebe IV, 399
Watson, Phebe IV, 452
Watson, Phebe IV, 476
Watson, Phebe IV, 478
Watson, Phebe IV, 501
Watson, Phebe IV, 502
Watson, Phebe IV, 555
Watson, Phebe IV, 664
Watson, Phebe Ann II, 1079
Watson, Phebe Ann II, 1082
Watson, Phebe Ann IV, 664
Watson, Phebe Beal II, 1035
Watson, Phebe E. IV, 502
Watson, Phebe Eva IV, 300
Watson, Phebe Eva IV, 502
Watson, Phebe Eva IV, 852
Watson, Phebe Eva IV, 1266
Watson, Pheby II, 1035
Watson, Pheby IV, 502
Watson, Philip L. II, 1082
Watson, Polly VI, 1011
Watson, Polly Ann VI, 1011
Watson, Priscilla II, 326
Watson, Rachel II, 433
Watson, Rachel II, 499
Watson, Rachel II, 627
Watson, Rachel II, 679
Watson, Rachel II, 971
Watson, Rachel II, 1013
Watson, Rachel II, 1035
Watson, Rachel II, 1036
Watson, Rachel II, 1079
Watson, Rachel II, 1080
Watson, Rachel II, 1082
Watson, Rachel IV, 785
Watson, Rachel Ann II, 1056
Watson, Rachel C. II, 1067
Watson, Rachel C. II, 1082
Watson, Rachel V. III, 419
Watson, Rachel V. III, 464
Watson, Raymond I, 950
Watson, Raymond W. I, 935
Watson, Rebecca II, 187
Watson, Rebecca II, 257
Watson, Rebecca II, 270
Watson, Rebecca II, 814
Watson, Rebecca II, 824
Watson, Rebecca II, 972

Watson, Rebecca II, 980
Watson, Rebecca II, 1036
Watson, Rebecca IV, 171
Watson, Rebecca IV, 463
Watson, Rebecca IV, 502
Watson, Rebecca IV, 520
Watson, Rebecca IV, 555
Watson, Rebecca IV, 1120
Watson, Rebecca VI, 1011
Watson, Rebecka II, 433
Watson, Rebeckah II, 971
Watson, Rebeckah II, 997
Watson, Rebeckah II, 1035
Watson, Rebekah II, 644
Watson, Rebekah II, 679
Watson, Rhoda VI, 1011
Watson, Robert II, 679
Watson, Robert II, 1024
Watson, Rose A. V, 649
Watson, Rudolph Burnie III, 419
Watson, Rudolph Burnie III, 464
Watson, Ruth II, 980
Watson, Ruth II, 1035
Watson, Samuel II, 187
Watson, Samuel II, 433
Watson, Samuel II, 627
Watson, Samuel II, 679
Watson, Samuel II, 680
Watson, Samuel C. II, 1056
Watson, Samuel I. II, 936
Watson, Samuel J. II, 936
Watson, Samuel Thomasson IV, 500
Watson, Samuel Thomasson IV, 502
Watson, Sarah II, 731
Watson, Sarah II, 773
Watson, Sarah II, 1003
Watson, Sarah II, 1035
Watson, Sarah II, 1036
Watson, Sarah IV, 356
Watson, Sarah IV, 470
Watson, Sarah IV, 501
Watson, Sarah IV, 502
Watson, Sarah V, 137
Watson, Sarah V, 138
Watson, Sarah V, 649
Watson, Sarah VI, 883
Watson, Sarah VI, 1005
Watson, Sarah A. IV, 502
Watson, Sarah E. B. VI, 824
Watson, Sarah M. VI, 1011
Watson, Shepherd Arthur V, 718
Watson, Silas II, 1036
Watson, Stephen II, 479
Watson, Susan B. II, 1080
Watson, Susan V. II, 773
Watson, Susan V. II, 936
Watson, Susan W. II, 773
Watson, Susanna II, 622
Watson, Susanna II, 680
Watson, Susannah II, 823
Watson, Susannah M. II, 953
Watson, Tacy II, 1027
Watson, Tacy II, 1030
Watson, Tacy II, 1036
Watson, Tamer II, 977
Watson, Tamer II, 1035
Watson, Temperance II, 107
Watson, Temperance II, 110
Watson, Thomas II, 433
Watson, Thomas II, 680
Watson, Thomas II, 773
Watson, Thomas II, 971
Watson, Thomas II, 972
Watson, Thomas II, 980
Watson, Thomas II, 1003
Watson, Thomas II, 1023
Watson, Thomas II, 1024
Watson, Thomas II, 1035
Watson, Thomas V, 718
Watson, Thomas VI, 948
Watson, Thomas VI, 1011
Watson, Thomas, Jr. II, 679
Watson, Thomas, Jr. II, 1027
Watson, Thomas, Jr. II, 1035
Watson, Thos. S. II, 722
Watson, Thressa M. IV, 1013
Watson, Thurman V, 718
Watson, Uriah A. VI, 1011
Watson, Wade I, 935
Watson, Walter IV, 1266
Watson, Walter E. II, 1082
Watson, Wd. Abigail II, 552
Watson, Wd. Caroline Moore II, 826
Watson, Wd. Hannah II, 270
Watson, Wd. Mary II, 479
Watson, Wd. Mary II, 680
Watson, Wd. Sarah II, 1035
Watson, William I, 598
Watson, William II, 187
Watson, William II, 197
Watson, William II, 270
Watson, William II, 971
Watson, William IV, 300
Watson, William IV, 356
Watson, William IV, 452
Watson, William IV, 500
Watson, William IV, 501
Watson, William IV, 502
Watson, William IV, 599
Watson, William IV, 664
Watson, William IV, 1013
Watson, William IV, 1266
Watson, William V, 210
Watson, William VI, 871
Watson, William VI, 956
Watson, William VI, 957
Watson, William VI, 1011
Watson, William E. II, 1067
Watson, William Newbold II, 1067
Watson, William O. VI, 973
Watson, William O. VI, 1011
Watson, William W. VI, 863
Watson, William, Jr. VI, 1011
Watson, William, Sr. VI, 1011
Watson, Wm. II, 679
Watson, Wm. II, 680
Watson, Wm. II, 936
Watson, Wm. II, 1035
Watson, Wm. II, 1036
Watson, Wm. IV, 291
Watson, Wm. IV, 300
Watson, Wm. IV, 476
Watson, Wm. IV, 1013
Watson, Wm. E. II, 1080
Watson, Wm. E. II, 1082
Watson, Wm. G. II, 1082
Watson, Wm. H. II, 1056
Watson, Wm. Newbold II, 1082
Watson, Wm. W. IV, 1013
Watson, Wyatt J. VI, 872
Watson, Wyatt J. VI, 1011
Watson, Zachariah J. VI, 1011
Watt, Anna Maria IV, 376
Watt, Anna Maria IV, 452
Watterbury, Mildred IV, 1323
Watterbury, Mildred IV, 1342
Watterbury, Ralph IV, 1323
Watterbury, Ralph IV, 1342
Watterman, Fanny II, 842
Watterman, Fanny II, 936
Watterman, Hannah II, 936
Watterman, Humphrey J. II, 842
Watterman, Humphrey J. II, 936
Watterman, John II, 842
Watterman, John II, 936
Watterman, Margaretta C. II, 842
Watterman, Margaretta C. II, 936
Watters, Clara IV, 1013
Watters, Genevieve Avon IV, 1013
Watters, Juanita Elaine IV, 1013
Watters, Martha M. IV, 300
Watters, Rogers I, 580
Watters, Russell B. IV, 1013
Watters, Sarah VI, 437
Watters, Sarah VI, 455
Watterson, Martha T. IV, 300
Watterworth, Elizabeth IV, 698
Watterworth, Elizabeth IV, 785
Watterworth, William IV, 698
Watterworth, William IV, 785
Wattkins, Lydia I, 771
Wattles, Mary E. F. V, 138
Watton, Eliza VI, 835
Watton, Stacey P. III, 343
Watts, Alias VI, 852
Watts, Ann VI, 872
Watts, Ann VI, 1011
Watts, Ann Mariah VI, 821
Watts, Annie C. V, 1024
Watts, Benj. VI, 1000
Watts, Benjamin VI, 936
Watts, Benjamin VI, 984
Watts, Benjamin VI, 1011
Watts, Benjamin VI, 1021
Watts, Charity V, 754
Watts, Charity V, 772
Watts, Demsy VI, 88
Watts, E. VI, 842
Watts, Edward VI, 801
Watts, Edward VI, 852
Watts, Elisa M. VI, 978
Watts, Elizabeth V, 288
Watts, Elizabeth VI, 801
Watts, Elizabeth VI, 927
Watts, Elizabeth VI, 943
Watts, Elizabeth VI, 1000
Watts, Elizabeth R. VI, 990
Watts, Flora Cook V, 364
Watts, Frances VI, 943
Watts, Isabella E. VI, 943
Watts, James VI, 1021
Watts, James D. VI, 908
Watts, James D. VI, 927
Watts, James D. VI, 978
Watts, Jane VI, 928
Watts, Jas. VI, 978
Watts, John II, 448
Watts, John VI, 32
Watts, John VI, 35
Watts, John VI, 990
Watts, John H. VI, 863
Watts, Lucia IV, 502
Watts, Lucinda C. VI, 1011
Watts, Margaret IV, 502
Watts, Margaret C. VI, 863
Watts, Mary II, 762
Watts, Mary II, 773
Watts, Mary II, 1063
Watts, Mary IV, 502
Watts, Mary VI, 801
Watts, Mary VI, 842
Watts, Mary VI, 852
Watts, Mary VI, 1011
Watts, Mary F. D. VI, 943
Watts, Maud V, 288
Watts, Minnie V, 1024
Watts, Mitchell VI, 1021
Watts, Mrs. Mary VI, 842
Watts, Nellie V, 940
Watts, Paulina A. VI, 927
Watts, Raymond V, 288
Watts, Rhoda A. V, 1024
Watts, Richard D. VI, 943
Watts, Richard D. VI, 978
Watts, Richard D. VI, 1020
Watts, Sally VI, 1011
Watts, Sally VI, 1021
Watts, Sarah II, 596
Watts, Sarah II, 680
Watts, Sarah VI, 936
Watts, Sarah A. VI, 863
Watts, Shepherd VI, 1011
Watts, Susannah V, 1024
Watts, Thomas W. VI, 863
Watts, Thos. W. V, 1024
Watts, W. W. VI, 1012
Watts, Wd. Hester II, 448
Watts, William VI, 908
Watts, William VI, 918
Watts, William VI, 1011
Watts, William W. VI, 982
Watts, William W. VI, 990
Watts, Wm. Wesley V, 1024
Wattson, Joseph II, 433
Waturbury, Dorothy E. IV, 1342
Waturbury, Kenneth L. IV, 1342
Waturbury, Maria IV, 1342
Waturbury, Mildred IV, 1342
Waturbury, Nellie S. IV, 1342
Waturbury, Nellie Sylvia IV, 1342
Waturbury, Ralph IV, 1342
Waturbury, Ralph H. IV, 1342
Waturbury, Ralph P. IV, 1342
Waturbury, Sylvia IV, 1342
Waturbury, Wm. H. IV, 1342
Waugh, Abner VI, 1011
Waugh, Alexander VI, 974
Waugh, Alexander VI, 1011
Waugh, David H. IV, 1384
Waugh, Elizabeth VI, 1011
Waugh, Hannah IV, 1384
Waugh, Huldah IV, 1384
Waugh, Keziah IV, 1384
Waugh, Levi IV, 1384
Waugh, Lydia IV, 1384
Waugh, Mary J. VI, 903
Waugh, Matilda VI, 1011
Waugh, Nicholas VI, 903
Waugh, Nicholas VI, 1011
Waugh, Phebe IV, 1384
Waugh, Polly VI, 1011
Waugh, Rachel VI, 789
Waugh, Reuben IV, 1384
Waugh, Thomas VI, 1011
Waugh, William H. VI, 903
Waugh, Wm. H. VI, 1021
Wauters, Rebekah II, 74
Wauters, Rebekah II, 110
Waxsmith, Elaine IV, 785
Waxsmith, Joise IV, 785
Waxsmith, Lee IV, 785
Waxsmith, Mrs. Mary IV, 785
Waxsmith, Opal IV, 785
Way, ??? III, 343
Way, ??? IV, 1085
Way, ??? V, 965
Way, Abbigal I, 1072
Way, Abigail I, 670
Way, Abigail I, 685
Way, Abigail I, 691
Way, Abigail I, 736
Way, Abigail I, 1066
Way, Abigail I, 1069
Way, Abigail I, 1072
Way, Abigail IV, 378
Way, Abigail IV, 452
Way, Abigail IV, 599
Way, Abigail IV, 1081
Way, Abigail IV, 1120
Way, Abigail IV, 1139
Way, Abigail V, 138
Way, Abigail V, 142
Way, Abigail V, 288
Way, Abigail V, 289
Way, Abigail V, 313
Way, Abigail V, 364
Way, Abigail V, 871
Way, Abigail V, 873
Way, Abigail V, 962
Way, Abigail V, 978
Way, Abigal I, 1072
Way, Abner III, 343
Way, Abner P. III, 121
Way, Abner P. III, 343
Way, Achsach I, 736
Way, Achsah I, 1066
Way, Achsah I, 1071
Way, Achsah I, 1072
Way, Agness I, 1071
Way, Agness I, 1072
Way, Agnis I, 1069
Way, Albert M. II, 937
Way, Alfancy Marian IV, 1140
Way, Alfancy Marion IV, 1081
Way, Alfoncy Marion IV, 1140
Way, Alfred II, 936
Way, Alfred II, 937
Way, Alfred H. VI, 789
Way, Alfred H. VI, 790
Way, Alice IV, 452
Way, Alice IV, 502
Way, Alice IV, 599
Way, Alice Hannah IV, 502
Way, Amos Vernon IV, 452
Way, Ann II, 680
Way, Ann IV, 452
Way, Ann IV, 502
Way, Ann IV, 598
Way, Ann IV, 599
Way, Ann IV, 600
Way, Ann IV, 785
Way, Ann IV, 1099
Way, Ann IV, 1111
Way, Ann IV, 1120
Way, Ann IV, 1139
Way, Anna I, 669
Way, Anna I, 736
Way, Anna I, 1066
Way, Anna V, 210
Way, Anna VI, 718
Way, Anna H. VI, 789
Way, Anna K. II, 937
Way, Anne IV, 452
Way, Anthony I, 669
Way, Anthony V, 849
Way, Anthony V, 873
Way, Benjamin IV, 378
Way, Benjamin IV, 452
Way, Benjamin IV, 502
Way, Benjamin IV, 503
Way, Benjamin IV, 578
Way, Benjamin IV, 599
Way, Benjamin IV, 1081
Way, Benjamin IV, 1120
Way, Benjamin IV, 1139
Way, Carlene A. III, 145
Way, Carline A. III, 343
Way, Caroline I, 736
Way, Caroline I, 1066
Way, Charity I, 426
Way, Charles II, 936
Way, Charles C. VI, 652
Way, Charles C. VI, 653
Way, Charles C. VI, 718
Way, Charles C. VI, 719
Way, Charles C. VI, 749
Way, Charles C. VI, 789
Way, Charles C. VI, 790
Way, Charles E. V, 718
Way, Charles Eugene V, 718
Way, Charles F. III, 386
Way, Charles Farrington III, 343
Way, Charles Farrington III, 386
Way, Charles Harvey IV, 1081
Way, Charles Harvey IV, 1139
Way, Charles Harvey IV, 1140
Way, Charlotte I, 669
Way, Charlotte I, 673
Way, Charlotte I, 691
Way, Charlotte V, 210
Way, Charlotte M. III, 343
Way, Charlottee V, 210
Way, Charlotty I, 580
Way, Charlotty V, 210
Way, Chas. C. II, 937
Way, Chas. C. VI, 790
Way, D. L. V, 718
Way, Daniel L. V, 718
Way, David IV, 452
Way, David IV, 502
Way, David IV, 587
Way, David IV, 598
Way, David IV, 599
Way, David IV, 600
Way, David IV, 1081
Way, David IV, 1099
Way, David IV, 1120
Way, David IV, 1139
Way, David V, 313
Way, David VI, 455
Way, David L. IV, 452
Way, David L. IV, 599
Way, David L. V, 138
Way, David L. V, 718
Way, David L. V, 962
Way, David Leroy V, 718
Way, Deborah IV, 1081
Way, Deborah IV, 1139
Way, Deborah VI, 653
Way, Deborah VI, 718
Way, Deborah VI, 775
Way, Deborah VI, 789
Way, Deborah VI, 790
Way, Dempsey IV, 1140
Way, Dorothy V, 209
Way, Dr. Nicholas II, 433
Way, Dr. Samuel J. V, 138
Way, Dunbar III, 386
Way, Edith VI, 790
Way, Edward W. IV, 579
Way, Elam IV, 579
Way, Eli J. VI, 718
Way, Elias V, 138
Way, Elias V, 313
Way, Elias H. V, 138
Way, Elias H. V, 313
Way, Eliz. III, 344
Way, Eliz. Lancaster III, 344
Way, Eliza D. I, 426
Way, Eliza Pleasant VI, 718
Way, Elizabeth I, 426
Way, Elizabeth I, 427
Way, Elizabeth II, 433
Way, Elizabeth II, 680
Way, Elizabeth II, 826
Way, Elizabeth II, 936
Way, Elizabeth III, 343
Way, Elizabeth III, 386
Way, Elizabeth IV, 452
Way, Elizabeth IV, 502
Way, Elizabeth IV, 579
Way, Elizabeth IV, 599
Way, Elizabeth IV, 1112
Way, Elizabeth IV, 1120
Way, Elizabeth VI, 455
Way, Elsie VI, 718
Way, Elsie J. VI, 789
Way, Esther III, 343
Way, Esther III, 428
Way, Esther III, 464
Way, Esther IV, 579
Way, Fannie E. V, 138
Way, Fanny V, 138
Way, Frances C. III, 145
Way, Frances C. III, 343
Way, Frances Elizabeth V, 138
Way, Francis D. II, 826
Way, Francis W. II, 937
Way, Francis W. VI, 789
Way, Francis W. VI, 790
Way, Francis Way II, 936
Way, Frank Troth VI, 790
Way, Geo. Pierce III, 145
Way, Geo. Pierce III, 343
Way, George II, 433
Way, George II, 936
Way, George B. II, 937
Way, George B. VI, 789
Way, George B. VI, 790
Way, George Washington IV, 108
Way, George Washington IV, 113
Way, George Washington IV, 114
Way, Hannah I, 1069
Way, Hannah I, 1071
Way, Hannah I, 1072
Way, Hannah II, 845
Way, Hannah II, 936
Way, Hannah IV, 452
Way, Hannah IV, 502

Hannah IV, 599
Hannah IV, 600
Hannah IV, 1081
Hannah IV, 1120
Hannah IV, 1121
Hannah IV, 1139
Hannah IV, 1140
Hannah V, 288
Hannah V, 539
Hannah VI, 392
Hannah VI, 455
Hannah G. VI, 455
Hannah Jane II, 781
Helen III, 121
Helen III, 343
Henriette V, 138
Henry I, 580
Henry I, 669
Henry I, 691
Henry I, 736
Henry I, 1066
Henry I, 1069
Henry I, 1072
Henry V, 210
Henry V, 539
Homer IV, 579
Howard Sharpless II, 937
Huldah I, 669
Huldah I, 685
Huldah I, 691
Huldah V, 873
Isadora Ann IV, 1081
Isaac A. I, 426
Isadora Ann IV, 1140
Jacob III, 343
Jacob IV, 452
Jacob IV, 502
Jacob IV, 599
Jacob IV, 1140
Jacob H. III, 343
Jacob W. V, 138
Jacob W. V, 313
James II, 817
James II, 826
James III, 343
James IV, 579
Jane II, 826
Jane III, 428
Jane III, 464
Jane IV, 451
Jane IV, 452
Jane IV, 502
Jane IV, 578
Jane IV, 598
Jane IV, 599
Jane IV, 1120
Jane IV, 1139
Jasper C. II, 936
Jasper C. II, 937
Jasper C. VI, 653
Jasper C. VI, 718
Jasper C. VI, 765
Jasper C. VI, 775
Jasper C. VI, 789
Jasper C. VI, 790
Jasper Chester VI, 790
Jasper Cope II, 826
Jehu Lewis IV, 66
Jemima III, 107
Jemima III, 343
Joel V, 210
John I, 426
John I, 669
John I, 670
John I, 679
John I, 691
John I, 1069
John I, 1072
John II, 680
John II, 845
John II, 936
John III, 55
John III, 115
John III, 343
John III, 344
John III, 454
John III, 464
John IV, 452
John IV, 579
John IV, 660
John IV, 1081
John IV, 1120
John IV, 1121
John IV, 1139
John IV, 1140
John B. IV, 1120
John B. IV, 1140
John Cloud II, 826
John D. III, 386
John H. I, 426
John Taylor IV, 579
Way, John, Jr. III, 343
Way, Jonathan V, 210
Way, Jordan III, 386
Way, Joseph I, 669
Way, Joseph I, 685
Way, Joseph I, 691
Way, Joseph I, 1058
Way, Joseph II, 433
Way, Joseph II, 561
Way, Joseph II, 680
Way, Joseph II, 689
Way, Joseph II, 826
Way, Joseph II, 845
Way, Joseph II, 936
Way, Joseph III, 343
Way, Joseph IV, 579
Way, Joseph V, 210
Way, Joseph V, 539
Way, Joseph C. II, 897
Way, Joseph C. II, 936
Way, Joseph C. IV, 579
Way, Joseph, Jr. II, 680
Way, Josiah G. II, 826
Way, Josiah G. II, 937
Way, Josiah G. VI, 790
Way, Judith III, 123
Way, Judith III, 343
Way, Judith III, 386
Way, Julia A. I, 426
Way, Katharine E. II, 937
Way, Lavina H. IV, 579
Way, Levina I, 545
Way, Levina I, 580
Way, Levinah V, 539
Way, Lindley H. IV, 579
Way, Lydia I, 669
Way, Lydia I, 679
Way, Lydia I, 691
Way, Lydia I, 1069
Way, Lydia I, 1070
Way, Lydia I, 1072
Way, Lydia II, 801
Way, Lydia II, 826
Way, Lydia II, 937
Way, Lydia IV, 333
Way, Lydia IV, 356
Way, Lydia IV, 452
Way, Lydia IV, 568
Way, Lydia IV, 579
Way, Lydia IV, 599
Way, Lydia IV, 1081
Way, Lydia IV, 1120
Way, Lydia IV, 1140
Way, Lydia V, 539
Way, Lydia Ann IV, 579
Way, Lydia Ann VI, 652
Way, Lydia Ann VI, 719
Way, Lydia Ann VI, 789
Way, Lydia Anna VI, 653
Way, Lydia Anna VI, 718
Way, Lydia Anna VI, 749
Way, Lydia Anna VI, 789
Way, Mabel VI, 718
Way, Mabel H. VI, 789
Way, Malinda V, 19
Way, Malinda V, 891
Way, Malinda V, 940
Way, Margaret I, 426
Way, Margaret I, 429
Way, Margaret IV, 1120
Way, Margaret E. I, 426
Way, Margaret J. IV, 1120
Way, Margaret J. IV, 1140
Way, Margaret W. IV, 579
Way, Marianne V, 978
Way, Mariannie V, 313
Way, Martha IV, 1031
Way, Martha W. IV, 1026
Way, Mary I, 426
Way, Mary I, 669
Way, Mary I, 670
Way, Mary I, 673
Way, Mary I, 674
Way, Mary I, 691
Way, Mary I, 1069
Way, Mary I, 1072
Way, Mary II, 448
Way, Mary III, 146
Way, Mary III, 314
Way, Mary III, 343
Way, Mary III, 344
Way, Mary III, 386
Way, Mary IV, 452
Way, Mary IV, 502
Way, Mary IV, 579
Way, Mary IV, 599
Way, Mary IV, 660
Way, Mary IV, 1140
Way, Mary V, 210
Way, Mary VI, 718
Way, Mary A. VI, 789
Way, Mary Anita VI, 790
Way, Mary Ann IV, 452
Way, Mary Ann IV, 599
Way, Mary Ann IV, 1081
Way, Mary Ann IV, 1140
Way, Mary Anne V, 288
Way, Mary D. III, 344
Way, Mary E. I, 426
Way, Mary Emily I, 426
Way, Mary Emily V, 718
Way, Mary Grace V, 718
Way, Mary H. VI, 786
Way, Mary H. VI, 789
Way, Mary H. VI, 790
Way, Mary Jane IV, 1081
Way, Mary Jane IV, 1139
Way, Mary Jane IV, 1140
Way, Mary Victoria I, 427
Way, Maryann IV, 452
Way, Maryanne V, 364
Way, Matilda IV, 45
Way, Matthew I, 670
Way, Matthew I, 1069
Way, Matthew I, 1071
Way, Matthew I, 1072
Way, Milicent IV, 452
Way, Milicent IV, 599
Way, Millicent IV, 452
Way, Millicent IV, 599
Way, Millicent IV, 1081
Way, Millicent IV, 1120
Way, Milton IV, 1120
Way, Milton IV, 1140
Way, Miriame V, 364
Way, Monroe IV, 599
Way, Moorman I, 736
Way, Moorman I, 1066
Way, Moorman I, 1069
Way, Moses VI, 775
Way, Moses VI, 789
Way, Nathan I, 669
Way, Nathan I, 685
Way, Nathan I, 691
Way, Nathan V, 873
Way, Nathaniel S. II, 936
Way, Nathaniel S. II, 937
Way, Nathaniel S. VI, 786
Way, Nathaniel S. VI, 789
Way, Nathaniel S. VI, 790
Way, Nicholas II, 680
Way, Paschal V, 138
Way, Patience I, 679
Way, Patience I, 691
Way, Patience I, 736
Way, Patience I, 1066
Way, Patience I, 1072
Way, Paul I, 426
Way, Paul I, 545
Way, Paul I, 580
Way, Paul I, 669
Way, Paul I, 670
Way, Paul I, 673
Way, Paul I, 691
Way, Paul I, 1069
Way, Paul I, 1071
Way, Paul I, 1072
Way, Paul V, 539
Way, Paul Hillman VI, 790
Way, Penina IV, 579
Way, Peninah IV, 579
Way, Phatran V, 288
Way, Phebe III, 197
Way, Phebe III, 344
Way, Phebe III, 454
Way, Phebe III, 464
Way, Phebe IV, 664
Way, Phebe E. II, 936
Way, Phebe Elizabeth II, 900
Way, Phebe Elizabeth II, 936
Way, Phebe M. II, 936
Way, Phebe Moore II, 826
Way, Phocian R. V, 313
Way, Phocion V, 313
Way, Phocion R. V, 138
Way, Phocion R. V, 940
Way, Phosian R. V, 138
Way, Photian V, 364
Way, Rachel I, 426
Way, Rachel I, 669
Way, Rachel III, 343
Way, Rachel IV, 587
Way, Rachel IV, 599
Way, Rachel IV, 1137
Way, Rachel IV, 1140
Way, Rachel V, 210
Way, Rachel Ann III, 343
Way, Rebecca III, 386
Way, Rebecca IV, 660
Way, Rebecca IV, 664
Way, Rebecca IV, 858
Way, Rebecca IV, 860
Way, Rebecca J. I, 426
Way, Rhoda V, 849
Way, Rhoda V, 873
Way, Robert IV, 356
Way, Robert IV, 452
Way, Robert IV, 502
Way, Robert IV, 568
Way, Robert IV, 599
Way, Robert IV, 1081
Way, Robert IV, 1120
Way, Robert IV, 1140
Way, Robert V, 138
Way, Robert V, 142
Way, Robert V, 288
Way, Robert V, 289
Way, Robert V, 313
Way, Robert V, 364
Way, Robert V, 539
Way, Robert V, 962
Way, Robert V, 978
Way, Robert Fink III, 343
Way, Ruth IV, 579
Way, Ruth VI, 790
Way, Ruth L. II, 800
Way, Ruthanna IV, 1132
Way, Ruthanna IV, 1139
Way, Ruthanna IV, 1140
Way, Sally II, 845
Way, Sally II, 936
Way, Sally C. II, 936
Way, Samuel II, 680
Way, Samuel III, 146
Way, Samuel III, 343
Way, Samuel III, 344
Way, Samuel III, 428
Way, Samuel III, 464
Way, Samuel IV, 1120
Way, Samuel IV, 1139
Way, Samuel V, 288
Way, Samuel C. V, 138
Way, Samuel C. V, 313
Way, Samuel Marsh III, 343
Way, Samuel, Jr. III, 344
Way, Samuel, Jr. III, 464
Way, Samuel, Jr. VI, 392
Way, Samuel, Jr. VI, 455
Way, Sarah I, 685
Way, Sarah I, 691
Way, Sarah I, 1058
Way, Sarah II, 680
Way, Sarah II, 689
Way, Sarah II, 817
Way, Sarah II, 826
Way, Sarah III, 55
Way, Sarah III, 115
Way, Sarah III, 343
Way, Sarah III, 344
Way, Sarah III, 386
Way, Sarah IV, 55
Way, Sarah IV, 452
Way, Sarah IV, 502
Way, Sarah IV, 599
Way, Sarah IV, 968
Way, Sarah IV, 1081
Way, Sarah IV, 1099
Way, Sarah IV, 1120
Way, Sarah IV, 1140
Way, Sarah V, 210
Way, Sarah V, 539
Way, Sarah C. II, 936
Way, Sarah L. II, 937
Way, Sarah S. II, 826
Way, Sarah S. II, 897
Way, Sarah S. VI, 765
Way, Sarah S. VI, 790
Way, Sarah, Jr. III, 115
Way, Seth I, 669
Way, Seth V, 539
Way, Susanna II, 680
Way, Susanna II, 936
Way, Susanna IV, 45
Way, Susanna IV, 66
Way, Susannah I, 736
Way, Susannah I, 1066
Way, Susannah I, 1069
Way, Susannah II, 936
Way, Susie S. V, 718
Way, Sydney Elizabeth II, 936
Way, Temperance III, 428
Way, Thomas III, 343
Way, Thomas V, 539
Way, Tilman IV, 579
Way, Valentine III, 464
Way, Wd. Ann B. II, 817
Way, Widow Mary I, 691
Way, William I, 580
Way, William I, 669
Way, William I, 670
Way, William I, 685
Way, William I, 691
Way, William I, 736
Way, William I, 1066
Way, William I, 1069
Way, William I, 1072
Way, William II, 433
Way, William IV, 579
Way, William V, 210
Way, William V, 718
Way, William, Jr. I, 736
Way, Wm. I, 736
Way, Wm. II, 680
Wayman, Anna E. I, 1163
Wayman, Edmund I, 1163
Wayman, Eliza I, 1163
Wayman, Eliza S. I, 1163
Wayman, Helen Bentley III, 344
Wayman, Isaac I. I, 1163
Wayman, Martha E. I, 1163
Wayman, Mary A. I, 1163
Wayman, Nancy Jane I, 1163
Wayman, Nora S. I, 1163
Wayman, Peter Edwin III, 103
Wayman, Rachel L. I, 1163
Wayman, Rebecca L. I, 1163
Wayman, Susannah I, 1161
Wayman, Susannah I, 1163
Wayman, Suzanne III, 103
Wayman, Suzanne III, 344
Waymire, Andrew V, 772
Waymire, Dorothy V, 772
Waymire, Elizabeth I, 721
Waymire, Elizabeth I, 736
Waymire, Elizabeth V, 772
Waymire, Frederic V, 772
Waymire, Frederick I, 736
Waymire, Frederick V, 772
Waymire, Frederick, Jr. V, 772
Waymire, Huldah I, 736
Waymire, Huldah V, 764
Waymire, Huldah V, 772
Waymire, John V, 772
Waymire, Melinda V, 793
Waymire, Rebecca V, 772
Wayn, John II, 433
Wayn, William II, 433
Wayne, Betsy VI, 852
Wayne, Caroline VI, 826
Wayne, Catharine II, 930
Wayne, Elisabeth II, 269
Wayne, Elisabeth II, 270
Wayne, Eliza II, 826
Wayne, Eliza II, 930
Wayne, Eliza II, 937
Wayne, Elizabeth II, 433
Wayne, Elizabeth II, 722
Wayne, Elizabeth II, 773
Wayne, Elizabeth II, 826
Wayne, Elizabeth II, 930
Wayne, Elizabeth II, 937
Wayne, Elizabeth V, 940
Wayne, Henry II, 826
Wayne, Henry II, 937
Wayne, Isaac Potts II, 433
Wayne, Jacob II, 269
Wayne, Jacob II, 270
Wayne, Jacob II, 722
Wayne, Jacob II, 826
Wayne, Jacob II, 930
Wayne, Jacob II, 937
Wayne, Jacob L. II, 826
Wayne, Jesse R. II, 930
Wayne, John II, 433
Wayne, John VI, 852
Wayne, John VI, 856
Wayne, John VI, 863
Wayne, John A. VI, 863
Wayne, Joseph VI, 863
Wayne, Joseph W. II, 433
Wayne, Joseph W. II, 773
Wayne, Joseph W. II, 937
Wayne, Joseph W. V, 940
Wayne, Leonard VI, 813
Wayne, Leonard VI, 826
Wayne, Lydia Tomlinson II, 826
Wayne, Manuel VI, 842
Wayne, Margaret VI, 863
Wayne, Margaret W. II, 433
Wayne, Margaret W. II, 773
Wayne, Margaret W. II, 937
Wayne, Margaret Walker II, 826
Wayne, Martha II, 930
Wayne, Martha VI, 842
Wayne, Martha J. II, 937
Wayne, Martha Jones II, 826
Wayne, Mary II, 826
Wayne, Mary II, 937
Wayne, Mary VI, 863
Wayne, Mary Elizabeth II, 930
Wayne, Mary L. II, 782
Wayne, Nancy VI, 813
Wayne, Naomi P. II, 930
Wayne, Patience IV, 66

Wayne, Rebecca II, 269
Wayne, Rebecca II, 270
Wayne, Rebecca II, 433
Wayne, Rebecca II, 782
Wayne, Rebecca II, 785
Wayne, Rebecca II, 826
Wayne, Rebecca II, 844
Wayne, Rebecca II, 937
Wayne, Rebecca P. II, 837
Wayne, Rebecca P. II, 844
Wayne, Rebecca P. II, 937
Wayne, Rebecca Potts II, 785
Wayne, Rebecca W. II, 433
Wayne, Rebecca W. II, 680
Wayne, Rebecca W. II, 722
Wayne, Rebecca W. II, 773
Wayne, Rebecca W. II, 844
Wayne, Reuben II, 930
Wayne, Ruth Anna II, 782
Wayne, Ruth Anna II, 837
Wayne, Ruth Anna II, 937
Wayne, Ruthanna II, 782
Wayne, Samuel VI, 842
Wayne, Samuel G. II, 270
Wayne, Sarah II, 433
Wayne, Sarah II, 680
Wayne, Sarah II, 930
Wayne, Sarah II, 1036
Wayne, Sarah Ann II, 433
Wayne, Sarah Ann II, 731
Wayne, Sarah Ann II, 773
Wayne, Sarah Ann II, 785
Wayne, Sarah Ann II, 844
Wayne, Sarah Ann II, 937
Wayne, Sarah G. II, 270
Wayne, Sarah G. II, 680
Wayne, Sarah G. II, 773
Wayne, Sarah G. II, 937
Wayne, Sarah Gillingham II, 826
Wayne, Sarah W. II, 782
Wayne, Susan II, 930
Wayne, Susanna II, 930
Wayne, Thomas VI, 831
Wayne, William II, 269
Wayne, William II, 270
Wayne, William II, 433
Wayne, William II, 826
Wayne, William VI, 826
Wayne, William, Jr. II, 433
Wayne, Wm. II, 680
Wayne, Wm. II, 773
Wayne, Wm. II, 782
Wayne, Wm. II, 785
Wayne, Wm. II, 837
Wayne, Wm. II, 844
Wayne, Wm. II, 930
Wayne, Wm. II, 937
Wayne, Wm., Jr. II, 680
Wayne, Wm., Jr. II, 785
Wayne, Wm., Jr. II, 826
Wayne, Wm., Jr. II, 937
Waynwright, Mary II, 430
Ways, Ann II, 558
Ways, Ann II, 680
Ways, Joseph II, 433
Ways, William II, 433
Waystaf, Sarah II, 34
Waytes, Mary IV, 66
Wayts, Joseph Sopher IV, 66
Wayts, Mary IV, 66
Wayts, Mary IV, 134
Wayts, Sarah IV, 60
Wayts, Sarah IV, 66
Wayts, Sarah IV, 133
Wayts, Sarah IV, 134
Wayts, Sarah Sopher IV, 66
Wayts, Shaedlock IV, 133
Wayts, Shaidlock IV, 134
Wayts, Shaidlock N. IV, 66
Wayts, Shaidlock N. IV, 134
Wayts, Susanna IV, 60
Wayts, Susanna IV, 66
Wayts, Susanna IV, 133
Wayts, Susanna IV, 134
Wayts, Susannah IV, 134
Wayts, William IV, 134
Wayts, Wm. IV, 134
Wd, ??? II, 643
Wd, Alice II, 644
Wd, Rebecca II, 644
Wd. Sanders, Sarah II, 643
Wd. Saunders, Sarah II, 643
Wd. Shirley, Lydia II, 642
Wead, James A. V, 539
Weade, James A. V, 537
Weadon, Mary I, 904
Weadon, Mary I, 905
Weagley, Hiley V, 1024
Weakes, Benjamin I, 1039
Weaks, Elijah VI, 863
Weaks, James I, 1039
Weaks, Joseph VI, 1012
Weaks, Margaret VI, 863
Weaks, Mary VI, 1012
Wealdon, Alfred IV, 302
Wealdon, Ann IV, 302
Wealdon, Isaac IV, 302
Wealdon, Meriba IV, 302
Wealdon, Nathan IV, 302
Wealdon, Rachel IV, 302
Wealdon, Ruth IV, 66
Wean, Arthur V, 210
Wean, Charles V, 210
Wean, Charles A. V, 210
Wean, Gertrude V, 210
Wean, Mrs. Chas. V, 210
Wean, Pearl Lucile V, 210
Wear, Carrie May I, 919
Wear, Ellen I, 919
Wear, Ellen I, 920
Wear, Etta Belle I, 920
Wear, Hugh I, 1163
Wear, Janie I, 1163
Wear, Jennie I, 1163
Wear, Joseph W. I, 1163
Wear, Margaret J. I, 1163
Wear, Matilda C. I, 1163
Wear, Nancy J. I, 1163
Wear, Pleas I, 919
Wear, Pleas I, 920
Wear, Reuben F. I, 1163
Wear, Sarah J. I, 1163
Wear, William C. I, 1163
Weare, Edith III, 61
Weare, Edith III, 344
Weare, Fred Lincoln III, 61
Weare, Fred Lincoln III, 344
Weare, John III, 344
Weare, Ruth Jane III, 344
Weasner, Abigail I, 843
Weasner, Rachel I, 843
Weatherald, Sarah Eleanor VI, 573
Weatherald, Sarah Eleanor VI, 578
Weatherall, Nancy Catherine VI, 507
Weatherall, Nancy Catherine VI, 543
Weatherber, Anna II, 864
Weatherber, Anna II, 937
Weatherby, Elizabeth V, 951
Weatherby, Hannah V, 951
Weatherby, Melville IV, 1226
Weatherby, Mevlville IV, 1226
Weatherby, Wm. V, 951
Weatherford, Anderson VI, 863
Weatherford, Ann E. M. VI, 863
Weatherford, Buchanan VI, 808
Weatherford, Jane VI, 838
Weatherford, John VI, 844
Weatherford, John VI, 863
Weatherford, John B. VI, 863
Weatherford, June VI, 844
Weatherford, Nancy VI, 863
Weatherhead, Anna C. V, 138
Weatherill, Joseph II, 683
Weatherill, Mary II, 569
Weatherite, Mary II, 680
Weatherly, Lydia I, 691
Weatherly, Melville IV, 1226
Weatherly, Sarah I, 936
Weatherson, Margaret IV, 300
Weatherson, Myrtle M. IV, 300
Weaver, ??? VI, 787
Weaver, ??? VI, 790
Weaver, Abigail II, 536
Weaver, Abigail II, 680
Weaver, Abraham IV, 66
Weaver, Abraham IV, 114
Weaver, Adaline Smith IV, 785
Weaver, Alfretta V, 649
Weaver, Ann II, 110
Weaver, Ann II, 433
Weaver, Ann II, 536
Weaver, Ann II, 680
Weaver, Benjamin II, 433
Weaver, Bessie V, 467
Weaver, Beulah A. II, 848
Weaver, Beulah A. II, 937
Weaver, Cassio O. IV, 1013
Weaver, Catharine V, 1024
Weaver, Catherine V, 1024
Weaver, Cecile Inez V, 1024
Weaver, Charles IV, 1384
Weaver, Charles V, 288
Weaver, Charles A. V, 288
Weaver, Charles B. II, 680
Weaver, Charles H. IV, 1384
Weaver, Clara IV, 785
Weaver, David IV, 1000
Weaver, David Cassia IV, 1013
Weaver, David Smith II, 110
Weaver, Deborah IV, 452
Weaver, Deborah IV, 456
Weaver, Dorothy VI, 787
Weaver, Dorothy VI, 790
Weaver, Earl Ray V, 1024
Weaver, Edna Elnora V, 1024
Weaver, Edward II, 270
Weaver, Edwin A. II, 680
Weaver, Edwin A. IV, 300
Weaver, Elijah II, 536
Weaver, Elijah II, 680
Weaver, Elisha F. IV, 1384
Weaver, Elisha T. IV, 1384
Weaver, Elizabeth II, 110
Weaver, Elizabeth II, 270
Weaver, Elizabeth II, 796
Weaver, Ella IV, 785
Weaver, Emma IV, 1044
Weaver, Emma J. E. VI, 790
Weaver, Esther Opal V, 1024
Weaver, Eva V, 1024
Weaver, Eve II, 110
Weaver, Florence Eyster VI, 741
Weaver, Florence Eyster VI, 791
Weaver, Gale V, 1024
Weaver, George W. II, 680
Weaver, Gilbert IV, 1384
Weaver, Girard W. II, 722
Weaver, Gulielma II, 82
Weaver, Gulielma II, 110
Weaver, Gulielma IV, 785
Weaver, Harold V, 1024
Weaver, Helen Delilah V, 1024
Weaver, Isaac II, 433
Weaver, Isaac IV, 66
Weaver, Isaac, Jr. II, 680
Weaver, Isaac, Jr. IV, 66
Weaver, James IV, 66
Weaver, James IV, 114
Weaver, Jane V, 288
Weaver, Jane V, 422
Weaver, Jane V, 436
Weaver, Jane T. IV, 1384
Weaver, Jennie Mercile V, 1024
Weaver, John II, 433
Weaver, John II, 680
Weaver, John IV, 1384
Weaver, John H. IV, 1355
Weaver, John H. IV, 1384
Weaver, John Philip VI, 935
Weaver, John W. IV, 1384
Weaver, Jonathan II, 110
Weaver, Joseph IV, 1044
Weaver, Joseph M. IV, 1044
Weaver, Joshua P. IV, 440
Weaver, Josiah II, 110
Weaver, Juday VI, 849
Weaver, Julia F. II, 722
Weaver, Kate V, 772
Weaver, Katharine V, 772
Weaver, Littleberry VI, 863
Weaver, Lucinda IV, 440
Weaver, Lucinda IV, 452
Weaver, Lucinda M. IV, 785
Weaver, Lucretia V, 772
Weaver, Lucy VI, 863
Weaver, Lydia IV, 1355
Weaver, Lydia IV, 1384
Weaver, Mackay R. B. VI, 863
Weaver, Margaret IV, 1044
Weaver, Martha VI, 420
Weaver, Mary I, 304
Weaver, Mary I, 319
Weaver, Mary II, 110
Weaver, Mary II, 270
Weaver, Mary II, 722
Weaver, Mathew VI, 863
Weaver, Mervin IV, 785
Weaver, Pearl IV, 1000
Weaver, Phebe IV, 1355
Weaver, Phebe IV, 1384
Weaver, Polly VI, 863
Weaver, Rebecca IV, 768
Weaver, Rebecca IV, 785
Weaver, Rebecca A. II, 680
Weaver, Rebekah I, 999
Weaver, Robert H. IV, 785
Weaver, Rose V, 772
Weaver, Samuel VI, 863
Weaver, Sarah II, 680
Weaver, Sarah IV, 66
Weaver, Sarah IV, 109
Weaver, Sarah IV, 114
Weaver, Sarah Ann IV, 1384
Weaver, Sarah W. VI, 863
Weaver, Susanna II, 110
Weaver, Susannah II, 110
Weaver, Thomas II, 100
Weaver, Thomas II, 110
Weaver, Thomas II, 536
Weaver, Thomas II, 680
Weaver, Thomas V, 772
Weaver, Vera Bruella IV, 785
Weaver, Vera Buella IV, 785
Weaver, W. W. VI, 817
Weaver, Walter IV, 785
Weaver, Walter W. IV, 785
Weaver, William IV, 66
Weaver, William IV, 114
Weaver, William VI, 826
Weaver, William B. II, 722
Weaver, William N. IV, 1384
Weaver, William W. VI, 831
Weaver, William W. VI, 849
Weaver, William W. VI, 863
Weaver, Wilson VI, 863
Weaver, Wm. W. II, 680
Web, Richard II, 680
Webb, ??? IV, 785
Webb, Adelia IV, 1351
Webb, Adelia IV, 1384
Webb, Adrian IV, 1384
Webb, Alice V, 1024
Webb, Alice Ryder V, 963
Webb, Allice V, 1024
Webb, Amanda J. VI, 1011
Webb, Amos Hoag IV, 1384
Webb, Ann I, 50
Webb, Ann I, 77
Webb, Ann II, 629
Webb, Ann II, 680
Webb, Ann IV, 747
Webb, Ann IV, 785
Webb, Ann VI, 545
Webb, Anna B. II, 826
Webb, Anna Barnitz VI, 755
Webb, Anne B. II, 882
Webb, Anne B. II, 937
Webb, Anney VI, 863
Webb, Annie E. V, 1024
Webb, Bathsheba II, 792
Webb, Benina IV, 785
Webb, Benjamin II, 680
Webb, Benjamin IV, 727
Webb, Benjamin IV, 785
Webb, Benjamin IV, 1013
Webb, Bessie V, 467
Webb, Betsy VI, 820
Webb, Betsy VI, 1011
Webb, Betsy Ann VI, 863
Webb, Betty VI, 607
Webb, Burd S. VI, 1011
Webb, Carrie E. IV, 1266
Webb, Cassandra T. II, 845
Webb, Cassandra T. II, 937
Webb, Cassandra Turner II, 786
Webb, Cassandra Turner II, 826
Webb, Cassie I, 1163
Webb, Catharin V, 963
Webb, Catharine II, 820
Webb, Catharine IV, 1384
Webb, Catharine V, 963
Webb, Charlotte IV, 1384
Webb, Charlotte V, 1024
Webb, Cornelia Needles II, 826
Webb, Daniel VI, 1011
Webb, Dorcas IV, 1384
Webb, Edith II, 680
Webb, Edmund VI, 807
Webb, Edmund VI, 820
Webb, Edmund VI, 825
Webb, Edmund VI, 836
Webb, Edmund VI, 848
Webb, Edmund VI, 863
Webb, Edmund, Jr. VI, 863
Webb, Edwin IV, 1384
Webb, Edwin Lorenzo IV, 1384
Webb, Eli VI, 607
Webb, Elias V, 1024
Webb, Elijah N. I, 1163
Webb, Elisha IV, 1384
Webb, Eliza III, 344
Webb, Eliza. II, 238
Webb, Elizabeth II, 270
Webb, Elizabeth II, 433
Webb, Elizabeth II, 633
Webb, Elizabeth II, 680
Webb, Elizabeth II, 800
Webb, Elizabeth II, 876
Webb, Elizabeth II, 937
Webb, Elizabeth IV, 747
Webb, Elizabeth IV, 783
Webb, Elizabeth IV, 785
Webb, Elizabeth VI, 13
Webb, Elizabeth VI, 545
Webb, Elizabeth Yardley II, 826
Webb, Ella V, 1024
Webb, Emeline IV, 1368
Webb, Emeline IV, 1384
Webb, Emma II, 815
Webb, Emma II, 826
Webb, Emma II, 912
Webb, Emma II, 937
Webb, Esther Ann II, 712
Webb, Esther Hattie I, 1163
Webb, Ezekiel IV, 1351
Webb, Ezekiel IV, 1368
Webb, Ezekiel IV, 1384
Webb, Ezekiel D. IV, 1384
Webb, Fanny IV, 1351
Webb, Fanny IV, 1368
Webb, Fanny IV, 1384
Webb, Fanny Louisa IV, 138
Webb, Frances V, 963
Webb, Frances VI, 955
Webb, Frances Maria III, 34
Webb, Frank Thomas III, 26
Webb, Frank Thomas III, 34
Webb, Geo. V, 1024
Webb, George VI, 863
Webb, Hannah II, 433
Webb, Hannah II, 451
Webb, Hannah II, 563
Webb, Hannah II, 680
Webb, Hannah II, 731
Webb, Hannah II, 773
Webb, Hannah III, 344
Webb, Hannah III, 394
Webb, Hannah III, 398
Webb, Hannah IV, 97
Webb, Hannah IV, 114
Webb, Harriet II, 773
Webb, Harriet P. II, 937
Webb, Harriett II, 937
Webb, Harriett VI, 737
Webb, Harriett VI, 757
Webb, Helen II, 712
Webb, Helen Marguerite IV,
Webb, Helen Marguerite IV,
Webb, Henry II, 448
Webb, Isaac III, 344
Webb, Isaac James IV, 885
Webb, Isabella II, 552
Webb, Isabella II, 681
Webb, Issabella II, 681
Webb, J. W. V, 467
Webb, Jacob III, 344
Webb, James II, 681
Webb, James II, 826
Webb, James VI, 1011
Webb, James Barber II, 826
Webb, James Knap IV, 1384
Webb, James L. II, 773
Webb, James L. II, 826
Webb, James L. II, 937
Webb, Jane V, 963
Webb, Jesse I, 427
Webb, Jesse I, 695
Webb, Jesse I, 736
Webb, Jesse I, 1051
Webb, Jesse VI, 455
Webb, Jesse VI, 817
Webb, Jesse VI, 838
Webb, Jesse VI, 863
Webb, Jesse VI, 992
Webb, Jno. II, 681
Webb, Job III, 344
Webb, Job III, 394
Webb, Job III, 398
Webb, Job III, 476
Webb, John II, 177
Webb, John II, 433
Webb, John II, 540
Webb, John II, 599
Webb, John II, 680
Webb, John III, 344
Webb, John III, 476
Webb, John IV, 747
Webb, John V, 436
Webb, John VI, 455
Webb, John VI, 847
Webb, John VI, 863
Webb, John W. V, 467
Webb, John W. V, 963
Webb, Joseph I, 427
Webb, Joseph II, 433
Webb, Joseph II, 451
Webb, Joseph II, 563
Webb, Joseph II, 680
Webb, Joseph Chittenden IV, 1384
Webb, Josephine V, 1024
Webb, Julia Maria IV, 1384
Webb, Leah IV, 727
Webb, Leah IV, 743
Webb, Leah IV, 785
Webb, Leah IV, 874
Webb, Leah IV, 885
Webb, Leah James IV, 885
Webb, Lucina IV, 1002
Webb, Lucina IV, 1013
Webb, Lucy VI, 838

, Lucy VI, 863
, Lucy VI, 1011
, Lydia IV, 727
, Lydia IV, 785
, Lydia IV, 885
, Lydia IV, 886
, Margaretta T. II, 731
, Margaretta T. II, 773
, Maria IV, 300
, Martha VI, 992
, Mary II, 193
, Mary II, 433
, Mary II, 451
, Mary II, 540
, Mary II, 622
, Mary II, 680
, Mary II, 681
), Mary II, 826
), Mary V, 604
), Mary Albino III, 261
b, Mary Albino III, 344
b, Mary H. J. III, 344
b, Mary Jones VI, 863
b, Milly VI, 863
b, Nancy VI, 833
b, Nancy VI, 863
b, Naomi VI, 607
b, Nathan H. IV, 1384
b, Nathan Hall IV, 1384
b, Nicholas Pyle II, 680
b, Oliver V, 604
b, Onie May I, 1163
b, Pauline IV, 300
b, Penina IV, 785
b, Penina IV, 1013
b, Peninah IV, 885
b, Phebe IV, 657
b, Phebe VI, 607
b, Polly VI, 847
b, Polly VI, 848
b, Polly E. VI, 1011
b, Priscilla III, 186
b, Priscilla III, 344
b, Raisin IV, 1384
b, Ralph V, 604
b, Ralph Dale V, 604
b, Rebecca II, 177
bb, Rebecca II, 826
bb, Rebecca II, 877
bb, Rebecca II, 937
bb, Rebecca S. II, 826
bb, Rebecca S. II, 877
bb, Rebecca S. II, 937
bb, Rebecca Sinclair VI, 749
bb, Rebecca Sinclair VI, 790
bb, Rebecca T. II, 845
bb, Rebecca T. II, 877
bb, Rebecca T. II, 912
bb, Rebecca T. VI, 749
bb, Rebecca T. VI, 790
bb, Reuben II, 773
bb, Reuben II, 826
bb, Reuben II, 876
ebb, Reuben II, 937
ebb, Reuben VI, 1011
ebb, Richard II, 680
ebb, Richard III, 344
ebb, Robert II, 224
ebb, Robert II, 270
ebb, Robert II, 433
ebb, Robert II, 448
ebb, Roy V, 604
ebb, Ruth II, 680
ebb, Sallie V, 467
ebb, Sally VI, 836
Vebb, Sarah II, 96
Vebb, Sarah II, 110
Vebb, Sarah II, 433
Vebb, Sarah II, 826
Vebb, Sarah III, 344
Vebb, Sarah IV, 750
Vebb, Sarah IV, 785
Vebb, Sarah IV, 1351
Vebb, Sarah IV, 1384
Vebb, Sarah VI, 1011
Vebb, Sarah Ann II, 826
Vebb, Sarah Ann II, 937
Vebb, Sarah J. II, 876
Vebb, Sarah J. II, 937
Vebb, Stephen II, 731
Vebb, Stephen II, 773
Webb, Sumantha Vienna I, 1163
Webb, Susan R. II, 826
Webb, Susanah II, 599
Webb, Susanah II, 680
Webb, Susannah VI, 864
Webb, Sylvia V, 604
Webb, Tacy VI, 622
Webb, Tacy VI, 688
Webb, Thomas III, 344
Webb, Thomas VI, 607
Webb, Thomas VI, 863
Webb, Thos. Dutton III, 344
Webb, Veda Mae V, 718
Webb, Veda U. V, 718
Webb, Viresta VI, 817
Webb, Virgene May V, 604
Webb, Wd. Edith II, 561
Webb, Wd. Edith II, 680
Webb, Wd. Eliza W. II, 177
Webb, Wd. Hannah III, 476
Webb, William II, 433
Webb, William VI, 1011
Webb, William Barber II, 826
Webb, Wm. II, 681
Webb, Wm. V, 1024
Webb, Wm. B. II, 845
Webb, Wm. B. II, 846
Webb, Wm. B. II, 877
Webb, Wm. B. II, 882
Webb, Wm. B. II, 912
Webb, Wm. B. II, 924
Webb, Wm. B. II, 937
Webb, Wm. B. VI, 749
Webb, Wm. B. VI, 790
Webb, Wm. John II, 712
Webber, ??? III, 344
Webber, Anne II, 212
Webber, Benjamin II, 110
Webber, Benjamin II, 681
Webber, Catherine VI, 860
Webber, Edith III, 344
Webber, Edith III, 354
Webber, Elizabeth II, 270
Webber, Ellean III, 344
Webber, Henry VI, 806
Webber, Henry VI, 841
Webber, Henry VI, 842
Webber, Henry Headford III, 344
Webber, Jacob II, 212
Webber, James VI, 1011
Webber, James B. VI, 839
Webber, Jane VI, 848
Webber, Jeffrey III, 344
Webber, Lucinda Catharine VI, 1011
Webber, Luminar VI, 839
Webber, Martin VI, 824
Webber, Martin VI, 839
Webber, Martin VI, 848
Webber, Mary Ann II, 136
Webber, Mrs. Anna IV, 1342
Webber, Nancy VI, 1011
Webber, Nathaniel VI, 1011
Webber, Peter VI, 817
Webber, Peter VI, 841
Webber, Rachel VI, 806
Webber, Rachel VI, 848
Webber, Sally VI, 816
Webber, Stanley II, 774
Weber, Adam VI, 863
Weber, Ann II, 270
Weber, Bethuel Gifford II, 722
Weber, Caroline II, 722
Weber, Casper VI, 827
Weber, Casper VI, 863
Weber, Catharine VI, 802
Weber, Charles W. II, 722
Weber, Effie Belle II, 722
Weber, Elizabeth II, 270
Weber, Elizabeth VI, 863
Weber, Elizabeth M. VI, 863
Weber, Hannah VI, 863
Weber, Henry VI, 863
Weber, Jacob II, 270
Weber, Jane VI, 863
Weber, Jennie C. IV, 1226
Weber, John VI, 806
Weber, John VI, 816
Weber, John VI, 846
Weber, John VI, 853
Weber, John VI, 855
Weber, John VI, 863
Weber, John, Jr. VI, 816
Weber, John, Jr. VI, 863
Weber, Keturah VI, 863
Weber, Louis II, 722
Weber, Margaret VI, 806
Weber, Martin VI, 810
Weber, Martin VI, 816
Weber, Martin VI, 835
Weber, Martin VI, 863
Weber, Mary VI, 816
Weber, Mary A. II, 774
Weber, Mary Ann II, 722
Weber, Mildred VI, 863
Weber, Nancy VI, 863
Weber, Olivia VI, 419
Weber, Peggy VI, 846
Weber, Peggy VI, 863
Weber, Peter VI, 802
Weber, Peter VI, 815
Weber, Peter VI, 856
Weber, Peter VI, 863
Weber, Polly VI, 835
Weber, Rachel VI, 827
Weber, Rachel VI, 855
Weber, Rose II, 722
Weber, Rose II, 774
Weber, Ruth VI, 853
Weber, Ruth VI, 863
Weber, Stanley II, 774
Weber, Stanley K. II, 722
Weber, Stanley K. II, 774
Weber, William VI, 816
Weber, William VI, 827
Weber, William VI, 863
Weber, William H. VI, 836
Weblus, Antonia III, 280
Weblus, Antonia III, 344
Weblus, Helen III, 280
Weblus, Helen III, 344
Weblus, John C. III, 280
Weblus, John C. III, 344
Webster, ??? V, 313
Webster, ??? V, 965
Webster, A. W. I, 736
Webster, Abigail P. IV, 315
Webster, Abner IV, 301
Webster, Abner IV, 452
Webster, Abner IV, 453
Webster, Abner V, 772
Webster, Agnes II, 722
Webster, Albert D. R. IV, 453
Webster, Albert S. II, 722
Webster, Albert S. II, 774
Webster, Albina IV, 331
Webster, Albina IV, 356
Webster, Albina IV, 452
Webster, Albina IV, 453
Webster, Albinah IV, 396
Webster, Alexandria III, 197
Webster, Alexandria III, 344
Webster, Alfred L. II, 774
Webster, Ann II, 433
Webster, Ann II, 804
Webster, Ann III, 145
Webster, Ann III, 344
Webster, Ann IV, 163
Webster, Ann IV, 378
Webster, Ann IV, 415
Webster, Ann IV, 452
Webster, Ann IV, 453
Webster, Ann IV, 1081
Webster, Ann Catharine III, 344
Webster, Ann P. IV, 301
Webster, Ann P. IV, 424
Webster, Ann P. IV, 453
Webster, Anna III, 205
Webster, Anna IV, 395
Webster, Anna IV, 399
Webster, Anna IV, 452
Webster, Anna IV, 453
Webster, Anna IV, 1342
Webster, Anne IV, 331
Webster, Anne IV, 356
Webster, Anne IV, 399
Webster, Anne H. II, 125
Webster, Annie IV, 453
Webster, Annie H. II, 125
Webster, Annie L. IV, 383
Webster, Annie L. IV, 454
Webster, Asenath P. IV, 380
Webster, Asenath P. IV, 453
Webster, Aurelius V, 1024
Webster, Benjamin II, 986
Webster, Benjamin II, 1036
Webster, Betsy Ann VI, 1011
Webster, Beulah M. II, 882
Webster, Beulah M. II, 937
Webster, Caleb II, 722
Webster, Caleb II, 774
Webster, Caroline II, 775
Webster, Charles I, 920
Webster, Charles IV, 301
Webster, Charles IV, 453
Webster, Charles P. IV, 452
Webster, Charles P. IV, 453
Webster, Charley V, 1024
Webster, Christiana II, 882
Webster, Clarkson L. II, 937
Webster, Clarkson Lukens II, 826
Webster, Daniel II, 882
Webster, Daniel II, 937
Webster, David D. III, 156
Webster, David D. III, 344
Webster, Debora Ann IV, 453
Webster, Deborah II, 986
Webster, Deborah II, 1036
Webster, Deborah IV, 378
Webster, Deborah IV, 399
Webster, Deborah IV, 405
Webster, Deborah IV, 452
Webster, Deborah IV, 453
Webster, Deborah Ann IV, 453
Webster, Deborah Chambers IV, 452
Webster, Deborah Harriet IV, 453
Webster, Delia I, 920
Webster, Doris Blackburn IV, 1342
Webster, Eden III, 344
Webster, Eden S. III, 344
Webster, Edith II, 125
Webster, Edith II, 826
Webster, Edith II, 937
Webster, Edith III, 300
Webster, Edmund II, 920
Webster, Edmund II, 937
Webster, Edson C. IV, 453
Webster, Edson C. IV, 454
Webster, Edward III, 344
Webster, Edward B. II, 937
Webster, Edward Burrough II, 826
Webster, Eli IV, 163
Webster, Eli IV, 447
Webster, Eli IV, 452
Webster, Eli IV, 453
Webster, Eli IV, 578
Webster, Eli IV, 599
Webster, Elisabeth II, 681
Webster, Elisha VI, 664
Webster, Eliza V, 957
Webster, Eliza V, 962
Webster, Eliza Jane IV, 301
Webster, Eliza Jane IV, 426
Webster, Eliza Jane IV, 453
Webster, Elizabeth II, 433
Webster, Elizabeth II, 713
Webster, Elizabeth II, 722
Webster, Elizabeth II, 826
Webster, Elizabeth II, 920
Webster, Elizabeth II, 937
Webster, Elizabeth III, 84
Webster, Elizabeth III, 197
Webster, Elizabeth III, 206
Webster, Elizabeth III, 344
Webster, Elizabeth IV, 301
Webster, Elizabeth IV, 433
Webster, Elizabeth IV, 452
Webster, Elizabeth IV, 453
Webster, Elizabeth V, 288
Webster, Elizabeth V, 312
Webster, Elizabeth V, 313
Webster, Elizabeth V, 772
Webster, Elizabeth Alice M. II, 783
Webster, Elizabeth D. VI, 736
Webster, Elizabeth H. II, 937
Webster, Ellen III, 344
Webster, Ellen V, 1024
Webster, Emily II, 722
Webster, Emily T. II, 722
Webster, Emily T. II, 774
Webster, Emma A. IV, 442
Webster, Emma A. IV, 453
Webster, Emma C. IV, 453
Webster, Florence IV, 453
Webster, Florence V, 138
Webster, Florence A. II, 882
Webster, Florence A. II, 937
Webster, Florence W. IV, 368
Webster, Florence W. IV, 453
Webster, Franklin P. IV, 454
Webster, Franklin T. IV, 453
Webster, George C. II, 722
Webster, George C. II, 774
Webster, George J. IV, 301
Webster, George Robert II, 774
Webster, George T. II, 775
Webster, Hannah II, 270
Webster, Hannah II, 433
Webster, Hannah II, 681
Webster, Hannah II, 704
Webster, Hannah II, 713
Webster, Hannah II, 774
Webster, Hannah IV, 66
Webster, Hannah IV, 144
Webster, Hannah IV, 147
Webster, Hannah IV, 163
Webster, Hannah IV, 301
Webster, Hannah IV, 315
Webster, Hannah IV, 356
Webster, Hannah IV, 378
Webster, Hannah IV, 385
Webster, Hannah IV, 393
Webster, Hannah IV, 452
Webster, Hannah IV, 453
Webster, Hannah IV, 555
Webster, Hannah IV, 574
Webster, Hannah IV, 599
Webster, Hannah IV, 1081
Webster, Hannah V, 138
Webster, Hannah Ann IV, 399
Webster, Hannah Ann IV, 453
Webster, Hannah P. II, 722
Webster, Hannah P. II, 774
Webster, Hannah P. II, 775
Webster, Hannah W. II, 722
Webster, Hannah W. II, 774
Webster, Harlan S. IV, 454
Webster, Harlan Stanton IV, 453
Webster, Harriet G. IV, 453
Webster, Henry IV, 301
Webster, Henry IV, 453
Webster, Henry H. IV, 453
Webster, Horner J. IV, 453
Webster, Howard J. II, 937
Webster, Howard Jeffries II, 826
Webster, Hugh III, 344
Webster, Hugh V, 313
Webster, Hugh V, 772
Webster, Huth V, 138
Webster, Isaac IV, 163
Webster, Isaac IV, 453
Webster, Isaac IV, 555
Webster, Isaac IV, 1081
Webster, Isaac VI, 292
Webster, Isabel IV, 301
Webster, Isabella IV, 484
Webster, James III, 344
Webster, James IV, 301
Webster, Jamima IV, 484
Webster, Jemima IV, 301
Webster, Jemima IV, 314
Webster, Jemima IV, 315
Webster, Jemima M. IV, 315
Webster, Jephtha IV, 301
Webster, Jeptha IV, 452
Webster, Jeptha L. IV, 399
Webster, Jeptha L. IV, 452
Webster, Jeptha L. IV, 453
Webster, Jesse III, 344
Webster, Jesse IV, 555
Webster, Jesse IV, 1081
Webster, John II, 433
Webster, John II, 681
Webster, John III, 205
Webster, John IV, 66
Webster, John IV, 114
Webster, John IV, 144
Webster, John IV, 147
Webster, John IV, 163
Webster, John IV, 301
Webster, John IV, 331
Webster, John IV, 356
Webster, John IV, 378
Webster, John IV, 396
Webster, John IV, 405
Webster, John IV, 426
Webster, John IV, 433
Webster, John IV, 452
Webster, John IV, 453
Webster, John IV, 599
Webster, John V, 138
Webster, John VI, 982
Webster, John VI, 1011
Webster, John B. III, 300
Webster, John V. IV, 301
Webster, John, Jr. II, 681
Webster, Joseph II, 433
Webster, Joseph II, 775
Webster, Joseph III, 197
Webster, Joseph IV, 1384
Webster, Joseph V, 1024
Webster, Joseph G. IV, 301
Webster, Joseph G. IV, 452
Webster, Joseph G. IV, 453
Webster, Joshua IV, 163
Webster, Joshua IV, 452
Webster, Joshua P. II, 937
Webster, Joshua Percy II, 826
Webster, Joshua R. II, 775
Webster, Laura IV, 453
Webster, Louis Alton IV, 453
Webster, Lukens II, 826
Webster, Lukens II, 937
Webster, Lydia II, 720
Webster, Lydia IV, 301
Webster, Lydia IV, 452
Webster, Lydia IV, 453
Webster, Lydia V, 539
Webster, Lydia Ann IV, 421
Webster, Lydia Ann IV, 453
Webster, Lydia Maria IV, 301
Webster, Lydia P. IV, 432
Webster, Lydia P. IV, 453
Webster, Lydia P. IV, 1075
Webster, Lydia P. IV, 1081
Webster, Lydia R. V, 539
Webster, Lydia Smedley II, 770
Webster, Lydia Smedley II, 774
Webster, Madison I, 736
Webster, Maggy VI, 1011

Webster, Margaret II, 681
Webster, Margaret III, 185
Webster, Margaret III, 344
Webster, Marion II, 125
Webster, Marner L. IV, 453
Webster, Martha IV, 418
Webster, Martha IV, 453
Webster, Martha E. IV, 453
Webster, Mary II, 448
Webster, Mary III, 344
Webster, Mary IV, 301
Webster, Mary IV, 400
Webster, Mary IV, 405
Webster, Mary IV, 406
Webster, Mary IV, 453
Webster, Mary V, 978
Webster, Mary VI, 982
Webster, Mary A. III, 300
Webster, Mary Alice IV, 453
Webster, Mary Ann III, 344
Webster, Mary Avice IV, 440
Webster, Mary C. II, 937
Webster, Mary Elinor II, 774
Webster, Mary Jane IV, 1163
Webster, Mary Jane IV, 1192
Webster, Mary Lydia IV, 453
Webster, Mary M. IV, 301
Webster, Mary Melissa IV, 453
Webster, Mary V. IV, 301
Webster, Melissa IV, 397
Webster, Melissa IV, 453
Webster, Mercy IV, 447
Webster, Mercy IV, 452
Webster, Mercy IV, 453
Webster, Mercy IV, 599
Webster, Mery IV, 578
Webster, Minerva V, 138
Webster, Minerva G. V, 138
Webster, Mira V, 1024
Webster, Nailor IV, 301
Webster, Nathan IV, 163
Webster, Nathan IV, 301
Webster, Nathan IV, 452
Webster, Nathan T. IV, 453
Webster, Nathan Thomas IV, 453
Webster, Naylor IV, 315
Webster, Naylor IV, 484
Webster, Nelson P. III, 84
Webster, Nelson P. III, 197
Webster, Nelson P. III, 206
Webster, Nelson P. III, 344
Webster, Nelson P. VI, 736
Webster, Nelson P. VI, 790
Webster, Patience II, 806
Webster, Peter II, 1036
Webster, Peter II, 1038
Webster, Phebe IV, 61
Webster, Phebe IV, 66
Webster, Phebe IV, 147
Webster, Phebe IV, 163
Webster, Phebe IV, 398
Webster, Phebe IV, 399
Webster, Phebe IV, 400
Webster, Phebe IV, 412
Webster, Phebe IV, 447
Webster, Phebe IV, 448
Webster, Phebe IV, 452
Webster, Phebe IV, 453
Webster, Rachel Elizabeth III, 344
Webster, Raymond Nathan IV, 453
Webster, Rebecca III, 344
Webster, Rebecca IV, 66
Webster, Rebecca N. II, 920
Webster, Rebecca N. II, 937
Webster, Rev. Calvary M. III, 344
Webster, Richard VI, 982
Webster, Richard VI, 1011
Webster, Richard G. II, 125
Webster, Rollin IV, 1384
Webster, Ruth II, 824
Webster, Ruth IV, 1120
Webster, Ruth IV, 1122
Webster, Ruth Ann IV, 301
Webster, Ruthanna II, 699
Webster, Ruthanna II, 713
Webster, Sallie I, 920
Webster, Samuel II, 269
Webster, Samuel II, 270
Webster, Samuel II, 681
Webster, Samuel IV, 301
Webster, Samuel IV, 399
Webster, Samuel IV, 453
Webster, Samuel VI, 1011
Webster, Samuel C. II, 722
Webster, Samuel C. II, 774
Webster, Samuel C., Jr. II, 774
Webster, Sarah II, 267
Webster, Sarah II, 269
Webster, Sarah II, 270
Webster, Sarah II, 433
Webster, Sarah II, 986
Webster, Sarah II, 1036
Webster, Sarah III, 146
Webster, Sarah III, 344
Webster, Sarah IV, 193
Webster, Sarah IV, 301
Webster, Sarah IV, 315
Webster, Sarah IV, 370
Webster, Sarah IV, 385
Webster, Sarah IV, 387
Webster, Sarah IV, 399
Webster, Sarah IV, 400
Webster, Sarah IV, 452
Webster, Sarah IV, 453
Webster, Sarah IV, 555
Webster, Sarah IV, 574
Webster, Sarah IV, 1081
Webster, Sarah C. IV, 315
Webster, Sarah Eliz. III, 156
Webster, Sarah Eliz. III, 344
Webster, Sarah Ellen II, 722
Webster, Sarah Ellen II, 774
Webster, Sarah Ellen W. II, 774
Webster, Sarah Jane IV, 301
Webster, Sarah W. IV, 439
Webster, Sarah W. IV, 453
Webster, Stephen III, 344
Webster, Susan III, 344
Webster, Susan IV, 433
Webster, Susan IV, 452
Webster, Susan Catharine VI, 664
Webster, Susan L. III, 344
Webster, Susanna III, 344
Webster, Susanna IV, 66
Webster, Susanna IV, 106
Webster, Susannah III, 205
Webster, Susannah III, 287
Webster, Susannah III, 344
Webster, Susannah IV, 114
Webster, Taylor IV, 66
Webster, Taylor IV, 71
Webster, Taylor IV, 114
Webster, Taylor V, 288
Webster, Taylor V, 772
Webster, Thomas II, 269
Webster, Thomas II, 270
Webster, Thomas IV, 163
Webster, Thomas IV, 301
Webster, Thomas IV, 331
Webster, Thomas IV, 356
Webster, Thomas IV, 395
Webster, Thomas IV, 399
Webster, Thomas IV, 432
Webster, Thomas IV, 452
Webster, Thomas IV, 453
Webster, Thomas IV, 1075
Webster, Thomas IV, 1081
Webster, Thomas M. II, 722
Webster, Thomas M. II, 774
Webster, Thomas P. IV, 301
Webster, Thomas, Jr. IV, 453
Webster, Walter A. IV, 454
Webster, Walter Alva IV, 453
Webster, Warner IV, 452
Webster, Warner IV, 453
Webster, Wd Hannah IV, 114
Webster, Wd. Elizabeth III, 206
Webster, Wd. Elizabeth D. VI, 790
Webster, Wd. Margaret III, 185
Webster, William II, 722
Webster, William III, 145
Webster, William III, 146
Webster, William III, 197
Webster, William III, 344
Webster, William IV, 66
Webster, William VI, 114
Webster, William IV, 453
Webster, William IV, 1384
Webster, William V, 138
Webster, William V, 288
Webster, William V, 313
Webster, William V, 772
Webster, William R. IV, 301
Webster, William R. V, 138
Webster, William R. V, 539
Webster, William S. III, 344
Webster, Willimay II, 125
Webster, Willis V. IV, 442
Webster, Willis V. IV, 453
Webster, Willis William IV, 453
Webster, Wm. II, 713
Webster, Wm. II, 722
Webster, Wm. II, 920
Webster, Wm. II, 937
Webster, Wm. II, 986
Webster, Wm. II, 1036
Webster, Wm. IV, 163
Webster, Wm. V, 962
Webster, Wm. S. III, 185
Weden, Daniel II, 448
Weden, Rachel II, 448
Wedge, Chas. V, 1024
Wedge, Hannah V, 1024
Wedge, John V, 1024
Wedge, Mary V, 1024
Wedge, Sarah V, 1024
Wedge, Susan V, 1024
Weece, William V, 288
Weed, Emma West V, 718
Weeden, Abigail III, 344
Weeden, Anna Anthony III, 344
Weeden, George Anthony III, 344
Weeden, Holder C. III, 344
Weeden, John Lewis II, 826
Weeden, Joseph A. III, 344
Weeden, Mary II, 826
Weeden, Rachel I, 889
Weedon, John II, 433
Weedon, Mary I, 904
Weedon, Mary W. II, 937
Weedon, Rachel I, 904
Week, Alderson VI, 1018
Week, Benjamin V, 772
Weeke, Adeline III, 50
Weeke, Jas. III, 50
Weeke, Lydia H. III, 50
Weeke, William, Jr. I, 1039
Weekes, Alderson VI, 1009
Weekes, Elijah VI, 917
Weekes, Elizabeth VI, 1011
Weekes, George VI, 917
Weekes, Mary VI, 917
Weekes, Mary VI, 1021
Weekes, Peggy VI, 1009
Weekes, William VI, 1011
Weekley, Martha A. V, 164
Weekley, Martha A. V, 210
Weeks, ??? III, 75
Weeks, ??? III, 346
Weeks, Abbie S. III, 344
Weeks, Abbie S. III, 358
Weeks, Abigail I, 580
Weeks, Abigail I, 1016
Weeks, Abigail I, 1028
Weeks, Abigail I, 1039
Weeks, Abigail III, 454
Weeks, Abigail III, 476
Weeks, Abigail V, 799
Weeks, Abigail V, 819
Weeks, Abraham III, 345
Weeks, Abraham H. III, 345
Weeks, Ada Louise III, 345
Weeks, Adaline III, 345
Weeks, Adeline III, 345
Weeks, Adrian III, 345
Weeks, Agness Witt VI, 908
Weeks, Alderosn VI, 967
Weeks, Alderson VI, 869
Weeks, Alderson VI, 871
Weeks, Alderson VI, 875
Weeks, Alderson VI, 878
Weeks, Alderson VI, 885
Weeks, Alderson VI, 886
Weeks, Alderson VI, 889
Weeks, Alderson VI, 890
Weeks, Alderson VI, 891
Weeks, Alderson VI, 894
Weeks, Alderson VI, 897
Weeks, Alderson VI, 898
Weeks, Alderson VI, 902
Weeks, Alderson VI, 904
Weeks, Alderson VI, 906
Weeks, Alderson VI, 907
Weeks, Alderson VI, 908
Weeks, Alderson VI, 911
Weeks, Alderson VI, 913
Weeks, Alderson VI, 914
Weeks, Alderson VI, 917
Weeks, Alderson VI, 922
Weeks, Alderson VI, 923
Weeks, Alderson VI, 924
Weeks, Alderson VI, 925
Weeks, Alderson VI, 926
Weeks, Alderson VI, 927
Weeks, Alderson VI, 928
Weeks, Alderson VI, 931
Weeks, Alderson VI, 932
Weeks, Alderson VI, 933
Weeks, Alderson VI, 935
Weeks, Alderson VI, 936
Weeks, Alderson VI, 937
Weeks, Alderson VI, 938
Weeks, Alderson VI, 939
Weeks, Alderson VI, 941
Weeks, Alderson VI, 942
Weeks, Alderson VI, 945
Weeks, Alderson VI, 946
Weeks, Alderson VI, 948
Weeks, Alderson VI, 949
Weeks, Alderson VI, 952
Weeks, Alderson VI, 956
Weeks, Alderson VI, 957
Weeks, Alderson VI, 959
Weeks, Alderson VI, 961
Weeks, Alderson VI, 962
Weeks, Alderson VI, 963
Weeks, Alderson VI, 965
Weeks, Alderson VI, 968
Weeks, Alderson VI, 969
Weeks, Alderson VI, 971
Weeks, Alderson VI, 972
Weeks, Alderson VI, 977
Weeks, Alderson VI, 982
Weeks, Alderson VI, 983
Weeks, Alderson VI, 984
Weeks, Alderson VI, 985
Weeks, Alderson VI, 986
Weeks, Alderson VI, 993
Weeks, Alderson VI, 994
Weeks, Alderson VI, 996
Weeks, Alderson VI, 997
Weeks, Alderson VI, 998
Weeks, Alderson VI, 1004
Weeks, Alderson VI, 1006
Weeks, Alderson VI, 1007
Weeks, Alderson VI, 1008
Weeks, Alderson VI, 1009
Weeks, Alderson VI, 1010
Weeks, Alderson VI, 1011
Weeks, Alderson VI, 1012
Weeks, Alderson VI, 1013
Weeks, Alderson VI, 1014
Weeks, Alderson VI, 1015
Weeks, Alderson VI, 1016
Weeks, Alderson VI, 1017
Weeks, Alderson VI, 1019
Weeks, Alderson VI, 1021
Weeks, Alex. B. III, 129
Weeks, Alexander B. III, 345
Weeks, Alexander N. III, 191
Weeks, Alice III, 345
Weeks, Alice H. III, 73
Weeks, Alice H. III, 345
Weeks, Alice L. III, 346
Weeks, Alice L. III, 464
Weeks, Allithena III, 346
Weeks, Alvah III, 345
Weeks, Amy III, 420
Weeks, Anderson VI, 911
Weeks, Anderson VI, 918
Weeks, Anderson VI, 920
Weeks, Ann III, 101
Weeks, Ann III, 345
Weeks, Ann III, 464
Weeks, Ann III, 465
Weeks, Ann H. III, 346
Weeks, Anna I, 867
Weeks, Anna III, 52
Weeks, Anna III, 346
Weeks, Anna III, 398
Weeks, Anna III, 407
Weeks, Anna III, 464
Weeks, Anna B. III, 53
Weeks, Anna B. III, 345
Weeks, Anna B. III, 346
Weeks, Anna B. III, 464
Weeks, Anna Bertha III, 346
Weeks, Anna L. III, 38
Weeks, Anna L. III, 334
Weeks, Anne III, 345
Weeks, Anne III, 435
Weeks, Augustine III, 464
Weeks, Benj. III, 346
Weeks, Benj. V, 819
Weeks, Benj. R. III, 369
Weeks, Benjamin I, 580
Weeks, Benjamin I, 843
Weeks, Benjamin I, 867
Weeks, Benjamin I, 1016
Weeks, Benjamin I, 1028
Weeks, Benjamin I, 1039
Weeks, Benjamin III, 345
Weeks, Benjamin III, 346
Weeks, Benjamin V, 793
Weeks, Benjamin V, 799
Weeks, Benjamin K. III, 345
Weeks, Benjamin K. III, 346
Weeks, Beulah III, 464
Weeks, Beulah III, 465
Weeks, Beulah III, 475
Weeks, Caron Happock I, 580
Weeks, Caron Happock I, 1016
Weeks, Catharine P. VI, 1012
Weeks, Charity III, 345
Weeks, Charity III, 398
Weeks, Charity III, 476
Weeks, Charles Melville III, 73
Weeks, Charles Melville III, 345
Weeks, Charlotte III, 63
Weeks, Charlotte III, 178
Weeks, Charlotte VI, 1021
Weeks, Clabourn VI, 908
Weeks, Clarissa I, 904
Weeks, Clary I, 580
Weeks, Clary I, 1016
Weeks, Columbus VI, 1012
Weeks, Cornelius III, 345
Weeks, Cornelius III, 464
Weeks, Cuthbert W. VI, 101
Weeks, Cynthia III, 345
Weeks, Daniel S. III, 345
Weeks, Deborah III, 345
Weeks, Deborah III, 461
Weeks, Deborah III, 464
Weeks, Dorinda E. III, 346
Weeks, Dorinda Eloise III, 3
Weeks, Dorothy III, 345
Weeks, Dorothy III, 465
Weeks, Dorothy III, 503
Weeks, Dr. ??? I, 1
Weeks, Dr. ??? I, 91
Weeks, Dr. ??? I, 92
Weeks, Dr. ??? I, 206
Weeks, Dr. ??? I, 279
Weeks, Dr. ??? I, 1015
Weeks, Dr. ??? I, 1074
Weeks, Dr. Stephen B. I, 1
Weeks, Dr. Stephen B. I, 101
Weeks, Edmund III, 345
Weeks, Edward L. III, 427
Weeks, Edwin W. III, 345
Weeks, Edwin W. III, 464
Weeks, Edwin W. III, 475
Weeks, Edwin Willets III, 34
Weeks, Eleanor VI, 1012
Weeks, Elijah VI, 1012
Weeks, Eliza III, 60
Weeks, Eliza III, 64
Weeks, Eliza III, 345
Weeks, Eliza III, 346
Weeks, Elizabeth III, 344
Weeks, Elizabeth III, 345
Weeks, Elizabeth III, 346
Weeks, Elizabeth III, 358
Weeks, Elizabeth III, 406
Weeks, Elizabeth III, 415
Weeks, Elizabeth III, 459
Weeks, Elizabeth III, 464
Weeks, Elizabeth III, 503
Weeks, Elizabeth VI, 1011
Weeks, Elizabeth J. III, 501
Weeks, Elwood V, 138
Weeks, Emma III, 53
Weeks, Emma III, 345
Weeks, Emma III, 346
Weeks, Emma III, 353
Weeks, Emma III, 464
Weeks, Emma III, 465
Weeks, Emma III, 468
Weeks, Emma B. IV, 785
Weeks, Emma Jane III, 61
Weeks, Emma Jane III, 345
Weeks, Evelyn III, 464
Weeks, Evelyn T. III, 406
Weeks, Florence V, 605
Weeks, Freelove III, 346
Weeks, Freelove III, 436
Weeks, Freelove III, 437
Weeks, Freelove III, 464
Weeks, George III, 151
Weeks, George III, 405
Weeks, George III, 435
Weeks, George VI, 932
Weeks, George VI, 972
Weeks, George VI, 992
Weeks, George N. III, 464
Weeks, Hannah I, 580
Weeks, Hannah I, 804
Weeks, Hannah I, 843
Weeks, Hannah I, 1016
Weeks, Hannah I, 1039
Weeks, Hannah III, 92
Weeks, Hannah III, 305
Weeks, Hannah III, 345
Weeks, Hannah III, 346
Weeks, Hannah III, 420
Weeks, Hannah III, 427
Weeks, Hannah III, 464
Weeks, Hannah III, 503
Weeks, Hannah J. IV, 785
Weeks, Hannah T. III, 369
Weeks, Henrietta III, 229
Weeks, Henrietta III, 345
Weeks, Henrietta III, 427
Weeks, Henrietta III, 464
Weeks, Henry H. III, 285
Weeks, Henry H. III, 345
Weeks, Henry H. III, 346
Weeks, Herietta W. III, 464
Weeks, Hester III, 345
Weeks, Ida III, 464

s, Ida L. III, 346
s, Isaac III, 345
s, Isaac III, 464
s, Isaac D. III, 464
s, Jacob III, 459
s, Jacob M. III, 411
s, Jacob M. III, 464
s, James I, 843
s, James I, 867
s, James I, 1039
s, James III, 92
s, James III, 345
s, James III, 346
s, James III, 464
s, James Edward III, 61
s, James Edward III, 345
s, James L. III, 464
s, Jane I, 867
s, Jane I, 904
s, Jane I, 906
s, Jane III, 345
s, Jane III, 465
s, Jane Ann III, 346
s, Jane M. III, 406
s, Jane M. III, 464
s, Jane S. III, 60
s, Jane S. III, 62
s, Jane S. III, 345
s, Janet Burling III, 464
s, Jas. L. III, 415
s, Jemima III, 503
s, Jerusha III, 436
s, Jerusha III, 437
s, Jesse III, 80
s, Jesse III, 345
s, Jesse III, 511
s, Jesse K. III, 60
s, Jesse K. III, 64
s, Jesse K. III, 345
s, Jesse K. III, 346
s, Johanna D. VI, 1012
s, John I, 843
s, John I, 867
s, John I, 904
s, John I, 906
s, John I, 1039
s, John III, 464
s, John III, 465
s, John III, 503
s, John VI, 908
s, John D. III, 346
s, Joseph III, 344
s, Joseph III, 358
s, Joseph III, 420
s, Joseph III, 501
s, Joseph VI, 1012
s, Josephine III, 221
s, Josephine III, 361
s, Joshua III, 345
s, Julia III, 511
s, Julia Ann VI, 1012
s, Leonard K. III, 345
s, Leonard K. III, 346
s, Louise III, 285
ks, Louise J. III, 345
ks, Louise Ruth III, 465
ks, Louise Ruth F. III, 463
ks, Luke B. III, 511
ks, Lydia I, 867
ks, Lydia I, 1066
ks, Lydia III, 345
ks, Lydia III, 346
ks, Lydia H. III, 345
ks, Lydia M. III, 345
ks, Lydia M. III, 369
ks, Lydia S. II, 832
ks, Lydia S. II, 937
ks, Margaret III, 456
ks, Margaret III, 464
ks, Margaret M. III, 464
ks, Margarett III, 464
ks, Maria IV, 785
ks, Mariah G. IV, 785
ks, Marion III, 17
ks, Marion III, 346
ks, Martha III, 346
ks, Martha III, 406
ks, Martha III, 441
ks, Martha III, 449
ks, Martha III, 454
ks, Martha III, 464
ks, Martha III, 473
ks, Mary I, 580
ks, Mary I, 1016
ks, Mary III, 95
ks, Mary III, 101
ks, Mary III, 120
ks, Mary III, 134
ks, Mary III, 218
ks, Mary III, 345
ks, Mary III, 346
Weeks, Mary III, 370
Weeks, Mary III, 402
Weeks, Mary III, 449
Weeks, Mary III, 464
Weeks, Mary V, 799
Weeks, Mary V, 819
Weeks, Mary V, 1024
Weeks, Mary VI, 1012
Weeks, Mary C. III, 461
Weeks, Mary Catharine III, 345
Weeks, Mary Ella III, 464
Weeks, Mary H. III, 345
Weeks, Mary H. III, 346
Weeks, Melissa III, 345
Weeks, Minna VI, 992
Weeks, Minnie Wright V, 718
Weeks, Moses H. III, 345
Weeks, Moses K. III, 346
Weeks, Nancey VI, 994
Weeks, Nancy VI, 972
Weeks, Nancy VI, 1009
Weeks, Nancy VI, 1012
Weeks, Nath. III, 394
Weeks, Nathaniel M. III, 18
Weeks, Nathaniel M. III, 346
Weeks, Nathaniel M. III, 394
Weeks, Nathaniel M. III, 464
Weeks, Octavus VI, 1012
Weeks, Peggy VI, 932
Weeks, Peninah III, 98
Weeks, Peninah III, 346
Weeks, Peter VI, 1012
Weeks, Phebe III, 80
Weeks, Phebe III, 345
Weeks, Phebe III, 346
Weeks, Phebe III, 490
Weeks, Phebe I. III, 226
Weeks, Phebe Jane III, 191
Weeks, Phebe Jane III, 346
Weeks, Phebe M. III, 464
Weeks, Phebe Merritt III, 503
Weeks, Phebe S. III, 64
Weeks, Phebe S. III, 345
Weeks, Phebe S. III, 346
Weeks, Phebe T. III, 402
Weeks, Phebe T. III, 464
Weeks, Polly Howard VI, 908
Weeks, Rachel III, 464
Weeks, Rachel III, 503
Weeks, Raisin IV, 1384
Weeks, Rebecca III, 345
Weeks, Rebecca III, 346
Weeks, Refine III, 456
Weeks, Refine III, 464
Weeks, Richard III, 223
Weeks, Richard III, 346
Weeks, Richard III, 406
Weeks, Richard III, 441
Weeks, Richard III, 449
Weeks, Richard III, 454
Weeks, Richard III, 464
Weeks, Richard III, 503
Weeks, Richard Henry III, 345
Weeks, Robert III, 425
Weeks, Robert H. III, 345
Weeks, Robert H. III, 346
Weeks, Robert S. III, 346
Weeks, Sally VI, 1012
Weeks, Sam'l III, 406
Weeks, Sam'l III, 464
Weeks, Samantha III, 223
Weeks, Samantha III, 464
Weeks, Samantha IV, 1384
Weeks, Samuel III, 345
Weeks, Samuel III, 398
Weeks, Samuel III, 408
Weeks, Samuel III, 454
Weeks, Samuel III, 461
Weeks, Samuel III, 464
Weeks, Samuel III, 465
Weeks, Samuel III, 476
Weeks, Samuel C. III, 52
Weeks, Samuel C. III, 346
Weeks, Samuel D. III, 464
Weeks, Samuel M. III, 346
Weeks, Samuel W. III, 464
Weeks, Sandford H. III, 336
Weeks, Sandford H., Jr. III, 346
Weeks, Sanford III, 346
Weeks, Sarah I, 172
Weeks, Sarah III, 59
Weeks, Sarah III, 61
Weeks, Sarah III, 63
Weeks, Sarah III, 80
Weeks, Sarah III, 345
Weeks, Sarah III, 346
Weeks, Sarah III, 369
Weeks, Sarah III, 454
Weeks, Sarah III, 464
Weeks, Sarah III, 465
Weeks, Sarah III, 511
Weeks, Sarah Ann III, 345
Weeks, Sarah Ann IV, 1384
Weeks, Sarah C. III, 464
Weeks, Sarah Cromwell III, 346
Weeks, Sarah Elizabeth III, 18
Weeks, Sarah Elizabeth III, 346
Weeks, Sarah Elizabeth III, 394
Weeks, Sarah Elizabeth III, 464
Weeks, Sarah H. III, 346
Weeks, Sarah Jane IV, 163
Weeks, Sarah Louisa III, 345
Weeks, Sarah R. III, 408
Weeks, Sarah R. III, 464
Weeks, Semantha III, 345
Weeks, Semantha III, 346
Weeks, Silas III, 464
Weeks, Silas III, 465
Weeks, Silas III, 468
Weeks, Silas B. III, 53
Weeks, Silas B. III, 345
Weeks, Silas B. III, 346
Weeks, Silas B. III, 353
Weeks, Silas Burling III, 463
Weeks, Silas Burling III, 464
Weeks, Silas Burling III, 465
Weeks, Silas D. III, 464
Weeks, Silas D. III, 465
Weeks, Siner VI, 1012
Weeks, Stephen III, 346
Weeks, Stephen III, 464
Weeks, Stephen VI, 39
Weeks, Stephen VI, 348
Weeks, Susan V, 884
Weeks, Susan V, 887
Weeks, Susan E. VI, 909
Weeks, Susan M. III, 346
Weeks, Susanna I, 580
Weeks, Susanna I, 843
Weeks, Susanna I, 1016
Weeks, Susanna IV, 1386
Weeks, Susannah I, 904
Weeks, Susannah IV, 1384
Weeks, Theodore III, 346
Weeks, Thomas VI, 1012
Weeks, Thomas F. III, 346
Weeks, Thomas T. III, 345
Weeks, Thomas T. III, 346
Weeks, Thos. T. III, 345
Weeks, Thos. T. III, 346
Weeks, Washington W. III, 345
Weeks, Wd. Ann III, 464
Weeks, Wd. Mary III, 151
Weeks, Wd. Mary III, 345
Weeks, Wd. Rachel III, 75
Weeks, Willet III, 346
Weeks, Willet III, 465
Weeks, William I, 843
Weeks, William I, 867
Weeks, William I, 904
Weeks, William VI, 1011
Weeks, William VI, 1012
Weeks, William VI, 1021
Weeks, William D. VI, 1012
Weeks, William M. III, 461
Weeks, William, Jr. I, 1039
Weeks, Williams VI, 909
Weeks, Wm. Bunting III, 17
Weeks, Wm. Burling III, 346
Weeks, Wm. M. III, 402
Weeks, Wm. M. III, 464
Weeks, Zeno III, 346
Weeksham, Jehu, Jr. I, 905
Weekss, Robert III, 464
Weells, Ann I, 454
Weels, Polly VI, 1009
Weels, Sarah VI, 1009
Weely, Mary I, 423
Weely, Mary I, 427
Weems, Frances VI, 764
Weems, Frances VI, 790
Weesner, Jemima V, 788
Weesner, John I, 427
Weesner, Joseph I, 914
Weesner, Josiah I, 427
Weesner, Micajah I, 427
Weesner, Michael V, 788
Weesner, Phebe I, 427
Weesner, Rachel I, 427
Weesner, Rachel I, 843
Weever, Edward II, 264
Weever, Edward II, 270
Weever, Mary II, 264
Weever, Mary II, 270
Weger, Anna Frances III, 339
Weger, Gottlieb III, 346
Weger, Joseph III, 346
Weger, Mary III, 346
Weger, Philip III, 339
Weger, Renee III, 339
Weger, Renee III, 346
Wehking, Caroline VI, 751
Wehmier, Frederick V, 940
Wehmier, Lottie V, 940
Weider, Addie IV, 1342
Weider, Adelaide M. IV, 1321
Weider, Adelaide M. IV, 1342
Weidle, Sophia VI, 985
Weigel, Clifford IV, 1342
Weigle, Charles F. IV, 1266
Weigle, Chas. IV, 1266
Weigles, Chas. IV, 1266
Weikert, Emma Johnson III, 347
Weikert, Emma Johnson V, 940
Weil, Harriett R. IV, 1342
Weiler, Wm. IV, 1342
Weiler, Wm. Smith IV, 1342
Weimer, Cora V, 649
Weimer, Gladys V, 649
Weimer, Gladys S. V, 649
Weimer, J. H. V, 649
Weimer, J. W. V, 649
Weimer, J. W. V, 718
Weimer, Karl John III, 269
Weimer, Karl John III, 347
Weimer, Karl John, Jr. III, 347
Weimer, Leo V, 649
Weimer, Leo V, 718
Weimer, Mary E. III, 269
Weimer, Robert A. III, 347
Weimer, Rosa V, 649
Weimer, Ruby S. III, 347
Weimer, S. Ruby III, 269
Weiner, Gladys S. V, 649
Weingart, Anna IV, 1039
Weingart, Anna Jackson IV, 1044
Weintz, Chas. V, 940
Weintz, Chas. H. V, 940
Weinwurm, Anna III, 347
Weinwurm, Grace III, 347
Weinwurm, Maurice III, 347
Weir, Absalom IV, 1342
Weir, Adolphus Gus VI, 1012
Weir, Annie E. III, 465
Weir, Charles Lorell IV, 301
Weir, Denzlon IV, 503
Weir, Elizabeth VI, 718
Weir, Elizabeth VI, 719
Weir, Eva Rose IV, 301
Weir, George III, 465
Weir, George IV, 503
Weir, George IV, 1192
Weir, Gretta E. IV, 301
Weir, Gretta Elizabeth IV, 301
Weir, Jane VI, 718
Weir, Jane VI, 719
Weir, Jessie IV, 503
Weir, Martha IV, 503
Weir, Martha VI, 1012
Weir, Martha H. IV, 1192
Weir, Robert VI, 718
Weir, Sarah VI, 718
Weir, Sarah VI, 719
Weir, William VI, 718
Weir, William VI, 719
Weirman, Nickolas I, 1163
Weisenborn, Billy V, 1024
Weisenborn, Clara V, 1024
Weisenborn, Clarissa V, 1024
Weisenborn, Cordelia V, 1024
Weisenborn, Thos. V, 1024
Weisenborn, Wm. V, 1024
Weisman, Harriet III, 347
Weisner, Abigail I, 367
Weisner, Abigail I, 395
Weisner, Abigail I, 427
Weisner, Abigail I, 810
Weisner, Abigail I, 843
Weisner, Abigail I, 910
Weisner, Ann I, 843
Weisner, Ann I, 910
Weisner, Ann I, 914
Weisner, Benj. I, 367
Weisner, Bennajaw I, 367
Weisner, Cyrenius I, 367
Weisner, Deborah I, 910
Weisner, Deborah I, 914
Weisner, Elizabeth I, 367
Weisner, Elizabeth I, 828
Weisner, Elizabeth I, 843
Weisner, Elizabeth I, 914
Weisner, Elizabeth I, 1039
Weisner, Elizabeth IV, 785
Weisner, Emeline I, 367
Weisner, Frederick IV, 785
Weisner, Isaac I, 1039
Weisner, Jabez I, 367
Weisner, Jacob I, 1039
Weisner, Jamima I, 559
Weisner, Jamima I, 580
Weisner, Jemima I, 580
Weisner, Jemima I, 907
Weisner, Jemima I, 914
Weisner, Jesse I, 823
Weisner, Jesse I, 843
Weisner, Jesse I, 907
Weisner, Jesse I, 910
Weisner, Jesse I, 914
Weisner, John I, 367
Weisner, John I, 427
Weisner, John I, 843
Weisner, John Pike I, 580
Weisner, Jonathan I, 910
Weisner, Joseph I, 910
Weisner, Joseph I, 914
Weisner, Josiah I, 367
Weisner, Josiah I, 423
Weisner, Josiah I, 427
Weisner, Lydai I, 823
Weisner, Lydai I, 843
Weisner, Lydia I, 907
Weisner, Lydia I, 914
Weisner, Macajah I, 914
Weisner, Malon I, 910
Weisner, Margaret Forney IV, 785
Weisner, Mary I, 1039
Weisner, Matilda I, 367
Weisner, Micael I, 843
Weisner, Micajah I, 367
Weisner, Micajah I, 395
Weisner, Micajah I, 427
Weisner, Micajah I, 559
Weisner, Micajah I, 580
Weisner, Micajah I, 843
Weisner, Micajah I, 914
Weisner, Micajah, Jr. I, 914
Weisner, Micha-torn I, 427
Weisner, Michael I, 427
Weisner, Michael I, 828
Weisner, Michael I, 843
Weisner, Michael I, 910
Weisner, Michael I, 914
Weisner, Milicent I, 367
Weisner, Phebe I, 423
Weisner, Phebe I, 427
Weisner, Rachel I, 367
Weisner, Rachel I, 410
Weisner, Rachel I, 427
Weisner, Rachel I, 843
Weisner, Rebecca I, 907
Weisner, Rebecca I, 914
Weisner, Rebecca Menhall I, 843
Weisner, Rebeccah I, 910
Weisner, Ruth I, 427
Weisner, Ruth I, 546
Weisner, Ruth I, 580
Weisner, Ruth I, 843
Weisner, Ruth I, 910
Weisner, Widow Ruth I, 580
Weisner, William I, 427
Weisner, William I, 843
Weisner, Wm I, 427
Weisner, Wm. I, 367
Weisner, Wm. I, 410
Weiss, Anna C. III, 151
Weiss, Caroline III, 196
Weiss, Lillian V, 210
Weitsel, Elizabeth IV, 785
Welbaum, Glenn V, 772
Welbaum, Mrs. Della V, 726
Welbaum, Paul V, 772
Welborn, Abigail I, 932
Welborn, Daniel I, 843
Welborn, Henry Rufus I, 843
Welborn, Julia B. I, 843
Welborn, Julia R. I, 807
Welborn, Julia R. I, 843
Welborn, Leanna S. I, 843
Welborn, Louisa I, 853
Welborn, Romulus I, 843
Welborn, Sarah I, 843
Welburn, Choica I, 930
Welch, ??? I, 32
Welch, ??? VI, 348
Welch, A. B. IV, 1266
Welch, A. R. IV, 1266
Welch, Abner II, 1036
Welch, Abner IV, 301
Welch, Abner IV, 1266
Welch, Adaline VI, 1012
Welch, Adda B. V, 139
Welch, Addo Bell V, 138
Welch, Agness II, 1013
Welch, Agness II, 1036
Welch, Alice IV, 301
Welch, Alice IV, 1266
Welch, Alice VI, 1012
Welch, Alice A. IV, 938
Welch, Alice A. IV, 1013
Welch, Allen IV, 1266
Welch, Alonzo V, 1024
Welch, Amanda V, 1024
Welch, Amos I, 979

Welch, Amos V, 54
Welch, Amos V, 138
Welch, Amos V, 139
Welch, Amos V, 364
Welch, Amos V, 560
Welch, Amos V, 604
Welch, Ann II, 1010
Welch, Ann II, 1036
Welch, Ann IV, 785
Welch, Ann V, 138
Welch, Ann V, 139
Welch, Ann V, 141
Welch, Ann V, 541
Welch, Ann M. V, 139
Welch, Ann M. V, 604
Welch, Anna M. V, 604
Welch, Betsey I, 979
Welch, Betsy V, 139
Welch, Betsy V, 364
Welch, Buddell V, 963
Welch, Carrie Smith IV, 1192
Welch, Catharine V, 1024
Welch, Catharine VI, 987
Welch, Catharine Karns VI, 1012
Welch, Catherine VI, 945
Welch, Charles V, 1024
Welch, Chloe I, 979
Welch, Chloe I, 999
Welch, Chloe I, 1000
Welch, Chloe V, 25
Welch, Chloe V, 121
Welch, Chloe V, 138
Welch, Chloe V, 139
Welch, Chloe V, 364
Welch, Chloe V, 793
Welch, Chloe VI, 313
Welch, Chloe VI, 344
Welch, Clara D. IV, 1192
Welch, Daniel VI, 808
Welch, Daniel VI, 812
Welch, Domanack VI, 945
Welch, Dominie VI, 1012
Welch, Dora IV, 1013
Welch, Edw. VI, 808
Welch, Edward VI, 859
Welch, Elcie V, 1024
Welch, Eli M. I, 627
Welch, Elisabeth I, 19
Welch, Elisabeth I, 32
Welch, Elisabeth I, 172
Welch, Eliza IV, 1298
Welch, Eliza V, 139
Welch, Eliza V, 141
Welch, Eliza E. IV, 1279
Welch, Eliza E. IV, 1298
Welch, Elizabeth I, 815
Welch, Elizabeth I, 843
Welch, Elizabeth II, 1036
Welch, Elizabeth IV, 1266
Welch, Elizabeth V, 138
Welch, Elizabeth V, 793
Welch, Elizabeth V, 963
Welch, Elizabeth V, 1024
Welch, Elizabeth VI, 856
Welch, Elizabeth Cooper V, 107
Welch, Elizabeth Cooper V, 139
Welch, Elizabeth H. V, 121
Welch, Elizabeth H. V, 138
Welch, Emma Alice I, 627
Welch, Emma Alice I, 642
Welch, Emmerson IV, 1192
Welch, Esther II, 225
Welch, Esther II, 270
Welch, Esther V, 34
Welch, Esther V, 138
Welch, Esther V, 139
Welch, Esther V, 539
Welch, Esther V, 604
Welch, Esther P. V, 139
Welch, Eva IV, 1192
Welch, Eva E. C. IV, 1192
Welch, F. E. IV, 1192
Welch, Fanny VI, 1012
Welch, Frances J. V, 139
Welch, Francis A. IV, 1192
Welch, Francis J. V, 139
Welch, Frank V, 1024
Welch, Frank C. IV, 1192
Welch, Frank Corbitt IV, 1192
Welch, Frank Leslie I, 627
Welch, Geo. W. V, 1024
Welch, George II, 1010
Welch, George II, 1036
Welch, George VI, 972
Welch, George VI, 1012
Welch, George VI, 1017
Welch, George C. I, 904
Welch, Gilbert M. V, 139
Welch, Hannah I, 43
Welch, Hannah II, 682
Welch, Hannah Copeland I, 78
Welch, Harriett L. V, 139
Welch, Harriett Lydia V, 138
Welch, Harvey B. IV, 1266
Welch, Harvey R. IV, 301
Welch, Harvey R. IV, 1266
Welch, Hilda Rose I, 642
Welch, Horace G. IV, 727
Welch, Horace G. IV, 785
Welch, Horace G. V, 139
Welch, Horace Greeley V, 138
Welch, Howard G. IV, 1298
Welch, Iredell I, 1000
Welch, Isaac V, 139
Welch, Isaac V, 793
Welch, Isaiah V, 139
Welch, Isaiah V, 479
Welch, Isaiah V, 539
Welch, Isaiah F. V, 34
Welch, Isham I, 1000
Welch, Jacob V, 963
Welch, James II, 1010
Welch, James II, 1036
Welch, James V, 139
Welch, James V, 539
Welch, James VI, 1012
Welch, James C. I, 904
Welch, Jane I, 904
Welch, Jane IV, 114
Welch, Jane IV, 265
Welch, Jane IV, 301
Welch, Jemimy VI, 1012
Welch, Jessie IV, 1192
Welch, Jessie E. IV, 1192
Welch, John I, 979
Welch, John I, 999
Welch, John I, 1000
Welch, John II, 1036
Welch, John IV, 785
Welch, John IV, 1013
Welch, John V, 138
Welch, John V, 139
Welch, John V, 141
Welch, John V, 539
Welch, John V, 541
Welch, John V, 604
Welch, John VI, 1012
Welch, John F. IV, 1298
Welch, John T. IV, 1298
Welch, Jonah V, 139
Welch, Joseph II, 225
Welch, Joseph II, 240
Welch, Joseph II, 270
Welch, Joseph II, 972
Welch, Josephine IV, 727
Welch, Josephine IV, 785
Welch, Josiah F. V, 138
Welch, Judeth I, 979
Welch, Judith V, 32
Welch, Judith V, 33
Welch, Judith V, 139
Welch, Judith V, 364
Welch, Kezia I, 924
Welch, Kezia I, 928
Welch, Leah V, 34
Welch, Leah V, 139
Welch, Leah V, 479
Welch, Leah V, 539
Welch, Leah C. V, 139
Welch, Leah E. V, 138
Welch, Leslie I, 642
Welch, Lettice II, 682
Welch, Lizzie IV, 1013
Welch, Lucy VI, 1012
Welch, Lucy E. IV, 301
Welch, Lucy E. IV, 1266
Welch, Lydia II, 240
Welch, Lydia II, 270
Welch, Lydia L. VI, 812
Welch, Lyman IV, 1192
Welch, Mahlon II, 1036
Welch, Margaret I, 611
Welch, Margaret IV, 1013
Welch, Margaret V, 150
Welch, Margaret V, 649
Welch, Martha I, 979
Welch, Martha II, 1036
Welch, Martha V, 34
Welch, Martha V, 138
Welch, Martha V, 139
Welch, Martha V, 364
Welch, Martha V, 604
Welch, Martha A. V, 139
Welch, Martha A. V, 539
Welch, Martha Ann V, 539
Welch, Mary I, 888
Welch, Mary I, 904
Welch, Mary I, 979
Welch, Mary I, 999
Welch, Mary II, 270
Welch, Mary IV, 301
Welch, Mary V, 43
Welch, Mary V, 138
Welch, Mary V, 139
Welch, Mary V, 539
Welch, Mary V, 604
Welch, Mary V, 780
Welch, Mary V, 1024
Welch, Mary VI, 885
Welch, Mary VI, 945
Welch, Mary VI, 1012
Welch, Mary Ann V, 139
Welch, Mary Elisabeth I, 19
Welch, Mary Esther V, 139
Welch, Matilda I, 996
Welch, Matilda I, 1000
Welch, Matilda IV, 1298
Welch, Mattie I, 627
Welch, Meribah II, 270
Welch, Meribah II, 972
Welch, Meribah II, 1036
Welch, Milton IV, 1298
Welch, Moses I, 979
Welch, Nancy VI, 1012
Welch, Nathan I, 1163
Welch, Olive V, 718
Welch, Oliver M. V, 139
Welch, Oliver M. V, 718
Welch, Payton VI, 898
Welch, Payton VI, 900
Welch, Payton VI, 906
Welch, Payton VI, 916
Welch, Payton VI, 920
Welch, Payton VI, 926
Welch, Payton VI, 947
Welch, Payton VI, 989
Welch, Payton VI, 997
Welch, Payton VI, 1007
Welch, Payton VI, 1008
Welch, Payton VI, 1015
Welch, Payton VI, 1016
Welch, Payton H. IV, 301
Welch, Payton H. IV, 1266
Welch, Pearl I, 642
Welch, Pearl Olive I, 627
Welch, Peyton VI, 870
Welch, Peyton VI, 872
Welch, Peyton VI, 874
Welch, Peyton VI, 877
Welch, Peyton VI, 878
Welch, Peyton VI, 893
Welch, Peyton VI, 899
Welch, Peyton VI, 900
Welch, Peyton VI, 907
Welch, Peyton VI, 928
Welch, Peyton VI, 939
Welch, Peyton VI, 947
Welch, Peyton VI, 967
Welch, Peyton VI, 971
Welch, Peyton VI, 982
Welch, Peyton VI, 1007
Welch, Peyton VI, 1008
Welch, Peyton VI, 1012
Welch, Peyton VI, 1014
Welch, Phebe V, 121
Welch, Polly VI, 1012
Welch, Precilla I, 999
Welch, Precilla I, 1000
Welch, Priscilla V, 139
Welch, Rachel IV, 301
Welch, Rachel IV, 1266
Welch, Rachel IV, 1298
Welch, Rachel V, 54
Welch, Rachel V, 138
Welch, Rachel V, 139
Welch, Rachel V, 142
Welch, Rachel V, 560
Welch, Rachel V, 604
Welch, Rayton H. IV, 301
Welch, Richard VI, 1008
Welch, Robert Barclay V, 139
Welch, Robert Barclay V, 539
Welch, Roswell IV, 1192
Welch, Ruth I, 979
Welch, Ruth I, 999
Welch, Ruth I, 1000
Welch, Ruth II, 160
Welch, Ruth V, 136
Welch, Ruth V, 1024
Welch, Ruth P. V, 1024
Welch, Sabry I, 1000
Welch, Salley I, 979
Welch, Sally V, 364
Welch, Sally VI, 891
Welch, Sally Webster V, 139
Welch, Samantha IV, 1192
Welch, Samuel I, 971
Welch, Samuel I, 979
Welch, Samuel I, 999
Welch, Samuel I, 1000
Welch, Samuel V, 121
Welch, Samuel V, 138
Welch, Samuel V, 139
Welch, Samuel V, 142
Welch, Samuel V, 364
Welch, Samuel V, 793
Welch, Samuel VI, 313
Welch, Samuel VI, 344
Welch, Samuel, Jr. V, 138
Welch, Sarah I, 1163
Welch, Sarah II, 152
Welch, Sarah II, 160
Welch, Sarah II, 1036
Welch, Sarah V, 121
Welch, Sarah V, 138
Welch, Sarah V, 963
Welch, Sarah V, 1024
Welch, Sarah VI, 880
Welch, Savilla Emma V, 138
Welch, Susan VI, 808
Welch, Susan VI, 880
Welch, Susan M. VI, 1012
Welch, Susannah VI, 1012
Welch, Tacy L. IV, 1192
Welch, Theodore IV, 1192
Welch, Theodore K. IV, 1192
Welch, Theodore M. IV, 1192
Welch, Thomas VI, 356
Welch, Thomas VI, 1012
Welch, Thomas C. V, 139
Welch, Thomas W. V, 139
Welch, Turner I, 979
Welch, Turner I, 999
Welch, Turner I, 1000
Welch, Turner V, 34
Welch, Turner V, 138
Welch, Turner V, 139
Welch, Turner V, 539
Welch, Turner V, 604
Welch, Viola V, 1024
Welch, Warren T. V, 139
Welch, Webster I, 979
Welch, Webster V, 139
Welch, Webster V, 364
Welch, Webster V, 780
Welch, Webster V, 793
Welch, Webster G. V, 43
Welch, Webster G. V, 138
Welch, Webster G. V, 139
Welch, William I, 19
Welch, William VI, 1012
Welch, William Hamilton, Jr. I, 19
Welch, Wm. II, 1036
Welch, Wm. V, 1024
Welch, Wm. Lyman IV, 1192
Weld, Angelina E. G. II, 743
Weld, Angelina E. G. II, 774
Welden, Isabella II, 681
Welding, Alice V, 968
Welding, Alice V, 978
Welding, Anna H. III, 21
Welding, Anna H. III, 347
Welding, Anne H. II, 833
Welding, Anne H. II, 937
Welding, Charles F. III, 347
Welding, Emily V, 978
Welding, Isabel II, 483
Welding, Isabell II, 681
Welding, Micajah VI, 790
Welding, Sarah H. II, 833
Welding, Sarah H. II, 937
Welding, Sarah H. III, 21
Welding, Sarah H. III, 347
Welding, Sarah J. II, 774
Welding, Watson J. II, 774
Welding, Watson J. II, 833
Welding, Watson J. II, 937
Welding, Watson J. III, 21
Welding, Watson J. III, 347
Welding, William H. III, 347
Welding, Wm. H. III, 347
Weldon, Ann IV, 356
Weldon, Elizabeth IV, 356
Weldon, Hannah III, 26
Weldon, Hannah G. III, 347
Weldon, Isaac IV, 356
Weldon, Isabel II, 483
Weldon, Isabel II, 681
Weldon, Isabell II, 681
Weldon, Isabella II, 681
Weldon, John IV, 356
Weldon, John Carver II, 681
Weldon, Joseph IV, 356
Weldon, Josiah III, 347
Weldon, Martha IV, 302
Weldon, Mary Ann IV, 527
Weldon, Mary Ann IV, 555
Weldon, Nathan IV, 356
Weldon, Phebe III, 347
Weldon, Rachel IV, 301
Weldon, Tabitha IV, 555
Weldy, Fern V, 772
Weldy, Mary IV, 486
Weldy, Mary IV, 503
Weleasy, Chas. V, 1024
Welford, Charles V, 604
Welford, Julia V, 604
Welhoff, Flora IV, 1316
Welker, Charles IV, 1192
Welker, Gertrude I, 625
Welker, Mary IV, 882
Welker, Mary IV, 886
Welker, Ruth Madona V, 102
Welker, Walter Edwin V, 102
Well, Leah James IV, 886
Well, Lydia IV, 886
Well, Mary II, 433
Wellam, Abby Lucy Mary A. I, 580
Wellam, Elizabeth I, 580
Wellan, Mary IV, 301
Wellans, Ada VI, 51
Wellans, Peter VI, 51
Weller, Ada Pyle V, 604
Weller, Anna V, 604
Weller, Carrie E. V, 210
Weller, Catharine V, 210
Weller, Catherine V, 210
Weller, Earl V, 649
Weller, Ella J. V, 649
Weller, Ernest V, 649
Weller, Homer V, 649
Weller, Letitia B. V, 714
Weller, Louiza V, 467
Weller, Lucile V, 696
Weller, Lucile V, 718
Weller, Oscar V, 604
Weller, Peter S. V, 467
Weller, Roy V, 696
Weller, Roy V, 718
Weller, Samuel V, 210
Weller, Sarah Louiza V, 467
Weller, Verna V, 694
Weller, Verna V, 718
Weller, Wm. J. V, 649
Welling, Emily V, 978
Wellington, Jesse I, 277
Wellington, Lydia I, 277
Wellins, Asenath IV, 573
Wellins, Asenath IV, 599
Wellis, Wm. V, 650
Wellons, Ada VI, 88
Wellons, Floyd W. VI, 88
Wellons, Mary IV, 454
Wellons, Peter VI, 88
Wellons, Robert L. VI, 88
Wells, ??? II, 448
Wells, A. II, 938
Wells, Aaron L. I, 472
Wells, Aaron Lindley I, 486
Wells, Aaron Lindly I, 486
Wells, Abigail I, 427
Wells, Abigail II, 433
Wells, Abigail II, 537
Wells, Abigail II, 681
Wells, Abigail II, 722
Wells, Abigail II, 774
Wells, Abner IV, 163
Wells, Abner IV, 301
Wells, Abner IV, 357
Wells, Abner IV, 454
Wells, Abner IV, 1299
Wells, Albert IV, 1299
Wells, Alpheus I, 428
Wells, Amos P. IV, 163
Wells, Amos P. IV, 357
Wells, Amos Peasley IV, 163
Wells, Anderson I, 919
Wells, Ann I, 427
Wells, Ann I, 428
Wells, Ann I, 454
Wells, Ann I, 486
Wells, Ann II, 448
Wells, Ann IV, 1081
Wells, Ann B. IV, 163
Wells, Ann B. IV, 357
Wells, Ann Craig II, 681
Wells, Ann M. IV, 163
Wells, Ann M. IV, 1081
Wells, Anna II, 433
Wells, Anna II, 511
Wells, Anna II, 681
Wells, Anna V, 288
Wells, Anna C. II, 826
Wells, Anna C. II, 937
Wells, Anna Craige II, 681
Wells, Anne Craig II, 511
Wells, Annie V, 288
Wells, Annie Jane I, 427
Wells, Arthur II, 448
Wells, Arthur II, 568
Wells, Arthur II, 681
Wells, Arthur II, 722
Wells, Arthur II, 774

B. W. IV, 1266
Barnabas H. III, 476
Belle V, 1024
Benj. I, 367
Benj. I, 427
Benjamin I, 367
Benjamin I, 373
Benjamin I, 427
Burford VI, 863
Catharine I, 424
Catharine I, 427
Catharine II, 1001
Catharine II, 1036
Catharine IV, 163
Catharine IV, 301
Catherine II, 1036
Catherine IV, 114
Catherine T. IV, 150
Catherine T. IV, 163
Charity I, 352
Charity I, 367
Charity I, 389
Charity I, 417
Charity I, 427
Charity I, 691
Charity VI, 481
Charity VI, 577
Charles H. II, 826
Charles H. II, 938
Charlotte Elizabeth
, 465
Charlotte Elizabeth
, 476
Chas. Edward IV, 1298
Clara E. IV, 1013
Cordelia I, 935
Cordelia I, 950
Cordelia K. I, 950
Cyrus C. I, 472
Cyrus Clarkson I, 486
Cyrus Newton I, 486
Daniel II, 110
Daniel IV, 1299
David IV, 163
David IV, 357
David IV, 1298
David J. VI, 1012
David T. IV, 357
Deborah II, 589
Deborah II, 681
Deborah III, 449
Deborah III, 465
Deborah IV, 163
Deborah IV, 301
Deborah IV, 357
Deborah IV, 454
Deborah IV, 1151
Deborah IV, 1192
Dorcas I, 367
Dorcas I, 373
Dorcas I, 427
Edna III, 449
Edna III, 465
Edward II, 433
Edward II, 681
Edwin N. II, 826
Elisabeth I, 55
Elisabeth I, 77
Elisha II, 1082
Elisha IV, 163
Elisha IV, 301
Elisha IV, 357
Elisha IV, 1081
Elisha M. IV, 163
Eliza IV, 1384
Eliza A. III, 476
Eliza C. IV, 1384
Eliza Ellen IV, 1192
Eliza R. IV, 1377
Elizabeth I, 373
Elizabeth I, 376
Elizabeth I, 426
Elizabeth I, 427
Elizabeth I Sup 1, 7
Elizabeth II, 270
Elizabeth II, 433
Elizabeth IV, 114
Elizabeth IV, 163
Elizabeth IV, 196
Elizabeth IV, 911
Elizabeth IV, 917
Elizabeth V, 139
Elizabeth C. II, 937
Elizabeth Done IV, 301
Elizabeth W. II, 826
Ella V, 436
Emily I, 428
Emily II, 722
Emily II, 774
Ernest III, 347
Esther I, 427
Wells, Esther II, 974
Wells, Esther II, 1036
Wells, Esther IV, 354
Wells, Esther IV, 357
Wells, Esther IV, 1080
Wells, Esther IV, 1081
Wells, Eva IV, 1342
Wells, Florentine W. VI, 1012
Wells, Frances VI, 999
Wells, Francis I, 42
Wells, Francis I, 77
Wells, Francis I Sup 1, 6
Wells, Francis I Sup 1, 7
Wells, Francis II, 433
Wells, Francis II, 774
Wells, George V, 604
Wells, George V, 1024
Wells, Gideon II, 270
Wells, Gideon II, 537
Wells, Gideon II, 549
Wells, Gideon II, 681
Wells, Gideon Hill II, 681
Wells, Gideon Hill III, 347
Wells, Gilbert II, 433
Wells, Hannah II, 110
Wells, Hannah II, 232
Wells, Hannah II, 239
Wells, Hannah II, 270
Wells, Hannah II, 273
Wells, Hannah II, 537
Wells, Hannah II, 681
Wells, Hannah IV, 163
Wells, Hannah IV, 261
Wells, Hannah IV, 301
Wells, Hannah IV, 357
Wells, Hannah IV, 413
Wells, Hannah IV, 454
Wells, Hannah IV, 459
Wells, Hannah IV, 1081
Wells, Hannah V, 49
Wells, Hannah V, 139
Wells, Hannah V, 436
Wells, Hannah Hill II, 433
Wells, Hannah L. IV, 163
Wells, Hannah L. IV, 357
Wells, Hannah L. W. IV, 156
Wells, Hannah L. W. IV, 163
Wells, Hannah Louisa IV, 1298
Wells, Harpalynce H. VI, 1012
Wells, Harriett VI, 1012
Wells, Henry Hill II, 433
Wells, Hester I, 427
Wells, Howard II, 937
Wells, Howard II, 938
Wells, Hugh II, 937
Wells, Hughs II, 938
Wells, Isaac I, 367
Wells, Isaac I, 427
Wells, Isaac I, 474
Wells, Isaac I, 486
Wells, Isaac I, 674
Wells, Isaac I, 691
Wells, Isaac II, 826
Wells, Isaac IV, 141
Wells, Isaac IV, 163
Wells, Isaac IV, 301
Wells, Isaac IV, 357
Wells, Isaac IV, 555
Wells, Isaac IV, 1081
Wells, Isaac N. II, 937
Wells, Isaac Newton II, 826
Wells, Isaiah IV, 114
Wells, Isaiah IV, 163
Wells, Israel IV, 301
Wells, James II, 270
Wells, James F. V, 288
Wells, James H. VI, 1012
Wells, Jane II, 512
Wells, Jane II, 681
Wells, Jesse I, 427
Wells, Joel I, 427
Wells, John I, 427
Wells, John I, 428
Wells, John I, 472
Wells, John I, 486
Wells, John IV, 114
Wells, John IV, 163
Wells, John IV, 301
Wells, John IV, 1081
Wells, John IV, 1298
Wells, John VI, 455
Wells, John VI, 578
Wells, John C. I, 486
Wells, John Calvin I, 472
Wells, John Craig II, 681
Wells, John F. V, 288
Wells, John T. IV, 354
Wells, John T. IV, 357
Wells, John T. IV, 454
Wells, John T. IV, 1080
Wells, John T. IV, 1081
Wells, John William I, 427
Wells, Jonathan IV, 163
Wells, Jonathan IV, 301
Wells, Jonathan IV, 357
Wells, Jonathan IV, 555
Wells, Jonathan IV, 1081
Wells, Joseph I, 77
Wells, Joseph I, 201
Wells, Joseph I, 343
Wells, Joseph I, 352
Wells, Joseph I, 367
Wells, Joseph I, 385
Wells, Joseph I, 427
Wells, Joseph I, 691
Wells, Joseph II, 433
Wells, Joseph VI, 577
Wells, Joseph, Jr. I, 427
Wells, Joseph, Jr. VI, 481
Wells, Joseph, Jr. VI, 577
Wells, Joseph, Sr. I, 427
Wells, Josiah IV, 163
Wells, Josiah IV, 357
Wells, Josiah IV, 555
Wells, Julia I, 465
Wells, Julia A. IV, 1384
Wells, Julia Ann IV, 1384
Wells, Katharine F. II, 938
Wells, Lamar G. III, 347
Wells, Levi IV, 114
Wells, Levi IV, 137
Wells, Levi IV, 163
Wells, Levi IV, 301
Wells, Levi IV, 454
Wells, Levi IV, 555
Wells, Levi IV, 1081
Wells, Levi G. IV, 1081
Wells, Levi J. IV, 1081
Wells, Lewis IV, 163
Wells, Louisa I, 371
Wells, Louisa I, 935
Wells, Louisa J. I, 919
Wells, Lucinda J. VI, 947
Wells, Lydia II, 551
Wells, Lydia II, 681
Wells, Lydia IV, 577
Wells, Lydia IV, 599
Wells, Margaret I, 42
Wells, Margaret I, 52
Wells, Margaret I, 77
Wells, Margaret I, 156
Wells, Margaret I, 172
Wells, Margaret I, 352
Wells, Margaret I, 369
Wells, Margaret I, 385
Wells, Margaret I, 390
Wells, Margaret I, 427
Wells, Margaret IV, 163
Wells, Margaret IV, 301
Wells, Margaret IV, 357
Wells, Margaret IV, 395
Wells, Margaret IV, 454
Wells, Margaret IV, 1081
Wells, Margaret VI, 573
Wells, Margaret VI, 577
Wells, Margaret VI, 578
Wells, Martha I, 427
Wells, Martha II, 448
Wells, Martha IV, 143
Wells, Martha IV, 163
Wells, Martha IV, 357
Wells, Martha Emma II, 826
Wells, Mary I, 367
Wells, Mary I, 370
Wells, Mary I, 373
Wells, Mary I, 427
Wells, Mary I, 474
Wells, Mary I, 486
Wells, Mary I, 674
Wells, Mary I, 691
Wells, Mary I, 771
Wells, Mary II, 270
Wells, Mary II, 433
Wells, Mary II, 448
Wells, Mary II, 603
Wells, Mary II, 681
Wells, Mary II, 1036
Wells, Mary IV, 114
Wells, Mary IV, 150
Wells, Mary IV, 329
Wells, Mary IV, 357
Wells, Mary IV, 1299
Wells, Mary IV, 1384
Wells, Mary VI, 1012
Wells, Mary A. I, 371
Wells, Mary Ann I, 486
Wells, Mary Emma II, 938
Wells, Mary F. I, 428
Wells, Mary Gideon II, 681
Wells, Mary Griffitts II, 722
Wells, Mary Griffitts II, 774
Wells, Mary Ida II, 826
Wells, Matilda E. V, 288
Wells, Meriba IV, 1377
Wells, Meriba IV, 1384
Wells, Meribah IV, 1384
Wells, Minta Caroline I, 486
Wells, Molly VI, 859
Wells, Moses II, 270
Wells, Moses IV, 163
Wells, Moses IV, 301
Wells, Moses IV, 555
Wells, Moses IV, 1081
Wells, Moses B. IV, 163
Wells, Moses D. IV, 301
Wells, Nancey I, 201
Wells, Nancy I, 195
Wells, Nancy I, 201
Wells, Nancy I, 472
Wells, Nancy E. VI, 863
Wells, Nathan I, 427
Wells, Nellie IV, 1266
Wells, Nellie IV, 1299
Wells, Nellie W. IV, 1299
Wells, Phebe II, 1036
Wells, Philip II, 512
Wells, Philip II, 681
Wells, Pricilla II, 270
Wells, Rachel I, 425
Wells, Rachel I, 427
Wells, Rachel II, 270
Wells, Rachel II, 433
Wells, Rachel II, 549
Wells, Rachel II, 603
Wells, Rachel II, 681
Wells, Rachel VI, 585
Wells, Rachel Moore II, 681
Wells, Reba Emma II, 887
Wells, Reba Emma II, 938
Wells, Rebecca I, 367
Wells, Rebecca II, 448
Wells, Rebecca IV, 268
Wells, Rebecca IV, 301
Wells, Rebecca IV, 314
Wells, Rebecca IV, 315
Wells, Rebeckah II, 681
Wells, Rebekah II, 568
Wells, Rebekah II, 663
Wells, Rebekah II, 681
Wells, Richard II, 270
Wells, Richard II, 433
Wells, Richard II, 549
Wells, Richard II, 603
Wells, Richard II, 681
Wells, Richard II, 722
Wells, Richard II, 774
Wells, Richard Hill II, 433
Wells, Richard M. VI, 947
Wells, Richard M. VI, 1009
Wells, Richard M. VI, 1012
Wells, Richard W. II, 774
Wells, Richard Waln II, 537
Wells, Richard Waln II, 681
Wells, Robert II, 681
Wells, Robert II, 774
Wells, Robert V, 139
Wells, Russel IV, 1384
Wells, Russel Thomas IV, 1384
Wells, Russell IV, 1377
Wells, Russell IV, 1384
Wells, Ruth I, 371
Wells, Ruth I, 427
Wells, Ruth II, 270
Wells, Ruth IV, 163
Wells, Ruth IV, 357
Wells, Ruth Anna II, 937
Wells, Ruth Ellen I, 422
Wells, Ruth Ellen I, 427
Wells, Ruth L. IV, 1342
Wells, Ruth T. IV, 163
Wells, Sally I, 371
Wells, Sally I, 427
Wells, Samuel I, 367
Wells, Samuel II, 433
Wells, Samuel II, 681
Wells, Samuel IV, 413
Wells, Samuel IV, 454
Wells, Samuel Griffitts II, 433
Wells, Samuel Griffitts II, 681
Wells, Samuel Griffitts II, 774
Wells, Samuel Preston II, 433
Wells, Sarah I, 190
Wells, Sarah I, 201
Wells, Sarah I, 427
Wells, Sarah I, 679
Wells, Sarah I, 691
Wells, Sarah I, 919
Wells, Sarah II, 270
Wells, Sarah II, 542
Wells, Sarah II, 616
Wells, Sarah II, 681
Wells, Sarah II, 826
Wells, Sarah IV, 114
Wells, Sarah IV, 163
Wells, Sarah IV, 413
Wells, Sarah IV, 414
Wells, Sarah IV, 454
Wells, Sarah VI, 947
Wells, Sarah VI, 999
Wells, Sarah Ann IV, 152
Wells, Sarah Ann IV, 163
Wells, Sarah Ann IV, 357
Wells, Sarah E. V, 288
Wells, Sarah G. IV, 454
Wells, Sarah Gilbert IV, 301
Wells, Sarah H. IV, 1384
Wells, Sherman III, 449
Wells, Sherman III, 465
Wells, Simon I, 371
Wells, Slisha IV, 163
Wells, Stephen I, 427
Wells, Susan IV, 1081
Wells, Susanna I, 427
Wells, Susanna IV, 114
Wells, Susanna IV, 141
Wells, Susanna IV, 163
Wells, Susanna IV, 207
Wells, Susanna IV, 301
Wells, Susanna IV, 555
Wells, Susannah IV, 114
Wells, Susannah IV, 163
Wells, Susannah IV, 357
Wells, Susannah VI, 455
Wells, Thomas I, 427
Wells, Thomas II, 433
Wells, Thomas II, 681
Wells, Thomas II, 774
Wells, Thomas IV, 114
Wells, Thomas IV, 163
Wells, Thomas IV, 454
Wells, Thomas V, 49
Wells, Thomas V, 139
Wells, Thomas V, 436
Wells, Thomas M. IV, 314
Wells, Thomas M. IV, 315
Wells, Thos. V, 940
Wells, Virginia I, 428
Wells, W. C. I, 935
Wells, W. C. I, 950
Wells, Wd. Elizabeth II, 448
Wells, Wd. Mary II, 513
Wells, Wilberforce II, 937
Wells, Wilberforce II, 938
Wells, William I, 427
Wells, William I, 428
Wells, William II, 270
Wells, William II, 433
Wells, William II, 448
Wells, William IV, 163
Wells, William IV, 301
Wells, William IV, 357
Wells, William IV, 454
Wells, William IV, 555
Wells, William IV, 1081
Wells, William IV, 1299
Wells, William VI, 1012
Wells, Wm. II, 448
Wells, Wm. II, 511
Wells, Wm. II, 681
Wells, Wm. IV, 150
Wells, Wm. IV, 163
Wells, Wm. IV, 357
Wells, Wm. IV, 1081
Wells, Wm. Benjamin IV, 1298
Wells, Zachariah I, 427
Wellson, Phetheny I, 172
Wellson, Phetheny I, 176
Wellstood, James III, 347
Wels, Joseph I, 534
Wels, Joseph I, 580
Wels, Mary I, 580
Wels, Widow Mary I, 534
Welsch, Ruth II, 160
Welsch, Wm. V, 1024
Welsh, Albina VI, 719
Welsh, Amos V, 139
Welsh, Ann III, 347
Welsh, Ann M. V, 139
Welsh, Anna M. V, 568
Welsh, Barbara May VI, 642
Welsh, Benjamin VI, 719
Welsh, Betsy V, 139
Welsh, Chloe V, 139
Welsh, Constance M. VI, 719
Welsh, Daniel VI, 831
Welsh, Edward Bently VI, 719
Welsh, Elisabeth I, 50
Welsh, Elisabeth I, 77
Welsh, Elizabeth II, 974
Welsh, Elizabeth II, 1036
Welsh, Emelia L. III, 347
Welsh, Emelie III, 357
Welsh, Emma Alice I, 642
Welsh, Enoch II, 681

Welsh, Fayett VI, 719
Welsh, Fayette G. VI, 626
Welsh, Fayette G. VI, 628
Welsh, Fayette G. VI, 700
Welsh, George VI, 965
Welsh, Hannah I, 78
Welsh, Hannah II, 682
Welsh, Hannah Copeland I, 78
Welsh, Helen E. VI, 700
Welsh, Helen E. VI, 719
Welsh, Helen Elizabeth VI, 719
Welsh, Hilda Rose I, 642
Welsh, Howard L. VI, 700
Welsh, Howard L. VI, 719
Welsh, James II, 1036
Welsh, Jane I, 904
Welsh, Jane I, 906
Welsh, Jemima II, 590
Welsh, Jemima II, 682
Welsh, John Hallock III, 347
Welsh, John S. III, 347
Welsh, Joseph B. III, 347
Welsh, Joseph B. III, 357
Welsh, Judith V, 139
Welsh, Lena III, 347
Welsh, Lettice II, 681
Welsh, Lettice II, 682
Welsh, Lewis E. III, 347
Welsh, Martha V, 108
Welsh, Martha V, 139
Welsh, Martha A. V, 139
Welsh, Mary III, 347
Welsh, Mary III, 357
Welsh, Mary VI, 831
Welsh, May VI, 719
Welsh, Nellie VI, 687
Welsh, Nellie VI, 719
Welsh, Pearl I, 642
Welsh, Rachel V, 139
Welsh, Ruth II, 161
Welsh, Sally Webster V, 139
Welsh, Samuel V, 139
Welsh, Samuel B. VI, 642
Welsh, Samuel B. VI, 719
Welsh, Sarah I, 1007
Welsh, Sarah I, 1013
Welsh, Sarah II, 1036
Welsh, Susan Parthenia VI, 626
Welsh, Susan Parthenia VI, 628
Welsh, Susan Parthenia VI, 700
Welsh, Susan Parthenia VI, 719
Welsh, Therese Marie III, 347
Welsh, William VI, 687
Welsh, William H. VI, 831
Welsh, Wm. II, 1036
Welte, Mabel IV, 1342
Welte, Mabel F. IV, 1342
Welti, Mabel IV, 1342
Welton, Elizabeth II, 682
Welton, Hannah II, 682
Welton, John II, 678
Welton, John II, 682
Welton, Mary II, 678
Welton, Mary II, 682
Welty, J. Jerome IV, 1299
Weltz, Anna R. V, 719
Wemmell, A. Andrew III, 187
Wemmell, A. Andrew III, 347
Wemmell, Andrew III, 347
Wemmell, Ann E. III, 347
Wemmell, Sarah Rebecca III, 187
Wemmell, Sarah Rebecca III, 347
Wendall, Abigail H. II, 938
Wendall, Reba Emma II, 938
Wendall, Winfield S. II, 938
Wenger, Eva IV, 649
Wenger, Susanna IV, 961
Wentworth, Mary III, 212
Wentworth, Mary III, 347
Wenworn, Sarah II, 434
Werfield, Elmer IV, 1342
Werlim, Charles IV, 1192
Werner, ??? III, 372
Werner, Augusta III, 223
Werner, Edgar Schell III, 318
Werner, Edgar Schell III, 347
Werner, Helen Ethel III, 372
Werner, Mary M. III, 347
Werner, Melle Stanleyetta III, 318
Werner, Melle Stanleyetta III, 347
Werner, Philip P. III, 347
Werniecke, Sarah IV, 589
Werniecke, Sarah IV, 599
Werrilow, Jane II, 1002
Werrilow, Jane II, 1035
Werrilow, Thomas II, 1002
Werrilow, Thomas II, 1035
Wert, Fanny V, 1024
Wert, Jennie V, 1024
Wert, Nancy V, 1024
Wertnz, Katherine M. V, 139
Wertnz, Laura V, 139
Wertnz, Laura A. V, 139
Werton, Thomas II, 1033
Werts, Charles V, 772
Werts, Lola IV, 1226
Wertsel, Lydia V, 288
Wertz, Charles H. IV, 1384
Wertz, Delilah V, 793
Wertz, Delilah V, 794
Wertz, Elmer V, 1025
Wertz, Fanny V, 1024
Wertz, Jennie V, 1024
Wertz, Lucy V, 1025
Wertz, Nancy V, 1024
Wertz, Susanna V, 1024
Wesbster, Chas. IV, 453
Wesbster, Lewis IV, 453
Wesbster, Sarah C. IV, 453
Wesbster, Sarah Jane IV, 453
Weseman, Amelia V, 436
Weseman, Betty Ethel V, 436
Wesley, Enoch Arden VI, 790
Wesley, Isabella Skillman VI, 782
Wesley, Isabelle Skillman VI, 780
Wesley, Isabelle Skillman VI, 790
Wesley, Lofton Stuart VI, 780
Wesley, Lofton Stuart VI, 782
Wesley, Lofton Stuart VI, 790
Wesley, Lofton Stuart, Jr. VI, 790
Wesley, Rhoda VI, 790
Wesley, Rhoda Margaret VI, 790
Wesly, Pheby II, 1036
Wesner, Ann I, 827
Wesner, Jesse I, 827
Wesner, Jesse I, 843
Wesner, Micajah I, 914
Wesner, Micajah, Jr. I, 914
Wessels, Anna Maria II, 1068
Wessels, Anna Maria II, 1082
West, ??? V, 940
West, ??? VI, 39
West, Abigail II, 682
West, Abigail V, 322
West, Abigail V, 365
West, Abigail V, 377
West, Abigail V, 437
West, Abigail V, 438
West, Abigail V, 439
West, Abigail C. V, 365
West, Abigail C. V, 437
West, Abigail C. V, 438
West, Abigal VI, 956
West, Abner VI, 864
West, Abraham IV, 1379
West, Abraham IV, 1383
West, Abraham IV, 1384
West, Abraham IV, 1385
West, Abram IV, 1385
West, Addie Lewis V, 210
West, Adelbert C. V, 437
West, Adrian IV, 1385
West, Alce II, 434
West, Alma Blanche IV, 715
West, Alpheus V, 604
West, Alpheus T. V, 604
West, Alsom IV, 786
West, Amelia V, 365
West, Amos III, 100
West, Amos III, 182
West, Amos III, 347
West, Amy II, 218
West, Amy II, 271
West, Andrew S. V, 439
West, Ann I, 454
West, Ann VI, 88
West, Ann VI, 863
West, Anna II, 906
West, Anna IV, 301
West, Anna IV, 307
West, Anna IV, 1384
West, Anna IV, 1385
West, Anna V, 390
West, Anna V, 436
West, Anna V, 437
West, Anna V, 438
West, Anna V, 439
West, Anna V, 649
West, Anna VI, 1012
West, Anna M. II, 906
West, Anna M. II, 938
West, Anna M. IV, 1266
West, Anna M. V, 609
West, Anna M. V, 650
West, Anna Marie IV, 1266
West, Anna Mary II, 938
West, Anne VI, 123
West, Anne VI, 124
West, Annie V, 438
West, Annie M. V, 439
West, Arthur W. V, 437
West, Arthur W. V, 438
West, Asenath V, 139
West, Asenath N. V, 54
West, Asenath N. V, 139
West, Austin VI, 814
West, Austin VI, 864
West, Benedict IV, 1385
West, Benjamin II, 434
West, Benjamin V, 365
West, Benjamin V, 436
West, Benjamin V, 438
West, Benjamin VI, 863
West, Benjamin, Jr. II, 434
West, Betsey VI, 1012
West, Betsy VI, 863
West, Betsy Jane V, 437
West, Bettie J. V, 438
West, Beulah II, 187
West, Beulah II, 271
West, Beulah II, 682
West, C. V, 438
West, C. Roy V, 437
West, Caleb II, 682
West, Calishta VI, 814
West, Calphurnia VI, 864
West, Carey V, 439
West, Carl V, 439
West, Carl V, 719
West, Carol C. V, 438
West, Caroline III, 335
West, Caroline III, 347
West, Caroline IV, 31
West, Caroline IV, 66
West, Caroline E. V, 412
West, Caroline E. V, 436
West, Caroline S. IV, 1132
West, Caroline S. IV, 1140
West, Carrie V, 210
West, Cassius J. V, 438
West, Catharine V, 438
West, Charles II, 434
West, Charles II, 678
West, Charles II, 682
West, Charles V, 139
West, Charles V, 210
West, Charles V, 364
West, Charles V, 437
West, Charles V, 438
West, Charles V, 539
West, Charles V, 540
West, Charles VI, 818
West, Charles VI, 864
West, Charles VI, 1012
West, Charles C. II, 682
West, Charles C. II, 774
West, Charles O. V, 365
West, Charles O. V, 367
West, Charles O. V, 377
West, Charles O. V, 437
West, Charles O. V, 438
West, Charles, Jr. II, 434
West, Charlotte F. V, 439
West, Chas. V, 210
West, Chas. C. II, 938
West, Christopher II, 434
West, Christopher V, 436
West, Christopher V, 438
West, Christopher VI, 818
West, Clara V, 437
West, Clara V, 439
West, Clara Myrta V, 437
West, Clara Myrta V, 438
West, Clarence V, 438
West, Clarence??? V, 438
West, Clary V, 439
West, Cona VI, 863
West, Cora Garner V, 439
West, Cordelia IV, 1385
West, Cornelia II, 129
West, Daniel II, 972
West, Daniel V, 436
West, Daniel V, 438
West, Daniel V, 649
West, Daniel V, 650
West, Daniel VI, 1012
West, Daniel C. V, 437
West, Daniel H. V, 437
West, Daniel Win V, 719
West, Daniel Wynne V, 719
West, David II, 826
West, David V, 139
West, David V, 210
West, David V, 416
West, David V, 436
West, David V, 438
West, David V, 649
West, David L. IV, 1385
West, Deborah II, 448
West, Deborah II, 534
West, Deborah II, 682
West, Denny VI, 933
West, Dianna V, 437
West, Eadeth V, 395
West, Eady VI, 996
West, Earl V, 439
West, Edgar C. V, 437
West, Edith V, 395
West, Edith V, 438
West, Edith H. V, 436
West, Edward II, 434
West, Edward II, 682
West, Edward V, 540
West, Edwin P. V, 437
West, Edwin P. V, 438
West, Edwin Quinn V, 365
West, Effie V, 365
West, Eldon IV, 786
West, Eleanor II, 191
West, Eleanor II, 271
West, Eli III, 316
West, Eli III, 347
West, Elial V, 436
West, Eliel V, 437
West, Eliel W. V, 423
West, Eliel W. V, 437
West, Eliel W. V, 438
West, Elijah IV, 1385
West, Elijah F. IV, 1385
West, Elisabeth IV, 1384
West, Elisha VI, 816
West, Elisha B. V, 436
West, Elisha B. V, 437
West, Elisha B. V, 438
West, Elisha B. V, 439
West, Eliz. III, 182
West, Eliz. III, 347
West, Eliza V, 405
West, Eliza V, 436
West, Eliza V, 438
West, Eliza A. V, 437
West, Eliza A. V, 438
West, Eliza Ann V, 438
West, Eliza E. V, 423
West, Eliza E. V, 438
West, Eliza Ellen V, 437
West, Elizabeth II, 187
West, Elizabeth II, 271
West, Elizabeth II, 434
West, Elizabeth II, 555
West, Elizabeth II, 682
West, Elizabeth II, 826
West, Elizabeth II, 938
West, Elizabeth III, 100
West, Elizabeth III, 347
West, Elizabeth IV, 66
West, Elizabeth IV, 664
West, Elizabeth IV, 874
West, Elizabeth IV, 886
West, Elizabeth IV, 1379
West, Elizabeth IV, 1385
West, Elizabeth V, 365
West, Elizabeth V, 393
West, Elizabeth V, 436
West, Elizabeth V, 437
West, Elizabeth V, 438
West, Elizabeth V, 527
West, Elizabeth V, 539
West, Elizabeth V, 566
West, Elizabeth V, 624
West, Elizabeth V, 649
West, Elizabeth V, 650
West, Elizabeth VI, 701
West, Elizabeth VI, 864
West, Elizabeth VI, 901
West, Elizabeth VI, 940
West, Elizabeth VI, 1012
West, Elizabeth C. II, 774
West, Elizabeth C. II, 938
West, Elizabeth J. II, 906
West, Elizabeth J. II, 938
West, Elizabeth Jones II, 826
West, Elizabeth W. II, 878
West, Elizabeth W. II, 938
West, Ellen II, 165
West, Elwood H. V, 604
West, Emilia V, 393
West, Emilia V, 438
West, Emily V, 437
West, Emma III, 259
West, Emma III, 263
West, Emma V, 437
West, Emma V, 439
West, Emma V, 719
West, Emma F. II, 938
West, Emma Florence II, 938
West, Emory VI, 864
West, Enos V, 210
West, Enos V, 438
West, Erick IV, 1266
West, Ernest F. IV, 1266
West, Ernest Fullerton IV, 1266
West, Esther J. V, 435
West, Esther J. V, 437
West, Esther J. V, 439
West, Esther Jane V, 436
West, Esther Jane V, 438
West, Ethel V, 439
West, Ettie M. V, 289
West, Eva V, 438
West, Eva V, 719
West, Eva Mather V, 604
West, Eva Mather V, 719
West, Ezra V, 649
West, Fanny VI, 864
West, Flora B. V, 439
West, Florella V, 437
West, Frances I, 123
West, Frances VI, 809
West, Frances VI, 827
West, Frances VI, 901
West, Frances W. V, 437
West, Francis V, 437
West, Frank M. V, 365
West, Fred V, 439
West, Genevia V, 439
West, Genevra V, 437
West, Gennette VI, 864
West, Geo. V, 438
West, Geo. W. III, 335
West, Geo. W. III, 347
West, George II, 172
West, George II, 176
West, George II, 187
West, George II, 271
West, George IV, 66
West, George IV, 664
West, George IV, 874
West, George IV, 886
West, George IV, 1385
West, George V, 426
West, George V, 436
West, George V, 437
West, George V, 438
West, George V, 439
West, George VI, 344
West, George VI, 875
West, George VI, 940
West, George VI, 991
West, George VI, 1005
West, George VI, 1012
West, George W. VI, 864
West, George, Jr. II, 271
West, Giles VI, 196
West, Giles VI, 217
West, Ginevra V, 439
West, Grace V, 719
West, Grace Ann III, 125
West, Hannah II, 208
West, Hannah II, 270
West, Hannah II, 434
West, Hannah II, 488
West, Hannah II, 647
West, Hannah II, 682
West, Hannah IV, 664
West, Hannah IV, 785
West, Hannah IV, 870
West, Hannah IV, 886
West, Hannah V, 436
West, Hannah V, 438
West, Hannah VI, 455
West, Hannah VI, 994
West, Hannah Ann V, 539
West, Hannah M. V, 436
West, Harley V, 437
West, Harrison V, 288
West, Harry V, 437
West, Harvey V, 139
West, Hattie D. V, 437
West, Hattie E. V, 437
West, Hazel V, 719
West, Helen V, 313
West, Helena V, 305
West, Helena V, 313
West, Helena V, 406
West, Helena V, 437
West, Helena V, 438
West, Hellena V, 406
West, Hellena V, 438
West, Henry V, 539
West, Henry Paxon II, 682
West, Huldah IV, 1367
West, Huldah IV, 1385
West, Ichabad IV, 1385
West, Ira IV, 1385
West, Isaac II, 434
West, Isaac III, 347
West, Isaac V, 139
West, Isaac A. V, 539
West, Isaac C. V, 437
West, Isaac C. V, 467
West, Isaiah V, 438
West, Isaiah V, 649

Isaiah M. V, 607
Isaiah M. V, 650
Iven J. VI, 1012
J. M. V, 365
J. Peirce II, 906
J. Peirce II, 938
Jacob IV, 1372
James II, 434
James II, 682
James II, 972
James IV, 503
James V, 365
James V, 437
James V, 438
James VI, 796
James VI, 864
James Asa V, 437
James H. V, 436
James H. V, 438
James Harvey V, 439
James M. V, 365
James P. IV, 503
James W. VI, 948
Jane II, 187
Jane II, 234
Jane II, 271
Jane II, 682
Jane III, 316
Jane IV, 1367
Jane IV, 1385
Jane V, 288
Jane VI, 279
Jane VI, 344
Jane VI, 539
Jane VI, 578
Jane VI, 684
Jean VI, 279
Jehiel V, 365
Jehiel V, 437
Jehiel V, 438
Jehiel G. V, 365
Jehiel G. V, 437
Jehiel G. V, 438
Jennie V, 289
Jenny VI, 864
t, Jeremiah V, 437
t, Jeremiah V, 438
t, Jeremiah V, 649
t, Jeremiah A. V, 649
t, Jeremiah H. V, 436
t, Jeremiah H. V, 438
st, Jesse IV, 785
t, Jesse V, 436
t, Jesse V, 438
st, Jesse VI, 809
st, Jesse VI, 843
st, Jesse VI, 850
st, Jesse VI, 864
st, Jesse B. V, 437
st, Jesse Waterman II, 682
st, Jno. II, 271
st, Joanna V, 438
st, Joanna V, 439
st, Joel II, 434
st, Joel VI, 1012
st, John II, 165
st, John II, 270
st, John II, 271
st, John II, 434
st, John II, 517
st, John II, 682
st, John V, 365
st, John V, 436
st, John V, 438
st, John V, 439
est, John V, 940
est, John VI, 818
est, John VI, 827
est, John VI, 870
est, John VI, 947
est, John VI, 951
est, John VI, 994
est, John VI, 996
est, John VI, 1012
est, John A. VI, 864
est, John L. V, 54
est, John L. V, 139
est, John L. V, 539
est, John L. V, 540
est, John M. V, 437
est, John M. V, 438
est, John M. V, 439
est, John W. V, 437
est, John W. V, 438
est, John W. V, 940
Vest, John W. VI, 864
Vest, John William V, 437
Vest, John William V, 438
Vest, Jonathan II, 434
Vest, Jordan VI, 936
Vest, Jordan VI, 996
West, Jos. V, 438
West, Joseph II, 271
West, Joseph II, 434
West, Joseph III, 347
West, Joseph IV, 785
West, Joseph IV, 786
West, Joseph V, 436
West, Joseph V, 438
West, Joseph VI, 539
West, Joseph VI, 545
West, Joseph VI, 578
West, Joseph VI, 684
West, Joseph VI, 956
West, Joseph Milton V, 365
West, Joseph Milton V, 438
West, Josephine III, 347
West, Josephine IV, 1266
West, Josephine A. III, 314
West, Josephine A. III, 347
West, Joshua Peirce II, 826
West, Josiah E. V, 437
West, Josiah M. V, 436
West, Jourdan VI, 933
West, Lafayette V, 365
West, Lana IV, 1372
West, Lana IV, 1385
West, Larena A. V, 437
West, Lena III, 76
West, Lena III, 77
West, Lena III, 347
West, Lenna V, 437
West, Leota J. IV, 1266
West, Leota Josephine IV, 1266
West, Leslie V, 289
West, Leslie Mellie V, 439
West, Letitia V, 139
West, Letitia V, 539
West, Letty VI, 846
West, Levi IV, 1385
West, Levi VI, 864
West, Levi VI, 936
West, Levi G. II, 938
West, Levi Gheen II, 938
West, Lewis H. IV, 1266
West, Lillian V, 719
West, Lindley A. V, 365
West, Lindley O. V, 437
West, Lindley O. V, 439
West, Linley H. V, 437
West, Lizzie V, 365
West, Lizzie V, 439
West, Lizzie V, 467
West, Lizzie B. V, 437
West, Lizzie Bell V, 438
West, Locky VI, 1012
West, Louie V, 438
West, Louis Monroe IV, 1266
West, Louisa V, 437
West, Louisa V, 438
West, Louisa V, 439
West, Louisa V, 719
West, Louisa VI, 825
West, Louisa K. V, 539
West, Lovie V, 439
West, Lt. Col. John VI, 11
West, Lucy Ann VI, 1012
West, Lydia II, 434
West, Lydia II, 682
West, Lydia IV, 785
West, Lydia IV, 786
West, Lydia IV, 1385
West, Lydia Ann IV, 1385
West, Lydia Jane IV, 1374
West, Lydia Jane IV, 1385
West, M. A. IV, 1339
West, M. E. V, 437
West, Malinda J. VI, 1012
West, Margaret V, 437
West, Margaret V, 438
West, Margaret V, 634
West, Margaret V, 650
West, Margaret Ellen V, 649
West, Margaret Ellen V, 698
West, Margaret Emaly V, 438
West, Margaret Emely V, 365
West, Margaret Moon V, 438
West, Margaretta V, 719
West, Maria IV, 1372
West, Maria IV, 1385
West, Maria V, 139
West, Marianna V, 437
West, Marietta V, 437
West, Marietta V, 438
West, Marion V, 437
West, Martha VI, 196
West, Martha VI, 217
West, Martha VI, 830
West, Martha VI, 843
West, Martha VI, 947
West, Martha VI, 991
West, Martin V, 322
West, Martin V, 365
West, Martin V, 377
West, Martin V, 437
West, Martin V, 438
West, Mary II, 176
West, Mary II, 187
West, Mary II, 271
West, Mary II, 434
West, Mary II, 483
West, Mary II, 578
West, Mary II, 682
West, Mary II, 712
West, Mary II, 784
West, Mary II, 1036
West, Mary III, 335
West, Mary III, 347
West, Mary IV, 567
West, Mary IV, 599
West, Mary IV, 664
West, Mary IV, 886
West, Mary IV, 1379
West, Mary IV, 1383
West, Mary IV, 1385
West, Mary V, 123
West, Mary V, 139
West, Mary V, 322
West, Mary V, 364
West, Mary V, 377
West, Mary V, 400
West, Mary V, 411
West, Mary V, 426
West, Mary V, 436
West, Mary V, 437
West, Mary V, 438
West, Mary V, 539
West, Mary V, 649
West, Mary V, 650
West, Mary V, 873
West, Mary V, 1025
West, Mary VI, 545
West, Mary VI, 864
West, Mary A. VI, 864
West, Mary A. VI, 960
West, Mary Amney V, 262
West, Mary Amney V, 288
West, Mary Ann IV, 1383
West, Mary Ann IV, 1384
West, Mary Ann IV, 1385
West, Mary Ann V, 210
West, Mary Ann V, 212
West, Mary Ann V, 288
West, Mary Ann V, 438
West, Mary Ann V, 440
West, Mary Anna II, 434
West, Mary Anna II, 774
West, Mary Anna II, 938
West, Mary Anne V, 437
West, Mary Anne V, 438
West, Mary Ash II, 176
West, Mary D. V, 613
West, Mary D. V, 650
West, Mary E. V, 437
West, Mary E. V, 439
West, Mary E. V, 540
West, Mary Elizabeth V, 365
West, Mary Elizabeth V, 439
West, Mary Iona V, 437
West, Mary M. V, 288
West, Mary Margaret V, 288
West, Mary Margaret V, 438
West, Mary T. II, 682
West, Mary T. II, 722
West, Maxine V, 438
West, May IV, 664
West, Melcena V, 437
West, Merl V, 439
West, Merle V, 437
West, Merle V, 439
West, Mildred V, 439
West, Mildred V, 719
West, Millie V, 313
West, Milly VI, 818
West, Milly VI, 1008
West, Milton E. V, 437
West, Morris V, 288
West, Morris V, 289
West, Mr. Frank IV, 786
West, Mrs. ??? IV, 786
West, Muretta P. V, 438
West, Musa V, 437
West, Nancy V, 426
West, Nancy V, 436
West, Nancy V, 438
West, Nancy VI, 875
West, Nancy VI, 936
West, Nancy VI, 951
West, Nancy A. VI, 796
West, Nathaniel IV, 1385
West, Nathaniel VI, 933
West, Nathaniel VI, 940
West, Nathaniel VI, 1012
West, Obadiah VI, 996
West, Obediah VI, 863
West, Obediah VI, 1008
West, Oliver V, 437
West, Oliver H. V, 437
West, Oliver H. V, 438
West, Oliver H. V, 439
West, Orpha L. V, 437
West, Orpha L. V, 940
West, Orva L. V, 438
West, Otis T. V, 437
West, Otis T. V, 438
West, Owen V, 322
West, Owen V, 364
West, Owen V, 365
West, Owen V, 377
West, Owen V, 393
West, Owen V, 436
West, Owen V, 437
West, Owen V, 438
West, Owen V, 439
West, Owen Lindley V, 365
West, Paxton V, 439
West, Payton V, 365
West, Perry II, 448
West, Peyton V, 389
West, Peyton V, 395
West, Peyton V, 412
West, Peyton V, 435
West, Peyton V, 436
West, Peyton V, 437
West, Peyton V, 438
West, Peyton V, 439
West, Peyton V, 719
West, Peyton Gale V, 719
West, Peyton M. V, 436
West, Peyton M. V, 438
West, Polly VI, 864
West, Polly VI, 870
West, Polly VI, 875
West, Polly VI, 1012
West, Priscilla IV, 664
West, Prudence II, 434
West, Prudence II, 678
West, Prudence II, 682
West, R. E. IV, 1266
West, Rachel II, 656
West, Rachel II, 682
West, Rachel IV, 664
West, Rachel IV, 874
West, Rachel IV, 886
West, Rachel V, 365
West, Rachel V, 377
West, Rachel V, 439
West, Rachel D. V, 365
West, Rachel D. V, 367
West, Rachel D. V, 393
West, Rachel D. V, 437
West, Rachel D. V, 438
West, Raymond J. V, 437
West, Rebecca II, 434
West, Rebecca IV, 785
West, Rebecca V, 365
West, Rebecca V, 387
West, Rebecca V, 437
West, Rebecca V, 438
West, Rebecca V, 540
West, Rebecca VI, 863
West, Rebecca T. II, 682
West, Rebecca T. II, 774
West, Rebecca T. II, 938
West, Rebecca Trotter II, 938
West, Rebekah VI, 701
West, Reuben VI, 863
West, Rev. H. T. IV, 1339
West, Rhoda V, 437
West, Rhoda Ellen V, 364
West, Rhoda Emley V, 437
West, Richard V, 540
West, Robert I, 120
West, Robert V, 437
West, Robert V, 438
West, Robert V, 467
West, Robert K. V, 139
West, Robert K. V, 539
West, Robert Paul V, 719
West, Roda V, 388
West, Roda V, 437
West, Rosa V, 438
West, Rosalie V, 437
West, Rosilla V, 438
West, Roy V, 365
West, Russell V, 439
West, Ruth V, 210
West, Ruth V, 416
West, Ruth V, 436
West, Ruth V, 437
West, Ruth V, 438
West, Ruth V, 649
West, Ruth Ann V, 288
West, Ruth E. IV, 1266
West, Ruth Elizabeth IV, 1266
West, Sadie Shepert V, 289
West, Sadie Shubert V, 719
West, Sally VI, 809
West, Sally VI, 864
West, Sally VI, 901
West, Sally VI, 1012
West, Sally Ann VI, 1012
West, Samuel II, 271
West, Samuel II, 682
West, Samuel IV, 664
West, Samuel V, 436
West, Samuel V, 438
West, Samuel VI, 875
West, Samuel VI, 960
West, Samuel VI, 968
West, Samuel VI, 1012
West, Samuel L. V, 437
West, Sarah II, 434
West, Sarah II, 453
West, Sarah II, 457
West, Sarah II, 517
West, Sarah II, 524
West, Sarah II, 682
West, Sarah II, 972
West, Sarah II, 1036
West, Sarah III, 347
West, Sarah IV, 813
West, Sarah IV, 852
West, Sarah IV, 1339
West, Sarah IV, 1385
West, Sarah V, 365
West, Sarah V, 383
West, Sarah V, 388
West, Sarah V, 389
West, Sarah V, 395
West, Sarah V, 412
West, Sarah V, 435
West, Sarah V, 436
West, Sarah V, 437
West, Sarah V, 438
West, Sarah V, 540
West, Sarah V, 604
West, Sarah V, 641
West, Sarah V, 649
West, Sarah VI, 940
West, Sarah VI, 996
West, Sarah VI, 1012
West, Sarah A. V, 389
West, Sarah Ann V, 436
West, Sarah Ann V, 437
West, Sarah H. V, 437
West, Sarah J. V, 288
West, Sarah J. V, 441
West, Sarah Jane V, 288
West, Sarah Jane V, 338
West, Sarah Jane V, 365
West, Sarah Jane V, 437
West, Sarah Jane V, 438
West, Sarah L. III, 100
West, Sarah L. V, 29
West, Sarah L. V, 139
West, Sarah Margaret V, 437
West, Sarah Plummer VI, 545
West, Sarah T. V, 594
West, Sarah T. V, 604
West, Sarah W. VI, 799
West, Sarah, Sr. II, 434
West, Sary I, 120
West, Sidney IV, 785
West, Sophia IV, 1379
West, Sophia IV, 1385
West, Sophia V, 390
West, Sophia V, 567
West, Sophia V, 604
West, Stella V, 437
West, Stella V, 439
West, Stella V, 719
West, Stella J. V, 719
West, Stephen IV, 664
West, Stephen IV, 886
West, Stephen Eric IV, 1266
West, Stephen R. IV, 1266
West, Stephen Rosenkrants IV, 1266
West, Sue III, 420
West, Susan VI, 968
West, Susan P. III, 347
West, Susan T. II, 938
West, Susan Trotter II, 938
West, Susanna I, 428
West, Susanna II, 434
West, Susanna T. II, 434
West, Susanna T. II, 774
West, Susannah II, 270
West, Susannah IV, 1360
West, Susannah IV, 1385
West, Sylvia A. V, 437
West, Sylvia A. V, 940
West, Sylvia C. V, 438
West, Sylvia C. V, 940

West, Tabathy Jane IV, 1385
West, Tacey VI, 684
West, Tacy VI, 539
West, Tacy VI, 578
West, Tacy VI, 648
West, Tamar V, 436
West, Tamar V, 649
West, Tamar V, 719
West, Tamer V, 438
West, Tamer V, 607
West, Tamer V, 624
West, Tamer V, 650
West, Tamor V, 641
West, Thomas II, 271
West, Thomas II, 434
West, Thomas II, 555
West, Thomas II, 682
West, Thomas V, 139
West, Thomas V, 289
West, Thomas V, 365
West, Thomas V, 436
West, Thomas V, 438
West, Thomas V, 624
West, Thomas V, 641
West, Thomas VI, 701
West, Thomas VI, 816
West, Thomas VI, 825
West, Thomas VI, 830
West, Thomas VI, 863
West, Thomas VI, 1012
West, Thomas C. V, 467
West, Thomas Elwood V, 437
West, Thos. V, 649
West, Virgil V, 719
West, Walter V, 365
West, Walter V, 437
West, Wd. Matilda VI, 11
West, Wd. Sarah W. II, 172
West, Wd. Susan P. III, 182
West, Webster V, 439
West, Webster B. V, 437
West, Webster B. V, 438
West, Wendall P. V, 437
West, Willard V, 439
West, Willard W. V, 437
West, William II, 270
West, William II, 271
West, William II, 434
West, William II, 453
West, William V, 210
West, William V, 212
West, William V, 364
West, William V, 365
West, William V, 369
West, William V, 388
West, William V, 390
West, William V, 436
West, William V, 438
West, William V, 439
West, William V, 440
West, William V, 604
West, William V, 649
West, William V, 873
West, William VI, 818
West, William VI, 864
West, William VI, 1012
West, William A. III, 314
West, William A. III, 347
West, William Allen V, 139
West, William E. V, 604
West, William H. V, 438
West, William W. IV, 1385
West, William, Jr. II, 271
West, Willie V, 313
West, Wilson V, 365
West, Wilson W. V, 365
West, Winnie V, 437
West, Winnie V, 439
West, Wm. II, 517
West, Wm. II, 647
West, Wm. II, 682
West, Wm. V, 210
West, Wm. V, 365
West, Wm. V, 437
West, Wm. V, 567
West, Wm. V, 604
West, Wm. V, 650
West, Wm. V, 1025
West, Wm. E. V, 604
West, Wm. H. V, 439
West, Wm. Pusey II, 938
West, Wm. Waterman II, 682
Westall, Catherine S. III, 347
Westall, Elizabeth III, 76
Westall, Elizabeth III, 347
Westall, George W. III, 76
Westall, George W. III, 347
Westall, John W. III, 347
Westbrook, Albert IV, 1165
Westbrook, Albert IV, 1192
Westbrook, Albert E. IV, 1192
Westbrook, Albert Warren IV, 1192
Westbrook, Anna Etta IV, 1192
Westbrook, Annetta IV, 1165
Westbrook, Annetta IV, 1192
Westbrook, Annette IV, 1192
Westbrook, Catherine IV, 1192
Westbrook, Daniel IV, 1192
Westbrook, Daryl Richard IV, 1192
Westbrook, Della A. I, 259
Westbrook, Etta W. IV, 1192
Westbrook, Gussie IV, 1192
Westbrook, Helen C. IV, 1165
Westbrook, Huber IV, 1192
Westbrook, Joy IV, 1192
Westbrook, Kent IV, 1192
Westbrook, Laurence L. IV, 1192
Westbrook, Lawrence IV, 1192
Westbrook, Lawrence Kent IV, 1192
Westbrook, Louisa E. III, 280
Westbrook, Louisa E. III, 302
Westbrook, Mabel I, 213
Westbrook, Margaret IV, 1192
Westbrook, Rosa Theodosia IV, 1192
Westbrook, Ruth Anna IV, 1192
Westbrook, Sarah I, 927
Westbrook, Theodosia IV, 1192
Westbrooks, Sarah I, 1133
Westcomb, Chas. T. V, 940
Westcombe, Chas. T. V, 940
Westenberg, Anna IV, 1315
Westenberg, Anna Fistler IV, 1342
Westenberg, Dorothy Mildred IV, 1342
Westenberg, J. C. IV, 1342
Westenberg, John Clarence IV, 1342
Westenberg, Laura R. IV, 1342
Westenberg, Mabel IV, 1342
Westenhaver, Annie M. IV, 1266
Westenhaver, Cleveland IV, 1266
Westenhaver, Elizabeth IV, 1266
Westenhaver, Margaret IV, 1266
Westenhaver, W. P. IV, 1266
Westenhour, Cleveland IV, 1266
Westenhour, Margaret IV, 1266
Westenhour, W. P. IV, 1266
Wester, Benjamin VI, 88
Wester, Hannah IV, 268
Wester, Levina VI, 54
Wester, Levina VI, 88
Wester, Martha VI, 88
Wester, Mary VI, 88
Westerfield, Ida V, 1025
Westerfield, Manerva V, 1025
Westerfield, Minesca V, 1025
Westerfield, Wm. V, 1025
Westerfield, Wm. F. V, 1025
Westervelt, Edward H. III, 348
Westervelt, Eleanor III, 100
Westervelt, Eleanor Jane III, 348
Westervelt, Elenor III, 348
Westervelt, Theodore W. III, 348
Westfahl, Mildred IV, 1342
Westfield, Manerva V, 1025
Westgate, Albert IV, 1385
Westgate, Amanda IV, 1385
Westgate, Amy IV, 1353
Westgate, Amy IV, 1385
Westgate, Austin IV, 1385
Westgate, Charles H. IV, 1385
Westgate, Dorcas IV, 1353
Westgate, Dorcas IV, 1367
Westgate, Dorcas IV, 1385
Westgate, Esther IV, 1385
Westgate, Fanny IV, 1385
Westgate, Fanny M. IV, 1385
Westgate, Hannah E. IV, 1363
Westgate, Hannah E. IV, 1385
Westgate, Henry G. IV, 1385
Westgate, Jeremiah IV, 1353
Westgate, Jeremiah IV, 1367
Westgate, Jeremiah IV, 1385
Westgate, Jeremiah Jun. IV, 1385
Westgate, Jonathan IV, 1353
Westgate, Jonathan IV, 1363
Westgate, Jonathan IV, 1385
Westgate, Mary IV, 1385
Westgate, Mary S. IV, 1385
Westgate, Nancy IV, 1385
Westgate, Nelson IV, 1385
Westgate, Orlando IV, 1385
Westgate, Pamelia IV, 1385
Westgate, Pamilia IV, 1353
Westgate, Pamilia IV, 1385
Westgate, Samuel IV, 1385
Westgate, Sylvanus IV, 1347
Westgate, Sylvanus IV, 1385
Westgate, Sylvanus W. IV, 1385
Westgate, Wanton IV, 1385
Westgate, William IV, 1385
Westhermer, Mildred T. V, 34
Westhermer, Mildred T. V, 140
Westlake, Emma V, 1025
Westland, ??? VI, 356
Westland, Ephraim VI, 381
Westmoreland, F. G. I, 921
Westmoreland, F. J. I, 925
Weston, Amelia III, 322
Weston, Amy J. III, 322
Weston, Ara I, 950
Weston, Clarence IV, 1343
Weston, Clarence D. IV, 1343
Weston, Daniel II, 682
Weston, Edward II, 540
Weston, Edward II, 682
Weston, Elizabeth III, 64
Weston, Elizabeth IV, 916
Weston, Hannah II, 434
Weston, Hannah II, 540
Weston, Hannah II, 682
Weston, John IV, 916
Weston, Lelia I, 212
Weston, Lewis II, 682
Weston, Margaret IV, 916
Weston, Mary II, 448
Weston, Mary II, 449
Weston, Peter I, 227
Weston, Peter I, 259
Weston, Peterson I, 259
Weston, Robert II, 448
Weston, Samuel III, 322
Weston, Susannah II, 449
Weston, Thomas II, 448
Weston, Thomas II, 449
Westpfohl, Florence IV, 1342
Westpfohl, Mildred IV, 1342
Westpfohl, Minnie IV, 1342
Westpfohl, Theodore IV, 1342
Westpfohl, Thomas IV, 1342
Westray, Elizabeth VI, 88
Westray, Joseph VI, 88
Westray, Lemuel VI, 88
Westray, Michel VI, 64
Westray, Michel VI, 88
Westray, Samuel I, 259
Westray, Willis VI, 88
Westre, Achsah I, 319
Westre, Benjamin I, 304
Westre, Benjamin I, 319
Westre, Elizabeth I, 304
Westre, Elizabeth I, 319
Westrick, Willis V, 1025
Wetheral, Sarah Eleanor VI, 578
Wetherald, Ann II, 938
Wetherald, Ann VI, 790
Wetherald, Elizabeth II, 799
Wetherald, Elizabeth V, 940
Wetherald, Esther VI, 790
Wetherald, George III, 348
Wetherald, Haworth II, 799
Wetherald, Haworth V, 940
Wetherald, James III, 348
Wetherald, Jonathan H. V, 940
Wetherald, Joseph II, 799
Wetherald, Joseph V, 940
Wetherald, Joseph E. VI, 790
Wetherald, Mary II, 799
Wetherald, Mary V, 940
Wetherald, Mary VI, 790
Wetherald, Mary Anne III, 348
Wetherald, Samuel B. VI, 790
Wetherald, Sarah V, 940
Wetherald, Susan H. V, 940
Wetherald, Susannah H. V, 940
Wetherald, Thomas VI, 727
Wetherald, Thomas VI, 790
Wetherald, Thomas, Jr. VI, 790
Wetherald, Wm. V, 940
Wetherall, Nancy VI, 719
Wetherall, Nancy Catharine VI, 506
Wetherall, Nancy Catharine VI, 578
Wetherall, Nancy Catharine VI, 654
Wetherall, Nancy Catherine VI, 508
Wetherall, Sarah Eleanor VI, 498
Wetherall, Sarah Eleanor VI, 578
Wetherall, Sarah Eleanor VI, 790
Wetherals, Silas II, 212
Wetherals, Thos. II, 212
Wetherbon, Polly IV, 1182
Wetherbon, Polly IV, 1192
Wetherby, Edmond II, 110
Wetherby, Edmund II, 110
Wetherby, Margit II, 110
Wetherby, Sarah II, 110
Wethered, Mary L. III, 292
Wethered, Mary L. III, 311
Wethered, Mary Lewin III, 31
Wetherell, Joseph, Jr. II, 271
Wetheril, John II, 271
Wetheril, John II, 1036
Wetheril, Mary II, 1036
Wetheril, Sarah II, 1036
Wetheril, Thomas II, 271
Wetheril, Wm. II, 1036
Wetherill, Ann II, 187
Wetherill, Ann II, 271
Wetherill, Ann II, 434
Wetherill, Ann II, 480
Wetherill, Ann II, 682
Wetherill, Ann Eliza II, 187
Wetherill, Anna II, 271
Wetherill, Anna II, 722
Wetherill, Anna S. II, 305
Wetherill, Anna S. II, 306
Wetherill, Anne II, 187
Wetherill, Anne II, 220
Wetherill, Avalina H. II, 187
Wetherill, Avolina H. II, 187
Wetherill, Benjamin II, 271
Wetherill, Catharine II, 187
Wetherill, Charles II, 305
Wetherill, Charles S. II, 305
Wetherill, Christopher II, 187
Wetherill, Christopher II, 250
Wetherill, Christopher II, 257
Wetherill, Christopher II, 271
Wetherill, Christopher II, 272
Wetherill, Christopher II, 480
Wetherill, Christopher II, 682
Wetherill, Christopher II, 695
Wetherill, Deborah E. II, 187
Wetherill, Deborah E. II, 305
Wetherill, Edward Agustus II, 305
Wetherill, Elizabeth II, 187
Wetherill, Elizabeth II, 250
Wetherill, Elizabeth II, 434
Wetherill, Elizabeth Virginia II, 305
Wetherill, Isaac II, 187
Wetherill, John II, 187
Wetherill, John II, 199
Wetherill, John II, 257
Wetherill, John II, 271
Wetherill, John II, 683
Wetherill, Joseph II, 187
Wetherill, Joseph II, 271
Wetherill, Joseph II, 274
Wetherill, Joseph II, 434
Wetherill, Joseph II, 480
Wetherill, Joseph II, 682
Wetherill, Joseph II, 683
Wetherill, Joseph, Jr. II, 271
Wetherill, Joshua II, 683
Wetherill, Lydia II, 305
Wetherill, Lydia Ann II, 305
Wetherill, Margaret Ethel II, 305
Wetherill, Mary II, 187
Wetherill, Mary II, 212
Wetherill, Mary II, 235
Wetherill, Mary II, 271
Wetherill, Mary II, 274
Wetherill, Mary II, 434
Wetherill, Mary II, 608
Wetherill, Mary II, 682
Wetherill, Mary Crispin II, 271
Wetherill, Mary Elizabeth II, 271
Wetherill, May Georgia II, 305
Wetherill, Mercy II, 187
Wetherill, Mercy II, 271
Wetherill, Mercy II, 274
Wetherill, Mordecai II, 683
Wetherill, Penelope S. II, 305
Wetherill, Phebe II, 257
Wetherill, Phebe II, 271
Wetherill, Rebecca II, 187
Wetherill, Rebecca II, 239
Wetherill, Rebecca II, 271
Wetherill, Samuel II, 187
Wetherill, Samuel II, 271
Wetherill, Samuel II, 434
Wetherill, Samuel II, 608
Wetherill, Samuel II, 682
Wetherill, Samuel II, 683
Wetherill, Samuel R. II, 187
Wetherill, Samuel R. II, 271
Wetherill, Samuel R. II, 274
Wetherill, Samuel R. II, 305
Wetherill, Samuel, Jr. II, 434
Wetherill, Samuel, Jr. II, 682
Wetherill, Samuel, Jr. II, 695
Wetherill, Samuel, Sr. II, 434
Wetherill, Sarah II, 187
Wetherill, Sarah II, 199
Wetherill, Sarah II, 271
Wetherill, Sarah II, 582
Wetherill, Sarah II, 682
Wetherill, Sarah II, 683
Wetherill, Sarah II, 695
Wetherill, Silas Crispen II,
Wetherill, Thomas II, 187
Wetherill, Thomas II, 220
Wetherill, Thomas II, 271
Wetherill, Thomas II, 434
Wetherill, Thomas II, 608
Wetherill, Thomas II, 682
Wetherill, Thomas, Jr. II, 4
Wetherill, Thomasin II, 257
Wetherill, Thos. II, 212
Wetherill, William II, 187
Wetherill, William II, 305
Wetherill, William A. II, 187
Wethrell, John II, 1036
Wethrell, John II, 1041
Wethrell, Sarah II, 1036
Wethrell, Sarah II, 1041
Wetmore, Eliza IV, 1342
Wetmore, Henry IV, 1342
Wetmore, Nellie S. IV, 1342
Wetsel, Sarah IV, 84
Wetsel, Sarah IV, 114
Wetzel, Helen M. IV, 1343
Wetzel, J. E. IV, 301
Wetzel, Mrs. Margaret IV, 13
Wetzley, Alice V, 772
Wever, Martha VI, 455
Wever, Olivia VI, 455
Wey, Alice IV, 588
Wey, Alice IV, 599
Wey, Ann IV, 588
Wey, David IV, 588
Wey, Metilda IV, 239
Weyer, Daniel V, 467
Weyer, Ella V, 467
Weyer, Lizzie V, 467
Weyer, Lydia A. V, 467
Weyer, Wm. V, 467
Weyman, Isabella II, 494
Weyman, Isabella II, 683
Weyman, Rebekah II, 471
Weyman, Rebekah II, 683
Weymire, Frederick I, 695
Weymire, Frederick I, 736
Weymire, Huldah I, 709
Weymire, Huldah I, 736
Weymont, Isabella II, 683
Weymore, Margaret IV, 95
Weymore, Margaret IV, 114
Whalen, Bertha IV, 1343
Whalen, Carrie IV, 1343
Whalen, Carrie B. IV, 1343
Whalen, Carrie Bell IV, 1343
Whalen, Eleanor S. IV, 1343
Whalen, Frankie A. IV, 1343
Whalen, Isabella IV, 1343
Whalen, Mary II, 683
Whalen, Mary Ann IV, 1131
Whalen, Mary Ann IV, 1140
Whalen, Sarah IV, 1343
Whaley, Elwood L. VI, 89
Whaley, Gaida VI, 92
Whaley, Lewis E. VI, 89
Whaley, Louis VI, 65
Whaley, Louis E. VI, 89
Whaley, Ruth VI, 89
Whaley, Winifred B. VI, 89
Whaley, Winifred W. VI, 89
Whaley, Zada VI, 65
Whaley, Zada Verlinda VI, 65
Whaley, Zada Verlinda VI, 89
Whallen, Sarah IV, 1343
Whalley, Amelia IV, 1385
Whallin, Bertha IV, 1343
Whallin, Isabella IV, 1343
Whallon, Bertha IV, 1343
Whallon, Carrie B. IV, 1343
Whallon, Carrie Bell IV, 1343
Whallon, Frankie A. IV, 1343
Whalton, Elizabeth II, 675
Wharnaby, Elizabeth II, 683
Wharten, Ann II, 722
Whartenaby, Elizabeth II, 434
Whartnaby, Elizabeth II, 672
Whartnaby, Elizabeth II, 683
Wharto, Mary III, 307
Wharton, ??? III, 70
Wharton, Abi II, 972
Wharton, Abi II, 1063
Wharton, Abi II, 1076
Wharton, Abi II, 1083
Wharton, Abigail II, 972
Wharton, Abigail II, 1001
Wharton, Abigail II, 1027
Wharton, Abigail II, 1036
Wharton, Abigail II, 1037

rton, Abigail II, 1040
rton, Abigail II, 1063
rton, Abigail II, 1074
rton, Abigail II, 1083
rton, Abigail IV, 141
rton, Abigail IV, 163
rton, Abigail IV, 301
rton, Abigail IV, 514
rton, Abigail IV, 555
rton, Abigail IV, 556
rton, Abigail B. IV, 555
rton, Abijah IV, 163
rton, Abner II, 1036
rton, Abner VI, 578
rton, Abraham II, 835
rton, Albert V, 140
rton, Albert V, 605
rton, Amos IV, 301
rton, Amos C. V, 64
rton, Ann II, 237
rton, Ann II, 271
rton, Ann II, 722
rton, Ann II, 972
rton, Ann II, 1037
rton, Ann II, 1063
arton, Ann V, 52
arton, Ann V, 140
arton, Ann A. VI, 988
arton, Ann E. V, 64
arton, Anna III, 224
arton, Anna III, 348
arton, Anna IV, 301
arton, Anna IV, 302
arton, Anna IV, 311
arton, Anna IV, 315
arton, Anna C. II, 892
arton, Anna C. II, 938
arton, Anna L. II, 938
arton, Benjamin II, 434
arton, Bethia IV, 521
arton, Bethia IV, 556
arton, Bethiah IV, 302
arton, Betty V, 64
arton, Capt. ??? VI, 953
arton, Carpenter II, 434
arton, Carpenter II, 683
arton, Catharine VI, 953
arton, Charles II, 434
arton, Charles II, 512
arton, Charles II, 683
arton, Charles W. II, 938
arton, Charlotte E. VI, 941
arton, Chas. II, 938
arton, Chas. W. II, 892
arton, Chas. W. II, 938
arton, Christian II, 972
arton, Christian II, 1037
arton, Daniel II, 972
arton, Daniel II, 979
harton, Daniel II, 1001
harton, Daniel II, 1006
harton, Daniel II, 1027
harton, Daniel II, 1036
harton, Daniel II, 1037
harton, Daniel II, 1040
harton, Daniel II, 1063
harton, Daniel II, 1067
harton, Daniel II, 1083
harton, Daniel IV, 301
harton, Daniel IV, 302
harton, Daniel V, 140
harton, David II, 972
harton, Deborah II, 826
harton, Deborah F. II, 892
harton, Deborah F. II, 906
harton, Deborah F. II, 938
harton, Deborah T. II, 938
harton, Delitha Ann IV, 555
harton, Dixon V, 140
harton, Dixon V, 210
Vharton, Dorcas III, 70
Vharton, Dorcas III, 348
harton, Edward II, 972
Vharton, Edward II, 1036
Vharton, Eli IV, 301
Vharton, Eliza II, 722
Vharton, Elizabeth II, 501
Vharton, Elizabeth II, 502
Vharton, Elizabeth II, 683
Vharton, Elizabeth II, 972
Vharton, Elizabeth II, 1037
Vharton, Elizabeth II, 1063
Vharton, Elizabeth II, 1076
Vharton, Elizabeth II, 1083
Vharton, Elizabeth V, 62
Vharton, Elizabeth V, 87
Vharton, Elizabeth V, 140
Wharton, Elizabeth V, 1025
Wharton, Emma V, 210
Wharton, Enos V, 64
Wharton, Esther V, 64
Wharton, Ezra II, 972
Wharton, Ezra II, 1037
Wharton, Ezra IV, 163
Wharton, Ezra IV, 212
Wharton, Ezra IV, 301
Wharton, Ezra IV, 555
Wharton, Ezra IV, 556
Wharton, Fannie V, 540
Wharton, Florence VI, 738
Wharton, Florence VI, 790
Wharton, Franklin II, 434
Wharton, Freeman V, 64
Wharton, George II, 434
Wharton, Hannah II, 434
Wharton, Hannah II, 482
Wharton, Hannah II, 683
Wharton, Hannah II, 938
Wharton, Hannah II, 972
Wharton, Hannah II, 980
Wharton, Hannah II, 1037
Wharton, Hannah IV, 212
Wharton, Hannah IV, 301
Wharton, Hannah V, 76
Wharton, Hannah V, 140
Wharton, Hannah B. II, 917
Wharton, Hannah B. II, 938
Wharton, Hannah B. V, 140
Wharton, Harley V, 439
Wharton, Hester V, 64
Wharton, Hudson II, 434
Wharton, Hulda V, 540
Wharton, Huldah V, 439
Wharton, Huldah V, 540
Wharton, Isaac II, 434
Wharton, Isaac II, 683
Wharton, Isaac V, 439
Wharton, Israel II, 972
Wharton, Israel II, 1036
Wharton, Israel V, 64
Wharton, Jacob II, 434
Wharton, Jacob II, 595
Wharton, James II, 434
Wharton, James II, 683
Wharton, James II, 1037
Wharton, James IV, 301
Wharton, James IV, 302
Wharton, James V, 140
Wharton, James Dixon V, 210
Wharton, Jemima II, 434
Wharton, Jemima II, 512
Wharton, Jemima II, 683
Wharton, Jesse V, 1025
Wharton, Joel IV, 141
Wharton, Joel IV, 163
Wharton, Joel IV, 301
Wharton, Joel IV, 514
Wharton, Joel IV, 555
Wharton, John II, 434
Wharton, John II, 498
Wharton, John II, 683
Wharton, John II, 972
Wharton, John II, 979
Wharton, John II, 992
Wharton, John II, 1036
Wharton, John V, 64
Wharton, John VI, 578
Wharton, John VI, 903
Wharton, John VI, 951
Wharton, John VI, 988
Wharton, John VI, 1004
Wharton, John VI, 1012
Wharton, John A. VI, 988
Wharton, John W. I, 622
Wharton, John, Jr. II, 683
Wharton, John, Jr. II, 1036
Wharton, Johnson II, 1037
Wharton, Johnson II, 1063
Wharton, Johnson II, 1083
Wharton, Johnston II, 972
Wharton, Joice II, 1036
Wharton, Joice VI, 578
Wharton, Jonathan V, 140
Wharton, Joseph II, 219
Wharton, Joseph II, 266
Wharton, Joseph II, 271
Wharton, Joseph II, 434
Wharton, Joseph II, 482
Wharton, Joseph II, 595
Wharton, Joseph II, 683
Wharton, Joseph II, 892
Wharton, Joseph II, 938
Wharton, Joseph II, 972
Wharton, Joseph II, 979
Wharton, Joseph II, 992
Wharton, Joseph II, 1036
Wharton, Joseph Talmon II, 434
Wharton, Joseph, Jr. II, 434
Wharton, Joseph, Jr. II, 683
Wharton, Joseph, Sr. II, 434
Wharton, Joshua V, 64
Wharton, Josiah IV, 556
Wharton, Josiah Bundy IV, 555
Wharton, Kansas V, 210
Wharton, Lena I, 622
Wharton, Lena I, 637
Wharton, Lena I, 642
Wharton, Levi IV, 301
Wharton, Levi IV, 302
Wharton, Linton IV, 301
Wharton, Linton IV, 302
Wharton, Lucy V, 97
Wharton, Lucy V, 140
Wharton, Mahlon II, 1036
Wharton, Mahlon V, 64
Wharton, Mahlon VI, 578
Wharton, Margaret II, 774
Wharton, Margaret V, 64
Wharton, Margery II, 1036
Wharton, Margery VI, 578
Wharton, Martha II, 722
Wharton, Martha II, 1037
Wharton, Martha IV, 163
Wharton, Martha IV, 207
Wharton, Martha IV, 212
Wharton, Martha IV, 301
Wharton, Martha IV, 302
Wharton, Martha IV, 555
Wharton, Martha IV, 556
Wharton, Martha L. VI, 988
Wharton, Mary II, 434
Wharton, Mary II, 461
Wharton, Mary II, 683
Wharton, Mary II, 823
Wharton, Mary II, 826
Wharton, Mary II, 892
Wharton, Mary II, 938
Wharton, Mary II, 972
Wharton, Mary II, 992
Wharton, Mary II, 1006
Wharton, Mary II, 1019
Wharton, Mary II, 1036
Wharton, Mary II, 1037
Wharton, Mary III, 198
Wharton, Mary III, 224
Wharton, Mary III, 348
Wharton, Mary V, 62
Wharton, Mary V, 63
Wharton, Mary V, 64
Wharton, Mary V, 76
Wharton, Mary V, 101
Wharton, Mary V, 140
Wharton, Mary VI, 578
Wharton, Mary Elizabeth V, 64
Wharton, Mary Ellen II, 1067
Wharton, Mary Ellen II, 1083
Wharton, Mary Frances III, 348
Wharton, Mary L. II, 938
Wharton, Matilda IV, 541
Wharton, Matilda IV, 555
Wharton, Matilda IV, 556
Wharton, Minnie V, 605
Wharton, Moore II, 434
Wharton, Moses II, 1027
Wharton, Moses II, 1037
Wharton, Moses II, 1063
Wharton, Moses II, 1067
Wharton, Moses II, 1079
Wharton, Moses II, 1083
Wharton, Nancy VI, 1012
Wharton, Narcissa V, 64
Wharton, Nehemiah II, 972
Wharton, Nehemiah II, 1036
Wharton, Nehemiah II, 1037
Wharton, Nehemiah V, 140
Wharton, Phebe II, 972
Wharton, Phebe II, 979
Wharton, Phebe II, 981
Wharton, Phebe II, 1036
Wharton, Phebe II, 1059
Wharton, Phebe II, 1063
Wharton, Phebe II, 1079
Wharton, Phebe II, 1083
Wharton, Phebe V, 140
Wharton, Phebe VI, 578
Wharton, Phebe Ann II, 1063
Wharton, Phebe Ann II, 1079
Wharton, Phebe Ann II, 1083
Wharton, Phebe N. V, 37
Wharton, Phebe N. V, 140
Wharton, Phineas II, 972
Wharton, Phineas II, 1063
Wharton, Rachel II, 434
Wharton, Rachel II, 451
Wharton, Rachel II, 498
Wharton, Rachel II, 595
Wharton, Rachel II, 665
Wharton, Rachel II, 683
Wharton, Rachel II, 972
Wharton, Rachel IV, 301
Wharton, Rachel IV, 555
Wharton, Rachel IV, 556
Wharton, Rebecca II, 110
Wharton, Rebecca II, 434
Wharton, Rebecca II, 972
Wharton, Rebecca II, 979
Wharton, Rebecca II, 1034
Wharton, Rebecca II, 1036
Wharton, Rebecca V, 63
Wharton, Rebecca V, 140
Wharton, Rheuben V, 64
Wharton, Rhoda M. VI, 1004
Wharton, Richard II, 434
Wharton, Rodman II, 826
Wharton, Rodman II, 906
Wharton, Rodman II, 938
Wharton, Royal VI, 1012
Wharton, Sally VI, 941
Wharton, Sally VI, 1012
Wharton, Samuel II, 434
Wharton, Samuel II, 683
Wharton, Samuel II, 972
Wharton, Samuel III, 348
Wharton, Samuel Fisher II, 826
Wharton, Samuel Fisher II, 938
Wharton, Samuel, Jr. II, 434
Wharton, Sarah I, 622
Wharton, Sarah II, 219
Wharton, Sarah II, 266
Wharton, Sarah II, 271
Wharton, Sarah II, 434
Wharton, Sarah II, 683
Wharton, Sarah II, 938
Wharton, Sarah II, 972
Wharton, Sarah II, 1027
Wharton, Sarah II, 1028
Wharton, Sarah II, 1036
Wharton, Sarah II, 1037
Wharton, Sarah II, 1063
Wharton, Sarah II, 1083
Wharton, Sarah V, 64
Wharton, Sarah VI, 578
Wharton, Sarah A. V, 140
Wharton, Sarah J. V, 140
Wharton, Sarah Jane V, 210
Wharton, Sarah W. II, 835
Wharton, Silas II, 1037
Wharton, Silas IV, 301
Wharton, Silas IV, 302
Wharton, Silas V, 37
Wharton, Silas V, 62
Wharton, Silas V, 63
Wharton, Silas V, 76
Wharton, Silas V, 140
Wharton, Silas W. V, 64
Wharton, Sophia H. VI, 903
Wharton, Stacey V, 64
Wharton, Stephen II, 434
Wharton, Susanna II, 434
Wharton, Susanna II, 583
Wharton, Susanna II, 683
Wharton, Susanna IV, 519
Wharton, Susanna IV, 556
Wharton, Susannah II, 595
Wharton, Susannah II, 683
Wharton, Susannah Dillwyn II, 826
Wharton, Susannah Dillwyn II, 906
Wharton, Susannah Dillwyn II, 938
Wharton, Susannah Parrish II, 826
Wharton, Tabitha Ann IV, 556
Wharton, Talitha Ann IV, 302
Wharton, Talitha Ann IV, 514
Wharton, Talitha Ann IV, 556
Wharton, Talitha Ann IV, 628
Wharton, Thomas II, 434
Wharton, Thomas II, 482
Wharton, Thomas II, 595
Wharton, Thomas II, 665
Wharton, Thomas II, 683
Wharton, Thomas II, 972
Wharton, Thomas, Jr. II, 434
Wharton, Thomas, Jr. II, 583
Wharton, Thomas, Jr. II, 683
Wharton, Walter V, 439
Wharton, Walter V, 540
Wharton, Wd. Hannah II, 609
Wharton, William II, 434
Wharton, William II, 826
Wharton, William II, 972
Wharton, William VI, 738
Wharton, William VI, 790
Wharton, William Redwood, Jr. II, 826
Wharton, William Rodman II, 826
Wharton, William, Jr. II, 826
Wharton, William, Jr. II, 972
Wharton, Wm. II, 595
Wharton, Wm. II, 683
Wharton, Wm. II, 892
Wharton, Wm. II, 906
Wharton, Wm. II, 938
Wharton, Wm. II, 1019
Wharton, Wm. II, 1037
Wharton, Wm. II, 1063
Wharton, Wm. II, 1076
Wharton, Wm. II, 1083
Wharton, Wm., Jr. II, 1006
Wharton, Wm., Jr. II, 1036
Wharton, Wm., Jr. III, 224
Wharton, Wm., Jr. III, 348
Whartonby, Edward II, 683
Whartonby, Elizabeth II, 683
Whathall, Elizabeth H. V, 491
Whayne, Ann VI, 864
Whayne, Benjamin VI, 864
Whayne, Judith VI, 864
Whayne, Leonard VI, 864
Whayne, Milly VI, 812
Whealdon, ??? IV, 302
Whealdon, Abel IV, 562
Whealdon, Alfred IV, 302
Whealdon, Alfred IV, 556
Whealdon, Alfred IV, 562
Whealdon, Alphred IV, 302
Whealdon, Ann IV, 44
Whealdon, Ann IV, 66
Whealdon, Ann IV, 302
Whealdon, Ann IV, 556
Whealdon, Ann IV, 562
Whealdon, Elizabeth IV, 544
Whealdon, Elizabeth IV, 556
Whealdon, Elizabeth IV, 562
Whealdon, Isaac IV, 167
Whealdon, Isaac IV, 302
Whealdon, Isaac IV, 556
Whealdon, Isaac IV, 562
Whealdon, Isaac, Jr. IV, 556
Whealdon, John IV, 556
Whealdon, John IV, 562
Whealdon, Jonathan IV, 562
Whealdon, Joseph IV, 556
Whealdon, Martha IV, 66
Whealdon, Martha IV, 302
Whealdon, Martha S. IV, 1014
Whealdon, Martha Smith IV, 66
Whealdon, Martha Smith IV, 302
Whealdon, Mary Ann IV, 556
Whealdon, Marybe IV, 562
Whealdon, Matilda IV, 1014
Whealdon, Meriba IV, 302
Whealdon, Meriba IV, 556
Whealdon, Meriha IV, 302
Whealdon, Nathan IV, 44
Whealdon, Nathan IV, 66
Whealdon, Nathan IV, 302
Whealdon, Nathan IV, 556
Whealdon, Nathan IV, 562
Whealdon, Rachel IV, 66
Whealdon, Rachel IV, 302
Whealdon, Rachel IV, 556
Whealdon, Rebecca IV, 66
Whealdon, Rebecca IV, 302
Whealdon, Ruth IV, 66
Whealdon, Ruth IV, 302
Whealdon, Ruth IV, 556
Whealdon, Tabitha IV, 556
Whealer, David I, 867
Whealer, Jesse I, 867
Whealer, John I, 867
Whealer, Jonathan I, 867
Whealer, Mary I, 867
Whealer, Nathan I, 867
Whealer, Phebe I, 867
Whealer, Solomon I, 867
Whealing, Lavina VI, 848
Whealing, Martha VI, 848
Whealler, Gould I, 201
Whealers, Gould I, 201
Whealon, Dr. Geo VI, 657
Whealon, Frederick IV, 664
Whealon, George IV, 636
Whealon, George IV, 664
Whealon, Jane IV, 664
Whealon, Mary IV, 636
Whealon, Mary IV, 664
Whealon, Mary VI, 657
Wheat, Basil VI, 881
Wheat, Basil VI, 1012
Wheat, Benjamin II, 271
Wheat, Betsey VI, 1012
Wheat, Clementina VI, 1012
Wheat, Clementine Louisa VI, 1013
Wheat, Dooley VI, 1013
Wheat, Edith B. VI, 951
Wheat, Eli VI, 1012
Wheat, Eliza VI, 1013
Wheat, Eliza M. VI, 1013
Wheat, Elizabeth L. VI, 940
Wheat, Forest VI, 940

Wheat, Forest VI, 1011
Wheat, Forest VI, 1012
Wheat, Frances VI, 1012
Wheat, Hazael VI, 972
Wheat, Hazael VI, 1011
Wheat, Hazael VI, 1013
Wheat, Jack C. VI, 951
Wheat, Jack C. VI, 1013
Wheat, Jane VI, 972
Wheat, Jane VI, 1012
Wheat, John VI, 927
Wheat, John VI, 1020
Wheat, Joseph VI, 881
Wheat, Joseph VI, 891
Wheat, Joseph VI, 998
Wheat, Joseph VI, 1012
Wheat, Levi VI, 1012
Wheat, Lydda VI, 891
Wheat, Lydia VI, 991
Wheat, Martha A. VI, 1013
Wheat, Martha M. VI, 1013
Wheat, Mary II, 216
Wheat, Mary II, 271
Wheat, Mary Harrison VI, 1012
Wheat, Massay VI, 951
Wheat, Nancy VI, 881
Wheat, Nancy VI, 1011
Wheat, Nelly VI, 939
Wheat, Perthania VI, 1012
Wheat, Polly VI, 998
Wheat, Polly VI, 1011
Wheat, Rachel VI, 1020
Wheat, Sally VI, 1012
Wheat, Z. VI, 951
Wheat, Z. L. VI, 1005
Wheat, Zachariah VI, 912
Wheat, Zachariah VI, 972
Wheat, Zachariah VI, 991
Wheat, Zachariah VI, 1011
Wheat, Zachariah VI, 1012
Wheat, Zachariah J. VI, 1013
Wheat, Zadack VI, 951
Wheat, Zadock VI, 891
Wheate, Benjamin II, 187
Wheate, Elizabeth II, 187
Wheate, Mary II, 187
Wheatley, Ada R. IV, 1266
Wheatley, Miriam Anna IV, 1343
Wheaton, Amos II, 826
Wheaton, Rachel II, 938
Wheaton, Rachel V, 467
Wheaton, Wd. Rachel II, 826
Wheeler, ??? IV, 302
Wheeler, Aaron I, 794
Wheeler, Agnes VI, 1013
Wheeler, Alfred I, 844
Wheeler, Alfred A. I, 844
Wheeler, Alonzo L. I, 844
Wheeler, Alonzo S. I, 844
Wheeler, Amy I, 428
Wheeler, Anderson VI, 908
Wheeler, Anderson VI, 1013
Wheeler, Ann II, 110
Wheeler, Ann II, 434
Wheeler, Ann II, 501
Wheeler, Ann II, 525
Wheeler, Ann II, 569
Wheeler, Ann II, 683
Wheeler, Anna L. III, 348
Wheeler, Anny VI, 1013
Wheeler, Aquila V, 940
Wheeler, Aquilla V, 940
Wheeler, Aquilla J. V, 940
Wheeler, B. C. III, 96
Wheeler, B. C. III, 348
Wheeler, Benjamin I, 367
Wheeler, Benjamin I, 428
Wheeler, Benjamin I, 691
Wheeler, Betsey VI, 954
Wheeler, Blanch Ross V, 719
Wheeler, Caroline VI, 864
Wheeler, Celia I, 794
Wheeler, Celia I, 818
Wheeler, Celia I, 844
Wheeler, Charity I, 794
Wheeler, Charity I, 811
Wheeler, Charity I, 843
Wheeler, Charity I, 867
Wheeler, Charity I, 904
Wheeler, Charlotte VI, 1013
Wheeler, Clara V, 1025
Wheeler, Clark III, 348
Wheeler, Cornelia I, 844
Wheeler, Cynthia I, 887
Wheeler, Cynthia I, 905
Wheeler, Daniel III, 348
Wheeler, David I, 844
Wheeler, David I, 869
Wheeler, David I, 905
Wheeler, Dobson II, 110
Wheeler, Dora Sapp V, 650
Wheeler, Edith II, 434
Wheeler, Edna I, 642
Wheeler, Edna Lena I, 627
Wheeler, Edna V. III, 348
Wheeler, Eli Junius Horney I, 844
Wheeler, Eli P. I, 844
Wheeler, Elias III, 348
Wheeler, Elijah VI, 1013
Wheeler, Eliza D. I, 829
Wheeler, Eliza D. I, 844
Wheeler, Elizabeth I, 367
Wheeler, Elizabeth I, 414
Wheeler, Elizabeth I, 428
Wheeler, Elizabeth I, 520
Wheeler, Elizabeth I, 689
Wheeler, Elizabeth I, 691
Wheeler, Elizabeth I, 784
Wheeler, Elizabeth I, 794
Wheeler, Elizabeth I, 818
Wheeler, Elizabeth I, 843
Wheeler, Elizabeth I, 844
Wheeler, Elizabeth II, 569
Wheeler, Elizabeth IV, 481
Wheeler, Elizabeth IV, 503
Wheeler, Elizabeth V, 866
Wheeler, Elizabeth V, 873
Wheeler, Elizabeth VI, 1013
Wheeler, Ellen IV, 503
Wheeler, Ellis IV, 114
Wheeler, Emily I, 794
Wheeler, Floyd IV, 1299
Wheeler, Francis F. I, 844
Wheeler, Gabriel VI, 884
Wheeler, Gabriel VI, 897
Wheeler, Gabriel VI, 904
Wheeler, Gabriel VI, 917
Wheeler, Gabriel VI, 1013
Wheeler, Gabriel, Jr. VI, 948
Wheeler, Gabriel, Sr. VI, 1013
Wheeler, George VI, 864
Wheeler, George VI, 1013
Wheeler, George C. VI, 830
Wheeler, Gould I, 172
Wheeler, Gould I, 201
Wheeler, Gould IV, 66
Wheeler, Gould V, 940
Wheeler, Hannah I, 562
Wheeler, Hannah I, 580
Wheeler, Hannah I, 794
Wheeler, Hannah I, 841
Wheeler, Hannah I, 843
Wheeler, Hannah IV, 315
Wheeler, Hannah IV, 334
Wheeler, Hannah IV, 357
Wheeler, Henry I, 784
Wheeler, Henry I, 794
Wheeler, Henry I, 843
Wheeler, Henry I, 844
Wheeler, Henry VI, 864
Wheeler, Honor C. IV, 98
Wheeler, Honor C. IV, 114
Wheeler, Isabella VI, 799
Wheeler, Jane I, 794
Wheeler, Jane I, 827
Wheeler, Jane I, 843
Wheeler, Jane I, 867
Wheeler, Jesse I, 843
Wheeler, Jesse I, 844
Wheeler, Jesse I, 905
Wheeler, Joel VI, 884
Wheeler, John I, 366
Wheeler, John I, 367
Wheeler, John I, 414
Wheeler, John I, 428
Wheeler, John I, 580
Wheeler, John I, 794
Wheeler, John I, 829
Wheeler, John I, 843
Wheeler, John I, 844
Wheeler, John I, 867
Wheeler, John I, 905
Wheeler, John VI, 876
Wheeler, John VI, 947
Wheeler, John VI, 981
Wheeler, John VI, 1013
Wheeler, Joice VI, 901
Wheeler, Jonathan I, 794
Wheeler, Jonathan I, 827
Wheeler, Jonathan I, 843
Wheeler, Jonathan I, 844
Wheeler, Jonathan I, 847
Wheeler, Jonathan I, 867
Wheeler, Jonathan I, 905
Wheeler, Joseph I, 367
Wheeler, Joseph I, 691
Wheeler, Joseph III, 348
Wheeler, Judith IV, 230
Wheeler, Judith J. IV, 230
Wheeler, Judith J. D. IV, 302
Wheeler, Julia Antoinette I, 844
Wheeler, Julia C. III, 96
Wheeler, Julia C. III, 348
Wheeler, Kezia I, 794
Wheeler, Kezia I, 843
Wheeler, Keziah I, 837
Wheeler, Keziah I, 843
Wheeler, Keziah I, 867
Wheeler, Keziah I, 904
Wheeler, Keziah IV, 1343
Wheeler, Leah I, 784
Wheeler, Leah I, 794
Wheeler, Leah I, 844
Wheeler, Lucinda VI, 1013
Wheeler, Lydia I, 794
Wheeler, Lydia I, 818
Wheeler, Lydia I, 839
Wheeler, Lydia I, 843
Wheeler, Lydia I, 844
Wheeler, Lydia C. I, 844
Wheeler, Mamie V, 1025
Wheeler, Manlove I, 562
Wheeler, Manlove I, 580
Wheeler, Manlove I, 773
Wheeler, Manlove I, 794
Wheeler, Manlove I, 827
Wheeler, Manlove I, 843
Wheeler, Manlove, Jr. I, 843
Wheeler, Margaret I, 867
Wheeler, Margaret I, 894
Wheeler, Margaret I, 905
Wheeler, Margaret VI, 825
Wheeler, Martha I, 930
Wheeler, Mary I, 366
Wheeler, Mary I, 367
Wheeler, Mary I, 426
Wheeler, Mary I, 428
Wheeler, Mary I, 580
Wheeler, Mary I, 691
Wheeler, Mary I, 794
Wheeler, Mary I, 811
Wheeler, Mary I, 818
Wheeler, Mary I, 843
Wheeler, Mary I, 844
Wheeler, Mary I, 882
Wheeler, Mary I, 905
Wheeler, Mary VI, 830
Wheeler, Mary VI, 864
Wheeler, Mary Flower II, 569
Wheeler, Mary Jones II, 569
Wheeler, Mary P. V, 862
Wheeler, Mary P. V, 873
Wheeler, Matilda III, 123
Wheeler, Melissa I, 844
Wheeler, Milly I, 844
Wheeler, Mrs. E. IV, 1343
Wheeler, Mrs. Emma IV, 1343
Wheeler, Nancy IV, 1203
Wheeler, Nancy IV, 1226
Wheeler, Nancy VI, 884
Wheeler, Nancy VI, 947
Wheeler, Nancy VI, 981
Wheeler, Nancy R. IV, 1226
Wheeler, Nathan I, 894
Wheeler, Nathan I, 905
Wheeler, Noah V, 146
Wheeler, Olga IV, 1226
Wheeler, Phebe I, 575
Wheeler, Phebe I, 580
Wheeler, Phebe I, 798
Wheeler, Phebe I, 844
Wheeler, Phebe I, 905
Wheeler, Priscilla VI, 917
Wheeler, Rachel I, 794
Wheeler, Rachel I, 829
Wheeler, Rachel I, 843
Wheeler, Rebecca II, 236
Wheeler, Rebecca II, 271
Wheeler, Rhoda VI, 799
Wheeler, Rhoda VI, 864
Wheeler, Rhoda VI, 904
Wheeler, Rhoda VI, 1013
Wheeler, Richard I, 794
Wheeler, Robert II, 236
Wheeler, Robert II, 271
Wheeler, Roland VI, 1013
Wheeler, Ruth I, 798
Wheeler, Ruth I, 844
Wheeler, Ruth I, 905
Wheeler, Ruth C. I, 869
Wheeler, Ruth C. I, 905
Wheeler, Sally VI, 876
Wheeler, Samuel II, 434
Wheeler, Samuel II, 569
Wheeler, Samuel II, 683
Wheeler, Samuel III, 348
Wheeler, Samuel VI, 830
Wheeler, Samuel P. VI, 864
Wheeler, Sarah I, 366
Wheeler, Sarah I, 367
Wheeler, Sarah I, 384
Wheeler, Sarah I, 394
Wheeler, Sarah I, 428
Wheeler, Sarah I, 520
Wheeler, Sarah I, 627
Wheeler, Sarah I, 804
Wheeler, Sarah I, 835
Wheeler, Sarah I, 843
Wheeler, Sarah I, 844
Wheeler, Sarah I, 845
Wheeler, Sarah II, 579
Wheeler, Sarah II, 683
Wheeler, Sarah III, 348
Wheeler, Sarah V, 210
Wheeler, Sarah V, 719
Wheeler, Sarah VI, 825
Wheeler, Sarah VI, 864
Wheeler, Sarah VI, 901
Wheeler, Sarah VI, 1013
Wheeler, Sarah J. III, 465
Wheeler, Sarah, Jr. III, 438
Wheeler, Sary VI, 908
Wheeler, Solomon I, 905
Wheeler, Solomon VI, 1013
Wheeler, Susan F. II, 739
Wheeler, Susan F. II, 774
Wheeler, Tamer Ann V, 167
Wheeler, Tamer Ann V, 210
Wheeler, Thomas II, 449
Wheeler, Thomas V, 1025
Wheeler, Thomas VI, 1013
Wheeler, Widow Mary I, 827
Wheeler, Will IV, 1226
Wheeler, William I, 428
Wheeler, William I, 794
Wheeler, William I, 839
Wheeler, William I, 843
Wheeler, William VI, 1013
Wheeler, William Henry I, 627
Wheeler, Wilson VI, 864
Wheeler, Wm. I, 520
Wheeler, Wm. IV, 302
Wheeler, Wm. IV, 1226
Wheeler, Wm. J. IV, 1343
Wheeler???, Ann Louisa III, 305
Wheeling, Eliza VI, 1013
Wheeling, Elizabeth VI, 1013
Wheeling, John VI, 1013
Wheelr, Agnes VI, 1013
Wheelr, Elizabeth VI, 1013
Wheelr, Gabriel, Jr. VI, 1013
Wheelr, James VI, 1013
Wheelr, John VI, 1013
Wheelr, Nancy VI, 1013
Wheelr, Sukey VI, 1013
Wheelr, Wilson VI, 1013
Wheilden, Experience II, 221
Wheilden, Joseph II, 221
Wheildon, Experience II, 271
Wheildon, Joseph II, 271
Whelan, Ann II, 434
Whelan, Israel II, 434
Whelan, Israel II, 435
Whelan, Jane II, 435
Whelan, Margaret VI, 848
Whelan, Martha VI, 848
Whelan, Mary II, 435
Whelan, Mary VI, 839
Whelan, Rachel VI, 840
Whelan, Thomas VI, 839
Whelan, Thomas VI, 840
Whelan, Townsend II, 435
Wheldon, Martha IV, 302
Wheldon, Martha S. IV, 1014
Wheldon, Tabitha IV, 555
Whelen, Isaac II, 683
Whelen, Israel II, 434
Whelen, Joseph II, 683
Whelen, Mary II, 683
Whelen, Townsend II, 683
Whelon, Betsy VI, 828
Whelon, Israel II, 435
Whelon, Jane II, 435
Wherey, Rachel I Sup 1, 4
Wherey, Rachel I Sup 1, 6
Wherley, Abraham III, 348
Wherrit, Bertha IV, 1343
Wherry, Rachel IV, 527
Wherry, Rachel IV, 556
Wherry, Sarah IV, 533
Wherry, Sarah IV, 556
Wheson, Thomas III, 348
Whetherby, Sarah II, 110
Whetheril, Mary II, 1036
Whetheril, Sarah II, 1036
Whetley, Alexander V, 365
Whetson, ??? V, 823
Whetstone, Mary C. V, 1025
Whetton, George IV, 852
Whetton, Minnie IV, 852
Whetton, Sarah Jane IV, 852
Whetzel, Addie V, 467
Whevit, John S. IV, 1343
Whible, Margaret II, 145
Whible, Margret II, 160
Whicher, Mary IV, 503
Whicker, Mary I, 580
Whicker, Mary I, 608
Whicker, Rhoda I, 580
Whidbee, R. Emma I, 78
Whidbee, Rachel M. I, 78
Whidbee, Sarah I, 76
Whidbee, Sarah I, 78
Whigam, Wm. C. IV, 1343
Whigham, Wm. C. IV, 1343
Whight, John VI, 1013
Whight, Lucy VI, 1013
Whiley, David VI, 1013
Whiley, Patsy VI, 1013
Whinery, Aaron IV, 251
Whinery, Aaron IV, 302
Whinery, Abigail IV, 66
Whinery, Abigail IV, 302
Whinery, Abigail IV, 664
Whinery, Abigail IV, 786
Whinery, Abigail IV, 838
Whinery, Abigail IV, 843
Whinery, Abigail IV, 852
Whinery, Abigail IV, 853
Whinery, Abigail V, 508
Whinery, Abigail V, 540
Whinery, Abigail V, 541
Whinery, Abraham C. IV, 852
Whinery, Achilles V, 540
Whinery, Achilles V, 541
Whinery, Adelaide V, 541
Whinery, Albert V, 289
Whinery, Albert V, 540
Whinery, Albert V, 541
Whinery, Albin V, 540
Whinery, Alfred L. IV, 302
Whinery, Allen V, 540
Whinery, Allen C. V, 140
Whinery, Almira IV, 852
Whinery, Almira IV, 853
Whinery, Alpheus V, 540
Whinery, Alpheus V, 541
Whinery, Alvaretta V, 540
Whinery, Amelia IV, 816
Whinery, Amelia IV, 845
Whinery, Amelia IV, 852
Whinery, Amelia P. IV, 1014
Whinery, Amy IV, 852
Whinery, Amy IV, 853
Whinery, Amy IV, 1000
Whinery, Angeline IV, 798
Whinery, Angeline IV, 852
Whinery, Angeline IV, 853
Whinery, Ann IV, 685
Whinery, Ann IV, 786
Whinery, Ann IV, 804
Whinery, Ann IV, 852
Whinery, Ann IV, 853
Whinery, Ann V, 540
Whinery, Ann V, 541
Whinery, Anna IV, 838
Whinery, Anna IV, 852
Whinery, Anna IV, 854
Whinery, Anna IV, 856
Whinery, Anna IV, 1000
Whinery, Anna E. IV, 854
Whinery, Anna Margarete IV, 1014
Whinery, Anna P. V, 140
Whinery, Anne IV, 1014
Whinery, Annie Jane V, 540
Whinery, Arthur V, 439
Whinery, Arthur V, 541
Whinery, Arthur V, 605
Whinery, Arthur D. IV, 1014
Whinery, Arthur Dallas IV, 1014
Whinery, Arthur Enos V, 605
Whinery, Asenath IV, 201
Whinery, Asenath IV, 291
Whinery, Asenath IV, 302
Whinery, Asenath IV, 583
Whinery, Asenath IV, 984
Whinery, Asenath H. IV, 219
Whinery, Asenath H. IV, 302
Whinery, Barby Dallis IV, 852
Whinery, Barby Dallis IV, 854
Whinery, Benjamin IV, 1014
Whinery, Benjamin V, 511
Whinery, Benjamin V, 540
Whinery, Benjamin V, 541
Whinery, Benjamin M. IV, 853
Whinery, Benjamin M. IV, 1014
Whinery, Bertram IV, 854
Whinery, Byron IV, 854
Whinery, Calvin V, 540
Whinery, Calvin V, 541
Whinery, Camille IV, 1014
Whinery, Celesta V, 719
Whinery, Charles IV, 852

ery, Charles IV, 853
ery, Charles L. IV, 853
ery, Charles L. IV, 1014
ery, Charles Leech IV, 852
ery, Charles Rollin V, 540
nery, Chas. L. IV, 853
ery, Chas. L. IV, 1014
ery, Chas. Leech IV, 1014
nery, Chester IV, 302
nery, Chester E. IV, 302
nery, Clara May IV, 1014
nery, Clara R. IV, 214
nery, Clara R. IV, 302
nery, Cyrus IV, 852
nery, Cyrus IV, 1000
nery, Cyrus IV, 1014
nery, David IV, 804
nery, David IV, 852
nery, David IV, 853
nery, David IV, 854
nery, David IV, 930
nery, David IV, 1014
inery, David V, 540
inery, David, Jr. IV, 854
inery, Debora IV, 302
inery, Deborah IV, 192
inery, Deborah IV, 302
inery, Deborah IV, 838
inery, Deborah IV, 853
inery, Deborah IV, 945
inery, Deborah IV, 1014
inery, Edith IV, 302
inery, Edith IV, 852
inery, Edna IV, 854
inery, Edna B. IV, 854
inery, Edna H. IV, 854
inery, Edna H. IV, 1266
inery, Edna H. V, 650
inery, Edward IV, 357
inery, Edward IV, 853
inery, Edward B. V, 540
inery, Edwin V, 501
inery, Edwin V, 540
inery, Edwin V, 541
inery, Edwin T. V, 541
inery, Elijah IV, 853
inery, Eliza V, 540
inery, Eliza Ann IV, 853
hinery, Elizabeth IV, 797
hinery, Elizabeth IV, 853
hinery, Elizabeth IV, 978
hinery, Elizabeth IV, 984
hinery, Elizabeth IV, 1014
hinery, Elizabeth V, 380
hinery, Elizabeth V, 439
hinery, Elizabeth V, 482
hinery, Elizabeth V, 541
hinery, Ellsworth V, 541
hinery, Elma T. IV, 201
hinery, Elma T. IV, 302
hinery, Elsworth V, 540
hinery, Elwood IV, 302
hinery, Elwood IV, 853
hinery, Elwood D. IV, 201
hinery, Elwood D. IV, 219
hinery, Elwood D. IV, 302
hinery, Elwood D. IV, 583
hinery, Elwood D. IV, 852
hinery, Elwood D. IV, 853
hinery, Elwood D. IV, 854
hinery, Emaline IV, 1014
hinery, Emaline P. IV, 1014
hinery, Emeline P. IV, 853
hinery, Emeline P. IV, 1014
Vhinery, Emilia V, 540
Vhinery, Emily B. IV, 852
Vhinery, Emily B. IV, 853
Vhinery, Emily B. IV, 1006
Vhinery, Enos V, 540
Vhinery, Enos V, 541
Vhinery, Enos V, 605
Vhinery, Esther V, 540
Vhinery, Esther V, 541
Vhinery, Eunice IV, 698
Vhinery, Eunice IV, 786
Whinery, Eva V, 540
Whinery, Eva V, 541
Whinery, Eva M. V, 541
Whinery, Evan IV, 852
Whinery, Evan IV, 853
Whinery, Ezra V, 514
Whinery, Ezra V, 540
Whinery, Ezra V, 541
Whinery, Ezra V, 605
Whinery, Fileta IV, 854
Whinery, Fileta V, 650
Whinery, Florence IV, 854
Whinery, Florence L. IV, 786
Whinery, Florence L. IV, 854
Whinery, Florence L. IV, 1014
Whinery, Florence S. IV, 1014
Whinery, Francis IV, 302
Whinery, Frank V, 540
Whinery, Frank G. V, 719
Whinery, Frank Garwood V, 541
Whinery, George IV, 302
Whinery, George IV, 853
Whinery, Halland V, 540
Whinery, Hanna IV, 302
Whinery, Hannah IV, 251
Whinery, Hannah IV, 302
Whinery, Hannah IV, 811
Whinery, Hannah IV, 829
Whinery, Hannah IV, 852
Whinery, Hannah IV, 853
Whinery, Hannah IV, 856
Whinery, Hannah V, 266
Whinery, Hannah V, 289
Whinery, Hannah V, 501
Whinery, Hannah V, 514
Whinery, Hannah V, 519
Whinery, Hannah V, 541
Whinery, Hannah V, 605
Whinery, Hannah L. V, 540
Whinery, Hannah Loretta V, 541
Whinery, Hannah M. V, 540
Whinery, Hannah M. V, 719
Whinery, Hannah Morris V, 289
Whinery, Harold Clifton IV, 854
Whinery, Harriet IV, 847
Whinery, Harriet IV, 853
Whinery, Harriet IV, 854
Whinery, Harriet V, 514
Whinery, Harriet V, 540
Whinery, Harriet V, 541
Whinery, Helen IV, 990
Whinery, Henry V, 541
Whinery, Henry V, 605
Whinery, Hervey M. IV, 302
Whinery, Hiram IV, 852
Whinery, Hiram IV, 853
Whinery, Holland IV, 853
Whinery, Holland V, 540
Whinery, Holland G. V, 540
Whinery, Howard E. Stratton IV, 556
Whinery, Hubbard IV, 852
Whinery, Huldah IV, 814
Whinery, Huldah IV, 852
Whinery, Huldah IV, 853
Whinery, Ida IV, 1014
Whinery, Ida M. IV, 1014
Whinery, Isaac IV, 853
Whinery, Isabella V, 541
Whinery, Isabella V, 543
Whinery, Isabella A. V, 540
Whinery, Isaiah IV, 852
Whinery, Isaiah IV, 853
Whinery, Isaiah IV, 854
Whinery, Isaiah V, 541
Whinery, Isaiah V, 719
Whinery, J. H. IV, 854
Whinery, J. H. IV, 1266
Whinery, Jacob C. IV, 853
Whinery, James IV, 805
Whinery, James IV, 853
Whinery, James IV, 860
Whinery, James IV, 1014
Whinery, James V, 417
Whinery, James V, 439
Whinery, James V, 541
Whinery, James V, 605
Whinery, James L. V, 540
Whinery, James Morris V, 289
Whinery, Jane IV, 804
Whinery, Jane IV, 810
Whinery, Jane IV, 852
Whinery, Jane IV, 853
Whinery, Jane Ann IV, 853
Whinery, Jane Ann V, 540
Whinery, Jediah IV, 853
Whinery, Jemima R. V, 540
Whinery, Jeremiah IV, 852
Whinery, Jeremiah H. IV, 853
Whinery, John IV, 832
Whinery, John IV, 852
Whinery, John IV, 853
Whinery, John IV, 984
Whinery, John IV, 1014
Whinery, John V, 540
Whinery, John C. IV, 853
Whinery, John E. IV, 853
Whinery, John E. H. IV, 852
Whinery, John Leach IV, 852
Whinery, John, Jr. IV, 786
Whinery, John, Jr. IV, 853
Whinery, John, Jr. IV, 978
Whinery, John, Jr. IV, 1014
Whinery, Jonathan M. V, 540
Whinery, Joseph IV, 798
Whinery, Joseph IV, 810
Whinery, Joseph IV, 852
Whinery, Joseph IV, 853
Whinery, Joseph V, 140
Whinery, Joseph V, 500
Whinery, Joseph V, 540
Whinery, Joseph B. IV, 852
Whinery, Joseph B. IV, 853
Whinery, Joseph H. IV, 852
Whinery, Joseph H. IV, 854
Whinery, Joseph H. IV, 1266
Whinery, Joseph H. V, 650
Whinery, Joseph W. IV, 854
Whinery, Joshua S. IV, 852
Whinery, Joshua S. IV, 853
Whinery, Josiah IV, 852
Whinery, Josiah V, 540
Whinery, Josiah V, 541
Whinery, Jr. Wm. IV, 853
Whinery, Judith IV, 786
Whinery, Judith IV, 790
Whinery, Judith IV, 853
Whinery, Judith IV, 857
Whinery, Judith V, 439
Whinery, Judith V, 540
Whinery, Judith V, 541
Whinery, Judith V, 605
Whinery, Judith E. V, 540
Whinery, Judith E. V, 605
Whinery, Leander IV, 786
Whinery, Leander IV, 852
Whinery, Leander IV, 854
Whinery, Leander IV, 1014
Whinery, Leech IV, 852
Whinery, Lenna V, 439
Whinery, Lenna L. V, 439
Whinery, Leora May IV, 854
Whinery, Lesley IV, 854
Whinery, Lewis Alfred IV, 302
Whinery, Lorenza V, 541
Whinery, Lorenza V. V, 541
Whinery, Lorenzo V. V, 540
Whinery, Louisa M. IV, 302
Whinery, Luella IV, 854
Whinery, Lydia I, 753
Whinery, Lydia I, 771
Whinery, Lydia IV, 664
Whinery, Lydia IV, 801
Whinery, Lydia IV, 802
Whinery, Lydia IV, 852
Whinery, Lydia IV, 853
Whinery, Lydia V, 102
Whinery, Lydia V, 140
Whinery, Lydia V, 523
Whinery, Lydia V, 540
Whinery, Lydia V, 541
Whinery, Lydia A. IV, 1014
Whinery, Lydia Ann IV, 1014
Whinery, Lydia B. IV, 979
Whinery, Lydia B. IV, 1014
Whinery, Lydia Ellen V, 540
Whinery, Lydia Emely V, 540
Whinery, Lydia Emily V, 514
Whinery, Lydia Emily V, 540
Whinery, Lydia Emily V, 541
Whinery, Mabel IV, 302
Whinery, Mabel IV, 553
Whinery, Mabel IV, 556
Whinery, Mahlon IV, 302
Whinery, Mahlon IV, 811
Whinery, Mahlon IV, 852
Whinery, Mahlon IV, 853
Whinery, Mahlon IV, 856
Whinery, Margaret IV, 854
Whinery, Margary IV, 853
Whinery, Margery IV, 853
Whinery, Mark V, 140
Whinery, Mark V, 540
Whinery, Mark V, 541
Whinery, Martha IV, 798
Whinery, Martha IV, 810
Whinery, Martha IV, 847
Whinery, Martha IV, 852
Whinery, Martha IV, 853
Whinery, Martha IV, 854
Whinery, Martha Emily IV, 848
Whinery, Martha Emily IV, 852
Whinery, Martha J. IV, 845
Whinery, Martha J. IV, 846
Whinery, Martha J. IV, 852
Whinery, Martha J. IV, 854
Whinery, Mary IV, 302
Whinery, Mary IV, 675
Whinery, Mary IV, 786
Whinery, Mary IV, 800
Whinery, Mary IV, 832
Whinery, Mary IV, 852
Whinery, Mary IV, 853
Whinery, Mary IV, 854
Whinery, Mary IV, 927
Whinery, Mary IV, 1014
Whinery, Mary V, 417
Whinery, Mary V, 439
Whinery, Mary V, 541
Whinery, Mary V, 605
Whinery, Mary Ann IV, 952
Whinery, Mary Ann IV, 1014
Whinery, Mary B. IV, 786
Whinery, Mary B. IV, 852
Whinery, Mary B. IV, 853
Whinery, Mary B. IV, 1006
Whinery, Mary B. IV, 1014
Whinery, Mary B. IV, 1031
Whinery, Mary Bell V, 540
Whinery, Mary Bell V, 541
Whinery, Mary E. V, 439
Whinery, Mary Edith IV, 219
Whinery, Mary Edith IV, 406
Whinery, Mary Edith IV, 583
Whinery, Mary Elizabeth V, 405
Whinery, Mary Elizabeth V, 439
Whinery, Mary H. IV, 854
Whinery, Mary Jane IV, 852
Whinery, Mary Jane IV, 853
Whinery, Mary V. IV, 786
Whinery, Mary V. IV, 1014
Whinery, Matilda I, 753
Whinery, Melva Rachel IV, 302
Whinery, Minor IV, 853
Whinery, Nathan IV, 797
Whinery, Nathan IV, 816
Whinery, Nathan IV, 852
Whinery, Nathan IV, 853
Whinery, Nathan H. V, 540
Whinery, Nathen IV, 845
Whinery, Newton IV, 786
Whinery, Newton IV, 853
Whinery, Olive IV, 990
Whinery, Olive R. IV, 184
Whinery, Olive R. IV, 302
Whinery, Olive R. IV, 931
Whinery, Olive R. IV, 1014
Whinery, Oliver IV, 852
Whinery, Oliver M. V, 540
Whinery, Orval H. IV, 1014
Whinery, Orvil IV, 1014
Whinery, Patricia Ann IV, 302
Whinery, Phebe IV, 66
Whinery, Phebe IV, 664
Whinery, Phebe IV, 799
Whinery, Phebe IV, 801
Whinery, Phebe IV, 852
Whinery, Phebe IV, 853
Whinery, Phebe IV, 854
Whinery, Phebe IV, 1014
Whinery, Phebe V, 540
Whinery, Phebe B. IV, 799
Whinery, Phebe Ellen IV, 827
Whinery, Phebe Ellen IV, 852
Whinery, Phebe Ellen IV, 854
Whinery, Phebe Jane IV, 853
Whinery, Phebe Jane IV, 1012
Whinery, Phebe Jane IV, 1014
Whinery, Phebe R. V, 540
Whinery, Phileta IV, 854
Whinery, Rachel IV, 824
Whinery, Rachel IV, 831
Whinery, Rachel IV, 834
Whinery, Rachel Jane V, 540
Whinery, Rachel Jane V, 541
Whinery, Rachel M. V, 541
Whinery, Rachel S. IV, 816
Whinery, Rachel S. IV, 852
Whinery, Rachel S. IV, 854
Whinery, Raymond IV, 854
Whinery, Raymond V, 650
Whinery, Rebecca IV, 810
Whinery, Rebecca IV, 852
Whinery, Rebecca IV, 853
Whinery, Rebecca Ann IV, 852
Whinery, Rebecca Ann V, 515
Whinery, Rebecca Ann V, 541
Whinery, Rhoda IV, 786
Whinery, Rhoda IV, 852
Whinery, Rhoda IV, 854
Whinery, Robert I, 753
Whinery, Robert IV, 66
Whinery, Robert IV, 801
Whinery, Robert IV, 814
Whinery, Robert IV, 852
Whinery, Robert IV, 853
Whinery, Robert IV, 1014
Whinery, Robert V, 719
Whinery, Robert B. IV, 852
Whinery, Robert B. IV, 853
Whinery, Robert C. V, 719
Whinery, Ruth IV, 843
Whinery, Ruth IV, 852
Whinery, Ruth IV, 853
Whinery, Ruth V, 511
Whinery, Ruth V, 540
Whinery, Ruth V, 541
Whinery, Ruth L. V, 541
Whinery, Ruth M. V, 140
Whinery, Sallie V, 140
Whinery, Sally IV, 805
Whinery, Sally IV, 853
Whinery, Samuel IV, 852
Whinery, Samuel V, 514
Whinery, Samuel V, 540
Whinery, Samuel V, 541
Whinery, Samuel D. IV, 854
Whinery, Samuel D. IV, 990
Whinery, Samuel G. V, 540
Whinery, Sara IV, 302
Whinery, Sara IV, 852
Whinery, Sarah IV, 804
Whinery, Sarah IV, 807
Whinery, Sarah IV, 852
Whinery, Sarah IV, 853
Whinery, Sarah IV, 854
Whinery, Sarah IV, 922
Whinery, Sarah IV, 930
Whinery, Sarah IV, 1014
Whinery, Sarah V, 140
Whinery, Sarah V, 500
Whinery, Sarah V, 501
Whinery, Sarah V, 517
Whinery, Sarah V, 529
Whinery, Sarah V, 540
Whinery, Sarah V, 541
Whinery, Sarah Elsie IV, 854
Whinery, Sarah Jane IV, 852
Whinery, Sarah Jane V, 502
Whinery, Sarah Jane V, 541
Whinery, Sarah Leota IV, 1014
Whinery, Sarah M. V, 540
Whinery, Sarah Whinery V, 289
Whinery, Stephen IV, 852
Whinery, Stephen IV, 853
Whinery, Susan IV, 814
Whinery, Susan IV, 852
Whinery, Susan IV, 853
Whinery, Susan L. IV, 1266
Whinery, Susan Lydia V, 140
Whinery, Susanna IV, 810
Whinery, Susanna IV, 853
Whinery, Susanna V, 605
Whinery, Susannah IV, 852
Whinery, Susannah IV, 853
Whinery, Susannah M. V, 541
Whinery, Thomas IV, 800
Whinery, Thomas IV, 852
Whinery, Thomas IV, 853
Whinery, Thomas IV, 927
Whinery, Thomas IV, 1006
Whinery, Thomas IV, 1014
Whinery, Thomas V, 140
Whinery, Thomas V, 540
Whinery, Thomas B. I, 753
Whinery, Thomas B. IV, 302
Whinery, Thomas Hiatt V, 140
Whinery, Thomas Milton V, 540
Whinery, Thomas, Jr. V, 541
Whinery, Thos. IV, 1014
Whinery, Thos. A. IV, 302
Whinery, Thos. B. IV, 214
Whinery, Thos. B. IV, 302
Whinery, Vincent IV, 853
Whinery, Vincent V, 540
Whinery, Walter IV, 302
Whinery, Walter N. IV, 192
Whinery, Walter N. IV, 302
Whinery, Walter N. IV, 945
Whinery, Walter N. IV, 1014
Whinery, Walter P. V, 540
Whinery, Walter T. V, 541
Whinery, Walter, Jr. IV, 302
Whinery, Warren V, 439
Whinery, Wesley IV, 854
Whinery, William IV, 853
Whinery, William V, 541
Whinery, William D. IV, 786
Whinery, William H. V, 540
Whinery, William H. V, 719
Whinery, William Henry V, 541
Whinery, William J. IV, 852
Whinery, Willis IV, 852
Whinery, Willis IV, 854
Whinery, Wilmer IV, 854
Whinery, Wilmer D. IV, 786
Whinery, Wilmer D. IV, 854
Whinery, Wilmer D. IV, 1014
Whinery, Wilson J. IV, 302
Whinery, Wm. IV, 786
Whinery, Wm. IV, 853
Whinery, Wm. IV, 854
Whinery, Wm. H. V, 719
Whinery, Wm. J. IV, 854
Whinery, Wright V, 540
Whinery, Zalinda IV, 852
Whinery, Zimri IV, 786
Whinery, Zimri IV, 790
Whinery, Zimri IV, 853
Whinery, Zimri IV, 857

Whinery, Zimri IV, 1031
Whinery, Zimri V, 439
Whinery, Zimri V, 496
Whinery, Zimri V, 540
Whinery, Zimri V, 541
Whinery, Zimri W. V, 541
Whinnery, Abigail IV, 66
Whinnery, Abigail IV, 786
Whinnery, Amy IV, 1044
Whinnery, Ann H. IV, 732
Whinnery, Ann H. IV, 786
Whinnery, Anna IV, 1044
Whinnery, Anna Mary IV, 1044
Whinnery, Arthur J. Hartley IV, 454
Whinnery, Clara IV, 689
Whinnery, Clara H. IV, 285
Whinnery, Clarah Amy IV, 1044
Whinnery, Cyrus IV, 1044
Whinnery, Edna IV, 786
Whinnery, Edna H. IV, 786
Whinnery, Eleanor I, 428
Whinnery, Elijah IV, 732
Whinnery, Elijah IV, 786
Whinnery, Ethel L. IV, 786
Whinnery, Eunice IV, 786
Whinnery, Fileta IV, 786
Whinnery, Florence L. IV, 786
Whinnery, Helen IV, 786
Whinnery, Ida IV, 1044
Whinnery, James IV, 786
Whinnery, Jane IV, 786
Whinnery, John I, 428
Whinnery, John IV, 1044
Whinnery, John, Jr. IV, 786
Whinnery, Joseph IV, 786
Whinnery, Joseph H. IV, 786
Whinnery, Judith IV, 786
Whinnery, Leander IV, 786
Whinnery, Leona IV, 786
Whinnery, Leora May IV, 1044
Whinnery, Lillian H. IV, 1044
Whinnery, Lucella IV, 786
Whinnery, Lydia I, 771
Whinnery, Lydia IV, 786
Whinnery, Mabel IV, 285
Whinnery, Mary I, 410
Whinnery, Mary I, 428
Whinnery, Mary IV, 689
Whinnery, Mary IV, 786
Whinnery, Mary B. IV, 786
Whinnery, Mary Edith IV, 407
Whinnery, Mary Edith IV, 454
Whinnery, Mary H. IV, 1044
Whinnery, Mary V. IV, 786
Whinnery, Newton IV, 786
Whinnery, Phebe IV, 66
Whinnery, Rachel IV, 786
Whinnery, Raymond E. IV, 786
Whinnery, Rhoda IV, 786
Whinnery, Robert IV, 66
Whinnery, Sarah IV, 786
Whinnery, Susan E. IV, 1044
Whinnery, Thomas I, 428
Whinnery, Thomas I, 771
Whinnery, Thomas IV, 786
Whinnery, Thomas V, 540
Whinnery, Thomas B. IV, 285
Whinnery, William IV, 786
Whinnery, William D. IV, 786
Whinnery, Wilmer IV, 786
Whinnery, Wilmer D. IV, 786
Whinnery, Wm. IV, 689
Whinnery, Wm. IV, 786
Whinnery, Wm. J. IV, 1044
Whinnery, Zimri IV, 786
Whinney, Elizabeth II, 683
Whinney, Elizabeth Wyatt II, 560
Whinney, Elizabeth Wyatt II, 683
Whinney, John II, 560
Whinney, John II, 683
Whinney, Richard II, 560
Whinney, Richard II, 683
Whinry, Thomas I, 771
Whinslow, Ann I, 199
Whinslow, Ann I, 203
Whipp, Alice Louise V, 605
Whipp, Thelma Elizabeth V, 605
Whipple, Alice II, 683
Whipple, Clark IV, 1192
Whipple, Ernest IV, 1192
Whipple, Helen III, 446
Whipple, Helen III, 448
Whipple, John III, 348
Whipple, Joseph II, 683
Whipple, Lyman IV, 1226
Whipple, Marion U. III, 150
Whipple, Marion U. III, 151
Whipple, Pearl IV, 1192
Whipple, Pearl IV, 1226
Whipple, W. Ernest IV, 1192
Whippo, Deborah III, 194
Whippo, Deborah III, 269
Whippo, Deborah III, 348
Whippo, John III, 348
Whippo, Laurence III, 348
Whippo, Maria III, 348
Whippo, Priscilla III, 348
Whippo, Wd. Deborah III, 348
Whippoe, Elizabeth II, 435
Whipps, Nina Cook V, 719
Whips, Ann I, 347
Whips, George I, 347
Whips, Jean I, 347
Whirley, Eshter VI, 992
Whirley, Joel VI, 1020
Whirley, John VI, 843
Whirley, Sinthia VI, 1020
Whirley, William VI, 992
Whiston, Elizabeth II, 683
Whistor, Sarah II, 111
Whit, Rella I, 935
Whit, Sarah I, 90
Whitacer, Reva V, 210
Whitacher, Hannah IV, 1299
Whitacor, Andrew VI, 607
Whitacor, Aquilla VI, 607
Whitacor, Jane VI, 607
Whitacor, John VI, 607
Whitacor, Jonas VI, 607
Whitacor, Moses VI, 607
Whitacor, Patience VI, 607
Whitacor, Priscilla VI, 607
Whitacor, Rhoda VI, 607
Whitacor, Robert VI, 607
Whitacre, Abner VI, 719
Whitacre, Abraham V, 140
Whitacre, Achsa IV, 854
Whitacre, Achsah IV, 786
Whitacre, Achsah VI, 578
Whitacre, Achsah VI, 719
Whitacre, Acquilla V, 74
Whitacre, Ada L. V, 141
Whitacre, Addie V, 141
Whitacre, Albert V, 140
Whitacre, Albert V, 141
Whitacre, Albinah VI, 632
Whitacre, Albinah VI, 719
Whitacre, Alice VI, 578
Whitacre, Alice VI, 579
Whitacre, Alma IV, 854
Whitacre, Alma J. IV, 786
Whitacre, Amos VI, 719
Whitacre, Amos C. V, 140
Whitacre, Amos C. V, 141
Whitacre, Andrew V, 88
Whitacre, Andrew V, 98
Whitacre, Andrew V, 140
Whitacre, Andrew V, 141
Whitacre, Andrew VI, 607
Whitacre, Andrew VI, 720
Whitacre, Ann IV, 163
Whitacre, Ann IV, 454
Whitacre, Ann IV, 664
Whitacre, Ann V, 138
Whitacre, Ann V, 140
Whitacre, Ann V, 141
Whitacre, Ann V, 541
Whitacre, Ann VI, 564
Whitacre, Ann VI, 578
Whitacre, Ann VI, 658
Whitacre, Ann VI, 719
Whitacre, Anna IV, 430
Whitacre, Anna IV, 454
Whitacre, Anna IV, 854
Whitacre, Anne IV, 854
Whitacre, Annie V, 1025
Whitacre, Aquilla V, 37
Whitacre, Aquilla V, 112
Whitacre, Aquilla V, 117
Whitacre, Aquilla V, 138
Whitacre, Aquilla V, 140
Whitacre, Aquilla V, 141
Whitacre, Aquilla VI, 607
Whitacre, Aquilla VI, 720
Whitacre, Asa V, 141
Whitacre, Asael IV, 664
Whitacre, Asahel IV, 67
Whitacre, Asahel IV, 854
Whitacre, Benjamin VI, 578
Whitacre, Benjamin F. V, 1025
Whitacre, Bethia II, 722
Whitacre, Bethia B. II, 737
Whitacre, Bethia B. II, 774
Whitacre, Bethula V, 873
Whitacre, Bethulah V, 858
Whitacre, Bethuly V, 873
Whitacre, Caleb IV, 22
Whitacre, Caleb IV, 67
Whitacre, Caleb IV, 683
Whitacre, Caleb IV, 786
Whitacre, Caleb IV, 854
Whitacre, Caleb IV, 926
Whitacre, Caleb IV, 1014
Whitacre, Caleb VI, 494
Whitacre, Caleb VI, 578
Whitacre, Caleb VI, 641
Whitacre, Caleb VI, 719
Whitacre, Calvin V, 873
Whitacre, Charles V, 141
Whitacre, Chas. R. IV, 786
Whitacre, Christopher V, 873
Whitacre, Cornelius IV, 854
Whitacre, Cornelius IV, 860
Whitacre, Daniel IV, 854
Whitacre, David IV, 786
Whitacre, David VI, 578
Whitacre, David VI, 719
Whitacre, Dora IV, 854
Whitacre, Dora IV, 1014
Whitacre, Edward IV, 66
Whitacre, Edward IV, 67
Whitacre, Edward IV, 664
Whitacre, Edward IV, 854
Whitacre, Edward V, 140
Whitacre, Edward VI, 719
Whitacre, Edward P. V, 141
Whitacre, Elbridge IV, 854
Whitacre, Eldora IV, 854
Whitacre, Eliza V, 139
Whitacre, Eliza V, 141
Whitacre, Eliza V, 1025
Whitacre, Eliza Ann V, 140
Whitacre, Eliza T. V, 141
Whitacre, Elizabeth II, 1004
Whitacre, Elizabeth II, 1038
Whitacre, Elizabeth IV, 886
Whitacre, Elizabeth Rachel IV, 664
Whitacre, Ella IV, 786
Whitacre, Ella IV, 854
Whitacre, Emily S. V, 140
Whitacre, Emmerson V, 439
Whitacre, Ephraim V, 873
Whitacre, Eva IV, 786
Whitacre, Eva Marie IV, 786
Whitacre, Frank IV, 786
Whitacre, Frank IV, 854
Whitacre, Franklin T. V, 141
Whitacre, George VI, 578
Whitacre, Gulielma IV, 917
Whitacre, H. B. IV, 1014
Whitacre, Hannah II, 991
Whitacre, Hannah II, 1038
Whitacre, Hannah IV, 854
Whitacre, Hannah V, 115
Whitacre, Hannah V, 141
Whitacre, Hannah VI, 519
Whitacre, Hannah VI, 520
Whitacre, Hannah VI, 579
Whitacre, Hannah VI, 661
Whitacre, Hannah VI, 665
Whitacre, Hannah VI, 719
Whitacre, Hannah VI, 720
Whitacre, Hannah P. V, 140
Whitacre, Harlan V, 1025
Whitacre, Harold W. V, 141
Whitacre, Harriet B. V, 141
Whitacre, Harriett V, 140
Whitacre, Heneretta IV, 904
Whitacre, Heneretta IV, 917
Whitacre, Herbert Martin IV, 1014
Whitacre, Horace J. V, 141
Whitacre, Ida V, 141
Whitacre, Isaac IV, 67
Whitacre, Isaac IV, 664
Whitacre, Isaac IV, 854
Whitacre, Isaac VI, 719
Whitacre, Isaac Painter VI, 607
Whitacre, James Cowgle VI, 607
Whitacre, Jane V, 105
Whitacre, Jane V, 117
Whitacre, Jane V, 140
Whitacre, Jane V, 141
Whitacre, Jane V, 310
Whitacre, Jane V, 313
Whitacre, Jane VI, 578
Whitacre, Jane VI, 607
Whitacre, Jane VI, 720
Whitacre, John II, 1038
Whitacre, John IV, 67
Whitacre, John IV, 664
Whitacre, John IV, 854
Whitacre, John IV, 886
Whitacre, John V, 140
Whitacre, John V, 141
Whitacre, John V, 858
Whitacre, John V, 873
Whitacre, John VI, 494
Whitacre, John VI, 519
Whitacre, John VI, 520
Whitacre, John VI, 553
Whitacre, John VI, 578
Whitacre, John VI, 579
Whitacre, John VI, 607
Whitacre, John VI, 641
Whitacre, John VI, 665
Whitacre, John VI, 719
Whitacre, John VI, 720
Whitacre, John, Jr. VI, 578
Whitacre, Jonas V, 141
Whitacre, Jonas VI, 579
Whitacre, Jonas VI, 607
Whitacre, Jonas VI, 720
Whitacre, Jonas. Robert VI, 579
Whitacre, Jonathan IV, 664
Whitacre, Jonathan IV, 886
Whitacre, Jonathan VI, 719
Whitacre, Jonathan Lupton VI, 607
Whitacre, Joseph IV, 664
Whitacre, Joseph IV, 854
Whitacre, Joseph IV, 886
Whitacre, Joseph V, 141
Whitacre, Joseph VI, 578
Whitacre, Joseph VI, 582
Whitacre, Joseph H. V, 719
Whitacre, Joseph R. II, 722
Whitacre, Joshua VI, 564
Whitacre, Joshua VI, 578
Whitacre, Joshua VI, 579
Whitacre, Joshua VI, 719
Whitacre, Jr. Edward IV, 854
Whitacre, Kesiah IV, 67
Whitacre, Kezia IV, 664
Whitacre, Keziah IV, 67
Whitacre, Keziah VI, 719
Whitacre, Levi IV, 886
Whitacre, Levi Samuel IV, 664
Whitacre, Lewis R. II, 737
Whitacre, Lewis R. II, 774
Whitacre, Lidia V, 140
Whitacre, Lindley V, 140
Whitacre, Louis R. II, 722
Whitacre, Loverna V, 141
Whitacre, Lydia IV, 825
Whitacre, Lydia IV, 854
Whitacre, Lydia IV, 917
Whitacre, Lydia V, 37
Whitacre, Lydia V, 141
Whitacre, Lydia S. V, 79
Whitacre, Lydia S. V, 141
Whitacre, Mahlon IV, 20
Whitacre, Mahlon IV, 66
Whitacre, Mahlon IV, 67
Whitacre, Mahlon IV, 664
Whitacre, Mahlon IV, 854
Whitacre, Mahlon VI, 719
Whitacre, Marcy II, 1006
Whitacre, Marcy II, 1038
Whitacre, Margaret V, 27
Whitacre, Margaret V, 140
Whitacre, Margaret V, 141
Whitacre, Maria IV, 51
Whitacre, Maria IV, 67
Whitacre, Maria IV, 163
Whitacre, Maria IV, 302
Whitacre, Maria IV, 926
Whitacre, Maria IV, 1014
Whitacre, Marianna V, 141
Whitacre, Marion V, 141
Whitacre, Martha II, 1014
Whitacre, Martha IV, 66
Whitacre, Martha IV, 67
Whitacre, Martha IV, 664
Whitacre, Martha IV, 826
Whitacre, Martha IV, 854
Whitacre, Martha V, 873
Whitacre, Martha VI, 719
Whitacre, Mary IV, 67
Whitacre, Mary IV, 664
Whitacre, Mary IV, 854
Whitacre, Mary IV, 886
Whitacre, Mary V, 74
Whitacre, Mary V, 88
Whitacre, Mary V, 98
Whitacre, Mary V, 141
Whitacre, Mary V, 873
Whitacre, Mary VI, 719
Whitacre, Mary VI, 722
Whitacre, Mary Ann II, 722
Whitacre, Mary Ethel V, 141
Whitacre, Mary Jane V, 95
Whitacre, Mary Jane V, 98
Whitacre, Mary Jane V, 140
Whitacre, Mary Jane V, 141
Whitacre, Mary P. V, 141
Whitacre, Mary Potts V, 140
Whitacre, Mary W. II, 722
Whitacre, Mary W. II, 737
Whitacre, Mary W. II, 774
Whitacre, Mattie II, 722
Whitacre, Maud IV, 854
Whitacre, Maurice V, 140
Whitacre, Maurice V, 141
Whitacre, Moses V, 140
Whitacre, Moses V, 141
Whitacre, Moses VI, 607
Whitacre, Moses VI, 720
Whitacre, Moses M. IV, 447
Whitacre, Moses M. IV, 454
Whitacre, Moses M. V, 131
Whitacre, Moses M. V, 140
Whitacre, Moses M. V, 141
Whitacre, Myra IV, 854
Whitacre, N. Reece II, 722
Whitacre, N. Reece II, 737
Whitacre, Nancy V, 141
Whitacre, Nancy V, 1025
Whitacre, Nannie V, 439
Whitacre, Naomi II, 1038
Whitacre, Naomi IV, 67
Whitacre, Naomi VI, 494
Whitacre, Naomi VI, 519
Whitacre, Naomi VI, 520
Whitacre, Naomi VI, 553
Whitacre, Naomi VI, 578
Whitacre, Naomi VI, 579
Whitacre, Naomi VI, 607
Whitacre, Naomi VI, 641
Whitacre, Naomi VI, 644
Whitacre, Naomi VI, 665
Whitacre, Naomi VI, 719
Whitacre, Patience IV, 454
Whitacre, Patience V, 33
Whitacre, Patience V, 74
Whitacre, Patience V, 105
Whitacre, Patience V, 140
Whitacre, Patience V, 141
Whitacre, Patience VI, 579
Whitacre, Patience VI, 600
Whitacre, Patience VI, 607
Whitacre, Patience VI, 720
Whitacre, Phebe IV, 20
Whitacre, Phebe IV, 67
Whitacre, Phebe IV, 664
Whitacre, Phebe IV, 810
Whitacre, Phebe IV, 854
Whitacre, Phebe IV, 917
Whitacre, Phebe VI, 494
Whitacre, Phebe VI, 578
Whitacre, Phebe VI, 641
Whitacre, Phebe VI, 719
Whitacre, Precilla IV, 447
Whitacre, Precilla IV, 454
Whitacre, Priscilla IV, 454
Whitacre, Priscilla V, 33
Whitacre, Priscilla V, 131
Whitacre, Priscilla V, 140
Whitacre, Priscilla V, 141
Whitacre, Priscilla VI, 607
Whitacre, Priscilla VI, 720
Whitacre, Rachel IV, 854
Whitacre, Rachel IV, 886
Whitacre, Rachel IV, 1014
Whitacre, Rachel V, 125
Whitacre, Rachel V, 141
Whitacre, Rachel V, 873
Whitacre, Rachel VI, 719
Whitacre, Rachel VI, 722
Whitacre, Ralph IV, 786
Whitacre, Ralph C. IV, 786
Whitacre, Ray IV, 854
Whitacre, Rebecca II, 1001
Whitacre, Rebecca II, 1038
Whitacre, Rebecca IV, 22
Whitacre, Rebecca IV, 67
Whitacre, Rebecca IV, 664
Whitacre, Rebecca IV, 786
Whitacre, Rebecca IV, 886
Whitacre, Rebecca IV, 926
Whitacre, Rebecca V, 37
Whitacre, Rebecca V, 94
Whitacre, Rebecca V, 140
Whitacre, Rebecca V, 141
Whitacre, Rebecca VI, 578
Whitacre, Rebecca VI, 719
Whitacre, Rebecca Potts V, 140
Whitacre, Reece II, 774
Whitacre, Reva C. V, 210
Whitacre, Rhoda V, 74
Whitacre, Rhoda V, 140
Whitacre, Rhoda V, 141
Whitacre, Rhoda VI, 607
Whitacre, Rhoda VI, 720
Whitacre, Rhoda N. V, 140
Whitacre, Richard VI, 720
Whitacre, Robert II, 1006
Whitacre, Robert II, 1038
Whitacre, Robert IV, 454
Whitacre, Robert V, 33
Whitacre, Robert V, 74
Whitacre, Robert V, 105
Whitacre, Robert V, 140

acre, Robert V, 141
acre, Robert V, 469
acre, Robert VI, 519
acre, Robert VI, 520
acre, Robert VI, 553
acre, Robert VI, 578
acre, Robert VI, 579
acre, Robert VI, 600
acre, Robert VI, 607
acre, Robert VI, 661
acre, Robert VI, 665
acre, Robert VI, 719
acre, Robert VI, 720
acre, Robert Miller VI, 607
acre, Rossana V, 141
acre, Ruth Ann V, 141
acre, Ruth Anna V, 141
acre, Ruthann V, 117
acre, Ruthann V, 138
acre, Ruthanna V, 37
acre, Ruthanna V, 74
acre, Ruthanna V, 112
acre, Ruthanna V, 140
acre, Ruthanna V, 141
acre, Samuel IV, 664
acre, Samuel IV, 886
acre, Samuel V, 873
acre, Samuel B. V, 1025
acre, Samuel Kelly V, 140
acre, Samuel Kelly V, 141
acre, Sara B. V, 141
acre, Sarah IV, 917
acre, Sarah V, 141
acre, Sarah VI, 553
acre, Sarah VI, 578
acre, Sarah VI, 579
acre, Sarah VI, 649
acre, Sarah VI, 719
acre, Sarah VI, 720
acre, Sarah B. V, 140
acre, Sarah B. V, 887
acre, Sarah C. V, 140
acre, Sarah C. V, 141
acre, Sarah E. II, 722
acre, Sarah G. IV, 786
acre, Sidney V, 141
acre, Sidney T. V, 140
acre, Susanna IV, 854
acre, Susanna V, 873
acre, Susannah IV, 854
acre, Thomas IV, 67
acre, Thomas IV, 786
acre, Thomas IV, 854
acre, Thomas VI, 719
acre, Thornton IV, 786
acre, Thornton VI, 578
acre, Thorton VI, 719
acre, W. L. V, 210
acre, Walter H. V, 141
acre, Walter L. V, 141
acre, William IV, 664
acre, William IV, 886
acre, William V, 141
acre, William B. V, 141
acre, William T. V, 140
acre, William T. V, 141
acre, Wm. S. II, 722
aker, Asa V, 141
aker, Charles V, 141
aker, Daniel VI, 864
aker, Edward IV, 67
aker, Frances VI, 864
aker, Frances F. III, 348
aker, Ida V, 141
aker, Isaac IV, 67
aker, James VI, 840
aker, James VI, 841
aker, John IV, 67
aker, John V, 141
aker, Kesiah IV, 67
aker, Louise III, 18
aker, Mahlon IV, 67
aker, Martha IV, 67
aker, Martha VI, 864
aker, Mary VI, 352
aker, Mary VI, 356
aker, Mary Ethel V, 141
aker, Mary J. V, 210
aker, Mary V. VI, 839
aker, Nancy VI, 840
aker, Nancy W. VI, 864
aker, Rachel V, 597
aker, Rachel V, 605
aker, Rachel VI, 841
aker, Reva V, 210
aker, Reva C. V, 210
aker, Rossana V, 141
aker, Samuel VI, 356
aker, Samuel VI, 839
aker, Sarah IV, 917
aker, Sarah V, 141
Whitaker, Sarah E. I, 1134
Whitaker, Thomas IV, 67
Whitaker, Thomas A. III, 18
Whitaker, Thomas A. III, 348
Whitaker, Thos. III, 348
Whitaker, W. L. V, 210
Whitaker, William VI, 864
Whitakre, Ella IV, 786
Whitall, Abraham II, 110
Whitall, Alice III, 348
Whitall, Alice B. III, 348
Whitall, Alice E. III, 123
Whitall, Alice E. III, 348
Whitall, Anna II, 718
Whitall, Anna II, 774
Whitall, Anna M. III, 123
Whitall, Anna M. III, 348
Whitall, Anna Maria II, 774
Whitall, Anna Maria II, 777
Whitall, Caroline III, 199
Whitall, Caroline III, 348
Whitall, Charles D. III, 348
Whitall, Dr. Samuel III, 348
Whitall, Israel III, 123
Whitall, Israel III, 348
Whitall, Israel F. III, 348
Whitall, James II, 435
Whitall, James II, 570
Whitall, James II, 684
Whitall, Job I, 1098
Whitall, Job I, 1099
Whitall, John II, 396
Whitall, John II, 435
Whitall, John M. II, 757
Whitall, John M. II, 770
Whitall, Joseph II, 684
Whitall, Joseph, Jr. II, 774
Whitall, Lydia II, 435
Whitall, Lydia II, 570
Whitall, Lydia II, 684
Whitall, Mary II, 435
Whitall, Mary Clark II, 757
Whitall, Mary Clark II, 770
Whitall, Rebecca II, 570
Whitall, Rebecca II, 684
Whitall, Richard II, 774
Whitall, Susan B. II, 774
Whitall, Tatthu II, 570
Whitall, Tatthu II, 684
Whitall, Wm. C. II, 684
Whitall, Zatthu II, 684
Whitam, Mary IV, 133
Whitam, Mary IV, 134
Whitby, Nancy V, 289
Whitby, William V, 289
Whitcare, John VI, 530
Whitcare, Naomi VI, 530
Whitcare, Robert VI, 530
Whitcher, H. B. IV, 1014
Whitcher, Herbert Martin IV, 1014
Whitcraft, Daisy V, 1025
Whitcraft, Dora V, 1025
Whitcraft, Jane IV, 400
Whitcraft, Nancy IV, 400
White, ??? I, 22
White, ??? III, 263
White, ??? III, 348
White, ??? III, 349
White, ??? III, 386
White, ??? III, 388
White, ??? IV, 1014
White, ??? IV, 1386
White, ??? VI, 455
White, ??? VI, 520
White, ??? VI, 661
White, Aaron I, 49
White, Aaron I, 79
White, Aaron I, 80
White, Aaron I, 87
White, Aaron I, 123
White, Aaron I, 173
White, Aaron I, 175
White, Aaron II, 1037
White, Aaron III, 348
White, Aaron IV, 164
White, Aaron IV, 357
White, Aaron IV, 454
White, Aaron IV, 599
White, Aaron V, 141
White, Aaron VI, 720
White, Abagail I, 844
White, Abel III, 134
White, Abel III, 350
White, Abi II, 972
White, Abi II, 981
White, Abi II, 1037
White, Abigail I, 35
White, Abigail I, 78
White, Abigail I, 79
White, Abigail I, 82
White, Abigail I, 87
White, Abigail I, 123
White, Abigail I, 163
White, Abigail I, 164
White, Abigail I, 174
White, Abigail I, 175
White, Abigail I, 794
White, Abigail I, 814
White, Abigail I, 844
White, Abigail I, 890
White, Abigail I, 905
White, Abigail II, 46
White, Abigail II, 482
White, Abigail II, 684
White, Abigail VI, 383
White, Abigail VI, 456
White, Abigail B. I, 604
White, Abigail W. II, 880
White, Abigail W. II, 938
White, Abner VI, 455
White, Abraham I, 124
White, Abraham I, 144
White, Abraham I, 172
White, Abraham I, 173
White, Abraham I, 174
White, Abraham I, 196
White, Abraham I, 202
White, Absalom G. B. I, 20
White, Absalom G. B. I, 83
White, Absila I, 260
White, Absilla I, 244
White, Absilla I, 298
White, Absoley I, 244
White, Achsah I, 23
White, Achsah I, 65
White, Achsah I, 81
White, Ada Jackson I, 22
White, Adam VI, 864
White, Addison Thomas I, 604
White, Adelaide E. I, 951
White, Adelaide Everett I, 22
White, Adeline I, 23
White, Adeline IV, 664
White, Adeline VI, 978
White, Adrian A. IV, 664
White, Adrian C. IV, 664
White, Agatha I, 520
White, Agnes I, 581
White, Agnes IV, 964
White, Agnes Heston IV, 1015
White, Aileen I, 928
White, Albert I, 123
White, Albert I, 175
White, Albert I, 604
White, Alberta III, 465
White, Albertson I, 81
White, Alethia I, 20
White, Alfred I, 82
White, Alfred I, 123
White, Alfred I, 163
White, Alfred I, 175
White, Alfred I, 176
White, Alfred I, 440
White, Alfred I, 454
White, Alfred R. VI, 80
White, Alfred R. VI, 89
White, Alfred R. VI, 90
White, Alice I, 25
White, Alice I, 84
White, Alice I, 520
White, Alice I, 547
White, Alice I, 581
White, Alice I, 613
White, Alice I, 905
White, Alice I, 930
White, Alice I, 951
White, Alice III, 137
White, Alice III, 349
White, Alice IV, 1227
White, Alice B. III, 348
White, Alice Browning I, 947
White, Alice Browning III, 245
White, Alice E. I, 23
White, Alice E. W. I, 930
White, Alice Eva I, 19
White, Alice Everett I, 25
White, Alice Everett I, 85
White, Alice Everett I, 936
White, Alice Everett I, 946
White, Alice Everett I, 951
White, Alice L. I, 24
White, Alice L. N. I, 936
White, Alice Lanton I, 14
White, Alice Lauton I, 64
White, Alice Lauton I, 84
White, Alice Mary V, 940
White, Alice N. I, 84
White, Alice N. I, 85
White, Alice N. I, 931
White, Alice N. I, 951
White, Alice Nicholson I, 951
White, Alice P. I, 936
White, Alice Paige I, 951
White, Alice W. I, 85
White, Alla E. J. I, 670
White, Allen III, 348
White, Allen Jay I, 21
White, Allice I, 441
White, Allie E. VI, 89
White, Allison Osmond I, 26
White, Alpheus I, 20
White, Alpheus I, 82
White, Alpheus W. I, 387
White, Alpheus W. I, 428
White, Alvah I, 951
White, Alza Gertrude I, 85
White, Amanda Catharine I, 440
White, Amanda Catharine I, 454
White, Ambros I, 202
White, Ambrose I, 175
White, Ambrose M. I, 844
White, Amelia I, 21
White, Amelia Amelda I, 83
White, Amos II, 271
White, Amos III, 36
White, Amos III, 303
White, Amos III, 348
White, Amos III, 349
White, Amos O. VI, 740
White, Amos O. VI, 790
White, Amy I, 370
White, Amy I, 428
White, Amy I, 440
White, Amy I, 454
White, Amy IV, 357
White, Amy V, 456
White, Amy C. I, 422
White, Amy C. I, 428
White, Amy C. I, 440
White, Amy C. I, 691
White, Amy T. VI, 864
White, Anabel I, 23
White, Anabella IV, 164
White, Analiza S. IV, 357
White, Anderson I, 25
White, Anderson I, 30
White, Anderson I, 175
White, Anderson VI, 864
White, Anderson M. I, 83
White, Andrew I, 23
White, Andrew Dickson II, 895
White, Andrew Dickson II, 939
White, Ann I, 20
White, Ann I, 23
White, Ann I, 63
White, Ann I, 80
White, Ann I, 81
White, Ann I, 102
White, Ann I, 123
White, Ann I, 124
White, Ann I, 147
White, Ann I, 161
White, Ann I, 163
White, Ann I, 172
White, Ann I, 173
White, Ann I, 174
White, Ann I, 175
White, Ann I, 201
White, Ann I, 228
White, Ann I, 240
White, Ann I, 260
White, Ann I, 427
White, Ann I, 428
White, Ann I, 520
White, Ann I, 604
White, Ann I, 608
White, Ann I, 905
White, Ann I, 1134
White, Ann II, 120
White, Ann II, 125
White, Ann II, 187
White, Ann II, 435
White, Ann II, 972
White, Ann III, 36
White, Ann III, 222
White, Ann III, 303
White, Ann III, 348
White, Ann III, 349
White, Ann IV, 67
White, Ann IV, 76
White, Ann IV, 114
White, Ann IV, 163
White, Ann IV, 295
White, Ann IV, 302
White, Ann IV, 355
White, Ann IV, 398
White, Ann IV, 454
White, Ann IV, 503
White, Ann IV, 786
White, Ann VI, 89
White, Ann VI, 105
White, Ann VI, 124
White, Ann VI, 143
White, Ann VI, 376
White, Ann VI, 455
White, Ann VI, 517
White, Ann VI, 579
White, Ann VI, 703
White, Ann VI, 720
White, Ann E. I, 225
White, Ann Elesabeth I, 84
White, Ann Elisabeth I, 24
White, Ann Elisabeth I, 68
White, Ann Eliza IV, 342
White, Ann Eliza IV, 357
White, Ann Elizabeth Peele I, 951
White, Ann Elizabeth W. I, 932
White, Ann Gertrude I, 84
White, Ann L. VI, 1004
White, Ann M. I, 22
White, Ann M. I, 83
White, Ann Missouri I, 24
White, Ann V. VI, 940
White, Anna I, 23
White, Anna I, 25
White, Anna I, 71
White, Anna I, 81
White, Anna I, 84
White, Anna I, 123
White, Anna I, 124
White, Anna I, 187
White, Anna I, 604
White, Anna I, 905
White, Anna II, 435
White, Anna III, 349
White, Anna III, 350
White, Anna IV, 164
White, Anna IV, 369
White, Anna IV, 454
White, Anna IV, 503
White, Anna V, 916
White, Anna VI, 720
White, Anna C. III, 465
White, Anna D. III, 263
White, Anna D. III, 348
White, Anna Deborah II, 827
White, Anna Deborah II, 939
White, Anna E. II, 835
White, Anna E. II, 939
White, Anna J. III, 348
White, Anna M. I, 712
White, Anna M. I, 736
White, Anna M. I, 757
White, Anna M. I, 771
White, Anna Maria II, 435
White, Anna Maria II, 774
White, Anna Maria II, 801
White, Anna Maria II, 938
White, Anna Mary I, 24
White, Anna N. I, 23
White, Anna N. I, 82
White, Anna N. I, 88
White, Anna Nicholson I, 32
White, Anna Perisho I, 21
White, Anna T. II, 1083
White, Anna T. V, 126
White, Anna T. V, 141
White, Anne I, 36
White, Anne I, 78
White, Anne I, 172
White, Anne IV, 164
White, Anne IV, 357
White, Anne VI, 1013
White, Anne Gertrude I, 17
White, Anne Gertrude I, 24
White, Anne Gertrude I, 25
White, Annie I, 20
White, Annie I, 951
White, Annie II, 909
White, Annie II, 939
White, Annie III, 465
White, Annie E. V, 605
White, Annie Lee I, 611
White, Annie Lee I, 935
White, Annie Lucile VI, 740
White, Annie Lucile VI, 790
White, Archie Bell I, 19
White, Archie Bell I, 21
White, Archie Bell I, 29
White, Armager I, 260
White, Armaiger I, 298
White, Armecia I, 844
White, Armiger I, 228
White, Armiger I, 244
White, Armiger I, 260
White, Arnold I, 123
White, Arnold I, 124
White, Arnold, Jr. I, 123
White, Arnold, Jr. I, 172
White, Arnold, Sr. I, 123
White, Arnould I, 91
White, Arnould I, 92

White, Arnould I, 123
White, Arnould I, 156
White, Arnould I, 161
White, Arnould I, 172
White, Arnould I, 176
White, Arthur I, 23
White, Arthur I, 24
White, Arthur IV, 303
White, Arthur V, 365
White, Arthur B. IV, 303
White, Arthur O. I, 19
White, Arthur R. IV, 1227
White, Asenath I, 520
White, Asenath I, 581
White, Asenath I, 608
White, Asenath IV, 164
White, Asenath IV, 855
White, Asenath Arabella IV, 164
White, Asenath B. I, 604
White, Asenath C. I, 661
White, Asenath C. I, 670
White, Asenath C. I, 684
White, Asenath O. I, 691
White, Asenith I, 581
White, Asenith IV, 786
White, Asenith IV, 855
White, Asenith Arabella IV, 786
White, Ashley V, 541
White, Augustus I, 124
White, Augustus E. I, 82
White, Augustus E. I, 134
White, Augustus E. I, 176
White, Augustus Edwin I, 24
White, Banff III, 465
White, Barbara III, 465
White, Barbara J. III, 465
White, Barbara Jane III, 465
White, Barbary Ellen I, 33
White, Barclay II, 435
White, Barclay II, 774
White, Barclay II, 827
White, Barclay II, 869
White, Barclay II, 934
White, Barclay II, 938
White, Barclay, Jr. II, 939
White, Beale III, 349
White, Beck VI, 124
White, Belinda IV, 303
White, Benj. I, 521
White, Benj. IV, 1192
White, Benja. I, 80
White, Benjamin I, 19
White, Benjamin I, 22
White, Benjamin I, 25
White, Benjamin I, 53
White, Benjamin I, 78
White, Benjamin I, 79
White, Benjamin I, 80
White, Benjamin I, 81
White, Benjamin I, 117
White, Benjamin I, 123
White, Benjamin I, 124
White, Benjamin I, 125
White, Benjamin I, 138
White, Benjamin I, 142
White, Benjamin I, 161
White, Benjamin I, 173
White, Benjamin I, 174
White, Benjamin I, 175
White, Benjamin I, 201
White, Benjamin I, 520
White, Benjamin I, 581
White, Benjamin I, 844
White, Benjamin II, 271
White, Benjamin II, 276
White, Benjamin II, 807
White, Benjamin II, 972
White, Benjamin II, 1037
White, Benjamin IV, 357
White, Benjamin IV, 854
White, Benjamin IV, 1192
White, Benjamin V, 324
White, Benjamin V, 365
White, Benjamin V, 439
White, Benjamin VI, 124
White, Benjamin VI, 143
White, Benjamin VI, 911
White, Benjamin A. I, 83
White, Benjamin Alonzo I, 25
White, Benjamin F. III, 348
White, Benjamin F. III, 349
White, Benjamin Galette I, 84
White, Benjamin H. I, 22
White, Benjamin P. I, 125
White, Benjamin, Jr. I, 79
White, Benjamin, Jr. I, 173
White, Benjamin, Jr. I, 174
White, Bennoni I, 174
White, Benoni I, 123
White, Benoni I, 174
White, Berkley VI, 456
White, Bert Thomas I, 642
White, Bertha Maie I, 20
White, Bessie I, 630
White, Bessie VI, 664
White, Bessie Lee I, 22
White, Bessie Lee I, 28
White, Bethuel I, 520
White, Betsey I, 81
White, Betsy I, 80
White, Betsy I, 82
White, Betsy I, 163
White, Betsy I, 228
White, Betsy I, 319
White, Betsy I, 604
White, Betsy Ann I, 81
White, Betty I, 72
White, Betty I, 80
White, Betty I, 174
White, Betty I, 201
White, Betty I, 905
White, Beulah II, 110
White, Beulah II, 684
White, Beulah May I, 22
White, Beulah S. II, 869
White, Beulah S. II, 938
White, Blanche Roundtree I, 19
White, Blanche Roundtree I, 29
White, Borden I, 520
White, Borden I, 548
White, Borden I, 581
White, Borden C. I, 604
White, Bordon I, 521
White, Briton III, 349
White, Brittain II, 827
White, Brittain III, 349
White, Britton III, 348
White, Britton, Jr. III, 348
White, Burt Thomas I, 642
White, Caleb I, 19
White, Caleb I, 20
White, Caleb I, 25
White, Caleb I, 76
White, Caleb I, 78
White, Caleb I, 79
White, Caleb I, 80
White, Caleb I, 84
White, Caleb I, 114
White, Caleb I, 123
White, Caleb I, 125
White, Caleb I, 173
White, Caleb I, 174
White, Caleb I, 175
White, Caleb I, 176
White, Caleb I, 187
White, Caleb I, 201
White, Caleb I, 202
White, Caleb I, 203
White, Caleb I, 520
White, Caleb I, 581
White, Caleb I, 905
White, Caleb Toms I, 25
White, Carlton I, 19
White, Carlton Francis I, 935
White, Carlton Francis I, 951
White, Caroline I, 450
White, Caroline I, 454
White, Caroline VI, 1013
White, Caroline H. I, 84
White, Catharine I, 22
White, Catharine I, 24
White, Catharine I, 82
White, Catharine I, 123
White, Catharine I, 228
White, Catharine I, 254
White, Catharine I, 260
White, Catharine I, 275
White, Catharine I, 277
White, Catharine I, 367
White, Catharine I, 404
White, Catharine I, 428
White, Catharine I, 440
White, Catharine I, 520
White, Catharine I, 558
White, Catharine I, 581
White, Catharine I, 691
White, Catharine II, 684
White, Catharine III, 221
White, Catharine IV, 454
White, Catharine IV, 458
White, Catharine IV, 599
White, Catharine VI, 864
White, Catharine VI, 929
White, Catharine VI, 962
White, Catharine C. I, 628
White, Catharine C. I, 642
White, Catharine E. VI, 966
White, Catharine E. VI, 1013
White, Catharine J. III, 386
White, Catharine Ricks I, 21
White, Catharine S. VI, 1014
White, Catherine I, 29
White, Catherine I, 58
White, Catherine I, 260
White, Catherine II, 435
White, Catherine J. III, 389
White, Celia A. IV, 490
White, Celine VI, 930
White, Chalkey I, 81
White, Chalkley IV, 1385
White, Charity I, 428
White, Charles I, 14
White, Charles I, 19
White, Charles I, 21
White, Charles I, 22
White, Charles I, 23
White, Charles I, 79
White, Charles I, 80
White, Charles I, 82
White, Charles I, 83
White, Charles I, 84
White, Charles I, 123
White, Charles I, 138
White, Charles I, 173
White, Charles I, 174
White, Charles I, 176
White, Charles I, 187
White, Charles I, 202
White, Charles I, 225
White, Charles II, 435
White, Charles B. III, 349
White, Charles C. I, 604
White, Charles E. III, 349
White, Charles F. I, 15
White, Charles F. I, 19
White, Charles F. I, 67
White, Charles F. I, 84
White, Charles F. I, 85
White, Charles F. I, 932
White, Charles Francis I, 24
White, Charles H. I, 32
White, Charles H. I, 41
White, Charles H. I, 59
White, Charles H. I, 83
White, Charles H. I, 84
White, Charles H. I, 85
White, Charles H. VI, 51
White, Charles Henry I, 19
White, Charles Henry I, 83
White, Charles Henry I, 89
White, Charles Nicholson I, 25
White, Charles Nicholson I, 85
White, Charles Nicholson I, 936
White, Charles Raymond I, 19
White, Charles Raymond I, 85
White, Charles Raymond I, 935
White, Charles Raymond I, 951
White, Charles T. I, 951
White, Charles T. II, 140
White, Charles Thomas I, 19
White, Charles W. I, 951
White, Charlot I, 201
White, Charlotte I, 21
White, Charlotte I, 138
White, Charlotte I, 175
White, Charlotte I, 197
White, Charlotte I, 623
White, Charlotte I, 931
White, Charlotte VI, 1013
White, Charlotte C. I, 228
White, Charlotte C. I, 260
White, Charlotte McA. I, 15
White, Charlotte McAdams I, 22
White, Charlotte McAdams I, 67
White, Charlotte McAdams I, 83
White, Chas. E. III, 137
White, Chas. Farnum III, 349
White, Chas. N. I, 951
White, Christiana VI, 675
White, Christiana VI, 720
White, Christopher II, 17
White, Christopher II, 45
White, Christopher II, 435
White, Christopher II, 547
White, Christopher II, 659
White, Christopher II, 684
White, Clara II, 895
White, Clara II, 939
White, Clara Mable I, 20
White, Clara Pauline I, 23
White, Clarence C. II, 939
White, Clarence O. I, 20
White, Clarence Osmond I, 19
White, Clarence Osmond I, 20
White, Clarence Osmond I, 22
White, Clarence Osmond I, 29
White, Clarinda I, 20
White, Clarinda II, 684
White, Clarkson I, 25
White, Clarsanda I, 82
White, Clifford Burr III, 258
White, Clifford Burr III, 349
White, Clifford Burr III, 494
White, Clifford Burr III, 503
White, Clothilda VI, 124
White, Colvin III, 350
White, Content I, 124
White, Cora I, 935
White, Cora I, 937
White, Cora I, 951
White, Cora E. I, 21
White, Cora E. I, 84
White, Cora E. I, 85
White, Cora E. I, 947
White, Cora E. I, 951
White, Cora Ella I, 24
White, Cornelia III, 100
White, Cornelia III, 223
White, Cornelia III, 349
White, Cornelius I, 19
White, Cornelius I, 81
White, Cornelius Francis I, 25
White, Crawford E. VI, 929
White, Crawford E. VI, 941
White, Crawford E. VI, 1013
White, Cynthia Burr III, 349
White, Cyrus IV, 1014
White, Cyrus IV, 1015
White, Daida I, 1134
White, Damaris I, 61
White, Damaris I, 78
White, Damaris I, 124
White, Damaris I, 166
White, Damaris I, 172
White, Daniel I, 80
White, Daniel I, 125
White, Daniel II, 110
White, Daniel II, 435
White, Daniel II, 972
White, Daniel II, 1037
White, Daniel VI, 1013
White, Daniel S. II, 938
White, Daniel S., Jr. II, 869
White, Daniel S., Jr. II, 938
White, Daniel Smith II, 684
White, Daniel Smith II, 774
White, Dave III, 465
White, Dave, Jr. III, 465
White, David I, 8
White, David I, 18
White, David I, 20
White, David I, 21
White, David I, 23
White, David I, 24
White, David I, 80
White, David I, 81
White, David I, 82
White, David I, 83
White, David I, 84
White, David I, 87
White, David I, 123
White, David I, 176
White, David I, 177
White, David I, 260
White, David I, 581
White, David I, 628
White, David I, 642
White, David IV, 357
White, David F. I, 228
White, David F. I, 260
White, David Francis I, 23
White, David Francis I, 83
White, David G. IV, 164
White, David G. IV, 855
White, David Goucher IV, 163
White, David J. I, 628
White, David J. I, 642
White, David Jordan I, 23
White, David Ralph I, 931
White, David Underhill III, 349
White, David, Jr. I, 82
White, David, Jr. I, 83
White, David, Jr. I, 176
White, Davis I, 81
White, Davis I, 626
White, Davis Bassett II, 110
White, Davis Bassett II, 684
White, Deborah I, 159
White, Deborah I, 173
White, Deborah I, 174
White, Deborah I, 367
White, Deborah I, 388
White, Deborah I, 428
White, Deborah II, 972
White, Deborah II, 1037
White, Deborah VI, 412
White, Deborah VI, 455
White, Deborah VI, 456
White, Deborah Bertha I, 19
White, Deborah Bertha I, 35
White, Deborah Bertha I, 84
White, Deborah Bertha VI, 51
White, Deborah Bertha VI, 89
White, Deborah Peele I, 21
White, Deborah, Jr. VI, 456
White, Debrah I, 173
White, Dedida I, 905
White, Deida I, 888
White, Deida I, 905
White, Delphina I, 22
White, Delphina I, 23
White, Delphina I, 83
White, Dempsey I, 19
White, Dempsey I, 44
White, Dempsey I, 83
White, Dempsey C. I, 25
White, Dempsey E. I, 83
White, Dempsey H. I, 20
White, Dempsey H. I, 22
White, Dempsey H. I, 84
White, Demsey I, 20
White, Demsey I, 72
White, Demsey I, 80
White, Demsey I, 176
White, Demsey Henley I, 25
White, Dinah Ann IV, 691
White, Dinah Ann IV, 786
White, Diza VI, 104
White, Docton I, 80
White, Doctrine I, 20
White, Doctron I, 202
White, Dora I, 928
White, Dora I, 929
White, Dora Elisabeth I, 19
White, Dora W. I, 10
White, Dorcas V, 456
White, Dorothea IV, 1385
White, Dorothy I, 22
White, Dorothy I, 76
White, Dorothy I, 78
White, Dorothy Atlessa I, 25
White, Dorothy Holmes VI,
White, Dorothy Holmes VI,
White, Dosha VI, 966
White, Drine Linwood I, 19
White, Drine??? Linwood I, 1
White, Easter II, 77
White, Easter II, 110
White, Edith I, 23
White, Edith IV, 454
White, Edith IV, 1385
White, Edith R. IV, 331
White, Edith R. IV, 357
White, Editha L. VI, 915
White, Edm T. VI, 579
White, Edmon I, 123
White, Edmond I, 175
White, Edmund I, 79
White, Edmund I, 87
White, Edmund I, 123
White, Edmund I, 124
White, Edmund I, 149
White, Edmund I, 173
White, Edmund I, 175
White, Edmund I, 176
White, Edmund I, 187
White, Edmund I, 198
White, Edmund I, 202
White, Edmund III, 349
White, Edmund Alden III, 34
White, Edmund P. VI, 863
White, Edna III, 349
White, Edna III, 369
White, Edna V, 541
White, Edney VI, 977
White, Edw VI, 579
White, Edward I, 82
White, Edward I, 176
White, Edward I, 201
White, Edward II, 125
White, Edward III, 85
White, Edward III, 349
White, Edward IV, 1015
White, Edward IV, 1226
White, Edward VI, 455
White, Edward B. I, 176
White, Edward F. VI, 89
White, Edward H. III, 349
White, Edward N. III, 349
White, Edward Nelson, Jr. III, 349
White, Edward Y. IV, 1192
White, Edward, Jr. I, 173
White, Edwin Saunders I, 21
White, Effie IV, 684
White, Effie IV, 787
White, Elbert Scott I, 20
White, Eleanor I, 440
White, Eleanor G. VI, 1013
White, Elen Mildred I, 936
White, Elener I, 448
White, Elener Jones I, 454
White, Elenor I, 431
White, Elenor I, 440
White, Elezabeath I, 137

te, Elezabeath I, 172
te, Elgar Toms V, 289
te, Eli I, 79
te, Eli I, 147
te, Eli I, 173
te, Eli I, 175
te, Eli I, 520
te, Eli I, 970
te, Elias I, 14
te, Elias I, 81
te, Elias I, 124
te, Elias I, 160
te, Elias A. I, 202
ite, Elias G. IV, 1192
ite, Elias G. IV, 1227
ite, Elihu I, 604
ite, Elihu II, 435
ite, Elihu A. I, 20
ite, Elihu A. I, 83
ite, Elihu A. I, 84
ite, Elihu Anthony I, 20
ite, Elihu M. I, 20
ite, Elijah I, 19
ite, Elijah I, 604
ite, Elinder I, 367
ite, Elis I, 581
ite, Elisabeth I, 14
ite, Elisabeth I, 20
ite, Elisabeth I, 21
ite, Elisabeth I, 22
ite, Elisabeth I, 23
ite, Elisabeth I, 24
ite, Elisabeth I, 25
ite, Elisabeth I, 29
ite, Elisabeth I, 34
ite, Elisabeth I, 51
ite, Elisabeth I, 56
ite, Elisabeth I, 62
ite, Elisabeth I, 69
ite, Elisabeth I, 70
ite, Elisabeth I, 71
ite, Elisabeth I, 76
ite, Elisabeth I, 78
ite, Elisabeth I, 79
ite, Elisabeth I, 80
ite, Elisabeth I, 81
ite, Elisabeth I, 82
ite, Elisabeth I, 85
ite, Elisabeth I, 86
ite, Elisabeth I, 124
ite, Elisabeth I, 137
ite, Elisabeth I, 139
ite, Elisabeth I, 142
ite, Elisabeth I, 159
ite, Elisabeth I, 167
ite, Elisabeth I, 168
ite, Elisabeth I, 169
hite, Elisabeth I, 172
hite, Elisabeth I, 173
hite, Elisabeth I, 174
hite, Elisabeth I, 175
hite, Elisabeth I, 176
hite, Elisabeth I, 177
hite, Elisabeth I, 201
hite, Elisabeth I, 202
hite, Elisabeth I, 260
hite, Elisabeth I, 520
hite, Elisabeth I, 615
hite, Elisabeth A. I, 64
hite, Elisabeth A. I, 84
hite, Elisabeth A. I, 85
hite, Elisabeth Ann I, 22
hite, Elisabeth Ann I, 82
hite, Elisabeth C. I, 83
hite, Elisabeth C. I, 88
hite, Elisabeth Catherine I, 21
hite, Elisabeth E. I, 20
hite, Elisabeth E. I, 24
hite, Elisabeth E. I, 27
hite, Elisabeth E. I, 84
hite, Elisabeth E. I, 85
hite, Elisabeth J. I, 21
hite, Elisabeth J. I, 24
hite, Elisabeth J. I, 28
hite, Elisabeth J. I, 84
hite, Elisabeth M. M. I, 21
hite, Elisabeth M. M. I, 84
hite, Elisabeth Parker I, 124
hite, Elisabeth R. I, 23
hite, Elisabeth W. I, 23
hite, Elisabeth W. I, 83
hite, Elisha I, 80
hite, Elisha I, 174
hite, Elisha I, 201
hite, Elisha I, 604
hite, Elisha I, 608
hite, Elisha Burke I, 20
hite, Eliz. III, 134
hite, Eliz. III, 219
hite, Eliz. III, 316
hite, Eliza I, 24
White, Eliza I, 81
White, Eliza I, 520
White, Eliza I, 604
White, Eliza IV, 163
White, Eliza IV, 164
White, Eliza IV, 454
White, Eliza IV, 1014
White, Eliza IV, 1015
White, Eliza IV, 1343
White, Eliza Ann I, 82
White, Eliza Ann IV, 855
White, Eliza Ann IV, 1202
White, Eliza Deans I, 20
White, Eliza E. I, 81
White, Eliza Elliott I, 54
White, Eliza Elliott I, 81
White, Eliza F. VI, 940
White, Eliza Jane I, 22
White, Eliza Jane I, 24
White, Eliza Jane I, 82
White, Eliza Jane IV, 947
White, Eliza R. VI, 92
White, Elizabeth I, 1
White, Elizabeth I, 8
White, Elizabeth I, 20
White, Elizabeth I, 81
White, Elizabeth I, 82
White, Elizabeth I, 99
White, Elizabeth I, 107
White, Elizabeth I, 123
White, Elizabeth I, 124
White, Elizabeth I, 125
White, Elizabeth I, 141
White, Elizabeth I, 152
White, Elizabeth I, 172
White, Elizabeth I, 177
White, Elizabeth I, 187
White, Elizabeth I, 228
White, Elizabeth I, 277
White, Elizabeth I, 298
White, Elizabeth I, 520
White, Elizabeth I, 521
White, Elizabeth I, 545
White, Elizabeth I, 581
White, Elizabeth I, 604
White, Elizabeth I, 682
White, Elizabeth I, 691
White, Elizabeth I, 736
White, Elizabeth I, 738
White, Elizabeth I, 844
White, Elizabeth I, 902
White, Elizabeth I, 905
White, Elizabeth I, 936
White, Elizabeth I, 969
White, Elizabeth I Sup 1, 7
White, Elizabeth II, 46
White, Elizabeth II, 65
White, Elizabeth II, 80
White, Elizabeth II, 110
White, Elizabeth II, 125
White, Elizabeth II, 143
White, Elizabeth II, 271
White, Elizabeth II, 276
White, Elizabeth II, 435
White, Elizabeth II, 671
White, Elizabeth II, 684
White, Elizabeth II, 722
White, Elizabeth II, 762
White, Elizabeth II, 774
White, Elizabeth II, 827
White, Elizabeth II, 938
White, Elizabeth II, 1010
White, Elizabeth II, 1037
White, Elizabeth III, 86
White, Elizabeth III, 348
White, Elizabeth III, 349
White, Elizabeth III, 350
White, Elizabeth IV, 47
White, Elizabeth IV, 67
White, Elizabeth IV, 164
White, Elizabeth IV, 335
White, Elizabeth IV, 357
White, Elizabeth IV, 404
White, Elizabeth IV, 454
White, Elizabeth IV, 599
White, Elizabeth IV, 786
White, Elizabeth V, 204
White, Elizabeth V, 211
White, Elizabeth V, 289
White, Elizabeth V, 365
White, Elizabeth V, 439
White, Elizabeth V, 812
White, Elizabeth VI, 45
White, Elizabeth VI, 46
White, Elizabeth VI, 84
White, Elizabeth VI, 88
White, Elizabeth VI, 89
White, Elizabeth VI, 90
White, Elizabeth VI, 279
White, Elizabeth VI, 456
White, Elizabeth VI, 579
White, Elizabeth VI, 720
White, Elizabeth VI, 810
White, Elizabeth VI, 886
White, Elizabeth VI, 929
White, Elizabeth VI, 967
White, Elizabeth Ann I, 22
White, Elizabeth Ann IV, 1202
White, Elizabeth Ann IV, 1226
White, Elizabeth Ann IV, 1227
White, Elizabeth B. III, 350
White, Elizabeth H. VI, 89
White, Elizabeth H. VI, 265
White, Elizabeth H. VI, 279
White, Elizabeth M. I, 945
White, Elizabeth M. I, 950
White, Elizabeth M. I, 951
White, Elizabeth R. I, 454
White, Elizabeth R. VI, 89
White, Elizabeth Rosela I, 440
White, Elizabeth S. III, 349
White, Elizabeth W. I, 604
White, Elizabeth W. VI, 1013
White, Elizabeth, Jr. II, 774
White, Elkanah I, 124
White, Ella I, 24
White, Ella I, 628
White, Ella I, 642
White, Ella Aline I, 670
White, Ella E. I, 22
White, Ella E. I, 85
White, Ella J. Smith V, 719
White, Ella Newby I, 24
White, Ellen I, 84
White, Ellen K. II, 877
White, Ellen K. II, 938
White, Ellen M. I, 21
White, Ellen M. VI, 89
White, Ellen M. VI, 90
White, Ellen M. W. I, 931
White, Ellen Margaret I, 83
White, Ellen Mildred I, 25
White, Ellen Mildred I, 85
White, Ellen Mildred I, 951
White, Ellis I, 581
White, Elma IV, 303
White, Elma IV, 1099
White, Elma IV, 1120
White, Elmer C. I, 25
White, Elmina I, 568
White, Elmina I, 581
White, Elnora IV, 303
White, Elsberry Lee I, 20
White, Elsberry Lee I, 21
White, Elva I, 202
White, Elvey I, 779
White, Elvira I, 548
White, Elvira I, 581
White, Elvira Ida I, 440
White, Elvy I, 191
White, Elvy I, 202
White, Elwood Quinton I, 20
White, Elwood Quinton??? I, 20
White, Emaline IV, 1014
White, Emaline IV, 1015
White, Emily I, 624
White, Emily I, 628
White, Emily I, 806
White, Emily I, 844
White, Emily I, 905
White, Emily E. I, 867
White, Emily E. I, 878
White, Emily E. I, 905
White, Emma Elisabeth I, 24
White, Emma H. I, 20
White, Emma H. I, 84
White, Emma J. I, 21
White, Emma J. I, 29
White, Emma J. I, 30
White, Emma Laura I, 20
White, Emma Laura I, 83
White, Emma Pearl I, 21
White, Emmons III, 349
White, Emmons III, 503
White, Enock C. VI, 951
White, Ernest I, 20
White, Ernest I, 21
White, Ernest I, 85
White, Ernest W. I, 24
White, Ernest W. I, 84
White, Estelle III, 253
White, Estelle III, 349
White, Ester I, 581
White, Estey R. III, 465
White, Esther I, 23
White, Esther I, 80
White, Esther I, 81
White, Esther I, 155
White, Esther I, 174
White, Esther I, 225
White, Esther I, 228
White, Esther I, 257
White, Esther I, 260
White, Esther I, 264
White, Esther II, 17
White, Esther II, 45
White, Esther II, 46
White, Esther II, 684
White, Esther II, 972
White, Esther II, 983
White, Esther II, 990
White, Esther II, 1037
White, Esther III, 349
White, Esther E. I, 19
White, Esther E. I, 67
White, Esther E. I, 83
White, Esther E. I, 84
White, Esther J. I, 21
White, Esther Jane I, 29
White, Esther Jane IV, 786
White, Esther May I, 21
White, Eugene T. I, 85
White, Eunice I, 84
White, Eunice I, 581
White, Eunice Lavinia I, 24
White, Evalyn Banks I, 24
White, Evelyn Novella I, 25
White, Everett IV, 1014
White, Everett Stanley IV, 1015
White, Exum I, 23
White, Exum I, 80
White, Exum I, 81
White, Exum I, 82
White, Exum VI, 56
White, Exum VI, 89
White, Exum VI, 90
White, Exum N. I, 21
White, Exum N. I, 83
White, Exum N. I, 84
White, Exum N. VI, 55
White, Exum N. VI, 78
White, Exum N. VI, 89
White, Exum N. VI, 90
White, Exum Newby I, 21
White, Exum Newby I, 83
White, Exum W. I, 82
White, Ezra M. I, 21
White, Fernando I, 84
White, Fernando C. I, 21
White, Fernando C. I, 84
White, Fernando L. I, 670
White, Fernando Murry I, 21
White, Flora W. I, 670
White, Florence I, 56
White, Florence I, 84
White, Florence I, 922
White, Frances I, 26
White, Frances I, 201
White, Frances VI, 1014
White, Frances Alice V, 940
White, Frances B. VI, 929
White, Francis I, 20
White, Francis I, 21
White, Francis I, 22
White, Francis I, 24
White, Francis I, 25
White, Francis I, 32
White, Francis I, 55
White, Francis I, 56
White, Francis I, 76
White, Francis I, 79
White, Francis I, 80
White, Francis I, 81
White, Francis I, 83
White, Francis I, 124
White, Francis I, 125
White, Francis I, 144
White, Francis I, 154
White, Francis I, 173
White, Francis I, 174
White, Francis I, 175
White, Francis I, 176
White, Francis I, 180
White, Francis I, 187
White, Francis I, 195
White, Francis I, 197
White, Francis I, 201
White, Francis I, 202
White, Francis I, 844
White, Francis I, 905
White, Francis I, 921
White, Francis III, 348
White, Francis V, 289
White, Francis V, 299
White, Francis V, 313
White, Francis VI, 121
White, Francis Carlton I, 85
White, Francis T. V, 940
White, Francis T. V, 941
White, Francis William I, 20
White, Frank IV, 503
White, Frank J. V, 650
White, Frank L. IV, 503
White, Freddie IV, 503
White, Frederica IV, 503
White, Fredrick I, 81
White, Geo. F. II, 938
White, Geo. F. III, 223
White, Geo. F. III, 349
White, George I, 21
White, George I, 79
White, George I, 82
White, George I, 175
White, George I, 937
White, George I, 951
White, George II, 187
White, George II, 271
White, George II, 272
White, George II, 684
White, George II, 774
White, George III, 349
White, George IV, 163
White, George IV, 303
White, George IV, 786
White, George V, 204
White, George V, 211
White, George VI, 456
White, George VI, 967
White, George VI, 1013
White, George VI, 1014
White, George B. V, 541
White, George B. V, 605
White, George F. II, 934
White, George F. II, 938
White, George F. III, 349
White, George Foster II, 827
White, George T. III, 159
White, George W. I, 84
White, George Wilson I, 24
White, George Wilson I, 642
White, Gertie IV, 503
White, Gertrude IV, 503
White, Geulielma I, 307
White, Geulielma I, 319
White, Gilly I, 202
White, Granderson VI, 895
White, Guleemus I, 280
White, Guli I, 260
White, Gulielma I, 260
White, Gulielma Atlee II, 883
White, Gulielma Atlee II, 939
White, Guly I, 260
White, Gulyelma I, 228
White, Gurela I, 779
White, H. A. VI, 1016
White, H. M. VI, 1005
White, Halford Elihu I, 20
White, Hanah I, 124
White, Hanah E. I, 440
White, Hannah I, 175
White, Hannah I, 361
White, Hannah I, 367
White, Hannah I, 411
White, Hannah I, 428
White, Hannah I, 440
White, Hannah I, 520
White, Hannah I, 521
White, Hannah I, 537
White, Hannah I, 540
White, Hannah I, 558
White, Hannah I, 581
White, Hannah I, 670
White, Hannah I, 691
White, Hannah I, 844
White, Hannah I, 872
White, Hannah I, 905
White, Hannah II, 46
White, Hannah II, 93
White, Hannah II, 110
White, Hannah II, 187
White, Hannah II, 251
White, Hannah II, 271
White, Hannah II, 435
White, Hannah II, 450
White, Hannah II, 547
White, Hannah II, 637
White, Hannah II, 659
White, Hannah II, 684
White, Hannah II, 762
White, Hannah II, 774
White, Hannah II, 972
White, Hannah II, 976
White, Hannah II, 1013
White, Hannah II, 1021
White, Hannah II, 1023
White, Hannah II, 1028
White, Hannah II, 1031
White, Hannah II, 1037
White, Hannah II, 1042
White, Hannah III, 134
White, Hannah III, 223
White, Hannah III, 226
White, Hannah III, 231
White, Hannah III, 293

White, Hannah III, 303
White, Hannah III, 348
White, Hannah III, 349
White, Hannah III, 350
White, Hannah III, 490
White, Hannah III, 503
White, Hannah IV, 140
White, Hannah IV, 163
White, Hannah IV, 164
White, Hannah IV, 454
White, Hannah IV, 459
White, Hannah IV, 575
White, Hannah IV, 599
White, Hannah IV, 786
White, Hannah IV, 854
White, Hannah IV, 855
White, Hannah IV, 1015
White, Hannah IV, 1176
White, Hannah IV, 1192
White, Hannah V, 904
White, Hannah VI, 124
White, Hannah VI, 217
White, Hannah VI, 456
White, Hannah A. V, 940
White, Hannah Amelia V, 899
White, Hannah Amelia V, 901
White, Hannah Amelia V, 926
White, Hannah Amelia V, 941
White, Hannah B. I, 604
White, Hannah D. III, 23
White, Hannah D. III, 100
White, Hannah D. III, 349
White, Hannah D. III, 350
White, Hannah E. I, 689
White, Hannah E. I, 691
White, Hannah E. III, 227
White, Hannah E. III, 449
White, Hannah E. IV, 599
White, Hannah G. III, 23
White, Hannah G. III, 350
White, Hannah Howell V, 963
White, Hannah Jane IV, 1186
White, Hannah Jane IV, 1192
White, Hannah S. III, 349
White, Hannah T. III, 159
White, Hannah T. III, 349
White, Hannah T. IV, 786
White, Hannah Y. IV, 1192
White, Hannah, Jr. II, 637
White, Hannah, Jr. II, 684
White, harles Francis I, 935
White, Harriet H. I, 83
White, Harriett Susannah I, 82
White, Harrison I, 844
White, Hazel Elisabeth I, 21
White, Helen II, 895
White, Helen II, 939
White, Helen II, 1070
White, Helen II, 1083
White, Helen Comley II, 939
White, Helen Comly II, 938
White, Helen Lawson V, 904
White, Helen Lawson V, 940
White, Helen Magill II, 939
White, Helen Trump II, 827
White, Helena G. II, 140
White, Henrietta I, 611
White, Henrietta I, 935
White, Henrietta IV, 1015
White, Henrietta Henly I, 20
White, Henrietta S. IV, 1015
White, Henry I, 1
White, Henry I, 61
White, Henry I, 70
White, Henry I, 78
White, Henry I, 80
White, Henry I, 91
White, Henry I, 92
White, Henry I, 107
White, Henry I, 124
White, Henry I, 131
White, Henry I, 135
White, Henry I, 137
White, Henry I, 144
White, Henry I, 151
White, Henry I, 161
White, Henry I, 166
White, Henry I, 172
White, Henry I, 173
White, Henry I, 174
White, Henry I, 175
White, Henry I, 176
White, Henry I, 201
White, Henry I, 203
White, Henry I, 520
White, Henry I, 581
White, Henry I, 600
White, Henry I, 604
White, Henry I, 608
White, Henry I, 736
White, Henry I Sup 1, 4
White, Henry I Sup 1, 5
White, Henry III, 348
White, Henry IV, 1192
White, Henry V, 365
White, Henry VI, 11
White, Henry VI, 904
White, Henry VI, 1000
White, Henry VI, 1014
White, Henry VI, 1019
White, Henry A. I, 21
White, Henry A. I, 84
White, Henry A. I, 951
White, Henry Alva I, 24
White, Henry Alva I, 936
White, Henry Alva I, 947
White, Henry Alva I, 951
White, Henry Alva III, 245
White, Henry Beale III, 349
White, Henry E. I, 21
White, Henry E. I, 24
White, Henry E. I, 29
White, Henry E. I, 83
White, Henry E. I, 84
White, Henry H. I, 604
White, Henry Haydock III, 350
White, Henry J. IV, 1192
White, Henry Kirk III, 349
White, Henry M. VI, 940
White, Henry M. VI, 977
White, Henry M. VI, 994
White, Henry M. VI, 1004
White, Henry M. VI, 1013
White, Henry M. VI, 1014
White, Henry W. V, 439
White, Henry Walter VI, 89
White, Henry Walton I, 23
White, Henry Wilson V, 439
White, Henry, Jr. I, 124
White, Henry, Sr. I, 172
White, Henryanna I, 628
White, Henryanna C. I, 633
White, Henryanna C. I, 642
White, Henryette IV, 1014
White, Hephzabeth I, 173
White, Herbert I, 931
White, Herman Ray I, 22
White, Hester II, 46
White, Hettie I, 24
White, Hope I, 277
White, Hope I, 520
White, Hope I, 581
White, Hopewell I, 581
White, Horace II, 895
White, Horace II, 939
White, Horace G. II, 877
White, Horace G. II, 938
White, Horace Wilson I, 19
White, Horace Wilson I, 85
White, Horace Wilson I, 935
White, Horace Wilson I, 951
White, Howard II, 435
White, Howard II, 774
White, Howard II, 827
White, Howard II, 835
White, Howard II, 938
White, Howard II, 939
White, Howard II, 1067
White, Howard II, 1083
White, Howard, Jr. II, 938
White, Howard, Jr. II, 939
White, Howard, Jr. II, 1083
White, Howson S. VI, 1013
White, Hugh D. I, 670
White, Hugh P. I, 21
White, Hugh Peele I, 19
White, Hulda I, 173
White, Huldah I, 45
White, Huldah I, 50
White, Huldah I, 78
White, Huldah I, 125
White, Huldah I, 173
White, Huldah II, 80
White, Huldah II, 110
White, Ida May VI, 740
White, Ida May VI, 790
White, Inez Mary I, 21
White, Irene I, 22
White, Irvin P. I, 85
White, Irvin P. I, 935
White, Irvin Peelle I, 19
White, Irvine P. I, 951
White, Isaac I, 79
White, Isaac I, 124
White, Isaac I, 172
White, Isaac I, 275
White, Isaac I, 277
White, Isaac I, 520
White, Isaac I, 529
White, Isaac I, 581
White, Isaac I, 600
White, Isaac I, 604
White, Isaac I, 628
White, Isaac I, 772
White, Isaac I, 867
White, Isaac IV, 163
White, Isaac IV, 164
White, Isaac IV, 355
White, Isaac IV, 454
White, Isaac IV, 786
White, Isaac IV, 854
White, Isaac IV, 855
White, Isaac VI, 579
White, Isaac VI, 703
White, Isaac VI, 720
White, Isaac C. VI, 89
White, Isaac H. I, 844
White, Isaac J. I, 604
White, Isabella I, 18
White, Isabella I, 20
White, Isabella I, 23
White, Isabella I, 82
White, Isabella I, 83
White, Isabella I, 84
White, Isabella I, 176
White, Isabella I, 177
White, Isabella I, 260
White, Isabella I, 581
White, Isabella I, 626
White, Isabella I, 628
White, Isabella VI, 92
White, Isabella Parker I, 19
White, Isabelle I, 176
White, Isabelle I, 177
White, Isack I, 124
White, Isadora IV, 786
White, Isaiah T. I, 905
White, Israel II, 1037
White, Israel IV, 67
White, Israel IV, 164
White, Israel IV, 454
White, Israel IV, 458
White, Israel IV, 503
White, Israel IV, 855
White, Israel IV, 1015
White, Israel VI, 456
White, J. F. I, 84
White, J. H. Thomas I, 22
White, J. H. Thomas I, 85
White, J. Robert I, 623
White, J. Thomas I, 85
White, Jabaze M. I, 670
White, Jabez I, 867
White, Jabez M. I, 670
White, Jabez Melvin I, 670
White, Jacob I, 21
White, Jacob I, 64
White, Jacob I, 71
White, Jacob I, 78
White, Jacob I, 80
White, Jacob I, 81
White, Jacob I, 844
White, Jacob II, 435
White, Jacob IV, 164
White, Jacob IV, 454
White, Jacob IV, 599
White, Jacob VI, 903
White, Jacob VI, 908
White, Jacob VI, 915
White, Jacob VI, 929
White, Jacob VI, 951
White, Jacob VI, 966
White, Jacob VI, 977
White, Jacob VI, 986
White, Jacob VI, 1002
White, Jacob VI, 1013
White, Jacob S. VI, 940
White, Jacob S. VI, 1004
White, Jacob S. VI, 1014
White, Jacob W. VI, 929
White, Jacob W. VI, 950
White, Jacob W. VI, 1013
White, James I, 22
White, James I, 79
White, James I, 80
White, James I, 123
White, James I, 124
White, James I, 128
White, James I, 144
White, James I, 163
White, James I, 167
White, James I, 172
White, James I, 173
White, James I, 174
White, James I, 176
White, James I, 191
White, James I, 201
White, James I, 706
White, James I, 736
White, James I, 867
White, James I, 905
White, James I, 931
White, James II, 125
White, James II, 271
White, James II, 499
White, James II, 574
White, James II, 683
White, James II, 684
White, James IV, 67
White, James IV, 302
White, James IV, 303
White, James IV, 454
White, James IV, 786
White, James IV, 854
White, James VI, 456
White, James VI, 720
White, James VI, 883
White, James VI, 1002
White, James VI, 1013
White, James A. I, 84
White, James Carson I, 20
White, James D. I, 794
White, James D. I, 844
White, James Edward I, 123
White, James F. I, 19
White, James F. I, 20
White, James F. I, 29
White, James F. I, 59
White, James F. I, 84
White, James F. I, 85
White, James F., Jr. I, 24
White, James Francis I, 21
White, James Henry I, 19
White, James Hugh I, 21
White, James M. I, 176
White, James N. V, 1025
White, James P. I, 84
White, James P. I, 89
White, James Robert I, 931
White, James Thurston I, 24
White, James W. II, 684
White, James, Sr. VI, 951
White, Jane I, 24
White, Jane I, 123
White, Jane I, 172
White, Jane I, 176
White, Jane I, 189
White, Jane I, 202
White, Jane I, 440
White, Jane I, 441
White, Jane I, 446
White, Jane I, 454
White, Jane I, 661
White, Jane I, 670
White, Jane I, 691
White, Jane I, 692
White, Jane I, 891
White, Jane I, 895
White, Jane I, 905
White, Jane I, 1134
White, Jane III, 348
White, Jane III, 349
White, Jane III, 350
White, Jane III, 386
White, Jane III, 388
White, Jane III, 389
White, Jane IV, 22
White, Jane IV, 54
White, Jane IV, 67
White, Jane IV, 164
White, Jane IV, 295
White, Jane IV, 302
White, Jane IV, 355
White, Jane IV, 357
White, Jane IV, 454
White, Jane IV, 855
White, Jane VI, 456
White, Jane VI, 703
White, Jane VI, 720
White, Jane VI, 851
White, Jane VI, 1013
White, Jane VI, 1018
White, Jane S. II, 877
White, Jane S. II, 938
White, Jane Susannah I, 1134
White, Jane, Jr. IV, 454
White, Jas. F. I, 30
White, Jeames I, 202
White, Jean VI, 455
White, Jemima I, 23
White, Jemima I, 24
White, Jemima I, 25
White, Jemima I, 29
White, Jemima I, 32
White, Jemima I, 42
White, Jemima I, 71
White, Jemima I, 80
White, Jemima I, 81
White, Jemima I, 82
White, Jemima I, 84
White, Jemima I, 173
White, Jemima I, 604
White, Jemimah I, 175
White, Jennie B. III, 101
White, Jennie E. III, 349
White, Jennie Sullivan Nora I, 21
White, Jephthah I, 82
White, Jeptha I, 8
White, Jeptha I, 14
White, Jeptha I, 15
White, Jeptha I, 21
White, Jeptha I, 22
White, Jeptha I, 82
White, Jeptha I, 83
White, Jeptha I, 84
White, Jeptha McAdams I, 93
White, Jeptha T. I, 83
White, Jeremiah VI, 1013
White, Jeremiah C. VI, 962
White, Jesse I, 19
White, Jesse I, 35
White, Jesse I, 72
White, Jesse I, 79
White, Jesse I, 80
White, Jesse I, 81
White, Jesse I, 88
White, Jesse I, 123
White, Jesse I, 124
White, Jesse I, 134
White, Jesse I, 174
White, Jesse I, 176
White, Jesse I, 188
White, Jesse I, 201
White, Jesse I, 520
White, Jesse I, 608
White, Jesse I, 794
White, Jesse I, 844
White, Jesse IV, 67
White, Jesse IV, 137
White, Jesse IV, 139
White, Jesse IV, 156
White, Jesse IV, 163
White, Jesse IV, 164
White, Jesse IV, 370
White, Jesse IV, 454
White, Jesse IV, 503
White, Jesse IV, 595
White, Jesse IV, 599
White, Jesse IV, 786
White, Jesse IV, 854
White, Jesse V, 211
White, Jesse VI, 456
White, Jesse VI, 720
White, Jesse VI, 864
White, Jesse VI, 1014
White, Jesse VI, 1019
White, Jesse Elliott I, 80
White, Jesse Jessop I, 19
White, Jesse Jessop I, 85
White, Jesse Jessop I, 935
White, Jesse Jessop I, 951
White, Jesse Osmond I, 20
White, Jesse White VI, 720
White, Jesse, Jr. I, 80
White, Jesse, Jr. IV, 454
White, Jessey VI, 967
White, Jessie F. IV, 474
White, Jethro I, 84
White, Jethro Thomas I, 25
White, Jno. I, 79
White, Jno. VI, 373
White, Joel I, 867
White, Joel I, 905
White, Joel IV, 1014
White, Joel IV, 1015
White, Joel IV, 1385
White, Joel VI, 455
White, John I, 10
White, John I, 19
White, John I, 21
White, John I, 22
White, John I, 24
White, John I, 25
White, John I, 30
White, John I, 50
White, John I, 55
White, John I, 73
White, John I, 78
White, John I, 79
White, John I, 81
White, John I, 82
White, John I, 83
White, John I, 87
White, John I, 90
White, John I, 92
White, John I, 99
White, John I, 111
White, John I, 124
White, John I, 125
White, John I, 134
White, John I, 142
White, John I, 152
White, John I, 159
White, John I, 172

:e, John I, 173
:e, John I, 174
:e, John I, 175
:e, John I, 176
te, John I, 187
te, John I, 201
:e, John I, 202
te, John I, 260
te, John I, 440
te, John I, 454
te, John I, 520
te, John I, 581
te, John I, 661
te, John I, 670
te, John I, 691
te, John I, 692
te, John I, 736
te, John I, 794
te, John I, 844
te, John I, 867
te, John I, 905
te, John I, 969
ite, John I Sup 1, 3
ite, John I Sup 1, 6
te, John II, 46
te, John II, 65
te, John II, 80
ite, John II, 110
ite, John II, 187
ite, John II, 228
ite, John II, 271
ite, John II, 435
ite, John II, 449
ite, John II, 684
ite, John II, 972
ite, John II, 1037
ite, John III, 86
ite, John III, 117
ite, John III, 247
ite, John III, 348
ite, John III, 349
ite, John III, 386
ite, John III, 389
ite, John IV, 54
ite, John IV, 67
ite, John IV, 164
ite, John IV, 295
ite, John IV, 302
ite, John IV, 855
ite, John IV, 1385
ite, John V, 211
ite, John VI, 37
ite, John VI, 105
ite, John VI, 124
ite, John VI, 365
ite, John VI, 455
ite, John VI, 456
ite, John VI, 879
hite, John VI, 903
hite, John VI, 986
hite, John VI, 1006
hite, John VI, 1014
hite, John A. I, 22
hite, John A. I, 85
hite, John A. I, 428
hite, John A. V, 211
hite, John Ambrose I, 22
hite, John Anderson I, 20
hite, John B. III, 349
hite, John C. I, 71
hite, John C. I, 81
hite, John C. I, 670
hite, John Christopher II, 435
hite, John Comley II, 939
hite, John Comly II, 827
hite, John Corlies III, 25
hite, John Cornwell I, 22
hite, John Duke I, 228
hite, John E. I, 174
hite, John Earl I, 80
hite, John F. II, 938
hite, John F. III, 349
hite, John G. I, 604
hite, John H. III, 349
hite, John H., Jr. I, 84
hite, John Henry Thomas I, 21
hite, John Henry Thomas I, 83
hite, John I. II, 938
hite, John J. I, 176
hite, John J. I, 794
hite, John J. II, 774
hite, John J. II, 880
hite, John J. II, 938
hite, John J. G. I, 670
hite, John Jordan I, 124
hite, John L. I, 8
hite, John L. I, 19
hite, John L. I, 22
hite, John L. I, 23
hite, John L. I, 25
hite, John L. I, 28
White, John L. I, 84
White, John L. Winslow I, 22
White, John L. Winslow I, 25
White, John M. I, 454
White, John M. I, 604
White, John M. IV, 855
White, John Milton I, 440
White, John Milton I, 441
White, John Milton I, 450
White, John Milton I, 454
White, John O. I, 23
White, John O. I, 77
White, John O. I, 83
White, John Osmund I, 22
White, John Osmund I, 24
White, John R. I, 21
White, John R. I, 33
White, John R. I, 82
White, John Richard I, 82
White, John Richard I, 124
White, John S. I, 21
White, John S. I, 22
White, John S. I, 31
White, John S. I, 84
White, John S. I, 125
White, John T. I, 20
White, John T. I, 82
White, John T. I, 106
White, John T. I, 125
White, John T. I, 151
White, John T. I, 175
White, John T. I, 187
White, John T. I, 202
White, John T., Jr. V, 941
White, John V. I, 670
White, John W. I, 440
White, John W. I, 691
White, John Wesley I, 691
White, John Wilson I, 23
White, John Winslow I, 24
White, John Winslow I, 201
White, John, Jr. I, 80
White, Joicey VI, 1010
White, Jonah II, 722
White, Jonathan I, 23
White, Jonathan I, 63
White, Jonathan I, 71
White, Jonathan I, 79
White, Jonathan I, 80
White, Jonathan I, 81
White, Jonathan I, 87
White, Jonathan I, 124
White, Jonathan I, 161
White, Jonathan I, 172
White, Jonathan I, 173
White, Jonathan I, 771
White, Jonathan II, 110
White, Jonathan II, 125
White, Jonathan VI, 89
White, Jonathan VI, 821
White, Jonathan VI, 854
White, Jonathan VI, 864
White, Jonathan Thomas I, 26
White, Jonnie Quinton I, 20
White, Jordan I, 22
White, Jordan I, 25
White, Jordan I, 76
White, Jordan I, 78
White, Jordan I, 124
White, Jordan I, 174
White, Jordan I, 175
White, Jordan I, 201
White, Jordan I, 779
White, Jordan I, 931
White, Jordon I, 173
White, Jordon I, 174
White, Jordon I, 187
White, Jordon I, 202
White, Joseph I, 21
White, Joseph I, 22
White, Joseph I, 23
White, Joseph I, 24
White, Joseph I, 25
White, Joseph I, 29
White, Joseph I, 32
White, Joseph I, 36
White, Joseph I, 71
White, Joseph I, 78
White, Joseph I, 80
White, Joseph I, 81
White, Joseph I, 84
White, Joseph I, 123
White, Joseph I, 124
White, Joseph I, 125
White, Joseph I, 152
White, Joseph I, 172
White, Joseph I, 173
White, Joseph I, 176
White, Joseph I, 177
White, Joseph I, 202
White, Joseph I, 228
White, Joseph I, 260
White, Joseph I, 298
White, Joseph I, 307
White, Joseph I, 319
White, Joseph I, 521
White, Joseph I, 867
White, Joseph I, 905
White, Joseph I, 922
White, Joseph I, 935
White, Joseph I, 1134
White, Joseph II, 46
White, Joseph II, 99
White, Joseph II, 110
White, Joseph II, 272
White, Joseph II, 435
White, Joseph II, 683
White, Joseph II, 722
White, Joseph II, 801
White, Joseph II, 972
White, Joseph II, 981
White, Joseph II, 983
White, Joseph II, 984
White, Joseph II, 997
White, Joseph II, 1023
White, Joseph II, 1028
White, Joseph II, 1031
White, Joseph II, 1037
White, Joseph III, 348
White, Joseph IV, 855
White, Joseph V, 650
White, Joseph VI, 455
White, Joseph VI, 456
White, Joseph VI, 897
White, Joseph VI, 900
White, Joseph VI, 904
White, Joseph VI, 997
White, Joseph VI, 1013
White, Joseph VI, 1018
White, Joseph Addison I, 670
White, Joseph Baker III, 253
White, Joseph Baker III, 349
White, Joseph Baker III, 350
White, Joseph D. I, 19
White, Joseph D. I, 428
White, Joseph Ellis I, 23
White, Joseph G. I, 23
White, Joseph H. I, 22
White, Joseph H. VI, 89
White, Joseph J. I, 21
White, Joseph J. VI, 90
White, Joseph J. G. VI, 89
White, Joseph John Gurney I, 83
White, Joseph L. I, 21
White, Joseph M. I, 81
White, Joseph M. I, 176
White, Joseph Morris I, 123
White, Joseph N. D. I, 670
White, Joseph R. I, 83
White, Joseph W. I, 124
White, Joseph W. II, 880
White, Joseph W. II, 938
White, Joseph W. IV, 855
White, Joseph, Jr. I, 78
White, Joseph, Jr. I, 87
White, Joseph, Jr. I, 260
White, Joseph, Sr. I, 78
White, Joseph, Sr. I, 260
White, Josepheus I, 81
White, Josephine I, 931
White, Josephine V, 365
White, Josephine V, 439
White, Josephine E. V, 422
White, Josephine E. V, 439
White, Josephus I, 22
White, Josephus I, 82
White, Josephus I, 88
White, Josephus I, 125
White, Josephus I, 175
White, Joshua I, 25
White, Joshua I, 79
White, Joshua I, 81
White, Joshua I, 123
White, Joshua I, 125
White, Joshua I, 154
White, Joshua I, 157
White, Joshua I, 172
White, Joshua I, 173
White, Joshua I, 174
White, Joshua IV, 1176
White, Joshua IV, 1192
White, Joshua IV, 1226
White, Joshua VI, 45
White, Joshua VI, 46
White, Joshua Theodore I, 23
White, Josiah I, 19
White, Josiah I, 20
White, Josiah I, 22
White, Josiah I, 23
White, Josiah I, 47
White, Josiah I, 62
White, Josiah I, 78
White, Josiah I, 79
White, Josiah I, 80
White, Josiah I, 81
White, Josiah I, 82
White, Josiah I, 84
White, Josiah I, 123
White, Josiah I, 125
White, Josiah I, 174
White, Josiah I, 187
White, Josiah I, 201
White, Josiah I, 209
White, Josiah I, 228
White, Josiah I, 232
White, Josiah I, 260
White, Josiah I, 628
White, Josiah I, 905
White, Josiah II, 46
White, Josiah II, 93
White, Josiah II, 110
White, Josiah II, 187
White, Josiah II, 251
White, Josiah II, 252
White, Josiah II, 271
White, Josiah II, 435
White, Josiah II, 684
White, Josiah II, 722
White, Josiah II, 762
White, Josiah II, 774
White, Josiah V, 365
White, Josiah E. I, 82
White, Josiah R. I, 25
White, Josiah R. I, 84
White, Josiah T. I, 20
White, Josiah T. I, 23
White, Josiah T. I, 82
White, Josiah T. I, 83
White, Josiah T. I, 176
White, Josiah T. I, 177
White, Josiah T. I, 228
White, Josiah Thomas I, 20
White, Josias II, 46
White, Josias II, 271
White, Judith III, 406
White, Judith III, 465
White, Juley I, 80
White, Julia I, 8
White, Julia I, 14
White, Julia I, 15
White, Julia I, 20
White, Julia I, 21
White, Julia I, 22
White, Julia I, 30
White, Julia I, 82
White, Julia I, 83
White, Julia I, 84
White, Julia I, 89
White, Julia A. I, 24
White, Julia A. I, 30
White, Julia An I, 454
White, Julia Ann I, 440
White, Julia Emma I, 22
White, Julia S. I, 84
White, Julia S. I, 85
White, Julia Scott I, 22
White, Julia V. I, 21
White, Julia V. I, 84
White, Julia W. IV, 303
White, Julian VI, 1014
White, July I, 260
White, Kate C. I, 850
White, Katharine I, 277
White, Katharine I, 367
White, Katharine I, 431
White, Katharine I, 605
White, Katharine I, 608
White, Katherine I, 361
White, Katherine I, 520
White, Kittie Ida I, 21
White, Kittie Ida I, 84
White, Lacy VI, 1014
White, Laura A. I, 84
White, Laura A. I, 89
White, Laura Ann I, 20
White, Laura B. I, 951
White, Laura Brim I, 951
White, Lavena V, 439
White, Lavina V, 365
White, Lemuel VI, 89
White, Lemuel VI, 131
White, Lemuel VI, 143
White, Lemuel VI, 864
White, Lenora P. I, 21
White, Lenora P. I, 31
White, Leola I, 20
White, Leola White I, 21
White, Leota I, 85
White, Leslie Brown I, 20
White, Leslie Cartland I, 642
White, Levina V, 324
White, Levina V, 365
White, Levina V, 439
White, Lewis I, 81
White, Lewis IV, 503
White, Lewis C. I, 691
White, Lewis Edward I, 123
White, Lewis Edward I, 187
White, Lewis Edward I, 202
White, Lewis K. IV, 1014
White, Lewis Parker IV, 1015
White, Lewis S. IV, 840
White, Lewis S. IV, 854
White, Lida I, 145
White, Lida I, 173
White, Liddia II, 435
White, Lidey I, 70
White, Lidey I, 78
White, Lillie IV, 303
White, Lillie Maie I, 21
White, Lillie May I, 23
White, Lillie R. I, 84
White, Lilly Rebecca I, 23
White, Lindon Oriella I, 19
White, Lindsey IV, 841
White, Littleberry VI, 1013
White, Livina J. I, 922
White, Lloyd Wilson I, 642
White, Lorenzo I, 608
White, Lorenzo D. I, 520
White, Lorenzo D. I, 604
White, Lorenzo D. I, 608
White, Lorenzo D. I, 706
White, Lorenzo D. I, 736
White, Lorenzo D. I, 738
White, Lottie I, 623
White, Louesa E. I, 686
White, Louesa E. I, 691
White, Louisa I, 83
White, Louisa I, 529
White, Louisa I, 581
White, Louisa I, 670
White, Louisa I, 928
White, Louisa B. II, 733
White, Louisa B. II, 774
White, Louisa D. VI, 51
White, Louisa D. VI, 89
White, Louiza L. I, 85
White, Lucanic I, 81
White, Lucinda I, 202
White, Lucinda VI, 951
White, Lucinda VI, 1013
White, Lucinda H. VI, 893
White, Lucinda H. VI, 970
White, Lucretia IV, 664
White, Lucy I, 642
White, Lucy VI, 104
White, Lucy VI, 124
White, Lucy VI, 864
White, Lucy VI, 972
White, Lucy VI, 1013
White, Lucy Lenora I, 17
White, Lucy Lenora I, 84
White, Lucy McD. VI, 1014
White, Lucy McDaniel VI, 951
White, Lucy O'Brian I, 20
White, Ludena I, 24
White, Luella IV, 841
White, Luezer I, 670
White, Lycurgus B. I, 21
White, Lyda I, 173
White, Lyddia I, 78
White, Lydia I, 8
White, Lydia I, 10
White, Lydia I, 19
White, Lydia I, 21
White, Lydia I, 22
White, Lydia I, 24
White, Lydia I, 25
White, Lydia I, 30
White, Lydia I, 37
White, Lydia I, 44
White, Lydia I, 50
White, Lydia I, 78
White, Lydia I, 79
White, Lydia I, 80
White, Lydia I, 81
White, Lydia I, 82
White, Lydia I, 83
White, Lydia I, 84
White, Lydia I, 86
White, Lydia I, 87
White, Lydia I, 88
White, Lydia I, 89
White, Lydia I, 125
White, Lydia I, 175
White, Lydia I, 225
White, Lydia I, 260
White, Lydia I, 441
White, Lydia I, 520
White, Lydia I, 524
White, Lydia I, 581
White, Lydia I, 613
White, Lydia I, 618

White, Lydia I, 626
White, Lydia I, 771
White, Lydia I, 929
White, Lydia I, 932
White, Lydia I, 935
White, Lydia I, 936
White, Lydia II, 435
White, Lydia II, 684
White, Lydia II, 827
White, Lydia II, 938
White, Lydia II, 984
White, Lydia II, 997
White, Lydia II, 1037
White, Lydia IV, 164
White, Lydia IV, 454
White, Lydia IV, 583
White, Lydia IV, 599
White, Lydia IV, 786
White, Lydia IV, 1127
White, Lydia IV, 1140
White, Lydia IV, 1221
White, Lydia IV, 1227
White, Lydia V, 211
White, Lydia V, 365
White, Lydia V, 407
White, Lydia V, 439
White, Lydia VI, 89
White, Lydia VI, 455
White, Lydia Elisabeth I, 22
White, Lydia Elisabeth I, 24
White, Lydia F. V, 211
White, Lydia J. I, 454
White, Lydia Jane I, 440
White, Lydia Jane IV, 334
White, Lydia Jane IV, 357
White, Lydia Jane V, 289
White, Lydia L. I, 83
White, Lydia L. I, 88
White, Lydia Louisa I, 24
White, Lydia Louise I, 83
White, Lydia Mourning I, 25
White, Lydia N. I, 631
White, Lydia N. I, 642
White, Lydia Nicholson I, 25
White, Lydia Nicholson I, 40
White, M ary I, 188
White, M. Ellen I, 232
White, M. Ellen I, 260
White, M. Ellen B. I, 228
White, M. Florence I, 19
White, M. Florence I, 83
White, Mabel III, 490
White, Maggie IV, 474
White, Maggie Olive I, 21
White, Mahala I, 581
White, Mahala I, 600
White, Mahala I, 604
White, Mahala I, 608
White, Mar??? IV, 854
White, Marcia I, 123
White, Marcia I, 175
White, Margaret I, 20
White, Margaret I, 22
White, Margaret I, 23
White, Margaret I, 35
White, Margaret I, 49
White, Margaret I, 60
White, Margaret I, 64
White, Margaret I, 72
White, Margaret I, 76
White, Margaret I, 78
White, Margaret I, 79
White, Margaret I, 80
White, Margaret I, 81
White, Margaret I, 82
White, Margaret I, 88
White, Margaret I, 91
White, Margaret I, 123
White, Margaret I, 124
White, Margaret I, 154
White, Margaret I, 160
White, Margaret I, 161
White, Margaret I, 162
White, Margaret I, 173
White, Margaret I, 174
White, Margaret I, 175
White, Margaret I, 176
White, Margaret I, 187
White, Margaret I, 198
White, Margaret I, 201
White, Margaret I, 202
White, Margaret I, 228
White, Margaret I, 260
White, Margaret I, 905
White, Margaret I, 921
White, Margaret I, 926
White, Margaret II, 435
White, Margaret II, 684
White, Margaret IV, 503
White, Margaret IV, 786
White, Margaret IV, 817
White, Margaret IV, 854
White, Margaret IV, 1192
White, Margaret V, 141
White, Margaret VI, 89
White, Margaret VI, 419
White, Margaret VI, 455
White, Margaret VI, 456
White, Margaret VI, 1013
White, Margaret A. I, 84
White, Margaret A. I, 134
White, Margaret A. I, 176
White, Margaret A. IV, 1266
White, Margaret Adeline I, 77
White, Margaret Adeline I, 83
White, Margaret Ann I, 23
White, Margaret Ann I, 124
White, Margaret Beale III, 349
White, Margaret Bertha Allie I, 20
White, Margaret C. I, 24
White, Margaret C. III, 25
White, Margaret E. I, 20
White, Margaret E. I, 83
White, Margaret E. I, 84
White, Margaret E. IV, 750
White, Margaret E. IV, 786
White, Margaret Ellen I, 23
White, Margaret Ellen I, 84
White, Margaret Ellen I, 209
White, Margaret Ellen I, 260
White, Margaret Ellen I, 628
White, Margaret Elma IV, 163
White, Margaret Elma IV, 164
White, Margaret Elma IV, 786
White, Margaret Jordan I, 82
White, Margaret M. I, 20
White, Margaret M. I, 83
White, Margaret Milicent I, 25
White, Margaret S. I, 81
White, Margaret Scott I, 138
White, Margaret Scott I, 175
White, Margaret Susan VI, 89
White, Margaret W. I, 18
White, Margaret W. I, 20
White, Margaret W. I, 75
White, Margaret W. I, 83
White, Margaret Wharton II, 767
White, Margaret Wilson I, 23
White, Margaret Wilson I, 84
White, Margaret Wilson I, 260
White, Margaret Wilson I, 626
White, Margaret Winslow I, 86
White, Margret I, 49
White, Margrete I, 172
White, Maria I, 55
White, Maria I, 81
White, Mariah VI, 679
White, Mariah VI, 700
White, Mariam I, 201
White, Marian I, 202
White, Marianna I, 25
White, Marianna I, 85
White, Marianna I, 944
White, Marianna D. II, 891
White, Marianna D. II, 938
White, Marianna Nicholson I, 936
White, Marianna W. I, 951
White, Marjorie Lelia I, 25
White, Marry II, 99
White, Marry II, 110
White, Marshall III, 349
White, Martha I, 14
White, Martha I, 20
White, Martha I, 21
White, Martha I, 22
White, Martha I, 30
White, Martha I, 66
White, Martha I, 80
White, Martha I, 81
White, Martha I, 82
White, Martha I, 112
White, Martha I, 117
White, Martha I, 123
White, Martha I, 124
White, Martha I, 125
White, Martha I, 151
White, Martha I, 157
White, Martha I, 162
White, Martha I, 164
White, Martha I, 172
White, Martha I, 173
White, Martha I, 174
White, Martha I, 176
White, Martha I, 177
White, Martha I, 187
White, Martha I, 201
White, Martha I, 202
White, Martha I, 450
White, Martha I, 454
White, Martha I, 831
White, Martha I, 844
White, Martha I, 905
White, Martha I, 921
White, Martha I, 930
White, Martha II, 972
White, Martha II, 1007
White, Martha II, 1037
White, Martha IV, 21
White, Martha IV, 67
White, Martha IV, 786
White, Martha IV, 854
White, Martha VI, 89
White, Martha A. VI, 1014
White, Martha Ann VI, 970
White, Martha Ann VI, 998
White, Martha D. I, 604
White, Martha E. I, 24
White, Martha E. I, 25
White, Martha E. I, 26
White, Martha E. I, 29
White, Martha E. I, 84
White, Martha E. I, 454
White, Martha Ellen I, 440
White, Martha Emmeline I, 22
White, Martha G. I, 85
White, Martha J. I, 45
White, Martha J. I, 83
White, Martha J. I, 84
White, Martha Jane I, 8
White, Martha Jane I, 22
White, Martha Jane I, 440
White, Martha Jane IV, 163
White, Martha Jane IV, 164
White, Martha Jane IV, 165
White, Martha Jane VI, 1019
White, Martha M. I, 32
White, Martha M. I, 85
White, Martha N. I, 21
White, Martha N. I, 83
White, Martha N. I, 84
White, Martha N. I, 85
White, Martha N. I, 89
White, Martha P. I, 59
White, Martha P. VI, 89
White, Martha P. VI, 90
White, Martha P. Durham I, 84
White, Martha Parker I, 21
White, Martha Penelope I, 83
White, Martha R. I, 81
White, Martha R. VI, 89
White, Martha R. VI, 279
White, Martha Rix I, 63
White, Martha Rix I, 81
White, Martha Victoria I, 22
White, Martha W. I, 19
White, Mary I, 19
White, Mary I, 20
White, Mary I, 21
White, Mary I, 22
White, Mary I, 23
White, Mary I, 24
White, Mary I, 25
White, Mary I, 26
White, Mary I, 31
White, Mary I, 32
White, Mary I, 42
White, Mary I, 46
White, Mary I, 47
White, Mary I, 54
White, Mary I, 55
White, Mary I, 57
White, Mary I, 61
White, Mary I, 63
White, Mary I, 65
White, Mary I, 70
White, Mary I, 72
White, Mary I, 74
White, Mary I, 78
White, Mary I, 79
White, Mary I, 80
White, Mary I, 81
White, Mary I, 83
White, Mary I, 87
White, Mary I, 88
White, Mary I, 91
White, Mary I, 111
White, Mary I, 123
White, Mary I, 124
White, Mary I, 125
White, Mary I, 134
White, Mary I, 139
White, Mary I, 143
White, Mary I, 145
White, Mary I, 147
White, Mary I, 149
White, Mary I, 153
White, Mary I, 154
White, Mary I, 155
White, Mary I, 159
White, Mary I, 172
White, Mary I, 173
White, Mary I, 174
White, Mary I, 175
White, Mary I, 176
White, Mary I, 177
White, Mary I, 180
White, Mary I, 187
White, Mary I, 195
White, Mary I, 197
White, Mary I, 199
White, Mary I, 201
White, Mary I, 202
White, Mary I, 228
White, Mary I, 260
White, Mary I, 367
White, Mary I, 440
White, Mary I, 454
White, Mary I, 455
White, Mary I, 520
White, Mary I, 581
White, Mary I, 600
White, Mary I, 604
White, Mary I, 608
White, Mary I, 642
White, Mary I, 691
White, Mary I, 732
White, Mary I, 736
White, Mary I, 875
White, Mary I, 905
White, Mary I, 906
White, Mary I, 970
White, Mary I, 1114
White, Mary I, 1134
White, Mary II, 46
White, Mary II, 110
White, Mary II, 113
White, Mary II, 125
White, Mary II, 187
White, Mary II, 235
White, Mary II, 271
White, Mary II, 272
White, Mary II, 435
White, Mary II, 449
White, Mary II, 499
White, Mary II, 630
White, Mary II, 659
White, Mary II, 683
White, Mary II, 684
White, Mary II, 774
White, Mary II, 799
White, Mary II, 909
White, Mary II, 972
White, Mary II, 1023
White, Mary II, 1037
White, Mary III, 26
White, Mary III, 349
White, Mary III, 350
White, Mary IV, 41
White, Mary IV, 67
White, Mary IV, 139
White, Mary IV, 142
White, Mary IV, 163
White, Mary IV, 164
White, Mary IV, 302
White, Mary IV, 303
White, Mary IV, 370
White, Mary IV, 454
White, Mary IV, 595
White, Mary IV, 599
White, Mary IV, 1008
White, Mary IV, 1014
White, Mary IV, 1015
White, Mary IV, 1192
White, Mary IV, 1343
White, Mary V, 211
White, Mary V, 365
White, Mary V, 439
White, Mary V, 901
White, Mary V, 962
White, Mary VI, 45
White, Mary VI, 46
White, Mary VI, 60
White, Mary VI, 73
White, Mary VI, 89
White, Mary VI, 92
White, Mary VI, 99
White, Mary VI, 121
White, Mary VI, 124
White, Mary VI, 369
White, Mary VI, 371
White, Mary VI, 376
White, Mary VI, 444
White, Mary VI, 447
White, Mary VI, 455
White, Mary VI, 456
White, Mary VI, 579
White, Mary VI, 720
White, Mary VI, 864
White, Mary VI, 947
White, Mary VI, 951
White, Mary VI, 1013
White, Mary A. I, 82
White, Mary A. I, 83
White, Mary A. I, 151
White, Mary A. I, 176
White, Mary A. I, 202
White, Mary A. I, 844
White, Mary A. V, 134
White, Mary A. V, 141
White, Mary A. VI, 1013
White, Mary A. C. VI, 92
White, Mary Abigail I, 25
White, Mary Adaline IV, 164
White, Mary Adaline IV, 786
White, Mary Adaline IV, 855
White, Mary Adeline IV, 163
White, Mary Alice I, 24
White, Mary Ann I, 21
White, Mary Ann I, 32
White, Mary Ann I, 83
White, Mary Ann I, 88
White, Mary Ann II, 120
White, Mary Ann II, 125
White, Mary Ann II, 684
White, Mary Ann II, 774
White, Mary Ann II, 877
White, Mary Ann II, 938
White, Mary Ann III, 349
White, Mary Anna III, 350
White, Mary B. III, 33
White, Mary B. III, 36
White, Mary B. III, 348
White, Mary B. III, 349
White, Mary C. I, 454
White, Mary C. VI, 90
White, Mary Catharine I, 440
White, Mary D. II, 909
White, Mary D. II, 939
White, Mary D. III, 85
White, Mary E. I, 10
White, Mary E. I, 20
White, Mary E. I, 22
White, Mary E. I, 23
White, Mary E. I, 24
White, Mary E. I, 25
White, Mary E. I, 26
White, Mary E. I, 27
White, Mary E. I, 28
White, Mary E. I, 44
White, Mary E. I, 54
White, Mary E. I, 67
White, Mary E. I, 83
White, Mary E. I, 84
White, Mary E. I, 85
White, Mary E. I, 642
White, Mary E. I, 670
White, Mary E. I, 932
White, Mary E. VI, 90
White, Mary Elisabeth I, 25
White, Mary Elisabeth I, 45
White, Mary Elisabeth I, 83
White, Mary Eliza I, 8
White, Mary Eliza I, 15
White, Mary Eliza I, 19
White, Mary Eliza I, 21
White, Mary Eliza I, 83
White, Mary Eliza I, 935
White, Mary Eliza I, 951
White, Mary Elizabeth I, 931
White, Mary Ellen I, 215
White, Mary Elma I, 7
White, Mary Emmiline I, 125
White, Mary Eunice I, 23
White, Mary H. II, 938
White, Mary H. II, 1083
White, Mary Hayes II, 835
White, Mary Hayes II, 939
White, Mary I. I, 84
White, Mary I. VI, 89
White, Mary I. VI, 90
White, Mary Irma I, 24
White, Mary Isabella I, 21
White, Mary Isabella I, 23
White, Mary Isabella I, 83
White, Mary Isabella I, 84
White, Mary Isabella I, 89
White, Mary Isabella I, 228
White, Mary Isabella I, 260
White, Mary Isabelle I, 30
White, Mary J. I, 19
White, Mary J. I, 20
White, Mary J. I, 21
White, Mary J. I, 24
White, Mary J. I, 59
White, Mary J. I, 83
White, Mary J. I, 84
White, Mary J. I, 85
White, Mary J. I, 89
White, Mary J. I, 624
White, Mary J. I, 794
White, Mary J. I, 899
White, Mary J. I, 905
White, Mary J. II, 934

te, Mary J. II, 938
te, Mary J. V, 650
te, Mary Jane I, 440
te, Mary Jarvis II, 271
te, Mary Jeanes II, 827
te, Mary Jordan I, 22
te, Mary Jordan I, 84
ite, Mary N. I, 19
ite, Mary Neal V, 141
ite, Mary O. I, 10
ite, Mary O. I, 22
te, Mary O. I, 24
ite, Mary O. I, 81
ite, Mary Parker I, 124
ite, Mary Pleasant I, 22
ite, Mary R. I, 22
ite, Mary R. I, 23
ite, Mary R. I, 24
ite, Mary R. I, 30
ite, Mary R. I, 82
ite, Mary R. I, 83
ite, Mary R. I, 84
ite, Mary R. V, 211
ite, Mary R. VI, 89
ite, Mary S. I, 83
ite, Mary Sabra I, 24
ite, Mary Sabra I, 28
ite, Mary Sabra I, 32
ite, Mary Sabra I, 83
ite, Mary Symons I, 8
ite, Mary Symons I, 20
ite, Mary Symons I, 22
ite, Mary Symons I, 48
ite, Mary Symons I, 81
ite, Mary U. V, 141
ite, Mary W. II, 125
ite, Mary, Sr. I, 83
ite, Massey IV, 855
ite, Massey VI, 897
ite, Matilda IV, 345
ite, Matilda IV, 357
ite, Matilda IV, 599
ite, Matilda IV, 1014
ite, Matilda IV, 1015
ite, Matilda VI, 720
ite, Matilda VI, 930
ite, Matilda VI, 1003
ite, Matilda VI, 1013
ite, Matilda VI, 1016
ite, Matthew I, 23
ite, Matthew I, 25
ite, Matthew I, 70
ite, Matthew I, 78
ite, Matthew I, 79
ite, Matthew I, 173
ite, Matthew I, 174
ite, Matthew I, 176
ite, Matthew I, 604
ite, Mattie VI, 89
ite, Mattie VI, 91
ite, Mattie P. VI, 55
ite, Mattie W. VI, 51
ite, Maud Lee I, 19
ite, Maud Leigh I, 85
ite, Maud Leigh I, 935
ite, Maude Leigh I, 951
hite, Maxamillan I, 201
hite, Maximilian I, 905
hite, Maximilion I, 187
hite, May I, 80
hite, Melissa I, 852
hite, Mercy IV, 1015
hite, Mercy IV, 1176
hite, Mercy IV, 1192
hite, Meriam I, 71
hite, Meriam I, 78
hite, Merriet M. VI, 1013
hite, Merva IV, 1343
hite, Micah I, 174
hite, Micah I, 201
hite, Micajah I, 520
hite, Mildred Esther IV, 1014
hite, Mildred Esther IV, 1015
hite, Milea I, 70
hite, Milea I, 80
hite, Miles I, 34
hite, Miles I, 81
hite, Miles I, 175
hite, Miles I, 176
hite, Miles I, 187
hite, Miles I, 202
hite, Milesant I, 197
hite, Milesant I, 201
hite, Miley I, 25
hite, Miley I Sup 1, 7
hite, Milicent I, 19
hite, Milicent I, 53
hite, Milicent I, 78
hite, Milicent I, 79
hite, Milicent I, 81
hite, Milicent I, 87
White, Milicent I, 142
White, Milicent I, 173
White, Miliscent I, 154
White, Miliscent I, 173
White, Milisent I, 79
White, Millie Elisabeth I, 26
White, Milton I, 520
White, Miriam I, 25
White, Miriam I, 34
White, Miriam I, 76
White, Miriam I, 79
White, Miriam I, 82
White, Miriam I, 123
White, Miriam I, 124
White, Miriam I, 144
White, Miriam I, 147
White, Miriam I, 161
White, Miriam I, 172
White, Miriam I, 173
White, Miriam I, 174
White, Miriam I, 175
White, Miriam I, 180
White, Miriam I, 187
White, Miriam I, 931
White, Miriam IV, 855
White, Miriam IV, 1015
White, Moody I, 23
White, Mordecai I, 80
White, Mordecai John I, 25
White, Mordecai M. V, 941
White, Mordecai Morris V, 899
White, Mordecai Morris V, 901
White, Mordecai Morris V, 904
White, Mordecai Morris V, 926
White, Mordecai Morris V, 940
White, Mordecai Morris V, 941
White, Morris I, 123
White, Moses IV, 786
White, Moses V, 211
White, Mourning I, 22
White, Mourning I, 30
White, Mourning I, 35
White, Mourning I, 79
White, Mourning I, 82
White, Mourning I, 202
White, Mourning VI, 105
White, Mourning VI, 131
White, Mourning VI, 143
White, Mrs. Effie IV, 787
White, Mrs. Matilda VI, 978
White, Murray M. I, 951
White, Murray M., Jr. I, 951
White, Murray Meader I, 936
White, Myrtle Elisabeth I, 21
White, Nancy VI, 518
White, Nancy VI, 664
White, Nancy VI, 862
White, Nancy VI, 864
White, Nancy VI, 870
White, Nancy VI, 986
White, Nancy VI, 997
White, Nancy VI, 1013
White, Nancy VI, 1014
White, Nancy A. I, 604
White, Nancy Jane V, 650
White, Nancy Virginia I, 25
White, Naomi I, 25
White, Naomi I, 60
White, Naomi I, 63
White, Naomi I, 84
White, Naomi I, 132
White, Naomi I, 152
White, Naomi I, 172
White, Naomi I, 173
White, Naomi I, 563
White, Naomi I, 581
White, Naomi I, 622
White, Naomi VI, 458
White, Naomi VI, 626
White, Naomi VI, 680
White, Naomi VI, 681
White, Naomi VI, 720
White, Naomi VI, 723
White, Naomia I, 277
White, Naomiah I, 107
White, Naomy I, 124
White, Nathan I, 22
White, Nathan I, 23
White, Nathan I, 24
White, Nathan I, 34
White, Nathan I, 78
White, Nathan I, 79
White, Nathan I, 81
White, Nathan I, 82
White, Nathan I, 83
White, Nathan I, 88
White, Nathan I, 173
White, Nathan I, 174
White, Nathan I, 175
White, Nathan I, 176
White, Nathan I, 201
White, Nathan I, 260
White, Nathan I, 706
White, Nathan IV, 503
White, Nathan IV, 712
White, Nathan IV, 786
White, Nathan VI, 73
White, Nathan VI, 89
White, Nathan Edward I, 24
White, Nathaniel II, 972
White, Nathaniel IV, 163
White, Nathaniel V, 165
White, Nathaniel V, 211
White, Nathaniel VI, 369
White, Nathaniel VI, 371
White, Nathaniel VI, 376
White, Nathaniel VI, 445
White, Nathaniel VI, 455
White, Nathaniel VI, 456
White, Nathaniel VI, 462
White, Nathaniel VI, 562
White, Nathaniel VI, 579
White, Nathaniel VI, 584
White, Nathaniel, Jr. VI, 456
White, Ned. I, 260
White, Nehemiah I, 112
White, Nehemiah I, 114
White, Nehemiah I, 123
White, Nehemiah I, 125
White, Nehemiah I, 157
White, Nehemiah I, 162
White, Nehemiah I, 172
White, Nehemiah I, 173
White, Nellie I, 628
White, Neomi I, 520
White, Neomi I, 581
White, Newton I, 441
White, Newton I, 454
White, Nicon I, 82
White, Nixon I, 123
White, Nixon I, 202
White, Noami VI, 682
White, Novella I, 25
White, Obed I, 19
White, Obed I, 82
White, Olive IV, 664
White, Olive B. IV, 664
White, Oliver I, 22
White, Oliver I, 23
White, Oliver I, 83
White, Oliver I, 123
White, Oliver III, 350
White, Oliver H. I, 84
White, Orpah I, 23
White, Orpah I, 36
White, Orpah I, 78
White, Orpha I, 71
White, Orpha I, 80
White, Orpha I, 81
White, Oscar I, 905
White, Oscar W. II, 909
White, Oscar W. II, 939
White, Osmond I, 22
White, Osmond I, 23
White, Osmond I, 30
White, Osmund I, 24
White, Osmund I, 25
White, Osmund I, 82
White, Osmund I, 83
White, Oswin I, 24
White, Oswin I, 82
White, Oswin I, 83
White, Oswin VI, 84
White, Oswin VI, 89
White, Oswin VI, 265
White, Oswin VI, 279
White, Ottis J. I, 24
White, Pacy VI, 967
White, Pamely VI, 864
White, Parkey VI, 1013
White, Parthena I, 80
White, Parthena I, 905
White, Partheney I, 123
White, Parthenia I, 79
White, Parthenia I, 187
White, Pasco I, 23
White, Patheney I, 123
White, Patience II, 271
White, Patience III, 349
White, Patience III, 350
White, Patsa I, 319
White, Patsy I, 175
White, Patsy VI, 967
White, Pattie E. I, 22
White, Paul I, 123
White, Paul I, 125
White, Paul IV, 503
White, Paul IV, 840
White, Paul IV, 855
White, Paul Jay I, 21
White, Paul Jay I, 24
White, Paul Whitter I, 670
White, Pauline E. V, 650
White, Peggy I, 319
White, Penelope I, 124
White, Penelope I, 201
White, Penelope I, 736
White, Penelope I, 905
White, Penelope I, 931
White, Penelope VI, 1013
White, Penina I, 70
White, Penina I, 79
White, Penina I, 771
White, Penina I, 844
White, Peninah I, 191
White, Peninah I, 202
White, Peninah I, 844
White, Peninnah I, 162
White, Peninnah I, 173
White, Penninah I, 11
White, Penninah I, 58
White, Penninah I, 82
White, Penninah I, 114
White, Penninah I, 174
White, Penninah I, 736
White, Penninah I, 771
White, Percival B. I, 25
White, Perciville C. VI, 1014
White, Permelia E. VI, 1003
White, Perthena I, 201
White, Perthenia I, 201
White, Peter II, 271
White, Peter III, 348
White, Peter III, 350
White, Pethena I, 125
White, Pethenea I, 123
White, Petheney I, 173
White, Petheny I, 174
White, Pethey I, 175
White, Pharaba I, 206
White, Pharaba Wilson I, 83
White, Pharaby I, 79
White, Pharaby I, 237
White, Pharaby I, 260
White, Pharebee I, 173
White, Phariba Wilson I, 23
White, Pharibe I, 173
White, Phebe I, 794
White, Phebe I, 805
White, Phebe I, 844
White, Phebe III, 350
White, Phebe III, 406
White, Phebe III, 465
White, Phebe IV, 67
White, Phebe IV, 163
White, Phebe IV, 164
White, Phebe IV, 247
White, Phebe IV, 302
White, Phebe IV, 303
White, Phebe IV, 786
White, Phebe V, 165
White, Phebe V, 211
White, Phebe VI, 445
White, Phebe VI, 455
White, Phebe VI, 456
White, Phebe VI, 462
White, Phebe C. III, 23
White, Phebe C. III, 210
White, Phebe S. IV, 763
White, Phebe S. IV, 786
White, Phebe S. V, 211
White, Phebe, Jr. VI, 445
White, Phebe, Jr. VI, 462
White, Pherby I, 228
White, Phetheny I, 172
White, Phetheny I, 176
White, Philander III, 349
White, Philiman I, 123
White, Phillip McFarland I, 22
White, Phinehas I, 81
White, Pleasant I, 22
White, Pleasant I, 25
White, Pleasant I, 63
White, Pleasant I, 79
White, Pleasant I, 82
White, Pleasant I, 174
White, Pleasant I, 201
White, Pleasant VI, 975
White, Pleasant VI, 1013
White, Pliny Earl I, 670
White, Polly I, 175
White, Polly I, 201
White, Polly VI, 864
White, Polly VI, 900
White, Polly VI, 929
White, Polly VI, 937
White, Polly VI, 938
White, Polly VI, 1013
White, Polly J. I, 604
White, Polly P. VI, 1013
White, Priscilla I, 82
White, Priscilla I, 123
White, Priscilla I, 202
White, Priscilla IV, 320
White, Priscilla IV, 330
White, Priscilla IV, 357
White, Priscilla B. I, 642
White, Priscilla Henryanna I, 628
White, Pritchard I, 82
White, Prudence G. IV, 786
White, Prudence H. IV, 712
White, Prudence H. IV, 786
White, Rachel I, 22
White, Rachel I, 23
White, Rachel I, 25
White, Rachel I, 40
White, Rachel I, 55
White, Rachel I, 71
White, Rachel I, 72
White, Rachel I, 74
White, Rachel I, 76
White, Rachel I, 78
White, Rachel I, 79
White, Rachel I, 80
White, Rachel I, 81
White, Rachel I, 87
White, Rachel I, 123
White, Rachel I, 124
White, Rachel I, 138
White, Rachel I, 172
White, Rachel I, 173
White, Rachel I, 228
White, Rachel I, 367
White, Rachel I, 520
White, Rachel I, 867
White, Rachel I, 872
White, Rachel I, 905
White, Rachel II, 60
White, Rachel II, 110
White, Rachel II, 326
White, Rachel II, 972
White, Rachel II, 983
White, Rachel II, 1037
White, Rachel III, 350
White, Rachel IV, 67
White, Rachel IV, 139
White, Rachel IV, 163
White, Rachel IV, 164
White, Rachel IV, 265
White, Rachel IV, 293
White, Rachel IV, 302
White, Rachel IV, 303
White, Rachel VI, 31
White, Rachel VI, 37
White, Rachel VI, 45
White, Rachel VI, 46
White, Rachel VI, 455
White, Rachel VI, 456
White, Rachel VI, 720
White, Rachel VI, 1013
White, Rachel Ann IV, 163
White, Rachel C. III, 23
White, Rachel C. III, 349
White, Rachel C. III, 350
White, Rachel J. I, 20
White, Rachel J. I, 83
White, Rachel M. A. R. I, 20
White, Rachel M. A. R. I, 83
White, Rachel, Jr. I, 162
White, Rachel, Jr. I, 174
White, Rains II, 110
White, Randolph VI, 521
White, Randolph VI, 522
White, Randolph VI, 579
White, Raymond N. I, 26
White, Raymond Travis I, 20
White, Rayne II, 99
White, Rayne II, 110
White, Rebeca I, 81
White, Rebeca I, 124
White, Rebeca I, 125
White, Rebecah I, 124
White, Rebecca I, 23
White, Rebecca I, 34
White, Rebecca I, 72
White, Rebecca I, 76
White, Rebecca I, 78
White, Rebecca I, 79
White, Rebecca I, 80
White, Rebecca I, 81
White, Rebecca I, 82
White, Rebecca I, 125
White, Rebecca I, 156
White, Rebecca I, 172
White, Rebecca I, 175
White, Rebecca I, 176
White, Rebecca I, 201
White, Rebecca I, 202
White, Rebecca I, 581
White, Rebecca I, 600
White, Rebecca I, 922
White, Rebecca II, 187
White, Rebecca II, 228

White, Rebecca II, 251
White, Rebecca II, 252
White, Rebecca II, 271
White, Rebecca II, 276
White, Rebecca II, 435
White, Rebecca II, 684
White, Rebecca II, 722
White, Rebecca II, 774
White, Rebecca II, 801
White, Rebecca II, 934
White, Rebecca II, 938
White, Rebecca IV, 275
White, Rebecca IV, 303
White, Rebecca VI, 412
White, Rebecca VI, 456
White, Rebecca Ann II, 272
White, Rebecca Ann II, 684
White, Rebecca Ann II, 774
White, Rebecca H. VI, 903
White, Rebecca Lamb II, 827
White, Rebecca Merritt II, 294
White, Rebecca Merritt II, 305
White, Rebecca S. II, 684
White, Rebecca S. II, 774
White, Rebecca S. II, 880
White, Rebecca S. II, 938
White, Rebecca W. II, 938
White, Rebeccah I, 125
White, Rebeccah I, 164
White, Rebeccah I, 174
White, Rebeccah I, 187
White, Rebeccah II, 187
White, Rebeckah I, 78
White, Rebeckah I, 149
White, Rebeckah I, 150
White, Rebeckah I, 174
White, Rebeckah II, 542
White, Rebeckah II, 684
White, Rebekah I, 156
White, Rebekah I, 172
White, Rebekah I, 187
White, Rebekah I, 188
White, Rebekah I, 202
White, Rebekah I, 520
White, Rebekah I, 581
White, Rebekah I, 604
White, Rebekah II, 110
White, Rebekah II, 684
White, Rebekah VI, 420
White, Reines II, 46
White, Reuben I, 174
White, Rhoda IV, 164
White, Rhoda IV, 454
White, Rhoda IV, 583
White, Rhoda IV, 599
White, Rhoda Jane I, 604
White, Richard I, 84
White, Richard I, 175
White, Richard I, 969
White, Richard I, 970
White, Richard III, 350
White, Richard V, 134
White, Richard V, 141
White, Richard Everett I, 24
White, Richard Henry I, 25
White, Richardson VI, 864
White, Ro VI, 89
White, Robert I, 21
White, Robert I, 22
White, Robert I, 23
White, Robert I, 80
White, Robert I, 82
White, Robert I, 124
White, Robert I, 128
White, Robert I, 137
White, Robert I, 156
White, Robert I, 172
White, Robert I, 173
White, Robert I, 174
White, Robert I, 187
White, Robert I, 188
White, Robert I, 201
White, Robert I, 202
White, Robert I, 520
White, Robert I, 581
White, Robert II, 450
White, Robert II, 547
White, Robert II, 684
White, Robert III, 23
White, Robert III, 134
White, Robert III, 350
White, Robert VI, 19
White, Robert VI, 89
White, Robert VI, 851
White, Robert B. I, 604
White, Robert B. III, 33
White, Robert B. III, 349
White, Robert Barnes III, 350
White, Robert Bowne III, 350
White, Robert Cornell III, 350
White, Robert Howard I, 23
White, Robert J. I, 21
White, Robert J. I, 24
White, Robert J. I, 27
White, Robert J. I, 28
White, Robert J. I, 83
White, Robert J. I, 84
White, Robert J. III, 350
White, Robert J. Cornell III, 350
White, Robert J., Jr. I, 84
White, Robert J., Sr. I, 25
White, Robert J., Sr. I, 29
White, Robert J., Sr. I, 84
White, Robert Jones I, 83
White, Robert Jordan I, 20
White, Robert Jordan I, 24
White, Robert L. IV, 503
White, Robert L. IV, 786
White, Robert Ralph I, 21
White, Robert Ralph I, 24
White, Robert, Jr. III, 23
White, Robertson I, 175
White, Robinson I, 81
White, Robinson I, 82
White, Robinson I, 175
White, Robt. Brown III, 350
White, Robt. Cornell III, 23
White, Robt. Cornell III, 100
White, Robt. Cornell III, 348
White, Robt. Cornell III, 349
White, Robt. J. Cornell III, 350
White, Robt., Jr. III, 350
White, Rollo Peaslie I, 21
White, Rosa I, 428
White, Rosa B. IV, 320
White, Rosa B. IV, 357
White, Rosa Bell IV, 357
White, Rosa Elma I, 642
White, Rose B. IV, 357
White, Roselle III, 349
White, Rowlan I, 441
White, Rowland H. I, 450
White, Rowland H. I, 454
White, Roxanna I, 930
White, Roxie I, 387
White, Roxie I, 428
White, Roxie I, 670
White, Roxie D. I, 428
White, Roxie Dixon I, 691
White, Ruby I, 24
White, Rufus I, 19
White, Rufus I, 20
White, Rufus I, 21
White, Rufus I, 24
White, Rufus I, 68
White, Rufus I, 82
White, Rufus I, 83
White, Rufus I, 84
White, Rufus I, 85
White, Rufus I, 87
White, Rufus I, 225
White, Rufus I, 642
White, Rufus I, 932
White, Rufus I, 935
White, Rufus I, 936
White, Rufus F. I, 794
White, Rufus J. I, 17
White, Rufus J. I, 24
White, Rufus J. I, 25
White, Rufus Jay I, 21
White, Ruth I, 123
White, Ruth I, 124
White, Ruth I, 144
White, Ruth I, 172
White, Ruth I, 277
White, Ruth I, 367
White, Ruth I, 520
White, Ruth I, 523
White, Ruth I, 581
White, Ruth I, 905
White, Ruth I, 932
White, Ruth III, 349
White, Ruth III, 503
White, Ruth IV, 1299
White, Ruth IV, 1300
White, Ruth IV, 1329
White, Ruth V, 1025
White, Ruth Alice III, 258
White, Ruth Alice III, 349
White, Ruth Alice III, 494
White, Ruth Alice III, 503
White, Ruth E. I, 85
White, Ruth E. I, 440
White, Ruth E. I, 691
White, Ruth E. I, 935
White, Ruth Etna I, 19
White, Ruth Matchett IV, 1343
White, S. W. I, 670
White, S. W. I, 691
White, Sa??? I, 90
White, Sabillah V, 541
White, Sabina II, 808
White, Sabra I, 21
White, Sabra I, 51
White, Sabra I, 82
White, Sabra A. I, 21
White, Sabra Allen I, 30
White, Salley VI, 902
White, Salley VI, 904
White, Sallie I, 25
White, Sally V, 650
White, Sally VI, 908
White, Sally J. I, 604
White, Samira I, 809
White, Samira I, 844
White, Samira IV, 841
White, Saml. D. VI, 982
White, Samuel I, 22
White, Samuel I, 24
White, Samuel I, 25
White, Samuel I, 79
White, Samuel I, 81
White, Samuel I, 82
White, Samuel I, 83
White, Samuel I, 84
White, Samuel I, 123
White, Samuel I, 124
White, Samuel I, 125
White, Samuel I, 168
White, Samuel I, 173
White, Samuel I, 176
White, Samuel I, 201
White, Samuel I, 202
White, Samuel I, 367
White, Samuel I, 428
White, Samuel I, 440
White, Samuel I, 454
White, Samuel I Sup 1, 7
White, Samuel II, 46
White, Samuel II, 187
White, Samuel II, 272
White, Samuel II, 449
White, Samuel II, 976
White, Samuel II, 1023
White, Samuel II, 1037
White, Samuel IV, 664
White, Samuel VI, 862
White, Samuel Crawford II, 187
White, Samuel O. I, 23
White, Samuel S. I, 80
White, Samuel S. I, 81
White, Samuel Scott I, 23
White, Sarah I, 14
White, Sarah I, 19
White, Sarah I, 20
White, Sarah I, 22
White, Sarah I, 23
White, Sarah I, 25
White, Sarah I, 29
White, Sarah I, 46
White, Sarah I, 47
White, Sarah I, 56
White, Sarah I, 58
White, Sarah I, 62
White, Sarah I, 63
White, Sarah I, 64
White, Sarah I, 70
White, Sarah I, 73
White, Sarah I, 75
White, Sarah I, 78
White, Sarah I, 79
White, Sarah I, 80
White, Sarah I, 81
White, Sarah I, 82
White, Sarah I, 84
White, Sarah I, 87
White, Sarah I, 88
White, Sarah I, 90
White, Sarah I, 109
White, Sarah I, 119
White, Sarah I, 123
White, Sarah I, 124
White, Sarah I, 125
White, Sarah I, 128
White, Sarah I, 136
White, Sarah I, 138
White, Sarah I, 144
White, Sarah I, 147
White, Sarah I, 150
White, Sarah I, 152
White, Sarah I, 172
White, Sarah I, 173
White, Sarah I, 174
White, Sarah I, 175
White, Sarah I, 176
White, Sarah I, 177
White, Sarah I, 187
White, Sarah I, 188
White, Sarah I, 191
White, Sarah I, 201
White, Sarah I, 202
White, Sarah I, 228
White, Sarah I, 260
White, Sarah I, 319
White, Sarah I, 386
White, Sarah I, 428
White, Sarah I, 454
White, Sarah I, 520
White, Sarah I, 572
White, Sarah I, 581
White, Sarah I, 600
White, Sarah I, 608
White, Sarah I, 642
White, Sarah I, 670
White, Sarah I, 706
White, Sarah I, 736
White, Sarah I, 844
White, Sarah I, 905
White, Sarah I Sup 1, 3
White, Sarah I Sup 1, 6
White, Sarah II, 51
White, Sarah II, 110
White, Sarah II, 271
White, Sarah II, 435
White, Sarah II, 479
White, Sarah II, 684
White, Sarah II, 774
White, Sarah II, 938
White, Sarah II, 972
White, Sarah II, 976
White, Sarah II, 997
White, Sarah II, 1001
White, Sarah II, 1037
White, Sarah III, 50
White, Sarah III, 290
White, Sarah III, 349
White, Sarah III, 350
White, Sarah IV, 163
White, Sarah IV, 164
White, Sarah IV, 339
White, Sarah IV, 352
White, Sarah IV, 357
White, Sarah IV, 454
White, Sarah IV, 490
White, Sarah IV, 503
White, Sarah IV, 595
White, Sarah IV, 599
White, Sarah IV, 664
White, Sarah V, 165
White, Sarah V, 211
White, Sarah V, 289
White, Sarah V, 541
White, Sarah V, 605
White, Sarah V, 950
White, Sarah V, 962
White, Sarah VI, 55
White, Sarah VI, 89
White, Sarah VI, 369
White, Sarah VI, 455
White, Sarah VI, 456
White, Sarah VI, 720
White, Sarah VI, 928
White, Sarah VI, 1013
White, Sarah VI, 1014
White, Sarah A. I, 70
White, Sarah A. I, 83
White, Sarah Abigail I, 21
White, Sarah Ann I, 187
White, Sarah Ann III, 348
White, Sarah Ann III, 350
White, Sarah Ann VI, 528
White, Sarah Ann VI, 579
White, Sarah Ann VI, 1019
White, Sarah B. I, 29
White, Sarah Baker III, 350
White, Sarah Bertha I, 19
White, Sarah Bertha I, 20
White, Sarah E. I, 19
White, Sarah E. I, 84
White, Sarah E. I, 844
White, Sarah Elizabeth I, 23
White, Sarah F. I, 89
White, Sarah F. V, 541
White, Sarah Frances VI, 1016
White, Sarah G. VI, 521
White, Sarah G. VI, 522
White, Sarah G. VI, 579
White, Sarah G. VI, 791
White, Sarah H. III, 349
White, Sarah H. V, 299
White, Sarah H. V, 313
White, Sarah I. III, 349
White, Sarah I. III, 503
White, Sarah I. VI, 78
White, Sarah I. VI, 89
White, Sarah I. VI, 90
White, Sarah Isabella I, 21
White, Sarah Isabella I, 23
White, Sarah Isabella I, 83
White, Sarah Isabella I, 84
White, Sarah J. I, 21
White, Sarah J. I, 89
White, Sarah J. V, 211
White, Sarah J. VI, 89
White, Sarah Jane I, 24
White, Sarah Jane I, 75
White, Sarah Jane I, 83
White, Sarah Jane Tamer I, 8
White, Sarah Newby I, 22
White, Sarah Penelope I, 23
White, Sarah Rufina V, 552
White, Sarah W. I, 19
White, Sarah W. I, 64
White, Sarah W. I, 82
White, Sarah W. III, 86
White, Sarah, Jr. I, 79
White, Sarrah IV, 156
White, Semira A. I, 604
White, Sension I, 190
White, Sension I, 202
White, Serena B. II, 869
White, Serena B. II, 938
White, Seth I, 25
White, Sheldon II, 938
White, Shirley Nathaniel I, 6
White, Shirley Nathaniel I, 6
White, Shirley Nathaniel I, 6
White, Sidney M. I, 84
White, Sidney Murray I, 951
White, Silas I, 78
White, Silvia Ann I, 21
White, Simeon I, 520
White, Simeon I, 521
White, Simeon A. VI, 905
White, Simeon A. VI, 960
White, Simeon A. VI, 975
White, Simeon A. VI, 983
White, Simeon A. VI, 1007
White, Simon I, 367
White, Simon I, 370
White, Simon I, 386
White, Simon I, 428
White, Simon I, 440
White, Simon I, 454
White, Simon I, 670
White, Simon I, 691
White, Simon III, 406
White, Simon III, 465
White, Simon A. VI, 1014
White, Simon W. I, 670
White, Solomon II, 435
White, Solomon II, 450
White, Solomon II, 637
White, Solomon II, 684
White, Solomon II, 722
White, Solomon II, 1010
White, Sopha I, 201
White, Sophia I, 174
White, Stanton I, 277
White, Stanton I, 520
White, Stanton I, 572
White, Stanton I, 581
White, Stanton I, 600
White, Stanton I, 608
White, Steaphen I, 201
White, Stephen I, 72
White, Stephen I, 80
White, Stephen I, 125
White, Stephen I, 164
White, Stephen I, 174
White, Stephen I, 624
White, Stephen I, 628
White, Stephen I, 642
White, Stephen VI, 888
White, Stephen VI, 953
White, Stephen VI, 962
White, Stephen VI, 987
White, Stephen VI, 1013
White, Stephen D. I, 428
White, Stephen P. I, 642
White, Stephen P. I, 905
White, Stephen Stapler II, 684
White, Stephen V. I, 428
White, Steven I, 260
White, Susan III, 348
White, Susan VI, 89
White, Susan VI, 1014
White, Susan B. P. III, 33
White, Susan B. P. III, 349
White, Susan Morris V, 926
White, Susan Morris V, 940
White, Susana I, 172
White, Susana I, 905
White, Susanah I, 969
White, Susanna I, 125
White, Susanna I, 142
White, Susanna I, 172
White, Susanna I, 428
White, Susanna I, 904
White, Susanna I, 905
White, Susannah I, 80
White, Susannah I, 82
White, Susannah I, 106
White, Susannah I, 123
White, Susannah I, 125

ite, Susannah I, 151
ite, Susannah I, 159
ite, Susannah I, 174
ite, Susannah I, 175
ite, Susannah I, 202
ite, Susannah I, 772
ite, Susannah I, 905
ite, Susannah I, 1134
ite, Susannah VI, 365
ite, Susannah VI, 455
ite, Susannah VI, 456
ite, Susannah VI, 888
ite, Susannah M. VI, 77
ite, Susannah M. VI, 89
ite, Sylvanus IV, 303
ite, Tabitha I, 128
ite, Tabitha I, 172
ite, Tabitha II, 272
ite, Tabitha IV, 840
ite, Tabitha IV, 855
ite, Tabitha V, 141
ite, Taby VI, 987
ite, Tacy S. II, 827
ite, Tamar IV, 1014
ite, Tamer I, 21
ite, Tamer I, 794
ite, Tamer IV, 840
ite, Tamer IV, 854
ite, Teresa III, 349
ite, Thaddeus I, 25
ite, Thaddeus I, 81
ite, Thaddeus I, 82
ite, Thaddeus I, 163
ite, Thamar IV, 854
ite, Theodosia A. VI, 951
ite, Theophelous I, 201
ite, Theophetas I, 201
ite, Theophies I, 905
ite, Theophilas I, 80
ite, Theophilas I, 844
ite, Theophilus I, 25
ite, Theophilus I, 80
ite, Theophlus I, 844
ite, Thomas I, 11
ite, Thomas I, 19
ite, Thomas I, 21
ite, Thomas I, 22
ite, Thomas I, 23
ite, Thomas I, 25
ite, Thomas I, 36
ite, Thomas I, 51
ite, Thomas I, 63
ite, Thomas I, 72
ite, Thomas I, 78
ite, Thomas I, 79
ite, Thomas I, 80
ite, Thomas I, 81
ite, Thomas I, 82
ite, Thomas I, 109
ite, Thomas I, 119
ite, Thomas I, 124
ite, Thomas I, 159
ite, Thomas I, 172
ite, Thomas I, 174
ite, Thomas I, 175
ite, Thomas I, 228
ite, Thomas I, 237
ite, Thomas I, 260
ite, Thomas I, 277
ite, Thomas I, 298
ite, Thomas I, 367
ite, Thomas I, 428
ite, Thomas I, 520
ite, Thomas I, 521
ite, Thomas I, 581
ite, Thomas I, 600
ite, Thomas I, 604
ite, Thomas I, 608
ite, Thomas I, 682
ite, Thomas I, 691
ite, Thomas I, 905
ite, Thomas I, 929
ite, Thomas I, 1134
ite, Thomas II, 45
ite, Thomas II, 271
ite, Thomas II, 435
ite, Thomas II, 542
ite, Thomas II, 684
ite, Thomas II, 972
ite, Thomas II, 1037
ite, Thomas III, 349
ite, Thomas IV, 142
ite, Thomas IV, 163
ite, Thomas IV, 164
ite, Thomas IV, 302
ite, Thomas IV, 303
ite, Thomas IV, 357
ite, Thomas IV, 454
ite, Thomas IV, 503
ite, Thomas IV, 786
ite, Thomas IV, 854
White, Thomas V, 541
White, Thomas VI, 31
White, Thomas VI, 37
White, Thomas VI, 279
White, Thomas VI, 455
White, Thomas VI, 456
White, Thomas VI, 579
White, Thomas VI, 584
White, Thomas VI, 703
White, Thomas VI, 720
White, Thomas VI, 1013
White, Thomas A. V, 650
White, Thomas C. I, 794
White, Thomas Chalkley II, 938
White, Thomas D. I, 20
White, Thomas D. I, 25
White, Thomas D. I, 82
White, Thomas D. I, 83
White, Thomas D. I, 151
White, Thomas D. I, 176
White, Thomas E. I, 89
White, Thomas J. I, 228
White, Thomas J. I, 428
White, Thomas N. I, 81
White, Thomas N. VI, 89
White, Thomas Newby I, 20
White, Thomas Newby I, 81
White, Thomas P. I, 21
White, Thomas P. I, 84
White, Thomas P. VI, 60
White, Thomas P. VI, 89
White, Thomas P. VI, 90
White, Thomas P., Jr. VI, 89
White, Thomas Pailen I, 124
White, Thomas Parker I, 83
White, Thomas S. I, 23
White, Thomas T. VI, 1013
White, Thomas W. I, 10
White, Thomas W. VI, 89
White, Thomas William IV, 163
White, Thomas Winfred I, 19
White, Thomas Winfred I, 85
White, Thomas Winfred I, 951
White, Thomas, Jr. I, 260
White, Thomas, Jr. I, 581
White, Thophilus I, 76
White, Thophilus I, 78
White, Thos. I, 228
White, Thos. II, 877
White, Thos. II, 938
White, Thos. IV, 454
White, Thos. IV, 474
White, Thos. V, 650
White, Thos. Chalkley II, 827
White, Thos., Jr. V, 940
White, Timothy I, 23
White, Timothy I, 80
White, Timothy I, 81
White, Timothy VI, 88
White, Timothy VI, 89
White, Timothy B. IV, 664
White, Timothy, Jr. IV, 664
White, Tomes I, 201
White, Toms I, 49
White, Toms I, 74
White, Toms I, 79
White, Toms I, 125
White, Toms I, 173
White, Toms I, 174
White, Toms I, 187
White, Toms I, 201
White, Toms I, 202
White, Tracis I, 202
White, Uriah IV, 21
White, Uriah IV, 67
White, Uriah IV, 786
White, Uriah IV, 854
White, Uriah VI, 456
White, Uriah VI, 720
White, Uriah VI, 864
White, Vera IV, 786
White, Vivian I, 623
White, Vivian Jordan I, 931
White, Vivian Robert I, 21
White, W. Winfred I, 935
White, Walter I, 14
White, Walter I, 24
White, Walter I, 25
White, Walter I, 64
White, Walter I, 84
White, Walter I, 85
White, Walter I, 613
White, Walter I, 930
White, Walter I, 931
White, Walter I, 936
White, Walter I, 951
White, Walter Rhoades II, 827
White, Warren IV, 1299
White, Watson I, 82
White, Wayland I, 23
White, Wayland I, 25
White, Wd. Charlotte II, 807
White, Wd. Mary Woodrow VI, 562
White, Wesley J. I, 25
White, Wesley J. I, 84
White, Widow Anne I, 172
White, Widow Charlotte I, 175
White, Widow Charlotte I, 201
White, Widow Damaris I, 124
White, Widow Damaris I, 172
White, Widow Elizabeth I, 164
White, Widow Elizabeth I, 172
White, Widow Jane I, 161
White, Widow Lydia I, 79
White, Widow Margaret I, 56
White, Widow Margaret I, 176
White, Widow Martha R. I, 82
White, Widow Mary I, 21
White, Widow Mary I, 197
White, Widow Mary I, 201
White, Widow Mary VI, 579
White, Widow Mary Jordan I, 82
White, Widow Pleasant Winslow I, 43
White, Widow Sarah I, 440
White, Wilfred F. VI, 732
White, Wilfred F. VI, 791
White, Willard Moody I, 215
White, William I, 22
White, William I, 23
White, William I, 25
White, William I, 43
White, William I, 78
White, William I, 79
White, William I, 81
White, William I, 83
White, William I, 124
White, William I, 125
White, William I, 164
White, William I, 173
White, William I, 175
White, William I, 176
White, William I, 298
White, William I, 428
White, William I, 440
White, William I, 441
White, William I, 446
White, William I, 454
White, William I, 520
White, William I, 608
White, William I, 794
White, William I, 844
White, William I, 905
White, William I, 953
White, William I, 969
White, William I, 1134
White, William II, 187
White, William II, 235
White, William II, 271
White, William II, 435
White, William II, 972
White, William II, 1037
White, William IV, 164
White, William IV, 357
White, William VI, 455
White, William VI, 456
White, William VI, 720
White, William VI, 945
White, William VI, 1013
White, William A. I, 85
White, William A. I, 454
White, William A. I, 670
White, William A. I, 691
White, William A. VI, 798
White, William A. VI, 951
White, William A. VI, 1013
White, William A. VI, 1014
White, William A. B. VI, 940
White, William Adison I, 440
White, William Albertson I, 202
White, William Allison I, 22
White, William Allison I, 25
White, William Allison I, 26
White, William C. I, 604
White, William C. III, 350
White, William C., Jr. III, 350
White, William E. I, 670
White, William F. I, 21
White, William F. I, 83
White, William F. I, 84
White, William Frances I, 26
White, William Francis I, 24
White, William Freshwater I, 25
White, William Freshwater I, 81
White, William H. III, 349
White, William H. VI, 887
White, William H. VI, 908
White, William Hambleton IV, 786
White, William Luther I, 84
White, William M. VI, 823
White, William M. VI, 864
White, William O. I, 22
White, William O. I, 84
White, William Odis I, 20
White, William Overman I, 82
White, William Rufus I, 24
White, William Wilson I, 83
White, William, Jr. I, 36
White, William, Jr. I, 78
White, William, Jr. I, 79
White, William, Jr. I, 87
White, William, Jr. II, 271
White, William, Sr. II, 722
White, Willis Farnum III, 349
White, Wilson I, 928
White, Wilson V, 365
White, Winona V, 650
White, Wm. I, 361
White, Wm. I, 367
White, Wm. I, 404
White, Wm. I, 428
White, Wm. II, 125
White, Wm. II, 479
White, Wm. II, 684
White, Wm. II, 1031
White, Wm. II, 1037
White, Wm. IV, 490
White, Wm. IV, 786
White, Wm. IV, 855
White, Wm. IV, 1202
White, Wm. V, 456
White, Wm. V, 605
White, Wm. A. I, 670
White, Wm. A. V, 211
White, Wm. A. VI, 929
White, Wm. A. VI, 1013
White, Wm. A. VI, 1018
White, Wm. A., Jr. I, 670
White, Wm. Alexander I, 21
White, Wm. C. III, 26
White, Wm. C. III, 350
White, Wm. Davis VI, 881
White, Wm. Fracis I, 7
White, Wm. Hamilton IV, 164
White, Wm. Joseph I, 611
White, Wm. W. I, 23
White, Wm., Jr. II, 125
White, Wyke I, 63
White, Wyot I, 604
White, Zacha. I, 63
White, Zachariah I, 42
White, Zachariah I, 78
White, Zachariah I, 79
White, Zachariah I, 154
White, Zachariah I, 201
White, Zebulon Donald I, 20
White, Zephaniah I, 172
White, Zephemiah I, 172
Whiteacer, Jane II, 1029
Whiteacer, Jane II, 1038
Whiteacre, Mary IV, 664
Whiteall, Caroline V, 917
Whiteall, Charles II, 435
Whiteall, James II, 435
Whiteall, James II, 609
Whiteall, James II, 684
Whiteall, James, Jr. II, 684
Whiteall, John II, 435
Whiteall, Joseph II, 684
Whiteall, Louisa II, 684
Whiteall, Lydia II, 684
Whiteall, Mary II, 435
Whiteall, Mary II, 609
Whiteall, Mary II, 684
Whiteall, Rebecca II, 684
Whiteall, Tatthu II, 684
Whiteall, Wm. C. II, 684
Whiteall, Zatthu II, 684
Whitealls, John II, 435
Whiteborn, Frances VI, 933
Whitebread, Sarah II, 578
Whitebread, Sarah II, 684
Whitechar, Joseph II, 1000
Whitechar, Joseph II, 1038
Whitechar, Robert II, 1000
Whitechar, Robert II, 1038
Whitechar, Sarah II, 1000
Whitechar, Sarah II, 1038
Whitecor, Ann IV, 664
Whitecor, Asael IV, 664
Whitecor, Edward IV, 664
Whitecor, Isaac IV, 664
Whitecor, John IV, 664
Whitecor, Kezia IV, 664
Whitecor, Mahlon IV, 664
Whitecor, Martha IV, 664
Whitecor, Phebe IV, 664
Whitecre, Rebecca IV, 886
Whitefield, Benjam VI, 90
Whitefield, Benjamin VI, 90
Whitefield, Sarah II, 684
Whiteford, Eliz. III, 440
Whitehall, Abraham II, 435
Whitehall, Charles II, 435
Whitehall, Esther II, 435
Whitehall, James II, 435
Whitehall, John II, 435
Whitehall, Louisa II, 632
Whitehall, Louisa II, 684
Whitehall, Lydia II, 435
Whitehall, Mary II, 435
Whitehall, Samuel II, 435
Whitehall, Sarah II, 435
Whitehead, Ann III, 399
Whitehead, Ann III, 465
Whitehead, Benjamin II, 449
Whitehead, Charlotte V, 211
Whitehead, David III, 350
Whitehead, David IV, 164
Whitehead, David IV, 303
Whitehead, Edward II, 435
Whitehead, Elias G. V, 211
Whitehead, Elisha III, 350
Whitehead, Elisha IV, 164
Whitehead, Eliz. III, 350
Whitehead, Elizabeth III, 113
Whitehead, Elizabeth III, 350
Whitehead, Elizabeth A. VI, 864
Whitehead, Esther II, 464
Whitehead, Esther II, 684
Whitehead, Gertrude V, 211
Whitehead, Hannah III, 350
Whitehead, Hannah IV, 156
Whitehead, Hannah IV, 164
Whitehead, Henry II, 684
Whitehead, James II, 435
Whitehead, Jane I, 376
Whitehead, Jane I, 428
Whitehead, Jesse III, 350
Whitehead, Jesse IV, 164
Whitehead, Joan II, 272
Whitehead, John I, 61
Whitehead, John I, 85
Whitehead, John III, 350
Whitehead, John III, 399
Whitehead, John III, 465
Whitehead, Jos. III, 350
Whitehead, Joseph III, 350
Whitehead, Joseph B. VI, 58
Whitehead, Joseph B. VI, 90
Whitehead, Josiah I, 428
Whitehead, Lina I, 30
Whitehead, Lulu VI, 65
Whitehead, Lulu VI, 90
Whitehead, Lusetta I, 597
Whitehead, Lusetta I, 598
Whitehead, Martha J. VI, 65
Whitehead, Martin VI, 864
Whitehead, Mary I, 193
Whitehead, Mary I, 202
Whitehead, Mary III, 350
Whitehead, Mary IV, 156
Whitehead, Mary IV, 164
Whitehead, Mary V, 211
Whitehead, Miriam I, 61
Whitehead, Miriam I, 85
Whitehead, Penelope II, 435
Whitehead, Rachel III, 350
Whitehead, Raleigh VI, 864
Whitehead, Ralph IV, 164
Whitehead, Rebecca V, 211
Whitehead, Roy V, 772
Whitehead, Samuel III, 350
Whitehead, Samuel IV, 164
Whitehead, Sarah I, 425
Whitehead, Sarah I, 428
Whitehead, Serena VI, 864
Whitehead, Thomas II, 684
Whitehead, William III, 350
Whitehead, William IV, 164
Whitehead, William A. VI, 65
Whitehead, Wm. V, 467
Whitehouse, Catharine III, 350
Whitehouse, John III, 350
Whitehouse, John III, 503
Whitehouse, Sarah I, 627
Whitehurst, ??? I, 31
Whitehurst, Berthel I, 628
Whitehurst, Lena I, 628
Whitehurst, Luther I, 628
Whitehurst, Richard VI, 11
Whitehurst, Sallie E. I, 31
Whitehurst, William VI, 11
Whiteker, Martha II, 1037
Whiteleather, Anna E. IV, 929
Whiteleather, Blanch Elizabeth IV, 1015
Whiteleather, Blanche E. IV, 1015
Whiteleather, Bye IV, 855
Whiteleather, Elizabeth IV, 821
Whiteleather, Elizabeth IV, 855

Whiteleather, Idella IV, 917
Whiteleather, Idella IV, 1044
Whiteleather, Joseph IV, 929
Whiteleather, Katharine IV, 1015
Whiteleather, Lawrence IV, 917
Whiteleather, Lawrence IV, 1044
Whiteleather, Leah IV, 929
Whiteleather, Thelma IV, 1044
Whiteleather, Thelma Marrietta IV, 917
Whiteleather, Winfred B. IV, 1015
Whiteley, Caroline II, 722
Whiteley, George T. II, 722
Whiteley, Joseph II, 722
Whiteley, Joseph II, 774
Whiteley, Joshua R. II, 722
Whiteley, Mary II, 722
Whiteley, Mary Ann II, 722
Whiteley, Mary Ann II, 774
Whiteley, Mary J. II, 722
Whiteley, Sarah E. II, 722
Whiteley, Sarah Ellen II, 722
Whiteley, Sarah Ellen II, 774
Whiteley, Thomas II, 722
Whitelick, Ann II, 685
Whitelick, Martha II, 685
Whitelick, Mary II, 685
Whitelick, Rumford Dawes II, 685
Whitell, James II, 435
Whitell, Sarah II, 435
Whitelock, Ann II, 797
Whitelock, Ann II, 1083
Whitelock, Anna S. II, 1083
Whitelock, Daniel II, 685
Whitelock, Elizabeth II, 685
Whitelock, Isaac II, 435
Whitelock, Isaac II, 685
Whitelock, Isaac II, 797
Whitelock, Jane II, 814
Whitelock, Jane S. II, 1083
Whitelock, Martha II, 685
Whitelock, Mary II, 557
Whitelock, Mary II, 685
Whitelock, Sarah II, 435
Whitelow, William VI, 862
Whitely, Annie V, 888
Whitely, Caroline II, 774
Whitely, Elmira J. V, 141
Whitely, George T. II, 774
Whitely, Joseph II, 774
Whitely, Joshua R. II, 774
Whitely, Mary Ann II, 774
Whitely, Mary J. II, 774
Whitely, Milley VI, 1014
Whitely, Nancy VI, 938
Whitely, Sarah E. II, 774
Whitely, Sarah Ellen II, 774
Whitely, Susan Jane VI, 938
Whitely, William VI, 959
Whitely, William VI, 1014
Whitemore, Francis W. IV, 67
Whitenot, Jane VI, 385
Whitenot, Jane VI, 456
Whitepain, Sarah II, 643
Whitepain, Sarah II, 685
Whitesell, Susie II, 134
Whiteside, Bertha P. III, 277
Whiteside, Frederick W. III, 277
Whiteside, Jennie Ross V, 719
Whiteside, Margaretta V, 719
Whitesides, Hannah IV, 67
Whitesides, Henry II, 1037
Whiteson, Hannah III, 447
Whiteson, Joseph III, 447
Whiteson, Mary Esther III, 448
Whiteson, Phebe III, 448
Whiteson, Samuel III, 448
Whitey, Esra VI, 881
Whitezell, Elizabeth IV, 664
Whitfield, Jane III, 350
Whitfield, Margaret VI, 45
Whitfield, Margaret VI, 46
Whitfield, Rebecca III, 106
Whitfield, Rebecca III, 350
Whitfield, Selena Grace III, 58
Whitfield, Selena Grace III, 351
Whitfield, Susan III, 264
Whitfield, Susan III, 351
Whithead, Lewis VI, 46
Whithead, Mary VI, 45
Whithead, Mary VI, 46
Whiticar, John II, 1025
Whiticar, John II, 1037
Whiticar, Thomas IV, 786
Whitiker, Mary IV, 67
Whiting, Anna IV, 1217
Whiting, Claretta III, 65
Whiting, Clariss III, 65
Whiting, Judith C. IV, 1224
Whiting, Judith C. IV, 1227
Whiting, Molly III, 65
Whiting, Phebe III, 351
Whiting, Samuel III, 65
Whiting, Sarah S. IV, 1217
Whiting, Sarah S. IV, 1227
Whiting, Thomas IV, 1217
Whitingdon, Josie V, 211
Whitlack, Sarah S. V, 289
Whitley, ??? III, 35
Whitley, ??? III, 351
Whitley, Ann C. VI, 1014
Whitley, Barsheba VI, 1014
Whitley, Benjamin I, 340
Whitley, Bettie I, 340
Whitley, Charles VI, 1014
Whitley, Edgar III, 351
Whitley, Eliza I, 340
Whitley, Elizabeth III, 351
Whitley, Emma I, 340
Whitley, Hansford I, 176
Whitley, James H. III, 351
Whitley, Jane I, 340
Whitley, Jesse, Jr. I, 340
Whitley, John I, 340
Whitley, John VI, 1014
Whitley, John D. I, 340
Whitley, Lola I, 340
Whitley, Louisa I, 340
Whitley, Louise I, 340
Whitley, Lydia I, 340
Whitley, Malinda VI, 810
Whitley, Martha III, 35
Whitley, Martha III, 351
Whitley, Milley VI, 1014
Whitley, Pemelia VI, 1014
Whitley, Sarah I, 340
Whitley, William VI, 1014
Whitley, Willie I, 340
Whitlock, Charles E. VI, 279
Whitlock, Eliza Catherine VI, 266
Whitlock, H. Virginia VI, 265
Whitlock, H. Virginia VI, 279
Whitlock, Harriet Virginia VI, 279
Whitlock, James G. VI, 279
Whitlock, James Gilbert VI, 279
Whitlock, Jane VI, 74
Whitlock, Jane VI, 90
Whitlock, Jane VI, 217
Whitlock, Jane VI, 279
Whitlock, Jane C. VI, 266
Whitlock, Jane C. VI, 279
Whitlock, Joel Cook VI, 90
Whitlock, Lottie I, 929
Whitlock, Lydia III, 351
Whitlock, Martha II, 685
Whitlock, Martha VI, 265
Whitlock, Martha S. VI, 266
Whitlock, Martha S. VI, 279
Whitlock, Mary J. VI, 58
Whitlock, Mary J. VI, 90
Whitlock, Mary Jane VI, 235
Whitlock, Mary Jane VI, 279
Whitlock, Octavia VI, 279
Whitlock, Octavia A. VI, 279
Whitlock, Richard VI, 279
Whitlock, Richard H. VI, 235
Whitlock, Richard H. VI, 266
Whitlock, Richard H. VI, 279
Whitlock, Susannah VI, 864
Whitlock, Thomas VI, 864
Whitlock, Wm. IV, 1343
Whitlock, Wm. E. IV, 1343
Whitlocke, George VI, 1014
Whitlocke, Harriet VI, 1014
Whitlocke, Martha B. VI, 974
Whitlocke, Mary D. VI, 966
Whitlow, ??? V, 719
Whitlow, Alexander VI, 800
Whitlow, Andrew VI, 800
Whitlow, Andrew VI, 841
Whitlow, Andrew VI, 864
Whitlow, Andrew S. VI, 803
Whitlow, Andrew S., Jr. VI, 800
Whitlow, Charlotte VI, 839
Whitlow, Charlotte VI, 864
Whitlow, Delilih P. VI, 800
Whitlow, Delina VI, 862
Whitlow, Henry VI, 798
Whitlow, Henry VI, 862
Whitlow, J. H. VI, 839
Whitlow, Josiah VI, 825
Whitlow, Josiah H. VI, 808
Whitlow, Louisa VI, 864
Whitlow, Margaret M. VI, 800
Whitlow, Martha VI, 862
Whitlow, Martha Smith VI, 798
Whitlow, Nettie V, 710
Whitlow, Nettie V, 719
Whitlow, Patsy VI, 798
Whitlow, Sarah II, 435
Whitlow, Sarah VI, 864
Whitlow, Sarah P. VI, 815
Whitlow, William VI, 798
Whitlow, William VI, 815
Whitlow, William VI, 841
Whitlow, William VI, 851
Whitlow, William VI, 864
Whitlow, Wm. P. VI, 864
Whitman, Charity V, 719
Whitman, Charles V, 719
Whitman, Ella V, 719
Whitman, Isaac III, 351
Whitman, Martha III, 435
Whitman, Martha III, 437
Whitman, Martha III, 465
Whitman, Nancy III, 351
Whitmore, Martin II, 110
Whitner, Annie VI, 279
Whitner, James VI, 279
Whitner, Virginia VI, 279
Whitner, Virginia Barna VI, 279
Whitney, Amy I, 486
Whitney, Chas. B. III, 299
Whitney, Chas. B. III, 351
Whitney, D. III, 452
Whitney, Dan D. III, 455
Whitney, Daniel D. III, 452
Whitney, Daniel D. III, 455
Whitney, Daniel D. III, 465
Whitney, Demsey I, 298
Whitney, Ebanezar I, 692
Whitney, Ebenezar I, 298
Whitney, Ebenezar I, 679
Whitney, Eli I, 298
Whitney, Eli I, 670
Whitney, Eli I, 692
Whitney, Elizabeth I, 298
Whitney, Elizabeth III, 451
Whitney, Elizabeth III, 452
Whitney, Elizabeth III, 465
Whitney, Elnathan I, 692
Whitney, Esther III, 351
Whitney, George G. III, 351
Whitney, Henrietta III, 452
Whitney, Henrietta III, 455
Whitney, Henrietta III, 465
Whitney, James H. III, 351
Whitney, Janet E. III, 351
Whitney, Jemima I, 298
Whitney, Jemima I, 692
Whitney, Jemimah I, 319
Whitney, Joseph R. II, 775
Whitney, Joseph Rankin II, 775
Whitney, Katie Gould III, 299
Whitney, Katie Gould III, 351
Whitney, Nella III, 299
Whitney, Nella III, 351
Whitney, Ramsom I, 298
Whitney, Ray IV, 1044
Whitney, Richard A. III, 351
Whitney, Sarah III, 319
Whitney, Sarah III, 351
Whitney, Sarah III, 452
Whitney, Sarah III, 455
Whitney, Sarah T. III, 351
Whitney, Sarah W. III, 465
Whitney, Scudder V. III, 451
Whitney, Scudder V. III, 452
Whitney, Scudder V. III, 465
Whitney, Widow Jemima I, 679
Whitney, William Gillett III, 351
Whitney, William H. A. III, 351
Whitpain, Jehu II, 685
Whitpain, John II, 435
Whitpain, Mary II, 435
Whitpain, Mary II, 685
Whitpain, Sarah II, 435
Whitpain, Sarah II, 656
Whitpain, Sarah II, 685
Whitpain, Wd. Ann II, 435
Whitpain, William II, 435
Whitpain, Zachariah II, 435
Whitpain, Zachary II, 656
Whitpain, Zachary II, 685
Whitpain, Zechariah II, 435
Whitpaine, Jehu II, 590
Whitpaine, John II, 435
Whitpaine, John II, 440
Whitpaine, Mary II, 590
Whitpane, Sarah II, 454
Whitpane, Sarah II, 685
Whitpayne, John II, 404
Whitpayne, Zachariah II, 404
Whitsal, Susannah V, 141
Whitsall, Susannah V, 141
Whitsel, Adda Rachel V, 289
Whitsel, Adda Rachel V, 605
Whitsel, Emma M. V, 141
Whitsel, Inis V, 289
Whitsel, Lida F. V, 289
Whitsel, Lida F. V, 605
Whitsel, Martha Ann V, 83
Whitsel, Martha M. V, 141
Whitsel, Matilda V, 116
Whitsel, Matilda V, 141
Whitsel, Susan J. V, 289
Whitsel, Susan J. V, 605
Whitsel, Susannah V, 141
Whitsel, Susannah V, 605
Whitsel, Susannah J. V, 602
Whitsel, Susannah J. V, 605
Whitson, ??? III, 351
Whitson, ??? V, 147
Whitson, Abbie III, 466
Whitson, Abi II, 722
Whitson, Abigail III, 437
Whitson, Abigail P. III, 351
Whitson, Abraham III, 322
Whitson, Abraham III, 351
Whitson, Abraham III, 386
Whitson, Abraham III, 387
Whitson, Abraham III, 468
Whitson, Abraham III, 486
Whitson, Abraham III, 503
Whitson, Abraham III, 504
Whitson, Abraham U. III, 386
Whitson, Abraham W. III, 386
Whitson, Abram Underhill III, 465
Whitson, Abram Underhill III, 466
Whitson, Abrm. III, 421
Whitson, Abrm. III, 465
Whitson, Abrm. III, 468
Whitson, Amey III, 465
Whitson, Amos II, 722
Whitson, Amos III, 411
Whitson, Amos III, 465
Whitson, Amos III, 467
Whitson, Amos III, 479
Whitson, Amos III, 482
Whitson, Amos III, 503
Whitson, Amos III, 505
Whitson, Amy III, 386
Whitson, Amy III, 387
Whitson, Amy III, 411
Whitson, Amy III, 465
Whitson, Amy III, 466
Whitson, Amy III, 467
Whitson, Amy III, 468
Whitson, Amy III, 479
Whitson, Amy III, 482
Whitson, Amy III, 503
Whitson, Amy III, 504
Whitson, Amy III, 505
Whitson, Ann I, 1037
Whitson, Ann I, 1039
Whitson, Ann I, 1058
Whitson, Ann I, 1059
Whitson, Ann III, 166
Whitson, Ann III, 351
Whitson, Ann III, 386
Whitson, Ann III, 388
Whitson, Ann III, 389
Whitson, Ann III, 465
Whitson, Ann III, 500
Whitson, Ann III, 503
Whitson, Ann III, 504
Whitson, Ann III, 505
Whitson, Ann III, 506
Whitson, Ann V, 199
Whitson, Ann V, 211
Whitson, Ann VI, 587
Whitson, Ann Eliza III, 169
Whitson, Ann Eliza III, 351
Whitson, Anna III, 386
Whitson, Anna III, 387
Whitson, Anna III, 465
Whitson, Anna III, 468
Whitson, Anna IV, 833
Whitson, Anna IV, 855
Whitson, Anna R. II, 722
Whitson, Anna R. II, 775
Whitson, Anne III, 467
Whitson, Barbara V, 211
Whitson, Barbara V, 526
Whitson, Barbara V, 541
Whitson, Barbara V, 544
Whitson, Benj. F. IV, 833
Whitson, Benjamin F. IV, 855
Whitson, Charity V, 211
Whitson, Charles III, 351
Whitson, Charles III, 386
Whitson, Charles III, 503
Whitson, Clemence III, 393
Whitson, Clemence III, 406
Whitson, Clemence III, 466
Whitson, Clement III, 406
Whitson, Clement III, 435
Whitson, Clement III, 460
Whitson, Clement III, 465
Whitson, Clement III, 466
Whitson, Clement III, 481
Whitson, Clementine III, 479
Whitson, Clementine III, 486
Whitson, Clementine III, 501
Whitson, Clementine III, 502
Whitson, Clementine III, 503
Whitson, Clemmy III, 503
Whitson, Clemmy III, 504
Whitson, Cyrus II, 722
Whitson, Cyrus II, 775
Whitson, Daniel III, 351
Whitson, Daniel III, 503
Whitson, Daniel III, 504
Whitson, David I, 1039
Whitson, David I, 1058
Whitson, David I, 1059
Whitson, David I, 1062
Whitson, David I, 1063
Whitson, David I Sup 1, 11
Whitson, David III, 351
Whitson, David III, 386
Whitson, David III, 435
Whitson, David III, 465
Whitson, David III, 466
Whitson, David III, 503
Whitson, David V, 142
Whitson, David V, 159
Whitson, David V, 211
Whitson, David V, 469
Whitson, David VI, 587
Whitson, David, Jr. V, 211
Whitson, Deborah III, 116
Whitson, Deborah III, 351
Whitson, Deborah III, 410
Whitson, Deborah III, 437
Whitson, Deborah III, 441
Whitson, Deborah III, 465
Whitson, Deborah III, 466
Whitson, Deborah III, 467
Whitson, Deborah III, 487
Whitson, Deborah III, 496
Whitson, Deborah III, 500
Whitson, Deborah III, 503
Whitson, Deborah III, 504
Whitson, Deborah III, 505
Whitson, Deborah V, 472
Whitson, Deborah V, 541
Whitson, Dinah V, 542
Whitson, Dinah V, 549
Whitson, Dinah V, 605
Whitson, Edmund Hicks III,
Whitson, Edward III, 351
Whitson, Elenor V, 506
Whitson, Elenor V, 542
Whitson, Eliphalet III, 503
Whitson, Elizabeth II, 1037
Whitson, Elizabeth III, 466
Whitson, Elizabeth III, 495
Whitson, Elizabeth III, 503
Whitson, Elizabeth III, 504
Whitson, Elizabeth V, 541
Whitson, Ellen Jane V, 541
Whitson, Emma II, 939
Whitson, Esther III, 281
Whitson, Esther III, 351
Whitson, Esther III, 353
Whitson, Esther III, 360
Whitson, Esther III, 361
Whitson, Esther III, 386
Whitson, Esther III, 387
Whitson, Esther III, 421
Whitson, Esther III, 443
Whitson, Esther III, 465
Whitson, Esther III, 466
Whitson, Esther III, 468
Whitson, Esther III, 470
Whitson, Eugene III, 386
Whitson, Eugene III, 389
Whitson, Eunice V, 542
Whitson, Eunice V, 605
Whitson, Eva T. V, 211
Whitson, Ezekiel V, 483
Whitson, Florence Edna III, 4
Whitson, Florence Edna III, 3
Whitson, Franklin B. III, 504
Whitson, George, Jr. V, 542
Whitson, Gilbert III, 351
Whitson, Gilbert III, 504
Whitson, Gilbert E. III, 351
Whitson, Gilbert E. III, 465
Whitson, Hannah II, 292
Whitson, Hannah III, 59
Whitson, Hannah III, 166
Whitson, Hannah III, 351
Whitson, Hannah III, 403
Whitson, Hannah III, 411
Whitson, Hannah III, 435
Whitson, Hannah III, 437
Whitson, Hannah III, 465

tson, Hannah III, 466
tson, Hannah III, 482
tson, Hannah III, 499
tson, Hannah III, 503
tson, Hannah III, 504
tson, Hannah III, 505
tson, Hannah W. III, 500
tson, Hannah W. III, 503
tson, Hannah W. III, 504
tson, Helen F. III, 504
tson, Henry II, 1037
tson, Henry III, 48
tson, Henry III, 230
tson, Henry III, 351
tson, Henry III, 393
tson, Henry III, 403
tson, Henry III, 406
tson, Henry III, 435
tson, Henry III, 437
tson, Henry III, 460
tson, Henry III, 465
tson, Henry III, 466
tson, Henry III, 479
tson, Henry III, 481
tson, Henry III, 486
tson, Henry III, 501
tson, Henry III, 502
tson, Henry III, 503
tson, Henry III, 504
tson, Ida M. IV, 855
tson, Jacob III, 504
tson, Jacob H. III, 351
tson, Jacob H. III, 386
tson, Jacob H. III, 504
tson, Jacob S. III, 351
tson, Jacob S. III, 465
tson, James V, 474
tson, James V, 542
tson, James L. V, 549
tson, James L. V, 605
tson, James Lindley V, 541
tson, Jane V, 542
tson, Jarvis III, 466
tson, Jennie B. III, 504
tson, Jervis P. III, 466
tson, Joel V, 211
tson, John I, 1059
tson, John III, 351
tson, John III, 436
tson, John III, 437
tson, John III, 441
tson, John III, 443
tson, John III, 453
tson, John III, 465
tson, John III, 466
tson, John III, 487
tson, John III, 491
tson, John III, 496
tson, John III, 500
tson, John III, 503
tson, John V, 142
tson, John V, 211
tson, John V, 474
tson, John V, 534
tson, John V, 541
tson, John V, 542
tson, John V, 549
tson, John V, 605
tson, John V, 873
tson, John VI, 456
tson, Jonah R. III, 504
tson, Jonathan III, 487
tson, Jordan I, 1039
tson, Jordan I, 1059
tson, Jordan V, 171
tson, Jordan V, 211
tson, Jordan VI, 587
tson, Jordon V, 141
tson, Jordon V, 142
tson, Jordon V, 541
tson, Jos. III, 59
tson, Jos. III, 351
tson, Joseph III, 166
tson, Joseph III, 230
tson, Joseph III, 351
tson, Joseph III, 465
tson, Joseph III, 499
tson, Joseph III, 503
tson, Joseph III, 504
tson, Kezia III, 465
tson, Kezia III, 479
tson, Keziah III, 393
tson, Keziah III, 403
tson, Keziah III, 466
tson, Keziah III, 479
tson, Keziah III, 504
tson, Ludlow III, 351
tson, Margaret III, 351
tson, Margaret III, 466
tson, Margaret V, 541
tson, Margaret VI, 456
Whitson, Maria III, 351
Whitson, Maria III, 504
Whitson, Mariah III, 465
Whitson, Martha III, 285
Whitson, Martha III, 353
Whitson, Martha III, 355
Whitson, Martha III, 465
Whitson, Martha III, 466
Whitson, Martha III, 467
Whitson, Martha III, 491
Whitson, Martha III, 504
Whitson, Martha III, 505
Whitson, Martha C. III, 495
Whitson, Mary I, 924
Whitson, Mary I, 1058
Whitson, Mary I, 1059
Whitson, Mary I, 1062
Whitson, Mary I, 1063
Whitson, Mary I Sup 1, 11
Whitson, Mary II, 1012
Whitson, Mary II, 1037
Whitson, Mary III, 322
Whitson, Mary III, 386
Whitson, Mary III, 387
Whitson, Mary III, 389
Whitson, Mary III, 421
Whitson, Mary III, 436
Whitson, Mary III, 453
Whitson, Mary III, 465
Whitson, Mary III, 466
Whitson, Mary III, 468
Whitson, Mary III, 486
Whitson, Mary III, 487
Whitson, Mary III, 500
Whitson, Mary III, 501
Whitson, Mary III, 503
Whitson, Mary III, 504
Whitson, Mary III, 505
Whitson, Mary III, 506
Whitson, Mary V, 142
Whitson, Mary V, 159
Whitson, Mary V, 171
Whitson, Mary V, 211
Whitson, Mary V, 469
Whitson, Mary V, 483
Whitson, Mary V, 534
Whitson, Mary V, 541
Whitson, Mary VI, 587
Whitson, Mary Ann V, 211
Whitson, Mary E. III, 309
Whitson, Mary E. III, 351
Whitson, Mary Esther III, 466
Whitson, Mary H. II, 939
Whitson, Mary J. III, 465
Whitson, Mary M. III, 466
Whitson, Mary Thomas V, 483
Whitson, Mary W. III, 465
Whitson, Matilda II, 939
Whitson, Maud III, 466
Whitson, Maud E. III, 420
Whitson, Maud E. III, 466
Whitson, Milton S. III, 387
Whitson, Mrs. Clara IV, 1343
Whitson, Mrs. Clara E. IV, 1343
Whitson, Naomi V, 211
Whitson, Naomi V, 541
Whitson, Naomy V, 171
Whitson, Naomy V, 211
Whitson, Nathaniel III, 421
Whitson, Nathaniel III, 436
Whitson, Nathaniel III, 465
Whitson, Nathaniel III, 466
Whitson, Nathaniel III, 504
Whitson, Phebe I, 1039
Whitson, Phebe I, 1053
Whitson, Phebe I, 1058
Whitson, Phebe I, 1059
Whitson, Phebe I, 1063
Whitson, Phebe III, 48
Whitson, Phebe III, 230
Whitson, Phebe III, 351
Whitson, Phebe III, 386
Whitson, Phebe III, 406
Whitson, Phebe III, 422
Whitson, Phebe III, 436
Whitson, Phebe III, 466
Whitson, Phebe III, 473
Whitson, Phebe III, 481
Whitson, Phebe III, 503
Whitson, Phebe III, 504
Whitson, Phebe V, 141
Whitson, Phebe V, 142
Whitson, Phebe V, 159
Whitson, Phebe V, 171
Whitson, Phebe V, 211
Whitson, Phebe V, 544
Whitson, Phebe VI, 587
Whitson, Phebe C. III, 386
Whitson, Phebe C. III, 388
Whitson, Phebe J. III, 309
Whitson, Phebe J. III, 386
Whitson, Phebe J. III, 389
Whitson, Phebe J. III, 465
Whitson, Phebe J. III, 466
Whitson, Phebe W. III, 230
Whitson, Phebe, Jr. III, 351
Whitson, Phila G. III, 230
Whitson, Phoebe I, 1059
Whitson, Phoebe P. II, 702
Whitson, Rachel III, 491
Whitson, Rachel III, 504
Whitson, Rebecca III, 465
Whitson, Rebecca III, 466
Whitson, Rebecca III, 479
Whitson, Rebecca III, 503
Whitson, Rebecca III, 504
Whitson, Rebekah V, 40
Whitson, Rebekah V, 141
Whitson, Rebekah V, 873
Whitson, Retta V, 751
Whitson, Retta V, 772
Whitson, Robert III, 465
Whitson, Robert III, 503
Whitson, Robert III, 504
Whitson, Robert Furnas, Jr. V, 211
Whitson, Rowland I, 1059
Whitson, Rowland V, 211
Whitson, Ruth III, 465
Whitson, Ruth III, 504
Whitson, Sam'l III, 389
Whitson, Sam'l III, 465
Whitson, Samuel I, 1039
Whitson, Samuel I, 1059
Whitson, Samuel III, 309
Whitson, Samuel III, 351
Whitson, Samuel III, 386
Whitson, Samuel III, 422
Whitson, Samuel III, 466
Whitson, Samuel III, 503
Whitson, Samuel III, 504
Whitson, Samuel V, 141
Whitson, Samuel V, 211
Whitson, Samuel V, 526
Whitson, Samuel V, 541
Whitson, Samuel V, 544
Whitson, Samuel VI, 587
Whitson, Samuel S. III, 351
Whitson, Sarah II, 702
Whitson, Sarah III, 165
Whitson, Sarah III, 206
Whitson, Sarah III, 318
Whitson, Sarah III, 328
Whitson, Sarah III, 329
Whitson, Sarah III, 330
Whitson, Sarah III, 351
Whitson, Sarah III, 386
Whitson, Sarah III, 421
Whitson, Sarah III, 460
Whitson, Sarah III, 466
Whitson, Sarah III, 485
Whitson, Sarah III, 502
Whitson, Sarah III, 503
Whitson, Sarah III, 504
Whitson, Sarah V, 211
Whitson, Sarah V, 541
Whitson, Sarah Ann III, 504
Whitson, Sarah P. III, 386
Whitson, Sarah P. III, 389
Whitson, Sarah W. III, 331
Whitson, Silas Willis I, 1059
Whitson, Silas Willis V, 211
Whitson, Solomon I, 1039
Whitson, Solomon I, 1058
Whitson, Solomon I, 1059
Whitson, Solomon I, 1063
Whitson, Solomon III, 465
Whitson, Solomon III, 466
Whitson, Solomon III, 473
Whitson, Solomon V, 141
Whitson, Solomon V, 211
Whitson, Solomon V, 541
Whitson, Solomon V, 544
Whitson, Solomon V, 772
Whitson, Solomon VI, 587
Whitson, Susan III, 466
Whitson, Susan H. III, 351
Whitson, Susan W. III, 59
Whitson, T. Clarkson II, 939
Whitson, Tamson VI, 456
Whitson, Thomas III, 351
Whitson, Thomas III, 386
Whitson, Thomas III, 388
Whitson, Thomas III, 410
Whitson, Thomas III, 465
Whitson, Thomas III, 466
Whitson, Thomas III, 467
Whitson, Thomas III, 500
Whitson, Thomas III, 503
Whitson, Thomas III, 504
Whitson, Thomas III, 505
Whitson, Thomas III, 506
Whitson, Thomas V, 211
Whitson, Thomas V, 541
Whitson, Thomas Clarkson II, 939
Whitson, Thomas H. II, 702
Whitson, Thomas H. II, 950
Whitson, Thomas U. III, 351
Whitson, Thomas, Jr. III, 116
Whitson, Thomas, Jr. III, 351
Whitson, Thos. III, 389
Whitson, Thos. III, 465
Whitson, Thos. III, 468
Whitson, Thos. III, 505
Whitson, Underhill III, 386
Whitson, Underhill III, 503
Whitson, Unice V, 542
Whitson, Willet III, 504
Whitson, Willet P. III, 495
Whitson, Willet P. III, 504
Whitson, William V, 211
Whitson, William E. III, 386
Whitson, William Edward III, 420
Whitson, Willis I, 1039
Whitson, Willis I, 1059
Whitson, Willis V, 40
Whitson, Willis V, 141
Whitson, Willis V, 211
Whitson, Willis V, 873
Whitson, Willis VI, 587
Whitson, Wm. E. III, 466
Whitson, Wm. Edward III, 466
Whitson, Wyllis V, 141
Whitt, Elizabeth II, 111
Whittachar, Sarah II, 1037
Whittacre, Dora IV, 1014
Whittacre, Elizabeth II, 1038
Whittacre, Eva IV, 786
Whittacre, Hannah II, 1038
Whittacre, Jane II, 1038
Whittacre, John II, 1037
Whittacre, John II, 1038
Whittacre, John, Jr. II, 1037
Whittacre, Joseph II, 1038
Whittacre, Marcy II, 1038
Whittacre, Martha II, 1037
Whittacre, Mary II, 1026
Whittacre, Mary II, 1038
Whittacre, Naomi II, 1038
Whittacre, Naomy II, 1037
Whittacre, Ralph IV, 786
Whittacre, Rebecca II, 1038
Whittacre, Robert II, 1038
Whittacre, Sarah II, 1009
Whittacre, Sarah II, 1037
Whittacre, Sarah II, 1038
Whittacre, Sidney V, 112
Whittacre, Sidney V, 141
Whittaker, Edwin VI, 860
Whittaker, George II, 722
Whittaker, Harry H. III, 351
Whittaker, Jane II, 722
Whittaker, Martha I, 935
Whittaker, Mary VI, 356
Whittaker, Mary VI, 1014
Whittaker, Mary Ann II, 722
Whittaker, Robert II, 1038
Whittaker, Robert II, 1040
Whittaker, Samuel VI, 356
Whittaker, Samuel VI, 1014
Whittaker, Sarah II, 1038
Whittaker, Sarah II, 1040
Whittall, Esther II, 435
Whittall, James II, 435
Whittall, Mary II, 435
Whittan, Ann II, 46
Whittan, James II, 46
Whittan, Joseph II, 46
Whittan, Sarah II, 46
Whittecar, Nancy W. VI, 864
Whittecar, William VI, 864
Whittecur, Elliner II, 111
Whitted, Ann I, 455
Whitten, Alwilda IV, 503
Whitten, Ann Elizabeth VI, 874
Whitten, Anna IV, 503
Whitten, Annis W. IV, 495
Whitten, Annis W. IV, 503
Whitten, Arabella Jane VI, 980
Whitten, Bery C. IV, 503
Whitten, Catharine II, 685
Whitten, Catherine II, 685
Whitten, Cleopatra A. VI, 953
Whitten, Elisha VI, 919
Whitten, Elisha VI, 941
Whitten, Elisha VI, 997
Whitten, Elisha VI, 1002
Whitten, Elisha VI, 1005
Whitten, Elisha, Jr. VI, 934
Whitten, Eliza Ann VI, 1014
Whitten, Elizabeth II, 562
Whitten, Elizabeth II, 685
Whitten, Elizabeth IV, 503
Whitten, Elizabeth VI, 803
Whitten, Elizabeth VI, 864
Whitten, Florence IV, 503
Whitten, Forrest IV, 303
Whitten, Frank IV, 503
Whitten, Glenn IV, 303
Whitten, Glennie IV, 503
Whitten, Golda IV, 503
Whitten, Henry John III, 351
Whitten, James II, 112
Whitten, James II, 685
Whitten, Jane VI, 1014
Whitten, Jane G. VI, 967
Whitten, Jeremiah VI, 1014
Whitten, John IV, 503
Whitten, John J. IV, 503
Whitten, Joseph VI, 864
Whitten, Joseph VI, 874
Whitten, Joseph VI, 949
Whitten, Joseph VI, 967
Whitten, Joseph VI, 1004
Whitten, Joseph VI, 1014
Whitten, Juliann VI, 953
Whitten, Kathrine II, 685
Whitten, Lemuel IV, 503
Whitten, Lizzie IV, 503
Whitten, Lucinda A. VI, 1002
Whitten, Lucy IV, 303
Whitten, Margaret VI, 979
Whitten, Margaret Elizabeth IV, 503
Whitten, Maria L. VI, 1014
Whitten, Mary IV, 503
Whitten, Mary J. IV, 503
Whitten, Mary V. IV, 503
Whitten, Orwell IV, 303
Whitten, Polly VI, 1005
Whitten, Richard II, 562
Whitten, Richard II, 685
Whitten, Robert II, 685
Whitten, Sadie R. IV, 503
Whitten, Sarah VI, 921
Whitten, Sarah J. IV, 503
Whitten, Sherod VI, 1014
Whitten, Susan M. VI, 1014
Whitten, Walter IV, 503
Whitten, William IV, 303
Whitten, William IV, 503
Whitten, William VI, 979
Whitten, William A. VI, 874
Whitten, William A. VI, 1014
Whitten, William B. VI, 880
Whitten, William B. VI, 893
Whitten, William B. VI, 919
Whitten, William B. VI, 927
Whitten, William E. VI, 947
Whitten, Wm. VI, 921
Whitten, Wm. VI, 944
Whitten, Wm. VI, 995
Whitten, Wm. B. VI, 949
Whitten, Wm. B. VI, 964
Whitten, Wm. E. VI, 934
Whitten, Wm. T. IV, 503
Whitten, Wm., Jr. IV, 503
Whittenton, Elizabeth VI, 1014
Whittenton, John VI, 1014
Whitter, John I, 1076
Whitter, Mary I, 1076
Whittesley, Charles R. VI, 791
Whittesley, Charles Terrill VI, 791
Whittesley, Mary Weaver VI, 791
Whittesley, Penelope VI, 791
Whitticer, Mary IV, 854
Whittichar, John, Jr. II, 1037
Whittier, Mary H. I, 1163
Whittier, Mary Hammer I, 1163
Whittin, Elisha, Jr. VI, 1014
Whittin, Emily VI, 1014
Whittington, Adaline VI, 990
Whittington, Addison B. VI, 1014
Whittington, C. L. I, 627
Whittington, C. L. I, 628
Whittington, C. L. I, 642
Whittington, Eliza V, 650
Whittington, Eliza Ann VI, 967
Whittington, Elizabeth VI, 864
Whittington, Elizabeth VI, 910
Whittington, Elizabeth VI, 1014
Whittington, Fetna I, 628
Whittington, Fetney I, 627
Whittington, Fetney I, 642
Whittington, Fetnie I, 642
Whittington, Finetta J. VI, 1014
Whittington, George M. VI, 897
Whittington, George M. VI, 901
Whittington, George M. VI, 996
Whittington, George M. VI, 1014
Whittington, James VI, 864

Whittington, James VI, 910
Whittington, James VI, 944
Whittington, James VI, 967
Whittington, James VI, 990
Whittington, James L. VI, 990
Whittington, John VI, 864
Whittington, John VI, 910
Whittington, John VI, 932
Whittington, John VI, 956
Whittington, John VI, 966
Whittington, John VI, 986
Whittington, John VI, 1014
Whittington, John VI, 1017
Whittington, Judith VI, 990
Whittington, Kenneth Thornlow I, 628
Whittington, Keziah VI, 878
Whittington, Lemira B. VI, 996
Whittington, Luettie V, 650
Whittington, Margaret Lucile I, 628
Whittington, Margaret Lucile I, 642
Whittington, Martha VI, 1014
Whittington, Martha J. VI, 932
Whittington, Mary VI, 901
Whittington, Nancy VI, 864
Whittington, Nancy VI, 944
Whittington, Patsy VI, 919
Whittington, Rhoda VI, 990
Whittington, Stark VI, 996
Whittington, Susanna VI, 956
Whittington, Susanna VI, 1014
Whittington, William VI, 878
Whittington, Wm. VI, 956
Whittlesey, Charles Raymond VI, 741
Whittlesey, Mary Weaver VI, 741
Whitton, Bert IV, 787
Whitton, Catharine II, 685
Whitton, Catherine II, 461
Whitton, Chas. IV, 787
Whitton, Elisha VI, 941
Whitton, Elisha VI, 1014
Whitton, Elisha, Jr. VI, 1014
Whitton, Eliza Ann VI, 1014
Whitton, Emily VI, 1014
Whitton, George B. IV, 855
Whitton, Irene IV, 787
Whitton, James II, 461
Whitton, James II, 685
Whitton, Jane VI, 1014
Whitton, Jenny VI, 1014
Whitton, Jeremiah VI, 942
Whitton, Jeremiah VI, 1014
Whitton, Joanna VI, 954
Whitton, Joseph IV, 787
Whitton, Joseph VI, 1014
Whitton, Margaret IV, 787
Whitton, Maria L. VI, 1014
Whitton, Mary II, 271
Whitton, Mary II, 272
Whitton, Mary IV, 787
Whitton, Nancy VI, 941
Whitton, Nancy VI, 999
Whitton, Robert II, 685
Whitton, Sarah VI, 1014
Whitton, Sarah J. IV, 855
Whitton, Sherod VI, 1014
Whitton, Susan M. VI, 1014
Whitton, William VI, 954
Whitton, William VI, 1014
Whitton, William A. VI, 1014
Whitworth, Abraham VI, 1014
Whitworth, Alexander I, 508
Whitworth, Fanny VI, 1014
Whitworth, Francis VI, 874
Whitworth, Gustavus VI, 1014
Whitworth, Hannah I, 508
Whitworth, Hannah I, 521
Whitworth, Hannah I, 581
Whitworth, Henrietta VI, 874
Whitworth, Jemima I, 576
Whitworth, Jemima I, 581
Whitworth, John VI, 1001
Whitworth, John VI, 1014
Whitworth, Louisa VI, 1014
Whitworth, Martha E. IV, 1343
Whitworth, Mary VI, 1014
Whitworth, Nancy VI, 1014
Whitworth, W. Alexander I, 521
Whitzell, Elizabeth IV, 871
Whitzell, Elizabeth IV, 886
Whoard, Mary Ann VI, 940
Whollan, Eleanor S. IV, 1343
Whooten, Thomas, Sr. II, 435
Whooton, Gulielma I, 43
Whorley, Caroline VI, 876
Whorley, David VI, 963
Whorley, Dosha VI, 932
Whorley, Eliza VI, 1020
Whorley, Francis VI, 1020
Whorley, Henry VI, 895
Whorley, Lucy VI, 1006
Whorley, Lurany VI, 1020
Whorley, Martha VI, 876
Whorley, Martha Ann VI, 976
Whorley, Mary VI, 1005
Whorley, Maxey VI, 880
Whorley, Nancy VI, 984
Whorley, Permelia VI, 895
Whorley, Permelia A. VI, 880
Whorley, Polley R. VI, 880
Whorley, Rainey VI, 876
Whorley, Rhoda VI, 901
Whorley, Rodah VI, 1020
Whorley, Sarah E. VI, 901
Whorley, Talbert VI, 1020
Whorley, Thomas VI, 901
Whorley, Thomas VI, 1020
Whorley, William VI, 880
Whorley, William VI, 976
Whorley, William VI, 1020
Whorley, Z. VI, 1006
Whorly, Hannah VI, 456
Whormann, Frederick III, 30
Whormann, Fredericka III, 323
Whoton, Albert V, 144
Whtie, Joseph VI, 886
Whyland, Fred S. V, 719
Whypple, Alice II, 683
Whyte, Alberta III, 465
Whyte, Annie III, 465
Whyte, Banff III, 465
Whyte, Barbara III, 398
Whyte, Barbara III, 465
Whyte, Barbara J. III, 465
Whyte, Barbara Jane III, 465
Whyte, Dave III, 465
Whyte, Dave, Jr. III, 398
Whyte, Dave, Jr. III, 465
Wiar, Mary II, 275
Wiar, Sarah II, 275
Wiat, Elizabeth II, 48
Wiat, Sarah II, 48
Wiatt, Benjamin VI, 828
Wiatt, Clarissa A. VI, 864
Wiatt, Elizabeth II, 113
Wiatt, Mary II, 113
Wiatt, Robert H. VI, 864
Wiatt, Sally VI, 864
Wiatt, Thomas VI, 864
Wiatt, Thomas VI, 926
Wiatte, Arnold VI, 796
Wibal, Emma IV, 1343
Wibal, Evert IV, 1343
Wibel, Emma IV, 1343
Wibel, Everett IV, 1343
Wibel, Evert IV, 1343
Wibel, L. Everet IV, 855
Wibel, Mrs. Emma IV, 1343
Wible, Helen A. II, 136
Wible, John J. V, 1025
Wible, Margaretta II, 160
Wible, Margret II, 160
Wical, Clara B. V, 719
Wical, Elizabeth V, 719
Wical, Noel V, 719
Wicher, Cylla I, 936
Wicher, Eulas Monroe I, 936
Wicher, Everett Elwood I, 936
Wicher, Jettie Gertrude I, 936
Wicher, John Hiram I, 936
Wicher, Mehitable I, 936
Wicher, William I, 936
Wicherly, Edward IV, 309
Wichersham, David IV, 641
Wichersham, Rebecca IV, 641
Wichwin, Ella A. III, 189
Wick, ??? III, 136
Wick, ??? III, 351
Wick, Martha B. III, 136
Wick, Martha B. III, 351
Wick, Peter VI, 217
Wickel, Arabell V, 1025
Wickel, Leuretta V, 1025
Wickel, Rebecca V, 1025
Wickel, Rosa Ellen V, 1025
Wicker, Alma I, 922
Wicker, Alma I, 951
Wicker, Anna IV, 1343
Wicker, Bertie I, 627
Wicker, Dora G. I, 951
Wicker, Hazel I, 951
Wicker, J. H. I, 951
Wicker, James M. VI, 821
Wicker, James W. I, 922
Wicker, Lillie I, 922
Wickerham, Catherine VI, 384
Wickersham, ??? V, 142
Wickersham, Abbie T. IV, 653
Wickersham, Abbie T. IV, 665
Wickersham, Abby F. IV, 787
Wickersham, Abby T. IV, 665
Wickersham, Abel I, 521
Wickersham, Abel I, 794
Wickersham, Abigail VI, 456
Wickersham, Abigail VI, 607
Wickersham, Abner IV, 665
Wickersham, Abner V, 542
Wickersham, Adams VI, 456
Wickersham, Amos II, 435
Wickersham, Amos II, 546
Wickersham, Amos II, 629
Wickersham, Amos II, 685
Wickersham, Amos IV, 855
Wickersham, Amos IV, 1343
Wickersham, Amos, Jr. II, 685
Wickersham, Amos, Jr. III, 351
Wickersham, Amy IV, 855
Wickersham, Anice IV, 1299
Wickersham, Ann I, 521
Wickersham, Ann II, 685
Wickersham, Ann II, 816
Wickersham, Ann IV, 556
Wickersham, Ann IV, 606
Wickersham, Ann IV, 613
Wickersham, Ann IV, 622
Wickersham, Ann IV, 643
Wickersham, Ann IV, 654
Wickersham, Ann IV, 664
Wickersham, Ann IV, 665
Wickersham, Ann IV, 787
Wickersham, Ann IV, 877
Wickersham, Ann IV, 886
Wickersham, Anna I, 794
Wickersham, Anna I, 844
Wickersham, Anna V, 502
Wickersham, Anna V, 542
Wickersham, Anne II, 629
Wickersham, Anne V, 544
Wickersham, Asaph H. V, 542
Wickersham, B. Franklin II, 722
Wickersham, Caleb I, 521
Wickersham, Caleb I, 794
Wickersham, Caleb I, 810
Wickersham, Caleb I, 844
Wickersham, Caleb V, 873
Wickersham, Catharine VI, 456
Wickersham, Cyrus IV, 665
Wickersham, Cyrus IV, 1015
Wickersham, David IV, 534
Wickersham, David IV, 556
Wickersham, David IV, 636
Wickersham, David IV, 665
Wickersham, David IV, 713
Wickersham, David IV, 787
Wickersham, David IV, 831
Wickersham, David V, 142
Wickersham, David V, 542
Wickersham, David E. II, 722
Wickersham, David E. II, 775
Wickersham, David Evans IV, 114
Wickersham, Edward J. V, 542
Wickersham, Eli II, 685
Wickersham, Elijah IV, 114
Wickersham, Elijah IV, 115
Wickersham, Elijah V, 941
Wickersham, Elis IV, 665
Wickersham, Elis. IV, 646
Wickersham, Eliza II, 435
Wickersham, Eliza IV, 646
Wickersham, Eliza IV, 665
Wickersham, Eliza IV, 855
Wickersham, Eliza IV, 886
Wickersham, Eliza V, 142
Wickersham, Eliza V, 542
Wickersham, Eliza Ann IV, 665
Wickersham, Eliza Ann IV, 886
Wickersham, Eliza Ann IV, 1012
Wickersham, Eliza Ann IV, 1015
Wickersham, Eliza Emeline IV, 855
Wickersham, Elizabeth II, 435
Wickersham, Elizabeth II, 546
Wickersham, Elizabeth II, 629
Wickersham, Elizabeth II, 685
Wickersham, Elizabeth IV, 67
Wickersham, Elizabeth IV, 164
Wickersham, Elizabeth IV, 503
Wickersham, Elizabeth IV, 643
Wickersham, Elizabeth IV, 664
Wickersham, Elizabeth IV, 895
Wickersham, Elizabeth V, 542
Wickersham, Elizabeth VI, 456
Wickersham, Elizabeth E. IV, 892
Wickersham, Elizabeth E. IV, 895
Wickersham, Elizabeth Emeline IV, 886
Wickersham, Elizabeth Emeline IV, 895
Wickersham, Ellis IV, 665
Wickersham, Ellis IV, 855
Wickersham, Ellis IV, 886
Wickersham, Ellis IV, 895
Wickersham, Ellis IV, 1015
Wickersham, Ellis T. IV, 855
Wickersham, Ellis Taylor IV, 895
Wickersham, Elmira W. II, 705
Wickersham, Emma IV, 803
Wickersham, Enna IV, 855
Wickersham, Enoch I, 521
Wickersham, Enoch I, 794
Wickersham, Enoch I, 844
Wickersham, Enoch V, 142
Wickersham, Enoch V, 211
Wickersham, Enoch V, 469
Wickersham, Enoch V, 520
Wickersham, Enoch V, 532
Wickersham, Enoch V, 542
Wickersham, Enoch V, 544
Wickersham, Enoch VI, 456
Wickersham, Evans IV, 115
Wickersham, Florence II, 435
Wickersham, Florence II, 685
Wickersham, Florence L. V, 542
Wickersham, George II, 685
Wickersham, George IV, 114
Wickersham, George V, 719
Wickersham, Hannah II, 788
Wickersham, Hannah IV, 606
Wickersham, Hannah IV, 665
Wickersham, Hannah IV, 1015
Wickersham, Hannah V, 520
Wickersham, Hannah V, 542
Wickersham, Hannah V, 544
Wickersham, Harriet V, 211
Wickersham, Horace V, 211
Wickersham, Isaac II, 435
Wickersham, Isaac IV, 67
Wickersham, Isaac IV, 114
Wickersham, Isaac IV, 164
Wickersham, Isaac V, 142
Wickersham, Isaac VI, 456
Wickersham, James I, 521
Wickersham, James V, 211
Wickersham, James V, 542
Wickersham, James V, 544
Wickersham, James VI, 456
Wickersham, Jane VI, 365
Wickersham, Jane VI, 456
Wickersham, Jane M. V, 542
Wickersham, Jehu I, 521
Wickersham, Jehu I, 581
Wickersham, Jehu I, 794
Wickersham, Jehu I, 844
Wickersham, Jehu I, 905
Wickersham, Jehu I, 1039
Wickersham, Jehu, Jr. I, 844
Wickersham, Jehu, Jr. I, 905
Wickersham, Jemima IV, 1068
Wickersham, Jemima IV, 1081
Wickersham, Jesse V, 542
Wickersham, Job IV, 665
Wickersham, Job IV, 886
Wickersham, Joel IV, 622
Wickersham, Joel IV, 665
Wickersham, Joel IV, 787
Wickersham, Joel IV, 886
Wickersham, John II, 435
Wickersham, John II, 685
Wickersham, John II, 775
Wickersham, John IV, 114
Wickersham, John IV, 665
Wickersham, John B. II, 775
Wickersham, Jonathan VI, 365
Wickersham, Jonathan VI, 456
Wickersham, Jonathan VI, 607
Wickersham, Jonathan Marsh IV, 886
Wickersham, Joseph IV, 665
Wickersham, Joseph IV, 886
Wickersham, Joseph IV, 1015
Wickersham, Joseph C. V, 542
Wickersham, Joseph C. V, 719
Wickersham, Joseph L. IV, 895
Wickersham, Joseph P. IV, 665
Wickersham, Josiah VI, 456
Wickersham, Kennett I, 581
Wickersham, Leah V, 527
Wickersham, Leah V, 542
Wickersham, Levi V, 542
Wickersham, Levi B. IV, 665
Wickersham, Lewis IV, 855
Wickersham, Lewis IV, 886
Wickersham, Lidia VI, 456
Wickersham, Lydia I, 521
Wickersham, Lydia I, 794
Wickersham, Lydia I, 806
Wickersham, Lydia I, 810
Wickersham, Lydia I, 844
Wickersham, Lydia V, 542
Wickersham, Lydia VI, 398
Wickersham, Lydia VI, 456
Wickersham, Lydia E. IV, 895
Wickersham, Lydia Elma IV, 8
Wickersham, Lydia elma IV, 8
Wickersham, Lydia Elma IV,
Wickersham, Margaret II, 685
Wickersham, Margaret IV, 665
Wickersham, Margaret IV, 886
Wickersham, Margaret IV, 10
Wickersham, Margaret V, 142
Wickersham, Margaret V, 532
Wickersham, Margaret V, 542
Wickersham, Margaret V, 544
Wickersham, Maria IV, 665
Wickersham, Maria IV, 787
Wickersham, Mariah IV, 665
Wickersham, Marium IV, 665
Wickersham, Mary I, 521
Wickersham, Mary I, 794
Wickersham, Mary I, 844
Wickersham, Mary II, 435
Wickersham, Mary II, 685
Wickersham, Mary IV, 665
Wickersham, Mary IV, 886
Wickersham, Mary IV, 1015
Wickersham, Mary V, 142
Wickersham, Mary V, 542
Wickersham, Mary VI, 362
Wickersham, Mary VI, 382
Wickersham, Mary VI, 456
Wickersham, Mary A. V, 542
Wickersham, Mary Ann IV, 79
Wickersham, Mary Ann IV, 85
Wickersham, Mary ann IV, 88
Wickersham, Mary C. V, 534
Wickersham, Mary C. V, 542
Wickersham, Mary J. IV, 1015
Wickersham, Mary R. VI, 454
Wickersham, Mary R. VI, 456
Wickersham, Mary S. II, 939
Wickersham, Miriam W. IV, 61
Wickersham, Miriam W. IV, 66
Wickersham, Morgan IV, 855
Wickersham, Morgan IV, 886
Wickersham, Nantilla V, 542
Wickersham, Nathan Hunt IV, 665
Wickersham, Noah V, 542
Wickersham, Pearce IV, 665
Wickersham, Pearce IV, 1015
Wickersham, Phebe II, 698
Wickersham, Phebe II, 801
Wickersham, Phebe IV, 622
Wickersham, Phebe IV, 639
Wickersham, Phebe IV, 665
Wickersham, Phebe IV, 787
Wickersham, Phebe IV, 951
Wickersham, Phebe IV, 1015
Wickersham, Phebe F. IV, 787
Wickersham, Phebe Flovilla IV, 665
Wickersham, Phoebe IV, 886
Wickersham, Pierce IV, 1015
Wickersham, Priscilla I, 521
Wickersham, Priscilla I, 794
Wickersham, Priscilla I, 833
Wickersham, Priscilla I, 844
Wickersham, Priscilla II, 705
Wickersham, Priscilla II, 814
Wickersham, Rachel I, 794
Wickersham, Rachel V, 142
Wickersham, Rachel V, 508
Wickersham, Rachel V, 542
Wickersham, Rachel C. IV, 627
Wickersham, Rachel C. IV, 665
Wickersham, Rachel C. IV, 713
Wickersham, Rachel C. IV, 831
Wickersham, Rachel E. IV, 641
Wickersham, Rebecca IV, 665
Wickersham, Rebecca IV, 787
Wickersham, Rebecca IV, 1299
Wickersham, Rebecca VI, 384
Wickersham, Rebecca VI, 420
Wickersham, Rebecca VI, 456
Wickersham, Rebecca B. IV, 53
Wickersham, Rebecca B. IV, 55
Wickersham, Rebecca B. IV, 66
Wickersham, Rebecca B. IV, 71
Wickersham, Rebecca B. IV, 83
Wickersham, Rebecca C. V, 542
Wickersham, Rebecca R. IV, 63
Wickersham, Rebecca R. IV, 66
Wickersham, Richard II, 435
Wickersham, Richard II, 685
Wickersham, Richard VI, 456
Wickersham, Robert V, 542
Wickersham, Robert VI, 454
Wickersham, Robert A. VI, 454
Wickersham, Robert A. VI, 456
Wickersham, Ruth I, 844
Wickersham, Ruth Anna IV, 66

ersham, Ruth Anna IV, 787
ersham, Sampson IV, 643
ersham, Sampson IV, 664
ersham, Samuel VI, 456
ersham, Sarah I, 521
ersham, Sarah I, 794
ersham, Sarah I, 844
ersham, Sarah II, 452
ersham, Sarah II, 685
ersham, Sarah IV, 114
ersham, Sarah IV, 613
ersham, Sarah IV, 665
ersham, Sarah IV, 667
ersham, Sarah IV, 677
ersham, Sarah IV, 787
ersham, Sarah V, 512
ersham, Sarah V, 542
ersham, Sarah V, 544
ersham, Sarah Evans II, 435
ersham, Sarah Evans II, 685
kersham, Sarah Evans IV, 114
kersham, Sarah Hayes II, 435
kersham, Sarah J. V, 542
kersham, Sarah R. II, 435
kersham, Sarah R. II, 722
kersham, Sarah R. II, 775
kersham, Sophie VI, 799
kersham, Susanna IV, 114
kersham, Susanna V, 542
kersham, Susannah V, 514
kersham, Susannah V, 542
kersham, Susannah H. V, 544
kersham, Thomas II, 685
kersham, Thomas II, 705
kersham, Thomas IV, 114
kersham, Thomas IV, 556
kersham, Thomas IV, 622
kersham, Thomas IV, 654
kersham, Thomas IV, 664
ckersham, Thomas IV, 665
kersham, Thomas IV, 787
ckersham, Thomas IV, 886
ckersham, Thomas IV, 1015
ckersham, Thomas IV, 1299
ckersham, Thomas V, 542
ckersham, Thomas VI, 579
ckersham, Thomas Bartlet II, 685
ickersham, Thomas Bartlett IV, 114
ickersham, Thomas E. IV, 665
ickersham, Thomas M. IV, 895
ickersham, Thomas, Jr. II, 685
ickersham, Thomas, Sr. IV, 787
ickersham, Thos. IV, 606
ickersham, Thos. IV, 613
ickersham, William V, 542
ickersham, William VI, 456
ickersham, William Morrison IV, 115
ickersham, William Quimby IV, 895
ickersham, William, Jr. V, 542
ickersham, Wm. M. II, 775
ickershaw, Joseph IV, 1015
Vickes, George F. III, 352
Vickes, M. Louisa III, 352
Vickesham, Elizabeth VI, 366
Vickliffe, Eliza II, 707
Vickliffe, Elizabeth II, 722
Vickliffe, Hannah II, 774
Vickliffe, Mary II, 260
Vickliffe, Mary II, 272
Vickward, Rachel II, 272
Vickwire, Ella A. III, 216
Vickwire, Ella A. III, 277
Vickworm, Samuel II, 272
Widas, Jane II, 686
Widdefield, Chas. II, 939
Widdefield, Eleanor II, 827
Widdefield, Eleanor II, 939
Widdefield, Elizabeth II, 827
Widdefield, Elizabeth II, 939
Widdefield, George II, 939
Widdefield, Hannah II, 814
Widdefield, Hannah II, 827
Widdefield, Hannah II, 939
Widdefield, Hannah, Jr. II, 939
Widdefield, James II, 814
Widdefield, James II, 827
Widdefield, James II, 909
Widdefield, James II, 939
Widdefield, Joseph II, 827
Widdefield, Joseph II, 939
Widdefield, Mary II, 827
Widdefield, Mary II, 939
Widdefield, Rebecca II, 909
Widdefield, Rebecca II, 939
Widdefield, Rebecca W. II, 939
Widdefield, Rebecca W. Penrose II, 939
Widdefield, Samuel II, 939
Widdefield, Samuel E. II, 939
Widdefield, Samuel S. II, 814
Widdefield, Sarah II, 789
Widdefield, Sarah II, 806
Widdefield, Sarah II, 827
Widdefield, Sarah II, 939
Widdefield, Sarah M. II, 827
Widdefield, Sarah M. II, 939
Widdefield, Wd. Elizabeth II, 789
Widdefield, Wd. Rebecca II, 814
Widdefield, William II, 827
Widdefield, Wm. II, 789
Widdefield, Wm. II, 939
Widdefield, Wm. A. II, 939
Widders, Martha II, 685
Widdifield, Amy II, 435
Widdifield, Ann T. II, 890
Widdifield, Bertha B. II, 890
Widdifield, Charles II, 435
Widdifield, Charles II, 775
Widdifield, Charles III, 352
Widdifield, Deborah II, 435
Widdifield, Deborah II, 686
Widdifield, Eleanor II, 685
Widdifield, Eleanor II, 775
Widdifield, Elisabeth II, 685
Widdifield, Elizabeth II, 435
Widdifield, Elizabeth II, 685
Widdifield, Elizabeth II, 686
Widdifield, Elizabeth II, 775
Widdifield, Elizabeth II, 853
Widdifield, Elizabeth II, 939
Widdifield, Emily T. II, 890
Widdifield, George II, 435
Widdifield, George II, 686
Widdifield, George II, 890
Widdifield, Gulielma II, 435
Widdifield, Gulielma II, 685
Widdifield, Gulielma II, 722
Widdifield, Hannah II, 564
Widdifield, Hannah II, 685
Widdifield, Isabella H. II, 890
Widdifield, James II, 435
Widdifield, John II, 435
Widdifield, John II, 564
Widdifield, John II, 577
Widdifield, John II, 595
Widdifield, John II, 685
Widdifield, Joseph II, 435
Widdifield, Joseph II, 775
Widdifield, Joseph II, 939
Widdifield, Lizzie T. II, 890
Widdifield, Mary II, 435
Widdifield, Mary II, 577
Widdifield, Mary II, 685
Widdifield, Mary II, 939
Widdifield, Mary A. II, 890
Widdifield, Massey II, 435
Widdifield, Massey II, 685
Widdifield, Peter II, 435
Widdifield, Peter II, 595
Widdifield, Peter II, 685
Widdifield, Rebecca II, 435
Widdifield, Rebecca II, 685
Widdifield, Rebekah II, 595
Widdifield, Rebekah II, 685
Widdifield, Samuel II, 435
Widdifield, Samuel II, 939
Widdifield, Samuel III, 352
Widdifield, Sarah II, 435
Widdifield, Sarah II, 452
Widdifield, Sarah II, 685
Widdifield, Sarah II, 853
Widdifield, Sarah II, 939
Widdifield, William II, 435
Widdifield, William, Jr. II, 435
Widdifield, Wm. II, 685
Widdifield, Wm. II, 686
Widdifield, Wm. II, 775
Widdifield, Wm. II, 853
Widdifield, Wm. A. II, 685
Widdifield, Wm. A. II, 775
Widdifield, Wm. A. II, 939
Widdifield, Wm., Jr. II, 685
Widdin, Daniel II, 449
Widdin, Rachel II, 449
Widdin, Sarah II, 449
Widdow, Esther II, 435
Widdowfield, Amy II, 435
Widdowfield, Deborah II, 686
Widdowfield, Eleanor II, 685
Widdowfield, Elisabeth II, 620
Widdowfield, Elisabeth II, 685
Widdowfield, Elizabeth II, 435
Widdowfield, Elizabeth II, 686
Widdowfield, George II, 435
Widdowfield, George II, 686
Widdowfield, Gulielma II, 685
Widdowfield, John II, 435
Widdowfield, John II, 660
Widdowfield, John II, 685
Widdowfield, Joseph II, 435
Widdowfield, Mary II, 563
Widdowfield, Mary II, 600
Widdowfield, Mary II, 660
Widdowfield, Mary II, 685
Widdowfield, Massey II, 685
Widdowfield, Peter II, 435
Widdowfield, Peter II, 685
Widdowfield, Rebecca II, 685
Widdowfield, Sarah II, 435
Widdowfield, Sarah II, 685
Widdowfield, Wm. II, 685
Widdowfield, Wm. II, 686
Widdowfield, Wm. A. II, 685
Widdowfield, Wm., Jr. II, 685
Widdows, Elen I, 890
Widdows, Elen I, 905
Widdows, Jane II, 686
Widdows, Jane R. I, 331
Widdows, Jane Ruth I, 341
Widdows, Mary II, 827
Widdows, Mary II, 939
Widdows, Milla I, 905
Widdows, Millia I, 905
Widdows, Peter II, 686
Widdows, Peter II, 827
Widdows, Peter II, 939
Widdows, Peter III, 504
Widdows, Winston Salem I, 341
Widmayer, Hannah II, 46
Widmayer, Martin II, 46
Widmayer, Martin II, 64
Widmayer, Martin II, 111
Widmayer, Mary II, 46
Widmayer, Mary II, 64
Widmayer, Mary II, 111
Widmayer, Virgin II, 46
Widop, Charles Augustine I, 844
Widowfield, Elizabeth II, 620
Widowfield, Elizabeth II, 685
Widowfield, Peter II, 435
Widowfield, Rebecca II, 435
Widows, Elen I, 905
Widows, Isaac I, 581
Widows, Isaac, Jr. I, 581
Widows, Mary I, 905
Widows, Melica I, 581
Widows, Melissa I, 581
Widows, Milla I, 905
Widows, Millia I, 905
Widows, Nathan I, 905
Widows, Peter II, 686
Widows, Samira I, 905
Widows, Sarah I, 905
Widows, Sarah I, 931
Widup, Charles Augustine I, 844
Widup, Charles Y. I, 844
Widup, John P. I, 844
Wieat, Bartholomew II, 51
Wieat, Bartholomew II, 113
Wieat, John II, 46
Wieat, Sarah II, 51
Wieat, Sarah II, 113
Wiebert, Catherine S. III, 347
Wieder, Addie IV, 1342
Wieder, Edna II, 131
Wiegand, Tryphosia II, 262
Wiegel, Clifford IV, 1342
Wier, Daniel V, 467
Wier, Denslow IV, 1242
Wier, Eliza IV, 303
Wier, George IV, 1192
Wier, George IV, 1242
Wier, George M. IV, 303
Wier, Jessie IV, 1242
Wier, Martha IV, 1242
Wier, Sadie IV, 303
Wierman, Alexander IV, 714
Wierman, Joel II, 322
Wierman, Joel II, 326
Wierman, Lydia S. II, 322
Wierman, Lydia S. II, 326
Wierman, Mary IV, 714
Wierman, Mary A. IV, 714
Wierman, Mary A. IV, 787
Wiesner, Abigail I, 794
Wiesner, Abigail I, 843
Wiesner, Deborah I, 794
Wiesner, Elizabeth I, 828
Wiesner, Elizabeth I, 843
Wiesner, Jesse I, 794
Wiesner, Macajah I, 914
Wiesner, Micaijah I, 794
Wiesner, Micajah I, 794
Wiesner, Micajah I, 828
Wiesner, Micajah I, 843
Wiesner, Michael I, 794
Wiesner, Ruth I, 794
Wiesner, Ruth I, 831
Wiesner, Ruth I, 843
Wiesner, William I, 794
Wigam, ??? III, 352
Wigam, Isaac III, 352
Wigam, John S. III, 352
Wigand, Tryphosa II, 272
Wigenton, George VI, 1014
Wigert, Arthur III, 352
Wigert, Mary F. II, 740
Wigert, Mary F. II, 775
Wigert, Mary F. III, 352
Wigg, Emma I, 319
Wigg, Henry VI, 30
Wigg, Lillie I, 319
Wigg, Mary A. I, 285
Wigg, Rufus I, 285
Wigg, Sallie I, 305
Wigg, Sallie I, 319
Wigganton, Susannah I, 1076
Wiggens, Margery IV, 112
Wiggens, Margery IV, 115
Wiggenton, Ann VI, 920
Wiggenton, Ann E. VI, 880
Wiggenton, Benjamin VI, 880
Wiggenton, Benjamin VI, 1012
Wiggenton, Celia VI, 920
Wiggenton, Elizabeth VI, 897
Wiggenton, George VI, 1014
Wiggenton, Isack VI, 938
Wiggenton, John VI, 897
Wiggenton, John VI, 1014
Wiggenton, Martha VI, 1012
Wiggenton, Mary Jane VI, 938
Wiggenton, Nancy VI, 1014
Wiggenton, Stella VI, 1014
Wiggins, ??? III, 428
Wiggins, Abel B. III, 437
Wiggins, Abel B. III, 466
Wiggins, Amy III, 428
Wiggins, Amy III, 466
Wiggins, Ann II, 314
Wiggins, Arthur I, 341
Wiggins, Benjamin II, 972
Wiggins, Benjamin III, 466
Wiggins, Carrie I, 341
Wiggins, Cuthbert II, 985
Wiggins, Cuthbert II, 1038
Wiggins, Cuthbert IV, 115
Wiggins, Deborah III, 437
Wiggins, Deborah III, 466
Wiggins, Dessie Kaiser IV, 787
Wiggins, Effie I, 341
Wiggins, Eliza IV, 84
Wiggins, Eliza IV, 115
Wiggins, Elizabeth B. II, 972
Wiggins, Ella I, 341
Wiggins, Ellen R. III, 466
Wiggins, Emily II, 314
Wiggins, Estelle I, 341
Wiggins, Florence V, 650
Wiggins, George Walter III, 466
Wiggins, Hannah IV, 99
Wiggins, Hannah IV, 115
Wiggins, Harrison IV, 115
Wiggins, Harry T. II, 314
Wiggins, Henry III, 504
Wiggins, Herman I, 341
Wiggins, Herman L. I, 341
Wiggins, Isaac I, 341
Wiggins, Isabella Amanda III, 466
Wiggins, James I, 331
Wiggins, Jane V, 650
Wiggins, John I, 341
Wiggins, John Bryant I, 341
Wiggins, John T. I, 341
Wiggins, John W. I, 341
Wiggins, Joseph I, 341
Wiggins, Joseph II, 985
Wiggins, Joseph II, 1038
Wiggins, Julia E. III, 504
Wiggins, Lewis I, 341
Wiggins, Lillian R. I, 341
Wiggins, Louis I, 341
Wiggins, Margaret II, 985
Wiggins, Margaret II, 1038
Wiggins, Margaret IV, 115
Wiggins, Margaret B. II, 972
Wiggins, Margery IV, 115
Wiggins, Martha IV, 90
Wiggins, Martha IV, 115
Wiggins, Mary Ann II, 972
Wiggins, Mary Ann III, 466
Wiggins, Mary D. III, 437
Wiggins, Max II, 314
Wiggins, Mollie I, 341
Wiggins, Nancy V, 650
Wiggins, Norman Stone II, 314
Wiggins, Sarah I, 331
Wiggins, Sarah II, 985
Wiggins, Sarah II, 1038
Wiggins, Sarah II, 1063
Wiggins, Teresa IV, 99
Wiggins, Teresa IV, 115
Wiggins, Vara I, 341
Wiggins, William S. III, 466
Wigginton, Benjamin VI, 864
Wigginton, Benjamin VI, 896
Wigginton, Caroline VI, 1014
Wigginton, Catherine C. VI, 896
Wigginton, Elizabeth N. VI, 1014
Wigginton, George VI, 1014
Wigginton, Harriett B. VI, 864
Wigginton, Isaac VI, 1014
Wigginton, John VI, 908
Wigginton, John VI, 916
Wigginton, John VI, 1014
Wigginton, John, Sr. VI, 871
Wigginton, Marget VI, 1014
Wigginton, Martha VI, 916
Wigginton, Nancy VI, 892
Wigginton, Nancy VI, 1014
Wigginton, Patsey VI, 1014
Wigginton, Peggy VI, 871
Wigginton, Peyton VI, 1014
Wigginton, Sisley VI, 1014
Wigginton, Stella VI, 1014
Wigginton, Thos. VI, 892
Wigginton, William VI, 1014
Wiggonton, Elizabeth VI, 916
Wiggonton, Jean VI, 876
Wiggonton, John VI, 916
Wiggs, ??? VI, 39
Wiggs, Elizabeth VI, 27
Wiggs, Elizabeth VI, 37
Wiggs, Emma I, 319
Wiggs, Henry VI, 7
Wiggs, Henry VI, 8
Wiggs, Henry VI, 15
Wiggs, Henry VI, 23
Wiggs, Henry VI, 27
Wiggs, Henry VI, 37
Wiggs, Henry VI, 38
Wiggs, Henry VI, 41
Wiggs, Henry VI, 42
Wiggs, Katheren VI, 37
Wiggs, Katheren VI, 38
Wiggs, Kathren VI, 37
Wiggs, Lidia VI, 46
Wiggs, Mary VI, 37
Wiggs, Sara VI, 37
Wiggs, William VI, 8
Wiggs, William VI, 37
Wiggs, William VI, 42
Wiggs, William VI, 46
Wiggs, Wm. VI, 46
Wigham, Dorothy III, 504
Wigham, Elizabeth III, 352
Wigham, Isaac III, 352
Wigham, Isaac III, 498
Wigham, Isaac III, 504
Wigham, John S. III, 352
Wigham, Mary III, 504
Wigham, Mary Caroline III, 352
Wigham, Mary L. III, 352
Wigham, Mary L. III, 498
Wigham, Mary L. III, 504
Wigham, Mary S. III, 352
Wigham, Thomas III, 352
Wigham, Thomas III, 504
Wight, Sarah II, 592
Wight, Sarah II, 686
Wight, Thos. II, 592
Wight, Thos. II, 686
Wigine, Meriam IV, 904
Wigine, Meriam IV, 917
Wigington, John VI, 1014
Wigington, Marget VI, 1014
Wigle, Elizabeth IV, 1299
Wigle, Harry IV, 1299
Wigle, Jessie IV, 1299
Wikall, Arabella V, 542
Wikall, Lemella V, 542
Wikall, Rebecca V, 542
Wikall, Rosa Ella V, 542
Wilaby, Matilda IV, 1015
Wilbacks, Stephen III, 352
Wilber, Emma F. III, 352
Wilber, Hannah IV, 503
Wilber, Hannah K. IV, 503
Wilber, William III, 352
Wilber, William IV, 503
Wilberforce, Anna Mary II, 306
Wilberforce, William II, 306
Wilbern, Virena Elma I, 772
Wilborn, Ann E. VI, 824
Wilborn, L. S. VI, 824
Wilborn, Virena Elma I, 763
Wilborn, Virena Elma I, 772

Wilbour, Amy R. III, 352
Wilbour, Israel III, 352
Wilbourn, Richard VI, 918
Wilbourn, Robert G. VI, 824
Wilbourne, Ferdinand VI, 825
Wilbur, Allen E. III, 167
Wilbur, Allen E. III, 352
Wilbur, Ann III, 352
Wilbur, Anna V, 941
Wilbur, Anna B. V, 941
Wilbur, Dorinda III, 82
Wilbur, Dorothy I, 638
Wilbur, Dorothy I, 642
Wilbur, Eliza III, 352
Wilbur, Eliza M. III, 296
Wilbur, Eliza M. III, 352
Wilbur, Elizabeth III, 167
Wilbur, Elizabeth III, 352
Wilbur, Ernest III, 352
Wilbur, Henry III, 352
Wilbur, Henry VI, 720
Wilbur, Henry W. III, 296
Wilbur, Henry W. III, 352
Wilbur, Humphrey III, 352
Wilbur, Jane III, 167
Wilbur, Jane III, 352
Wilbur, John Finch III, 352
Wilbur, Widow Eliza VI, 720
Wilbur, William Pierce III, 352
Wilburn, Bessie V, 1025
Wilburn, Elizabeth VI, 864
Wilburn, Fannie VI, 864
Wilburn, Julia B. I, 843
Wilburn, Nancy VI, 864
Wilburn, R. B. VI, 839
Wilburn, R. G. VI, 864
Wilburn, Richard VI, 864
Wilburn, Robert L. VI, 864
Wilcher, ??? VI, 846
Wilcher, John VI, 1014
Wilcher, Lindsey VI, 1014
Wilcher, Lucy VI, 974
Wilcher, Martha VI, 1014
Wilcher, Polly VI, 1014
Wilchire, Francis II, 449
Wilckinson, Rebecca V, 1025
Wilckinson, Sirus V, 1025
Wilcocks, Elizabeth II, 272
Wilcomb, Anna III, 387
Wilcomb, Charles III, 387
Wilcomb, Charles K. III, 352
Wilcomb, Hannah III, 352
Wilcomb, John III, 352
Wilcomb, John III, 387
Wilcomb, John Wilcomb III, 387
Wilcomb, Margaret III, 387
Wilcomb, Mary III, 387
Wilcomb, Sarah III, 387
Wilcomb, William III, 387
Wilcox, ??? III, 352
Wilcox, Abigail II, 626
Wilcox, Abigail II, 686
Wilcox, Ann II, 449
Wilcox, Ann II, 625
Wilcox, Barnabas II, 436
Wilcox, Benjamin IV, 1242
Wilcox, Catharine IV, 1031
Wilcox, Charles IV, 1026
Wilcox, Charles IV, 1031
Wilcox, Clara M. II, 722
Wilcox, Clara M. II, 775
Wilcox, Clement IV, 1031
Wilcox, Daniel II, 436
Wilcox, Daniel II, 449
Wilcox, Deborah II, 533
Wilcox, Deborah IV, 1242
Wilcox, Deborah Godfrey II, 686
Wilcox, Elizabeth II, 722
Wilcox, Elizabeth M. IV, 1026
Wilcox, Elizabeth M. IV, 1031
Wilcox, Frances H. VI, 864
Wilcox, G. Elldaah II, 722
Wilcox, Gideon II, 707
Wilcox, Gideon II, 722
Wilcox, Gideon II, 746
Wilcox, Gideon II, 775
Wilcox, Hannah II, 632
Wilcox, Hannah II, 686
Wilcox, Hester II, 449
Wilcox, Issachar II, 686
Wilcox, Jane IV, 1242
Wilcox, Joseph II, 435
Wilcox, Joseph II, 449
Wilcox, Joseph II, 625
Wilcox, Joseph II, 686
Wilcox, Lucinda V, 274
Wilcox, Lucinda V, 289
Wilcox, Maria III, 352
Wilcox, Martha V, 289
Wilcox, Martha Jane V, 289
Wilcox, Mary II, 746
Wilcox, Mary E. II, 707
Wilcox, Mary E. II, 722
Wilcox, Mary E. II, 775
Wilcox, Phebe E. IV, 363
Wilcox, Phebe E. IV, 454
Wilcox, Sarah II, 686
Wilcox, Sarah II, 707
Wilcox, Sarah II, 722
Wilcox, Sarah II, 746
Wilcox, Sarah II, 775
Wilcox, Sarah III, 352
Wilcox, Sarah IV, 367
Wilcox, Sarah IV, 454
Wilcox, Sidney III, 262
Wilcox, Sidney III, 352
Wilcox, Thomas VI, 1014
Wilcox, Thomas W. VI, 864
Wilcox, Wd. Ann II, 435
Wilcox, Wd. Sarah II, 436
Wilcox, Winifred VI, 1014
Wilcoxen, Edith IV, 503
Wilcoxen, Elizabeth II, 213
Wilcoxen, Elizabeth II, 272
Wilcoxen, Eloise IV, 503
Wilcoxen, Nancy E. IV, 503
Wilcoxen, Thomas O. IV, 503
Wilcuts, Benjamin I, 844
Wilcuts, Christian I, 844
Wilcuts, Christian I, 1070
Wilcuts, Christian I, 1072
Wilcuts, Clark I, 844
Wilcuts, Clark I, 1072
Wilcuts, Daniel I, 1070
Wilcuts, John I, 844
Wilcuts, Milley I, 844
Wilcuts, Milly I, 1072
Wilcuts, Rachel I, 844
Wilcuts, Thomas I, 844
Wilcuts, Thomas I, 1072
Wilcutts, Clark I, 844
Wilcutts, Clark I Sup 1, 10
Wilcutts, Thomas I Sup 1, 10
Wild, Thomas VI, 279
Wilde, ??? III, 352
Wilde, Charles III, 352
Wilde, Eleanor III, 195
Wilde, Eleanor III, 234
Wilde, Eleanor III, 242
Wilde, Eleanor III, 352
Wilde, Elizabeth III, 352
Wilde, Harriet III, 352
Wilde, Herbert III, 352
Wilde, Jane III, 234
Wilde, Jane III, 352
Wilde, Jennet III, 234
Wilde, Jennet III, 352
Wilde, John III, 195
Wilde, John III, 234
Wilde, John III, 352
Wilde, Jonathan III, 352
Wilde, Mary III, 352
Wilde, Mary W. III, 195
Wilde, Patience III, 352
Wilde, Richard III, 352
Wilde, Sarah Ann III, 352
Wilde, Wd. Elizabeth III, 352
Wilde, William III, 352
Wilder, Carson I, 614
Wilder, Fatima I, 55
Wilder, Fatima I, 85
Wilder, Joseph T. I, 85
Wilder, Margaret Jewel I, 614
Wildes, Elizabeth II, 436
Wildey, ??? III, 352
Wildey, Elizabeth II, 713
Wildey, Emily III, 26
Wildey, Emily III, 303
Wildey, Patience III, 352
Wildey, Richard III, 309
Wildey, Richard III, 352
Wildey, Wd. Elizabeth III, 352
Wildman, Abraham IV, 753
Wildman, Abraham IV, 787
Wildman, Abraham VI, 344
Wildman, Abraham VI, 345
Wildman, Abraham VI, 521
Wildman, Abraham VI, 579
Wildman, Albert L. Pierce II, 939
Wildman, Almeda V, 183
Wildman, Almeda M. V, 211
Wildman, Almedia V, 211
Wildman, Amy IV, 787
Wildman, Amy VI, 344
Wildman, Amy VI, 345
Wildman, Ana I, 1013
Wildman, Ann I, 970
Wildman, Ann II, 974
Wildman, Ann II, 975
Wildman, Ann II, 988
Wildman, Ann II, 1015
Wildman, Ann II, 1038
Wildman, Ann II, 1039
Wildman, Ann II, 1049
Wildman, Ann V, 211
Wildman, Ann V, 565
Wildman, Ann V, 567
Wildman, Ann V, 605
Wildman, Ann V, 952
Wildman, Ann V, 962
Wildman, Ann VI, 356
Wildman, Ann VI, 499
Wildman, Ann VI, 579
Wildman, Ann VI, 968
Wildman, Ann C. II, 959
Wildman, Ann C. II, 972
Wildman, Ann C. II, 1057
Wildman, Ann C. II, 1063
Wildman, Anna II, 827
Wildman, Anna II, 939
Wildman, Anna V, 953
Wildman, Baker II, 1038
Wildman, Benj. A. II, 787
Wildman, Benjamin II, 939
Wildman, Benjamin V, 172
Wildman, Benjamin V, 211
Wildman, Benjamin V, 962
Wildman, Benjamin V, 963
Wildman, Benjamin A. II, 939
Wildman, Benjamin A. II, 1083
Wildman, Benjamin Albertson II, 827
Wildman, Bertha E. V, 963
Wildman, Chalkley A. II, 1083
Wildman, Charles II, 939
Wildman, Charles II, 1038
Wildman, Charles II, 1063
Wildman, Charles II, 1068
Wildman, Charles II, 1070
Wildman, Charles II, 1083
Wildman, Charlotte VI, 899
Wildman, Chas. II, 827
Wildman, Chas. II, 939
Wildman, Cinthy IV, 115
Wildman, Cinthy V, 365
Wildman, Cora V, 963
Wildman, Cynthia V, 351
Wildman, Cynthia V, 365
Wildman, David Baker IV, 303
Wildman, David Baker IV, 315
Wildman, Deborah I, 1006
Wildman, Deborah IV, 67
Wildman, Deborah IV, 753
Wildman, Deborah IV, 787
Wildman, Deborah V, 211
Wildman, Deborah V, 959
Wildman, Deborah V, 962
Wildman, Deborah VI, 344
Wildman, Deborah VI, 345
Wildman, Deborah VI, 579
Wildman, Deborah VI, 968
Wildman, Earnest Adkins V, 963
Wildman, Edward I, 1006
Wildman, Edward V, 142
Wildman, Edward V, 211
Wildman, Edward V, 214
Wildman, Edward V, 953
Wildman, Edward V, 960
Wildman, Edward V, 962
Wildman, Elias II, 972
Wildman, Elias II, 1038
Wildman, Elias II, 1063
Wildman, Elias II, 1083
Wildman, Eliza II, 1022
Wildman, Eliza II, 1038
Wildman, Eliza V, 953
Wildman, Eliza V, 962
Wildman, Elizabeth I, 970
Wildman, Elizabeth I, 1006
Wildman, Elizabeth I, 1013
Wildman, Elizabeth II, 975
Wildman, Elizabeth II, 988
Wildman, Elizabeth II, 996
Wildman, Elizabeth II, 997
Wildman, Elizabeth II, 1015
Wildman, Elizabeth II, 1022
Wildman, Elizabeth II, 1025
Wildman, Elizabeth II, 1038
Wildman, Elizabeth II, 1063
Wildman, Elizabeth II, 1083
Wildman, Elizabeth IV, 303
Wildman, Elizabeth IV, 315
Wildman, Elizabeth IV, 787
Wildman, Elizabeth V, 209
Wildman, Elizabeth V, 211
Wildman, Elizabeth V, 214
Wildman, Elizabeth V, 605
Wildman, Elizabeth V, 952
Wildman, Elizabeth V, 959
Wildman, Elizabeth V, 962
Wildman, Elizabeth V, 963
Wildman, Elizabeth VI, 344
Wildman, Elizabeth VI, 345
Wildman, Elizabeth, Jr. II, 1063
Wildman, Ellwood II, 827
Wildman, Ellwood II, 939
Wildman, Ellwood II, 1083
Wildman, Elwood II, 939
Wildman, Elwood II, 1070
Wildman, Elwood II, 1083
Wildman, Emma II, 796
Wildman, Esther L. II, 827
Wildman, Esther L. II, 847
Wildman, Esther L. II, 939
Wildman, Frances Ann VI, 1014
Wildman, Frank IV, 1192
Wildman, Georgianna II, 309
Wildman, Hannah I, 1006
Wildman, Hannah II, 827
Wildman, Hannah II, 908
Wildman, Hannah II, 939
Wildman, Hannah II, 1011
Wildman, Hannah II, 1038
Wildman, Hannah IV, 1127
Wildman, Hannah IV, 1140
Wildman, Hannah V, 142
Wildman, Hannah V, 211
Wildman, Hannah V, 214
Wildman, Hannah V, 289
Wildman, Hannah V, 290
Wildman, Hannah V, 953
Wildman, Hannah V, 960
Wildman, Hannah V, 962
Wildman, Hannah V, 963
Wildman, Hannah Jane IV, 303
Wildman, Hannah Jane IV, 315
Wildman, Hiram V, 605
Wildman, Horace Peirce II, 827
Wildman, Israel VI, 899
Wildman, Israel VI, 928
Wildman, Israel VI, 972
Wildman, Israel VI, 980
Wildman, Israel VI, 1010
Wildman, Israel VI, 1014
Wildman, Jane V, 567
Wildman, Jane V, 605
Wildman, Jesse IV, 787
Wildman, Jesse VI, 344
Wildman, Jesse VI, 345
Wildman, John I, 970
Wildman, John I, 1006
Wildman, John I, 1013
Wildman, John II, 959
Wildman, John II, 972
Wildman, John II, 996
Wildman, John II, 1049
Wildman, John II, 1057
Wildman, John II, 1063
Wildman, John II, 1068
Wildman, John II, 1082
Wildman, John II, 1083
Wildman, John IV, 62
Wildman, John IV, 67
Wildman, John IV, 115
Wildman, John V, 112
Wildman, John V, 142
Wildman, John V, 211
Wildman, John V, 605
Wildman, John V, 945
Wildman, John V, 952
Wildman, John V, 956
Wildman, John V, 959
Wildman, John V, 962
Wildman, John VI, 356
Wildman, John VI, 579
Wildman, John VI, 718
Wildman, John VI, 864
Wildman, John H. II, 1083
Wildman, John K. II, 827
Wildman, John K. II, 908
Wildman, John K. II, 939
Wildman, John M. II, 972
Wildman, Jonah IV, 787
Wildman, Jonah VI, 344
Wildman, Jonah VI, 345
Wildman, Jonah VI, 1014
Wildman, Jonathan H. V, 605
Wildman, Jos. IV, 303
Wildman, Joseph II, 975
Wildman, Joseph II, 988
Wildman, Joseph II, 1015
Wildman, Joseph II, 1022
Wildman, Joseph II, 1038
Wildman, Joseph II, 1063
Wildman, Joseph II, 1083
Wildman, Joseph IV, 303
Wildman, Joseph IV, 315
Wildman, Joseph, Jr. II, 975
Wildman, Joseph, Jr. II, 1038
Wildman, Joshua II, 1063
Wildman, Joshua II, 1083
Wildman, Joshua IV, 303
Wildman, Joshua IV, 315
Wildman, Leticia VI, 344
Wildman, Leticia VI, 521
Wildman, Letitia IV, 753
Wildman, Letitia VI, 299
Wildman, Letitia VI, 344
Wildman, Letitia VI, 345
Wildman, Letitia VI, 579
Wildman, Lettitia IV, 787
Wildman, Lilla V, 365
Wildman, Loren II, 827
Wildman, Lydia IV, 303
Wildman, Lydia IV, 314
Wildman, Lydia IV, 315
Wildman, Lydia Ann V, 605
Wildman, Lydia Anne V, 605
Wildman, Mahlon II, 1025
Wildman, Mahlon II, 1038
Wildman, Mahlon IV, 787
Wildman, Mahlon VI, 344
Wildman, Mahlon VI, 345
Wildman, Margaret II, 1063
Wildman, Margaret V, 952
Wildman, Margaret V, 962
Wildman, Margarett II, 1038
Wildman, Maria L. V, 172
Wildman, Maria L. V, 211
Wildman, Maria L. V, 962
Wildman, Maria L. V, 963
Wildman, Mariah L. V, 962
Wildman, Marion V, 183
Wildman, Marion V, 209
Wildman, Marion V, 211
Wildman, Marion V, 214
Wildman, Marion V, 963
Wildman, Martha II, 847
Wildman, Martha II, 939
Wildman, Martha II, 1063
Wildman, Martha II, 1083
Wildman, Martha IV, 303
Wildman, Martha IV, 315
Wildman, Martha IV, 454
Wildman, Martha K. II, 827
Wildman, Martin II, 988
Wildman, Martin II, 1021
Wildman, Martin II, 1038
Wildman, Martin II, 1063
Wildman, Mary II, 827
Wildman, Mary II, 867
Wildman, Mary II, 939
Wildman, Mary II, 972
Wildman, Mary II, 1015
Wildman, Mary II, 1038
Wildman, Mary II, 1063
Wildman, Mary II, 1068
Wildman, Mary II, 1082
Wildman, Mary II, 1083
Wildman, Mary IV, 250
Wildman, Mary IV, 303
Wildman, Mary IV, 315
Wildman, Mary IV, 454
Wildman, Mary IV, 787
Wildman, Mary IV, 1081
Wildman, Mary IV, 1140
Wildman, Mary VI, 344
Wildman, Mary VI, 345
Wildman, Mary VI, 579
Wildman, Mary VI, 582
Wildman, Mary VI, 687
Wildman, Mary VI, 718
Wildman, Mary VI, 720
Wildman, Mary VI, 864
Wildman, Mary Ann II, 827
Wildman, Mary Ann II, 939
Wildman, Mary Ann II, 1070
Wildman, Mary Ann II, 1083
Wildman, Mary C. II, 972
Wildman, Mary C. II, 1057
Wildman, Mary C. II, 1063
Wildman, Mary L. II, 939
Wildman, Mary Lloyd II, 827
Wildman, Mary T. V, 112
Wildman, Mary T. V, 142
Wildman, Mary T. V, 963
Wildman, Mercy II, 1038
Wildman, Murry S. V, 963
Wildman, Myrtle M. V, 963
Wildman, Myrtle Maddeville V, 963
Wildman, Nancy IV, 787
Wildman, Nancy VI, 344
Wildman, Nancy VI, 345
Wildman, Nancy A. VI, 928
Wildman, Olive V, 963
Wildman, Oliver V, 605
Wildman, Phebe VI, 579
Wildman, Phebe VI, 586
Wildman, Phebe VI, 723
Wildman, Phebe VI, 724
Wildman, Rachel II, 1038
Wildman, Rachel II, 1063
Wildman, Rachel C. II, 972
Wildman, Rachel C. II, 1063

nan, Rachel E. V, 953
nan, Rachel E. V, 962
nan, Rachel T. V, 963
nan, Rebecca IV, 62
nan, Rebecca IV, 67
nan, Rebecca IV, 115
nan, Rebecca V, 605
nan, Rebecca Helen V, 568
nan, Rebecca Helen V, 605
nan, Rebeckah V, 365
nan, Robert B. II, 1038
nan, Robert Elder V, 963
nan, Ruth V, 584
nan, Ruth V, 605
nan, Samuel II, 847
nan, Samuel II, 939
nan, Samuel II, 1038
nan, Samuel II, 1063
nan, Samuel Cary II, 1038
nan, Sarah II, 974
nan, Sarah II, 996
nan, Sarah II, 997
nan, Sarah II, 1038
nan, Sarah II, 1063
nan, Sarah IV, 787
nan, Sarah VI, 344
nan, Sarah VI, 345
nan, Sarah VI, 1014
nan, Sarah Ann II, 1082
nan, Sarah Ann II, 1083
nan, Sarah M. II, 959
nan, Sarah M. II, 972
nan, Sarah M. II, 996
nan, Sarah M. II, 1038
nan, Sarah M. II, 1050
nan, Sarah M. Flowers
I, 1063
nan, Senaca I, 1006
nan, Seneca V, 211
nan, Seneca V, 567
nan, Seneca V, 605
nan, Seneca V, 963
nan, Soloman II, 1038
nan, Soloman II, 1083
nan, Solomin IV, 454
nan, Solomon II, 974
nan, Solomon II, 997
nan, Solomon II, 1038
nan, Solomon II, 1063
nan, Solomon IV, 303
nan, Solomon IV, 315
nan, Solomon IV, 454
nan, Susanna S. II, 1068
nan, Susanna S. II, 1070
nan, Susanna S. II, 1083
nan, Susannah II, 827
nan, Thomas II, 972
nan, Thomas II, 1015
nan, Thomas II, 1038
nan, Thomas II, 1063
nan, Thomas V, 605
nan, Thomas Smith IV, 303
nan, Thomas Smith IV, 315
nan, Thomas Winder V, 289
nan, Thomas Winder V, 963
nan, Townsend IV, 115
nan, Townsend V, 365
nan, Walter II, 1038
nan, Walter II, 1063
nan, Walter V, 963
nan, Walter B. II, 1083
nan, Walter B. IV, 303
nan, Walter B. IV, 315
nan, Wd. Esther Lloyd
homas II, 787
nan, Wilbur IV, 1192
nan, William I, 1006
nan, William II, 1038
nan, William IV, 67
nan, William IV, 303
nan, William V, 211
nan, William V, 605
nan, William VI, 344
nan, William VI, 356
nan, William VI, 499
nan, William VI, 579
nan, William VI, 967
nan, William W. VI, 899
nan, William W. VI, 973
nan, Wm. I, 970
nan, Wm. II, 1015
nan, Wm. II, 1038
nan, Wm. II, 1063
nan, Wm. V, 953
nan, Wm. V, 962
nan, Wm. VI, 579
nan, Wm. H. V, 605
nan, Wm. W. VI, 1018
nan, Zillah IV, 115
nan, Zillah V, 363
nan, Zillah V, 365
Wilds, Dina V, 542
Wilds, Dinah V, 532
Wile, Emma V, 1025
Wile, Eva V, 1025
Wile, Rebecca V, 491
Wile, Rebecca V, 542
Wile, W. A. V, 1025
Wile, Wm. V, 1025
Wileman, Abraham IV, 164
Wileman, Abraham IV, 357
Wileman, Abraham IV, 738
Wileman, Abraham IV, 787
Wileman, Abraham IV, 895
Wileman, Amy IV, 787
Wileman, Amy IV, 1031
Wileman, Ann I, 970
Wileman, Ann V, 211
Wileman, Ann VI, 968
Wileman, Benjamin V, 211
Wileman, Deborah IV, 787
Wileman, Deborah V, 211
Wileman, Deborah VI, 968
Wileman, Edward V, 211
Wileman, Elizabeth I, 960
Wileman, Elizabeth I, 970
Wileman, Elizabeth IV, 303
Wileman, Elizabeth IV, 787
Wileman, Elizabeth IV, 893
Wileman, Elizabeth IV, 895
Wileman, Elizabeth V, 211
Wileman, Esther H. IV, 895
Wileman, Hannah V, 211
Wileman, Jesse IV, 332
Wileman, Jesse IV, 357
Wileman, Jesse IV, 787
Wileman, John I, 960
Wileman, John I, 970
Wileman, John V, 211
Wileman, Jonah IV, 787
Wileman, Jos. IV, 303
Wileman, Joshua IV, 303
Wileman, Latitia IV, 164
Wileman, Letitia IV, 357
Wileman, Letitia IV, 738
Wileman, Letitia IV, 895
Wileman, Lettitia IV, 787
Wileman, Lydia IV, 332
Wileman, Lydia IV, 357
Wileman, Mahlon IV, 787
Wileman, Mahlon IV, 893
Wileman, Mahlon IV, 895
Wileman, Martha IV, 303
Wileman, Martha IV, 454
Wileman, Martin II, 1021
Wileman, Mary IV, 303
Wileman, Mary IV, 738
Wileman, Mary IV, 787
Wileman, Mary IV, 1120
Wileman, Nancy IV, 787
Wileman, Sarah IV, 787
Wileman, Seneca V, 211
Wileman, Solomon IV, 303
Wileman, Solomon IV, 454
Wileman, William IV, 303
Wileman, William V, 211
Wileman, Wm. I, 970
Wiles, A. VI, 935
Wiles, A. VI, 956
Wiles, A. VI, 967
Wiles, Aaron I, 979
Wiles, Aaron I, 1000
Wiles, Alton III, 420
Wiles, Alton III, 466
Wiles, Amelia I, 983
Wiles, Amelia I, 1000
Wiles, Burford VI, 864
Wiles, Diana V, 650
Wiles, Dina V, 542
Wiles, Dinah V, 542
Wiles, Edith A. IV, 406
Wiles, Edith A. IV, 440
Wiles, Edith A. IV, 821
Wiles, Elizabeth I, 979
Wiles, Elizabeth I, 981
Wiles, Elizabeth I, 987
Wiles, Elizabeth I, 1000
Wiles, Emaline IV, 1015
Wiles, Eunice Ann V, 745
Wiles, Eunice Ann V, 772
Wiles, Frances I, 979
Wiles, Frances I, 1000
Wiles, Frances I, 1013
Wiles, John I, 979
Wiles, John I, 1000
Wiles, Joseph II, 272
Wiles, Joseph II, 274
Wiles, Julia G. III, 420
Wiles, Julia G. III, 466
Wiles, Luke I, 979
Wiles, Luke I, 1000
Wiles, Luke I, 1008
Wiles, Luke I, 1013
Wiles, Luke, Jr. I, 1000
Wiles, Luke, Sr. I, 1000
Wiles, Milley I, 979
Wiles, Moses I, 979
Wiles, Moses I, 1000
Wiles, Nancy E. VI, 864
Wiles, Nathan I, 979
Wiles, Rebecca V, 542
Wiles, Rhoda I, 1000
Wiles, Rhoda I, 1008
Wiles, Rhoda I, 1013
Wiles, Sally B. I, 994
Wiles, Sally B. I, 1000
Wiles, Sarah V, 542
Wiles, Thomas I, 979
Wiles, Thomas I, 987
Wiles, Thomas I, 1000
Wiley, ??? III, 353
Wiley, ??? VI, 791
Wiley, ??? VI, 794
Wiley, Abel IV, 314
Wiley, Abel IV, 315
Wiley, Abel IV, 503
Wiley, Abigail IV, 1015
Wiley, Abigail G. IV, 1015
Wiley, Ann IV, 479
Wiley, Ann IV, 503
Wiley, Ann V, 451
Wiley, Ann V, 830
Wiley, Ann V, 873
Wiley, Ann V, 888
Wiley, Ann W. V, 888
Wiley, Ann Wright V, 873
Wiley, Ann Wright V, 941
Wiley, Avarilla IV, 1015
Wiley, Bartlett VI, 864
Wiley, Bartley VI, 848
Wiley, Benjamin IV, 503
Wiley, Cynthia IV, 787
Wiley, Cynthia IV, 1015
Wiley, David IV, 599
Wiley, David IV, 665
Wiley, David IV, 765
Wiley, David IV, 787
Wiley, David IV, 1015
Wiley, David V, 888
Wiley, Deborah V, 873
Wiley, Deborah V, 888
Wiley, Deborah V, 941
Wiley, Deborah Ann Waight
V, 941
Wiley, Drusilla IV, 1015
Wiley, Eliza. VI, 839
Wiley, Elizabeth I, 428
Wiley, Elizabeth IV, 599
Wiley, Elizabeth IV, 765
Wiley, Elizabeth IV, 787
Wiley, Elizabeth IV, 1015
Wiley, Elizabeth IV, 1081
Wiley, Elizabeth V, 873
Wiley, Elizabeth V, 888
Wiley, Elizabeth VI, 819
Wiley, Elizabeth VI, 864
Wiley, Ella V, 289
Wiley, Ellen S. II, 723
Wiley, Ellen S. II, 775
Wiley, Elmira A. V, 941
Wiley, Esther IV, 1031
Wiley, Frank IV, 503
Wiley, Geo. W. V, 888
Wiley, George V, 873
Wiley, Gulia Elma IV, 315
Wiley, Gulielma IV, 303
Wiley, Hannah IV, 164
Wiley, Hannah IV, 454
Wiley, Hannah IV, 472
Wiley, Hannah IV, 503
Wiley, Hannah IV, 1081
Wiley, Hannah V, 873
Wiley, Hannah V, 888
Wiley, Isaac V, 873
Wiley, Isaac V, 888
Wiley, Isaac V, 941
Wiley, Isaac, Jr. V, 888
Wiley, James IV, 787
Wiley, James IV, 1015
Wiley, James VI, 864
Wiley, Jane IV, 886
Wiley, Jemima V, 888
Wiley, Jemima C. V, 888
Wiley, Jemima E. V, 885
Wiley, Jemima E. V, 888
Wiley, John II, 686
Wiley, John IV, 503
Wiley, John IV, 1015
Wiley, John VI, 851
Wiley, John VI, 859
Wiley, John VI, 865
Wiley, Joseph IV, 599
Wiley, Joseph IV, 787
Wiley, Joseph IV, 1015
Wiley, Joseph IV, 1044
Wiley, Joseph V, 451
Wiley, Lucy VI, 851
Wiley, Margaret II, 797
Wiley, Margaret V, 873
Wiley, Margery IV, 1015
Wiley, Maria Louisa Thomas
V, 888
Wiley, Maria Louise Thomas
V, 888
Wiley, Mary II, 686
Wiley, Mary III, 414
Wiley, Mary IV, 503
Wiley, Mary IV, 787
Wiley, Mary IV, 1015
Wiley, Mary V, 888
Wiley, Mary VI, 791
Wiley, Mary VI, 794
Wiley, Mary G. IV, 1015
Wiley, Mary J. VI, 865
Wiley, Mary Jane V, 451
Wiley, Mary W. V, 888
Wiley, Matilda IV, 479
Wiley, Matilda IV, 503
Wiley, May Latimer IV, 1343
Wiley, Nancy VI, 819
Wiley, Ora IV, 503
Wiley, Owen H. II, 723
Wiley, Phebe III, 353
Wiley, Philip P. V, 888
Wiley, Rachel I, 428
Wiley, Rachel IV, 503
Wiley, Rebecca II, 436
Wiley, Rebecca IV, 503
Wiley, Rebecca IV, 1081
Wiley, Rebecca Ann IV, 1015
Wiley, Richard IV, 503
Wiley, Richard IV, 1015
Wiley, Richard S. IV, 503
Wiley, Ruth I, 428
Wiley, Ruth V, 211
Wiley, Ruth V, 508
Wiley, Ruth V, 542
Wiley, Sally VI, 839
Wiley, Sally VI, 864
Wiley, Samuel II, 686
Wiley, Sarah IV, 599
Wiley, Sarah IV, 787
Wiley, Sarah IV, 886
Wiley, Sarah IV, 984
Wiley, Sarah IV, 1015
Wiley, Sarah V, 873
Wiley, Sarah V, 888
Wiley, Sarah V, 941
Wiley, Sarah A. II, 723
Wiley, Sarah M. IV, 1015
Wiley, Susan II, 828
Wiley, Thomas I, 428
Wiley, Thomas II, 436
Wiley, Thomas V, 873
Wiley, Thomas V, 885
Wiley, Thomas V, 888
Wiley, Thomas V, 941
Wiley, Thos. V, 941
Wiley, Vincent J. V, 873
Wiley, William I, 428
Wiley, William III, 353
Wiley, William IV, 665
Wiley, William IV, 886
Wiley, William IV, 1015
Wiley, William F. IV, 503
Wiley, William T. IV, 503
Wiley, William, Jr. IV, 886
Wiley, Wm. IV, 886
Wiley, Wm. F. IV, 503
Wilgus, Mary II, 977
Wilgus, Mary II, 1038
Wilgus, Mary V, 772
Wilgus, Rachel E. IV, 1299
Wilgus, Thomas IV, 1299
Wilgus, Thomas V, 772
Wilhelm, Anna IV, 787
Wilhelm, Charles IV, 787
Wilhelm, Chas. IV, 787
Wilhelm, Chas. Herman IV, 787
Wiliams, John IV, 426
Wiliams, Sarah IV, 426
Wilies, Eunice Ann V, 772
Wilkens, Hannah III, 353
Wilkens, Hannah A. III, 353
Wilkens, J. G. III, 353
Wilkens, J. G. H. III, 353
Wilkens, James III, 353
Wilkens, James De Voe III, 353
Wilkens, Sarah IV, 841
Wilkenson, Elizabeth VI, 45
Wilkenson, Elizabeth VI, 46
Wilkersham, Jehu I, 1039
Wilkerson, Aaron V, 142
Wilkerson, Aaron V, 978
Wilkerson, Aaron V, 979
Wilkerson, Abiah V, 142
Wilkerson, America H. VI, 1015
Wilkerson, Ann VI, 803
Wilkerson, Anna VI, 865
Wilkerson, Betsey VI, 886
Wilkerson, Caroline M. VI, 895
Wilkerson, Catherine VI, 865
Wilkerson, Col. Peter VI, 865
Wilkerson, Cynthia VI, 1011
Wilkerson, Daniel VI, 865
Wilkerson, David VI, 1015
Wilkerson, Doshia VI, 896
Wilkerson, Drury VI, 937
Wilkerson, Edwin Legrand V, 605
Wilkerson, Edwin LeGrand
V, 605
Wilkerson, Eliza VI, 895
Wilkerson, Elizabeth V, 142
Wilkerson, Elizabeth V, 978
Wilkerson, Elizabeth VI, 1015
Wilkerson, Elizabeth
Blazebrook VI, 1014
Wilkerson, Elizabeth Burks
VI, 895
Wilkerson, Frances VI, 946
Wilkerson, Frank V, 605
Wilkerson, Henrietta L. I, 643
Wilkerson, James VI, 1003
Wilkerson, James VI, 1015
Wilkerson, Jefferson VI, 1015
Wilkerson, Jemima W. VI, 1015
Wilkerson, Jesse VI, 803
Wilkerson, John VI, 323
Wilkerson, John VI, 345
Wilkerson, John VI, 878
Wilkerson, John VI, 893
Wilkerson, John VI, 946
Wilkerson, John VI, 968
Wilkerson, John VI, 1014
Wilkerson, John VI, 1015
Wilkerson, John VI, 1017
Wilkerson, John D. VI, 1015
Wilkerson, Joseph VI, 865
Wilkerson, Joseph VI, 893
Wilkerson, Joseph VI, 956
Wilkerson, Joseph VI, 1014
Wilkerson, Joseph VI, 1015
Wilkerson, Judith VI, 1017
Wilkerson, Katharine I, 453
Wilkerson, Katharine Rightsmon
I, 455
Wilkerson, Kesiah VI, 1015
Wilkerson, Louisa VI, 1015
Wilkerson, Lydia VI, 1017
Wilkerson, Lythea VI, 865
Wilkerson, Magdaline S. VI, 1015
Wilkerson, Mahlon V, 142
Wilkerson, Malinda VI, 873
Wilkerson, Malinda VI, 1015
Wilkerson, Margaret M. VI, 1015
Wilkerson, Martha Maria VI, 934
Wilkerson, Mary VI, 457
Wilkerson, Mary VI, 1015
Wilkerson, Milly VI, 865
Wilkerson, Milly VI, 946
Wilkerson, Myrtle V, 605
Wilkerson, Nancy VI, 852
Wilkerson, Nancy VI, 865
Wilkerson, Nancy VI, 963
Wilkerson, Nancy VI, 968
Wilkerson, Nancy VI, 1015
Wilkerson, Nelly VI, 956
Wilkerson, Nicholas VI, 873
Wilkerson, Nicholas VI, 895
Wilkerson, Nicholas VI, 905
Wilkerson, Nicholas VI, 1003
Wilkerson, Nicholas VI, 1011
Wilkerson, Nicholas VI, 1015
Wilkerson, Nichols VI, 1015
Wilkerson, Owen VI, 896
Wilkerson, Owen VI, 1015
Wilkerson, Owen, Jr. VI, 1015
Wilkerson, Parson VI, 865
Wilkerson, Parson VI, 895
Wilkerson, Parson VI, 896
Wilkerson, Parson VI, 956
Wilkerson, Parson VI, 968
Wilkerson, Parson VI, 1010
Wilkerson, Parson VI, 1015
Wilkerson, Parsons VI, 1015
Wilkerson, Perry V, 605
Wilkerson, Philip VI, 1010
Wilkerson, Philip VI, 1015
Wilkerson, Polly VI, 1015
Wilkerson, Rachel V, 142
Wilkerson, Rachel V, 978
Wilkerson, Rachel VI, 1015
Wilkerson, Rebecca VI, 1015
Wilkerson, Rhoda VI, 1015
Wilkerson, Sally VI, 895

Wilkerson, Sally VI, 961
Wilkerson, Sarah VI, 105
Wilkerson, Sarah VI, 124
Wilkerson, Sarah VI, 1015
Wilkerson, Sarah M. VI, 1015
Wilkerson, Sophia VI, 1010
Wilkerson, Suckey VI, 1003
Wilkerson, Suckey VI, 1015
Wilkerson, Susan VI, 893
Wilkerson, Susaner Thomas VI, 922
Wilkerson, Susanna VI, 323
Wilkerson, Susanna VI, 345
Wilkerson, Susanna VI, 852
Wilkerson, Susanna VI, 893
Wilkerson, Susanna VI, 1014
Wilkerson, Susanna VI, 1015
Wilkerson, Tacy V, 142
Wilkerson, Tacy V, 974
Wilkerson, Tacy V, 978
Wilkerson, Vinea VI, 922
Wilkerson, William VI, 865
Wilkerson, William VI, 957
Wilkerson, William VI, 1015
Wilkerson, William L. VI, 967
Wilkerson, William L. VI, 978
Wilkerson, William O. VI, 1015
Wilkes, Archibald VI, 928
Wilkes, Cathanders VI, 899
Wilkes, Elizabeth Ann VI, 898
Wilkes, Henry VI, 873
Wilkes, Henry VI, 899
Wilkes, Henry VI, 906
Wilkes, Laura I, 926
Wilkes, Luetta I, 922
Wilkes, Luretta I, 929
Wilkes, Luretta Lea I, 926
Wilkes, Rufus V. B. I, 926
Wilkes, Sally VI, 878
Wilkes, Samuel VI, 906
Wilkes, Samuel VI, 968
Wilkes, Samuel VI, 1015
Wilkes, Samuel H. VI, 873
Wilkes, Samuel H. VI, 888
Wilkes, Sarah VI, 1015
Wilkes, Timandra VI, 873
Wilkes, William C. VI, 899
Wilkeson, Thomas II, 272
Wilkings, Sarah IV, 836
Wilkings, Sarah IV, 855
Wilkins, Agnes IV, 1151
Wilkins, Amos IV, 67
Wilkins, Amos IV, 115
Wilkins, Amos VI, 280
Wilkins, Amy II, 686
Wilkins, Ann II, 534
Wilkins, Ann II, 686
Wilkins, Ann IV, 855
Wilkins, Anna II, 723
Wilkins, Anna H. II, 775
Wilkins, Betsy Ann II, 284
Wilkins, Betsy Ann II, 305
Wilkins, Caleb II, 436
Wilkins, Caleb II, 686
Wilkins, Caroline M. II, 936
Wilkins, Caroline M. II, 939
Wilkins, Catharine I, 419
Wilkins, Catharine I, 428
Wilkins, Cert VI, 217
Wilkins, Charles II, 686
Wilkins, Chas. II, 826
Wilkins, Chas. II, 936
Wilkins, Chas. II, 939
Wilkins, Daniel IV, 115
Wilkins, Daniel IV, 665
Wilkins, Daniel IV, 787
Wilkins, Daniel IV, 810
Wilkins, Daniel IV, 855
Wilkins, Daniel VI, 279
Wilkins, Daniel VI, 280
Wilkins, Deborah B. II, 723
Wilkins, Elisabeth IV, 665
Wilkins, Elizabeth II, 272
Wilkins, Elizabeth IV, 115
Wilkins, Elizabeth IV, 787
Wilkins, Elizabeth IV, 843
Wilkins, Elizabeth IV, 855
Wilkins, Elizabeth V, 837
Wilkins, Elizabeth VI, 280
Wilkins, Elizabeth Deborah II, 723
Wilkins, Enoch I, 428
Wilkins, Enoch II, 686
Wilkins, Esther II, 490
Wilkins, Esther II, 686
Wilkins, Esther S. II, 686
Wilkins, Frances V, 313
Wilkins, Francis II, 436
Wilkins, Francis V, 289
Wilkins, Francisco V, 289
Wilkins, George I, 428
Wilkins, Hannah IV, 787
Wilkins, Hannah IV, 842
Wilkins, Hannah IV, 855
Wilkins, Hannah V, 224
Wilkins, Hannah V, 289
Wilkins, Hannah V, 313
Wilkins, Hannah A. III, 353
Wilkins, Hannah Augusta III, 100
Wilkins, Harvey II, 775
Wilkins, Henry H. II, 723
Wilkins, J. G. III, 100
Wilkins, J. G. III, 353
Wilkins, James I, 428
Wilkins, James II, 686
Wilkins, John II, 272
Wilkins, John IV, 115
Wilkins, John IV, 665
Wilkins, John IV, 787
Wilkins, John V, 289
Wilkins, John V, 313
Wilkins, John V, 448
Wilkins, John VI, 280
Wilkins, Jonathan I, 428
Wilkins, Joseph IV, 115
Wilkins, Joseph IV, 665
Wilkins, Joseph IV, 787
Wilkins, Joseph IV, 855
Wilkins, Joseph V, 289
Wilkins, Joseph V, 313
Wilkins, Joseph VI, 279
Wilkins, Joseph VI, 280
Wilkins, Joseph Sarah VI, 280
Wilkins, Joseph, Jr. IV, 855
Wilkins, Joseph, Jr. V, 289
Wilkins, Keturah II, 219
Wilkins, Keturah II, 272
Wilkins, Louisa V, 719
Wilkins, Mary IV, 855
Wilkins, Mary V, 27
Wilkins, Mary M. II, 305
Wilkins, Norma IV, 886
Wilkins, Patience II, 305
Wilkins, Phebe IV, 810
Wilkins, Phebe IV, 855
Wilkins, Rachel II, 674
Wilkins, Rachel II, 686
Wilkins, Rachel IV, 115
Wilkins, Rachel IV, 665
Wilkins, Rachel V, 142
Wilkins, Rachel V, 962
Wilkins, Rachel VI, 279
Wilkins, Rachel VI, 280
Wilkins, Rebecca V, 289
Wilkins, Richard I, 428
Wilkins, Robert II, 436
Wilkins, Robert Hilyard II, 723
Wilkins, S. Harvey II, 723
Wilkins, Sarah II, 490
Wilkins, Sarah II, 686
Wilkins, Sarah IV, 115
Wilkins, Sarah IV, 665
Wilkins, Sarah IV, 787
Wilkins, Sarah IV, 836
Wilkins, Sarah IV, 855
Wilkins, Sarah V, 289
Wilkins, Sarah V, 313
Wilkins, Sarah V, 837
Wilkins, Sarah VI, 279
Wilkins, Sarah VI, 280
Wilkins, Sarah Ann II, 775
Wilkins, Sarah B. II, 826
Wilkins, Sarah B. II, 936
Wilkins, Sarah B. II, 939
Wilkins, Sarah Elizabeth Tamson VI, 279
Wilkins, Sarah J. IV, 303
Wilkins, Susanna IV, 115
Wilkins, Susanna VI, 280
Wilkins, Susannah IV, 646
Wilkins, Susannah IV, 665
Wilkins, Susannah IV, 787
Wilkins, Susannah VI, 279
Wilkins, Tamson IV, 115
Wilkins, Tamson IV, 787
Wilkins, Tamzon IV, 665
Wilkins, Tamzon V, 289
Wilkins, Tamzon V, 313
Wilkins, Tamzon VI, 280
Wilkins, Thomas IV, 787
Wilkins, Thomas V, 289
Wilkins, Thos. V, 313
Wilkins, Wd. Caroline Moore II, 826
Wilkins, William II, 436
Wilkins, William IV, 115
Wilkins, William IV, 665
Wilkins, William IV, 787
Wilkins, William V, 289
Wilkins, William VI, 279
Wilkins, William VI, 280
Wilkins, William J. V, 837
Wilkins, Wm. V, 313
Wilkins, Wm. Wood II, 686
Wilkinson Fenton, John VI, 406
Wilkinson Fenton, Rachel VI, 406
Wilkinson Fenton, Ruth VI, 406
Wilkinson, ??? VI, 501
Wilkinson, Aaron V, 978
Wilkinson, Aaron VI, 579
Wilkinson, Agnes VI, 579
Wilkinson, Amey II, 508
Wilkinson, Amey II, 686
Wilkinson, Amos II, 686
Wilkinson, Ann I, 367
Wilkinson, Ann I, 405
Wilkinson, Ann II, 464
Wilkinson, Ann II, 686
Wilkinson, Ann II, 723
Wilkinson, Anna VI, 457
Wilkinson, Anna VI, 720
Wilkinson, Anna Eliza VI, 730
Wilkinson, Anna M. VI, 733
Wilkinson, Anna M. VI, 791
Wilkinson, Anna Mary II, 939
Wilkinson, Barbara VI, 496
Wilkinson, Barbara VI, 500
Wilkinson, Barbara VI, 579
Wilkinson, Barbara VI, 580
Wilkinson, Barbary VI, 579
Wilkinson, Barbary VI, 584
Wilkinson, Calvert IV, 855
Wilkinson, Catharine I, 367
Wilkinson, Charles VI, 730
Wilkinson, Clura IV, 1193
Wilkinson, Daniel I, 367
Wilkinson, David M. VI, 1015
Wilkinson, Elisabeth I, 441
Wilkinson, Elizabeth I, 367
Wilkinson, Elizabeth V, 978
Wilkinson, Elizabeth VI, 398
Wilkinson, Elizabeth VI, 496
Wilkinson, Elizabeth VI, 545
Wilkinson, Elizabeth VI, 579
Wilkinson, Elizabeth VI, 580
Wilkinson, Elmore IV, 1193
Wilkinson, Ester II, 449
Wilkinson, Francis I, 367
Wilkinson, Francis I, 441
Wilkinson, Francis V, 448
Wilkinson, Francis VI, 729
Wilkinson, Francis H. VI, 730
Wilkinson, Francis H. VI, 791
Wilkinson, George James IV, 855
Wilkinson, George R. IV, 556
Wilkinson, Gertrude V, 650
Wilkinson, Hannah II, 46
Wilkinson, Hannah II, 109
Wilkinson, Hannah II, 111
Wilkinson, Hannah II, 827
Wilkinson, Hannah II, 1063
Wilkinson, Hannah VI, 720
Wilkinson, Henry VI, 37
Wilkinson, James I, 367
Wilkinson, James IV, 357
Wilkinson, Jesse VI, 579
Wilkinson, John I, 367
Wilkinson, John II, 449
Wilkinson, John II, 1034
Wilkinson, John II, 1038
Wilkinson, John V, 448
Wilkinson, John VI, 41
Wilkinson, John VI, 579
Wilkinson, Joseph II, 109
Wilkinson, Joseph II, 111
Wilkinson, Joseph V, 448
Wilkinson, Joseph VI, 496
Wilkinson, Joseph VI, 500
Wilkinson, Joseph VI, 579
Wilkinson, Joseph VI, 580
Wilkinson, Joseph VI, 720
Wilkinson, Joseph VI, 917
Wilkinson, Joseph, Jr. VI, 496
Wilkinson, Joseph, Jr. VI, 579
Wilkinson, Joseph, Jr. VI, 580
Wilkinson, Magdaline S. VI, 1015
Wilkinson, Mahlon V, 142
Wilkinson, Mahlon VI, 580
Wilkinson, Margrat I, 367
Wilkinson, Mari II, 436
Wilkinson, Mary I, 1056
Wilkinson, Mary II, 1036
Wilkinson, Mary II, 1038
Wilkinson, Mary IV, 544
Wilkinson, Mary IV, 556
Wilkinson, Mary V, 808
Wilkinson, Mary V, 818
Wilkinson, Mary VI, 457
Wilkinson, Mary VI, 579
Wilkinson, Mary Alice VI, 729
Wilkinson, Mary Alice VI, 730
Wilkinson, Mary Alice VI, 791
Wilkinson, Minna V, 650
Wilkinson, Morris R. VI, 733
Wilkinson, Morris R. VI, 760
Wilkinson, Morris R. VI, 791
Wilkinson, Nathaniel II, 827
Wilkinson, Norris II, 827
Wilkinson, Norris II, 939
Wilkinson, Phineas VI, 580
Wilkinson, Polly B. VI, 1015
Wilkinson, R. L. VI, 997
Wilkinson, Rachel V, 978
Wilkinson, Rachel VI, 579
Wilkinson, Rachel VI, 580
Wilkinson, Rebecca II, 436
Wilkinson, Rebecca VI, 34
Wilkinson, Rebecca VI, 37
Wilkinson, Rebecca VI, 505
Wilkinson, Rebecca VI, 580
Wilkinson, Rebecca V. VI, 1015
Wilkinson, Ruth VI, 553
Wilkinson, Ruth VI, 580
Wilkinson, Samuel I, 367
Wilkinson, Sarah II, 939
Wilkinson, Sarah V, 448
Wilkinson, Sarah VI, 499
Wilkinson, Sarah VI, 500
Wilkinson, Sarah VI, 579
Wilkinson, Sarah VI, 580
Wilkinson, Sarah VI, 733
Wilkinson, Sarah VI, 791
Wilkinson, Sarah H. VI, 760
Wilkinson, Sarah H. VI, 791
Wilkinson, Sidney H. II, 827
Wilkinson, Tacy V, 978
Wilkinson, Tacy VI, 579
Wilkinson, Thomas I, 367
Wilkinson, Thomas H. VI, 1015
Wilkinson, Thomas M. IV, 1299
Wilkinson, William I, 367
Wilkinson, William II, 436
Wilkinson, William VI, 34
Wilkinson, William VI, 37
Wilkinson, William VI, 580
Wilkinson, William VI, 1015
Wilkinson, Wm. II, 1038
Wilkinson, Wm. C. II, 939
Wilkinson, Wm. M. II, 939
Wilkison, Ann I, 428
Wilkison, Dorcas I, 428
Wilkison, Elizabeth I, 428
Wilkison, Francis I, 428
Wilkison, John I, 428
Wilkison, Thomas I, 428
Wilkisson, John I, 428
Wilkisson, Thomas I, 343
Wilkisson, Thomas I, 428
Wilks, Ann VI, 961
Wilks, Anne VI, 1015
Wilks, Archibald VI, 1015
Wilks, Barberry VI, 1015
Wilks, Benjamin VI, 1015
Wilks, Betsy VI, 1015
Wilks, Elizabeth VI, 533
Wilks, Elizabeth VI, 580
Wilks, Elizabeth VI, 1015
Wilks, Emily VI, 1015
Wilks, Faney VI, 1015
Wilks, Francis VI, 1015
Wilks, Henry VI, 909
Wilks, Henry VI, 968
Wilks, Henry VI, 1015
Wilks, James VI, 1015
Wilks, Jesse VI, 1015
Wilks, John VI, 1015
Wilks, Julia Ann VI, 968
Wilks, Lucy VI, 1015
Wilks, Margaret VI, 1015
Wilks, Margaret VI, 1019
Wilks, Mary Sophia VI, 972
Wilks, Matilda VI, 1015
Wilks, Olga E. IV, 1343
Wilks, Peyton VI, 1015
Wilks, Polly VI, 1015
Wilks, Samuel VI, 900
Wilks, Samuel VI, 968
Wilks, Samuel VI, 1015
Wilks, Samuel N. VI, 1015
Wilks, Samuel W. VI, 1015
Wilks, Sarah VI, 1015
Wilks, Sophia VI, 972
Wilks, Susanna VI, 1015
Wilks, Thomas VI, 1015
Wilks, William C. VI, 968
Wilks, William C. VI, 1015
Wilkson, Hannah II, 111
Will, Augusta V, 941
Will, Augusta L. V, 941
Will, Eliza V, 941
Will, Elizabeth VI, 1017
Will, Elsie V, 907
Will, Israel A. V, 1025
Will, Mary V, 1025
Will, Milley VI, 1018
Will, Mrs. ??? IV, 1245
Will, Richard V, 907
Will, Wm. VI, 1017
Willaims, Daniel W. VI, 101
Willaims, Rebecca VI, 1016
Willaman, C. D. IV, 787
Willaman, Ellen IV, 787
Willaman, Frank IV, 787
Willaman, Joseph IV, 787
Willaman, Lucy IV, 787
Willaman, Martha IV, 787
Willan, Dr. Robert II, 436
Willan, Dr. Robert II, 686
Willard, Abraham IV, 1266
Willard, Anna II, 958
Willard, Cassandria VI, 865
Willard, Clarkey I, 187
Willard, Clarky I, 202
Willard, Cyprian I, 202
Willard, Daniel I, 187
Willard, Daniel I, 202
Willard, Dorothy Everett VI
Willard, Edward VI, 431
Willard, Elisabeth I, 9
Willard, Elisabeth I, 48
Willard, Elisabeth I, 85
Willard, Elisabeth I, 202
Willard, Elizabeth I, 187
Willard, Elva I, 187
Willard, Elva I, 202
Willard, Exum I, 187
Willard, Exum I, 202
Willard, Frances V, 244
Willard, Frank IV, 1343
Willard, Ida IV, 1343
Willard, John I, 187
Willard, John VI, 848
Willard, John VI, 856
Willard, John VI, 860
Willard, John VI, 864
Willard, Joseph I, 187
Willard, Joseph I, 195
Willard, Joseph I, 202
Willard, Margaret I, 202
Willard, Margaret VI, 1015
Willard, Martha VI, 815
Willard, Martin I, 202
Willard, Mary I, 187
Willard, Mary I, 202
Willard, Mary Jane VI, 912
Willard, Miriam I, 192
Willard, Miriam I, 202
Willard, Mrs. IV, 1343
Willard, Nancy VI, 815
Willard, Peninah I, 195
Willard, Peninah I, 202
Willard, Penninah I, 187
Willard, Polly VI, 864
Willard, R. G. VI, 912
Willard, Rachel I, 187
Willard, Rebekah I, 187
Willard, Rebekah I, 192
Willard, Rebekah I, 202
Willard, Rhoda I, 192
Willard, Rhoda I, 202
Willard, Richard VI, 865
Willard, Richard VI, 912
Willard, Sally VI, 856
Willard, Sarah I, 187
Willard, Sarah I, 192
Willard, Sarah I, 202
Willard, Susanah I, 187
Willard, Susanna I, 202
Willard, Susanna II, 939
Willard, Thomas I, 187
Willard, Thomas I, 202
Willard, Winfrey VI, 1015
Willcox, Abigail II, 686
Willcox, Ann II, 449
Willcox, Daniel II, 436
Willcox, Elizabeth II, 272
Willcox, Frederick II, 901
Willcox, Frederick II, 921
Willcox, John L. IV, 1299
Willcox, Joseph II, 449
Willcox, Mary II, 46
Willcox, Robert II, 46
Willcut, Milly I, 581
Willcuts, Benj. Thomas I, 106
Willcuts, Christian I, 1069
Willcuts, Clark I, 795
Willcuts, Clark I, 1069
Willcuts, David I, 1069
Willcuts, Hursley I, 1069
Willcuts, John Thomas I, 106
Willcuts, Jonathan I, 1069
Willcuts, Joseph I, 1069
Willcuts, Milley I, 795

ıts, Milley I, 1069
ıts, Rachel I, 1069
uts, Tabitha I, 1069
uts, Thomas I, 795
ıts, Thomas I, 1066
ıts, Thomas I, 1069
, Eliza V, 941
, Richard V, 941
man, Adam A. V, 467
man, Huldah V, 467
man, M. Belle V, 467
rson, Wd. Sarah II, 436
rson, William II, 436
s, Ruth IV, 338
s, Ruth IV, 358
t, ??? IV, 1141
t, Aaron I, 428
t, Daniel III, 139
t, Deliverance IV, 1386
t, Eliza III, 43
t, Germetta I, 428
t, Grace III, 134
t, Hannah III, 139
t, John V, 439
t, John W. I, 428
t, Mary I, 428
t, Mary II, 813
t, Mary E. I, 428
t, Minnie R. I, 428
t, Rebecca A. I, 428
t, Stephen W. I, 428
t, Thomas I, 428
t, Thomas Prickney I, 428
t, Ulysses G. I, 428
ts, ??? III, 40
ts, ??? III, 199
ts, ??? III, 246
ts, ??? III, 355
ts, ??? III, 356
ts, ??? III, 417
ts, ??? III, 427
ts, ??? III, 457
ts, ??? III, 472
ts, ??? III, 493
ts, Abbe III, 466
ts, Abbie III, 491
ts, Abbie III, 506
s, Abigail II, 272
s, Abigail III, 387
s, Abigail III, 389
s, Abigail III, 442
s, Abigail III, 466
s, Abigail III, 470
s, Abigail III, 471
s, Abigail III, 487
s, Abigail III, 504
s, Abigail III, 505
s, Abigail III, 506
s, Abraham III, 353
s, Abraham III, 354
s, Abraham III, 411
s, Abraham III, 466
s, Abraham III, 468
s, Abraham III, 469
s, Abraham III, 506
s, Albert III, 504
s, Alice A. III, 469
s, Almira IV, 1198
s, Amelia III, 197
s, Amelia III, 216
s, Amelia III, 225
s, Amelia III, 325
s, Amelia III, 353
s, Amelia III, 354
s, Amelia III, 355
s, Amelia III, 382
s, Amelia III, 387
s, Amelia III, 418
s, Amelia III, 466
s, Amey III, 465
s, Ammi IV, 115
s, Ammi IV, 1193
s, Amos II, 46
s, Amos II, 272
s, Amos III, 353
s, Amos III, 355
s, Amos III, 369
s, Amos III, 379
s, Amos III, 387
s, Amos III, 396
s, Amos III, 408
s, Amos III, 433
s, Amos III, 436
s, Amos III, 439
s, Amos III, 459
s, Amos III, 466
s, Amos III, 467
s, Amos III, 468
s, Amos III, 470
s, Amos III, 471
s, Amos III, 504
Willets, Amos III, 505
Willets, Amy III, 270
Willets, Amy III, 354
Willets, Amy III, 386
Willets, Amy III, 387
Willets, Amy III, 433
Willets, Amy III, 435
Willets, Amy III, 450
Willets, Amy III, 458
Willets, Amy III, 467
Willets, Amy III, 468
Willets, Amy III, 469
Willets, Amy III, 470
Willets, Amy III, 472
Willets, Amy III, 482
Willets, Amy III, 493
Willets, Amy III, 496
Willets, Amy III, 501
Willets, Amy III, 503
Willets, Amy III, 504
Willets, Amy III, 505
Willets, Amy III, 506
Willets, Andrew III, 276
Willets, Andrew III, 353
Willets, Andrew III, 354
Willets, Andrew III, 355
Willets, Andrew III, 469
Willets, Andrew III, 471
Willets, Andrew III, 496
Willets, Andrew III, 505
Willets, Andrew III, 506
Willets, Anmi IV, 91
Willets, Ann II, 272
Willets, Ann II, 1050
Willets, Ann III, 353
Willets, Ann III, 354
Willets, Ann III, 355
Willets, Ann III, 356
Willets, Ann III, 369
Willets, Ann III, 383
Willets, Ann III, 387
Willets, Ann III, 460
Willets, Ann III, 467
Willets, Ann III, 504
Willets, Ann III, 505
Willets, Ann III, 506
Willets, Ann IV, 216
Willets, Ann IV, 1193
Willets, Ann V, 880
Willets, Ann V, 888
Willets, Ann M. III, 354
Willets, Ann P. III, 387
Willets, Ann P. III, 388
Willets, Ann P. III, 390
Willets, Anna III, 185
Willets, Anna III, 353
Willets, Anna III, 354
Willets, Anna III, 386
Willets, Anna III, 387
Willets, Anna III, 424
Willets, Anna III, 461
Willets, Anna III, 465
Willets, Anna III, 467
Willets, Anna III, 468
Willets, Anna III, 470
Willets, Anna III, 472
Willets, Anna III, 505
Willets, Anna V, 289
Willets, Anna C. III, 450
Willets, Anna C. III, 469
Willets, Anna L. II, 704
Willets, Anna L. II, 775
Willets, Anna L. III, 469
Willets, Anna Maria II, 786
Willets, Anna W. III, 469
Willets, Anna W. III, 505
Willets, Anna W. III, 506
Willets, Anne III, 354
Willets, Anne III, 355
Willets, Anne III, 387
Willets, Anne III, 467
Willets, Annie III, 469
Willets, Annie IV, 504
Willets, Annie Ann III, 353
Willets, Annie Ann III, 355
Willets, Annie Ann III, 356
Willets, Annie Ann F. III, 356
Willets, Annie C. III, 467
Willets, Annie C. III, 469
Willets, Annie E. III, 505
Willets, Annie J. III, 356
Willets, Annie K. III, 469
Willets, Annie L. III, 382
Willets, Annie L. III, 387
Willets, Anny III, 354
Willets, Anson III, 356
Willets, Asa IV, 115
Willets, Azuba II, 272
Willets, Benj. Arnold III, 469
Willets, Benjamin F. III, 387
Willets, Caleb W. III, 354
Willets, Caleb W. III, 356
Willets, Caroline II, 311
Willets, Caroline III, 213
Willets, Caroline III, 353
Willets, Caroline III, 354
Willets, Caroline III, 379
Willets, Caroline III, 380
Willets, Caroline III, 387
Willets, Caroline III, 468
Willets, Caroline III, 505
Willets, Caroline F. III, 353
Willets, Carrie III, 148
Willets, Carrie III, 334
Willets, Carrie S. III, 334
Willets, Carrie S. III, 353
Willets, Carrie S. III, 356
Willets, Cath. III, 468
Willets, Catharine III, 354
Willets, Catharine III, 387
Willets, Catharine III, 435
Willets, Catharine III, 437
Willets, Catharine III, 443
Willets, Catharine III, 445
Willets, Catharine III, 466
Willets, Catharine III, 467
Willets, Catharine III, 468
Willets, Catharine III, 505
Willets, Catherine III, 459
Willets, Catherine III, 469
Willets, Charity III, 467
Willets, Charity III, 505
Willets, Charity IV, 454
Willets, Charity IV, 578
Willets, Charity IV, 600
Willets, Charity IV, 1179
Willets, Charity IV, 1193
Willets, Charity IV, 1198
Willets, Charity V, 448
Willets, Charity V, 760
Willets, Charity V, 772
Willets, Charity, Jr. V, 448
Willets, Charles II, 723
Willets, Charles III, 353
Willets, Charles III, 354
Willets, Charles III, 387
Willets, Charles III, 435
Willets, Charles III, 467
Willets, Charles III, 471
Willets, Charles III, 505
Willets, Charles IV, 1193
Willets, Charles D. III, 505
Willets, Charles D. III, 506
Willets, Charles Edwin III, 353
Willets, Charles Edwin III, 356
Willets, Charles F. III, 467
Willets, Charles F. III, 468
Willets, Charles H. III, 467
Willets, Charlotte III, 356
Willets, Charlotte M. III, 505
Willets, Chas. Luther III, 213
Willets, Clar III, 19
Willets, Clara III, 29
Willets, Clara III, 334
Willets, Clara III, 353
Willets, Clara III, 354
Willets, Clara III, 356
Willets, Clara III, 468
Willets, Clara H. III, 353
Willets, Clara L. III, 356
Willets, Clara Louise III, 19
Willets, Clara Louise III, 353
Willets, Clayton IV, 1227
Willets, Clayton N. IV, 1227
Willets, Clemence III, 458
Willets, Clemence III, 467
Willets, Clemence III, 468
Willets, Clement III, 471
Willets, Col. Thomas III, 354
Willets, Col. Thos III, 355
Willets, Cornelia III, 355
Willets, Cornelia III, 398
Willets, Cornelia III, 467
Willets, Cornelia III, 471
Willets, Cornelia A. III, 93
Willets, Cornelia A. III, 140
Willets, Cornelia A. III, 353
Willets, Cornelia A. III, 354
Willets, Cornelia P. III, 59
Willets, Cornelia P. III, 355
Willets, Cornelia R. III, 109
Willets, Cornelia W. III, 353
Willets, Cynthia IV, 1146
Willets, Cynthia IV, 1171
Willets, Cynthia IV, 1193
Willets, Cynthia IV, 1202
Willets, Cynthia IV, 1227
Willets, D. J. III, 185
Willets, Daniel III, 185
Willets, Daniel III, 353
Willets, Daniel III, 354
Willets, Daniel III, 387
Willets, Daniel III, 413
Willets, Daniel III, 435
Willets, Daniel III, 444
Willets, Daniel III, 458
Willets, Daniel III, 467
Willets, Daniel III, 468
Willets, Daniel III, 469
Willets, Daniel III, 470
Willets, Daniel III, 491
Willets, Daniel III, 493
Willets, Daniel III, 498
Willets, Daniel III, 499
Willets, Daniel III, 501
Willets, Daniel III, 505
Willets, Daniel T. III, 202
Willets, Daniel T. III, 353
Willets, Daniel T. III, 377
Willets, Daniel T. III, 387
Willets, Daniel T. III, 396
Willets, Daniel T. III, 467
Willets, David II, 272
Willets, David III, 465
Willets, David III, 468
Willets, David III, 469
Willets, David III, 472
Willets, David III, 503
Willets, David III, 505
Willets, David IV, 303
Willets, David IV, 1193
Willets, David P. IV, 214
Willets, David P. IV, 303
Willets, David P. IV, 1193
Willets, Deborah III, 105
Willets, Deborah III, 290
Willets, Deborah III, 353
Willets, Deborah III, 354
Willets, Deborah III, 458
Willets, Deborah III, 465
Willets, Deborah III, 467
Willets, Deborah III, 468
Willets, Deborah III, 469
Willets, Deborah III, 470
Willets, Deborah III, 472
Willets, Deborah III, 503
Willets, Deborah III, 505
Willets, Deborah III, 506
Willets, Deborah IV, 1193
Willets, Deborah V, 888
Willets, Dinah III, 330
Willets, Dinah III, 354
Willets, Dinah III, 458
Willets, Dinah III, 466
Willets, Dinah III, 467
Willets, Dinah III, 470
Willets, Dinah III, 471
Willets, Dorothy III, 467
Willets, Dorothy J. III, 467
Willets, Edgar III, 467
Willets, Edith III, 344
Willets, Edith III, 354
Willets, Edmond III, 353
Willets, Edmond III, 355
Willets, Edmond III, 467
Willets, Edmund II, 775
Willets, Edmund III, 285
Willets, Edmund III, 353
Willets, Edmund III, 355
Willets, Edmund III, 430
Willets, Edmund III, 446
Willets, Edmund III, 466
Willets, Edmund III, 467
Willets, Edmund III, 469
Willets, Edmund III, 471
Willets, Edmund III, 504
Willets, Edmund III, 505
Willets, Edmund R. III, 467
Willets, Edw. III, 409
Willets, Edw. III, 471
Willets, Edw. S. III, 471
Willets, Edw. S. III, 472
Willets, Edward III, 93
Willets, Edward III, 353
Willets, Edward III, 355
Willets, Edward III, 387
Willets, Edward III, 452
Willets, Edward III, 467
Willets, Edward III, 470
Willets, Edward B. III, 60
Willets, Edward B. III, 353
Willets, Edward G. III, 386
Willets, Edward S. III, 386
Willets, Edward S. III, 387
Willets, Edward S. III, 468
Willets, Edward S. III, 470
Willets, Edwin C. III, 393
Willets, Edwin C. III, 468
Willets, Elbert S. III, 353
Willets, Eli IV, 115
Willets, Eli IV, 303
Willets, Eli IV, 1193
Willets, Eli V, 962
Willets, Eliakim II, 253
Willets, Eliakim II, 272
Willets, Elias III, 506
Willets, Elikum II, 787
Willets, Elis IV, 504
Willets, Eliz. III, 134
Willets, Eliz. III, 194
Willets, Eliz. III, 354
Willets, Eliz. III, 355
Willets, Eliz. III, 496
Willets, Eliz. III, 504
Willets, Eliz. III, 505
Willets, Eliz. III, 506
Willets, Eliz. F. III, 185
Willets, Eliz. F. III, 353
Willets, Eliz. T. III, 353
Willets, Eliza III, 202
Willets, Eliza III, 353
Willets, Eliza III, 457
Willets, Eliza III, 468
Willets, Eliza IV, 227
Willets, Eliza IV, 303
Willets, Eliza B. III, 353
Willets, Eliza Elma IV, 1157
Willets, Eliza Elma IV, 1193
Willets, Eliza Jane IV, 216
Willets, Eliza K. III, 469
Willets, Elizabeth II, 272
Willets, Elizabeth III, 43
Willets, Elizabeth III, 194
Willets, Elizabeth III, 197
Willets, Elizabeth III, 202
Willets, Elizabeth III, 353
Willets, Elizabeth III, 354
Willets, Elizabeth III, 355
Willets, Elizabeth III, 356
Willets, Elizabeth III, 377
Willets, Elizabeth III, 396
Willets, Elizabeth III, 417
Willets, Elizabeth III, 453
Willets, Elizabeth III, 454
Willets, Elizabeth III, 466
Willets, Elizabeth III, 467
Willets, Elizabeth III, 468
Willets, Elizabeth III, 470
Willets, Elizabeth III, 471
Willets, Elizabeth III, 496
Willets, Elizabeth III, 504
Willets, Elizabeth III, 505
Willets, Elizabeth III, 506
Willets, Elizabeth III, 507
Willets, Elizabeth IV, 86
Willets, Elizabeth IV, 106
Willets, Elizabeth IV, 115
Willets, Elizabeth IV, 303
Willets, Elizabeth IV, 454
Willets, Elizabeth IV, 504
Willets, Elizabeth IV, 1157
Willets, Elizabeth IV, 1193
Willets, Elizabeth C. III, 153
Willets, Elizabeth E. III, 468
Willets, Elizabeth F. III, 40
Willets, Elizabeth F. III, 353
Willets, Elizabeth F. III, 396
Willets, Elizabeth F. III, 467
Willets, Elizabeth P. III, 401
Willets, Elizabeth P. III, 451
Willets, Elizabeth P. III, 470
Willets, Elizabeth P. IV, 115
Willets, Elizabeth P. IV, 504
Willets, Elizabeth P. IV, 1193
Willets, Elizabeth T. III, 387
Willets, Elizabeth W. III, 270
Willets, Elizabeth W. III, 356
Willets, Ellen IV, 1193
Willets, Ellen IV, 1202
Willets, Ellen IV, 1227
Willets, Elli IV, 1157
Willets, Ellis IV, 115
Willets, Ellis IV, 303
Willets, Ellis IV, 358
Willets, Ellis IV, 478
Willets, Ellis IV, 1157
Willets, Ellis IV, 1171
Willets, Ellis IV, 1174
Willets, Ellis IV, 1178
Willets, Ellis IV, 1193
Willets, Ellis V, 772
Willets, Ellis C. IV, 303
Willets, Ellis Campbell IV, 303
Willets, Ellis, Jr. IV, 1193
Willets, Elma III, 29
Willets, Elma A. III, 356
Willets, Elma C. III, 29
Willets, Elma C. III, 353
Willets, Elma C. III, 356
Willets, Elma H. III, 167
Willets, Elvira IV, 1193
Willets, Emily III, 387
Willets, Emma III, 53
Willets, Emma III, 345

Willets, Emma III, 346
Willets, Emma III, 353
Willets, Emma III, 464
Willets, Emma III, 468
Willets, Esther III, 76
Willets, Esther III, 139
Willets, Esther III, 351
Willets, Esther III, 353
Willets, Esther III, 354
Willets, Esther III, 355
Willets, Esther III, 386
Willets, Esther III, 387
Willets, Esther III, 435
Willets, Esther III, 467
Willets, Esther III, 468
Willets, Esther III, 470
Willets, Esther III, 471
Willets, Esther III, 472
Willets, Esther III, 493
Willets, Esther III, 505
Willets, Esther III, 506
Willets, Esther A. IV, 1227
Willets, Esther Ann IV, 1227
Willets, Esther G. III, 403
Willets, Esther G. III, 426
Willets, Esther G. III, 468
Willets, Esther G. III, 469
Willets, Eugene K. III, 468
Willets, Everet F. III, 468
Willets, Ezra IV, 115
Willets, Ezra IV, 1193
Willets, Ezra C. IV, 115
Willets, Fannie III, 469
Willets, Fannie A. III, 355
Willets, Fannie Amelia III, 426
Willets, Fannie Amelia III, 468
Willets, Florence III, 468
Willets, Florence III, 469
Willets, Florence III, 505
Willets, Florence Elizabeth III, 468
Willets, Florence Elizabeth III, 469
Willets, Florence Mary III, 354
Willets, Florence May III, 23
Willets, Frances III, 354
Willets, Frances III, 505
Willets, Franklin F. III, 505
Willets, Fred'k III, 387
Willets, Frederick III, 353
Willets, Frederick III, 386
Willets, Frederick III, 387
Willets, Frederick III, 465
Willets, Frederick III, 468
Willets, Frederick E. III, 468
Willets, Frederick E. III, 505
Willets, G. Grafton IV, 1193
Willets, George III, 354
Willets, George III, 468
Willets, Gideon III, 470
Willets, Gloriana M. III, 383
Willets, Gloriana M. III, 387
Willets, Grace C. III, 212
Willets, Grace Caroline III, 212
Willets, Grace Caroline III, 213
Willets, Grace Caroline III, 354
Willets, Grace Carolyn III, 213
Willets, Grace O. III, 467
Willets, Guliann IV, 478
Willets, Hannah II, 46
Willets, Hannah II, 111
Willets, Hannah III, 153
Willets, Hannah III, 330
Willets, Hannah III, 331
Willets, Hannah III, 353
Willets, Hannah III, 354
Willets, Hannah III, 355
Willets, Hannah III, 387
Willets, Hannah III, 409
Willets, Hannah III, 413
Willets, Hannah III, 417
Willets, Hannah III, 422
Willets, Hannah III, 424
Willets, Hannah III, 435
Willets, Hannah III, 437
Willets, Hannah III, 443
Willets, Hannah III, 445
Willets, Hannah III, 451
Willets, Hannah III, 455
Willets, Hannah III, 458
Willets, Hannah III, 460
Willets, Hannah III, 465
Willets, Hannah III, 466
Willets, Hannah III, 467
Willets, Hannah III, 468
Willets, Hannah III, 469
Willets, Hannah III, 470
Willets, Hannah III, 471
Willets, Hannah III, 496
Willets, Hannah III, 497
Willets, Hannah III, 498
Willets, Hannah III, 500
Willets, Hannah III, 503
Willets, Hannah III, 504
Willets, Hannah III, 505
Willets, Hannah III, 506
Willets, Hannah III, 507
Willets, Hannah IV, 303
Willets, Hannah IV, 358
Willets, Hannah IV, 478
Willets, Hannah IV, 504
Willets, Hannah IV, 1171
Willets, Hannah IV, 1193
Willets, Hannah IV, 1215
Willets, Hannah IV, 1227
Willets, Hannah B. III, 452
Willets, Hannah K. III, 471
Willets, Hannah R. IV, 303
Willets, Hannah W. III, 270
Willets, Harold Reginald III, 23
Willets, Harold Reginald III, 354
Willets, Harold Reginald III, 356
Willets, Harrison III, 211
Willets, Helen T. III, 409
Willets, Helen T. III, 467
Willets, Helena III, 354
Willets, Henrietta II, 723
Willets, Henrietta III, 411
Willets, Henrietta III, 466
Willets, Henrietta III, 468
Willets, Henry III, 354
Willets, Henry III, 355
Willets, Henry III, 356
Willets, Henry III, 359
Willets, Henry III, 468
Willets, Henry III, 471
Willets, Henry III, 506
Willets, Henry IV, 454
Willets, Henry V, 448
Willets, Henry G. III, 354
Willets, Henry Griffen III, 344
Willets, Henry Griffen III, 353
Willets, Henry T. III, 331
Willets, Henry T. III, 354
Willets, Henry T. III, 470
Willets, Henry T. III, 505
Willets, Hilma Kindlund III, 213
Willets, Hope III, 354
Willets, Hope III, 469
Willets, Hope III, 470
Willets, Howard III, 216
Willets, Howard III, 354
Willets, Howard III, 355
Willets, Iaaiah IV, 115
Willets, Ida III, 76
Willets, Ida III, 354
Willets, Ida III, 393
Willets, Ida III, 403
Willets, Ida III, 468
Willets, Ida III, 469
Willets, Ida E. III, 355
Willets, Ida E. III, 403
Willets, Ida E. III, 468
Willets, Isaac III, 270
Willets, Isaac III, 354
Willets, Isaac III, 453
Willets, Isaac III, 458
Willets, Isaac III, 464
Willets, Isaac III, 467
Willets, Isaac III, 472
Willets, Isaac III, 482
Willets, Isaac III, 496
Willets, Isaac III, 501
Willets, Isaac III, 504
Willets, Isaac III, 505
Willets, Isaac III, 506
Willets, Isaac U. III, 346
Willets, Isaac U. III, 353
Willets, Isaac U. III, 406
Willets, Isaac U. III, 446
Willets, Isaac U. III, 451
Willets, Isaac U. III, 467
Willets, Isaac U. III, 468
Willets, Isaac U. III, 470
Willets, Isaac U. III, 471
Willets, Isaiah IV, 115
Willets, Isaiah IV, 303
Willets, Isaiah IV, 1193
Willets, Israel III, 501
Willets, Israel IV, 115
Willets, Jackson III, 501
Willets, Jacob III, 202
Willets, Jacob III, 212
Willets, Jacob III, 353
Willets, Jacob III, 354
Willets, Jacob III, 356
Willets, Jacob III, 387
Willets, Jacob III, 435
Willets, Jacob III, 437
Willets, Jacob III, 443
Willets, Jacob III, 455
Willets, Jacob III, 466
Willets, Jacob III, 468
Willets, Jacob III, 469
Willets, Jacob III, 470
Willets, Jacob III, 471
Willets, Jacob III, 487
Willets, Jacob III, 496
Willets, Jacob III, 497
Willets, Jacob III, 500
Willets, Jacob III, 504
Willets, Jacob III, 505
Willets, Jacob III, 506
Willets, Jacob III, 507
Willets, Jacob H. III, 354
Willets, Jacob H. III, 380
Willets, Jacob H. III, 387
Willets, Jacob H. III, 437
Willets, Jacob H. III, 467
Willets, Jacob H. III, 469
Willets, Jacob Hicks III, 355
Willets, Jacob S. III, 354
Willets, Jacob Valentine III, 472
Willets, Jacob, Jr. III, 469
Willets, James III, 354
Willets, James III, 452
Willets, James III, 454
Willets, James III, 468
Willets, James III, 469
Willets, James III, 470
Willets, James III, 505
Willets, James Parnel II, 723
Willets, James R. III, 353
Willets, James R. III, 354
Willets, James R. III, 450
Willets, James R. III, 469
Willets, James W. III, 422
Willets, James W. III, 469
Willets, Jane III, 115
Willets, Jane III, 354
Willets, Jane III, 355
Willets, Jane III, 441
Willets, Jane III, 450
Willets, Jane III, 466
Willets, Jane III, 469
Willets, Jane III, 470
Willets, Jane III, 471
Willets, Jane III, 506
Willets, Jane IV, 1365
Willets, Jane IV, 1386
Willets, Jane F. III, 355
Willets, Jane H. III, 469
Willets, Jane P. III, 468
Willets, Jane P. III, 471
Willets, Jane P. III, 506
Willets, Jane R. III, 445
Willets, Jane R. III, 469
Willets, Jane R. III, 505
Willets, Jane R. III, 506
Willets, Jas. III, 468
Willets, Jas. R. III, 468
Willets, Jehu IV, 1174
Willets, Jehu IV, 1193
Willets, Jemima III, 466
Willets, Jeremiah, Jr. II, 723
Willets, Jessa IV, 115
Willets, Jesse III, 469
Willets, Jesse IV, 115
Willets, Jesse IV, 1193
Willets, Joanna III, 452
Willets, Joanna III, 469
Willets, Job III, 468
Willets, Job III, 469
Willets, Job III, 505
Willets, Joel IV, 115
Willets, Joel IV, 303
Willets, Joel IV, 1146
Willets, Joel IV, 1171
Willets, Joel IV, 1193
Willets, Joel IV, 1202
Willets, Joel IV, 1227
Willets, Johanna III, 452
Willets, John III, 43
Willets, John III, 273
Willets, John III, 353
Willets, John III, 468
Willets, John III, 470
Willets, John III, 505
Willets, John IV, 81
Willets, John IV, 86
Willets, John IV, 106
Willets, John IV, 115
Willets, John IV, 303
Willets, John IV, 504
Willets, John IV, 1193
Willets, John IV, 1227
Willets, John A. IV, 216
Willets, John C. III, 355
Willets, John E. V, 962
Willets, John Eliot IV, 1193
Willets, John Elliott IV, 1193
Willets, John F. II, 305
Willets, John Gill II, 1050
Willets, John J. III, 387
Willets, John M. IV, 115
Willets, John M. IV, 1193
Willets, John N. IV, 216
Willets, John T. III, 197
Willets, John T. III, 216
Willets, John T. III, 325
Willets, John T. III, 354
Willets, John T. III, 355
Willets, John, Jr. III, 505
Willets, Jonah III, 433
Willets, Jonah III, 466
Willets, Jonah III, 467
Willets, Jonah III, 469
Willets, Jonah III, 470
Willets, Jonah III, 505
Willets, Jonathan III, 354
Willets, Jonathan III, 355
Willets, Jonathan III, 469
Willets, Jos. III, 426
Willets, Jos. III, 468
Willets, Joseph III, 48
Willets, Joseph III, 76
Willets, Joseph III, 115
Willets, Joseph III, 139
Willets, Joseph III, 290
Willets, Joseph III, 353
Willets, Joseph III, 354
Willets, Joseph III, 355
Willets, Joseph III, 356
Willets, Joseph III, 387
Willets, Joseph III, 403
Willets, Joseph III, 417
Willets, Joseph III, 419
Willets, Joseph III, 447
Willets, Joseph III, 451
Willets, Joseph III, 465
Willets, Joseph III, 466
Willets, Joseph III, 467
Willets, Joseph III, 468
Willets, Joseph III, 469
Willets, Joseph III, 470
Willets, Joseph III, 471
Willets, Joseph III, 503
Willets, Joseph IV, 454
Willets, Joseph IV, 1193
Willets, Joseph V, 289
Willets, Joseph C. III, 355
Willets, Joseph C. IV, 1193
Willets, Joseph Clarence III, 356
Willets, Joseph J. III, 353
Willets, Josephine Louisa III, 356
Willets, Joshua III, 417
Willets, Joshua III, 469
Willets, Joshua III, 484
Willets, Joshua III, 506
Willets, Judith Ann VI, 236
Willets, Juleann IV, 504
Willets, Katharine III, 468
Willets, Katharine III, 471
Willets, Katharine Valerie III, 445
Willets, Katherine III, 469
Willets, Kezia III, 433
Willets, Kezia III, 466
Willets, Kitty III, 499
Willets, Kitty III, 505
Willets, Lamira IV, 1157
Willets, Lamira IV, 1193
Willets, Lamira IV, 1198
Willets, Latitia III, 411
Willets, Latitia III, 461
Willets, Latitia III, 469
Willets, Latitia III, 470
Willets, Latitia III, 471
Willets, Latitia V. III, 354
Willets, Laura G. F. III, 424
Willets, Laura G. F. III, 471
Willets, Leah III, 250
Willets, Leah III, 355
Willets, Leah III, 356
Willets, Leah III, 387
Willets, Leah III, 393
Willets, Leah III, 466
Willets, Leah III, 471
Willets, Leah III, 505
Willets, Lee IV, 115
Willets, Lemira IV, 358
Willets, Lemira IV, 1193
Willets, Leonard III, 466
Willets, Letitia III, 354
Willets, Lewis IV, 1179
Willets, Lewis IV, 1193
Willets, Lewis V, 760
Willets, Lewis V, 772
Willets, Lorraine III, 469
Willets, Louisa A. III, 469
Willets, Lydia III, 59
Willets, Lydia III, 353
Willets, Lydia III, 354
Willets, Lydia III, 355
Willets, Lydia III, 356
Willets, Lydia III, 453
Willets, Lydia III, 471
Willets, Lydia III, 472
Willets, Lydia III, 491
Willets, Lydia III, 505
Willets, Lydia III, 506
Willets, Lydia IV, 303
Willets, Lydia IV, 1174
Willets, Lydia IV, 1193
Willets, Lydia V, 817
Willets, Lydia M. III, 498
Willets, Lydia Orthodox III,
Willets, Lydia P. III, 247
Willets, Lydia S. IV, 289
Willets, Lydia S. IV, 303
Willets, Mabel M. III, 355
Willets, Mabel Maria III, 15
Willets, Mabel Maria III, 35
Willets, Mahlon V, 142
Willets, Margaret I, 1007
Willets, Margaret I, 1013
Willets, Margaret III, 414
Willets, Margaret IV, 216
Willets, Margaret IV, 303
Willets, Margaret IV, 475
Willets, Margaret IV, 504
Willets, Margaret IV, 1193
Willets, Margaret Ann III, 3
Willets, Maria III, 81
Willets, Maria III, 355
Willets, Maria III, 356
Willets, Maria III, 471
Willets, Maria IV, 91
Willets, Maria IV, 115
Willets, Maria IV, 1193
Willets, Marietta III, 451
Willets, Marietta III, 468
Willets, Marietta III, 470
Willets, Mark IV, 227
Willets, Mark IV, 289
Willets, Mark IV, 303
Willets, Mark IV, 355
Willets, Mark IV, 358
Willets, Mark IV, 501
Willets, Mark IV, 504
Willets, Martha III, 211
Willets, Martha III, 285
Willets, Martha III, 353
Willets, Martha III, 354
Willets, Martha III, 355
Willets, Martha III, 359
Willets, Martha III, 387
Willets, Martha III, 403
Willets, Martha III, 430
Willets, Martha III, 439
Willets, Martha III, 444
Willets, Martha III, 446
Willets, Martha III, 448
Willets, Martha III, 466
Willets, Martha III, 467
Willets, Martha III, 469
Willets, Martha III, 470
Willets, Martha III, 471
Willets, Martha III, 472
Willets, Martha III, 486
Willets, Martha III, 487
Willets, Martha III, 496
Willets, Martha III, 504
Willets, Martha III, 505
Willets, Martha III, 506
Willets, Martha III, 507
Willets, Martha IV, 1193
Willets, Martha Amanda III
Willets, Martha E. S. III, 21
Willets, Martha E. T. III, 35
Willets, Martha Ellen IV, 11
Willets, Martha H. III, 353
Willets, Martha H. III, 467
Willets, Martha T. III, 356
Willets, Martha V. III, 468
Willets, Martha V. III, 480
Willets, Martha V. III, 506
Willets, Martin V, 962
Willets, Mary I, 914
Willets, Mary II, 272
Willets, Mary III, 43
Willets, Mary III, 67
Willets, Mary III, 194
Willets, Mary III, 246
Willets, Mary III, 258
Willets, Mary III, 273
Willets, Mary III, 331
Willets, Mary III, 346
Willets, Mary III, 353
Willets, Mary III, 354
Willets, Mary III, 355
Willets, Mary III, 356
Willets, Mary III, 369
Willets, Mary III, 387
Willets, Mary III, 406

s, Mary III, 433
s, Mary III, 434
s, Mary III, 453
s, Mary III, 456
s, Mary III, 459
s, Mary III, 462
ts, Mary III, 464
ts, Mary III, 466
ts, Mary III, 467
ts, Mary III, 468
ts, Mary III, 469
ts, Mary III, 470
ts, Mary III, 471
ts, Mary III, 495
ts, Mary III, 501
ts, Mary III, 502
ts, Mary III, 504
ts, Mary III, 505
ts, Mary III, 506
ts, Mary IV, 115
ts, Mary IV, 303
ts, Mary IV, 1178
ts, Mary IV, 1193
ts, Mary IV, 1375
ts, Mary V, 968
ets, Mary V, 979
ets, Mary A. III, 489
ets, Mary Ann III, 331
ets, Mary Ann IV, 216
ets, Mary C. III, 446
ets, Mary C. III, 451
ets, Mary C. III, 470
ets, Mary C. III, 471
ets, Mary E. III, 467
ets, Mary E. III, 471
ets, Mary E. IV, 216
ets, Mary F. I, 611
ets, Mary H. IV, 1193
ets, Mary J. III, 468
ets, Mary J. III, 470
ets, Mary J. III, 501
ets, Mary J. IV, 1174
ets, Mary J. IV, 1193
ets, Mary Jane III, 418
ets, Mary Jane III, 466
ets, Mary Jane III, 468
lets, Mary K. M. III, 355
lets, Mary Kingsland III, 216
lets, Mary Kingsland III, 354
lets, Mary P. II, 305
lets, Mary P. III, 186
lets, Mary P. III, 387
lets, Mary P. III, 388
lets, Mary R. III, 505
lets, Mary R. Titus III, 470
llets, Mary S. III, 355
llets, Mary S. III, 356
llets, Mary S. III, 468
llets, Mary S. III, 470
llets, Mary S. IV, 303
llets, Mary T. III, 401
llets, Mary T. III, 468
llets, Mary T. III, 470
llets, Mary T. III, 472
llets, Mary U. III, 354
llets, Mary U. III, 411
llets, Mary V. III, 445
llets, Mary V. III, 469
llets, Mary V. III, 480
llets, Mary V. III, 498
llets, Mary V. III, 505
illets, Mary V. III, 506
illets, Mary Valentine III, 472
illets, Matilda III, 445
illets, Matilda III, 498
illets, Matilda III, 506
illets, Mercy III, 470
illets, Mercy Griffith IV, 216
illets, Milford IV, 1193
illets, Milton IV, 115
illets, Milton IV, 1193
illets, Minnie III, 505
illets, Morton IV, 1193
Villets, Morton H. IV, 1193
Villets, Nancy III, 469
Villets, Nancy III, 506
Villets, Nancy V, 289
Villets, Nathan IV, 216
Villets, Obadiah III, 194
Villets, Obadiah III, 355
Villets, Obadiah III, 407
Villets, Obadiah III, 408
Villets, Obadiah III, 470
Villets, Obadiah III, 496
Villets, Obadiah III, 504
Villets, Obadiah III, 505
Villets, Obadiah III, 506
Villets, Obediah III, 354
Villets, Obediah III, 355
Villets, Oliver H. IV, 1193
Villets, Peter III, 470
Willets, Phebe II, 253
Willets, Phebe II, 272
Willets, Phebe II, 787
Willets, Phebe III, 48
Willets, Phebe III, 354
Willets, Phebe III, 355
Willets, Phebe III, 356
Willets, Phebe III, 359
Willets, Phebe III, 417
Willets, Phebe III, 436
Willets, Phebe III, 438
Willets, Phebe III, 454
Willets, Phebe III, 455
Willets, Phebe III, 456
Willets, Phebe III, 458
Willets, Phebe III, 466
Willets, Phebe III, 467
Willets, Phebe III, 468
Willets, Phebe III, 469
Willets, Phebe III, 470
Willets, Phebe III, 471
Willets, Phebe III, 472
Willets, Phebe III, 482
Willets, Phebe III, 484
Willets, Phebe III, 497
Willets, Phebe III, 500
Willets, Phebe III, 501
Willets, Phebe III, 505
Willets, Phebe III, 506
Willets, Phebe III, 507
Willets, Phebe IV, 1193
Willets, Phebe V, 888
Willets, Phebe Ann III, 354
Willets, Phebe Elma IV, 1193
Willets, Phebe J. III, 470
Willets, Phebe M. III, 353
Willets, Phebe P. III, 491
Willets, Phebe P. III, 506
Willets, Phebe, Jr. III, 447
Willets, Phebe, Jr. III, 469
Willets, Priscilla III, 355
Willets, Priscilla III, 506
Willets, Rachel III, 250
Willets, Rachel III, 355
Willets, Rachel III, 356
Willets, Rachel III, 387
Willets, Rachel III, 417
Willets, Rachel III, 419
Willets, Rachel III, 453
Willets, Rachel III, 469
Willets, Rachel III, 470
Willets, Rachel III, 471
Willets, Rachel IV, 67
Willets, Rachel IV, 81
Willets, Rachel IV, 86
Willets, Rachel IV, 113
Willets, Rachel IV, 115
Willets, Rachel IV, 303
Willets, Rachel IV, 504
Willets, Rachel IV, 1157
Willets, Rachel IV, 1171
Willets, Rachel IV, 1174
Willets, Rachel IV, 1178
Willets, Rachel IV, 1193
Willets, Rachel V, 772
Willets, Rachel H. III, 468
Willets, Rachel L. IV, 1193
Willets, Rachel S. III, 48
Willets, Rachel S. III, 354
Willets, Rachel S. III, 355
Willets, Rebecca III, 355
Willets, Rebecca III, 439
Willets, Rebecca III, 466
Willets, Rebecca III, 468
Willets, Rebecca III, 470
Willets, Rebecca III, 471
Willets, Rebecca IV, 115
Willets, Rebecca IV, 1193
Willets, Rebecca M. II, 1050
Willets, Rebeccah IV, 115
Willets, Richard II, 111
Willets, Richard II, 272
Willets, Richard III, 354
Willets, Richard III, 355
Willets, Richard III, 387
Willets, Richard III, 414
Willets, Richard III, 442
Willets, Richard III, 453
Willets, Richard III, 458
Willets, Richard III, 460
Willets, Richard III, 466
Willets, Richard III, 467
Willets, Richard III, 468
Willets, Richard III, 469
Willets, Richard III, 470
Willets, Richard III, 471
Willets, Richard III, 505
Willets, Richard III, 506
Willets, Richard R. III, 504
Willets, Richard R. III, 506
Willets, Richard, Jr. III, 506
Willets, Robert III, 353
Willets, Robert III, 355
Willets, Robert III, 383
Willets, Robert III, 387
Willets, Robert III, 456
Willets, Robert III, 467
Willets, Robert III, 469
Willets, Robert III, 470
Willets, Robert III, 471
Willets, Robert III, 495
Willets, Robert III, 505
Willets, Robert III, 506
Willets, Robert Henry III, 424
Willets, Robert Henry III, 471
Willets, Robert Hicksite III, 355
Willets, Robert Pitfield I, 611
Willets, Robert R. III, 15
Willets, Robert R. III, 59
Willets, Robert R. III, 211
Willets, Robert R. III, 247
Willets, Robert R. III, 353
Willets, Robert R. III, 354
Willets, Robert R. III, 355
Willets, Robert R. III, 356
Willets, Robert R. III, 453
Willets, Robert R. III, 471
Willets, Robert R. III, 472
Willets, Robert R., Jr. III, 355
Willets, Robert Tabor III, 471
Willets, Roberts R. III, 431
Willets, Robt. III, 387
Willets, Robt. R. III, 355
Willets, Roy III, 471
Willets, Ruth III, 466
Willets, Ruth III, 470
Willets, Ruth III, 471
Willets, Ruth III, 505
Willets, Ruth IV, 86
Willets, Ruth IV, 115
Willets, Ruth W. III, 506
Willets, S. Phebe III, 471
Willets, Samira IV, 389
Willets, Samira IV, 454
Willets, Samira IV, 1193
Willets, Samuel II, 272
Willets, Samuel III, 153
Willets, Samuel III, 225
Willets, Samuel III, 331
Willets, Samuel III, 353
Willets, Samuel III, 354
Willets, Samuel III, 355
Willets, Samuel III, 356
Willets, Samuel III, 382
Willets, Samuel III, 387
Willets, Samuel III, 419
Willets, Samuel III, 443
Willets, Samuel III, 450
Willets, Samuel III, 466
Willets, Samuel III, 468
Willets, Samuel III, 469
Willets, Samuel III, 470
Willets, Samuel III, 471
Willets, Samuel III, 497
Willets, Samuel III, 506
Willets, Samuel IV, 115
Willets, Samuel IV, 303
Willets, Samuel IV, 1193
Willets, Samuel IV, 1227
Willets, Samuel C. IV, 1193
Willets, Samuel Lawrence III, 353
Willets, Samuel P. III, 387
Willets, Samuel P. III, 468
Willets, Samuel S. II, 1050
Willets, Samuel S. III, 353
Willets, Samuel S. III, 355
Willets, Sarah II, 272
Willets, Sarah III, 28
Willets, Sarah III, 81
Willets, Sarah III, 225
Willets, Sarah III, 247
Willets, Sarah III, 276
Willets, Sarah III, 285
Willets, Sarah III, 353
Willets, Sarah III, 355
Willets, Sarah III, 356
Willets, Sarah III, 377
Willets, Sarah III, 393
Willets, Sarah III, 419
Willets, Sarah III, 440
Willets, Sarah III, 446
Willets, Sarah III, 466
Willets, Sarah III, 470
Willets, Sarah III, 471
Willets, Sarah III, 473
Willets, Sarah III, 496
Willets, Sarah III, 505
Willets, Sarah III, 506
Willets, Sarah IV, 81
Willets, Sarah IV, 115
Willets, Sarah IV, 289
Willets, Sarah IV, 303
Willets, Sarah IV, 355
Willets, Sarah IV, 358
Willets, Sarah IV, 501
Willets, Sarah IV, 504
Willets, Sarah IV, 712
Willets, Sarah IV, 1184
Willets, Sarah IV, 1193
Willets, Sarah IV, 1222
Willets, Sarah IV, 1372
Willets, Sarah IV, 1386
Willets, Sarah V, 365
Willets, Sarah VI, 249
Willets, Sarah A. III, 380
Willets, Sarah A. III, 387
Willets, Sarah A. III, 437
Willets, Sarah A. III, 467
Willets, Sarah A. III, 469
Willets, Sarah A. III, 471
Willets, Sarah Ann IV, 303
Willets, Sarah C. III, 446
Willets, Sarah C. III, 468
Willets, Sarah C. III, 471
Willets, Sarah E. III, 202
Willets, Sarah E. III, 356
Willets, Sarah Ellen IV, 1227
Willets, Sarah F. III, 60
Willets, Sarah F. III, 353
Willets, Sarah H. III, 225
Willets, Sarah H. III, 353
Willets, Sarah H. III, 355
Willets, Sarah H. III, 356
Willets, Sarah H. III, 387
Willets, Sarah H. III, 469
Willets, Sarah Jane III, 354
Willets, Sarah M. III, 446
Willets, Sarah M. III, 471
Willets, Sarah M. III, 505
Willets, Sarah Maria III, 353
Willets, Sarah Maria III, 467
Willets, Sarah P. III, 356
Willets, Sarah Parry III, 355
Willets, Sarah V. IV, 227
Willets, Sarah V. IV, 303
Willets, Seaman III, 383
Willets, Seaman III, 387
Willets, Seaman III, 388
Willets, Seth Barrows III, 471
Willets, Seth C. C. III, 471
Willets, Sina W. IV, 214
Willets, Sina W. IV, 303
Willets, Sophia III, 331
Willets, Sophia III, 354
Willets, Sophia III, 468
Willets, Sophia III, 505
Willets, Sophia III, 506
Willets, Sophia U. III, 468
Willets, Stephen III, 81
Willets, Stephen III, 355
Willets, Stephen III, 356
Willets, Stephen III, 471
Willets, Stephen E. III, 471
Willets, Stephen T. III, 356
Willets, Stephen T. III, 471
Willets, Susan III, 356
Willets, Susan V, 888
Willets, Susan A. III, 213
Willets, Susan A. III, 353
Willets, Susan A. III, 354
Willets, Susan A. III, 356
Willets, Susannah III, 239
Willets, Susannah III, 356
Willets, Susannah Morris III, 470
Willets, T. Henry III, 354
Willets, Tacey III, 247
Willets, Tacie III, 15
Willets, Tacie III, 355
Willets, Tacie III, 431
Willets, Tacie P. III, 211
Willets, Tacie P. III, 355
Willets, Tacie P. III, 471
Willets, Taylor IV, 115
Willets, Taylor IV, 303
Willets, Taylor IV, 1193
Willets, Thomas III, 246
Willets, Thomas III, 258
Willets, Thomas III, 330
Willets, Thomas III, 353
Willets, Thomas III, 354
Willets, Thomas III, 355
Willets, Thomas III, 356
Willets, Thomas III, 387
Willets, Thomas III, 393
Willets, Thomas III, 422
Willets, Thomas III, 445
Willets, Thomas III, 466
Willets, Thomas III, 468
Willets, Thomas III, 470
Willets, Thomas III, 471
Willets, Thomas III, 506
Willets, Thomas S. III, 387
Willets, Thomas W. III, 353
Willets, Thomas W. III, 467
Willets, Thomas W. III, 471
Willets, Thos. III, 250
Willets, Thos. III, 355
Willets, Thos. III, 504
Willets, Thos. III, 505
Willets, Thos. W. III, 424
Willets, Tristram III, 470
Willets, Unity III, 355
Willets, Valentine III, 441
Willets, Valentine III, 471
Willets, Wait III, 356
Willets, Wait III, 434
Willets, Wait III, 506
Willets, Walter III, 387
Willets, Walter R. III, 270
Willets, Walter R. III, 356
Willets, Walter R. III, 387
Willets, Walter R. III, 471
Willets, Wd. Ann F. III, 198
Willets, Wd. Deborah III, 353
Willets, Wd. Katharine III, 469
Willets, Wd. Margaret III, 470
Willets, Wd. Mary II, 787
Willets, Wendill P. IV, 1227
Willets, Willet III, 213
Willets, Willet III, 469
Willets, Willet III, 505
Willets, William III, 401
Willets, William III, 411
Willets, William III, 438
Willets, William III, 445
Willets, William III, 451
Willets, William III, 461
Willets, William III, 462
Willets, William III, 467
Willets, William III, 468
Willets, William III, 469
Willets, William III, 470
Willets, William III, 471
Willets, William III, 472
Willets, William III, 498
Willets, William III, 505
Willets, William III, 506
Willets, William III, 507
Willets, William IV, 1193
Willets, William V, 142
Willets, William V, 289
Willets, William H. III, 468
Willets, William H. III, 472
Willets, William Henry III, 355
Willets, William Henry III, 356
Willets, William Henry III, 468
Willets, William Henry III, 472
Willets, William J. III, 356
Willets, William Jackson III, 354
Willets, William P. III, 427
Willets, William P. III, 467
Willets, William P. III, 472
Willets, William R. III, 356
Willets, William Rufus III, 213
Willets, William Russell III, 356
Willets, William S. III, 505
Willets, William U. III, 167
Willets, William U. III, 354
Willets, William U. III, 356
Willets, William W. III, 471
Willets, Wm. III, 354
Willets, Wm. III, 445
Willets, Wm. III, 469
Willets, Wm. III, 471
Willets, Wm. III, 480
Willets, Wm. III, 505
Willets, Wm. III, 506
Willets, Wm. III, 507
Willets, Wm. IV, 1227
Willets, Wm. E. III, 468
Willets, Wm. Edgar III, 469
Willets, Wm. Henry III, 448
Willets, Wm. J. III, 198
Willets, Wm. J. III, 353
Willets, Wm. J. III, 355
Willets, Wm. J. III, 356
Willets, Wm. P. III, 418
Willets, Wm. P. III, 466
Willets, Wm. Rufus III, 213
Willets, Wm. T. III, 202
Willets, Wm. U. III, 19
Willets, Wm. U. III, 29
Willets, Wm. U. III, 334
Willets, Wm. U. III, 353
Willets, Wm. U. III, 354
Willets, Zebulon III, 356
Willets, Zebulon III, 387
Willets, Zebulun III, 468
Willets, Zebulun III, 471
Willett, ??? II, 813
Willett, Abraham III, 273
Willett, Abraham III, 353
Willett, Andrew III, 398

Willett, Beatrice IV, 1343
Willett, Col. Thos III, 355
Willett, Col. Thos. III, 273
Willett, Deborah III, 353
Willett, Elbert S. III, 387
Willett, Helena III, 273
Willett, Jonathan III, 354
Willett, Mary III, 273
Willett, Mary III, 355
Willett, Mary III, 398
Willett, Sarah III, 79
Willett, Sarah III, 86
Willett, Sarah W. II, 781
Willett, William III, 273
Willetts, Anna W. II, 940
Willetts, Caroline II, 880
Willetts, Daniel III, 446
Willetts, Deborah III, 61
Willetts, Edith W. II, 940
Willetts, Elizabeth II, 787
Willetts, Elizabeth IV, 164
Willetts, Henry I, 845
Willetts, Henry V, 365
Willetts, Jacob III, 61
Willetts, Jacob III, 140
Willetts, Jacob III, 491
Willetts, James II, 723
Willetts, Jane W. III, 61
Willetts, John H. II, 939
Willetts, John H. II, 940
Willetts, Leah III, 444
Willetts, Martha III, 446
Willetts, Mary II, 787
Willetts, Mary P. II, 305
Willetts, Rachel C. II, 940
Willetts, Sarah V, 365
Willetts, Susan A. III, 140
Willetts, Thomas III, 444
Willey, Dora V, 1025
Willey, Florence III, 463
Willey, Samuel V, 1025
Willgans, Thomas IV, 1299
Willhite, Mary V, 719
Willhous, Sally I, 1062
William, ??? IV, 447
William, Ann I, 1039
William, Caroline F. VI, 735
William, Ebelus II, 436
William, Jacob R. III, 358
William, James, Jr. VI, 484
William, Jane M. III, 358
William, Mary II, 436
William, Mary V, 511
William, Mary Elizabeth III, 358
William, Penina IV, 579
William, Salley VI, 885
William, William VI, 457
William, Wm. D. III, 358
Williaman, Frank IV, 787
Williaman, Lucy IV, 748
Williams, ??? II, 437
Williams, ??? III, 282
Williams, ??? III, 314
Williams, ??? III, 358
Williams, ??? III, 439
Williams, ??? IV, 303
Williams, ??? IV, 1047
Williams, ??? V, 315
Williams, ??? V, 965
Williams, ??? VI, 574
Williams, A. J. V, 719
Williams, Aaron IV, 164
Williams, Aaron IV, 454
Williams, Aaron IV, 456
Williams, Aaron Hackney I, 1163
Williams, Abba IV, 409
Williams, Abba IV, 455
Williams, Abbie IV, 454
Williams, Abbie IV, 557
Williams, Abbot II, 188
Williams, Abbot II, 226
Williams, Abbot II, 272
Williams, Abbott II, 436
Williams, Abby IV, 164
Williams, Abel I, 368
Williams, Abel I, 970
Williams, Abel I, 1134
Williams, Abel Lewis I, 1112
Williams, Abigail I, 368
Williams, Abigail I, 692
Williams, Abigail I, 737
Williams, Abigail I, 844
Williams, Abigail I, 1051
Williams, Abigail I, 1112
Williams, Abigail II, 272
Williams, Abigail II, 274
Williams, Abigail II, 955
Williams, Abigail III, 357
Williams, Abigail IV, 303
Williams, Abigail IV, 304
Williams, Abigail IV, 534
Williams, Abigail IV, 535
Williams, Abigail IV, 556
Williams, Abigail IV, 557
Williams, Abigail IV, 718
Williams, Abigail IV, 855
Williams, Abigail IV, 1386
Williams, Abigail V, 138
Williams, Abigail V, 142
Williams, Abigail V, 288
Williams, Abigail V, 289
Williams, Abigail Perdue V, 467
Williams, Abijah VI, 580
Williams, Abner II, 687
Williams, Abner IV, 304
Williams, Abner IV, 455
Williams, Abner IV, 456
Williams, Abner IV, 599
Williams, Abner IV, 600
Williams, Abner IV, 1078
Williams, Abner IV, 1082
Williams, Abner VI, 580
Williams, Abner VI, 581
Williams, Abner VI, 582
Williams, Abner VI, 583
Williams, Abner W. V, 962
Williams, Abraham I, 429
Williams, Abraham I, 1099
Williams, Abraham II, 305
Williams, Abraham IV, 67
Williams, Abraham IV, 303
Williams, Abraham IV, 665
Williams, Abraham IV, 855
Williams, Abraham VI, 721
Williams, Abram I, 429
Williams, Abram I, 1099
Williams, Absalom VI, 1016
Williams, Achellis I, 958
Williams, Achillas I, 521
Williams, Achillas I, 579
Williams, Achillas I, 582
Williams, Achilles I, 582
Williams, Achilles I, 970
Williams, Achilles V, 142
Williams, Achilles VI, 345
Williams, Achilles VI, 356
Williams, Achsah IV, 1194
Williams, Achsah P. IV, 1194
Williams, Addison IV, 1120
Williams, Agatha VI, 217
Williams, Aggetha VI, 954
Williams, Agness VI, 993
Williams, Albert IV, 304
Williams, Albert VI, 911
Williams, Albert VI, 1016
Williams, Albert B. II, 882
Williams, Albert B. II, 940
Williams, Albert J. II, 940
Williams, Alesanna IV, 449
Williams, Alesanna IV, 456
Williams, Alexander I, 429
Williams, Alexander I, 1134
Williams, Alexander V, 873
Williams, Alfred K. V, 941
Williams, Alfred W. VI, 865
Williams, Alice II, 940
Williams, Alice V, 650
Williams, Alice Bertha IV, 1044
Williams, Alice J. V, 941
Williams, Allen I, 1099
Williams, Allen V, 289
Williams, Allen V, 467
Williams, Alta T. V, 543
Williams, Amanda C. III, 357
Williams, Amelia IV, 1266
Williams, Ameret Jane VI, 865
Williams, Americus V. V, 941
Williams, Amey VI, 998
Williams, Amos I, 582
Williams, Amy I, 1046
Williams, Amy II, 449
Williams, Amy III, 357
Williams, Amy III, 362
Williams, Amy III, 467
Williams, Amy III, 472
Williams, Amy B. IV, 358
Williams, Amy B. IV, 556
Williams, Amy B. IV, 557
Williams, Anderson V, 439
Williams, Anderson VI, 807
Williams, Anderson VI, 817
Williams, Anderson VI, 819
Williams, Anderson VI, 858
Williams, Anderson VI, 864
Williams, Anderson VI, 865
Williams, Andrew I, 905
Williams, Andrew II, 436
Williams, Andrew IV, 1299
Williams, Andrew V, 1025
Williams, Ann I, 26
Williams, Ann I, 277
Williams, Ann I, 521
Williams, Ann I, 553
Williams, Ann I, 582
Williams, Ann I, 1016
Williams, Ann II, 272
Williams, Ann II, 273
Williams, Ann II, 274
Williams, Ann II, 302
Williams, Ann II, 305
Williams, Ann II, 408
Williams, Ann II, 436
Williams, Ann II, 449
Williams, Ann II, 491
Williams, Ann II, 625
Williams, Ann II, 665
Williams, Ann II, 687
Williams, Ann II, 723
Williams, Ann II, 804
Williams, Ann II, 827
Williams, Ann II, 837
Williams, Ann II, 940
Williams, Ann III, 357
Williams, Ann III, 433
Williams, Ann III, 472
Williams, Ann IV, 67
Williams, Ann IV, 116
Williams, Ann IV, 246
Williams, Ann IV, 304
Williams, Ann IV, 357
Williams, Ann IV, 410
Williams, Ann IV, 436
Williams, Ann IV, 455
Williams, Ann IV, 456
Williams, Ann IV, 549
Williams, Ann IV, 557
Williams, Ann IV, 591
Williams, Ann IV, 600
Williams, Ann IV, 665
Williams, Ann IV, 787
Williams, Ann IV, 826
Williams, Ann IV, 855
Williams, Ann V, 142
Williams, Ann V, 340
Williams, Ann V, 365
Williams, Ann V, 406
Williams, Ann V, 439
Williams, Ann V, 941
Williams, Ann VI, 46
Williams, Ann VI, 484
Williams, Ann VI, 513
Williams, Ann VI, 580
Williams, Ann VI, 581
Williams, Ann VI, 721
Williams, Ann VI, 865
Williams, Ann E. IV, 788
Williams, Ann Eliza IV, 304
Williams, Ann Elizabeth IV, 788
Williams, Ann Elizabeth IV, 1031
Williams, Ann H. II, 940
Williams, Ann Lynch V, 142
Williams, Ann P. IV, 1120
Williams, Ann Shoebridge IV, 115
Williams, Ann W. VI, 865
Williams, Anna I, 277
Williams, Anna I, 521
Williams, Anna I, 545
Williams, Anna I, 582
Williams, Anna I, 643
Williams, Anna II, 188
Williams, Anna II, 272
Williams, Anna II, 687
Williams, Anna II, 703
Williams, Anna III, 357
Williams, Anna III, 358
Williams, Anna IV, 67
Williams, Anna IV, 164
Williams, Anna IV, 304
Williams, Anna IV, 405
Williams, Anna IV, 428
Williams, Anna IV, 443
Williams, Anna IV, 454
Williams, Anna IV, 455
Williams, Anna IV, 1120
Williams, Anna IV, 1140
Williams, Anna V, 80
Williams, Anna V, 81
Williams, Anna V, 142
Williams, Anna V, 772
Williams, Anna V, 793
Williams, Anna V, 907
Williams, Anna V, 941
Williams, Anna V, 957
Williams, Anna VI, 345
Williams, Anna VI, 1016
Williams, Anna H. II, 827
Williams, Anna H. II, 940
Williams, Anna K. III, 357
Williams, Anna L. V, 142
Williams, Anna L. V, 941
Williams, Anna M. V, 142
Williams, Anna Marie V, 543
Williams, Anna Martin IV, 1343
Williams, Anna R. II, 436
Williams, Anna R. II, 775
Williams, Anna R. III, 356
Williams, Anna R. III, 357
Williams, Anna Rhoads II, 723
Williams, Anna Rhoads II, 775
Williams, Anna S. II, 887
Williams, Anna S. II, 916
Williams, Anna S. II, 940
Williams, Anna W. V, 772
Williams, Annabella II, 940
Williams, Anne I, 61
Williams, Anne I, 85
Williams, Anne I, 277
Williams, Anne II, 436
Williams, Anne IV, 146
Williams, Anne IV, 164
Williams, Anne IV, 455
Williams, Anne IV, 456
Williams, Anne IV, 600
Williams, Anne V, 941
Williams, Anne Nicholson III, 356
Williams, Annes I, 1092
Williams, Annes I, 1099
Williams, Annie V, 126
Williams, Annie V, 142
Williams, Annie M. IV, 304
Williams, Anthony IV, 455
Williams, Antoinette I, 26
Williams, Antoinette I, 85
Williams, Anzonetta IV, 1299
Williams, Arabella Durham I, 1163
Williams, Aranah VI, 865
Williams, Archibald VI, 802
Williams, Archibald VI, 865
Williams, Archibald N. VI, 809
Williams, Arthur III, 356
Williams, Arthur III, 357
Williams, Arthur III, 358
Williams, Arthur IV, 855
Williams, Arthur IV, 1266
Williams, Arthur E. IV, 1194
Williams, Asa I, 521
Williams, Asa I, 970
Williams, Asa IV, 304
Williams, Asa IV, 687
Williams, Asa IV, 787
Williams, Asa IV, 855
Williams, Asa IV, 1193
Williams, Asa IV, 1194
Williams, Asa IV, 1299
Williams, Asa V, 962
Williams, Asher Ellwood III, 356
Williams, Asher Ellwood III, 357
Williams, Audren IV, 1267
Williams, Augusta S. III, 356
Williams, Avis V, 289
Williams, Avis V, 962
Williams, Azariah I, 367
Williams, Azariah I, 737
Williams, Azariah I, 1134
Williams, Azariah I, 1163
Williams, Azariah V, 873
Williams, Azeriah I, 737
Williams, Azeriah I, 1137
Williams, Azeriah I, 1163
Williams, Beatrix V, 898
Williams, Beatrix V, 941
Williams, Becca IV, 412
Williams, Becca IV, 456
Williams, Bekah IV, 454
Williams, Benaja I, 737
Williams, Benajah I, 521
Williams, Benajah I, 958
Williams, Benajah I, 1163
Williams, Benazette IV, 1296
Williams, Benazette IV, 1299
Williams, Benejah V, 142
Williams, Benezet IV, 1299
Williams, Benj. IV, 677
Williams, Benjamin I, 737
Williams, Benjamin II, 436
Williams, Benjamin II, 440
Williams, Benjamin II, 449
Williams, Benjamin II, 687
Williams, Benjamin III, 357
Williams, Benjamin III, 472
Williams, Benjamin IV, 67
Williams, Benjamin IV, 115
Williams, Benjamin IV, 116
Williams, Benjamin IV, 303
Williams, Benjamin IV, 304
Williams, Benjamin IV, 357
Williams, Benjamin IV, 456
Williams, Benjamin IV, 600
Williams, Benjamin IV, 665
Williams, Benjamin IV, 787
Williams, Benjamin IV, 788
Williams, Benjamin IV, 855
Williams, Benjamin IV, 917
Williams, Benjamin IV, 1082
Williams, Benjamin IV, 1386
Williams, Benjamin V, 941
Williams, Benjamin VI, 580
Williams, Benjamin VI, 721
Williams, Benjamin F. V, 543
Williams, Bertha Virginia II,
Williams, Bertha Virginia II,
Williams, Bertrand IV, 1299
Williams, Betsey VI, 1016
Williams, Betsy V, 365
Williams, Betsy VI, 1016
Williams, Beulah I, 582
Williams, Beulah V, 142
Williams, Billy I, 368
Williams, Billy I, 1112
Williams, Binaja I, 1000
Williams, Birtie L. I, 1163
Williams, Boid I, 368
Williams, Boid I, 1112
Williams, Boyd I, 368
Williams, Branson D. IV, 557
Williams, Buley I, 579
Williams, Burch V, 700
Williams, Burch V, 719
Williams, C. F. I, 951
Williams, C. J. I, 933
Williams, Caleb I, 368
Williams, Caleb I, 521
Williams, Caleb I, 845
Williams, Caleb I, 970
Williams, Caleb I, 1112
Williams, Carie Alice V, 650
Williams, Carl I, 845
Williams, Caroline III, 356
Williams, Caroline III, 357
Williams, Caroline IV, 357
Williams, Caroline V, 941
Williams, Caroline VI, 1016
Williams, Caroline F. II, 940
Williams, Caroline F. VI, 738
Williams, Caroline French II, 8
Williams, Caroline Matilda V, 365
Williams, Caroline Williams III, 356
Williams, Carrie Belle III, 220
Williams, Carrie Belle III, 320
Williams, Carroll VI, 581
Williams, Carroll R. II, 940
Williams, Carroll Rupert I, 26
Williams, Caspar IV, 73
Williams, Caspar IV, 117
Williams, Casper IV, 456
Williams, Casper IV, 787
Williams, Casper IV, 788
Williams, Casper IV, 855
Williams, Cassandra V, 543
Williams, Cassandria VI, 811
Williams, Catharine I, 408
Williams, Catharine I, 429
Williams, Catharine I, 795
Williams, Catharine I, 844
Williams, Catharine I, 845
Williams, Catharine I, 1112
Williams, Catharine II, 510
Williams, Catharine II, 827
Williams, Catharine IV, 170
Williams, Catharine IV, 358
Williams, Catharine IV, 556
Williams, Catharine IV, 557
Williams, Catharine IV, 697
Williams, Catharine IV, 787
Williams, Catharine IV, 788
Williams, Catharine IV, 917
Williams, Catharine VI, 581
Williams, Catharine VI, 957
Williams, Catharine Boyd II, 940
Williams, Catharine Dunwick II, 687
Williams, Catherine II, 365
Williams, Catherine II, 436
Williams, Catherine II, 473
Williams, Catherine IV, 82
Williams, Catherine IV, 116
Williams, Catherine IV, 677
Williams, Catherine V, 142
Williams, Catherine V, 289
Williams, Catheron I, 368
Williams, Cathron I, 368
Williams, Caty I, 521
Williams, Caty VI, 927
Williams, Celina VI, 1016
Williams, Charity I, 429
Williams, Charity I, 521
Williams, Charity I, 544
Williams, Charity I, 581
Williams, Charity I, 737
Williams, Charity I, 1000
Williams, Charity I, 1163

ms, Charity II, 272
ms, Charity IV, 429
ms, Charity IV, 454
ms, Charity IV, 456
ms, Charles I, 1134
ms, Charles I, 1163
ms, Charles II, 272
ms, Charles II, 325
ms, Charles II, 326
ms, Charles II, 436
ms, Charles II, 687
ms, Charles II, 688
ms, Charles III, 356
ms, Charles III, 357
ms, Charles IV, 304
ms, Charles IV, 562
ms, Charles IV, 787
ms, Charles IV, 788
ms, Charles IV, 855
ms, Charles IV, 856
ms, Charles IV, 1194
ms, Charles V, 873
ms, Charles VI, 887
ms, Charles VI, 1016
ms, Charles A. V, 543
ms, Charles B. II, 436
ms, Charles B. II, 775
ms, Charles B. VI, 1016
ms, Charles C. IV, 1266
ms, Charles G. V, 366
ms, Charles Gustavus
366
ms, Charles H. IV, 357
ms, Charles Havila V, 962
ms, Charles Henry V, 941
ms, Charles K. IV, 304
ms, Charles M. IV, 1140
ms, Charles Mortimer
, 1140
ms, Charles R. II, 775
ms, Charles R. III, 356
ms, Charles R. III, 357
ms, Charles Rhoads II, 723
ms, Charles S. IV, 788
ms, Charles S. IV, 856
ms, Charles S. IV, 1016
ms, Charles S. IV, 1299
ms, Charles T. III, 356
ms, Charley O. V, 366
ms, Charlotte III, 472
ms, Charlotte VI, 1016
ms, Chas C. IV, 855
ms, Chas. II, 838
ms, Chas. III, 265
ms, Chas. IV, 304
ms, Chas. IV, 1194
ms, Chas. V, 650
ms, Chas. H. IV, 353
ms, Chas. H. V, 936
ms, Chas. H. V, 941
ms, Chas. O. V, 365
ms, Chas. R. III, 357
ms, Chas. S. II, 940
ms, Chas. S. IV, 787
ms, Chester IV, 1266
ms, Christopher V, 365
ms, Cicero Franklin, Jr.
951
ms, Cidney Eliza IV, 556
ms, Cilas I, 1013
ms, Cilas, Jr. I, 1013
ms, Clara V, 543
ms, Clara V, 941
ms, Clarence II, 827
ms, Clarence II, 940
ms, Clarissa Elizabeth
951
ms, Clark I, 706
ms, Clark V, 142
ms, Clark V, 289
ms, Clark V, 365
ms, Clark V, 941
ms, Clark V, 962
ms, Clark V, 979
ms, Clarkay IV, 455
ms, Clarke V, 131
ms, Clarke V, 142
ms, Clayton N. IV, 1194
ms, Clement P. IV, 557
ms, Cleopatra I, 429
ms, Clide Burtrum I, 26
ms, Clyde V, 605
ms, Constance IV, 455
ms, Constant IV, 436
ms, Constant IV, 455
ms, Cora V, 365
ms, Cora A. V, 650
ms, Cornelia A. VI, 1016
ms, Cyrus M. V, 941
ms, Cyrus M. V, 979
ms, Cyrus Milton V, 941

Williams, Daisy H. III, 356
Williams, Daisy M. IV, 1194
Williams, Daisy Miller IV, 1168
Williams, Daniel I, 368
Williams, Daniel I, 429
Williams, Daniel I, 521
Williams, Daniel I, 582
Williams, Daniel I, 737
Williams, Daniel I, 1046
Williams, Daniel I, 1051
Williams, Daniel II, 436
Williams, Daniel II, 522
Williams, Daniel II, 610
Williams, Daniel II, 686
Williams, Daniel II, 811
Williams, Daniel II, 827
Williams, Daniel III, 472
Williams, Daniel IV, 117
Williams, Daniel IV, 147
Williams, Daniel IV, 385
Williams, Daniel IV, 391
Williams, Daniel IV, 392
Williams, Daniel IV, 399
Williams, Daniel IV, 409
Williams, Daniel IV, 434
Williams, Daniel IV, 437
Williams, Daniel IV, 455
Williams, Daniel IV, 493
Williams, Daniel IV, 504
Williams, Daniel IV, 519
Williams, Daniel IV, 524
Williams, Daniel IV, 548
Williams, Daniel IV, 556
Williams, Daniel IV, 600
Williams, Daniel IV, 697
Williams, Daniel IV, 746
Williams, Daniel IV, 787
Williams, Daniel IV, 788
Williams, Daniel IV, 836
Williams, Daniel IV, 1082
Williams, Daniel IV, 1097
Williams, Daniel IV, 1120
Williams, Daniel V, 962
Williams, Daniel VI, 345
Williams, Daniel VI, 582
Williams, Daniel M. IV, 1082
Williams, Daniel M. IV, 1120
Williams, Daniel Melton IV, 600
Williams, Daniel T. IV, 1299
Williams, Daniel W. III, 472
Williams, Daphene I, 845
Williams, Darkis I, 737
Williams, Darkis I, 1000
Williams, David I, 367
Williams, David I, 429
Williams, David I, 737
Williams, David I, 1000
Williams, David I, 1134
Williams, David I, 1163
Williams, David II, 594
Williams, David II, 686
Williams, David III, 64
Williams, David III, 356
Williams, David III, 357
Williams, David IV, 445
Williams, David IV, 455
Williams, David IV, 456
Williams, David IV, 600
Williams, David IV, 1015
Williams, David IV, 1082
Williams, David IV, 1123
Williams, David IV, 1194
Williams, David IV, 1266
Williams, David V, 873
Williams, David VI, 457
Williams, David VI, 484
Williams, David VI, 580
Williams, David VI, 581
Williams, David VI, 1015
Williams, David Brown II, 1039
Williams, David E. V, 142
Williams, David Gordon III, 358
Williams, David J. IV, 455
Williams, David J. IV, 456
Williams, David Milton IV, 1081
Williams, David W. IV, 455
Williams, David, Jr. VI, 580
Williams, Dearman IV, 304
Williams, Dearman IV, 788
Williams, Dearman IV, 855
Williams, Dearman IV, 904
Williams, Dearman IV, 917
Williams, Dearman IV, 1082
Williams, Dearmon IV, 303
Williams, Deborah I, 367
Williams, Deborah I, 429
Williams, Deborah I, 737
Williams, Deborah I, 1134
Williams, Deborah I, 1163
Williams, Deborah II, 491
Williams, Deborah II, 522

Williams, Deborah II, 625
Williams, Deborah II, 687
Williams, Deborah II, 688
Williams, Deborah IV, 303
Williams, Deborah IV, 304
Williams, Deborah IV, 381
Williams, Deborah IV, 455
Williams, Deborah IV, 456
Williams, Deborah IV, 600
Williams, Deborah IV, 855
Williams, Deborah IV, 1082
Williams, Deborah IV, 1120
Williams, Deborah IV, 1177
Williams, Deborah IV, 1194
Williams, Deborah IV, 1299
Williams, Deborah V, 873
Williams, Deborah Ann III, 356
Williams, Deborah Ann IV, 1299
Williams, Debroah I, 1112
Williams, Deerman IV, 1081
Williams, Della I, 951
Williams, Devorah I, 429
Williams, Dicie M. I, 1163
Williams, Dinah II, 440
Williams, Dinah II, 491
Williams, Dinah IV, 67
Williams, Dinah IV, 539
Williams, Dinah IV, 557
Williams, Dinah IV, 665
Williams, Dinah IV, 787
Williams, Dinah VI, 721
Williams, Dolores Nail IV, 1044
Williams, Don H. V, 290
Williams, Don L. V, 290
Williams, Dora B. I, 1163
Williams, Dorcas I, 521
Williams, Dorcas I, 547
Williams, Dorcas I, 582
Williams, Dorcas I, 737
Williams, Dorothy Gladys
IV, 1194
Williams, Doshia VI, 1009
Williams, Downing III, 207
Williams, Dr. A. J. V, 719
Williams, Drucilla I, 1163
Williams, Druzilla IV, 337
Williams, Druzilla IV, 358
Williams, Duncan IV, 304
Williams, Earl IV, 1266
Williams, Ebelus II, 436
Williams, Ebenezer VI, 457
Williams, Edgar V, 212
Williams, Edgar V, 543
Williams, Edgar V, 772
Williams, Edith II, 272
Williams, Edith II, 687
Williams, Edith IV, 687
Williams, Edith IV, 787
Williams, Edith IV, 788
Williams, Edith IV, 1282
Williams, Edith IV, 1299
Williams, Edith P. IV, 1194
Williams, Edith Roberts II, 940
Williams, Edith S. IV, 556
Williams, Edna Pusey II, 940
Williams, Edw. P. III, 357
Williams, Edward I, 1046
Williams, Edward I Sup 1, 9
Williams, Edward II, 436
Williams, Edward II, 437
Williams, Edward II, 449
Williams, Edward II, 610
Williams, Edward II, 686
Williams, Edward III, 472
Williams, Edward IV, 931
Williams, Edward IV, 978
Williams, Edward IV, 1015
Williams, Edward IV, 1267
Williams, Edward V, 605
Williams, Edward VI, 1016
Williams, Edward C. III, 398
Williams, Edward C. III, 472
Williams, Edward D. VI, 928
Williams, Edward D. VI, 987
Williams, Edward E. IV, 1299
Williams, Edward H. IV, 788
Williams, Edward H. IV, 855
Williams, Edward H. IV, 1266
Williams, Edward H. IV, 1299
Williams, Edward R. IV, 1267
Williams, Edwards I, 429
Williams, Edwin VI, 81
Williams, Edwin Franklin IV, 917
Williams, Edwin S. II, 940
Williams, Edwin Satterthwait
II, 887
Williams, Edwin Satterthwait
II, 940
Williams, Effalina III, 472
Williams, Eleanor I, 521
Williams, Eleanor I, 554

Williams, Eleanor I, 581
Williams, Eleanor I, 582
Williams, Eleanor I, 1134
Williams, Eleanor II, 940
Williams, Eleanor III, 300
Williams, Eleanor III, 357
Williams, Eleanor III, 363
Williams, Eleanor VI, 553
Williams, Eleanor VI, 580
Williams, Eleanor H. III, 357
Williams, Elener VI, 903
Williams, Eli VI, 1016
Williams, Elias IV, 164
Williams, Elias IV, 454
Williams, Elias IV, 456
Williams, Elias IV, 600
Williams, Elias IV, 1082
Williams, Elias IV, 1120
Williams, Elisabeth I, 26
Williams, Elisabeth I, 44
Williams, Elisabeth I, 85
Williams, Elisabeth I, 1112
Williams, Elisabeth II, 234
Williams, Elisabeth II, 272
Williams, Elisabeth VI, 457
Williams, Elisabeth Ashton
II, 686
Williams, Elisha VI, 953
Williams, Elisha VI, 959
Williams, Elisha J. IV, 554
Williams, Eliz. I. III, 177
Williams, Eliz. J. III, 78
Williams, Eliza III, 356
Williams, Eliza IV, 304
Williams, Eliza IV, 456
Williams, Eliza IV, 556
Williams, Eliza IV, 1120
Williams, Eliza IV, 1156
Williams, Eliza IV, 1194
Williams, Eliza V, 941
Williams, Eliza VI, 743
Williams, Eliza VI, 947
Williams, Eliza E. V, 719
Williams, Eliza F. IV, 455
Williams, Eliza F. IV, 456
Williams, Eliza G. III, 357
Williams, Eliza J. V, 365
Williams, Eliza M. IV, 410
Williams, Eliza Williams III, 356
Williams, Elizabeth I, 277
Williams, Elizabeth I, 368
Williams, Elizabeth I, 415
Williams, Elizabeth I, 428
Williams, Elizabeth I, 429
Williams, Elizabeth I, 521
Williams, Elizabeth I, 682
Williams, Elizabeth I, 692
Williams, Elizabeth I, 795
Williams, Elizabeth I, 913
Williams, Elizabeth I, 914
Williams, Elizabeth I, 958
Williams, Elizabeth I, 1046
Williams, Elizabeth I, 1051
Williams, Elizabeth I, 1088
Williams, Elizabeth I, 1099
Williams, Elizabeth I, 1134
Williams, Elizabeth II, 77
Williams, Elizabeth II, 111
Williams, Elizabeth II, 224
Williams, Elizabeth II, 231
Williams, Elizabeth II, 272
Williams, Elizabeth II, 436
Williams, Elizabeth II, 449
Williams, Elizabeth II, 626
Williams, Elizabeth II, 686
Williams, Elizabeth II, 688
Williams, Elizabeth II, 719
Williams, Elizabeth II, 723
Williams, Elizabeth II, 793
Williams, Elizabeth II, 806
Williams, Elizabeth II, 850
Williams, Elizabeth II, 972
Williams, Elizabeth II, 1003
Williams, Elizabeth II, 1038
Williams, Elizabeth III, 123
Williams, Elizabeth III, 357
Williams, Elizabeth III, 398
Williams, Elizabeth III, 408
Williams, Elizabeth III, 416
Williams, Elizabeth III, 439
Williams, Elizabeth III, 448
Williams, Elizabeth III, 472
Williams, Elizabeth IV, 67
Williams, Elizabeth IV, 115
Williams, Elizabeth IV, 116
Williams, Elizabeth IV, 146
Williams, Elizabeth IV, 164
Williams, Elizabeth IV, 178
Williams, Elizabeth IV, 303
Williams, Elizabeth IV, 304
Williams, Elizabeth IV, 357

Williams, Elizabeth IV, 379
Williams, Elizabeth IV, 394
Williams, Elizabeth IV, 437
Williams, Elizabeth IV, 438
Williams, Elizabeth IV, 455
Williams, Elizabeth IV, 456
Williams, Elizabeth IV, 493
Williams, Elizabeth IV, 504
Williams, Elizabeth IV, 556
Williams, Elizabeth IV, 573
Williams, Elizabeth IV, 574
Williams, Elizabeth IV, 578
Williams, Elizabeth IV, 579
Williams, Elizabeth IV, 585
Williams, Elizabeth IV, 594
Williams, Elizabeth IV, 599
Williams, Elizabeth IV, 600
Williams, Elizabeth IV, 665
Williams, Elizabeth IV, 746
Williams, Elizabeth IV, 787
Williams, Elizabeth IV, 788
Williams, Elizabeth IV, 815
Williams, Elizabeth IV, 836
Williams, Elizabeth IV, 844
Williams, Elizabeth IV, 855
Williams, Elizabeth IV, 1081
Williams, Elizabeth IV, 1082
Williams, Elizabeth IV, 1120
Williams, Elizabeth IV, 1193
Williams, Elizabeth V, 142
Williams, Elizabeth V, 282
Williams, Elizabeth V, 289
Williams, Elizabeth V, 361
Williams, Elizabeth V, 365
Williams, Elizabeth V, 629
Williams, Elizabeth V, 637
Williams, Elizabeth V, 650
Williams, Elizabeth V, 926
Williams, Elizabeth V, 941
Williams, Elizabeth V, 962
Williams, Elizabeth VI, 473
Williams, Elizabeth VI, 490
Williams, Elizabeth VI, 525
Williams, Elizabeth VI, 538
Williams, Elizabeth VI, 580
Williams, Elizabeth VI, 581
Williams, Elizabeth VI, 582
Williams, Elizabeth VI, 859
Williams, Elizabeth VI, 863
Williams, Elizabeth VI, 865
Williams, Elizabeth VI, 898
Williams, Elizabeth VI, 926
Williams, Elizabeth VI, 951
Williams, Elizabeth VI, 958
Williams, Elizabeth VI, 1006
Williams, Elizabeth VI, 1015
Williams, Elizabeth VI, 1016
Williams, Elizabeth A. VI, 865
Williams, Elizabeth Ann II, 940
Williams, Elizabeth Ann IV, 1082
Williams, Elizabeth Ann VI, 1016
Williams, Elizabeth E. V, 719
Williams, Elizabeth F. II, 882
Williams, Elizabeth Frances
VI, 981
Williams, Elizabeth J. II, 850
Williams, Elizabeth J. II, 940
Williams, Elizabeth J. III, 357
Williams, Elizabeth Jane II, 940
Williams, Elizabeth P. III, 357
Williams, Elizabeth S. VI, 581
Williams, Elizabeth T. VI, 1016
Williams, Ella I, 455
Williams, Ella IV, 1299
Williams, Ella H. III, 207
Williams, Ella Hansell III, 357
Williams, Ella S. I, 455
Williams, Elleda L. V, 719
Williams, Ellen Hannah III, 472
Williams, Ellen M. I, 928
Williams, Ellen M. I, 936
Williams, Ellen P. II, 723
Williams, Ellener I, 958
Williams, Ellis II, 827
Williams, Elma I, 845
Williams, Elma IV, 1299
Williams, Elmer IV, 1267
Williams, Elmerton IV, 1299
Williams, Elonner I, 958
Williams, Elonner I, 970
Williams, Elsie III, 48
Williams, Elsie III, 358
Williams, Elsie C. III, 357
Williams, Elsie Cromwell III, 358
Williams, Elwood I, 1112
Williams, Elwood I, 1115
Williams, Elwood III, 356
Williams, Elwood IV, 456
Williams, Elwood IV, 600
Williams, Elwood IV, 1082
Williams, Elwood IV, 1120

Williams, Elwood T. IV, 1081
Williams, Elwood Williams I, 1134
Williams, Elzabeth IV, 600
Williams, Elzey P. IV, 1343
Williams, Emaretta IV, 1299
Williams, Emily IV, 339
Williams, Emily Rebecca I, 620
Williams, Emma III, 357
Williams, Emma III, 362
Williams, Emma IV, 1299
Williams, Emma V, 212
Williams, Emma V, 366
Williams, Emma V, 605
Williams, Emma F. R. II, 940
Williams, Emma P. IV, 1299
Williams, Emmaretta V, 873
Williams, Emmor II, 940
Williams, Enion II, 234
Williams, Enion II, 272
Williams, Enion II, 686
Williams, Enion II, 972
Williams, Enion V, 142
Williams, Enion V, 266
Williams, Enion V, 288
Williams, Enion V, 289
Williams, Enneon I, 695
Williams, Ennian I, 844
Williams, Ennion I, 688
Williams, Ennion I, 692
Williams, Ennion I, 706
Williams, Ennion I, 737
Williams, Ennion I, 844
Williams, Ennion I, 1051
Williams, Ennion II, 234
Williams, Ennion II, 272
Williams, Ennion II, 686
Williams, Ennion II, 688
Williams, Ennion II, 827
Williams, Ennion II, 861
Williams, Ennion II, 940
Williams, Ennion II, 1003
Williams, Ennion II, 1038
Williams, Ennion V, 211
Williams, Ennion V, 215
Williams, Ennion V, 289
Williams, Ennion V, 962
Williams, Enoch I, 368
Williams, Enoch I, 844
Williams, Enoch I, 845
Williams, Enoch IV, 1299
Williams, Enos Wilson V, 212
Williams, Ephraim IV, 304
Williams, Ephraim IV, 436
Williams, Ephraim IV, 455
Williams, Ephraim IV, 456
Williams, Ephraim IV, 549
Williams, Ephraim IV, 600
Williams, Ephraim IV, 788
Williams, Erma Stiner IV, 1194
Williams, Ernest Daniel IV, 557
Williams, Erzekiah I, 368
Williams, Erzekiah I, 1112
Williams, Ester VI, 865
Williams, Esther I, 521
Williams, Esther I, 536
Williams, Esther I, 582
Williams, Esther II, 436
Williams, Esther II, 655
Williams, Esther II, 687
Williams, Esther II, 723
Williams, Esther III, 445
Williams, Esther III, 472
Williams, Esther IV, 455
Williams, Esther IV, 458
Williams, Esther IV, 1015
Williams, Esther IV, 1147
Williams, Esther IV, 1272
Williams, Esther IV, 1299
Williams, Esther V, 289
Williams, Esther Ann IV, 1299
Williams, Esther B. IV, 1194
Williams, Esther B. IV, 1299
Williams, Esther M. I, 643
Williams, Esther P. V, 467
Williams, Etta V, 289
Williams, Etta V, 290
Williams, Ettie V, 289
Williams, Eugene IV, 1299
Williams, Euly I, 914
Williams, Eunice II, 703
Williams, Evan VI, 580
Williams, Everette V, 142
Williams, Ezekial VI, 1016
Williams, Ezra IV, 456
Williams, Ezra IV, 599
Williams, Ezra IV, 600
Williams, Ezra IV, 1120
Williams, Fannie M. I, 1163
Williams, Florence IV, 1267
Williams, Floy I, 845
Williams, Floy I, 928
Williams, Floy I, 936
Williams, Floy I, 951
Williams, Frances I, 620
Williams, Frances Ann IV, 787
Williams, Frances E. III, 356
Williams, Francis IV, 438
Williams, Francis V, 365
Williams, Francis VI, 865
Williams, Francis Baker II, 940
Williams, Francis Edward V, 439
Williams, Francis H. IV, 410
Williams, Francis R. IV, 455
Williams, Frank H. II, 940
Williams, Franklin Howard II, 940
Williams, Frederick V, 439
Williams, Fredk. W. III, 357
Williams, Gabriel I, 1163
Williams, Garret II, 940
Williams, Garrett II, 827
Williams, Garrett II, 940
Williams, Garrison IV, 1031
Williams, Genetta IV, 1299
Williams, Geneva IV, 1267
Williams, Geo. II, 224
Williams, Geo. V, 142
Williams, Geo. R. III, 356
Williams, George I, 581
Williams, George I, 845
Williams, George II, 188
Williams, George II, 272
Williams, George II, 274
Williams, George II, 302
Williams, George II, 305
Williams, George II, 436
Williams, George II, 449
Williams, George II, 465
Williams, George II, 687
Williams, George II, 723
Williams, George II, 775
Williams, George II, 817
Williams, George II, 828
Williams, George II, 841
Williams, George II, 864
Williams, George II, 955
Williams, George III, 357
Williams, George IV, 456
Williams, George IV, 1266
Williams, George IV, 1299
Williams, George VI, 469
Williams, George VI, 581
Williams, George VI, 865
Williams, George VI, 897
Williams, George VI, 1016
Williams, George A. V, 142
Williams, George C. II, 188
Williams, George C. II, 325
Williams, George C. II, 326
Williams, George C. II, 775
Williams, George G. II, 688
Williams, George G. II, 723
Williams, George G. III, 357
Williams, George N. III, 357
Williams, George T. VI, 824
Williams, George W. I, 845
Williams, George, Jr. II, 775
Williams, Gerard Rhodes III, 356
Williams, Gershom V, 467
Williams, Gladys Martha I, 951
Williams, Gomery I, 1163
Williams, Gomery Williams I, 1163
Williams, Goodman VI, 90
Williams, Grace I, 387
Williams, Grace I, 429
Williams, Grace I, 691
Williams, Grace I, 692
Williams, Grace I, 1051
Williams, Grace II, 436
Williams, Grace II, 465
Williams, Grace II, 687
Williams, Grace II, 723
Williams, Grace III, 356
Williams, Grace IV, 532
Williams, Grace IV, 557
Williams, Grace V, 266
Williams, Grace V, 289
Williams, Grace D. III, 357
Williams, Grace Deborah II, 723
Williams, Grace Deborah II, 775
Williams, Grace E. III, 356
Williams, Grace Laurence V, 543
Williams, Granville Sharp V, 941
Williams, Guli Ann IV, 545
Williams, Gulie A. IV, 557
Williams, Guy V, 289
Williams, Guy V, 290
Williams, H. A. V, 719
Williams, Hannah I, 521
Williams, Hannah I, 582
Williams, Hannah I, 737
Williams, Hannah I, 958
Williams, Hannah I, 959
Williams, Hannah I, 968
Williams, Hannah I, 970
Williams, Hannah I, 1000
Williams, Hannah I, 1010
Williams, Hannah I, 1013
Williams, Hannah I, 1112
Williams, Hannah I, 1134
Williams, Hannah II, 202
Williams, Hannah II, 272
Williams, Hannah II, 302
Williams, Hannah II, 305
Williams, Hannah II, 325
Williams, Hannah II, 326
Williams, Hannah II, 436
Williams, Hannah II, 478
Williams, Hannah II, 483
Williams, Hannah II, 624
Williams, Hannah II, 661
Williams, Hannah II, 686
Williams, Hannah II, 687
Williams, Hannah II, 775
Williams, Hannah II, 821
Williams, Hannah II, 827
Williams, Hannah II, 828
Williams, Hannah II, 837
Williams, Hannah II, 926
Williams, Hannah II, 940
Williams, Hannah III, 357
Williams, Hannah III, 407
Williams, Hannah III, 472
Williams, Hannah IV, 67
Williams, Hannah IV, 109
Williams, Hannah IV, 115
Williams, Hannah IV, 116
Williams, Hannah IV, 304
Williams, Hannah IV, 338
Williams, Hannah IV, 339
Williams, Hannah IV, 357
Williams, Hannah IV, 456
Williams, Hannah IV, 504
Williams, Hannah IV, 556
Williams, Hannah IV, 562
Williams, Hannah IV, 599
Williams, Hannah IV, 600
Williams, Hannah IV, 665
Williams, Hannah IV, 787
Williams, Hannah IV, 788
Williams, Hannah IV, 815
Williams, Hannah IV, 836
Williams, Hannah IV, 855
Williams, Hannah IV, 931
Williams, Hannah IV, 978
Williams, Hannah IV, 1015
Williams, Hannah IV, 1082
Williams, Hannah IV, 1105
Williams, Hannah IV, 1120
Williams, Hannah IV, 1299
Williams, Hannah V, 38
Williams, Hannah V, 142
Williams, Hannah V, 941
Williams, Hannah VI, 483
Williams, Hannah VI, 510
Williams, Hannah VI, 513
Williams, Hannah VI, 525
Williams, Hannah VI, 526
Williams, Hannah VI, 546
Williams, Hannah VI, 553
Williams, Hannah VI, 580
Williams, Hannah VI, 581
Williams, Hannah VI, 582
Williams, Hannah B. II, 861
Williams, Hannah B. II, 940
Williams, Hannah C. II, 305
Williams, Hannah C. IV, 357
Williams, Hannah C. IV, 556
Williams, Hannah C. IV, 600
Williams, Hannah C. IV, 1081
Williams, Hannah C. IV, 1082
Williams, Hannah C. VI, 452
Williams, Hannah C. VI, 457
Williams, Hannah C. VI, 580
Williams, Hannah Clendennon IV, 600
Williams, Hannah Conrow VI, 457
Williams, Hannah Cooper II, 188
Williams, Hannah Francena IV, 519
Williams, Hannah Francena IV, 557
Williams, Hannah N. II, 838
Williams, Hannah N. II, 940
Williams, Hannah P. IV, 746
Williams, Hannah P. IV, 787
Williams, Hannah P. IV, 819
Williams, Hannah P. IV, 836
Williams, Hannah Roberts II, 554
Williams, Hannah S. IV, 728
Williams, Hannah S. IV, 787
Williams, Hannah S. IV, 788
Williams, Hannah S. IV, 855
Williams, Hannah S. IV, 1266
Williams, Harriett IV, 1266
Williams, Harriett P. VI, 1016
Williams, Helen III, 38
Williams, Helen III, 48
Williams, Helen III, 357
Williams, Helen III, 358
Williams, Helen W. II, 940
Williams, Henery VI, 457
Williams, Henry I, 1051
Williams, Henry I, 1099
Williams, Henry I, 1134
Williams, Henry III, 48
Williams, Henry III, 357
Williams, Henry III, 358
Williams, Henry IV, 164
Williams, Henry IV, 304
Williams, Henry IV, 405
Williams, Henry IV, 409
Williams, Henry IV, 454
Williams, Henry IV, 455
Williams, Henry IV, 599
Williams, Henry IV, 600
Williams, Henry IV, 1140
Williams, Henry VI, 457
Williams, Henry VI, 826
Williams, Henry B. III, 357
Williams, Henry Borton II, 940
Williams, Henry C. II, 723
Williams, Henry C. II, 775
Williams, Henry D. IV, 382
Williams, Henry D. IV, 455
Williams, Henry D. IV, 456
Williams, Henry D. IV, 572
Williams, Henry Glenn V, 289
Williams, Henry Noyes III, 357
Williams, Henry Thomas I, 26
Williams, Henry W. II, 305
Williams, Henry Wills II, 188
Williams, Herbert L. I, 26
Williams, Herbert L. I, 31
Williams, Herbert Lee I, 26
Williams, Herbert T. I, 85
Williams, Hester VI, 580
Williams, Hezekiah I, 368
Williams, Hezekiah I, 429
Williams, Hezekiah I, 970
Williams, Hezekiah I, 1113
Williams, Hezekiah I, 1134
Williams, Hezekiah I, 1163
Williams, Hezekiah II, 272
Williams, Hezekiah II, 436
Williams, Hezekiah II, 465
Williams, Hezekiah II, 636
Williams, Hezekiah II, 723
Williams, Hezekiah III, 52
Williams, Hezekiah III, 215
Williams, Hezekiah III, 216
Williams, Hezekiah III, 299
Williams, Hezekiah III, 356
Williams, Hezekiah III, 357
Williams, Hezikiah I, 1134
Williams, Homer IV, 1299
Williams, Horace E. III, 357
Williams, Howard II, 827
Williams, Howard II, 940
Williams, Huldah II, 188
Williams, Huldah II, 273
Williams, Huldah Ellen V, 650
Williams, Huldah J. V, 650
Williams, Humphrey I, 429
Williams, Humphrey I Sup 1, 9
Williams, Humphrey II, 687
Williams, Humphrey VI, 570
Williams, Humphrey VI, 580
Williams, Humphrey VI, 581
Williams, Hunphrey I, 428
Williams, Huston IV, 1299
Williams, Ida IV, 263
Williams, Ida IV, 304
Williams, Ida B. IV, 1299
Williams, Inez V, 290
Williams, Iona May I, 26
Williams, Isaac I, 176
Williams, Isaac I, 368
Williams, Isaac I, 415
Williams, Isaac I, 429
Williams, Isaac I, 581
Williams, Isaac I, 773
Williams, Isaac I, 844
Williams, Isaac I, 845
Williams, Isaac I, 959
Williams, Isaac I, 970
Williams, Isaac I, 1101
Williams, Isaac I, 1112
Williams, Isaac I, 1134
Williams, Isaac I, 1137
Williams, Isaac II, 188
Williams, Isaac II, 241
Williams, Isaac II, 272
Williams, Isaac II, 436
Williams, Isaac II, 554
Williams, Isaac II, 625
Williams, Isaac II, 686
Williams, Isaac II, 687
Williams, Isaac II, 688
Williams, Isaac II, 691
Williams, Isaac II, 703
Williams, Isaac III, 270
Williams, Isaac III, 357
Williams, Isaac III, 362
Williams, Isaac III, 472
Williams, Isaac IV, 600
Williams, Isaac IV, 1120
Williams, Isaac V, 251
Williams, Isaac V, 289
Williams, Isaac V, 365
Williams, Isaac V, 439
Williams, Isaac V, 962
Williams, Isaac VI, 582
Williams, Isaac VI, 1016
Williams, Isaac B. IV, 1194
Williams, Isaac C. IV, 599
Williams, Isaac C. IV, 600
Williams, Isaac E. VI, 582
Williams, Isaac U. III, 472
Williams, Isaac Walker VI, 58
Williams, Isaac, Jr. I, 1134
Williams, Isaac, Jr. II, 625
Williams, Isaac, Jr. II, 688
Williams, Isaachar IV, 456
Williams, Isabella II, 827
Williams, Isabella II, 940
Williams, Isachar IV, 455
Williams, Isaiah IV, 67
Williams, Isaiah IV, 164
Williams, Isaiah IV, 428
Williams, Isaiah IV, 454
Williams, Isaiah IV, 455
Williams, Isaiah IV, 456
Williams, Isaiah IV, 599
Williams, Isaiah IV, 600
Williams, Isaiah IV, 665
Williams, Isaiah IV, 787
Williams, Isaiah IV, 1082
Williams, Isaiah IV, 1120
Williams, Isaiah IV, 1140
Williams, Isaiah VI, 721
Williams, Israel V, 650
Williams, Israel VI, 580
Williams, Israel VI, 721
Williams, J. Cadwallader IV, 1299
Williams, J. Edgar I, 643
Williams, J. Edgar V, 772
Williams, J. R. III, 281
Williams, Jacob I, 429
Williams, Jacob I, 737
Williams, Jacob IV, 455
Williams, Jacob IV, 456
Williams, Jacob V, 289
Williams, Jacob VI, 1006
Williams, Jacob VI, 1016
Williams, Jacob Paul II, 940
Williams, Jacob R. III, 254
Williams, Jacob R. III, 281
Williams, Jacob R. III, 356
Williams, Jacob R. III, 357
Williams, Jacob T. II, 837
Williams, Jacob T. II, 940
Williams, Jacob Tomkins II, 827
Williams, James I, 85
Williams, James I, 368
Williams, James I, 535
Williams, James I, 582
Williams, James I, 737
Williams, James I, 844
Williams, James I, 845
Williams, James I, 914
Williams, James I, 970
Williams, James I, 1134
Williams, James II, 436
Williams, James III, 357
Williams, James IV, 304
Williams, James IV, 600
Williams, James IV, 917
Williams, James V, 366
Williams, James VI, 125
Williams, James VI, 143
Williams, James VI, 580
Williams, James VI, 865
Williams, James VI, 957
Williams, James VI, 958
Williams, James VI, 1016
Williams, James E. IV, 1140
Williams, James Edward VI, 582
Williams, James Ezra IV, 1140
Williams, James F. VI, 1016

ms, James G. Oldham
962
ms, James H. V, 439
ms, James Harvey V, 439
ms, James K. V, 365
ms, James K. V, 366
ms, James L. V, 542
ms, James L. V, 543
ms, James M. III, 242
ms, James M. III, 357
ms, James M. VI, 1016
ms, James W. VI, 457
ms, James W. VI, 581
ms, James W. VI, 582
ms, James Walker VI, 483
ms, James Walker VI, 581
ms, Jane I, 428
ms, Jane I, 521
ms, Jane II, 436
ms, Jane II, 522
ms, Jane II, 610
ms, Jane II, 636
ms, Jane II, 686
ms, Jane II, 687
ms, Jane II, 811
ms, Jane II, 827
ms, Jane III, 102
ms, Jane III, 186
ms, Jane III, 356
ms, Jane III, 357
ms, Jane III, 416
ms, Jane III, 507
ms, Jane IV, 173
ms, Jane IV, 178
ms, Jane IV, 304
ms, Jane IV, 357
ms, Jane IV, 399
ms, Jane IV, 437
ms, Jane IV, 455
ms, Jane IV, 456
ms, Jane IV, 589
ms, Jane IV, 600
ms, Jane IV, 697
ms, Jane IV, 787
ms, Jane IV, 1082
ms, Jane IV, 1123
ms, Jane Garret II, 827
ms, Jane J. IV, 600
ms, Jane M. III, 254
ms, Jane M. III, 357
ms, Jane Maria III, 281
ms, Jane Maria III, 357
ms, Jane T. IV, 456
ms, Jane W. III, 102
ms, Jas. IV, 556
ms, Jasen IV, 556
ms, Jason IV, 535
ms, Jason IV, 556
ms, Jason IV, 557
ms, Jean I, 368
ms, Jean VI, 582
ms, Jean VI, 1016
ms, Jene VI, 1016
ms, Jennie V, 365
ms, Jennie Gayle IV, 1044
ms, Jennie M. III, 300
ms, Jennie M. III, 357
ms, Jennie M. III, 363
ms, Jephthah IV, 1120
ams, Jephthann Fawcett
V, 1121
ams, Jeptha IV, 456
ams, Jeptha Anna IV, 557
ams, Jepthaann IV, 1097
ams, Jeremiah II, 686
ams, Jeremiah III, 221
ams, Jeremiah III, 407
ams, Jeremiah III, 472
ams, Jeremiah IV, 1194
ams, Jesse I, 368
ams, Jesse I, 521
ams, Jesse I, 554
ams, Jesse I, 577
ams, Jesse I, 581
ams, Jesse I, 582
ams, Jesse I, 795
ams, Jesse I, 847
ams, Jesse I, 914
ams, Jesse I, 953
ams, Jesse I, 958
ams, Jesse I, 970
ams, Jesse I, 971
ams, Jesse I, 1112
ams, Jesse II, 775
ams, Jesse II, 806
ams, Jesse IV, 304
ams, Jesse IV, 357
ams, Jesse IV, 455
ams, Jesse IV, 599
ams, Jesse IV, 600
ams, Jesse IV, 1299
Williams, Jesse V, 142
Williams, Jesse V, 941
Williams, Jesse VI, 345
Williams, Jesse VI, 356
Williams, Jesse Davis IV, 1120
Williams, Jesse Davis IV, 1140
Williams, Jesse Lynch V, 142
Williams, Jesse Turner I, 521
Williams, Joan VI, 581
Williams, Joan VI, 582
Williams, Job IV, 164
Williams, Job IV, 304
Williams, Job IV, 455
Williams, Job IV, 599
Williams, Job IV, 600
Williams, Job M. IV, 379
Williams, Job M. IV, 454
Williams, Job M. IV, 1082
Williams, Job M. IV, 1120
Williams, Joel I, 1134
Williams, Joel IV, 455
Williams, John I, 26
Williams, John I, 76
Williams, John I, 85
Williams, John I, 90
Williams, John I, 368
Williams, John I, 428
Williams, John I, 429
Williams, John I, 521
Williams, John I, 581
Williams, John I, 582
Williams, John I, 682
Williams, John I, 692
Williams, John I, 706
Williams, John I, 795
Williams, John I, 843
Williams, John I, 844
Williams, John I, 845
Williams, John I, 958
Williams, John I, 968
Williams, John I, 970
Williams, John I, 1006
Williams, John I, 1013
Williams, John I, 1051
Williams, John I, 1112
Williams, John I Sup 1, 6
Williams, John I Sup 1, 9
Williams, John II, 436
Williams, John II, 449
Williams, John II, 723
Williams, John II, 850
Williams, John II, 882
Williams, John III, 357
Williams, John III, 408
Williams, John III, 469
Williams, John III, 472
Williams, John III, 507
Williams, John III, 511
Williams, John IV, 67
Williams, John IV, 115
Williams, John IV, 116
Williams, John IV, 156
Williams, John IV, 164
Williams, John IV, 357
Williams, John IV, 381
Williams, John IV, 454
Williams, John IV, 455
Williams, John IV, 456
Williams, John IV, 600
Williams, John IV, 665
Williams, John IV, 855
Williams, John IV, 1016
Williams, John IV, 1109
Williams, John IV, 1299
Williams, John V, 142
Williams, John V, 289
Williams, John V, 365
Williams, John V, 941
Williams, John VI, 42
Williams, John VI, 457
Williams, John VI, 462
Williams, John VI, 538
Williams, John VI, 576
Williams, John VI, 581
Williams, John VI, 822
Williams, John VI, 854
Williams, John VI, 907
Williams, John VI, 951
Williams, John VI, 981
Williams, John VI, 1009
Williams, John VI, 1015
Williams, John VI, 1016
Williams, John Abbot II, 188
Williams, John Abbot II, 272
Williams, John Abbott II, 687
Williams, John Alvin IV, 1299
Williams, John B. VI, 131
Williams, John B. VI, 143
Williams, John Bouvier IV, 115
Williams, John Donald II, 940
Williams, John Earl IV, 1044
Williams, John F. IV, 917
Williams, John F. IV, 1081
Williams, John F. IV, 1082
Williams, John G. IV, 787
Williams, John G. IV, 788
Williams, John G. IV, 1031
Williams, John H. IV, 304
Williams, John J. VI, 978
Williams, John J. VI, 1016
Williams, John M. IV, 600
Williams, John P. IV, 455
Williams, John P. IV, 456
Williams, John P. IV, 1120
Williams, John Paul J. III, 347
Williams, John Paul J. III, 357
Williams, John Pennington
IV, 1015
Williams, John S. IV, 116
Williams, John S. IV, 357
Williams, John S. IV, 455
Williams, John S. IV, 456
Williams, John S. V, 941
Williams, John, Jr. I, 85
Williams, John, Jr. VI, 981
Williams, Johnathan I, 1134
Williams, Jonathan I, 343
Williams, Jonathan I, 367
Williams, Jonathan I, 428
Williams, Jonathan I, 429
Williams, Jonathan I, 521
Williams, Jonathan I, 737
Williams, Jonathan I, 1163
Williams, Jonathan II, 188
Williams, Jonathan II, 272
Williams, Jonathan II, 687
Williams, Jonathan IV, 556
Williams, Jonathan V, 142
Williams, Jonathan V, 289
Williams, Jonathan V, 365
Williams, Jonathan V, 873
Williams, Jonathan VI, 457
Williams, Jonathan G. II, 188
Williams, Jonathan G. II, 436
Williams, Jonathan G. II, 688
Williams, Jonathan G. III, 357
Williams, Jonithan I, 958
Williams, Jos. IV, 225
Williams, Joseph I, 429
Williams, Joseph I, 692
Williams, Joseph I, 706
Williams, Joseph I, 1046
Williams, Joseph I, 1051
Williams, Joseph I, 1134
Williams, Joseph II, 436
Williams, Joseph II, 440
Williams, Joseph II, 449
Williams, Joseph II, 688
Williams, Joseph II, 775
Williams, Joseph III, 357
Williams, Joseph IV, 164
Williams, Joseph IV, 357
Williams, Joseph IV, 415
Williams, Joseph IV, 455
Williams, Joseph IV, 456
Williams, Joseph IV, 536
Williams, Joseph IV, 542
Williams, Joseph IV, 545
Williams, Joseph IV, 552
Williams, Joseph IV, 556
Williams, Joseph IV, 743
Williams, Joseph IV, 787
Williams, Joseph IV, 788
Williams, Joseph IV, 1120
Williams, Joseph IV, 1194
Williams, Joseph V, 289
Williams, Joseph V, 365
Williams, Joseph V, 941
Williams, Joseph V, 962
Williams, Joseph Addison
IV, 1140
Williams, Joseph F. II, 940
Williams, Joseph Franklin II, 827
Williams, Joseph H. IV, 556
Williams, Joseph J. II, 940
Williams, Joseph J. IV, 788
Williams, Joseph John IV, 358
Williams, Joseph John IV, 556
Williams, Joseph John IV, 557
Williams, Joseph Jonathan
II, 827
Williams, Joseph Kirkbride
II, 436
Williams, Joseph S. II, 887
Williams, Joseph S. II, 916
Williams, Joseph S. II, 940
Williams, Joseph Stokes II, 827
Williams, Joshua I, 368
Williams, Joshua I, 429
Williams, Joshua I, 1112
Williams, Joshua IV, 417
Williams, Joshua VI, 1016
Williams, Josia I, 368
Williams, Josiah I, 368
Williams, Josiah I, 795
Williams, Josiah I, 1112
Williams, Josiah V, 142
Williams, Josiah V, 365
Williams, Josiah V, 473
Williams, Josiah V, 542
Williams, Josiah V, 544
Williams, Josiah G. II, 940
Williams, Josiah Garrett II, 827
Williams, Julia IV, 1194
Williams, Julia IV, 1299
Williams, Julia Ann IV, 787
Williams, Julia Ann IV, 788
Williams, Julia Ann IV, 856
Williams, Julia Ann IV, 1016
Williams, Julia Matilda III, 281
Williams, Julia Matilda III, 357
Williams, Justin Cadwalader
III, 356
Williams, Justin Cadwalader
III, 357
Williams, Katharine I, 383
Williams, Katharine I, 429
Williams, Katharine I, 795
Williams, Katharine V, 341
Williams, Katharine V, 365
Williams, Katherine II, 505
Williams, Katherine II, 686
Williams, Katherine VI, 582
Williams, Katie H. V, 941
Williams, Ketturah V, 962
Williams, Ketura Ann IV, 1082
Williams, Keturah V, 202
Williams, Keturah V, 211
Williams, Keturah V, 212
Williams, Keturah V, 289
Williams, Keturah Ann IV, 917
Williams, Keturah Ann IV, 1082
Williams, Kitturah V, 289
Williams, Latha IV, 1267
Williams, Latitia II, 625
Williams, Latitia II, 687
Williams, Laura III, 64
Williams, Laura III, 357
Williams, Laura IV, 1194
Williams, Laura IV, 1227
Williams, Laura B. IV, 1194
Williams, Laura E. V, 366
Williams, Laura Emma V, 365
Williams, Laverne IV, 1300
Williams, Lavernen IV, 1299
Williams, Lavina IV, 456
Williams, Lavisa IV, 404
Williams, Lavisa IV, 456
Williams, Leander Perry VI, 791
Williams, Lena IV, 1267
Williams, Lena IV, 1299
Williams, Letitia II, 436
Williams, Levi IV, 1082
Williams, Levi IV, 1120
Williams, Levinah I, 521
Williams, Levy IV, 456
Williams, Lewis VI, 580
Williams, Lewis VI, 954
Williams, Lewis VI, 1016
Williams, Lewis E. VI, 865
Williams, Liddy VI, 899
Williams, Lidiah III, 472
Williams, Lilla F. III, 265
Williams, Lilla F. III, 356
Williams, Lilla F. III, 357
Williams, Lindley IV, 456
Williams, Lindley IV, 600
Williams, Lindley IV, 1082
Williams, Lindley IV, 1120
Williams, Lindley M. IV, 304
Williams, Lindley M. IV, 788
Williams, Lindley M. IV, 1081
Williams, Lindley Murray IV, 787
Williams, Lisborn V, 439
Williams, Lizie IV, 1278
Williams, Lizie IV, 1299
Williams, Lizzie I, 429
Williams, Lizzie IV, 788
Williams, Lizzie IV, 1299
Williams, Lloyd L. IV, 856
Williams, Lloyd L. IV, 1016
Williams, Lon I, 933
Williams, Lott V, 962
Williams, Lott G. IV, 1299
Williams, Lottie IV, 1327
Williams, Lottie IV, 1343
Williams, Louah Cadwalader
IV, 1299
Williams, Louella V, 212
Williams, Louella V, 213
Williams, Louisa V, 941
Williams, Lovice IV, 455
Williams, Loyd L. IV, 788
Williams, Lucinda III, 242
Williams, Lucinda III, 357
Williams, Lucinda IV, 1118
Williams, Lucinda IV, 1120
Williams, Luckey VI, 858
Williams, Lucretia M. IV, 1031
Williams, Lucy V, 142
Williams, Lucy VI, 1006
Williams, Lucy C. V, 142
Williams, Lucy J. VI, 1016
Williams, Lucy L. VI, 865
Williams, Lumley II, 686
Williams, Luvenia IV, 1299
Williams, Lydia I, 1007
Williams, Lydia I, 1013
Williams, Lydia II, 202
Williams, Lydia II, 272
Williams, Lydia II, 436
Williams, Lydia II, 664
Williams, Lydia II, 687
Williams, Lydia II, 688
Williams, Lydia II, 775
Williams, Lydia II, 817
Williams, Lydia II, 861
Williams, Lydia II, 940
Williams, Lydia III, 52
Williams, Lydia III, 216
Williams, Lydia III, 357
Williams, Lydia IV, 164
Williams, Lydia IV, 357
Williams, Lydia IV, 378
Williams, Lydia IV, 379
Williams, Lydia IV, 417
Williams, Lydia IV, 439
Williams, Lydia IV, 454
Williams, Lydia IV, 455
Williams, Lydia IV, 456
Williams, Lydia IV, 542
Williams, Lydia IV, 554
Williams, Lydia IV, 557
Williams, Lydia IV, 600
Williams, Lydia IV, 743
Williams, Lydia IV, 787
Williams, Lydia IV, 998
Williams, Lydia IV, 1015
Williams, Lydia IV, 1081
Williams, Lydia IV, 1082
Williams, Lydia IV, 1120
Williams, Lydia IV, 1299
Williams, Lydia VI, 457
Williams, Lydia VI, 462
Williams, Lydia VI, 538
Williams, Lydia VI, 576
Williams, Lydia VI, 581
Williams, Lydia VI, 584
Williams, Lydia A. III, 299
Williams, Lydia Ann IV, 524
Williams, Lydia Ann IV, 557
Williams, Lydia Ann IV, 1097
Williams, Lydia Ann IV, 1120
Williams, Lydia Ann IV, 1121
Williams, Lydia J. IV, 1296
Williams, Lydia J. IV, 1299
Williams, Lydia Jane IV, 788
Williams, Lydia M. IV, 304
Williams, Lydia M. IV, 357
Williams, Lydia M. IV, 358
Williams, Lydia M. IV, 556
Williams, Lydia M. IV, 557
Williams, Lydia M. IV, 788
Williams, Lydia M. IV, 1108
Williams, Lydia M. IV, 1121
Williams, Lydia Neill VI, 582
Williams, Lydia P. II, 940
Williams, Lydia Parry II, 916
Williams, Lydia Parry II, 940
Williams, Lydia W. II, 739
Williams, Lydia W. II, 775
Williams, Lyman V, 366
Williams, Mabel V, 700
Williams, Mable V, 719
Williams, Madora I, 845
Williams, Mahlon P. IV, 1299
Williams, Malenda VI, 865
Williams, Malinda V, 543
Williams, Manoah IV, 455
Williams, Margareat I, 368
Williams, Margaret I, 347
Williams, Margaret I, 364
Williams, Margaret I, 368
Williams, Margaret I, 376
Williams, Margaret I, 378
Williams, Margaret I, 426
Williams, Margaret I, 428
Williams, Margaret I, 429
Williams, Margaret I, 737
Williams, Margaret I, 795
Williams, Margaret I, 796
Williams, Margaret I, 844
Williams, Margaret I, 845
Williams, Margaret I, 970

Williams, Margaret I, 1112
Williams, Margaret I, 1134
Williams, Margaret II, 188
Williams, Margaret II, 224
Williams, Margaret II, 226
Williams, Margaret II, 272
Williams, Margaret II, 437
Williams, Margaret II, 539
Williams, Margaret II, 686
Williams, Margaret II, 687
Williams, Margaret II, 688
Williams, Margaret II, 817
Williams, Margaret II, 827
Williams, Margaret II, 828
Williams, Margaret IV, 303
Williams, Margaret IV, 384
Williams, Margaret IV, 455
Williams, Margaret V, 543
Williams, Margaret VI, 504
Williams, Margaret VI, 574
Williams, Margaret VI, 581
Williams, Margaret VI, 582
Williams, Margaret VI, 810
Williams, Margaret Ann IV, 1044
Williams, Margaret C. IV, 407
Williams, Margaret C. IV, 456
Williams, Margarett II, 272
Williams, Margaretta IV, 1031
Williams, Margot VI, 951
Williams, Margrett II, 436
Williams, Margrett II, 449
Williams, Maria III, 357
Williams, Maria III, 358
Williams, Maria Louisa III, 357
Williams, Maria Louise III, 254
Williams, Maria P. VI, 865
Williams, Mariam IV, 1120
Williams, Mariam IV, 1121
Williams, Marian IV, 456
Williams, Marjorie I, 643
Williams, Marjorie III, 265
Williams, Marjorie III, 357
Williams, Marjorie F. III, 356
Williams, Marjory IV, 1194
Williams, Martha I, 382
Williams, Martha I, 429
Williams, Martha I, 688
Williams, Martha I, 692
Williams, Martha I, 695
Williams, Martha I, 706
Williams, Martha I, 737
Williams, Martha I, 927
Williams, Martha I, 1000
Williams, Martha I, 1163
Williams, Martha II, 436
Williams, Martha II, 470
Williams, Martha II, 686
Williams, Martha II, 940
Williams, Martha III, 357
Williams, Martha III, 469
Williams, Martha III, 472
Williams, Martha IV, 67
Williams, Martha IV, 417
Williams, Martha IV, 419
Williams, Martha IV, 434
Williams, Martha IV, 435
Williams, Martha IV, 455
Williams, Martha IV, 456
Williams, Martha IV, 548
Williams, Martha IV, 552
Williams, Martha IV, 556
Williams, Martha IV, 557
Williams, Martha IV, 561
Williams, Martha IV, 562
Williams, Martha IV, 594
Williams, Martha IV, 600
Williams, Martha IV, 648
Williams, Martha IV, 665
Williams, Martha IV, 771
Williams, Martha IV, 788
Williams, Martha IV, 855
Williams, Martha IV, 1194
Williams, Martha V, 142
Williams, Martha V, 211
Williams, Martha V, 215
Williams, Martha V, 266
Williams, Martha V, 281
Williams, Martha V, 288
Williams, Martha V, 289
Williams, Martha V, 290
Williams, Martha V, 311
Williams, Martha V, 313
Williams, Martha V, 941
Williams, Martha V, 948
Williams, Martha V, 962
Williams, Martha VI, 45
Williams, Martha VI, 46
Williams, Martha VI, 513
Williams, Martha VI, 580
Williams, Martha VI, 721
Williams, Martha VI, 854
Williams, Martha VI, 865
Williams, Martha VI, 1016
Williams, Martha A. VI, 865
Williams, Martha A. VI, 999
Williams, Martha Ann VI, 81
Williams, Martha Bell IV, 456
Williams, Martha Bell V, 941
Williams, Martha Belle V, 941
Williams, Martha E. VI, 808
Williams, Martha Fannie I, 933
Williams, Martha J. III, 314
Williams, Martha M. W. II, 175
Williams, Martha P. II, 940
Williams, Martha Paul II, 827
Williams, Martha S. IV, 556
Williams, Martha S. IV, 557
Williams, Martha S. VI, 814
Williams, Mary I, 26
Williams, Mary I, 31
Williams, Mary I, 85
Williams, Mary I, 348
Williams, Mary I, 367
Williams, Mary I, 368
Williams, Mary I, 410
Williams, Mary I, 428
Williams, Mary I, 429
Williams, Mary I, 521
Williams, Mary I, 535
Williams, Mary I, 547
Williams, Mary I, 549
Williams, Mary I, 581
Williams, Mary I, 582
Williams, Mary I, 795
Williams, Mary I, 800
Williams, Mary I, 844
Williams, Mary I, 845
Williams, Mary I, 958
Williams, Mary I, 968
Williams, Mary I, 970
Williams, Mary I, 1001
Williams, Mary I, 1012
Williams, Mary I, 1013
Williams, Mary I, 1046
Williams, Mary I, 1051
Williams, Mary I, 1112
Williams, Mary I, 1134
Williams, Mary I, 1155
Williams, Mary I, 1163
Williams, Mary II, 109
Williams, Mary II, 111
Williams, Mary II, 188
Williams, Mary II, 234
Williams, Mary II, 241
Williams, Mary II, 272
Williams, Mary II, 408
Williams, Mary II, 436
Williams, Mary II, 449
Williams, Mary II, 520
Williams, Mary II, 582
Williams, Mary II, 594
Williams, Mary II, 686
Williams, Mary II, 687
Williams, Mary II, 691
Williams, Mary II, 827
Williams, Mary II, 940
Williams, Mary III, 347
Williams, Mary III, 356
Williams, Mary III, 357
Williams, Mary III, 379
Williams, Mary III, 408
Williams, Mary III, 416
Williams, Mary III, 469
Williams, Mary III, 472
Williams, Mary III, 511
Williams, Mary IV, 67
Williams, Mary IV, 117
Williams, Mary IV, 147
Williams, Mary IV, 164
Williams, Mary IV, 357
Williams, Mary IV, 391
Williams, Mary IV, 409
Williams, Mary IV, 410
Williams, Mary IV, 438
Williams, Mary IV, 442
Williams, Mary IV, 454
Williams, Mary IV, 455
Williams, Mary IV, 456
Williams, Mary IV, 536
Williams, Mary IV, 552
Williams, Mary IV, 556
Williams, Mary IV, 557
Williams, Mary IV, 562
Williams, Mary IV, 582
Williams, Mary IV, 589
Williams, Mary IV, 600
Williams, Mary IV, 665
Williams, Mary IV, 787
Williams, Mary IV, 788
Williams, Mary IV, 840
Williams, Mary IV, 844
Williams, Mary IV, 855
Williams, Mary IV, 904
Williams, Mary IV, 917
Williams, Mary IV, 1031
Williams, Mary IV, 1081
Williams, Mary IV, 1082
Williams, Mary IV, 1120
Williams, Mary IV, 1194
Williams, Mary IV, 1227
Williams, Mary IV, 1267
Williams, Mary IV, 1299
Williams, Mary V, 131
Williams, Mary V, 142
Williams, Mary V, 212
Williams, Mary V, 354
Williams, Mary V, 365
Williams, Mary V, 542
Williams, Mary V, 543
Williams, Mary V, 605
Williams, Mary V, 941
Williams, Mary V, 958
Williams, Mary V, 962
Williams, Mary V, 979
Williams, Mary VI, 431
Williams, Mary VI, 457
Williams, Mary VI, 570
Williams, Mary VI, 580
Williams, Mary VI, 581
Williams, Mary VI, 582
Williams, Mary VI, 583
Williams, Mary VI, 721
Williams, Mary VI, 865
Williams, Mary VI, 867
Williams, Mary VI, 932
Williams, Mary VI, 937
Williams, Mary VI, 1006
Williams, Mary VI, 1016
Williams, Mary A. VI, 802
Williams, Mary Ann I, 736
Williams, Mary Ann I, 737
Williams, Mary Ann II, 305
Williams, Mary Ann II, 436
Williams, Mary Ann II, 688
Williams, Mary Ann IV, 304
Williams, Mary Ann IV, 327
Williams, Mary Ann IV, 357
Williams, Mary Ann IV, 388
Williams, Mary Ann IV, 556
Williams, Mary Ann IV, 576
Williams, Mary Ann IV, 579
Williams, Mary Ann IV, 588
Williams, Mary Ann IV, 1078
Williams, Mary Ann IV, 1082
Williams, Mary Ann VI, 886
Williams, Mary Ann VI, 1016
Williams, Mary Anne IV, 1299
Williams, Mary B. IV, 787
Williams, Mary B. IV, 1031
Williams, Mary C. III, 472
Williams, Mary C. IV, 1194
Williams, Mary E. I, 26
Williams, Mary E. I, 85
Williams, Mary E. IV, 557
Williams, Mary E. IV, 1194
Williams, Mary E. VI, 582
Williams, Mary E. VI, 851
Williams, Mary Eliz. III, 219
Williams, Mary Eliza IV, 225
Williams, Mary Eliza IV, 304
Williams, Mary Eliza IV, 557
Williams, Mary Eliza IV, 917
Williams, Mary Elizabeth VI, 483
Williams, Mary Elizabeth VI, 576
Williams, Mary Elizabeth VI, 581
Williams, Mary Elizabeth VI, 582
Williams, Mary Elizabeth VI, 875
Williams, Mary Ellen IV, 556
Williams, Mary Ellen IV, 557
Williams, Mary F. IV, 917
Williams, Mary F. IV, 1082
Williams, Mary F. V, 439
Williams, Mary G. III, 356
Williams, Mary H. I, 628
Williams, Mary H. I, 643
Williams, Mary H. II, 940
Williams, Mary H. III, 270
Williams, Mary I. VI, 805
Williams, Mary Jane II, 827
Williams, Mary Jane II, 940
Williams, Mary Louisa IV, 456
Williams, Mary Louisa V, 941
Williams, Mary M. IV, 438
Williams, Mary O. IV, 1299
Williams, Mary Ruth VI, 576
Williams, Mary Ruth VI, 582
Williams, Mary S. IV, 535
Williams, Mary S. VI, 557
Williams, Mary S. IV, 1299
Williams, Mary T. III, 357
Williams, Mary T. IV, 556
Williams, Mary V. VI, 807
Williams, Mary W. IV, 1177
Williams, Mary W. IV, 1193
Williams, Mary W. IV, 1288
Williams, Mary W. IV, 1299
Williams, Mary W. V, 605
Williams, Mary Weaver VI, 786
Williams, Mary Wood II, 686
Williams, Mary, Jr. VI, 1016
Williams, Maryette III, 511
Williams, Mathew I, 1134
Williams, Mathias VI, 837
Williams, Matilda I, 985
Williams, Matilda I, 1000
Williams, Matilda II, 436
Williams, Matilda II, 674
Williams, Matilda II, 688
Williams, Matilda VI, 1016
Williams, Mattheas I, 958
Williams, Matthew I, 582
Williams, Matthew V, 142
Williams, Matthew VI, 832
Williams, Matthew M. VI, 1016
Williams, Matthias I, 521
Williams, Matthias I, 582
Williams, Matthias V, 142
Williams, Mattie IV, 1299
Williams, Mattie Lou I, 26
Williams, Mattie Lou I, 31
Williams, Mattie Low I, 85
Williams, Maynard E. V, 543
Williams, Mehiah Ann V, 543
Williams, Micaijah I, 970
Williams, Micajah I, 582
Williams, Micajah I, 970
Williams, Micajah VI, 356
Williams, Micajah J. IV, 338
Williams, Micajah J. IV, 357
Williams, Micajah T. IV, 357
Williams, Micajah T. V, 941
Williams, Micajah Terrell I, 521
Williams, Micajah Terrell V, 142
Williams, Micajah Terrell V, 941
Williams, Micajah Terrell VI, 345
Williams, Mifflin IV, 1299
Williams, Milicent J. I, 729
Williams, Milicent J. I, 737
Williams, Minchel VI, 457
Williams, Minnie I, 628
Williams, Minnie I, 643
Williams, Minsher VI, 457
Williams, Miriam IV, 456
Williams, Miriam IV, 1082
Williams, Miriam IV, 1108
Williams, Mock I, 845
Williams, Mock S. I, 845
Williams, Mock S. I, 928
Williams, Mock S. I, 936
Williams, Morris II, 202
Williams, Morris II, 272
Williams, Morris L. II, 940
Williams, Morris R. III, 300
Williams, Morris R. III, 357
Williams, Morris R. III, 363
Williams, Morris R. III, 472
Williams, Moses I, 429
Williams, Mouning VI, 1002
Williams, Mrs. E. P. IV, 1343
Williams, Mrs. Jennie IV, 1343
Williams, Mrs. Samuel IV, 1300
Williams, Murphy I, 429
Williams, Myrtle IV, 1016
Williams, Myrtle Elvira IV, 557
Williams, Myrtle L. III, 64
Williams, Myrtle L. III, 357
Williams, Myrtle May IV, 1015
Williams, Nancy I, 1134
Williams, Nancy I, 1163
Williams, Nancy V, 212
Williams, Nancy V, 289
Williams, Nancy V, 290
Williams, Nancy V, 439
Williams, Nancy V, 873
Williams, Nancy V, 958
Williams, Nancy V, 962
Williams, Nancy VI, 817
Williams, Nancy VI, 886
Williams, Nancy VI, 911
Williams, Nancy VI, 944
Williams, Nancy VI, 967
Williams, Nancy VI, 1016
Williams, Nancy A. VI, 817
Williams, Nancy A. VI, 1016
Williams, Nancy B. V, 400
Williams, Nancy B. V, 439
Williams, Narcissa V, 924
Williams, Narcissa V, 941
Williams, Nathan I, 260
Williams, Nathan I, 368
Williams, Nathan I, 521
Williams, Nathan I, 737
Williams, Nathan I, 970
Williams, Nathan I, 1000
Williams, Nathan I, 1112
Williams, Nathan I, 1163
Williams, Nathan II, 561
Williams, Nathan II, 940
Williams, Nathan IV, 224
Williams, Nathan IV, 303
Williams, Nathan IV, 455
Williams, Nathan IV, 456
Williams, Nathan IV, 1120
Williams, Nathan V, 142
Williams, Neither Humphrey VI, 581
Williams, Nelly I, 1112
Williams, Neola IV, 1299
Williams, Nicholas I, 958
Williams, Nicholas II, 449
Williams, Nicholas III, 357
Williams, Nicholas VI, 1002
Williams, Nicholas VI, 1016
Williams, Nimrod IV, 415
Williams, Nimrod IV, 455
Williams, Nimrod IV, 456
Williams, Obediah IV, 1299
Williams, Obidah IV, 787
Williams, Obie IV, 1299
Williams, Odell Windall I, 9
Williams, Oliver II, 436
Williams, Ora IV, 1299
Williams, Orlander I, 1163
Williams, Orpha V, 542
Williams, Oscar Elmer V, 54
Williams, Otho F. IV, 456
Williams, Otho F. IV, 600
Williams, Owen I, 368
Williams, Owen I, 429
Williams, Owen I, 795
Williams, Owen I, 844
Williams, Owen I, 845
Williams, Owen I, 1163
Williams, Owen II, 449
Williams, Owen V, 289
Williams, Owen V, 365
Williams, Owen VI, 457
Williams, Owen VI, 581
Williams, Owen VI, 582
Williams, Owen C. I, 1163
Williams, Owen, Jr. I, 845
Williams, Owin I, 383
Williams, Owin I, 429
Williams, P. A. I, 486
Williams, P. B. V, 1025
Williams, Paul IV, 1016
Williams, Paul V, 719
Williams, Paul H. I, 1163
Williams, Paul Paton IV, 101
Williams, Pegga I, 845
Williams, Peggy VI, 959
Williams, Penelope IV, 1299
Williams, Penina IV, 579
Williams, Penina IV, 601
Williams, Peninah IV, 164
Williams, Peninah IV, 456
Williams, Peninah IV, 573
Williams, Peninah IV, 579
Williams, Peninah IV, 594
Williams, Peninah IV, 600
Williams, Peninah IV, 1120
Williams, Peninnah IV, 456
Williams, Percilla I, 368
Williams, Percilla I, 1112
Williams, Peter I, 706
Williams, Peter V, 142
Williams, Peter V, 212
Williams, Peter V, 289
Williams, Peter V, 290
Williams, Peter V, 945
Williams, Peter V, 958
Williams, Peter V, 962
Williams, Peter V, 963
Williams, Peter VI, 213
Williams, Peter VI, 217
Williams, Peter T., Jr. V, 941
Williams, Phebe I, 795
Williams, Phebe I, 827
Williams, Phebe I, 845
Williams, Phebe II, 188
Williams, Phebe II, 272
Williams, Phebe II, 305
Williams, Phebe II, 625
Williams, Phebe II, 688
Williams, Phebe II, 775
Williams, Phebe III, 282
Williams, Phebe III, 357
Williams, Phebe III, 408
Williams, Phebe III, 466
Williams, Phebe III, 469
Williams, Phebe III, 472
Williams, Phebe IV, 415
Williams, Phebe IV, 419
Williams, Phebe IV, 455
Williams, Phebe IV, 456

ns, Phebe IV, 1082
ms, Phebe IV, 1120
ms, Phebe V, 142
ms, Phebe V, 215
ms, Phebe V, 289
ms, Phebe V, 340
ms, Phebe V, 341
ms, Phebe V, 354
ms, Phebe V, 361
ms, Phebe V, 365
ms, Phebe V, 490
ms, Phebe V, 543
ms, Phebe V, 544
ms, Phebe H. IV, 357
ms, Phebe H. IV, 358
ms, Phebe H. IV, 516
ms, Phebe H. IV, 556
ms, Phebe H. IV, 557
ams, Phebe H. IV, 1090
ams, Phebe H. IV, 1121
ams, Phebe J. IV, 73
ams, Phebe J. IV, 116
ams, Phebe J. IV, 117
ams, Phebe J. IV, 788
ams, Phebe J. IV, 855
ams, Phebe J. IV, 1015
ams, Phebe J. IV, 1227
ams, Phebe J. IV, 1266
ams, Philadelphia III, 221
ams, Philadelphia III, 357
ams, Philena IV, 1117
ams, Philena IV, 1120
ams, Philena IV, 1140
ams, Philip Strahl IV, 456
ams, Polly VI, 799
ams, Polly VI, 837
ams, Polly VI, 865
ams, Polly VI, 982
iams, Preston IV, 456
iams, Preston IV, 1120
iams, Priscilla I, 364
iams, Priscilla I, 368
iams, Priscilla I, 429
iams, Priscilla I, 845
iams, Priscilla I, 1119
iams, Priscilla I, 1134
iams, Priscilla VI, 582
iams, Priscillia I, 1134
iams, Prissilla I, 368
iams, Prudance I, 1112
iams, Prudence I, 368
liams, Prudence I, 488
liams, Prudence I, 521
liams, Prudence I, 525
liams, Prudence I, 532
liams, Prudence I, 581
liams, Prudence I, 582
liams, Prudence I, 845
liams, Prudence I, 958
liams, Prudence I, 1013
liams, Prudence I, 1148
liams, Prudence I, 1163
liams, Prudence IV, 455
lliams, Prudence IV, 456
lliams, Prudence IV, 458
lliams, Prudence VI, 469
lliams, Prudence VI, 581
illiams, Purdy III, 357
lliams, Rachel I, 85
illiams, Rachel I, 348
illiams, Rachel I, 367
illiams, Rachel I, 368
illiams, Rachel I, 378
illiams, Rachel I, 387
illiams, Rachel I, 402
illiams, Rachel I, 415
illiams, Rachel I, 428
illiams, Rachel I, 429
illiams, Rachel I, 521
illiams, Rachel I, 545
illiams, Rachel I, 582
illiams, Rachel I, 682
Villiams, Rachel I, 692
Villiams, Rachel I, 712
Villiams, Rachel I, 736
Villiams, Rachel I, 844
Villiams, Rachel I, 970
Villiams, Rachel I, 1101
Williams, Rachel I, 1112
Williams, Rachel I, 1126
Williams, Rachel I, 1134
Williams, Rachel I, 1137
Williams, Rachel I, 1163
Williams, Rachel II, 305
Williams, Rachel II, 436
Williams, Rachel II, 608
Williams, Rachel II, 626
Williams, Rachel II, 655
Williams, Rachel II, 686
Williams, Rachel II, 688
Williams, Rachel III, 358
Williams, Rachel IV, 357
Williams, Rachel IV, 358
Williams, Rachel IV, 364
Williams, Rachel IV, 382
Williams, Rachel IV, 392
Williams, Rachel IV, 455
Williams, Rachel IV, 456
Williams, Rachel IV, 539
Williams, Rachel IV, 557
Williams, Rachel IV, 572
Williams, Rachel IV, 579
Williams, Rachel IV, 600
Williams, Rachel IV, 952
Williams, Rachel IV, 1015
Williams, Rachel IV, 1082
Williams, Rachel IV, 1123
Williams, Rachel IV, 1299
Williams, Rachel V, 61
Williams, Rachel V, 139
Williams, Rachel V, 142
Williams, Rachel V, 650
Williams, Rachel V, 962
Williams, Rachel VI, 582
Williams, Rachel Ann II, 188
Williams, Rachel F. II, 827
Williams, Rachel F. II, 940
Williams, Rachel G. IV, 556
Williams, Rachel H. II, 940
Williams, Rachel L. IV, 456
Williams, Rachel P. IV, 455
Williams, Rachel S. IV, 456
Williams, Rachel S. IV, 600
Williams, Rachel S. V, 142
Williams, Rachel Tilton III, 358
Williams, Ramson A. I, 1163
Williams, Ransom Andrew I, 620
Williams, Reachel I, 1112
Williams, Reachel I, 1134
Williams, Reason VI, 1016
Williams, Rebbecca IV, 327
Williams, Rebecca I, 1046
Williams, Rebecca I, 1112
Williams, Rebecca I, 1113
Williams, Rebecca I, 1134
Williams, Rebecca II, 272
Williams, Rebecca II, 365
Williams, Rebecca IV, 147
Williams, Rebecca IV, 164
Williams, Rebecca IV, 170
Williams, Rebecca IV, 357
Williams, Rebecca IV, 358
Williams, Rebecca IV, 456
Williams, Rebecca IV, 516
Williams, Rebecca IV, 554
Williams, Rebecca IV, 556
Williams, Rebecca IV, 557
Williams, Rebecca IV, 917
Williams, Rebecca IV, 1082
Williams, Rebecca IV, 1109
Williams, Rebecca IV, 1120
Williams, Rebecca IV, 1121
Williams, Rebecca V, 350
Williams, Rebecca V, 365
Williams, Rebecca VI, 581
Williams, Rebecca VI, 582
Williams, Rebecca J. II, 940
Williams, Rebecca Jane VI, 582
Williams, Rebecca P. IV, 455
Williams, Rebecca T. II, 882
Williams, Rebecca T. II, 940
Williams, Rebecka II, 436
Williams, Rebeckah I, 521
Williams, Rebeckah II, 436
Williams, Rebeckah II, 562
Williams, Rebeckah II, 686
Williams, Rebeckah IV, 455
Williams, Rebekah I, 1013
Williams, Rebekah I, 1134
Williams, Rebekah II, 1038
Williams, Rebekah IV, 415
Williams, Rebekah IV, 455
Williams, Reed II, 436
Williams, Reed II, 687
Williams, Reed A. II, 940
Williams, Rehoboath VI, 581
Williams, Reid A. II, 940
Williams, Reuben VI, 865
Williams, Rhoda IV, 454
Williams, Rhoda IV, 456
Williams, Rich I, 582
Williams, Richard I, 198
Williams, Richard I, 202
Williams, Richard I, 266
Williams, Richard I, 269
Williams, Richard I, 276
Williams, Richard I, 277
Williams, Richard I, 368
Williams, Richard I, 487
Williams, Richard I, 521
Williams, Richard I, 523
Williams, Richard I, 525
Williams, Richard I, 540
Williams, Richard I, 570
Williams, Richard I, 581
Williams, Richard I, 582
Williams, Richard I, 845
Williams, Richard I, 958
Williams, Richard I, 970
Williams, Richard I, 1111
Williams, Richard I, 1112
Williams, Richard I, 1126
Williams, Richard I, 1134
Williams, Richard I, 1163
Williams, Richard I Sup 1, 10
Williams, Richard II, 436
Williams, Richard II, 575
Williams, Richard II, 687
Williams, Richard II, 688
Williams, Richard II, 723
Williams, Richard II, 775
Williams, Richard III, 472
Williams, Richard IV, 164
Williams, Richard IV, 303
Williams, Richard IV, 304
Williams, Richard IV, 600
Williams, Richard IV, 787
Williams, Richard IV, 855
Williams, Richard IV, 917
Williams, Richard IV, 1015
Williams, Richard IV, 1386
Williams, Richard VI, 464
Williams, Richard VI, 469
Williams, Richard VI, 581
Williams, Richard VI, 582
Williams, Richard Downing III, 357
Williams, Richard J. II, 723
Williams, Richard J. II, 775
Williams, Richard, Jr. I, 582
Williams, Riley V, 650
Williams, Riley W. III, 357
Williams, Robert I, 176
Williams, Robert I, 266
Williams, Robert I, 277
Williams, Robert I, 795
Williams, Robert I, 970
Williams, Robert II, 436
Williams, Robert IV, 115
Williams, Robert IV, 116
Williams, Robert IV, 146
Williams, Robert IV, 164
Williams, Robert IV, 357
Williams, Robert IV, 454
Williams, Robert IV, 456
Williams, Robert IV, 600
Williams, Robert IV, 1194
Williams, Robert V, 142
Williams, Robert V, 365
Williams, Robert V, 941
Williams, Robert VI, 947
Williams, Robert Seal I, 628
Williams, Rodger VI, 840
Williams, Roger VI, 865
Williams, Roger VI, 898
Williams, Roger VI, 937
Williams, Roger VI, 967
Williams, Roger VI, 977
Williams, Roger VI, 1016
Williams, Roses I, 845
Williams, Ruth I, 368
Williams, Ruth I, 521
Williams, Ruth I, 541
Williams, Ruth I, 582
Williams, Ruth I, 845
Williams, Ruth I, 1046
Williams, Ruth I, 1112
Williams, Ruth II, 436
Williams, Ruth II, 688
Williams, Ruth II, 723
Williams, Ruth II, 775
Williams, Ruth IV, 391
Williams, Ruth IV, 455
Williams, Ruth IV, 1266
Williams, Ruth VI, 581
Williams, Ruth VI, 582
Williams, Ruth Ann IV, 456
Williams, Ruth Anna IV, 403
Williams, Sabelia I, 26
Williams, Sabelia E. I, 85
Williams, Salinda V, 212
Williams, Salley VI, 1016
Williams, Sallie V, 1025
Williams, Sallie B. III, 229
Williams, Sallie B. III, 270
Williams, Sallie B. III, 357
Williams, Sally I, 1112
Williams, Sally IV, 164
Williams, Sally IV, 456
Williams, Sally IV, 569
Williams, Sally IV, 600
Williams, Sally VI, 865
Williams, Sally VI, 1016
Williams, Sally C. K. IV, 304
Williams, Sam'l B. III, 357
Williams, Sam'l B. VI, 805
Williams, Samuel I, 277
Williams, Samuel II, 185
Williams, Samuel II, 188
Williams, Samuel II, 272
Williams, Samuel II, 302
Williams, Samuel II, 305
Williams, Samuel II, 436
Williams, Samuel II, 437
Williams, Samuel II, 625
Williams, Samuel II, 636
Williams, Samuel II, 665
Williams, Samuel II, 687
Williams, Samuel II, 723
Williams, Samuel II, 827
Williams, Samuel II, 838
Williams, Samuel II, 940
Williams, Samuel III, 358
Williams, Samuel III, 472
Williams, Samuel IV, 67
Williams, Samuel IV, 139
Williams, Samuel IV, 164
Williams, Samuel IV, 455
Williams, Samuel IV, 456
Williams, Samuel IV, 569
Williams, Samuel IV, 582
Williams, Samuel IV, 591
Williams, Samuel IV, 600
Williams, Samuel IV, 728
Williams, Samuel IV, 787
Williams, Samuel IV, 788
Williams, Samuel IV, 855
Williams, Samuel IV, 856
Williams, Samuel V, 289
Williams, Samuel V, 962
Williams, Samuel VI, 802
Williams, Samuel VI, 817
Williams, Samuel VI, 827
Williams, Samuel VI, 865
Williams, Samuel VI, 981
Williams, Samuel VI, 999
Williams, Samuel VI, 1016
Williams, Samuel B. III, 38
Williams, Samuel B. III, 48
Williams, Samuel B. III, 357
Williams, Samuel Borton II, 940
Williams, Samuel Byron, Jr. III, 357
Williams, Samuel E. VI, 826
Williams, Samuel J. IV, 1044
Williams, Samuel Leeke IV, 562
Williams, Samuel Reeve II, 436
Williams, Samuel Reeve II, 775
Williams, Samuel T. VI, 924
Williams, Samuel T. VI, 1000
Williams, Samuel W. VI, 981
Williams, Samuel W. VI, 999
Williams, Samuel W. VI, 1016
Williams, Samuel, Jr. II, 625
Williams, Samuel, Jr. II, 687
Williams, Sarah I, 9
Williams, Sarah I, 26
Williams, Sarah I, 90
Williams, Sarah I, 266
Williams, Sarah I, 269
Williams, Sarah I, 276
Williams, Sarah I, 277
Williams, Sarah I, 367
Williams, Sarah I, 397
Williams, Sarah I, 426
Williams, Sarah I, 428
Williams, Sarah I, 429
Williams, Sarah I, 455
Williams, Sarah I, 521
Williams, Sarah I, 523
Williams, Sarah I, 570
Williams, Sarah I, 572
Williams, Sarah I, 577
Williams, Sarah I, 582
Williams, Sarah I, 736
Williams, Sarah I, 737
Williams, Sarah I, 795
Williams, Sarah I, 843
Williams, Sarah I, 845
Williams, Sarah I, 914
Williams, Sarah I, 958
Williams, Sarah I, 1006
Williams, Sarah I, 1013
Williams, Sarah I, 1046
Williams, Sarah I, 1051
Williams, Sarah I, 1112
Williams, Sarah I, 1134
Williams, Sarah I Sup 1, 4
Williams, Sarah I Sup 1, 6
Williams, Sarah I Sup 1, 9
Williams, Sarah II, 188
Williams, Sarah II, 272
Williams, Sarah II, 436
Williams, Sarah II, 573
Williams, Sarah II, 575
Williams, Sarah II, 625
Williams, Sarah II, 626
Williams, Sarah II, 627
Williams, Sarah II, 629
Williams, Sarah II, 686
Williams, Sarah II, 688
Williams, Sarah II, 723
Williams, Sarah II, 779
Williams, Sarah II, 799
Williams, Sarah II, 806
Williams, Sarah II, 811
Williams, Sarah II, 816
Williams, Sarah II, 823
Williams, Sarah II, 955
Williams, Sarah II, 964
Williams, Sarah II, 972
Williams, Sarah II, 982
Williams, Sarah II, 1039
Williams, Sarah II, 1044
Williams, Sarah II, 1055
Williams, Sarah III, 103
Williams, Sarah III, 358
Williams, Sarah III, 462
Williams, Sarah IV, 115
Williams, Sarah IV, 116
Williams, Sarah IV, 139
Williams, Sarah IV, 156
Williams, Sarah IV, 164
Williams, Sarah IV, 191
Williams, Sarah IV, 214
Williams, Sarah IV, 224
Williams, Sarah IV, 303
Williams, Sarah IV, 304
Williams, Sarah IV, 339
Williams, Sarah IV, 357
Williams, Sarah IV, 380
Williams, Sarah IV, 399
Williams, Sarah IV, 415
Williams, Sarah IV, 445
Williams, Sarah IV, 455
Williams, Sarah IV, 456
Williams, Sarah IV, 556
Williams, Sarah IV, 569
Williams, Sarah IV, 574
Williams, Sarah IV, 579
Williams, Sarah IV, 582
Williams, Sarah IV, 591
Williams, Sarah IV, 600
Williams, Sarah IV, 787
Williams, Sarah IV, 855
Williams, Sarah IV, 917
Williams, Sarah IV, 931
Williams, Sarah IV, 1015
Williams, Sarah IV, 1082
Williams, Sarah IV, 1167
Williams, Sarah IV, 1266
Williams, Sarah IV, 1299
Williams, Sarah V, 142
Williams, Sarah V, 212
Williams, Sarah V, 251
Williams, Sarah V, 289
Williams, Sarah V, 365
Williams, Sarah V, 439
Williams, Sarah V, 473
Williams, Sarah V, 488
Williams, Sarah V, 530
Williams, Sarah V, 542
Williams, Sarah V, 543
Williams, Sarah V, 544
Williams, Sarah V, 802
Williams, Sarah V, 873
Williams, Sarah V, 941
Williams, Sarah VI, 345
Williams, Sarah VI, 356
Williams, Sarah VI, 385
Williams, Sarah VI, 457
Williams, Sarah VI, 553
Williams, Sarah VI, 582
Williams, Sarah VI, 875
Williams, Sarah VI, 981
Williams, Sarah VI, 1015
Williams, Sarah A. III, 358
Williams, Sarah Ann VI, 1016
Williams, Sarah B. III, 191
Williams, Sarah B. IV, 978
Williams, Sarah B. IV, 979
Williams, Sarah B. IV, 1015
Williams, Sarah B. IV, 1016
Williams, Sarah Baldwin I, 582
Williams, Sarah Boyer II, 436
Williams, Sarah C. IV, 353
Williams, Sarah C. IV, 357
Williams, Sarah C. IV, 410
Williams, Sarah E. IV, 304
Williams, Sarah E. V, 936
Williams, Sarah E. V, 941
Williams, Sarah Elizabeth V, 941
Williams, Sarah Elizabeth VI, 81
Williams, Sarah Elizabeth VI, 90
Williams, Sarah Ellen V, 439

Williams, Sarah Esther IV, 267
Williams, Sarah Esther IV, 304
Williams, Sarah Esther IV, 1290
Williams, Sarah Esther IV, 1299
Williams, Sarah Frances VI, 1016
Williams, Sarah Jane IV, 456
Williams, Sarah Jane V, 941
Williams, Sarah L. I, 1000
Williams, Sarah Louisa II, 436
Williams, Sarah M. IV, 456
Williams, Sarah M. IV, 1109
Williams, Sarah M. VI, 544
Williams, Sarah M. VI, 582
Williams, Sarah M. VI, 827
Williams, Sarah S. IV, 557
Williams, Sarah S. V, 365
Williams, Sarah T. IV, 215
Williams, Sarah T. IV, 304
Williams, Sarah W. II, 185
Williams, Sarah W. II, 302
Williams, Sarah W. II, 305
Williams, Sarah W. IV, 304
Williams, Sarah, Jr. IV, 600
Williams, Selia I, 260
Williams, Sena VI, 899
Williams, Septimus L. VI, 1016
Williams, Seth I, 706
Williams, Seth IV, 455
Williams, Seth IV, 600
Williams, Seth IV, 1117
Williams, Seth IV, 1120
Williams, Seth IV, 1121
Williams, Seth IV, 1140
Williams, Seth V, 142
Williams, Seth V, 202
Williams, Seth V, 211
Williams, Seth V, 289
Williams, Sibbilla I, 1046
Williams, Sidney IV, 1299
Williams, Sidwell IV, 557
Williams, Silas I, 521
Williams, Silas I, 549
Williams, Silas I, 581
Williams, Silas I, 582
Williams, Silas I, 970
Williams, Silas I, 1013
Williams, Silas IV, 1299
Williams, Simeon V, 605
Williams, Solomon I, 1163
Williams, Sophia I, 1132
Williams, Sophia I, 1134
Williams, Stella IV, 1343
Williams, Stephen IV, 304
Williams, Stephen V, 142
Williams, Stephen G. V, 142
Williams, Stillborn II, 436
Williams, Strangeman I, 1000
Williams, Susan II, 302
Williams, Susan II, 305
Williams, Susan II, 838
Williams, Susan II, 940
Williams, Susan IV, 1177
Williams, Susan IV, 1194
Williams, Susan IV, 1227
Williams, Susan V, 962
Williams, Susan VI, 822
Williams, Susan A. VI, 865
Williams, Susan Jane IV, 1242
Williams, Susan M. IV, 1194
Williams, Susan R. VI, 865
Williams, Susan T. VI, 431
Williams, Susan T. VI, 432
Williams, Susan T. VI, 457
Williams, Susan T. VI, 544
Williams, Susan T. VI, 580
Williams, Susan T. VI, 582
Williams, Susan W. II, 325
Williams, Susan W. II, 326
Williams, Susanna I, 402
Williams, Susanna I, 413
Williams, Susanna I, 429
Williams, Susanna I, 521
Williams, Susanna I, 551
Williams, Susanna I, 582
Williams, Susanna I, 737
Williams, Susanna I, 1000
Williams, Susanna I, 1013
Williams, Susanna I, 1112
Williams, Susanna II, 550
Williams, Susanna II, 686
Williams, Susanna IV, 67
Williams, Susanna IV, 665
Williams, Susanna VI, 832
Williams, Susanna VI, 1016
Williams, Susanna L. VI, 835
Williams, Susannah I, 198
Williams, Susannah I, 202
Williams, Susannah I, 1013
Williams, Susannah II, 508
Williams, Susannah II, 686
Williams, Susannah VI, 582
Williams, Susannah VI, 721
Williams, Sybbilla I, 1051
Williams, Tabitha I, 737
Williams, Tabitha I, 1000
Williams, Tabitha I, 1163
Williams, Tace IV, 665
Williams, Tacy II, 463
Williams, Tacy IV, 67
Williams, Tacy IV, 855
Williams, Tacy VI, 721
Williams, Tacy F. II, 1083
Williams, Talbat IV, 600
Williams, Tasa IV, 665
Williams, Temperance IV, 385
Williams, Temperance IV, 392
Williams, Temperance IV, 455
Williams, Temperance IV, 456
Williams, Temperance IV, 600
Williams, Tennison IV, 1266
Williams, Terrell I, 582
Williams, Terrell VI, 356
Williams, Thankful III, 358
Williams, Theodosha V, 543
Williams, Thomas I, 970
Williams, Thomas I, 1134
Williams, Thomas I, 1163
Williams, Thomas II, 197
Williams, Thomas II, 257
Williams, Thomas II, 272
Williams, Thomas II, 436
Williams, Thomas II, 437
Williams, Thomas II, 449
Williams, Thomas II, 626
Williams, Thomas II, 655
Williams, Thomas II, 665
Williams, Thomas II, 686
Williams, Thomas II, 687
Williams, Thomas II, 688
Williams, Thomas II, 827
Williams, Thomas II, 978
Williams, Thomas II, 1038
Williams, Thomas III, 358
Williams, Thomas III, 416
Williams, Thomas III, 436
Williams, Thomas III, 442
Williams, Thomas III, 445
Williams, Thomas III, 472
Williams, Thomas IV, 455
Williams, Thomas IV, 456
Williams, Thomas IV, 458
Williams, Thomas IV, 562
Williams, Thomas IV, 787
Williams, Thomas IV, 788
Williams, Thomas IV, 1194
Williams, Thomas IV, 1227
Williams, Thomas IV, 1299
Williams, Thomas IV, 1343
Williams, Thomas V, 439
Williams, Thomas V, 490
Williams, Thomas V, 543
Williams, Thomas V, 962
Williams, Thomas VI, 721
Williams, Thomas VI, 808
Williams, Thomas VI, 827
Williams, Thomas VI, 851
Williams, Thomas VI, 863
Williams, Thomas VI, 865
Williams, Thomas VI, 898
Williams, Thomas VI, 998
Williams, Thomas VI, 1016
Williams, Thomas B. V, 542
Williams, Thomas B. V, 544
Williams, Thomas C. IV, 1193
Williams, Thomas E. IV, 357
Williams, Thomas E. IV, 556
Williams, Thomas Elwood IV, 557
Williams, Thomas G. IV, 358
Williams, Thomas L. I, 26
Williams, Thomas L. I, 85
Williams, Thomas R. III, 358
Williams, Thomas Reed II, 827
Williams, Thomas W. VI, 865
Williams, Thomas, Jr. VI, 818
Williams, Thomas, Jr. VI, 856
Williams, Thos. II, 821
Williams, Thos. II, 827
Williams, Thos. II, 837
Williams, Thos. II, 926
Williams, Thos. II, 940
Williams, Thos. III, 357
Williams, Thos. III, 469
Williams, Thos. III, 472
Williams, Thos. IV, 455
Williams, Thos. VI, 814
Williams, Thos. C. IV, 1015
Williams, Thos. C. IV, 1177
Williams, Thos. C. IV, 1288
Williams, Thos. C. IV, 1299
Williams, Thos. Clarkson IV, 1147
Williams, Thos. Clarkson IV, 1272
Williams, Thos. Clarkson IV, 1299
Williams, Thos. D. VI, 865
Williams, Thos. R. II, 940
Williams, Timothy D. III, 358
Williams, Tylee III, 358
Williams, Tyrrel I, 970
Williams, Ulia I, 845
Williams, V. IV, 1267
Williams, Velina A. IV, 455
Williams, Velma IV, 1267
Williams, Verna IV, 856
Williams, Verna Louise IV, 788
Williams, Vernia L. IV, 788
Williams, Viola M. I, 1163
Williams, W. W. IV, 788
Williams, W. W. VI, 829
Williams, W. W. VI, 863
Williams, Walter III, 357
Williams, Walter III, 358
Williams, Walter III, 472
Williams, Walter IV, 1016
Williams, Walter VI, 890
Williams, Walter VI, 905
Williams, Walter VI, 1016
Williams, Walter H. III, 356
Williams, Walter Rollin IV, 1015
Williams, Walter T. IV, 855
Williams, Walter T. IV, 1266
Williams, Washington III, 472
Williams, Wd. Elizabeth III, 472
Williams, Wd. Elizabeth VI, 526
Williams, Wd. Elizabeth VI, 549
Williams, Wd. Jane II, 554
Williams, Wd. Lydia III, 357
Williams, Wd. Mary III, 442
Williams, Wd. Mary III, 472
Williams, Wd. Mary Ann II, 188
Williams, Webster V, 605
Williams, Welmet I, 396
Williams, Welmet I, 429
Williams, Widow Joan Williams VI, 581
Williams, Widow Rachel I, 76
Williams, Widow Rachel I, 85
Williams, Willet IV, 456
Williams, Willet IV, 1120
Williams, William I, 26
Williams, William I, 368
Williams, William I, 428
Williams, William I, 429
Williams, William I, 521
Williams, William I, 706
Williams, William I, 795
Williams, William I, 827
Williams, William I, 844
Williams, William I, 845
Williams, William I, 970
Williams, William I, 1010
Williams, William I, 1013
Williams, William I, 1101
Williams, William I, 1112
Williams, William I, 1134
Williams, William I, 1137
Williams, William I, 1163
Williams, William II, 437
Williams, William II, 449
Williams, William III, 358
Williams, William IV, 357
Williams, William IV, 455
Williams, William IV, 456
Williams, William IV, 600
Williams, William IV, 1299
Williams, William V, 142
Williams, William V, 215
Williams, William V, 289
Williams, William V, 290
Williams, William V, 354
Williams, William V, 361
Williams, William V, 365
Williams, William V, 772
Williams, William V, 962
Williams, William VI, 431
Williams, William VI, 457
Williams, William VI, 483
Williams, William VI, 490
Williams, William VI, 525
Williams, William VI, 526
Williams, William VI, 538
Williams, William VI, 544
Williams, William VI, 549
Williams, William VI, 576
Williams, William VI, 580
Williams, William VI, 581
Williams, William VI, 582
Williams, William VI, 583
Williams, William VI, 838
Williams, William VI, 865
Williams, William VI, 867
Williams, William VI, 911
Williams, William VI, 915
Williams, William VI, 1015
Williams, William VI, 1016
Williams, William A. V, 439
Williams, William C. IV, 357
Williams, William C. IV, 556
Williams, William C. V, 941
Williams, William C. VI, 865
Williams, William D. III, 357
Williams, William Howard I, 26
Williams, William Minor V, 543
Williams, William R. VI, 1016
Williams, William Talbott IV, 304
Williams, William W. VI, 865
Williams, William Walker VI, 865
Williams, William, Jr. I, 1163
Williams, Willit IV, 456
Williams, Wisper IV, 562
Williams, Wm. I, 348
Williams, Wm. I, 364
Williams, Wm. I, 368
Williams, Wm. I, 402
Williams, Wm. I, 429
Williams, Wm. I, 1112
Williams, Wm. II, 483
Williams, Wm. II, 686
Williams, Wm. IV, 379
Williams, Wm. IV, 576
Williams, Wm. IV, 600
Williams, Wm. IV, 665
Williams, Wm. IV, 1081
Williams, Wm. IV, 1082
Williams, Wm. IV, 1120
Williams, Wm. IV, 1327
Williams, Wm. IV, 1343
Williams, Wm. V, 340
Williams, Wm. V, 341
Williams, Wm. V, 544
Williams, Wm. V, 650
Williams, Wm. V, 962
Williams, Wm. Anderson V, 439
Williams, Wm. C. IV, 170
Williams, Wm. C. IV, 327
Williams, Wm. C. IV, 357
Williams, Wm. C. IV, 358
Williams, Wm. C. IV, 516
Williams, Wm. C. IV, 554
Williams, Wm. C. IV, 556
Williams, Wm. C. IV, 557
Williams, Wm. C. IV, 1120
Williams, Wm. C. IV, 1121
Williams, Wm. C. V, 365
Williams, Wm. C. VI, 839
Williams, Wm. Clinton IV, 1299
Williams, Wm. D. III, 219
Williams, Wm. Henry IV, 1140
Williams, Wm. K. IV, 304
Williams, Wm. R. III, 360
Williams, Worth R. V, 365
Williams, Yearsly IV, 339
Williams, Zachariah II, 437
Williams, Zaddock I, 737
Williams, Zadoc I, 1163
Williams, Zadoc V, 142
Williams, Zadock I, 1163
Williams, Zalinda V, 575
Williams, Zalinda V, 605
Williams, Zilpah IV, 454
Williams, Zilpha IV, 405
Williams, Zilpha IV, 409
Williams, Zilpha IV, 455
Williams, Zilpha IV, 600
Williams, Zilphah IV, 164
Williams, Zodock I, 1000
Williamson, A. Jackson V, 290
Williamson, Abbie III, 358
Williamson, Abbie S. III, 358
Williamson, Abigail V, 769
Williamson, Abigail V, 773
Williamson, Abraham IV, 304
Williamson, Adam J. V, 290
Williamson, Adam Jackson V, 290
Williamson, Alvah III, 345
Williamson, Alvah III, 358
Williamson, Amoret VI, 1017
Williamson, Ann VI, 562
Williamson, Ann VI, 701
Williamson, Ann VI, 703
Williamson, Ann VI, 705
Williamson, Ann VI, 707
Williamson, Ann VI, 826
Williamson, Ann VI, 865
Williamson, Ann L. II, 723
Williamson, Ann L. II, 775
Williamson, Ann M. VI, 957
Williamson, Anna II, 255
Williamson, Anna II, 273
Williamson, Anna II, 775
Williamson, Anna III, 358
Williamson, Anna IV, 1267
Williamson, Anna V, 142
Williamson, Anna V, 143
Williamson, Anna VI, 1016
Williamson, Anna C. V, 941
Williamson, Anna L. III, 30
Williamson, Anne VI, 496
Williamson, Anne VI, 561
Williamson, Anne VI, 562
Williamson, Anne VI, 563
Williamson, Anne VI, 642
Williamson, Archa VI, 811
Williamson, Archer VI, 815
Williamson, Archer VI, 823
Williamson, Archer VI, 850
Williamson, Archer VI, 861
Williamson, Archie VI, 801
Williamson, Arthur M. III,
Williamson, Barnabas D. V
Williamson, Benjamin III, 6
Williamson, Benjamin III, 3
Williamson, Benjamin M. V
Williamson, Benjamin M. V
Williamson, Benjamin M. VI, 1016
Williamson, Benjamin M. VI, 1017
Williamson, Betsey VI, 1016
Williamson, Betsy VI, 879
Williamson, Blanche V, 440
Williamson, Caleb VI, 914
Williamson, Caleb VI, 940
Williamson, Caleb VI, 951
Williamson, Caleb VI, 952
Williamson, Caleb VI, 992
Williamson, Caleb VI, 1016
Williamson, Calvin VI, 865
Williamson, Caroline III, 61
Williamson, Caroline III, 35
Williamson, Celesta M. IV,
Williamson, Celesta M. IV,
Williamson, Charity V, 290
Williamson, Charles D. III,
Williamson, Chas. D. III, 35
Williamson, Clara May III,
Williamson, Cora J. V, 290
Williamson, Daniel VI, 865
Williamson, Deborah VI, 10
Williamson, Deborah M. II,
Williamson, Deborah M. II,
Williamson, Debrix VI, 865
Williamson, Edith IV, 1267
Williamson, Edith C. IV, 12
Williamson, Edmund IV, 30
Williamson, Eleanor II, 437
Williamson, Elisha VI, 865
Williamson, Elisha VI, 993
Williamson, Elisha VI, 1016
Williamson, Elisha VI, 1017
Williamson, Eliza W. VI, 95
Williamson, Elizabeth II, 43
Williamson, Elizabeth II, 72
Williamson, Elizabeth II, 77
Williamson, Elizabeth III, 1
Williamson, Elizabeth III, 3
Williamson, Elizabeth IV, 8
Williamson, Elizabeth VI, 8
Williamson, Elizabeth VI, 8
Williamson, Elizabeth VI, 8
Williamson, Elizabeth VI, 9
Williamson, Elizabeth VI, 9
Williamson, Elizabeth VI, 9
Williamson, Elizabeth VI, 1
Williamson, Elizabeth VI, 1
Williamson, Elizabeth D. IV
Williamson, Elizabeth D. IV
Williamson, Elizabeth Dillon IV, 895
Williamson, Elizabeth L. IV
Williamson, Elizabeth R. VI
Williamson, Florence IV, 12
Williamson, Florence V, 440
Williamson, Frances VI, 81
Williamson, Frances VI, 10
Williamson, Frances C. VI,
Williamson, Francis VI, 836
Williamson, Frank IV, 304
Williamson, Frank H. III, 3
Williamson, Frank H. III, 3
Williamson, George A. V, 29
Williamson, George F. III, 3
Williamson, George F., Jr. III, 358
Williamson, Gracey VI, 889
Williamson, Hannah II, 792
Williamson, Hannah II, 796
Williamson, Harriet M. V, 2
Williamson, Harriet P. VI, 8
Williamson, Harrison V, 290
Williamson, Harvey R. III,
Williamson, Henry IV, 304
Williamson, Henry VI, 345

nson, Henry VI, 867
mson, Henry VI, 881
mson, Henry VI, 943
mson, Henry VI, 1007
nson, Henry VI, 1016
mson, Henry P. VI, 881
mson, Henry P. VI, 943
mson, Henry P. VI, 1016
mson, Henry P. VI, 1017
mson, Hohn II, 688
mson, Ines IV, 304
mson, Isaac II, 723
mson, Isaac II, 775
mson, Isaac IV, 894
mson, James VI, 889
mson, James VI, 927
mson, James VI, 936
mson, James VI, 957
mson, James VI, 961
mson, James VI, 974
mson, James VI, 1016
mson, James L. VI, 957
amson, Jane VI, 1003
amson, Jane VI, 1017
amson, Jean Margaret
I, 271
amson, Jean Margaret
II, 358
amson, Jennie IV, 304
amson, Jennie V, 467
amson, Jenny VI, 1016
amson, Jesse VI, 1016
amson, John II, 437
amson, John II, 688
amson, John III, 358
amson, John V, 941
amson, John VI, 810
amson, John VI, 902
amson, John VI, 925
amson, John VI, 969
amson, John VI, 1016
amson, John VI, 1017
amson, John A. IV, 304
amson, John McC. V, 290
amson, John, Sr. VI, 984
amson, Jonah VI, 1017
amson, Joseph III, 358
amson, Joseph V, 941
iamson, Joseph C. IV, 304
iamson, Joshua VI, 1016
iamson, Judith R. VI, 940
iamson, Kate V, 773
iamson, Keziah VI, 607
iamson, Lauretta III, 69
iamson, Laurette III, 358
iamson, Laurette W. III, 304
iamson, Leoanrd H. VI, 887
iamson, Leonard VI, 1016
iamson, Leonard H. VI, 879
iamson, Leonard H. VI, 884
iamson, Leonard H. VI, 1016
liamson, Leonard H. VI, 1017
liamson, Lillie May IV, 304
liamson, Lindora IV, 1204
liamson, Linora Conant
IV, 1227
liamson, Littleberry VI, 1016
liamson, Littlebury VI, 981
liamson, Louisa V, 467
liamson, Louisa Semour
VI, 951
liamson, Lucinda H. VI, 1017
liamson, Lucretia III, 303
liamson, Lucy C. VI, 762
lliamson, Lucy C. VI, 791
lliamson, Lucy H. VI, 1016
lliamson, Lydia H. III, 358
lliamson, M. IV, 1267
illiamson, Magdalene VI, 1007
illiamson, Mahalon H. VI, 1016
illiamson, Mahalon L. VI, 912
illiamson, Mahlon H. VI, 941
illiamson, Mahlon H. VI, 957
illiamson, Margaret VI, 1017
illiamson, Margaret B. II, 1083
illiamson, Mariam V, 543
illiamson, Marjorie V, 440
illiamson, Marshall VI, 867
illiamson, Martha VI, 1016
illiamson, Mary II, 437
illiamson, Mary II, 556
illiamson, Mary II, 688
illiamson, Mary II, 775
illiamson, Mary IV, 304
illiamson, Mary IV, 877
Villiamson, Mary IV, 886
Villiamson, Mary VI, 831
Villiamson, Mary VI, 984
Villiamson, Mary Ann E.
VI, 1022
Villiamson, Mary E. III, 358
Williamson, Mary E. V, 34
Williamson, Mary Emma III, 358
Williamson, Mary G. VI, 1022
Williamson, Mary Louise III, 358
Williamson, Mathew II, 437
Williamson, Matilda VI, 1017
Williamson, Mattie A. IV, 1267
Williamson, Maud IV, 1267
Williamson, Milborn VI, 1016
Williamson, Milburn VI, 1016
Williamson, Milburn VI, 1017
Williamson, Milley VI, 993
Williamson, Milley VI, 1016
Williamson, Minerva S. IV, 304
Williamson, Minor V, 467
Williamson, Miriam V, 142
Williamson, Miriam V, 524
Williamson, Miriam V, 543
Williamson, Nancy VI, 872
Williamson, Nancy VI, 957
Williamson, Nancy VI, 1016
Williamson, Nancy A. VI, 1017
Williamson, Nathan VI, 832
Williamson, Nathaniel VI, 865
Williamson, Ollie V, 543
Williamson, Orpah II, 688
Williamson, Passmore II, 775
Williamson, Patsey VI, 865
Williamson, Patsy VI, 836
Williamson, Permelia VI, 957
Williamson, Peter S. IV, 304
Williamson, Phebe II, 775
Williamson, Phebe W. II, 737
Williamson, Phebe W. II, 775
Williamson, Polly M. VI, 943
Williamson, Priscilla VI, 943
Williamson, Rachel H. III, 358
Williamson, Rachel H. III, 360
Williamson, Rachel H. III, 468
Williamson, Rachel H. III, 472
Williamson, Raymond V, 440
Williamson, Rhoda VI, 865
Williamson, Rhoda A. V, 290
Williamson, Richard V, 142
Williamson, Richard P. V, 142
Williamson, Robt VI, 291
Williamson, S. Heaton III, 358
Williamson, Sally VI, 838
Williamson, Sally VI, 980
Williamson, Sally VI, 1016
Williamson, Sally M. VI, 865
Williamson, Sally W. VI, 884
Williamson, Samuel A. V, 290
Williamson, Sarah II, 1024
Williamson, Sarah II, 1039
Williamson, Sarah III, 358
Williamson, Sarah V, 1025
Williamson, Sarah VI, 1016
Williamson, Sarah VI, 1017
Williamson, Sarah Estella V, 290
Williamson, Solomon VI, 1017
Williamson, Sophia VI, 1016
Williamson, Susan V, 773
Williamson, Susanna VI, 902
Williamson, Temperance V, 773
Williamson, Temperance VI, 881
Williamson, Thomas II, 723
Williamson, Thomas II, 775
Williamson, Thomas VI, 1017
Williamson, Thomas D. VI, 865
Williamson, Virginia IV, 788
Williamson, Virginia J. VI, 914
Williamson, Walter II, 796
Williamson, William II, 437
Williamson, William VI, 814
Williamson, William VI, 831
Williamson, William VI, 1017
Williamson, William M. VI, 894
Williamson, William R. III, 358
Williamson, William T. V, 290
Williamson, Wm. III, 358
Williamson, Wm. VI, 826
Williamson, Wm. R. III, 468
Williamson, Wm. R. III, 472
Williard, Judith II, 437
Williard, Miriam I, 9
Williard, Nancy Marie I, 951
Williard, Samuel II, 273
Williard, Thomas II, 437
Willice, Jemima VI, 1008
Willie, Jane III, 431
Willie, Mary III, 431
Willie, Samuel III, 431
Williman, Abraham VI, 345
Williman, Amy VI, 345
Williman, Deborah VI, 345
Williman, Elizabeth VI, 345
Williman, Jesse VI, 345
Williman, Jonah VI, 345
Williman, Letitia VI, 344
Williman, Letitia VI, 345
Williman, Mahlon VI, 345
Williman, Mary VI, 345
Williman, Nancy VI, 345
Williman, Sarah VI, 345
Willims, Deborah IV, 452
Willims, Mary II, 111
Willis, ??? III, 359
Willis, ??? III, 360
Willis, ??? III, 387
Willis, ??? III, 399
Willis, ??? III, 503
Willis, ??? III, 507
Willis, ??? IV, 1125
Willis, Abigail III, 422
Willis, Abigail III, 436
Willis, Abigail III, 444
Willis, Abigail III, 450
Willis, Abigail III, 466
Willis, Abigail III, 472
Willis, Abigail III, 473
Willis, Abigail III, 474
Willis, Abigail III, 476
Willis, Abigail III, 487
Willis, Abigail III, 490
Willis, Abigail III, 500
Willis, Abigail III, 501
Willis, Abigail III, 507
Willis, Abner I, 1088
Willis, Achsa II, 606
Willis, Achsa II, 688
Willis, Achsah I, 521
Willis, Achsah I, 545
Willis, Achsah I, 582
Willis, Achsah I, 845
Willis, Achsah II, 437
Willis, Adam III, 473
Willis, Alfred III, 236
Willis, Alfred III, 358
Willis, Alfred III, 359
Willis, Alfred III, 360
Willis, Alfred R. III, 358
Willis, Alfred R. III, 507
Willis, Alice V, 650
Willis, Amey III, 508
Willis, Amos II, 111
Willis, Amos IV, 562
Willis, Amy III, 302
Willis, Amy III, 358
Willis, Amy III, 429
Willis, Amy III, 472
Willis, Amy III, 474
Willis, Amy III, 496
Willis, Amy III, 507
Willis, Amy L. III, 442
Willis, Andrew V, 212
Willis, Andrew V, 963
Willis, Ann I, 521
Willis, Ann I, 845
Willis, Ann I, 1134
Willis, Ann III, 249
Willis, Ann III, 302
Willis, Ann III, 358
Willis, Ann III, 433
Willis, Ann III, 472
Willis, Ann III, 473
Willis, Ann III, 474
Willis, Ann Augusta III, 74
Willis, Ann Augusta III, 358
Willis, Ann Elizabeth III, 358
Willis, Anna I, 1124
Willis, Anna I, 1134
Willis, Anna III, 358
Willis, Anna III, 359
Willis, Anna III, 433
Willis, Anna III, 501
Willis, Anna III, 507
Willis, Anna V, 212
Willis, Anna F. III, 358
Willis, Anna Jessop I, 578
Willis, Anna Jessop I, 582
Willis, Anna Maria II, 688
Willis, Anna Maria II, 775
Willis, Anna Maria II, 921
Willis, Anna Maria II, 940
Willis, Anna Maria Shoemaker
II, 940
Willis, Anna W. III, 360
Willis, Anne II, 437
Willis, Anne III, 358
Willis, Anne III, 443
Willis, Anne III, 473
Willis, Anne III, 474
Willis, Anne III, 507
Willis, Anne III, 508
Willis, Anne V, 202
Willis, Anne V, 212
Willis, Annie III, 360
Willis, Annie III, 472
Willis, Annie III, 508
Willis, Annie R. IV, 978
Willis, Arthur III, 502
Willis, Benj. H. III, 429
Willis, Benjamin H. III, 472
Willis, Beth III, 433
Willis, Betsey V, 313
Willis, Brown IV, 1242
Willis, Caroline III, 507
Willis, Caroline H. III, 507
Willis, Casandra IV, 95
Willis, Cath. M. III, 393
Willis, Catharine III, 473
Willis, Catharine III, 474
Willis, Catharine III, 507
Willis, Catharine M. III, 433
Willis, Catharine M. III, 473
Willis, Catharine M. III, 474
Willis, Catharine M. III, 492
Willis, Catharine M. III, 508
Willis, Catherine M. III, 393
Willis, Charity I, 845
Willis, Charles I, 614
Willis, Charles I, 631
Willis, Charles I, 643
Willis, Charles III, 472
Willis, Charles III, 490
Willis, Charles C. III, 472
Willis, Charles H. IV, 358
Willis, Chas. H. IV, 344
Willis, Chas. P. II, 879
Willis, Chas. P. II, 886
Willis, Chas. P. II, 940
Willis, Clara I, 936
Willis, Clara Harmon I, 951
Willis, Cora E. I, 936
Willis, Cornelia III, 358
Willis, Cornelia G. III, 358
Willis, Cornelia Grinnell III, 358
Willis, Cornell III, 417
Willis, Cornell III, 429
Willis, Cornell III, 472
Willis, Cornwell III, 472
Willis, Cornwell III, 473
Willis, Daniel III, 359
Willis, David I, 1088
Willis, David I, 1099
Willis, David I, 1124
Willis, David I, 1134
Willis, David II, 437
Willis, David II, 688
Willis, David II, 1039
Willis, David III, 473
Willis, Dinah II, 688
Willis, Edmond III, 508
Willis, Edmond P. III, 507
Willis, Edmund III, 359
Willis, Edmund III, 360
Willis, Edmund III, 450
Willis, Edmund III, 473
Willis, Edmund III, 474
Willis, Edmund III, 500
Willis, Edmund III, 501
Willis, Edmund III, 507
Willis, Edmund P. III, 473
Willis, Edmund P. III, 507
Willis, Edward III, 74
Willis, Edward III, 358
Willis, Edward III, 359
Willis, Edward III, 497
Willis, Edward III, 502
Willis, Edward III, 507
Willis, Edward Hillman VI, 791
Willis, Edward K. I, 936
Willis, Edward Mott VI, 791
Willis, Edward Mott, Jr. VI, 747
Willis, Edward Mott, Jr. VI, 763
Willis, Edward Mott, Jr. VI, 791
Willis, Elijah V, 212
Willis, Elijah V, 979
Willis, Elijah C. V, 963
Willis, Elijah C. V, 979
Willis, Eliz. III, 474
Willis, Eliz. III, 508
Willis, Eliza III, 121
Willis, Eliza III, 358
Willis, Eliza V, 650
Willis, Elizabeth I, 582
Willis, Elizabeth I, 845
Willis, Elizabeth II, 249
Willis, Elizabeth II, 252
Willis, Elizabeth II, 273
Willis, Elizabeth II, 437
Willis, Elizabeth II, 688
Willis, Elizabeth III, 327
Willis, Elizabeth III, 359
Willis, Elizabeth III, 417
Willis, Elizabeth III, 428
Willis, Elizabeth III, 429
Willis, Elizabeth III, 433
Willis, Elizabeth III, 444
Willis, Elizabeth III, 472
Willis, Elizabeth III, 473
Willis, Elizabeth III, 474
Willis, Elizabeth III, 497
Willis, Elizabeth III, 502
Willis, Elizabeth III, 507
Willis, Elizabeth C. III, 393
Willis, Elizabeth C. III, 473
Willis, Elizabeth H. III, 507
Willis, Elwood II, 827
Willis, Emaline IV, 1044
Willis, Emilie II, 886
Willis, Emilie II, 940
Willis, Emily II, 827
Willis, Emily III, 358
Willis, Emily III, 359
Willis, Emily Marian II, 940
Willis, Epenetus III, 472
Willis, Epinetus A. III, 473
Willis, Erma IV, 1227
Willis, Esther II, 75
Willis, Esther II, 111
Willis, Esther III, 16
Willis, Esther III, 358
Willis, Esther III, 359
Willis, Esther III, 473
Willis, Esther III, 474
Willis, Flora M. IV, 344
Willis, Flora M. IV, 358
Willis, Forest IV, 1227
Willis, Frances III, 359
Willis, Francis III, 359
Willis, Fry III, 443
Willis, Fry III, 473
Willis, Fry III, 474
Willis, Fry III, 507
Willis, Fry III, 508
Willis, Geo. G. V, 941
Willis, Geo. W. IV, 1343
Willis, George II, 437
Willis, George II, 688
Willis, George II, 879
Willis, George II, 940
Willis, George III, 507
Willis, George IV, 1194
Willis, George IV, 1242
Willis, George VI, 1008
Willis, George G. III, 358
Willis, George Henry III, 360
Willis, George T. III, 358
Willis, George T. III, 507
Willis, George W. IV, 1242
Willis, Grinnell III, 358
Willis, Grinnell III, 359
Willis, Hannah I, 521
Willis, Hannah I, 578
Willis, Hannah I, 582
Willis, Hannah II, 46
Willis, Hannah II, 99
Willis, Hannah II, 111
Willis, Hannah II, 437
Willis, Hannah II, 688
Willis, Hannah III, 396
Willis, Hannah III, 422
Willis, Hannah III, 435
Willis, Hannah III, 437
Willis, Hannah III, 448
Willis, Hannah III, 472
Willis, Hannah III, 473
Willis, Hannah III, 474
Willis, Hannah III, 487
Willis, Hannah III, 498
Willis, Hannah III, 500
Willis, Hannah III, 502
Willis, Hannah III, 503
Willis, Hannah III, 507
Willis, Hannah III, 508
Willis, Hannah V, 290
Willis, Hannah V, 313
Willis, Hannah V, 448
Willis, Hannah C. III, 429
Willis, Hannah C. III, 473
Willis, Hannah H. III, 358
Willis, Hannah Haydock III, 358
Willis, Hannah, Jr. I, 582
Willis, Hannah, Sr. I, 582
Willis, Hempstead III, 358
Willis, Henrietta III, 502
Willis, Henrietta III, 507
Willis, Henrietta V, 202
Willis, Henrietta V, 212
Willis, Henrietta V, 289
Willis, Henrietta V, 290
Willis, Henrietta V, 953
Willis, Henrietta V, 960
Willis, Henrietta V, 962
Willis, Henry II, 688
Willis, Henry III, 16
Willis, Henry III, 221
Willis, Henry III, 251
Willis, Henry III, 282
Willis, Henry III, 318
Willis, Henry III, 358
Willis, Henry III, 359

Willis, Henry III, 408
Willis, Henry III, 414
Willis, Henry III, 435
Willis, Henry III, 436
Willis, Henry III, 437
Willis, Henry III, 444
Willis, Henry III, 452
Willis, Henry III, 473
Willis, Henry III, 474
Willis, Henry III, 493
Willis, Henry III, 507
Willis, Henry III, 508
Willis, Henry IV, 116
Willis, Henry IV, 184
Willis, Henry IV, 304
Willis, Henry Stuart I, 936
Willis, Henry T. III, 502
Willis, Hester II, 75
Willis, Hester II, 111
Willis, Hester III, 359
Willis, Hiram I, 582
Willis, Isaac I, 1088
Willis, Isaac I, 1099
Willis, Isaac I, 1124
Willis, Isaac I, 1134
Willis, Isaac II, 111
Willis, Isaac III, 473
Willis, Isaac III, 498
Willis, Isaac III, 503
Willis, Isaac III, 507
Willis, Isaac III, 508
Willis, Isaac V, 448
Willis, Isaac V, 650
Willis, J. P. III, 474
Willis, Jacob III, 359
Willis, Jacob III, 474
Willis, Jacob B. III, 464
Willis, Jacob B. III, 473
Willis, Jacob, Jr. III, 473
Willis, James II, 827
Willis, James II, 940
Willis, James III, 358
Willis, James III, 474
Willis, James C. II, 940
Willis, James C. III, 472
Willis, Jane III, 121
Willis, Jane III, 199
Willis, Jane III, 359
Willis, Jane III, 473
Willis, Jane III, 474
Willis, Jane III, 491
Willis, Jane III, 507
Willis, Jane Ann III, 359
Willis, Jarvis Pharo II, 273
Willis, Jericho III, 358
Willis, Jesse I, 521
Willis, Jesse I, 1077
Willis, Jesse I, 1088
Willis, Jesse I, 1099
Willis, Jesse I, 1134
Willis, Jesse I, 1137
Willis, Jesse V, 313
Willis, Jesse V, 448
Willis, Jno. III, 488
Willis, Joel I, 521
Willis, Joel I, 582
Willis, Joel IV, 67
Willis, Joel IV, 116
Willis, Joel IV, 260
Willis, Joel IV, 304
Willis, Joel V, 290
Willis, Joel V, 313
Willis, Joel V, 448
Willis, John I, 1088
Willis, John I, 1099
Willis, John I, 1134
Willis, John II, 111
Willis, John II, 688
Willis, John III, 428
Willis, John III, 436
Willis, John III, 444
Willis, John III, 466
Willis, John III, 471
Willis, John III, 472
Willis, John III, 473
Willis, John III, 474
Willis, John III, 476
Willis, John III, 484
Willis, John III, 489
Willis, John III, 507
Willis, John III, 508
Willis, John Chamberlain VI, 791
Willis, John James III, 358
Willis, John P. III, 358
Willis, John P. III, 507
Willis, John R. III, 327
Willis, John R. III, 355
Willis, John R. III, 358
Willis, John R. III, 359
Willis, John S. IV, 1044
Willis, John W. V, 963
Willis, Jonathan I, 521
Willis, Jonathan I, 578
Willis, Jonathan I, 582
Willis, Jonathan II, 437
Willis, Jonathan II, 592
Willis, Jonathan II, 688
Willis, Jonathan II, 809
Willis, Jonathan II, 940
Willis, Jonathan II, 1039
Willis, Jonathan II, 1042
Willis, Jonathan V, 448
Willis, Jonathan Carmalt II, 827
Willis, Jonathan, II I, 521
Willis, Jonathan, Jr. II, 688
Willis, Jonathan, Jr. II, 1039
Willis, Jonathan, Jr. II, 1042
Willis, Jordan III, 359
Willis, Jordan III, 474
Willis, Joseph II, 688
Willis, Joseph III, 474
Willis, Joseph IV, 456
Willis, Joseph Grinnell III, 358
Willis, Joseph Grinnell III, 359
Willis, Joshua III, 359
Willis, Josiah E. II, 940
Willis, Jourdan II, 111
Willis, Jourdon II, 46
Willis, Justinian VI, 934
Willis, Katharine III, 414
Willis, Katharine III, 473
Willis, Kezia III, 474
Willis, Laetitia II, 688
Willis, Latitia II, 437
Willis, Latitia II, 592
Willis, Latitia II, 809
Willis, Latitia II, 1039
Willis, Latitia II, 1042
Willis, Latitia III, 475
Willis, Laura II, 827
Willis, Laura II, 940
Willis, Leatitia II, 1039
Willis, Leonard S. III, 473
Willis, Letitia III, 408
Willis, Letitia Ann III, 507
Willis, Levi V, 212
Willis, Levi V, 963
Willis, Lina I, 1072
Willis, Lizzie T. III, 360
Willis, Lucretia M. III, 507
Willis, Lydia I, 521
Willis, Lydia I, 578
Willis, Lydia I, 582
Willis, Lydia I, 1132
Willis, Lydia I, 1134
Willis, Lydia III, 342
Willis, Lydia III, 359
Willis, Lydia IV, 95
Willis, Lydia IV, 101
Willis, Lydia IV, 116
Willis, Lydia IV, 184
Willis, Lydia IV, 229
Willis, Lydia IV, 304
Willis, Lydia V, 290
Willis, Lydia H. IV, 260
Willis, Lydia H. IV, 304
Willis, Lydia Jenkins IV, 116
Willis, Lydia M. IV, 116
Willis, Marcy III, 359
Willis, Margaret I, 614
Willis, Margaret I, 631
Willis, Margaret I, 643
Willis, Margaret III, 359
Willis, Margaret III, 472
Willis, Margret I, 845
Willis, Maria III, 473
Willis, Maria VI, 791
Willis, Maria Phebe III, 507
Willis, Maria T. III, 360
Willis, Marian II, 827
Willis, Marjorie Mae III, 490
Willis, Marjorie Mae III, 508
Willis, Martha III, 355
Willis, Martha III, 358
Willis, Martha III, 359
Willis, Martha III, 464
Willis, Martha III, 473
Willis, Martha III, 474
Willis, Martha III, 501
Willis, Martha III, 507
Willis, Martha IV, 358
Willis, Martha F. III, 359
Willis, Martha R. III, 473
Willis, Mary I, 582
Willis, Mary I, 845
Willis, Mary I, 904
Willis, Mary I, 905
Willis, Mary I, 1088
Willis, Mary I, 1134
Willis, Mary II, 49
Willis, Mary II, 63
Willis, Mary II, 111
Willis, Mary II, 252
Willis, Mary II, 273
Willis, Mary II, 437
Willis, Mary II, 592
Willis, Mary II, 688
Willis, Mary II, 792
Willis, Mary II, 809
Willis, Mary II, 829
Willis, Mary III, 16
Willis, Mary III, 87
Willis, Mary III, 221
Willis, Mary III, 251
Willis, Mary III, 282
Willis, Mary III, 318
Willis, Mary III, 358
Willis, Mary III, 359
Willis, Mary III, 387
Willis, Mary III, 399
Willis, Mary III, 412
Willis, Mary III, 416
Willis, Mary III, 421
Willis, Mary III, 422
Willis, Mary III, 427
Willis, Mary III, 429
Willis, Mary III, 435
Willis, Mary III, 438
Willis, Mary III, 444
Willis, Mary III, 451
Willis, Mary III, 452
Willis, Mary III, 472
Willis, Mary III, 473
Willis, Mary III, 474
Willis, Mary III, 476
Willis, Mary III, 491
Willis, Mary III, 498
Willis, Mary III, 499
Willis, Mary III, 501
Willis, Mary III, 507
Willis, Mary III, 508
Willis, Mary A. II, 879
Willis, Mary A. II, 886
Willis, Mary A. II, 940
Willis, Mary Ann II, 827
Willis, Mary Ann II, 879
Willis, Mary Ann II, 940
Willis, Mary Augusta III, 359
Willis, Mary B. III, 358
Willis, Mary B. III, 359
Willis, Mary B. H. III, 358
Willis, Mary Crete VI, 747
Willis, Mary Crete VI, 791
Willis, Mary Crete Hatch VI, 763
Willis, Mary D. III, 473
Willis, Mary E. IV, 1242
Willis, Mary Esther III, 508
Willis, Mary F. III, 236
Willis, Mary F. III, 358
Willis, Mary F. III, 359
Willis, Mary F. III, 360
Willis, Mary F. III, 365
Willis, Mary F. III, 418
Willis, Mary F. III, 473
Willis, Mary F. III, 484
Willis, Mary F. III, 507
Willis, Mary H. III, 473
Willis, Mary H. III, 507
Willis, Mary Katherine VI, 791
Willis, Mary P. III, 393
Willis, Mary P. III, 473
Willis, Mary S. III, 486
Willis, Mary S. III, 507
Willis, Mary W. III, 474
Willis, Mary W. III, 484
Willis, Mary W. III, 488
Willis, Mary W. III, 489
Willis, Mary W. III, 507
Willis, Mary W. III, 508
Willis, Matilda I, 1124
Willis, Matilda I, 1134
Willis, Mercy III, 399
Willis, Mercy III, 473
Willis, Mildred V, 212
Willis, Mildred K. V, 953
Willis, Millay I, 845
Willis, Milley I, 1070
Willis, Milley I, 1072
Willis, Mordecai III, 359
Willis, Mordecai III, 399
Willis, Mordecai III, 473
Willis, Mordecai III, 474
Willis, Nancy V, 289
Willis, Nancy V, 290
Willis, Nancy V, 960
Willis, Nancy V, 962
Willis, Nathaniel P. III, 358
Willis, Newel I, 845
Willis, Obadiah S. III, 358
Willis, Oliver III, 360
Willis, Pamelia T. III, 502
Willis, Patience II, 204
Willis, Patience II, 273
Willis, Pauline III, 490
Willis, Pauline III, 507
Willis, Pauline Elizabeth IV, 1016
Willis, Peggy III, 359
Willis, Peter IV, 358
Willis, Phebe III, 66
Willis, Phebe III, 150
Willis, Phebe III, 359
Willis, Phebe III, 387
Willis, Phebe III, 408
Willis, Phebe III, 435
Willis, Phebe III, 436
Willis, Phebe III, 437
Willis, Phebe III, 438
Willis, Phebe III, 446
Willis, Phebe III, 466
Willis, Phebe III, 473
Willis, Phebe III, 474
Willis, Phebe III, 476
Willis, Phebe III, 480
Willis, Phebe III, 493
Willis, Phebe III, 499
Willis, Phebe III, 507
Willis, Phebe III, 508
Willis, Phebe E. III, 474
Willis, Phebe M. III, 358
Willis, Phebe M. III, 359
Willis, Phebe P. III, 474
Willis, Phebe W. III, 434
Willis, Priscilla III, 507
Willis, Prudence II, 90
Willis, Prudence II, 111
Willis, Rachel I, 1088
Willis, Rachel I, 1134
Willis, Rachel III, 282
Willis, Rachel III, 359
Willis, Rachel III, 432
Willis, Rachel III, 433
Willis, Rachel III, 434
Willis, Rachel III, 444
Willis, Rachel III, 472
Willis, Rachel III, 473
Willis, Rachel III, 474
Willis, Rachel III, 484
Willis, Rachel III, 492
Willis, Rachel III, 493
Willis, Rachel III, 496
Willis, Rachel III, 507
Willis, Rachel III, 508
Willis, Rachel V, 979
Willis, Rachel W. III, 419
Willis, Raymond S. IV, 1016
Willis, Rebecca III, 259
Willis, Rebecca III, 359
Willis, Rebecca A. III, 472
Willis, Richard II, 204
Willis, Richard II, 273
Willis, Richard III, 358
Willis, Richard III, 433
Willis, Richard III, 473
Willis, Richard III, 474
Willis, Richard III, 500
Willis, Richard III, 507
Willis, Richard V, 650
Willis, Richard C. III, 507
Willis, Richard J. III, 507
Willis, Richard Troth VI, 791
Willis, Richardson III, 359
Willis, Richardson C. III, 359
Willis, Richmond C. III, 359
Willis, Robert II, 273
Willis, Robert II, 688
Willis, Robert III, 359
Willis, Robert IV, 95
Willis, Robert IV, 116
Willis, Robert VI, 345
Willis, Robert S. III, 507
Willis, Rowland III, 433
Willis, Ruth III, 416
Willis, Ruth III, 474
Willis, Ruth IV, 358
Willis, Sam'l III, 393
Willis, Sam. III, 412
Willis, Samuel I, 936
Willis, Samuel II, 314
Willis, Samuel II, 437
Willis, Samuel III, 422
Willis, Samuel III, 427
Willis, Samuel III, 429
Willis, Samuel III, 432
Willis, Samuel III, 433
Willis, Samuel III, 434
Willis, Samuel III, 438
Willis, Samuel III, 470
Willis, Samuel III, 472
Willis, Samuel III, 473
Willis, Samuel III, 474
Willis, Samuel III, 476
Willis, Samuel III, 491
Willis, Samuel III, 492
Willis, Samuel III, 493
Willis, Samuel III, 496
Willis, Samuel III, 507
Willis, Samuel III, 508
Willis, Samuel C. III, 472
Willis, Samuel, Jr. III, 474
Willis, Sarah I, 845
Willis, Sarah I, 1088
Willis, Sarah I, 1099
Willis, Sarah I, 1134
Willis, Sarah II, 46
Willis, Sarah II, 111
Willis, Sarah II, 437
Willis, Sarah II, 688
Willis, Sarah III, 318
Willis, Sarah III, 359
Willis, Sarah III, 399
Willis, Sarah III, 427
Willis, Sarah III, 451
Willis, Sarah III, 452
Willis, Sarah III, 466
Willis, Sarah III, 471
Willis, Sarah III, 473
Willis, Sarah III, 474
Willis, Sarah III, 496
Willis, Sarah III, 502
Willis, Sarah III, 507
Willis, Sarah III, 508
Willis, Sarah IV, 116
Willis, Sarah VI, 959
Willis, Sarah A. III, 429
Willis, Sarah A. III, 472
Willis, Sarah J. I, 582
Willis, Sarah Leah III, 472
Willis, Sarah R. III, 359
Willis, Sarah R. III, 507
Willis, Sarah S. III, 508
Willis, Sarah S. III, 509
Willis, Sarah W. III, 359
Willis, Seth II, 360
Willis, Silas II, 46
Willis, Silas II, 111
Willis, Silas III, 249
Willis, Silas III, 260
Willis, Silas III, 359
Willis, Silas III, 432
Willis, Silas III, 438
Willis, Silas III, 466
Willis, Silas III, 473
Willis, Silas III, 474
Willis, Silas III, 508
Willis, Stephen II, 111
Willis, Stephen III, 473
Willis, Steven II, 111
Willis, Stewart I, 951
Willis, Stuart I, 951
Willis, Susan IV, 116
Willis, Susan IV, 184
Willis, Susan IV, 304
Willis, Susan IV, 1051
Willis, Susan IV, 1082
Willis, Susan Ann II, 940
Willis, Susan Ann P. II, 827
Willis, Susanna II, 437
Willis, Susanna II, 688
Willis, Tacy IV, 1120
Willis, Tacy IV, 1121
Willis, Thomas I, 1072
Willis, Thomas III, 387
Willis, Thomas III, 433
Willis, Thomas III, 446
Willis, Thomas III, 473
Willis, Thomas III, 474
Willis, Thomas III, 480
Willis, Thomas III, 499
Willis, Thomas III, 502
Willis, Thomas III, 507
Willis, Thomas III, 508
Willis, Thomas C. III, 358
Willis, Thomas Hallett III, 508
Willis, Thomas Y. II, 688
Willis, Thomas Yardley II, 437
Willis, Townsend III, 396
Willis, Townsend III, 422
Willis, Townsend III, 472
Willis, Townsend III, 474
Willis, Townsend III, 486
Willis, Townsend III, 487
Willis, Townsend III, 507
Willis, Valentine III, 490
Willis, Valentine III, 508
Willis, Valina I, 688
Willis, Valina I, 692
Willis, Virginia Alice III, 508
Willis, W. III, 359
Willis, W. III, 473
Willis, Walter III, 359
Willis, Walter Hudson II, 827
Willis, Walter Hudson II, 940
Willis, Wd. Ann III, 260
Willis, Wd. Hannah III, 472
Willis, Wd. Phebe III, 508

Westley V, 212
William I, 521
William I, 1088
William I, 1099
William I, 1134
William II, 437
William III, 121
William III, 318
William III, 358
William III, 359
William III, 408
William III, 416
William III, 435
William III, 473
William III, 474
William III, 501
William III, 507
William V, 202
William V, 212
William V, 215
William V, 289
William V, 290
William V, 945
William A. III, 360
William Alfred III, 475
William Daniel III, 475
William Henry III, 359
William Thomas III, 360
Wm. II, 49
Wm. II, 111
Wm. II, 1039
Wm. III, 302
Wm. III, 358
Wm. III, 437
Wm. III, 451
Wm. III, 473
Wm. III, 474
Wm. III, 501
Wm. III, 507
Wm. V, 650
Wm. V, 953
Wm. V, 960
Wm. V, 962
Wm. V, 963
Wm. Henry III, 342
Wm. Henry III, 359
Wm. Mott III, 358
Wm. Mott III, 360
Wm., Jr. II, 111
Wm., Jr. V, 963
Wm., Sr. V, 963
Zebulon S. III, 360
n, Anna Mae V, 720
n, Eliza V, 440
n, Ercy Earl V, 720
n, Lizzie V, 440
n, Lizzie V, 720
n, Margaret III, 360
n, Wm. V, 720
, Achsah I, 845
, Andrew P. V, 951
, Ann I, 845
, Anna V, 959
, Charity I, 845
, Elijah C. V, 962
, Elizabeth I, 845
, Henrietta V, 959
, Margret I, 845
, Mariah V, 951
, Mary I, 845
, Newel I, 845
, Rachel V, 962
, Sarah I, 845
, Wm. V, 959
on, Elisha I, 277
on, Sarah II, 437
on, Thomas II, 437
, ??? III, 360
, ??? III, 472
, Abigail I, 582
, Abigail I, 795
, Abigail I, 910
, Abigail I, 914
, Abigail III, 39
, Abigail III, 257
, Abigail III, 333
, Abigail III, 360
, Abigail III, 396
, Abigail III, 407
, Abigail III, 435
, Abigail III, 437
, Abigail III, 466
, Abigail III, 473
, Abigail III, 474
, Abigail III, 476
, Abigail III, 489
, Abigail III, 503
, Abigail III, 504
, Abigail III, 506
, Abraham III, 360
, Abraham III, 512
Willits, Achsah I, 795
Willits, Achsah I, 845
Willits, Adelaide III, 360
Willits, Adelaide O. III, 122
Willits, Adelaide O. III, 361
Willits, Albert III, 504
Willits, Alfred C. II, 775
Willits, Alice A. III, 469
Willits, Ammi IV, 115
Willits, Ammi IV, 474
Willits, Ammi IV, 504
Willits, Amos II, 272
Willits, Amos III, 408
Willits, Amos III, 414
Willits, Amos III, 450
Willits, Amos III, 466
Willits, Amos III, 467
Willits, Amos III, 468
Willits, Amos III, 470
Willits, Amos III, 471
Willits, Amos III, 504
Willits, Amos III, 505
Willits, Amos, Jr. II, 111
Willits, Amy III, 408
Willits, Amy III, 465
Willits, Amy III, 467
Willits, Amy III, 472
Willits, Ann I, 795
Willits, Ann I, 807
Willits, Ann I, 845
Willits, Ann II, 272
Willits, Ann II, 688
Willits, Ann III, 26
Willits, Ann III, 360
Willits, Ann III, 503
Willits, Ann III, 506
Willits, Ann IV, 584
Willits, Ann H. III, 454
Willits, Ann P. III, 360
Willits, Anna II, 738
Willits, Anna II, 1063
Willits, Anna III, 330
Willits, Anna III, 450
Willits, Anna III, 452
Willits, Anna III, 467
Willits, Anna III, 505
Willits, Anna K. III, 360
Willits, Anna L. II, 775
Willits, Anna W. II, 845
Willits, Anna W. II, 940
Willits, Anna W. III, 360
Willits, Anna W. III, 505
Willits, Anna W. III, 506
Willits, Anne III, 450
Willits, Anne III, 467
Willits, Annie IV, 504
Willits, Annie E. III, 505
Willits, Annie K. III, 332
Willits, Asa II, 688
Willits, Asa IV, 115
Willits, Benj. Arnold III, 469
Willits, Benjamin I, 834
Willits, Benjamin III, 360
Willits, Catharine III, 434
Willits, Catharine III, 467
Willits, Catherine III, 146
Willits, Catherine III, 360
Willits, Catherine VI, 280
Willits, Charity I, 795
Willits, Charity I, 845
Willits, Charity I, 910
Willits, Charity I, 914
Willits, Charity III, 360
Willits, Charity IV, 600
Willits, Charity IV, 1198
Willits, Charity, Jr. I, 845
Willits, Charles II, 723
Willits, Charles II, 775
Willits, Charles D. III, 505
Willits, Charles D. III, 508
Willits, Charles F. III, 447
Willits, Charlotte II, 723
Willits, Clara D. II, 723
Willits, Clara D. II, 775
Willits, Clara Dilworth II, 775
Willits, Clayton N. IV, 1227
Willits, Clement III, 413
Willits, Cynthia IV, 1193
Willits, Cynthia IV, 1227
Willits, Daniel III, 398
Willits, Daniel T. III, 467
Willits, David II, 272
Willits, David II, 723
Willits, David III, 470
Willits, David IV, 504
Willits, Deborah I, 834
Willits, Deborah III, 199
Willits, Deborah III, 360
Willits, Deborah III, 443
Willits, Deborah III, 467
Willits, Deborah III, 469
Willits, Deborah III, 470
Willits, Deborah III, 501
Willits, Deborah III, 505
Willits, Deliverance IV, 1386
Willits, Dinah III, 437
Willits, Dinah III, 471
Willits, Dorothy J. III, 447
Willits, Edith W. II, 845
Willits, Edmund II, 723
Willits, Edmund II, 775
Willits, Edmund III, 360
Willits, Edmund S. III, 358
Willits, Edmund, Jr. III, 434
Willits, Edw. S. III, 471
Willits, Edw. S. III, 472
Willits, Edward III, 443
Willits, Edward S. III, 281
Willits, Edward S. III, 360
Willits, Edward S. III, 361
Willits, Edward S. III, 465
Willits, Edward S. III, 468
Willits, Eli IV, 115
Willits, Eli IV, 328
Willits, Eli IV, 358
Willits, Eli IV, 1193
Willits, Eliakim II, 272
Willits, Elis IV, 504
Willits, Elisabeth I, 845
Willits, Eliz. III, 504
Willits, Eliz. III, 505
Willits, Eliz. III, 506
Willits, Eliza IV, 503
Willits, Eliza IV, 504
Willits, Elizabeth I, 795
Willits, Elizabeth I, 910
Willits, Elizabeth I, 912
Willits, Elizabeth I, 914
Willits, Elizabeth II, 272
Willits, Elizabeth III, 114
Willits, Elizabeth III, 360
Willits, Elizabeth III, 410
Willits, Elizabeth III, 440
Willits, Elizabeth III, 468
Willits, Elizabeth III, 488
Willits, Elizabeth III, 495
Willits, Elizabeth III, 504
Willits, Elizabeth III, 505
Willits, Elizabeth III, 506
Willits, Elizabeth IV, 115
Willits, Elizabeth IV, 358
Willits, Elizabeth IV, 391
Willits, Elizabeth IV, 454
Willits, Elizabeth IV, 494
Willits, Elizabeth IV, 503
Willits, Elizabeth IV, 504
Willits, Elizabeth IV, 1193
Willits, Elizabeth P. IV, 504
Willits, Elizabeth P. IV, 1193
Willits, Ella III, 122
Willits, Ella III, 244
Willits, Ella III, 360
Willits, Ella III, 361
Willits, Ellen IV, 1148
Willits, Ellen IV, 1193
Willits, Ellen E. II, 723
Willits, Ellis IV, 115
Willits, Ellis IV, 358
Willits, Ellis IV, 494
Willits, Ellis IV, 503
Willits, Ellis IV, 504
Willits, Ellis IV, 545
Willits, Esther II, 723
Willits, Esther III, 281
Willits, Esther III, 358
Willits, Esther III, 360
Willits, Esther III, 361
Willits, Esther III, 443
Willits, Esther III, 468
Willits, Esther III, 471
Willits, Esther III, 472
Willits, Esther V, 863
Willits, Esther Ann IV, 1227
Willits, Ezra C. IV, 115
Willits, Florence III, 401
Willits, Florence III, 421
Willits, Florence III, 486
Willits, Florence III, 505
Willits, Florence Eliz. III, 401
Willits, Florence Elizabeth III, 468
Willits, Frances H. III, 342
Willits, Franklin F. III, 505
Willits, Fred'k E. III, 360
Willits, Fred'k E. III, 506
Willits, Frederick E. III, 467
Willits, Frederick E. III, 505
Willits, Gabriel I, 795
Willits, Gabriel I, 834
Willits, Gabriel I, 845
Willits, Gabriel I, 907
Willits, Gabriel I, 910
Willits, Gabriel I, 911
Willits, Gabriel I, 914
Willits, Grace O. III, 447
Willits, Guli Ann IV, 503
Willits, Guliann IV, 504
Willits, Hannah II, 111
Willits, Hannah III, 65
Willits, Hannah III, 330
Willits, Hannah III, 360
Willits, Hannah III, 434
Willits, Hannah III, 448
Willits, Hannah III, 466
Willits, Hannah III, 468
Willits, Hannah III, 470
Willits, Hannah III, 500
Willits, Hannah III, 502
Willits, Hannah III, 504
Willits, Hannah III, 505
Willits, Hannah IV, 358
Willits, Hannah IV, 494
Willits, Hannah IV, 503
Willits, Hannah IV, 504
Willits, Hannah IV, 545
Willits, Hannah R. II, 775
Willits, Hannah R. IV, 504
Willits, Henrietta II, 723
Willits, Henrietta II, 775
Willits, Henrietta R. II, 723
Willits, Henrietta R. II, 775
Willits, Henry I, 795
Willits, Henry I, 845
Willits, Henry I, 910
Willits, Henry I, 913
Willits, Henry I, 914
Willits, Henry III, 360
Willits, Henry III, 471
Willits, Henry IV, 600
Willits, Henry T. III, 403
Willits, Henry T. III, 434
Willits, Henry Willits VI, 582
Willits, Hope III, 114
Willits, Hope III, 198
Willits, Hope III, 268
Willits, Hope III, 360
Willits, Hope III, 469
Willits, Isaac III, 413
Willits, Isaiah IV, 115
Willits, Isaiah IV, 1193
Willits, Israel IV, 115
Willits, Jacob III, 182
Willits, Jacob III, 468
Willits, Jacob III, 472
Willits, Jacob III, 488
Willits, Jacob III, 503
Willits, Jacob III, 505
Willits, Jacob III, 507
Willits, James II, 688
Willits, James II, 723
Willits, James III, 332
Willits, James III, 360
Willits, James III, 401
Willits, James III, 421
Willits, James III, 450
Willits, James III, 486
Willits, James III, 505
Willits, James Parnel II, 723
Willits, James R. III, 454
Willits, Jane III, 436
Willits, Jane III, 471
Willits, Jane III, 506
Willits, Jas. III, 452
Willits, Jemima I, 795
Willits, Jemima I, 845
Willits, Jeremiah II, 723
Willits, Jeremiah VI, 280
Willits, Jeremiah, Jr. II, 723
Willits, Jeremiah, Jr. II, 775
Willits, Jericho III, 360
Willits, Jessa IV, 115
Willits, Jesse I, 910
Willits, Jesse III, 469
Willits, Jesse IV, 86
Willits, Jesse IV, 115
Willits, Jesse IV, 504
Willits, Jesse V, 862
Willits, Jesse V, 863
Willits, Jesse VI, 280
Willits, Job III, 501
Willits, Job III, 505
Willits, Joel IV, 115
Willits, Joel IV, 474
Willits, Joel IV, 504
Willits, Joel IV, 1193
Willits, Joel IV, 1227
Willits, John II, 688
Willits, John III, 199
Willits, John III, 360
Willits, John IV, 115
Willits, John IV, 494
Willits, John IV, 503
Willits, John IV, 504
Willits, John IV, 1386
Willits, John VI, 582
Willits, John Elliott IV, 1193
Willits, John F. II, 188
Willits, John Gill II, 1063
Willits, John H. II, 845
Willits, John M. IV, 115
Willits, John M. IV, 1193
Willits, Jos. III, 472
Willits, Joseph I, 795
Willits, Joseph I, 845
Willits, Joseph I, 910
Willits, Joseph III, 360
Willits, Joseph III, 361
Willits, Joseph III, 434
Willits, Joseph III, 443
Willits, Joseph III, 469
Willits, Joseph III, 472
Willits, Joseph IV, 600
Willits, Joseph V, 289
Willits, Judith II, 114
Willits, Judith II, 125
Willits, Judith A. VI, 237
Willits, Juleann IV, 504
Willits, Katharine III, 414
Willits, Katharine III, 471
Willits, Katherine III, 469
Willits, Lamira IV, 328
Willits, Lamira IV, 358
Willits, Leah I, 834
Willits, Leah III, 360
Willits, Leah III, 409
Willits, Lee IV, 115
Willits, Lemira IV, 358
Willits, Lemira IV, 1193
Willits, Levi I, 910
Willits, Lorraine III, 469
Willits, Lucy VI, 280
Willits, Lydia III, 500
Willits, Lydia III, 506
Willits, Lydia IV, 503
Willits, Lydia IV, 504
Willits, Lydia IV, 600
Willits, Lydia Ann II, 817
Willits, Lydia S. IV, 504
Willits, Margaret I, 795
Willits, Margaret I, 845
Willits, Margaret IV, 504
Willits, Maria III, 81
Willits, Maria III, 360
Willits, Maria III, 453
Willits, Maria III, 471
Willits, Maria IV, 474
Willits, Maria IV, 504
Willits, Maria Louisa III, 512
Willits, Mark IV, 358
Willits, Mark IV, 503
Willits, Mark IV, 504
Willits, Martha II, 114
Willits, Martha II, 125
Willits, Martha III, 333
Willits, Martha III, 360
Willits, Martha III, 469
Willits, Martha III, 472
Willits, Martha III, 488
Willits, Martha III, 489
Willits, Martha III, 506
Willits, Martha III, 507
Willits, Martha VI, 280
Willits, Martha A. II, 125
Willits, Martha T. III, 430
Willits, Mary I, 795
Willits, Mary I, 813
Willits, Mary I, 845
Willits, Mary I, 913
Willits, Mary I, 914
Willits, Mary II, 252
Willits, Mary II, 272
Willits, Mary II, 688
Willits, Mary III, 114
Willits, Mary III, 129
Willits, Mary III, 182
Willits, Mary III, 238
Willits, Mary III, 268
Willits, Mary III, 360
Willits, Mary III, 361
Willits, Mary III, 403
Willits, Mary III, 404
Willits, Mary III, 414
Willits, Mary III, 437
Willits, Mary III, 439
Willits, Mary III, 440
Willits, Mary III, 443
Willits, Mary III, 444
Willits, Mary III, 467
Willits, Mary III, 468
Willits, Mary III, 470
Willits, Mary III, 471
Willits, Mary III, 493
Willits, Mary III, 506
Willits, Mary IV, 115

Willits, Mary IV, 474
Willits, Mary IV, 504
Willits, Mary V, 862
Willits, Mary VI, 280
Willits, Mary F. I, 629
Willits, Mary F. I, 643
Willits, Mary H. IV, 504
Willits, Mary Jane III, 434
Willits, Mary P. II, 305
Willits, Mary R. III, 434
Willits, Mary R. III, 488
Willits, Mary S. III, 281
Willits, Mary S. III, 360
Willits, Mary S. III, 443
Willits, Mary T. III, 430
Willits, Mary T. III, 453
Willits, Mary V. III, 505
Willits, Mercy III, 198
Willits, Mercy III, 360
Willits, Mildred Keane V, 842
Willits, Mildred Keane V, 873
Willits, Milton IV, 115
Willits, Milton IV, 504
Willits, Morton IV, 1193
Willits, Nancy III, 469
Willits, Nathan I, 795
Willits, Nathan I, 910
Willits, Nathan I, 914
Willits, Nathan II, 114
Willits, Nathan II, 125
Willits, Newel I, 795
Willits, Newel I, 845
Willits, Obadiah III, 482
Willits, Obadiah III, 488
Willits, Obadiah III, 495
Willits, Obadiah III, 502
Willits, Obadiah III, 504
Willits, Obadiah III, 505
Willits, Obadiah III, 506
Willits, Pamela III, 502
Willits, Patience III, 360
Willits, Peter III, 467
Willits, Phebe I, 834
Willits, Phebe I, 910
Willits, Phebe II, 272
Willits, Phebe II, 688
Willits, Phebe II, 723
Willits, Phebe III, 360
Willits, Phebe III, 361
Willits, Phebe III, 398
Willits, Phebe III, 409
Willits, Phebe III, 436
Willits, Phebe III, 466
Willits, Phebe III, 472
Willits, Phebe III, 476
Willits, Phebe III, 482
Willits, Phebe III, 488
Willits, Phebe III, 502
Willits, Phebe III, 504
Willits, Phebe III, 505
Willits, Phebe III, 506
Willits, Phebe III, 507
Willits, Phebe V, 862
Willits, Phebe V, 863
Willits, Phebe V, 873
Willits, Phoebe B. II, 715
Willits, Priscilla I, 795
Willits, Priscilla I, 834
Willits, Priscilla I, 845
Willits, Priscilla I, 907
Willits, Priscilla I, 910
Willits, Priscilla I, 914
Willits, Rachel III, 361
Willits, Rachel III, 436
Willits, Rachel III, 437
Willits, Rachel IV, 115
Willits, Rachel IV, 481
Willits, Rachel IV, 503
Willits, Rachel IV, 504
Willits, Rachel VI, 582
Willits, Rachel H. III, 358
Willits, Rachel H. III, 360
Willits, Rachel H. III, 472
Willits, Rebecca III, 361
Willits, Rebecca III, 466
Willits, Rebecca III, 468
Willits, Rebecca III, 470
Willits, Rebecca IV, 86
Willits, Rebecca IV, 115
Willits, Rebecca IV, 504
Willits, Rebecca M. II, 1063
Willits, Rich. III, 437
Willits, Rich. III, 443
Willits, Richard II, 111
Willits, Richard III, 39
Willits, Richard III, 65
Willits, Richard III, 129
Willits, Richard III, 257
Willits, Richard III, 330
Willits, Richard III, 333
Willits, Richard III, 342
Willits, Richard III, 360
Willits, Richard III, 396
Willits, Richard III, 403
Willits, Richard III, 430
Willits, Richard III, 435
Willits, Richard III, 436
Willits, Richard III, 444
Willits, Richard III, 448
Willits, Richard III, 453
Willits, Richard III, 466
Willits, Richard III, 468
Willits, Richard III, 469
Willits, Richard III, 470
Willits, Richard III, 471
Willits, Richard III, 473
Willits, Richard III, 476
Willits, Richard III, 489
Willits, Richard III, 502
Willits, Richard III, 506
Willits, Richard R. III, 500
Willits, Richard R. III, 504
Willits, Richard R. III, 506
Willits, Richard, Jr. III, 506
Willits, Robert III, 440
Willits, Robert III, 467
Willits, Robert III, 471
Willits, Robert III, 506
Willits, Robert P. I, 629
Willits, Robert Pitfield I, 643
Willits, Ruth I, 910
Willits, Ruth III, 463
Willits, Ruth III, 470
Willits, Ruth III, 471
Willits, Ruth IV, 115
Willits, Ruth W. III, 503
Willits, Ruth W. III, 506
Willits, Samira IV, 1193
Willits, Samuel III, 436
Willits, Samuel III, 471
Willits, Samuel III, 506
Willits, Samuel IV, 115
Willits, Samuel IV, 358
Willits, Samuel IV, 503
Willits, Samuel S. II, 114
Willits, Samuel S. II, 125
Willits, Samuel S. II, 1063
Willits, Sarah I, 795
Willits, Sarah I, 834
Willits, Sarah I, 845
Willits, Sarah I, 910
Willits, Sarah I, 914
Willits, Sarah II, 111
Willits, Sarah II, 272
Willits, Sarah II, 723
Willits, Sarah III, 81
Willits, Sarah III, 361
Willits, Sarah III, 471
Willits, Sarah III, 508
Willits, Sarah IV, 115
Willits, Sarah IV, 358
Willits, Sarah IV, 494
Willits, Sarah IV, 503
Willits, Sarah IV, 504
Willits, Sarah IV, 534
Willits, Sarah IV, 545
Willits, Sarah A. III, 471
Willits, Sarah Ann IV, 504
Willits, Sarah Ellen IV, 1227
Willits, Sarah M. III, 505
Willits, Sarah T. III, 360
Willits, Sarah V. IV, 358
Willits, Stephen III, 81
Willits, Stephen III, 453
Willits, Stephen III, 471
Willits, Susannah I, 910
Willits, Taylor IV, 115
Willits, Thomas II, 723
Willits, Thomas III, 146
Willits, Thomas III, 360
Willits, Thomas III, 409
Willits, Thomas III, 436
Willits, Thomas III, 437
Willits, Thomas III, 471
Willits, Thomas III, 506
Willits, Thos. III, 414
Willits, Timothy III, 360
Willits, Wait III, 493
Willits, Wait III, 506
Willits, Wendill P. IV, 1227
Willits, Widow Elizabeth I, 911
Willits, Widow Elizabeth I, 914
Willits, William I, 834
Willits, William III, 472
Willits, William III, 502
Willits, William III, 505
Willits, William III, 506
Willits, William III, 507
Willits, William H. III, 244
Willits, Wm. II, 723
Willits, Wm. H. III, 122
Willits, Wm. H. III, 360
Willits, Wm. H. III, 361
Willits, Zebulon III, 361
Willitt, ??? III, 360
Willitt, Abraham III, 360
Willitt, Charity III, 360
Willitt, Desiah S. IV, 1386
Willitt, John III, 360
Willitt, Judith IV, 1386
Willitt, Richard IV, 1386
Willitt, Stephen IV, 1386
Willitts, Adrian IV, 1386
Willitts, Ammi IV, 115
Willitts, Anna II, 1063
Willitts, Anna Maria II, 827
Willitts, Benjamin IV, 1386
Willitts, Deliverance IV, 1386
Willitts, Desiah S. IV, 1386
Willitts, Edith Wood II, 827
Willitts, Elizabeth IV, 1386
Willitts, Emma II, 827
Willitts, Hannah II, 827
Willitts, James II, 688
Willitts, Jane IV, 1386
Willitts, Jesse II, 827
Willitts, John IV, 1386
Willitts, John H. II, 939
Willitts, John Hutton II, 827
Willitts, Joseph I, 845
Willitts, Judith IV, 1386
Willitts, Leah III, 446
Willitts, Margaret II, 827
Willitts, Maria IV, 115
Willitts, Martha II, 180
Willitts, Mary I, 643
Willitts, Mary II, 485
Willitts, Mary II, 688
Willitts, Mary F. I, 643
Willitts, Mary Hutton II, 827
Willitts, Micajah IV, 1386
Willitts, Phebe II, 437
Willitts, Phebe II, 723
Willitts, Phebe II, 827
Willitts, Richard IV, 1386
Willitts, Robert P. I, 643
Willitts, Robert Pitfield I, 643
Willitts, Robert T. II, 180
Willitts, Ruth IV, 1386
Willitts, Samuel IV, 1386
Willitts, Samuel Leeds IV, 1386
Willitts, Sophia T. II, 180
Willitts, Stephen IV, 1386
Willlard, John VI, 816
Willlard, Richard VI, 816
Willlets, Hannah III, 462
Willmott, Henry IV, 788
Willmott, Robert R. III, 361
Willoby, Henry II, 449
Willoby, Lidia II, 449
Willoby, Robert II, 449
Willots, Elizabeth II, 252
Willots, Richard II, 252
Willotts, Elizabeth II, 272
Willotts, Richard II, 272
Willoughby, Robert C. III, 361
Willoum, Ann II, 1015
Willoum, Ann II, 1040
Willoum, Jane II, 1015
Willoum, Jane II, 1040
Wills, ??? II, 175
Wills, Aaron II, 188
Wills, Aaron II, 273
Wills, Aaron II, 274
Wills, Aaron II, 281
Wills, Aaron II, 285
Wills, Aaron II, 306
Wills, Abel II, 188
Wills, Abigail II, 300
Wills, Abigail II, 306
Wills, Abner VI, 1017
Wills, Agness VI, 1001
Wills, Albert II, 306
Wills, Alfred II, 188
Wills, Alfred II, 306
Wills, Alfred II, 314
Wills, Amy II, 273
Wills, Ann II, 171
Wills, Ann II, 188
Wills, Ann II, 207
Wills, Ann II, 272
Wills, Ann II, 273
Wills, Ann II, 274
Wills, Ann II, 285
Wills, Ann II, 295
Wills, Ann II, 306
Wills, Ann II, 437
Wills, Ann II, 527
Wills, Ann II, 688
Wills, Ann D. II, 288
Wills, Ann D. II, 306
Wills, Ann D. III, 361
Wills, Anna II, 188
Wills, Anna II, 306
Wills, Anna II, 711
Wills, Anna II, 716
Wills, Anna II, 965
Wills, Anna D. III, 166
Wills, Anna D. III, 361
Wills, Anna Deacon III, 131
Wills, Anna Dean III, 131
Wills, Anna Elizabeth II, 866
Wills, Anna Elizabeth II, 940
Wills, Anna T. II, 306
Wills, Anna T. III, 361
Wills, Asa II, 866
Wills, Asa II, 940
Wills, Asuba II, 212
Wills, Asuba II, 274
Wills, Benjamin II, 437
Wills, Benjamin D. III, 361
Wills, Betsy VI, 1017
Wills, Betty VI, 806
Wills, Beulah II, 306
Wills, Caroline S. II, 318
Wills, Caroline S. II, 326
Wills, Chalkley II, 188
Wills, Chalkley J. II, 171
Wills, Chalkley J. II, 285
Wills, Chalkley J. II, 288
Wills, Chalkley J. II, 306
Wills, Chalkley J. III, 361
Wills, Charles II, 188
Wills, Charles II, 306
Wills, Charles III, 361
Wills, Charles VI, 1017
Wills, Charles Henry II, 188
Wills, Charles T. III, 361
Wills, Clayton II, 188
Wills, Clayton N. II, 306
Wills, Creed T. VI, 862
Wills, Daniel II, 188
Wills, Daniel II, 198
Wills, Daniel II, 204
Wills, Daniel II, 216
Wills, Daniel II, 219
Wills, Daniel II, 246
Wills, Daniel II, 273
Wills, Daniel II, 274
Wills, Daniel II, 276
Wills, Daniel II, 292
Wills, Daniel II, 295
Wills, Daniel II, 300
Wills, Daniel II, 306
Wills, Daniel II, 688
Wills, Daniel II, 866
Wills, Daniel III, 361
Wills, Daniel J. II, 188
Wills, Daniel J. II, 306
Wills, Daniel J. III, 361
Wills, Daniel, Jr. II, 239
Wills, Daniel, Jr. II, 273
Wills, David II, 273
Wills, Dillwyn II, 188
Wills, Edward II, 688
Wills, Edward D. III, 361
Wills, Edwin M. VI, 1017
Wills, Elijah VI, 1017
Wills, Elisabeth II, 238
Wills, Eliz. III, 361
Wills, Eliz. R. III, 175
Wills, Elizabeth II, 168
Wills, Elizabeth II, 188
Wills, Elizabeth II, 198
Wills, Elizabeth II, 203
Wills, Elizabeth II, 222
Wills, Elizabeth II, 233
Wills, Elizabeth II, 234
Wills, Elizabeth II, 236
Wills, Elizabeth II, 273
Wills, Elizabeth II, 274
Wills, Elizabeth II, 275
Wills, Elizabeth II, 276
Wills, Elizabeth II, 306
Wills, Elizabeth II, 1039
Wills, Elizabeth III, 361
Wills, Elizabeth V, 827
Wills, Elizabeth VI, 869
Wills, Elizabeth VI, 920
Wills, Elizabeth VI, 1017
Wills, Elizabeth G. III, 361
Wills, Elizabeth H. II, 306
Wills, Elizabeth H. III, 361
Wills, Elizabeth R. II, 292
Wills, Elizabeth R. II, 306
Wills, Elizabeth R. III, 166
Wills, Elkinton II, 306
Wills, Elmer IV, 1267
Wills, Emily II, 870
Wills, Emma W. II, 287
Wills, Emma W. II, 306
Wills, Euclid VI, 806
Wills, Euclid VI, 926
Wills, Euclid VI, 1017
Wills, Frances VI, 979
Wills, George II, 273
Wills, George II, 437
Wills, George Elkinton II, 8
Wills, George J. II, 306
Wills, George J. III, 361
Wills, George W. II, 188
Wills, Grace II, 188
Wills, Grace II, 210
Wills, Grace II, 273
Wills, Grace II, 274
Wills, Hannah II, 111
Wills, Hannah II, 188
Wills, Hannah II, 210
Wills, Hannah II, 213
Wills, Hannah II, 232
Wills, Hannah II, 237
Wills, Hannah II, 270
Wills, Hannah II, 273
Wills, Hannah II, 274
Wills, Hannah II, 437
Wills, Hannah II, 688
Wills, Hannah II, 705
Wills, Hannah B. II, 188
Wills, Hannah B. II, 290
Wills, Hannah B. II, 306
Wills, Hannah C. II, 188
Wills, Hannah C. II, 300
Wills, Hannah C. II, 306
Wills, Harriet B. VI, 865
Wills, Henry II, 306
Wills, Henry W. II, 124
Wills, Henry W. II, 125
Wills, Henry W. II, 188
Wills, Henry W. II, 306
Wills, Hester II, 188
Wills, Hester II, 214
Wills, Hester II, 273
Wills, Hope II, 188
Wills, Hope II, 215
Wills, Hope II, 238
Wills, Hope II, 273
Wills, Hope II, 779
Wills, Howard II, 188
Wills, Howard H. II, 306
Wills, Hudson II, 203
Wills, Ignatious VI, 979
Wills, Ignatius VI, 1017
Wills, Jacob II, 273
Wills, James II, 111
Wills, James II, 188
Wills, James II, 273
Wills, James II, 274
Wills, James II, 276
Wills, James II, 437
Wills, James II, 688
Wills, James VI, 1017
Wills, James C. VI, 869
Wills, James, Sr. II, 437
Wills, Jane II, 219
Wills, Jane II, 273
Wills, Jane II, 437
Wills, Jarrett II, 188
Wills, Jemima II, 188
Wills, Jemima II, 216
Wills, Jemima II, 267
Wills, Jemima II, 273
Wills, Jemima II, 274
Wills, Jemima II, 306
Wills, Jemima II, 827
Wills, John II, 188
Wills, John II, 213
Wills, John II, 215
Wills, John II, 219
Wills, John II, 222
Wills, John II, 233
Wills, John II, 236
Wills, John II, 238
Wills, John II, 240
Wills, John II, 258
Wills, John II, 268
Wills, John II, 273
Wills, John II, 275
Wills, John II, 779
Wills, John VI, 69
Wills, John VI, 90
Wills, John VI, 806
Wills, John B. II, 188
Wills, John B. II, 283
Wills, John B. II, 306
Wills, John B. VI, 935
Wills, John B. VI, 1017
Wills, John Bishop II, 188
Wills, John, Jr. II, 273
Wills, Joseph II, 188
Wills, Joseph II, 265
Wills, Joseph II, 274
Wills, Joseph II, 283
Wills, Joseph II, 306
Wills, Joseph V, 827
Wills, Joseph Henry II, 188

Joseph Henry II, 306
Joseph P. II, 188
Joseph P. II, 274
Joseph Powell II, 188
Joshua II, 188
Joshua S. II, 124
Joshua S. II, 125
Joshua S. II, 306
Josiah II, 314
Justinian VI, 869
Justinian VI, 892
Justinian VI, 920
Justinian VI, 979
Justinian VI, 1017
Justinian VI, 1018
Justinian, Sr. VI, 920
Katey VI, 812
Lettice II, 273
Lettice II, 274
Lidia VI, 1017
Lizzie S. III, 361
Lucy VI, 1017
Lydia II, 188
Lydia II, 267
Lydia II, 274
Lydia D. II, 315
Lydia E. II, 188
Lydia E. II, 306
Lydia P. II, 306
Lydia S. II, 124
Lydia S. II, 125
Lydia S. II, 188
Lydia S. II, 306
Margaret II, 219
Margaret II, 225
Margaret II, 228
Margaret II, 237
Margaret II, 242
Margaret II, 273
Margaret II, 274
Margaret VI, 69
Margaret VI, 90
Margarot II, 188
Marie B. II, 285
Marie B. II, 306
Martha II, 188
Martha II, 273
Martha II, 274
Martha II, 281
Martha II, 285
Martha II, 306
Martha II, 314
Martha B. II, 314
Martha B. II, 315
Martha Emma II, 306
Martha Eyre II, 188
Martha M. III, 166
Martha M. III, 361
Mary II, 188
Mary II, 203
Mary II, 204
Mary II, 228
Mary II, 240
Mary II, 246
Mary II, 273
Mary II, 274
Mary II, 306
Mary II, 437
Mary V, 827
Mary V, 1025
Mary Ann II, 866
Mary Ann II, 940
Mary B. II, 188
Mary B. II, 285
Mary B. II, 306
Mary E. VI, 1017
Mary Ella II, 288
Mary Ella II, 306
Mary R. VI, 1017
Mercy II, 203
Meredith VI, 891
Meredith VI, 1017
Meriba II, 239
Meriba II, 273
Meriba II, 274
Meribah II, 188
Micajah R. III, 166
Micajah R. III, 361
Mildred VI, 1017
Mina A. VI, 806
Minerva VI, 921
Molly VI, 926
Moses II, 168
Moses II, 188
Moses II, 203
Moses II, 228
Moses II, 237
Moses II, 242
Moses II, 273
Moses II, 274
Moses II, 688
Wills, Nancy VI, 916
Wills, Rachael II, 203
Wills, Rachel II, 188
Wills, Rachel II, 242
Wills, Rachel II, 273
Wills, Rachel II, 274
Wills, Rachel II, 437
Wills, Rachel II, 779
Wills, Rachel A. II, 188
Wills, Rachel A. II, 265
Wills, Rachel A. II, 274
Wills, Rachel A. II, 306
Wills, Rachel Ann II, 188
Wills, Rebecca II, 188
Wills, Rebecca II, 268
Wills, Rebecca II, 273
Wills, Rebecca II, 274
Wills, Rebecca II, 276
Wills, Rebecca II, 283
Wills, Rebecca II, 306
Wills, Rebecca II, 779
Wills, Rebecca Ann II, 175
Wills, Rebecca Ann II, 290
Wills, Rebecca Ann II, 306
Wills, Rebecca P. II, 283
Wills, Rebecca P. II, 306
Wills, Rebecca Powell II, 188
Wills, Rebecca W. II, 124
Wills, Rebecca W. II, 125
Wills, Richard II, 203
Wills, Richard Albert II, 188
Wills, Robert C. II, 318
Wills, Robert C. II, 326
Wills, Ruth II, 188
Wills, Sally VI, 1017
Wills, Samuel II, 188
Wills, Samuel II, 210
Wills, Samuel II, 216
Wills, Samuel II, 267
Wills, Samuel II, 272
Wills, Samuel II, 274
Wills, Samuel II, 827
Wills, Samuel J. II, 315
Wills, Samuel, Jr. II, 273
Wills, SamuelJ. II, 306
Wills, Sarah I, 427
Wills, Sarah II, 240
Wills, Sarah II, 273
Wills, Sarah II, 274
Wills, Sarah II, 306
Wills, Sarah II, 314
Wills, Sarah VI, 979
Wills, Sarah Ann II, 316
Wills, Sarah Ann II, 326
Wills, Sarah F. II, 188
Wills, Sarah F. II, 306
Wills, Sarah S. II, 188
Wills, Sarepta II, 306
Wills, Seth II, 273
Wills, Susanna II, 188
Wills, Susanna II, 281
Wills, Susanna II, 306
Wills, Susanna W. II, 292
Wills, Susanna W. II, 306
Wills, Susannah II, 188
Wills, Susannah II, 295
Wills, Susannah II, 300
Wills, Susannah II, 306
Wills, Susannah N. II, 188
Wills, Virgin II, 188
Wills, Virgin II, 265
Wills, Virgin II, 274
Wills, Virgin II, 283
Wills, Virgin II, 306
Wills, William II, 437
Wills, William VI, 70
Wills, William VI, 881
Wills, William VI, 921
Wills, William VI, 979
Wills, William VI, 1017
Wills, William James VI, 821
Wills, William R. II, 188
Wills, Willis VI, 90
Wills, Willis VI, 1017
Wills, Winston VI, 865
Wills, Winston VI, 1017
Wills, Woodson VI, 881
Wills, Woodson VI, 1017
Wills, Zenith VI, 1017
Willsey, Ann W. V, 874
Willsford, Abraham II, 274
Willsford, Rebecca II, 230
Willson, Abigail II, 274
Willson, Abraham II, 274
Willson, Abram P. IV, 1121
Willson, Amos VI, 582
Willson, Ann I, 86
Willson, Ann Eliza V, 719
Willson, Ann Elizabeth IV, 1121
Willson, Annabella II, 802
Willson, Annabella Laing II, 816
Willson, Arthur H. IV, 1121
Willson, Benjamin I Sup 1, 3
Willson, Benjamin I Sup 1, 5
Willson, Benjamin I Sup 1, 6
Willson, Benjamin II, 274
Willson, Catharine II, 802
Willson, Christian I, 558
Willson, Christian I, 582
Willson, Christian II, 274
Willson, Christiana II, 274
Willson, David VI, 582
Willson, Dewit C. IV, 1121
Willson, Dinah VI, 928
Willson, Edward F. V, 719
Willson, Elisabeth I, 85
Willson, Elizabeth I, 68
Willson, Elizabeth IV, 1121
Willson, Elizabeth VI, 582
Willson, Elizabeth J. V, 719
Willson, Fanny VI, 982
Willson, George II, 437
Willson, George L. IV, 1121
Willson, Hannah IV, 1121
Willson, Harmon T. IV, 1121
Willson, Henry I, 1000
Willson, Hester V, 301
Willson, Hopey I, 277
Willson, Howland E. I, 583
Willson, Isaac I, 68
Willson, Isaac I, 85
Willson, Isaac IV, 1121
Willson, Jacob I Sup 1, 7
Willson, Jacob P. IV, 1121
Willson, James VI, 887
Willson, James VI, 977
Willson, James VI, 982
Willson, James VI, 1017
Willson, James A. VI, 879
Willson, James H. V, 719
Willson, Jane II, 1039
Willson, Jane VI, 582
Willson, Jeremiah V, 143
Willson, John I, 85
Willson, John I, 86
Willson, John I Sup 1, 7
Willson, John II, 437
Willson, John II, 689
Willson, John II, 823
Willson, John II, 1039
Willson, John II, 1089
Willson, John III, 361
Willson, John Bryan I, 277
Willson, John R. II, 1089
Willson, Joseph I, 62
Willson, Joseph I, 85
Willson, Joseph I, 86
Willson, Joseph I, 277
Willson, Joseph IV, 788
Willson, Joseph IV, 1121
Willson, Joseph VI, 721
Willson, Joseph G. I, 277
Willson, Joseph T. V, 942
Willson, Joshua V, 719
Willson, Judah I Sup 1, 3
Willson, Judey VI, 1017
Willson, Laura E. V, 719
Willson, Lavinia II, 1089
Willson, Lavinia A. II, 1089
Willson, Margaret III, 361
Willson, Margarett VI, 582
Willson, Martha I, 50
Willson, Martha I, 85
Willson, Martha I, 331
Willson, Martha VI, 686
Willson, Martha VI, 850
Willson, Mary I, 62
Willson, Mary I, 85
Willson, Mary I, 455
Willson, Mary VI, 525
Willson, Mary VI, 582
Willson, Mourning I, 66
Willson, Mourning I, 85
Willson, Nathan I, 86
Willson, Nathan IV, 1121
Willson, Nathaniel VI, 977
Willson, Peggy VI, 977
Willson, Rachel I, 40
Willson, Rachel I, 85
Willson, Rachel I, 87
Willson, Rachel I Sup 1, 7
Willson, Rachel II, 274
Willson, Rebecah I, 455
Willson, Rebecca II, 823
Willson, Rebecca II, 1039
Willson, Rebeckah I, 68
Willson, Rebeckah I, 85
Willson, Rebeckah II, 999
Willson, Rebeckah II, 1039
Willson, Rebeckah VI, 582
Willson, Robert I, 50
Willson, Robert I, 85
Willson, Robert I, 90
Willson, Robert I Sup 1, 5
Willson, Robert I Sup 1, 7
Willson, Robert II, 689
Willson, Robert II, 1039
Willson, Robert VI, 582
Willson, Robert A. IV, 1121
Willson, Ruth I, 583
Willson, Ruth II, 274
Willson, Ruth VI, 582
Willson, Sally A. VI, 887
Willson, Samuel I, 86
Willson, Samuel I, 277
Willson, Sarah I, 331
Willson, Sarah II, 111
Willson, Sarah II, 274
Willson, Sarah IV, 1121
Willson, Sarah VI, 582
Willson, Sarah VI, 583
Willson, Sarah VI, 686
Willson, Sarah B. IV, 1121
Willson, Silvanus I, 68
Willson, Silvanus I, 85
Willson, Stephen II, 999
Willson, Stephen II, 1039
Willson, Stephen VI, 686
Willson, Stephen VI, 722
Willson, Thomas I, 582
Willson, Thomas II, 274
Willson, Thomas II, 437
Willson, Thomas VI, 582
Willson, Thomas, Jr. II, 274
Willson, Thos. VI, 582
Willson, Viney VI, 879
Willson, Watty IV, 1386
Willson, Wd. Annabella L. II, 823
Willson, Wd. Sarah II, 1015
Willson, Wd. Sarah II, 1039
Willson, William I, 85
Willson, William II, 274
Willson, William IV, 1121
Willson, William VI, 582
Willson, Wm. IV, 1121
Willson, Wm. F. IV, 1121
Willson, Wm. Finley IV, 1121
Willward, Sarah I, 48
Willward, Sarah I, 85
Wilman, Mary IV, 1121
Wilmarth, Bettie VI, 634
Wilmarth, Bettie VI, 721
Wilmarth, Bettie VI, 738
Wilmarth, Betty VI, 634
Wilmerton, Paul II, 188
Wilmerton, Rebecca II, 188
Wilmerton, Rebecca II, 274
Wilmeth, Emily IV, 1194
Wilmeth, Henry IV, 1194
Wilmiatt, Cynthia I, 798
Wilmiatt, Cynthia I, 845
Wilmiatt, James I, 845
Wilmiatt, Mary I, 845
Wilmore, Luther IV, 1343
Wilmore, Luther G. IV, 1343
Wilmorton, Katherine II, 1007
Wilmorton, Katherine II, 1039
Wilmorton, Paul II, 992
Wilmorton, Paul II, 1007
Wilmorton, Paul II, 1039
Wilmott, Harold E. III, 361
Wilmott, Robert R. III, 361
Wilmouth, Betsy VI, 855
Wilsee, Henry V, 874
Wilsen, Margaret W. I, 86
Wilsey, George III, 361
Wilsey, George W. III, 361
Wilsey, Henry V, 874
Wilsey, Ida III, 361
Wilsey, Lydia V, 834
Wilsey, Lydia V, 874
Wilsey, Marietta III, 163
Wilsey, Marietta III, 361
Wilsey, Marietta Bellows III, 163
Wilsey, Marietta Bellows III, 361
Wilsey, William I, 905
Wilsey, Wm. III, 163
Wilsey, Wm. III, 361
Wilsferd, John II, 975
Wilsferd, John II, 1039
Wilsfird, Sarah II, 991
Wilsford, John II, 1039
Wilsford, Mary II, 1039
Wilsford, Sarah II, 1039
Wilson, ??? III, 95
Wilson, ??? III, 102
Wilson, ??? III, 113
Wilson, ??? III, 362
Wilson, ??? IV, 304
Wilson, ??? IV, 1125
Wilson, ??? V, 147
Wilson, ??? V, 965
Wilson, Aaron IV, 358
Wilson, Aaron IV, 456
Wilson, Aaron IV, 457
Wilson, Aaron V, 143
Wilson, Aaron V, 979
Wilson, Abbie I, 1163
Wilson, Abigail I, 125
Wilson, Abigail I, 737
Wilson, Abigail I, 741
Wilson, Abigail I, 769
Wilson, Abigail I, 772
Wilson, Abigail II, 265
Wilson, Abigail II, 274
Wilson, Abigail II, 437
Wilson, Abigail II, 573
Wilson, Abigail II, 604
Wilson, Abigail II, 689
Wilson, Abigail II, 828
Wilson, Abigail II, 855
Wilson, Abigail II, 941
Wilson, Abigail V, 417
Wilson, Abigail B. IV, 557
Wilson, Abraham I, 71
Wilson, Abraham I, 85
Wilson, Abraham II, 274
Wilson, Abraham IV, 289
Wilson, Abraham IV, 305
Wilson, Abraham P. IV, 1140
Wilson, Absilla I, 75
Wilson, Absilla I, 86
Wilson, Achilles II, 689
Wilson, Achilles II, 1039
Wilson, Achsah III, 361
Wilson, Ada Catharine IV, 1300
Wilson, Adaline I, 341
Wilson, Adda B. I, 671
Wilson, Adda B. I, 692
Wilson, Adline B. VI, 1018
Wilson, Agnes II, 828
Wilson, Agnes II, 1030
Wilson, Agnes II, 1039
Wilson, Agnes III, 206
Wilson, Agnes III, 240
Wilson, Agness II, 1039
Wilson, Agness VI, 865
Wilson, Agness, Jr. II, 1039
Wilson, Albert V, 213
Wilson, Alberta VI, 791
Wilson, Alex H. VI, 804
Wilson, Alexander II, 689
Wilson, Alexander II, 690
Wilson, Alexander VI, 804
Wilson, Alexander VI, 865
Wilson, Alexander M. VI, 1018
Wilson, Alfred I, 187
Wilson, Alfred I, 203
Wilson, Alfred V, 567
Wilson, Alfred V, 605
Wilson, Alice II, 922
Wilson, Alice II, 941
Wilson, Alice III, 225
Wilson, Alice III, 362
Wilson, Alicean IV, 649
Wilson, Alicean IV, 666
Wilson, Allen I, 521
Wilson, Almira V, 567
Wilson, Almira V, 605
Wilson, Alta V, 543
Wilson, Alta V, 773
Wilson, Amelia IV, 330
Wilson, Amelia IV, 358
Wilson, Amelia IV, 557
Wilson, Amelia IV, 558
Wilson, Amos I, 1059
Wilson, Amos IV, 68
Wilson, Amos IV, 344
Wilson, Amos IV, 358
Wilson, Amos IV, 460
Wilson, Amos V, 202
Wilson, Amos V, 212
Wilson, Amos V, 213
Wilson, Amos, Jr. V, 213
Wilson, Amy II, 271
Wilson, Amy II, 274
Wilson, Amy II, 767
Wilson, Amy II, 776
Wilson, Ann I, 1
Wilson, Ann I, 26
Wilson, Ann I, 86
Wilson, Ann I, 163
Wilson, Ann I, 176
Wilson, Ann I, 1059
Wilson, Ann I Sup 1, 6
Wilson, Ann II, 39
Wilson, Ann II, 40
Wilson, Ann II, 233
Wilson, Ann II, 240
Wilson, Ann II, 274
Wilson, Ann II, 437
Wilson, Ann II, 614
Wilson, Ann II, 689
Wilson, Ann II, 690

Wilson, Ann II, 828
Wilson, Ann II, 972
Wilson, Ann II, 990
Wilson, Ann II, 1017
Wilson, Ann II, 1038
Wilson, Ann II, 1039
Wilson, Ann II, 1063
Wilson, Ann IV, 180
Wilson, Ann IV, 304
Wilson, Ann IV, 305
Wilson, Ann IV, 447
Wilson, Ann IV, 457
Wilson, Ann IV, 460
Wilson, Ann IV, 504
Wilson, Ann IV, 520
Wilson, Ann IV, 558
Wilson, Ann IV, 600
Wilson, Ann IV, 818
Wilson, Ann IV, 856
Wilson, Ann IV, 1227
Wilson, Ann V, 143
Wilson, Ann V, 166
Wilson, Ann V, 208
Wilson, Ann V, 212
Wilson, Ann V, 213
Wilson, Ann V, 544
Wilson, Ann V, 942
Wilson, Ann VI, 823
Wilson, Ann VI, 865
Wilson, Ann Eliza IV, 305
Wilson, Ann Eliza IV, 387
Wilson, Ann Eliza IV, 457
Wilson, Ann Eliza IV, 557
Wilson, Ann Eliza IV, 558
Wilson, Ann Eliza V, 719
Wilson, Ann Eliza V, 720
Wilson, Ann Elizabeth IV, 457
Wilson, Ann Jane Mary I, 905
Wilson, Ann Jefferis II, 941
Wilson, Ann Jeffris II, 827
Wilson, Ann W. II, 828
Wilson, Ann W. II, 941
Wilson, Ann Walker II, 828
Wilson, Anna I, 737
Wilson, Anna II, 437
Wilson, Anna II, 573
Wilson, Anna II, 689
Wilson, Anna II, 941
Wilson, Anna III, 361
Wilson, Anna IV, 305
Wilson, Anna IV, 344
Wilson, Anna IV, 358
Wilson, Anna IV, 504
Wilson, Anna IV, 558
Wilson, Anna V, 213
Wilson, Anna V, 942
Wilson, Anna V, 1025
Wilson, Anna VI, 722
Wilson, Anna B. III, 270
Wilson, Anna D. II, 928
Wilson, Anna D. II, 941
Wilson, Anna Elizabeth III, 361
Wilson, Anna J. II, 1059
Wilson, Anna Jane I, 522
Wilson, Anna Mae V, 720
Wilson, Anna Maria II, 437
Wilson, Anna Maria II, 690
Wilson, Anna Maria II, 941
Wilson, Anna Maria IV, 305
Wilson, Anna S. II, 305
Wilson, Anna S. II, 306
Wilson, Anne II, 689
Wilson, Anne II, 1039
Wilson, Anne IV, 358
Wilson, Anne IV, 558
Wilson, Anne VI, 1017
Wilson, Anne, Jr. II, 1039
Wilson, Annie II, 818
Wilson, Annie IV, 305
Wilson, Annie Dewees II, 822
Wilson, Anslum VI, 1018
Wilson, Anthony I, 1134
Wilson, Archelaus II, 689
Wilson, Argus V, 212
Wilson, Arka D. I, 671
Wilson, Arkadelpha I, 692
Wilson, Arthur H. IV, 1140
Wilson, Arzilli V, 630
Wilson, Arzilli V, 650
Wilson, Asa IV, 305
Wilson, Asa V, 605
Wilson, Asa V, 942
Wilson, Asa VI, 1015
Wilson, Asa VI, 1017
Wilson, Asenath I, 673
Wilson, Asenath I, 692
Wilson, Azaliah IV, 1386
Wilson, B. F. VI, 280
Wilson, Benjamin I, 26
Wilson, Benjamin I, 86
Wilson, Benjamin I Sup 1, 6
Wilson, Benjamin II, 274
Wilson, Benjamin II, 690
Wilson, Benjamin II, 708
Wilson, Benjamin II, 1013
Wilson, Benjamin II, 1039
Wilson, Benjamin IV, 48
Wilson, Benjamin IV, 68
Wilson, Benjamin IV, 116
Wilson, Benjamin IV, 536
Wilson, Benjamin IV, 557
Wilson, Benjamin IV, 558
Wilson, Benjamin IV, 708
Wilson, Benjamin IV, 788
Wilson, Benjamin F. VI, 280
Wilson, Benjamin Kid IV, 68
Wilson, Benjamin S. II, 275
Wilson, Benjamin S. II, 690
Wilson, Benjamin S. II, 776
Wilson, Bertha V, 212
Wilson, Beryl Star II, 827
Wilson, Bessie I, 632
Wilson, Bessie I, 643
Wilson, Bethena IV, 408
Wilson, Bethena IV, 457
Wilson, Betsey VI, 1007
Wilson, Betsey VI, 1016
Wilson, Bettie I, 670
Wilson, Bettie H. I, 643
Wilson, Betty I, 151
Wilson, Betty I, 176
Wilson, Betty I, 1059
Wilson, Betty II, 111
Wilson, Betty IV, 68
Wilson, Betty V, 212
Wilson, Betty V, 469
Wilson, Betty V, 508
Wilson, Betty V, 543
Wilson, Betty V, 544
Wilson, Betty Woodnutt II, 111
Wilson, Beulah II, 46
Wilson, Beulah II, 100
Wilson, Beulah II, 111
Wilson, Beulah II, 139
Wilson, Beulah II, 140
Wilson, Beulah II, 177
Wilson, Beulah II, 690
Wilson, Beulah II, 749
Wilson, Beulah II, 776
Wilson, Beulah E. IV, 289
Wilson, Beulah E. IV, 305
Wilson, Bevan V, 182
Wilson, Blanch IV, 788
Wilson, Bob Draughn I, 951
Wilson, C. Victor III, 508
Wilson, Caleb I, 86
Wilson, Caleb II, 1059
Wilson, Caleb IV, 116
Wilson, Caleb IV, 1082
Wilson, Caroline I, 154
Wilson, Caroline I, 176
Wilson, Caroline III, 361
Wilson, Caroline C. IV, 305
Wilson, Caroline J. III, 222
Wilson, Caroline J. III, 361
Wilson, Caroline L. II, 941
Wilson, Caroline Laing II, 828
Wilson, Caroline Louisa II, 828
Wilson, Carrie I, 341
Wilson, Catharine I, 563
Wilson, Catharine I, 582
Wilson, Catharine II, 690
Wilson, Catharine III, 102
Wilson, Catharine III, 361
Wilson, Catharine IV, 305
Wilson, Catharine IV, 387
Wilson, Catharine IV, 449
Wilson, Catharine IV, 457
Wilson, Catharine IV, 520
Wilson, Catharine IV, 551
Wilson, Catharine IV, 557
Wilson, Catharine IV, 558
Wilson, Catharine IV, 600
Wilson, Catharine IV, 788
Wilson, Catharine VI, 457
Wilson, Catharine VI, 791
Wilson, Catharine VI, 1017
Wilson, Catharine Maria III, 362
Wilson, Catherine I, 1134
Wilson, Catherine IV, 1082
Wilson, Catherine V, 143
Wilson, Catherine VI, 457
Wilson, Catrain I, 847
Wilson, Celia VI, 833
Wilson, Champion VI, 814
Wilson, Champion VI, 974
Wilson, Champness VI, 974
Wilson, Champy VI, 955
Wilson, Charles I, 1059
Wilson, Charles II, 972
Wilson, Charles II, 1039
Wilson, Charles III, 512
Wilson, Charles IV, 305
Wilson, Charles IV, 457
Wilson, Charles IV, 558
Wilson, Charles IV, 600
Wilson, Charles V, 212
Wilson, Charles V, 213
Wilson, Charles VI, 852
Wilson, Charles H. IV, 1300
Wilson, Charles Henry III, 512
Wilson, Charles M. II, 942
Wilson, Charles S. II, 941
Wilson, Charles S. VI, 721
Wilson, Charles Waring II, 437
Wilson, Charles Waring II, 690
Wilson, Charles William Lytle VI, 457
Wilson, Charles Wm. II, 1059
Wilson, Charlotte I, 921
Wilson, Chas. V, 1025
Wilson, Chas. L. VI, 448
Wilson, Chas. M. II, 942
Wilson, Chas. M. V, 1025
Wilson, Chas. S. II, 827
Wilson, Chas. W. II, 941
Wilson, Chlorine V, 543
Wilson, Chlorine V, 605
Wilson, Christian I, 582
Wilson, Christian I, 671
Wilson, Christian I, 687
Wilson, Christian I, 692
Wilson, Christian II, 274
Wilson, Christian H. II, 942
Wilson, Christiana II, 274
Wilson, Christiana IV, 1300
Wilson, Christopher I, 14
Wilson, Christopher I, 26
Wilson, Christopher I, 86
Wilson, Christopher I, 164
Wilson, Christopher I, 176
Wilson, Christopher I, 177
Wilson, Christopher I, 187
Wilson, Christopher I, 203
Wilson, Christopher I, 1025
Wilson, Christopher I, 1056
Wilson, Christopher I, 1059
Wilson, Christopher I, 1060
Wilson, Christopher I, 1063
Wilson, Christopher IV, 68
Wilson, Christopher V, 155
Wilson, Christopher V, 159
Wilson, Christopher V, 204
Wilson, Christopher V, 212
Wilson, Cladora I, 628
Wilson, Clara IV, 788
Wilson, Clarky S. I, 1000
Wilson, Clasky I, 893
Wilson, Clasky I, 906
Wilson, Claybon V, 366
Wilson, Clyde V, 605
Wilson, Col. Joshua VI, 865
Wilson, Connell V, 707
Wilson, Connell V, 719
Wilson, Cora V, 1025
Wilson, Cornelius A. III, 222
Wilson, Cornelius A. III, 242
Wilson, Cornelius A. III, 361
Wilson, Curtis Jolife VI, 723
Wilson, Cyrus I, 737
Wilson, Cyrus IV, 304
Wilson, Cyrus IV, 305
Wilson, Cyrus IV, 358
Wilson, Cyrus IV, 457
Wilson, Cyrus C. I, 670
Wilson, Cyrus C. I, 671
Wilson, Cyrus C. I, 692
Wilson, Cyrus J. III, 270
Wilson, Cyrus J. III, 361
Wilson, Daniel IV, 143
Wilson, Daniel IV, 164
Wilson, Daniel IV, 188
Wilson, Daniel IV, 279
Wilson, Daniel IV, 305
Wilson, Daniel IV, 384
Wilson, Daniel IV, 457
Wilson, Daniel IV, 600
Wilson, Daniel IV, 1059
Wilson, Daniel IV, 1082
Wilson, Daniel V, 440
Wilson, Daniel D. V, 440
Wilson, Daniel P. V, 962
Wilson, Daniel P. VI, 722
Wilson, Daniel Pope V, 962
Wilson, Daniel Pope VI, 722
Wilson, Darcon V, 873
Wilson, Darkin II, 46
Wilson, Darkin II, 111
Wilson, Darkin V, 143
Wilson, David I, 671
Wilson, David II, 680
Wilson, David II, 689
Wilson, David II, 775
Wilson, David II, 776
Wilson, David II, 827
Wilson, David II, 922
Wilson, David II, 926
Wilson, David II, 941
Wilson, David II, 944
Wilson, David II, 1039
Wilson, David IV, 68
Wilson, David IV, 358
Wilson, David IV, 510
Wilson, David IV, 557
Wilson, David IV, 558
Wilson, David IV, 666
Wilson, David VI, 457
Wilson, David VI, 509
Wilson, David VI, 752
Wilson, David VI, 791
Wilson, David VI, 1017
Wilson, David A. I, 671
Wilson, David F. I, 582
Wilson, David F. I, 583
Wilson, David Franklin I, 521
Wilson, David H. IV, 666
Wilson, David P. V, 962
Wilson, David Pope V, 962
Wilson, David Pope VI, 722
Wilson, Deborah I, 875
Wilson, Deborah I, 905
Wilson, Deborah II, 437
Wilson, Deborah IV, 215
Wilson, Deborah IV, 305
Wilson, Deborah IV, 412
Wilson, Deborah IV, 427
Wilson, Deborah IV, 457
Wilson, Deborah IV, 528
Wilson, Deborah IV, 557
Wilson, Deborah IV, 558
Wilson, Deborah IV, 1194
Wilson, Deborah VI, 869
Wilson, Deborah VI, 958
Wilson, Deborough VI, 1017
Wilson, Demsey IV, 457
Wilson, Dewey I, 643
Wilson, Dewit C. IV, 1096
Wilson, Dewitt C. IV, 1140
Wilson, Dewitt Clinton IV, 1140
Wilson, Dicey VI, 865
Wilson, Dinah I, 1039
Wilson, Dinah I, 1053
Wilson, Dinah I, 1056
Wilson, Dinah I, 1057
Wilson, Dinah I, 1058
Wilson, Dinah I, 1059
Wilson, Dinah I, 1063
Wilson, Dinah IV, 68
Wilson, Dinah IV, 70
Wilson, Dinah IV, 856
Wilson, Dinah V, 17
Wilson, Dinah V, 198
Wilson, Dinah V, 204
Wilson, Dinah V, 212
Wilson, Dinah V, 213
Wilson, Dinah V, 214
Wilson, Dinah VI, 976
Wilson, Dinnah I, 1024
Wilson, Dora I, 670
Wilson, Dorothy III, 361
Wilson, Dr. Franklin D. VI, 280
Wilson, E. Clarkson VI, 721
Wilson, E. P. VI, 976
Wilson, E. P. VI, 995
Wilson, E. P. VI, 996
Wilson, E. Willard Janney VI, 723
Wilson, Earl IV, 788
Wilson, Earl V, 1025
Wilson, Ebenezer III, 113
Wilson, Ebenezer III, 361
Wilson, Edgar Jesse V, 213
Wilson, Edith II, 827
Wilson, Edith II, 922
Wilson, Edith II, 926
Wilson, Edith II, 941
Wilson, Edith II, 944
Wilson, Edith IV, 68
Wilson, Edith IV, 116
Wilson, Edith IV, 328
Wilson, Edith IV, 358
Wilson, Edith IV, 557
Wilson, Edith IV, 558
Wilson, Edith V, 143
Wilson, Edith V, 942
Wilson, Edith I. II, 941
Wilson, Edith J. II, 903
Wilson, Edith J. II, 941
Wilson, Edw. Clark I, 951
Wilson, Edward II, 197
Wilson, Edward II, 274
Wilson, Edward II, 437
Wilson, Edward II, 690
Wilson, Edward IV, 358
Wilson, Edward V, 719
Wilson, Edward VI, 722
Wilson, Edward B. II, 827
Wilson, Edward C. II, 942
Wilson, Edward C. VI, 787
Wilson, Edward Carroll VI, 7
Wilson, Edward Clarkson VI
Wilson, Edward Clarkson VI
Wilson, Edward F. V, 719
Wilson, Edward H. II, 941
Wilson, Edward S. V, 962
Wilson, Edward S. VI, 722
Wilson, Edward Stabler V, 96
Wilson, Edward W. II, 876
Wilson, Edward W. II, 941
Wilson, Edward Warner II, 8
Wilson, Edwin II, 827
Wilson, Edwin IV, 305
Wilson, Edwin IV, 427
Wilson, Edwin IV, 457
Wilson, Edwina Luke II, 827
Wilson, Eleanor Jane I, 674
Wilson, Eleanor Jane I, 692
Wilson, Eleanor Ruby I, 628
Wilson, Eleazar I, 737
Wilson, Eley VI, 838
Wilson, Eli I, 1059
Wilson, Eli V, 212
Wilson, Eli V, 213
Wilson, Elias E. I, 795
Wilson, Elias E. I, 905
Wilson, Elias Ely II, 723
Wilson, Elias Ely II, 776
Wilson, Elijah V, 730
Wilson, Elijah C. VI, 971
Wilson, Elijah C. VI, 1018
Wilson, Elinor Jane I, 612
Wilson, Elisabeth I, 26
Wilson, Elisabeth I, 60
Wilson, Elisabeth I, 62
Wilson, Elisabeth I, 66
Wilson, Elisabeth I, 71
Wilson, Elisabeth I, 79
Wilson, Elisabeth I, 85
Wilson, Elisabeth I, 86
Wilson, Elisabeth I, 87
Wilson, Elisabeth I, 125
Wilson, Elisabeth I, 176
Wilson, Elisabeth I, 177
Wilson, Elisabeth I, 195
Wilson, Elisabeth I, 203
Wilson, Elisabeth I, 261
Wilson, Elisabeth I, 628
Wilson, Elisha IV, 557
Wilson, Elisha IV, 1300
Wilson, Eliza I, 455
Wilson, Eliza I, 583
Wilson, Eliza I, 737
Wilson, Eliza II, 789
Wilson, Eliza II, 814
Wilson, Eliza III, 362
Wilson, Eliza III, 512
Wilson, Eliza IV, 305
Wilson, Eliza IV, 313
Wilson, Eliza IV, 315
Wilson, Eliza IV, 513
Wilson, Eliza IV, 520
Wilson, Eliza IV, 528
Wilson, Eliza IV, 557
Wilson, Eliza IV, 558
Wilson, Eliza IV, 788
Wilson, Eliza IV, 1194
Wilson, Eliza V, 383
Wilson, Eliza V, 440
Wilson, Eliza VI, 448
Wilson, Eliza VI, 1017
Wilson, Eliza A. V, 440
Wilson, Eliza Ann VI, 1018
Wilson, Eliza Ann B. VI, 217
Wilson, Eliza Jane II, 828
Wilson, Elizabeth I, 261
Wilson, Elizabeth I, 319
Wilson, Elizabeth I, 521
Wilson, Elizabeth I, 582
Wilson, Elizabeth I, 670
Wilson, Elizabeth I, 671
Wilson, Elizabeth I, 674
Wilson, Elizabeth I, 677
Wilson, Elizabeth I, 692
Wilson, Elizabeth I, 718
Wilson, Elizabeth I, 737
Wilson, Elizabeth I, 845
Wilson, Elizabeth I, 905
Wilson, Elizabeth I, 1008
Wilson, Elizabeth I, 1013
Wilson, Elizabeth I, 1059
Wilson, Elizabeth I, 1134
Wilson, Elizabeth I, 1135
Wilson, Elizabeth II, 46
Wilson, Elizabeth II, 86
Wilson, Elizabeth II, 111

on, Elizabeth II, 240
on, Elizabeth II, 275
on, Elizabeth II, 437
on, Elizabeth II, 522
on, Elizabeth II, 643
on, Elizabeth II, 659
on, Elizabeth II, 688
on, Elizabeth II, 689
on, Elizabeth II, 690
on, Elizabeth II, 807
on, Elizabeth II, 919
on, Elizabeth II, 1013
on, Elizabeth II, 1039
on, Elizabeth II, 1086
on, Elizabeth III, 231
on, Elizabeth III, 361
on, Elizabeth IV, 17
on, Elizabeth IV, 38
on, Elizabeth IV, 39
on, Elizabeth IV, 46
on, Elizabeth IV, 48
on, Elizabeth IV, 67
on, Elizabeth IV, 161
on, Elizabeth IV, 274
on, Elizabeth IV, 279
on, Elizabeth IV, 296
on, Elizabeth IV, 304
on, Elizabeth IV, 305
on, Elizabeth IV, 358
on, Elizabeth IV, 385
on, Elizabeth IV, 456
on, Elizabeth IV, 457
on, Elizabeth IV, 578
on, Elizabeth IV, 600
on, ELizabeth IV, 600
on, Elizabeth IV, 601
on, Elizabeth IV, 631
on, Elizabeth IV, 666
on, Elizabeth IV, 788
on, Elizabeth V, 143
on, Elizabeth V, 204
on, Elizabeth V, 212
on, Elizabeth V, 213
on, Elizabeth V, 313
on, Elizabeth V, 417
on, Elizabeth V, 440
on, Elizabeth V, 480
on, Elizabeth V, 675
on, Elizabeth V, 679
on, Elizabeth V, 719
on, Elizabeth V, 720
on, Elizabeth V, 942
on, Elizabeth V, 979
on, Elizabeth VI, 13
on, Elizabeth VI, 457
on, Elizabeth VI, 509
on, Elizabeth VI, 510
on, Elizabeth VI, 512
on, Elizabeth VI, 583
on, Elizabeth VI, 625
on, Elizabeth VI, 627
on, Elizabeth VI, 642
on, Elizabeth VI, 643
on, Elizabeth VI, 645
on, Elizabeth VI, 679
on, Elizabeth VI, 680
on, Elizabeth VI, 691
on, Elizabeth VI, 698
on, Elizabeth VI, 708
on, Elizabeth VI, 714
on, Elizabeth VI, 718
on, Elizabeth VI, 721
on, Elizabeth VI, 722
on, Elizabeth VI, 723
on, Elizabeth VI, 804
on, Elizabeth VI, 837
on, Elizabeth VI, 862
on, Elizabeth VI, 865
on, Elizabeth VI, 867
on, Elizabeth VI, 971
on, Elizabeth VI, 973
on, Elizabeth VI, 1016
on, Elizabeth VI, 1017
on, Elizabeth VI, 1018
on, Elizabeth A. II, 866
on, Elizabeth A. II, 919
on, Elizabeth A. II, 926
on, Elizabeth A. II, 941
on, Elizabeth A. II, 942
on, Elizabeth A. IV, 288
on, Elizabeth Agester II, 827
on, Elizabeth Ann IV, 305
on, Elizabeth Ann VI, 1018
on, Elizabeth Ann B. VI, 217
on, Elizabeth B. II, 690
on, Elizabeth B. VI, 695
on, Elizabeth B. VI, 702
on, Elizabeth B. VI, 721
on, Elizabeth B. VI, 723
on, Elizabeth C. V, 213
on, Elizabeth C. VI, 625
Wilson, Elizabeth C. VI, 643
Wilson, Elizabeth C. VI, 645
Wilson, Elizabeth C. VI, 721
Wilson, Elizabeth C. VI, 723
Wilson, Elizabeth Caroline V, 212
Wilson, Elizabeth E. II, 321
Wilson, Elizabeth E. II, 327
Wilson, Elizabeth G. IV, 601
Wilson, Elizabeth G. VI, 1017
Wilson, Elizabeth J. V, 719
Wilson, Elizabeth M. II, 941
Wilson, Elizabeth N. II, 876
Wilson, Elizabeth P. III, 79
Wilson, Elizabeth P. III, 357
Wilson, Elizabeth P. III, 361
Wilson, Elizabeth Pearson II, 776
Wilson, Elizabeth Pierson II, 776
Wilson, Elizabeth T. II, 942
Wilson, Elizabeth T. VI, 787
Wilson, Elizabeth W. VI, 787
Wilson, Elizabeth W. VI, 791
Wilson, Elizabeth W. T. VI, 791
Wilson, Ella V, 605
Wilson, Ella A. IV, 1194
Wilson, Ellanora V, 213
Wilson, Ellen I, 890
Wilson, Ellen I, 906
Wilson, Ellen III, 361
Wilson, Ellen IV, 598
Wilson, Ellen IV, 601
Wilson, Ellen V, 382
Wilson, Ellen G. II, 327
Wilson, Ellen I. I, 670
Wilson, Elmira III, 361
Wilson, Elmira IV, 478
Wilson, Elmira IV, 504
Wilson, Elsie V, 440
Wilson, Elsie V, 543
Wilson, Elviria I, 261
Wilson, Elvy I, 299
Wilson, Elvy I, 319
Wilson, Emeline II, 46
Wilson, Emeline II, 111
Wilson, Emeline II, 126
Wilson, Emeline II, 140
Wilson, Emeline II, 775
Wilson, Emeline II, 776
Wilson, Emeline V, 1025
Wilson, Emeline VI, 1017
Wilson, Emily III, 361
Wilson, Emily E. VI, 721
Wilson, Emily L. I, 678
Wilson, Emily L. I, 692
Wilson, Emily W. III, 201
Wilson, Emma V, 773
Wilson, Emma C. V, 366
Wilson, Emma S. II, 866
Wilson, Emma S. II, 941
Wilson, Emma Stratton II, 795
Wilson, Emmaline II, 125
Wilson, Emmeline II, 690
Wilson, Emmerson V, 543
Wilson, Emory Kirk V, 720
Wilson, Enamuel VI, 1007
Wilson, Enoch IV, 1300
Wilson, Enoch V, 143
Wilson, Enoch V, 942
Wilson, Enoch V, 979
Wilson, Enoch VI, 457
Wilson, Enoch VI, 791
Wilson, Enoch VI, 792
Wilson, Enos V, 151
Wilson, Enos V, 210
Wilson, Enos V, 212
Wilson, Enos V, 213
Wilson, Enos V, 474
Wilson, Enos V, 543
Wilson, Enos V, 544
Wilson, Enos B. V, 212
Wilson, Ephraim I, 125
Wilson, Ephraim II, 723
Wilson, Ephraim II, 776
Wilson, Ephraim T. I, 228
Wilson, Ephraim Trublood I, 177
Wilson, Ephraim Trueblood I, 261
Wilson, Ephriam II, 828
Wilson, Ercy Earl V, 720
Wilson, Essie V, 605
Wilson, Estella May IV, 1267
Wilson, Ester II, 437
Wilson, Esther I, 86
Wilson, Esther I, 1025
Wilson, Esther I, 1056
Wilson, Esther I, 1059
Wilson, Esther I, 1061
Wilson, Esther I, 1063
Wilson, Esther IV, 305
Wilson, Esther IV, 457
Wilson, Esther IV, 510
Wilson, Esther IV, 524
Wilson, Esther IV, 558
Wilson, Esther IV, 704
Wilson, Esther IV, 788
Wilson, Esther V, 212
Wilson, Esther V, 313
Wilson, Esther C. V, 213
Wilson, Ethan II, 690
Wilson, Eunice I, 359
Wilson, Eunice I, 671
Wilson, Eunice I, 692
Wilson, Eunice I, 845
Wilson, Eunice I, 1000
Wilson, Eunice I, 1101
Wilson, Eunice I, 1134
Wilson, Eunice I, 1135
Wilson, Eunice II, 941
Wilson, Eunice V, 720
Wilson, Eunice C. I, 846
Wilson, Euphamy V, 213
Wilson, Euphemia V, 166
Wilson, Euphemia V, 212
Wilson, Eva H. VI, 721
Wilson, Ezekiel I, 737
Wilson, Ezra V, 735
Wilson, Fannie II, 919
Wilson, Fannie A. II, 919
Wilson, Fannie A. II, 941
Wilson, Fereby I, 905
Wilson, Fletcher V, 1025
Wilson, Florence III, 122
Wilson, Florence III, 361
Wilson, Florence V, 440
Wilson, Florence Inez VI, 721
Wilson, Floy Gennetta IV, 1300
Wilson, Floyd I, 951
Wilson, Folger VI, 691
Wilson, Folger P. VI, 721
Wilson, Frances V, 687
Wilson, Frances V, 719
Wilson, Frances E. V, 182
Wilson, Frances E. V, 213
Wilson, Frances E. M. VI, 869
Wilson, Francis I, 1163
Wilson, Francis II, 437
Wilson, Francis IV, 305
Wilson, Francis IV, 457
Wilson, Francis IV, 558
Wilson, Francis Stokes II, 941
Wilson, Frank II, 828
Wilson, Frank II, 942
Wilson, Frank IV, 788
Wilson, Frank Earl IV, 788
Wilson, Franklin IV, 288
Wilson, Franklin IV, 305
Wilson, Franklin D. VI, 280
Wilson, Franklin J. II, 941
Wilson, Franklin Pope VI, 721
Wilson, Franklin S. II, 855
Wilson, Franklin S. II, 941
Wilson, Franklin Stokes II, 828
Wilson, Franklin Stokes II, 941
Wilson, Gabriel II, 437
Wilson, Gabriel IV, 116
Wilson, Gabriel V, 143
Wilson, Gabriel V, 942
Wilson, Gabril V, 143
Wilson, Georganna I, 341
Wilson, George I, 582
Wilson, George I, 1134
Wilson, George II, 46
Wilson, George II, 111
Wilson, George II, 437
Wilson, George II, 522
Wilson, George II, 553
Wilson, George II, 604
Wilson, George II, 610
Wilson, George II, 614
Wilson, George II, 629
Wilson, George II, 688
Wilson, George II, 689
Wilson, George II, 775
Wilson, George II, 776
Wilson, George II, 941
Wilson, George II, 1039
Wilson, George II, 1063
Wilson, George V, 143
Wilson, George V, 382
Wilson, George V, 979
Wilson, George VI, 6
Wilson, George VI, 13
Wilson, George VI, 40
Wilson, George VI, 217
Wilson, George VI, 983
Wilson, George VI, 1017
Wilson, George H. VI, 961
Wilson, George J. IV, 558
Wilson, George W. VI, 1018
Wilson, Gerald V, 213
Wilson, Gideon I, 1059
Wilson, Gideon V, 212
Wilson, Gideon V, 213
Wilson, Grace II, 689
Wilson, Grace V, 773
Wilson, Gulia E. I, 690
Wilson, Gulia E. I, 692
Wilson, Gulielma I, 671
Wilson, Hampton II, 1039
Wilson, Hampton II, 1063
Wilson, Hannah I, 408
Wilson, Hannah I, 429
Wilson, Hannah I, 670
Wilson, Hannah I, 680
Wilson, Hannah I, 692
Wilson, Hannah I, 1025
Wilson, Hannah I, 1056
Wilson, Hannah I, 1059
Wilson, Hannah I, 1061
Wilson, Hannah I, 1063
Wilson, Hannah II, 46
Wilson, Hannah II, 111
Wilson, Hannah II, 160
Wilson, Hannah II, 233
Wilson, Hannah II, 274
Wilson, Hannah II, 437
Wilson, Hannah II, 553
Wilson, Hannah II, 642
Wilson, Hannah II, 689
Wilson, Hannah II, 690
Wilson, Hannah II, 822
Wilson, Hannah II, 985
Wilson, Hannah II, 1039
Wilson, Hannah IV, 59
Wilson, Hannah IV, 67
Wilson, Hannah IV, 68
Wilson, Hannah IV, 164
Wilson, Hannah IV, 180
Wilson, Hannah IV, 214
Wilson, Hannah IV, 221
Wilson, Hannah IV, 274
Wilson, Hannah IV, 304
Wilson, Hannah IV, 305
Wilson, Hannah IV, 319
Wilson, Hannah IV, 336
Wilson, Hannah IV, 358
Wilson, Hannah IV, 457
Wilson, Hannah IV, 528
Wilson, Hannah IV, 557
Wilson, Hannah IV, 558
Wilson, Hannah IV, 1189
Wilson, Hannah IV, 1194
Wilson, Hannah V, 31
Wilson, Hannah V, 143
Wilson, Hannah V, 145
Wilson, Hannah V, 155
Wilson, Hannah V, 212
Wilson, Hannah V, 536
Wilson, Hannah V, 543
Wilson, Hannah V, 544
Wilson, Hannah V, 834
Wilson, Hannah V, 873
Wilson, Hannah VI, 457
Wilson, Hannah VI, 583
Wilson, Hannah VI, 691
Wilson, Hannah VI, 722
Wilson, Hannah VI, 752
Wilson, Hannah VI, 771
Wilson, Hannah VI, 791
Wilson, Hannah VI, 792
Wilson, Hannah VI, 898
Wilson, Hannah VI, 901
Wilson, Hannah B. IV, 358
Wilson, Hannah Fell II, 817
Wilson, Hannah M. III, 361
Wilson, Hannah Maria II, 776
Wilson, Hannah P. V, 942
Wilson, Hannah P. V, 952
Wilson, Hannah P. V, 962
Wilson, Hannah P. VI, 457
Wilson, Hannah P. VI, 623
Wilson, Hannah P. VI, 625
Wilson, Hannah P. VI, 721
Wilson, Hannah P. VI, 722
Wilson, Hannah P. VI, 723
Wilson, Hannah T. II, 941
Wilson, Hanson Z. III, 361
Wilson, Harold L. III, 79
Wilson, Harold Lincoln III, 361
Wilson, Harriet Ann VI, 643
Wilson, Harriet Ann VI, 721
Wilson, Harriett V, 213
Wilson, Harriett Ann VI, 723
Wilson, Hartshorne II, 828
Wilson, Hartshorne II, 941
Wilson, Hattie IV, 1267
Wilson, Hattie V, 143
Wilson, Henry I, 125
Wilson, Henry I, 319
Wilson, Henry I, 582
Wilson, Henry I, 737
Wilson, Henry I, 845
Wilson, Henry I, 875
Wilson, Henry I, 905
Wilson, Henry I, 1000
Wilson, Henry II, 689
Wilson, Henry II, 1039
Wilson, Henry II, 1043
Wilson, Henry IV, 68
Wilson, Henry IV, 116
Wilson, Henry IV, 358
Wilson, Henry V, 143
Wilson, Henry V, 290
Wilson, Henry V, 366
Wilson, Henry V, 942
Wilson, Henry B. III, 221
Wilson, Henry B. III, 361
Wilson, Henry B. VI, 721
Wilson, Henry M. IV, 1267
Wilson, Henry, Jr. II, 689
Wilson, Hepzibah III, 113
Wilson, Hepzibah III, 361
Wilson, Hester III, 95
Wilson, Hester III, 97
Wilson, Hester V, 313
Wilson, Hester M. III, 361
Wilson, Hester Maria V, 143
Wilson, Hiram I, 454
Wilson, Hiram I, 455
Wilson, Hiram I, 653
Wilson, Hiram I, 670
Wilson, Hiram I, 675
Wilson, Hiram I, 692
Wilson, Hiram A. I, 671
Wilson, Hope I, 845
Wilson, Hopey I, 277
Wilson, Hopy I, 583
Wilson, Hopy I, 795
Wilson, Hopy I, 905
Wilson, Hosey I, 74
Wilson, Howland E. I, 583
Wilson, Howland Embree I, 522
Wilson, Hubbard II, 816
Wilson, Hugh IV, 164
Wilson, Hugh IV, 358
Wilson, Hugh IV, 457
Wilson, Huldah I, 52
Wilson, Huldah I, 74
Wilson, Huldah I, 86
Wilson, Huldah I, 1059
Wilson, Huldah IV, 1300
Wilson, Huldah V, 212
Wilson, Huldah V, 213
Wilson, Ida May V, 166
Wilson, Ida May V, 212
Wilson, Idena V, 212
Wilson, Inez V, 707
Wilson, Inez V, 719
Wilson, Inez Ridgeway V, 720
Wilson, Ira III, 361
Wilson, Isaac I, 1
Wilson, Isaac I, 26
Wilson, Isaac I, 40
Wilson, Isaac I, 47
Wilson, Isaac I, 85
Wilson, Isaac I, 86
Wilson, Isaac I, 90
Wilson, Isaac I, 92
Wilson, Isaac I, 444
Wilson, Isaac I, 455
Wilson, Isaac I, 582
Wilson, Isaac I, 670
Wilson, Isaac I, 692
Wilson, Isaac I, 1059
Wilson, Isaac I Sup 1, 6
Wilson, Isaac II, 265
Wilson, Isaac II, 274
Wilson, Isaac II, 689
Wilson, Isaac II, 973
Wilson, Isaac II, 1039
Wilson, Isaac II, 1043
Wilson, Isaac II, 1063
Wilson, Isaac IV, 68
Wilson, Isaac IV, 139
Wilson, Isaac IV, 164
Wilson, Isaac IV, 319
Wilson, Isaac IV, 358
Wilson, Isaac IV, 385
Wilson, Isaac IV, 456
Wilson, Isaac IV, 457
Wilson, Isaac IV, 600
Wilson, Isaac IV, 666
Wilson, Isaac V, 166
Wilson, Isaac V, 212
Wilson, Isaac V, 313
Wilson, Isaac V, 544
Wilson, Isaac V, 942
Wilson, Isaac VI, 217
Wilson, Isaac VI, 457
Wilson, Isaac VI, 625
Wilson, Isaac VI, 690
Wilson, Isaac VI, 691
Wilson, Isaac VI, 721
Wilson, Isaac VI, 722
Wilson, Isaac VI, 723

Wilson, Isaac VI, 791
Wilson, Isaac VI, 865
Wilson, Isaac B. V, 942
Wilson, Isaac Blackfan V, 942
Wilson, Isaac J. IV, 1194
Wilson, Isaac, Jr. I, 86
Wilson, Isaac, Jr. IV, 164
Wilson, Isaac, Jr. IV, 358
Wilson, Isaac, Jr. IV, 457
Wilson, Isabel I, 261
Wilson, Isabel IV, 1044
Wilson, Isabella I, 20
Wilson, Isabella I, 77
Wilson, Isabella I, 86
Wilson, Isabella I, 139
Wilson, Isabella I, 176
Wilson, Isabella I, 177
Wilson, Isabella I, 331
Wilson, Isabella I, 626
Wilson, Isabella I, 628
Wilson, Isabella V, 541
Wilson, Isabella V, 543
Wilson, Isabella VI, 217
Wilson, Isabelle I, 176
Wilson, Isabelle I, 177
Wilson, Isaiah IV, 116
Wilson, Isaiah IV, 856
Wilson, Isbel I, 125
Wilson, Isbel I, 177
Wilson, Isbel I, 228
Wilson, Israel IV, 24
Wilson, Israel IV, 67
Wilson, Israel IV, 68
Wilson, Israel IV, 167
Wilson, Israel IV, 180
Wilson, Israel IV, 304
Wilson, Israel IV, 305
Wilson, Israel IV, 328
Wilson, Israel IV, 358
Wilson, Israel IV, 387
Wilson, Israel IV, 449
Wilson, Israel IV, 457
Wilson, Israel IV, 507
Wilson, Israel IV, 520
Wilson, Israel IV, 551
Wilson, Israel IV, 557
Wilson, Israel IV, 558
Wilson, Israel IV, 627
Wilson, Israel IV, 788
Wilson, Israel V, 143
Wilson, Israel V, 942
Wilson, Israel V, 979
Wilson, Israel I. IV, 457
Wilson, Israel J. IV, 457
Wilson, Israel J. IV, 557
Wilson, Israel T. IV, 305
Wilson, Israel, Jr. IV, 305
Wilson, Israel, Jr. IV, 557
Wilson, Israel, Jr. IV, 558
Wilson, Isral VI, 457
Wilson, J. Clark I, 643
Wilson, J. Clarkson I, 670
Wilson, J. Floyd I, 670
Wilson, J. Frank II, 919
Wilson, J. Frank II, 941
Wilson, J. Franklin II, 941
Wilson, J. H. V, 366
Wilson, J. W. V, 1025
Wilson, Jabez I, 692
Wilson, Jacob I, 26
Wilson, Jacob I, 70
Wilson, Jacob I, 85
Wilson, Jacob I, 86
Wilson, Jacob I, 193
Wilson, Jacob I, 202
Wilson, Jacob I, 233
Wilson, Jacob I, 261
Wilson, Jacob I, 845
Wilson, Jacob II, 689
Wilson, Jacob II, 828
Wilson, James I, 86
Wilson, James I, 582
Wilson, James I, 1059
Wilson, James II, 46
Wilson, James II, 100
Wilson, James II, 111
Wilson, James II, 125
Wilson, James II, 140
Wilson, James II, 274
Wilson, James II, 437
Wilson, James II, 450
Wilson, James II, 644
Wilson, James II, 689
Wilson, James II, 690
Wilson, James II, 776
Wilson, James II, 779
Wilson, James II, 810
Wilson, James II, 828
Wilson, James II, 941
Wilson, James II, 1039
Wilson, James III, 361
Wilson, James III, 362
Wilson, James IV, 305
Wilson, James IV, 457
Wilson, James IV, 666
Wilson, James V, 143
Wilson, James V, 204
Wilson, James V, 212
Wilson, James V, 213
Wilson, James V, 650
Wilson, James V, 942
Wilson, James VI, 143
Wilson, James VI, 217
Wilson, James VI, 280
Wilson, James VI, 791
Wilson, James VI, 796
Wilson, James VI, 798
Wilson, James VI, 828
Wilson, James VI, 854
Wilson, James VI, 901
Wilson, James VI, 906
Wilson, James VI, 961
Wilson, James VI, 973
Wilson, James VI, 987
Wilson, James VI, 1014
Wilson, James VI, 1016
Wilson, James VI, 1017
Wilson, James A. VI, 879
Wilson, James C. V, 213
Wilson, James Clark III, 361
Wilson, James H. V, 366
Wilson, James H. V, 719
Wilson, James Jefferis II, 941
Wilson, James K. IV, 305
Wilson, James M. I, 845
Wilson, James M. I, 906
Wilson, James M. VI, 1017
Wilson, James Pope VI, 722
Wilson, James R. II, 275
Wilson, James R. II, 767
Wilson, James R. II, 775
Wilson, James R. II, 776
Wilson, James S. II, 941
Wilson, James Smith II, 160
Wilson, James W. I, 845
Wilson, James W. I, 846
Wilson, James W. V, 942
Wilson, James W. VI, 1017
Wilson, Jane I, 583
Wilson, Jane I, 670
Wilson, Jane I, 691
Wilson, Jane I, 692
Wilson, Jane I, 845
Wilson, Jane I, 905
Wilson, Jane I, 925
Wilson, Jane II, 46
Wilson, Jane II, 111
Wilson, Jane II, 437
Wilson, Jane II, 621
Wilson, Jane II, 689
Wilson, Jane II, 975
Wilson, Jane II, 1039
Wilson, Jane II, 1063
Wilson, Jane III, 303
Wilson, Jane IV, 304
Wilson, Jane IV, 305
Wilson, Jane IV, 312
Wilson, Jane IV, 315
Wilson, Jane IV, 457
Wilson, Jane IV, 557
Wilson, Jane V, 143
Wilson, Jane V, 719
Wilson, Jane V, 838
Wilson, Jane V, 873
Wilson, Jane VI, 371
Wilson, Jane VI, 435
Wilson, Jane VI, 457
Wilson, Jane VI, 578
Wilson, Jane VI, 583
Wilson, Jane VI, 734
Wilson, Jane VI, 752
Wilson, Jane VI, 791
Wilson, Jane VI, 865
Wilson, Jane C. I, 676
Wilson, Jane C. I, 692
Wilson, Jane Elwood V, 720
Wilson, Jane H. II, 942
Wilson, Jas. IV, 557
Wilson, Jeain II, 111
Wilson, Jean I, 582
Wilson, Jeanette V, 213
Wilson, Jefferies II, 776
Wilson, Jefferis II, 775
Wilson, Jefferis II, 776
Wilson, Jefferis II, 941
Wilson, Jehu I, 1025
Wilson, Jehu I, 1059
Wilson, Jehu I, 1061
Wilson, Jehu I, 1063
Wilson, Jehu II, 822
Wilson, Jehu II, 828
Wilson, Jehu II, 941
Wilson, Jehu IV, 68
Wilson, Jehu V, 17
Wilson, Jehu V, 212
Wilson, Jehu V, 213
Wilson, Jehu V, 469
Wilson, Jennie V, 213
Wilson, Jennie M. V, 213
Wilson, Jennie Maria V, 212
Wilson, Jeremiah I, 692
Wilson, Jeremiah IV, 68
Wilson, Jeremiah IV, 116
Wilson, Jeremiah V, 143
Wilson, Jeremiah V, 941
Wilson, Jeremiah V, 942
Wilson, Jeremiah, Sr. V, 942
Wilson, Jesse I, 26
Wilson, Jesse I, 86
Wilson, Jesse I, 92
Wilson, Jesse I, 176
Wilson, Jesse I, 203
Wilson, Jesse I, 444
Wilson, Jesse I, 455
Wilson, Jesse I, 628
Wilson, Jesse I, 670
Wilson, Jesse I, 671
Wilson, Jesse I, 674
Wilson, Jesse I, 692
Wilson, Jesse I, 737
Wilson, Jesse II, 46
Wilson, Jesse II, 86
Wilson, Jesse II, 111
Wilson, Jesse II, 274
Wilson, Jesse II, 437
Wilson, Jesse II, 680
Wilson, Jesse II, 689
Wilson, Jesse III, 122
Wilson, Jesse III, 361
Wilson, Jesse V, 143
Wilson, Jesse V, 480
Wilson, Jesse V, 979
Wilson, Jesse VI, 702
Wilson, Jesse VI, 721
Wilson, Jesse VI, 722
Wilson, Jesse Clarkson I, 628
Wilson, Jesse F. I, 670
Wilson, Jesse Lois I, 628
Wilson, Jesse M. I, 583
Wilson, Jesse Milton I, 522
Wilson, Jesse S. III, 361
Wilson, Jesse S. VI, 708
Wilson, Jesse S. VI, 721
Wilson, Jesse S. VI, 723
Wilson, Jesse S. VI, 791
Wilson, Jessey VI, 878
Wilson, Jessie Louise I, 643
Wilson, Jethro I, 671
Wilson, Jethro I, 737
Wilson, Jethro I, 845
Wilson, Jethro I, 1134
Wilson, Jethro I, 1135
Wilson, Joanna IV, 68
Wilson, Joanna IV, 116
Wilson, Joanna V, 143
Wilson, Joanna V, 941
Wilson, John I, 26
Wilson, John I, 59
Wilson, John I, 85
Wilson, John I, 86
Wilson, John I, 125
Wilson, John I, 154
Wilson, John I, 170
Wilson, John I, 176
Wilson, John I, 177
Wilson, John I, 187
Wilson, John I, 203
Wilson, John I, 228
Wilson, John I, 261
Wilson, John I, 277
Wilson, John I, 359
Wilson, John I, 521
Wilson, John I, 522
Wilson, John I, 582
Wilson, John I, 583
Wilson, John I, 600
Wilson, John I, 671
Wilson, John I, 737
Wilson, John I, 845
Wilson, John I, 1024
Wilson, John I, 1025
Wilson, John I, 1039
Wilson, John I, 1056
Wilson, John I, 1057
Wilson, John I, 1058
Wilson, John I, 1059
Wilson, John I, 1063
Wilson, John I, 1134
Wilson, John II, 46
Wilson, John II, 111
Wilson, John II, 188
Wilson, John II, 240
Wilson, John II, 251
Wilson, John II, 274
Wilson, John II, 437
Wilson, John II, 688
Wilson, John II, 689
Wilson, John II, 690
Wilson, John II, 776
Wilson, John II, 807
Wilson, John II, 941
Wilson, John II, 975
Wilson, John II, 1039
Wilson, John III, 361
Wilson, John IV, 68
Wilson, John IV, 116
Wilson, John IV, 305
Wilson, John IV, 330
Wilson, John IV, 358
Wilson, John IV, 557
Wilson, John IV, 558
Wilson, John IV, 1044
Wilson, John V, 143
Wilson, John V, 212
Wilson, John V, 213
Wilson, John V, 313
Wilson, John V, 467
Wilson, John V, 719
Wilson, John V, 720
Wilson, John V, 873
Wilson, John V, 1025
Wilson, John VI, 357
Wilson, John VI, 791
Wilson, John VI, 804
Wilson, John VI, 812
Wilson, John VI, 814
Wilson, John VI, 837
Wilson, John VI, 838
Wilson, John VI, 855
Wilson, John VI, 862
Wilson, John VI, 865
Wilson, John VI, 867
Wilson, John VI, 877
Wilson, John VI, 941
Wilson, John VI, 976
Wilson, John VI, 1017
Wilson, John VI, 1018
Wilson, John B. I, 845
Wilson, John B. I, 905
Wilson, John B. II, 437
Wilson, John B. II, 690
Wilson, John B. II, 776
Wilson, John B. II, 828
Wilson, John B. II, 886
Wilson, John B. II, 941
Wilson, John Bailey II, 689
Wilson, John Brion I, 582
Wilson, John Bryan I, 277
Wilson, John Bryan I, 795
Wilson, John Bryant I, 905
Wilson, John C. I, 737
Wilson, John C. II, 776
Wilson, John C. III, 361
Wilson, John C. IV, 558
Wilson, John C. V, 440
Wilson, John C. V, 719
Wilson, John Calvin I, 521
Wilson, John Calvin I, 522
Wilson, John Cyrus III, 361
Wilson, John French IV, 558
Wilson, John French IV, 788
Wilson, John Hirst IV, 558
Wilson, John Howell V, 962
Wilson, John I. II, 827
Wilson, John Iredel II, 723
Wilson, John J. VI, 1018
Wilson, John L. IV, 305
Wilson, John M. I, 737
Wilson, John Mc VI, 721
Wilson, John N. VI, 869
Wilson, John Pierson II, 690
Wilson, John R. II, 1086
Wilson, John R. II, 1087
Wilson, John R. II, 1089
Wilson, John R. VI, 1017
Wilson, John R. VI, 1018
Wilson, John S. VI, 980
Wilson, John S. VI, 1017
Wilson, John W. III, 361
Wilson, John W. IV, 305
Wilson, John Warden VI, 457
Wilson, John Warder VI, 457
Wilson, John Warder VI, 791
Wilson, John Webster II, 828
Wilson, John Webster IV, 666
Wilson, John Wilson I, 81
Wilson, John, Jr. I, 582
Wilson, John, Jr. VI, 804
Wilson, John, Sr. I, 1059
Wilson, Jonathan I, 52
Wilson, Jonathan I, 86
Wilson, Jonathan I, 671
Wilson, Jonathan II, 690
Wilson, Jonathan II, 972
Wilson, Jonathan II, 1017
Wilson, Jonathan II, 1039
Wilson, Jonathan IV, 59
Wilson, Jonathan IV, 67
Wilson, Jonathan IV, 68
Wilson, Jonathan IV, 137
Wilson, Jonathan IV, 180
Wilson, Jonathan IV, 221
Wilson, Jonathan IV, 234
Wilson, Jonathan IV, 255
Wilson, Jonathan IV, 274
Wilson, Jonathan IV, 304
Wilson, Jonathan IV, 305
Wilson, Jonathan IV, 358
Wilson, Jonathan IV, 557
Wilson, Jonathan William VI, 457
Wilson, Joseph I, 42
Wilson, Joseph I, 85
Wilson, Joseph I, 86
Wilson, Joseph I, 125
Wilson, Joseph I, 127
Wilson, Joseph I, 135
Wilson, Joseph I, 176
Wilson, Joseph I, 177
Wilson, Joseph I, 277
Wilson, Joseph I, 563
Wilson, Joseph I, 582
Wilson, Joseph I, 583
Wilson, Joseph I, 671
Wilson, Joseph I, 706
Wilson, Joseph I, 737
Wilson, Joseph I, 772
Wilson, Joseph I, 845
Wilson, Joseph I, 847
Wilson, Joseph I, 905
Wilson, Joseph I, 1134
Wilson, Joseph I Sup 1, 10
Wilson, Joseph II, 46
Wilson, Joseph II, 111
Wilson, Joseph II, 139
Wilson, Joseph II, 140
Wilson, Joseph II, 437
Wilson, Joseph II, 493
Wilson, Joseph II, 689
Wilson, Joseph II, 690
Wilson, Joseph II, 789
Wilson, Joseph II, 972
Wilson, Joseph II, 1039
Wilson, Joseph IV, 68
Wilson, Joseph IV, 305
Wilson, Joseph IV, 456
Wilson, Joseph IV, 457
Wilson, Joseph IV, 513
Wilson, Joseph IV, 528
Wilson, Joseph IV, 557
Wilson, Joseph IV, 600
Wilson, Joseph IV, 788
Wilson, Joseph IV, 1189
Wilson, Joseph IV, 1194
Wilson, Joseph V, 143
Wilson, Joseph V, 313
Wilson, Joseph V, 417
Wilson, Joseph V, 536
Wilson, Joseph V, 543
Wilson, Joseph V, 544
Wilson, Joseph V, 1025
Wilson, Joseph VI, 129
Wilson, Joseph VI, 143
Wilson, Joseph VI, 583
Wilson, Joseph VI, 721
Wilson, Joseph VI, 803
Wilson, Joseph VI, 814
Wilson, Joseph VI, 824
Wilson, Joseph VI, 826
Wilson, Joseph VI, 837
Wilson, Joseph VI, 851
Wilson, Joseph VI, 852
Wilson, Joseph VI, 859
Wilson, Joseph VI, 958
Wilson, Joseph VI, 983
Wilson, Joseph VI, 1007
Wilson, Joseph VI, 1017
Wilson, Joseph A. Branson I,
Wilson, Joseph D. IV, 457
Wilson, Joseph D. IV, 557
Wilson, Joseph E. V, 962
Wilson, Joseph E. VI, 722
Wilson, Joseph Eby VI, 722
Wilson, Joseph Ely V, 962
Wilson, Joseph F. II, 866
Wilson, Joseph F. II, 926
Wilson, Joseph F. II, 941
Wilson, Joseph Franklin II, 8
Wilson, Joseph G. I, 277
Wilson, Joseph G. I, 583
Wilson, Joseph G. I, 795
Wilson, Joseph G. I, 845
Wilson, Joseph G. I, 905
Wilson, Joseph G. I, 906
Wilson, Joseph G. IV, 305

on, Joseph G. IV, 558
on, Joseph H. II, 100
on, Joseph H. II, 111
on, Joseph H. II, 177
on, Joseph H. II, 690
on, Joseph H. II, 749
on, Joseph H. II, 776
on, Joseph Hinchman II, 689
on, Joseph Hinchman II, 690
on, Joseph John II, 776
on, Joseph T. V, 942
on, Joseph Taylor V, 942
on, Joshua V, 212
on, Joshua V, 213
on, Joshua V, 719
on, Joshua V, 720
on, Joshua B. IV, 358
on, Josiah II, 437
on, Josiah II, 690
on, Josie V, 212
on, Judah I Sup 1, 6
on, Judey VI, 1017
on, Judith VI, 1017
on, Julianah I, 46
on, Julianah I, 86
on, Julianna VI, 791
on, Julius H. II, 941
on, Julius Howard II, 828
on, Katharine VI, 457
on, Katherine V, 543
on, Kermit IV, 788
on, Kesiah I, 86
on, Kezia I, 57
on, Kezia I, 66
on, Kezia I, 86
on, Kezia II, 690
on, Laura I, 737
on, Laura V, 719
on, Laura V, 720
on, Laura V, 1025
on, Laura C. IV, 358
on, Laura E. V, 719
on, Laura E. V, 962
on, Lavinia II, 1086
on, Lavinia II, 1087
on, Lawrence Pope VI, 723
on, Lawson VI, 971
on, Lelah V, 213
on, Lemuel IV, 305
on, Letitia II, 1039
on, Levi IV, 305
on, Levi F. IV, 457
on, Levi F. IV, 558
on, Levi Fawcett IV, 558
on, Levis III, 475
on, Liddia I, 127
on, Liddia I, 176
on, Liddia II, 999
on, Linda Alice II, 941
on, Lindley IV, 557
on, Lindsey I, 737
on, Lindsey I, 925
on, Lizzie IV, 305
on, Lizzie IV, 1044
on, Lizzie V, 440
on, Lizzie V, 720
on, Lizzie Lukens II, 827
on, Lockey Ann VI, 888
on, Louella V, 213
on, Louisa II, 46
on, Louisa II, 139
on, Louisa II, 140
on, Louisa II, 157
on, Louisa II, 160
on, Louisa III, 113
on, Louisa III, 361
on, Louisa IV, 584
on, Louisa IV, 600
on, Louisa V, 440
on, Louisa Emily I, 670
on, Louisa Jane VI, 721
on, Louisa Richards II, 827
on, Louise Emily I, 653
on, Louissa II, 125
on, Lucretia II, 828
on, Lucretia Crispin II, 789
on, Lucy V, 885
on, Lucy VI, 826
on, Lucy VI, 865
on, Lucy T. IV, 305
on, Lucy W. IV, 288
on, Lucy W. IV, 305
on, Lyda I, 176
on, Lydda I, 125
on, Lyddia I, 48
on, Lyddia I, 86
on, Lyddia II, 1039
on, Lydia I, 24
on, Lydia I, 25
on, Lydia I, 71
on, Lydia I, 82
Wilson, Lydia I, 85
Wilson, Lydia I, 86
Wilson, Lydia I, 87
Wilson, Lydia I, 177
Wilson, Lydia I, 228
Wilson, Lydia I, 261
Wilson, Lydia I, 418
Wilson, Lydia I, 429
Wilson, Lydia I, 670
Wilson, Lydia I, 671
Wilson, Lydia I, 682
Wilson, Lydia I, 692
Wilson, Lydia I, 772
Wilson, Lydia I, 932
Wilson, Lydia I, 935
Wilson, Lydia I, 936
Wilson, Lydia I, 1008
Wilson, Lydia I, 1013
Wilson, Lydia II, 689
Wilson, Lydia II, 1022
Wilson, Lydia II, 1039
Wilson, Lydia IV, 645
Wilson, Lydia IV, 666
Wilson, Lydia IV, 1386
Wilson, Lydia V, 212
Wilson, Lydia V, 213
Wilson, Lydia V, 925
Wilson, Lydia V, 942
Wilson, Lydia VI, 457
Wilson, Lydia VI, 723
Wilson, Lydia VI, 1017
Wilson, Lydia Ellen V, 202
Wilson, Lydia Ellen V, 212
Wilson, Lydia Folger V, 941
Wilson, Lydia L. V, 952
Wilson, Lydia L. V, 962
Wilson, Lydia L. VI, 722
Wilson, Lydia Lovegrove V, 962
Wilson, Lydia Lovegrove VI, 722
Wilson, Lydia N. VI, 642
Wilson, Lydia N. VI, 644
Wilson, Lydia N. VI, 682
Wilson, Lydia N. VI, 722
Wilson, Lydia Pusey II, 790
Wilson, Lynah P. VI, 798
Wilson, Lyndon Floyd I, 951
Wilson, Mabel II, 708
Wilson, Mabel B. IV, 412
Wilson, Mabel B. IV, 457
Wilson, Mabel B. IV, 536
Wilson, Mabel B. IV, 558
Wilson, Mabel F. IV, 1267
Wilson, Mable V. VI, 82
Wilson, Mable V. VI, 90
Wilson, Mack V, 1025
Wilson, Macy IV, 1300
Wilson, Madge V, 543
Wilson, Madge V, 605
Wilson, Mahala VI, 958
Wilson, Mardon II, 828
Wilson, Mardon II, 941
Wilson, Mardon, Jr. II, 941
Wilson, Margaret I, 81
Wilson, Margaret I, 86
Wilson, Margaret I, 125
Wilson, Margaret I, 187
Wilson, Margaret I, 195
Wilson, Margaret I, 202
Wilson, Margaret I, 203
Wilson, Margaret I, 1134
Wilson, Margaret II, 251
Wilson, Margaret II, 274
Wilson, Margaret II, 767
Wilson, Margaret II, 776
Wilson, Margaret II, 786
Wilson, Margaret II, 827
Wilson, Margaret II, 967
Wilson, Margaret II, 1059
Wilson, Margaret III, 361
Wilson, Margaret IV, 47
Wilson, Margaret IV, 67
Wilson, Margaret IV, 134
Wilson, Margaret IV, 305
Wilson, Margaret IV, 346
Wilson, Margaret IV, 351
Wilson, Margaret IV, 356
Wilson, Margaret IV, 358
Wilson, Margaret IV, 457
Wilson, Margaret IV, 1082
Wilson, Margaret IV, 1140
Wilson, Margaret IV, 1386
Wilson, Margaret Ann IV, 1044
Wilson, Margaret D. IV, 253
Wilson, Margaret D. IV, 305
Wilson, Margaret D. IV, 457
Wilson, Margaret J. II, 1059
Wilson, Margaret J. II, 1063
Wilson, Margaret S. II, 776
Wilson, Margaret S. II, 972
Wilson, Margaret W. I, 86
Wilson, Margaret W. I, 203
Wilson, Margaret W. IV, 305
Wilson, Margaret Winslow I, 86
Wilson, Margarett II, 1039
Wilson, Maria III, 361
Wilson, Maria IV, 221
Wilson, Maria IV, 305
Wilson, Maria IV, 519
Wilson, Maria IV, 530
Wilson, Maria IV, 557
Wilson, Maria IV, 558
Wilson, Maria IV, 618
Wilson, Maria IV, 666
Wilson, Mariah IV, 180
Wilson, Mariah IV, 305
Wilson, Mariah W. VI, 961
Wilson, Mariam I, 319
Wilson, Mariam I, 730
Wilson, Mariam I, 737
Wilson, Mariam I, 905
Wilson, Marie V, 543
Wilson, Marion V, 543
Wilson, Marion V, 605
Wilson, Martha I, 59
Wilson, Martha I, 85
Wilson, Martha I, 176
Wilson, Martha I, 200
Wilson, Martha I, 203
Wilson, Martha I, 331
Wilson, Martha I, 628
Wilson, Martha I, 692
Wilson, Martha I, 1059
Wilson, Martha II, 689
Wilson, Martha II, 1039
Wilson, Martha IV, 24
Wilson, Martha IV, 48
Wilson, Martha IV, 67
Wilson, Martha IV, 68
Wilson, Martha IV, 116
Wilson, Martha IV, 139
Wilson, Martha IV, 164
Wilson, Martha IV, 279
Wilson, Martha IV, 304
Wilson, Martha IV, 305
Wilson, Martha IV, 328
Wilson, Martha IV, 358
Wilson, Martha IV, 442
Wilson, Martha IV, 456
Wilson, Martha IV, 457
Wilson, Martha IV, 528
Wilson, Martha IV, 551
Wilson, Martha IV, 557
Wilson, Martha IV, 558
Wilson, Martha IV, 594
Wilson, Martha IV, 627
Wilson, Martha IV, 1059
Wilson, Martha IV, 1082
Wilson, Martha V, 212
Wilson, Martha V, 213
Wilson, Martha V, 290
Wilson, Martha V, 543
Wilson, Martha V, 953
Wilson, Martha V, 962
Wilson, Martha VI, 371
Wilson, Martha VI, 457
Wilson, Martha VI, 583
Wilson, Martha VI, 679
Wilson, Martha VI, 691
Wilson, Martha VI, 698
Wilson, Martha VI, 721
Wilson, Martha VI, 722
Wilson, Martha VI, 734
Wilson, Martha VI, 750
Wilson, Martha VI, 791
Wilson, Martha VI, 792
Wilson, Martha VI, 804
Wilson, Martha VI, 837
Wilson, Martha VI, 1018
Wilson, Martha A. IV, 558
Wilson, Martha Ann I, 86
Wilson, Martha Ann IV, 557
Wilson, Martha Ann V, 212
Wilson, Martha Ann V, 213
Wilson, Martha Ann VI, 642
Wilson, Martha Ann VI, 643
Wilson, Martha Ann VI, 722
Wilson, Martha Ann VI, 1018
Wilson, Martha Chappell IV, 788
Wilson, Martha J. I, 671
Wilson, Martha R. III, 56
Wilson, Martha R. III, 361
Wilson, Martha T. III, 194
Wilson, Martha W. I, 670
Wilson, Martha, Jr. IV, 68
Wilson, Marthann V, 213
Wilson, Martin W. IV, 1386
Wilson, Mary I, 35
Wilson, Mary I, 47
Wilson, Mary I, 60
Wilson, Mary I, 75
Wilson, Mary I, 85
Wilson, Mary I, 86
Wilson, Mary I, 125
Wilson, Mary I, 160
Wilson, Mary I, 176
Wilson, Mary I, 177
Wilson, Mary I, 405
Wilson, Mary I, 429
Wilson, Mary I, 444
Wilson, Mary I, 454
Wilson, Mary I, 455
Wilson, Mary I, 521
Wilson, Mary I, 522
Wilson, Mary I, 582
Wilson, Mary I, 583
Wilson, Mary I, 653
Wilson, Mary I, 670
Wilson, Mary I, 671
Wilson, Mary I, 675
Wilson, Mary I, 681
Wilson, Mary I, 692
Wilson, Mary I, 737
Wilson, Mary I, 802
Wilson, Mary I, 845
Wilson, Mary I, 867
Wilson, Mary I, 905
Wilson, Mary I, 924
Wilson, Mary I, 925
Wilson, Mary I, 1000
Wilson, Mary I, 1024
Wilson, Mary I, 1029
Wilson, Mary I, 1039
Wilson, Mary I, 1056
Wilson, Mary I, 1058
Wilson, Mary I, 1059
Wilson, Mary I, 1060
Wilson, Mary I, 1063
Wilson, Mary I, 1119
Wilson, Mary I, 1134
Wilson, Mary I, 1135
Wilson, Mary II, 100
Wilson, Mary II, 111
Wilson, Mary II, 271
Wilson, Mary II, 274
Wilson, Mary II, 437
Wilson, Mary II, 450
Wilson, Mary II, 480
Wilson, Mary II, 493
Wilson, Mary II, 528
Wilson, Mary II, 596
Wilson, Mary II, 600
Wilson, Mary II, 610
Wilson, Mary II, 614
Wilson, Mary II, 629
Wilson, Mary II, 644
Wilson, Mary II, 688
Wilson, Mary II, 689
Wilson, Mary II, 690
Wilson, Mary II, 779
Wilson, Mary II, 810
Wilson, Mary II, 827
Wilson, Mary II, 844
Wilson, Mary II, 941
Wilson, Mary II, 972
Wilson, Mary II, 977
Wilson, Mary II, 990
Wilson, Mary II, 1039
Wilson, Mary II, 1063
Wilson, Mary III, 56
Wilson, Mary III, 195
Wilson, Mary III, 237
Wilson, Mary III, 250
Wilson, Mary III, 361
Wilson, Mary III, 362
Wilson, Mary IV, 68
Wilson, Mary IV, 131
Wilson, Mary IV, 134
Wilson, Mary IV, 143
Wilson, Mary IV, 164
Wilson, Mary IV, 188
Wilson, Mary IV, 279
Wilson, Mary IV, 305
Wilson, Mary IV, 315
Wilson, Mary IV, 323
Wilson, Mary IV, 358
Wilson, Mary IV, 427
Wilson, Mary IV, 457
Wilson, Mary IV, 557
Wilson, Mary IV, 600
Wilson, Mary IV, 631
Wilson, Mary IV, 665
Wilson, Mary IV, 1082
Wilson, Mary IV, 1194
Wilson, Mary V, 143
Wilson, Mary V, 155
Wilson, Mary V, 159
Wilson, Mary V, 204
Wilson, Mary V, 212
Wilson, Mary V, 213
Wilson, Mary V, 366
Wilson, Mary V, 474
Wilson, Mary V, 543
Wilson, Mary V, 605
Wilson, Mary V, 979
Wilson, Mary V, 1025
Wilson, Mary VI, 454
Wilson, Mary VI, 457
Wilson, Mary VI, 579
Wilson, Mary VI, 583
Wilson, Mary VI, 719
Wilson, Mary VI, 722
Wilson, Mary VI, 741
Wilson, Mary VI, 779
Wilson, Mary VI, 792
Wilson, Mary VI, 814
Wilson, Mary VI, 823
Wilson, Mary VI, 909
Wilson, Mary VI, 1017
Wilson, Mary A. I, 680
Wilson, Mary A. I, 692
Wilson, Mary A. II, 708
Wilson, Mary A. IV, 536
Wilson, Mary A. IV, 558
Wilson, Mary A. IV, 708
Wilson, Mary A. IV, 788
Wilson, Mary A. VI, 1018
Wilson, Mary Alice IV, 1267
Wilson, Mary Ann II, 274
Wilson, Mary Ann II, 804
Wilson, Mary Ann II, 824
Wilson, Mary Ann II, 828
Wilson, Mary Ann II, 855
Wilson, Mary Ann II, 886
Wilson, Mary Ann II, 941
Wilson, Mary Ann IV, 305
Wilson, Mary Ann IV, 339
Wilson, Mary Ann IV, 358
Wilson, Mary Ann IV, 558
Wilson, Mary Ann IV, 600
Wilson, Mary Ann V, 210
Wilson, Mary Ann V, 212
Wilson, Mary Ann V, 438
Wilson, Mary Ann V, 440
Wilson, Mary Ann V, 716
Wilson, Mary Ann VI, 721
Wilson, Mary B. IV, 446
Wilson, Mary B. IV, 457
Wilson, Mary B. V, 202
Wilson, Mary B. V, 212
Wilson, Mary B. V, 467
Wilson, Mary C. IV, 1140
Wilson, Mary C. V, 942
Wilson, Mary Clarissa IV, 1140
Wilson, Mary Corbit II, 941
Wilson, Mary D. II, 723
Wilson, Mary Dorotha II, 776
Wilson, Mary Dorothea II, 776
Wilson, Mary E. V, 366
Wilson, Mary E. VI, 457
Wilson, Mary E. VI, 766
Wilson, Mary E. VI, 791
Wilson, Mary Elsie V, 213
Wilson, Mary Felen II, 828
Wilson, Mary G. II, 941
Wilson, Mary H. II, 125
Wilson, Mary H. II, 140
Wilson, Mary H. II, 177
Wilson, Mary H. II, 749
Wilson, Mary H. II, 775
Wilson, Mary H. II, 776
Wilson, Mary H. IV, 557
Wilson, Mary Hinchman II, 46
Wilson, Mary Hinchman II, 111
Wilson, Mary J. VI, 808
Wilson, Mary Jane I, 549
Wilson, Mary Jane I, 583
Wilson, Mary Jane I, 795
Wilson, Mary Jane I, 845
Wilson, Mary Jane V, 382
Wilson, Mary Jane V, 942
Wilson, Mary Jane VI, 865
Wilson, Mary Jane VI, 1001
Wilson, Mary Jane VI, 1017
Wilson, Mary Kathryn V, 213
Wilson, Mary M. III, 508
Wilson, Mary Maude VI, 721
Wilson, Mary N. VI, 718
Wilson, Mary N. VI, 722
Wilson, Mary N. VI, 723
Wilson, Mary P. V, 605
Wilson, Mary Rahamah I, 522
Wilson, Mary Say II, 689
Wilson, Mary Susan I, 628
Wilson, Mary Susan I, 643
Wilson, Mary T. II, 941
Wilson, Mary T. II, 972
Wilson, Mary T. II, 1059
Wilson, Mary T. II, 1063
Wilson, Mary Thornton II, 828
Wilson, Mary W. I, 359
Wilson, Mary, Jr. II, 690
Wilson, Mary, Jr. V, 213
Wilson, Mathew VI, 859
Wilson, Mathew VI, 865

Wilson, Matilda I, 1000
Wilson, Matilda I, 1134
Wilson, Matilda I, 1135
Wilson, Matilda IV, 788
Wilson, Matthew VI, 837
Wilson, Maud Carter I, 628
Wilson, Maud S. V, 963
Wilson, McCaul II, 437
Wilson, Mercy II, 326
Wilson, Mercy II, 1039
Wilson, Mercy II, 1063
Wilson, Mercy IV, 80
Wilson, Mercy IV, 116
Wilson, Mercy IV, 234
Wilson, Mercy IV, 305
Wilson, Mercy V, 39
Wilson, Metilda I, 845
Wilson, Micahel I, 582
Wilson, Micajah I, 737
Wilson, Mical I, 582
Wilson, Michael I, 582
Wilson, Michael V, 313
Wilson, Michael Clarkson I, 522
Wilson, Michael S. IV, 1386
Wilson, Milicent I, 86
Wilson, Milicent I, 261
Wilson, Milicent V, 313
Wilson, Milicent Wilson I, 228
Wilson, Miliscent I, 125
Wilson, Miliscent I, 177
Wilson, Milisent I, 170
Wilson, Milisent I, 177
Wilson, Minerva R. V, 212
Wilson, Minnie V, 208
Wilson, Minnie V, 543
Wilson, Minnie V, 773
Wilson, Mirall I, 176
Wilson, Mireanna IV, 666
Wilson, Miriam I, 56
Wilson, Miriam I, 76
Wilson, Miriam I, 86
Wilson, Miriam I, 170
Wilson, Miriam I, 177
Wilson, Miriam I, 203
Wilson, Miriam I, 583
Wilson, Miriam I, 670
Wilson, Miriam I, 675
Wilson, Miriam I, 692
Wilson, Miriam I, 808
Wilson, Miriam I, 820
Wilson, Miriam I, 845
Wilson, Miriam IV, 557
Wilson, Miriam V, 480
Wilson, Miriam V, 553
Wilson, Miriam VI, 714
Wilson, Miriam VI, 722
Wilson, Miriam VI, 723
Wilson, Miriam Ann I, 795
Wilson, Miriam Ann I, 845
Wilson, Miriam, Jr. I, 193
Wilson, Miriam, Jr. I, 203
Wilson, Mirriam I, 86
Wilson, Morgan IV, 1044
Wilson, Morgan V, 143
Wilson, Mornen I, 670
Wilson, Morning I, 687
Wilson, Morning I, 692
Wilson, Morris A. IV, 358
Wilson, Morris Herbert V, 942
Wilson, Mournin I, 682
Wilson, Mourning I, 46
Wilson, Mourning I, 85
Wilson, Mourning I, 86
Wilson, Mourning I, 319
Wilson, Mourning I, 692
Wilson, Mrs. Floyd I, 951
Wilson, Myrtle V, 143
Wilson, N. Jeanette VI, 721
Wilson, N. Jeanette VI, 723
Wilson, Nancy I, 14
Wilson, Nancy I, 198
Wilson, Nancy I, 203
Wilson, Nancy I, 737
Wilson, Nancy V, 440
Wilson, Nancy VI, 583
Wilson, Nancy VI, 722
Wilson, Nancy VI, 804
Wilson, Nancy VI, 933
Wilson, Nancy VI, 1017
Wilson, Naomi I, 643
Wilson, Nathan I, 86
Wilson, Nathan I, 125
Wilson, Nathan I, 583
Wilson, Nathan I, 670
Wilson, Nathan I, 737
Wilson, Nathan II, 437
Wilson, Nathan II, 689
Wilson, Nathan IV, 457
Wilson, Nathan V, 143
Wilson, Nathan H. D. I, 583
Wilson, Nathan Hunt I, 522
Wilson, Nathan M. I, 795
Wilson, Nathan M. I, 905
Wilson, Nathaniel VI, 865
Wilson, Nathaniel VI, 928
Wilson, Nathaniel VI, 1017
Wilson, Neill Robinson VI, 723
Wilson, Nellie V, 1025
Wilson, Nettie V, 720
Wilson, Newby I, 671
Wilson, Nora IV, 1267
Wilson, Norman Bell I, 628
Wilson, O. Dewey I, 670
Wilson, Oline V, 1025
Wilson, Olive Emily V, 213
Wilson, Olive M. III, 361
Wilson, Oliver II, 658
Wilson, Oliver II, 689
Wilson, Oliver II, 690
Wilson, Oliver II, 723
Wilson, Oliver II, 776
Wilson, Oliver II, 828
Wilson, Oliver II, 922
Wilson, Oliver II, 941
Wilson, Oliver IV, 116
Wilson, Oliver IV, 358
Wilson, Oliver VI, 727
Wilson, Oliver VI, 791
Wilson, Oliver H. II, 941
Wilson, Oliver Howard II, 776
Wilson, Oliver Howard II, 828
Wilson, Oliver Howard II, 936
Wilson, Oliver N. I, 670
Wilson, Ora E. V, 366
Wilson, Oriana I, 621
Wilson, Orianna R. I, 726
Wilson, Orianna R. I, 737
Wilson, Orreana VI, 855
Wilson, Orville Dewey I, 628
Wilson, Osborn V, 212
Wilson, Otie Foland V, 720
Wilson, Owen IV, 305
Wilson, Owen IV, 600
Wilson, Owen IV, 1082
Wilson, Paul Victor III, 508
Wilson, Paulina VI, 1018
Wilson, Pearl V, 143
Wilson, Penina IV, 600
Wilson, Peninah I, 70
Wilson, Peninah I, 85
Wilson, Permillia VI, 865
Wilson, Perrin V, 366
Wilson, Peter VI, 865
Wilson, Peter VI, 867
Wilson, Peter Dobson III, 361
Wilson, Peter H. VI, 911
Wilson, Peter H. VI, 1018
Wilson, Pharaba I, 169
Wilson, Pharaba I, 177
Wilson, Pharaba G. V, 474
Wilson, Pharaba G. V, 543
Wilson, Pharaby I, 164
Wilson, Pharaby I, 176
Wilson, Pharaby I, 845
Wilson, Phariba I, 14
Wilson, Phariba I, 26
Wilson, Phariba A. I, 87
Wilson, Phariba J. V, 549
Wilson, Phariba J. V, 605
Wilson, Pharriba I, 203
Wilson, Phebe I, 1025
Wilson, Phebe I, 1057
Wilson, Phebe I, 1059
Wilson, Phebe I, 1061
Wilson, Phebe I, 1063
Wilson, Phebe II, 689
Wilson, Phebe II, 1039
Wilson, Phebe IV, 304
Wilson, Phebe IV, 305
Wilson, Phebe IV, 335
Wilson, Phebe IV, 358
Wilson, Phebe IV, 457
Wilson, Phebe V, 212
Wilson, Phebe V, 313
Wilson, Phebe V, 829
Wilson, Phebe Alice III, 490
Wilson, Phebe Alice III, 508
Wilson, Phebe Jane IV, 305
Wilson, Phebe Mara II, 776
Wilson, Phebe Mira II, 723
Wilson, Phebe W. II, 828
Wilson, Pheraba I, 203
Wilson, Pherabe I, 86
Wilson, Phereby I, 583
Wilson, Pheriba I, 125
Wilson, Pheriba I, 692
Wilson, Pheriba I, 795
Wilson, Pheriba V, 605
Wilson, Pheribah I, 670
Wilson, Pheribee I, 177
Wilson, Phetheny I, 176
Wilson, Phineas I, 692
Wilson, Pink VI, 765
Wilson, Pink VI, 792
Wilson, Polley VI, 983
Wilson, Polly VI, 854
Wilson, Polly VI, 865
Wilson, Polly VI, 898
Wilson, Polly VI, 1017
Wilson, Poole II, 776
Wilson, R. B., Jr. VI, 82
Wilson, R. B., Jr. VI, 90
Wilson, Rachel I, 38
Wilson, Rachel I, 85
Wilson, Rachel I, 86
Wilson, Rachel I, 90
Wilson, Rachel I, 125
Wilson, Rachel I, 176
Wilson, Rachel I, 261
Wilson, Rachel I, 582
Wilson, Rachel I, 583
Wilson, Rachel I, 670
Wilson, Rachel I, 686
Wilson, Rachel I, 692
Wilson, Rachel I, 845
Wilson, Rachel I, 905
Wilson, Rachel I Sup 1, 8
Wilson, Rachel II, 46
Wilson, Rachel II, 111
Wilson, Rachel II, 274
Wilson, Rachel II, 437
Wilson, Rachel II, 689
Wilson, Rachel II, 706
Wilson, Rachel II, 931
Wilson, Rachel II, 986
Wilson, Rachel II, 1039
Wilson, Rachel IV, 46
Wilson, Rachel IV, 67
Wilson, Rachel IV, 68
Wilson, Rachel IV, 212
Wilson, Rachel IV, 214
Wilson, Rachel IV, 221
Wilson, Rachel IV, 304
Wilson, Rachel IV, 305
Wilson, Rachel IV, 315
Wilson, Rachel IV, 358
Wilson, Rachel IV, 399
Wilson, Rachel IV, 457
Wilson, Rachel IV, 528
Wilson, Rachel IV, 557
Wilson, Rachel IV, 558
Wilson, Rachel IV, 600
Wilson, Rachel IV, 627
Wilson, Rachel IV, 1069
Wilson, Rachel IV, 1082
Wilson, Rachel V, 143
Wilson, Rachel V, 962
Wilson, Rachel V, 979
Wilson, Rachel VI, 23
Wilson, Rachel VI, 284
Wilson, Rachel VI, 457
Wilson, Rachel VI, 583
Wilson, Rachel VI, 719
Wilson, Rachel VI, 722
Wilson, Rachel VI, 812
Wilson, Rachel D. IV, 355
Wilson, Rachel D. IV, 358
Wilson, Rachel D. IV, 449
Wilson, Rachel D. IV, 457
Wilson, Rachel D. IV, 557
Wilson, Rachel D. IV, 558
Wilson, Rachel Elizabeth I, 522
Wilson, Rachel Kirk V, 720
Wilson, Rachel W. IV, 1194
Wilson, Rachell I, 233
Wilson, Rachell I, 261
Wilson, Rachell II, 689
Wilson, Ralph IV, 1044
Wilson, Rathmel II, 437
Wilson, Rathmel II, 690
Wilson, Raymond V, 213
Wilson, Raymond H. V, 212
Wilson, Rebeca VI, 414
Wilson, Rebeca VI, 457
Wilson, Rebeca Littler VI, 457
Wilson, Rebecah I, 455
Wilson, Rebecca I, 42
Wilson, Rebecca I, 86
Wilson, Rebecca I, 628
Wilson, Rebecca I, 670
Wilson, Rebecca I, 671
Wilson, Rebecca I, 692
Wilson, Rebecca I, 1072
Wilson, Rebecca II, 689
Wilson, Rebecca II, 793
Wilson, Rebecca II, 815
Wilson, Rebecca II, 828
Wilson, Rebecca II, 973
Wilson, Rebecca II, 1039
Wilson, Rebecca III, 122
Wilson, Rebecca III, 361
Wilson, Rebecca IV, 116
Wilson, Rebecca IV, 139
Wilson, Rebecca IV, 164
Wilson, Rebecca IV, 358
Wilson, Rebecca IV, 431
Wilson, Rebecca IV, 456
Wilson, Rebecca IV, 457
Wilson, Rebecca IV, 600
Wilson, Rebecca V, 151
Wilson, Rebecca V, 213
Wilson, Rebecca V, 313
Wilson, Rebecca V, 440
Wilson, Rebecca V, 474
Wilson, Rebecca V, 543
Wilson, Rebecca V, 544
Wilson, Rebecca V, 730
Wilson, Rebecca V, 798
Wilson, Rebecca V, 800
Wilson, Rebecca V, 801
Wilson, Rebecca V, 942
Wilson, Rebecca VI, 792
Wilson, Rebecca A. II, 941
Wilson, Rebecca A. II, 944
Wilson, Rebecca A. IV, 1140
Wilson, Rebecca Ann II, 941
Wilson, Rebecca Ann IV, 1140
Wilson, Rebecca B. V, 210
Wilson, Rebecca B. V, 212
Wilson, Rebecca B. V, 213
Wilson, Rebecca B. V, 543
Wilson, Rebecca D. III, 361
Wilson, Rebecca D. VI, 702
Wilson, Rebecca D. VI, 721
Wilson, Rebecca D. VI, 722
Wilson, Rebecca D. VI, 723
Wilson, Rebecca E. I, 671
Wilson, Rebecca E. I, 682
Wilson, Rebecca E. I, 692
Wilson, Rebecca Jane IV, 1140
Wilson, Rebecka I, 47
Wilson, Rebeckah I, 85
Wilson, Rebeckah I, 444
Wilson, Rebeckah I, 455
Wilson, Rebeckah II, 1039
Wilson, Rebeckah IV, 319
Wilson, Rebeckah IV, 358
Wilson, Rebeka I, 86
Wilson, Rebekah IV, 116
Wilson, Rebekah V, 39
Wilson, Rebekah V, 143
Wilson, Rebekah VI, 457
Wilson, Rebekah VI, 573
Wilson, Reuben I, 42
Wilson, Reuben I, 85
Wilson, Reuben I, 86
Wilson, Reuben I, 202
Wilson, Reuben I, 845
Wilson, Reuben V, 773
Wilson, Rhichama I, 583
Wilson, Rhoda I, 40
Wilson, Rhoda I, 86
Wilson, Richard IV, 788
Wilson, Richard Harker I, 522
Wilson, Richard Harlan II, 46
Wilson, Richard Harlan II, 125
Wilson, Richard Harlan II, 140
Wilson, Richard Harlem II, 160
Wilson, Richard Roberts III, 361
Wilson, Richard S. III, 361
Wilson, Robeart I, 90
Wilson, Robeart I Sup 1, 8
Wilson, Robert I, 1
Wilson, Robert I, 26
Wilson, Robert I, 67
Wilson, Robert I, 85
Wilson, Robert I, 86
Wilson, Robert I, 90
Wilson, Robert I, 163
Wilson, Robert I, 176
Wilson, Robert I, 905
Wilson, Robert I Sup 1, 3
Wilson, Robert I Sup 1, 4
Wilson, Robert I Sup 1, 6
Wilson, Robert II, 39
Wilson, Robert II, 46
Wilson, Robert II, 111
Wilson, Robert II, 689
Wilson, Robert II, 972
Wilson, Robert II, 1039
Wilson, Robert III, 56
Wilson, Robert III, 361
Wilson, Robert IV, 116
Wilson, Robert IV, 305
Wilson, Robert IV, 1194
Wilson, Robert V, 39
Wilson, Robert V, 143
Wilson, Robert VI, 27
Wilson, Robert VI, 37
Wilson, Robert VI, 827
Wilson, Robert VI, 852
Wilson, Robert VI, 862
Wilson, Robert VI, 865
Wilson, Robert VI, 934
Wilson, Robert VI, 1017
Wilson, Robert Armitage III,
Wilson, Robert B. IV, 1194
Wilson, Robert Darkin II, 46
Wilson, Robert M. V, 440
Wilson, Robert, Jr. II, 111
Wilson, Roberts II, 1039
Wilson, Robt. VI, 855
Wilson, Roxana IV, 648
Wilson, Roxana IV, 666
Wilson, Ruben I, 845
Wilson, Ruby IV, 1343
Wilson, Ruetha VI, 909
Wilson, Ruth I, 38
Wilson, Ruth I, 62
Wilson, Ruth I, 67
Wilson, Ruth I, 85
Wilson, Ruth I, 86
Wilson, Ruth I, 107
Wilson, Ruth I, 583
Wilson, Ruth I, 643
Wilson, Ruth I, 735
Wilson, Ruth I, 737
Wilson, Ruth I, 745
Wilson, Ruth I, 1059
Wilson, Ruth I, 1134
Wilson, Ruth II, 89
Wilson, Ruth II, 111
Wilson, Ruth II, 251
Wilson, Ruth II, 274
Wilson, Ruth III, 512
Wilson, Ruth IV, 68
Wilson, Ruth IV, 160
Wilson, Ruth IV, 164
Wilson, Ruth IV, 305
Wilson, Ruth IV, 358
Wilson, Ruth IV, 444
Wilson, Ruth IV, 457
Wilson, Ruth IV, 552
Wilson, Ruth IV, 557
Wilson, Ruth IV, 558
Wilson, Ruth IV, 600
Wilson, Ruth IV, 1052
Wilson, Ruth IV, 1082
Wilson, Ruth IV, 1176
Wilson, Ruth IV, 1194
Wilson, Ruth V, 143
Wilson, Ruth V, 212
Wilson, Ruth V, 1025
Wilson, Ruth VI, 1017
Wilson, Ruth Millard I, 628
Wilson, Ruth Pierce II, 274
Wilson, Ruth W. II, 46
Wilson, S. Allen II, 1063
Wilson, Sallie I, 341
Wilson, Sallie B. II, 800
Wilson, Sallie B. II, 876
Wilson, Sallie B. II, 941
Wilson, Sallie B. VI, 657
Wilson, Sallie H. II, 323
Wilson, Sally IV, 422
Wilson, Sally IV, 457
Wilson, Sally VI, 853
Wilson, Samantha V, 467
Wilson, Samuel I, 57
Wilson, Samuel I, 86
Wilson, Samuel I, 125
Wilson, Samuel I, 277
Wilson, Samuel I, 671
Wilson, Samuel I, 687
Wilson, Samuel I, 692
Wilson, Samuel I, 735
Wilson, Samuel I, 737
Wilson, Samuel II, 827
Wilson, Samuel II, 828
Wilson, Samuel II, 972
Wilson, Samuel II, 973
Wilson, Samuel II, 977
Wilson, Samuel II, 1026
Wilson, Samuel II, 1039
Wilson, Samuel III, 512
Wilson, Samuel IV, 164
Wilson, Samuel IV, 305
Wilson, Samuel IV, 332
Wilson, Samuel IV, 358
Wilson, Samuel IV, 456
Wilson, Samuel IV, 457
Wilson, Samuel IV, 1194
Wilson, Samuel V, 212
Wilson, Samuel V, 213
Wilson, Samuel V, 544
Wilson, Samuel VI, 457
Wilson, Samuel VI, 558
Wilson, Samuel VI, 583
Wilson, Samuel VI, 698
Wilson, Samuel VI, 722
Wilson, Samuel VI, 723
Wilson, Samuel VI, 792
Wilson, Samuel VI, 863
Wilson, Samuel VI, 865
Wilson, Samuel VI, 895

, Samuel VI, 901
, Samuel VI, 909
, Samuel VI, 1017
, Samuel A. II, 972
, Samuel A. II, 1059
n, Samuel A. II, 1063
, Samuel Allen II, 1063
n, Samuel C. I, 737
n, Samuel D. III, 508
n, Samuel L. II, 690
n, Samuel Livezey II, 689
n, Samuel M. V, 1025
n, Samuel, Jr. II, 1039
n, Samuel, Jr. VI, 583
n, Samuell I, 277
n, Sarah I, 1
n, Sarah I, 35
n, Sarah I, 36
n, Sarah I, 38
n, Sarah I, 42
n, Sarah I, 85
n, Sarah I, 86
n, Sarah I, 125
on, Sarah I, 135
on, Sarah I, 168
on, Sarah I, 175
on, Sarah I, 176
on, Sarah I, 177
on, Sarah I, 308
on, Sarah I, 319
on, Sarah I, 328
on, Sarah I, 331
on, Sarah I, 341
on, Sarah I, 671
on, Sarah I, 706
son, Sarah I, 737
son, Sarah I, 772
son, Sarah I, 887
son, Sarah I, 905
son, Sarah I, 1025
son, Sarah I, 1057
son, Sarah I, 1059
son, Sarah I, 1061
son, Sarah I, 1063
son, Sarah II, 111
son, Sarah II, 140
son, Sarah II, 197
son, Sarah II, 251
son, Sarah II, 265
son, Sarah II, 274
son, Sarah II, 437
lson, Sarah II, 472
lson, Sarah II, 680
lson, Sarah II, 689
lson, Sarah II, 690
lson, Sarah II, 723
lson, Sarah II, 775
lson, Sarah II, 776
lson, Sarah II, 811
lson, Sarah II, 827
lson, Sarah II, 886
lson, Sarah II, 902
lson, Sarah II, 941
ilson, Sarah II, 950
ilson, Sarah II, 972
ilson, Sarah II, 1026
ilson, Sarah II, 1039
ilson, Sarah III, 301
ilson, Sarah IV, 38
ilson, Sarah IV, 67
ilson, Sarah IV, 68
ilson, Sarah IV, 164
ilson, Sarah IV, 305
ilson, Sarah IV, 332
ilson, Sarah IV, 358
ilson, Sarah IV, 456
Vilson, Sarah IV, 457
Vilson, Sarah IV, 600
Vilson, Sarah IV, 1082
Vilson, Sarah IV, 1140
Vilson, Sarah V, 143
Vilson, Sarah V, 212
Wilson, Sarah V, 213
Wilson, Sarah V, 467
Wilson, Sarah V, 469
Wilson, Sarah V, 543
Wilson, Sarah V, 605
Wilson, Sarah V, 942
Wilson, Sarah VI, 27
Wilson, Sarah VI, 37
Wilson, Sarah VI, 91
Wilson, Sarah VI, 129
Wilson, Sarah VI, 457
Wilson, Sarah VI, 530
Wilson, Sarah VI, 558
Wilson, Sarah VI, 583
Wilson, Sarah VI, 627
Wilson, Sarah VI, 681
Wilson, Sarah VI, 686
Wilson, Sarah VI, 698
Wilson, Sarah VI, 722
Wilson, Sarah VI, 792
Wilson, Sarah VI, 877
Wilson, Sarah VI, 911
Wilson, Sarah VI, 1017
Wilson, Sarah A. IV, 188
Wilson, Sarah A. IV, 305
Wilson, Sarah Alvaretta IV, 1300
Wilson, Sarah Ann II, 776
Wilson, Sarah Ann IV, 368
Wilson, Sarah Ann IV, 457
Wilson, Sarah Ann IV, 615
Wilson, Sarah Ann IV, 666
Wilson, Sarah B. IV, 1096
Wilson, Sarah B. IV, 1140
Wilson, Sarah C. II, 125
Wilson, Sarah C. II, 140
Wilson, Sarah C. II, 152
Wilson, Sarah C. II, 160
Wilson, Sarah Chamles II, 46
Wilson, Sarah E. I, 429
Wilson, Sarah E. I, 671
Wilson, Sarah E. I, 692
Wilson, Sarah Edna IV, 558
Wilson, Sarah Elizabeth VI, 1017
Wilson, Sarah Ellen II, 828
Wilson, Sarah Ellen II, 942
Wilson, Sarah H. II, 326
Wilson, Sarah H. II, 876
Wilson, Sarah H. II, 942
Wilson, Sarah H. III, 247
Wilson, Sarah J. V, 212
Wilson, Sarah J. V, 605
Wilson, Sarah Jane VI, 723
Wilson, Sarah L. II, 941
Wilson, Sarah Lancaster II, 827
Wilson, Sarah M. III, 512
Wilson, Sarah P. II, 941
Wilson, Sarah P. IV, 358
Wilson, Sarah P. VI, 1018
Wilson, Sarah Poole II, 941
Wilson, Sarah S. IV, 255
Wilson, Sarah S. IV, 305
Wilson, Seth I, 1025
Wilson, Seth I, 1029
Wilson, Seth I, 1039
Wilson, Seth I, 1059
Wilson, Seth IV, 68
Wilson, Seth V, 212
Wilson, Seth V, 543
Wilson, Sherman IV, 1300
Wilson, Sidnah II, 972
Wilson, Sidney II, 1039
Wilson, Silvanus I, 85
Wilson, Silvanus I, 86
Wilson, Silvaus I, 85
Wilson, Silvester I, 737
Wilson, Skidmore IV, 164
Wilson, Spencer B. V, 212
Wilson, Stanley Kirk V, 720
Wilson, Stella IV, 1267
Wilson, Stephen I, 692
Wilson, Stephen II, 274
Wilson, Stephen II, 828
Wilson, Stephen II, 855
Wilson, Stephen II, 941
Wilson, Stephen II, 973
Wilson, Stephen II, 975
Wilson, Stephen II, 1039
Wilson, Stephen IV, 164
Wilson, Stephen IV, 358
Wilson, Stephen IV, 456
Wilson, Stephen IV, 457
Wilson, Stephen V, 942
Wilson, Stephen V, 952
Wilson, Stephen V, 962
Wilson, Stephen V, 963
Wilson, Stephen VI, 457
Wilson, Stephen VI, 558
Wilson, Stephen VI, 583
Wilson, Stephen VI, 679
Wilson, Stephen VI, 698
Wilson, Stephen VI, 721
Wilson, Stephen VI, 722
Wilson, Stephen VI, 771
Wilson, Stephen VI, 792
Wilson, Stephen B. V, 962
Wilson, Stephen R. II, 1086
Wilson, Stephen, Jr. V, 962
Wilson, Stephen, Jr. V, 963
Wilson, Stephen, Jr. VI, 457
Wilson, Stephen, Jr. VI, 722
Wilson, Steven II, 265
Wilson, Steven II, 274
Wilson, Susan II, 828
Wilson, Susan II, 941
Wilson, Susan IV, 557
Wilson, Susan V, 720
Wilson, Susan VI, 961
Wilson, Susan I. II, 941
Wilson, Susan J. II, 849
Wilson, Susan J. II, 941
Wilson, Susan McLoren V, 366
Wilson, Susan R. III, 113
Wilson, Susan R. III, 361
Wilson, Susanna II, 599
Wilson, Susanna II, 689
Wilson, Susanna IV, 1386
Wilson, Susannah II, 689
Wilson, Susannah IV, 666
Wilson, Susannah IV, 1384
Wilson, Sylvanus I, 737
Wilson, T. G. I, 341
Wilson, Tabitha II, 828
Wilson, Tacy IV, 788
Wilson, Tamar I, 1056
Wilson, Tamar I, 1059
Wilson, Tamar V, 159
Wilson, Tamar V, 212
Wilson, Tamar Owen I, 1056
Wilson, Teresa III, 361
Wilson, Teresa L. III, 361
Wilson, Terese L. III, 221
Wilson, Theodata VI, 625
Wilson, Theodate VI, 690
Wilson, Theodate VI, 691
Wilson, Theodate VI, 721
Wilson, Theodate VI, 723
Wilson, Theodore V, 1025
Wilson, Theodore F. IV, 1194
Wilson, Theophilus V, 941
Wilson, Thomas I, 62
Wilson, Thomas I, 85
Wilson, Thomas I, 86
Wilson, Thomas I, 203
Wilson, Thomas I, 261
Wilson, Thomas I, 429
Wilson, Thomas I, 582
Wilson, Thomas I, 583
Wilson, Thomas I, 671
Wilson, Thomas I, 692
Wilson, Thomas I, 737
Wilson, Thomas I, 845
Wilson, Thomas I, 1059
Wilson, Thomas I, 1134
Wilson, Thomas I, 1135
Wilson, Thomas II, 233
Wilson, Thomas II, 249
Wilson, Thomas II, 251
Wilson, Thomas II, 274
Wilson, Thomas II, 437
Wilson, Thomas II, 670
Wilson, Thomas II, 688
Wilson, Thomas II, 689
Wilson, Thomas II, 690
Wilson, Thomas II, 776
Wilson, Thomas II, 1013
Wilson, Thomas II, 1017
Wilson, Thomas II, 1039
Wilson, Thomas III, 361
Wilson, Thomas IV, 304
Wilson, Thomas IV, 305
Wilson, Thomas IV, 339
Wilson, Thomas IV, 358
Wilson, Thomas IV, 457
Wilson, Thomas IV, 600
Wilson, Thomas IV, 1082
Wilson, Thomas IV, 1386
Wilson, Thomas V, 143
Wilson, Thomas V, 212
Wilson, Thomas V, 440
Wilson, Thomas VI, 147
Wilson, Thomas VI, 371
Wilson, Thomas VI, 421
Wilson, Thomas VI, 435
Wilson, Thomas VI, 454
Wilson, Thomas VI, 457
Wilson, Thomas VI, 723
Wilson, Thomas VI, 734
Wilson, Thomas VI, 752
Wilson, Thomas VI, 791
Wilson, Thomas VI, 792
Wilson, Thomas VI, 823
Wilson, Thomas VI, 837
Wilson, Thomas VI, 865
Wilson, Thomas VI, 928
Wilson, Thomas VI, 1016
Wilson, Thomas VI, 1017
Wilson, Thomas Arnet I, 522
Wilson, Thomas C. VI, 1018
Wilson, Thomas Erwin VI, 457
Wilson, Thomas H. IV, 457
Wilson, Thomas Irwin VI, 457
Wilson, Thomas Irwin VI, 791
Wilson, Thomas Jefferson V, 213
Wilson, Thomas, Jr. II, 251
Wilson, Thomas, Jr. II, 274
Wilson, Thomas, Jr. II, 1039
Wilson, Thomas, Jr. IV, 304
Wilson, Thomas, Sr. I, 86
Wilson, Thos. II, 690
Wilson, Thos. II, 827
Wilson, Thos. IV, 305
Wilson, Thos. V, 213
Wilson, Thos. L. IV, 1300
Wilson, Timothy I, 187
Wilson, Timothy I, 203
Wilson, Timothy IV, 288
Wilson, Timothy IV, 305
Wilson, Townsend IV, 305
Wilson, Vergie V, 1025
Wilson, Victor III, 225
Wilson, Victor C. III, 490
Wilson, Vincent VI, 1017
Wilson, Vincent B. VI, 898
Wilson, Viola Foland V, 543
Wilson, W. Albion I, 643
Wilson, W. H. I, 628
Wilson, W. N. VI, 843
Wilson, W. S. I, 341
Wilson, W. W. V, 650
Wilson, Walter II, 188
Wilson, Walter II, 271
Wilson, Walter II, 274
Wilson, Walter II, 767
Wilson, Walter II, 776
Wilson, Walter V, 212
Wilson, Walter V, 213
Wilson, Walter T. V, 212
Wilson, Warren IV, 788
Wilson, Warren Kirk V, 720
Wilson, Watson F. II, 941
Wilson, Watty IV, 1386
Wilson, Wd Elizabeth IV, 644
Wilson, Wd Elizabeth IV, 667
Wilson, Wd. Amy II, 188
Wilson, Wd. Hannah II, 828
Wilson, Wd. Margaret II, 968
Wilson, Wd. Mary Ann II, 807
Wilson, Wd. Rebecca D. VI, 721
Wilson, Wd. Sarah II, 689
Wilson, Wd. Sarah II, 1039
Wilson, Wd. Susannah II, 810
Wilson, Weldon V, 213
Wilson, Widow Elisabeth I, 203
Wilson, Wilbur V, 212
Wilson, Wilbur V, 213
Wilson, Wilhelmina II, 776
Wilson, Wilhelmina C. II, 941
Wilson, Wilhelmina W. II, 753
Wilson, Wilhelmina W. II, 776
Wilson, Wilhemina II, 894
Wilson, Wilhemina C. II, 941
Wilson, Willa VI, 439
Wilson, Willa VI, 457
Wilson, Willa VI, 695
Wilson, Willa VI, 723
Wilson, Willard V, 720
Wilson, Willet III, 512
Wilson, William I, 20
Wilson, William I, 24
Wilson, William I, 25
Wilson, William I, 60
Wilson, William I, 82
Wilson, William I, 85
Wilson, William I, 86
Wilson, William I, 87
Wilson, William I, 125
Wilson, William I, 151
Wilson, William I, 160
Wilson, William I, 175
Wilson, William I, 176
Wilson, William I, 177
Wilson, William I, 203
Wilson, William I, 331
Wilson, William I, 429
Wilson, William I, 628
Wilson, William I, 670
Wilson, William I, 671
Wilson, William I, 692
Wilson, William I, 737
Wilson, William I, 845
Wilson, William I, 1134
Wilson, William II, 46
Wilson, William II, 140
Wilson, William II, 178
Wilson, William II, 233
Wilson, William II, 274
Wilson, William II, 437
Wilson, William IV, 17
Wilson, William IV, 38
Wilson, William IV, 39
Wilson, William IV, 67
Wilson, William IV, 68
Wilson, William IV, 116
Wilson, William IV, 305
Wilson, William IV, 358
Wilson, William IV, 457
Wilson, William IV, 557
Wilson, William IV, 558
Wilson, William IV, 600
Wilson, William IV, 1082
Wilson, William IV, 1140
Wilson, William V, 143
Wilson, William V, 440
Wilson, William V, 873
Wilson, William V, 942
Wilson, William VI, 457
Wilson, William VI, 625
Wilson, William VI, 642
Wilson, William VI, 643
Wilson, William VI, 645
Wilson, William VI, 679
Wilson, William VI, 714
Wilson, William VI, 718
Wilson, William VI, 721
Wilson, William VI, 722
Wilson, William VI, 888
Wilson, William VI, 895
Wilson, William VI, 911
Wilson, William VI, 958
Wilson, William VI, 1001
Wilson, William VI, 1017
Wilson, William A. I, 632
Wilson, William A. I, 692
Wilson, William Albion I, 628
Wilson, William Albion I, 671
Wilson, William B. II, 326
Wilson, William B. II, 327
Wilson, William B. VI, 457
Wilson, William B. VI, 1017
Wilson, William C. IV, 305
Wilson, William C. IV, 457
Wilson, William Curtis VI, 723
Wilson, William Findley IV, 1140
Wilson, William H. VI, 721
Wilson, William H. VI, 723
Wilson, William L. I, 670
Wilson, William L. I, 671
Wilson, William L. I, 692
Wilson, William R. I, 87
Wilson, William S. IV, 1386
Wilson, William S. V, 440
Wilson, William Smith II, 46
Wilson, William, Jr. V, 873
Wilson, Williams II, 1039
Wilson, Willis IV, 1194
Wilson, Willis L. IV, 1194
Wilson, Willis S. IV, 1194
Wilson, Wm H. VI, 702
Wilson, Wm. I, 359
Wilson, Wm. II, 89
Wilson, Wm. II, 111
Wilson, Wm. II, 140
Wilson, Wm. II, 160
Wilson, Wm. II, 573
Wilson, Wm. II, 604
Wilson, Wm. II, 688
Wilson, Wm. II, 689
Wilson, Wm. II, 775
Wilson, Wm. II, 942
Wilson, Wm. III, 361
Wilson, Wm. IV, 46
Wilson, Wm. IV, 134
Wilson, Wm. IV, 279
Wilson, Wm. IV, 631
Wilson, Wm. IV, 1082
Wilson, Wm. IV, 1300
Wilson, Wm. V, 313
Wilson, Wm. V, 440
Wilson, Wm. V, 720
Wilson, Wm. V, 942
Wilson, Wm. VI, 642
Wilson, Wm. VI, 645
Wilson, Wm. VI, 680
Wilson, Wm. VI, 691
Wilson, Wm. VI, 708
Wilson, Wm. VI, 721
Wilson, Wm. VI, 722
Wilson, Wm. A. I, 643
Wilson, Wm. C. IV, 457
Wilson, Wm. C. IV, 524
Wilson, Wm. C. IV, 704
Wilson, Wm. C. IV, 788
Wilson, Wm. Curtis VI, 439
Wilson, Wm. Curtis VI, 457
Wilson, Wm. Curtis VI, 695
Wilson, Wm. Curtis VI, 723
Wilson, Wm. H. V, 650
Wilson, Wm. H. VI, 695
Wilson, Wm. H. VI, 721
Wilson, Wm. H. VI, 723
Wilson, Wm. P. II, 776
Wilson, Wm. Pool II, 941
Wilson, Wm. Poole II, 941
Wilson, Wm. S. I, 341
Wilson, Wm. S. II, 125
Wilson, Wm. S. II, 775
Wilson, Wm. S. II, 941
Wilson, Wm. Savery II, 690
Wilson, Wm. Smith II, 111
Wilson, Wm. Smith II, 690
Wilson, Wm., Jr. IV, 134
Wilson, Woodard Albion I, 628
Wilson, Worth I, 643

Wilson, Worth H. I, 670
Wilson, Worth Hardin I, 628
Wilson, Wugh V, 942
Wilson, Yarnal IV, 305
Wilson, Yarnal IV, 457
Wilson, Yarnall IV, 304
Wilson, Yarnel IV, 358
Wilson, Zachariah I, 86
Wilson, Zeruah I, 674
Wilson, Zeruah I, 692
Wilsown, Sarah I, 176
Wilstach, Cornelius V, 290
Wilstach, Sarah V, 290
Wilt, Elizabeth IV, 1016
Wilt, Frank IV, 1016
Wilt, Jane Elizabeth IV, 1016
Wilt, Mary VI, 537
Wilt, Mary VI, 583
Wilt, Robert IV, 1016
Wilt, Robert R. IV, 1016
Wilt, Ruth Paxton IV, 1016
Wilt, William Franklin IV, 1016
Wiltbank, Mary II, 828
Wiltbank, Robert II, 828
Wiltbank, Sallie M. II, 828
Wiltberger, Ann II, 437
Wiltberger, Peter II, 437
Wilton, Elizabeth II, 437
Wilton, Jane II, 690
Wilton, John II, 437
Wilton, Mathew II, 437
Wilton, Wm. II, 690
Wiltse, Ann W. V, 874
Wiltse, Elizabeth V, 874
Wiltse, George V, 874
Wiltse, Henry V, 874
Wiltse, Henry V, 888
Wiltse, John C. V, 874
Wiltse, Lydia V, 874
Wiltse, Martin V, 874
Wiltse, Rachel V, 874
Wiltse, Rachel V, 882
Wiltse, Rachel V, 888
Wiltse, Simeon V, 874
Wiltse, Simeon V, 882
Wiltse, Simeon V, 888
Wiltse, Simeon, Jr. V, 874
Wiltse, William V, 874
Wiltsee, Elizabeth V, 143
Wiltsee, Henry V, 143
Wiltsee, Henry V, 888
Wiltsee, John V, 143
Wiltsee, Martin V, 143
Wiltsee, Simeon V, 143
Wiltsee, William V, 143
Wiltsey, Henry V, 888
Wiltsher, Sarah V, 604
Wily, Ann W. V, 880
Wily, David V, 888
Wily, Elizabeth V, 884
Wily, Elizabeth V, 888
Wily, Hannah V, 886
Wily, Hannah V, 888
Wily, Isaac V, 873
Wily, Isaac, Jr. V, 888
Wily, Jemima V, 888
Wily, Jemima C. V, 888
Wily, John VI, 607
Wily, Maria Louisa Thomas V, 888
Wily, Maria Louise Thomas V, 888
Wily, Mary W. V, 883
Wily, Philip P. V, 888
Wily, Rachel I, 389
Wily, Rachel I, 428
Wily, Ruth I, 428
Wily, Samuel II, 686
Wily, Thomas V, 888
Wimbish, Abraham VI, 865
Wimbish, Judith VI, 865
Wimer, Hannah II, 828
Wimer, Hannah II, 911
Wimer, Margaret II, 911
Wimer, Rachel K. II, 789
Wimer, Sarah II, 828
Wimer, Thomas II, 828
Wimer, Thos. II, 828
Wimer, Thos. II, 911
Win, Florence IV, 1300
Win, Ruth IV, 1299
Win, Ruth IV, 1300
Winans, Carrie B. III, 76
Winans, Carrie B. III, 362
Winans, Luella IV, 1343
Winborn, Elisabeth I, 261
Winborn, James VI, 90
Winborn, Mary VI, 90
Winborn, Sarah I, 233
Winborn, Sarah I, 261
Winborne, Elisabeth I, 261
Winborrow, Barbara VI, 11
Winborrow, John VI, 11
Winbourn, Esther VI, 19
Winburn, Mary VI, 70
Winburn, Mary VI, 90
Winchester, Hannah Frances II, 724
Winchester, Mary Lou I, 626
Winchester, Mattie M. I, 615
Windell, Maud V, 773
Winder, ??? IV, 795
Winder, Aaron II, 1040
Winder, Aaron IV, 918
Winder, Aaron IV, 1300
Winder, Aaron V, 287
Winder, Aaron V, 290
Winder, Aaron V, 312
Winder, Aaron V, 313
Winder, Abigail IV, 788
Winder, Abigail IV, 908
Winder, Abigail IV, 918
Winder, Abner II, 1040
Winder, Abner IV, 68
Winder, Abner IV, 1300
Winder, Abner V, 290
Winder, Abner Webster IV, 1300
Winder, Abner, Jr. V, 290
Winder, Ada IV, 457
Winder, Ada IV, 918
Winder, Adah IV, 789
Winder, Adah IV, 856
Winder, Adah IV, 908
Winder, Adah IV, 917
Winder, Adah IV, 918
Winder, Adah B. IV, 789
Winder, Adah B. IV, 902
Winder, Adah B. IV, 918
Winder, Adah B. IV, 942
Winder, Adah B. IV, 1016
Winder, Aedah IV, 903
Winder, Agness V, 287
Winder, Alfred III, 121
Winder, Alfred III, 157
Winder, Alfred III, 362
Winder, Alfred IV, 1300
Winder, Alice IV, 1242
Winder, Alice R. IV, 1016
Winder, Alice Rebecca IV, 856
Winder, Alice Rebecca IV, 1016
Winder, Allen V, 290
Winder, Amy IV, 789
Winder, Amy IV, 847
Winder, Amy IV, 856
Winder, Amy V, 290
Winder, Ann II, 1040
Winder, Ann IV, 68
Winder, Ann IV, 789
Winder, Ann IV, 809
Winder, Ann IV, 856
Winder, Ann IV, 918
Winder, Ann V, 287
Winder, Ann Elizabeth IV, 1016
Winder, Anna Elizabeth IV, 856
Winder, Anna Elizabeth IV, 1016
Winder, Anna H. IV, 819
Winder, Anna H. IV, 856
Winder, Anna H. IV, 918
Winder, Anna May IV, 1300
Winder, Asenath IV, 856
Winder, Asenath IV, 857
Winder, Asenath IV, 918
Winder, Benj. IV, 899
Winder, Benjamin IV, 371
Winder, Benjamin IV, 457
Winder, Benjamin IV, 788
Winder, Benjamin IV, 789
Winder, Benjamin IV, 900
Winder, Benjamin IV, 908
Winder, Benjamin IV, 917
Winder, Benjamin IV, 918
Winder, Bessie III, 121
Winder, Bessie III, 362
Winder, Caleb V, 290
Winder, Charles Blish IV, 1300
Winder, Charlott IV, 1300
Winder, Clearance IV, 1300
Winder, David IV, 579
Winder, David IV, 601
Winder, David IV, 789
Winder, David IV, 856
Winder, David IV, 1300
Winder, David V, 290
Winder, David Russell II, 973
Winder, Davidson V, 290
Winder, Deborah IV, 19
Winder, Deborah IV, 68
Winder, Deborah IV, 1300
Winder, Deborah Ann IV, 1300
Winder, Dorothy Emily IV, 856
Winder, Dorothy Emily IV, 1016
Winder, Edmond II, 1040
Winder, Edna Ruth II, 973
Winder, Edna Ruth II, 1063
Winder, Edward IV, 1300
Winder, Edward V, 290
Winder, Efphama IV, 856
Winder, Efphama IV, 902
Winder, Efphama IV, 918
Winder, Efphame IV, 856
Winder, Efphema IV, 856
Winder, Efphema IV, 857
Winder, Eleanor IV, 789
Winder, Eleanor IV, 811
Winder, Eleanor IV, 856
Winder, Eleanor IV, 903
Winder, Eleanor IV, 918
Winder, Eliza IV, 1300
Winder, Eliza Jane IV, 1300
Winder, Elizabeth II, 690
Winder, Elizabeth II, 978
Winder, Elizabeth II, 1040
Winder, Elizabeth IV, 68
Winder, Elizabeth IV, 579
Winder, Elizabeth IV, 601
Winder, Elizabeth V, 290
Winder, Elizabeth C. II, 973
Winder, Elizabeth L. V, 976
Winder, Elizabeth L. V, 979
Winder, Elizabeth W. II, 1060
Winder, Elizabeth W. II, 1063
Winder, Elizabeth Wilma II, 1063
Winder, Ephama IV, 789
Winder, Ephama IV, 918
Winder, Esther IV, 789
Winder, Esther IV, 808
Winder, Esther IV, 856
Winder, Esther IV, 902
Winder, Esther IV, 918
Winder, Esther Ann IV, 1300
Winder, Esther L. IV, 856
Winder, Esther L. IV, 1016
Winder, Esther Lydia IV, 856
Winder, Esther Lydia IV, 1016
Winder, Esther W. IV, 808
Winder, Eunice IV, 1300
Winder, Eunice H. IV, 1300
Winder, Eunice N. IV, 1227
Winder, Euphema IV, 856
Winder, Hannah II, 981
Winder, Hannah II, 1040
Winder, Hannah IV, 25
Winder, Hannah IV, 68
Winder, Hannah IV, 789
Winder, Hannah IV, 827
Winder, Hannah IV, 856
Winder, Hannah IV, 899
Winder, Hannah IV, 908
Winder, Hannah IV, 917
Winder, Hannah IV, 918
Winder, Hannah IV, 1300
Winder, Hannah V, 290
Winder, Hannah V, 963
Winder, Harriet Jane IV, 1300
Winder, Helen Lorene II, 973
Winder, Helen Lorene II, 1060
Winder, Helen Lorene II, 1063
Winder, Henry V, 290
Winder, Hope IV, 1300
Winder, Hope V, 290
Winder, Howard IV, 1300
Winder, James II, 1040
Winder, James IV, 19
Winder, James IV, 68
Winder, James IV, 116
Winder, James IV, 1300
Winder, James V, 290
Winder, James V, 979
Winder, James A. V, 290
Winder, James Joseph II, 973
Winder, John II, 1018
Winder, John II, 1040
Winder, John IV, 25
Winder, John IV, 68
Winder, John IV, 1300
Winder, John V, 251
Winder, John V, 290
Winder, John A. Cope IV, 1016
Winder, John Elwood IV, 1300
Winder, John J. IV, 856
Winder, John Richard II, 973
Winder, John Richard II, 1063
Winder, John W. V, 942
Winder, John, Jr. II, 1040
Winder, Joseph II, 978
Winder, Joseph II, 983
Winder, Joseph II, 1040
Winder, Joseph III, 362
Winder, Joseph IV, 457
Winder, Joseph IV, 601
Winder, Joseph IV, 789
Winder, Joseph IV, 808
Winder, Joseph IV, 856
Winder, Joseph IV, 857
Winder, Joseph IV, 902
Winder, Joseph IV, 911
Winder, Joseph IV, 918
Winder, Joseph IV, 1016
Winder, Joseph A. IV, 1300
Winder, Joseph C. II, 973
Winder, Joseph C. II, 1060
Winder, Joseph C. II, 1063
Winder, Joseph C. IV, 457
Winder, Joseph C. IV, 856
Winder, Joseph John IV, 1300
Winder, Joseph M. III, 362
Winder, Joshua V, 290
Winder, Katherine V, 287
Winder, Leah IV, 856
Winder, Leah IV, 857
Winder, Lenard IV, 457
Winder, Leonard II, 973
Winder, Leonard IV, 789
Winder, Leonard IV, 809
Winder, Leonard IV, 856
Winder, Leonard IV, 1016
Winder, Levi IV, 1300
Winder, Levi V, 290
Winder, Lewis V, 942
Winder, Lucinda V, 287
Winder, Lucy IV, 894
Winder, Lucy IV, 895
Winder, Lucy V, 287
Winder, Lydia IV, 601
Winder, Lydia IV, 789
Winder, Lydia IV, 808
Winder, Lydia IV, 856
Winder, Lydia IV, 902
Winder, Lydia IV, 911
Winder, Lydia IV, 918
Winder, Lydia IV, 1016
Winder, Lydia Ann IV, 789
Winder, Lydia Ann IV, 856
Winder, Lydia Ann IV, 918
Winder, Marcy IV, 68
Winder, Margaret II, 1040
Winder, Margaret IV, 68
Winder, Margaret V, 284
Winder, Margaret V, 290
Winder, Margaret L. IV, 1300
Winder, Maria IV, 1289
Winder, Maria IV, 1300
Winder, Martha L. III, 121
Winder, Martha L. III, 157
Winder, Martha L. III, 362
Winder, Marthy J. IV, 1300
Winder, Mary II, 1040
Winder, Mary IV, 789
Winder, Mary IV, 914
Winder, Mary IV, 918
Winder, Mary IV, 1300
Winder, Mary E. IV, 1016
Winder, Mary Esther II, 973
Winder, Mary Esther II, 1063
Winder, Mary Ida IV, 856
Winder, Mary Ida IV, 1016
Winder, Mary Jane IV, 1300
Winder, Mary V. V, 290
Winder, Moses II, 1040
Winder, Moses IV, 1300
Winder, Moses V, 290
Winder, Nancy A. IV, 1300
Winder, Olivia IV, 1300
Winder, Phebe IV, 1300
Winder, Phebe V, 287
Winder, Phebe V, 290
Winder, Phebe V, 312
Winder, Phebe V, 313
Winder, Phinehas IV, 1300
Winder, Phinehas M. IV, 1300
Winder, Rachel IV, 789
Winder, Rachel IV, 917
Winder, Rebecca II, 1040
Winder, Rebecca II, 1063
Winder, Rebecca IV, 1300
Winder, Rebecca H. III, 362
Winder, Rebecca H. V, 143
Winder, Rebeckah II, 1018
Winder, Rebeckah II, 1040
Winder, Ruth II, 978
Winder, Ruth II, 983
Winder, Ruth II, 1040
Winder, Ruth II, 1063
Winder, Ruth Anna II, 973
Winder, Ruth Anna IV, 457
Winder, Ruth Anna IV, 809
Winder, Ruth Anna IV, 856
Winder, Ruth Anna IV, 1016
Winder, Ruth R. II, 973
Winder, Ruthanna IV, 856
Winder, Ruthanna IV, 1016
Winder, Ruthanna C. IV, 856
Winder, Samuel Chambers IV, 358
Winder, Samuel Charles IV
Winder, Sarah II, 977
Winder, Sarah II, 1040
Winder, Sarah IV, 918
Winder, Sarah IV, 1300
Winder, Sarah V, 251
Winder, Sarah V, 290
Winder, Sarah Elizabeth V,
Winder, Sarah Esther IV, 1
Winder, Sarah S. IV, 371
Winder, Sarah S. IV, 457
Winder, Sarah S. IV, 789
Winder, Sarah S. IV, 856
Winder, Sarah S. IV, 900
Winder, Sarah S. IV, 918
Winder, Senneca IV, 1300
Winder, Sewel IV, 1300
Winder, Sewell V, 290
Winder, Susan IV, 1300
Winder, Susannah IV, 918
Winder, Tamar IV, 901
Winder, Tamar IV, 918
Winder, Thomas IV, 1300
Winder, Thomas V, 290
Winder, Thomas V, 963
Winder, William IV, 457
Winder, William IV, 789
Winder, William IV, 897
Winder, William IV, 903
Winder, William IV, 908
Winder, William IV, 917
Winder, William IV, 918
Winder, William Leonard II,
Winder, Wm. IV, 856
Winder, Wm. IV, 918
Winders, Aaron V, 290
Winders, Abner IV, 116
Winders, Abner V, 290
Winders, Allen V, 290
Winders, Amy V, 230
Winders, Amy V, 290
Winders, Ann IV, 30
Winders, Ann IV, 97
Winders, Ann IV, 116
Winders, Caleb V, 290
Winders, Elizabeth IV, 116
Winders, Elizabeth V, 290
Winders, Hannah IV, 68
Winders, Hannah IV, 116
Winders, Hannah V, 962
Winders, Henry V, 290
Winders, Hope V, 290
Winders, James IV, 116
Winders, James V, 290
Winders, John IV, 116
Winders, John V, 290
Winders, Joshua V, 290
Winders, Levi V, 290
Winders, Margaret IV, 116
Winders, Mercy IV, 116
Winders, Moses V, 290
Winders, Sarah V, 290
Winders, Sarah S. IV, 789
Winders, Thomas V, 290
Winders, Thomas V, 962
Windham, Mercy IV, 352
Windham, Mercy IV, 358
Windham, Mercy IV, 359
Windham, Mercy IV, 457
Windham, Mercy IV, 1194
Windle, Amy IV, 1016
Windle, Anna VI, 792
Windle, Anna B. VI, 792
Windle, Anna Bailey II, 1083
Windle, Anna Bailey VI, 736
Windle, Anna Bailey VI, 792
Windle, Bertha IV, 1016
Windle, Bertha M. IV, 1016
Windle, Charles II, 1083
Windle, Charles T. II, 1083
Windle, Charles T. VI, 736
Windle, Charles T. VI, 792
Windle, Clara B. II, 942
Windle, David C. VI, 792
Windle, Dorothy VI, 497
Windle, Dorothy VI, 559
Windle, Dorothy VI, 562
Windle, Edward Howell II, 1083
Windle, Edward Howell VI, 764
Windle, Edward Howell VI, 792
Windle, Edwin D. IV, 1016
Windle, Emma IV, 856
Windle, Emma IV, 1016
Windle, Emma M. IV, 1016
Windle, Emma Pettit IV, 1016
Windle, Frederick VI, 1015
Windle, Geo. IV, 1016
Windle, Joseph J. IV, 856
Windle, Louise K. VI, 764
Windle, Louise K. VI, 792
Windle, Lydia II, 795

, Milton E. IV, 1016
, Paris IV, 1016
, Phebe D. IV, 813
, Phebe D. IV, 856
, Susan IV, 830
, Susan IV, 856
es, ??? III, 508
es, Bertha III, 486
es, Bertha III, 508
es, Carolyn Louise III, 486
es, Carolyn Louise III, 508
es, Morton M. III, 486
es, Morton M. III, 508
r, Edmund II, 437
r, Elizabeth II, 437
r, James IV, 116
w, Ann II, 1040
ow, Edmund II, 437
ow, Elizabeth II, 1010
ow, Elizabeth II, 1040
w, Hannah II, 1040
ow, James II, 977
ow, James II, 1040
ow, John II, 1008
ow, John II, 1040
ow, Sarah II, 977
ow, Sarah II, 1038
ow, Sarah II, 1040
ows, James V, 979
son, Bida IV, 1194
son, Wm. Arthur IV, 1194
sor, Alvin E. IV, 1194
sor, Bida IV, 1194
sor, Charles L. IV, 1194
sor, Charles T. IV, 1194
sor, Emma Louisa IV, 1194
sor, Huber IV, 1192
sor, Myrta B. IV, 1194
sor, Pearl IV, 1192
dsor, Ralph Leroy IV, 1194
dsor, Ruth IV, 1194
dsor, Will IV, 1194
dsor, Wm. Arthur IV, 1194
e, ??? III, 362
e, Abigail III, 379
e, Abigail III, 387
e, Ann VI, 667
e, Ann VI, 674
e, Charles III, 362
e, Elizabeth III, 387
e, James III, 387
e, Jane L. III, 362
e, Jane L. III, 379
e, Jane L. III, 388
e, John III, 362
e, John III, 379
e, John III, 387
e, Mary III, 388
e, Thomas III, 362
ebrenner, Edgar IV, 1343
ebrenner, Edgar IV, 1344
ebrenner, Frank IV, 1343
ebrenner, Minnie IV, 1343
ebrenner, Mr. ??? IV, 1344
ebrenner, Mrs. ??? IV, 1344
ebrenner, Philbert IV, 1343
ebrenner, Philbert IV, 1344
nebrenner, Rachel IV, 1343
nebrenner, Rachel IV, 1344
negar, A. J. V, 467
negar, Ed V, 440
negar, Isaac V, 440
negar, Isabel V, 467
negar, Richard V, 467
negar, Taylor V, 467
neiger, Jonathan IV, 747
neinger, Malisa IV, 747
neland, Bessie IV, 789
neland, C. M. IV, 789
neland, Margaret L. IV, 789
ner, Eva IV, 1300
iner, Hittie IV, 1300
ines, Abigail III, 387
ines, Bessie M. IV, 1344
ines, Edward S. III, 388
ines, Edward S. III, 390
ines, Eliza T. III, 387
ines, Elizabeth III, 387
ines, Elizabeth T. III, 390
ines, Gilbert H. III, 387
ines, Gilbert H. III, 388
ines, Gilbert H. III, 390
ines, Gilbert S. III, 390
ines, James III, 387
Wines, Jane III, 387
Wines, Jane L. III, 388
Wines, Jane L. III, 390
Wines, John III, 387
Wines, John III, 388
Wines, John III, 390
Wines, Johnn III, 381
Wines, Mary III, 388
Wines, Robert C. III, 388
Winfield, Addie V, 605
Winfield, Alice A. V, 440
Winfield, Alice A. V, 605
Winfield, Alice A. V, 720
Winfield, Charles V, 143
Winfield, Charles V, 605
Winfield, Charles V, 606
Winfield, Charles A. V, 440
Winfield, Charles A. V, 720
Winfield, Effie L. V, 213
Winfield, Elanor J. V, 605
Winfield, Emma V, 606
Winfield, Frank V, 605
Winfield, Frank V, 606
Winfield, Frank J. V, 720
Winfield, Frank Y. V, 440
Winfield, Jessie B. V, 143
Winfield, John V, 605
Winfield, John V, 720
Winfield, John V, 1025
Winfield, John D. V, 440
Winfield, Joseph V, 605
Winfield, Margaret III, 411
Winfield, Margaret III, 475
Winfield, Marie V, 605
Winfield, Mary C. V, 605
Winfield, Mary Y. V, 440
Winfield, Pearl May V, 605
Winfield, Robert L. V, 143
Winfield, Robert L. V, 606
Winfield, T. J. V, 605
Winfield, Thelma V, 213
Winfield, Thomas J. V, 605
Winfield, Vergil E. V, 213
Winfield, W. E. V, 1025
Winford, Jane VI, 865
Winford, Joshua VI, 865
Winfred, Thomas I, 583
Winfree, Charles VI, 844
Winfree, Charlotte VI, 1018
Winfree, Chris VI, 849
Winfree, Chris. VI, 801
Winfree, Chris. VI, 828
Winfree, Chris. VI, 836
Winfree, Christopher VI, 843
Winfree, Fanny VI, 1018
Winfree, Israel VI, 1018
Winfree, Jane M. VI, 801
Winfree, Louisa A. VI, 849
Winfree, Lucy A. VI, 843
Winfree, Martha C. VI, 836
Winfree, Mary C. VI, 828
Winfree, Nancy VI, 844
Winfree, Samuel VI, 1018
Winfrey, Charles VI, 796
Winfrey, Charlotte VI, 1018
Winfrey, Fanny VI, 1018
Winfrey, Isaac VI, 1018
Winfrey, Israel VI, 998
Winfrey, Israel VI, 1018
Winfrey, Lucy VI, 1018
Winfrey, Saml. VI, 1003
Winfrey, Samuel VI, 1018
Winfrey, Sarah VI, 959
Winfrey, Sarah VI, 1018
Winfrey, Susannah VI, 796
Winfrey, Thomas VI, 1018
Winfry, Fanny VI, 1018
Winfry, Israel VI, 1018
Wing, ??? III, 362
Wing, Achsah III, 498
Wing, Achsah III, 508
Wing, Alice V, 832
Wing, Alice V, 833
Wing, Alvira IV, 1386
Wing, Ann Maria III, 234
Wing, Anna I, 936
Wing, Anna Maria III, 362
Wing, Catharine M. III, 366
Wing, Charles V, 942
Wing, Chas. V, 942
Wing, Clara V, 865
Wing, Cornelius V, 942
Wing, Cynthia T. III, 362
Wing, Daniel III, 498
Wing, Daniel III, 508
Wing, Dedan A. V, 865
Wing, Edward V, 942
Wing, Eliza V, 906
Wing, Eliza V, 942
Wing, Elizabeth V, 232
Wing, Elizabeth V, 290
Wing, Elizabeth V, 942
Wing, Elizabeth C. II, 942
Wing, Elvira IV, 1386
Wing, Emma O. III, 362
Wing, Francis III, 234
Wing, Hannah III, 362
Wing, Hannah J. III, 362
Wing, Hannah S. III, 362
Wing, Irene III, 362
Wing, John III, 366
Wing, John D. III, 362
Wing, Jonas III, 362
Wing, Joseph III, 362
Wing, Joseph K. III, 362
Wing, Julia A. III, 362
Wing, Lydia II, 914
Wing, Lydia II, 942
Wing, Lydia IV, 457
Wing, Lydia IV, 504
Wing, Lydia R. II, 942
Wing, Margaret III, 362
Wing, Mary II, 690
Wing, Mary III, 28
Wing, Mary III, 32
Wing, Mary III, 255
Wing, Mary III, 362
Wing, Mary III, 498
Wing, Mary III, 508
Wing, Mary Alice III, 362
Wing, Mary Elizabeth III, 362
Wing, Mary R. III, 366
Wing, Oliver III, 362
Wing, Oliver H. III, 255
Wing, Oliver H. III, 362
Wing, Phebe IV, 458
Wing, Phebe H. IV, 1147
Wing, Phebe H. IV, 1194
Wing, Rachel H. III, 255
Wing, Rachel H. III, 362
Wing, Sarah IV, 457
Wing, Sarah IV, 458
Wing, Sarah IV, 504
Wing, Sarah IV, 1194
Wing, Stephen R. II, 942
Wing, Stephen Roger, Jr. II, 914
Wing, Stephen Rogers II, 942
Wing, Walter IV, 1386
Wing, William G. III, 362
Wing, William George III, 362
Wing, Wm. V, 942
Wingate, Charles III, 106
Wingate, Charles III, 272
Wingate, Charles III, 362
Wingate, Ella W. III, 106
Wingate, Ella W. III, 272
Wingate, Ella W. III, 362
Wingate, Emma III, 357
Wingate, Emma III, 362
Wingate, General George W. III, 362
Wingate, George III, 218
Wingate, George W. III, 218
Wingate, Hannah W. III, 362
Wingate, Joseph Phelps III, 357
Wingate, Joseph Phelps III, 362
Wingate, Mary III, 106
Wingate, Mary P. III, 272
Wingate, Mary P. III, 362
Wingate, Susan P. III, 218
Wingate, Susan P. III, 362
Winger, Anna IV, 1344
Wingfield, A. G. VI, 1018
Wingfield, Charlotte VI, 1018
Wingfield, Eliza A. VI, 965
Wingfield, Elizabeth H. VI, 865
Wingfield, Frances W. VI, 1018
Wingfield, G. A. VI, 879
Wingfield, G. A. VI, 922
Wingfield, G. A. VI, 949
Wingfield, G. A. VI, 1003
Wingfield, G. A. VI, 1011
Wingfield, G. A. VI, 1017
Wingfield, Gustavus A. VI, 939
Wingfield, Gustavus A. VI, 1018
Wingfield, Harriet E. VI, 1018
Wingfield, J. L. VI, 878
Wingfield, James L. VI, 938
Wingfield, James L. VI, 1018
Wingfield, Jemima VI, 1018
Wingfield, John VI, 1018
Wingfield, John H. VI, 878
Wingfield, Leftwich, Jr. VI, 1018
Wingfield, Lewis VI, 965
Wingfield, Lewis B. VI, 1018
Wingfield, Lucy G. VI, 878
Wingfield, Mary VI, 1018
Wingfield, Mary W. VI, 1018
Wingfield, Nelson D. VI, 1018
Wingfield, Pauline E. VI, 878
Wingfield, Sarah B. VI, 882
Wingfield, Susan L. VI, 874
Wingfield, Thomas H. VI, 865
Wingfield, William VI, 874
Wingfield, William A. VI, 1018
Wingfield, Wm. A. VI, 965
Wingo, Edmud T. VI, 1018
Wingo, Mary Jane VI, 1018
Winker, Louise I, 927
Winkle, Almira B. V, 290
Winkle, Barbara Alta V, 720
Winkle, Betty Joanne V, 720
Winkle, Catharine V, 1025
Winkle, Cecil Ross V, 290
Winkle, Dwight V, 720
Winkle, Elizabeth V, 290
Winkle, Emma V, 720
Winkle, Georgiana V, 720
Winkle, James V, 290
Winkle, James P. V, 290
Winkle, James P. V, 366
Winkle, Lillian V, 720
Winkle, Loren Fay V, 290
Winkle, Oral Guy V, 290
Winkle, Robert Eugene V, 720
Winkle, Samuel V, 290
Winkler, Helen IV, 1344
Winkler, John A. VI, 1018
Winkler, Mary T. VI, 1018
Winkles, John A. VI, 1018
Winkles, Levi VI, 883
Winkles, Levi VI, 1018
Winkles, Mary T. VI, 1018
Winkles, Sally VI, 1018
Winkley, Joel IV, 1300
Winn, ??? IV, 929
Winn, Annabella II, 723
Winn, Annabella II, 738
Winn, Annabella II, 776
Winn, Annabella E. II, 776
Winn, Daisy IV, 306
Winn, Deborah II, 437
Winn, Elizabeth II, 258
Winn, Elizabeth II, 275
Winn, Elizabeth II, 723
Winn, Elizabeth II, 738
Winn, Elizabeth II, 776
Winn, Elizabeth C. II, 776
Winn, Elliott II, 776
Winn, Isaac II, 438
Winn, John VI, 865
Winn, Lydia S. II, 723
Winn, Lydia S. II, 776
Winn, Margaret II, 1040
Winn, Mary II, 438
Winn, Mary II, 511
Winn, Mary II, 695
Winn, Mathilda V, 290
Winn, Nancy VI, 865
Winn, Roselia IV, 929
Winn, Samuel II, 738
Winn, Samuel II, 776
Winn, Thomas II, 437
Winn, Thomas II, 438
Winn, Thomas II, 723
Winn, Thomas II, 738
Winn, Thomas II, 776
Winn, William A. IV, 306
Winn, William, Sr. VI, 345
Winner, Andrew IV, 1227
Winner, Andrew C. IV, 1227
Winner, Arthur Jay IV, 1344
Winner, Charles IV, 1227
Winner, Daniel IV, 1227
Winner, Daniel W. IV, 1227
Winner, Ellis IV, 789
Winner, Ellis IV, 1227
Winner, Henry IV, 1227
Winner, Henry C. IV, 1227
Winner, Lemuel IV, 1227
Winner, Mary IV, 1227
Winner, Miriam E. II, 283
Winner, Miriam E. II, 306
Winner, Mrs. Gladys IV, 1344
Winner, Simon IV, 1227
Winner, Simon P. IV, 1227
Winner, Susan II, 704
Winner, Susan II, 714
Winner, Susanna III, 244
Winnicot, Richd. VI, 1004
Winnicot, Sally VI, 1004
Winrod, Phebe Ann Greenfield IV, 542
Winrod, Phebe Ann Greenfield IV, 558
Winser, Elisabeth II, 690
Winsloe, Easter I, 90
Winsloe, John I, 90
Winslow, ??? I, 13
Winslow, ??? I, 16
Winslow, ??? I, 26
Winslow, ??? I, 28
Winslow, ??? I Sup 1, 7
Winslow, Abigail I, 32
Winslow, Abigail I, 78
Winslow, Abigail I, 87
Winslow, Abner I, 846
Winslow, Abner F. I, 328
Winslow, Abner F. I, 331
Winslow, Abner G. I, 738
Winslow, Abner T. I, 738
Winslow, Achsah I, 30
Winslow, Achsah I, 88
Winslow, Ada Muriel I, 29
Winslow, Adalin Elisabeth I, 31
Winslow, Addison E. I, 26
Winslow, Addison E. I, 27
Winslow, Addison E. I, 89
Winslow, Adelbert Vincent I, 26
Winslow, Adliza J. I, 721
Winslow, Adliza J. I, 738
Winslow, Albert I, 30
Winslow, Alcora Elisabeth I, 32
Winslow, Alcora Lane I, 26
Winslow, Alice I, 70
Winslow, Alice Pearl IV, 1344
Winslow, Alice W. I, 27
Winslow, Alice W. I, 29
Winslow, Allen Jay I, 29
Winslow, Allen Ulysses I, 26
Winslow, Allen Ulysses I, 89
Winslow, Allen Williamson I, 32
Winslow, Alma M. I, 29
Winslow, Alma May I, 28
Winslow, Alvin Curtis I, 738
Winslow, Alvin Luther I, 29
Winslow, Amelia I, 27
Winslow, Amelia I, 28
Winslow, Amelia I, 29
Winslow, Amelia I, 89
Winslow, Ann I, 17
Winslow, Ann I, 23
Winslow, Ann I, 26
Winslow, Ann I, 27
Winslow, Ann I, 30
Winslow, Ann I, 31
Winslow, Ann I, 68
Winslow, Ann I, 72
Winslow, Ann I, 87
Winslow, Ann I, 203
Winslow, Ann I, 319
Winslow, Ann I, 738
Winslow, Anna I, 12
Winslow, Anna I, 27
Winslow, Anna I, 28
Winslow, Anna I, 706
Winslow, Anna I, 709
Winslow, Anna I, 729
Winslow, Anna I, 732
Winslow, Anna I, 738
Winslow, Anna Barbara I, 628
Winslow, Anna G. I, 89
Winslow, Anna Gertrude I, 89
Winslow, Anna L. I, 89
Winslow, Anna N. I, 82
Winslow, Anna N. I, 88
Winslow, Anna Nicholson I, 32
Winslow, Anne E. I, 846
Winslow, Arba I, 26
Winslow, Arno Ed White I, 27
Winslow, Arthur M. I, 26
Winslow, Asa Paul I, 27
Winslow, Atlessa Manola I, 28
Winslow, Barbary Ellen I, 33
Winslow, Benjamin I, 28
Winslow, Benjamin I, 78
Winslow, Benjamin I, 87
Winslow, Benjamin I, 89
Winslow, Benjamin I, 203
Winslow, Benjamin I, 228
Winslow, Benjamin C. I, 27
Winslow, Benjamin C. I, 33
Winslow, Benjamin C. I, 41
Winslow, Benjamin C. I, 88
Winslow, Benjamin J. I, 89
Winslow, Benjamin P. I, 5
Winslow, Bennoni I, 671
Winslow, Berna Alphine I, 26
Winslow, Berna Alphine??? I, 26
Winslow, Berna??? Alphine I, 26
Winslow, Berna??? Alphine??? I, 26
Winslow, Bernard Everett I, 28
Winslow, Bernice Lucille I, 27
Winslow, Bertha Clarissa I, 32
Winslow, Bessie Clara I, 28
Winslow, Bessie Lee I, 22
Winslow, Bessie Lee I, 28
Winslow, Bethana I, 706
Winslow, Bethany I, 738
Winslow, Beula I, 33
Winslow, Blanche Roundtree I, 19
Winslow, Blanche Roundtree I, 29
Winslow, Branning Thomas I, 30
Winslow, Caleb I, 23
Winslow, Caleb I, 27
Winslow, Caleb I, 28
Winslow, Caleb I, 31
Winslow, Caleb I, 39

Winslow, Caleb I, 66
Winslow, Caleb I, 68
Winslow, Caleb I, 87
Winslow, Caleb I, 88
Winslow, Caleb I, 203
Winslow, Caleb D. I, 29
Winslow, Caleb J. I, 27
Winslow, Caleb J. I, 88
Winslow, Caleb M. I, 27
Winslow, Caleb M. I, 29
Winslow, Caleb M. I, 33
Winslow, Caleb M. I, 89
Winslow, Carol Vernon I, 28
Winslow, Caroline I, 177
Winslow, Caroline I, 671
Winslow, Caroline I, 685
Winslow, Caroline I, 692
Winslow, Caroline I, 695
Winslow, Caroline I, 706
Winslow, Caroline I, 707
Winslow, Caroline I, 713
Winslow, Caroline I, 728
Winslow, Caroline I, 737
Winslow, Caroline I, 738
Winslow, Carrie Amelia I, 29
Winslow, Carrol Talmage I, 33
Winslow, Carroll Talmage I, 27
Winslow, Cassie Rebecca I, 33
Winslow, Catharine I, 43
Winslow, Catharine I, 88
Winslow, Catharine Ida I, 32
Winslow, Catherine I, 7
Winslow, Catherine I, 30
Winslow, Catherine Ida I, 27
Winslow, Cecil Calvert I, 26
Winslow, Charity I, 16
Winslow, Charity I, 30
Winslow, Charity I, 43
Winslow, Charity I, 87
Winslow, Charity I, 180
Winslow, Charity I, 203
Winslow, Charles I, 26
Winslow, Charles I, 27
Winslow, Charles I, 31
Winslow, Charles E. I, 27
Winslow, Charles Edmund I, 32
Winslow, Charles Ellis I, 29
Winslow, Charles Everett I, 27
Winslow, Charles J. I, 28
Winslow, Charles J. I, 89
Winslow, Charles Kenneth I, 27
Winslow, Charles T. I, 27
Winslow, Charles T. I, 28
Winslow, Charles T. I, 89
Winslow, Charles Wilford I, 33
Winslow, Charlotte I, 32
Winslow, Chas T. I, 24
Winslow, Christinea I, 731
Winslow, Christinea I, 737
Winslow, Clara Alberta I, 19
Winslow, Clara Alberta I, 30
Winslow, Clara May I, 27
Winslow, Clarence Ray I, 28
Winslow, Clarence Vivian I, 27
Winslow, Clemma Adell I, 26
Winslow, Clinton R. I, 27
Winslow, Cora Geneva I, 29
Winslow, Cyrus C. I, 738
Winslow, Cyrus J. I, 20
Winslow, Cyrus J. I, 84
Winslow, Cyrus J. I, 89
Winslow, Cyrus J. I, 738
Winslow, Cyrus J. I, 846
Winslow, Daniel I, 707
Winslow, Daniel Allen I, 89
Winslow, Daniel Alonzo I, 32
Winslow, Daniel Alonzo I, 89
Winslow, David A. I, 27
Winslow, David A. I, 33
Winslow, David M. I, 18
Winslow, David M. I, 27
Winslow, David M. I, 32
Winslow, David M. I, 88
Winslow, David Morris I, 27
Winslow, David Morris I, 30
Winslow, David Morris I, 33
Winslow, Delia I, 31
Winslow, Della V. I, 27
Winslow, Delphina I, 32
Winslow, Delphina I, 89
Winslow, Dempsey I, 28
Winslow, Dempsey I, 31
Winslow, Dempsey I, 88
Winslow, Dempsey Allen I, 31
Winslow, Dempsey E. I, 13
Winslow, Dempsey E. I, 26
Winslow, Dempsey E. I, 27
Winslow, Dempsey E. I, 28
Winslow, Dempsey E. I, 29
Winslow, Dempsey E. I, 31
Winslow, Dempsey E. I, 89
Winslow, Dempsey E., Jr. I, 89
Winslow, Dempsey Eugene I, 28
Winslow, Dempsey Eugenia I, 88
Winslow, Dillie I, 32
Winslow, Dorcas I, 30
Winslow, Easter I, 90
Winslow, Edna Elizabeth I, 30
Winslow, Edward W. I, 88
Winslow, Elbert L. I, 28
Winslow, Elbert L. I, 89
Winslow, Elbert Worth I, 28
Winslow, Eleazar I, 671
Winslow, Eleazar I, 689
Winslow, Eleazar I, 692
Winslow, Eleazar I, 706
Winslow, Eleazar I, 738
Winslow, Eleazar I, 772
Winslow, Eleazer I, 737
Winslow, Elesabeth I, 33
Winslow, Eli W. I, 28
Winslow, Eli Wilson I, 32
Winslow, Elias I, 31
Winslow, Elias Benjamin I, 33
Winslow, Elias P. I, 27
Winslow, Elias S. W. I, 30
Winslow, Elihu I, 29
Winslow, Elisa J. I, 738
Winslow, Elisabeth I, 7
Winslow, Elisabeth I, 8
Winslow, Elisabeth I, 16
Winslow, Elisabeth I, 19
Winslow, Elisabeth I, 27
Winslow, Elisabeth I, 28
Winslow, Elisabeth I, 30
Winslow, Elisabeth I, 31
Winslow, Elisabeth I, 32
Winslow, Elisabeth I, 37
Winslow, Elisabeth I, 50
Winslow, Elisabeth I, 55
Winslow, Elisabeth I, 62
Winslow, Elisabeth I, 64
Winslow, Elisabeth I, 66
Winslow, Elisabeth I, 69
Winslow, Elisabeth I, 87
Winslow, Elisabeth I, 88
Winslow, Elisabeth I, 89
Winslow, Elisabeth I, 143
Winslow, Elisabeth I, 154
Winslow, Elisabeth I, 177
Winslow, Elisabeth A. I, 28
Winslow, Elisabeth A. I, 85
Winslow, Elisabeth A. I, 89
Winslow, Elisabeth C. I, 33
Winslow, Elisabeth C. I, 83
Winslow, Elisabeth C. I, 88
Winslow, Elisabeth Catherine I, 21
Winslow, Elisabeth May I, 27
Winslow, Elisha I, 31
Winslow, Elisha S. I, 24
Winslow, Elisha S. I, 26
Winslow, Elisha S. I, 27
Winslow, Elisha S. I, 28
Winslow, Elisha S. I, 29
Winslow, Elisha S. I, 30
Winslow, Elisha S. I, 31
Winslow, Elisha S. I, 88
Winslow, Elisha S. I, 89
Winslow, Elisha S., Jr. I, 28
Winslow, Eliza I, 89
Winslow, Eliza I, 733
Winslow, Eliza I, 738
Winslow, Eliza E. I, 28
Winslow, Eliza E. I, 89
Winslow, Eliza Jane I, 3
Winslow, Eliza Jane I, 30
Winslow, Elizabeth I, 12
Winslow, Elizabeth I, 28
Winslow, Elizabeth I, 31
Winslow, Elizabeth I, 87
Winslow, Elizabeth I, 89
Winslow, Elizabeth I, 126
Winslow, Elizabeth I, 177
Winslow, Elizabeth I, 319
Winslow, Elizabeth I, 331
Winslow, Elizabeth I, 671
Winslow, Elizabeth I, 689
Winslow, Elizabeth I, 692
Winslow, Elizabeth I, 706
Winslow, Elizabeth I, 718
Winslow, Elizabeth I, 727
Winslow, Elizabeth I, 736
Winslow, Elizabeth I, 737
Winslow, Elizabeth I, 738
Winslow, Elizabeth I, 757
Winslow, Elizabeth I, 772
Winslow, Elizabeth I, 846
Winslow, Elizabeth I Sup 1, 3
Winslow, Elizabeth I Sup 1, 6
Winslow, Elizabeth I Sup 1, 7
Winslow, Elizabeth W. I, 706
Winslow, Elmer R. I, 22
Winslow, Elmer R. I, 28
Winslow, Elsie Alcora I, 28
Winslow, Elsie Alcora I, 32
Winslow, Elwood I, 30
Winslow, Emily Ann I, 707
Winslow, Emily F. I, 714
Winslow, Emily F. I, 738
Winslow, Emily Lavina I, 772
Winslow, Emma Dora I, 29
Winslow, Emma J. I, 30
Winslow, Emma R. I, 16
Winslow, Emma R. I, 33
Winslow, Emmett Thomas Love I, 26
Winslow, Ernest Calvin I, 28
Winslow, Ernest Calvin I, 31
Winslow, Ernest Melvin I, 27
Winslow, Ervin Timothy I, 31
Winslow, Estella J. I, 738
Winslow, Esther I, 12
Winslow, Esther I, 27
Winslow, Esther I, 28
Winslow, Esther I, 30
Winslow, Esther I, 43
Winslow, Esther I, 68
Winslow, Esther I, 87
Winslow, Esther I, 88
Winslow, Esther I, 228
Winslow, Esther I Sup 1, 6
Winslow, Esther Ann I, 6
Winslow, Esther Ann I, 44
Winslow, Esther Ann I, 89
Winslow, Esther Burnett I, 30
Winslow, Esther E. I, 30
Winslow, Esther E. I, 88
Winslow, Esther Jane I, 29
Winslow, Esther Jane I, 31
Winslow, Esther May I, 31
Winslow, Esther P. I, 5
Winslow, Esther P. I, 27
Winslow, Esther P. I, 41
Winslow, Esther P. I, 88
Winslow, Ethel May I, 26
Winslow, Etta Rebecca I, 28
Winslow, Eugene I, 25
Winslow, Eugene I, 26
Winslow, Eugene I, 28
Winslow, Eugene I, 31
Winslow, Eugene E. I, 29
Winslow, Eugene Earle I, 28
Winslow, Eula I, 89
Winslow, Eula Stallings I, 30
Winslow, Eunice I, 26
Winslow, Eunice V, 650
Winslow, Eunice C. I, 738
Winslow, Eunice C. I, 846
Winslow, Eva Wrae I, 33
Winslow, Evie Bernell I, 29
Winslow, Exum I, 16
Winslow, Exum I, 30
Winslow, Exum I, 88
Winslow, Exum B. I, 12
Winslow, Exum B. I, 29
Winslow, Exum B. I, 31
Winslow, Exum B. I, 89
Winslow, Exum Bell I, 28
Winslow, Exum Ralph I, 31
Winslow, Eza Marunda I, 33
Winslow, Ezra I, 126
Winslow, Fannie May I, 27
Winslow, Fannie May I, 89
Winslow, Florence Irene I, 29
Winslow, Flotilla I, 30
Winslow, Flotilla I, 32
Winslow, Flotilla I, 89
Winslow, Frances I, 88
Winslow, Francis I, 3
Winslow, Francis I, 7
Winslow, Francis I, 24
Winslow, Francis I, 28
Winslow, Francis I, 33
Winslow, Francis I, 87
Winslow, Francis I, 88
Winslow, Francis Osmond I, 30
Winslow, Francis T. K. I, 32
Winslow, Garden Layden I, 33
Winslow, George Benjamin I, 27
Winslow, George Gilbert I, 33
Winslow, George H. I, 89
Winslow, George Henry I, 89
Winslow, George R. I, 28
Winslow, George T. I, 28
Winslow, George T. I, 29
Winslow, George T. I, 32
Winslow, George T. I, 85
Winslow, George T. I, 89
Winslow, George T., Jr. I, 28
Winslow, George Thomas I, 32
Winslow, George Wilbur I, 32
Winslow, Georgietta I, 30
Winslow, Gerald Stanley I, 26
Winslow, Gertrude L. I, 29
Winslow, Grace Eliza III, 362
Winslow, Gulielma I, 228
Winslow, Gulielma P. I, 219
Winslow, Guy I, 26
Winslow, H. K. I, 707
Winslow, Halford I, 32
Winslow, Hannah I, 29
Winslow, Hannah I, 50
Winslow, Hannah I, 87
Winslow, Hariett I, 88
Winslow, Harold Brenton I, 31
Winslow, Harriet P. I, 88
Winslow, Harriett A. I, 89
Winslow, Harriett Ann I, 27
Winslow, Harriett Ellen I, 30
Winslow, Harriett P. I, 30
Winslow, Harriett P. I, 33
Winslow, Haywood I, 32
Winslow, Helen Catharine I, 28
Winslow, Henrietta I, 89
Winslow, Henrietta S. I, 89
Winslow, Henry I, 27
Winslow, Henry I, 126
Winslow, Henry I, 671
Winslow, Henry I, 707
Winslow, Henry I, 727
Winslow, Henry I, 737
Winslow, Henry I, 738
Winslow, Henry I, 951
Winslow, Henry E. I, 24
Winslow, Henry E. I, 28
Winslow, Henry E. I, 31
Winslow, Henry Edgar I, 88
Winslow, Henry Elson I, 29
Winslow, Henry Elson I, 31
Winslow, Henry Willard I, 27
Winslow, Henry, Jr. I, 738
Winslow, Herbert Paul I, 29
Winslow, Howard I, 89
Winslow, Hugh I, 738
Winslow, Hugh P. I, 27
Winslow, Ida Beatrice I, 29
Winslow, Ida L. I, 28
Winslow, Ira Sankey I, 28
Winslow, Ira Sankey I, 29
Winslow, Irene I, 29
Winslow, Irene I, 31
Winslow, Irene I, 32
Winslow, Isa Gladys I, 28
Winslow, Isabella I, 28
Winslow, Isabella I, 738
Winslow, Isabella A. I, 69
Winslow, Isabella A. I, 89
Winslow, Isabella A. I, 846
Winslow, Isabelle I, 16
Winslow, Israel I, 87
Winslow, Iva G. I, 228
Winslow, J. Calvin I, 70
Winslow, J. Edward I, 27
Winslow, J. Luther I, 29
Winslow, Jacob I, 33
Winslow, Jacob I, 50
Winslow, Jacob I, 79
Winslow, Jacob I, 80
Winslow, Jacob I, 87
Winslow, Jacob I, 177
Winslow, Jacob W. I, 64
Winslow, Jacob W. I, 88
Winslow, James I, 104
Winslow, James I, 126
Winslow, James I, 177
Winslow, James I, 708
Winslow, James I, 737
Winslow, James Alton I, 29
Winslow, James Alvah I, 26
Winslow, James Claudius I, 27
Winslow, James H. I, 29
Winslow, James P. I, 3
Winslow, James P. I, 31
Winslow, James P. I, 39
Winslow, James P. I, 89
Winslow, James Peele I, 32
Winslow, James Ruffin I, 738
Winslow, James T. I, 30
Winslow, Jamie I, 33
Winslow, Jane I, 7
Winslow, Jane I, 706
Winslow, Jane I, 738
Winslow, Jane I, 772
Winslow, Jane I, 906
Winslow, Jane I, 936
Winslow, Jane P. I, 88
Winslow, Jane Rebecca I, 31
Winslow, Jane Rebecca I, 89
Winslow, Jasper James I, 29
Winslow, Jennie I, 33
Winslow, Jennie F. I, 27
Winslow, Jesse I, 87
Winslow, Jesse I, 88
Winslow, Jesse I, 177
Winslow, Jesse I, 706
Winslow, Jesse I, 718
Winslow, Jesse I, 738
Winslow, Jesse B. I, 12
Winslow, Jesse B. I, 19
Winslow, Jesse B. I, 29
Winslow, Jesse B. I, 31
Winslow, Jesse B. I, 33
Winslow, Jesse B. I, 44
Winslow, Jesse B. I, 82
Winslow, Jesse B. I, 88
Winslow, Jesse B. I, 89
Winslow, Jesse Calvin I, 28
Winslow, Jesse Eugene I, 28
Winslow, Jesse F. I, 28
Winslow, Jesse L. I, 89
Winslow, Jesse T. I, 18
Winslow, Jesse T. I, 27
Winslow, Jesse T. I, 28
Winslow, Jesse T. I, 29
Winslow, Jesse T. I, 89
Winslow, Jesse White I, 88
Winslow, Jessie B. I, 6
Winslow, Jessie Belle I, 29
Winslow, Job I, 87
Winslow, Joe J. I, 89
Winslow, John I, 7
Winslow, John I, 22
Winslow, John I, 29
Winslow, John I, 30
Winslow, John I, 33
Winslow, John I, 36
Winslow, John I, 43
Winslow, John I, 67
Winslow, John I, 72
Winslow, John I, 78
Winslow, John I, 87
Winslow, John I, 88
Winslow, John I, 90
Winslow, John I, 125
Winslow, John I, 126
Winslow, John I, 177
Winslow, John I, 203
Winslow, John I, 671
Winslow, John I, 685
Winslow, John I, 692
Winslow, John I, 706
Winslow, John I, 707
Winslow, John I, 718
Winslow, John I, 738
Winslow, John I, 741
Winslow, John I Sup 1, 6
Winslow, John Allen I, 28
Winslow, John Allen I, 30
Winslow, John Allen I, 88
Winslow, John Allen I, 89
Winslow, John D. I, 89
Winslow, John DeWitt I, 30
Winslow, John Dewitt I, 33
Winslow, John E. I, 17
Winslow, John E. I, 27
Winslow, John E. I, 28
Winslow, John E. I, 30
Winslow, John E. I, 31
Winslow, John E. I, 32
Winslow, John E. I, 88
Winslow, John F. I, 16
Winslow, John F. I, 19
Winslow, John Francis I, 30
Winslow, John Hubbard I, 738
Winslow, John L. I, 27
Winslow, John L. I, 30
Winslow, John L. I, 31
Winslow, John L. I, 88
Winslow, John McClarin I, 738
Winslow, John Oliver I, 32
Winslow, John Osmund I, 32
Winslow, John R. I, 31
Winslow, John R. I, 88
Winslow, John T. I, 30
Winslow, John T. I, 88
Winslow, John T. I, 739
Winslow, John T. I, 951
Winslow, John Thomas I, 738
Winslow, John Thomas I, 936
Winslow, John Thomas I, 951
Winslow, John W. I, 89
Winslow, John W. I, 723
Winslow, John W. I, 737
Winslow, John William I, 27
Winslow, John, Sr. I, 706
Winslow, Jonathan I, 126
Winslow, Jonathan I, 738
Winslow, Jonathan P. I, 738
Winslow, Jonathan P. I, 772
Winslow, Jonathan P. I, 906
Winslow, Jordan I, 87
Winslow, Joseph I, 30
Winslow, Joseph I, 31
Winslow, Joseph I, 76

slow, Joseph I, 78
slow, Joseph I, 79
slow, Joseph I, 87
slow, Joseph I, 163
slow, Joseph I, 177
slow, Joseph I, 671
slow, Joseph I, 707
slow, Joseph I, 737
slow, Joseph I, 738
slow, Joseph V, 650
slow, Joseph Benjamin I, 32
slow, Joseph D. I, 28
slow, Joseph D. I, 89
slow, Joseph Henry I, 27
slow, Joseph John I, 29
slow, Joseph Robert I, 32
slow, Joseph, Sr. I, 87
slow, Joshua C. I, 16
slow, Joshua C. I, 28
slow, Joshua C. I, 29
slow, Joshua C. I, 89
slow, Joshua Calvin I, 26
slow, Joshua Calvin I, 31
slow, Joshua Calvin I, 32
slow, Joshua E. I, 32
slow, Josiah I, 27
slow, Josiah I, 30
slow, Josiah I, 31
slow, Josiah I, 125
slow, Josiah I, 126
slow, Josiah I, 177
slow, Josiah I, 737
nslow, Josiah Francis I, 33
nslow, Josiah P. I, 33
nslow, Josiah P. I, 88
nslow, Josieh I, 177
nslow, Julia I, 19
nslow, Julia I, 30
nslow, Julia I, 84
nslow, Julia I, 88
nslow, Julia I, 89
nslow, Julia A. I, 30
nslow, Julia E. I, 27
nslow, Julia E. I, 33
nslow, Julia E. I, 89
nslow, Julia M. I, 29
nslow, Julian I, 7
nslow, Julian I, 27
nslow, Julian I, 33
nslow, Juliana I, 251
nslow, Juliana I, 261
nslow, Juliana R. I, 88
nslow, Julianna I, 88
inslow, Katherine Emma I, 26
inslow, Lancelot I, 22
inslow, Lancelot I, 28
inslow, Lancelot I, 29
inslow, Lancelot I, 30
inslow, Lancelot I, 31
inslow, Lancelot I, 32
inslow, Lancelot I, 43
inslow, Lancelot I, 87
inslow, Lancelot I, 88
inslow, Lancelot B. I, 28
inslow, Lancelot B. I, 31
inslow, Lancelott I, 88
inslow, Lancelott B. I, 89
inslow, Laura I, 738
inslow, Laura A. I, 84
inslow, Laura A. I, 89
inslow, Laura A. I, 738
inslow, Laura A. I, 846
inslow, Laura Ann I, 20
Winslow, Leah I, 29
Winslow, Leah I, 90
Winslow, Leah E. I, 18
Winslow, Leah Elizabeth I, 27
Winslow, Lebens Leverett I, 26
Winslow, Lee Ora I, 228
Winslow, Leland Joshua I, 29
Winslow, Leland White I, 30
Winslow, Lelia I, 25
Winslow, Lelia I, 26
Winslow, Lelia I, 28
Winslow, Lelia I, 31
Winslow, Lelia Manola I, 28
Winslow, Lena Bell I, 30
Winslow, Lenora P. I, 31
Winslow, Lenora Virginia I, 32
Winslow, Lenora Virginia I, 89
Winslow, Leonard F. I, 228
Winslow, Leonard Frances I, 32
Winslow, Leonora Virginia I, 89
Winslow, Leslie Newlin I, 31
Winslow, Lettice I, 177
Winslow, Levert I, 16
Winslow, Lidia I, 31
Winslow, Lillian Emma I, 29
Winslow, Lillie Hanna I, 951
Winslow, Lina I, 30
Winslow, Linda I, 28
Winslow, Lindley J. I, 89
Winslow, Lindley Jay I, 31
Winslow, Lindley Jay Franklin I, 28
Winslow, Lindsay I, 643
Winslow, Lindsey I, 26
Winslow, Linford I, 26
Winslow, Linford I, 31
Winslow, Linford I, 33
Winslow, Linwood I, 26
Winslow, Lottie H. IV, 1267
Winslow, Lottie Holding IV, 1267
Winslow, Louis Theodore I, 28
Winslow, Louisa I, 723
Winslow, Louisa I, 738
Winslow, Louise I, 738
Winslow, Loys Virgelle I, 31
Winslow, Loyyd Edward I, 29
Winslow, Lucille I, 24
Winslow, Lucinda I, 12
Winslow, Lucinda I, 28
Winslow, Lucinda E. I, 59
Winslow, Lucinda E. I, 89
Winslow, Lucinda Lane I, 12
Winslow, Lucius E. I, 31
Winslow, Lucius E. I, 33
Winslow, Luna I, 29
Winslow, Luther J. I, 29
Winslow, Luther J. I, 89
Winslow, Lyda I, 707
Winslow, Lydia I, 22
Winslow, Lydia I, 30
Winslow, Lydia I, 32
Winslow, Lydia I, 33
Winslow, Lydia I, 39
Winslow, Lydia I, 71
Winslow, Lydia I, 78
Winslow, Lydia I, 82
Winslow, Lydia I, 87
Winslow, Lydia I, 88
Winslow, Lydia I, 89
Winslow, Lydia I, 738
Winslow, Lydia A. I, 17
Winslow, Lydia Ann I, 30
Winslow, Lydia Anna I, 32
Winslow, Lydia Anna I, 89
Winslow, Lydia L. I, 83
Winslow, Lydia L. I, 88
Winslow, Lydia Louisa I, 24
Winslow, Lydia Louisa I, 28
Winslow, Lydia M. I, 8
Winslow, Lydia M. I, 27
Winslow, Lydia V. I, 6
Winslow, Lydia V. I, 32
Winslow, M. Catharine I, 88
Winslow, M. Levert I, 70
Winslow, Mafia I, 28
Winslow, Mafra E. I, 73
Winslow, Mafra E. I, 89
Winslow, Maggie W. I, 846
Winslow, Margaret I, 7
Winslow, Margaret I, 16
Winslow, Margaret I, 17
Winslow, Margaret I, 27
Winslow, Margaret I, 28
Winslow, Margaret I, 29
Winslow, Margaret I, 30
Winslow, Margaret I, 31
Winslow, Margaret I, 36
Winslow, Margaret I, 40
Winslow, Margaret I, 72
Winslow, Margaret I, 77
Winslow, Margaret I, 81
Winslow, Margaret I, 82
Winslow, Margaret I, 87
Winslow, Margaret I, 88
Winslow, Margaret I, 89
Winslow, Margaret A. I, 30
Winslow, Margaret A. I, 59
Winslow, Margaret A. I, 88
Winslow, Margaret Ann I, 88
Winslow, Margaret C. I, 30
Winslow, Margaret E. I, 18
Winslow, Margaret E. I, 29
Winslow, Margaret E. I, 30
Winslow, Margaret F. I, 88
Winslow, Margaret F. VI, 90
Winslow, Margaret Isabella I, 29
Winslow, Margaret J. I, 18
Winslow, Margaret Jane I, 33
Winslow, Margaret Louise I, 27
Winslow, Margaret P. I, 89
Winslow, Marietta I, 33
Winslow, Marietta I, 89
Winslow, Martha I, 3
Winslow, Martha I, 13
Winslow, Martha I, 30
Winslow, Martha I, 31
Winslow, Martha I, 43
Winslow, Martha I, 46
Winslow, Martha I, 64
Winslow, Martha I, 88
Winslow, Martha I, 173
Winslow, Martha I, 177
Winslow, Martha I, 197
Winslow, Martha I, 203
Winslow, Martha I, 706
Winslow, Martha I, 709
Winslow, Martha I, 738
Winslow, Martha A. I, 27
Winslow, Martha Caroline I, 89
Winslow, Martha D. I, 16
Winslow, Martha D. I, 26
Winslow, Martha D. I, 28
Winslow, Martha D. I, 31
Winslow, Martha Delphina I, 28
Winslow, Martha Delphina I, 29
Winslow, Martha Delphina I, 88
Winslow, Martha E. I, 24
Winslow, Martha E. I, 29
Winslow, Martha E. J. I, 33
Winslow, Martha Elisabeth I, 43
Winslow, Martha Elisabeth I, 88
Winslow, Martha Elsie I, 31
Winslow, Martha Emma I, 28
Winslow, Martha Emma I, 31
Winslow, Martha Gabrilla I, 32
Winslow, Martha Grace I, 26
Winslow, Martha Iris I, 32
Winslow, Martha Jane I, 28
Winslow, Martha Jane I, 32
Winslow, Martha L. I, 12
Winslow, Martha Lueza I, 32
Winslow, Martha M. I, 32
Winslow, Martha N. I, 83
Winslow, Martha N. I, 89
Winslow, Martha S. I, 26
Winslow, Martha S. I, 27
Winslow, Martha S. I, 28
Winslow, Martha S. I, 29
Winslow, Martha S. I, 30
Winslow, Martha S. I, 88
Winslow, Martha W. I, 19
Winslow, Mary I, 8
Winslow, Mary I, 12
Winslow, Mary I, 18
Winslow, Mary I, 28
Winslow, Mary I, 29
Winslow, Mary I, 30
Winslow, Mary I, 31
Winslow, Mary I, 33
Winslow, Mary I, 40
Winslow, Mary I, 62
Winslow, Mary I, 66
Winslow, Mary I, 67
Winslow, Mary I, 70
Winslow, Mary I, 72
Winslow, Mary I, 77
Winslow, Mary I, 78
Winslow, Mary I, 81
Winslow, Mary I, 87
Winslow, Mary I, 88
Winslow, Mary I, 90
Winslow, Mary I, 105
Winslow, Mary I, 125
Winslow, Mary I, 126
Winslow, Mary I, 173
Winslow, Mary I, 177
Winslow, Mary I, 197
Winslow, Mary I, 203
Winslow, Mary I, 319
Winslow, Mary I, 583
Winslow, Mary I, 671
Winslow, Mary I, 706
Winslow, Mary I, 707
Winslow, Mary I, 708
Winslow, Mary I, 715
Winslow, Mary I, 716
Winslow, Mary I, 718
Winslow, Mary I, 728
Winslow, Mary I, 737
Winslow, Mary I, 738
Winslow, Mary A. I, 5
Winslow, Mary A. I, 6
Winslow, Mary A. I, 11
Winslow, Mary A. I, 27
Winslow, Mary A. I, 28
Winslow, Mary A. I, 29
Winslow, Mary A. I, 31
Winslow, Mary A. I, 58
Winslow, Mary A. I, 88
Winslow, Mary A. I, 89
Winslow, Mary A. I, 261
Winslow, Mary Ann I, 11
Winslow, Mary Ann I, 15
Winslow, Mary Ann I, 19
Winslow, Mary Ann I, 27
Winslow, Mary Ann I, 31
Winslow, Mary Ann I, 32
Winslow, Mary Ann I, 33
Winslow, Mary Ann I, 83
Winslow, Mary Ann I, 88
Winslow, Mary Ann I, 89
Winslow, Mary Ann I, 254
Winslow, Mary Ann I, 261
Winslow, Mary Bell I, 88
Winslow, Mary D. I, 30
Winslow, Mary E. I, 24
Winslow, Mary E. I, 27
Winslow, Mary E. I, 28
Winslow, Mary E. I, 29
Winslow, Mary E. I, 30
Winslow, Mary E. I, 31
Winslow, Mary E. I, 32
Winslow, Mary E. I, 88
Winslow, Mary E. I, 89
Winslow, Mary E. I, 738
Winslow, Mary E. I, 846
Winslow, Mary Elisabeth I, 26
Winslow, Mary Elisabeth I, 27
Winslow, Mary Elisabeth I, 28
Winslow, Mary Elisabeth I, 32
Winslow, Mary Elizabeth I, 33
Winslow, Mary Etta I, 27
Winslow, Mary Iona I, 31
Winslow, Mary Irma I, 24
Winslow, Mary Isabella I, 83
Winslow, Mary Isabella I, 89
Winslow, Mary Isabelle I, 30
Winslow, Mary J. I, 28
Winslow, Mary J. I, 83
Winslow, Mary J. I, 89
Winslow, Mary J. T. I, 27
Winslow, Mary Jane I, 7
Winslow, Mary Jane I, 88
Winslow, Mary Jane I, 738
Winslow, Mary Jemima I, 29
Winslow, Mary Lee I, 28
Winslow, Mary Londa I, 772
Winslow, Mary O. I, 846
Winslow, Mary Olive I, 32
Winslow, Mary P. I, 32
Winslow, Mary Pleasant I, 32
Winslow, Mary S. I, 31
Winslow, Mary S. I, 32
Winslow, Mary Sabra I, 28
Winslow, Mary Sabra I, 29
Winslow, Mary Sabra I, 32
Winslow, Mary Sabra I, 89
Winslow, Mary Verna I, 12
Winslow, Mary Vernon I, 26
Winslow, Mathew I, 709
Winslow, Mathew I, 738
Winslow, Matthew I, 738
Winslow, Matthew R. I, 26
Winslow, Mattie I, 12
Winslow, Mattie I, 29
Winslow, Mattie Lou I, 26
Winslow, Mattie Lou I, 31
Winslow, Maud I, 31
Winslow, Maud I, 89
Winslow, Mavis Catharine I, 31
Winslow, Mavis Leana I, 28
Winslow, Meriam I, 30
Winslow, Meriam I, 35
Winslow, Meriam I, 87
Winslow, Meriam I, 737
Winslow, Merrill E. I, 228
Winslow, Merrill White I, 29
Winslow, Miles I, 30
Winslow, Milicent I, 57
Winslow, Milicent I, 79
Winslow, Milicent I, 87
Winslow, Milicent I, 88
Winslow, Milicent I, 706
Winslow, Milicent I, 721
Winslow, Milicent I, 736
Winslow, Milicent I, 737
Winslow, Milicent I, 738
Winslow, Milicent Henby I, 88
Winslow, Milisent I, 53
Winslow, Milisent I, 87
Winslow, Millicent N. I, 707
Winslow, Milton I, 707
Winslow, Milton I, 738
Winslow, Mineola I, 31
Winslow, Minneola I, 89
Winslow, Miriam I, 46
Winslow, Miriam I, 87
Winslow, Miriam I, 115
Winslow, Miriam I, 125
Winslow, Miriam I, 126
Winslow, Miriam I, 162
Winslow, Miriam I, 177
Winslow, Miriam I, 671
Winslow, Miriam I, 690
Winslow, Miriam I, 692
Winslow, Miriam I, 713
Winslow, Miriam I, 738
Winslow, Mollie I, 18
Winslow, Morris I, 8
Winslow, Myrta W. I, 643
Winslow, Myrtle Clarine I, 28
Winslow, Myrtle Gladys I, 26
Winslow, Nancy I, 707
Winslow, Nancy I, 720
Winslow, Nancy I, 738
Winslow, Nancy A. I, 31
Winslow, Nathan I, 31
Winslow, Nathan I, 87
Winslow, Nathan I, 88
Winslow, Nathan I, 89
Winslow, Nathan I, 331
Winslow, Nathan I, 706
Winslow, Nathan I, 707
Winslow, Nathan I, 738
Winslow, Nathan I, 757
Winslow, Nathan I, 772
Winslow, Nathan I, 846
Winslow, Nathan VI, 90
Winslow, Nathan B. I, 89
Winslow, Nathan Benjamin I, 31
Winslow, Nathan E. I, 31
Winslow, Nathan E. I, 89
Winslow, Nathan Elisha I, 32
Winslow, Nathan F. I, 27
Winslow, Nathan, Jr. I, 738
Winslow, Nereus Arthur I, 28
Winslow, Nettie Lee I, 16
Winslow, Nettie Lee I, 33
Winslow, Nina I, 28
Winslow, Nixon I, 738
Winslow, Nora I, 32
Winslow, Nora A. I, 32
Winslow, Nora A. I, 33
Winslow, Norman Newlin I, 32
Winslow, Novella I, 25
Winslow, O. Roy I, 33
Winslow, Obed I, 30
Winslow, Obed I, 31
Winslow, Obed I, 32
Winslow, Obed I, 33
Winslow, Obed I, 63
Winslow, Obed I, 88
Winslow, Obed I, 261
Winslow, Odessa May I, 30
Winslow, Olive Leora I, 27
Winslow, Onella Rebecca I, 32
Winslow, Ora I, 27
Winslow, Orris Warren I, 33
Winslow, Oscar I, 31
Winslow, Oscar I, 33
Winslow, Oscar Roy I, 29
Winslow, Otho Iverton I, 33
Winslow, Paul J. I, 29
Winslow, Pearl IV, 1344
Winslow, Peggy I, 30
Winslow, Peggy I, 87
Winslow, Peninah I, 706
Winslow, Peninah I, 737
Winslow, Peninah T. I, 261
Winslow, Penninah I, 163
Winslow, Penninah I, 177
Winslow, Penninah I, 228
Winslow, Penninah I, 707
Winslow, Penninah I, 718
Winslow, Penninah I, 738
Winslow, Penninah Terretta I, 213
Winslow, Percy E. I, 29
Winslow, Percy E. I, 31
Winslow, Percy E. I, 32
Winslow, Percy Lancelot I, 32
Winslow, Phariba I, 30
Winslow, Phebe I, 723
Winslow, Phebe I, 737
Winslow, Pheriba I, 51
Winslow, Pheriba I, 88
Winslow, Pininiah I, 738
Winslow, Pinniah I, 738
Winslow, Pleasant I, 30
Winslow, Pleasant I, 31
Winslow, Pleasant I, 32
Winslow, Pleasant I, 33
Winslow, Pleasant I, 43
Winslow, Pleasant I, 76
Winslow, Pleasant I, 79
Winslow, Pleasant I, 87
Winslow, Pleasant I, 88
Winslow, Pleasant I, 261
Winslow, Pleasant I, 319
Winslow, Pleasant A. I, 30
Winslow, Pleasant A. I, 88
Winslow, Preston Claud I, 28
Winslow, Rachel I, 3
Winslow, Rachel I, 7
Winslow, Rachel I, 23
Winslow, Rachel I, 27
Winslow, Rachel I, 28
Winslow, Rachel I, 30
Winslow, Rachel I, 63
Winslow, Rachel I, 76
Winslow, Rachel I, 78
Winslow, Rachel I, 79

Winslow, Rachel I, 85
Winslow, Rachel I, 87
Winslow, Rachel I, 88
Winslow, Randolph I, 89
Winslow, Randolph Pinkney I, 26
Winslow, Randolph W. I, 88
Winslow, Ravis Clarine I, 31
Winslow, Raymond Alexis I, 26
Winslow, Rebecca I, 12
Winslow, Rebecca I, 19
Winslow, Rebecca I, 24
Winslow, Rebecca I, 29
Winslow, Rebecca Jane I, 19
Winslow, Rebecca Jane I, 29
Winslow, Rebecca Jane I, 31
Winslow, Reby Constance I, 31
Winslow, Robert I, 30
Winslow, Robert I, 81
Winslow, Robert I, 87
Winslow, Robert I, 88
Winslow, Robert I, 738
Winslow, Robert Elisha I, 27
Winslow, Robert J. I, 30
Winslow, Robert J. I, 32
Winslow, Roland I, 89
Winslow, Rubie Marie I, 26
Winslow, Rufus H. I, 31
Winslow, Rufus H. I, 32
Winslow, Rufus H. I, 89
Winslow, Ruth I, 49
Winslow, Ruth I, 87
Winslow, Ruth I, 125
Winslow, Ruth I, 126
Winslow, Ruth I, 148
Winslow, Ruth I, 177
Winslow, Ruth I, 706
Winslow, Ruth I, 723
Winslow, Ruth I, 738
Winslow, Ruth Alice I, 32
Winslow, Ruth Elsie I, 27
Winslow, Sabelia I, 26
Winslow, Sabra Allen I, 30
Winslow, Sallie E. I, 31
Winslow, Sallie F. I, 89
Winslow, Samuel I, 6
Winslow, Samuel I, 27
Winslow, Samuel I, 28
Winslow, Samuel I, 30
Winslow, Samuel I, 31
Winslow, Samuel I, 32
Winslow, Samuel I, 49
Winslow, Samuel I, 83
Winslow, Samuel I, 87
Winslow, Samuel I, 88
Winslow, Samuel I, 89
Winslow, Samuel I, 125
Winslow, Samuel I, 126
Winslow, Samuel I, 177
Winslow, Samuel E. I, 32
Winslow, Samuel M. I, 32
Winslow, Samuel Martin I, 31
Winslow, Samuel R. I, 32
Winslow, Samuel S. I, 738
Winslow, Samuel Stanton I, 738
Winslow, Samuel T. I, 738
Winslow, Samuel W. I, 31
Winslow, Sarah I, 12
Winslow, Sarah I, 13
Winslow, Sarah I, 22
Winslow, Sarah I, 27
Winslow, Sarah I, 29
Winslow, Sarah I, 30
Winslow, Sarah I, 31
Winslow, Sarah I, 32
Winslow, Sarah I, 33
Winslow, Sarah I, 36
Winslow, Sarah I, 57
Winslow, Sarah I, 63
Winslow, Sarah I, 65
Winslow, Sarah I, 78
Winslow, Sarah I, 82
Winslow, Sarah I, 87
Winslow, Sarah I, 88
Winslow, Sarah I, 89
Winslow, Sarah I, 90
Winslow, Sarah I, 126
Winslow, Sarah I, 177
Winslow, Sarah I, 201
Winslow, Sarah I, 203
Winslow, Sarah I, 261
Winslow, Sarah I, 706
Winslow, Sarah I, 707
Winslow, Sarah I, 737
Winslow, Sarah I, 738
Winslow, Sarah I, 772
Winslow, Sarah A. I, 33
Winslow, Sarah A. I, 74
Winslow, Sarah A. I, 88
Winslow, Sarah Alberta I, 89
Winslow, Sarah Ann I, 17
Winslow, Sarah Ann I, 33
Winslow, Sarah B. I, 29
Winslow, Sarah B. I, 89
Winslow, Sarah Bertha I, 19
Winslow, Sarah C. I, 88
Winslow, Sarah C. I, 89
Winslow, Sarah E. I, 28
Winslow, Sarah E. I, 29
Winslow, Sarah E. I, 429
Winslow, Sarah E. I, 738
Winslow, Sarah E. R. I, 32
Winslow, Sarah Elisabeth I, 58
Winslow, Sarah Elisabeth I, 88
Winslow, Sarah Elisabeth I, 89
Winslow, Sarah Elizabeth I, 29
Winslow, Sarah Elizabeth I, 88
Winslow, Sarah F. I, 31
Winslow, Sarah F. I, 32
Winslow, Sarah F. I, 39
Winslow, Sarah Francis I, 3
Winslow, Sarah Ida I, 27
Winslow, Sarah J. I, 15
Winslow, Sarah J. I, 32
Winslow, Sarah J. I, 67
Winslow, Sarah Maie I, 31
Winslow, Sarah S. I, 88
Winslow, Sarah W. I, 328
Winslow, Sarah W. I, 331
Winslow, Seth I, 707
Winslow, Seth I, 738
Winslow, Sherill Sanford I, 26
Winslow, Sibyl Jane I, 29
Winslow, Sidney Arthur I, 26
Winslow, Sobelia I, 33
Winslow, Stanton I, 706
Winslow, Stella Maie I, 28
Winslow, Susan A. I, 32
Winslow, Susan F. I, 26
Winslow, Susanna J. I, 738
Winslow, Susannah I, 713
Winslow, Susannah I, 738
Winslow, T. Grellet I, 28
Winslow, Tamer I, 17
Winslow, Tamer I, 18
Winslow, Tamer I, 21
Winslow, Tamer I, 27
Winslow, Tamer I, 33
Winslow, Tamer I, 43
Winslow, Tamer I, 88
Winslow, Theresa May I, 29
Winslow, Thomas I, 27
Winslow, Thomas I, 29
Winslow, Thomas I, 31
Winslow, Thomas I, 69
Winslow, Thomas I, 87
Winslow, Thomas I, 89
Winslow, Thomas I, 90
Winslow, Thomas I, 125
Winslow, Thomas I, 126
Winslow, Thomas I, 173
Winslow, Thomas I, 177
Winslow, Thomas I, 319
Winslow, Thomas I, 671
Winslow, Thomas I, 692
Winslow, Thomas I, 695
Winslow, Thomas I, 706
Winslow, Thomas I, 707
Winslow, Thomas I, 709
Winslow, Thomas I, 729
Winslow, Thomas I, 737
Winslow, Thomas I, 738
Winslow, Thomas I, 936
Winslow, Thomas I, 953
Winslow, Thomas I Sup 1, 3
Winslow, Thomas I Sup 1, 6
Winslow, Thomas I Sup 1, 7
Winslow, Thomas A. I, 12
Winslow, Thomas A. I, 27
Winslow, Thomas A. I, 28
Winslow, Thomas A. I, 32
Winslow, Thomas A. I, 82
Winslow, Thomas A. I, 88
Winslow, Thomas A. I, 89
Winslow, Thomas Alexander I, 27
Winslow, Thomas Claude I, 32
Winslow, Thomas E. I, 11
Winslow, Thomas E. I, 15
Winslow, Thomas E. I, 19
Winslow, Thomas E. I, 31
Winslow, Thomas E. I, 32
Winslow, Thomas E. I, 88
Winslow, Thomas E. I, 89
Winslow, Thomas E. I, 254
Winslow, Thomas E. I, 261
Winslow, Thomas Edward I, 29
Winslow, Thomas Elwood I, 88
Winslow, Thomas Elwood Grellet I, 27
Winslow, Thomas Floyd I, 27
Winslow, Thomas Graft I, 32
Winslow, Thomas Grellett I, 32
Winslow, Thomas H. I, 18
Winslow, Thomas Lloyd I, 27
Winslow, Thomas N. I, 89
Winslow, Thomas Newby I, 32
Winslow, Thomas R. I, 28
Winslow, Thomas R. I, 32
Winslow, Thomas R. I, 33
Winslow, Thomas W. I, 17
Winslow, Thomas W. I, 21
Winslow, Thomas W. I, 30
Winslow, Thomas W. I, 33
Winslow, Thomas W. I, 43
Winslow, Thomas W. I, 88
Winslow, Thos. A. I, 31
Winslow, Timothy I, 12
Winslow, Timothy I, 27
Winslow, Timothy I, 30
Winslow, Timothy I, 62
Winslow, Timothy I, 85
Winslow, Timothy I, 87
Winslow, Timothy I Sup 1, 6
Winslow, Ulysses I, 12
Winslow, Ulysses Crafton I, 26
Winslow, Velum C. I, 33
Winslow, Vera Valentine I, 33
Winslow, Verna Louise I, 26
Winslow, Wallace Fentress I, 28
Winslow, Wallace J. I, 29
Winslow, Walter I, 89
Winslow, Walter C. I, 29
Winslow, Walter Raleigh I, 29
Winslow, Widow Jemima I, 39
Winslow, Widow Jemima I, 87
Winslow, Widow Martha I, 87
Winslow, Widow Rachel I, 28
Winslow, Widow Ruth I, 104
Winslow, William I, 27
Winslow, William I, 30
Winslow, William I, 33
Winslow, William I, 79
Winslow, William I, 80
Winslow, William I, 87
Winslow, William I, 88
Winslow, William I, 251
Winslow, William I, 261
Winslow, William I, 739
Winslow, William C. I, 429
Winslow, William C. I, 738
Winslow, William Elihu I, 33
Winslow, William F. I, 33
Winslow, William F. I, 88
Winslow, William Herbert I, 31
Winslow, William Julius I, 30
Winslow, William Lewis I, 26
Winslow, William O. I, 30
Winslow, William O. I, 33
Winslow, William O. I, 88
Winslow, William O. I, 89
Winslow, William T. I, 26
Winslow, William T. I, 27
Winslow, William T. I, 29
Winslow, William T. I, 30
Winslow, William T. I, 31
Winslow, William T. I, 33
Winslow, William T. I, 89
Winslow, William U. I, 261
Winslow, William W. I, 27
Winslow, William W. I, 89
Winslow, William W. I, 213
Winslow, William W. I, 219
Winslow, William W. I, 228
Winslow, Willis J. I, 27
Winslow, Willis J. I, 89
Winslow, Winford Samuel I, 28
Winslow, Winnie Evans I, 26
Winslow, Winston Josiah I, 31
Winslow, Wm. I, 7
Winslow, Wm. C. Roland I, 33
Winslow, Wm. Charles Roland I, 27
Winslow, Wm. T. I, 16
Winslow, Wm. T. I, 31
Winson, Ruth V, 662
Winston, ??? VI, 223
Winston, Alanson VI, 866
Winston, Alice VI, 802
Winston, Amelia VI, 212
Winston, Amelia VI, 217
Winston, Amelia VI, 218
Winston, Amey VI, 262
Winston, Amey VI, 280
Winston, Amy VI, 280
Winston, Ann VI, 84
Winston, Ann VI, 90
Winston, Ann VI, 217
Winston, Ann VI, 218
Winston, Ann VI, 280
Winston, Ann VI, 281
Winston, Anthony VI, 217
Winston, Anthony VI, 280
Winston, Benjamin A. VI, 800
Winston, Bolling VI, 218
Winston, Bowling VI, 230
Winston, Bowling VI, 265
Winston, Bowling VI, 281
Winston, Bowling H. VI, 266
Winston, Bowling H. VI, 280
Winston, Bowling H. VI, 281
Winston, Bowling Henry VI, 281
Winston, Charlotte E. VI, 866
Winston, Cornelia VI, 281
Winston, Deborah Ann IV, 244
Winston, Edmond VI, 217
Winston, Edmond VI, 280
Winston, Edmund VI, 802
Winston, Edmund VI, 873
Winston, Elizabeth VI, 218
Winston, Elizabeth VI, 280
Winston, Elizabeth VI, 281
Winston, Elizabeth C. VI, 218
Winston, Elizabeth C. VI, 280
Winston, Elizabeth C. VI, 866
Winston, Elizabeth H. VI, 217
Winston, Ella T. VI, 281
Winston, Frances VI, 866
Winston, George VI, 179
Winston, George VI, 180
Winston, George VI, 210
Winston, George VI, 217
Winston, George VI, 218
Winston, George VI, 280
Winston, George VI, 345
Winston, Henry VI, 19
Winston, Henry VI, 218
Winston, Isaac VI, 218
Winston, Isaac VI, 280
Winston, James VI, 84
Winston, James VI, 90
Winston, James VI, 197
Winston, James VI, 217
Winston, James VI, 218
Winston, James VI, 280
Winston, Jemima VI, 157
Winston, Jemima VI, 217
Winston, Jemima VI, 280
Winston, Jemimah VI, 280
Winston, John VI, 217
Winston, John VI, 218
Winston, John VI, 262
Winston, John VI, 280
Winston, John VI, 281
Winston, John C. VI, 265
Winston, John C. VI, 280
Winston, John C. VI, 281
Winston, John G. VI, 281
Winston, John H. VI, 854
Winston, John H. VI, 866
Winston, Judith IV, 288
Winston, Judith VI, 179
Winston, Judith VI, 180
Winston, Judith VI, 210
Winston, Judith VI, 217
Winston, Judith VI, 218
Winston, Judith VI, 345
Winston, Julia W. VI, 265
Winston, Julia W. VI, 266
Winston, Julia W. VI, 280
Winston, Julia W. VI, 281
Winston, Laura I, 628
Winston, Laura A. I, 643
Winston, Lindley M. VI, 280
Winston, Lindley M. VI, 281
Winston, Lucy A. VI, 217
Winston, Lucy A. VI, 280
Winston, Lucy A. VI, 281
Winston, Lucy Ann VI, 218
Winston, Margaret Ann VI, 215
Winston, Margaret Ann VI, 218
Winston, Martha VI, 280
Winston, Mary IV, 244
Winston, Mary IV, 736
Winston, Mary VI, 217
Winston, Mary VI, 218
Winston, Mary VI, 233
Winston, Mary VI, 280
Winston, Mary H. VI, 210
Winston, Mary H. VI, 217
Winston, Mary H. VI, 218
Winston, Mary L. VI, 266
Winston, Mary L. VI, 281
Winston, Mrs. Samuel VI, 280
Winston, Nancy VI, 230
Winston, Nathan VI, 280
Winston, Nathan VI, 287
Winston, Nathaniel IV, 306
Winston, Nathaniel V, 942
Winston, Nathaniel VI, 157
Winston, Nathaniel VI, 217
Winston, Nathaniel VI, 218
Winston, Nathaniel VI, 280
Winston, Nathaniel VI, 281
Winston, Nathaniel VI, 287
Winston, Nathaniel VI, 329
Winston, Nathaniel VI, 330
Winston, Nathaniel VI, 345
Winston, Peggy VI, 90
Winston, Pleasant VI, 19
Winston, Pleasant VI, 217
Winston, Pleasant VI, 218
Winston, Pleasant VI, 280
Winston, Pleasant VI, 281
Winston, Pleasant VI, 866
Winston, Pleasant, Sr. VI, 28
Winston, Rebecca VI, 280
Winston, Salley VI, 280
Winston, Samuel VI, 217
Winston, Samuel VI, 218
Winston, Samuel VI, 280
Winston, Sarah VI, 802
Winston, Thomas VI, 217
Winston, William VI, 218
Winston, William VI, 281
Winston, Zalinda IV, 306
Winston, Zalinda VI, 281
Winston, Zalinda VI, 329
Winston, Zalinda VI, 330
Winston, Zalinda VI, 345
Winter, Catharine III, 362
Winter, Daniel I, 429
Winter, Ella III, 269
Winter, Ella III, 362
Winter, Gabriell II, 438
Winter, Geo. C. III, 362
Winter, Hannah I, 429
Winter, Hannah II, 605
Winter, Hannah II, 690
Winter, Harry W. III, 269
Winter, Harry W. III, 362
Winter, Henrietta II, 690
Winter, Henrietta II, 776
Winter, James II, 690
Winter, James II, 776
Winter, John III, 362
Winter, Jonathan IV, 165
Winter, Jonathan IV, 359
Winter, Luzena C. V, 942
Winter, Luzina C. V, 904
Winter, Michael II, 438
Winter, Sarah I, 386
Winter, Sarah I, 429
Winter, Sarah II, 438
Winters, Agathy IV, 379
Winters, Agathy IV, 458
Winters, Alven I, 846
Winters, Alveran I, 795
Winters, Alvin I, 846
Winters, Anna B. III, 73
Winters, Avary I, 846
Winters, Avery I, 846
Winters, Daniel I, 351
Winters, Florence L. III, 73
Winters, Gabriell II, 438
Winters, Geo. L. V, 1025
Winters, Geo. W. III, 73
Winters, Gertrude V, 440
Winters, James II, 723
Winters, John I, 846
Winters, John IV, 1300
Winters, John A. I, 795
Winters, John C. V, 440
Winters, John W. I, 795
Winters, Joseph IV, 1300
Winters, Joseph R. IV, 1300
Winters, Kennet V, 720
Winters, Kenneth V, 672
Winters, Laura B. I, 795
Winters, Laura B. I, 846
Winters, Louetta E. I, 846
Winters, Lowetta E. I, 795
Winters, Lucy IV, 1300
Winters, Lucy Elizabeth V, 440
Winters, Luzena V, 942
Winters, Luzena C. V, 942
Winters, Malvina I, 846
Winters, Margaret I, 951
Winters, Margaret A. I, 846
Winters, Margaret Ann I, 936
Winters, Mariah E. V, 213
Winters, Mary Ruth V, 672
Winters, Mary Ruth V, 720
Winters, Melvina I, 795
Winters, Melvina I, 835
Winters, Melvina I, 846
Winters, Myrtle V, 213
Winters, Nancy IV, 1300
Winters, Nancy V, 366
Winters, Nancy Ilo IV, 1300
Winters, R. Alma V, 213
Winters, Regina E. I, 795
Winters, Regina E. I, 846
Winters, Ruby V, 366
Winters, Ruth A. V, 213
Winters, Sarah I, 351
Winters, W. IV, 1344

ers, Wm. IV, 1344
rs, Woot IV, 1300
erstein, Charles A. IV, 1194
erstein, Susan C. IV, 1194
hrop, Henry III, 410
n, Elizabeth Daniel II, 46
on, Hannah II, 46
on, Hannah II, 53
on, Hannah II, 111
n, John II, 46
on, John II, 53
on, John II, 111
on, Samuel II, 111
ingham, Bertrand III, 297
ingham, Clement V. III, 362
ingham, David Lawton
I, 362
ingham, Eliz. III, 362
ingham, Eliz. V. III, 362
ingham, Elizabeth III, 333
ingham, Elizabeth V.
I, 362
ingham, Ellen III, 297
ingham, Hannah III, 362
ingham, Helen E. III, 362
ingham, Helen Eliz.
I, 297
ingham, Helen Eliz.
I, 362
ingham, Jere. III, 362
ingham, Jeremiah III, 333
ingham, Jeremiah III, 362
ingham, John III, 362
ingham, Louise V. III, 362
ingham, Lucien B. III, 297
ingham, Ruth III, 72
ingham, Ruth III, 202
ingham, Ruth III, 362
ingham, Ruth L. III, 72
ingham, Ruth L. III, 362
ingham, Sidney III, 362
ingham, Thomas III, 202
ingham, Thos. III, 72
ingham, Thos. III, 362
ingham, Valentine III, 362
om, Daniel V, 773
om, Ida V, 773
om, Sarah V, 773
ton, Susanna II, 438
Daniel V, 467
Harrison V, 467
Huldah V, 467
Mary II, 275
Mary II, 723
Mary II, 776
Mary Ann V, 554
Mary Ann V, 606
Nancy V, 309
Nancy V, 313
Permelia V, 580
Permelia V, 606
Sarah II, 275
an, ??? IV, 1300
an, Amy I, 430
an, Catharine I, 415
an, Catharine I, 429
an, Charlotte IV, 1300
an, John W. IV, 1300
an, Martha Jane IV, 1300
an, Mary Alexander
, 856
an, Nicholas Alexander
, 1300
an, Sidney Rebecca
, 1300
an, Thomas IV, 1300
an, William I, 429
an, William I, 430
Annie May IV, 1300
Kate IV, 1300
, Anna M. IV, 1300
, Annie May IV, 1300
, Caroline IV, 1300
, Kate IV, 1300
hing, Lorena IV, 947
hing, Lorena Crum IV, 1016
l, Ann IV, 292
l, Ann IV, 306
ll, Sarah E. IV, 308
, Elsa II, 720
, Irmgard II, 720
, Richard II, 720
m, Sarah II, 690
Albertine IV, 789
Alfred S. II, 942
Anna I, 298
Armilda V, 366
Arwilda V, 366
Caroline V, 366
Charles N. IV, 1044
Chas. II, 828
Wise, Chas. II, 859
Wise, Chas. II, 913
Wise, Chas. II, 942
Wise, Chas. S. II, 942
Wise, Clara M. IV, 1016
Wise, Clara M. IV, 1044
Wise, Cora IV, 1037
Wise, Cornelia IV, 789
Wise, Daniel IV, 1300
Wise, Edward V, 291
Wise, Edward V, 467
Wise, Edward S. V, 291
Wise, Eliza V, 366
Wise, Eliza M. V, 963
Wise, Elizabeth I, 707
Wise, Elizabeth I, 711
Wise, Elizabeth I, 739
Wise, Elizabeth IV, 23
Wise, Elizabeth IV, 68
Wise, Elizabeth I. II, 913
Wise, Elizabeth I. II, 942
Wise, Ellen IV, 1300
Wise, Emily II, 859
Wise, Emily II, 942
Wise, Emily E. II, 942
Wise, Franklin B. IV, 1044
Wise, Geo. C. IV, 789
Wise, George C. IV, 789
Wise, George C. VI, 90
Wise, George C., Jr. IV, 789
Wise, George C., Jr. VI, 281
Wise, H. F. V, 291
Wise, Hannah IV, 1016
Wise, Hannah Laura IV, 1044
Wise, Harvey V, 366
Wise, Horace E. II, 942
Wise, Hugh V, 366
Wise, Jacob II, 913
Wise, Jacob II, 942
Wise, James V, 366
Wise, James, Jr. V, 366
Wise, James, Sr. V, 366
Wise, John I, 707
Wise, John V, 963
Wise, John Milton I, 707
Wise, John S. I, 739
Wise, Joseph II, 913
Wise, Joseph II, 942
Wise, Joseph IV, 789
Wise, Joseph V, 963
Wise, Joseph F. V, 366
Wise, Josie V, 291
Wise, Josie R. V, 291
Wise, Katharine S. IV, 789
Wise, Katherine VI, 90
Wise, Linsey Jordan I, 707
Wise, Louey V, 467
Wise, Louie V, 467
Wise, Lydia II, 828
Wise, Lydia II, 913
Wise, Lydia II, 942
Wise, Lydia II, 1001
Wise, Lydia II, 1040
Wise, Lydia P. II, 859
Wise, Lydia P. II, 942
Wise, Margaret IV, 23
Wise, Margaret IV, 1044
Wise, Mary II, 913
Wise, Mary II, 942
Wise, Mary V, 366
Wise, Mary Reiff II, 802
Wise, May V, 467
Wise, Melissa V, 366
Wise, Miriam C. IV, 789
Wise, Miriam C. VI, 90
Wise, Nancy I, 298
Wise, Nora V, 366
Wise, Olive V, 366
Wise, Pusey IV, 1016
Wise, Rodna V, 366
Wise, Rodney V, 366
Wise, Ruth IV, 666
Wise, Ruth IV, 910
Wise, Ruth IV, 918
Wise, Ruth Anna V, 963
Wise, Ruth S. IV, 789
Wise, Susan V, 1025
Wise, W. F. V, 291
Wiseman, Anna III, 363
Wiseman, Anne III, 97
Wiseman, Anne III, 368
Wiseman, Annie III, 363
Wiseman, Elizabeth III, 97
Wiseman, Elizabeth III, 363
Wiseman, Harriet III, 363
Wiseman, Harriet III, 368
Wiseman, Lottie IV, 1227
Wiseman, William III, 363
Wiseman, William III, 368
Wiseman, Wm. III, 97
Wisenbarger, Christopher VI, 845
Wisenbarger, Peggy VI, 845
Wisenborn, Clara V, 1025
Wisenborn, Cordelia V, 1025
Wisenborn, Thos. V, 1025
Wisenborn, Wm. V, 1025
Wisener, Abigail I, 367
Wisener, Anthony V, 754
Wisener, Elizabeth IV, 755
Wisener, Elizabeth IV, 789
Wisener, Elizy J. IV, 789
Wisener, Isaac V, 143
Wisener, Isaac V, 773
Wisener, Jacob V, 143
Wisener, Jacob V, 773
Wisener, John I, 367
Wisener, John V, 773
Wisener, Mary V, 143
Wisener, Mary V, 773
Wisener, Micajah I, 367
Wisener, Michael I, 367
Wisener, Ruth I, 367
Wisener, Ruth V, 143
Wisener, Sarah V, 143
Wisener, Sarah V, 728
Wisener, Sarah V, 773
Wisener, Susanna V, 754
Wisener, Susannah V, 725
Wisener, Susannah V, 773
Wisener, Thomas V, 143
Wisener, William I, 367
Wiser, Lydia II, 1083
Wishart, Ann II, 438
Wishart, Ann II, 461
Wishart, Ann II, 690
Wishart, Joseph II, 438
Wishart, Peter II, 438
Wishart, Peter II, 461
Wishart, Peter II, 690
Wishart, Thomas II, 438
Wishart, Thomas Betson II, 690
Wishart, William II, 438
Wismer, Mary II, 825
Wismer, Mary II, 826
Wisner, Elizy J. IV, 789
Wisnor, Rachel I, 427
Wison, William VI, 457
Wissinger, Alma Lockner V, 773
Wistar, ??? II, 46
Wistar, Alice P. II, 126
Wistar, Alice Parry II, 47
Wistar, Amie A. II, 116
Wistar, Amie A. II, 126
Wistar, Anistacia II, 438
Wistar, Anna II, 47
Wistar, Anna B. II, 119
Wistar, Anna B. II, 126
Wistar, Anna H. II, 47
Wistar, Anna H. II, 126
Wistar, Anna Mary II, 279
Wistar, Anna Mary II, 306
Wistar, Annabella II, 776
Wistar, Annabella C. II, 723
Wistar, Annabella C. II, 776
Wistar, Annabella E. II, 735
Wistar, Annabella E. II, 776
Wistar, Annie A. II, 47
Wistar, Annie A. II, 126
Wistar, B. Wyatt II, 723
Wistar, B. Wyatt IV, 1344
Wistar, Bart IV, 1340
Wistar, Bart IV, 1344
Wistar, Bartholomew II, 46
Wistar, Bartholomew II, 47
Wistar, Bartholomew II, 111
Wistar, Bartholomew II, 438
Wistar, Bartholomew II, 691
Wistar, Bartholomew II, 723
Wistar, Bartholomew II, 732
Wistar, Bartholomew II, 735
Wistar, Bartholomew II, 776
Wistar, Bartholomew W. II, 188
Wistar, Bartholomew Wyatt
II, 735
Wistar, Bartholomew Wyatt
II, 776
Wistar, Bessie L. D. IV, 1322
Wistar, Bessie L. D. IV, 1344
Wistar, Bessie Louisa IV, 1344
Wistar, Caleb Cresson II, 723
Wistar, Caleb Cresson II, 776
Wistar, Caspar II, 46
Wistar, Caspar II, 47
Wistar, Caspar II, 438
Wistar, Caspar II, 536
Wistar, Caspar II, 538
Wistar, Caspar II, 571
Wistar, Caspar II, 690
Wistar, Caspar II, 691
Wistar, Caspar II, 723
Wistar, Caspar II, 743
Wistar, Caspar II, 767
Wistar, Caspar II, 776
Wistar, Caspar III, 126
Wistar, Caspar, Jr. II, 46
Wistar, Caspar, Jr. II, 126
Wistar, Caspar, Jr. II, 591
Wistar, Caspar, Jr. II, 691
Wistar, Casper II, 19
Wistar, Casper II, 47
Wistar, Casper II, 55
Wistar, Casper II, 72
Wistar, Casper II, 111
Wistar, Casper II, 114
Wistar, Casper II, 115
Wistar, Casper II, 116
Wistar, Casper II, 124
Wistar, Casper II, 126
Wistar, Casper II, 438
Wistar, Casper II, 691
Wistar, Casper III, 363
Wistar, Casper, Jr. II, 691
Wistar, Catharine II, 46
Wistar, Catharine II, 47
Wistar, Catharine II, 72
Wistar, Catharine II, 111
Wistar, Catharine II, 117
Wistar, Catharine II, 126
Wistar, Catharine II, 438
Wistar, Catharine II, 690
Wistar, Catharine II, 691
Wistar, Catharine II, 723
Wistar, Catharine III, 363
Wistar, Catherine II, 438
Wistar, Catherine III, 272
Wistar, Cathrine II, 536
Wistar, Cathrine II, 690
Wistar, Charles II, 126
Wistar, Charles IV, 1344
Wistar, Charles E. IV, 1344
Wistar, Charles Jones II, 691
Wistar, Charlotte II, 22
Wistar, Charlotte II, 46
Wistar, Charlotte II, 47
Wistar, Charlotte II, 55
Wistar, Charlotte II, 65
Wistar, Charlotte II, 101
Wistar, Charlotte II, 111
Wistar, Charlotte II, 117
Wistar, Charlotte II, 118
Wistar, Charlotte II, 126
Wistar, Charlotte W. II, 114
Wistar, Charlotte W. II, 126
Wistar, Clayton II, 47
Wistar, Clayton II, 101
Wistar, Clayton II, 111
Wistar, Clayton II, 112
Wistar, Clayton II, 114
Wistar, Clayton II, 126
Wistar, Clayton N. II, 126
Wistar, Clayton Newbold II, 47
Wistar, Cleaton II, 114
Wistar, Cleaton II, 126
Wistar, Cleaton II, 140
Wistar, Cleayton II, 47
Wistar, Cornelia II, 144
Wistar, Cornelia II, 160
Wistar, Cornelia B. II, 140
Wistar, Cornelia B. II, 160
Wistar, Daniel II, 438
Wistar, Daniel II, 690
Wistar, Dilalwyn II, 776
Wistar, Dillwyn II, 723
Wistar, Dillwyn IV, 1344
Wistar, Dillwyn C. IV, 1332
Wistar, Dr. Casper II, 279
Wistar, Dr. Casper II, 306
Wistar, Elizabeth II, 47
Wistar, Elizabeth II, 438
Wistar, Elizabeth II, 555
Wistar, Elizabeth II, 598
Wistar, Elizabeth II, 691
Wistar, Elizabeth II, 767
Wistar, Elizabeth II, 776
Wistar, Elizabeth W. II, 47
Wistar, Elizabeth W. II, 124
Wistar, Elizabeth W. II, 126
Wistar, Elizabeth Waln II, 438
Wistar, Elizabeth Waln II, 700
Wistar, Emma II, 306
Wistar, Emma II, 438
Wistar, Emma II, 723
Wistar, Emma II, 776
Wistar, Emma Alderson II, 306
Wistar, Emma Mabel IV, 1344
Wistar, Esther II, 767
Wistar, Esther F. II, 723
Wistar, Esther F. II, 776
Wistar, Esther Fisher II, 776
Wistar, Francis II, 126
Wistar, Francis II, 776
Wistar, Hannah II, 22
Wistar, Hannah II, 46
Wistar, Hannah II, 47
Wistar, Hannah II, 55
Wistar, Hannah II, 111
Wistar, Hannah J. II, 723
Wistar, Hannah J. II, 743
Wistar, Hannah J. II, 776
Wistar, Harvey Langhorne
II, 438
Wistar, Henry II, 438
Wistar, Isaac C. J. II, 776
Wistar, Isaac C. Jones II, 723
Wistar, Isabella II, 438
Wistar, Isabella II, 591
Wistar, Isabella II, 691
Wistar, Jennie IV, 1332
Wistar, Jennie IV, 1344
Wistar, John II, 22
Wistar, John II, 46
Wistar, John II, 47
Wistar, John II, 55
Wistar, John II, 65
Wistar, John II, 101
Wistar, John II, 111
Wistar, John II, 114
Wistar, John II, 117
Wistar, John II, 118
Wistar, John II, 119
Wistar, John II, 126
Wistar, John II, 438
Wistar, John II, 555
Wistar, John II, 691
Wistar, John Dorland IV, 1344
Wistar, John, Jr. II, 691
Wistar, Joseph II, 46
Wistar, Joseph B. II, 47
Wistar, Joseph B. II, 116
Wistar, Joseph B. II, 126
Wistar, Joseph E. II, 46
Wistar, Joshua II, 438
Wistar, Josiah II, 47
Wistar, Josiah II, 114
Wistar, Josiah II, 126
Wistar, Katharine II, 115
Wistar, Katharine II, 126
Wistar, Katharine J. II, 776
Wistar, Katherine II, 114
Wistar, Laetitia M. II, 47
Wistar, Langhorne II, 438
Wistar, Laura II, 306
Wistar, Laura II, 723
Wistar, Laura II, 776
Wistar, Leatitia II, 47
Wistar, Leatitia M. II, 114
Wistar, Leatitia M. II, 126
Wistar, Letitia M. II, 119
Wistar, Letitia M. II, 126
Wistar, Lottie Maud II, 47
Wistar, Lottie Maude II, 126
Wistar, Lowrie II, 438
Wistar, Lowry II, 438
Wistar, Lowry II, 690
Wistar, Lydia II, 571
Wistar, Lydia II, 691
Wistar, Lydia II, 723
Wistar, Lydia III, 190
Wistar, Lydia III, 363
Wistar, Lydia J. II, 279
Wistar, Lydia J. II, 306
Wistar, Lydia J. II, 723
Wistar, Lydia J. II, 743
Wistar, Lydia J. II, 776
Wistar, Lydia J., Jr. II, 776
Wistar, Mabel IV, 1340
Wistar, Margaret II, 126
Wistar, Margaret II, 438
Wistar, Margaret II, 538
Wistar, Margaret II, 690
Wistar, Margaret N. II, 126
Wistar, Margaret U. II, 743
Wistar, Margaret U. II, 776
Wistar, Margaret Vaux II, 723
Wistar, Mariann II, 732
Wistar, Mariann II, 776
Wistar, Martha II, 47
Wistar, Martha II, 114
Wistar, Martha II, 126
Wistar, Mary II, 46
Wistar, Mary II, 47
Wistar, Mary II, 65
Wistar, Mary II, 72
Wistar, Mary II, 101
Wistar, Mary II, 111
Wistar, Mary II, 114
Wistar, Mary II, 124
Wistar, Mary II, 126
Wistar, Mary II, 306
Wistar, Mary II, 438
Wistar, Mary II, 531
Wistar, Mary II, 555
Wistar, Mary II, 571
Wistar, Mary II, 691

Wistar, Mary II, 723
Wistar, Mary II, 776
Wistar, Mary III, 126
Wistar, Mary III, 363
Wistar, Mary Ann II, 47
Wistar, Mary Ann II, 114
Wistar, Mary Ann II, 126
Wistar, Mary Ann II, 438
Wistar, Mary Emeline IV, 1344
Wistar, Mary S. II, 47
Wistar, Mary S. II, 126
Wistar, Mary Waln II, 700
Wistar, Mary Waln II, 723
Wistar, Mary Waln II, 730
Wistar, Mary Waln II, 776
Wistar, May IV, 1344
Wistar, May D. IV, 1340
Wistar, May Dorland IV, 1344
Wistar, Mifflin II, 723
Wistar, Mifflin II, 767
Wistar, Mifflin II, 776
Wistar, R. Wyatt IV, 1344
Wistar, Rachel II, 438
Wistar, Rebecca II, 19
Wistar, Rebecca II, 46
Wistar, Rebecca II, 47
Wistar, Rebecca II, 55
Wistar, Rebecca II, 111
Wistar, Rebecca II, 114
Wistar, Rebecca II, 115
Wistar, Rebecca II, 116
Wistar, Rebecca II, 124
Wistar, Rebecca II, 126
Wistar, Rebecca II, 159
Wistar, Rebecca II, 160
Wistar, Rebecca II, 438
Wistar, Rebecca II, 691
Wistar, Rebecca I. II, 140
Wistar, Rebecca, Jr. II, 46
Wistar, Richard II, 47
Wistar, Richard II, 72
Wistar, Richard II, 111
Wistar, Richard II, 113
Wistar, Richard II, 114
Wistar, Richard II, 126
Wistar, Richard II, 140
Wistar, Richard II, 438
Wistar, Richard II, 531
Wistar, Richard II, 591
Wistar, Richard II, 690
Wistar, Richard II, 691
Wistar, Richard Waln II, 438
Wistar, Richard, Jr. II, 47
Wistar, Richard, Jr. II, 126
Wistar, Robert III, 363
Wistar, Robert IV, 1344
Wistar, Robert Warder IV, 1344
Wistar, Samuel II, 691
Wistar, Sarah II, 46
Wistar, Sarah II, 47
Wistar, Sarah II, 111
Wistar, Sarah II, 113
Wistar, Sarah II, 114
Wistar, Sarah II, 126
Wistar, Sarah II, 438
Wistar, Sarah II, 591
Wistar, Sarah II, 690
Wistar, Sarah II, 691
Wistar, Sarah II, 723
Wistar, Sarah II, 776
Wistar, Sarah III, 363
Wistar, Sarah Harlan II, 126
Wistar, Sarah Harlen II, 47
Wistar, Sarah W. II, 19
Wistar, Sarah Wyatt II, 438
Wistar, Sarah, Jr. II, 438
Wistar, Sarah, Jr. II, 691
Wistar, Susan II, 306
Wistar, Susan II, 438
Wistar, Susan II, 723
Wistar, Susan II, 776
Wistar, Susan N. II, 306
Wistar, Susan N. II, 438
Wistar, Susan N. II, 691
Wistar, Susan N. II, 732
Wistar, Susan N. II, 735
Wistar, Susan N. II, 776
Wistar, Susanna II, 627
Wistar, Susanna II, 691
Wistar, Thomas II, 438
Wistar, Thomas II, 571
Wistar, Thomas II, 691
Wistar, Thomas II, 723
Wistar, Thomas II, 776
Wistar, Thomas III, 363
Wistar, Virginia III, 363
Wistar, Virtinia IV, 1344
Wistar, W. Wilburforce II, 776
Wistar, Wd. Martha II, 47
Wistar, Wd. Mary II, 111
Wistar, Wd. Susan N. II, 188
Wistar, William II, 438
Wistar, William Wilberforce II, 279
Wistar, William Wilberforce II, 306
Wistar, William Wynne II, 438
Wistar, Wm. Henry II, 126
Wistar, Wm. Wilberforce II, 723
Wistar, Wm. Wilberforce II, 776
Wistar, Wyatt II, 438
Wister, Anistacia II, 438
Wister, Bartholomew II, 438
Wister, Bessie IV, 1322
Wister, Caspar II, 438
Wister, Caspar II, 691
Wister, Casper II, 438
Wister, Casper II, 691
Wister, Catharine II, 690
Wister, Catherine II, 438
Wister, Charlotte II, 111
Wister, Daniel II, 438
Wister, Harvey Langhorne II, 438
Wister, Henry II, 438
Wister, Isabella II, 438
Wister, John II, 438
Wister, John II, 691
Wister, Joshua II, 438
Wister, Lydia II, 691
Wister, Rachel II, 438
Wister, Richard II, 438
Wister, Sarah II, 438
Wister, Sarah, Jr. II, 438
Wister, Thomas II, 438
Wister, William II, 438
Wister, Wyatt II, 438
Wisterd, Catherine II, 438
Wiston, Mary VI, 205
Wistra, Samuel I, 261
Witbee, Julia Ann II, 809
Witchel, Bathsheba IV, 359
Witchel, Bathsheba IV, 558
Witchel, Bethsheba IV, 359
Witchel, Hannah IV, 558
Witchel, Isaac IV, 359
Witchel, Isaac IV, 558
Witchel, Jane IV, 558
Witchel, John IV, 165
Witchel, John IV, 359
Witchel, John IV, 558
Witchel, John, Jr. IV, 359
Witchel, Laban IV, 558
Witchel, Lydia S. IV, 558
Witchel, Mary IV, 165
Witchel, Mary IV, 359
Witchel, Mary IV, 558
Witchel, Sarah II, 193
Witchell, Barton IV, 562
Witchell, Bathsheba IV, 359
Witchell, Bathsheba IV, 558
Witchell, Bathsheba IV, 562
Witchell, Hannah IV, 558
Witchell, Isaac IV, 558
Witchell, Isaac IV, 562
Witchell, Jane IV, 558
Witchell, Jane IV, 562
Witchell, John IV, 359
Witchell, John IV, 558
Witchell, John IV, 562
Witchell, Laban IV, 558
Witchell, Lydia S. IV, 558
Witchell, Mary IV, 359
Witchell, Mary IV, 558
Witchell, Mary IV, 562
Witchell, Sarah II, 275
Witcher, Dora G. I, 951
Witcher, J. H. I, 951
Witcher, John VI, 988
Witcher, Sarah VI, 988
Witcraft, Amos IV, 1300
Witcraft, James IV, 1300
Witcraft, James H. IV, 1300
Witcraft, John S. II, 275
Witcraft, Mary IV, 1300
Witcraft, Rebecca II, 275
Witham, Ruthanna V, 33
Witham, Ruthanna V, 143
Witherbee, Anna V, 490
Witherbee, Anna V, 543
Withero, Lloyd V, 1025
Withers, Edward B. VI, 833
Withers, Edward B. VI, 866
Withers, Elizabeth D. II, 306
Withers, Elizabeth W. II, 285
Withers, Elizabeth W. II, 306
Withers, Elvira W. VI, 866
Withers, Flora V. VI, 866
Withers, Grace II, 47
Withers, Grace II, 54
Withers, Grace II, 112
Withers, Janet VI, 833
Withers, Jennette E. VI, 833
Withers, John F. VI, 866
Withers, Mary II, 47
Withers, Mary II, 107
Withers, Mary II, 112
Withers, Phillip T. VI, 866
Withers, Robert W. VI, 833
Withers, Robert W. VI, 866
Withers, Samuel II, 47
Withers, Samuel II, 54
Withers, Samuel II, 112
Withers, Susan D. VI, 866
Withey, Samuel J. II, 723
Withington, Lydia I, 277
Withpain, John II, 685
Withpain, Zecheriah II, 685
Withrow, Emma V, 852
Withrow, Rae IV, 789
Withrow, Thelma L. IV, 789
Withrow, Virginia IV, 789
Withy, Elizabeth V, 45
Withy, Elizabeth V, 143
Withy, Jacob V, 143
Withy, James V, 143
Withy, Jonathan V, 143
Withy, Lee III, 300
Withy, Mary V, 143
Withy, Samuel J. II, 777
Witman, Eliz. D. III, 207
Witson, Esther III, 358
Witson, Jane V, 537
Witson, Thomas III, 505
Witt, Abner VI, 1018
Witt, Abraham VI, 1018
Witt, Adaline A. VI, 962
Witt, Albert M. VI, 1019
Witt, Alcy VI, 1018
Witt, Alice VI, 1019
Witt, Alsinda VI, 1018
Witt, Amanda VI, 866
Witt, Angeline VI, 897
Witt, Ann VI, 894
Witt, Ann VI, 898
Witt, Ann VI, 1021
Witt, Benj. VI, 899
Witt, Benjamin VI, 894
Witt, Benjamin VI, 910
Witt, Benjamin VI, 1019
Witt, Benjamin B. VI, 1019
Witt, Bethani VI, 1018
Witt, Bethenia VI, 996
Witt, Betsey VI, 1018
Witt, Booker VI, 1018
Witt, Burrel G. VI, 900
Witt, Caleb VI, 866
Witt, Caleb VI, 1008
Witt, Catharine VI, 1018
Witt, Charles VI, 1018
Witt, Daisy VI, 729
Witt, David VI, 891
Witt, David VI, 1018
Witt, Dennel VI, 970
Witt, Elisibeth VI, 892
Witt, Eliza Ann VI, 910
Witt, Elizabeth VI, 889
Witt, Elizabeth VI, 978
Witt, Elizabeth VI, 1018
Witt, Elizabeth Ann VI, 948
Witt, Elizabeth S. VI, 980
Witt, Ellis R. VI, 866
Witt, Elvira VI, 1018
Witt, Elvirah F. VI, 998
Witt, Emeline VI, 1019
Witt, Frances VI, 1019
Witt, George VI, 948
Witt, George W. VI, 1019
Witt, Gincy VI, 999
Witt, Hannah II, 449
Witt, Hannah VI, 1019
Witt, Henry L. VI, 866
Witt, Jack VI, 897
Witt, James VI, 1018
Witt, James VI, 1019
Witt, Jane VI, 866
Witt, Jane VI, 898
Witt, Jane VI, 900
Witt, Jane VI, 910
Witt, Jane VI, 1018
Witt, Jesse VI, 1018
Witt, Jesse, Jr. VI, 928
Witt, Jesse, Sr. VI, 978
Witt, Joannah VI, 967
Witt, John II, 449
Witt, John VI, 884
Witt, John VI, 898
Witt, John VI, 899
Witt, John VI, 900
Witt, John VI, 925
Witt, John VI, 948
Witt, John VI, 967
Witt, John VI, 977
Witt, John VI, 999
Witt, John VI, 1007
Witt, John VI, 1011
Witt, John VI, 1018
Witt, John VI, 1019
Witt, John B. VI, 899
Witt, John B. VI, 1018
Witt, John E. VI, 1019
Witt, Judith VI, 925
Witt, Juliann VI, 1019
Witt, Keziah VI, 1009
Witt, Lewis VI, 1018
Witt, Lockey VI, 914
Witt, Locky VI, 900
Witt, Lucy Ann VI, 1019
Witt, Lyndney J. VI, 866
Witt, Margaret VI, 1015
Witt, Margaret C. VI, 1019
Witt, Marinda B. VI, 958
Witt, Martha VI, 998
Witt, Martha VI, 1018
Witt, Martha A. VI, 1018
Witt, Martha Jane VI, 884
Witt, Martha Jane VI, 899
Witt, Mary VI, 892
Witt, Mary VI, 927
Witt, Mary VI, 963
Witt, Mary VI, 1018
Witt, Mary A. VI, 866
Witt, Mary Ann VI, 899
Witt, Milley VI, 972
Witt, Mills VI, 996
Witt, Mills VI, 1018
Witt, Milly VI, 1018
Witt, Nancey VI, 977
Witt, Nancy VI, 894
Witt, Nancy VI, 970
Witt, Nancy VI, 978
Witt, Nancy VI, 999
Witt, Nancy VI, 1018
Witt, Nancy R. VI, 866
Witt, Polly VI, 898
Witt, Polly VI, 1018
Witt, Rebecca VI, 1019
Witt, Reuben VI, 898
Witt, Reuben VI, 958
Witt, Reuben VI, 962
Witt, Reuben VI, 996
Witt, Reuben VI, 1018
Witt, Reuben VI, 1019
Witt, Reubin VI, 866
Witt, Robert II, 449
Witt, Robert VI, 914
Witt, Robert VI, 948
Witt, Robert VI, 1018
Witt, Robt. VI, 982
Witt, Roland VI, 866
Witt, Roland VI, 972
Witt, Rowland VI, 889
Witt, Rowland VI, 927
Witt, Rowland VI, 978
Witt, Rowland VI, 1009
Witt, Rowland VI, 1018
Witt, Ruth II, 449
Witt, Sally VI, 866
Witt, Sally VI, 948
Witt, Sally VI, 1018
Witt, Saluda Ann VI, 1018
Witt, Sarah II, 449
Witt, Sarah VI, 899
Witt, Sarah A. VI, 808
Witt, Sophia VI, 1018
Witt, Suckey VI, 898
Witt, Susan VI, 808
Witt, Susan VI, 1018
Witt, Susannah VI, 1019
Witt, William VI, 980
Witt, William VI, 989
Witt, William VI, 998
Witt, William VI, 1018
Witt, William H. VI, 948
Witt, William H. VI, 1019
Witt, Zachariah VI, 808
Witt, Zachariah VI, 866
Witte, Mabel III, 508
Witten, Catharine VI, 1019
Witten, John VI, 1019
Witten, Richard II, 685
Witten, Wm. II, 942
Witter, Anne I, 1076
Witter, Elizabeth I, 1076
Witter, Geo. Henry III, 395
Witter, Geo. Henry III, 475
Witter, Grant D. IV, 1242
Witter, James I, 1076
Witter, John I, 1076
Witter, Jonathan I, 1076
Witter, Jonathan V, 291
Witter, Margaret Shepard III, 395
Witter, Margaret Shephard III, 475
Witter, Martha I, 1076
Witter, Mary I, 1076
Witter, Maud III, 475
Witter, Maud B. III, 395
Witter, Norwood I, 1076
Witter, Samuel I, 1076
Witter, Thomas I, 1076
Witteto, John VI, 1005
Witteto, Mary VI, 1005
Witteto, Polly VI, 1005
Wittichar, Naomy II, 1037
Wittig, Emma V, 1026
Wittig, Wm. V, 1026
Wittig, Wm. H. V, 1026
Wittman, Bertha IV, 1344
Wittman, Elizabeth IV, 1334
Wittman, Elizabeth IV, 1344
Witton, James II, 64
Witton, James II, 112
Witton, Sarah II, 64
Witton, Sarah II, 112
Witty, ??? III, 475
Witty, Charles IV, 1344
Witty, Elizabeth I, 522
Witty, Elizabeth I, 583
Witty, Ella III, 475
Witty, Emma V, 1026
Witty, Hannah I, 522
Witty, Hannah I, 583
Witty, James I, 522
Witty, James I, 583
Witty, James V, 291
Witty, Jennie IV, 1344
Witty, Jennie M. III, 363
Witty, John I, 522
Witty, John I, 583
Witty, Lee III, 357
Witty, Lee III, 363
Witty, Lee III, 475
Witty, Mary I, 522
Witty, Mary I, 583
Witty, May IV, 1344
Witty, Rebecca I, 522
Witty, Rebecca I, 583
Witty, William I, 522
Witty, William I, 583
Wivell, Margaret II, 601
Wivell, Margarett II, 691
Wlaton, Deborah V, 183
Wlaton, Moses V, 183
Woaton, Susanna VI, 821
Wodell, Claud I, 951
Wodell, Cloud I, 430
Wodell, Cornelia I, 951
Wodell, E.C. I, 430
Wodin, Daniel II, 449
Woelfler, Bertha III, 32
Woelfler, Bertha III, 363
Woelfler, Clara III, 32
Woelfler, Clara III, 363
Woelfler, Ludwig III, 32
Woelfler, Ludwig III, 363
Woffington, Esther I, 906
Wohman, Samuel IV, 919
Woland, Catherine VI, 976
Wolary, Hanna M. V, 543
Wolary, John A. V, 543
Wolbert, Medora Smith II, 7
Wolcott, ??? III, 363
Wolcott, Ann O. III, 363
Wolcott, Charles Henry III,
Wolcott, Henrietta III, 186
Wolcott, Henrietta III, 363
Wolcott, Henry L. III, 363
Wolcott, Henry W. III, 186
Wolcott, Henry W. III, 363
Wolcott, Jos. III, 363
Wolcott, Joseph III, 196
Wolcott, Joseph III, 363
Wolcott, Mary III, 196
Wolcott, Mary III, 363
Wolcott, Samuel P. III, 363
Wolcott, Sarah L. III, 196
Wolcott, Sarah L. III, 363
Wolcott, Sybillah III, 186
Wolcott, Sybillah III, 363
Wolf, Albert V, 1026
Wolf, Amy IV, 903
Wolf, Amy IV, 918
Wolf, Angeline V, 400
Wolf, Angeline V, 440
Wolf, Anna V, 467
Wolf, Atlanta V, 606
Wolf, Atlanta G. V, 606
Wolf, Atlanta Georga V, 606
Wolf, Benjamin V, 606
Wolf, Benjamin F. V, 606
Wolf, Bertha May V, 1026
Wolf, Charley N. V, 606
Wolf, Charlie Henry V, 606
Wolf, Clyde V, 468

Eli IV, 504
Elizabeth J. IV, 930
, Elsie V, 313
, Elsie V, 468
Emma V, 143
, Eva May V, 606
, Eveline V, 313
, Evelyn V, 468
Fred V, 467
, Frederick IV, 789
, G. Wesley V, 1026
, Grace V, 1026
, Jean E. V, 313
, Joel V, 291
, John V, 606
, John S. V, 606
, Lida J. V, 291
, Lucile V, 468
, Maggie F. V, 606
, Margaret V, 591
, Margaret V, 606
, Margaret F. V, 440
, Margaret F. V, 606
, Mariam V, 779
f, Mariam V, 793
f, Martha IV, 1344
f, Martha Helen IV, 1344
f, Martha Star V, 1026
f, Mary IV, 489
f, Mary IV, 504
f, Mary VI, 814
f, Mildred E. V, 313
f, Myrtie B. V, 606
f, Myrtie Belle V, 606
f, Nancy IV, 789
f, Otto V, 773
lf, Pearl E. V, 313
lf, Richa IV, 789
lf, Sarah II, 1040
lf, Velara E. V, 606
lf, Velora Eliza V, 606
lf, W. W. V, 313
lf, William A. V, 606
lf, William Alonzo V, 606
lf, Wm. IV, 789
lf, Wm. V, 467
lfard, Felix V, 213
lfard, Josephine V, 213
lfard, Lewis V, 213
olfe, Beulah III, 464
olfe, Beulah III, 475
olfe, Frederick IV, 789
olfe, Lettie III, 464
olfe, Lettie III, 475
olfe, Levi B. III, 464
olfe, Levi B. III, 475
olfe, Mary L. I, 612
olfe, Richa IV, 789
olfe, Sarah II, 1040
olfe, Susan V, 566
olfe, Thomas II, 1040
olfe, Wm. IV, 789
olff, Emma II, 967
olfgang, Clara IV, 789
olfgang, Henry E. IV, 789
olfgang, Mr. ??? IV, 789
olfgang, Mrs. ??? IV, 789
olfgang, Thelma L. IV, 789
olfgang, Warren IV, 789
olfington, Esther I, 906
olford, Arthur V, 963
Volford, Edward VI, 457
Volford, Ella II, 831
Volford, Ella II, 942
Volford, Frank IV, 1300
Volford, Irene Maurice VI, 448
Volford, Irene Maurice VI, 457
Volford, Julia IV, 1300
Volford, Sarah VI, 457
Volford, Susan V, 1026
Volford, W. M. V, 1026
Volfrann, Marion V, 143
Volfrann, Wilhelm V, 143
Volfrann, William H. V, 143
Wollam, Alfred V, 874
Wollam, Arthur IV, 506
Wollam, Arthur J. IV, 506
Wollam, Arthur J. V, 874
Wollam, Arthur James V, 874
Wollam, Clara M. V, 874
Wollam, Edgar IV, 1344
Wollam, Edgar A. IV, 1344
Wollam, Edgar A. V, 874
Wollam, Emma IV, 506
Wollam, Emma V, 874
Wollam, Hiram IV, 506
Wollam, Hiram V, 874
Wollam, Hiram S. IV, 506
Wollam, Hiram S. V, 874
Wollam, Julia IV, 1194
Wollam, Nancy V, 874
Wollam, Roy IV, 506
Wollam, Roy H. IV, 506
Wollam, Roy H. V, 874
Wollam, Roy Hiram V, 874
Wollam, Rubie IV, 506
Wollam, Ruby V, 874
Wollam, Ruby F. V, 874
Wollam, Ruby Frances IV, 506
Wollard, Martyn I Sup 1, 7
Wollard, Rhoda V, 240
Wollard, Rhoda V, 291
Wollary, Calvin V, 720
Wollary, Elva V, 720
Wollary, J. A. V, 720
Wollary, John A. V, 720
Wollary, Malinda V, 720
Wollary, Melinda J. V, 720
Wollaston, Dorothy I, 425
Wollaston, Dorothy I, 430
Wollaston, George W. II, 943
Wollaston, Joshua II, 568
Wollaston, Martha II, 631
Wollaston, Priscilla II, 568
Wollenburg, M. Edith V, 213
Woller, Oliver `IV, 306
Wollet, Owen V, 1026
Wollet, Robert Owen V, 1026
Wolley, Cicely II, 693
Wolley, Hannah II, 439
Wolley, Thomas II, 439
Wollis, Elizabeth I, 583
Wollison, Dorothy I, 430
Wolliston, Ellinor II, 439
Wolliston, Priscilla II, 439
Wolliston, Thomas II, 439
Wolliston, Wd. Martha II, 439
Wollom, Arthur V, 773
Wollom, Lea V, 773
Wollom, Rev. J. Arthur V, 773
Wolloston, Eleanor II, 693
Wolloston, Thomas II, 693
Wollower, Helen III, 501
Wollston, John II, 163
Wolston, Martha L. II, 1074
Wolston, Martha L. II, 1083
Woltz, Ann M. VI, 1019
Woltz, James H. VI, 1019
Woltz, Mary M. VI, 1019
Woltz, William F. VI, 1019
Wolverton, Charles II, 275
Wolverton, Hettie F. II, 826
Wolves, Thos. VI, 93
Womack, ??? VI, 293
Womack, Achillis VI, 1019
Womack, Alexander VI, 839
Womack, Allen VI, 1019
Womack, Anna VI, 927
Womack, Edmund VI, 942
Womack, Edmund VI, 1019
Womack, Edward VI, 807
Womack, Edward VI, 990
Womack, Elizabeth VI, 866
Womack, Jesse VI, 887
Womack, Joel VI, 866
Womack, John W. VI, 831
Womack, Julia B. VI, 887
Womack, Leroy VI, 866
Womack, Mary VI, 916
Womack, Mathew VI, 810
Womack, Molissa VI, 942
Womack, Nancey VI, 1019
Womack, Nancy VI, 887
Womack, Nancy VI, 921
Womack, Nancy VI, 942
Womack, Nancy G. VI, 810
Womack, Nancy Jane VI, 921
Womack, Peyton A. VI, 140
Womack, Peyton A. VI, 144
Womack, Polly VI, 839
Womack, Polly VI, 1019
Womack, Rachel VI, 1019
Womack, Robert VI, 1019
Womack, Salley VI, 927
Womack, Sally VI, 866
Womack, Sarah VI, 916
Womack, Sarah VI, 927
Womack, Sarah VI, 1019
Womack, Sarah F. VI, 1019
Womack, William VI, 1019
Womax, Ann VI, 959
Womax, Rody VI, 959
Womax, Sarah VI, 884
Womax, Sarah VI, 959
Womble, Elizabeth VI, 97
Womble, Elizabeth VI, 98
Womble, Elizabeth VI, 125
Womble, Jane I, 424
Womble, Jane I, 430
Wommack, Isham VI, 345
Womsley, Rachel II, 109
Wonell, Helen E. III, 71
Wong, Dow III, 363
Wong, Yow III, 363
Wood, ??? II, 449
Wood, ??? III, 173
Wood, ??? III, 192
Wood, ??? III, 296
Wood, ??? III, 359
Wood, ??? III, 363
Wood, ??? III, 365
Wood, ??? III, 366
Wood, ??? III, 508
Wood, ??? IV, 1047
Wood, ??? IV, 1082
Wood, ??? IV, 1141
Wood, ??? IV, 1227
Wood, Aaron I, 970
Wood, Aaron III, 363
Wood, Aaron III, 366
Wood, Aaron IV, 165
Wood, Aaron IV, 454
Wood, Aaron IV, 458
Wood, Aaron IV, 601
Wood, Aaron VI, 356
Wood, Abel III, 508
Wood, Abigail I, 200
Wood, Abigail I, 203
Wood, Abigail I, 583
Wood, Abigail II, 591
Wood, Abigail II, 691
Wood, Abigail II, 723
Wood, Abigail II, 777
Wood, Abigail III, 212
Wood, Abigail III, 284
Wood, Abigail III, 363
Wood, Abigail III, 364
Wood, Abigail III, 365
Wood, Abigail III, 366
Wood, Abigail III, 437
Wood, Abigail III, 475
Wood, Abigail III, 508
Wood, Abigail IV, 102
Wood, Abigail IV, 116
Wood, Abigail IV, 165
Wood, Abigail IV, 258
Wood, Abigail IV, 306
Wood, Abigail IV, 1189
Wood, Abigail IV, 1195
Wood, Abigail IV, 1228
Wood, Abigail IV, 1296
Wood, Abigail IV, 1300
Wood, Abigail VI, 543
Wood, Abigail VI, 580
Wood, Abigail VI, 583
Wood, Abigail VI, 624
Wood, Abigail VI, 723
Wood, Abigail S. III, 365
Wood, Abraham IV, 458
Wood, Abraham IV, 1082
Wood, Absillit V, 851
Wood, Absillit V, 874
Wood, Addeson IV, 558
Wood, Addison IV, 505
Wood, Addison IV, 558
Wood, Addison IV, 1082
Wood, Adison IV, 505
Wood, Ajah III, 363
Wood, Alan II, 838
Wood, Alan II, 877
Wood, Alan II, 942
Wood, Alan Wood II, 828
Wood, Albert III, 365
Wood, Albert III, 475
Wood, Albert G. III, 475
Wood, Alfred III, 363
Wood, Alfred III, 365
Wood, Alfred IV, 504
Wood, Alfred IV, 505
Wood, Alfred IV, 789
Wood, Alfred IV, 1016
Wood, Alfred IV, 1082
Wood, Alfred IV, 1121
Wood, Alice IV, 946
Wood, Alice IV, 1220
Wood, Alice IV, 1228
Wood, Alice VI, 583
Wood, Alice E. II, 942
Wood, Alice Elizabeth II, 828
Wood, Alice S. III, 363
Wood, Allen II, 942
Wood, Allen IV, 307
Wood, Allen D. IV, 601
Wood, Alliance IV, 918
Wood, Allinson II, 828
Wood, Almeda IV, 307
Wood, Almedia IV, 382
Wood, Almedia IV, 458
Wood, Almedia IV, 572
Wood, Almedia IV, 601
Wood, Almira IV, 1016
Wood, Alvira IV, 1228
Wood, Amanda J. IV, 1103
Wood, Amanda J. IV, 1121
Wood, Amanda J. IV, 1267
Wood, Amanda Jane IV, 1121
Wood, Amos IV, 116
Wood, Amos IV, 458
Wood, Amos IV, 1195
Wood, Amos IV, 1196
Wood, Anderson VI, 1019
Wood, Anderson S. VI, 858
Wood, Andrew VI, 866
Wood, Angeline IV, 1386
Wood, Ann I, 608
Wood, Ann II, 112
Wood, Ann II, 438
Wood, Ann II, 454
Wood, Ann II, 506
Wood, Ann II, 691
Wood, Ann III, 394
Wood, Ann IV, 93
Wood, Ann IV, 116
Wood, Ann IV, 130
Wood, Ann IV, 134
Wood, Ann IV, 373
Wood, Ann IV, 458
Wood, Ann IV, 504
Wood, Ann IV, 505
Wood, Ann IV, 506
Wood, Ann IV, 559
Wood, Ann IV, 601
Wood, Ann IV, 1082
Wood, Ann V, 928
Wood, Ann V, 942
Wood, Ann VI, 371
Wood, Ann VI, 457
Wood, Ann VI, 458
Wood, Ann VI, 583
Wood, Ann Augusta III, 364
Wood, Ann B. IV, 531
Wood, Ann B. IV, 558
Wood, Ann B. IV, 559
Wood, Ann Eliza III, 363
Wood, Ann Eliza III, 365
Wood, Ann Etta IV, 1196
Wood, Ann H. II, 838
Wood, Ann H. II, 942
Wood, Ann Hunter II, 828
Wood, Ann L. V, 440
Wood, Ann M. III, 364
Wood, Ann Maria IV, 306
Wood, Ann Maria IV, 504
Wood, Ann R. II, 942
Wood, Ann R. III, 365
Wood, Anna III, 47
Wood, Anna III, 363
Wood, Anna III, 364
Wood, Anna III, 365
Wood, Anna III, 496
Wood, Anna III, 508
Wood, Anna IV, 32
Wood, Anna IV, 68
Wood, Anna IV, 301
Wood, Anna IV, 306
Wood, Anna IV, 307
Wood, Anna IV, 505
Wood, Anna IV, 506
Wood, Anna IV, 1171
Wood, Anna IV, 1194
Wood, Anna IV, 1195
Wood, Anna IV, 1227
Wood, Anna V, 942
Wood, Anna B. III, 167
Wood, Anna B. III, 364
Wood, Anna B. III, 365
Wood, Anna B. III, 366
Wood, Anna B., Jr. III, 364
Wood, Anna Buckley III, 366
Wood, Anna C. II, 438
Wood, Anna C. III, 366
Wood, Anna Cynthia IV, 1196
Wood, Anna E. III, 79
Wood, Anna E. III, 321
Wood, Anna E. IV, 1228
Wood, Anna Eugenia VI, 664
Wood, Anna H. III, 310
Wood, Anna H. III, 366
Wood, Anna Maria II, 438
Wood, Anna Maria II, 692
Wood, Anna Maria II, 774
Wood, Anna Maria II, 777
Wood, Anna Maria IV, 487
Wood, Anna Maria IV, 506
Wood, Anna Mott III, 365
Wood, Anna U. IV, 307
Wood, Annetta IV, 1165
Wood, Annetta IV, 1192
Wood, Annette IV, 1192
Wood, Annie P. IV, 505
Wood, Arbenah VI, 458
Wood, Arbina IV, 558
Wood, Arbinah VI, 607
Wood, Archibald VI, 866
Wood, Arnold III, 363
Wood, Arnold III, 366
Wood, Arthur G. IV, 1195
Wood, Arthur King III, 363
Wood, Arthur King III, 366
Wood, Arthur P. IV, 559
Wood, Asa VI, 218
Wood, Asa VI, 345
Wood, Asa M. IV, 1195
Wood, Asa M. IV, 1196
Wood, Asaph IV, 179
Wood, Asaph IV, 306
Wood, Asaph IV, 1121
Wood, Ascenath IV, 559
Wood, Asenath IV, 558
Wood, Asenath VI, 458
Wood, Asenith IV, 359
Wood, Beaulah II, 112
Wood, Bell V, 291
Wood, Bell V, 720
Wood, Belle V, 720
Wood, Benjamin I, 126
Wood, Benjamin I, 177
Wood, Benjamin II, 438
Wood, Benjamin III, 366
Wood, Benjamin IV, 165
Wood, Benjamin IV, 306
Wood, Benjamin IV, 307
Wood, Benjamin IV, 1195
Wood, Benjamin IV, 1196
Wood, Benjamin B. III, 366
Wood, Benjamin, Jr. III, 363
Wood, Bernice C. II, 942
Wood, Betsey VI, 963
Wood, Beulah I, 598
Wood, Beulah Swain I, 598
Wood, Billen II, 449
Wood, Bird VI, 885
Wood, Bird VI, 1015
Wood, Bird VI, 1019
Wood, Blagdon VI, 1016
Wood, Blagdon VI, 1019
Wood, Blanche E. III, 333
Wood, Blanche E. III, 363
Wood, Caleb II, 47
Wood, Caleb II, 94
Wood, Caleb II, 112
Wood, Caleb II, 126
Wood, Caleb II, 140
Wood, Caleb II, 723
Wood, Caleb II, 942
Wood, Caleb III, 363
Wood, Caleb III, 508
Wood, Caleb IV, 495
Wood, Caleb IV, 504
Wood, Caleb IV, 505
Wood, Caleb IV, 1082
Wood, Caleb IV, 1103
Wood, Caleb IV, 1121
Wood, Caleb H. II, 140
Wood, Caleb H. II, 160
Wood, Caleb H. II, 942
Wood, Callie V, 720
Wood, Capt. Abraham VI, 289
Wood, Carolina II, 1040
Wood, Caroline II, 275
Wood, Caroline II, 1040
Wood, Caroline III, 363
Wood, Caroline III, 365
Wood, Caroline III, 366
Wood, Caroline IV, 1068
Wood, Caroline A. IV, 1196
Wood, Caroline B. II, 726
Wood, Caroline B. II, 777
Wood, Caroline S. II, 942
Wood, Caroline T. IV, 1227
Wood, Carrie IV, 1196
Wood, Carrie IV, 1267
Wood, Carrie A. IV, 1196
Wood, Carrie C. V, 213
Wood, Carrie C. V, 720
Wood, Cassandra VI, 639
Wood, Cassandra VI, 676
Wood, Catharine II, 438
Wood, Catharine II, 569
Wood, Catharine II, 692
Wood, Catharine II, 712
Wood, Catharine II, 777
Wood, Catharine III, 192
Wood, Catharine IV, 116
Wood, Catharine IV, 165
Wood, Catharine IV, 454
Wood, Catharine IV, 458
Wood, Catharine IV, 1177
Wood, Catharine IV, 1195
Wood, Catharine IV, 1196
Wood, Catharine VI, 458
Wood, Catharine VI, 978
Wood, Catharine H. III, 121
Wood, Catharine H. III, 363
Wood, Catharine M. III, 219

Wood, Catharine M. III, 364
Wood, Catharine M. III, 366
Wood, Catherine I, 1131
Wood, Catherine I, 1135
Wood, Catherine II, 384
Wood, Catherine II, 438
Wood, Catherine III, 211
Wood, Catherine IV, 93
Wood, Catherine IV, 95
Wood, Catherine IV, 116
Wood, Catherine IV, 1195
Wood, Catherine IV, 1228
Wood, Catherine VI, 356
Wood, Catherine VI, 414
Wood, Catherine VI, 457
Wood, Catherine VI, 858
Wood, Catherine VI, 1019
Wood, Caty VI, 866
Wood, Charity II, 449
Wood, Charity IV, 268
Wood, Charity IV, 306
Wood, Charity IV, 504
Wood, Charity IV, 505
Wood, Charity IV, 506
Wood, Charity IV, 521
Wood, Charity IV, 529
Wood, Charity IV, 531
Wood, Charity IV, 559
Wood, Charity IV, 1016
Wood, Charles II, 47
Wood, Charles II, 126
Wood, Charles II, 438
Wood, Charles II, 1040
Wood, Charles III, 121
Wood, Charles III, 172
Wood, Charles III, 363
Wood, Charles III, 364
Wood, Charles III, 365
Wood, Charles III, 366
Wood, Charles III, 508
Wood, Charles IV, 1195
Wood, Charles IV, 1196
Wood, Charles IV, 1228
Wood, Charles VI, 951
Wood, Charles VI, 1019
Wood, Charles A. II, 942
Wood, Charles A. III, 475
Wood, Charles A. VI, 1020
Wood, Charles D. IV, 505
Wood, Charles F. III, 508
Wood, Charles J. II, 140
Wood, Charles J. II, 160
Wood, Charles J. II, 828
Wood, Charles J. II, 942
Wood, Charles L. VI, 458
Wood, Charles L. VI, 459
Wood, Charles L. VI, 618
Wood, Charles L. VI, 723
Wood, Charles S. II, 723
Wood, Charles S. II, 761
Wood, Charles S. II, 777
Wood, Charles Sumner IV, 1228
Wood, Charles W. IV, 306
Wood, Charles W. VI, 1020
Wood, Charlotte VI, 866
Wood, Chas. E. IV, 1155
Wood, Chas. J. II, 942
Wood, Cidney IV, 458
Wood, Clara B. VI, 459
Wood, Clara Virginia VI, 458
Wood, Clarence IV, 1228
Wood, Clarkey IV, 403
Wood, Clarkey IV, 458
Wood, Clarkson IV, 1196
Wood, Clarry IV, 458
Wood, Clement III, 93
Wood, Clement III, 363
Wood, Cora IV, 506
Wood, Cornelia III, 109
Wood, Cornelia III, 366
Wood, Cornelia I. IV, 505
Wood, Cornelia J. IV, 306
Wood, Cornelia J. IV, 307
Wood, Cornelia J. IV, 505
Wood, Cornelia J. IV, 506
Wood, Cornelia W. III, 326
Wood, Cornelius VI, 457
Wood, Cornelius VI, 458
Wood, Daniel II, 828
Wood, Daniel III, 363
Wood, Daniel III, 365
Wood, Daniel IV, 306
Wood, Daniel IV, 1082
Wood, Daniel IV, 1143
Wood, Daniel IV, 1147
Wood, Daniel IV, 1171
Wood, Daniel IV, 1190
Wood, Daniel IV, 1194
Wood, Daniel IV, 1195
Wood, Daniel IV, 1228
Wood, Daniel B. IV, 1234
Wood, Daniel B. IV, 1242
Wood, Daniel C. V, 720
Wood, Daniel H. IV, 1195
Wood, Daniel H. IV, 1196
Wood, Daniel H. IV, 1267
Wood, Daniel M. III, 366
Wood, Daniel P. II, 94
Wood, Daniel T. IV, 1195
Wood, Daniel T. IV, 1228
Wood, Daniel T. IV, 1242
Wood, Daniel T. VI, 385
Wood, Daniel T. VI, 426
Wood, Daniel T. VI, 449
Wood, Daniel T. VI, 459
Wood, Daniel T. VI, 681
Wood, Daniel T. VI, 682
Wood, Daniel T. VI, 723
Wood, Daniel T., Jr. VI, 458
Wood, David II, 47
Wood, David II, 94
Wood, David II, 112
Wood, David II, 126
Wood, David II, 160
Wood, David II, 438
Wood, David II, 723
Wood, David II, 777
Wood, David II, 1005
Wood, David II, 1040
Wood, David III, 365
Wood, David IV, 1189
Wood, David IV, 1195
Wood, David IV, 1219
Wood, David IV, 1227
Wood, David VI, 458
Wood, David VI, 583
Wood, David VI, 817
Wood, David VI, 827
Wood, David VI, 866
Wood, David C. II, 692
Wood, David John IV, 1195
Wood, David John M. IV, 1228
Wood, David R. II, 140
Wood, David R. II, 160
Wood, David R. II, 942
Wood, David S. III, 363
Wood, David S. III, 365
Wood, David Shove III, 365
Wood, Deademi III, 508
Wood, Deadicini V, 942
Wood, Deborah I, 69
Wood, Deborah I, 126
Wood, Deborah I, 177
Wood, Deborah II, 692
Wood, Deborah II, 985
Wood, Deborah II, 1040
Wood, Deborah III, 364
Wood, Deborah Ann II, 828
Wood, Deborah Ann II, 915
Wood, Deborah Ann II, 942
Wood, Deborah M. II, 692
Wood, Deborah M. II, 915
Wood, Deborah M. II, 919
Wood, Deborah M. II, 942
Wood, Deborah Malandra II, 828
Wood, Demartha VI, 889
Wood, Desire IV, 1177
Wood, Desire IV, 1195
Wood, Diana VI, 1019
Wood, Direxa IV, 1155
Wood, Direxa IV, 1195
Wood, Dr. James R. III, 364
Wood, E. VI, 1019
Wood, Ebeneezer V, 213
Wood, Ebenezer W. VI, 741
Wood, Edmund III, 364
Wood, Edmund III, 366
Wood, Edmund VI, 811
Wood, Edmund VI, 830
Wood, Edmund VI, 851
Wood, Edmund VI, 866
Wood, Edmund B. VI, 818
Wood, Edna IV, 1121
Wood, Edna IV, 1139
Wood, Edna IV, 1140
Wood, Edw. H. III, 364
Wood, Edward III, 364
Wood, Edward III, 365
Wood, Edward Bond VI, 584
Wood, Edward H. III, 176
Wood, Edward H. III, 364
Wood, Edward H. III, 365
Wood, Edward Randolph II, 724
Wood, Edwin VI, 807
Wood, Effie M. IV, 1228
Wood, Elam IV, 307
Wood, Elam IV, 458
Wood, Elam IV, 601
Wood, Eleanor II, 466
Wood, Eleanor II, 691
Wood, Eleanor II, 712
Wood, Eleanor II, 979
Wood, Eleanor II, 1040
Wood, Eleanor III, 364
Wood, Eleanor III, 366
Wood, Eleanor H. IV, 110
Wood, Eleanor H. IV, 116
Wood, Eleanor H. VI, 568
Wood, Eleanor H. VI, 583
Wood, Eleanor K. III, 219
Wood, Eleanor K. III, 364
Wood, Eliajh IV, 458
Wood, Elijah IV, 458
Wood, Elisha IV, 1082
Wood, Elisha IV, 1121
Wood, Elisha M. IV, 306
Wood, Elisha M. IV, 566
Wood, Elisha M. IV, 601
Wood, Elisha M. IV, 1087
Wood, Elisha M. IV, 1121
Wood, Eliza III, 364
Wood, Eliza IV, 1195
Wood, Eliza IV, 1196
Wood, Eliza VI, 820
Wood, Eliza VI, 1019
Wood, Eliza Ann III, 363
Wood, Eliza Ann III, 365
Wood, Eliza J. III, 364
Wood, Eliza J. III, 366
Wood, Eliza Jane IV, 501
Wood, Eliza Jane IV, 505
Wood, Eliza Jane IV, 558
Wood, Eliza Jane IV, 1023
Wood, Eliza Jane IV, 1031
Wood, Eliza Jane IV, 1228
Wood, Eliza L. III, 366
Wood, Eliza Mary IV, 1228
Wood, Elizabeth I, 172
Wood, Elizabeth I, 177
Wood, Elizabeth I, 751
Wood, Elizabeth II, 56
Wood, Elizabeth II, 112
Wood, Elizabeth II, 152
Wood, Elizabeth II, 160
Wood, Elizabeth II, 274
Wood, Elizabeth II, 275
Wood, Elizabeth II, 306
Wood, Elizabeth II, 438
Wood, Elizabeth II, 449
Wood, Elizabeth II, 477
Wood, Elizabeth II, 555
Wood, Elizabeth II, 643
Wood, Elizabeth II, 691
Wood, Elizabeth II, 692
Wood, Elizabeth II, 723
Wood, Elizabeth II, 761
Wood, Elizabeth II, 777
Wood, Elizabeth II, 781
Wood, Elizabeth II, 809
Wood, Elizabeth II, 1040
Wood, Elizabeth III, 192
Wood, Elizabeth III, 308
Wood, Elizabeth III, 347
Wood, Elizabeth III, 364
Wood, Elizabeth III, 365
Wood, Elizabeth III, 447
Wood, Elizabeth III, 475
Wood, Elizabeth IV, 68
Wood, Elizabeth IV, 105
Wood, Elizabeth IV, 116
Wood, Elizabeth IV, 165
Wood, Elizabeth IV, 306
Wood, Elizabeth IV, 307
Wood, Elizabeth IV, 424
Wood, Elizabeth IV, 442
Wood, Elizabeth IV, 454
Wood, Elizabeth IV, 458
Wood, Elizabeth IV, 468
Wood, Elizabeth IV, 482
Wood, Elizabeth IV, 485
Wood, Elizabeth IV, 504
Wood, Elizabeth IV, 505
Wood, Elizabeth IV, 506
Wood, Elizabeth IV, 558
Wood, Elizabeth IV, 601
Wood, Elizabeth IV, 637
Wood, Elizabeth IV, 918
Wood, Elizabeth IV, 1082
Wood, Elizabeth IV, 1121
Wood, Elizabeth IV, 1143
Wood, Elizabeth IV, 1147
Wood, Elizabeth IV, 1195
Wood, Elizabeth IV, 1196
Wood, Elizabeth IV, 1209
Wood, Elizabeth IV, 1228
Wood, Elizabeth IV, 1296
Wood, Elizabeth IV, 1300
Wood, Elizabeth VI, 37
Wood, Elizabeth VI, 356
Wood, Elizabeth VI, 580
Wood, Elizabeth VI, 583
Wood, Elizabeth VI, 723
Wood, Elizabeth VI, 797
Wood, Elizabeth VI, 818
Wood, Elizabeth VI, 827
Wood, Elizabeth VI, 830
Wood, Elizabeth VI, 845
Wood, Elizabeth VI, 851
Wood, Elizabeth VI, 865
Wood, Elizabeth VI, 866
Wood, Elizabeth VI, 900
Wood, Elizabeth VI, 935
Wood, Elizabeth VI, 953
Wood, Elizabeth VI, 986
Wood, Elizabeth VI, 995
Wood, Elizabeth VI, 1019
Wood, Elizabeth A. IV, 494
Wood, Elizabeth A. IV, 505
Wood, Elizabeth A. VI, 867
Wood, Elizabeth Ann IV, 469
Wood, Elizabeth Ann IV, 500
Wood, Elizabeth Ann IV, 505
Wood, Elizabeth Ann IV, 1082
Wood, Elizabeth C. III, 202
Wood, Elizabeth C. III, 257
Wood, Elizabeth C. III, 364
Wood, Elizabeth C. III, 365
Wood, Elizabeth C. IV, 306
Wood, Elizabeth C. IV, 307
Wood, Elizabeth C. IV, 505
Wood, Elizabeth F. II, 284
Wood, Elizabeth G. IV, 1189
Wood, Elizabeth G. IV, 1196
Wood, Elizabeth G. IV, 1225
Wood, Elizabeth G. IV, 1227
Wood, Elizabeth H. II, 726
Wood, Elizabeth H. II, 777
Wood, Elizabeth Hull III, 364
Wood, Elizabeth J. VI, 866
Wood, Elizabeth K. III, 364
Wood, Elizabeth K. III, 366
Wood, Elizabeth L. IV, 234
Wood, Elizabeth L. IV, 306
Wood, Elizabeth L. IV, 481
Wood, Elizabeth L. IV, 504
Wood, Elizabeth L. IV, 505
Wood, Elizabeth P. IV, 1121
Wood, Elizabeth P. IV, 1158
Wood, Elizabeth P. IV, 1196
Wood, Elizabeth R. III, 241
Wood, Elizabeth R. III, 365
Wood, Elizabeth R. VI, 1019
Wood, Elizabeth Schooley VI, 584
Wood, Elizabeth T. III, 364
Wood, Elizabeth T. IV, 1196
Wood, Elizabeth T. VI, 792
Wood, Elizabeth U. III, 308
Wood, Elizabeth U. III, 364
Wood, Elizabeth U. III, 366
Wood, Elizabeth W. IV, 1177
Wood, Elkanah III, 364
Wood, Elkanah III, 475
Wood, Elkanah III, 496
Wood, Elkanah III, 508
Wood, Ellen V, 291
Wood, Ellen Collins II, 723
Wood, Ellen L. III, 82
Wood, Elma III, 363
Wood, Elma III, 364
Wood, Elmary VI, 1019
Wood, Elmer C. IV, 1228
Wood, Elva IV, 383
Wood, Elva IV, 458
Wood, Elvira IV, 1217
Wood, Elvira IV, 1227
Wood, Elvira IV, 1228
Wood, Elvy IV, 458
Wood, Emily III, 365
Wood, Emily F. VI, 866
Wood, Emily H. III, 508
Wood, Emma III, 132
Wood, Emma III, 363
Wood, Emma III, 364
Wood, Emma III, 365
Wood, Emma III, 366
Wood, Emma IV, 505
Wood, Emma IV, 506
Wood, Emma C. III, 366
Wood, Emma M. IV, 506
Wood, Emmor IV, 458
Wood, Emmor IV, 1082
Wood, Enoch IV, 1121
Wood, Enoch IV, 1140
Wood, Enos IV, 68
Wood, Enos IV, 637
Wood, Enos IV, 918
Wood, Epenetus III, 455
Wood, Ernest W. III, 364
Wood, Ernest W. III, 366
Wood, Esther IV, 373
Wood, Esther IV, 448
Wood, Esther IV, 455
Wood, Esther IV, 458
Wood, Esther IV, 488
Wood, Esther IV, 496
Wood, Esther IV, 504
Wood, Esther IV, 505
Wood, Esther IV, 558
Wood, Esther IV, 601
Wood, Esther IV, 1072
Wood, Esther IV, 1082
Wood, Esther IV, 1189
Wood, Esther IV, 1195
Wood, Esther IV, 1219
Wood, Esther IV, 1227
Wood, Esther VI, 371
Wood, Esther VI, 457
Wood, Esther VI, 626
Wood, Esther VI, 710
Wood, Esther B. IV, 1189
Wood, Esther B. IV, 1195
Wood, Esther B. IV, 1196
Wood, Esther De Benneville II, 828
Wood, Esther Maria IV, 505
Wood, Esther Mariah IV, 1082
Wood, Esther N. IV, 1196
Wood, Esther P. III, 475
Wood, Esther W. IV, 1218
Wood, Esther W. IV, 1228
Wood, Eugene IV, 1195
Wood, Eugene Beauhavnois VI, 583
Wood, Eunace IV, 1195
Wood, Eunice I, 608
Wood, Eva V, 667
Wood, Eva V, 720
Wood, Eva VI, 372
Wood, Eva C. IV, 946
Wood, Ezra III, 364
Wood, F. P. VI, 816
Wood, Fam IV, 1228
Wood, Fanny VI, 1019
Wood, Florence IV, 1228
Wood, Frances I, 352
Wood, Frances IV, 1195
Wood, Frances IV, 1228
Wood, Frances VI, 866
Wood, Frances VI, 950
Wood, Frances Adelaide III, 36
Wood, Frances T. IV, 1195
Wood, Frances T. IV, 1228
Wood, Francis II, 777
Wood, Francis III, 364
Wood, Francis III, 366
Wood, Francis VI, 935
Wood, Francis VI, 948
Wood, Francis VI, 1019
Wood, Francis Howgill III, 364
Wood, Francis M. V, 440
Wood, Francis Sydney III, 364
Wood, Francis T. IV, 1212
Wood, Frank V, 366
Wood, Frank Dutton VI, 584
Wood, Franklin II, 942
Wood, Franklin IV, 1082
Wood, Franklin VI, 792
Wood, Fred IV, 1196
Wood, Frederick III, 307
Wood, Frederick IV, 918
Wood, Frederick IV, 1195
Wood, Frederick M. III, 366
Wood, Frederick R. III, 364
Wood, Frederick R. III, 366
Wood, Frederick S. IV, 505
Wood, Frederick S. IV, 918
Wood, Frederick William III, 36
Wood, Furbay Eugene IV, 1228
Wood, G. W. II, 622
Wood, G. W. II, 691
Wood, Geo. A. V, 213
Wood, Geo. D. III, 365
Wood, George II, 438
Wood, George II, 449
Wood, George II, 692
Wood, George III, 364
Wood, George III, 365
Wood, George III, 366
Wood, George A. II, 723
Wood, George Albert IV, 1195
Wood, George B. II, 692
Wood, George B. II, 777
Wood, George B. IV, 1121
Wood, George B., Jr. II, 777
Wood, George C. IV, 601
Wood, George H. III, 243
Wood, George H. III, 364
Wood, George H., Jr. III, 364
Wood, George I. IV, 1195
Wood, George J. IV, 1195
Wood, George J. IV, 1196
Wood, George R. II, 777
Wood, George R. IV, 306
Wood, George R. IV, 1121
Wood, George R. V, 291

d, George S. III, 364
d, George S. III, 365
d, Gerard Hopkins IV, 505
d, Gerard Hopkins IV, 558
d, Gerard Hopkins IV, 1082
d, Gilbert Congdon III, 364
d, Gilbert Congdon III, 366
d, Gilpin II, 942
d, Governor James VI, 948
d, Grace III, 365
d, Grace IV, 1016
od, Grace IV, 1196
od, Grace VI, 458
od, Grace F. IV, 1196
od, Grace R. III, 157
od, Grace R. III, 364
od, Grandvil IV, 504
od, Granville IV, 506
od, Greenberry P. IV, 505
od, Greenberry P. IV, 789
od, Greenberry P. IV, 1006
od, Greenberry P. IV, 1016
od, Greenbury IV, 504
od, Griffith IV, 1228
od, Griffith L. IV, 1195
od, Griffith L. IV, 1228
od, Guilelema III, 307
od, H. III, 192
od, Hanna IV, 117
od, Hannah I, 126
od, Hannah II, 47
od, Hannah II, 65
od, Hannah II, 87
od, Hannah II, 112
od, Hannah II, 150
od, Hannah II, 160
od, Hannah II, 477
od, Hannah II, 691
od, Hannah II, 692
od, Hannah II, 723
ood, Hannah II, 792
ood, Hannah II, 802
ood, Hannah II, 827
ood, Hannah III, 365
ood, Hannah III, 429
ood, Hannah III, 475
ood, Hannah IV, 98
ood, Hannah IV, 116
ood, Hannah IV, 165
ood, Hannah IV, 207
ood, Hannah IV, 285
ood, Hannah IV, 306
ood, Hannah IV, 307
ood, Hannah IV, 326
ood, Hannah IV, 359
ood, Hannah IV, 360
Vood, Hannah IV, 558
Vood, Hannah IV, 634
Vood, Hannah IV, 789
Vood, Hannah IV, 1006
Vood, Hannah IV, 1016
Vood, Hannah IV, 1120
Vood, Hannah IV, 1121
Wood, Hannah IV, 1202
Wood, Hannah IV, 1227
Wood, Hannah IV, 1228
Wood, Hannah VI, 402
Wood, Hannah VI, 420
Wood, Hannah VI, 433
Wood, Hannah VI, 458
Wood, Hannah VI, 600
Wood, Hannah VI, 607
Wood, Hannah Ann II, 723
Wood, Hannah Ann II, 777
Wood, Hannah Ann II, 913
Wood, Hannah Ann II, 942
Wood, Hannah B. M. IV, 1195
Wood, Hannah Leggett III, 364
Wood, Hannah P. III, 508
Wood, Hannah S. IV, 482
Wood, Hannah S. IV, 483
Wood, Hannah S. IV, 505
Wood, Hannah Z. III, 508
Wood, Hanson IV, 458
Wood, Harold B. II, 189
Wood, Harold B. II, 307
Wood, Harriet III, 475
Wood, Harriet A. III, 365
Wood, Harriet V. S. III, 284
Wood, Harriet V. S. III, 364
Wood, Harriet V. S. III, 366
Wood, Harriett M. IV, 1227
Wood, Harry IV, 1227
Wood, Harry IV, 1228
Wood, Hazel III, 243
Wood, Hazel III, 364
Wood, Hazel V, 720
Wood, Helen III, 307
Wood, Helen III, 501
Wood, Helen III, 508
Wood, Helen V, 468
Wood, Helen L. IV, 918
Wood, Helen Louise V, 313
Wood, Henry II, 47
Wood, Henry II, 87
Wood, Henry II, 112
Wood, Henry II, 622
Wood, Henry II, 686
Wood, Henry II, 691
Wood, Henry II, 692
Wood, Henry II, 777
Wood, Henry III, 167
Wood, Henry III, 192
Wood, Henry III, 363
Wood, Henry III, 365
Wood, Henry III, 366
Wood, Henry IV, 306
Wood, Henry IV, 307
Wood, Henry IV, 1195
Wood, Henry IV, 1228
Wood, Henry V, 366
Wood, Henry VI, 643
Wood, Henry C. IV, 306
Wood, Henry C. IV, 505
Wood, Henry C. IV, 506
Wood, Henry Clay VI, 584
Wood, Henry D. VI, 885
Wood, Henry M. III, 364
Wood, Henry S. II, 942
Wood, Henry T. III, 364
Wood, Henry T. III, 366
Wood, Herbert IV, 505
Wood, Herbert Stephen III, 366
Wood, Hope II, 942
Wood, Horatio C. II, 284
Wood, Horatio C. II, 306
Wood, Horatio C. II, 723
Wood, Horatio C. II, 777
Wood, Horation C. II, 726
Wood, Howard II, 838
Wood, Howard II, 942
Wood, Howard III, 366
Wood, Huntington III, 475
Wood, Ida May III, 363
Wood, Irene VI, 866
Wood, Irene B. III, 95
Wood, Irene B. III, 364
Wood, Isaac II, 222
Wood, Isaac II, 275
Wood, Isaac III, 364
Wood, Isaac III, 365
Wood, Isaac IV, 306
Wood, Isaac IV, 403
Wood, Isaac IV, 458
Wood, Isaac IV, 505
Wood, Isaac V, 543
Wood, Isaac V, 720
Wood, Isaac VI, 395
Wood, Isaac VI, 457
Wood, Isaac VI, 618
Wood, Isaac VI, 682
Wood, Isaac VI, 723
Wood, Isaac, Sr. VI, 458
Wood, Isabel IV, 68
Wood, Isaiah IV, 504
Wood, Isaiah IV, 505
Wood, Isaiah IV, 789
Wood, Israel I, 970
Wood, Israel III, 508
Wood, Israel IV, 165
Wood, Israel IV, 306
Wood, Israel IV, 424
Wood, Israel IV, 458
Wood, Israel IV, 601
Wood, Israel IV, 1082
Wood, Israel IV, 1195
Wood, Israel IV, 1196
Wood, Israel IV, 1204
Wood, Israel IV, 1205
Wood, Israel IV, 1212
Wood, Israel IV, 1218
Wood, Israel IV, 1223
Wood, Israel IV, 1225
Wood, Israel IV, 1227
Wood, Israel IV, 1228
Wood, Israel VI, 356
Wood, Israel C. IV, 1195
Wood, J. Densmore V, 720
Wood, Jacob II, 47
Wood, Jacob II, 87
Wood, Jacob II, 112
Wood, Jacob II, 150
Wood, Jacob II, 160
Wood, Jacob III, 364
Wood, Jacob III, 365
Wood, Jacob III, 366
Wood, Jacob III, 457
Wood, Jacob III, 475
Wood, Jacob IV, 68
Wood, Jacob IV, 70
Wood, Jacob IV, 346
Wood, Jacob IV, 359
Wood, Jacob IV, 558
Wood, Jacob IV, 666
Wood, Jacob VI, 458
Wood, Jacob VI, 607
Wood, James II, 47
Wood, James II, 112
Wood, James II, 189
Wood, James II, 438
Wood, James II, 449
Wood, James II, 569
Wood, James II, 622
Wood, James II, 691
Wood, James II, 692
Wood, James II, 777
Wood, James II, 807
Wood, James II, 828
Wood, James II, 915
Wood, James II, 919
Wood, James II, 942
Wood, James III, 508
Wood, James IV, 306
Wood, James IV, 307
Wood, James IV, 458
Wood, James IV, 946
Wood, James VI, 866
Wood, James VI, 914
Wood, James VI, 995
Wood, James VI, 1019
Wood, James D. II, 828
Wood, James F. II, 284
Wood, James F. II, 306
Wood, James F. II, 777
Wood, James Francis II, 777
Wood, James P. II, 942
Wood, James Pancoast II, 828
Wood, James R. III, 353
Wood, James R. III, 364
Wood, Jane I, 352
Wood, Jane I, 799
Wood, Jane I, 846
Wood, Jane II, 47
Wood, Jane II, 438
Wood, Jane II, 449
Wood, Jane III, 366
Wood, Jane IV, 306
Wood, Jane IV, 458
Wood, Jane IV, 504
Wood, Jane IV, 585
Wood, Jane IV, 601
Wood, Jane IV, 1082
Wood, Jane VI, 458
Wood, Jane VI, 807
Wood, Jane VI, 817
Wood, Jane VI, 827
Wood, Jane VI, 858
Wood, Jane VI, 866
Wood, Jane VI, 1019
Wood, Jane Jones IV, 601
Wood, Jane L. IV, 468
Wood, Jane L. IV, 505
Wood, Jane M. IV, 1016
Wood, Janet III, 363
Wood, Janett VI, 1019
Wood, Jemima IV, 1165
Wood, Jemima IV, 1195
Wood, Jenett VI, 1019
Wood, Jennett S. VI, 1019
Wood, Jenny VI, 866
Wood, Jeremiah III, 475
Wood, Jeremiah VI, 889
Wood, Jeremiah VI, 907
Wood, Jeremiah VI, 981
Wood, Jeremiah VI, 1019
Wood, Jesse IV, 116
Wood, Jesse IV, 165
Wood, Jesse IV, 306
Wood, Jesse IV, 348
Wood, Jesse IV, 359
Wood, Jesse IV, 360
Wood, Jesse VI, 458
Wood, Jesse VI, 583
Wood, Jesse VI, 607
Wood, Jesse VI, 935
Wood, Jesse VI, 946
Wood, Jesse VI, 987
Wood, Jesse VI, 1019
Wood, Jesse Atkinson IV, 1016
Wood, Jesse M. IV, 558
Wood, Jesse M. V, 143
Wood, Jessie IV, 1016
Wood, Jessie E. IV, 506
Wood, Jno. VI, 806
Wood, Joanna II, 136
Wood, Joel IV, 306
Wood, Joel IV, 307
Wood, Joel IV, 312
Wood, Joel IV, 315
Wood, Joel IV, 485
Wood, Joel IV, 504
Wood, Joel IV, 505
Wood, Joel IV, 506
Wood, John I, 352
Wood, John I, 628
Wood, John II, 222
Wood, John II, 275
Wood, John II, 438
Wood, John II, 449
Wood, John II, 643
Wood, John II, 691
Wood, John II, 752
Wood, John II, 777
Wood, John III, 36
Wood, John III, 173
Wood, John III, 237
Wood, John III, 257
Wood, John III, 363
Wood, John III, 364
Wood, John III, 365
Wood, John III, 366
Wood, John III, 508
Wood, John IV, 68
Wood, John IV, 70
Wood, John IV, 93
Wood, John IV, 98
Wood, John IV, 116
Wood, John IV, 117
Wood, John IV, 165
Wood, John IV, 306
Wood, John IV, 373
Wood, John IV, 448
Wood, John IV, 455
Wood, John IV, 458
Wood, John IV, 493
Wood, John IV, 497
Wood, John IV, 504
Wood, John IV, 585
Wood, John IV, 601
Wood, John IV, 666
Wood, John IV, 789
Wood, John IV, 1082
Wood, John V, 942
Wood, John VI, 37
Wood, John VI, 414
Wood, John VI, 457
Wood, John VI, 458
Wood, John VI, 583
Wood, John VI, 796
Wood, John VI, 835
Wood, John VI, 839
Wood, John VI, 845
Wood, John VI, 865
Wood, John VI, 866
Wood, John VI, 889
Wood, John VI, 963
Wood, John VI, 1019
Wood, John B. II, 723
Wood, John B. II, 777
Wood, John B. VI, 900
Wood, John B. VI, 1019
Wood, John B., Jr. II, 942
Wood, John F. IV, 1016
Wood, John F. VI, 817
Wood, John F. VI, 866
Wood, John G. VI, 458
Wood, John Henry III, 364
Wood, John Jay III, 365
Wood, John King III, 366
Wood, John M. III, 492
Wood, John M. III, 508
Wood, John M. VI, 863
Wood, John Milton IV, 1121
Wood, John P. IV, 505
Wood, John P. IV, 1082
Wood, John P. IV, 1121
Wood, John P. IV, 1158
Wood, John P. IV, 1196
Wood, John Richard VI, 583
Wood, John S. I, 643
Wood, John S. III, 366
Wood, John T. VI, 1020
Wood, John Thornton III, 363
Wood, John W. III, 366
Wood, John W. IV, 307
Wood, John W. IV, 382
Wood, John W. IV, 458
Wood, John W. IV, 572
Wood, John W. IV, 601
Wood, John, Jr. III, 365
Wood, John, Jr. IV, 116
Wood, Jonah IV, 116
Wood, Jonas III, 365
Wood, Jonas III, 398
Wood, Jonas III, 408
Wood, Jonas III, 412
Wood, Jonas III, 475
Wood, Jonathan I, 934
Wood, Jonathan II, 438
Wood, Jonathan II, 691
Wood, Jonathan IV, 306
Wood, Jonathan IV, 307
Wood, Jonathan IV, 1016
Wood, Jonathan IV, 1176
Wood, Jonathan IV, 1177
Wood, Jonathan IV, 1195
Wood, Jonathan IV, 1196
Wood, Jonathan IV, 1225
Wood, Jonathan IV, 1227
Wood, Jonathan IV, 1228
Wood, Jonathan B. IV, 1195
Wood, Jonathan B. IV, 1228
Wood, Jonathan, Jr. IV, 864
Wood, Jonathan, Jr. IV, 886
Wood, Jonathan, Jr. IV, 1143
Wood, Jonathan, Jr. IV, 1195
Wood, Jonathan, Jr. IV, 1228
Wood, Jos. VI, 502
Wood, Jos., Jr. VI, 583
Wood, Joseph I, 126
Wood, Joseph I, 177
Wood, Joseph II, 438
Wood, Joseph II, 449
Wood, Joseph II, 508
Wood, Joseph II, 555
Wood, Joseph II, 596
Wood, Joseph II, 625
Wood, Joseph II, 691
Wood, Joseph II, 692
Wood, Joseph II, 777
Wood, Joseph II, 828
Wood, Joseph II, 915
Wood, Joseph II, 942
Wood, Joseph III, 363
Wood, Joseph III, 365
Wood, Joseph III, 406
Wood, Joseph III, 475
Wood, Joseph IV, 68
Wood, Joseph IV, 102
Wood, Joseph IV, 116
Wood, Joseph IV, 152
Wood, Joseph IV, 165
Wood, Joseph IV, 306
Wood, Joseph IV, 307
Wood, Joseph IV, 458
Wood, Joseph IV, 558
Wood, Joseph IV, 601
Wood, Joseph IV, 1082
Wood, Joseph IV, 1120
Wood, Joseph IV, 1121
Wood, Joseph IV, 1140
Wood, Joseph IV, 1228
Wood, Joseph IV, 1386
Wood, Joseph VI, 371
Wood, Joseph VI, 416
Wood, Joseph VI, 457
Wood, Joseph VI, 458
Wood, Joseph VI, 476
Wood, Joseph VI, 580
Wood, Joseph VI, 624
Wood, Joseph VI, 723
Wood, Joseph VI, 817
Wood, Joseph VI, 866
Wood, Joseph VI, 867
Wood, Joseph M. IV, 1195
Wood, Joseph M. IV, 1196
Wood, Joseph M. IV, 1296
Wood, Joseph M. IV, 1300
Wood, Joseph M. VI, 792
Wood, Joseph R. III, 241
Wood, Joseph R. III, 363
Wood, Joseph R. III, 365
Wood, Joseph Symons I, 177
Wood, Joseph U. IV, 307
Wood, Joseph, Jr. II, 691
Wood, Joseph, Jr. III, 394
Wood, Joseph, Jr. III, 475
Wood, Joseph, Jr. IV, 1140
Wood, Josephine II, 724
Wood, Josephine II, 828
Wood, Joshua IV, 68
Wood, Joshua IV, 110
Wood, Joshua IV, 116
Wood, Joshua IV, 306
Wood, Joshua IV, 326
Wood, Joshua IV, 359
Wood, Joshua IV, 360
Wood, Joshua IV, 488
Wood, Joshua IV, 496
Wood, Joshua IV, 504
Wood, Joshua IV, 505
Wood, Joshua IV, 558
Wood, Joshua IV, 666
Wood, Joshua IV, 1072
Wood, Joshua IV, 1082
Wood, Joshua VI, 420
Wood, Joshua VI, 458
Wood, Joshua VI, 568
Wood, Joshua VI, 583
Wood, Joshua VI, 600
Wood, Joshua VI, 607
Wood, Josiah IV, 116
Wood, Josiah IV, 167
Wood, Josiah IV, 306
Wood, Josiah IV, 1082

Wood, Josiah VI, 583
Wood, Josiah VI, 723
Wood, Josiah VI, 953
Wood, Josiah VI, 1019
Wood, Judith VI, 890
Wood, Julia I, 934
Wood, Julia III, 366
Wood, Juliana F. II, 761
Wood, Juliana F. II, 777
Wood, Juliann II, 723
Wood, Juliann VI, 1019
Wood, Julianna II, 724
Wood, Julianna R. II, 777
Wood, Juriah VI, 1020
Wood, Kate IV, 1147
Wood, Kate E. IV, 1196
Wood, Katharine Murray III, 364
Wood, Katharine Virginia IV, 1016
Wood, Katherine VI, 356
Wood, Katy VI, 1019
Wood, Keester IV, 306
Wood, Kessiah VI, 866
Wood, Kester IV, 306
Wood, Kester IV, 1082
Wood, Keziah III, 162
Wood, Keziah III, 366
Wood, Kinsey IV, 1196
Wood, L. Hollingsworth III, 501
Wood, L. Hollingsworth III, 508
Wood, Lamira IV, 1016
Wood, Lamira IV, 1227
Wood, Lamira IV, 1228
Wood, Latitia II, 47
Wood, Latitia II, 87
Wood, Latitia II, 112
Wood, Laura VI, 458
Wood, Laura G. II, 877
Wood, Laura G. II, 942
Wood, Leander III, 508
Wood, Lenora IV, 1196
Wood, Levi IV, 306
Wood, Levi IV, 1194
Wood, Levi IV, 1196
Wood, Lewcy IV, 481
Wood, Lewcy IV, 492
Wood, Lewis IV, 68
Wood, Lewis IV, 306
Wood, Lewis IV, 307
Wood, Lewis IV, 458
Wood, Lewis IV, 505
Wood, Lewis IV, 558
Wood, Lewis IV, 559
Wood, Lewis V, 313
Wood, Libius IV, 1195
Wood, Libius IV, 1196
Wood, Libius IV, 1228
Wood, Lindley H. IV, 1195
Wood, Lindley H. IV, 1228
Wood, Lizzie C. IV, 307
Wood, Lizzie C. IV, 506
Wood, Lorena IV, 918
Wood, Lou F. V, 468
Wood, Louisa III, 192
Wood, Louisa V, 942
Wood, Louisa C. II, 942
Wood, Louisa K. III, 365
Wood, Louisa M. III, 365
Wood, Louisa M. IV, 1097
Wood, Louisa M. IV, 1121
Wood, Louisa T. IV, 1227
Wood, Louise III, 475
Wood, Louise C. II, 942
Wood, Louise Moyer III, 475
Wood, Lucinda VI, 908
Wood, Lucretia VI, 458
Wood, Lucretia N. VI, 459
Wood, Lucretia Nichols VI, 385
Wood, Lucretia Nichols VI, 458
Wood, Lucy IV, 306
Wood, Lucy IV, 307
Wood, Lucy IV, 468
Wood, Lucy IV, 473
Wood, Lucy IV, 476
Wood, Lucy IV, 505
Wood, Lucy VI, 951
Wood, Lucy J. IV, 306
Wood, Lucy L. IV, 483
Wood, Lucy L. IV, 504
Wood, Lucy L. IV, 506
Wood, Lumina VI, 866
Wood, Lydia II, 47
Wood, Lydia II, 94
Wood, Lydia II, 112
Wood, Lydia II, 1063
Wood, Lydia II, 1064
Wood, Lydia III, 363
Wood, Lydia III, 365
Wood, Lydia IV, 75
Wood, Lydia IV, 116
Wood, Lydia IV, 306
Wood, Lydia IV, 464
Wood, Lydia IV, 476
Wood, Lydia IV, 495
Wood, Lydia IV, 497
Wood, Lydia IV, 504
Wood, Lydia IV, 505
Wood, Lydia IV, 506
Wood, Lydia IV, 558
Wood, Lydia IV, 1016
Wood, Lydia IV, 1061
Wood, Lydia IV, 1068
Wood, Lydia IV, 1082
Wood, Lydia IV, 1083
Wood, Lydia IV, 1084
Wood, Lydia IV, 1103
Wood, Lydia IV, 1121
Wood, Lydia IV, 1143
Wood, Lydia IV, 1177
Wood, Lydia IV, 1195
Wood, Lydia IV, 1196
Wood, Lydia V, 143
Wood, Lydia V, 543
Wood, Lydia VI, 395
Wood, Lydia VI, 457
Wood, Lydia VI, 458
Wood, Lydia VI, 565
Wood, Lydia VI, 567
Wood, Lydia VI, 583
Wood, Lydia VI, 624
Wood, Lydia VI, 723
Wood, Lydia VI, 1020
Wood, Lydia Ann IV, 497
Wood, Lydia Ann IV, 505
Wood, Lydia B. IV, 306
Wood, Lydia B. IV, 494
Wood, Lydia B. IV, 505
Wood, Lydia B. IV, 550
Wood, Lydia B. IV, 559
Wood, Lydia C. II, 723
Wood, Lydia E. IV, 895
Wood, Lydia Emma VI, 584
Wood, Lydia H. III, 363
Wood, Lydia H. III, 365
Wood, Lydia O. IV, 1227
Wood, Lydia V. VI, 458
Wood, Lydie VI, 556
Wood, M. H. IV, 918
Wood, Mahala VI, 1019
Wood, Maida IV, 505
Wood, Margaret II, 304
Wood, Margaret II, 438
Wood, Margaret II, 692
Wood, Margaret III, 36
Wood, Margaret III, 365
Wood, Margaret III, 366
Wood, Margaret IV, 32
Wood, Margaret IV, 68
Wood, Margaret IV, 306
Wood, Margaret IV, 384
Wood, Margaret IV, 426
Wood, Margaret IV, 458
Wood, Margaret IV, 478
Wood, Margaret IV, 492
Wood, Margaret IV, 504
Wood, Margaret IV, 505
Wood, Margaret IV, 1082
Wood, Margaret VI, 37
Wood, Margaret VI, 437
Wood, Margaret VI, 458
Wood, Margaret VI, 607
Wood, Margaret VI, 792
Wood, Margaret VI, 1019
Wood, Margaret H. IV, 263
Wood, Margaret H. IV, 306
Wood, Margaret H. IV, 307
Wood, Margaret H. IV, 492
Wood, Margaret H. IV, 504
Wood, Margaret H. IV, 505
Wood, Margaret L. VI, 459
Wood, Margaret Logan VI, 449
Wood, Margaret Logan VI, 458
Wood, Margaret M. VI, 643
Wood, Margaret R. VI, 458
Wood, Margaret, Jr. II, 692
Wood, Maria III, 296
Wood, Maria III, 365
Wood, Maria IV, 80
Wood, Maria IV, 116
Wood, Maria VI, 618
Wood, Maria VI, 682
Wood, Maria VI, 723
Wood, Maria N. VI, 459
Wood, Maria Nichols VI, 458
Wood, Mariam G. VI, 459
Wood, Mariana III, 363
Wood, Marianna III, 47
Wood, Marianna III, 365
Wood, Marianna III, 366
Wood, Marianna M. III, 366
Wood, Marie C. IV, 1228
Wood, Marietta IV, 1227
Wood, Mariette IV, 1227
Wood, Marion III, 492
Wood, Marion III, 508
Wood, Mark II, 47
Wood, Martha II, 691
Wood, Martha II, 752
Wood, Martha II, 777
Wood, Martha III, 257
Wood, Martha III, 359
Wood, Martha III, 363
Wood, Martha III, 364
Wood, Martha III, 365
Wood, Martha III, 366
Wood, Martha III, 455
Wood, Martha III, 475
Wood, Martha III, 508
Wood, Martha IV, 306
Wood, Martha IV, 391
Wood, Martha IV, 458
Wood, Martha IV, 468
Wood, Martha IV, 505
Wood, Martha IV, 566
Wood, Martha IV, 601
Wood, Martha IV, 1082
Wood, Martha IV, 1087
Wood, Martha IV, 1121
Wood, Martha IV, 1196
Wood, Martha IV, 1227
Wood, Martha V, 358
Wood, Martha V, 366
Wood, Martha V, 720
Wood, Martha V, 939
Wood, Martha V, 942
Wood, Martha VI, 811
Wood, Martha VI, 829
Wood, Martha VI, 866
Wood, Martha VI, 1019
Wood, Martha A. IV, 1196
Wood, Martha Ann VI, 993
Wood, Martha Ann VI, 1019
Wood, Martha Elizabeth IV, 1195
Wood, Martha Elizabeth IV, 1227
Wood, Martha Jane VI, 1019
Wood, Martha M. VI, 839
Wood, Martha T. IV, 1196
Wood, Martha W. IV, 1147
Wood, Mary I, 126
Wood, Mary I, 583
Wood, Mary II, 47
Wood, Mary II, 73
Wood, Mary II, 126
Wood, Mary II, 248
Wood, Mary II, 275
Wood, Mary II, 438
Wood, Mary II, 449
Wood, Mary II, 555
Wood, Mary II, 569
Wood, Mary II, 582
Wood, Mary II, 622
Wood, Mary II, 625
Wood, Mary II, 671
Wood, Mary II, 686
Wood, Mary II, 691
Wood, Mary II, 692
Wood, Mary II, 694
Wood, Mary II, 723
Wood, Mary II, 724
Wood, Mary II, 838
Wood, Mary II, 936
Wood, Mary II, 942
Wood, Mary II, 1040
Wood, Mary III, 152
Wood, Mary III, 284
Wood, Mary III, 363
Wood, Mary III, 364
Wood, Mary III, 365
Wood, Mary III, 366
Wood, Mary III, 394
Wood, Mary III, 398
Wood, Mary III, 406
Wood, Mary III, 408
Wood, Mary III, 412
Wood, Mary III, 437
Wood, Mary III, 457
Wood, Mary III, 475
Wood, Mary IV, 165
Wood, Mary IV, 207
Wood, Mary IV, 251
Wood, Mary IV, 291
Wood, Mary IV, 306
Wood, Mary IV, 307
Wood, Mary IV, 308
Wood, Mary IV, 384
Wood, Mary IV, 458
Wood, Mary IV, 464
Wood, Mary IV, 466
Wood, Mary IV, 474
Wood, Mary IV, 482
Wood, Mary IV, 500
Wood, Mary IV, 504
Wood, Mary IV, 505
Wood, Mary IV, 506
Wood, Mary IV, 517
Wood, Mary IV, 558
Wood, Mary IV, 559
Wood, Mary IV, 573
Wood, Mary IV, 601
Wood, Mary IV, 864
Wood, Mary IV, 886
Wood, Mary IV, 1016
Wood, Mary IV, 1056
Wood, Mary IV, 1074
Wood, Mary IV, 1082
Wood, Mary IV, 1091
Wood, Mary IV, 1120
Wood, Mary IV, 1121
Wood, Mary IV, 1139
Wood, Mary IV, 1140
Wood, Mary IV, 1143
Wood, Mary IV, 1195
Wood, Mary IV, 1204
Wood, Mary IV, 1212
Wood, Mary IV, 1218
Wood, Mary IV, 1223
Wood, Mary IV, 1225
Wood, Mary IV, 1227
Wood, Mary IV, 1228
Wood, Mary V, 304
Wood, Mary V, 313
Wood, Mary V, 720
Wood, Mary V, 922
Wood, Mary V, 942
Wood, Mary VI, 453
Wood, Mary VI, 458
Wood, Mary VI, 565
Wood, Mary VI, 567
Wood, Mary VI, 580
Wood, Mary VI, 582
Wood, Mary VI, 583
Wood, Mary VI, 838
Wood, Mary VI, 855
Wood, Mary VI, 984
Wood, Mary VI, 1015
Wood, Mary VI, 1019
Wood, Mary Ann IV, 306
Wood, Mary Ann IV, 458
Wood, Mary Ann IV, 505
Wood, Mary Ann IV, 1079
Wood, Mary Ann IV, 1082
Wood, Mary Ann IV, 1111
Wood, Mary Ann IV, 1121
Wood, Mary Ann IV, 1140
Wood, Mary Ann IV, 1228
Wood, Mary Ann VI, 1020
Wood, Mary Ann B. II, 724
Wood, Mary Ann B. II, 777
Wood, Mary Ann E. III, 364
Wood, Mary Anna III, 47
Wood, Mary Anna III, 51
Wood, Mary Anna III, 364
Wood, Mary Anna III, 365
Wood, Mary Anna III, 366
Wood, Mary Arnold, Jr. I, 177
Wood, Mary Augusta III, 364
Wood, Mary B. II, 160
Wood, Mary B. III, 363
Wood, Mary B. IV, 1196
Wood, Mary Biddle II, 942
Wood, Mary Bulah IV, 1227
Wood, Mary C. IV, 1386
Wood, Mary C. VI, 459
Wood, Mary Caroline IV, 306
Wood, Mary Catharine VI, 583
Wood, Mary Catherine VI, 556
Wood, Mary Conard VI, 458
Wood, Mary E. III, 364
Wood, Mary E. IV, 90
Wood, Mary E. IV, 116
Wood, Mary E. IV, 306
Wood, Mary E. IV, 473
Wood, Mary E. IV, 504
Wood, Mary E. IV, 505
Wood, Mary E. IV, 1227
Wood, Mary E. IV, 1228
Wood, Mary E. VI, 1020
Wood, Mary Elizabeth III, 307
Wood, Mary Elizabeth IV, 1155
Wood, Mary Ellen IV, 1196
Wood, Mary Elma III, 365
Wood, Mary F. III, 365
Wood, Mary Frances IV, 1195
Wood, Mary Frances IV, 1196
Wood, Mary Gertrude II, 942
Wood, Mary H. III, 365
Wood, Mary H. IV, 505
Wood, Mary H. IV, 506
Wood, Mary H. IV, 1195
Wood, Mary H. IV, 1205
Wood, Mary H. IV, 1227
Wood, Mary H. VI, 553
Wood, Mary H. VI, 583
Wood, Mary Henrietta VI, 583
Wood, Mary Henrietta VI, 58
Wood, Mary Jane III, 212
Wood, Mary Jane III, 364
Wood, Mary Jane III, 365
Wood, Mary Jane III, 366
Wood, Mary Jane VI, 521
Wood, Mary Jane VI, 583
Wood, Mary L. II, 189
Wood, Mary L. II, 284
Wood, Mary L. II, 307
Wood, Mary M. IV, 504
Wood, Mary M. VI, 884
Wood, Mary P. II, 828
Wood, Mary P. IV, 464
Wood, Mary P. IV, 504
Wood, Mary R. II, 150
Wood, Mary R. II, 160
Wood, Mary R. IV, 504
Wood, Mary R. IV, 506
Wood, Mary R. IV, 559
Wood, Mary R. IV, 601
Wood, Mary R. King III, 366
Wood, Mary S. III, 308
Wood, Mary S. III, 330
Wood, Mary S. III, 364
Wood, Mary S. III, 366
Wood, Mary T. IV, 1196
Wood, Mary T. V, 720
Wood, Mary U. III, 132
Wood, Mary U. III, 365
Wood, Mary U. III, 446
Wood, Mary U. III, 475
Wood, Mary Underhill III, 36
Wood, Mary V. IV, 506
Wood, Mary V. V, 942
Wood, Mary V. VI, 704
Wood, Mary V. VI, 723
Wood, Mary W. IV, 1196
Wood, Mary, Jr. I, 128
Wood, Mary, Jr. VI, 458
Wood, Maryann IV, 458
Wood, Maryann IV, 1082
Wood, Mathew IV, 458
Wood, Matilda IV, 306
Wood, Matilda IV, 1073
Wood, Matilda IV, 1150
Wood, Matilda IV, 1195
Wood, Matilda IV, 1242
Wood, Matilda A. IV, 1234
Wood, Matilda A. IV, 1242
Wood, Matthew IV, 384
Wood, Matthew IV, 426
Wood, Matthew IV, 458
Wood, May VI, 804
Wood, Merab II, 438
Wood, Mildred III, 93
Wood, Mildred III, 363
Wood, Mildred VI, 833
Wood, Mildred VI, 835
Wood, Mildred Ann VI, 1019
Wood, Milison II, 112
Wood, Milly VI, 897
Wood, Milly VI, 909
Wood, Milton IV, 504
Wood, Milton IV, 1082
Wood, Miner VI, 820
Wood, Miram G. VI, 681
Wood, Miriam G. VI, 385
Wood, Miriam G. VI, 426
Wood, Miriam G. VI, 449
Wood, Miriam G. VI, 458
Wood, Miriam G. VI, 682
Wood, Miriam G. VI, 723
Wood, Moming VI, 897
Wood, Morris III, 365
Wood, Morton IV, 1228
Wood, Moses I, 970
Wood, Moses IV, 165
Wood, Moses IV, 458
Wood, Moses VI, 356
Wood, Moses Q. III, 365
Wood, Mourning I, 126
Wood, Mourning VI, 897
Wood, Moyer III, 447
Wood, Moyer III, 475
Wood, Nancy IV, 1195
Wood, Nancy VI, 817
Wood, Nancy VI, 836
Wood, Nancy VI, 851
Wood, Nancy VI, 866
Wood, Nancy VI, 963
Wood, Nancy VI, 984
Wood, Nancy VI, 1019
Wood, Nancy L. VI, 811
Wood, Naomi II, 47
Wood, Naomi II, 94
Wood, Naomi II, 112
Wood, Naomi II, 126
Wood, Naomi II, 140
Wood, Naomi II, 160
Wood, Naomi II, 723

d, Naomi II, 866
d, Naomi II, 942
d, Naomi IV, 116
d, Naomi VI, 583
d, Nathan I, 203
d, Nathan IV, 116
d, Nathan IV, 306
d, Nathan IV, 458
d, Nathan IV, 478
d, Nathan IV, 504
d, Nathan IV, 1082
d, Nathan IV, 1121
d, Nathan VI, 458
d, Nathan L. IV, 306
d, Nathan L. IV, 307
d, Nathan L. IV, 474
d, Nathan L. IV, 504
d, Nathan L. IV, 505
d, Nathan L. IV, 506
d, Nathan L. IV, 918
d, Nathan R. IV, 504
d, Nathan R. IV, 506
d, Nathen IV, 505
d, Neomi IV, 102
d, Neomi IV, 116
d, Newton IV, 505
d, Olive B. VI, 792
d, Oliver R. IV, 306
d, Orlando IV, 1227
d, Orlando IV, 1228
d, Orpha IV, 372
d, Orpha IV, 458
d, Oscar IV, 1195
d, Oscar IV, 1196
d, Patience VI, 946
d, Patsey VI, 796
d, Patsey VI, 866
d, Patsey Sleep VI, 838
d, Patsy VI, 856
d, Pattey VI, 959
d, Paul II, 942
d, Paul VI, 818
d, Paul VI, 866
d, Paul VI, 951
d, Paul VI, 997
d, Paul VI, 1019
d, Pearly Miars V, 720
d, Peleg IV, 1228
d, Peleg P. IV, 1195
d, Pemberton VI, 664
d, Peninah I, 203
d, Peru Elizabeth K. III, 364
d, Peter III, 347
d, Peter III, 364
d, Peter VI, 959
d, Phebe I, 379
d, Phebe I, 430
d, Phebe III, 152
d, Phebe III, 363
d, Phebe III, 364
d, Phebe III, 365
d, Phebe III, 408
d, Phebe IV, 179
d, Phebe IV, 306
d, Phebe IV, 346
d, Phebe IV, 359
d, Phebe IV, 417
d, Phebe IV, 458
d, Phebe IV, 558
d, Phebe IV, 1165
d, Phebe IV, 1171
d, Phebe IV, 1190
d, Phebe IV, 1194
d, Phebe IV, 1227
d, Phebe VI, 981
d, Phebe Ann V, 957
d, Phebe B. IV, 307
d, Phebe B. IV, 1195
d, Phebe B. IV, 1219
d, Phebe C. III, 176
d, Phebe E. III, 365
d, Phebe E. III, 366
d, Phebe H. III, 364
d, Phebe Jane III, 365
d, Phianah III, 365
d, Philip Hopkins III, 366
d, Pininah I, 195
d, Pininah I, 203
d, Polly VI, 817
d, Polly VI, 866
d, Polly VI, 1019
d, Priscilla II, 47
d, Priscilla II, 96
d, Priscilla II, 112
d, Priscilla IV, 1195
d, Priscilla IV, 1196
d, Priscilla VI, 866
d, Priscilla H. IV, 1196
d, Priscilla H. IV, 1227
d, Priscilla H. IV, 1228
d, Prudence IV, 373
Wood, Prudence IV, 458
Wood, Prudence IV, 601
Wood, Pusey IV, 268
Wood, Pusey IV, 306
Wood, Pusey IV, 307
Wood, Pusey IV, 463
Wood, Pusey IV, 504
Wood, Pusey IV, 505
Wood, Pusey IV, 506
Wood, Pusey IV, 521
Wood, Pusey IV, 529
Wood, Pusey IV, 531
Wood, Pusey IV, 558
Wood, Pusey IV, 559
Wood, Pusey IV, 1016
Wood, Pusy IV, 504
Wood, Rachel I, 54
Wood, Rachel I, 126
Wood, Rachel I, 177
Wood, Rachel II, 808
Wood, Rachel II, 1088
Wood, Rachel II, 1089
Wood, Rachel IV, 68
Wood, Rachel IV, 152
Wood, Rachel IV, 165
Wood, Rachel IV, 306
Wood, Rachel IV, 326
Wood, Rachel IV, 359
Wood, Rachel IV, 367
Wood, Rachel IV, 438
Wood, Rachel IV, 458
Wood, Rachel IV, 504
Wood, Rachel IV, 506
Wood, Rachel IV, 521
Wood, Rachel IV, 558
Wood, Rachel IV, 559
Wood, Rachel IV, 598
Wood, Rachel IV, 601
Wood, Rachel IV, 762
Wood, Rachel IV, 1082
Wood, Rachel IV, 1121
Wood, Rachel IV, 1190
Wood, Rachel IV, 1195
Wood, Rachel IV, 1228
Wood, Rachel VI, 416
Wood, Rachel VI, 457
Wood, Rachel VI, 458
Wood, Rachel VI, 607
Wood, Rachel VI, 866
Wood, Rachel Ann IV, 488
Wood, Rachel Ann IV, 505
Wood, Rachel Ann IV, 558
Wood, Rachel Ann IV, 1195
Wood, Rachel Ann IV, 1225
Wood, Rachel Ann IV, 1227
Wood, Rachel Ann VI, 458
Wood, Rachel H. IV, 1205
Wood, Rachel H. IV, 1227
Wood, Rachel H. IV, 1228
Wood, Rachel Jr. IV, 1163
Wood, Rachel, Jr. IV, 1195
Wood, Rachell II, 671
Wood, Rachell II, 691
Wood, Raymond III, 365
Wood, Raymond A. III, 202
Wood, Raymond A. III, 365
Wood, Raymond Albert III, 365
Wood, Re IV, 1228
Wood, Realy Ann VI, 986
Wood, Rebecca II, 261
Wood, Rebecca II, 275
Wood, Rebecca II, 384
Wood, Rebecca III, 364
Wood, Rebecca IV, 70
Wood, Rebecca IV, 116
Wood, Rebecca IV, 348
Wood, Rebecca IV, 359
Wood, Rebecca IV, 360
Wood, Rebecca IV, 463
Wood, Rebecca IV, 505
Wood, Rebecca IV, 506
Wood, Rebecca IV, 559
Wood, Rebecca IV, 1016
Wood, Rebecca IV, 1227
Wood, Rebecca VI, 458
Wood, Rebecca VI, 618
Wood, Rebecca VI, 723
Wood, Rebecca VI, 989
Wood, Rebecca Ann IV, 1082
Wood, Rebecca C. IV, 1121
Wood, Rebecca K. IV, 1227
Wood, Rebecca M. IV, 1227
Wood, Rebecca P. IV, 558
Wood, Rebecca R. IV, 1228
Wood, Rebeccah VI, 580
Wood, Rebeckah II, 112
Wood, Rebeka II, 112
Wood, Rebekah I, 126
Wood, Rebekah I, 137
Wood, Rebekah I, 177
Wood, Rebekah II, 691
Wood, Redstone VI, 458
Wood, Reuben IV, 1195
Wood, Reuben IV, 1227
Wood, Reuben E. IV, 1217
Wood, Reuben E. IV, 1228
Wood, Reubin IV, 306
Wood, Rhea V, 720
Wood, Rhea E. V, 720
Wood, Rhoda I, 126
Wood, Rhoda I, 583
Wood, Rhoda IV, 1176
Wood, Rhoda IV, 1195
Wood, Rhoda IV, 1225
Wood, Rhoda IV, 1227
Wood, Rhoda IV, 1228
Wood, Rhoda VI, 799
Wood, Rhoda VI, 866
Wood, Rhoda VI, 879
Wood, Rhoda VI, 978
Wood, Rhoda E. IV, 1195
Wood, Rhoda E. IV, 1218
Wood, Rhoda E. IV, 1227
Wood, Rhoda M. IV, 1228
Wood, Richard I, 126
Wood, Richard I, 148
Wood, Richard I, 177
Wood, Richard I, 203
Wood, Richard II, 47
Wood, Richard II, 65
Wood, Richard II, 112
Wood, Richard II, 438
Wood, Richard II, 449
Wood, Richard II, 691
Wood, Richard II, 724
Wood, Richard II, 761
Wood, Richard II, 777
Wood, Richard III, 173
Wood, Richard III, 365
Wood, Richard IV, 306
Wood, Richard IV, 505
Wood, Richard IV, 1195
Wood, Richard IV, 1196
Wood, Richard VI, 556
Wood, Richard VI, 565
Wood, Richard VI, 567
Wood, Richard B. II, 942
Wood, Richard C. II, 692
Wood, Richard D. II, 112
Wood, Richard D. II, 692
Wood, Richard D. II, 724
Wood, Richard D. II, 777
Wood, Richard, Jr. II, 112
Wood, Ritta VI, 879
Wood, Ritta VI, 989
Wood, Robert II, 438
Wood, Robert II, 555
Wood, Robert II, 691
Wood, Robert II, 723
Wood, Robert III, 157
Wood, Robert III, 364
Wood, Robert III, 366
Wood, Robert III, 367
Wood, Robert IV, 165
Wood, Robert IV, 207
Wood, Robert IV, 306
Wood, Robert IV, 601
Wood, Robert IV, 1082
Wood, Robert IV, 1121
Wood, Robert IV, 1195
Wood, Robert IV, 1196
Wood, Robert V, 543
Wood, Robert VI, 458
Wood, Robert VI, 583
Wood, Robert VI, 824
Wood, Robert VI, 866
Wood, Robert H. III, 364
Wood, Robert Walter III, 364
Wood, Robert, Jr. IV, 1082
Wood, Roberts VI, 583
Wood, Rollin IV, 1386
Wood, Rosa IV, 1228
Wood, Rosa V, 313
Wood, Rosa V, 468
Wood, Rosamond II, 1005
Wood, Rosamond Iden II, 1040
Wood, Rose IV, 307
Wood, Rosina IV, 307
Wood, Roxie Johnson IV, 1267
Wood, Rubin IV, 1227
Wood, Ruth II, 47
Wood, Ruth II, 87
Wood, Ruth II, 112
Wood, Ruth II, 438
Wood, Ruth II, 509
Wood, Ruth II, 672
Wood, Ruth II, 691
Wood, Ruth III, 475
Wood, Ruth III, 493
Wood, Ruth III, 508
Wood, Ruth IV, 68
Wood, Ruth IV, 89
Wood, Ruth IV, 116
Wood, Ruth IV, 1196
Wood, Ruth V, 143
Wood, Ruth VI, 458
Wood, Ruth Etta IV, 1228
Wood, Ruth L. IV, 1179
Wood, Ruth L. IV, 1196
Wood, Ruth M. V, 720
Wood, Ruth R. IV, 1195
Wood, Ruth T. IV, 1195
Wood, Ruth T. V, 958
Wood, Sabina IV, 117
Wood, Sallie I, 935
Wood, Sallie Thompson I, 934
Wood, Sally VI, 866
Wood, Sally VI, 933
Wood, Sally VI, 938
Wood, Sally VI, 963
Wood, Sally W. IV, 295
Wood, Sally W. IV, 307
Wood, Samuel I, 126
Wood, Samuel II, 692
Wood, Samuel II, 1040
Wood, Samuel III, 152
Wood, Samuel III, 284
Wood, Samuel III, 363
Wood, Samuel III, 364
Wood, Samuel III, 365
Wood, Samuel III, 366
Wood, Samuel III, 446
Wood, Samuel III, 475
Wood, Samuel IV, 306
Wood, Samuel IV, 307
Wood, Samuel IV, 458
Wood, Samuel IV, 468
Wood, Samuel IV, 473
Wood, Samuel IV, 481
Wood, Samuel IV, 483
Wood, Samuel IV, 492
Wood, Samuel IV, 504
Wood, Samuel IV, 505
Wood, Samuel IV, 1195
Wood, Samuel IV, 1196
Wood, Samuel IV, 1227
Wood, Samuel VI, 866
Wood, Samuel A. II, 942
Wood, Samuel A. IV, 1242
Wood, Samuel Allinson II, 828
Wood, Samuel B. VI, 459
Wood, Samuel Brown VI, 458
Wood, Samuel C. II, 692
Wood, Samuel C. II, 724
Wood, Samuel H. IV, 1195
Wood, Samuel McPherson VI, 583
Wood, Samuel N. IV, 1228
Wood, Samuel P. III, 363
Wood, Samuel S. III, 365
Wood, Samuel W. IV, 1195
Wood, Sarah I, 126
Wood, Sarah I, 148
Wood, Sarah I, 177
Wood, Sarah II, 112
Wood, Sarah II, 222
Wood, Sarah II, 438
Wood, Sarah II, 622
Wood, Sarah II, 691
Wood, Sarah II, 786
Wood, Sarah II, 796
Wood, Sarah II, 1040
Wood, Sarah III, 172
Wood, Sarah III, 237
Wood, Sarah III, 363
Wood, Sarah III, 364
Wood, Sarah III, 365
Wood, Sarah III, 367
Wood, Sarah III, 404
Wood, Sarah III, 508
Wood, Sarah IV, 105
Wood, Sarah IV, 116
Wood, Sarah IV, 165
Wood, Sarah IV, 173
Wood, Sarah IV, 295
Wood, Sarah IV, 306
Wood, Sarah IV, 307
Wood, Sarah IV, 359
Wood, Sarah IV, 438
Wood, Sarah IV, 458
Wood, Sarah IV, 504
Wood, Sarah IV, 505
Wood, Sarah IV, 539
Wood, Sarah IV, 558
Wood, Sarah IV, 559
Wood, Sarah IV, 569
Wood, Sarah IV, 585
Wood, Sarah IV, 601
Wood, Sarah IV, 789
Wood, Sarah IV, 1016
Wood, Sarah IV, 1082
Wood, Sarah IV, 1140
Wood, Sarah IV, 1147
Wood, Sarah IV, 1195
Wood, Sarah IV, 1356
Wood, Sarah IV, 1386
Wood, Sarah V, 942
Wood, Sarah VI, 356
Wood, Sarah VI, 458
Wood, Sarah VI, 804
Wood, Sarah VI, 866
Wood, Sarah A. V, 100
Wood, Sarah Amelia III, 475
Wood, Sarah Ann III, 366
Wood, Sarah Ann IV, 1228
Wood, Sarah Ann IV, 1242
Wood, Sarah Ann VI, 1019
Wood, Sarah B. II, 160
Wood, Sarah B. IV, 307
Wood, Sarah E. IV, 1143
Wood, Sarah E. IV, 1195
Wood, Sarah E. IV, 1198
Wood, Sarah E. V, 967
Wood, Sarah E. V, 979
Wood, Sarah Ellen II, 828
Wood, Sarah Ellen IV, 1195
Wood, Sarah Ellen IV, 1196
Wood, Sarah Ellen IV, 1228
Wood, Sarah M. III, 36
Wood, Sarah M. III, 173
Wood, Sarah M. III, 365
Wood, Sarah M. III, 366
Wood, Sarah M. III, 475
Wood, Sarah M. III, 505
Wood, Sarah S. III, 363
Wood, Sarah T. IV, 1223
Wood, Sarah T. IV, 1227
Wood, Sarahann IV, 1227
Wood, Septimus II, 438
Wood, Seth IV, 458
Wood, Sidney III, 365
Wood, Sidney IV, 448
Wood, Sidney IV, 458
Wood, Sidney IV, 597
Wood, Sidney IV, 601
Wood, Silas III, 365
Wood, Silas III, 366
Wood, Silas VI, 800
Wood, Silas VI, 836
Wood, Silas VI, 866
Wood, Silas VI, 984
Wood, Silas VI, 1019
Wood, Simeon III, 366
Wood, Simeon IV, 558
Wood, Simmons III, 366
Wood, Sophia VI, 800
Wood, Stella III, 157
Wood, Stella III, 364
Wood, Stephen II, 712
Wood, Stephen III, 192
Wood, Stephen III, 219
Wood, Stephen III, 310
Wood, Stephen III, 364
Wood, Stephen III, 365
Wood, Stephen III, 366
Wood, Stephen IV, 1195
Wood, Stephen IV, 1196
Wood, Stephen IV, 1227
Wood, Stephen IV, 1228
Wood, Stephen VI, 871
Wood, Stephen VI, 872
Wood, Stephen VI, 875
Wood, Stephen VI, 876
Wood, Stephen VI, 877
Wood, Stephen VI, 883
Wood, Stephen VI, 884
Wood, Stephen VI, 893
Wood, Stephen VI, 900
Wood, Stephen VI, 913
Wood, Stephen VI, 924
Wood, Stephen VI, 936
Wood, Stephen VI, 940
Wood, Stephen VI, 956
Wood, Stephen VI, 960
Wood, Stephen VI, 967
Wood, Stephen VI, 969
Wood, Stephen VI, 989
Wood, Stephen VI, 993
Wood, Stephen VI, 996
Wood, Stephen VI, 1002
Wood, Stephen VI, 1004
Wood, Stephen A. IV, 1228
Wood, Stephen J. III, 363
Wood, Stephen M. IV, 1195
Wood, Stephen, Jr. III, 364
Wood, Stephen, Jr. III, 366
Wood, Sterling Alex. III, 363
Wood, Susan IV, 505
Wood, Susan IV, 1109
Wood, Susan IV, 1121
Wood, Susan IV, 1158
Wood, Susan VI, 674
Wood, Susan VI, 723
Wood, Susan VI, 836

Wood, Susan VI, 866
Wood, Susan A. IV, 1072
Wood, Susan A. IV, 1082
Wood, Susan A. IV, 1111
Wood, Susan A. IV, 1121
Wood, Susan Amos IV, 1082
Wood, Susan E. IV, 1237
Wood, Susan E. IV, 1242
Wood, Susan L. II, 818
Wood, Susan Louisa II, 818
Wood, Susan P. IV, 1196
Wood, Susanna I, 430
Wood, Susanna II, 752
Wood, Susanna II, 777
Wood, Susanna IV, 165
Wood, Susanna IV, 306
Wood, Susanna IV, 458
Wood, Susanna IV, 463
Wood, Susanna IV, 464
Wood, Susanna IV, 465
Wood, Susanna IV, 478
Wood, Susanna IV, 493
Wood, Susanna IV, 501
Wood, Susanna IV, 504
Wood, Susanna IV, 505
Wood, Susanna IV, 1082
Wood, Susanna IV, 1121
Wood, Susanna V, 942
Wood, Susanna VI, 1019
Wood, Susanna A. IV, 501
Wood, Susanna A. IV, 505
Wood, Susanna L. II, 724
Wood, Susanna L. II, 777
Wood, Susannah I, 38
Wood, Susannah II, 222
Wood, Susannah IV, 227
Wood, Susannah IV, 306
Wood, Susannah IV, 363
Wood, Susannah IV, 376
Wood, Susannah IV, 414
Wood, Susannah IV, 438
Wood, Susannah IV, 458
Wood, Susannah IV, 504
Wood, Susannah IV, 505
Wood, Susannah IV, 1121
Wood, Susannah IV, 1196
Wood, Susannah V, 313
Wood, Susannah V, 942
Wood, Susannah VI, 356
Wood, Susannah VI, 560
Wood, Susannah VI, 583
Wood, Susannah L. II, 919
Wood, Susannah L. II, 942
Wood, Sydney M. II, 828
Wood, Sylvanus IV, 666
Wood, Sylvanus IV, 789
Wood, Tacy II, 807
Wood, Tacy II, 828
Wood, Tacy IV, 1195
Wood, Tacy IV, 1196
Wood, Tamer I, 126
Wood, Temperance IV, 1016
Wood, Temperance B. IV, 927
Wood, Temperance B. IV, 1016
Wood, Temperance B. IV, 1228
Wood, Thamer I, 177
Wood, Theodocia V, 942
Wood, Theodosia III, 508
Wood, Theresa I, 643
Wood, Theresa V. I, 628
Wood, Theresa York I, 643
Wood, Thirsa VI, 458
Wood, Thirsah VI, 379
Wood, Thirsah VI, 458
Wood, Thomas II, 438
Wood, Thomas II, 449
Wood, Thomas II, 692
Wood, Thomas II, 1040
Wood, Thomas III, 363
Wood, Thomas III, 364
Wood, Thomas III, 365
Wood, Thomas III, 366
Wood, Thomas III, 437
Wood, Thomas IV, 165
Wood, Thomas IV, 306
Wood, Thomas IV, 307
Wood, Thomas IV, 458
Wood, Thomas IV, 464
Wood, Thomas IV, 494
Wood, Thomas IV, 504
Wood, Thomas IV, 505
Wood, Thomas IV, 506
Wood, Thomas IV, 601
Wood, Thomas IV, 1082
Wood, Thomas IV, 1147
Wood, Thomas IV, 1177
Wood, Thomas IV, 1196
Wood, Thomas IV, 1227
Wood, Thomas VI, 458
Wood, Thomas VI, 799
Wood, Thomas VI, 933
Wood, Thomas VI, 963
Wood, Thomas VI, 981
Wood, Thomas VI, 995
Wood, Thomas VI, 1019
Wood, Thomas VI, 1020
Wood, Thomas A. IV, 1195
Wood, Thomas A. IV, 1225
Wood, Thomas A. IV, 1227
Wood, Thomas A. IV, 1228
Wood, Thomas B. III, 366
Wood, Thomas C. VI, 866
Wood, Thomas C. VI, 964
Wood, Thomas C. VI, 993
Wood, Thomas C. VI, 1019
Wood, Thomas E. IV, 1195
Wood, Thomas Herbert IV, 506
Wood, Thomas J. VI, 839
Wood, Thomas M. II, 942
Wood, Thomas M. IV, 458
Wood, Thomas, Jr. IV, 505
Wood, Thos. IV, 306
Wood, Thos. IV, 468
Wood, Thos. IV, 469
Wood, Thos. IV, 494
Wood, Thos. IV, 500
Wood, Thos. IV, 504
Wood, Thos. IV, 505
Wood, Thos. IV, 1196
Wood, Thos. V, 942
Wood, Thos. C. VI, 866
Wood, Thos. S. II, 942
Wood, Tilghman A. VI, 1019
Wood, Triphina IV, 789
Wood, Usley VI, 806
Wood, Vincent IV, 1386
Wood, Vincent A. III, 365
Wood, Violet VI, 1019
Wood, Virginia III, 366
Wood, W. III, 366
Wood, Wager H. III, 364
Wood, Walter III, 364
Wood, Walter III, 365
Wood, Walter III, 366
Wood, Walter IV, 1016
Wood, Walter IV, 1227
Wood, Walter IV, 1228
Wood, Walter R. III, 47
Wood, Walter R. III, 51
Wood, Walter R. III, 365
Wood, Walter R. III, 366
Wood, Wd. Ann II, 449
Wood, Wd. Catharine Davis II, 807
Wood, Wd. Laura II, 801
Wood, Wd. Martha VI, 882
Wood, Wd. Sarah Doyle II, 596
Wood, Wd. Susannah VI, 778
Wood, Wesley VI, 1019
Wood, Willett III, 366
Wood, William I, 126
Wood, William I, 128
Wood, William I, 167
Wood, William I, 177
Wood, William II, 248
Wood, William II, 275
Wood, William II, 438
Wood, William II, 1040
Wood, William III, 162
Wood, William III, 173
Wood, William III, 330
Wood, William III, 365
Wood, William III, 366
Wood, William III, 404
Wood, William III, 475
Wood, William IV, 306
Wood, William IV, 307
Wood, William IV, 359
Wood, William IV, 458
Wood, William IV, 463
Wood, William IV, 505
Wood, William IV, 558
Wood, William IV, 559
Wood, William IV, 1195
Wood, William IV, 1228
Wood, William IV, 1301
Wood, William VI, 457
Wood, William VI, 458
Wood, William VI, 565
Wood, William VI, 583
Wood, William VI, 607
Wood, William VI, 866
Wood, William VI, 898
Wood, William VI, 938
Wood, William VI, 1019
Wood, William A. V, 440
Wood, William Allen IV, 307
Wood, William C. IV, 504
Wood, William Congdon III, 366
Wood, William E. II, 723
Wood, William G. I, 935
Wood, William Greeser I, 935
Wood, William H. III, 366
Wood, William H. IV, 1227
Wood, William H. S. III, 109
Wood, William H. S. III, 326
Wood, William Henry S. III, 366
Wood, William K. III, 364
Wood, William K. III, 366
Wood, William L. III, 366
Wood, William M. II, 189
Wood, William M. II, 307
Wood, William O. VI, 1019
Wood, William R. III, 363
Wood, William S. III, 366
Wood, William S. VI, 584
Wood, William Schooley Dutton VI, 584
Wood, William T. IV, 505
Wood, William T. IV, 506
Wood, William, Jr. IV, 505
Wood, Wilmouth VI, 898
Wood, Wilson IV, 458
Wood, Wilson IV, 601
Wood, Wilson IV, 1082
Wood, Winneford I, 126
Wood, Wm. II, 506
Wood, Wm. II, 569
Wood, Wm. II, 691
Wood, Wm. II, 692
Wood, Wm. III, 308
Wood, Wm. III, 349
Wood, Wm. III, 364
Wood, Wm. IV, 165
Wood, Wm. IV, 306
Wood, Wm. IV, 363
Wood, Wm. IV, 458
Wood, Wm. IV, 464
Wood, Wm. IV, 482
Wood, Wm. IV, 501
Wood, Wm. IV, 504
Wood, Wm. IV, 505
Wood, Wm. IV, 1082
Wood, Wm. IV, 1121
Wood, Wm. IV, 1227
Wood, Wm. VI, 567
Wood, Wm. VI, 900
Wood, Wm. Congdon III, 366
Wood, Wm. E. II, 777
Wood, Wm. E. II, 942
Wood, Wm. H. S. III, 82
Wood, Wm. H. S. III, 132
Wood, Wm. H. S. III, 363
Wood, Wm. Henry S. III, 365
Wood, Wm. Henry S. III, 366
Wood, Wm. K. IV, 1227
Wood, Wm. M. II, 126
Wood, Wm. Pitts III, 366
Wood, Wm. S. III, 212
Wood, Wm. S. III, 284
Wood, Wm. S. III, 363
Wood, Wm. S. III, 364
Wood, Wm. S. III, 365
Wood, Wm. S. III, 366
Wood, Wm. S. VI, 556
Wood, Wm. W. II, 126
Wood, Wm. W. II, 777
Wood, Wm. Wood II, 692
Wood, Worthington IV, 458
Wood, Zachariah IV, 165
Wood, Zachariah IV, 458
Wood, Zemah IV, 312
Wood, Zemah IV, 315
Wood, Zeruah IV, 306
Woodall, B. Harfield VI, 866
Woodall, Becky VI, 815
Woodall, Elisha VI, 866
Woodall, Elizabeth VI, 813
Woodall, Elizabeth VI, 862
Woodall, Jacob VI, 815
Woodall, Jacob VI, 848
Woodall, Jacob VI, 849
Woodall, Jacob VI, 862
Woodall, Jacob H. VI, 808
Woodall, James VI, 866
Woodall, James H. VI, 866
Woodall, Mary VI, 825
Woodall, Mary VI, 848
Woodall, Nancy VI, 862
Woodall, Phebe VI, 849
Woodall, Sally VI, 866
Woodall, Sampson VI, 813
Woodall, Sampson VI, 825
Woodall, Samuel VI, 866
Woodall, Sarah VI, 825
Woodall, Sarah VI, 866
Woodall, Susan VI, 813
Woodard, Abashai V, 143
Woodard, Abisha V, 143
Woodard, Abisha V, 291
Woodard, Abishai V, 291
Woodard, Absellit I, 304
Woodard, Absellit I, 320
Woodard, Absilit I, 320
Woodard, Absillet I, 298
Woodard, Adaline V, 291
Woodard, Alisha V, 650
Woodard, Avis I, 298
Woodard, Avis I, 303
Woodard, Avis I, 320
Woodard, Avis V, 291
Woodard, Cadar I, 298
Woodard, Cader I, 248
Woodard, Cader I, 261
Woodard, Cedar I, 320
Woodard, Charles E. IV, 307
Woodard, Clarenda V, 291
Woodard, Clarinda V, 282
Woodard, Clarinda V, 291
Woodard, Clarinda V, 466
Woodard, Clarissa V, 291
Woodard, Cornelius I, 320
Woodard, Dr. Matthew VI, 281
Woodard, Dr. Matthew F. VI, 281
Woodard, Eleanor V, 466
Woodard, Elizabeth I, 312
Woodard, Elizabeth I, 319
Woodard, Elizabeth V, 143
Woodard, Elizabeth V, 647
Woodard, Elizabeth V, 650
Woodard, Elizabeth Manerva V, 650
Woodard, Emily IV, 217
Woodard, Emily C. IV, 217
Woodard, Emily C. IV, 307
Woodard, Hannah II, 678
Woodard, Inez D. VI, 281
Woodard, Isaac I, 298
Woodard, Isaac I, 311
Woodard, Isaac I, 319
Woodard, Isaac I, 320
Woodard, Isaac IV, 217
Woodard, Isaac V, 143
Woodard, Isaac V, 466
Woodard, Isaac M. V, 143
Woodard, Isaac M. V, 291
Woodard, Isaac Parker I, 298
Woodard, Isaac Parker I, 320
Woodard, Jane V, 143
Woodard, Jane V, 239
Woodard, Jane V, 291
Woodard, Jane V, 650
Woodard, John I, 320
Woodard, Joseph Foster VI, 281
Woodard, Josiah I, 320
Woodard, Josiah O. I, 298
Woodard, Levi V, 243
Woodard, Levi V, 291
Woodard, Luke I, 261
Woodard, Luke I, 298
Woodard, Luke I, 303
Woodard, Luke I, 314
Woodard, Luke I, 319
Woodard, Luke I, 320
Woodard, Luke V, 291
Woodard, Lydia I, 298
Woodard, Lydia I, 319
Woodard, Lydia I, 320
Woodard, Margaret V, 286
Woodard, Margaret V, 291
Woodard, Mary I, 298
Woodard, Mary I, 304
Woodard, Mary I, 311
Woodard, Mary I, 313
Woodard, Mary I, 319
Woodard, Mary I, 320
Woodard, Mary II, 692
Woodard, Mary V, 143
Woodard, Mary V, 291
Woodard, Mary Adaline V, 143
Woodard, Mary Adaline V, 650
Woodard, Mary Inez VI, 281
Woodard, Mary Olive VI, 244
Woodard, Mary Olive VI, 281
Woodard, Matthew F. VI, 281
Woodard, Minerva V, 143
Woodard, Minerva V, 291
Woodard, Minerva V, 650
Woodard, Paul D. VI, 244
Woodard, Paul D. VI, 281
Woodard, Paul Davis VI, 281
Woodard, Paul Davis, Jr. VI, 281
Woodard, Peninah I, 298
Woodard, Peninah I, 312
Woodard, Peninah I, 320
Woodard, Pininah I, 320
Woodard, Rachel I, 248
Woodard, Rachel I, 261
Woodard, Rachel I, 298
Woodard, Rachel I, 320
Woodard, Sallie I, 294
Woodard, Sarah I, 296
Woodard, Sarah I, 298
Woodard, Sarah I, 303
Woodard, Sarah I, 306
Woodard, Sarah I, 311
Woodard, Sarah I, 314
Woodard, Sarah I, 319
Woodard, Sarah I, 320
Woodard, Sarah Ann IV, 307
Woodard, Sarah Ann V, 243
Woodard, Sarah Ann V, 291
Woodard, Sarah W. VI, 69
Woodard, Sarah W. VI, 90
Woodard, Silas Hollowell I, 3
Woodard, Thomas I, 298
Woodard, Thomas I, 319
Woodard, Thomas I, 320
Woodard, Thomas Cox I, 298
Woodard, Thomas Cox I, 320
Woodard, Warren I, 294
Woodard, William V, 143
Woodard, William V, 291
Woodard, William V, 650
Woodard, William E. I, 298
Woodard, William Morris I, 3
Woodard, William V. B. VI, 6
Woodard, Zachariah I, 320
Woodart, Bartlit VI, 887
Wooday, Martha VI, 251
Woodbridge, E. T. III, 367
Woodbridge, Elsa III, 367
Woodbridge, Eugenie III, 275
Woodbridge, J. L. III, 367
Woodbridge, Mary A. IV, 789
Woodburn, Emma C. I, 739
Woodburn, Emma Cornelia I,
Woodburn, Emma Cornelia I,
Woodburn, Martha I, 613
Woodburn, Thedore I, 613
Woodcock, Anne VI, 1020
Woodcock, Anthony II, 439
Woodcock, Anthony II, 692
Woodcock, Bancroft II, 692
Woodcock, Catharine II, 439
Woodcock, Elizabeth II, 808
Woodcock, Elizabeth VI, 102
Woodcock, Henry VI, 978
Woodcock, Jacob II, 692
Woodcock, Jane II, 439
Woodcock, John II, 439
Woodcock, Nancy VI, 989
Woodcock, Nelley VI, 978
Woodcock, Rachel II, 275
Woodcock, Rachel II, 692
Woodcock, Rebecca II, 459
Woodcock, Rebecca II, 692
Woodcock, Robert II, 692
Woodcock, Robert VI, 902
Woodcock, Robert VI, 965
Woodcock, Robert VI, 989
Woodcock, Robert VI, 1020
Woodcock, Robt. VI, 926
Woodcock, Ruth II, 439
Woodcock, Ruth II, 692
Woodcock, Sarah VI, 978
Woodcock, William VI, 1020
Wooddell, Cornelia I, 951
Wooddy, Elizabeth I, 368
Wooddy, Hugh I, 368
Wooddy, James I, 368
Wooddy, Joshua I, 368
Wooddy, Mary I, 368
Wooddy, Robert I, 368
Wooddy, Ruth I, 368
Wooddy, Thomas I, 368
Woodell, Angie V, 366
Wooden, James III, 442
Woodes, Rebeckah II, 112
Woodes, Rebeka II, 60
Woodes, Rebeka II, 112
Woodey, James VI, 220
Woodey, Martha VI, 185
Woodey, Martha VI, 220
Woodey, Mary Ann VI, 1020
Woodey, Patience VI, 1020
Woodey, Randolph VI, 1020
Woodey, Richard VI, 1020
Woodford, Amarilla F. VI, 10
Woodford, Ann II, 1018
Woodford, Ann II, 1040
Woodford, Catharine VI, 982
Woodford, Eliza S. VI, 906
Woodford, Elizabeth VI, 958
Woodford, Elizabeth VI, 1015
Woodford, Hannah VI, 900
Woodford, Henry VI, 906
Woodford, Henry VI, 958
Woodford, Henry VI, 963
Woodford, Henry VI, 1020
Woodford, Henry A. VI, 1015
Woodford, Henry, Jr. VI, 102
Woodford, Jacob VI, 898
Woodford, Jacob VI, 985
Woodford, Jacob VI, 1015

ford, Jacob VI, 1020
ford, James VI, 872
ford, James VI, 906
ford, James VI, 968
ford, Jane VI, 906
ford, Lucy VI, 1020
ford, Mary VI, 963
ford, Matilda VI, 1015
ford, Nancy E. VI, 1020
ford, Parthena Jane VI, 963
ford, Sally VI, 1020
ford, Shepard VI, 1020
ford, Shepherd VI, 1015
ford, Shepherd VI, 1020
ford, Thomas II, 1018
ford, Thomas II, 1040
ford, Thomas VI, 345
ford, Thomas VI, 356
ford, Thomas VI, 900
ford, Thomas VI, 906
ford, Thomas VI, 958
ford, Thomas VI, 982
ford, William VI, 877
ford, William VI, 900
ford, William VI, 963
ford, Wm. II, 1018
ford, Wm. II, 1040
ford, Wm. VI, 1015
ham, Edward VI, 342
ham, Edward VI, 872
ham, Edward VI, 1020
ham, Winifred VI, 1020
house, Elizabeth II, 202
house, Elizabeth II, 275
house, Sarah II, 415
in, Archibald V, 942
land, Jasper IV, 1301
land, Lizzie IV, 1301
land, Mary A. IV, 1301
le, Cloud I, 430
ley, Andrew VI, 58
ley, Andrew VI, 90
ley, Mary I, 61
ley, Mary II, 483
ley, Mary II, 692
ley, Wd. Mary II, 692
ly, Elisabeth I, 52
ly, Elizabeth I, 100
ly, William II, 439
man, Agnes VI, 643
man, Agnes VI, 645
man, Agness VI, 643
man, Agness VI, 723
man, Henry II, 692
man, Henry VI, 723
man, Margaret M. VI, 723
mancey, Wm. II, 644
mancy, Charles V, 291
mancy, Wm. II, 692
manse, Edna V, 291
mansee, Ada V, 720
mansee, Betsy V, 306
mansee, Betsy V, 313
mansee, Charles V, 291
mansee, Delilah IV, 151
mansee, Delilah Ann
V, 165
lmansee, Edith V, 366
lmansee, Edna V, 291
mansee, Edna Emily V, 711
mansee, Edna Emily V, 720
lmansee, Edna M. V, 291
lmansee, Eland L. V, 291
mansee, Ella V, 366
mansee, Geneva V, 291
lmansee, Gulielma V, 358
lmansee, Gulielma V, 366
mansee, Herman V, 291
mansee, Herman V, 711
lmansee, Herman V, 720
lmansee, Louisa V, 291
lmansee, Mary Ann V, 355
mansee, Mary Ann V, 366
lmansee, Mary S. V, 650
lmansee, Wilbur E. V, 291
dmansey, Dorothy II, 439
dmansey, Mary II, 439
dmansey, Mary II, 692
dmansey, Thomas II, 439
dmansey, William II, 439
dmansey, Wm. II, 692
dmansie, Louisa V, 284
dmansie, Louisa V, 291
dnut, Abbie M. V, 942
dnut, Ann II, 73
dnut, Ann II, 109
dnut, Ann II, 112
dnut, Anna III, 367
dnut, Anna III, 508
dnut, Anna Elizabeth III, 411
dnut, Anna F. III, 388
Woodnut, Anna F. III, 475
Woodnut, Anne Elizabeth III, 475
Woodnut, Catharine A. III, 508
Woodnut, Clement V, 942
Woodnut, Clement A. II, 942
Woodnut, Clement A. V, 942
Woodnut, Clement Acton II, 828
Woodnut, Elizabeth II, 75
Woodnut, Elizabeth II, 112
Woodnut, Elizabeth II, 126
Woodnut, Grace II, 88
Woodnut, Grace II, 112
Woodnut, Grace Anna III, 486
Woodnut, Grace Anna III, 508
Woodnut, H. C., Jr. III, 486
Woodnut, Hannah V, 942
Woodnut, Hannah Hallowy
II, 828
Woodnut, Henry II, 112
Woodnut, Henry III, 508
Woodnut, Henry C. III, 411
Woodnut, Henry C. III, 475
Woodnut, Henry C. III, 508
Woodnut, Henry C., Jr. III, 486
Woodnut, Henry C., Jr. III, 508
Woodnut, Jonathan II, 86
Woodnut, Jonathan II, 112
Woodnut, Jonathan II, 828
Woodnut, Joseph II, 63
Woodnut, Joseph II, 112
Woodnut, Josephine J. III, 508
Woodnut, Mary II, 828
Woodnut, Rachell II, 63
Woodnut, Rachell II, 112
Woodnut, Rebecka II, 95
Woodnut, Rebecka II, 112
Woodnut, Richard II, 75
Woodnut, Richard II, 95
Woodnut, Richard II, 109
Woodnut, Richard II, 112
Woodnut, Richard II, 126
Woodnut, Sarah II, 86
Woodnut, Sarah II, 112
Woodnut, Thomas II, 828
Woodnut, Thomas V, 942
Woodnut, Thos. V, 942
Woodnut, William V, 942
Woodnut, William K. II, 828
Woodnut, Wm. II, 692
Woodnut, Wm. V, 942
Woodnutt, Abbie M. V, 942
Woodnutt, Abigail II, 942
Woodnutt, Abigail M. II, 899
Woodnutt, Ann II, 112
Woodnutt, Ann Elizabeth II, 128
Woodnutt, Anna Elizabeth II, 140
Woodnutt, Betty II, 112
Woodnutt, Betty Wilson II, 112
Woodnutt, Clement V, 942
Woodnutt, Clement A. II, 140
Woodnutt, Clement A. II, 161
Woodnutt, Clement A. II, 942
Woodnutt, Clement Acton II, 942
Woodnutt, Edward II, 47
Woodnutt, Edward H. II, 140
Woodnutt, Elizabeth II, 28
Woodnutt, Elizabeth II, 47
Woodnutt, Elizabeth II, 72
Woodnutt, Elizabeth II, 75
Woodnutt, Elizabeth II, 112
Woodnutt, Elizabeth II, 115
Woodnutt, Elizabeth II, 126
Woodnutt, Elizabeth II, 128
Woodnutt, Elizabeth II, 132
Woodnutt, Elizabeth II, 140
Woodnutt, Elizabeth II, 154
Woodnutt, Elizabeth II, 160
Woodnutt, Elizabeth F. II, 144
Woodnutt, Elizabeth F. II, 161
Woodnutt, Elizabeth G. II, 47
Woodnutt, Elizabeth G. II, 140
Woodnutt, Emily Conrow II, 140
Woodnutt, Esther C. II, 140
Woodnutt, Esther C. II, 161
Woodnutt, Grace II, 47
Woodnutt, Grace II, 51
Woodnutt, Grace II, 112
Woodnutt, Hannah II, 47
Woodnutt, Hannah II, 49
Woodnutt, Hannah II, 60
Woodnutt, Hannah II, 112
Woodnutt, Hannah II, 127
Woodnutt, Hannah II, 797
Woodnutt, Hannah V, 942
Woodnutt, Hannah Ann II, 47
Woodnutt, Hannah Ann II, 126
Woodnutt, Hannah Ann II, 140
Woodnutt, Hannah Ann II, 161
Woodnutt, Hannah H. II, 899
Woodnutt, Hannah H. II, 942
Woodnutt, Henry II, 47
Woodnutt, Henry II, 112
Woodnutt, Howard Conrow
II, 140
Woodnutt, James II, 72
Woodnutt, James II, 75
Woodnutt, James II, 112
Woodnutt, James II, 126
Woodnutt, James II, 132
Woodnutt, James II, 140
Woodnutt, James M. II, 47
Woodnutt, James M. II, 140
Woodnutt, James M. II, 161
Woodnutt, James Mason II, 47
Woodnutt, James Mason II, 60
Woodnutt, James Mason II, 72
Woodnutt, James Mason II, 112
Woodnutt, James Mason II, 154
Woodnutt, James Mason II, 160
Woodnutt, Jas. II, 127
Woodnutt, Jas. II, 140
Woodnutt, Jonathan II, 47
Woodnutt, Jonathan II, 72
Woodnutt, Jonathan II, 112
Woodnutt, Jonathan II, 126
Woodnutt, Jonathan II, 140
Woodnutt, Jonathan II, 144
Woodnutt, Jonathan II, 161
Woodnutt, Joseph II, 47
Woodnutt, Joseph II, 112
Woodnutt, Joseph B. II, 140
Woodnutt, Joseph B. II, 161
Woodnutt, Joseph Bassett II, 140
Woodnutt, Lydia II, 140
Woodnutt, Lydia II, 161
Woodnutt, Lydia P. II, 132
Woodnutt, Margaret II, 47
Woodnutt, Margaret II, 49
Woodnutt, Margaret II, 60
Woodnutt, Margaret II, 72
Woodnutt, Margaret II, 75
Woodnutt, Margaret II, 97
Woodnutt, Margaret II, 112
Woodnutt, Margaret II, 127
Woodnutt, Margaret II, 132
Woodnutt, Margaret II, 140
Woodnutt, Margaret II, 154
Woodnutt, Margaret II, 160
Woodnutt, Margaret M. II, 140
Woodnutt, Margaret M. II, 161
Woodnutt, Martha II, 47
Woodnutt, Martha II, 126
Woodnutt, Martha II, 140
Woodnutt, Martha II, 161
Woodnutt, Martha W. II, 156
Woodnutt, Mary II, 47
Woodnutt, Mary II, 72
Woodnutt, Mary II, 112
Woodnutt, Mary II, 140
Woodnutt, Mary II, 144
Woodnutt, Mary II, 154
Woodnutt, Mary II, 160
Woodnutt, Mary II, 161
Woodnutt, Mary E. II, 142
Woodnutt, Mary E. II, 161
Woodnutt, Mary Elizabeth II, 140
Woodnutt, Mary M. II, 132
Woodnutt, Mary M. II, 140
Woodnutt, Mary, Sr. II, 126
Woodnutt, Preston II, 72
Woodnutt, Preston II, 112
Woodnutt, Preston II, 126
Woodnutt, Preston II, 154
Woodnutt, Preston II, 160
Woodnutt, Preston C. II, 47
Woodnutt, Preston C. II, 140
Woodnutt, Preston C. II, 161
Woodnutt, Preston Carpenter
II, 47
Woodnutt, Preston Harbert
II, 140
Woodnutt, Rachel II, 47
Woodnutt, Rachel II, 72
Woodnutt, Rachel II, 112
Woodnutt, Rachel II, 154
Woodnutt, Rachel II, 160
Woodnutt, Rachell II, 112
Woodnutt, Rebecka II, 112
Woodnutt, Richard II, 28
Woodnutt, Richard II, 47
Woodnutt, Richard II, 51
Woodnutt, Richard II, 112
Woodnutt, Richard II, 126
Woodnutt, Richard II, 132
Woodnutt, Richard II, 140
Woodnutt, Richard II, 161
Woodnutt, Richard Henry II, 140
Woodnutt, Richard Henry II, 161
Woodnutt, Sarah II, 47
Woodnutt, Sarah II, 112
Woodnutt, Sarah II, 161
Woodnutt, Sarah C. II, 140
Woodnutt, Sarah H. II, 140
Woodnutt, Sarah H. II, 161
Woodnutt, Thomas II, 47
Woodnutt, Thomas II, 112
Woodnutt, Thomas II, 126
Woodnutt, Thomas II, 140
Woodnutt, Thomas II, 161
Woodnutt, Thomas II, 942
Woodnutt, Thomas W. II, 140
Woodnutt, Thomas W. II, 161
Woodnutt, Thos. II, 899
Woodnutt, Thos. II, 942
Woodnutt, Thos. V, 942
Woodnutt, William II, 47
Woodnutt, William G. II, 47
Woodnutt, William G. II, 140
Woodnutt, Wm. II, 112
Woodnutt, Wm. II, 128
Woodnutt, Wm. V, 942
Woodnutt, Wm. G. II, 126
Woodnutt, Wm. G. II, 140
Woodnutt, Wm. G. II, 144
Woodnutt, Wm. G. II, 161
Woodnutt, Wm. W. II, 140
Woodnutt, Wm. W. II, 942
Woodnutt, Wm. W., Jr. II, 161
Woodridge, Patsy VI, 956
Woodrofe, Joseph II, 275
Woodroff, Edmund L. VI, 1020
Woodroff, Polly VI, 1020
Woodroof, Edmund L. VI, 1020
Woodroof, Elizabeth VI, 983
Woodroof, Elizabeth VI, 1020
Woodroof, Emmy VI, 1020
Woodroof, James VI, 1020
Woodroof, John Henry VI, 1020
Woodroof, Matilda E. VI, 949
Woodroof, Polly VI, 1020
Woodroof, Thomas II, 439
Woodroof, Thomas VI, 1020
Woodroofe, Edith II, 48
Woodroofe, Isaac II, 48
Woodroofe, John II, 48
Woodroofe, Mary II, 48
Woodroofe, Thomas II, 48
Woodrow, Abraham VI, 459
Woodrow, Allen III, 367
Woodrow, Ann V, 291
Woodrow, Ann V, 366
Woodrow, Ann VI, 459
Woodrow, Benjamin II, 943
Woodrow, Clara V, 291
Woodrow, David V, 366
Woodrow, David V, 943
Woodrow, David T. V, 943
Woodrow, Elisabeth VI, 607
Woodrow, Eliz. III, 367
Woodrow, Eliza III, 217
Woodrow, Elizabeth V, 291
Woodrow, Elizabeth V, 366
Woodrow, Elizabeth VI, 375
Woodrow, Elizabeth VI, 459
Woodrow, Elizabeth VI, 594
Woodrow, Grace III, 217
Woodrow, Grace III, 367
Woodrow, Grace VI, 459
Woodrow, Grace VI, 584
Woodrow, Grace VI, 607
Woodrow, Hellena V, 366
Woodrow, Henry VI, 459
Woodrow, Henry VI, 584
Woodrow, Henry VI, 607
Woodrow, Henry VI, 792
Woodrow, Henry H. III, 217
Woodrow, Henry H. III, 367
Woodrow, Isaac VI, 459
Woodrow, Isaac, Jr. VI, 459
Woodrow, John V, 366
Woodrow, John VI, 459
Woodrow, John VI, 584
Woodrow, John VI, 607
Woodrow, Joseph II, 275
Woodrow, Joseph V, 291
Woodrow, Joseph VI, 459
Woodrow, Joseph Innes II, 777
Woodrow, Joseph, Jr. II, 777
Woodrow, Joshua V, 138
Woodrow, Joshua V, 291
Woodrow, Joshua V, 366
Woodrow, Joshua VI, 459
Woodrow, Joshua VI, 594
Woodrow, Joshua VI, 607
Woodrow, Joshua, Jr. V, 366
Woodrow, Joshua, Jr. VI, 459
Woodrow, Joshua, Jr. VI, 599
Woodrow, Lidia VI, 459
Woodrow, Lyddia VI, 459
Woodrow, Lydia VI, 459
Woodrow, Lydia VI, 584
Woodrow, Lydia VI, 594
Woodrow, Lydia VI, 607
Woodrow, Lydia VI, 608
Woodrow, Lydia, Jr. VI, 459
Woodrow, Lydia, Jr. VI, 607
Woodrow, Lydia, Sr. VI, 608
Woodrow, Mahala V, 138
Woodrow, Mary IV, 68
Woodrow, Mary IV, 165
Woodrow, Mary VI, 455
Woodrow, Mary VI, 459
Woodrow, Mary VI, 584
Woodrow, Mary VI, 607
Woodrow, Mary VI, 764
Woodrow, Mary VI, 792
Woodrow, Mary Joyce II, 823
Woodrow, Phebe VI, 379
Woodrow, Phebe VI, 459
Woodrow, Rachel V, 286
Woodrow, Rachel V, 291
Woodrow, Rachel V, 366
Woodrow, Rachel VI, 459
Woodrow, Rachel VI, 607
Woodrow, Sarah II, 275
Woodrow, Sarah II, 823
Woodrow, Sarah II, 943
Woodrow, Sarah V, 943
Woodrow, Simeon VI, 444
Woodrow, Simeon VI, 455
Woodrow, Simeon VI, 459
Woodrow, Simeon VI, 562
Woodrow, Simeon VI, 579
Woodrow, Simeon VI, 584
Woodrow, Thos. II, 823
Woodrow, Watson V, 291
Woodrow, Widow Mary VI, 579
Woodrow-White, Mary VI, 562
Woodruff, Alice Irene V, 874
Woodruff, Anna F. III, 475
Woodruff, Benjamin III, 367
Woodruff, Bethia IV, 1051
Woodruff, Bethiah IV, 1083
Woodruff, Charles S. II, 777
Woodruff, Charles S. III, 367
Woodruff, Delia P. VI, 792
Woodruff, Elizabeth I, 984
Woodruff, Elizabeth I, 1000
Woodruff, Hannah IV, 982
Woodruff, Hannah IV, 1016
Woodruff, Henrietta W. III, 475
Woodruff, Hollie IV, 790
Woodruff, James E. VI, 792
Woodruff, Margaret O. III, 475
Woodruff, Marvin V, 874
Woodruff, Maud M. II, 777
Woodruff, Maude G. III, 367
Woodruff, Phebe VI, 792
Woodruff, Thomas VI, 1020
Woods, ??? IV, 886
Woods, Aaron I, 1013
Woods, Agness VI, 955
Woods, Albert IV, 666
Woods, Albert G. IV, 666
Woods, Almira IV, 1016
Woods, Ann IV, 607
Woods, Ann IV, 666
Woods, Anne IV, 666
Woods, David IV, 666
Woods, Deborah I, 69
Woods, Ealenor I, 455
Woods, Edith Elnora IV, 968
Woods, Eliza IV, 624
Woods, Eliza IV, 666
Woods, Eliza Mary IV, 1213
Woods, Elizabeth I, 1013
Woods, Elizabeth IV, 68
Woods, Elizabeth IV, 605
Woods, Elizabeth IV, 666
Woods, Elizabeth IV, 856
Woods, Elizabeth IV, 886
Woods, Enos IV, 68
Woods, Enos IV, 666
Woods, Enos IV, 856
Woods, Enos IV, 886
Woods, Enos L. IV, 666
Woods, Enos Lewis IV, 666
Woods, Esther IV, 605
Woods, Esther IV, 634
Woods, Esther IV, 646
Woods, Esther IV, 666
Woods, Grace IV, 1016
Woods, Hannah IV, 666
Woods, Hannah IV, 856
Woods, Hazel V, 701
Woods, Isaac II, 208
Woods, Isabel IV, 68
Woods, Isabel IV, 654
Woods, Isabel IV, 666
Woods, Isabel IV, 856
Woods, Isabella IV, 666
Woods, Israel IV, 886
Woods, Iva V, 1026
Woods, Jacob IV, 68

Woods, Jacob IV, 70
Woods, Jacob IV, 666
Woods, Jacob IV, 856
Woods, James IV, 666
Woods, James IV, 856
Woods, James IV, 886
Woods, James IV, 968
Woods, James VI, 1019
Woods, Jane M. IV, 1016
Woods, Janet McCutcheon IV, 1344
Woods, Jessie IV, 1344
Woods, John IV, 29
Woods, John IV, 68
Woods, John IV, 70
Woods, John IV, 605
Woods, John IV, 666
Woods, John F. IV, 1016
Woods, John L. IV, 666
Woods, Jonathan IV, 1016
Woods, Jonathan, Jr. IV, 886
Woods, Joseph IV, 68
Woods, Joseph IV, 666
Woods, Joseph IV, 856
Woods, Joseph IV, 886
Woods, Joshua IV, 68
Woods, Joshua IV, 666
Woods, Josie IV, 1344
Woods, Joweph IV, 666
Woods, Kesiah IV, 666
Woods, Kezia IV, 666
Woods, Lewis IV, 68
Woods, Lewis IV, 666
Woods, Lorana B. IV, 1344
Woods, Loreno M. IV, 1344
Woods, Lydia IV, 666
Woods, Lydia Ann IV, 631
Woods, Lydia Ann IV, 666
Woods, Mary II, 208
Woods, Mary II, 275
Woods, Mary II, 1040
Woods, Mary IV, 886
Woods, Mary IV, 1016
Woods, Mary IV, 1217
Woods, Mary VI, 822
Woods, Mary Ann IV, 666
Woods, Mary R. IV, 542
Woods, Matilda IV, 856
Woods, Matilda IV, 886
Woods, Matilda IV, 911
Woods, Maud IV, 1344
Woods, Maude IV, 1344
Woods, Melvin V, 1026
Woods, Mildred VI, 899
Woods, Mildred Ann VI, 1019
Woods, Piney I, 1
Woods, Princess V, 1026
Woods, Rachel VI, 822
Woods, Rebecca IV, 29
Woods, Rebecca IV, 70
Woods, Rebecca IV, 605
Woods, Rebecca IV, 666
Woods, Rebecca IV, 873
Woods, Rebecca IV, 886
Woods, Rebecca IV, 921
Woods, Rebecca IV, 1016
Woods, Rebeccah IV, 666
Woods, Roxy Johnson IV, 1344
Woods, Ruth IV, 646
Woods, Ruth IV, 666
Woods, Samuel IV, 605
Woods, Samuel IV, 634
Woods, Samuel IV, 646
Woods, Samuel IV, 666
Woods, Samuel Hole IV, 886
Woods, Sarah II, 691
Woods, Sarah II, 1040
Woods, Sarah IV, 641
Woods, Sarah IV, 666
Woods, Sarah IV, 968
Woods, Susanna I, 423
Woods, Susanna I, 430
Woods, Sylvanus IV, 666
Woods, Triphenia IV, 638
Woods, Triphenia IV, 666
Woods, Tryphena IV, 666
Woods, William IV, 666
Woods, Wm. IV, 666
Woods, Wm. IV, 1217
Woodside, Sarah II, 591
Woodside, Sarah II, 692
Woodsley, James VI, 281
Woodson, ??? III, 367
Woodson, ??? VI, 220
Woodson, Agnes VI, 173
Woodson, Agnes VI, 174
Woodson, Agnes VI, 219
Woodson, Agnes VI, 220
Woodson, Agness VI, 210
Woodson, Anderson VI, 823
Woodson, Anderson VI, 824
Woodson, Anderson VI, 865
Woodson, Anderson VI, 866
Woodson, Anderson, Jr. VI, 810
Woodson, Ann VI, 215
Woodson, Ann VI, 220
Woodson, Ann VI, 281
Woodson, Benj. VI, 208
Woodson, Benja. VI, 148
Woodson, Benjamin VI, 208
Woodson, Benjamin VI, 218
Woodson, Benjamin VI, 219
Woodson, Benjamin VI, 866
Woodson, Caroline Matilda VI, 220
Woodson, Charles VI, 149
Woodson, Charles VI, 173
Woodson, Charles VI, 177
Woodson, Charles VI, 203
Woodson, Charles VI, 205
Woodson, Charles VI, 206
Woodson, Charles VI, 210
Woodson, Charles VI, 218
Woodson, Charles VI, 219
Woodson, Charles VI, 220
Woodson, Charles VI, 281
Woodson, Charles, Jr. VI, 215
Woodson, Charles, Jr. VI, 218
Woodson, Charles, Jr. VI, 220
Woodson, Charles, Jr. VI, 281
Woodson, Edward VI, 815
Woodson, Elijah VI, 823
Woodson, Elijah VI, 824
Woodson, Elijah VI, 826
Woodson, Elisa VI, 219
Woodson, Elizabeth VI, 157
Woodson, Elizabeth VI, 203
Woodson, Elizabeth VI, 204
Woodson, Elizabeth VI, 218
Woodson, Elizabeth VI, 219
Woodson, Elizabeth VI, 865
Woodson, Elizabeth VI, 866
Woodson, Frances VI, 810
Woodson, Frederick VI, 220
Woodson, Genito VI, 263
Woodson, George VI, 220
Woodson, Henrico VI, 214
Woodson, Henry Turrell VI, 219
Woodson, Jacob VI, 206
Woodson, Jacob VI, 219
Woodson, Jacob VI, 220
Woodson, Jacob VI, 281
Woodson, Jacob VI, 866
Woodson, James VI, 220
Woodson, James VI, 263
Woodson, Jane VI, 148
Woodson, Jane VI, 218
Woodson, Jane VI, 219
Woodson, John VI, 8
Woodson, John VI, 19
Woodson, John VI, 148
Woodson, John VI, 208
Woodson, John VI, 219
Woodson, John VI, 281
Woodson, John VI, 810
Woodson, John E. VI, 828
Woodson, John E. VI, 866
Woodson, John Pleasants VI, 219
Woodson, John, Jr. VI, 218
Woodson, John, Junior VI, 219
Woodson, John, Senior VI, 219
Woodson, Joseph VI, 36
Woodson, Joseph VI, 37
Woodson, Joseph VI, 207
Woodson, Joseph VI, 218
Woodson, Joseph VI, 219
Woodson, Joseph VI, 220
Woodson, Joseph VI, 281
Woodson, Joseph, Jr. VI, 219
Woodson, Josiah III, 367
Woodson, Judith VI, 148
Woodson, Judith VI, 163
Woodson, Judith VI, 218
Woodson, Judith VI, 219
Woodson, Lucy B. VI, 866
Woodson, Martha VI, 866
Woodson, Mary VI, 19
Woodson, Mary VI, 36
Woodson, Mary VI, 37
Woodson, Mary VI, 201
Woodson, Mary VI, 203
Woodson, Mary VI, 205
Woodson, Mary VI, 218
Woodson, Mary VI, 219
Woodson, Mary VI, 220
Woodson, Mary VI, 866
Woodson, Mary E. VI, 826
Woodson, Melville P. F. VI, 853
Woodson, Minnie F. VI, 853
Woodson, Nancy VI, 823
Woodson, Obediah VI, 866
Woodson, Rachel VI, 216
Woodson, Rachel VI, 219
Woodson, Rachel VI, 866
Woodson, Richard VI, 219
Woodson, Richard VI, 802
Woodson, Richard VI, 866
Woodson, Robert VI, 218
Woodson, Robert, Jr. VI, 219
Woodson, Robert, Sr. VI, 219
Woodson, Samll Tucker VI, 219
Woodson, Sarah VI, 208
Woodson, Sarah VI, 214
Woodson, Sarah VI, 215
Woodson, Sarah VI, 218
Woodson, Sarah VI, 219
Woodson, Sarah VI, 220
Woodson, Sarah VI, 264
Woodson, Sarah VI, 824
Woodson, Sarah VI, 866
Woodson, Sarah A. VI, 857
Woodson, Stephen VI, 157
Woodson, Stephen VI, 161
Woodson, Stephen VI, 219
Woodson, Stephen VI, 220
Woodson, Susanna VI, 203
Woodson, Susanna VI, 220
Woodson, Susannah VI, 204
Woodson, Susannah VI, 218
Woodson, Susannah VI, 219
Woodson, Tarlton VI, 176
Woodson, Tarlton VI, 203
Woodson, Tarlton VI, 214
Woodson, Tarlton VI, 219
Woodson, Tarlton VI, 220
Woodson, Tarlton VI, 263
Woodson, Tarlton VI, 264
Woodson, Tarlton VI, 281
Woodson, Tarlton, Jr. VI, 85
Woodson, Tarlton, Jr. VI, 219
Woodson, Tarlton, Jr. VI, 281
Woodson, Tarlton, Sr. VI, 85
Woodson, Tarlton, Sr. VI, 219
Woodson, Thomas VI, 835
Woodson, Thomas VI, 866
Woodson, Thomas A. VI, 867
Woodson, Thomas Cheadle VI, 219
Woodson, Thos. A. VI, 857
Woodson, Tucker VI, 219
Woodson, Urselah VI, 176
Woodson, Urselah VI, 218
Woodson, William VI, 209
Woodson, William VI, 847
Woodson, William VI, 866
Woodson, William Penn III, 367
Woodson, William, Jr. VI, 218
Woodward, ??? IV, 307
Woodward, Aaron I, 671
Woodward, Aaron I, 970
Woodward, Abashai V, 143
Woodward, Abraham I, 583
Woodward, Abraham I, 671
Woodward, Abraham I, 692
Woodward, Abraham I, 970
Woodward, Abraham I, 1101
Woodward, Abraham I, 1112
Woodward, Abraham I, 1135
Woodward, Abraham, Jr. I, 1135
Woodward, Abraham, Sr. I, 1112
Woodward, Alice I, 671
Woodward, Alice I, 1118
Woodward, Alice I, 1135
Woodward, Americus H. II, 140
Woodward, Americus Hodge II, 140
Woodward, Ann I, 1109
Woodward, Ann I, 1112
Woodward, Ann II, 804
Woodward, Anna C. III, 367
Woodward, Benajah B. II, 307
Woodward, Benjamin I, 1112
Woodward, Benjamin III, 367
Woodward, Bertha III, 367
Woodward, Bertha C. III, 202
Woodward, Bertha C. III, 367
Woodward, Bessie IV, 1044
Woodward, Cader I, 261
Woodward, Caleb A. II, 307
Woodward, Caroline II, 140
Woodward, Caroline D. II, 161
Woodward, Carolyn Freeman VI, 792
Woodward, Celia VI, 1020
Woodward, Charity T. II, 140
Woodward, Charity T. II, 161
Woodward, Charles E. II, 777
Woodward, Charles E. IV, 307
Woodward, Charles Eli IV, 307
Woodward, Clara E. IV, 307
Woodward, Cornelia III, 266
Woodward, Cornelia III, 367
Woodward, Daniel C. III, 367
Woodward, Daniel M. III, 140
Woodward, David C. IV, 68
Woodward, Donald V, 943
Woodward, Dorothy II, 140
Woodward, Edgar III, 367
Woodward, Edgar H. III, 202
Woodward, Edgar H. III, 367
Woodward, Edgar Hunt III, 367
Woodward, Elenora II, 140
Woodward, Eli I, 671
Woodward, Elisabeth II, 307
Woodward, Eliz. III, 179
Woodward, Eliz. III, 266
Woodward, Eliz. III, 367
Woodward, Eliza I, 671
Woodward, Eliza II, 825
Woodward, Elizabeth I, 685
Woodward, Elizabeth I, 692
Woodward, Elizabeth I, 970
Woodward, Elizabeth I, 1099
Woodward, Elizabeth I, 1101
Woodward, Elizabeth I, 1112
Woodward, Elizabeth I, 1118
Woodward, Elizabeth I, 1135
Woodward, Elizabeth II, 631
Woodward, Elizabeth II, 692
Woodward, Elizabeth III, 91
Woodward, Elizabeth III, 140
Woodward, Elizabeth III, 367
Woodward, Elizabeth V, 143
Woodward, Elizabeth A. II, 828
Woodward, Elizabeth Ann II, 140
Woodward, Elizabeth C. III, 367
Woodward, Elizabeth Lippincott II, 828
Woodward, Ella II, 828
Woodward, Ella II, 897
Woodward, Ella Jane II, 140
Woodward, Ella Mattson II, 943
Woodward, Elza I, 1119
Woodward, Elza I, 1135
Woodward, Emily C. IV, 307
Woodward, Emma III, 367
Woodward, Eugene S. II, 140
Woodward, Florence Hopkins VI, 792
Woodward, Floy O. IV, 784
Woodward, Floyd III, 367
Woodward, Francis III, 367
Woodward, George VI, 1020
Woodward, Gilbert III, 367
Woodward, Guy IV, 401
Woodward, Guy IV, 459
Woodward, H. Wells VI, 792
Woodward, Hannah I, 671
Woodward, Hannah I, 692
Woodward, Hannah I, 1101
Woodward, Hannah I, 1112
Woodward, Hannah I, 1126
Woodward, Hannah I, 1135
Woodward, Hannah II, 692
Woodward, Hannah S. II, 140
Woodward, Hannah S. II, 161
Woodward, Hannah, Sr. I, 1112
Woodward, Harriet II, 140
Woodward, Harriett II, 140
Woodward, Henrietta II, 635
Woodward, Henrietta II, 692
Woodward, Henrietta II, 720
Woodward, Henrietta II, 723
Woodward, Henrietta R. II, 723
Woodward, Henry E. III, 367
Woodward, Hope IV, 108
Woodward, Hope IV, 116
Woodward, Irene Adelaide II, 897
Woodward, Irene Adelaide II, 943
Woodward, Isaac II, 439
Woodward, Isaac IV, 307
Woodward, Isaac V, 143
Woodward, Isaac W. II, 140
Woodward, Isaac W. II, 161
Woodward, Israel II, 635
Woodward, Israel II, 692
Woodward, Jacob VI, 883
Woodward, James IV, 790
Woodward, James IV, 856
Woodward, Jane I, 671
Woodward, Jane I, 1112
Woodward, Jane I, 1121
Woodward, Jane I, 1135
Woodward, Jane III, 367
Woodward, Jane V, 143
Woodward, Jane VI, 515
Woodward, Jane VI, 584
Woodward, Jesse I, 1112
Woodward, Jesse VI, 515
Woodward, Jesse VI, 584
Woodward, Jocelyn VI, 792
Woodward, John I, 671
Woodward, John IV, 790
Woodward, John IV, 856
Woodward, John IV, 918
Woodward, John VI, 584
Woodward, John D. III, 140
Woodward, John D. III, 367
Woodward, John E. II, 307
Woodward, John E. II, 943
Woodward, John Everman II,
Woodward, John L. IV, 307
Woodward, John S. IV, 307
Woodward, John T. IV, 307
Woodward, John, Jr. II, 307
Woodward, Jophet II, 275
Woodward, Joseph Donald II,
Woodward, Josephine V, 943
Woodward, Joshua II, 723
Woodward, Judith IV, 955
Woodward, Judith IV, 1017
Woodward, Lance VI, 888
Woodward, Lance VI, 926
Woodward, Lance VI, 970
Woodward, Lena Caroline VI, 792
Woodward, Lettice IV, 790
Woodward, Lettice IV, 856
Woodward, Lizzie III, 367
Woodward, Louisa J. IV, 459
Woodward, Marian II, 140
Woodward, Marie H. III, 367
Woodward, Marietta S. II, 152
Woodward, Marietta S. II, 161
Woodward, Martha III, 140
Woodward, Martha III, 367
Woodward, Mary II, 635
Woodward, Mary II, 641
Woodward, Mary II, 692
Woodward, Mary II, 723
Woodward, Mary III, 367
Woodward, Mary Adaline V, 14
Woodward, Mary Ann II, 439
Woodward, Mary D. III, 179
Woodward, Mary D. III, 367
Woodward, Mary E. II, 720
Woodward, Mary E. IV, 216
Woodward, Mary E. IV, 307
Woodward, Mary Eva IV, 401
Woodward, Mary Eva IV, 459
Woodward, Maryetta II, 140
Woodward, Miles IV, 459
Woodward, Morris III, 367
Woodward, Nancy VI, 1020
Woodward, Nathaniel III, 367
Woodward, Orlando J. V, 943
Woodward, Oscar IV, 1044
Woodward, Prudence VI, 515
Woodward, Prudence VI, 584
Woodward, Prudence, Jr. VI, 58
Woodward, Rachel II, 439
Woodward, Rachel II, 692
Woodward, Rachel II, 787
Woodward, Rachel Ann II, 867
Woodward, Rachel Ann II, 943
Woodward, Ralph V, 943
Woodward, Rebecca II, 282
Woodward, Rebecca II, 307
Woodward, Rebecca II, 692
Woodward, Rebecca II, 723
Woodward, Rebecca Atmore II, 828
Woodward, Rebeckah VI, 919
Woodward, Rhoda I, 1129
Woodward, Rhoda I, 1135
Woodward, Ric'd VI, 919
Woodward, Richard VI, 1020
Woodward, Richard Halliday VI, 772
Woodward, Richard Halliday VI, 792
Woodward, Roenna VI, 58
Woodward, Roenna VI, 90
Woodward, Samuel I, 1099
Woodward, Samuel I, 1112
Woodward, Samuel I, 1135
Woodward, Samuel II, 635
Woodward, Samuel II, 692
Woodward, Samuel II, 720
Woodward, Samuel II, 723
Woodward, Samuel II, 804
Woodward, Samuel VI, 965
Woodward, Samuel VI, 1020
Woodward, Samuel L. II, 307
Woodward, Sara B. II, 140
Woodward, Sarah I, 1126
Woodward, Sarah I, 1135
Woodward, Sarah II, 821
Woodward, Sarah IV, 291
Woodward, Sarah IV, 307
Woodward, Sarah IV, 313
Woodward, Sarah IV, 315
Woodward, Sarah VI, 482
Woodward, Sarah VI, 584
Woodward, Sarah Ann IV, 307

dward, Sarah B. II, 161
dward, Sarah J. II, 897
dward, Sarah J. II, 943
dward, Sarah T. IV, 307
dward, Sarah W. VI, 90
dward, Susan II, 307
dward, Susanna I, 671
dward, Susanna I, 678
dward, Susanna I, 692
dward, Susanna II, 692
dward, Susannah IV, 856
odward, Sylvia Belle VI, 772
odward, Sylvia Belle VI, 792
odward, Theodore Bolton II, 828
odward, Thomas III, 140
odward, Thomas III, 367
odward, Thomas W. III, 367
odward, Thomas, Jr. III, 91
odward, Thomas, Jr. III, 367
odward, Thos. III, 179
odward, Thos. III, 367
odward, Thos. J. II, 828
odward, Thos., Jr. III, 266
odward, Thos., Jr. III, 367
odward, Usly VI, 926
odward, W. V. B. VI, 58
odward, W. V. B. VI, 90
odward, Walter J. IV, 307
odward, Wd. Margaret II, 804
odward, Widow Elizabeth I, 1135
odward, William I, 671
oodward, William I, 685
oodward, William I, 692
oodward, William I, 1099
oodward, William I, 1101
oodward, William I, 1112
oodward, William I, 1135
oodward, William IV, 790
oodward, William IV, 856
oodward, William V, 143
Voodward, William VI, 919
Voodward, William Van Buren VI, 90
Voodward, Wm. IV, 856
Voodward, Wm. Henry II, 897
Voodward, Wm. Henry II, 943
Voodworth, Anna IV, 790
Voodworth, Anna IV, 1017
Voodworth, Charles IV, 1017
Voodworth, Elisha IV, 790
Voodworth, Elisha IV, 1017
Voodworth, Esther IV, 737
Voodworth, Esther IV, 790
Woodworth, George M. IV, 790
Woodworth, Joshua IV, 737
Woodworth, Lizzie IV, 737
Woodworth, Lizzie E. IV, 790
Woodworth, Lizzie R. IV, 1044
Woodworth, Maria B. IV, 1044
Woodworth, Mary IV, 790
Woodworth, Mary E. IV, 790
Woodworth, Philo H. IV, 1044
Woodworth, Richard II, 693
Woody, Abigail I, 556
Woody, Abigail I, 583
Woody, Abigail L. I, 441
Woody, Abigail L. I, 453
Woody, Abigail L. I, 455
Woody, Abigail L. I, 522
Woody, Achsah A. I, 328
Woody, Achsah A. I, 331
Woody, Achsah A. I, 441
Woody, Agness VI, 220
Woody, Albert L. I, 430
Woody, Alson I, 430
Woody, Amy I, 430
Woody, Amy E. I, 441
Woody, Ann I, 430
Woody, Anthony I, 430
Woody, Arvest I, 455
Woody, Asenath I, 430
Woody, Betsey VI, 1003
Woody, Catharine I, 441
Woody, Catharine I, 455
Woody, Catharine E. I, 441
Woody, Cecelia VI, 220
Woody, Cecile I, 949
Woody, Cecile I, 951
Woody, Cecile VI, 220
Woody, Charity I, 369
Woody, Charity I, 441
Woody, Cicile VI, 185
Woody, Cicilia VI, 173
Woody, Cisilia VI, 173
Woody, Cisilia VI, 174
Woody, Cisilia VI, 220
Woody, Cleopatra I, 386
Woody, Cleopatra I, 430
Woody, Constantia VI, 220
Woody, Cynthia A. I, 936
Woody, Daniel W. I, 430
Woody, Daniel Wheeler I, 369
Woody, Eleanor I, 446
Woody, Eleanor I, 455
Woody, Eleanor I, 692
Woody, Elenor I, 430
Woody, Elenor I, 441
Woody, Elenor I, 452
Woody, Elenor I, 455
Woody, Elisabeth I, 441
Woody, Elizabeth I, 369
Woody, Elizabeth I, 378
Woody, Elizabeth I, 430
Woody, Elizabeth I, 450
Woody, Elizabeth I, 455
Woody, Elizabeth VI, 884
Woody, Ella I, 441
Woody, Ellener I, 583
Woody, Enos I, 455
Woody, Enos S. I, 441
Woody, Enos S. I, 455
Woody, Eva V, 720
Woody, Eva T. V, 720
Woody, Eva Terrell V, 366
Woody, Fernando I, 455
Woody, Frank I, 441
Woody, Gelia I, 455
Woody, Hannah I, 369
Woody, Hannah I, 371
Woody, Hannah I, 430
Woody, Hannah I, 441
Woody, Hannah I, 444
Woody, Hannah I, 455
Woody, Harriett I, 430
Woody, Harvey I, 455
Woody, Herman Clayton V, 720
Woody, Horace Herman I, 583
Woody, Hugh I, 350
Woody, Hugh I, 368
Woody, Hugh I, 369
Woody, Hugh I, 372
Woody, Hugh I, 399
Woody, Hugh I, 430
Woody, Hugh I, 441
Woody, Hugh I, 446
Woody, Hugh I, 455
Woody, Hugh I, 583
Woody, Irene I, 430
Woody, J. Waldo IV, 1344
Woody, J. Waldo V, 720
Woody, James I, 346
Woody, James I, 357
Woody, James I, 363
Woody, James I, 369
Woody, James I, 386
Woody, James I, 430
Woody, James I, 441
Woody, James I, 455
Woody, James I, 522
Woody, James I, 556
Woody, James I, 583
Woody, James VI, 147
Woody, James VI, 220
Woody, Jane I, 441
Woody, Jane I, 443
Woody, Jane I, 455
Woody, Jean I, 369
Woody, Jemima VI, 220
Woody, Jessie IV, 1344
Woody, Joanna I, 369
Woody, Johanah I, 369
Woody, John I, 369
Woody, John I, 441
Woody, John I, 447
Woody, John I, 455
Woody, John I, 1163
Woody, John VI, 1020
Woody, John Milton I, 369
Woody, John W. I, 441
Woody, John W. I, 455
Woody, John W. I, 583
Woody, John Waldo I, 583
Woody, Joseph I, 441
Woody, Joseph I, 455
Woody, Joshua I, 368
Woody, Joshua I, 430
Woody, Judith VI, 185
Woody, Judith VI, 186
Woody, Judith VI, 220
Woody, Katharine I, 445
Woody, Katharine I, 455
Woody, Leanna L. I, 383
Woody, Leanna L. I, 430
Woody, Leona I, 951
Woody, Leona A. I, 936
Woody, Leona A. I, 951
Woody, Lurany VI, 220
Woody, Mahlon I, 441
Woody, Mahlon I, 455
Woody, Malen I, 441
Woody, Malon I, 455
Woody, Margaret I, 331
Woody, Margaret I, 441
Woody, Margaret I, 455
Woody, Margaret I, 677
Woody, Margaret I, 692
Woody, Martha VI, 185
Woody, Martha VI, 220
Woody, Martha Jay I, 441
Woody, Mary I, 346
Woody, Mary I, 350
Woody, Mary I, 357
Woody, Mary I, 363
Woody, Mary I, 369
Woody, Mary I, 372
Woody, Mary I, 386
Woody, Mary I, 416
Woody, Mary I, 430
Woody, Mary I, 431
Woody, Mary I, 441
Woody, Mary I, 447
Woody, Mary I, 455
Woody, Mary VI, 185
Woody, Mary VI, 187
Woody, Mary VI, 220
Woody, Mary A. I, 430
Woody, Mary A. I, 739
Woody, Mary Ann I, 441
Woody, Mary Ann I, 611
Woody, Mary Ann VI, 1020
Woody, Mary C. I, 441
Woody, Mary C. I, 583
Woody, Mary E. I, 455
Woody, Mary Edith V, 720
Woody, Massie VI, 220
Woody, Micajah VI, 173
Woody, Micajah VI, 185
Woody, Micajah VI, 186
Woody, Micajah VI, 220
Woody, Milton J. I, 383
Woody, Milton J. I, 430
Woody, Nathan I, 369
Woody, Nathan I, 441
Woody, Nathan D. I, 371
Woody, Nathan D. I, 430
Woody, Nathan Dixon I, 369
Woody, Nathaniel I, 331
Woody, Nathaniel I, 399
Woody, Nathaniel I, 430
Woody, Nathaniel I, 441
Woody, Nathaniel I, 455
Woody, Nathaniel I, 677
Woody, Nathaniel I, 692
Woody, Octavia F. I, 430
Woody, R. Cecil I, 951
Woody, Rachel I, 441
Woody, Rachel H. I, 441
Woody, Rebecca I, 363
Woody, Rebecca I, 369
Woody, Rebecca I, 452
Woody, Rebecca I, 455
Woody, Richard VI, 1020
Woody, Robert I, 386
Woody, Robert I, 430
Woody, Robert I, 936
Woody, Ruth I, 350
Woody, Ruth I, 368
Woody, Ruth I, 369
Woody, Ruth I, 378
Woody, Ruth I, 430
Woody, Ruth I, 441
Woody, Ruth I, 446
Woody, Ruth I, 447
Woody, Ruth I, 451
Woody, Ruth I, 455
Woody, Ruth Cecile I, 936
Woody, Ruth E. I, 441
Woody, Sally I, 399
Woody, Sally I, 430
Woody, Sally I, 455
Woody, Saml. I, 430
Woody, Samuel I, 369
Woody, Samuel I, 416
Woody, Samuel I, 430
Woody, Samuel I, 441
Woody, Samuel I, 446
Woody, Samuel I, 447
Woody, Samuel I, 455
Woody, Samuel I, 583
Woody, Samuel I, 692
Woody, Samuel E. I, 328
Woody, Samuel E. I, 331
Woody, Samuel E. I, 441
Woody, Sarah I, 357
Woody, Sarah I, 369
Woody, Sarah I, 401
Woody, Sarah I, 430
Woody, Sarah I, 441
Woody, Sarah I, 452
Woody, Sarah I, 455
Woody, Sarah VI, 220
Woody, Sarah J. I, 441
Woody, Sarah Winter I, 369
Woody, Silas Earnest I, 441
Woody, Sophia I, 369
Woody, Sophia I, 386
Woody, Sophia I, 430
Woody, Susanna I, 446
Woody, Susanna I, 455
Woody, Susanna VI, 201
Woody, Susanna VI, 220
Woody, Susannah I, 369
Woody, Susannah VI, 201
Woody, Thomas I, 430
Woody, Thomas I, 441
Woody, Thomas I, 455
Woody, Ursula VI, 220
Woody, Waldo V, 720
Woody, William VI, 220
Woody, William VI, 937
Woody, William VI, 947
Woody, William N. I, 441
Woody, Williams VI, 884
Woody, Zachariah Hornaday I, 430
Woody, Zeno I, 441
Woodyard, Elma V, 351
Woodyard, Elma V, 366
Woodyard, Elma Murphey V, 366
Woodyard, Joseph V, 366
Woodyard, Ruth V, 366
Woodyard, Wilbur V, 351
Woodyard, Wilbur V, 366
Wooften, Tibet VI, 989
Woofter, Tibet VI, 989
Woolam, Arthur IV, 506
Woolam, Arthur J. IV, 506
Woolam, Emma IV, 506
Woolam, Hiram IV, 506
Woolam, Hiram S. IV, 506
Woolam, Roy IV, 506
Woolam, Roy H. IV, 506
Woolam, Rubie IV, 506
Woolam, Ruby Frances IV, 506
Woolard, Clara V, 213
Woolard, Daniel V, 291
Woolard, Edgar V. V, 291
Woolard, Edgar Vernon V, 291
Woolard, Elizabeth V, 291
Woolard, Elizabeth M. V, 291
Woolard, Frances V, 291
Woolard, Frances Olive V, 291
Woolard, Frank V, 291
Woolard, Harry Delbert V, 291
Woolard, Horace Clinton V, 291
Woolard, James V, 291
Woolard, Jennie V, 291
Woolard, John V, 291
Woolard, Joseph V, 291
Woolard, Lewis V, 143
Woolard, Lewis Glenn V, 291
Woolard, Mary V, 291
Woolard, Mary J. V, 291
Woolard, Merab V, 291
Woolard, Mertie V, 291
Woolard, Milton V, 291
Woolard, Milton S. V, 291
Woolard, Myrta M. V, 291
Woolard, Nancy J. I, 1128
Woolard, Nancy J. I, 1135
Woolard, Rhoda V, 291
Woolard, Sarah Elizabeth V, 291
Woolard, William V, 291
Woolard, William F. V, 291
Woolard, Wilson V, 291
Woolard, Wilson P. V, 291
Woolary, Elva V, 718
Woolary, Eva V, 718
Woolary, Louisa V, 543
Woolary, Nathaniel V, 638
Woolary, Nathaniel V, 650
Woolaston, Aquilla II, 439
Woolaston, Eleanor II, 693
Woolaston, Ellinor II, 439
Woolaston, Hannah II, 439
Woolaston, Jeremiah II, 439
Woolaston, Joshua II, 568
Woolaston, Joshua II, 693
Woolaston, Martha II, 693
Woolaston, Mary II, 675
Woolaston, Mary II, 693
Woolaston, Mary II, 822
Woolaston, Priscilla II, 439
Woolaston, Priscilla II, 568
Woolaston, Priscilla II, 693
Woolaston, Samuel II, 439
Woolaston, Thomas II, 439
Woolaston, Thomas II, 693
Woolaston, Wd. Martha II, 439
Woolcot, Benjamin II, 189
Woolcot, Jane II, 189
Woolcot, Peeter II, 189
Woolcot, Peter II, 189
Woolcott, ??? III, 367
Woolcott, Jason IV, 1386
Woolcott, Joane II, 275
Woolcott, Joane II, 277
Woolcott, Joseph III, 367
Woolcott, Joseph H. III, 367
Woolcott, Lydia IV, 1386
Woolcott, Mary N. III, 367
Wooldridge, Daniel VI, 866
Wooldridge, Dick VI, 837
Wooldridge, E. V. VI, 856
Wooldridge, Eada VI, 867
Wooldridge, Edmund VI, 867
Wooldridge, Elizabeth VI, 804
Wooldridge, Elizabeth VI, 866
Wooldridge, Elizabeth VI, 867
Wooldridge, Emily VI, 820
Wooldridge, Fanny VI, 867
Wooldridge, Fleming VI, 866
Wooldridge, Frances VI, 809
Wooldridge, Geo. VI, 867
Wooldridge, George VI, 866
Wooldridge, George VI, 867
Wooldridge, Hannah VI, 842
Wooldridge, Harker VI, 823
Wooldridge, James VI, 825
Wooldridge, John VI, 866
Wooldridge, John VI, 867
Wooldridge, Lewallen VI, 867
Wooldridge, Lucy VI, 809
Wooldridge, Margaret VI, 867
Wooldridge, Martha VI, 867
Wooldridge, Mary II, 1040
Wooldridge, Mary VI, 837
Wooldridge, Mary VI, 866
Wooldridge, Milly VI, 866
Wooldridge, Peter VI, 867
Wooldridge, Polly VI, 825
Wooldridge, Polly VI, 837
Wooldridge, Rhoda VI, 846
Wooldridge, Richard VI, 820
Wooldridge, Richard VI, 825
Wooldridge, Richard VI, 842
Wooldridge, Richard VI, 867
Wooldridge, Richard D. VI, 867
Wooldridge, Robert VI, 866
Wooldridge, Sally VI, 804
Wooldridge, Sarah VI, 867
Wooldridge, Simeon VI, 825
Wooldridge, Thomas VI, 866
Wooldridge, Virlinchege VI, 820
Wooldridge, William VI, 821
Wooldridge, William VI, 823
Wooldridge, William VI, 867
Wooldridge, William F. VI, 833
Wooldridge, William S. VI, 837
Wooldridge, William S. VI, 867
Woolem, Angeline IV, 879
Woolem, Angeline IV, 886
Woolem, Joseph V, 1026
Woolery, Carl V, 543
Woolery, Edward V, 543
Woolery, Ethel V, 543
Woolery, Flora V, 543
Woolery, Hanna M. V, 543
Woolery, Hannah V, 543
Woolery, Hannah M. V, 543
Woolery, J. A. V, 543
Woolery, J. A. V, 720
Woolery, J. Asberry V, 543
Woolery, J. Asbury V, 543
Woolery, Jemima Parlott V, 650
Woolery, John A. V, 543
Woolery, Lindley V, 543
Woolery, Lindley J. V, 543
Woolery, Loren V, 543
Woolery, Loren C. V, 543
Woolery, Louisa V, 543
Woolery, Malinda V, 720
Woolery, Martha E. V, 543
Woolery, Naomi B. V, 543
Woolery, Nathaniel V, 650
Woolery, Rachel V, 622
Woolery, Rachel V, 650
Wooleston, Thomas II, 439
Wooley, Abigail II, 823
Wooley, Amos IV, 1301
Wooley, Ann II, 136
Wooley, Ann II, 693
Wooley, Anna V, 143
Wooley, Charles IV, 1242
Wooley, Cicely II, 693
Wooley, Curlis V, 144
Wooley, Curtis L. V, 143
Wooley, Douglas V, 143
Wooley, Ella V, 144
Wooley, Emmerson D. V, 143
Wooley, Finley IV, 1301
Wooley, Florence V, 143
Wooley, George II, 136

Wooley, George II, 439
Wooley, George IV, 1242
Wooley, Hannah II, 439
Wooley, Henrietta M. IV, 1301
Wooley, James V, 143
Wooley, James A. V, 143
Wooley, John II, 693
Wooley, John Albert IV, 1301
Wooley, Joshua Tittery II, 693
Wooley, Leonidas V, 143
Wooley, Martha Culver IV, 1242
Wooley, Mary IV, 1301
Wooley, Mary V. III, 323
Wooley, Phebe Eliza III, 463
Wooley, Phebe J. II, 786
Wooley, Robert II, 693
Wooley, Sarah II, 693
Wooley, Sarah III, 393
Wooley, Sarah A. III, 475
Wooley, Sarah E. IV, 1301
Wooley, Thomas II, 439
Wooley, Thomas II, 693
Wooley, Wardell III, 323
Wooley, William III, 393
Wooley, William III, 475
Wooley, William IV, 1301
Wooley, Wm. IV, 1301
Woolf, Marietta IV, 1017
Woolfe, Paul II, 693
Woolfe, Sarah II, 989
Woolfe, Sarah II, 1040
Woolfolk, George VI, 1020
Woolfolk, Mary C. VI, 1020
Woolford, Phelix V, 213
Woolington, Sarah VI, 969
Woolison, Dorothy I, 425
Woollens, Thomas II, 693
Woolley, ??? III, 367
Woolley, Anna V, 143
Woolley, Cicely II, 668
Woolley, Elizabeth III, 119
Woolley, Elizabeth III, 367
Woolley, Helen Justina III, 367
Woolley, Huldah II, 994
Woolley, Huldah II, 1040
Woolley, Jacob B. III, 106
Woolley, Jacob B. III, 367
Woolley, Jacob, Jr. III, 367
Woolley, James A. V, 143
Woolley, John III, 119
Woolley, John III, 367
Woolley, Joseph C. III, 367
Woolley, Julia A. III, 367
Woolley, Letitia III, 367
Woolley, Margaret III, 194
Woolley, Margaret III, 280
Woolley, Margaret III, 367
Woolley, Mary U. III, 367
Woolley, Mary V. III, 194
Woolley, Mary V. III, 367
Woolley, Robt. H. III, 367
Woolley, Sarah III, 413
Woolley, Sidney III, 367
Woolley, Susan Louisa III, 106
Woolley, Susan Louisa III, 367
Woolley, Wardell III, 194
Woolley, Wardell III, 367
Woolley, William III, 413
Woollman, Elizabeth II, 189
Woollman, John II, 189
Woollman, Mary II, 189
Woollman, Samuel II, 189
Woollston, John II, 163
Woollstone, Benjamin II, 693
Woollstone, Elizabeth II, 693
Woollstone, Grace II, 1007
Woollstone, Grace II, 1040
Woollstone, Hannah II, 693
Woollstone, Jeremiah II, 693
Woollstone, Jonathan II, 1007
Woollstone, Margery II, 1040
Woollstone, Martha II, 693
Woollstone, Sarah II, 693
Woolman, Aaron II, 276
Woolman, Aaron IV, 667
Woolman, Aaron A. IV, 1017
Woolman, Aaron Aaronson IV, 790
Woolman, Aaron Airison IV, 790
Woolman, Aaron T. IV, 789
Woolman, Aaronson II, 276
Woolman, Abbie II, 932
Woolman, Abigail II, 126
Woolman, Abigail II, 140
Woolman, Abigail II, 161
Woolman, Abigail II, 189
Woolman, Abigail II, 265
Woolman, Abigail II, 276
Woolman, Abigail II, 313
Woolman, Abigail II, 828
Woolman, Abigail II, 943
Woolman, Abigail C. II, 307
Woolman, Abner II, 189
Woolman, Abner II, 193
Woolman, Abner II, 257
Woolman, Abner II, 275
Woolman, Abner II, 276
Woolman, Abner II, 307
Woolman, Abner II, 1063
Woolman, Abner IV, 627
Woolman, Abner IV, 667
Woolman, Abner IV, 690
Woolman, Abner IV, 727
Woolman, Abner IV, 781
Woolman, Abner IV, 789
Woolman, Abner IV, 790
Woolman, Abner IV, 827
Woolman, Abner IV, 856
Woolman, Abner IV, 935
Woolman, Abner IV, 945
Woolman, Abner IV, 961
Woolman, Abner IV, 997
Woolman, Abner IV, 1017
Woolman, Abner IV, 1018
Woolman, Abner S. IV, 965
Woolman, Abner S. IV, 1017
Woolman, Abner S. IV, 1018
Woolman, Abner, Jr. IV, 1018
Woolman, Abraham II, 126
Woolman, Abraham II, 275
Woolman, Abraham IV, 1017
Woolman, Abraham S. II, 276
Woolman, Addison M. IV, 856
Woolman, Addison N. IV, 1017
Woolman, Alice II, 126
Woolman, Alice II, 315
Woolman, Alice II, 1083
Woolman, Alice A. IV, 965
Woolman, Alice A. IV, 966
Woolman, Alice A. IV, 1017
Woolman, Alice A. IV, 1018
Woolman, Allen IV, 1017
Woolman, Allen Abraham IV, 1017
Woolman, Alva IV, 1017
Woolman, Alva IV, 1018
Woolman, Alvira IV, 856
Woolman, Amy IV, 789
Woolman, Amy IV, 1017
Woolman, Amy IV, 1018
Woolman, Ann II, 189
Woolman, Ann II, 269
Woolman, Ann II, 276
Woolman, Ann II, 303
Woolman, Ann II, 307
Woolman, Ann IV, 690
Woolman, Ann IV, 789
Woolman, Ann IV, 1017
Woolman, Ann IV, 1018
Woolman, Anna II, 276
Woolman, Anna II, 327
Woolman, Anna IV, 789
Woolman, Anna IV, 790
Woolman, Anna IV, 838
Woolman, Anna IV, 854
Woolman, Anna IV, 856
Woolman, Anna IV, 1017
Woolman, Anna V, 888
Woolman, Anna F. II, 973
Woolman, Anna F. II, 1064
Woolman, Anne II, 202
Woolman, Anne II, 275
Woolman, Annie V, 888
Woolman, Annie L. II, 314
Woolman, Aron Aronson II, 189
Woolman, Asher II, 189
Woolman, Asher II, 205
Woolman, Asher II, 228
Woolman, Asher II, 265
Woolman, Asher II, 267
Woolman, Asher II, 275
Woolman, Asher II, 276
Woolman, Asher II, 303
Woolman, Asher II, 307
Woolman, Asher II, 313
Woolman, Asher II, 314
Woolman, Asher IV, 790
Woolman, Asher IV, 1017
Woolman, Asher IV, 1018
Woolman, Ashur II, 245
Woolman, Benjamin IV, 789
Woolman, Benjamin IV, 1017
Woolman, Benjamin H. II, 307
Woolman, Benjamin Hollingshead II, 189
Woolman, Bertha II, 1083
Woolman, Bertha S. IV, 1017
Woolman, Beulah II, 189
Woolman, Beulah II, 205
Woolman, Beulah II, 275
Woolman, Beulah V, 887
Woolman, Beulah V, 888
Woolman, Brancille S. II, 315
Woolman, Burr II, 189
Woolman, Burr II, 276
Woolman, Caroline IV, 827
Woolman, Caroline IV, 1017
Woolman, Caroline B. II, 314
Woolman, Caroline H. IV, 968
Woolman, Caroline H. IV, 1018
Woolman, Caroline W. IV, 727
Woolman, Charles II, 189
Woolman, Charles II, 276
Woolman, Charles Burton II, 1064
Woolman, Charles H. II, 189
Woolman, Charles H. II, 276
Woolman, Charles H. II, 315
Woolman, Charles H. IV, 1044
Woolman, Charles L. II, 189
Woolman, Charles S. II, 169
Woolman, Charles S. II, 189
Woolman, Charles S. II, 307
Woolman, Christian II, 189
Woolman, Christian II, 276
Woolman, Christian II, 1037
Woolman, Christian II, 1040
Woolman, Christian II, 1059
Woolman, Christian II, 1063
Woolman, Clara Rosella IV, 790
Woolman, Clyde IV, 1044
Woolman, Daniel II, 189
Woolman, Daniel II, 276
Woolman, Daniel Howard II, 314
Woolman, Daniel L. II, 314
Woolman, Daniel L. II, 315
Woolman, Daniel L. II, 327
Woolman, David II, 275
Woolman, David II, 276
Woolman, Eber II, 189
Woolman, Eber II, 275
Woolman, Eber V, 213
Woolman, Eber V, 543
Woolman, Edith II, 189
Woolman, Edith II, 228
Woolman, Edith II, 275
Woolman, Edith IV, 856
Woolman, Edmund H. II, 189
Woolman, Edward J. IV, 699
Woolman, Edward J. IV, 789
Woolman, Edward J. IV, 812
Woolman, Edward J. IV, 838
Woolman, Edward J. IV, 854
Woolman, Edward J. IV, 856
Woolman, Edward J. IV, 1017
Woolman, Edward J. IV, 1018
Woolman, Elisabeth II, 203
Woolman, Eliza II, 240
Woolman, Eliza II, 276
Woolman, Eliza IV, 1018
Woolman, Eliza V, 881
Woolman, Eliza V, 888
Woolman, Eliza W. II, 716
Woolman, Elizabeth II, 126
Woolman, Elizabeth II, 189
Woolman, Elizabeth II, 199
Woolman, Elizabeth II, 229
Woolman, Elizabeth II, 247
Woolman, Elizabeth II, 265
Woolman, Elizabeth II, 275
Woolman, Elizabeth II, 276
Woolman, Elizabeth II, 285
Woolman, Elizabeth II, 307
Woolman, Elizabeth II, 314
Woolman, Elizabeth II, 315
Woolman, Elizabeth II, 787
Woolman, Elizabeth II, 821
Woolman, Elizabeth IV, 789
Woolman, Elizabeth IV, 1017
Woolman, Elizabeth V, 886
Woolman, Elizabeth V, 888
Woolman, Elizabeth V, 943
Woolman, Elizabeth S. II, 973
Woolman, Elizabeth S. II, 1045
Woolman, Elizabeth S. II, 1064
Woolman, Elizabeth W. II, 324
Woolman, Elizabeth W. II, 327
Woolman, Elizabeth, Jr. II, 275
Woolman, Ellis IV, 789
Woolman, Ellis IV, 1017
Woolman, Elvira IV, 627
Woolman, Elvira IV, 667
Woolman, Elvira IV, 727
Woolman, Elvira IV, 961
Woolman, Elvira IV, 1017
Woolman, Elvira IV, 1018
Woolman, Elvira H. IV, 667
Woolman, Elvira H. IV, 827
Woolman, Elvira H. IV, 1017
Woolman, Elvira H. IV, 1018
Woolman, Elvirah IV, 789
Woolman, Emely II, 276
Woolman, Emily II, 307
Woolman, Emily IV, 838
Woolman, Emily IV, 856
Woolman, Emily N. II, 315
Woolman, Emily N. II, 324
Woolman, Emily N. II, 327
Woolman, Emily N. II, 819
Woolman, Enoch IV, 789
Woolman, Enoch IV, 1017
Woolman, Enoch IV, 1018
Woolman, Esther II, 275
Woolman, Esther II, 693
Woolman, Esther IV, 946
Woolman, Esther IV, 1017
Woolman, Eva J. V, 943
Woolman, Florence Martha IV, 699
Woolman, Florence Martha IV, 790
Woolman, Florence Martha IV, 856
Woolman, Franklin II, 189
Woolman, Franklin II, 307
Woolman, G. II, 310
Woolman, George II, 189
Woolman, George II, 276
Woolman, George IV, 790
Woolman, George IV, 1121
Woolman, Gertrude IV, 1017
Woolman, Giles S. II, 973
Woolman, Giles S. II, 1064
Woolman, Granvil II, 314
Woolman, Granvil S. II, 314
Woolman, Granville II, 189
Woolman, Granville II, 240
Woolman, Granville II, 242
Woolman, Granville II, 265
Woolman, Granville II, 269
Woolman, Granville II, 275
Woolman, Granville II, 276
Woolman, Granville S. II, 314
Woolman, Granville S. II, 327
Woolman, Granville, Jr. II, 307
Woolman, Hannah II, 189
Woolman, Hannah II, 224
Woolman, Hannah II, 240
Woolman, Hannah II, 242
Woolman, Hannah II, 265
Woolman, Hannah II, 269
Woolman, Hannah II, 275
Woolman, Hannah II, 276
Woolman, Hannah II, 314
Woolman, Hannah II, 693
Woolman, Hannah Ann II, 310
Woolman, Hannah Ann II, 314
Woolman, Hannah Ann II, 319
Woolman, Hannah Ann II, 327
Woolman, Helen II, 1054
Woolman, Helena S. II, 134
Woolman, Henry IV, 1017
Woolman, Henry IV, 1018
Woolman, Henry M. II, 315
Woolman, Isaac C. V, 888
Woolman, Isaac L. II, 315
Woolman, Isaac L. II, 327
Woolman, James II, 189
Woolman, James Ezra IV, 699
Woolman, James Ezra IV, 790
Woolman, James Ezra IV, 856
Woolman, Jane II, 189
Woolman, Jane II, 193
Woolman, Jane II, 271
Woolman, Jane II, 275
Woolman, Jane II, 276
Woolman, Jane II, 282
Woolman, Jane II, 294
Woolman, Jane II, 307
Woolman, Jane II, 1037
Woolman, Jane IV, 240
Woolman, Jane IV, 764
Woolman, Jane IV, 784
Woolman, Jane IV, 789
Woolman, Jane IV, 790
Woolman, Jane IV, 1017
Woolman, Jane IV, 1018
Woolman, Jane R. II, 276
Woolman, Jane R. II, 315
Woolman, Jane R. II, 321
Woolman, Jane R. II, 327
Woolman, Jas. II, 134
Woolman, Jemima Elizabeth V, 943
Woolman, Jervis II, 315
Woolman, Jervis S. II, 315
Woolman, Jervis S. II, 327
Woolman, Jesse IV, 1044
Woolman, Jesse Hall IV, 699
Woolman, Jesse Hall Dewees IV, 790
Woolman, Jesse Hall Deweese IV, 856
Woolman, Jesse J. IV, 1044
Woolman, Jessie IV, 856
Woolman, Job II, 189
Woolman, Joel II, 189
Woolman, Joel II, 275
Woolman, Joel II, 276
Woolman, Joel II, 282
Woolman, Joel II, 307
Woolman, Joel II, 1037
Woolman, Joel II, 1059
Woolman, Joel II, 1063
Woolman, Joel IV, 789
Woolman, Joel IV, 1017
Woolman, John I, 177
Woolman, John II, 126
Woolman, John II, 189
Woolman, John II, 199
Woolman, John II, 203
Woolman, John II, 217
Woolman, John II, 234
Woolman, John II, 247
Woolman, John II, 275
Woolman, John II, 276
Woolman, John II, 693
Woolman, John II, 716
Woolman, John II, 724
Woolman, John II, 777
Woolman, John IV, 1017
Woolman, John VI, 281
Woolman, John A. II, 189
Woolman, John A. II, 267
Woolman, John A. II, 276
Woolman, John A. V, 888
Woolman, John Aaronson II,
Woolman, John Aaronson II,
Woolman, John Aronson II, 1
Woolman, John Aronson II, 2
Woolman, John Aronson II, 2
Woolman, John C. V, 888
Woolman, John J. II, 189
Woolman, John J. II, 307
Woolman, John S. II, 276
Woolman, John Stavonsin V,
Woolman, John W. II, 777
Woolman, Jonah II, 189
Woolman, Jonah II, 274
Woolman, Jonah II, 275
Woolman, Jonah II, 276
Woolman, Jonah II, 315
Woolman, Jonathan II, 189
Woolman, Jonathan II, 307
Woolman, Jonathan H. II, 31
Woolman, Jonathan H. II, 32
Woolman, Joseph II, 276
Woolman, Joseph II, 307
Woolman, Joseph II, 315
Woolman, Joseph IV, 1017
Woolman, Joseph A. II, 276
Woolman, Joseph A. IV, 789
Woolman, Joseph B. II, 189
Woolman, Joseph B. II, 276
Woolman, Joseph B. II, 307
Woolman, Joseph B. II, 315
Woolman, Joseph B. II, 327
Woolman, Joseph B. V, 879
Woolman, Joseph B. V, 881
Woolman, Joseph B. V, 888
Woolman, Joseph Burr II, 32
Woolman, Joseph Howard IV,
Woolman, Joseph Howard IV,
Woolman, Joseph Howard IV,
Woolman, Joseph J. IV, 1017
Woolman, Josiah II, 189
Woolman, Josiah II, 276
Woolman, Josiah H. II, 276
Woolman, Josiah H. II, 307
Woolman, Josiah H. II, 315
Woolman, Josiah H. II, 327
Woolman, Judith IV, 1017
Woolman, Judith Ann IV, 101
Woolman, Judith Ann IV, 101
Woolman, Julia S. II, 315
Woolman, Julietta V, 888
Woolman, Kezia II, 276
Woolman, Keziah II, 189
Woolman, Keziah II, 275
Woolman, Keziah IV, 784
Woolman, Keziah IV, 789
Woolman, Keziah IV, 790
Woolman, Leah II, 189
Woolman, Leah II, 201
Woolman, Leah II, 257
Woolman, Leah II, 267
Woolman, Leah II, 275
Woolman, Leah IV, 1017
Woolman, Lewis A. IV, 692
Woolman, Lewis A. IV, 789
Woolman, Lewis A. IV, 1017
Woolman, Lewis A. IV, 1018
Woolman, Lewis C. II, 1054
Woolman, Lydia II, 189
Woolman, Lydia II, 228

man, Lydia II, 276
man, Lydia II, 307
man, Lydia II, 315
man, Lydia II, 321
man, Lydia II, 327
man, Lydia A. IV, 692
man, Lydia A. IV, 789
man, Lydia A. IV, 790
man, Lydia A. IV, 1004
man, Lydia A. IV, 1017
man, Lydia A. IV, 1018
man, Margaret IV, 867
man, Margaret IV, 886
man, Margaret Hanna
V, 856
man, Margaret Hannah
V, 699
man, Margaret Hannah
V, 790
man, Margaret L. II, 314
man, Margaret L. II, 321
man, Margaret L. II, 327
man, Maria II, 265
man, Maria II, 267
man, Maria II, 276
man, Maria II, 307
man, Maria II, 315
man, Maria II, 323
man, Maria II, 327
man, Maria IV, 790
man, Maria IV, 1017
man, Maria Taylor IV, 1017
man, Maria Taylor IV, 1018
man, Marietta IV, 1017
man, Marietta IV, 1018
man, Martha II, 189
man, Martha II, 193
man, Martha II, 274
man, Martha II, 275
man, Martha II, 276
man, Martha II, 281
man, Martha II, 307
man, Martha II, 315
man, Martha II, 710
man, Martha IV, 690
man, Martha IV, 781
man, Martha IV, 789
man, Martha IV, 790
man, Martha IV, 935
man, Martha IV, 945
man, Martha IV, 997
man, Martha IV, 1017
man, Martha B. II, 311
man, Martha B. II, 314
man, Martha B. II, 315
man, Martha B. II, 327
man, Martha Etta V, 888
man, Martha L. II, 315
man, Martha W. II, 314
man, Martin IV, 1017
man, Mary II, 126
man, Mary II, 131
man, Mary II, 140
man, Mary II, 189
man, Mary II, 201
man, Mary II, 209
man, Mary II, 232
man, Mary II, 234
man, Mary II, 275
man, Mary II, 276
man, Mary II, 307
man, Mary II, 315
man, Mary II, 327
man, Mary II, 787
man, Mary II, 828
man, Mary II, 957
man, Mary II, 1004
man, Mary II, 1040
man, Mary II, 1047
man, Mary II, 1054
man, Mary II, 1063
man, Mary II, 1064
man, Mary IV, 789
man, Mary IV, 790
man, Mary IV, 945
man, Mary IV, 1017
man, Mary IV, 1018
man, Mary V, 881
man, Mary V, 888
man, Mary V, 943
man, Mary VI, 513
man, Mary VI, 524
man, Mary A. II, 973
man, Mary Ann II, 122
man, Mary Ann II, 126
man, Mary Ann II, 134
man, Mary Ann II, 276
man, Mary Ann II, 307
man, Mary Ann IV, 764
man, Mary Ann IV, 789
man, Mary Ann IV, 790
Woolman, Mary Anna II, 315
Woolman, Mary C. IV, 699
Woolman, Mary C. IV, 789
Woolman, Mary C. IV, 790
Woolman, Mary C. IV, 812
Woolman, Mary C. IV, 856
Woolman, Mary Dewees IV, 699
Woolman, Mary Dewees IV, 790
Woolman, Mary E. II, 189
Woolman, Mary E. II, 281
Woolman, Mary E. II, 307
Woolman, Mary E. II, 315
Woolman, Mary E. II, 316
Woolman, Mary E. II, 327
Woolman, Mary Edith II, 315
Woolman, Mary Elizabeth
IV, 1044
Woolman, Mary Ella V, 943
Woolman, Mary Ellen V, 943
Woolman, Mary Elsa V, 888
Woolman, Mary Etta IV, 1018
Woolman, Mary H. II, 315
Woolman, Mary Jane II, 134
Woolman, Mary W. II, 963
Woolman, Mary W. II, 1054
Woolman, Mary W. IV, 667
Woolman, Mary W. IV, 789
Woolman, Mary W. IV, 790
Woolman, Maryetta IV, 1017
Woolman, Matilday II, 315
Woolman, Maurice II, 1083
Woolman, Meriba D. II, 325
Woolman, Meriba D. II, 327
Woolman, Meribah II, 276
Woolman, Meribah II, 307
Woolman, Meribah II, 315
Woolman, Micajah IV, 1017
Woolman, Micajah IV, 1018
Woolman, Micajah IV, 1044
Woolman, Mildred Rebecca
Dewees IV, 790
Woolman, Minnie IV, 1044
Woolman, Moses II, 189
Woolman, Naomi II, 716
Woolman, Naomi II, 777
Woolman, Nathan II, 189
Woolman, Nathan II, 307
Woolman, Nathaniel II, 247
Woolman, Nathaniel II, 275
Woolman, Orien Clayton V, 888
Woolman, Patience II, 242
Woolman, Patience II, 275
Woolman, Patience II, 283
Woolman, Patience II, 307
Woolman, Patience M. II, 169
Woolman, Patience M. II, 189
Woolman, Phebe II, 282
Woolman, Phebe II, 307
Woolman, Phebe II, 309
Woolman, Phebe II, 314
Woolman, Phebe II, 315
Woolman, Phebe IV, 1017
Woolman, Phebe IV, 1018
Woolman, Phebe V, 885
Woolman, Phebe V, 888
Woolman, Phebe L. II, 314
Woolman, Phebe M. II, 327
Woolman, Phebe W. II, 308
Woolman, Phebe W. II, 311
Woolman, Phebe W. II, 314
Woolman, Phebe W. II, 315
Woolman, Phebe W. II, 317
Woolman, Phebe W. II, 327
Woolman, Priscilla IV, 1009
Woolman, Priscilla IV, 1017
Woolman, Priscilla IV, 1018
Woolman, Rachael II, 205
Woolman, Rachael II, 276
Woolman, Rachel II, 189
Woolman, Rachel II, 205
Woolman, Rachel II, 228
Woolman, Rachel II, 242
Woolman, Rachel II, 245
Woolman, Rachel II, 265
Woolman, Rachel II, 275
Woolman, Rachel II, 276
Woolman, Rachel II, 313
Woolman, Rachel II, 314
Woolman, Rachel IV, 1005
Woolman, Rachel IV, 1017
Woolman, Rachel IV, 1018
Woolman, Rachel E. II, 189
Woolman, Rachel E. II, 303
Woolman, Rachel E. II, 307
Woolman, Rachel P. IV, 769
Woolman, Rachel P. IV, 790
Woolman, Rachel R. IV, 1018
Woolman, Rachel, Sr. II, 275
Woolman, Rebecca II, 189
Woolman, Rebecca II, 271
Woolman, Rebecca II, 274
Woolman, Rebecca II, 275
Woolman, Rebecca II, 276
Woolman, Rebecca II, 281
Woolman, Rebecca II, 285
Woolman, Rebecca II, 307
Woolman, Rebecca IV, 667
Woolman, Rebecca IV, 789
Woolman, Rebecca IV, 935
Woolman, Rebecca IV, 1017
Woolman, Rebecca IV, 1018
Woolman, Rebecca V, 947
Woolman, Rebecca D. II, 189
Woolman, Rebecca H. IV, 789
Woolman, Rebecca H. IV, 1017
Woolman, Reuben II, 131
Woolman, Reuben II, 140
Woolman, Reuben II, 787
Woolman, Reuben II, 828
Woolman, Robert S. II, 973
Woolman, Russell J. IV, 856
Woolman, Ruth V, 154
Woolman, Ruth V, 213
Woolman, Ruth V, 543
Woolman, Ruth V, 879
Woolman, Ruth V, 943
Woolman, Ruth Adams V, 888
Woolman, S. Robert II, 1064
Woolman, Samuel II, 189
Woolman, Samuel II, 193
Woolman, Samuel II, 203
Woolman, Samuel II, 217
Woolman, Samuel II, 242
Woolman, Samuel II, 271
Woolman, Samuel II, 274
Woolman, Samuel II, 275
Woolman, Samuel II, 276
Woolman, Samuel II, 281
Woolman, Samuel II, 282
Woolman, Samuel II, 285
Woolman, Samuel II, 307
Woolman, Samuel II, 1037
Woolman, Samuel IV, 667
Woolman, Samuel IV, 764
Woolman, Samuel IV, 784
Woolman, Samuel IV, 789
Woolman, Samuel IV, 790
Woolman, Samuel IV, 955
Woolman, Samuel IV, 1017
Woolman, Samuel IV, 1018
Woolman, Samuel B. II, 307
Woolman, Samuel C. II, 307
Woolman, Samuel E. II, 973
Woolman, Samuel E. II, 1059
Woolman, Samuel E. II, 1063
Woolman, Samuel E. II, 1064
Woolman, Samuel F. II, 189
Woolman, Samuel F. II, 228
Woolman, Samuel F. II, 276
Woolman, Samuel F. II, 315
Woolman, Samuel Garrett II, 314
Woolman, Samuel Jarrett II, 327
Woolman, Samuel, Jr. II, 271
Woolman, Samuel, Jr. II, 276
Woolman, Samuel, Jr. IV, 789
Woolman, Samuel, Jr. IV, 1017
Woolman, Samuel, Sr. IV, 1017
Woolman, Sarah II, 189
Woolman, Sarah II, 217
Woolman, Sarah II, 275
Woolman, Sarah II, 276
Woolman, Sarah II, 307
Woolman, Sarah II, 315
Woolman, Sarah II, 316
Woolman, Sarah II, 327
Woolman, Sarah II, 777
Woolman, Sarah IV, 789
Woolman, Sarah IV, 790
Woolman, Sarah IV, 997
Woolman, Sarah IV, 1017
Woolman, Sarah IV, 1018
Woolman, Sarah Ann V, 861
Woolman, Sarah Ann V, 874
Woolman, Sarah Ann V, 886
Woolman, Sarah Ann V, 888
Woolman, Sarah G. II, 724
Woolman, Sarah G. II, 777
Woolman, Sarah Jane II, 1067
Woolman, Sarah Jane II, 1071
Woolman, Sarah Jane II, 1083
Woolman, Sarah L. II, 1064
Woolman, Sarahetta IV, 982
Woolman, Sarahetta IV, 1017
Woolman, Sarahetta IV, 1018
Woolman, Susan II, 276
Woolman, Susan II, 307
Woolman, Susan II, 315
Woolman, Susan II, 326
Woolman, Susan II, 327
Woolman, Susanna II, 276
Woolman, Susanna IV, 781
Woolman, Susanna IV, 850
Woolman, Susanna IV, 856
Woolman, Susanna IV, 1017
Woolman, Susanna V, 888
Woolman, Susanna B. V, 887
Woolman, Susanna B. V, 888
Woolman, Susanna L. II, 1064
Woolman, Susanna S. II, 1064
Woolman, Susannah II, 478
Woolman, Susannah II, 693
Woolman, Susannah II, 1059
Woolman, Susannah II, 1063
Woolman, Susannah IV, 789
Woolman, Susannah IV, 790
Woolman, Susannah V, 888
Woolman, Susannah S. II, 973
Woolman, Thomas II, 276
Woolman, Thomas II, 307
Woolman, Thomas Arthur IV, 790
Woolman, Thomas B. IV, 790
Woolman, Thomas B. IV, 1017
Woolman, Thomas B. IV, 1018
Woolman, Thomas F. IV, 1018
Woolman, Thomas T. IV, 1017
Woolman, Thos. B. IV, 789
Woolman, Thos. B. IV, 997
Woolman, Thos. Leonard IV, 1017
Woolman, Thos. Tucker IV, 789
Woolman, Unity IV, 955
Woolman, Unity IV, 1018
Woolman, Uriah II, 189
Woolman, Uriah II, 201
Woolman, Uriah II, 275
Woolman, Uriah II, 276
Woolman, Uriah II, 478
Woolman, Uriah II, 693
Woolman, Uriah V, 888
Woolman, Uriah V, 943
Woolman, Uriah, Jr. V, 888
Woolman, Urish II, 693
Woolman, Wd. Hannah S. II, 189
Woolman, Wd. Martha II, 189
Woolman, Wd. Mary II, 189
Woolman, Wd. Mary II, 780
Woolman, Wd. Patience II, 189
Woolman, Wd. Rachel II, 189
Woolman, Wd. Rebecca II, 189
Woolman, William II, 189
Woolman, William II, 275
Woolman, William V, 888
Woolman, William S. II, 973
Woolman, Wm. IV, 1017
Woolman, Wm. V, 888
Woolman, Wm. B. V, 886
Woolman, Wm. B. V, 888
Woolman, Wm. Henry IV, 1017
Woolman, Wm. R. V, 888
Woolman, Wm. R. V, 943
Woolman, Wm. S. II, 1064
Woolman, Wm. V. V, 888
Woolman, Zella IV, 1044
Woolrich, Thomas II, 693
Woolridge, Ann J. T. VI, 1020
Woolridge, Martha M. VI, 1020
Woolridge, Mary II, 1002
Woolridge, Pryor S. VI, 1020
Woolridge, Thomas II, 693
Woolridge, Thomas VI, 1020
Woolsey, Benjamin III, 367
Woolsey, Benjamin III, 368
Woolsey, Catharine III, 368
Woolsey, Charlotte III, 367
Woolsey, Charlotte III, 368
Woolsey, Elizabeth III, 368
Woolsey, Gardner III, 368
Woolsey, Grennette III, 368
Woolsey, Hannah III, 367
Woolsey, Hannah III, 368
Woolsey, Hannah V, 943
Woolsey, Isaac III, 367
Woolsey, Jere. III, 367
Woolsey, Jeremiah III, 367
Woolsey, Jeremiah III, 368
Woolsey, Laura III, 60
Woolsey, Laura W. III, 60
Woolsey, Margaret III, 368
Woolsey, Marianne V, 291
Woolsey, Peter III, 368
Woolsey, Sarah III, 244
Woolsey, Sarah III, 368
Woolsey, Susanna III, 368
Woolsey, Wm. S. III, 60
Woolson, John II, 1064
Woolstin, Samuel II, 1040
Woolston, Abigail II, 322
Woolston, Abigail II, 327
Woolston, Abigail L. II, 315
Woolston, Ann II, 957
Woolston, Ann II, 990
Woolston, Ann II, 1041
Woolston, Ann II, 1083
Woolston, Ann S. II, 1064
Woolston, Anna E. II, 943
Woolston, Anna S. II, 943
Woolston, Benjamin II, 693
Woolston, Benjamin II, 973
Woolston, Benjamin II, 1064
Woolston, Benjamin S. II, 1078
Woolston, Benjamin S. II, 1083
Woolston, Cyrus III, 363
Woolston, Cyrus III, 368
Woolston, Daniel II, 315
Woolston, Daniel II, 322
Woolston, Daniel II, 327
Woolston, Daniel III, 368
Woolston, Deborah II, 943
Woolston, Edwin A. II, 943
Woolston, Eliza II, 1068
Woolston, Eliza II, 1083
Woolston, Eliza B. II, 1041
Woolston, Eliza B. II, 1042
Woolston, Eliza B. II, 1064
Woolston, Eliza W. II, 828
Woolston, Eliza W. II, 943
Woolston, Elizabeth II, 190
Woolston, Elizabeth II, 276
Woolston, Elizabeth II, 693
Woolston, Elizabeth II, 828
Woolston, Elizabeth II, 968
Woolston, Elizabeth II, 987
Woolston, Elizabeth II, 1000
Woolston, Elizabeth II, 1018
Woolston, Elizabeth II, 1025
Woolston, Elizabeth II, 1029
Woolston, Elizabeth II, 1040
Woolston, Elizabeth II, 1041
Woolston, Elizabeth II, 1064
Woolston, Elizabeth II, 1078
Woolston, Elizabeth II, 1083
Woolston, George W. II, 943
Woolston, Grace II, 1040
Woolston, Hannah II, 190
Woolston, Hannah II, 210
Woolston, Hannah II, 219
Woolston, Hannah II, 276
Woolston, Hannah II, 277
Woolston, Hannah II, 693
Woolston, Hannah II, 1000
Woolston, Hannah II, 1027
Woolston, Hannah II, 1040
Woolston, Harriet III, 363
Woolston, Harriet III, 368
Woolston, Jabez II, 276
Woolston, Jabez II, 277
Woolston, Jane II, 1009
Woolston, Jane II, 1041
Woolston, Jane II, 1042
Woolston, Jane II, 1064
Woolston, Jane L. II, 1083
Woolston, Jane S. II, 1083
Woolston, Jeremiah II, 276
Woolston, Jeremiah II, 439
Woolston, Jeremiah II, 693
Woolston, Jeremiah II, 1018
Woolston, Jeremiah II, 1040
Woolston, John II, 190
Woolston, John II, 194
Woolston, John II, 207
Woolston, John II, 210
Woolston, John II, 218
Woolston, John II, 219
Woolston, John II, 230
Woolston, John II, 276
Woolston, John II, 1008
Woolston, John II, 1040
Woolston, John II, 1042
Woolston, John II, 1064
Woolston, John H. II, 973
Woolston, John W. II, 1083
Woolston, Jonathan II, 190
Woolston, Jonathan II, 276
Woolston, Jonathan II, 968
Woolston, Jonathan II, 1000
Woolston, Jonathan II, 1040
Woolston, Jonathan II, 1041
Woolston, Jonathan II, 1042
Woolston, Joseph L. II, 943
Woolston, Joshua II, 780
Woolston, Joshua II, 957
Woolston, Joshua II, 987
Woolston, Joshua II, 1009
Woolston, Joshua II, 1041
Woolston, Joshua II, 1042
Woolston, Joshua II, 1064
Woolston, Joshua II, 1083
Woolston, Joshua W. II, 828
Woolston, Joshua W. II, 943
Woolston, Joshua W. II, 1068
Woolston, Joshua W. II, 1083
Woolston, Joshua, Jr. II, 1041
Woolston, Joshua, Jr. II, 1042
Woolston, Lydia II, 973
Woolston, Lydia II, 1041

Woolston, Lydia II, 1064
Woolston, Lydia II, 1083
Woolston, Lydia VI, 459
Woolston, Lydia Ann II, 289
Woolston, Lydia Ann II, 307
Woolston, Margaretta II, 1083
Woolston, Margery II, 112
Woolston, Margery II, 277
Woolston, Margery II, 984
Woolston, Margery II, 1008
Woolston, Margery II, 1040
Woolston, Margery II, 1041
Woolston, Maria II, 973
Woolston, Marjery II, 112
Woolston, Martha II, 307
Woolston, Martha II, 693
Woolston, Martha II, 1064
Woolston, Mary II, 190
Woolston, Mary II, 276
Woolston, Mary II, 957
Woolston, Mary II, 1009
Woolston, Mary II, 1032
Woolston, Mary II, 1041
Woolston, Mary II, 1042
Woolston, Mary W. II, 1083
Woolston, Rachel II, 1041
Woolston, Rachel B. II, 1078
Woolston, Rachel B. II, 1083
Woolston, Rebecca II, 190
Woolston, Rebecca II, 276
Woolston, Samuel II, 190
Woolston, Samuel II, 439
Woolston, Samuel II, 984
Woolston, Samuel II, 1000
Woolston, Samuel II, 1040
Woolston, Samuel II, 1041
Woolston, Samuel S. II, 1083
Woolston, Sarah II, 190
Woolston, Sarah II, 276
Woolston, Sarah II, 693
Woolston, Sarah II, 1030
Woolston, Sarah II, 1041
Woolston, Stephen II, 828
Woolston, Stephen II, 1009
Woolston, Stephen II, 1029
Woolston, Stephen II, 1041
Woolston, Stephen II, 1042
Woolston, Stephen II, 1064
Woolston, Stephen II, 1078
Woolston, Stephen II, 1083
Woolston, Susan II, 795
Woolston, Susan II, 1075
Woolston, Susan II, 1083
Woolston, Tacy F. II, 1083
Woolston, Thomas II, 190
Woolston, Thomas II, 1083
Woolston, Thomas L. II, 1064
Woolston, Thomas L. II, 1083
Woolston, Wd. Hannah II, 1043
Woolston, Wm. II, 1083
Woolstone, Elizabeth II, 273
Woolstone, Elizabeth II, 276
Woolstone, Hannah II, 245
Woolstone, Hannah II, 260
Woolstone, Hannah II, 276
Woolstone, Hannah II, 1018
Woolstone, Hannah II, 1040
Woolstone, John II, 202
Woolstone, John II, 273
Woolstone, John II, 276
Woolstone, Jonathan II, 276
Woolstone, Mary II, 202
Woolstone, Mary II, 276
Woolstone, Rebecca II, 261
Woolstone, Rebecca II, 276
Woolstone, Samuel II, 202
Woolstone, Samuel II, 213
Woolstone, Samuel II, 276
Woolstone, Samuel II, 1018
Woolstone, Samuel II, 1040
Woolstone, Sarah II, 196
Woolstone, Sarah II, 276
Woolsy, Hannah V, 923
Woolten, Samuel VI, 584
Woolten, Sarah VI, 584
Woolverton, Charles II, 275
Woolwine, Eliza I, 746
Woolwine, Eliza I, 754
Wooly, Andrew VI, 33
Wooly, Andrew VI, 38
Woory, Joseph VI, 29
Woosincraft, William II, 449
Woosley, Lillie V, 366
Wooster, Addie IV, 307
Wooster, Amos IV, 1354
Wooster, Amos IV, 1368
Wooster, Amos IV, 1386
Wooster, Hinman VI, 979
Wooster, J. F. IV, 307
Wooster, Lodema IV, 1354
Wooster, Lodema IV, 1368
Wooster, Lodema IV, 1386
Wooster, Mercy IV, 1354
Wooster, Mercy IV, 1386
Wooster, Sylvester IV, 1354
Wooster, Sylvester IV, 1386
Wooten, ??? I, 279
Wooten, A. E. IV, 1228
Wooten, Abijah V, 144
Wooten, Abijah V, 874
Wooten, Albert V, 144
Wooten, Andrew V, 874
Wooten, Arthur I, 250
Wooten, Arthur I, 261
Wooten, Carrie Gulielma I, 33
Wooten, Charles N. I, 1135
Wooten, Daniel V, 874
Wooten, Dillen Moody IV, 1228
Wooten, Dillon V, 144
Wooten, Elmer V, 213
Wooten, Elmer O. V, 213
Wooten, Ernest C. I, 33
Wooten, Esther V, 213
Wooten, Gilbert Gurney IV, 1228
Wooten, Gurney V, 144
Wooten, Harriet R. III, 261
Wooten, Harriet R. III, 368
Wooten, Helen V, 144
Wooten, Helen Pauline IV, 1228
Wooten, Henry V, 874
Wooten, Irvine Tavis I, 33
Wooten, Isam V, 874
Wooten, Isam C. IV, 1228
Wooten, Isham V, 874
Wooten, Isom V, 144
Wooten, Isom P. V, 874
Wooten, Itasca F. V, 213
Wooten, James V, 874
Wooten, James C. I, 1135
Wooten, Joel V, 874
Wooten, John M. I, 1135
Wooten, Jonathan I, 261
Wooten, Joseph A. I, 1135
Wooten, Lewis V, 874
Wooten, Lucetta IV, 1228
Wooten, Lucetta V, 144
Wooten, Lucretta IV, 1228
Wooten, Martha IV, 566
Wooten, Martha IV, 601
Wooten, Martha V, 874
Wooten, Martha Gertrude I, 33
Wooten, Mary Jane V, 874
Wooten, Nathan I, 261
Wooten, Nathan E. I, 33
Wooten, Nathan Y. I, 1135
Wooten, Nellie V, 144
Wooten, Nellie V, 720
Wooten, Nellie Ruth IV, 1228
Wooten, Pharaba I, 33
Wooten, Rachel I, 250
Wooten, Rachel I, 261
Wooten, Rachel I, 1115
Wooten, Rachel I, 1135
Wooten, Rebecca IV, 601
Wooten, Rebecca IV, 1121
Wooten, Sarah I, 66
Wooten, Sarah I, 308
Wooten, Sarah I, 320
Wooten, Sarah E. I, 1135
Wooten, Thomas V, 874
Wooten, Wilfrid E. III, 368
Wooten, Wilfrid E. Harriet III, 261
Wooten, William V, 874
Wooten, William J. I, 1135
Wooten, William S. V, 874
Wooten, Wm. Clarence I, 33
Wooten, Wm. N. I, 33
Wooters, Bessie I, 612
Wooters, Bessie I, 628
Wooters, Bessie I, 630
Wooters, Bessie I, 643
Wooters, J. K. I, 643
Wooters, John Keener I, 612
Wooters, John Kerner I, 628
Wooters, John Thomas I, 628
Wooters, Keens C. I, 630
Wooters, Keens C. I, 643
Wooters, Mary I, 628
Wooters, William Henry I, 628
Wootin, Martin IV, 1196
Wooting, Martin IV, 1196
Wooton, Abijah V, 874
Wooton, Amelia J. III, 131
Wooton, Amelia J. III, 368
Wooton, Andrew V, 874
Wooton, Arthur I, 178
Wooton, Daniel V, 874
Wooton, Ellen V, 606
Wooton, Harriet III, 368
Wooton, Harriet R. III, 368
Wooton, Henry V, 874
Wooton, Isom P. V, 874
Wooton, James V, 874
Wooton, Joel V, 874
Wooton, John VI, 867
Wooton, Jonathan I, 261
Wooton, Martha V, 874
Wooton, Mary Jane V, 874
Wooton, Nancy VI, 867
Wooton, Nathan I, 261
Wooton, Pharabe I, 3
Wooton, Rebecca IV, 366
Wooton, Rebecca IV, 459
Wooton, Robert VI, 867
Wooton, Thomas V, 874
Wooton, Wilfred Edward III, 368
Wooton, Wilfrid E. III, 368
Wooton, William S. V, 874
Wooton, Wm. I, 3
Wootring, Martin IV, 1196
Wootton, Wilfred Edward III, 368
Worcester, Amos IV, 1386
Worcester, Edith Scott VI, 765
Worcester, Eunice IV, 1386
Worcester, Lodema IV, 1386
Worcester, Mercy IV, 1386
Worcester, Sylvester IV, 1386
Word, John H. VI, 1020
Word, Joshua VI, 1020
Word, Sally VI, 1020
Wordly, Nancy VI, 867
Wordly, Raney VI, 867
Wordon, Anna V, 1026
Woreley, Mary VI, 867
Woreley, Nehemiah VI, 867
Work, Anna IV, 1267
Work, Daniel IV, 1267
Work, Elizabeth IV, 1083
Workman, Ida M. I, 951
Workman, Mary I, 421
Workman, Mary I, 430
Workman, Oma Marie IV, 1344
Workman, Sarah IV, 105
Workman, Sarah IV, 116
Workman, Vergie V, 720
Works, Abram VI, 584
Works, Betsey VI, 584
Works, James VI, 548
Works, James W. VI, 548
Works, James W. VI, 584
Works, Sarah E. VI, 584
Works, Sarah Esther VI, 548
Worldly, John VI, 867
Worldly, Nancy VI, 867
Worley, Aaron IV, 117
Worley, Aaron IV, 134
Worley, Ann IV, 116
Worley, Ann IV, 117
Worley, Aron IV, 117
Worley, Asa IV, 117
Worley, Beulah Elma VI, 584
Worley, Bland V, 720
Worley, C. Bland V, 606
Worley, C. Bland V, 720
Worley, Caleb IV, 117
Worley, Cephalonia VI, 895
Worley, Charles B. V, 606
Worley, Charles B., Jr. V, 606
Worley, Charles Bland V, 606
Worley, Chas. Bland V, 720
Worley, Chas. W. V, 213
Worley, Clarence M. IV, 1267
Worley, Daniel VI, 867
Worley, Dorcas VI, 905
Worley, Effie V, 213
Worley, Eliza VI, 584
Worley, Eliza VI, 1020
Worley, Elizabeth II, 439
Worley, Elizabeth IV, 114
Worley, Elizabeth IV, 117
Worley, Elizabeth VI, 987
Worley, Elizabeth VI, 1015
Worley, Elizabeth VI, 1020
Worley, Ella V, 291
Worley, Ellen J. II, 911
Worley, Ellen J. II, 943
Worley, Ellen J. VI, 584
Worley, Ellen Janney II, 815
Worley, Emily VI, 1020
Worley, Florence II, 861
Worley, Florence II, 943
Worley, Florence VI, 584
Worley, Florence W. II, 861
Worley, Florence W. II, 943
Worley, Frances VI, 1020
Worley, Francis II, 439
Worley, Francis VI, 962
Worley, Francis VI, 1020
Worley, Freda V, 606
Worley, Freda O. V, 606
Worley, Freda O. V, 720
Worley, Freda Osborn V, 720
Worley, George H. VI, 886
Worley, George W. VI, 1020
Worley, Hannah II, 815
Worley, Hannah VI, 533
Worley, Hannah VI, 584
Worley, Hannah VI, 944
Worley, Hannah B. II, 943
Worley, Hannah M. II, 943
Worley, Hannah M. VI, 584
Worley, Henry I, 583
Worley, Henry II, 439
Worley, Henry VI, 931
Worley, Henry VI, 984
Worley, Henry VI, 1005
Worley, Henry VI, 1020
Worley, Henry A. VI, 900
Worley, Henry A. VI, 975
Worley, Hiram V, 144
Worley, Hiram V, 313
Worley, Jacob I, 963
Worley, Jacob I, 970
Worley, Jacob IV, 117
Worley, Jacob V, 144
Worley, Jacob V, 291
Worley, Jacob, Jr. V, 313
Worley, James B. V, 606
Worley, James M. VI, 1015
Worley, Jane VI, 584
Worley, Jane Walker VI, 487
Worley, Jane Walker VI, 584
Worley, Jemima VI, 1005
Worley, Joel VI, 944
Worley, Joel VI, 1020
Worley, John IV, 68
Worley, John IV, 114
Worley, John IV, 117
Worley, John V, 144
Worley, John V, 313
Worley, John VI, 1020
Worley, John C. VI, 953
Worley, John C. VI, 1020
Worley, John M. VI, 1020
Worley, Joseph VI, 867
Worley, Joshua VI, 847
Worley, Katy V, 144
Worley, Katy V, 313
Worley, Lewis Deardorff II, 815
Worley, Louisa VI, 1015
Worley, Lucinda V, 213
Worley, Lucy VI, 1020
Worley, Lurany VI, 1020
Worley, Lurena VI, 945
Worley, Luveney E. VI, 931
Worley, Lydia I, 550
Worley, Lydia I, 583
Worley, Lydia IV, 98
Worley, Lydia IV, 117
Worley, Lydia V, 465
Worley, Lydia VI, 584
Worley, Mariana VI, 584
Worley, Marianna II, 943
Worley, Martha G. VI, 983
Worley, Martha Susan VI, 923
Worley, Mary I, 963
Worley, Mary I, 970
Worley, Mary II, 439
Worley, Mary VI, 867
Worley, Mary VI, 987
Worley, Mary A. M. VI, 975
Worley, Mary Ann IV, 114
Worley, Mary Ann IV, 116
Worley, Mary Ann IV, 117
Worley, Mary Anna VI, 584
Worley, Mary B. VI, 1020
Worley, Mary Elizabeth IV, 1267
Worley, Mary Jane VI, 1021
Worley, Mary L. VI, 916
Worley, Mathew VI, 1015
Worley, Matthew VI, 961
Worley, Matthew VI, 987
Worley, Matthew VI, 1020
Worley, Milley VI, 1020
Worley, Milly V, 144
Worley, Milly V, 313
Worley, Moses VI, 867
Worley, Nathan II, 439
Worley, Nehemiah VI, 795
Worley, Nehemiah VI, 867
Worley, Patcy VI, 944
Worley, Patty V, 144
Worley, Phebe I, 963
Worley, Phebe I, 970
Worley, Phebe V, 144
Worley, Phebe V, 305
Worley, Phebe V, 313
Worley, Polley VI, 1015
Worley, Polly V, 313
Worley, Polly VI, 1020
Worley, Rachel I, 959
Worley, Rachel I, 970
Worley, Rachel VI, 867
Worley, Rachel VI, 1020
Worley, Rebecca V, 144
Worley, Rebecca V, 606
Worley, Rebeckah V, 222
Worley, Rebeckah V, 291
Worley, Rhoda VI, 867
Worley, Richard A. VI, 975
Worley, Richard A. VI, 1020
Worley, Rodah VI, 1020
Worley, Ruth V, 291
Worley, Sadie V, 144
Worley, Sally H. VI, 1020
Worley, Sarah II, 693
Worley, Sarah VI, 958
Worley, Sarah E. V, 133
Worley, Sarah E. V, 144
Worley, Sarah E. VI, 584
Worley, Sinthia VI, 1020
Worley, Stephen V, 313
Worley, Stephen V, 465
Worley, Susan R. II, 943
Worley, Susan R. VI, 584
Worley, Susanna VI, 1015
Worley, Susannah V, 468
Worley, Talbert VI, 1020
Worley, Thomas II, 693
Worley, Thomas V, 213
Worley, Thomas VI, 1020
Worley, William VI, 931
Worley, William VI, 975
Worley, William VI, 987
Worley, William VI, 1015
Worley, William VI, 1020
Worley, William D. VI, 1021
Worley, Wm. Mack V, 468
Worley, Z. VI, 922
Worley, Z. VI, 923
Worley, Z. VI, 952
Worley, Z. VI, 960
Worley, Z. VI, 963
Worley, Z. VI, 985
Worley, Z. VI, 996
Worley, Z. VI, 1008
Worley, Z. VI, 1009
Worley, Z. VI, 1014
Worley, Zach. VI, 974
Worley, Zachariah VI, 895
Worley, Zachariah VI, 905
Worley, Zachariah VI, 1020
Worline, Ida B. IV, 1196
Wormaldorf, David V, 291
Wormaldurf, David V, 291
Wormwag, Emma B. VI, 574
Wormwag, Emma B. VI, 584
Worner, Mary V, 288
Wornicks, Lettie A. V, 468
Wornstaff, Guy V, 468
Wornstaff, Mrs. M. L. IV, 119
Worral, Ann IV, 233
Worral, Anna Mariah II, 1041
Worral, Benjamin, Sr. IV, 308
Worral, Elizabeth II, 1041
Worral, Elizabeth IV, 1065
Worral, Elizabeth IV, 1083
Worral, Elwood II, 1041
Worral, George II, 1041
Worral, Isaac R. IV, 68
Worral, Jane II, 1041
Worral, Joseph C. II, 1041
Worral, Maria S. II, 1041
Worral, Martha II, 981
Worral, Martha II, 1041
Worral, Penn II, 1041
Worral, Sarah II, 318
Worral, Sarah II, 327
Worral, Thomas II, 981
Worral, Thomas II, 1041
Worral, Wd. Mary II, 1041
Worral, Wm. II, 694
Worrall, Aaron IV, 1122
Worrall, Abigail II, 817
Worrall, Alfred IV, 1122
Worrall, Amos IV, 1083
Worrall, Ann IV, 308
Worrall, Ann IV, 1083
Worrall, Ann Dillwyn II, 277
Worrall, Anna B. II, 943
Worrall, Anna Maria II, 1064
Worrall, Anna R. II, 943
Worrall, Benj. IV, 206
Worrall, Benjamin IV, 307
Worrall, Benjamin IV, 1083
Worrall, Benjamin IV, 1121
Worrall, Benjamin, Sr. IV, 108
Worrall, Caleb Pierce II, 694
Worrall, Clarkson IV, 1122
Worrall, Deborah IV, 1112
Worrall, Deborah IV, 1122
Worrall, Deborah V, 874
Worrall, Deborah, Jr. V, 874
Worrall, Edward IV, 1122

all, Edward P. IV, 1122
all, Eleanor IV, 307
all, Eleanor IV, 308
all, Eleanor IV, 1083
all, Eleanor IV, 1107
all, Eleanor IV, 1122
all, Eliza IV, 1122
all, Elizabeth II, 694
all, Elizabeth II, 724
all, Elizabeth II, 1034
all, Elizabeth IV, 1083
all, Elizabeth IV, 1093
all, Elizabeth IV, 1106
all, Elizabeth IV, 1122
all, Elizabeth P. IV, 1122
rall, Elwood IV, 1083
rall, Elwood IV, 1122
rall, Elwood P. II, 1064
rall, Elwood R. IV, 1112
rall, Elwood R. IV, 1122
rall, Esther IV, 1083
rall, George II, 646
rall, George II, 694
rall, George F. II, 1064
rall, Hannah IV, 1078
rall, Hannah IV, 1083
rall, Hannah Ann II, 828
rall, Hannah Ann II, 943
rall, Howard II, 439
rall, Isaac II, 694
rall, Isaac IV, 308
rall, Isaac IV, 1083
rall, Isaac IV, 1088
rall, Isaac IV, 1122
rrall, Isaiah, Jr. II, 694
rrall, Jane II, 646
rrall, Jane II, 694
rrall, Jane II, 724
rrall, Jesse IV, 1122
rrall, John II, 693
rrall, John IV, 233
rrall, John IV, 307
rrall, John IV, 1083
rrall, John IV, 1112
rrall, John IV, 1121
rrall, John IV, 1122
rrall, Jonathan II, 439
rrall, Jonathan II, 694
rrall, Jonathan IV, 307
rrall, Jonathan IV, 308
rrall, Jonathan IV, 1083
rrall, Jonathan IV, 1122
orrall, Jonathan G. IV, 1083
orrall, Jonathan G. IV, 1122
orrall, Jonathan J. IV, 1121
orrall, Joseph IV, 1122
orrall, Joseph G. IV, 1121
orrall, Lucetta IV, 1094
orrall, Lucetta IV, 1121
orrall, Lucetta IV, 1122
orrall, Lydia IV, 1083
orrall, Lydia IV, 1094
orrall, Lydia IV, 1122
orrall, Margaret IV, 1083
orrall, Margaret IV, 1087
orrall, Margaret IV, 1101
orrall, Margaret IV, 1122
orrall, Martha II, 327
orrall, Martha IV, 266
orrall, Martha IV, 307
orrall, Martha IV, 1083
orrall, Martha IV, 1089
orrall, Martha IV, 1093
orrall, Martha IV, 1101
orrall, Martha IV, 1117
orrall, Martha IV, 1122
orrall, Mary II, 364
Vorrall, Mary II, 646
Vorrall, Mary II, 693
Vorrall, Mary II, 694
Vorrall, Mary II, 787
Vorrall, Mary II, 796
Vorrall, Mary II, 817
Vorrall, Mary IV, 1083
Vorrall, Mary IV, 1121
Vorrall, Mary IV, 1122
Vorrall, Mary Ann II, 828
Vorrall, Mary Ann II, 943
Vorrall, Mary E. IV, 1122
Vorrall, Mary Ellen IV, 1115
Worrall, Mary Ellen IV, 1122
Worrall, Miriam IV, 1083
Worrall, Mordecai IV, 308
Worrall, Mordecai IV, 1083
Worrall, Mordecai IV, 1088
Worrall, Mordecai IV, 1122
Worrall, Peninah IV, 1122
Worrall, Peninah F. IV, 1107
Worrall, Peter II, 190
Worrall, Peter II, 277
Worrall, Peter II, 506
Worrall, Peter II, 693
Worrall, Peter II, 817
Worrall, Priscilla IV, 206
Worrall, Priscilla IV, 307
Worrall, Priscilla IV, 1083
Worrall, Prissilla IV, 1121
Worrall, Rachel IV, 1088
Worrall, Rachel IV, 1122
Worrall, Rachel E. IV, 1122
Worrall, Rachel Emily IV, 1111
Worrall, Rachel Emily IV, 1122
Worrall, Rebecca IV, 233
Worrall, Rebecca IV, 307
Worrall, Rebecca IV, 308
Worrall, Rebecca IV, 1083
Worrall, Rebecca IV, 1089
Worrall, Rebecca IV, 1122
Worrall, Rebecca IV, 1123
Worrall, Rebecca B. IV, 1122
Worrall, Richard II, 693
Worrall, Richard T. II, 828
Worrall, Richard T. II, 943
Worrall, Robert II, 694
Worrall, Ruth IV, 1083
Worrall, Ruth IV, 1088
Worrall, Ruth IV, 1089
Worrall, Ruth IV, 1109
Worrall, Ruth IV, 1114
Worrall, Ruth IV, 1120
Worrall, Ruth IV, 1121
Worrall, Ruth IV, 1122
Worrall, Ruth Ann IV, 1112
Worrall, Ruth Ann IV, 1122
Worrall, Ruthann IV, 1122
Worrall, Sarah II, 693
Worrall, Sarah IV, 1071
Worrall, Sarah IV, 1083
Worrall, Sarah IV, 1088
Worrall, Sarah IV, 1122
Worrall, Sarah Ellen IV, 1122
Worrall, Sarah G. IV, 1122
Worrall, Susanna II, 693
Worrall, Susanna IV, 1083
Worrall, Susannah II, 190
Worrall, Susannah II, 277
Worrall, Susannah IV, 1107
Worrall, Susannah IV, 1122
Worrall, Thomas II, 439
Worrall, Thomas II, 646
Worrall, Thomas II, 693
Worrall, Thomas II, 694
Worrall, Wd. Susannah II, 506
Worrall, William IV, 1122
Worrall, William P. IV, 1122
Worrall, Winfield S. II, 943
Worrall, Wm. IV, 1122
Worrall, Wm. P. IV, 1122
Worrall, Zebulon IV, 266
Worrall, Zebulon IV, 307
Worrall, Zebulon IV, 1083
Worrall, Zebulon IV, 1089
Worrall, Zebulon IV, 1093
Worrall, Zebulon IV, 1101
Worrall, Zebulon IV, 1117
Worrall, Zebulon IV, 1122
Worrall, Zebulon, Jr. IV, 1122
Worrel, Ann IV, 307
Worrel, Benjamin IV, 117
Worrel, Benjamin IV, 165
Worrel, Benjamin IV, 307
Worrel, Bettie I, 320
Worrel, Edward VI, 90
Worrel, Edward E. VI, 90
Worrel, Eleanor IV, 68
Worrel, Eleanor IV, 117
Worrel, Eleanor IV, 165
Worrel, Eleanor IV, 307
Worrel, Elijah VI, 90
Worrel, Elizabeth VI, 459
Worrel, George IV, 307
Worrel, Isaac R. IV, 68
Worrel, Isaac R. IV, 308
Worrel, Jacob IV, 307
Worrel, Jane II, 439
Worrel, John IV, 307
Worrel, Jonathan II, 583
Worrel, Jonathan II, 694
Worrel, Jonathan IV, 165
Worrel, Jonathan IV, 307
Worrel, Jonathan VI, 459
Worrel, Joseph IV, 307
Worrel, Kezia VI, 459
Worrel, Keziah VI, 459
Worrel, Mary VI, 90
Worrel, Nathaniel IV, 165
Worrel, Nathaniel IV, 307
Worrel, Sarah II, 583
Worrel, Sarah II, 694
Worrel, Sarah IV, 165
Worrel, Sarah IV, 290
Worrel, Sarah IV, 307
Worrel, Sarah IV, 308
Worrel, Susanna II, 693
Worrel, William VI, 90
Worrell, ??? IV, 307
Worrell, Abigail II, 694
Worrell, Amos IV, 308
Worrell, Amos IV, 1083
Worrell, Ann IV, 307
Worrell, Ann IV, 308
Worrell, Ann IV, 466
Worrell, Ann IV, 506
Worrell, Ann IV, 1083
Worrell, Anna B. II, 943
Worrell, Anna R. II, 943
Worrell, Benjamin IV, 117
Worrell, Benjamin IV, 307
Worrell, Benjamin IV, 308
Worrell, Benjamin IV, 790
Worrell, Benjamin IV, 1083
Worrell, Benjamin, Jr. IV, 308
Worrell, Benjamin, Sr. IV, 308
Worrell, Bettie I, 320
Worrell, Burgess IV, 308
Worrell, Caleb Pierce II, 694
Worrell, Chas. D. II, 828
Worrell, Comly II, 327
Worrell, Daniel IV, 307
Worrell, Daniel IV, 466
Worrell, Daniel IV, 506
Worrell, Daniel L. II, 327
Worrell, David IV, 473
Worrell, David IV, 506
Worrell, Deborah V, 829
Worrell, Deborah V, 873
Worrell, Demas II, 327
Worrell, Demas C. II, 327
Worrell, Edward VI, 90
Worrell, Eleanor IV, 307
Worrell, Eleanor IV, 308
Worrell, Eleanor IV, 790
Worrell, Eleanor IV, 1083
Worrell, Eleanor IV, 1103
Worrell, Elenor IV, 790
Worrell, Eliza Ann IV, 307
Worrell, Elizabeth II, 439
Worrell, Elizabeth II, 693
Worrell, Elizabeth II, 694
Worrell, Elizabeth IV, 307
Worrell, Elizabeth IV, 308
Worrell, Elizabeth IV, 506
Worrell, Elizabeth IV, 790
Worrell, Elizabeth IV, 1083
Worrell, Elizabeth IV, 1103
Worrell, Elizabeth VI, 384
Worrell, Elizabeth S. II, 439
Worrell, Elizanne IV, 506
Worrell, Elmina IV, 482
Worrell, Elmina IV, 506
Worrell, Elwood IV, 308
Worrell, Esther IV, 308
Worrell, Esther IV, 1050
Worrell, Esther IV, 1083
Worrell, George II, 694
Worrell, George II, 1016
Worrell, George II, 1041
Worrell, George IV, 307
Worrell, George IV, 308
Worrell, George IV, 790
Worrell, George V, 829
Worrell, George V, 873
Worrell, Grace II, 439
Worrell, Grace II, 694
Worrell, Hannah II, 439
Worrell, Hannah II, 693
Worrell, Hannah II, 694
Worrell, Hannah IV, 308
Worrell, Hannah IV, 1083
Worrell, Hannah Ann II, 828
Worrell, Hannah Ann II, 943
Worrell, Helen E. III, 212
Worrell, Howard II, 439
Worrell, Isaac II, 694
Worrell, Isaac IV, 307
Worrell, Isaac IV, 308
Worrell, Isaac IV, 1083
Worrell, Isaac R. IV, 308
Worrell, Isaiah II, 693
Worrell, Isaiah II, 694
Worrell, Isaiah IV, 307
Worrell, Isaiah IV, 506
Worrell, Isaiah, Jr. II, 694
Worrell, Isaiah, Jr. IV, 506
Worrell, Jacob IV, 307
Worrell, James C. IV, 506
Worrell, Jane II, 439
Worrell, Jane II, 476
Worrell, Jane II, 693
Worrell, Jane II, 694
Worrell, Jane II, 1016
Worrell, Jane II, 1041
Worrell, John II, 693
Worrell, John IV, 307
Worrell, John IV, 308
Worrell, John IV, 790
Worrell, Jonathan II, 439
Worrell, Jonathan II, 694
Worrell, Jonathan IV, 307
Worrell, Jonathan IV, 308
Worrell, Jonathan IV, 790
Worrell, Jonathan IV, 1083
Worrell, Jonathan IV, 1103
Worrell, Jonathan VI, 384
Worrell, Joseph II, 327
Worrell, Joseph IV, 307
Worrell, Joseph IV, 308
Worrell, Joseph IV, 790
Worrell, Joseph C. II, 1016
Worrell, Joseph C. II, 1041
Worrell, Joseph Cicero II, 694
Worrell, Joseph L. II, 327
Worrell, Josephus C. II, 828
Worrell, Keziah VI, 384
Worrell, Lydia IV, 308
Worrell, Lydia IV, 1083
Worrell, Margaret IV, 307
Worrell, Margaret IV, 308
Worrell, Maria S. II, 1016
Worrell, Maria S. II, 1041
Worrell, Maris II, 805
Worrell, Martha II, 327
Worrell, Martha IV, 307
Worrell, Martha IV, 308
Worrell, Martha L. II, 327
Worrell, Mary II, 693
Worrell, Mary II, 694
Worrell, Mary II, 1027
Worrell, Mary IV, 278
Worrell, Mary IV, 308
Worrell, Mary Ann II, 828
Worrell, Mary Ann II, 943
Worrell, Mary E. V, 291
Worrell, Mary Sermon II, 694
Worrell, Mary T. II, 327
Worrell, Mercy II, 439
Worrell, Mercy II, 694
Worrell, Miriam IV, 308
Worrell, Miriam IV, 1083
Worrell, Mordecai IV, 307
Worrell, Mordecai IV, 308
Worrell, Mordecai IV, 1083
Worrell, Nancy I, 320
Worrell, Nathaniel IV, 307
Worrell, Nathaniel IV, 308
Worrell, Nathaniel IV, 790
Worrell, Peter II, 190
Worrell, Peter II, 693
Worrell, Priscilla IV, 307
Worrell, Priscilla IV, 308
Worrell, Priscilla IV, 1083
Worrell, Rachel II, 439
Worrell, Rachel II, 694
Worrell, Rachel Ann IV, 1131
Worrell, Rachel Ann IV, 1140
Worrell, Rebecca II, 439
Worrell, Rebecca II, 476
Worrell, Rebecca II, 694
Worrell, Rebecca IV, 307
Worrell, Rebecca IV, 308
Worrell, Rebecca IV, 1058
Worrell, Rebecca IV, 1083
Worrell, Richard II, 439
Worrell, Richard II, 693
Worrell, Richard T. II, 828
Worrell, Richard T. II, 943
Worrell, Robert II, 439
Worrell, Robert II, 476
Worrell, Robert II, 693
Worrell, Robert II, 694
Worrell, Ruth IV, 308
Worrell, Ruth IV, 1050
Worrell, Ruth IV, 1083
Worrell, Ruth V, 291
Worrell, Samuel II, 439
Worrell, Sarah II, 327
Worrell, Sarah II, 693
Worrell, Sarah II, 694
Worrell, Sarah IV, 307
Worrell, Sarah IV, 308
Worrell, Sarah IV, 473
Worrell, Sarah IV, 506
Worrell, Sarah IV, 790
Worrell, Sarah IV, 1083
Worrell, Sarah IV, 1122
Worrell, Sarah V, 873
Worrell, Sarah G. IV, 506
Worrell, Sarah L. II, 327
Worrell, Sarah, Jr. IV, 506
Worrell, Sarah, Sr. IV, 506
Worrell, Susanna II, 693
Worrell, Susanna IV, 506
Worrell, Susannah II, 190
Worrell, Susannah IV, 506
Worrell, Thomas II, 439
Worrell, Thomas II, 693
Worrell, Thomas II, 694
Worrell, Thomas IV, 307
Worrell, Thomas IV, 308
Worrell, Thomas IV, 1050
Worrell, Warrick IV, 506
Worrell, Wd. Elvira Matilda II, 805
Worrell, Wd. Mary II, 1041
Worrell, Wd. Rachel II, 439
Worrell, Wd. Susanna II, 439
Worrell, William B. V, 291
Worrell, William P. IV, 307
Worrell, Winfield S. II, 943
Worrell, Wm. II, 694
Worrell, Zebulon IV, 307
Worrell, Zebulon IV, 308
Worrell, Zebulon IV, 310
Worrick, Hannah II, 68
Worrick, Hannah II, 112
Worrick, Thomas II, 68
Worrick, Thomas II, 112
Worril, Abigail II, 694
Worril, Elizabeth II, 675
Worril, Elizabeth II, 693
Worril, Hannah II, 633
Worril, Hannah II, 693
Worril, Jane II, 693
Worril, Rachel II, 580
Worril, Rachel II, 694
Worril, Richard II, 503
Worril, Richard II, 633
Worril, Richard II, 675
Worril, Richard II, 693
Worril, Robert II, 503
Worril, Robert II, 675
Worril, Robert II, 693
Worril, Robert II, 694
Worril, Wd. Jane II, 503
Worrill, Elizabeth II, 694
Worrill, Elizabeth II, 696
Worrill, Hannah II, 694
Worrill, Martha II, 992
Worrill, Martha II, 1041
Worrill, Rachel II, 694
Worrill, Rachel II, 696
Worrill, Robert II, 439
Worrill, Robert II, 694
Worrill, Robert II, 696
Worrill, Sarah II, 693
Worrill, Wd. Rachel II, 439
Worriloe, Elizabeth II, 461
Worriloe, Elizabeth II, 694
Worriloe, Susanna II, 694
Worriloe, Thomas II, 694
Worrilow, Susanna II, 694
Worrilow, Thomas II, 472
Worrilow, Thomas II, 694
Worrils, Thomas II, 439
Worrils, Wd. Susanna II, 439
Worron, David I, 1111
Worron, Hannary I, 1111
Worron, Henry I, 1111
Worron, James I, 1111
Worron, James, Sr. I, 1111
Worron, Margreat I, 1111
Worron, Reachel I, 1111
Worron, Sarah I, 1111
Worron, Tabitha I, 1111
Worsham, Lon I, 933
Worsham, Martha VI, 808
Worsham, William VI, 808
Worshburn, Benjamin IV, 1146
Worshburn, Huldah IV, 1146
Worshburn, Lavina B. IV, 1146
Worshburn, Mary IV, 1187
Worshburn, Philena IV, 1162
Worshburn, Philena IV, 1191
Worstal, Ann II, 1006
Worstal, Ann II, 1041
Worstall, Ann II, 1041
Worstall, Anna II, 783
Worstall, James II, 694
Worstall, James II, 1064
Worstall, James, Jr. II, 1064
Worstall, Jane II, 1064
Worstall, John II, 973
Worstall, John II, 1041
Worstall, John II, 1064
Worstall, Joseph II, 1064
Worstall, Mary II, 1064
Worstall, Mary M. II, 1064
Worstall, Rachel II, 1064
Worstall, Robert II, 973
Worstall, Ruth II, 973
Worstall, Ruth II, 1041
Worstall, Ruth II, 1064
Worstall, Samuel II, 1041
Worstall, Sarah II, 694
Worstall, Susanna II, 1064

Worstel, Ann IV, 308
Worstel, Susannah IV, 1117
Worstel, Susannah IV, 1122
Worstell, Ann IV, 308
Worstell, Clarence IV, 308
Worstell, John IV, 308
Worstell, Lucinda IV, 1122
Worstell, Mary IV, 1117
Worstell, Mary IV, 1122
Worstell, Ruth IV, 308
Worstell, Ruth Ann IV, 308
Worstell, Sarah C. IV, 308
Worstell, Sarah E. IV, 308
Worstell, Susan IV, 1122
Worstell, Susannah IV, 1122
Worster, Eunice IV, 1386
Worth, Abigail I, 693
Worth, Abigail I, 810
Worth, Abigail I, 846
Worth, Achsa I, 843
Worth, Achsa I, 846
Worth, Achsah I, 598
Worth, Achsah I, 846
Worth, Adrian I, 671
Worth, Andrew G. V, 291
Worth, Anna I, 522
Worth, Anna I, 583
Worth, Anna I, 672
Worth, Anna I, 693
Worth, Anna III, 225
Worth, Anna III, 368
Worth, Anna V. III, 368
Worth, Annie H. I, 643
Worth, Annie Henley I, 628
Worth, Archibald Swain I, 522
Worth, Barzilla G. I, 693
Worth, Belinda I, 693
Worth, Benjamin III, 368
Worth, Caroline IV, 980
Worth, Caroline H. III, 368
Worth, Charles I, 643
Worth, Charles I, 846
Worth, Clara I, 951
Worth, Cora I, 523
Worth, Cora I, 931
Worth, Cora M. I, 522
Worth, Cora M. I, 583
Worth, Cora Worth I, 583
Worth, D. Adrian I, 522
Worth, Daniel I, 522
Worth, Daniel I, 523
Worth, Daniel I, 529
Worth, Daniel I, 544
Worth, Daniel I, 583
Worth, Daniel I, 671
Worth, Daniel I, 672
Worth, Daniel I, 692
Worth, Daniel I, 693
Worth, Daniel I, 846
Worth, Daniel A. I, 522
Worth, Daniel A. I, 583
Worth, David I, 671
Worth, David I, 810
Worth, David I, 846
Worth, David W. I, 544
Worth, David W. I, 583
Worth, David W. I, 906
Worth, Dr. David W. I, 906
Worth, Edgar W. I, 522
Worth, Edgar W. I, 583
Worth, Edward H. III, 368
Worth, Edward Hallowell III, 225
Worth, Elihu I, 671
Worth, Elma IV, 1196
Worth, Emily Ann I, 671
Worth, Emily L. I, 522
Worth, Emily L. I, 529
Worth, Emily L. I, 583
Worth, Eunice I, 522
Worth, Eunice I, 523
Worth, Eunice I, 583
Worth, Eunice I, 625
Worth, Eunice I, 640
Worth, Eunice I, 643
Worth, Eunice I, 671
Worth, Eunice I, 672
Worth, Eunice I, 692
Worth, Eunice I, 810
Worth, Eunice I, 846
Worth, Eunice E. R. I, 522
Worth, Eunice E. R. I, 583
Worth, Eunice Hussey I, 671
Worth, Eunice L. I, 643
Worth, Eunice N. I, 762
Worth, Eunice N. I, 772
Worth, Eveline I, 693
Worth, Flora I, 867
Worth, Flora I, 936
Worth, Flora I, 951
Worth, Flora M. I, 874
Worth, Flora M. I, 906
Worth, Florina I, 944
Worth, Florina I, 951
Worth, Florina G. I, 867
Worth, Francis I, 522
Worth, Francis I, 583
Worth, George I, 846
Worth, George S. VI, 792
Worth, Herbert T. I, 867
Worth, Hiram I, 690
Worth, Hiram I, 693
Worth, Hiram I, 772
Worth, Hiram B. I, 643
Worth, Hiram C. I, 583
Worth, Hiram C. I, 693
Worth, Hiram C. I, 867
Worth, Hiram C. I, 906
Worth, Hiram C. I, 936
Worth, Hiram Coffin I, 628
Worth, Hiram Coffin I, 671
Worth, Jethro I, 795
Worth, Jethro I, 797
Worth, Jethro I, 846
Worth, Joane II, 275
Worth, Joane II, 277
Worth, Job I, 457
Worth, Job I, 583
Worth, Job I, 671
Worth, Job I, 672
Worth, Job I, 684
Worth, Job I, 692
Worth, Job I, 693
Worth, Job I, 906
Worth, Jonah I, 583
Worth, Joseph I, 583
Worth, Joseph I, 671
Worth, Joseph I, 692
Worth, Joseph I, 867
Worth, Joseph I, 951
Worth, Joseph S. I, 693
Worth, Joseph S. I, 867
Worth, Joseph S. I, 874
Worth, Joseph S. I, 906
Worth, Joseph S. I, 936
Worth, Joseph S. I, 951
Worth, Joseph Swain I, 671
Worth, Joseph, Jr. I, 692
Worth, Joseph, Jr. I, 951
Worth, Judith I, 583
Worth, Judith I, 692
Worth, Kezia I, 1000
Worth, Keziah I, 971
Worth, Laura Ann I, 693
Worth, Laura D. I, 671
Worth, Laura D. B. I, 522
Worth, Laura D. B. I, 583
Worth, Louisa I, 743
Worth, Lula IV, 1196
Worth, Lydia I, 598
Worth, Lydia I, 671
Worth, Lydia I, 672
Worth, Lydia I, 690
Worth, Lydia I, 692
Worth, Lydia I, 693
Worth, Lydia I, 846
Worth, Lydia I, 907
Worth, Margaret III, 368
Worth, Martha Jane I, 671
Worth, Mary I, 522
Worth, Mary I, 672
Worth, Mary I, 797
Worth, Mary I, 846
Worth, Mary I, 936
Worth, Mary II, 260
Worth, Mary V, 943
Worth, Mary Cladora I, 671
Worth, Mary Ella I, 671
Worth, Matilda I, 558
Worth, Matilda I, 583
Worth, Matilda I, 678
Worth, Matilda I, 692
Worth, Matilda I, 846
Worth, Matilda I, 907
Worth, Matilda V, 788
Worth, Minnie I, 951
Worth, Miriam I, 676
Worth, Miriam I, 693
Worth, Nettie V, 1026
Worth, Norah Leland VI, 792
Worth, Paul I, 915
Worth, Percy I, 522
Worth, Phebe I, 583
Worth, Phebe I, 628
Worth, Phebe I, 673
Worth, Phebe I, 690
Worth, Phebe I, 693
Worth, Phebe I, 772
Worth, Phebe I, 867
Worth, Phebe I, 906
Worth, Phebe I, 915
Worth, Phebe I, 936
Worth, Phebe III, 368
Worth, Phebe A. I, 867
Worth, Phebe Gertrude I, 951
Worth, Phebe S. I, 693
Worth, Phebe Swain I, 671
Worth, Phoeby I, 951
Worth, Rachel I, 544
Worth, Rachel I, 583
Worth, Rachel I, 671
Worth, Rachel I, 906
Worth, Rachel I, 977
Worth, Randolph I, 583
Worth, Reuben I, 672
Worth, Reuben I, 690
Worth, Reuben I, 693
Worth, Rhoda I, 457
Worth, Rhoda I, 598
Worth, Rhoda I, 671
Worth, Rhoda I, 672
Worth, Rhoda I, 684
Worth, Rhoda I, 690
Worth, Rhoda I, 692
Worth, Rhoda I, 693
Worth, Rhoda M. I, 583
Worth, Rhoda M. I, 643
Worth, Rhoda M. I, 693
Worth, Rhoda Macy I, 628
Worth, Rhoda Macy I, 671
Worth, Roda I, 846
Worth, Rodah I, 846
Worth, Ruben I, 672
Worth, Ruth I, 622
Worth, Ruth I, 624
Worth, Ruth I, 639
Worth, Ruth I, 643
Worth, Ruth M. I, 643
Worth, Sallie I, 643
Worth, Sallie M. I, 583
Worth, Sallie M. I, 624
Worth, Sallie M. I, 625
Worth, Sallie M. I, 643
Worth, Sallie M. I, 762
Worth, Sallie M. I, 772
Worth, Sallie Mallette I, 628
Worth, Sarah I, 274
Worth, Sarah I, 583
Worth, Sarah I, 671
Worth, Sarah I, 693
Worth, Sarah I, 906
Worth, Sarah IV, 1196
Worth, Sarah J. IV, 1196
Worth, Silas I, 558
Worth, Silas I, 583
Worth, Silas I, 846
Worth, Silas I, 907
Worth, Silas V, 788
Worth, Stephen I, 671
Worth, Susanna II, 255
Worth, Susanna II, 277
Worth, Thaddeus M. I, 583
Worth, Thomas I, 672
Worth, Thomas C. I, 693
Worth, W. H. I, 643
Worth, William I, 341
Worth, William I, 522
Worth, William I, 583
Worth, William I, 643
Worth, William I, 671
Worth, William I, 672
Worth, William I, 673
Worth, William I, 692
Worth, William I, 693
Worth, William II, 260
Worth, William II, 275
Worth, William II, 277
Worth, William C. I, 867
Worth, William H. I, 331
Worth, William H. I, 625
Worth, William H. I, 643
Worth, William H. I, 671
Worth, William H. I, 693
Worth, William H. I, 762
Worth, William H. I, 772
Worth, William Henry I, 624
Worth, William Henry I, 628
Worth, Williard Turner I, 951
Worth, Wm. P. III, 368
Worth, Zeno I, 671
Worth, Zeno I, 693
Worthenton, Sarah II, 1036
Worthenton, Sarah II, 1041
Worthin, Richard II, 449
Worthing, Edmund II, 449
Worthing, Elizabeth II, 449
Worthing, Richard II, 449
Worthing, Sarah I, 935
Worthington, ???ildred IV, 1083
Worthington, Alice II, 694
Worthington, Amanda A. IV, 1122
Worthington, Amy Leanna IV, 459
Worthington, Andrew Conard II, 828
Worthington, Ann IV, 1055
Worthington, Ann IV, 1064
Worthington, Ann IV, 1067
Worthington, Ann IV, 1080
Worthington, Ann IV, 1083
Worthington, Ann IV, 1122
Worthington, Anna IV, 359
Worthington, Anna IV, 1080
Worthington, Anna IV, 1083
Worthington, Anna IV, 1084
Worthington, Armelda V, 292
Worthington, Armilla V, 292
Worthington, Arthur V, 292
Worthington, Caleb Engle IV, 1140
Worthington, Daniel II, 439
Worthington, Daniel II, 691
Worthington, Daniel II, 694
Worthington, Easther II, 85
Worthington, Easther II, 112
Worthington, Edwin IV, 1123
Worthington, Edwin T. IV, 1122
Worthington, Edwin T. IV, 1123
Worthington, Elisabeth II, 694
Worthington, Elisha IV, 1058
Worthington, Eliza A. IV, 1123
Worthington, Eliza A. IV, 1133
Worthington, Eliza A. IV, 1140
Worthington, Eliza Ann IV, 1083
Worthington, Eliza Ann IV, 1084
Worthington, Eliza Ann IV, 1123
Worthington, Eliza J. IV, 1098
Worthington, Eliza J. IV, 1122
Worthington, Eliza J. IV, 1123
Worthington, Elizabeth II, 58
Worthington, Elizabeth II, 112
Worthington, Elizabeth II, 439
Worthington, Elizabeth IV, 1050
Worthington, Elizabeth IV, 1056
Worthington, Elizabeth IV, 1067
Worthington, Elizabeth IV, 1072
Worthington, Elizabeth IV, 1073
Worthington, Elizabeth IV, 1083
Worthington, Elizabeth IV, 1084
Worthington, Elizabeth IV, 1089
Worthington, Elizabeth IV, 1096
Worthington, Elizabeth IV, 1122
Worthington, Elizabeth IV, 1123
Worthington, Elizabeth IV, 1133
Worthington, Elizabeth IV, 1372
Worthington, Elizabeth IV, 1386
Worthington, Elizabeth Brown IV, 1084
Worthington, Elizabeth Brown IV, 1123
Worthington, Elizabeth T. VI, 792
Worthington, Elma IV, 1083
Worthington, Elma IV, 1095
Worthington, Elma IV, 1123
Worthington, Ephraim I, 754
Worthington, Ephraim I, 772
Worthington, Ephraim II, 58
Worthington, Ephraim II, 112
Worthington, Esther II, 783
Worthington, Evaline IV, 1119
Worthington, Evaline IV, 1123
Worthington, Frederick IV, 1123
Worthington, Grace B. IV, 1123
Worthington, Grace T. IV, 1055
Worthington, Grace T. IV, 1083
Worthington, Grace T. IV, 1084
Worthington, Hannah II, 810
Worthington, Hannah II, 943
Worthington, Henry W. II, 777
Worthington, Isaac V, 606
Worthington, Isaac V, 720
Worthington, J. Kent III, 150
Worthington, J. Kent III, 368
Worthington, Jacob IV, 420
Worthington, Jacob IV, 1050
Worthington, Jacob IV, 1083
Worthington, Jacob IV, 1084
Worthington, Jael II, 126
Worthington, James IV, 1228
Worthington, Jeremiah IV, 1372
Worthington, Jeremiah IV, 1386
Worthington, Jesse IV, 1073
Worthington, Jesse IV, 1083
Worthington, Jesse IV, 1084
Worthington, Jesse IV, 1095
Worthington, Jesse IV, 1122
Worthington, Jesse J. IV, 1123
Worthington, John II, 810
Worthington, Joseph II, 439
Worthington, Joseph II, 694
Worthington, Josephine III, 368
Worthington, Josephine G. III, 150
Worthington, Josephine G. III, 368
Worthington, Joshua H. III,
Worthington, Joshua H. III,
Worthington, Leanna IV, 459
Worthington, Louisa M. IV, 1
Worthington, Lydia IV, 420
Worthington, Lydia IV, 580
Worthington, Lydia IV, 601
Worthington, Lydia IV, 1058
Worthington, Lydia IV, 1083
Worthington, Lydia IV, 1084
Worthington, Lydia Gibbons IV, 1084
Worthington, Lydia S. IV, 108
Worthington, Lydia S. IV, 112
Worthington, Malissa J. V, 60
Worthington, Margaret Elizabe VI, 667
Worthington, Mary II, 691
Worthington, Mary II, 694
Worthington, Mary IV, 1083
Worthington, Mary IV, 1084
Worthington, Mary IV, 1096
Worthington, Mary IV, 1123
Worthington, Mary V, 606
Worthington, Mary J. IV, 420
Worthington, Mary J. IV, 459
Worthington, Mary J. IV, 580
Worthington, Mary J. IV, 601
Worthington, Mary J. IV, 1084
Worthington, Mary T. IV, 1131
Worthington, Mary T. IV, 1140
Worthington, Mildred IV, 1072
Worthington, Mildred IV, 1111
Worthington, Mildred IV, 1123
Worthington, Mildreth IV, 108
Worthington, Nancy V, 292
Worthington, Priscilla IV, 420
Worthington, Priscilla IV, 1067
Worthington, Priscilla IV, 1083
Worthington, Rachel II, 784
Worthington, Rachel IV, 1073
Worthington, Rachel IV, 1083
Worthington, Rachel IV, 1084
Worthington, Rachel IV, 1095
Worthington, Rachel IV, 1114
Worthington, Rachel IV, 1122
Worthington, Rachel IV, 1123
Worthington, Rachel V, 292
Worthington, Rachel Schofield IV, 1123
Worthington, Rachell II, 439
Worthington, Rebecca II, 112
Worthington, Rebecca II, 715
Worthington, Rebecca IV, 430
Worthington, Rebecca IV, 444
Worthington, Rebecca IV, 1073
Worthington, Rebecca IV, 1083
Worthington, Rebecca IV, 1122
Worthington, Rebecca IV, 1123
Worthington, Rebecca P. IV, 112
Worthington, Reuben IV, 601
Worthington, Reuben E. IV, 108
Worthington, Rheuben IV, 1084
Worthington, Rhoda C. V, 606
Worthington, Rhoda C. V, 720
Worthington, Robert II, 112
Worthington, Robert II, 439
Worthington, Robert IV, 1228
Worthington, Robert, Jr. VI, 459
Worthington, Samuel I, 754
Worthington, Samuel I, 772
Worthington, Samuel II, 112
Worthington, Samuel W. I, 772
Worthington, Sarah II, 112
Worthington, Sarah II, 439
Worthington, Sarah II, 694
Worthington, Sarah II, 977
Worthington, Sarah II, 1041
Worthington, Sarah III, 81
Worthington, Sarah III, 368
Worthington, Sarah IV, 308
Worthington, Sarah IV, 1058
Worthington, Sarah IV, 1064
Worthington, Sarah IV, 1083
Worthington, Sarah IV, 1122
Worthington, Sarah IV, 1372
Worthington, Sarah IV, 1386
Worthington, Sarah V, 226
Worthington, Sarah V, 292
Worthington, Sarah Ann IV, 1083
Worthington, Sarah Ann IV, 1084
Worthington, Sarah C. III, 368
Worthington, Sarah E. V, 566
Worthington, Sarah Ellen V, 606
Worthington, Sarah Ellen V, 676
Worthington, Sarah Ellin V, 568
Worthington, Sarah Ellin V, 606
Worthington, Sarah W. IV, 1097
Worthington, Sarah W. IV, 1123

hington, Susannah H.
II, 368
hington, Thomas
efferson IV, 1122
hington, Walter IV, 1123
hington, Walter Guy
V, 1123
hington, Wd. Hannah
ohnson II, 828
hington, Wd. Margaret
I, 810
hington, William IV, 1083
hington, William IV, 1096
hington, Wm. IV, 1067
hington, Wm. IV, 1072
hington, Wm. IV, 1073
thington, Wm. IV, 1083
thington, Wm. IV, 1084
thington, Wm. IV, 1123
thington, Wm. IV, 1133
thington, Wm. C. III, 368
thington, Wm. C. V, 606
thington, Wm. Clark V, 606
thington, Wm. E. IV, 1123
thington, Wm. H. IV, 1123
thington, Zenas IV, 601
thington, Zenas IV, 1055
thington, Zenas IV, 1080
thington, Zenas IV, 1083
thington, Zenas IV, 1084
thington, Zinas Ruben
Sarah Ann IV, 601
thy, Edith IV, 308
thy, Edith IV, 506
rthy, Edward IV, 308
rthy, Edward IV, 506
rthy, Elizabeth IV, 308
rthy, Franklin IV, 308
rthy, Franklin IV, 506
rthy, Jane IV, 501
rthy, John IV, 308
rthy, John IV, 501
rthy, John IV, 506
rthy, Margaret IV, 308
rthy, Margaret IV, 501
rthy, Margaret IV, 506
rtman, Elva V, 1026
rtman, Lester V, 1026
ssencroft, Grace II, 449
ssencroft, William II, 449
ssoncraft, Charles II, 449
ten, Abijah V, 874
ten, Andrew V, 874
ten, Henry V, 874
ten, Isam V, 874
ten, James V, 874
ten, Joel V, 874
ten, Martha V, 874
ten, Mary Jane V, 874
ten, Rachel I, 261
oten, Thomas V, 874
oten, William V, 874
oton, Joel V, 874
oton, Thomas V, 874
raight, Mabel IV, 1324
rathwell, Thomas II, 449
ratliall, Frederic A. IV, 1344
ray, ??? III, 263
ray, Agness VI, 867
ray, Alec I, 898
ray, Alfred III, 368
ray, Alfred Bussell III, 368
ray, Alfred Bussell III, 369
ray, Alfred Busselle III, 368
ray, Ann III, 45
ray, Ann III, 368
ray, Anna C. III, 263
ray, Anna M. III, 168
ray, Anna M. III, 368
Vray, Anna Maria III, 368
Vray, Cecil Masters III, 369
Vray, Chris III, 168
Vray, Chris. III, 368
Vray, Chris. III, 369
Vray, Christopher III, 45
Vray, Christopher III, 57
Wray, Christopher III, 168
Wray, Christopher III, 263
Wray, Christopher III, 368
Vray, Christopher, Jr. III, 368
Wray, Creed F. VI, 796
Wray, Edith Sophia III, 169
Wray, Edith Sophia III, 368
Wray, Edith Sophie III, 368
Wray, Edward III, 368
Wray, Edward M. III, 368
Wray, Edward Marshall III, 368
Wray, Eliz. III, 45
Wray, Eliz. III, 368
Wray, Elizabeth III, 263
Wray, Elizabeth III, 368
Wray, Elizabeth III, 369
Wray, Elizabeth C. III, 368
Wray, Elizabeth C. III, 369
Wray, Elizabeth Daw III, 368
Wray, Elizabeth L. III, 368
Wray, Emeline I, 898
Wray, Emma IV, 688
Wray, Francis H. III, 263
Wray, Frank A. III, 263
Wray, Hannah III, 121
Wray, Hannah III, 368
Wray, Hannah III, 369
Wray, Hannah B. III, 368
Wray, Helen III, 369
Wray, Helen B. III, 221
Wray, Helen B. III, 369
Wray, Henry III, 368
Wray, Henry VI, 798
Wray, Henry VI, 835
Wray, Henry VI, 841
Wray, Ida III, 369
Wray, Jabez VI, 867
Wray, John III, 368
Wray, John III, 369
Wray, John VI, 798
Wray, John VI, 839
Wray, John VI, 867
Wray, Jos. B. III, 368
Wray, Joseph III, 368
Wray, Joseph B. III, 121
Wray, Joseph B. III, 368
Wray, Joseph B. III, 369
Wray, Joseph Bowman III, 368
Wray, Josephine III, 121
Wray, Josephine B. III, 369
Wray, Kate III, 263
Wray, Lewis VI, 867
Wray, Lucinda VI, 839
Wray, Lucy W. III, 263
Wray, Luke VI, 938
Wray, Luke VI, 998
Wray, Mahala VI, 867
Wray, Margaret III, 263
Wray, Marjorie Rebecca III, 369
Wray, Martha III, 263
Wray, Martha III, 368
Wray, Mary III, 368
Wray, Mary Emma IV, 688
Wray, Mary Emma IV, 790
Wray, Mary H. III, 368
Wray, Mary H. III, 369
Wray, Nancy VI, 798
Wray, Nancy VI, 815
Wray, Sally VI, 998
Wray, Samuel Bussell III, 221
Wray, Samuel Bussell III, 369
Wray, Samuel Daw III, 368
Wray, Sarah II, 113
Wray, Sarah III, 149
Wray, Sarah III, 279
Wray, Sarah III, 280
Wray, Sarah III, 368
Wray, Sarah VI, 867
Wray, Senah VI, 938
Wray, Sophia III, 368
Wray, Sophia J. III, 168
Wray, Sophia J. III, 368
Wray, Sophia J. III, 369
Wray, Sophia Jane III, 57
Wray, Sophia Jane III, 368
Wray, Susan E. III, 368
Wray, Thelma I, 627
Wray, Thomas IV, 68
Wray, William III, 368
Wray, William H. III, 368
Wray, William H. III, 369
Wray, Wm. Anthony III, 263
Wren, Anna IV, 1018
Wren, Anna M. IV, 1301
Wren, Elijah IV, 1018
Wren, Elijah VI, 144
Wren, Esther IV, 1031
Wren, Francis VI, 15
Wren, John IV, 1301
Wren, Julie VI, 133
Wren, Lydia IV, 895
Wren, Lydia IV, 1018
Wren, Mary IV, 1018
Wren, Rebecca IV, 1301
Wren, Richard VI, 19
Wren, Sarah IV, 895
Wren, William IV, 895
Wren, William IV, 1018
Wren, Wm. IV, 895
Wren, Wm. VI, 96
Wrenn, Alfred VI, 125
Wrenn, Anna VI, 144
Wrenn, Anne VI, 125
Wrenn, Bailey VI, 125
Wrenn, Deborah VI, 125
Wrenn, Deborah VI, 144
Wrenn, Delitha VI, 125
Wrenn, Elijah VI, 125
Wrenn, Elijah VI, 144
Wrenn, Elitha VI, 125
Wrenn, Eliza IV, 1031
Wrenn, Elizabeth VI, 125
Wrenn, Esther IV, 1031
Wrenn, Evans VI, 125
Wrenn, Fanny VI, 125
Wrenn, Francis VI, 41
Wrenn, Hannah VI, 125
Wrenn, Henry I, 430
Wrenn, Jesse VI, 125
Wrenn, Julia VI, 125
Wrenn, Lemuel IV, 1031
Wrenn, Levi IV, 1031
Wrenn, Lidia VI, 144
Wrenn, Lindley IV, 1031
Wrenn, Lucy VI, 125
Wrenn, Lydia VI, 125
Wrenn, Lydia VI, 144
Wrenn, Marey VI, 144
Wrenn, Mary I, 430
Wrenn, Mary VI, 125
Wrenn, Paul E. I, 951
Wrenn, Richard VI, 125
Wrenn, Sally VI, 125
Wrenn, Sarah IV, 1031
Wrenn, Suckey VI, 113
Wrenn, Suckey VI, 125
Wrenn, Sukey VI, 125
Wrenn, William IV, 1031
Wrenn, William VI, 125
Wrenn, Wm. VI, 125
Wrenn, Wm. VI, 144
Wrenn, Wm. Bailey, Sr. VI, 125
Wrigh, Ann VI, 460
Wrigh, James VI, 460
Wrigh, Lucy VI, 460
Wrigh, Micajah VI, 460
Wrigh, Ralph VI, 460
Wrigh, Susanah VI, 460
Wright, ??? II, 48
Wright, ??? II, 829
Wright, ??? III, 369
Wright, ??? III, 370
Wright, ??? III, 371
Wright, ??? III, 377
Wright, ??? III, 379
Wright, ??? III, 388
Wright, ??? IV, 308
Wright, ??? IV, 603
Wright, ??? IV, 1141
Wright, ??? VI, 348
Wright, ??? VI, 460
Wright, ??? VI, 746
Wright, A. Wright III, 67
Wright, Aaron III, 67
Wright, Aaron III, 355
Wright, Aaron III, 369
Wright, Aaron III, 475
Wright, Aaron IV, 68
Wright, Aaron IV, 359
Wright, Aaron IV, 1197
Wright, Aaron V, 144
Wright, Aaron V, 979
Wright, Aaron VI, 608
Wright, Abadigs II, 277
Wright, Abigail II, 277
Wright, Abigail II, 505
Wright, Abigail II, 694
Wright, Abigail II, 695
Wright, Abigail II, 698
Wright, Abigail IV, 165
Wright, Abigail IV, 194
Wright, Abigail IV, 308
Wright, Abigail IV, 332
Wright, Abigail IV, 359
Wright, Abigail IV, 459
Wright, Abigail V, 271
Wright, Abigail V, 292
Wright, Abigail V, 293
Wright, Abigail V, 486
Wright, Abigail V, 531
Wright, Abigail V, 544
Wright, Abigail V, 650
Wright, Abigail M. II, 724
Wright, Abraham I, 1099
Wright, Abraham III, 388
Wright, Abraham V, 144
Wright, Abraham V, 543
Wright, Achsah II, 815
Wright, Achsah L. III, 369
Wright, Ada B. III, 371
Wright, Adam II, 190
Wright, Addison V, 440
Wright, Aggy VI, 1021
Wright, Agnes VI, 1013
Wright, Agness VI, 867
Wright, Agness VI, 959
Wright, Albert V, 293
Wright, Albert Aiken III, 370
Wright, Alberta IV, 1301
Wright, Alexander II, 439
Wright, Alexander III, 388
Wright, Alexander T. IV, 739
Wright, Alfred IV, 740
Wright, Alfred IV, 790
Wright, Alfred IV, 791
Wright, Alfred IV, 1026
Wright, Alice II, 1029
Wright, Alice II, 1041
Wright, Alice IV, 309
Wright, Alice V, 715
Wright, Alice V, 720
Wright, Alice V, 773
Wright, Alice Ann IV, 739
Wright, Alice G. VI, 459
Wright, Alice G. VI, 461
Wright, Alice G. White VI, 375
Wright, Alice G. White VI, 460
Wright, Alice J. V, 1026
Wright, Alla J. V, 214
Wright, Allen V, 963
Wright, Almeda III, 403
Wright, Almeda III, 475
Wright, Alonzo IV, 1301
Wright, Alonzo V, 367
Wright, Alpheus L. I, 906
Wright, Alpheus Linsey I, 867
Wright, Amanda V, 105
Wright, Amanda V, 144
Wright, Amanda V, 943
Wright, Amanda VI, 1021
Wright, Amanda Ann V, 144
Wright, Ambrose F. VI, 836
Wright, Ambrose S. VI, 846
Wright, Amelia III, 114
Wright, Amelia III, 370
Wright, Amelia III, 388
Wright, Amelia III, 390
Wright, Amelia IV, 1026
Wright, Amelia Eliza III, 370
Wright, Amelia Howell VI, 1021
Wright, Amelia R. IV, 740
Wright, Amelia R. IV, 790
Wright, Amey V, 440
Wright, Amey V, 543
Wright, Amon V, 293
Wright, Amos II, 48
Wright, Amos II, 113
Wright, Amos II, 822
Wright, Amos IV, 68
Wright, Amos IV, 359
Wright, Amos IV, 559
Wright, Amos IV, 1344
Wright, Amos V, 440
Wright, Amos VI, 400
Wright, Amos VI, 416
Wright, Amos VI, 461
Wright, Amos VI, 608
Wright, Amos F. IV, 1344
Wright, Amos Willets III, 369
Wright, Amy V, 292
Wright, Angeline Elizabeth
VI, 1021
Wright, Angie P. I, 441
Wright, Ann I, 430
Wright, Ann I, 583
Wright, Ann I, 868
Wright, Ann I, 1034
Wright, Ann I, 1039
Wright, Ann I, 1088
Wright, Ann I, 1091
Wright, Ann I, 1099
Wright, Ann I, 1100
Wright, Ann I, 1112
Wright, Ann I, 1125
Wright, Ann I, 1135
Wright, Ann II, 95
Wright, Ann II, 113
Wright, Ann II, 277
Wright, Ann II, 278
Wright, Ann II, 307
Wright, Ann II, 315
Wright, Ann II, 439
Wright, Ann II, 649
Wright, Ann II, 694
Wright, Ann II, 695
Wright, Ann II, 1041
Wright, Ann II, 1064
Wright, Ann III, 369
Wright, Ann III, 387
Wright, Ann III, 474
Wright, Ann III, 475
Wright, Ann III, 476
Wright, Ann IV, 156
Wright, Ann IV, 165
Wright, Ann IV, 346
Wright, Ann IV, 359
Wright, Ann IV, 524
Wright, Ann IV, 559
Wright, Ann IV, 857
Wright, Ann IV, 1123
Wright, Ann IV, 1162
Wright, Ann IV, 1196
Wright, Ann IV, 1197
Wright, Ann V, 23
Wright, Ann V, 144
Wright, Ann V, 285
Wright, Ann V, 292
Wright, Ann V, 293
Wright, Ann V, 324
Wright, Ann V, 366
Wright, Ann V, 447
Wright, Ann V, 448
Wright, Ann V, 468
Wright, Ann V, 543
Wright, Ann V, 943
Wright, Ann V, 979
Wright, Ann VI, 377
Wright, Ann VI, 424
Wright, Ann VI, 459
Wright, Ann VI, 460
Wright, Ann VI, 461
Wright, Ann VI, 585
Wright, Ann VI, 608
Wright, Ann VI, 902
Wright, Ann VI, 1011
Wright, Ann VI, 1021
Wright, Ann B. IV, 308
Wright, Ann Eliza II, 943
Wright, Ann Eliza III, 249
Wright, Ann L. II, 753
Wright, Ann L. II, 777
Wright, Ann M. VI, 746
Wright, Ann M. VI, 792
Wright, Ann O'Neel VI, 1021
Wright, Anna II, 113
Wright, Anna II, 829
Wright, Anna II, 892
Wright, Anna II, 943
Wright, Anna III, 370
Wright, Anna IV, 309
Wright, Anna IV, 791
Wright, Anna V, 233
Wright, Anna V, 278
Wright, Anna V, 292
Wright, Anna V, 293
Wright, Anna V, 394
Wright, Anna V, 441
Wright, Anna V, 943
Wright, Anna VI, 375
Wright, Anna VI, 378
Wright, Anna VI, 459
Wright, Anna VI, 460
Wright, Anna B. V, 26
Wright, Anna B. V, 144
Wright, Anna C. V, 943
Wright, Anna E. II, 943
Wright, Anna H. II, 829
Wright, Anna H. II, 873
Wright, Anna H. II, 943
Wright, Anna Longstreth II, 829
Wright, Anna Louisa III, 369
Wright, Anna Louise III, 259
Wright, Anna M. V, 220
Wright, Anna M. V, 293
Wright, Anna M. V, 468
Wright, Anna S. VI, 788
Wright, Anna S. VI, 789
Wright, Anna S. VI, 793
Wright, Anna, Jr. IV, 791
Wright, Anne IV, 525
Wright, Anne IV, 559
Wright, Anne VI, 867
Wright, Anne Jane IV, 759
Wright, Annetta W. II, 903
Wright, Annetta W. II, 943
Wright, Annie V, 441
Wright, Annie VI, 461
Wright, Annie A. III, 106
Wright, Annie A. III, 221
Wright, Annie A. III, 369
Wright, Annie Augusta III, 221
Wright, Annie Augusta III, 370
Wright, Annie B. IV, 309
Wright, Annie Eyre II, 816
Wright, Anthony III, 19
Wright, Anthony III, 369
Wright, Anthony IV, 359
Wright, Anthony V, 367
Wright, Anthony VI, 875
Wright, Anthony VI, 921
Wright, Anthony VI, 935
Wright, Anthony VI, 1013
Wright, Anthony VI, 1021
Wright, Anthony VI, 1022
Wright, Anthony P. VI, 875
Wright, Anthony P. VI, 913
Wright, Anthony P. VI, 954
Wright, Anthony P. VI, 1013
Wright, Anthony P. VI, 1022

Wright, Anthony, Sr. VI, 959
Wright, Aquilla V, 943
Wright, Archibald VI, 1021
Wright, Arena III, 371
Wright, Arena Jane I, 867
Wright, Arthur III, 369
Wright, Arthur V, 721
Wright, Artless V, 441
Wright, Ashley V, 293
Wright, Ashley J. V, 293
Wright, Ashley Johnson V, 292
Wright, Augustus III, 371
Wright, Barbara II, 439
Wright, Barbara II, 621
Wright, Barbara II, 694
Wright, Barbarah II, 439
Wright, Barbary VI, 579
Wright, Barbary VI, 584
Wright, Barnabas III, 148
Wright, Barnabas III, 369
Wright, Barsheba VI, 993
Wright, Bartlett VI, 1022
Wright, Bell V, 367
Wright, Benj. IV, 308
Wright, Benj. IV, 506
Wright, Benj. H. V, 977
Wright, Benj. H. V, 979
Wright, Benjamin II, 31
Wright, Benjamin II, 48
Wright, Benjamin II, 60
Wright, Benjamin II, 113
Wright, Benjamin II, 130
Wright, Benjamin II, 277
Wright, Benjamin II, 307
Wright, Benjamin II, 315
Wright, Benjamin II, 327
Wright, Benjamin II, 439
Wright, Benjamin II, 621
Wright, Benjamin II, 694
Wright, Benjamin II, 990
Wright, Benjamin II, 1041
Wright, Benjamin II, 1083
Wright, Benjamin II, 1084
Wright, Benjamin IV, 68
Wright, Benjamin IV, 165
Wright, Benjamin IV, 308
Wright, Benjamin IV, 309
Wright, Benjamin IV, 667
Wright, Benjamin IV, 739
Wright, Benjamin IV, 790
Wright, Benjamin IV, 1228
Wright, Benjamin V, 366
Wright, Benjamin V, 544
Wright, Benjamin V, 979
Wright, Benjamin VI, 345
Wright, Benjamin VI, 356
Wright, Benjamin VI, 459
Wright, Benjamin VI, 461
Wright, Benjamin VI, 584
Wright, Benjamin VI, 608
Wright, Benjamin VI, 949
Wright, Benjamin VI, 1021
Wright, Benjamin F. IV, 309
Wright, Benjamin F. V, 367
Wright, Benjamin G. IV, 359
Wright, Benjamin H. IV, 165
Wright, Benjamin H. IV, 285
Wright, Benjamin H. IV, 308
Wright, Benjamin H. IV, 309
Wright, Benjamin H. IV, 1267
Wright, Benjamin H. VI, 1022
Wright, Benjamin Townsend IV, 790
Wright, Benjamin Townsend IV, 857
Wright, Benjamin, Jr. II, 48
Wright, Benjamin, Jr. II, 113
Wright, Benjamin, Jr. IV, 309
Wright, Bernard IV, 1267
Wright, Bert E. V, 367
Wright, Bertha V, 367
Wright, Bertha E. V, 367
Wright, Bessie V, 293
Wright, Betsey I, 1112
Wright, Betsey III, 370
Wright, Betsey V, 313
Wright, Betsey V, 943
Wright, Betsy I, 1135
Wright, Betsy I Sup 1, 12
Wright, Betsy IV, 857
Wright, Betsy V, 440
Wright, Betsy V, 773
Wright, Betsy V, 943
Wright, Betty I, 1039
Wright, Betty V, 292
Wright, Betty V, 486
Wright, Betty V, 543
Wright, Beulah II, 694
Wright, Beulah II, 695
Wright, Beulah IV, 309
Wright, Beulah VI, 448
Wright, Beulah VI, 460
Wright, Beulah VI, 566
Wright, Beulah VI, 584
Wright, Beulah R. IV, 308
Wright, Bond VI, 1007
Wright, Bowater VI, 585
Wright, Boyater VI, 459
Wright, Buelah R. II, 777
Wright, Bulah VI, 461
Wright, C. III, 369
Wright, Callie V, 721
Wright, Calvin I, 486
Wright, Calvin E. I, 472
Wright, Camden G. VI, 845
Wright, Camden G. VI, 867
Wright, Camilla Susan VI, 1022
Wright, Campbell VI, 867
Wright, Carl W. I, 951
Wright, Carline I, 472
Wright, Caroline III, 370
Wright, Caroline IV, 739
Wright, Caroline IV, 790
Wright, Caroline IV, 791
Wright, Caroline V, 283
Wright, Caroline V, 292
Wright, Caroline V, 293
Wright, Caroline V, 1026
Wright, Caroline E. III, 388
Wright, Caroline E. III, 390
Wright, Carolyn IV, 309
Wright, Carrie V, 721
Wright, Carrie Edith V, 721
Wright, Carrie Louisa III, 84
Wright, Carrie Louisa III, 369
Wright, Carrie Louisa III, 370
Wright, Catharine I, 1088
Wright, Catharine II, 253
Wright, Catharine II, 277
Wright, Catharine III, 229
Wright, Catharine III, 384
Wright, Catharine III, 388
Wright, Catharine IV, 256
Wright, Catharine IV, 308
Wright, Catharine IV, 739
Wright, Catharine V, 213
Wright, Catharine V, 543
Wright, Catharine VI, 993
Wright, Catharine VI, 1021
Wright, Catharine F. III, 370
Wright, Catherine I, 1097
Wright, Catherine I, 1099
Wright, Catherine III, 219
Wright, Catherine V, 292
Wright, Catherine V, 293
Wright, Catherine V, 963
Wright, Cecelia II, 919
Wright, Cecelia II, 943
Wright, Cecilia II, 811
Wright, Cecilia A. II, 943
Wright, Celia VI, 1021
Wright, Charity I, 369
Wright, Charity I, 430
Wright, Charity I, 1039
Wright, Charity I, 1088
Wright, Charity I, 1098
Wright, Charity I, 1099
Wright, Charity I, 1100
Wright, Charity I, 1112
Wright, Charity IV, 68
Wright, Charity IV, 667
Wright, Charity IV, 738
Wright, Charity IV, 790
Wright, Charity V, 144
Wright, Charity V, 486
Wright, Charity V, 544
Wright, Charity VI, 356
Wright, Charity VI, 585
Wright, Charity Balinder VI, 1021
Wright, Charles I, 522
Wright, Charles I, 583
Wright, Charles II, 439
Wright, Charles III, 369
Wright, Charles III, 370
Wright, Charles III, 388
Wright, Charles III, 509
Wright, Charles IV, 165
Wright, Charles IV, 306
Wright, Charles IV, 308
Wright, Charles IV, 309
Wright, Charles IV, 506
Wright, Charles IV, 1197
Wright, Charles IV, 1228
Wright, Charles V, 468
Wright, Charles VI, 796
Wright, Charles VI, 817
Wright, Charles VI, 899
Wright, Charles VI, 1021
Wright, Charles A. III, 311
Wright, Charles A. III, 369
Wright, Charles A. IV, 1196
Wright, Charles A. IV, 1197
Wright, Charles F. V, 144
Wright, Charles H. III, 382
Wright, Charles H. III, 388
Wright, Charles Henry III, 388
Wright, Charles Stroud IV, 308
Wright, Charles W. V, 367
Wright, Charlotte III, 369
Wright, Charlotte V, 157
Wright, Charlotte V, 213
Wright, Charlotte VI, 585
Wright, Charlotte VI, 911
Wright, Charlotte VI, 1021
Wright, Charlotte B. II, 1064
Wright, Charlotty V, 213
Wright, Chas. IV, 265
Wright, Chas. IV, 308
Wright, Chas. IV, 505
Wright, Chas. Stroud IV, 309
Wright, Chas. W. V, 367
Wright, Chauncey III, 149
Wright, Chauncey III, 369
Wright, Clarry VI, 1021
Wright, Claud S. V, 367
Wright, Clement III, 486
Wright, Clement III, 509
Wright, Clifford V, 293
Wright, Cornelia II, 903
Wright, Cornelia Jenkins II, 829
Wright, Cornelia Jenkins II, 943
Wright, Cornelia N. II, 891
Wright, Cynthia I, 868
Wright, Cynthia I, 906
Wright, D. VI, 948
Wright, D. D. III, 390
Wright, D. Henry II, 943
Wright, Daisy D. V, 721
Wright, Daniel II, 70
Wright, Daniel II, 277
Wright, Daniel III, 370
Wright, Daniel III, 387
Wright, Daniel III, 395
Wright, Daniel III, 475
Wright, Daniel V, 293
Wright, Daniel VI, 459
Wright, Daniel VI, 460
Wright, Daniel VI, 461
Wright, Daniel VI, 608
Wright, Daniel D. III, 388
Wright, Daniel Dodge III, 388
Wright, Daniel L. II, 277
Wright, Daniel P. VI, 858
Wright, Daniel P. VI, 867
Wright, Daniel Webster V, 292
Wright, Daniel Zelley II, 315
Wright, Daniel, Jr. VI, 461
Wright, David I, 867
Wright, David I, 951
Wright, David I, 1088
Wright, David II, 277
Wright, David III, 370
Wright, David IV, 857
Wright, David V, 236
Wright, David V, 239
Wright, David V, 292
Wright, David V, 293
Wright, David V, 366
Wright, David V, 403
Wright, David V, 440
Wright, David V, 773
Wright, David V, 963
Wright, David VI, 393
Wright, David VI, 459
Wright, David VI, 460
Wright, David VI, 461
Wright, David VI, 608
Wright, David VI, 894
Wright, David VI, 907
Wright, David Cattell IV, 117
Wright, David D. V, 468
Wright, David H. V, 367
Wright, David H. V, 721
Wright, David Hadley I, 867
Wright, David Harold V, 721
Wright, David Henry II, 944
Wright, David L. I, 441
Wright, David L. I, 455
Wright, David M. VI, 1021
Wright, David Sands V, 293
Wright, David, Jr. II, 277
Wright, David, Jr. V, 293
Wright, Davis S. V, 367
Wright, Deborah II, 614
Wright, Deborah II, 694
Wright, Deborah V, 514
Wright, Deborah J. V, 544
Wright, Deborough VI, 1017
Wright, Delilah VI, 1021
Wright, Della S. IV, 1267
Wright, Delpha IV, 1301
Wright, Delphia IV, 1301
Wright, Delphina L. I, 472
Wright, Dicy VI, 893
Wright, Dillen V, 144
Wright, Dillon V, 650
Wright, Doctor J. V, 292
Wright, Doctor J. V, 293
Wright, Dora IV, 1344
Wright, Dora J. I, 472
Wright, Dora Jane I, 486
Wright, Dorothy IV, 309
Wright, Dorothy VI, 788
Wright, Dorothy Eileen IV, 790
Wright, Dorothy Ellen IV, 791
Wright, Dorothy Evelyn IV, 309
Wright, Dorothy Evelyn V, 144
Wright, Dosia II, 113
Wright, Dr. Alfred V, 144
Wright, Dr. Emily V, 144
Wright, Dr. F. O. V, 720
Wright, Dr. Frank O. V, 293
Wright, Dunbar III, 388
Wright, Dusia II, 113
Wright, Eadith I, 906
Wright, Easter II, 231
Wright, Easter II, 277
Wright, Easton III, 371
Wright, Ebenezer II, 48
Wright, Ebenezer II, 70
Wright, Ebenezer II, 113
Wright, Ebenezer II, 126
Wright, Ebenezer II, 140
Wright, Ebenezer II, 161
Wright, Ebenezer II, 277
Wright, Ebenezer Miller II, 161
Wright, Edatha L. VI, 1022
Wright, Edgar III, 345
Wright, Edgar III, 369
Wright, Edgar III, 370
Wright, Edgar S. III, 259
Wright, Edgar S. III, 369
Wright, Edith I, 867
Wright, Edith I, 906
Wright, Edith M. II, 315
Wright, Edith M. II, 322
Wright, Edith M. II, 327
Wright, Edith M. II, 1084
Wright, Edith Virginia III, 311
Wright, Edith Virginia III, 369
Wright, Edna III, 349
Wright, Edna III, 369
Wright, Edward II, 161
Wright, Edward II, 943
Wright, Edward III, 240
Wright, Edward III, 370
Wright, Edward IV, 309
Wright, Edward V, 249
Wright, Edward V, 292
Wright, Edward V, 293
Wright, Edward V, 440
Wright, Edward V, 468
Wright, Edward VI, 460
Wright, Edward VI, 461
Wright, Edward VI, 532
Wright, Edward A. III, 369
Wright, Edward B. IV, 309
Wright, Edward B. IV, 1228
Wright, Edward Betts II, 944
Wright, Edward Bonsall IV, 308
Wright, Edward Dearing VI, 1022
Wright, Edward E. III, 264
Wright, Edward N. II, 873
Wright, Edward N. II, 943
Wright, Edward Needles II, 828
Wright, Edward Needles II, 829
Wright, Edward R. IV, 1196
Wright, Edward S. II, 140
Wright, Edward S. II, 161
Wright, Edward S. V, 293
Wright, Edward W. V, 292
Wright, Edwin III, 369
Wright, Edwin V, 293
Wright, Edwin Wadkins V, 292
Wright, Eldora V, 367
Wright, Eleanor I, 455
Wright, Eleanor III, 371
Wright, Eleanor V, 292
Wright, Eleanor V, 293
Wright, Eleanor C. V, 293
Wright, Eleanor C. V, 367
Wright, Eleanor E. VI, 1021
Wright, Elenor IV, 199
Wright, Elenor IV, 308
Wright, Elenor IV, 1088
Wright, Elenor IV, 1123
Wright, Elijah I, 522
Wright, Elijah I, 583
Wright, Elijah I, 795
Wright, Elijah I, 867
Wright, Elijah I, 906
Wright, Elijah V, 76
Wright, Elijah V, 144
Wright, Elijah VI, 1021
Wright, Elijah A. VI, 867
Wright, Elinor II, 209
Wright, Elinor II, 277
Wright, Elisabeth II, 694
Wright, Elisabeth IV, 667
Wright, Elisabeth VI, 608
Wright, Elisha IV, 559
Wright, Elisha F. VI, 867
Wright, Eliz VI, 460
Wright, Eliza I, 936
Wright, Eliza II, 724
Wright, Eliza II, 856
Wright, Eliza II, 943
Wright, Eliza III, 295
Wright, Eliza III, 369
Wright, Eliza III, 370
Wright, Eliza III, 371
Wright, Eliza III, 388
Wright, Eliza V, 954
Wright, Eliza VI, 861
Wright, Eliza VI, 1021
Wright, Eliza Jane VI, 893
Wright, Eliza Nailer Morgan IV, 790
Wright, Eliza Nailor IV, 857
Wright, Eliza Nailor Morgan IV, 790
Wright, Elizabeth I, 369
Wright, Elizabeth I, 522
Wright, Elizabeth I, 528
Wright, Elizabeth I, 583
Wright, Elizabeth I, 846
Wright, Elizabeth I, 1088
Wright, Elizabeth I, 1092
Wright, Elizabeth I, 1099
Wright, Elizabeth I, 1112
Wright, Elizabeth I, 1135
Wright, Elizabeth I Sup 1, 12
Wright, Elizabeth II, 31
Wright, Elizabeth II, 48
Wright, Elizabeth II, 52
Wright, Elizabeth II, 78
Wright, Elizabeth II, 113
Wright, Elizabeth II, 190
Wright, Elizabeth II, 200
Wright, Elizabeth II, 226
Wright, Elizabeth II, 227
Wright, Elizabeth II, 234
Wright, Elizabeth II, 277
Wright, Elizabeth II, 439
Wright, Elizabeth II, 694
Wright, Elizabeth II, 695
Wright, Elizabeth II, 724
Wright, Elizabeth II, 777
Wright, Elizabeth II, 817
Wright, Elizabeth II, 822
Wright, Elizabeth II, 1027
Wright, Elizabeth II, 1041
Wright, Elizabeth II, 1073
Wright, Elizabeth II, 1083
Wright, Elizabeth II, 1084
Wright, Elizabeth III, 369
Wright, Elizabeth III, 370
Wright, Elizabeth III, 371
Wright, Elizabeth III, 378
Wright, Elizabeth III, 380
Wright, Elizabeth III, 388
Wright, Elizabeth III, 450
Wright, Elizabeth III, 451
Wright, Elizabeth III, 475
Wright, Elizabeth III, 508
Wright, Elizabeth III, 509
Wright, Elizabeth IV, 68
Wright, Elizabeth IV, 165
Wright, Elizabeth IV, 308
Wright, Elizabeth IV, 309
Wright, Elizabeth IV, 349
Wright, Elizabeth IV, 351
Wright, Elizabeth IV, 359
Wright, Elizabeth IV, 374
Wright, Elizabeth IV, 739
Wright, Elizabeth IV, 742
Wright, Elizabeth IV, 786
Wright, Elizabeth IV, 790
Wright, Elizabeth IV, 857
Wright, Elizabeth IV, 1228
Wright, Elizabeth V, 119
Wright, Elizabeth V, 144
Wright, Elizabeth V, 254
Wright, Elizabeth V, 293
Wright, Elizabeth V, 347
Wright, Elizabeth V, 367
Wright, Elizabeth V, 394
Wright, Elizabeth V, 440
Wright, Elizabeth V, 441
Wright, Elizabeth V, 469
Wright, Elizabeth V, 533
Wright, Elizabeth V, 544
Wright, Elizabeth V, 721

nt, Elizabeth V, 726
ht, Elizabeth V, 773
ht, Elizabeth V, 814
ht, Elizabeth V, 826
ht, Elizabeth V, 864
ht, Elizabeth V, 874
ht, Elizabeth V, 875
ht, Elizabeth V, 930
ht, Elizabeth V, 938
ht, Elizabeth V, 943
ht, Elizabeth VI, 220
ht, Elizabeth VI, 345
ht, Elizabeth VI, 356
ht, Elizabeth VI, 459
ht, Elizabeth VI, 491
ht, Elizabeth VI, 514
ht, Elizabeth VI, 531
ht, Elizabeth VI, 532
ht, Elizabeth VI, 585
ght, Elizabeth VI, 608
ght, Elizabeth VI, 817
ght, Elizabeth VI, 819
ght, Elizabeth VI, 867
ght, Elizabeth VI, 875
ght, Elizabeth VI, 893
ght, Elizabeth VI, 896
ght, Elizabeth VI, 913
ght, Elizabeth VI, 927
ght, Elizabeth VI, 955
ght, Elizabeth VI, 982
ght, Elizabeth VI, 1001
ght, Elizabeth VI, 1020
ght, Elizabeth VI, 1021
ght, Elizabeth A. II, 724
ght, Elizabeth A. II, 828
ght, Elizabeth A. III, 370
ght, Elizabeth A. VI, 867
ght, Elizabeth A. A. VI, 880
ght, Elizabeth Ann II, 828
ght, Elizabeth C. III, 146
ght, Elizabeth E. V, 293
ght, Elizabeth E. V, 468
ight, Elizabeth F. V, 874
ight, Elizabeth G. VI, 461
ight, Elizabeth J. I, 1097
ight, Elizabeth J. I, 1100
ight, Elizabeth Jane I, 1088
ight, Elizabeth Jane IV, 1197
ight, Elizabeth M. II, 113
ight, Elizabeth M. IV, 309
ight, Elizabeth M. IV, 760
ight, Elizabeth P. II, 828
ight, Elizabeth P. II, 943
right, Elizabeth P. IV, 1267
ight, Elizabeth R. VI, 958
right, Elizabeth S. II, 1064
right, Elizabeth T. II, 724
right, Ella I, 441
right, Ella III, 264
right, Ella III, 369
right, Ella III, 371
right, Ella A. Werntz V, 721
right, Ella M. II, 1084
right, Ella V. IV, 1026
right, Ella V. IV, 1031
right, Ellen V, 293
right, Ellen V, 533
right, Ellen V, 544
right, Ellen V, 721
right, Ellen C. V, 367
right, Ellen S. IV, 308
right, Ellen S. IV, 309
Vright, Ellener I, 584
Vright, Ellis VI, 1021
Vright, Elsie V, 367
Vright, Elsie A. V, 367
Vright, Elva N. V, 441
Vright, Elva N. V, 721
Vright, Elwood I, 455
Vright, Elwood V, 366
Vright, Elwood B. IV, 309
Vright, Elwood Osborne I, 441
Vright, Emaline I, 1088
Vright, Emeline III, 369
Vright, Emeline IV, 1018
Wright, Emily II, 724
Wright, Emily II, 828
Wright, Emily II, 943
Wright, Emily III, 61
Wright, Emily III, 108
Wright, Emily III, 369
Wright, Emily III, 371
Wright, Emily V, 280
Wright, Emily V, 293
Wright, Emily V, 978
Wright, Emily V, 979
Wright, Emma IV, 790
Wright, Emma V, 366
Wright, Emma V, 367
Wright, Emma V, 1026
Wright, Emma E. V, 721
Wright, Emma L. V, 367
Wright, Emmett IV, 359
Wright, Emsley I, 472
Wright, Emsley I, 486
Wright, Ephier VI, 1021
Wright, Esley V, 492
Wright, Esly V, 544
Wright, Esther I, 906
Wright, Esther IV, 790
Wright, Esther IV, 856
Wright, Esther IV, 857
Wright, Esther V, 874
Wright, Esther VI, 371
Wright, Esther VI, 399
Wright, Esther VI, 416
Wright, Esther VI, 438
Wright, Esther VI, 459
Wright, Esther VI, 460
Wright, Esther VI, 461
Wright, Esther B. II, 1073
Wright, Esther B. II, 1084
Wright, Esther C. V, 293
Wright, Etta IV, 1301
Wright, Eunice I, 868
Wright, Eunice IV, 336
Wright, Eunice IV, 351
Wright, Eunice V, 293
Wright, Eunice VI, 369
Wright, Eunice VI, 459
Wright, Eunice VI, 608
Wright, Eunice B. V, 293
Wright, Ezekiel II, 113
Wright, F. O. V, 721
Wright, Fanny IV, 68
Wright, Fanny IV, 359
Wright, Fanny VI, 894
Wright, Flora V, 214
Wright, Florence III, 371
Wright, Florence V, 214
Wright, Florence C. V, 721
Wright, Florence L. III, 223
Wright, Frances II, 829
Wright, Frances II, 837
Wright, Frances II, 904
Wright, Frances II, 943
Wright, Frances IV, 1228
Wright, Frances VI, 460
Wright, Frances VI, 867
Wright, Frances VI, 1021
Wright, Frances P. II, 903
Wright, Frances Palmer II, 829
Wright, Francis II, 277
Wright, Francis IV, 308
Wright, Francis IV, 309
Wright, Francis IV, 1228
Wright, Francis VI, 1021
Wright, Francis D. IV, 309
Wright, Francis T. III, 369
Wright, Francis T. III, 371
Wright, Frank IV, 1344
Wright, Frank V, 314
Wright, Frank V, 440
Wright, Frank C. V, 367
Wright, Frank M. V, 441
Wright, Frank M. V, 721
Wright, Frank O. V, 293
Wright, Frank O. V, 721
Wright, Frank Winsor IV, 1344
Wright, Frankie V, 367
Wright, Franky VI, 922
Wright, Fred V, 367
Wright, Fred'k Willets III, 475
Wright, Frederick VI, 450
Wright, Frederick VI, 459
Wright, Frederick W. III, 369
Wright, Fretwel II, 277
Wright, Fretwell II, 277
Wright, G. W. V, 1026
Wright, Gabriel V, 144
Wright, Gardiner Harrison II, 695
Wright, Geo. VI, 795
Wright, Geo. VI, 951
Wright, Geo. P. IV, 309
Wright, Georganna I, 486
Wright, George II, 48
Wright, George II, 113
Wright, George II, 307
Wright, George II, 724
Wright, George III, 369
Wright, George III, 370
Wright, George IV, 1196
Wright, George V, 213
Wright, George V, 214
Wright, George V, 292
Wright, George V, 367
Wright, George V, 650
Wright, George V, 715
Wright, George V, 720
Wright, George V, 963
Wright, George VI, 858
Wright, George VI, 867
Wright, George VI, 1021
Wright, George A. II, 777
Wright, George A. III, 369
Wright, George A. VI, 861
Wright, George Edward III, 369
Wright, George F. V, 875
Wright, George M. I, 486
Wright, George Mead III, 371
Wright, George P. IV, 308
Wright, George T. VI, 585
Wright, George W. I, 470
Wright, George W. I, 472
Wright, George W. V, 214
Wright, George W. V, 874
Wright, Georgeanna I, 472
Wright, Gilbert V, 721
Wright, Glenn V, 773
Wright, Grace F. VI, 461
Wright, Grace L. V, 144
Wright, Grace L. V, 721
Wright, Grace L. VI, 368
Wright, Grace Lillian VI, 367
Wright, Grace Lillian VI, 460
Wright, Grace, Jr. VI, 461
Wright, Grief VI, 900
Wright, Grief VI, 944
Wright, Grief VI, 1021
Wright, Griffith V, 543
Wright, Gurney V, 367
Wright, Gurney V, 721
Wright, Gurney C. V, 721
Wright, Gustavus W. VI, 979
Wright, Hanah V, 650
Wright, Hannah I, 369
Wright, Hannah I, 795
Wright, Hannah I, 846
Wright, Hannah I, 847
Wright, Hannah I, 867
Wright, Hannah I, 868
Wright, Hannah I, 906
Wright, Hannah I, 1026
Wright, Hannah I, 1039
Wright, Hannah I, 1135
Wright, Hannah II, 33
Wright, Hannah II, 48
Wright, Hannah II, 85
Wright, Hannah II, 87
Wright, Hannah II, 113
Wright, Hannah II, 126
Wright, Hannah II, 140
Wright, Hannah II, 161
Wright, Hannah II, 248
Wright, Hannah II, 277
Wright, Hannah II, 653
Wright, Hannah II, 656
Wright, Hannah II, 694
Wright, Hannah II, 695
Wright, Hannah III, 369
Wright, Hannah III, 371
Wright, Hannah III, 379
Wright, Hannah III, 388
Wright, Hannah III, 475
Wright, Hannah III, 508
Wright, Hannah IV, 68
Wright, Hannah IV, 165
Wright, Hannah IV, 308
Wright, Hannah IV, 309
Wright, Hannah IV, 319
Wright, Hannah IV, 332
Wright, Hannah IV, 359
Wright, Hannah IV, 506
Wright, Hannah IV, 559
Wright, Hannah IV, 739
Wright, Hannah IV, 790
Wright, Hannah IV, 791
Wright, Hannah IV, 857
Wright, Hannah IV, 1123
Wright, Hannah IV, 1196
Wright, Hannah V, 144
Wright, Hannah V, 185
Wright, Hannah V, 213
Wright, Hannah V, 214
Wright, Hannah V, 248
Wright, Hannah V, 249
Wright, Hannah V, 264
Wright, Hannah V, 292
Wright, Hannah V, 293
Wright, Hannah V, 297
Wright, Hannah V, 313
Wright, Hannah V, 324
Wright, Hannah V, 366
Wright, Hannah V, 367
Wright, Hannah V, 440
Wright, Hannah V, 451
Wright, Hannah V, 468
Wright, Hannah V, 486
Wright, Hannah V, 543
Wright, Hannah V, 544
Wright, Hannah V, 773
Wright, Hannah V, 958
Wright, Hannah V, 979
Wright, Hannah VI, 369
Wright, Hannah VI, 376
Wright, Hannah VI, 383
Wright, Hannah VI, 412
Wright, Hannah VI, 416
Wright, Hannah VI, 430
Wright, Hannah VI, 437
Wright, Hannah VI, 445
Wright, Hannah VI, 459
Wright, Hannah VI, 460
Wright, Hannah VI, 461
Wright, Hannah VI, 585
Wright, Hannah VI, 603
Wright, Hannah VI, 608
Wright, Hannah A. IV, 1123
Wright, Hannah A. VI, 400
Wright, Hannah A. VI, 461
Wright, Hannah A. V. VI, 1022
Wright, Hannah B. V, 144
Wright, Hannah C. III, 369
Wright, Hannah C. T. III, 148
Wright, Hannah E. V, 293
Wright, Hannah Frances II, 724
Wright, Hannah G. II, 321
Wright, Hannah G. II, 327
Wright, Hannah H. II, 113
Wright, Hannah Lydia V, 292
Wright, Hannah M. III, 371
Wright, Hannah M. IV, 308
Wright, Hannah M. IV, 309
Wright, Hannah T. III, 369
Wright, Hannah W. IV, 265
Wright, Hannah W. IV, 308
Wright, Hannah W. VI, 400
Wright, Hannah, Jr. I, 906
Wright, Harriet E. VI, 875
Wright, Harriet T. III, 388
Wright, Harrison II, 137
Wright, Harrison II, 141
Wright, Harrison II, 161
Wright, Harrison VI, 916
Wright, Harrison Cooke II, 695
Wright, Harry Noble III, 349
Wright, Harry Noble III, 369
Wright, Hattie V, 367
Wright, Helen V, 692
Wright, Helen V, 720
Wright, Helen V, 721
Wright, Henrietta H. II, 912
Wright, Henrietta H. II, 943
Wright, Henrietta Hoskins II, 829
Wright, Henrietta M. IV, 1344
Wright, Henry I, 522
Wright, Henry I, 583
Wright, Henry II, 694
Wright, Henry II, 695
Wright, Henry IV, 790
Wright, Henry IV, 1197
Wright, Henry C. IV, 308
Wright, Henry C. IV, 309
Wright, Henry C. V, 293
Wright, Henry C. V, 367
Wright, Henry P. V, 367
Wright, Hester II, 231
Wright, Hester II, 277
Wright, Hester II, 990
Wright, Hester II, 1041
Wright, Hester II, 1083
Wright, Homer V, 692
Wright, Homer V, 720
Wright, Homer Elroy V, 721
Wright, Horace III, 475
Wright, Howard II, 1084
Wright, Howard III, 370
Wright, Hugh V, 441
Wright, Huldah VI, 1021
Wright, Ida IV, 431
Wright, Ida J. III, 382
Wright, Ida J. III, 388
Wright, Ida May V, 558
Wright, Ida R. IV, 1301
Wright, Ida Rosella IV, 1301
Wright, Inez Ellen V, 721
Wright, Inis V, 1026
Wright, Isaac I, 1039
Wright, Isaac I, 1088
Wright, Isaac I, 1099
Wright, Isaac I, 1112
Wright, Isaac I, 1135
Wright, Isaac II, 113
Wright, Isaac III, 311
Wright, Isaac III, 369
Wright, Isaac III, 370
Wright, Isaac III, 371
Wright, Isaac III, 455
Wright, Isaac III, 475
Wright, Isaac V, 144
Wright, Isaac V, 313
Wright, Isaac V, 440
Wright, Isaac V, 441
Wright, Isaac V, 486
Wright, Isaac V, 543
Wright, Isaac V, 606
Wright, Isaac V, 650
Wright, Isaac V, 826
Wright, Isaac V, 874
Wright, Isaac V, 875
Wright, Isaac VI, 459
Wright, Isaac VI, 461
Wright, Isaac VI, 608
Wright, Isaac VI, 917
Wright, Isaac VI, 1021
Wright, Isaac A. IV, 359
Wright, Isaac A. IV, 1123
Wright, Isaac M. III, 369
Wright, Isaac M. III, 371
Wright, Isaac N. IV, 791
Wright, Isaac R. IV, 1196
Wright, Isaac S. II, 315
Wright, Isaac S. II, 1084
Wright, Isaac S. V, 440
Wright, Isaac Walton III, 370
Wright, Isabella V, 144
Wright, Israel V, 144
Wright, Israel V, 943
Wright, Iva V, 1026
Wright, J. D. V, 293
Wright, J. D. V, 441
Wright, J. Gurney I, 262
Wright, J. H. V, 468
Wright, J. Howard III, 84
Wright, J. Howard III, 221
Wright, J. Howard III, 369
Wright, J. Robert VI, 867
Wright, J. W. V, 1026
Wright, Jacob I, 1088
Wright, Jacob I, 1097
Wright, Jacob I, 1099
Wright, Jacob I, 1100
Wright, Jacob II, 724
Wright, Jacob V, 144
Wright, Jacob V, 292
Wright, Jacob V, 543
Wright, Jacob V, 943
Wright, Jacob H. V, 292
Wright, Jain I, 867
Wright, James I, 369
Wright, James I, 583
Wright, James I, 795
Wright, James I, 846
Wright, James I, 867
Wright, James I, 906
Wright, James I, 970
Wright, James I, 1039
Wright, James I, 1077
Wright, James I, 1088
Wright, James I, 1099
Wright, James I, 1112
Wright, James II, 614
Wright, James II, 694
Wright, James III, 370
Wright, James IV, 165
Wright, James IV, 359
Wright, James IV, 559
Wright, James IV, 562
Wright, James IV, 739
Wright, James V, 144
Wright, James V, 213
Wright, James V, 292
Wright, James V, 394
Wright, James V, 404
Wright, James V, 440
Wright, James V, 441
Wright, James V, 531
Wright, James V, 543
Wright, James V, 544
Wright, James V, 650
Wright, James V, 773
Wright, James V, 874
Wright, James V, 875
Wright, James V, 963
Wright, James VI, 357
Wright, James VI, 358
Wright, James VI, 428
Wright, James VI, 430
Wright, James VI, 445
Wright, James VI, 459
Wright, James VI, 460
Wright, James VI, 461
Wright, James VI, 463
Wright, James VI, 468
Wright, James VI, 532
Wright, James VI, 561
Wright, James VI, 585
Wright, James VI, 586
Wright, James VI, 603
Wright, James VI, 608
Wright, James VI, 609
Wright, James VI, 702
Wright, James VI, 903

Wright, James VI, 944
Wright, James VI, 959
Wright, James VI, 1021
Wright, James A. II, 943
Wright, James Allen V, 213
Wright, James Anderson I, 906
Wright, James Anderson I, 1016
Wright, James Anderson II, 828
Wright, James B. III, 386
Wright, James B. III, 388
Wright, James B. III, 390
Wright, James D. IV, 359
Wright, James D. IV, 459
Wright, James D. VI, 847
Wright, James E. V, 367
Wright, James E. VI, 1022
Wright, James Hunnicutt VI, 221
Wright, James M. III, 371
Wright, James M. VI, 877
Wright, James M. VI, 880
Wright, James M. VI, 1022
Wright, James O. VI, 1022
Wright, James, Jr. I, 583
Wright, James, Jr. I, 1099
Wright, James, Jr. VI, 459
Wright, James, Jr. VI, 460
Wright, James, Jr. VI, 461
Wright, James, Jr. VI, 585
Wright, James, Sr. VI, 461
Wright, Jamima IV, 1228
Wright, Jane I, 486
Wright, Jane I, 795
Wright, Jane I, 846
Wright, Jane I, 904
Wright, Jane I, 906
Wright, Jane I, 1088
Wright, Jane I, 1096
Wright, Jane I, 1099
Wright, Jane III, 320
Wright, Jane III, 369
Wright, Jane III, 370
Wright, Jane III, 386
Wright, Jane III, 388
Wright, Jane III, 508
Wright, Jane III, 509
Wright, Jane IV, 68
Wright, Jane IV, 309
Wright, Jane IV, 322
Wright, Jane IV, 359
Wright, Jane V, 144
Wright, Jane V, 213
Wright, Jane V, 224
Wright, Jane V, 292
Wright, Jane V, 293
Wright, Jane V, 468
Wright, Jane VI, 890
Wright, Jane VI, 938
Wright, Jane VI, 1011
Wright, Jane A. II, 777
Wright, Jane A. IV, 308
Wright, Jane D. IV, 309
Wright, Jane E. III, 46
Wright, Jane E. VI, 986
Wright, Jane F. V, 144
Wright, Jane M. III, 371
Wright, Jane Maria III, 370
Wright, Jane P. IV, 308
Wright, Jane Richardson II, 717
Wright, Janetta F. VI, 1021
Wright, Jas. B. III, 386
Wright, Jeams I, 583
Wright, Jeane Louise IV, 791
Wright, Jeanne Louise IV, 790
Wright, Jemima I, 1031
Wright, Jemima I, 1039
Wright, Jemima I, 1088
Wright, Jemima I, 1099
Wright, Jemima IV, 68
Wright, Jemima IV, 972
Wright, Jemima IV, 1018
Wright, Jemima IV, 1228
Wright, Jemima V, 17
Wright, Jemima V, 144
Wright, Jemima V, 215
Wright, Jemima V, 234
Wright, Jemima V, 292
Wright, Jemima V, 302
Wright, Jemima V, 313
Wright, Jemima V, 440
Wright, Jemima V, 441
Wright, Jemima V, 963
Wright, Jemima Ruth I, 1088
Wright, Jemima Ruth I, 1100
Wright, Jemimah IV, 68
Wright, Jemimah V, 292
Wright, Jenkinson IV, 359
Wright, Jenkinson IV, 459
Wright, Jericho III, 172
Wright, Jesse I, 1039
Wright, Jesse I, 1088
Wright, Jesse I, 1091
Wright, Jesse I, 1099
Wright, Jesse I, 1100
Wright, Jesse V, 440
Wright, Jesse V, 544
Wright, Jesse V, 650
Wright, Jesse VI, 366
Wright, Jesse VI, 378
Wright, Jesse VI, 393
Wright, Jesse VI, 459
Wright, Jesse VI, 460
Wright, Jesse VI, 461
Wright, Jesse R. I, 472
Wright, Jesse S. R. I, 1088
Wright, Jesse Samuel VI, 460
Wright, Jesse, Jr. I, 1088
Wright, Jesse, Jr. I, 1098
Wright, Jesse, Jr. I, 1099
Wright, Jessie IV, 1197
Wright, Jessie V, 468
Wright, Jessie F. III, 403
Wright, Jessie F. III, 475
Wright, Jessie L. V, 441
Wright, Jessie L. V, 721
Wright, Jno. T. VI, 461
Wright, Joab IV, 68
Wright, Joab V, 144
Wright, Joab V, 213
Wright, Joab V, 292
Wright, Joab V, 440
Wright, Joab, Jr. V, 292
Wright, Joale V, 543
Wright, Joanna V, 294
Wright, Joannah III, 369
Wright, Job III, 95
Wright, Job III, 301
Wright, Job III, 369
Wright, Job III, 370
Wright, Job IV, 68
Wright, Joel I, 1088
Wright, Joel II, 694
Wright, Joel IV, 1228
Wright, Joel V, 23
Wright, Joel V, 144
Wright, Joel V, 253
Wright, Joel V, 292
Wright, Joel V, 469
Wright, Joel V, 533
Wright, Joel V, 543
Wright, Joel V, 544
Wright, Joel V, 938
Wright, Joel V, 943
Wright, Joel V, 963
Wright, Joel VI, 491
Wright, Joel VI, 585
Wright, Joel VI, 793
Wright, Joel VI, 958
Wright, Joel VI, 1021
Wright, Joel B. I, 1090
Wright, Joel B. I, 1100
Wright, Joel F. V, 293
Wright, Joel H. V, 293
Wright, Joel M. VI, 881
Wright, Joel M. VI, 1022
Wright, Joel T. V, 292
Wright, Joel T. V, 293
Wright, Joel T. V, 468
Wright, Joel T. V, 720
Wright, Joel T. V, 721
Wright, Joel, Jr. V, 943
Wright, John I, 343
Wright, John I, 344
Wright, John I, 347
Wright, John I, 369
Wright, John I, 375
Wright, John I, 430
Wright, John I, 441
Wright, John I, 455
Wright, John I, 472
Wright, John I, 583
Wright, John I, 795
Wright, John I, 867
Wright, John I, 1025
Wright, John I, 1031
Wright, John I, 1039
Wright, John I, 1088
Wright, John I, 1097
Wright, John I, 1099
Wright, John I, 1100
Wright, John I Sup 1, 10
Wright, John II, 113
Wright, John II, 449
Wright, John II, 694
Wright, John II, 695
Wright, John II, 698
Wright, John II, 815
Wright, John III, 56
Wright, John III, 209
Wright, John III, 333
Wright, John III, 369
Wright, John III, 370
Wright, John III, 412
Wright, John III, 444
Wright, John III, 459
Wright, John III, 475
Wright, John III, 489
Wright, John III, 498
Wright, John III, 508
Wright, John III, 509
Wright, John IV, 68
Wright, John IV, 165
Wright, John IV, 308
Wright, John IV, 359
Wright, John IV, 559
Wright, John IV, 667
Wright, John IV, 739
Wright, John IV, 790
Wright, John IV, 857
Wright, John IV, 1018
Wright, John IV, 1157
Wright, John IV, 1179
Wright, John IV, 1196
Wright, John IV, 1197
Wright, John IV, 1301
Wright, John V, 144
Wright, John V, 213
Wright, John V, 234
Wright, John V, 271
Wright, John V, 292
Wright, John V, 293
Wright, John V, 294
Wright, John V, 366
Wright, John V, 369
Wright, John V, 388
Wright, John V, 440
Wright, John V, 468
Wright, John V, 543
Wright, John V, 544
Wright, John V, 864
Wright, John V, 874
Wright, John V, 943
Wright, John V, 1026
Wright, John VI, 345
Wright, John VI, 356
Wright, John VI, 362
Wright, John VI, 436
Wright, John VI, 459
Wright, John VI, 460
Wright, John VI, 461
Wright, John VI, 464
Wright, John VI, 491
Wright, John VI, 514
Wright, John VI, 585
Wright, John VI, 586
Wright, John VI, 608
Wright, John VI, 802
Wright, John VI, 867
Wright, John VI, 873
Wright, John VI, 877
Wright, John VI, 893
Wright, John VI, 917
Wright, John VI, 935
Wright, John VI, 938
Wright, John VI, 944
Wright, John VI, 955
Wright, John VI, 969
Wright, John VI, 993
Wright, John VI, 999
Wright, John VI, 1011
Wright, John VI, 1018
Wright, John VI, 1021
Wright, John A. VI, 960
Wright, John C. III, 370
Wright, John C. IV, 1228
Wright, John D. III, 114
Wright, John D. III, 329
Wright, John D. III, 370
Wright, John D. III, 378
Wright, John D. III, 388
Wright, John D. III, 390
Wright, John D. IV, 308
Wright, John D. IV, 319
Wright, John D. IV, 359
Wright, John D. IV, 459
Wright, John D. IV, 1123
Wright, John D. VI, 375
Wright, John D. VI, 459
Wright, John D. VI, 460
Wright, John D. VI, 461
Wright, John Dunbar, Jr. III, 370
Wright, John Eldridge III, 146
Wright, John Eldridge III, 370
Wright, John Elwood I, 1088
Wright, John H. III, 370
Wright, John H. V, 367
Wright, John H. VI, 922
Wright, John H. VI, 1020
Wright, John H. VI, 1022
Wright, John Howard III, 85
Wright, John Howard III, 106
Wright, John Howard III, 221
Wright, John Howard III, 341
Wright, John Howard III, 369
Wright, John Howard III, 370
Wright, John Jordan III, 388
Wright, John Lewis I, 867
Wright, John M. I, 1088
Wright, John M. VI, 830
Wright, John McAmis I, 1100
Wright, John Mills I, 906
Wright, John Mills I, 1016
Wright, John P. VI, 867
Wright, John Q. A. VI, 968
Wright, John Q. A. VI, 1022
Wright, John R. V, 875
Wright, John S. I, 486
Wright, John S. II, 880
Wright, John S. II, 943
Wright, John T. VI, 461
Wright, John W. II, 724
Wright, John W. III, 295
Wright, John W. III, 369
Wright, John W. III, 370
Wright, John W. III, 371
Wright, John W. IV, 1301
Wright, John William III, 370
Wright, John Wm. III, 370
Wright, John, Jr. I, 1039
Wright, John, Jr. V, 293
Wright, John, Jr. VI, 585
Wright, John-Prier I, 1112
Wright, Jonah V, 144
Wright, Jonah V, 282
Wright, Jonah V, 292
Wright, Jonathan I, 795
Wright, Jonathan I, 867
Wright, Jonathan I, 906
Wright, Jonathan II, 209
Wright, Jonathan II, 226
Wright, Jonathan II, 231
Wright, Jonathan II, 277
Wright, Jonathan II, 439
Wright, Jonathan II, 627
Wright, Jonathan II, 694
Wright, Jonathan II, 904
Wright, Jonathan III, 369
Wright, Jonathan IV, 790
Wright, Jonathan IV, 1171
Wright, Jonathan V, 119
Wright, Jonathan V, 144
Wright, Jonathan V, 213
Wright, Jonathan V, 292
Wright, Jonathan V, 293
Wright, Jonathan V, 313
Wright, Jonathan V, 366
Wright, Jonathan V, 367
Wright, Jonathan V, 440
Wright, Jonathan V, 441
Wright, Jonathan V, 469
Wright, Jonathan V, 514
Wright, Jonathan V, 544
Wright, Jonathan V, 650
Wright, Jonathan V, 773
Wright, Jonathan V, 889
Wright, Jonathan V, 930
Wright, Jonathan V, 965
Wright, Jonathan V, 979
Wright, Jonathan VI, 369
Wright, Jonathan VI, 373
Wright, Jonathan VI, 376
Wright, Jonathan VI, 416
Wright, Jonathan VI, 437
Wright, Jonathan VI, 445
Wright, Jonathan VI, 459
Wright, Jonathan VI, 460
Wright, Jonathan VI, 461
Wright, Jonathan VI, 585
Wright, Jonathan VI, 608
Wright, Jonathan B. V, 144
Wright, Jonathan B. V, 366
Wright, Jonathan B. V, 367
Wright, Jonathan B. V, 721
Wright, Jonathan B. VI, 367
Wright, Jonathan H. V, 440
Wright, Jonathan, Jr. V, 86
Wright, Jonathan, Jr. V, 543
Wright, Jonathan, Jr. V, 943
Wright, Jonathan, Sr. V, 943
Wright, Jonothan V, 144
Wright, Jonothan, Jr. V, 144
Wright, Jordan III, 107
Wright, Jordan III, 370
Wright, Jordan III, 378
Wright, Jordan III, 384
Wright, Jordan III, 387
Wright, Jordan III, 388
Wright, Jordan III, 390
Wright, Jordan III, 451
Wright, Jordan III, 475
Wright, Jordan III, 508
Wright, Jordan III, 509
Wright, Joseph I, 369
Wright, Joseph I, 430
Wright, Joseph I, 472
Wright, Joseph I, 1099
Wright, Joseph II, 113
Wright, Joseph II, 140
Wright, Joseph II, 161
Wright, Joseph II, 257
Wright, Joseph II, 277
Wright, Joseph II, 694
Wright, Joseph II, 695
Wright, Joseph III, 303
Wright, Joseph III, 370
Wright, Joseph III, 425
Wright, Joseph III, 474
Wright, Joseph III, 475
Wright, Joseph III, 476
Wright, Joseph III, 508
Wright, Joseph IV, 68
Wright, Joseph IV, 156
Wright, Joseph IV, 165
Wright, Joseph IV, 167
Wright, Joseph IV, 308
Wright, Joseph IV, 332
Wright, Joseph IV, 346
Wright, Joseph IV, 359
Wright, Joseph IV, 524
Wright, Joseph IV, 559
Wright, Joseph IV, 739
Wright, Joseph IV, 742
Wright, Joseph IV, 760
Wright, Joseph IV, 786
Wright, Joseph IV, 790
Wright, Joseph IV, 857
Wright, Joseph IV, 860
Wright, Joseph IV, 893
Wright, Joseph IV, 896
Wright, Joseph IV, 1018
Wright, Joseph IV, 1228
Wright, Joseph V, 144
Wright, Joseph V, 292
Wright, Joseph V, 293
Wright, Joseph V, 301
Wright, Joseph V, 313
Wright, Joseph V, 324
Wright, Joseph V, 326
Wright, Joseph V, 366
Wright, Joseph V, 367
Wright, Joseph V, 440
Wright, Joseph VI, 345
Wright, Joseph VI, 354
Wright, Joseph VI, 356
Wright, Joseph VI, 459
Wright, Joseph VI, 460
Wright, Joseph VI, 461
Wright, Joseph VI, 491
Wright, Joseph VI, 585
Wright, Joseph VI, 903
Wright, Joseph VI, 924
Wright, Joseph VI, 952
Wright, Joseph VI, 954
Wright, Joseph VI, 959
Wright, Joseph VI, 993
Wright, Joseph VI, 996
Wright, Joseph VI, 1021
Wright, Joseph A. IV, 1018
Wright, Joseph A. IV, 1044
Wright, Joseph D. IV, 308
Wright, Joseph D. IV, 459
Wright, Joseph Dew IV, 359
Wright, Joseph Dew IV, 459
Wright, Joseph H. IV, 857
Wright, Joseph H. V, 468
Wright, Joseph H. VI, 748
Wright, Joseph Hicks IV, 790
Wright, Joseph M. IV, 1196
Wright, Joseph P. VI, 880
Wright, Joseph R. VI, 460
Wright, Joseph Richd VI, 460
Wright, Joseph, Jr. VI, 356
Wright, Joseph, Sr. IV, 165
Wright, Joshua I, 846
Wright, Joshua I, 906
Wright, Joshua I, 970
Wright, Joshua I, 1099
Wright, Joshua I, 1112
Wright, Joshua I, 1135
Wright, Joshua II, 190
Wright, Joshua II, 247
Wright, Joshua II, 277
Wright, Joshua IV, 68
Wright, Joshua V, 144
Wright, Joshua V, 281
Wright, Joshua V, 292
Wright, Joshua V, 293
Wright, Joshua V, 313
Wright, Joshua V, 440
Wright, Joshua V, 726
Wright, Josia II, 113
Wright, Josiah II, 200
Wright, Josiah II, 694
Wright, Josiah V, 144
Wright, Josiah V, 979
Wright, Josias II, 277

t, Jubal VI, 891
t, Jubal VI, 893
t, Judah IV, 1228
t, Judith I, 1030
t, Judith I, 1039
t, Judith IV, 68
t, Judith IV, 667
t, Judith IV, 786
t, Judith IV, 790
t, Judith IV, 853
t, Judith IV, 857
t, Judith V, 213
t, Judith V, 292
t, Judith V, 963
t, Judith VI, 356
t, Judith VI, 954
t, Jules VI, 900
t, Julia V, 367
t, Julia VI, 895
t, Julia Amelia IV, 791
t, Juliann V, 543
t, Justice IV, 857
t, Justice V, 943
t, Justus III, 370
t, Justus V, 943
t, Kate V, 293
t, Kate V, 720
t, Kate V, 721
t, Katharine I, 267
t, Katharine I, 277
t, Katharine III, 475
t, Katharine VI, 1022
t, Katherine V, 293
t, Katie V, 367
t, Kessiah VI, 867
t, Kezia I, 578
t, Kezia I, 584
t, Keziah I, 584
t, Keziah II, 277
t, Keziah III, 56
t, Keziah III, 397
t, Keziah III, 476
t, Keziah V, 367
t, Latitia IV, 667
t, Latitia VI, 1021
t, Laura III, 67
t, Lavina IV, 68
t, Lavina IV, 349
t, Lavina IV, 359
t, Lavina IV, 559
t, Lavina IV, 1152
t, Lavina IV, 1171
t, Lavina IV, 1197
t, Lavina VI, 608
t, Lavina H. IV, 459
t, Lavina H. IV, 525
t, Lavini VI, 608
t, Lavinia H. IV, 394
t, Lawrence IV, 1301
t, Le Anna I, 262
t, Leah I, 422
t, Leah I, 430
t, Leah I, 472
t, Leah I, 486
t, Leah I, 1025
t, Leah I, 1039
t, Leah III, 95
t, Leah III, 370
t, Leander I, 522
t, Leanna V, 721
t, Leatitia II, 113
t, Leatitia II, 126
t, Lenna VI, 1022
t, Leslie V, 441
t, Leslie V, 721
t, Letitia IV, 667
t, Letitia V, 366
t, Letticia V, 366
t, Levan I, 583
t, Levi II, 772
t, Levi IV, 1229
t, Levi V, 213
t, Levi V, 292
t, Levi V, 293
t, Levi V, 367
t, Levi V, 721
t, Levi VI, 460
t, Levi VI, 461
t, Levi, Jr. V, 367
t, Levin I, 522
t, Levina IV, 68
t, Levina VI, 598
t, Levina VI, 608
t, Levincy VI, 461
t, Levitt V, 596
t, Lewis VI, 846
t, Lewis VI, 893
t, Lewis VI, 922
t, Lewis A. I, 472
t, Lindley H. IV, 559
t, Lindley H. IV, 1197
Wright, Lindley M. IV, 1197
Wright, Lindley M. V, 293
Wright, Lindley Murray V, 292
Wright, Linnetta M. IV, 1344
Wright, Littleberry VI, 1021
Wright, Lizzie V, 721
Wright, Lizzie Gustin V, 367
Wright, Lot V, 293
Wright, Louis Senat II, 829
Wright, Louisa II, 1082
Wright, Louisa V, 116
Wright, Louisa V, 144
Wright, Louisa V, 367
Wright, Louisa V, 440
Wright, Louisa V, 721
Wright, Louisa A. II, 1084
Wright, Louisa Ann VI, 1021
Wright, Louisa Caroline I, 486
Wright, Louisa G. IV, 359
Wright, Louisa S. V, 144
Wright, Louisa S. V, 721
Wright, Louisa Sabin VI, 367
Wright, Louise I, 486
Wright, Louiza V, 144
Wright, Lovey A. I, 472
Wright, Lovey Ann I, 486
Wright, Lovin A. VI, 867
Wright, Lovina H. IV, 1197
Wright, Luce VI, 459
Wright, Lucinda VI, 867
Wright, Lucurgus B. V, 367
Wright, Lucy I, 846
Wright, Lucy I, 1112
Wright, Lucy I, 1135
Wright, Lucy I Sup 1, 12
Wright, Lucy II, 277
Wright, Lucy II, 492
Wright, Lucy II, 695
Wright, Lucy V, 347
Wright, Lucy V, 367
Wright, Lucy V, 773
Wright, Lucy V, 929
Wright, Lucy V, 943
Wright, Lucy VI, 460
Wright, Lucy VI, 585
Wright, Lucy VI, 905
Wright, Lucy VI, 1021
Wright, Lucy A. VI, 867
Wright, Lundy II, 1084
Wright, Lycurgus B. V, 367
Wright, Lydia I, 795
Wright, Lydia I, 867
Wright, Lydia II, 694
Wright, Lydia II, 695
Wright, Lydia II, 777
Wright, Lydia III, 171
Wright, Lydia III, 370
Wright, Lydia IV, 308
Wright, Lydia IV, 309
Wright, Lydia IV, 790
Wright, Lydia IV, 857
Wright, Lydia IV, 893
Wright, Lydia IV, 896
Wright, Lydia V, 144
Wright, Lydia V, 213
Wright, Lydia V, 265
Wright, Lydia V, 292
Wright, Lydia V, 293
Wright, Lydia V, 301
Wright, Lydia V, 313
Wright, Lydia V, 326
Wright, Lydia V, 366
Wright, Lydia V, 367
Wright, Lydia V, 440
Wright, Lydia V, 838
Wright, Lydia V, 874
Wright, Lydia V, 943
Wright, Lydia VI, 460
Wright, Lydia VI, 895
Wright, Lydia VI, 1021
Wright, Lydia A. V, 468
Wright, Lydia Allen VI, 608
Wright, Lydia Ann V, 292
Wright, Lydia E. III, 329
Wright, Lydia E. III, 370
Wright, Lydia H. IV, 791
Wright, Lydia H. VI, 366
Wright, Lydia H. VI, 378
Wright, Lydia H. VI, 393
Wright, Lydia H. VI, 460
Wright, Lydia H. VI, 461
Wright, Lydia M. III, 345
Wright, Lydia M. III, 369
Wright, Lydia S. III, 303
Wright, Lydia S. III, 370
Wright, Lydia S. V, 943
Wright, M. Fisher II, 943
Wright, Madge V, 293
Wright, Mahala I, 1112
Wright, Mahala I, 1135
Wright, Mahala V, 367
Wright, Mahala V, 440
Wright, Mahala V, 773
Wright, Mahala Ann V, 773
Wright, Mahlon I, 472
Wright, Mahlon I, 486
Wright, Mahlon V, 144
Wright, Mahlon V, 979
Wright, Mahlon B. II, 1064
Wright, Malhala Ann I Sup 1, 12
Wright, Malinda VI, 959
Wright, Malinda Margaret I, 1088
Wright, Malinda Margaret I, 1100
Wright, Margaret I, 369
Wright, Margaret I, 846
Wright, Margaret I, 1088
Wright, Margaret I, 1097
Wright, Margaret I, 1099
Wright, Margaret II, 695
Wright, Margaret III, 203
Wright, Margaret III, 486
Wright, Margaret III, 509
Wright, Margaret IV, 79
Wright, Margaret IV, 117
Wright, Margaret V, 144
Wright, Margaret V, 236
Wright, Margaret V, 292
Wright, Margaret V, 543
Wright, Margaret V, 544
Wright, Margaret V, 874
Wright, Margaret VI, 185
Wright, Margaret VI, 220
Wright, Margaret VI, 376
Wright, Margaret VI, 437
Wright, Margaret VI, 460
Wright, Margaret VI, 585
Wright, Margaret VI, 1021
Wright, Margaret Ann III, 388
Wright, Margarett VI, 532
Wright, Margery III, 370
Wright, Margret II, 113
Wright, Maria V, 943
Wright, Maria S. III, 371
Wright, Mariah V, 943
Wright, Mariah VI, 867
Wright, Mariah VI, 1022
Wright, Mariana W. III, 67
Wright, Marilla I, 1088
Wright, Marillia L. IV, 309
Wright, Mark II, 990
Wright, Mark II, 1041
Wright, Mark II, 1064
Wright, Mark II, 1073
Wright, Mark II, 1074
Wright, Mark II, 1075
Wright, Mark II, 1079
Wright, Mark II, 1083
Wright, Martha I, 455
Wright, Martha I, 906
Wright, Martha I, 1016
Wright, Martha II, 695
Wright, Martha II, 828
Wright, Martha II, 990
Wright, Martha II, 1014
Wright, Martha II, 1041
Wright, Martha II, 1064
Wright, Martha II, 1075
Wright, Martha II, 1079
Wright, Martha II, 1083
Wright, Martha II, 1084
Wright, Martha III, 388
Wright, Martha IV, 68
Wright, Martha IV, 208
Wright, Martha IV, 308
Wright, Martha IV, 309
Wright, Martha IV, 359
Wright, Martha IV, 459
Wright, Martha IV, 647
Wright, Martha IV, 667
Wright, Martha IV, 742
Wright, Martha IV, 790
Wright, Martha IV, 1228
Wright, Martha V, 222
Wright, Martha V, 253
Wright, Martha V, 292
Wright, Martha V, 293
Wright, Martha V, 367
Wright, Martha V, 441
Wright, Martha V, 650
Wright, Martha V, 943
Wright, Martha VI, 356
Wright, Martha VI, 442
Wright, Martha VI, 459
Wright, Martha VI, 460
Wright, Martha VI, 586
Wright, Martha VI, 867
Wright, Martha Ann V, 858
Wright, Martha Ann V, 875
Wright, Martha Ann VI, 881
Wright, Martha Ann VI, 1022
Wright, Martha C. II, 1079
Wright, Martha C. II, 1084
Wright, Martha E. VI, 366
Wright, Martha E. VI, 460
Wright, Martha E. VI, 1022
Wright, Martha Elizabeth VI, 460
Wright, Martha Jane III, 370
Wright, Martha L. IV, 243
Wright, Martha L. IV, 309
Wright, Martha P. IV, 1219
Wright, Martha T. II, 943
Wright, Martha W. VI, 460
Wright, Martin VI, 1021
Wright, Martitia I, 470
Wright, Martitia I, 472
Wright, Mary I, 344
Wright, Mary I, 347
Wright, Mary I, 369
Wright, Mary I, 375
Wright, Mary I, 430
Wright, Mary I, 584
Wright, Mary I, 608
Wright, Mary I, 867
Wright, Mary I, 868
Wright, Mary I, 899
Wright, Mary I, 905
Wright, Mary I, 906
Wright, Mary I, 1016
Wright, Mary I, 1035
Wright, Mary I, 1038
Wright, Mary I, 1039
Wright, Mary I, 1112
Wright, Mary II, 48
Wright, Mary II, 60
Wright, Mary II, 70
Wright, Mary II, 113
Wright, Mary II, 190
Wright, Mary II, 202
Wright, Mary II, 226
Wright, Mary II, 277
Wright, Mary II, 278
Wright, Mary II, 439
Wright, Mary II, 694
Wright, Mary II, 695
Wright, Mary II, 724
Wright, Mary II, 777
Wright, Mary II, 783
Wright, Mary II, 829
Wright, Mary II, 1041
Wright, Mary III, 19
Wright, Mary III, 67
Wright, Mary III, 172
Wright, Mary III, 240
Wright, Mary III, 249
Wright, Mary III, 311
Wright, Mary III, 355
Wright, Mary III, 369
Wright, Mary III, 370
Wright, Mary III, 371
Wright, Mary III, 377
Wright, Mary III, 378
Wright, Mary III, 387
Wright, Mary III, 388
Wright, Mary III, 406
Wright, Mary III, 459
Wright, Mary III, 474
Wright, Mary III, 475
Wright, Mary III, 476
Wright, Mary III, 501
Wright, Mary IV, 68
Wright, Mary IV, 306
Wright, Mary IV, 308
Wright, Mary IV, 309
Wright, Mary IV, 331
Wright, Mary IV, 359
Wright, Mary IV, 505
Wright, Mary IV, 506
Wright, Mary IV, 559
Wright, Mary IV, 737
Wright, Mary IV, 791
Wright, Mary IV, 1107
Wright, Mary IV, 1196
Wright, Mary IV, 1197
Wright, Mary IV, 1228
Wright, Mary IV, 1344
Wright, Mary V, 144
Wright, Mary V, 239
Wright, Mary V, 282
Wright, Mary V, 292
Wright, Mary V, 293
Wright, Mary V, 366
Wright, Mary V, 419
Wright, Mary V, 441
Wright, Mary V, 535
Wright, Mary V, 543
Wright, Mary V, 544
Wright, Mary V, 979
Wright, Mary VI, 345
Wright, Mary VI, 354
Wright, Mary VI, 356
Wright, Mary VI, 361
Wright, Mary VI, 378
Wright, Mary VI, 393
Wright, Mary VI, 394
Wright, Mary VI, 445
Wright, Mary VI, 450
Wright, Mary VI, 459
Wright, Mary VI, 460
Wright, Mary VI, 461
Wright, Mary VI, 468
Wright, Mary VI, 491
Wright, Mary VI, 514
Wright, Mary VI, 532
Wright, Mary VI, 585
Wright, Mary VI, 608
Wright, Mary VI, 867
Wright, Mary VI, 917
Wright, Mary VI, 924
Wright, Mary VI, 935
Wright, Mary VI, 960
Wright, Mary VI, 1011
Wright, Mary VI, 1021
Wright, Mary A. I, 470
Wright, Mary A. II, 883
Wright, Mary A. II, 892
Wright, Mary A. II, 904
Wright, Mary A. II, 912
Wright, Mary A. II, 943
Wright, Mary A. III, 95
Wright, Mary A. III, 370
Wright, Mary A. IV, 308
Wright, Mary Anderson II, 829
Wright, Mary Ann I, 472
Wright, Mary Ann I, 486
Wright, Mary Ann II, 137
Wright, Mary Ann II, 141
Wright, Mary Ann II, 156
Wright, Mary Ann II, 161
Wright, Mary Ann II, 694
Wright, Mary Ann II, 695
Wright, Mary Ann II, 777
Wright, Mary Ann III, 369
Wright, Mary Ann IV, 309
Wright, Mary Ann IV, 790
Wright, Mary Ann VI, 913
Wright, Mary B. III, 85
Wright, Mary B. III, 99
Wright, Mary B. III, 180
Wright, Mary B. III, 370
Wright, Mary B. III, 373
Wright, Mary B. III, 388
Wright, Mary B. III, 390
Wright, Mary B. IV, 285
Wright, Mary B. IV, 308
Wright, Mary B. L. IV, 309
Wright, Mary C. VI, 927
Wright, Mary Crulet V, 293
Wright, Mary Crute V, 293
Wright, Mary Crute V, 367
Wright, Mary D. III, 388
Wright, Mary E. II, 1084
Wright, Mary E. IV, 308
Wright, Mary E. IV, 309
Wright, Mary Eliza IV, 333
Wright, Mary Eliza IV, 359
Wright, Mary Elizabeth VI, 1022
Wright, Mary Ellen II, 315
Wright, Mary Ellen II, 327
Wright, Mary Ellen II, 1074
Wright, Mary Ellen II, 1084
Wright, Mary Ellin II, 1084
Wright, Mary Emily V, 543
Wright, Mary Evaline I, 1100
Wright, Mary Eveline I, 1088
Wright, Mary F. III, 370
Wright, Mary F. III, 388
Wright, Mary F. III, 509
Wright, Mary Frances I, 951
Wright, Mary Gilbert IV, 308
Wright, Mary Gilbert IV, 359
Wright, Mary H. IV, 1267
Wright, Mary I. IV, 359
Wright, Mary J. II, 883
Wright, Mary J. II, 943
Wright, Mary J. IV, 359
Wright, Mary J. V, 404
Wright, Mary J. VI, 897
Wright, Mary J. VI, 952
Wright, Mary Jane II, 943
Wright, Mary Jane V, 286
Wright, Mary Jane V, 293
Wright, Mary Jane V, 627
Wright, Mary Jane V, 650
Wright, Mary Jane VI, 460
Wright, Mary Jane VI, 461
Wright, Mary Jenkinson IV, 1123
Wright, Mary L. VI, 944
Wright, Mary Lane V, 963
Wright, Mary Luiza I, 867
Wright, Mary N. III, 369
Wright, Mary N. III, 370

Wright, Mary P. III, 387
Wright, Mary P. III, 388
Wright, Mary P. VI, 916
Wright, Mary R. I, 472
Wright, Mary S. II, 1074
Wright, Mary S. II, 1083
Wright, Mary S. VI, 986
Wright, Mary Seal II, 837
Wright, Mary Seal II, 943
Wright, Mary Susan VI, 378
Wright, Mary Susan VI, 460
Wright, Mary Susanna VI, 460
Wright, Mary T. VI, 1022
Wright, Mary Thomas IV, 1123
Wright, Mary Timberlake V, 292
Wright, Mary W. III, 67
Wright, Mary W. III, 475
Wright, Mary, Jr. VI, 461
Wright, Maryann K. IV, 739
Wright, Matilda IV, 790
Wright, Matilda IV, 857
Wright, Matilda V, 440
Wright, Matilda VI, 1022
Wright, Matilda A. V, 721
Wright, Matthew VI, 890
Wright, Matthew VI, 895
Wright, Matthew VI, 942
Wright, Matthew VI, 960
Wright, Mattie I, 441
Wright, Mattie V, 721
Wright, Maud V, 360
Wright, Maud H. V, 367
Wright, May IV, 309
Wright, Md. Hannah VI, 468
Wright, Melissa F. V, 367
Wright, Melvina V, 367
Wright, Meredith VI, 867
Wright, Meredith VI, 1021
Wright, Meriam IV, 733
Wright, Meriam IV, 791
Wright, Micaiah I, 583
Wright, Micajah I, 583
Wright, Micajah I, 867
Wright, Micajah I, 868
Wright, Micajah I, 906
Wright, Micajah I Sup 1, 10
Wright, Micajah V, 874
Wright, Micajah V, 875
Wright, Micajah VI, 459
Wright, Micajah VI, 460
Wright, Micajah VI, 585
Wright, Miers Fisher II, 829
Wright, Mildred V, 354
Wright, Mildred V, 366
Wright, Mildred V, 367
Wright, Mildred VI, 867
Wright, Milton II, 829
Wright, Milton V, 293
Wright, Milton V, 440
Wright, Minerva V, 214
Wright, Minnie V, 721
Wright, Minnie A. V, 441
Wright, Minnie O. V, 721
Wright, Miriam I, 868
Wright, Miriam IV, 733
Wright, Miriam IV, 790
Wright, Miriam IV, 791
Wright, Mirium IV, 857
Wright, Molley VI, 867
Wright, Morris English IV, 309
Wright, Morris P. IV, 308
Wright, Morris P. IV, 309
Wright, Moses I, 1088
Wright, Moses V, 943
Wright, Moses VI, 1021
Wright, Moses D. V, 943
Wright, Moses Walton V, 214
Wright, Mrs. Carl B. I, 951
Wright, Mrs. Katharine VI, 994
Wright, Myra IV, 1197
Wright, Myra F. II, 944
Wright, Myra F. IV, 359
Wright, Myrtle IV, 1267
Wright, Nancy I, 441
Wright, Nancy I, 455
Wright, Nancy I, 522
Wright, Nancy VI, 161
Wright, Nancy VI, 220
Wright, Nancy VI, 221
Wright, Nancy VI, 345
Wright, Nancy VI, 352
Wright, Nancy VI, 356
Wright, Nancy VI, 867
Wright, Nancy VI, 873
Wright, Nancy VI, 875
Wright, Nancy VI, 891
Wright, Nancy VI, 917
Wright, Nancy VI, 942
Wright, Nancy VI, 959
Wright, Nancy VI, 969
Wright, Nancy VI, 1017
Wright, Nancy VI, 1021
Wright, Nancy A. VI, 955
Wright, Nanny VI, 1021
Wright, Naomi I, 1112
Wright, Narcissa V, 282
Wright, Narcissa V, 293
Wright, Narcissa A. V, 293
Wright, Nathan I, 369
Wright, Nathan I, 584
Wright, Nathan I, 906
Wright, Nathan I, 1016
Wright, Nathan I, 1039
Wright, Nathan II, 48
Wright, Nathan II, 113
Wright, Nathan II, 226
Wright, Nathan II, 277
Wright, Nathan II, 695
Wright, Nathan II, 724
Wright, Nathan II, 777
Wright, Nathan II, 943
Wright, Nathan III, 369
Wright, Nathan IV, 886
Wright, Nathan IV, 1018
Wright, Nathan V, 293
Wright, Nathan VI, 461
Wright, Nathaniel II, 783
Wright, Nehemiah IV, 165
Wright, Nehemiah IV, 194
Wright, Nehemiah IV, 308
Wright, Nehemiah IV, 331
Wright, Nehemiah IV, 359
Wright, Nehemiah IV, 459
Wright, Nehemiah IV, 1088
Wright, Nehemiah IV, 1123
Wright, Nellie V, 367
Wright, Nellie VI, 461
Wright, Nellie S. VI, 405
Wright, Nellie S. VI, 460
Wright, Nettie IV, 1267
Wright, Noah V, 773
Wright, Nora IV, 1344
Wright, Obadiah III, 370
Wright, Oney VI, 877
Wright, Opha E. V, 144
Wright, Orilla E. V, 773
Wright, Orpha IV, 309
Wright, Orpha P. V, 144
Wright, Owen V, 293
Wright, Owen V, 440
Wright, Owen V, 773
Wright, Owen W. V, 293
Wright, P. Brelsford II, 1084
Wright, Palmyra IV, 1197
Wright, Parker VI, 867
Wright, Parvin IV, 165
Wright, Parvin IV, 285
Wright, Parvin IV, 308
Wright, Parvin IV, 309
Wright, Parvin V, 533
Wright, Parvin V, 544
Wright, Patience II, 694
Wright, Patience III, 425
Wright, Patience III, 475
Wright, Patricia Ellen V, 720
Wright, Patrick II, 439
Wright, Paul V, 144
Wright, Paul H. V, 144
Wright, Paul H. V, 721
Wright, Paul Howard IV, 309
Wright, Paxon VI, 586
Wright, Paxson IV, 308
Wright, Paxson IV, 1196
Wright, Paxton IV, 359
Wright, Peace IV, 1176
Wright, Peace IV, 1197
Wright, Pearl IV, 1344
Wright, Pearl W. IV, 1344
Wright, Peggy VI, 875
Wright, Pemelia IV, 1197
Wright, Percy English IV, 1267
Wright, Permelia IV, 1160
Wright, Permelia VI, 1022
Wright, Peter II, 48
Wright, Peter II, 113
Wright, Peter II, 829
Wright, Peter II, 831
Wright, Peter II, 837
Wright, Peter II, 883
Wright, Peter II, 892
Wright, Peter II, 904
Wright, Peter II, 912
Wright, Peter II, 943
Wright, Peter III, 370
Wright, Peter F. II, 943
Wright, Peter Harmon I, 1088
Wright, Peter Harmon I, 1100
Wright, Peter M. VI, 877
Wright, Peter M. VI, 897
Wright, Peter M. VI, 917
Wright, Peter M. VI, 955
Wright, Peter M. VI, 1021
Wright, Peter M. VI, 1022
Wright, Peter T. II, 844
Wright, Peter T. II, 903
Wright, Peter T. II, 904
Wright, Peter T. II, 941
Wright, Peter T. II, 943
Wright, Peter Troth II, 829
Wright, Peter Troth II, 837
Wright, Peter Troth II, 943
Wright, Peter Troth, Jr. II, 829
Wright, Pheba VI, 881
Wright, Phebe III, 209
Wright, Phebe III, 370
Wright, Phebe III, 387
Wright, Phebe III, 395
Wright, Phebe III, 406
Wright, Phebe III, 412
Wright, Phebe III, 444
Wright, Phebe III, 475
Wright, Phebe III, 476
Wright, Phebe III, 489
Wright, Phebe III, 498
Wright, Phebe III, 508
Wright, Phebe III, 509
Wright, Phebe IV, 165
Wright, Phebe IV, 514
Wright, Phebe IV, 559
Wright, Phebe IV, 790
Wright, Phebe IV, 791
Wright, Phebe V, 97
Wright, Phebe V, 388
Wright, Phebe V, 440
Wright, Phebe V, 543
Wright, Phebe VI, 362
Wright, Phebe VI, 368
Wright, Phebe VI, 428
Wright, Phebe VI, 445
Wright, Phebe VI, 459
Wright, Phebe VI, 461
Wright, Phebe VI, 561
Wright, Phebe VI, 586
Wright, Phebe VI, 608
Wright, Phebe VI, 702
Wright, Phebe VI, 893
Wright, Phebe VI, 911
Wright, Phebe A. IV, 791
Wright, Phebe Ann I, 1088
Wright, Phebe Ann I, 1100
Wright, Phebe C. III, 386
Wright, Phebe C. III, 388
Wright, Phebe J. III, 370
Wright, Phebe J. V, 367
Wright, Phebe Jane V, 721
Wright, Phebe L. IV, 524
Wright, Phebe L. IV, 559
Wright, Phila III, 370
Wright, Phila III, 371
Wright, Phila Eliz. III, 371
Wright, Pierson Brelsford II, 1084
Wright, Pleasant V, 292
Wright, Pleasant V, 293
Wright, Polly V, 440
Wright, Polly VI, 796
Wright, Polly VI, 921
Wright, Polly VI, 959
Wright, Polly VI, 1011
Wright, Polly VI, 1021
Wright, Polly M. VI, 917
Wright, Price VI, 1021
Wright, Pricilla M. II, 161
Wright, Priscilla II, 85
Wright, Priscilla II, 87
Wright, Priscilla II, 113
Wright, Priscilla II, 140
Wright, Priscilla II, 777
Wright, Prudence II, 126
Wright, Pryor VI, 867
Wright, Pryor B. VI, 867
Wright, Rachael VI, 491
Wright, Rachel I, 343
Wright, Rachel I, 347
Wright, Rachel I, 369
Wright, Rachel I, 375
Wright, Rachel I, 407
Wright, Rachel I, 430
Wright, Rachel I, 584
Wright, Rachel I, 906
Wright, Rachel I, 1016
Wright, Rachel I, 1025
Wright, Rachel I, 1030
Wright, Rachel I, 1031
Wright, Rachel I, 1036
Wright, Rachel I, 1039
Wright, Rachel I, 1088
Wright, Rachel I, 1097
Wright, Rachel I, 1099
Wright, Rachel II, 663
Wright, Rachel II, 694
Wright, Rachel II, 943
Wright, Rachel II, 1041
Wright, Rachel II, 1074
Wright, Rachel II, 1082
Wright, Rachel II, 1083
Wright, Rachel II, 1084
Wright, Rachel III, 56
Wright, Rachel III, 301
Wright, Rachel III, 369
Wright, Rachel III, 370
Wright, Rachel III, 448
Wright, Rachel III, 476
Wright, Rachel IV, 208
Wright, Rachel IV, 308
Wright, Rachel IV, 790
Wright, Rachel IV, 1171
Wright, Rachel IV, 1196
Wright, Rachel IV, 1197
Wright, Rachel V, 213
Wright, Rachel V, 292
Wright, Rachel V, 293
Wright, Rachel V, 440
Wright, Rachel V, 441
Wright, Rachel V, 451
Wright, Rachel V, 468
Wright, Rachel V, 595
Wright, Rachel V, 596
Wright, Rachel V, 606
Wright, Rachel V, 613
Wright, Rachel V, 650
Wright, Rachel VI, 183
Wright, Rachel VI, 184
Wright, Rachel VI, 220
Wright, Rachel VI, 221
Wright, Rachel VI, 281
Wright, Rachel VI, 335
Wright, Rachel VI, 345
Wright, Rachel VI, 400
Wright, Rachel VI, 416
Wright, Rachel VI, 445
Wright, Rachel VI, 460
Wright, Rachel VI, 461
Wright, Rachel VI, 490
Wright, Rachel VI, 585
Wright, Rachel VI, 586
Wright, Rachel VI, 608
Wright, Rachel VI, 867
Wright, Rachel A. VI, 411
Wright, Rachel A. VI, 460
Wright, Rachel Adeline I, 1088
Wright, Rachel Adeline I, 1100
Wright, Rachel Ann V, 292
Wright, Rachel Ann VI, 460
Wright, Rachel E. V, 468
Wright, Rachel Edith IV, 791
Wright, Rachel Elva V, 292
Wright, Rachel H. V, 468
Wright, Rachel M. V, 61
Wright, Rachel M. V, 144
Wright, Rachel N. II, 880
Wright, Rachel Rebecca III, 149
Wright, Rachel W. II, 1084
Wright, Ralph I, 583
Wright, Ralph I, 795
Wright, Ralph I, 847
Wright, Ralph I, 867
Wright, Ralph I, 868
Wright, Ralph I, 906
Wright, Ralph I, 936
Wright, Ralph V, 144
Wright, Ralph V, 721
Wright, Ralph V, 773
Wright, Ralph VI, 459
Wright, Ralph VI, 460
Wright, Ralph VI, 585
Wright, Ralph B. V, 721
Wright, Ralph Elliott V, 144
Wright, Ranuel I, 584
Wright, Rebecah I, 584
Wright, Rebecca I, 936
Wright, Rebecca II, 70
Wright, Rebecca II, 98
Wright, Rebecca II, 113
Wright, Rebecca II, 126
Wright, Rebecca II, 257
Wright, Rebecca II, 277
Wright, Rebecca II, 695
Wright, Rebecca II, 705
Wright, Rebecca II, 777
Wright, Rebecca II, 822
Wright, Rebecca II, 829
Wright, Rebecca II, 943
Wright, Rebecca III, 107
Wright, Rebecca III, 370
Wright, Rebecca III, 384
Wright, Rebecca III, 388
Wright, Rebecca III, 390
Wright, Rebecca IV, 68
Wright, Rebecca IV, 165
Wright, Rebecca IV, 359
Wright, Rebecca IV, 739
Wright, Rebecca IV, 790
Wright, Rebecca IV, 1122
Wright, Rebecca IV, 1123
Wright, Rebecca V, 91
Wright, Rebecca V, 144
Wright, Rebecca V, 292
Wright, Rebecca V, 313
Wright, Rebecca V, 366
Wright, Rebecca V, 440
Wright, Rebecca V, 895
Wright, Rebecca V, 943
Wright, Rebecca VI, 459
Wright, Rebecca VI, 460
Wright, Rebecca Ann II, 106
Wright, Rebecca Ann II, 107
Wright, Rebecca Ann II, 108
Wright, Rebecca K. IV, 1227
Wright, Rebecca M. VI, 368
Wright, Rebecca M. VI, 460
Wright, Rebecca M. VI, 731
Wright, Rebecca S. VI, 460
Wright, Rebecca Tharesa VI
Wright, Rebecca W. IV, 1123
Wright, Rebeccah I, 543
Wright, Rebeccah II, 94
Wright, Rebeccah II, 113
Wright, Rebeckah IV, 539
Wright, Rebeckah V, 281
Wright, Rebeckah V, 292
Wright, Rebeckah V, 726
Wright, Rebeckah V, 773
Wright, Rebeckah VI, 460
Wright, Rebeka I, 868
Wright, Rebekah I, 1112
Wright, Rebekah I, 1135
Wright, Rebekah I Sup 1, 12
Wright, Rebekah VI, 608
Wright, Reliance II, 783
Wright, Reuben III, 370
Wright, Reuben III, 371
Wright, Reuben, Jr. III, 370
Wright, Rev. John I. V, 1026
Wright, Rhoda II, 614
Wright, Rhoda II, 694
Wright, Rhoda IV, 559
Wright, Rhoda V, 333
Wright, Rhoda V, 366
Wright, Rhoda V, 367
Wright, Rhoda VI, 938
Wright, Rhoda VI, 1021
Wright, Rice V, 440
Wright, Richard II, 126
Wright, Richard II, 140
Wright, Richard II, 161
Wright, Richard II, 724
Wright, Richard III, 370
Wright, Richard III, 371
Wright, Richard V, 213
Wright, Richard V, 721
Wright, Richard V, 945
Wright, Richard V, 963
Wright, Richard VI, 437
Wright, Richard VI, 445
Wright, Richard VI, 460
Wright, Richard VI, 461
Wright, Richards IV, 739
Wright, Richardson I, 795
Wright, Richardson I, 867
Wright, Richardson I, 868
Wright, Richardson I, 906
Wright, Rite VI, 993
Wright, Rithy VI, 920
Wright, Robert II, 190
Wright, Robert II, 234
Wright, Robert II, 277
Wright, Robert II, 439
Wright, Robert III, 67
Wright, Robert III, 370
Wright, Robert III, 388
Wright, Robert III, 390
Wright, Robert IV, 165
Wright, Robert IV, 208
Wright, Robert IV, 308
Wright, Robert IV, 347
Wright, Robert IV, 359
Wright, Robert IV, 1196
Wright, Robert IV, 1197
Wright, Robert V, 367
Wright, Robert V, 441
Wright, Robert VI, 345
Wright, Robert VI, 586
Wright, Robert VI, 802
Wright, Robert VI, 819
Wright, Robert VI, 855
Wright, Robert VI, 858
Wright, Robert VI, 861
Wright, Robert VI, 867
Wright, Robert B. VI, 865
Wright, Robert B. VI, 867
Wright, Robert K. II, 829
Wright, Robert K. II, 892
Wright, Robert K. II, 912
Wright, Robert K. II, 943

t, Robert K., Jr. II, 943
t, Robert Kemp II, 829
t, Robert P. VI, 1021
t, Robert W. S. VI, 1022
t, Robert Willets III, 388
t, Rodema E. I, 441
t, Ronald V, 721
t, Rosella V, 213
t, Rowena V, 721
t, Rowena Berlin V, 721
t, Rozettia I, 472
t, Ruth I, 867
t, Ruth I, 1025
t, Ruth I, 1088
t, Ruth I, 1098
t, Ruth I, 1099
t, Ruth II, 31
t, Ruth II, 48
t, Ruth II, 60
t, Ruth II, 113
t, Ruth II, 130
t, Ruth II, 141
t, Ruth II, 160
t, Ruth II, 161
t, Ruth V, 292
t, Ruth V, 293
t, Ruth V, 403
t, Ruth V, 440
t, Ruth V, 441
t, Ruth V, 468
t, Ruth V, 499
t, Ruth V, 543
t, Ruth V, 963
t, Ruth VI, 381
t, Ruth VI, 388
t, Ruth VI, 404
t, Ruth VI, 445
t, Ruth VI, 459
t, Ruth VI, 460
t, Ruth VI, 461
t, Ruth VI, 491
t, Ruth VI, 561
t, Ruth VI, 586
t, Ruth VI, 608
t, Ruth VI, 678
t, Ruth VI, 702
t, Ruth VI, 705
t, Ruth Ann II, 1084
t, Ruthy VI, 955
t, Salley VI, 1021
t, Sally IV, 790
t, Sally IV, 791
t, Sally IV, 1018
t, Sally VI, 445
t, Sally VI, 460
t, Sally VI, 795
t, Sally VI, 944
t, Sally VI, 999
t, Sally VI, 1020
t, Sally VI, 1021
t, Sally Ann IV, 285
t, Sally Ann IV, 308
t, Sally Ann IV, 309
t, Sally Ann V, 977
t, Sally Ann V, 979
t, Sally H. VI, 1020
t, Sally S. VI, 1021
t, Sally Salina I, 867
t, Sam'l Kelley Gaunt 1100
t, Sampson V, 292
t, Sampson V, 441
t, Samuel II, 113
t, Samuel II, 190
t, Samuel II, 227
t, Samuel II, 277
t, Samuel II, 439
t, Samuel II, 694
t, Samuel II, 695
t, Samuel II, 772
t, Samuel II, 777
t, Samuel II, 1041
t, Samuel III, 370
t, Samuel III, 371
t, Samuel IV, 308
t, Samuel IV, 559
t, Samuel IV, 739
t, Samuel V, 596
t, Samuel VI, 459
t, Samuel VI, 460
t, Samuel B. VI, 460
ht, Samuel C. II, 277
ht, Samuel G. II, 695
ht, Samuel Gardiner II, 695
t, Samuel L. III, 370
ht, Samuel, Jr. II, 694
ht, Sarah I, 369
ht, Sarah I, 430
ht, Sarah I, 472
nt, Sarah I, 584
ht, Sarah I, 899
Wright, Sarah I, 906
Wright, Sarah I, 990
Wright, Sarah I, 1000
Wright, Sarah I, 1016
Wright, Sarah I, 1031
Wright, Sarah I, 1039
Wright, Sarah I, 1088
Wright, Sarah I, 1099
Wright, Sarah I, 1112
Wright, Sarah I, 1127
Wright, Sarah I, 1135
Wright, Sarah II, 143
Wright, Sarah II, 161
Wright, Sarah II, 277
Wright, Sarah II, 315
Wright, Sarah II, 327
Wright, Sarah II, 579
Wright, Sarah II, 641
Wright, Sarah II, 665
Wright, Sarah II, 694
Wright, Sarah II, 695
Wright, Sarah II, 777
Wright, Sarah II, 829
Wright, Sarah II, 943
Wright, Sarah III, 108
Wright, Sarah III, 311
Wright, Sarah III, 333
Wright, Sarah III, 343
Wright, Sarah III, 369
Wright, Sarah III, 370
Wright, Sarah III, 371
Wright, Sarah III, 412
Wright, Sarah III, 455
Wright, Sarah III, 475
Wright, Sarah III, 476
Wright, Sarah III, 509
Wright, Sarah IV, 68
Wright, Sarah IV, 165
Wright, Sarah IV, 336
Wright, Sarah IV, 347
Wright, Sarah IV, 359
Wright, Sarah IV, 531
Wright, Sarah IV, 533
Wright, Sarah IV, 534
Wright, Sarah IV, 543
Wright, Sarah IV, 551
Wright, Sarah IV, 559
Wright, Sarah IV, 918
Wright, Sarah IV, 1179
Wright, Sarah IV, 1196
Wright, Sarah IV, 1197
Wright, Sarah V, 59
Wright, Sarah V, 144
Wright, Sarah V, 239
Wright, Sarah V, 282
Wright, Sarah V, 292
Wright, Sarah V, 293
Wright, Sarah V, 313
Wright, Sarah V, 440
Wright, Sarah V, 441
Wright, Sarah V, 499
Wright, Sarah V, 543
Wright, Sarah V, 544
Wright, Sarah V, 650
Wright, Sarah V, 721
Wright, Sarah V, 912
Wright, Sarah V, 943
Wright, Sarah VI, 166
Wright, Sarah VI, 170
Wright, Sarah VI, 183
Wright, Sarah VI, 220
Wright, Sarah VI, 221
Wright, Sarah VI, 460
Wright, Sarah VI, 608
Wright, Sarah VI, 789
Wright, Sarah VI, 793
Wright, Sarah VI, 867
Wright, Sarah VI, 1013
Wright, Sarah VI, 1021
Wright, Sarah A. II, 161
Wright, Sarah A. II, 723
Wright, Sarah A. III, 371
Wright, Sarah Amanda V, 293
Wright, Sarah Ann I, 1088
Wright, Sarah Ann III, 371
Wright, Sarah Ann IV, 333
Wright, Sarah Ann IV, 359
Wright, Sarah Ann IV, 1196
Wright, Sarah Ann IV, 1197
Wright, Sarah Ann V, 294
Wright, Sarah C. V, 367
Wright, Sarah Catherine II, 804
Wright, Sarah D. II, 698
Wright, Sarah E. I, 486
Wright, Sarah E. V, 214
Wright, Sarah E. VI, 736
Wright, Sarah E. VI, 793
Wright, Sarah Elizabeth II, 1053
Wright, Sarah Elizabeth II, 1064
Wright, Sarah Emeline VI, 438
Wright, Sarah Emeline VI, 445
Wright, Sarah Emeline VI, 461
Wright, Sarah Emiline VI, 460
Wright, Sarah F. I, 472
Wright, Sarah G. II, 724
Wright, Sarah G. II, 777
Wright, Sarah H. II, 904
Wright, Sarah H. VI, 1021
Wright, Sarah Helen III, 370
Wright, Sarah J. I, 1090
Wright, Sarah J. I, 1100
Wright, Sarah J. III, 84
Wright, Sarah J. III, 106
Wright, Sarah J. III, 221
Wright, Sarah J. III, 370
Wright, Sarah Jane I, 1100
Wright, Sarah Jane III, 85
Wright, Sarah Jane III, 221
Wright, Sarah Jane III, 341
Wright, Sarah Jane III, 369
Wright, Sarah Jane III, 370
Wright, Sarah Jane V, 943
Wright, Sarah Jane VI, 1022
Wright, Sarah L. V, 468
Wright, Sarah M. IV, 1157
Wright, Sarah M. IV, 1196
Wright, Sarah M. V, 367
Wright, Sarah M. V, 441
Wright, Sarah P. IV, 1018
Wright, Sarah, Jr. V, 440
Wright, Sary V, 388
Wright, Scholey II, 277
Wright, Scholey VI, 598
Wright, Scholey VI, 608
Wright, Scholy VI, 608
Wright, Schooley IV, 68
Wright, Schooley IV, 349
Wright, Schooley IV, 359
Wright, Schooley IV, 559
Wright, Schooly VI, 460
Wright, Schooly VI, 461
Wright, Schooly VI, 608
Wright, Seaman III, 371
Wright, Seaman H. III, 370
Wright, Sherwood IV, 1123
Wright, Sidney V, 144
Wright, Sidney V, 249
Wright, Sidney V, 256
Wright, Sidney V, 292
Wright, Sidney V, 293
Wright, Sidney VI, 423
Wright, Sidney VI, 430
Wright, Sidney VI, 459
Wright, Sidney VI, 460
Wright, Sidney VI, 461
Wright, Sidney L. II, 943
Wright, Sidney M. III, 371
Wright, Silisia M. IV, 1344
Wright, Solomon III, 369
Wright, Solomon III, 370
Wright, Solomon III, 371
Wright, Solomon V, 144
Wright, Solomon V, 543
Wright, Solomon VI, 460
Wright, Solomon VI, 461
Wright, Solomon M. VI, 1022
Wright, Sophia I, 906
Wright, Sophia I, 1016
Wright, Sophia I, 1025
Wright, Sophia I, 1036
Wright, Sophia I, 1039
Wright, Sophia VI, 1018
Wright, Sparel B. VI, 935
Wright, Sparel B. VI, 1022
Wright, Stephen II, 48
Wright, Stephen II, 52
Wright, Stephen II, 85
Wright, Stephen II, 87
Wright, Stephen II, 113
Wright, Stephen II, 126
Wright, Stephen II, 140
Wright, Stephen II, 277
Wright, Stephen III, 388
Wright, Stephen H. II, 161
Wright, Sudney VI, 460
Wright, Susan III, 370
Wright, Susan III, 378
Wright, Susan III, 388
Wright, Susan IV, 308
Wright, Susan IV, 1158
Wright, Susan IV, 1197
Wright, Susan V, 117
Wright, Susan V, 144
Wright, Susan VI, 586
Wright, Susan VI, 1021
Wright, Susan B. V, 943
Wright, Susan J. VI, 877
Wright, Susan S. IV, 308
Wright, Susan S. IV, 309
Wright, Susanah VI, 460
Wright, Susanna I, 583
Wright, Susanna I, 1112
Wright, Susanna I, 1135
Wright, Susanna I Sup 1, 12
Wright, Susanna II, 724
Wright, Susanna III, 371
Wright, Susanna V, 72
Wright, Susanna V, 119
Wright, Susanna V, 144
Wright, Susanna V, 292
Wright, Susanna V, 293
Wright, Susanna V, 366
Wright, Susanna V, 544
Wright, Susanna V, 728
Wright, Susanna V, 773
Wright, Susanna VI, 459
Wright, Susanna VI, 877
Wright, Susannah I, 369
Wright, Susannah I, 1031
Wright, Susannah I, 1039
Wright, Susannah I, 1112
Wright, Susannah II, 694
Wright, Susannah III, 370
Wright, Susannah III, 509
Wright, Susannah IV, 520
Wright, Susannah IV, 559
Wright, Susannah V, 76
Wright, Susannah V, 144
Wright, Susannah V, 292
Wright, Susannah V, 366
Wright, Susannah V, 469
Wright, Susannah V, 544
Wright, Susannah V, 773
Wright, Susannah V, 809
Wright, Susannah V, 943
Wright, Susannah VI, 460
Wright, Susannah VI, 461
Wright, Susannah VI, 585
Wright, Susannah VI, 608
Wright, Susannah VI, 802
Wright, Susannah B. V, 86
Wright, Susannah B. V, 144
Wright, Sydney Longstreth II, 829
Wright, Sylvia VI, 861
Wright, Synthia VI, 1021
Wright, T. III, 369
Wright, Tacy VI, 369
Wright, Tacy VI, 460
Wright, Tacy VI, 620
Wright, Tacy VI, 732
Wright, Tacy VI, 749
Wright, Tamar III, 343
Wright, Temperance III, 508
Wright, Thaddeus V, 943
Wright, Thadeus W. V, 367
Wright, Theodore II, 828
Wright, Theodore II, 943
Wright, Theodore V, 441
Wright, Theodore V, 721
Wright, Thomas I, 267
Wright, Thomas I, 277
Wright, Thomas I, 1039
Wright, Thomas II, 48
Wright, Thomas II, 113
Wright, Thomas II, 277
Wright, Thomas II, 278
Wright, Thomas II, 307
Wright, Thomas II, 315
Wright, Thomas II, 327
Wright, Thomas II, 439
Wright, Thomas III, 343
Wright, Thomas III, 371
Wright, Thomas III, 387
Wright, Thomas IV, 857
Wright, Thomas V, 366
Wright, Thomas V, 874
Wright, Thomas VI, 166
Wright, Thomas VI, 183
Wright, Thomas VI, 220
Wright, Thomas VI, 345
Wright, Thomas VI, 356
Wright, Thomas VI, 367
Wright, Thomas VI, 371
Wright, Thomas VI, 399
Wright, Thomas VI, 438
Wright, Thomas VI, 459
Wright, Thomas VI, 460
Wright, Thomas VI, 461
Wright, Thomas VI, 736
Wright, Thomas VI, 789
Wright, Thomas VI, 793
Wright, Thomas VI, 986
Wright, Thomas VI, 1011
Wright, Thomas VI, 1021
Wright, Thomas C. V, 293
Wright, Thomas Clarkson V, 292
Wright, Thomas H. VI, 161
Wright, Thomas H. VI, 184
Wright, Thomas H. VI, 221
Wright, Thomas K. IV, 1228
Wright, Thomas L. III, 371
Wright, Thomas P. VI, 857
Wright, Thomas S. III, 388
Wright, Thomas Searing III, 388
Wright, Thomas Shepherd VI, 793
Wright, Thomas T. III, 370
Wright, Thomas, Jr. II, 277
Wright, Thomas, Jr. III, 387
Wright, Thomas, Sr. VI, 220
Wright, Thomasin II, 247
Wright, Thomasin II, 277
Wright, Thos. III, 371
Wright, Thos. V, 943
Wright, Thos. VI, 986
Wright, Thos. T. III, 369
Wright, Tillman A. VI, 1022
Wright, Tomazon II, 277
Wright, Tommey VI, 891
Wright, Tommey VI, 896
Wright, Tommey VI, 959
Wright, Tommey VI, 1020
Wright, Tommy VI, 873
Wright, Tommy VI, 1021
Wright, Unice IV, 165
Wright, Unice VI, 608
Wright, Vashti V, 144
Wright, Victor Leon V, 720
Wright, Viley IV, 359
Wright, Viley IV, 459
Wright, Viley W. IV, 331
Wright, Viley W. IV, 359
Wright, Vincent I, 1088
Wright, Virgil A. V, 721
Wright, Virginia IV, 309
Wright, W. A. V, 293
Wright, W. S. Lundy II, 327
Wright, Walter IV, 308
Wright, Walter V, 440
Wright, Walter A. V, 441
Wright, Walter A. V, 721
Wright, Walter B. IV, 309
Wright, Walter L. II, 1084
Wright, Warren V, 773
Wright, Wd Elizabeth II, 627
Wright, Wd. Barberah II, 439
Wright, Wd. Elizabeth II, 694
Wright, Wd. Esther IV, 857
Wright, Wd. Esther VI, 396
Wright, Wd. Hannah II, 190
Wright, Wd. Mary II, 694
Wright, Wd. Rebecca II, 815
Wright, Webster VI, 586
Wright, Wellmett I, 1112
Wright, Welmet I, 1135
Wright, Welmet I Sup 1, 12
Wright, Welmet V, 773
Wright, Wendall V, 721
Wright, Widower David VI, 1021
Wright, Wilbur Leed III, 223
Wright, Wilbur Teed III, 371
Wright, Wilbur Teed, Jr. III, 371
Wright, Willard H. VI, 788
Wright, William I, 369
Wright, William I, 422
Wright, William I, 430
Wright, William I, 472
Wright, William I, 522
Wright, William I, 583
Wright, William I, 584
Wright, William I, 795
Wright, William I, 867
Wright, William I, 906
Wright, William I, 951
Wright, William I, 1015
Wright, William I, 1016
Wright, William I, 1025
Wright, William I, 1035
Wright, William I, 1039
Wright, William I, 1041
Wright, William I, 1088
Wright, William I, 1099
Wright, William I, 1100
Wright, William II, 48
Wright, William II, 277
Wright, William II, 307
Wright, William II, 315
Wright, William II, 327
Wright, William II, 724
Wright, William II, 829
Wright, William III, 61
Wright, William III, 108
Wright, William III, 369
Wright, William III, 370
Wright, William III, 371
Wright, William III, 509
Wright, William IV, 68
Wright, William IV, 165
Wright, William IV, 308
Wright, William IV, 309
Wright, William IV, 351
Wright, William IV, 359
Wright, William IV, 459

Wright, William IV, 790
Wright, William IV, 1123
Wright, William IV, 1196
Wright, William V, 214
Wright, William V, 292
Wright, William V, 468
Wright, William V, 486
Wright, William V, 773
Wright, William V, 874
Wright, William VI, 22
Wright, William VI, 185
Wright, William VI, 186
Wright, William VI, 220
Wright, William VI, 369
Wright, William VI, 459
Wright, William VI, 532
Wright, William VI, 585
Wright, William VI, 586
Wright, William VI, 608
Wright, William VI, 961
Wright, William VI, 992
Wright, William VI, 1021
Wright, William A. V, 293
Wright, William B. IV, 559
Wright, William C. II, 277
Wright, William Dillen V, 292
Wright, William E. V, 292
Wright, William M. IV, 308
Wright, William M. IV, 309
Wright, William M. VI, 867
Wright, William P. III, 370
Wright, William P. V, 440
Wright, William P. VI, 817
Wright, William Penn III, 370
Wright, William Redwood II, 829
Wright, William S. III, 371
Wright, William S. VI, 1021
Wright, William S. Lundy II, 315
Wright, William T. II, 1067
Wright, William W. IV, 309
Wright, William W. IV, 1197
Wright, William, Jr. III, 371
Wright, Wilson III, 371
Wright, Wilson VI, 837
Wright, Wilson VI, 867
Wright, Wingfield VI, 1021
Wright, Winifred IV, 790
Wright, Wm. II, 98
Wright, Wm. II, 113
Wright, Wm. II, 253
Wright, Wm. II, 614
Wright, Wm. II, 694
Wright, Wm. II, 695
Wright, Wm. II, 891
Wright, Wm. II, 903
Wright, Wm. II, 943
Wright, Wm. III, 370
Wright, Wm. III, 371
Wright, Wm. IV, 165
Wright, Wm. IV, 336
Wright, Wm. IV, 525
Wright, Wm. IV, 790
Wright, Wm. IV, 1123
Wright, Wm. IV, 1197
Wright, Wm. V, 214
Wright, Wm. V, 451
Wright, Wm. V, 468
Wright, Wm. V, 544
Wright, Wm. VI, 1001
Wright, Wm. VI, 1021
Wright, Wm. A. V, 943
Wright, Wm. B. III, 403
Wright, Wm. B. III, 475
Wright, Wm. B. V, 1026
Wright, Wm. Edwin IV, 1267
Wright, Wm. H. III, 371
Wright, Wm. H. IV, 165
Wright, Wm. H. IV, 1018
Wright, Wm. Harrison III, 371
Wright, Wm. Henry IV, 1196
Wright, Wm. John IV, 1267
Wright, Wm. Lewelling I, 867
Wright, Wm. Mosher IV, 1196
Wright, Wm. Redwood II, 943
Wright, Wm. S. V, 943
Wright, Wm. T. II, 1084
Wright, Wright H. VI, 942
Wright, Zebulun III, 509
Wright, Zelly II, 277
Wrightman, Sarah IV, 1295
Wrightman, Sarah IV, 1301
Wrights, J. H. III, 221
Wrightsman, Abigail V, 650
Wrightsman, David I, 472
Wrightsman, David I, 486
Wrightsman, Deborah I, 376
Wrightsman, Deborah I, 430
Wrightsman, Lennard I, 472
Wrightsman, Leonard I, 465
Wrightsman, Leonard I, 486
Wrightsman, Mary A. I, 465
Wrightsman, Mary Ann I, 472
Wrightsman, Mary Ann I, 486
Wrightsman, Rachel I, 430
Wrightsman, Sophia I, 486
Wrigley, Grace IV, 745
Wrigley, Ida IV, 745
Wrigley, J. L. IV, 745
Wrigth, Amos VI, 368
Wrigth, Rachel VI, 368
Wrintingham, Eliz. V. III, 297
Wrintingham, Jere. III, 297
Writ, Margret II, 90
Writ, Margret II, 113
Write, Elizabeth V, 144
Write, Hannah II, 53
Write, Hannah II, 113
Write, John II, 53
Write, John II, 113
Write, Robert VI, 345
Writer, Hannah C. IV, 309
Writter, Margaretta W. II, 156
Wronsley, John I, 430
Wroth, Kenneth V, 1026
Wroth, Mary V, 1026
Wulfeck, Ora V, 694
Wulfeck, Ora V, 721
Wulfeck, Wallace V, 694
Wulfeck, Wallace V, 721
Wunderlin, Mrs. Margaret IV, 791
Wurts, Anna C. III, 180
Wurts, Anna C. III, 371
Wurts, Anna Virginia III, 371
Wurts, Augusta III, 371
Wurts, Henry III, 371
Wurts, Lionel III, 180
Wurts, Lionel III, 371
Wurts, Richard III, 371
Wuthrick, Effie Marie IV, 1018
Wyant, Isaac IV, 309
Wyant, Nettie IV, 309
Wyar, Barzillai III, 371
Wyar, Elizabeth III, 371
Wyatt, Bartholomew II, 48
Wyatt, Bartholomew II, 113
Wyatt, Bartholomew II, 438
Wyatt, Bartholomew II, 695
Wyatt, Bartholomew, Jr. II, 113
Wyatt, Benjamin VI, 865
Wyatt, Benjamin VI, 867
Wyatt, Catharine VI, 867
Wyatt, Elisabeth II, 261
Wyatt, Elisabeth II, 277
Wyatt, Elisabeth II, 695
Wyatt, Elizabeth II, 35
Wyatt, Elizabeth II, 48
Wyatt, Elizabeth II, 60
Wyatt, Elizabeth II, 99
Wyatt, Elizabeth II, 113
Wyatt, Geo. IV, 1344
Wyatt, Geo. H. IV, 1344
Wyatt, George VI, 867
Wyatt, John III, 371
Wyatt, Margaret VI, 867
Wyatt, Mary I, 34
Wyatt, Mary II, 48
Wyatt, Mary II, 110
Wyatt, Mary II, 113
Wyatt, Mary II, 840
Wyatt, Mary A. VI, 917
Wyatt, Sarah II, 48
Wyatt, Sarah II, 111
Wyatt, Sarah II, 113
Wyatt, Sarah II, 438
Wyatt, Susanne VI, 1022
Wyatt, Thomas VI, 917
Wyatt, Thomas VI, 1022
Wyatt, William V, 293
Wyckoff, Frances III, 100
Wyckoff, Frances III, 300
Wyckoff, S. Maria III, 303
Wycoff, Mariah III, 448
Wyer, Barzillai III, 371
Wyer, Elizabeth III, 371
Wyeth, Eliza II, 439
Wyeth, Joan II, 439
Wyeth, John II, 439
Wyley, David IV, 787
Wyley, Elizabeth I, 418
Wyley, Elizabeth I, 428
Wyley, Elizabeth IV, 787
Wyley, Joseph IV, 787
Wyley, Mary IV, 787
Wyley, Rachel I, 428
Wyley, Sarah IV, 787
Wylie, David IV, 459
Wylie, Elizabeth IV, 459
Wylie, Ethel IV, 459
Wylie, Frank IV, 506
Wylie, Grace M. IV, 459
Wylie, Grace Martha IV, 459
Wylie, Hannah IV, 459
Wylie, J. Alberta IV, 459
Wylie, James VI, 851
Wylie, Jane IV, 506
Wylie, Jessie Alberta IV, 459
Wylie, Joseph IV, 459
Wylie, Joseph W. IV, 459
Wylie, M. Ethel IV, 459
Wylie, Myrtle E. IV, 459
Wylie, Myrtle Ellen IV, 459
Wylie, Sarah IV, 459
Wylie, Wm. IV, 506
Wyllie, Allen L. VI, 867
Wyllie, Allen S. VI, 804
Wyllie, Martha VI, 867
Wyly, John II, 686
Wyman, Nerva IV, 309
Wyman, Ruby IV, 1344
Wymer, Charles IV, 1267
Wymer, Edgar F. IV, 1267
Wymer, Elizabeth IV, 1267
Wymer, Frank IV, 1267
Wymer, Hannah II, 944
Wymer, James IV, 1267
Wymer, Leo V, 649
Wymer, Margaret II, 944
Wymer, Thomas II, 944
Wymer, Thos. II, 944
Wymond, E. Paul V, 943
Wymond, Edward Paul V, 943
Wymond, Edwin Paul V, 943
Wymond, Ella V, 943
Wymond, Grace A. V, 943
Wymond, Harry V, 943
Wymond, Laura V, 943
Wymond, Laura F. V, 943
Wymond, Laura H. V, 943
Wymond, Laura Harding V, 943
Wymond, Wm. V, 943
Wymond, Wm. W. V, 943
Wyncopp, Elsie VI, 679
Wynkoop, Elsie VI, 682
Wynkoop, Elsie VI, 723
Wynkoop, Rachel II, 96
Wynkoop, Rachel II, 113
Wynn, Ann II, 695
Wynn, John VI, 856
Wynn, John J. VI, 1006
Wynn, Joseph S. II, 944
Wynn, Martha Ann VI, 1006
Wynn, Mary II, 438
Wynn, Mary II, 677
Wynn, Mary II, 695
Wynn, Susanna VI, 713
Wynn, Susanna VI, 723
Wynn, Thomas II, 677
Wynn, Thomas II, 695
Wynn, Venia VI, 811
Wynne, Amanda VI, 867
Wynne, Christina VI, 806
Wynne, Elizabeth Newlin II, 829
Wynne, James VI, 867
Wynne, John VI, 867
Wynne, Jones VI, 856
Wynne, Joseph Sharp II, 829
Wynne, Leviney VI, 806
Wynne, Mary II, 695
Wynne, Mourning VI, 856
Wynne, Phebe II, 829
Wynne, Polly St. John VI, 867
Wynne, Samuel C. II, 829
Wyrick, John A. I, 584
Wysong, Alfred V, 144
Wysong, Alfred V, 214
Wysong, Alphred V, 214
Wysong, Carl V, 606
Wysong, Carl E. V, 606
Wysong, Eleanor S. V, 943
Wysong, Elnora V, 606
Wysong, Elnora V, 943
Wysong, Emma V, 606
Wysong, Etha V, 671
Wysong, Etha V, 721
Wysong, Etha May V, 721
Wysong, Eugene V, 606
Wysong, Eva V, 144
Wysong, Eva V, 214
Wysong, George W. VI, 1022
Wysong, Lauren V, 721
Wysong, Levi V, 144
Wysong, Levi V, 214
Wysong, Loren Adelbert V, 606
Wysong, Mary V, 606
Wysong, Mary VI, 1022
Wysong, Raymond V, 606
Wytcherly, Edward IV, 309

Y???, Hannah IV, 286
Yacoubi, Martha IV, 1344
Yader, George IV, 309
Yale, Caroline C. III, 37
Yale, Caroline C. III, 337
Yancey, Betsy VI, 867
Yancey, Catharine Louisa VI, 998
Yancey, Charles VI, 1022
Yancey, Elizabeth VI, 867
Yancey, Elizabeth I. M. VI, 875
Yancey, Jeremiah VI, 816
Yancey, Joel VI, 845
Yancey, Joel VI, 867
Yancey, Joel VI, 986
Yancey, Joel VI, 998
Yancey, Layton VI, 1022
Yancey, Louisa H. VI, 1022
Yancey, Martha Ann VI, 986
Yancey, Nancy VI, 867
Yancey, Nelly VI, 875
Yancey, R. VI, 801
Yancey, Sarah VI, 1022
Yancey, Smith H. VI, 816
Yancey, Wm. T. VI, 887
Yancy, Harriet VI, 859
Yancy, James VI, 858
Yancy, Jeremiah VI, 859
Yancy, Patsey C. VI, 858
Yaple, Rachel III, 294
Yaratt, William VI, 15
Yarby, Isabella IV, 309
Yarby, Morrison IV, 309
Yard, Angelina C. II, 881
Yard, Angelina C. II, 944
Yard, Henry H. II, 881
Yard, Henry H. II, 944
Yard, Henry Herbert II, 829
Yard, Israel II, 829
Yard, Jacob S. II, 881
Yard, Jacob S. II, 944
Yard, Jane II, 829
Yard, Joseph II, 449
Yard, Mary II, 449
Yard, Sarah II, 829
Yard, Sarah II, 881
Yard, Sarah II, 944
Yardley, Achsah II, 1042
Yardley, Achsah II, 1064
Yardley, Acsah II, 1029
Yardley, Ann II, 973
Yardley, Ann II, 1011
Yardley, Ann II, 1041
Yardley, Ann II, 1042
Yardley, Ann II, 1082
Yardley, Ann II, 1084
Yardley, Ann VI, 516
Yardley, Anne II, 973
Yardley, Anne II, 1034
Yardley, Anne II, 1042
Yardley, Charles II, 829
Yardley, Charles II, 944
Yardley, Charles II, 1064
Yardley, Charles II, 1082
Yardley, Charles II, 1084
Yardley, Chas. F. II, 944
Yardley, Courtland II, 1064
Yardley, Edward II, 1041
Yardley, Edward II, 1042
Yardley, Edward II, 1064
Yardley, Edward T. II, 944
Yardley, Edward Thomas II, 829
Yardley, Eliza P. II, 190
Yardley, Eliza P. II, 307
Yardley, Eliza P. II, 1064
Yardley, Elizabeth II, 522
Yardley, Elizabeth II, 695
Yardley, Elizabeth II, 806
Yardley, Elizabeth II, 829
Yardley, Elizabeth II, 944
Yardley, Elizabeth II, 982
Yardley, Elizabeth II, 984
Yardley, Elizabeth II, 1009
Yardley, Elizabeth II, 1011
Yardley, Elizabeth II, 1020
Yardley, Elizabeth II, 1042
Yardley, Elizabeth II, 1064
Yardley, Elizabeth II, 1082
Yardley, Elizabeth II, 1084
Yardley, Elizabeth P. II, 1064
Yardley, Ella J. II, 944
Yardley, Ella Jane II, 944
Yardley, Ellen II, 1046
Yardley, Ellen II, 1064
Yardley, Enoch II, 1041
Yardley, Ester II, 981
Yardley, Ester II, 1041
Yardley, Esther II, 1054
Yardley, Esther II, 1064
Yardley, Florence II, 1066
Yardley, George II, 1064
Yardley, Hannah II, 784
Yardley, Hannah II, 977
Yardley, Hannah II, 1029
Yardley, Hannah II, 1042
Yardley, Hannah, Jr. II, 984
Yardley, Hannah, Jr. II, 104
Yardley, Harriet II, 1046
Yardley, Harriet II, 1064
Yardley, Harriet III, 371
Yardley, Henry A. II, 944
Yardley, Henry Albert II, 94
Yardley, Howard II, 829
Yardley, Howard II, 944
Yardley, Isaac II, 1042
Yardley, Isaac II, 1064
Yardley, Isaac III, 371
Yardley, James Martin II, 8
Yardley, Jane II, 1041
Yardley, Jane VI, 661
Yardley, John II, 1064
Yardley, John Seymour II, 7
Yardley, John Seymour II, 8
Yardley, John Seymour II, 9
Yardley, Joseph II, 1042
Yardley, Joseph II, 1064
Yardley, Joseph Warner II,
Yardley, Latitia II, 809
Yardley, Latitia II, 1039
Yardley, Latitia II, 1042
Yardley, Latitia II, 1064
Yardley, Lucilla II, 973
Yardley, Lucilla II, 1042
Yardley, Lydia II, 1042
Yardley, Lydia II, 1064
Yardley, Lydia IV, 268
Yardley, Lydia IV, 309
Yardley, Lydia H. II, 944
Yardley, Lydia Hart II, 724
Yardley, Lydia Hart II, 777
Yardley, Lydia Hart II, 944
Yardley, Mahlon II, 982
Yardley, Mahlon II, 1011
Yardley, Mahlon II, 1020
Yardley, Mahlon II, 1042
Yardley, Mahlon II, 1064
Yardley, Mahlon II, 1082
Yardley, Mahlon II, 1084
Yardley, Mahlon, Jr. II, 984
Yardley, Margaret II, 1061
Yardley, Margaret II, 1064
Yardley, Margaret Ann II, 1
Yardley, Margaretta II, 973
Yardley, Margaretta II, 1064
Yardley, Margarette II, 1042
Yardley, Margretta II, 1042
Yardley, Mary II, 805
Yardley, Mary II, 809
Yardley, Mary II, 829
Yardley, Mary II, 1003
Yardley, Mary II, 1005
Yardley, Mary II, 1041
Yardley, Mary II, 1042
Yardley, Mary II, 1064
Yardley, Mary VI, 474
Yardley, Mary VI, 493
Yardley, Mary VI, 515
Yardley, Mary VI, 516
Yardley, Mary VI, 517
Yardley, Mary VI, 519
Yardley, Mary VI, 521
Yardley, Mary VI, 522
Yardley, Mary VI, 546
Yardley, Mary VI, 735
Yardley, Mary L. II, 896
Yardley, Mary L. II, 944
Yardley, Mary Letitia II, 829
Yardley, Mary S. II, 829
Yardley, Mary S. II, 944
Yardley, Mary W. II, 1042
Yardley, Mercy II, 1011
Yardley, Mercy II, 1042
Yardley, Oliver H. II, 944
Yardley, Oliver Hough II, 82
Yardley, Rebecca II, 1018
Yardley, Rebecca II, 1042
Yardley, Richard II, 973
Yardley, Richard II, 1042
Yardley, Robert II, 1041
Yardley, Robert II, 1064
Yardley, Samuel II, 277
Yardley, Samuel II, 829
Yardley, Samuel II, 1042
Yardley, Samuel, Jr. II, 1042
Yardley, Sarah II, 522
Yardley, Sarah II, 695
Yardley, Sarah II, 829
Yardley, Sarah II, 982
Yardley, Sarah II, 1008
Yardley, Sarah II, 1020
Yardley, Sarah II, 1029
Yardley, Sarah II, 1042
Yardley, Sarah II, 1064
Yardley, Sarah S. II, 724
Yardley, Sarah S. II, 745
Yardley, Sarah S. II, 777

ey, Sarah S. II, 829
ey, Sarah S. II, 944
ey, Sarah Warner II, 829
ey, Susan J. II, 731
ey, Susan J. II, 777
ey, Susan J. II, 944
ey, Susan Josephine II, 724
ey, Susan, Jr. II, 1064
ey, Susanna II, 745
ey, Susanna II, 777
ey, Susanna II, 1045
ey, Susanna II, 1064
ey, Susanna, Sr. II, 1064
ey, Susannah II, 829
ey, Susannah II, 896
ey, Susannah II, 944
ey, Susannah II, 982
ey, Susannah II, 1011
ey, Susannah II, 1041
ey, Susannah II, 1042
ley, Thomas II, 745
ley, Thomas II, 777
ley, Thomas II, 944
ley, Thomas II, 975
lley, Thomas II, 982
lley, Thomas II, 1011
lley, Thomas II, 1041
lley, Thomas II, 1042
lley, Thomas VI, 516
lley, Thomas H. II, 944
lley, Thomas W. II, 1064
lley, Thomas W. II, 1084
dley, Thomas, Jr. II, 1042
dley, Thos. II, 829
dley, Thos. II, 896
dley, Thos. II, 944
dley, Thos. H. II, 944
dley, Thos. Hart II, 829
dley, Thos., Jr. II, 1042
dley, William II, 724
dley, William II, 829
dley, William II, 952
dley, William II, 973
dley, William W. III, 371
dley, Wm, Jr. II, 777
dley, Wm. II, 522
dley, Wm. II, 695
dley, Wm. II, 829
dley, Wm. II, 944
rdley, Wm. II, 982
rdley, Wm. II, 1008
rdley, Wm. II, 1029
rdley, Wm. II, 1034
rdley, Wm. II, 1041
rdley, Wm. II, 1042
rdley, Wm., Jr. II, 695
rdley, Wm., Jr. II, 745
rdley, Wm., Jr. II, 829
rdley, Wm., Jr. II, 944
rdly, Ann II, 1010
rdly, Hannah II, 1037
rdly, Hannah II, 1042
rger, America V, 468
rger, Edward V, 721
rger, Edward E. V, 721
rger, Estella V, 699
rger, Estella V, 721
rger, John L. V, 721
rger, Mary Alice V, 721
rger, Nellie V, 721
rger, Nellie Marie V, 661
rger, Nellie Marie V, 721
arnal, Adah VI, 489
arnal, Adah VI, 586
arnal, Asenath VI, 586
arnal, Elizabeth VI, 489
arnal, Elizabeth VI, 586
arnal, Elizabeth, Jr. VI, 586
arnal, Geo. IV, 309
arnal, George IV, 69
arnal, George IV, 309
arnal, Hannah IV, 309
arnal, James II, 695
arnal, James II, 696
Yarnal, Lydia IV, 309
Yarnal, Mordecai IV, 309
Yarnal, Mordecai, Jr. II, 695
Yarnal, Phebe IV, 69
Yarnal, Phebe IV, 309
Yarnal, Phebe VI, 410
Yarnal, Rachel D. II, 944
Yarnal, Reuben II, 944
Yarnal, Sarah VI, 586
Yarnal, Susanna IV, 309
Yarnall, Aaron IV, 117
Yarnall, Agnes II, 722
Yarnall, Albin II, 829
Yarnall, Albin II, 944
Yarnall, Amos IV, 117
Yarnall, Amy II, 439
Yarnall, Ann II, 439
Yarnall, Ann II, 440
Yarnall, Ann II, 525
Yarnall, Ann II, 696
Yarnall, Benj. II, 695
Yarnall, Benjamin II, 439
Yarnall, Benjamin II, 695
Yarnall, Benjamin H. II, 696
Yarnall, Caroline R. II, 734
Yarnall, Caroline R. II, 777
Yarnall, Catharine II, 440
Yarnall, Catherine II, 440
Yarnall, Catherine II, 503
Yarnall, Catherine II, 695
Yarnall, Charles II, 439
Yarnall, Deborah II, 440
Yarnall, Deborah II, 503
Yarnall, Deborah II, 696
Yarnall, Deborah P. II, 705
Yarnall, Edward II, 439
Yarnall, Edward II, 440
Yarnall, Edward II, 734
Yarnall, Edward II, 777
Yarnall, Eli II, 637
Yarnall, Eli II, 696
Yarnall, Eli IV, 117
Yarnall, Elizabeth II, 439
Yarnall, Elizabeth II, 440
Yarnall, Elizabeth II, 476
Yarnall, Elizabeth II, 656
Yarnall, Elizabeth II, 695
Yarnall, Elizabeth II, 696
Yarnall, Elizabeth II, 724
Yarnall, Elizabeth C. II, 439
Yarnall, Elizabeth C. II, 696
Yarnall, Elizabeth W. II, 734
Yarnall, Ellen II, 440
Yarnall, Ellen II, 593
Yarnall, Ellen II, 695
Yarnall, Ellis II, 439
Yarnall, Ellis II, 440
Yarnall, Ellis II, 525
Yarnall, Ellis II, 554
Yarnall, Ellis II, 694
Yarnall, Ellis II, 696
Yarnall, Ellis II, 734
Yarnall, Ellis II, 777
Yarnall, Ellis H. II, 439
Yarnall, Ellis, Jr. II, 696
Yarnall, Enoch II, 705
Yarnall, Esther II, 696
Yarnall, Esther II, 777
Yarnall, Ezeble II, 439
Yarnall, Ezekiel II, 440
Yarnall, Francis II, 439
Yarnall, Francis II, 695
Yarnall, George IV, 117
Yarnall, George IV, 601
Yarnall, George, Jr. IV, 103
Yarnall, George, Jr. IV, 117
Yarnall, Hannah II, 440
Yarnall, Hannah II, 554
Yarnall, Hannah II, 637
Yarnall, Hannah II, 694
Yarnall, Hannah II, 695
Yarnall, Hannah II, 696
Yarnall, Hannah II, 705
Yarnall, Hannah IV, 309
Yarnall, Hannah IV, 459
Yarnall, Hannah IV, 601
Yarnall, Howard II, 777
Yarnall, Isaac II, 695
Yarnall, Isaac II, 696
Yarnall, Israel II, 440
Yarnall, Israel II, 696
Yarnall, Jacob II, 439
Yarnall, Jacob II, 695
Yarnall, James II, 695
Yarnall, James II, 696
Yarnall, Jane II, 440
Yarnall, Jane II, 656
Yarnall, Jane II, 695
Yarnall, Jane II, 696
Yarnall, Jenny II, 439
Yarnall, Job II, 586
Yarnall, Job II, 695
Yarnall, John II, 695
Yarnall, John II, 696
Yarnall, Joseph II, 439
Yarnall, Joseph II, 440
Yarnall, Joseph II, 656
Yarnall, Joseph II, 695
Yarnall, Joseph II, 696
Yarnall, Joshua II, 696
Yarnall, Josiah II, 724
Yarnall, Lydia II, 439
Yarnall, Lydia II, 440
Yarnall, Lydia IV, 117
Yarnall, Marmaduke C. II, 734
Yarnall, Mary II, 439
Yarnall, Mary II, 440
Yarnall, Mary II, 476
Yarnall, Mary II, 507
Yarnall, Mary II, 554
Yarnall, Mary II, 636
Yarnall, Mary II, 695
Yarnall, Mary II, 696
Yarnall, Mary II, 777
Yarnall, Mary IV, 117
Yarnall, Mary, Jr. II, 696
Yarnall, Mordecai II, 439
Yarnall, Mordecai II, 440
Yarnall, Mordecai II, 507
Yarnall, Mordecai II, 593
Yarnall, Mordecai II, 682
Yarnall, Mordecai II, 695
Yarnall, Mordecai II, 696
Yarnall, Mordecai IV, 117
Yarnall, Mordecai IV, 309
Yarnall, Mordecai IV, 459
Yarnall, Mordecai IV, 601
Yarnall, Mordecai, Jr. II, 695
Yarnall, Mordicai II, 476
Yarnall, Mordicai II, 696
Yarnall, Nathan II, 439
Yarnall, Nathan II, 525
Yarnall, Nathan II, 554
Yarnall, Nathan II, 637
Yarnall, Nathan II, 694
Yarnall, Nathan II, 695
Yarnall, Nathan II, 696
Yarnall, Peter II, 440
Yarnall, Peter II, 696
Yarnall, Phebe II, 440
Yarnall, Phebe II, 696
Yarnall, Phebe IV, 165
Yarnall, Phebe IV, 309
Yarnall, Phebe IV, 459
Yarnall, Phebe VI, 462
Yarnall, Phebe VI, 608
Yarnall, Phebe G. II, 944
Yarnall, Pheobe VI, 491
Yarnall, Philena II, 718
Yarnall, Philip II, 586
Yarnall, Philip II, 695
Yarnall, Rachel II, 439
Yarnall, Rachel II, 440
Yarnall, Rachel II, 525
Yarnall, Rachel II, 694
Yarnall, Rachel II, 696
Yarnall, Rachel II, 944
Yarnall, Rachel D. II, 944
Yarnall, Rachel Davis II, 829
Yarnall, Rachel T. II, 944
Yarnall, Rebecca II, 440
Yarnall, Rebecca II, 586
Yarnall, Rebecca II, 612
Yarnall, Rebecca II, 695
Yarnall, Rebeckah II, 612
Yarnall, Rebeckah II, 696
Yarnall, Rebekah II, 695
Yarnall, Reuben II, 829
Yarnall, Reuben II, 944
Yarnall, Robert II, 439
Yarnall, Robert II, 440
Yarnall, Samuel II, 784
Yarnall, Sarah II, 439
Yarnall, Sarah II, 440
Yarnall, Sarah II, 682
Yarnall, Sarah II, 695
Yarnall, Sarah II, 734
Yarnall, Sarah IV, 103
Yarnall, Sarah IV, 117
Yarnall, Susanna IV, 117
Yarnall, Susanna IV, 309
Yarnall, Susannah IV, 117
Yarnall, Susannah IV, 459
Yarnall, Susannah IV, 601
Yarnall, Susannah Edmondson II, 784
Yarnall, Sydney S. II, 944
Yarnall, Thamzin II, 637
Yarnall, Thamzin II, 696
Yarnall, Thamzin II, 829
Yarnall, Thamzin II, 944
Yarnall, Thomas Coffin II, 439
Yarnall, Thomas Coffin II, 696
Yarnall, Thomasin II, 696
Yarnall, William II, 439
Yarnall, Winnie V, 650
Yarnall, Wm. II, 696
Yarnel, Asenath VI, 506
Yarnel, Asenath VI, 586
Yarnel, Mary IV, 117
Yarnel, Mordecai IV, 187
Yarnel, Phebe IV, 187
Yarnel, Phebe VI, 462
Yarnel, Susannah IV, 92
Yarnell, Beulah V, 651
Yarnell, Eli IV, 117
Yarnell, Eugene V, 651
Yarnell, George IV, 117
Yarnell, Hannah II, 695
Yarnell, Hannah V, 875
Yarnell, Hannah VI, 593
Yarnell, J. H. III, 371
Yarnell, J. Howard III, 371
Yarnell, James II, 695
Yarnell, Job II, 695
Yarnell, M. Francis III, 371
Yarnell, Mordecai II, 695
Yarnell, Thamzin II, 829
Yarnell, Winnie V, 650
Yarnsey, Edmund II, 449
Yarratt, William VI, 22
Yarratt, William VI, 23
Yarratt, William VI, 29
Yarret, Katheren VI, 23
Yarret, William VI, 41
Yarrett, ??? VI, 40
Yarrett, Elizabeth VI, 38
Yarrett, Katheren VI, 37
Yarrett, Katheren VI, 38
Yarrett, Katherine VI, 7
Yarrett, Kathren VI, 38
Yarrett, Margarett VI, 38
Yarrett, Margrett VI, 38
Yarrett, William VI, 38
Yarrett, William VI, 40
Yarrett, Wm. VI, 7
Yarrett???, Elizabeth VI, 33
Yarrett???, William VI, 33
Yarus, Della Louise III, 224
Yarus, Della Louise III, 371
Yarus, Edna L. III, 371
Yarus, Edna Louise III, 224
Yarus, Westley F. III, 224
Yarus, Westley F. III, 371
Yater, Lillie IV, 309
Yates, ??? IV, 857
Yates, Abigail IV, 825
Yates, Abigail IV, 857
Yates, Alice VI, 479
Yates, Alice VI, 481
Yates, Alice VI, 586
Yates, Alice, Jr. VI, 537
Yates, Ann IV, 20
Yates, Ann IV, 69
Yates, Ann IV, 165
Yates, Ann IV, 857
Yates, Ann IV, 925
Yates, Ann H. VI, 462
Yates, Anna I, 313
Yates, Anna I, 320
Yates, Anna IV, 157
Yates, Anna IV, 165
Yates, Anna IV, 359
Yates, Anna Mary IV, 791
Yates, Anna Mary IV, 902
Yates, Anna Mary IV, 918
Yates, Asenath IV, 791
Yates, Asenath IV, 856
Yates, Asenath IV, 857
Yates, Asenath IV, 918
Yates, Belle IV, 1229
Yates, Benjamin IV, 20
Yates, Benjamin IV, 69
Yates, Benjamin IV, 791
Yates, Benjamin IV, 857
Yates, Benjamin VI, 579
Yates, Benjamin VI, 586
Yates, Benjamin VI, 723
Yates, Benjamin VI, 724
Yates, Benjamin, Jr. VI, 724
Yates, Callin W. VI, 905
Yates, Callin W. VI, 960
Yates, Charles IV, 857
Yates, Clara J. IV, 836
Yates, Clara J. IV, 857
Yates, Clara Jane IV, 791
Yates, Clerky I, 739
Yates, Clerky I, 1135
Yates, Clerky V, 145
Yates, Collin W. VI, 966
Yates, Dinah III, 194
Yates, Dinah III, 371
Yates, Effama IV, 857
Yates, Efphema IV, 856
Yates, Efphema IV, 857
Yates, Elias VI, 872
Yates, Elias VI, 1021
Yates, Elias VI, 1022
Yates, Elizabeth I, 1135
Yates, Elizabeth III, 371
Yates, Elizabeth IV, 857
Yates, Elizabeth V, 145
Yates, Elizabeth VI, 586
Yates, Elizabeth Jane IV, 857
Yates, Elphamy IV, 857
Yates, Emelina IV, 902
Yates, Emeline IV, 791
Yates, Emeline IV, 918
Yates, Enoch V, 145
Yates, Francis III, 372
Yates, Hannah III, 372
Yates, Hannah J. IV, 799
Yates, Hannah J. IV, 857
Yates, Henry VI, 462
Yates, Hesley IV, 791
Yates, Isaac VI, 586
Yates, James IV, 69
Yates, James IV, 791
Yates, James VI, 724
Yates, James VI, 1022
Yates, Jamima VI, 724
Yates, Jane III, 248
Yates, Jane VI, 959
Yates, Jany VI, 1021
Yates, Jemima IV, 69
Yates, Jemima IV, 791
Yates, John III, 248
Yates, John IV, 791
Yates, John IV, 856
Yates, John IV, 857
Yates, John IV, 918
Yates, Jonathan VI, 1022
Yates, Joseph VI, 586
Yates, Leah IV, 856
Yates, Leah IV, 857
Yates, Louisa IV, 1018
Yates, Lucy L. VI, 1022
Yates, Margaret IV, 857
Yates, Mary I, 739
Yates, Mary I, 1135
Yates, Mary IV, 69
Yates, Mary IV, 708
Yates, Mary IV, 791
Yates, Mary IV, 857
Yates, Mary V, 145
Yates, Mary VI, 724
Yates, Mary VI, 960
Yates, Mary VI, 966
Yates, Mary B. I, 643
Yates, Mary Ballinger I, 643
Yates, Mrs. ??? VI, 11
Yates, Nancy VI, 1022
Yates, Patrick I, 1135
Yates, Patrick V, 145
Yates, Phebe IV, 20
Yates, Phebe IV, 69
Yates, Phebe IV, 791
Yates, Phebe IV, 857
Yates, Phebe IV, 925
Yates, Phebe VI, 579
Yates, Phebe VI, 586
Yates, Phebe VI, 723
Yates, Phebe VI, 724
Yates, Polly VI, 935
Yates, Polly VI, 1022
Yates, Rachel IV, 821
Yates, Rachel IV, 857
Yates, Rebecca IV, 825
Yates, Rebecca IV, 857
Yates, Rhoda VI, 1021
Yates, Richard VI, 11
Yates, Richard VI, 12
Yates, Robert IV, 791
Yates, Robert IV, 918
Yates, Robert IV, 925
Yates, Robert VI, 586
Yates, Ruth IV, 20
Yates, Ruth IV, 69
Yates, Ruth VI, 724
Yates, Samuel II, 696
Yates, Sarah IV, 65
Yates, Sarah IV, 69
Yates, Sarah IV, 821
Yates, Sarah IV, 857
Yates, Sarah VI, 586
Yates, Sarah VI, 724
Yates, Sarah VI, 872
Yates, Sarah VI, 959
Yates, Shelton IV, 1018
Yates, Susanna I, 878
Yates, Susanna I, 906
Yates, Sylvanus IV, 791
Yates, Sylvanus IV, 857
Yates, Tilford VI, 966
Yates, William I, 739
Yates, William I, 1135
Yates, William III, 372
Yates, William VI, 586
Yates, William VI, 966
Yates, William VI, 1022
Yates, William, Jr. VI, 586
Yates, Wilson VI, 960
Yatkins, Hiram IV, 1267
Yatkins, Hiram V, 214
Yatkins, Marcus IV, 1267
Yatkins, Sarah IV, 1267
Yatkins, Sarah V, 214
Yatkins, William IV, 1267
Yeager, Adolph IV, 791
Yeager, Alice IV, 791
Yeager, Henrietta IV, 791

Yeakley, Florence Latiner IV, 1344
Yeakley, Henry I, 1100
Yeakley, William Penn I, 1100
Yealall, Susannah II, 440
Yeardley, Acsah II, 973
Yeardley, Ann II, 973
Yeardley, Ann II, 979
Yeardley, Ann II, 1041
Yeardley, Ann II, 1042
Yeardley, Ann VI, 499
Yeardley, Ann VI, 586
Yeardley, Anna II, 973
Yeardley, Anne II, 973
Yeardley, Eliza II, 327
Yeardley, Elizabeth II, 1021
Yeardley, Elizabeth II, 1042
Yeardley, Enoch II, 973
Yeardley, Hannah II, 973
Yeardley, Hester II, 973
Yeardley, Jane II, 973
Yeardley, Jane II, 999
Yeardley, Jane II, 1041
Yeardley, Jane VI, 499
Yeardley, Jane VI, 500
Yeardley, Jane VI, 519
Yeardley, Jane VI, 531
Yeardley, Jane VI, 555
Yeardley, Jane VI, 586
Yeardley, John II, 973
Yeardley, Joseph II, 973
Yeardley, Joyce II, 973
Yeardley, Leatitia II, 973
Yeardley, Lucilla II, 973
Yeardley, Mahlon II, 973
Yeardley, Margaretta II, 973
Yeardley, Margarette II, 1021
Yeardley, Margarette II, 1042
Yeardley, Mary II, 973
Yeardley, Mary II, 996
Yeardley, Mary II, 1007
Yeardley, Mary II, 1041
Yeardley, Mary II, 1042
Yeardley, Mary VI, 586
Yeardley, Rebecca II, 973
Yeardley, Richard II, 973
Yeardley, Samuel II, 973
Yeardley, Samuel II, 1042
Yeardley, Sarah II, 973
Yeardley, Sarah II, 987
Yeardley, Sarah II, 1031
Yeardley, Sarah II, 1042
Yeardley, Thomas II, 973
Yeardley, Thomas II, 1021
Yeardley, Thomas II, 1042
Yeardley, Thomas VI, 499
Yeardley, Thomas VI, 586
Yeardley, Thomas, Jr. II, 996
Yeardley, Thomas, Jr. II, 1042
Yeardley, Thos., Jr. II, 1042
Yeardley, William II, 973
Yeardley, Wm. II, 695
Yeardley, Wm. II, 1021
Yeardley, Wm. II, 1031
Yearsley, Abigail IV, 459
Yeates, ??? VI, 726
Yeates, Alice VI, 537
Yeates, Alice VI, 586
Yeates, Ann III, 372
Yeates, Ann IV, 459
Yeates, Ann VI, 793
Yeates, Ann Humphrey VI, 733
Yeates, Ann Humphrey VI, 793
Yeates, Anna III, 372
Yeates, Anna Smith III, 137
Yeates, Anna Smith III, 371
Yeates, Anne II, 184
Yeates, Benjamin IV, 65
Yeates, Clerky V, 145
Yeates, Dinah III, 371
Yeates, Edman II, 696
Yeates, Edman II, 944
Yeates, Elizabeth III, 371
Yeates, Elizabeth IV, 117
Yeates, Elizabeth V, 145
Yeates, Elizabeth VI, 586
Yeates, Elizabeth VI, 793
Yeates, Enoch V, 145
Yeates, Francis III, 372
Yeates, Hannah III, 372
Yeates, Hannah IV, 78
Yeates, Hannah IV, 117
Yeates, Hannah VI, 793
Yeates, Henry VI, 733
Yeates, Henry VI, 793
Yeates, Hepzabah I, 584
Yeates, Jane III, 38
Yeates, Jane III, 117
Yeates, Jane III, 371
Yeates, Jane III, 372
Yeates, John III, 372
Yeates, Jonas IV, 117
Yeates, Margaret Lamb VI, 793
Yeates, Mary IV, 815
Yeates, Mary V, 145
Yeates, Mary Abbey III, 372
Yeates, Mary Abby III, 117
Yeates, Mary Abby III, 372
Yeates, Patrick V, 145
Yeates, Phebe II, 696
Yeates, Phebe IV, 65
Yeates, Phebe Jane III, 372
Yeates, Rachel I, 584
Yeates, Rachel VI, 793
Yeates, Samuel II, 696
Yeates, Samuel III, 117
Yeates, Samuel III, 371
Yeates, Samuel III, 372
Yeates, Sarah II, 975
Yeates, Sarah III, 372
Yeates, Sarah VI, 467
Yeates, Sarah VI, 481
Yeates, Sarah VI, 586
Yeates, Sarah VI, 736
Yeates, Sarah VI, 793
Yeates, Thomas II, 696
Yeates, William III, 372
Yeates, William IV, 78
Yeates, William IV, 117
Yeates, William VI, 467
Yeates, William VI, 481
Yeates, William VI, 586
Yeates, William VI, 793
Yeates, William, Jr. VI, 586
Yeates, William, Jr. VI, 793
Yeates, William, Sr. VI, 736
Yeates, William, Sr. VI, 793
Yeates, Wm. VI, 736
Yeates, Wm. VI, 793
Yeates, Wm., Jr. VI, 793
Yeatman, John IV, 69
Yeatman, John IV, 117
Yeatman, John D. VI, 828
Yeatman, John P. VI, 867
Yeatman, Susan VI, 867
Yeats, Ann VI, 793
Yeats, Ann W. IV, 801
Yeats, Charles IV, 801
Yeats, Clerky I, 1135
Yeats, Dinah III, 194
Yeats, Dinah III, 371
Yeats, Eliza V, 943
Yeats, Elizabeth I, 1135
Yeats, Elizabeth VI, 793
Yeats, Hannah IV, 117
Yeats, Hannah IV, 801
Yeats, Hannah VI, 793
Yeats, Henry VI, 793
Yeats, Hepzabah I, 584
Yeats, Hiram IV, 801
Yeats, Isaac IV, 801
Yeats, Jane III, 372
Yeats, John III, 372
Yeats, Joseph IV, 801
Yeats, Margaret IV, 800
Yeats, Mary I, 1135
Yeats, Mary IV, 801
Yeats, Nancy VI, 959
Yeats, Patrick I, 1135
Yeats, Rachel VI, 793
Yeats, Sarah II, 1042
Yeats, Sarah VI, 793
Yeats, Thomas G. IV, 801
Yeats, William I, 1135
Yeats, William, Jr. VI, 793
Yei, Lewis V, 214
Yeigh, H. B. V, 214
Yeigh, Lewis V, 214
Yeildhall, ??? II, 449
Yeildhall, Anthony II, 449
Yeildhall, John II, 449
Yeildhall, Mary II, 449
Yeildhall, Susanna II, 449
Yeildhall, Wm. II, 449
Yeisley, John C. V, 1026
Yeisley, John P. V, 1026
Yellott, ??? III, 372
Yellott, Bethia G. III, 372
Yellott, Bethiah III, 372
Yellott, Caroline M. III, 372
Yellott, Edward F. III, 372
Yellott, George III, 372
Yellott, John G. III, 372
Yellott, John J. III, 330
Yellott, John J. III, 372
Yellott, John, Jr. III, 372
Yellott, Phebe T. III, 330
Yellott, Phebe T. III, 372
Yellott, Sophia B. III, 78
Yellott, William III, 372
Yellott, Worthington III, 372
Yelverton, John B. VI, 793
Yelverton, John DeWitt VI, 765
Yelverton, John Dewitt VI, 793
Yelverton, Margaret Lamb VI, 765
Yelverton, Sarah A. VI, 793
Yengling, Willard Lee IV, 791
Yeo, Alice V, 214
Yeo, Amanda V, 214
Yeo, Elizabeth V, 606
Yeo, Elizabeth V, 721
Yeo, Emma V, 214
Yeo, Jary Jane II, 893
Yeo, Martha Ann V, 214
Yeo, Mary Jane II, 944
Yeo, William H. V, 606
Yeo, William H. V, 721
Yeo, Wm. V, 606
Yeomans, ??? III, 372
Yeomans, Charles C. III, 372
Yeomans, Charles E. III, 328
Yeomans, Charles E. III, 329
Yeomans, Esther W. III, 372
Yeomans, Hannah Louisa III, 328
Yeomans, Hannah Louisa III, 372
Yeomans, Louisa III, 329
Yergan, Lucinda I, 934
Yerkas, Joseph II, 696
Yerkes, Amelia H. II, 944
Yerkes, Anthony II, 461
Yerkes, Anthony II, 696
Yerkes, Anthony II, 787
Yerkes, Anthony II, 804
Yerkes, Arnold Phipps VI, 767
Yerkes, Arnold Phipps VI, 793
Yerkes, Arthur W. VI, 793
Yerkes, Carolyn Margaret VI, 793
Yerkes, Catharine Canby II, 804
Yerkes, Chas. T. II, 829
Yerkes, Elizabeth II, 789
Yerkes, Ellen III, 361
Yerkes, Emily T. II, 890
Yerkes, Emily T. II, 944
Yerkes, George S. II, 829
Yerkes, Hannah II, 461
Yerkes, Hannah II, 696
Yerkes, Hannah II, 810
Yerkes, Hannah Littler II, 787
Yerkes, Harman II, 829
Yerkes, Henrietta II, 890
Yerkes, Henrietta II, 944
Yerkes, Isaac II, 829
Yerkes, John Keith II, 890
Yerkes, John Keith II, 944
Yerkes, Joseph II, 461
Yerkes, Joseph II, 696
Yerkes, Julia II, 935
Yerkes, Julia II, 944
Yerkes, Margaret H. VI, 793
Yerkes, Rebecca II, 829
Yerkes, Rebecca VI, 767
Yerkes, Rebecca VI, 793
Yerkes, Susannah II, 787
Yerkes, Susannah II, 804
Yerkes, Virginia Moon VI, 793
Yerkes, Wm. Austin II, 890
Yerkes, Wm. Austin II, 944
Yerks, Affa III, 372
Yewdall, Margaretta II, 944
Yewdall, Margaretta P. II, 944
Yewdall, Margaretta Price II, 829
Yewdall, Margaretta S. II, 829
Yewdall, Margaretta S. II, 944
Yewdall, Samuel Price II, 944
Yewdall, Samuel W. II, 829
Yewdall, Samuel W. II, 944
Yewdall, Sarah II, 829
Yewdall, Sarah S. II, 944
Yhost, Hannah IV, 310
Yhost, Margaret IV, 310
Yhost, Mary IV, 310
Yhost, Rachel IV, 310
Yhost, Sarah IV, 310
Yieldhall, Joan II, 440
Yieldhall, Mary II, 440
Yieldhall, Robert II, 440
Yieldhall, Susannah II, 440
Yieldhall, Wd. Jane II, 440
Yoakum, Anne VI, 1022
Yoakum, Michael VI, 1022
Yoarex, Elijah II, 973
Yoarex, Fannie II, 973
Yoarex, Florence Eva II, 973
Yoarex, Lewis Edwin II, 973
Yoarex, Moses II, 973
Yoarex, Patience II, 973
Yoars, Julia E. I, 929
Yocom, Anna IV, 1049
Yocom, Anna IV, 1084
Yocom, Edward IV, 1084
Yocom, Elizabeth S. IV, 1084
Yocom, Hannah IV, 459
Yocom, Jacob IV, 598
Yocom, Jacob IV, 601
Yocom, Joshua IV, 1084
Yocom, Lydia IV, 598
Yocom, Lydia IV, 601
Yocom, Mary Jane IV, 1084
Yocom, Mary P. IV, 1084
Yocom, Rachel IV, 1084
Yocom, Rebecca IV, 309
Yocom, Rebecca IV, 601
Yocom, Samuel IV, 601
Yocom, Sarah IV, 384
Yocom, Sarah IV, 1064
Yocom, Sarah IV, 1084
Yocom, Sarah Ann IV, 1084
Yocom, Thomas IV, 384
Yocom, Thomas IV, 1084
Yocom, Thomas Austin IV, 1084
Yocom, Thomas D. IV, 1084
Yocom, Thos. D. IV, 1084
Yocum, ??? IV, 309
Yocum, Aaron D. IV, 360
Yocum, David IV, 459
Yocum, Elizabeth S. IV, 1073
Yocum, Elizabeth S. IV, 1084
Yocum, Gainer IV, 395
Yocum, Gainer IV, 459
Yocum, Hannah IV, 309
Yocum, Hannah IV, 454
Yocum, Hannah IV, 459
Yocum, Hannah T. IV, 359
Yocum, Hannah T. IV, 397
Yocum, Hannah T. IV, 459
Yocum, Isaac IV, 459
Yocum, Jacob IV, 309
Yocum, Jacob IV, 459
Yocum, Jane IV, 359
Yocum, Jane IV, 459
Yocum, Jesse IV, 395
Yocum, Jesse IV, 459
Yocum, John IV, 309
Yocum, John IV, 459
Yocum, John D. IV, 359
Yocum, John D. IV, 397
Yocum, John D. IV, 459
Yocum, John H. V, 1026
Yocum, Joseph IV, 359
Yocum, Joseph IV, 459
Yocum, Joshua IV, 1084
Yocum, Lindley IV, 459
Yocum, Lindly IV, 359
Yocum, Lydia IV, 411
Yocum, Lydia IV, 459
Yocum, Maria IV, 459
Yocum, Mark IV, 309
Yocum, Mark IV, 459
Yocum, Martha V, 1026
Yocum, Mary IV, 459
Yocum, Mary J. IV, 359
Yocum, Mary P. IV, 1084
Yocum, Nathan G. IV, 359
Yocum, Nathan G. IV, 459
Yocum, Phebe IV, 459
Yocum, Rebecca IV, 309
Yocum, Rebecca IV, 459
Yocum, Rebecca, Jr. IV, 459
Yocum, Rebeckah IV, 459
Yocum, Samuel IV, 309
Yocum, Samuel IV, 359
Yocum, Samuel IV, 411
Yocum, Samuel IV, 459
Yocum, Samuel, Jr. IV, 459
Yocum, Samuel, Sr. IV, 360
Yocum, Sarah IV, 459
Yocum, Thomas IV, 309
Yocum, Thomas IV, 459
Yocum, Thomas D. IV, 1084
Yocus, Bertha IV, 686
Yocus, Etta IV, 686
Yocus, Nicholas IV, 686
Yoe, Thomas B. VI, 793
Yoe, Wm. V, 606
Yoh, Ruby V, 1026
Yoh, Savilla V, 1026
Yokeley, Addie I, 903
Yokely, Addie I, 906
Yokum, Anna V, 293
Yokum, Hannah T. IV, 359
Yokum, John D. IV, 359
Yokum, Nathan G. IV, 359
Yonce, Martha I, 878
Yonce, Martha I, 906
Yong, Mary II, 440
Yong, Morgan II, 440
Yong, Thomas II, 696
Yonge, Susan III, 343
Yonkerman, Annis IV, 1344
Yonkerman, John IV, 1344
Yonley, Rebecca VI, 417
Yonnaly, Rebecca VI, 462
Yont, Eva V, 145
Yore, Lovie IV, 310
York, Anna I, 683
York, Anna I, 693
York, Bartlett I, 643
York, Bartlett W. I, 613
York, Charlotta V, 367
York, Charlotte V, 367
York, Clara K. IV, 1242
York, Dewey R. V, 367
York, Dewey Raymond V, 36
York, Emilie IV, 1242
York, Emily D. IV, 1242
York, Ethel I, 613
York, Ethel I, 630
York, Ethel I, 643
York, George IV, 1242
York, George J. IV, 1242
York, Harley E. V, 367
York, Harley Edward V, 367
York, Harriet J. IV, 1242
York, John I, 754
York, John T. V, 367
York, John Theodore V, 367
York, John W. I, 772
York, Leander I, 472
York, Leander I, 486
York, Leota F. V, 367
York, Lewis H. V, 367
York, Lola Fern V, 367
York, Lula I, 613
York, Lula I, 628
York, Mary II, 582
York, Mary II, 696
York, Nancy I, 693
York, Nancy I, 772
York, Phebe Ann IV, 1242
York, Rebecca II, 440
York, Sally I, 754
York, Sarah I, 772
York, Susan Jane Williams IV, 1242
York, Theresa I, 643
York, Theresa V. I, 628
York, Thomas I, 693
York, Walter L. V, 367
York, Walter Lewis V, 367
York, William Bartlette I, 628
Yorke, William I, 1051
Yorty, John Wagginer V, 773
Yorty, Nancy V, 773
Yost, Eliza V, 850
Yost, Ellen IV, 215
Yost, Ellen IV, 310
Yost, Hannah IV, 254
Yost, Hannah IV, 310
Yost, Margaret IV, 310
Yost, Margaret IV, 313
Yost, Margaret IV, 315
Yost, Margaret V, 306
Yost, Margaret V, 314
Yost, Martha IV, 310
Yost, Mary IV, 310
Yost, Mary IV, 312
Yost, Mary IV, 315
Yost, Michel IV, 254
Yost, Myrtle G. IV, 1267
Yost, Rachel IV, 254
Yost, Rachel IV, 310
Yost, Sarah IV, 310
Yost, Sarah IV, 312
Yost, Sarah IV, 315
Yost, Sarah M. IV, 1267
Yost, W. W. IV, 1267
Yost, Wallice W. IV, 1267
Yott, Edith M. III, 347
Yott, Elliot Ives III, 372
Yott, Helen III, 347
Yott, Helen Edith III, 347
Yott, Helen Ethel III, 372
Yott, Lillian M. III, 372
Yott, Malcolm C. III, 347
Yott, Malcolm C. III, 372
Youdle, Susannah III, 372
Younce, Mary Ann V, 773
Younce, Mary Ann V, 774
Young, ??? III, 118
Young, ??? III, 373
Young, ??? IV, 791
Young, ??? IV, 861
Young, Abby Jane III, 118
Young, Abby Jane III, 372
Young, Abi V, 145
Young, Abigail III, 118
Young, Abigail VI, 453
Young, Abram VI, 755
Young, Adam VI, 942
Young, Albert IV, 1267
Young, Alex. III, 372
Young, Alexander III, 175
Young, Alexander III, 372

, Alexander III, 476
, Alfred V, 145
, Alice B. V, 145
, Allice B. V, 145
, Amos IV, 791
, Amos IV, 792
, Amos IV, 918
, Amos IV, 1018
, Amos IV, 1019
g, Ann IV, 80
g, Ann IV, 117
g, Ann IV, 510
g, Ann IV, 559
g, Ann IV, 667
g, Ann IV, 675
g, Ann IV, 708
g, Ann IV, 791
g, Ann IV, 866
g, Ann IV, 886
g, Ann IV, 1011
g, Ann IV, 1018
g, Ann IV, 1019
g, Ann VI, 329
g, Ann VI, 345
g, Ann VI, 1022
g, Ann B. IV, 791
ng, Ann Elizabeth III, 372
ng, Ann Lorena IV, 792
ng, Ann, Jr. IV, 791
ng, Anna III, 372
ng, Anna IV, 791
ng, Anna Lorena IV, 680
ng, Annie IV, 792
ng, Annie B. IV, 708
ng, Annie B. IV, 791
ng, Arda Ray IV, 1267
ng, Arthur VI, 823
ng, Benj. M. IV, 866
ng, Benj. P. III, 476
ng, Benj., Jr. IV, 791
ng, Benjamin IV, 791
ng, Benjamin IV, 792
ung, Benjamin IV, 918
ung, Benjamin IV, 1019
ung, Benjamin M. IV, 886
ung, Benjamin M. IV, 1018
ung, Benjamin Morgan IV, 886
ung, Beth Stones III, 509
ung, Burton V, 773
ung, C. A. IV, 310
ung, C. B. V, 1026
ung, Caleb H. Lewis V, 145
ung, Carleton Garretson VI, 742
ung, Carleton Garretson VI, 793
ung, Carleton Garrettson VI, 741
ung, Carleton Garrettson VI, 742
ung, Caroline IV, 946
ung, Caroline IV, 1018
ung, Caroline IV, 1019
ung, Catherine V, 145
ung, Charles III, 372
oung, Charles IV, 791
oung, Charles A. III, 373
oung, Charles Alexander III, 372
oung, Charles C. V, 145
oung, Charles H. V, 145
oung, Charles Wager III, 372
oung, Charlotte Elizabeth III, 465
oung, Charlotte Elizabeth III, 476
Young, Chas. B. V, 1026
Young, Christiana IV, 60
Young, Christiana IV, 69
Young, Christina IV, 1267
Young, Cordelia III, 15
Young, Daisy J. V, 145
Young, Daniel IV, 886
Young, Daniel IV, 1011
Young, Daniel IV, 1018
Young, Daniel IV, 1019
Young, Daniel IV, 1301
Young, Daniel V, 563
Young, Daniel V, 606
Young, Daniel Test IV, 791
Young, Daniel Test IV, 792
Young, David IV, 791
Young, David IV, 1019
Young, Dessie V, 773
Young, Dina IV, 117
Young, Dinah IV, 69
Young, Dinah IV, 559
Young, Dinah VI, 543
Young, Dinah VI, 587
Young, Don C. IV, 310
Young, Drusilla IV, 692
Young, Drusilla IV, 791
Young, Duncan VI, 345
Young, Duncan VI, 1022
Young, Edward III, 372
Young, Edward IV, 1301
Young, Edward B. V, 145
Young, Edward C. IV, 1301
Young, Edward C. V, 944
Young, Edward Carnegy V, 944
Young, Edward Cummings III, 372
Young, Edwin IV, 1019
Young, Eli IV, 117
Young, Eli IV, 559
Young, Eliz. III, 175
Young, Eliz. III, 372
Young, Elizabeth II, 614
Young, Elizabeth II, 696
Young, Elizabeth II, 941
Young, Elizabeth II, 944
Young, Elizabeth III, 372
Young, Elizabeth IV, 559
Young, Elizabeth IV, 653
Young, Elizabeth IV, 791
Young, Elizabeth IV, 1301
Young, Elizabeth VI, 647
Young, Elizabeth VI, 724
Young, Elizabeth VI, 867
Young, Elizabeth C. V, 773
Young, Elizabeth D. III, 476
Young, Elizabeth L. III, 372
Young, Elizabeth Marion II, 944
Young, Elizabeth N. IV, 1301
Young, Elizabeth N. R. VI, 867
Young, Ella V. II, 887
Young, Ella V. II, 944
Young, Ellen V, 367
Young, Ellen L. II, 854
Young, Ellen L. II, 944
Young, Elma Jones IV, 1267
Young, Emily Grace III, 310
Young, Emily Grace III, 372
Young, Ernest V, 721
Young, Ernest H. III, 509
Young, Evan IV, 69
Young, Fleming IV, 1018
Young, Fleming C. IV, 1019
Young, Florence L. II, 701
Young, Florence Louella II, 732
Young, Florence Louella II, 778
Young, Frank C. III, 509
Young, Franklin III, 465
Young, Franklin III, 476
Young, Fred IV, 1045
Young, Fred W. IV, 1044
Young, Geo. V, 1026
Young, Geo. E. IV, 282
Young, Geo. E. IV, 310
Young, Geo. F. III, 263
Young, Geo. F. P. III, 310
Young, Geo. F. P. III, 372
Young, Geo. H. V, 944
Young, Geo. P. III, 372
Young, George III, 372
Young, George V, 606
Young, George V, 1026
Young, George H. III, 372
Young, Hannah I, 1163
Young, Hannah II, 998
Young, Hannah II, 1042
Young, Hannah III, 476
Young, Hannah IV, 117
Young, Hannah IV, 559
Young, Hannah IV, 876
Young, Hannah IV, 886
Young, Hannah VI, 478
Young, Hannah VI, 586
Young, Hannah VI, 587
Young, Hannah VI, 628
Young, Hannah VI, 700
Young, Hannah VI, 724
Young, Hannah H. IV, 1003
Young, Hannah H. IV, 1018
Young, Hannah H. IV, 1019
Young, Hannah M. IV, 1301
Young, Hannah Sophia V, 182
Young, Hannah Sophia V, 214
Young, Hannah Sulphia V, 214
Young, Harrison III, 494
Young, Harrison III, 509
Young, Harvey V, 1026
Young, Henry II, 941
Young, Henry II, 944
Young, Henry IV, 1019
Young, Henry IV, 1301
Young, Henry V, 145
Young, Henry VI, 132
Young, Henry VI, 144
Young, Henry C. II, 944
Young, Henry D. III, 372
Young, Henry H. III, 372
Young, Henry S. IV, 1301
Young, Henry S. VI, 793
Young, Hercules IV, 117
Young, Hercules IV, 559
Young, Hercules VI, 478
Young, Hercules VI, 586
Young, Hercules VI, 628
Young, Hercules VI, 724
Young, Herculus IV, 117
Young, Hiram III, 372
Young, Hiram V, 944
Young, Huldah V, 420
Young, Huldah V, 421
Young, J. Francis V, 875
Young, J. M. IV, 717
Young, Jacob VI, 586
Young, James IV, 69
Young, James IV, 791
Young, James V, 145
Young, James V, 182
Young, James V, 773
Young, James VI, 543
Young, James VI, 587
Young, James E. V, 145
Young, James E. V, 214
Young, James F. III, 476
Young, James T. V, 773
Young, James W. IV, 1267
Young, James, Jr. IV, 69
Young, Jane III, 476
Young, Jane IV, 702
Young, Jane IV, 791
Young, Jane IV, 792
Young, Jane IV, 816
Young, Jane IV, 886
Young, Jane IV, 918
Young, Jane IV, 953
Young, Jane IV, 988
Young, Jane IV, 1018
Young, Jane IV, 1019
Young, Jane V, 798
Young, Jane VI, 823
Young, Janet VI, 627
Young, Janet VI, 734
Young, Jehu IV, 1301
Young, Jehu W. IV, 1019
Young, Jennie V, 1026
Young, Jesse IV, 791
Young, Jesse IV, 886
Young, Jesse IV, 918
Young, Jesse IV, 1018
Young, Jesse IV, 1019
Young, Job IV, 310
Young, John II, 440
Young, John II, 614
Young, John II, 696
Young, John III, 509
Young, John IV, 69
Young, John IV, 117
Young, John IV, 559
Young, John VI, 8
Young, John VI, 38
Young, John VI, 329
Young, John VI, 462
Young, John VI, 867
Young, John VI, 950
Young, John VI, 1012
Young, John VI, 1022
Young, John A. II, 854
Young, John A. II, 944
Young, John J. IV, 1018
Young, John J. IV, 1019
Young, John S. III, 151
Young, John S. III, 373
Young, Joseph II, 696
Young, Joseph III, 372
Young, Joseph IV, 667
Young, Joseph IV, 791
Young, Joseph IV, 866
Young, Joseph IV, 886
Young, Joseph IV, 1018
Young, Joseph IV, 1019
Young, Joseph VI, 852
Young, Joseph E. IV, 791
Young, Joseph M. IV, 1019
Young, Joseph W. V, 944
Young, Joseph, Jr. IV, 886
Young, Joseph, Jr. IV, 946
Young, Joseph, Jr. IV, 1018
Young, Joshua C. IV, 1018
Young, Joshua C. IV, 1019
Young, Larkin I, 1163
Young, Laura B. V, 606
Young, Laura Bell IV, 1267
Young, Laurence III, 372
Young, Lavina IV, 1019
Young, Lawrence IV, 310
Young, Lawrence N. IV, 310
Young, Lelia A. V, 145
Young, Lelia Abi V, 145
Young, Lewis V, 721
Young, Lila IV, 310
Young, Lilia I, 643
Young, Lillie V, 1026
Young, Lizzie V, 293
Young, Lizzie M. II, 944
Young, Lorena IV, 679
Young, Lowell V, 1026
Young, Lowell H. V, 1026
Young, Lydia IV, 1019
Young, Lydia A. IV, 282
Young, Lydia A. IV, 310
Young, Lydia S. VI, 793
Young, M. Alma III, 372
Young, M. C. V, 721
Young, Mansfield III, 339
Young, Mansfield III, 373
Young, Margaret III, 263
Young, Margaret III, 372
Young, Margaret IV, 366
Young, Margaret IV, 459
Young, Margaret VI, 487
Young, Margaret VI, 587
Young, Margaret M. V, 1026
Young, Margaret Sylvia IV, 791
Young, Margaret Sylvia IV, 792
Young, Margit VI, 940
Young, Maria IV, 1301
Young, Martha III, 372
Young, Martha S. II, 854
Young, Martha S. II, 944
Young, Martin Clarkson IV, 1301
Young, Martin Clarkson V, 145
Young, Mary I, 904
Young, Mary I, 906
Young, Mary I, 1080
Young, Mary I, 1127
Young, Mary I, 1135
Young, Mary II, 440
Young, Mary II, 701
Young, Mary II, 778
Young, Mary II, 1030
Young, Mary II, 1042
Young, Mary III, 476
Young, Mary IV, 866
Young, Mary IV, 886
Young, Mary IV, 1018
Young, Mary IV, 1019
Young, Mary IV, 1267
Young, Mary V, 182
Young, Mary V, 1026
Young, Mary VI, 837
Young, Mary A. III, 310
Young, Mary A. V, 1026
Young, Mary Amanda III, 263
Young, Mary Amanda III, 372
Young, Mary B. IV, 310
Young, Mary B. IV, 848
Young, Mary C. IV, 1019
Young, Mary Cowgill IV, 1267
Young, Mary E. IV, 1301
Young, Mary E. V, 145
Young, Mary Elizabeth IV, 791
Young, Mary Elizabeth IV, 1345
Young, Mary M. II, 732
Young, Mary M. V, 1026
Young, Mary Wilson II, 1064
Young, Matilda V, 1026
Young, Matthew VI, 867
Young, Maude IV, 310
Young, Merrill IV, 1267
Young, Michal V, 810
Young, Mildred Binns IV, 792
Young, Mildred M. IV, 791
Young, Milley IV, 1018
Young, Miranda V, 1026
Young, Morgan II, 440
Young, Morgan IV, 117
Young, Morgan IV, 559
Young, Mourning V, 227
Young, Mourning V, 293
Young, Mrs. C. N. IV, 310
Young, Mrs. Marian V, 1026
Young, Myra V, 1026
Young, Nancy VI, 329
Young, Nancy VI, 950
Young, Narcisa IV, 1018
Young, Narcissa IV, 1019
Young, Nathaniel VI, 867
Young, Newton V, 1026
Young, Nora V, 773
Young, Olive VI, 627
Young, Olive VI, 734
Young, Oliver H. II, 854
Young, Oliver H. II, 944
Young, Omar H. V, 875
Young, Omer V, 875
Young, Phebe III, 372
Young, Phebe III, 494
Young, Phebe III, 509
Young, Phebe IV, 644
Young, Phebe IV, 886
Young, Phebe V, 721
Young, Phebe V, 822
Young, Phebe B. III, 175
Young, Phebe B. III, 372
Young, Phebe C. III, 509
Young, Phebe R. IV, 1386
Young, Polly VI, 1012
Young, Polly H. VI, 812
Young, Rachel III, 372
Young, Rachel III, 373
Young, Rachel IV, 92
Young, Rachel IV, 117
Young, Rachel IV, 866
Young, Rachel IV, 886
Young, Rachel IV, 918
Young, Rachel IV, 1018
Young, Rachel IV, 1019
Young, Rachel Ella IV, 791
Young, Rebecca II, 944
Young, Rebecca III, 372
Young, Rebecca III, 373
Young, Rebecca V, 944
Young, Rebecca A. II, 941
Young, Rebecca A. II, 944
Young, Rebecca Eva IV, 1301
Young, Reuben V, 367
Young, Rhoda IV, 1301
Young, Rhoda V, 563
Young, Rhoda V, 606
Young, Rhoda V, 721
Young, Rhoda Ann V, 145
Young, Robert W. III, 372
Young, Robert W. III, 373
Young, Robert W. V, 944
Young, Robert W., Jr. V, 944
Young, Robert, Jr. III, 372
Young, Roy Dwight V, 875
Young, Ruby F. V, 875
Young, Ruby Frances V, 875
Young, Ruth I, 1061
Young, Ruth I, 1063
Young, Ruth V, 721
Young, Ruth VI, 543
Young, Ruth Elizabeth V, 651
Young, Salley VI, 1022
Young, Sally VI, 867
Young, Samuel IV, 1344
Young, Samuel IV, 1345
Young, Sarah I, 1163
Young, Sarah III, 372
Young, Sarah III, 373
Young, Sarah III, 476
Young, Sarah III, 509
Young, Sarah IV, 46
Young, Sarah IV, 69
Young, Sarah IV, 791
Young, Sarah IV, 886
Young, Sarah IV, 1018
Young, Sarah IV, 1019
Young, Sarah VI, 462
Young, Sarah VI, 478
Young, Sarah VI, 586
Young, Sarah VI, 587
Young, Sarah VI, 628
Young, Sarah VI, 724
Young, Sarah VI, 867
Young, Sarah Bell IV, 1345
Young, Sarah C. V, 145
Young, Sarah C. V, 214
Young, Sarah Catherine V, 145
Young, Sarah Chace VI, 793
Young, Sarah Chace Franklin VI, 741
Young, Sarah M. III, 151
Young, Sarah M. III, 305
Young, Sarah M. III, 373
Young, Sarah Marie III, 373
Young, Sarah S. III, 372
Young, Sarah T. III, 339
Young, Scott V, 1026
Young, Silas IV, 69
Young, Silas VI, 462
Young, Susan III, 254
Young, Susanna IV, 69
Young, Susanna IV, 886
Young, Susanna B. VI, 669
Young, Susanna B. VI, 724
Young, Susanna H. VI, 852
Young, Susannah VI, 867
Young, Tamar IV, 918
Young, Tamar IV, 1018
Young, Tamer IV, 769
Young, Tamer IV, 791
Young, Tamer IV, 792
Young, Tamer IV, 1019
Young, Tamor IV, 791
Young, Thomas II, 696
Young, Thomas IV, 675
Young, Thomas IV, 791
Young, Thomas IV, 886
Young, Thomas IV, 918

Young, Thomas IV, 1018
Young, Thomas IV, 1019
Young, Thomas VI, 831
Young, Thomas VI, 867
Young, Thomas S. IV, 1018
Young, Thomas W. IV, 1301
Young, Thomas Winder IV, 1301
Young, Thomas, Jr. IV, 792
Young, Thos. IV, 708
Young, Thos. M. VI, 804
Young, Wd. Sarah M. III, 151
Young, Wd. Sarah R. II, 825
Young, Will V, 1026
Young, Will VI, 852
Young, William IV, 886
Young, William VI, 812
Young, William VI, 867
Young, William VI, 1022
Young, William A. V, 773
Young, William L. III, 372
Young, William L. III, 373
Young, William L. V, 944
Young, William P. II, 701
Young, William Robert IV, 792
Young, William T. V, 145
Young, Wilmer IV, 791
Young, Wm. II, 696
Young, Wm. II, 998
Young, Wm. II, 1042
Young, Wm. V, 1026
Young, Wm. L. V, 944
Young, Wm. P. II, 732
Young, Wm. P. II, 778
Youngblood, Jacob I, 430
Younge, Charles H. V, 145
Younger, Amanda IV, 792
Younger, Ann VI, 902
Younger, Ann VI, 978
Younger, Aurelius IV, 792
Younger, Benjamin IV, 792
Younger, Jenny VI, 902
Younger, Lucy VI, 868
Younger, Margaret II, 267
Younger, Margaret II, 277
Younger, Susanna VI, 978
Younger, Wm. S. VI, 868
Youngger, Margaret II, 277
Younghusband, Elizabeth T. VI, 208
Younghusband, Elizabeth T. VI, 221
Younghusband, Henrico VI, 281
Younghusband, Isaac VI, 206
Younghusband, Isaac VI, 221
Younghusband, Mary VI, 164
Younghusband, Mary VI, 221
Younghusband, Mary VI, 281
Younghusband, Mary VI, 474
Younghusband, Mary P., Jr. VI, 281
Youngs, Alexander III, 404
Youngs, Alexander III, 451
Youngs, Alexander III, 476
Youngs, Gilbert III, 451
Youngs, Hannah III, 476
Youngs, Mary III, 451
Youngs, Phebe III, 400
Youngs, Richard III, 400
Youngs, Sarah III, 404
Youngs, Sarah III, 451
Youngs, Sarah III, 476
Youngs, Susannah III, 400
Younker, Hannah II, 520
Younker, Hannah II, 696
Yount, Amelia V, 750
Yount, Amelia V, 774
Yount, Andrew I, 672
Yount, Andrew V, 145
Yount, Andrew V, 774
Yount, Andrew V, 794
Yount, Ann V, 794
Yount, Caroline V, 774
Yount, Catharine I, 672
Yount, Catherine V, 76
Yount, Catherine V, 145
Yount, Clifford V, 774
Yount, Dale Eugene V, 774
Yount, Dan V, 145
Yount, Daniel I, 672
Yount, Daniel I, 739
Yount, Daniel V, 774
Yount, Davis V, 794
Yount, Delilah V, 774
Yount, Delilah V, 793
Yount, Delilah V, 794
Yount, Edgar V, 774
Yount, Edgar W. V, 774
Yount, Effie V, 774
Yount, Elam V, 773
Yount, Elim V, 774
Yount, Elizabeth I, 672
Yount, Elizabeth I, 722
Yount, Elizabeth I, 739
Yount, Elizabeth V, 739
Yount, Elizabeth V, 746
Yount, Elizabeth V, 773
Yount, Elizabeth V, 774
Yount, Elizabeth V, 785
Yount, Elizabeth V, 793
Yount, Elizabeth V, 794
Yount, Emma V, 774
Yount, Enos V, 773
Yount, Enos V, 774
Yount, Enos V, 794
Yount, Eva V, 145
Yount, Eve V, 145
Yount, Eve V, 774
Yount, Frederic V, 774
Yount, Frederick V, 145
Yount, Frederick V, 773
Yount, Frederick V, 774
Yount, Frederick V, 793
Yount, Frederick V, 794
Yount, Frederick, Jr. V, 774
Yount, Golda V, 774
Yount, Goldie V, 774
Yount, H V, 773
Yount, H??? V, 773
Yount, Harold V, 774
Yount, Harry V, 774
Yount, Harvey V, 774
Yount, Henry I, 672
Yount, Henry I, 707
Yount, Henry I, 739
Yount, Henry V, 145
Yount, Henry V, 745
Yount, Henry V, 746
Yount, Henry V, 773
Yount, Henry V, 774
Yount, Henry V, 785
Yount, Henry V, 793
Yount, Henry V, 794
Yount, Herman V, 774
Yount, Howard V, 774
Yount, Insco V, 794
Yount, Jacob V, 773
Yount, Jacob V, 774
Yount, Jesse V, 793
Yount, Jesse V, 794
Yount, Joanna V, 794
Yount, John I, 739
Yount, John V, 145
Yount, John V, 744
Yount, John V, 773
Yount, John V, 774
Yount, John V, 793
Yount, John V, 794
Yount, John C. V, 794
Yount, John H. V, 774
Yount, Josie V, 774
Yount, Juanita V, 774
Yount, Katharine V, 774
Yount, Leroy V, 774
Yount, Mahala V, 773
Yount, Mahala V, 774
Yount, Mary I, 672
Yount, Mary I, 707
Yount, Mary I, 739
Yount, Mary V, 145
Yount, Mary V, 744
Yount, Mary V, 745
Yount, Mary V, 773
Yount, Mary V, 774
Yount, Mary V, 793
Yount, Mary V, 794
Yount, Mary Ann V, 773
Yount, Mary Ann V, 774
Yount, Mary Ann V, 794
Yount, Merlin Leroy V, 774
Yount, Micah V, 774
Yount, Michael V, 773
Yount, Milly V, 773
Yount, Milly V, 774
Yount, Noah V, 773
Yount, Rebecca V, 744
Yount, Rebecca V, 774
Yount, Rebeckah V, 793
Yount, Rebeckah V, 794
Yount, Rettie V, 774
Yount, Rosanna V, 794
Yount, Samuel V, 774
Yount, Sarah I, 707
Yount, Sarah V, 145
Yount, Sarah V, 745
Yount, Sarah V, 746
Yount, Sarah V, 773
Yount, Sarah V, 774
Yount, Sarah V, 785
Yount, Sarah V, 793
Yount, Sarah V, 794
Yount, Solomon V, 773
Yount, Solomon V, 774
Yount, Solomon V, 793
Yount, Solomon V, 794
Yount, Theresa V, 761
Yount, Theresa V, 774
Yount, Tressie V, 774
Yount, William H. V, 774
Younts, Carl A. I, 643
Younts, Edgar I, 643
Younts, Iona Deboe I, 643
Younts, Ione I, 643
Younts, Joseph W. I, 621
Younts, Martha D. I, 621
Younts, Mildred Deboe I, 643
Younts, Pearl I, 621
Younts, Pearl I, 637
Younts, Pearl I, 643
Younts, Sarah Margaret I, 643
Yourex, Fannie II, 1064
Yourex, Florence Eva II, 1064
Yourex, Golda IV, 459
Yourex, Golda B. H. IV, 403
Yourex, Golda B. H. IV, 459
Yourex, Lewis Edwin II, 1064
Yourex, Mary Arline IV, 459
Yourex, Moses II, 1064
Yourex, Moses IV, 459
Yourex, Moses R. IV, 459
Yourex, Moses Richard II, 1064
Yourex, Paul Hall IV, 459
Youst, Mary IV, 310
Youst, Rachel IV, 310
Yow, Alfred L. I, 614
Yow, Elsie I, 638
Yow, Elsie I, 643
Yow, Enoch G. I, 486
Yow, Enoch S. I, 472
Yow, Frances I, 733
Yow, Frances I, 739
Yow, Martha J. I, 614
Yow, Mary J. I, 614
Yow, Phebe I, 486
Yowell, Mary Willa V, 651
Yuen, Chang III, 373
Yuille, Amanda VI, 868
Yuille, George VI, 868
Yunt, Andrew IV, 69
Yunt, Catharine IV, 69
Yunt, Daniel I, 739
Yunt, Henry I, 695
Yunt, Henry I, 739
Yunt, Henry IV, 69
Yunt, John I, 739
Yunt, Mary I, 695
Yunt, Mary I, 733
Yunt, Mary I, 739
Yunt, Mary IV, 69
Yunt, Sarah IV, 69
Z???, Bessie III, 103
Z???, Bessie III, 373
Z???, Mary III, 373
Zabriskie, Mary II, 944
Zachary, A. E. I, 923
Zachary, Alfred I, 442
Zachary, Alfred L. I, 455
Zachary, Coy I, 952
Zachary, Coy B. I, 952
Zachary, Coy Bernice I, 936
Zachary, Daniel II, 440
Zachary, Daniel II, 583
Zachary, Daniel II, 696
Zachary, David I, 1000
Zachary, Deborah I, 442
Zachary, Deborah I, 455
Zachary, Edith E. Fay I, 936
Zachary, Edna B. I, 952
Zachary, Edna Bertha I, 936
Zachary, Edw'd I, 951
Zachary, Edward A. I, 952
Zachary, Edward Alfred I, 936
Zachary, Edward Lyndon I, 936
Zachary, Effie I, 923
Zachary, Effie Beatrice I, 936
Zachary, Effie Beatrice I, 951
Zachary, Eliza Jane I, 442
Zachary, Elizabeth II, 440
Zachary, Hannah E. I, 442
Zachary, Hannah E. I, 455
Zachary, Helen Maris I, 936
Zachary, Iris May I, 936
Zachary, Ivan Ray I, 936
Zachary, James I, 442
Zachary, James I, 455
Zachary, Jane I, 442
Zachary, Jemima I, 846
Zachary, Jemima VI, 281
Zachary, John I, 846
Zachary, John I, 1000
Zachary, Jonathan I, 442
Zachary, Jonathan I, 455
Zachary, Jonathan I, 936
Zachary, Jonathan, Jr. I, 455
Zachary, Julia I, 455
Zachary, Lillie I, 455
Zachary, Lizzie R. I, 442
Zachary, Lloyd II, 696
Zachary, Lora Edna I, 951
Zachary, Lura I, 923
Zachary, Lura I, 952
Zachary, Lura Edna I, 936
Zachary, Lyndon E. I, 952
Zachary, Martha I, 442
Zachary, Martha E. I, 442
Zachary, Mary I, 455
Zachary, Mary I, 936
Zachary, Mary I, 998
Zachary, Mary I, 1000
Zachary, Mary Ann I, 442
Zachary, Mary E. I, 442
Zachary, Nancy Garden I, 442
Zachary, Nannie I, 455
Zachary, Paul M. I, 936
Zachary, Paul M. I, 952
Zachary, Sarah I, 455
Zachary, William I, 442
Zachary, William I, 455
Zachary, William I, 846
Zachary, William I, 1000
Zachary, William H. I, 455
Zachary, William, Jr. I, 1000
Zachery, William I, 971
Zachrah, Mary I, 455
Zacry, Jemima I, 971
Zakery, David I, 979
Zakery, Elizabeth I, 979
Zakery, James I, 979
Zakery, Jemima I, 979
Zakery, John I, 979
Zakery, Joseph I, 979
Zakery, Mary I, 979
Zakery, William I, 979
Zame, Mrs. Elma IV, 792
Zane, Alis II, 191
Zane, Alis II, 277
Zane, Ann II, 440
Zane, Ann II, 697
Zane, Daniel II, 440
Zane, Deborah II, 440
Zane, Easter III, 407
Zane, Easter III, 476
Zane, Ebenezer II, 440
Zane, Ebenezer II, 696
Zane, Elizabeth II, 440
Zane, Elizabeth III, 473
Zane, Elizabeth Tatum II, 806
Zane, Elnathan II, 696
Zane, Esther II, 697
Zane, Esther II, 778
Zane, Esther II, 868
Zane, Esther II, 944
Zane, Grace II, 629
Zane, Hannah II, 440
Zane, Hannah II, 564
Zane, Hannah II, 619
Zane, Hannah II, 697
Zane, Hester II, 944
Zane, Isaac II, 440
Zane, Isaac II, 513
Zane, Isaac II, 619
Zane, Isaac II, 696
Zane, Isaac II, 697
Zane, Isaac, Jr. II, 696
Zane, Jesse II, 440
Zane, Jesse II, 697
Zane, Jesse S. II, 469
Zane, Jesse S. II, 697
Zane, Joel II, 440
Zane, Joel II, 697
Zane, John II, 440
Zane, John Ferriss II, 697
Zane, Jonathan II, 440
Zane, Jonathan II, 522
Zane, Jonathan II, 564
Zane, Jonathan II, 696
Zane, Jonathan II, 697
Zane, Jonathan, Jr. II, 440
Zane, Jonathan, Jr. II, 564
Zane, Jonathan, Jr. II, 696
Zane, Joseph II, 113
Zane, Joseph II, 806
Zane, Liddia II, 440
Zane, Lidya II, 522
Zane, Lidya II, 697
Zane, Lydia II, 440
Zane, Lydia II, 522
Zane, Lydia II, 697
Zane, Maria II, 603
Zane, Maria II, 697
Zane, Mary II, 440
Zane, Mary II, 522
Zane, Mary II, 696
Zane, Mary II, 697
Zane, Mary H. II, 469
Zane, Mary H. II, 697
Zane, Nathan II, 81
Zane, Nathan II, 113
Zane, Nathan II, 440
Zane, Nathan S. II, 697
Zane, Nathaniel II, 440
Zane, Nathaniel II, 513
Zane, Nathaniel II, 629
Zane, Nathaniel II, 696
Zane, Phebe II, 440
Zane, Rachel II, 81
Zane, Rachel II, 113
Zane, Rachel III, 255
Zane, Rachel III, 373
Zane, Rachel III, 433
Zane, Rachel III, 476
Zane, Rebecca II, 440
Zane, Rebeckah, Jr. II, 72
Zane, Rebeckah, Jr. II, 113
Zane, Robert II, 18
Zane, Robert II, 55
Zane, Robert II, 61
Zane, Robert II, 63
Zane, Robert II, 80
Zane, Robert II, 191
Zane, Robert II, 277
Zane, Robert III, 473
Zane, Sarah II, 440
Zane, Sarah II, 513
Zane, Sarah II, 696
Zane, Sarah II, 697
Zane, Sarah II, 805
Zane, Sarah VI, 462
Zane, Susanna II, 469
Zane, Susanna II, 697
Zane, Timothy H. II, 697
Zane, William II, 440
Zane, Wm. II, 697
Zaner, Anna V, 1026
Zaner, Annie V, 1026
Zanes, Daniel II, 440
Zanes, Ebenezer II, 440
Zanes, Elizabeth II, 440
Zanes, Isaac II, 440
Zanes, Jonathan II, 440
Zanes, Joseph II, 113
Zanes, Mary II, 440
Zanes, Phebe II, 440
Zanes, Rachel II, 113
Zanes, Rebecca II, 440
Zaney, Whankey II, 510
Zaney, Whankey II, 697
Zankee, Martha II, 595
Zankee, Martha II, 697
Zappernick, Lavina IV, 844
Zealey, Margaret II, 665
Zeally, John II, 277
Zealy, Ann II, 227
Zealy, Ann II, 277
Zealy, John II, 440
Zealy, Margaret II, 697
Zealy, Margarett II, 440
Zealy, Martha II, 440
Zealy, Martha II, 697
Zealy, Sylvanus II, 227
Zealy, Sylvanus II, 277
Zean, Sarah VI, 608
Zeanes, Jonathan II, 696
Zeans, Ann II, 449
Zeans, Elnathan II, 449
Zeans, Jonathan II, 440
Zeans, Mary II, 440
Zeans, Sarah II, 449
Zebley, Anna Beeson II, 309
Zebley, Elwood II, 309
Zebley, Georgianna II, 309
Zebley, Jacob S. III, 509
Zebley, Sarah S. III, 509
Zebulun, ??? III, 471
Zehister, Jane V, 1026
Zehister, Joseph V, 1026
Zeigler, Charles F. IV, 1267
Zeigler, Charles T. IV, 1267
Zeigler, Geo. M. V, 721
Zeigler, George V, 721
Zeigler, Martin V, 606
Zeitler, Edith IV, 1019
Zeitler, Edward IV, 1019
Zeitler, Ella IV, 1019
Zeitler, Walter IV, 1019
Zelee, Damarus II, 204
Zelee, Damarus II, 277
Zelee, Daniel II, 204
Zelee, Daniel II, 277
Zell, Blanch V, 145
Zell, Blanch Rachel V, 145
Zell, Edna V, 145
Zell, Edna Phoebe V, 145
Zell, Elsie V, 145
Zell, Elsie Rua V, 145
Zell, Emma II, 697

:unice V, 184
:unice V, 214
Iannah II, 697
Iannah II, 829
Iannah II, 944
.ida V, 145
.ida T. V, 145
.ouisa J. V, 81
.ouisa J. V, 145
.ouiza J. V, 145
Mary V, 214
Thomas V, 145
Thos II, 944
Thos. II, 829
Thos. Ellwood II, 829
Thos. Ellwood II, 944
Walter V, 145
Warren V, 145
Warren Truman V, 145
Wm. II, 945
n, Anna IV, 1345
r, Ada M. V, 690
r, Ada M. V, 721
r, Etta V, 468
rs, Anna IV, 1345
y, ??? II, 315
y, Abigail S. II, 315
y, Agnes II, 315
y, Albert II, 315
y, Albert II, 327
y, Ann II, 277
y, Ann II, 278
y, Ann II, 315
ey, Ann II, 325
ey, Ann II, 327
ey, Anne S. II, 327
ey, Anne W. II, 315
ey, Annie S. II, 318
ey, Annie S. II, 327
ey, Bathsheba II, 315
ey, Benjamin II, 278
ey, Benjamin II, 315
ey, Benjamin II, 327
ey, Caleb S. II, 315
ey, Chalkley II, 307
ey, Chalkley II, 315
ey, Chalkley II, 327
ey, Charles II, 126
ley, Charles E. II, 126
ley, Charles S. II, 315
ley, Clayton II, 307
ley, Clayton II, 315
ley, Clayton II, 327
ley, Clayton B. II, 327
ley, Daniel II, 277
ley, Daniel II, 278
ley, Daniel II, 307
ley, Daniel II, 315
ley, Daniel II, 327
ley, Daniel S. II, 325
lley, Daniel S. II, 327
lley, Daniel Shreeve II, 315
lley, Daniel Stokes II, 315
lley, Edith IV, 673
lley, Edith IV, 704
lley, Edith IV, 792
lley, Elizabeth II, 315
lley, Elizabeth B. II, 315
elley, Elizabeth B. II, 327
elley, Elizabeth H. II, 278
elley, Elizabeth S. II, 318
elley, Elizabeth S. II, 327
elley, Enoch S. IV, 792
elley, Ernest L. II, 315
elley, Ethel W. II, 315
elley, Franklin S. II, 315
elley, Franklin S. II, 327
elley, George II, 278
elley, George W. S. II, 315
elley, Gervis S. II, 315
elley, Hannah II, 277
elley, Hannah II, 278
elley, Hannah II, 315
elley, Howard IV, 704
Zelley, J. Howard IV, 673
Zelley, Jervis S. II, 327
Zelley, Job II, 278
Zelley, John II, 307
Zelley, John II, 315
Zelley, John II, 327
Zelley, Joseph II, 307
Zelley, Joseph II, 315
Zelley, Joseph Howard IV, 792
Zelley, Josiah II, 315
Zelley, Josiah II, 327
Zelley, Leander S. II, 315
Zelley, Leander Shreve II, 315
Zelley, Martha II, 315
Zelley, Mary B. II, 315
Zelley, Mary B. II, 327
Zelley, Mary Elizabeth II, 315
Zelley, Nathaniel F. II, 315
Zelley, Nathaniel F. II, 327
Zelley, Noah II, 278
Zelley, Penelope II, 315
Zelley, Penelope II, 327
Zelley, Rachael II, 315
Zelley, Rachel W. II, 325
Zelley, Rachel W. II, 327
Zelley, Rebecca II, 327
Zelley, Rebecca W. II, 712
Zelley, Rehoboam II, 315
Zelley, Rehoboam II, 327
Zelley, Ridgway II, 307
Zelley, Samuel Stockton II, 315
Zelley, Samuel Stockton II, 327
Zelley, Sarah II, 327
Zelley, Sarah B. IV, 792
Zelley, Sarah Edith IV, 673
Zelley, Sarah Edith IV, 792
Zelley, Silvanus II, 315
Zelley, Silvenus II, 315
Zelley, Sylvanus II, 327
Zelley, William II, 278
Zelley, William Braddock II, 315
Zelley, William H. II, 327
Zelley, William Henry II, 315
Zelli, Giuseppina VI, 743
Zelly, Aaron II, 190
Zelly, Aaron II, 278
Zelly, Aaron L. II, 190
Zelly, Abraham II, 277
Zelly, Agnes H. II, 924
Zelly, Agnes H. II, 945
Zelly, Albert II, 945
Zelly, Ann II, 190
Zelly, Ann II, 277
Zelly, Ann II, 278
Zelly, Ann II, 307
Zelly, Bathsheba II, 190
Zelly, Bathsheba II, 278
Zelly, Bathsheba II, 307
Zelly, Bathsheba II, 1041
Zelly, Bathsheba II, 1042
Zelly, Benjamin II, 190
Zelly, Benjamin II, 278
Zelly, Benjamin II, 307
Zelly, Benjamin II, 327
Zelly, Benjamin II, 945
Zelly, Chalkley II, 307
Zelly, Clayton II, 307
Zelly, Clayton II, 327
Zelly, Damarus II, 277
Zelly, Daniel II, 190
Zelly, Daniel II, 277
Zelly, Daniel II, 278
Zelly, Daniel II, 307
Zelly, Daniel S. II, 327
Zelly, Daniel, Jr. II, 277
Zelly, Daniel, Jr. II, 278
Zelly, Eliza II, 1042
Zelly, Eliza B. II, 1041
Zelly, Eliza B. II, 1042
Zelly, Elizabeth II, 278
Zelly, Elizabeth H. II, 190
Zelly, Elizabeth H. II, 278
Zelly, Elizabeth L. II, 924
Zelly, Elizabeth L. II, 945
Zelly, Franklin S. II, 924
Zelly, Franklin S. II, 945
Zelly, George II, 278
Zelly, Hannah II, 190
Zelly, Hannah II, 277
Zelly, Hannah II, 278
Zelly, Jemima II, 190
Zelly, Jemima II, 278
Zelly, Job II, 277
Zelly, Job II, 278
Zelly, John II, 277
Zelly, John II, 307
Zelly, John II, 556
Zelly, John II, 697
Zelly, John R. II, 190
Zelly, Jon II, 311
Zelly, Joseph II, 307
Zelly, Josiah II, 307
Zelly, Josiah II, 327
Zelly, Leander Shreve II, 924
Zelly, Leander Shreve II, 945
Zelly, Margaret II, 190
Zelly, Margaret II, 556
Zelly, Margarett II, 697
Zelly, Martha II, 190
Zelly, Martha II, 278
Zelly, Mary II, 249
Zelly, Mary II, 278
Zelly, Noah II, 190
Zelly, Noah II, 278
Zelly, Penelope II, 190
Zelly, Penelope II, 278
Zelly, Penelope II, 307
Zelly, Rachel II, 277
Zelly, Rachel II, 302
Zelly, Rachel II, 307
Zelly, Rachel II, 311
Zelly, Rachel W. II, 327
Zelly, Rebecca II, 278
Zelly, Rebecca II, 307
Zelly, Rehoboam II, 307
Zelly, Rehoboam II, 327
Zelly, Richard R. II, 307
Zelly, Ridgway II, 307
Zelly, S. Stockton II, 945
Zelly, Samuel II, 277
Zelly, Samuel Stockton II, 327
Zelly, Sarah II, 277
Zelly, Sarah II, 278
Zelly, Sarah II, 327
Zelly, Sylvanus II, 190
Zelly, Sylvanus II, 277
Zelly, Sylvanus II, 278
Zelly, Sylvanus II, 307
Zelly, Sylvanus II, 327
Zelly, Sylvanus II, 1041
Zelly, Sylvanus II, 1042
Zelly, Sylvanus, Jr. II, 278
Zelly, Sylvennus II, 190
Zelly, William II, 278
Zelly, William Braddock II, 278
Zentmeyer, Elizabeth V, 145
Zentmeyer, Enos V, 145
Zentmeyer, Olive Branch V, 145
Zentmeyer, Samuel V, 145
Zentmeyer, Sophronia V, 145
Zeppernick, Andrew IV, 857
Zeppernick, Cary IV, 857
Zeppernick, Francis A. IV, 857
Zeppernick, Harmon C. IV, 857
Zeppernick, Harmon E. IV, 857
Zeppernick, Jonathan IV, 857
Zeppernick, Lavina IV, 857
Zeppernick, Marion C. IV, 857
Zeppernick, Martha IV, 844
Zeppernick, Martha IV, 857
Zerns, Anna Jane II, 829
Zerns, Elizabeth II, 139
Zerns, Elizabeth W. II, 128
Zerns, Elizabeth W. II, 141
Zerns, Elizabeth W. II, 159
Zerns, Elizabeth W. II, 161
Zerns, John R. II, 141
Zerns, John Righter II, 829
Zerns, Lydia II, 141
Zerns, Lydia Freidland II, 829
Zerns, Mary II, 141
Zerns, William II, 141
Zerns, Wm. II, 161
Zerns, Wm. M. II, 945
Zerns, Wm. Morris II, 141
Zerns, Wm. Morris II, 829
Zetta, Viola V, 99
Zeverly, Rachel VI, 618
Zeverly, Rachel VI, 724
Zeverly, Rachel Hannah VI, 617
Zeverly, W. VI, 617
Ziegler, Della V, 822
Ziemer, Augusta III, 339
Zigler, Elizabeth V, 794
Zigler, Tacy VI, 403
Zigler, Tacy VI, 462
Zilboorg, Anna III, 373
Zilboorg, Gregory III, 373
Zilboorg, Moses III, 373
Zilboorg, Ray III, 373
Zilley, Aaron II, 278
Zilley, Daniel II, 278
Zilley, Daniel II, 307
Zilley, John II, 277
Zilly, Abraham II, 277
Zilly, Daniel II, 278
Zilly, Edith II, 239
Zilly, Edith II, 278
Zilly, Eliza II, 1042
Zilly, Penelope II, 278
Zilly, Rachel II, 263
Zilly, Rachel II, 277
Zimble, Anthony VI, 1012
Zimmer, Tacy IV, 1267
Zimmerman, Annie V, 468
Zimmerman, Charles M. V, 145
Zimmerman, Cora IV, 1345
Zimmerman, Dinah II, 440
Zimmerman, Edward IV, 1301
Zimmerman, Edward, Sr. IV, 1301
Zimmerman, Eliza VI, 637
Zimmerman, Eliza VI, 724
Zimmerman, Elizabeth IV, 781
Zimmerman, Floyd IV, 1301
Zimmerman, Grace IV, 310
Zimmerman, Helene Smith IV, 1079
Zimmerman, Helene Smith IV, 1123
Zimmerman, Henry IV, 1079
Zimmerman, Henry IV, 1123
Zimmerman, Henry Smith IV, 1123
Zimmerman, Henry Timmerman IV, 1079
Zimmerman, Homer IV, 781
Zimmerman, Iva McCoy IV, 1301
Zimmerman, J. Grace IV, 310
Zimmerman, Jacob V, 468
Zimmerman, John Frederick IV, 1079
Zimmerman, John Frederick IV, 1123
Zimmerman, Lydia V, 456
Zimmerman, M. D. V, 1026
Zimmerman, Maggie V, 468
Zimmerman, Margaret IV, 781
Zimmerman, Maria IV, 1079
Zimmerman, Maria IV, 1123
Zimmerman, Mary II, 440
Zimmerman, Mary D. V, 1026
Zimmerman, Norah V, 1026
Zimmerman, Olive V, 468
Zimmerman, R. L. V, 1026
Zimmerman, Rebecca V, 468
Zimmerman, Ruth S. V, 145
Zimmerman, S. Anna V, 293
Zimmerman, Thaddeus E. V, 145
Zimmerman, William IV, 886
Zimmerman, Wm. IV, 1079
Zimmerman, Wm. IV, 1123
Zimmerman, Wm. P. V, 468
Zimmerman, Zatharine V, 293
Zimmers, Alliance IV, 1345
Zimmers, Clyde IV, 1345
Zimmers, Jno., Jr. IV, 1345
Zimmers, Lillian IV, 1345
Zimmers, Lottie IV, 1345
Zimmers, Mamie IV, 1345
Zink, ??? V, 774
Zink, Agnes IV, 506
Zink, Ann V, 764
Zink, Anna V, 764
Zink, George V, 723
Zink, John IV, 506
Zink, Mary IV, 506
Zink, Mary V, 723
Zink, Moses IV, 506
Zink, Susie IV, 506
Zink, Wm. IV, 506
Zinnbeck, Dora Collins V, 1026
Zippernick, Andrew IV, 811
Zippernick, Martha IV, 811
Zoll, Jacob VI, 1022
Zoll, Rebecca VI, 1022
Zollars, Elizabeth IV, 792
Zollickoffer, Henry M. II, 945
Zollickoffer, Henry W. II, 945
Zook, ??? IV, 310
Zook, Esther IV, 310
Zook, Jacob IV, 310
Zook, Lindley IV, 310
Zook, Paul IV, 310
Zook, Paul L. IV, 310
Zook, Sadie E. IV, 310
Zorn, Hannah E. II, 718
Zorn, Israel S. II, 718
Zorn, Matilda Ann II, 718
Zorns, Elizabeth W. II, 139
Zorns, Hannah II, 137
Zorns, Israel II, 137
Zorns, John F. II, 161
Zorns, John R. II, 139
Zorns, John R. II, 144
Zorns, John R. II, 161
Zorns, Lydia II, 139
Zorns, Lydia F. II, 144
Zorns, Lydia F. II, 161
Zorns, Mary II, 144
Zorns, Mary II, 161
Zorns, Matilda II, 137
Zorns, Wm. II, 144
Zorns, Wm. II, 161
Zucker, Mary III, 60
Zucker, Mary III, 373
Zucker, Mary E. III, 60
Zucker, Mary E. III, 373
Zucker, Richard III, 373
Zucker, Richard D. III, 60
Zuercher, Blanch IV, 1019
Zuercher, Blanche IV, 1019
Zuercher, Blanche Mae IV, 1019
Zuercher, Corinne Mae IV, 1019
Zuercher, Harrison IV, 1019
Zuercher, Harrison Raymond IV, 1019
Zuercher, Harrison Wm. IV, 1019
Zuercher, Loris William IV, 1019
Zumbro, Martha IV, 1095
Zumbro, Martha IV, 1123
Zurface, Bertha Adams V, 721
Zurface, Carl V, 721
Zurface, Harold V, 721
Zurface, Harold Eugene V, 651
Zurface, Harold Eugene V, 721
Zurface, Malva V, 721
Zurface, Mattie Walker V, 721
Zurface, Melba V, 721
Zurface, Melba May V, 651
Zurface, Ruth V, 721
Zurface, Ruth Elizabeth V, 651
Zurface, Virginia V, 721
Zurface, Virginia Eilene V, 651
Zurface, Virginia Ellene V, 721